W9-DCA-857

# Webster's Third New International Dictionary

OF THE ENGLISH LANGUAGE

UNABRIDGED

A Merriam-Webster

REG. U.S. PAT. OFF.

WITH SEVEN LANGUAGE DICTIONARY

## VOLUME II

# H to R

ENCYCLOPÆDIA BRITANNICA, INC.

*Chicago, London, Toronto, Geneva, Sydney, Tokyo, Manila*

HELEN HEMINGWAY BENTON, *Publisher*

Standard Book Numbers:
0-87779-001-9 (buff buckram)
0-87779-002-7 (dark tan Fabrikoid)
0-87779-003-5 (2 volumes, buff buckram)
0-87779-005-1 (tan buckram, India paper)
0-87779-006-X (dark brown Fabrikoid, India paper)

MADE IN THE U. S. A.

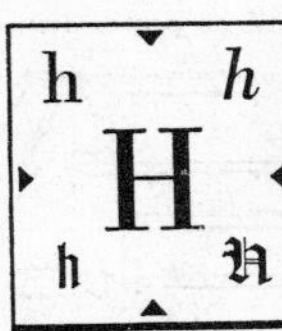

**¹h** \'āch\ *n, pl* **h's** *or* **hs** \'āchəz\ *often cap, often attrib* **1 a :** the eighth letter of the English alphabet **b :** an instance of this letter printed, written, or otherwise represented **c :** a speech counterpart of orthographic *h* (as *h* in *hoe, ahead,* or German *hügel*) **2 :** a printer's type, a stamp, or some other instrument for reproducing the letter *h* **3 :** someone or something arbitrarily or conveniently designated *h* esp. as the eighth in order or class **4 :** something having the shape of the letter H ⟨grooved and slotted to receive H bronze members —Kenneth Cheesman⟩

**²h** *abbr, often cap* **1** hail **2** haler **3** half **4** hall **5** handily **6** harbor **7** hard; hardness **8** [Ger *hauch*] film **9** haze **10** headquarters **11** heat **12** hecto- **13** height **14** helicopter **15** heller **16** hence **17** henry **18** [L *heres*] heir **19** heroin **20** high **21** hit **22** holy **23** home **24** honor **25** horizon; horizontal **26** horn **27** horse **28** hot **29** hour **30** house **31** humidity **32** hundred **33** husband **34** hydrant

**³h** *symbol* **1** *cap* hydrogen **2** *cap* enthalpy **3** *cap* intensity of magnetic field **4** Planck constant

**H³** *or* **³H** \(')āch¦thrē\ *symbol* tritium

**H²** *or* **²H** \(')āch¦tü\ *symbol* deuterium

**¹ha** *or* **hah** \'hä, 'hȧ\ *interj* [ME *ha*] — used to express surprise, joy, or grief or sometimes doubt or hesitation

**²ha** \"\ *vi* -ED/-ING/-S **:** to utter the exclamation *ha*

**³ha** *or* **hah** \"\ *n* -S **:** an utterance of the exclamation *ha*

**⁴ha** *or* **ha'** \hə, (')hȧ\ *var of* A

**⁵ha** *dial Brit pres 1st & 2d sing & pres pl of* HAVE

**ha** *abbr* hectare

**HA** *abbr* **1** heavy artillery **2** high-angle **3** *often not cap* [L *hoc anno*] in this year; [L *huius anni*] of this year **4** horse artillery **5** hot air **6** hour angle

**ha'** \'hȯ, 'hȧ\ *Scot var of* HALL

**HAA** *abbr* heavy antiaircraft

**haab** \'häb\ *n* -S [Maya] **1 :** TUN **2 :** the 365-day year of the Maya calendar — often distinguished from *tun*

**haak-en-steek** \'häkən,stēk\ *n* -S [Afrik, lit., hook and sting; fr. the fact that it has some curved and some straight thorns] **:** UMBRELLA THORN

**haar** \'(h)är\ *n* -S [prob. fr. a LG or D dial. word akin to D dial. *harig* damp, misty, MD *hare* sharp wind, piercing cold, Fris *harig* misty, ON *hārr* gray, hoary — more at HOAR] *dial Brit* **:** a cold wet sea fog

**haar·der** *var of* ²HARDER

**haar·lem** \'härləm, 'hȧl-\ *adj, usu cap* [fr. *Haarlem*, Netherlands] **:** of or from the city of Haarlem, Netherlands **:** of the kind or style prevalent in Haarlem

**haas·tia** \'häst̄ēə\ *n* -S [NL, fr. Sir John F. J. von *Haast* †1887 German-born geologist and explorer in New Zealand + NL *-ia*] **:** RAOULIA 2

**hab** *abbr* habitat

**HAB** *abbr* high-altitude bombing

**ha·ba** \'(h)äbə\ *n* -S [Sp, fr. L *faba* bean — more at BEAN] **:** BROAD BEAN

**ha·bab** \hə'bäb, 'hä,bäb\ *n, pl* **habab** *usu cap* **1 a :** a nomadic people of the Red sea region in Africa **b :** a member of such people **2 :** the Semitic language of the Habab

**ha·ba·ne·ra** \,(h)äbə'nerə, *often* ÷ -bən'ye- *although the fifth letter in Spanish is n not ñ*\ *n* -S [Sp (*danza*) *habanera*, lit., Havanan dance, fr. *danza* dance + *habanera*, fem. of *habanero* Havanan, fr. La *Habana*, Cuba + *-ero* -er] **1 :** a Cuban dance of voluptuous character in slow duple time **2 :** a slow Cuban dance tune in duple time with the distinctive rhythm of a dotted eighth note, a sixteenth note, and two eighth notes throughout

**ha·ba·ne·ro** \-e(,)rō\ *n* -S *cap* [Sp, fr. La *Habana* (Havana), Cuba + *-ero* -er] **:** a native or inhabitant of Havana, Cuba

**hab·ble** \'häbəl\ *Scot var of* HOBBLE

**hab·da·lah** *or* **hav·da·lah** \,hävdə'lä, häv'dōlə\ *n* -S [Heb *habhdālāh* separation, division] **:** a Jewish religious ceremony marking the close of a Sabbath or of holidays and consisting of the recital by the head of a household of appropriate benedictions over a cup esp. of wine, a spice box, and a newly lighted special candle

**ha·be·as cor·pus** \'hābēə'skȯrpəs, -biə'-, -kȯ(ə)p-\ *n* [ME, fr. ML, lit., you should have the body (the opening words of the writ)] **1 :** any of several common-law writs that have for their object the bringing of a party before a court or judge and that are issued out of court or awarded by a judge in vacation; *esp* **:** HABEAS CORPUS AD SUBJICIENDUM ⟨the privilege of the writ of *habeas corpus* shall not be suspended, unless when in cases of rebellion or invasion the public safety may require it —*U.S. Constitution*⟩ **2 :** the right of a citizen to obtain a writ of habeas corpus as a protection against illegal imprisonment

**habeas corpus ad fa·ci·en·dum et re·cip·i·en·dum** \-ad-,fāshē'endəm·e·trə,sipē'endəm\ *n* [NL, lit., you should have the body for doing and receiving] **:** a writ issued from a superior court to an inferior court requiring that a defendant be produced with the cause of his being taken and held

**habeas corpus ad pro·se·quen·dum** \-,präsə'kwendəm\ *n* [NL, lit., you should have the body for prosecuting] **:** a writ for removing a prisoner for trial to the jurisdiction in which the offense was committed

**habeas corpus ad sub·ji·ci·en·dum** \-(,)səb,jisē'endəm\ *n* [NL, lit., you should have the body for submitting] **:** a writ for inquiring into the lawfulness of the restraint of a person who is imprisoned or detained in another's custody

**habeas corpus ad tes·ti·fi·can·dum** \-,testəfə'kandəm\ *n* [NL, lit., you should have the body for testifying] **:** a writ for bringing a person in custody into court as a witness

**habeas corpus cum cau·sa** \-(,)kəm'kȯzə\ *n* [NL, lit., you should have the body with the cause] **:** HABEAS CORPUS AD FACIENDUM ET RECIPIENDUM

**hab·e·nar·ia** \,habə'na(a)rēə\ *n* [NL, fr. L *habena* strap, thong (fr. *habēre* to have, hold) + NL *-aria*; fr. the shape of parts of the flowers — more at GIVE] **1** *cap* **:** a very large genus of somewhat glabrous orchids chiefly of the northern hemisphere with usu. small flowers having the lip lobed, entire, or fringed and borne in racemes or spikes — see FRINGED ORCHIS, REIN ORCHIS **2** -S **:** any plant of the genus *Habenaria* or its flower

**ha·ben·dum** \hə'bendəm\ *n* -S [NL, fr. L, to be had, neut. of *habendus*, gerundive of *habēre* to have, to hold (the first word of this part of the deed)] **:** the part of a deed that formerly limited and defined an estate and the extent of ownership granted and sometimes the type of tenancy by which the grantees would hold an estate but that is now rarely encountered or is merely formal in deeds in which a fee simple absolute is presumed granted

**ha·ben·u·la** \hə'benyələ\ *n, pl* **habenu·lae** \-yə(,)lē\ [L, dim. of *habena* strap, thong] **1** *also* **ha·ben·u·lar trigone** \-lə(r)-\ **:** an anatomic structure in the form of a band; *esp* **:** a small triangular area of the surface of the epithalamus on either side of the base of the pineal body **2** *also* **habenular nucleus :** a nucleus underlying each habenula and connected by commissural fibers that forms a correlation center for olfactory stimuli — called also *nucleus habenulae*

**haber** *var of* HAVER

**haberah** *var of* HAVERAH

**hab·er·dash·er** \'habə(r),dashə(r)\ *n* -S [ME *haberdassher*, fr. modif. of AF *hapertas* petty merchandise + ME *-er*] **1** *Brit* **:** a dealer in small wares or notions (as needles, thread, buttons, trimmings) **2 :** a dealer in men's furnishings (as shirts, ties, hats, gloves)

**hab·er·dash·ery** \-sh(ə)rē, -ri\ *n* -ES [ME *haberdassherie*, fr. *haberdassher* + *-ie* -y] **1 :** the goods sold by a haberdasher **2 :** a haberdasher's shop

**haberdine** *n* -S [ME, fr. MF *habordean*, by false division (the *l* being taken as the definite article) fr. *labordean*, fr. *Labourd*, Basque district in France] *obs* **:** a cod salted and dried

**ha·be·re fa·ci·as pos·ses·si·o·nem** \hə'birē'fāshēəspə,zesē'ō,nem\ *n* [ML, you should cause to have possession (the opening words of the writ)] **:** a writ of execution in ejectment orig. in England in cases of chattels real

**habere facias sei·si·nam** \-'sēzə,nam\ *n* [ML, you should cause to have seisin] **:** a common-law writ formerly used in real actions to recover seisin

**hab·er·geon** \'habərjən, hə'bərj(ē)ən\ *or* **hau·ber·geon** \'hȯb-, hȯ'-\ *n* -S [ME *haubergeoun*, fr. MF *haubergeon*, dim. of *hauberc* — more at HAUBERK] **1 :** a medieval jacket of mail shorter than a hauberk **2 :** HAUBERK

**haber process** \'häbə(r)-\ *n, usu cap H* [after Fritz *Haber* †1934 Ger. chemist] **:** a catalytic process for synthesizing ammonia from nitrogen and hydrogen at elevated temperature and pressure

**hab·ile** \'habəl\ *adj* [F, fr. L *habilis* — more at ABLE] **1** *obs* **:** FIT, SUITABLE **2 :** ABLE, ADROIT, SKILLFUL ⟨that astonishing ~ use of his lean little hands —J.G.Cozzens⟩

**ha·bil·i·ment** \hə'biləmənt\ *n* -S [MF *habillement*, fr. *abillier*, *habiller* to prepare a log for working, prepare, dress (fr. *bille* log, trunk) + *-ment* — more at BILLET] **1 habiliments** *pl* **:** TRAPPINGS, EQUIPMENT, GEAR ⟨the disintegrative process of the frontier . . . stripping them of the ~*s* of civilization —W.P. Webb⟩ ⟨all the psychological trappings and ~*s* of a crusade —W.A.White⟩ **2 habiliments** *pl, archaic* **:** necessary equipment and material (as for war) **:** OUTFITTING **3 a :** the dress suited to or characteristic of a calling, occupation, or occasion **:** GARB, COSTUME, VESTMENT — usu. used in pl. ⟨dressed in shabby gaucho ~*s* —W.H.Hudson †1922⟩ ⟨~*s* of a priest⟩ ⟨the antique forms and ~*s* which their Roman ancestors had found congenial —G.C.Sellery⟩ **b :** CLOTHES, GARMENT, DRESS — usu. used in pl. ⟨pointed in silence to my torn and muddied ~*s* —Hugh McCrae⟩ ⟨seize a buttonhole, or any little bit of the ~*s*, of the man she was addressing —George Meredith⟩

**ha·bil·i·men·ta·tion** \hə,bilə(,)men'tāshən\ *n* -S **:** the arts and industries connected with the manufacture and use of clothes

**ha·bil·i·ment·ed** \hə'bilə,mentəd\ *adj* **:** CLOTHED

**ha·bil·i·tate** \hə'bilə,tāt, *usu* -ād·+V\ *vb* -ED/-ING/-S [LL *habilitatus*, past part. of *habilitare*, fr. L *habilitas* aptness, ability — more at ABILITY] *vt* **1** *archaic* **:** QUALIFY, ENTITLE **2 :** to fit out (as a mine) **:** equip for working **3 :** CLOTHE, DRESS ~ *vi* **:** to qualify oneself (as for teaching in a university) ⟨had just *habilitated* as a privatdocent in the theological faculty —Jack Finegan⟩

**ha·bil·i·ta·tion** \hə,bilə'tāshən\ *n* -S [ML *habilitation-*, *habilitatio*, fr. LL *habilitatus* + L *-ion-*, *-io* -ion] **:** the act of habilitating **:** QUALIFICATION ⟨thesis for ~ as docent⟩ **:** CAPACITATION ⟨~ of cerebral palsy patients⟩

**ha·bil·i·ty** \hə'bilədē\ *n* -ES **:** the quality of being habile **:** EXPERTNESS

**ha·bi·ru** \'häbē,rü, hə'bē(,)rü\ *also* **ha·bi·ri** \-ē(,)rē\ *n pl, usu cap* [Bab *khabiru*] **:** a nomadic people mentioned in Assyro-Babylonian literature from 2000 B.C. on and often identified as the Hebrews of the Bible

**¹hab·it** \'habət, *usu* -əd·+V\ *n* -S [ME *habit, abit*, fr. OF, fr. L *habitus* condition, appearance, attire, character, disposition, habit, fr. *habēre* to have, hold — more at GIVE] **1** *archaic* **a :** CLOTHING, APPAREL ⟨costly thy ~ as thy purse can buy —Shak.⟩ **:** mode of dress ⟨in the vile ~ of a village slave —Alexander Pope⟩ **b :** a garment or a suit of clothes **:** OUTFIT **2 a :** a costume indicative or characteristic of a calling, rank, or function ⟨monk's ~⟩ **b :** RIDING HABIT **3 :** BEARING, CONDUCT, BEHAVIOR — used esp. in Scots law in the phrase *habit and repute* ⟨marriage by ~ and repute⟩ **4 a :** bodily appearance or makeup **:** physical type **:** PHYSIQUE ⟨his corpulent ~ of body, natural both to the vigor of his type and to a sedentary way of life —Osbert Sitwell⟩ **b** *obs* **:** the body as a physiological organism **:** the system of bodily processes **c** *obs* **:** the body's surface **5 :** the prevailing disposition or character of a person's thoughts and feelings **:** mental makeup ⟨where he has gone to indulge a contemplative ~ —L.J.Halle⟩ ⟨a whole ~ of sensibility —F.R.Leavis⟩ **6 a** *of a person* **:** a settled tendency of behavior or normal manner of procedure **:** CUSTOM, PRACTICE, WAY ⟨contributed letters to the newspapers — a ~ that became a lifelong one —B.J.Hendrick⟩ ⟨the local ~ of building in perishable materials —Bernard Newman⟩ **b** *of a thing* **:** a usual manner of occurrence or behavior **:** TENDENCY ⟨black clouds there have a ~ of sitting right on the water —Ira Wolfert⟩ ⟨paste has a ~ of going hard and lumpy once opened⟩ **7 a :** a behavior pattern acquired by frequent repetition or developed as a physiologic function and showing itself in regularity ⟨the daily bowel ~⟩ or increased facility of performance or in a decreased power of resistance ⟨a drug ~⟩ **b :** an acquired or developed mode of behavior or function that has become nearly or completely involuntary ⟨put the keys back in his pocket through force of ~⟩ **8** *of an organism* **:** characteristic mode of growth or occurrence ⟨elms have a spreading ~⟩ ⟨a grass ubiquitous in its ~⟩ **9** *of a crystal* **:** characteristic or common assemblage of forms at crystallization leading to a usual appearance **10** *obs* **:** close acquaintance **:** FAMILIARITY ⟨he inclines to a sort of disgust . . . with the system and he has few . . . ~*s* with any of its professors —Edmund Burke⟩ **11 :** a generic entity occurring as an external or supernatural reality or force constitutive of or acting on an individual **12 :** ADDICTION 2a

**syn** HABITUDE, PRACTICE, USAGE, CUSTOM, USE, WONT: these all have in common the sense of a way of behaving that has become more or less fixed; in most cases they have the sense of such a way considered collectively or in the abstract. HABIT, usu. applying to individuals, signifies a way of acting or thinking done frequently enough to have become unconscious or unpremeditated in each repetition or to have become compulsive ⟨the *habit* of dawdling on the way to school⟩ ⟨a persistent *habit* of coughing⟩ ⟨*habits* of mind⟩ ⟨speech *habits*⟩ HABITUDE usu. suggests habitual or usual state of mind or attitude ⟨you who are so sincere with me are never quite sincere with others. You have contracted this bad *habitude* from your custom of addressing the people —W.S.Landor⟩ ⟨a confusion of assertions, viewpoints, personal motives and prejudices, and local *habitudes* can serve only to darken counsel —*Yale Rev.*⟩ PRACTICE suggests an act, often habitual, repeated with regularity and usu. by choice ⟨the team made a *practice* of leaving their scenarios unfinished until actual production —*Current Biog.*⟩ ⟨promised the people that he would establish democratic *practices* —*Collier's Yr. Bk.*⟩ ⟨the *practice* of supplementing poultry and hog feeds with antibiotics —*Americana Annual*⟩ ⟨the *practice* of self-examination —Anne Fremantle⟩ USAGE suggests more a customary action, a practice followed so generally that it has become a social norm ⟨an unwritten constitution comprising ancient British conventions and *usage* —*Americana Annual*⟩ ⟨earn a living in a business community without yielding to its *usages* —W.H.Hamilton⟩ ⟨better versed in diplomatic *usage* than any of his colleagues —F.A.Ogg & Harold Zink⟩ CUSTOM can apply to habit, practice, or usage that has become public and associated with an individual or group because of its long continuance, its uniformity, and often, its morally compulsive quality ⟨it is the Arabian *custom* to date, if possible, the birth of sons by unusual events —*Current Biog.*⟩ ⟨in contemporary society it is not a fashion that men wear trousers; it is the *custom* —Edward Sapir⟩ ⟨the *custom* — and this is all that it can be properly called — according to which Congress and the President tacitly agree to abide by the interpretation of the Court —M.R.Cohen⟩ USE, rare in current speech, signifies a customary act or practice more or less distinctive of an individual or particular group ⟨the polite *uses* of society⟩ ⟨the religious *use* and wont of the country people⟩ WONT applies to a habitual or customary manner, method, or practice distinguishing an individual or group; it differs from USE only in extending to manner ⟨intended to come oftener to church than had been his *wont* of late —William Black⟩ ⟨this nice balance between sovereignty and liberty is maintained by use and *wont* —V.L.Parrington⟩ ⟨a people living by *wont* in a natural atmosphere of suspicion and mistrust, and consumed by fantasies —V.S.Pritchett⟩ **syn** see in addition PHYSIQUE

**²habit** \"\ *vt* -ED/-ING/-S **:** CLOTHE, DRESS ⟨the nature of such pedantry to ~ itself in a harsh and crabbed style —R.M. Weaver⟩

**³habit** \"\ *vb* -ED/-ING/-S [ME *habiten* to dwell, reside, fr. MF *habiter*, fr. L *habitare* to have possession of, inhabit, dwell, abide, fr. *habitus*, past part. of *habēre* to have, hold — more at GIVE] *vi, obs* **:** LIVE, ABIDE ~ *vt* **1** *archaic* **:** INHABIT **2** *archaic* **:** ACCUSTOM, HABITUATE

**hab·it·abil·i·ty** \,habədə'bilədē\ *n* **:** the state of being habitable

**hab·it·able** \'habədəbəl, -bətəb-\ *adj* [ME *abitable*, fr. OF *habitable, abitable*, fr. L *habitabilis*, fr. *habitare* + *-abilis* -able] **:** capable of being inhabited **:** that may be inhabited or dwelt in ⟨the ~ world⟩; *specif, of a dwelling* **:** reasonably fit for occupation by a tenant of the class for which it was let or of the class ordinarily occupying such a dwelling — **hab·it·able·ness** *n* -ES — **hab·it·ably** \-blē, -li\ *adv*

**habitacle** *n* -S [ME, fr. OF, fr. L *habitaculum* — more at BINNACLE] **1** *obs* **:** a dwelling place **2** *obs* **:** a niche in a wall (as for a statue)

**hab·it·al·ly** \'habəd·ᵊlē\ *adv* [irreg. fr. *habitat* + *-ly*] **:** with respect to habitat

**hab·it·ancy** \'habəd·ənsē\ *n* -ES **1 :** the fact of residence **:** INHABITANCY **2 :** the whole number of inhabitants **:** POPULATION

**¹hab·i·tant** \'habəd·ənt\ *n* -S [MF, fr. pres. part. of *habiter* to dwell, inhabit — more at HABIT] **1 :** INHABITANT, RESIDENT **2** *or* **ha·bi·tan** \,(h)abē¦täⁿ\ [CanF *habitant*, fr. F, inhabitant] **:** a settler or descendant of a settler of French origin belonging to the farming class in Canada

**²ha·bi·tant** \,(h)abē¦täⁿ\ *adj* **:** relating to, characteristic of, or produced by the French farmers of Canada ⟨~ furniture⟩ ⟨~ homespun⟩

**hab·i·tat** \'habə,tat, *usu* -ad·+V\ *n* -S [L, it inhabits, 3d pers. sing. pres. indic. of *habitare* to inhabit (the initial word in Latin descriptions of species of fauna and flora in old natural histories) — more at HABIT] **1 a :** the place where a plant or animal species naturally lives and grows ⟨found as weeds throughout the tropics, but their original ~ has not been determined —Walter Bally⟩ **b :** the kind of site or region with respect to physical features (as soil, weather, elevation) naturally or normally preferred by a biological species ⟨provides three main kinds of ~, namely rocks, sand, and mud —W.H.Dowdeswell⟩ ⟨shell opaque and dull, varying in solidity according to the ~⟩ **c :** the purely physical environment of a locality occupied by a human group ⟨unable to maintain themselves as rulers in the steppe ~ of the nomads —Owen & Eleanor Lattimore⟩ **2 :** the place where something is commonly found ⟨has its natural ~ in university, in government, or in industrial laboratories —B.B.Watson⟩

**habitat form** *n* **:** ECAD

**habitat group** *n* **:** a museum exhibit showing plant and animal specimens in such attitudes and with their natural surroundings so reproduced as to picture their habits and habitat

**hab·i·ta·tion** \,habə'tāshən\ *n* -S [ME *habitacioun*, fr. MF *habitation*, fr. L *habitation-*, *habitatio*, fr. *habitatus* (past part. of *habitare* to inhabit, dwell) + *-ion-*, *-io* -ion — more at HABIT] **1 a :** the act of inhabiting **:** state of inhabiting or dwelling or of being inhabited **:** OCCUPANCY **b :** the right of one with his family to occupy the residential property of another as a home **2 a :** a dwelling place **:** HOUSE, HOME, RESIDENCE ⟨a map showing towns, villages, and scattered ~*s*⟩ ⟨his notebooks . . . gave his ideas a local ~ —Van Wyck Brooks⟩ **3 :** SETTLEMENT, COLONY ⟨their ~*s* were usually spoken of as camps, sometimes composed of 200 tents —Clark Wissler⟩ — **hab·i·ta·tion·al** \¦=;=¦tāshənᵊl, -shnəl\ *adj*

**habit clinic** *n* **:** a clinic dealing with the prevention and treatment of behavior problems in young children

**habited** *adj* **1** *obs* **:** fixed by habit **:** ACCUSTOMED **2** *archaic* **:** INHABITED **3 :** CLOTHED; *esp* **:** dressed in a habit ⟨the monasteries were gone, the ~ men and women were but memories —Sigmund Beale⟩

**habit-forming** \'=;=,=\ *adj* **:** inducing the formation of a habit or an addiction ⟨a *habit-forming* drug⟩

**habiting** *pres part of* HABIT

**habits** *pl of* HABIT, *pres 3d sing of* HABIT

**habit spasm** *n* **:** TIC 1

**¹ha·bit·u·al** \hə'bich(ə)wəl, -chəl\ *adj* [ML *habitualis*, fr. L *habitus* condition, habit + *-alis* -al — more at HABIT] **1 :** of the nature of a habit **:** according to habit **:** established by or repeated by force of habit **:** CUSTOMARY ⟨~ smoking⟩ ⟨~ courtesy⟩ ⟨~ morning walk⟩ **2 :** doing, practicing, or acting in some manner by force of habit **:** customarily doing a certain thing ⟨a ~ drunkard⟩ ⟨~ playgoer⟩ ⟨his ~ position by the door⟩ **3 :** used or involved in the practice of a habit **:** USUAL ⟨~ topic⟩ **4 :** existing as a part of the inward constitution or habit **:** inherent in an individual ⟨~ faith⟩ ⟨~ grace⟩; *also* **:** NATIVE, INBORN ⟨~ tact⟩ **syn** see USUAL

**²habitual** \"\ *n* -S **:** an habitual offender; *esp* **:** an habitual drunkard, criminal, or user of drugs **:** ADDICT

**habitual abortion** *n* **:** recurrent abortion in successive pregnancies

**habitual criminal** *n* **:** one convicted of a crime who has a certain number of prior convictions for offenses of a character specified by statute (as felonies) and is thereby under some statutes subject to an increased penalty (as life imprisonment)

**ha·bit·u·al·i·ty** \hə,bichə'waləd·ē\ *n* -ES **:** the state of being controlled (as in thinking) by old habits

**ha·bit·u·al·ly** \-lē, -li\ *adv* **1 :** by habit **:** CUSTOMARILY, UNTHINKINGLY **2 :** CONSISTENTLY, PERSISTENTLY, REPEATEDLY, USUALLY

**ha·bit·u·al·ness** *n* -ES **:** the quality or state of being habitual

**¹habituate** *adj* [LL *habituatus*] *obs* **:** formed by habit **:** HABITUAL

**²ha·bit·u·ate** \hə'bichə,wāt, *usu* -ād·+V\ *vt* -ED/-ING/-S [LL *habituatus*, past part. of *habituare*, fr. L *habitus* condition, appearance, habit — more at HABIT] **1 :** to make used to **:** ACCUSTOM, FAMILIARIZE ⟨*habituated* to courtly rhetoric —Francis Hackett⟩ ⟨trying to substitute coeducation, to ~ one sex to another so that difference of sex will be lost sight of —Margaret Mead⟩ **2** *obs* **:** to make (an action) habitual **3** *archaic* **:** to go to or be in frequently **:** FREQUENT

**ha·bit·u·a·tion** \=,=;=wāshən\ *n* -S [ME *habituacioun*, fr. ML *habituation-*, *habituatio*, fr. LL *habituatus* + L *-ion-*, *-io* -ion] **1 :** the act or process of making habitual or accustomed ⟨the essence of the tragedy of Macbeth — the ~ to crime —T.S. Eliot⟩ **2 a :** tolerance to the effects of a drug acquired through continued use and manifested by decreasing effectiveness of the same amount of drug administered in successive doses ⟨cathartic ~⟩ ⟨narcotic ~⟩ **b :** the psychic or emotional counterpart of acquired tolerance that is manifested by psychologic dependence upon a drug after a period of use — often distinguished from *addiction*

**¹ha·bit·u·a·tive** \=';=,wād·iv\ *adj* [²*habituate* + *-ive*] *of a grammatical form* **:** expressing habitual action or condition — compare INCIPIATIVE

**²habituative** \"\ *n* -S **:** an habituative form

**hab·i·tude** \'habə,tüd, -ə,tyüd\ *n* -S [ME *abitude*, fr. MF *habitude*, fr. L *habitudo*, fr. *habitus*, past part. of *habēre* to have, hold — more at GIVE] **1 a** *archaic* **:** native or essential character **:** normal constitution **b** *obs* **:** RELATION, RESPECT **2** *obs* **:** habitual association **:** FAMILIARITY **3 a :** habitual disposition or mode of behavior or procedure ⟨the sense of fitness and proportion that comes from years of ~ in the practice of an art —B.N.Cardozo⟩ **b :** HABIT, CUSTOM ⟨congressional investigation . . . has acquired the sanction of ~ —R.H.Rovere⟩ **syn** see HABIT

**hab·i·tu·di·nal** \,habə¦tüd(ᵊ)nəl, -ə¦tyü-\ *adj* [L *habitudin-*, *habitudo* + E *-al*] **:** relating to or associated with a habitude ⟨occupational and ~ diseases, such as . . . lead poisoning and extreme obesity —*Quarterly Rev.*⟩

**ha·bi·tué** \hə'bichə,wā, =;=¦=\ *n* -S [F, fr. past part. of *habituer* to frequent, fr. LL *habituare* — more at HABITUATE] **1 :** one who frequents a place ⟨Paris ~*s*⟩ or class of places ⟨an ~ of the theater⟩ **2 :** a drug addict

**hab·i·tus** \'habəd·əs\ *n, pl* **habitus** [NL, fr. L, condition, appearance, habit, character — more at HABIT] **1 a :** the body build and constitution esp. as related to predisposition to disease ⟨ulcer ~⟩ **:** HABIT 4a — see CONSTITUTIONAL TYPE **b :** HABIT 8 **2 a :** a mental power or faculty **b :** HABIT 6a

**hab·nab** \'(h)ab,nab\ *also* **hab** *or* **nab** \'(h)abə(r)'nab\ *adv* [fr. (assumed) ME dial. *habbe nabbe, habbe or nabbe* whether he (she, I) have or does (do) not have, fr. ME dial. *habbe*, 1st & 3d pers. sing. pres. subj. of *habben* to have (fr. OE *habban*) + ME *or* + ME dial. *nabbe*, 1st & 3d pers. sing. pres. subj. of *nabben* not to have, fr. OE *nabban*, fr. *ne* not + *habban* to have — more at HAVE, OR, NO] *now dial Brit* **:** in one way or another **:** by hook or crook

**ha·boob** \hə'büb\ *n* -S [Ar *habūb* violent wind] **:** a violent dust storm or sandstorm of northern Africa or India

**habro-** *comb form* [NL, fr. L, fr. Gk, fr. *habros*] **:** graceful — in generic names in zoology ⟨*Habronema*⟩

**hab·ro·brac·on** \ˌhabrōˈbrakən\ *n* [NL, fr. *habro-* + *Bracon* genus of ichneumon flies — more at BRACONIDAE] **1** *cap* **:** a genus of very small wasps (family Braconidae) that are parasitic on caterpillars and that are valuable for laboratory studies of genetics **2** -S *often cap* **:** any insect of the genus *Habrobracon*

**hab·ro·ne·ma** \-ˈnēmə\ *n, cap* [NL, fr. *habro-* + *-nema*] **:** a genus of parasitic nematode worms (family Spiruridae) having developmental stages in flies of the genera *Musca* and *Stomoxys* and adult stages in the stomach of the horse or the proventriculus of various birds — see HABRONEMIASIS, SUMMER SORES

**hab·ro·ne·mi·a·sis** \ˌhabrōnēˈmīəsəs\ *also* **hab·ro·ne·mo·sis** \-ˈmōsəs\ *n* -ES [NL, fr. *Habronema* + *-iasis* or *-osis*] **:** infestation with or disease caused by roundworms of the genus *Habronema* and characterized in the horse by gastric tumors and inflammation or by summer sores

**hab·ro·ne·mic** \ˌhabrōˈnēmik\ *adj* [NL *Habronema* + E *-ic*] **:** relating to or caused by worms of the genus *Habronema*

**ha·bu** \ˈhä(ˌ)bü\ *n* -S [native name in the Ryukyu islands] **:** a dangerously venomous pit viper (*Trimeresurus flavoviridis*) common in the Ryukyu islands

**ha·bu·ka** \ˈhäˌbükə\ *var of* HAPUKU

**ha·bu·tai** *or* **ha·bu·tae** \ˈhäbəˌtī\ *n* -S [Jap *habutae*, lit., glossy silk] **:** a soft lightweight Japanese silk in plain weave

**há·ček** \ˈhaˌchek\ *n* -S [Czech] **:** a diacritic ˇ placed over a letter (as in *č, ě, ğ, š*) to modify it **:** an inverted circumflex — called also *wedge*

**ha·cen·da·do** \ˌ(h)äsenˈdä(ˌ)dō\ *also* **ha·ci·en·da·do** \-sēe-\ *n* -S [Sp, fr. *hacienda*] **:** the owner or proprietor of a hacienda **:** rural landlord **:** LANDOWNER

**ha·cen·de·ro** \ˌ(h)äsenˈde(ˌ)rō\ *also* **ha·ci·en·de·ro** \-sēen-\ *n* -S [Sp. fr. *hacienda* + *-ero* -er] **:** HACENDADO

**ha·ché** \(h)äˈshā\ *adj* [F, fr. past part. of *hacher* to chop up, mince, hash, hatch (a map) — more at HASH] **:** MINCED, HASHED

¹**ha·chure** \haˈshů(ə)r, ˈhashər\ *also* **hatch·ure** \ˈhachə(r)\ *n* -S [F, *hachure*, fr. *hacher* + *-ure*] **:** a short line used for shading and denoting surfaces in relief (as in map drawing) and drawn in the direction of slope, being short, broad, and close together for a steep slope and long, narrow, and far apart for a gentle slope — compare CONTOUR LINE

²**hachure** \"\ *also* **hatchure** \"\ *vt* -ED/-ING/-S **:** to shade with or show by hachures — compare CROSSHATCH

**h acid** *n, usu cap H* **:** a crystalline acid $H_2NC_{10}H_4(OH)(SO_3H)_2$ made from naphthalene and used as a dye intermediate; 8-amino-1-naphthol-3,6-disulfonic acid

**ha·ci·en·da** \ˌ(h)äsēˈendə, ˌ(h)as-\ *n* -S [Sp, fr. L *facienda*, things to be done, neut. pl. of *faciendus*, fut. passive part. of *facere* to do, make — more at DO] **1 a :** a large estate (as a ranch or farm) in present or formerly Spanish-speaking countries **:** PLANTATION **b :** the main building of a farm or ranch **c :** the buildings of a mining or manufacturing establishment **2** *chiefly Southwest* **:** a ranch dwelling typically with low rambling lines and wide porches **3 :** the state revenue or its administration in a Spanish-speaking country ⟨was appointed minister of ∼⟩

¹**hack** \ˈhak\ *vb* -ED/-ING/-S [ME *hakken*, fr. OE *-haccian* (attested in *tōhaccian* to chop to pieces); akin to MLG *hacken* to hack, OHG *hacchōn*, OE *haca* door fastener, ON *haka* chin — more at HOOK] *vt* **1 a :** to cut with repeated irregular or unskillful blows ⟨was ∼*ed* to pieces with swords⟩ ⟨plaster had been ∼*ed* out of the wall⟩ **b :** to sever with repeated blows ⟨∼*ed* off a bough with his hunting knife⟩ **c :** to mangle or mutilate with or as if with cutting blows ⟨we ∼*ed* reputations to pieces —H.J.Laski⟩ ⟨the original story had been ∼*ed* almost beyond recognition⟩ **d :** to trim or shape by or as if by crude or ruthless strokes ⟨lyrical expressions ∼*ed* out with broad strokes of a brush charged with pure color —F.J.Mather⟩ ⟨huge sums were ∼*ed* off the original appropriation⟩ **2 :** to clear (a path or area) by cutting away vegetation ⟨∼*ed* their way through the jungle⟩ ⟨farms ∼*ed* out of the wilderness⟩ **3 a :** to break up the surface of (land) **b :** to break up the soil and sow (seed) at the same operation — used with *in* ⟨∼ in wheat⟩ **c :** to cut, trim, or uproot with a hack, hook, or sickle **4 :** CHIP *vt* **4** **5 a :** to roughen or dress (stone or concrete) with a hack hammer **b :** to tilt (a face brick) slightly in a wall so that the bottom is set in to prevent shadows **c :** to interrupt (a course of stones) by the use of two smaller courses in walling **6 :** to kick the shins of (an opposing player) in rugby **7** *chiefly Midland* **a :** ACHIEVE, MANAGE ⟨I can't quite ∼ it⟩ **b :** to put up with **:** TOLERATE ⟨I can't ∼ something like stealing —B.J.Friedman⟩ **8 :** to call out or give directions to (a bird dog) **9 :** to enter (a gamecock) in a single match **10** *chiefly Midland* **:** to disconcert and embarrass esp. by teasing **:** HECKLE ⟨he was so ∼*ed* he could hardly talk⟩ ∼ *vi* **1 :** to make cutting blows or rough cuts **:** CHOP ⟨∼*ing* away at the vines and shrubs⟩ **2** *now dial Eng* **:** to speak haltingly **:** STAMMER **3 :** to cough in a short dry manner **:** cause short dry coughing ⟨a ∼*ing* asthma⟩ **4 a :** to kick or kick at a rugby opponent's shins deliberately **b :** to strike or hold the arm of a basketball opponent with the hand **5** *slang* **:** LOAF, IDLE, KNOCK — used with *around* ⟨∼*ing* around at the corner drugstore —Ruth McKenney⟩

²**hack** \"\ *n* -S [ME *hak;* akin to MHG & MD *hacke* mattock, hoe, pickax; derivatives fr. the root of E ¹*hack*] **1 :** a tool or implement for hacking (as a pick, mattock, or hoe) **2 :** CUT, NICK, NOTCH; *esp* **:** a blaze cut in a tree **3** *now dial Eng* **:** a stumbling or stammering in speech **4 :** a short dry cough **5 a :** a hacking blow ⟨a vicious ∼ across the neck stunned him⟩ **b :** TRY, ATTEMPT, TURN, WHACK ⟨let me take a ∼ at it⟩ **c :** an individual match of gamecocks **6 :** a kick on the shins in rugby **7 :** a foothold cut in the ice four yards behind the tee in curling **8 a** *chiefly Midland* **:** a state of embarrassed confusion — often used with *under* ⟨he put Joe under ∼ teasing him about his girl⟩ **b :** restriction to quarters as punishment for naval officers — usu. used with *under* ⟨he had some of the officers under ∼ and some of the crew grumbling —Fletcher Pratt⟩

³**hack** \"\ *n* -S [blend of ¹*hatch* and ¹*heck*] **1 a :** the board on which a falcon's meat is served **b :** the state of partial liberty in which a falcon is kept before training — used chiefly with *at* ⟨kept at ∼⟩ ⟨flying at ∼⟩ **2 :** FRAME, GRATING: as **a :** a frame for drying fish or cheese **b :** a rack for feeding cattle **c :** a grating in a millrace or above a dam **3 :** a long low pile into which bricks are built for drying after being molded

⁴**hack** \"\ *vt* -ED/-ING/-S **1 :** to keep (a hawk) in a state of partial liberty **2 :** to put (fish or cheese) on a frame for drying

⁵**hack** \"\ *n* -S [short for *hackney*] **1 a** (1) **:** a horse let out for common hire (2) **:** a horse used in all kinds of work **b :** a horse worn out in service **:** JADE **c :** a light easy saddle horse; *esp* **:** a three-gaited saddle horse **2 a :** a coach or carriage let for hire **:** HACKNEY ⟨on horse, on foot, in ∼*s* and gilded chariots —Alexander Pope⟩ **b** *slang* **:** HEARSE **c** (1) **:** TAXICAB (2) **:** CABDRIVER **d** *slang* **:** CABOOSE **3 a :** one who hires out his professional service **:** one who forfeits individual freedom of action or initiative or professional integrity in exchange for wages or other assured reward **:** HIRELING, MERCENARY ⟨party ∼*s* have replaced earnest New Dealers —*New Republic*⟩; *esp* **:** a writer who works on order from publishers **b :** a writer whose writings aim mainly at commercial success rather than literary quality **c** *slang* **:** a prison guard or custodian **4 :** a watch or inferior chronometer for use in place of the standard chronometer in marking time when taking observations at sea

⁶**hack** \"\ *adj* **1 :** working for hire ⟨∼ attorney⟩ ⟨∼ critic⟩ **2 :** performed by, suited to, or characteristic of a hack **:** MEDIOCRE, UNINSPIRED ⟨∼ writing⟩ ⟨the staging and lighting were mostly on a ∼ level —*New Republic*⟩ **3 :** HACKNEYED, TRITE ⟨∼ dramatic scenes⟩

⁷**hack** \"\ *vb* -ED/-ING/-S *vt* **1 :** to make trite and commonplace by frequent and indiscriminate use ⟨the word "remarkable" has been so ∼*ed* —J.H.Newman⟩ **2** *archaic* **:** to employ as a hack writer **3 :** to use as a hack **:** let out (as a horse) for hire ∼ *vi* **1 :** to ride or drive at an ordinary pace or over the roads as distinguished from racing or riding across country **2 :** to become exposed or offered to common use for hire ⟨was then ∼*ed* in the park for a year before going to stud —Dennis Craig⟩ **3 :** to live the life of a literary drudge or hack **:** do hack writing **4 :** to ride in a hackney coach or in a taxicab **5 :** to operate a taxicab

**hackamatak** *var of* HACKMATACK

**hack·a·more** \ˈhakəˌmō(ə)r, -ˌó(ə)r, -ōə, -ˌó(ə)\ *n* -S [by folk etymology fr. Sp *jáquima*, fr. OSp *xaquima*, fr. Ar *shakīmah*] **1 :** a bridle that consists of a halter often of soft rope or braided horsehair, has a loop capable of being tightened about the nose in place of a bit, and is used esp. in breaking and training horses **2 :** a primitive or emergency bridle consisting of a continuous length of rope or rawhide with a slip noose at one end that is passed over the lower jaw, the free end being looped over the head behind the ears and slipped through the noose on the opposite side so as to serve as a single rein

**hackamore knot** *n* **:** a knot that consists of a loop formed by concentric hitches and is used as a sling for a jug or bottle or as a rope bridle for a horse

hackamore knot

**hackbarrow** \ˈ⸗,⸗(ˌ)⸗\ *n* [³*hack* + *barrow*] **:** a barrow for taking bricks from the molders to the hacks

**hackberry** \ˈhak- — *see* BERRY\ *n* [alter. of *hagberry*] **1 :** any of several No. American trees or shrubs of the genus *Celtis; esp* **:** a large round-headed tree (*C. occidentalis*) of eastern and central U.S. that has dark purple edible berries and is sometimes planted for shade or in shelterbelts — called also *sugarberry* **2 :** the pale to grayish or greenish yellow moderately hard tough wood of hackberry (esp. *C. occidentalis*)

**hack·but** \ˈhakˌbət\ *or* **hag·but** \-ag,-\ *n* -S [MF *haguebute, hacquebute*, modif. of MD *hakebusse* — more at HARQUEBUS] **:** HARQUEBUS

**hack·but·eer** \ˌhakbəˈti(ə)r\ *or* **hack·but·ter** \ˈhakˌbəd·ə(r)\ *n* -S [MF *haquebutier, hacquebutier*, fr. *haquebute, hacquebute* + *-ier* -er] **:** a soldier armed with a hackbut

**hacked** *past of* HACK

**hacked bolt** *n* [fr. past part. of ¹*hack*] **:** JAG BOLT

**hack·ee** \ˈhakē\ *n* -S [prob. of imit. origin] **:** CHIPMUNK

¹**hack·er** \ˈhakə(r)\ *n* -S [¹*hack* + *-er* (n. suffix)] **1 :** one that hacks: as **a** *dial Eng* **:** a hand implement or hooked fork for grubbing out roots **b :** one that handles green brick in ceramics manufacturing **c :** CHIPPER **d** **2 :** one who is inexperienced or unskilled in a sport ⟨an insouciance and grace in the man's movements which mean the difference between a willing courageous ∼ . . . and a great artist —Barnaby Conrad⟩

²**hacker** \"\ *vi* -ED/-ING/-S [¹*hack* + *-er* (v. suffix)] *dial Eng* **:** to hesitate in speaking **:** STAMMER

³**hacker** \"\ *n* -S [⁵*hack* + *-er*] **:** CABDRIVER

**hack·ery** \ˈhakərē\ *n* -ES [perh. fr. Bengali *hākārī* shouting (of drivers), fr. *hākā* shout] *India* **:** a bullock cart

**hack hammer** *n* [²*hack*] **:** a hammer that resembles an adz and is used in dressing stone and roughening

**hack·ia** \ˈhakēə\ *n* -S [fr. a native name in Brit. Guiana] **:** any of several tropical American trees (as of the genus *Tabebuia*) that yield notably hard heavy durable timber

**hack·ie** \ˈhakē, -ki\ *n* -S [⁵*hack* + *-ie*] **:** CABDRIVER

**hacking** *n* -S [fr. gerund of ¹*hack*] **:** the system of low cuts or scratches and grooves in a lap to hold diamond powder for cutting and polishing gems

**hacking coat** *or* **hacking jacket** *n* [fr. pres. part. of ⁷*hack*] **:** a riding jacket with slits at the side or at the back and slanted flap pockets

**hacking knife** *n* [fr. pres. part. of ¹*hack*] **:** a knife with a short blade and stout handle used for rough work (as removing old putty)

**hack·ing·ly** *adv* **:** in a hacking manner

¹**hack·le** \ˈ(h)akəl\ *n* -S [ME *hakel*, fr. OE *hacele* cloak; akin to OHG *hachul* mantle, ON *hökoll*, Goth *hakuls*, and prob. to OE *hēcen* kid, MLG *hōken* kid, OSlav *koza* goat] *now dial Eng* **:** any of various coverings: as **a :** the natural coat of an animal **b :** a bird's plumage **c :** a straw covering for a bee skep

²**hackle** \"\ *vt* -ED/-ING/-S *dial Eng* **:** to cover with a hackle

³**hack·le** \ˈhakəl\ *n* -S [ME *hakell, hekele* — more at HATCHEL] **1 :** a comb or board with long metal teeth for dressing flax, hemp, or jute **2 a :** one of the long narrow feathers on the neck or saddle of a bird (as the domestic fowl) **b :** the neck plumage of the male domestic fowl — see COCK illustration **3 hackles** *pl* **a :** erectile hairs along the neck and back of a dog or other animal **b :** TEMPER, DANDER ⟨don't get your ∼*s* up about nothing⟩ **4 a** *or* **hackle fly :** an artificial fishing fly made chiefly of the filaments of a cock's neck feathers **b :** filaments of cock feather projecting downward from the head of an artificial fly — see FLY illustration

⁴**hackle** \"\ *vt* **hackled; hackled; hackling** \-k(ə)liŋ\ **hackles 1 :** to separate the long fibers of (flax, hemp, or jute) from waste material and from each other by combing with a hackle **2 :** to furnish (a fishing fly) with a hackle

⁵**hackle** \"\ *vt* -ED/-ING/-S [freq. of ¹*hack*] **:** to chop up or chop off roughly **:** HACK

⁶**hackle** \"\ *n* -S *often attrib* **:** fracture (as of glass) that results in hackly edges ⟨the coarser the ∼ the more violent and sudden was the parting of the glass —C.J.Phillips⟩ ⟨∼ marks⟩ ⟨∼ structure⟩

**hackleback** \ˈ⸗⸗,⸗\ *n* -S [³*hackle* + *back*] **1** *also* **hackleback sturgeon** [so called fr. the projecting scales on its back] **:** SHOVELNOSE STURGEON **2 :** an untrimmed barrel stave

**hack·ler** \ˈhak(ə)lə(r)\ *n* -S [⁴*hackle* + *-er*] **:** one that hackles; *esp* **:** a worker who hackles hemp, flax, or broomcorn

**hacklog** \ˈ⸗,⸗\ *n* [¹*hack* + *log*] **:** CHOPPING BLOCK

**hack·ly** \ˈhak(ə)lē, -li\ *adj, sometimes* -ER/-EST [⁵*hackle* + *-y*] **:** looking as if hacked **:** ROUGH, JAGGED, BROKEN ⟨∼ fracture surface of a mineral⟩

**hack·man** \ˈhakmən\ *n, pl* **hackmen** [⁵*hack* + *man*] **:** CABDRIVER

**hack·man·ite** \ˈhakməˌnīt\ *n* -S [Victor *Hackman*, 19th cent. Finnish scientist + E *-ite*] **:** a sodalite containing a little sulfur and usu. fluorescing orange or red under ultraviolet light

¹**hack·ma·tack** \ˈhakməˌtak\ *n* -S [of Algonquian origin; akin to Abnaki *akemantak* snowshoe wood] **1 :** any of several coniferous trees: as **a :** a tamarack (*Larix laricina*) **b :** COMMON JUNIPER **2 :** the wood of hackmatack **3 :** BALSAM POPLAR

²**hackmatack** \"\ *also* **hack·a·ma·tak** \-kəm-\ *n* -S [alter. of *tacamahac*] **:** a tree (*Calophyllum tacamahaca*) that produces tacamahac

¹**hack·ney** \ˈhaknē, -ni\ *n* [ME *hakeney, hakenai*, prob. fr. *Hakeneye* Hackney, formerly a town, now a metropolitan borough of London, England] **1** -S **a :** a horse suitable for ordinary riding or driving **:** NAG **b :** a trotting horse used chiefly for driving **2 a** *usu cap* **:** a breed of rather compact usu. chestnut, bay, or brown horses with a conspicuously high knee and hock flexion in stepping that originated in and about Norfolk, England as a result of interbreeding local trotting mares with Thoroughbred and Arabian sires **b** -S *often cap* **:** a horse of this breed **3** -S **a** *obs* **:** a horse or pony kept for hire **b** *obs* **:** one that works for hire **:** DRUDGE, SLAVE **c** *obs* **:** PROSTITUTE **4** -S **:** a carriage or automobile kept for hire **:** HACK, CAB

²**hackney** \"\ *adj* **1 :** kept for public hire ⟨∼ cab⟩ ⟨∼ carriage⟩ **2 :** HACKNEYED **3** *archaic* **:** done or suitable for doing by a drudge

³**hackney** \"\ *vt* -ED/-ING/-S **1 a :** to make common or frequent use of (as a horse) **:** wear out in common service **b :** to make trite, vulgar, or commonplace **2** *obs* **:** to drive hard **:** wear out by driving **3** *archaic* **a :** to make coarse (the sensibilities) **b :** to make sophisticated or jaded (as through worldly experience) ⟨∼*ed* as he was in the ways of life —Tobias Smollett⟩

**hackney coach** *n* **:** a coach used as a hackney carriage; *esp* **:** a four-wheeled carriage drawn by two horses and having seats for six persons

**hackneyed** *adj* [fr. past part. of ³*hackney*] **:** COMMONPLACE ⟨∼ phrase⟩ ⟨∼ metaphor⟩ ⟨histrionic rhetoric and ∼ gesture —H.V.Gregory⟩ **syn** see TRITE

**hack·ney·man** \ˈhaknēmən, -nim-\ *n, pl* **hackneymen** [ME *hakeneyman*, fr. *hakeney* + *man*] **:** a man who hires out horses and carriages

**hackney pony** *n, often cap H* **:** a Hackney horse less than 14.2 hands high

**hacks** *pres 3d sing of* HACK, *pl of* HACK

**hacksaw** \ˈ⸗,⸗\ *n* [¹*hack* + *saw*] **:** a hand or power-driven fine-tooth saw with blade under tension in a bow-shaped frame for cutting metal or other hard materials

hacksaws

**hackster** *n* -S [¹*hack* + *-ster*] **1** *obs* **:** RUFFIAN, ASSASSIN **2** *obs* **:** PROSTITUTE

**hack·thorn** \ˈhakˌthórn\ *n* [part modif., part trans. of Afrik *haakdoring*, fr. *haak* hook + *doring* thorn] **:** a southern African wattle (*Acacia detinens*)

**hacktree** \ˈ⸗,⸗\ *n* [*hack*berry + *tree*] **:** HACKBERRY 1

**hack watch** *n* [⁵*hack*] **:** a watch having a device for stopping the balance so that the hour, minute, and sweep-second hands may be reset at a desired instant — compare ⁵HACK 4

**hackwork** \ˈ⸗,⸗\ *n* [⁶*hack* + *work*] **:** literary, artistic, or other professional work done on order or according to formula or conformity with commercial standards of quality; *esp* **:** work done by a hack writer ⟨the evil effect of ∼ and two wars upon an outstanding talent —V.S.Pritchett⟩

**hacky** \ˈhakē\ *adj* -ER/-EST [¹*hack* + *-y*] **:** HACKING ⟨a ∼ cough⟩

**hacqueton** *var of* HAQUETON

**had** *past of* HAVE — see PAST PERFECT

**ha·da·da** \ˈhädədə\ *n* -S [Afrik *hadida*, of imit. origin] **:** HADEDAH IBIS

**hadarim** *pl of* HEDER

**had·bot** *or* **had·bote** \ˈhädˌbōt\ *n* s [OE *hādbōt*, fr. *hād* person, degree + *bōt* remedy, recompense — more at -HOOD, BOOT] **:** recompense demanded under old English law for violence or insult to a person in holy orders

**hadden** *Scot past part of* HOLD

**had·der** \ˈhädər\ *chiefly Scot var of* HEATHER

**haddest** *archaic past 2d sing of* HAVE

**had·die** \ˈhädi\ *n* -S [by alter.] *Scot* **:** HADDOCK

**had·ding·ton·shire** \ˈhadiŋtənˌshi(ə)r, -ˌshər\ *or* **haddington** *adj, usu cap* [fr. *Haddingtonshire* or *Haddington* county (now usu. called *East Lothian*), Scotland] **:** EAST LOTHIAN

**had·do** \ˈha(ˌ)dō\ *n* -S [Nisqualli *huddoh*] **:** HUMPBACK SALMON

**had·dock** \ˈhadək\ *n, pl* **haddock** *also* **haddocks** [ME *haddok*] **1 :** an important food fish (*Melanogrammus aeglefinus*) of the family Gadidae that is usu. smaller than the common cod, has a black lateral line and a dark spot just behind the gills, and occurs on both sides of the Atlantic from Iceland south to the Mediterranean and Cape Hatteras **2 a :** HAKE **b :** ROSEFISH

**had·dock·er** \-kə(r)\ *n* -S **:** one that fishes for haddock

¹**hade** \ˈ(h)ād\ *n* -S [origin unknown] *now dial Eng* **:** an unplowed strip left between plowed parts of a field

²**hade** \ˈhād\ *vi* -ED/-ING/-S [origin unknown] **:** to deviate from the vertical (as of a vein, fault, or lode)

³**hade** \"\ *n* -S **:** the angle made by a rock fault plane or a vein with the vertical

**ha·de·an** \(ˈ)hāˈdēən\ *adj, usu cap* **:** of, relating to, or characteristic of Hades

**ha·de·dah ibis** \ˈhadədə-\ *n* [Afrik *hadida*, of imit. origin] **:** a largely grayish brown African ibis (*Hagedashia hagedash*) having the wing coverts tinged with iridescent green

**ha·den·doa** *or* **ha·den·do·wa** \həˈdendəwə\ *n, pl* **hadendoa** *or* **hadendoas** *or* **hadendowa** *or* **hadendowas** *usu cap* **1 :** a chiefly nomadic Beja-speaking people of Nubia between the Nile and the Red sea related to the Beni Amer and Bisharin **2 :** a member of the Hadendoa people

**ha·des** \ˈhāˌdēz\ *n, pl* **hades** *usu cap* [fr. *Hades*, god of the underworld, abode of the dead in Greek mythology, fr. Gk *Haidēs, Aidēs*] **1 :** the abode or state of the dead **:** the place of departed spirits — compare NETHERWORLD, SHEOL **2 :** HELL ⟨go to ∼⟩ ⟨hotter than ∼ out on the firing range⟩ ⟨what in ∼ are you doing here⟩

**hadfield manganese steel** \ˈhadˌfēl(d)-\ *n, usu cap H* [after Sir Robert *Hadfield* †1940 Eng. metallurgist] **:** a wear-resistant austenitic steel containing about 12 percent manganese and 1.2 percent carbon

¹**ha·dhra·mau·tian** *or* **ha·dra·mau·tian** \ˌhädrəˈmóshən\ *adj, usu cap* [*Hadhramaut, Hadramaut*, region of southeastern Arabia + E *-ian*] **:** of, relating to, or characteristic of the land, people, or dialect of Hadhramaut in southeastern Arabia

²**hadhramautian** *or* **hadramautian** \"\ *n* -S *usu cap* **:** HADHRAMI

**ha·dhra·mau·tic** \-ód·ik\ *n* -S *usu cap* [*Hadhramaut* + E *-ic*] **:** the Arabic dialect of Hadhramaut

**ha·dhra·mi** *or* **ha·dra·mi** \ˈhädrəmē\ *n, pl* **hadhrami** *also* **hadhramis** *or* **hadrami** *also* **hadramis** *usu cap* **1 :** an Arabian theocratic people living in the region between Aden and Oman in southern Arabia **2 :** a member of the Hadhrami people

**hading** *n* -S [fr. gerund of ²*hade*] **:** ³HADE

**ha·dith** \həˈdēth\ *also* **ha·dit** \-ēt\ *n, pl* **hadith** *or* **hadiths** *also* **hadit** *or* **hadits** *often cap* [Ar *ḥadīth*] **1 :** a narrative record of the sayings or customs of Muhammad and his companions **2 :** the collective body of traditions relating to Muhammad and his companions

**hadj** *var of* HAJJ

**hadj·e·mi** *or* **haj·e·mi** \ˈhajəmē\ *n* -S *cap* [Per] **:** a Persian of mixed Iranian and Turkish or Turkic stock

**hadji** *var of* HAJI

**had·land** \ˈ(h)adlənd\ *dial Eng var of* HEADLAND

**had·ley chest** \ˈhadlē-\ *n, usu cap H* [fr. *Hadley*, Mass.] **:** an Early American chest that has three panels in the front, a well, and one, two, or rarely three drawers and that is ornamented over the entire front with flat carving usu. involving a tulip motif and sometimes including the initials of the owner

**had·na** \ˈhadnə\ [by alter.] *Scot* **:** had not

**hadn't** \ˈhadᵊn(t)\ [by contr.] **:** had not

**hadn't ought** *chiefly dial* **:** ought not — usu. used with *to* ⟨you really *hadn't ought* to do that⟩

**had ought** *chiefly dial* **:** OUGHT — usu. used with *to* ⟨I *had ought* to go but I don't want to⟩

**hadr-** *or* **hadro-** *comb form* [NL, fr. L, fr. Gk, fr. *hadros* thick, bulky; akin to Gk *hadēn* enough — more at SAD] **:** thick ⟨*hadrome*⟩ **:** heavy ⟨*Hadrosaurus*⟩

**had·rome** \ˈhaˌdrōm\ *also* **had·rom** \ˈhadrəm\ *n* -S [G *hadrom*, fr. *hadr-* + *-om* -ome] **1 :** the part of the mestome that conducts water **2 :** the somewhat rudimentary xylem in cryptogams

**had·ro·me·ri·na** \ˌhadrōməˈrīnə\ *n pl, cap* [NL, fr. *hadr-* + *mer-* (part) + *-ina*] **:** an order of Demospongiae including the boring sponges

**had·ro·mycosis** \ˌhadrō+\ *n* [NL, fr. *hadr-* + *mycosis*] **:** infestation of the xylem of a plant by a fungus; *also* **:** a plant disease due to such a cause

**had·ro·my·cot·ic** \ˌhadrō(ˌ)mīˈkäd·ik\ *adj* [fr. NL *hadromycosis*, after such pairs as NL *psychosis:* E *psychotic*] **:** relating to or caused by hadromycosis

**had·ro·saur** \ˈhadrəˌsó(ə)r, -ó(ə)\ *n* -S [NL *Hadrosaurus*] **:** a dinosaur of the genus *Hadrosaurus* or family Hadrosauridae **:** DUCK-BILLED DINOSAUR

**had·ro·sau·rus** \ˌ⸗⸗ˈsórəs\ *n, cap* [NL, fr. *hadr-* + *-saurus*] **:** a genus (the type of a family Hadrosauridae) of heavy herbivorous dinosaurs found in the Cretaceous of No. America that attained a length of over thirty feet and had a large head with a broad bill like that of a duck and numerous small teeth

**hadst** *archaic past 2d sing of* HAVE

**hae** *chiefly Scot var of* HAVE & *chiefly Scot pres 1st sing & pres pl & Scot pres 2d sing of* HAVE

**haec·ce·i·tas** \hekˈsēəˌtas, hēk-\ *n* -ES [ML] **:** HAECCEITY

**haec·ce·i·ty** *or* **hec·ce·i·ty** \-əd·ē\ *n* -ES [ML *haecceitas*, fr. L *haec, haecce*, fem. of *hic, hicce* this + *-itas* -ity] **:** the status of being an individual or a particular nature **:** INDIVIDUALITY, SPECIFICITY, THISNESS; *specif* **:** what makes something to be an ultimate reality different from any other — compare QUIDDITY 2

¹**haeck·e·li·an** \(ˈ)heˈkēlēən\ *adj, usu cap* [Ernst H. *Haeckel* †1919, Ger. biologist + E *-ian*] **:** relating to Haeckel or his theories — compare RECAPITULATION THEORY

²**haeckelian** \"\ *n* -S *usu cap* **:** a believer in Haeckel's theories

**haeck·el·ism** \ˈhekə,lizəm\ *n* -s *usu cap* [Ernst H. *Haeckel* + E *-ism*] **:** Haeckel's theories and speculations
**haed** *past of* HA, *Scot past of* HAVE
**haeing** *Scot pres part of* HAVE
**haeltzuk** *usu cap, var of* HEILTSUK
**haem** *var of* HEME
**haem-** *or* **haemo-** — see HEM-
**haema-** — see HEMA-
**hae·ma·dip·sa** \,hēmə'dipsə, ,hem-\ *n, cap* [NL, fr. *hem-* + Gk *dipsa* thirst] **:** a genus of small tropical land leeches that are troublesome to men and animals esp. because their bites result in prolonged bleeding
**hae·ma·go·gus** \-'gōgəs\ *n, cap* [NL, fr. LL, adj., drawing off blood, fr. Gk *haimagōgos*, fr. *haim-* hem- + *-agōgos* (fr. *agein* to lead, drive) — more at AGENT] **:** a genus of strong-flying diurnal Neotropical mosquitoes including several vectors of jungle yellow fever
**hae·ma·moe·ba** \-'mēbə\ [NL, fr. *hem-* + *amoeba*] *syn of* PLASMODIUM
**hae·man·thus** \hē'man(t)thəs\ *n, cap* [NL, fr. *hem-* + *-anthus*; fr. the color of some of the flowers] **:** a genus of African bulbous herbs (family Amaryllidaceae) comprising the blood lilies and having flowers in a dense head with a whorl of colored spathes
**hae·ma·phy·sa·lis** \,hēmə'fīsələs, ,hem-\ *n, cap* [NL, fr. *hem-* + Gk *physallis* bladder] **:** a cosmopolitan genus of small eyeless ticks (family Ixodidae) some of which are disease carriers
**haemat-** *or* **haemato-** — see HEMAT-
**hae·mat·i·num** \hē'madənəm\ *also* **hae·mat·i·non** \-d-ə-,nän\ *n* -s [NL, fr. neut. of L *haematinus* blood-colored, fr. Gk *haimatinos* bloody, fr. *haimat-* hemat- + *-inos* -ine] **:** a hard opaque red glass made by the ancients; *also* **:** a modern imitation of this
**hae·ma·to·bran·chia** \,hēməd·ō'braŋkēə, ,hem-\ *n pl, cap* [NL, fr. *hemat-* + *-branchia*] *in some classifications* **:** a division of arthropods consisting of the trilobites, eurypterids, and king crabs — **hae·ma·to·branch·i·ate** \¦==¦braŋkēət, -ē,āt\ *adj*
**hae·ma·to·do·cha** \,hēməd·ō'dōkə, ,hem-, hē,mad·ə'-\ *n* -s [NL, fr. *hemat-* + Gk *dochē* receptacle] **:** a fibrous elastic sac in the palpus of male spiders that is distended with hemolymph during pairing
**hae·ma·to·pi·nus** \-'pīnəs\ *n, cap* [NL, fr. *hemat-* + *-pinus* (fr. Gk *pinein* to drink)] **:** a genus of sucking lice including various serious pests of domestic animals
**hae·mat·o·pus** \hē'madəpəs\ *n, cap* [NL, fr. *hemat-* + *-pus*] **:** a genus (the type of the family Haematopodidae) of shorebirds consisting of the oyster catchers
**hae·ma·tox·y·lon** \,hēmə'täksə,län, ,hem-\ *n* [NL, fr. *hemat-* + *-xylon*; fr. its red color] **1** *cap* **:** a genus of tropical American bushy and usu. thorny trees (family Leguminosae) having pinnate leaves and small yellow flowers borne in showy axillary racemes — see LOGWOOD **2** -s **:** the wood or dye of logwood
**-hae·mia** \'hēmēə\ — see -EMIA
**haemin** *var of* HEMIN
**hae·mo·bartonella** \¦hēmō, ¦hemō+\ *n* [NL, fr. *hemat-* + *Bartonella*] **1** *cap* **:** a genus of blood parasites (family Bartonellaceae) of various mammals believed to be rickettsiae related to the organism causing Oroya fever in man but not known to multiply in the host tissues or to cause any cutaneous eruption **2** *pl* **haemobartonellae :** any organism of the genus *Haemobartonella*
**hae·mo·do·ra·ce·ae** \,hēmōdə'rāsē,ē, ,hem-\ *n pl, cap* [NL, fr. *Haemodorum*, type genus (fr. *hem-* + Gk *dōron* gift) + *-aceae*] **:** a family of chiefly tropical plants (order Liliales) having flowers with three stamens and an inferior ovary arranged in a complex panicled inflorescence — **hae·mo·do·ra·ceous** \¦===¦rāshəs\ *adj*
**haemoglobin** *var of* HEMOGLOBIN
**hae·mo·gregarina** \¦hēmō, ¦hemō+\ *n, cap* [NL, fr. *hem-* + *Gregarina*] **:** a genus (the type of the family Haemogregarinidae) of coccidia that are parasites at different stages of their life cycle of the circulatory system of vertebrates and of the digestive tract of invertebrates — **hae·mo·gregarine** *or* **he·mo·gregarine** \"+\ *adj or n*
**hae·mon·cho·sis** \,hē,mäŋ'kōsəs\ *or* **hae·mon·chi·a·sis** \,hē,mäŋ'kīəsəs\ *n* -ES [NL, fr. *Haemonchus* + *-osis* or *-iasis*] **:** infestation with or disease caused by worms of the genus *Haemonchus* (esp. *H. contortus*), being typically characterized by anemia, digestive disturbances, and emaciation resulting from the bloodsucking habits of the worms
**hae·mon·chus** \hē'mäŋkəs\ *n, cap* [NL, fr. *hem-* + *-onchus* (irreg. fr. Gk *onkos* barb of an arrow)] **:** a widely distributed genus of nematode worms (family Trichostrongylidae) comprising chiefly a parasite (*H. contortus*) of the abomasum of sheep and other ruminants and rarely in man — see HAEMONCHOSIS
**haem·op·is** \hē'mäpəs\ *n, cap* [NL, fr. *hem-* + *-opis*] **:** a genus of large aquatic leeches (family Hirudinidae) that have few teeth or none and feed chiefly on small aquatic invertebrates
**hae·mo·pro·te·id** \,hēmō'prōd·ēəd, ,hem-\ *adj* [NL *Haemoproteidae*] **:** of or relating to the Haemoproteidae or to protozoans of this family
**hae·mo·pro·te·i·dae** \,hēmō(,)prō'tēə,dē, ,hem-\ *n pl, cap* [NL, fr. *Haemoproteus*, type genus + *-idae*] **:** a family of Haemosporidia related to the malarial parasites but having the schizogenous phases typically in visceral endothelium of various birds and including the two genera *Haemoproteus* and *Leucocytozoon*
**hae·mo·proteus** \¦hēmō, ¦hemō+\ *n, cap* [NL, fr. *hem-* + *Proteus*] **:** a genus of protozoan parasites occurring in the blood of certain birds (as pigeons)
**haem·or·rha·gia** \,hemə'rājēə\ *n* -s [L — more at HEMORRHAGE] **:** HEMORRHAGE
**hae·mo·spo·rid·ia** \,hēmōspə'ridēə, ,hem-\ *n pl, cap* [NL, fr. *hem-* + *-sporidia*] **:** an order of minute telosporidian protozoans parasitic at some stage of the life cycle in the blood cells of vertebrates that includes the malaria parasites (family Plasmodiidae), numerous bird parasites (family Haemoproteidae), and the piroplasms and related pathogens of cattle (family Babesiidae) — **hae·mo·spo·rid·i·an** \¦===¦ridēən\ *adj or n*
**hae·mu·li·dae** \hē'mjülə,dē\ [NL, fr. *Haemulon*, type genus (fr. *hem-* + Gk *oulon* gum) + *-idae*] *syn of* POMADASIDAE
**haen** *chiefly Scot past part of* HAVE
**haereditas** *var of* HEREDITAS
**ha·e·re·mai** \'hīä,rä'mä(,)ē, 'hīərə,mī\ *interj* [Maori, lit., come here] *Austral & NewZeal* — used to express welcome
**haeres** *var of* HERES
**haes** *Scot pres 3d sing of* HAVE
**haet** \'hāt\ *n* -s [contr. of *hae it* (in such phrases as *Deil hae it!* Devil take it!)] *chiefly Scot* **:** a small quantity **:** PARTICLE **:** WHIT
**haff** \'häf\ *n* -s [G, fr. LG, fr. MLG *haf* sea — more at HAVEN] **:** a long shallow lagoon separated from the open sea by a narrow sandbar or barrier beach (as on the Baltic coast of Germany)
**haf·fet** *or* **haf·fit** \'hafət\ *n* -s [ME (Sc dial.) *halfheid*, fr. *half* + *heid*, Sc var. of *hed* head — more at HEAD] *Scot* **:** CHEEK, TEMPLE; *esp* **:** the hair growing at the temple
**haff·lins** \'häflənz\ *var of* HALFLINGS
**ha·fiz** \'häfəz\ *n, pl* **hafiz** *or* **hafis** \-əs\ [Ar *ḥāfiẓ*, lit., one who remembers] **:** a Muslim who knows the Koran by heart — used as a title of respect
**haf·ner ware** \'häfnə(r)-\ *n, usu cap H* [G *hafnerware* pottery fr. *hafner* potter + *ware*] **:** mid-16th century German earthenware often in the form of stove tiles and heavy vessels
**haf·ni·um** \'hafnēəm\ *n* -s [NL, fr. *Hafnia* (Copenhagen), Denmark] **:** a high-melting gray tetravalent metallic element closely resembling zirconium chemically, occurring in most zirconium minerals, and useful because of its ready emission of electrons (as in filaments for incandescent lamps) — symbol *Hf*; see ELEMENT table
**¹haft** \'haft, 'häft\ *n* -s [ME, fr. OE *hæft*; akin to OE *hæft* bond, fetter, captive, OHG *haft* fetter, captivity, *hefti* handle, ON *hapt* fetter, *hepti* handle, Goth *hafts* burdened, *hafjan* to carry — more at HEAVE] **:** the handle of a weapon (as a sword or dagger) or tool (as a sickle, awl, file)
**²haft** \"\ *vt* -ED/-ING/-S [ME *haften*, fr. *haft*, n.] **:** to set in or furnish with a haft ⟨~ a dagger⟩
**³haft** \'(h)aft\ *vb* -ED/-ING/-S [prob. of Scand origin; akin to ON *heftha* to gain (land) by right of occupation, *hefth* possession, act of gaining by occupation, ON *hafa* to have — more at HAVE] *vt, dial Brit* **:** to accustom (sheep) to a different pasture ~ *vi, dial Brit* **:** to become settled or established esp. in a place of residence ⟨we are now nicely ~*ed* here⟩
**⁴haft** \"\ *n* -s **1** *dial Brit* **:** an established pasture **2** *dial Brit* **:** a dwelling place
**haf·ta·rah** *or* **haph·ta·rah** *or* **haf·to·rah** *or* **haph·to·rah** \,häftə'rä, häf'tōrə\ *n, pl* **hafta·roth** \,häftə'rōth\ *or* **hafta·rot** \-ōt\ *or* **haftarahs** *or* **haphtaroth** *or* **haphtarot** *or* **haphtarahs** *or* **haftoroth** *or* **haftorot** *or* **haftorahs** *or* **haphtoroth** *or* **haphtorot** *or* **haphtorahs** [Heb *haphṭārāh* conclusion] **:** one of the biblical selections esp. from the Books of the Prophets bearing on and read immediately after the parashah at the conclusion of the Jewish synagogue service on sabbaths, festivals, and fast days
**¹hag** \'hag, -aa(ə)g, -aig\ *n* -s [ME *hagge*, *hegge*, prob. fr. a shortened form of OE *hægtesse* harpy, witch; akin to MD *haghetisse* witch, OHG *hagzissa*, *hagazussa* harpy, witch; all fr. a prehistoric WGmc compound whose components are akin respectively to OE *haga* hedge and to G dial. (Westphalia) *dūs* devil; akin to Norw *tysja* elf, crippled woman, Gaulish *dusius* demon, incubus, Corn *dus*, *diz* devil, OE *dūst* dust — more at HEDGE, DUST] **1** *archaic* **a :** a female demon **:** FURY, HARPY **b :** an evil or frightening spirit **:** ELF, BOGEY, HOBGOBLIN ⟨blue meager ~, or stubborn unlaid ghost —John Milton⟩ **c :** NIGHTMARE **2 :** a woman who has compacted with the devil **:** WITCH ⟨you secret, black and midnight ~*s* —Shak.⟩ **3 a :** an ugly or evil-looking old woman **b :** a woman of haggard or slatternly appearance **c** *obs* **:** an old man **4 :** HAGFISH **5** [by shortening] **:** HAGDON
**²hag** \'(h)ag\ *vt* **hagged; hagged; hagging; hags 1** *dial Brit* **:** HARASS, HARRY **2** *dial Brit* **:** to urge on **:** GOAD **3** *dial Brit* **:** to tire out **:** FATIGUE
**³hag** \"\ *n* -s [ME, prob. fr. ON *hagi* enclosed pasture; akin to OE *haga* hedge] *dial Eng* **:** an enclosed wooded area **:** WOODS
**⁴hag** \"\ *vt* **hagged; hagged; hagging; hags** [ME *haggen*, of Scand origin; akin to ON *höggva* to chop — more at HEW] *dial Brit* **:** HACK, CHOP, HEW
**⁵hag** \"\ *n* -s [of Scand origin; akin to ON *högg* stroke (as of an ax or sword), blow, ravine, *höggva* to chop] **1** *dial Brit* **:** NOTCH, HACK **2** *dial Brit* **a :** a section of timber marked off for felling **b :** felled timber or brushwood **3** *dial Brit* **:** QUAGMIRE, MARSH, BOG **4** *dial Brit* **:** a firm spot in a bog **5** *dial Brit* **a :** the projection of peat where cutting has stopped **b :** the overhanging edge of a stream
**hag·berry** \'(h)agbəri\ *n* [*hag-* (of Scand origin; akin to ON *heggr* bird cherry, Sw *hägg*, Dan *hæg*) + berry — more at HEDGE] *dial Brit* **:** EUROPEAN BIRD CHERRY
**hagborn** \'=,=\ *adj* [¹*hag* + *born*] **:** born of a witch
**hagbut** *var of* HACKBUT
**hag·don** \'hagdən\ *n* -s [origin unknown] **:** any of several seabirds chiefly of the No. Atlantic: as **a :** SHEARWATER **b :** FULMAR
**ha·gen** \'hägən\ *adj, usu cap* [fr. *Hagen*, Germany] **:** of or from the city of Hagen, Germany **:** of the kind or style prevalent in Hagen
**ha·ge·nia** \hə'jēnēə\ *n, cap* [NL, fr. Karl Gottfried *Hagen* †1829 Ger. botanist + NL *-ia*] **:** a genus of pinnate-leaved Ethiopian trees (family Rosaceae) having large panicles of flowers — see BRAYERA
**hagfish** \'=,=\ *n* [¹*hag* + *fish*] **:** any of several marine cyclostomes (order Hyperotreta) that are related to the lampreys and in general resemble eels but have a round mouth surrounded by eight tentacles, a single nostril opening behind the pharynx, a tongue with horny teeth, and rudimentary eyes and labyrinthine apparatus and that feed upon fishes by boring into their bodies and consuming their viscera and flesh
**hagg** \'(h)ag\ *var of* ⁵HAG
**hag·ga·da** *or* **hag·ga·dah** \hə'gäd|ə, -gō|\ *n, pl* **hagga·doth** *or* **hagga·dot** \-|,dōt(h), -ōs\ *usu cap* [Heb *haggādhāh*, fr. *higgidh* to tell] **1** *or* **ag·ga·da** \ə'g-\ **:** explanatory matter occurring in rabbinical literature, often taking the form of story, anecdote, legend, or parable, and treating such varied subjects as astronomy, astrology, magic, medicine, mysticism **2 :** explanatory matter in the Talmud interpreting the Scriptures as distinguished from that regulating religious practice — compare HALAKAH, MIDRASH — **hag·gadic** \-'gadik, -'gäd-\ *also* **hag·gadi·cal** \-dəkəl\ *adj, often cap*
**hag·ga·dist** \hə'gädəst\ *n* -s *often cap* **:** a haggadic writer **:** a student of the Haggada — **hag·ga·dis·tic** \¦hagə¦distik\ *adj, often cap*
**¹hag·gard** \'hagə(r)d, 'haig- *sometimes* 'haag-\ *adj* [MF *hagard*] **1 a** *of a hawk* **:** caught after acquiring adult plumage **:** UNTAMED **b** *obs* **:** INTRACTABLE, WILLFUL **c** *obs* **:** WANTON, UNCHASTE ⟨if I do prove her ~ . . . I'll whistle her off —Shak.⟩ **2 :** wild in appearance: as **a** *of the eyes* **:** wild and staring **b** *of a person* **:** WILD-EYED ⟨staring his eyes, and ~ was his look —John Dryden⟩ **c :** having a worn or emaciated appearance caused by privation, suffering, anxiety, or age **:** HARROWED, GAUNT ⟨thin and worn, ~ from sleeplessness —Adria Langley⟩ — **hag·gard·ly** *adv* — **hag·gard·ness** *n* -ES
**²haggard** \"\ *n* -s **1 :** an adult hawk caught wild — compare EYAS **2** *obs* **:** an intractable person; *esp* **:** a woman reluctant to yield to wooing ⟨I have loved this proud disdainful ~ —Shak.⟩
**³hag·gard** \'(h)agəd\ *n* -s [of Scand origin; akin to ON *heygarthr* stockyard, fr. *hey* hay + *garthr* yard — more at HAY, YARD] *dial Brit* **:** a small plot of farm land; *esp* **:** an open area between the house and barn for keeping cattle or storing grain
**hagged** \'(h)agd\ *adj* [¹*hag* + *-ed*] **1** *dial Brit* **a :** BEWITCHED **:** ENCHANTED **b :** resembling a witch or a hag **2** *dial Brit* **:** HAGGARD, GAUNT
**hagging** *pres part of* HAG
**hag·gis** \'hagəs\ *n* -ES [ME *hagese*, *hagws*, *hagas*, prob. fr. *haggen* to hack, chop — more at HAG] **:** a pudding esp. popular in Scotland made of the heart, liver, and lungs of a sheep or a calf minced with suet, onions, oatmeal, and seasonings and boiled in the stomach of the animal
**hag·gish** \'hagish\ *adj* [¹*hag* + *-ish*] **:** resembling or characteristic of a hag — **hag·gish·ly** *adv* — **hag·gish·ness** *n* -ES
**¹hag·gle** \'hagəl, -aig-\ *vb* **haggled; haggled; haggling** \-g(ə)liŋ\ **haggles** [freq. of ⁴*hag*] *vt* **1 :** to cut roughly or clumsily **:** HACK ⟨~ a branch off⟩ **2** *archaic* **:** to annoy or exhaust with wrangling or heckling **:** NAG ~ *vi* **1 :** to cut roughly or clumsily **:** HACK ⟨~ at a branch of the tree⟩ **2 :** to bargain or make difficulties in reaching a bargain **:** WRANGLE ⟨when it comes to making peace, we must not ~ over trifles —H.J.Laski⟩ **3** *now chiefly dial* **:** to go wearily or haltingly
**²haggle** \"\ *n* -s **:** an act or instance of haggling
**³hag·gle** \'(h)agəl\ *n* -s [ME *hagel* — more at HAIL] *dial Eng* **:** HAIL
**hag·gler** \'hag(ə)lə(r), -aig-\ *n* -s **1 :** one that haggles **2** *dial chiefly Brit* **:** HUCKSTER 1
**hag·gy** \'hagē\ *adj* -ER/-EST [⁵*hag* + *-y*] *chiefly Scot* **:** boggy and uneven
**ha·gi** \'häge\ *n* -s [Jap] **:** a Japanese bush clover (*Lespedeza bicolor*)
**hagi-** *or* **hagio-** *comb form* [LL, fr. Gk, fr. *hagios*] **1 :** holy ⟨*hagio*grapha⟩ ⟨*hagio*scope⟩ **2 :** saints ⟨*hagio*graphy⟩
**ha·gia** \'hāgēə\ *n pl* [LGk, fr. neut. pl. of Gk *hagios*] **:** consecrated eucharistic elements in the Eastern Church
**ha·gi·gah** \hə'gēgə\ *or* **cha·gi·gah** \kə'-\ *n pl* [Heb *hăghīghāh*] **:** the voluntary sacrifices offered with the paschal lamb at the Passover and on other festivals by Jews on their pilgrimages to the temple at Jerusalem
**hag·i·oc·ra·cy** \,hagē'äkrəsē, ,hājē-\ *n* -ES [*hagi-* + *-cracy*] **:** government by a body of persons regarded as holy; *also* **:** a state so governed
**hag·i·og·ra·pher** \-fə(r)\ *n* -s [ML *hagiographus* (fr. LGk *hagiographos*) + E *-er*] **1 :** one of the writers of the 13 books forming the third division of the Hebrew Scriptures **2 :** a writer of hagiography
**hag·i·o·graph·ic** \¦hagēə¦grafik, ¦hājē-\ *or* **hag·i·o·graph·i·cal** \-fəkəl\ *adj* **:** of or relating to the 13 books forming the third division of the Hebrew Scriptures **:** of or relating to hagiography
**hag·i·og·ra·phist** \,hagē'ägrəfəst, ,hājē-\ *n* -s [LL *hagiographus* + E *ist*] **:** HAGIOGRAPHER
**hag·i·og·ra·phy** \-fē, -fi\ *n* -ES [*hagi-* + *-graphy*] **:** biography of saints **:** saints' lives **:** biography of an idealizing or idolizing character ⟨the tone is one of personal affection rather than of ~ or impartial assessment —*Times Lit. Supp.*⟩
**hag·i·ol·a·ter** \,hagē'älәd·ə(r), ,hājē-\ *n* -s [*hagi-* + *-later*] **:** one that invokes or worships saints
**hag·i·ol·a·trous** \¦==¦älə·trəs\ *adj* **:** of or relating to the invocation or worship of saints
**hag·i·ol·a·try** \-,=='älə·trē\ *n* -ES [*hagi-* + *-latry*] **:** the invocation or worship of saints
**hag·i·o·lith** \'hagēə,lith, 'hājē-\ *n* -s [*hagi-* + *-lith*] **:** a stone monument or edifice (as a dolmen, a menhir, or an obelisk) erected for religious or ceremonial purposes — **hag·i·o·lith·ic** \¦===¦lithik\ *adj*
**hag·i·o·log·ic** \¦hagēə¦läjik, ¦hājē-\ *or* **hag·i·o·log·i·cal** \-jəkəl\ *adj* **:** of or relating to hagiology
**hag·i·ol·o·gist** \,hagē'äləjəst, ,hājē-\ *n* -s **:** one skilled in hagiology
**hag·i·ol·o·gy** \-jē\ *n* -ES [*hagi-* + *-logy*] **:** the history or description of sacred writings or of sacred persons: as **a :** a narrative of the lives of saints **b :** a catalog of saints
**hag·i·o·scope** \'hagēə,skōp, 'hājē-\ *n* -s [*hagi-* + *-scope*] **:** an opening in the interior walls of a cruciform church so placed as to afford a view of the altar to those in the transept — called also *squint* — **hag·i·o·scop·ic** \¦===¦skäpik\ *adj*
**hag·let** \'haglət\ *n* -s [origin unknown] **:** SHEARWATER
**hag·me·na** \,hägmə'nä\ *sometimes cap, var of* HOGMANAY
**hag moth** *n* [¹*hag*] **:** a No. American eucleid moth (*Phobetron pithecium*) whose larva feeds on trees and shrubs
**hagride** \'=,=\ *vt* [¹*hag* + *ride*] **1 :** to afflict with or as if with a nightmare **:** oppress with dread or anxiety **:** HARASS, TORMENT ⟨the great martian panic which showed how *hagridden* the American public had become —D.W.Brogan⟩ **2 :** to burden unduly ⟨families *hagridden* by poverty would find . . . a better life —Dixon Wecter⟩ **:** OBSESS ⟨*hagridden* by social prejudice and suspicion —J.E.P.Grigg⟩
**hags** *pl of* HAG, *pres 3rd sing of* HAG
**hagseed** \'=,=\ *n* [¹*hag* + *seed*] **:** the offspring of a witch
**hag's taper** \'hagz-\ *also* **hagtaper** \'=,==\ *n, pl* **hag's tapers** *also* **hagtapers** [alter. of earlier *higgis taper*, *hickis taper*, *hightaper*, fr. *higgis*, *hickis*, *hig* (origin unknown) + *taper* (candle)] **:** MULLEIN **:** GREAT MULLEIN
**hagstone** \'=,=\ *n* **:** a naturally perforated stone used as an amulet against witchcraft
**hague** \'hāg\ *adj, usu cap* [fr. (*The*) *Hague*, Netherlands] **:** of or from The Hague, capital of the Netherlands **:** of the kind or style prevalent in the Hague
**hag·worm** \'(h)ag,wərm, -,wōm\ *n* [ME, prob. fr. *hagge* hag + *worm*] **1** *dial Eng* **:** a common snake (as an adder or viper) **2** *dial Eng* **:** BLINDWORM
**hah** *var of* HA
**¹ha-ha** \(')hä¦hä\ *interj* [ME, fr. OE *ha ha*, of imit. origin] — used to express amusement or derision
**²ha-ha** \'hä,hä, =¦=\ *also* **haw-haw** \'hȯ,hȯ, =¦=\ *n* -s [F *haha*, prob. fr. *haha*, interj. used to express surprise] **:** SUNK FENCE
**haham** *var of* HAKAM
**hahn·e·mann·ism** \'hänəmə,nizəm\ *n* -s *usu cap* [Samuel *Hahnemann* †1843 Ger. physician + E *-ism*] **:** HOMEOPATHY
**hai·a·ri** \hī'ärē\ *n* -s [native name in British Guiana] **1 :** FISH POISON **2 :** a plant of the genus *Lonchocarpus* that contains rotenone
**hai·a·tha·lah** \,hīə'tälə\ *n, pl* **haiathalah** *usu cap* **:** EPHTHALITE
**hai·da** \'hīdə\ *n, pl* **haida** *or* **haidas** *usu cap* **1 a :** a Skittagetan people of the Queen Charlotte islands, British Columbia, and Prince of Wales Island, Alaska **b :** a member of such people **2 :** the language of the Haida people **3 :** a language stock of the Na-dene phylum comprising Haida only — called also *Skittagetan* — **hai·dan** \-d°n\ *adj, usu cap*
**hai·ding·er·ite** \'hīdiŋə,rīt\ *n* -s [Wilhelm Karl von *Haidinger* †1871 Austrian mineralogist + E *-ite*] **:** a mineral $HCaAsO_4 \cdot H_2O$ consisting of white hydrous calcium arsenate
**hai·duk** \'hī,dük\ *n* -s [G *heiduck*, *haiduck*, fr. Hung *hajdúk*, pl. of *hajdú* robber] **1 :** a Balkan outlaw opposed to Turkish rule **2 :** a Hungarian mercenary foot soldier of a class eventually elevated to noble rank **3 :** a male attendant or servant in various European countries dressed in livery resembling the costume of Hungarian haiduks
**hai·fa** \'hīfə\ *adj, usu cap* [fr. *Haifa*, Israel] **:** of or from the city of Haifa, Israel **:** of the kind or style prevalent in Haifa
**hai·gle** \'hāgəl\ *var of* HAGGLE *vi* 3
**¹haik** *also* **haick** \'hīk, 'hāk\ *n, pl* **haiks** *or* **haika** *also* **haicks** [Ar *ḥā'ik*, *ḥayk*] **:** a voluminous piece of usu. white cloth worn as an outer garment by men and women in northern Africa
**²haik** *var of* HAKE
**hai·kai** \'hī,kī\ *n, pl* **haikai** [Jap] **:** an often playful type of Japanese verse or prose cultivated in the later feudal ages — compare HAIKU, HOKKU
**hai·kal** \'hī,käl, 'hā,-\ *n* -s [Syriac *haykal* & Heb *hēkhāl*, fr. Assyr-Bab *ēkallu*, fr. Sumerian *e gal* temple, palace, fr. *e* house + *gal* great] **1 :** a sanctuary of a Coptic church cut off from the nave by a screen and containing three altars **2 :** the main altar
**hai·ku** \'hī(,)kü\ *n, pl* **haiku** [Jap] **:** an unrhymed Japanese poem of three lines containing 5, 7, and 5 syllables respectively, referring in some way to one of the seasons of the year, and constituting a late 19th century development of the hokku
**hai·kwan tael** \'hī'kwän-\ *n* [*haikwan* fr. Chin (Pek) *hai³ kuan¹* maritime customs, lit., gate of the sea] **:** a unit of value used by the Chinese for reckoning customs duties **:** customs tael
**¹hail** \'hāl, *esp before pause or consonant* -āəl\ *n* -s [ME *hail*, *hagel*, *hawel*, fr. OE *hægl*, *hagol*; akin to OHG *hagal* hail, ON *hagl*, Runic Goth *haal* (name of a rune), Gk *kachlēx* pebble] **1 a :** precipitation in the form of small balls or lumps usu. consisting of concentric layers of clear ice and compact snow produced by the oscillation of raindrops within cumulonimbus clouds or by the freezing of raindrops from nimbus clouds **b** *archaic* **:** a shower of hail **:** HAILSTORM ⟨a very considerable portion of this country has been desolated by a ~ —Thomas Jefferson⟩ **2 :** something that gives the effect of falling hail ⟨a ~ of applause⟩ ⟨a ~ of shot kicked up river sand —F.B. Gipson⟩
**²hail** \"\ *vi* -ED/-ING/-S [ME *haylen*, *hawelen*, fr. OE *hagalian*, fr. *hagol*, n.] **1 :** to precipitate hail ⟨it rained and ~*ed*⟩ **2 :** to pour down like hail **:** strike in the manner of hail ⟨flak ~s upon the plane —*Science Yr. Bk.*⟩
**³hail** \"\ *interj* [ME *hail*, *heil*, fr. ON *heill*, fr. *heill*, adj., healthy — more at WHOLE] **1** — used to express acclamation ⟨~ to the chief —Sir Walter Scott⟩ ⟨~, King of the Jews —Mk 15:18 (RSV)⟩ **2** *archaic* — used as a salutation ⟨all ~, sweet madam, and fair time of day —Shak.⟩ ⟨good morrow to you both. *Hail* to your grace —Shak.⟩ **3 :** HURRAH — used to express good feeling or enthusiasm ⟨*hail*, *hail*, the gang's all here⟩
**⁴hail** \"\ *vb* -ED/-ING/-S [ME *hailen*, *heilen*, fr. *hail*, *heil*, interj.] *vt* **1 a :** SALUTE, GREET, ACCOST ⟨~*ed* the report with undisguised satisfaction —J.B.Matthews⟩ ⟨~*ed* him and gave him her hand —P.B.Kyne⟩ **b :** to greet with enthusiastic approval **:** ACCLAIM ⟨~ him as a hero⟩ ⟨~ the advances audio has made —R.D.Darrell⟩ **2 :** to greet or summon by calling to ⟨~ a passing ship⟩ ⟨~ a taxi⟩ **3** *chiefly Scot* **:** to reach (the goal) esp. in a game of shinny ~ *vi* **1 :** to call out; *esp* **:** to call a greeting to a passing ship ⟨the ship ~*ed* as we passed⟩ — **hail from :** to have origin or home base in **:** come from ⟨he *hails from* the hill country⟩
**⁵hail** \"\ *n* -s **1 :** an exclamation of greeting **:** SALUTATION ⟨he heard a ~ and his own name called —George Meredith⟩; *specif* **:** a shout of acclamation ⟨greeted the emperor with a ~⟩ **2 :** a calling to attract attention **:** act of hailing ⟨after such ~, the windward yacht shall at once allow the leeward yacht room to tack —Guy Pennant⟩ **3** *chiefly Scot* **a :** the cry uttered when a goal is struck in a game (as shinny) **b :** GOAL ⟨defeated by four ~*s*⟩ — **within hail :** within hearing distance ⟨*within hail* of the telephone —Nevil Shute⟩

**⁶hail** \"\ *var of* HALE

**hail columbia** *n, usu cap H&C* [euphemism; fr. *Hail Columbia* (1798), patriotic song by Joseph Hopkinson †1842 Am. jurist] **:** HELL ⟨give them *Hail Columbia*⟩

**hail·er** \'hālə(r)\ *n* -s **:** one that hails

**¹hail-fellow** \'=,=(,)=\ *or* **hail-fellow-well-met** \'=,=(,)='='\ *adj* [fr. the archaic salutations *hail, fellow!* & *hail, fellow! well met!*] **:** heartily informal **:** COMRADELY ⟨extended a *hail-fellow* hand —Edith Wharton⟩ ⟨a giant of a man — rough, hearty, violent, *hail-fellow-well-met* —Kenneth Roberts⟩

**²hail-fellow** \"\ *or* **hail-fellow-well-met** \"\ *n, pl* **hail-fellows** *or* **hail-fellows-well-met** **1 :** a boon companion **:** PAL ⟨all were *hail-fellows-well-met* by the time the convention opened —*Typewriter Topics*⟩ **2 :** the quality or state of comradeship ⟨there was a *hail-fellow-well-met*, a camaraderie, a gregariousness about it —*N.Y. Times*⟩

**hailing distance** *n* [fr. gerund of ⁴*hail*] **1 :** the limit to which a human voice is heard ⟨when a patron lives within *hailing distance* —*U.S. Post Office Manual*⟩ **2 :** a close proximity **:** short reach ⟨within *hailing distance* of knowledge —H.J. Muller⟩

**hail insurance** *n* [¹*hail*] **:** insurance against loss resulting from damage by hail esp. to growing crops

**hail mary** *n, usu cap H&M* [ME *hail Marie, heil Marie;* trans. of ML *Ave Maria* 1, 3

**hailproof** \'=,=\ *adj* **:** impervious to hail ⟨~ netting over tobacco plants⟩

**hails** *pl of* HAIL, *pres 3d sing of* HAIL

**hailshot** \'=,=\ *n, pl* **hailshot** [ME *hayle shotte*] *archaic* **:** small shot that scatters like hail

**hailstone** \'=,=\ *n* [ME, fr. OE *hagolstān* (akin to ON *haglsteinn* hailstone), fr. *hagol* hail + *stān* stone — more at HAIL, STONE] **:** a single ball or lump of ice falling from a cloud **:** a pellet of hail

**hailstorm** \'=,=\ *n* -s **1 :** a storm accompanied by hail **:** a shower of hail ⟨the rain changed to a violent ~ —*McClure's*⟩ **2 :** something that resembles a hailstorm in concentrated violence ⟨a ~ of contempt —William James⟩

**haily** \'hālē\ *adj* **:** made of or accompanied by hail

**haim** \'hām\ *chiefly dial var of* HAME

**haim·suck·en** \'hām,səkən\ *var of* HAMESUCKEN

**¹hain** \'(h)ān\ *vt* -ED/-ING/-S [ME *hanen, haynen,* fr. ON *hegna* to enclose; akin to MLG *hegenen* to enclose, MHG *heinen* to enclose, OHG *hagan* thornbush, ON *hagi* enclosed pasture — more at HAG] *dial Brit* **1 :** to fence or enclose (a tract of land) for grass **2 :** to put aside **:** SAVE, SPARE

**²hain** \"\ *vt* -ED/-ING/-S [ME *heyen, heynen* to raise, fr. OE *hēan,* fr. *hēah* high — more at HIGH] *dial Eng* **:** to cause (a price or fee) to be increased **:** RAISE

**hai·nai** \'(h)ī,nī\ *n, pl* **hainai** *or* **hainais** *usu cap* **1 :** a Caddo people of the Texas panhandle **2 :** a member of such people — compare HASINAI

**hai·nan·ese** \,hīnə¦nēz, -ēs\ *n, pl* **hainanese** *cap* [*Hainan,* island in the So. China Sea + E *-ese*] **:** a native or inhabitant of the Chinese island of Hainan

**hainch** \'(h)ānsh\ *dial Brit var of* HAUNCH

**haing** *pres part of* HA

**hain't** \(')(h)ānt\ [partly contr. of *have not, has not;* partly alter. of *ain't*] **:** AIN'T

**hai·phong** \'hī'fȯŋ\ *adj, usu cap* [fr. *Haiphong,* northern Vietnam] **:** of or from the city of Haiphong, northern Vietnam **:** of the kind or style prevalent in Haiphong

**¹hair** \'ha(a)(ə)r, 'he|, |ə\ *n* -s *often attrib* [ME *her, heer, hare, heir, hair,* fr. OE *hǣr;* akin to OFris *hēr* hair, OHG & ON *hār,* and perh. to MIr *carrach* scurfy, mangy, Lith *šerys* bristle, Skt kapucchala hair on the back of the head] **1 :** a slender threadlike outgrowth of the epidermis of an animal; *esp* **:** one of the usu. pigmented filaments that form the characteristic coat of a mammal, contain neither blood vessels nor nerves, and are composed chiefly of elongated and modified epidermal cells covered by a cuticle of flat imbricated cells that produce a rough surface — compare BRISTLE, HAIR FOLLICLE, ROOT, SPINE **2 a :** the hairy covering of an animal or of some particular part of him; *specif* **:** the coating of fairly coarse and relatively straight individual hairs on a human head — distinguished from *fur* and *wool* **b :** HAIRCLOTH **3 a** (1) **:** a minute distance or amount **:** TRIFLE ⟨won by a ~⟩ (2) **:** a precise degree **:** NICETY ⟨aligned to a ~⟩ **b :** something likened to hair ⟨~*s* of fire came up through the busted plates —Saul Bellow⟩ ⟨eucalyptus . . . tossed their purple-black ~ of leaves in the air —Eve Langley⟩ **4** *obs* **:** KIND, NATURE, CHARACTER ⟨the quality and ~ of our attempt brooks no division —Shak.⟩ **5 a :** a filamentous structure that resembles hair ⟨leaf ~⟩ **b :** BOW HAIR — **against the hair** *archaic* **:** contrary to the normal tendency **:** against the grain ⟨if you should fight, you go *against the hair* of your professions —Shak.⟩ — **hair of the dog :** a small amount of the cause of an ill used as a remedy for it; *specif* **:** a drink of liquor the morning after a drinking bout ⟨I'd fetched a bottle — a little of the *hair of the dog* would do me good —Ross Santee⟩ — **in one's hair :** persistently annoying ⟨people could be friendly without getting *in each other's hair* —J.R.Chamberlain⟩ — **in the hair 1** *of raw furs* **:** with the fur outward **2** *of hides* **:** with the hair on — **one's hair down :** one's normal reserve in abeyance ⟨management with *its hair down* —*Time*⟩ **:** one's guard down ⟨that doesn't mean you have to let *your hair down* and tell him all the innermost secrets of your business —Franklin Spier⟩ ⟨they took *their hair down* and we felt that we made progress . . . in getting the type of information we are after —J.P.Richards⟩ — **out of one's hair :** eliminated as an annoying factor ⟨keep the children of the guests occupied and *out of their mothers' hair* —Marvin Schwartz⟩

**²hair** \"\ *vb* -ED/-ING/-S *vt* **1 :** to remove hair from ⟨~ a hide⟩ **2 :** to apply hair to ⟨~ a doll⟩ ⟨~ a fiddlestick⟩ **:** cover with or as if with hair ⟨a thick, white hand . . . ~*ed* over with fine reddish fuzz —William Faulkner⟩ ~ *vi* **:** to produce hair or something resembling hair ⟨these woods would not ~ up —*Scientific American*⟩

**hair ball** \'=,=\ *n* **1 :** a compact mass of hair in the stomach occurring esp. during shedding in an animal (as a cat) that cleanses its coat by licking **2 :** PHYTOBEZOAR

**hairbeard** \'=,=\ *n* **:** a wood rush (*Luzula campestris*)

**hairbell** *n* **:** HAREBELL

**hairbird** \'=,=\ *n* [so called fr. its use of horsehair in its nest] **:** CHIPPING SPARROW

**¹hairbrain** \'=,=\ *n* -s [by folk etymology] **:** HAREBRAIN

**²hairbrain** \"\ *adj* **:** HAREBRAINED

**hairbrained** \'=¦=\ *adj* [by folk etymology] **:** HAREBRAINED

**hair-branch tree** *n* **:** an African shrub (*Trichocladus crinitus*) of the family Hamamelidaceae

**hair brand** *n* **:** a temporary cattle brand made by scorching or picking out the hair without scarring the skin and used esp. by rustlers

**¹hairbreadth** *or* **hairsbreadth** \'=,=\ *n* **1 :** a narrow margin ⟨lost the governorship by a ~ —W.V.Shannon⟩ **2 :** HAIR 3a

**²hairbreadth** \"\ *adj* **:** having the breadth of a hair **:** very narrow ⟨~ escape⟩

**hair brown** *n* **:** a dark gray to brownish gray that is lighter and slightly redder than beaver gray — called also *argali, limestone, quail*

**hairbrush** \'=,=\ *n* **1 :** a brush for the hair **2 :** a brush made of hair

**hair calf** *n* **:** SLINK 1

**haircap moss** *n* **:** a moss of the genus *Polytrichum* (esp. *P. juniperinum*)

**hair cell** *n* **:** a cell with hairlike processes; *esp* **:** one of the sensory cells in the auditory epithelium of the organ of Corti

**¹hair-check** \'=,=\ *n* **:** a fine crack resulting from shrinkage on the surface of concrete or paint — **hair-checking** \'=,==\ *n*

**²hair-check** \"\ *vi* **:** CRAZE *vi* 3

**haircloth** \'=,=\ *n* -s **1 :** any of various stiff wiry fabrics having a hair weft esp. of horsehair or camel's hair and a cotton, linen, or wool warp and being used for upholstery or stiffening in garments **2 :** an article of haircloth; *esp* **:** HAIR SHIRT

**haircomb** \'=,=\ *n* **:** a way of combing the hair ⟨this form of ~ was almost a tradition among old-time bartenders —Herman Goodman⟩

**hair compass** *n* **:** a compass that permits of minute adjustment

**haircut** \'=,=\ *n* **1 :** the act or process of cutting and shaping the hair **2 :** a hairstyle achieved by cutting and shaping

**haircutter** \'=,==\ *n* **:** one that cuts hair

**haircutting** \'=,==\ *n* **:** the art or occupation of a barber

**hair dividers** *n pl* **:** HAIR COMPASS

**hairdo** \'=,=\ *n* -s **:** a way of dressing the hair ⟨go in for elaborate ~*s* —Agnes M. Miall⟩; *esp* **:** a modish coiffure for women ⟨season's favorite ~ —*N.Y. Times*⟩

**hair-drawn** \'=¦=\ *adj* **:** HAIRSPLITTING ⟨impatient of such *hair-drawn* distinctions —S.H.Adams⟩

**hairdress** \'=,=\ *n* **:** COIFFURE

**hairdresser** \'=,==\ *n* **1 :** one whose business or occupation is hairdressing and giving beauty treatments **:** COSMETOLOGIST **2** *Brit* **:** BARBER ⟨having a shave at the *hairdresser's* —A.J. Liebling⟩

**hairdressing** \'=,==\ *n* **1 a :** the action or process of washing, cutting, curling, or arranging the hair **b :** the occupation of a hairdresser **c :** HAIRDO **2 :** a dressing (as a pomade) for the hair

**haired** \'ha(a)|(ə)rd, 'he|, |əd\ *adj* [ME *hered,* fr. *her, heer* + *-ed*] **:** having hair — usu. preceded by a descriptive term ⟨corn ~⟩ ⟨*fair-haired*⟩ ⟨wavy ~⟩ ⟨sparsely ~ leaves⟩

**hair·en** \'harən\ *adj* [ME *heren,* fr. OE *hǣren,* fr. *hǣr* hair + *-en* — more at HAIR] *chiefly dial* **:** made of hair

**hair fern** *n* [short for *maidenhair fern*] **:** MAIDENHAIR

**hair-fibered** \'=¦=\ *adj, of plaster* **:** containing fiber as a binder

**hair follicle** *n* **:** the tubular epithelial sheath surrounding the lower part of a hair shaft and enclosing at the bottom a vascular papilla that supplies the growing basal part of the hair with nourishment — compare ROOT

**hair grass** *n* **1 :** any of several grasses having slender wiry stems or leaves: as **a :** ROUGH BENT **b :** any of several grasses of the genera *Deschampsia, Muhlenbergia,* and *Aira* **2 :** any of several fine-leaved strictly aquatic spike rushes including some that are popular as aerators for the balanced aquarium

**hair grip** *n, chiefly Brit* **:** BOBBY PIN

**hairhound** \'=,=\ *n* [by folk etymology] **:** HOREHOUND

**hair hygrometer** *n* **:** an absorption hygrometer with a sensitive element of human hair

**hairier** *comparative of* HAIRY

**hairies** *pl of* HAIRY

**hairiest** *superlative of* HAIRY

**hair·i·ness** \'ha(a)rēnəs, 'her-, -rin-\ *n* -ES [ME *heryness,* fr. *hery, heeri* hairy + *-ness*] **:** the quality or state of being hairy

**hairing** *pres part of* HAIR

**hair kiln** *n* **:** a kiln floor which consists of open-woven horsehair cloth supported on laths of wood and on which hops are placed to dry

**hairlace** *n* [ME *harlas,* fr. *har, heer* hair + *las* lace] *obs* **:** a fillet (as of net) for the hair

**hair·less** \'ha(a)|(ə)rləs, 'he|, |əl-\ *adj* **:** lacking hair — **hair·less·ness** *n* -ES

**hairlike** \'=,=\ *adj* **:** resembling a hair **:** elongated, slender, and filamentous ⟨~ appendages of a crustacean⟩

**¹hairline** \'=,=\ *n* **1** *archaic* **:** a cord (as a fishline) made of hair **2 a :** a very slender line ⟨faint ~ of light around the edges of the windows —Shirley A. Grau⟩; *specif* **:** a tiny line or crack on a surface (as of paint) **b :** a very small difference **:** narrow margin ⟨the ~ that divides the comic from the grotesque —Wolcott Gibbs⟩ **c** (1) **:** a fine line connecting thicker strokes in a printed letter — called also *thin stroke* (2) **:** a fine line on a printer's rule or ornament (3) **:** a fine line drawn or etched for reproduction (as on a steel engraving) (4) **:** a fine strand of surplus metal on the face of newly cast type or slugs **:** WHISKER **d** (1) **:** a printed or woven textile design consisting of lengthwise or crosswise lines usu. one thread wide (2) **:** a fabric with such a design **3 a :** the line at which the hair meets the scalp ⟨receding ~⟩ **b :** the way the hair frames the face ⟨has a nice ~⟩ — **to a hairline** *adv* **:** to a nicety **:** with exactitude ⟨matched *to a hairline*⟩

**²hairline** \"\ *adj* **1 :** of or relating to a very slender line **:** THIN ⟨~ mustache⟩ ⟨~ shading⟩ **2 a :** hinging on very small differences **:** CLOSE ⟨~ victory⟩ **b :** marked by exactitude **:** PRECISE ⟨~ accuracy⟩

**hair man** *n* **:** an operator of a machine in which cattle hair is washed, dried, and baled

**hair moss** *n* [by shortening] **:** HAIRCAP MOSS

**hair moth** *n* **:** a moth that destroys goods made of hair or fur; *esp* **:** WEBBING CLOTHES MOTH

**hairn** \'härn\ *var of* HARN

**hairnet** \'=,=\ *n* **:** an open-meshed net made usu. of human hair or silk and worn over the hair to keep it in place

**hair orchid** *n* **:** a Himalayan orchid (*Trichosma suavis*) with yellowish purple-streaked flowers

**hair pencil** *n* **1 :** a brush or pencil made of fine hair (as of a camel) and used in painting **2 :** a close tuft of hairs occurring on parts of the body of certain caterpillars

**hairpiece** \'=,=\ *n* **:** TOUPEE 2

**¹hairpin** \'=,=\ *n* **1 :** a pin to hold the hair in place; *specif* **:** a two-pronged U-shaped pin made of wire, plastic, or bone **2 a :** something shaped like a hairpin; *specif* **:** a sharp turn in a road having relatively parallel approaches ⟨at the top of a long swinging ~ he looked back and saw the moving lights of a car —Wallace Stegner⟩ **b :** two closed slalom gates placed one immediately below the other on a ski slope

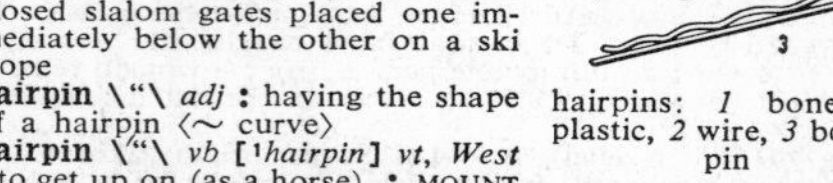


hairpins: *1* bone or plastic, *2* wire, *3* bobby pin

**²hairpin** \"\ *adj* **:** having the shape of a hairpin ⟨~ curve⟩

**³hairpin** \"\ *vb* [¹*hairpin*] *vt, West* **:** to get up on (as a horse) **:** MOUNT ⟨*hairpinning* . . . at sight anything on four hoofs —P.A.Rollins⟩ ~ *vi* **:** to make a hairpin turn ⟨the road ~*s* up the mountainside —Tom Marvel⟩

**hairpin lace** *n* **:** a lace with looped edges made by crocheting around the prongs of a U-shaped needle

**hair pyrites** *n* [so called fr. its interwoven capillary crystals that suggest a wad of hair] **:** MILLERITE

**hair-raiser** \'=,==\ *n* **:** one that is hair-raising **:** CHILLER ⟨the ingredients for an old-fashioned *hair-raiser* —*Theatre Arts*⟩

**hair-raising** \'=,==\ *adj* **:** making the hair stand on end: **a :** causing fear or shock **:** TERRIFYING ⟨have listened to some *hair-raising* confessions in my time —Mary R. Rinehart⟩ **b :** causing surprise or excitement **:** THRILLING ⟨no vivid or brilliant or *hair-raising* item of song or dance —*Dance News*⟩ — **hair-rais·ing·ly** *adv*

**hairs** *pl of* HAIR, *pres 3d sing of* HAIR

**hair salt** *n* [trans. of G *haarsalz*] **1 :** ALUNOGEN **2 :** epsomite when in silky fibers

**hairsbreadth** *var of* HAIRBREADTH

**hair seal** *n* **1 :** a seal whose coat lacks underfur **2 a :** the fur of the hair seal **b :** an article made of this fur

**hairsheep** \'=,=\ *n* [so called fr. the fact that the hide comes fr. a sheep that grows hair instead of wool] **:** a leather used in bookbinding — compare CABRETTA

**hair shirt** *n* **1 :** a shirt made of coarse rough animal hair worn next to the skin as a penance ⟨led him . . . to give himself to fasting, a *hair shirt,* and prayer —K.S.Latourette⟩ **2 :** one that flagellates **:** SCOURGE ⟨the *hair shirt* of duty —L.D.Lewis⟩ ⟨uncomfortable to live with — a regular *hair shirt* of a man —E.B.White⟩ — **hairshirted** *adj*

**hair sieve** *n* [ME *herseve,* fr. *her, heer* hair + *seve* sieve] **:** a strainer with a haircloth bottom

**hairslip** \'=,=\ *n* **:** loosening of the hair from a hide due to improper or inadequate curing

**hair snake** *n* **:** HORSEHAIR SNAKE

**hair sofa** *n* **:** a sofa upholstered in haircloth

**hair space** *n* **:** a very thin space used in printing (as the ½-point copper space or the 1-point brass space)

**hairspace** \'=,=\ *vt* [*hair space*] **:** to set with hair spaces

**hairsplitter** \'=,==\ *n* **:** one that indulges in hairsplitting **:** QUIBBLER

**¹hairsplitting** \'=,==\ *adj* **:** making excessively fine or trivial distinctions in reasoning ⟨ancient ~ technicalities of special pleading —Charles Sumner⟩ ⟨tricky ~ statesmen —Weston La Barre⟩

**²hairsplitting** \"\ *n* **:** hairsplitting reasoning or argument ⟨an excessive penchant for intellectual and verbal ~ —J.W. Beach⟩

**hairspring** \'=,=\ *n* **:** a slender spiraled recoil spring that regulates the motion of the balance wheel of a timepiece — called also *balance spring*

**hairst** \'hārst\ *chiefly Scot var of* HARVEST

**hair·stane** \'hār,stān\ *Scot var of* HOARSTONE

**hairstone** \'=,=\ *n* [prob. trans. of G *haarstein*] **:** quartz thickly penetrated with hairlike crystals of rutile, actinolite, or other mineral

**hair straightener** *n* **:** an agent (as heat or a chemical preparation) used for straightening kinky hair

**hairstreak** \'=,=\ *n* **:** any of various small butterflies of *Strymon* and related genera usu. having striped markings under the wings and thin filamentous projections from the hind wings

**hair stroke** *n* **1 :** a delicate stroke in writing **2 :** SERIF

**hairstyle** \'=,=\ *n* **:** a way of wearing the hair **:** COIFFURE

**hairstyling** \'=,==\ *n* **:** the art or practice of a hair stylist

**hair stylist** *n* **:** one who designs individualized hairdos esp. for women and often dresses the hair in the suggested style

**hairtail** \'=,=\ *n* [so called fr. the fact that the tail ends in a hairlike filament] **:** CUTLASS FISH

**hair trigger** *n* **:** a gun trigger so delicately adjusted that it releases the cock at the slightest touch

**hair-trigger** \'=,==\ *or* **hair-triggered** \'=,==\ *adj* [*hair trigger*] **1 a :** disposed to react quickly ⟨*hair-trigger* children who needed only a leader . . . to break into happy riot —John Steinbeck⟩ **b :** immediately responsive to the slightest stimulus ⟨*hair-trigger* nerves⟩ ⟨there is a *hair-trigger* ferocity about leopards —Alan Moorehead⟩ **c :** marked by promptness **:** INSTANTANEOUS ⟨*hair-trigger* service on inquiries —J.J. Canavan⟩ **2 :** delicately adjusted or easily disrupted ⟨*hair-trigger* schedule⟩ ⟨*hair-trigger* balance⟩

**hair-trigger flower** *n* **:** an Australian plant of the genus *Stylidium* (esp. *S. graminifolium*) whose column of stamens reacts sensitively to the touch

**hair trunk** *n* **:** a trunk covered with hide from which the hair has not been removed

**hairweed** \'=,=\ *n* **1 :** a filamentous green alga **2 :** any of several plants of the genus *Cuscuta; esp* **:** CLOVER DODDER

**hairwood** \'=,=\ *n* [by alter.] **:** HAREWOOD 2

**hairwork** \'=,=\ *n* **1 :** the making of wigs, switches, and other articles from hair **2 :** articles made of hair

**hair worker** *n* **:** one that combs, sorts, and washes hair for use in hairwork

**hairworm** \'=,=\ *n* **:** any of various very slender elongated worms: as **a :** a worm of the nematode genus *Capillaria* **b :** a worm of the order Gordioidea **:** HORSEHAIR SNAKE

**¹hairy** \'ha(a)rē, 'her-, -ri\ *adj* -ER/-EST [ME *heery,* fr. *heer* hair + *-y*] **1 :** covered with or as if with hair ⟨~ ape⟩ ⟨~ overcoat⟩; *specif* **:** having a downy fuzz on the stems and leaves ⟨~ lotus⟩ **2 :** made of or resembling hair ⟨~ gown and mossy cell —John Milton⟩ **3 a :** rough and broken **:** RUGGED ⟨we are getting into some ~ country —Adrian Bell⟩ **b :** CRUDE, FRIGHTENING, UNPLEASANT ⟨~ bodyguard⟩ ⟨had some pretty ~ moments —L.A.Viereck⟩

**²hairy** \"\ *n* -ES **:** one that is hairy; *specif* **:** a draft horse with heavy feathering on the legs

**hairy armadillo** *n* **:** a peludo (*Euphractus villosus*)

**hairy arum** *n* **:** a foul-smelling aroid (*Helicodiceros muscivorus*) of southern Europe with hairy purple spadix

**hairy-bait** \'=,=\ *n* **:** LUGWORM

**hairy-chested** \'=¦==\ *adj* **:** full of strength or vigor **:** ROBUST ⟨*hairy-chested* mining history —Phil Spelman⟩

**hairy china cardamom** *n, usu cap 1st C* **:** an aromatic seed of a Chinese herb (*Amomum villosum*) used as a substitute for true cardamom

**hairy chinch bug** *n* **:** a bug closely related to and possibly a short-winged variety of the chinch bug that is sometimes destructive to turf in the northeastern U.S.

**hairy crab** *n* **:** a subglobose crab of the group Dromiacea having the body partially covered with bits of algae and debris

**hairy crabgrass** *n* **:** CRABGRASS 1a

**hairy-foot** \'=,=\ *n, pl* **hairy-foots** [so called fr. the hairy down at the base of the stem] **:** an inedible mushroom (*Marasmius personatus*) related to the fairy-ring mushroom

**hairy frog** *n* **:** any of three large western African frogs of the genus *Astylosternus* (family Ranidae) having hairlike outgrowths of skin on the sides of the trunk and thighs

**hairy grama** *n* **:** a grama (*Bouteloua hirsuta*) having the rachis prolonged beyond the spikelets as a naked point and the leaf blades sparsely hairy — called also *black grama*

**hairy greenweed** *n* **:** a southern European shrub (*Genista pilosa*) cultivated as forage for sheep

**hairy head** *also* **hairy crown** *n* **1 :** HOODED MERGANSER **2 :** RED-BREASTED MERGANSER

**hairy honeysuckle** *n* **:** a twining shrub (*Lonicera hirsuta*) of moist woodlands of the northern and eastern U.S. and adjacent Canada with dull dark green leaves that are sessile or short-petioled and pubescent on both surfaces and with crowded terminal spikes of orange or yellow flowers

**hairy indigo** *n* **:** a shrubby perennial (*Indigofera hirsuta*) with hirsute stems and foliage, flowers in dense clusters, and the calyx lobes often nearly as long as the petal that is native to Asia, Africa, and Australia and has been introduced into the southern U.S. as a forage and soil-improvement crop

**hairy lip fern** *n* **:** WOOLLY LIP FERN

**hairy-nosed wombat** \'==,=-\ *n* **:** a southern Australian wombat (*Lasiorhinus latrifrons*) distinguished by an extremely hairy rhinarium

**hairy pipewort** *n* **:** a low herb (*Lachnocaulon anceps*) of the family Eriocaulaceae of the southeastern U.S. having a 3-angled hairy scape

**hairy rat** *n* **:** a long-tailed Australian rat (*Mesembryomys hirsutus*)

**hairy root** *n* **:** a phase of the crown-gall disease esp. in apples characterized by abnormal development of fine fibrous roots

**hairy saki** *n* **:** a tropical American monkey (*Pithecia monacha*) with a purplish brown face covered with short white hair and a body coat that varies from black to brown and yellowish white

**hairy shore crab** *n* **:** YELLOW SHORE CRAB

**hairy solomon's seal** *n, usu cap 1st S* **:** a pubescent alternate-leaved perennial herb (*Polygonatum pubescens*) of eastern No. America

**hairy spurge** *n* **:** a much-branched hirsute weed (*Euphorbia hirsuta*) that has decumbent or prostrate stems in a dense mat and is native to northeastern No. America

**hairy sumac** *n* **:** STAGHORN SUMAC

**hairy-tailed mole** \'==,=-\ *n* **:** BREWERS' MOLE

**hairy vetch** *or* **hairy tare** *n* **:** a European vetch (*Vicia villosa*) extensively cultivated as a cover and early forage crop

**hairy willow herb** *n* **:** a European willow herb (*Epilobium hirsutum*) with a stout hairy stem and rose-purple flowers

**hairy woodpecker** *n* **:** a common No. American woodpecker (*Dendrocopos villosus*) closely resembling but larger than the downy woodpecker

**hais·la** \'hīslə\ *n, pl* **haisla** *or* **haislas** *usu cap* **1 :** a Kwakiutl people of British Columbia — compare WAKASHAN **2 :** a member of the Kwakiutl people

**hait** \'hāt\ *interj* [ME] *chiefly Scot* — used to urge on an animal

**haith** \'hāth\ *interj* [prob. euphemism for *faith*] *chiefly Scot* — used as a mild oath

**hai·thal** \'hī,täl\ *n, usu cap* **:** EPHTHALITE

**hai·ti** \'hād·|ē, -āt|, |i\ *adj, usu cap* [fr. *Haiti,* country in the West Indies] **:** of or from Haiti **:** of the kind or style prevalent in Haiti **:** HAITIAN

**¹hai·tian** \'hāshən, 'hād·|ēən, -āt|, |iən\ *adj, usu cap* [*Haiti* + E *-an*] **1 :** of, relating to, or characteristic of the island of Haiti **2 :** of, relating to, or characteristic of the people of Haiti

**²haitian** \"\ *n* -s **1** *cap* **:** a native or inhabitant of Haiti — compare TAINO **2** *or* **haitian creole** *usu cap H&C* **:** CREOLE 4b

**hai·tsai** \'hī'tsī\ *n* -s [Chin (Pek) *hai³-t'sai⁴,* fr. *hai³* sea + *t'sai⁴* herb, green vegetable] **1 :** a transparent gelatinous substance prepared from a red alga (*Gloiopeltis tenax*) and used by the Chinese for lanterns and windows and for stiffening cloth **2 :** the alga that yields haitsai

**hai·ver** \'hāvə(r)\ *var of* HAVER

**ha·je** \'hājē\ *n* -s [Ar *ḥayyah* snake] **:** an Egyptian cobra (*Naja haje*)

**hajemi** *cap, var of* HADJEMI

**haji** *or* **hadji** *or* **hajji** \ˈhajē\ *n* -s [Ar *ḥajjī*, fr. *ḥajj*] **:** one who has made a pilgrimage to Mecca — often used as a title

**ha·jib** \ˈhä,jib\ *n* -s [Ar *ḥājib*, lit., one who prevents from entering] **:** a Muslim court official often corresponding to a chamberlain or a prime minister

**hajj** *or* **hadj** *or* **haj** \ˈhaj\ *n* -ES [Ar *ḥajj*] **:** the pilgrimage to Mecca prescribed as a religious duty for Muslims

**ha·ka** \ˈhä(,)kä\ *n* -s [Maori] **:** a Maori posture dance accompanied by rhythmic chanting

**ha·ka·foth** *or* **ha·ka·fot** *or* **hak·ka·foth** *or* **hak·ka·fot** \ˈhäkə,fōth, -ōs, -ōt\ *n pl* [Heb *haqqāphōth*, pl. of *haqqāphāh* circuit] **:** a ceremony in the Jewish synagogue typically on Simhath Torah in which members of the congregation carrying the scrolls of the Torah make seven processional circuits around the bimah to the accompaniment of traditional hymns and songs

**ha·kam** *or* **ha·ham** \ˈhäkäm\ *also* **cho·chem** \ˈkōkəm\ *n, pl* **haka·mim** *or* **haha·mim** \,käkäˈmēm\ [Heb *ḥākhām* wise, wise man; *chochem* fr. Yiddish *khokhem*, fr. Heb *ḥākhām*] **1 :** one learned in Jewish law **:** WISE MAN; *specif, pl* **:** the rabbinical interpreters of biblical law of the first two Christian centuries whose interpretations are recorded in the Mishnah and contemporary works **2 :** a title given to a rabbi by the Sephardic Jews

[1]**hake** \ˈhāk\ *n, pl* **hake** *also* **hakes** [ME] **1 :** any of several fishes (the genus *Merluccius*) that are related to the cods but often regarded as forming a separate family and several of which are of importance as food fishes **2 :** any of various marine fishes of *Urophycis* and related genera (family Gadidae) resembling the cod and having narrow filamentous pelvic fins placed under the throat — called also *codling;* compare SILVER HAKE, SQUIRREL HAKE, STOCKFISH, WHITE HAKE **3 :** NORTHERN WHITING

[2]**hake** \ˈ"\ *vi* -ED/-ING/-S **:** to fish for hake

[3]**hake** \ˈ"\ *vi* -ED/-ING/-S [ME *haken*] **1** *chiefly Scot* **:** to wander around idly **:** LOAF **2** *chiefly Scot* **:** to trudge or tramp — often used with *about* or *around*

[4]**hake** \ˈ"\ *n* -s **:** a person in the habit of haking

[5]**hake** \ˈ(h)āk\ *n* -s [prob. of Scand origin; akin to Icel *haki* hook — more at HOOK] **1** *dial Eng* **:** HOOK; *esp* **:** POTHOOK 1 **2** *dial Eng* **:** a clevis of a plow

[6]**hake** *or* **haik** \ˈhāk\ *n* -s [prob. by alter.] **:** [3]HACK 2

**ha·kea** \ˈhākēə, ˈhāk-\ *n, cap* [NL, after C. L. von *Hake* †1818 Ger. horticulturist] **:** a genus of Australian shrubs and small trees (family Proteaceae) having evergreen often spiny leaves and showy flowers in dense clusters — see CUSHION-FLOWER

**ha·ken·kreuz** \ˈhäkən,krȯits\ *n, pl* **hakenkreu·ze** \-tsə\ *or* **hakenkreuzes** *often cap* [G, fr. *haken* hook (fr. OHG *hācko, hāko*) + *kreuz* cross, fr. OHG *krūzi*, fr. L *cruc-, crux* — more at HOOK, CROSS] **:** the swastika used as a symbol of German anti-Semitism or of German under Nazi government

**ha·ken·kreuz·ler** \-tslə(r)\ *n, pl* **hakenkreuzler** *or* **hakenkreuzlers** *usu cap* [G, fr. *hakenkreuz*] **:** a member of any German-speaking organization in Europe after World War I using the swastika as an emblem of anti-Semitism or of extreme nationalist sentiment

[1]**ha·kim** \həˈkēm\ *n, pl* **hakims** \-mz\ *also* **hu·ka·ma** \,hakəˈmä\ [Ar *ḥakīm*, lit., wise one] **:** a Muslim physician

[2]**ha·kim** \ˈhä,kēm\ *n, pl* **hakim** *or* **hakims** [Ar *ḥākim*] **:** a Muslim ruler, governor, or judge

**hak·ka** \ˈhäkˈkä, ˈhakə\ *n, pl* **hakka** *or* **hakkas** *usu cap* **1 a :** a people of the Yellow River plain that migrated into the hilly areas of southeastern China possibly during the T'ang dynasty **b :** a member of such people **2 :** a dialect of Chinese spoken in part of Kwangtung province

**hakkafot** *or* **hakkafoth** *var of* HAKAFOTH

**ha·ko** \ˈhä(,)kō\ *n* -s [Pawnee] **:** a Pawnee Indian ceremony representing the union of Heaven and Earth and the birth of life performed with prayers, invocation by pipe, and eagle dances to ensure long life and posterity to the participants

**ha·ko·da·te** \,häkəˈdädā\ *adj, usu cap* [fr. *Hakodate*, Japan] **:** of or from the city of Hakodate, Japan **:** of the kind or style prevalent in Hakodate

**hal-** *or* **halo-** *comb form* [F, fr. Gk, fr. *hals* salt — more at SALT] **1 :** of or relating to a salt ⟨*halo*chromism⟩ **2** [ISV, fr. *halogen*] **a :** halogen ⟨*hal*ide⟩ **b** *now usu* **halo-** **:** containing halogen ⟨*halo*alkyl groups⟩ — compare CHLOR- 3

**ha·la** \ˈhälə\ *n* -s [Hawaiian] **:** a screw pine (*Pandanus odoratissimus* syn. *P. tectorius*) native from southern Asia west to Hawaii having a trunk supported by a clump of slanting aerial roots, branches ending in spiral tufts of long narrow leaves which are used for plaiting mats, baskets, and hats, and fruits resembling pineapples but falling apart on ripening into many wedge-shaped yellow to red sections which are used as food in Micronesia and for leis in Polynesia

**hal·a·car·i·dae** \,haləˈkarə,dē\ *n pl, cap* [NL, fr. *Halacarus*, type genus (fr. *hal-* + *Acarus*) + *-idae*] **:** a small family of leathery-bodied free-living mites (group Hydrachnellae) that frequent marine algae

**ha·laf·ian** \həˈläfēən\ *also* **ha·laf** \həˈläf\ *adj, usu cap* [fr. Tell *Halaf*, site in northeastern Syria on the Turkish border near the village of Ras el 'Ain] **:** of or belonging to an early Aeneolithic culture of Syria and north Mesopotamia characterized by the use of stone as well as copper, adobe buildings, and a fine polychrome pottery

**ha·la·kah** *or* **ha·la·chah** *or* **ha·la·cha** \häˈläkä, ,häläˈkä, həˈläkə\ *n, pl* **ha·la·kahs** \-käz, -kəz\ *or* **ha·la·koth** *or* **ha·la·choth** \häˈlä,kōth, ,häläˈkōth, -ōt, -ōs\ *often cap* [Heb *hălākhāh*, lit., way] **:** the body of Jewish oral laws supplementing written law or both oral and written law together or any particular law or custom prescribed by the legal codices

**ha·lak·ic** *or* **ha·lach·ic** \həˈlakik\ *adj, often cap* **:** of or relating to the halakah

**ha·lal** \həˈläl\ *vt* **halalled; halalled; halalling; halals** [Ar *ḥalāl* that which is lawful] **:** to slaughter for food according to Moslem law

**ha·lal·cor** \-,kō(ə)r\ *n* -s [Hindi *halālkhor*, fr. Per, fr. Ar *ḥalāl* + Per *khor* eating] **:** a person in Iran and India to whom any food is lawful

**ha·la·pe·pe** \,häləˈpāpē\ *n* -s [Hawaiian] **:** a tree (*Dracaena aurea*) of the Pacific islands having flowers resembling lilies and yielding a wood used for carving

**hal·ate** \ˈha,lāt\ *n* -s [*hal-* + *-ate*] **:** a salt of chloric, bromic, or iodic acid

**ha·la·tion** \hāˈlāshən, hə-, ha-\ *n* -s [*halo* + *-ation*] **1 :** the spreading of light beyond its proper boundaries in a developed photographic image (as around a window facing the sky in an interior view or around other bright objects) caused principally by reflection from the back of the film or plate **2 :** a bright ring that sometimes encompasses the point at which a bright light shows on a television screen

**halavah** *var of* HALVAH

**hal·a·zone** \ˈhalə,zōn\ *n* -s [*hal-* + *az-* + *-one*] **:** a white crystalline powdery acid $C_6H_4(SO_2NCl_2)COOH$ used as a disinfectant for drinking water; *para-(N,N'*-dichloro-sulfamyl)-benzoic acid

**hal·berd** \ˈhalbərd, ˈhȯlb-, ˈhäl-\ *or* **hal·bert** \-rt\ *n* -s [ME *haubert, halberd*, fr. MF *hallebarde*, fr. MHG *helmbarte*, fr. *helm* handle + *barte* ax, fr. OHG *barta*, fr. *bart* beard; akin to OHG *halb* handle — more at HELVE, BEARD] **:** a weapon used esp. in the 15th and 16th centuries that consists typically of a battle-ax and pike mounted on a shaft about six feet long

heads of halberds

**hal·berd·ier** \ˈ==ˈdi(ə)r\ *n* -s [MF *hallebardier*, fr. *hallebarde* + *-ier* -er] **:** a person armed with a halberd; *esp* **:** a guard who carries a halberd as a symbol of his duty

**hal·chid·ho·ma** \,halchəˈdōmə\ *n, pl* **halchidhoma** *or* **halchidhomas** *usu cap* **1 :** an Indian people in the Colorado River valley near the mouth of the Gila allied with the Maricopa **2 :** a member of the Halchidhoma

[1]**hal·cy·on** \ˈhalsēən\ *n* [ME *alceon, alicion*, fr. L *halcyon, alcyon*, fr. Gk *halkyōn, alkyōn*] **1 -s a :** a bird identified with the kingfisher that was fabled by the ancients to nest at sea in a floating nest about the time of the winter solstice and to calm the waves during incubation **b :** KINGFISHER **2** [NL, fr. L *halcyon, alcyon*] *cap* **:** a genus of large kingfishers widely distributed in warmer parts of the Old World

[2]**halcyon** \ˈ"\ *adj* **1 :** belonging to or suggestive of the period commonly reckoned as 14 days assumed by the ancients to occur at the time of the winter solstice during the nesting period of the halcyon ⟨~ calm⟩ **2 a :** pleasingly or idyllically calm or peaceful **:** SERENE ⟨a ~ atmosphere⟩ **b :** HAPPY, GOLDEN ⟨a ~ era⟩ ⟨the ~ days of youth⟩ **c :** PROSPEROUS, AFFLUENT ⟨the ~ days of the clipper-ship trade⟩ **syn** see CALM

**hal·dane's law** *or* **haldane's rule** \ˈhȯl,dānz-\ *n, usu cap H* [after John B. S. *Haldane* b1892 Scottish geneticist] **:** a principle in genetics: when in an interspecific cross one sex is absent, rare, or sterile in the offspring, that sex is heterogametic

**hal·dan·ite** \ˈhȯl(,)dä,nīt, -,də,-\ *n* -s *usu cap* [James Alexander *Haldane* †1851 and Robert *Haldane* †1842, his brother, Scot. clergymen and evangelists + E *-ite*] **:** a follower of an evangelical movement in Scotland led by the Haldane brothers

**hal·du** \ˈhäl(,)dü\ *n* -s [Hindi *haldū*] **1 :** a timber tree (*Adina cordifolia*) of the family Rubiaceae with light-yellow even-grained wood **2 :** the wood of haldu

[1]**hale** *also* **hail** \ˈhāl, *esp before pause or consonant* -āəl\ *adj* -ER/-EST [partly fr. ME (northern dial.) *hal, hale*, fr. OE *hāl*; partly fr. ME *hail, heil*, fr. ON *heill* — more at WHOLE] **1 :** free from defect, disease, or infirmity **:** SOUND, HEALTHY, ROBUST ⟨a ~ body⟩ ⟨~ in youth⟩ **2** *chiefly Scot* **:** WHOLE **syn** see HEALTHY

[2]**hale** \ˈ"\ *adv* [partly fr. ME *hal, hale*, fr. *hal, hale*, adj.; partly fr. ME *hail, heil*, fr. *hail, heil*, adj.] *now dial Brit* **:** WHOLLY

[3]**hale** \ˈ"\ *vb* -ED/-ING/-S [ME *halen*, fr. MF *haler* — more at HAUL] *vt* **1 :** HAUL, PULL, DRAW **2 :** to compel (a person) to go ⟨~ a vagrant into court⟩ **3** *obs* **:** VEX, ANNOY ~ *vi* **1** *obs* **:** to move briskly (as of a ship) **2** *now dial Brit* **:** to pour or flow copiously ⟨the sweat was *haling* off him⟩ **3 :** to pull or tug ⟨*haling* at the plow⟩ **syn** see PULL

[4]**ha·le** \ˈhä(,)lā\ *n* -s [Hawaiian] *in Hawaii* **:** HOUSE

**hal·e·co·mor·phi** \,haləkōˈmȯr,fī\ *n pl, cap* [NL, fr. L *Halec*, genus of fish (fr. L *halec, halex, alec, allec* fish brine) + NL *-o-* + *-morphi*] *syn of* CYCLOGANOIDEI

**hal·e·cos·to·mi** \,haləˈkästə,mī\ *n pl, cap* [NL, fr. *Halec* + NL *-o-* + *-stomi*] **:** an order of extinct ganoid fishes resembling herrings

**hale·ness** *n* -ES **:** the quality or state of being hale ⟨the ~ of the old man at 90 was surprising⟩

**ha·le·nia** \həˈlēnēə\ *n, cap* [NL, fr. Johann *Halen*, 19th cent. Ger. botanist + NL *-ia*] **:** a genus of herbs (family Gentianaceae) with opposite leaves and spurred flowers — see SPURRED GENTIAN

[1]**hal·er** \ˈhālə(r)\ *n* -s [[3]*hale* + *-er*] **:** one that hales

[2]**ha·ler** \ˈhälər, -,le(ə)r\ *n, pl* **halers** \-rz\ *or* **hale·ru** \-,lə,rü\ [Czech, fr. MHG *hallære, haller, heller* — more at HELLER] **:** a monetary unit of Czechoslovakia equal to 1/100 of the koruna — see MONEY table

**hales** \ˈālz\ *n pl* [prob. of Scand origin; akin to ON *hali* tail, pointed end; akin to Gk *kēlon* arrow, MIr *cail* spear, Skt *śala* stick, porcupine quill] *dial Eng* **:** handles on an implement (as a plow or a wheelbarrow)

**ha·le·sia** \həˈlēzh(ē)ə, hāˈ-\ *n* [NL, fr. Stephen *Hales* †1761 Eng. physiologist + NL *-ia*] **1** *cap* **:** a genus of small trees (family Styracaceae) of southeastern No. America having alternate leaves and white bell-shaped flowers borne in great profusion before the leaves — see SILVER BELL **2** -s **:** any plant of the genus *Halesia*

**hale·some** \ˈhālsəm\ *adj* [ME (northern dial.) *halsum*, fr. *hal, hale* healthy + *-sum* -some — more at HALE] *chiefly Scot* **:** WHOLESOME

**hale water** *n, chiefly Scot* **:** a heavy rainfall

**ha·ley-over** \ˈhālē==\ *n* [origin unknown] **:** ANTONY OVER

[1]**half** \ˈhaf, haa(ə)f, hai|, hȧ|, hä|; *in sense 2b the f is often lost when "past" follows*\ *n, pl* **halves** \|vz\ [ME, fr. OE *healf*; akin to OHG & Goth *halba* side, half, ON *halfa*, L *scalpere* to cut, scratch, Gk *skalops* mole (animal), OE *sciell* shell — more at SHELL] **1** *obs* **:** PART, SIDE **2 a :** one of two equal parts into which a thing is divisible ⟨~ of it⟩ ⟨~ of the profits⟩; *also* **:** a part of a thing approximately equal to the remainder ⟨the larger ~ of the fortune⟩ **:** a sizable portion ⟨the bottom ~ of the social pyramid —N.E.Eliason⟩ — often used without *of* esp. when a quantitative word follows ⟨~ the money⟩ **b :** half an hour — used in designation of time ⟨~ past ten⟩ ⟨~ after five⟩ **3 :** one of a pair: as **a :** PARTNER **b :** SEMESTER, TERM **c** (1) **:** one of the two playing periods usu. separated by an interval that together make up the playing time of certain games (as football) — see QUARTER 21b (2) **:** the turn of one team to bat in baseball ⟨first ~ of the eighth inning⟩ **4 a :** HALF CROWN **b :** HALF-DOLLAR **5 :** significant part **:** CRUX, WHOLE — used with a negative ⟨that's not the ~ of it⟩ **6** [by shortening] **:** HALFBACK **7 :** HALF TIME — **and a half** *slang* **:** of great size, importance, difficulty, or perplexity ⟨a job *and a half*⟩ — **by half** *adv* **:** by a great deal **:** far and away ⟨too stupid *by half*⟩ — **by halves** *adv* **:** inadequately or incompletely **:** HALFHEARTEDLY ⟨let's not do things *by halves*⟩ — **half a mind :** more or less of an intention ⟨*have half a mind* to go swimming⟩ **:** more or less intending ⟨am *half a mind* to go swimming⟩ — **in half** *adv* **:** into two equal or nearly equal parts ⟨cut an apple *in half*⟩

[2]**half** \ˈ"\ *adj* [ME, fr. OE *healf*; akin to OHG *halb* half, ON *halfr*, Goth *halbs*, OE *healf*, n.] **1 a :** being one of two equal parts ⟨a ~ share⟩ ⟨a ~ sheet of paper⟩ **b** (1) **:** amounting to nearly half **:** approximately a half (2) **:** PARTIAL, IMPERFECT ⟨~ knowledge of a subject⟩ **2 a :** reaching only half the normal distance ⟨a ~ gunshot away⟩ **b :** extending or covering only half (as of the regular or normal area) ⟨a ~ window⟩ ⟨a ~ mask⟩ **c :** covering the backbone and one quarter of the boards away from the backbone and sometimes the corners ⟨a book bound in ~ leather⟩ ⟨a *half*-vellum binding⟩ — compare FULL 12c **d :** PART-TIME ⟨working only ~ days⟩ ⟨~ shift⟩ **3** *chiefly Brit* **:** of a species of small size — used of birds and sometimes of fish

[3]**half** \ˈ"\ *adv* [ME, fr. *half*, adj.] **1 a :** in an equal part or degree **b :** only partially **:** not completely **:** IMPERFECTLY ⟨~ digested⟩ ⟨~ persuaded⟩ **2 a :** at all **:** REALLY — used with a negative ⟨a performance that wasn't ~ bad⟩ **b :** used with a negative and before a verb to imply the opposite of what is expressed ⟨didn't ~ beat up the policeman⟩ **3 a :** by half an hour less ⟨~ ten o'clock⟩ — used chiefly in Scotland and Ireland **b :** used before a numeral in designating soundings to add one half to the numeral ⟨~ six fathoms⟩ **c :** used in the nomenclature of points of the compass between the names of two points to designate a position or direction half a point from the first compass point in the direction of the second

**hal·fa** \ˈhalfə\ *var of* ALFA

**half-a-crown** \ˈ==ˈ=\ *n* **1 :** HALF CROWN **2 :** the sum of two shillings and sixpence

**half a dollar** *n* **:** HALF-DOLLAR

[1]**half-and-half** \ˈ==ˈ=\ *n* **:** something that is half one thing and half another: as **a :** a mixture of two malt beverages (as porter and ale or beer and stout) **b :** solder made of equal parts of lead and tin

[2]**half-and-half** \ˈ"\ *adj* **1 :** half one thing and half another ⟨a *half-and-half* mixture⟩ **2 a :** EQUAL ⟨a job demanding *half-and-half* cooperation⟩ **b :** demanding equal participation on the part of two persons ⟨a *half-and-half* proposition⟩ **3 :** PARTIAL ⟨*half-and-half* enthusiasm⟩

[3]**half-and-half** \ˈ"\ *adv* **1 :** into two equal parts ⟨divided *half-and-half*⟩ **2 :** EQUALLY ⟨a duty shared *half-and-half* by husband and wife⟩

**half an eye** *n* **:** partial vision; *esp* **:** a casual or careless glance

**half-ape** \ˈ=ˈ=\ *n* **:** one of the lower primates (as a lemur or tarsier)

**half-armor** \ˈ=ˈ==\ *n* **:** armor protecting only a part of the body

**half-assed** \ˈ=ˈ=\ *adj* **1** *slang* **:** lacking significance, adequacy, or completeness **:** DEFICIENT ⟨wasn't going to do a *half-assed* job —R.O.Bowen⟩ **2** *slang* **:** lacking intelligence, ability, or experience **:** STUPID ⟨those *half-assed* women on Quality Hill want to kick it out of town —Conrad Richter⟩

**half aunt** *n* **:** the half sister of a parent

**halfback** \ˈ=,=\ *n* **1 :** one of the backs stationed near either flank in football **2 :** a player stationed immediately behind the forward line (as in field hockey or soccer or rugby)

**half-baked** \ˈ=ˈ=\ *adj* **1 :** only imperfectly baked **:** UNDERDONE **2 a :** not well planned **:** poorly contrived ⟨a *half-baked* plan⟩ **b :** lacking judgment, intelligence, or common sense ⟨a *half-baked* individual⟩ ⟨dramatic ideas that are often trivial or *half-baked* —Winthrop Sargeant⟩

**half-ball stroke** *n* **:** a stroke in billiards in which the center of the striker's ball is made to hit the extreme edge of an object ball

**half bat** *n* **:** one half of a brick

**halfbeak** \ˈ=,=\ *n* **:** any of a family (Hemiramphidae) of small elongate fishes resembling the gar, closely allied to the flying fishes and like these often moving some distance through the air above the water, having on the lower jaw an extension like a beak, and inhabiting chiefly warm seas

**half-beam** \ˈ=,=\ *n* **:** a beam in a ship extending from one of the sides to a deck opening (as a hatchway)

**half-bent** \ˈ=,=\ *n* **:** the first notch in the tumbler of a gunlock for the sear point to enter to half-cock the piece

**half binding** *n* **:** a book binding in which one kind of material (as leather, cloth, or vellum) covers the backbone, one quarter of the boards away from the backbone, and sometimes the corners while another kind of material covers the rest — compare FULL BINDING, QUARTER BINDING, THREE-QUARTER BINDING

**half bishop** *n* **:** an artist's canvas measuring 45 by 56 inches — compare BISHOP'S LENGTH

**half blood** *n* **1 a :** the relation between persons having one parent but not both in common — compare BLOOD 2, CONSANGUINEOUS, DEMISANG, UTERINE, WHOLE BLOOD **b :** a person so related to another **2 :** HALF-BREED 1 **3 :** a grade of wool next below fine in a descending scale of fineness — compare BLOOD 7, BRAID 2, QUARTER BLOOD **4 a :** an animal tracing from a pure breed or strain through one parent only **b :** an individual heterozygous for a specified character **:** GRADE 5

**half-blooded** \ˈ=ˈ==\ *also* **half-blood** \ˈ=,=\ *adj* **1 :** having half blood or being a half-breed **2 :** having one parent of good and one of inferior stock ⟨a *half-blooded* sheep⟩

**half board** *n* **:** a maneuver of luffing a boat sailing close-hauled so that it shoots into the wind but before it has quite lost headway of putting the helm up again and letting the boat fill away on the same tack

**half bog soil** *n* **:** an interzonal group of soils developed under swamp-forest types of vegetation, having mucky or peaty surface soil underlain by gray mineral soil, and appearing mostly in humid or subhumid climates

**half boot** *n* **:** a boot with a top reaching somewhat above the ankle

**half-bound** \ˈ=ˈ=\ *adj* **:** having a half binding ⟨a *half-bound* book⟩

**half-box** \ˈ=,=\ *n* **:** a section of a page of a newspaper or periodical being usu. rectangular and marked off at the top and bottom by rules or an ornamental border — see BOX 9a

**half-breadth plan** *n* **:** a plan of one side of a ship showing by horizontal longitudinal sections the forms of the various waterlines, rail and deck lines at the side, the frame stations, and the buttock lines

[1]**half-bred** \ˈ=ˈ=\ *adj* **:** HALF-BLOODED

[2]**half-bred** \ˈ=,=\ *n* -s **:** a half-blooded animal

[1]**half-breed** \ˈ=,=\ *n* -s **1 :** the offspring of parents of different races; *esp* **:** the offspring of an American Indian and a white person **2 a** *usu cap* **:** a member of the faction of the Republican party that supported President Garfield in his controversy in 1881 with Senators Conkling and Platt of New York State over a civil-service appointment **b :** an insurgent faction in a political party **3 :** an animal or plant produced by crossing two distinct forms — often used to distinguish the product of such a cross within a species; compare HYBRID

[2]**half-breed** \ˈ"\ *adj* **:** HALF-BLOODED

**half brother** *n* [ME] **:** a brother by one parent only

**half-bull** \ˈ=,=\ *n* **:** a male fur seal not fully adult

**half cadence** *or* **half close** \-ˈklōz\ *n* **:** a musical chord sequence giving a sense of partial harmonic completion (as tonic to dominant) — see CADENCE illustration

[1]**half-caste** \ˈ=,=\ *n* **:** a person of mixed racial or cultural descent **:** HALF-BREED

[2]**half-caste** \ˈ"\ *adj* **:** of the rank of or relating to a half-caste

**half-castrate** \ˈ=ˈ==, ˈ=ˈ==\ *vt* **:** to remove the descended testis of (a unilateral ridgeling) to prevent breeding

**half-cell** \ˈ=,=\ *n* **:** a device consisting of a single electrode immersed in an electrolytic solution and thus developing a definite potential difference

**half cent** *n* **:** a coin representing one half a cent (as the copper half cent coined by the U. S. 1793–1857)

**half chronometer** *n* **:** a watch having an escapement compounded of the lever and chronometer escapements; *also* **:** a fine lever-escapement watch adjusted for temperature

**half-close** \ˈ=ˈklōs\ *adj* **:** MID 3

**half cock** *n* **1 :** the position of the hammer of a firearm when about half retracted and held by the sear so that it cannot be operated by a pull on the trigger **2 :** a state of inadequate preparation or mental confusion — used with *at* ⟨the whole project went off at *half cock*⟩

**half-cock** \ˈ=ˈ=\ *vt* **:** to place the hammer of (a firearm) at half cock

**half-cocked** \ˈ=ˈ=\ *adj* **1 :** being at half cock **2 :** lacking clear or rational preparation, knowledge, or intention ⟨go off *half-cocked*⟩; *also* **:** STUPID, FOOLISH ⟨*half-cocked* public officials⟩

**half column** *n* **:** an engaged column which projects from a wall by approximately half its diameter

**half cone** *n* **:** the part of a cone formed by half lines from the vertex — opposed to *double cone*

**half-course** \ˈ=,=\ *n* **:** a course at a school, college, or university having fewer weekly meetings than the regular course and carrying correspondingly fewer credits

**half cousin** *n* **:** the child of a half uncle or half aunt

**half-cracked** \ˈ=ˈ=\ *adj* **:** HALF-WITTED

**half crown** *n* **:** a British coin worth *2s 6d* being in the 16th cent. of gold, from 1601–1946 of silver, and then of cupronickel; *sometimes* **:** the sum of *2s 6d*

**half deck** *n* **1 :** an incomplete deck; *specif* **:** a portion of the deck of a sailing ship next below the spar deck between mainmast and cabin **2 :** a slipper limpet of the genus *Crepidula*

**half-decked** \ˈ=ˈ=\ *adj* **:** partly decked and partly open ⟨*half-decked* craft . . . used by the later Vikings —C.I.Elton⟩

**half-deck·er** \ˈ=ˈdekə(r)\ *n* **:** a half-decked ship

**half-diamond indention** *n* **:** a style of display typesetting in which succeeding lines are indented at each end, each line being shorter than the preceding line — called also *inverted-pyramid indention*

**half dime** *n* **:** a silver five-cent coin struck by the U. S. mint in 1792 and from 1794 to 1873

**half disme** *n* **:** a half dime struck in 1792

**half-dollar** \ˈ=ˈ==\ *n* **1 :** a coin representing one half of a dollar ⟨a U. S. or Canadian *half-dollar*⟩ **2 :** the sum of fifty cents or one half of a dollar

**half door** *n* **1 :** either part of a Dutch door **2 :** a swing door that fills only a part of the doorway

**half eagle** *n* **:** the five-dollar gold piece issued by the U. S. 1795–1916 and in 1929 — compare EAGLE

**half-evergreen** \ˈ=ˈ===\ *adj, of a plant* **:** incompletely evergreen: **a :** having foliage that is functional and persistent during part of the winter or dry season **b :** tending to be evergreen in the milder but deciduous in the more rigorous part of the range

**half-faced** \ˈ=ˈ=\ *adj* **1 :** showing a profile **2 :** closed or protecting on three sides but open on the front ⟨a *half-faced* tent⟩ ⟨a *half-faced* cabin⟩

**half fare** *n* **:** a reduced fare (as on railroads or buses) available to underage children, to employees, or to passengers who ride at a particular time or under certain circumstances

**half gainer** *n* **:** a gainer in which the diver executes a half-backward somersault and enters the water headfirst and facing the board

**half gerund** *n* **:** the gerund in *-ing* when taking certain constructions suggestive of the participle (as *coming* in "I don't like him coming here" and *climbing* in "he tears his shirt climbing trees")

**half-hardy** \ˈ=ˈ==\ *adj, of a plant* **:** able to withstand a moderately low temperature but injured by severe freezing and surviving the winter in cold climates only if carefully protected

**half-hardy annual** *n* **:** a plant that may endure a few degrees of frost but is killed at lower temperatures (as China aster or zinnia)

**half hatchet** *n* **:** a hatchet with a straight edge broader than the edge of a lathing hatchet and with a flat hammer face on the end opposite the cutting edge — see HATCHET illustration

**halfhead bedstead** \ˈ⸗,⸗-\ *n* **:** a bedstead with posts lower than the headboard

**half header** *n* **:** half a brick used to close a course

**halfhearted** \ˈ⸗¦⸗⸗\ *adj* **:** lacking heart, spirit, or interest ⟨a ~ try⟩ — **half·heart·ed·ly** *adv* — **half·heart·ed·ness** *n* -ES

**half hitch** *n* **:** a knot usu. tied double and used for temporarily securing a rope to an object by making a turn around the object, around the standing part, under the turn, and when double, around the standing part again and through the last bight

half hitch

**half-holiday** \ˈ⸗¦⸗⸗\ *n* **:** a holiday limited to half a day

**half hose** *n* **:** men's socks reaching halfway to the knee

**half hour** *n* [ME] **1 :** thirty minutes **2 :** the midpoint of an hour — **half-hourly** \ˈ⸗¦⸗⸗\ *adv (or adj)*

**half-hour glass** \ˈ⸗¦⸗-\ *n* **:** an instrument for measuring time in half-hour intervals

**half hunter** *n* **:** a watch having the outer half of the crystal protected by a metal casing

**halfies** *pl of* HALFY

**half-inferior** \ˈ⸗⸗¦⸗⸗⸗\ *adj* **:** borne below the androecium in a concave receptacle but free from the axis — used of the ovary (as in perigynous flowers)

**half island** *or* **half isle** *n* **:** PENINSULA

**half joe** \ˈ⸗¦jō\ *n, pl* **half joes** [*half* + *joe*, short for *johannes*] **:** JOHANNES

**half-knot** \ˈ⸗¦⸗\ *n* **:** a knot joining the ends of two cords and used in tying other knots (as the square knot); *also* **:** OVERHAND KNOT

**half lap** *n* **:** END LAP

**half-length** \ˈ⸗¦⸗\ *n* **:** something that is or represents only half the complete length (as a portrait showing only the upper half of a person)

**half-life** \ˈ⸗¦⸗\ *also* **half-life period** *n* **1 :** the time required for half of the atoms of a radioactive substance present at the beginning to become disintegrated ⟨rays from uranium have a *half-life* of millions of years —F.B.Colton⟩ ⟨this isotope has *half-life* of twenty-three minutes —L.J.Levert⟩ ⟨there will still be one quarter of the element left at the end of two *half-life periods* —G.E.Owen⟩ **2 :** the time required for half the amount of a substance (as a drug or radioactive tracer) in or introduced into a living system to be eliminated whether by excretion, metabolic decomposition, or other natural process

**half-light** \ˈ⸗,⸗\ *n* **:** grayish light (as of dim interiors, evening, or mist); *also* **:** the portion of a work of art showing such light

**half line** *n* **:** a straight line in mathematics beginning at a given point and extending indefinitely in one direction only — called also *half ray*

1**half·ling** *pronunc at* HALF + lən *or* liŋ\ *or* **half·lin** \-lən\ *n* -s [*half* + *-ling*] **1** *chiefly Scot* **:** a half-grown person **2** *chiefly Scot* **:** half of a silver penny

2**halfling** \ˈ"\ *or* **halflin** \ˈ"\ *adj, chiefly Scot* **:** not fully grown **:** IMMATURE

**half·lings** \-nz,-ŋz\ *adv* [ME *halfling, halflings*, fr. *half* + *-ling, -lings*] *Scot* **:** half or approximately half **:** PARTIALLY ⟨while Jennie ~ is afraid to speak —Robert Burns⟩

**half-long** \ˈ⸗¦⸗\ *adj, of a speech sound* **:** intermediate in duration between long and short

**half-loop** \ˈ⸗¦⸗\ *n* **:** a flight maneuver in which an aircraft pulls up in an inside loop but continues upside down in level flight in the direction from which it came

**half·ly** *adv* [ME, fr. *half* + *-ly*] **:** 3HALF

**half-marrow** \ˈ⸗¦(,)⸗\ *n, now dial Brit* **:** a partner or mate; *specif* **:** SPOUSE

1**half-mast** \ˈ⸗¦⸗\ *n* **:** a point some distance but not necessarily halfway down below the top of a mast or staff or the peak of a gaff ⟨a flag flown at *half-mast* as a token of mourning⟩

2**half-mast** \ˈ⸗¦⸗\ *adj* **:** located below the top of the mast ⟨a *half-mast* position⟩

3**half-mast** \ˈ"\ *vt* [1*half-mast*] **:** to cause to hang at half-mast ⟨*half-mast* a flag⟩

**half measure** *n* **:** a partial, halfhearted, or weak line of action ⟨victory is seldom won by *half measures*⟩

**half·mens** \ˈhälf,men(t)s\ *n, pl* **halfmens** \ˈ"\ *or* **half·men·se** \-n(t)sə\ [Afrik, fr. *half* + *mens* human being, person] **:** a southern African plant (*Pachypodium namaquam*) of the family Apocynaceae having an upright naked stem surmounted by a crown of leaves and suggesting in outline the figure of a human

**half-minded** \ˈ⸗¦⸗⸗\ *adj* **:** being of an undecided or partial intent, desire, or will ⟨*half-minded* to do something desperate⟩

**half-monitor** \ˈ⸗ˈ⸗⸗⸗\ *n* **:** a roof for hog or poultry houses shaped like a saw tooth

**half-moon** \ˈ⸗,⸗ *also* ⸗ˈ⸗\ *n* **1 :** the moon at the quarters when half its disk appears illuminated — see MOON illustration **2 :** a figure or object that is pointed at both ends, is about a fourth as wide as it is long, and in plane outline is half of a circle with the straight section curved in so that one side is concave while the other is convex ⟨an island *half-moon*⟩ **3 :** the lunule of a fingernail **4 a :** a bluish black California marine food fish (*Medialuna californiensis*) of the family Scorpididae — called also *blue perch* **b :** SCALARE

**half-mooned** \ˈ⸗,münd\ *adj* **:** shaped like a half-moon ⟨in his *half-mooned* chair —Thomas Coryat⟩

**half mourning** *n* **1 :** a period of mourning succeeding that of deep mourning **2 :** mourning dress lightened by the use of white, gray, or lavender

**half nelson** *n* **:** a wrestling hold in which one arm is thrust under the corresponding arm of the opponent generally from behind and the hand placed upon the back of his neck — compare FULL NELSON, QUARTER NELSON, THREE-QUARTER NELSON

**half nephew** *n* **:** the son of a half brother or half sister

**half·ness** *n* -ES **:** the quality or state of being half

**half niece** *n* **:** the daughter of a half brother or half sister

**half note** *n* **:** a musical note of half the value of a whole note — called also *minim*

**half nut** *n* **:** a screw nut split lengthwise so that either one part may be arranged to ride on a screw or the two parts may be arranged to clamp about a screw

half notes

**half-one** \ˈ⸗,⸗, *in sense 2* ˈ⸗,⸗\ *n* **1 :** a golf handicap of one stroke subtracted on alternate holes **2** *Irish* **:** a half a glass of whiskey

**half-open** \ˈ⸗¦⸗⸗\ *adj* **:** MID 3

**half-orphan** \ˈ⸗¦⸗⸗\ *n* **:** a child with only one parent living

**half·pace** *pronunc at* HALF + ,pās\ *n* [by folk etymology fr. MF *haut pas*, lit., high step] **1 :** a raised floor or dais or a platform or footpace at the top of steps (as for a throne or an altar) **2 :** a landing of a staircase like a broad step between two half flights — compare QUARTERPACE

**half·pen·ny** \ˈhāp(ə)nē\ *n, pl* **half·pence** \-pən(t)s\ *or* **halfpennies** \-p(ə)nēz\ [ME *halfpeny, halfpeni*, fr. *half* + *peny, peni* penny] **1 :** a coin or token representing one half of a penny (as a British coin issued from the time of Edward I) **2 :** the sum of half a penny **3 :** a small amount ⟨not a ~ less⟩

**halfpenny post** *n, Brit* **:** second-class mail

**half·pen·ny·worth** \-i,wərth, ˈhāpəth\ *n* **:** something that is worth or costs a halfpenny ⟨a ~ of fish⟩

**half-pike** \ˈ⸗,⸗\ *n* **:** a pike with a short shaft — compare BOARDING PIKE, SPONTOON

**half-pint** \ˈ⸗¦⸗\ *n* **1 :** half a pint **2** *slang* **:** a short, small, or inconsequential person

**half-pitch** \ˈ⸗¦⸗\ *adj* **:** having a gradient of one to two ⟨a *half-pitch* slope⟩

**half plane** *n, math* **:** the part of a plane on one side of an indefinitely extended straight line drawn in it

**half principal** *n* **:** a principal roof rafter that does not extend to the ridge

**half-rat·er** \ˈ⸗¦⸗⸗\ *n* **:** a small sailing yacht of about 15-ft. waterline built under the rating rule in use in Great Britain about the end of the 19th century

**half ray** *n* **:** HALF LINE

**half rest** *n* **:** a rest in music corresponding in value with a half note

**half rhyme** *n* **:** a terminal consonance other than rhyme in two or more words (as in the unstressed final syllables of *hollow* and *shallow* or the matching terminal consonant clusters of *stopped* and *wept*)

**half ring** *n* **:** one of the incomplete cartilaginous rings that support the upper part of the bronchial tubes of most birds and in singing birds form a part of the syrinx

**half-ripe** \ˈ⸗¦⸗\ *or* **half-ripened** \ˈ⸗¦⸗⸗\ *adj* **:** of, relating to, or consisting of the current growth of a tree, shrub, or woody plant that has not yet reached the mature wood stage ⟨*half-ripe* part⟩

1**half-roll** \ˈ⸗¦⸗\ *n* **:** a flight maneuver in which an airplane rolls halfway over and then flies upside down along its original line of flight

2**half-roll** \ˈ"\ *vi, of an airplane* **:** to perform a half-roll

**half-round** \ˈ⸗¦⸗\ *adj* **1 :** semicircular or approximately so; *also* **:** flat on one side and round on the other **2** *of veneer* **:** cut from a log placed off center in a lathe so that it comes into contact with the blade on rotation only when the projecting portion reaches the blade

**half round** \ˈ"\ *n* **:** something half-round (as a chisel or molding)

**half-round file** *n* **:** a file made flat on one side and convex on the other

**half run** *n* **:** a contract purchased from an advertising agency whereby a card of a type suitable for bus, subway, or train advertising is required to be placed in half of the cars in a specified district

**half-saved** \ˈ⸗¦⸗\ *adj, now dial Eng* **:** HALF-WITTED

**half-seas over** \ˈ⸗,⸗¦⸗⸗\ *adj, slang* **:** DRUNK

**half sheet** *n* **:** a sheet imposed and printed by the work-and-turn method

**half shell** *n* **:** either of the valves of a bivalve — **on the half shell :** in either of the halves of a shell ⟨oysters *on the half shell*⟩

**half shirt** *n* **:** a man's shirtfront or a woman's chemisette worn in the late 17th century; *also* **:** STOMACHER

**half-shot** \ˈ⸗¦⸗\ *adj, slang* **:** partially drunk

**half-shrub** \ˈ⸗,⸗\ *n* **:** a perennial plant in which the stems are more or less woody esp. at the base — **half-shrubby** \ˈ⸗¦⸗⸗\ *adj*

**half-sib** \ˈ⸗¦⸗\ *also* **half-sibling** \ˈ⸗¦⸗⸗\ *n* **:** a half brother or half sister — compare SIB

**half-silvered** \ˈ⸗¦⸗⸗\ *adj, of a mirror or glass block* **:** having a metallic film backing of such thinness that only half the incident light is reflected with the remainder being transmitted through the backing

**half sister** *n* [ME] **:** a sister by one parent only

**half size** *n* **:** a size in suits, coats, or dresses for short or short-waisted women with full figures

**half sleeve** *n* **:** any of various sleeves that reach to a little above the elbow or to a little below the elbow

1**half-slip** \ˈ⸗,⸗\ *n* **:** PETTICOAT 1c

2**half-slip** \ˈ⸗¦⸗\ *adj* **:** of or relating to the degree of ripeness of a melon when the peduncle is separated from the fruit by pulling or pressure

**half-snap** \ˈ⸗¦⸗\ *n* **:** a quick movement of a shotgun to the shoulder followed by a rapid check on the alignment of the piece before it is fired

**half snipe** *n* **:** JACKSNIPE

**half sole** *n* **:** a shoe sole extending from the shank forward **:** TAP

**half-sole** \ˈ⸗¦⸗\ *vt* [*half sole*] **:** to attach a half sole to esp. in repairing (a shoe)

**half sovereign** *n* **:** a British gold coin worth ten shillings or ½ pound sterling regularly issued up to 1916 and since then only occasionally (as in 1937)

**half space** *n* **:** a halfpace in a stair

**half-staff** \ˈ⸗¦⸗\ *n* **:** HALF-MAST — used of a flag on a flagpole

**half step** *n* **1 :** a walking step of 15 inches or in double time of 18 inches **2 :** the pitch interval in music between two adjacent keys on a keyboard instrument — called also *semitone*

**half-stopped** \ˈ⸗¦⸗\ *adj* **:** partly covered at the top — used of an organ pipe

**half story** *n* **:** an uppermost story which is usu. lighted by dormer windows and in which a sloping roof replaces the upper part of the front wall

**half-stripe** \ˈ⸗,⸗\ *n* **:** the narrow ¼-inch stripe which together with the full ½-inch stripe makes up the sleeve and shoulder-board rank insignia of naval officers below flag rank

**half stuff** *or* **half stock** *n* **:** paper pulp; *esp* **:** paper pulp from rags partly processed (as by washing, bleaching, and draining) and ready for the beater

**half sweep** *n* **:** a sweep with a blade on only one side for use in cultivating close to a crop row

**half-sword** *n* **1** *obs* **:** a sword of small size **2** *obs* **:** half the length of a sword — **at half-sword** *adv, obs* **:** at close quarters

**half tester bed** *n* **:** a bed with a low foot and a canopy projecting from the posts at the head

**half tide** *n* **:** the time or state halfway between flood and ebb

**half timber** \ˈ⸗¦⸗⸗\ *or* **half-timbered** \ˈ⸗¦⸗⸗\ *adj* **:** being of the Tudor or Elizabethan construction employing wood framing with spaces filled with masonry — **half-timbering** \ˈ⸗¦(⸗)⸗\ *n*

**half time** *n* **:** time marking the completion of half of a game or contest; *also* **:** the intermission between the second and third quarters of a game (as football and basketball)

**half-timer** \ˈ⸗¦⸗⸗\ *n* **1 :** one that spends only half the usual time at anything **2** *Brit* **:** a child who is permitted to work half his time at some employment

**half tint** *n* **:** DEMITINT

**half title** *n* **1 :** the title of a book usu. standing alone on a right-hand page directly preceding the title page — called also *bastard title* **2 :** the title of a book standing alone on a usu. right-hand page immediately preceding the first page of text or at the head of the first page of text

**half-toe** \ˈ⸗,⸗\ *n* **:** the ball of the foot as the base of support in a dance step

**halftone** \ˈ⸗,⸗\ *n, often attrib* **1 :** HALF STEP 2 **2 a :** any of the shades of gray between the darkest and the lightest parts of a photographic image — called also *middletone* **b** [so called fr. the fact that this process was the first that was successful in reproducing the halftones of a photo] **:** a photoengraving made from an image photographed through a screen having a lattice of horizontal and vertical lines and then etched so that the details of the image are reproduced in fine dots with the darker areas appearing as heavy and concentrated dots and the lighter areas as fine and diffused dots; *also* **:** a print made from a halftone — compare DROPOUT

**half-tongue** \ˈ⸗,⸗\ *n* [ME *half tong*; intended as trans. of ML *medietas linguae*] **:** a jury de medietate linguae in English law

1**half-track** \ˈ⸗,⸗\ *n* -s **1 :** a chain-track drive system serving to propel a vehicle supported in front by a pair of wheels and consisting of an endless metal belt on each side of the vehicle driven by one of two inside sprockets, running on bogie wheels mounted on the frame, and laying down on the ground as it revolves a flexible track of cleated steel or hard-rubber plates **2 :** a motor vehicle equipped with half-tracks in the rear and wheels in the front; *specif* **:** such a vehicle lightly armored for military use

2**half-track** \ˈ⸗,⸗\ *also* **half-tracked** \ˈ⸗,⸗\ *adj* **:** equipped with half-tracks

**half-truth** \ˈ⸗,⸗\ *n* **:** a partially true or partially fabricated statement made to deceive or to escape censure ⟨a public led astray by the *half-truths* of a dictator⟩

**half-turn** \ˈ⸗,⸗\ *n* **:** reversal of direction (as in a staircase) either by one 180-degree turn or two right-angle turns

**half twist** *n* **1 :** a dive done in either pike or layout position from a springboard or platform in which the diver executes a half turn of the body on a longitudinal axis before entering the water — compare FULL TWIST **2 :** a half turn of the body in the air on a longitudinal axis executed alone or in conjunction with other maneuvers (as on a trampoline, from a springboard, or in vaulting)

**half uncial** *n* **:** a book hand formed by combining uncial characters with carefully written cursive forms and used as the typical book hand from the earliest times in Ireland and from the 7th century to the Norman Conquest in England

half uncials

**half uncle** *n* **:** the half brother of a parent

**half-value layer** *n* **:** the thickness of an absorbing substance necessary to reduce by one half the initial intensity of the radiation traversing it

**half volley** *n* **:** a ball that is stroked or batted at the instant it rebounds from the ground: as **a :** a kick in soccer taken on the run as a ball rebounds from the ground **b :** a dropkick in rugby **c :** a bowled cricket ball that lands near enough to the blockhole to be readily hit as soon as it leaves the ground

**half-volley** \ˈ⸗¦⸗⸗\ *vb* [*half volley*] *vt* **:** to drive (a tennis ball) as a half volley ~ *vi* **:** to play a half volley in tennis

**half-wave plate** *n* **:** a crystal plate that reduces by ½ cycle the phase difference between the two components of polarized light traversing it — compare QUARTER-WAVE PLATE

**half-wave rectifier** *n* **:** a rectifier that utilizes one half cycle of alternating current and suppresses the other

1**halfway** \ˈ⸗¦⸗\ *adv* [ME, fr. *half* + *way*] **1 :** at a point at or near the middle **:** MIDWAY ⟨two ships passing ~ across the ocean⟩ **2 :** with concessions **:** in a state of readiness to negotiate **:** AMENABLY ⟨the revolutionists met the national government ~⟩ **3 a :** PARTIALLY, ALMOST **:** very nearly ⟨the fighter ~ yielded⟩ **b :** MORE OR LESS ⟨a ~ kind remark⟩

2**halfway** \ˈ"\ *adj* **1 :** equally distant from the extremes of a space or course **:** midway between two points ⟨a ~ point⟩ **2 :** PARTIAL ⟨~ measures⟩

**halfway covenant** *n, cap H&C* **:** a form of church membership among the Congregational churches of New England allowed by decisions in 1657 and 1662 and permitting baptized persons of moral life and orthodox faith to enjoy privileges of full membership except the partaking of the Lord's Supper

**halfway house** *n* **:** an inn or place of call midway on a journey; *also* **:** any halfway place in a progress

**half wellington** *n, usu cap W* **:** a loose-topped leather boot similar to the Wellington but shorter and usu. worn under trousers

**half-wit** \ˈ⸗,⸗\ *n* **:** a foolish person **:** DOLT, BLOCKHEAD

**half-witted** \ˈ⸗¦⸗⸗\ *adj* **1 :** SILLY, SENSELESS **2 :** mentally deficient **:** FOOLISH, IMBECILE — **half-wit·ted·ly** *adv* — **half-wit·ted·ness** *n* -ES

**half-world** \ˈ⸗,⸗\ *n* **1 :** HEMISPHERE ⟨will prevent economic development of our *half-world* —Hamish Hamilton⟩ **2 :** DEMIMONDE ⟨the painted hussies of the *half-world* . . . in pinchbeck finery —Donn Byrne⟩ **3 :** UNDERWORLD ⟨a criminal not previously connected with the *half-world* —Frank Mullady⟩

half Wellington

**halfy** *pronunc at* HALF + ē *or* i\ *n* -ES *slang* **:** a beggar who has had both legs amputated

**half year** *n* [ME] **1 :** one half of a year (as January to June or July to December) **2 :** one of two academic terms **:** SEMESTER — **half-yearly** \ˈ⸗¦⸗⸗\ *adv (or adj)*

**hali-** *comb form* [NL, fr. Gk, fr. *hals* salt, sea — more at SALT] **1 :** sea ⟨*hali*plankton⟩ **2 :** salt **:** a salt ⟨*hali*steresis⟩

**hal·i·ae·e·tus** \,halēˈēədəs\ *n, cap* [NL, fr. Gk *haliaetos, haliaietos*, a bird (prob. the osprey), fr. *hali-* + *aetos, aietos* eagle] **:** a genus of eagles including the bald eagle and many sea eagles

**hal·i·but** \ˈhaləbət *also* ˈhäl-; *usu* -bəd.+V\ *n, pl* **halibut** *also* **halibuts** [ME *halybutte*, fr. *haly, holy* holy + *butte* flatfish, fr. its being eaten on holy days — more at HOLY, BUTT] **:** the largest of the flatfishes formerly regarded as forming a single species but now usu. divided into an Atlantic species (*Hippoglossus hippoglossus*) and a Pacific (*H. stenolepis*), being an inhabitant of all northern seas, and constituting one of the largest of teleost fishes, the female sometimes weighing several hundred pounds though the male rarely weighs over 50 pounds — see ARROW-TOOTHED HALIBUT, CALIFORNIA HALIBUT

**hal·i·but·er** \-(,)bəd·ə(r), -ətə-\ *n* -s **:** one that fishes for halibut; *also* **:** a boat used in such fishing

**halibut-liver oil** *n* **:** a yellowish to brownish fatty oil from the liver of the halibut used chiefly as a source of vitamin A

**hal·i·car·nas·si·an** *also* **hal·i·car·nas·se·an** \¦halə(,)kär-ˈnasēən\ *adj, cap* [*Halicarnassus*, ancient city in Asia Minor + E *-ian* or *-ean*] **:** of or belonging to ancient Halicarnassus

**hal·i·choe·rus** \,haləˈkirəs, -kēr-\ *n, cap* [NL, fr. *hali-* + Gk *choiros* young pig] **:** the genus comprising the gray seal

**hal·i·clys·tus** \-ˈklistəs\ *n, cap* [NL, fr. *hali-* + *-clystus* (prob. fr. Gk *klystēr* syringe)] **:** a widely distributed genus of stauromedusan jellyfishes (class Scyphozoa)

**ha·lic·o·re** \həˈlikə(,)rē\ [NL, fr. *hali-* + Gk *korē* girl] *syn of* DUGONG

**ha·lic·ti·dae** \həˈliktə,dē\ *n pl, cap* [NL, fr. *Halictus*, type genus + *-idae*] **:** a cosmopolitan family of small black or brightly metallic solitary bees including many pollinators valuable to agriculture — **ha·lic·tine** \-,tīn, -tən\ *adj*

**ha·lic·tus** \həˈliktəs\ *n, cap* [NL, irreg. fr. Gk *halizein* to gather, assemble, fr. *halēs* assembled, pressed together] **:** a cosmopolitan genus of gregarious but not social burrowing bees that provision the larval cells with pollen and nectar and include important pollinators of economic plants — see SWEAT BEE

**halide** \ˈha,līd,ˈhā,-,-ləd\ *n* -s [*hal-* + *-ide*] **:** a binary compound of a halogen with a more electropositive element or radical

**hal·i·dom** \ˈhalədəm\ *or* **hal·i·dome** \-,dōm\ *n* -s [ME, fr. OE *hāligdōm*, fr. *hālig* holy + *-dōm* -dom — more at HOLY] *archaic* **:** a holy place or relic — often used in the phrase *by my halidom*

**hal·i·eu·tic** \,halēˈ(y)üd·ik\ *also* **hal·i·eu·ti·cal** \-d·əkəl\ *adj* [LL *halieuticus*, fr. Gk *halieutikos*, fr. (assumed) *halieutos* verbal of *halieuein* to fish, fr. *hals* salt, sea) + *-ikos* -ic — more at SALT] **:** of or relating to fishing — **hal·i·eu·ti·cal·ly** \-d·ək(ə)lē\ *adv*

**hal·i·eu·tics** \-d·iks\ *n pl but sing in constr* **:** the art or practice of fishing; *also* **:** a treatise on fishes or fishing

**hal·i·fax** \ˈhalə,faks\ *adj, usu cap* **1** [fr. *Halifax*, county borough in England] **:** of or from the county borough of Halifax, England **:** of the kind or style prevalent in Halifax **2** [fr. *Halifax*, N. S.] **:** of or from Halifax, the capital of Nova Scotia **:** of the kind or style prevalent in Halifax

1**hal·i·go·ni·an** \,haləˈgōnēən\ *n* -s *cap* [ML *Haligonia* Halifax + E *-an*] **:** a native or inhabitant of Halifax, Nova Scotia or Halifax, England

2**haligonian** \ˈ⸗¦⸗⸗⸗\ *adj, usu cap* **:** of or belonging to Haligonians

**hal·i·me·da** \,haləˈmēdə\ *n, cap* [NL, after *Halimede*, a nereid, fr. Gk *Halimēdē*] **:** a genus (family Codiaceae) of calcareous marine green algae remarkable for the jointed coenocytic thallus which in most of the species (as *H. tuna*) resembles a prickly-pear cactus in miniature

**haling** *pres part of* HALE

**hal·ing hands** \ˈhāliŋ,-\ *n pl* [*haling* fr. gerund of 3*hale*] **:** heavy woolen gloves or mittens worn esp. by sailors

**hal·i·o·tis** \,halēˈōdəs\ *n* [NL, fr. *hali-* + Gk *ōt-, ous* ear] **1** *cap* **:** a genus (the type of the family Haliotidae) of gastropod mollusks comprising the abalones **2** *pl* **haliotis :** any mollusk of the genus *Haliotis* **:** ABALONE — **hal·i·o·toid** \ˈ⸗⸗¦ōd,-ōid\ *adj*

**hali·plankton** \¦halə+\ *n* [ISV *hali-* + *plankton*] **:** oceanic plankton

**hal·i·se·ri·tes** \,haləsəˈrīd·(,)ēz, hə,lis-\ *n, cap* [NL, fr. *hali-* + Gk *seris* endive + NL *-ites*] **:** a genus of Old World cretaceous fossil plants of uncertain relationship possibly related to the dicotyledonous genus *Fontainea* but by some considered thallophytes because of the dichotomous flat leaves

**ha·lis·i·do·ta** \hə,lisəˈdōdə\ *n, cap* [NL] **:** a genus of arctiid moths several of which have larvae that feed on the foliage of trees

**hal·i·ste·re·sis** \,haləstəˈrēsəs, hə,lis-\ *n, pl* **halistere·ses**

\-ē(ˌ)sēz\ [NL, fr. *hali-* + Gk *-steresis* loss] **:** loss of salts esp. of lime from bone (as in osteomalacia)

**hal·i·ste·ret·ic** \ˌhaləstəˈred·ik, həˌlis-\ *adj* **:** affected with or constituting halisteresis

**halite** \ˈhaˌlīt, ˈhā-\ *n* -s [NL *halites*, fr. *hal-* + *-ites* -ite] **:** a mineral NaCl consisting of sodium chloride **:** native salt **:** ROCK SALT

**hal·i·the·ri·um** \ˌhaləˈthirēəm\ *n, cap* [NL, fr. *hali-* + *-therium*] **:** a genus of sirenians that is known from remains found in the Oligocene and Miocene of southern Europe and the Oligocene of Madagascar and is made type of a separate family or included in Dugongidae

**hal·i·to·sis** \ˌhaləˈtōsə̇s\ *n, pl* **halito·ses** \-ōˌsēz\ [NL, fr. L *halitus* breath (fr. *halare* to breathe) + NL *-osis* — more at EXHALE] **:** a condition of having fetid breath

**hall** \ˈhȯl\ *n* -s *often attrib* [ME *halle, hal*, fr. OE *heall;* akin to OHG *halla* hall, ON *höll*, L *cella* small room, Gk *kalia* hut, nest, Skt *śālā* hut, OE *helan* to conceal — more at HELL] **1 a :** the castle or house of a medieval king or noble **b :** the chief living room in such a structure used for eating, sleeping, and entertaining **c** *chiefly dial* **:** the living room or parlor of a house **2 :** the manor house or residence of a landed proprietor — often used in proper names ⟨Locksley *Hall*⟩ ⟨Headlong *Hall*⟩ **3** *sometimes cap* **:** a large usu. imposing building used for public or semipublic purposes; *specif* **:** TOWN HALL — now used chiefly in proper names ⟨Westminster *Hall*⟩ ⟨Faneuil *Hall*⟩ **4 a** (1) **:** a building used by a college or university for teaching or research ⟨~s of learning⟩ — often used in proper names ⟨Goodheart *Hall*⟩ (2) **:** DORMITORY **b :** a college or a division of a college at some universities **c** (1) **:** the common dining room of an English college (2) **:** a meal served there **5 a** *archaic* **:** a cleared passageway through a crowd — used in the exclamation *a hall, a hall* **b** (1) **:** the entrance room or passageway of a residence or other building **:** FOYER, LOBBY ⟨the front ~ of the house⟩ ⟨left his rubbers in the back ~⟩ (2) **:** a corridor or passage in a building **6 :** a large room for assembly usu. equipped with seats (as for lectures or concerts) **:** AUDITORIUM ⟨a lecture ~⟩ ⟨a concert ~⟩ **7 :** a place used for public entertainment: as **a :** a building or room used for a particular kind of amusement or play ⟨a pool ~⟩ ⟨a gambling ~⟩ **b :** a building with an auditorium used for public musical entertainments; *specif* **:** MUSIC HALL **8 :** a building belonging to or used as the place of assembly, social center, or headquarters of a fraternal society or trade union ⟨his office was the union ~ —R.F.Mirvish⟩ — often used in proper names ⟨Hungarian *Hall*⟩

**hal·lah** *or* **chal·lah** \ˈkälə, käˈlä\ *n, pl* **hal·loth** *or* **hal·lot** \ˈkäˌlōt(h), -ōs, ⸗ˈ⸗\ *or* **hal·lahs** \ˈkäləz\ [Heb *ḥallāh*] **:** a loaf of white bread often baked in braided or twisted form and used among Jews esp. at a Friday evening meal inaugurating the Sabbath and on holidays

**hal·la·li** \ˌhaləˈlē\ *n* -s [imit.] **:** a huntsman's bugle call ⟨his ~ rang high —George Meredith⟩

**hal·lan** \ˈhalən, ˈhäl-\ *n* -s [origin unknown] *dial Brit* **:** a partition in a cottage esp. between the door and the fireplace

**hal·lan·shak·er** \-ˌshākər, -ˌshak-\ *n* **1** *chiefly Scot* **:** a wandering beggar **2** *chiefly Scot* **:** RASCAL, SCOUNDREL

**hall bedroom** *n* **:** a small narrow bedroom formed by a partition at one end of a hall

**hallboy** \ˈ⸗ˌ⸗\ *n* **1 :** CALLBOY **2 :** a boy employed to clean the halls of a hotel

**hall church** *n* [trans. of G *hallenkirche*] **:** a Gothic church esp. in Germany in which in place of the clerestory the aisles are carried up to nearly the height of the nave

**hallcist** \ˈ⸗ˌ⸗\ *n* -s [*hall* + *cist* (grave)] **:** a large rectangular earth-covered corridor made of rock slabs and used in ancient times as a tomb

**hall clock** *n* **:** GRANDFATHER CLOCK

**hall coefficient** \ˈhȯl-\ *or* **hall constant** *n, usu cap H* [after Edwin H. *Hall* †1938 Am. physicist] **:** the quotient of the potential difference per unit width of metal strip in the Hall effect divided by the product of the magnetic intensity and the longitudinal current density

**hal·le** \ˈhälə\ *adj, usu cap* [fr. *Halle*, Germany] **:** of or from the city of Halle, Germany **:** of the kind or style prevalent in Halle

**hall effect** *n, usu cap H* [after Edwin H. *Hall*] **:** a potential difference observed between the edges of a strip of metal carrying a longitudinal current when placed in a magnetic field perpendicular to the plane of the strip

**häl·le·flin·ta** \ˌheləˈflintə\ *n* -s [Sw, fr. *hälle-* slab, rock (fr. OSw *hællo-, hælla*) + *flinta* flint, fr. OSw; akin to ON *hella* cliff, mountain, Goth *hallus* cliff, and to OE *flint* — more at HILL, FLINT] **:** a very compact banded rock resembling felsite and consisting of minute particles of feldspar and quartz with fine scales of mica and chlorite — **häl·le·flin·toid** \-nt,ȯid\ *adj*

**hal·lel** \häˈläl, ˈhäˌläl, ˈhaˌlel\ *n, usu cap* [Heb *hallēl* praise] **:** a selection of psalms of praise chanted on Passover, Shabuoth, Sukkoth, Hanukkah, and Rosh Hodesh

1**hal·le·lu·jah** \ˌhaləˈlüyə\ *interj, sometimes cap* [Heb *hallĕlūyāh* praise (ye) the Lord] — used to express praise, joy, or thanks ⟨the mighty voice of a great multitude in heaven, crying, "*Hallelujah!*" —Rev 19:1 (RSV)⟩

2**hallelujah** \"\ *n* -s **:** a shout or song of praise or thanksgiving ⟨jubilant ~s for . . . the Minister of Housing —Mollie Panter-Downes⟩

3**hallelujah** \"\ *adj* [2*hallelujah*] **:** of or belonging to the Salvation Army ⟨~ lass⟩ ⟨~ bonnet⟩ ⟨~ meeting⟩

**hal·len** *var of* HALLAN

**hal·len·kir·che** \ˈhälənˌkirkə\ *n, pl* **hallenkir·chen** \-rkən\ *usu cap* [G, fr. *halle* hall + *kirche* church] **:** HALL CHURCH

**hal·ley's method** \ˈha\|lēz- *also* ÷ˈhā\|\ *n, cap H* [after Edmund *Halley* †1742 Eng. astronomer] **:** a method of finding the parallax of Venus and hence the sun's distance by observing the duration of a transit of Venus from stations widely separated in latitude

**hallgirl** \ˈ⸗ˌ⸗\ *n* **:** a girl employed to clean the halls of a hotel

**hall house** *n, chiefly Scot* **:** MANOR HOUSE

**halliard** *var of* HALYARD

**hal·ling** \ˈhäliŋ, ˈhal-\ *n* -s [Norw, fr. *Hallingdal* a valley in southern Norway] **1 :** an acrobatic Norwegian dance in duple measure for one to three single dancers **2 :** a lively dance tune written in a major key usu. in 2/4 time and usu. played on the Hardanger fiddle

**hal·lion** \ˈhalyən\ *n* -s [origin unknown] *chiefly Scot* **:** SCAMP, SCOUNDREL

1**hall·mark** \ˈhȯlˌmärk, -mȧk\ *n* [Goldsmiths' *Hall*, London, England, where gold and silver articles were assayed and stamped + E *mark*] **1 a** *in England* **:** an official mark stamped on gold and silver articles to attest their purity and comprised of the king's or queen's mark, the maker's mark, the assayer's mark, and a letter of the alphabet for the year, a new style being used when the alphabet in one style is exhausted **b :** a mark stamped on gold and silver articles consisting of the word "sterling" accompanied by the name or mark of the manufacturer **c :** a mark or device placed or stamped upon an article of trade to indicate origin, purity, or genuineness ⟨the ~ of a potter of the Ming dynasty⟩ **d :** the identifying mark or device (as of a company) ⟨the new ~ will be a small, bright spot on company letterheads —*Bull. Standard Oil of Calif.*⟩ **2 :** a distinguishing or identifying characteristic, trait, or feature ⟨avoidance of such constructions . . . has become a ~ of social respectability —Thomas Pyles⟩ ⟨the ~ of the adult human being is responsibility —Weston La Barre⟩ ⟨his solicitude for the poor . . . is the ~ of his best stories —Hakon Stangerup⟩

2**hallmark** \"\ *vt* **1 :** to stamp with a hallmark **2 a :** to constitute a distinguishing or identifying feature or trait of ⟨two great faults and two great virtues ~*ed* the work of the late . . . associate justice —Fred Rodell⟩ **b :** to have or display the distinguishing, validating, or identifying traits or features of ⟨a host of inconspicuous but ~*ed* spinsters —*Times Lit. Supp.*⟩ ⟨my one genuine ~*ed* ghost story —Rudyard Kipling⟩

**hall·moot** \ˈhȯlˌmüt\ *n* [ME *halimot*, fr. *hal* hall + *-imot* (fr. OE *gemōt* assembly) — more at HALL, GEMOT] **:** a private court of the lord of a manor **:** COURT BARON

1**hal·lo** *or* **hal·loa** \həˈlō, haˈ-, ˈha(ˌ)lō\ *or* **hal·loo** \-lü\ *or* **hul·loo** \(ˌ)həˈlü, ˈhə(ˌ)lü\ *interj* [origin unknown] **1** — used to attract attention **2** — used as a call of encouragement or jubilation

2**hallo** *or* **halloa** *or* **halloo** *or* **hulloo** \"\ *vb* -ED/-ING/-S *vi* **:** to cry *hallo* **:** call out **:** HOLLER ~ *vt* **1 a :** to call or cry *hallo* to **:** attract the attention of **b :** to call encouragement to **2 :** to utter loudly **:** HOLLER

3**hallo** *or* **halloa** *or* **halloo** *or* **hulloo** \"\ *n, pl* **hallos** *or* **halloes** *or* **halloas** *or* **halloos** *or* **hulloos :** an exclamation or call of *hallo* **:** a halloing or shouting

4**hallo** \"\ *chiefly Brit var of* HELLO

**hal·lock** \ˈhalək\ *n* -s [after *Hallock*, 19th cent. Am. box manufacturer] **:** a rectangular wood veneer berry box with straight sides and a raised bottom

**hall of fame** *usu cap H&F* **1 :** a hall, building, room, or other structure housing statues, busts, tablets, or other memorials commemorating famous or illustrious persons usu. selected for inclusion by a qualified group of electors ⟨a *Hall of Fame* honoring great merchants of America was inaugurated tonight —*Springfield (Mass.) Union*⟩ ⟨ground-breaking ceremonies were held today for the national cowboy *Hall of Fame* here —*N.Y. Times*⟩ **2 :** a group of individuals in some particular category formally selected by a group of qualified electors or informally adjudged by popular opinion as most illustrious or meriting immortal fame ⟨earned herself a permanent place in the trotters' *Hall of Fame* —R.E.Meyer⟩

**halloth** *or* **hallot** *pl of* HALLAH

1**hal·low** \ˈha\|(ˌ)lō, \|lə, *often* -ləw + V *sometimes* ˈhä\|\ *vt* **hal·lowed** \\|(ˌ)lōd, \|ləd\ **hal·lowed** \", *in the Lord's Prayer* " *or* \|ləwə̇d *or* \|lōə̇d\ **hallowing; hallows** [ME *halowen*, fr. OE *hālgian*, fr. *hālig* holy — more at HOLY] **1 :** to make holy **:** set apart for holy or religious use **:** treat or keep as sacred **:** CONSECRATE ⟨~*ed* be thy name —Mt 6:9 (RSV)⟩ **2 :** to respect greatly **:** VENERATE, REVERE ⟨institutions ~*ed* for their classical learning —*Loyola Univ. Bull.*⟩ ⟨the most ~*ed* of all law-enforcement agencies —Dwight MacDonald⟩

2**hal·low** \"\ *vb* -ED/-ING/-S [ME *halowen*, fr. MF *halloer*, fr. *hallo*, interj.] **:** HALLO ⟨~*ed* at several to explain himself —A.E.Fife⟩

3**hal·low** \ˈhalə, +V " *or* -ləw\ *dial var of* HOLLOW

**hal·low·day** \ˈhaləˌdā, -lōˌ-\ *n* [short for *All Hallow Day*, fr. ME *all halowen day*, lit., all the saints' day] **1** *dial Eng, usu cap* **:** ALL SAINTS' DAY **2** *dial Eng* **:** a saint's day **:** HOLIDAY

**hallowed** *see* 1HALLOW\ *adj* [ME *halowed*, fr. past part. of *halowen* to hallow — more at HALLOW] **1 :** CONSECRATED, BLESSED **2 :** REVERED, VENERATED, SACRED ⟨the ~ heroes of the past —Oscar Fraley⟩ ⟨the ~ customs of our group —M.R. Cohen⟩

**hal·lowed·ly** *adv* **:** in a hallowed manner

**hal·lowed·ness** *n* -ES **:** the quality or state of being hallowed **:** HOLINESS

**hal·low·een** *also* **hal·low·e'en** \ˌhaləˈwēn, ÷ˌhäl-\ *n* -s *usu cap* [short for *All Hallow E'en*] **:** the evening preceding All Saints' Day **:** the evening of October 31 which is often devoted by young people to merrymaking (as with jack-o'-lanterns) and playing pranks sometimes involving petty damage to property

**hal·low·mas** \ˈhalō\|ˌmas, -lə\|, \|ˌmaa(ə)s, \|ˌmais, \|ˌməs *sometimes* \|ˌmȧs\ *n* -ES *cap* [short for *Allhallowmass*] **:** the feast of All Saints

**hal·loy·site** \həˈlȯiˌsīt, haˈ-, -ˌzīt\ *n* -s [F, fr. Omalius d'*Halloy* †1875 Belg. geologist + F *-ite*] **:** a clay mineral $Al_2Si_2O_5(OH)_4.nH_2O$ occurring in soft white or light-colored masses and in at least two states of hydration $n=2$, $n=4$

**hall porter** *n, chiefly Brit* **:** a porter or attendant who carries the luggage of patrons and performs other chores at a hotel

**hall process** \ˈhȯl-\ *n, usu cap H* [after Charles M. *Hall* †1914 Am. chemist] **:** the process by which aluminum is produced consisting of electrolysis of a molten solution of purified alumina in cryolite at a temperature of about 950°C

**halls** *pl of* HALL

**hall scale** *n, usu cap H* [after Maurice C. *Hall* b1886 Amer. zoologist] **:** an Asiatic scale (*Nilotaspis halli*) that has been introduced into California where it is a serious pest of stone fruit trees

**hall's honeysuckle** *n, usu cap 1st H* [after G. R. *Hall*, 20th cent. Am. physician who introduced the plant from China] **:** a honeysuckle (*Lonicera japonica halliana*) that is a vining variety of Japanese honeysuckle with flowers initially pure white but yellowing with age, is often used as an ornamental climber or ground cover, and has established itself as an aggressive escape in much of the southeastern U. S.

**hallstand** \ˈ⸗ˌ⸗\ *n* **:** a tall piece of furniture with a mirror, several pegs or arms for hats and other articles of clothing, a rack for umbrellas, and a compartment for storage

hallstand

**hall·statt** *or* **hall·stadt** \ˈhȯlˌstat, ˈhälˌshtät\ *adj, usu cap* [fr. *Hallstatt*, village in Austria] **1 :** of or belonging to Hallstatt, Austria or the archaeological remains there **2 :** of or relating to the earlier period of the Iron Age in Europe characterized by transition from the use of bronze to iron, possession of domestic animals, agriculture, and skill in the making of pottery and ornaments — compare LA TÈNE

**hall·statt·an** *also* **hall·stadt·an** \(ˈ)hȯlˌstad·ēn, (ˈ)hälˌshtäd-\ *adj, usu cap* [*Hallstatt*, Austria + E *-an*] **:** HALLSTATT

**hall tree** *n* **:** CLOTHES TREE

**hal·lu·ci·nate** \həˈlüsᵊnˌāt *also* həlˈyü-\ *vb* -ED/-ING/-S [L *hallucinatus, alucinatus*, past part. of *hallucinari, alucinari* to talk idly, prate, dream, prob. fr. Gk *halyein, alyein* to be distraught, to wander] *vt* **:** to affect with visions or imaginary perceptions ⟨they are not *hallucinated*, they know that the object is not really there —R.S.Woodworth⟩ ⟨a poor *hallucinated* invalid —Marguerite Young⟩ ~ *vi* **:** to have hallucinations ⟨most normal persons have occasionally *hallucinated* —William McDougall⟩

**hal·lu·ci·na·tion** \⸗ˌ⸗⸗ˈāshən\ *n* -s [L *hallucination-, hallucinatio, alucination-, alucinatio*, fr. *hallucinatus, alucinatus* + *-ion-, -io* -ion] **1 a :** perception of objects with no reality **:** experience of sensations with no external cause usu. arising from disorder of the nervous system (as in delirium tremens or in functional psychosis without known neurological disease) **b :** the object of a hallucinatory perception **2 :** a completely unfounded or mistaken impression or notion **:** DELUSION ⟨that popular ~, from which not even great scientists are . . . free —Lewis Mumford⟩ — **hal·lu·ci·na·tion·al** \⸗ˌ⸗⸗ˈāshənᵊl, -āshnəl\ *adj* — **hal·lu·ci·na·tive** \⸗ˈ⸗⸗ˌād·iv, ⸗ˈ⸗⸗ˌəd·iv\ *adj*

**hal·lu·ci·na·to·ry** \⸗ˈ⸗⸗əˌtōrē\ *adj* **:** partaking of or tending to produce hallucination **:** not objectively perceived **:** IMAGINED, UNREAL ⟨fleeing in terror from a ~ wolf —Mark Kanzer⟩ ⟨succumbed to ~ rhetoric —Irving Howe⟩ ⟨the bizarre, ~ dreams of fever —Jean Stafford⟩

**hal·lu·cino·gen** \⸗ˈ⸗⸗əˌjen, -jən, ˌhalyəˈsinə-\ *n* -s [*hallucination* + *-o-* + *-gen*] **:** a substance that induces hallucinations; *esp* **:** one taken orally ⟨mescaline is a ~⟩ — **hal·lu·ci·no·gen·ic** \həˌlüsᵊnəˈjenik *also* həlˌyü-\ *adj*

**hal·lu·ci·no·sis** \həˌlüsᵊnˈōsə̇s *also* həlˌyü-\ *n, pl* **hallucino·ses** \-ōˌsēz\ [NL, fr. L *hallucinatio* + NL *-osis*] **:** a pathological mental state occurring esp. as a manifestation of alcoholism in which awareness consists largely or exclusively of hallucinations

**hal·lux** \ˈhaləks\ *n, pl* **hallu·ces** \-l(y)əˌsēz -ləˌs-\ [NL, fr. L *hallus, hallux* big toe] **:** the first or preaxial digit of the hind limb **:** BIG TOE

**hallux val·gus** \-ˈvalgəs\ *n* [NL, lit., wry big toe] **:** an abnormal deviation of the big toe toward the outside of the foot associated esp. with the wearing of ill-fitting shoes — compare BUNION

**hall·wachs effect** \ˈhälˌväks-\ *n, usu cap H* [after Wilhelm *Hallwachs* †1922 Ger. physicist] **:** a photoelectric effect in which a negatively charged body in a vacuum is discharged upon exposure to ultraviolet radiation

**hallway** \ˈ⸗ˌ⸗\ *n* **:** HALL; *esp* **:** an entrance hall

**halm** *var of* HAULM

**Hal·ma** \ˈhalmə\ *trademark* — used for a game played by two or four players on a board having 256 squares with the object being for each player to move or jump his men from their home corner to a corresponding position in the opposite corner

1**ha·lo** \ˈhā(ˌ)lō\ *n, pl* **halos** *or* **haloes** [L *halos* halo of the sun, fr. Gk *halōs* threshing floor, disk of the sun or the moon, halo around the sun or moon; akin to Gk *halōn* threshing floor, and perh. to *lyein* to loosen — more at LOSE] **1 :** a circle, arc, or splotch of light either white or prismatically colored and definitely situated with reference to a luminous body and resulting from the reflection or refraction or both of its light; *specif* **:** circles round the sun or moon caused by the presence of ice particles in the atmosphere and differing from coronas in being of definite size usu. of about 22° or 46° radius and if colored in showing red on the side nearest to the luminary **2 :** something resembling a halo: as **a :** NIMBUS **b :** a differentiated zone surrounding a central object ⟨the ~ around a boil⟩ ⟨the presence of a ~ of alteration has been used as a guide to ore finding —A.M.Bateman⟩; *specif* **:** a zone usu. of lighter colored tissue characteristically surrounding the lesions in certain plant diseases esp. of bacterial origin **c :** a circlet of flowers, a ribbon, or a small hat worn off the face and back on the head by women **3 :** the aura of glory, veneration, prestige, or sentiment surrounding an idealized person or thing ⟨a . . . positive ~ surrounds scientific endeavors —John Dewey⟩ ⟨put a romantic ~ about the old plantation life —Oscar Handlin⟩ ⟨the exclusiveness of the institute . . . gave it a ~ —Romola Nijinsky⟩

2**halo** \"\ *vt* -ED/-ING/-ES **:** to form or surround with a halo **:** encircle as if with a halo ⟨red-gold hair . . . ~*ing* a slim face —Frank Yerby⟩ ⟨the ~*ed* lights burned her eyes —John Dos Passos⟩ ⟨~*ed* by publicity —F.L.Allen⟩

3**halo** \ˈha(ˌ)lō\ *adj* [*hal-*] **:** containing halogen — used esp. of organic compounds ⟨~ aldehydes⟩

**halo-** — see HAL-

**ha·lob·a·tes** \həˈläbəˌtēz\ *n, cap* [NL, fr. *hal-* + *-bates*] **:** a genus of small wingless marine water striders having the thorax large and the abdomen very small

**hal·o·bi·ont** \ˌhalōˈbīˌänt\ *n* -s *often attrib* [*hal-* + *-biont*] **:** an organism (as a plant) that flourishes in a saline habitat

**halo blight** *n* **1** *also* **halo spot :** a blight of beans and occas. other legumes that is caused by a bacterium (*Pseudomonas phaseolicola*) and typically produces on the leaves, stems, and pods round water-soaked lesions surrounded by a yellowish zonation, the lesions finally turning brick red **2 :** blight affecting the leaves of oats and other grasses caused by a bacterium (*Pseudomonas coronafaciens*) characterized by oval water-soaked lesions turning gray to brownish and surrounded by a pale zonation

**hal·o·chro·mism** \ˌhaləˈkrōˌmizəm\ *n* -s [*hal-* + *chrom-* + *-ism*] **:** the phenomenon or property of the formation of strongly colored salts by addition of acids to colorless or faintly colored compounds

**halo effect** *n* **:** a tendency for a general opinion or attitude derived from rating an individual as high or low on one item of a test to exert an influence upon the rating of other and separate items, traits, or responses; *esp* **:** generalization from the perception of one outstanding personality trait to an overevaluation of the whole personality

**hal·o·form** \ˈhaləˌfȯrm\ *n* [*hal-* + *-form* (as in *chloroform*)] **:** a compound $CHX_3$ (as chloroform) derived from methane by replacement of three atoms of hydrogen by halogen

**hal·o·gen** \-jən, -ˌjen\ *n* -s [Sw, fr. *halo-* hal- + *-gen*] **:** any of the five elements fluorine, chlorine, bromine, iodine, and astatine forming part of group VII A of the periodic table and existing in the free state normally as diatomic molecules — compare PSEUDOHALOGEN — **ha·log·e·nous** \(ˈ)haˈläjənəs\ *adj*

**hal·o·gen·ate** \ˈhaləjə̇ˌnāt, haˈläj-\ *vt* -ED/-ING/-S **:** to treat or cause to combine with a halogen **:** introduce a halogen into (as an organic compound) — **hal·o·gen·a·tion** \ˌhaləjə̇ˈnāshən, haˌläj-\ *n* -s

**hal·o·gen·ide** \ˈhaləjə̇ˌnīd, haˈläj-\ *n* -s [ISV *halogen* + *-ide*] **:** HALIDE — used in the nomenclature adopted by the International Union of Pure and Applied Chemistry

**hal·o·gen·oid** \-ˌnȯid\ *n* -s **:** PSEUDOHALOGEN

**hal·o·ge·ton** \ˌhaləˈjēᵊn\ *n* [NL, fr. *hal-* + Gk *geitōn* neighbor] **1** *cap* **:** a small genus of Mediterranean and central Asian herbs and shrubs (family Chenopodiaceae) with fleshy semicylindrical leaves and axillary clusters of flowers — see BARILLA 1b **2** -s **:** any plant of the genus *Halogeton; esp* **:** a coarse annual herb (*H. glomeratus*) introduced into No. America from Siberia and now a noxious weed in western American rangelands dangerous to sheep and cattle because of its high oxalate content

**hal·o·hy·drin** \-ˈhīdrə̇n\ *n* -s [ISV *hal-* + *-hydrin*] **:** any of a class of organic compounds derived from glycols or polyhydroxy alcohols (as glycerol) by substitution of halogen for part of the hydroxyl groups — compare CHLOROHYDRIN

**halolike** \ˈ⸗(ˌ)⸗ˌ⸗\ *adj* **:** resembling a halo

**hal·o·lim·nic** \ˌhalōˈlimnik\ *adj* [ISV *hal-* + *limn-* + *-ic*] *of a marine organism* **:** capable of living in fresh water

**ha·lom·e·ter** \haˈlämə̇d·ə(r)\ *n* [ISV *hal-* + *-meter*] **:** an instrument for measuring the forms of crystals of salts

**hal·o·mor·phic** \ˌhaləˈmȯrfik\ *adj* [*hal-* + *-morphic*] **:** of or relating to intrazonal soils characterized by the presence of either neutral or alkali salts or both — compare CALOMORPHIC, HYDROMORPHIC — **hal·o·mor·phism** \ˌ⸗⸗ˈ⸗ˌfizəm\ *n* -s

**hal·o·phile** \ˈhaləˌfīl\ *n* -s [ISV *hal-* + *-phile;* prob. orig. formed as Sw *halofil*] **:** a halophilic organism

**hal·o·phil·ic** \ˌ⸗⸗ˈfilik\ *or* **ha·loph·i·lous** \(ˈ)haˈläfələs\ *also* **hal·o·phile** \ˈhaləˌfīl\ *or* **hal·o·phil** \-ˌfil\ *adj* [*hal-* + *-philic* or *-philous* or *-phile, -phil*] *of an organism* **:** flourishing in a salty environment

**hal·o·phyte** \ˈhaləˌfīt\ *n* -s [ISV *hal-* + *-phyte*] **:** a plant that grows naturally in soils having a high content of various salts, that usu. resembles a true xerophyte and that occurs in many families (as Chenopodiaceae, Compositae, Plumbaginaceae) — compare MESOPHYTE — **hal·o·phyt·ic** \ˌ⸗⸗ˈfid·ik\ *adj*

**hal·o·ra·ga·ce·ae** \ˌhalərəˈgāsēˌē, həˌlȯr-\ *n pl, cap* [NL, fr. *Haloragis*, type genus + *-aceae*] **:** a family (order Myrtales) of usu. monoecious plants having predominantly unisexual flowers with 4 or 8 stamens and an inferior ovary

**hal·o·rag·i·da·ce·ae** *or* **hal·or·rhag·i·da·ce·ae** \ˌhaləˌrajəˈdāsēˌē\ [NL, fr. *Haloragid-, Haloragis* + *-aceae*] *syn of* HALORAGACEAE

**hal·o·ra·gis** \ˌhaləˈrājə̇s\ *n, cap* [NL, irreg. fr. *hal-* + Gk *rhag-, rhax* berry] **:** the type genus of Haloragaceae — see SEABERRY

**halos** *pl of* HALO

**hal·o·saur** \ˈhaləˌsȯ(ə)r\ *n* -s [NL *Halosaurus*] **:** a member of the Halosauridae

**hal·o·sau·rid** \ˌ⸗⸗ˈsȯrəd\ *adj* [NL *Halosauridae*] **:** of or relating to the Halosauridae

**hal·o·sau·ri·dae** \ˌ⸗⸗ˈ⸗rəˌdē\ *n pl, cap* [NL, fr. *Halosaurus*, type genus + *-idae*] **:** a family (order Heteromi) of mostly extinct deep-sea fishes having cycloid scales

**hal·o·sau·rus** \-rəs\ *n, cap* [NL, fr. *hal-* + *-saurus*] **:** the type genus of the Halosauridae

**hal·o·sere** \ˈhaləˌsi(ə)r\ *n* [*hal-* + *sere*] **:** an ecological sere originating in a saline habitat

**halo spot** *n* **:** HALO BLIGHT 1

**halo·tolerant** \ˌhalō+\ *adj* [*hal-* + *tolerant*] **:** HALOXENE

**ha·lot·ri·chite** \haˈlä·trəˌkīt\ *n* -s [G *halotrichit*, fr. *hal-* + *trich-* + *-it* -ite] **1 :** a mineral $FeAl_2(SO_4)_4.22H_2O$ consisting of a hydrous iron aluminum sulfate **2 :** any of several sulfates similar to halotrichite in construction and habit

**halo·tyd·e·us** \ˌhalōˈtidēəs, -tid-, tīˌd(y)üs\ *n, cap* [NL, fr. *hal-* + *Tydeus*, genus of mites, after *Tydeus*, Greek mythological hero] **:** a genus of soft-bodied phytophagous mites that have the front pair of legs modified as sensory organs and that are destructive to legumes and certain other crops in southern Africa and Australia — see SANDMITE

**hal·oxene** \(ˈ)haˈläkˌsēn, ˈhaləˌzēn\ *adj* [*hal-* + Gk *xenos* foreign — more at XEN-] *of an organism* **:** tolerating but not preferring a saline habitat — compare HALOPHILIC

**hals** *or* **halse** \'hȯs, -å-,-a-\ *n, pl* **halses** [ME *hals*, fr. OE *heals* — more at COLLAR] **1** *now dial Brit* **:** NECK **2** *now dial Brit* **a :** THROAT, WINDPIPE **b :** PASS, DEFILE, COL

**halse** \"\ *vt* -ED/-ING/-S [ME *halsen*, fr. *hals*, n.] *now dial Brit* **:** EMBRACE, HUG

**hal·sen** \'älzən, 'ȯz³n\ *vt* -ED/-ING/-S [ME *halsnen* to adjure, conjure, fr. *halsen* to adjure, conjure, entreat, greet (fr. OE *hālsian*) + *-nen* -en; akin to OHG *heilisōn* to predict, adjure, conjure, ON *heilsa* to greet; derivatives fr. the root of OE *hāl* healthy, whole — more at WHOLE] *now dial Eng* **:** DIVINE, PREDICT

**halsh** \'(h)alsh\ *vt* -ED/-ING/-ES [ME *halchen* to embrace, tie, knot, prob. alter. of *halsen*] *dial Eng* **:** KNOT

**¹halt** \'hȯlt\ *adj* [ME, fr. OE *healt*; akin to OHG *halz* lame, ON *haltr*, Goth *halts* lame, L *clades* destruction, disaster, Gk *klan* to break, *kolos* docked, hornless, *kolobos* docked, curtailed, Lith *kalti* to beat, forge; basic meaning: beating, hewing] **:** having a halting walk **:** LAME ⟨gave alms to the ~ and . . . the poor —Jean Stafford⟩ ⟨a place for everyone . . . old and young, hale and ~ —Sir Winston Churchill⟩

**²halt** \"\ *vi* -ED/-ING/-S [ME *halten*, fr. OE *healtian*; akin to OHG *halzēn* to be lame, limp; derivatives fr. the root of E ¹*halt*] **1 :** to walk or proceed lamely **:** LIMP ⟨so lamely . . . that dogs bark at me as I ~ by them —Shak.⟩ **2 :** to stand in perplexity or doubt between alternate courses **:** WAVER **3 :** to display weakness or imperfection (as in argument, development, or meter) **:** proceed raggedly or falteringly **:** FALTER, LAPSE ⟨the translation ~s now and then —*Brit. Book News*⟩ ⟨the verse that ~s in places⟩ ⟨the argument often ~s and sometimes breaks down completely⟩

**³halt** \"\ *n* -s [G, fr. MHG, fr. *halt!*, imp. of *halten* to hold, stop, fr. OHG *haltan* — more at HOLD] **1 :** a temporary or definitive stop in marching or walking or in any action or process **:** arrest of progress ⟨the car came to a sudden ~⟩ ⟨economic progress was brought to a ~⟩ ⟨a ~, rather than a complete stoppage, in the flow of talent —*Irish Digest*⟩ ⟨time to call a ~ in a useless struggle⟩ **2** *chiefly Brit* **:** a stopping place for public transport; *esp* **:** a railway flag stop ⟨a slow train stopping at every station including ~s —*Punch*⟩

**⁴halt** \"\ *vb* -ED/-ING/-S [G *halten* to hold, stop, fr. OHG *haltan*] *vi* **1 :** to cease marching or journeying **:** stop for a longer or shorter period **:** stand still ⟨ordered his troops to ~⟩ ⟨made two or three . . . paces about the room, and suddenly ~*ed* —W.J.Locke⟩ ⟨many families ~*ed* and took up land in the mountain valleys —*Amer. Guide Series: Tenn.*⟩ **2 :** to discontinue temporarily or permanently **:** TERMINATE, END, SUSPEND ⟨hostilities ~*ed* while the generals conferred⟩ ⟨the project ~*ed* because of inadequate financial support⟩ ~ *vt* **1 :** to cause to cease marching or journeying **:** bring to a stop ⟨~*ed* the wagon train at a small settlement⟩ ⟨~*ed* the advance of his troops⟩ ⟨slid the bowl back down the bar and ~*ed* it before the soldier —Kay Boyle⟩ ⟨marshes that would have ~*ed* any vehicle —*Amer Guide Series: N.C.*⟩ **2 :** to cause the discontinuance of **:** terminate the existence or progress of **:** END ⟨did the best he could to ~ the erosion —D.L.Graham⟩ ⟨consumer spending . . . rose and ~*ed* the decline —*Dun's Rev.*⟩ ⟨~ hostilities⟩ ⟨sought to ~ corruption and increase efficiency⟩

**¹hal·ter** \'hȯltə(r)\ *n* -s *often attrib* [ME, fr. OE *hælftre*; akin to OHG *halftra* halter, MLG *halchter*, MD *halfter, halchter*; derivatives fr. the root of E *helve*] **1 a :** a rope or strap with or without a headstall for leading or tying a horse or other animal **b :** a headstall of rope or leather and usu. with noseband and throatlatch to which a lead may be attached **2 :** a rope for hanging criminals **:** NOOSE; *also* **:** death by hanging **3 a :** a woman's or girl's waist typically held in place by bands or straps around the neck and across the back and leaving the back, arms, and midriff bare **b :** an adaptation of this style for the necklines of other garments (as blouses, dresses, bathing suits) **c** *or* **halter strap :** SLING 3a(3)

halter 1b

**²halter** \"\ *vt* **haltered; haltered; haltering** \-ltəriŋ, -l·triŋ\ **halters 1 a :** to catch with or as if with a halter **:** put a halter on (as a horse) **b :** to put a hangman's halter on **:** HANG **2 :** to put restraint upon **:** BRIDLE, FETTER, HAMPER, RESTRAIN ⟨~ his conscience⟩ ⟨always afraid of the effect of ~*ing* the daily press⟩

**³hal·ter** \", 'hal- *or* **hal·tere** \-,ti(ə)r, -iə\ *n, pl* **hal·teres** \=ˈti(,)rēz; 'hȯl,ti(ə)rz, -iəz\ [NL, fr. L, jumping weight, fr. Gk *haltēr*, fr. *hallesthai* to jump — more at SALLY] **:** one of the modified second pair of wings in Diptera and the first pair in Strepsiptera that are reduced to club-shaped organs and that function as flight instruments — called also *balancer, poiser*

**halterbreak** \'==,=\ *vt* **:** to break (as a colt) to a halter

**hal·te·rid·i·um** \,haltə'ridēəm\ [NL, fr. L *halter* + NL *-idium*] *syn of* HAEMOPROTEUS

**hal·ti·ca** \'haltikə\ [NL, prob. fr. Gk *haltikos* good at leaping — more at ALTICA] *syn of* ALTICA

**halting** *adj* [ME, fr. pres. part. of *halten* to limp — more at HALT] **1 a :** marked by a limp **:** LAME, LIMPING ⟨recognized the cripple's ~ walk⟩ **b :** slow and hesitant or reluctant **:** DRAGGING, UNCERTAIN ⟨walked home with heavy heart and ~ steps⟩ **c :** lacking smoothness, facility, verve, or display of easy command in delivery **:** marked by abrupt halts and starts **:** FALTERING, AWKWARD, UNGRACEFUL ⟨his speaking voice . . . is thin and ~ —*Current Biog.*⟩ ⟨too wise to let his ~ utterance weaken the impression of his facile pen —John Buchan⟩ ⟨his ~ delivery of the play's longest speech —Henry Hewes⟩ **2 a :** displaying weakness or imperfection (as in argument, development, or meter) **:** marked by lapses (as of grammar, interest, continuity) **:** proceeding raggedly or falteringly ⟨a very ~ argument⟩ ⟨the poem's weak and ~ rhymes⟩ ⟨the ~ development of this thin plot⟩ **b :** lacking in sureness (as of purpose, drive, or continuity) **:** proceeding by fits and starts **:** FUMBLING, INDECISIVE, VACILLATING, INEFFECTIVE ⟨development of the military intelligence service . . . was slow and ~ —G.F.Ashworth⟩ ⟨the season got off to a ~ start⟩ ⟨made ~ advance toward solving their difficulties —C.L.Jones⟩ — **halt·ing·ly** *adv*

**halt·ing·ness** *n* -ES **:** DEFECTIVENESS, FAULTINESS

**halts** *pres 3d sing of* HALT, *pl of* HALT

**hal·uck·et** \'haləkət\ *adj* [fr. past part. of Sc *hallock, haluck* to behave in a giddy or foolish manner, fr. *hallock, haluck* giddy, foolish girl] *Scot* **:** wild and giddy **:** HALF-WITTED

**ha·luk·kah** *or* **cha·luk·kah** *also* **ha·lu·kah** *or* **ha·lu·ka** *or* **cha·lu·ka** \ˌkälüˈkä, kəˈlükə\ *n* -s [Heb *hăluqqāh* portion, division] **:** a fund collected from Jews throughout the world for support of the needy in Palestine

**ha·lutz** *or* **cha·lutz** \kä'lüts\ *n, pl* **ha·lutz·im** *or* **cha·lutz·im** \,kä,lüt'sēm, kä'lütsim\ [NHeb *hālūṣ*, fr. Heb, warrior, vanguard] **:** a Jewish immigrant to Palestine who works in the Jewish settlements at tasks contributing to the development of the country as a Jewish homeland **:** PIONEER

**ha·lutza** *or* **cha·lutza** \ˌkä,lütˈsä\ *n, pl* **halutz·oth** *or* **halutz·ot** *or* **chalutz·oth** *or* **chalutz·ot** \ˌkä,lüt,sōt(h), -ōs, =ˈ=,=\ [NHeb *hălūṣāh*, fem. of *hālūṣ*] **:** a female halutz

**ha·lutz·i·ut** *or* **cha·lutz·i·ut** \ˌkälütsēˈüt\ *n* -s [NHeb *hālūṣiut*, fr. *hālūṣ*] **:** PIONEERING; *specif* **:** the pioneer movement of the halutzim in Palestine

**hal·vah** *or* **hal·va** *or* **halavah** \hˈäl'vä, kˈ, ˈäl'vä; 'häl(,)vä, 'hȧl(,)vȧ, -l(ə)və, -lə,v-; 'halvə\ *n* -s [Yiddish *halva*, fr. Romanian, fr. Turk *helva*, fr. Ar *ḥalwā* sweetmeat] **:** a flaky confection of crushed sesame seeds in a base of honey or other syrup

**¹halve** \'hav, -aa(ə)-,-ai-,-å-,-ä-\ *vt* -ED/-ING/-S [ME *halven, halfen*, fr. *half*, n. — more at HALF] **1 a :** to divide into two equal parts **:** separate into halves ⟨~ an apple⟩ ⟨ripe walnuts, *halved* and picked from the shell —Nora Waln⟩ **b :** to reduce to one half ⟨*halving* the purchase tax on cotton goods —*New Republic*⟩ ⟨doubling the profit by *halving* the cost⟩ **c :** to share equally ⟨was it the double of my dream . . . or did we ~ a dream? —W.B.Yeats⟩ ⟨it didn't much matter that he was here to ~ my triumph —Max Beerbohm⟩ **2 :** to join two pieces of (timber) by cutting away each for half its thickness at the joining place and fitting together **3 :** to play (as a hole, round, match) in the same number of strokes as one's opponent at golf

**²halve** \"\ *n* -s **:** a tie score on a hole or a round of golf ⟨salvaged a ~ on the 147-yard third —*N.Y. Herald Tribune*⟩

**halved** *adj* **1 :** reduced to one half ⟨had to get along with a ~ income⟩ **2 :** appearing as if one side or one half were cut away **:** DIMIDIATE

**halv·ers** \-və(r)z\ *n pl* **:** half shares **:** HALVES ⟨went ~ on the price⟩

**halves** *pl of* HALF

**hal·yard** *or* **hal·liard** \'halyə(r)d\ *also* **haul·yard** \'hȯl-\ *n* -s [alter. of ME *halier*, fr. *halen* to pull — more at HALE] **:** a rope or tackle for hoisting and lowering (as a yard, spar, sail, flag) — see *ship* illustration

**hal·yik·wa·mai** \hal'yikwə,mī\ *n, pl* **halyikwamai** *or* **halyikwamais** *usu cap* **1 :** an Indian people in the Colorado river valley below the mouth of the Gila allied with the Cocopa **2 :** a member of the Halyikwamai people

**hal·y·si·tes** \,halə'sīd·(,)ēz\ *n, cap* [NL, fr. Gk *halysis* chain + NL *-ites*] **:** a genus consisting of the chain corals

**hal·zoun** \(')hal¦zün\ *n* -s [prob. fr. Ar *ḥalzūn* snail] **:** infestation of the larynx and pharynx by worms esp. of the genus *Fasciola* consumed in raw liver

**¹ham** \'am\ *n* -s [ME (attested only in place names), fr. OE *hamm*; akin to MLG *ham* enclosed land, OE *hemm* border — more at HEM] *now dial Eng* **:** a piece of grassland

**²ham** \'ham, -aa(ə)-\ *n* -s [ME *hamme*, fr. OE *hamm*; akin to OHG *hamma* popliteal space, thigh, haunch, ON *hǫm* haunch, Gk *knēmē* shinbone, OIr *cnāim* bone, leg] **1 a :** the part of the leg behind the knee **:** the hollow of the knee **:** POPLITEAL SPACE ⟨such a case as yours constrains a man to bow in the ~s —Shak.⟩ **b :** a buttock with its associated thigh or with the hinder part of a thigh — usu. used in pl. ⟨squatted submissively on his ~s —Joseph Conrad⟩ **c :** a hock or the hinder part of a hock **2 a :** the thigh of an animal prepared for food ⟨deer or elk ~s —R.R.Camp⟩; *esp* **:** the thigh of a hog either fresh or cured by salting and smoking ⟨~s . . . from . . . peanut-fed hogs —*U.S. Code*⟩ — see PORK illustration **b :** something that resembles such a ham in shape; *specif* **:** a cushion used esp. by tailors for pressing curved areas of garments **3** [short for *hamfatter*] **a :** an unskillful but flamboyant performer **:** EXHIBITIONIST, STRUTTER ⟨a wrestling match between a couple of ~s⟩ ⟨an oratorical ~⟩ ⟨the basset is a natural ~ —Charlotte Paul⟩; *esp* **:** an inept or ineffective actor esp. in an overtheatrical style ⟨a typical down-and-out vaudeville ~ —Bennett Cerf⟩ **b :** an inexperienced or incompetent telegraph operator **c :** a government-licensed operator of an amateur radio station ⟨once on the air, he got in touch with ~s on the mainland and they in turn warned ships away from the dangerous coast —R.B. Gehman⟩ **4 a :** melodrama or mawkish sentimentality **:** overdone theatricality ⟨a film scenario full of tears and ~ —V.S.Pritchett⟩ **b :** a tendency to histrionics **:** theatrical streak ⟨dignity may suffer as the ~ emerges in response to the camera's grinding —Walter Goodman⟩

**³ham** \"\ *adj* **1 :** HAMMY ⟨~ actor⟩ ⟨less ~ than its rivals —William Empson⟩ ⟨in all his life he had never been in any situation so corny, so ~ —Charles Jackson⟩ **2 :** of or relating to amateur radio ⟨~ operator⟩ ⟨~ radio band⟩ ⟨~ shack⟩

**⁴ham** \"\ *vb* **hammed; hammed; hamming; hams** *vt* **1 :** to execute with exaggerated speech or gestures **:** OVERACT ⟨spoofed the story and *hammed* the action —Paul Jaretzki⟩ — often used with *up* ⟨~ it up in beer-hall fashion —*Metronome*⟩ **2 :** to infuse with melodrama or mawkish sentimentality ⟨the narration was overly *hammed* in the writing —*Billboard*⟩ ~ *vi* **:** to overplay a part ⟨~s and mugs and . . . misses most of his best effects by underestimating his own simple power —Virgil Thomson⟩

**hamada** *var of* HAMMADA

**¹ha·ma·dan** \'hamə,dan, ¦hamə¦dän\ *n* -s *usu cap* [fr. *Hamadan*, Iran] **:** a Persian rug made in and around Hamadan usu. of wool mixed with camels' hair, tied with the Ghiordes knot, and characterized by muted colors and small angular all-over patterns **2 :** a Kurdish rug marketed in Hamadan

**²hamadan** \"\ *adj, usu cap* [fr. *Hamadan*, Iran] **:** of or from the city of Hamadan, Iran **:** of the kind or style prevalent in Hamadan

**ham·a·dry·ad** \,hamə'drīəd, -ī,ad\ *n* -s [L *Hamadryad-, Hamadryas*, fr. Gk, fr. *hama* together with + *Dryad-, Dryas* Dryad — more at DRYAD] **1 :** a nymph of trees and woods; *esp* **:** a nymph whose life begins and ends with that of a particular tree **2 a** [trans. of NL *hamadryas* (specific epithet of *Naja hamadryas*), fr. L *Hamadryas*] **:** KING COBRA **b** [trans. of NL *hamadryas* (specific epithet of *Papio hamadryas*), fr. L *Hamadryas*] **:** SACRED BABOON

**ham·a·dry·as baboon** \¦==¦drīəs-\ *n* [NL *hamadryas*, specific epithet of *Papio hamadryas*] **:** SACRED BABOON

**ha·mal** *also* **ham·mal** \hə'mäl, -mȯl\ *n* -s [Ar *ḥammāl* porter] **:** a burden bearer in Turkey and other countries of the eastern Mediterranean **:** PORTER

**ha·ma·ma·tsu** \¦hämə¦mät(,)sü\ *adj, usu cap* [fr. *Hamamatsu*, Japan] **:** of or from the city of Hamamatsu, Japan **:** of the kind or style prevalent in Hamamatsu

**ham·a·mel·i·da·ce·ae** \,hamə,melə'dāsē,ē\ *n pl, cap* [NL, fr. *Hamamelid-, Hamamelis*, type genus + *-aceae*] **:** a family of shrubs and trees (order Rosales) having small often clustered flowers and a bicarpellate bilocular ovary and comprising the witch hazels and related plants — see FOTHERGILLA, HAMAMELIS — **ham·a·mel·i·da·ceous** \¦=¦==¦dāshəs\ *adj*

**ham·a·mel·i·dan·the·mum** \,==,==ˈdan(t)thəməm\ *n, cap* [NL, fr. *Hamamelid-, Hamamelis* + *-anthemum*] **:** a genus of fossil plants having flowers resembling those of the witch hazel and found in amber of Oligocene age in the region of the Baltic sea

**ham·a·mel·i·dox·y·lon** \-'däksə,län\ *n, cap* [NL, fr. *Hamamelid-, Hamamelis* + *-o-* + *-xylon*] **:** a genus of fossil plants having wood identical with or similar to that of the witch hazel

**ham·a·me·lis** \-'mēləs\ *n, cap* [NL, fr. Gk *hamamēlis* medlar, fr. *hama* together with + *mēlon* apple, fruit — more at MELON] **:** a genus of shrubs or small trees (family Hamamelidaceae) having pinnately veined leaves and clustered flowers with elongated ribbon-shaped petals — see WITCH HAZEL

**ham·a·mel·i·tes** \,hamə'melə,tēz, -,mə'līd·(,)ēz\ *n, cap* [NL, fr. *Hamamelis* + *-ites*] **:** a genus of fossil plants having leaves similar to those of the witch hazel

**ha·man·tasch** *also* **ha·man·tash** \'hämən,täsh, 'həm-\ *n, pl* **hamantasch·en** \-shən\ [Yiddish *homentash*, fr. *Homen*, biblical chief minister of Ahasuerus and enemy of the Jews (Esth 3–7) + *tash* pocket, bag, fr. OHG *tasca*, fr. (assumed) VL *tasca* task, compensation, purse — more at TASK] **:** a three-cornered cake with a poppy-seed or prune filling traditionally eaten in Jewish households at Purim

**ha·mar·tia** \,hä,mär'tēə, hə'märd·ēə\ *n* -s [Gk, fr. *hamartanein* to err] **1 :** a defect of character **:** error, guilt, or sin esp. of the tragic hero in a literary work **2 :** HAMARTOMA — **ha·mar·ti·al** \¦hä,mär¦tēəl, hə'märd·ēəl\ *adj*

**ha·mar·ti·ol·o·gy** \hə,märd·ē'äləjē\ *n* -ES [Gk *hamartia* sin + E *-o-* + *-logy*] **:** a part of theology treating the doctrine of sin — compare PONEROLOGY

**ham·ar·to·ma** \,hamə(r)'tōmə\ *n, pl* **hamartomas** *or* **hamartomata** [NL, fr. Gk *hamartia* + NL *-oma*] **:** a mass resembling a tumor assumed to represent anomalous development of tissue natural to a part or organ rather than a true tumor — **ham·ar·toma·tous** \¦hamə(r)¦tämәd·əs, -tōm-\ *adj*

**ha·mate** \'hā,māt\ *adj* [L *hamatus*, fr. *hamus* hook + *-atus* -ate; perh. akin to Gk *chamos* bent] **:** bent at the end into a hook **:** HOOKED

**ha·mat·ed** \-,mād·əd\ *adj* [L *hamatus* + E *-ed*] **:** HAMATE

**¹ha·math·ite** \'hāmə,thīt, -,ma,-\ *n* -s *usu cap* [*Hamath* (Hama), Syria + E *-ite*] **:** a native or inhabitant of the ancient city of Hamath in western Syria

**²hamathite** \"\ *adj, usu cap* **1 :** of, relating to, or characteristic of Hamath **2 :** of, relating to, or characteristic of the people of Hamath

**ha·ma·tum** \hə'mād·əm, -hā'-\ *n, pl* **hama·ta** \-d·ə\ *or* **hamatums** [NL, fr. neut. of L *hamatus* hooked] **:** a bone on the inner side of the second row of the carpus in mammals that apparently represents a fusion of the fourth and fifth carpal bones — called also *unciform*

**ham beetle** *n* **:** any of several small beetles that feed in cured or dried food products; *esp* **:** RED-LEGGED HAM BEETLE

**ham·berg·ite** \'ham(,)bər,gīt\ *n* -s [Sw *hambergit*, fr. Axel *Hamberg* †1933 Swed. mineralogist + Sw *-it* -ite] **:** a mineral $Be_2(OH)BO_3$ consisting of beryllium borate and occurring as grayish white prismatic crystals (hardness 7.5, sp. gr. 2.35)

**ham·ble** \'am(b)əl\ *vi* -ED/-ING/-S [perh. akin to LG *humpeln* to limp, OIr *camm* crooked — more at CHANGE] *dial Eng* **:** to limp or stumble in walking

**ham·ble·to·nian** \,hambəl'tōnēən, -ōnyən\ *adj, usu cap* [after *Hambletonian*, 19th cent. Am. stallion from which this strain has descended] **:** a strain of American trotting horses

**ham·bo** \'häm(,)bü\ *n* -s [Sw, fr. *Hambo*, parish in Hälsingland, Sweden] **:** a Swedish round dance to various melodies in triple time

**hambone** \'=,=\ *n* [²*ham* + *bone*] *slang* **:** a performer using a spurious Negro dialect

**ham·bro·line** \'hambrə,līn, -,lən\ *also* **ham·ber·line** \-bə(r),-\ *or* **ham·ber** \-bə(r)\ *n* -s [*hambroline, hamberline* fr. E *hambro-, hamber-* (irreg. fr. *Hamburg*, Germany) + E *line*; *hamber* short for *hamberline*] **:** right-handed 3-strand usu. tarred hemp or jute marine cordage used for small seizings — compare ROUNDLINE

**¹ham·burg** \'ham,bərg, 'haam-, -bōg,-bəig\ *n* -s [fr. *Hamburg*, Germany] **1** *sometimes cap* **:** a machine-embroidered usu. fine cotton edging for trimming women's clothes **2** *usu cap* **:** a European breed of rather small domestic fowls with plumage usu. spangled or penciled with white, rose combs, and lead-blue legs **3** [short for *Hamburg steak*] **:** HAMBURGER

**²hamburg** \", 'häm,bür|g, 'håm-, -üə|, |k\ *adj, usu cap* [fr. *Hamburg*, Germany] **:** of or from the city of Hamburg, Germany **:** of the kind or style prevalent in Hamburg

**hamburg brandy** *n, usu cap H* **:** an imitation grape brandy made by adding flavoring to potato or beet spirit

**ham·burg·er** \'ham,bərgər, 'haam-, -bōgə(r, -bəigə(r\ *n* -s *often attrib* [short for *Hamburger steak*] **1 a :** ground beef **b :** a cooked patty of ground beef — compare SALISBURY STEAK **2 :** a sandwich made of a hamburger patty in a split round bun

**hamburg parsley** *n, usu cap H* **:** a parsley (*Petroselinum crispum* var. *tuberosum*) having smooth uncurled foliage and being cultivated primarily for its enlarged edible taproot which resembles a small very savory parsnip

**hamburg steak** *pronunc at* ¹HAMBURG +\ *or* **hamburger steak** *n, sometimes cap H* [²*Hamburg* or G *Hamburger* of Hamburg, fr. *Hamburg*, Germany] **:** HAMBURGER

**¹hame** \'hām\ *n* -s [ME, prob. fr. MD; akin to OE *ham* undergarment, *hame* covering, OHG *hama*, ON *hamr* covering, shape, Skt *śāmulya* woolen shirt] **:** one of the two curved wooden or metal projections which are attached to or form part of the collar of a draft horse and to which the traces are fastened

**²hame** \"\ *Scot var of* HOME

**ha·meil** \'hāməl\ *adj* [of Scand origin; akin to ON *heimill, heimall* domestic, at one's disposal, fr. *heimr* home, homeland — more at HOME] *Scot* **:** domestic and homelike

**¹hamel** *or* **hamil** \'aməl, '(h)ām-\ *n* -s [MF *hamel* — more at HAMLET] *now dial Eng* **:** HAMLET

**²ham·el** \'haməl\ *n* -s [Afrik, fr. MD; akin to OE *hamola* man with cropped hair, OHG *hamal* wether, *hamal* castrated, ON *hamla* to castrate, *skammr* short, Skt *śamala* error, damage; basic meaning: castrated] *Africa* **:** WETHER

**ha·me·lia** \hə'mēlyə\ *n* [NL, fr. Henri L. Duhamel-Dumonceau †1782 Fr. agriculturist + NL *-ia*] **1** *cap* **:** a genus (family Rubiaceae) of tropical American shrubs having flowers in scorpioid cymes with the corolla distinctly 5-ribbed **2** -s **:** any plant of the genus *Hamelia*

**hame·suck·en** *also* **haim·suck·en** \'hām,səkən\ *n* -s [ME *hamsoken*, fr. OE *hāmsōcn*, fr. *hām* home + *sōcn* attack; akin to ON *sōkn* attack, OE *sēcan* to attack, seek — more at HOME, SEEK] **1** *Scots law* **:** the assaulting of a person in his own house or dwelling place **2** *Old Eng law* **a** (1) **:** a franchise of trying persons charged with assaulting a person in his own home and receiving the fines or damages imposed (2) **:** such fines or damages **b :** BURGLARY, HOUSEBREAKING

**ha·metz** *or* **cha·metz** *or* **cho·metz** \ḵō'māts, 'ḵō,mets\ *n* -ES [Heb *ḥāmēṣ*] **:** leaven or leavened food banned during Passover

**hame·with** \'hāmwəth\ *adv (or adj)* [alter. of earlier *hameward*, fr. ²*hame* + *-ward*] *Scot* **:** HOMEWARD

**ham·fare** \'ham,fa(ə)(ə)r, -fe|\ *n* [ME *hamfare*, fr. *ham* home + *fare* journey, expedition — more at FARE] **:** HAMESUCKEN

**ham·fat·ter** \'ham,fad·ə(r)\ *n* -s [fr. "The Ham-fat Man," Negro minstrel song + E *-er*] *slang* **:** ²HAM 3a

**ham–fisted** \'=¦==\ *adj, chiefly Brit* **:** HAM-HANDED 2

**ham–handed** \'=¦==\ *adj* **1 :** having especially large hands ⟨a *ham-handed* companion who looked like a heavyweight wrestler —W.M.Swann⟩ **2 :** HEAVY-HANDED, CLUMSY ⟨*ham-handed* dramatist —J.C.Trewin⟩ ⟨teams made up of ponderous or *ham-handed* players —H.N.Maclean⟩

**hami** *pl of* HAMUS

**ha·mi·form** \'hāmə,fȯrm\ *adj* [L *hamus* hook + E *-iform* — more at HAMATE] **:** HOOKED 1

**ha·milt** \'hāmәlt, -ld\ *var of* HAMEIL

**ham·il·ton** \'haməlt³n, -tən\ *adj, usu cap* [fr. *Hamilton*, Ontario] **:** of or from the city of Hamilton, Ontario **:** of the kind or style prevalent in Hamilton

**¹ham·il·to·ni·an** \¦==¦tōnēən, -ōnyən\ *adj, usu cap* **1** [Alexander *Hamilton* †1804 Am. statesman + E *-ian*] **1 :** of or relating to the statesman Hamilton or to his political and social doctrines or program characterized by advocacy of a strong central government of a unitary type, protection of industrial and commercial interests, and a general distrust of the political capacity or wisdom of the common man ⟨the *Hamiltonian* creed of selective suffrage —S.H.Adams⟩ ⟨the *Hamiltonian* tradition in the U.S. —Alexander Brady⟩ ⟨the clash of Jeffersonian and *Hamiltonian* America —R.M.Weaver⟩ ⟨the *Hamiltonian* realistic concern with . . . the protection of American industries —T.I.Cook & Malcolm Moos⟩ **2** [James *Hamilton* †1829 Brit. language teacher + E *-ian*] **:** of or relating to the scholar Hamilton or his system of language teaching **3** [Sir William *Hamilton* †1856 Scottish philosopher + E *-ian*] **:** of or relating to the philosopher Hamilton or his theories — compare HAMILTONISM **4** [Sir William R. *Hamilton* †1865 Brit. mathematician + E *-ian*] **:** of or relating to the mathematician Hamilton or his system of dynamics

**²hamiltonian** \"\ *n* -s *usu cap* **:** a follower or exponent of Hamiltonian doctrines or theories; *esp* **:** a follower or advocate of the social or political doctrines of Alexander Hamilton

**ham·il·to·ni·an·ism** \,haməl'tōnēə,nizəm, -ōnyə,-\ *n* -s *usu cap* [¹*Hamiltonian* + E *-ism*] **:** the body of social and political doctrines held by or associated with the statesman Hamilton **:** the Hamiltonian program or ideology

**ham·il·ton·ism** \'haməlt³n,izəm, -ltə,ni-\ *n* -s *usu cap* [Sir William *Hamilton* + E *-ism*] **:** the philosophical and logical teachings of Sir William Hamilton esp. concerning the doctrine of natural realism and the quantification of the predicate

**ham·i·noea** \,hamə'nēə\ *n, cap* [NL] **:** a common genus of bubble shells (family Akeridae) of the Pacific coast of No. America with a shell so thin that the pulsation of the heart of the translucent yellowish brown animal within is commonly visible through it

**ham·ite** \'ha,mīt, *usu* -īd·+V\ *n* -s *usu cap* [*Ham*, son of Noah, eponymous ancestor of the Hamites (Gen 10:6–20) + E *-ite*] **1 :** a descendant of Ham, one of the sons of Noah **2 a :** a member of a group of African peoples including the Berber peoples north of the Sahara, the Tuaregs and Tibbu in the Sudan, possibly the extinct Guanches of the Canaries, the ancient Egyptians and their descendants, and the Galla of east Africa that are mostly Muslims, are highly variable in appearance but mainly Caucasoid, and are believed by many to be late-Paleolithic or post-Paleolithic colonists of western Europe **b :** a native speaker of a Hamitic language — compare COPT, ETHIOPIAN

**ha·mi·tes** \hə'mīd·(,)ēz\ *n, cap* [NL, fr. L *hamus* hook + NL *-ites* — more at HAMATE] **:** a genus of extinct Cretaceous ammonoids with a shell forming repeated V-shaped loops in one plane

**1ham·it·ic** \(ˈ)haˈmid·ik, həˈm-, -mitik\ *adj, usu cap* [*Hamite* + *-ic*] **1** : of, relating to, or characteristic of the Hamites **2** : of, relating to, or characteristic of one of the Hamitic languages

**2hamitic** \"\ *n* -s *usu cap* : HAMITIC LANGUAGES ⟨an authority on *Hamitic*⟩

**ham·i·ti·cized** \haˈmid·ə,sīzd, həˈm-\ *adj, usu cap* : conjectured or presumed to have acquired through interbreeding certain traits hypothetically characteristic of the ancient ancestors of the Hamitic-speaking peoples

**hamitic languages** *n pl, usu cap H* : the Berber, Cushitic, and sometimes Egyptian branches of the Afro-Asiatic or Hamito-Semitic languages formerly regarded as constituting an independent language family or as constituting one of two coordinate subfamilies of the Hamito-Semitic languages

**ham·i·tism** \ˈhamə,tizəm\ *n* -s *usu cap* : the quality or state of being Hamitic

**hamito-** *comb form, usu cap* [*Hamitic*] : Hamitic and ⟨*Hamito*-Bantu⟩ ⟨*Hamito*-Semitic⟩ — usu. with hyphen

**1hamito-semitic** \ˌhamə,tō+\ *adj, usu cap H&S* [*Hamito-* + *Semitic*] : of, relating to, or characteristic of the Hamito-Semitic languages

**2hamito-semitic** \"\ *n, usu cap H&S* : HAMITO-SEMITIC LANGUAGES

**hamito-semitic languages** *n pl, usu cap H&S* : AFRO-ASIATIC LANGUAGES

**1ham·let** \ˈhamlət, *usu* -əd·+V\ *n* -s [ME, fr. MF *hamelet,* dim. of *hamel,* dim. of *ham,* of Gmc origin; akin to OE *hām* homeland, village, house — more at HOME] **1** : a small village ⟨performances are being contemplated in cities, in towns, and even in ~*s* —Joseph Wechsberg⟩ ⟨a ~ in the town of Readsboro —J.H.Buffum⟩ **2** : the smallest incorporated unit of municipal government ⟨incorporation into a ~, the bottom rung of the municipal ladder —*N.Y.Times*⟩

**2hamlet** \"\ *n* -s [origin unknown] **1 a** : a large grouper (*Epinephelus striatus*) common from Florida to Brazil and in the Caribbean and important as a food fish — called also *Nassau grouper* **b** *Bahamas* : any young grouper **2** : a yellow and black thickly spotted moray (*Gymnothorax moringa*) used for food in the West Indies

**3hamlet** \"\ *n* -s *usu cap* [after *Hamlet,* chief character of the tragedy *Hamlet* (1600–1601) by William Shakespeare †1616 English dramatist] : a brooding indecisive person ⟨the very *Hamlet* of our age . . . a philosopher thrust into power at a time of violence —Michael Amrine⟩ ⟨tortured by indecision, a *Hamlet* in politics —*Newsweek*⟩

**hamlike** \ˈ≈,≈\ *adj* : resembling a ham ⟨swung a ~ fist toward the west window of the kitchen —Kenneth Roberts⟩

**ham·ma·da** *or* **ha·ma·da** \həˈmädə\ *n* -s [Ar *ḥammādah*] : a rock-floored or rock-strewn desert region esp. in the Sahara

**hammal** *var of* HAMAL

**ham·mar·ite** \ˈhamə,rīt\ *n* -s [Sw *hammarit,* fr. Gladhammar, Sweden, its locality + Sw *-it* -ite] : a mineral prob. $Pb_2Cu_2Bi_4S_9$ consisting of lead, copper, and bismuth sulfide

**hammed** *past of* HAM

**1ham·mer** \ˈhamə(r)\ *n* -s *often attrib* [ME *hamer,* fr. OE *hamor;* akin to OHG *hamar* hammer, ON *hamarr* hammer, crag, Gk *akmōn* anvil, Skt *áśma* stone, Gk *akmē* edge — more at EDGE] **1 a** : a hand tool consisting of a solid head set crosswise on a handle and used for pounding (as in driving nails, breaking stone, beating metal surfaces) — see BALL PEEN HAMMER, CLAW HAMMER, SLEDGEHAMMER; compare MALLET **b** : a power tool that often substitutes a metal block or a drill for the hammerhead (as in driving posts, stamping or forging metal, or breaking up rock surfaces) — see AIR HAMMER, DROP HAMMER, JACKHAMMER; compare PILE DRIVER **2** : one that strikes like a hammer ⟨we need a concerted, vigorous voice; we need a ~ —Harvey Breit⟩ ⟨wielding this problem as the ~ with which they must smash the last vestiges of Christian thought —L.J. Shehan⟩ ⟨the ~ thrust of radio and television —*Saturday Rev.*⟩ **3** : something that resembles a hammer in form or action: as **a** : a lever with a striking head for ringing a bell or striking a gong (as in a clock or an electric bell) **b** *obs* : a door knocker **c** (1) : a steel cover for the powder pan of a flintlock gun against which the flint strikes to ignite the powder; *also* : an arm that holds the flint for striking : 1COCK 4 (2) : an arm that strikes the cap in a percussion lock to ignite the propelling charge (3) : a part of the action of a modern gun that strikes the primer of the cartridge in firing or that strikes the firing pin to ignite the cartridge **d** : MALLEUS 1a **e** : GAVEL; *specif* : a gavel with which an auctioneer indicates that an article is sold to the last bidder **f** (1) : a padded mallet in a piano action for striking a string (2) : a hand mallet for playing on a percussion instrument of fixed pitch (as a dulcimer or a xylophone) **4** : a metal sphere hurled in the hammer throw that usu. weighs 16 pounds and together with its flexible wire handle measures not more than four feet in length — **under the hammer** *adv* : for sale at auction ⟨priceless heirlooms went *under the hammer*⟩

**2hammer** \"\ *vb* **hammered; hammered; hammering** \-m(ə)riŋ\ **hammers** [ME *hameren,* fr. *hamer,* n.] *vi* **1 a** : to strike blows esp. repeatedly with or as if with a hammer : POUND ⟨the impounded water ~*s* at the weak spots —Russell Lord⟩ ⟨his pulses ~*ing* in his head —Clive Arden⟩ **b** : WATER-HAMMER **2** : to become insistent or urgent : be in or keep up a state of agitation ⟨these thoughts . . . ~*ed* in her indignant consciousness —J.C.Powys⟩ **3** : to make repeated efforts as if shaping with a hammer: **a** : to reiterate an opinion or attitude repeatedly and emphatically : to place emphasis by constant repetition or discussion ⟨continually ~*s* on the danger of intrigue —O.M.Green⟩ — often used with *away* ⟨letters and pamphlets all ~*ed* away at the same point —Nathan Kelne⟩ **b** : to work persistently or tirelessly : TOIL, LABOR ⟨Beethoven thought of an air, ~*ed* at it, altered it again and again —C.W.H.Johnson⟩ **4** *now dial Eng* : to speak haltingly : STAMMER ~ *vt* **1 a** : to strike with a hammer : beat, drive, or shape with repeated blows ⟨~ a nail⟩ ⟨~ a horseshoe⟩ ⟨~ out a tray⟩ **b** : to fasten with a hammer (as by nailing) ⟨~ down a lid⟩ **c** : to build with hammer and nails — usu. used with *together* ⟨~ together a cold frame⟩ **2** : to strike as if with a hammer: **a** : to hit or drive with the force of a hammer ⟨~*ed* in three home runs in one game —Bob Broeg⟩ ⟨the incoming train ~*ed* the rear of the shorter train —*Springfield (Mass.) Union*⟩ **b** : to strike with repeated blows : POUND, THUMP ⟨~ a typewriter⟩ ⟨~*ing* a rather hard pillow into a more comfortable shape —Dorothy Sayers⟩ **c** : to bring or keep under attack : BELABOR ⟨the State Department is being badly ~*ed* on this issue —*New Republic*⟩ **3** : to produce or bring about as if by means of repeated blows: **a** : to shape or put together by persevering effort ⟨~ our words to fit a song —Charles Fox⟩ ⟨~*ed* together an alliance —*Newsweek*⟩ — often used with *out* ⟨~ out a policy⟩ ⟨~ out an empire⟩ ⟨sat at the piano for hours . . . trying to ~ out an original tune —Noel Coward⟩ **b** : to force or drive into the consciousness by reiteration ⟨~*ing* in day after day the same few and relatively simple beliefs —John Dewey⟩ — often used with *home* ⟨~*s* home the theme of freedom to think —Brooks Atkinson⟩ **c** : to level off : make smooth : ADJUST — usu. used with *out* ⟨differences are ~*ed* out in discussion —Walter Moberly⟩ **d** (1) : to force down the price of (a stock) by selling short ⟨told the broker whom I had been using to ~ down the stock to continue his operations —B.M.Baruch⟩ (2) : to declare (a member of the London stock exchange) to be a defaulter ⟨broke away to the stock exchange and at twenty-four was insolvent and ~*ed* —*Times Lit. Supp.*⟩

**ham·mer–ai·toff projection** \ˈhämə(r)ī,tȯf-\ *n, usu cap H&A* [after Ernst von *Hammer* †1925 Ger. geographer and David *Aitoff* †1933 Russ. geographer] : AITOFF PROJECTION

**hammer and sickle** *n, sometimes cap H&S* [fr. its adoption (1923) by the U.S.S.R. on its national flag] **1** : an emblem consisting of a crossed sickle and hammer used as a symbol of peasant and worker **2** : a flag bearing the insignia of the hammer and sickle

**hammer and tongs** *adv (or adj)* : with the force and violence of a blacksmith pounding iron : with all one's strength : in a rough-and-tumble manner ⟨the wedding party going it *hammer and tongs* down the road —Richard Llewellyn⟩ ⟨go after a witness in the old *hammer-and-tongs* style —Mitchell Dawson⟩ ⟨has gone at his job in a *hammer-and-tongs* way that has annoyed — and offended — a good many businessmen —*Newsweek*⟩

**hammer beam** *n* : either of the short horizontal beams or cantilevers projecting from the top of a pair of opposite walls to support a roof principal for a Gothic roof and thus dispense with the necessity for a tie beam

*l* hammer beams

**hammerbird** \ˈ≈,≈\ *n* : HAMMERKOP

**hammerblow** \ˈ≈,≈\ *n* : a stroke of or as if of a hammer; *specif* : a pounding of the rails by the driving wheels of a locomotive caused by the inertia of unbalanced parts

**hammer brace** *n* : a bracket under a hammer beam

**hammer butt** *n* : a block into which the base of a hammer shank in a piano action is fitted

**hammercloth** \ˈ≈,≈\ *n* [ME *hamerclothe*] : an ornamented often fringed cloth hung over the coachman's seat esp. of a ceremonial coach

**hammerdress** \ˈ≈,≈\ *vt* : to dress or face (stone) with a hammer

**hammer drill** *n* : a percussion rock drill in which a plunger or hammer strikes rapid blows on the shank of a loosely held drill — compare PISTON DRILL

**hammered** *adj* : having surface indentations produced or appearing to have been produced by hammering ⟨a bracelet of dark ~ metal —Douglass Wallop⟩

**hammered glass** *n* : rolled glass made nontransparent by embossing it on one side to resemble beaten metal

**ham·mer·er** \ˈhamərə(r)\ *n* -s : one that hammers

**hammerhead** \ˈ≈,≈\ *n* **1** : the striking part of a hammer; *specif* : a part of a hammer in a piano action that strikes the strings **2** : one that is dense or stupid : BLOCKHEAD, NUMSKULL ⟨a big ~ but even if he had had a smart head, a no-good horse —Richard Wormser⟩ **3** : something that resembles the striking part of a hammer: as **a** : any of various medium-sized sharks that with the shovelheads constitute the family Sphyrnidae, have the eyes at the ends of lateral extensions of the flattened head, are active voracious fishes sometimes considered man-eaters, are widely distributed in warm seas, and include some (as *Sphyrna zygaena* and *S. tudes*) which are fished for their hides and vitamin-rich livers **b** (1) : HOG SUCKER (2) : HAMMERHEADED BAT (3) *or* **hammerheaded stork** \ˈ≈,≈≈-\ : HAMMERKOP

**hammerhead crane** *n* : a heavy-duty crane with a horizontal counterbalanced jib

**hammerheaded** \ˌ≈≈ˈ≈≈\ *adj* **1** : having a head shaped like that of a hammer **2** : DENSE, STUPID, THICKHEADED

**hammerheaded bat** *n* : a West African epaulet bat (*Epomorphus monstrosus* or *Hypsegnathus monstrosus*) with greatly enlarged larynx and distinctive voice

**hammerhead shark** *also* **hammerheaded shark** *n* : HAMMERHEAD 3a

**hammerhead stall** *n* : a maneuver in which an airplane pulls up in a vertical climb until it almost stalls and then drops the nose in a wingover so that direction of flight is reversed

**hammering** *n* -s **1** : the act or process of beating or pounding with or as if with a hammer ⟨the art of silver ~⟩ ⟨slow ~ of heavy guns —Kenneth Roberts⟩ ⟨under ~*s* from me . . . the legislature passed a bill —F.D.Roosevelt⟩ **2** : a pattern of shallow indentations produced with a hammer

**ham·mer·ing·ly** *adv* : in a hammering manner

**ham·mer·kop** \ˈhamə(r),käp\ *also* **hammerkop bird** *or* **hammerkop stork** *n* -s [Afrik *hamerkop,* fr. *hamer* hammer + *kop* head] : a chiefly dusky brown African wading bird (*Scopus umbretta*) intermediate in some respects between storks and herons but distinguished by its large head with heavy bill and thick dorsal crest and by its huge domed nest

**ham·mer·less** \-ləs\ *adj* **1** : lacking a hammer **2** : having the hammer concealed — used of a gun having the hammer enclosed within the receiver

**hammerlock** \ˈ≈,≈\ *n* : a wrestling hold in which an opponent's arm is held bent behind his back

**ham·mer·man** \-mən, -,man\ *n, pl* **hammermen** [ME, fr. *hamer* hammer + *man*] : one that works with a hammer; *esp* : an operator of a power-driven hammer (as a jackhammer)

**hammer mill** *n* **1** : a grinder in which feed and other products are pulverized by several rows of thin steel hammers revolving at high speed **2** : a crusher in which minerals (as ores, rock, coal) are broken up by the impact of swinging hammer bars hinged to a rapidly rotating shaft

**hammer oyster** *n* : any of several bivalve mollusks of *Malleus* and related genera of Chinese and Australian waters having elongated handle-shaped shells that resemble an oyster on the interior and that are prolonged in both directions at the dorsal margin to suggest the head of a hammer

**hammer post** *n* : a pendant in the shape of a pilaster that serves as impost to a hammer brace

**hammer price** *n* : the price at which a defaulter's contract is settled on the London stock exchange

**hammer rail** *n* : a padded strip of wood supporting the hammers in a piano action when at rest

**hammers** *pl of* HAMMER, *pres 3d sing of* HAMMER

**hammer scale** *n* : a scale that forms on heated metal when it is hammered

**hammer shank** *n* : a wooden dowel onto which a hammer in a piano action is fitted

**hammer shell** *n* : HAMMER OYSTER; *also;* its shell

**hammersmith** \ˈ≈,≈\ *n* **1** : a smith who works with a hammer **2** : one who supervises work done with drop hammers or power presses

**hammer spring** *n* : a spring that actuates a hammer (as in a gun or a piano action)

**hammer spur** *n* : a projection on the hammer of a gun by which it is cocked

**hammerstone** \ˈ≈,≈\ *n* : a prehistoric hammering implement consisting of a rounded stone

**hammer throw** *n* : a field event in which a metal sphere attached to a flexible handle is hurled for distance from inside a circle with a 7-foot diameter

**hammertoe** \ˈ≈,≈\ *n* : a toe (as the second) deformed by permanent angular flexion of the second and third joints resulting in an incurved form resembling a claw

**hammer tongs** *n* : blacksmith's tongs having projecting lugs for engaging holes of hammerheads during forging

**hammer-weld** \ˈ≈ˌ≈\ *vt* : to weld by blows with a hammer

**hammer welding** *n* : forge welding by mechanical hammering

**hammerwort** \ˈ≈,≈\ *n* : PELLITORY 1

**hammer-wrought** \ˈ≈ˈ≈\ *adj* : shaped with a hammer

**hamming** *pres part of* HAM

**1ham·mock** \ˈhamək *also* -mik *or* -mēk\ *n* -s *often attrib* [Sp *hamaca,* fr. Taino] **1** : a swinging couch or bed usu. made of netting or canvas and slung by cords from supports at each end ⟨two trees just wide enough apart to swing a ~⟩ **2** : something that resembles a hammock (as the suspended nest of an oriole); *specif* : a length of light twine netting hung along or across a sleeping-car berth to hold wearing apparel and other personal belongings

hammock 1

**2hammock** \"\ *vt* -ED/-ING/-S : to suspend in or as if in a hammock ⟨~*ed* him in her shawl in a loop that placed him close to her breast —John Steinbeck⟩ ⟨content to ~ himself passively in the amplitude of enveloping time —Victoria Sackville-West⟩

**3hammock** \"\ *n* -s *often attrib* [origin unknown] **1** : HUMMOCK **2** : a fertile area in the southern U.S. (as Florida) that is often somewhat higher than its surroundings and is characterized by hardwood vegetation and soil of greater depth and containing more humus than that of the flatwoods or pinelands; *specif* : an island of dense tropical undergrowth in the Everglades

**hammock batten** *n* **1** : one of the battens on a ship's beam from which a hammock is slung **2** : a bar used for spreading hammock clews

**hammock clew** *n* [1*hammock*] : CLEW 3b

**hammock cloth** *n* : a tarpaulin or piece of canvas used on a ship to cover stowed hammocks or to place over the openings in hammock nettings — called also *top cloth*

**hammock hickory** *n* [3*hammock*] : a Florida tree (*Carya floridana* or *C. magnifloridana*) having gray bark, reddish brown to gray twigs, leaves with 5 to 7 leaflets, and fruit that is broadly ellipsoid to pyriform

**hammock netting** *also* **hammock berthing** *n* : a net or a box trough to hold sailors' hammocks when not in use

**ham·my** \ˈhamē, ˈhaam-, -mi\ *adj* -ER/-EST **1 a** : flavored with or tasting of ham **b** : resembling ham in flavor or appearance **2** : like or characteristic of a ham actor : exaggeratedly and usu. self-consciously theatrical : OVERACTED ⟨children are not dismayed by ~ acting provided the story is good —Rose M. Daly⟩

**ha·mo·tzi** \häˈmōtsē\ *n* -s [Heb *hammōṣī,* lit., the one who brings forth; fr. the concluding words of the benediction] : the recital of the Hebrew benediction over bread before meals

**1ham·per** \ˈhampə(r), ˈhaam-, ˈhaim-\ *vt* **hampered; hampered; hampering** \-p(ə)riŋ\ **hampers** [ME *hamperen;* perh. akin to Flem *hampern* to stutter, MD *hāperen*] **1 a** : to restrict the movement of by bonds or obstacles : FETTER, IMPEDE ⟨elaborate ~*ing* clothes —James Laver⟩ ⟨icebergs ~*ed* the progress of the ship⟩ ⟨pitching . . . violently in the seaway, ~*ed* by her heavy tow —R.S.Porteous⟩ **b** : to interfere with the operation of : DISRUPT ⟨radio communications ~*ed* by static —*Globe & Mail*⟩ **2 a** : CURB, RESTRAIN, LIMIT ⟨the view . . . that rhyme and meter ~ the poet's free expression —J.L. Lowes⟩ ⟨did nothing to ~ the boisterousness of the occasion —Silas Spitzer⟩ **b** : to interfere with : ENCUMBER, HANDICAP, OBSTRUCT ⟨an obsolete ideology can ~ an economy —V.G. Childe⟩ ⟨~*ed* by lack of money as often as by lack of initiative —H.J.Hanham⟩

**syn** CLOG, TRAMMEL, FETTER, SHACKLE, MANACLE, HOG-TIE: HAMPER, the most general of these terms, can imply any impediment or restraining agent that encumbers, delays, or interferes with an action ⟨like other branches of science, history is now encumbered and *hampered* by its own mass —Henry Adams⟩ ⟨his principle was to choose competent lieutenants, and then to leave them to work without *hampering* interference —*Irish Digest*⟩ ⟨*hampered* in his progress by the weight of a large bundle on his back⟩ CLOG usu. implies a foreign useless impediment that clings, gums up, or obstructs ⟨all common ambitions, rank, possessions, power, the things which *clog* man's feet —John Buchan⟩ ⟨his mind is *clogged* with the strangest miscellany of truth and marvel —V.L. Parrington⟩ ⟨waved the traffic away from the *clogged* thoroughfare —Ralph Gustafson⟩ TRAMMEL suggests entanglement by or confinement within a net ⟨had now become *trammeled* in events —Ethel Wilson⟩ ⟨a landscape of increasing strangeness, replete with things shocking to a culture-*trammeled* understanding —B.L.Whorf⟩ FETTER suggests the total or almost total crippling restraint of chains or manacles ⟨a tendency toward introversion . . . had slowly mastered him, *fettering* his actions and segregating him in an unhappy little world —I.V.Morris⟩ ⟨watched a world prepare for war while he was *fettered* by the nation's propensity for isolationism —Estes Kefauver⟩ SHACKLE and MANACLE are very similar to although stronger than FETTER, usu. suggesting a total impeding of action ⟨if the power of the courts stereotypes legislation within the forms and limits . . . expedient in the 19th or perhaps the 18th century, it *shackles* progress and breeds distrust and suspicion of the courts —B.N.Cardozo⟩ ⟨keep Rome *manacled* hand and foot: no fear of unruliness —Robert Browning⟩ HOG-TIE implies a making completely helpless or a total thwarting ⟨as soon as the senator can get us *hog-tied* to that extent, he will . . . ram these unconstitutional measures down our throats —*Congressional Record*⟩ ⟨accuse Americans of being *hog-tied* to business —*advt*⟩

**2hamper** \"\ *n* -s **1** : something that impedes : OBSTRUCTION, SHACKLE ⟨if the Fourteenth Amendment is not to be a greater ~ . . . than I think was intended —O.W.Holmes †1935⟩ **2** : TOP-HAMPER

**3hamper** \"\ *n* -s [ME *hampere,* alter. of *hanaper* — more at *hanaper*] : a basket or box usu. with a cover for packing, storing, or transporting food and other articles: as **a** : a basket often of wickerwork for carrying food or drink ⟨a picnic ~⟩ ⟨helped . . . the yardman to pack the game in ~*s* —Adrian Bell⟩ **b** : a container of standardized capacity for shipping fruits and vegetables that is of splint, stave, or fiberboard construction and is circular, elliptical, or polygonal in shape with a top diameter usu. greater than the bottom, with slatted sides, and with a bottom that may be loose, stapled, or nailed in place or formed by a continuation of the sides — compare BASKET 1 **c** : a small ventilated receptacle for laundry made of wood, plastic, or metal and usu. having a flat side to fit against a wall **d** : a large canvas container on casters used for sorting and moving mail in a post office

hamper b

**4hamper** \"\ *vt* **hampered; hampered; hampering** \-p(ə)riŋ\ **hampers** *chiefly Brit* **1** : to pack in a hamper ⟨trifles . . . ~*ed* up together —T.A.Browne⟩ **2** : to present with a hamper of food or wine ⟨something particularly charming about being ~*ed* at Christmas time —*Westminster Gazette*⟩

**hamp·race** \ˈham,prās\ *n usu cap* [1*Hampshire* + Land*race*] : MONTANA 2a

**1hamp·shire** \ˈham(p),shi(ə)r, ˈhaam-, -,shiə, -,shə(r)\ *n* [fr. *Hampshire,* England] **1** *usu cap* : an American breed of black, white-belted swine with white forelegs, rather long head, and straight face **2** -s *often cap* : an animal of the Hampshire breed

**2hampshire** \"\ *adj, usu cap* [fr. *Hampshire,* England] : of or from Hampshire, England : of a kind or style prevalent in Hampshire

**3hampshire** \"\ *also* **hampshire down** \ˌ≈(,)≈ˈdau̇n\ *n* [2*Hampshire*] **1** *usu cap H&D* : a British breed of medium-wooled mutton-type sheep that are large, thick-fleshed, and hornless and have dark faces and legs **2** -s *usu cap H often cap D* : a sheep of the Hampshire breed

**hams** *pl of* HAM, *pres 3d sing of* HAM

**ham·socn** \ˈhäm,sōkən\ *n* -s [OE *hāmsōcn* — more at HAMESUCKEN] : HAMESUCKEN

**ham·ster** \ˈhamztə(r), ˈhaam-, -m(p)st-\ *n* -s [G, fr. OHG *hamustro* (akin to OS *hamustra* hamster), of Slavic origin; akin to OSlav *choměstorŭ* hamster] : any of numerous Old World rodents of *Cricetus* and related genera having very large cheek pouches and somewhat resembling the American white-footed mouse but short-tailed and commonly larger and of burrowing habits — see GOLDEN HAMSTER

**ham·stery** \-tərē\ *n* -ES : an establishment for breeding and raising hamsters

**1hamstring** \ˈ≈,≈\ *n* [2*ham* (popliteal space) + *string*] **1 a** : either of two groups of tendons bounding the upper part of the popliteal space at the back of the knee and forming the tendons of insertion of certain muscles of the back of the thigh **b** : the large tendon above and behind the hock of a quadruped : ACHILLES' TENDON **2** : a restrictive power : regulatory control ⟨fend for itself . . . among myriad regulations, restrictions, and government ~*s* —*Atlantic*⟩

**2hamstring** \"\ *vt* **hamstrung; hamstrung; hamstringing; hamstrings 1 a** : to deprive of the power of locomotion by cutting the leg tendons : CRIPPLE, DISABLE ⟨wolf packs ~ and destroy many moose —Frank Dufresne⟩ **b** : to cut the muscle or tendons in the small of a whale ⟨it is sometimes the custom when fast to a whale more than commonly powerful and alert, to seek to ~ him —Herman Melville⟩ **2** : to make ineffective or powerless : limit or destroy the effectiveness of : HINDER, IMPAIR ⟨supporting rather than ~*ing* our negotiators —F.L. Allen⟩ ⟨talents *hamstrung* by respectability —Cyril Connolly⟩ ⟨~ . . . arms production by wresting away raw-material sources —Virginia Prewett⟩

**ham·u·lar** \ˈhamyələ(r)\ *adj* [L *hamulus* + E *-ar*] : HAMATE

**ham·u·lus** \-ləs\ *n, pl* **hamu·li** \-,lī\ [NL, fr. L, little hook, dim. of *hamus*] : a hook or hooklike process; *esp* : a little hook terminating the barbule of a feather

**ha·mus** \ˈhāməs\ *n, pl* **ha·mi** \-,mī\ [NL, fr. L, hook — more at HAMATE] *biol* : a hook or curved process

**ham·za** or **ham·zah** \ˈhamzə\ *n* -s [Ar *hamzah*, lit., compression (as of the larynx)] **1 :** the sign for a glottal stop in Arabic orthography — usu. represented in English by an apostrophe **2 :** the sound for which the hamza stands

**ham·zat·ed** \-ˌzād·əd\ *adj* **:** bearing a hamza — used of a letter of the Arabic alphabet or of a word written in the Arabic alphabet ⟨a ~ alif⟩

**¹han** *dial Brit pres pl of* HAVE

**²han** \ˈhän, -a-\ *adj, usu cap* [*Han,* Chin. dynasty (206 B.C.–A.D. 220)] **1 :** of, relating to, or having the characteristics of the period of the Han dynasty ⟨*Han* pottery⟩ **2 :** of, relating to, or being a nationality group in China descended from the original Chinese and constituting an overwhelming majority of the population and the dominant cultural group **:** belonging to the Chinese proper as distinguished from other nationality groups (as the Manchu or Mongols) ⟨the *Han* race⟩

**³han** \ˈ"\ *n, pl* **han** *or* **hans** *usu cap* **1 :** an Athapaskan people of the Yukon river district in east central Alaska and the Yukon Territory of Canada **2 :** a member of the Han people

**han'** \ˈ(h)an, ˈhȯn\ *Scot var of* HAND

**han·a·fi** \ˈhanə(ˌ)fē\ *n* -s *usu cap* [Ar *ḥanafīy,* after abu-*Hanifah* †767 Muslim jurist] **1 :** an orthodox school of Muslim jurisprudence predominating in Turkey and India — compare HANBALI, MALIKI, SHAFI'I **2** *or* **han·a·fite** \-ˌfīt\ **:** a follower of the Hanafi school

**han·a·hill** *or* **han·na·hill** \ˈhanəˌhil\ *n* -s [origin unknown] **:** a sea bass (*Centropristes striatus*) of the Atlantic coast

**han·ap** \ˈhaˌnap, -ˌnəp\ *n* -s [ME, fr. MF *hanap, henap,* of Gmc origin; akin to OE *hnæpp* bowl, drinking vessel, OS *hnapp,* MD & MLG *nap,* OHG *hnapf,* ON *hnappr*] **:** an elaborate medieval goblet or standing cup usu. having a cover

**han·a·per** \ˈhanəpə(r)\ *n* -s [ME (also, case to hold hanaps), fr. MF *hanapier* case to hold hanaps, fr. *hanap* + *-ier* -er] *Brit* **:** a small wicker case used as a repository for legal documents

**han·a·ster** \ˈhanəstə(r)\ *n* -s [ME *hanster,* fr. *hans* hansa + *-ster* — more at HANSA] **:** a person admitted to the merchant guild in Oxford, England

**han·ba·li** \ˈhanbə(ˌ)lē\ *n* -s *usu cap* [Ar *ḥanbalīy,* after ibn-*Hanbal* †855 Arab jurist] **1 :** an orthodox school of Muslim jurisprudence predominating in Saudi Arabia — compare HANAFI, MALIKI, SHAFI'I **2** *or* **han·ba·lite** \-əˌlīt\ **:** a follower of the Hanbali school

**hance** \ˈhan(t)s\ *n* -s [obs. E *hance, haunce* lintel, fr. *hance, haunce* to raise, fr. ME *hauncen,* prob. short for *enhauncen* — more at ENHANCE] **1 :** a curved contour on a ship (as the fall of the fife rail to the deck) **2 a** (1) **:** the arc of minimum radius at the springing of an elliptical or similar arch (2) **:** the haunch of an arch **b :** a small arch joining a straight lintel to a jamb

**hance arch** *n* **:** an arch having greater curvature at its springings than at the crown

**hanch** \ˈhanch\ *vb* [ME *hanchen,* fr. MF *hancher*] *vt, now dial Eng* **:** to snap at noisily or greedily ~ *vi, now dial Eng* **:** to snap noisily and greedily

**han·cock·ite** \ˈhanˌkäˌkīt\ *n* -s [E. P. *Hancock,* 19th cent. Am. mineralogist + E *-ite*] **:** a complex silicate that contains lead, calcium, strontium, and other metals and is isomorphous with epidote

**¹hand** \ˈhand, -aa(ə)-\ *n* -s *often attrib* [ME, fr. OE *hand, hond*; akin to OHG *hant* hand, ON *hönd,* Goth *handus*] **1 a** (1) **:** the terminal part of the vertebrate forelimb when modified (as in man) as a grasping organ being made up of wrist, metacarpus, terminal fingers, and opposable thumb or of these parts excluding the wrist and exhibiting unusual mobility and flexibility both of the digits and the whole organ (2) **:** the segment of the forelimb of a vertebrate below the fishes that corresponds to the hand (as the pinion of a bird) irrespective of its form or functional specialization ⟨a kangaroo's forearms seem undeveloped, but the powerful five-fingered ~s are skilled at feinting and clouting —*Springfield (Mass.) Union*⟩ **b :** a part serving the function of or resembling a hand: as (1) **:** the hind foot of an ape (2) **:** the chela of a crustacean (3) **:** the tarsus of either forelimb of an insect (as a fly) **c :** something resembling a hand in appearance, shape, function, or use or suggesting the fingers of a hand in shape, arrangement, or number: as (1) **:** an indicator or pointer on a dial ⟨the ~s of a clock⟩ (2) **:** a stylized figure of a hand with forefinger extended to point a direction or call attention to something; *specif* **:** INDEX 9 (3) **:** five articles (as oranges) of the same kind sold together (4) **:** a bunch of 8 to 20 bananas attached together on their stem (5) **:** a palmate form of gingerroot (6) **:** a bunch of large leaves tied together usu. with another leaf; *esp* **:** a bunch of 5 to 20 uniform leaves of tobacco tied together by a tie leaf at the butt end of the leaves **2 a :** personal possession — usu. used in pl. ⟨anxious not to let the property get out of his ~s⟩ **b** (1) **:** CONTROL, DIRECTION, SUPERVISION ⟨guided the proceedings from the front row with a very helpful ~ —*Sydney (Australia) Bull.*⟩ — usu. used in pl. ⟨kept the management of the firm in his own ~s⟩ ⟨the reception was already in the ~s of the florists and caterers⟩ (2) **:** right or privilege in controlling or directioning ⟨allowed the teacher a free ~ in her treatment of the children⟩ **3 a :** SIDE, DIRECTION ⟨armed men were running and fighting on either ~⟩ **b :** one of two sides of an issue or argument **:** one of two or more aspects of a subject or matter of consideration ⟨on the one ~ we can appeal for peace, or on the other declare war⟩ ⟨on the one ~ I should like to give the child a great deal of freedom but on the other ~ I don't want him totally out of my control⟩ **c** (1) **:** the manner of twisting or going round whether right-handed or left-handed ⟨the ~ of a spiral⟩ ⟨a right-*hand* screw⟩ (2) **:** the characteristic of a door determining whether it opens to the right or to the left as viewed from the outside (as of a cupboard or closet) or from the inside (as of a room) with door opening away — compare LEFT-HAND, LEFT-HAND REVERSE BEVEL, RIGHT-HAND, RIGHT-HAND REVERSE BEVEL (3) **:** the characteristic of a hinge determining whether it is to be fitted to a right-handed or left-handed door — compare LEFT-HAND, RIGHT-HAND (4) **:** the characteristic of a lock determining whether it throws to the right or left — compare LEFT-HAND, RIGHT-HAND **4 a :** a pledge or indication of agreement or of satisfaction with terms (as of a contract) ⟨without further talk he gave me his ~ on the deal and we closed it⟩ **b :** a pledge of betrothal or bestowal in marriage ⟨asked the man for his daughter's ~⟩ **5 hands** *pl* **:** skill in handling the reins in horsemanship ⟨he didn't ride well, he hadn't good ~s —H.G.Wells⟩ **6 a :** style of penmanship **:** HANDWRITING ⟨a handsome ~⟩ ⟨a crabbed ~⟩ ⟨left behind her twenty-six volumes written in her own ~ —Elizabeth Bowen⟩ ⟨in the cuneiform ~ —J.H.Breasted⟩ **b :** SIGNATURE ⟨some writs require a judge's ~⟩ **7 a :** SKILL, ABILITY ⟨wished to try his ~ at painting⟩ ⟨the comedienne tries her ~ at singing and dancing . . . for the first time —*Theatre Arts*⟩ **b :** an instrumental part ⟨several men had a ~ in the crime⟩ ⟨letting private industry have a bigger ~ in developing nuclear energy —*Wall Street Jour.*⟩ **8 :** a unit of measure equal to 4 inches used esp. for the height of horses — compare HANDBREADTH **9 a :** assistance or aid esp. involving physical effort ⟨gave the old man a ~ with his heavy bundles⟩ **b :** PARTICIPATION, INTEREST, CONCERN ⟨a project in which several people had a ~⟩ ⟨took a ~ in planning the new curriculum⟩ **c :** a round of applause ⟨won a good ~ for his acting⟩ ⟨gave the singer quite a ~⟩ **10 a** (1) **:** a player in a card game or board game (2) **:** the cards or pieces held by a player after a deal or distribution (3) **:** a set of cards or pieces in a player's possession at any point during a game (4) **:** the period of a game during which all cards or pieces distributed at one time are played (5) **:** a portion of undealt cards available for play in solitaire **b :** the force or solidity of one's position usu. as a negotiator against an opposing force ⟨these developments greatly strengthened the ~ of union policymakers —*Collier's Yr. Bk.*⟩ — often used in pl. **11 a :** one who performs or executes a particular work ⟨two portraits by the same ~⟩ ⟨essays by various ~s in praise of her work —*Collier's Yr. Bk.*⟩ **b** (1) **:** one employed at manual labor or general tasks ⟨a ranch ~⟩ (2) **:** WORKER, EMPLOYEE ⟨business was so successful the company soon was employing over a hundred ~s⟩ **c :** a member of a ship's crew ⟨all ~s on deck⟩ **d :** one relatively skilled in or disposed to perform a particular action or engage in a particular pursuit ⟨quite a ~ at figures⟩ ⟨a great ~ at carpentry⟩ **e :** a specialist in a usu. designated activity or region ⟨a Latin America ~⟩ — compare OLD HAND **12** *archaic* **:** one that is a source of information **13 a** *archaic* **:** a touch or stroke esp. of a brush on a painting **b :** HANDIWORK ⟨the destruction showed the ~ of vandals⟩ **c :** style of execution **:** WORKMANSHIP ⟨the very brushstrokes showed the ~ of a master⟩ **:** manner of handling **:** TOUCH ⟨in all the masques and pageants . . . his ~ was heavy and his invention flat —Francis Hackett⟩ ⟨treated the child with a light ~⟩ **14 :** the pawl that rotates the cylinder of a revolver **15** *dial* **:** the near horse **16** *dial Brit* **:** a locality or neighborhood ⟨he comes from over near Kendal ~⟩ **17** *or* **hand game :** a gambling game played by American Indians consisting of guessing the whereabouts of pieces of bone or other small objects which are passed rapidly from hand to hand **18** [trans. of L *manus*] **:** MANUS 2 **19 :** a turn of play in which there is an opportunity to score in a game **:** INNING **20 :** the feel of cloth or leather or tactile reaction to its textural qualities of smoothness, flexibility, softness ⟨the warm, dry, luxurious ~ of silk —*Collier's Yr. Bk.*⟩ **21** *also* **hand cheese :** any of several cheeses of a kind orig. molded by hand — **at close hand** *adv* **:** in close proximity **:** NEARBY ⟨as a personal friend he saw the great man *at close hand* on many occasions⟩ — **at first hand** *adv* **:** FIRSTHAND ⟨got the facts *at first hand* by going in person to the scene of the accident⟩ — **at hand :** near in time or place ⟨rather than buy more wood we used what was *at hand*⟩ ⟨the day of reckoning was *at hand*⟩ — **at second hand** *adv* **:** through an intermediary **:** INDIRECTLY ⟨got all his information *at second hand* rather than from original sources⟩ — **at the hands of** *or* **at the hand of :** by the act or instrumentality of ⟨the old way of life became totally outdated *at the hand of* the new technology and psychology⟩ **:** from the hands of ⟨received bad treatment *at the hands of* his master⟩ — **at third hand** *adv* **:** from a thirdhand source **:** in thirdhand condition **:** through more than one intermediary ⟨an account that was as unreliable as most information got *at third hand*⟩ — **by hand** *adv* **1 :** with the hands **:** by manual labor ⟨tilled the garden *by hand*⟩ **2 :** in handwriting ⟨a typewritten letter with a note added *by hand*⟩ **3 :** with personal care and attention ⟨bring a child up *by hand*⟩ **4 :** without the use of a machine that is usu. used for the purpose ⟨became disgusted with the adding machine so added the figures *by hand*⟩ — **for one's own hand :** for one's own advantage ⟨the group refused to work cooperatively, each member rather playing *for his own hand*⟩ — **from hand to hand :** from possession by one person to that of another **:** through successive possession by a number of people ⟨a bauble of little worth that went *from hand to hand*⟩ — **from hand to mouth :** with provision sufficient only for present needs **:** PRECARIOUSLY ⟨always poor and living *from hand to mouth*⟩ ⟨vagrants who live happily *from hand to mouth* —Brooks Atkinson⟩ — **in hand** *adv* **1 a :** in one's possession ⟨when he had enough money *in hand* he bought a car⟩ **b :** in control ⟨kept the children *in hand* by a system of rewards and punishments⟩ **c :** at one's disposal ⟨for a poor man he had a large amount of property *in hand* because of his position⟩ **:** to spare ⟨a race won with plenty of time *in hand*⟩ **2** *obs* **:** with one or accompanying one often on a leash **3 a :** in preparation ⟨a new play *in hand*⟩ **:** under consideration ⟨took the matter *in hand* at a board meeting⟩ **:** in course of transaction ⟨a business deal *in hand*⟩ **b :** under effective control or management ⟨got the business *in hand* before planning new sales campaigns⟩ **4 :** HAND IN HAND **5** *of a ball* **:** not yet in play or put out of play by the rules of the game — opposed to *in play* — **into hand** *adv* **:** into control or supervision ⟨the most troublesome children were taken *into hand* by special counselors⟩ — **lift a hand** *or* **raise a hand :** to make an effort **:** WORK — **of all hands** *obs* **:** on all sides **:** on every side — **off one's hands :** out of one's care or charge ⟨relieved to get so great a responsibility *off his hands*⟩ — **of one's hands** *obs* **:** of valor, skill, or ability esp. in fighting — **on all hands** *adv* **:** on every hand ⟨in the dark of the woods he could hear twittering and scurrying *on all hands*⟩ — **on every hand** *adv* **:** in or from every direction **:** EVERYWHERE ⟨as I . . . went into business, I found *on every hand* that quantity counted for more than quality —Edward Bok⟩ — **on hand** *adv* **1 :** in present possession and easily available ⟨a large stock of goods *on hand*⟩ **2 :** about to appear **:** PENDING, AFOOT ⟨reported there was trouble *on hand*⟩ **3 :** in attendance **:** PRESENT ⟨I will be *on hand* when you call⟩ — **on one's hands :** in one's possession, care, or management, often as a responsibility or a burden ⟨a lot of worthless property *on his hands*⟩ ⟨a problem child *on her hands* for a week⟩ ⟨a whole afternoon *on his hands* to do with as he wished⟩ — **out of hand** *adv* **1 :** without delay, hesitation, or preparation **:** FORTHWITH, PROMPTLY ⟨hanged the man *out of hand* without waiting for trial⟩ ⟨dismissed the traditional logic *out of hand* —J.A.Passmore⟩ **2 :** done with ⟨the business was finally *out of hand*⟩ **3 :** out of control ⟨let his temper get *out of hand*⟩ ⟨the children got *out of hand* and had to be spanked⟩ — **put one's hand on** *or* **lay one's hand on :** FIND, LOCATE ⟨arranged the files so he could *put his hand on* any fact he wanted in a moment⟩ — **put one's hand to** *or* **set one's hand to 1 :** to take hold of ⟨*put his hand to* the plow⟩ **2 :** to engage in **:** UNDERTAKE ⟨knew he would succeed in whatever he *put his hand to*⟩ — **to hand** *adv* **1 :** into possession ⟨used whatever came *to hand* and didn't cost anything⟩ **2 :** within reach **:** easily available ⟨weapons ready *to hand*⟩ ⟨convenient local ammunition lying *to hand* —Mollie Panter-Downes⟩ **3 :** into control or subjection ⟨the insurgents were brought quickly *to hand*⟩ — **to one's hand :** already prepared to appeal to one's taste or special talents ⟨a subject matter for a playwright just made *to his hand*⟩ — **under the hand of :** authenticated by the handwriting or signature of ⟨a deed executed *under the hand of* the owner⟩ — **with a heavy hand 1 :** with little mercy **:** STERNLY, RIGOROUSLY ⟨put down a revolt *with a heavy hand*⟩ **2 :** without grace, delicacy, or sensitivity **:** CLUMSILY ⟨went at the task *with a heavy hand* neglecting essential distinctions⟩ — **with clean hands :** UNCORRUPTED, INNOCENT ⟨although the opportunity to profit by dishonesty was always near he came out *with clean hands*⟩

**²hand** \ˈ"\ *vb* -ED/-ING/-S *vt* **1 a** *obs* **:** to manage with the hands **:** MANIPULATE; *also* **:** to lay hands on **b :** FURL ⟨~*ed* the mainsail —Thomas Horgan⟩ **2 :** to lead, guide, or assist with the hand **:** CONDUCT ⟨~ a lady into a bus⟩ ⟨~*ed* herself along the life line and followed her shipmates to the poop —Roland Barker⟩ **3 :** to give, pass, or transmit with the hand ⟨~ a person a letter⟩ **4 :** to make (one's way) by means of or by swinging with the hands ⟨an animal that ~s its way through the trees —Weston La Barre⟩ **5 :** to compel a person to submit to **:** administer forcefully to a person ⟨the smaller boy ~*ed* the bully a terrible beating⟩ ~ *vi* **:** to hand a sail — **hand it to :** to give credit to **:** concede the excellence of ⟨had to *hand it to* the committee for doing such a good job in getting out the vote⟩

**hand-adz** \ˈ=,=\ *n* **:** a prehistoric celt-shaped tool usu. of stone having one flat and one curved surface and an adz type of cutting edge

**hand alphabet** *n* **:** MANUAL ALPHABET

**hand and foot** *adv* [ME, fr. OE *hand and fōt*] **1 :** in a way to prevent escape or totally impede action ⟨bound the prisoner *hand and foot*⟩ **2 :** TOTALLY, COMPLETELY, ASSIDUOUSLY ⟨a woman who waited on her husband *hand and foot*⟩

**hand apple** *n* **:** an apple suitable for eating without cooking

**handarm** \ˈ=,=\ *n* **:** HANDGUN

**hand ax** *n* **:** a prehistoric stone implement consisting of a biface core having one end pointed for cutting and the other end rounded for holding in the hand

**handbag** \ˈ=,=\ *n* **1 :** TRAVELING BAG **2 :** a woman's bag made in various shapes of fabric, leather, or plastic, held in the hand or looped by handles over the shoulder, and used for carrying usu. small personal articles and accessories

**handball** \ˈ=,=\ *n* **1 :** a small hollow black rubber ball used in the game of handball **2 :** a game similar to squash played in a walled court or against a single wall or board by two or four players who use their hands to strike the ball

**handbank** \ˈ=,=\ *vt* **:** to haul (logs) to be banked for further transportation — **hand·bank·er** \ˈ=,=ə(r)\ *n*

**handbarrow** \ˈ=,=(ˌ)=\ *n* [ME *handberwe,* fr. *hand* + *berwe, barew, barowe* barrow — more at BARROW] **:** a flat rectangular frame with handles at both ends that is carried by two persons — compare WHEELBARROW

**handbasin** \ˈ=,==\ *n* **:** WASHBOWL

**handbell** \ˈ=,=\ *n* **:** a small bell with a handle; *esp* **:** one of a set tuned in a scale for musical performance

handbell

**handbill** \ˈ=,=\ *n* **:** a small printed sheet to be distributed (as for advertising) by hand and often doubling as a poster

**handbook** \ˈ=,=\ *n* [trans. of G *handbuch*] **1 a :** a book capable of being conveniently carried as a ready reference **:** MANUAL **b :** a concise reference book covering a particular subject or field of knowledge ⟨a ~ of geology⟩ ⟨a ~ of fungi⟩ ⟨a ~ of scouting⟩ ⟨a Milton ~⟩ **c :** a book of directions and information for travelers ⟨a ~ of France⟩ **2 a :** a bookmaker's book of bets **b :** a place where bookmaking is carried on

**hand·book·ing** \ˈ=,=iŋ\ *n* **:** BOOKMAKING 2

**handbow** \ˈ=,=\ *n* **:** a bow drawn by hand as distinguished from a crossbow

**hand brake** *n* **:** a brake (as on an automobile) operated by hand

**hand·breadth** \ˈhan(d)ˌ=\ *or* **hands·breadth** \-n(d)z,=\ *n* **:** the breadth of a hand; *also* **:** any of various units of length based on the breadth of a hand varying from about 2½ to 4 inches — compare HAND 8

**hand·breed** \ˈhanˌbrēd, ˈhȯn-\ *n* [ME *handbrede,* fr. OE *handbred,* fr. *hand, hond* hand + *bred* surface, board; akin to OE *bord* piece of sawed lumber — more at HAND, BOARD] *chiefly Scot* **:** HANDBREADTH

**hand breeding** *n* **:** controlled mating in which both the time and the mating individuals are selected by the breeder — called also *hand mating;* opposed to *pasture breeding*

**H and C** *abbr, often not cap* hot and cold running water

**handcar** \ˈ=,=\ *n* **:** a small four-wheeled car propelled by a hand-operated mechanism or by a small motor or fastened as a trailer to a motor-propelled car and used on railroad tracks for transporting men and materials in railroad-track construction and maintenance work

**handcart** \ˈ=,=\ *n* **:** a cart drawn or pushed by hand

**hand cheese** *n* **:** HAND 21

**handclap** \ˈ=,=\ *n* **:** a clap of the hands in indication of approval or praise ⟨a flurry of ~s greeted his appearance as the featured pianist⟩

handcart

**handclasp** \ˈ=,=\ *n* **:** a clasping of hands usu. by two people during an introduction of one to the other done as a formality upon meeting or parting or as a sign of friendship, affection, unanimity, or good wishes **:** HANDSHAKE

**hand composition** *n* **:** the work of a hand compositor

**hand compositor** *n* **:** one that sets type by hand esp. as contrasted with a typesetting-machine keyboard operator

**¹handcraft** \ˈ=,=\ *n* [ME, fr. OE *handcræft,* fr. *hand* + *cræft* craft] **:** HANDICRAFT

**²handcraft** \ˈ"\ *vt* **:** to fashion by handicraft ⟨a distinguished weathervane ~*ed* of heavy aluminum —*House Beautiful*⟩ ⟨~*ed* dress materials —*New Yorker*⟩ ⟨a ~*ed* chassis that uses no production shortcuts —*advt*⟩

**hand·craft·man** \ˈ=,=mən\ *or* **hand·crafts·man** \-f(t)sm-\ *n, pl* **handcraftmen** *or* **handcraftsmen :** one who is skilled in handicraft

**¹handcuff** \ˈ=,=\ *vt* **1 :** to apply handcuffs to **:** MANACLE **2 :** to restrain esp. completely or so as to prevent action by or as if by means of handcuffs ⟨the wording of the present charter would ~ the present parliament by preventing any revisions —*Current History*⟩

**²handcuff** \ˈ"\ *n* **:** a metal fastening that can be locked around a wrist and that is usu. connected by a chain or bar with another such fastening which can be locked about the other wrist of the same person or the wrist of another person **:** MANACLE — usu. used in pl. and often with *pair*

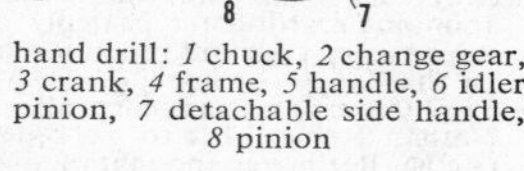
handcuffs, open and closed

**hand cultivator** *n* **:** WHEEL CULTIVATOR 2

**h and d curve** \ˌāchan'dē-\ *n, usu cap H&D* [after Ferdinand Hurter *and* Charles Driffield *fl* 1890 Brit. photographers] **:** CHARACTERISTIC CURVE a

**hand down** *vt* **1 :** to transmit in succession (as from father to son or from predecessor to successor) ⟨the family property was *handed down* from generation to generation⟩ **2 a :** to deliver to the proper office of an inferior court (the decision or opinion of an appellate court) **b :** to make official formulation of and express (the opinion of any court) **c :** to promulgate (as a policy) with authoritative force brooking no opposition ⟨the dictator *handed down* his decision⟩

**hand-down** \ˈ=,=\ *n* -s [by shortening] **:** HAND-ME-DOWN

**hand drill** *n* **1 :** a small portable drilling machine resembling a breast drill but designed to be held and operated by hand **2 :** a primitive drill consisting of a shaft carrying a point of stone, bone, shell, or metal and revolved usu. by the palms of the hands

hand drill: *1* chuck, *2* change gear, *3* crank, *4* frame, *5* handle, *6* idler pinion, *7* detachable side handle, *8* pinion

**h and d speed** \ˌāchən-ˈdē-\ *n, usu cap H&D* [after Ferdinand Hurter *and* Charles Driffield *fl* 1890] **:** a number indicating the sensitivity of a photographic emulsion determined by the method of Hurter and Driffield

**h and d system** *n, usu cap H&D* [after Ferdinand Hurter *and* Charles Driffield *fl* 1890] **:** a system for determining the speed of photographic materials that is based on the characteristic curve and related to the inertia of the material

**hand·ed** \ˈhandəd, ˈhaan-\ *adj* **1 :** having hands ⟨a ~, vertical, tree-living animal —Weston La Barre⟩ **2 :** being either right-hand, left-hand, right-hand reverse bevel, or left-hand reverse bevel — used of doors, hinges, locks, screws

**hand·ed·ness** *n* -ES **1 :** the quality or state of being handed **2 :** a tendency to use one hand rather than the other ⟨a test for ~⟩

**han·de·lian** \(ˈ)hanˈdēlyən, -lēən\ *adj, usu cap* [George F. *Handel,* (Händel) †1759 Ger. composer + E *-ian*] **:** of or relating to the German composer Handel or belonging to, befitting, or suggesting his music

**hand·er** \ˈhandə(r), ˈhaan-\ *n* -s **1** *dial Brit* **:** a blow on the hand **2 :** one that drops tobacco hands to the prizer for packing in hogsheads

**hander-in** \ˈ=ˈ=\ *n, pl* **handers-in :** a textile worker who assists in the drawing-in of the warp

**¹handfast** \ˈ=,=\ *vt* [ME *handfesten, handfasten,* fr. ON *handfesta,* fr. *hand-, hönd* hand + *festa* to fasten, fr. *fastr* fast — more at HAND, FAST] *archaic* **:** to bind in contract by joining hands; *esp* **:** BETROTH

**²handfast** \ˈ"\ *n, archaic* **:** a contract or covenant esp. of betrothal or marriage

**³handfast** \ˈ"\ *adj* [¹*hand* + *fast*] *archaic* **:** having a firm or close grasp **:** CLOSEFISTED

**handfasting** *n* -s **1** *archaic* **:** BETROTHAL **2 :** an irregular or probationary marriage contracted by joining hands and agreeing to live together as man and wife; *also* **:** the living together under such an agreement

**hand-feed** \ˈ=,=\ *vt* **:** to provide and apportion rations to (animals) at regular intervals in quantities sufficient for a single feeding — compare SELF-FEED

**hand file** *n* **:** a file of rectangular section with parallel sides and slightly thicker than a mill file

**¹handfish** \ˈ=,=\ *n* [¹*hand* + *fish* (n.); fr. the pectoral fins that resemble hands] **:** a fish of the family Brachionichthyidae

**²handfish** \ˈ=,=\ *vi* [¹*hand* + *fish* (v.)] **:** to catch fish with the hands sometimes with bait as a lure **:** GUDDLE

**hand-fives** \ˈ=,=\ *n pl but sing in constr* **:** FIVES

**handflag** \ˈ=,=\ *n* **:** one of usu. two flags used in transmitting messages by semaphore

**handflower tree** \'≈,≈-\ *n* : HAND TREE

**hand fly** *n* [so called fr. its being nearest the angler's hand] : DROPPER 1a

**hand frame** *n* : a textile machine (as a knitting frame) worked by hand or foot power

**hand·ful** *also* **hand·full** \'han(d),fu̇l, 'haan-\ *n, pl* **hand·fuls** \-n(d),fu̇lz\ *or* **hands·ful** \-n(d)z,fu̇l\ [ME, fr. OE *handfull*, fr. *hand* hand + *full* full — more at HAND, FULL] **1** : as much or as many as the hand will grasp or contain ⟨the child grabbed a ~ of jelly beans⟩ **2** : a small quantity or number ⟨only a ~ of people have ever seen that great high region —*London Calling*⟩ ⟨bought for liquor and a ~ of pin money the huge tracts near the present Twin Cities —*Amer. Guide Series: Minn.*⟩ ⟨this figure had shrunk to only a ~ —Walter Sullivan⟩ ⟨only a few of our people are killers; only a ~ would take a man's life so greedily —Lillian Smith⟩ **3** : as much as one can control or manage using all one's effort ⟨the rearing of the children and the keeping of the house proved to be a ~ for one of her frail constitution⟩ ⟨a snake as savage as this one would be a ~ —W.L.Gresham⟩

**hand gallop** *n* [so called fr. the fact that the horse is kept well in hand to control his speed] : a fast pace in horseback riding between a canter and a gallop : a very fast easy canter : a moderate gallop

**hand game** *n* : HAND 17

**hand glass** *n* **1** : a small mirror with a handle **2** : a 14-second or 28-second sandglass used in timing the running out of a nautical log line

**handgrab** \'≈,≈\ *n* : a bar or handle (as on a ship) used for steadying or supporting oneself

**handgrasp** \'≈,≈\ *n* : HANDLE

**handgravure** \'≈≈,≈\ *n* : copperplate printing in which the inked plate is wiped by hand before each impression

**hand grenade** *n* : a grenade designed to be thrown by hand

**handgrip** \'≈,≈\ *n* [ME *hand grip*, fr. OE *handgripe*, fr. *hand* hand + *gripe* grip — more at HAND, GRIP] **1** : a grasping with the hand : HANDCLASP **2** : something that is attached to or forms part of an object and is designed to be grasped by the hand in lifting the object: as **a** : HANDLE ⟨the ~ of the revolver⟩ ⟨a pot with two small projecting ~*s*, one on each side⟩ **b** : HILT ⟨the ~ of a sword⟩ **c** : the outer usu. projecting end of the arm of an armchair ⟨it has nearly flat scrolled arms that . . . terminate in down-scrolled ~*s* —T.H.Ormsbee⟩ **3 handgrips** *pl* : close and usu. critical or desperate struggle : hand-to-hand combat — usu. used in the phrases *at handgrips* or *come to handgrips* ⟨before they lost the town the soldiers were at ~*s* with the enemy⟩ ⟨the struggle was so evenly matched the soldiers came to ~*s* before the issue was decided⟩

**handguard** \'≈,≈\ *n* **1 a** : a guard on a sword — compare CROSS GUARD **b** : a guard on a knife or dagger similar to that on a sword **2** : a wooden piece above the barrel of a rifle

**handgun** \'≈,≈\ *n* [ME *handgunne*, fr. *hand* + *gunne* gun — more at GUN] : a firearm held and fired with one hand

**¹hand·hab·end** \'≈,habənd\ *or* **handhaving** \'≈,≈≈\ *adj* [*handhabend* fr. ME, fr. OE *handhabbend*, fr. *hand*, *hond* hand + *habbend*, pres. part. of *habben* to have — more at HAND, HAVE] : having possession of stolen goods — used in Old English law of a thief caught with the loot

**²handhabend** \"\ *or* **handhaving** \"\ *n* -s : the jurisdiction to try a handhabend thief

**handhold** \'≈,≈\ *n* **1** : HOLD, GRIP ⟨got a ~ on the edge of the dock and pulled himself out of the water⟩ ⟨has a ~ on a rich chunk of the empire and he will not let go —*Time*⟩ **2** : something to hold on to (as in mountain climbing) ⟨swinging from one ~ to the next in a line⟩; *specif* : the part of an implement fashioned for grasping with the hand

**handhole** \'≈,≈\ *n* **1** : a hole large enough only for insertion of a hand (as for lifting) or of a hand and arm (as for cleaning out otherwise inaccessible places or giving access to enclosed parts) **2** : a shallow form of manhole giving access to a top row of ducts in an underground electrical system

**hand·hol·er** \'≈,≈ə(r)\ *n* : an operator of a machine for cutting handholes in the ends of wooden boxes

**hand horn** *n* : a natural French horn whose pitch a player can modify or alter by inserting his hand in the bell

**hand horse** *n, dial* : the near horse

**¹hand·i·cap** \'handē,kap, 'haan-, -də,-\ *n* -s *often attrib* [fr. obs. E. a game of forfeits and exchanges in which the players held forfeit money in a cap, alter. of *hand in cap*] **1** : a race or any contest of agility, strength, or skill in which in order to equalize chances of winning an artificial disadvantage is imposed on a supposedly superior contestant or an artificial advantage is given to one supposedly inferior **2 a** : an advantage given a weaker contestant or a disadvantage imposed upon a stronger contestant in the form of points, strokes, weight to be carried, or distance from the target or goal in order to equalize chances of winning **b** : a disadvantage that makes achievement unusually difficult; *esp* : a physical disability that limits the capacity to work

**²handicap** \"\ *vb* **handicapped; handicapped; handicapping; handicaps** *vt* **1 a** : to give a handicap to **b** : to assign handicaps to in order to equalize chances of success ⟨the horses were admirably *handicapped* in the race⟩ **2** : to put at a disadvantage ⟨*handicapped* in his job by worries over debts⟩ ~ *vi* : to engage in handicapping

**hand·i·cap·per** \-pə(r)\ *n* -s : one that handicaps in racing: **a** : the official (as of a jockey club) who assigns the weights to be carried by the horses in a handicap **b** : one whose job is handicapping ⟨earned some money as a ~ for a local newspaper⟩

**handicapping** *n* -s : the occupation of predicting winners in horse races usu. for publication

**hand·i·craft** \-,kraft, -aa(ə)-,-ai-,-á-\ *n* [ME *handie-crafte*, alter. (influenced by *handiwerk* handiwork) of *handcraft*, fr. *hand* + *craft*] **1 a** : an occupation in which articles are fashioned totally or chiefly by hand esp. with manual and often artistic skill usu. as either a trade or a hobby **b** : the articles fashioned by those engaged in such an occupation **2** *archaic* : one living by handicraft : HANDICRAFTSMAN

**hand·i·craft·er** \-tə(r)\ *n* -s : one that engages in a handicraft usu. as a hobby or avocation

**hand·i·crafts·man** \-f(t)smən\ *n, pl* **handicraftsmen** : one that engages in a handicraft : ARTISAN

**hand·i·cuff** \'≈≈,kəf\ *n* -s [¹*hand* + -*icuff*, as in *fisticuff*] *archaic* : a blow with the hand : FISTICUFF

**handier** *comparative of* HANDY

**handiest** *superlative of* HANDY

**Handie–Talkie** \¦handē¦tȯkē\ *trademark* — used for a small portable radio transmitter-receiver

**hand·i·grips** \'handē,grips\ *archaic var of* HANDGRIPS

**hand·i·ly** \'handəlē, 'haan-, -li\ *adv* [*handy* + -*ly*] **1** : in a handy manner: as **a** : DEXTEROUSLY ⟨applied the brush ~ and finished the painting in a few minutes⟩ **b** : EASILY ⟨despite the handicap the horse won the race ~⟩ **c** : CONVENIENTLY ⟨kept the eraser ~ beside him as he wrote⟩ **2** *Midland* : JUSTLY, FAIRLY, RIGHTLY ⟨you can't ~ tell him to go home⟩

**hand in** *vt* : SUBMIT ⟨his thoughts were concentrated on *handing in* reports that would injure nobody —Alfred Burmeister⟩

**hand–in** \'≈,≈\ *n* -s [*hand in*] *in squash or badminton* : the player who serves the ball or his period of service

**hand·i·ness** \'handēnəs, 'haan-, -din-\ *n* -ES [*handy* + -*ness*] : the quality or state of being handy

**handing** *pres part of* HAND

**hand in glove** *or* **hand and glove** *adv* : in extremely close relationship or agreement esp. for nefarious purposes ⟨mass production is the outgrowth of the so-called industrial revolution and has had a part *hand in glove* with it —A.H.Compton⟩ ⟨the police were found to be working *hand in glove* with the racketeers⟩

**hand in hand** *adv* **1** *of two people* : with hands clasped usu. in affection or intimacy **2** : in the manner of things that are inseparably interrelated : in union : CONJOINTLY ⟨freedom of speech and true democratic government go *hand in hand*⟩ ⟨more and more architecture and landscape architecture go *hand in hand* —*Collier's Yr. Bk.*⟩ ⟨illness and bad housing go *hand in hand* —*Times Lit. Supp.*⟩

**hand–in–hand** \'≈≈'≈\ *adj* [*hand in hand*] **1** *of two people* : having the hands clasped usu. in affection or intimacy **2** : being close or intimate : going side by side or in close relationship

**handiron** \'≈,≈\ *n* [by folk etymology] *dial* : ANDIRON

**hand·i·work** \'handē,-, 'haan-, -di,-\ *n* [ME *handiwerk*, fr. OE *handgeweorc*, fr. *hand* hand + *geweorc*, fr. *ge-* (collective and perfective prefix) + *weorc* work — more at HAND, CO-, WORK] **1 a** : work done by the hands ⟨occupied his time around the house with ~ of various kinds⟩ **b** : work done personally : personal or individual achievement ⟨his fortune is his own ~ —S.N.Behrman⟩ ⟨showed the ~ of a master criminal⟩ **2** : the product of handiwork ⟨the fiddle was . . . the ~ of the great Italian master violin maker —*Fortnight*⟩ ⟨selling baskets, ~, and curios to tourists —*Amer. Guide Series: Maine*⟩

**handjar** *var of* KHANJAR

**hand·ker·cher** \'haŋkə(r)chə(r), 'haiŋ-\ *dial var of* HANDKERCHIEF

**hand·ker·chief** \'haŋkə(r)chə̇f, 'haiŋ-, -(,)chi̇f, -,chēf\ *n, pl* **handkerchiefs** *also* **handkerchieves** \|fs, |vz; *many whose pl is* -ēvz *have* ə *or* i *as a last-syllable vowel in the sing*\ [*hand* + *kerchief*] **1** : a piece of cloth usu. square and often printed, edged, or embroidered that is used for various usu. personal purposes (as the wiping of the nose or eyes) or as a costume accessory **2** : KERCHIEF 1

**handkerchief dance** *n* : a dance in which kerchiefs are waved or in which dancers are linked by the kerchiefs they hold in their hands

**handkerchief table** *n* : a folding triangular table that becomes square when the drop leaf supported by a swinging leg is raised

**hand–kissing** \'≈,≈≈\ *n* -s : the custom in some countries (as France) of a gentleman's pressing his lips to the back of a woman's hand as a gesture of courtesy (as in an introduction) or of affection

**hand labor** *n* : manual labor as distinct from machine work

**handlaid** \'≈,≈\ *adj* **1** *of paper* : HANDMADE **2** *of a rope or line* : laid by hand

**hand language** *n* : communication by means of a manual alphabet : DACTYLOLOGY

**¹han·dle** \'handᵊl, 'haan-, *rapid* -nᵊl\ *n* -s [ME *handel*, fr. OE *handle*; akin to MLG *hantel* handle; derivatives fr. the root of E ¹*hand*] **1** : a part that is designed esp. to be grasped by the hand or that may be grasped by the hand (as for lifting or steering) **2 a** : something that resembles a handle in appearance, use, or function **b** : something (as a pretext or opportunity) that may be figuratively seized as a means of dealing with some larger abstract unit ⟨the only ~ he has for laying hold of the future —Dixon Wecter⟩ ⟨the ~ by which the writer grasps reality —Max Lerner & Edwin Mims⟩ **3 a** *slang* : NAME ⟨bore an odd ~⟩ ⟨with the heavenly ~ of St. Thomas —*Newsweek*⟩ : TITLE ⟨an Englishman with a ~ to his name—Baron or something⟩ **b** *dial* : a given name that is somewhat unusual ⟨what did they go and give the poor kid a ~ like that for —Edna Reynolds⟩ **4** : HAND 20 ⟨a well-scoured acetate fabric will have a soft springy ~ —*Dyestuffs*⟩ **5** [²*handle*] : the total amount of money bet on a race, game, or event or over a period of time (as a season) **6** *chiefly NewZeal* : a measure of beer approximately one pint — **off the handle** *adv* : into a state marked esp. by sudden and violent anger ⟨her nerves were so bad that she flew *off the handle* at the least provocation⟩

**²handle** \"\ *vb* **handled; handled; handling** \-(ᵊ)liŋ\ **handles** [ME *handelen*, fr. OE *handlian*; akin to OHG *hantalōn* to take with the hands, ON *höndla* to handle, seize; derivatives fr. the root of E ¹*hand*] *vt* **1 a** : to touch, feel, hold, take up, move, or otherwise affect with the hand : use the hands upon ⟨~ a material to find out how rough it is⟩ ⟨please do not ~ the merchandise⟩ **b** : to manage in using with the hands (as a spade or a weapon) : PLY, MANIPULATE, WIELD ⟨~ a scythe⟩ ⟨~ a gun with precision⟩ ⟨excellent at *handling* a horse⟩ **c** *of a batsman in cricket* : to pick up or touch with the hand (a ball in play) except at the request of the fielding side — used esp. in the phrase *out, handled the ball* **2 a** : to deal with or treat of in writing or speaking or in the plastic arts (as a theme, subject, argument, or objection) ⟨the writer ~*s* the matter briefly and concisely⟩ ⟨told him how to ~ color in using oil paints⟩ **b** : to conduct oneself in relation to : assume an attitude to **c** (1) : MANAGE, CONTROL, DIRECT ⟨was asked to ~ the staff of researchers in the absence of the director⟩ ⟨a lawyer who ~*s* the affairs of several corporations⟩ (2) : to have immediate physical charge in the care and training of (an animal) ⟨a good man to ~ his stable of horses⟩; *also* : to hold and incite (a sporting animal or bird) in a match (3) : to train (a pugilist) and act as the second during a fight (4) : to engage professionally in showing or exhibiting (an animal) in a show-ring **d** : to supervise, oversee, or control (as a worker) in such a way as to encourage a maximum of work output or persuade to a particular course of action or conduct ⟨a boss whose special gift was an ability to ~ men⟩ **e** : to deal with : act upon : dispose of : perform some function with regard to ⟨a period in which to ~ the day's mail and clear up back business⟩ ⟨told how much freight was *handled* at the port of New York⟩ ⟨a disposal unit that could ~ the city's garbage⟩ **f** : to trade in : engage in the buying, selling, or distributing of (a commodity) ⟨will be *handling* new and used cars⟩ : have or cause to pass through one's hands in commercial transactions **g** (1) : to perform or do to the point of completeness or success ⟨a man who would really ~ the job⟩ (2) : to drink (intoxicating drinks) without losing the normal control of one's faculties or actions or acting in foolish ways ⟨could not ~ liquor and always began to giggle and get maudlin after two drinks⟩ **3** *in hunting* : KILL **4** : to move up and down or draw out and replace (hides) in the pit in the process of tanning — see HANDLER 3 **5** : to be competent enough or fit to act upon, perform, manage, direct, solve, or deal with successfully in some other way ⟨a singer unable to ~ the difficult passages of the score⟩ ⟨equal to *handling* any amount of business that came along⟩ ⟨unable to ~ the boys⟩ ⟨his inability to ~ so difficult a problem —Sherwood Anderson⟩ ⟨a faucet that ~*s* hot and cold water simultaneously⟩ ⟨a typewriter that can ~ almost any number of carbons⟩ **6** : to have within its jurisdiction ⟨a court that ~*s* only probate matters⟩ ~ *vi* : to act, behave, or feel in a certain way when handled or directed ⟨bought a car that ~*s* well⟩ ⟨the schooner . . . ~*s* easily —Kenneth Roberts⟩ ⟨the dog ~*s* well in field trials⟩; *specif* : to submit obediently to direction or control ⟨the dog *handled* well in the trials⟩

**syn** HANDLE, MANIPULATE, WIELD, SWING, and PLY can mean in common to deal with as with the hands, esp. in an easy or dexterous manner. HANDLE implies at the least enough skill, and usu. a specified degree more, to accomplish one's end ⟨knew better than most men how to *handle* a blade —L.C. Douglas⟩ ⟨able to *handle* a foreign language with proficiency⟩ ⟨doubted that their economy could ever *handle* more than the natural population increase —*Time*⟩ MANIPULATE implies dexterity and adroitness in handling, esp. a mechanical or technical skill, and extends to suggest, in figurative use, a dealing with something in a crafty, artful, often fraudulent way ⟨the kind of courage required for mountaineering, for *manipulating* an aeroplane, or for managing a small ship in a gale —Bertrand Russell⟩ ⟨was able to *manipulate* sequences of words in blank verse in a manner which is quite his own —T.S.Eliot⟩ ⟨agencies by which some human beings *manipulate* other human beings for their own advantage —John Dewey⟩ ⟨a genius of legal dishonesty in *manipulating* stocks⟩ WIELD implies mastery and vigor in the handling of a tool, weapon, or other implement ⟨the longbow, which was so tall that the man *wielding* it had to pull the string back to his eye or ear —Tom Wintringham⟩ ⟨a past master in *wielding* a golf club⟩ ⟨*wield* the scalpel —G.B.Shaw⟩ ⟨*wield* tremendous political power —Green Peyton⟩ ⟨he *wields* . . . a very capable scholarship that gives backbone to his work —N.L.Rothman⟩ SWING in literal use implies a wide sweep of action ⟨*swing* a ball bat⟩ ⟨being able to *swing* an oar —H.A.Chippendale⟩ but in an extended figurative use it can imply the successful handling of something large or difficult in relation to one's capacities ⟨a task too hard for him to *swing*⟩ ⟨*swing* a deal in high finance⟩ PLY is interchangeable with HANDLE or WIELD when great diligence or industry is implied ⟨tell them where it will best repay them to *ply* their pickaxes and spades —F.R. Leavis⟩ ⟨the experts *plied* their pens —R.F.Harrod⟩ **syn** see in addition TREAT

—**handle with gloves on** *or* **handle with kid gloves** : to treat with extreme care

**han·dle·able** \-ᵊləbəl\ *adj* : capable of being handled ⟨bucket feeding . . . makes the heifers gentle and ~ —*Australian Home Beautiful*⟩ ⟨a set of ~ . . . and inexpensive volumes —Margaret Marshall⟩

**hand lead** \-,led\ *n* : a small lead for sounding in shallow water

**handlebar** \'≈≈,≈\ *n* **1** : a straight or bent bar with a handle or serving as a handle **2 a** (1) *or* **handlebars** *pl* : the shaped bar that forms part of a cycle's steering mechanism and that is grasped by the hands — see BICYCLE illustration (2) : one end of such a bar usu. grasped by one hand while riding (3) : a part of a steering mechanism suggesting or shaped like such a bar or one end of such a bar **b handlebars** *pl* : HANDLEBAR MOUSTACHE

**handlebar moustache** *n* : a man's heavy moustache with long slightly curved sections at each end

**handle blank** *n* : a piece of dimension lumber often of hickory and suitable for making handles

**han·dled** \¦handᵊld, ¦haan-, *rapid* -nᵊld\ *adj* : having a usu. specified type of handle ⟨a pearl-*handled* penknife⟩ ⟨a long-*handled* knife⟩

**handled cross** *n* : ANKH

**han·dle·less** \'han(d)ᵊl(l)ə̇s, 'haan-\ *adj* : having no handle

**hand lens** *n* : a magnifying glass designed to be held in the hand

**han·dler** \'hand(ᵊ)lə(r), 'haan-, *rapid* -n(ᵊ)l-\ *n* -s [ME, fr. *handelen* to handle + -*er*] **1** : one that handles ⟨all ~*s* of food in restaurants require a health certificate⟩ ⟨the railroad was one of the largest ~*s* of coal in the world⟩: as **a** : a worker whose task it is to move, carry, stow, or arrange materials or objects by hand or chiefly by hand **b** : one in immediate physical charge of an animal **c** : one that holds and incites a dog, gamecock, or other sporting animal in a match or hunt **d** : one that helps to train a pugilist or acts as his second during a match **e** : one professionally engaged in exhibiting animals in the show ring **f** : one that guides, directs, and acts as publicity man and general agent for another (as for a political candidate during a campaign) **2** : a worker who affixes handles (as to pottery or baskets) **3** : a pit containing tanning liquor in which hides are worked over or handled in the tanning process

**handles** *pl of* HANDLE, *pres 3d sing of* HANDLE

**hand·less** \'handlə̇s, 'haan-, *rapid* -nl-\ *adj* [ME, fr. ¹*hand* + -*less*] **1** : having no hands ⟨a ~ war veteran⟩ **2** : inefficient, clumsy, or incompetent in manual tasks ⟨could hardly empty a scuttle of ashes, so ~ was the poor creature —Mary H. Vorse⟩

**hand letter** *n* : a single letter usu. cut in brass that is applied by hand to the binding of a book

**hand–letter** \'≈¦≈≈\ *vb* [*hand letter*] *vt* **1** : to print by hand ⟨a *hand-lettered* notice in chalk on the wall⟩ **2** : to apply hand letters to (a book or its binding) ~ *vi* : PRINT

**hand level** *n* : a surveyor's level designed to be held in the hand and consisting of a telescope with a bubble tube so attached that the position of the bubble can be seen when looking through the telescope

**h and l hinge** *n, cap 1st H&L* : a door hinge resembling a ligature of a capital H and L

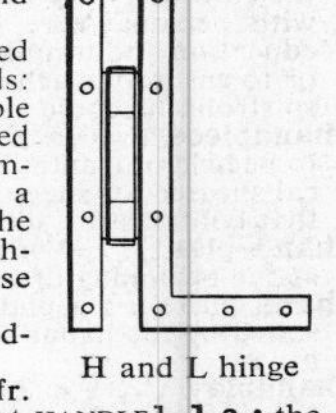

H and L hinge

**handlike** \'≈,≈\ *adj* : shaped like a hand or grasping in the manner of a hand

**¹handline** \'≈,≈\ *n* **1** : a line managed chiefly by direct contact with the hands: as **a** : any of several comparatively simple arrangements of hooks and line designed for use in the hands of or under the immediate and continuous supervision of a fisherman — opposed to *setline* **b** : the line on a hand lead **c** : a line used without rod or reel for fishing **2** : a fire hose of small diameter

**²handline** \'≈,≈\ *vi* : to fish with a handline — **hand·lin·er** \'≈,≈ə(r)\ *n*

**handling** *n* -s [ME, fr. OE *handlung*, fr. *handlian* to handle + -*ung* -ing — more at HANDLE] **1 a** : the action of one that handles something ⟨a child who needed a good deal of ~⟩ ⟨the horses seemed to thrive under his ~⟩ **b** : a process by which something is handled esp. in a commercial transaction ⟨the problem was not the sales but the ~ of the merchandise⟩; *esp* : the packaging and shipping of an object or a material (as to a consumer) ⟨made a small ~ charge for all deliveries of goods outside the city limits⟩ **2** : the manner in which something is handled ⟨the coach liked his ball ~ and made him captain of the team⟩ ⟨improved in his ~ of language⟩; *esp* : the mode or style of treatment or presentation (as of a theme) in a musical, literary, or art work ⟨the dramatist's ~ of the climax of the action was ineffective⟩ **3** : the manner in which something acts when handled ⟨the ~ of the automobile was smooth and effortless⟩

**handling room** *n* : a compartment opening into magazines and shell rooms in which ammunition is arranged and placed on hoists to be sent directly to the guns of a naval vessel

**hand–lining** \'≈,≈≈\ *n* : fishing with a handline

**handlist** \'≈,≈\ *n* : a handy orig. fairly brief list (as of newspapers or manuscripts) for purposes of reference or check ⟨a ~ of 100 books on warfare⟩ ⟨a ~ of plays produced between 1850 and 1900⟩

**¹handload** \'≈¦≈\ *vt* : to load (ammunition) by hand ~ *vi* : to handload ammunition — **handloading** \'≈¦≈≈\ *adj*

**²handload** \"\ *n* : a cartridge that has been loaded by hand

**handloader** \'≈¦≈≈\ *n* : one that loads his own cartridges

**handlock** \'≈¦≈\ *vt* [fr. obs. E *handlock* handcuff (n.)] *archaic* : HANDCUFF, MANACLE

**handloom** \'≈¦≈\ *n* : any of various looms or weaving devices operated wholly or partly by hand or foot power

**handloomed** \'≈¦≈\ *adj* : woven on a handloom

**¹handmade** \'≈¦≈\ *adj* **1** : made by hand or a hand process esp. as distinguished from a machine or mechanical process ⟨~ paper⟩ ⟨~ furniture⟩ **2** : simulating something that is handmade ⟨paper with a ~ finish⟩; *also* : used in the fabrication of such simulation ⟨~ felt⟩

**²handmade** \"\ *n* -s : something that is handmade; *esp* : a handmade fabric or dress

**handmaid** \'≈,≈\ *n* [ME, fr. *hand* + *maid*] **1** : a personal maid or female servant or attendant **2** : something whose essential function is to serve and assist ⟨holds that the state . . . must become the servant or ~ of the church —*Times Lit. Supp.*⟩ ⟨even philosophy and logic . . . were in his eyes the mere ~*s* of the critical spirit —Richard Wollheim⟩

**handmaiden** \'≈,≈≈\ *n* [ME, fr. *hand* + *maiden*] : HANDMAID ⟨good sense which . . . is the indispensable ~ of the critical art —Carlos Baker⟩ ⟨literature must never become the ~ of the history program or the science program —A.S.Artley⟩ ⟨ethics is not the ~ of theology —Brand Blanshard⟩ — **hand·maid·en·ly** \-lē\ *adj*

**handmaid moth** *n* : a moth of the genus *Datana* (esp. *D. ministra*)

**hand mast** *n* : a mast made from one timber : POLE MAST

**hand mating** *n* : HAND BREEDING

**¹hand–me–down** \'≈≈,≈\ *adj* **1** *of clothing* : ready-made and usu. cheap and shoddy ⟨cheap store clothes of the *hand-me-down* variety for export to the Southwest —Dixon Wecter⟩ **2 a** : put in use by one person or group after being already used and discarded by another : SECOND-HAND ⟨not just any old *hand-me-down* philosophy of education —*Atlantic*⟩ **b** : already having been worn or used and discarded by another (as an older brother) ⟨wearing their older sisters' *hand-me-down* evening dresses —Peter Taylor⟩

**²hand–me–down** \"\ *n* -s : something that is hand-me-down ⟨the terms . . . are *hand-me-downs* from former generations of businessmen —W.H.Whyte⟩ ⟨are our diet beliefs more *hand-me-downs* from the previous generation —C.R.Stackhouse⟩; *esp* : a hand-me-down garment or suit ⟨uniforms . . . had the unmistakable fit of *hand-me-downs* —Hamilton Basso⟩ ⟨wore *hand-me-downs* until he was 16 and then was allowed to buy himself a new suit⟩

**hand–minded** \'≈¦≈≈\ *adj* : naturally disposed primarily to manual activities ⟨those who are so exclusively *hand-minded* as to suggest the wisdom of drawing them off into manual or technical schools —B.P.Fowler〉 — **hand-mind·ed·ness** *n* -ES

**hand money** *n* : EARNEST MONEY

**hand mower** *n* : a lawn mower designed to be pushed by hand — distinguished from *power mower*

**hand nut** *n* : WING NUT, THUMB NUT

**hand off** *vt* **1** : to hand (the ball) to a nearby teammate during a football play **2** : to force (a tackler) away with the open palm of the hand while carrying the ball esp. in rugby

**hand-off** \'=,=\ *n* -S [*hand off*] **1** : a football play in which the ball is handed by one player to another nearby 〈scored on a ~〉; *also* : a ball that is transferred in this manner 〈take a ~〉 **2** : an act of handing off an opponent esp. in rugby

**hand of pork** *dial Eng* : a shoulder of pork without the blade bone

**hand of write** *Scot* : HANDWRITING

**hand on** *vt* : HAND DOWN 1 〈the father *handed on* his good reputation to his son〉 〈*handed on* the tradition of French classical painting to the generation who followed him —Robert Richman〉

**hand orchis** *n* [so called fr. the fingerlike tubers] : SPOTTED ORCHIS 1

**hand organ** *n* : a barrel organ operated by a hand crank

**hand out** *vt* **1** : to give free 〈*handing out* free samples of a new breakfast food〉 〈*handing out* passes to a movie〉 or as a master or proprietor to an inferior or one he may patronize 〈make a bow and accept anything the king wanted to *hand out* —Dorothy C. Fisher〉 **2** : to give freely 〈a politician *handing out* compliments to his constituents〉 〈*handing out* advice to all prospective buyers〉 **3** : ADMINISTER 〈reconciled to any punishment *handed out* to him〉

hand organ

**handout** \'=,=\ *n* -S [*hand out*] **1** : something handed out or designed to be handed out: as **a** : a portion of food, clothing, or money given to or as if to a beggar **b** : a folder or circular of information for free distribution (as an advertising throwaway) **c** (1) : a mimeographed or printed press release by a news service (2) : a prepared statement released to the press by advertisers, government agencies or officials, or publicity agencies **2** : [5]DOWN 2c

**hand over** *vt* **1** : to yield control of : deliver up 〈the thief *handed over* the stolen watch to the policeman〉 **2** : hand on to another 〈*handed over* the perquisites of office to his successor〉 〈such privileges may be *handed over* as a dowry —Edward Sapir〉

**hand over fist** *adv* : quickly and in large amounts 〈began to make money *hand over fist*〉

**hand over hand** *adv* : by grasping with the hands moving alternately one before or above the other 〈climb a rope *hand over hand*〉 〈haul in a line *hand over hand*〉

**hand over head** *adv* [ME *hand ovyr hedd*] *archaic* : without heed of what one is really doing : RASHLY, RECKLESSLY

**hand phone** *n* : HANDSET

**handpick** \'='=\ *vt* **1** : to pick by hand as opposed to a machine process 〈machines supplanted the workers who ~*ed* the cotton〉 〈~*ing* the insects from the plants〉 **2 a** : to select with personal care for quality 〈~ the man because of his education and training —T.M.Landy〉 **b** : to select personally or to ensure the achievement of personal ends 〈a party leader so strong he could ~ the political candidates〉 〈a ~*ed* jury〉

**handpiece** \'=,=\ *n* : the part of a mechanized device designed to be held or manipulated by hand; *esp* : the part of a mechanical shearer for sheep that is manipulated by the operator and that contains the shearing blades

**hand-plant** \'=,=\ *n* : the tobacco plant set in the starting hill at the beginning of a row in a tobacco field

**hand plate** *n* : a plate placed on a door to prevent its being soiled by the hands — called also *push plate;* compare FINGER PLATE

**handplay** \'=,=\ *n* **1** : an exchange of blows in hand-to-hand fighting **2** : the act of playing as high bidder in a game of skat with the cards dealt without using the skat

**hand plow** *n* : a light plow propelled by hand for use in gardens — called also *garden plow*

**hand-pollinate** \'=ˌ==,=\ *vt* : to pollinate by hand usu. with a camel's-hair brush — **hand-pollination** \ˌ=,==ˈ==\ *n*

**handpress** \'=,=\ *n* : a hand-operated printing or proving press

**hand prop** *n* : a small and movable property used by an actor during the performance of a play or a small property (as a cushion or drinking glass) capable of being carried on and off a set easily

**hand pump** *n* : a pump operated by hand; *esp* : one for emergency use when a power-operated pump fails

**hand puppet** *n* : a puppet constructed with a hollow head and arms attached to a costume fitting over the puppeteer's hand and activated by movements of the fingers and thumb inserted in the head and arms — called also *glove doll*

**handrail** \'=,=\ *n* : a narrow rail for grasping with the hand as a support

**handrailing** \'=,==\ *n* : HANDRAILS; *also* : material designed for a handrail

**handreader** \'=,==\ *n* : PALMIST

**handreading** \'=,==\ *n* : PALMISTRY

**handrest** \'=,=\ *n* : a rest or support for the hand or for a hand tool (as on a lathe)

hand puppet

**hand ride** *n* : an act of hand-riding; *also* : the ride in a race in which the jockey hand-rides

**hand-ride** \'=,=\ *vb* [*hand ride*] *vt* : to ride (a horse) without using a whip or spurs during a race ~ *vi* : to hand-ride a racehorse

**hand rope** *n* **1** : GUEST ROPE 2 **2** : a very flexible wire rope made up of usu. six strands about a hemp center and used for signal pulls, steering lines, elevator-controlling devices

**hand-run** \'=,=\ *adj, of lace* : machine-made but finished by hand

**hand running** *adv* : in unbroken succession : CONSECUTIVELY 〈won three games *hand running*〉 〈could chin a pole twenty times *hand running* —W.A.White〉

**hands** *pl of* HAND, *pres 3d sing of* HAND

**handsale** \'=,=\ *n* **1** : a form of sale made binding by a handshake and customary among the early Teutonic races **2** : money paid as earnest money to bind a sale

**hands around** *n pl* : a movement in square dancing in which the dancers join hands and circle left

**handsaw** \'=,=\ *n* : a saw used with one hand and operated by a backward and forward drive of the arm; *esp* : the common saw consisting of a wide blade with a handle at one end — compare CROSSCUT SAW, HACKSAW, RIPSAW

**handsaw fish** *n* [so called fr. the finely serrated edge of the dorsal ray] : a fish of the genus *Alepisaurus*

**handsbreadth** *var of* HANDBREADTH

**hand-schül·ler-chris·tian disease** \ˌhan(d),shülə(r)'kris(h)chən-\ *n, usu cap H&S&C* [after Alfred J. *Hand* b1868 Am. physician + Artur *Schüller* b1874 Austrian neurologist + Henry *Christian* b1876 Am. physician] : an inflammatory histiocytosis associated with disturbances in cholesterol metabolism that occurs chiefly in young children and is marked by cystic defects of the skull, exophthalmos, and diabetes insipidus

[1]**hand-screen** \'=,=\ *n* : a small usu. ornamented screen designed to be held in the hand and used formerly as a shade against heat or light

[2]**hand-screen** \'=,=\ *vt* : to print by the silk-screen process

**hand screw** *n* : a screw or screw device turned by hand — compare THUMBSCREW

**hand-screw clamp** *n* : a woodworker's clamp with two hardwood jaws joined by a pair of right-hand and left-hand threaded screws that maintain parallel adjustment of the jaws when their handles are turned in the same direction

**hands down** *adv* **1** : without much effort : EASILY 〈won the race *hands down*〉 **2** : without question or the possibility of dispute 〈is *hands down* the most competent craftsman in his field〉

**hands-down** \'='=\ *adj* [*hands down*] **1** : achieved without great effort : EASY 〈won a *hands-down* victory〉 **2** : UNQUESTIONABLE, UNDISPUTED 〈was the *hands-down* popular choice for the presidency〉 〈books that were *hands-down* favorites of the editors and critics —Raymond Walters b.1912〉

[1]**hand·sel** *also* **han·sel** \'han(t)səl\ *n* -S [ME *hansell*, prob. fr. ON *handsal* obligation confirmed by a handshake, handshake, promise, fr. *hand-*, *hond* hand + *sal* payment, payday; akin to ON *selja* to give, sell — more at HAND, SELL] **1** *obs* **a** : a token of luck : LUCK **b** : AUGURY **2** : a gift made as a token of good wishes or luck esp. at the beginning of a new course of action or upon someone's entering upon a new condition: as **a** : a bridegroom's present to the bride on her wedding day **b** : money given at the new year **3** : something received first (as in a day of trading or at a shop newly opened) and taken to be a token of good luck **4 a** : a first installment or earnest money **b** : EARNEST, FORETASTE 〈our present tears . . . are but the ~s of our joys hereafter —Robert Herrick †1674〉

[2]**handsel** \"\ *also* **hansel** \"\ *vt* **handseled** *or* **handselled; handseled** *or* **handselled; handseling** *or* **handselling** \-s(ə)liŋ\ **handsels** [ME *handsellen*, fr. *handsel*, n.] **1** *chiefly Brit* : to give a handsel to **2** *chiefly Brit* : to celebrate the beginning of the existence or use of : inaugurate with a token or gesture of luck or pleasure 〈~ a new house with a banquet〉 **3** *chiefly Brit* : to use or do for the first time : be the first to try or experience

**handsel monday** *n, usu cap H&M* : the first Monday of the new year when handsels are given (as to servants, children) esp. in Scotland

**handservant** \'=,==\ *n* : HANDMAID

**handset** \'=,=\ *n* : a telephone mouthpiece and earpiece and the respective microphone and speaker mounted on a single handle — called also *French telephone*

**hand-set** \'=,=\ *adj* : consisting of or printed or cast from individual pieces of type assembled by hand

**hand-setting** \'=,==\ *n* : the setting or casting of hand-set printed matter

**handshake** \'=,=\ *n* : a grasping with the right hand of another's right hand or a grasping of right hands by two people often with a slight up and down shake of the hands usu. upon meeting or taking leave as a sign of friendship, affection, or good wishes or as a mere polite formality : HANDCLASP

**handshaker** \'=,==\ *n* **1** : one that makes capital of shaking hands or showing extreme politic friendliness 〈money raisers, speechmakers, ~s, and official greeters —H.S.Commager〉 **2** : one that is usu. naively fond of meeting people 〈a natural ~ in the good sense of that abused word —S.H.Adams〉

**handsheet** \'=,=\ *n* : a single sheet of paper made by a hand process for testing purposes (as to determine qualities of paper to be made from a given batch of pulp)

**handshield** \'=,=\ *n* : a welder's protective mask designed to be held up before the face by hand

**handsled** \'=,=\ *or* **handsleigh** \'=,=\ *n* : a sled that can be pulled by hand and that is usu. suitable for only one to ride : a small sled : a child's sled

**hands-off** \'='=\ *adj* [*hands off*] : practicing noninterference 〈preserved their *hands-off* policy toward the internal affairs of other countries〉 : advocating or insisting upon noninterference 〈showed a rather belligerent *hands-off* attitude when people came near his possessions〉

**hands off** *v imper* : refrain from touching : refrain from interference : leave (one) alone

[1]**hand·some** \'han(t)səm, 'haan-,'hain-\ *adj, usu* -ER/-EST [ME *handsom, handsum* easy to manipulate, perh. fr. (assumed) MD *handsaem* (whence D *handzaam*), fr. *hand* + *-saem* -some (akin to OHG *-sam*)] **1** *now dial* **a** : HANDY **b** : easy to handle or maneuver : suitable for handling **c** : conveniently near : ready and at hand **2** *chiefly dial* **a** : APPROPRIATE, SUITABLE **b** : of good quality 〈~ vegetables〉 **3 a** : of considerable value or of scope large enough to gratify highly : SIZABLE, AMPLE 〈a very considerable, I may say a very ~, inheritance —Ngaio Marsh〉 〈the soil, everywhere of ~ depth and finest quality —Thomas Carlyle〉 〈winning the election by a ~ margin〉 **b** : marked by or calling for skillful execution : ADROIT, ACCOMPLISHED, APT 〈combining scholarship, imagination, literary flair, practical aptitude and personal gusto in the *handsomest* proportions —Richard Watts〉 **4 a** : marked by or given with becoming graciousness, generosity, largess, magnanimity : not sparing : not merely equable or proper 〈~ contributions to charities〉 〈assuredly, the archbishop . . . leaves something ~ for the servants —George Borrow〉 **b** : given to graceful commendation or laudation 〈passed a ~ resolution in my favor —R.M.Lovett〉 **5** : having an impressive and pleasing appearance: **a** : attractive, well-proportioned, and good-looking usu. in a way suggesting poise, dignity, and strength 〈with reddish brown hair, bright brown eyes, fine forehead, and firm mouth and chin, he was exceptionally ~ —Allan Nevins & H.S.Commager〉 〈though she had lost long ago her virginal loveliness, she had ripened . . . into a ~ and fruitful-looking woman —Ellen Glasgow〉 **b** : imposing or noticeable through some combination of symmetry, proportion, size, or color 〈a very ~ house with white marble steps . . . and a delicate silver knocker —Frances Trollope〉 〈a very ~ . . . saddle, quilted on the seat with green plush, garnished with a double row of silver-headed studs —Laurence Sterne〉 〈the red lizard, a ~ . . . form of the common olive-brown newt —*Amer. Guide Series: N.H.*〉 **syn** see BEAUTIFUL, LIBERAL

[2]**handsome** \"\ *adv* -ER/-EST [ME *handsom*, fr. *handsom, handsum*, adj.] *now dial* : HANDSOMELY 〈handsome is as ~ does〉

**handsome har·ry** \ˌ==ˈharē\ *n, pl* **handsome harrys** *usu cap 2d H* : a deer grass (*Rhexia virginica*) having stems with pubescent internodes

**hand·some·ly** *adv* **1** : in a handsome manner 〈a ~ bound book〉 〈a ~ large donation to charity〉 **2** *naut* **a** : slowly and carefully 〈ease off a line ~〉 **b** : in a shipshape manner 〈the yacht hove alongside ~〉

**hand·some·ness** *n* -ES : the quality or state of being handsome 〈the man's ~ excused a slight slowness of wit〉

**hand·span** \'=,=\ *n* : a distance equal to or an area equivalent in its circumference to a span 〈a ~ waist〉

**hand·speak** \'hanz,pēk, -n,sp-, -pik\ *dial var of* HANDSPIKE

**hand specimen** *n* **1** : a fragment of rock trimmed and shaped to dimensions of about 4x3x1 inches **2** : a fragment of rock with at least one freshly broken surface and small enough to be easily handled for megascopic study

[1]**hand·spike** \'han(d)z,pīk, -),sp-, 'haan-\ *n* [by folk etymology fr. D *handspaak*, fr. *hand* + *spaak* pole] : a wooden bar or pole used as a lever (as in turning a windlass) or as a support (as for carrying timber)

[2]**handspike** \'=,=\ *vt* **1** : to use a handspike on **2** : to move with a handspike

**handspoke** \'=,=\ *n, now dial Brit* : either of two bars used to carry a coffin at a funeral

**handspring** \'=,=\ *n* : an act or a feat esp. in tumbling in which the body turns forward or backward in a full circle from a standing position and lands first on the hands and then on the feet

**hand stack** *n, chiefly Midland* : a small pile of hay : HAYCOCK

[1]**handstamp** \'=,=\ *n* **1** : a stamp (as of rubber) that is operated by hand **2** : a stamping (as a postal marking) that has been made by hand

[2]**handstamp** \'=,=\ *vt* **1** : to stamp by hand **2** : to impress (a marking) by means of a handstamp

**handstamper** \'=,==\ *n* : HANDSTAMP 1

**handstand** \'=,=\ *n* : an act of supporting the body on the hands with the trunk and legs balanced in air

**handstick** \'=,=\ *n, Midland* : HANDSPIKE

**handstone** \'=,=\ *n* **1** : COUP DE POING **2** : a stone held in the hand and applied to a milling stone for the grinding of seeds or grain

**handstroke** \'=,=\ *n* **1** : a blow with the hand **2** : a bell ringer's pull on the rope that swings a church bell to its mouth-up position : the sounding stroke — compare BACKSTROKE 2

**handstruck** \'=,=\ *adj, Brit* : HANDSTAMPED 〈a ~ postage stamp or overprint〉

**hand's turn** *n* : an act of manual labor; *esp* : a single usu. small expenditure of effort 〈would not do a *hand's turn* to save himself from starvation〉

**hands up** *v imper* : put (one's) hands up in the air and hold them up : SURRENDER

**hand-tailor** \'='==\ *vt* **1** : to make chiefly by individual workmanship or by a specified number of hand operations to individual specifications 〈a *hand-tailored* suit〉 **2** : to make to order 〈a truck or trailer *hand-tailored* to his own specifications —*Steelways*〉

**hand tap** *n* : a tap for forming screw threads that is turned by hand

**hand-tight** \'='=\ *adj* : being as tight as can be made by the hand alone : moderately tight

**hand to hand** *adv* [ME — more at HAND] : at very close quarters 〈fought the bear *hand to hand* to the death —*Amer. Guide Series: Oreg.*〉

**hand-to-hand** \ˌ==ˈ=\ *adj* [*hand to hand*] **1** : being at very close quarters 〈*hand-to-hand* combat〉 **2** : passed from person to person 〈*hand-to-hand* delivery . . . of registered mail —*U.S. Post Office Manual*〉

**hand-to-mouth** \ˌ==ˈ=\ *adj* : having or providing nothing to spare or having or providing barely enough esp. of money or the necessities of existence : PRECARIOUS 〈leading a *hand-to-mouth* existence〉 〈found employment in shoveling sidewalks, sawing wood, and other *hand-to-mouth* jobs —Dixon Wecter〉 〈steel users . . . report that they are operating on a *hand-to-mouth* basis with less than a week's supply —*Newsweek*〉

**hand-tool** \'='=\ *vt* : TOOL *vt* 1

**hand tooling** *n* : the operation or product of hand-tooling

**hand torch** *n, Brit* : FLASHLIGHT

**hand towel** *n* : a small towel for the hands and usu. the face

**handtrap** \'=,=\ *n* : a mechanical device held in the hand and used to hurl clay targets into the air for shooting practice

**hand-traverse** \'=,==, '=ˌ==, ˌ=ˈ==\ *n* : a method used in mountaineering to cross a ledge that lacks standing room in which a climber grasps the ledge and moves along using his hands and allowing his body and legs to hang free

**hand tree** *n* : a tree (*Chiranthodendron pentadactylon*) of the family Sterculiaceae that is cultivated for its showy flowers whose spreading stamens suggest an open hand

**hand truck** *n* **1** : a small hand-propelled truck or wheelbarrow; *esp* : one consisting of a rectangular frame having at one end a pair of handles and at the other end a pair of small heavy wheels and a projecting edge or nose plate to slide under a load (as a trunk or box) and hold it in place **2** : a small truck having a motor for propulsion or lifting the load and controlled by a walking or riding operator

**hand tub** *n* : a fire-fighting apparatus consisting of an often tub-shaped reservoir of water pumped out through a hose by means of a pump with brakes that are rocked up and down by a number of men on each side of the apparatus; *also* : such an apparatus together with the wagon it is mounted on

hand truck 1

**hand vise** *n* : a small clamp or vise on a handle designed for holding small objects while they are being worked usu. by hand

**hand vote** *n* : a vote taken by counting the raised right hands of voters

**hand wagon** *n* : HANDCART

**handwaled** \'='=\ *adj* [[1]*hand* + *waled* past part. of *wale* (to choose)] *chiefly Scot* : individually selected : HANDPICKED

**handweave** \'='=\ *vt* : to produce (fabric) on a handloom; *often* : to produce (fabric) on a loom on which the shuttle is actually thrown by hand — **handweaver** \'='==\ *n*

**handweaving** \'='==\ *n* : the occupation of one that hand weaves or the product of hand weaving

**handwheel** \'=,=\ *n* : a wheel worked by hand; *esp* : one whose rim serves as the handle by which a valve, lathe feed, or other part is operated

**handwhile** \'=,=\ *n* [ME, fr. OE *handhwīl*, fr. *hand, hond* hand + *hwīl* while — more at HAND, WHILE] *now Scot* : MOMENT, INSTANT

**handwork** \'=,=\ *n* [ME *handwerk*, fr. OE *hand-weorc*] : work done with the hands as distinguished from work done by a machine : HANDIWORK

**handworked** \'='=\ *adj* : formed by hand or chiefly by hand processes 〈~ lace〉 〈a ~ iron railing〉

**handworker** *or* **handworkman** \'=,==\ *n, pl* **handworkers** *or* **handworkmen** [[1]*hand* + *worker* or *workman*] : one who is skilled at working with the hands

**handwoven** \'='==\ *adj* : produced on a handloom on which the shuttle is often actually thrown by hand 〈a ~ fabric〉

**handwrist** \'=,=\ *n* [ME, fr. OE *hand-wyrst*, fr. *hand* + *wyrst* wrist — more at WRIST] *now dial Brit* : WRIST

**handwrit** \'=,=\ *n* [ME, fr. *hand* + *writ*] *now dial* : HANDWRITING

[1]**handwrite** \'=,=\ *vt* [back-formation fr. *handwriting*] : to write by hand 〈words in a written contract may be *handwritten* —E.M.Robinson〉 〈these *handwritten* missives —Amy Lowell〉

[2]**handwrite** \'=,=\ *n* -S **1** *now dial* : HANDWRITING **2** *now dial* : a person's signature

**handwriting** \'=,==\ *n* [[1]*hand* + *writing*] **1** : writing in which the hand forms the letters with a pen, pencil, stylus, or similar writing implement; *also* : the cast or form of such writing peculiar to a particular person **2** : something written by hand : MANUSCRIPT — **the handwriting on the wall** [so called fr. the mysterious handwriting in the Bible that appeared on the wall of Belshazzar's palace to foretell his doom (Dan 5)] : a doom foreshadowed : an omen of one's fate usu. unpleasant

**handwriting analysis** *n* : GRAPHOLOGY

**handwrought** \'='=\ *adj* : fashioned by hand or chiefly by hand processes 〈~ nails〉 〈~ silver〉 〈~ details〉

[1]**handy** \'handē, 'haan-, -di\ *adj* -ER/-EST [[1]*hand* + *-y*] **1** *obs* : performed by hand 〈~ strokes —John Milton〉 **2 a** : ready to the hand : conveniently near and accessible 〈a ~ restaurant just around the corner〉 〈kept his gun ~ as long as danger was near〉 **b** : convenient for handling, for use, or for reference 〈a ~ volume〉; *also* : convenient for or adaptable to a variety of uses 〈a ~ tool in the kitchen〉 **c** *of a ship* : easily handled : obedient to the helm **3** : clever in using the hands esp. in a variety of convenient ways 〈a man who is ~ around the house〉 : ADROIT, DEXTEROUS 〈~ with a paintbrush〉 **syn** see DEXTEROUS

[2]**handy** \"\ *adv, dial* : HANDILY

**handy-an·dy** \ˌ=='andē, -'aan-, -di\ *n* -ES [after *Handy Andy* Rooney, hero of the novel *Handy Andy* by Samuel Lover †1868 Irish novelist] : HANDYMAN 1, 2

**handy-bil·ly** \'==,bilē, -li\ *n* -ES **1** : WATCH TACKLE **2** : a small portable pump used chiefly aboard ship

**handy boy** *n* : a boy whose work is the doing of general tasks (as around a farm)

**handycuff** *var of* HANDICUFF

[1]**handy-dan·dy** \ˌ=='dandē, -'daan-, -ndi\ *n* [ME, something held in a clasped hand, by redupl. fr. *hand*] *now dial Eng* : a child's game in which one child guesses in which closed hand another holds some small object

[2]**handy-dandy** \"\ *adv, dial Brit* : with quick alternation of place, circumstance, or condition

**handy·man** \-,man, -aa(ə)-\ *n, pl* **handymen** **1** : one whose work is the doing of general miscellaneous tasks; *esp* : one who performs miscellaneous or routine tasks (as about a home, public building, factory, laboratory) **2** : one that is competent in a variety of small skills or inventive or ingenious in repair or maintenance work (as around a house) or in the construction of handy devices **3** : one who has sufficient training to take responsibility for one or more phases of a trade (as in the shipbuilding industry) but who is not proficient enough to perform all its work phases **4** : JUMPER 1f

**handy-pan·dy** \ˌhandi'pandi\ *or* **handy-span·dy** \-'sp-\ *dial Brit var of* HANDY-DANDY

**handy·weight** \'==,=\ *adj, of a market animal* : intermediate in weight

**handywoman** \'==,==\ *n, pl* **handywomen** : a female handyman

**handywork** *archaic var of* HANDIWORK

**¹hang** \ˈhaŋ, ˈhaiŋ *sometimes* ˈheŋ\ *vb* **hung** \ˈhəŋ\ *also* **hanged**; **hung** *also* **hanged**; **hanging**; **hangs** [partly fr. ME *hon* (past, *heng, hing, hang, hong;* past part. *hangen, hongen*), fr. OE *hōn* (vt); partly fr. ME *hangen, hongen*, fr. OE *hangian* (vi & vt); partly fr. ME *hengen, hingen*, fr. ON *hengja* (vt), causative fr. the root of ON *hanga* to hang; all akin to OHG *hāhan* to hang (vt), *hangēn* (vi), Goth *hāhan* to hang, and prob. to L *cunctari* to hesitate, Skt *śaṅkate* he wavers, doubts, fears, Hitt *ganki* he hangs] *vt* **1 a :** to fasten to some elevated point without support from below **:** SUSPEND ⟨~ a coat on a hook⟩ ⟨~ a pan from a beam over a stove⟩ ⟨~ meat to ripen⟩ ⟨a picture *hung* on the wall⟩ **b** (1) **:** to put to death by suspending from a cross, gibbet, or gallows — sometimes *hanged* in the past ⟨condemned to be ~*ed* by the neck until dead⟩ (2) **:** to bring to justice or doom **:** expose in evil actions or objectionable ways in such a manner as to bring to punishment or an appropriate fate ⟨the criminal's very brazenness will ~ him sooner or later⟩ ⟨the chef's arrogant manner finally *hung* him and he lost his job⟩ — often used interjectionally as a mild imprecation ⟨I'll be ~*ed*⟩ ⟨~ it all⟩ **c :** to fasten so as to allow free motion within given limits upon a point of suspension ⟨~ a pendulum⟩; *also* **:** to install by fastening in such a way ⟨can fit and ~ 20 doors in less than two hours —*Amer. Builder*⟩ **d :** to fit or fix in position or at a proper angle (a part of an implement that is swung in use) ⟨~ an ax to its helve⟩ **e :** to adjust the hem of (a skirt) so as to hang evenly and at a proper height when worn ⟨spent an hour ~*ing* a skirt⟩ **2 :** to cover, decorate, or furnish by hanging pictures, trophies, drapery, or other decorations ⟨*hung* the room with evergreen boughs⟩ ⟨able to ~ themselves . . . with a variety of ostentatious ornaments —Jacquetta & Christopher Hawkes⟩ **3 :** to hold or bear in a suspended or inclined manner ⟨~ her head in embarrassment⟩ **4 a :** to fasten (as with glue or paste) to a wall ⟨~ wallpaper⟩ ⟨~ tile in the bathroom⟩ **b :** to cause (a name) to stick ⟨*hung* several nasty nicknames on him during the campaign⟩ **5 a :** to style or set (as a paragraph) in printing with a hanging indention ⟨~ each boldface entry word one em⟩ **b :** to place below the foot of a type page (overset type matter) **6 a :** to append or attach (as a rider) additionally to a legislative bill **b :** to impose (as an idea) upon a convenient form or medium for artistic expedience ⟨*hung* his sardonic and sometimes savage satire on romantic opera —*Time*⟩ **7 :** to prevent (as a jury) from reaching a decision (as by one member's refusal to join in a verdict which must be unanimous) **8 a :** to display (an exhibition of pictures) in a gallery or hall **b :** to display the works of (an artist) in a gallery **9 :** to catch (a fish) with a hook **10 :** to strike a blow with ⟨*hung* that left on the Dutchman's jaw —Ring Lardner⟩ **11 :** to give no further consideration to **:** neglect totally ⟨would ~ the responsibility and go fishing⟩ ~ *vi* **1 a :** to become suspended or fastened to some point above without support from below **:** DANGLE ⟨a purse ~*ing* from a strap⟩ ⟨a sign ~*ing* from a nail⟩ ⟨meat ~*ing* to ripen⟩ ⟨a picture ~*ing* on the wall⟩ **b** (1) **:** to die or become dead by hanging —sometimes *hanged* in the past ⟨he ~*ed* for his crimes⟩ (2) **:** to come to justice **:** become subjected to an appropriate unpleasant doom **c** (1) **:** to remain poised or stationary in midair round about or overhead as if suspended ⟨a dim, oblong patch of light ~*ing* slantwise in the darkness —Liam O'Flaherty⟩ ⟨clouds ~*ing* low overhead⟩ ⟨the bird *hung* in the air a moment and then swooped⟩ ⟨musty air *hung* in the alleyway⟩ ⟨foggy weather had been ~*ing* over the prairie —O.E.Rölvaag⟩ **:** HOVER ⟨around each *hung* a spirit, an emanation —Anton Vogt⟩ (2) **:** to have only a precarious hold ⟨meadows ~*ing* on ridge and mountain slopes —John Muir †1914⟩ (3) **:** to stay with persistence ⟨the notion *hung* in his mind for days⟩ (4) **:** to await as if exposed ⟨that Indian property . . . ~*s* as a rich prize for the taking —D'Arcy McNickle⟩ **d** (1) **:** to become fastened so as to allow free motion on the point of suspension ⟨the door ~*s* on its hinges⟩ (2) **:** to be in a specified position on a point of suspension ⟨the casement window *hung* open over the street⟩ **e :** to be imminent **:** IMPEND ⟨evils ~ over the nation⟩ **f :** to be circumstantially relevant ⟨thereby ~*s* a tale —Shak.⟩ **g :** to fall or droop from a usu. tense or taut position ⟨his lower lip *hung* open —J.D.Wall⟩ ⟨the reins *hung* loose on the horse's back⟩ **2 :** to rest or depend for authority or resolution ⟨an election often ~*s* on one vote⟩ ⟨the question of unity ~*s* on what the writer deems the veritable topic of his work —H.O. Taylor⟩ **3 :** to support things that are suspended or attached or that incline over or downward ⟨trees ~*ing* with festoons of moss⟩ **4 a** (1) **:** to take hold for support **:** CLING, CLEAVE, ADHERE ⟨the woman seemed faint and *hung* on his arm⟩ ⟨*hung* to the trolley-car strap⟩ (2) **:** to keep persistent contact ⟨the dogs *hung* to the trail of the fox⟩ **b :** to be burdensome **:** act as an oppressive weight or care ⟨the worry *hung* on his mind until he was frantic⟩ ⟨time ~*s* on his hands and he is unutterably bored⟩ **c :** LEAN ⟨~*ing* on the rail of the ship watching the sea⟩ **5 a :** to be indecisive or uncertain **:** be in suspense **:** suffer delay ⟨the decision is still ~*ing*⟩ **b :** to occupy an uncertain mid-position ⟨his career *hung* for several years between law and medicine⟩ **6 :** to lean, incline, or jut over or downward ⟨high above it ~*s* the rocky pinnacle —*Hot-Metal Magic*⟩ **7 :** to be in a state of rapt attention — usu. used with *on* ⟨*hung* on his every word⟩ **8 :** IDLE, LOITER ⟨found the boys ~*ing* around poolrooms⟩ ⟨making the acquaintance of quiet gentlemen ~*ing* about the fringes of tourist parties —Louis Bromfield⟩ — compare HANG AROUND **9 :** to have the charge stuck or arched in one part while the part underneath falls away so as to leave a gap — used esp. of a blast furnace for iron **10 :** to fit or fall from the figure in easy lines ⟨the coat ~*s* loosely⟩ **11 a** *of a ball* **:** to rebound unexpectedly or unusually slowly (as in a game of cricket or tennis) **b** *of a racehorse* **:** to run at less than top speed **syn** see DEPEND — **hang fire 1 :** to be slow in the explosion of a charge after its primer has been discharged **2 :** to delay or be delayed usu. momentarily or temporarily ⟨the love of a young man who *hung fire* about carrying out his pledges —William de Morgan⟩ ⟨the plans had to *hang fire* until the city council approved them⟩ — **hang in the air :** to be uncompleted, unverified, or inadequately authorized ⟨something to be done, tested, made accurate, not left *hanging in the air* —A.N.Whitehead⟩ — **hang in the balance :** to be doubtful or uncertain ⟨the prisoner's fate *hangs in the balance*⟩ — **hang one on 1** *slang* **:** to inflict a heavy blow upon ⟨*hung one on* him and he was taken off in an ambulance⟩ **2** *slang* **:** to get very drunk — **hang over one's head :** to be an imminent threat or danger to one ⟨a charge of treason *hung over his head* for some time⟩ ⟨depression and insecurity *hanging over the head* of the entire nation⟩

**²hang** \"\ *n* -s **1 a :** the manner in which a thing hangs ⟨the ~ of the ax on its helve⟩ ⟨the ~ of the gown⟩ **b :** a position taken on any piece of gymnastics apparatus in which the center of gravity of a gymnast is below the point of support **2 :** DECLIVITY, SLOPE; *also* **:** DROOP ⟨the ~ of his lower lip⟩ **3 a :** the peculiar and significant order or meaning ⟨can't get the ~ of the discourse⟩ ⟨get the ~ of harmony singing —Dinah Shore⟩ **b :** the special method of doing, using, or dealing with something **:** KNACK ⟨took some time to get the ~ of driving the tractor⟩ **4 :** a hesitation, pause, or slackening in motion or in a course ⟨a marked ~ of the oar in the air before it dipped⟩ **5 :** the action of a furnace that hangs — called also *hanging* — **give a hang** *or* **care a hang :** to be concerned or worried ⟨does not *give a hang* whether he wins or not⟩

**hang·able** \-ŋəbəl\ *adj* **1 :** capable of being hanged esp. legally ⟨a person not ~ according to the law until he is of a certain age⟩ **2 :** punishable by hanging ⟨a ~ offense⟩

**¹hangar** \ˈhaŋə(r), ˈhaiŋ-, -ŋgə- *sometimes* ˈheŋ- *or* -ŋ,gär *or* ŋ,gä(r\ *n* -s [F, fr. MF, prob. fr. ML *angarium* shed for shoeing horses, perh. fr. *angaria* carriage, wagon, fr. LL, compulsory service — more at ANGARIA] **:** SHELTER, SHED; *esp* **:** a covered and usu. enclosed area or a large shed for housing and repairing aircraft (as airplanes)

**²hangar** \"\ *vt* -ED/-ING/-S **:** to place or store in a hangar

**hangar deck** *n* **:** a deck on an aircraft carrier that is below the flight deck and that is used as a hangar

**hang around** *vi* **1 a :** to pass time or stay around a particular place aimlessly **:** loiter idly ⟨found nothing to do so spent his time just *hanging around* in the house⟩ ⟨*hanging around* in poolrooms⟩ **b :** to wait or occupy oneself in some adventitious way because of delay ⟨my ship was not ready to sail so that I was forced to *hang around* for several hours impatiently⟩ **2 :** to spend one's time in company esp. idly ⟨if you want to *hang around* with a bunch of football players that's your business —R.H.Newman⟩

**hang back** *vi* **1 a :** to drag behind others ⟨a small child following the older children but *hanging back* a little⟩ **b :** to delay purposely in advancing to a particular point ⟨we came almost alongside the ship but *hung back* until the captain's signal to come close⟩ **2 :** to be reluctant **:** HESITATE, FALTER

**hang behind** *vi* **:** to hang back

**hangbird** \ˈ=,=\ *n* [so called fr. its habit of suspending its nest from a branch] **:** BALTIMORE ORIOLE

**hang·by** \ˈ=,bī\ *n* [fr. *hang by*, v.] *now dial Eng* **:** a flattering hanger-on **:** SYCOPHANT

**hang·chow** \ˈhaŋ¦chau̇, ˈhäŋ¦jō\ *adj, usu cap* [fr. *Hangchow*, China] **:** of or from the city of Hangchow, China **:** of the kind or style prevalent in Hangchow

**¹hangdog** \ˈ=,=\ *adj* [¹*hang* + *dog*] **1 :** befitting a hangdog ⟨your manners have been of that silent and sullen and ~ kind —Charles Dickens⟩ **2 a :** ASHAMED, GUILTY ⟨had a ~ air about him even though he didn't get caught in the theft⟩ **b :** DEJECTED, COWED, PITIFUL ⟨the child's ~ look when told to go in the house⟩

**²hangdog** \"\ *n* [¹*hang* + *dog*] **:** a despicable or miserable fellow

**hange** \ˈhanj\ *n* -s [ME *henge, hinge*, fr. *hengen, hingen* to hang — more at HANG] *dial Eng* **:** ²PLUCK 2a

**hanged** *past of* HANG

**hang·er** \ˈhaŋə(r), ˈhaiŋ- *sometimes* ˈheŋ-\ *n* -s [ME, fr. *hangen* to hang + *-er* — more at HANG] **1 :** one that hangs: as **a :** HANGMAN **b :** a workman who hangs up articles to make them easily accessible or to position them for inspection or processing (as smoking, drying) **c :** a member of a hanging committee at an art exhibit **2 :** something that hangs, overhangs, or is suspended: as **a :** a decorative strip of cloth (as on a costume or a wall) **b :** a steep wooded declivity **c :** a depending part containing a bearing for a revolving piece; *esp* **:** a metal frame secured to the ceiling and carrying a bearing for overhead shafting **d :** a layer of tobacco leaves or stalks hung on sticks in a curing barn **3 :** a device or contrivance by which or to which something is hung or hangs: as **a :** a strap or loop on a sword belt by which a sword or dagger can be suspended **b :** a loop or chain (as on a collar) by which a garment is hung up **c :** a chain or S-shaped rod on which a pot is hung by a pothook **d :** a usu. metal or wooden device that fits inside a garment (as a suit) from shoulder to shoulder for hanging from a hook or rod (as in a closet) **e :** a metal strap used to hold an eaves in place **f :** a dangling leather loop or wooden handle that standing passengers in a moving trolley car, bus, or subway train may hold on to for keeping balance **g :** one of the devices upon which a sliding door is sometimes suspended **4 :** the written character 2 resembling a pothanger and used as an exercise in teaching beginners to write — used chiefly in the phrase *pothooks and hangers* **5 :** a bobbin in bobbin lace holding a thread in one position **6 :** a vertical tension member receiving its stress only from the part of a structure directly attached to it **7 :** an iron box secured to and projecting from a wall or beam to carry one end of a joist or girder **8 :** ³TANGLE **9 :** a metal frame for holding photographic film in tank development

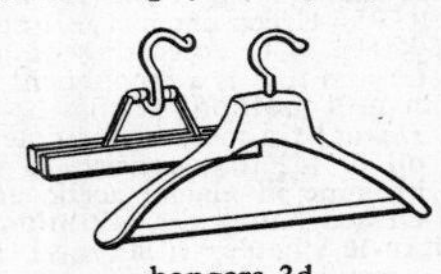
hangers 3d

**hanger bolt** *n* **:** a bolt made with a tapered lag-screw thread on one end and a machine-bolt thread on the other and used in timber construction

hanger bolt

**hanger case** *n* **:** a traveling bag with hangers and space for one or two suits

**hang·er·man** \-,man, -mən\ *n, pl* **hangermen :** one who installs hangers and brackets for supporting pipelines on ships — called also *bracketman*

**hanger-off** \ˈ=¦=\ *n, pl* **hangers-off** *or* **hanger-offs** [*hang off*, v. + *-er*] **:** a slaughterhouse worker who suspends finished sheep carcasses from an overhead trolley and puts inspection stamps on them

**hanger-on** \ˈ=¦=\ *n, pl* **hangers-on** *or* **hanger-ons** [*hang on* + *-er*] **:** one that hangs around a person, place, or institution in hope of personal gain (as patronage or preferment) ⟨soldiers became *hangers-on* of saloons and free-lunch bars —Dixon Wecter⟩ ⟨czars, princes and aristocracy, and their *hanger-ons* —F.D.Roosevelt⟩; *often* **:** one that hangs around in this manner with annoying persistence **syn** see PARASITE

**hangersmith** \ˈ=,=\ *n* **:** one who makes hangers and brackets for supporting pipelines on ships

**hanger wood** *n* **:** drooping branches on a fruit tree (as peach)

**hang-fair** \ˈ=,=\ *n, now dial Eng* **:** a public execution ⟨come to attend the *hang-fair* next day —Thomas Hardy⟩

**hangfire** \ˈ=,=\ *n* [fr. the phrase *hang fire*] **:** a delay in the explosion of the charge of a gun after the primer has been fired **:** the temporary failure of a primer or igniter

**hangi** \ˈhäŋē\ *n* -s [Maori] **:** an underground oven used by the Maoris that consists of a pit in which stones are heated, wrapped food is placed on stones, and branches, wet sacks, and earth are used to cover the stones and food

**hang·ie** \ˈhaŋi\ *n* -s [¹*hang* + *-ie*] *dial Brit* **:** HANGMAN

**¹hanging** *n* -s [ME, fr. *hangen* to hang + *-ing* — more at HANG] **1 a :** the act of suspending something ⟨requested that the entire exhibition committee be at the ~ to assist in positioning the pictures⟩ **b :** a killing or execution in which a noose at the end of a suspended rope is placed around a person's neck and then the support under him quickly removed so that he drops or swings free and dies from a broken neck or from asphyxiation ⟨sentenced to ~⟩ — see GALLOWS; compare GIBBET 1 **2 :** something hung: as **a :** CURTAIN — usu. used in pl. **b :** a covering (as a tapestry or wallpaper) for a wall — usu. used in pl. **3 :** a downward slope or inclination **:** DECLIVITY ⟨the ~ of a ship's deck⟩ **4 :** HANG 5

**²hanging** *adj* **1 :** situated or lying on steeply sloping ground ⟨a ~ meadow on the mountainside⟩ or on top of some high place (as a wall or roof) ⟨a fine ~ garden aloft on breezy inaccessible heights —John Muir †1914⟩ **2 a :** leaning over or downward **:** drooping or jutting out and downward **:** OVERHANGING ⟨a ~ rock⟩ ⟨~ wood⟩ **b :** SUSPENDED, PENDENT **c :** supported only by the wall on one side ⟨a ~ staircase⟩ ⟨a ~ balcony⟩ **d :** situated at or having a discordant junction ⟨a ~ cirque⟩ **3** *obs* **:** being in suspense or abeyance **4** *archaic* **:** downcast or dejected in appearance **5 :** adapted for sustaining a hanging object **6 a :** deserving, likely to cause, or prone to inflict death by hanging ⟨a ~ crime⟩ ⟨a ~ judge⟩ **b :** being of great moment or significance ⟨not disposed to make a ~ matter of it —*Manchester Guardian Weekly*⟩ **7** *of a chess pawn* **:** connected and abreast

**hanging barrel** *n* **:** the going barrel in a watch whose arbor is supported by attachment to the upper plate only allowing the movement to be made very thin

**hanging basket** *n* **:** a container made (as of wood or wire) to resemble a basket to hold a plant hung up for decoration or for greenhouse cultivation (as of orchids)

**hanging block** *n* **:** a preparation like a hanging drop but with agar replacing the liquid medium

**hanging bog** *n* **:** QUAKING BOG

**hanging buttress** *n* **:** a buttress usu. supported on a corbel

**hanging clamp** *n* **:** a clamp that can be fixed to various parts of a ship to serve as a fixed iron for attachments (as for a tackle block or a stage)

**hanging committee** *n* **:** a committee having charge of the hanging of pictures in an exhibition

**hanging drop** *n* **:** a drop of liquid suspended from a cover glass usu. placed over the cavity of a depression slide and containing microorganisms or cells for microscopic study (as in an agglutination test)

**hanging fly** *n* **:** a mecopterous insect of the family Bittacidae

**hanging glacier** *n* **:** a body of ice or névé that breaks off abruptly at the edge of a precipice or steep slope

**hanging indention** *n* **:** indention in which the first word of the first line of a passage is set flush with the left-hand margin and the first words of the second and subsequent lines are set to the right of the left-hand margin

**hanging keel** *n* **:** BAR KEEL

**hanging lie** *n* **:** the position of a golf ball which comes to rest on ground sloping downward in the direction it is to be played

**hanging moss** *n* **1 :** a lichen of the genus *Usnea* **2 :** SPANISH MOSS

**hanging paper** *n* **:** partly processed paper that is to be converted (as by coating and printing) into wallpaper

**hanging participle** *n* **:** a participle that dangles syntactically

**hanging rail** *n* **:** the rail of a door or casement to which hinges are attached

**hanging side** *n* **:** the hanging-wall side of a geologic vein, fault, or bed

**hanging sleeve** *n* **1 :** an ornamental straight-hanging oversleeve of the 15th century usu. set in or tied on at the armhole **2 :** a loose open sleeve on a child's garment

**hanging stairs** *n pl* **:** stairs that are or appear to be supported along one side only (as by brackets projecting from an adjacent wall or by having one end of each step built into a wall, the front edge of each step being supported along the back edge of the step below)

**hanging stile** *n* **1** *also* **hanging head** *or* **hanging post :** the stile of a door to which hinges are secured **2 :** the upright of a window frame to which casements are hinged or in which the pulleys for sash windows are fastened

**hanging valley** *n* **:** a valley whose lower end is notably higher than the level of the valley or the shore to which it leads

**hanging wall** *n* **:** the upper or overhanging wall of an inclined vein, fault, or other geologic structure — opposed to *footwall*

**hang·le** \ˈhaŋəl\ *n* -s [¹*hang* + *-le* (suffix denoting an instrument)] *dial Eng* **:** an iron pothook

**hang·man** \ˈhaŋmən, ˈhaiŋ-, -,man, -,maa(ə)n *sometimes* ˈheŋ-\ *n, pl* **hangmen** [ME *hangeman*, fr. *hangen* to hang + *man*] **1 :** one who hangs another; *esp* **:** a public executioner **2 :** a game in which one player chooses a word and the others try to guess it one letter at a time, a part of a picture of a hanged man being drawn for each wrong guess

**hangman's halter** *or* **hangman's knot** *n* **:** a slip noose usu. made with eight or nine turns for hanging a condemned person

hangman's halter

**hang·man·ship** \ˈ==,ship\ *n* **:** the office or the occupation of a hangman

**hang·ment** \ˈhaŋ,ment\ *n* -s [ME *hangement*, fr. *hangen* to hang + *-ment*] *now dial chiefly Eng* **:** HANGING

**hang·nail** \ˈhaŋ,nāl, ˈhaiŋ- *sometimes* ˈheŋ-\ *n* [by folk etymology fr. *agnail, angnail* — more at AGNAIL] **:** a piece of skin from the nail fold hanging loose at the side or root of a fingernail

**hangnest** \ˈ=,=\ *n* [so called fr. its habit of suspending its nest from a branch] **:** BALTIMORE ORIOLE

**hang off** *vi* **:** to hang back

**hang on** *vi* **1 a :** to keep hold **:** hold onto something usu. tightly ⟨the truck was bouncing so much we had to *hang on* to save ourselves from being thrown against the sides⟩ **b :** to persist tenaciously in an enterprise **:** refuse to give up ⟨even at the end of his life he was still *hanging on*, still seeking justice⟩ **2 :** to continue to cause suffering **:** resist getting better in health ⟨a winter cold that seemed to *hang on* all spring⟩ **3 a** *of a sound* **:** to continue to sound ⟨the strains of music *hung on* for a long time⟩ **b :** to continue listening on a telephone **:** keep a telephone connection open ⟨*hang on* a minute while I look it up⟩ — **hang on to :** to hold, grip, or keep tenaciously ⟨the child *hung on to* the lollipop for dear life⟩ ⟨swore he would *hang on to* the job until they fired him⟩

**hang out** *vi* **1** *obs* **:** to protrude in a downward direction **2 a** *slang* **:** LIVE, RESIDE ⟨*hung out* at a boardinghouse in town⟩ **b :** to spend one's time idly or in loitering around or in a particular place ⟨did a lot of *hanging out* in barrooms⟩ ~ *vt* **:** to suspend from something outside in order to display usu. to the public ⟨*hung out* a sign advertising his products⟩ ⟨*hung* Christmas decorations *out* around the windows⟩

**hangout** \ˈ=,=\ *n* -s [*hang out*] **1 :** a place where one resides, stays, or tends to frequent or lounge around ⟨adopts the corner drugstore as his ~ —C.C.Scott⟩ **2 :** an often low-class place of entertainment ⟨got a beer at the ~ in the next block⟩

**hang over** *vi* **:** to remain to be handled or completed (as of unfinished business at the end of a meeting) ⟨the meeting adjourned and left the plans *hanging over*⟩ ⟨let the case *hang over* for the new administration —*Time*⟩

**hangover** \ˈ=,==\ *n* -s [*hang over*] **1 :** something that remains from what is past (as a surviving trait or custom) ⟨manners that were really a ~ from an earlier day⟩ **2 a :** disagreeable physical effects (as headache, stupor, or nausea) following heavy consumption of alcohol **b :** disagreeable aftereffects from the use of drugs **c :** a letdown or deflation following great excitement or excess ⟨an exhausted silence seemed to come down over the capitol, a colossal election ~ —Mollie Panter-Downes⟩ **3 :** undue prolongation and indistinct articulation of bass notes from a loudspeaker because of poor design or inadequate damping

**hangrod** \ˈ=,=\ *n* **:** a horizontal rod on which clothing is hung by means of coat hangers

**hangs** *pres 3d sing of* HANG, *pl of* HANG

**hangtag** \ˈ=,=\ *n* **:** a tag attached to an article of merchandise giving information about the quality of its material and about its proper care

**hang together** *vi* **1 :** to remain united **:** stand by one another ⟨the boys felt a strong loyalty and *hung together* when in strange company⟩ ⟨the immigrant races had tended to *hang together*, united by language, a foreign-language press —F.L. Paxson⟩ **2 :** to form a consistent or coherent whole ⟨a set of facts that seem to *hang* well *together* —Edward Clodd⟩ **:** have unity (as of artistic construction) ⟨the story *hangs together* pretty well⟩

**¹han·gul** \ˈhäŋgəl\ *n* -s [Kashmiri *hāngul*] **:** a deer (*Cervus cashmiriensis*) of Kashmir closely related to the red deer of Europe

**²hangul** *usu cap, var of* HANKUL

**hang up** *vt* **1 a :** to place on a hook or hanger designed for the purpose ⟨told the child to *hang up* his coat⟩ **b :** to place (a telephone receiver or earpiece) back on the hook or cradle so that the connection is broken **c** *Austral* **:** to tie (a horse) to a ring or post **d :** to cause (a tree) to catch in another tree in falling **2 :** to keep delayed, suspended, or held up ⟨the negotiations were *hung up* for a week by the illness of the prime minister⟩ **3 :** to cause (a record) to be set **:** ACHIEVE ⟨has *hung up* a record for the hundred-yard dash⟩ **4 :** to cause to stick or snag immovably ⟨the ship was *hung up* on a sandbar for two hours⟩ ~ *vi* **1 :** to hang up a telephone receiver or earpiece ⟨the speaker said goodbye and *hung up* abruptly⟩ **2 :** to become stuck or snagged so as to be immovable ⟨if the ship *hangs up* on a sandbar, we remove the passengers in lifeboats⟩ **3 :** to break a trip (as by automobile) for a night's rest

**hang-up** \ˈ=,=\ *n* -s [*hang up*] **1 :** a tree caught in another tree in felling **2 :** an immovable obstacle (as a tree stump) in a skid road

**ha·nif** \ha'nēf, hä'-\ *n* -s [Ar *ḥanīf*, prob. fr. Aram *ḥănēf* hypocrite, heretic] **:** a pre-Islamic hermit of Arabia that lived a wandering ascetic life and professed a vague form of monotheism

**hani·fite** \ˈhanə,fīt, ha'nē,f-\ *n* -s *usu cap* [*Abū-Ḥanīfah* †767 Muslim jurist + E *-ite*] **:** HANAFI 2

**ha·nis** \ˈhänəs\ *n, pl* **hanis** *or* **hanises** *usu cap* **1 :** a Kusan people on the shores of the Coos river and Coos Bay, Oregon **2 :** a member of the Hanis people

**¹hank** \ˈhaŋk, ˈhaiŋk\ *vt* -ED/-ING/-S [ME *hanken*, of Scand origin; akin to ON *hanka* to coil, fasten, fr. *hank-, hönk*, n.] **1 :** to fasten with a hank **2 :** to fold, loop, or coil into a hank

**²hank** \"\ *n* -s [ME, of Scand origin; akin to ON *hönk* hank, coil, skein, clasp, *hanki* clasp; fr. or akin to MLG *hank* handle, fr. the stem of OHG *hengen, henken* to hang, causative fr. the root of *hāhan* to hang — more at HANG] **1 :** a coil, loop, or ring esp. of rope: as **a** *dial Eng* **:** a loop used to fasten or suspend something (as a strap on a door) **b :** a coiled or looped bundle (as of yarn, rope, wire) usu. containing a definite yardage ⟨a ~ of cotton yarn contains 840 yards⟩ —

see COUNT 8a; compare SKEIN 1 **c :** a ring (as of wood, iron, or rope) attached to the edge of a jib or staysail and running on a stay **2** *now chiefly dial* **:** ADVANTAGE, POWER, HOLD ⟨shouldn't let them get such a ~ over you⟩

¹**han·ker** \'haŋkə(r), 'haiŋ-\ *vb* **hankered; hankered; han·kering** \-k(ə)riŋ\ **hankers** [prob. fr. Flem. *hankeren* (akin to D *hunkeren*), freq. of *hangen* to hang; akin to OHG *hāhan* to hang — more at HANG] *vi* **1** *now chiefly dial* **:** to linger or hang around esp. in anticipation or desire ⟨used to ~ around the stillroom —Thomas Hughes⟩ **2 a :** to desire strongly and yearn in distress ⟨a thirsty man ~*ing* for water⟩ **b :** to experience a controlled but persistent desire — usu. used with *for* or *after* ⟨~ to spend an evening in general conversation —Clifton Fadiman⟩ ⟨has always ~*ed* to do a bit of acting —Bennett Cerf⟩ ⟨spend a lot of time ~*ing* after forbidden pleasures⟩ ⟨~*ed* for a good cup of coffee⟩ **3** *chiefly Scot* **:** to hesitate or pause esp. in speaking ⟨he hums and he ~*s* —Robert Burns⟩ ~ *vt* **:** to yearn for **:** want badly ⟨it supplies what we have long ~*ed* —*Saturday Rev.*⟩ **syn** see LONG

²**hanker** \"\ *n* -S **:** HANKERING

**han·ker·er** \-kərə(r)\ *n* -S **:** one that hankers ⟨~*s* after pleasure⟩

**hankering** *n* -S **:** the experience of one that hankers: **a :** strong desire **:** great yearning ⟨the same ~ for swift success, the same hasty greed —*Times Lit. Supp.*⟩ **b :** a controlled but persistent desire ⟨push out of his consciousness the ~ to spend an evening alone⟩

**han·ker·ing·ly** *adv* **:** in the manner of one that hankers ⟨kept thinking ~ about seeing his family again⟩

**hank for hank** *adv, of boats* **:** on the same tack together and making equal speed ⟨sail *hank for hank*⟩

**han·kie** *or* **han·ky** *also* **han·key** \'haŋkē, 'haiŋ-, -ki\ *n, pl* **hankies** [by shortening & alter.] **:** HANDKERCHIEF

**han·kle** \'haŋkəl\ *vt* -ED/-ING/-S [freq. of ¹*hank*] *now dial Eng* **1 :** TWIST, ENTANGLE **2 :** to involve (a person) in something by luring or enticing — usu. used with *in* or *on* ⟨didn't want to join but they *hankled* him on⟩

**han·kow** \'haŋ'kau̇, 'han'kau̇, -kō; 'hän'kō\ *adj, usu cap* [fr. *Hankow*, China] **:** of or from the city of Hankow, China **:** of the kind or style prevalent in Hankow

**hanks·ite** \'haŋk,sīt\ *n* -S [Henry G. *Hanks* †1907 Am. mineralogist + E *-ite*] **:** a mineral $Na_{22}K(SO_4)_9(CO_3)_2Cl$ consisting of white or yellow sulfate-carbonate-chloride of sodium and potassium occurring in hexagonal crystals

**han·kul** \'häŋ,kül\ *also* **han·gul** \-ŋ,gül\ *n* -S *usu cap* [Korean] **:** the alphabet of 24, formerly 25, characters invented in the 15th century in which Korean is usu. written — called also *onmun*

**han·ky-pank** \'haŋkē,paŋk\ *adj* [short for *hanky-panky*] **:** marked by or derived from hanky-panky ⟨*hanky-pank* joints —*Life*⟩ ⟨their pockets full of *hanky-pank* money —Herbert Gold⟩

**han·ky-pan·ky** \-'paŋkē\ *also* **hankey-pankey** *n, pl* **hanky-pankies** *also* **hankey-pankeys** [alter. (perh. influenced by *handkerchief*) of *hocus-pocus*] **1 :** questionable, deceitful, or fraudulent activity **:** TRICKERY **:** MISCHIEF ⟨there's been some *hanky-panky* going on, and we haven't got to the bottom of it —F.W.Crofts⟩ ⟨wanted things to be completely above board —and no *hanky-panky*⟩ ⟨while the philandering physician was playing *hanky-panky* with his patients —Alan Hynd⟩ **2 :** meaningless or foolish activity or talk ⟨people went in for too much hullabaloo and *hanky-panky* —John Steinbeck⟩ ⟨had a thorough grasp of the political and social *hanky-panky* of his period —*Time*⟩

**han·na** \'hanə\ *dial Brit* **:** have not

**hannahill** *var of* HANAHILL

**han·nay·ite** \'hanē,īt\ *n* -S [G *hannayit*, fr. J. B. *Hannay*, 19th cent. Scot. chemist + G *-it* -ite] **:** a mineral $Mg_3(NH_4)_2H_4(PO_4)_4.8H_2O$ consisting of a hydrous acid ammonium magnesium phosphate occurring in guano

**han·ni·bal·ic** \'hanə'balik\ *also* **han·ni·ba·lian** \-'bālyən, -lēən\ *adj, usu cap* [*Hannibal* †183 B.C. Carthaginian general who made war against Rome + E *-ic* or *-ian*] **:** of or relating to the Carthaginian general Hannibal

**ha·no** \'hä,nō, 'ha,-\ *n, pl* **hano** *or* **hanos** *usu cap* [Sp, of AmerInd origin] **1 :** a Tanoan people occupying a pueblo in Arizona **2 :** a member of the Hano people

**ha·noi** \(')ha'nȯi *also* hə'n-\ *adj, usu cap* [fr. *Hanoi*, North Vietnam] **:** of or from Hanoi, the capital of North Vietnam **:** of the kind or style prevalent in Hanoi

**hano·ver** *or* **han·no·ver** \'ha(,)nōvə(r), -anəv-, *G* hä'nōvər *or* hä'nōfər\ *adj, usu cap* [fr. *Hanover* (Hannover), Germany] **:** of or from the city of Hanover, Germany **:** of the kind or style prevalent in Hanover

¹**han·o·ve·ri·an** \'hanō'virēən, -anə'- *also* -ver-\ *adj, usu cap* [*Hanover*, province of Prussia, Germany (fr. G *Hannover*) + E *-ian*] **1 a :** of, relating to, or subject to the Prussian province of Hanover **b :** of, relating to, or supporting the former ducal house of Hanover **c :** of, relating to, or supporting the British House of Hanover **2 :** of, relating to, or being a period of architectural development in western Europe usu. held to be equivalent to the 18th century

²**hanoverian** \"\ *n* **1** -S *cap* **a :** a native or inhabitant of Hanover, Germany **b :** a member of the former ducal house of Hanover **c :** a member or supporter of the British House of Hanover **2 a** *usu cap* **:** a breed of horses developed by crossing heavy cold-blooded German horses with Thoroughbreds **b** -S *often cap* **:** any animal of this breed

**hans** *pl of* HAN

**han·sa** \'han(t)sə, 'hän(,)zä\ *or* **hanse** \'han(t)s, 'hänzə\ *n* -S *usu cap* [*hansa*, fr. ML, fr. MLG *hanse*; *hanse* fr. ME *hans, hanze*, fr. MF & MLG; MF *hanse* fr. MLG; akin to OE *hōs* company, OHG *hansa* troop of warriors, Goth, company, multitude] **1 a :** a merchant guild in a medieval town **b :** an association for trading in foreign countries; *esp* **:** the league first constituted of merchants of various free German cities dealing abroad in the medieval period and later of the cities themselves and organized to secure greater safety and privileges in trading and mutual defense against foreign aggression either by law or arms **2 a :** the entrance fee to a merchant guild **b :** the tax levied upon traders not belonging to a guild

¹**han·sard** \'han(t)sərd, -n,särd, -nzərd, -n,zärd\ *n* -S *usu cap* [*hansa* + *-ard*] **:** a merchant of one of the Hansa towns

²**han·sard** \'han(t)sərd, -n,särd\ *n* -S *usu cap* [after Luke *Hansard* †1828 Eng. printer who printed the journals of the House of Commons] **:** the official published report of proceedings in the British parliament

¹**han·se·at·ic** \'han(t)sē'ad·ik, 'haan-, -at\, ēk *also* -nzē-\ *adj, usu cap* [ML *Hanseaticus*, fr. *hansa* — more at HANSA] **:** of or relating to the Hansa (sense 1b)

²**hanseatic** \"\ *n* -S *usu cap* **:** a member of the Hansa (sense 1b)

**hansel** *var of* HANDSEL

**han·sen·osis** \,han(t)sə'nōsəs\ *n* -ES [NL, fr. A. G. H. *Hansen* + NL *-osis*] **:** LEPROSY

**han·sen·ot·ic** \;==;näd·ik\ *adj* [fr. NL *hansenosis*, after such pairs as NL *neurosis*: E *neurotic*] **:** LEPROUS 1

**han·sen's bacillus** \'han(t)sənz-\ *n, usu cap H* [after Armauer G. H. *Hansen* †1912 Norw. physician who discovered the bacillus] **:** the bacterium (*Mycobacterium leprae*) that causes leprosy

**hansen's disease** *n, usu cap H* [after A. G. H. *Hansen*] **:** LEPROSY

**hansh** *var of* HANCH

**han·som** \'han(t)səm, 'haan-, 'hain-\ *or* **hansom cab** *n* -S [after Joseph Aloysius *Hansom* †1882 Eng. architect who designed such a vehicle] **:** a light two-wheeled covered carriage with the driver's seat elevated behind and with the reins passed over the top

hansom

**hans·wurst** \(')hän(t)s,vu̇(ə)rst\ *n* -S *usu cap* [G, fr. LG *Hanswurst*, lit., Jack sausage] **:** a broadly farcical or burlesque stock character common in German comedy in the 16th to the 18th centuries

**han't** \(')(h)ānt, *chiefly Brit* (')(h)ȧnt\ [by contraction] *dial* **:** have not **:** has not

**hant** \'hant, -aa(ə)-,-ai-,-ȧ-,-ā-\ *var of* HAUNT

**h antigen** *n, usu cap H* [G, fr. *hauchantigen*, fr. *hauch* breath + *antigen*] **:** FLAGELLAR ANTIGEN

**han·tik** \'hän,tēk\ *n, pl* **hantik** *or* **hantiks** *usu cap* [native name on Panay] **1 a :** a Bisayan people inhabiting western Panay, Philippines **b :** a member of such people **2 :** an Austronesian language of the Hantik people that is sometimes considered a dialect of Bisayan

**han·tle** \'hant°l\ *n* -S [prob. alter. of *handful*] *chiefly Scot* **1 :** HANDFUL **2 :** QUANTITY, AMOUNT; *esp* **:** a sizable or considerable amount ⟨a ~ of money⟩ ⟨a good ~ of people⟩

**ha·nuk·kah** *or* **ha·nu·kah** *or* **cha·nu·kah** *also* **cha·nuk·kah** \'k\änəkə, 'h\, \än-, -nük-, -,kä, -nikə, -nēkə\ *n* -S *usu cap* [Heb *hănukkāh* dedication] **:** the eight-day Jewish festival of lights beginning on the 25th of Kislev and commemorating the victory of the Maccabees over Antiochus of Syria and their rededication of the defiled Temple of Jerusalem

**hanum** *var of* KHANUM

**hanu·man** \'hənu̇,män, 'hən-, ,==\'=\ *n* -S [Hindi *Hanumān*, a monkey god, hanuman, fr. nom. of Skt *hanumant*, lit., possessing (large) jaws, fr. *hanu* jaw — more at CHIN] **:** a common Indian monkey (*Presbytis entellus*) protected in its homeland as a protégé of a monkey god

**ha·nu·nóo** \'hänə'nō\ *n, pl* **hanunóo** *or* **hanunóos** *usu cap* **1 a :** a predominantly pagan people inhabiting southern Mindoro, Philippines **b :** a member of such people **2 :** an Austronesian language of the Hanunóo people

**ha·nus·ite** \'hänə,s(h)īt\ *n* -S [Czech *hanušit*, fr. Josef *Hanuš* †1956 Czech chemist + Czech *-it* -ite] **:** a mineral $Mg_2Si_3O_7(OH)_2.H_2O$ consisting of a hydrous basic silicate of magnesium that is a component of pectolite

**ha·nus method** \'hänəs(h)-, -,nu̇sh-\ *n, usu cap H* [after J. *Hanuš*] **:** a method for determining the iodine number of an oil or fat that consists in adding a mixture of iodine and bromine in glacial acetic acid and estimating the excess of unused halogen by titration with sodium thiosulfate

**hao·le** \'hau̇lē, -(,)lā\ *n* -S [Hawaiian] *Hawaii* **:** one who is not a member of the native race of Hawaii; *esp* **:** a member of the white race

**hao·ma** \'hau̇mə\ *n* -S [Av — more at SOMA (intoxicant)] **:** a sacred drink used ritually in Zoroastrianism and sometimes personified as a deified being — compare SOMA

**hao·ri** \'hau̇rē\ *n* -S [Jap] **:** a loose outer garment resembling a coat and extending to the knee and worn in Japan

¹**hap** \'hap\ *n* -S [ME *hap, happe*, fr. ON *happ* good luck; akin to OE *gehæp* suitable, Sw dial. *happa* (*sig*) to take place, Norw *heppa* to take place, OIr *cob* victory, OSlav *kobĭ* augury] **1 :** something that happens or befalls without plan, apparent cause, or predictability ⟨odd little ~*s* and mishaps of domestic life⟩ **2 :** a force which shapes events unpredictably **:** CHANCE, LUCK, FORTUNE ⟨by some bad tide or ~ . . . the ill-made catamaran was overset —Herman Melville⟩ ⟨the fish of evil ~ . . . had been caught and frozen fast —Llewelyn Powys⟩ **syn** see CHANCE

²**hap** \"\ *vi* **happed; happed; happing; haps** [ME *happen*, fr. *hap, happe*, n.] **1 :** to have the fortune **:** HAPPEN, CHANCE ⟨what's to be done, if a man ~*s* to go wrong⟩ ⟨if ~ it must, that I must see thee lie —Robert Herrick †1674⟩ **2 :** to come by chance **:** LIGHT — used with *on* or *upon* ⟨*happed* upon the very book he was looking for⟩

³**hap** \"\ *vt* **happed; happed; happing; haps** [ME *happen*] *dial* **:** to wrap up for warmth **:** CLOTHE, COVER ⟨at the kitchen fire, *happed* in an old overcoat —Michael Murphy⟩

⁴**hap** \"\ *n* -S *dial* **:** something that serves as a covering or wrap (as a bed quilt or cloak)

**ha·pa haole** \'häpə'hau̇lē, -(,)lā\ *adj* [Hawaiian, fr. *hapa* half (fr. E *half*) + *haole* white person] *Hawaii* **:** of part-white ancestry or origin; *esp* **:** Hawaiian-Caucasian

**hap·a·lo·nych·ia** \,hapəlō'nikēə\ *n* -S [NL, fr. Gk *hapalos* soft + NL *-onychia*] **:** abnormal softness of the fingernails or toenails

**hapax** *n* -ES [by shortening] **:** HAPAX LEGOMENON

**ha·pax le·go·me·non** \,ha,paksl̇ə'gämə,nän, ,hā,pak-, ,hä-,päk-, -,non\ *n, pl* **hapax legome·na** \-,nə, -,nä\ [Gk, something said only once] **:** a word or form evidenced by a single citation **:** a word or form occurring once and only once in a document or corpus

**hapchance** \'=,=\ *n* [¹*hap* + *chance*] **:** a fortuitous or chance event or circumstance ⟨the ~ of a sounding word —Richard Llewellyn⟩ ⟨this ~ . . . enterprise is nothing to sneeze at —Dave Roberts⟩

**ha'·pen·ny** \'hāp(ə)nī\ *n* [by contr.] **:** HALFPENNY

**hap-harlot** \'=,==\ *n* [³*hap* + *harlot* (knave)] *now dial Eng* **:** a coarse coverlet

¹**haphazard** \(')=;==\ *n* [¹*hap* + *hazard*] CHANCE, ACCIDENT, RANDOM ⟨this little remnant preserved by the ~ of chance —Edith Hamilton⟩ ⟨take our principles at ~ —John Locke⟩

²**haphazard** \"\ *adj* **:** marked by lack of plan, regularity, order, guidance, or direction **:** made, performed, or selected according to chance, whim, or speculation rather than on the basis of considered judgment or firm knowledge **:** AIMLESS, RANDOM ⟨his ~ untidy ways —Virginia Woolf⟩ ⟨not . . . a collection of ~ schemes, but rather the orderly component parts of a connected and logical whole —F.D.Roosevelt⟩ ⟨there must be some guidance unless selection is to be ~ —Muna Lee⟩ ⟨the room was . . . filled with ~ furniture —Howard Griffin⟩ ⟨~ ascriptions have been made —A.M.Young⟩ **syn** see RANDOM

³**haphazard** \"\ *adv* [²*haphazard*] **:** HAPHAZARDLY ⟨were built . . . without any regard to their situation, placed ~, wherever it was convenient —Edith Hamilton⟩

**hap·haz·ard·ly** *adv* **:** in a haphazard manner ⟨a little cluster of islands grouped ~ about a bigger green island —Louis Bromfield⟩

**hap·haz·ard·ness** *n* -ES **:** the quality or state of being haphazard

**hap·haz·ard·ry** \-rē\ *n* -ES **:** haphazard character or order **:** CHANCINESS, FORTUITY ⟨the good things in his work always have an air of ~ —*Manchester Guardian Weekly*⟩ ⟨whose forebears had known only the ~ of idol and fetish worship —Galbraith Welch⟩

**haphtarah** *or* **haphtorah** *var of* HAFTARAH

**hapl-** *or* **haplo-** *also* **apl-** *or* **aplo-** *comb form* [NL, fr. Gk *hapl-, haplo-*, fr. *haploos, haplous, haplos*, fr. *ha-* one (akin to Gk *homos* same) + *-ploos, -plous, -plos* multiplied by; akin to L *-plus* multiplied by — more at SAME, DOUBLE] **1 :** single **:** simple ⟨*haploscope*⟩ **2** [*haploid*] **:** of or relating to the haploid generation or condition

**hap·less** \'hapləs\ *adj* [¹*hap* + *-less*] **:** marked by the absence of good luck **:** UNFORTUNATE ⟨~ beings caught in the grip of forces we can do little about —W.H.Whyte⟩ **syn** see UNLUCKY

**hap·less·ly** *adv* **:** in a hapless manner

**hap·less·ness** *n* -ES **:** the quality or state of being hapless

**haplite** *var of* APLITE

**hap·lo·bi·ont** \'haplō'bī,änt, ha'plōbē,änt\ *n* -S [*hapl-* + *-biont*] **:** a plant producing only sexual haploid individuals — compare DIPLOBIONT, HAPLONT — **hap·lo·bi·on·tic** \'hap(,)lō,bī'äntik, ha'plōbē'äntik\ *adj*

**hap·lo·caulescent** \'ha(,)plō+\ *adj* [*hapl-* + *caulescent*] **:** having a simple axis — used of a plant (as the poppy) capable of developing reproductive organs on the primary axis: compare DIPLOCAULESCENT, TRIPLOCAULESCENT

**hap·lo·chlamydeous** \"+\ *adj* [*hapl-* + *chlamydeous*] **:** having rudimentary perianth leaves protecting the sporophylls (as in pistillate flowers of a walnut tree) — compare HOMOCHLAMYDEOUS

¹**hap·lo·diploid** \"+\ *adj* [*hapl-* + *diploid*] **:** of, relating to, or characterized by haplodiploidy

²**haplodiploid** \"\ *n* **:** an individual produced by haplodiploidy

**hap·lo·diploidy** \"+\ *n* [*hapl-* + *diploidy*] **:** sex differentiation in which haploid males are produced from unfertilized eggs and diploid females from fertilized eggs (as in certain insects)

**hap·lo·diplont** \"+\ *n* [*hapl-* + *diplont*] **:** a haploid plant reproducing by spores

**hap·lod·o·ci** \ha'pläda,sī\ *n pl, cap* [NL, fr. *hapl-* + *-doci* (fr. Gk *dokos* beam, bar)] **:** an order of spiny-finned fishes comprising the toadfishes

**hap·lo·dont** \'haplə,dänt\ *adj* [*hapl-* + *-odont*] **:** having or constituting molar teeth with simple crowns without tubercles — **hap·lo·don·ty** \-ntē\ *n* -ES

**hap·lo·dri·li** \,haplə'drī,lī\ [NL, fr. *hapl-* + *-drili* (fr. Gk *drilos* worm)] *syn of* ARCHIANNELIDA

**hap·log·ra·phy** \ha'plägrəfē\ *n* -ES [*hapl-* + *-graphy*] **:** the omission in writing or copying of one of two or more adjacent and similar letters, syllables, words, or lines

¹**hap·loid** \'ha,plȯid\ *adj* [ISV, fr. Gk *haploeidēs* single, fr. *hapl-* + *-oeidēs* -oid] **1 :** having the gametic number of chromosomes or half the number characteristic of the somatic cells **2 :** MONOPLOID

²**haploid** \"\ *n* -S **:** a haploid individual

**hap·loi·dy** \'ha,plȯidē\ *n* -ES **:** the condition of being haploid

¹**hap·lo·lep·id** \,haplə'lepəd, ha'pläləp-\ *adj* [NL *Haplolepidae*] **:** of or relating to the family Haplolepidae

²**haplolepid** \"\ *n* -S **:** a fish of the family Haplolepidae

**hap·lo·lep·i·dae** \,haplə'lepə,dē\ *n pl, cap* [NL, fr. *Haplolepis*, type genus + *-idae*] **:** a family of small primitive Upper Carboniferous bony fishes with large scales

**hap·lo·lep·is** \,haplə'lepəs, ha'pläləp-\ *n, cap* [NL, fr. *hapl-* + Gk *lepis* scales of a fish] **:** the type genus of the family Haplolepidae

**hap·lol·o·gy** \ha'pläləjē\ *n* -ES [ISV *hapl-* + *-logy*] **:** contraction of a word by the omission of one or more similar sounds or syllables in pronunciation (as in \'lībrē\ for *library* or \'präblē\ for *probably*)

**hap·lo·mi** \ha'plō,mī\ *n pl, cap* [NL, fr. *hapl-* + *-omi* (fr. Gk *ōmos* shoulder)] **:** a small order of teleost fishes having cycloid scales, abdominal pelvic fins, a persistent air duct, and typically no mesocoracoid arch that is now usu. restricted to the pikes, the Alaska blackfish, and a few related forms but formerly included also the Microcyprini and some other fishes — **hap·lo·mous** \-məs\ *adj*

¹**hap·lo·mid** \-məd\ *adj* [NL *Haplomi* + E *-id*] **:** of or relating to the order Haplomi

²**haplomid** \"\ *n* -S **:** a fish of the order Haplomi

**hap·lo·mitosis** \,ha(,)plō+\ *n* [NL, fr. *hapl-* + *mitosis*] **:** a primitive mitosis occurring in certain flagellates in which chromosomes are imperfectly differentiated and the endosome functions as a division center — compare MESOMITOSIS, PROMITOSIS

**hap·lont** \'ha,plänt\ *n* -S [ISV *hapl-* + *-ont*] **:** an organism having somatic cells with the haploid chromosome number and only the zygote diploid — compare DIPLONT, GAMETOPHYTE — **hap·lon·tic** \(')ha'pläntik\ *adj*

**hap·lo·pap·pus** \,haplō'papəs\ *n, cap* [NL, fr. *hapl-* + *pappus*] **:** a large genus of perennial herbs (family Compositae) of the western U. S. with mostly alternate rigid leaves and yellow flowers

**hap·lo·peristomic** *also* **hap·lo·peristomous** \'ha(,)plō+\ *adj* [*hapl-* + *peristome* + *-ic* or *-ous*] **:** APLOPERISTOMATOUS

**hap·lo·phase** \'haplō,fāz\ *n* [ISV *hapl-* + *phase*] **:** the haploid phase (as the gametophyte) in the life cycle of certain plants

¹**hap·lo·polyploid** \'ha(,)plō+\ *adj* [*hapl-* + *polyploid*] *of a polyploid* **:** having the gametic number of chromosomes

²**haplo-polyploid** \"\ *n* **:** a haplo-polyploid individual

**hap·lor·chis** \ha'plȯrkəs\ *n, cap* [NL, fr. *hapl-* + Gk *orchis* testicle — more at ORCHIS] **:** a genus of minute digenetic trematodes (family Heterophyidae) infesting the intestines of flesh-eating birds and mammals and occas. man in tropical areas

**hap·lo·scope** \'haplə,skōp\ *n* [ISV *hapl-* + *-scope*] **:** a simple stereoscope used in the study of depth perception — **hap·lo·scop·ic** \;==;skäpik\ *adj*

**hap·lo·sis** \ha'plōsəs\ *n, pl* **haplo·ses** \-ō,sēz\ [NL, fr. *hapl-* + *-osis*] **:** the halving of the somatic chromosome number by meiosis — compare DIPLOSIS

**hap·lo·spo·rid·ia** \,hap(,)lōspə'ridēə\ *n pl, cap* [NL, fr. pl. of *Haplosporidium* genus of Acnidosporidia, fr. *hapl-* + *sporidium*] **:** a small order of Acnidosporidia comprising parasites in invertebrates and lower vertebrates and being of no known economic importance

¹**hap·lo·spo·rid·i·an** \;=(,)=;=;ridēən\ *adj* [NL *Haplosporidia* + E *-an*] **:** of or relating to the order Haplosporidia

²**haplosporidian** \"\ *n* -S **:** a member of the order Haplosporidia

**hap·lo·stemo·nous** \;haplō;stēmənəs, -tem-\ *adj* [ISV *hapl-* + *-stemonous*] **:** ISOSTEMONOUS

**hap·lo·thrips** \'haplō,thrips\ *n, cap* [NL, fr. *hapl-* + L *thrips* — more at THRIPS] **:** a widespread genus of thrips including forms extremely destructive to cultivated plants

**hap·lo·type** \-,tīp\ *n* [*hapl-* + *type*] **:** the sole species included in the original description of a genus **:** ORTHOTYPE — **hap·lo·typ·ic** \;==;tipik\ *adj*

**hap·ly** \'haplē, -li\ *adv* [ME, fr. *hap, happe* hap + *-ly* — more at HAP] **:** by chance, luck, or accident ⟨the sound of many a word in mocking echoes ~ overheard —George Santayana⟩

**hap'orth** *or* **ha'porth** \-s\ [by contr.] **:** HALFPENNYWORTH

**happed** *past of* HAP

¹**hap·pen** \'hapən, -pᵊm\ *vb* **happened** \-pənd, -pᵊnd\ **happening** \-p(ə)niŋ\ **happens** \-pənz, -pᵊmz\ [ME *happenen, hapnen*, fr. *hap, happe*, n., hap + *-enen* -en — more at HAP] *vi* **1 a :** to occur fortuitously, casually, or coincidentally **:** come about without previous design — often used with impersonal *it* ⟨it ~*s* the 500-mile auto race is in progress —Bruce Westley⟩ ⟨as it ~*s*, I have the book right here⟩ **b :** to come into existence spontaneously or as if spontaneously without causal necessity, effort, or other process ⟨no success in life merely ~*s* —Katharine F. Gerould⟩ ⟨we were together and love ~*ed* —Galway Kinnell⟩ **2 a :** to present itself as an event or process **:** become a reality **:** come into being **:** take place **:** OCCUR ⟨a study of what ~*s* when we sleep⟩ ⟨accidents are continually ~*ing*⟩ ⟨cloudbursts do not ~ . . . often —G. W.Murray⟩ ⟨hurried to the scene . . . where the shooting ~*ed* —*Current Biog.*⟩ **b** (1) **:** to present itself as an experience or effect — used with *to* ⟨creep is what ~*s* to a hot metal when you pull it —R.P.Lister⟩ ⟨all sorts of pleasant things ~*ed* to him⟩ (2) **:** to present itself by way of injury or harm — used with *to* ⟨the tickbirds . . . make sure that nothing ~*s* to their rhino —Jule Mannix⟩ ⟨I'd have something ~ to me if I did —Rose Macaulay⟩ **3 :** to have the luck or fortune ⟨he ~*s* to be a very rich man⟩ ⟨forms of life which ~ to be adjusted to their environment —W.R.Inge⟩ ⟨I ~*ed* to hear it⟩ **4 :** to chance to come **:** FALL, LIGHT ⟨while leafing through a journal . . . I ~*ed* across this passage —R.A.Hall b.1911⟩ ⟨~*ed* on a cottage almost hidden in elm tree boughs —*Times Lit. Supp.*⟩ ⟨~*ed* upon a remarkable and neglected volume —Charlton Laird⟩ **5 :** to come or go casually **:** make an appearance **:** turn up **:** drop in ⟨he ~*ed* into the typists' room to borrow a stamp —Dorothy Sayers⟩ ⟨hoping that no wayfarer would ~ along the lane —Joseph Conrad⟩ ⟨any person who might ~ by was expected to . . . visit —*Amer. Guide Series: Texas*⟩ ~ *vt, dial* **:** to become of **:** occur to **:** BEFALL ⟨little I mind what ~*s* me —Augusta Gregory⟩ ⟨what would ~ my little business if I . . . married her —Frank O'Connor⟩

**syn** CHANCE, OCCUR, TRANSPIRE, BEFALL, BETIDE: HAPPEN is a general term without special connotation and signifies to take place either with or without plan, motivation, or apparent or assignable cause. CHANCE, perhaps somewhat archaic or literary in suggestion, stresses lack of plan or causation ⟨a novel that *chanced* to be local and concrete and true —Sinclair Lewis⟩ ⟨he *chanced* to sit banqueting with the mariners about the hour of tierce —G.G.Coulton⟩ OCCUR, often interchangeable with HAPPEN, has the additional meaning of be found, be met with, exist, may more strongly suggest an event which commands attention or consideration, and is more frequent than HAPPEN with negatives ⟨a sluggish, smoke-colored animal, *occurring* in shallow swamp waters —L.P.Schultz⟩ ⟨a bismuth bearing vein *occurs* on Charley Creek —*Encyc. Americana*⟩ ⟨when once a certain detachment from possessive vice and objective ambition has *occurred* in the mind —J.C. Powys⟩ ⟨this is possible in theory, but, actually, never seemed to *occur* —V.G.Heiser⟩ TRANSPIRE means to leak out and become known; by semantic change it has come to mean simply OCCUR, although it is likely to be used of events of some importance ⟨all memorable events . . . *transpire* in morning time and in a morning atmosphere —H.D.Thoreau⟩ ⟨no clear-cut issue developed and no real contest *transpired* —E.E.Robinson⟩ BEFALL and BETIDE, both rather literary, may suggest occurring because of destiny or fate and may be used esp. with reference to unpleasant matters ⟨a . . . piece of ill fortune, which about this time *befell* me —Charles Lamb⟩ ⟨the fate which Beria meted out to so many should now have *befallen* him —Malcolm Muggeridge⟩ ⟨woe *betide* a known traitor⟩

**²happen** \"\ *adv, now dial* : MAYBE, PERHAPS ⟨and ~ they'll tell him so too —Angus Wilson⟩

**happenchance** \'==,=\ *n* [¹*happen* + *chance*] : HAPPENSTANCE

**happening** *n* -s : OCCURRENCE ⟨~*s* of major significance⟩

**happen-so** \'==,=\ *n, dial* : chance occurrence : HAPPENSTANCE

**hap·pen·stance** \'hapənz(,)-, -pᵊmz(,)-, -ən(,)s-, -ᵊm(,)s- — *last syllable as at* CIRCUMSTANCE\ *n* -s [*happen* + *circumstance*] : a circumstance regarded as due to chance

**hap·per** \'hapər\ *Scot var of* HOPPER

**happied** *past of* HAPPY

**happier** *comparative of* HAPPY

**happies** *pres 3d sing of* HAPPY

**happiest** *superlative of* HAPPY

**hap·pi·fy** \'hapə,fī, -pē,f-\ *vt* -ED/-ING/-ES [*happy* + *-fy*] : to make happy ⟨~ existence by constant intercourse with those adapted to elevate it —Mary B. Eddy⟩

**hap·pi·ly** \-pəlē, -li\ *adv* [ME, fr. *happy* + *-ly*] **1** : by good fortune : FORTUNATELY, LUCKILY ⟨the date . . . has been ~ preserved for posterity —Sydney Race⟩ **2** *archaic* : by chance : HAPLY **3** : in a happy manner or state : with feelings of contentment ⟨I was driving ~ along —Richard Joseph⟩ **4** : in an adequate or fitting manner : APTLY, SUCCESSFULLY, APPROPRIATELY, FELICITOUSLY ⟨poetry writing and breadwinning do not go ~ together —Kenneth Mackenzie⟩ ⟨chances are he will mix the two very ~ —Leslie Check⟩ ⟨a matured poetic intelligence . . . ~ fused with the creative heat of poetic imagination —H.V.Gregory⟩

**hap·pi·ness** \-pēnəs, -pən-\ *n* -ES [*happy* + *-ness*] **1** *archaic* : good fortune : good luck : PROSPERITY ⟨all ~ bechance to thee —Shak.⟩ **2 a** (1) : a state of well-being characterized by relative permanence, by dominantly agreeable emotion ranging in value from mere contentment to deep and intense joy in living, and by a natural desire for its continuation (2) : a pleasurable or enjoyable experience ⟨I had the ~ of seeing you —W.S.Gilbert⟩ **b** *Aristotelianism* : EUDAEMONIA **3** : APTNESS, FELICITY ⟨his examples lack ~⟩ ⟨a striking ~ of expression⟩ **syn** FELICITY, BEATITUDE, BLESSEDNESS, BLISS: HAPPINESS is the general term denoting enjoyment of or pleasurable satisfaction in well-being, security, or fulfillment of wishes ⟨pleasures may come about through chance contact and stimulation; such pleasures are not to be despised in a world full of pain. But *happiness* and delight are a different sort of thing. They come to be through a fulfillment that reaches to the depths of our being — one that is an adjustment of our whole being with the conditions of existence —John Dewey⟩ FELICITY, a more bookish or elevated word, may denote a higher, more lasting, or more perfect happiness ⟨all the *felicity* which a marriage of true affection could bestow —Jane Austen⟩ ⟨*felicity* or continued happiness consists not in having prospered, but in the process of prospering —Frank Thilly⟩ BEATITUDE refers in this sense to the highest happiness, the felicity of the blessed ⟨the years of loving sacrifice in scraping that boxful without letting Patty go short were amply crowned for John by this one moment. He sat down again in the corner wrapped in *beatitude* —Mary Webb⟩ ⟨a sense of deep *beatitude* — a strange sweet foretaste of Nirvana —Max Beerbohm⟩ BLESSEDNESS suggests the deep joy of pure affection or of acceptance by a god ⟨the *blessedness* of the saints⟩ BLISS may apply to a complete and assured felicity ⟨all my life's *bliss* from thy dear life was given —Emily Brontë⟩ ⟨now safely lodged in perfect *bliss*; and with spirits elated to rapture —Jane Austen⟩

**happing** *pres part of* HAP

**¹hap·py** \'hapē, -pi\ *adj, usu* -ER/-EST [ME, fr. *hap, happe* hap + *-y* — more at HAP] **1** : favored by luck or fortune : FORTUNATE, PROSPEROUS, PROPITIOUS, FAVORABLE ⟨perennially ~ dice should be inspected to discover whether they are loaded —J.R.Newman⟩ ⟨scientific discoveries . . . seem to drop out of the blue, the gift of ~ chance —*Lamp*⟩ ⟨they experiment in color . . . with results sometimes ~, sometimes disastrous —Roger Fry⟩ **2** : notably well adapted or fitting : markedly effective : APT, FELICITOUS, APPROPRIATE, JUST ⟨he will seek to establish by law the ~ mean —G.L.Dickinson⟩ ⟨the ~ diction, and the graceful phrase —E.G.Bulwer-Lytton⟩ ⟨the passage in the finale was particularly ~ —Virgil Thomson⟩ ⟨television is an especially ~ medium —Irving Kolodin⟩ ⟨the attendants had a ~ thought —Jeremiah Dowling⟩ **3 a** : having the feeling arising from the consciousness of well-being ⟨would forbid any novelist to represent a good man as ever miserable or a wicked man as ever ~ —Havelock Ellis⟩ **b** : characterized or attended by happiness : expressing, reflecting, or suggestive of happiness : not tragic : PLEASANT, JOYOUS ⟨the ~ years of childhood⟩ ⟨a ~ family life⟩ ⟨a book with a ~ ending⟩ ⟨it had been a merciful passing, even a ~ one —S.H.Adams⟩ ⟨the ~ noises of prolonged mastication —C.H. Rickword⟩ ⟨paints a ~ picture of rural life⟩ ⟨past ~ brooks flashing to the sun —G.D.Brown⟩ **c** : GLAD, PLEASED ⟨I am ~ to meet you⟩ ⟨I would be ~ for the president to declare his policy —*Time*⟩ **d** : having or marked by an atmosphere of good fellowship or camaraderie : HARMONIOUS, CONGENIAL, FRIENDLY ⟨sailormen prefer a ~ to a taut ship, where strict discipline is the only diet —A.R.Griffin⟩ ⟨I know that they will find . . . a ~ welcome on the Canadian shore —F.D. Roosevelt⟩ ⟨its ~ industrial relations and the loyal spirit of its workers —Sam Pollock⟩ **4** *obs* : BLESSED **5** : having a feeling of well-being as a result of drink ⟨came home a bit ~⟩ **6 a** : characterized by a dazed irresponsible state — used as a terminal element in combination with the cause of the condition indicated ⟨a punch-*happy* prizefighter⟩ ⟨the gold-*happy* miners decided to have a horse race —J.A.Michener⟩ **b** : impulsively, nervously, or obsessively quick to use something — used as a terminal element in combinations with the object indicated ⟨they'll be gun-*happy* and . . . let go at anything that moves —William Wright⟩ ⟨trigger-*happy* soldiers⟩ **c** : enthusiastic to the point of obsession : OBSESSED — used as a terminal element in combinations with the object of the feeling indicated ⟨I know your type . . . publicity-*happy* —Ellery Queen⟩ ⟨that guy is stripe-*happy* —Norman Mailer⟩ ⟨sailor-*happy* girls who move around after the fleet —Katharine T. Kinkead⟩ **syn** see FIT, GLAD, LUCKY

**²happy** \"\ *vt* -ED/-ING/-ES *now dial* : to make happy ⟨it don't ~ me up any —Howard Troyer⟩

**happy dust** *n, slang* : COCAINE; *also* : HEROIN

**happy family** *n, Austral* : an Australian babbler (genus *Pomatostomus*) of sociable habits; *esp* : GRAY-CROWNED BABBLER

**happy-go-lucky** \'==,=,'==\ *adj* : marked by blithe lack of concern, care, plan, or serious forethought : disposed to accept cheerfully whatever happens : CAREFREE, EASYGOING ⟨on carefully prepared lines rather than as a *happy-go-lucky* venture —*Country Life*⟩ ⟨his amiable but *happy-go-lucky* household —*Amer. Guide Series: Fla.*⟩ **syn** see RANDOM

**happy hunting ground** *n* **1** : the No. American Indian paradise conceived as a region to which the souls of warriors and hunters pass after death for the purpose of spending a happy hereafter in hunting and feasting **2** : a choice or profitable area of operation or exploitation ⟨the reef limestones . . . have been the *happy hunting ground* for fossil collectors —*Jour. of Geol.*⟩ ⟨a *happy hunting ground* for crooks of all nationalities —David Masters⟩ ⟨junkyards . . . have become *happy hunting grounds* for the man in search of spare parts —G.H.Waltz⟩

**happy jack** *n, Austral* : HAPPY FAMILY

**happy warrior** *n* [so called fr. the use of the term in *Character of the Happy Warrior* (1807), poem by William Wordsworth †1850 Eng. poet] : one who is undaunted by difficulties : CRUSADER ⟨the *happy warrior* who . . . was to fight for all the revolution had stood for —Van Wyck Brooks⟩

**¹haps** *pl of* HAP, *pres 3d sing of* HAP

**²haps** \'haps\ *dial Eng var of* HASP

**hapt-** *or* **hapto-** *comb form* [ISV, fr. Gk *haptein* to fasten — more at APSIS] : contact : combination ⟨*hapto*phore⟩

**hap·ten** \'hap,ten\ *also* **hap·tene** \-tēn\ *n* -s [G *hapten*, fr. *hapt-* + *-en* -ene] **1** : a nonantigenic or very weakly antigenic substance that reacts in vitro with an antibody **2** : a substance not antigenic in itself that in combination with a carrier antigen confers specificity or antigenicity or both — **hap·ten·ic** \(')hap¦tenik\ *adj*

**hap·tere** \'hap,ti(ə)r\ *n* -s [NL *hapteron*] : HAPTERON

**hap·ter·on** \'haptə,rän\ *n, pl* **hap·tera** \-tərə\ [NL, fr. Gk *haptein* to fasten] : a discoid outgrowth or swelling of the stem by which a plant is fixed to its substratum (as in many rock-inhabiting seaweeds) : HOLDFAST

**hap·tic** \'haptik\ *or* **hap·ti·cal** \-təkəl\ *adj* [ISV *hapt-* + *-ic, -ical*] **1** : relating to or based on the sense of touch ⟨~ impressions⟩ **2** : characterized by a predilection for the sense of touch ⟨a ~ person⟩

**hap·to·phore** \'haptə,fō(ə)r\ *adj* [ISV *hapt-* + *-phore* (fr. Gk *-phoros* -phorous)] *immunol* : having an ability to enter into combination

**hap·to·po·da** \hap'täpədə\ *n pl, cap* [NL, fr. *hapt-* + *-poda*] : an order of extinct arachnids not closely related to any living group

**hap·tor** \'haptər *also* -,tō(ə)r\ *n* -s [NL, fr. *hapt-* + *-or*] : an organ of attachment in a parasitic worm; *esp* : a complex organ usu. with multiple suckers and strong hooks on the posterior end of many monogenetic trematodes — **hap·to·ral** \-tərəl\ *adj*

**hap·to·trop·ic** \¦haptə¦träpik\ *adj* [ISV *hapt-* + *-tropic*] : exhibiting haptotropism — **hap·to·trop·i·cal·ly** \-pək(ə)lē\ *adv*

**hap·tot·ro·pism** \hap'tä·trə,pizəm\ *n* [ISV *hapt-* + *-tropism*] : positive stereotropism esp. of plants

**ha·pu** \'hä(,)pü\ *n* -s [Maori] : a Maori clan or tribal subdivision

**ha·pu·ku** *or* **ha·pu·ka** \'hä,pükə\ *n, pl* **hapuku** *or* **hapuka** [Maori *hapuku*] *NewZeal* : GROPER 1b

**haque·ton** \'haktən\ *n* -s [ME *hacton*, alter. of *aketoun* — more at ACTON] *archaic* : ACTON

**har** *var of* HAAR

**har** *abbr* harbor

**ha·ra·ke·ke** \'härə,kākē\ *n* -s [Maori] : NEW ZEALAND FLAX

**hara-kari** *also* **hari-kari** \,harē'kirē, ,hari'kiri, -arə'k-, -'kar- *also* ,her- *or* -'ker-\ *n* -s [Jap *harakiri*, fr. *hara* belly + *kiri* ending, cutting] **1** : suicide by disembowelment formerly practiced by the Japanese samurai or decreed to one of its members by the feudal court in consideration of his social status in lieu of the ordinary death penalty **2** : suicide by any means

**haram** *var of* HAREM

**¹ha·rangue** \hə'raŋ, -raiŋ\ *n* -s [ME *arang*, fr. MF *arenge, harenge, harangue*, fr. OIt *aringa, arenga* public address, fr. *aringare* to make a speech, fr. *aringo* public square, prob. fr. an (assumed) Gmc compound whose components are akin respectively to Goth *harjis* host and to OHG *hring* ring — more at HARRY, RING] **1 a** : a speech addressed to a public assembly : ORATION, DECLAMATION ⟨listening to his capacious ~ and its immaculate delivery —Sir Winston Churchill⟩ **b** : a bombastic ranting speech or writing ⟨found it a subject for rabble-rousing ~*s* —W.F.Jenkins⟩ ⟨embark on emotional and frequently violent ~*s* —K.E.Read⟩ ⟨the long, tiresome ~ so characteristic of . . . books on the subject —J.H.Donnelly⟩ **c** : a didactic, scolding, or hortatory talk or discussion : LECTURE ⟨launch into a brilliant ~ on the habits of trout —Honor Tracy⟩ ⟨gave me a ~ on the subject of my poor grades⟩ **2** : an animated discussion or conversation ⟨neglected to call up in the evening for our nightly ~ —Vli Beigel⟩ ⟨the morning ~*s* of husband-and-wife teams —M.G.Faught⟩

**²harangue** \"\ *vb* -ED/-ING/-S [F *haranguer*, fr. MF, fr. *harangue*] *vi* : to make a harangue : DECLAIM ⟨poets . . . and philosophers recited their works, and *harangued* for diversion —Tobias Smollett⟩ ~ *vt* : to address in a harangue ⟨that lady was still *haranguing* the girl —F.M.Ford⟩

**ha·rangu·er** \-ŋə(r)\ *n* -s : one that harangues

**ha·rap·pa** \hə'rapə\ *also* **ha·rap·pan** \-pən\ *adj, usu cap* [*Harappa* fr. *Harappa*, locality in West Punjab, Pakistan; *Harappan* fr. *Harappa* + E *-an*] : of or relating to a city culture of the Indus valley in the third and second millenniums B.C. characterized by a complex social and economic structure and an art largely concerned with the reproduction of animal forms

**ha·ra·ri** \hə'rärē\ *n, pl* **harari** *or* **hararis** *usu cap* [fr. *Harar*, region of Ethiopia] **1 a** : a people of eastern Ethiopia now mixed with the Somali but orig. Himyaritic Semites **b** : a member of such people **2** : a Semitic language of the Harari people

**ha·ras** \a'rä, ä'rä\ *n, pl* **haras** \-rä(z)\ [ME *harace, haras*, fr. OF *haraz*] **1** *archaic* : a horse-breeding establishment : stud farm **2** : HARRAS

**¹harass** \hə'ras, 'harəs, -raa(ə)s,-'rais *also* 'herəs *or* ha'r-\ *vt* -ED/-ING/-ES [F *harasser*, fr. MF, fr. *harer* to set a dog on, fr. OF *hare*, interj. used to incite dogs, of Gmc origin; akin to OHG *hara, hera* hither; akin to OHG *hiar* here — more at HERE] **1 a** : to lay waste (as an enemy's country) : RAID, HARRY ⟨hostile Indians ~*ed* the frontier⟩ **b** : to worry and impede by repeated attacks ⟨his guerrilla forces cooperated with United States parachute troops in ~*ing* the Japanese —*Current Biog.*⟩ ⟨~*ed* the enemy retreat⟩ **2 a** : to tire out (as with physical or mental effort) : EXHAUST, FATIGUE ⟨I have been ~*ed* with the toil of verse —William Wordsworth⟩ **b** : to vex, trouble, or annoy continually or chronically (as with anxieties, burdens, or misfortune) : PLAGUE, BEDEVIL, BADGER ⟨sciatica occasionally ~*ed* her —Arnold Bennett⟩ ⟨~ the pilot and thus keep him in a constant state of . . . upset —H.G.Armstrong⟩ ⟨~*ed* . . . by lack of funds —Henry Miller⟩ **syn** see WORRY

**²harass** \"\ *n* -ES *archaic* : WORRY, HARASSMENT

**harassed** \-st\ *adj* **1** : WORN-OUT, EXHAUSTED, FATIGUED ⟨breathless and ~ at the end of the climb —Wyn Roberts⟩ **2 a** : sorely troubled, vexed, or burdened (as with cares, importunities, misfortune) : BADGERED ⟨looked like a ~ draper's clerk⟩ ⟨one of the . . . busiest and most ~ men in the country —S.H.Adams⟩ ⟨led a ~ life⟩ **b** : expressing or reflecting harassment ⟨wrote a series of ~ letters⟩ ⟨wore a ~ look on his face⟩

**harassed·ly** \-sədlē, -stlē, -li\ *adv* : in a harassed manner

**harass·ing** *adj* : causing or tending to cause harassment ⟨a series of ~ lawsuits —T.W.Arnold⟩ ⟨I've had many a ~ disappointment —E.B.Barrett⟩

**harassing fire** *n* : fire designed to disturb the rest, curtail the movement, or lower the morale of enemy troops; *esp* : artillery fire having these objects

**harass·ing·ly** *adv* : in a harassing manner

**harass·ment** \-smənt\ *n* -s **1** : the act or an instance of harassing : VEXATION, ANNOYANCE ⟨the ~ of unions . . . will become more difficult —T.W.Arnold⟩ ⟨chafed by the ~*s* of travel —R.L.Taylor⟩ ⟨the weather, taxes, . . . and various ~*s* of a more personal nature —*New Yorker*⟩ ⟨border incidents . . . no longer have the character of mere ~ —*Atlantic Monthly*⟩ **2** : the condition of being harassed ⟨showed signs of ~ —E.M.Lustgarten⟩ ⟨his continuing ~ may have been due in great part to his own . . . contentious personality —Stuart MacClintock⟩

**harateen** *var of* HARRATEEN

**har·a·tin** *also* **har·ra·tin** \¦harə¦tēn\ *n, pl* **haratin** *or* **haratins** *usu cap* **1 a** : a negroid Berber people of the southern slope of the Atlas mountains **b** : a member of such people **2** : a half-breed of Berber and Sudanese Negro parentage

**har·bin** \'härbən, (')här¦bin\ *adj, usu cap* [fr. *Harbin*, Manchuria] : of or from the city of Harbin, Manchuria : of the kind or style prevalent in Harbin

**¹har·bin·ger** \'härbənjər, 'häbənjə(r\ *n* -s [ME *herbergere, herbergeour, herbengar* (also, one who provides lodging, host), fr. OF *herbergere, herbergeor* one that makes camp, one that provides lodgings, host, fr. *herberge* army encampment, hostelry, of Gmc origin; akin to OHG *heriberga* army encampment, hostelry — more at HARBOR] **1** : a person sent before to provide lodgings; *esp* : an officer of the English royal household formerly sent ahead to prepare lodgings (as on a royal progress) **2 a** *archaic* : a person sent before to announce the coming of someone : HERALD ⟨be myself the ~ and make joyful the hearing of my wife —Shak.⟩ **b** : one who pioneers in or initiates a major change (as in art, science, or doctrine) : PRECURSOR, FORERUNNER, TRAILBLAZER, APOSTLE ⟨the ~*s* of organized religion in Oregon were four . . . Indians —*Amer. Guide Series: Oregon*⟩ ⟨the great legal ~ of the New Deal revolution —*Time*⟩ ⟨the ~*s* of peace to a hitherto distracted . . . people —David Livingstone⟩ **c** : something that presages or foreshadows what is to come : PORTENT, OMEN, SIGN, INDICATION, SYMBOL ⟨robins are revered . . . as ~*s* of spring —E.A.Bauer⟩ ⟨the sinister white owl . . . the ~ of destruction —Alan Moorehead⟩ ⟨a proper wife is the surest ~ of success for the soldier —H.H. Arnold & I.C.Eaker⟩ ⟨winter's sad ~*s*, the yellow leaves —J.G.Frazer⟩

**²harbinger** \"\ *vt* -ED/-ING/-S : to be a harbinger of : PRESAGE

**harbinger-of-spring** \'====='=\ *n, pl* **harbingers-of-spring** : a small tuberous early-blooming No. American herb (*Erigenia bulbosa*) of the family Umbelliferae with ternate leaves and umbellate white flowers

**¹har·bor** \'härbər, 'häbə(r\ *n* -s *see -or in Explan Notes, often attrib* [ME *herberge, herberwe, herber, harborowe*; akin to OHG & OS *heriberga* army encampment, hostelry, MLG *herberge* hostelry, ON *herbergi*; all fr. a prehistoric WGmc-NGmc compound whose components are akin respectively to OHG *heri* army and to OHG *bergan* to shelter, hide — more at HARRY, BURY] **1 a** : a place of security and comfort : HAVEN, ASYLUM, REFUGE, SHELTER ⟨the . . . Loyalists found ~ in the same areas —W.G.Hardy⟩ ⟨a very ~ from the raging streets —Charles Dickens⟩ ⟨the beauty and the ~ of a snug house —Meridel Le Sueur⟩ **b** : the resting place or lair of a wild animal (as a deer) **2 a** : a small bay or other sheltered part of a considerable body of water usu. well protected either naturally or artificially (as by jetties) against high waves and strong currents and deep enough to furnish anchorage for ships or other craft; *esp* : such a place in which port facilities are provided ⟨Halifax ~⟩ ⟨a yacht ~⟩ **b** : INLET ⟨Pearl *Harbor*, Hawaii⟩ ⟨Otago *Harbor*, N.Z.⟩ ⟨Grays *Harbor*, Wash.⟩ ⟨Charlotte *Harbor*, Fla.⟩ ⟨Little Egg *Harbor*, N.J.⟩ **syn** HAVEN, PORT: HARBOR applies to a part of a body of water (as a sea or lake) partially or almost totally enclosed so that ships or boats entering it may be protected when they are moored, and by extension applies to any place of protection ⟨the boat arrived safely in the *harbor* by nightfall⟩ ⟨two promontories of land forming a natural *harbor*⟩ ⟨find a *harbor* until the financial panic had passed⟩ HAVEN, now chiefly literary except in names, adds to HARBOR the idea of refuge or place of peace ⟨a blessed *haven* into which convoys could slip from the submarine-infested Atlantic —Stewart Beach⟩ ⟨the colony acquired an unsavory reputation for providing a friendly *haven* for pirates —*Amer. Guide Series: R.I.*⟩ ⟨leave for a while their own crowded homes and find a calm cozy *haven* where they can talk without interruption —Ernest & Pearl Beaglehole⟩ ⟨an excellent *haven* for game birds and deer —*Amer. Guide Series: Minn.*⟩ PORT signifies a place, usu. both harbor and adjacent town or city, suitable for landing men or goods, and by extension applies to a destination or goal ⟨transatlantic steamers docked in the *port* of New York⟩ ⟨the home *port* of steamers formerly navigating the waters of the lake —*Amer. Guide Series: N.H.*⟩ ⟨steamboat *ports* on the Columbia —Dayton Kohler⟩ ⟨unload a damaged ship at the first available *port*⟩

**²harbor** \"\ *vb* **harbored**; **harbored**; **harboring** \-b(ə)riŋ\ **harbors** *see -or in Explan Notes* [ME *herbergen, herberwen, herberen, harborowen*, fr. *herberge, herberwe, herber, harborowe*, n.] *vt* **1 a** (1) : to give shelter or refuge to : take in ⟨benefited by ~*ing* and absorbing displaced European psychiatrists —Lauretta Bender⟩ ⟨~*ed* white renegades and strays from hostile tribes —*Amer. Guide Series: Tenn.*⟩ ⟨return of Greek children ~*ed* in other countries —*Americana Annual*⟩ (2) : to receive clandestinely and conceal ⟨a fugitive from justice⟩ (3) : to have (an animal) in one's keeping ⟨may not ~ a dog without a permit⟩ **b** (1) : to be the home or habitat of : CONTAIN ⟨the pool normally ~*s* several large trout —Alexander MacDonald⟩ ⟨her home . . . had ~*ed* her family for four generations —*Current Biog.*⟩ ⟨this structure ~*s* a mirror and bookrest —*New Yorker*⟩ ⟨the . . . buildings ~ a maze of ducts and pipes —Lewis Mumford⟩ ⟨caves which . . . certainly ~ bats —Thomas Barbour⟩ ⟨the same county that ~*s* the depressing cotton towns —L.D.Stamp⟩ (2) : to be the host of (a parasite) ⟨one of the pigs ~*ed* . . . kidney worms —J.E.Alicata⟩ **c** : to track (an animal) to lair or hiding place **2** : CHERISH, ENTERTAIN ⟨~ thoughts⟩ ⟨~ feelings⟩ ⟨~ a deep resentment against the U. S. —Winifred Raushenbush⟩ ⟨any power which might ~ aggressive designs —C.A.Fisher⟩ ⟨~*ed* a mistrust of expressed emotion —Stewart Cockburn⟩ **3** : to place (a ship) for shelter ~ *vi* **1 a** : to find or take shelter : be present ⟨it was quite thinkable that dreadful heresies might ~ there —G.W.Johnson⟩ **b** (1) *of an animal* : to rest or hide away esp. habitually ⟨fierce boars ~*ed* in the dense wood⟩ (2) : LIVE ⟨parasites that ~ in the blood⟩ **2** : to take shelter or come to anchor in a harbor **3** : to conceal a fugitive from justice ⟨you can be shot for ~*ing*, she thought —Ion Braby⟩

**har·bor·age** \-b(ə)rij\ *n* -s **1 a** : SHELTER, REFUGE ⟨talking as if he had a right to ~, attention, and affection —Clemence Dane⟩ ⟨for this ~ . . . hostility seemed to her a little price to pay —Katherine Freeman⟩ **b** : a place of shelter or refuge : RESTING-PLACE ⟨the island was a ~ for privateersmen and runaway slaves⟩ **c** : a place offering favorable environmental conditions for growth and life ⟨to reduce a rat population, competition must be increased by reducing food or ~ —*Wildlife Rev.*⟩ ⟨weedy hedgerows . . . are thus a ~ for many troublesome pests —F.D.Smith & Barbara Wilcox⟩ **2 a** : shelter for ships : harbor facilities ⟨the long indented coast offers excellent ~⟩ **b** : HARBOR ⟨the ship . . . was lifted over the sandbars into the safe ~ of Matanzas —J.B.Cabell & A.J. Hanna⟩

**har·bor·er** \-bərə(r)\ *n* -s **1** : one that harbors ⟨the ~ of suspicion does not inspire faith in himself —L.P.Stryker⟩ **2** : a person who tracks a deer to its harbor and keeps watch on it there

**harbor gasket** *n* : a canvas or sennit band used to secure a sail

**harbor line** *n* : a line defining the limits of a harbor

**harbor master** *n* **1** : an officer charged with the duty of executing the regulations respecting the use of a harbor esp. as to berthing and mooring **2** : an officer who directs the policing of a harbor area by members of a municipal police force

**harbor porpoise** *n* : a common porpoise (*Phocaena phocaena*) of the north Atlantic and Pacific

**harbor seal** *n* : a small seal (*Phoca vitulina*) about four feet long living along the north Atlantic coasts, occas. occurring as far south as the Mediterranean and New Jersey, usu. keeping near land, and often ascending rivers; *also* : a similar seal (*P. richardii*) of the north Pacific coasts

**¹har·bor·ward** \-bə(r)wə(r)d\ *adv* [¹*harbor* + *-ward*] : toward the harbor ⟨a pleasant little frame house . . . looking ~ —*New Yorker*⟩

**²harborward** \"\ *adj* : facing the harbor ⟨lined on both the ~ and landward sides by residences —Lewis Mumford⟩

**harbour** *Brit var of* HARBOR

**¹hard** \'härd, 'häd\ *adj* -ER/-EST [ME, fr. OE *heard*; akin to OHG *hart* hard, ON *harthr* hard, Goth *hardus* severe, Gk *kratos* strength, *kratys* strong, and prob. to Skt *karkara* hard] **1 a** (1) : not easily penetrated, cut, or separated into parts : not easily yielding to pressure : FIRM, SOLID, COMPACT ⟨an extremely ~ stone⟩ ⟨wriggled uncomfortably in his ~ chair⟩ ⟨these apples are very ~⟩ (2) : having rigid boards on the sides covered in cloth or paper ⟨a ~ binding⟩ ⟨selling methods . . . to fit the ~ books —Henry Garfinkle⟩ (3) : HARDWOOD 2 **b** *of liquor* (1) : having a harsh, sharp, or acid taste ⟨a ~ wine⟩ (2) : STRONG, SPIRITUOUS, INTOXICATING; *specif* : having an alcoholic content of more than 22.5 percent **c** (1) : characterized by the presence of dissolved substances (as salts of magnesium and calcium) that prevent the formation of lather with soap — used of water and water solutions (2) *of oil* : too thick to pour at ordinary temperatures (3) : characterized by radiation of relatively high penetrating power ⟨~ X rays⟩; *also* : relating to or constituting a high-vacuum tube that produces such radiation ⟨~ tube⟩ (4) : having or producing relatively great photographic contrast ⟨a ~ negative⟩ ⟨~ paper⟩ (5) : difficult to fuse or soften ⟨a ~ glass⟩ ⟨a ~ enamel⟩ **d** (1) *of money* : metallic as distinct from paper ⟨the colonies suffered from a shortage of ~ money⟩ ⟨ranchers . . . who were known to keep their wealth in the form of ~ money —W.H.Breen⟩ (2) *of currency* : convertible into gold or heavily backed by a gold reserve and typically stable, high, or appreciating in value ⟨the period of the eighteen-nineties witnessed a bitter struggle between the *hard*-money and the cheap-money groups —C.B.Swisher⟩; *also* : available to borrowers in limited supply and at high interest rates ⟨a *hard*-money policy⟩ (3) *of a currency* : soundly backed and usu. readily convertible into foreign currencies without restrictions or large discounts ⟨they require payment in dollars, pounds, or other ~ . . . currency —Joseph Wechsberg⟩ (4) : constituting currency as distinct from promissory notes or other documents of contingent value — often used as an intensive in the phrase *hard cash* ⟨he has to be paid in *hard* cash⟩ ⟨pay the writing schools ~ cash to liberate their muse —Edward Uhlan⟩ (5) *of prices* : high and firm **e** (1) : TIGHT — used esp. of yarns with many twists per inch (2) : NAPLESS — used esp. of woolen and worsted fabrics with a smooth clear finish (3) *of plumage* : close-fitting and firm in texture (4) *of individual feathers* : uniformly colored **2 a** (1) : capable of great physical exertion or endurance : not flabby or soft : physically fit ⟨nice animals in good ~ condition —R.M.Daw⟩ ⟨all likely lads in ~ condition —John Buchan⟩ (2) : resistant esp. to stress or disease : HARDY ⟨children of ~*er* stock —Ernest Beaglehole⟩ **b** : free of weakness or other flaw : STRONG, UNYIELDING, TEMPERED ⟨brought out of the war a character austere and not a little ~ —Edmund Wilson⟩ ⟨a man of ~ unbending will⟩ **c** (1) : not tentative or contingent : FIXED, DEFINITE, BINDING, CONCRETE ⟨failure . . . to make ~, firm decisions at high levels —*Science*⟩ ⟨the continuing lack of a ~ agreement with the U.S. —Benjamin Welles⟩ (2) : not speculative or conjectural : based on fact : objectively existent : FACTUAL, ACTUAL, RELIABLE ⟨backed by evidence which he considers ~ —*American Anthropologist*⟩ ⟨a comprehensive set of ~ figures emerged for the first time —*Time*⟩ ⟨most facts are independent of our volitions; that is why they are called ~ —Bertrand Russell⟩ ⟨~ evidence that the government's optimism is not unfounded —Sydney Gruson⟩ (3) : HARD-AND-FAST ⟨there can be no ~ line of division between these two groups of changes —Edward Sapir⟩ (4) : CLOSE, SEARCHING, CONCENTRATED ⟨took a last ~ look at the old homestead⟩ ⟨at a later date I will take a ~ look at my political future —*N.Y.Times*⟩ (5) *of news* : not trivial, diverting, or sensational : important in its economic, political, or other large bearing ⟨~ news refers to the less exciting and more analytical stories of public affairs, economics, social problems —F.L.Mott⟩ — compare SOFT **d** : free from sentimentality or illusions : viewing objectively or coolly : REALISTIC, PRACTICAL ⟨the ~ modern mind —*College English*⟩ ⟨the later version is ~*er*, less "poetic" in the Romantic sense, less sentimental —Louis MacNeice⟩ ⟨the most practical place to teach ~ practical thinking is in . . . sociology —*Nat'l Catholic Educational Assoc. Bull.*⟩ ⟨a Scotsman's ~, keen sense of the practical —R.W. Chapman⟩ ⟨notable for his ~ sense, frugality, and industry⟩ **3 a** (1) : difficult to bear or endure : not easy to put up with or consent to : GRIEVOUS, UNPLEASANT, DISTRESSING, BAD ⟨you've had very ~ luck⟩ ⟨the dory was . . . in ~ shape —G.W.Brace⟩ ⟨the ~ years dragged by⟩ ⟨too much reading is ~ on the eyes⟩ ⟨that traffic cop gave me a ~ time⟩; *specif* : economically depressed ⟨~ times followed, and domestic creditors suffered equally with the foreign —S.E.Morison & H.S.Commager⟩ ⟨the Alaska gold rush . . . put an end to ~ times —*Amer. Guide Series: Wash.*⟩ (2) : OPPRESSIVE, INEQUITABLE, UNJUST ⟨musicians also find it ~ that they must pay heavy duty . . . on orchestral instruments —*Report: (Canadian) Royal Commission on Nat'l Development*⟩ ⟨the ~ system of apprenticeship, virtual peonage, was failing rapidly —*Amer. Guide Series: Tenn.*⟩ **b** (1) : harsh or severe in one's dealings : lacking compassion or gentleness : UNFEELING, CALLOUS ⟨he was a stern, ~, cruel man —Anthony Trollope⟩ ⟨people who are ~, grasping, selfish —G.B.Shaw⟩ ⟨don't be too ~ on the boy⟩ (2) : INTRACTABLE, HARDENED, INCORRIGIBLE, TOUGH ⟨my first real assignment was as a sort of scoutmaster to a ~ gang of boys —R.M.Lovett⟩ ⟨a prison warden of long standing and accustomed to dealing with ~ cases⟩ (3) : devoid of fine or refined feelings : impudently bold : BRAZEN, SHAMELESS ⟨a ~, cheap, frightened floozy —Arthur Knight⟩ **c** (1) : harsh, severe, or offensive in tendency or effect : UNPALATABLE, CRUEL ⟨this is a ~ saying to people who have worked so much —Clement Attlee⟩ ⟨said some very ~ things to me⟩ : HOSTILE, RESENTFUL ⟨no ~ feelings, I'm sure⟩ : ROUGH, COARSE ⟨~ and frugal fare, yet we throve upon it⟩ : making no concession : STRICT, UNRELENTING ⟨he drives a very ~ bargain⟩ ⟨a credit to the ~ religious system under which they were bred —G.M. Trevelyan⟩ (2) : tending to put in a bad or sinister light : UNFAVORABLE, FORBIDDING ⟨~ stories too were told about him; something . . . concerning an hereditary propensity to eat men —Herman Melville⟩ (3) : RIGOROUS, INCLEMENT, VIOLENT ⟨one of the ~*est* winters in men's memories⟩ ⟨a ~, driving rain⟩ ⟨in ~ weather he stayed in his . . . house —Mary Webb⟩ **d** (1) : intense in force, manner, or degree : SHARP, PROFOUND, DEEP ⟨a ~ spell of coughing —Ellen Glasgow⟩ ⟨dealt him a ~ blow⟩ ⟨fell into a ~ sleep⟩ ⟨going at a ~ trot down that steep hill —Rachel Henning⟩ (2) : carried on, performed, or waged with great intensity, exertion, or energy : ARDUOUS, STRENUOUS, UNREMITTING ⟨got where he is by ~ work⟩ ⟨this question requires ~ thinking —W.H.Whyte⟩ ⟨with some the sell is ~, with big advertising budgets . . . and platoons of agents on the road —Blake Ehrlich⟩ (3) : performing or carrying on an activity or one's work with great energy, intensity, or persistence ⟨a ~ drinker⟩ ⟨one of the ~*est* workers on the floor⟩ ⟨a very ~ smoker —Tadhg Murphy⟩ (4) : subjecting to a severe strain : INTENSIVE, PUNISHING ⟨was nearing a century of ~ wear when it lost a cover —R.W.Chapman⟩ ⟨this garment will stand ~ use⟩ (5) : useful for a long time : DURABLE ⟨~ merchandise⟩ **e** : giving the impression of or suggesting hardness: as (1) : lacking in shading, delicacy, or subtlety : HARSH, STRIDENT ⟨this is for ~ big tone —Warwick Braithwaite⟩ ⟨it has a ~ but brilliant note —Robert Donington⟩ (2) : characterized by sharp or harsh outline, rigid execution, and stiff drawing ⟨exaggerated shadows to intensify crisp outlines and ~ forms —Katharine Kuh⟩ ⟨a portrait in the ~ but sincere and living fashion of the period —G.K.Chesterton⟩ (3) : sharply defined : STARK, CRISP, PRECISE ⟨looking . . . at the ~ shadows we cast on the ground —John Skölle⟩ ⟨in the early twilight the outlines of the castle loomed ~ and clear⟩ (4) : not softened or shaded in any way : GLARING, VIVID ⟨~ bright sunlight at the water's edge —Oscar Handlin⟩ ⟨the light is so ~ and brilliant that . . . you have to screw up your eyes —Thomas Wood †1950⟩ ⟨had the ~ dull flush of the steady heavy drinker —Thomas Wolfe⟩ ⟨staring at the ceiling in the ~ light of the one unshaded lamp —Nevil Shute⟩ (5) : sounding as in *arcing* and *geese* respectively — used of *c* and *g* or their sound (6) *of a consonant* : VOICELESS (7) : constituting a vowel before which there is no \y\ sound and no \y\-like modification of a consonant or constituting a consonant in whose articulation there is no \y\-like modification and which is not followed by a \y\ sound (as in Russian) — compare PALATALIZE (8) : indicative or suggestive of severity, firmness, toughness, or insensitivity of temperament or character ⟨the same faint, ~ smile around the edges of her mouth —Thomas Wolfe⟩ ⟨with a rather ~ mouth and a supercilious manner —Scott Fitzgerald⟩ ⟨a fund of English openness and good nature legible in his ~ features —William Heath⟩ ⟨a ~ pair of eyes that belied his unmanly, almost effeminate face —Barnaby Conrad⟩ — often used in combination ⟨a *hard*-faced businessman who knows all the latest salacious limericks —Harold Wincott⟩ ⟨a *hard*-eyed little man⟩ **4** : presenting difficulties, obstacles, or perplexities: as **a** (1) : difficult to accomplish, master, resolve, or acquire : not easy : TROUBLESOME, PERPLEXING ⟨this ailment is ~ to cure⟩ ⟨the American habit of tipping . . . is a ~ one to break —Richard Joseph⟩ ⟨of course all languages are ~ —Bernard Bloch⟩ ⟨a ~ decision⟩ ⟨she's playing ~ to get⟩ ⟨a distinctly ~ problem⟩ (2) : difficult to comprehend or explain : OBSCURE, DARK, THORNY ⟨a ~ saying, no doubt, . . . but it has its meaning —Havelock Ellis⟩ ⟨this is at first sight a very ~ saying, but a little consideration will show that it is only natural —J.A.Todd⟩ ⟨a book full of long, ~ words⟩ (3) : difficult to untie or unravel ⟨he tied his shoelaces in ~ knots —Erskine Caldwell⟩ **b** *archaic* : having difficulty in doing something **c** : attended or marked by drudgery, hardship, or other painful experience ⟨many perished on the long ~ march to safety⟩ ⟨fishing and lumbering . . . are ~ trades —Upton Sinclair⟩ ⟨the birth was ~ —Farley Mowat⟩

**syn** DIFFICULT, ARDUOUS: HARD is a general antonym for *easy* and is applicable to any activity requiring great exertion ⟨a *hard* task⟩ ⟨the *hard* work of digging the shaft⟩ ⟨a subject *hard* to teach⟩ ⟨inspirations such as these do not necessarily eliminate all the *hard* work that goes into developing them and putting them down on paper —J.D.Cook⟩ DIFFICULT may imply obstacles to be surmounted, problems to be solved, complications to be removed, simplifications to be made, or trials to be faced by skill, ingenuity, or resolution ⟨to climb a mountain which, as all who have climbed it testify, is long, steep, and *difficult* —W.R.Inge⟩ ⟨business of a delicate and *difficult* nature, which might get people into trouble —Charles Dickens⟩ ⟨trying to write things that have not been written before, and that were very *difficult* to write —Havelock Ellis⟩ ⟨the more *difficult* task of changing the ways of thinking, the habits, and the practices of the Japanese people —*Collier's Yr. Bk.*⟩ ARDUOUS may suggest need for perseverance and resolute exertion ⟨the local railways . . . worked their *arduous* ways up the mining valleys —O.S.Nock⟩ ⟨the *arduous* task of formulating legislation necessary to the country's welfare —F.D. Roosevelt⟩ ⟨the scientific spirit, like the spirit of sanctity, can be acquired only by the *arduous* methodical discipline —M.R. Cohen⟩ **syn** see in addition FIRM

— **hard up 1** : short of money : economically distressed ⟨he managed to pay his way although awfully *hard up* at the time⟩ ⟨the region was perennially *hard up*⟩ **2** : experiencing an acute want or deprivation of any kind ⟨far past the age when any woman, however *hard up*, would look at him twice —Ruth Park⟩ ⟨he's very *hard up* for friends⟩ — **the hard way** *adv* **1** : in a manner difficult to bear or accomplish : RIGOROUSLY, LABORIOUSLY ⟨had come up *the hard way*, through modeling, the chorus line, dramatic school, little theaters and bit parts in screen and TV shows —Fergus McGill⟩ **2** : by throwing a doublet in craps (as when the point is 4, 6, 8, or 10 and is made respectively by 2-2, 3-3, 4-4, or 5-5) ⟨to make 8 *the hard way* —C.B.Davis⟩

**²hard** \"\ *adv* -ER/-EST [ME *harde*, fr. OE *hearde*; akin to OHG *harto* extremely, ON *hartha*; derivative fr. the root of E ¹*hard*] **1 a** : with great or utmost effort or energy : VIGOROUSLY, STRENUOUSLY, EARNESTLY ⟨the men were ~ at work⟩ ⟨the lumbermen lived and played ~⟩ ⟨you've been going too ~ the last six months⟩ ⟨it forces one to think ~⟩ **b** : VIOLENTLY, FIERCELY ⟨drove the muzzle ~ into the gangster's face⟩ ⟨the rain came down ~⟩ ⟨the wind is blowing ~⟩ **c** (1) : to the full extent or the extreme limit — used in nautical directions esp. to the helmsman ⟨~ right⟩ ⟨~ alee⟩ ⟨~ aport⟩ (2) : to a considerable extent : MASSIVELY, LARGELY ⟨if . . . you wish to persevere with the present tree, cut it back ~ —*Sydney (Australia) Bull.*⟩ ⟨the strike cut production back ~⟩ **d** : in an immoderate manner : to an extreme degree : INTENSIVELY, UNREMITTINGLY ⟨he is hitting the bottle ~⟩ **e** : in a searching, close, or concentrated manner : INTENTLY ⟨looked ~ at him⟩ ⟨listen ~ to what I have to say⟩ **f** : in a sharp or emphatic manner : POINTEDLY ⟨the incident brought home to him ~ his inadequate grasp of the subject⟩ **2 a** : in such a manner as to cause hardship, difficulty, or pain : HARSHLY, SEVERELY, CRUELLY, BADLY ⟨the Stamp Act and other laws which bore ~ on colonial prosperity —H.E.Scudder⟩ ⟨such levies hit the poor ~*er* than the rich —*Collier's Yr. Bk.*⟩ ⟨things have gone very ~ with us⟩ **b** : with extreme rancor, bitterness, or grief : with animus or resentment of — often used with *take* ⟨this expansion of Russia's . . . was taken very ~ in the liberal Western world —*New Republic*⟩ ⟨it was his first taste of defeat . . . he took it ~ —S.H.Adams⟩ **c** : AUSTERELY, FRUGALLY ⟨they deserved to live ~ even if it deprived them of . . . leisure in which to think high —F.M.Ford⟩ **3** : TIGHTLY, FIRMLY, FAST ⟨hold on ~⟩ **4** : to the point of hardness ⟨like my eggs boiled ~⟩ ⟨the river froze ~⟩ **5** : with difficulty : LABORIOUSLY ⟨breathing ~ after that long run⟩ **6** : in close or immediate proximity in time or space ⟨caught the fish ~ in to the shore⟩ ⟨the house stood ~ by the river⟩ ⟨~ on the heels of the Supreme Court decision⟩ ⟨darkness was ~ at hand⟩ ⟨steamships berth ~ up against the main streets —William Sansom⟩

**³hard** \"\ *n* -S [ME, something that is hard, fr. *hard*, adj.] **1** *chiefly Brit* : a firm foreshore or landing place **2** *slang chiefly Brit* : HARD LABOR ⟨ten years ~ . . . for clouting some bloke —Richard Llewellyn⟩ **3** : ERECTION 2 — used in the phrase *hard on*; usu. considered vulgar

**hard-and-fast** \ˈ=ˌ=ˈ=\ *adj* : not subject to deviation, revision, or modification : rigidly binding : FIXED, CATEGORICAL, ABSOLUTE ⟨*hard-and-fast* rules⟩ ⟨*hard-and-fast* distinctions⟩ ⟨a *hard-and-fast* line⟩

**har·dang·er** \härˈdäŋər\ *n* -S [Hardanger, district in Norway] : embroidery of Norwegian origin worked over counted threads in a geometrical design

**hardanger fiddle** *n, usu cap H* [trans. of Norw *hardangerfele*, fr. *Hardanger* + Norw *fele* fiddle] : a fiddle of Norwegian origin with four stopped and four sympathetic strings used to accompany the halling and other Scandinavian dances

**¹hardback** \ˈ=ˌ=\ *adj* : HARD 1a (2)

**²hardback** \"\ *n* : a book bound in hard covers

**hardbake** \ˈ=ˌ=\ *n, Brit* : a sweetmeat of sugar or molasses and almonds

**hardball** \ˈ=ˌ=\ *n* : BASEBALL

**hard-bark hickory** *n* : MOCKERNUT

**hard beech** *n* : a tall beech (*Nothofagus truncata*) with very hard wood found in south temperate regions esp. in New Zealand

**hard-bill** \ˈ=ˌ=\ *n* : any of numerous birds with a hard strong bill adapted to cracking seeds and nuts — compare SOFT-BILL

**hard-bitten** \ˈ=ˈ==\ *adj* [*hard* + *-bitten* having (such) a bite (fr. *bitten*, past part. of *bite*)] **1** : having a hard bite : inclined to bite hard ⟨so *hard-bitten* an animal that all the torture you can use will not make him leave his hold —Martin Hunter⟩ **2 a** : seasoned or steeled in battle : tough in fighting ⟨*hard-bitten* tribesmen, their . . . faces flecked with the blood of the fighting —T.E.Lawrence⟩ ⟨the rangers . . . were a *hard-bitten* lot, and they went after outlaws in a businesslike way —W.M. Raine⟩ **b** (1) : seasoned or steeled in struggle or experience of any kind : having the qualities appropriate to a veteran ⟨this genial but *hard-bitten* career diplomat —*Newsweek*⟩ (2) : CONFIRMED, INVETERATE ⟨*hard-bitten* amateur high-fidelity operators —R.S.Lanier⟩ ⟨*hard-bitten* bachelors complained that they were too shy to approach women —*Atlantic*⟩ **3 a** (1) : marked by severity or austerity of character : of tough moral fiber : UNYIELDING, INDOMITABLE, RUGGED ⟨a *hard-bitten*, granite-faced, Scotch-Irish Presbyterian —*Newsweek*⟩ ⟨his *hard-bitten* New England independence —Edwin Clark⟩ ⟨one of those *hard-bitten* ruggedly individualistic men —Pamela Taylor⟩ (2) : full of difficulties or hardships : HARSH ⟨the life of the farmer was all too often a lonely *hard-bitten* existence —*Amer. Guide Series: Ind.*⟩ **b** : lacking polish or refinement : rough or coarse in manner or appearance : TOUGH, HARD-BOILED ⟨patronized by roistering, *hard-bitten* seafarers —*Amer. Guide Series: Fla.*⟩ **c** : lacking sensitivity or compassion : CALLOUS, RUTHLESS, HARD ⟨the typical story of the *hard-bitten* man who clawed his way to the top —V.P.Hass⟩ **d** : free of sentimentality or illusions : not credulous or naïve : TOUGH-MINDED, REALISTIC, PRACTICAL ⟨this *hard-bitten* gentleman has an aesthetic and romantic side —Stanley Walker⟩ ⟨a somewhat more *hard-bitten* scholarly segment . . . squared off for wordy battles with the faithful —M.W.Fishwick⟩ ⟨realistic, *hard-bitten*, and unrhetorical —*Saturday Rev.*⟩

**hardboard** \ˈ=ˌ=\ *n* : a composition board made by shredding wood chips by sudden release of high steam pressure and then compressing them with or without added binders or other materials at high temperatures

**hard-boil** \ˈ=ˌ=\ *vt* [back-formation fr. *hard-boiled*] : to cook (an egg) until hard-boiled

**hard-boiled** \ˈ=ˈ=\ *adj* [²*hard* + *boiled*] **1** : boiled until both white and yolk have solidified — used of an egg **2** : heavily starched : STIFF ⟨wore a double-breasted, dark suit and a collar . . .; it was one of those *hard-boiled* old-timers —F.C. Othman⟩ — compare BOILED SHIRT **3 a** : devoid of sentimentality or weakness : CALLOUS, TOUGH ⟨I, a *hard-boiled* South Sea trader, was genuinely shocked —*Atlantic*⟩ ⟨*hard-boiled* politicians⟩ ⟨a *hard-boiled* outfit under a *hard-boiled* leader —E.J.Fitzgerald⟩ **b** : of or relating to a literary form or production characterized by impersonal matter-of-fact presentation of naturalistic or violent themes or incidents, by a generally unemotional or stoic tone, and often by a total absence of explicit or implied moral judgments ⟨the *hard-boiled* tradition of detective fiction —John Paterson⟩ ⟨the novels of the *hard-boiled* school —George Stevens⟩ **c** : DOWN-TO-EARTH, PRACTICAL, HARDHEADED, REALISTIC ⟨from the *hardest-boiled* examination of the American system, this is a blueprint for disaster —A.A.Berle⟩ ⟨handle aid programs on a friendly but *hard-boiled* business basis —*N.Y. Times*⟩ ⟨a fundamentally *hard-boiled* permanently businesslike people —*Times Lit. Supp.*⟩

**hard-boiled·ness** *n* -ES : the quality or state of being hard-boiled

**hardboot** \ˈ=ˌ=\ *n* : a person devoted to horse racing ⟨the local ~*s* tramped or rode trolleys —*Newsweek*⟩ — used esp. of Kentuckians

**hardbought** \ˈ=ˈ=\ *adj* : gained or won by hard or intensive effort ⟨the ~ battle for political control —Allan Nevins⟩ ⟨lest the silent ~ knowledge show in his eyes —Ross Lockridge⟩

**hardbound** \ˈ=ˈ=\ *adj* : HARD 1a (2)

**hard brick** *or* **hard-burned brick** \ˈ=ˌ=-\ *n* : brick that has received the proper amount of burning in the kiln

**hard candy** *n* : candy made of sugar and corn syrup boiled without crystallizing and usu. fruit-flavored

**hardcase** \ˈ=ˌ=\ *n, often attrib* **1** : a person by nature incorrigible or intractable : a tough customer; *esp* : a hardened criminal ⟨small-time ~ —Mickey Spillane⟩ ⟨ran with a ~ crowd —Luke Short⟩ ⟨remained at peace with local ~*s* by giving demonstrations of his . . . gunnery —W.L.Gresham⟩ **2** : a person in a pitiful plight : a case of hardship ⟨my ~*s* were all of the literary sort —F.M.Ford⟩

**hard cherry** *n* : BIGARREAU CHERRY

**hard cider** *n* : fermented apple juice containing usu. less than 10 percent alcohol

**hard clam** *n* : a clam with a thick hard shell; *specif* : QUAHOG

**hard coal** *n* : ANTHRACITE

**hard-coated** \ˈ=ˈ==\ *adj, of a dog* : having a crisp harsh-textured coat

**hard core** *n* **1** *usu* **hardcore** \ˈ=ˌ=\ *chiefly Brit* : brick rubbish, clinker, broken stone, or other hard material in pieces used as a bottom (as in making roads and in foundations) **2** : an esp. resistant or enduring structural and usu. basic or central part of a larger entity: as **a** : the most militant, die-hard, or loyal element or nucleus of a group, organization, or movement ⟨this group, whose *hard core* . . . is the trade unions —C.J. Friedrich⟩ ⟨the party's *hard core* of stubborn ultraconservatives —*N.Y. Times*⟩ **b** : a group of refugees or displaced persons not readily sponsored or resettled because of physical or other incapacities; *specif* : a group of refugees requiring institutional care wherever they go ⟨*hard-core* cases — incurably sick people, bedridden old people, inevitable charges of the state —John Hersey⟩

**hard court** *n* : a lawn-tennis court with a paved surface (as of asphalt or concrete) — distinguished from *clay court* and *grass court*

**hard-cover** \ˈ=ˌ==\ *adj* : HARD 1a (2)

**hard crab** *n* : HARD-SHELL CRAB

**hard-drawn** \ˈ=ˈ=\ *adj* : drawn so as to produce great hardness and strength — used esp. of copper wire and tubing

**¹hard·en** \ˈhärdᵊn, ˈhȧdᵊn\ *vb* **hardened; hardened; hardening** \-d(ᵊ)niŋ\ **hardens** [ME *hardnen*, fr. ¹*hard* + *-nen* -en] *vt* **1** : to make hard or harder : make firm, tight, or compact: as **a** : to convert into solid or stiffer solid form ⟨~ an unsaturated oil by catalytic hydrogenation⟩ **b** : to make hard (as steel) by heat treatment, esp. heating and quenching in water, brine, or oil **c** : to compact (felt) by applying moisture, heat, friction, and pressure **d** : to decrease the swelling and raise the melting point of (the emulsion layer of a photographic material) by chemical treatment **2** *dial Eng* **a** : to make bold : urge on : ENCOURAGE **b** : to strengthen or confirm esp. in disposition, feelings, or a course of action : REINFORCE ⟨~*ed* him in his determination to leave at once⟩ ⟨a development that only ~*ed* his conviction that he was right⟩ **3** : to make callous or unfeeling ⟨~*ed* his heart against me⟩ ⟨its influence did not ~ him; he has always risen above cynicism —L.A. Triebel⟩ **4** : to make hardy or robust : INURE, TOUGHEN ⟨~ troops by long marches⟩ ⟨coarse foods . . . help to ~ the gums —Morris Fishbein⟩; *specif* : to inure to cold or other unfavorable environmental conditions (as by gradual exposure to lower temperatures or by decreasing the water supply) — often used with *off* **5** : to signify that the pronunciation of (a consonant letter) is plosive rather than fricative ~ *vi* **1** : to become hard or harder : acquire solidity, compactness, or rigidity ⟨mortar ~*s* by drying⟩ ⟨deviations ~ into modes of action —John Dewey⟩ **2 a** : to become confirmed or strengthened (as in feeling, disposition, or course of action) ⟨opposition began to ~ —L.S.B.Leakey⟩ **b** : to become hard in temper or disposition ⟨it was enough . . . to set up resistance in her: she ~*ed* —Elizabeth Bowen⟩ **c** : to assume an appearance or give an impression of harshness or severity ⟨her face ~*ed* instantly —Margaret Deland⟩ ⟨his face ~*ed* into anger —Liam O'Flaherty⟩ **3** : to become higher or less subject to fluctuations downward : FIRM, STRENGTHEN, STIFFEN ⟨prices . . . ~*ed* quickly and drastically —R.F.Yates⟩ ⟨~*ing* commodity markets⟩

**syn** INURE, SEASON, ACCLIMATIZE, ACCLIMATE: HARDEN, in the sense pertinent here, is to habituate or toughen, usu. by degrees, to what generally causes pain or discomfort, or to make slowly callous to what usu. affects the feelings ⟨frontier life *hardened* most men quickly to rough conditions, often to extreme privations⟩ ⟨not yet *hardened* to the wicked world of international politics —Dexter Perkins⟩ To INURE one is to cause one to submit unwillingly, to harden one to patient endurance of the objectionable ⟨they were *inured* to hardship and unafraid of the wilderness —*Amer. Guide Series: Tenn.*⟩ ⟨an experienced judge is more or less *inured* to criticism —W.F. Brown b.1903⟩ SEASON suggests a gradual bettering of condition or increase in ability brought about by time or experience, a maturing (of a thing) to a sound, reliable condition, or a maturing (of a person or a talent) to a greater efficiency or perfection in a particular activity or calling ⟨old wood, *seasoned* by the sea wind for many decades —*Amer. Guide Series: N.Y. City*⟩ ⟨a soldier, *seasoned* by many campaigns⟩ ⟨the chapters which follow have all been tried out and *seasoned* with discussion —H.A.Overstreet⟩ To ACCLIMATIZE or to ACCLIMATE is to adapt or to accustom to new and hitherto alien conditions, ACCLIMATIZE more frequently suggesting a human agency ⟨to help *acclimatize* the new arrivals to conditions on the continent —Hanama Tasaki⟩ ⟨sheep . . . *acclimatized* to the hills —F.D.Smith & Barbara Wilcox⟩ ⟨they were *acclimatized* now to the cool atmosphere of professional life —Mary Lavin⟩ ⟨I became so well *acclimated* to German customs —David Fairchild⟩ ⟨*acclimating* the disabled veteran to the job and adjusting the job to the veteran —*Current Biog.*⟩

**²harden** \ˈ(h)ä(r)dən\ *n* -S *often attrib* [ME *herdyng, herden, harden*, irreg. fr. *herdes, hardes* hurds — more at HURDS] *dial Brit* : a fabric made of the coarser parts of flax or hemp

**hard·en·abil·i·ty** \ˌhärdᵊnəˈbiləd·ē\ *n* -ES : the property determining the depth to which a ferrous alloy can be hardened by quenching

**har·den·ber·gia** \ˌhärdᵊnˈbərjēə\ *n, cap* [NL, fr. Franziska von *Hardenberg*, 19th cent. Austrian noblewoman + NL *-ia*] : a small genus of Australian woody climbers (family Leguminosae) with small violet-blue flowers

**hardened** *adj* [ME *hardned*, fr. past part. of *hardnen* to harden] **1** : made hard or harder ⟨~ brass⟩ ⟨~ roads⟩ **2 a** : grown unfeeling or callous ⟨~ as I am, I felt a thrill of horror —Allen Upward⟩ **b** : CONFIRMED, INVETERATE, VETERAN ⟨many of the findings will hardly appeal except to ~ Johnsonians —*Times Lit. Supp.*⟩ ⟨~ fishermen protested —L.F. Ranlett⟩ ⟨a commercial or otherwise ~ traveler —W.C. Brownell⟩; *specif* : confirmed in error or vice ⟨a ~ little reprobate —W.M.Thackeray⟩ ⟨a ~ heretic⟩ ⟨~ criminals⟩ **c** : grown or become inured or steeled ⟨the duty was easy for a ~ horseman —S.H.Adams⟩ ⟨~ fighting men⟩

**hard·en·er** \ˈhärd(ᵊ)nər, ˈhȧd(ᵊ)nə(r\ *n* -S : one that hardens: as **a** (1) : a worker who hardens steel objects by heating and quick cooling (2) : a preliminary alloy added to a melt in order to introduce alloying elements **b** (1) : a worker who hardens felt (2) : a machine for hardening felt **c** : a substance added (as to a paint or varnish) to impart greater hardness to the film **d :** a substance (as alum or formaldehyde) used in a gelatin film, emulsion, or processing bath to prevent swelling and softening during processing

**hardening** *n* -s [fr. gerund of ¹*harden*] **1 :** something (as a material used for converting the surface of iron into steel) that hardens **2 :** INDURATION 1d ⟨~ of the arteries⟩

**hardens** *pres 3d sing of* HARDEN

¹**harder** *comparative of* HARD

²**har·der** \ˈhärdə(r)\ *n* -s [Afrik, fr. D] *Africa* **:** GRAY MULLET

**har·de·ri·an gland** \(ˈ)härˈdirēən-\ *also* **harder's gland** *n, sometimes cap H* [after Johann J. *Harder* †1711 Swiss anatomist] **:** an accessory lacrimal gland on the inner side of the orbit in reptiles and birds but usu. degenerate in mammals

**hardest** *superlative of* HARD

**hard-face** \ˈ=,=\ *vt* **:** to weld a wear-resistant metal onto the surface of (a metal part)

**hard-favored** \ˈ=ˈ==\ *adj* **:** HARD-FEATURED — **hard-fa·vored·ness** *n* -ES

**hard-featured** \ˈ=ˈ==\ *adj* **:** having coarse, unattractive, or stern features

**hard fern** *n* **:** DEER FERN; *broadly* **:** any of several ferns of the genus *Blechnum*

**hard fescue** *n* **:** a European fescue (*Festuca ovina duriuscula*) that is a variety of sheep fescue and is sometimes used in permanent pasture and lawn mixtures

**hard-fiber** \ˈ=ˈ==\ *adj* [¹*hard* + *fiber*, n.] **:** vulcanized with zinc chloride — used of paper or boards

**hard fiber** *n* [¹*hard* + *fiber*, n.] **:** leaf fiber with heavily lignified walls that is hard and stiff in texture and is used in making cordage, twine, and textiles

**hard finish** *n* **:** a smooth finishing coat of hard fine plaster applied to the surface of rough plastering

**hardfisted** \ˈ=ˈ==\ *adj* **1 a :** having hard or strong hands esp. from labor **:** capable of hard physical labor **:** hardened to or by labor **:** STRONG ⟨had a ~ hired girl to help with the work —Floyd Dell⟩ ⟨~ sons of toil —Robert Grant †1940⟩ **b :** hard of will or temper **:** free of weakness **:** TOUGH, TOUGH-MINDED, RUTHLESS ⟨a ~ ruler and a demanding father —Diana Chang⟩ ⟨~ men of affairs⟩ **2 :** CLOSEFISTED, STINGY, MEAN ⟨as ~ . . . as any Boston landlord —G.W.Johnson⟩ — **hard·fist·ed·ness** *n* -ES

**hard goods** *n pl* **:** DURABLES

**hard-grained** \ˈ=ˈ=\ *adj* **1 :** having a close firm grain **2 :** of a hard nature **:** UNATTRACTIVE

**hard grass** *n* **:** any of several different grasses (as orchard grass and members of the genera *Sclerochloa* and *Glyceria*)

**hard ground** *n* **:** etching ground melted from a ball or cake onto a heated plate and spread while soft by means of a roller or dabber

**hardhack** \ˈ=,=\ *n* [¹ *hard* + *hack*, v.] **1 :** an American shrub (*Spiraea tomentosa*) with rusty tomentose leaves and dense terminal panicles of pink or occas. white flowers **2 :** HOP HORNBEAM **3 :** SHRUBBY CINQUEFOIL

**hardhanded** \ˈ=ˈ==\ *adj* **:** HARDFISTED — **hard·hand·ed·ness** *n* -ES

**hard hat** *n* **1** *Brit* **:** DERBY **2 :** a protective hat usu. with a metal crown worn esp. by construction workers

**hardhead** \ˈ=,=\ *n* **1 a :** a shrewd practical hardheaded person ⟨a prospect that moves ~s as well as visionaries⟩ **b :** BLOCKHEAD **2 a :** any of several fishes: as (1) *also* **hardhead trout :** STEELHEAD TROUT (2) **:** ATLANTIC CROAKER (3) **:** a small cyprinid fish (*Mylopharodon conocephalus*) of California streams; *also* **:** the related greaser blackfish **b :** GRAY WHALE **3 a :** RUDDY DUCK **b** *or* **hardheaded duck** \ˈ=ˈ==-\ **:** WHITE-EYED DUCK **4 a :** KNAPWEED — usu. used in pl. **b :** RIBGRASS **c :** SNEEZEWORT 2 **d :** CORN COCKLE **5 :** HARDHEAD SPONGE **6 a :** a hard brittle white residue obtained in refining tin by liquation and containing tin, iron, arsenic, and copper **b :** a refractory lump of ore only partly smelted

**hardheaded** \ˈ=ˈ==\ *adj* [¹*hard* + *headed*] **1 :** STUBBORN, WILLFUL ⟨always was ~ about what she wanted —Erskine Caldwell⟩ **2 :** not moved by sentiment or impulse **:** having no illusions **:** PRACTICAL, SOBER, REALISTIC ⟨a ~ appraisal of our position in Asia today —*N. Y. Times*⟩ ⟨~ realists⟩ — **hard·head·ed·ly** *adv* — **hard·head·ed·ness** *n* -ES

**hardhead sponge** *n* **:** any of several commercial sponges having a harsh but elastic and fairly durable fiber that occur off the West Indies and Central America

**hardhearted** \ˈ=ˈ==\ *adj* [ME *hardherted*, fr. ¹*hard* + *herted* hearted] **:** UNSYMPATHETIC, UNFEELING, CALLOUS, CRUEL, PITILESS — **hard·heart·ed·ly** *adv* — **hard·heart·ed·ness** *n* -ES

**hard-hitting** \ˈ=ˈ==\ *adj* **:** ENERGETIC, VIGOROUS, AGGRESSIVE, EFFECTIVE, INTENSIVE ⟨a *hard-hitting* advertising campaign⟩ ⟨writes a fast, *hard-hitting* prose —E.J.Fitzgerald⟩

**har·die** *or* **har·dy** \ˈhärdē\ *n, pl* **hardies** [prob. fr. ¹*hard* + *-ie* or *-y*] **:** a blacksmith's fuller or chisel having a square shank for insertion into a hole in the anvil

**hardie hole** *or* **hardy hole** *n* **:** a square hole in a blacksmith's anvil for insertion of the shank of a hardie

**hardier** *comparative of* HARDY

**hardiest** *superlative of* HARDY

**har·di·head** \ˈhärdē,hed\ *var of* HARDYHEAD

**har·di·hood** \ˈhärdē,hu̇d, ˈhȧd-, -di,-\ *n* [¹*hardy* + *-hood*] **1 a :** resolute courage and fortitude **:** strong will to prevail, withstand, or survive ⟨~ is the fisherman's talent by which he wins his living from the sea —Richard Jefferies⟩ **b :** self-assured resolute audacity or disdainful insolence ⟨no historian will have the ~ to maintain that he commands this . . . view —A.J.Toynbee⟩ **2 :** VIGOR, ROBUSTNESS ⟨a man of action . . . who greatly prized and honored physical ~ —J.D.Adams⟩ **syn** see TEMERITY

**har·di·ly** \-dᵊlē, -li\ *adv* [ME, fr. ¹*hardy* + *-ly*] **:** in a hardy manner **:** BOLDLY, STOUTLY ⟨stared back ~ —Clemence Dane⟩

**har·dim** \ˈhär,dim\ *n* -s [modif. of Ar *ḥirdhawn*] **:** STARRED LIZARD

**har·di·ment** \ˈhärdēmənt\ *n* -s [ME, fr. MF, fr. OF *hardiment*, *hardement*, fr. *hardi* bold + *-ment* — more at HARDY] **1** *archaic* **:** HARDIHOOD, BOLDNESS, COURAGE **2** *obs* **:** a bold deed

**har·di·ness** \ˈhärdēnəs, ˈhȧd-, -din-\ *n* -ES [ME *hardinesse*, fr. ¹*hardy* + *-nesse* -ness] **:** the quality or state of being hardy: as **a :** the condition of being inured to fatigue or hardship **:** capability of endurance or resistance ⟨a race of great ~⟩; *specif* **:** the ability of a plant to survive under adverse conditions esp. of low temperatures **b :** BOLDNESS, AUDACITY, TEMERITY ⟨somewhere ~ failed her —Elizabeth Bowen⟩

**har·ding·grass** \ˈhärdiŋ,gras\ *n, often cap* [prob. fr. the name *Harding*] **:** a perennial canary grass (*Phalaris tuberosa stenoptera*) of Australia and southern Africa introduced into No. America as a forage grass

**hard·ish** \ˈhärdish\ *adj* **:** rather hard ⟨the seats, though cushioned, were ~ —Lucien Price⟩

**har·di·shrew** \ˈhȧdi,shrü\ *n* [¹*hardy* + *shrew*] *Brit* **:** a common shrew (*Sorex araneus*)

**hard labor** *n* **:** compulsory labor imposed upon imprisoned criminals as a part of the prison discipline but not necessarily more severe nor greater in amount than that customarily performed by ordinary laborers

**hard-laid** \ˈ=ˈ=\ *adj, of rope* **:** twisted tightly so that the angle of the strands is about 45 degrees

**hard lay** *n* **:** a lay in which the strands of a rope are hard-laid for greater firmness and resistance to abrasive wear

**hard lead** *n* **1 :** unrefined lead made hard by impurities esp. of copper, antimony, and arsenic **2 :** ANTIMONIAL LEAD; *specif* **:** an alloy containing about 5 percent antimony — compare GRID METAL

**hard lines** *n pl, chiefly Brit* **:** hard luck ⟨it's damned *hard lines* to have a lot of planning . . . go for nothing —F.V.W.Mason⟩ — often used with *on* ⟨*hard lines* on the kid, I say —G.A. Wagner⟩

**hard liquor** *n* **:** DISTILLED LIQUOR

**hard liver** *or* **hard liver disease** *n* **:** a toxic hepatic cirrhosis of swine and cattle due to ingestion of the seeds of a tarweed (*Amsinckia intermedia*) in the northwestern U. S.

**hard·ly** *adv* [ME *hardely, hardly*, fr. OE *heardlīce*, adv. of *heardlīc* severe, bold, fr. *heard* hard + *-līc* -ly (adj. suffix)] **1 :** with force or energy **:** VIOLENTLY, VIGOROUSLY ⟨turquoise . . . earrings jangling down ~ on diminutive gold chains —Osbert Sitwell⟩ **2 a :** in a severe or harsh manner **:** ROUGHLY, UNFAIRLY, UNPLEASANTLY, BADLY ⟨things may go ~ with us . . . before the war is over —Nevil Shute⟩ **b :** with great or excessive grief or resentment ⟨had not believed that he would take it so ~⟩ **3 :** in a difficult manner **:** by hard work or struggle **:** with trouble **:** PAINFULLY ⟨the right to play croquet had been a ~ won concession —Osbert Lancaster⟩ ⟨wondering why the lesson had to be learned so ~ —Kamala Markandaya⟩ ⟨means of existence wrung so ~ from the soil —Sir Winston Churchill⟩ **4 :** only just **:** not quite **:** not altogether **:** BARELY, SCARCELY ⟨men who were ~ literate⟩ ⟨why, I ~ know him⟩ ⟨~ knew what to say⟩ ⟨this is ~ the time to discuss such matters⟩ — sometimes used in nonstandard construction with a superfluous negative ⟨horse thieves was so bad that a man couldn't ~ keep a . . . horse —J.F.Dobie⟩

**hardly ever** *adv* **:** almost never **:** very seldom ⟨we *hardly ever* see them anymore⟩

**hard maple** *n* **1 :** a maple with notably hard wood; *esp* **:** SUGAR MAPLE **2 :** the wood of a hard maple

**hardmouthed** \ˈ=ˈ=\ *adj* **1 a** *of a horse* **:** not sensitive to the bit **b :** OBSTINATE, STUBBORN ⟨~ women who laid down the law —John Galsworthy⟩ **2** *of a dog* **:** given to biting down hard on a retrieved bird

**hard·ness** *n* -ES [ME *hardnesse*, fr. OE *heardnes*, fr. *heard* hard + *-nes* -ness] **1 :** the quality or state of being hard: as **a** (1) **:** a property of solids, plastics, and very viscous liquids that is indicated by their solidity and firmness (2) **:** resistance of metal to indentation by an indenter of fixed shape and size under a static load or to scratching (as by a file or diamond cutting point) (3) **:** ability of a metal to cause rebound of a small standard object dropped from a fixed height (4) **:** the cohesion of the particles on the surface of a mineral as determined by its capacity to scratch another or be itself scratched — compare MOHS' SCALE **b :** a quality exhibited by water containing various dissolved salts (as of calcium and magnesium) that prevent soap from lathering by giving rise to an insoluble curdy precipitate and that cause incrustations in boilers or kettles — see PERMANENT HARDNESS, TEMPORARY HARDNESS; compare SOFTNESS **c :** a quality of radiation (as of X rays) that determines its penetrating power **d :** excessive contrast in a photographic negative or print **e** (1) **:** HARSHNESS, SEVERITY, CALLOUSNESS ⟨a ~ toward shop assistants by customers —Lucien Price⟩ ⟨free from all resentment, ~, and scorn —Oscar Wilde⟩ (2) **:** RIGOR, INCLEMENCY, DIFFICULTY ⟨the poverty of the country, the ~ of life —Felix Gilbert⟩ ⟨happier than the townsman . . . in spite of the ~ of his lot —G.E.Fussell⟩ (3) **:** freedom from sentimentality, weakness, or slackness ⟨it was Yeats's dryness and ~ that excited us —Louis MacNeice⟩ ⟨that doctrine of ~ which distinguishes the work of the best imagist poets —Jacob Isaacs⟩ **2 :** something hard to do or bear **:** HARDSHIP

**hard-nosed** \ˈ=ˈ=\ *adj* **:** HARD-BITTEN, STUBBORN ⟨a *hard-nosed* scrapping breed —Breck Porter⟩

**hardock** \ˈhär,dăk\ *n* -s [origin unknown] **:** BURDOCK

**hard-of-hearing** *adj* **:** of, relating to, or characterized by a defective but functional sense of hearing

**hard oil** *n* **:** an interior varnish that dries with a relatively hard surface

**hard pad** *or* **hard pad disease** *n* **:** a serious and frequently fatal virus disease of dogs related to and sometimes indistinguishable from common distemper but typically involving bronchopneumonia, severe diarrhea, and a peculiar thickening and hardening of the skin of the pads and nose which commonly peels away as the acute stage of the disease subsides

**hard palate** *n* **:** a part of the human palate supported by the maxillary and palatine bones

**hardpan** \ˈ=,=\ *n* **1 :** a cemented or compacted and often clayey layer in soil that hampers root penetration and results from accumulation of cementing material or may be caused by repeated plowing to the same depth — compare PLOW SOLE **2 :** a firm substantial fundamental part or quality of something **:** BEDROCK ⟨gets down to the ~ of the question⟩

**hard paste** *n* **:** a ceramic body consisting of kaolin together with china stone or with feldspar and flint **2** *or* **hard-paste porcelain :** true high-fired porcelain made with a hard-paste body — compare SOFT PASTE

**hard patch** *n* **:** a plate riveted or welded over another to cover a break

**hard pear** *n* **1 :** a southern African shrub (*Olinia cymosa*) having square stems, cymose white flowers, red drupaceous fruit, and hard wood that is used for making musical instruments **2 :** a southern African tree (*Strychnos henningsii*) with elliptical leaves and spherical one-seeded fruit about ¾ inch in diameter

**hard pine** *n* **:** a pine (as longleaf pine or a pitch pine) having hard wood and leaves usu. in groups of two or three; *also* **:** the wood of a hard pine

**hard put** *adj* [*put* fr. past part. of *put*, v.] **:** faced with difficulty or perplexity **:** being in a quandary **:** barely or hardly able ⟨was *hard put* to find a satisfactory answer⟩ ⟨were *hard put* to meet mortgage payments —*Current Biog.*⟩ — often used in the phrase *hard put to it* to ⟨*hard put* to it to account for the differences between the ancient Chinese and the ancient Egyptians —Bertrand Russell⟩

**hard road** *n* **:** a road that has been paved or otherwise hard-surfaced

**hard-rock** \ˈ=,=\ *adj, of a miner* **:** experienced in underground work in hard massive formations

**hard rot** *n* **:** any of several plant diseases characterized by lesions with hard surfaces and rotted tissue; *esp* **:** a disease of the gladiolus caused by a fungus (*Septoria gladioli*) that produces lesions on both leaves and corms

**hard rubber** *n* **:** a firm relatively inextensible rubber or rubber product: as **a :** a normally black substance having the texture of horn and made by vulcanizing natural rubber with high percentages (as about 30 to 50 percent) of sulfur and with or without other compounding ingredients **b :** a similar substance made from certain synthetic rubbers (as GR-S and nitrile rubber) and sulfur **c :** a similar substance made from natural or certain synthetic rubbers by the use of organic vulcanizing agents without elemental sulfur

**hard rush** *n* **:** a common rush (*Juncus effusus*)

¹**hards** \ˈhärdz\ *n pl* [ME *hardes, herdes* — more at HURDS] **:** HURDS

²**hards** *pl of* HARD

**hard sauce** *n* **:** a creamed mixture of butter and powdered sugar often with added cream and flavoring

¹**hardscrabble** \ˈ=ˈ==\ *adj* [¹*hard* + *scrabble*, n.] **:** yielding or gaining a bare or meager living with greatest difficulty or hardest labor **:** BARREN, IMPOVERISHED, MARGINAL ⟨ranges from ~ farms in the hilly portions . . . to productive farms on prairie land —*Social Forces*⟩ ⟨a rather ~ life . . . among people who had few comforts and amenities —Henry Beston⟩ ⟨a ~ farmer⟩ ⟨till their ~ acres . . . intensively —*Pa. Game News*⟩

²**hardscrabble** \ˈ"\ *n* **:** hardscrabble land ⟨homestead of field, stream, hayfield, and ~ —S.T.Williamson⟩

**hard seed** *n* **:** seed in which the testa is unusually hard and impervious to moisture and which is therefore slow in germinating unless treated mechanically or chemically

**hard sell** *n* **:** aggressive high-pressure selling or salesmanship — often used with *the* ⟨everyone had keyed himself up to the *hard sell* —*Business Week*⟩; compare SOFT SELL

**hard-set** \ˈ=ˈ=\ *adj* [ME *harde sette*, fr. *harde* hard (adv.) + *sette, set*, past part. of *setten* to set — more at SET] **1 :** hard pressed **:** HARD PUT ⟨it's *hard set* I am to walk —J.M.Synge⟩ **2 a :** fixed in rigidity **:** HARD, FIRM ⟨there is a *hard-set* line about his mouth —*Nation*⟩ **b :** subjected to the process of incubation by setting ⟨frightened a . . . gull from her *hard-set* eggs —E.A.Armstrong⟩

¹**hard-shell** \ˈ=ˈ=\ *adj* **1 a :** having a hard shell **b :** UNYIELDING, CONFIRMED, UNCOMPROMISING ⟨a *hard-shell* conservative⟩ **2** *often cap H&S* **:** of, relating to, or characteristic of the Hard-Shell Baptists

²**hard-shell** \ˈ=,=\ *n* **1 :** HARD-SHELL CRAB **2** *often cap H&S* **:** a Hard-Shell Baptist

**hard-shell baptist** *n, usu cap H&S&B* **1 :** PRIMITIVE BAPTIST **2 :** a strict and uncompromising Baptist

**hard-shell clam** *also* **hard-shelled clam** *n* **:** QUAHOG

**hard-shell crab** *or* **hard-shelled crab** *n* **:** a crab that has not recently shed its shell and hence has the shell rigid — used chiefly of edible crabs (as the blue crab)

**hard-shelled** \ˈ=ˈ=\ *adj* [¹*hard* + *shelled*, adj.] **:** HARD-SHELL

**hard·ship** \ˈhärd,ship, ˈhȧd-\ *n* [ME *hardshipe*, fr. ¹*hard* + *-shipe* -ship] **1 a :** SUFFERING, PRIVATION ⟨years of danger and ~⟩ ⟨inflation was a cause of ~⟩ ⟨a life of ~⟩ **b :** a particular instance or type of suffering or privation ⟨the losses and ~s . . . entailed by war —Bertrand Russell⟩ ⟨enduring cold, hunger, and other ~s⟩ **2 :** something that causes or entails suffering or privation ⟨cannot help thinking it a ~ that more indulgence is allowed to men than to women —James Boswell⟩ ⟨one of the ~s of town life . . . is the absence of spring water —*Amer. Guide Series: N. C.*⟩ ⟨all the ~s of the northern passage — head winds, fog —L.B.Schmidt⟩ **syn** see DIFFICULTY

**hard-sized** \ˈ=ˈ=\ *adj, of paper* **:** sufficiently sized to be relatively impermeable by water — compare SLACK-SIZED

**hard smut** *n* **:** a disease of wheat caused by nematodes of the genus *Tylenchus* that transform the kernels into galls resembling the smut balls of bunt

**hard soap** *n* **:** soap made by using sodium hydroxide or sodium carbonate — compare CASTILE SOAP

**hard solder** *n* [¹*hard* + *solder*, n.] **:** a solder that contains copper, requires a red heat to melt, and is used for brazing

**hard-solder** \ˈ=ˈ==\ *vb* [*hard solder*] **:** to solder with hard solder **:** BRAZE

**hard sponge** *n* **:** ZIMOCCA

**hardstand** \ˈ=,=\ *also* **hardstanding** \ˈ=ˈ==\ *n* **:** a hard-surfaced area (as at an airfield) for parking an airplane

**hardstem bulrush** *or* **hard-stemmed bulrush** \ˈ=,=-\ *n* **:** a widely distributed No. American bulrush (*Scirpus acutus*) that has hard rigid olive green culms and a rather stiff panicle; *also* **:** any of several closely related bulrushes

**hard-surface** \ˈ=ˈ==\ *vt* [¹*hard* + *surface*, v.] **1 :** to treat (as by paving or macadamizing) the surface of (as a road) to prevent muddiness **2 :** HARD-FACE

**hardtack** \ˈ=,=\ *n* **1 :** a hard biscuit or loaf bread made of flour and water without salt and baked in large or small forms — called also *pilot bread, ship biscuit* **2 :** any of several mountain mahoganies; *esp* **:** a spreading shrub or small tree (*Cercocarpus betuloides*) that has obovate distally serrate leaves dark green above and whitish below

**hardtail** \ˈ=,=\ *n* **1 a :** BLUE RUNNER **b :** a fish related to the blue runner **2 :** MULE

**hard tick** *n* **:** a tick of the family Ixodidae — compare SOFT TICK

**hard-times token** *n* **:** one of the tokens issued during the controversy between the Jacksonian administration and the Bank of the U. S. — called also *Jackson cent*

**hardtop** \ˈ=,=\ *n* [¹*hard* + *top*, n.] **1 :** an automobile with a metal roof **2** *also* **hardtop convertible :** an automobile similar to a convertible in lacking vertical posts between windows but differing in having a rigid top of metal or plastic that in some models is fixed and in others is either lowerable into the rear deck or demountable

¹**hard-top** \ˈ=,=\ *n* [¹*hard* + *top*, n.] **:** a hard-surfaced area or road

²**hard-top** \ˈ=,=\ *vt* **:** HARD-SURFACE

**hard tussock** *n* **:** a fescue (*Festuca novae-zealandiae*) common in New Zealand as a forage grass

**hard wall plaster** *n* **:** CEMENT PLASTER

**hardware** \ˈ=,=\ *n* **1 :** ware (as fittings, trimmings, cutlery, tools, parts of machines and appliances, metal building equipment, utensils) made of metal **2 a :** FIREARMS ⟨while the men spoke politely . . . most of them wore ~ —*Amer. Guide Series: Ariz.*⟩ ⟨riding up with plenty of ~ in sight —F.B.Gipson⟩ **b :** metal items of military equipment for combat use (as ships, guns, tanks, airplanes, and their parts) and major support items (as trucks, jeeps, radar)

**hardware cloth** *n* **:** galvanized screening of steel wire woven with a close mesh commonly ⅛ inch to ¾ inch

**hardware disease** *n* **:** traumatic damage to the viscera of cattle due to ingestion of a foreign body (as a nail or barbed wire)

**hardwareman** \ˈ=,=mən\ *n, pl* **hardwaremen :** a person who makes or deals in hardware

**hard waste** *n* **:** textile waste rejected during manufacturing processes after spinning and consisting usu. of twisted yarns

**hard wheat** *n* **:** a wheat with hard flinty kernels high in gluten and yielding a strong flour esp. suitable for bread and macaroni — compare DURUM WHEAT, SOFT WHEAT

**hard·wick·ia** \härˈdwikēə\ *n, cap* [NL, fr. Thomas *Hardwicke* †1835 Eng. artillery officer in India + NL *-ia*] **:** a small genus of Indian trees (family Leguminosae) having pinnate leaves and flowers in panicled racemes

¹**hardwood** \ˈ=,=\ *n* [¹*hard* + *wood*] **1 :** the wood of an angiospermous tree as distinguished from that of a coniferous tree, known orig. from hard European woods (as beech and oak) but including both the softest and the hardest of woods **2 :** a tree that yields hardwood **:** an arborescent angiosperm

²**hardwood** \ˈ"\ *adj* **1 :** having hardwood or made of hardwood **2 :** consisting of mature woody tissue ⟨~ cuttings⟩

**hard-wooded** \ˈ=ˈ==\ *adj* [¹*hard* + *wood* + *-ed*] **1 :** having hard wood that is difficult to work or finish **2 :** HARDWOOD 1

**hardworking** \ˈ=ˈ==\ *adj* **:** INDUSTRIOUS, LABORIOUS ⟨learned and ~ men —G.H.Turnbull⟩

¹**har·dy** \ˈhärdē, ˈhȧd-, -di\ *adj* -ER/-EST [ME *hardy, hardi*, fr. OF *hardi*, fr. past part. of (assumed) OF *hardir* to make hard, of Gmc origin; akin to OE *hierdan* to make hard, MD *harden, herden*, OHG *herten*, ON *hertha*, Goth *gahardjan*; causative-denominative fr. the root of E ¹*hard*] **1 :** BOLD, DARING, BRAVE, RESOLUTE ⟨displayed a ~ intrepid spirit⟩ **2 :** full of assurance or presumption **:** AUDACIOUS, BRAZEN **3 a :** inured to fatigue or hardships **:** capable of endurance **:** STRONG, ROBUST ⟨the boys were ~, robust . . . little fellows —Samuel Butler †1902⟩ ⟨small and ~ ponies —*Amer. Guide Series: La.*⟩ **b :** capable of living outdoors over winter without artificial protection or of withstanding other adverse conditions (as insufficient or excessive light, excessive moisture, drought, lack of nourishing food) ⟨~ plants⟩ ⟨a ~ breed of cattle⟩ — compare HALF-HARDY, TENDER

²**hardy** *var of* HARDIE

**hardy annual** *n* **:** an annual (as radish or spinach) capable of resisting frosts or light freezing — compare TENDER ANNUAL

**hardy border** *n* **:** an ornamental or decorative planting of hardy herbaceous perennials (as peony, iris, phlox)

**hardy catalpa** *n* **:** WESTERN CATALPA

**hardyhead** \ˈ=ˌ=,=\ *n* [prob. fr. ¹*hardy* + *head*, n.] *Austral* **:** SILVERSIDES

**hardy orange** *n* **:** TRIFOLIATE ORANGE

**hardy perennial** *n* **:** something that lasts from year to year or appears afresh from time to time ⟨the Borgias have been among the *hardy perennials* of historical literature —C.M.L. Beuf⟩ ⟨the climatic theory . . . one of those *hardy perennials* that the frosts of scholarship do not much discourage —Charlton Laird⟩

**har·dy·ston·ite** \ˈhärdēstə,nīt\ *n* -s [*Hardyston*, Sussex County, northern New Jersey + E *-ite*] **:** a mineral $Ca_2ZnSi_2O_7$ consisting of a zinc calcium silicate

¹**hare** \ˈha(a)(ə)r, ˈhel, |ə\ *n, pl* **hares** *also* **hare** [ME, fr. OE *hara*; akin to OHG *haso* hare, ON *heri*, W *ceinach*, Skt *śaśa* hare, OE *hasu* gray, OHG *hasan*, ON *hǫss* gray, L *canus* gray, white, hoary] **1 a :** any of various timid long-eared gnawing mammals (order Lagomorpha) with a divided upper lip, long strong hind legs adapted to leaping, and a short cocked tail that have soft usu. gray or brown fur turning white in some northern species in winter, usu. live in the open, feed chiefly on vegetation and bark, bear furred young with eyes open at birth, and are native to most parts of the world except Central and So. America, Australia, and Madagascar — compare COTTONTAIL, JACKRABBIT, RABBIT **b :** the fur or pelt of a hare often sheared and dyed to imitate more valuable furs **c :** a member of the family Leporidae — often used with a qualifying term ⟨African rock ~⟩ ⟨Asiatic harsh-furred ~⟩ **d :** an animal resembling a true hare in appearance or behavior **2 a :** one that is likened

European hare

to a hare: as (1) : a ridiculous person : FOOL ⟨made a ~ of him one time in my column —Sean O'Faolain⟩ (2) : the object of pursuit in a game of hare and hounds ⟨a flushed little ~ bounds past us, distributing the paper scent in his course —W.H.Rideine⟩ (3) *slang Brit* : a passenger traveling without a ticket ⟨the conductor came round and searched under the seats for ~*s* —Stephen Graham⟩ **b** : a topic for discussion or pursuit ⟨first raised this ~ about the decline of the novel —Harold Nicolson⟩ **3** *usu cap* **a** : an Athapaskan people west and northwest of Great Bear Lake, Canada **b** : a member of such people **c** : the language of the Hare people

**²hare** \"\ *vi* -ED/-ING/-S : to move swiftly : RUN ⟨scrambled down the wall and *hared* along the lane, my heart in my mouth —James Edwards⟩ — often used with *off* ⟨whichever team is called turns about and ~*s* off for base —J.B.Pick⟩

**³hare** \"\ *vt* -ED/-ING/-S [prob. alter. of ¹*harry*] *archaic* : to tease or harass esp. by frightening

**hare and hounds** *n* : a game in which two or more of the players start out first, scatter bits of paper for a trail, and try to keep ahead of the others who try to catch them before they reach a designated place

**harebell** \'=,=\ *n* [ME *harebelle*, fr. ¹*hare* + *belle* bell] **1** : a slender herb (*Campanula rotundifolia*) having blue flowers, cordate or ovate basal leaves, and linear stem leaves — called also *bluebell* **2** : WOOD HYACINTH

**¹harebrain** \'=,=\ *n* [¹*hare* + *brain*] : one who is flighty or foolish : CRACKPOT

**²harebrain** \"\ *adj* : HAREBRAINED

**harebrained** \'=¦=\ *adj* [¹*hare* + *brained*] : FLIGHTY, FOOLISH, CRACKBRAINED — **hare·brained·ness** \'=¦brānd̸nəs *also* -ndnəs\ *n* -ES

**hared up** *adj* [perh. alter. (influenced by ¹*hair*) of *het up*; fr. the tendency of the hair on a person's head or an animal's back to stand on end as a result of extreme excitement] *dial* : being in a state of angry excitement : IRATE

**hare-finder** \'=,==\ *n*, *Brit* : one that goes ahead of a coursing party in order to start the hare ⟨you stare about like a *hare-finder* —Thomas Shadwell⟩

**harefoot** \'=,=\ *n* : a long narrow close-toed foot characteristic of some dogs, esp. the American foxhound

**harefooted** \'=¦==\ *adj* [¹*hare* + *footed*] **1** : moving swiftly : FLEET **2** : having a harefoot

**harehearted** \'=¦==\ *adj* : easily frightened : TIMID

**hare kangaroo** *n* : HARE WALLABY

**harelip** \'=¦=\ *n* **1** : a lip congenitally cleft usu. in the center of the upper one but sometimes cleft both sides of center **2** : the deformity that a harelip exhibits

**harelipped** \'=¦=\ *adj* : having a harelip

**harelipped bat** *n* : a large tropical American fish-eating bat (genus *Noctilio*) exhibiting marked sexual dichromatism with the males orange-rufous and the females dark brown to drab

**¹ha·rem** *or* **ha·ram** *also* **ha·rim** \'harəm, 'her- *sometimes* 'hār-, 'här-, hə'rēm\ *n* -S [Ar *ḥarīm* harem, anything forbidden or sacred & Ar *ḥaram* harem, sanctuary] **1 a** : a house or part of a house allotted to women in a Muslim household and usu. designed for maximum seclusion — called also *seraglio*, *zenana* **b** : the family of wives, concubines, female relatives, and servants occupying a harem **2** : a group usu. of women associated with one man ⟨a literary lion with his ~⟩ **3** : a Muslim sacred place (as a mosque) forbidden to non-Muslims **4** : a group of females controlled by one male — used of polygamous animals (as the fur seal, pheasant, wild horse)

**²harem** \"\ *adj* : of a style or design resembling that associated with a Turkish harem — used esp. of a woman's dress having a full skirt with the lower edge gathered on a narrow band and then turned under

**ha·rem·lik** \-m,lik\ *n* -S [Turk *haremlik*, fr. *harem* (fr. Ar *ḥarīm* & Ar *ḥaram*) + -*lik* place] : HAREM 1a

**harem slipper** *n* : BABOUCHE

**ha·ren·gi·form** \hə'renjə,fȯrm\ *adj* [*harengi-* (fr. NL *harengus* — specific epithet of the herring *Clupea harengus* —, fr. ML *harengus* herring, of Gmc origin and akin to MD *harinc*, *hareng* herring) + -*form* — more at HERRING] : having the shape of a herring

**ha·ren·gu·la** \hə'rengyələ\ *n*, *cap* [NL, fr. ML *harengus* herring + NL -*ula*] : a nearly cosmopolitan genus of small herrings (family Clupeidae)

**hares** *pl of* HARE, *pres 3d sing of* HARE

**hare's apparatus** \'ha(a)(ə)rz-\ *n*, *usu cap H* [after Robert *Hare* †1858 Am. chemist] : an apparatus for comparing the densities of liquids in two separate vessels by means of their rise in two graduated vertical tubes immersed at their lower ends in the liquids and connected at the top by a third tube to which suction is applied

**hare's-beard** \'=,=\ *n*, *pl* **hare's-beards** : MULLEIN

**hare's-ear** \'=,=\ *n*, *pl* **hare's-ears** **1** : a European annual herb (*Bupleurum rotundifolium*) with perfoliate leaves that resemble rabbit ears and small yellowish flowers **2** *also* **hare's-ear mustard** : a glabrous annual herb (*Conringia orientalis*) having sessile entire leaves with prominent basal lobes

**hare's eye** *n* : LAGOPHTHALMOS

**hare's-foot** \'=,=\ *or* **hare's-foot clover** *n*, *pl* **hare's-foots** *or* **hare's-foot clovers** : RABBIT-FOOT CLOVER

**hare's-foot fern** *n*, *pl* **hare's-foot ferns** **1** : a fern (*Davallia canariensis*) of the Canary islands and Madeira having a soft gray hairy rootstock **2** : an Australian fern (*Davallia pyxidata*) **3** : a bristle fern (*Trichomanes boschianum*) **4** : SERPENT FERN

**hare's-foot trefoil** *n*, *pl* **hare's-foot trefoils** : RABBIT-FOOT CLOVER

**hare's-lettuce** \'=,==\ *n*, *pl* **hare's-lettuces** : an annual sow thistle (*Sonchus oleraceus*)

**hare's-tail** \'=,=\ *n*, *pl* **hare's-tails** **1** : HARE'S-TAIL GRASS **2** : COTTON GRASS

**hare's-tail grass** *n*, *pl* **hare's-tail grasses** : a European grass (*Lagurus ovatus*) with florets in a spike that resembles a hare's tail naturalized in California and New Zealand and used for dry bouquets

**hare's-tail rush** *n*, *pl* **hare's-tail rushes** : COTTON GRASS

**hare system** \'ha(a)(ə)r- 'he|, |ə-\ *n* [after Thomas *Hare* †1891 Eng. political reformer] : a system of proportional representation that aims to achieve party representation in the closest proportion to actual voting strength by transferring votes beyond those needed to elect a candidate from him to the next indicated choice — compare LIST SYSTEM, PREFERENTIAL VOTING, SINGLE TRANSFERABLE VOTE

**hare wallaby** *n* : any of several small Australian wallabies (genus *Lagorchestes*) that resemble hares and have hairy noses

**harewood** \'=,=\ *n* [alter. of earlier *aire-wood*, fr. obs. E *ayre*, *ayer* harewood (perh. fr. Friulian *ayar* maple tree, fr. L *acer*) + E *wood* — more at ACER] **1** : a greenish gray figured cabinet wood obtained by chemical treatment and dyeing of sycamore maple and sometimes other maples — called also *gray harewood* **2** : a strongly figured tropical American wood initially yellow but seasoning to silvery gray with greenish markings, obtained from a tree of the genus *Xanthoxylum*, and much used by 18th century cabinetmakers but now rarely available

**har·fang** \'här,faŋ\ *n* -S [Sw *harfång*, lit., hare catcher, fr. *hare* (fr. OSw *hari*) + *fånga* to catch, fr. OSw *fanga*, fr. MLG *vangen*; akin to OE *hara* hare and to OHG *fāhan* to catch — more at HARE, PACT] : SNOWY OWL

**har·grave kite** \'här,grāv-\ *n*, *usu cap H* [after Lawrence *Hargrave* †1915 Australian pioneer in aviation] : BOX KITE

**ha·ri·a·li grass** \,härē'ālē-\ *also* **ha·ri·a·li grass** \-lē-\ *n* [Hindi *hariyālī*, fr. Skt *haritālikā*] *India* : BERMUDA GRASS

**ha·ri·a·na** \,härē'änə\ *n* [fr. *Hariana*, town in northwest India] **1** *usu cap* : an Indian breed of large rugged milk and draft cattle included among the Brahmans in American studbooks **2** -S *often cap* : an animal of the Hariana breed

**¹har·i·cot** \'harə,kō, -,kät, *usu* -äd·+V\ *or* **haricot bean** *n* -S [F, perh. fr. *haricot* stew] : the ripe seed or the unripe pod of any of several beans of the genus *Phaseolus* (esp. *P. vulgaris*) used as a vegetable

**²haricot** \"\ *n* -S [F, fr. MF, prob. irreg. fr. *harigoter* to cut in pieces, fr. OF, perh. of Gmc origin; akin to OHG *heriōn* to lay waste — more at HARRY] : a stew esp. of mutton or lamb and vegetables

**har·i·jan** \'harə,jan\ *n* -S *often cap* [Skt *harijana* person belonging to the god Vishnu, fr. *Hari* Vishnu + *jana* person — more at KIN] : a member of the outcaste group in India : UNTOUCHABLE — used esp. by followers of Gandhi

**hari-kari** *var of* HARA-KIRI

**harim** *var of* HAREM

**haring** *pres part of* HARE

**har·i·o·la·tion** \,harēə'lāshən\ *n* -S [L *hariolation-*, *hariolatio* action of prophesying, fr. *hariolatus* (past part of *hariolari* to prophesy, divine) + -*ion-*, -*io* -ion; prob. akin to L *haruspex* soothsayer, diviner — more at YARN] : the act or process of deduction : GUESSWORK ⟨facts as distinguished from what classical scholars call ~*s* —George Saintsbury⟩

**har·i·son's yellow rose** \'harəsənz-\ *n*, *usu cap H* [after Mr. *Harison*, 19th cent. Am. horticulturist] : a hybrid rose (*Rosa harisonii*) with yellow flowers originating as a cross between the Scotch rose and the Austrian brier

**¹hark** \'härk, 'hȧk\ *vb* -ED/-ING/-S [ME *herken*; akin to OFris *herkia*, *harkia* to listen, MD *horken*, *hoorken*, OHG *hōrechen*, and perh. to OHG *hōren* to hear — more at HEAR] *vt* **1** *archaic* : to give ear to : listen to ⟨~ what he himself here saith —William Beveridge⟩ **2** *Brit* : to urge to go ahead or to return — used with directional adverb ⟨~*ed* forward his pack of hounds —G.W.Dasent⟩ ⟨there is but one that ~*s* me back —Henry Taylor⟩ **~** *vi* **1** : to pay close attention : LISTEN ⟨when . . . some far cry came faintly through the wooded hills I have seen him lift his hand and bid us ~ —Irving Bacheller⟩ — often used with *to* ⟨only natural for them to ~ to him —G.G. Black⟩ **2** *chiefly Scot* : WHISPER

**²hark** \"\ *n* -S : a shout of encouragement or guidance to hounds

**hark back** *vi* **1** *of a hunting dog* : to retrace a course until a scent is regained **2 a** : to turn back to an earlier topic or circumstance ⟨*hark back* . . . to a passage already quoted —Susanne K. Langer⟩ ⟨don't *hark back* to the old days unless you can be amusing about them —Agnes Rogers⟩ **b** : to go back to something as an origin or source ⟨archaisms that *hark back* to the early days of colonialism —C.J.Crowley⟩ ⟨this proposition *harks back* to Locke and Smith —*Quarterly Jour. of Economics*⟩

**hark-back** \'=,=\ *n* -S [*hark back*] : a reversion or reference to something past ⟨this *hark-back* to the caveman code —Philip Gibbs⟩ ⟨*hark-backs* to the yesteryear lore of the theater —Abel Green⟩

**harken** *var of* HEARKEN

**¹harl** *or* **harle** \'(h)ärl, '(h)ȧl\ *vb* -ED/-ING/-S [ME *harlen* to drag] *vt* **1** *dial Brit* : to drag, scrape, or pull (an object) usu. along the ground **2** *chiefly Scot* : to plaster (a surface) with roughcast ⟨the ~*ed* walls with which for many generations the Scots had finished their houses —Ian Finlay⟩ **~** *vi*, *chiefly Brit* : to troll for fish ⟨~*ing* for spring salmon —*Atlantic*⟩

**²harl** *or* **harle** \'hȧl\ *n* -S *Brit* : roughcast wall facing

**³harl** \'(h)ärl, '(h)ȧl\ *vt* -ED/-ING/-S [ME *harlen* to entangle] *dial Eng* **1** : to snarl up : ENTANGLE **2** *or* **harle** : to thread one leg of (a dead rabbit) through the other for ease in carrying

**⁴harl** \"\ *n* -S *dial Eng* : a tangled mass : SNARL

**⁵harl** \'härl\ *n* -S [ME *herle*, prob. fr. MLG *herle*, *harle*] **1** *or* **harle** : a fiber in a stalk of flax or hemp **2** : HERL

**har·lan's hawk** \'härlənz-\ *n*, *usu cap 1st H* [after Richard *Harlan* †1843 Am. physician and naturalist] : a hawk (*Buteo harlani*) of the southern U.S. that is similar to but darker than the red-tailed hawk

**har·lech** \'här,lek\ *adj*, *usu cap* [fr. *Harlech*, Wales] : of, relating to, or constituting a subdivision of the European Cambrian — see GEOLOGIC TIME table

**har·lem blue** \'härləm-\ *n*, *usu cap H* [*Haarlem*, city in the Netherlands] : ANTWERP BLUE

**har·lem·ite** \'härlə,mīt\ *n* -S *usu cap* [*Harlem*, a district of Manhattan borough, New York City + E -*ite*] : a native or resident of the district of Manhattan borough, New York City, north of Central Park between 8th Avenue and the East and Harlem rivers

**¹har·le·quin** \'härlək(w)ən, 'hȧl-\ *n* -S [alter. (influenced by obs. F *harlequin*, fr. MF, fr. OIt *arlecchino*) of earlier *harlicken*, modif. of OIt *arlecchino*, fr. MF *Helquin*, *Hannequin*, *Hennequin*, leader of a troop of malevolent spirits popularly believed to fly through the air at night, fr. OF *Hellequin*, *Hielekin*, *Hierlekin*, prob. fr. (assumed) ME *Herle king* (whence ML *Herla rex*) King Herle, mythical figure who may orig. have been identical with Woden, chief god of the Germanic peoples] **1 a** *usu cap* : a quick-witted zany servant who is a stock character in commedia dell'arte, appears variously in European and American pantomime and ballet as a clown, a foppish simpleton, a magician, and the languishing lover of Columbine, and usu. wears a mask and parti-colored tights and carries a lath sword **b** : BUFFOON **2** : HARLEQUIN DUCK **3 a** : a variegated pattern (as of a textile) **b** : a combination of colors in patches on a solid ground (as in the coats of some dogs) ⟨a Great Dane's handsome ~⟩

harlequin 1a

**²harlequin** \"\ *vt* -ED/-ING/-S : to make a patchwork of : MOTTLE ⟨his face was ~*ed* with patches of some white cream he used for his complexion —Frederick Buechner⟩

**³harlequin** \"\ *adj* **1** : of a type or style inspired by or characteristic of Harlequin ⟨~ hat⟩ ⟨a ~ day, a strayed reveler from April, in glittering lozenges of blue and silver —Elinor Wylie⟩ **2** : of variegated usu. brilliant color and pattern ⟨~ fish⟩

**har·le·quin·ade** \,härlək(w)ə'nād, ,hȧl-\ *n* -S [modif. (influenced by *harlequin*) of F *arlequinade*, fr. *arlequin* harlequin (fr. MF, fr. OIt *arlecchino*) + -*ade*] **1 a** : a play or pantomime in which the harlequin has a leading role; *esp* : an introductory burlesque scene dominated by a clown and a harlequin **b** : an extravaganza ballet that features a dancing clown and other figures of fantasy **2** : a plotless comedy : FARCE ⟨incomparably at his best in the audacious ~ —*Atlantic*⟩ ⟨life is . . . a ~ written by a madman —H.J.Laski⟩

**harlequin beetle** *n* : a very large tropical American longicorn beetle (*Acrocinus longimanus*) having very long legs and antennae and intricately patterned red, black, and gray wing covers

**harlequin bug** *also* **harlequin cabbage bug** *n* : a black stinkbug (*Murgantia histrionica*) brilliantly marked with red, orange, and yellow that is destructive to cabbage and related plants in tropical America and the warmer parts of the U.S.

**harlequin duck** *n* : a small variegated sea duck (*Histrionicus histrionicus*) chiefly of northern No. America, Iceland, and Siberia with the male being chiefly blue with many white markings and red-brown sides

**har·le·quin·ism** \'härlək(w)ə,nizəm\ *n* -S : an action or expression characteristic of a harlequin

**harlequin opal** *n* : an opal with small angular patches of brilliant color on a reddish ground

**harlequin pigeon** *n* : FLOCK PIGEON

**harlequin quail** *n* **1** : a small African quail (*Coturnix delegorguei*) that frequents low-lying grassy tropical areas and is a highly regarded game and table bird **2** : any of various chiefly tropical American quails (genus *Cyrtonyx*) having the sides of the head conspicuously patterned in black and white

**harlequin snake** *n* : CORAL SNAKE; *esp* : BEAD SNAKE

**harlequin table** *n* [prob. so called fr. a resemblance between the movable set of drawers and some of the stage machinery of the commedia dell'arte] : a little 18th century English table convertible into a writing desk by means of a set of drawers pulled up from the level top

**harling** *n* -S [fr. gerund of ¹*harl*] *Brit* : a method of angling for salmon in a large river by trailing a fly behind a boat while it is rowed back and forth from bank to bank

**¹har·lot** \'härlət, 'hȧl-, *usu* -əd·+V\ *n* -S [ME *harlot*, *herlot*, fr. OF *herlot*] **1** *obs* : one of the riffraff : ROGUE, VAGABOND, KNAVE ⟨called him openly "beggarly ~ and cutthroat" —*Durham Depositions*⟩; *specif* : FORNICATOR ⟨the ~ king is quite beyond my arm —Shak.⟩ **2** : a disreputable woman; *specif* : PROSTITUTE

**²harlot** \"\ *adj* **1** : of or relating to a harlot ⟨~ house⟩ **2** : not subject to control : FICKLE ⟨pursuing the ~ goddess Fame —W.A.White⟩

**³harlot** \"\ *vi* -ED/-ING/-S : PROSTITUTE

**har·lot·ry** \-lətrē, -ri\ *n* -ES [ME *harlotrie*, fr. ¹*harlot* + -*rie* -ry] **1** *obs* : coarse or ribald speech or action : OBSCENITY **2** : PROSTITUTION **3** : an unprincipled or immoral woman : BAGGAGE 4 ⟨he sups tonight with a ~ —Shak.⟩ **4** : tawdry attractiveness : VULGARITY ⟨brightly rouged and painted — but without ~, with a careful art —William Sansom⟩

**harls** *pres 3d sing of* HARL, *pl of* HARL

**¹harm** \'härm, 'hȧm\ *n* -S [ME, fr. OE *hearm*; akin to OHG *harm* disgrace, injury, ON *harmr* grief, OSlav *sramŭ* shame] **1 a** : physical or mental damage : INJURY ⟨safety glass protects passengers from ~⟩ ⟨where the dune belt and the beach are both wide the sea did little ~ —J.A.Steers⟩ **b** : MISCHIEF, HURT, DISSERVICE ⟨his preelection declaration of independence had done him no ~ —Virginia Prewett⟩ **2** : an act or instance of injury ⟨guess at intents and assume ~*s* —Burges Johnson⟩; *specif* : a material and tangible detriment or loss to a person, whether or not the law grants a remedy — distinguished from *injury* **syn** see INJURY — **out of harm's way** : in a safe place : remote from sources of injury ⟨a loudspeaker set high *out of harm's way* —Evelyn Waugh⟩

**²harm** \"\ *vt* -ED/-ING/-S [ME *harmen*, fr. OE *hearmian*, fr. *hearm*, n.] : to cause hurt or damage to : INJURE ⟨the national interest . . . was gravely ~*ed* by this attack —Elmer Davis⟩ **syn** see INJURE

**³harm** \"\ *adj* [¹*harm*] *South* : DISRESPECTFUL, UNKIND, HARMFUL ⟨never said a ~ word against your daddy —T.H.Phillips⟩

**har·mal** \'härməl\ *or* **har·ma·la** \-lə\ *or* **har·mel** \-məl\ *n* -S [NL *harmala*, fr. Gk, perh. of Sem origin; akin to Ar *harmalah* harmal] : an herb (*Peganum harmala*) of India and the Levant with strong-scented seeds that yield several alkaloids and are used as a vermifuge and stimulant

**har·ma·line** \'härmə,lēn, -lən\ *n* -S [ISV *harmal* + -*ine*] : a crystalline alkaloid $C_{13}H_{14}N_2O$ found in harmal seeds; dihydro-harmine

**har·ma·lol** \-,lȯl, -,lōl\ *n* -S [ISV *harmal* + -*ol*] : a brown crystalline phenolic alkaloid $C_{12}H_{12}N_2O$ found in harmal seeds

**har·man** \'härmən\ *also* **harman beck** *n* -S [origin unknown] *archaic* : CONSTABLE, BEADLE ⟨not the lad to betray anyone to the *harman beck* —Sir Walter Scott⟩

**har·mat·tan** \,härmə'tan, här'mad·ᵊn\ *n* -S [Twi *haramata*, perh. fr. Ar *harām* forbidden or evil thing; akin to Ar *ḥaram* harem] : a dry dust-laden wind blowing from the interior on the Atlantic coast of Africa in some seasons

**harm·er** \'härmər\ *n* -S : one that harms

**harm·ful** \'härmfəl, 'hȧm-\ *adj* [ME, fr. ¹*harm* + -*ful*] : DAMAGING, TROUBLESOME, INJURIOUS ⟨~ drug⟩ ⟨~ influence⟩

**harm·ful·ly** \-f(ə)lē, -li\ *adv* : in a harmful manner

**harm·ful·ness** *n* -ES : the quality or state of being harmful

**har·mine** \'här,mēn, -mən\ *n* -S [ISV *harmal* + -*ine*] : a white crystalline alkaloid $C_{13}H_{12}N_2O$ found in harmal seeds; harmalol methyl ether

**harm·less** \'härmləs, 'hȧm-\ *adj* [ME *harmles*, fr. ¹*harm* + -*les*, -*lees* -less] **1** : free from harm : UNHURT **2** : free of guilt : INNOCENT ⟨any child or ~ thing —W.H.Davies⟩ **3** : free from liability or loss — often used in the phrase *to save harmless* or *to hold harmless* ⟨the company shall indemnify and save ~ each member of the committee against any and all expenses —C.M.Winslow⟩ **4** : free of or lacking capacity or intent to injure : INNOCUOUS ⟨the first ball was ~ —Dorothy Sayers⟩ ⟨~ craze for the small lions of literary society —W.S.Maugham⟩ ⟨~ joke⟩

**harmless error** *n* : a trivial technical error of law not requiring in the interests of justice a reversal of a judgment or the setting aside of a verdict or a new trial

**harm·less·ly** *adv* : in a harmless manner

**harm·less·ness** *n* -ES : the quality or state of being harmless

**har·mol·i·ta** \här'mäləd·ə\ *n*, *cap* [NL] : a genus of chalcid flies (family Eurytomidae) including numerous forms with larvae that feed in the stems of cereal grasses and weaken and distort them — see WHEAT JOINTWORM

**har·mo·nia** \här'mōnēə, -nyə\ *n* -S [NL, fr. Gk, harmonic suture, joint — more at HARMONY] : HARMONIC SUTURE

**harmoniacal** *adj* [LL *harmoniacus* musical (fr. L *harmonia* harmony) + E -*al*] *obs* : HARMONIOUS

**har·mo·ni·al** \här'mōnēəl\ *adj* [L *harmonia* + E -*al*] *archaic* : HARMONIOUS

**¹har·mon·ic** \(')här'mänik, (')hȧ'-, -nēk\ *or* **har·mon·i·cal** \-nəkəl\ *adj* [*harmonic* fr. L *harmonicus*, fr. Gk *harmonikos*, fr. *harmonia* harmony + -*ikos* -ic; *harmonical* fr. L *harmonicus* + E -*al*] **1** *archaic* : of or relating to music : MUSICAL ⟨where the ~ meetings take place —Charles Dickens⟩; *specif* : relating to the melody of ancient music as distinct from its rhythm **2** : of or relating to harmony as distinguished from melody or rhythm ⟨subtleties of ~ change and tonality —Ralph Hill⟩ **3 a** : of agreeable musical consonance : HARMONIOUS ⟨~ chant⟩ **b** : pleasing to the ear : HARMONIZED ⟨great ~ orchestral effects of the older verse —J.L.Lowes⟩ **4** : expressible in terms of sine or cosine functions — see HARMONIC PROGRESSION **5** : of an integrated nature : CONGRUOUS ⟨a creative, ~, loving human being —M.F.A.Montagu⟩; *specif* : having the general proportions of the body in harmony with each other (as elongated face with elongated skull) **6** : of or relating to harmonics ⟨size of the resonating cavity cannot be the only determinant of the ~ response —Robert Donington⟩; *specif* : sounding an octave or more higher than another organ stop of similar length ⟨~ flute⟩

**²harmonic** \'=¦==\ *n* -S **1 a** : one of a series of overtones or upper partials; *esp* : one produced by a vibration frequency which is an integral multiple of the vibration rate producing the fundamental ⟨the ear possesses the very odd characteristic of imagining the existence of the fundamental even when it is not present, if the ~*s* are strong —Oliver Read⟩ — compare NODE 5 **b** : a flutelike tone produced on a stringed instrument (as violin or harp) by touching a vibrating string at a nodal point causing one of the vibrating sections to determine the higher pitch in the harmonic series in direct proportion to the vibration frequency of the vibrating segment — called also *flageolet tone* **2** : a component frequency of a harmonic motion (as of an electromagnetic wave) that is an integral multiple of the fundamental frequency ⟨the second ~ has a frequency that is two times that of the fundamental⟩ ⟨if the current wave is analyzed mathematically, it is found to have a third ~ about one-third the amplitude of the fundamental 60-cycle wave —B.F.Bailey & J.S.Gault⟩ ⟨at the frequencies used for television signals, more so than on the broadcast bands, the second, third, and fourth ~*s* of the local oscillator in a superheterodyne receiver are liable to interfere with other sections of the receiver —*Television & Radar Encyc.*⟩

**har·mon·i·ca** \här'mänəkə, hȧ'-, -nēkə\ *n* -S [alter. (influenced by ¹*harmonic*) of *armonica*] **1** : GLASS HARMONICA **2** : an instrument of graduated strips of glass or metal struck with hammers **3** : a small rectangular wind instrument with free metallic reeds recessed in adjacent air slots along its length from which alternate tones of the scale are sounded by exhaling and inhaling and chords or single notes are produced depending on the number of slots covered by the mouth — called also *mouth organ*

harmonica 3

**har·mon·i·cal·ly** \-nək(ə)lē, -nēk-, -li\ *adv* **1** *obs* : HARMONIOUSLY ⟨the same spirit ~ works in all believers through the world —John Flavel⟩ **2** : in respect to relations or properties bearing some resemblance to those of musical consonances **3** : in respect to harmony as distinguished from melody ⟨feels music melodically before he feels it ~ —Neville Cardus⟩ **4** : in harmonic progression or division

**har·mon·i·cal·ness** *n* -ES : the quality or state of being harmonic

**harmonic analysis** *n* : the approximate expression of a periodic function known only for some values of the independent variable in a finite series of sines and cosines

**harmonic analyzer** *n* : a machine for the automatic resolution of periodic curves into the component sine curves of which they may be regarded as the resultants

**harmonic close** *n* : CADENCE 2b

**harmonic conjugates** *n pl* : the two points that divide a line segment internally and externally in the same ratio

**harmonic distortion** *n* : distortion in which harmonics of an

input signal are produced in an amplifier and appear in the output along with the amplified input signal
**harmonic division** *n* **:** the division of a line segment at two points internally and externally in the same ratio — compare HARMONIC CONJUGATES
**har·mon·i·chord** \här'mänə,kȯrd\ *n* -s [F *harmonicorde*, fr. *harmonie* harmony (fr. OF *armonie*) + *-corde* -chord — more at HARMONY] **:** a keyboard instrument in which a sustained string tone is produced by the action of a rotating wooden cylinder on the strings — compare SOSTINENTE PIANOFORTE
**harmonic interval** *n* **:** the pitch relation between simultaneous musical tones
**har·mon·i·cism** \här'mänə,sizəm\ *n* -s **:** the quality or state of being harmonic
**harmonic law** *n* **:** the third of Kepler's laws of planetary motion
**harmonic mean** *n* **1 :** the reciprocal of the arithmetic mean of the reciprocals of two or more quantities **2 :** one of the terms between the first and last terms of a harmonic progression
**harmonic minor scale** *n* **:** a minor scale like the natural form except that the 7th tone is raised by a half step (as A-B-C-D-E-F-G♯-A)
**harmonic motion** *n* **:** a vibratory motion that has one frequency or amplitude (as that of a sounding violin string or swinging pendulum) or a vibratory motion that is composed of two or more such simple vibratory motions— see SIMPLE HARMONIC MOTION
**har·mon·i·con** \här'mänəkən, hä'-, -nē,kän\ *n, pl* **harmoni·ca** \-kə\ [Gk *harmonikon*, neut. of *harmonikos* musical — more at HARMONIC] **1 :** HARMONICA **2 :** ORCHESTRION
**harmonic progression** *n* **:** a progression the reciprocals of whose terms form an arithmetic progression
**harmonic row** *or* **harmonic range** *n* **:** a set of four collinear points — compare HARMONIC CONJUGATES
**har·mon·ics** \här'mäniks, hä'-, -nēks\ *n pl but usu sing in constr* **:** the doctrine or science of musical sounds
**harmonic sequence of vowels :** VOWEL HARMONY
**harmonic series** *n* **1 :** the divergent series 1+½+⅓+¼+⅕+ . . . **2 :** a series of partial tones consisting of a fundamental tone or first harmonic and all the overtones whose frequency ratio to it can be expressed in whole numbers, these harmonics usu. being consecutively numbered

C c g c′ e′ g′ ♭b′ c″d″e″♯f″g″
1 2 3 4 5 6 7 8 9 10 11 12

harmonic series with C as the fundamental

**harmonic sign** *or* **harmonic mark** *n* **:** a small circle ○ placed over a note in stringed-instrument music to indicate that it is to be played as a harmonic
**harmonic stop** *n* **:** a pipe-organ stop composed of pipes so constructed as to sound an octave or more higher than regular pipes of similar length
**harmonic suture** *n* **:** an immovable body joint formed by the contact of relatively smooth surfaces (as bones of the skull)
**harmonic synthesizer** *n* **:** a mechanical device (as a tide-predicting machine) that combines differing harmonics and graphs the result
**harmonic theory** *n* **:** a postulate in phonetics: the reinforcing vibrations produced in the superglottic cavities in vowel articulation are harmonics of the fundamental vocal-cord note — compare FORMANT, INHARMONIC THEORY
**harmonies** *pl of* HARMONY
**har·mo·ni·ous** \(')här¦mōnēəs, (')hä¦-, -nyəs\ *adj* [MF *armonieux, harmonieux*, fr. *armonie, harmonie* harmony — more at HARMONY] **1 :** musically concordant **:** agreeably consonant **2 :** having the component parts agreeably related to each other **:** CONGRUOUS ⟨~ medley of small vaulted chambers —Norman Douglas⟩ **3 :** marked by accord in sentiment or action **:** COMPATIBLE ⟨~ relationship between church and state —H.D.Hazeltine⟩ — **har·mo·ni·ous·ness** *n* -ES
**har·mo·ni·ous·ly** *adv* **:** in a harmonious manner **:** COMPATIBLY ⟨for such a large group of relatives to coexist ~ . . is an accomplishment —Freeman Lincoln⟩
**har·mon·i·phon** \här'mänə,fän\ *also* **har·mon·i·phone** \-,fōn\ *n* -s [prob. fr. F *harmoniphon*, fr. *harmonie* harmony (fr. OF *armonie*) + *-phon* (fr. Gk *phōnē* sound) — more at HARMONY, BAN] **:** an obsolete wind instrument consisting of a series of reed pipes blown with a single mouthpiece and controlled by means of a keyboard, the tone resembling that of the oboe
**har·mo·nist** \'härmənəst, 'häm-\ *n* -s [*harmony* + *-ist*] **1 a :** a member of a school of theorists in ancient Greece basing the principles of music on the subjective effects of tones rather than on their mathematical relations **b :** one who composes or performs music **c :** one skilled in harmony **2 :** one who shows the agreement or harmony of corresponding passages of different literary works (as the Gospels) ⟨editorial ~s of the Pentateuch —*Interpreter's Bible*⟩ **3 :** HARMONIZER **4** *usu cap* [*Harmony*, community in Pennsylvania + E *-ist*] **:** HARMONITE
**har·mo·nis·tic** \¦==¦nistik, -tēk\ *adj* **:** of, relating to, or characteristic of a harmony or harmonist ⟨~ methods⟩ — **har·mo·nis·ti·cal·ly** \-tək(ə)lē\ *adv*
**har·mo·nite** \'härmə,nīt\ *n* -s *usu cap* [*Harmony*, community in Pennsylvania founded in 1803 by the Harmonites + E *-ite*] **:** a member of an 18th century German communal religious sect that settled in Pennsylvania in 1803 — called also *Rappist*
**har·mo·ni·um** \här'mōnēəm, hä'-, -nyəm\ *n* -s [F, fr. *harmonie* harmony, fr. OF *armonie*] **:** REED ORGAN; *specif* **:** a keyboard instrument in which the tones are produced by forcing air through free metallic reeds by means of a bellows — contrasted with *American organ*
**har·mo·niz·able** \'härmə,nīzəbəl\ *adj* **:** capable of being brought into harmony
**har·mo·ni·za·tion** \,härmənə'zāshən, ,häm-, -nī-\ *n* -s **1 :** the quality or state of being in harmony ⟨style of ~⟩ **2 :** an act or instance of producing harmony ⟨has developed a wonderful faculty for ~ —Herbert Read⟩; *specif* **:** a piece of harmonized music ⟨~ for string quartet⟩
**har·mo·nize** \'härmə,nīz, 'häm-\ *vb* -ED/-ING/-S *see -ize in Explan Notes* [MF *harmoniser* to bring into harmony, fr. *armonie, harmonie* + *-iser* -ize] *vi* **1 :** to play or sing in harmony ⟨four small children who have been *harmonizing* in the next compartment since 6:00 a.m. —Bennett Cerf⟩ **2 a :** to be in accord **:** CORRELATE ⟨designed to ~ with normal feeding operations —W.F.Brown b.1903⟩ **b :** to become pleasingly related **:** BLEND ⟨furnishings and architecture ~ —Edgar Kaufmann⟩; *specif* **:** to unite in harmony ⟨the tenor and alto parts ~⟩ ~ *vt* **1 :** to bring into consonance **:** relate harmoniously ⟨~ the interests of his various properties —J.B. Hedges⟩ **2 :** to bring into accord **:** RECONCILE ⟨~ its practices . . . with its professed ideals —Vera M. Dean⟩ **3 :** to provide or accompany with harmony (as a melody) **syn** see AGREE
**har·mo·niz·er** \-zə(r)\ *n* -s **:** one that harmonizes
**har·mon·o·graph** \här'mänə,graf\ *n* [ISV *harmono-* (fr. Gk *harmonia* concord, harmony) + *-graph*] **:** an instrument for combining two or more vibrations usu. of two pendulums at right angles to each other and recording them in a single curve — compare LISSAJOUS FIGURE
**har·mo·ny** \'härmənē, 'häm-, -ni\ *n* -ES [ME *armonye*, fr. MF *armonie*, fr. OF, fr. L *harmonia*, fr. Gk, joint, concord, harmony, fr. *harmos* joint, fastening — more at ARM] **1 a** *archaic* **:** tuneful sound **:** MELODY ⟨ten thousand harps that tuned angelic *harmonies* —John Milton⟩ **b :** musicality of language ⟨tonal ~ of the poem —C.S.Kilby⟩ **2 a :** the combination of simultaneous musical notes into a chord (as a triad) **b :** the structure of a piece of music according to the composition and progression of its chords — compare MELODY, RHYTHM **c :** the science of the structure, relation, and progression of chords in homophonic composition **3 :** combination into a consistent whole **:** INTEGRATION ⟨~ of man and the machine in modern war —George Barrett⟩ **4 a :** CORRESPONDENCE, AGREEMENT, ACCORD ⟨the fullest freedom . . . comes when our desires are in ~ with those of our neighbors —A.H.Compton⟩ **b :** internal calm **:** TRANQUILLITY ⟨the moral task for man, if he is to achieve ~, is to . . . assure the supremacy of the good —Norman Kelman⟩ **5 :** a systematic arrangement of parallel literary passages (as of the Gospels) for the purpose of showing agreement or harmony **6 :** HARMONIC SUTURE **7 :** the arrangement of parts in pleasing relation to each other ⟨~ of his face —Alvin Redman⟩; *specif* **:** the orderly combination of colors resulting in an aesthetically pleasing general effect ⟨relations of contrast and ~ —John Dewey⟩ — compare COLOR BALANCE
**harmony of the spheres :** a doctrine promulgated by the Pythagoreans that the celestial spheres are separated by intervals corresponding to the relative lengths of strings that produce harmonious tones — compare MUSIC OF THE SPHERES
**harmony of vowels :** VOWEL HARMONY
**har·most** \'här,mäst\ *n* -s [Gk *harmostēs*, fr. *harmozein* to join together, govern; akin to Gk *harmos* joint, fastening — more at ARM] **:** a governor appointed by the Spartans over subject towns and people
**har·mo·tome** \'härmə,tōm\ *n* [F, fr. Gk *harmos* joint + *tomē* section, fr. *temnein* to cut; fr. its occurrence in crystalline form with an octahedron dividing parallel to the plane that passes through the terminal edges — more at TOME] **:** a mineral $(Ba,K)(Al,Si)_2Si_6O_{16}.6H_2O$ consisting of a hydrous silicate of aluminum, barium, and potassium
**harms** *pl of* HARM, *pres 3d sing of* HARM
[1]**harn** \'härn\ *n* -s [ME *hernes, harnes* (pl.), of Scand origin; akin to ON *hjarni* brain; akin to OHG *hirni* brain, MD *hersene* brain, ON *hjarsi* crown of the head — more at CEREBRAL] *chiefly Scot* **:** BRAIN **:** BRAINS — usu. used in pl.
[2]**harn** \"\ *n* -s [by contr.] **:** [2]HARDEN
[1]**har·ness** \'härnəs, 'hän-\ *n* -ES *often attrib* [ME *herneis, harneis* baggage of an army or of a group of travelers, gear of a riding horse, armor, furniture, equipment, fr. OF, prob. fr. (assumed) ON *hernest* provisions for an army, fr. ON *herr* army + *nest* provisions; akin to OE *nest* food, provisions, OHG *-nest* food, *ginesan* to survive — more at HARRY, NOSTALGIA] **1 a** (1) **:** the gear or tackle other than a yoke of a draft animal (as a horse, dog, or goat) (2) **:** TACKLE, GEAR, EQUIPMENT **:** the mounting or finishing parts (as of the mechanism and gear by which a large bell is suspended and rung) **b** (1) **:** occupational surroundings **:** work routine ⟨get back into ~ after a vacation⟩ ⟨many girls . . . take on the formidable task of running in double ~, embracing both marriage and a career —Robert Reid⟩ (2) **:** close association ⟨ability to work in ~ with others —R.P.Brooks⟩ **c :** something that resembles a harness ⟨knee ~⟩ ⟨parachute ~⟩ ⟨window-washer's ~⟩ ⟨toddler on a ~⟩; *specif* **:** a prefabricated system of wiring with the necessary insulation and terminals ready to be attached (as in an ignition or lighting system) **2 :** defensive military equipment for horse or man; *specif* **:** ARMOR ⟨smote the king of Israel between the joints of the ~ —1 Kings 22:34 (AV)⟩ **3 :** clothing esp. of a specialized type ⟨a policeman's ~⟩ ⟨haven't seen her in anything but hospital ~ for a long time —L.C.Douglas⟩ **4 :** a part of the loom which holds the heddles and controls their motion and by which the warp threads are raised or depressed to form a shed — called also *leaf* — **in harness** *adv* **:** on duty ⟨constantly on call even when not *in harness*⟩ — compare *die in harness* at [1]DIE

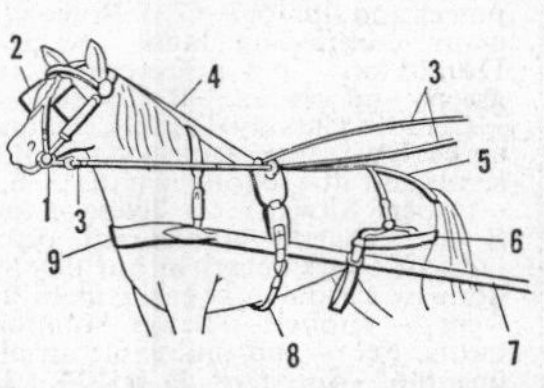

harness: *1* bit, *2* blinder, *3, 3* reins, *4* checkrein, *5* crupper, *6* breeching, *7* trace, *8* bellyband or girth, *9* breast collar

[2]**harness** \"\ *vt* -ED/-ING/-ES [ME *herneisen, harneisen*, fr. *herneis, harneis*, n.] **1** *archaic* **:** to dress or equip for battle **:** ARM ⟨~ yourselves for the war —John Bunyan⟩ **2 a :** to put a harness on ⟨~ a horse⟩ **b :** to attach by means of a harness ⟨the yellow wagon ~*ed* to . . . two stout grays —Ellen Glasgow⟩ **c :** to tie together **:** YOKE ⟨must ~ his mechanical apparatus to his creative mind —Andrew Buchanan⟩ **3 :** to put to work **:** UTILIZE ⟨~ the atom for constructive purposes —*Mech. Engineering*⟩ ⟨~ words to convey ideas —*advt*⟩ ⟨they who have ~*ed* contemporary social forces —W.H.Whyte⟩ ⟨*harnessing* the limitless power of the sun —*advt*⟩
**harness bull** *or* **harness cop** *n, slang* **:** a uniformed policeman ⟨the *harness bulls* just stood at attention —Mickey Spillane⟩
**harness cask** *n* **:** a tub on shipboard for storing or soaking salt meat preparatory to use
**harnessed antelope** *n* [*harnessed* fr. past part. of [2]*harness*] **:** any of several antelopes of the genus *Tragelaphus* having striped markings that resemble a harness — see BUSHBUCK, GUIB
**har·ness·er** \-sə(r)\ *n* -s **:** one that harnesses
**harness hitch** *n* **:** MAN-HARNESS KNOT
**harness horse** *n* **1 :** a horse for racing in harness — compare PACER, TROTTER **2 :** DRAFT HORSE — distinguished from *saddle horse*
**harness leather** *n* **:** a strong pliable oil-finished leather made from cattle hides
**harness plate** *n* **:** electroplated hardware used on harness
**harness race** *n* **:** a trotting or pacing race between Standard-bred horses harnessed to 2-wheeled sulkies
**harn·pan** \'härn,pan\ *n* [ME *hernepanne, harnepanne*, fr. *herne-, harne-* (fr. *hernes, harnes* brains) + *panne* pan — more at HARN, PAN] *chiefly Scot* **:** casing for the brain **:** SKULL
**harns** *pl of* HARN
**haro** *var of* HARROW
**ha·ro·seth** *or* **ha·ro·set** *or* **ha·ro·ses** \hə'rōs(h)əth, -ət, -əs\ *or* **cha·ro·sety** *or* **cha·ro·set** *or* **cha·ro·ses** \kə'-\ *n pl but usu sing in constr* [Heb *ḥaroseth, ḥaroset*, fr. *ḥarsith, ḥarsit* clay or earthen pot] **:** a pastelike mixture of apples, nuts, cinnamon, and wine used during the seder meal on the Passover and symbolic of the clay from which the Israelites made bricks during their Egyptian slavery
[1]**harp** \'härp, 'häp\ *n* -s [ME *harpe*, fr. OE *hearpe;* akin to OHG *harpha* harp, ON *harpa* harp, Gk *karphos* dry stalk, stick, Russ *korobit'* to bend, warp, and prob. to L *curvus* curved — more at CROWN] **1 a :** a musical instrument (as the clarsach, lyre) of ancient origin with strings set usu. in an open frame and plucked with the fingers **b :** an orchestral instrument with a triangular frame consisting of a large, hollow, and tapering back which is the sounding board, a vertical pillar, a curved neck to which the strings are attached by wrest pins, a base or pedestal equipped with seven pedals each of which when depressed one notch raises all strings of the same letter names one half step and when depressed two notches raises them a whole step, having usu. 46 strings tuned diatonically in C-flat major with a compass of 6½ octaves above C flat and with all C and F strings colored for ease of recognition **c :** JEW'S HARP 1 **d :** HARMONICA **e :** a percussion pipe-organ stop of metal or wooden bars with resonators sounded by electric hammer action **2 :** HARPER 2 **3 :** something that resembles a harp: as **a :** a forked fitting for holding a trolley wheel or shoe in contact with a power-supplying wire or cable **b :** a many-stringed implement used in cutting the curd of Swiss cheese **c :** a metal hoop or arch that supports a lampshade **4 :** HARP SEAL **5** *often cap* **:** a person of Irish birth or descent — often taken to be offensive


modern harp 1b: *1* base, *2* pillar, *3* neck, *4* body, *5* sound board, *6* pedals, *7* feet

[2]**harp** \"\ *vb* -ED/-ING/-S [ME *harpen*, fr. OE *hearpian*, fr. *hearpe*, n.] *vi* **1 :** to play on a harp **2 :** to dwell on a subject **:** repeat a theme with tiresome frequency ⟨continues to ~ on higher wages and shorter hours —G.W.Johnson⟩ ⟨if I seem to be ~*ing* away at the value of variety —Alistair Cooke⟩ **3** *obs* **:** to form an opinion on insufficient evidence **:** GUESS ⟨only to ~ at the matter —John Cotgrave⟩ **4 :** to make a sound like a harp ⟨hear the wind ~ —E.J.Schoettle⟩ ~ *vt* **1** *obs* **:** to play on or recite to the accompaniment of a harp ⟨a tale . . . ~*ed* in hall and bower —Thomas Warton⟩ **2** *archaic* **:** to attract or compel by playing sweetly on the harp ⟨could ~ his wife up out of hell —Alfred Tennyson⟩ **3** *archaic* **:** to discuss or refer to repeatedly and tediously **4** *archaic* **:** to guess at or give expression to ⟨thou hast ~*ed* my fear aright —Shak.⟩ **5 :** to cut and mix curd of (Swiss cheese) with a harp
**har·pa** \'härpə\ *n, cap* [NL, fr. LL, harp, of Gmc origin; akin to OE *hearpe* harp] **:** the sole genus of the Harpidae
**har·pac·toph·a·gous** \¦här(,)pak¦täfəgəs\ *adj* [*harpacto-* (fr. Gk *harpaktos* stolen, got by plundering, fr. *harpazein* to snatch, seize) + *-phagous;* akin to Gk *harpagē* hook, rake — more at ASSART] **:** PREDATORY — used esp. of insects
**har·pa·go** \'härpə,gō\ *n, pl* **harpago·nes** \,härpə'gō,nēz\ [NL *harpagon-, harpago*, fr. L, grappling iron, irreg. fr. Gk *harpagē* hook, rake] **:** an element of the male copulatory apparatus of many insects that forms part of a clasper; *esp* **:** a modified stylus of the ninth segment forming one lateral half of a clasper — usu. used in pl.
**har·pa·goph·y·tum** \,härpə'gäfəd·əm\ *n, cap* [NL, fr. L *harpago* grappling hook + Gk *phyton* plant — more at PHYT-] **:** a small genus of southern African herbs (family Pedaliaceae) including the grapple plant
**har·pa·gor·nis** \,härpə'gȯrnəs\ *n, cap* [NL, fr. Gk *harpag-, harpax* rapacious + NL *-ornis;* akin to Gk *harpagē* hook, rake] **:** a genus of extinct birds (family Accipitridae) much larger than any existing eagle and found in the Pleistocene of New Zealand
**harp·er** \'härpər, 'häpə(r\ *n* -s [ME, fr. OE *hearpere*, fr. *hearpe* harp + *-ere* -er] **1 :** one that plays on a harp **2 :** any of several Irish coins of the 16th and 17th centuries having a harp on one side; *esp* **:** a silver shilling piece worth nine English pence — called also *harp shilling* **3 :** TOAD CRAB
**har·pes** \'här,pēz\ *n pl* [NL *harpe* (sing.), fr. Gk *harpē* sickle; akin to Gk *harpagē* hook, rake] **:** the claspers of a male moth or butterfly
**harp guitar** *or* **harp lute** *n* **:** a large guitar with triangular body and two extra bass strings — compare DITAL HARP
**har·pi·dae** \'härpə,dē\ *n pl, cap* [NL, fr. *Harpa* + *-idae*] **:** a family of tropical marine gastropod mollusks (suborder Stenoglossa) comprising the harp shells — see HARPA
**harpies** *pl of* HARPY
**harp·in** \'härpən\ *also* **harp·ing** \-piŋ\ *n* -s [prob. fr. [1]*harp* + *-ing*] **1** *archaic* **:** a wale around a ship's bow stouter than the rest of the strakes **2 :** one of the timbers used during construction of a ship to regulate and hold in place the cant frames
**harping iron** *or* **harping spear** *n* [*harping* prob. fr. MF *harper* to grapple, grasp + E *-ing*] *archaic* **:** HARPOON
**harping johnny** *n, usu cap J* [*harping* prob. fr. pres. part. of [2]*harp*] **:** ORPINE
**harp·ist** \'härpəst, 'häp-\ *n* -s **:** a harp player
**harp·less** \-pləs\ *adj* **:** lacking a harp
[1]**har·poon** \här'pün, hä'-\ *n* -s [prob. fr. D *harpoen*, fr. MD, fr. OF *harpon* brooch, fr. *harper* to grapple, grasp, prob. of Scand origin; akin to Icel *harpa* to pinch, squeeze together; prob. akin to ON *harpa* harp, OE *hearpe* — more at HARP] **1 :** a throwing weapon used in hunting large fish and sea animals; *specif* **:** a barbed whaling spear thrown by hand or shot from a gun that has a flat triangular head usu. detachable and sharpened at both edges, a long shaft, and a strong line for making the whale fast to the pursuing boat — compare TOGGLE IRON **2 :** a medical instrument with a barbed head used for removing bits of living tissue for examination
[2]**harpoon** \"\ *vt* -ED/-ING/-S **:** to strike or capture with or as if with a harpoon ⟨~ a whale⟩ ⟨~ an olive⟩
**har·poon·er** \-nə(r)\ *also* **har·poon·eer** \¦här(,)pü¦ni(ə)r\ *n* -s [[1]*harpoon* + *-er* or *-eer*] **:** one that throws or fires a harpoon **:** BOATSTEERER
**harpoon fork** *n* **:** a fork for loading and unloading hay **:** HAYFORK
**harpoon gun** *n* **:** a machine for hurling a harpoon
**harpoon line** *n* **:** a light strong manila rope with a flexible lay now used principally for purse lines
**harpoon log** *n* **:** a log consisting of a rotator and a distance-registering device combined in a cylindrical case and towed astern — compare TAFFRAIL LOG
**harpoon oar** *n* **:** a forward oar pulled by the harpooner as a whaling ship approaches a whale

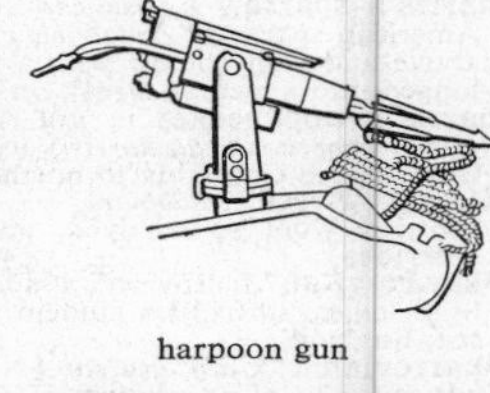
harpoon gun

**harps** *pl of* HARP, *pres 3d sing of* HARP
**harp seal** *n* **:** a common arctic seal (*Phoca groenlandica*) sometimes found as far south as the Maine coast, the adults being grayish above and white below, the male having a black crescent suggesting a harp along each side and a black face and throat, and the newborn young being all white
**harp shell** *n* **:** a tropical gastropod mollusk of the genus *Harpa* having a large variegated shell with prominent ribs
**harp shilling** *n* **:** HARPER
**harpsical** *also* **harpsicall** *n* -s [by alter.] *n, obs* **:** HARPSICHORD
**harpsichon** *also* **harpsicon** *n* -s [by alter.] *n, obs* **:** HARPSICHORD
**harp·si·chord** \'härpsə,kȯrd, 'häpsə,kō(ə)d\ *n* -s [modif. of It *arpicordo*, fr. *arpi-* (fr. *arpa* harp, fr. LL *harpa*) + *-cordo* (fr. *corda* cord, string, fr. L *chorda* cord) — more at HARPA, CORD] **:** a wire-stringed musical instrument resembling in shape the grand piano, usu. having two keyboards with one to four strings for each key and seven stops or pedals, and producing its tones by the plucking of its strings with quills or leather points set in jacks operated from the keyboards and capable of gradation of tone only by alternating the stops or keyboards

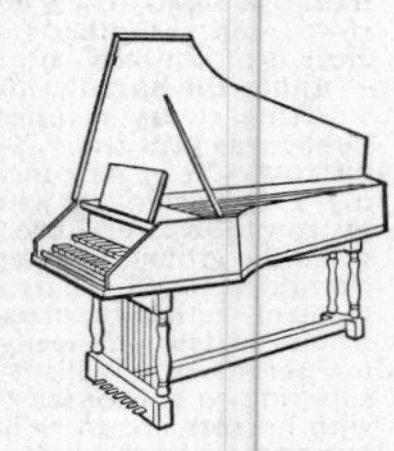
harpsichord

**harp·si·chord·ist** \-dəst\ *n* -s **:** one who plays the harpsichord
**harp turtle** *n* **:** LEATHERBACK
**har·pu·la** \'härpyələ\ *n* -s [native name in Bengal] **:** a fast-growing tree (*Harpullia cupanioides*) of India and the East Indies that yields a wood used esp. for building
**har·pul·lia** \här'pəlēə\ *n* [NL, fr. native name in Bengal] **1** *cap* **:** a genus of tropical Asiatic and African trees (family Sapindaceae) having pinnate leaves, panicles of greenish flowers and red or orange fruit **2** -s **:** any tree of the genus *Harpullia*
**harpway tuning** \'=,=-\ *n* [*harpway* fr. [1]*harp* + *way*] **:** a tuning of a viol (as in fifths and fourths: A-E-A-E-A-D) to facilitate arpeggio playing
**har·py** \'härpē, 'häp-, -pi\ *n* -ES [L *Harpyia*, fr. Gk] **1 :** a predatory monster in chiefly classical mythology represented as having a woman's head and the body and claws of a vulture and as being an instrument of divine vengeance **2 a :** a predatory person **:** LEECH, SWINDLER ⟨homesteaders had managed to escape other *harpies* — such as land agents offering to harry claims through —Dixon Wecter⟩ **b :** a shrewish or depraved woman ⟨gin shops . . . crowded by day as well as by night with screaming *harpies* —Kenneth Roberts⟩
**harpy bat** *also* **harpy** *n* -ES **1 :** any of various East Indian fruit bats having prominent tubular nostrils and constituting the genus *Nyctimene* **2 :** an East Indian insectivorous bat (*Harpiocephalus harpia*)
**harpy eagle** *also* **harpy** *n* -ES **:** either of two large eagles: **a :** a largely black-and-white eagle (*Harpia harpyja*) having a double crest on the head and remarkably strong bill and claws, found in northern So. and Central America where it is believed to prey on large forest birds and various mammals **b :** a rare eagle (*Pithecophaga jefferyi*) of the Philippines held to live chiefly on monkeys

**har·que·bus** *or* **ar·que·bus** \'(h)ärk(w)əbəs, '(h)äk-\ *n* -ES [MF *harquebuse, arquebuse,* modif. of MD *hakebusse,* fr. *hake* hook + *busse* box, tube, gun, fr. LL *buxis* box; akin to MD *hoec* corner — more at HOOK, BOX] **1 :** a portable but heavy matchlock gun invented about the middle of the 15th century and fired from a support to which it was attached by a fixed hook, later wheel-lock or flintlock modifications being lightened and provided with a bent stock and a longer butt so that they could be fired from the shoulder **2 harquebuses** *pl, obs* **:** soldiers armed with the harquebus

**har·que·bus·ade** \,==bə'sād\ *n* -S [MF, fr. *harquebuse* + *-ade*] **1** *obs* **:** a shot from a harquebus **2** *archaic* **:** a volley from harquebuses

**har·que·bus·ier** *or* **ar·que·bus·ier** \-'si(ə)r, -'siə\ *n* -S [MF, fr. *harquebuse, arquebuse* + *-ier* -er] **:** a soldier armed with a harquebus or sometimes with a musket or other gun ⟨at the head of a company of ~s —Frank Yerby⟩

**harr** \'(h)är\ *n* -S [ME *herre, harre,* fr. OE *heorra;* akin to ON *hjarri* hinge and perh. to L *cardin-, cardo* hinge — more at CARDINAL] **1** *obs* **:** a gate or door hinge **2** *now dial Eng* **:** an upright to which hinges are fastened and from which a door or gate swings

**har·ras** \'harəs\ *n* -ES [ME *haras* herd of stud horses, enclosure for a herd of stud horses, fr. OF *haras, haraz*] **:** a herd of stud horses

**har·ra·teen** *or* **har·a·teen** \'harə,tēn\ *n* -S [origin unknown] **:** an English fabric of linen or wool used chiefly for curtains and bed hangings in the 18th and early 19th centuries

**harratin** *usu cap, var of* HARATIN

**harri** *usu cap, var of* HURRI

**har·ri·cane** \'harə,kān\ *dial var of* HURRICANE

**har·ri·dan** \'harədən *also* 'her-, -dᵊn\ *n* -S [perh. modif. of F *haridelle* worn-out horse, tall lean ugly woman] **:** a haggard old woman **:** HAG; *esp* **:** a worn-out strumpet

**harried** *adj* [fr. past part. of ¹*harry*] **:** beset by disturbing problems or anxieties **:** HARASSED ⟨as ~ as innkeepers coping with a full house —Mary McGrory⟩ ⟨a rather ~ journalist trying to produce a maximum of copy —Edmund Wilson⟩

¹**har·ri·er** \'harēə(r), -riə- *also* 'her-\ *n* -S [irreg. fr. ¹*hare* + *-ier*] **1 :** a hunting dog from 19 to 21 inches high resembling a small foxhound and used for hunting rabbits and other small game **2 :** a runner on a cross-country team

²**harrier** \"\ *n* -S [¹*harry* + *-er*] **1 :** one that harries **2** [alter. (influenced by ¹*harry*) of earlier *harrower,* fr. ¹*harrow* + *-er*] **:** any of various slender hawks with long angled wings and long legs that constitute a genus (*Circus*), feed chiefly on small mammals, reptiles, and insects which they hunt by flying low over open ground, and usu. nest on the ground — see HEN HARRIER, MARSH HARRIER, MARSH HAWK

**harrier eagle** *n* **:** any of numerous rather large Old World hawks constituting a genus (*Circaetus*) and intermediate in some respects between typical hawks and typical eagles — called also *short-toed eagle*

**harries** *pres 3d sing of* HARRY, *pl of* HARRY

**har·ring·ton** \'hariŋtən\ *n* -S *usu cap* [after John, 1st Baron *Harington* of Exton †1613 Eng. nobleman who coined such tokens under a patent granted by James I] **:** a copper token worth a farthing in 17th century England

**har·ris buck** \'harəs-\ *n, usu cap H* [after Sir William C. *Harris* †1848 Eng. traveler] **:** SABLE ANTELOPE

**har·ris·burg** \'harəs,bərg, -,bəg *also* 'her-\ *adj, usu cap* [fr. *Harrisburg,* capital of Pennsylvania] **:** of or from Harrisburg, the capital of Pennsylvania ⟨*Harrisburg* residents⟩ **:** of the kind or style prevalent in Harrisburg

**har·ris·ia** \hə'risēə\ *n, cap* [NL, fr. William *Harris,* Jamaican botanist + NL *-ia*] **:** a genus of slender spiny tropical American cacti with solitary showy white or pink flowers

**har·ri·son red** \'harəsᵊn-\ *n, often cap H* [perh. after Birge *Harrison* †1929 Am. landscape painter] **:** CHINESE VERMILION

**harris's hawk** *or* **harris hawk** *n, usu cap 1st H* [after Edward *Harris* †1863 Am. naturalist] **:** a common hawk (*Parabuteo unicinctus harrisi*) of the deserts and prairies of southwestern U.S., Mexico, and Central America chiefly dark brown with conspicuous white markings on the tail

**harris's sparrow** *n, usu cap H* **:** a widely distributed No. American sparrow (*Zonotrichia querula*) largely dusky brown above and white below with a black cap and black bib prolonged into a median streak on the breast

**harris's woodpecker** *n, usu cap H* **:** a hairy woodpecker (*Dendrocopos villosus harrisi*) occurring along the Pacific coast from British Columbia to northern California

**Harris Tweed** *trademark* — used for a tweed made of Scottish wool spun, dyed, and handwoven in the Outer Hebrides

¹**har·ro·vi·an** \hə'rōvēən\ *n* -S *usu cap* [NL *Harrovia* Harrow + E *-an,* n. suffix] **:** a student of Harrow School in Middlesex, England

²**harrovian** \"\ *adj, usu cap* [NL *Harrovia* Harrow + E *-an,* adj. suffix] **:** of or relating to Harrow School

¹**har·row** \'ha(,)rō, -rə *also* 'he(-, *often* -,raw+V\ *vt* -ED/-ING/-S [ME *harwen, herwen,* fr. OE *hergian* to harry — more at HARRY] **1** *archaic* **:** to descend into (hell) in order to bring away the souls of the righteous ⟨Christ hath ~*ed* hell —J.M. Neale⟩ **2** *archaic* **:** ROB, PILLAGE, PLUNDER ⟨long ~*ed* by oppressor's hand —Sir Walter Scott⟩

²**harrow** \"\ *n* -S *often attrib* [ME *harwe;* perh. akin to OSw *harf* harrow, Gk *keirein* to cut — more at SHEAR] **1 :** a cultivating implement used primarily for pulverizing or smoothing the soil and sometimes for mulching, covering seed, or removing weeds — compare BOG HARROW, BRUSH HARROW, DISC HARROW, DRAG 1d **2 a :** an implement that resembles a harrow; *specif:* a toothed framework drawn over an oyster bed to clear it of seaweed **b :** a formation that resembles a harrow — **under the harrow** *adv* **:** under constant threat of penalty or suffering ⟨every manifestation of initiative in the educated public was kept *under the harrow* —Bernard Pares⟩

³**harrow** \"\ *vt* -ED/-ING/-S [ME *harwen, harowen,* fr. *harwe,* n.] **1 a :** to cultivate with a harrow ⟨plowed and ~*ed* and laid his rows —Russell Lord⟩ **b :** to cultivate as if with a harrow ⟨~*ed* the ground for literature —Van Wyck Brooks⟩ **2 a :** to cut into as if with a harrow ⟨the whole thing looked ~*ed* in the pigment, rather than painted —F.J.Mather⟩ **b** *archaic* **:** to wound or tear physically **:** LACERATE ⟨~*ing* his cheeks with a few scratches —William Beckford⟩ **3 :** to cause distress or suffering to **:** AGONIZE ⟨has not set out to appall the reader with horrors nor to ~ him with miseries —Douglas Stewart⟩

⁴**har·row** *or* **haro** \'ha(,)rō, hə'rō\ *interj* [ME *harrow, harow,* fr. MF *haro, harou,* fr. OF, prob. of Gmc origin; akin to OHG *hara* hither; akin to OE *hēr* here, OHG *hier* — more at HERE] — used to express alarm or distress

⁵**har·row** \'ha(,)rō\ *adj, usu cap* [fr. *Harrow* on the Hill, urban district, Middlesex, England] **:** of or from the urban district of Harrow on the Hill, England **:** of the kind or style prevalent in Harrow on the Hill

**har·row·er** \'harəwə(r), *also* 'her-\ *n* -S [ME *haroer, harower,* fr. *harwen, harowen* to cultivate with a harrow + *-er*] **:** one that harrows

**harrowing** *adj* [fr. pres. part. of ³*harrow*] **:** acutely distressing or painful **:** AGONIZING ⟨~ tales of unfortunates who had lost limbs or had been frozen to death —V.G.Heiser⟩ — **har·row·ing·ly** *adv*

**harrow-plow** \'=(,)=,=\ *n* [²*harrow*] **:** ONE-WAY DISC PLOW

**harrs** *pl of* HARR

**har·rumph** \hə'rəm(p)f\ *vi* -ED/-ING/-S [imit.] **1 :** to make a pompous throat-clearing sound ⟨several students chuckled and one or two professorial alumni good-naturedly ~*ed* —W.H.Nelson⟩ **2 :** to comment disapprovingly **:** PROTEST ⟨the state department ~*ed* and . . . oil companies stood on their legal, unenforceable rights —*Time*⟩

¹**har·ry** \'harē, -ri *also* 'her-\ *vb* -ED/-ING/-ES [ME *harien, herien,* fr. OE *hergian;* akin to OHG *heriōn* to lay waste, ON *herja;* denominative fr. the noun represented by OE *here* army, OHG *heri,* ON *herr* army, Goth *harjis* host; akin to Gk *koiranos* commander, OPer *kāra* army] *vi* **:** to attack and loot **:** RAID ⟨had *harried* widely and laid siege to Paris —Charlton Laird⟩ ~ *vt* **1 a :** ASSAULT, DEVASTATE, RAVAGE ⟨ordered his troops to ~ the town⟩ ⟨shabby trees *harried* by fire —G.R. Stewart⟩ **b** *chiefly Scot* **:** to engage in robbing or plundering ⟨shame lassie for ~*ing* birds' nests —J.M.Barrie⟩ **2 a :** ATTACK ⟨~ a person⟩ ⟨the cat reached out a big fat paw and *harried* the boy —Erskine Caldwell⟩ **b :** to force (a person) to move along ⟨saga of migratory laborers *harried* across the continent —J.D.Hart⟩ **3** *now dial Brit* **:** to drag off as plunder — usu. used with *off* or *out* ⟨the devil came and *harried* off his soul —Emily Brontë⟩ **4 a :** to keep under constant attack or threat of attack **:** HARASS ⟨*harried* by guerrillas and occasionally invaded by organized forces —T.M.Spaulding⟩ **b :** to goad by constant demands or annoyances **:** TORMENT ⟨three renegade boys who came to ~ a couple of farm women —James Kelly⟩ ⟨*harries* the doctor by telephone —Mary B. Spahr⟩ **syn** see WORRY

²**harry** \"\ *n* -ES **1 :** harrying action ⟨teased and broken by the ~ of the following gale —J.D.Beresford⟩ **2 :** VEXATION ⟨cut off from the hurries and *harries* of the daily world —Roger Angell⟩

¹**harsh** \'härsh, 'hȧsh\ *adj* -ER/-EST [alter. of earlier *harsk,* fr. ME, of Scand origin; akin to Norw *harsk* rancid, harsh, Sw *härsk* rancid; akin to MLG *harsch* rough, and prob. to L *carrere* to card — more at CHARD] **1 :** having a coarse or uneven surface **:** rough to the touch **:** SHAGGY ⟨a small terrier with a ~ dense coat —*Dict. of Sports*⟩ ⟨granite stones ~ with lichen —Nancy Hale⟩; *specif* **:** difficult to manipulate and finish because of too many large particles of aggregate in proportion to the amount of fine particles ⟨~ mortar⟩ ⟨~ concrete⟩ **2 a :** disagreeable to taste or smell **:** RAW, ACRID, IRRITATING ⟨the cognac was ~ —Winifred Bambrick⟩ ⟨a very irritating, pungent, ~ smoke —W.W.Garver⟩ **b :** disagreeable to the ear **:** GRATING, STRIDENT, JARRING ⟨her ~ voice was full of power and humor —G.W.Brace⟩ ⟨music . . . requires sounds of many contrasting kinds: ~ as well as mellow —Robert Donington⟩ **c :** disagreeable to the eye **:** STARK ⟨~ dull greens and blacks —Roger Fry⟩ ⟨a ~, almost a violent, face —Claudia Cassidy⟩; *specif, photog* **:** HARD **d :** physically disagreeable **:** UNCOMFORTABLE ⟨wild and ~ country, full of hot sand and the cholla cactus —S.H.Adams⟩ ⟨~ north wind —Osbert Sitwell⟩ ⟨~ lives of toil in sweatshops and mines⟩ **3 a :** sharply unpleasant or rigorous **:** STERN ⟨the ~ facts of court delays in our city —S.H.Hofstadter⟩ ⟨could be done by a woman as easily as by a man . . . provided discipline were ~ enough —Lewis Mumford⟩ **b :** SEVERE, EXACTING, CRUEL ⟨as ~ and unlovable an old tyrant as one could well imagine —*Sat. Eve. Post*⟩ **4 :** lacking in aesthetic grace or refinement **:** CRUDE ⟨a ~ and sometimes unpleasant book, barren of pretty touches —Brendan Gill⟩ **syn** see ROUGH

²**harsh** \"\ *adv* **:** HARSHLY ⟨with *harsh*-resounding trumpets' dreadful bray —Shak.⟩

**harsh·en** \-shən\ *vb* -ED/-ING/-S *vt* **:** to make harsh ⟨a great gravity that ~*ed* his soft voice —*Scribner's*⟩ ~ *vi* **:** to become harsh ⟨saw the grain of his skin ~*ing* over face bones —Elizabeth Bowen⟩

**harsh-furred hare** \'=,=-\ *n* **:** a small hare (*Caprolagus hispidus* or *Lepus hispidus*) of the eastern Himalayan foothills with a massive skull, short ears, and a dull dark coat in which whitish bristly hairs are mingled

**harsh·ly** *adv* **:** in a harsh manner: **a :** coarsely to the touch **:** ROUGHLY ⟨rubbed herself ~ with a towel —I.V.Morris⟩ **b :** offensively to the senses **:** DISAGREEABLY ⟨houses on the far side, ~ white in this straight hard glare —Thomas Wood †1950⟩ **c :** unfeelingly to the sensibilities **:** RIGOROUSLY, CRUELLY ⟨~ limits the freedom of the creative imagination —Philip Toynbee⟩ ⟨he was made prisoner and ~ treated —E.M.Coulter⟩ **d :** ungracefully by aesthetic standards **:** CRUDELY ⟨a number of his canvases are slightly repellent — notably one of a ~ drawn, bedraggled mother and child —R.M.Coates⟩

**harsh·ness** *n* -ES [alter. of earlier *harsknes,* fr. ME, fr. *harsk* harsh + *-nes* -ness] **:** the quality or state of being harsh

**hars·let** \'härslət\ *dial var of* HASLET

**hars·tig·ite** \'härstə,gīt\ *n* -S [Sw *harstigit,* fr. *Harstig* mine, Sweden + Sw *-it* -ite] **:** a mineral $Be_2Ca_3Si_3O_{11}$ consisting of a silicate of beryllium and calcium (hardness 5.5, sp. gr. 3.05)

**hart** \'härt, 'hȧt, *usu* -d·+V\ *n, pl* **harts** *also* **hart** [ME *hert,* fr. OE *heort, heorot;* akin to OHG *hiruz* hart, ON *hjörtr,* L *cervus* hart, stag, Gk *keras* horn — more at HORN] *chiefly Brit* **:** the male of the red deer esp. over five years old **:** STAG — compare HIND

**har·tal** \hər'täl\ *n* -S [Hindi *haṛtāl,* fr. *hāṭ* shop + *tālā* lock] **:** concerted cessation of work and business esp. as a protest against a political situation or an act of government — compare NONCOOPERATION

**har·te·beest** \'här|d·ə,bēst, 'hȧ|, |tə,-, |t,-\ *n, pl* **hartebeests** *also* **hartebeest** [obs. Afrik (now *hartbees*), fr. D *hartebeest, hertebeest* deer, fr. *hart, hert* deer, stag (fr. MD *hert*) + *beest* beast, fr. MD *beeste, beest,* fr. OF *beste;* akin to OE *heort, heorot* hart — more at HART, BEAST] **1 :** a large nearly exterminated African antelope (*Alcelaphus caama*) that is grayish brown in color with a yellow patch on the buttocks, black markings on the face, and ringed divergent horns bent back at the tips — compare SASSABY **2 :** any of several other African antelopes of the genus *Alcelaphus* — compare NORTHERN HARTEBEEST

**hart·ford** \'härtfərd, 'hȧtfəd\ *adj, usu cap* [fr. *Hartford,* capital of Connecticut] **:** of or from Hartford, the capital of Connecticut ⟨*Hartford* insurance companies⟩ **:** of the kind or style prevalent in Hartford

**hartford fern** *n, usu cap H* **:** CLIMBING FERN

**hart·ford·ite** \-,dīt\ *n* -S *cap* **:** a native or resident of Hartford, Connecticut

**hart·ite** \'härd·,īt\ *n* -S [G *hartit,* fr. *Oberhart,* Austria + G *-it* -ite] **:** a white fossil resin perhaps $C_{19}H_{32}$ occurring in peat beds

**hart·le·ian** *also* **hart·ley·an** \'härtlēən, =ˈ==\ *adj, usu cap* [David *Hartley* †1757 Eng. philosopher, founder of the doctrine of associationism + E *-an*] **:** of or relating to the doctrine of associationism or its founder

**hart·man·nia** \härt'manēə\ *n, cap* [NL, fr. Emanuel *Hartmann,* 19th cent. Am. botanist + NL *-ia*] *in some classifications* **:** a small genus of American herbs (family Onagraceae) with alternate leaves and showy flowers in spikes or racemes that are usu. included in the genus *Oenothera*

¹**har·to·gia** \här'tōjēə\ [NL, fr. J. *Hartog,* 18th cent. Du. traveler + NL *-ia*] *syn of* AGATHOSMA

²**hartogia** \"\ *n, cap* [NL, fr. J. *Hartog* + NL *-ia*] **:** a genus of southern African plants (family Rutaceae) having white or purplish flowers with long-clawed petals, five stamens, and five conspicuous staminodia

**hart's-eye** \'=,=\ *n, pl* **hart's-eyes 1 :** CRETAN DITTANY **2 :** PARSNIP

**harts·horn** \'=,=\ *n* -S [ME *hertes horn,* fr. OE *heortes horn,* fr. *heortes* (gen. of *heort* hart) + *horn*] **1 :** a hart's horn or antler **2** *archaic* **a :** AMMONIA WATER **b :** AMMONIUM CARBONATE c **3** *or* **hartshorn plantain :** BUCKHORN 3b(1)

**hartshorn bush** *n* **:** ROYAL FERN

**hartshorn plant** *n* **:** an American pasqueflower (*Anemone patens*)

**hart's-thorn** \'=,=\ *n, pl* **hart's-thorns :** COMMON BUCKTHORN

**hart's-tongue** \'=,=\ *or* **hart's-tongue fern** *n, pl* **hart's-tongues** *or* **hart's-tongue ferns** [*hart's-tongue* fr. ME *hertestonge,* fr. *hertes* (gen. of *hert* hart) + *tonge* tongue; *hart's-tongue fern* fr. *hart's-tongue* + *fern;* fr. the shape of the fronds] **1 :** a chiefly Eurasian fern (*Phyllitis scolopendrium*) with simple lanceolate fronds often auriculate at the base **2 :** a tropical American fern (*Polybotria cervina*) of the family Polypodiaceae **3 :** STRAP FERN

**hart's truffle** *n* **:** an ascomycetous fungus of the genus *Elaphomyces* that resembles a puffball — compare LYCOPERDON NUT

¹**har·um-scar·um** \ˌharəm'skarəm, *also* ˌherəm'skerəm\ *adv* (*or adj*) [perh. alter. (perh. influenced by ¹*hare*) of ¹*helter-skelter*] **:** in a rash or heedless way **:** RECKLESSLY ⟨trucks whizzing *harum-scarum* along clay streets —Allan Ashbolt⟩ ⟨dashing *harum-scarum* from one rooftop to another⟩

²**harum-scarum** \"\ *n* -S **:** one that is rash or heedless **:** SCATTERBRAIN ⟨do you really expect those wild young *harum-scarums* to live up to their oath —S.H.Adams⟩ — **har·um-scar·um·ness** *n*

**ha·rus·pex** *or* **arus·pex** \(h)ə'rə,speks, '(h)ar-\ *n, pl* **ha·ruspi·ces** *or* **aruspices** \-'rəspə,sēz\ [L *haruspic-, haruspex,* fr. *haru-* (akin to Gk *chordē* gut, cord) + *-spic-, -spex* (fr. *spicere, specere* to look) — more at YARN, SPY] **1 :** one that foretells events by interpreting natural phenomena (as lightning) **:** SOOTHSAYER; *esp* **:** a diviner in ancient Rome basing his predictions on inspection of the entrails of sacrificial animals — compare AUGUR **2 :** one that prophesies **:** PROGNOSTICATOR ⟨our forecast has proven far more accurate than the divinations of the Democrat ~ —O.D.Heck⟩

**ha·rus·pi·cal** \-'rəspəkəl\ *adj* **:** of, relating to, or having the characteristics of an haruspex

**ha·rus·pi·ca·tion** \(h)ə,rəspə'kāshən\ *n* -S [L *haruspic-, haruspex* + E *-ation*] **1 :** HARUSPICY **2 :** an act or instance of foretelling events **:** PROPHECY ⟨it's the best job of social ~ that's been done in years —Christopher Morley⟩

**ha·rus·pi·cy** *or* **arus·pi·cy** \-'rəspəsē\ *n* -ES [L *haruspicium,* fr. *haruspic-, haruspex*] **:** the art or practice of divination — compare HARUSPEX

**harvard beets** *n pl, usu cap H* [*Harvard* University, Cambridge, Massachusetts] **:** diced or sliced cooked beets served in a vinegar sauce thickened with cornstarch

**harvard crimson** *n, often cap H* **1 :** a moderate red that is slightly darker than cerise, darker than claret, darker, very slightly bluer, and less strong than average strawberry (sense 2a), and bluer and very slightly darker than Turkey red — called also *jockey* **2** *of textiles* **:** a deep purplish red that is redder and paler than hollyhock or magenta (sense 2a) and stronger and slightly bluer and lighter than American beauty

**har·ve·ian** \'härvēən, =ˈ==\ *adj, usu cap* [William *Harvey* †1657 Eng. physician and anatomist + E *-an*] **:** of, relating to, or commemorating William Harvey

¹**har·vest** \'härvəst, 'hȧv-\ *n* -S *often attrib* [ME *hervest* autumn, fr. OE *hærfest;* akin to OHG *herbist* autumn, ON *haust* autumn, L *carpere* to gather, pluck, Gk *karpos* fruit, Skt *kṛpāṇa* sword, Gk *keirein* to cut — more at SHEAR] **1 :** the season for gathering in agricultural crops ⟨he who has seen ten winters or ~s is ten years old —M.P.Nilsson⟩ ⟨considerable variation in the Territory as regards the date of the ~ —*Tanganyika Territory*⟩ **2 a :** the act or process of gathering in a crop ⟨the hay ~⟩ ⟨reduce the numbers of fish . . . through more intensive and efficient ~ by anglers —L.S. Marceau⟩ **b :** the gathering in of something other than a crop ⟨more to these poems than just the . . . ~ of a trained eye —*Times Lit. Supp.*⟩ **3 a :** a mature crop of grain or fruit **:** YIELD ⟨bountiful ~s of corn —John Bird⟩ **b :** the quantity of any natural product gathered usu. from a single area within a single season ⟨~ of elk⟩ ⟨~ of beaver skins⟩ ⟨salt ~⟩ ⟨ice ~⟩ **4 :** an accumulated store or productive result **:** ACHIEVEMENT, INGATHERING ⟨one's total ~ of thinking, feeling, living, and observing —T.S.Eliot⟩ ⟨the final ~ of the theocracy —V.L. Parrington⟩ ⟨~ of the guillotine —Alfred Cobban⟩ ⟨~ of half crowns —W.J.MacQueen-Pope⟩ **5** *or* **harvest brown :** a brownish orange to light brown that is lighter than sorrel or tawny, redder and lighter than raw sienna, and slightly yellower and lighter than caramel

²**harvest** \"\ *vb* -ED/-ING/-S [ME *hervesten,* fr. *hervest,* n.] *vt* **1 a :** to gather in (a crop) **:** REAP ⟨when all the beets are ~*ed* a steam shovel loads them on trucks —*Amer. Guide Series: Minn.*⟩ **b :** to gather (a natural product) as if by harvesting ⟨~ honey⟩ ⟨~ timber⟩ ⟨~ whales⟩ **2 a :** to accumulate a store of ⟨~ news leads and witticisms —Bennett Cerf⟩ **b :** to win as a result of achievements ⟨~*ed* rewards in fame and wealth . . . simply undreamed of —*N. Y. Herald Tribune*⟩ ~ *vi* **:** to gather in a food crop ⟨sold it standing in the field to save himself the trouble of ~*ing* —Pearl Buck⟩ ⟨the husky black bear ~s upon both soil and water —George Heinold⟩ **syn** see REAP

**har·vest·able** \-təbəl\ *adj* **:** capable of or subject to being harvested

**harvest bug** *n* **:** CHIGGER 2

**harvest doll** *or* **harvest mother** *or* **harvest queen** *n* **:** a doll decorated with grain and flowers or an image made from the last sheaf cut in the harvest and used in European celebrations of the harvest home — called also *kirn baby, mell-doll*

**har·vest·er** \-tə(r)\ *n* -S **:** one that harvests: as **a :** HARVESTMAN **b :** a machine for harvesting field crops — compare COMBINE 3, CORN BINDER, COTTON PICKER **c :** a gatherer of something other than crops ⟨semimonthly ~ of noteworthy pronouncements —*Official Catholic Yearbook*⟩

**harvester ant** *n* **:** an ant that gathers and stores up seeds for food: as **a :** a member of an Old World genus (*Messor*) common around the Mediterranean **b :** any of several western No. American ants; *esp* **:** a common ant (*Pogonomyrmex barbatus*) of southwestern U.S. — called also *agricultural ant*

**harvester-thresher** \'===ˈ==\ *n* **:** COMBINE 3

**harvest fish** *n* **:** any of various butterfishes of the family Stromateidae: as **a :** a small marine fish (*Peprilus paru*) having a narrow deep body and being found along the Atlantic coast of America from Brazil to Cape Cod **b :** DOLLARFISH 1

**harvest fly** *n* **:** CICADA; *specif* **:** DOG-DAY CICADA

**harvest home** *n* **1 :** the gathering and bringing home of the harvest; *also* **:** the time of harvest — see HARVEST DOLL **2 :** a feast made at the close of the harvest — called also *hockey, kirn, mell, mell supper* **3 :** the song sung by the reapers at the close of the harvest

**harvesting** *n* -S [fr. gerund of ²*harvest*] **:** an act or instance of gathering in a crop or store ⟨what crops survived the drought are rotted in the ~ —Oliver La Farge⟩ ⟨deer . . . are controlled by heavy ~ —Robert Crichton⟩

**har·vest·less** \'härvəstləs\ *adj* **:** lacking a harvest **:** UNPRODUCTIVE

**harvest-lice** \'=,=\ *n pl but sing or pl in constr* **1 :** a hooked or barbed fruit that readily adheres to things (as clothing or the fur of an animal) which come in contact with it **2 :** a plant (as cleavers, agrimonia, or beggar-ticks of the genus *Bidens*) bearing fruits that are harvest-lice

**har·vest·man** \'==mən\ *n, pl* **harvestmen 1 :** one who harvests agricultural crops **:** harvest hand **2 :** an arachnid of the order Phalangida that superficially resembles a true spider but has a small rounded body composed of an indistinctly segmented cephalothorax to which the short broad abdomen showing nine dorsal plates is broadly joined, very long slender legs, chelate chelicerae, and rather short leglike pedipalpi — called also *daddy longlegs*

**harvest mite** *n* **:** CHIGGER 2

**harvest moon** *n* **:** the full moon nearest the time of the September equinox when for mid-northern latitudes its daily delay in rising is much shorter than usual by reason of the relatively small angle the moon's orbit makes with the eastern horizon

**harvest mouse** *n* **1 :** a small European field mouse (*Micromys minutus*) that builds a globular nest on the stems of wheat or other plants **2 :** any of several small field mice (genus *Reithrodontomys*) of the southern U.S.

**harvests** *pl of* HARVEST, *pres 3d sing of* HARVEST

**harvest spider** *n* **:** HARVESTMAN 2

**harvesttime** \'==,=\ *n* [ME *hervest-time,* fr. *hervest* harvest, autumn + *time*] **:** the time during which an annual crop (as wheat) is harvested

**harz·burg·ite** \'härts,bər,gīt\ *n* -S [G *harzburgit,* fr *Harzburg,* Germany + G *-it* -ite] **:** a rock of the peridotite group consisting essentially of olivine and orthopyroxene

¹**has** *pres 3d sing of* HAVE

²**has** *pres 3d sing of* HA, *pl of* HA

**has-been** \'haz,bin\ *n* -S [fr. *has been,* 3d pers. sing. perf. indic. of *be*] **1 :** one that has passed the peak of effectiveness or popularity ⟨a seedy *has-been* of an actor traveling a comeback trail —Gordon Allison⟩ ⟨that little, dried-up *has-been* of a town —J.B.Benefield⟩ ⟨obsolete, a *has-been* as a warplane —*Springfield (Mass.) Daily News*⟩ **2 has-beens** *pl* **:** old times or past events ⟨just for *has-beens* I took him to lunch —W.H.Smith⟩

**haschisch** *var of* HASHISH

**ha·sen·pfef·fer** \'häzᵊn,(p)fefə(r)\ *or* **has·sen·pfef·fer** \'häs-\ *n* -S [G *hasenpfeffer,* fr. *hase* hare (fr. OHG *haso*) + *pfeffer* pepper, fr. OHG *pfeffar* — more at HARE, PEPPER] **1 :** a stew made of rabbit meat which has been soaked for two days in vinegar and pickling spices and to which sour cream is added before serving **2 :** a card game similar to euchre

¹**hash** \'hash, -aa(ə)sh, -aish\ *vb* -ED/-ING/-ES [F *hacher,* fr. OF *hachier,* fr. *hache* battle-ax, of Gmc origin; akin to OHG *häppa* sickle, pruning knife; akin to Gk *koptein* to smite, cut off — more at CAPON] *vt* **1 a :** to chop to pieces; *specif* **:** to prepare for use in a meat and vegetable dish by cutting into

small pieces ⟨~ the leftover pot roast⟩ **b :** to make a confused muddle of **:** JUMBLE ⟨in both dates and geography he pretty well ~*es* the history of the . . . company —Bernard De Voto⟩ **2 :** to cut with long strokes **:** SLASH ⟨they are . . . ~*ing* them down, and their blood is running down like water —Patrick Walker⟩ **3 :** to talk about **:** REVIEW ⟨~ and rehash the evidence —D.W.Peck⟩ ~ *vi* **1** *slang* **:** to serve food in a restaurant **:** wait table ⟨got my job back ~*ing* —R.P.Warren⟩ **2 :** to marshal facts **:** CONSIDER ⟨we've ~*ed* and rehashed enough —Hamilton Basso⟩

**2hash** \"\ *n* -ES **1 a :** chopped food; *specif* **:** a dish usu. consisting of leftover meat chopped into small pieces, mixed with potatoes, and browned by baking or frying **b** *slang* **:** a meal esp. in a cafeteria or at a lunch counter **:** FOOD ⟨called last week and took ~ with us —*Gringo & Greaser*⟩ ⟨waiter in a ~ joint —Scott Fitzgerald⟩ **2 :** a restatement of something that is already known ⟨this much is old ~, but the . . . tabulation goes on to supply some curious verification —*N.Y. Herald Tribune*⟩ **3 :** MIXTURE, JUMBLE, HODGEPODGE: as **a :** a confused muddle **:** MESS ⟨made rather a ~ of her life —Clive Arden⟩ ⟨one basic style of architecture with a ~ of every other style slapped on by successive owners —Sam Boal⟩ **b :** an undesired signal or combination of signals in a radio, radar, or television receiver due to set noise, radio noise, interference, or other cause **c :** a medley of miscellaneous steps and figures in square dancing **4** *chiefly Scot* **:** a careless or stupid person of slovenly speech or habits **:** worthless fellow

**3hash** \'(h)ash\ *dial var of* HARSH

**hash·ab** \'ha,shab\ *n* -S [Ar *khashab*] **:** a gray-barked acacia tree (*Acacia senegal*) found in the Sudan that is the source of a white or light-colored variety of gum arabic

**hashed brown potatoes** \'=,=-\ *also* **hash·browns** \'hash-,braunz\ *or* **hashed-browns** \-sht,-\ *n pl* **:** chopped cooked potatoes packed into a skillet and fried brown on both sides

**hash·er** \'hashə(r), -aash-, -aish-\ *n* -S **1** *slang* **:** WAITER, WAITRESS ⟨a ~ in the Shanghai Café —*N.Y. Times*⟩ **2 a :** COOKEE **b :** a worker who feeds into a hashing machine unmarketable meat that may be used for by-products

**hash·ery** \-shərē\ *n* -ES [*2hash* + *-ery*] *slang* **:** HASH HOUSE

**hash house** *n, slang* **:** an inexpensive eating place **:** BEANERY ⟨at an all-night *hash house* . . . he nurses a cup of coffee and a doughnut —Norman Mailer⟩

**1hash·im·ite** *or* **hash·em·ite** \'hashə,mīt\ *n* -S *usu cap* [*Hashim*, great-grandfather of Muhammad (founder of the Muslim religion) + E *-ite*] **:** a member of an Arabic family having common ancestry with Muhammad and founding dynasties in countries of the eastern Mediterranean

**2hashimite** *or* **hashemite** \"\ *adj, usu cap* **:** of, relating to, or ruled by the Hashimites

**hash·ish** *also* **hash·eesh** *or* **hasch·isch** \'ha|(,)shēsh, 'haa|, 'hai|, |shish *sometimes* =ˈshēsh *or* hə'shēsh\ *n* -ES [Ar *hashīsh* dry herbage, hashish] **1 :** a narcotic drug derived from the hemp (*Cannabis sativa*) that is smoked, chewed, or drunk for its intoxicating effect ⟨inhaled the ~ of his words with which he puffed dreamlike clouds about her head —Helen Howe⟩ — compare BHANG, CANNABIS, CHARAS, GANJA, MARIHUANA **2 :** an intoxicating liquor prepared from cannabis

**hash·ka·bah** \häsh'käbə\ *n* -S *sometimes cap* [MHeb *hashkābhāh*, lit., lying down, fr. Heb *hashkībh* to lie down, die] **:** a recital of the memorial prayer for the dead esp. among Sephardic Jews

**hash mark** *n* **:** a military service stripe ⟨it takes a soldier or airman three years, and a sailor or marine four, to get a *hash mark* —*Armed Forces Talk*⟩

**hash out** *vt* **:** to thrash out ⟨invited by a faculty committee . . . to *hash out* their views on education theory —*Saturday Rev.*⟩

**hash over** *vt* **:** to talk over **:** DISCUSS ⟨*hash over* old times⟩ ⟨*hash over* a ball game⟩ ⟨plunged into the subject under discussion and *hashed it over* —E.J.Kahn⟩

**hashslinger** \'=,==\ *n* **:** WAITER, WAITRESS

**hash up** *vt* **1 :** to make a mess of **:** mutilate almost beyond recognition ⟨*hashed up* the account of the accident⟩ ⟨a concept that has *hashed up* remedial legislation⟩ **2 :** to warm up **:** give fresh existence to **:** REANIMATE ⟨*hashing up* ancient quarrels —*Times Lit. Supp.*⟩ ⟨*hash up* novel interpretations of men and events based on little more than the findings of their predecessors —*Listener*⟩

**ha·sid** *or* **cha·sid** *or* **has·sid** *or* **chas·sid** \'hasəd, 'käs-\ *n, pl* **ha·sid·im** *or* **has·sid·im** \'hasədəm, kə'sēd-\ *usu cap* [Heb *hāsīdh* pious, one who is pious (pl. *hāsīdhīm*)] **1 :** a member of a pious Jewish sect founded about the 3d century B.C. by opponents of Hellenistic innovations and devoted to the strict observance of the ritual of purification and separation — called also *assidean* **2 :** a member of a Jewish sect devoted to mysticism and opposed to secular studies and Jewish rationalism that was founded in Poland about 1750 by Rabbi Israel ben Eliezer to revive the strict practices of the earlier Hasidim — **ha·sid·ic** *or* **cha·sid·ic** *or* **has·sid·ic** *or* **chas·sid·ic** \hə'sidik, kə'-\ *adj, usu cap*

**hasidean** *or* **hasidaean** *usu cap, var of* ASSIDEAN

**has·i·dism** *or* **chas·i·dism** *or* **hass·i·dism** *or* **chass·i·dism** \'hasə,dizəm, 'käs-\ *n* -S *usu cap* **:** the practices and beliefs of the Hasidim

**ha·si·nai** \'häsə,nī\ *n, pl* **hasinai** *usu cap* **1 :** one of the three principal confederations of the Caddo Indians inhabiting northeastern Texas **2 :** a member of the Hasinai Confederacy

**hask** \'(h)ask\ *adj* [ME, harsh, alter. of *harsk* — more at HARSH] **1** *now dial Eng, of weather* **:** cold and dry **2** *now dial Eng* **a :** rough and harsh to the touch **b :** harsh to the taste **3** *now dial Eng* **:** coarse and dry in texture

**has·ka·lah** \,haskə'lä, häs'kōlə\ *n* -S *usu cap, often attrib* [NHeb *haśkālāh*, lit., intellect, enlightenment] **:** an intellectual enlightenment movement among Jews of eastern Europe in the 18th and 19th centuries that attempted to acquaint the masses with European and Hebrew languages and secular education and culture to supplement talmudic studies — see MASKIL

**has·let** *or* **hass·let** \'haslət, 'hās-, -āzl-\ *n* -S [ME *hastlet, hastelet*, fr. MF *hastelet* piece of meat roasted on a spit, dim. of *haste* piece of meat roasted on a spit, fr. OF, modif. (influenced by OF *haste* shaft of a spear, fr. L *hasta* spear) of a Gmc word represented by OHG *harsta* frying pan; akin to OE *hierstan, hyrstan* to fry, roast, MHG *harst* gridiron, OE *heorth* hearth — more at HEARTH, YARD] **1 :** the edible viscera (as the heart or liver) of a butchered animal (as a hog) **2 :** a braised dish made of edible viscera

**has·mo·nae·an** *or* **has·mo·ne·an** \,hazmə'nēən\ *or* **as·mo·nae·an** *or* **as·mo·ne·an** \,az-\ *n* -S *usu cap* [LL *Asmonaeus* Hasmon, ancestor of the Maccabees (fr. Gk *Asamōnaios*) + E *-an*] **:** a member of a dynasty or family of Jewish patriots to which the Maccabees belonged

**has·na** \'haznə\ [by contr.] *dial Brit* **:** has not

**hasn't** \'haz°n(t)\ [by contr.] **:** has not

**1hasp** \'hasp, 'haa(ə)sp, 'haisp, 'häsp\ *n* -S [ME *hasp, haspe*, fr. OE *hæsp, hæpse*; akin to MHG *haspe* hasp, ON *hespa*, and perh. to L *capsa* chest, case — more at CASE] **1 a :** a fastener esp. for a door or lid consisting of a hinged metal strap that fits over a staple and is secured by a pin or padlock **b :** a similar strap having a projecting knob that snaps into a lock and that is much used on luggage **c :** any of several other devices (as a latch) for fastening a door or window ⟨the spring of the window ~ —G.M.Fenn⟩ **2 :** a clasp for a book or an article of clothing ⟨a ledger bound with metal ~*s* —William Fifield⟩ ⟨cape with a ~ at the throat⟩ **3** *now dial Eng* **a :** a skein or hank of yarn, thread, or silk **b :** a fourth part of a spindle of such material

hasps 1

**2hasp** \"\ *vt* -ED/-ING/-S [ME *haspen*, fr. OE *hæpsian*, fr. *hæpse*, n.] **1 :** to fasten with or as if with a hasp ⟨~ the door⟩ **2** *obs* **:** to confine in a small space — often used with *up* ⟨~*ed up* with thee in this small vehicle —*Spectator*⟩

**hasp lock** *n* **1 :** a prison lock attached permanently to the hasp of a door and adapted to secure the door **2 :** a detachable lock (as a padlock) to secure a hasp

**has·sall's corpuscle** *also* **has·sal's corpuscle** \'hasəlz-\ *n, usu cap H* **:** CORPUSCLE OF HASSALL

**has·sar** \'hasə(r)\ *n* -S [Arawak *asa*] **:** any of several armored catfishes (family Callichthyidae) of the Orinoco and its tributaries that are remarkable for their nest-building habits and for being able to leave the water and travel some distance on land

**hassenpfeffer** *var of* HASENPFEFFER

**hassid** *usu cap, var of* HASID

**hassidean** *or* **hassidaean** *usu cap, var of* ASSIDEAN

**1has·sle** *also* **has·sel** \'hasəl, 'haas-, 'hais-, 'häs-\ *n* -S [perh. blend of *2haggle* and *2tussle*] **1 a :** a heated argument **:** WRANGLE ⟨embroiling myself in a long, exasperating ~ with masons —S.J.Perelman⟩ **b :** a violent skirmish **:** FIGHT ⟨small units and small patrols, but for those in each ~ . . . it is still a tense, blood-curdling exchange of bullets —*N.Y. Times*⟩ **2 :** a protracted debate **:** CONTROVERSY ⟨an extremely esoteric ~ over . . . ideas and concepts —Philip Hamburger⟩ **3 a :** a state of confusion or commotion **:** TURMOIL ⟨all ~ and hurly-burly —Ellery Queen⟩ **b :** a strenuous effort **:** STRUGGLE ⟨it's been a real ~ digging up new talent —Benny Goodman⟩

**2hassle** \"\ *vi* **hassled; hassled; hassling** \-s(ə)liŋ\ **hassles :** ARGUE, FIGHT, DISPUTE ⟨*hassled* with the umpires a time or two too many —Leo Durocher⟩ ⟨a lot of *hassling* back and forth over the telephone —*Sports Illustrated*⟩

**hasslet** *var of* HASLET

**has·sock** \'hasək, -aas-\ *n* -S [ME, fr. OE *hassuc*] **1 :** a rank tuft of bog grass or sedge **:** TUSSOCK **2 a :** a small kneeling cushion or footstool ⟨an old-fashioned church ~ with flaps at the ends —Anna Kavan⟩ **b :** a bulky upholstered cushion used as an article of household furniture: as (1) **:** a large stuffed cushion that serves as a seat or leg rest — compare OTTOMAN, POUF (2) **:** a similar cushion or backless padded seat mounted on legs or having a hollow center for storage

hassocks 2b(1)

**hassock fan** *n* **:** an electric fan operating in a cylindrical hassock-shaped frame and propelling air upward from the floor

**hassock grass** *n* **:** TUFTED HAIR GRASS 2

**has·socky** \-kē\ *adj* **:** full of hassocks

**has·su·na** \hə'sünə\ *or* **has·su·nan** \-nən\ *adj, usu cap* [*hassuna* fr. *Hassuna*, archaeological site in northern Iraq; *hassunan* fr. *Hassuna* + E *-an*] **:** of or relating to an Aeneolithic culture of Mesopotamia earlier than the Halafian and characterized by the use of sometimes painted pottery, the manufacture of small clay figurines of women, and urn burial

**hast** *archaic pres 2d sing of* HAVE

**has·ta** \'hastə\ [contr. of *hast thou*] *dial Brit* **:** have you

**has·tate** \'ha,stāt\ *adj* [NL *hastatus*, fr. L *hasta* spear — more at YARD] **1 :** shaped like an arrow with flaring barbs **2** *of a leaf* **:** triangular with sharp basal lobes spreading away from the petiole — see LEAF illustration — **has·tate·ly** *adv*

**hastato-** *comb form* [NL, fr. *hastatus*] **:** hastately **:** hastate and ⟨*hastato*lanceolate⟩ ⟨*hastato*sagittate⟩

**1haste** \'hāst\ *n* -S [ME, fr. OF, of Gmc origin; akin to OE *hǣst* violence, OHG *heisti* violent, *heiftig* impetuous, ON *heipt, heifst* feud, war, hatred, Goth *haifsts* strife, conflict, fight; perh. akin to Skt *śībham* quickly] **1 :** rapidity of motion **:** SPEED ⟨out of breath from ~ —Jane Austen⟩ **2 :** rash or headlong action **:** PRECIPITATENESS ⟨~ makes waste⟩ ⟨the beauty of speed uncontaminated by ~ —*Harper's*⟩ **3 :** over-eagerness to act **:** HURRY ⟨I feel no ~ and no reluctance to depart —Edna S. V. Millay⟩

**syn** HURRY, SPEED, EXPEDITION, DISPATCH: HASTE indicates quickness or swiftness, often careless, on the part of persons impelled by urgency, pressure, eagerness ⟨"Why this mad *haste*?" I asked. "Bandits", he shouted. —W.O.Douglas⟩ HURRY may imply haste with confusion, agitation, and hustle ⟨there was a great *hurry* in the streets, of people speeding away to get shelter before the storm broke —Charles Dickens⟩ ⟨for whom all these women worked with such a sense of frantic *hurry* —Winifred Bambrick⟩ SPEED may focus attention on the fact of quickness, with very occasional implications of success ⟨such developments are bound to increase the *speed* of the social and economic revolution —R.W.Steel⟩ ⟨accused of slowness and undue deliberation, yet he built an adequate navy from nothing with surprising *speed* —H.K.Beale⟩ EXPEDITION and DISPATCH both designate efficient speed, the former with a suggestion of smooth efficiency, the latter of brisk promptness ⟨to move with reasonable *expedition* along the narrow pavements of Rotting Hill is impossible —Wyndham Lewis⟩ ⟨proceed with great *dispatch* and arrest the people involved —Dean Acheson⟩

**2haste** \"\ *vb* -ED/-ING/-S [ME *hasten*, fr. OF *haster*, fr. *haste*, n.] *vt, archaic* **:** to urge on **:** HASTEN ⟨with our fair entreaties ~ them on —Shak.⟩ ⟨~ thee, nymph, and bring with thee jest and youthful jollity —John Milton⟩ ~ *vi* **:** to move or act swiftly **:** HURRY ⟨~ to correct a seeming impression —O.W. Holmes †1935⟩ ⟨these minutes even now *hasting* into eternity —Winston Churchill⟩

**haste·ful** \-tfəl\ *adj* **:** full of haste **:** HASTY — **haste·ful·ly** \-fəlē\ *adv*

**haste·less** \-tləs\ *adj* **:** being without haste **:** UNHURRIED

**has·ten** \'hās°n\ *vb* **hastened; hastened; hastening** \-s(°)niŋ\ **hastens** [alter. of *2haste*] *vt* **1 a :** to urge on **:** HURRY ⟨~*ed* her to the door —A.J.Cronin⟩ **b :** to speed up **:** ACCELERATE ⟨~ the coming of a new order —D.W.Brogan⟩ **2** *obs* **:** to send or bring quickly ⟨I pray . . . the king . . . to ~ his effectual letters —Edward Nicholas⟩ ~ *vi* **:** to move or act quickly **:** make haste **:** HURRY ⟨must ~ on to the bull ring —Mary Webb⟩ ⟨let me ~ to add that I do not mean absolute values —Kemp Malone⟩ **syn** see SPEED

**has·ten·er** \-s(°)nə(r)\ *n* -S **:** one that hastens

**hast·er** \'hāstə(r)\ *n* -S [*2haste* + *-er*] **:** HASTENER

**has·ti·lude** \'hastə,lüd\ *n, pl* **hastiludes** \-dz\ *or* **hastilu·dia** \,=='lüdēə\ [ML *hastiludium*, fr. LL *hasti-* (fr. L *hasta* spear) + *-ludium* (fr. L *ludus* play, sport) — more at YARD, LUDICROUS] **:** a medieval joust **:** spear play ⟨one sport called ~*s* was no less dangerous than war itself —W.H.Dixon⟩

**hast·i·ly** \'hāstəlē, -li\ *adv* [ME, fr. *hasty* + *-ly*] **1 :** rapidly and often with little attention to detail **:** HURRIEDLY ⟨read it ~⟩ ⟨wartime factories were ~ built⟩ **2 :** without thorough consideration **:** RASHLY ⟨sold ~ and at a sacrifice —Raymond Weaver⟩

**hast·i·ness** \-tēnəs\ *n* -ES [ME *hastinesse*, fr. *hasty* + *-nesse* -ness] **:** the quality or state of being hasty

**hast·ings** \'(h)āstənz\ *n pl* [pl. of obs. E *hasting* early fruit or vegetable, fr. *hasting*, adj., ripening early, fr. pres. part. of E *2haste*] *now dial Eng* **:** early fruit or vegetables; *esp* **:** early peas

**has·tings·ite** \'hāstiŋ,zīt\ *n* -S [*Hastings* county, Ontario, Canada, its locality + E *-ite*] **:** a sodium-calcium-iron amphibole ideally $NaCa_2Fe_5Al_2Si_6O_{22}(OH)_2$ but generally containing a little potassium and magnesium

**has·tu·la** \'haschələ\ *n* -S [NL, fr. L, small spear, dim. of *hasta* spear] **:** a flat often triangular expansion at the upper surface of the petiole of a palm leaf where it joins the blade

**hasty** \'hāstē, -ti\ *adj* -ER/-EST [ME, fr. OF *hasti, hastif*, fr. *haste*, n. + *-if* -ive] **1 a :** rapid in action or movement **:** SPEEDY ⟨a ~ traveler⟩ **b :** made in a hurry **:** QUICK ⟨~ city-street snapshots —R.B.Heilman⟩ **c :** fast and often superficial **:** HURRIED ⟨a ~ smoke⟩ **2 :** being in a hurry **:** EAGER, IMPATIENT ⟨too passionate and ~ to keep pace with the deliberate steps of his leader —Philip Marsh⟩ **3 :** ill-considered **:** PRECIPITATE, RASH ⟨warning against ~ enterprises and partial solutions —M.R.Cohen⟩ **4 :** prone to anger **:** IRRITABLE ⟨a man of ~ temper —G.B.Shaw⟩ **syn** see FAST, PRECIPITATE

**hasty pudding** *n* **1** *Brit* **:** a porridge or pudding made of oatmeal or flour boiled in water **2** *NewEng* **:** cornmeal mush usu. served hot with milk and maple sugar or molasses — compare INDIAN PUDDING

**1hat** \'hat, *usu* -ad·+V\ *n* -S *often attrib* [ME, fr. OE *hæt*; akin to ON *hǫttr* head covering — more at HOOD] **1 :** a covering for the head: as **a :** a head covering typically having a shaped crown and brim and made of felt, straw, or silk and worn by men — distinguished from *cap*; compare DERBY, FELT, STETSON, STRAW HAT **b :** a decorative accessory in a wide variety of shapes and materials worn by women — compare BONNET, CARTWHEEL, CLOCHE, PILLBOX, SAILOR, TOQUE **2 a :** a head covering of distinctive color or shape worn as a symbol of office ⟨cardinal's ~⟩ **b :** an office symbolized by or as if by the wearing of a special hat ⟨the two principal ~*s* a president wears are those of ceremonial head of state and chief executive —Cabell Phillips⟩ **3 :** a layer of bark spread on the hides in a tanning pit **4 :** a container used for taking up a collection of voluntary contributions (as of money) ⟨go round with the ~⟩ ⟨pass the ~⟩ — **have one's hat in the ring** *or* **throw one's hat in the ring** *or* **toss one's hat in the ring :** to announce one's entry or readiness to enter into a fight or contest (as for elective office) — **take one's hat off to :** to acknowledge the achievement or superiority of **:** COMPLIMENT ⟨the way was colossal and I *take my hat off to* him —H.J.Laski⟩

**2hat** \"\ *vb* **hatted; hatted; hatting; hats** *vt* **1 :** to furnish or provide with a hat ⟨smartly gowned, *hatted*, and gloved for the journey —A.N.Whitehead⟩ **2 :** to bestow a cardinal's hat on ~ *vi* **:** to make or supply hats

**3hat** *dial past of* HIT

**4hat** *dial Eng var of* HIT

**hatable** *var of* HATEABLE

**hat ball** *n* **:** a game of roly-poly in which the ball is rolled into hats placed on the ground

**hatband** \'=,=\ *n* [ME, fr. *1hat* + *band*, n.] **:** a band of fabric, leather, or cord around the crown of a hat just above the brim

**hatbox** \'=,=\ *n* **1 :** a box for holding hats **2 :** a piece of hand luggage that is usu. round and deep, has a handle, and is designed esp. for carrying hats though it is often used as a traveling bag by women

**1hatch** \'hach\ *n* -ES [ME *hache, hacche*, fr. OE *hæc*; akin to MD *hecke* trapdoor, grating, MLG *heck* fence] **1 a** *obs* **:** the lower half of a divided door ⟨in at the window or else o'er the ~ —Shak.⟩ **b :** a small door, wicket, or serving counter ⟨equipped with an escape ~ for use in case of fire —W.H. Goodenough⟩ ⟨shop through a ~ in the wall —*Time*⟩ ⟨snatched up two plates of cold tongue . . . from the serving-room ~ —Margaret Kennedy⟩ **2 a** *obs* (1) **:** movable planking over the cargo hold of a ship — usu. used in pl. (2) **:** DECK — usu. used in pl. ⟨upon the giddy footing of the ~*es* —Shak.⟩ **b :** a door or grated cover giving vertical access down into a compartment ⟨smoke rose through the same ~ where . . . men could climb to the cannon deck —J.H.Cutler⟩ ⟨luggage disappears through the big plane's ~⟩ ⟨the inspector lifts the ~ in the top of the oil storage tank⟩; *specif* **:** the cover of a tank turret ⟨one of the .50-caliber guns can be . . . fired from inside without opening the turret ~ —*Military Rev.*⟩ **c :** HATCHWAY **d :** an enclosed space **:** COMPARTMENT ⟨her ~*es* were enlarged and her lumber-carrying career . . . resumed —H.G.Peterson⟩ ⟨device . . . the airman is placing in its release ~ —*N.Y. Times Mag.*⟩ **3 :** something that resembles a hatch: as **a :** FLOODGATE, SLUICE GATE **b :** an opening or door in the deck or fuselage of an airplane (as for a means of escape in an emergency or for loading cargo) **c :** a frame or weir in a river for catching fish

**2hatch** \'(h)ach\ *vt* -ED/-ING/-ES *now dial Eng* **:** to close (a door) with a hatch

**3hatch** \'hach\ *vb* -ED/-ING/-ES [ME *hacchen*; akin to MHG *hecken* to mate (said of birds)] *vi* **1 :** to produce young from an egg by incubation ⟨the hen ~*ed* today⟩ **2 :** to emerge from an egg or chrysalis ⟨watched the chickens ~⟩ ⟨begins to ~ from the chrysalis in early July —E.B.Ford⟩ — often used with *off* or *out* ⟨hens' eggs take 21 days to ~ out —*Jeyes' Poultry Bk.*⟩ **3 :** to incubate eggs **:** BROOD ⟨the old hen is ~*ing*⟩ ~ *vt* **1** *archaic* **:** BREED, PROPAGATE ⟨what monsters now doth nature ~ —*Mirour for Magistrates*⟩ ⟨serving as a nursery bed to ~ . . . the infant plant —William Bartram⟩ **2 a :** to produce (young) from an egg by applying natural or artificial heat ⟨a duck . . . which ~*ed* chickens —Margaret Deland⟩ ⟨an incubator can ~ more eggs at a time than a hen⟩ **b :** to cause to incubate ⟨turtle eggs are ~*ed* by the sun⟩ **3 :** to bring into being **:** ORIGINATE, PRODUCE ⟨~*ing* a program of economic aid —E.K.Lindley⟩ ⟨they repair to the little summer place to garden and smoke pipes, they ~ books, they go fishing —George Spelvin⟩; *esp* **:** to concoct in secret ⟨~ a conspiracy⟩ — often used with *up* ⟨when was all this ~*ed up* —Ann Bridge⟩

**4hatch** \"\ *n* -ES **1 a :** an act of hatching ⟨congregate in family groups soon after the ~ —W.W.Haines⟩ **b :** the transformation of a swarm of insects from a water-dwelling to a winged phase ⟨trout were rising freely to a ~ of small gray flies —F.C. Craighead b. 1916 & J.J.Craighead⟩ **2 :** a product of hatching **:** brood of young ⟨the entire ~ in an incubator —J.E.Shillinger & L.C.Morley⟩

**5hatch** \"\ *vt* -ED/-ING/-ES [ME *hachen*, fr. MF *hacher*, fr. OF *hachier* to chop up — more at HASH] **1 :** to inlay in fine lines **:** apply narrow bands of a different color or material to **2 :** to mark with fine closely spaced parallel or crisscrossed lines in drawing or engraving chiefly to represent shading — see 3HATCHING

**6hatch** \"\ *n* -ES **:** STROKE, LINE; *esp* **:** one used in engraving or drawing to give the effect of shading

**hatch·abil·i·ty** \,hachə'bilədē\ *n* **1 :** the quality or state of being hatchable ⟨low ~ generally means low vitality in the chicks that do hatch —*Reliable Poultry Jour.*⟩ **2 :** the ability to produce hatchable eggs ⟨turkey hens which become broody during the laying season show higher . . . ~ than nonbroody hens —*Agric. Research in S. Dak.*⟩

**hatch·able** \'hachəbəl\ *adj* [*3hatch* + *-able*] *of an egg* **:** capable of being hatched

**hatch bar** *n* **:** a bar across a hatch to batten it down

**hatch beam** *n* **:** a heavy portable beam across a large hatch to support the cover

**hatch deck** *n* **:** a temporary deck of removable planking or covers over the hold

**hatcheck** \'=,=\ *adj* **1 :** that checks hats and other articles of clothing ⟨~ girl⟩ **2 :** used in the checking of hats and other articles of clothing ⟨~ stand⟩

**1hatch·el** \'hachəl\ *also* **hetch·el** \'hech-\ *n* -S [*hatchel* alter. of *hetchel*, fr. ME *hechele, hekele, hakell*; akin to MD *hekele* hackle, MHG *hechel, hachel* hackle, OHG *hāko* hook — more at HOOK] **:** 3HACKLE 1

**2hatchel** \"\ *vt* **hatcheled** *or* **hatchelled; hatcheled** *or* **hatchelled; hatcheling** *or* **hatchelling; hatchels** [alter. of earlier *hetchel*, fr. ME *hechelen*, fr. *hechele*, n.] **1 :** 4HACKLE 1 **2 :** HECKLE 2

**hatch·er** \'hachə(r)\ *n* -S **1 :** one that hatches; *specif* **:** a device to which eggs are transferred from the incubator shortly before they are due to hatch **2 :** one that produces or originates

**hatch·ery** \-ch(ə)rē, -ri\ *n* -ES **1 :** a place for hatching eggs (as of poultry or fish) **2 :** a place for the large-scale production of weanling feeder pigs

**hatch·ery·man** \'=(=)=,=\ *n, pl* **hatcherymen :** one who operates a hatchery

**hatches** *pl of* HATCH, *pres 3d sing of* HATCH

**1hatch·et** \'hachət, *usu* -əd·+V\ *n* -S *often attrib* [ME *hachet, hacchet* small ax, fr. MF *hachette*, fr. *hache* battle-ax + *-ette* — more at HASH] **1 a :** a short-handled ax with a hammerhead to be used with one hand either for cutting or hammering **b :** TOMAHAWK **2 :** a dental excavator

**2hatchet** \"\ *vt* -ED/-ING/-S **1 :** to cut or kill with a hatchet ⟨~ a tree⟩ ⟨~ an enemy⟩ **2 :** to dispatch as if with a hatchet ⟨~ proposal⟩

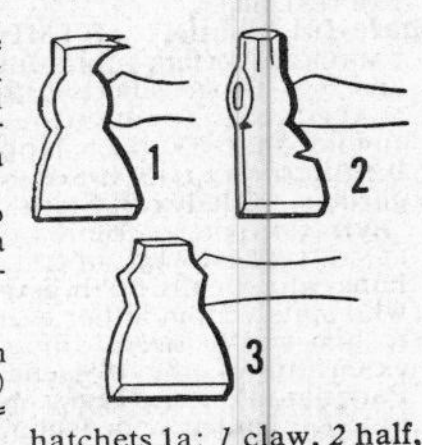

hatchets 1a: *1* claw, *2* half, *3* broad

**hatchet cactus** *n* **:** a small Mexican cactus (*Pelecyphora aselliformis*) with white flowers and hatchet-shaped tubercles

**hatchet face** *n* **1 :** a long narrow face with sharp features **2 :** a person having a thin sharp face — **hatchet-faced** \'=,='=\ *adj*

**hatchetfish** \'=,=,=\ *n* **:** any of several small So. American characin fishes with enlarged pectoral fins and thin wedge-shaped bodies that are often seen in tropical aquariums

**hatchet job** *n* **:** an act of defamation **:** malicious attack ⟨turned traitor to his class and performed a *hatchet job* on the commuting world —*Time*⟩

**hatchet man** *n* **1 :** a professional killer **:** TRIGGERMAN, HIGHBINDER ⟨the hooded cult retaliated and four . . . *hatchet men* were found dead in a ditch —W.M.Swann⟩ **2 a :** one who transmits orders or maintains discipline for a superior **:** HENCHMAN ⟨needed a competent and senior foreign service *hatchet man* to keep the . . . career boys under control —*Harper's*⟩; *specif* **:** an ideological watchdog or party disciplinarian ⟨served his party as chief *hatchet man* —Robert Bendiner⟩ **b** (1) **:** a writer who specializes in denunciation and invective often on orders from an employer and without regard to personal scruples ⟨our present journalistic *hatchet man* —B.R.Redman⟩ (2) **:** CRITIC ⟨a literary *hatchet man* —S.E.Hyman⟩

**hatchet stake** *n* **:** a sharp-edged stake on which to bend sheet metal — see STAKE illustration

**hatch·ett·ine** \ˈhachəd·ˌēn, -d·ən\ *or* **hatch·ett·ite** \-d·ˌīt\ *n* -s [Charles *Hatchett* †1847 Eng. chemist + E *-ine* or *-ite*] **:** a mineral paraffin wax $C_{38}H_{78}$ melting at 55° to 65° C in the natural state and at 79° C when pure — called also *mineral tallow*

**hatch·et·to·lite** \-d·ō,līt\ *n* -s [Charles *Hatchett* †1847 + E *-o-* + *-lite*] **:** a uranium-bearing pyrochlore

**hatchet work** *n* **:** the work of a hatchet man

**hatchgate** \ˈ=,=\ *n* **1 :** WICKET **2 :** ¹HATCH 3a

¹**hatching** *n* -s [ME *hacchynge*, fr. gerund of ME *hacchen* to produce young from an egg by incubation — more at HATCH (verb)] **:** ⁴HATCH

²**hatching** *n* -s [fr. gerund of ⁵*hatch*] **1 a :** the engraving or drawing of fine lines in close proximity to each other chiefly to give an effect of shading **b :** the pattern so created **2 :** the process or result of weaving threads of one color into an adjoining area of another color in a tapestry so as to produce an effect of shading or highlights **3 :** a fine concentric line of pores in the tangential section of some woods

**hatching spine** *n* **:** a spine on the unhatched young of various insects used to break the embryonic envelope

**hatch·ite** \ˈha,chīt\ *n* -s [Frederick H. *Hatch* †1932 Eng. mining engineer and geologist + E *-ite*] **:** a mineral consisting of a sulfide of lead and arsenic that occurs in triclinic crystals but whose exact composition is unknown

**hatch·ling** \ˈhachliŋ\ *n* -s **:** a recently hatched animal

**hatch·man** \ˈ=mən\ *also* **hatch·mind·er** \ˈ=,==\ *or* **hatch·way·man** \ˈ=,=mən\ *n, pl* **hatchmen** *also* **hatchminders** *or* **hatchwaymen :** one who stands by a ship's hatch to assist with the loading and unloading

**hatch·ment** \ˈhachmənt\ *n* -s [perh. alter. of *achievement*] **:** a panel having the shape of a square placed cornerwise or of a lozenge, bearing the coat of arms of a deceased person, and displayed temporarily usu. on the outside wall of his dwelling

**hatchure** *obs var of* HACHURE

**hatchway** \ˈ=,=\ *n* **:** an opening equipped with a hatch and giving access to a compartment, room, or cellar; *specif* **:** a passageway between the decks of a ship

**hatch whip** *n* **:** a block and tackle for hoisting cargo through a hatchway

**hat dance** *n* **:** a national courtship folk dance of Mexico performed by two people in which the man throws a sombrero on the ground and the girl signifies acceptance of him as her lover by dancing on its brim and then putting it on her head — compare JARABE

¹**hate** \ˈhāt, *usu* -ād·+V\ *n* -s *often attrib* [ME, alter. (prob. influenced by *haten*, v.) of *hete*, fr. OE; akin to OHG *haz* hate, ON *hatr* hate, Goth *hatis* wrath, Gk *kēdos* grief, mourning, Av *sādra* sorrow] **1 a :** intense hostility toward an object (as an individual) that has frustrated the release of an inner tension (as of a biological nature) ⟨quick dislike had ripened into ~ —I.V.Morris⟩ ⟨rid your mind of any hidden ~*s* or grudges —W.J.Reilly⟩; *specif* **:** a systematic esp. politically exploited expression of hate ⟨the forces of darkness, bigotry, and ~⟩ ⟨~ list⟩ ⟨~ bombings⟩ ⟨~ mail⟩ **b :** an habitual emotional attitude in which distaste is coupled with sustained ill will ⟨his life became increasingly dominated by ~⟩ **c :** a strong dislike or antipathy **:** DISTASTE ⟨developed a ~ for string quartets⟩ **2 :** an object of hatred ⟨a generation whose finest ~ had been big business —F.L.Paxson⟩

²**hate** \ˈ"\ *vb* -ED/-ING/-S [ME *haten*, fr. OE *hatian*; akin to OS *haton* to hate, OHG *hazzōn*, ON *hata*; denominative fr. the root of ¹*hate*] *vt* **1 :** to feel extreme enmity toward **:** regard with active hostility ⟨sit there *hating* one another and end up by cutting one another's throats —John Wain⟩ **2 a :** to have a strong aversion to **:** DETEST, RESENT ⟨~ what is evil, hold fast to what is good —Rom 12: 9 (RSV)⟩ ⟨they ~ being moved from one box to another —Henry Wynmalen⟩ **b :** to find distasteful **:** DISLIKE ⟨*hated* the cold and the snow —Harold Griffin⟩ ⟨so pretty she *hated* to get glasses when she needed them —John Steinbeck⟩ ⟨*hated* that young men should raise their hats to him out of respect for his superior age —Arnold Bennett⟩ **~** *vi* **:** to express or feel extreme enmity or active hostility ⟨harsh faces and *hating* eyes —Katherine A. Porter⟩

**syn** DETEST, LOATHE, ABHOR, ABOMINATE: HATE, the antonym of love, indicates an extreme of dislike, aversion, and enmity experienced often toward an equal with a possible accompanying feeling of grudging respect ⟨if there had been one atom of genuine passion in his duplicity, she might have despised him less even while she *hated* him more —Ellen Glasgow⟩ ⟨he *hates* Lucy Wales. I don't mean dislike, or find distasteful, or have an aversion for; I mean hate —Hamilton Basso⟩ Applied to things and qualities it indicates extreme dislike ⟨between the cruelty that we *hate* and the humor that we prize —Agnes Repplier⟩ DETEST indicates very strong aversion but may lack the actively hostile malevolence associated with HATE ⟨the boy glimpsed something of the system of slavery, and early came to *detest* it —C.E.Carter⟩ LOATHE may suggest disgust and revulsion rather than aversion and active antipathy ⟨except when I am listening to their music I *loathe* the whole race: great, stupid, brutal, immoral, sentimental savages —Rose Macaulay⟩ ⟨he is not hated, for in hate there is something of fear and something of respect, neither of which is present here. And you could not say *loathed*, for loathing is passive and this is an active feeling. Best say detested; vigorously disliked —T.O. Heggen⟩ ABHOR may suggest a revulsion or repugnance accompanied by a tendency to flinch from as though in fear or horror ⟨Rome had made herself *abhorred* throughout the world by the violence and avarice of her generals —J.A. Froude⟩ ⟨this temptation to *abhor* the flesh, which reached such a pitch that he was filled with a horror of all created life —Compton Mackenzie⟩ ⟨rats, who *abhor* light and crave privacy —V.G.Heiser⟩ ABOMINATE may indicate strong lasting hatred and loathing as of something foully unnatural ⟨the accused . . . protest, disclaim, *abominate* the honor —Robert Browning⟩ These words all weaken in hyperbolic usages.

— **hate one's guts :** to feel a particularly strong animosity or contempt for someone ⟨I don't dislike him, I *hate his guts* —E.S.Gardner⟩

³**hate** \ˈ"\ *var of* HAET

**hate·able** *or* **hat·able** \ˈhād·əbəl\ *adj* **:** subject to being hated **:** DETESTABLE

**hate·ful** \ˈhātfəl\ *adj* [ME, fr. ¹*hate* + *-ful*] **1 :** full of hate **:** MALICIOUS ⟨talk of an outbreak of the Sioux who were surly and ~ —Bruce Siberts⟩ **2 a :** exciting or deserving of hatred **:** REPULSIVE ⟨opinions ~ to the majority —M.R.Cohen⟩ ⟨avoid that ~ backslapping heartiness —R.B.McKerrow⟩ **b :** UNCONGENIAL, ANNOYING, DISTASTEFUL ⟨~ to be without a garden —Gladys B. Stern⟩

**syn** ABHORRENT, OBNOXIOUS, INVIDIOUS, REPUGNANT, REPELLENT, DISTASTEFUL: HATEFUL applies to that which arouses hate, which calls forth active hostility ⟨the *hateful* old cat . . . who spits venom in her every sentence —C.B.Tinker⟩ ⟨the war to him was a *hateful* thing, stupid and unjust, waged for the extension of the obscene system of negro slavery —V.L. Parrington⟩ ABHORRENT may characterize that which arouses hatred blended with feelings of horror or outrage ⟨to Greek thought the indefinite or limitless was as the monstrous and unformed, and therefore *abhorrent* to the classic ideals of perfection —H.O.Taylor⟩ ⟨they themselves consider sorcery as an *abhorrent* crime —W.J.Wallace & Edith S. Taylor⟩ OBNOXIOUS describes what is objectionable or extremely repulsive ⟨when mosquitoes grew *obnoxious* we packed up our dishes and went to the house —Della Lutes⟩ ⟨an opportunity to hang around the house and smoke too many cigars and aggravate his poor, patient wife, and exasperate his children, and make himself generally *obnoxious* to all —Simeon Ford⟩ ⟨resentment against the Stamp Act reached a climax . . . His Majesty's Ship Diligence was prevented from landing the *obnoxious* stamps —*Amer. Guide Series: N. C.*⟩ INVIDIOUS describes that which excites ill will, resentment, or hatred, and is likely to rankle ⟨bowed with an *invidious* curtness and insolently walked off the stage —Edmund Wilson⟩ ⟨the *invidious* task of improving other people's utterance —J.M.Barzun⟩ ⟨rogues, by which perhaps rather *invidious* name I designate persons who will do nothing unless they get something out of it for themselves —G.B.Shaw⟩ REPUGNANT applies to what is resisted, disliked, and shunned as incompatible with one's principles or tastes ⟨soon the pressures of male eyes, eyes expressing sex, the curious lamplike luminosity, became *repugnant* to her —Peggy Bennett⟩ ⟨the internationalism of the socialists found any barriers of race or nationality *repugnant* —Oscar Handlin⟩ ⟨the nonlegal methods of the magistrates in dispensing judgment, so *repugnant* to the spirit of the common law —V.L. Parrington⟩ REPELLENT, close to REPUGNANT, may apply to what is shunned as offensive to personal tastes and inclinations ⟨as *repellent* in form and abstract in substance as many of the German writers on aesthetics of the nineteenth century —Irving Babbitt⟩ ⟨as a cardinal's nephew he was accustomed to many and *repellent* smiles upon inimical lips —Elinor Wylie⟩ DISTASTEFUL, a somewhat less forceful term, applies to what one dislikes, usu. for strongly personal reasons ⟨don't like my letters shown about as curiosities: it is most *distasteful* to me —Oscar Wilde⟩ ⟨developed a keen interest in the purely scientific aspects of medicine, the more practical phases of a practitioner's routine being *distasteful* to him —J.F.Fulton⟩ ⟨plans to refurnish the bedrooms with her own personal belongings, since she finds it *distasteful* to think of using the personal belongings of its previous occupants —Kenneth Roberts⟩

**hate·ful·ly** \-fəlē, -li\ *adv* [ME, fr. *hateful* + *-ly*] **:** in a hateful manner

**hate·ful·ness** *n* -ES **:** the quality or state of being hateful

**hate·less** \ˈhātləs\ *adj* **:** being without hate — **hate·less·ness** *n* -ES

**hatemonger** \ˈ=,==\ *n* **:** one who enjoys or makes a practice of stirring up enmity **:** AGITATOR ⟨local ~s were probably financed and directed from outside the state —*Associated Press*⟩

**hatemongering** \ˈ=,=(=)=\ *n* **:** the act or practice of stirring up hatred or enmity

**hate out** *vt* **:** to drive out by hostility ⟨a common way of dealing with offenders was to *hate* them *out* of the community —C.M.Babcock⟩

**hat·er** \ˈhād·ə(r), -ātə-\ *n* -s [ME *hatere*, fr. *haten* to hate + *-ere* -er] **:** one that hates

**hates** *pl of* HATE, *pres 3d sing of* HATE

**hate sheet** *n* **:** a newspaper or periodical characterized by strong feelings against a race or a national or religious group ⟨the worst inflammatory *hate sheet* published —Walter Winchell⟩

**hat·field yew** \ˈhat,fēld-\ *n, sometimes cap H* [after T. D. *Hatfield* *fl*1900 Am. horticulturist] **:** an ornamental yew that is a variety (*Taxus cuspidata hatfieldii*) of Japanese yew with ascending branches and wide spreading leaves

**hat·ful** \ˈhat,fu̇l\ *n, pl* **hatfuls** *also* **hatsful** \-t,fu̇lz, ts,fu̇l\ **1 :** as much or as many as a hat will hold ⟨gathered a ~ of eggs⟩ **2 :** a considerable amount or number **:** PECK ⟨these dives can cost you a ~ of money —T.H.Fielding⟩ ⟨turned down a ~ of princes —Helen B. Woodward⟩

**hath** *archaic pres 3d sing of* HAVE

**hatha–yoga** \ˈhəd·əˈyōgə\ *n* [Skt *haṭha* force, persistence + *yoga* disciplined activity — more at YOGA] **:** a system of physical exercises for the control and perfection of the body that constitutes one of the four chief Hindu disciplines — see YOGA

**ha·thi gray** \ˈhäd·ē-\ *n* [Hindi *hāthī* elephant, fr. Skt *hastin*, fr. *hasta* hand, elephant's trunk; prob. akin to Lith *pažastė* armpit] **:** a greenish gray that is yellower, lighter, and slightly less strong than cabbage green

**hath·or column** \ˈhathə(r)-\ *n, usu cap H* [*Hathor*, ancient Egyptian goddess of love] **:** a type of Egyptian column usu. having a 4-faced capital carved with heads of the goddess Hathor

**hathor–headed** \ˈ==ˈ==\ *adj, usu cap H* **:** carved with masks of Hathor

**ha·thor·ic** \həˈthȯrik, -ˈthär-\ *adj, usu cap* [*Hathor* + E *-ic*] **:** of or relating to Hathor or to a column surmounted by her image

**ha·ti** \ˈhad·ē\ *n* -s [Egypt *ḥati*] *often cap, Egyptian relig* **:** the physical heart — compare ²AB

**hating** *pres part of* HATE

**hat in hand** *adv* **:** in an attitude of respectful humility ⟨have to apologize *hat in hand*⟩

**hat leather** *n* **:** leather (as sheepskin or calf) for making hat or cap sweatbands

**hat·less** \ˈhatləs\ *adj* [ME *hatles*, fr. ¹*hat* + *-les* -less] **:** being without a hat — **hat·less·ness** *n* -ES

**hat money** *n* **1 :** PRIMAGE 1a **2 :** money in the form of truncated tin obelisks used in Pahang, Malay Peninsula in the 19th century

**hat off** *n, pl* **hats off :** ADMIRATION, CONGRATULATIONS ⟨end these memories with my *hat off* to the leaders —J.J.Malloy⟩ ⟨if you can do that and come up smiling — well, then, it's *hats off* all round —Myrtle R. White⟩

**hat palm** *n* **:** any of various palms or plants resembling palms whose leaves are used for making hats: as **a :** JIPIJAPA **b :** a palm (*Coccothrinax argentea*) of Panama **c :** CARNAUBA **d :** any of several West Indian fan palms of the genus *Thrinax*; *esp* **:** CHIP HAT PALM **e** *Philippines* **:** any of various palms of the genera *Areca*, *Corypha*, *Livistona*, and *Pandanus*

**hat piece** *n, obs* **:** a protective metal skullcap worn under a hat

**hatpin** \ˈ=,=\ *n* **1 :** a long straight pin with an ornamented head that is used to keep a hat in place **2 :** a plant of the genus *Eriocaulon* (esp. *E. decangulare*)

**hat rack** *n* **1 a** (1) **:** a wooden framework with several projecting pegs that hangs against a wall and is used to hold hats and other articles of clothing (2) **:** CLOTHES TREE (3) **:** HALLSTAND **b :** a loop (as of wire) into which to slip the brim of a hat under a theater seat or shelf or against a wall **2 :** a thin low-quality meat animal

hat rack 1a(1)

**ha·tred** \ˈhā·trəd\ *n* -s [ME *hatred, hatered, hatereden*, fr. ¹*hate* + *-reden* (fr. OE *rǣden* condition) — more at KINDRED] **1 :** HATE **2 :** a general attitude of prejudiced hostility **:** group animosity ⟨the human race lives in a welter of organized ~s and threats of mutual extermination —Bertrand Russell⟩

**hats** *pl of* HAT, *pres 3d sing of* HAT

**hat·sa** \ˈhatsə\ *n, pl* **hatsa** *or* **hatsas** *usu cap* **1 a :** a Negro African people of northern Tanganyika **b :** a member of such people **2 :** the language spoken by the Hatsa people and related to Khoisan

**hatsful** *pl of* HATFUL

**hatstand** \ˈ=,=\ *n* **1 a :** CLOTHES TREE **b :** HALLSTAND **2 :** an accessory for a closet shelf that consists of a short rod set in a base topped with a knob or disk and used to support a hat so that it will keep its shape while not in use

**hatted** *adj* [fr. past part. of ²*hat*] **:** wearing a hat ⟨two neatly ~ and gloved old ladies —Claudia Cassidy⟩ ⟨a bearskin-*hatted* sentry⟩

¹**hat·ter** \ˈhad·ə(r), -atə-\ *n* -s [ME, fr. ¹*hat* + *-er*] **1 :** one that makes, sells, or cleans and repairs hats **2** [prob. so called fr. the presumed applicability of the proverbial expression "mad as a hatter"] *Austral* **a :** a solitary bush dweller **b :** a lone miner or prospector — often used of a person who has become eccentric from too much solitude **3 :** fur esp. of rabbits for making felt hats — usu. used in pl.

²**hatter** *vt* -ED/-ING/-S [ME (Sc) *hatteren*] **1** *now dial* **:** BATTER, BRUISE **2** *archaic* **:** to wear out **:** worry and harass — sometimes used with *out*

¹**hat·te·ria** \həˈtirēə\ [NL] *syn of* SPHENODON

²**hatteria** \ˈ"\ *n* -s **:** TUATARA

**hat·ti** \ˈhad·ē\ *or* **khat·ti** \ˈka-\ *n, pl* **hatti** *or* **hattis** *or* **khatti** *or* **khattis** *usu cap* [Akkadian *ḫatti, khatti*] **1 :** a pre-Hittite people of central Anatolia **2 :** a member of such people — **hat·ti·an** \ˈhad·ēən\ *adj, usu cap*

¹**hat·tic** \ˈhad·ik\ *adj, usu cap* [*Hatti* + *-ic*] **:** of or relating to the Hatti people

²**hattic** \ˈ"\ *n* -s *usu cap* **:** a language known from quotations in Hittite documents and assumed to be that of the Hatti

**hatting** *n* -s [fr. gerund of ²*hat*] **1 a :** the making of hats **b :** the material from which hats are made **2 :** HAT 3

**hat·tock** \ˈ(h)ad·ək\ *n* -s [¹*hat* + *-ock*] **1** *obs* **:** a small hat **2** *dial Eng* **a :** a grain shock with the top protected by sheaves leaned slantingly against it heads down **b :** one of the two protecting sheaves

**hat tree** *n* **1 a :** CLOTHES TREE **b :** HALLSTAND **2 :** either of two Australian trees (*Sterculia discolor* and *S. lurida*) that produce strong bast fibers

**hat trick** *n* **1 a :** a sleight-of-hand trick performed with a hat **b :** a skillful maneuver ⟨a remarkable political *hat trick* —Mollie Panter-Downes⟩ **2 a** [prob. so called fr. a former practice of rewarding this feat with a present of a new hat] **:** the dismissal by a bowler of three batsmen with three consecutive balls in cricket **b :** a similar outstanding feat in another sport: as (1) **:** the winning of three consecutive horse races (2) **:** the scoring of three goals in one game by a hockey player (3) **:** the hitting by one player of a single, double, triple, and home run in a game of baseball

**hau** \ˈhau̇\ *n* -s [Hawaiian & Marquesan] **:** MAJAGUA a

**haubergeon** *var of* HABERGEON

**hau·ber·get** \ˈhōbə(r)ˌjet\ *n* -s [ML *haubergettum*] **:** an early English woolen cloth

**hau·berk** \ˈhȯ(ˌ)bərk\ *n* -s [ME, fr. OF *hauberc*, of Gmc origin; akin to OE *healsbeorg* neck armor, OHG *halsberg*, ON *halsbjörg*; all fr. a prehistoric WGmc-NGmc compound whose constituents are represented respectively by OE *heals* neck and OE *beorg* protection; akin to OE *beorgan* to preserve, defend — more at COLLAR, BURY] **1 :** a long tunic of ring or chain mail that with a close-fitting helmet and a shield constituted the main defensive armor of the 12th to 14th centuries **2 :** HABERGEON

hauberk

**haud** \ˈhȯd\ *chiefly Scot var of* HOLD

**hau·er·ite** \ˈhau̇ə,rīt\ *n* -s [G *hauerit*, fr. Franz von *Hauer* †1899 Austrian geologist + G *-it* -ite] **:** a mineral $MnS_2$ consisting of native manganese sulfide and occurring as reddish brown or brownish black octahedral or pyritohedral crystals or massive (sp. gr. 3.46)

**hauf** \ˈhäf, ˈhȯf\ *dial Brit var of* HALF

**haugh** \ˈhȯ(k̟), ˈhä(k̟)\ *n* -s [ME (Sc dial.) *holch, hawch*, fr. OE *heolh* corner of land; akin to OE *holh* cave, *hol* hollow — more at HOLE] *chiefly Scot* **:** a low-lying meadow by the side of a river **:** an alluvial plain

**haught** *adj* [alter. (influenced by such words as *caught*, *taught*) of ME *haute*, fr. MF *haut*, lit., high, fr. L *altus* — more at OLD] **1** *obs* **:** HAUGHTY ⟨thou ~ insulting man —Shak.⟩ **2** *obs* **:** NOBLE, HIGH-MINDED, LOFTY

**haugh·ti·ly** \ˈhȯd·ᵊl·ē, \|t\|, \|ᵊli, \|əl- *also* ˈhä\|\ *adv* **:** in a haughty manner

**haugh·ti·ness** \\|ēnəs, \|in-\ *n* -ES **:** the quality or state of being haughty **:** ARROGANCE

**haugh·ty** \\|ē, \|i\ *adj* -ER/-EST [*haught* + *-y*] **1 :** disdainfully proud or overbearing **:** ARROGANT ⟨~ young beauty . . . never deigned to notice us —Herman Melville⟩ **2** *obs* **:** exalted in nature **:** NOBLE ⟨words . . . equal unto this ~ enterprise —Edmund Spenser⟩ **3 :** imposing in aspect **:** LOFTY ⟨~ cathedral⟩

**syn** see PROUD

¹**haul** \ˈhȯl\ *vb* -ED/-ING/-S [ME *halen* to pull, draw, fr. OF *haler*, of Gmc origin; akin to MD *halen* to pull; akin to OE *geholian* to obtain, OHG *halōn, holōn, holēn* to call, fetch, OS *halōn*, and perh. to OE *hlōwan* to low — more at LOW] *vt* **1 a :** to change the course of (a ship) esp. so as to sail closer to the wind — often used with directional adverb ⟨told the chief officer to ~ her off four points —*Mercantile Marine Mag.*⟩ **b :** to sail or hold on a course ⟨~*ed* his skiff all the way north —A.B.Mayse⟩ **2 a** (1) **:** to exert traction on **:** PULL ⟨~ a wagon⟩ — often followed by directional adverb ⟨~ out a stump⟩ ⟨~ up a lobster pot⟩ ⟨~ in an anchor⟩ ⟨~ down a flag⟩ (2) **:** to take by drawing in or up (as with a net) ⟨~ herring⟩ **b :** to exert influence on so as to achieve a desired end **:** DRAG ⟨his wife . . . will ~ him to a highbrow play —Francis Fergusson⟩ **c :** to transport from one place to another in a vehicle **:** CART ⟨~ passengers⟩ ⟨~ coal from the mines⟩ ⟨cattle are ~*ed* by rail⟩ **3 :** to bring before (an authority) for interrogation or punishment **:** HALE ⟨~ traffic violators into court⟩ — often used with *up* ⟨~ up a . . . president of the United States to explain his conduct in office to a congressional committee —Elmer Davis⟩ **~** *vi* **1 a :** to change course so as to sail closer to the wind — often used with *up* ⟨she ~*ed* up 'til the sails began to shiver⟩ **b :** to sail on a course ⟨decided to ~ south⟩ **2 a** (1) **:** to exert traction **:** PULL ⟨~ on a rope⟩ — often followed by directional adverb ⟨~ back on the reins⟩ ⟨~*ed* over to put a pilot aboard —H.A.Chippendale⟩ (2) **:** to take or seek a catch esp. of fish by hauling a net ⟨go ~*ing* for herring⟩ **b :** to propel oneself **:** COME, GO ⟨about three o'clock we ~*ed* into Moonridge —Kenneth Clark⟩ ⟨the bull ~*ed* back for another lunge —F.B.Gipson⟩ **c :** to carry from one place to another **:** furnish transportation ⟨nominal charge for ~*ing*⟩ **3** *of the wind* **:** to change direction **:** SHIFT ⟨the wind has ~*ed* more to the south —William Willis⟩ — often used with *around* ⟨~*ed* around to the starboard quarter⟩ **syn** see PULL — **haul down one's colors :** SURRENDER ⟨saw she was beaten and *hauled down her colors*⟩ — **haul in one's horns :** retreat from an arrogant or aggressive position ⟨admitted his error and *hauled in his horns*⟩ — **haul one over the coals :** to criticize or reprimand **:** take to task **:** CENSURE ⟨*hauled him over the coals* for loafing on the job⟩ — **haul one's wind :** head the bow of a ship closer into the wind **:** LUFF ⟨*hauled his wind* until the sail was trimmed in flat —Vincent McHugh⟩ — often used with *on, upon,* or *to*

²**haul** \ˈ"\ *n* -s **1 a :** an act of dragging **:** strong pull ⟨the rope stood up under the strain of the ~⟩ **b :** a mechanical device for pulling **:** CONVEYOR BELT ⟨mine cars on a car ~⟩ **2 :** the result of an effort to collect either legitimately or by theft **:** TAKE ⟨rich ~*s* of plankton —N.B.Marshall⟩ ⟨a mink coat ~ —Rose Thurburn⟩; *specif* **:** the fish taken in a single draft of a net **3** *ropemaking* **:** a bundle of yarns to be tarred **4 a :** an act of transporting ⟨a rail ~ meant that several hundred expensive . . . cars would have to be bought —N.M.Clark⟩ **b :** the distance or route over which a load is transported ⟨sand is normally taken from deposits within a reasonable ~ of the site of building —G.S.Brady⟩ ⟨ride first-class only on the short ~*s* —T.H.Fielding⟩ ⟨the long ~ round the Cape —Sir Winston Churchill⟩ **c :** the quantity of material transported **:** LOAD ⟨~*s* of unsifted ore —*Times Lit. Supp.*⟩

**haulabout** \ˈ==,=\ *n* -s [fr. *haul about*, v.] **:** a steel barge with large hatchways and coal transporters used for coaling ships

**haul·age** \ˈhȯlij\ *n* -s *often attrib* **1 :** the act or process of hauling **2 :** a charge made for hauling

**haulage rope** *n* **:** TRANSMISSION ROPE

**haulageway** \ˈ==,=\ *n* **:** a passage in a coal mine along which coal is transported **:** GANGWAY 4

**haulaway** \ˈ==,=\ *n* -s [fr. *haul away*, v.] **:** a motor truck designed for the transportation of new automobiles

haulaway

**haulback** \ˈ=,=\ *n* -s [fr. *haul back*, v.] **1 :** a small wire rope used to pull the main cable back to the timber after each haulage in logging **2 :** COMEBACK 4

**hauled** *past of* HAUL

**haul·er** \ˈhȯlə(r)\ *n* -s **:** one that hauls; *specif* **:** a commercial establishment whose business is hauling

**haul·ier** \ˈhȯlyə(r), -liə-\ *Brit var of* HAULER

**hauling** *n* -s [fr. gerund of ¹*haul*] **1 :** an act or instance of applying physical traction to move something **2 :** the act or occupation of transporting goods in a vehicle ⟨hired a trucker to do the ~⟩

**hauling ground** *n* **:** an area where young male seals congregate during the breeding season

**¹haulm** \'hȯm, 'hām\ *n* -s [ME *halm*, fr. OE *healm*; akin to OHG *halm* straw, stem, ON *halmr* straw, stem, L *culmus* stalk, Gk *kalamos* reed, OSlav *slama* straw] **1** *Brit* **:** the stems or tops of cultivated plants (as peas, beans, potatoes, and cereals) esp. after the crop has been gathered **:** STRAW, LITTER **2** *Brit* **:** an individual plant stem (as the culm of a grass)

**²haulm** \"\ *vt* -ED/-ING/-S *Brit* **:** to arrange (straw) for thatching

**haulmy** \-mi\ *adj* -ER/-EST *Brit* **:** having haulms

**haul off** *vi* **:** to get ready often on the spur of the moment ⟨*haul off* and hit him⟩ ⟨what makes you think you can *haul off* and leave here without paying me? —Erskine Caldwell⟩

**haulover** \'ˌ=,==\ *n* -s [fr. *haul over*, v.] **:** PORTAGE 4

**hauls** *pres 3d sing of* HAUL, *pl of* HAUL

**haul seine** *n* **:** a long net for commercial fishing one end of which is usu. attached to the land and the other run around a school of fish which are then drawn ashore

**haul seiner** *n* **:** one that fishes with a haul seine

**haul up** *vi* **:** to come to a stop ⟨the child circled the room and *hauled up* in front of the visitor⟩

**haul-up** \'ˌ=,=\ *n* -s [fr. *haul up*, v.] **:** a jack ladder having a V-shaped trough up which logs are drawn by a jack chain

**haulyard** *var of* HALYARD

**haunch** \'hȯnch, -ä-, -à-\ *n* -ES [ME *haunche*, fr. OF *hanche*, of Gmc origin; akin to MD *hanke* hip, haunch] **1 a :** the projecting region of the lateral parts of the pelvis and the hip joint **:** HIP ⟨his right arm resting forever on Eve's ~ —W.H.Auden⟩ **b :** the fleshy part of the buttock and top of the thigh **:** HINDQUARTER ⟨squatting first on one ~ and then on the other —William Humphrey⟩ — see HORSE illustration **2 :** a leg and loin of an animal for use as food ⟨~ of venison⟩ **3 :** either side of an arch between the springing and the crown **:** the part of an arch bounded by vertical lines drawn through the crown and the outer extremity of the extrados and by horizontal lines drawn through the crown and the spring point **4 :** the tapered end of a tenon **5 :** the shoulder of a highway — usu. used in pl.

**haunch bone** *n* **:** INNOMINATE BONE; *specif* **:** ILIUM

**haunched** \-cht\ *adj* **:** having haunches

**haunch·less** \-chləs\ *adj* **:** lacking haunches

**haunchy** \-chē\ *adj* -ER/-EST **:** having large haunches

**¹haunt** \ hȯnt, -ä-, -à-\ *vb* -ED/-ING/-S [ME *haunten*, fr. OF *hanter*, prob. of Gmc origin; akin to OE *hāmettan* to domicile, ON *heimta* to bring home, fetch, pull, claim; derivatives fr. the stem of E *home*] *vt* **1 a :** to visit often **:** linger in the vicinity of (a place) **:** FREQUENT ⟨loved and ~*ed* the theater —Carlos Baker⟩ ⟨knew . . . what coverts the pheasants ~*ed* —Adrian Bell⟩ **b :** to continually seek the company of (a person) **:** hang around ⟨impostors that ~ the official in foreign ports —Van Wyck Brooks⟩ **2 a :** to have a disquieting or harmful effect on **:** TROUBLE, MOLEST ⟨the gnawing question . . . ~*ed* the uneasy royal heart —Francis Hackett⟩ ⟨crisis was to ~ her days —Charles Lee⟩ ⟨mysterious illness that . . . would not go until the being it ~*ed* lay dead —Edith Sitwell⟩ ⟨icebergs . . . which drift out to sea to ~ mariners —Glen Jacobsen⟩ **b** (1) **:** to linger in the consciousness of **:** recur constantly to ⟨the possibility of the dairy farm ~*ed* her mind —Ellen Glasgow⟩ ⟨single lines of poetry often ~ people who cannot trace them to their source —Bennett Cerf⟩ (2) **:** to reappear continually in **:** recur constantly in ⟨a certain type of . . . woman who has already ~*ed* his poetry —Edmund Wilson⟩ **3 :** to visit or inhabit as a disembodied spirit ⟨spirits are supposed to ~ the places where their bodies most resorted —Charles Dickens⟩ ⟨the river is ~*ed* by certain malevolent water spirits —J.G.Frazer⟩ ~ *vi* **1 :** to stay around or persist **:** LINGER ⟨likes to ~ around the firehouse⟩ ⟨scent that can ~ for a lifetime —Flora Thompson⟩ **2 :** to appear habitually as a disembodied spirit ⟨not far from . . . where she ~*ed* appeared for a short time a much more remarkable spirit —W.B.Yeats⟩

**²haunt** \"\ *n* -s [ME, fr. *haunten*, v.] **1** *now dial Brit* **:** PRACTICE, CUSTOM, HABIT **2** *obs* **:** an act of frequenting in numbers **:** CONCOURSE ⟨our life, exempt from public ~, finds tongues in trees —Shak.⟩ **3 a :** a place habitually frequented **:** favorite resort **:** HOME ⟨sages in their sequestered ~*s* —Laurence Binyon⟩ ⟨own their own ships and fly them to weekend ~*s* —Phil Gustafson⟩ ⟨quiet ~*s* of beauty —S.P.B. Mais⟩ **b** (1) **:** the lair or feeding ground of an animal **:** area where an animal is usu. to be found ⟨~ of the tiger⟩ ⟨herring are most plentiful when the water in their favorite ~*s* is a degree or two warmer than average —J.P.Tully⟩ (2) **:** the favorite environment of a plant ⟨~ of the cardinal flower⟩ **4** *or* **hant** \'hant, -aa(ə)-,-ai-,-ā-,-ā-\ *chiefly dial* **:** a disembodied spirit **:** GHOST

**haunted** *adj* **1 :** FILLED, INFESTED — now usu. used in combination ⟨a sad, kindly, God-*haunted* man —S.N.Behrman⟩ ⟨seal-*haunted* isle —A.A.MacGregor⟩ ⟨moved . . . from one dust-*haunted* base to another —Martin Quigley⟩ **2 :** inhabited by or as if by apparitions **:** frequented by ghosts ⟨a ~ house⟩ ⟨as dusk comes on Kipling's study is the most ~ place I know —Christopher Morley⟩ **3 :** HARASSED, AFFLICTED, TROUBLED ⟨the deep ~ eyes of a man whose convictions have burned him hollow —T.H.White b. 1915⟩ — **haunt·ed·ness** *n* -ES

**haunt·er** \-tə(r)\ *n* -s [ME *hawntare*, fr. *hawnten, haunten* to haunt + *-are* -er] **:** one that haunts

**¹haunting** *n* -s [ME, fr. *haunten* + *-ing*] **:** an act of frequenting esp. by a disembodied spirit ⟨simply not the case that all incumbents vouched for ~*s* —*A.G.N.Flew*⟩

**²haunting** *adj* [ME, fr. pres. part. of *haunten* to haunt — more at HAUNT] **:** that haunts: as **a :** lingering in the consciousness **:** not readily forgotten ⟨the cathedral organ and the distant voices have a ~ beauty —Claudia Cassidy⟩ **b :** having a disquieting effect **:** DISTURBING ⟨from two handsome and talented young men to two ~ horrors of disintegration —Charles Lee⟩ — **haunt·ing·ly** *adv*

**haun·ty** \'hȯnti, 'hän-, 'han-\ *adj* -ER/-EST [origin unknown] *dial Eng* **:** UNRULY, RESTLESS

**hau·pia** \haủ'pēə\ *n* -s [Hawaiian] **:** a Hawaiian pudding made of cornstarch and coconut cream

**hau·ra·nit·ic** \ˌhaủrə¦nid·ik\ *adj, usu cap* [*Hauran*, region in southern Syria + E *-ite* + *-ic*] **:** of or relating to the region of Hauran

**hau·ri·ant** *also* **hau·ri·ent** \'hȯrēənt, 'haủr-\ *adj* [L *haurient-, hauriens*, pres. part. of *haurire* to draw (as water), drain, devour — more at EXHAUST] *heraldry, of a fish or water animal* **:** being in pale with the head up as if rising for air — compare URINANT

**haus** *pl of* HAU

**hau·sa** *also* **haus·sa** \'haủ¦sə, ¦zə\ *n, pl* **hausa** *or* **hausas** *usu cap* **1 a :** a highly variable negroid people of the Sudan between Lake Chad and the Niger numbering in the millions and united primarily by language **b :** a member of such people **2 :** the Chad language of the Hausa people that is widely used in west Africa as a trade language

**hause** \'hȯs, 'häs\ *chiefly Scot var of* HALS

**hau·sen** \'haủzᵊn\ *n* -s [G, fr. MHG *hūse, hūsen*, fr. OHG *hūso* — more at HUSO] **:** BELUGA 1

**haus·frau** \'haủs,fraủ\ *n, pl* **hausfraus** \-aủz\ *also* **hausfrau·en** \-aủən\ [G, fr. *haus* house (fr. OHG *hūs*) + *frau* wife, woman, fr. OHG *frouwa* lady, mistress — more at HOUSE, FROW] **:** the mistress of a household **:** HOUSEWIFE ⟨the women were dumpy, overworked ~*s* —Joanna Spencer⟩

**haus·mann·ite** \'haủsmə,nīt\ *n* -s [J. F. L. *Hausmann* †1859, Ger. mineralogist + E *-ite*] **:** an opaque mineral $Mn_3O_4$ consisting of manganese tetroxide

**hausse-col** \(ˈ)(h)ōs¦kül\ *n* -s [F, by folk etymology (influence of F *hausser* to raise) fr. MF *housecol, hochecol, hauscol*] **:** GORGET 1

**haust** *abbr* [L *haustus*] draft — used in pharmacy

**haus·tel·late** \(ˈ)hȯ¦stelət, 'hȯstə,lāt\ *adj* [NL *haustellum* + E *-ate*] **:** having a haustellum **:** SUCTORIAL

**haus·tel·lum** \hȯ'steləm\ *n, pl* **haustel·la** \-lə\ [NL, fr. *haustus* (past part. of *haurire* to draw, draw up) + *-ellum* (dim. suffix) — more at EXHAUST] **:** a proboscis adapted for sucking blood or the juices of plants

**haus·to·ri·al** \(ˈ)hȯ¦stōrēəl\ *adj* [NL *haustorium* + E *-al*] **:** HAUSTELLATE

**haus·to·ri·um** \=ˈ=rēəm\ *n, pl* **hausto·ria** \-rēə\ [NL, fr. L *haustus* + *-orium*] **:** a food-absorbing outgrowth of a hypha, stem, or other plant organ: as **a :** a projection from various fungous hyphae **b :** a cell of the embryo sac or embryo in some seed plants **c :** an outgrowth of the stem or root in a parasitic seed plant (as dodder)

**haus·tral** \'hȯstrəl\ *also* **haus·trat·ed** \-,strād·əd\ *adj* [NL *haustrum* + E *-al* or *-ated* (fr. *-ate* + *-ed*)] **:** of, relating to, or exhibiting haustra

**haus·tra·tion** \hȯ'strāshən\ *n* -s [NL *haustrum* + E *-ation*] **:** the quality or state of having haustra

**haus·trum** \'hȯstrəm\ *n, pl* **haus·tra** \-rə\ [NL, fr. L, machine for drawing water, fr. *haustus*, past part. of *haurire* to draw (as water) — more at EXHAUST] **:** a recess in the colon

**haus·tus** \'hȯstəs\ *n, pl* **haustus** [L, lit., action of drawing, fr. *haustus*, past part.] *Roman & civil law* **:** a right to draw water from a well or spring on another's land and a right of passage to and from the well or spring — compare SERVITUDE

**haut·bois** *also* **haut·boy** \'(h)ō,bȯi\ *n, pl* **hautbois** \-ȯiz\ *also* **hautboys** \"\ [MF *hautbois*, fr. *haut* high + *bois* wood, woods, of Gmc origin; akin to OHG *busc* bush, forest — more at HAUGHT, BUSH] **1 a :** OBOE **b :** a pipe-organ stop of 16, 8, and sometimes 4-foot pitch similar to an organ oboe **2 :** a strawberry (*Fragaria moschata*) native to Europe and early brought into cultivation having the calyx strongly recurved in fruit

**haut·boist** \-ōist\ *also* **haut·boy·ist** \"\ *n* -s [F *hautboïste*, fr. *hautbois* + *-iste*] **:** OBOIST

**haute cou·ture** \,ōt,kü'tủ(ə)r\ *n* [F, lit., high sewing] **1 :** the leading dressmaking establishments for the creation of exclusive often trend-setting fashions for women **2 a :** the art of creating high fashions for women **b :** the fashions created

**haute école** \,ōd·(,)ā'kōl\ *n* [F, lit., high school] **1 :** a method of training a horse in the more difficult feats of horsemanship **2 :** the technique of expert horsemanship

**haute-lisse** \(ˈ)ōt¦lēs\ *adj* [F] **:** HIGH-WARP

**hau·teur** \(ˈ)hō¦tər, (ˈ)(h)ō¦-\ *n* -s [F, fr. *haut* high, proud + *-eur* -or — more at HAUGHT] **:** an assumption of superiority or arrogant or condescending manner **:** HAUGHTINESS ⟨a cold ~ and disdain which infuriated his colleagues —J.H.Plumb⟩

**haut monde** \ō'mō"d, -mȯnd\ *n* [F, lit., high world] **:** the socially elect **:** high society

**haut pas** \ō'pä\ *n* [ME *hautepase*, fr. MF *haut pas*, lit., high step] **:** a raised part of a floor **:** DAIS — compare HALFPACE

**haut-relief** \¦ō, ¦ō+=ˌ=\ *n* [F] **:** HIGH RELIEF

**ha·uy·nite** \ä'wē,nīt\ *or* **ha·uyne** \ä'wēn\ *n* -s [*hauynite* fr. *hauyne* + *-ite*; *hauyne* fr. F *haüyne*, fr. Abbé René Just *Haüy* †1822 Fr. mineralogist + F *-ine*] **:** an isometric silicate mineral $(Na,Ca)_{4-8}Al_6Si_6O_{24}(SO_4)_{1-2}$ consisting of sulfate of aluminum, calcium, and sodium and occurring commonly as rounded grains in various igneous rocks (hardness 5.5–6, sp. gr. 2.4–2.5)

**hav** *abbr* haversine

**hav·age** \'(h)avij\ *n* -s [¹*have* + *-age*] *dial Eng* **:** familial descent **:** LINEAGE

**ha·vai·ki** \hə'vīkē\ *n, cap* [Marquesan & Tuamotuan] **:** a fabled original homeland from which the Polynesians believe themselves to have come and to which their spirits return after death

**¹ha·va·na** \hə'vanə\ *adj, usu cap* [fr. *Havana*, Cuba] **1 :** of or from Havana, the capital of Cuba ⟨a *Havana* cigar⟩ **:** of the kind or style prevalent in Havana **:** HAVANAN **2 a** *of tobacco* **:** grown in Cuba **b** *of a cigar* **:** made in Cuba or from Cuban tobacco

**²havana** \"\ *n* **1** -s *usu cap* [prob. fr. Sp *habano*, fr. *habano*, adj., of Havana, fr. La *Habana* (Havana), Cuba] **a :** a cigar made partly or wholly from Cuban tobacco ⟨a box of *Havanas*⟩ **b :** tobacco raised in Cuba ⟨*Havana* leaf⟩ **2** *or* **havana brown** -s *often cap H* **:** BISMARCK BROWN **3 a** *usu cap* **:** a breed of rather small brown rabbits originating in Holland **b** -s *often cap* **:** a rabbit of this breed

**¹ha·van·an** \-nən\ *adj, usu cap* [*Havana*, Cuba + E *-an*] **1 :** of, relating to, or characteristic of Havana, the capital of Cuba **2 :** of, relating to, or characteristic of the people of Havana

**²havanan** \"\ *n* -s *cap* **:** a native or resident of Havana

**havana seed** *n, usu cap H* **:** any of several U. S. cigar tobaccos derived from seed orig. imported from Cuba

**ha·va·su·pai** \ˌhävə'sü,pī\ *n, pl* **havasupai** *or* **havasupais** *usu cap* **1 a :** an Indian people of Cataract Canyon, a tributary of Grand Canyon, Arizona **b :** a member of such people **2 :** a Yuman language of the Havasupai people

**havdalah** *var of* HABDALAH

**¹have** \(ˈ)hav, (ˈ)hev; *as an auxiliary* " *or* ˌ(h)əv *or after a vowel* v; *before "to" usu* ¦haf *or* ¦hef\ *vb, past* **had** \(ˈ)had, (ˈ)hed; *as an auxiliary* " *or* ˌ(h)əd *or after a vowel* d\ *also archaic 2d sing* **hadst** \(ˈ)ha¦dzt, (ˈ)he¦, ˌ(h)əl, ¦dst, ¦tst\ *or* **had·dest** (with *thou*) \'hadəst, ¦hed-\ *past part* **had** *also chiefly Scot* **haen** \(ˈ)hān\ *pres part* **hav·ing** \'haviŋ, ¦hev-\ *pres 1st sing* **have** *also dial Brit* **ha** \(ˈ)ha, ˌ(h)ə\ *or chiefly Scot* **hae** \(ˈ)hā\ *2d sing* **have** *also archaic* **hast** (with *thou*) \(ˈ)hast, (ˈ)hest, ˌ(h)əst\ *or dial Brit* **ha**; *3d sing* **has** \(ˈ)haz, (ˈ)hez; *as an auxiliary* " *or* ˌ(h)əz *or after a vowel* z; *before "to" usu* ¦has *or* ¦hes\ *also archaic* **hath** \(ˈ)hath, (ˈ)heth, ˌ(h)əth\ *or dial Brit* **have**; *pl* **have** *also dial Brit* **ha** *or* **han** \(ˈ)han, (h)ən\ *or chiefly Scot* **hae** \(ˈ)hā\ [ME *haven, habben*, fr. OE *habban*; akin to OHG *habēn* to have, ON *hafa*, Goth *haban*, OE *hebban* to lift, raise — more at HEAVE] *vt* **1 a :** to hold in possession as property **:** OWN ⟨~ a cow⟩ ⟨~ a car⟩ ⟨~ a lot of money⟩ **b :** to hold, keep, or retain esp. in one's use, service, regard, or affection or at one's disposal ⟨can't ~ your cake and eat it too⟩ ⟨the chairman *has* all the tickets needed⟩ ⟨*has* some rare coins saved up⟩ ⟨~ him in fond remembrance⟩ ⟨~ no time to lose⟩ **c :** to consist of (as all one's elements or constituent parts) **:** CONTAIN, INCLUDE ⟨~ a subordinate part⟩ ⟨the car *has* a self-starter⟩ ⟨the lake *has* some large pickerel⟩ ⟨April *has* 30 days⟩ **d :** CARRY, BEAR, SUPPORT ⟨~ an essential part⟩ ⟨~ an attachment⟩ ⟨the house *has* a roof⟩ ⟨the dress *has* a label⟩ **:** WEAR ⟨*has* a blue suit⟩ ⟨*has* a tweed coat⟩ **e :** to be possessed by ⟨declaring she *had* a devil —Max Peacock⟩ **2 :** to feel compulsion, obligation, or necessity in regard to — used with a noun object followed by *to* and the infinitive ⟨~ a letter to write⟩ ⟨~ a task to perform⟩ ⟨~ nothing to do⟩ ⟨~ a deadline to meet⟩ **3 a :** to stand in any of several personal relationships to (as father to son, host to guest, friend to friend) ⟨the man *had* four daughters⟩ ⟨it is unpleasant to ~ enemies⟩ **b :** to be attended by or associated with often as an essential concomitant ⟨the king *has* many courtiers⟩ ⟨certain foods present special difficulties and so ~ rules of their own to make eating them easier —Agnes M. Miall⟩ ⟨the wine *had* no effect on me⟩ ⟨his proposal *had* many objections⟩ **c :** to stand or remain in any of several implicit physical, logical, or emotional relationships to ⟨as we sailed north we *had* Africa on our right⟩ ⟨*had* only six feet of water under the keel⟩ ⟨the word *has* no exact equivalent⟩ ⟨~ the voters on the right side⟩ **4 a** (1) **:** to acquire or get possession of **:** OBTAIN ⟨nothing to be *had* from the empty larder⟩ ⟨good meat could not be *had* at all during the food shortage⟩ (2) **:** GAIN ⟨*had* a lot from the trip⟩ ⟨*had* nothing from the experience⟩ (3) **:** to be able to avail oneself of or utilize (something already done or completed) ⟨in this field a student *has* many helpful monographs and handbooks⟩ (4) **:** WIN ⟨*had* the hole by two strokes⟩ ⟨ought to ~ the fight by the third round⟩ **b :** RECEIVE ⟨*had* news of the lost ship⟩ ⟨asked if the police *had* any information that might lead to an arrest⟩ ⟨*had* a letter from him⟩ **c :** ACCEPT ⟨so burnt no one would ~ a piece⟩; *specif* **:** to accept in marriage ⟨wished to marry but could find no one who would ~ him⟩ **d :** ACHIEVE ⟨believes a satisfactory peace can be *had* between the belligerent powers⟩ **e :** to copulate with ⟨rumor claimed he had never *had* a woman in his life —Norman Mailer⟩ **5 a :** to be marked, distinguished, or characterized by (as an attribute, quality, position, or a distinctive biographical fact) ⟨the cloth *has* a silky texture⟩ ⟨*had* a taste for exotic foods⟩ ⟨*has* a habit of nail biting⟩ ⟨the threat *had* the desired effect⟩ ⟨*had* a height of four feet⟩ ⟨the goods *had* a value of $1000⟩ ⟨the common law *had* its origin in a group of writs drawn from various uses —Curtis Bok⟩ **b :** EXHIBIT, SHOW, MANIFEST ⟨*had* the goodness to get a chair⟩ ⟨*had* the gall to refuse⟩ ⟨~ mercy on us⟩ **c :** USE, EXERCISE ⟨~ a care what you say to him⟩ **6 a :** to experience esp. by submitting to, undergoing, being affected by, enjoying, or suffering ⟨~ a rest⟩ ⟨~ a medical examination⟩ ⟨~ a cold⟩ ⟨the worst government they ever *had*⟩ ⟨~ an operation⟩ ⟨a book that will ~ a wide circulation⟩ **:** PASS ⟨~ a life full of suffering⟩ **b :** to carry on or engage in **:** PERFORM ⟨~ a standing feud with a political opponent⟩ ⟨~ a fight⟩ ⟨~ a talk with a friend⟩ ⟨~ a part in a play⟩; *also* **:** EXECUTE, TAKE ⟨*had* a punch at the assailant before he escaped⟩ ⟨*had* a look at the body⟩ **c :** to entertain in the mind or feelings **:** CHERISH ⟨*had* a great deal of affection for the children⟩ ⟨~ no doubt of success⟩ ⟨~ an opinion⟩ **7 a :** to cause to go **:** LEAD, CONVEY ⟨did not ~ the child anywhere where he could be exposed to measles⟩ ⟨the aunt *had* the child to live with her⟩ **b :** to cause to by persuasive or forceful means (as by inviting, ordering, compelling) — used with the infinitive without *to* ⟨*had* the chauffeur drive to town⟩ ⟨*had* the children go to bed early⟩ ⟨the court *had* him pay the man what he owed him⟩ ⟨you are going to pay for the damage and I'll ~ you know it⟩ **c :** to cause to be ⟨*has* people around at all times⟩ ⟨likes to ~ people in the office who are efficient⟩ ⟨*had* him sick with the details of the accident⟩ ⟨anxious to ~ you a satisfied customer —Richard Joseph⟩ ⟨nearly *had* the table over with her pushing and shoving⟩ ⟨*had* the tent poles down in a minute⟩ **d :** to cause to become ⟨I'll ~ him a good soldier before long⟩ **e** (1) **:** to cause to come by inviting ⟨~ friends over for an evening of bridge⟩ (2) **:** to receive as a guest ⟨I'll be over whenever you can ~ me⟩ **f :** to represent to be ⟨the author always *has* his characters doing foolish things⟩ **8 a :** to allow to or suffer to — used with the infinitive without *to* ⟨would not ~ him treat the dog so⟩ **b :** to allow to be or suffer to be ⟨will not ~ him chosen president⟩ ⟨~ women in the men's part of the building only once a month on visitors' day⟩ ⟨a strange man to ~ around⟩ **9 a** (1) **:** to be marked by an intellectual grasp of **:** KNOW, UNDERSTAND ⟨a student who *has* only a little French and no mathematics⟩ ⟨*having* no foreign language he was handicapped and ineffectual —Carl Van Doren⟩ (2) **:** to understand the character of ⟨you do not come to associate with him long before you ~ him⟩ (3) **:** to be able to handle adequately ⟨the job is so easy that in only a few days you ~ it⟩ **b :** to place in a scale of distinctions **:** CATEGORIZE ⟨sees with so many sense and other organs that you never know where to ~ him artistically —*Times Lit. Supp.*⟩ **10 a :** to maneuver into a position of disadvantage or cause to be at a disadvantage ⟨*had* his opponent at the point of defeat⟩ ⟨the criminal *had* the police nonplussed⟩ ⟨the team *had* their opponents beaten before the half⟩ **b :** to place or maneuver into a vulnerable or defenseless position or a position bringing certain defeat ⟨when he brought the charge before the court he *had* me since the evidence against me was in my own handwriting⟩ **c :** OUTWIT, OUTPLAY, OUTMANEUVER ⟨*had* his opponent in only three more moves of the chessmen⟩ **:** DEFEAT ⟨would like to play on but you ~ me steadily⟩ **:** to get the better of or triumph over by finding, achieving, getting ⟨*had* the laugh on me⟩ ⟨*had* the goods on me⟩ ⟨*had* the jump on me⟩ **d :** TRICK, CHEAT, FOOL, BAMBOOZLE ⟨in this enterprise the partners *had* him and left him without a penny⟩ ⟨the size of this bill convinces me I've been *had*⟩ **11 a :** to be in a position to exercise (as a right or privilege) ⟨as a friend he *has* the freedom of my house⟩ ⟨*has* no right to go⟩ **b :** to be in control of **:** be responsible for ⟨was put in charge and he *has* overall direction of the program —C.E.Black & E.C.Helmreich⟩ ⟨*has* the job of directing traffic⟩ **12 :** BEAR, BEGET ⟨she is going to ~ a baby⟩ ⟨the man *had* a son last week⟩ **13 :** to partake of **:** EAT, DRINK ⟨~ dinner at 7 o'clock⟩ ⟨~ coffee every morning⟩ **:** SMOKE ⟨~ a cigarette after breakfast⟩ **14 :** to give a job to **:** HIRE ⟨no shipowner will hire him, no captain will ~ him —P.J.Scharper⟩ **15 :** to associate oneself with **:** participate in ⟨won't ~ any part of the dirty business⟩ **16 a :** to cause to do one's bidding **:** CONTROL, DOMINATE ⟨the man with the money was always able to ~ him⟩ **b :** BUY 4, BRIBE, SUBORN ⟨as long as juries, judges and law enforcement officers can be *had* for a price —D.W. Maurer⟩ **17 :** to engage and hold (as the attention) ⟨the salesman *had* the interest of the buyer⟩ ⟨the political candidate *has* the ear of the farmers⟩ ~ *verbal auxiliary* **1 :** to be in a position or state marked by an action or state completed or ended or virtually completed or ended — used with the past participle to form the present perfect, past perfect, or future perfect ⟨*has* gone home⟩ ⟨~ been here already⟩ ⟨the army *had* already taken the town when we arrived⟩ ⟨will ~ finished dinner by the time the guests arrive⟩ **2 :** to be compelled or under obligation or necessity — used with the infinitive with *to* ⟨~ to see a doctor⟩ ⟨~ to pay taxes⟩ ⟨*had* to be home by six⟩ — compare ¹GET 12b

**syn** HOLD, OWN, POSSESS, ENJOY: HAVE is a very general term indicating any condition or action of control, retaining, keeping, regarding, or experiencing as one's own. HOLD suggests stronger control, grasp, or retention: *to hold to an opinion* suggests greater tenacity and resolution than *to have an opinion; to hold control* implies firm retention in contrast to *to have control*, which may imply the accidental or temporary; *to hold a job* suggests continuation, *to have one* occupation at the moment. OWN may suggest holding with power to use and dispose as a legal or natural right ⟨*own* one's own house⟩ ⟨the stockholders *own* the corporation, and the corporation *owns* the assets of the incorporated business —Harold Koontz & Cyril O'Donnell⟩ ⟨when a child is old enough, he should . . . be allowed to *own* books —Bertrand Russell⟩ POSSESS may be interchangeable with HAVE; similar to OWN, it may apply more widely to intangibles ⟨he *possesses*, through his experience, knowledge not possessed by those whose experience has been different —Bertrand Russell⟩ ⟨it must be a delightful city, and *possess* all the attractions of the next world —Oscar Wilde⟩ ENJOY implies having as one's own with all benefits and advantages, usu. pleasurable, or with other concomitants, perhaps unpleasant ⟨*enjoys* worldwide fame⟩ ⟨*enjoy* unlimited help and the best opportunities⟩ ⟨shorn of the remarkable privileges which he formerly *enjoyed* —J.G.Frazer⟩ **syn** see in addition OUGHT

— **had as good** *or* **had as well :** would benefit as much to or as well — used with the infinitive without *to* ⟨*had as good* throw his money away as spend it foolishly⟩ — **had as lief** *or* **had as soon :** would just as gladly — used with the infinitive without *to* ⟨*had as lief* stay home as go gadding about⟩ — **had better** *or* **had best 1 :** would be wise to — used with the infinitive without *to* ⟨*had better* try slow walks to start building up his strength⟩ **2 :** should for one's own welfare ⟨*had better* pay what the court tells him to⟩ — **had liefer** *or* **had sooner** *or* **had rather :** would rather — used with the infinitive without *to* ⟨*had liefer* sit at home than go to the dance⟩ ⟨*had sooner* drink than sleep⟩ — **had liefest** *or* **had soonest :** would like best to — used with the infinitive without *to* ⟨*had liefest* have the least seasoned dishes⟩ — **have a go :** to hit a bowled cricket ball vigorously with intent to score — **have a hand in :** to exercise some control over ⟨*have a hand in* the management of the business⟩ **:** significantly influence or direct ⟨*having a hand in* the control of American domestic corporations —T.W.Arnold⟩ — **have at :** to go at or deal with usu. hostilely ⟨flops the morning bale of poetry manuscripts upon my desk and I pull up my chair to *have at* them —H.L. Mencken⟩ ⟨the two men *had at* each other with fists and feet⟩ ⟨have seen four . . . characters *have at* each other for two very powerful concluding acts —*Theatre Arts*⟩ — **have done :** STOP, CEASE, DESIST ⟨wish you would *have done* before I go mad⟩ — used chiefly in the imperative — **have done with :** to finish doing, using, dealing with, working on, or handling ⟨when he *had done with* the pen he laid it down⟩ ⟨will he never *have done with* his persistent speechmaking⟩ — **have had it 1** *slang* **:** to have had or have done all one is going to be allowed to ⟨he's been cheating me for years but now he's *had it*⟩ **2** *slang* **:** to have experienced, endured, or suffered all one can or as much as one can ever expect to usu. of a particular kind of experience ⟨he felt he was capable of enduring pain but after that experience he'd *had it*⟩ ⟨if that's what it takes to make him happy, he *has had it* —*Nashville Tennessean*⟩ — **have it 1 a :** ASSERT, MAINTAIN, CLAIM ⟨rumor *has it* that there will be a marked change in women's fashions⟩ ⟨all their friends *have it* that they are secretly married⟩ — often used with *will* ⟨the enemy will *have it* that we are already defeated⟩ **b :** to conceive of and act in relation to a point under consideration ⟨which way do you want to *have it*⟩ ⟨*have it* your own way⟩ **2 :** to express or phrase it ⟨he was drunk as a lord, as his friends *have it*⟩ **3 :** to endure or suffer it — used with *will not* or *would not* ⟨tried to exploit him but he would not *have it*⟩ ⟨after his insult if he tries to explain I will not *have it*⟩ **4 :** to bring about **:** ARRANGE ⟨good fortune *had it* that we arrived early⟩ **5 a :** to gain or hold an advantage **:** WIN **b :** to gain the victory in a viva-voce vote ⟨the ayes *have it*⟩ **6 :** to receive or suffer a blow, punishment, or disaster ⟨the fighter let his opponent *have it* in the face⟩ **7 :** to have or have hit on a solution or a practicable or appropriate plan or method **8 :** to be so dealt with by fortune or circumstance that one's affairs or welfare are of a (particular favorable or unfavorable) character ⟨*had it* good in times of prosperity⟩ ⟨*has it* pretty tough since his wife died⟩ — **have it coming :** to deserve or merit what one gets, benefits by, or suffers ⟨so vicious a man that whatever evil things happen to him he will *have it coming*⟩ — **have it in for :** to intend to do harm to **:** wish evil to **:** plan to harm in some way ⟨*had it in for* all foreigners⟩ — **have it in one :** to have the capability or courage ⟨*has it in him* to do better than he did⟩ — **have it out :** to settle or clear up a matter of contention by free discussion or a fight — **have it over** *or* **have it all over :** to be in a more advantageous position than ⟨*has it over* one ignorant of the language⟩ — **have kittens :** to be in an agitated mood **:** become perturbed or upset ⟨company's coming and Ma's been *having kittens*⟩ — **have none of :** to refuse to allow, tolerate, or have anything to do with ⟨will *have none of* your sloppy ways around this house⟩ ⟨as soon as he found the business was dishonest he would *have none of* it⟩ — **have nothing on :** to have no advantage or superiority over ⟨the man was a crook but *had nothing on* the men he cheated who would have cheated him far more⟩; *esp* **:** to possess no incriminating or embarrassing information about ⟨felt at ease because he knew his opponents *had nothing on* him that they could use for blackmail⟩ — **have no use for :** to hold in contempt **:** DESPISE ⟨*has no use for* dishonest politicians⟩ **:** be unwilling to tolerate or deal with in any way — **have oneself :** to indulge in or go out of one's way to have (as a good time) **:** GET ⟨the boys *had themselves* a time while the parents were away⟩ — **have one's eye on :** to have marked intentions of acquiring or possessing ⟨*had his eye on* a little cottage up in the mountains⟩ ⟨*had his eye on* his neighbor's daughter⟩ — **have one's hands full :** to have in hand as much as or more than one can conveniently handle **:** be pressed with work, engagements, difficulties — **have one's head** *of a horse* **:** to move freely without restraint from the reins ⟨on the last stretch the trainer let the mare *have her head*⟩ — **have one's head** *or* **have one's hide :** to be extremely angry at or inflict severe punishment upon (as by beheading) ⟨he said that if I didn't stop bothering him he'd *have my hide*⟩ ⟨swore he'd *have the heads* of the outlaws⟩ — **have one's own back :** to get even — **have something on :** to possess incriminating or embarrassing information about ⟨*had something on* the police chief so that he felt safe from arrest⟩ — **have to do with 1 :** to have business or intercourse with **:** concern oneself with **:** deal with ⟨semantics *has to do with* the responses we have to words⟩ **2 :** to have (as something or nothing) in the way of connection or relation with, participation in, or effect on ⟨the lawyer would *have* nothing *to do with* the case⟩ ⟨your frame of mind *has* much *to do with* your physical wellbeing⟩ — **to have and to hold :** to possess by virtue of a lawful title (as under the habendum clause in a deed) — formerly used in deeds in English to introduce the tenendum

**²have** \'hav\ *n* -s **:** one that has material wealth as distinguished from one that is poor — compare HAVE-NOT ⟨conceived of war as a battle between the ~*s* and the have-nots for control of the world's wealth⟩ ⟨rich and poor, employer and employee, ~*s* and have-nots alike —*Engineering and Mining Jour.*⟩

**have·lock** \'hav,läk, -vlək\ *n* -s [after Sir Henry *Havelock* †1857 Eng. general in India] **:** a covering for a cap or hat with an extended back or back and sides to protect the neck from the sun or bad weather

**¹ha·ven** \'hāvən\ *n* -s [ME, fr. OE *hæfen, hæfene;* akin to OE *hæf* sea, MLG *havene* harbor, MHG *hap, habe, habene* sea, harbor, ON *haf* sea, *höfn* harbor, OE *hebban* to raise, lift — more at HEAVE] **1 :** a bay, recess, or inlet of the sea or the mouth of a river that affords anchorage and shelter for shipping **:** HARBOR, PORT **2 :** a place of safety **:** SHELTER, ASYLUM **syn** see HARBOR

**²haven** \" \ *vb* -ED/-ING/-S *vi, obs* **:** to take refuge in a haven ~ *vt* **:** to shelter in a haven

**ha·ven·less** \-nləs\ *adj* [ME *havenlesse,* fr. *haven* + *-lesse* -less] **:** having no harbor or haven ⟨a ~ sea⟩ ⟨a ~ life⟩

**have–not** \'hav,nät\ *n* -s **:** one that is poor in material wealth as distinguished from one that is rich ⟨ownership of the natural resources of the earth by individuals, groups or nations, causing a struggle between the haves and *have-nots* which is the major cause of war and destruction —*Science News Letter*⟩

**haven't** \'havənt, 'habᵊmt\ [by contr.] **:** have not

**have on** *vt* **1 :** WEAR ⟨the child *had* his best clothes *on* for the party⟩ ⟨*had on* a new suit⟩ **2 :** to plan to take part in **:** have (something) planned ⟨*have* a dance *on* for that night⟩ ⟨will see what he *has on* now⟩ ⟨if you don't *have* anything *on* tonight, come over⟩

**¹hav·er** \'havə(r)\ *n* -s [ME, fr. ON *hafri;* akin to OHG *habaro,* OS *haboro;* prob. derivatives fr. the root of ON *hafr* male goat; fr. its being used as food for goats — more at CAPRIOLE] **1** *chiefly Brit* **a :** OAT; *esp* **:** volunteer or uncultivated oats **b :** WILD OAT 1a **2** *chiefly Brit* **:** TALL OAT GRASS

**²hav·er** \'hävər\ *n* -s [ME, owner, fr. *haven* to have + *-er*] *Scots law* **:** the holder of a deed or other legal document

**³ha·ver** \'hāvə(r)\ *vi* -ED/-ING/-S [origin unknown] *chiefly Brit* **:** to hem and haw **:** stall for time (as by useless talk) ⟨waste no more time ~*ing* over a few missing guns —Marguerite Steen⟩

**⁴ha·ver** *or* **ha·ber** *or* **cha·ver** *or* **cha·ber** \'kävər\ *n, pl* **have·rim** *or* **habe·rim** \kä'vārim\ [Heb *ḥābhēr*] **:** COMRADE, ASSOCIATE

**ha·ve·rah** *or* **ha·be·rah** \'kävərə\ *n, pl* **have·roth** *or* **habe·roth** *or* **have·rot** *or* **habe·rot** \,kävə'rōth, -ōt\ [Heb *ḥăbhērāh,* fem. of *ḥābhēr*] **:** a female haver

**havercake** \'==,=\ *n* [¹*haver* + *cake*] *Scot* **:** OATCAKE

**ha·ver·el** \'hāv(ə)rəl\ *n* -s [³*haver* + *-el*] *chiefly Scot* **:** a garrulous half-wit

**havergrass** \'==,=\ *n* [¹*haver* + *grass*] **:** any of several chiefly European wild oats

**ha·ver·hill fever** \'hāv(ə)rəl-\ *n, usu cap H* [fr. *Haverhill,* Mass., where the disease appeared in epidemic proportions in 1926] **:** rat-bite fever not always contracted from the bite of a rat but sometimes from contaminated food

**ha·ver·ing** \'hāv(ə)riŋ\ *adj* [fr. pres. part. of ³*haver*] *dial Brit* **:** equivocal and devious ⟨some ~ jargon that might mean anything —J.C.Powys⟩

**ha·ver·ings** \-ŋz\ *n pl* [fr. pl. of *havering,* gerund of ³*haver*] *Brit* **:** absurd, pointless, or maundering talk **:** BABBLINGS ⟨a tone of fatherly impatience with my moony ~ —H.H.Richardson⟩

**havermeal** \'==,=\ *n* [¹*haver* + *meal*] *Scot* **:** OATMEAL

**ha·vers** \'hāvərz\ *n pl* [³*haver* + *-s*] *chiefly Scot* **:** stuff and nonsense **:** POPPYCOCK ⟨you're talking ~ —John Buchan⟩

**hav·er·sack** \'havə(r),sak\ *n* [F *havresac* (formerly, bag for oats), fr. G *habersack* bag for oats, fr. *haber* oat, oats (fr. OHG *habaro*) + *sack* bag, fr. OHG *sac* — more at HAVER, SACK] **:** a bag or case similar to a knapsack but usu. worn over one shoulder

**ha·ver·sian canal** \hə'vərzhən-, (')hä¦v… *sometimes* -rshən\ *n, sometimes cap H* [Clopton *Havers* †1702 Eng. physician and anatomist + E *-ian*] **:** any of the small canals through which the blood vessels ramify in bone

haversack

**haversian system** *n, sometimes cap H* **:** a haversian canal with the concentrically arranged laminae of bone that surround it

**hav·er·sine** \'havə(r),sīn\ *n* [*half versed sine*] **:** half of the versed sine — abbr. *hav*

**haves** *pl of* HAVE

**have up** *vt* **1 :** to bring before an authority (as a court) to answer a charge ⟨the man *had* the writer *up* for libel⟩ ⟨the room where new boys were examined and old ones *had up* for rebuke or punishment —Samuel Butler †1902⟩ ⟨the man swore he would *have* them *up* for defamation of character⟩ **2 :** to be aroused in ⟨father *had* his temper *up* and swore loudly⟩ ⟨the revolutionaries *had* their blood *up* for some action⟩

**¹ha·vey–ca·vey** \'(h)āvi'kāvi\ *adj* [origin unknown] *dial Eng* **:** precariously balanced **:** UNSTEADY

**²havey–cavey** \" \ *adv, dial Eng* **:** HELTER-SKELTER

**hav·i·land** \'havələnd\ *n* -s *usu cap, often attrib* [after David *Haviland,* 19th cent. Am. manufacturer in France, its originator] **:** porcelain tableware designed for the American trade and made by a factory founded in 1839 at Limoges, France

**hav·il·dar** \'havəl,där\ *n* -s [Hindi *hawāldār,* fr. Ar *hawāla* charge + Per *dār* having] **:** a noncommissioned officer in the Indian army corresponding to a sergeant

**havildar major** *n* **:** a sergeant major in the Indian army

**¹having** *n* -s [ME, fr. gerund of *haven* to have] **:** something one possesses or which belongs to one **:** PROPERTY — usu. used in pl.

**²having** *adj* [fr. pres. part. of ¹*have*] **:** GRASPING, AVARICIOUS ⟨she's got rather a ~ nature —John Galsworthy⟩

**ha·vings** \'hāvinz\ *n pl but sing in constr* [ME, fr. pl. of *having,* gerund of *haven* to have] *Scot* **:** DEPORTMENT, BEHAVIOR, MANNERS; *specif* **:** good manners ⟨a lady of gentle ~⟩

**hav·ior** \'hāvyə(r)\ *n* -s [ME *haviour* possession, alter. of *havour,* alter. (influenced by ME *haven* to have) of *aver, avoir,* fr. MF *aveir, avoir,* fr. OF, fr. *aveir, avoir,* v., to have, fr. L *habēre* — more at GIVE] *chiefly dial* **:** BEHAVIOR

**hav·la·gah** \,hävlə'gä\ *n* -s [Heb *habhlāghāh*] **:** SELF-RESTRAINT ⟨appeals by Zionist leaders for a policy of ~⟩

**hav·na** \'havnə\ *dial Brit* **:** have not

**¹hav·oc** \'havək, -vik,-vēk\ *n* -s [ME *havok,* fr. AF, modif. of OF *havot,* n., pillage & interj. used to signal start of pillage, perh. of Gmc origin; akin to Goth *hafjan* to lift — more at HEAVE] **1 :** wide and general damage or destruction **:** DEVASTATION, WASTE ⟨appalled by the ~ and loss of life caused by the earthquake —F.J.Crowley⟩ — see *cry havoc* at ¹CRY **2 :** great confusion and disorder ⟨several small children can create ~ in a house⟩ — **play havoc with** *or* **raise havoc with :** to do great damage to **:** render ineffectual **:** throw into disorder and confusion ⟨a weapon which could *play havoc with* land and sea defenses —Vera M. Dean⟩

**²havoc** \" \ *vb* **havocked; havocked; havocking; havocs :** to lay waste **:** DEVASTATE, DESTROY

**havre** *usu cap, var of* LE HAVRE

**¹haw** \'hȯ\ *n* -s [ME *hawe,* fr. OE *haga* hedge, hawthorn — more at HEDGE] **1 :** a piece of enclosed ground **:** YARD **2 a :** a hawthorn berry **b :** HAWTHORN **3 a :** the fruit of any of several shrubs or trees of the genus *Viburnum* **b :** a shrub or tree bearing such fruit

**²haw** \" \ *n* -s [origin unknown] **:** NICTITATING MEMBRANE; *esp* **:** an inflamed nictitating membrane of a domesticated mammal

**³haw** \" \ *vi* -ED/-ING/-S [imit.] **:** to inject a haw or a sound like it into one's speech during a hesitation or pause ⟨did a lot of hemming and ~*ing* during his talk⟩

**⁴haw** \" \ *n* -s **:** a sound often made by speakers during a pause while they are collecting their thoughts or trying to formulate them ⟨a long talk punctuated by hems and ~*s*⟩

**⁵haw** \" \ *v imper* [origin unknown] — used (1) as a command to a team or draft animal to turn to the left; (2) as a call in square dancing to progress to the left; compare ¹GEE ~ *vi* -ED/-ING/-S **1 :** to cry out the command *haw* to a draft animal ⟨we geed and ~*ed* until we were hoarse —A.M.Bailey⟩ **2 :** to turn to the near or left side ⟨the mare geed when she should have ~*ed*⟩ **3 :** to obey the command *haw* ⟨teaching a pair of young steers to ~⟩

**ha·waii** \hə'wä(,)(y)ē, -wī(,)(y)ē, -wȯ(,)(y)ē, -wä(,)(y)ē, -wäyə, -wȯyə, -wī(y)ə *also* hä'- *or* hä'- *or* 'vä(,)(y)ē *or* -vī(,)(y)ē *or* -vä(,)(y)ē *sometimes* -'və(,)(y)ē *or* -'wə(,)(y)ē; *a glottal stop often follows the 2d-syllable vowel when no y follows & when the last vowel is* ē\ *adj, usu cap* [*Hawaii,* state of the U.S., fr. Hawaiian *Hawai'i;* akin to Marquesan *Havaiki,* fabled original homeland of the Polynesians] **:** of or from Hawaii **:** of the kind or style prevalent in Hawaii **:** HAWAIIAN

**¹ha·wai·ian** \hə'wäyən, -wȯyən, -wī(y)ən\ *adj, usu cap* [*Hawaii* + E *-an*] **1 :** of or relating to Hawaii or the Hawaiian islands or the language of the Hawaiians **2 :** of or relating to a system of kinship terminology in which the terms for cross-cousins and parallel cousins are the same as those for sisters

**²hawaiian** \" \ *n* -s *cap* **1 :** a person of Hawaiian or part-Hawaiian ancestry **2 :** the Hawaiian language

**ha·waii·ana** *pronunc at* HAWAII *stressed* =,== + 'anə *or* 'änə *or* 'ānə *also* 'ānə\ *n pl, usu cap* [*Hawaii* + E *-ana*] **:** objects relating characteristically to Hawaii or of Hawaiian origin (as books or curios)

**hawaiian beet webworm** *n, usu cap H* **:** a grub that is the larva of a pyralidid moth (*Hymenia recurvalis*) and is destructive to beets and other green crops in much of the U.S.

**hawaiian crab** *n, usu cap H* **:** a large Pacific swimming crab (*Portunus sanguinolentus*) that is related to the Atlantic blue crab and is an important market crab in Hawaii

**hawaiian duck** *n, usu cap H* **:** a small drab duck (*Anas wyvilliana*) prized for food in the Hawaiian islands that is prob. an offshoot of the mallard

**hawaiian goose** *n, usu cap H* **:** NENE

**hawaiian guitar** *n, usu cap H* **:** a flat-bodied stringed musical instrument that has a long fretted neck and usu. 6 to 8 strings, that is held in a horizontal position either on the knees of the player or on an adjustable stand, and that is played by plucking the strings with thimbles, the desired pitch being obtained by sliding a small metal bar across the raised strings **2 :** UKULELE

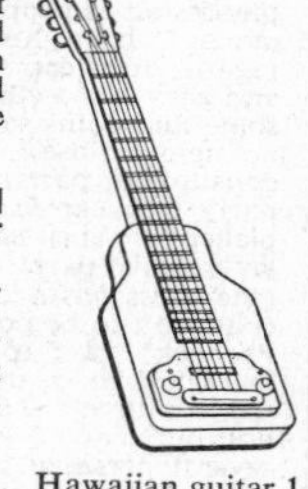

Hawaiian guitar 1

**hawaiian mahogany** *n, usu cap H* **:** KOA

**haw·er** \'hȯ(ə)r, -ȯə\ *n* -s [³*haw* + *-er*] **:** one that haws in speech ⟨one of your hemmers and ~*s*⟩

**hawfinch** \'=,=\ *n* [¹*haw* + *finch*] **:** a common finch (*Coccothraustes coccothraustes*) of Europe and Asia having a large heavy bill and short thick neck, and a male that is marked with black, white, and shades of brown

**¹haw–haw** *var of* HA-HA

**²haw–haw** \(')hȯ¦hȯ\ *n* -s [imit.] **:** a deep or esp. loud boisterous laugh **:** GUFFAW

**³haw–haw** \" \ *vi* -ED/-ING/-S **:** to laugh in haw-haws **:** GUFFAW

**⁴haw–haw** \'hȯ¦hȯ\ *adj* [redupl. of ⁴*haw*] **:** marked by or given to the use of frequent haws as a habit or affectation of speech often associated with a southern British upper-class speech ⟨that famous *haw-haw* English accent —J.B.Priestley⟩ ⟨a kind of *haw-haw* way of talking —Clements Ripley⟩

**¹hawk** \'hȯk\ *n* -s [ME *hauk,* fr. OE *hafoc, heafoc;* akin to OHG *habuh* hawk, ON *haukr* hawk, Russ *kobets,* a kind of falcon] **1 a :** any of numerous diurnal birds of prey belonging to the suborder Falcones of the order Falconiformes: (1) **:** any of the smaller members of this group (as falcons, buzzards, harriers, kites, caracaras, and ospreys) as distinguished from the notably larger eagles and Old World vultures (2) **:** any of various typical members of the family Accipitridae (as the New World Cooper's and sharp-shinned hawks and the Old World sparrow hawks) **:** ACCIPITER — see GOSHAWK; BILL illustration; compare OWL **b :** any of various birds that suggest hawks in appearance or behavior — used chiefly in combination; see NIGHTHAWK **2 :** one (as a swindler) who preys on his fellowmen **3 :** a small board or metal sheet with a handle on the underside used to hold mortar

hawk 3

**²hawk** \" \ *vb* -ED/-ING/-S [ME *hauken,* fr. *hauk,* n.] *vi* **1 :** to hunt birds by means of trained hawks **:** practice falconry **2 :** to soar and strike like a hawk ⟨birds ~*ing* after insects⟩ ~ *vt* **:** to hunt on the wing like a hawk ⟨the small bats ~ insects in midair —J.A.Thomson⟩

**³hawk** \" \ *vb* -ED/-ING/-S [back-formation fr. ²*hawker*] *vt* **:** to offer for sale by calling out or crying in the street **:** carry (merchandise) about from place to place for sale **:** PEDDLE **:** offer to various people for sale ⟨his works were ~*ed* in every street —Jonathan Swift⟩ ⟨small boys ~ large, luscious figs along the street —*Amer. Guide Series: N.C.*⟩ ⟨a dozen or so scripts which were currently being ~*ed* about town by various play agents —George Noble⟩ ~ *vi* **:** to peddle goods **:** hawk merchandise ⟨balloon-and-pennant man, ~*ing* by the grandstand gate —W.V.T.Clark⟩

**⁴hawk** \" \ *vb* -ED/-ING/-S [imit.] *vi* **:** to utter a harsh palatal or guttural sound in or as if in trying to clear the throat ~ *vt* **:** to raise (as phlegm) by hawking — often used with *up*

**⁵hawk** \" \ *n* -s **:** an audible effort to force up phlegm from the throat

**hawkbell** \'=,=\ *n* [ME *haukes bell, hauk bell*] **:** a small hollow spherical bell containing a free pellet and often attached to a hawk's leg

**¹hawkbill** \'=,=\ *or* **hawkbill turtle** *n* [¹*hawk* + *bill*] **:** HAWKSBILL TURTLE

**²hawkbill** \" \ *adj* [¹*hawk* + *bill*] **:** HAWK-BILLED

**hawk–billed** \'=¦=\ *adj* **1 :** having a bill or jaws like a hawk's beak **2 :** shaped like a hawk's bill

**hawkbit** \'=,=\ *n* [*hawkweed* + (*devil's*) *bit*] **:** any of various plants of the genus *Leontodon; esp* **:** FALL DANDELION

**hawk cuckoo** *n* **:** any of several Asiatic cuckoos of the genus *Cuculus* that outwardly resemble hawks — see BRAINFEVER BIRD

**hawk eagle** *n* **:** any of numerous eagles (as the African crowned eagle) exhibiting rather hawklike characters

**¹hawk·er** \'hȯkə(r)\ *n* -s [ME *hauker,* fr. OE *hafocere,* fr. *hafoc* hawk + *-ere* -er — more at HAWK] **1 :** FALCONER **2 :** an animal that captures its prey on the wing; *esp* **:** an insect that does this

**²hawker** \" \ *n* -s [by folk etymology fr. LG *hoker, höker* peddler, fr. MLG *hōker,* fr. *hōken, hūken* to peddle, bear on the back, squat + *-er;* akin to MD *hoken, hoeken* to peddle, squat, MHG *hūchen* to squat, ON *hūka* to squat, OE *hēah* high — more at HIGH] **1 :** one that hawks wares esp. in the streets **:** PEDDLER **2 :** one that hawks wares assisted by a beast of burden or private vehicle (as a carriage)

**³hawker** \" \ *n* -s [⁴*hawk* + *-er*] **:** one that hawks as if clearing his throat esp. constantly or habitually

**hawk·ery** \-kərē\ *n* -ES **:** a place where hawks are kept

**hawke's bay** \'hȯks-\ *adj, usu cap H&B* [fr. *Hawke's Bay,* provincial district in New Zealand] **:** of or from the provincial district of Hawke's Bay, New Zealand **:** of the kind or style prevalent in Hawke's Bay provincial district

**hawkeye** \'=,=\ *n* **1 :** an unceasing minute scrutiny ⟨keeping . . . a ~ on all strangers riding in and out of the little village —Howard Troyer⟩ **2 :** one whose vision is markedly keen or who is esp. good in the perception of details (as errors) ⟨the ~*s* who trap printed mistakes before they get out to a critical public — *Trip through Brown and Bigelow*⟩ **3** *usu cap* **:** IOWAN 1 — a nickname

**hawk–eyed** \'=¦=\ *adj* **:** having a keen eye **:** SHARP-SIGHTED

**haw·kie** *also* **haw·key** \'hȯki, 'häki\ *n, pl* **hawkies** *also* **hawkeys** [Sc dial. *hawkit, hawked* having white spots or streaks + *-ie, -ey*] *Scot* **:** a white-faced cow — often used as a pet name for any cow

**hawking** *n* -s [ME *hauking,* fr. gerund of *hauken* to hawk — more at HAWK] **:** FALCONRY

**hawk·ish** \'hȯkish, -kēsh\ *adj* **:** resembling or suggesting a hawk or the beak of a hawk in appearance ⟨a ~ face⟩ ⟨fishing boats with ~ prows —A.H.Leighton⟩

**hawklike** \'=,=\ *adj* **:** resembling or suggesting a hawk in appearance or character ⟨a ~ nose —Louis Bromfield⟩ ⟨~ eagerness —*Wall Street Jour.*⟩ ⟨~ vision⟩

**hawkmoth** \'=,=\ *n* **:** any of numerous rather large stout-bodied moths constituting a family (Sphingidae), having a long proboscis which at rest is kept coiled, long strong narrow fore wings more or less pointed at the ends, small hind wings, and stout antennae often hooked at the tip, and being usu. quiet in coloration but often handsomely patterned and graceful and hovering in flight — see HORNWORM

**hawk nose** *n* **:** a nose curved like a hawk's beak

**hawk–nosed** \'=¦=\ *adj* **:** having a markedly curved and more or less pointed nose suggesting a hawk's beak ⟨the strength of the *hawk-nosed* face —Louis Bromfield⟩

**hawk owl** *n* **1 :** a largely diurnal owl (*Surnia ulula*) of northern forests that somewhat resembles a hawk in appearance, having a long rounded tail and rather short pointed wings **2 :** a widespread owl (*Ninox scutulata*) of eastern Asia and the Pacific islands having the facial disk little differentiated; *also* **:** any of several congeners (as the boobook owls)

**hawk parrot** *n* **:** a So. American parrot (*Deroptyus accipitrinus*) with a large erectile nuchal crest

**hawks** *pl of* HAWK, *pres 3d sing of* HAWK

**hawk's–beard** \'=,=\ *n, pl* **hawk's–beards** [so called fr. the large bristly pappus] **:** a plant of the genus *Crepis*

**hawksbill turtle** \'=,=-\ *or* **hawksbill** *n* **:** a carnivorous sea turtle (*Eretmochelys imbricata*) of tropical and subtropical seas, having a shell that rarely exceeds two feet in length and is covered with large overlapping horny plates of a brown color marbled with yellow that furnish the best tortoiseshell of commerce

**hawk's–eye** \'=,=\ *n, pl* **hawk's–eyes 1 :** a blue variety of tigereye **2 :** GOLDEN PLOVER

**hawk·shaw** \'hȯk,shȯ\ *n* -s *usu cap* [after *Hawkshaw,* a detective in the play *The Ticket of Leave Man* (1863), by Tom Taylor †1880 Eng. dramatist and in the comic strip *Hawkshaw the Detective,* by Gus Mager †1956 Am. artist] **:** DETECTIVE

**hawk swallow** *n* **:** a common European swift (*Apus apus*)

**hawkweed** \'=,=\ *n* **:** any of several composite plants esp. of the genera *Hieracium, Picris,* and *Erechtites*

**hawky** \'hȯkē\ *adj* -ER/-EST **:** HAWKLIKE

**ha·wok** \'hä,wäk\ *n, pl* **hawok** [Maidu *howok*] **:** Indian money of California consisting of shell disks or buttons

**ha·wor·thia** \hȯ'(w)ərthēə, -thēə\ *n* [NL, fr. Adrian H. *Haworth* †1833 Eng. botanist + NL *-ia*] **1** *cap* **:** a genus of succulent plants (family Liliaceae) from the Cape of Good Hope with thick fleshy leaves mostly crowded in a basal rosette and white or greenish flowers in a terminal spike **2** -s **:** any plant of the genus *Haworthia*

**haws** *pl of* HAW, *pres 3d sing of* HAW

**hawse** \'hȯz *also* -ȯs\ *n* -s [ME *halse,* fr. ON *hals* neck, part of the bow of a ship — more at COLLAR] **1 a :** HAWSEHOLE **b :** the part of a ship's bow that contains the hawseholes **2 :** the position or arrangement of the anchor cables of a ship when both a port and starboard anchor are used — see FOUL HAWSE, OPEN HAWSE **3 :** the distance or the space between a ship's bows and her anchor **:** the space spanned by the anchor cables ⟨the small boat anchored in the large ship's ~⟩

**hawse bag** *n* **:** a bag stuffed with sawdust, shavings, or oakum and used for closing a hawsehole — called also *jackass*

**hawse bolster** *n* **:** a wooden or iron guard at the end of or around a hawsepipe as protection against the chafing of the cable and to facilitate its movement

**hawse–full** \'=,=\ *also* **hawse–fallen** \'=,==\ *adj* **:** having the hawseholes under water **:** having the sea breaking through the hawseholes ⟨a ship riding *hawse-full* at anchor⟩

**hawsehole** \'=,=\ *n* **:** one of the usu. metal-lined holes in the bow of a ship through which cables pass

**hawse hook** *n* **:** a breasthook above the hawseholes

**hawsepiece** \'=,=\ *n* **:** one of the timbers in the bow of a wooden ship through which a hawsehole is cut

**hawsepipe** \'=,=\ *n* **:** a cast-iron or steel pipe placed in the bows of a ship on each side of the stem for the anchor chains to pass through

**haw·ser** \'hȯzə(r) *also* -ȯsə-\ *n* -s [ME *haucer, hauser, hawser,* fr. AF *hauceour,* fr. MF *haucier* to raise, hoist (fr. — assumed — VL *altiare,* fr. L *altus* high) + *-our* -or — more at OLD] **:** a large rope for towing or mooring a ship or securing it at a dock

**hawser bend** *n* **:** a method of joining the ends of two heavy ropes by means of seizings

**hawser clamp** *n* **:** a device for gripping a hawser as it is paid out

**hawser–laid** \'=¦=\ *adj* **:** CABLE-LAID

**hawse timber** *n* **:** HAWSEPIECE

**hawsing iron** *n* **:** CAULKING IRON

**haw·thorn** \'hȯ,thȯrn, -th(ə)n\ *n* [ME *hawethorn,* fr. OE *hagathorn, haguthorn* fr. *haga* hedge, hawthorn + *thorn* thorn, thornbush — more at HEDGE, THORN] **:** a spring-flowering shrub or tree of the genus *Crataegus* (esp. the European *C.*

*oxyacantha* and the American *C. coccinea*) having usu. thorny branches, shining often lobed leaves, white or pink fragrant flowers, and small red fruits — see HAW, RED HAW

**hawthorn china** *n* **:** an oriental porcelain with a decoration of flowering plum-tree branches in white on a dark blue or black ground

**hawthorn pattern** *n* **:** the pattern on hawthorn china

**hawthorn rust** *n* **:** a rust fungus (*Gymnosporangium globosum*) in its aecial and pycnial stage

**haw tree** *n* **1** *obs* **:** HAWTHORN **2 :** WHITEBEAM **3 :** SERVICE TREE 1b

**¹hay** \ˈhā\ *n* -s [ME *haie, heie,* fr. OE *hege;* akin to OE *haga* hedge, hawthorn — more at HEDGE] **1** *archaic* **:** an enclosing fence **:** HEDGE **2** *archaic* **:** a place enclosed with a hay **:** PARK

**²hay** \ˈ"\ *n* -s [ME *hey,* fr. OE *hēg, hīg, hēg;* akin to OHG *hewi* hay, ON *hey,* Goth *hawi* hay, OE *hēawan* to hew — more at HEW] **1 :** grass ready for mowing or esp. cut and cured for fodder; *specif* **:** the entire herbage sometimes including the seeds of grasses and other forage plants (as legumes) harvested and dried esp. for feed **2 :** a grayish greenish yellow that is slightly less strong and very slightly lighter than absinthe yellow, greener and duller than dusty yellow, and slightly deeper than yellow stone **3 :** a rewarding result of careful effort, industriousness, or cultivation (as of friendships) ⟨got some political ~ out of his association with underworld characters⟩ **4** *slang* **:** BED — used with *the* ⟨drag out of the ~ at six-thirty to dress and serve breakfast —Margaret Long⟩ ⟨caught him in the ~ with one of her maids —H.A.Smith⟩ **5 :** a trifling sum of money ⟨sells over $250,000 worth of them a year — and in the book trade that is anything but ~ —J.C.Furnas⟩

**³hay** \ˈ"\ *vb* -ED/-ING/-S *vi* **:** to cut and cure grass for hay and usu. haul it from the field and store it ~ *vt* **1 :** to dry (a cut grass) so as to make hay **2 :** to grow grass on for making hay ⟨~ the lower meadow⟩ **3 :** to give hay to ⟨~ the horses⟩

**⁴hay** \ˈ"\ *n* -s [ME *haye,* fr. AF *haie*] *archaic* **:** a net used for catching a wild animal (as a rabbit)

**⁵hay** *or* **hey** \ˈ"\ *n* -s [MF *haye*] **1 :** a rustic dance with much interweaving of couples **2 :** a right and left performed in a figure eight, straight line, or circular pattern in a dance

**hay bacillus** *n* [so called fr. the fact that isolations were formerly made from boiled hay infusions] **:** a rod-shaped spore-forming chiefly aerobic bacterium (*Bacillus subtilis*) widely distributed in soil and decaying organic matter

**hay barrack** *n* **:** BARRACK 4

**haybird** \ˈ=,=\ *n* **1 :** any of various small European birds (as the blackcap or the garden warbler) that build nests largely of grass **2 :** PECTORAL SANDPIPER

**haybote** \ˈ=,=\ *n* -s [ME *haybote, heybote,* fr. *haie, heie* hedge + *bote* profit, advantage, repair — more at ¹HAY, BOOT] **1 :** the wood or thorns allowed to a tenant or commoner in English law for repairing his hedges or fences — called also *hedgebote* **2 :** the right to take haybote

**haybox** \ˈ=,=\ *n* **:** a box packed with hay as insulation and used as a fireless cooker

**hayburner** \ˈ=,==\ *n, slang* **:** HORSE; *esp* **:** a second-rate racehorse

**haycap** \ˈ=,=\ *n* **:** a covering for a haycock

**haycock** \ˈ=,=\ *n* [ME *hay kock,* fr. *hay, hey* hay + *kock, cok* cock (pile) — more at HAY, COCK] **:** a small rounded somewhat conical pile of hay

**hay cutter** *n* **:** a machine for cutting or chopping hay into short lengths

**hay·doo·dle** \ˈhā,düdᵊl\ *n* [euphemism, *doodle* (as in *cock-a-doodle-do*) being substituted for ⁶*cock,* associated with ¹*cock* (penis)] *chiefly Midland* **:** HAYCOCK

**hay down** *vt* **:** to dry (tobacco) too rapidly during curing

**haye** \ˈhā, ˈhī\ *n* -s [D *haai,* fr. MD *haey, haeye,* fr. ON *hār* thole, dogfish, shark; akin to OHG *huohili* small plow, Goth *hoha* plow, W *cainc* branch, OIr *cēcht* plow, Skt *śākhā* branch; basic meaning: branch] *archaic* **:** SHARK

**hay·er** \ˈhāə(r), ˈhe(ə)r, ˈheə\ *n* -s **:** one that hays

**hay fern** *n* **:** HAY-SCENTED FERN

**hay fever** *n* **:** an acute allergic nasal catarrh and conjunctivitis that is sometimes accompanied by asthmatic symptoms; *specif* **:** POLLINOSIS

**hay fe·ver·ite** \ˈhāˈfēvə,rīt\ *n* -s **:** one who is suffering from hay fever

**hay-fever weed** *n* **:** RAGWEED 2

**hayfield** \ˈ=,=\ *n* **:** a field where grasses or legumes for hay are grown

**hayfork** \ˈ=,=\ *n* **1 a :** a hand fork for pitching hay **b :** a mechanically operated fork for loading or unloading hay **2 :** an attachment to a hay tedder that stirs mowed hay

**hay hook** *n* **:** a steel hook held in the hand for dragging a bale of hay

**haying** *n* -s **:** the process or season of harvesting hay

**hay jack** *n* **:** HAYBIRD 1

**hay knife** *n* **:** a long-bladed knife with large rounded serrations on the edge for sawing off sections at the end of a stack or compact pile of hay

**haylift** \ˈ=,=\ *n* **:** an airlift engaged in dropping emergency food to farm animals isolated esp. by deep snow

**hay-loader** \ˈ=,==\ *n* **:** an implement for gathering hay from a windrow or swath and loading it into a wagon or trailer

hay-loader

**hayloft** \ˈ=,=\ *n* **:** a loft or scaffold for hay **:** HAYMOW

**haymaker** \ˈ=,==\ *n* **1 a :** a worker who cuts and cures hay **b :** a machine for curing hay **2 a :** a powerful blow with the fist often resulting in a knockout **b :** an action or statement that is a stunning setback **:** an attack that overthrows or puts in a dangerous or extremely unpleasant position ⟨a leading coffee user today prepared a ~ for its coffee suppliers and announced that it plans to begin dispensing free tea with meals to discourage the use of coffee —*Springfield (Mass.) Daily News*⟩ ⟨traded ~s of innuendo and insult across the courtroom —*Time*⟩

**haymaking** \ˈ=,==\ *n* **1 :** the operation or work of cutting grass and curing it for hay **2 :** the act of taking full advantage of an easy opportunity ⟨the ~ of the profiteer after the war —W.R.Inge⟩

**haymow** \ˈ=,=\ *n* [ME *hay moghte* haystack, fr. *hay, hey* hay + *moghte, mowe* mow — more at HAY, MOW] **:** a part of a barn where hay is stored

**hay plant** *n* **:** WOODRUFF

**hay press** *n* **:** a baler for hay

**hayrack** \ˈ=,=\ *n* **1 :** a frame mounted on the running gear of a wagon and used in hauling hay or straw — called also *hayrig* **2 :** a feeding rack that holds hay for cattle or horses

**hayrick** \ˈ=,=\ *n* [ME *heyrek,* fr. *hey* hay + *rek, reke* rick — more at HAY, RICK] **:** a relatively large sometimes thatched outdoor pile of hay **:** HAYSTACK

**hayride** \ˈ=,=\ *n* **:** a pleasure ride usu. at night by a group in a wagon, sleigh, or open truck partly filled with straw or hay

**hayrig** \ˈ=,=\ *or* **hayrigging** \ˈ=,==\ *n* **:** HAYRACK

**hays** *pl of* HAY, *pres 3d sing of* HAY

**hayscales** \ˈ=,=\ *n pl* **:** large often public scales utilizing a platform for the weighing of hay on wagons or trucks

**hay-scented fern** \ˈ=,==-\ *n* **:** a No. American fern (*Dennstaedtia punctilobula*) with fragrant pale green fronds and an aroma like hay

**hayseed** \ˈ=,=\ *n* **1 a :** seed shattered from hay **b :** the bits of straw or chaff from hay that cling to clothes **2 :** a person who is markedly rustic and unsophisticated **:** YOKEL **3 :** any of various minute crustaceans (as the red feed) which live at the surface of the sea and upon which herrings and many other fishes feed

**hay·sel** \ˈhāsəl\ *n* -s [²*hay* + *sele*] *dial Eng* **:** the haying season

**hayshaker** \ˈ=,==\ *n, slang* **:** HAYSEED 2

**hayshock** \ˈ=,=\ *n, chiefly South & Midland* **:** HAYCOCK

**haystack** \ˈ=,=\ *n* [ME *haystak,* fr. *hay, hey* hay + *stak* stack — more at HAY, STACK] **:** a stack of hay **:** HAYRICK

**hay sweep** *n* **:** BUCK RAKE

**hay-tal·let** *or* **hay-tal·lat** \ˈhā,talət\ *n, dial Eng* **:** HAYLOFT

**hay-time** \ˈ=,=\ *n* **:** the period in which haying is usu. done

**hayward** \ˈ=,=\ *n* [ME *hayward, heyward,* fr. *haie, heie* enclosure, hedge + *ward* — more at HAY, WARD] **1 a :** an officer appointed to keep cattle from breaking through from a town common or roadway into enclosed fields and to impound strays **b :** the keeper of a town's common herd of cattle **2 :** FIELD DRIVER

**¹haywire** \ˈ=,=\ *n* [²*hay* + *wire*] **:** wire used to bind bales (as of hay or straw)

**²haywire** \ˈ"\ *adj* [so called fr. the frequent use of baling wire to make makeshift repairs] **1 a :** inadequately equipped ⟨a ~ outfit⟩ **:** FLIMSY **b :** put together inexpensively or patched up tentatively from available odds and ends **:** JURY-RIGGED ⟨a ~ plant hurriedly built of secondhand tank cars and salvaged equipment —*Monsanto Mag.*⟩ **2 a :** being out of order **:** BROKEN-DOWN ⟨luckily for us, their range-finding and director gear must have been ~ . . . so her fire wasn't very accurate —*Outspan*⟩ **b :** tangled up **:** mixed up **:** not running or working normally **:** acting in an odd way ⟨a ~ train that came and went at the worst possible hours —*N.Y. Herald Tribune Bk. Rev.*⟩ ⟨~ development of western industrial culture —Marston Bates⟩ — often used in the predicate with *go* ⟨magnetic compasses won't work, radios go ~, and ordinary engine oil freezes —*All Hands*⟩ ⟨psychologists have gone so ~ with this new freedom that many interpretations are wild and bizarre —P.M. Symonds⟩ **3 :** emotionally excited **:** gone to pieces **:** UPSET ⟨she's pretty much ~ just now, but she'll have settled down by the time you get here —Mary R. Rinehart⟩ — often used with *go* ⟨went completely ~ and in one mad, exotic moment she bought the red pocketbook —Mary D. Gillies⟩ ⟨many boxing champions have gone ~ after winning a title —D.M. Daniel⟩ ⟨the danger that men in responsible executive positions might go ~ —Elmer Davis⟩

**³haywire** \ˈ"\ *n* [¹*haywire;* fr. the appearance of the leaves] **:** a sporadic disease of potatoes that is of unknown cause but considered by some to be due to a virus or viruses but by others to be due to unfavorable conditions during tuber development and that is characterized by the production of dwarfed plants with elongated stiff sometimes rolled leaves which finally turn yellow with purplish discoloration esp. at the tips and margins

**haz** *abbr* hazard

**ha·zan** *or* **haz·zan** *or* **cha·zan** *or* **chaz·zan** \ḵəˈzän, ˈḵäzᵊn\ *n, pl* **haza·nim** *or* **hazza·nim** \ḵəˈzänim\ [LHeb *ḥazzān*] **1 :** a synagogue official of the talmudic period **2 :** CANTOR 2

**ha·zan·ic** *or* **haz·zan·ic** *or* **cha·zan·ic** *or* **chaz·zan·ic** \-nik, -ˈnik\ *adj* **1 :** belonging to or characteristic of a hazan **:** CANTORIAL 2 **2 :** connected with or relating to hazanuth

**ha·za·nuth** *or* **ha·za·nut** *or* **haz·za·nuth** *or* **haz·za·nut** *or* **cha·za·nuth** *or* **cha·za·nut** *or* **chaz·za·nuth** *or* **chaz·za·nut** \ḵəˈzänət(h), -nəs\ *n* -s [LHeb *ḥazzānūth,* fr. *ḥazzan*] **1 :** cantorial singing or chanting **:** synagogal melodies **2 :** cantors of the synagogue; *collectively* **:** CANTORATE

**ha·za·ra** \həˈzärə\ *n, pl* **hazara** *or* **hazaras** *usu cap* **:** a Mongoloid people of Afghanistan

**¹haz·ard** \ˈhazə(r)d\ *n* -s [ME *hasard, hazard,* fr. MF *hasard,* fr. Ar *az-zahr* the die] **1 a :** a game of chance like craps played with two dice **b :** CHUCK-A-LUCK **2 a :** an adverse chance (as of being lost, injured, or defeated) **:** DANGER, PERIL ⟨the discovery of atomic fission brought into ~ the industrial potential of any state which could not destroy its enemy before it was itself destroyed —H.J.Laski⟩ **b :** a thing or condition that might operate against success or safety **:** a possible source of peril, danger, duress, or difficulty ⟨a coast visited by frequent dense fogs and mountains subject to violent storms constitute ~s to air travel —*Amer. Guide Series: Calif.*⟩ **c :** a condition that tends to create or increase the possibility of loss **3 a :** the effect of unpredictable, unplanned, and unanalyzable forces in determining events **:** CHANCE ⟨men and women danced together, women danced together, men danced together, as ~ had brought them together —Charles Dickens⟩ **b :** an event occurring without design, forethought, or direction **:** ACCIDENT ⟨looked like a fugitive, who had escaped from something in clothes caught up at ~ —Willa Cather⟩ **4 :** something risked (as stakes in gaming) **5 :** one of the winning openings in a court-tennis court — compare DEDANS, GRILLE, WINNING GALLERY **6 :** a stroke by which a pool ball is holed after contact with another ball — compare LOSING HAZARD, WINNING HAZARD **7 :** a golf-course obstacle restricting the player's stroke (as a bunker, sand trap, watercourse) **syn** see CHANCE, DANGER — **at hazard :** at stake

**²hazard** \ˈ"\ *vt* -ED/-ING/-S [ME *hasarder,* fr. *hasard*] **1 a :** to lay open to the risk of being lost, captured, or taken in or as if in a game of chance **:** GAMBLE, BET, VENTURE ⟨~*ed* a week's salary on a single turn of the cards⟩ ⟨asked him to ~ a small sum in a business venture⟩ **b :** to expose to possible risk of loss or damage ⟨so as not to ~ other buildings —*N.Y. City Fire Dept. Manual*⟩ **2 :** to take the risk of: **a :** to accept the chances and dangers of, venturing and daring to proceed or undertake despite them ⟨decided to ~ an open battle⟩ **b :** to have the courage to put forward or offer and expose to possible rebuff or censure (as a guess or suggestion) ⟨dares not ~ a prophecy —W.R.Sharp⟩ **syn** see VENTURE

**haz·ard·er** \-də(r)\ *n* -s [ME *hasardour, hasarder,* fr. MF *hasardeur,* fr. *hasarder* + *-eur* -or] **1 :** one that hazards **2** *archaic* **:** a player at hazard **:** GAMESTER

**haz·ard·less** \-dləs\ *adj* **:** not hazardous **:** marked by no hazard **:** involving no risk or danger

**haz·ard·ous** \-dəs\ *adj* [MF *hasardeux,* fr. *hasard* + *-eux* -ous] **1 :** depending on hazard or on chance; *specif* **:** ALEATORY **2 :** exposed or exposing one to hazard **:** involving risk of loss **:** RISKY **syn** see DANGEROUS

**haz·ard·ous·ly** *adv* **:** in a hazardous manner

**haz·ard·ous·ness** *n* -ES **:** the quality or state of being hazardous ⟨deterred by the ~ of the enterprise⟩

**hazardry** *n* -ES [ME *hasarderie, hasardrie,* fr. MF, fr. *hasarder* + *-erie* -ery] *obs* **:** GAMBLING

**hazard side** *n* **:** the side of a court-tennis court in which service is received — compare SERVICE SIDE

**¹haze** \ˈhāz\ *vb* -ED/-ING/-S [prob. back-formation fr. *hazy*] *vi* **1** *archaic* **:** to drizzle and fog **2 :** to become hazy or cloudy ⟨above the hotel the purple mountains *hazed* in the heat —William Sansom⟩ ~ *vt* **:** to make hazy **:** fog up **:** make dull or cloudy ⟨the purple night smoking up from the western water and *hazing* the world —Marjory S. Douglas⟩

**²haze** \ˈ"\ *n* -s [prob. back-formation fr. *hazy*] **1 a :** fine dust, salt particles, smoke, or particles of water finer and more scattered than those of fog causing lack of transparency of the air and making distant objects indistinct or invisible ⟨the fine ~ hanging lightly over the city and blurring its further outlines —Isolde Farrell⟩ ⟨a fog is likely soon to disappear by evaporation, while a ~ hangs on until washed out by rain, thinned by convection, or blown away by clear air —W.J.Humphreys⟩ **b :** a cloudy appearance in a transparent liquid or solid **c :** a dullness or cloudiness of finish (as on furniture) **:** BLOOM **2 :** something suggesting atmospheric haze: **a :** something giving the impression of clouds or cloudiness in the air or to the view ⟨the soft ~ of thickets of oaks —*Amer. Guide Series: Texas*⟩ ⟨a ~ of gnats danced under the bitten leaves —Elizabeth Taylor⟩ ⟨a ~ of greenery⟩ **b :** a state of mental dimness or obtuseness **:** haziness of mind or mental perception **c :** a state in which many things tend to merge and lose their separate identity ⟨looking back through the ~ of years —Allen Johnson⟩ **d :** a frame of mind vague or uncertain in its exact character but marked by strong generalized feeling dominating the reason ⟨a ~ of disbelief⟩ ⟨in a ~ of love⟩ or a set of conditions producing such a frame of mind ⟨its ~ of wine and waltz —Frederic Morton⟩

**³haze** \ˈ"\ *vt* -ED/-ING/-S [origin unknown] **1** *dial Eng* **:** to intimidate by physical punishment **2 a :** to harass (as a ship's crew) by exacting unnecessary, disagreeable, or difficult work **b** (1) **:** to harass or try to embarrass or disconcert by banter, ridicule, or criticism ⟨began to brood under the roughhouse play and built up a sullen resentment against the men who were *hazing* him —D.P.Mannix⟩ (2) **:** to subject (as a freshman or a fraternity pledge) to treatment intended to put in ridiculous or disconcerting positions **3** *West* **a :** to drive (animals) from horseback ⟨cowboys *hazed* herds slowly up north along an old Indian trail —S.E.Fletcher⟩ **b :** to separate (animals from a group) from horseback ⟨~ calves from a herd⟩ — often used with *out* ⟨~ out the dogies⟩

**⁴haze** \ˈ"\ *vt* -ED/-ING/-S [origin unknown] *dial Brit* **:** to season or mellow by drying in the sun

**haze blue** *n* **:** a pale purplish blue that is redder and paler than hydrangea blue, redder and slightly less strong than moonstone blue, and redder than starlight blue

**haze gray** *n* **:** a light gray similar to smoke gray

**¹ha·zel** \ˈhāzəl\ *n* -s [ME *hasel,* fr. OE *hæsel;* akin to OHG *hasal* hazel, ON *hasl,* OIr & OW *coll,* L *corulus*] **1 a :** a shrub or small tree of the genus *Corylus* (esp. *C. americana* and *C. cornuta* or in Europe *C. avellana*) — see FILBERT **b :** an Australian tree (*Pomaderris apetala*) grown for ornament and for its fine-grained wood **c :** the wood of either of these trees **d :** the wood of the sweet gum **2 a :** HAZELNUT 1 **b :** the fruit of the hawthorn **3 :** ASARABACCA **4** *also* **hazelnut :** a light brown to strong yellowish brown — called also *filbert, muffin, noisette*

**²hazel** \ˈ"\ *adj* [ME *hasel,* fr. *hasel,* n.] **1 :** consisting of hazels or of the wood of the hazel **:** relating to or derived from the hazel ⟨a ~ wand⟩ **2 :** of the color hazel **:** AVELLANEOUS

**hazel alder** *n* **:** SMOOTH ALDER

**hazel hen** *also* **hazel grouse** *n* **:** a European woodland grouse (*Tetrastes bonasia*) related to the American ruffed grouse

**hazel hoe** *n* **:** a large heavy grub hoe used in forests for trenching and clearing in fire fighting and for trimming small branches from tree trunks

**ha·zel·ly** \-zəlē\ *adj* **1 :** covered with or abounding in hazels **2 :** of the color hazel

**hazel mouse** *n* **:** a dormouse of the genus *Muscardinus*

**hazelnut** \ˈ==,=\ *n* [ME *haselnutte,* fr. OE *hæselhnutu,* fr. *hæsel* hazel + *hnutu* nut — more at HAZEL, NUT] **1 :** any of several nuts that are produced by the hazel and that have a husk little or no longer than the nut **2 :** HAZEL 4

**hazel pine** *n* **1 :** the wood of the sweet gum **2 :** SWEET GUM

**hazelwood** \ˈ==,=\ *n* **:** the wood of the sweet gum

**hazelwort** \ˈ==,=\ *n* **:** an asarabacca (*Asarum europaeum*)

**haz·er** \ˈhāzə(r)\ *n* -s **:** one that hazes: **a :** one of two cowboys who ride beside a bucking horse to protect both horse and broncobuster **b :** a rider who assists a cowboy bulldogging steers by riding on the opposite side of the steer to keep it from veering away

**hazes** *pres 3d sing of* HAZE, *pl of* HAZE

**ha·zi·ly** \ˈhāzəlē, -li\ *adv* **:** in a hazy manner ⟨saw the distant hills ~ through the field glasses⟩ ⟨remembered only ~ where he was going⟩

**ha·zi·ness** \-zēnəs, -zin-\ *n* -ES **:** the quality or state of being hazy ⟨the ~ of the smoky atmosphere⟩ ⟨a ~ in his mental processes⟩

**hazing** *n* -s **:** the action of one that hazes: **a :** the infliction of unnecessary or excessive work esp. on sailors in order to harass **b** (1) **:** an attempt to embarrass or disconcert by ridicule or persistent criticism (2) **:** the subjecting (as of a freshman or fraternity pledge) to treatment intended to put in ridiculous or disconcerting position

**ha·zle** \ˈhāzəl\ *vt* -ED/-ING/-S [freq. of ⁴*haze*] **:** HAZE

**ha·zy** \ˈhāzē, -zi\ *adj* -ER/-EST [fr. earlier *hawsey, heysey,* of unknown origin] **:** marked by haze: as **a :** obscured or made dim or cloudy with haze ⟨a ~ weather⟩ ⟨a ~ view of the mountains⟩ **b :** OBSCURE, VAGUE, INDEFINITE ⟨a ~ idea that he'd like to get married⟩ ⟨a somewhat ~ account of what he did⟩ ⟨~ logic⟩ **c :** CLOUDED ⟨a mirror ~ with steam⟩ ⟨some gasolines containing sulfur, when exposed to sunlight, become ~ —A.N.Sachanen⟩

**hazy blue** *n* **:** CAMEO GREEN

**hazzan** *var of* HAZAN

**hazzanuth** *or* **hazzanut** *var of* HAZANUTH

**HB** *abbr* **1** halfback **2** hard black **3** heavy bomber **4** His Beatitude; His Blessedness

**Hb** *symbol* hemoglobin

**h bar** *n, cap H* **:** a bar like an I bar but with wider flanges

**h beam** *n, cap H* **:** a beam like an I beam but with wider flanges

**h-bomb** \ˈ=,=\ *n, usu cap H* **:** HYDROGEN BOMB

**h bone** *n, cap H* **:** AITCHBONE

**hbr** *abbr* harbor

**h-budding** \ˈ=,==\ *n, cap H* **:** plate budding in which cuts in the bark of the stock are made in the form of an H

**HC** *abbr* **1** half calf **2** half chest **3** hand control **4** held covered; hold covered **5** high capacity **6** high church **7** high commissioner **8** high-compression **9** hockey club **10** Holy Communion **11** *often not cap* honoris causa **12** hot and cold **13** House of Commons **14** house of correction

**hcap** *abbr* handicap

**HCF** *abbr* highest common factor

**HCL** *abbr* high cost of living

**hcp** *abbr* handicap

**hd** *abbr* **1** hand **2** head **3** hogshead

**HD** *abbr* **1** harbor defense **2** heavy-duty **3** high density **4** home defense **5** horse-drawn

**hdbk** *abbr* handbook

**hdg** *abbr* heading

**hdkf** *abbr* handkerchief

**hdl** *abbr* **1** handle **2** headline

**hdlg** *abbr* handling

**hdqrs** *abbr* headquarters

**hdw** *abbr* hardware

**hdwd** *abbr* hardwood

**hdwe** *abbr* hardware

**¹he** \(ˈ)hē, ē, ,(h)i\ *pron* [ME, fr. OE *hē;* akin to OE *hēo, hīo* she, *hit* it, *hīe* they, OS *hē, hie* he, OHG *hē,* ON *hann* he, Goth *himma* (dat.) this, L *cis, citra* on this side, Gk *keinos, ekeinos* that (adj.), that person, Arm *sa* this, Hitt *ki;* basic meaning: this] **1 :** that male one ⟨I'll have no father, if you be not ~ —Shak.⟩ ⟨I spoke to the boy and ~ spoke to me⟩ **:** that one regarded as masculine (as by personification) ⟨last came Anarchy: ~ rode on a white horse —P.B.Shelley⟩ — used as nominative masculine pronoun of the third person singular usu. in reference to a previously specified subject or to someone indicated by some means (as pointing) ⟨~ heard me say it and so did ~⟩ ⟨~ with the beard is the one I mean⟩; sometimes in poetry and in substandard speech used pleonastically together with a noun as subject of a verb ⟨the Senator ~ said he'd have to have you —John Dos Passos⟩ ⟨Sir Oluf ~ rideth over the plain —H.W.Longfellow⟩ — see ¹HIM, ¹HIS; compare ³HIS, IT, SHE, THEY **2 :** that one whose sex is unknown or immaterial ⟨find out who is ringing the doorbell and what ~ wants⟩ ⟨~ that hath ears to hear, let him hear —Mt 11:15 (AV)⟩ — used as a nominative case form in general statements (as in statutes) to include females, fictitious persons (as corporations), and several persons collectively ⟨if a customer is dissatisfied ~ may return the goods⟩ ⟨one manufacturer is advertising . . . that ~ will sell cars freight-free —*Motor Trend*⟩ **3** *archaic* **:** the one **:** the other — used as a nominative masculine demonstrative pronoun in the expressions *he . . . he* and *he and he* **4 :** YOU — used as a nominative case form in speaking to or as if to a baby ⟨did ~ bump his little head⟩ and in some English dialects in addressing a boy or in addressing a person of higher or lower social status than the speaker **5 a** *substand* **:** HIM — used in a compound object ⟨between his wife and ~⟩ **b** *dial Eng* **:** HIM, IT — used emphatically as object of a verb or preposition ⟨don't give it to ~⟩

**²he** \ˈhē\ *n* -s *often attrib* [ME, fr. *he,* pron.] **1 :** a male person or animal ⟨the ~s would quarrel and fight with the females —Jonathan Swift⟩ — often used in combination ⟨a routine *he-* or *she* plot⟩ ⟨*he-*goat⟩ **2 a :** one that is strongly masculine or virile — used chiefly in combination ⟨a real *he-*man⟩ ⟨that's what I call *he-*literature —Sinclair Lewis⟩ **b** *dial* **:** a large or powerful one of its kind — used chiefly in combination ⟨a regular old *he-*blizzard —Wallace Stegner⟩ **3** *Brit* **:** ³TAG 1; *also* **:** the player who is it

**³he** *also* **heh** \ˈhā\ *n* -s [Heb *hē'*, perh. lit., window] **1 :** the fifth letter of the Hebrew alphabet — symbol ה; see ALPHABET table **2 :** the letter of the Phoenician alphabet or of any of the various Semitic alphabets corresponding to Hebrew he

**HE** *abbr* **1** high efficiency **2** high explosive **3** His Eminence **4** His Excellency; Her Excellency

**He** *symbol* helium

**¹head** \ˈhed\ *n* -s *see sense 6b* [ME *heved, hed,* fr. OE *hēafod;* akin to OHG *houbit* head, ON *hǫfuth,* Goth *haubith,* L *caput* head, Skt *kapucchala* hair at the back of the head] **1 :** the division of the human body that contains the brain, the eyes, the ears, the nose, and the mouth; *also* **:** the corresponding anterior division of the body of various animals including all vertebrates, most arthropods, and many mollusks and worms **2 a :** the seat of the intellect **:** the place where thought and inspiration originate **:** UNDERSTANDING, MIND ⟨two ~*s* are better than one⟩ ⟨he has some queer notions in his ~⟩ **b :** a person with respect to certain mental qualities ⟨let wiser ~*s* prevail⟩ **c :** natural aptitude or talent ⟨a good ~ for figures⟩ **d :** mental or emotional control **:** POISE ⟨can keep his ~ in a crisis⟩ ⟨level ~⟩ ⟨a situation calling for a cool ~⟩ **e :** HEADACHE ⟨it didn't give you a ~ like beer —R.O.Bowen⟩ **f :** the mouth as the organ of speech ⟨he'd better keep his ~ shut about this⟩ **3 a :** the hair on a head **b :** the hair as a head covering **:** COIFFURE, HEADDRESS **4 a :** a sculptured representation of a head ⟨a bronze ~ of Lincoln⟩ **b :** the obverse of a coin — compare HEAD OR TAIL **5 :** the antlers of a deer **6 a :** each one among a number **:** INDIVIDUAL ⟨count ~*s*⟩ ⟨a cost of $5 per ~⟩ **b** *pl* **head :** a unit of number (as of domestic animals) ⟨a thousand ~ of cattle⟩ **c** *Brit* **:** a herd or aggregation of game animals **7 a :** an end of something regarded as the upper or higher end ⟨~ of a valley⟩ ⟨~ of a slope⟩ ⟨~ of a staircase⟩ or as being the part most distant from an entrance ⟨~ of a bay⟩ or as being opposite the foot ⟨~ of a bed⟩ ⟨~ of a grave⟩ ⟨seated at the ~ of the table⟩ **b :** the source or beginning esp. of a stream ⟨the ~ of the Nile⟩ ⟨the ~ of navigation⟩ — compare FOUNTAINHEAD **c :** either end of something (as a bridge, cask, or drum) whose two ends may not or need not be distinguished **d :** an underground passage or level in a coal mine **e :** a position or direction of the set of parallel planes in a massive crystalline rock along which fracture is most difficult, being normal to the direction of strongest cohesion **f :** a round or inning played from one end of a course to the other in certain games (as bowls and curling) **8 :** one who stands in relation to others somewhat as the head does to the other members of the body **:** DIRECTOR, CHIEF: as **a :** HEADMASTER **b :** one in charge of a division or department in an office or institution; *esp* **:** one in charge of a department in a school, college, or university **c :** an officer in charge of a hall or college (as at Oxford or Cambridge) **9 a :** CAPITULUM 3b **b :** the top or foliaged part of a plant consisting of a compacted mass of leaves ⟨~ of lettuce⟩ ⟨~ of a tree⟩ or close fructification ⟨~ of grain⟩ **c :** a bunch or hank of flax, hemp, or jute packed for marketing **10 :** HEADLAND, PROMONTORY, CAPE — now used chiefly in place names **11 a :** the leading element of a military column or a procession **b :** the leader or the leading position in dancing **c :** the hottest and most active portion of an advancing forest fire or grass fire **d :** freedom to proceed on one's course or to have one's way — used chiefly in the phrases *give one his head* and *let one have his head* **e :** HEADWAY ⟨often she had to fight for her ~ as the press of sail buried her bow —C.V.Reilly⟩ **12 :** the uppermost extremity or projecting part of an object **:** TOP ⟨~ of a cane⟩ ⟨~ of a bolt⟩ ⟨~ of a mast⟩ ⟨~ of a doorway⟩: as **a :** the striking part of a weapon (as an arrow, spear, ax) or tool (as a hammer, hatchet, ram) **b :** the striking end of a racket, club, stick, or paddle — see GOLF illustration **c :** the point of a violin bow — see BOW illustration **d** *of a bowed instrument* **:** the pegbox and scroll **e :** HEAD JOINT 1 **f :** the rounded proximal end of a long bone (as the humerus) **g :** the end of a muscle nearest the origin **h :** the anterior end of an invertebrate **:** SCOLEX **i :** the end of a cigar that is placed in the mouth **j :** a protective covering for the ends of roll paper **k :** the oval part of a printed musical note **13 a :** a body of water kept in reserve at a height (as for a mill or in a reservoir); *also* **:** the containing bank, dam, or wall **b :** a mass of water in motion (as in a rip current) **c :** a sudden rush of liquid (as water through an irrigation ditch or oil from a well) **d :** the flow of water used in irrigating a field **e :** unconsolidated earth material moved by solifluction — compare CONGELITURBATE **14 a :** the difference in elevation between two points in a body or column of fluid (as between the surface and a submerged orifice at which the fluid flows outward or when pumping into an elevated tank flows inward) **b :** the resulting pressure of the fluid at the lower point expressible as this height; *broadly* **:** pressure of a fluid ⟨an engine with a full ~ of steam⟩ **15 :** the front or foremost part of something: as **a :** the bow and adjacent parts of a ship ⟨brought her ~ into the wind⟩ **b :** a ship's toilet — compare BEAKHEAD 1b **c :** a portion of a hide in front of the flare of the shoulder — see HIDE illustration **d :** the approximate length of the head of a horse ⟨won the race by a ~⟩ **16 :** the place of leadership or of honor or command **:** the most important or foremost position ⟨at the ~ of his class⟩ **17 a** (1) **:** a word or words often in larger letters placed above or at the beginning of a passage of written or printed matter in order to introduce or categorize — called also *heading, headline;* compare RUNNING HEAD, SHOULDER HEAD, SIDEHEAD (2) **:** a separate part or topic of a discourse or writing **:** POINT ⟨~*s* of a sermon⟩ ⟨you may rest easy on that ~⟩ **b :** a portion of a page or sheet that is above the first line of printing; *also* **:** the corresponding blank part of an imposed form — compare PAGE 1d **18 a :** the topmost edge of a book standing upright — compare FOOT, TAIL; BINDING EDGE, FORE EDGE **b :** the upper edge of a sail — see SAIL illustration **19 a :** the foam or scum rising on a fermenting or effervescing liquid **b :** the cream that rises on standing milk **c heads** *pl* **:** the first runnings **d heads** *pl* **:** crude ore fed to a concentrating plant — compare CONCENTRATE, MIDDLING, TAILING **20 a :** the part of a boil, pimple, or abscess at which it is likely to break **b :** culminating point of action or of tension **:** CRISIS, CLIMAX, ISSUE **c** *archaic* **:** a gathered force (as in rebellion) ⟨to save our heads by raising of a ~ —Shak.⟩ **21 a :** a cover for an alembic or other distilling apparatus — see ALEMBIC illustration **b :** the hood of a carriage **c** *Brit* **:** the top of an automobile **22 a** *or* **head metal :** an extra piece of metal on a foundry casting made by filling up a riser after the mold is full in order to supply loss from shrinkage and to permit slag or dross and unsound metal to rise clear of the casting **b :** a riser filled in in this manner **c :** a part of a railroad rail supported by a web and base that guides and provides a running surface for the flanged wheels of cars and locomotives — see T RAIL illustration **23 :** a part or attachment of an apparatus, machine, or machine tool containing a device (as a cutter, grinder, polisher, drill) for acting mechanically on something ⟨turret ~ of a lathe⟩ ⟨milling ~⟩ ⟨sheep-shearing ~⟩ ⟨safety-*head* centrifuge⟩; *also* **:** the part of an apparatus that performs the chief function ⟨the ~ of a photographic enlarging camera⟩ ⟨a shower ~⟩ ⟨a sprinkler ~⟩ ⟨welding ~⟩ **24 a :** CYLINDER HEAD **b :** a movable mount for attaching a camera to a tripod or other support **c :** a device used in recording sound for converting electrical signals into the recorded form, for converting the recorded form into electrical signals, or for removing recorded material from a record — see ERASE HEAD, MAGNETIC HEAD, RECORDING HEAD, REPRODUCING HEAD **25 :** an immediate constituent of an endocentric compound or construction having the same grammatical function as the whole (as the terms *polite old man, old man,* and *man* in "a polite old man") — **by the head :** drawing the greater depth of water forward — **off one's head :** CRAZY, DISTRACTED — **out of one's head :** unable to command one's mental powers **:** DELIRIOUS — **over one's head 1 :** beyond one's comprehension ⟨he liked pictures but art criticism was *over his head*⟩ ⟨the speech went *over the heads* of the audience⟩ **2 :** so as to pass over or ignore one's superior standing or authority ⟨quit when his juniors were promoted *over his head*⟩ ⟨went *over the head* of his boss to complain⟩ **3** *obs* **:** PAST, GONE-BY

²**head** \"\ *adj* [ME *heved, hed,* fr. *heved, hed,* n.] **1 :** of, relating to, or for a head or the head **2 :** PRINCIPAL, CHIEF, LEADING, FIRST ⟨~ chorister⟩ ⟨~ cook⟩ **3 :** situated at the head ⟨~ wall⟩ ⟨~ sails⟩ **4 :** coming from in front **:** meeting the head as it is moved forward ⟨~ sea⟩ ⟨~ tide⟩

³**head** \"\ *vb* -ED/-ING/-S [ME *hedden,* fr. *hed,* n.] *vt* **1 :** BEHEAD **2 a :** to lop off the top branches of **:** POLL ⟨~ a tree⟩ **b :** to cut back (the shoots of plants) to induce branching or check growth — often used with *in* or *back* **c :** to harvest (a crop) by cutting off the heads **3 a :** to put a head on **:** fit a head to ⟨~ an arrow⟩ ⟨~ a bolt⟩ ⟨~ a cask⟩ **b :** to form the head or top of ⟨the church tower was ~*ed* by a spire⟩ **4 :** to put oneself at the head of **:** act as leader to ⟨~ an expedition⟩ ⟨~ a revolt⟩ **5 a :** to face or oppose head on ⟨~ the waves⟩ ⟨~*ing* the driving rain⟩ **b :** to get in front of so as to hinder, stop, or turn back ⟨~ a herd of cattle⟩ **c :** to take a lead over (as in a race) **:** SURPASS **d :** to pass (a stream) by going round above the source **6 a :** to put something at the head of (as a list) **:** furnish with a heading ⟨each page was ~*ed* with the writer's name and the date⟩ **b :** to stand as the first or leading member of ⟨~*s* the list of local war heroes⟩ ⟨~*ed* his class all through school⟩ **7 :** to set the course or direct the progress of ⟨~ a ship northward⟩ ⟨~ a horse toward home⟩ **8 :** to drive or direct (as a soccer ball) by hitting with the head ~ *vi* **1 :** to form a head ⟨this cabbage ~*s* early⟩ ⟨the pimple ~*ed*⟩ **2 :** to point or proceed in a certain direction ⟨how does she ~, helmsman⟩ ⟨the fleet was ~*ing* out⟩ ⟨the dog ~*ed* for the woods⟩ ⟨the business seemed to be ~*ing* for trouble⟩ **3 a :** to have a source **:** ORIGINATE, RISE ⟨the more important rivers . . . ~ in the Rocky mountains or their foothills —*Scientific Monthly*⟩ **b :** to flow intermittently (as oil from a well)

**head·ache** \'he,dāk *sometimes* -,dik *or* -,dēk\ *n* [ME *hedache,* fr. OE *hēafodece,* fr. *hēafod* head + *ece, æce* ache — more at HEAD, ACHE] **1 :** pain inside the head **:** CEPHALALGIA **2** [so called fr. the effect of their odor] **:** any of several poppies **3 :** a vexatious situation **:** a baffling problem **:** a source of trouble or worry ⟨the lack of funds for financing the educational needs of our communities sooner or later proves to be the principal ~ —C.A.Herter⟩

**headache plant** *n* [so called fr. its use as a remedy for headache] **:** AMERICAN PASQUEFLOWER

**headache post** *n* **:** a post placed on an oil-well derrick floor in order to prevent the walking beam from accidentally striking a workman

**headache weed** *n* **:** a West Indian plant of the genus *Hedyosmum* (family Chloranthaceae) held to be a remedy for headache

**head-aching** \-,dākiŋ, -kēŋ\ *adj* **:** causing headache

**head·achy** \'he,dākē, -ki *sometimes* -,dik- *or* -,dēk-\ *adj* -ER/-EST **1 :** having headache **2 :** causing headache or attended by headache

**head and front** *n, archaic* **:** the foremost or essential feature or part ⟨the very *head and front* of my offending —Shak.⟩

**head and shoulders** *adv* **1** *archaic* **:** without good reason or excuse **:** by force **:** VIOLENTLY **2 :** beyond comparison **:** by far **:** OUTSTANDINGLY ⟨stood *head and shoulders* above the rest in character and ability⟩

**head-and-tail-light** \,=:=',=\ *also* **head-and-tail-light fish** *n* **:** a small So. American characin fish (*Hemigrammus ocellifer*) that is translucent green with orange-tinged black-tipped fins and shimmering red eyes and tail spots and is often kept in the tropical aquarium

¹**headband** \'=,=\ *n* [¹*head* + *band*] **1 :** a band worn on or around the head: as **a :** an ornamental band (as of cloth, flowers, jewels) **b :** a band connecting two earphones **2 :** ARCHIVOLT 1 **3 :** a plain or decorative band printed or engraved at the head of a page or a chapter **4 :** a narrow strip of cloth sewn or glued by hand to a book at the extreme ends of the backbone — compare FOOTBAND

²**headband** \"\ *vt* **:** to fasten headbands on (a book)

**head betony** *n* **:** WOOD BETONY 2

**head blight** *or* **head blighting** *n* **:** a blighting of the heads of a cereal; *esp* **:** such a blighting caused by a fungus (*Gibberella zeae*) — compare WHEAT SCAB

**headblock** \'=,=\ *n* **:** a block supporting the head of something: as **a :** a part of a sawmill carriage that supports the log **b :** a block of wood between the fifth wheel and the forward spring of a carriage or wagon **c :** one of a set of extra-long railroad ties used for supporting the operating mechanism of a point rail

**headboard** \'=,=\ *n* **1 a** (1) **:** a board stretching between the headposts of a bed (2) **:** an upright structure forming a head for a bed **b :** a light partition that separates one berth in a sleeping car from that next to it **2 :** a wooden board at the upper corner of a Bermudian mainsail to which the halyard is shackled

**headborough** \'=,=(,)=\ *n* [ME *hed borwe,* fr. *hed* head + *borwe* pledge, tithing — more at BORROW] **1 :** a chief of a frankpledge or tithing — compare TITHINGMAN **2 :** BORSHOLDER

**headbox** \'=,=\ *n* **1 :** a receptacle in a papermaking machine that holds the stuff and regulates its flow onto the wire **2 :** a case covering the operating mechanism of a venetian blind

**head boy** *n* **:** a head prefect in a British school

**head cabbage** *or* **heading cabbage** *n* **:** CABBAGE 1

**headcap** \'=,=\ *n* **:** the covering leather at the head and foot of the backbone of a hand-covered book shaped over the headbands

**head capsule** *n* **:** an exoskeleton of the head of an insect made up of fused chitinous plates in which the primitive segmentation is obscured

**head-cavity** \'=,===\ *n* **:** one of the transitory somites of the head of an early vertebrate embryo

**head cell** *n* **:** CAPITULUM 3a

**headcheese** \'=;=\ *n* **:** the meat of the head, feet, and sometimes the tongue and heart esp. of a pig cut up fine, seasoned and boiled, and either made into a large sausage or pressed into a firm jellied mass

**headchute** \'=,=\ *n* **:** a pipe for ejecting refuse from a ship's head

**headcloth** \'=,=\ *n* **1 :** a cloth forming a covering or screen for the head of a bed **2 :** any of various cloth coverings for the head (as a kerchief, a kaffiyeh, a turban) **3 headcloths** *pl, obs* **:** the pieces of a woman's headdress

**head cold** *n* **:** a common cold in which the symptoms are primarily centered in the nasal passages and adjacent mucous tissues

**head-collar** \'=,==\ *n, Brit* **:** HALTER 1b

**head couple** *n* **:** a couple in a square dance set whose backs are to the music or the caller; *also* **:** the couple opposite — compare FOOT COUPLE, SIDE COUPLE

**head court** *n* [ME *hed court*] **:** an obsolete Scottish county freeholders' court having charge for some time prior to 1832 of the registration of voters

**head ditch** *n* **:** an irrigation ditch across an upper slope from which water is drawn into basins or furrows

**head·dress** \'he(d),dres\ *n* **1 :** an often elaborate covering for the head (as for ceremonial or social occasions) **2 :** a manner of dressing the hair; *esp* **:** a fanciful arrangement of a woman's hair often with accessories (as flowers, veils, ribbons, combs)

**head dropper** *n* **:** a slaughterhouse worker who severs heads from carcasses and removes edible portions for processing

**head·ed** \'hedəd\ *adj* [ME *hedded,* fr. past part. of *hedden* to head — more at HEAD] **1 :** having a head or a heading ⟨a ~ bolt⟩ ⟨~ paragraphs⟩ **2 :** formed into a head **:** MATURED ⟨~ cabbage⟩ **3 :** having (such) a head or (so many) heads — often used in compounds ⟨curly-*headed* boy⟩ ⟨a cool-*headed* businessman⟩ ⟨a gold-*headed* cane⟩ **4** *of lumber* **:** tongued and grooved at the ends — usu. used in the phrase *dressed and headed*

**head end** *n* **1 :** the first few inches of fabric that are woven in a loom after new warp is started and that are often used for notations (as various marks of identification) **2 :** the cars of a passenger train that are immediately behind the locomotive and are commonly used for handling mail, express, and baggage

**head·end·er** \(')he'dendə(r)\ *n* -S [*head end* + *-er*] **:** a head-on collision

**head-end revenue** *n* **:** revenue from railroad traffic (as mail, express, milk) carried at the head end

**head-end system** *n* **:** an arrangement whereby electricity for a complete railroad train is furnished by a single generating plant located on the locomotive or tender or on a separate car

**head·er** \'hedə(r)\ *n* -S [ME *heder,* fr. *hed* head + *-er*] **1** *obs* **:** HEADSMAN **2 :** a worker or machine that removes heads; *esp* **:** a grain-harvesting machine that cuts off the grain heads and elevates them to a wagon **3 a :** a brick or stone laid in a wall with its end toward the face of the wall — opposed to *stretcher* **b :** a beam fitted between trimmers and across the ends of tail beams in a building frame **c :** a conduit or chamber (as the exhaust manifold of a multicylinder engine) into which a number of smaller conduits open **d :** a wall or barrier at either end of a motor truck or trailer body to prevent shifting of cargo on stopping or starting **4 a :** a worker or a machine that upsets rivets **b :** a cooper who puts heads on barrels by hand or by machine — called also *headerman* **5 :** an officer in charge of a whaleboat **6 :** a fall or dive head foremost ⟨tripped and took a ~ into a rosebush⟩ ⟨try a ~ off the high diving board⟩ **7 :** a dog trained to head cattle or sheep **8 :** a main shoot (as of a fruit tree) that tends to elongate with few side branches **9 :** SADDLE 12

**header and thresher** *n* **:** COMBINE 3

**header bond** *n* **:** a masonry bond in which all courses are header courses

**header-box** \'==,=\ *or* **header barge** *n* **:** a large wagon box with one side higher than the other into which cut grain is elevated by header

header bond

**header course** *n* **:** a masonry course in which all the bricks are laid as headers

**header fork** *n* **:** a fork with three or four tines for pitching grain heads with attached straw harvested with a header

**head·er·man** \-mən, -,man\ *n, pl* **headermen 1 :** HEADER 4b **2 :** an operator of a machine for making steel bends, offsets, bolt blanks, bolt heads, and rivet heads **3 :** one who forges hot or cold metal on a bulldozer **4 :** a worker who rivets together the fitted-up metal plates of oil-storage tanks

**header-up** \'==;=\ *n* -S [*head up,* v. + *-er*] **1 :** HEADERMAN 2 **2 :** HEADER 4b

**head fast** *n* **:** a mooring hawser or chain at the head of a ship

**headfirst** \'=;=\ *adv* **:** with the head foremost **:** HEADLONG, ABRUPTLY, RECKLESSLY ⟨had plunged ~ into the statehood fight —Edna Ferber⟩

**headfish** \'=,=\ *n* **:** OCEAN SUNFISH

**head-flattening** \'=,=(=)=\ *n* **:** a practice dating from prehistoric times and formerly engaged in by various peoples of No. America and So. America whereby the skull is caused to develop with a flattened top by the application of pressure during infancy

**head fold** *n* **:** an anterior thickening of the blastoderm immediately anterior to the neural plate of an amniotic embryo from which the anterior part of the body develops

**headforemost** \(')=',=\ *adv* **:** HEADFIRST, HEADLONG

**head form** *n* **:** the shape of a human head esp. with reference to the cephalic index

**headframe** \'=,=\ *n* **:** a frame structure over a mine shaft to support the hoisting sheaves — called also *gallows*

**head·ful** \'=,fu̇l\ *n* -S **:** a quantity (as of information) that fills the head

**head gate** *n* **1 :** a gate at the upper end of a canal lock **2 :** a gate for controlling the water flowing into a race, sluice, or irrigation ditch

**headgear** \'=,=\ *n* **1 a :** a covering for the head (as a hat, cap, bonnet) **b :** a protective device for the head (as a soldier's helmet or a welder's helmet) **c :** HEAD HARNESS **2 :** hoisting or drilling gear at the top of a mine shaft or oil well

**head harness** *n* **:** a part of a horse's harness worn on or depending from the head and including bridle, checkrein, reins, bit, and blinders

**headhouse** *n* **1 :** a structure in which the headframe of a mine is housed **2 :** a part of a railroad passenger terminal providing accommodations for persons waiting for trains **3 :** a service area or building attached to a greenhouse usu. for housing the central temperature-control equipment and providing working and storage room

¹**headhunt** \'=,=\ *n* **:** an expedition for securing heads as trophies

²**headhunt** \"\ *vi* **1 :** to kill and decapitate enemies and preserve their heads as trophies **2 :** to seek to deprive political enemies of position or influence ⟨an opportunity for local sniping and ~*ing* in individual states and districts —*N.Y. Times*⟩

**headhunter** \'=,==\ *n* **:** one that practices headhunting

**headier** *comparative of* HEADY

**headiest** *superlative of* HEADY

**head·i·ly** \'hedᵊlē, -ᵊli, -dəl-\ *adv* [ME *hedylyche,* fr. *hedy* heady + *-lyche, -liche* -ly] **1 :** RASHLY, HEADLONG **2 :** so as to cause exhilaration or dizziness

**head in** *vi* **:** to take a side track in order to give way to an approaching train

**head·i·ness** \-dēnəs, -din-\ *n* -ES [ME *hedinesse,* fr. *hedy* heady + *-nesse* -ness] **1 :** RASHNESS, HEADSTRONGNESS ⟨~ of youth⟩ **2 :** intoxicating quality ⟨the ~ of a spring morning⟩ ⟨a perfume with a ~ impossible to describe⟩

**head·ing** \'hediŋ, -dēŋ\ *n* -S [ME *hedding,* fr. gerund of *hedden* to head] **1** *archaic* **:** DECAPITATION **2 :** the compass direction in which the longitudinal axis of a ship or airplane points **3 :** something that forms or serves as a head: as **a :** HEAD 17a(1) **b :** a plain, colored, or patterned band woven at the beginning and end of a fabric **c** (1) **:** an edge of a ruffle above the line of gathering (2) **:** an edge of a curtain rising above a curtain rod (3) **:** FOOTING 8a **4 :** material for heads of casks or barrels **5 :** DRIFT 6a, 6b **6 :** an end of a stone or brick presented outward; *also* **:** HEADING COURSE **7** *South & Midland* **:** PILLOW, BOLSTER

**heading bond** *n* **:** a masonry bond that is formed by courses of headers

**heading broccoli** *n* **:** BROCCOLI 1

**heading course** *n* **:** a masonry course of headers only

**heading joint** *n* **1 :** a joint (as between two boards) at right angles to the grain **2 :** a masonry joint between two voussoirs in the same course

**heading stone** *n* **:** HEADER 3a

**head joint** *n* **1 :** the final joint of a flute containing the embouchure **2 :** a vertical masonry joint between the ends of stretchers

**head·ker·chief** \'=,== (*with last two syllables like* KERCHIEF) *or* '==(,)= (*with last two syllables as in* HANDKERCHIEF)\ *n* **:** KERCHIEF

**head kidney** *n* **1 :** PRONEPHROS **2 :** a nephridium often early developed in the cephalic segment of larval annelids and other invertebrates

**head knee** *n* **:** a timber in the frame of a ship fayed edgeways to the cutwater and stem

**head lamp** *n* **:** HEADLIGHT

**head·land** \'hedlənd, -,land, -,laa(ə)nd\ *n* [ME *hedeland,* fr. OE *hēafodlond,* fr. *hēafod* head + *lond* land — more at HEAD, LAND] **1 :** a ridge or strip of unplowed land at the ends of furrows or near a fence **2 :** a point or portion usu. of high land jutting out into the sea, a lake, or other body of water

**hea·dle** \'hedᵊl\ *var of* HEDDLE

**headledge** \'=,=\ *n* **1 :** either of the athwartship coamings of a hatchway or other deck opening **2 :** either of the upright end posts of a centerboard box

**head·less** \'hedləs\ *adj* [ME *hevedles, hedles,* fr. OE *hēafodlēas,* fr. *hēafod* head + *-lēas* -less — more at HEAD] **1 a :** having no head **b :** BEHEADED ⟨~ corpse⟩ **c** *of a line of verse* **:** lacking the normal first syllable **2 :** having no chief or leader **3 :** lacking good sense or prudence **:** FOOLISH, STUPID — **head·less·ness** *n* -ES

**headletter** \'=,==\ *n* **:** type or lettering suitable for use in heads or display

**head lettuce** *n* **:** any of various cultivated lettuces that constitute a distinct variety (*Lactuca sativa capitata*) and are distinguished by leaves arranged in a dense rosette which ultimately develops into a compact head suggesting that of cabbage — compare LEAF LETTUCE

**headlight** \'=,=\ *n* **:** a light usu. having a reflector and special lens and mounted on the front of a locomotive, streetcar, or motor vehicle for illuminating the road ahead

**headlighting** \'=,==\ *n* **:** the illumination in front of a vehicle supplied by the headlights

**head·like** \'=,=\ *adj* **:** resembling or suggesting a head in shape or function

**head line** *n, usu cap H* **:** LINE OF HEAD

¹**headline** \'=,=\ *n* [¹*head* + *line*] **1 :** HEADROPE 2, 3 **2 :** HEAD FAST **3 a :** HEAD 17a(1) **b :** a head of a newspaper story or article usu. printed in large type and devised to summarize, give essential information about, or interest readers in reading the story or article that follows **c :** BANNER 4

2**headline** \"\ *vt* **1 :** to provide (as a news story) with a headline ⟨the editor *headlined* the story quickly⟩ — often followed by a specified headline as a complementary object ⟨*headlined* the story *Man Bites Dog*⟩ **2 :** to publicize highly in or as if in headlines ⟨a *headlined* hero of World War II⟩ **3 :** to be engaged as a leading performer in (a show) ⟨a blues singer *headlined* the floor show⟩

**head·lin·er** \ˈ=,līnə(r)\ *n* -s **:** a performer whose name is printed in a headline in the bill **:** STAR

**headline schedule** *n* **:** HEAD SCHEDULE

**headlining** \ˈ=,==\ *n* [1*head* + *lining*] **:** material that covers the ceiling of an automobile interior

**headload** \ˈ=,=\ *n* **:** a load carried on the head ⟨women stagger under ~s that would shatter the spines of pack mules —*Time*⟩ ⟨the primitive method of ~s is still used to convey the cacao to road or rail —A.W.Knapp⟩

**headlock** \ˈ=,=\ *n* **:** a wrestling hold in which one encircles his opponent's head with one arm and secures the grip by interlocking his fingers

**head log** *n* **:** a front bottom log on a skidway

1**head·long** \ˈ=¦lȯŋ *also* -¦läŋ\ *adv* [ME *hedlong*, alter. of *hedling*, fr. *hed* head + *-ling*] **1 :** with the head foremost **:** HEADFIRST **2 :** without deliberation **:** RASHLY, RECKLESSLY, HEEDLESSLY **3 :** without delay or pause **:** in a rush **:** UNSWERVINGLY

2**headlong** \ˈ=,=\ *adj* **1 :** IMPETUOUS, RASH, PRECIPITATE, RECKLESS ⟨her childlikeness, her ~ sympathies, the impulsive traits that endeared —W.R.Benét⟩ ⟨such personal possessions as they had been able to carry with them in their ~ flight —E.J. Phelan⟩ **2 :** plunging headforemost ⟨a ~ dive into the pool⟩ **3** *archaic* **:** STEEP, PRECIPITOUS ⟨like a tower upon a ~ rock —Lord Byron⟩ **syn** see PRECIPITATE

**head·long·ness** \ˈ=¦=nəs\ *n* -ES **:** the quality or state of being headlong

**head louse** *n* **:** a sucking louse frequenting the head of its host; *esp* **:** a louse that is a variety (*Pediculus humanus capitis*) of the common louse of man, lives on the scalp, and attaches its eggs to hairs

**head maggot** *n* **:** the larva of the sheep botfly (*Oestrus ovis*)

**head·man** *in sense 1* ˈhed¦man *or* -maa(ə)n, *in sense 2* -mən\ *n, pl* **headmen** [ME *hevedman*, *hedman*, fr. OE *hēafodman*, fr. *hēafod* head + *man* — more at HEAD, MAN] **1 a :** OVERSEER, FOREMAN, CHIEF **b :** a lesser chief or subleader of a primitive community (as a clan, tribe, or village) **2 :** HEADSMAN

**headmark** \ˈ=,=\ *n* **1** *chiefly Scot* **:** the distinguishing characteristics esp. of the head that make one individual recognizable from another **2** *Midland* **:** a credit (as toward a prize to be awarded) given to a pupil for reaching the head position in an examination conducted with the pupils lined up and each pupil advancing toward the head of the line according to the proportionate number of his correct answers ⟨wanted to get the prize for the most ~s —J.H.Stuart⟩

**headmaster** \ˈ=¦==\ *n* **1 :** a man at the head of the staff of a private school usu. having some teaching duties but mainly concerned with administration, discipline, and counseling **2 :** the principal of a British secondary or elementary school

**head·mas·ter·ly** \-lē,-li\ *adj* **:** belonging to or characteristic of a headmaster

**head·mas·ter·ship** \-,ship\ *n* **:** the post of a headmaster

**head matter** *n* [so called fr. its being obtained fr. the head of the whale] **:** the contents of the case of the sperm whale that yield spermaceti and clear oil

**head metal** *n* **:** HEAD 22a

**head meter** *n* **:** a flowmeter whose operation is dependent upon change of pressure head

**headmistress** \ˈ=¦==\ *n* **:** a woman at the head of the staff of a private school — compare HEADMASTER

**head money** *n* **1 :** HEAD TAX **2 :** money paid for killing or capturing a person (as an outlaw) **:** BOUNTY

**head·most** \ˈ=,mōst *also chiefly Brit* -məst\ *adj* [1*head* + *-most*] **:** most advanced **:** most forward **:** LEADING ⟨the ~ ship in the line⟩

**headnote** \ˈ=,=\ *n* **1 :** a note of comment or explanation at the beginning (as of a page or chapter) **2 :** a summary prefixed to the report of a decided legal case stating the principles or rulings of the decision and usu. the main facts

**head note** *n* **:** HEAD TONE

**head off** *vt* **:** to turn back or turn aside **:** BLOCK, DIVERT, PREVENT ⟨a prime example of the way . . . troubleshooters *head off* strikes —*Time*⟩ ⟨police seemed to *head* me *off* in every direction —Adrian Bell⟩

**head of horns :** HEAD 5

**head on** \(ˈ)=¦=\ *adv* **1 :** with the head or front pointing directly toward an object ⟨the ship struck the rocks *head on*⟩ ⟨the cars collided *head on*⟩ **2 :** in direct opposition or contradiction ⟨to let his wife settle this question without his meeting it *head on* —Herbert Gold⟩ ⟨what happens to the savage when he meets civilization *head on* —J.F.McComas⟩

**head-on** \ˈ=,=\ *adj* [*head on*] **1 :** having the front facing in the direction of motion ⟨swerved to avoid a *head-on* crash⟩ or line of sight ⟨a *head-on* view of a building⟩ **2 :** directly opposite or opposing **:** FRONTAL ⟨a *head-on* attack on the committee's policy⟩

**head or tail** *n* **1 :** this side or that side — often used in pl. in tossing a coin to decide a choice, question, or stake — compare HEADS OR TAILS **2 :** beginning or end **:** one thing or another **:** something definite ⟨could not make *head or tail* of what he said⟩

**head over ears** *adv* **:** up to the ears **:** DEEPLY ⟨fell *head over ears* into English literature and history —Angela Thirkell⟩ ⟨*head over ears* in debt⟩

**head over heels** *adv* [alter. of *heels over head*] **1 a :** in or as if in a somersault ⟨fell *head over heels* down the hill⟩ ⟨a blow sent him *head over heels* into the pond⟩ **b :** upside down ⟨swung *head over heels* from the branch⟩ **2 :** HOPELESSLY, DEEPLY ⟨fell *head over heels* in love⟩ ⟨was *head over heels* in debt⟩

**headpenny** \ˈ=¦==\ *n* [ME *hed penny*, fr. *hed* head + *penny*] **1 :** HEAD TAX **2** *obs* **:** an individual or personal assessment or payment to church funds

**headphone** \ˈ=,=\ *n* **:** an earphone held over the ear by a band worn on the head

**headpiece** \ˈ=,=\ *n* **1 a :** a protective or defensive covering for the head; *esp* **:** any of the various helmets worn formerly by knights in armor and now by members of the armed forces, participants in some sports, and construction workers **b :** HAT, CAP **c :** HEADSTALL, HALTER **2 a :** HEAD **b :** UNDERSTANDING, BRAINS **3 a :** an ornament placed above the text matter of a page or at the beginning of a chapter — compare TAILPIECE **b :** HEADNOTE **4 :** a top part: as **a :** a headboard of a bed **b :** a lintel of a door or window

headphones

**headpin** \ˈ=,=\ *n* **1 :** a bowling pin that stands foremost in the arrangement of pins — called also *kingpin* **2 :** KINGPIN 2

**headpin bowling** *n* **:** bowling in which a bowler aims directly at the 1-3 pocket when attempting to make a strike — compare SPOT BOWLING

**headplate** \ˈ=,=\ *n* **:** a key plate for printing a design featuring a person's head

**headpost** \ˈ=,=\ *n* **1 :** one of the posts at the head of a bed **2 :** the post nearest the manger in a stall

**head post** *n* **:** a movable post supporting an imitation head of leather used as an object for saber exercise in a cavalry riding school

**head process** *n* **:** an axial strand of cells that extends forward from the primitive knot in the early vertebrate embryo and is the precursor of the notochord

**headquarter** \ˈ=,==, (ˈ)=¦==\ *vb* [back-formation fr. *headquarters*] *vi* **:** to make one's headquarters ~ *vt* **:** to place in headquarters

**headquarters** \ˈ=,==, (ˈ)=¦==\ *n pl but often sing in constr* **1 a :** a place from which a military commander issues orders and performs the functions of command **b :** the personnel associated with and assisting the commander in performing his function **2 :** a chief or usual place of business **:** the administrative center of an enterprise or activity ⟨turned the archbishop's palace into a busy ~, organizing the duties of the clergy of all ranks —J.A.Gade⟩

**headquarters company** *n* **:** an administrative and tactical unit furnishing the necessary specialist personnel for headquarters of a battalion or higher unit

**headrace** \ˈ=,=\ *n* **:** a race for conveying water to a point of industrial application (as a waterwheel or turbine)

1**head·rail** \ˈhe,drāl\ *n* **1 :** one of the elliptical rails at a wooden ship's head extending from the place of the figurehead to the bow **2 a :** the upper horizontal piece of a door **b :** a solid piece at the top of the back of a chair **c :** a crosspiece at the head of a bed

2**headrail** \"\ *n* [trans. of OE *hēafodhrægl*, fr. *hēafod* head + *hrægl* garment — more at HEAD, RAIL] **:** a medieval head covering for women consisting usu. of a cloth draped loosely over the head and hanging down in back

1**headreach** \ˈ=,=\ *vi* [1*head* + *reach*] **:** to move ahead into the wind by momentum (as in tacking)

2**headreach** \"\ *n* **:** the distance covered by headreaching

**head register** *n* **:** the upper division in the pitch range of the human voice beginning at the point where the vocal cords readjust to produce the higher musical tone and characterized by a lighter tone quality

**headrest** \ˈ=,=\ *n* **:** a shaped part or attachment (as on a barber's chair) for supporting the head

**head rhyme** *n* **:** BEGINNING RHYME

**head rice** *n* **:** unbroken grains of milled rice with the hull, bran, and germ removed

**headrig** \ˈ=,=\ *n* **:** the main saw in a mill with or without other saws or associated equipment

**headright** \ˈ=,=\ *n* **1 :** a grant (as of money or land) formerly given one who fulfilled certain conditions relating esp. to settling and developing land (as in Virginia in 1619 and in Texas in 1839) **2 :** a right belonging to an Indian member of a tribe to receive a per-capita share in the distribution of income earned by the tribal trust fund (as from the sale or lease of mineral rights) or a share of the fund on its termination; *also* **:** the right of a member to a share of tribal property

**headring** \ˈ=,=\ *n* **1 :** an often decorated ring formed on the head by building up the hair with vegetable or animal fibers and worn by married warriors of some Kaffir tribes **2 :** a pad (as of vegetable fiber) worn to facilitate carrying a load on the head

**head rod** *n* **:** the switch rod nearest the point of a railroad switch

**headroom** \ˈ=,=\ *n* **1 :** vertical space in which to stand or move **:** HEADWAY 2 **2 :** HEADSPACE 3

**headrope** \ˈ=,=\ *n* [ME *hedrope*, fr. *hed* head + *rope*] **1** *obs* **:** rope leading from a masthead as a stay **2 a :** a part of a boltrope that is sewed along the upper edge of a sail **b :** a rope along the upper edge of a fishnet **3 a :** a rope at the head of an animal (as for tying or leading it) **b :** HEADFAST **4 :** AGAL

**heads** *pl of* HEAD, *pres 3d sing of* HEAD

**head·sail** \ˈhedsəl (*usual nautical pronunc*), -,sāl\ *n* **:** a sail (as a jib or fore staysail) set forward of the foremast

**headsaw** \ˈ=,=\ *n* **:** a saw in a sawmill that cuts logs into planks, boards, and cants — compare RESAW

**head scab** *n* **:** sarcoptic mange of the head of sheep caused by a mite (*Sarcoptes scabiei* var. *ovis*)

**head schedule** *n* **:** a list of the type faces, type sizes, and headline forms approved for use in the headlines of a newspaper

**head sea** *n* **:** waves coming from directly ahead — compare FOLLOWING SEA, QUARTERING SEA

**headset** \ˈ=,=\ *n* **1 :** an attachment for holding an earphone and transmitter in place at one's head **2 :** a pair of headphones

**headshake** \ˈ=,=\ *n* **:** a shake of the head usu. signifying denial or distrust

**headshaker** \ˈ=,==\ *n* **:** SKEPTIC, PESSIMIST ⟨adventurers . . . knowing before they began that the mockers and ~s would have the laugh of them —Clemence Dane⟩

**headshaking** \ˈ=,==\ *n* **:** an act of shaking the head (as in disbelief or distrust)

**head·ship** \ˈhed,ship\ *n* **:** the position, office, or dignity of a head or chief **:** LEADERSHIP, PRIMACY

**headshrinker** \ˈ=,==\ *n* **1 :** a headhunter who shrinks the heads of his victims **2** *slang* **:** PSYCHIATRIST

**headsill** \ˈ=,=\ *n* **1 :** a horizontal member at the top of a doorframe or window frame **2 :** either of the pieces supporting the log at its ends in a saw pit

**headskin** \ˈ=,=\ *n* **:** a tough elastic fatty mass covering the head of a sperm whale beneath the skin

**heads·man** \ˈhedzmən\ *n, pl* **headsmen 1 :** an executioner who cuts off heads **2 :** HEADER 5 **3 :** PUSHER 1e

**head smut** *n* **1 :** a covered smut of corn and sorghum caused by a fungus (*Sphacelotheca reiliana*) **2 :** any smut affecting the heads of grains or grasses

**heads or tails** *n pl but sing in constr* **:** a simple gambling game in which a coin is tossed and won by the player who successfully calls the side that lands upward — compare HEAD OR TAIL

**head·space** \ˈ=,=\ *n* **1 :** a space between the breech and bolt face of a firearm using rimless ammunition **2 :** the space taken up by the cartridge rim in a firearm using rimmed ammunition **3 :** a space left between the contents and the ends or closure of a drum, barrel, can, or bottle in order to allow for variations in fill or expansion of contents — called also *outage*

**headspring** \ˈ=,=\ *n* [ME *hedspring*, fr. *hed* head + *spring*] **1 :** FOUNTAINHEAD, SOURCE **2 :** a tumbling skill similar to a handspring except that the spring is made from the head and hands instead of from the hands alone

**headstall** \ˈ=,=\ *n* [ME *hedstall*, fr. *hed* head + *stall*] **:** a part of a bridle or halter that encircles the head — see BRIDLE illustration

**headstamp** \ˈ=,=\ *n* **:** numbers or letters stamped into the base of a cartridge case by the manufacturer in order to identify the cartridge and its original loading

**headstand** \ˈ=,=\ *n* **:** an acrobatic feat of standing on one's head usu. with support from the hands

**head start** *n* [2*head*] **1 :** an advantage granted or achieved at the beginning of a race, a chase, or a competition **:** START ⟨a *head start* of 15 paces⟩ ⟨10-minute *head start*⟩ **2 :** a favorable or promising beginning **:** a good start

**head stay** *n* **:** FORESTAY

**headstick** \ˈ=,=\ *n* **:** a short stick fitted to the headrope of a jib-headed sail or an ensign to prevent twisting

**headstock** \ˈ=,=\ *n* **1 :** a bearing or pedestal for a revolving or moving part: as **a :** a part of a lathe that holds the revolving spindle and its attachments **b :** a part of a cylindrical grinding machine that rotates the work **c :** a part of a planing machine supporting the cutter **d :** a movable head in a measuring machine **e :** a framework containing a runway for the carriage in a spinning mule **f :** a headframe over a mine shaft **2 :** a pivoted crossbeam that supports a church bell

**headstone** \ˈ=,=\ *n* **1 :** the principal stone in a foundation **:** chief stone **:** CORNERSTONE **2 :** the stone at the head of a grave

**headstream** \ˈ=,=\ *n* **:** a stream that is the source or one of the sources of a river

**head string** *n* **:** a line connecting the second diamonds of the side rails at the head end of a billiard table that marks a limit on or within which the cue ball is placed in lagging for the break or beginning the game

**headstrong** \ˈ=,=\ *adj* [ME *hedstrong*, fr. *hed* head + *strong*] **1 :** not easily restrained **:** UNGOVERNABLE, OBSTINATE ⟨~ youth⟩ **2 :** directed by ungovernable will **:** proceeding from obstinacy ⟨violent ~ actions⟩ **syn** see UNRULY

**head·strong·ly** *adv* **:** in a headstrong manner

**head·strong·ness** *n* -ES **:** the quality of being headstrong

**heads up** *interj* — used as a warning to look out for danger overhead or to clear a passageway

**heads-up** \ˈ=,=\ *adj* [*heads up*] **:** ALERT, WIDE-AWAKE, RESOURCEFUL ⟨fast, aggressive, *heads-up* football⟩

**head tax** *n* **:** a tax usu. identical on every individual in a class or group: as **a :** POLL TAX **b :** a per-capita tax imposed on one (as a steamship company) bringing immigrants into the U.S.

**head tie** *n* **:** a kerchief for the head

**headtire** *n* [1*head* + *tire* (headdress)] *obs* **:** HEADDRESS

**head tone** *n* **:** a vocal tone produced in the head register

**head tree** *n* **:** the spar tree nearest the donkey engine in a skyline logging system

**head up** *vt* **1 :** to close (as a barrel) at the head or with a head **2 :** HEAD *vt* 4 ~ *vi* **1 :** HEAD *vi* 3a **2 :** to come to an apex **:** find a head ⟨a bureaucracy that *headed up* in the king —W.P. Webb⟩

**head voice** *n* **:** the vocal tones of the head register

**headwaiter** \ˈ=¦==\ *n* **:** the head of the dining-room staff of a restaurant or hotel

**headwall** \ˈ=,=\ *n* **1 a :** a precipice rising above the floor of a glacial cirque **b :** a steep slope forming the head of a valley **2 :** a wall of masonry or concrete built at the outlet of a drainpipe or culvert with the end of the conduit flush with the outer surface of the wall

1**head·ward** \ˈhedw(ə)rd\ *also* **head·wards** \-dz\ *adv* [1*head* + *-ward*, *-wards*] **:** toward the head **:** in the direction of the head ⟨a stream lengthens its course by eroding ~⟩

2**headward** \"\ *adj* **:** proceeding toward the head **:** occurring at or near the head ⟨~ erosion of a valley⟩ ⟨loss of consciousness caused by ~ acceleration of the body⟩

3**headward** \-,wȯrd, -ȯ(ə)d\ *n* -s [trans. of OE *hēafodweard*] **:** feudal service consisting in acting as a guard to the lord

**head·wark** \ˈ=,wärk\ *n* -s [ME *hedewerk*, fr. OE *hēafodwærc*, fr. *hēafod* head + *wærc* pain; akin to OE *weorc* work — more at HEAD, WARK] *chiefly dial Brit* **:** HEADACHE

**headwater** \ˈ=,==\ *n* **:** the source and upper part of a stream — usu. used in pl.

**headway** \ˈ=,=\ *n* **1 a :** motion or rate of motion in a forward direction (as of a ship) **b :** ADVANCE, PROGRESS ⟨make ~ in a profession⟩ ⟨a life in which the claims of spirit and emotion will make some ~ against the necessities of physical existence —Clive Bell⟩ **2 :** clear space (as under an arch or girder) sufficient to allow of easy passing underneath **:** HEADROOM **3 :** the time interval between two vehicles traveling in the same direction on the same route

**headwear** \ˈ=,=\ *n* **:** apparel for the head **:** HEADGEAR 1a

**head wind** *n* **:** a wind blowing in a direction opposite to a course esp. of a ship or airplane ⟨delayed by strong *head winds*⟩

**headword** \ˈ=,=\ *n* **1 :** a word or term often in distinctive type placed at the beginning of a chapter, paragraph, or entry (as in a dictionary or a catalog) **2 :** a word qualified by a modifier ⟨it is not always easy to state the precise kind of relation that exists between the modifier and its ~ —C.C.Fries⟩

**headwork** \ˈ=,=\ *n* **1 :** mental labor; *esp* **:** clever thinking **2 :** ornamentation for an arch keystone **3 :** a structure for controlling the quantity of water entering a channel **4 headworks** *pl* **:** a platform or raft with tackle for warping or kedging a log raft through still water

**headworker** \ˈ=¦==\ *n* [2*head* + *worker*] **:** a director of a social agency or settlement

**heady** \ˈhedē, -di\ *adj* -ER/-EST [ME *hevedy*, *hedy*, fr. *heved*, *hed* head + *-y* — more at HEAD] **1 a :** WILLFUL, RASH ⟨the flow of the story is interrupted by . . . the giving of ~ opinions —S.L.A.Marshall⟩ **b :** VIOLENT, IMPETUOUS ⟨~ waters of the swollen river⟩ ⟨~ tempest⟩ **2 a :** tending to make giddy or light-headed **:** INTOXICATING ⟨~ perfume⟩ ⟨~ triumphs⟩ ⟨the ~ air of spring⟩ **b :** GIDDY, INTOXICATED, EXHILARATED ⟨students showing themselves ~ with ideas —*Time*⟩ **3 :** having or showing good judgment **:** SHREWD, CLEVER, SMART ⟨ran a ~ race⟩ ⟨one of the nimblest and *headiest* . . . quarterbacks —*Time*⟩

**head yard** *n* **:** a yard on a foremast

**heaf** \ˈhēf\ *n* -s [alter. of 4*haft*, *heft*] *dial Eng* **:** a piece of ground used as a sheep pasture

1**heal** \ˈhēl, *esp before pause or consonant* -ēəl\ *vb* -ED/-ING/-S [ME *helen*, fr. OE *hǣlan*; akin to OHG *heilen* to heal, ON *heila*, Goth *hailjan*; causative denominatives fr. the root of OE *hāl* healthy, whole — more at WHOLE] *vt* **1 a :** to make sound or whole **:** restore to health **b :** to cure of disease or affliction ⟨a society to ~ convulsions or cramps —Ruth F. Kirk⟩ ⟨~ injured tissues⟩ **2 a :** to cause (an undesirable condition) to be overcome or eliminated **:** MEND ⟨the troubles . . . had not been forgotten, but they had been ~*ed* —William Power⟩ ⟨~ marital rifts and to ward off hasty divorce actions —*N.Y. Times*⟩; *specif* **:** to patch up (a rift or division) **:** CEMENT ⟨the conflicts between capital and labor . . . might temporarily be ~*ed* —J.A.Hobson⟩ ⟨~*ed* a breach between the two branches of the family —*Current Biog.*⟩ **b :** to restore to original purity or integrity **:** to make (a person) spiritually whole **:** to restore from evil ⟨~*ed* of his sins⟩ ⟨thus saith the Lord, I have ~*ed* these waters —2 Kings 2:21 (AV)⟩ ~ *vi* **1 :** to grow sound **:** return to a sound state ⟨the limb ~s⟩ ⟨the wound ~s⟩ **2 :** to effect a cure **syn** see CURE

2**heal** \"\ *vt* -ED/-ING/-S [ME *helen* to hide, conceal, cover, fr. OE *helan* — more at HELL] **1** *dial chiefly Eng* **:** to cover (as seeds) with earth **2** *dial chiefly Eng* **:** to cover with slates or tiles ⟨a leaky-roofed, tile-*healed* . . . cottage —F.M.Ford⟩

**heal·able** \ˈhēləbəl\ *adj* **:** capable of being healed

**heal-all** \ˈhēl,ȯl\ *n, pl* **heal-alls** \-,ȯlz\ *also* **heals-alls** \-lz,ȯlz\ **1 :** SELF-HEAL **2 :** a plant of the genus *Scrophularia* **3 :** GREAT GREEN ORCHIS **4 :** YELLOW CLINTONIA

**heald** \ˈhēld\ *n* -s [ME *helde*, fr. OE *hefeld*; akin to MLG *hevelte* heddle, ON *hafald*; derivatives fr. the root of OE *hebban* to raise, lift — more at HEAVE] *chiefly Brit* **:** HEDDLE

**heald·er** \ˈhēldə(r)\ *n* -s *Brit* **:** DRAWER-IN

**heal·er** \ˈhēlə(r)\ *n* -s [ME *helere*, fr. *helen* to heal + *-ere* -er — more at HEAL] **1 :** one that heals ⟨time is a great ~⟩; *specif* **:** a person who engages in healing through means not requiring medical training or licensing **2 :** a Christian Science practitioner

1**healing** *n* -s [ME *heling*, fr. OE *hǣling*, fr. *hǣlan* to heal + *-ing* — more at HEAL] **:** the act or process of curing or of restoring to health **:** the process of getting well

2**healing** *adj* [ME *heling*, fr. pres. part. of *helen* to heal] **:** tending to heal or cure **:** CURATIVE ⟨a ~ art⟩ — **heal·ing·ly** *adv*

**healing blade** *n* **:** BROAD-LEAVED PLANTAIN 1

**healing herb** *n* **1 :** COMFREY **2 :** HOARY PLANTAIN 1

**heal·some** \ˈhēlsəm\ *Scot var of* WHOLESOME

1**health** \ˈhelth *also* -ltth\ *n* -s [ME *helthe*, fr. OE *hǣlth*, fr. *hāl* whole, healthy — more at WHOLE] **1 a :** the condition of an organism or one of its parts in which it performs its vital functions normally or properly **:** the state of being sound in body or mind ⟨nursed him back to ~⟩ ⟨he is the picture of ~⟩ ⟨dental ~⟩ ⟨mental ~⟩ — compare DISEASE **b :** the condition of an organism with respect to the performance of its vital functions esp. as evaluated subjectively or nonprofessionally ⟨how is your ~ today⟩ ⟨never in better ~⟩ ⟨her ~ is very delicate⟩ ⟨broken in ~⟩ ⟨went traveling for his ~⟩ **2 :** flourishing condition **:** WELL-BEING, VITALITY, PROSPERITY ⟨one more indication of the ~ of this pulsating . . . art form —Harriet Johnson⟩ ⟨expected the capitalist system to retain some degree of ~ —F.C.Barghoorn⟩ ⟨a serious menace to our economic ~ —F.L.Allen⟩ **3 :** a toast to someone's health, well-being, or prosperity ⟨"to her Majesty!" he said . . . and drank a long ~ —Theodore Bonnet⟩ ⟨proposed the ~ of the ladies —B.A.Botkin & A.F.Harlow⟩

2**health** \"\ *adj* **1 :** of, relating to, or engaged in welfare work directed to the cure and prevention of disease ⟨a ~ center⟩ ⟨~ agencies⟩ **2 :** of, relating to, or conducive to health ⟨~ foods⟩ ⟨~ drinks⟩ ⟨~ education⟩

**health department** *n* **:** a division of a local or larger government responsible for the oversight and care of matters relating to public health

**health·ful** \-thfəl\ *adj* [ME *helthful*, fr. *helthe* health + *-ful*] **1 :** beneficial to health of body or mind **:** conducive to health **:** SALUTARY ⟨a ~ climate⟩ **2 :** HEALTHY ⟨a weird translation of Dickens' relatively ~ exuberance into a morbid . . . mysticism —*Writer*⟩ ⟨physical organization . . . which was at once ~ and exquisitely delicate —Nathaniel Hawthorne⟩

**syn** HEALTHY, WHOLESOME, SALUBRIOUS, SALUTARY, HYGIENIC, SANITARY: HEALTHFUL and HEALTHY are both used to mean conducive to or indicative of health or soundness, the former word being preferred in some quarters ⟨a *healthful* climate⟩ ⟨better nutrition, more *healthful* housing, sounder forms of recreation —Lewis Mumford⟩ ⟨one of the *healthiest* climates in England —Arnold Bennett⟩ ⟨extolled the *healthy* air of the hills as the best way to recover from fever —Hervey Allen⟩ ⟨*healthy* and normal outlets for youthful energies —Allan Nevins & H.S.Commager⟩ WHOLESOME may more strongly suggest beneficial, upbuilding, or sustaining capacities, physically, intellectually, or spiritually ⟨*wholesome* meats⟩ ⟨the warm rays of the sun, too, were *wholesome* for him in body and soul —Nathaniel Hawthorne⟩ ⟨one trade is healthier or cleanlier than another, that it is carried on in a more *wholesome* or pleasant locality —Alfred Marshall⟩ ⟨*wholesome*, fast-reading adaptations for teen-agers of the adult best sellers they want to read —*N.Y. Times Bk. Rev.*⟩ SALUBRIOUS may suggest the pleasantly invigorating or bracing ⟨these uplands are likewise often the most *salubrious* seat of living, with their fine scenery, their bracing ionized air, their range of recreation, from mountain-climbing and fishing to swimming and ice-skating —Lewis Mumford⟩ SALUTARY may describe something corrective, tonic, or otherwise beneficially effective although the thing in question may in itself be unpleasant ⟨in the open air, which is the most *salutary* of all things for both body and mind —R.L.Stevenson⟩ ⟨*salutary* was the tartness with which she protested, "You're the most conceited man that ever lived!" —Sinclair Lewis⟩ ⟨idle ladies and gentlemen are treated with *salutary* contempt, whilst the worker's blouse is duly honored —G.B.Shaw⟩ HYGIENIC is likely to suggest conformity with various health principles and laws ⟨anyone . . . who took the proper amount of balanced food, or consumed his excess heat units in regular exercise, and lived a reasonably *hygienic* life —V.G.Heiser⟩ SANITARY implies cleanly precaution against contamination, infection, or other unhealthful developments ⟨the *sanitary* appearance of the hospital kitchen⟩

**health·ful·ly** \-fəlē, -li\ *adv* [ME *helthfully*, fr. *helthful* + *-ly*] **:** in a healthful manner

**health·ful·ness** *n* -ES **:** the quality or state of being healthful

**health·i·ly** \-thəlē, -li\ *adv* **:** in a healthy manner

**health·i·ness** \-thēnəs, -thin-\ *n* -ES **:** the quality or state of being healthy

**health insurance** *n* **:** insurance against loss through illness of the insured

**health·less** \-thləs\ *adj* **1 :** lacking health of body or mind **:** INFIRM **2 :** not conducive to health **:** UNWHOLESOME

**health line** *n, usu cap H* **:** LINE OF MERCURY

**health officer** *n* **:** an officer charged with the enforcement of laws relating to health and sanitation **:** an executive officer under the direction of a health department or similar public body

**health physicist** *n* **:** a specialist in health physics

**health physics** *n pl but usu sing in constr* **:** physics dealing with the medical and hygienic aspects of and precautions against exposure to radioactive radiations

**health·some** \-thsəm\ *adj* **:** WHOLESOME, HEALTHFUL ⟨lent the street an air of good ~ quiet —William Sansom⟩

**healthy** \-thē, -thi\ *adj* -ER/-EST **1 a :** enjoying good health **:** free from disease **:** functioning properly or normally in its vital functions ⟨the examination revealed him to be a perfectly ~ man⟩ ⟨a ~ body⟩ ⟨~ eyes are a precious possession⟩ ⟨a ~ tree⟩ **b :** conducive to health **:** SALUTARY ⟨walk three miles every day . . . a beastly bore, but ~ —G.S.Patton⟩ ⟨his life recently had not been a ~ one —A. Conan Doyle⟩ ⟨the *healthiest* damned island in the Pacific —John Dos Passos⟩ **c :** indicating, reflecting, or suggestive of health ⟨a ~ color in his cheeks —Charles Dickens⟩ ⟨the ~ smell of grain —T.B. Costain⟩ ⟨stretched her arms over her head with a gesture of ~ fatigue —Ellen Glasgow⟩ **2 a :** morally or spiritually wholesome **:** not sickly, morbid, or sentimental **:** tending toward or indicating moral health ⟨their principal purpose of giving our children ~ entertainment —Coulton Waugh⟩ ⟨that's a good ~, cynical approach —James Street⟩ ⟨~ vulgarity inseparable from all vital human works —Albert Dasnoy⟩ ⟨in ~ reaction to the romantic fustian of the nineteenth century —Christopher Fry⟩ **b :** free from malfunctioning of any kind **:** VIABLE, PROSPEROUS, FLOURISHING, DESIRABLE ⟨the restoration of a ~ economy⟩ ⟨not a ~ state of affairs⟩ ⟨the negative plates are probably defective . . . requiring an extended period of charging and discharging to put them back in a ~ condition —A.L.Dyke⟩ ⟨a ~ book-publishing business —Harry Botsford⟩ **c :** productive of good of any kind **:** POSITIVE, BENEFICIAL ⟨showed his formidable ships of war . . . making a very ~ impression —C.S.Forester⟩ ⟨the creation of a ~ rivalry between the services —H.B.Hinton⟩ **d :** large in quantity or degree **:** CONSIDERABLE, MASSIVE ⟨repairs . . . account for a ~ bit of income —Bill Wolf⟩ ⟨the product carries a ~ price tag —*Printers' Ink*⟩ **e :** VIGOROUS, HEARTY ⟨a ~ appetite⟩ ⟨gives the boat a ~ shove . . . into deeper water —*All Hands*⟩ **3 :** SAFE — usu. used in negative construction ⟨not so ~ to be around . . . they might take a pop at us —Giorgio De Santillana⟩ ⟨not a ~ spot to be in at that time —H.A.Chippendale⟩

**syn** SOUND, WHOLESOME, ROBUST, HALE, WELL: HEALTHY can imply (1) the possession of full vigor of mind or body or (2) merely freedom from any sign of disease or morbidity ⟨a family with four *healthy*, active boys⟩ ⟨keep a child *healthy* during the winter⟩ ⟨a *healthy* outlook on life⟩ SOUND implies more strongly the absence of all defects of mind or body ⟨develop vigorous children, *sound* in mind and body⟩ ⟨*sound* of limb and healthy of mind⟩ WHOLESOME implies a healthiness that impresses others favorably, esp. as indicating physical, moral, or mental soundness or balance ⟨her hair carelessly pinned back, her eyes shining, her face aglow, looking oddly *wholesome* in a smeared white painter's smock —Herman Wouk⟩ ⟨a short, strongly made woman, *wholesome* and still youthful —C.B.Nordhoff & J.N.Hall⟩ ROBUST is the opposite of *delicate*, implying a vigor manifest in muscularity, solidity, strength of voice, power of endurance, and so on ⟨was looking *robust* and full of health and vigor —Samuel Butler †1902⟩ ⟨*robust* and tough in fiber —I.A.Gordon⟩ ⟨the giant zinnias are so *robust* here that you can transplant them in full bloom —Barrett McGurn⟩ HALE applies chiefly to elderly persons who still retain physical qualities of men in their prime ⟨this particular black panther was not old and sore, like many man-eaters. It was an exceedingly *hale* animal —David Walker⟩ ⟨his father, though an old man, was still *hale* —Sheila Kaye-Smith⟩ ⟨now in his 80th year but still alert, *hale* and hearty —*Western Farmers News*⟩ WELL merely implies freedom from disease ⟨stay *well* amidst disease and poverty⟩ ⟨seemingly doomed to constant illness, only once in a while did he feel really *well*⟩

**syn** see in addition HEALTHFUL

**healthy potato disease** *n* **:** LATENT VIRUS DISEASE

**¹heap** \ˈhēp\ *n* -S [ME *heep, hepe*, fr. OE *hēap*; akin to OHG *houf, hūfo* heap, OS *hōp*, MLG *hūpe* heap, OE *hēah* high — more at HIGH] **1 :** a collection of things laid or thrown one on another **:** PILE ⟨small ~*s* of stones at which . . . sacrifices are offered —J.G.Frazer⟩ **2 :** a great number or large quantity **:** LOT ⟨there would be a ~ of noise and excitement —S.H. Holbrook⟩ ⟨it took a ~ of work —Meridel Le Sueur⟩ ⟨made a ~ of money⟩ ⟨there must be ~*s* of young poets who adore you —G.B.Shaw⟩ **3 :** the totality of rivals or competitors — used in the phrase *the top of the heap* ⟨it's getting to the top of the ~ that saves a man —Louis Auchincloss⟩ ⟨remain at the top of the concert ~ indefinitely —*Time*⟩ **4** *slang* **:** AUTOMOBILE; *esp* **:** an old beat-up automobile ⟨that ~ wasn't worth more than thirty dollars —C.L.Lamson⟩ ⟨my old tin ~ wouldn't start —Christopher Morley⟩ — **heap sight** *dial* **:** a great deal ⟨I'd a *heap sight* rather stay⟩ — **of a heap** *or* **all of a heap 1 :** so as to be stupefied, amazed, or overcome ⟨a lot of people were also struck *all of a heap* because . . . the favorite could do no better than finish third —G.F.T.Ryall⟩ ⟨struck him so completely *of a heap* that he was almost a broken man —H.L.Davis⟩ **2 :** all of a sudden ⟨*all of a heap* they had given her perplexity, immobility, and a dreadful thought —F.M.Ford⟩

**²heap** \"\ *vb* -ED/-ING/-S [ME *hepen*, fr. OE *hēapian*; akin to OHG *houfōn* to heap; denominatives fr. the root of E ¹*heap*] *vt* **1 a :** to throw or lay in a heap **:** pile or collect in great quantity **:** lay up **:** AMASS, ACCUMULATE ⟨stacks of firewood were ~*ed* all about the store —F.V.W.Mason⟩ **b :** to fill, load, or cover with a heap or heaps ⟨dishes ~*ed* high with food⟩ ⟨fields ~*ed* high with stacks of grain⟩ **2 a :** to accord, assign, or bestow lavishly or in large quantities ⟨~*ed* scorn and reproaches upon him⟩ ⟨~*ing* work upon his shoulders⟩ **b :** to bestow lavishly or in large quantities upon ⟨~*ed* him with stewardships and sinecures —Francis Hackett⟩ **3 :** to form or round into a heap (as in measuring) **:** fill (a measure) more than even full ~ *vi* **:** to form in a heap ⟨the tall clouds of deep July ~*ed* mountainous in the blue —C.G.Glover⟩

**heaped measure** *or* **heaping measure** *n* **:** dry measure obtained by filling the container heaping full

**heap roasting** *or* **heap roast** *n* **:** a process in which high-sulfur ore piled in the open is roasted without fuel other than for ignition, the heat being furnished by the combustion of the sulfur in the ore

**heaps** \ˈhēps\ *adv* [fr. pl. of ¹*heap*] **:** very much **:** EXTREMELY ⟨thanks just ~⟩ — not often in formal use

**hear** \ˈhi(ə)r, -iə\ *vb* **heard** \ˈhərd, ˈhəd\ *also dial* **heared** *or* **heerd** *or* **heered** \ˈhi(ə)rd, -i(ə)d\ *or* **hearn** *or* **heern** \ˈhi(ə)rn, -i(ə)n\ **heard** *also dial* **heared** *or* **heerd** *or* **heered** *or* **hearn** *or* **heern**; **hearing; hears** [ME *heren*, fr. OE *hīeran, hȳran, hēran*; akin to OHG *hōren* to hear, ON *heyra*, Goth *hausjan* to hear, L *cavēre* to be on one's guard, Gk *akouein* to hear, *koein* to notice, hear, Skt *kavi* clever, wise] *vt* **1 :** to be made aware of by the ear **:** apprehend by the ear ⟨so great was the din that I could not ~ him⟩ ⟨he could ~ the distant rumble of the native drums⟩ **2 :** to be informed or gain knowledge of by hearing ⟨~ that business is picking up⟩ ⟨*heard* that you were ill⟩ ⟨*heard* nothing more about the affair⟩ — often used in the phrase *hear say* ⟨I've *heard* say that he has been married before⟩ and *heard tell* ⟨ain't *heard* tell of them since I don't know when —Hamilton Basso⟩ ⟨you may have *heard* tell of the wonder chemical, fluorine —*Amer. Girl*⟩ **3 a :** to listen to with favor or compliance **:** GRANT ⟨the Lord has *heard* my prayers⟩ **b :** to listen to with care or attention **:** give audience to ⟨won't you ~ my side of the story⟩ ⟨would not ~ the envoy, and angrily dismissed him⟩ ⟨would not ~ me through⟩ ⟨they *heard* him out, hiding their skepticism —F.D.Downey⟩ **c :** to attend and listen to ⟨~ a concert⟩ ⟨~ mass⟩ **d :** to listen to the recitation of ⟨he wants me to ~ him his part —Christopher Isherwood⟩ **4 a :** to give a legal hearing to ⟨~ a case⟩ ⟨the judge refused to ~ their claims⟩ **b** (1) **:** to take testimony from ⟨the committee *heard* 345 witnesses⟩ (2) **:** to take (testimony) usu. at a hearing ⟨the committee's decision to ~ testimony . . . on the condition of natives —*Current Biog.*⟩ ~ *vi* **1 :** to have the capacity of apprehending sound ⟨he can't ~ at all, poor fellow⟩ **2 a :** to gain information through oral communication **:** have a report **:** LEARN ⟨have *heard* about your doings⟩ ⟨who ever *heard* of such a thing⟩ **b :** to receive a message or letter ⟨haven't *heard* from him in two months⟩ **3 :** to entertain the idea **:** CONSENT, YIELD — used in negative construction with *of* ⟨will not ~ of my going⟩ or *to* ⟨would not ~ to it —Clyde Eagleton⟩ **4 :** to receive a scolding or tongue-lashing or punishment ⟨another complaint and you'll ~ from me⟩ **5 —** often used in the expression *Hear! Hear!* during a speech to call attention to the words of the speaker or in applause

**hear·able** \ˈhirəbəl\ *adj* [ME *herable*, fr. *heren* to hear + *-able*] **:** capable of being heard

**hear·er** \-rə(r)\ *n* -S [ME *herere*, fr. *heren* to hear + *-ere* -er] **1 :** one that hears **:** AUDITOR **2 :** AUDIENT 2

**hear·ing** \ˈhiriŋ, -rēŋ\ *n* -S [ME *heringe*, fr. *heren* + *-inge* -ing] **1 a** (1) **:** the act or power of apprehending sound; *specif* **:** one of the special senses of vertebrates that is concerned with the perception of sound, is mediated through the organ of Corti of the ear in mammals or through corresponding sensory receptors of the lagena in lower vertebrates, is normally sensitive in man to sound vibrations between 16 and 27,000 cycles per second but most receptive to those between 2000 and 5000 cycles per second, is conducted centrally by the cochlear branch of the auditory nerve, and is coordinated esp. in the medial geniculate body (2) **:** an analogous perception of vibration in other animals ⟨the katydid . . . whose ~ is in slits on the front legs —C.D. & Mary Michener⟩ **b :** the extent within which sound may be heard **:** EARSHOT ⟨within ~ —Shak.⟩ **2 a** (1) **:** the act or an instance of actively or carefully listening (as to a speaker or performer) **:** AUDITION, AUDIENCE ⟨a powerful version . . . and you should give it a ~ —*Jazz Jour.*⟩ ⟨a man knows by instinct whether he'll get a tender ~ —Eden Phillpotts⟩ ⟨the orchestra did not impress me in one ~ as being quite up to Eastern . . . standards —Virgil Thomson⟩ (2) *dial Eng* **:** a church service **:** PREACHING (3) **:** opportunity to be heard or to present one's side of a case ⟨at least give me a ~⟩ ⟨the worst of men is entitled to a ~⟩ (4) **:** opportunity (as for a book or doctrine) to be generally known, evaluated, or appreciated **:** public attention or patronage ⟨no other book of equal seriousness ever had so quick a ~ —J.D.Hart⟩ ⟨a new trend which is struggling for a ~ —Edward Sapir⟩ ⟨numerous and fantastic theories of sleep continue to find a ~ —Webb Garrison⟩ **b** (1) **:** a trial in equity practice (2) **:** a listening to arguments or proofs and arguments in interlocutory proceedings (3) **:** a preliminary examination in criminal procedure (4) **:** a trial before an administrative tribunal **c :** a session (as of a congressional committee) in which witnesses are heard and testimony is taken ⟨the committee will hold ~*s* in a number of major cities⟩ **3** *chiefly dial* **:** a piece of news **:** RUMOR; *esp* **:** a choice bit of gossip **4** *Scot* **:** SCOLDING, LECTURE

**hearing aid** *n* **:** a device that amplifies the sound reaching an auditor's receptor organs; *specif* **:** an instrument for this purpose that consists of microphone, amplifier, and reproducer and is fundamentally comparable to a miniature telephone

**hearing examiner** *also* **hearing officer** *n* **:** a referee appointed by an agency of government to conduct an investigation or a public or private hearing and to report his findings of fact and sometimes his recommendations so that the agency may exercise its statutory powers (as by establishing rules and regulations or deciding controversies)

**heark·en** *also* **hark·en** \ˈhärkən, ˈhäk-\ *vb* -ED/-ING/-S [ME *herken*, fr. OE *heorcnian, hyrcnian*; akin to OFris *herkia, harkia* to listen — more at HARK] *vi* **1 :** to give ear **:** LISTEN ⟨~*ed* without much mental comment —Theodore Dreiser⟩ ⟨~*ed* to all they said night after night —Glenway Wescott⟩ ⟨stopped to ~ to the distant sound of another dog barking —Winnie Fitch⟩ **2 :** to listen with attention, sympathy, or acceptance of what is said **:** give respectful attention ⟨the boy was ~*ing* to another —Fanny Butcher⟩ ⟨how was it possible . . . that nobody ~*ed* to Goethe's voice —J.P.Hodin⟩ ⟨the humble folk who ~*ed* to these evangelists —G.M.Stephenson⟩ ~ *vt, archaic* **:** to give heed to **:** HEAR

**hearken back** *vi* **:** to hark back ⟨*hearken back* to the good old days of a century ago —Bernard Berelson⟩

**hearn** *dial past of* HEAR

**hearsay** \ˈ=,=\ *n* -S *often attrib* [fr. the phrase *hear say*] **1 :** something heard from another **:** REPORT, RUMOR ⟨like the ~*s* bandied about by the medievalists —S.N.Behrman⟩ ⟨the qualifications and doubts that distinguish critical science from ~ knowledge —M.R.Cohen⟩ ⟨places off the route, but known from ~ —G.F.Hudson⟩ **2 :** HEARSAY EVIDENCE

**hearsay evidence** *n* **:** legal testimony that consists in a narration by one person of matters told him by another; *broadly* **:** evidence that does not derive its value solely from the credit given to the witness himself as such but that rests in part on the veracity and competency of some other person or sometimes of the witness at another time

**hearsay rule** *n* **:** a rule barring the admission of hearsay evidence as testimony by reason of the unavailability of the sanctions of cross-examination to test the accuracy of the statement

**¹hearse** \ˈhərs, ˈhəs\ *n* -S [ME *herse*, fr. MF *herce* harrow, frame for holding candles, fr. L *hirpic-, hirpex* harrow, prob. of Oscan origin; akin to Oscan *hirpus* wolf; akin to L *hircus* he-goat] **1 a :** a usu. triangular frame of wood or metal designed to hold usu. 15 candles and used esp. in the Tenebrae service in Holy Week **b :** an elaborate temporary or permanent framework erected over a coffin or tomb of a royal, noble, or distinguished person and often decorated with lighted candles, banners, heraldic devices, and hangings and with memorial verses or epitaphs attached to it **2 a** *archaic* **:** COFFIN **:** GRAVE **:** TOMB **:** MONUMENT **b** *obs* **:** BIER 2 **3 :** a vehicle for conveying the dead to the grave

hearse 1a

**²hearse** \"\ *vt* -ED/-ING/-S **1 a** *archaic* **:** to place on a bier or in a coffin **b :** to convey in a hearse **2 :** BURY, ENTOMB **3 :** to shroud as if with a hearse

**hears·ti·an** \ˈhərstēən\ *adj, usu cap* [William Randolph *Hearst* †1951 Am newspaper publisher + E *-ian*] **:** of, relating to, or resembling the journalistic style or methods or the intense nationalism associated with the publisher William R. Hearst and his publications ⟨as chauvinistic, or *Hearstian*, as ever —Ted Oster⟩ ⟨the comic strip and other variegated features of the *Hearstian* type —*Vanity Fair*⟩

**hearst·ling** \ˈhərstliŋ\ *n* -S *usu cap* [W. R. *Hearst* + E *-ling*] **:** a journalist employed by or sharing the views of W. R. Hearst **:** a reactionary journalist ⟨how the *Hearstlings* will howl at the call for the repeal of the ban —K.N.Stewart⟩

**¹heart** \ˈhärt, ˈhät, *usu* -d·+V\ *n* -S [ME *hert*, fr. OE *heorte*; akin to OHG *herza* heart, ON *hjarta*, Goth *hairto*, L *cord-, cor*, OIr *cride*, Gk *kardia*, Arm *sirt*, Hitt *karts*] **1 a :** a hollow muscular organ of vertebrate animals that by its rhythmic contraction acts as a force pump maintaining the circulation of the blood, is in the human adult about five inches long and three and one half broad, of conical form, is placed obliquely in the chest with the broad end upward and to the right and the apex opposite the interval between the cartilages of the fifth and sixth ribs on the left side, is enclosed in a serous pericardium, and consists as in other mammals and in birds of four chambers divided into an upper pair of rather thin-walled auricles which receive blood from the veins and a lower pair of thick-walled ventricles into which the blood is forced and which in turn pump it into the arteries, back flow being prevented by valves, or in lower forms is less perfectly differentiated, having usu. two auricles and one ventricle in reptiles and amphibians and but a single auricle and ventricle in most fishes **b :** a structure in an invertebrate animal functionally analogous to the vertebrate heart: as (1) **:** a contractile ventricle with one to four thin-walled auricles that circulates the body fluid of most mollusks (2) **:** a contractile tube in most arthropods that receives blood from an investing pericardial sinus through openings provided with valves and circulates it forward and peripherally in the body (3) **:** any of a series of paired pulsating anterior blood vessels connecting the main dorsal and ventral blood vessels of certain annelids **c :** BREAST, BOSOM ⟨could have hugged him to my ~ —W.M.Thackeray⟩ **d :** something resembling a heart in shape: (1) **:** a conventionalized representation of a heart (as a decorative figure or a trinket) (2) **:** a red conventionalized figure of a heart stamped on a playing card (3) **:** a heart-shaped block through which a lanyard is reeved to extend stays (4) **:** the heart-shaped part of a pound net placed at the end of the leader to direct fish into the pot (5) **:** a foundry molder's heart-shaped trowel (6) **hearts** *pl but sing in constr* **:** a wood sorrel (*Oxalis montana*) **2 a :** a playing card marked with a conventionalized figure of a heart **b hearts** *pl* **:** the suit comprising cards so marked **c :** an odd bridge trick won or contracted for when hearts are trumps **d hearts** *pl but sing in constr* **:** a game resembling whist in which the object is to avoid taking tricks containing hearts and often other specified cards **3 a** (1) **:** the whole personality including intellectual as well as emotional functions or traits ⟨come from the ~ that is gay, warm, friendly, and enthusiastic —Constance Foster⟩ ⟨I say what is in my ~⟩ ⟨deep in your own ~, you share my prejudice —Walter de la Mare⟩ ⟨each man knew in his ~ that it was a lie —L.B.Salomon⟩ (2) *obs* **:** INTELLECT, UNDERSTANDING (3) **:** MEMORY, ROTE — used in the phrase *by heart* ⟨got the whole poem by ~⟩ ⟨knew the town's 500 telephone numbers by ~ —Peg Bracken⟩ (4) **:** OPINION, ATTITUDE, POSTURE — used chiefly in the phrase *change of heart* ⟨two aspects to the Soviet change of ~ on the Austrian treaty —T.P.Whitney⟩ **b** (1) **:** the emotional or moral as distinguished from the intellectual nature **:** CONSCIENCE, CHARACTER, SPIRIT ⟨has a good ~ but a weak head⟩ ⟨who can look into the ~ of a man⟩ ⟨his ~ dictated one course, his reason another⟩ (2) **:** generous disposition **:** SENSIBILITY, COMPASSION, FEELINGS ⟨have you no ~⟩ ⟨Oh, have a ~, lend me a dollar⟩ (3) **:** hardness or flintiness of character or temper **:** unfeeling disposition — usu. used with *have* in negative construction ⟨he loved his wife; he had not the ~ to deny her anything —Clara Morris⟩ ⟨hadn't the ~ . . . to refuse to come —Ellen Glasgow⟩ (4) **:** TEMPERAMENT, DISPOSITION, MOOD ⟨went home with a heavy ~⟩ ⟨are not inclined to regard free-trade agitation with a light ~ —*Dun's Rev.*⟩ (5) **:** GOODWILL, WILLINGNESS, SINCERITY, ZEAL — used chiefly in the phrase *with all my heart* ⟨will do it for you with all my ~⟩ **c :** LOVE, AFFECTIONS ⟨he lost his ~ to her at once⟩ ⟨laid his ~ at her feet⟩ ⟨a free public-school system . . . was one thing that lay near his ~ —A.W.Long⟩ ⟨his speeches won him ~*s* from coast to coast —William Clark⟩ **d :** COURAGE, ARDOR, ENTHUSIASM ⟨don't lose ~; all will turn out well⟩ ⟨felt some sinking of the ~⟩ ⟨an unsatisfactory . . . student, for my ~ was not in it —W.S.Maugham⟩ ⟨put ~ into me by what you say —O.W.Holmes †1935⟩ ⟨at the sight of reinforcements, the dispirited soldiers took ~⟩ ⟨lost all ~ for my silly chase —Arthur Grimble⟩ ⟨many a people has kept itself in ~ when its statesmen have despaired —W.B.Adams⟩ **e** (1) **:** TASTE, LIKING ⟨likes music but has no ~ for grand opera⟩ — used chiefly in the phrase *after one's own heart* ⟨a man after his own ~⟩ (2) **:** fixed purpose or desire **:** ardent wish — now used chiefly in the phrase *set one's heart on* ⟨set his ~ on getting a new car⟩ (3) **:** intense concern, solicitude, or preoccupation — used chiefly in the phrase *at heart* ⟨people who are unaware of the issue which he has at ~ —J.H.Robinson⟩ ⟨with victory secured, there was one other thing that he had at ~⟩ **f :** one's innermost being **:** one's innermost or actual character, disposition, or feelings — used chiefly in the phrases *at heart* ⟨at ~ a

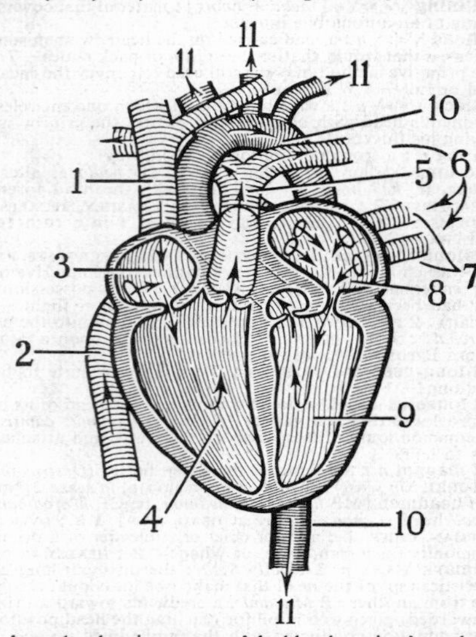


heart 1a, showing course of the blood coming from the extremities and entering from *1* superior vena cava and from *2* inferior vena cava; to *3* right auricle; to *4* right ventricle; to *5* pulmonary artery; to *6* lungs (not shown); to *7* pulmonary veins; to *8* left auricle; to *9* left ventricle; to *10* aorta; leaving by *11* to the extremities (not shown)

heart 1d(1)

sensitive high-strung man⟩ and *heart of hearts* ⟨assisting those who in their ~ of hearts are . . . implacably anti-American —Perry Miller⟩ ⟨in his ~ of hearts I do not think he ever really surrenders faith —Edward Wagenknecht⟩ **4 :** PERSON ⟨two young ~*s* had been freed . . . from the burden of guilt and suspicion —Agnes S. Turnbull⟩ — usu. used with a qualifier ⟨poor ~! who would relieve her wants now⟩ ⟨farewell, dear ~⟩ **5 :** the central or decisive part of something **:** CENTER: as **a :** an inner central area or region ⟨a system of waterways extending into the ~ of No. America⟩ **b :** an essential part **:** the part that determines the real nature of something or gives significance to the other parts **:** the determining aspect ⟨the discernment and understanding with which he penetrates to the ~ and essence of the problem —B.N.Cardozo⟩ ⟨those words of Jesus show us the ~ of Easter's meaning —W.F.Hambly⟩ **c :** the center of activity **:** a vital part on which continuing activity or existence depends ⟨Rome was the ~ and pulse of the empire —John Buchan⟩ **d :** HEARTWOOD **e :** CORE 1h **f :** a firm part (as of a head of lettuce); *also* **:** the center of a celery plant **6** *chiefly Brit* **:** condition for bearing crops **:** FERTILITY — used chiefly in the phrase *in good heart* ⟨the land has never been in better ~ —S.P.B.Mais⟩ **syn** see CENTER — **to heart** *adv* **:** under serious consideration **:** with deep concern **:** with hurt feelings ⟨took it *to heart*⟩ ⟨Sterne . . . laid the criticism *to heart* —Virginia Woolf⟩ — **to one's heart's content :** to the point of complete satisfaction or satiety **:** to the limits of one's will or pleasure ⟨eat *to your heart's content*⟩ ⟨printers imported any foreign books they thought would be popular . . . and reprinted them *to their heart's content* —Margaret Nicholson⟩

**²heart** \"\ *vb* -ED/-ING/-S [ME *herten*, fr. OE *hiertan*, fr. *heorte*, n.] *vt* **1** *archaic* **:** to give heart to **:** HEARTEN, ENCOURAGE, INSPIRIT **2 :** to fix or seat in the heart **3 :** to fill in (as a wall) with rubble or similar material ~ *vi* **:** to form a compact center or heart; *specif* **:** to develop a head (as of lettuce and cabbage)

**³heart** \"\ *dial var of* HEARTH

**heartache** \ˈ=,=\ *n* **:** anguish of mind **syn** see SORROW

**heart and soul** *adv* **:** without reservations **:** COMPLETELY, WHOLLY ⟨count on me to help *heart and soul*⟩

**heart attack** *n* **1 :** HEART FAILURE **2 :** a seizure of weak or abnormal functioning of the heart

**heart balm** *n* **:** compensation for breach of promise to marry or alienation of affections ⟨two days after the marriage . . . was sued by another woman for two hundred thousand dollars' *heart balm* —Carey McWilliams⟩

**heartbeat** \ˈ=,=\ *n* **1 :** one complete pulsation of the heart **2 :** the vital center or driving impulse ⟨the dining car is the real ~ and life of a train —Richard Barnitz⟩ ⟨the school is the ~ of our organic society —Agnes Meyer⟩

**heart block** *n* **:** incoordination of the heartbeat in which the auricles and ventricles beat independently due to defective transmission through the atrioventricular bundle and marked by decreased cardiac output often with cerebral ischemia

**heart bond** *n* **:** a masonry bond in which no header stone stretches across the wall but two headers meet in the middle and their joint is covered by another stone

**¹heartbreak** \ˈ=,=\ *n* **1 :** crushing grief ⟨the sorrow and the ~ which . . . abide in the homes of so many of our neighbors —H.S.Truman⟩ **2 :** something that causes heartbreak ⟨proved a . . . ~ to the authors of his being —C.G.Glover⟩ ⟨the spectacle of his gentle fortitude was . . . a ~ —John Buchan⟩

**²heartbreak** \"\ *vt* [back-formation fr. *heartbroken*] **:** to break the heart of

**heartbreaker** \ˈ=,==\ *n* **:** something that causes heartbreak ⟨arming merchant ships . . . has been another ~ —*Fortune*⟩

**heartbreaking** \ˈ=,==\ *adj* **:** causing overpowering or intense sorrow, anguish, or distress ⟨made progress only with the most ~ efforts —Farley Mowat⟩ ⟨it is ~ to see new schools going up without proper . . . planning —Cecile Starr⟩ — **heart·break·ing·ly** *adv*

**heartbroken** \ˈ=ˌ==\ *adj* [¹*heart* + *broken*] **:** overcome by sorrow — **heart·bro·ken·ly** *adv* — **heart·bro·ken·ness** \ˈhärt-ˌbrōkən(n)əs\ *n* -ES

**heartburn** \ˈ=,=\ *n* **1 :** a burning discomfort behind the lower part of the sternum usu. related to spasm of the lower end of the esophagus or of the cardia of the stomach — called also *cardialgia, pyrosis* **2 :** HEARTBURNING

**heartburning** \ˈ=,==\ *n* **:** intense or rancorous jealousy or resentment ⟨his promotion to ministerial rank is bound to cause much ~ —J.A.Stevenson⟩ ⟨the seniority rule . . . prevents bitter personal rivalries, factional sniping, and ~ —S.D. Bailey⟩

**heart cherry** *n* **:** any of several cultivated sweet cherries with rather soft-fleshed heart-shaped fruits — compare BIGARREAU CHERRY, DUKE 5

**heart cockle** *n* **:** ²COCKLE 1a; *esp* **:** a widely distributed burrowing cockle (*Isocardia cor*) with the umbones well separated giving the shell a heart-shaped appearance

**heart disease** *n* **:** an abnormal organic condition of the heart or of the heart and circulation

**heart·ed** \ˈhärd·əd, ˈhȧ|, |təd\ *adj* [ME *herted*, fr. *hert* heart + *-ed* — more at HEART] **1 :** having a (specified kind of) heart — often used in combination ⟨gave pleasure to lighter-*hearted* members of the staff —J.G.Cozzens⟩ **2 :** seated or laid up in the heart

**heart·ed·ness** *n* -ES **:** the condition of having a heart esp. of a specified kind — often used in combination ⟨hard*heartedness*⟩ ⟨cold*heartedness*⟩

**heart·en** \ˈhärtᵊn, ˈhȧt-\ *vb* **heartened; heartened; hearten·ing** \-t(ᵊ)niŋ\ **heartens** [¹*heart-* + *-en*] *vt* **1 :** to give heart to **:** inspire with fresh zeal, hope, or courage **:** rouse from indifference or discouragement ⟨people . . . whose presence either ~*ed* the spirit or kindled the mind —Jan Struther⟩ ⟨their supporters are enormously ~*ed* —Mollie Panter-Downes⟩ **2** *archaic* **:** to restore fertility or strength to (as land) ~ *vi* **:** to take courage **:** become imbued with fresh spirit and energy ⟨then the engine would ~ up and show off its paces —William Baucke⟩ **syn** see ENCOURAGE

**heartening** *adj* **:** tending or serving to hearten, inspire, or give fresh courage ⟨a ~ sign⟩ ⟨a ~ development⟩ — **heart·en·ing·ly** *adv*

**heart failure** *n* **1 :** a condition in which the heart is unable to pump blood at an adequate rate or in adequate volume — see CONGESTIVE HEART FAILURE, CORONARY FAILURE **2 :** cessation of the heartbeat **:** DEATH **3 :** a sudden feeling of faintness (as at a surprise or sudden shock)

**heartfelt** \ˈ=,=\ *adj* **:** profoundly felt **:** EARNEST ⟨~ sympathy⟩ ⟨~ thanks⟩ **syn** see SINCERE

**heart-free** \ˈ=,=\ *adj* **:** not committed or engaged in one's affections ⟨quite *heart-free* —George Meredith⟩

**heart·ful** \ˈhärtfəl\ *adj* [ME *hertful*, fr. *hert* heart + *-ful* — more at HEART] **:** full of heartfelt emotion **:** HEARTY ⟨~ prayers⟩ — **heart·ful·ly** \-fəlē\ *adv*

**hearth** \ˈhärth, ˈhȧth *sometimes* ˈharth, ˈhəth\ *n* -S [ME *herth*, fr. OE *heorth*; akin to OHG *herd* hearth, ON *hyrr* fire, Goth *hauri* coal, Skt *kūḍayāti* he singes, and perh. to L *carbo* ember, charcoal, *cremare* to burn up] **1 a :** a brick, stone, or cement area of floor in front of a fireplace; *also* **:** a corresponding projection resembling a shelf on a stove **b :** the floor of a fireplace or of a brick oven on which a fire may be built **c** (1) **:** the lowest section of a blast furnace at and below the tuyeres where the molten metal and slag are collected (2) **:** the bottom of a refinery, reverberatory, or open-hearth furnace on which the ore or metal is exposed to the flame (3) **:** BLOOMERY (4) **:** the inside bottom of a cupola (5) **:** the fuel floor of a smith's forge (6) **:** the bottom of a heat-treating furnace that usu. supports the work **d :** the bed of a furnace on which pots rest in glass manufacturing **e :** a fire-hardened earth floor upon which primitive man built fires (as in an ancient rock shelter or campsite) **f :** a piece of wood against which a hardwood stick is rubbed or into which it is twirled to make fire by friction — compare FIRE DRILL **2 :** HOUSE, HOME, FIRESIDE ⟨not rest . . . until every family has a ~ of its own —James Griffiths⟩ **3 :** a nuclear area (as of high culture) **:** a vital or creative center **:** ECUMENE ⟨the small group of . . . nations that constitute the central ~ of occidental civilization —A.L. Kroeber⟩ ⟨the south and southwest of Mexico constitute one of the great culture ~*s* of the world —C.O.Sauer⟩

**hearth·less** \-thləs\ *adj* **:** not having a hearth

**hearth money** *n* **1 :** PETER'S PENCE **2 :** a 17th century English tax of two shillings on hearths in all houses paying the church and poor rates — called also *chimney money*

**hearth-penny** \ˈ=,==\ *n* [ME *herthpeny*, fr. OE *heorthpenig*; fr. *heorth* hearth + *penig* penny — more at HEARTH, PENNY] **:** PETER PENNY

**hearthrug** \ˈ=,=\ *n* **:** a rug for the front of the hearth

**hearthside** \ˈ=,=\ *n* **:** FIRESIDE

**hearthstone** \ˈ=,=\ *n* [ME *herthstone*, fr. *herth* hearth + *stone*] **1 a :** stone forming a hearth **b :** FIRESIDE, HOME **2 :** a soft stone or composition of powdered stone and pipe clay used to whiten or scour hearths and doorsteps

**heartier** *comparative of* HEARTY

**heartiest** *superlative of* HEARTY

**heart·i·ly** \ˈhär|dᵊlē, ˈhȧ|, |tᵊ-, -li\ *adv* [ME *hertily*, fr. *herty* hearty + *-ly*] **1 :** in a hearty manner **2 a :** with all sincerity or goodwill **:** without reservations **:** WHOLEHEARTEDLY ⟨~ in sympathy with the essence of the liberal faith —M.R.Cohen⟩ **b :** with zest or gusto **:** VIGOROUSLY ⟨threw himself ~ into his work⟩ ⟨ate and drank ~⟩ **3 :** COMPLETELY, THOROUGHLY, EXCEEDINGLY ⟨~ sick of this idle debate⟩

**heart·i·ness** \|dēnəs, |din-\ *n* -ES **1 :** cordiality or geniality of manner **:** CHEERINESS, FRIENDLINESS ⟨detested his backslapping ~⟩ **2 :** ZEAL, ENTHUSIASM ⟨the music was sung with uninhibited ~ by the mountain folk —Herman Wouk⟩ ⟨enjoy themselves . . . with a ~ that makes the Londoner feel extremely envious —S.P.B.Mais⟩ **3 :** VIGOR, STRENGTH ⟨an air of rugged outdoor ~ —J.J.Godwin⟩

**hearting** *n* -S [fr. gerund of ²*heart*] **1 :** CORE 1l **2 :** PUDDLE WALL **3 :** BACKING 1a

**heart·land** \ˈhärt,land, ˈhȧt- -,laa(ə)nd, -,lənd\ *n* **:** an area of decisive importance **:** a pivotal or nuclear area ⟨the entire ~ of the country, the Mississippi Basin —A.W.Baum⟩ ⟨the German industrial ~ in the Ruhr valley —Henry Wallace⟩ ⟨the temperate highlands which are the ~ of the republic —A.P.Whitaker⟩ ⟨the ~ of Eastern duck and goose shooting —*Newsweek*⟩; *specif* **:** a central land area (as northern Eurasia from the Elbe to the Amur) conceived by geopoliticians to be capable of self-sufficiency as an economic and military unit, invulnerable to sea power, and therefore having strategic advantages for mastery of the world

**heartleaf** \ˈ=,=\ *n* **:** any of several wild gingers that have distinctly cordate leaves and are usu. included in the genus *Asarum* but are sometimes segregated in a separate genus

**heart-leaved aster** \ˈ=,=-\ *n* **:** a common blue aster (*Aster cordifolius*) of eastern No. America

**heart-leaved willow** *also* **heart-leafed willow** \ˈ=,=-\ *n* **:** a common broad-leaved American willow (*Salix cordata*) with cordate leaves

**heart·less** \ˈhärtləs, ˈhȧt-\ *adj* [ME *hertles*, fr. *hert* heart + *-les* -less] **1 :** devoid of heart **2 a** *archaic* **:** lacking courage or zeal **:** SPIRITLESS, DESPONDENT **b :** lacking feeling or affection **:** UNSYMPATHETIC, CRUEL ⟨it seems so ~ to leave her —G.B. Shaw⟩ ⟨a ~ mother, a false wife —W.M.Thackeray⟩ — **heart·less·ly** *adv* — **heart·less·ness** *n* -ES

**heart line** *n, usu cap H* **:** LINE OF HEART

**heart liverleaf** *or* **heart liverwort** *n* **:** a hepatica (*Hepatica triloba*)

**heart-lung machine** *n* **:** a mechanical pump that shunts the body's blood away from the heart and maintains the circulation during heart surgery

**heart murmur** *n* **:** MURMUR 4

**heartnut** \ˈ=,=\ *n* **:** JAPANESE WALNUT

**heart of palm :** the edible young terminal bud of various palms (as a cabbage palmetto) usu. served raw and dressed as a salad

**heartpea** \ˈ=,=\ *n* [so called fr. the shape of the seed] **:** BALLOON VINE

**heart pine** *n* **:** LONGLEAF PINE

**heart rate** *n* **:** a measure of cardiac activity usu. expressed as number of beats per minute

**heartrending** \ˈ=,==\ *adj* **:** causing intense grief, anguish, or pain ⟨gives a ~ description of his own days under a private tutor — G.G.Coveton⟩ ⟨his untimely death was . . . ~ —*Nation*⟩

**heart·rend·ing·ly** *adv* **:** in a heartrending manner

**heartrot** \ˈ=,=\ *n* **:** any of several rots involving the central part of a plant or plant organ: as **a :** disintegration of the heartwood of a tree (as by fungi of the genus *Fomes*) **b :** a disease of beets and rutabagas caused by a fungus (*Mycosphaerella tabifica*) that brings about decay of the heart and blighting of the leaves **c :** a rot of sugar beets caused by boron deficiency

**hearts** *pl of* HEART, *pres 3d sing of* HEART

**heart sac** *n* **:** PERICARDIUM

**hearts-and-flowers** *n pl but sing or pl in constr* **:** show of sentiment or sentimentality **:** cloying expressions of endearment ⟨cut out the *hearts-and-flowers* —Maritta Wolff⟩ ⟨I can't stand *hearts-and-flowers* stuff —Mary Miller⟩

**heart-scalded** \ˈhärt,skōdəd\ *adj, dial Brit* **:** tormented by sorrow or remorse **:** TROUBLED

**heart-searching** \ˈ=,==\ *n* **:** introspective analysis or self-examination ⟨the decision was reached only after prolonged *heart-searching* —*Times Lit. Supp.*⟩ ⟨of course these choices will not have been made without *heart-searchings* and reservations —A.J.Toynbee⟩

**hearts·ease** \ˈhärt,sēz, ˈhȧt-\ *n* [ME *herts ese*, fr. *herts* (gen. of *hert* heart) + *ese* ease] **1 :** peace of mind **:** TRANQUILLITY ⟨religion failed to bring him ~ —R.H.Bainton⟩ **2 a :** any of various violas: as (1) **:** WILD PANSY (2) **:** a common Old World viola (*Viola arvensis*) with creamy often violet-tinged flowers (3) **:** a violet (*V. ocellata*) of the Pacific coast of No. America with white petals tinged or marked with yellow and deep violet **b :** any of several smartweeds **3 :** a strong violet that is redder and paler than pansy or clematis and redder and lighter than royal purple (sense 2)

**heartseed** \ˈ=,=\ *n* [so called fr. the heart-shaped white spot on the black seed] **:** a plant of the genus *Cardiospermum*; *esp* **:** BALLOON VINE

**heart shake** *n* **:** a defect in timber consisting of shrinkage and separation of tissues across the annual rings usu. along the rays — compare RING SHAKE

**heart shell** *n* **1 :** any of numerous bivalve mollusks esp. of the families Cardiidae and Carditidae with shells that are heart-shaped in outline when viewed from the end **2 :** the shell of a heart-shell mollusk

**heartsick** \ˈ=,=\ *adj* **:** very despondent **:** DEPRESSED ⟨was too ~ to rise and fight —W.A.White⟩ **:** reflecting or marked by a feeling of sickness ⟨longed with a ~ yearning for the first few days to be over —W.M.Thackeray⟩

**heartsickening** *adj* **:** causing depression or despondency

**heartsickness** \ˈ=,==\ *n* **:** the quality or state of being heartsick ⟨died of . . . ~ after moving here and waiting for years for the man who never came —*Nat'l Geographic*⟩ ⟨the wild ~ of the desert —Lawrence Durrell⟩

**heart snakeroot** *n* [so called fr. the shape of the leaf] **:** WILD GINGER 2a

**heart·some** \ˈhertsəm\ *adj* [¹*heart* + *-some*] *chiefly Scot* **:** animating and enlivening **:** giving cheer ⟨a ~ thing, the smell of frying ham on a frosty morning —G.D.Brown⟩ — **heart·some·ly** *adv*

**heartsore** \ˈ=,=\ *adj* **:** HEARTSICK ⟨a ~ lover⟩

**heartstring** \ˈ=,=\ *n* [ME *hertstring*, fr. *hert* heart + *string*] **1** *obs* **:** a nerve or tendon supposed to support or sustain the heart **2 :** the deepest emotions or affections — usu. used in pl. ⟨tore at the ~*s* of memory —William Beebe⟩ ⟨could touch the ~*s* of the audience —E.H.Collis⟩

**heart-struck** \ˈ=,=\ *adj* **1 :** struck to the heart **2** *archaic* **:** driven to the heart **:** infixed in the mind

**heartthrob** \ˈ=,=\ *n* **1 :** the throb of a heart **2 a :** sentimental emotion **:** PASSION ⟨diary of ~*s* and rebuffs —*New Republic*⟩ **b :** SWEETHEART ⟨a girl on the . . . verge of giving her ~ the raspberry —P.G.Wodehouse⟩

**heart tie** *n* **:** a railroad crosstie with sapwood one fourth or less the width of the tie at the top measured at a point 20 inches to 40 inches from the middle of the tie

**heart-to-heart** \ˈ==ˈ=\ *adj* **:** SINCERE, FRANK ⟨a *heart-to-heart* talk⟩

**heart trefoil** *n* [so called fr. the shape of the leaves] **:** SPOTTED MEDIC

**heart urchin** *n* **:** a heart-shaped sea urchin

**heart wall** *n* **:** CORE 1l

**heartwarming** \ˈ=,==\ *adj* **:** inspiring a glow of sympathetic feeling **:** pleasantly moving or stirring **:** CHEERING ⟨her story of their experiences is entertaining and ~ —*Huntting's Monthly List*⟩ ⟨most ~ literary event of the year —*New Internat'l Yr. Bk.*⟩

**heartwater** \ˈ=,==\ *n* [so called fr. the accumulation of fluid in the pericardium] **:** a serious febrile disease of sheep, goats, and cattle in southern Africa caused by a rickettsial microorganism (*Cowdria ruminantium*) transmitted by a tick (*Amblyomma hebraeum*)

**heartweed** \ˈ=,=\ *n* **:** LADY'S THUMB

**heart-whole** \ˈ=ˈ=\ *adj* **1 :** not broken or depressed in spirit **:** UNDISMAYED ⟨so many clowns have been sunk . . . pathetic; here is one large and *heart-whole* —G.W.Stonier⟩ **2 :** having the affections free **:** not in love **3 :** free from deceit or hypocrisy **:** SINCERE, GENUINE ⟨a *heart-whole* friendship —George Meredith⟩

**heartwise** \ˈhärt,wīz\ *adv* [¹*heart* + *-wise*] **:** in the shape or manner of a heart ⟨her face . . . tapered ~ —T.B.Costain⟩

**heartwood** \ˈ=,=\ *n* **:** the older harder nonliving central portion of wood usu. being darker in color, denser, less permeable, and more durable than the surrounding sapwood but in some woods (as white spruce) lacking distinctive color and then being difficult to distinguish — called also *duramen*

**heartworm** \ˈ=,=\ *n* **1 :** a filarial worm (*Dirofilaria immitis*) that is esp. common in warm regions, lives as an adult in the right heart of dogs and some other carnivores, and discharges active larvae into the circulating blood whence they may be picked up by mosquitoes and transmitted to other hosts **2 :** infestation with or disease caused by the heartworm resulting typically in gasping, coughing, and nervous disorder and when severe commonly leading to death

**¹hearty** \ˈhär|dē, ˈhȧ|, |tē, -i\ *adj* -ER/-EST [ME *herty*, fr. *hert* heart + *-y*] **1 a :** giving unqualified support **:** unreservedly loyal **:** THOROUGHGOING, ENTHUSIASTIC ⟨a ~ Federalist —F.J. Klingberg⟩ ⟨a ~ assumer of its full share of . . . responsibilities —F.S.C.Northrop⟩ ⟨my ~ concurrence in everything you've done —T.B.Costain⟩ **b** (1) **:** exuberantly or unreservedly cordial or genial **:** not reserved or ceremonious in manner **:** JOVIAL ⟨had a bluff and ~ bearing, but he was a rogue —Ross Annett⟩ ⟨being a shade too ~ about it —Angus Mowat⟩ ⟨a wonderful ~ manner with a boy —G.D.Brown⟩ (2) **:** giving exuberant or unrestrained expression to one's feelings ⟨a ~ burst of laughter greeted his arrival⟩ ⟨a string of ~ curses⟩ (3) **:** APPROVING ⟨no one but a Chancery lawyer had a ~ word for the Chancery —F.W.Maitland⟩ ⟨some colleagues are distinctly less ~ about the General —Hal Lehrman⟩ **2 a :** exhibiting vigorous good health ⟨the mate was as ~ as a young lion —Herman Melville⟩ ⟨is my friend ~, now I am thin and pine —A.E.Housman⟩ **b** (1) **:** having a good appetite **:** consuming abundantly or with gusto ⟨a ~ eater⟩ ⟨a ~ drinker⟩ (2) **:** ABUNDANT, AMPLE ⟨ate a ~ meal⟩ ⟨took a ~ swig⟩ **c :** NOURISHING, INVIGORATING ⟨almost a meal in itself, with 15 tender vegetables in ~ beef stock —*Better Homes & Gardens*⟩ ⟨has a ~ flavor that is much livelier than our refined . . . variety —Silas Spitzer⟩ **:** FULL-BODIED ⟨a ~ Rhone with a full bouquet —*New Yorker*⟩ **3 :** vigorous or violent in manner or degree **:** VEHEMENT ⟨the breeze . . . was *heartier* . . . than before —Llewellyn Howland⟩ ⟨hooked a root and gave a ~ pull —C.S.Forester⟩ ⟨then came the rain in a ~ flood —John Muir †1914⟩ ⟨the wind had combed up some quite ~ waves —R.A.W.Hughes⟩ ⟨without any provocation at all give him a ~ kick —H.A.Chippendale⟩ **4** *chiefly Brit* **:** capable of bearing crops **:** FERTILE ⟨thistles so growing . . . signifieth the land to be ~ —Thomas Tusser⟩ **syn** see SINCERE

**²hearty** \"\ *n* -ES **1 a :** a bold brave fellow **:** COMRADE — used esp. in addressing sailors ⟨heave-ho, my *hearties*⟩ **b :** SAILOR ⟨the albatross mocked by the *hearties* —Stephen Spender⟩ **2** *chiefly Brit* **:** an individual of exuberant outgoing disposition or of athletic nonaesthetic tastes ⟨a Matisse reproduction could cause one's rooms to be wrecked . . . by rugger *hearties* —Jocelyn Brooke⟩

**heart yarn** *n* **:** yarn in the center of a rope

**¹heat** \ˈhēt, *usu* -ēd.+V\ *vb* **heated** \ˈhēd·əd, -ētəd\ *also dial* **het** \ˈhet, *usu* -ed.+V\ *or* **heated** *also dial* **het; heating; heats** [ME *heten*, fr. OE *hǣtan*; akin to OHG *heizen* to heat, MD *heten*, ON *heita*; causative-denominatives fr. the root of E *hot*] *vi* **1 a :** to become warm or hot **:** rise in temperature ⟨water ~*ing* in a large kettle⟩ ⟨the room slowly ~*ed*⟩ **b :** to become hot and spoil due to excessive or abnormal respiratory or fermentative activity ⟨grain containing excessive moisture may ~ seriously in the bin⟩ **2 :** to become excited, moved, or inflamed in mind or spirit ⟨cannot see injustice without ~*ing*⟩ ~ *vt* **1 :** to make warm or hot **:** raise the temperature of ⟨~ the oven to 350 degrees⟩ ⟨water ~*ed* by the sun⟩ **2 :** to arouse the emotion or spirit of **:** excite, move, or inflame usu. intensely or to a course of action ⟨his arrogance ~*s* me beyond enduring⟩ ⟨these stirring words ~*ed* us all⟩ **3 :** to make (as the human body) feverish or excessively hot ⟨wine ~*s* the blood⟩ ⟨he was ~*ed* by the long dry climb⟩ **4** *obs* **:** to run over (ground) **:** cover (ground) in or as if in a race

**²heat** \"\ *n* -S [ME *hete*, fr. OE *hǣte*, *hǣtu*; akin to OFris *hēte* heat, OHG *heizī*; derivatives fr. the root of E *hot*] **1 a :** the state of a body or of matter that is perceived as opposed to cold and is characterized by elevation of temperature **:** a condition of being hot **:** WARMTH, HOTNESS ⟨the iron lost its ~ in contact with the cold ground⟩; *usu* **:** a marked or notable degree of this state **:** high temperature ⟨the ~ was intense⟩ ⟨you'll need a good ~ to burn that damp rubbish⟩ ⟨midsummer ~⟩ ⟨a ~ of 500 degrees⟩ **b** (1) **:** a feverish state of the body **:** pathological excessive bodily temperature (as from inflammation) ⟨knew the throbbing ~ of an abscess⟩ ⟨sponged him with alcohol to relieve the ~ of the fever⟩ (2) **:** a warm flushed condition of the body (as after exercise) (2) **:** a sensation produced by or like that produced by contact with or approach to heated matter ⟨felt the ~ rise in her face as she returned his look⟩ **c :** a hot place or situation (as a fire) ⟨the legendary salamander dallying at the heart of the fire⟩ ⟨the ~ all afternoon long⟩ ⟨dormant flies coming out into the ~⟩ **d** (1) **:** a period of heat or of exposure to heat ⟨requires a ~ of several hours to get out all the moisture⟩ ⟨had an unbroken ~ since the first of June⟩ (2) **:** a single complete operation of heating (as at a forge or in a furnace); *also* **:** the quantity of material so heated **e** (1) **:** a form of energy the addition of which causes substances to rise in temperature, fuse, evaporate, expand, or undergo any of various other related changes, which flows to a body by contact with or radiation from bodies at higher temperatures, and which can be produced in a body (as by compression) (2) **:** the energy associated with the random motions of the molecules, atoms, or smaller structural units of which matter is composed **f :** an indication of temperature attained as manifested by the condition, appearance, or color of a body ⟨when the rod is at the proper welding ~⟩ — compare RED HEAT **g :** one of a series of discrete rates or intensities of heating ⟨an electric iron may have three ~*s*⟩ **2 a :** intensity of feeling or reaction (as in fury, vehemence, or agitation of mind) ⟨answered with considerable ~⟩ ⟨such a ~ of eloquence flowed forth⟩ **b :** the height or stress of an action or condition ⟨in the ~ of battle⟩ ⟨during the first ~ of the epidemic⟩ **c** (1) **:** sexual excitement esp. in a female mammal **:** ESTRUS **:** a state in which a female will accept service by a male — usu. used with *in* or *into* or, esp. Brit., with *on* ⟨ewes come on ~ soon after flushing⟩ ⟨like a bitch in ~⟩ (2) **:** the time or duration of heat **:** an episode of heat ⟨a mare is most likely to settle during the foal ~ that occurs two or three weeks after parturition⟩ **3 :** one of the fundamental qualities of bodies, elements, or humors recognized in medieval physiology **4 :** pungency of flavor ⟨cherry peppers have greater ~ than most⟩ ⟨the tangy ~ of crystallized ginger⟩ **5 :** a vigorous or violent uninterrupted action **:** a single continuous effort ⟨set down the outline of his paper at a single ~⟩: as **a** (1) **:** a single course in a race or other contest that consists of two or more courses for all contestants ⟨won two ~*s* out of three⟩ (2) **:** one of several preliminary races held to eliminate less competent contenders from the final race when contestants are too numerous to compete at once ⟨swam in the second ~ and won, but lost out in the final race⟩ **b :** a field trial event in which two dogs compete directly with each other and usu.

by comparison with other braces competing in the field trial **c** (1) *slang* **:** the intensification of law-enforcement activity or investigational pressure usu. with special concern for a particular kind of crime or criminal ⟨the bookies are out of business till the ~ is off⟩ (2) **:** pressure or coercion intended to influence a course of action or events ⟨taxpayers get relief by turning the ~ on their congressmen⟩ (3) **:** strain, tension, or difficulty resulting from the pressure of events ⟨weaken when the ~ is on⟩ **6 a :** a charge of metal made in a Bessemer converter or the steel scrap, pig, or molten iron, limestone, and fluxes in the open-hearth or electric furnace **b :** the resulting molten steel **c :** the ingots charged into the soaking pits or the blooms charged into the reheating furnace

**heat·able** \ˈhēd-əbəl, -ētəb-\ *adj* **:** capable of being heated **:** suitable for heating ⟨a compact ~ apartment⟩

**heat balance** *n* **:** the distribution of the heat energy supplied to a thermomechanical system (as a steam power plant) among the various drains upon it including both useful output and losses; *also* **:** an evaluation or record of such distribution

**heat barrier** *n* **:** THERMAL BARRIER

**heat-body** \ˈ=,==\ *vt* **:** to increase the viscosity of (an oil) by heating — compare BODIED OIL

**heat budget** *n* **:** the amount of heat required to raise the waters of a lake to their maximum summer temperature calculated from their minimum winter temperature of 0° C or 4° C and usu. expressed as gram calories of heat per square centimeter of lake surface

**heat canker** *n* **:** a canker of plant stems caused by high temperatures esp. of the surface soil ⟨flax is subject to *heat canker*⟩

**heat capacity** *n* **:** the quantity of heat required to raise the temperature of a body one degree — called also *thermal capacity*

**heat center** *n* **:** any of various areas in the central nervous system concerned with the regulation of the body temperature

**heat content** *n* **:** ENTHALPY

**heat cramps** *n pl* **:** a condition marked by the sudden development of cramps in skeletal muscles resulting from prolonged work in high temperatures accompanied by profuse perspiration with loss of sodium chloride from the body

**heat death** *n* **:** an ultimate state of thermal equilibrium implying conditions of maximum entropy and zero available energy that according to the laws of thermodynamics the material universe is apparently approaching

**heat devil** *n* **:** a shimmering appearance in the air above a heated surface

**heated** *adj* **1 :** made or become hot ⟨wiped his ~ face with a large bandanna⟩ **2 :** marked by emotional heat ⟨a ~ session of the conclave⟩ **:** IRATE, ANGRY ⟨an exchange of ~ words⟩

**heat·ed·ly** *adv* **:** in a heated manner **:** with heat ⟨denied the charges ~⟩

**heated term** *n* **:** the season of hot weather

**heat engine** *n* **:** a mechanism (as an external-combustion engine or an internal-combustion engine) for converting heat energy into mechanical energy

**heat equator** *n* **:** THERMAL EQUATOR

**heat·er** \ˈhēd·ə(r), -ētə-\ *n* -s [ME *heter,* fr. *heten* to heat + *-er* — more at HEAT] **1 :** something that heats **:** a contrivance that imparts heat or holds something to be heated: as **a :** a stove, furnace, radiator, or other device for giving off heat **b :** an iron core for heating box irons **c :** a wire or filament in an electron tube that heats the cathode indirectly **2 a :** one whose work is to heat something — often used in combination ⟨rivet ~⟩ ⟨tire ~⟩ **b :** one that heats metal billets to make them workable **c :** one that tends the burners that heat a petroleum-products still **3** *slang* **:** PISTOL

**heater car** *n* **:** a freight car with heating apparatus and insulation for transporting perishables in cold or freezing weather

**heater piece** *n* [*heater* (core for a box iron); fr. the shape] *NewEng* **:** a triangular plot of land

**heater-shaped** \ˈ==,=\ *also* **heater** *adj* [*heater* (core for a box iron)] **:** triangular or ogival in outline — used chiefly of a medieval shield

**heat exchanger** *n* **:** a device (as an automobile radiator, a regenerator, or an intercooler) for transferring heat from one fluid to another without allowing them to mix

**heat exhaustion** *n* **:** a condition characterized by faintness or fainting, palpitation, nausea, vomiting, headache, and profuse sweating and resulting from physical exertion in a hot environment — called also *heat prostration;* compare HEATSTROKE

**heat·ful** \ˈhētfəl\ *adj* **:** full of or producing heat; *esp* **:** capable of releasing abundant heat in combustion

**heath** \ˈhēth, *in Maine & adjacent Canada* ˈhāth\ *n* -s [ME *heth, heeth,* fr. OE *hǣth;* akin to OHG *heida* heather, MHG *heide* heath (field), heather, ON *heithr* field, plateau, Goth *haithi* field, OW *coit* forest] **1 a** *obs* **:** any of various low-growing shrubby plants of open wastelands **b :** a plant of the family Ericaceae esp. of the genera *Erica* and *Calluna* typically growing on open barren rather acid and frequently ill-drained soil **c :** any of various heathlike plants: as (1) **:** POVERTY GRASS (2) **:** a tamarisk (*Tamarix gallica*) that is native to Western Europe but established as an escape in parts of No. America (3) **:** CROWBERRY 1a (4) **:** a desert plant that was probably the savin juniper — referring to Jer 17:6 (AV) (5) **:** AUSTRALIAN HEATH **2 a :** a tract of wasteland **b :** an extensive area of rather level open uncultivated land that usu. has poor coarse soil, inferior drainage, and a surface rich in peat or peaty humus and that characteristically has plants of the family Ericaceae as the dominant floral element **c :** a plant community typically occurring on heath in cool climates and being characterized by paucity or absence of trees and dominance of plants of the family Ericaceae — **one's native heath :** the region where one was born or brought up

**heath aster** *n* **:** either of two common much-branched pubescent perennial No. American asters (*Aster ericoides* and *A. arenosus*) with heathlike foliage and small white crowded flower heads

**heat haze** *n* **:** air rising above a hot surface (as of sand or rock) with a shimmering effect that tends to obscure details of the landscape

**heath bell** *n* **:** BELL HEATHER

**heathbird** \ˈ=,=\ *n* **:** BLACK GROUSE

**heath-clad** \ˈ=,=\ *adj* **:** covered with heath ⟨a *heath-clad* slope⟩

**heath cock** *n* **:** the male black grouse **:** BLACKCOCK

**heath cypress** *n* **:** any of various mosses; *esp* **:** a ground fir (*Lycopodium alpinum*) that resembles a miniature cypress tree

**¹hea·then** \ˈhēthən\ *adj* [ME *hethen,* fr. OE *hǣthen,* adj. & n.; akin to OHG *heidan,* adj., heathen, *heidano,* n., ON *heithinn,* adj., heathen, Goth *haithno* heathen woman, prob. derivatives fr. the root of E *heath* (land)] **1 :** of or relating to the heathen, their religions, or their customs **:** PAGAN, UNENLIGHTENED **2 :** STRANGE, UNFAMILIAR, FOREIGN

**²heathen** \ˈ"\ *n, pl* **heathens** *or* **heathen** [ME *hethen,* fr. OE *hǣthen*] **1 a :** an unconverted member of a people or nation that does not acknowledge the God of the Bible **:** PAGAN ⟨I shall give thee the ~ for thine inheritance —Ps 2:8 (AV)⟩ **b** *biblical* **:** IDOLATER, GENTILE **2 a :** a person whose culture or enlightenment is of an inferior grade; *esp* **:** an irreligious person **b :** a person felt to resemble a heathen (as in nonconformity or ignorance) ⟨a grand old ~ who made his own place in life⟩

**hea·then·dom** \-dəm\ *n* -s **1 :** the part of the world where heathenism prevails; *collectively* **:** HEATHEN **2 :** HEATHENISM

**hea·then·esse** \ˌhēthəˌnes\ *n* -s [ME *hethenesse,* fr. OE *hǣthennes,* fr. *hǣthen* heathen + *-nes,* -ness] **:** HEATHENDOM

**hea·then·ish** \ˈ==,nish\ *adj* **1 :** of or relating to the heathen **:** resembling or thought to be characteristic of heathens ⟨worse than ~ crimes —John Milton⟩ **2** *obs* **:** of heathen race or belief **:** HEATHEN **3 :** tending to be or somewhat heathen ⟨this ~ rhythm⟩ — **hea·then·ish·ly** *adv* — **hea·then·ish·ness** *n* -ES

**hea·then·ism** \-,nizəm\ *n* -s **:** the religious system or rites of heathens **:** IDOLATRY, PAGANISM; *also* **:** manners or morals like those of the heathen

**hea·then·ize** \-,nīz\ *vb* -ED/-ING/-S *vt* **:** to make heathen or heathenish ~ *vi* **:** to become heathen or heathenish

**hea·then·ly** *adj* [ME *hethenly,* fr. *hethen* heathen + *-ly*] **:** in a heathen manner **:** HEATHENISHLY

**hea·then·ness** \-ən(n)əs\ *n* -ES **:** the state or quality of being heathen

**hea·then·ry** \-ənrē, -ri\ *n* -ES **1 :** the state, quality, or character of the heathen **:** HEATHENISM **2 :** heathen nations or people

**¹heath·er** \ˈhethə(r)\ *n* -s [ME (northern dial.) *hather, hadder,* prob. modif. of *heth, heeth* heath, heather — more at HEATH] **1 a :** HEATH 1b; *esp* **:** a common erect to almost prostrate evergreen heath (*Calluna vulgaris*) of northern and alpine regions that has small crowded sessile leaves and racemes of tiny usu. purplish pink flowers **b :** BEACH HEATHER **c :** CROWBERRY 1a **2 a** *also* **heather purple :** a grayish reddish purple that is bluer, stronger, and slightly lighter than campanula violet and bluer, lighter, and stronger than livid purple **b :** a grayish to moderate purplish red that is redder and darker than daphne red

**²heather** \ˈ"\ *adj* **1 :** of, relating to, prepared from, or like heather **2 :** having flecks or a mingling of various colors — used chiefly of woolen yarns and fabrics ⟨a soft ~ tweed⟩ **3 :** of the color heather

**heather ale** *n* **:** a Scottish traditional beverage brewed from an extract of heather blossoms with honey, spice, hops, and yeast

**heather bell** *n* **:** BELL HEATHER

**heather-bleat** \ˈ==,=\ *also* **heatherbleater** \ˈ==,==\ *or* **heather-blutter** \-,bləd·ər\ *n* -s *chiefly Scot* **:** a common Old World snipe (*Capella gallinago*)

**heather cat** *n, Scot* **:** VAGABOND, ROVER ⟨here today and gone tomorrow — a fair *heather cat* —R.L.Stevenson⟩

**heather cow** *n, chiefly Scot* **:** a tuft or twig of heath

**heath·ered** \ˈhethə(r)d\ *adj* **:** full of or covered with heather ⟨~ slopes⟩

**heather grass** *n* **:** HEATH GRASS

**heath·ery** \ˈheth(ə)rē, -ri\ *adj* **1 :** abounding in or covered with heather ⟨~ hillsides⟩ **2 :** suggesting or resembling heather ⟨a delicate ~ fragrance⟩; *esp* **:** HEATHER 2

**heath family** *n* **:** ERICACEAE

**heath-fowl** *or* **heath-game** \ˈ=,=\ *n* **1** *Brit* **:** BLACK GROUSE **2** *Brit* **:** RED GROUSE

**heath grass** *n* **:** a chiefly European perennial grass (*Sieglingia decumbens*) that grows commonly on heaths and moors and is indigenous in Newfoundland and in southwestern Nova Scotia

**heath grouse** *n* **:** BLACK GROUSE

**heath hen** *n* **1 :** the female black grouse **:** GRAY HEN **2 :** a grouse that was formerly abundant in the northeastern U.S. but is now completely extinct and that is usu. considered an eastern variety (*Tympanuchus cupido cupido*) of the prairie chicken

**heath·land** \ˈ=,land, -lənd\ *n* **:** HEATH 2a, MOOR 1

**heath·less** \ˈ=ləs\ *adj* **:** free from heath ⟨a ~ moor⟩

**heathlike** \ˈ=,=\ *adj* **:** resembling a heath; *usu* **:** similar to a plant of the genera *Erica* or *Calluna* in habits of growth or in having fine crowded leaves suggesting needles

**heath pea** *n* **:** a European leguminous herb (*Lathyrus tuberosus*) bearing small tubers used for food and in Scotland to flavor whiskey

**heath peat** *n* **:** peat formed chiefly from roots and stems of plants of the genera *Erica* and *Calluna*

**heath poult** *n* **:** the young of the black grouse

**heaths** *pl of* HEATH

**heathwort** \ˈ=,=\ *n* **:** HEATH 1b

**heath-wren** \ˈ=,=\ *n* **:** either of two warblers (*Hylacola pyrrhopygia* and *H. cauta*) that are shy ground-nesting birds of open rangelands of southern Australia and noted as songsters and mimics — called also *ground wren*

**heathy** \ˈhēthē, ˈhāth-\ *adj* -ER/-EST [ME *hethy,* fr. *heth, heeth* heath + *-y* — more at HEATH] **:** of, relating to, or resembling heath **:** abounding with heath

**heat hyperpyrexia** *n* **:** HEATSTROKE

**heating** *pres part of* HEAT

**heating element** *n* **:** the part of an electric heating appliance in which the electrical energy is transformed into heat

**heating furnace** *n* **:** REHEATING FURNACE

**heating load** *n* **:** the quantity of heat per unit time that must be supplied to maintain the temperature in a building or portion of a building at a given level

**heat·ing·ly** *adv* **:** in a heating manner **:** so as to make hot

**heating mantle** *n* **:** an apparatus consisting of resistance wire stitched into glass cloth or asbestos cloth and tailored to surround a vessel to which it supplies heat

**heating pad** *n* **:** a flexible pad for applying heat (as to the body) consisting of electric heating elements embedded in insulating material

**heating plant** *n* **:** the whole system (as of boiler, pipes, and radiators or of furnace, ducts, and registers) used for heating an enclosed space (as a building or group of buildings)

**heat lamp** *n* **:** INFRARED LAMP

**heat·less** \ˈ=ləs\ *adj* **:** lacking heat; *esp* **:** having no artificial heat provided ⟨a ~ apartment⟩ ⟨observing ~ days to conserve fuel⟩

**heat lightning** *n* **:** vivid and extensive flashes of electric light without thunder that are seen near the horizon esp. at the close of a hot day and are ascribed to far-off lightning reflected by high clouds

**heat of adsorption :** the heat evolved when a given amount of a substance is adsorbed

**heat of combustion :** the heat of reaction resulting from the complete burning of a substance and expressed variously (as in calories per gram or per mole or esp. for fuels in British thermal units per pound or per cubic foot)

**heat of condensation :** heat evolved when a vapor changes to a liquid; *specif* **:** the quantity of heat that is evolved when unit mass of a vapor is changed at a specified temperature to a liquid and that equals the heat of vaporization

**heat of decomposition :** the heat of reaction resulting from the decomposition of a compound into its elements or into other neutral compounds; *esp* **:** the quantity involved in the decomposition of a mole

**heat of dilution :** the heat evolved per mole of solute when a solution is greatly diluted

**heat of dissociation :** the heat of reaction resulting from dissociation of molecules of a compound into smaller molecules, fragments, or atoms

**heat of formation :** the heat of reaction resulting from the formation of a compound by direct union of its elements, usu. expressed in calories per mole of the compound

**heat of fusion :** heat required to melt a solid; *specif* **:** the amount required to melt unit mass of a substance at standard pressure

**heat of hydration :** the heat evolved or absorbed when hydration occurs; *esp* **:** the amount involved when one mole is hydrated

**heat of ionization :** the heat required to ionize a substance; *esp* **:** the amount required to ionize one mole

**heat of neutralization :** the heat of reaction resulting from the neutralization of an acid or base; *esp* **:** the quantity produced when a gram equivalent of a base or acid is neutralized with a gram equivalent of an acid or base in dilute solution

**heat of reaction :** the heat evolved or absorbed during a chemical reaction taking place under conditions of constant temperature and of either constant volume or more often constant pressure; *esp* **:** the quantity involved when gram equivalents of the substances enter into the reaction

**heat of solution :** the heat evolved or absorbed when a substance dissolves; *specif* **:** the amount involved when one mole or sometimes one gram dissolves in a large excess of solvent

**heat of sublimation :** the heat absorbed when a solid sublimes; *specif* **:** the heat required to sublime unit mass at a specified temperature

**heat of transition :** the heat evolved or absorbed when a substance changes from one physical form to another

**heat of vaporization :** heat absorbed when a liquid vaporizes; *specif* **:** the quantity of heat required at a specified temperature to convert unit mass of liquid into vapor

**heat of wetting :** the heat evolved when an insoluble solid is wetted by a liquid (as water)

**heat prostration** *n* **:** HEAT EXHAUSTION

**heat pump** *n* **:** a device for transferring heat energy from a low-temperature locality to a high-temperature locality by mechanical means involving the compression and expansion of a fluid (as in mechanical refrigeration); *specif* **:** an apparatus for heating or cooling a building by transferring heat from or to a reservoir outside the building (as the ground, water, or air)

**heat rash** *n* **:** PRICKLY HEAT

**heat ray** *n* **:** a ray producing thermal effects; *specif* **:** an infrared ray

**heat rigor** *n* **:** rigor of living tissue caused by exposure to excessive but not immediately lethal temperatures

**heat·ron·ic** \(ˈ)hēˈtränik, -ēt·ˈr-\ *adj* [blend of ²*heat* and *electronic*] **:** utilizing dielectric heating

**heats** *pres 3d sing of* HEAT, *pl of* HEAT

**heat-seal** \ˈ=ˈ=\ *vt* **:** to unite (two or more thermoplastic surfaces) by heat and pressure to make a seam, closure, or attachment

**heat seal** *n* **:** a seal made by or a method of union involving heat-sealing

**heat-set** \ˈ=ˈ=\ *vt* **:** to fix (as a plastic or pleats in fabric) in a permanent form through the action of heat

**heatstroke** \ˈ=,=\ *n* **:** a condition characterized by cessation of sweating with inadequate elimination of body heat, extremely high temperature, rapid pulse, hot dry skin, flaccid muscles, delirium, collapse, and coma and resulting from prolonged exposure to high environmental temperature which causes a breakdown of the temperature-regulating mechanism of the body — compare HEAT EXHAUSTION

**heat-treat** \ˈ=,=\ *vt* **:** to treat (as metals) by heating and cooling in a way that will produce desired properties (as hardness or ductility) — compare ANNEAL, HARDEN, NORMALIZE, PATENT, SPHEROIDIZE, TEMPER; MALLEABLEIZE; GRAPHITIZE

**heat-treater** \ˈ=,==\ *n* **:** one that heat-treats metals

**heat treatment** *n* **:** a process or an instance of heat-treating

**heat unit** *n* **1 :** BRITISH THERMAL UNIT **2 :** CALORIE

**heat up** *vt* **:** to cause to heat ~ *vi* **:** to become hot **:** HEAT

**heat wave** *n* **1 :** a wave of thermal radiation **2 :** HOT WAVE

**heaume** \ˈhōm\ *n* -s [MF, fr. OF *helme* — more at HELMET] **:** a large helmet chiefly of the 13th century worn over a hood of mail or close-fitting steel cap and supported by the shoulders rather than the head

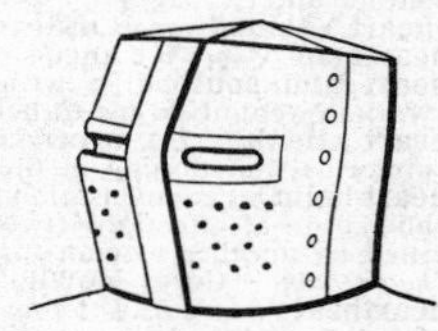
heaume

**heaum·er** \-mə(r)\ *n* -s **:** a maker of medieval helmets

**heau·ta·rit** \hōˈtärət, hyüˈt-\ *n* -s [Ar *ʿuṭārid*] *in alchemy* **:** MERCURY 1c

**he·au·toph·a·ny** \ˌhē,ȯˈtäfənē\ *n* -ES [Gk *heautou* of oneself (fr. *he* oneself + *autos* self) + E *-phany*] **:** manifestation of self

**¹heave** \ˈhēv\ *vb* **heaved** \-vd\ *or* **hove** \ˈhōv\ *or dial* **hoved** \ˈhōvd\ **heaved** *or* **hove** *or archaic & dial* **ho·ven** \ˈhōvən\ **heaving; heaves** [ME *hebben, heven,* fr. OE *hebban;* akin to OHG *heffen, hevan* to lift, raise, ON *hefja* to lift, raise, Goth *hafjan* to carry, L *capere* to take, seize, Gk *kaptein* to gulp down, *kōpē* handle, Alb *kap* I grasp, Skt *kapatī* two handfuls; basic meaning: grasping] *vt* **1** *obs* **a :** to raise or exalt in state or feeling **b :** BAPTIZE; *also* **:** to stand as sponsor for **c :** to offer or consecrate (a portion of a sacrifice) by symbolically lifting up or separating for special holy use — used of the action of an ancient Israelite priest **2 :** to cause to move upward or onward by a lifting effort **:** LIFT, RAISE; *usu* **:** to lift with exertion ⟨the wave *heaved* the boat on land⟩ **3** *obs* **:** to take up and remove **:** carry off **:** take away **4 :** THROW, CAST, TOSS, HURL ⟨he *hove* the lead⟩ ⟨*heaving* down the hay⟩ ⟨just ~ your books on the bed⟩ **5 a :** to utter with obvious effort or with a deep breath that causes the chest to heave visibly ⟨pulled off her shoes and *heaved* a sigh of relief⟩ **b :** VOMIT ⟨got carsick and *heaved* his lunch⟩ **6 a :** to cause to swell or rise ⟨the wind *heaved* the sea into mountainous waves⟩ ⟨a spent horse gasping and *heaving* his chest⟩ **b** *dial Brit* **:** to cause bloat in (a ruminant) ⟨sheep are often *hoven* by a sudden change to lush pasture⟩ **c :** to displace (as a mineral vein or a rock stratum) esp. by a fault; *usu* **:** to displace laterally or horizontally **7 a :** to draw, pull, or to haul on (as a rope) ⟨~ in the cable⟩ ⟨~ a line⟩ **b :** to cause (as a ship or sail) to move or to come into some position by or as if by hauling on a rope either as a means of propulsion or as a means of arranging for a particular kind of action ⟨~ a ship ahead, aback, or in stays⟩ ~ *vi* **1 a :** to rise or become thrown or raised up usu. as a result of the action of some external force (as pressure, wind, heat, or frost) ⟨the pavement *heaved* and buckled in the heat⟩ **b** *archaic* **:** to rise upward **:** TOWER, MOUNT **c** *of plants or roots* **:** to rise or become lifted out of the ground usu. by alternate freezing and thawing **2 :** to make an effort to raise, throw, or move something **:** strain to do something difficult **:** LABOR, STRUGGLE **3 a :** to rise and fall rhythmically or with alternate motions (as of waves, a ship at sea, or the chest in heavy breathing) ⟨waves *heaving* on a storm-tossed sea⟩ **b :** to pant for breath ⟨lay *heaving* from the strain of his effort⟩ **4 a :** GAG, RETCH ⟨could ~ from sheer disgust⟩ ⟨his stomach *heaved* at sight of the mess⟩ **b :** VOMIT — sometimes considered vulgar **5 a :** to haul or pull (as on a line) or push (as at a capstan); *specif* **:** to move a line or chain by the application of force through the interposition of a mechanical device (as a capstan) — compare HAUL **b :** to cause a ship to move in a specified direction or manner **c** *of a ship* **:** to move in an indicated way or direction ⟨the schooner *hove* alongside⟩ **6** *chiefly dial Brit, of livestock* **:** to become bloated **syn** see LIFT — **heave in stays** *of a sailing ship* **:** TACK — **heave one's gorge :** NAUSEATE **:** become nauseated — **heave the lead :** to make a sounding from a ship by means of a manual sounding line — **heave the log :** to cast the log over the stern to determine the speed of a ship

**²heave** \ˈ"\ *n* -s **1 a :** an effort to raise something (as a weight or oneself) or to move something heavy or resistant ⟨each ~ on the rope loosened the stump a bit more⟩ **b :** an act or instance of throwing **:** HURL, CAST ⟨skimmed the notice and gave it a ~ toward the wastebasket⟩ **2 :** an upward motion **:** RISING; *esp* **:** a rhythmical rising (as of the chest wall in difficult breathing or of the waves) **3 a :** the horizontal displacement by the faulting of a rock measured in a plane at right angles to the fault strike **b :** FROST HEAVE **4 heaves** *pl but usu sing in constr* **:** chronic pulmonary emphysema of the horse usu. associated with asthma, improper diet, or severe overexertion and marked by loss of elasticity of the lungs and distention of the air vesicles resulting in difficult expiration with heaving of the flanks and a persistent cough — called also *broken wind*

**heave-and-haul** \ˌ==ˈ=\ *vi* **heave-and-hauled; heave-and-hauled; heave-and-hauling; heave-and-hauls :** to fish with a handline by repeatedly throwing a hook out and drawing it back again

**heave down** *vt* **:** to careen (a ship) usu. for repairs or cleaning ~ *vi* **:** to careen a ship

**heave ho** \ˈ=ˈ=\ *interj* [ˈ*heave* + *ho*] — used esp. by sailors when heaving on a rope

**heave-ho** \ˈ=ˈ=\ *n* -s [*heave ho*] **:** DISMISSAL, REJECTION — used with *the* and often with *old* ⟨the voters finally got sick of the old guard and gave the mayor the old *heave-ho* at the polls⟩

**heave·less** \ˈ=ləs\ *adj* **:** free from heaves or heaving **:** QUIET ⟨a glassy ~ sea⟩

**¹heav·en** \ˈhevən *also* -evᵊm *or* -ebᵊm\ *n* -s [ME *heven, hevene,* fr. OE *heofon;* akin to OHG *himil,* OS *heban* sky, heaven, ON *himinn,* Goth *himins* sky, heaven, OE *hama* covering — more at HAME] **1 a :** the expanse of space surrounding the earth; *esp* **:** the expanse that seems to be over the earth like a great arch or dome **:** FIRMAMENT, CELESTIAL SPHERE — usu. used in pl. **b :** the part of the atmosphere in which clouds and winds occur and birds fly and from which rain and snow fall **:** the part of the atmosphere that is relatively dense and close to solid earth and that forms part of the biosphere ⟨a flock of geese crossing the bright ~⟩ **c** *archaic* **:** CLIMATE **d :** one of a series of realms represented (as in ancient and medieval cosmographies) as extending up or out from the earth **2** *often cap* **:** the dwelling place of the Deity **:** a celestial abode of bliss **:** the place or state of the blessed dead — compare ELYSIUM, HAPPY HUNTING GROUNDS, NIRVANA, PARADISE **3** *usu cap* **:** the sovereign of heaven **:** GOD; *also* **:** heavenly beings **:** the assembly of the blessed ⟨her prayers, whom *Heaven* delights to hear —Shak.⟩ **4 a :** a place or condition or period of utmost happiness, comfort, or delight **:** perfect felicity or contentment ⟨our week at the lake was ~ after the city's heat⟩ ⟨the mountain ~ to which we hope to retire one day⟩ ⟨this shabby proletarian ~⟩ **b :** a sublime or exalted condition ⟨the ~*s* of the imagination⟩ **c :** a transcendent cosmos or domain; *specif* **:** a realm of subsistent or eternal forms or entities ⟨a Platonic ~ of ideas⟩ **5 heavens** *pl but sing in constr* **:** a canopy or covering used over the stage in some Elizabethan theaters **6 :** a divine state and condition of immortality in the doctrine of Christian Science in which sin is absent and all manifestations of Mind are harmoniously ordered under the divine Principle **7** *in Chinese religion* **a :** universal law **b :** NATURE **c :** cosmic ethical principle **d :** inexorable fate **e :** a supreme personal power — **heaven knows :** CERTAINLY, UNDOUBTEDLY — used as an intensive ⟨*heaven knows* we need advice⟩ ⟨our efforts, *heaven knows*, have accomplished little enough⟩ — **in heaven** *or* **under heaven** *adv* **:** among innumerable possibilities **:** EVER — used as an intensive ⟨where *in heaven* were you⟩ ⟨what *in heaven* happened⟩ ⟨what *under heaven* possessed you to do such a thing⟩ ⟨who *under heaven* would have done such a thing⟩ — **to heaven** *or* **to heavens** *or* **to high heaven** *or* **to high heavens** *adv* **:** to an unusual and often an exaggerated or excessive level or degree ⟨the muddy tide flat smelled *to high heavens*⟩ ⟨complained *to heaven* about the tax burden⟩

**[2]heaven** \"\ *vt* **heavened; heavened; heavening** \-v(ə)niŋ, -vᵊmiŋ,-bᵊmiŋ\ **heavens 1** *obs* **:** to place in happiness or bliss **:** BEATIFY **2 :** to make heavenly or utterly happy in character

**heaven–born** \'==,=\ *adj* **:** of heavenly birth or origin **:** CELESTIAL, DIVINE ⟨*heaven-born* compassion⟩

**heaven–dust** \'==,=\ *n, slang* **:** COCAINE

**heav·en·less** \'==ləs\ *adj* **:** having no heaven **:** having no part or place in the heaven of the Deity ⟨heathens worshiping their ~ gods⟩

**heavenlike** \'==,=\ *adv (or adj)* **:** HEAVENLY

**heav·en·li·ness** \-‚lēnəs, -lin-\ *n* -ES **:** the quality or state of being heavenly

**[1]heav·en·ly** \'hevənlē, -li *also* -evᵊml- *or* -ebᵊml-\ *adj, sometimes* -ER/-EST [ME *hevenly*, fr. OE *heofonlīc*, fr. *heofon* heaven + *-līc* -ly — more at HEAVEN] **1 :** of or relating to the spatial heavens surrounding the earth **2 :** of, relating to, or dwelling in the heaven of God or of a god **:** CELESTIAL ⟨~ spirits⟩ **3 a :** fit for or characteristic of the divine heaven **:** appropriate to heaven **:** SACRED, BLESSED, DIVINE ⟨the ~ music of an angel choir⟩ ⟨turn your thoughts to ~ matters⟩ **b :** eminently pleasing **:** DELIGHTFUL, ENCHANTING **:** remarkably pleasant ⟨a ~ day for a picnic⟩ ⟨had a ~ time⟩ ⟨what a ~ necklace⟩

**[2]heavenly** \"\ *adv* [ME *hevenly*, fr. OE *heofonlīce*, fr. *heofonlīc*] **1 :** in a manner or to a degree resembling that of heaven **:** to the utmost **:** EXCEEDINGLY ⟨a maid most ~ pure⟩ ⟨were ~ happy there⟩ **2 :** by the influence or agency of heaven ⟨our ~ guided soul shall climb —John Milton⟩

**heavenly body** *n* **:** CELESTIAL BODY

**heavenly–minded** \¦===¦==\ *adj* **:** DEVOUT, GODLY, PIOUS — **heavenly–mindedness** *n*

**heavenly preceptor** *n, usu cap H&P* [trans. of Chin (Pek) *t'ien*[1] *shih*[1]] **:** a descendant of Chang Tao-ling chosen as the head of the Taoist organization — called also *celestial teacher;* used as a title

**heaven–sent** \'==,=\ *adj* **:** sent from heaven **:** PROVIDENTIAL **:** peculiarly apt or appropriate ⟨a *heaven-sent* opportunity⟩

**heaven tree** *n* **:** TREE OF HEAVEN

**heav·en·ward** \'==wə(r)d\ *adv (or adj)* [ME *hevenward*, fr. *heven* heaven + *-ward*] **:** toward or directed or tending toward heaven — **heav·en·ward·ly** *adv* — **heav·en·ward·ness** *n* -ES

**heav·en·wards** \-dz\ *adv* **:** HEAVENWARD

**heave offering** *n* **:** a separated portion of an ancient Israelite religious offering that was ceremonially raised and lowered in dedication to God and that afterward was reserved for the officiating priest's use

**heav·er** \'hēvə(r)\ *n* -S **:** one that heaves: as **a :** a laborer employed in handling freight or bulk goods ⟨a coal ~⟩ **b :** a bar used as a lever (as in twisting rope)

**heaves** *pres 3d sing of* HEAVE, *pl of* HEAVE

**heave to** \'='tü\ *vt* **:** to bring (a ship) by the wind with after sheets in and headsails aback so that it makes no headway but lies motionless except for drift **~** *vi* **:** to heave a ship to ⟨decided to *heave to* until daylight before attempting to pass the reef⟩

**heavied** *past of* HEAVY

**heavier–than–air** \¦====¦=\ *adj, of an aircraft* **:** having greater weight than displacement

**heavies** *pl of* HEAVY, *pres 3d sing of* HEAVY

**heav·i·ly** \'hevəlē, -li\ *adv* [ME *hevily*, fr. OE *hefiglīce*, fr. *hefig* heavy + *-līce* -ly] **1 :** in a heavy manner **:** with great weight ⟨the weight bore ~ on the beams⟩ **2 :** as if burdened with a great weight **:** slowly and laboriously **:** DULLY ⟨read the lesson ~⟩ **3** *archaic* **:** SORROWFULLY, DEJECTEDLY, GRIEVOUSLY ⟨why looks your grace so ~ today? —Shak.⟩ **4 :** to a great degree **:** INJURIOUSLY, SEVERELY ⟨~ punished for his fault⟩ ⟨crops ~ damaged by frost⟩

**heav·i·ness** \-vēnəs, -vin-\ *n* -ES [ME *hevynesse*, fr. OE *hefignes*, fr. *hefig* heavy + *-nes* -ness] **:** the quality or state of being heavy ⟨a metal of surprising ~⟩ ⟨the produce markets exhibited a seasonal ~⟩

**heaving** *pres part of* HEAVE

**heaving line** *n* [fr. gerund of [1]*heave*] **:** a light line that has a weight on the free end and the other end attached to a heavier line (as a hawser) and that can be thrown across intervening space and used to draw the heavier line to a desired position (as for mooring a ship at a wharf)

**heaving pile** *n* **:** a heavy pile on a wharf to which are led tackles from the mastheads of a ship to be hove down

**heav·i·side layer** \'hevē,sīd-\ *n, usu cap H* [after Oliver *Heaviside* †1925 Eng. physicist] **:** IONOSPHERE

**[1]heavy** \'hevē, -vi\ *adj* -ER/-EST [ME *hevy*, fr. OE *hefig*, OS *hēbig;* akin to OHG *hebīc* heavy, ON *höfugr* heavy, OE *hebban* to lift, raise — more at HEAVE] **1 a :** having great weight **:** being such as may be lifted or moved only with effort **:** WEIGHTY, PONDEROUS ⟨a ~ load⟩ **b :** having a high specific gravity and great weight in proportion to bulk — opposed to *light* ⟨gold is one of the *heavier* metals⟩ **c** (1) *of an isotope* **:** having or being atoms of greater than normal mass ⟨carbon 13 and carbon 14 are both ~ carbons⟩ (2) *of a compound* **:** characterized by heavy isotopes ⟨~ ammonia⟩ ⟨~ ice⟩ **2 a** *obs* **:** HARSH, OPPRESSIVE **b :** hard to bear, endure, accomplish, or fulfill **:** BURDENSOME ⟨suffering under the ~ exactions of this tyrant⟩; *often* **:** GRIEVOUS, AFFLICTIVE ⟨a ~ sorrow⟩ **3 :** of weighty import **:** SERIOUS, GRAVE, CONSEQUENTIAL ⟨~ news⟩ ⟨words ~ with meaning⟩ **4 :** DEEP, PROFOUND, INTENSE ⟨a ~ silence⟩ ⟨~ late frosts destroyed the crop⟩ **5 a :** laden or borne down by something weighty or oppressive **:** ENCUMBERED, BURDENED ⟨returned with ~ spirit from the conference⟩ ⟨today's world is ~ with so-called celebrities —J.P.Jones⟩ **:** bowed down (as with care, grief, sorrow) ⟨a light wife doth make a ~ husband —Shak.⟩ **b :** PREGNANT, GRAVID; *esp* **:** approaching parturition — used chiefly in the phrase *heavy with young* **6 a :** slow or dull from or as if from loss of vitality or resiliency **:** SLUGGISH, INACTIVE ⟨a tired ~ step⟩ ⟨a ~ countenance⟩ **b :** lacking sparkle or vivacity **:** DRAB, STUPID, INERT ⟨a dull ~ style lacking liveliness and appeal⟩ ⟨a ~ writer⟩ **c :** lacking mirth or gaiety **:** DOLEFUL, LEADEN ⟨~ cheer⟩ ⟨made ~ work of the conversation⟩ **d :** characterized by declining prices ⟨the market was slow and ~⟩ ⟨government bonds have been ~ for some time⟩ **7 a :** overcome or dulled with weariness **:** DROWSY, SLEEPY ⟨eyes ~ from prolonged study⟩ **b :** dull and confused due to interruption of sleep **:** having a feeling of disorientation due to the relaxation of sleep ⟨the children were ~ with sleep⟩ **8 :** greater in quantity or quality than the average of its kind or class: as **a :** unusually or exceptionally large ⟨a ~ fall of snow⟩ ⟨~ crops⟩ ⟨~ traffic⟩ **b :** of great force or momentum ⟨a ~ storm⟩ ⟨the *heaviest* sea in the last three seasons⟩ **c :** threatening to rain or snow **:** OVERCAST, LOWERING ⟨a ~ sky⟩ ⟨~ clouds⟩ **d :** impeding motion **:** CLOGGY, CLAYEY ⟨a ~ road⟩ ⟨cold ~ soils⟩ **e :** coming as if from a depth **:** LOUD, DEEP ⟨the ~ roll of thunder⟩ ⟨a ~ bass voice⟩ **f :** MASSIVE, COARSE ⟨a ~ scar⟩ ⟨a ~ growth of timber⟩ **g :** tending to produce dullness or sleepiness **:** OPPRESSIVE ⟨the ~ odor of tuberoses⟩ **h :** STEEP, ACUTE ⟨a ~ grade⟩ **i :** LABORIOUS, DIFFICULT ⟨a ~ task⟩ ⟨likely to be ~ sledding for a while⟩ **j :** being something specified to an exceptional degree ⟨a ~ drinker⟩ ⟨~ losers⟩ ⟨industry is a ~ user of electric power⟩; *broadly* **:** operating or dealing in large quantities ⟨~ buying of steel⟩ ⟨a ~ buyer⟩ **k :** having a high alcohol content **:** rich in malt and hop constituents and usu. dark in color ⟨~ ale⟩ **l :** of large capacity or output ⟨a ~ pump⟩ **m :** having a high boiling point — used esp. of distillates (as of petroleum) ⟨~ hydrocarbons⟩ ⟨~ ends present in gasoline⟩ **n** (1) **:** set or printed in boldface (2) **:** made with too much pressure of the sheet against the printing surface ⟨a ~ impression⟩ (3) **:** 11 points thick — used of the metal of an unmounted printing surface (as a copper engraving, stereotype, or electrotype) **o** *of a domino* **:** having a comparatively large number of pips ⟨the 6-6 is *heavier* than the 6-3⟩ **9 a :** digested slowly or with difficulty usu. because of excessive richness or seasoning ⟨a ~ fruitcake⟩ **b :** not properly raised or leavened ⟨~ bread⟩ **:** lacking in lightness ⟨rich dark cakes often tend to be ~⟩ **10 a :** belonging to or concerned with a class above a certain usual weight ⟨~ woolens⟩ ⟨~ trunk lines⟩ ⟨~ breeds⟩ **b :** producing metal, mineral, oil, or other basic substances and products derived from them ⟨~ industries⟩; *specif* **:** producing products on which other industries function **11 a :** heavily armed with guns of large caliber ⟨~ dragoons⟩ **b :** having maximally concentrated firepower often from a battery of medium-caliber guns ⟨~ antiaircraft emplacements⟩ **c :** heavily armored **12 a :** having stress or conspicuous sonority ⟨~ rhythm⟩ — used esp. of syllables in accentual verse; contrasted with *light* **b :** being the strongest of three degrees of stress in speech ⟨the ~ stress on the first syllable of *basketball*⟩ **c** *of a consonant* **:** VOICED — used esp. in connection with shorthand symbolization **13 :** relating or assigned to theatrical parts or scenes of a grave or somber nature ⟨played ~ roles for years⟩

**syn** WEIGHTY, PONDEROUS, CUMBROUS, CUMBERSOME, HEFTY: HEAVY implies literally of greater weight than the average of its kind or class and figuratively more or less depressing, effort-taking, or unendurable to the mind or spirits, or depressed or dispirited ⟨a *heavy* bag⟩ ⟨a *heavy* child⟩ ⟨a *heavy* volume of literary criticism⟩ ⟨a *heavy* scent of lilacs⟩ ⟨a *heavy* heart⟩ WEIGHTY implies actually and not relatively heavy; figuratively it implies of serious import ⟨a boy carrying *weighty* packages⟩ ⟨a *weighty* series of international decisions⟩ ⟨*weighty* questions about our future domestic policy⟩ PONDEROUS implies literally a weighty massiveness, usu. difficult to maneuver, or figuratively something complicatedly labored, usu. suggesting a certain slow and dull deliberateness of mental effort ⟨a *ponderous* elephant⟩ ⟨heavy concentrations of troops and weapons for *ponderous* operations overland —H.H.Martin⟩ ⟨a sober and somewhat *ponderous* analysis of the police work —Anthony Boucher⟩ ⟨a book dealing with the necessity for world organization and the fundamentals of world law might be dull or at least *ponderous* reading —A.E. Stevenson b.1900⟩ CUMBROUS and CUMBERSOME imply literally a heaviness and bulkiness difficult to move, carry, or otherwise deal with; figuratively, they apply to what is ponderous and unwieldy ⟨*cumbrous* old-fashioned wagons —Eddie Doherty⟩ ⟨one long and *cumbrous* sentence after another —M.W.Straight⟩ ⟨the camel . . . that lumbering and *cumbersome* beast —*Story of Camel Hair*⟩ ⟨the *cumbersome* amendment procedure of the outworn constitution —F.L.Paxson⟩ HEFTY implies, literally, heaviness or solid weightiness usu. as estimated by picking up in one's arms, holding in one's hand, or measuring by the eye against an imagined norm or, figuratively, weighty ⟨a *hefty* rock⟩ ⟨a *hefty* burden —A.J.Bruwer⟩ ⟨*hefty* peasants —*Time*⟩ ⟨*hefty* but handsome in her wedding dress —W.S.Maugham⟩ ⟨embodying so *hefty* a theme in a book —*Time*⟩

**[2]heavy** \"\ *vb* -ED/-ING/-ES [ME *hevyen*, fr. OE *hefigian*, fr. *hefig*, adj.] *vt, obs* **:** to make burdensome **:** weigh down **:** OPPRESS, BURDEN **~** *vi* **:** to play the role of a heavy **:** perform as a theatrical heavy

**[3]heavy** \"\ *adv* -ER/-EST [ME *hevy*, fr. OE *hefige*, fr. *hefig*, adj.] **:** in a heavy manner **:** HEAVILY ⟨time hung ~ on their hands⟩ ⟨a *heavy*-laden wagon⟩

**[4]heavy** \"\ *n* -ES [[1]*heavy*] **1 heavies** *pl* **a :** heavy cavalry **b :** HEAVY ARTILLERY **c :** heavy tanks of an army or other military force **d :** HEAVY BOMBERS **2 a :** HEAVYWEIGHT 1a **b :** a theatrical role or an actor representing a dignified or imposing person **c :** VILLAIN 4 **3 :** something (as underwear or cloth) heavy in comparison with typical members of its kind

**[5]heavy** \'hēvē, -vi\ *adj* -ER/-EST [[1]*heave* + *-y*] *of a horse* **:** affected with heaves

**heavy–armed** \¦==¦=\ *adj* **:** having or carrying heavy arms

**heavy artillery** *n* **1 a :** cannon of large caliber and great weight **b** *or* **heavy field artillery :** guns of 155 mm. or guns or howitzers of larger caliber **2 :** troops that serve heavy guns

**heavy bomber** *n* **:** a large long-range bomber designed primarily to carry large and heavy bomb loads to distant strategic targets — compare LIGHT BOMBER, MEDIUM BOMBER

**heavy chemical** *n* **:** a chemical produced and handled in large lots (as a ton or more a day) and often in a more or less crude state — used esp. of acids (as sulfuric acid), alkalies, and salts (as aluminum sulfate) — compare FINE CHEMICAL

**heavy concrete** *n* **:** concrete in which the usu. rock aggregates are partially or wholly replaced by aggregates of metal (as steel) and which is used esp. for counterweights or in shielding nuclear reactors

**heavy cream** *n* **:** cream that is markedly thick; *esp* **:** cream that by law contains not less than 36 percent butterfat

**heavy cruiser** *n* **:** a large naval cruiser whose principal armament usu. consists of 8-inch guns — compare LIGHT CRUISER

**heavy dactyl** *n* **:** a spondee resulting from substitution of a long syllable for the two short syllables in the thesis of a dactyl

**heavy–duty** \¦==¦==\ *adj* **:** able or designed to withstand unusual strain (as from heat, exposure, or wear) ⟨*heavy-duty* equipment⟩ ⟨a sturdy *heavy-duty* glove⟩

**heavy–footed** \¦==¦==\ *adj* **1 :** ponderous in or as if in movement ⟨a tired *heavy-footed* walk⟩ ⟨a *heavy-footed* literary style⟩ ⟨the conductor's rendering of the concerts was very *heavy-footed*⟩ **2** *dial* **:** PREGNANT **3 :** inclined to drive an automobile at excessive speeds ⟨issuing a few tickets to *heavy-footed* drivers —Robert Latimer⟩

**heavy going** *n* **:** difficult travel or progress

**heavy–handed** \¦==¦==\ *adj* **1 :** awkward or clumsy in or as if in the use of the hands: as **a :** having the hands seem heavy esp. from fatigue **b** *dial, of a cook or server* **:** inclined to be overgenerous ⟨*heavy-handed* with the potatoes⟩ ⟨much too *heavy-handed* with salt⟩ **c :** lacking or deficient in lightness, grace, or sparkle ⟨a *heavy-handed* didactic style⟩ **2 :** inclined to punish severely ⟨grandfather was *heavy-handed* with his own children but very indulgent with us grandchildren⟩; *broadly* **:** harshly oppressive ⟨*heavy-handed* tyranny⟩ — **heavy–handedly** *adv* — **heavy–handedness** *n* -ES

**heavy–headed** \¦==¦==\ *adj* **1 :** having a large or heavy head ⟨*heavy-headed* wheat⟩ **2 a :** DULL, STUPID **b :** DROWSY

**heavyhearted** \¦==¦==\ *adj* [ME *hevy herted*] **:** SADDENED, DISPIRITED, MELANCHOLY — **heavy·heart·ed·ly** *adv* — **heavy·heart·ed·ness** *n* -ES

**heavy hydrogen** *n* **:** an isotope of hydrogen having a mass number greater than 1; *esp* **:** DEUTERIUM

**heavy–laden** \¦==¦==\ *adj* **:** weighted down with or as if with a heavy burden **:** OPPRESSED, BURDENED ⟨a *heavy-laden* donkey⟩ ⟨*heavy-laden* with family cares⟩

**heavy liquid** *n* **:** a suspension of very fine particles of high specific gravity in water that forms a slurry with a specific gravity greater than that of water

**heavy man** *n, slang* **:** a professional criminal engaged in activities (as robbery or safecracking) that involve or may involve violence

**heavy metal** *n* **:** a metal of high specific gravity; *esp* **:** a metal having a specific gravity of 5.0 or over

**heavy mineral** *n* **:** a mineral of specific gravity higher than a standard (as 2.8 or 3.0) that commonly forms a minor component of a rock

**heavy nitrogen** *n* **:** an isotope of nitrogen having a mass member greater than 14; *esp* **:** nitrogen of mass 15

**heavy oil** *n* **:** an oil of high specific gravity; *specif* **:** a high-boiling distillate from tar

**heavy oil of wine :** a heavy yellow oily liquid obtained in the distillation of alcohol and sulfuric acid in making ether

**heavy oxygen** *n* **:** an isotope of oxygen having a mass number greater than 16; *esp* **:** oxygen of mass 18

**heavy pine** *or* **heavy–wooded pine** *n* **:** PONDEROSA PINE

**heavy racket** *n, slang* **:** a branch of crime that involves or may involve personal violence — compare HEAVY MAN

**heavyset** \¦==¦=\ *adj* **:** stocky and compact and sometimes tending to stoutness in build ⟨a ~ man⟩

**heavy solution** *n* **:** a liquid of high density (as a solution of mercury iodide in potassium iodide or of the cadmium salt of a borotungstic acid) used esp. in determining the specific gravities of minerals and in separating them when mechanically mixed

**heavy spar** *n* **:** BARITE

**heavy water** *n* **:** water containing more than the usual proportion of heavy hydrogen, heavy oxygen, or both; *esp* **:** water that is enriched in deuterium so that it consists either wholly or in larger than normal proportion of deuterium oxide and that is used in tracer studies and as a moderator in nuclear reactors

**heavy weapons company** *n* **:** an infantry company usu. equipped with mortars, heavy machine guns, and recoilless rifles in addition to lighter weapons

**heavyweight** \'==,=\ *n, often attrib* **1 :** one that is above average in weight: as **a :** a participant (as a boxer or wrestler) in a sport or athletic contest who belongs to the heaviest of the classes into which contestants are divided; *esp* **:** a boxer weighing not less than 175 pounds — compare FEATHERWEIGHT **b :** an exceptionally massive or heavy object (as a truck or naval vessel) **2 :** one that carries unusual weight (as an outstanding writer or philosopher or a political leader) ⟨the ~s of the party gathered in New York⟩

**hea·zle·wood·ite** \'hēzəl,wu̇,dīt\ *n* -S *usu cap* [*Heazlewood*, Tasmania, its locality + E *-ite*] **:** a mineral $Ni_3S_2$ consisting of sulfide of nickel

**heb** *abbr, usu cap* Hebrew

**he–balsam** \'=¦==\ *n* **1 :** BLACK SPRUCE 1 **2 :** RED SPRUCE

**heb·do·mad** \'hebdə,mad\ *n* -S [L *hebdomad-*, *hebdomas*, fr. Gk *hebdomad-*, *hebdomas*, fr. *hebdomos* seventh (fr. *hepta* seven) + *-ad-*, *-as* fem. suffix denoting connection with or descent from — more at SEVEN] **1 :** a group of seven ⟨a ~ of heavenly bodies⟩ **2 :** a period of seven days **:** WEEK **3** *gnosticism* **:** a group of seven aeons derived from the seven planetary deities who in most systems were half-hostile powers that created the world

**[1]heb·dom·a·dal** \(')heb¦dämədᵊl\ *adj* [LL *hebdomadalis*, fr. L *hebdomad-*, *hebdomas* + *-alis* -al] **1** *obs* **:** consisting of seven days **:** lasting seven days **2 :** occurring every seven days **:** WEEKLY

**[2]hebdomadal** \"\ *n* -S **:** a weekly newspaper or magazine

**heb·dom·a·dal·ly** \-dᵊlē\ *adv* **:** every week ⟨contributes ~ to the magazine⟩

**[1]heb·dom·a·dary** \heb'dämə,derē\ *n* -ES [ME *ebdomadary*, fr. LL *hebdomadarius*, fr. L *hebdomad-*, *hebdomas* + *-arius* -ary (n. suffix)] **:** a member of a Roman Catholic chapter or convent appointed for the week to sing the chapter mass and lead the recitation of the canonical hours

**[2]hebdomadary** \"\ *adj* [ML *hebdomadarius*, fr. L *hebdomad-*, *hebdomas* + *-arius* -ary (adj. suffix)] **:** occurring every seven days

**heb·dom·a·der** \-‚də(r)\ *n* -S [alter. of [1]*hebdomadary*] **:** a member of a Scottish university formerly appointed for the week to superintend student discipline

**[1]he·be** \'hē(,)bē\ *n* [NL, after *Hebe*, goddess of youth, fr. Gk *Hēbē*, fr. *hēbē*, youth; akin to Lith *pajėgà* power, ability] **1** *cap, in some classifications* **:** a genus comprising the shrubby evergreen veronicas of the southern hemisphere **2** -S **:** any veronica that can be placed in the genus *Hebe* including several of considerable horticultural interest

**[2]hebe** \'hēb\ *n* -S *often cap* [short for [2]*Hebrew*] **:** JEW — often taken to be offensive

**hebe-** *comb form* [Gk *hēbē* youth, pubes] **:** puberty ⟨*hebephrenia*⟩ **:** downy **:** hairy **:** pubescent ⟨*hebe*anthous⟩

**he·be·phre·nia** \,hēbə'frēnēə, ,heb-\ *n* -S [NL, fr. *hebe-* + *-phrenia*] **:** a schizophrenic reaction that is characterized by silliness, delusions, hallucinations, and regression and that has an early insidious onset and a usu. unfavorable prognosis — **he·be·phrenic** \¦==¦frenik *also* -rēn-\ *adj or n*

**heb·er·den's node** \'hebə(r)dᵊnz-\ *n, usu cap H* [after William *Heberden* †1801 Eng. physician] **:** any of the bony knots at joint margins (as at the terminal joints of the fingers) commonly associated with degenerative arthritis

**heb·e·tate** \'hebə,tāt\ *vb* -ED/-ING/-S [L *hebetatus*, past part. of *hebetare* to make dull (lit. & fig.), fr. *hebet-*, *hebes* dull] *vt* **:** to blunt the sensitivity or keenness of **:** make dull or obtuse ⟨desultory reading . . . ~*s* the brain —J.R.Lowell⟩ **~** *vi* **:** to become dull or obtuse — **heb·e·ta·tion** \,=='tāshən\ *n* -S

**heb·e·tude** \-ə,tüd, -ə·,tyüd\ *n* -S [LL *hebetudo*, fr. *hebēre* to be dull + *-tudo* -tude; akin to L *hebes* dull] **:** the absence of mental alertness or physical sensitivity **:** DULLNESS, LETHARGY ⟨her natural ~ must disgust him and eventually destroy all affection —Hugh McCrae⟩ — **heb·e·tu·di·nous** \¦==¦=(ᵊ)nəs\ *adj*

**he·brae·an** \(')hē¦brēən, hi'b-, (')he¦b-, hə'b-\ *n* -S *usu cap* [L *Hebraeus* Hebrew + E *-an* — more at HEBREW] *archaic* **:** a Hebrew scholar

**he·bra·ic** \-rāik,-rāēk\ *adj, usu cap* [ME *Ebrayke*, fr. LL *Hebraicus*, fr. Gk *Hebraikos*, fr. *Hebraios*, adj., Hebrew + *-ikos* -ic — more at HEBREW] **1 :** of, relating to, or characteristic of the Hebrews or of their language, literature, or religion ⟨those early Christians who were of *Hebraic* blood instead of Greek or Roman —C.J.Bulliet⟩ ⟨a Jewish house of worship ought to be . . . *Hebraic* —A.R.Katz⟩ **2 :** characterized by preoccupation with conscience and conduct ⟨was ardently *Hebraic*, exalting righteousness above love —V.L. Parrington⟩ ⟨the Hellenic and the *Hebraic* ways of looking at God, man, and the universe —Will Herberg⟩ — **he·bra·i·cal·ly** \-āək(ə)lē, -āēk-, -li\ *adv*

**he·bra·i·ca** \='=əkə, -ēkə\ *n pl, usu cap* [NL, fr. LL, neut. pl. of *Hebraicus*] **:** things Hebraic; *esp* **:** Hebraic literary or historical materials ⟨a collection of *Hebraica*⟩

**hebraic granite** *n, usu cap H* [so called fr. its supposed resemblance to letters of the Hebrew alphabet] **:** GRAPHIC GRANITE

**he·bra·ism** \'hē(,)brā\|,izəm, -‚brē\|, -‚brə\|\ *n* -S *usu cap* [*Hebraic* + *-ism*] **1 :** a characteristic feature of Hebrew occurring in another language or dialect ⟨the first half of the book of Acts . . . is replete with *Hebraisms* —S.M.Gilmour⟩ **2 a :** the thought, spirit, or practice characteristic of the Hebrews ⟨*Hebraism* related itself to centuries of literary and philosophical creativity —J.L.Teller⟩ — compare HELLENISM 4 **b :** the moral theory of life held to be characteristic of the Hebrews ⟨the governing idea of Hellenism is spontaneity of consciousness; that of *Hebraism*, strictness of conscience —Matthew Arnold⟩

**he·bra·ist** \\|‚əst\ *n* -S *usu cap* [*Hebraic* + *-ist*] **:** a specialist in Hebrew and Hebraic studies

**he·bra·is·tic** \¦=(,)=¦istik, -tēk\ *adj, usu cap* **1 :** HEBRAIC 1 ⟨*Hebraistic* culture⟩ **2 :** characterized by or given to the use of Hebraisms ⟨the least *Hebraistic* writer in the New Testament —B.M.Metzger⟩

**he·bra·iza·tion** \,hē,brāə'zāshən\ *n* -S *usu cap* **:** an act of hebraizing

**he·bra·ize** \'=(,)=,īz\ *vb* -ED/-ING/-S *often cap* [*Hebraic* + *-ize*] *vi* **1 :** to use Hebraisms ⟨must impeach him not only for atticizing but for *hebraizing* too —Richard Bentley †1742⟩ **2 :** to follow Hebraism ⟨here he is *hebraizing* and introducing an element . . . foreign to the law of our race —Frederick Pollock & F.W.Maitland⟩ **~** *vt* **:** to make Hebraic: **a :** to cause to become adapted to Hebraism ⟨~ this fact, erect a cosmology upon it, and we have the vital principle of Calvinism —V.L.Parrington⟩ **b :** to adapt (a foreign word) to Hebrew usage; *specif* **:** to change (a name) to a Hebrew equivalent ⟨*hebraized* his name when Israel was reborn —*Hadassah Newsletter*⟩

**[1]he·brew** \'hē(,)brü\ *adj, usu cap* [ME *Ebreu, Hebru, Hebrewe*, fr. OF *ebreu, ebrieu, hebreu, hebrieu*, fr. L *Hebraeus*, fr. Gk *Hebraios*, fr. Aram *'Ebrai*] **1 :** of, relating to, or characteristic of Hebrew **2 :** of, relating to, or characteristic of the Hebrews

**[2]hebrew** \"\ *n* -S *cap* [ME *Ebreu, Hebru, Hebrewe*, fr. OF *ebreu, ebrieu, hebreu, hebrieu*, fr. LL *Hebraeus*, fr. L, adj.] **1 :** a member of or descendant from one of a group of tribes of the northern branch of the Semites that includes the Israelites, Ammonites, Moabites, and Edomites; *esp* **:** ISRAELITE — compare JEW **2 a :** the Semitic language of the ancient Hebrews in which most of the Old Testament was written — called also *Biblical Hebrew* **b :** any of various later forms of this language (as Mishnaic Hebrew, rabbinical Hebrew, or modern Hebrew)

**hebrew alphabet** *n, usu cap H* **1 :** a Semitic alphabet used since about the 5th century B.C. for writing Hebrew and in medieval and modern times used also for Yiddish and on occasion other languages — called also *Aramaic alphabet;* see ALPHABET table **2 :** the Semitic alphabet used in writing Hebrew until about the 5th century B.C. and on occasion as late as the 2d century A.D. — called also *ancient Hebrew alphabet, early Hebrew alphabet, old Hebrew alphabet*

**he·brew·ism** \'hē(,)brü,izəm\ *n* -S *usu cap* **:** HEBRAISM

**he·bri·cian** \hē'brishən\ *n* -S *usu cap* [*Hebrew* + *-ician*] *archaic* **:** HEBRAIST

**¹heb·ri·de·an** \'hebrə'dēən, he'brid-\ *or* **he·brid·i·an** \he-'bridēən\ *adj, usu cap* [*Hebrides,* islands off the western coast of Scotland + E *-an, -ian*] **1 :** of, relating to, or characteristic of the Hebrides **2 :** of, relating to, or characteristic of the inhabitants of the Hebrides

**²hebridean** \"\ *or* **hebridian** \"\ *n* -S *cap* **:** a native or inhabitant of the Hebrides

**he·bron·ite** \'hēbrə,nīt\ *n* -S [*Hebron,* Maine, its locality + E *-ite*] **:** AMBLYGONITE

**hec·ate** \'hekə,tē, -kəd·ē, -kət\ *n* -S *usu cap* [after *Hecate,* Greek goddess of witchcraft, fr. L, fr. Gk *Hekatē*] *obs* **:** WITCH, HAG ⟨I speak not to that railing *Hecate* —Shak.⟩

**hecato-** *or* **hecaton-** *comb form* [Gk *hekato-,* fr. *hekaton* hundred — more at HUNDRED] **:** consisting of a hundred ⟨having a hundred (*hecato*phyllous)⟩

**hec·a·tomb** \'hekə,tōm *sometimes* -tüm *or* -tăm\ *n* -S [L *hecatombe,* fr. Gk *hekatombē,* fr. *hekaton* hundred + *-bē* (fr. stem of *bous* head of cattle, cow) — more at HUNDRED, COW] **1 :** an ancient Greek and Roman sacrifice consisting typically of 100 oxen or cattle **2 :** the sacrifice or slaughter of many victims ⟨make ourselves unhappy over the yearly ~ that follows the wake of the motor —Agnes Repplier⟩ **3 :** a large number or quantity ⟨the end of the war saw no ~s of officers slain by enfranchised privates —Dixon Wecter⟩

**hec·a·ton·tar·chy** \,hekə'tän,tärkē, ˈ=,=,=\ *n* -ES [Gk *hekatont-* hundred (fr. *hekaton*) + E *-archy*] **:** government by 100 persons

**hecceity** *var of* HAECCEITY

**hech** \'hek\ *interj* [imit.] — used esp. in Scots to express surprise, contempt, sorrow, or pain

**hechi·ma** \he'chēmə, 'hechəmə\ *n* -S [Jap] **:** DISHCLOTH GOURD

**hech·sher** \'hekshər\ *n, pl* **hech·she·rim** \hek'shārəm, -,rēm\ *or* **hech·shers** \'hekshərz\ [LHeb *hekhshēr,* lit., fitting] **:** a rabbinical endorsement or certification esp. of food products that conform with traditional Jewish dietary laws — compare KASHRUTH

**hecht** \'hekt\ *Scot var of* ¹HIGHT

**hech·tia** \'hektēə, -kshēə\ *n, cap* [NL, fr. J. G. H. *Hecht* †1837 Prussian counselor + NL *-ia*] **:** a genus of Mexican desert herbs (family Bromeliaceae) with rosettes of spiny leaves and ornamental floral bracts

**¹heck** \'hek\ *n* -S [ME *hek,* fr. OE *hæc, -hec* — more at HATCH] **1** *dial Eng* **a :** the lower half of a divided door **b :** an inner door **2** *chiefly Scot* **:** a wooden rack for holding fodder **3 a :** a wooden grating set across a stream to obstruct the passage of fish **b** *chiefly Scot* **:** a grating in a millrace **4 a :** a device on a vertical frame for controlling warp threads in textile manufacturing **b :** any of various attachments on spinning wheels or warping mills for guiding thread in textile manufacturing

**²heck** \"\ *n* -S [euphemism] **:** ¹HELL 2 ⟨that's the ~ of it⟩ ⟨~— he can't do that⟩ ⟨a ~ of a good fighter⟩

**heck·el·phone** \'hekəl,fōn\ *n* [G *heckelphon,* fr. Wilhelm *Heckel,* 20th cent. Ger. instrument maker, its inventor + G *-phon* -phone] **:** a woodwind instrument of the oboe family pitched an octave below the normal oboe

**heck·er·ism** \'hekə,rizəm\ *n* -S *usu cap* [Isaac Thomas *Hecker* †1888 Am. Roman Catholic clergyman + E *-ism*] **:** certain religious teachings (as the adaptation of traditional beliefs to the exigencies of modern culture, the exaltation of natural above supernatural virtues, the preference for active rather than passive virtue, the revision of traditional missionary technique) held to be erroneous by Pope Leo XIII — called also *Americanism*

**heck-how** \'hek,haü, -e,kaü\ *n* -S [origin unknown] **:** POISON HEMLOCK

**¹heck·le** \'hekəl\ *chiefly dial var of* HACKLE

**²heckle** \"\ *vt* **heckled; heckled; heckling** \-k(ə)liŋ\ **heckles** [ME *hekelen,* fr. *hakell, heckele* hackle — more at HATCHEL] **1 :** ⁴HACKLE 1 **2 a :** to harass with questions, challenges, gibes, or objections designed to embarrass and disconcert **:** BADGER ⟨would gather in front-row seats and ~ the performers with shouts —E.J.Kahn⟩ **b :** to interfere with unjustifiably or with hostile intent **:** meddle with so as to annoy, disturb, or injure **:** MOLEST ⟨*heckled* even by photographers who . . . set off flash bulbs as he was about to start —Claudia Cassidy⟩ ⟨seemed too harried and *heckled* by her life to spare love for the older children —John Dollard⟩ **syn** see BAIT

**³heckle** \"\ *var of* HICKWALL

**heck·ler** \-k(ə)lə(r)\ *n* -S **:** one that heckles ⟨spoke forcefully with a ready wit that took easy care of ~s —J.D.Hicks⟩

**hec·o·gen·in** \,hekō'jenən\ *n* -S [*heconin* saponin found in the juice of agaves (fr. *hec-* — fr. NL *Hectia,* genus name of *Hectia texensis* — + *-onin* — as in *saponin*) + *-genin*] **:** a crystalline steroid sapogenin $C_{27}H_{42}O_4$ obtained from a desert herb (*Hechtia texensis*) and many agaves and used in a synthesis of cortisone

**hect-** *or* **hecto-** *comb form* [F, irreg. fr. Gk *hekaton* — more at HUNDRED] **:** hundred ⟨*hect*are⟩ ⟨*hecto*graph⟩

**hect·ar·age** \'hek,ta(ə)rij, -tär-\ *n* -S [*hectare* + *-age*] **:** area in hectares

**hect·are** \'hek,ta(ə)(ə)r, -tär\ *n* -S [F, fr. *hect-* + *are*] **:** a metric unit of area equal to 100 ares or 10,000 square meters — see METRIC SYSTEM table

**hec·ta·style** \'hektə,stīl\ *n* [by alter.] **:** HEXASTYLE

**hec·te** \'hek(,)tē\ *n* -S [Gk *hektē,* fr. fem. of *hektos* sixth, fr. *hex* six — more at SIX] **:** an ancient Greek coin worth ⅙ stater; *esp* **:** an electrum coin of Phocaea and Lesbos

**¹hec·tic** \'hektik, -tēk\ *adj* [alter. (influenced by LL *hecticus*) of ME *etyk* (as in *fever etyk* hectic fever), fr. MF *etique,* fr. LL *hecticus,* fr. Gk *hektikos* habitual, habit-forming, consumptive, fr. *hekt-* (akin to *echein* to have) + *-ikos* -ic — more at SCHEME] **1 a :** HABITUAL, CONSTITUTIONAL, PERSISTENT; *specif, of a fever* **:** fluctuating but persistently recurrent ⟨~ fevers are characteristic of tuberculosis and septicemia⟩ **b :** characteristic of or habitually accompanying a hectic fever ⟨the ~ flush of tuberculosis⟩ **2 :** marked by a hectic condition **:** having a hectic fever **:** CONSUMPTIVE ⟨a ~ patient⟩ **3 :** having a glowing quality **:** FLUSHED, RED ⟨the ~ color had brightened in the boy's impatient face —Harriet La Barre⟩ **4 :** characterized by excitement, bustle, or feverish activity **:** RESTLESS ⟨the ~ years after oil was discovered —Harold Griffin⟩ ⟨~ travel through thirty different countries —Carveth Wells⟩ ⟨things were so ~ we couldn't even keep track of the people, let alone the material —N.O.Wahlstrom⟩ — **hec·ti·cal·ly** \-tək(ə)lē, -tēk-, -li\ *adv*

**²hectic** \"\ *n* -S [ME *etyk,* short for *fever etyk*] **1 :** a hectic fever **2 :** one affected by a hectic fever; *esp* **:** CONSUMPTIVE **3 :** hectic flush

**hec·ti·cal** \-təkəl, -tēk-\ *archaic var of* ¹HECTIC

**hec·tic·ness** *n* -ES **:** the quality or state of being hectic

**hective** *adj* [by alter.] *obs* **:** HECTIC

**hec·to·cot·y·lif·er·ous** \,hektə,käd·ᵊl;if(ə)rəs\ *adj* [NL *hectocotylus* + E *-i-* + *-ferous*] **:** bearing hectocotyli

**hec·to·cot·y·li·za·tion** \,==,==.əzāshən\ *n* -S **1 :** transformation into a hectocotylus **2 :** impregnation with a hectocotylus

**hec·to·cot·y·lize** \-'käd·ᵊl,īz\ *vt* -ED/-ING/-S [NL *hectocotylus* + E *-ize*] **1 :** to change into a hectocotylus **2 :** to impregnate with a hectocotylus

**hec·to·cot·y·lus** \-ᵊləs\ *n, pl* **hectocoty·li** \-ᵊl,ī\ [NL, fr. *hect-* + *-cotylus* (fr. Gk *kotylē* cup, anything hollow) — more at KETTLE] **:** a modified arm of a male cephalopod that is specially and variously adapted to effect the fertilization of the eggs; *esp* **:** an arm that in argonauts and some octopods receives the spermatophores, is inserted into the female mantle cavity, and then is broken free from the body of the male

**hec·to·cot·y·ly** \-ᵊlē\ *n* -ES **:** the quality or state of having or being converted into a hectocotylus

**hec·to·gram** *or* **hec·to·gramme** \'hektə,gram, -raa(ə)m\ *n* [F *hectogramme,* fr. *hecto-* hect- + *gramme* gram — more at GRAM] **:** a metric unit of mass and weight equal to 100 grams — see METRIC SYSTEM table

**¹hec·to·graph** *also* **hek·to·graph** \-,graf, -raa(ə)f, -raif, -rȧf\ *n* [G *hektograph,* fr. *hekto-* hect- + *-graph*] **:** a machine for making copies of a writing or drawing by transferring it to a slab of gelatin treated with glycerin and then taking impressions from the gelatin — **hec·to·graph·ic** \;==;grafik, -tēk\ *adj*

**²hectograph** \"\ *vt* **:** to copy with a hectograph

**hec·to·liter** \'hektə + ,-\ *n* [F *hectolitre,* fr. *hecto-* hect- + *litre* liter — more at LITER] **:** a metric unit of capacity equal to 100 liters — see METRIC SYSTEM table

**hec·to·meter** \'hektə,med·ə(r), hek'tämәd·-\ *n* [F *hectomètre,* fr. *hecto-* hect- + *mètre* meter — more at METER] **:** a metric unit of length equal to 100 meters — see METRIC SYSTEM table

**¹hec·tor** \'hektə(r)\ *n* -S [after *Hector,* a Trojan warrior in Homer's *Iliad,* fr. L, fr. Gk *Hektōr*] **:** one that hectors **:** BULLY, BRAGGART

**²hector** \"\ *vb* **hectored; hectored; hectoring** \-t(ə)riŋ\ **hectors** *vi* **:** to play the bully **:** SWAGGER **~** *vt* **:** to harass, intimidate, bully, or domineer over by bluster, scolding, or personal pressure ⟨domineering wives who ~ their husbands and in-laws to near distraction —Harrison Forman⟩ **syn** see BAIT

**hec·tor·ing·ly** *adv* **:** in a hectoring manner

**hec·tor·ite** \'hektə,rīt\ *n* -S [*Hector,* Calif., its locality + E *-ite*] **:** a mineral $(Mg,Li)_3Si_4O_{10}(OH)_2$ consisting of a hydrous silicate of magnesium and lithium — compare MONTMORILLONITE

**hed** \(;)hed, ,(h)əd\ *chiefly Scot past of* HAVE

**hed·dle** *also* **hea·dle** \'hedᵊl\ *n* -S [prob. alter. of ME *helde* — more at HEALD] **1 :** one of the sets of parallel cords or wires that with their mounting compose the harness used to guide warp threads and raise and lower them in weaving **2 :** a metal blade or twisted wire with an eyelet in the center through which warp threads pass in weaving

**hed·dler** \-d(ᵊ)lə(r)\ *n* -S **:** DRAWER-IN

**hed·e·bo** \'hedə,bō\ *n* -S [Dan. *hedebobroderi,* fr. *hedebo* dwelling on the heath (fr. *hede* heath + *bo* dwelling) + *broderi* embroidery] **:** an embroidery characterized by drawn-work and decorative stitching

**hed·en·berg·ite** \'hedᵊn,bər,gīt\ *n* -S [Sw *hedenbergit,* fr. Ludwig *Hedenberg* 19th cent. Swed. mineralogist + Sw *-it* -ite] **:** a mineral $CaFeSi_2O_6$ consisting of a calcium-iron pyroxene

**hede·o·ma** \,hedē'ōmə, ,hēd-\ *n* [NL, prob. irreg. fr. Gk *hēdys* sweet + *osmē* smell; fr. the fragrant blossoms — more at SWEET, ODOR] **1** *cap* **:** a small genus of American herbs (family Labiatae) having small flowers in axillary clusters and with bilabiate corolla and two stamens — see PENNYROYAL 2 **2** -S **:** any plant of the genus *Hedeoma*

**hedeoma oil** *n* **:** PENNYROYAL OIL

**¹he·der** \'hēdə(r)\ *n* -S [prob. fr. ²*he* + *deer* (animal)] *dial Eng* **:** a male sheep; *esp* **:** one past eight or nine months old that has not been sheared

**²he·der** *or* **che·der** *also* **che·dar** \'kädər, 'ked-\ *n, pl* **ha·da·rim** \kə'därəm, -dór-, -,rēm\ *or* **he·ders** \'kädərz, 'ked-\ [Yiddish *kheyder,* fr. Heb *hedher* room] **:** an elementary Jewish school in which children from about 7 to 13 years of age are taught to read the Pentateuch, the Prayer Book, and other books in Hebrew — compare TALMUD TORAH

**hed·era** \'hedərə\ *n, cap* [NL, fr. L, ivy; perh. akin to L *prehendere* to seize — more at GET] **:** a genus of Old World woody vines (family Araliaceae) usu. having palmate leaves but in adult form often becoming shrubby with unlobed leaves — see IVY

**hed·er·a·gen·in** \,hedərə'jenən; ,hedə'rajənən, -,nen\ *n* -S [ISV *hedera-* (fr. NL *Hedera*) + *-gen* + *-in*] **:** a crystalline triterpenoid saponin $C_{30}H_{48}O_4$ obtained by hydrolysis of hederin and other saponins (as from soap nuts)

**hed·er·in** \'hedərən\ *n* -S [ISV *heder-* (fr. NL *Hedera,* genus name of *Hedera helix*) + *-in*] **:** a crystalline antibiotic glycoside $C_{41}H_{64}O_{11}$ active against fungi and bacteria that is found esp. in ivy — called also *alpha-hederin, helixin*

**¹hedge** \'hej\ *n* -S [ME *hegge,* fr. OE *hecg;* akin to OE *haga* hedge, hawthorn, OHG *hag* hedge, hedged-in enclosure, *heckis* hedge, ON *heggr* bird cherry (tree), L *caulae* sheepfold, *colum* sieve, W *cae* field, Corn *kē* hedge, fence] **1 a :** a fence or boundary formed by a row of shrubs or low trees planted close together ⟨white farmhouses with faded red barns and fields bordered with ~s of green —Gordon Webber⟩ **b :** any fence or wall marking a boundary or forming a barrier ⟨the high stone ~ . . . encircled the enclosure —A.L.Rowse⟩ **2 a :** a line or array forming a barrier or marking a boundary ⟨pikemen . . . present a ~ of metal points from which any cavalry would flinch —Tom Wintringham⟩ **b :** a protective or defensive barrier ⟨regarded it as the main function of their existence to raise a ~ around the law —F.W.Farrar⟩ **3 a :** a means of protection or defense — usu. used with *against* ⟨proponents of using fluorides as a ~ against tooth decay —*N.Y.Times*⟩ **b :** any of several means of protection against financial loss: as (1) **:** a bet made against the side or chance already bet on (2) **:** a purchase or sale made not primarily for income or profit but as protection against a known risk ⟨realization that common stocks are the best ~ against inflation —C.E.Merrill⟩ (3) **:** a purchase or sale of commodity futures made to offset the risk of loss from market fluctuations **4 :** a statement so qualified or calculated as to be noncommittal or ambiguous ⟨bureaucratic literature . . . festooned with ~s and qualifications —*Fortune*⟩ **5 :** OSAGE ORANGE

**²hedge** \"\ *vb* -ED/-ING/-S [ME *heggen,* fr. *hegge,* n.] *vt* **1 :** to enclose with or separate by a hedge **:** fence with a row of shrubs or low trees planted close together ⟨its modest lot is *hedged* by . . . hibiscus —Frederick Simpich⟩ **2 a :** to enclose as if with a hedge **:** ENCIRCLE ⟨meandering through an immense meadow *hedged* by forest —S.H.Holbrook⟩ ⟨a small dance floor crowded with couples and *hedged* with waiting men —Edmund Wilson⟩ **b :** to surround so as to form a protective barrier **:** GUARD, PROTECT ⟨remembered that no great divinity ~s this sovereign —Graham Greene⟩ **c :** to surround so as to prevent freedom of movement or action **:** FENCE, HEM, RESTRICT ⟨the bulk and pressure of the rules that ~ him on every side —B.N.Cardozo⟩ — often used with *about* or *in* ⟨are *hedged* about with many special conditions, limitations, and restrictions —F.L.Mott⟩ ⟨*hedged* themselves in with a thousand dos and don'ts —A.L.Kroeber⟩ **3 :** to obstruct with or as if with a hedge or barrier **:** HINDER ⟨the difficulties which *hedged* all approach —D.G.Mitchell⟩ **4** *obs* **:** to introduce and include within something larger or more important — used with *in* or *into* ⟨when you are sent on an errand, be sure to ~ in some business of your own —Jonathan Swift⟩ **5 a :** to reduce or eliminate the risk of (a bet) by making a bet against the side or chance already bet on ⟨is *hedging* its bets in the all-important diplomatic poker game —*Newsweek*⟩ **b :** to protect oneself against financial loss from ⟨were advising clients to ~ the imminent inflation by buying farmland —*Forum*⟩ **6 :** to form into a hedge or barrier ⟨ye are *hedged* on the borders of my path —Adah I. Menken⟩ **7 :** to qualify or modify so as to allow for contingencies or avoid rigid commitment ⟨when he states a position, he is apt to ~ it round with careful qualifications —Colm Brogan⟩ **~** *vi* **1 :** to plant or trim hedges **2 a :** to evade risk or responsibility by avoiding an open or decisive course **:** TRIM ⟨having found . . . every incentive to cower and cringe and ~ and no incentive whatever to stand upright as a man —Van Wyck Brooks⟩ **b :** to qualify or modify a statement or position so as to allow for contingencies or avoid rigid commitment ⟨the paper for which he was responsible never *hedged* on public questions —H.K.Rowe⟩ ⟨no mathematician is infallible; he may make mistakes; but he must not ~ —A.S.Eddington⟩ **3 a :** to protect oneself financially — usu. used with *against* ⟨in order to ~ against inflation and save . . . a part of one's possessions —George Katona⟩ **b :** to reduce or eliminate the risk of a bet by making a bet against the side or chance already bet on **c :** to buy or sell commodity futures as a protection against loss due to price fluctuations **d :** to buy or sell forward exchange as a protection against loss due to foreign-exchange fluctuations **4 :** to form a hedge or barrier ⟨invested with the sanctity that once *hedged* about a king —Dumas Malone⟩

**³hedge** \"\ *adj* [¹*hedge*] **1 :** of, for, or relating to a hedge ⟨a ~ corner⟩ ⟨a ~ plant⟩ ⟨~ selling on the commodity exchanges⟩ **2 :** born, living, or made near or as if near hedges **:** ROADSIDE ⟨a ~ parson⟩ ⟨a ~ marriage⟩ **3 :** belonging to an inferior grade or class **:** THIRD-RATE ⟨a ~ tavern⟩

**hedge accentor** *n* **:** HEDGE SPARROW

**hedge apple** *or* **hedge ball** *n* **:** OSAGE ORANGE

**hedge·bet·ty** \'=,bed·ē\ *n* [¹*hedge* + *Betty,* the name] *dial Eng* **:** HEDGE SPARROW

**hedge bindweed** *n* **1 :** a common Eurasian and American wild convolvulus (*Convolvulus sepium*) — called also *wild morning glory* **2** *also* **hedge buckwheat :** CLIMBING FALSE BUCKWHEAT

**hedge bird** *n* **:** VAGRANT, VAGABOND

**hedge·bote** \'=,bōt\ *n* -S [¹*hedge* + *bote,* obs. var. of ¹*boot*] **:** HAYBOTE

**hedge cactus** *n* **:** a So. American white-flowered cactus (*Cereus peruvianus*) widely grown for hedges in the tropics

**hedge creeper** *n, obs* **:** HEDGE BIRD

**hedged** *past of* HEDGE

**hedge fence** *n* **:** a hedge that serves as a fence

**hedge fumitory** *n* **:** FUMITORY

**hedge garlic** *n* **:** GARLIC MUSTARD

**hedgehog** \'=,=\ *n, often attrib* [ME *hegge hogge,* fr. *hegge* hedge + *hogge* hog — more at HEDGE, HOG] **1 a :** any of several nocturnal Old World insectivorous mammals that constitute the genus *Erinaceus* (esp. *E. europaeus*), have the hair on the upper part of the body mixed with prickles or spines, and are able to roll themselves up so as to present the spines outwardly in every direction **b :** any of various other spine-bearing animals (as the tenrecs or the porcupines) **2 a :** any of various prickly fruits or seed pods (as those of *Ranunculus arvensis* and *Medicago echinus*) **b :** a plant bearing such a fruit **3 :** any of various coarse variably spinose West Indian sponges **4 a** (1) **:** a military defensive obstacle made of barbed wire bound around three poles, logs, or lengths of metal (2) **:** a military defensive obstacle that is made of three 6-foot angle irons bolted together, sometimes wound with barbed wire, and usu. embedded in concrete and that is designed to damage tanks and boats in beach landings **b :** a military defensive stronghold securely entrenched or fortified with minefields and pillboxes and equipped with supplies for sustained resistance to encirclement **c :** a multiple rocket-propelled weapon used against submarines

**hedgehog cactus** *n* **:** any of several cacti with stout sharp spines: as **a :** a cactus of the genus *Echinocactus* **b** *or*

**hedgehog cereus :** a cactus of the genus *Echinocereus*

**hedgehog caterpillar** *n* **:** the hairy larva of certain moths — compare WOOLLY BEAR

**hedgehog fish** *n* **:** PORCUPINE FISH

**hedgehog fruit** *n* **:** the prickly fruit of a maiden's-blush (*Echinocarpus australis*)

**hedgehog fungus** *also* **hedgehog mushroom** *n* [so called fr. the prickly hymenial surface] **:** a fungus of the genus *Hydnum* (esp. *H. erinaceum*)

**hedgehog gourd** *n* **:** an ornamental gourd (*Cucumis dipsaceus*) having a hairy fruit — called also *teasel gourd*

**hedgehog grass** *n* **:** BUR GRASS

**hedge·hog·gy** \'=,=ē, -i\ *adj* [*hedgehog* + *-y*] **:** tending to arouse aversion **:** FORBIDDING

**hedgehog medic** *n* **:** any of several plants of the genus *Medicago* (as *M. echinus*) having pods that resemble burs

**hedgehog parsley** *n* **:** a European herb (*Caucalis daucoides*) of the family Umbelliferae having fruit with prickly ribs

**hedgehog rat** *n* **:** SPINY RAT 1

**hedgehog shell** *n* **:** a spinose marine gastropod shell of *Murex* or related genera (as *M. tenuispina*)

**hedgehog skate** *n* **:** LITTLE SKATE

**hedgehog tenrec** *n* **:** a tenrec (*Setifer setosus*)

**hedgehop** \'=,=\ *vb* [back-formation fr. *hedgehopper*] *vi* **:** to fly an airplane at a low altitude; *specif* **:** to fly an airplane close to the ground and rise over obstacles as they appear ⟨went *hedgehopping* across Holland, dodging trees, telegraph poles and houses —*Life*⟩ ⟨~ over 12,000 miles of pipeline —*advt*⟩ **~** *vt* **1 a :** to transport by flying at a low altitude ⟨*hedgehopped* his passenger to the other end of the line —*Current Biog.*⟩ **b :** to fly an airplane close to the ground and rise so as to miss (an obstacle) ⟨was accused of *hedgehopping* three planes and a hangar and buzzing the control tower —*Newsweek*⟩ **2 :** to evade or elude as if by hedgehopping ⟨*hedgehopped* Soviet censors to carry a . . . message through the Iron Curtain —*N.Y. Times*⟩

**hedgehopper** \'=,==\ *n* **:** one that hedgehops: **a :** an airplane flying at a low altitude **b :** a pilot flying an airplane dangerously close to the ground

**hedge hyssop** *n* **1 :** an herb of the genus *Gratiola* (as the European *G. officinalis* or the American *G. aurea*) **2 :** any of several British plants resembling hedge hyssop (as *Scutellaria minor* and *Lythrum hyssopifolium*)

**hedge·less** \'hejləs\ *adj* **:** having no hedges

**hedge maple** *n* **:** a common low-growing Asiatic tree (*Acer campestre*) sometimes used as a hedge

**hedge mushroom** *n* **1 :** HORSE MUSHROOM **2 :** MEADOW MUSHROOM

**hedge mustard** *n* **:** a plant of the genus *Sisymbrium; esp* **:** a stiffly branching Old World annual herb (*S. officinale*) with pale yellow flowers that is widely naturalized in No. America and was formerly used in medicine as a diuretic and expectorant

**hedge nettle** *n* **:** a plant of the genus *Stachys:* as **a :** a perennial shade-loving Eurasiatic herb (*S. sylvatica*) with a green creeping rhizome having a foul odor when crushed **b :** a similar plant (*S. palustris*) with an odorless rhizome that is widespread in moist places in most of the northern hemisphere

**hedge parsley** *n* **:** any of several weedy plants of the family Umbelliferae with finely cut foliage resembling that of parsley; *esp* **:** an erect annual Eurasian weed (*Torilis japonica*) that has dense heads of white flowers, bristly fruits, and bipinnate leaves and is widely naturalized in eastern No. America

**hedgepig** \'=,=\ *n* **:** HEDGEHOG

**hedge pink** *n* **:** SOAPWORT 1

**hedge-priest** \'=,=\ *n* **:** an itinerant usu. uneducated priest

**hedg·er** \'hejə(r)\ *n* -S [in sense 1, fr. ¹*hedge* + *-er;* in sense 2, fr. ²*hedge* + *-er*] **1 :** one that plants or trims hedges **2 :** one that hedges (as in betting)

**hedge rose** *n* **:** any of various wild roses that tend to invade and thrive in hedgerows: as **a :** DOG ROSE **b :** SWEETBRIER **c :** MACARTNEY ROSE

**hedgerow** \'=,=\ *n* **:** a row of shrubs or trees enclosing or separating fields ⟨could see the white bursts of dogwood in the ~s —William Faulkner⟩

**hedges** *pl of* HEDGE, *pres 3d sing of* HEDGE

**hedge school** *n* [so called fr. the fact that in 17th and 18th cent. Ireland schools were held outside in out-of-the-way places to evade the law on Catholic education] **:** a school held out of doors esp. in Ireland

**hedge sparrow** *n* **:** a common European bird (*Prunella modularis* syn. *Accentor modularis*) that resembles a thrush, frequents hedges, and is reddish brown and ashen gray with the wing coverts tipped with white — called also *dunnock, hedge accentor*

**hedge-sparrow egg** *n* **:** a pale green to light yellowish green that is yellower and slightly lighter than cameo green

**hedge violet** *n* **:** a common European blue-flowered violet (*Viola sylvatica*) that grows in woods and hedgerows

**hedge willow** *n* **:** GREAT SALLOW

**hedging** *pres part of* HEDGE

**hedg·ing·ly** *adv* **:** in a hedging manner

**hedgy** \'hejē, -ji\ *adj* -ER/-EST **:** resembling or abounding in hedges ⟨~ growths⟩ ⟨a ~ countryside⟩

**he·di·on·di·lla** \,hedēən'dē(y)ə\ *n* -S [MexSp, fr. Sp *hediondo* stinking (fr. *heder* to stink, fr. L *foetēre, fetēre*) + *-illa* (dim. suffix) — more at FETID] **:** CREOSOTE BUSH

**hed·ley·ite** \'hedlē,īt\ *n* -S [*Hedley,* British Columbia, its locality + E *-ite*] **:** a mineral approximately $Bi_7Te_3$ consisting of an alloy of bismuth and tellurium

**he·don·ic** \(')hē¦dänik, -nēk\ *also* **he·don·i·cal** \-nəkəl, -nēk-\ *adj* [*hedonic* fr. Gk *hēdonikos,* fr. *hēdonē* pleasure +

-*ikos* -ic; *hedonical* fr. *hedonic* + *-al;* akin to Gk *hēdys* sweet — more at SWEET] **1 a :** of, relating to, or characterized by pleasure ⟨which might have shocked them, had they been in a less ~ state —Herman Wouk⟩ **b :** involving the psychological range of feelings from pleasant to unpleasant ⟨any particular color may undergo an alteration of ~ . . . effect —Hunter Mead⟩ **2 :** HEDONISTIC **3 :** of or relating to hedonics or to the states of consciousness that it deals with ⟨the relative pleasurableness of an intent as a whole can be determined with the help of some ~ calculus —F.E.Oppenheim⟩ **4 :** concerned with the production of pleasure or pleasurable sensation — **he·don·i·cal·ly** \-nək(ə)lē, -nēk-, -li\ *adv*

**hedonic gland** *n* **:** any of several glands of various salamanders and reptiles that produce a secretion believed to function in sexual attraction and stimulation

**he·don·ics** \hē'däniks, -nēks\ *n pl but usu sing in constr* **1 :** a theory of ethics dealing with or based on the relation of duty to pleasure **2 :** a branch of psychology that deals with pleasant and unpleasant states of consciousness and their relation to organic life

**he·do·nism** \'hēdᵊn,izəm, -də,ni-\ *n* -s [Gk *hēdonē* pleasure + E *-ism*] **1 :** an ethical doctrine taught by the ancient Epicureans and Cyrenaics and by the modern utilitarians that asserts that pleasure or happiness is the sole or chief good in life — called also *ethical hedonism;* distinguished from *psychological hedonism;* compare EGOISTIC HEDONISM, EPICUREANISM, EUDAEMONISM, UNIVERSALISTIC HEDONISM **2 :** a way of life based on or suggesting the principles of hedonism ⟨she was a perfect specimen of selfish ~ —Donald Armstrong⟩

**he·do·nist** \-dᵊnəst, -dənə-\ *n* -s [Gk *hēdonē* + E *-ist*] **1 :** an adherent of ethical or psychological hedonism **2 :** one who practices hedonism

**he·do·nis·tic** \,hēdᵊn'istik, -də,ni-, -tēk\ *also* **he·do·nis·ti·cal** \-tək·əl, -tēk-\ *adj* **1 :** of, relating to, or characterized by hedonism **2 :** of, relating to, or typical of hedonists — **he·do·nis·ti·cal·ly** \-tək(ə)lē, -tēk-, -li\ *adv*

**he·do·nom·e·ter** \,hēdᵊn'ämədə(r), -də'nä-\ *n* [Gk *hēdonē* + E *-o-* + *-meter*] **:** a device for measuring pleasure

**-he·dral** \'hēdrəl *sometimes chiefly Brit* 'hed-\ *adj comb form* [NL *-hedron* + E *-al*] **:** having a (specified) number of surfaces ⟨*dihedral*⟩ **:** having a (specified) kind of surface ⟨*euhedral*⟩

**hed·ri·oph·thal·ma** \,hedrē,äf'thalmə\ [NL, irreg. fr. Gk *hedraios* sedentary, stationary (fr. *hedra* seat) + NL *-ophthalma*] *syn of* EDRIOPHTHALMA

**-he·dron** \'hēdrən *sometimes* |,drän *or chiefly Brit* 'he|\ *n comb form, pl* **-hedrons** \-nz\ *or* **-he·dra** \|,drə\ [NL, fr. Gk *-edron,* fr. *hedra* seat — more at SIT] **:** geometrical figure or crystal having a (specified) form or number of surfaces ⟨holo*hedron*⟩ ⟨trapezo*hedron*⟩

**hedy-** *comb form* [NL, fr. Gk *hēdy-,* fr. *hēdys* — more at SWEET] **:** pleasant ⟨*hedy*phane⟩

**he·dych·i·um** \hē'dikēəm\ *n* [NL, fr. *hedy-* + Gk *chiōn* snow; fr. the white fragrant flowers — more at CHION-] **1** *cap* **:** a genus of tropical Asiatic herbs (family Zingiberaceae) having showy labiate flowers in a spike or spiky cluster — see BUTTERFLY LILY **1 2** -s **:** any plant of the genus *Hedychium*

**hed·y·phane** \'hedə,fān\ *n* -s [G *hedyphan,* fr. *hedy-* sweet + G *-phan* -phane] **:** a mineral $(Ca,Pb)_5Cl(AsO_4)_3$ consisting of a yellowish white monoclinic lead and calcium arsenate and chloride — compare APATITE

**he·dys·a·rum** \hē'disərəm\ *n* [NL, fr. Gk *hēdysaron* goutweed, fr. *hēdy-* hedy- + *saron* broom] **1** *cap* **:** a genus of herbs (family Leguminosae) of the north temperate zone and northern Africa with racemose flowers and flat pods that separate into nearly orbicular joints **2** -s **:** any plant of the genus *Hedysarum*

**hee·bie-jee·bies** *also* **hee·by-jee·bies** \'hēbē'jēbēz\ *n pl* [coined *ab* 1925 by Billy DeBeck †1942 Am. cartoonist] **:** a tense nervous jumpy condition produced by various causes (as strain, irritation, fear, worry) and sometimes marked by hallucinations **:** jangled nerves **:** JITTERS — used with *the* ⟨the unrelenting hollow beat of the jungle drums gave them the *heebie-jeebies*⟩

1**heed** \'hēd\ *vb* -ED/-ING/-S [ME *heden, heeden,* fr. OE *hēdan;* akin to OHG *huoten* to protect, guard; causative-denominatives fr. the root of OHG *huota* guard, protection — more at HOOD] *vi* **:** to concern oneself with or take notice of something **:** have regard or pay attention ⟨no sound save for the anxious telegraph machine, which was saying something important, although no one would ~ —Jean Stafford⟩ ~ *vt* **:** to concern oneself with or take notice of **:** have regard to **:** pay attention to **:** MIND ⟨had ~*ed* the call of a poor farmer —H.F.Wilkins⟩ ⟨unless the lessons of the experience are ~*ed* —Carl Spaatz⟩ ⟨will ~ only force —Rupert Emerson⟩

2**heed** \"\ *n* -s [ME *hede,* fr. *heden,* v.] **:** ATTENTION, NOTICE, REGARD, CARE ⟨no one paid any ~ to him —Upton Sinclair⟩ ⟨take ~ of what you do⟩ ⟨while he gives ~ to public opinion he is not unduly swayed by it —Victor Lewis⟩

**heed·ful** \'hēdfəl\ *adj* **:** taking heed **:** ATTENTIVE, MINDFUL, CAREFUL, OBSERVANT ⟨~ of what they were doing⟩ ⟨so ~ a writer —W.S.Maugham⟩ — **heed·ful·ly** \-fəlē, -li\ *adv* — **heed·ful·ness** *n* -ES

**heed·less** \'hēdləs\ *adj* **:** not taking heed **:** INATTENTIVE, UNMINDFUL, CARELESS, UNOBSERVANT, OBLIVIOUS ⟨the ~ younger lad's howling —Pearl Buck⟩ ⟨the ~ generosity and the spasmodic extravagance of persons used to large fortunes —Edith Wharton⟩ — **heed·less·ly** *adv* — **heed·less·ness** *n* -ES

1**hee-haw** \'hē,hȯ\ *n, pl* **hee-haws** [imit.] **1 :** the bray of a donkey **2 :** a loud rude laugh **:** GUFFAW

2**hee-haw** \"\ *vi* **1** *of a donkey* **:** BRAY **2 :** to laugh loudly and rudely **:** GUFFAW

**hee-hee** *var of* HE-HE

1**heel** \'hēl, *esp before pause or consonant* -ēəl\ *n* -s [ME *hele, heel,* fr. OE *hēla;* akin to OFris *hēl* heel, ON *hæll;* diminutives fr. the stem of OE *hōh* heel, hock — more at HOCK] **1 a :** the hind part of the foot of a human being below the ankle and behind the arch — opposed to *toe* **b :** the part of the hind limb of other vertebrates that is homologous with the human heel either occupying a similar situation (as in raccoons, bears, and other plantigrade animals) or relatively much raised above the ground (as in cows, horses, and other digitigrade animals) **:** HOCK **2 :** an anatomical structure suggestive of or associated with the hind part of the foot of a human being: as **a :** the hind part of a hoof **b :** the hind toe of a bird **c :** the spur of a cock **d :** either of the projections of a coffin bone **e :** the part of the palm of the hand nearest the wrist ⟨rubbed his eyes with the ~*s* of his hands —Warren Eyster⟩ **3 :** the foot as a symbol or instrument of violence or oppression ⟨even my bosom friend . . . has lifted his ~ against me —Ps 41:9 (RSV)⟩ ⟨under the ~ of a dictator⟩ **4 a :** one of the crusty ends of a loaf of bread **b :** one of the rind ends of a cheese **5 a :** the part of a shoe, boot, or slipper or of a sock or stocking that covers the heel of the human foot **b :** a solid part of a shoe or boot projecting downward and attached to or forming the back part of the sole under the heel of the foot — see SHOE illustration **6 a :** a latter or concluding part (as of a period of time) ⟨in the dismal ~ of . . . winter —Hamilton Basso⟩ **b :** REMAINDER, RESIDUE ⟨went to the nearest bottle of scotch and drained the ~ of it into his glass —Harry Sylvester⟩; *specif* **:** unburned and partially burned tobacco caked in the bowl of a pipe ⟨he knocked the ~ of his pipe of tobacco out on the palm of his hand —Seumas O'Kelly⟩ **7 :** a rear, low, or bottom part: as **a :** the after end of a ship's keel or the lower end of a mast **b :** the rear part of a plowshare **c :** the nut end of the bow of a musical instrument **d :** the part of a tool next to the tang or handle **e :** the crook of the head of a golf club where it joins the shaft — see GOLF illustration **f :** the base of a tuber or cutting or other part of a plant used for propagation of the plant **g :** the part of the rear extremity of a gun butt that is uppermost when the gun is held in firing position against the shoulder **h :** the rear end of a railroad frog **i :** a V-shaped piece of beef from the lower part of the round — called also *heel-of-round;* see BEEF illustration **j :** the base part of a ladder **k :** the lower end of a timber in a frame (as a post) **l :** the obtuse angle of the lower end of a rafter set sloping **8 :** a contemptible self-centered untrustworthy person **:** an altogether despicable individual; *esp* **:** a cheap double crosser ⟨a few ~*s* who appear to get away with it, but time eventually catches up with them —Frank Case⟩ **9** [2*heel*] **:** the act of heeling a ball in the game of rugby — **at heel** *adv* **:** close after **:** directly behind **:** in close pursuit ⟨the dog followed *at heel*⟩ — **by the heels :** in a tight grip **:** tightly constricted **:** securely confined ⟨the war, in which I'd hoped not to be caught, had me *by the heels* —Kenneth Roberts⟩ — **down at heel** *or* **down at the heel :** in or into a run-down, shabby, or slovenly condition ⟨old shoes which were *down at heel* —O.S.J.Gogarty⟩ ⟨they ran *down at the heel* somewhat as people will do anywhere when cut off from contact with a larger world —A.W.Long⟩ ⟨very *down at the heel* in appearance —Albert Hubbell⟩ — **on one's heels** *or* **upon one's heels :** following at heel — **on the heels of** *or* **upon the heels of :** close to the heels of **:** close after **:** immediately following ⟨*on the heels of* the news of what had happened —C.S.Forester⟩ **:** in close pursuit of ⟨stayed *on the heels of* the runaways⟩ — **to heel** *adv* **1 :** close to the heels **:** close behind ⟨at a word from his owner the dog moved *to heel*⟩ **2 :** into agreement, control, or subjection **:** into line ⟨the Commons, realizing that he was master still, came *to heel* —J.H.Plumb⟩ ⟨his disciplined mind, rejecting excuses, came heavily *to heel* —J.G.Cozzens⟩ ⟨it is hard to bring the eye *to heel* —D.L. Morgan⟩ — **under heel** *adv* **:** under control or subjection ⟨most of the continent was for a time brought *under heel* —A.L.Rowse⟩

2**heel** \"\ *vb* -ED/-ING/-S *vt* **1 a :** to furnish (as a shoe) with a heel **b (1) :** to fit (a gamecock) with a metal spur **(2) :** to arm (oneself) usu. with a gun ⟨wouldn't go through that territory without first ~*ing* himself⟩ **c (1) :** to supply or provide esp. with money or information ⟨a well-*heeled* customer⟩ ⟨better ~*ed* but still not flush⟩ ⟨I want to be ~*ed* when they book him —R.P.Warren⟩ **(2) :** to work for (a school newspaper or magazine) esp. as a reporter ⟨~*ed* the college paper —*Time*⟩ **2 :** to rope (as a steer) by the hind feet **3 a :** to follow closely after **:** follow at the heels of ⟨~*ed* them all the way up the ramp⟩ **b** *of a dog* **:** to urge (a lagging animal) onward by running after and nipping at the heels ⟨dogs ~*ed* the cattle and kept them on the move⟩ **4 a :** to exert pressure on with the heel: as **(1) :** to prod with the heel ⟨~*ed* his horse —A.B.Guthrie⟩ **(2) :** to crush with the heel ⟨~*ed* his cigarette out carefully —W.V.T.Clark⟩ **b :** to kick with the heel; *specif* **:** to pass (the ball) backward with the heel (as out of a scrum) in the game of rugby **5 :** to strike (a golf ball) with the heel of the club ~ *vi* **1 :** to move the heels rhythmically (as in dancing) **2 :** to move along at the heels of someone; *specif, of a dog* **:** to keep to heel ⟨a dog that ~*s* well⟩ **3 :** to move along rapidly **:** RUN ⟨~*ed* out of there as quick as he could⟩ **4 :** to heel a ball (as in the game of rugby) **5 :** to work for a school newspaper or magazine esp. as a reporter

3**heel** \"\ *vb* -ED/-ING/-S [alter. (prob. influenced by 1*heel* and 2*heel*) of earlier *heeld, hield,* fr. ME *helden, heelden, hielden,* fr. OE *hieldan, heldan, hyldan;* akin to OE *heald* inclined, OHG *hald* inclined, *helden* to bow, ON *hallr* inclined, *hella* to pour out, Goth *hulths* inclination, favor, grace, Lith *šalis* side, region] *vi* **:** to tilt to one side **:** TIP, LEAN, CANT, LIST ⟨the sleigh was on one runner, ~*ing* like a yacht in a gale —Hamlin Garland⟩ — used esp. of a boat ⟨in such a strong wind the sailboat kept ~*ing* to the left⟩ and sometimes with *over* ⟨the subchaser ~*ed* over —C.F.Mitchell⟩ ~ *vt* **:** to cause (as a boat) to tilt **:** cause to list ⟨~*ing* the sloop well over and skimming her along to windward —K.M.Dodson⟩

4**heel** \"\ *n* -s **1 :** a tilt (as of a boat) to one side **:** LIST **2 :** the extent of a tilt (as of a boat) ⟨a ~ of six degrees to starboard⟩

**heelaman** *var of* HIELEMAN

1**heel-and-toe** \',='=\ *adj* **:** marked by the alternating use of the heel and toe ⟨a *heel-and-toe* dance routine⟩; *specif* **:** marked by the use of a stride in which the heel of one foot touches the ground before the toe of the other foot leaves it and in which the leg is straight and the knee locked as each foot touches or leaves the ground ⟨a *heel-and-toe* walking race⟩

2**heel-and-toe** \"\ *n* -s **:** a heel-and-toe stride or dance step

**heel-and-toe watch** *n* **:** a deck watch alternating with an equal period of rest

**heelball** \'=,=\ *n* **1 :** the underpart of the heel of the foot **2 :** a composition of wax and lampblack used by shoemakers for polishing and by antiquaries in copying inscriptions on stone

**heel block** *n* **1 :** a block or last to support a shoe which is being heeled or from which heel lifts are being driven out **2 :** a filler block at the heel end of a railroad frog between the frog rails that reinforces the frog and that also serves as a foot guard

**heel bone** *n* **:** CALCANEUS

**heel boom** *or* **heeling boom** *n* **:** a log-loading boom against which the end of a log being loaded bears and is steadied as it is lifted and swung into position

**heeld** *var of* HIELD

**heel·er** \'hēlə(r)\ *n* -s [2*heel* + *-er*] **1 :** one that heels **2 :** a worker that puts heels on shoes **3 :** a dog that heels animals **4 :** a local worker for a political boss — called also *ward heeler*

**heel fly** *n* **:** a warble fly that attacks cattle; *esp* **:** a common warble fly (*Hypoderma lineata*) of warm parts of America

**heel in** *vt* [2*heel*] **:** to cover temporarily (the roots of a plant or often of several plants in one hole) with soil before setting permanently

**heeling error** *n* [fr. pres. part of 3*heel*] **:** a deviation of a compass due to a ship's heeling which causes vertical magnetic forces to have a horizontal component and transverse horizontal magnetic forces to have a vertical component

**heel·less** \'hēlləs\ *adj* **:** having no heel

**heel-of-round** \'=='=\ *n* **:** HEEL 7i

**heel pad** *n* **:** a pad (as of leather) fixed over an insole to provide a comfortable support for the heel of the foot

**heelpath** \'=,=\ *n* [1*heel* + *path;* fr. its being contrasted to *towpath,* the homophones *tow* and *toe* being punningly equated] **:** BERM d

**heelpiece** \'=,=\ *n* **:** a piece designed for, situated at, or forming the heel of something; *specif* **:** a piece of leather or other material used in making or repairing the heel of a shoe

**heel plate** *n* **1 :** BUTT PLATE **2 :** a metal plate (as one designed to protect against wear) for the heel of a shoe

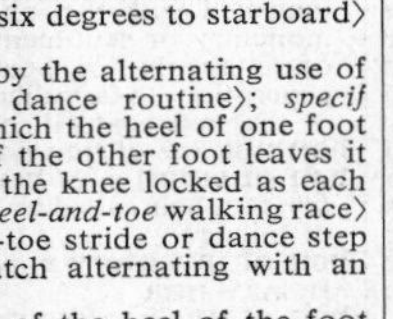

**heelpost** \'=,=\ *n* **1 :** a post to which a gate or door is hinged **2 :** the outer post of a stall partition in a stable

**heel rope** *n* **1 :** a rope fastened to the heel of a spar to control it **2 :** a rope used for hobbling a horse

**heels** *pl of* HEEL, *pres 3d sing of* HEEL

**heel seat** *n* **:** the part of a shoe to which the heel is attached

heel plates 2: *1* surface type, *2* insert type

**heels over head** *adv, archaic* **:** head over heels

**heel spur** *n* **:** the calcar of a bat's foot spreading the tail membrane

**heel stay** *n* **:** a piece of fabric or rough-surfaced leather cemented on the inside of the shoe at the back seam to prevent slipping at the heel

**heel string** *n, dial* **:** ACHILLES' TENDON

**heeltap** \'=,=\ *n* [1*heel* + *tap*] **1 :** a lift for the heel of a shoe **2 a (1) :** a small quantity of liquor remaining in a drinking glass **(2) :** a small quantity of liquor remaining in a bottle, cask, or other storage vessel **b :** DREGS **3 :** an imperfection in the glass bottom of a bottle marked by inequalities of thickness

**heeltree** \'=,=\ *n* [1*heel* + *tree*] **:** the whiffletree of a harrow

**heelwork** \'=,=\ *n* **:** dance technique emphasizing accents with the heels

**heem·raad** \'hām,räd, 'hēm-\ *n, pl* **heemra·den** \-dᵊn\ *often cap* [Afrik, fr. *heem* farm, village, home + *raad* council, councilman] **1 :** a council assisting a local Boer magistrate in the government of rural districts in So. Africa prior to the establishment of British administration **2 :** a member of a heemraad

**heer** \'hi(ə)r\ *n* -s [ME (Sc dial.) *heir, hair,* lit., hair — more at HAIR] **:** an old unit of yarn measure of about 600 yards or 1/24 of a spindle

**heerabol myrrh** *var of* HERABOL MYRRH

**heerd** *or* **heered** *or* **heern** *dial past of* HEAR

**heer·mann's gull** \'her,mänz-\ *also* **heermann gull** *n, usu cap H* [after A. L. *Heermann* †1865 Am. naturalist] **:** a white-headed bluish gray gull (*Larus heermanni*) of the Pacific coast of No. America

**heeze** \'hēz\ *vt* -ED/-ING/-S [alter. of earlier *heise* — more at HOISE] **1** *dial Brit* **:** HOIST **2** *dial Brit* **:** EXALT

**hef·ner candle** \'hefnə(r)-\ *n, usu cap H* [after Friedrich von *Hefner*-Alteneck †1904 Ger. electrical engineer] **:** a German standard unit of luminous intensity equal to about 0.92 of the candela

1**heft** \'heft\ *dial Brit var of* 3HAFT, 4HAFT

2**heft** \"\ *n* -s [fr. *heave,* after such pairs as E *weave: weft*] **1 :** WEIGHT, HEAVINESS ⟨his height and ~ varied a bit —A.J. Liebling⟩ ⟨plow horses of enormous ~ —Fannie Hurst⟩ **2** *archaic* **:** the greater part of something **:** BULK, MASS ⟨it's the ~ of their business —Mark Twain⟩

3**heft** \"\ *vb* -ED/-ING/-S *vt* **1 :** to heave up **:** HOIST, LIFT, RAISE ⟨~*ed* his pack higher on his broad shoulders —Norman Mailer⟩ **2 :** to test or ascertain the weight of by lifting or balancing ⟨picking the stone up and ~*ing* it —Emily Hahn⟩ ~ *vi* **:** to be heavy to a more or less clearly specified extent **:** WEIGH ⟨a box ~*ing* 15 pounds⟩ ⟨got an inch taller and ~*ed* heavier —C.T.Jackson⟩

**heft·er** \-tə(r)\ *n* -s **:** a worker who sorts and grades hides or leather

**heft·i·ly** \-təlē\ *adv* **:** in a hefty manner **:** STRONGLY, MIGHTILY ⟨~ attacked the suggestion⟩

**heft·i·ness** \-tēnəs\ *n* -ES **:** the quality or state of being hefty

**hefty** \-tē, -ti\ *adj, usu* -ER/-EST [2*heft* + *-y*] **1 :** having considerable weight **:** quite heavy ⟨a couple of big ~ books⟩ **2 a (1) :** large or bulky and usu. strong **:** BIG, RUGGED ⟨a ~ six-footer —*Time*⟩ ⟨a ~ fellow, in the habit of standing no nonsense from his customers —W.S.Maugham⟩ **(2) :** exhibiting considerable strength or force **:** POWERFUL, MIGHTY ⟨struck a ~ blow⟩ **b :** having a size or extent that is by no means small or negligible **:** not insignificant in size ⟨had a ~ hill to climb over⟩ or extent ⟨took a ~ hike⟩ **:** impressively large **:** good-sized ⟨a ~ majority —W.H.Whyte⟩ ⟨~ wage increases —*Time*⟩ ⟨paying up a pretty ~ sum for the settlement of certain debts —Claud Cockburn⟩ **:** IMPOSING ⟨tipped the scales at a ~ 224 pounds —Elizabeth Coatsworth⟩ **c :** quite rigorous or demanding by reason of size or extent ⟨received a ~ assignment that will take nearly all their time⟩ ⟨a ~ really tough job to do⟩ **3 :** generous in quantity **:** ABUNDANT, PLENTIFUL ⟨a ~ supply of ammunition —Clay Blair⟩ ⟨served up a ~ meal⟩ **syn** see HEAVY

**he·gari** \hə'garē, -'ger-, 'hegərē\ *n* -s [Ar (Sudan) *hegiri,* fr. Ar *hajari, hijāri* stony, stonelike] **:** any of several grain sorghums native to the Sudan region of Africa that resemble kafir and have chalky white seeds and of which one variety is grown in the southwestern U.S.

1**he·ge·li·an** \hā'gālēən, hə'-, hə'jēl-, -'gēl-\ *adj, usu cap* [Georg W.F.*Hegel* †1831 Ger. philosopher + E *-ian*] **:** of or relating to Hegel or his objective idealism or dialectic

2**hegelian** \"\ *n* -s *usu cap* **:** a follower of Hegel or adherent of Hegelianism

**he·ge·li·an·ism** \-ə,nizəm\ *n* -s *usu cap* **1 :** Hegel's objective idealism according to which the rational and the real are equatable so that reason can arrive through dialectic at a comprehension of an absolute idea of which all phenomena are held to be partial representations **2 :** a philosophical system marked by the acceptance of Hegel's objective idealism and the revision of his dialectic or by rejection of his objective idealism and acceptance of his dialectic

**he·ge·li·an·ize** \-,nīz\ *vt* -ED/-ING/-S *often cap* **:** to bring into conformity with Hegel's objective idealism or dialectic

**hegelian triad** *n, usu cap H* **:** the three dialectical stages of thesis, antithesis, and synthesis often held to be Hegel's characterization of the progress of history or of logical thought

**he·gel·ism** \'hāgə,lizəm\ *n* -s *usu cap* [G.W.F.*Hegel* + E *-ism*] **:** HEGELIANISM

**heg·e·mon** \'hejə,män, 'hēj-\ *n* -s [Gk *hēgemōn* guide, leader] **:** one (as a political state) possessing hegemony

**heg·e·mon·ic** \,==='mänik\ *also* **heg·e·mon·i·cal** \-nəkəl\ *adj* [Gk *hēgemonikos,* fr. *hēgemon-, hēgemōn* + *-ikos* -ic, -ical] **:** of, relating to, or exercising hegemony ⟨~ policies⟩ ⟨~ states⟩

**he·gem·o·nis·tic** \hə',jemə'nistik\ *adj* [*hegemony* + *-istic*] **:** HEGEMONIC

**he·gem·o·ny** \hə'jemənē, -ni *also* 'hejə,mōnē, -ni *sometimes* 'hegə,-\ *n* -ES [Gk *hēgemonia,* fr. *hēgemōn* guide, leader (fr. *hēgeisthai* to guide, lead) + *-ia* — more at SEEK] **1 :** preponderant influence or authority (as of a government or state) **:** LEADERSHIP, DOMINANCE ⟨aiming at world ~⟩ **2 :** a government or state possessing hegemony

**he·gi·ra** *also* **he·ji·ra** \hə'jīrə, 'hej(ə)rə\ *n* -s [fr. the *Hegira, Hejira,* the flight of Muhammad from Mecca in A.D. 622, fr. ML *hegira,* fr. Ar *hijrah,* lit., flight] **1** *usu cap* **:** the Muslim era **2 :** a journey or trip esp. when undertaken as a means of escaping from an undesirable or dangerous environment or as a means of arriving at a highly desirable destination ⟨the people wandered away on long ~*s* seeking new homesites near water —Frank Waters⟩; *specif* **:** a departure or flight made under such circumstances ⟨planning a ~ from the city to the cool peace of the mountains⟩ **3 :** EMIGRATION ⟨the ~ of many of the literati to Europe —C.I.Glicksberg⟩; *esp* **:** a mass exodus ⟨the ~ of farmers looking for new, cheap, fertile land —R.E.Riegel & G.D.Harmon⟩

**he·gu·men** \hə'gyümən\ *n* -s [LL *hegumenus,* fr. LGk *hēgoumenos,* fr. Gk *hēgoumenos* leader, president, fr. pres. part. of *hēgeisthai* to lead — more at SEEK] **:** the head of a religious community (as a small monastery) in the Eastern Church — used also as a title of honor for certain monks who are priests; compare ARCHIMANDRITE

1**heh** *like* EH\ *interj* [imit.] — used typically to indicate interrogation and often to express scorn, amusement, or surprise

2**heh** *var of* HE

**HEH** *abbr* Her Exalted Highness; His Exalted Highness

**he·he** \'hā(,)hā\ *n, pl* **hehe** *or* **hehes** *usu cap* **1 a :** a Bantu-speaking people of Tanganyika Territory **b :** a member of such people **2 :** a Bantu language of the Hehe people

**he-he** *or* **hee-hee** \'hē'hē\ *interj* [imit.] — used to express or as an imitation of derisive laughter or a senile or foolish giggle

**he-huckleberry** \'='==- — *see* BERRY\ *n* **1 :** an ironwood (*Cyrilla racemiflora*) of the southern U.S. **2 :** PRIVET ANDROMEDA

**HEI** *abbr* high explosive incendiary

**hei·au** \'hā,aù\ *n* -s [Hawaiian] **:** a pre-Christian Hawaiian temple or other place of worship (as a stone platform or an earthen terrace)

**heid** \'hēd\ *dial var of* HEAD

1**hei·deg·ge·ri·an** \,hī,de'girēən\ *adj, usu cap* [Martin *Heidegger* b1889 Ger. philosopher + E *-ian*] **:** of or relating to Heidegger or his existentialist philosophy

2**heideggerian** \"\ *n* -s *usu cap* **:** a follower of Heidegger or adherent of his existentialist philosophy

**hei·del·berg** \'hīdᵊl,bərg, -,bōg\ *adj, usu cap* [fr. *Heidelberg,* Germany] **:** of or from the city of Heidelberg, Germany **:** of the kind or style prevalent in Heidelberg

**heidelberg man** *or* **heidelberg race** *n, usu cap H* **:** an early Pleistocene man that is known from a massive chinless fossilized jaw with distinctly human dentition, that is the earliest hominoid generally assigned to the genus *Homo,* that is usu. placed in a distinct species (*H. heidelbergensis*), and that is considered to be closely related to Neanderthal man

**heif·er** \'hefə(r)\ *n* -s [ME *hayfare, hayfre, heyfre, heffre,* fr. OE *hēahfore,* perh. fr. *hēah* high + *-fore* (akin to OE *fearr* bull) — more at HIGH, PARE] **1 :** a young cow: **a :** one that is less than three years old and has freshened only once **b :** one that has never borne young or developed the proportions of a mature cow — used esp. in the meat trade **2 :** WOMAN; *esp* **:** a young woman

**heif·er·ette** \,hefə'ret\ *n* -s **:** a large heavy heifer having nearly the size and development of a mature cow

**heigh** \'hī, 'hā\ *interj* [origin unknown] — used to express cheeriness or exultation or to indicate interrogation or attract attention

**1heigh-ho** \ˈ=ˈ=\ *interj* [*heigh* + *ho*] — used typically to express boredom, weariness, or sadness and sometimes to serve as a cry of encouragement

**2heigh-ho** \ˈ=,=\ *n* -s : 3FLICKER

**1height** *also* **hight** \ˈhīt, *usu* -īd·+V *also* -ītth *sometimes* -īth\ *n* -s [ME *heighthe, heighte, heghte, heyeth*, fr. OE *hīehthu, hēhthu*; akin to OHG *hōhida* height, ON *hæth*, Goth *hauhitha*; derivatives fr. the root of E 1*high*] **1 a** : the highest part of something material ⟨finally reached the ~ of the mountain⟩ : uppermost section or area or region : top part : SUMMIT, APEX, PINNACLE ⟨plunged down from the ~ of the tower⟩ **b** : the highest point of something not material ⟨at the ~ of fame⟩ : most advanced point : ZENITH ⟨the ~ of culture⟩ : most extreme degree ⟨the ~ of stupidity⟩ : fullest possible degree ⟨at the ~ of success⟩ : CULMINATION ⟨the ~ of all their desires⟩ ⟨the ~ of passion⟩ : most active or intense part : CLIMAX ⟨the ~ of an argument⟩ ⟨at the very ~ of the storm⟩ **2 a** (1) : the distance extending from the bottom to the top of something standing upright ⟨measured the ~ of the building⟩ or from the bottom to an arbitrarily chosen upper point ⟨the tree has a ~ of five feet at its first branch⟩ (2) : the distance extending from the lowest point to the highest point of an animal body esp. of a human being in a natural standing position ⟨a man who is six feet in ~⟩ or from the lowest point to an arbitrarily chosen upper point ⟨a dog two feet in ~ at the shoulder⟩ : STATURE **b** (1) : the extent of elevation above a level ⟨the land reaches a ~ of 600 feet above sea level⟩ : distance extending upwards : ALTITUDE ⟨impossible to know the exact ~ reached by the rocket⟩ (2) : the degree of approximation of the tongue to the palate in pronouncing a vowel **3** : the quality of possessing sufficient or considerable or relatively great highness or stature or altitude ⟨a triumphal arch that would have been more impressive if it had had more ~⟩ **4 a** : an extent of land (as a hill, mountain, or plateau) rising to a considerable degree above the surrounding country : a lofty eminence **b** : a high place or point or position ⟨the ~s and depths of love⟩ **5 a** *obs* : an advanced degree of distinction (as in rank) : notable excellence : SUPERIORITY ⟨exceeded by the ~ of happier men —Shak.⟩ **b** (1) *obs* : HAUGHTINESS (2) *archaic* : loftiness of mind or spirit ⟨with something of the old Roman ~ about him —Charles Lamb⟩ **6** *obs* **a** : degree of geographical latitude **b** : position (as of a ship) off a coast

**2height** *also* **hight** \ˈhīt, ˈhikt\ *vt* -ED/-ING/-S *dial* : HEIGHTEN

**height·en** \ˈhītᵊn\ *vb* **heightened; heightened; heightening** \-t(ᵊ)niŋ\ **heightens** [1*height* + *-en*] *vt* **1 a** (1) : to increase the amount or degree or extent of : AUGMENT, AMPLIFY ⟨~*ing* his speed —Edith Sitwell⟩ ⟨conflict has ~*ed* citizens' awareness of what they want —Constance Green⟩ ⟨this only ~*s* our admiration —Edmund Wilson⟩ ⟨~*ed* their campaign against news censorship—*Americana Annual*⟩ (2) : to make (as a color, an emotional experience) brighter or more glowing or more intense : DEEPEN, INTENSIFY ⟨happiness ~*ed* the natural ruddiness of her cheeks⟩ (3) : to delineate more sharply : make more evident : bring out more strongly : point up : HIGHLIGHT ⟨shade ~*s* the brightness of light —Havelock Ellis⟩ ⟨the benevolent expression of his face was ~*ed* in later years by his white hair and beard —F.H.Dewey & E.S.Bates⟩ (4) : to make more acute : SHARPEN ⟨which had ~*ed* his appreciation of the more austere pleasures of the afternoon —Archibald Marshall⟩ (5) : to make more poignant ⟨their sorrow was ~*ed* by their forced absence from home⟩ (6) : to increase the impact of : STRENGTHEN ⟨rapid action ~*s* the effect of the drama⟩ **b** (1) : to give physical height to or increase the physical height of : raise high or higher : ELEVATE ⟨the building had been ~*ed* by the addition of a second story⟩ (2) : to raise above the ordinary or trite : make better by adding stature or distinction to ⟨how can we use this fact to ~ our civilization —C.A.Lindbergh b. 1902⟩ **2** *obs* : to cause to be elated or excited : EXALT ⟨being ~*ed* with this victory —James Ussher⟩ ~ *vi* **1** *archaic* : to become great or greater in physical height : GROW, RISE ⟨as we rode up the carriageway, the rock seemed to ~ marvelously —J.H. Newman⟩ **2 a** : to become great or greater in amount, degree, detail, or extent ⟨his youthful impatience ~*ed* —A.J.Cronin⟩ **b** : to become brighter (as of a color) or more glowing or more intense ⟨though the color had ~*ed* in his cheek, he did not flinch from his friend's gaze —James Joyce⟩ **syn** see INTENSIFY

**height finder** *n* : a device used to determine the height of an airborne object

**height gauge** *n* **1** : a gauge having a micrometer or a vernier scale for measuring heights **2** : a C-shaped metal device for measuring the foot-to-face height of printing type or mounted plates

**heighth** \ˈhī(t)th\ *chiefly dial var of* HEIGHT

**height measure** *n* : HYPSOMETER

**height of burst** : the vertical angle between the base of a target and the point of burst of artillery fire usu. as viewed from the firing point

**height of land** : 2DIVIDE 2a

**heights** *pl of* HEIGHT, *pres 3d sing of* HEIGHT

**height to paper** : the height of printing type measured from foot to face and standardized at 0.9186 inch in English-speaking countries — called also *type height*

**heil** \ˈhī(ə)l\ *vb* -ED/-ING/-S [G, interj., hail (used frequently by the Nazis in such phrases as *Heil Hitler!* Hail Hitler! and *Sieg heil!* Hail victory!), fr. MHG, fr. *heil*, adj., healthy, fr. OHG — more at WHOLE] : to salute with the German exclamation *heil*

**heilaman** *var of* HIELFMAN

**hei·li·gen·schein** \ˈhīləgən,shīn\ *n* -s [G, lit., halo, fr. *heiliger* saint (fr. *heilig* holy, fr. OHG *heilag*) + *schein* shine, light, fr. OHG *scīn*; akin to OHG *skīnan* to shine — more at HOLY, SHINE] : a bright light around the shadow of a person's head (as on a field or lawn) caused by diffraction and reflection of sunlight by dewdrops

**heils·ge·schich·te** \ˈhīlzgə,shiktə\ *n* -s *usu cap* [G, fr. *heil* salvation + *geschichte* history] : an interpretation of history emphasizing God's saving acts and viewing Jesus Christ as central in redemption

**heilt·suk** *or* **haelt·zuk** \ˈhā(ə)lt,sůk, -,zůk\ *n, pl* **heiltsuk** *or* **heiltsuks** *or* **haeltzuk** *or* **haeltzuks** *usu cap* **1** : a group of peoples including the Bellabella, China Hat, and Wikeno **2** : a member of the Heiltsuk group

**hei-mi·ao** \ˈhāmēˈau̇\ *n, pl* **hei-miao** *or* **hei-miaos** *usu cap H&M* [Chin (Pek) *hei*1 *miao*2, fr. *hei*1 black + *miao*2 sprouts, shoots, descendants] **1** : the principal division of the Miao peoples inhabiting the southeastern part of Kweichow province in southern China **2** : a member of the Hei-Miao

**hei·min** \ˈhāmən\ *n, pl* **heimin** [Jap, fr. *hei* common + *min* people] : the class of commoners consisting of peasants and laborers and traders in the Japanese social scale — compare KWAZOKU, SHIZOKU

**hei·nesque** \(ˈ)hī¦nesk\ *adj, usu cap* [Heinrich *Heine* †1856 Ger. poet and writer + E *-esque*] : of, relating to, or resembling the style of Heine

**1hei·nie** *also* **hei·ne** *or* **hei·ney** \ˈhīnē, -ni\ *n* -s [G *Heinrich* Henry (a common German name) + E *-ie*] : GERMAN; *esp* : a German soldier — usu. used disparagingly

**2heinie** \"\ *n* -s [alter. of 4*hinder*] *slang* : BUTTOCKS

**hei·nous** \ˈhānəs *sometimes* ˈhēn- *or* ˈhīn-\ *adj* [ME *heynous*, fr. MF *haineus* hateful, fr. *haine* hate (fr. *hair* to hate, of Gmc origin; akin to OS *haton* to hate) + *-eus* -ous — more at HATE] : hatefully or shockingly evil : grossly bad : enormously and flagrantly criminal : ABOMINABLE, EXECRABLE ⟨~ offenses⟩ ⟨a ~ act of treason⟩ ⟨a ~ accusation⟩ ⟨proposals of the most ~ nature —Elinor Wylie⟩ **syn** see OUTRAGEOUS

**hei·nous·ly** *adv* [ME *heynously*, fr. *heynous* + *-ly*] : in a heinous manner

**hei·nous·ness** *n* -ES : the quality or state of being heinous

**1heir** \ˈe(ə)r, ˈa(ə)l, |ə\ *n* -s [ME *eir, heir*, fr. OF, fr. L *hered-, heres*; akin to Gk *chēros* left, bereaved, OE *gān* to go — more at GO] **1 a** : one who inherits or is entitled to succeed to the possession of property after the death of its owner: as (1) : HEIR AT LAW (2) : HERES (3) : one who in modern civil codes based upon the civil law (as in Europe) succeeds to the entire estate of a person by operation of law or by testament and has a right of renunciation and usu. a right of entry with the benefit of inventory (4) *Scots law* : one taking heritable property by destination : one who succeeds only to movable estate (5) : one who receives some of the property of a deceased person by operation of law, by virtue of a will, or in any of various other ways **b** : one who receives or is entitled to receive property during the lifetime of a former owner ⟨made his friend ~ of the farm after deciding to live elsewhere⟩ **2** : one who inherits or is entitled to succeed to a hereditary rank, title, or office upon the death or removal from office by other cause (as abdication) of the holder ⟨~ to the principality of Monaco⟩ ⟨succession to the throne by the king's ~ following his abdication⟩ **3** : one to whom something other than property (as a position of leadership, participation in a tradition or culture, a natural talent, a quality of character) is transmitted or seems to be transmitted in accordance with or apart from the wish of a predecessor and with or without the necessity of direct succession ⟨looked upon himself as the logical ~ of the slain dictator⟩ ⟨was the ~ of the two chief traditions of scholarship in Europe —R.W.Southern⟩ ⟨~ of his father's virtues and vices⟩

**2heir** \"\ *vt* -ED/-ING/-S *now chiefly dial* : INHERIT

**heir apparency** *n, pl* **heir apparencies** : APPARENCY 3

**heir apparent** *n, pl* **heirs apparent** [ME] **1** : an heir whose right to an inheritance is indefeasible in law if he survives the legal ancestor ⟨became *heir apparent* to the throne when his grandfather . . . was killed —*Current Biog.*⟩ **2** : HEIR PRESUMPTIVE — not used technically **3** : one whose succession (as to a position or role) appears certain under existing circumstances ⟨*heir apparent* to Mr. Churchill as prime minister —*U.S. News & World Report*⟩ ⟨the Council of Europe, the parliamentary *heir apparent* of a federated Europe —J.R. Wike & A.Z.Rubinstein⟩

**heir at law** *n, pl* **heirs at law** **1** *Eng common law* : an heir in whom an intestate's real property as distinguished from his personal estate is vested by operation of law and not by will or by curtesy or by right of dower — called also *legal heir*; compare DEVISEE, LEGATEE **2** *usu* **heir-at-law** *Scots law* : an heir in whom by operation of the law of intestate succession the heritable estate and part or all of the movables of a decedent are vested — called also *heir of line, heir whatsoever, legal heir*

**heir·dom** \-rdəm\ *n* -s **1** *archaic* : HERITAGE **2** *archaic* : HEIRSHIP

**heir·ess** \ˈerəs, ˈar-\ *n* -ES : a female heir; *esp* : a female heir to great wealth

**heiress apparent** *n, pl* **heiresses apparent** **1** : a female heir apparent **2** : HEIRESS PRESUMPTIVE — not used technically

**heiress presumptive** *n, pl* **heiresses presumptive** : a female heir presumptive ⟨*heiress presumptive* to the British throne —*N.Y. Herald Tribune*⟩

**heir general** *n, pl* **heirs general** [ME *heire generall*] : HEIR AT LAW

**heir in tail** *n, pl* **heirs in tail** : one who expects to become or becomes a tenant in possession of a fee-tail estate in land upon the death of a tenant of the estate under special rules of common law or statute governing succession to such an estate as contrasted with the rules of inheritance under a statute of descent

**heir·less** \ˈ=ləs\ *adj* : having no heir

**heir·loom** \ˈ=,lüm\ *n* [ME *heirlome*, fr. *heir* + *lome* implement, tool — more at LOOM] **1** : a piece of property (as a deed or charter) that is viewed by law or special custom or will or settlement as an inseparable part of an inheritance and is so inherited with the inheritance **2** : something having special monetary or sentimental value or significance that is handed on either by or apart from formal inheritance from one generation to another ⟨the pin is a family ~⟩ ⟨a spiritual ~ that must, at all cost, be preserved intact —Edward Sapir⟩

**heirmos** *var of* HIRMOS

**heir of entail** *n, pl* **heirs of entail** **1** : HEIR IN TAIL **2** *Scots law* : an heir called to the succession by a destination : an heir of tailzie

**heir of inventory** *n, pl* **heirs of inventory** *Scots law* : BENEFICIARY HEIR

**heir of line** *n, pl* **heirs of line** *Scots law* : HEIR AT LAW 2

**heir of provision** *n, pl* **heirs of provision** *Scots law* : one who may or may not be an heir-at-law and who is called to succeed to property by the provisions of a deed or a contract or a bond : an heir by destination

**heir of the body** *n, pl* **heirs of the body** : a lineal heir esp. as contrasted with a collateral heir

**heir portioner** *n, pl* **heirs portioners** **1** *Scots law* : one of two or more female heirs coming in the absence of male issue into a succession to an estate and sharing equally according to degree of consanguinity, the share of any deceased female in the same degree going by representation to her heirs-at-law in the order of the eldest male, then other males, and finally the females **2** *Scots law* : one of two or more usu. female heirs in the same degree taking equal shares per capita

**heir presumptive** *n, pl* **heirs presumptive** **1** : an heir whose legal right to an inheritance may be defeated by the birth of a nearer relative ⟨*the heir presumptive* had been the king's brother —*Springfield (Mass.) Union*⟩ — compare HEIR APPARENT **2** : one whose succession (as to a position or role) appears likely but not certain ⟨*heir presumptive* at the foreign office —*New Statesman & Nation*⟩

**heirs** *pl of* HEIR, *pres 3d sing of* HEIR

**heir·ship** \ˈ=,ship\ *n* [ME *areschip*, fr. *are, eir* heir + *-schip, -ship* -ship] **1 a** : the condition of being an heir **b** : the right of inheritance **2** *archaic* : HERITAGE

**heir whatsoever** *n, pl* **heirs whatsoever** *Scots law* : HEIR AT LAW 2

**hei·sen·berg's principle** \ˈhīzᵊn,bərgz-\ *n, usu cap H* [after Werner K. *Heisenberg* b1901 Ger. physicist] : UNCERTAINTY PRINCIPLE

**1heist** \ˈhīst\ *vb* -ED/-ING/-S [alter. of 2*hoist*] *vt* **1** : *chiefly dial* : HOIST **2** *slang* : to appropriate unlawfully and usu. with violence : make off with : STEAL **3** *slang* : to commit armed robbery on : hold up; *specif* : to break into and rob ~ *vi, chiefly dial* : HOIST

**2heist** \"\ *n* -s **1** *slang* **a** : armed robbery : HOLDUP; *specif* : the act of breaking into and robbing an establishment (as a bank) **b** : THEFT **2** *slang* : something (as money, jewels) acquired by robbery or theft

**heist·er** \-tə(r)\ *n* -s **1** *chiefly dial* : one that hoists **2** *slang* : ROBBER, THIEF

**heit** \ˈhīt\ *var of* HAIT

**hei-ti·ki** \ˈhāˈtēkē\ *n, pl* **hei-tiki** *or* **hei-tikis** [Maori, fr. *hei* to hang + *Tiki*, the first man in Maori legend] : a greenstone charm in the shape of a human figure worn as a neck pendant by the Maoris

hei-tiki

**ˈhe·ja·zi** \ˈhejəzē\ *n* -s *cap* [Ar *hijāzīy*, fr. *Ḥijāz* Hejaz, kingdom of western Arabia] : a native or inhabitant of the Hejaz

**2hejazi** \"\ *adj, usu cap* **1** : of, relating to, or characteristic of the Hejaz **2** : of, relating to, or characteristic of the people of the Hejaz

**hejira** *var of* HEGIRA

**hektograph** *var of* HECTOGRAPH

**hel·arc·tos** \heˈlärktəs, -,täs\ *n, cap* [NL, irreg. fr. *heli-* + Gk *arktos* bear — more at ARCTIC] : a genus of mammals (family Ursidae)

**hel·beh** \ˈhelbə\ *n* -s [Ar *hulbah*] : fenugreek seed that is mixed with durra in a flour commonly used in Egypt

**held** *past of* HOLD

**held ball** *n* : TIE BALL

**hel·den·tenor** \ˈheldəntä¦nō(ə)r, -tä¦nō(ə)r, -¦tenər\ *n, pl* **helden·te·no·re** \-¸tä¦nōrə, -ˈnōrə\ *or* **heldentenors** [G, fr. *held* hero + *tenor*] : a tenor voice suited to heroic (as Wagnerian) roles : DRAMATIC TENOR

**hele** *var of* 2HEAL

**he·le·idae** \həˈlēə,dē\ [NL, fr. *Helea*, genus of flies (fr. Gk *heleia*, fem. of *heleios* of a marsh, marsh-dwelling, fr. *helos* marsh) + *-idae* — more at HELODES] *syn of* CERATOPOGONIDAE

**hel·e·na** \ˈhelənə\ *adj, usu cap* [fr. *Helena*, Mont.] : of or from Helena, the capital of Montana ⟨*Helena* businessmen⟩ : of the kind or style prevalent in Helena

**hel·e·nalin** \,heləˈnalən, -nāl-\ *n* -s [*helen-* (fr. NL *Helenium*, genus name of the sneezeweed *Helenium autumnale*) + *-al-* (fr. NL *autumnale*, specific epithet of the sneezeweed *Helenium autumnale*) + *-in*] : a poisonous bitter crystalline compound $C_{15}H_{18}O_4$ that is the active principle of sneezeweed

**hel·en flower** \ˈhelən-\ *also* **hel·en's flower** \-nz-\ *n, usu cap H* [NL *Helenium*] : a plant of the genus *Helenium*

**hele·nin** \ˈhelənən, həˈlēnən\ *n* -s [NL *Helenium* + E *-in*] **1** : alantolactone or a mixture from elecampane root containing it **2** : HELENALIN

**he·le·ni·um** \həˈlēnēəm\ *n* [NL, fr. L, a plant, elecampane, fr. Gk *helenion*, perh. fr. *helenē* wicker basket; akin to Gk *helix* (adj.) twisted, (n.) spiral, anything of spiral shape, *helissein* to turn, wind, *eilein* to roll, *eilyein* to enfold, enwrap — more at VOLUBLE] **1** *cap* : a genus of American herbs (family Compositae) with heads of yellow-rayed flowers and truncate-style branches — see SNEEZEWEED 1 **2** -s : any plant of the genus *Helenium*

**hel·e·och·a·ris** \,helēˈäkərəs\ [NL — more at ELEOCHARIS] *syn of* ELEOCHARIS

**hel·eo·plankton** \¦helē(,)ō+\ *n* [ISV *heleo-* (fr. Gk *heleos*, gen. of *helos* marsh) + *plankton* — more at HELODES] : plankton typical of small bodies of still fresh water

**hel·e·pole** \ˈhelə,pōl\ *also* **he·lep·o·lis** \həˈlepələs\ *n, pl* **helepoles** \ˈhelə,pōlz\ *also* **helepolises** \həˈlepələsəz\ [F & L; F *hélépole*, fr. L *helepolis*, fr. Gk *helepolis*, fr. *helein* to take + *polis* city — more at SELL, POLICE] : an ancient siege engine composed of a movable tower covering a battering ram

**helgramite** *or* **helgrammite** *var of* HELLGRAMMITE

**1heli-** *or* **helio-** *comb form* [L, fr. Gk *hēli-, hēlio-*, fr. *hēlios* — more at SOLAR] : sun ⟨*Heliornis*⟩ : the sun ⟨*heliocentric*⟩ ⟨*helioscope*⟩ : sunlight : solar energy ⟨*heliogravure*⟩ : sun and ⟨*heliolithic*⟩

**2heli-** *comb form* [by shortening] : helicopter ⟨*heliport*⟩ ⟨*helimail*⟩

**he·li·a·cal** \həˈlīəkəl, hē-,he-\ *adj* [LL *heliacos, heliacus* (fr. Gk *hēliakos*, fr. *hēlios* sun) + E *-al*] : relating to or near the sun — used esp. of the last setting of a star before and its first rising after invisibility due to conjunction with the sun — **he·li·a·cal·ly** \-ək(ə)lē\ *adv*

**heliacal cycle** *n* : SOLAR CYCLE

**heliacal year** *n* : a Sothic year

**he·li·am·pho·ra** \,hēlēˈam(p)fərə\ *n, cap* [NL, fr. *heli-* (fr. Gk *helissein* to roll, wind) + L *amphora*] : a genus of So. American pitcher plants (family Sarraceniaceae) native to the mountains of British Guiana and having scapes of nodding pink or white flowers

**he·li·an·tha·ceous** \¦hēlē,an¦thāshəs\ *adj* [NL *Helianthus* + E *-aceous*] : resembling, belonging to, or related to the genus *Helianthus*

**he·li·an·thate** \,hēlēˈan,thāt\ *n* -s [*helianth*in + *-ate*] : a salt of helianthin ⟨the ~ of streptomycin⟩

**he·li·an·the·mum** \,hēlēˈan(t)thəməm\ *n* [NL, fr. 1*heli-* + *-anthemum*] **1** *cap* : a genus of Eurasian herbs or undershrubs (family Cistaceae) having showy variously colored flowers with fugacious petals **2** -s : any plant of the genus *Helianthemum* — called also *rockrose, sunrose*

**he·li·an·thin** \,hēlēˈan(t)thən\ *also* **he·li·an·thine** \", -an-,thēn\ *n* -s [ISV *helianth-* (fr. NL *Helianthus*; fr. its color) + *-in, -ine*] **1** : a red compound $(CH_3)_2N^+{=}C_6H_4{=}NNH{-}C_6H_4SO_3^-$ of quinone structure obtained by acidifying methyl orange **2** : METHYL ORANGE

**he·li·an·thus** \-an(t)thəs\ *n* [NL, fr. 1*heli-* + *-anthus*] **1** *cap* : a genus of tall erect or sometimes much-branched American annual or perennial herbs (family Compositae) comprising the sunflowers and having flower heads with purple or yellow disk flowers and showy yellow sterile rays — see JERUSALEM ARTICHOKE **2** -ES : any plant of the genus *Helianthus*

**he·li·ast** \ˈhēlē,ast\ *n* -s [Gk *hēliastēs* member of the Heliaea, fr. *hēliazesthai* to be a member of the Heliaea, fr. *Hēliaia* Heliaea, supreme court at Athens, public place in which the court was held] : DICAST — **he·li·as·tic** \¦hēlē¦astik\ *adj*

**he·li·az·o·phyte** \,hēlēˈazə,fīt\ *n* -s [Gk *hēliazein* to bask in the sun (fr. *hēlios* sun) + E *-o-* + *-phyte* — more at SOLAR] : HELIOPHYTE

**helic-** *or* **helico-** *comb form* [Gk *helik-, heliko-*, fr. *helik-, helix* spiral — more at HELENIUM] : helix : spiral ⟨*helicine*⟩ ⟨*helicograph*⟩

**1heli·cal** \ˈheləkəl, -lēk- *also* ˈhēl-\ *adj* [*helic-* + *-al*] **1** : of, relating to, or having the form of a helix; *broadly* : SPIRAL 1a ⟨the ~ thread of a bolt⟩ ⟨metal tubing with annular or ~ fins⟩ **2** : having the angle of a helix formed about the pitch cylinder rather than being straight and parallel to the axis (as of a gear or milling cutter) ⟨~ teeth⟩ ⟨gears cut in a ~ rather than a spur shape for smoother operation⟩

**2helical** \"\ *n* -s : something helical in form (as a coil extension spring)

**helical gear** *also* **helical** *n* -s : a gear wheel having teeth set obliquely to the axis of rotation : SCREW WHEEL

**heli·cal·ly** \-k(ə)lē, -li\ *adv* **1** : in a helical manner ⟨thread is wound ~ on the spool⟩ ⟨~ cut gear wheels⟩ **2** : by use of a helical ⟨an iron cot with a link spring ~ attached to the angle-steel frame⟩

**helical milling** *n* : milling in which the work (as a helical gear) is given simultaneously a rotary motion and an endways motion — called also *spiral milling*

helical gears

**heliced** \ˈhelǝst, ˈhel-\ *adj* **1** : decorated with or having helices **2** : having the form of a low conical spiral (as the shell of a snail of the genus *Helix*)

**heli·cel·la** \,heləˈselə, -hēl-\ *n, cap* [NL, fr. *helic-* + *-ella*] : a genus of land snails (family Helicidae) including several snails of veterinary importance as intermediate hosts of flukes and of some nematode lungworms of sheep and other ruminants

**helices** *pl of* HELIX

**hel·i·chryse** \ˈhelə,krīs\ *n* -s [NL *Helichrysum*] : HELICHRYSUM 2

**hel·i·chry·sum** \,heləˈkrīsəm\ *n* [NL, fr. Gk *helichrysos*, fr. *helik-* helic- + *chrysos* gold — more at CHRYSALIS] **1** *cap* : a large genus of mostly African and Australian plants (family Compositae) with flower heads having shining involucres which retain their color when dried — see STRAWFLOWER **2** -s : any plant of the genus *Helichrysum*

**he·lic·i·dae** \həˈlisə,dē\ *n pl, cap* [NL, fr. *Helic-, Helix*, type genus + *-idae*] : a family of pulmonate land snails (suborder Stylommatophora) including the common edible snail and a number of pests — see 2HELIX

**he·lic·i·form** \-sə,fȯrm\ *adj* [ISV *helic-* + *-iform*] : SPIRAL

**hel·i·ci·na** \,heləˈsīnə\ *n* [NL, fr. *helic-* + *-ina*] **1** *cap* : a genus of operculate land snails (suborder Rhipidoglossa) that occur chiefly in warm regions and are distinguished by a short-spired shell, a single auricle, and a pulmonary chamber replacing the gill **2** -s : any mollusk shell of the genus *Helicina*

**heli·cit·ic** \¦heləˈsid·ik, ¦hel-\ *adj* [*helic-* + *-itic*] *of metamorphic rock* : marked by bands of inclusions showing the original bedding or schistosity of the rock and in many places cutting through the later formation

**hel·i·cline** \ˈhelə,klīn\ *n* -s [*heli-* (fr. Gk *helix* spiral) + *-cline*] : a gradually ascending and curving ramp

**helico-** — see HELIC-

**1hel·i·coid** \ˈhelə,kȯid\ *or* **hel·i·coi·dal** \¦heləˈkȯidᵊl\ *adj* [*helicoid* fr. Gk *helikoeidēs* of spiral form, fr. *helik-* helic- + *-oeidēs* -oid; *helicoidal* fr. *helicoid* + *-al*] **1** : having the properties of a helicoid **2** : forming or arranged in a spiral ⟨~ inflorescence⟩; *specif, of a gastropod shell* : having the form of a flat coil or flattened spiral ⟨*Planorbis* is characterized by a ~ shell⟩

**2helicoid** \"\ *n* -s : a surface resembling that of a screw thread that is generated by a curve which rotates about a straight line and moves in the direction of the line with a velocity whose ratio to the velocity of rotation is constant

**helicoidal saw** *n* : a stonecutter's saw consisting of an endless cable made of three steel wires twisted together, supplied with sand and water, and drawn along marble or other stone to cut it — called also *wire saw*

**helicoid cyme** *n* : BOSTRYX

**hel·i·con** \'helə,kän, -ləkən\ *n* -s [prob. fr. Gk *helik-*, *helix* spiral + E *-on* (as in *bombardon*)] **:** a very large bass tuba used in military bands that is made circular for carrying over the shoulder and around the body when marching

helicon

**hel·i·co·nia** \,helə'kōnēə, -nyə\ *n* [NL, fr. L, fem. of *Heliconius* of Helicon, fr. Gk *Helikōnios*, fr. *Helikōn* Helicon, mountain in Greece] **1** *cap* **:** a genus of tropical American perennial herbs (family Musaceae) that have inconspicuous flowers in terminal spikes often subtended by brightly colored bracts and large leaves often showily veined or mottled with red or yellow — see WILD PLANTAIN **2** -s **:** any plant of the genus *Heliconia*

**¹hel·i·co·nian** \,helə'kōnēən, -nyən\ *adj, usu cap* [L *Heliconius* + E *-an*] **:** of or relating to the Boeotian mountain Helicon supposed by the ancient Greeks to be the residence of Apollo and the Muses

**²heliconian** \"\ *n* -s [NL *Heliconius* + E *-an*] **:** a butterfly of *Heliconius* or a related genus

**hel·i·co·ni·idae** \,helәkə'nīə,dē\ *n pl, cap* [NL, fr. *Heliconius*, type genus + *-idae*] *in some classifications* **:** a family of chiefly tropical American butterflies with long fore wings and small rounded hind wings that is commonly included in the family Nymphalidae

**hel·i·co·ni·us** \,helə'kōnēəs\ *n* [NL, fr. L, of Helicon] **1** *cap* **:** a large Neotropical genus of long-winged butterflies that are often brilliantly colored or mimetic and that with related American butterflies constitute a subfamily of Nymphalidae or in some classifications the separate family Heliconiidae **2** *pl* **helico·nii** \-ē,ī\ **:** any butterfly of the genus *Heliconius*

**¹heli·cop·ter** \'helə,käptə(r), -lē,k- *also* 'hēl- *or sometimes substand* 'hēlə,k- *or* 'helyə,k- *sometimes* ,==(=)'==\ *n* -s *often attrib* [F *hélicoptère*, fr. *hélico-* (fr. Gk *heliko-* helic-) + *ptère* (fr. Gk *pteron* wing) — more at FEATHER] **:** an aircraft whose support in the air is derived chiefly from the aerodynamic forces acting on one or more rotors turning about substantially vertical axes

**²helicopter** \"\ *or* **heli·copt** \-pt\ *vb* -ED/-ING/-S *vi* **:** to travel by or as if by helicopter ⟨can ~ from the station to the airfield⟩ ⟨winged seeds that . . . come ~*ing* down —Richard Church⟩ ~ *vt* **:** to transport by helicopter ⟨~*ed* the officials aboard the ship⟩

**hel·i·co·ru·bin** \,helәkō'rübən\ *n* -s [*helico-* (fr. NL *Helic-*, *Helix*, genus name of *Helix pomatia*) + L *ruber* red + E *-in*] **:** a hemoprotein occurring in the intestine and hepatopancreas of pulmonate gastropods and in the hepatopancreas of the crayfish

**hel·i·co·trema** \-kō'trēmə\ *n* -s [NL, fr. *helic-* + *-trema*] **:** the minute opening by which the two scalae communicate at the top of the cochlea of the ear

**helic·te·res** \,helәk'tirēz, hә'liktә,r-\ *n, cap* [NL, fr. Gk *heliktēres*, pl. of *heliktēr* anything twisted, fr. *helik-*, *helix* spiral — more at HELENIUM] **:** a large genus of tropical trees and shrubs (family Sterculiaceae) with axillary flowers and fruits consisting of five twisted carpels — see SCREW TREE

**he·lic·tis** \hә'liktәs\ *n, cap* [NL, fr. *hel-* (prob. fr. Gk *helos* marsh) + Gk *iktis* yellow-breasted marten] **:** a genus of mammals (family Mustelidae) comprising the ferret-badgers

**he·lic·tite** \hә'lik,tīt, 'helәk-\ *n* -s [*helict-* (fr. Gk *heliktos* twisted, rolled, fr. *helik-*, *helix* spiral) + *-ite*] **:** an irregular stalactite with branching convolutions or spines

**hel·i·go·land trap** \'helәgō,land-\ *n, usu cap H* [fr. *Heligoland* (Helgoland), island in the North sea; fr. its original use there] **:** a large funnel-shaped structure of wire mesh opening into a smaller enclosure used for trapping birds (as for banding)

**heling** *pres part of* HELE

**¹he·lio** \'hēlē,ō\ *n* -s [by shortening] **:** HELIOGRAPH

**²helio** \"\ *n* -s [by shortening] **:** HELIOTROPE

**helio-** — see HELI-

**he·lio·centric** \,hēlēō+\ *adj* [¹*heli-* + *-centric*] **:** referred to or measured from the sun's center or appearing as if seen from it **:** having or relating to the sun as the center (as of the planetary system) ⟨the ~ theory of Copernicus⟩ — compare GEOCENTRIC

**heliocentric latitude** *n* **:** the celestial latitude of a celestial body as if seen from the center of the sun

**heliocentric longitude** *n* **:** the celestial longitude of a celestial body as if seen from the center of the sun — opposed to *geocentric longitude*

**heliocentric parallax** *n* **:** the parallax of a celestial body measured with the earth's orbit around the sun as a baseline **:** the angle subtended at the celestial body by the radius of the earth's orbit — called also *annual parallax*, *stellar parallax*

**he·lio·chrome** \'hēlēə,krōm\ *n* -s [¹*heli-* + *-chrome*] **:** a photograph in natural colors made orig. by use of a photohalide form of silver chloride

**he·lio·chromy** \-mē\ *n* -ES [F *héliochromie*, fr. *hélio-* ¹heli- + *-chromie* -chromy] **:** COLOR PHOTOGRAPHY

**he·li·o·don** \'hēlēə,dän\ *n* -s [NL, fr. ¹*heli-* + *-odon* (fr. Gk *hodos* way, path) — more at CEDE] **:** a device consisting of a pivoted platform and a spotlight on a vertical track used to simulate sun and shadow orientation for any latitude and day of year for a proposed building

**he·li·o·dor** \'hēlēə,dò(ə)r\ *n* -s [G] **:** a golden-yellow beryl found in southern Africa

**he·lio·gram** \-,gram\ *n* [¹*heli-* + *-gram*] **:** a message transmitted by a heliograph

**¹he·lio·graph** \-raf, -räf\ *n* [ISV ¹*heli-* + *-graph*] **1 a :** PHOTOENGRAVING 2b **b :** PHOTOGRAPH **c :** PHOTOHELIOGRAPH **2 :** an apparatus for telegraphing by means of the sun's rays thrown from a mirror — compare HELIOTROPE 3

**²heliograph** \"\ *vb* **:** to signal by means of a heliograph

**he·lio·graph·ic** \,hēlēə'grafik\ *adj* **1** [F *héliographique*, fr. *hélio-* ¹heli- + *-graphique* -graphic] **:** of, relating to, or by means of heliography or a heliograph ⟨~ communication⟩ **2** [¹*heli-* + *-graphic*] **:** SOLAR 1 ⟨~ latitude⟩

**he·li·og·ra·phy** \,hēlē'ägrəfē\ *n* -ES **1** [F *héliographie*, fr. *hélio-* ¹heli- + *-graphie* -graphy] **:** an early photographic process producing a photoengraving on a metal plate coated with an asphalt preparation; *broadly* **:** PHOTOGRAPHY **2** [¹*heli-* + *-graphy*] **:** the system, art, or practice of signaling with a heliograph

**he·lio·gra·vure** \,hēlēōgrə'vyů(ə)r\ *n* [F *héliogravure*, fr. *hélio-* ¹heli- + *gravure*] **:** PHOTOGRAVURE

**he·li·ol·a·try** \,hēlē'älə·trē\ *n* -ES [¹*heli-* + *-latry*] **:** sun worship

**¹he·li·o·lite** \'hēlēə,līt\ *n* -s [NL *Heliolites*, genus of corals, fr. ¹*heli-* + *-lites* (prob. fr. F *-lithe* -lite)] **:** a fossil coral of the family Heliolitidae

**²heliolite** \"\ *n* -s [F *héliolite*, fr. *hélio-* ¹heli- + *-lite*] **:** aventurine feldspar

**he·li·o·lith·ic** \,hēlēə'lithik\ *adj* [¹*heli-* + *-lithic*] **1 :** marked by, observing, or associated with practices (as sun worship and the erection of megaliths) held by some diffusionists to constitute a single widespread neolithic culture originating in Egypt ⟨~ culture⟩ ⟨~ peoples⟩ ⟨~ monuments⟩ **2 :** postulating an Egyptian origin for heliolithic traits found as the basis of higher culture in many parts of the world ⟨the ~ theory⟩

**he·li·o·lit·i·dae** \,hēlēō'lidə,dē\ *n pl, cap* [NL, fr. *Heliolites*, type genus + *-idae*] **:** a family of Paleozoic tabulate corals prob. related to the Helioporidae but having 12 radial septa in the large zooecia

**he·li·om·e·ter** \,hēlē'ämәd·ә(r)\ *n* [F *héliomètre*, fr. *hélio-* ¹heli- + *-mètre* -meter] **:** a visual telescope that has a divided objective with two movable parts which give a double image and that was orig. designed for measuring the apparent diameter of the sun and later used for measuring angles between stars but is now largely replaced by photographic methods

**he·lio·met·ric** \,hēlēō'me·trik\ *adj* [F *héliométrique*, fr. *hélio-* ¹heli- + *-métrique* -metric] **:** of, employing, or obtained by use of a heliometer ⟨~ observations⟩ ⟨~ results⟩ — **he·lio·met·ri·cal·ly** \-rək(ə)lē\ *adv*

**he·li·om·e·try** \,hēlē'ämə·trē\ *n* -ES **:** the art or practice of measuring with the heliometer

**he·lio·micrometer** \,hēlē(,)ō+\ *n* [¹*heli-* + *micrometer*] **:** an instrument for determining heliographic positions of spots and flocculi shown on direct photographs of the sun or on spectroheliograph plates

**he·li·oph·i·la** \,hēlē'äfələ\ *n, cap* [NL, fr. ¹*heli* + *-phila*] **:** a genus of southern African annual or partly woody perennial herbs (family Cruciferae) sometimes cultivated for their long showy racemes of bright blue flowers with white eyes

**he·lio·phile** \'hēlēə,fīl\ *n* -s [¹*heli-* + *-phile*] **:** one attracted or adapted to sunlight ⟨~*s* flocking to the beach⟩; *specif* **:** an aquatic alga adapted to attain maximum exposure to sunlight

**he·li·oph·i·lous** \,hēlē'äfələs\ *also* **he·lio·phil·ic** \,hēlēə'filik\ *adj* [¹*heli-* + *-philous* or *-philic*] **:** attracted by or adapted to sunlight

**he·lio·phobe** \'hēlēə,fōb\ *n* -s [¹*heli-* + *-phobe*] **:** one that is abnormally sensitive to the effect of sunlight

**he·li·oph·o·bous** \,hēlē'äfəbəs\ *also* **he·lio·pho·bic** \,hēlēə'fōbik *also* -fäb-\ *adj* [¹*heli-* + *-phobous* or *-phobic*] **:** avoiding the sun **:** shade loving ⟨~ plants⟩

**he·li·o·phyl·lite** \,hēlēō'fi,līt\ *n* -s [Sw *heliophyllit*, fr. ¹*heli-* + *-phyll* + *-it* -ite] **:** a mineral approximately $Pb_6As_2O_7Cl_4$ consisting of oxychloride of lead and arsenic that is apparently dimorphous with ecdemite

**he·li·o·phyte** \'hēlēə,fīt\ *n* -s [¹*heli-* + *-phyte*] **:** a plant thriving in or tolerating full sunlight

**¹he·li·o·pol·i·tan** \,hēlēə'pälət°n\ *adj, usu cap* [LL *Heliopolitanus*, fr. L *Heliopolites* Heliopolitan (fr. Gk *Hēliopolitēs*, fr. *Hēliopolis* Heliopolis, ancient city in Lower Egypt) + *-anus* -an] **:** of or relating to ancient Heliopolis, esp. Heliopolis, Egypt

**²heliopolitan** \"\ *n* -s *cap* [L *Heliopolitanus*, fr. *Heliopolites* + *-anus* -an] **:** a native or inhabitant of the ancient city of Heliopolis

**he·li·o·por·i·dae** \,hēlēə'pòrə,dē\ *n pl, cap* [NL, fr. *Heliopora*, type genus (fr. ¹*heli-* + *-pora*) + *-idae*] **:** a family of tabulate corals (order Coenothecalia) comprising the blue coral and extinct related forms and having the corallum composed of large zooecia interspersed with more numerous smaller tubes occupied by simple polyps without tentacles or reproductive organs

**he·li·op·sis** \,hēlē'äpsəs\ *n, cap* [NL, fr. ¹*heli-* + *-opsis*] **:** a small genus of American herbs (family Compositae) resembling a sunflower with fertile ray flowers and a conical receptacle

**he·li·or·nis** \-'òrnəs\ *n, cap* [NL, fr. *heli-* + *-ornis*] **:** the type genus of Heliornithidae including a single tropical American sun-grebe (*H. fulica*)

**he·li·or·nith·i·dae** \-,òr'nithə,dē\ *n pl, cap* [NL, fr. *Heliornith-*, *Heliornis*, type genus + *-idae*] **:** a family of tropical aquatic birds (order Gruiformes) comprising the sun-grebes and having a head and bill like those of a rail, a long body and tail, short legs, and lobed feet

**¹helios** *pl of* HELIO

**²he·li·os** \'hēlē,äs, -ēəs\ *n* -ES [NL, fr. Gk *hēlios* sun — more at SOLAR] **:** LUMINANCE 2

**he·li·o·sis** \,hēlē'ōsəs\ *n, pl* **helio·ses** \-ō,sēz\ [NL, fr. LL, exposure to the sun, fr. Gk *hēliōsis*, fr. *hēliousthai* to be exposed to the sun, be sunburned (fr. *hēlios* sun) + *-sis*] **:** SUNSTROKE

**he·li·o·stat** \'hēlēə,stat\ *n* -s [NL *heliostata*, fr. ¹*heli-* + *-stata* (fr. Gk *-statēs* -stat)] **1 :** an instrument consisting of a mirror mounted on an axis moved by clockwork by which a sunbeam is steadily reflected in one direction — compare COELOSTAT **2 :** a geodetic heliotrope — **he·li·o·stat·ic** \,hēlēə'stad·ik\ *adj*

**he·lio·tactic** \,hēlēō'taktik\ *adj* [¹*heli-* + *-tactic*] **:** of or relating to heliotaxis

**he·lio·tax·is** \,hēlēō'taksəs\ *n* [NL, fr. ¹*heli-* + *-taxis*] **:** phototaxis in which sunlight is the stimulus

**he·lio·therapy** \'hēlēō+,-\ *n* [¹*heli-* + *therapy*] **:** the use of sunlight or of an artificial source of ultraviolet, visible, or infrared radiation for therapeutic purposes

**he·li·o·this** \,hēlē'ōthəs\ *n, cap* [NL, irreg. fr. Gk *hēliōtis* (n.) dawn, (adj.) of the sun, fr. *hēlios* sun] **:** a genus of medium-sized noctuid moths including several forms having larvae that are destructive pests of cultivated crops — see CORN EARWORM

**heliothis moth** *n, Austral* **:** CORN EARWORM

**he·lio·trope** \'hēlēə,trōp, -lyə-, *Brit usu* 'hel-\ *n* -s [L *heliotropium*, fr. Gk *hēliotropion*, fr. *hēlios* sun + *-tropion* (fr. *tropos* turn) — more at SOLAR, TROPE] **1 a** *obs* **:** a plant of which the flower or stem turns toward the sun **b** [NL *Heliotropium*] **:** a plant of the genus *Heliotropium*; *esp* **:** GARDEN HELIOTROPE 2 **c :** GARDEN HELIOTROPE 1 **2 :** BLOODSTONE 1 **3 :** an instrument used in geodetic surveying for making long-distance observations by means of the sun's rays thrown from a mirror **4 a :** a variable color averaging a moderate purple that is bluer, lighter, and stronger than cobalt violet, manganese violet, or average amethyst, bluer and deeper than average lilac (sense 3a), and redder, stronger, and slightly lighter than mignon **b :** a moderate reddish purple that is redder and duller than bishop's violet **c :** any of various dyes imparting this color **5 :** a perfume imitating the scent of the garden heliotrope (sense 1)

heliotrope

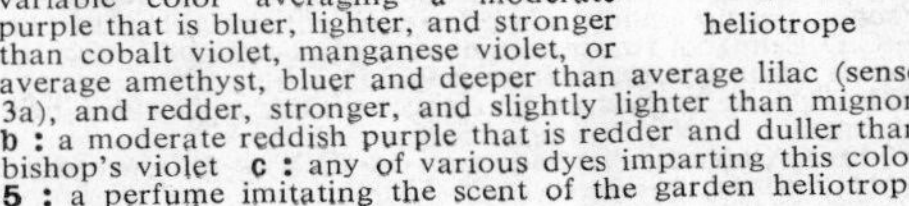

**heliotrope gray** *n* **:** a pale purple to purplish gray that is redder than plumbago gray

**heliotropian** *n* -s [modif. of Gk *hēliotropion*] *obs* **:** HELIOTROPE

**he·lio·tropic** \,=(=)='trōpik, -räp-\ *adj* [ISV ¹*heli-* + *-tropic*] **:** characterized by heliotropism ⟨spiders are negatively ~⟩ — **he·lio·tropi·cal·ly** \-pək(ə)lē\ *adv*

**he·lio·tro·pin** \,hēlēə·trōpən, ,hēlē'ä·trəp-\ *n* -s [ISV *heliotrop-* (fr. NL *Heliotropium*) + *-in*] **:** PIPERONAL

**he·lio·tro·pism** \,hēlē'ä·trə,pizəm, 'hēlēə·,trō,p-\ *n* [ISV ¹*heli-* + *-tropism*] **:** phototropism in which sunlight is the orienting stimulus (as in sunflower heads turning with the sun) — compare APHELIOTROPISM

**he·li·o·tro·pi·um** \,hēlēə'trōpēəm\ *n, cap* [NL, fr. Gk *hēliotropion* heliotrope — more at HELIOTROPE] **:** a genus of herbs and shrubs (family Boraginaceae) having small white or purple fragrant salver-shaped flowers in spikes — see HELIOTROPE 1b

**he·lio·type** \'hēlēə,tīp\ *n* [¹*heli-* + *type*] **:** COLLOTYPE

**he·lio·typography** \,hēlē(,)ō+\ *or* **he·lio·typy** \'hēlēə,tīpē\ *n* -ES [*heliotypography* fr. ¹*heli-* + *typography*; *heliotypy* ISV ¹*heli-* + *-typy*] **:** the collotype process

**he·lio·zoa** \,hēlēə'zōə\ *n pl, cap* [NL, fr. ¹*heli-* + *-zoa*] **:** an order of Actinopoda consisting of free-living holozoic usu. freshwater protozoans that reproduce by binary fission or budding and comprise the sun animalcules — see ACTINOPHRYS, ACTINOPODA, ACTINOSPHAERIUM — **he·lio·zo·an** \,hēlēə'zōən\ *adj or n* — **he·lio·zo·ic** \-ōik\ *adj*

**heli·port** \'helə *also* 'hēlə+,-\ *n, often attrib* [²*heli-* + *port*] **:** a landing and takeoff place for a helicopter (as on the roof of a building in the central area of a city)

**he·lip·ter·um** \hə'liptərəm\ *n, cap* [NL, fr. ¹*heli-* + Gk *pteron* wing — more at FEATHER] **:** a genus of African and Australian herbs (family Compositae) having a plumose pappus and densely silky hairy achenes and grown as an everlasting

**heli·so·ma** \,helə'sōmə, ,hel-\ *n, cap* [NL, fr. *heli-* (prob. fr. Gk *helix* spiral) + *-soma* — more at HELENIUM] **:** a genus of freshwater snails (family Planorbidae) including intermediate hosts of echinostomes and possibly other flukes of medical or veterinary importance

**he·li·um** \'hēlēəm\ *n* -s *often attrib* [NL, fr. Gk *hēlios* sun + NL *-ium* — more at SOLAR] **:** a very light colorless inert gaseous element that is the most difficult of all gases to liquefy, that occurs throughout the universe but in economically extractable amounts only in certain natural gases (as in the Texas panhandle and Kansas), and that is used chiefly in inflating airships and balloons, in arc welding and other metallurgical and chemical processes as an inert gaseous shield, and in diluting oxygen for breathing (as by patients with respiratory ailments and by divers) — symbol *He*; see ALPHA PARTICLE; ELEMENT table

**helium group** *n* **:** the group of elements forming group zero of the periodic table **:** the group of inert gases

**helium I** \,===,wən\ *n* **:** normal liquid helium boiling at 4.2°K under a pressure of 1 atmosphere and capable of existing between the critical point of 5.2°K and 2.26 atmosphere and the lambda point of 2.19°K

**helium II** \,===,tü\ *n* **:** superfluid helium formed from helium I by cooling below the lambda point and characterized by a very low viscosity and very high thermal conductivity

**¹helix** \'hēliks, 'hel-\ *n, pl* **heli·ces** \'helə,sēz, 'hēl-\ *also* **helix·es** \'hēliksəz, 'hel-\ [L, fr. Gk — more at HELENIUM] **1 :** something spiral in form: as **a :** an ornamental volute (as in an Ionic or Corinthian capital) **b :** a coil formed by winding wire around a uniform tube **2 :** the incurved rim of the external ear **3 :** a curve traced on a cylinder by the rotation of a point crossing its right sections at a constant oblique angle **:** a space curve with turns of constant slope from the base and constant distance from the axis **:** the curve described by the thread of a bolt or by a tubular coil spring; *broadly* **:** a three-dimensional curve with one or more turns around an axis (as the space curve described by a conical coil spring)

**²helix** \"\ *n, cap* [NL, fr. L, something spiral in form, volute] **:** a genus (the type of the family Helicidae) of orig. chiefly Eurasian and African pulmonate land snails having a coiled shell with a low conical spire and a wide reflexed lip and including the chief edible snails (as *H. pomatia*) as well as a number of pests of cultivated plants (as the brown snail)

**helix angle** *n* **:** the constant angle between the tangent to a helix and a generator of the cylinder upon which the helix lies

**helix·in** \'hēliksən, 'hel-\ *n* -s [NL *helix* (specific epithet of *Hedera helix*) (fr. L *helix* ivy, volute) + E *-in*] **:** HEDERIN

**helix·om·e·ter** \,==='sämәd·ә(r)\ *n* [*helix* + *-o-* + *-meter*] **:** a tubular instrument in which an electric light and a prism and lens system enable visual examination of a small-arms bore (as in criminal investigation)

**¹hell** \'hel\ *n* -s *often attrib* [ME, fr. OE; akin to OE *helan* to conceal, OHG *hella* hell, *helan* to conceal, ON *hel* heathen realm of the dead, Goth *halja* hell, L *celare* to hide, conceal, Gk *kalyptein* to cover, conceal, Skt *śaraṇa* screening, protecting; basic meaning: concealing] **1 a :** a place or state of the dead or of the damned: as (1) **:** a place usu. under the ground in which the dead continue to exist **:** NETHERWORLD, HADES, SHEOL ⟨I will slay the last of them with the sword . . . though they dig into ~ —Amos 9:1-2 (AV)⟩ ⟨spake of the resurrection of Christ that his soul was not left in ~ —Acts 2:31 (AV)⟩ — compare LIMBO (2) **:** a netherworld in which the damned must suffer everlasting punishment (as by fire) and malevolent beings live under the rule of the devil — called also *Gehenna;* compare PURGATORY (3) **:** a spiritual state of lasting separation from God or of complete isolation **:** eternal death **b** (1) **:** a nether domain of the devil and the demons (2) **:** the fallen angels headed by Satan **:** the devil and the demons of hell **:** the powers of evil **c** *Christian Science* **:** ERROR 2b, SIN **2 a :** a place or state of misery, torment, or wickedness ⟨hundreds of gallons of spilled gasoline turn the . . . wreckage into a concentrated ~ of searing flames —H.G. Armstrong⟩ ⟨condemned to go through the ~ of war —F.L. Allen⟩ — used interjectionally to express irritation, irony, incredulity, or surprise ⟨oh ~⟩ ⟨expert, ~! — he's no more an expert than I am⟩; often used as a generalized term of abuse ⟨go to ~⟩ or as a mild oath ⟨to ~ with it⟩ or as an intensive ⟨~ yes⟩; often used with *in* ⟨what in ~ are you doing⟩ or *the* ⟨get the ~ out of here⟩ or *to* ⟨lives way to ~ out in the sticks⟩ ⟨hope to ~ you're right⟩ or *as* ⟨cold as ~⟩ ⟨serious as all ~⟩ ⟨he sure as ~ did it⟩ or in the phrases *hell of a* ⟨in a ~ of a mess⟩ ⟨heard a ~ of a crash⟩ ⟨a good singer and one ~ of an actor⟩ and *hell out of* ⟨scared the ~ out of him⟩ ⟨the big guns smashed ~ out of them⟩ **b :** a place or state of turmoil, disorder, or destruction **:** PANDEMONIUM ⟨all ~ broke loose⟩ **:** HAVOC ⟨raise ~ with the true shape of the facts⟩ ⟨the wind played ~ with the garden⟩ **:** RUIN —John Lardner⟩ ⟨said the country was going to ~ in a hack⟩ **c :** a cause of torment, tumult, or havoc; *specif* **:** severe verbal castigation ⟨got ~ from his boss for being late⟩ **d** (1) **:** unrestrained fun or sportiveness **:** TOMFOOLERY ⟨the children were full of ~ and the house was soon a shambles⟩ (2) **:** the vexations or adventurous satisfaction of an activity — usu. used in the phrase *just for the hell of it* ⟨broke all the windows just for the ~ of it⟩ ⟨hopped a freight just for the ~ of it⟩ (3) **:** the most vexing, pleasing, or notable feature — used with *the* ⟨the ~ of it was that nobody could understand him⟩ ⟨the ~ of the plan is that it works⟩ **3 a** *archaic* **:** a receptacle into which a tailor throws his pieces **b :** HELLBOX **4 :** GAMBLING HOUSE **:** a cheap place of public resort **:** HALL, HOUSE, JOINT ⟨dining . . . in the cheap obscurity of a Soho eating ~ —Aldous Huxley⟩ — **hell and gone :** an extreme or inaccessible distance ⟨no sooner does one build sluice boxes . . . than a freshet occurs and carries them to *hell and gone* —S.E. Morison⟩ — often used for emphasis ⟨he would be the *hell and gone* away from here by now —G.B.Whitlaw⟩ — **hell and high water** *or* **hell or high water :** difficulties of whatever kind or size ⟨will stand by his convictions come *hell or high water*⟩ ⟨led his men through *hell and high water*⟩ — **hell for :** extremely concerned with or insistent on ⟨he was *hell for* efficiency and made life miserable for any man who could not fulfill his duties —H.A.Chippendale⟩ — **hell on :** extremely hard on or destructive to ⟨such a life was *hell on* his digestion and soon brought on an ulcer⟩ — **hell to pay :** the devil to pay ⟨if he's late there'll be *hell to pay*⟩ — **what the hell** — used interjectionally to express carefree indifference or cynical resignation ⟨*what the hell*, I may as well go⟩

**²hell** \"\ *vi* -ED/-ING/-S **1 :** to behave in a noisy and often dissolute way **:** CAROUSE ⟨Saturday night was their night to ~ a little —H.E.Giles⟩ ⟨come down to the city to ~ around for a weekend —Merle Miller⟩ **2 :** to travel at high speed ⟨a police radio car came ~*ing* down between the elevated pillars, siren blasting —Jack Jones b.1923⟩ ⟨with passengers numbering from two to nine, we ~*ed* all over the countryside —Bill Mauldin⟩

**hellaballoo** *var of* HULLABALOO

**hel·lad·ic** \he'ladik\ *adj, usu cap* [L *Helladicus* Greek, fr. Gk *Helladikos*, fr. *Hellad-*, *Hellas* Greece + *-ikos* -ic] **:** of or relating to the Bronze Age culture of the Greek mainland lasting from about 2500 to 1100 B.C. — compare AEGEAN, GREEK 1

**hel·la·do·the·ri·um** \,heladō'thirēəm\ *n, cap* [NL, fr. Gk *Hellad-*, *Hellas* Greece + NL *-o-* + *-therium*] **:** a genus of extinct Pliocene giraffes of Greece and Asia Minor

**hel·land·ite** \'helən,dīt\ *n* -s [G *hellandit*, fr. Amund *Helland* †1918 Norw. geologist + G *-it* -ite] **:** a mineral consisting of a silicate of the cerium metals with aluminum, iron, manganese, and calcium

**hell·ben·der** \'hel'bendə(r)\ *n* **1 a :** a large voracious aquatic salamander (*Cryptobranchus alleganiensis*) that is common in the streams of the Ohio valley and that attains a length of 18 inches **b :** a related species (*C. bishopi*) of the Ozark region **2** *slang* **:** one that is exceedingly reckless or otherwise extreme

**¹hell–bent** \'='=\ *adj* **1 :** stubbornly often recklessly determined **:** dead set ⟨they are *hell-bent* to cut taxes again before election —*New Republic*⟩ ⟨*hell-bent* on having his own way⟩ **2 :** moving at a reckless speed **:** going full tilt ⟨wonder if every next turn won't be good-bye after . . . meeting *hell-bent* trucks —Alfred Powers⟩; *broadly* **:** RECKLESS ⟨*hell-bent* adventure⟩ **3 :** moving willfully or speedily on the way to destruction ⟨*hell-bent* civilization is about to blow its top —Christopher Morley⟩

**²hell–bent** \"\ *also* **hell–bent for election** *adv* **:** in a hell-bent manner **:** at full tilt ⟨the 15 . . . mares raced *hell-bent* for the first turn —G.F.T.Ryall⟩

**hell–bind** \'=,=\ *n* [¹*hell* + *bind* (bine)] **:** DODDER

**hell bomb** *n, sometimes cap H* **:** HYDROGEN BOMB

**hellbox** \'=,=\ *n* **:** a receptacle into which a printer throws damaged or discarded type material

**hellbroth** \'=,=\ *n* **:** a brew for working black magic

**hellcat** \'=,=\ *n* **1 :** WITCH 1b(2) **2 :** one given to tormenting others; *esp* **:** SHREW

**hell–diver** \ˈ=,==\ *n* **:** a pied-billed grebe or other rather small grebe
**helldog** \ˈ=,=\ *n* **:** HELLHOUND
**hell driver** *n* **:** one that engages in hell driving esp. professionally
**hell driving** *n* **:** the performance of daredevil stunts with an automobile esp. for the entertainment of spectators
**hel·le·bore** \ˈhelə,bō(ə)r\ *n* -S [L *helleborus, elleborus,* fr. Gk *helleboros,* perh. fr. *hellos, ellos* fawn + *-boros* (fr. *bibrōskein* to devour); akin to Gk *elaphos* deer — more at ELK, VORACIOUS] **1 a :** a plant of the genus *Helleborus* — see BEAR'S-FOOT 1 **b :** a poisonous herb of the genus *Veratrum* **2 a :** the dried rhizome and root of any medicinal herb of the genus *Helleborus* (as the black hellebores *H. niger* and *H. orientalis* and the green hellebore *H. viridis*) or a powder or extract of this used by the ancient Greeks and Romans in treating mental and other disorders **b :** the dried rhizome and root of a white hellebore (*Veratrum album* or *V. viride*) or a powder or extract of this containing alkaloids (as protoveratrine) used as a cardiac and respiratory depressant and also as an insecticide
**hellebore green** *n* **:** a moderate olive green that is yellower, lighter, and stronger than forest green (sense 2), cypress, or Lincoln green and greener and stronger than holly green (sense 2)
**hellebore red** *n* **:** a moderate purplish red that is bluer and darker than average rose, redder and duller than violine pink, and redder and paler than magenta rose
**hel·lebo·rine** \ˈhelәbә,rīn, heˈlebərən\ *n* -S [NL (in older classifications, a genus of orchids), fr. L, a kind of hellebore, fr. Gk *helleborinē,* fr. *helleboros* + *-inē* (fr. fem. of *-inos* -ine)] **:** any of several orchids: as **a :** a plant of the genus *Cephalanthera* (as *C. rubra*) **b :** a plant of the genus *Epipactis* (as *E. helleborine*) **c :** RATTLESNAKE PLANTAIN
**hel·leb·o·rus** \heˈlebərəs\ *n, cap* [NL, fr. L, hellebore — more at HELLEBORE] **:** a genus of Eurasian perennial herbs (family Ranunculaceae) having deeply divided leaves and showy flowers with five petaloid sepals
**helled** *past of* HELL
**hel·lene** \ˈhe,lēn\ *n* -S [Gk *Hellēn*] **1** *cap* **:** a Greek of the Hellenic period **2** *cap* **:** a Greek of the modern kingdom of Greece **3** *usu cap* **:** a person marked by intellectual or artistic Hellenism
**¹hel·len·ic** \heˈlenik, -nēk *sometimes* -lēn-\ *adj, usu cap* [Gk *Hellēnikos,* fr. *Hellēn* + *-ikos* -ic] **1 :** GREEK; *specif* **:** of, relating to, or characteristic of Greek history or culture between the first Olympiad in 776 B.C. and the conquests of Alexander ending in 323 B.C. constituting a period of a growing sense of solidarity among the independent city states and of original and influential achievements in politics, art, literature, and philosophy **:** CLASSICAL ⟨the controlled intensity of thought and emotion of the *Hellenic* Athenians was not for the people of Hellenistic times —E.H.Short⟩ **2 :** marked by intellectual or artistic Hellenism ⟨the *Hellenic* temper of modern humanism⟩ — **hel·len·i·cal·ly** \-nək(ə)lē, -nēk-, -li\ *adv, often cap*
**²hellenic** \ˈ"\ *n* -S *usu cap* **:** classical Greek; *esp* **:** GREEK 2a
**hel·le·nism** \ˈhelə,nizəm\ *n* -S *usu cap* [Gk *Hellēnismos* imitation of things Greek, use of pure Greek language, fr. *hellēnizein* to speak Greek, imitate the Greeks, fr. *Hellēn* + *-izein* -ize] **1 :** GRECISM 1 **2 a :** conformity to or imitation of ancient Greek thought, customs, or styles ⟨the *Hellenism* of some Seleucid Jews with their Greek hats and gymnasium exercises⟩ ⟨*Hellenism* in the art of the classical revival of the 18th century⟩ **b :** devotion to Greece or to Greek culture or ideals ⟨an Attic poet noted for his intense *Hellenism*⟩ **3 :** Greek civilization esp. as modified in the Hellenistic period by oriental influences **4 :** a body of humanistic and classical ideals associated with ancient Greece and including reason, the pursuit of knowledge and the arts, moderation, civic responsibility, and bodily development ⟨a revival of *Hellenism* fostered by some British Victorians⟩ — compare HEBRAISM 2 **5 :** the Greeks as a national or cultural group
**¹hel·le·nist** \-nəst\ *n* -S *usu cap* [Gk *Hellēnistēs,* fr. *hellēnizein*] **1 :** a person living in Hellenistic times not Greek in ancestry but Greek in language, outlook, and way of life; *esp* **:** a hellenized Jew ⟨the *Hellenists* murmured against the Hebrews because their widows were neglected —Acts 6:1 (RSV)⟩ **2 :** a specialist in the language or culture of ancient Greece
**²hellenist** \ˈ"\ *adj, usu cap* **:** of or relating to Hellenism or Hellenists
**hel·le·nis·tic** \¦helə¦nistik, -tēk\ *adj, usu cap* **1 :** of, relating to, or characteristic of the cosmopolitan culture that developed after the conquests of Alexander the Great and passed into Roman culture in about the 2d century A.D., blended Greek and eastern elements (as in art, literature, and philosophy), and used Koine Greek as a common language ⟨the *Hellenistic* belief in the unity of mankind⟩ **2 :** of, relating to, or being the empires of Alexander the Great, the Antigonids, the Seleucids, and the Ptolemies representing an expansion of Greek power and influence eastward as far as India and southward to Egypt during the three centuries between the conquests of Alexander and the eastern conquests of Rome ⟨the *Hellenistic* period⟩ ⟨*Hellenistic* Athens⟩ ⟨the *Hellenistic* monarchies⟩ — compare GREEK 1 **3 :** conforming to or essentially influenced by Hellenistic culture ⟨the Scriptures in Greek for *Hellenistic* Jews⟩ ⟨the conflicting viewpoints of Jewish and *Hellenistic* Christianity⟩ — **hel·le·nis·ti·cal·ly** \-tək(ə)lē, -tēk-, -li\ *adv, often cap*
**hel·le·ni·za·tion** \,helənəˈzāshən, -,nīˈz-\ *n* -S *often cap* **1 :** the act or process of hellenizing **2 :** the quality or state of being hellenized
**hel·le·nize** \ˈhelə,nīz\ *vb* -ED/-ING/-S *often cap* [Gk *hellēnizein,* fr. *Hellēn* Greek + *-izein* -ize] *vi* **:** to become Greek or Hellenistic (as in cultural characteristics or language) ~ *vt* **:** to make Greek or Hellenistic in form or culture ⟨~ Roman sculpture⟩ ⟨~ a people⟩; *specif* **:** to alter (a word or phrase) so as to make conform to the distinctive language characteristics of Greek — **hel·le·niz·er** \-zə(r)\ *n* -S *often cap*
**helleno-** *comb form, usu cap* [Gk *hellēno-,* fr. *Hellēn* Greek] **1 :** the Greeks ⟨*Hellenocentric*⟩ ⟨*Hellenophile*⟩ **2 :** Greek and ⟨*Helleno*-Italic⟩
**¹hel·ler** \ˈhelə(r)\ *n, pl* **hellers** *or* **heller** [G, fr. MHG *hallære, haller, heller,* fr. *Hall,* town in Swabia, Germany where they were first minted + MHG *-ære, -er* -er] **1 :** an old small silver coin first issued in Germany in the 13th century, later debased to billon and finally to copper, and spreading to Austria and Switzerland **2 :** an Austrian unit of value 1893-1925 equal to ¹⁄₁₀₀ of the krone; *also* **:** a coin representing this unit last issued in 1916 **3 :** HALER
**²hell·er** \ˈ"\ *n* -S [¹*hell* + *-er*] *chiefly dial* **:** one that is hard to handle; *esp* **:** a person inclined to make trouble ⟨used to be a ~ — drank a lot and threw his weight around till he got in jail —Warren Leslie⟩
**hel·leri** \ˈhelə,rī, -,rē\ *n* -ES [NL (specific epithet of *Xiphophorus helleri*), after C. Heller, 20th cent. tropical fish collector] **1 :** SWORDTAIL **2 :** any of numerous brightly colored topminnows developed in the aquarium by hybridization between two tropical American fishes (*Xiphophorus helleri* and *Platypoecilus maculatus*)
**hel·les·pon·tine** \¦helə¦spänt³n, -än,tīn\ *adj, usu cap* [*Hellespont,* narrow strait between the Gallipoli peninsula in Europe and Turkey in Asia that connects the Sea of Marmara with the Aegean sea (fr. L *Hellespontus,* fr. Gk *Hellēspontos*) + E *-ine*] **:** of or relating to the Hellespont
**¹hellfire** \ˈ=,=\ *n* [ME, fr. *hell* + *fire*] **1 :** the fire of hell **:** FIRE AND BRIMSTONE ⟨an old-fashioned Calvinist sermon on ~⟩ **2 :** something that torments like the fire of hell (as burning spite or resentment)
**²hellfire** \ˈ"\ *adj* **:** FIRE-AND-BRIMSTONE ⟨a ~ preacher⟩ ⟨preached on a ~ topic⟩
**hell–fired** \ˈ=,=\ *adj* **:** DAMNED — used as an intensive ⟨is so *hell-fired* fussy⟩
**hell·flö·te** \ˈhel,flə(r)|də, -lā|\ *n* -S [G, fr. *hell* bright, clear + *flöte* flute] **:** a clear-toned flute organ stop sounding at 8-foot pitch
**¹hell–for–leather** \¦=¦=¦==\ *adv* **:** in a hell-for-leather manner **:** at full tilt **:** HELL-BENT ⟨galloped *hell-for-leather* down the trail⟩
**²hell–for–leather** \ˈ"\ *adj* [¹*hell-for-leather*] **:** marked by determined recklessness or great speed or force **:** RIP-ROARING ⟨she swept down the dizzying descent with the verve and *hell-for-leather* dash of a man —*Time*⟩
**³hell–for–leather** \ˈ"\ *n* **:** wild abandon or frantic haste ⟨became surer of his music . . . learned . . . to take it easy when the crowd did not demand *hell-for-leather* —Harold Sinclair⟩
**hell·gram·mite** *or* **hell·gra·mite** *or* **hel·gra·mite** *or* **hel·gram·mite** \ˈhelgrə,mīt, *usu* -īd.+V\ *n* -S [origin unknown] **:** a long-lived carnivorous aquatic larva of a large North American insect (*Corydalus cornutus*) or of various related insects that is much used as a fish bait by anglers — called also *dobson, toe-biter*
**hellhole** \ˈ=,=\ *n* **1 :** the pit of hell **2 :** a place of extreme discomfort or squalor **3 :** a place notorious for its vice or immoral activities
**hellhound** \ˈ=,=\ *n* [ME *hellehound,* fr. OE *hellehund,* fr. *hell* hell + *hund* dog — more at HELL, HOUND] **1 :** a dog represented in mythology (as of ancient Greece and Scandinavia) as standing guard in the underworld **2 :** a fiendishly evil person
**¹hel·li·cat** \ˈhelə,kat\ *n* [alter. (perh. influenced by E *hellcat*) of Sc *haloked,* fr. *halok* giddy girl + E *-ed*] *Scot* **:** an irresponsible and wild person
**²hellicat** \ˈ"\ *adj, Scot* **:** wild and giddy
**hel·lier** \ˈhelyə(r)\ *n* -S [ME *helyer,* fr. *helen* to hide, conceal, cover + *-yer, -ier* -er — more at HEAL] *dial Eng* **:** a tiler or slater of roofs
**helling** *pres part of* HELL
**hel·lion** \ˈhelyən\ *n* -S [prob. alter. (influenced by ¹*hell*) of *hallion*] **:** a disorderly, troublesome, or mischievous person ⟨the young ~s in my neighborhood are only interested in breaking windows and raising a row —*Camera*⟩ ⟨the difficult and usu. thankless work of teaching and mothering swarms of little ~s —J.A.MacEwen⟩
**¹hell·ish** \ˈhelish, -lēsh\ *adj* [¹*hell* + *-ish*] **:** of, resembling, or befitting hell **:** causing torment **:** DEVILISH ⟨nothing more ~ than warfare within the soul —Frank Yerby⟩ — **hell·ish·ly** \-lәshlē, -li\ *adv* — **hell·ish·ness** \-lishnәs, -lēsh-\ *n* -ES
**²hellish** \ˈ"\ *adv* **:** in an execrable manner ⟨the child acted ~ all day⟩ — sometimes used as an intensive ⟨a ~ cold day⟩
**hellkite** \ˈ=,=\ *n* **:** one that shows hellish cruelty
**hellmouth** \ˈ=,=\ *n, often cap* **:** a property in a medieval mystery or miracle play representing the entrance of hell as the gaping jaws sometimes with moving joints of a monster resembling a whale
**¹hel·lo** \həˈlō, heˈlō, ˈhe(,)lō, ˈheˈlō; *when a name follows, as in "Hello Bill", often* (,)=,=; *subject to wide intonational variation*\ *interj* [alter. of *hollo*] — used esp. as a familiar greeting or in answering the telephone or to express surprise
**²hello** \həˈlō, heˈlō, ˈhe(,)lō\ *vi* -ED/-ING/-S **:** to call or say hello
**³hello** \ˈ"\ *n* -S **:** an expression or gesture of greeting ⟨just dropped in to say ~⟩ ⟨never failed to wave a cheery ~ as he passed⟩
**hello girl** *n* **:** a female telephone operator
**hell on wheels :** one noted for hell raising
**hell–roaring** \ˈ=,==\ *adj* **:** marked by tumultuous violence or carousing
**hellroot** \ˈ=,=\ *n* **:** SMALL BROOMRAPE
**hells** *pl of* HELL, *pres 3d sing of* HELL
**hell's bells** *interj* — used esp. to express impatience or irritation
**hell ship** *n* **:** a ship characterized by brutal discipline or inhumane living conditions
**hell–vine** \ˈ=,=\ *n* **:** TRUMPET CREEPER
**hell·ward** \ˈhelwə(r)d\ *adv* [short for earlier *to hellward,* fr. ME, fr. *to* + *hell* + *-ward*] **:** toward hell
**hellweed** \ˈ=,=\ *n* **1 :** DODDER **2 :** CORN CROWFOOT **3 :** HEDGE BINDWEED
**hell week** *n* **:** a period of often rough initiation into a college fraternity
**helly** *adj, obs* **:** HELLISH
**hel·ly's fluid** \ˈhelēz-\ *n, usu cap H* [after Konrad *Helly* *b*1875 Swiss pathologist] **:** a fixing fluid consisting of an aqueous solution of mercuric chloride, potassium dichromate, sodium sulfate, and neutral formalin used in microscopy esp. for preservation of the cytoplasm and mitochondria
**¹helm** \ˈhelm, ˈheùm\ *n* -S [ME, fr. OE — more at HELMET] **1 :** HELMET 1; *specif* **:** HEAUME **2** *dial Eng* **a** *or* **helm cloud :** a heavy cloud lying over a mountain top **b** *or* **helm wind :** a gale of wind from the mountains accompanying a helm cloud **3** *dial Brit* **:** a rough shed or shelter for cattle
**²helm** \ˈ"\ *vt* -ED/-ING/-S [ME *helmen,* fr. OE *helmian,* fr. *helm,* n., helmet] **:** to cover or furnish with a helmet
**³helm** \ˈ"\ *n* -S [ME *helme,* fr. OE *helma;* akin to OHG *helmo* tiller, MHG *helm, halm, halme* handle, ON *hjalm* rudder, helm, and prob. to OE *sciell* shell — more at SHELL] **1 a :** a lever or wheel controlling the rudder of a ship for steering **:** the tiller or the wheel of a ship; *broadly* **:** the entire apparatus by which a ship is steered **b :** a position of a tiller attached forward of the rudder or a corresponding position of a wheel ⟨gave the command "up ~"⟩ ⟨with ~ hard aport⟩ — compare RIGHT RUDDER, WEATHER HELM **c :** deviation of the position of the helm from the amidships position ⟨15-degree ~⟩ ⟨sometimes no amount of opposite ~ will straighten the boat —C.D.Lane⟩ **2 a :** a position of control or of highest executive power (as in an organization) **:** HEAD
**⁴helm** \ˈ"\ *vt* -ED/-ING/-S **:** to direct with or as if with a helm **:** STEER
**hel·met** \ˈhelmət, ˈheùm-, *usu* -əd.+V\ *n* -S *often attrib* [MF *helmet, heaumet,* dim. of *helme, heaume* helmet, of Gmc origin; akin to OE & OHG *helm* helmet, ON *hjalmr,* Goth *hilms;* akin to OE *helan* to hide, conceal — more at HELL] **1 a :** a covering or enclosing headpiece of ancient or medieval armor — see ARMET, BASINET, MORION, SALLET; ARMOR illustration **b :** a piece of medieval head armor smaller than a heaume and resting on the head **:** CASQUE **c :** a heraldic representation of a helmet depicted above the shield in an achievement and supporting the crest **2 :** any of various protective head coverings usu. made of a hard material (as metal, heavy leather, fiber) to resist impact and supported by bands that prevent direct contact with the head for comfort and ventilation; *specif* **:** one covering the top, back, and sides of the head and often also the neck and having a window for the face and sometimes breathing or radio apparatus (as for a diver) — see CRASH HELMET, WELDER'S HELMET; compare GAS MASK, TOPEE **3 :** a variety of tumbler pigeon having a white ground color and a sharply defined cap and the tail of another color **4 :** something resembling a helmet in form or position: as **a :** a hood-shaped upper sepal or petal of some flowers (as monkshood or snapdragon) **b :** CASQUE 3 **c :** a galea of an insect **5 a :** a close-fitting cap (as of leather or knitted material) covering the top, back, and sides of the head and fastening under the chin — compare BALACLAVA **b :** a woman's small close-fitting brimless hat

helmets 2: *1* football, *2* lacrosse, *3* polo

**helmet bird** *n* **1 :** TOURACO **2 :** a Madagascan passerine bird (*Aerocharis prevostii*) having a swollen hooked beak and black-and-chestnut plumage
**helmet crab** *n* **:** KING CRAB 1
**hel·met·ed** \-məd.|əd, -mət|\ *adj* **1 :** wearing a helmet **2 :** having a helmet or a helmet-shaped form or structure
**helmeted guinea fowl** *n* **:** a guinea fowl (*Numida meleagris*) — used esp. of the wild African bird
**helmetflower** \ˈ==,=\ *n* **:** a plant having flowers with helmet-shaped petals or sepals or a flower of such a plant: as **a :** MONKSHOOD **b :** SKULLCAP **c :** a tropical American orchid of the genus *Coryanthes*
**helmetlike** \ˈ==,=\ *adj* **:** resembling a helmet in shape
**helmet liner** *n* **:** a stiff fabric or plastic headgear that fits inside a metal helmet and may be worn without the helmet
**helmet orchid** *n* **1 :** HELMETFLOWER c **2 :** an Australian orchid (*Pterostylis cucullata*) with a galeate lip
**helmetpod** \ˈ=,=\ *n* **:** TWINLEAF
**helmet quail** *n* **:** any of several American partridges (as the valley quail and Gambel quail) constituting a genus (*Lophortyx*) distinguished by a forwardly curving crest
**helmets** *pl of* HELMET
**helmet shell** *n* **1 :** a gastropod mollusk of the family Cassididae **2 :** the thick-walled shell of the helmet shell often used for cameos
**helmet shrike** *n* **:** any of various chiefly tropical Old World passerine birds related to and resembling the shrikes but usu. isolated in a separate family (Prionopidae)
**helm·holtz coil** \ˈhel|m,hōlts, ˈheù|\ *n, usu cap H* [after Hermann L.F. von *Helmholtz* †1894 Ger. physicist] **:** one of two equal parallel coaxial circular coils in series that are separated from each other by a distance equal to the radius of one coil for producing an approximately uniform magnetic field in the space between the coils
**helmholtz double layer** *n, usu cap H* [after H.L.F. von *Helmholtz*] **:** ELECTRIC DOUBLE LAYER
**helmholtz resonator** *n, usu cap H* [after H.L.F. von *Helmholtz*] **:** RESONATOR 1a
**helming** *pres part of* HELM
**hel·minth** \ˈhel,min(t)th, -,mən-\ *n, pl* **helminths** \-n(t)s, -n(t)ths\ [NL *Helminthes*] **:** a parasitic worm (as a roundworm, tapeworm, or leech); *esp* **:** one that parasitizes the intestine of a vertebrate
**helminth-** *or* **helmintho-** *comb form* [NL, fr. Gk, fr. *helminth-, helmis* intestinal worm, parasitic worm; akin to Gk *eulē* worm, maggot, Toch A *walyi* worms, Gk *eilein* to wind, roll — more at VOLUBLE] **1 :** helminth ⟨*helminth*iasis⟩ ⟨*helmintho*logy⟩ **2 :** shaped like a worm ⟨*helmintho*sporium⟩
**hel·min·thes** \helˈmin(t)thēz, -n,thēz\ *n pl, cap* [NL, fr. Gk *helminth-, helmis*] **:** the parasitic worms — used as though a taxon but without taxonomic implications
**hel·min·thi·a·sis** \,hel,minˈthīəsəs, -,mən-\ *n, pl* **helminthia·ses** \-ə,sēz\ [NL, fr. *helminth-* + *-iasis*] **:** infestation with or disease caused by parasitic worms
**hel·min·thic** \(ˈ)helˈmin(t)thik\ *adj* **:** of or caused by a helminth
**hel·min·tho·clad·i·a·ce·ae** \hel,min(t)thō,kladēˈāsē,ē, -lād-\ *n pl, cap* [NL, fr. *Helminthocladia,* type genus (fr. *helminth-* + Gk *klados* branch + NL *-ia*) + *-aceae* — more at GLADIATOR] **:** a family of red algae (order Nemalionales) having no envelope of vegetative cells formed about the reproductive filaments
**hel·min·thoid** \helˈmin,thȯid; ˈhelmən-, -,min-\ *adj* [*helminth-* + *-oid*] **:** resembling a helminth **:** WORMLIKE
**hel·min·tho·log·i·cal** \(¦)hel¦min(t)thə¦läjəkəl\ *adj* **:** of or relating to helminthology ⟨~ abstracts⟩
**hel·min·thol·o·gist** \,helmənˈthäləjəst, -,min-\ *n* -S **:** a specialist in helminthology
**hel·min·thol·o·gy** \-jē\ *n* -ES [*helminth-* + *-logy*] **:** a branch of zoology that is concerned with helminths; *esp* **:** the study of parasitic worms
**hel·min·tho·spo·rin** \(,)hel,min(t)thəˈspōrən\ *n* -S [NL *Helminthosporium* + E *-in*] **:** a dark maroon crystalline phenolic pigment $C_{15}H_{10}O_5$ derived from anthraquinone and formed by the action of certain molds (as *Helminthosporium gramineum*) on sugar
**hel·min·tho·spo·ri·um** \-rēəm\ *n* [NL, fr. *helminth-* + *-sporium*] **1** *cap* **:** a form genus of saprophytic or parasitic imperfect fungi (family Dematiaceae) having erect conidiophores and elongate, clavate or cylindric, several-septate spores — see BARLEY STRIPE **2** *pl* **helminthospo·ria** \-rēə\ *or* **helminthosporiums :** any fungus of the genus *Helminthosporium* — **hel·min·tho·spo·roid** \(¦)=¦==¦spō,rȯid\ *adj*
**helm·less** \ˈhelmləs, ˈheùm-\ *adj* **:** lacking a helm
**helm port** *n* **:** an opening in the counter of a ship for the rudder stock
**helm roof** *n* [¹*helm*] **:** a 4-faced steeply pitched roof rising to a point from a base of four gables
**helms** *pl of* HELM, *pres 3d sing of* HELM
**helms·man** \ˈhelmzmən, ˈheùm-\ *n, pl* **helmsmen :** a man at the helm who steers a ship **:** STEERSMAN
**helms·man·ship** \-,ship\ *n* **:** the art or practice of steering a ship
**¹helo-** *comb form* [NL, fr. Gk *helos* — more at HELODES] **:** marsh **:** bog ⟨*helo*bious⟩ ⟨*helo*phyte⟩
**²helo-** *comb form* [NL, fr. Gk *hēlo-,* fr. *hēlos;* perh. akin to L *vallus* stake, palisade — more at WALL] **:** nail ⟨*Helo*derma⟩ ⟨*Helo*tium⟩
**he·lo·bi·ae** \heˈlōbē,ē\ *syn of* NAIADALES
**he·lo·bi·ous** \-bēəs\ *adj* [¹*helo-* + *-bious* (fr. NL *-bius* having a — specified — mode of life) — more at -BIUS] **:** living in marshy places
**helo·der·ma** \,hēlōˈdərmə, ,hel-\ *n, cap* [NL, fr. ²*helo-* + *-derma*] **:** the type genus of the family Helodermatidae comprising the American gila monsters
**he·lo·der·mat·i·dae** \,==(,)dərˈmad.ə,dē\ *n pl, cap* [NL, fr. *Helodermat-, Heloderma,* type genus + *-idae*] **:** a small family of lizards having the dorsal scales replaced by rough tuberculated skin and including the American gila monsters and an obscure Bornean lizard

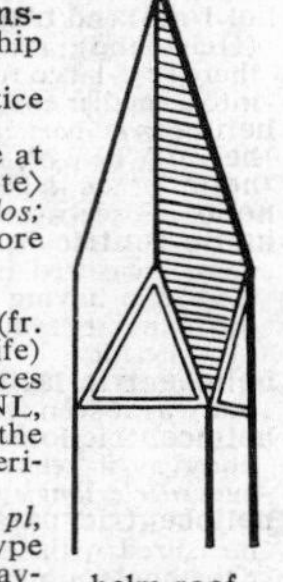

helm roof

**he·lo·des** \heˈlō(,)dēz\ *adj* [Gk *helōdēs,* fr. *helos* marsh; akin to Skt *saras* pond] **:** MARSHY
**hel·o·dri·lus** \,helōˈdrīləs\ *n, cap* [NL, fr. ¹*helo-* + Gk *drilos* worm] **:** a common No. American genus of earthworms (family Lumbricidae) found in rich soil or manure
**he·lo·ni·as** \həˈlōnēəs\ *n* [NL, irreg. fr. ¹*helo-* + *-ia*] **1** *cap* **:** a genus of bog herbs (family Melanthaceae) of the northeastern U.S. with basal leaves and purple racemose perfect flowers on a tall scape — see SWAMP PINK **2** -ES **:** the dried rhizome and roots of a blazing star (*Chamaelirium luteum*) formerly used as a vermifuge
**hel·o·pel·tis** \,helōˈpeltəs\ *n* [NL, fr. ¹*helo-* + *-peltis* (fr. Gk *peltē* shield)] **1** *cap* **:** a genus of tropical mirid bugs including several that attack economically important plants **2** -ES **:** any bug of the genus *Helopeltis; specif* **:** TEA MOSQUITO
**hel·o·phyte** \ˈhelə,fīt\ *n* -S [¹*helo-* + *-phyte*] **:** a bog plant; *esp* **:** a perennial marsh plant having its overwintering buds under water — compare HYDROPHYTE
**hel·ot** \ˈhelət\ *n* -S [L *Helotes,* pl., fr. Gk *Heilōtes*] **1** *usu cap* **:** a member of the lowest social and economic class of ancient Sparta thought to represent the conquered original population and constituting a body of serfs who were attached to the land, could not be sold, could be freed only by the state, were obliged to pay fixed portions of produce to the ruling Spartiates, and were required to serve in the armed forces — compare PERIOECI 2 **2 :** a member of any group of people deprived of rights and privileges and often exploited **:** SERF
**he·lo·ti·a·les** \hə,lōsheˈā(,)lēz, -ōd.ē-\ *n pl, cap* [NL, fr. *Helotium* + *-ales*] **:** an order of fungi (subclass Euascomycetes) that are characterized by inoperculate asci borne in a disk-shaped to goblet-shaped sessile or stalked apothecium which may be brilliantly colored or dark and dull and that include numerous saprophytes and a few parasites of economically important plants — compare PEZIZALES
**hel·ot·ism** \ˈhelәd.,izәm\ *n* -S **1 :** the quality or state of being a helot **:** SERFDOM **2 :** a symbiotic relation of plants or animals in which one functions as the slave of the other (as that between certain species of ants) — compare COMMENSALISM, PARASITISM, SYMBIOSIS
**he·lo·ti·um** \həˈlōshēəm, -ōd.ē-\ *n, cap* [NL, fr. LGk *hēlōtos* nail-shaped (fr. Gk *hēlos* nail) + NL *-ium*] **:** a genus (the type of the family Helotiaceae) comprising fungi that have inoperculate asci arranged in a hymenial layer in a cup-shaped apothecium with a colored rim of elongate thin-walled hyphae
**hel·ot·ry** \ˈhelətrē\ *n* -ES **1 :** the helots of a country or of an estate **2 :** the condition of a helot **:** SLAVERY, SERFDOM ⟨permanent white supremacy and permanent black ~ —Basil Davidson⟩
**¹help** \ˈhelp, ˈheùp, *chiefly in southern U S* ˈhep\ *vb* **helped** \-pt\ *or now chiefly dial* **holp** \ˈhō(l)p\ *or* **holped** \-pt\ **helped** *or now chiefly dial* **holp** *or* **holped** *or* **hol·pen** \ˈhō(l)pən\ **helping; helps** [ME *helpen,* fr. OE *helpan;* akin to OHG *helfan* to help, ON *hjalpa,* Goth *hilpan,* Lith *šelpti*] *vt* **1 a :** to give assistance or support to **:** AID ⟨agreed to ~ him with his

biography —Ruth P. Randall⟩ ⟨from the beginning she had ~*ed* and abetted him —Stuart Cloete⟩ — often used interjectionally ⟨*Help!* I'm drowning⟩ **b :** to assist in attaining ⟨good pitching ~*ed* the team to the American league championship⟩ **2 a :** REMEDY, CURE, RELIEVE ⟨bright curtains ~ a drab room⟩ ⟨aspirin ~*s* a headache⟩ ⟨humor often ~*s* a tense situation⟩ **b** *archaic* : to rescue from harm or misfortune : SAVE ⟨~ beer that beginneth to sour —Hugh Plat⟩ ⟨~ us from famine —Alfred Tennyson⟩ **c :** to get (oneself) out of a difficulty : EXTRICATE ⟨sometimes I fought when I couldn't ~ myself —John Reed⟩ **3 a :** to be of use to : BENEFIT ⟨a good speech should either amuse or ~ an audience⟩ ⟨one-way sailing was ~*ed* by monsoons —Anne Dorrance⟩ **b :** to further the advancement of : PROMOTE ⟨this dispute certainly did not ~ the negotiations —Theodore Hsi-En Chen⟩ ⟨~*ing* industrial development with two loans —Paul Bareau⟩ **4 a :** to change for the better : MEND ⟨people get used to what they can't ~ quicker than they think they're going to —Mary Austin⟩ **b :** to keep oneself from : refrain from : AVOID ⟨neither of us could ~ laughing —Oscar Wilde⟩ ⟨couldn't ~ seeing it was stuffed with newspaper clippings —James Hilton⟩ **c :** to keep from occurring : PREVENT ⟨scolded him for something he couldn't ~⟩ **d :** to be kept from : fail in ⟨the campaign against industrial accidents cannot ~ producing results —F.D.Roosevelt⟩ **5 a :** to dispense esp. at a meal : SERVE ⟨a loop of gold thread hung down from her sleeve as she ~*ed* the soup —Virginia Woolf⟩ **b :** to serve with food or drink esp. at a meal — often used with *to* ⟨~*ed* his neighbor to the wine⟩ ⟨~*ing* himself . . . to a slice of beef —T.L.Peacock⟩ **6 :** to appropriate for the use of (oneself) ⟨the company had ~*ed* itself to a generous supply of bicycles —P.W.Thompson⟩ ~ *vi* **:** to give aid or support : be of use : ASSIST ⟨to ~ rather than to blame —A.C.Benson⟩ ⟨every little bit ~*s*⟩ — often used with a following infinitive ⟨this principle may at least ~ to explain —A.O.Wolfers⟩

**syn** AID, ASSIST: these three verbs are virtually interchangeable in meaning to furnish another person or thing with what is needed to fill an insufficiency or what is needed for the attainment of an end. HELP implies more frequently than the others, however, an advance toward an end ⟨only money could *help* her through the worst of her ordeal —Marcia Davenport⟩ ⟨*help* a team to win a game⟩ ⟨will *help* to combat inflation⟩ ⟨*help* a wounded soldier back to camp⟩ AID often suggests the need of help or relief, often stressing weakness or insufficiency in the one aided and strength in the one aiding ⟨his undergraduate work . . . was *aided* by tuition grants —*Current Biog.*⟩ ⟨a wide variety of literature . . . that will broaden their horizons and *aid* them to sound, democratic decisions —C.M. Wieting⟩ ⟨to *aid* families in distress⟩ ASSIST usu. stresses the secondary role of the one assisting or the subordinate character of the assistance ⟨to *assist* visitors in finding places in hotels and auto courts —*Amer. Guide Series: Nev.*⟩ ⟨the president . . . is *assisted* by an 11-man cabinet —*Americana Annual*⟩ **syn** see in addition IMPROVE

— **cannot help but :** cannot but — **so help me :** on my word of honor : believe it or not ⟨dressed, *so help me,* in pink and purple tights⟩

**2help** \"\ *n* -S [ME, fr. OE; akin to OHG *helfa, hilfa* help, ON *hjalp* help, OE *helpan* to help] **1 a :** an act or instance of giving aid or support : ASSISTANCE ⟨offered his ~ in unloading the baggage⟩ ⟨generous to all who needed ~⟩ ⟨making . . . decisions with the ~ of all significant facts —*College & Univ. Business*⟩ ⟨always tried to be of ~⟩ **b :** the strength or resources employed in giving assistance ⟨the ~ comprised food, clothing, and medicine —J.A.McVann⟩ **2 a :** a useful adjunct : source of aid ⟨printed ~*s* to the memory —C.S.Braden⟩ ⟨the singer is a ~ but he is not essential —Deems Taylor⟩ **b :** DEALER HELP **3 :** a possibility of preventing or curing : REMEDY ⟨a situation for which there was no ~⟩ **4 a :** one who is in the pay or service of another: (1) : ASSISTANT, ALLY ⟨I could get you three or four rupees a month as my ~ —Attia S. Hosain⟩ ⟨now if the ~ of Norfolk and myself . . . will but amount to five-and-twenty thousand —Shak.⟩ (2) *or pl* **help :** a domestic worker or farmhand ⟨I've . . . scrubbed the bathroom floor when the ~ has quit —Ethel Merman⟩ ⟨hired ~ sat at table with the rest of the family —Sherwood Anderson⟩ ⟨the two extra ~*s* we always get in for the birthday —Ngaio Marsh⟩ (3) *pl* **help :** an office or factory worker : EMPLOYEE ⟨ran an ad in the ~ wanted column⟩ ⟨one of the ~ in . . . government agencies —*Antioch Rev.*⟩ **b :** the services of a paid worker ⟨they were without ~ again and she had all the work to do —Hamilton Basso⟩ **5 :** HELPING

**help·able** \-pəbəl\ *adj* : capable of being helped

**helped** *past of* HELP

**help·er** \-pə(r)\ *n* -S [ME, fr. *helpen* + *-er*] **1 :** one that helps ⟨the most idiomatic class of verbs are the ~*s* —Frederick Bodmer⟩; *specif* : an extra locomotive to assist a train (as on a grade) **2 :** HELP 4a; *specif* : a relatively unskilled worker who assists another esp. by manual labor ⟨first a ~ and then a journeyman —Walter Bernstein⟩ **3** *usu cap, Islam* : a member of the ansar — compare COMPANION 4c

**help·ful** \-pfəl\ *adj* [ME, fr. *help* + *-ful*] **1 :** of service or assistance : USEFUL, SALUTARY ⟨certain ideas are not only agreeable to think about . . . but they are also ~ in life's practical struggles —William James⟩ ⟨to the stomach it is pleasant, wholesome, and ~ —E.J.Banfield⟩ **2 :** CONSTRUCTIVE, ENCOURAGING ⟨a price control picture that is ~ —T.W.Arnold⟩ — **help·ful·ly** \-fəlē, -li\ *adv*

**help·ful·ness** \-fəlnəs\ *n* -ES : the quality or state of being helpful ⟨the . . . ~ of reference books —C.B.Shaw⟩

**1helping** *n* -S [ME, fr. *helpen* to help + *-ing*] **1** *archaic* : an act or instance of giving aid : HELP ⟨the law of all true ~ —R.C. Trench⟩ **2 a :** a portion of food : SERVING ⟨sent his plate back for a second ~⟩ **b :** something compared to a serving of food : PORTION ⟨only bona fide settlers . . . deserved ~*s* from the public domain —Dixon Wecter⟩

**2helping** *adj* [ME, fr. pres. part. of *helpen*] **1 :** giving aid or support **2 :** AUXILIARY ⟨~ verbs⟩ — **help·ing·ly** *adv*

**helping card** *n* : a queen or jack led in whist in an effort to promote the value of a card in a partner's hand

**helping hand** *n* **1 :** AID, ASSISTANCE ⟨always ready to lend a *helping hand*⟩ **2 :** a bridge hand containing some strength (as a queen or king) in each of at least three suits but with no biddable suit of its own and with too little strength for a no-trump bid

**help·less** \-pləs\ *adj* [ME *helples,* fr. *help* + *-les* -less] **1 :** lacking protection or support : DEFENSELESS ⟨as ~ as a flock of shepherdless sheep —W.H.Mallock⟩ **2 :** lacking in effectiveness : FUTILE ⟨a ~ medley of indecisions —Hugh Walpole⟩ **3 a :** lacking in strength or vigor : incapable of action : POWERLESS ⟨fell ill and lay ~ at the mouth of the river —Francis Parkman⟩ ⟨the government . . . drifted ~ in the conflicting currents —Charles & Mary Beard⟩ **b :** lacking power to resist : INVOLUNTARY ⟨the tiny spill of pebbles in ~ fall —Richard Llewellyn⟩ **4 :** lacking in comprehension : BEWILDERED ⟨blinked at the candle in a ~ way, like a young barn owl —Mary Webb⟩

**help·less·ly** *adv* : in a helpless manner

**help·less·ness** *n* -ES : the quality or state of being helpless

**help·mate** \-p,māt, *usu* -ād.+V\ *n* [by folk etymology (influence of *mate*) fr. *helpmeet*] : one serving as a companion, partner, or assistant; *specif* : WIFE ⟨proved a good and faithful ~, assisted me much by attending the shop —Benjamin Franklin⟩

**helpmeet** \'ˌ=ˌ=\ *n* [²*help* + *meet,* adj. (fitting) in *I will make an help meet for him* (Gen 2:18 AV)] : HELPMATE ⟨testify that their ~*s* retain that feminine tenderness and loyalty . . . no longer found in my own household —*Atlantic*⟩ ⟨chemistry . . . is the farmer's ~ —*Crops in Peace & War*⟩

**help out** *vi* : to render assistance : be of use ⟨won a scholarship which would *help out* —MacKinlay Kantor⟩ ~ *vt* : to give aid to ⟨*help* him *out*⟩

**helps** *pres 3d sing of* HELP, *pl of* HELP

**hel–shoes** \'hel,=\ *n pl, usu cap H* [part trans. of ON *helskōr,* fr. *hel* heathen realm of the dead + *skōr* shoes — more at HELL] *Norse mythol* : shoes placed on the dead before burial to aid them on the rough road to Hel

**hel·sing·fors** \'helsiŋ,fȯrz, -sēŋ-, -ö(ə)z\ *adj, usu cap* [fr. *Helsingfors* (Helsinki), Finland] : HELSINKI

**hel·sin·ki** \'hel,siŋkē, -ki, ='==\ *adj, usu cap* [fr. *Helsinki,* Finland] : of or from Helsinki, the capital of Finland : of the kind or style prevalent in Helsinki

**1hel·ter–skel·ter** \ˌheltə(r)ˈskeltə(r)\ *adv* [imit.] **1 :** in headlong disorder : PELL-MELL ⟨ran *helter-skelter,* getting in each other's way —F.V.W.Mason⟩ **2 :** in random order : HAPHAZARDLY ⟨magazines stacked *helter-skelter* on tables —T.H. White b. 1915⟩

**2helter–skelter** \"\ *n* -S **1 :** a disorderly confusion : TURMOIL ⟨the horses set off in a wild *helter-skelter* —J.M.Synge⟩ ⟨*helter-skelter* of conflict, emotion, and group activity —John Gould⟩ **2 :** an external spiral slide around a tower in an amusement park

**3helter–skelter** \"\ *adj* **1 :** confused and hurried : PRECIPITATE ⟨most companies are plagued with *helter-skelter* disorder when that five o'clock whistle blows —*Modern Industry*⟩ **2 a :** HIT-OR-MISS : HAPHAZARD ⟨shocked at the *helter-skelter* arrangement of the papers, all mussed and frayed —Jean Stafford⟩ ⟨the *helter-skelter* nondirectional nature of the discussion —John Withall⟩ **b :** FLIGHTY, SCATTERBRAINED ⟨*helter-skelter* attitude of the younger generation —Erle Stanley Gardner⟩

**1helve** \'helv, 'heu̇v\ *n* -S [ME, fr. OE *hielfe*; akin to OHG *halb* handle, OE *healf* half — more at HALF] **1 :** a handle of a tool or weapon (as an ax) : HAFT **2 :** a lever in a helve hammer that has the hammerhead at its end

**2helve** \"\ *vt* -ED/-ING/-S [ME *helven,* fr. *helve,* n.] : to furnish or fit with a helve

**helve hammer** *n* : a power hammer consisting essentially of a heavy head at one end of a lever lifted by power and dropping by its own weight on work that rests on an anvil — compare STRAP HAMMER, TRIP-HAMMER

**hel·vel·la** \hel'velə\ *n* [NL, fr. L, a small potherb, fr. *helvus* light-bay-colored + *-ella* (dim. suffix) — more at YELLOW] **1** *cap* : a genus (the type of the family Helvellaceae) comprising ascomycetous fungi with the ascocarps stalked, pileate, or saddle-shaped and often thrown into folds **2** -S : any fungus of the genus *Helvella* — **hel·vel·lic** \(')=ˈvelik\ *adj*

**hel·vel·la·ce·ae** \ˌhelvəˈlāsē,ē\ *n pl, cap* [NL, fr. *Helvella,* type genus + *-aceae*] : a family of fungi (order Pezizales) that includes various important edible fungi (as the morels) — see HELVELLA — **hel·vel·la·ceous** \ˌ==ˈlāshəs\ *adj*

**hel·vel·la·les** \-ˈlā(,)lēz\ *n pl, cap* [NL, fr. *Helvella* + *-ales*] *in some classifications* : an order of fungi including the Helvellaceae and Geoglossaceae

**hel·ve·tia blue** \(')helˈvēsh(ē)ə-\ *n, often cap H* [NL *Helvetia* Switzerland] : NAPOLEON BLUE

**1hel·ve·tian** \-shən\ *adj, usu cap* [NL *Helvetia* land of the Helvetii, Switzerland (fr. L *Helvetii,* ancient people of Switzerland + *-ia* -y) + E *-an*] : of or relating to the Helvetii or Helvetia : SWISS

**2helvetian** \"\ *n* -S *cap* : a native or inhabitant of Switzerland : SWISS; *specif* : a member of the ancient Helvetii

**1hel·vet·ic** \(')helˈved·ik\ *adj, usu cap* [L *Helveticus* of the Helvetii, fr. *Helvetii* + *-icus* -ic] : HELVETIAN

**2helvetic** \"\ *n* -S *usu cap* : a Swiss Protestant : a follower of Zwingli

**hel·ve·tii** \helˈvēshē,ī\ *n pl, usu cap* [L] : an early Celtic people of western Switzerland in the time of Julius Caesar

**hel·vid·i·an** \(')helˈvidēən\ *adj, usu cap* [*Helvidius* fl.A.D.380 Roman heretic + E *-an*] : of or relating to the teachings of the Roman layman Helvidius who held that Mary bore children after Jesus

**hel·vite** \'hel,vīt\ *also* **hel·vin** \-,vən\ *or* **hel·vine** \", -,vēn\ *n* -S [*helvite* alter. (influenced by *-ite*) of *helvin*; *helvin, helvine* fr. G *helvin,* fr. L *helvus* light-bay-colored + G *-in* — more at YELLOW] : a silicate mineral $(Mn,Fe,Zn)_8Be_6O_{24}S_2$ consisting of sulfide of manganese and beryllium and usu. containing also iron and zinc that is isomorphous with danalite and genthelvite

**hel·volic acid** \helˈväl|ik-, -vōl\ *n* [ISV *helvol-* (fr. L *helvolus, helveolus* pale yellow, fr. *helvus* light-bay-colored) + *-ic*] : FUMIGACIN

**helxi·ne** \helkˈsīnē, -lˈzī-\ *n, cap* [NL, fr. Gk *helxinē* pellitory, bindweed, fr. *helkein* to drag, pull — more at SULCUS] : a genus of plants (family Urticaceae) native to Corsica and Sardinia and cultivated elsewhere as pot plants with small leaves and tiny solitary flowers that form dense mossy mats — see BABY'S TEARS

**hel·zel** \'helzəl\ *n* -S [Yiddish, dim. of *hals* neck, fr. OHG — more at COLLAR] : a skin of the neck of poultry stuffed usu. with fat and flour

**1hem** \'hem\ *pron* [ME, fr. OE *him, heom,* dat. of *hīe* they — more at HE] **1** *dial* : THEM **2** *obs* : THEMSELVES

**2hem** \"\ *n* -S [ME *hem, hemm,* fr. OE; akin to ON *hemja* to hem in, restrain, OFris *hemma* to hinder, MHG *hemmen* to hem in, restrain, *hamen* to hem in, restrain, Arm *kamel* to press, squeeze, Russ *kom* lump, ball] **1 a :** a finished edge of a cloth article (as a skirt, sleeve, curtain, napkin, stocking) made by rolling or folding back an edge and stitching it down **b :** an edge usu. folded back and fastened down on articles of sheet metal, plastic, rubber, leather **2 a :** BORDER ⟨bright green ~ of reeds about the ponds —R.M.Lockley⟩ **b :** EDGE ⟨~ of the sea —Shak.⟩ ⟨the polar ~ —Emily Dickinson⟩ **3 :** the raised rim of a volute of an Ionic capital

**3hem** \"\ *vb* **hemmed; hemmed; hemming; hems** [ME *hemmen,* fr. *hem, hemm,* n.] *vt* **1 a :** to finish with a plain or decorative hem ⟨*hemmed* just above the ankle —*Women's Wear Daily*⟩ **b :** BORDER, EDGE **2 :** to enclose or confine with or as if with a ring around or arc before usu. preventing or hindering access, free activity, growth, or escape — usu. used with *in* ⟨body of water, *hemmed in* on all sides by evergreen forests —*Amer. Guide Series: N. H.*⟩ ⟨the regiment now found itself *hemmed* in by its own mine fields —P.W.Thompson⟩ ~ *vi* : to make hems in sewing **syn** see SURROUND

**4hem** \"; *as an interjection a throat-clearing sound*\ *n* -S [imit.] : a vocalized pause in speaking ⟨after clearing the husk in his throat with two or three ~*s* —T.L.Peacock⟩ : an instance of uttering this sound ⟨would use a peculiar rap at the door, and give four loud ~*s* —Oliver Goldsmith⟩ — often used interjectionally to call attention, to warn, or to express hesitation or doubt; compare ³HUM

**5hem** \'hem\ *vi* **hemmed; hemmed; hemming; hems :** to utter the sound represented by *hem* ⟨*hemmed* ominously as he always did when he was about to relieve his mind —W.A. White⟩ — often used with *haw* ⟨~ and haw and put it off, apparently in the hope that things will pick up —Clifford Aucoin⟩ ⟨*hemmed* and hawed, and then pointed out that the trouble was obviously connected with our consignment —F.W. Crofts⟩

**6hem** \"\ *archaic and dial var of* HIM

**7hem** \"\ *dial Eng var of* HAME

**8hem** \"\ *var of* HEME

**hem-** *or* **hemo-** *or* **hemi-** *or* **haem-** *or* **haemo-** *comb form* [MF *hemo-,* fr. L *haem-, haemo-,* fr. Gk *haim-, haimo-,* fr. *haima*; perh. akin to ON *seimr* honeycomb, OHG *seim* virgin honey, W *hufen* cream] : blood ⟨*hemarthrosis*⟩ ⟨*hemagglutination*⟩ ⟨*hemocyte*⟩ — the forms *haem-* or *haemo-* are preferred in taxonomic names ⟨*Haemanthus*⟩ ⟨*Haemogregarina*⟩

**hema-** *or* **haema-** *comb form* [NL, fr. Gk *haima* blood] : HEM- ⟨*hemacytometer*⟩ ⟨*hemapoiesis*⟩ — *haema-* preferred in taxonomic names in biology ⟨*Haemastoma*⟩

**hem·a·chate** \'hemə,kāt\ *n* -S [L *haemachates,* fr. (assumed) Gk *haimachatēs,* fr. Gk *haima* blood + *achatēs* agate — more at AGATE] : a light-colored agate like bloodstone with red jasper spots

**he·ma·cy·tom·e·ter** \ˌhēmə(ˌ)sīˈtäməd·ə(r), ˌhem-\ *n* [*hema-* + *cyt-* + *-meter*] : an instrument for counting blood cells

**he·ma·cy·to·zo·on** \-mə,sīd·əˈzō,än\ *n* [NL, fr. *hema-* + *cyt-* + *-zoon*] : HEMOCYTOZOON

**he·mad** \'hē,mad\ *adv* [*hem-* + ²*-ad*] : toward the hemal side

**he·ma·dynamometer** \ˌhēmə, ˌhemə+\ *n* [*hema-* + *dynamometer*] : a device for measuring blood pressure

**he·ma·fi·brite** \ˌhēməˈfī,brīt, ˌhem-\ *n* -S [ISV *hema-* + *fibr-* + *-ite*] : a mineral $Mn_3(AsO_4)(OH)_3.H_2O$ consisting of basic manganese arsenate

**he·mag·glut·i·nate** \ˌhēməˈglüd·ə,nāt, ˌhem-\ *vt* [*hem-* + *agglutinate*] : to cause hemagglutination of

**he·mag·glu·ti·na·tion** \ˌ==ˌ=='nāshən\ *n* [ISV *hem-* + *agglutination*] : agglutination of red blood cells

**he·mag·glu·ti·nin** \ˌ=='glüd·ənən\ *or* **he·mo·agglutinin** \ˌhē(ˌ)mō, ˌhe(ˌ)mō+\ *n* [ISV *hem-* + *agglutinin*] : an agglutinin that causes hemagglutination

**he·mal** \'hēməl\ *adj* [*hem-* + *-al*] **1 :** of or relating to the blood or blood vessels **2 :** situated on or belonging to the side of the spinal cord where the heart and chief blood vessels are placed : VENTRAL — used of vertebrate parts or organs

**hemal arch** *n* : a bony or cartilaginous arch extending ventrally from the spinal column: **a :** the arch formed by a vertebra and an associated pair of ribs **b** (1) : an arch on the ventral surface of each caudal vertebra of a lower vertebrate (as a fish or reptile) usu. considered to consist of the extended and ventrally fused parapophyses of the vertebra (2) : such an arch together with its dependent hemal spine forming a V-shaped or Y-shaped ventral prolongation of a caudal vertebra — called also *chevron bone*

**he·mal·bu·men** \ˌhēmalˈbyümən, ˌhem-\ *n* [ISV *hem-* + *albumen*] : a preparation of blood containing iron albuminate and used in chlorosis and anemia

**hemal node** *or* **hemal gland** *n* : HEMOLYMPH GLAND

**he·ma·moe·ba** \ˌhēməˈmēbə, ˌhem-\ *n* [NL, fr. *hem-* + *amoeba*] **1 :** an organism like an amoeba living in the blood; *esp* : MALARIA PARASITE **2 :** LEUKOCYTE

**he–man** \'=ˌ=\ *n, pl* **he–men :** an obviously strong virile man ⟨the great open spaces, where red-blooded *he-men* still roam —H.L.Mencken⟩ ⟨peppy, poker-playing, sales-hustling *he-men* who are our most characteristic Americans —Sinclair Lewis⟩ ⟨the tough, assured, half-humorous *he-man* who can take his women or leave them alone —Arthur Knight⟩

**he·man·gi·ec·ta·sis** \hē¦manjē+\ *n* -ES [NL, fr. *hem-* + *angi-* + *ectasis*] : dilatation of blood vessels

**he·man·gi·o·endothelioma** \hē¦manjē(,)ō+\ *n* [NL, fr. *hemangio-* (fr. *hemangioma*) + *endothelioma*] : an often malignant tumor originating by proliferation of capillary endothelium

**he·man·gi·oma** \hē,manjēˈōmə\ *n, pl* **hemangiomas** *also* **hemangio·ma·ta** \-məd·ə\ [NL, fr. *hem-* + *angioma*] : a usu. benign tumor made up of blood vessels and typically occurring as a purplish or reddish slightly elevated area of skin overlying a network of intercommunicating capillaries — see PORT-WINE STAIN, STRAWBERRY MARK

**he·man·gi·o·ma·to·sis** \=ˌ=ˌ=ōmə'tōsəs\ *n, pl* **hemangioma·to·ses** \-ō,sēz\ [NL, fr. *hemangiomat-, hemangioma* + *-osis*] : a condition in which hemangiomas are present in several parts of the body

**he·man·gi·o·sarcoma** \hē¦manjē(,)ō+\ *n* [NL, fr. *hemangio-* (fr. *hemangioma*) + *sarcoma*] : a malignant hemangioma

**he·ma·po·di·um** \ˌhēməˈpōdēəm, ˌhem-\ *or* **he·ma·pod** \ˈhēmə,päd, ˈhem-\ *n, pl* **hemapodia** *also* **hemapodiums** *or* **hemapods** [*hemapodium,* NL, fr. *hema-* + *-podium*; *hemapod* fr. *hema-* + *-pod*; fr. its proximity to the dorsal blood vessel] : the dorsal lobe of a parapodium

**he·map·o·dous** \hē'mapədəs\ *adj* [*hema-* + *-podous*] : of or relating to a hemapodium : having hemapodia

**he·ma·poi·e·sis** \ˌhēmə(ˌ)pȯiˈēsəs, ˌhem-\ *n* [NL, fr. *hema-* + *-poiesis*] : HEMATOPOIESIS

**he·mar·thro·sis** \ˌhēmärˈthrōsəs, ˌhem-\ *n* [NL, fr. *hem-* + *arthrosis*] : hemorrhage into a joint

**hemat-** *or* **hemato-** *or* **haemat-** *or* **haemato-** *comb form* [L *haemat-, haemato-,* fr. Gk *haimat-, haimato-,* fr. *haimat-, haima* blood — more at HEM-] : HEM- ⟨*hematoid*⟩ ⟨*hematocrit*⟩ — the forms *haemat-* or *haemato-* are preferred in taxonomic names ⟨*Haematozoon*⟩ ⟨*Haematogaster*⟩

**he·ma·tal** \'hēməd·əl, 'hem-\ *adj* [*hemat-* + *-al*] : relating to the blood or blood vessels

**he·ma·te·in** \ˌhēməˈtēən, ˌhem-\ *n* -S [ISV *hemat-* + *-ein*] : a reddish brown crystalline phenolic quinonoid compound $C_{16}H_{12}O_6$ constituting the essential dye in logwood extracts — see HEMATOXYLIN

**he·ma·tem·e·sis** \-ˈteməsəs\ *n* -ES [NL, fr. *hemat-* + Gk *emesis* vomiting — more at EMESIS] : the vomiting of blood

**he·ma·te·met·ic** \ˌhēməd·əˈmed·ik, ˌhem-\ *adj* [fr. NL *hematemesis,* after NL *emesis*: E *emetic*] : of or relating to hematemesis

**he·ma·therm** \'hēmə,thərm, 'hem-\ *n* -S [NL *Hematherma* (pl.), fr. *hema-* + *-therma* (fr. Gk *therma,* neut. pl. of *thermos* warm, hot) — more at WARM] : HOMOIOTHERM

**he·ma·ther·mal** \ˌ=='thərməl\ *or* **he·ma·ther·mous** \-məs\ *adj* [*hematherm* + *-al* or *-ous*] : HOMOIOTHERMIC

**1he·mat·ic** \hē'mad·|ik, -at|, |ēk\ *adj* [Gk *haimatikos,* fr. *haimat-* hemat- + *-ikos* -ic] **1 :** of or relating to blood **2 :** containing blood ⟨a ~ cyst⟩ **3 :** involving or affecting the blood ⟨a ~ crisis⟩ **4 :** having the color of blood : SANGUINEOUS

**2hematic** \"\ *n* -S : HEMATINIC

**he·ma·tid** \'hēməd·əd, 'hem-\ *n* -S [*hemat-* + *-id*] : a mature nonnucleated red blood cell

**he·ma·ti·dro·sis** \ˌhēməd·əˈdrōsəs, ˌhem-\ *n* -ES [NL, fr. *hemat-* + *-idrosis*] : the excretion through the skin of blood or blood pigments

**hem·a·tin** \'heməd·ən, 'hēm-\ *n* -S [ISV *hemat-* + *-in*] **1** *or* **hem·a·tine** \-ə,tēn, -əd·ən\ : HEMATEIN ⟨~ extract crystals⟩ — used esp. of preparations for use in dyeing; see DYE table I (under *Natural Black 1*) **2 a :** a compound derived from oxidized heme and usu. obtained in aqueous alkaline solutions or as a brownish black or bluish black solid $C_{34}H_{32}N_4O_4FeOH$ by treatment of hemin chloride with alkali; ferriprotoporphyrin hydroxide **b :** any of several similar compounds regarded as formed by the breakdown of hemoglobin esp. in some pathological conditions **c :** any of various similar iron-porphyrin derivatives or closely related pyrrole derivatives — compare HEME 2

**1hem·a·tin·ic** \ˌheməˈtinik, ˌhēm-\ *n* -S [*hematin* + *-ic*] : an agent that tends to stimulate blood-cell formation or to increase the hemoglobin in the blood

**2hematinic** \"\ *adj* : functioning as a hematinic ⟨the ~ value of certain iron salts⟩

**hem·a·tin·om·e·ter** \ˌheməd·ənˈäməd·ə(r), ˌhēm-\ *n* [ISV *hematin* + *-o-* + *-meter*] : HEMOGLOBINOMETER — **hem·a·tin·o·met·ric** \ˌ==d·ənō¦me·trik\ *adj*

**hem·a·tite** \'hemə,tīt, 'hēm-\ *n* -S [L *haematites,* fr. Gk *haimatitēs* resembling blood, fr. *haimat-, haima* blood — more at HEM-] : a mineral $Fe_2O_3$ consisting of ferric oxide and constituting an important iron ore that occurs in splendent metallic-looking rhombohedral crystals, in massive forms, and in red earthy forms (hardness of crystals 5.5–6.5, sp. gr. of crystals about 5.20) — called also *specular iron*; see LIMONITE, RED OCHER

**hematite red** *n* : a dark to dark grayish red

**hem·a·tit·ic** \ˌ=='tid·ik\ *adj* : of, containing, relating to, or resembling hematite in substance and color

**he·ma·to·bic** \ˌ=='tōbik\ *or* **he·ma·to·bi·ous** \-bēəs\ *adj* [NL *hematobium* + E *-ic* or *-ous*] : living in blood : parasitic in blood

**he·ma·to·bi·um** \ˌhēməˈtōbēəm, ˌhem-\ *n, pl* **hemato·bia** \-bēə\ [NL, fr. *hemat-* + *-bium* (fr. Gk *bios* mode of life) — more at QUICK] : an organism living in blood

**hem·a·to·blast** \'hemәd·ō,blast, 'hēm-\ *n* [ISV *hemat-* + *-blast*] **1 :** BLOOD PLATELET **2 :** an immature blood cell; *esp* : an immature red blood cell — **hem·a·to·blas·tic** \ˌ===ˈblastik\ *adj*

**hem·a·to·cele** \'===,sēl\ *n* -S [ISV *hemat-* + *-cele*] : a blood-filled cavity of the body; *also* : the effusion of blood into a body cavity (as the scrotum)

**hem·a·to·chrome** \-,krōm\ *n* [*hemat-* + *-chrome*] : an orange or reddish coloring matter found in various algae (as red snow)

**hem·a·to·col·pos** \ˌheməd·ōˈkäl,päs, ˌhēm-, -pəs\ *or* **hem·a·to·col·pus** \-lpəs\ *n* -ES [NL, fr. *hemat-* + *-colpos* or *-colpus*] : an accumulation of blood within the vagina

**he·mat·o·crit** \hi'mad·əkrət, -,krit\ *n* -S [ISV *hemat-* + *-crit* (fr. Gk *kritēs* judge) — more at CRITERION] **1 :** an instrument for determining the relative amounts of plasma and corpuscles in blood usu. by means of centrifugation **2** *or* **hematocrit value :** a percentile ratio of volume of packed red blood cells to volume of whole blood centrifuged by a hematocrit

**hem·a·to·cryal** \ˌheməd·ō¦krīəl, ˌhēm-\ *adj* [*hemat-* + *cry-* + *-al*] : COLD-BLOODED

**hem·a·to·cyte** \'===,sīt\ *n* -S [*hemat-* + *-cyte*] : HEMOCYTE

**hem·a·to·ge·nous** \ˌheməˈtäjənəs, ˌhēm-\ *adj* [*hemat-* + *-genous*] **1 :** concerned with the production of blood or of one or more of its constituents ⟨~ functions of the liver⟩ **2 a :** taking place by way of the blood ⟨~ metastasis of a tumor⟩ **b :** spread by way of the blood stream ⟨~ focal infection⟩ ⟨~ tuberculosis⟩

**hem·a·to·gone** \ˈhemәd·ә,gōn, ˈhēm-\ or **hem·a·to·go·nia** \,≈≈ˈgōnēә\ n -s [NL *hematogonia*, fr. *hemat-* + *-gonia* (fr. Gk *gonē* generation, offspring, seed) — more at GONE (germ cell)] : HEMOCYTOBLAST

**he·ma·toid** \ˈhēmә,tȯid, ˈhem-\ adj [Gk *haimatoeidēs*, fr. *haimat-* hemat — + *-eidēs* -oid] : resembling blood

**he·ma·toi·din** \,≈≈ˈtȯidәn\ n -s [ISV *hematoid* + *-in*] : BILIRUBIN

**hem·a·to·lite** \ˈhemәd·ō,līt, ˈhēm-\ n -s [ISV *hemat-* + *-lite;* fr. its color; orig. formed as Sw or G *aimatolit*] : a mineral $(Mn,Mg)_4Al(AsO_4)(OH)_8$ consisting of a brownish red aluminum manganese arsenate in rhombohedral crystals (sp.gr. 3.3–3.4)

**hem·a·to·log·ic** \¦hemәd·ō¦läjik, ¦hēm-\ or **hem·a·to·log·i·cal** \-jәkәl\ adj : of, relating to, or involving blood

**he·ma·tol·o·gist** \,hēmәˈtäləjәst, ,hem-\ n -s : one that specializes in the study of the blood

**he·ma·tol·o·gy** \-jē\ n -ES [*hemat-* + *-logy*] : a branch of biology that deals with the blood and blood-forming organs

**he·ma·tol·y·sis** \-ˈtäləsәs\ n [NL, fr. *hemat-* + *-lysis*] : HEMOLYSIS — **hem·a·to·lyt·ic** \¦hemәd·ō¦lid·ik, ¦hēm-\ adj

**he·ma·to·ma** \,hēmәˈtōmә, ,hem-\ n, pl **hematomas** \-ōmәz\ also **hematomata** \-ōmәd·ә\ [NL, fr. *hemat-* + *-oma*] : a tumor or swelling containing blood

**he·ma·tom·e·ter** \-ˈtämәd·ә(r)\ n [ISV *hemat-* + *-meter*] : HEMACYTOMETER

**hem·a·to·metra** \,hemәd·ōˈmē·trә, ,hēm-\ n -s [NL, fr. *hemat-* + *-metra*] : an accumulation of blood or menstrual fluid in the uterus

**hem·a·to·my·e·lia** \-d·ō,mīˈēlēә\ n -s [NL, fr. *hemat-* + *-myelia*] : a hemorrhage into the spinal cord

**hem·a·to·pericardium** \¦hemәd·ō, ¦hēm-+\ n [NL, fr. *hemat-* + *pericardium*] : HEMOPERICARDIUM

**hem·a·to·peritoneum** \"+\ n [NL, fr. *hemat-* + *peritoneum*] : HEMOPERITONEUM

**he·ma·toph·a·gous** \¦hēmә¦täfәgәs, ¦hem-\ adj [ISV *hemat-* + *-phagous*] : feeding on blood ⟨~ insects⟩ ⟨~ vampire bats⟩

**he·ma·toph·a·nite** \,≈≈ˈtäfә,nīt\ n -s [ISV *hemat-* + *phan-* (prob. fr. Gk *phanos* light, bright) + *-ite;* orig. formed as G *hämatophanit*] : a mineral $Pb_5Fe_4O_{10}(Cl,OH)_2$ consisting of oxychloride lead and iron

**hem·a·to·phyte** \ˈhemәd·ō,fīt, ˈhēm-\ n -s [*hemat-* + *-phyte*] : a plant parasite (as a bacterium) of the blood

**hem·a·to·plast** \-,plast\ n -s [*hemat-* + *-plast*] : HEMATOBLAST

**hem·a·to·poi·e·sis** \,hemәd·ō(,)pȯiˈēsәs, ,hēm-\ n -ES [NL, fr. *hemat-* + *-poiesis*] : formation of blood or of blood cells within the living body

**hem·a·to·poi·et·ic system** \¦≈≈≈(,)≈¦ed·ik-\ n [ISV *hemat-* + *-poietic*] : an organic system of the body consisting of the blood and the structures that function in its production

**hem·a·to·porphyrin** \¦hemәd·ō, ¦hēm-+\ n [ISV *hemat-* + *porphyrin*] : any of several isomeric porphyrins $C_{20}H_6N_4$-$(CH_3)_4(CHOHCH_3)_2(CH_2CH_2COOH)_2$ that are hydrated derivatives of protoporphyrins; *esp* : the deep red crystalline pigment obtained by treating hematin or heme with acid

**hem·a·to·por·phy·ri·nu·ria** \,hemәd·ō,pȯrfәrәˈn(y)u̇rēә, ,hēm-\ n -s [NL, fr. ISV *hematoporphyrin* + NL *-uria*] : PORPHYRINURIA

**hem·a·tor·rha·chis** \,hemәˈtȯrәkәs, ,hēm-\ n -ES [NL, fr. *hemat-* + *-rrhachis*] : hemorrhage into the spinal canal

**hem·a·to·salpinx** \¦hemәd·ō, ¦hēm-+\ n [NL, fr. *hemat-* + *salpinx*] : accumulation of blood in a fallopian tube

**hem·a·to·scope** \ˈhemәd·ō,skōp, ˈhēm-\ n [ISV *hemat-* + *-scope*] : an instrument for the spectroscopic examination of blood

**hem·a·to·thermal** \¦hemәd·ō, ¦hēm-+\ adj [*hemat-* + *thermal*] : WARM-BLOODED

**he·ma·tox·y·lin** \,hēmәˈtäksәlәn, ,hem-\ n -s [ISV *hematoxyl-* (fr. NL *Haematoxylon*, genus of plants, fr. *haemat-* hemat- + *-xylon*) + *-in*] : a colorless to yellowish crystalline phenolic compound $C_{16}H_{14}O_6$ found in logwood and used chiefly as a biological stain because of its ready oxidation to hematein; hydroxy-brazilin

**hem·a·to·zoal** \¦hemәd·ә¦zōәl, ¦hēm-\ adj : of or relating to hematozoa; *also* : blood-dwelling

**hem·a·to·zoan** \,≈≈≈ˈzōәn\ n -s [*hematozoon* + *-an*] : HEMATOZOON

**hem·a·to·zo·on** \-ō,än\ n, pl **hemato·zoa** \-ōә\ [NL, fr. *hemat-* + *-zoon*] : a blood-dwelling animal parasite

**he·ma·tu·ria** \,hēmәˈtu̇rēә, -ә·tyu̇-, ,hem-\ n -s [NL, fr *hemat-* + *-uria*] : the presence of blood or blood cells in the urine — compare HEMOGLOBINURIA

**he·mau·to·graph** \hēˈmȯd·ә,graf, heˈ-\ n [*hem-* + *auto-* + *-graph*] : a curve that is obtained when a stream of blood from an artery strikes against a piece of moving paper and that is indicative of the variations in blood pressure — **he·mau·to·graph·ic** \≈¦≈≈¦grafik\ adj — **he·mau·tog·ra·phy** \,hēmȯˈtägrәfē, ,hem-\ n -ES

**heme** \ˈhēm\ also **hem** \ˈhem\ or **haem** \ˈhēm, ˈhem\ n -s [ISV, fr. *hematin*] **1 :** a deep red iron-containing pigment $C_{34}H_{32}N_4O_4Fe$ that is obtained from hemoglobin by treatment with acid to remove the globin, that is a ferrous derivative of protoporphyrin, and that readily oxidizes to hematin or hemin — called also *ferroprotoporphyrin, protoheme, reduced hematin* **2 :** any of several compounds that are derived from protoporphyrin and iron in either the ferrous or ferric state and that constitute the nonprotein groups of some hemoproteins — compare HEMATIN 2c, HEMIN 2

**hem·el·y·tral** \heˈmelә·trәl\ adj : of or relating to a hemelytron or to hemelytra

**hem·el·y·tron** \-ә·,trän\ also **hem·el·y·trum** \-ә·trәm\ n, pl **hemely·tra** \-ә·trә\ [NL, fr. *hem-* (fr. *hemi-*) + *elytron* or *elytrum*] **1 :** one of the basally thickened anterior wings of various insects (as of Hemiptera) **2 :** one of the elytra of a chaetopod worm

**hem·en** \ˈhemәn\ pron [ME, alter. of *hem* — more at HEM (them)] *now dial Brit* : THEM — compare 1HEM

**hem·era** \ˈhemәrә\ n, pl **hemerae** \-ә(,)rē\ also **hemera** [NL, fr. Gk *hēmera* day; akin to Gk *ēmar* day, Arm *aur*] **1 :** a stratigraphic zone comprising the time range of a particular fossil species **2 :** a period of time during which a race of organisms is at the apex of its evolution

**hem·er·a·lope** \-rә,lōp\ n -s [F *héméralope*, fr. Gk *hēmeralōp-*, *hēmeralōps*] : one affected with hemeralopia

**hem·er·a·lo·pia** \,≈≈≈ˈlōpēә\ n -s [NL, fr. Gk *hēmeralōp-*, *hēmeralōps* (fr. *hēmera* day + *alaos* blind + *ōp-*, *ōps* eye) + NL *-ia*] **1 :** a defect of vision characterized by reduced visual capacity in bright lights — called also *day blindness* **2 :** NYCTALOPIA — **hem·er·a·lopic** \¦≈≈≈¦läpik\ adj

**hem·er·o·baptist** \¦hemәrō+\ n [ML *Hemerobaptista*, fr. Gk *Hēmerobaptistēs*, fr. *hēmero-* (fr. *hēmera* day) + *baptistēs* baptizer — more at BAPTIST] *usu cap* : one who practices daily or frequent baptism or ceremonial ablution; *specif* : a member of an ancient Jewish sect

**1hem·er·o·bi·id** \¦hemәrō¦bīәd\ adj [NL *Hemerobiidae*, family of flies, fr. *Hemerobius*, type genus + *-idae*] : of or relating to the genus *Hemerobius* or the family Hemerobiidae

**2hemerobiid** \"\ n -s : a hemerobiid fly

**hem·er·o·bi·us** \,hemәˈrōbēәs\ n, cap [NL, fr. Gk *hēmerobios* living for a day, fr. *hēmero-* + *-bios* (fr. *bios* mode of life) — more at QUICK] : a genus (the type of the family Hemerobiidae) of small usu. dark-colored lacewings with wings mottled with smoky brown — compare APHIS LION

**hem·er·o·cal·lis** \,hemәrōˈkalәs\ n, cap [NL, fr. Gk *hēmerokalles*, a kind of lily, fr. *hēmero-* (fr. *hēmera* day) + *-kalles* (fr. *kallos* beauty); fr. the fact that the blossoms close at night — more at CALLI-] : a genus of Eurasian herbs of the family Liliaceae with fibrous fleshy roots, basal linear leaves, and showy flowers in small clusters on naked scapes

**he·me·ryth·rin** \,hēmәˈrithrәn, ,hem-\ n -s [*hem-* + *erythr-* + *-in*] : an iron-containing respiratory pigment in the blood of various invertebrates

**1hemi-** *in pronunciations below*, ¦≈≈=¦hemē or (*usu not before vowels*) ¦hemә *sometimes* ¦he,mī\ *prefix* [ME, fr. L, fr. Gk *hēmi-* — more at SEMI-] **1 :** half of; *esp* : a lateral half of ⟨*hemi*centrum⟩ ⟨*hemi*cerebrum⟩ ⟨*hemi*cardia⟩ **2 :** relating to or affecting a half (as a lateral half) of an organ or part or of the whole body ⟨*hemi*plegia⟩ ⟨*hemi*atrophy⟩ **3** *chem* **a :** half in respect to combining ratio ⟨*hemi*basic⟩ **b :** having one half of the molecular weight of a (specified) compound or class of compounds **c :** having one half the number of characteristic groups in a (specified) compound or class of compounds ⟨*hemi*cyanine⟩ **4** *crystallog* : having one half the number of faces ⟨*hemi*hedron⟩

**2hemi-** — see HEM-

**-he·mia** \ˈhēmēә, *esp Brit* ˈhēmyә\ — see -EMIA

**hemi·acetal** \¦≈≈ *at* HEMI-+\ n [1*hemi-* + *acetal*] : any of a class of compounds characterized by the grouping >C(OH)-(OR) and usu. formed as intermediate products in the preparation of acetals from aldehydes or ketones ⟨an aldose is a favorable compound for the study of ~s —C.D.Hurd⟩ — see GLYCOSIDE, MONOSACCHARIDE

**hemi·anatropous** \"+\ adj [1*hemi-* + *anatropous*] : AMPHITROPOUS

**hemi·anesthesia** \"+\ n [NL, fr. 1*hemi-* + *anesthesia*] : loss of sensation in either lateral half of the body

**hemi·a·nop·sia** \,≈≈+әˈnäpsēә\ also **hem·i·a·no·pia** \-ˈnōpēә\ n -s [NL, fr. 1*hemi-* + *an-* 2*a-* + *-opsia* or *-opia*] : blindness in one half of the visual field and affecting one or both eyes

**hemi·a·nop·tic** \¦≈≈≈¦näptik\ adj [NL *hemianopsia* + E *optic*] : of or relating to hemianopsia

**hemi·ascomycetes** \¦≈≈ *at* HEMI-+\ n pl, cap [NL, fr. 1*hemi-* + *Ascomycetes*] : a subclass of Ascomycetes comprising simple ascomycetous fungi that lack an ascocarp and have asci arising directly from the fertile ascogonium and each containing an indefinite number of spores — see ENDOMYCETALES, TAPHRINALES; compare PROTOASCOMYCETES

**hemi·as·co·my·cet·i·dae** \"+,a(,)skō,mī¦sed·ә,dē\ *syn of* HEMIASCOMYCETES

**hemi·atrophy** \"+\ n -ES [NL *hemiatrophia*, fr. 1*hemi-* + LL *atrophia* atrophy — more at ATROPHY] : atrophy of one half of an organ or part or of the whole body ⟨facial ~⟩ — opposed to *hemihypertrophy*

**hemi·auxin** \"+\ n [1*hemi* + *auxin*] : an auxin precursor

**hemi·azygous vein** \"+ . . . -\ n [NL *hemiazygos*, fr. 1*hemi-* + *azygos*] : the left azygous vein passing up on the left side, crossing ventral to the vertebral column, and joining the right azygous vein

**hemi·ballism** *also* **hemi·ballismus** \"+\ n, pl **hemiballisms** *also* **hemiballismuses** [NL *hemiballismus*, fr. 1*hemi-* + *ballismus*] : violent uncontrollable movements of one lateral half of the body usu. due to hemorrhage in the opposite side of the brain

**hemi·ba·sid·i·ae** \,≈≈+bәˈsidē,ē\ [NL, fr. 1*hemi-* + *-basidiae* (fr. *basidium*)] *syn of* HEMIBASIDII

**hemi·ba·sid·i·a·les** \,≈≈≈,sidēˈā(,)lēz\ [NL, fr. *hemibasidium* + *-ales*] *syn of* USTILAGINALES

**hemi·ba·sid·ii** \,≈≈≈ˈsidē,ī\ n pl, cap [NL, fr. 1*hemi-* + *-basidii* (fr. *basidium*)] *in some classifications* : a subclass of Basidiomycetes comprising fungi with the basidium produced from a resting spore and including the order Ustilaginales or this together with the Uredinales — compare EUBASIDII, HETEROBASIDIOMYCETES

**hemi·basidiomycetes** \¦≈≈ *at* HEMI-+\ [NL, fr. *hemi-* + *Basidiomycetes*] *syn of* HEMIBASIDII

**hemi·basidium** \"+\ n [NL, fr. 1*hemi-* + *basidium*] : the transversely septate promycelium of a smut fungus — compare AUTOBASIDIUM, PROTOBASIDIUM

**hemi·benthic** *also* **hemi·benthonic** \"+\ adj [1*hemi-* + *benthic* or *benthonic*] : having a planktonic stage or phase ⟨~ animals⟩

**hemi·branch** \ˈ≈≈+,braŋk\ n **1** [NL *Hemibranchii*] : one of the Hemibranchii **2** [1*hemi-* + *-branch*] : a gill having lamellae or filaments only on one side; *collectively* : the lamellae or filaments on one side of a gill

**hemi·branchiate** \¦≈≈ *at* HEMI-+\ adj [1*hemi-* + *branchiate*] **1 :** having an incomplete or reduced branchial apparatus **2 :** of or relating to the Hemibranchii

**hemi·bran·chii** \,≈≈+ˈbraŋkē,ī\ n pl, cap [NL, fr. 1*hemi-* + *-branchii* (fr. L *branchia* gill) — more at BRANCHIA] *in some classifications* : a suborder of Thoracostei comprising fishes with an incomplete or reduced branchial apparatus and usu. including the sticklebacks, cornetfishes, bellows fishes, and shrimpfishes

**he·mic** \ˈhēmik, ˈhem-, -mēk\ adj [*hem-* + *-ic*] : of or relating to blood

**hemi·car·dia** \¦≈≈ *at* HEMI-+¦kärdēә\ n -s [NL, fr. 1*hemi-* + Gk *kardia* heart — more at HEART] : a lateral half of a 4≈chambered heart

**hemi·cellulose** \¦≈≈+\ n [ISV 1*hemi-* + *cellulose*] : any of various polysaccharides that accompany cellulose and lignin in the skeletal substances of wood and green plants and that resemble cellulose in being insoluble in water and hydrolyzable to simple sugar units by acids but differ from it in being soluble in alkali and presumably of smaller molecular dimensions, in undergoing acid hydrolysis more easily, and in giving rise on hydrolysis not only to glucose but also to uronic acids, xylose, galactose, and other carbohydrates — compare CELLULOSAN, PENTOSAN, POLYURONIDE — **hemi·cellulosic** \"+\ adj

**hemi·centrum** \"+\ n [NL, fr. 1*hemi-* + *centrum*] : a lateral half of the centrum of a vertebra

**hemi·ceph·a·lous** \"+¦sefәlәs\ or **hemi·ce·phal·ic** \"+sә¦falik\ adj [1*hemi-* + *-cephalous* or *-cephalic*] : having a poorly differentiated but distinct head — used of the larvae of various flies; compare EUCEPHALOUS

**hemi·cerebrum** \"+\ n [NL, fr. 1*hemi-* + *cerebrum*] : a lateral half of the cerebrum : CEREBRAL HEMISPHERE

**hemi·chorda** \"+\ [NL, fr. 1*hemi-* + *chorda* (notochord)] *syn of* HEMICHORDATA

**hemi·chordata** \"+\ n pl, cap [NL, fr. 1*hemi-* + *chordata*] : a division of Chordata usu. considered both subphylum and class, including the Enteropneusta and Pterobranchia and in some classifications the Phoronidea, and comprising a group of vermiform marine animals that have in the proboscis an outgrowth of the pharyngeal wall which suggests and is probably homologous with the notochord of higher chordates — **hemi·chordate** \"+\ n or adj

**hemi·cra·nia** \,≈≈ˈkrānēә\ n -s [LL — more at MIGRAINE] : pain in one side of the head — opposed to *amphicrania*

**hemi·cryptophyte** \¦≈≈ *at* HEMI-+\ n [ISV 1*hemi-* + *cryptophyte*] : a perennial plant having its overwintering buds located at the soil surface — **hemi·cryptophytic** \"+\ adj

**hemi·crystalline** \"+\ adj [ISV 1*hemi* + *crystalline*] : partly crystalline : characterized by crystals embedded in an amorphous groundmass

**he·mic·tic** \hēˈmiktik\ adj [fr. NL *hemixis*, after such pairs as NL *apomixis*: E *apomictic*] : of or relating to hemixis

**hemi·cy·cle** \ˈ≈≈ *at* HEMI- + ,sīkәl\ n [F *hémicycle*, modif. of L *hemicyclium*, fr. Gk *hēmikyklion*, fr. *hēmi-* 1hemi- + *kyklos* circle + *-ion* -ium — more at CYCLE] **1 :** a half circle : SEMICIRCLE **2 :** a curved or approximately semicircular structure or arrangement (as in an arena) : a curving or semicircular form (as of a driveway) ⟨a simple ~ containing the altar —W.K.Sturges⟩ ⟨the ~ of our modern civilization, the horseshoe area where nomadic man first settled down to tend crops —*Nat'l Geographic*⟩

**hemi·cyclic** \"+\ adj [1*hemi-* + *cyclic*] : having floral leaves partly in whorls and partly in spirals ⟨~ flowers⟩

**hemi·dactylous** \"+\ adj [NL *Hemidactylus* + E *-ous*] : of or relating to the genus *Hemidactylus*

**hemi·dactylus** \"+\ n, cap [NL, fr. 1*hemi-* + *dactylus*] : a widely distributed genus of geckos having the digits dilated and provided with two rows of lamellae on the underside

**hemi·demisemiquaver** \"+\ n [1*hemi-* + *demisemiquaver*] : SIXTY-FOURTH NOTE

**hemi·dome** \ˈ≈≈+,dōm\ n [ISV 1*hemi-* + *dome*] **1 :** a pinacoid parallel to the orthoaxis and cutting the vertical axes and clinoaxes in a crystal **2 :** a dome that has only two like faces (as an orthodome of a monoclinic crystal)

**hemi·dystrophy** \¦≈≈ *at* HEMI- +\ n [1*hemi-* + *dystrophy*] : an unequal development of the two lateral halves of the body

**hemi·elytral** \"+\ adj [NL *hemielytron* + E *-al*] : HEMELYTRAL

**hemi·elytron** *also* **hemi·elytrum** \"+\ n [NL, fr. 1*hemi-* + *elytron* or *elytrum*] : HEMELYTRON

**hemi·ep·es** \,≈≈+ˈe(,)pēz\ n, pl **hemiepe** [LL, fr. LGk *hēmiepes*, fr. Gk *hēmi-* 1hemi- + *-epes* (neut. of *-epēs*, fr. *epos* verse, line, word) — more at VOICE] : a dactylic tripody having a spondaic third foot or lacking the two short syllables of the third foot

**hemi·facial** \¦≈≈ *at* HEMI- +\ adj [1*hemi-* + *facial*] : involving or affecting one lateral half of the face ⟨~ spasm⟩

**hemi·form** \ˈ≈≈+,-\ n [1*hemi-* + *form*] : a rust in which only the uredinial and telial stages are known

**he·mig·a·lus** \hēˈmigәlәs\ n, cap [NL, fr. 1*hemi-* + *-galus* (fr. Gk *galē* weasel) — more at GALEA] : a genus of East Indian civets comprising the banded palm civets (as *H. hardwickii*)

**hemi·globin** \¦≈≈ *at* HEMI- +\ n [*hem-* + *globin*] : METHEMOGLOBIN

**hemi·glyph** \ˈ≈≈+,-\ n [1*hemi-* + *glyph*] : the half channel or groove on each edge of a triglyph

**hemi·he·dral** \¦≈≈+¦hēdrәl\ or **hemi·he·dric** \-rik\ adj [1*hemi-* + *-hedron* + *-al* or *-ic*] **1** *of a crystal* : having half the faces required by complete symmetry — compare HOLOHEDRAL **2 :** having the symmetry appropriate to a hemihedral form — **hemi·he·dral·ly** \-rәlē\ adv

**hemi·he·drism** \,≈≈+ˈhē,drizәm\ also **hemi·he·dry** \-ˈhēdrē\ n, pl **hemihedrisms** also **hemihedries** [1*hemi-* + *-hedron* + *-ism* or *-y*] : the property of crystallizing hemihedrally

**hemi·he·dron** \-ˈhēdrәn\ n, pl **hemihedrons** or **hemihedra** [NL, fr. 1*hemi-* + *-hedron*] : a hemihedral form or crystal

**hemi·holohedral** \¦≈≈ *at* HEMI- +\ adj [1*hemi-* + *holohedral*] *of a crystal* : having a hemihedral form in which half the octants have the full number of planes ⟨~ tetrahedron ⟨~ sphenoid⟩

**hemi·hydrate** \"+\ n [1*hemi-* + *hydrate*] : a hydrate containing half a molecule of water to one of the compound forming the hydrate — compare PLASTER OF PARIS — **hemi·hydrated** \"+\ adj

**hemi·hypertrophy** \"+\ n [NL *hemihypertrophia*, fr. 1*hemi-* + *hypertrophia* hypertrophy — more at HYPERTROPHY] : hypertrophy of one half of an organ or part or of the whole body ⟨facial ~⟩ — opposed to *hemiatrophy*

**hemi·karyon** \"+\ n [ISV 1*hemi-* + *karyon;* orig. formed in G] : a cell nucleus containing the haploid number of chromosomes — opposed to *amphikaryon* — **hemi·kar·y·ot·ic** \"+,karē¦äd·ik\ adj

**hemi·lateral** \"+\ adj [ISV 1*hemi-* + *lateral*] : of or affecting one lateral half of the body

**hemi·leia** \,≈≈+ˈlīә\ n, cap [NL, fr. 1*hemi-* + *-leia* (fr. Gk *leios* smooth, flat); fr. the shape of the spores — more at LIME] : a genus of rusts (order Uredinales) producing both urediospores and teliospores from a compound spore-bearing stalk

**hemi·mel·li·tene** \-ˈmelә,tēn\ n -s [ISV 1*hemi-* + *mellite* + *-ene*] : a liquid hydrocarbon $C_6H_3(CH_3)_3$ obtained from coal tar and petroleum; 1,2,3-trimethylbenzene

**hemi·mellitic acid** \¦≈≈ *at* HEMI- +. . .-\ n [ISV 1*hemi-* + *mellitic*] : a crystalline acid $C_6H_3(COOH)_3$ derived from benzene and having half as many carboxyl groups as mellitic acid; 1,2,3-benzene-tricarboxylic acid

**hem·im·er·id** \heˈmimәrәd\ n -s [NL *Hemimeridae*, family of insects, fr. *Hemimerus*, type genus + *-idae*] : an insect of the genus *Hemimerus*

**hem·im·er·oi·dea** \he,mimәˈrȯidēә\ [NL, fr. *Hemimerus* + *-oidea*] *syn of* DIPLOGLOSSATA

**hem·im·er·us** \heˈmimәrәs\ n, cap [NL, fr. 1*hemi-* + *-merus* (fr. Gk *meros* part) — more at MERIT] : a genus (coextensive with the family Hemimeridae and the order or suborder Diploglossata) comprising small wingless viviparous African insects parasitic on rodents

**hemi·metabola** \¦≈≈ *at* HEMI- +\ n pl, cap [NL, fr. 1*hemi-* + *Metabola*] : insects characterized by hemimetabolism

**hemi·metabolism** *also* **hemi·metabole** *or* **hemi·metaboly** \"+\ n [1*hemi-* + *metabolism* or *metabole* or *metaboly*] : incomplete metamorphosis; *esp* : incomplete metamorphosis in various insects with aquatic larvae in which the young does not resemble the adult

**hemi·metabolous** *also* **hemi·metabolic** \"+\ adj **1** [1*hemi-* + *metabolous* or *metabolic*] : of or relating to hemimetabolism **2** [NL *Hemimetabola* + E *-ous* or *-ic*] : of or relating to the Hemimetabola

**hemi·metamorphic** *or* **hemi·metamorphous** \"+\ adj [1*hemi-* + *metamorphic* or *metamorphous*] : of, relating to, or being marked by hemimetamorphosis

**hemi·metamorphosis** \"+\ n, pl **hemimetamorphoses** [NL, fr. 1*hemi-* + *metamorphosis*] : HEMIMETABOLISM

**hemimixis** *var of* HEMIXIS

**hemi·morph** \ˈ≈≈+,mȯrf\ n -s [1*hemi-* + *-morph*] : a hemimorphic form or crystal

**hemi·mor·phic** \¦≈≈+¦mȯrfik\ adj [ISV 1*hemi-* + *-morphic*] : unsymmetrical in form as regards the two ends of an axis : having a singular and polar axis

**hemi·mor·phism** \,≈≈+ˈmȯr,fizәm\ or **hemi·mor·phy** \ˈ≈≈+,mȯrfē\ n, pl **hemimorphisms** or **hemimorphies** [ISV 1*hemi-* + *-morphism* or *-morphy*] : the quality or state of being hemimorphic

**hemi·mor·phite** \,≈≈+ˈmȯr,fīt\ n -s [ISV *hemimorphic* + *-ite;* orig. formed as G *hemimorphit*] **1 :** a mineral $Zn_4$-$Si_2O_7OH.H_2O$ consisting of a basic zinc silicate in usu. white or colorless transparent orthorhombic crystals **2 :** SMITHSONITE

**hemi·my·aria** \"+mīˈa(a)rēә\ n pl, cap [NL, fr. 1*hemi-* + *-myaria*] : a suborder of Thaliacea that is coextensive in recent classifications with the family Salpidae

**he·min** *also* **hae·min** \ˈhēmәn\ n -s [ISV *hem-* + *-in*] **1 a** *also* **hemin chloride** : a red-brown to blue-black crystalline salt $C_{34}H_{32}N_4O_4FeCl$ derived from oxidized heme but usu. obtained in a characteristic crystalline form from hemoglobin by treatment with hot glacial acetic acid containing sodium chloride; ferriprotoporphyrin chloride — called also *protohemin;* compare BLOOD CRYSTAL, HEMATIN 2a, TEICHMANN'S CRYSTAL **b :** any of a series of salts of which hemin chloride is a member **2 :** any of several iron-porphyrin derivatives similar to hemin chloride — compare HEME 2

**hem·i·o·la** \,hemēˈōlә\ or **hem·i·o·lia** \-lēә\ n -s [LL *hemiolia*, fr. Gk *hēmiolia* ratio of one and a half to one (3:2), fr. *hēmiolia*, fem. of *hēmiolios* in the ratio of one and a half to one (3:2), fr. *hēmi-* 1hemi- + *-olios* (fr. *holos* whole) — more at SAFE] **1 :** the interval of a fifth in medieval music **2 :** the rhythmic alteration consisting of three notes in place of two or two notes in place of three

**hem·i·ol·ic** \¦≈≈¦älik\ adj [L *hemiolius* (fr. Gk *hēmiolios*) + E *-ic*] *in classical prosody* : of, relating to, or characterized by the proportion of three to two; *esp* : characterized by such a proportion between thesis and arsis ⟨a ~ foot⟩

**hemi·o·pia** \,≈≈ *at* HEMI- + ˈōpēә\ or **hemi·op·sia** \-ˈäpsēә\ n -s [NL, fr. 1*hemi-* + *-opia, -opsia*] : HEMIANOPSIA — **hemi·op·ic** \¦≈≈+¦äpik, -¦ōp-\ adj

**hemi·orthotype** \¦≈≈ *at* HEMI- +\ adj [*hemi-* + *orth-* + *type*] : MONOCLINIC

**hemi·parasite** \"+\ n [ISV 1*hemi-* + *parasite*] **1 :** a facultative parasite — compare HOLOPARASITE **2 :** a parasitic plant that contains some chlorophyll and is therefore capable of photosynthesis (as the mistletoe) — **hemi·parasitic** \"+\ adj

**hemi·paresis** \"+\ n [NL, fr. 1*hemi-* + *paresis*] : muscular weakness or partial paralysis restricted to one side of the body usu. of neural or psychic origin and often transitory — **hemi·paretic** \"+\ adj

**hemi·penis** \"+\ n [NL, fr. 1*hemi-* + *penis*] : one of the paired copulatory organs of lizards and snakes

**hemi·plankton** \"+\ n [NL, fr. 1*hemi-* + *plankton*] : plankton composed of predominantly plant organisms that at certain seasons come to rest on the bottom — compare HOLOPLANKTON

**hemi·ple·gia** \,≈≈+ˈplēj(ē)ә\ n -s [NL, fr. MGk *hēmiplēgia* paralysis, fr. *hēmi-* 1hemi- + *-plēgia* -plegia] : paralysis of one lateral half of the body or part of it resulting from injury (as by hemorrhage or disease) to the motor centers of the brain

**1hemi·ple·gic** \¦≈≈+¦plējik, -jēk\ adj [*hemiplegia* + *-ic*] : relating to or marked by hemiplegia

**2hemiplegic** \"\ n -s : a hemiplegic individual

**hemi·pode** \ˈ≈≈+,pōd\ also **hemi·pod** \-,päd\ n -s [NL *Hemipodius*, genus of birds, fr. Gk *hēmipod-*, *hēmipous* half foot, fr. *hēmi-* 1hemi- + *pod-*, *pous* foot — more at FOOT] : BUTTON QUAIL

**he·mip·pe** \hēˈmipē\ n -s [NL *hemippus* (specific epithet of *Equus hemippus*), fr. 1*hemi-* + *-ippus* (fr. Gk *hippos* horse) —

more at EQUINE] : a small wild ass (*Equus hemippus*) of Syria and Iraq

**hemi·prism** \ˈ⸗⸗ *at* HEMI- + ˌ-\ *n* [ISV ¹*hemi-* + *prism*] : a prism consisting of only two parallel faces (as in the triclinic system) : a pinacoid cutting two crystallographic axes

**he·mip·tera** \heˈmiptərə\ *n pl, cap* [NL, fr. ¹*hemi-* + *-ptera*] **1** : a large order of insects that comprise the true bugs (as the bedbug, squash bug, and chinch bug) and various related insects (as the aphids and mealybugs), that are generally more or less flattened, that have mouthparts adapted to piercing and sucking and usu. two pairs of wings of which the basal part of the anterior pair is thickened and coriaceous and the distal part membranous while the posterior pair is wholly membranous, that undergo an incomplete metamorphosis, and that include many important pests — see HETEROPTERA, HOMOPTERA **2 a** *in some classifications* : an order coextensive with Heteroptera **b** *in some esp former classifications* : an order including Hemiptera (sense 1) together with Anoplura and Thysanoptera

**he·mip·ter·oid** \-təˌrȯid\ *adj* [NL *Hemiptera* + E *-oid*] : characteristic of or resembling the Hemiptera ⟨~ insect⟩ ⟨~ mouthparts⟩

**he·mip·ter·ol·o·gy** \⸗ˌ⸗⸗ˈräləjē\ *n* -ES [NL *Hemiptera* + E *-o-* + *-logy*] : a branch of entomology that deals with Hemiptera

**he·mip·ter·on** \⸗ˈ⸗⸗ˌrän\ *also* **he·mip·ter·an** \-rən\ *n* -S [*hemipteron*, NL, back-formation fr. *Hemiptera; hemipteran* fr. NL *Hemiptera* + E *-an*] : one of the Hemiptera

**he·mip·ter·ous** \-rəs\ *adj* [NL *Hemiptera* + E *-ous*] : of or relating to the Hemiptera

**hemi·pyramid** \ˈ⸗⸗ *at* HEMI- + \ *n* [ISV ¹*hemi-* + *pyramid*] : a crystallographic pyramid or inclined prism consisting of only two pairs of parallel faces (as in the monoclinic system)

**hemi·quinonoid** *or* **hemi·quinoid** \"+\ *adj* [¹*hemi-* + *quinonoid* or *quinoid*] : having or relating to a quinonoid arrangement of bonds but only one carbonyl group instead of two

**hemi·ramph** \ˈ⸗⸗ˌram(p)f\ *n* -S [NL *Hemiramphus*] : a halfbeak of the genus *Hemiramphus*

**hem·i·ram·phid** \ˌ⸗⸗ˈram(p)fəd\ *adj* [NL *Hemiramphidae*, family of halfbeaks, fr. *Hemiramphus*, type genus + *-idae*] : HEMIRAMPHINE

**hemi·ram·phine** \-)ˌfīn, -ˌfən\ *adj* [NL *Hemiramphus* + E *-ine*] : of or relating to the genus *Hemiramphus* or the family Hemiramphidae

**hemi·ram·phus** \ˌ⸗⸗ˈram(p)fəs\ *n, cap* [NL, fr. ¹*hemi-* + *-ramphus* (irreg. fr. Gk *rhamphos* crooked beak, beak)] : a widely distributed genus of halfbeaks now usu. made the type of a separate family (Hemirhamphidae) but sometimes esp. formerly included in the family Exocoetidae

**hemirhamphus** \"\ [NL, fr. ¹*hemi-* + Gk *rhamphos* crooked beak, beak] *syn of* HEMIRAMPHUS

**hemi·saprophyte** \ˈ⸗⸗ *at* HEMI- + \ *n* [ISV ¹*hemi-* + *saprophyte*] : a partial saprophyte: **a** : an organism usu. a saprophyte but capable of existing as a parasite — compare HOLOSAPROPHYTE **b** : a plant containing a small amount of chlorophyll but obtaining most of its food material from humus — **hemi·saprophytic** \"+\ *adj*

**hemi·sect** \ˌ⸗⸗+ˈsekt\ *vt* -ED/-ING/-S [¹*hemi-* + *-sect*] : to divide along the mesial plane

**hemi·section** \ˈ⸗⸗ *at* HEMI- +\ *n* [¹*hemi-* + *section*] : a division or dividing along the mesial plane

**hemi·sphaeriales** \"+\ [NL, fr. ¹*hemi-* + *Sphaeriales*] *syn of* MICROTHYRIALES

**hem·i·spher·al** \ˌheməˈsfirəl, -fer-\ *adj* : HEMISPHERIC

**hem·i·sphere** \ˈheməˌsfi(ə)r, -iə\ *n* [alter. (influenced by MF *emisphere*) of ME *hemisphere, hemisperie*, fr. L *hemisphaerium*, fr. Gk *hēmisphairion*, fr. *hēmi-* ¹hemi- + *sphairion* small sphere (dim. of *sphaira* sphere, ball)] **1 a** : a half of the celestial sphere divided into two halves by the horizon, the celestial equator, or the ecliptic **b** *obs* : the sky above the horizon or overhead **c** : a projection on a plane surface of half of the celestial sphere **2** : REALM, PROVINCE ⟨a ~ of special knowledge⟩ ⟨a ~ of life heretofore unknown to us⟩ ⟨a discovery that was to have important repercussions in the ~s of French literary life —*Times Lit. Supp.*⟩ **3 a** : a half of the terrestrial globe esp. as divided by the equator ⟨sailed down over the equator into the southern ~⟩ or into halves one of which contains Europe, Asia, and Africa and the other the Americas ⟨sailed from Europe for the western ~⟩ **b** : a map or projection of one of these halves¶ **c** : the inhabitants of one of these halves of the earth ⟨America's plans did not seem to interest the eastern ~⟩ **4** : either of two half spheres formed by a plane through a sphere's center **5** : CEREBRAL HEMISPHERE

**hemi·spher·ec·to·my** \ˌ⸗⸗ˌsfiˈrektəmē\ *n* -ES [*hemisphere* + *-ectomy*] : surgical removal of a cerebral hemisphere

**hem·i·sphered** \ˈheməˌsfi(ə)rd\ *adj* : having a hemisphere or hemispheric form

**hem·i·spher·ic** \ˌheməˈsfirik, -fer-, -rēk\ *or* **hem·i·spher·i·cal** \-rəkəl, -rēk-\ *adj* [*hemisphere* + *-ic* or *-ical*] : of, relating to, or resembling a hemisphere ⟨a ~ bowl⟩ ⟨~ solidarity⟩ — **hem·i·spher·i·cal·ly** \-rək(ə)lē, -rēk-, -li\ *adv*

**hemispherical scale** *n* : a cosmopolitan soft scale (*Saissetia coffeae*) found in warm countries or as a greenhouse pest

**hem·i·sphe·roid** \ˌ⸗⸗ˈsfiˌrȯid\ *n* [¹*hemi-* + *spheroid*] : one of the halves into which a plane of symmetry cuts a spheroid — **hem·i·sphe·roi·dal** \ˌ⸗⸗ˌsfiˈrȯidᵊl\ *adj*

**hem·i·stich** \ˈheməˌstik\ *n* [L *hemistichium*, fr. Gk *hēmistichion*, fr. *hēmi-* ¹hemi- + *stichos* line, verse + *-ion* -ium; akin to Gk *steichein* to go — more at STAIR] : half a poetic line usu. divided by a caesura (as a metrically independent colon or group of feet of less than regular length)

**hem·i·stich·al** \ˌ⸗⸗ˈstikəl\ *adj* : of, relating to, or written in hemistichs ⟨a ~ division of a verse⟩

**hemi·symmetrical** \ˈ⸗⸗ *at* HEMI- +\ *adj* : HEMIHEDRAL

**hemi·symmetry** \"+\ *n* [¹*hemi-* + *symmetry*] : the quality or state of being hemisymmetrical

**hemi·terpene** \"+\ *n* [ISV ¹*hemi-* + *terpene*] : a compound $C_5H_8$ whose formula represents half that of a terpene; *esp* : ISOPRENE

**hemi·thorax** \"+\ *n* [NL, fr. ¹*hemi-* + *thorax*] : a lateral half of the thorax

**he·mit·ro·pal** \heˈmi·trəpəl\ *adj* : HEMITROPOUS

¹**hemi·trope** \ˈ⸗⸗ *at* HEMI- + ˌtrōp\ *adj* [F *hémitrope*, adj. & n., fr. *hémi-* ¹hemi- + *-trope*] : half turned round : half inverted; *specif* : HEMITROPIC

²**hemitrope** \"\ *n* -S [F *hémitrope*] : a hemitropic crystal

**hemi·trop·ic** \ˌ⸗⸗ˈträpik\ *adj, crystallog* : having a twinned structure such that one part would be parallel to the other if it were rotated 180 degrees

**hemi·tro·pism** \ˈ⸗⸗ˌtrōˌpizəm\ *or* **he·mit·ro·py** \heˈmi·trəpē\ *n, pl* **hemitropisms** *or* **hemitropies** [*hemitropism* fr. ¹*hemitrope* + *-ism; hemitropy* fr. F *hémitropie*, fr. *hémi-* ¹hemi- + *tropie* -tropy] : the quality or state of being hemitropic

**he·mit·ro·pous** \⸗ˈ⸗⸗pəs\ *adj* **1** [¹*hemitrope* + *-ous*] : HEMITROPIC **2** [¹*hemi-* + *-tropous*] : AMPHITROPOUS

**hemi·type** \ˈ⸗⸗ *at* HEMI- + ˌ-\ *n* [¹*hemi-* + *type*] : one that is hemitypic

¹**hemi·typic** \ˌ⸗⸗+\ *adj* [¹*hemi-* + *typic*] : imperfectly typical

²**hemitypic** \"+\ *n* -S : one that is hemitypic

**he·mix·is** \heˈmiksəs\ *also* **hemi·mix·is** \ˌ⸗⸗ *at* HEMI- + ˈmiksəs\ *n* -ES [*hemixis*, NL, contr. of *hemimixis; hemimixis*, NL, fr. ¹*hemi-* + *-mixis*] : a reorganization process in various ciliated protozoans in which the macronucleus breaks up and a new macronucleus is reconstituted from the fragments without accompanying micronuclear changes — compare ENDOMIXIS

**hemi·zo·ic** \ˌ⸗⸗+ˈzōik\ *adj* [¹*hemi-* + *-zoic*] : having chlorophyll-bearing chromatophores but also ingesting solid food ⟨~ green flagellates⟩ — compare HOLOPHYTIC, HOLOZOIC

**hemi·zygote** \"+\ *n* [¹*hemi-* + *zygote*] : one that is hemizygous

**hemi·zygotic** \"+\ *adj* : HEMIZYGOUS

**hemi·zy·gous** \ˌ⸗⸗+ˈzīgəs, heˈmizəgəs\ *adj* [¹*hemi-* + *-zygous*] : having or characterized by unpaired genes or a haploid organism or generation ⟨a ~ sex chromosome⟩

**hemline** \ˈ⸗ˌ⸗\ *n* [²*hem* + *line*] : the line formed by the lower edge of a dress, skirt, or coat

**hem·lock** \ˈhemˌläk\ *n, often attrib* [ME *hemeluc, hemlok, homelok*, fr. OE *hemlic, hymlic*, perh. fr. *hymele* hop plant; akin to MLG *homele* hop plant, ON *humli;* all prob. of Finno-Ugric origin akin to Finn *humala* hop plant & Vogul *qumlix*] **1 a** : any of several poisonous herbs having finely cut leaves and small white flowers; *esp* : any of the water hemlocks or the poison hemlock **b** : CONIUM 2 **2** *also* **hemlock fir** *or* **hemlock spruce a** : a tree of the genus *Tsuga* — see CAROLINA HEMLOCK, EASTERN HEMLOCK, MOUNTAIN HEMLOCK, WESTERN HEMLOCK; TREE illustration **b** : the soft coarse light splintery wood of a hemlock tree **3** : any of several prostrate evergreens of the genus *Taxus*

**hemlock chervil** *n* : a hedge parsley (*Torilis japonica*) that is native to Eurasia but naturalized widely in No. America

**hemlock green** *n* : a dark grayish green that is bluer and deeper than average ivy and bluer and darker than Persian green

**hemlock leather** *n* : leather tanned with hemlock bark or extract

**hemlock looper** *also* **hemlock spanworm** *n* : a greenish looper that is the larva of a rather plain buff or gray geometrid moth (*Lambdina fiscellaria*) of most of No. America, that feeds on hemlock and other conifers and oak, and that is sometimes a serious defoliator

**hemlock parsley** *n* : any of several plants of the genus *Conioselinum* (esp. *C. chinense*) that resemble the poisonous hemlocks but are themselves innocuous

**hemlock pitch** *n* : CANADA PITCH

**hemlock sawfly** *n* : a sawfly (*Neodiprion tsugae*) of western No. America having a larva that is a serious defoliator of western hemlock and occas. other conifers

**hemlock storksbill** *n* : ALFILARIA

**hemmed** *past of* HEM

**hem·mel** \ˈheməl\ *n* -S [perh. alter. of ¹*helm* (rough shed)] *dial Brit* : a simple shelter usu. in a field for cattle or hay

¹**hem·mer** \ˈhemə(r)\ *n* -S [ME, fr. *hemmen* to hem, border + *-er* — more at ³HEM] : one that hems: **a** : a worker who makes hems by hand or machine **b** : a sewing machine attachment for turning under and stitching hems **c** : a tool for turning over the edge of sheet metal

²**hemmer** \"\ *n* -S [⁵*hem* + *-er*] : one that hems in speech

**hemming** *n* -S [fr. gerund of ³*hem*] : the act or process of one that hems; *also* : HEM ⟨ran a wide ~ around the bottom of the cloth⟩

**hemo-** — see HEM-

**he·mo·blast** \ˈhēməˌblast, ˈhem-\ *n* [ISV *hem-* + *-blast*] : HEMATOBLAST

**he·mo·chorial** \ˌhēmō, ˌhemō+\ *adj* [*hem-* + *chorial*] *of a placenta* : having fetal epithelium bathed in maternal blood ⟨the lower rodents, bats, some insectivores, and most primates including man are ~⟩ — compare ENDOTHELIOCHORIAL, EPITHELIOCHORIAL, SYNDESMOCHORIAL

**he·mo·chromatosis** \"+\ *n* [NL, fr. *hem-* + *chromatosis*] : a disease characterized by widespread deposition of iron-containing pigments (as hemosiderin) in the tissues resulting in bronzing of the skin, associated with cirrhosis of the liver and pancreas and frequently with diabetic symptoms, and occurring usu. in males — called also *bronze diabetes*

**he·mo·chrome** \ˈhēməˌkrōm, ˈhem-\ *n* -S [ISV *hem-* + *-chrome*] : HEMOCHROMOGEN

**he·mo·chro·mo·gen** \ˌ⸗⸗ˈkrōməjən, -ˌjen\ *n* -S [ISV *hemochromo-* (fr. *hemochrome*) + *-gen*] **1** : a colored compound formed from or related to hemoglobin; *esp* : a bright red combination of a nitrogen base (as globin or pyridine) with heme — compare HEMOPROTEIN **2** : a colored compound of a nitrogenous base with a metal-porphyrin derivative esp. when in the reduced form

**he·mo·clas·tic crisis** \ˌ⸗⸗ˈklastik-\ *n* [ISV *hem-* + *-clastic* (disintegrating)] : an acute transitory alteration of the blood that sometimes accompanies anaphylactic shock and is marked by intense leukopenia with relative lymphocytosis, alteration in blood coagulability, and fall in blood pressure

**he·mo·coel** *also* **he·mo·coele** \ˈhēməˌsēl, ˈhem-\ *n* -S [*hem-* + *-coele*] : a body cavity (as in arthropods) formed by the expansion of parts of the blood-vascular system — **he·mo·coe·lic** \ˌ⸗⸗ˈsēlik\ *adj* — **he·mo·coe·lous** \-ləs\ *adj*

**he·mo·coelom** \ˌhēmō, ˌhemō+\ *n* [*hem-* + *coelom*] **1** : the part of the embryonic coelom in which the heart develops **2** : HEMOCOEL

**he·mo·concentration** \"+\ *n* [ISV *hem-* + *concentration*] : increased concentration of cells and solids in the blood usu. resulting from loss of fluid to the tissues — compare HEMODILUTION

**he·mo·co·nia** *also* **he·mo·ko·nia** \ˌhēməˈkōnēə, ˌhem-\ *n* -S [NL, fr. *hem-* + Gk *konia* dust — more at INCINERATE] : small refractive colorless particles in the blood that are believed to be castoff granules from the cells in the blood or minute globules of fat — called also *blood dust*

**he·mo·co·ni·o·sis** \ˌ⸗⸗ˌkōnēˈōsəs\ *n, pl* **hemoconio·ses** \-ˈōˌsēz\ [NL, fr. *hemoconia* + *-osis*] : a condition in which there is an abnormally high content of hemoconia in the blood

**he·mo·culture** \ˌhēmō, ˌhemō+\ *n* [ISV *hem-* + *culture*] : a culture made from blood to detect the presence of pathogenic microorganisms by providing conditions likely to further their multiplication

**he·mo·cu·pre·in** \ˌhēməˈk(y)üprēən, ˌhem-\ *n* -S [ISV *hem-* + *cupr-* + *-ein*] : a blue copper-containing protein obtained from red blood cells

**he·mo·cy·a·nin** \ˌ⸗⸗ˈsīənən\ *n* [ISV *hem-* + *cyan-* + *-in*] : a colorless copper-containing respiratory pigment found in solution in the blood plasma of various arthropods and mollusks and converted by oxygen to blue oxyhemocyanin

**he·mo·cyte** \ˈ⸗⸗ˌsīt\ *n* -S [ISV *hem-* + *-cyte*] : a blood cell esp. of an invertebrate animal

**he·mo·cy·to·blast** \ˌ⸗⸗ˈsīdəˌblast\ *n* -S [ISV *hemocyto-* (fr. *hemocyte*) + *-blast*] : a stem cell for blood-cellular elements; *esp* : one considered competent to produce all types of blood cell — **he·mo·cy·to·blas·tic** \ˌ⸗⸗ˌ⸗⸗ˈblastik\ *adj*

**he·mo·cy·to·blas·to·sis** \ˌhēməˌsīdəˌblaˈstōsəs, ˌhem-\ *n, pl* **hemocytoblasto·ses** \-ōˌsēz\ [NL, fr. ISV *hemocytoblast* + NL *-osis*] : lymphocytomatosis of chickens

**he·mo·cy·to·gen·e·sis** \-dəˈjenəsəs\ *n* [NL, fr. *hemocyto-* (fr. ISV *hemocyte*) + L *genesis*] : the part of hematopoiesis concerned with the formation of blood cells

**he·mo·cy·tol·y·sis** \-ˌsīˈtäləsəs\ *n, pl* **hemocytoly·ses** \-əˌsēz\ [NL, fr. *hemocyto-* (fr. ISV *hemocyte*) + NL *-lysis*] : a breaking down or dissolution of red blood cells esp. by the action of hypotonic solutions

**he·mo·cy·tom·e·ter** \-ˈtäməd-ə(r)\ *n* [ISV *hem-* + *cyt-* + *-meter*] : HEMACYTOMETER

**he·mo·cy·to·zo·on** \ˌsīd-əˈzōˌän\ *n* -S [NL, fr. *hemocyto-* (fr. ISV *hemocyte*) + NL *-zoon*] : an animal parasite (as the plasmodium of malaria) living within a blood corpuscle

**he·mo·dilution** \ˌhēmō, ˌhemō+\ *n* [*hem-* + *dilution*] : decreased concentration of cells and solids in the blood usu. resulting from gain of fluid from the tissues (as after hemorrhage) — compare HEMOCONCENTRATION

**he·mo·dynamic** \"+\ *adj* [ISV *hem-* + *dynamic*] **1** : of, relating to, or involving hemodynamics **2** : concerned with or functioning in the mechanics of blood circulation

**he·mo·dynamics** \"+\ *n pl but sing or pl in constr* [ISV *hem-* + *dynamics*] **1** : a branch of physiology that deals with circulatory movements and the forces involved in circulation of the blood **2 a** : the forces involved in circulation (as of a particular body part) ⟨renal ~⟩ **b** : hemodynamic effect (as of a drug)

**he·mo·endothelial** \"+\ *adj* [*hem-* + *endothelial*] *of a placenta* : having the fetal villi reduced to bare capillary loops that are bathed in maternal blood ⟨higher rodents are ~⟩

**hemoflagellate** \"+\ *n* [*hem-* + *flagellate*] : a flagellate (as a trypanosome) that is a blood parasite

**he·mo·fus·cin** \ˌhēməˈfəsən, ˌhem-\ *n* [ISV *hem-* + *fusc-* (fr. L *fuscus* dark brown) + *-in* — more at DUSK] : a yellowish brown pigment found in small amount in some normal tissues and increased amount in certain pathological states (as hemochromatosis)

**he·mo·glo·bic** \ˌ⸗⸗ˈglōbik\ *adj* [*hemoglobin* + *-ic*] : HEMOGLOBINIC

**he·mo·glo·bin** *also* **hae·mo·glo·bin** \ˈ⸗⸗ˌglōbən, ˌ⸗⸗ˈ⸗⸗\ *n* -S [ISV, short for earlier *hematoglobulin*, fr. *hemato-* (fr. *hematin*) + *globulin*] **1 a** : an iron-containing protein pigment occurring in the red blood cells of vertebrates and functioning primarily in the transport of oxygen from the lungs to the tissues of the body **b** : the dark purplish crystallizable form of this pigment that is found chiefly in the venous blood of vertebrates, that is a conjugated protein composed of heme and globin commonly in a ratio of four molecules of heme to one of globin but that may vary somewhat in different species and in different physiological and pathological states (as in some anemias), that combines loosely and reversibly with oxygen in the lungs or gills to form oxyhemoglobin and with carbon dioxide in the tissues to form carbhemoglobin, that in man is present normally in blood to the extent of 14 to 16 gm. in 100 ml. expressed sometimes on a scale of 0 to 100 with an average normal value (as 15 gm.) taken as 100, and that is determined in blood either colorimetrically or by quantitative estimation of the iron present — symbol *Hb;* called also *ferrohemoglobin, reduced hemoglobin;* compare CARBONYLHEMOGLOBIN, METHEMOGLOBIN **c** : any of numerous chemically similar iron-containing respiratory pigments that occur in cells or usu. free in the plasma of many annelid worms and certain other invertebrates, in some yeasts and other fungi, in the nodules formed on the roots of leguminous plants by nitrogen-fixing bacteria, and elsewhere — compare HEMOPROTEIN **2** : any of various respiratory pigments consisting of a conjugated protein that has as the nonprotein group either heme or an analogous compound containing a metal — compare MYOGLOBIN — **he·mo·glo·bin·ic** \ˌ⸗⸗ˌglōˈbinik\ *adj* — **he·mo·glo·bi·nous** \ˌ⸗⸗ˈglōbənəs\ *adj*

**hemoglobin A** *n* : the hemoglobin in the red blood cells of normal adult human beings

**he·mo·glo·bi·ne·mia** \ˌ⸗⸗ˌglōbəˈnēmēə\ *n* -S [NL, fr. ISV *hemoglobin* + NL *-emia*] **1** : the presence of free hemoglobin in the blood plasma resulting from the solution of hemoglobin out of the red blood cells or from disintegration of the red cells **2** : AZOTEMIA

**he·mo·glo·bi·nom·e·ter** \-ˈnäməd-ə(r)\ *n* [ISV *hemoglobin* + *-o-* + *-meter*] : an instrument for the colorimetric determination of hemoglobin in blood ⟨visual and photoelectric ~s⟩ — **he·mo·glo·bi·nom·e·try** \-mə·trē\ *n* -ES

**hemoglobin S** *n* : the hemoglobin occurring in the red blood cells in sickle-cell anemia and sicklemia and differing from hemoglobin A in its lower solubility and lower isoelectric point

**he·mo·glo·bi·nu·ria** \-ˈn(y)u̇rēə\ *n* -S [NL, fr. ISV *hemoglobin* + NL *-uria*] : the presence of free hemoglobin in the urine — compare HEMATURIA — **he·mo·glo·bi·nu·ric** \ˌ⸗⸗-ˌ⸗⸗ˈn(y)u̇rik\ *adj*

**he·mo·gram** \ˈhēməˌgram, ˈhem-\ *n* [ISV *hem-* + *-gram*] : a systematic report of the findings from a blood examination

**hemogregarine** *var of* HAEMOGREGARINE

**he·mo·his·ti·o·blast** \ˌhēmōˈhistēōˌblast, ˌhem-\ *n* [ISV *hem-* + *histi-* + *-blast*] : a hemocytoblast that is a derivative of the reticuloendothelial system

**he·moid** \ˈhēˌmȯid\ *adj* [ISV *hem-* + *-oid*] : resembling blood : HEMATOID

**hemokonia** *var of* HEMOCONIA

**he·mo·lymph** \ˈhēmə, ˈhemə+ˌ-\ *n* [ISV *hem-* + *lymph*] : the circulatory fluid of various invertebrate animals that is functionally comparable to the blood and lymph of vertebrates

**he·mo·lymphatic** \ˌ⸗⸗+\ *adj* [fr. *hemolymph*, after E *lymph: lymphatic*] : of, like, or relating to hemolymph or to a hemolymph gland

**hemolymph gland** *or* **hemolymph node** *n* : any of several small chiefly retroperitoneal nodes of tissue resembling lymph nodes but having the lymph spaces replaced in whole or in part by blood sinuses

**he·mo·ly·sin** \ˌhēməˈlīsᵊn, ˌhem-\ *n* [ISV *hem-* + *lysin*] : a substance (as an antibody) that esp. in conjunction with complement causes the dissolution of red blood cells with liberation of the contained hemoglobin

**he·mol·y·sis** \hēˈmäləsəs\ *n, pl* **hemoly·ses** \-əˌsēz\ [NL, fr. *hem-* + *-lysis*] : liberation of hemoglobin from red blood cells; *specif* : such a liberation brought about by a specific hemolysin usu. interacting with complement

**he·mo·lyt·ic** \ˌhēməˈlid-ik, ˌhem-\ *adj* [ISV *hem-* + *-lytic*] : of, relating to, involving, or inducing hemolysis ⟨~ antigens⟩

**hemolytic anemia** *n* : anemia characterized by excessive destruction of red blood cells caused by chemical poisoning (as by certain sulfonamide compounds), infections (as malaria or sepsis), cell abnormalities (as sickle-cell anemia), or other agents or factors (as endogenous hemolysins)

**hemolytic disease of the newborn** : ERYTHROBLASTOSIS FETALIS

**hemolytic jaundice** *or* **hemolytic icterus** *n* : a condition characterized by excessive destruction of red blood cells accompanied by jaundice; *specif* : a rare familial anemia characterized by small thick fragile red blood cells which are extremely susceptible to hemolysis, by enlargement of the spleen, and by more or less marked jaundice

**he·mo·lyze** \ˈhēməˌlīz, ˈhem-\ *vb* -ED/-ING/-S [fr. *hemolysis*, after such pairs as E *analysis: analyze*] *vt* : to cause (red blood cells) to dissolve : induce hemolysis of ~ *vi* : to undergo hemolysis

**he·mom·e·ter** \heˈmäməd-ə(r)\ *n* [ISV *hem-* + *-meter*] : an instrument for measuring some quality of blood: as **a** : HEMOGLOBINOMETER **b** : HEMADYNAMOMETER **c** : HEMACYTOMETER — **he·mo·met·ric** \ˌhēməˈme·trik, ˌhem-\ *adj* — **he·mom·e·try** \heˈmäməˌtrē\ *n* -ES

**he·mo·parasite** \ˌhēmō, ˌhemō+\ *n* [*hem-* + *parasite*] : an animal parasite (as a hemoflagellate or a filarial worm) living in the blood of a vertebrate

**he·mop·a·thy** \hēˈmäpəthē\ *n* -ES [ISV *hem-* + *-pathy*] : a pathological state (as anemia or agranulocytosis) of the blood or blood-forming tissues

**he·mo·pericardium** \ˌhēmō, ˌhemō+\ *n* [NL, fr. *hem-* + *pericardium*] : blood in the pericardial cavity

**he·mo·peritoneum** \"+\ *n* [NL, fr. *hem-* + *peritoneum*] : blood in the peritoneal cavity

**he·mo·phage** \ˈhēməˌfāj, ˈhem-\ *n* -S [*hem-* + *-phage*] : ERYTHROPHAGE

**he·mo·pha·gia** \ˌ⸗⸗ˈfājēə\ *n* -S [NL, fr. *hem-* + *-phagia*] **1** : an ingestion of blood **2** : phagocytosis of red blood cells — **he·moph·a·gous** \hēˈmäfəgəs\ *adj*

**he·mo·phagocyte** \ˌhēmō, ˌhemō+\ *n* [*hem-* + *phagocyte*] **1** : HEMOPHAGE **2** : a phagocytic cell of the bloodstream — **he·mo·phagocytic** \"+\ *adj*

¹**he·mo·phile** \ˈhēməˌfīl, ˈhem-\ *adj* [*hem-* + *-phile*] : HEMOPHILIC

²**hemophile** \"\ *n* -S [ISV *hem-* + *-phile*] **1** : HEMOPHILIAC **2** : a hemophilic organism (as a bacterium)

**he·mo·phil·ia** \ˌ⸗⸗ˈfilēə\ *n* -S [NL, fr. *hem-* + *-philia*] : a tendency to uncontrollable bleeding; *esp* : a sex-linked hereditary blood defect of males characterized by delayed clotting of the blood and consequent difficulty in controlling hemorrhage even after minor injuries — compare PSEUDOHEMOPHILIA

¹**he·mo·phil·i·ac** \-lēˌak\ *n* -S [*hemophilia* + *-ac* (fr. Gk *-akos*, adj. suffix)] : one affected with hemophilia

²**hemophiliac** \ˌ⸗⸗ˌ⸗⸗\ *adj* [*hemophilia* + *-ac* (fr. Gk *-akos*, adj. suffix)] : HEMOPHILIC

**he·mo·phil·ic** \-ˈfilik\ *adj* **1** [*hemophilia* + *-ic*] : of, like, or affected with hemophilia **2** [*hem-* + *-philic*] : blood-loving — used of an organism (as a bacterium) that grows best in a medium containing blood

**he·mo·phil·i·oid** \-ˈfilēˌȯid\ *also* **he·moph·i·loid** \hēˈmäfəˌlȯid\ *adj* [*hemophili-* or *hemophil-* (fr. *hemophilia*) + *-oid*] : resembling hemophilia esp. in exhibiting a tendency to uncontrollable bleeding ⟨a ~ state⟩

**he·moph·i·lus** \hēˈmäfələs\ *n, cap* [NL, fr. *hem-* + *-philus*] : a genus of minute nonmotile gram-negative strictly parasitic hemophilic bacteria (family Parvobacteriaceae) including several important pathogens (as *H. influenzae* associated with human respiratory infections, conjunctivitis, and meningitis, *H. suis* of swine influenza, or *H. ducreyi* of chancroid)

**he·mo·poi·e·sis** \ˌhēmōˌpȯiˈēsəs, ˌhem-\ *n* [NL, fr. *hem-* + *-poiesis*] : HEMATOPOIESIS — **he·mo·poi·et·ic** \ˌ⸗⸗ˌpȯiˈed·ik\ *adj*

**he·mo·poi·e·tin** \ˌ⸗⸗ˌpȯiˈētᵊn\ *n* -S [ISV *hemopoietic* + *-in;* prob. orig. formed as F *hémopoïétine*] : a hypothetical stimulant to blood-cell production possibly equivalent to the antianemic factor or one of its precursors

**he·mo·proteidae** \ˌhēmō, ˌhemō+\ *syn of* HAEMOPROTEIDAE

**he·mo·protein** \"+\ *n* [*hem-* + *protein*] : a conjugated protein (as hemoglobin, catalase, peroxidase, or cytochrome) whose nonprotein portion is heme or a heme : a hemochromogen with a protein combined with heme — compare CHROMOPROTEIN

**he·mo·proteus** \"+\ *syn of* HAEMOPROTEUS

**he·mop·toe** \hēˈmäptəwē\ *n* -s [NL, alter. of *hemoptysis*] : hemorrhage from the lungs

**he·mop·to·ic** \-wik\ *adj* [prob. fr. LL *haemoptoicus* spitting blood, fr. LGk *haimoptoikos*, alter. of Gk *haimoptyikos*, fr. *haimo-* hem- + *-ptyikos* (fr. *ptyein* to spit + *-ikos* -ic) — more at SPEW] : of or produced by hemoptysis

**he·mop·ty·sis** \-təsə̇s\ *n, pl* **hemopty·ses** \-ə,sēz\ [NL, fr. *hem-* + *-ptysis*] : expectoration of blood from some part of the respiratory tract — compare HEMATEMESIS

**he·mo·pyrrole** \ˌhēmō, ˌhemō+\ *n* [ISV *hem-* + *pyrrole*] : a low-melting solid or liquid homologue $C_8H_{13}N$ of pyrrole formed during reduction of hemin or phylloporphyrin with hydriodic acid; 2,3-dimethyl-4-ethyl-pyrrole

**¹hem·or·rhage** \ˈhem(ə)rij, -rēj\ *n* -s [F & L; F *hémorrhagie*, fr. L *haemorrhagia*, fr. Gk *haimorrhagia*, fr. *haimo-* hem- + *-rrhagia*] : a copious discharge of blood from the blood vessels

**²hemorrhage** \"\ *vi* -ED/-ING/-S : BLEED

**hem·or·rhag·ic** \ˌheməˈrajik\ *adj* [Gk *haimorrhagikos*, fr. *haimorrhagia* hemorrhage + *-ikos* -ic] : involving, associated with, or tending to cause hemorrhage ⟨~ retinitis⟩ ⟨~ toxemia⟩ ⟨~ agent⟩

**hemorrhagic diathesis** *n* : a constitutional tendency to spontaneous often severe bleeding — compare HEMOPHILIA, PURPURA HEMORRHAGICA

**hemorrhagic septicemia** *n* : pasteurellosis of domestic animals usu. due to a bacterium (*Pasteurella multocida*) and typically marked by internal hemorrhages, fever, mucopurulent discharges, and often pneumonia and diarrhea, typical forms being swine plague, shipping fever of cattle and lambs, and fowl cholera

**hem·or·rhag·in** \ˌ==ˈrajə̇n\ *n* -s [ISV *hemorrhage* + *-in*] : a toxic substance occurring usu. as a component of various snake venoms and capable of destroying the blood cells and the walls of small blood vessels — compare HEMOLYSIN

**hem·or·rhoid** \ˈhem(ə),rȯid\ *n* -s [MF *hemorrhoides*, pl, fr. L *haemorrhoidae*, fr. Gk *haimorrhoides*, fr. *haimorrhoos* flowing with blood, fr. *haimo-* hem- + *-rrhoos* (fr. *rhein* to flow) — more at STREAM] : a mass of dilated tortuous veins in swollen tissue situated at the anal margin or within the anal canal — usu. used in pl.; called also *piles*

**¹hem·or·rhoi·dal** \ˌ==ˈrȯidᵊl\ *adj* [F *hémorroidal*, fr. MF, fr. *hemorrhoides* hemorrhoids + *-al*] **1** : of, relating to, or involving hemorrhoids **2** : RECTAL

**²hemorrhoidal** \"\ *n* -s : a hemorrhoidal part (as an artery or vein)

**hemorrhoidal artery** *n* : one of the arteries supplying the rectal and anal region that consists of a superior which is a continuation of the inferior mesenteric and a middle and inferior which are usu. branches of the hypogastric and pudendal respectively

**hemorrhoidal vein** *n* : any of the veins corresponding to the hemorrhoidal arteries and forming a plexus at the lower rectum and anus

**hem·or·rhoid·ec·to·my** \ˌhem(ə)ˌrȯiˈdektəmē\ *n* -ES [*hemorrhoid* + *-ectomy*] : surgical removal of a hemorrhoid

**he·mo·salpinx** \ˌhēmō, ˌhemō+\ *n* [NL, fr. *hem-* + *salpinx*] : HEMATOSALPINX

**he·mo·sid·er·in** \ˌhēmōˈsidərə̇n, ˌhem-\ *n* -s [ISV *hem-* + *sider-* + *-in*] : a yellowish brown granular pigment formed by breakdown of hemoglobin, found in phagocytes and in tissues esp. in disturbances of iron metabolism (as in hemochromatosis, hemosiderosis, or some anemias), and composed essentially of colloidal ferric oxide — compare FERRITIN

**he·mo·sid·er·o·sis** \ˌ==ˌsidəˈrōsə̇s\ *n, pl* **hemosidero·ses** \-ō,sēz\ [NL, fr. ISV *hemosiderin* + NL *-osis*] : a pathological condition marked by the deposition of hemosiderin in the tissues as a result of the breakdown of red blood cells — compare HEMOCHROMATOSIS — **he·mo·sid·er·ot·ic** \ˌ==ˌ==ˈrädˌik\ *adj*

**he·mo·spo·rid·ia** \ˌhēmōspəˈridēə, ˌhem-\ *syn of* HAEMOSPORIDIA

**he·mo·sta·sis** \ˌhēməˈstāsə̇s\ *n, pl* **hemosta·ses** \-ə,sēz\ [NL, fr. Gk *haimostasis* styptic, fr. *haimo-* hem- + *-stasis*] **1** : stoppage or sluggishness of blood flow **2** : arrest of bleeding (as by a hemostatic agent)

**he·mo·stat** \ˈhēməˌstat, ˈhem-\ *n* -s **1** [by shortening] : HEMOSTATIC **2** [*hem-* + *-stat*] : an instrument for compressing a bleeding vessel

**¹he·mo·stat·ic** \ˌ==ˈstadˌik\ *n* -s [LGk *haimostatikos*, n. & adj.] : an agent that checks bleeding; *esp* : one that shortens the clotting time of blood — compare HEMOSTAT

**²hemostatic** \"\ *adj* [LGk *haimostatikos* good for stopping blood, fr. Gk *haimo-* hem- + *-statikos* -static] **1** : of or caused by hemostasis **2** : serving to check bleeding ⟨a ~ agent⟩

**he·mo·thorax** \ˌhēmō, ˌhemō+\ *n* [NL, fr. *hem-* + *thorax*] : blood in the pleural cavity

**he·mo·toxin** \"+\ *n* [ISV *hem-* + *toxin*] : HEMOLYSIN

**he·mot·ro·phe** \hēˈmä·trəfē\ *n* -s [*hem-* + *-trophe* (as in *embryotrophe*)] : the nutrients supplied to the embryo in placental mammals by the maternal bloodstream after formation of the placenta — compare EMBRYOTROPH, HISTOTROPH

**he·mo·zo·on** \ˌhēməˈzōˌän, ˌhem-\ *n, pl* **hemo·zoa** \-ōə\ [NL, fr. *hem-* + *-zoon*] : HEMATOZOON

**hemp** \ˈhemp\ *n* -s *often attrib* [ME *hemp, hempe*, fr. OE

hemp: flowering shoots of *1* staminate plant, of *2* pistillate plant; *3* staminate flower; *4* pistillate flower; *5* fruit

*hænep, henep*; akin to MD *hennep* hemp, OHG *hanaf, hanif*, ON *hampr*; prob. all of non-IE origin; akin to the source of Gk *kannabis* hemp & Arm *kanap*] **1 a** : a tall widely cultivated Asiatic herb (*Cannabis sativa*) with tough bast fiber that is used for making cloth, floor covering, and cordage — see BHANG, CANNABIDIOL, CANNABIN, CANNABINOL, CANNABIS, CHARAS, HASHISH; compare GANJA **b** : the fiber of this plant prepared for commercial use **c** : a narcotic drug (as hashish) from hemp **2** : the useful fiber of any of numerous plants (as jute, abaca, ramie) other than hemp; *also* : the plant producing such fiber **3** *archaic* **a** : a gallows rope **b** : HANGING **4** : a light grayish olive color that is redder and deeper than twine, Quaker gray, or average citron gray

**hemp agrimony** *n* : a coarse European herb (*Eupatorium cannabinum*) with reddish flower heads and sessile leaves

**hemp-brake** \ˈ=,=\ *n* : ⁴BRAKE 1

**hemp dogbane** *n* : INDIAN HEMP 1

**hem·pel column** \ˈhempəl-\ *n, usu cap H* [after Walter *Hempel* †1916 Ger. chemist] : a vertical column for fractional distillation filled with glass beads and provided with a side tube for exit of the vapors

**hemp·en** \ˈhempən\ *adj* [ME, fr. *hemp* + ¹*-en*] **1** : of, relating to, made of, or like hemp **2** *archaic* : of or relating to a hangman's noose or a hanging

**hemp family** *n* : URTICACEAE

**hemp nettle** *n* : a plant of the genus *Galeopsis*; *esp* : a coarse bristly Eurasian herb (*G. tetrahit*) having foliage resembling that of the nettle and being common as a weed in the U. S.

**hemp palm** *n* : either of two dwarf fan palms (*Chamaerops humilis* of the Mediterranean region and *Trachycarpus excelsa* of China) the leaves of which yield the fiber African hair

**hempseed** \ˈ=,=\ *n* [ME, fr. *hemp* + *seed*] : the seed of hemp

**hempseed oil** *n* : a light green to brownish yellow drying fatty oil obtained from hempseed and used chiefly in soft soap, paints, and varnishes and in Asia in foods

**hemp tree** *n* : AGNUS CASTUS

**hempweed** \ˈ=,=\ *n* **1** : HEMP AGRIMONY **2** *also* **hemp vine** : CLIMBING HEMPWEED

**¹hempy** *or* **hemp·ie** \ˈhempi\ *n, pl* **hempies** [*hemp* + *-y* or *-ie*] **1** *chiefly Scot* : ROGUE, GALLOWS BIRD **2** *chiefly Scot* : a lively mischievous young person

**²hempy** *or* **hempie** \"\ *adj, Scot* : full of deviltry : MISCHIEVOUS

**hems** *pl of* HEM, *pres 3d sing of* HEM

**¹hemstitch** \ˈ=,=\ *vt* [²*hem* + *stitch*] : to embroider (fabric) by drawing out parallel threads and stitching the exposed threads in groups to form various designs

**²hemstitch** \"\ *n* **1** *or* **hemstitching** \ˈ=,==\ : decorative needlework similar to drawnwork that is often used on or near stitching lines of hems **2** : a stitch used in hemstitching

hemstitch 1

**hemstitcher** \ˈ=,==\ *n* **1** : a worker who hemstitches by hand or machine **2** : a sewing-machine attachment for making hemstitching

**hen** \ˈhen\ *n* -s *often attrib* [ME, fr. OE *henn*; akin to OHG *henna* hen, OE *hana* rooster — more at CHANT] **1 a** : the female of the domestic fowl; *esp* : one that is more than a year old **b** : the female of any of various other birds (as most gallinaceous or domesticated birds) **c** : one who behaves like a hen ⟨there were younger children at home and Minnie was their devoted mother ~ —R.T.Moriarty⟩ **2 a** : the female of various marine animals (as the lobster) and some fishes **b** : HEN FISH **3** : an esp. older woman who is fussy or officious ⟨grown into a cantankerous old ~⟩ — **a hen on** : a secret plan in preparation : something hatching ⟨the higher officials knew there was *a hen on* —Jo Mora⟩

**henad** \ˈheˌnad, ˈhē,-\ *n* -s [Gk *henad-, henas*, fr. *hen*, neut. of *heis* one + *-ad-, -as* (fem. suffix denoting connection with); akin to Gk *homos* same — more at SAME, -AD] : MONAD 1a

**hen and chickens** *n, pl* **hens and chickens** : any of several plants having offsets, runners, or proliferous flowers: as **a** : HOUSELEEK **b** : GROUND IVY **c** : an English daisy with proliferous flowers **d** : a plant of the genus *Echeveria*

**henbane** \ˈ=,=\ *n* [ME, fr. *hen* + *bane*] **1 a** : a fetid Old World herb (*Hyoscyamus niger*) having clammy-pubescent dentate leaves and yellowish brown flowers, containing a poison that is deadly esp. to fowls, and yielding from its leaves an extract that is used in medicine and has properties similar to those of belladonna — called also *black henbane* **b** : YELLOW HENBANE **2** : EGYPTIAN HENBANE

**henbill** \ˈ=,=\ *n* **1** : PIED-BILLED GREBE **2** : AMERICAN COOT

**henbit** \ˈ=,=\ *n* [*hen* + *bit* (morsel)] **1** : an annual dead nettle (*Lamium amplexicaule*) with reniform leaves and flowers that are arranged in whorls of 6 to 10 or more and have connivent calyx teeth — called also *bee nettle* **2** : IVY-LEAVED SPEEDWELL **3** : BLACK HOREHOUND

**hence** \ˈhen(t)s\ *adv* [ME *hennes*, fr. *henne* hence (fr. OE *heonan*) + *-s* (adv. suffix); akin to OS *hinan, hinana* away from here, OHG *hina* & *hinnan, hinana*, OE *hēr* here — more at HERE] **1 a** : from this place : AWAY ⟨how churlishly I bid Lucretia ~ —Shak.⟩ ⟨get thee ~, Satan⟩; *specif* : from this world or life ⟨before I go ~ and be no more —Ps 39:13 (AV)⟩ **b** *obs* : at an interval in space : DISTANT ⟨three quarters of a mile ~ —Shak.⟩ — often used imperatively for *go hence* or *get (you) hence* ⟨*hence* with your little ones —Shak.⟩ **2 a** *archaic* : from now on : HENCEFORTH ⟨from ~ I'll love no friend —Shak.⟩ **b** : from this time : in the future ⟨a generation ~⟩ **3** : because of a preceding fact or premise : THEREFORE ⟨unorthodox and ~ unpopular doctrines —J.B.Conant⟩ **4** : from this source or origin ⟨~ the desire to impress public opinion —Hugh Gaitskell⟩ — **from hence** *adv, archaic* : HENCE : from this place ⟨a fortnight since we set out *from hence* upon a little excursion —Thomas Gray⟩ ⟨will not depart *from hence* —Robert Southey⟩

**henceforth** \(ˈ)=ˈ=\ *or* **henceforward** \(ˈ)=ˈ==\ *adv* [*henceforth* fr. ME *hennesforth*, fr. *hennes* + *forth*; *henceforward*, fr. ME *hennesforward*, fr. *hennes* + *forward*] : from this point on — **from henceforth** *or* **from henceforward** *adv, archaic* : HENCEFORTH ⟨*from henceforth* bear his name whose form thou bearest —Shak.⟩

**henchboy** *n* [*hench-* (as in *henchman*) + *boy*] *obs* : a boy attendant : PAGE

**hench·man** \ˈhenchmən\ *n, pl* **henchmen** [ME *hengestman, henxtman, henxman* groom, squire, fr. *hengest* stallion, gelding (fr. OE) + *man*; akin to OFris *hanxt, hengst* horse, OHG *hengist* gelding, ON *hestr* stallion, horse, and perh. to W *caseg* mare, Gk *kēkiein* to gush forth, Lith *šokti* to jump, dance; basic meaning: jumping, bubbling] **1 a** *obs* : a squire or page to a person of high rank ⟨a little changeling boy to be my ~ —Shak.⟩ **b** : a household servant : RETAINER ⟨hear my ~ . . . about to ring the bell for luncheon —William Black⟩ **2 a** : the head gillie of a Scottish chief **b** : a subordinate who is heavily relied upon : RIGHT-HAND MAN ⟨the significant look that passes between the suave mastermind and his black-browed ~ —Richard Mallett⟩ **3 a** : a loyal supporter : ADHERENT ⟨the *henchmen* of German political and economic reaction —Hillel Silver⟩ **b** : a political follower giving active support; *esp* : one whose support is chiefly a matter of personal advantage ⟨a fat, easygoing minor ~ who held a judgeship —Hodding Carter⟩ **c** : an unscrupulous often violent member of a gang : HATCHET MAN ⟨a third car full of his armed *henchmen* following behind —F.L.Allen⟩

**hen clam** *n* [so called fr. the belief that such clams are female only] **1** : SURF CLAM **2** : PISMO CLAM

**hen curlew** *n* : a long-billed No. American curlew (*Numenius americanus*) now rare because of excessive hunting

**hendeca-** *or* **hendec-** *comb form* [Gk *hendeka-, hendek-*, fr. *hendeka*, fr. *hen* (neut. of *heis* one) + *deka* ten — more at HENAD, TEN] : eleven ⟨*hendecasyllable*⟩ ⟨*hendecane*⟩

**hen·deca·colic** \(ˌ)henˌdekəˈkōlik, -ˈkäl-\ *adj* [*hendeca-* + ²*colon* + *-ic*] *Greek & Latin prosody* : made up of eleven cola

**hen·de·cane** \ˈhendəˌkān, henˈdeˌk-\ *n* -s [*hendeca-* + *-ane*] : UNDECANE

**hen·deca·se·mic** \(ˌ)henˌdekəˈsēmik\ *adj* [*hendeca-* + Gk *sēma* sign + E *-ic*] *Greek & Latin prosody* : containing or equivalent to eleven short syllables — compare MORA

**hen·deca·syllabic** \(ˌ)henˌdekə+\ *or* **en·deca·syllabic** \(ˌ)en-\ *adj* [L *hendecasyllabus* + E *-ic*] **1** : having eleven syllables **2** : composed of eleven-syllable lines

**hen·deca·syllable** \henˈdekə+, (ˌ)henˌdekə+ˈ-\ *n* [modif. (influenced by *syllable*) of L *hendecasyllabus*, fr. Gk *hendeka* eleven + *syllabē* syllable — more at SYLLABLE] : a line of eleven syllables ⟨the ~ is the principal verse in Italian poetry⟩

**hen·decyl** \(ˈ)hen+\ *n* -s [*hendecane* + *-yl*] : UNDECYL

**hen·di·a·dys** \henˈdīədə̇s\ *n* -ES [LL *hendiadys, hendiadyoin*, modif. of Gk *hen dia dyoin* one through two] : the expression of an idea by two nouns connected by *and* (as *cups and gold*) instead of by a noun and an adjective (as *golden cups*)

**hen·don** \ˈhendən\ *adj, usu cap* [fr. *Hendon*, England] : of or from the urban district of Hendon, England : of the kind or style prevalent in Hendon

**hen·eicosane** \(ˈ)hen+\ *n* -s [ISV *heneicos-* (fr. *hen-* — fr. Gk *hen*, neut. of *heis* one — + *eicosa-*) + *-ane*] : a paraffin hydrocarbon $C_{21}H_{44}$; *esp* : the white waxy normal heneicosane $CH_3(CH_2)_{19}CH_3$

**hen·e·quen** *also* **hen·i·quen** \ˈhenəkə̇n, ˌ==ˈken\ *n* -s [Sp *henequén, heniquén, jeniquén*, prob. fr. Taino] **1** : a strong yellowish or reddish hard fiber derived from the leaves of a tropical American agave, produced chiefly in Yucatán, and used largely in the production of binder twine — see SISAL **2** : the agave (*Agave fourcroydes*) that yields henequen

**hen feather** *n* : a feather on the shaft of an arrow set at an angle of 120 degrees from the cock feather

**hen-feathered** \ˈ=ˌ==\ *adj* : having plumage like that of a hen — used of a male bird that lacks sickle or hackle feathers; distinguished from *cock-feathered*

**hen-feathering** \ˈ=,=(=)=\ *n* : plumage on a cock resembling that of the hen

**hen fish** *n* **1** : any of various marine fishes (as the pomfret) **2** : an adult female fish

**hen flea** *n* : STICKTIGHT FLEA

**hen fruit** *n, slang* : a hen's egg

**henge** \ˈhenj\ *n* -s [back-formation fr. *Stonehenge*, an assemblage of upright bronze age monuments on Salisbury Plain, near Salisbury, England] : a circular Bronze Age structure (as of wood) with a surrounding bank and ditch found in England

**hen gorse** *n, dial Eng* : RESTHARROW

**heng·yang** \ˈhəŋˈyäŋ, ˈheŋ-; ˈheŋˈyaŋ\ *adj, usu cap* [fr. *Hengyang*, China] : of or from the city of Hengyang, China : of the kind or style prevalent in Hengyang

**hen harrier** *n* : a common harrier (*Circus cyaneus*) of which the adult male is largely bluish gray and the female and young male brown above and buff with dark streaks below, the two types differing so much that they are sometimes mistaken for members of different species — compare MARSH HAWK

**hen hawk** *n* : any of several large buteonine hawks that sometimes attack poultry (as the red-tailed hawk and the red-shouldered hawk)

**henhearted** \ˈ=ˌ==\ *adj* : TIMID, FEARFUL, COWARDLY

**hen·ism** \ˈheˌnizəm\ *n* -s [G *henismus*, fr. Gk *hen* (neut. of *heis* one) + G *-ismus* -ism — more at HENAD] : SINGULARISM, MONISM 1a

**henle's loop** *n, usu cap H* : LOOP OF HENLE

**henle's sheath** *n, usu cap H* : SHEATH OF HENLE

**¹hen·na** \ˈhenə\ *n* -s [Ar *ḥinnā'* alcanna (*Lawsonia inermis*)] **1** : an Old World tropical shrub or small tree (*Lawsonia inermis*) with small opposite leaves and axillary panicles of fragrant white flowers used by Buddhists and Muslims in religious ceremonies — called also *Egyptian henna* **2 a** : a reddish brown dye obtained from leaves of the henna plant and used in tinting or dyeing the hair red **b** : a liquid, powder, or paste made by mixing henna with other coloring agents (as metallic lakes, tannin, lampblack) — called also *compound henna* **3** : a variable color averaging a strong and moderate reddish brown to strong brown

**²henna** \"\ *vt* -ED/-ING/-S : to dye with henna

**henne·bique** \ˌhenəˈbēk, (ˈ)enˈb-\ *adj, usu cap* [after François *Hennebique* †1927 Fr. structural engineer] : relating to concrete reinforced with steel or iron

**hen·nery** \ˈhenərē\ *n* -ES [*hen* + *-ery*] **1** : a poultry farm **2** : an enclosure or house for poultry

**hen·nin** \ˈhenə̇n\ *n* -s [MF] : a high cone-shaped headdress usu. with a thin veil pendent from the top worn by European women in the 15th century — called also *steeple headdress*

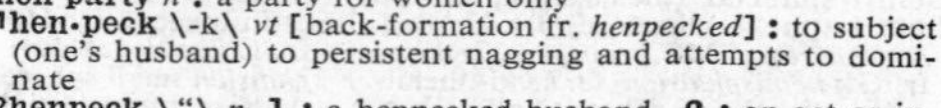

hennin

**hen·ny** \ˈhenē\ *adj* [*hen* + *-y*] : HEN-FEATHERED

**heno-** *comb form* [Gk, fr. *hen-, heis* — more at HENAD] : one ⟨*henotheism*⟩

**hen·o·the·ism** \ˈhenōthēˌizəm, ˌ==ˈ==ˌ=\ *n* [G *henotheismus*, fr. *heno-* + *-theismus* -theism] : the worship of one god without denying the existence of other gods — called also *monolatry*; compare KATHENOTHEISM

**hen·o·the·ist** \ˈhenōˌthēə̇st\ *n* [*heno-* + *-theist*] : one who practices henotheism — **hen·o·the·is·tic** \ˌ==ˌthēˈistik\ *adj*

**hen party** *n* : a party for women only

**¹hen·peck** \-k\ *vt* [back-formation fr. *henpecked*] : to subject (one's husband) to persistent nagging and attempts to dominate

**²henpeck** \"\ *n* **1** : a henpecked husband **2** : an act or instance of henpecking

**hen·pecked** \ˈhenˌpekt\ *adj* : subject to domination or persistent nagging by a wife

**hen pepper** *n* : SHEPHERD'S PURSE

**hen pigeon** *n* : a long-legged erect pigeon with a short tail carried high

**hen plant** *n* : either of two common plantains: **a** : BROAD-LEAVED PLANTAIN 1 **b** : RIBGRASS

**¹hen·ri·cian** \henˈrishən\ *n* -s *usu cap* [in sense 1, fr. ML *Henricianus*, fr. *Henricus* (Henry of Lausanne), 12th cent. Fr. heresiarch + L *-ianus* -ian; in sense 2, fr. NL *Henricianus*, fr. *Henricus* (Henry VIII) †1547 king of England + L *-ianus* -ian] **1** : a member of a 12th century religious sect in Switzerland and southern France holding that the sacraments are valid only when administered by a priest who lives up to his monastic vows **2** : an advocate of secular supremacy over the church and of the ecclesiastical reforms instituted during the reign of Henry VIII of England

**²henrician** \(ˈ)=ˈ==\ *adj, usu cap* **1** : of, relating to, or associated with Henry of Lausanne **2** : of or relating to Henry VIII of England or the ecclesiastical measures taken during his reign

**hen·ri deux faïence** \ˌäⁿ(ˌ)rēˈdə(r)\|-, -dēl-, =ˈ=ˈ=-\ *n, usu cap H&D* [after Henry II (*Henri Deux*) †1559 king of France] : SAINT-PORCHAIRE FAÏENCE

**hen·ri·et·ta** \ˌhenrēˈedˌə\ *or* **henrietta cloth** \ˌ==ˈ==-\ *n* -s *usu cap H* [after *Henrietta* Maria †1669 queen consort of Charles I of England] : a fine soft twilled fabric for dresses made of wool and sometimes with a silk warp

**henroost** \ˈ=,=\ *n* : a place where fowls roost

**hen·ry** \ˈhenrē, -ri\ *n, pl* **henrys** *or* **henries** [after Joseph *Henry* †1878 Am. physicist] **1** : the practical mks unit of inductance equal to the self-inductance of a circuit or the mutual inductance of two circuits in which the variation of one ampere per second results in an induced electromotive force of one volt, the unit being taken as standard in the U. S. **2** : a unit of inductance that is equal to 1.00049 henries and that was formerly taken as the standard in the U. S. — called also *international henry*

**henry's law** *n, usu cap H* [after William Henry †1836 Eng. chemist] : a fact in physical chemistry: the weight of a gas dissolved by a liquid is proportional to the pressure of the gas

**henry system** *n, usu cap H* [after Sir Edward *Henry* †1931 Brit. government official] : a system of numerical and letter classification of fingerprint patterns that treats the ten fingers as a unit and forms the basis of the majority of identification systems employed in English-speaking countries

**hens** *pl of* HEN

**hens·low's sparrow** \ˈhenzˌlōz-\ *n, usu cap H* [after J. S. *Henslow* †1875 Am. botanist] : a common No. American sparrow (*Passerherbulus henslowii*) found in old fields

**¹hent** \ˈhent\ *vt* **hent; hent; henting; hents** [ME *henten*, fr. OE *hentan* — more at HUNT] **1** *dial* **a** : to lay hold on : SEIZE, CATCH **b** : to take away : carry off **2** *obs* : to arrive at : REACH ⟨have ~ the gates —Shak.⟩

**²hent** *n* -s [*obs.* E *hent* art of seizing, fr. ¹*hent*] *obs* : conception of an idea or plan : INTENT ⟨up, sword, and know thou a more horrid ~ —Shak.⟩

**hen·te·ni·an** \(ˈ)henˈtēnēən\ *adj, usu cap* [John Hentenius (Henten) †1566 Fr. theologian who prepared the 1547 edition of the Vulgate + E *-an*] : of or relating to the 1547 edition of the Vulgate used for some time as the standard text of the Roman Catholic Church

**hen track** *or* **hen scratch** *n* : an illegible or scarcely legible mark intended as handwriting ⟨covering page after page of ruled yellow foolscap with his inky *hen tracks* —Bruce Bliven b. 1889⟩

**hen·tri·a·con·tane** \ˌhenˌtrīəˈkänˌtān, -ˌtrēə-\ *n* -s [ISV *hentriacont-* (fr. *hen-* — fr. Gk *hen*, neut. of *heis* one — + *triacont-* — fr. Gk *triakonta* thirty) + *-ane*] : a solid paraffin hydrocarbon $C_{31}H_{64}$; *esp* : normal hentriacontane $CH_3(CH_2)_{29}CH_3$ found in many natural waxes

**henware** \ˈ=,=\ *n* : BADDERLOCKS

**henwife** \ˈ=,=\ *n, pl* **henwives** : a woman who raises poultry

**he-oak** \ˈ=,=\ *n* : BEEFWOOD 1

**he·or·to·log·i·cal** \(ˌ)hēˌȯ(r)dᵊlˈäjə̇kəl\ *adj* : of or relating to heortology

**he·or·tol·o·gy** \ˌhēˌȯ(r)ˈtäləjē\ *n* -ES [Gk *heortē* feast + E *-o-* + *-logy*] : a study of religious calendars; *esp* : a study of the history and the meaning of the seasons and festivals of the church year

¹hep \ˈhep\ *var of* HIP

²hep \ˈhep, ˈhəp\ *interj* [origin unknown] — used to mark the cadence when troops are marching at attention

³hep \ˈhep\ *or* hip \ˈhip\ *adj* [origin unknown] **1 :** characterized by a keen informed awareness of or interest in what is new or smart **:** extremely alert and knowing ⟨astronautics, to which the small fry have been ~ for quite some time —C.J.Rolo⟩ ⟨you'll go crazy if you start using all that *hip* talk —Stanford Whitmore⟩ **2 :** characterized by a keen interest in and ready responsiveness to jazz ⟨each night after playing with his quintet before ~ audiences he studies classical compositions —Bob Thomas⟩ ⟨listening to recorded jazz with *hip* friends —*Metronome*⟩

**HEP** *abbr* hydroelectric power

**he·par** \ˈhē,pär\ *n* -s **1** [NL, fr. LL, liver (organ), fr. Gk *hēpar*] **:** LIVER 6 **2** [LL] **:** LIVER 1

**hep·a·rin** \ˈhepərən\ *n* -s [ISV *hepar* (organ) + *-in*] **:** a polysaccharide sulfuric acid ester found in liver, lung, and other tissues that prolongs the clotting time of blood by preventing the formation of fibrin and that is used in vascular surgery and in treatment of postoperative thrombosis and embolism

**hep·a·rin·iza·tion** \,hepərənə̇ˈzāshən, -,nīˈz-\ *n* -s **:** the process of heparinizing

**hep·a·rin·ize** \ˈhepərə,nīz\ *vt* -ED/-ING/-S [*heparin* + *-ize*] **:** to treat with heparin so as to make the blood nonclotting

**hepat-** *or* **hepato-** *comb form* [ML, fr. L, fr. Gk *hēpat-*, *hēpato-*, fr. *hēpat-*, *hēpar*] **1 :** liver ⟨*hepat*ectomy⟩ ⟨*hepato*logy⟩ **2 :** liver and ⟨*hepato*colic⟩ ⟨*hepato*splenomegaly⟩

**hep·a·tec·to·mize** \,hepəˈtektə,mīz\ *vt* -ED/-ING/-S **:** to excise the liver of

**hep·a·tec·to·my** \-,mē\ *n* -ES [*hepat-* + *-ectomy*] **:** excision of the liver or of a part of the liver

¹**he·pat·ic** \hə̇ˈpad·ik, -atl, |ēk\ *adj* [L *hepaticus*, fr. Gk *hēpatikos*, fr. *hēpat-*, *hēpar* liver + *-ikos* -ic; akin to L *jecur* liver, Skt *yakṛt*, Lith *jãknos*, *jeknos*] **1 a :** of, relating to, or affecting the liver ⟨~ cirrhosis⟩ **b :** resembling the liver in color or form ⟨~ aloes⟩ **2** *archaic* **:** of, relating to, or resembling a liver (sense 6) **3** [NL *Hepaticae*] **:** of or relating to the class Hepaticae

²**hepatic** \"\ *n* -s [NL *Hepaticae*] **:** a plant of the class Hepaticae **:** LIVERWORT

¹**he·pat·i·ca** \|ə̇kə, |ēkə\ *n* [NL, fr. ML, liverwort, fr. L *hepatica*, fem. of *hepaticus* of the liver; fr. the shape of the lobed leaves] **1 a** *cap* **:** a small genus of perennial herbs (family Ranunculaceae) of the north temperate zone that flower in the early spring and have lobed basal partly evergreen leaves and delicate white, pink, blue, or purplish flowers **b** -s **:** any plant or flower of the genus *Hepatica* **2** -s [ML] **:** a common liverwort (*Marchantia polymorpha*)

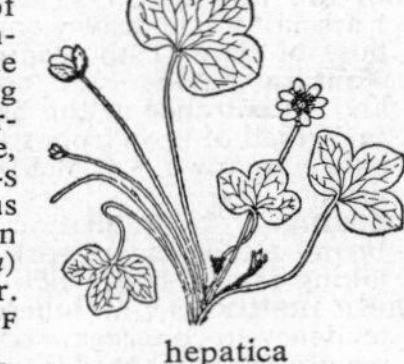
hepatica

²**hepatica** \"\ *n* -s *usu cap* [NL, fr. L, fem. of *hepaticus*] **:** LINE OF MERCURY

**he·pat·i·cae** \|ə,sē\ *n pl, cap* [NL fr. ML *hepaticae*, pl. of *hepatica* liverwort] **:** a class of Bryophyta comprising the liverworts and being distinguished from Musci by the presence of a usu. thalloid gametophyte that is not produced from a protonema, unicellular rhizoids and elaters, and antheridia and archegonia that are borne on the thallus and produce a short-lived and simple sporophyte — compare ANTHOCERATALES, JUNGERMANNIALES, MARCHANTIALES, SPHAEROCARPALES

**hepatic artery** *n* **:** the branch of the coeliac artery that supplies the liver with arterial blood

**hepatic cell** *n* **:** one of the polygonal epithelial cells of the liver that secrete bile

**hepatic duct** *n* **:** a duct conveying the bile away from the liver and in man and many other vertebrates uniting with the cystic duct to form the common bile duct — see DIGESTION illustration

**hepatic line** *n*, *usu cap H* **:** LINE OF MERCURY

**he·pat·i·col·o·gist** \hə̇,pad·əˈkäləjə̇st\ *n* -s **:** a specialist in hepaticology

**he·pat·i·col·o·gy** \-jē\ *n* -ES [NL *Hepaticae* + E *-o-* + *-logy*] **:** a branch of botany that deals with the Hepaticae

**hepatic tanager** *n* **:** a common tanager (*Piranga flava hepatica*) of the southwestern U. S. and Mexico

**hepatic vein** *n* **:** one of the veins that carry the blood received from the hepatic artery and from the portal vein away from the liver and that in man are usu. three in number and open into the inferior vena cava

**hep·a·tite** \ˈhepə,tīt\ *n* -s [G *hepatit*, fr. *hepat-* (fr. Gk *hēpat-* hepat-) + *-it* -ite; fr. its odor] **:** a barite that becomes fetid when rubbed or heated

**hep·a·ti·tis** \,hepəˈtīd·ə̇s, -ītə̇s\ *n* -ES [NL, fr. *hepat-* + *-itis*] **:** inflammation of the liver or a condition characterized by such inflammation — see INFECTIOUS HEPATITIS

**hep·a·ti·za·tion** \,hepəd·əˈzāshən, -pə,tīˈz-\ *n* -s [*hepat-* + *-ization*] **:** conversion of tissue (as of the lungs in pneumonia) into a substance resembling liver tissue in which the affected tissue may become solidified

**hep·a·tize** \ˈhepə,tīz\ *vt* -ED/-ING/-S [*hepat-* + *-ize*] **:** to cause to undergo hepatization ⟨a *hepatized* area of lung tissue⟩

**hepato-** — see HEPAT-

**hep·a·to·cellular** \ˈhepəd·ō+\ *adj* [*hepat-* + *cellular*] **:** of or involving hepatic cells ⟨~ jaundice⟩

**hep·a·to·cu·pre·in** \,hepəd·ōˈk(y)üprēən\ *n* -s [*hepat-* + *cupr-* + *-ein*] **:** a copper-containing protein isolated from ox liver

**hep·a·to·fla·vin** \-ˈflāvə̇n *also* -lav-\ *n* [*hepat-* + *flavin*] **:** RIBOFLAVIN

**hep·a·to·gen·ic** \ˈhepəd·ōˈjenik\ *or* **hep·a·tog·e·nous** \ˈhepəˈtäjənəs\ *adj* [*hepat-* + *-genic* or *-genous*] **:** produced or originating in the liver

**hep·a·to·ma** \,hepəˈtōmə\ *n*, *pl* **hepatomas** \-məz\ *or* **hepatoma·ta** \-məd·ə\ [NL, fr. *hepat-* + *-oma*] **:** a tumor of the liver that is usu. malignant — **hep·a·toma·tous** \ˈ=ˈtäməd·əs, -ˈtōm-\ *adj*

**hep·a·to·me·gal·ic** \ˈhepəd·ōməˈgalik\ *adj* **:** of, relating to, or resembling hepatomegaly

**hep·a·to·meg·a·ly** \,===ˈmegəlē\ *n* -ES [*hepat-* + *-megaly*] **:** enlargement of the liver

**hep·a·to·pancreas** \ˈhepəd·ō+\ *n* [NL *hepat-* + *pancreas*] **:** a glandular structure (as that of various crustaceans) that combines the digestive function of the vertebrate liver and pancreas — **hep·a·to·pancreatic** \"+\ *adj*

**hep·a·to·portal** \"+\ *adj* [*hepat-* + *portal*] **:** of or relating to the portal circulation of the liver as distinguished from that of the kidneys

**hep·a·tos·co·py** \,hepəˈtäskəpē\ *n* -ES [Gk *hēpatoskopia* inspection of the liver, fr. *hēpatoskopein* to inspect the liver (fr. *hēpat-* hepat- + *skopein* to inspect, contemplate, view) + *-ia* -y — more at SPY] **:** divination by inspecting the liver of animals

**hep·a·to·splenomegaly** \ˈhepəd·ō+\ *n* [*hepat-* + *splenomegaly*] **:** coincident enlargement of the liver and spleen

**hep·a·to·toxic** \"+\ *adj* [*hepat-* + *toxic*] **:** causing injury to the liver ⟨~ drugs⟩

**hepcat** \ˈ=,=\ *n* [³*hep* + *cat*] **:** one who is extremely hep ⟨horn-rimmed intellectual ~s with wild black hair —Jack Kerouac⟩; *specif* **:** a player or devotee of hot jazz

**hephthalite** *usu cap, var of* EPHTHALITE

**heph·the·mim·er·al caesura** \ˈhefthəˈmimərəl, ˈhepth-\ *n* [LL *hephthemimeris*, fr. Gk *hephthēmimerēs*, adj., containing seven halves, containing three feet and a half (fr. *hepta-* + *hēmi-* hemi- + *meros* part) + E *-al* — more at MERIT] **:** a caesura in classical verse occurring after the seventh half foot

**hepi·al·i·dae** \,hēpēˈalə,dē, ,hep-\ *n pl*, *cap* [NL, fr. *Hepialus*, type genus (irreg. fr. Gk *hēpiolos* moth) + *-idae*] **:** a family of lepidopterous insects comprising the ghost moths and having larvae burrow in wood or feed on roots

**hepped up** \ˈhepˈtəp\ *adj* **1 :** marked by intense interest or enthusiasm **:** HIPPED — usu. used with *about* ⟨was all *hepped up* about buying some silverware —E.G.Grening⟩ **2 :** marked by lively motion or tempo **:** pepped up **:** JAZZED ⟨*hepped-up* dinner music —*Saturday Rev.*⟩

**hep·pen** \ˈhepən\ *adj*, *usu* -ER/-EST [of Scand origin; akin to ON *heppinn* lucky, *happ* good luck — more at HAP (chance)] **1** *dial Brit* **:** neat and comfortable **:** ATTRACTIVE **2** *dial Brit* **:** CLEVER, DEFT, HANDY

¹**hep·ple·white** \ˈhepəl,(h)wīt\ *adj*, *usu cap* [after George *Hepplewhite* †1786 Eng. cabinetmaker] **:** of, relating to, or closely imitating a light and elegant style of furniture originating in late 18th century England that is often distinguishable from Sheraton by its greater use of curves (as in the favored shield and heart backs of its chairs), in its preference for concave curves esp. at sideboard corners, in its characteristic detachment of chair backs from the seat rail except for short side posts, and in the sweep of the high arms of its chairs to meet the line of the front legs

²**hepplewhite** \"\ *n* -s *usu cap* **:** an article of Hepplewhite furniture

**hep·ster** \ˈhepstə(r)\ *or* **hip·ster** \ˈhip-\ *n* -s [³*hep* or *hip* + *-ster*] **1 :** a devotee of jazz ⟨the orchestra's free style in improvising has impressed at least one longhair as well as the ~s —*Newsweek*⟩ **2** *usu hipster* **:** one who professes hep attitudes or tastes ⟨the ladies and gentlemen of the late watch — the *hipsters* who take the sun as a personal affront —Billy Rose⟩ ⟨the colorful dialogue of the *hipster* —*Saturday Rev.*⟩

Hepplewhite chair

**hepta-** *or* **hept-** *comb form* [Gk, fr. *hepta* — more at SEVEN] **1 :** seven ⟨*hepta*gon⟩ **2** *chem* **:** containing seven atoms, groups, or equivalents ⟨*hepta*acetate⟩

**hep·ta·chlor** \ˈheptə,klō(ə)r\ *n* -s [*heptachloro-*, fr. *hepta-* + *chlor-*] **:** a solid insecticide $C_{10}H_5Cl_7$ similar to chlordane

**hep·ta·chord** \-,kȯrd\ *n* [LL *heptachordus* with seven strings, fr. Gk *heptachordos*, fr. *hepta-* + *-chordos* stringed — more at -CHORD] **1 :** a 7-stringed lyre of ancient Greece **2 :** a diatonic scale of seven notes or tones **3 :** the interval of a seventh

**hep·tac·o·sane** \hepˈtakə,sān\ *n* -s [ISV *heptacos-* (fr. *hepta-* + *-cos-* — fr. *eicosa-*) + *-ane*] **:** a solid paraffin hydrocarbon $C_{27}H_{56}$; *esp* **:** the normal hydrocarbon $CH_3(CH_2)_{25}CH_3$ occurring in many waxes

**hep·tad** \ˈhep,tad\ *n* -s [Gk *heptad-*, *heptas* the number seven, fr. *hepta* seven] **:** a group of seven ⟨a ~ of litanies⟩

**hep·ta·dec·ane** \,heptəˈde,kān\ *n* -s [ISV *heptadec-* (fr. *hepta-* + *deca-*) + *-ane*] **:** any of several isomeric paraffin hydrocarbons $C_{17}H_{36}$; *esp* **:** the low-melting crystalline normal hydrocarbon $CH_3(CH_2)_{15}CH_3$

**hep·ta·dec·a·no·ic acid** \ˈheptə,dekəˈnōik-\ *n* [ISV *heptadecane* + *-oic*] **:** MARGARIC ACID

**hep·ta·decyl** \,heptəˈdesəl, -dēs-\ *n* [*heptadecane* + *-yl*] **:** any of several univalent radicals $C_{17}H_{35}$ derived from the heptadecanes by removal of one hydrogen atom; *esp* **:** the normal radical $CH_3(CH_2)_{15}CH_2$–

**hep·ta·gon** \ˈheptə,gän *sometimes* -təgən\ *n* -s [Gk *heptagōnos* heptagonal, fr. *hepta* seven + *-gōnos* (fr. *gōnia* corner, angle) — more at -GON] **:** a plane polygon having seven angles and therefore seven sides

**hep·tag·o·nal** \(ˈ)hepˈtagənᵊl, -taig-\ *adj* **:** having seven angles or sides

heptagons

**hep·ta·hydrate** \ˈheptə+\ *n* [*hepta-* + *hydrate*] **:** a compound with seven molecules of water — **hep·ta·hydrated** \"+\ *adj*

**hep·ta·kai·decagon** \ˈheptə,kī+\ *n* -s [Gk *heptakaideka* seventeen (fr. *hepta-* + *kai* and + *deka* ten) + E *-gon* — more at TEN] **:** a plane polygon having seventeen angles and therefore seventeen sides

**hept·aldehyde** \(ˈ)hept+\ *n* [ISV *hepta-* + *aldehyde*] **:** ENANTHALDEHYDE

**hep·tam·e·ter** \hepˈtaməd·ə(r)\ *n* [*hepta-* + *-meter*] **:** a poetic line of seven feet — **hep·ta·met·ri·cal** \ˈheptəˈmetrə̇kəl\ *adj*

**hep·ta·nal** \ˈheptə,nal\ *n* -s [*heptane* + *-al*] **:** ENANTHALDEHYDE

**hep·tane** \ˈhep,tān\ *n* -s [ISV *hepta-* + *-ane*] **:** any of nine isomeric paraffin hydrocarbons $C_7H_{16}$; *esp* **:** the liquid normal hydrocarbon $CH_3(CH_2)_5CH_3$ occurring in petroleum and as the chief constituent of some pine oils

**hep·ta·no·ic acid** \ˈheptəˈnōik-\ *n* [*heptane* + *-oic*] **:** ENANTHIC ACID

**hep·ta·none** \ˈheptə,nōn\ *n* -s [ISV *heptane* + *-one*] **:** a ketone $C_7H_{14}O$ derived from normal heptane

**hep·ta·phyllite** \ˈheptə+\ *n* [*hepta-* + *phyllite*] **:** any of a group of micas (as muscovite and other light-colored micas) with seven metallic ions per ten oxygen and two hydroxyl ions — compare OCTAPHYLLITE

¹**hep·ta·ploid** \ˈheptə,plȯid\ *adj* [*hepta-* + *-ploid*] **:** having seven times the monoploid number of chromosomes

²**heptaploid** \"\ *n* -s **:** a heptaploid individual, group, or generation

**hep·ta·ploi·dy** \ˈ==,plȯidē\ *n* -ES **:** the condition of being heptaploid

**hep·tarch** \ˈhep,tärk\ *n* -s [*hepta-* + ¹*-arch*] **:** one of the rulers of a heptarchy

**hep·tar·chal** \(ˈ)hepˈtärkəl\ *or* **hep·tar·chic** \-kik\ *or* **hep·tar·chi·cal** \-kə̇kəl\ *adj* **:** of, relating to, or constituting a heptarchy

**hep·tar·chy** \ˈhep,tärkē\ *n* -ES [*hepta-* + *-archy*] **1 :** a government by seven persons **2 :** a confederacy of seven Anglo-Saxon kingdoms held to have existed in the 7th and 8th centuries with each kingdom having its own ruler and one of the seven heptarchs sometimes being recognized as overlord

**hep·ta·stich** \ˈheptə,stik\ *n* -s [*hepta-* + *-stich*] **:** a group, stanza, or poem of seven lines

**hep·ta·style** \-,stīl\ *also* **hep·ta·sty·lar** \ˈ==ˈstīlə(r)\ *adj* [*hepta-* + *-style*, *-stylar*] **:** marked by columniation with seven columns across the front — compare DISTYLE

**hep·ta·sulfide** \ˈheptə+\ *n* [*hepta-* + *sulfide*] **:** a sulfide containing seven atoms of sulfur in the molecule

**hep·ta·syllabic** \ˈheptə+\ *adj* [*hepta-* + *syllabic*] **:** consisting of or having seven syllables ⟨a ~ line⟩

**hep·ta·syllable** \"+\ *n* [*hepta-* + *syllable*] **:** a poetic line of seven syllables

**hept·atomic** \ˈhept+\ *adj* [*hepta-* + *atomic*] **1 :** consisting of seven atoms **2 :** having seven replaceable atoms or radicals

**hep·ta·tonic** \ˈheptə+\ *adj* [*hepta-* + *tonic*] **:** composed of seven musical tones

**hep·ta·valent** \ˈheptə+\ *adj* [*hepta-* + *valent*] **:** having a valence of seven

**hep·tene** \ˈhep,tēn\ *n* -s [ISV *hepta-* + *-ene*] **:** any of the three straight-chain heptylenes

**hep·ti·tol** \ˈheptə,tȯl, -,tōl\ *n* -s [*hepta-* + *-itol*] **:** a heptahydroxy alcohol that is obtained by reducing a heptose or that exists naturally

**hep·tode** \ˈhep,tōd\ *n* -s [ISV *hepta-* + *-ode*] **:** a vacuum tube with seven electrodes including a cathode, an anode, a control grid, and four additional grids or other electrodes

**hep·to·ic acid** \(ˈ)hepˈtōik-\ *n* [*heptane* + *-oic*] **:** any of the monocarboxylic acids $C_6H_{13}COOH$ (as enanthic acid) derived from the heptanes

**hep·tose** \ˈhep,tōs *also* -ōz\ *n* -s [ISV *hepta-* + *-ose*] **:** any of a class of monosaccharides $C_7H_{14}O_7$ containing seven carbon atoms in the molecule and obtainable in various ways from lower sugars

**hept·ox·ide** \ˈhept+\ *n* [ISV *hepta-* + *oxide*] **:** an oxide containing seven oxygen atoms in the molecule

**hep·tran·chi·as** \hepˈtraŋkēəs\ *n*, *cap* [NL, prob. irreg. fr. *hepta-* + *branchiae*] **:** a genus of sharks (family Hexanchidae) having seven pairs of branchial clefts

**hep·tu·lose** \ˈheptə,lōs, -pchə- *also* -ōz\ *n* -s [*hepta-* + *-ulose*] **:** a ketose $C_7H_{14}O_7$ containing seven carbons in the molecule; *esp* **:** the isomer having the carbonyl group in the beta or 2-position ⟨D-*manno-heptulose* is found in avocados⟩

**hep·tyl** \ˈheptəl\ *n* -s [ISV *hepta-* + *-yl*] **:** any of several isomeric alkyl radicals $C_7H_{15}$ derived from the heptanes; *esp* **:** the normal radical $CH_3(CH_2)_5CH_2$–

**hep·tyl·ene** \ˈheptə,lēn\ *n* -s [ISV *heptyl* + *-ene*] **:** any of several liquid isomeric hydrocarbons $C_7H_{14}$ belonging to the ethylene series and including the heptenes

**hep·tyl·ic acid** \(ˈ)hepˈtilik-\ *n* [ISV *heptyl* + *-ic*] **:** HEPTOIC ACID

**hep·tyne** *also* **hep·tine** \ˈhep,tīn\ *n* -s [ISV *hepta-* + *-yne* or *-ine*] **:** any of three isomeric straight-chain liquid hydrocarbons $C_7H_{12}$ of the acetylene series

¹**her** [ME *hire*, fr. OE *hiere*, *hire*, *hyre*, gen. of *hēo*, *hīo* she — more at HE] *obs possessive of* ¹SHE

²**her** *R* (h)ər, ˈhər, +V ˈhər·; *-R* (h)ə(r, ˈhə, +V ˈhər· *or* ˈhə *also* ˈhər\ *adj* [ME *hire*, fr. OE *hiere*, *hire*, *hyre*, gen. of *hēo*, *hīo*] **1 a :** of or relating to her or herself as possessor **:** due to her **:** inherent in her **:** associated or connected with her ⟨before she has ~ floor swept —Edna S. V. Millay⟩ ⟨you have not seen Maine until you have seen ~ islands —R.W. Hatch⟩ — compare ¹SHE **b :** of or relating to her or herself as author, doer, giver, or agent **:** effected by her **:** experienced by her as subject **:** that she is capable of ⟨~ paintings⟩ ⟨~ research⟩ ⟨the reason for ~ winning the game⟩ ⟨she did ~ best⟩ **c :** of or relating to her or herself as object of an action **:** experienced by her as object ⟨~ rescuer⟩ ⟨~ exclusion from the club⟩ **d :** that she has to do with or is supposed to possess or to have knowledge or a share of or some interest in ⟨she plays ~ waltzes beautifully⟩ **e :** that is esp. significant for her **:** that brings her good fortune or prominence — used with *day* or sometimes with other words indicating a division of time ⟨it's not only her birthday, it's ~ day⟩ **2** *now dial* **:** -'s — used after a noun or noun phrase designating a female person or something personified as female in place of the possessive ending *'s* ⟨Jane Doe ~ book⟩

³**her** \"\ *pron*, *objective case of* SHE [ME *hire*, fr. OE *hiere*, *hire*, *hyre*, dat. of *hēo*, *hīo*] **1 :** ¹SHE 1, 2, 3: **a** — used as indirect object of a verb ⟨tell ~ the news⟩ **b** — used as object of a preposition ⟨a gift for ~⟩ **c** — used as direct object of a verb ⟨lifted the skiff and slid ~ into the water —Ernest Hemingway⟩ **d** — used in comparisons after *than* and *as* when the first term in the comparison is the direct or indirect object of a verb or the object of a preposition ⟨the dress fits her sister as well as ~⟩ ⟨give me the book rather than ~⟩ ⟨this course of study would be more useful to you than ~⟩ **e** — used in absolute constructions esp. together with a prepositional phrase, adjective, or participle ⟨she was invited to go dancing two or three times a week, and ~ without half as many nice dresses as she really needed⟩ ⟨and ~ being my own child⟩ **f** — used by speakers on all educational levels and by many reputable writers, though disapproved by some grammarians, in the predicate after forms of *be*, in comparisons after *than* and *as* when the first term in the comparison is the subject of a verb, and in other positions where it is itself neither the subject of a verb nor the object of a verb or preposition ⟨it was not ~ one hated but the idea of her —Virginia Woolf⟩ ⟨her sister sings better than ~⟩ ⟨~ and her excuses⟩ **g** — used in substandard speech as the subject of a verb which it does not immediately precede or as part of the compound subject of a verb ⟨~ and John got married⟩ **h** — used with a gerund in combination with other pronouns (as *him*) in the objective case ⟨I can't imagine ~ doing that any more than I can imagine him doing it⟩ **2 :** HERSELF — used reflexively as indirect object of a verb ⟨she bought ~ a hat⟩, object of a preposition ⟨she took her son with ~⟩, or direct object of a verb ⟨she sat ~ down⟩

⁴**her** *like stressed pronunciations at* ²HER\ *n* -s **:** WOMAN, GIRL ⟨four hims and a ~ —Charles Dickens⟩

**her** *abbr* **1** heraldic; heraldry **2** [L *heres*] heir

**hera** \ˈherə\ *n*, *pl* **hera** *or* **heras** *usu cap* **1 :** the peasant segment of the Nyoro people presumed to be cognate with the Bairu **2 :** a member of the Hera people

**her·a·bol myrrh** *or* **heer·a·bol myrrh** \ˈherə,bōl-\ *n* [origin unknown] **:** the true myrrh of commerce said to be obtained from an East African and Arabian tree (*Commiphora myrrha*)

**her·a·cle·an** \ˈherəˈklēən\ *or* **her·a·cleian** \-lē(y)ən, -līən\ *adj*, *usu cap* [*Heraclean* fr. L *Heracleus*, (fr. Gk *Hērakleios*, fr. *Hēraklēs*, Heracles, legendary Greek hero) + E *-an*; *Heracleian* fr. Gk *Hērakleios* + E *-an*] **:** of or relating to the hero Heracles

**he·rac·le·on·ite** \hə̇ˈraklēə,nīt\ *n* -s *usu cap* [*Heracleon*, 2d cent. Gnostic Christian + E *-ite*] **:** a follower of the Gnostic Heracleon of Alexandria

¹**her·a·cle·o·pol·i·tan** \ˈherə,klēəˈpälətᵊn\ *or* **her·a·cle·op·o·lite** \,==,klēˈäpə,līt\ *adj*, *usu cap* [*Heracleopolit-*, *Heracleopolis*, ancient city of Egypt + E *-an* or *-ite*] **:** of or relating to the ancient city of Heracleopolis in northern Egypt — often used of the kings of the IXth and Xth dynasties in Egypt

²**heracleopolitan** \"\ *n* -s *usu cap* **:** a native or inhabitant of Heracleopolis in northern Egypt

**her·a·cle·um** \ˈherəˈklēəm\ *n*, *cap* [NL, irreg. fr. Gk *hērakleia*, a plant, fr. *Hēraklēs* Hercules] **:** a widely distributed genus of plants (family Umbelliferae) having wing-margined fruit and large umbels of white flowers — see COW PARSNIP

¹**her·a·cli·te·an** \ˈherəˈklīd·ēən, -,klīˈtēən\ *also* **her·a·clitic** \-ˈkli|d·ik, -lī|\ *adj*, *usu cap* [L *Heracliteus* (fr. Gk *Hērakleiteios*, fr. *Hērakleitos* Heraclitus, 6th-5th cent. B.C. Greek philosopher) + E *-an* or *-ic*] **:** of or relating to the philosopher Heraclitus or his theories

²**heraclitean** \"\ *also* **heraclitic** \"\ *n* -s *usu cap* **:** a follower of Heraclitus

**her·a·cli·te·an·ism** \,==ˈklīd·ēə,nizəm, -klīˈtē-\ *n* -s *usu cap* **:** a philosophy based on the theory that everything is in flux and nothing remains fixed except the logos which is at once law and a ruling element identified with fire and that the world is made of the four elements fire, water, earth, and air which are continually transmuted into one another in fixed measures

¹**her·ald** \ˈherəld\ *n* -s [ME *heraud*, *herald*, fr. MF *hiraut*, *heraut*, fr. an (assumed) Gmc compound (akin to the name *Chariovolda* attested in Tacitus) whose first component is akin to OHG *heri* army, and whose 2d component is akin to OHG *waltan* to have power over, rule — more at HARRY, WIELD] **1 a :** an official at a tournament of arms whose duties consisting orig. of making announcements came to include keeping the scores, interpreting the rules, and marshaling the combatants **b :** an officer whose original duties of a tournament official came to include also the marshaling of other chivalric ceremonials, the making of official announcements, and the carrying of messages to or from rulers or commanders esp. in war with the status of ambassador **c :** such an officer of a monarch or government also having the responsibility for devising, granting, registering, and confirming armorial bearings, this responsibility coming to constitute his chief function as earlier functions became obsolete **:** OFFICER OF ARMS **d :** a member of the second of three grades of officers of arms ranking above a pursuivant and below a king of arms **2 a :** an official crier or messenger having duties similar in one or more respects to those of the herald of medieval and modern Europe ⟨Mercury was the gods' ~⟩ **b :** one (as a soldier) who signals with a trumpet ⟨more chieftains came, with ~s who blew on trumpets that were twelve feet long —Hector Bolitho⟩ **c :** AVANT-COURIER **3 a :** one that precedes or foreshadows **:** HARBINGER, FORERUNNER ⟨flights of ravens . . . are the sure ~s of the approach of the deer —Farley Mowat⟩ ⟨exciting novels . . . were the ~s of social changes —R.W.Livingstone⟩ **b** (1) **:** one that conveys news or proclaims **:** ANNOUNCER ⟨hark the ~ angels sing —George Whitefield⟩ ⟨it was the lark, the ~ of the morn —Shak.⟩ (2) **:** one that supports or advocates **:** SPOKESMAN ⟨conspicuous ~ of this enfranchising movement —C.A. Dinsmore⟩ **4 :** a specialist in heraldry **:** HERALDIST **5 :** a European noctuid moth (*Scoliopteryx libatrix*) **6 :** the identifying symbol or monogram of a railroad usu. displayed on its freight cars

²**herald** \"\ *vt* -ED/-ING/-S **1 :** to give notice of **:** ANNOUNCE, SIGNAL ⟨the publisher ~s a second series —J.N.Hazard⟩ ⟨the approach of a cold air mass . . . is ~*ed* by a shift of the wind —P.E.James⟩ **2 a :** to bring to public notice **:** PUBLICIZE ⟨one of the most ~*ed* and most exciting events in the country —T.H.Fielding⟩ **b :** to greet esp. with enthusiasm **:** HAIL ⟨the show was ~*ed* with a glum essay —E.R.Bentley⟩ ⟨automation has been extravagantly ~*ed* by some as the threshold to a new Utopia —John Diebold⟩ **3 :** to signal the approach of **:** PRECEDE, FORESHADOW ⟨~*ed* by a man ringing a bell and

esquired by his clerk —Adrian Bell› ‹an increase in . . . local quakes in a volcanic region is fairly sure to ~ an eruption —Howel Williams›
**he·ral·dic** \he'raldik, hə'-, -dēk\ *adj* [F *héraldique*, fr. ML *heraldus* (fr. MF *hiraut, heraut*) + F *-ique* -ic] **:** of or relating to heralds or heraldry ‹the ~ emblem of the emperor —Ethel Lewis› ‹the ~ procession moved on in gilded coaches —*Time*› — **he·ral·di·cal·ly** \-dək(ə)lē, -dēk-, -li\ *adv*
**her·ald·ist** \'herəldəst\ *n* -s **:** a specialist in heraldry
**herald of arms** *also* **herald at arms :** [1]HERALD 1
**her·ald·ry** \'herəldrē, -ri\ *n* -ES [[1]*herald* + *-ry*] **1 a :** the art or practice of an officer of arms including the devising, blazoning, and granting of armorial insignia, the investigation of persons' rights to use arms or particular armorial ensigns, the tracing and recording of pedigrees, the settling of questions of precedence, the marshaling of processions, and the supervision of public ceremonies **b :** pomp and elaborate ceremony esp. with display of armorial ensigns **:** PAGEANTRY ‹historic ~ of a British coronation› **c :** a branch of knowledge that deals with the history and practice of bearing and displaying armorial ensigns and with the art of describing them **:** ARMORY **2 a :** armorial ensigns ‹methods of painting ~ have changed very little —G.W.Eve› **b :** insignia (as military badges or Japanese mons) that resemble or are likened to armorial ensigns ‹brands are the ~ of the range —J.F. Dobie› **3** *archaic* **:** the office of an official crier or messenger ‹I trust my next ~ will be to a more friendly court —E.G. Bulwer-Lytton› **4** *obs* **:** social rank or precedence ‹you are more saucy . . . than the commission of your birth and virtue gives you ~ —Shak.› **5 :** advance notice or publicity ‹the play opened with no ~ to speak of›
**heralds' college** *n, cap H&C* **:** COLLEGE OF ARMS
**heralds' office** *n, cap H & usu cap O* **:** COLLEGE OF ARMS
**heraldy** *n* -ES [ME *heraldie*, fr. *heraud, herald* + *-ie* -y] *obs* **:** HERALDRY
**her·a·path·ite** \'herə,pa,thīt, -pȧ,-\ *n* -s [William B. *Herapath* †1868 Eng. chemist + E *-ite*] **:** a salt of quinine that is obtained by treating the sulfate with iodine in the form of rhomboidal plates capable of polarizing light and that is used as a polarizing agent usu. in the form of small crystals oriented in the same direction in a transparent film
**heras** *pl of* HERA
**he·rat** \he'rät\ *or* **he·rati** \-ädē\ *n* -s *usu cap* [fr. *Herat*, Afghanistan, where such rugs are made] **1 :** a usu. heavy cotton, silk, or occas. wool Oriental rug of loose texture that is tied with the Ghiordes knot and characterized by a basic pattern of a rosette between two curved leaves that is often much elaborated — compare KHORASSAN **2 :** an Ispahan of the 16th and 17th centuries
**herb** \'(h)ərb, '(h)əb, '(h)əib\ *n* -s *often attrib* [ME *erbe, herbe*, fr. OF, fr. L *herba*] **1 :** a seed-producing annual, biennial, or herbaceous perennial that does not develop persistent woody tissue but dies down at the end of a growing season — compare SHRUB, TREE **2 :** a plant or plant part valued for its medicinal, savory, or aromatic qualities ‹under ~s I have included laurel leaves —J.W.Parry› **3** *archaic* **:** GRASS, VEGETATION ‹underfoot the ~ was dry —Alfred Tennyson› **4 :** the leafy top of an herbaceous plant considered separately from the root
**her·ba·ce·ae** \,(h)ər'bāsē,ē\ *n pl, cap* [NL, fr. fem. pl. of L *herbaceus*] *in some esp former classifications* **:** a phylum comprising all plants that are fundamentally herbaceous and remain so — compare LIGNOSAE
**her·ba·ceous** \(')(h)ər'bāshəs\ *adj* [L *herbaceus* grassy, fr. *herba* grass, herb + *-aceus* -aceous] **1 a :** of, relating to, or having the characteristics of an herb **b** *of a stem* **:** having little or no woody tissue and persisting usu. for a single growing season **2 :** having the texture, color, or appearance of a leaf ‹~ sepals› — **her·ba·ceous·ly** *adv* — **her·ba·ceous·ness** *n* -ES
**herbaceous border** *n* **:** a permanent flower border consisting primarily of hardy herbaceous perennials but frequently including annuals and biennials
**herbaceous grafting** *n* **:** grafting in which both stock and scion are herbaceous (as in grafting a scion of double-flowered gypsophila onto a stock of single-flowered gypsophila)
**herbaceous perennial** *n* **:** a plant whose top growth dies down annually but whose crowns, roots, bulbs, or rhizomes survive the winter
**herb·age** \'(h)ərbij, -)əb-, -)əib-, -bēj\ *n* -s [ME, fr. MF, fr. *herbe, erbe* + *-age*] **1 :** grass and other herbaceous vegetation esp. when used for grazing animals **:** PASTURE **2 :** the succulent parts (as the foliage and young stems) of herbaceous plants **3 :** an easement of pasturage on another's ground
**her·ba im·pia** \,(h)ərbə'impēə\ *n* [L, lit., undutiful or unfilial herb; fr. the fact that small branches shoot out from the top of the main stem and on top of the parent stem] **:** a cotton rose (*Filago germanica*)
[1]**herb·al** \'(h)ərbəl, -)əb-, -)əib-\ *n* -s [*herb* + *-al* (n. suffix)] **1 :** a book in which plants are named, described, and often pictured usu. with special reference to their officinal properties **2** *archaic* **:** HERBARIUM 1
[2]**herbal** \"\ *adj* [*herb* + *-al* (adj. suffix)] **:** of, relating to, or made of herbs
**herb·al·ist** \-ləst\ *n* -s **1 a :** one that collects, grows, or deals in herbs, esp. medicinal herbs **b :** HERB DOCTOR ‹described herself as an ~ and dresser of sores —C.J.Brown› **2** *obs* **:** BOTANIST
**herb·al·ize** \-,līz\ *vi* -ED/-ING/-S **:** to collect plants (as medicinal herbs)
**her·ba·rism** \-bə,rizəm\ *n* -s [L *herbaria* botany (fr. *herba* grass, herb + *-aria* -ary) + E *-ism*] *archaic* **:** BOTANY
**herbarist** *n* -s [L *herbaria* + E *-ist*] *obs* **:** HERBALIST
**her·bar·i·um** \,(h)ər'ba(a)rēəm, ,(h)ə'-, ,(h)əi'-, ,(h)ə(r)'-, -ber-, -bär-\ *n, pl* **herbaria** [LL, fr. L *herba* + *-arium* -ary] **1 :** a collection of dried plant specimens usu. mounted and systematically arranged for botanical reference **2 :** a room, building, or institution housing an herbarium
**her·ba·rize** \'hərbə,rīz\ *vi* -ED/-ING/-S [L *herbaria* + E *-ize*] *archaic* **:** BOTANIZE
[1]**her·bar·ti·an** \(')her¦bärd-ēən, ¦hər'-\ *adj, usu cap* [Johann F. *Herbart* †1841 Ger. philosopher + E *-ian*] **:** of or relating to the German philosopher Herbart, his doctrines, or esp. the educational system outlined by him and developed by his disciples
[2]**herbartian** \"\ *n* -s *usu cap* **:** one who supports or believes in Herbartian doctrines
**her·bar·ti·an·ism** \(,)≈'≈≈ə,nizəm\ *n* -s *usu cap* **:** the doctrines advocated by the German philosopher Herbart and his followers
**herb·a·ry** \'(h)ərbərē, -)əb-, -)əib-, -ri\ *n* -ES [*herb* + *-ary*] *archaic* **:** a garden of herbs or vegetables
**herbbane** \'≈,≈\ *n* **:** BROOMRAPE
**herb bar·ba·ra** \-'bärb(ə)rə, -'bȧb-\ *n, pl* **herbs barbara** *or* **herb barbaras** *usu cap B* [trans. of ML or NL *herba* (*Sanctae*) *Barbarae*, fr. *Barbara* (St. Barbara) 3d cent. Christian martyr] **:** WINTER CRESS
**herb ben·net** \-'benət\ *n, pl* **herbs bennet** *or* **herb bennets** [ME *herbe beneit*, fr. MF *herbe beneite, herbe benoite*, fr. ML *herba benedicta*, lit., blessed herb] **:** a European herb (*Geum urbanum*) with pinnatifid leaves and yellow flowers
**herb chris·to·pher** \-'kristəfə(r)\ *n, pl* **herbs christopher** *or* **herb christophers** *usu cap C* [trans. of NL or ML *herba* (*Sancti*) *Christophori*, after *Christophorus* (St. Christopher) 3d cent. Christian martyr] **1 :** a common European baneberry (*Actaea spicata*) **2 :** either of two American baneberries: **a :** WHITE BANEBERRY **b :** RED BANEBERRY **3 :** ROYAL FERN **4 :** FLEABANE **a 5 :** MEADOWSWEET 2
**herb doctor** *n* **:** one who practices healing by the use of herbs — called also *herbalist*
**her·bert river cherry** \'hərbərt-\ *n, usu cap H&R* [fr. the *Herbert river*, Australia] **:** QUEENSLAND CHERRY
**herb gerard** \-jə'rärd, -'je,rärd\ *n, pl* **herbs gerard** *or* **herb gerards** *usu cap G* [trans. of ML or NL *herba* (*Sancti*) *Gerardi*, after *Gerardus* (St. Gerard) †1120 founder of the Knights of St. John] **:** GOUTWEED
**her·bi·ci·dal** \¦(h)ərbə¦sīd°l\ *adj* **1 :** of or relating to an herbicide **2 :** having the ability to destroy plants ‹~ agents›
**her·bi·cide** \'≈≈,sīd\ *n* -s [ISV *herbi-* (fr. L, fr. *herba* grass, herb) + *-cide*] **:** an agent (as a chemical) used to destroy or inhibit plant growth; *specif* **:** a selective weed killer that is not injurious to crop plants
**herbier** *comparative of* HERBY
**herbiest** *superlative of* HERBY
**herb·ish** \'(h)ərbish\ *adj, now dial* **:** of, relating to, or resembling herbs
**her·biv·o·ra** \(,)(h)ər'bivərə\ *n pl* [NL, fr. neut. pl. of *herbivorus*] **1** *cap, in former classifications* **:** a group of mammals nearly or exactly equivalent to Ungulata and feeding mainly on herbage **2 :** herbivorous animals; *esp* **:** members of the Herbivora
**her·bi·vore** \'(h)ərbə,vō(ə)r\ *n* -s [NL *Herbivora*] **:** a plant-eating animal; *esp* **:** one of the Herbivora
**her·bi·vor·i·ty** \,(h)ərbə'vórəd-ē\ *n* -ES [*herbivorous* + *-ity*] **:** the quality or state of being herbivorous ‹the form of the molar teeth . . . is recognizable, but the ~ of the fossil is not thereby determined —Richard Owen›
**her·biv·o·rous** \¦(h)ər¦bivərəs, ,(h)ər'b-\ *adj* [NL *herbivorus*, fr. L *herbi-* (fr. *herba* grass, herb) + *-vorus* -vorous] **1 :** feeding on plants **:** PHYTOPHAGOUS — used esp. of mammals; compare CARNIVOROUS, OMNIVOROUS **2 :** having a stout body-build and a long small intestine **:** ENDOMORPHIC — opposed to *carnivorous* — **her·biv·o·rous·ly** *adv*
**herb·less** \'(h)ərbləs\ *adj* **:** lacking herbs or herbage
**herb·let** \-lət\ *n* -s *archaic* **:** a small herb
**herblike** \'≈,≈\ *adj* **:** resembling an herb
**herb lily** *n* **:** a plant of the genus *Alstroemeria*
**herb mercury** *n, pl* **herbs mercury** *or* **herb mercuries :** a Eurafrican annual herb (*Mercurialis annua*) widely naturalized as a weed and having inconspicuous greenish flowers
**herb of grace** *n, pl* **herbs of grace** [so called fr. the association of *rue* (plant) with *rue* (repentance)] **:** RUE
**herb-of-the-cross** \,≈≈≈'≈\ *n, pl* **herbs-of-the-cross :** EUROPEAN VERVAIN
**her·bo·rist** \'(h)ərbərəst\ *n* -s [MF *herboriste, herboliste*, irreg. fr. *herbe* herb (fr. L *herba*) + *-iste* -ist] **:** HERBALIST
**her·bo·ri·za·tion** \,≈rə'zāshən, -,rī'z-\ *n* -s **:** an excursion for the study or collection of plants
**her·bo·rize** \'≈≈,rīz\ *vi* -ED/-ING/-S [F *herboriser*, fr. *herboriste* + *-iser* -ize] **:** BOTANIZE
**herb·ous** \'(h)ərbəs\ *or* **her·bose** \-,bōs\ *adj* [L *herbosus*, fr. *herba* grass, herb + *-osus* -ous, -ose] **:** HERBY
**herb par·is** \-'parəs\ *n, pl* **herbs paris** *or* **herb parises** *usu cap P* [by folk etymology (influence of *Paris*, France) fr. ML or NL *herba paris*, lit., herb of a couple; fr. the resemblance of its four leaves on a stalk to a true lover's knot] **:** a European herb (*Paris quadrifolia*) resembling and closely related to the trilliums and commonly reputed to be poisonous
**herb patience** *n, pl* **herbs patience :** PATIENCE 3
**herb rob·ert** \-'räbə(r)t\ *n, pl* **herbs robert** *or* **herb roberts** *usu cap R* [trans. of ML *herba Roberti*, prob. *Robertus* (St. Robert) †1067 Fr. ecclesiastic] **:** a sticky low herb (*Geranium robertianum*) with small reddish purple flowers
**herbs** *pl of* HERB
**herb st. bar·ba·ra** \-(,)sānt'bärb(ə)rə, ,sənt-, -'bȧb-\ *n, pl* **herbs st. barbara** *or* **herb st. barbaras**, *usu cap S&B* [trans. of ML or NL *herba* (*Sanctae*) *Barbarae* — more at HERB BARBARA] **:** WINTER CRESS
**herb she·rard** \-shə'rärd\ *n, pl* **herbs sherard** *or* **herb sherards** [NL *Sherardia*] **:** FIELD MADDER
**herb so·phia** \-sə'fīə, -sō'-, -fēə\ *n, pl* **herbs sophia** *or* **herb sophias** *usu cap S* [prob. fr. NL *sophia* (specific epithet of *Descurainia sophia*), fr. the name *Sophia*] **:** a hedge mustard (*Descurainia sophia*) with long linear pods
**herbst's corpuscle** \'herps(t)s-\ *n, usu cap H* **:** CORPUSCLE OF HERBST
**herb tobacco** *n* **:** a mixture of herbs containing coltsfoot (*Tussilago farfara*) and smoked for relieving coughs
**herb trinity** *n, pl* **herbs trinity** *or* **herb trinities** [trans. of ML or NL *herba trinitatis*] **1** [so called fr. the three-colored flowers] **:** PANSY **2** [so called fr. the three lobes of the leaf] **:** HEPATICA 1b
**herbwoman** \'≈,≈≈\ *or* **herbwife** \'≈,≈\ *n, pl* **herbwomen** *or* **herbwives :** a woman who sells herbs
**herby** \'(h)ərbē\ *adj* -ER/-EST [*herb* + *y*] **1 :** abounding in herbaceous vegetation **2 :** relating to, resembling, or tasting like an herb ‹a rich ~ flavor›
**her·cog·a·mous** \¦hər¦kägəməs\ *adj* [Gk *herkos* fence, barrier + E *-gamous*] **:** incapable of self-fertilization
**her·cog·a·my** \,hər'kägəmē\ *n* -ES [Gk *herkos* + E *-gamy*] **:** a state in which self-pollination is made impossible by structural obstacles (as in the flowers of orchids)
**her·cu·la·ne·an** \¦hərkyə¦lānēən\ *adj, usu cap* [*Herculaneum*, ancient city in southwestern Italy + E *-an*] **:** of or relating to the ancient Roman city of Herculaneum
**her·cu·le·an** \¦hər¦kyə¦lēən, ¦hər¦kyülēən, ¦hə̄¦, ¦həi¦, hə(r)-'kyül-\ *adj, usu cap* [*Hercules* + E *-an*] **1 :** of or relating to Hercules or his feats ‹*Herculean* labors› **2 a :** of heroic proportions **:** very large and strong ‹*Herculean* longshoreman› ‹the bed was a wide and *Herculean* piece —Ellery Queen› **b :** of extraordinary might or tremendous difficulty **:** displaying or requiring the strength of a Hercules ‹*Herculean* exertions› ‹*Herculean* task› **syn** see HUGE
**her·cu·les** \'hərkyə,lēz, 'hək-, 'həik-\ *n* -ES *usu cap* [after *Hercules*, Greco-Roman mythological hero noted for his great strength and for having accomplished twelve gigantic tasks imposed upon him, fr. L, fr. Gk *Hēraklēs*] **:** a man of great physical strength ‹said of him that it was greedy and unfair to be an Adonis and a *Hercules* as well —E.V.Lucas›
**hercules' allheal** \-,lē'zȯl,hēl\ *n, usu cap H* **:** a European herb (*Opopanax chironium*) — compare WOUNDWORT
**hercules beetle** *n, usu cap H* **1 :** a very large beetle (*Dynastes hercules*) native to tropical America of which the male being prob. the largest existing insect attains a length of over five inches and bears a long forwardly projecting horn on the thorax and another on the head **2 :** RHINOCEROS BEETLE
**hercules club** *n, usu cap H* **:** a large Australian whelk (*Pyrazus ebeninus*) with a dark brown nodose shell
**hercules'-club** \'≈≈,≈'≈\ *n, pl* **hercules'-clubs** *usu cap* **1 :** any of several prickly shrubs or trees: **a :** an ornamental tree (*Zanthoxylum clava-herculis*) of the southeastern U. S. and the West Indies **b :** either of two shrubs of the Bahamas (*Zanthoxylum coreaceum* or *Caesalpinia bahamensis*) **2 :** a gourd (*Lagenaria vulgaris*) with fruit sometimes exceeding five feet in length **3 :** a small prickly tree (*Aralia spinosa*) of eastern U. S. — called also *angelica tree, devil's-walking-stick*
**hercules stone** *n, usu cap H* **:** LODESTONE
**her·cyn·i·an** \(¦)hər¦sinēən\ *adj, usu cap* [L *Hercynia* (*silva*) Hercynian forest + E *-an*] **1 :** of or relating to an extensive mountain range covered with forests in ancient Germany **2 :** of or relating to the folding and mountain building that took place in the eastern hemisphere in late Paleozoic time — see GEOLOGIC TIME table
**her·cy·nite** \'hərs°n,īt\ *n* -s [G *hercynit*, fr. L *Hercynia* (*silva*), its locality + G *-it* -ite] **:** a black mineral $FeAl_2O_4$ consisting of an oxide of iron and aluminum and constituting a member of the spinel series
[1]**herd** \'hərd, 'hə̄d, 'həid\ *n* -s [ME *herde, herd*, fr. OE *heord*; akin to OHG *herta* herd, ON *hjörth*, Goth *hairda* herd, MW *cordd* troop, Gk *korthys* heap, Skt *śardha* herd, troop] **1 a :** a number of one kind of animal kept together under human care or control: as (1) **:** a company of one of the larger domestic animals ‹a ~ of horses› ‹~s of swine›; *esp* **:** such a company of domestic oxen — often contrasted with *flock* ‹patriarchs rich in ~s of cattle and flocks of sheep and goats› (2) **:** a company of one kind of wild or semi-domesticated animals kept or bred for human use ‹a ~ of ranch mink› ‹a ~ of laboratory mice› **b :** a congregation of gregarious wild animals: as (1) **:** a group of one or more kinds of usu. large herbivorous mammals ‹a ~ of elephants› ‹~s of antelopes darkening the African veldt› or of marine mammals ‹the dolphin ~ playing through the swell —Sacheverell Sitwell› ‹~s of seal coming ashore to bear young› (2) **:** a school of large fish ‹grazing on the bottom in ~s like the haddock —Rachel L. Carson› (3) **:** a flock of large and usu. chiefly terrestrial or aquatic birds ‹a ~ of swans› ‹a large ~ of wild turkeys› **2 a :** a group of people usu. having a common bond ‹entered the troop with the midwinter ~ of tenderfeet —MacKinlay Kantor› **b :** the whole body of mankind **:** the undistinguished masses **:** MOB ‹isolate the individual prophets from the ~ —Norman Cousins›; *esp* **:** society viewed as clinging to a blind conformity of standards and behavior ‹the ~ of mankind can hardly be said to think; their notions are almost all adoptive —Earl of Chesterfield› ‹a boarding school where the thirteen-year-old . . . helplessly watches the ~ tearing to shreds the spirit of a nonconformist student —Rose Feld› **3 :** a considerable quantity **:** large number ‹~s of new cars from America —Christopher Rand›
[2]**herd** \"\ *vi* -ED/-ING/-S [ME *herden*, fr. *herde, herd*, n.] **1 a :** to come together in a herd **:** feed or run together ‹animals are in general fond of ~*ing* and grazing in company —Oliver Goldsmith› **b :** to assemble or move in a group ‹New Yorkers . . . ~*ing* resignedly on subway platforms —Charlotte Devree› ‹when the bell rang they ~*ed* in together —Oliver La Farge› **2 :** to place oneself in a group **:** ASSOCIATE ‹it is desirable that young noblemen should ~ —Sir Walter Scott›
[3]**herd** \"\ *n* -s [ME *hierde, hirde, herde*, fr. OE *hyrde, hierde*; akin to OHG *hirti* herdsman, ON *hirthir*, Goth *hairdeis*; derivatives fr. the root of E [1]*herd*] **1 a :** one that herds domestic animals **:** HERDSMAN — now used chiefly in combination ‹cow*herd*› ‹swine*herd*› **b** *dial Brit* **:** SHEPHERD **2** [[4]*herd*] *West* **:** a tour of duty as a herdsman ‹a new ranch hand, on ~ for the first time› ‹cook had flapjacks ready for the men coming off night ~›
[4]**herd** \"\ *vt* -ED/-ING/-S [ME *herden*, fr. *hierde, herde*, n.] **1 a :** to keep (animals) together **:** LEAD, DRIVE ‹dogs are often trained to ~ sheep› **b :** to gather, lead, or drive as if in a herd ‹a nation that ~s fifteen millions of its own citizens into slave labor camps —James Burnham› ‹seventy-five boys and girls were ~*ed* by six or eight teachers —W.A.White› **2 :** to place in a group **:** ASSOCIATE ‹~ us with their kindred fools —Jonathan Swift›
**herdbook** \'≈,≈\ *n* **:** a book containing the records of one or more herds **:** an official record of the individuals and pedigrees of a recognized breed esp. of cattle or swine
**herdboy** \'≈,≈\ *n* **1 :** a boy who tends herd or assists a herder **2 :** COWBOY 3a
**herd·er** \-də(r)\ *n* -s [[4]*herd* + *-er*] **1 :** HERDSMAN **2 :** FLUME RUNNER **3 :** a worker who couples and uncouples locomotives in a railroad yard
**her·der·ite** \'hərdə,rīt, 'her-\ *n* -s [Baron Siegmund A. W. von *Herder* †1838 Ger. mining official + E *-ite*] **:** a mineral $CaBe(PO_4)(F,OH)$ consisting of phosphate and fluoride of beryllium and calcium
**her·dic** \'hərdik\ *n* -s [after Peter *Herdic* †1888 Am. inventor] **:** a small horse-drawn omnibus of late 19th century America having side seats and an entrance at the back ‹a ~ load of boys from some dance in town —C.M.Flandrau›

herdic

**herding** *n* -s [fr. gerund of [4]*herd*] **:** the act or work of taking care of livestock
**herd instinct** *n* **:** an inherent tendency to congregate or to react in unison ‹*herd instinct* of wild horses› ‹the startled cows obeyed the *herd instinct* to stampede›; *esp* **:** a theoretical human instinct toward gregariousness and conformity
**herds** *pl of* HERD, *pres 3d sing of* HERD
**herd's-grass** *also* **herd grass** \'≈,≈\ *n, pl* **herd's-grasses** [after John *Herd*, who in 1700 found timothy growing in N. H.] **1 :** TIMOTHY **2** [so called fr. its being frequently sown in mixtures with timothy] **:** REDTOP 1
**herds·man** \'hərdzmən, 'hə̄d-,'həid-\ *n, pl* **herdsmen** [alter. of earlier *herdman*, fr. ME *hirdman, herdman*, fr. OE *hyrdeman*, fr. *hierde, hyrde* herdsman + *man* — more at HERD] **:** a manager, breeder, or tender of livestock (as cattle or sheep)
**herd·wick** \'hər,dwik\ *n* [fr. obs. *herdwick* pasture ground, fr. ME, fr. *hierde, herde* herdsman + *wick*; fr. the breed's having been developed on the herdwicks of the Abbey of Furness in Lancashire, England] **1** *usu cap* **:** a British breed of very hardy coarse-wooled mountain sheep **2** -s *often cap* **:** an animal of the Herdwick breed
[1]**here** \'hi(ə)r, -iə; "*Come here!*" *is often* kə'mi-\ *adv* [ME, fr. OE *hēr*; akin to OHG *hiar, hier* here, ON & Goth *hēr*, OE *hē* he — more at HE] **1 a :** at this point in space **:** in this location ‹turn ~› ‹if they mean to have a war, let it begin ~ —John Parker› **:** in this very spot ‹he is not ~, for he has risen —Mt 28:6 (RSV)› — opposed to *there;* often used interjectionally esp. in answering a roll call or in calling a domestic animal **b :** at this point in time **:** NOW ‹~ it's August and summer's nearly over› **2 a :** at this critical point esp. of an argument or development **:** at this juncture ‹~ it becomes necessary to bring our concepts together —R.M.Weaver› **b :** in the matter in question **:** in this case or particular ‹the essential fact ~ was the division of the Roman empire —Gilbert Highet› **3 :** in the present life or state **:** on earth ‹happy ~, and more happy hereafter —Francis Bacon› — often used with *below* ‹implies some endeavor to improve conditions ~ below instead of a single-minded concentration on . . . the next world —Elmer Davis› **4 :** to or into this place **:** HITHER ‹bring the book ~› **5 —** used interjectionally and often reduplicated as an admonitory rebuke ‹~, that's enough› or soothing encouragement ‹~ ~, don't cry› — **here goes —** used interjectionally to express resolution or resignation esp. at the beginning of a rash, difficult, or unpleasant undertaking — **neither here nor there :** having no interest or relevance **:** of no consequence ‹matters of comfort and convenience that are *neither here nor there* to a real sailing fan›
[2]**here** \"\ *adj* [ME, fr. *here*, adv.] **1 —** used for emphasis esp. after a demonstrative pronoun or after a noun modified by a demonstrative adjective ‹this boy ~ knows what happened› **2** *now substand* **—** used for emphasis after a demonstrative adjective but before the noun modified ‹with regard to this ~ robbery —Charles Dickens›
[3]**here** \"\ *n* -s [ME, fr. *here*, adv.] **1 :** the present location or juncture **:** this place ‹where do we go from ~› ‹from ~ on the story gets more interesting› — opposed to *there* **2 :** immediacy in space abstracted from the other qualities and relations of the immediate experience ‹a ~ to which we relate all theres —James Ward›
[4]**he·re** \'he,re\ *n* -s [OE *here* army — more at HARRY] **:** an army in Anglo-Saxon times; *esp* **:** an army of invaders
**hereabouts** *or* **hereabout** \¦≈≈¦≈\ *adv* [ME *her abute*, fr. *her, here* here + *abute, about* about] **:** about or near this place ‹in this vicinity ‹the countryside ~› ‹somewhere ~›
[1]**hereafter** \(')≈'≈≈\ *adv* [ME *here after*, fr. OE *hēræfter*, fr. *hēr* here + *æfter* after — more at HERE, AFTER] **:** after this: **a :** after this in order or sequence ‹here and ~ I am following . . . her own version —S.H.Adams› **b :** after this in time ‹devise the agencies . . . that will make them impossible ~ —B.N.Cardozo› **c :** in some future time or state ‹this life is a preparation for life ~ —F.B.Artz› **d :** at the time of taking effect — used with this meaning in a statute and expressly so construed by law in some states of the U. S.
[2]**hereafter** \≈'≈≈\ *n* -s *sometimes cap* **1 :** a time to come **:** FUTURE **2 :** an existence or state beyond this life — often used with *the* ‹a belief in the ~ is shown in gifts and articles left with the dead in many burials —P.I.Wellman›
[3]**hereafter** \(')≈'≈≈\ *adj, archaic* **:** FUTURE ‹that ~ ages may behold what ruin happened in revenge of him —Shak.›
**here and now** *n* **:** the immediately present space and time **:** this day and age — used with *the* ‹although Omar was entirely negative in describing the joys of the hereafter, he was completely positive in enumerating the less doubtful joys of the *here and now* —H. W. Van Loon› ‹man's obligation is in the *here and now* —W.H.Whyte›
**here and there** *adv* [ME] **1 a :** in one place and another **:** IRREGULARLY ‹hills topped *here and there* by white buildings —Fred Zimmer› **b :** from time to time **:** now and then ‹only caught a word *here and there*› **2 :** hither and thither ‹roamed *here and there* looking for blueberries›
**hereat** \≈'≈\ *adv, archaic* [ME *her at*, fr. *here* + *at* (prep.)] **:** at or because of this
**hereaway** \¦≈≈¦≈\ *or* **here·aways** \¦≈≈,wāz\ *adv* [ME *hereaway*, fr. *here* + *away*] *now dial* **:** HEREABOUT
**hereby** \(')≈'≈\ *adv* [ME, fr. *here* + *by* (prep.)] **:** by this

**a** *obs* : by this place : near here ⟨~ upon the edge of yonder coppice —Shak.⟩ **b** : by this means; *esp* : by means of this act or document ⟨the sum of $800 is ~ authorized to be appropriated for this purpose —*Congressional Record*⟩

**heredes** *pl of* HERES

**he·red·i·ta·ble** \hə'redədəbəl, he'-, ¦herə¦did-\ *adj* [MF, fr. LL *hereditare* to inherit (fr. L. *hered-, heres* heir) + *-abilis* -able — more at HEIR] : HERITABLE

**her·e·dit·a·ment** \,herə'didəmənt; hə'redəd-, he'-\ *n* -s [ML *hereditamentum*, fr. LL *hereditare* + L *-mentum* -ment] *law* : heritable property : lands, tenements, any property corporeal or incorporeal, real, personal, or mixed, that may descend to an heir

**he·red·i·tar·i·an** \hə,redə'terēən, he,-\ *n* -s [*hereditary* + *-an*] : an advocate of hereditarianism

**he·red·i·tar·i·an·ism** \-ēə,nizəm\ *n* -s : a doctrine that individual differences may be accounted for primarily on the basis of genetics — compare ENVIRONMENTALISM

**he·red·i·tar·i·ly** \-¦=¦==terəlē, -li\ *adv* : in an hereditary manner ⟨the members of society who are ~ predisposed toward mental illness —J.F.Cuber & R.A.Harper⟩

**he·red·i·tar·i·ness** \-rēnəs, -rin-\ *n* -ES : the quality or state of being hereditary

**he·red·i·tary** \hə'redə,terē, -ri *also* he'-\ *adj* [L *hereditarius*, fr. *hereditas* inheritance + *-arius* -ary — more at HEREDITY] **1 a** : genetically transmitted or capable of being genetically transmitted from parent to offspring ⟨~ factor⟩ ⟨~ disease⟩ — see HEREDITY 2; compare ACQUIRED, CONGENITAL, FAMILIAL **b** : characteristic of or fostered by one's predecessors : ANCESTRAL ⟨~ pride⟩ ⟨~ bravery⟩ ⟨~ feud⟩ **2 a** : descended or capable of descending from an ancestor to an heir at law : received or passing by inheritance or required to pass by inheritance ⟨~ wealth⟩ ⟨~ monarchy⟩ **b** : having title or possession through inheritance ⟨~ sovereign⟩ ⟨~ nobility⟩ **3** : of a kind or status established by tradition ⟨~ enemy⟩ ⟨a ~ reputation for liberality and kindness —Louise P. Kellogg⟩ **4** : of or relating to inheritance or heredity ⟨unless he had the ~ dispositions which he has, he would not behave the way he does —Arthur Pap⟩ ⟨the ~ principle, once a business has been founded, has proved . . . a serviceable method of ensuring fresh supplies of managerial talent —Roy Lewis & Angus Maude⟩ **syn** see INNATE

**he·re·di·tas** *also* **hae·re·di·tas** \hə'redə,tas\ *n, pl* **heredita·tes** \-,==='tād·(,)ēz\ [L] *Roman & civil law* : inheritance or succession : the rights and liabilities to which an heir succeeds : an estate of a deceased person regarded as a juridical person

**hereditas ja·cens** \-'jā,senz\ *n* [L, lit., lying (inactive) inheritance] *Roman & civil law* : an inheritance not entered upon by the heir : a vacant succession

**he·red·i·ty** \hə'redədē, -ətē, -i *also* he'-\ *n* -ES [MF *heredité*, fr. L *hereditat-, hereditas*, fr. *hered-, heres* heir + *-itat-, -itas* -ity — more at HEIR] **1 a** : INHERITANCE ⟨their fathers were of yeoman rank, both by ~ and as large freeholders —Charles Partridge⟩ **b** : TRADITION ⟨Bretons are fishermen by ~⟩ **2 a** : the sum of the qualities and potentialities of an individual that are genetically derived from its ancestors : the germinal constitution of an individual **b** : the transmission of qualities from ancestor to descendant (as from parent to child) through a mechanism lying primarily in the chromosomes of the germ cells that in sexually reproducing organisms sorts out in meiosis the genes accumulated in past generations and recombines them during fertilization to produce a new individual conforming to the general pattern of its kind but exhibiting variations dependent both on specific recombination of factors and on interaction between the hereditary potentialities and the environment — compare GALTON'S LAW OF INHERITANCE, LAMARCKISM, MENDEL'S LAW, PANGENESIS, PHENOCOPY, WEISMANNISM

**heredo-** *comb form* [NL, fr. L *hered-, heres* heir — more at HEIR] : hereditary : hereditarily ⟨*heredo*ataxia⟩ ⟨*heredo*familial⟩

**her·e·ford** \'hərfərd, 'hōfəd, 'həifəd *sometimes* 'herəf-\ *n* [fr. county of *Hereford*, England] **1 a** *usu cap* : a breed of hardy red beef cattle with white faces and markings and either horned or polled that originated in Herefordshire, England, but are now extensively raised in the western U.S. and other grazing regions **b** -s *often cap* : an animal of this breed **2a** *usu cap* : an American breed of red and white swine typically having markings similar to those of Hereford cattle **b** -s *often cap* : a hog of this breed

**hereford disease** *n, cap H* : GRASS TETANY

**her·e·ford·shire** \'herəfərd,shi(ə)r, -fəd,shiə, -,shə(r), *US* " *or* 'hərf- *or* 'hōf- *or* 'həif-\ *or* **hereford** *adj, usu cap* [fr. *Herefordshire* or county of *Hereford*, Eng.] : of or from the county of Hereford, England : of the kind or style prevalent in Hereford

**herefrom** \(')=¦=\ *adv* [¹*here* + *from* (prep.)] *archaic* : from this: **a** : from this place **b** : from this source

**he·re·geld** \'herə,geld, -,ye-\ *n* -s [OE *heregeld, heregild*, fr. *here* army + *gield, geld, gild* payment, tribute — more at HARRY, GELD] **1** : DANEGELD **2** [ME (Sc dial.) *heregeld, hereyeld, hereʒeld*, prob. fr. OE *heregeld*] *old Scots law* : a due or payment corresponding to the English heriot

**herehence** *adv* [¹*here* + *hence*] *obs* : from or away from this point or source

**herein** \(,)=¦=\ *adv* [ME *herinne, herin*, fr. OE *hērinne*, fr. *hēr* here + *inne* in — more at HERE, IN] : in this: **a** : in this place ⟨~ were many vaulted . . . walks hewn out of the rock —John Ray⟩ ⟨enclosed ~ you will find my check⟩ **b** : in this passage, book, or document ⟨all legislative powers ~ granted —*U.S.Constitution*⟩ **c** : in this fact or particular ⟨~ you war against your reputation —Shak.⟩

**hereinabove** \=¦==¦=, ¦=(,)==¦=\ *adv* [*herein* + *above*] : above this : at a prior point in this writing or document ⟨payments due said fund, as ~ described —*Nat'l Bituminous Coal Wage Agreement*⟩

**hereinafter** \¦==¦==\ *adv* [*herein* + *after*] : after this : in the following part of this writing or document ⟨a behavior to be ~ defined —Edward Sapir⟩ ⟨subject to conditions of this policy as ~ specified⟩

**hereinbefore** \=¦==¦=, ¦=(,)==¦=\ *adv* [*herein* + *before*] : before this : in the preceding part of this writing or document ⟨oaths ~ directed to be taken by the governor —Martin Wight⟩

**hereinbelow** \=¦==¦=, ¦=(,)==¦=\ *adv* [*herein* + *below*] : below this : at a subsequent point in this writing or document ⟨which report is ~ set forth in full —*U.S.Code*⟩

**he·rem** *or* **che·rem** \'kārəm, 'ker-\ *n* -s [Heb *ḥērem*] : one of three forms of ecclesiastical excommunication pronounced by a rabbi or by the officials of a synagogue or community

**he·rend porcelain** \'he,rend-\ *n, usu cap H* [fr. *Herend*, town in Hungary where it was made] : Hungarian hard-paste porcelain made since the 18th century and often imitative of other wares

**here·ness** *n* -ES [*here* + *-ness*] : the state of being here

**her·eni·ging** *also* **her·ee·ni·ging** \hə'rēnəkiŋ, -ə̄kiŋ\ *n* -s *sometimes cap* [Afrik *hereniging* (formerly spelled *hereeniging*), lit., reunion, reuniting, fr. *herenig* to reunite + *-ing*] : an amalgamation of So. African political parties

**hereof** \(')=¦=\ *sometimes* -¦äf\ *adv* [ME *herof*, fr. OE *hērof*, fr. *hēr* here + *of* (prep.) — more at HERE, OF] : of this ⟨the twigs ~ are physic —Thomas Fuller⟩; *specif* : of this writing or document ⟨shown in the schedule on the last page ~⟩

**hereon** \(')=¦=\ *adv* [ME *heron*, fr. OE *hēron*, fr. *hēr* here + *on* (prep.)] : on this: **a** *archaic* : on this fact or basis ⟨happiness grounded ~ —Nehemiah Grew⟩ **b** : on this writing or document ⟨endorsed ~⟩

**hereout** \(')=¦=\ *adv* [ME *herout, herut*, fr. *here* + *out, ut* out (prep.) — more at HERE, OUT] *archaic* : out of this: **a** : out of this place : from here **b** : out of this premise : HENCE

**here-right** \(')=¦=\ *adv, dial Eng* : on the spot : right here ⟨let's settle it *here-right* —F.T.Elworthy⟩

**he·re·ro** \hə're(,)rō, 'herə,rō\ *n, pl* **herero** *or* **hereros** *usu cap* **1 a** : a Bantu people of the central part of South-West Africa — compare DAMARA **b** : a member of the Herero people **2** : the Bantu language of the Herero people

**-heres** *pl of* HERE

**²he·res** \'hā,rās\ *or* **hae·res** \'hī,-\ *n, pl* **here·des** *or* **haere·des** \=='rā,dās\ [L — more at HEIR] *civil law* : the universal successor of a deceased person — called also *heir*

**he·re·si·arch** \hə'rēzē,ärk, he'-, -rēsē-; 'herəsē,-\ *n* -s [LL *haeresiarcha*, fr. LGk *hairesiarchēs* leader of a sect, leader of a group of heretics, fr. Gk *hairesis* sect & LGk, heresy + Gk *-archēs* -arch — more at HERESY] : an originator or chief advocate of a heresy : leader of a group of heretics ⟨it is not only the lives of saints who leave their mark . . . but the lives of ~s and sinners as well —D.H.Wiest⟩ ⟨became the chief Communist ~ —E.J.Simmons⟩

**he·re·si·mach** \hə'rēzə,mak, he'-, -rēsə-; 'herəsē,-\ *n* -s [LGk *hairesimachos*, fr. *hairesis* heresy + Gk *-machos* (fr. *machesthai* to fight) — more at HERESY, -MACHY] : an active opponent of heresy and heretics

**he·re·si·og·ra·phy** \hə,rēzē'ägrəfē, he,-, -rēsē-; ,herəsē-\ *n* -ES [*heresio-* (fr. *heresy*) + *-graphy*] : a treatise on heresy

**he·re·si·ol·o·gist** \-'äləjəst\ *n* -s : a writer against heresies

**he·re·si·ol·o·gy** \-jē\ *n* -ES [*heresio-* (fr. *heresy*) + *-logy*] **1** : the study of heresies **2** : a treatise on heresies

**he·res ne·ces·sa·ri·us** \'hā,rā,snekə'särēəs\ *n* [NL, lit., heir of necessity] *Roman law* : a slave who is instituted by his master as his heir and who upon his master's death automatically attains his freedom and becomes his heir

**her·e·sy** \'herəsē, -si\ *n* -ES [ME *eresie, heresie*, fr. OF, fr. LL *haeresis*, fr. LGk *hairesis*, fr. Gk, action of taking, choice, sect, fr. *hairein* to take + *-sis*; perh. akin to Gk *hormē* assault, attack — more at SERUM] **1 a** : adherence to a religious opinion that is contrary to an established dogma of a church : HETERODOXY ⟨was convicted of ~ . . . because of his belief in the preexistence of souls —H.E.Starr⟩ — opposed to *orthodoxy* **b** : a deliberate and obstinate denial of a revealed truth by a baptized member of the Roman Catholic Church — compare INQUISITION 3a **c** : an opinion or doctrine contrary to church dogma ⟨all the great *heresies* . . . in Christianity have been specifically concerned with the relationship of the Son to the Father —Weston La Barre⟩ **2 a** : dissent from a dominant theory or opinion in any field ⟨so much that used to be scientific ~ is now regarded as scientific truth —Elmer Davis⟩ ⟨preaching ~ to the good Jeffersonian progressives of his day —C.B.Forcey⟩ **b** : an opinion or doctrine contrary to the truth or to generally accepted beliefs ⟨our democratic ~ which holds that . . . truth is to be found by majority vote —M.W. Straight⟩ **3** : a group or school of thought centering around a particular heresy ⟨favoring the German school of historians and other *heresies* of similar nature —A.G.Mayous⟩

**¹her·e·tic** \'herə,tik\ *n* -s [ME *eretik, heretik*, fr. MF *eretique, heretique*, adj. & n., fr. LL *haereticus*, fr. LGk *hairetikos*, fr. Gk, able to choose, fr. *hairetos* (verbal of *hairein* to take, *haireisthai* to choose) + *-ikos* -ic] **1 a** : a dissenter from established church dogma : DEVIATIONIST — distinguished from *infidel* **b** : a baptized member of the Roman Catholic Church who deliberately and obstinately disavows a revealed truth **2** : one that dissents from an accepted belief or doctrine of any kind : INNOVATOR, NONCONFORMIST ⟨to delete from history its ~s and its radicals would be to deprive it of that rare quality known as independence of mind —F.C.Neff⟩ ⟨the who resists a mania may be trodden under foot like any other ~ —W.G. Sumner⟩

**²heretic** \", hə'red·|ik, he'-, -ret|, |ēk\ *adj* [ME *eretik, heretik*, fr. MF *eretique, heretique*] : HERETICAL

**he·ret·i·cal** \hə'red·|əkəl, he'-, -ret|, 'ēk-\ *adj* [ML *haereticalis*, fr. LL *haereticus* + L *-alis* -al] **1** : of, relating to, or characterized by religious heresy : HETERODOX ⟨let a church member in good standing dare to utter ~ opinions on theology . . . his scalp is in danger —L.L.Rice⟩ — opposed to *orthodox* **2** : of, relating to, or characterized by departure from accepted beliefs or standards : RADICAL, UNORTHODOX ⟨we must have a spirit of tolerance which allows the expression of all opinions, however ~ they may appear —J.B.Conant⟩ ⟨many critics regard individualism in art as an ~ innovation —John Dewey⟩ — **he·ret·i·cal·ly** \-k(ə)lē, -li\ *adv* — **he·ret·i·cal·ness** \-kəlnəs\ *n* -ES

**he·ret·i·cate** \-,kāt\ *vt* -ED/-ING/-S [ML *haereticatus*, past part. of *haereticare*, fr. LL *haereticus*] **1** : to pronounce or denounce as heretical **2** : to denounce as a heretic : make a heretic of — **he·ret·i·ca·tion** \=,=='kāshən\ *n* -s

**he·ret·i·ca·tor** \'=='==,kād·ə(r)\ *n* -s : one that hereticates

**hereto** \(,)=¦=\ *adv* [ME *herto*, fr. *her, here* here + *to* (prep.)] : to this writing or document ⟨the chart ~ attached⟩

**¹here·to·fore** \¦hir|d·ə¦fō(ə)r, ¦hiə|, |tə-, -fō(ə)r, -ōə, -ó(ə)\ *adv* [ME *heretofore, heretoforn*, fr. *here* + *tofore, toforn* before, fr. OE *tōforan*, fr. *tō* to + *foran* before, fr. *fore* — more at TO, FORE] : before this : up to this time : HITHERTO ⟨I tell you now what we have ~ kept secret from you —A.C. Whitehead⟩

**²heretofore** \"\ *adj* [ME *heretoforn*, fr. *heretoforn*, adv.] *archaic* : PREVIOUS ⟨in his ~ voyages —Nathaniel Hawthorne⟩

**he·re·to·ga** \,herə'tōgə, '==,==\ *also* **her·e·togh** \'herə,tōk\ *n* -s [ME & OE; ME *heretogh*, fr. OE *heretoga*; akin to OFris *hertoga* leader of an army, duke, OS *heritogo*, OHG *herizoho, herizogo*, ON *hertogi*; all fr. a prehistoric Gmc compound whose constituents are akin respectively to OE *here* army and to OE *togian* to draw, drag, and that is prob. a trans. of Gk *stratēlatēs* leader of an army — more at HARRY, TOW] : the leader of an army or commander of militia in Anglo-Saxon England

**heretrix** *var of* HERITRIX

**hereunder** \(,)=¦==\ *adv* [ME, fr. *here* + *under* (prep.)] : under this: **a** : under this written statement : subsequently in this writing or document : BELOW ⟨I subjoin ~ a brief description of the seven-year bean —*Farmer's Weekly*⟩ **b** : under this agreement : in accordance with the terms of this document ⟨registration of copyright . . . ~ shall not exempt the copyright proprietor from the deposit of copies —Richard Wincor⟩

**hereunto** \=¦=(,)=, ¦=(,)=¦=\ *adv* [¹*here* + *unto* (prep.)] : to this; *esp* : to this writing or document ⟨we ~ affix our signatures⟩

**hereupon** \¦==¦=\ *adv* [ME *herupon*, fr. *her, here* here + *upon* (prep.)] : on this : at or as a sequel to this : immediately after this ⟨the warning whistle sounded and ~ the last passengers scrambled aboard⟩

**herewith** \(,)=¦=\ *adv* [ME *herwith*, fr. OE *hērwith*, fr. *hēr* here + *with*] : with this: **a** : with this communication : accompanying this writing or document; *specif* : enclosed in this envelope ⟨you will find my check ~⟩ **b** : with this proof : by this : in this way ⟨~ the principle is established —A. L.Kroeber⟩

**he·rez** \hə'rez\ *n* -ES *usu cap* [fr. *Herez*, Iran, where such rugs are made] : a usu. large heavy cotton or wool Oriental rug of coarse texture and variable quality made in northwestern Iran and characterized by strong angular design and an ivory background

**he·re·zeld** \'herə,yeld\ *n* -s [alter. (ʒ being taken as *z*) of ME (Sc dial.) *heregeld, hereyeld, hereʒeld* — more at HEREGELD] : HEREGELD 2

**heried** *past of* HERY

**heries** *pres 3d sing of* HERY

**herile** *adj* [L *herilis, erilis*, fr. *herus, erus* master + *-ilis* -ile] *obs* : of or relating to a master

**he·ring image** \'hāl|riŋ-, 'he|\ *n, usu cap H* [after Ewald *Hering* †1918 Ger. physiologist and psychologist] : a first positive afterimage in a succession of visual afterimages resulting from a brief light stimulus and appearing in the same hue as the original sensation

**her·i·ot** \'herēət\ *n* -s [ME *heriet, heriot*, fr. OE *heregeatwe, heregeatwa*, pl., military equipment, fr. *here* army + *geatwe, geatwa*, pl., equipment — more at HARRY] *Eng law* : a feudal duty or tribute due under English law to a lord upon the death of a tenant and consisting orig. of the horses and arms lent by the lord to his man, later of the best beast or chattel of the tenant, and in modern times (as surviving in copyhold tenures) of such a chattel as the custom of the manor enables the lord to take or of a money payment — distinguished from *relief*; compare HEREGELD 2, THIRDINGS

**her·i·ot·able** \-ēəd·əbəl\ *adj* : subject to payment of a heriot

**heriot service** *n* : a heriot reserved as an incident of the tenure of an estate in fee simple granted in free tenure before 1290

**her·i·ta·bil·i·ty** \,herəd·ə'bilədē, -rətə-, -lətē, -i\ *n* : the quality or state of being heritable

**¹her·i·ta·ble** \'herəd·əbəl, -rətə-\ *adj* [ME, fr. MF, fr. *heriter* to inherit + *-able*] **1** : capable of being inherited or of passing by inheritance : INHERITABLE **2** *Scots law* : of or relating to heritage or heritables **3** : HEREDITARY ⟨~ character⟩ ⟨~ office⟩ ⟨a viruslike agent transmitting ~ mammary tumors to young sucklings —*Lancet*⟩

**²heritable** \"\ *n* -s : a piece of heritable property — usu. used in pl.

**heritable bond** *or* **heritable security** *n, Scots law* : a form of bond or obligation carrying a yearly profit, secured upon land, treated as heritable, and now essentially like the English and American mortgage of real property

**her·i·ta·bly** \-blē, -bli\ *adv* : by right of inheritance

**her·i·tage** \'herəd·ij, -ətij *sometimes* -rə,täj\ *n* -s [ME, fr. MF, fr. *heriter* to inherit (fr. LL *hereditare*, fr. L *hered-, heres* heir) + *-age* — more at HEIR] **1 a** *law* : real and other property that descends to an heir as distinguished from personal property that passes to an executor or administrator : PATRIMONY **b** *Scots law* : immovable property as distinguished from movable or personal property **2 a** : something transmitted by or acquired from a predecessor : INHERITANCE, LEGACY ⟨rich ~ of folklore⟩ ⟨a ~, a shrine, their history in stone —*Britain Today*⟩ ⟨war had left its ~ of poverty —Rose Macaulay⟩ ⟨the corn crop is a ~ from the Indians —*Annual Report of Ill. Power Co.*⟩ **b** : TRADITION ⟨a . . . party whose ~ is vision and boldness —M.W.Straight⟩ ⟨institutions . . . adapted to varying national ~s —S.P.Hayes b.1910⟩ **3** : BIRTHRIGHT ⟨the ~ of natural freedom was long since cast away —V.L.Parrington⟩

**her·i·tance** \-rəd·ən(t)s, -ətə-\ *n* -s [ME *heritaunce*, fr. MF *heritance*, fr. *heriter* + *-ance*] *archaic* : HERITAGE, INHERITANCE

**her·i·tie·ra** \,herə'tirə\ *n, cap* [NL, after C.L.L'*Héritier* de Brutelle †1800 Fr. botanist] : a small genus of Australasian trees (family Sterculiaceae) yielding hard heavy durable wood

**her·i·tor** \'herəd·ə(r), -rətə-\ *n* -s [alter. of ME *heriter*, fr. MF *eretier, heritier*, fr. L *hereditarius*, hereditary — more at HEREDITARY] **1** : INHERITOR **2** *Scots law* : the owner in fee of heritable property or in parochial law of such real property in a parish as is subject to public burdens

**her·i·trix** *or* **her·e·trix** \'herə·(,)triks\ *n, pl* **heritri·ces** \,herə·'trī(,)sēz\ *or* **heritrix·es** \'herə·,triksəz\ : a female heritor

**herl** \'hər(·ə)l\ *n* -s [ME *herle* — more at HARL] **1** : a barb of a feather used in dressing an artificial fly **2** : an artificial fly containing a herl

**her·ling** \'hərlən, 'her-, -liŋ\ *n* -s [origin unknown] *chiefly Scot* : SEA TROUT 1; *esp* : a young sea trout

**herm** \'hərm\ *n* -s [L *herma, hermes*, fr. Gk *hermēs* statue of Hermes, herm, fr. *Hermēs*, messenger of the gods] : a statue in the form of a square stone pillar surmounted by a bust or head ⟨a ~ of Themistocles which has been identified by its inscription —*New Internat'l Yr. Bk.*⟩; *esp* : a pillar surmounted by a usu. bearded head of Hermes — compare TERM

**her·ma** \'hərmə\ *n, pl* **her·mae** \-,mē, -,mī *or* **her·mai** \-,mī\ [L] : HERM

**her·mae·an** \¦hər¦mēən\ *adj, often cap* [L *Hermaeus* (fr. Gk *Hermaios*, fr. *Hermēs*) + E *-an*] : of or relating to Hermes or a herm

**her·ma·ic** \-'māik\ *adj, usu cap* [Gk *Hermaikos*, fr. *Hermaios* + *-ikos* -ic] **1** : HERMETIC 1a **2** : HERMAEAN

**her·man·dad** \,ermən'dä(th)\ *n, pl* **hermanda·des** \-'ä(,)thās\ *sometimes cap* [Sp, brotherhood, fr. *hermano* brother (fr. L *germanus*, fr. *germanus*, adj., having the same parents) + *-dad* (fr. L *-tat-, -tas* -ty) — more at GERMAN] : one of several voluntary organizations formed in Spain during the 13th, 14th, and 15th centuries to maintain public order and resist the depredations of the nobles and later to exercise general police functions

**her·mann's fluid** \'hərmənz-, 'her,mänz-\ *n, usu cap H* [after Friedrich *Hermann* †1920 Ger. anatomist] : a fixing solution of platinic chloride, osmic acid, and acetic acid used in microscopy for cytological preparations

**her·maph·ro·dism** \hə(r)'mafrə,dizəm, ,hər'-, hə̄'-, həi'-\ *n* -s [F *hermaphrodisme*, fr. *hermaphrodite* (fr. L *hermaphroditus*) + *-isme* -ism] : HERMAPHRODITISM

**¹her·maph·ro·dite** \-dīt, *usu* -īd·+V\ *n* -s [ME *hermofrodite*, fr. L *hermaphroditus*, fr. Gk *hermaphroditos*, fr. *Hermaphroditos*, mythological son of Hermes and Aphrodite who became joined in body with the nymph Salmacis] **1 a** : an abnormal individual esp. among the higher vertebrates having both male and female reproductive organs — called also *androgyne* **b** : HOMOSEXUAL **2** : a combination of diverse elements; *specif* : HERMAPHRODITE BRIG **3** : an animal or plant that is normally equipped with both male and female reproductive organs : BISEXUAL ⟨the hydra . . . is a true ~ —Alpheus Hyatt⟩

**²hermaphrodite** \"\ *adj* : HERMAPHRODITIC

**hermaphrodite brig** *n* : a 2-masted vessel square-rigged forward and schooner-rigged aft — called also *brigantine*

**hermaphrodite caliper** *n* : a drawing instrument having one caliper and one divider leg

**hermaphrodite duct** *n* : a duct for the passage of both eggs and sperm in mollusks having an ovotestis

hermaphrodite brig

**her·maph·ro·dit·ic** \(,)=¦==¦did·|ik, ¦hər,m-, ¦hə̄,m-, ¦həi,m-, -¦dit|, |ēk\ *also* **her·maph·ro·dit·i·cal** \|əkəl, |ēk-\ *adj* **1** : of, relating to, or characterized by hermaphroditism **2** : MONOCLINOUS — **her·maph·ro·dit·i·cal·ly** \|ək(ə)lē, |ēk-, -li\ *adv*

**her·maph·ro·dit·ish** \-¦dīd·|ish, -īt|, |ēsh\ *adj* : HERMAPHRODITIC

**her·maph·ro·dit·ism** \(,)=¦==,dīd·,izəm, -,dī,tiz-\ *n* -s : the condition of being a hermaphrodite — compare DIOECISM

**her·me·neut** \'hərmə,n(y)üt\ *n* -s [Gk *hermēneutēs*, fr. *hermēneuein*] : an interpreter esp. in the early church

**her·me·neu·tic** \¦hərmə¦n(y)üd·ik\ *or* **her·me·neu·ti·cal** \-d·əkəl\ *adj* [*hermeneutic* fr. Gk *hermēneutikos*, fr. (assumed) *hermēneutos* (verbal of *hermēneuein* to interpret, translate, fr. *hermēneus* interpreter, prob. of non-IE origin) + *-ikos* -ic; *hermeneutical* fr. Gk *hermēneutikos* + E *-al*] : of or relating to hermeneutics : INTERPRETATIVE ⟨use of the ~ principle in the sociology of religion⟩ — **her·me·neu·ti·cal·ly** \-d·ək(ə)lē\ *adv*

**her·me·neu·tics** \¦hərmə¦n(y)üd·iks\ *n pl but usu sing in constr, also* **her·me·neu·tic** [Gk *hermēneutikē*, fr. fem. of *hermēneutikos*] : the study of the methodological principles of interpretation and explanation; *specif* : the study of the general principles of biblical interpretation ⟨~ became a weapon in ecclesiastical controversies —J.H.Summers⟩

**her·mes** \'hər(,)mēz\ *n, pl* **her·mae** \-,mē, -,mī\ *or* **her·mai** \-,mī\ *usu cap* [L — more at HERM] : HERM

**¹her·met·ic** \hə(r)'med·|ik, ¦hər¦m-, (')hə̄¦m-, (')həi¦m-, -et|, |ēk\ *or* **her·met·i·cal** \|əkəl, |ēk-\ *adj* [NL *hermeticus*, fr. *Hermet-, Hermes Trismegistus* Thoth, the Egyptian god of wisdom, fabled author of a number of mystical, philosophical, and alchemistic writings, fr. Gk *Hermēt-, Hermēs trismegistos*, lit., thrice-great Hermes (with whom the Greeks identified Thoth) + L *-icus* -ic, *-ical*] **1** *sometimes cap* **a** : of or relating to the mystical and alchemical writings or teachings of Thoth, the Egyptian god of wisdom ⟨~ sciences⟩ **b** : relating to or characterized by occultism, alchemy, magic, or whatever is obscure and mysterious : RECONDITE ⟨~ poetry⟩ **2** [so called fr. the belief that Hermes Trismegistus invented a magic seal to keep vessels airtight] **a** : impervious to air : AIRTIGHT ⟨~ seal⟩ ⟨~ compass⟩ **b** : impervious to external influence ⟨as ~ as a nunnery —Eugene MacCown⟩ **3** : of or relating to a herm : HERMAEAN

**²hermetic** \"\ *n* -s **1** : ALCHEMIST **2** : an expounder of hermetic teachings

**her·met·i·cal·ly** \|ək(ə)lē, |ēk-, -li\ *adv* **1 a** : in an airtight manner ⟨~ sealed suit for use in high-altitude flying —H.G. Armstrong⟩ **b** : in a manner that prevents entry or change ⟨doors ~ sealed to less illustrious callers —Marguerite Steen⟩

⟨two gentlemen of decided and ~ opposite views —Philip Hamburger⟩ **2 :** in an obscure or mystical manner ⟨~ painted in the Cubist discipline —Janet Flanner⟩

**her·met·i·cism** \(,)ᵊ'med·ə,sizəm, -etə-\ *n* -s *often cap* **:** HERMETISM

**hermetic powder** *n* **:** SYMPATHETIC POWDER

**her·met·ics** \(,)ᵊ'med·|iks, -et|, |ēks\ *n pl but usu sing in constr, usu cap* **:** HERMETISM

**her·me·tism** \'hərmə,tizəm\ *n* -s [*hermetic* + *-ism*] **1** *usu cap* **:** a system of ideas based on hermetic teachings **2 :** adherence to or practice of hermetic doctrine ⟨it is not . . . willful ~ if the message of their art is veiled and indirect —R.J. Goldwater⟩

**her·me·tist** \-məd·əst\ *n* -s *usu cap* **:** an adherent to hermetic doctrine or practices

**her·mi·no·nes** \,hərmə'nō(,)nēz\ *or* **her·mi·o·nes** \-mē'ō-, -,mī'ō-\ *n pl, usu cap* [L] **:** a division of ancient Teutons described by Tacitus as occupying central and eastern Germany and including interior tribes (as the Hermunduri, Heruli, Suevians, Quadi, Lombards, Vandals)

**her·mit** \'hərmət, 'hēm-,'həim-, *usu* -əd·+V\ *n* -s *often attrib* [ME *ermite, eremite, hermite, heremite*, fr. OF, fr. LL *eremita*, fr. LGk *erēmitēs*, fr. Gk *erēmitēs*, adj., living in the desert, fr. *erēmia* desert (fr. *erēmos* desolate, lonely + *-ia* -y) + *-itēs* -ite — more at RETINA] **1 a :** one that retires from society and lives in solitude **:** ANCHORITE, RECLUSE ⟨seclusive ~s whether in mountain shacks or shuttered brownstone houses⟩ ⟨a ~ nation⟩; *specif* **:** a Christian ascetic living alone in an isolated place in order to devote himself to religious exercises ⟨Christian monasticism from the third century ~s of the Egyptian deserts⟩ — compare MONK **b :** a member of a monastic order (as the Carthusians) whose members lead a chiefly eremitical life or of the Hermits of St. Augustine **c** *obs* **:** BEADSMAN ⟨for . . . the late dignities heaped up to them we rest your ~s —Shak.⟩ **2 a** (1) **:** any of various plainly colored forest-dwelling tropical hummingbirds constituting the genus *Phaethornis* (2) **:** any of several related hummingbirds **b :** HERMIT CRAB **3 :** a spiced molasses cookie often containing chopped raisins and nuts

**¹her·mit·age** \-əd·ij,-ətij\ *n* -s [ME *ermitage, hermitage*, fr. OF, fr. *ermite, hermite* + *-age*] **1 a :** the habitation of a hermit ⟨some forlorn and naked ~ remote from all the pleasures of the world —Shak.⟩ **b :** a secluded residence or private retreat **:** HIDEAWAY ⟨retirement to some country ~ —John Buchan⟩ **c :** a house of various monastic orders **:** MONASTERY ⟨Carthusian ~⟩ **2 :** the life or condition of a hermit ⟨when public places like theaters and restaurants are an integral part of city life . . . it is sheer ~ to be forced to forgo both —Evelyn Barkins⟩

**²her·mi·tage** \¦(h)ermē¦täzh\ *n* -s *usu cap* [fr. Tain-l'*Ermitage*, commune in Drôme dept., France] **1 :** a chiefly red Rhone Valley wine made from grapes grown above the commune of Tain-l'Ermitage **2 :** a wine similar to Hermitage made elsewhere

**hermit crab** *n* [so called fr. its living in the empty shells of gastropods, like a hermit in a cave] **1 :** any of numerous chiefly marine decapod crustaceans of the families Paguridae and Parapaguridae having somewhat elongated bodies and soft and more or less asymmetrical abdomens, occupying the empty shells of gastropods, and seeking larger shells as they increase in size — compare PURSE CRAB **2 :** one that behaves like a hermit crab ⟨creep out of that shell of gentility, you little *hermit crab* —W.J.Locke⟩

hermit crab in shell

**hermit crow** *n* [so called fr. its nongregarious habits] **:** CHOUGH

**her·mit·ess** \'hərməd·əs\ *or* **her·mi·tress** \-mə·trəs\ *n* -ES **:** a female hermit

**her·mit·ic** \(')hər¦mid·ik\ *or* **her·mit·i·cal** \-d·əkəl\ *adj* **:** of, relating to, or suited for a hermit — **her·mit·i·cal·ly** \-d·ək(ə)lē\ *adv*

**her·mit·ize** \'hərməd·,īz\ *vi* -ED/-ING/-S [*hermit* + *-ize*] **:** to live a solitary life

**hermit of st. au·gus·tine** \-ə'gəstən, -,ȯ'g-, -'ȯgə,stēn\ *usu cap H&S&A* [after *St. Augustine* — more at AUGUSTINIAN] **:** a member of an order of friars established in 1256 by Pope Alexander IV

**her·mit·ry** \'hərmətrē\ *n* -ES [*hermit* + *-ry*] **:** the quality or state of being a hermit **:** ISOLATION

**hermits** *pl of* HERMIT

**her·mit·ship** \'ᵊᵊ,ship\ *n* [*hermit* + *-ship*] **:** HERMITRY

**hermit thrush** *n* **:** a thrush (*Hylocichla guttata faxoni*) of eastern No. America that is dull brown above becoming rufous on the tail and spotted on the breast and is noted for its song; *broadly* **:** any of several related thrushes of western No. America

**hermit warbler** *n* **:** a warbler (*Dendroica occidentalis*) found from the Rocky mountains to the Pacific and having in the adult male a yellow head, black throat, and gray back

**her·mo·dac·tyl** \'hərmə,dakt°l, ,ᵊᵊ'ᵊᵊ\ *n, pl* **hermodactyls** \-t°lz\ *or* **her·mo·dac·ty·lus** \,ᵊᵊ'taləs\ *n, pl* **hermodactyls** *or* **hermodacty·li** \-tə,lī\ [ML *hermodactylus*, fr. Gk *hermodaktylon*, fr. *hermo-* (fr. *Hermēs*, messenger of the gods) + *-daktylon* (fr. *daktylos* finger)] **1 :** a root formerly used as a cathartic or for the relief of gout that was prob. derived from an Asiatic colchicum (*Colchicum luteum*) but has been often considered to be or confused with the root of the Mediterranean snake's-head iris **2 :** a plant producing hermodactyls; *broadly* **:** any of various colchicums — compare COLCHICINE

**her·mo·ge·nian** \,hərmə'jēnēən, -nyən\ *n, usu cap* [*Hermogenes*, 2d cent. A.D. Greek rhetorician (fr. L, fr. Gk *Hermogenēs*) + E *-ian*] **:** a disciple of Hermogenes in developing Marcion's doctrine of the eternity of matter

**her·mo·glyph·ic** \'hərmə¦glifik\ *also* **her·mog·ly·phist** \(,)hər'mägləfəst; 'hərmə,glif-, ,ᵊᵊ'ᵊᵊ\ *n* -s [*hermoglyphic* fr. Gk *hermoglyphikos* of statuary, fr. *hermoglypheus* statuary (fr. *hermēs* herm + *-glypheus*, fr. *glyphein* to carve) + *-ikos* -ic; *hermoglyphist* fr. Gk *hermoglyphikos* + E *-ist* — more at HERM, CLEAVE] **:** one that carves statues; *esp* **:** one that engraves inscriptions on herms

**her·mo·sa pink** \(,)hər'mōsə-\ *n* [prob. fr. *hermosa* (*rose*) bourbon rose, fr. Sp *hermosa*, fem. of *hermoso* beautiful, fr. L *formosus* — more at FORMOSITY] **:** a moderate to strong pink that is yellower and lighter than nymph pink and bluer and darker than peachblossom (sense 1)

**herms** *pl of* HERM

**¹hern** \'hərn\ *n* -s [ME *herne, hirne*, fr. OE *hyrne*; akin to OFris *horne* corner, MLG *hörne*, ON *hyrni* corner, OE *horn* horn — more at HORN] *now dial Eng* **:** NOOK, CORNER

**²hern** \'hərn, 'hər·ən\ *pron* [ME *hiren*, alter. (influenced by the *-n* in *min* mine, *thin* thine) of *hire* — more at HER] *dial* **:** HERS

**³hern** *also* **herne** \'hərn, 'hern\ *dial Brit var of* HERON

**her·nan·dia** \(,)hər'nandēə\ *n, cap* [NL, fr. Francisco *Hernández* †1578 Span. botanist + NL *-ia*] **:** a genus (the type of the family Hernandiaceae of the order Ranales) of tropical trees having light combustible wood, alternate entire leaves, small paniculate flowers, and drupaceous fruits — **her·nan·di·a·ceous** \(,)¦ᵊᵊ'āshəs\ *adj*

**her·ne** \'he(ə)rnə\ *adj, usu cap* [fr. *Herne*, Germany] **:** of or from the city of Herne, Germany **:** of the kind or style prevalent in Herne

**her·nia** \'hərnēə, 'hən-,'həin-, -nyə\ *n, pl* **herni·as** \-nēəz, -nyəz\ *or* **herni·ae** \-nē,ē\ [L — more at YARN] **:** a protrusion esp. of one of the abdominal viscera through connective tissue or through a wall of the cavity in which it is normally enclosed — called also *rupture* — **her·nial** \-nēəl,-nyəl\ *adj*

**her·ni·ar·i·a** \,hərnē'a(a)rēə\ *n, cap* [NL, fr. L *hernia* rupture + NL *-aria* — more at HERNIA] **:** a genus of small Old World herbs (family Caryophyllaceae) with minute green flowers — see RUPTUREWORT

**her·ni·ar·in** \-rən\ *n* -s [ISV *herniar-* (fr. NL *Herniaria*, genus name of *Herniaria hirsuta*) + *-in*] **:** a crystalline compound $C_{10}H_8O_3$ found esp. in a rupturewort (*Herniaria hirsuta*); the methyl ether of umbelliferone

**¹her·ni·ary** \'ᵊᵊ,erē, -ri\ *adj* [*hernia* + *-ary*] **:** of or relating to hernia or its treatment

**²herniary** \"\ *n* -ES [NL *Herniaria*] **:** a plant of the genus *Herniaria*

**her·ni·ate** \-,āt, *usu* -,ād·+V\ *vi* -ED/-ING/-S [*hernia* + *-ate*] **:** to protrude through an abnormal body opening **:** RUPTURE

**her·ni·a·tion** \,ᵊᵊ'āshən\ *n* -s **1 :** the act or process of herniating **:** formation of a hernia **2 :** HERNIA

**hernio-** *comb form* [F, fr. L *hernia* — more at YARN] **:** hernia ⟨*hernio*rrhaphy⟩ ⟨*hernio*tomy⟩

**her·ni·or·rha·phy** \,hərnē'ȯrəfē\ *n* -ES [ISV *hernio-* + *-rrhaphy*] **:** an operation for hernia that involves opening the coverings, returning the contents to their normal place, obliterating the hernial sac, and closing the opening with strong sutures

**her·ni·ot·o·my** \-'äd·əmē\ *n* -ES [F *herniotomie*, fr. *hernio-* + *-tomie* -tomy] **:** the operation of cutting through a band of tissue that constricts a strangulated hernia

**he·ro** \'hē(,)rō, 'hi(-\ *n* -ES [back-formation fr. *heroes*, pl., fr. ME, fr. L, fr. Gk *hērōes*, pl. of *hērōs*; perh. akin to L *servare* to protect — more at SERVE] **1 a :** a mythological or legendary figure endowed with great strength, courage, or ability, favored by the gods, and often believed to be of divine or partly divine descent — compare CULTURE HERO, DEMIGOD **b :** a man of courage and nobility famed for his military achievements **:** an illustrious warrior **c :** a man admired for his achievements and noble qualities and considered a model or ideal **d :** the principal male character in a drama, novel, story, or narrative poem **:** PROTAGONIST **e :** the central figure in an event, action, or period **2** *New York* **:** POOR BOY

**¹he·ro·di·an** \hə'rōdēən, he'-\ *n* -s *usu cap* [ME, fr. LL *Herodianus*, fr. *Herodes* (Herod) †4 B.C. king of Judea + L *-ianus* -ian] **:** a member of a political party of biblical times consisting of Jews who were apparently partisans of the Herodian house and together with the Pharisees opposed Jesus

**²herodian** \"\ *adj, usu cap* **:** of or relating esp. to Herod the Great, king of Judea (37–4 B.C.)

**he·rod·o·te·an** \hə¦rädə¦tēən\ *adj, usu cap* [*Herodotus*, 5th cent. B.C. Greek historian (fr. L, fr. Gk *Hērodotos*) + E *-ean*] **:** of, relating to, or suggestive of the historian Herodotus

**heroess** *n* -ES [*hero* + *-ess*] *obs* **:** HEROINE

**¹he·ro·ic** \hə'rōik, he'-,hē'-, -ōek\ *also* **he·ro·i·cal** \-ōəkəl, -ōek-\ *adj* [L *heroicus*, fr. Gk *hērōikos*, fr. *hērōs* hero + *-ikos* -ic, -ical] **1 a :** belonging to or representative or suggestive of the heroes of antiquity ⟨a ~ culture⟩ ⟨~ society⟩ ⟨the ~ age⟩ **b :** treating of or suitable to or used in the treatment of the heroes of antiquity ⟨~ legends⟩ ⟨~ material⟩ **2 a** (1) **:** arising from, exhibiting, or suggestive of boldness, spirit, or daring ⟨a ~ cavalry charge⟩ ⟨a ~ enterprise⟩ (2) **:** such as is likely to be undertaken only to save life ⟨~ surgery⟩ **:** EXTREME, RADICAL ⟨~ treatment⟩ **b :** supremely noble, altruistic, or self-sacrificing ⟨a ~ gesture⟩ ⟨~ deeds⟩ **3 a :** of impressively generous proportion, size, or volume ⟨a ~ voice⟩ ⟨~ contributions to charity⟩ **b :** larger than life but smaller than colossal ⟨a ~ statue⟩ **c :** having a pronounced effect **:** LARGE, POWERFUL — used chiefly of medicaments or dosage ⟨~ doses⟩ ⟨a ~ drug⟩ **4 :** belonging to or inspired by the literary conventions of Restoration England esp. as found in the works of John Dryden ⟨~ drama⟩

**²heroic** \"\ *n* -s **1 :** HEROIC VERSE, HEROIC POEM **2 heroics** *pl* **:** vainglorious, unnaturally extravagant, or shamelessly flamboyant conduct, behavior, or expression ⟨avoids all ~s . . . in its delineation of a man of dignity —*Newsweek*⟩

**he·ro·i·cal·ly** \-ōək(ə)lē, -ōek-, -li\ *also* **he·ro·ic·ly** \-kl-\ *adv* **:** in a heroic manner ⟨struggling ~⟩ ⟨~ generous⟩

**he·ro·i·cal·ness** *n* -ES **:** the quality or state of being heroic **:** HEROICNESS

**heroic couplet** *n* **:** a couplet of rhyming iambic pentameters often forming a distinct rhetorical as well as metrical unit

**he·ro·ic·ness** *n* -ES **:** the quality or state of being heroic

**he·roi·comic** *or* **he·roi·comical** \hə¦rōə, he¦-, hē¦-, -ōe+\ *adj* [F *héroïcomique*, blend of *héroïque* heroic (fr. L *heroicus*) and *comique* comic, comical, fr. L *comicus* — more at HEROIC, COMIC] **:** comic by being ludicrously noble, bold, or elevated

**heroic poem** *n* **:** an epic or a poem in epic style

**heroic poetry** *n* **:** epic poetry esp. celebrating the deeds of a hero

**heroic stanza** *or* **heroic quatrain** *n* **:** a rhymed quatrain in heroic verse with rhyme scheme *abab*

**heroic verse** *or* **heroic meter** *n* **1 :** dactylic hexameter — usu. used with special reference to epic verse of classical times **2** *or* **heroic line :** the verse form in which the heroic poetry of a particular language is or according to critical opinion should be composed (as the alexandrine in French and the hendecasyllabic line in Italian) **3 :** the iambic pentameter in rising rhythm used in epic and other serious English poetry during the 17th and 18th centuries

**her·oin** *also* **her·oine** \'he|rəwən *sometimes* 'hi| *or* |,rōin\ *n* -s [fr. *Heroin*, a trademark] **:** a bitter white crystalline narcotic $C_{21}H_{23}NO_5$ made from morphine but more potent than morphine and because of its addictive properties prohibited by law from being manufactured in or imported into the U.S. and many other countries — called also *diacetylmorphine, diamorphine*

**her·o·ine** \'herəwən *sometimes* 'hir-\ *n* -s [L *heroina, heroine*, fr. Gk *hērōinē*, fem. of *hērōs* hero — more at HERO] **1 a :** a mythological or legendary woman having the qualities of a hero **b :** a woman admired for her achievements and noble qualities and considered a model or ideal **2 a :** the principal female character in a drama, novel, story, or narrative poem **b :** the central female figure in an event, action, or period

**her·oin·ism** \'he|rəwə,nizəm *sometimes* 'hi| *or* |,rōi,ni-\ *n* -s [*heroin* + *-ism*] **:** addiction to heroin **:** habitual use of heroin

**hero·ism** \'herə,wizəm *also* 'hir- *or* 'hēr-\ *n* -s [F *héroïsme*, fr. *héros* hero (fr. L *heros*, fr. Gk *hērōs*) *-isme* -ism — more at HERO] **1 :** heroic conduct ⟨the ~ of a regiment defending a position⟩ **2 :** the qualities (as courage, bravery, self-sacrifice, unselfishness) of a hero **:** heroic characteristics ⟨a nation famous for the ~ of its leaders⟩

**hero·ize** \'hē(,)rō,īz, 'hi(-\ *vb* -ED/-ING/-S [*hero* + *-ize*] *vt* **:** to make heroic **:** treat or represent as a hero ⟨politicians *heroizing* themselves to their constituents⟩ ⟨*heroized* their leader⟩ ~ *vi* **:** to play the hero **:** represent oneself as a hero

**he·ro·la** \hə'rōlə\ *n* -s [origin unknown] **:** a large yellowish tawny African antelope (*Damaliscus hunteri*) with markings on face and tail

**her·on** \'herən\ *n, pl* **herons** *also* **heron** [ME *heiroun, heroun*, fr. MF *hairon, heron*, of Gmc origin; akin to OE *hrāgra* heron, OHG *heigaro, hreigaro*, ON *hegri*; akin to W *cryg* hoarse, Gk *krikē* it creaked, Lith *krykšti* to shriek, OHG *scrīan* to scream, cry — more at SCREAM] **:** any of various wading birds constituting the family Ardeidae that have a long neck and legs, a long tapering bill with a sharp point and sharp cutting edges, large wings and soft plumage, and the inner edge of the claw of the middle toe pectinate, that exhibit in some species dichromatism and develop in many species special plumes in the breeding season, that frequent chiefly the vicinity of water and feed mostly on aquatic animals which they capture by quick thrusts of the sharp bill, that usu. nest in trees often in communities, and that vary much in size among different species but are not as large as some of the cranes — see GREAT BLUE HERON, GREAT WHITE HERON, LITTLE BLUE HERON; compare EGRET

great blue heron

**her·on·ry** \-rē,-ri\ *n* -ES [*heron* + *-ry*] **:** a place where herons breed; *also* **:** a community of herons

**heron's-bill** \'ᵊᵊ,ᵊ\ *also* **heronbill** \'ᵊᵊ,ᵊ\ *n, pl* **heron's-bills** *also* **heronbills :** ERODIUM 2

**her·on·sew** \'herən,sō, -sü\ *n* -s [ME *heronsewe*, fr. MF *heroncel, heronceau* young heron, dim. of *hairon, heron*] *dial Brit* **:** HERON

**He·roult** \(')ā¦rü\ *trademark* — used for an arc furnace that heats both by radiation and by resistance of the bath and is widely used for making electric steel

**hero worship** *n* **1 :** veneration of heroes; *specif* **:** the recognition and just evaluation of illustrious individuals as the chief promoters of cultural advance **2 :** foolish or excessive adulation

**hero-worship** \¦ᵊᵊ¦ᵊᵊ\ *vt* [*hero worship*] **:** to feel, show, or express hero worship for — **hero-worshiper** \'ᵊ,ᵊ,ᵊᵊᵊ\ *n*

**her·pan·gi·na** \,hər,pan'jīnə, ,hər'panjənə\ *n* [NL, fr. *herpes* + *angina*] **:** a contagious disease of children characterized by fever, headache, and a vesicular eruption in the throat and caused by a strain of the Coxsackie virus

**her·pes** \'hər(,)pēz\ *n* -ES [L, fr. Gk *herpēs*, fr. *herpein* to creep — more at SERPENT] **:** any of several virus diseases characterized by the formation of blisters on the skin or mucous membranes — see HERPES SIMPLEX, HERPES ZOSTER

**herpes sim·plex** \¦ᵊᵊ'sim,pleks\ *n* [NL, lit., simple herpes] **:** a virus disease characterized by groups of blisters containing clear fluid formed on the skin or mucous membranes (as on the lips, mouth, genitals) — compare HERPES ZOSTER

**her·pes·tes** \,hər'pe(,)stēz\ *n, cap* [NL, fr. Gk *herpēstēs* animal that walks on all four feet, fr. *herpēstēs*, adj., creeping, fr. *herpein* to creep] **:** a genus of Old World carnivorous mammals (family Viverridae) comprising typical mongooses and sometimes placed in a separate family — **her·pes·tine** \-,stən, 'hərpə,stīn\ *adj or n*

**her·pes·toi·dea** \,hər,pe'stȯidēə\ [NL, fr. *Herpestes* + *-oidea*] *syn of* AELUROIDEA

**herpes zos·ter** \¦ᵊᵊ'zästər, -'zōs-\ *n* [NL, lit., girdle herpes; *zoster* fr. Gk *zōstēr* girdle; akin to Gk *zōnē* girdle, belt — more at ZONE] **:** an acute inflammation of the sensory ganglia of spinal and cranial nerves caused by a virus infection and associated with a vesicular eruption and neuralgic pains along the course of those nerves arising in the affected ganglia — called also *shingles*; compare HERPES SIMPLEX

**herpet-** *or* **herpeto-** *comb form* [partly fr. Gk *herpeton* animal that goes on all fours, snake, fr. neut. of *herpetos* creeping, fr. *herpein* to creep; partly fr. L *herpet-, herpes* herpes (also, a kind of animal, prob. a snake), fr. Gk *herpēt-, herpēs*; partly fr. Gk *herpetos* creeping — more at SERPENT] **1 :** reptile or reptiles ⟨*herpeto*fauna⟩ ⟨*herpeto*logy⟩ **2 :** herpes ⟨*herpeti*form⟩ **3 :** creeping ⟨*herpeto*monas⟩

**her·pet·ic** \(,)hər'ped·ik\ *adj* [*herpet-* + *-ic*] **:** of or relating to herpes ⟨~ virus⟩ ⟨~ pain⟩ **:** resembling herpes ⟨~ lesions⟩

**her·pet·i·form** \-d·ə,fȯrm\ *adj* [ISV *herpet-* + *-iform*] **:** resembling herpes

**her·pe·to·fauna** \,hərpəd·ō+\ *n* [NL, fr. *herpet-* + *fauna*] **:** reptiles or reptile life esp. of a particular region

**her·pe·to·log·ic** \¦hərpəd·ə¦läjik\ *adj or* **her·pe·to·log·i·cal** \-jəkəl\ *adj* **:** of or relating to herpetology — **her·pe·to·log·i·cal·ly** \-jək(ə)lē\ *adv*

**her·pe·tol·o·gist** \,hərpə'tälə̇jəst\ *n* -s **:** a specialist in herpetology

**her·pe·tol·o·gy** \-jē\ *n* -ES [*herpet-* + *-logy*] **:** a branch of zoology that treats of reptiles and amphibians

**¹her·pe·tom·o·nad** \,hərpə'tämə,nad\ *adj* [NL *Herpetomonad-, Herpetomonas*] **:** of or relating to the genus *Herpetomonas*

**²herpetomonad** \"\ *n* -s **:** a flagellate of the genus *Herpetomonas*

**her·pe·tom·o·nas** \-nəs, -,nas\ *n* [NL, fr. *herpet-* + *-monas*] **1** *cap* **:** a genus of flagellates (family Trypanosomatidae) morphologically similar to *Trypanosoma* but exclusively parasites of the gut of insects **2** -ES **:** any flagellate of the genus *Herpetomonas*; *also* **:** any member of the Trypanosomatidae that appears to have two flagella due to precocious duplication of the locomotor apparatus

**her·pob·del·li·da** \,hər,päb'delədə\ [NL, fr. *Herpobdella* genus of leeches (fr. Gk *herpein* to creep + NL *-o-* + *-bdella*) + *-ida*] *syn of* PHARYNGOBDELLIDA

**her·po·trich·ia** \,hərpə'trikēə\ *n, cap* [NL, fr. Gk *herpein* to creep + NL *-o-* + *-trichia*] **:** a genus of fungi (family Sphaeriaceae) having perithecia on a brown mycelial layer and including a form (*Herpotrichia nigra*) that is a parasite on conifers

**her·ren·volk** \'herən,fōk, -fōlk\ *n* -s *often cap* [G, fr. *herr* lord, master + *volk* people, nation] **:** a nationalistic group that believes itself to be racially preeminent and hence fitted to rule over inferior groups ⟨told the German people they were a *Herrenvolk* . . . destined to rule the inferior peoples of Europe —J.C.Harsch⟩

**her·ring** \'heriŋ, -rēŋ\ *n, pl* **herring** *or* **herrings** [ME *hering*, fr. OE *hǣring*; akin to OS *hering* herring, MD *harinc, hareng, herinc*, OHG *hārinc, hering*] **1 :** a valuable food fish (*Clupea harengus*) that reaches a length of about one foot, is extraordinarily abundant in the temperate and colder parts of the north Atlantic where it swims in great schools, feeds chiefly on small crustaceans, and approaches the coasts for spawning where it is caught and preserved in the adult state by smoking or salting and in the young state is extensively canned as sardines; *broadly* **:** a fish of the family Clupeidae — often used in combination ⟨California ~⟩; see ALEWIFE, FALL HERRING, GLUT HERRING **2 :** any of various fishes of families other than Clupeidae that resemble the north Atlantic herring — usu. used in combination; see FRESHWATER HERRING, LAKE HERRING, RAINBOW HERRING

**¹herringbone** \'ᵊᵊ,ᵊ\ *n, often attrib* [*herring* + *bone*] **1 :** a pattern resembling the lateral skeletal configuration of a herring; *specif* **:** a pattern (as on a fabric) made up of adjacent rows of parallel lines where any two adjacent rows slope slightly in reverse directions **2 a :** a twilled fabric with a herringbone pattern; *also* **:** a suit made of such a fabric **b :** a herringbone arrangement of materials (as of bricks in a wall) **3 :** a method in skiing of ascending a slope by herringboning; *also* **:** a series of herringbone steps made by herringboning

bricks laid in herringbone pattern

**²herringbone** \"\ *vt* **1 :** to produce a herringbone pattern on **2 :** to arrange in a herringbone pattern ~ *vi* **1 :** to produce herringbone configurations **2 :** to ascend a slope by toeing out with the skis and placing the weight on the inner border of the skis

**herringbone bond** *n* **:** a bond in masonry in which the bricks form a herringbone pattern

**herringbone gear** *n* **:** a gear with double helical teeth inclined in reverse directions and making a herringbone pattern

**herringbone stitch** *n* **:** an ornamental catch stitch

**herringbone strutting** *n* **:** crossed struts between floor joists

**her·ring-cale** *or* **her·ring-kale** \'ᵊᵊ,kāl\ *n* -s **:** a common fish (*Olisthops cyanomelas*) that resembles a wrasse and is found in Australian coastal waters

**her·ring·er** \-ŋə(r)\ *n* -s [*herring* + *-er*] **:** one that fishes for herrings

**herring gull** *n* **:** a common large gull (*Larus argentatus*) of the northern hemisphere that in the adult state is largely white with blue-gray mantle and dark wing tips and pink feet and in the immature state is mainly dark brown

**herring gutted** *adj, of a horse* **:** having a form usu. indicative of inferior quality where the abdomen or barrel narrows sharply toward the flanks

**herring hog** *n* **:** HARBOR PORPOISE

**herring king** *n* **:** OARFISH

**herring oil** *n* **:** a pale yellow to dark-colored fatty oil obtained from herring and used in making soap and fat-liquoring leather

**herring pond** *n* **:** a great body of water (as the Atlantic ocean or English channel) ⟨have been in perils on the great salt *herring pond* —David Humphreys⟩

**herrn·hut·er** \'hern,hüd·ər, ᵊ'ᵊᵊ\ *n* -s *usu cap* [G, fr. *Herrnhut* (lit., Lord's protection), town near Dresden, Germany founded by the Moravians in 1722] **:** MORAVIAN

**hers** \¦hərz, ¦həz\ *pron, sing or pl in constr* [ME *hires, hirs*, fr. *hire* her + *-s* -'s — more at HER] **1 :** her one or her ones — used without a following noun as a pronoun equivalent in meaning to the adjective *her* ⟨what a stricken look was ~ —S.T.Coleridge⟩ ⟨the eternal years of God are ~ —W.C.Bryant⟩; often used after *of* to single out one or more members of a class belonging to or connected with a particular female person or animal ⟨a favorite dessert of ~⟩ ⟨some friends of ~⟩ or merely to identify something or someone as belonging to or connected with a particular female person or animal without any implication of membership in a more extensive class ⟨that face of ~ —Shak.⟩ ⟨those charming manners of ~⟩ **2 :** something that belongs to her **:** what belongs to her ⟨all that is his is ~⟩

²hers *pl of* HER

³hers \"\ *adj, obs* : ²HER 1 — used as the first of two possessive adjectives modifying the same noun ⟨~ and mine adultery —Shak.⟩

**her·schel effect** \'hərshəl-\ *n, usu cap H* [after John F.W. *Herschel* †1871 Eng. astronomer] : a partial destruction of the latent image in photography by action of long wave radiation which is either red or infrared

**her·schelian** \ˌhər'shelēən, -shēl-\ *adj, usu cap* [Sir William *Herschel* †1822 Eng. astronomer + E *-ian*] : of or relating to the astronomer Herschel

**herschelian telescope** *n, usu cap H* : a reflecting telescope in which the need for a secondary mirror is avoided by tilting the primary mirror slightly and thereby throwing the focused image to the side where it can be observed without obstruction to the incoming light rays — called also *off-axis reflector*

**her·schel·ite** \'hərshəˌlīt\ *n* -s [Sir John F. W. *Herschel* + E *-ite*] : a chabazite that consists of glassy crystals of complex twinned structure

**herse** *obs var of* HEARSE

**her·self** \(h)ə(r)'‡\ *pron* [ME *hire self*, fr. OE *hiere self, hire self, hyre self*, dat. of *hēo self, hīo self* she herself — more at HE, SELF] **1** : that identical female one : that identical one regarded as feminine (as by personification) — compare ¹SHE 1; used (1) reflexively as object of a preposition or direct or indirect object of a verb ⟨she devotes a lot of time to her children and very little to ~⟩ ⟨she bought ~ some clothes⟩ ⟨she considers ~ lucky⟩ (2) for emphasis in apposition with *she, who, that*, or a noun ⟨she ~ painted the room⟩ ⟨she did it ~⟩ ⟨the housewife ~ bought the groceries⟩ ⟨the housewife bought the groceries ~⟩ ⟨armies threatened Rome ~⟩ ⟨my mother, who was young once ~⟩ (3) for emphasis instead of nonreflexive *her* as object of a preposition or direct or indirect object of a verb ⟨I looked beside me then, and I saw ~ —Padraic Colum⟩ (4) for emphasis instead of *she* or instead of *she herself* as subject of a verb ⟨she told me that neither her husband nor ~ could attend the meeting⟩ or as predicate nominative ⟨it's ~ she's trying to convince⟩ or in comparisons after *than* or *as* ⟨she met another woman as tall as ~⟩ (5) in absolute constructions ⟨~ an orphan, the authoress shows deep understanding of the problems of the orphan girl whose story she tells⟩ **2** : her normal, healthy, or sane condition ⟨she came to ~⟩ : her normal, healthy, or sane self ⟨ill for a week, she is now ~ again⟩ **3** *Scot* : MYSELF, YOURSELF, HIMSELF, ITSELF — used esp. in literary representations of the English spoken by Scottish Highlanders; compare ¹SHE 2 **4** *Irish & Scot* : a woman of consequence; *esp* : the mistress of the house ⟨where's ~⟩ **5** : YOURSELF ⟨did she hurt ~⟩ — compare HIMSELF 4

**hership** *n* [ME, fr. *herien* to harry + *-ship* — more at HARRY] **1** *obs* : a warlike raid esp. to steal cattle; *also* : the distress caused by such a raid **2** *obs* : the loot stolen in a hership

**hert·ford·shire** *Brit* 'hä(t)fədshiə(r), -shə(r), *US* " *or* 'härtfərd,shi(ə)r *or* 'hərt- *or* 'hät- *or* 'hərt-\ *or* **hertford** *adj, usu cap* [fr. *Hertfordshire* or county of *Hertford*, England] : of or from the county of Hertford, England : of the kind or style prevalent in Hertford

**hertfordshire kindness** *n, usu cap H* : a favor of the same kind in return

**hertz** \'hərts, 'hōts, 'hōits; 'he(ə)rts, 'heəts\ *n, pl* **hertz** *or* **hertzes** [after Heinrich R. *Hertz* †1894 Ger. physicist] : a unit of frequency of a periodic process equal to one cycle per second — abbr. *Hz*

**hertz·ian** \-sēən\ *adj, sometimes cap* [H. R. *Hertz* + E *-ian*] : of, relating to, or developed by the physicist Hertz

**hertzian telegraphy** *n* : telegraphy by means of Hertzian waves : RADIOTELEGRAPH

**hertzian wave** *n, usu cap H* : an electromagnetic wave produced by the oscillation of electricity in a conductor (as a radio antenna) and of a length ranging from a few millimeters to many kilometers

**hertz oscillator** *or* **hertzian oscillator** *n* : an inductive and capacitive circuit in which electric oscillations resulting in the emission of Hertzian waves are set up by passage of a spark or otherwise

**her·va ma·té** \ˌervə'mä(ˌ)tā, -mäd·ə\ *n* [Pg *herva mate, erva mate*, lit., maté plant] : MATÉ

**herx·hei·mer reaction** \'herksˌhīmər-\ *n, usu cap H* [after Karl *Herxheimer* †1944 Ger. dermatologist] : an increase in the symptoms of syphilis occurring in some persons when treatment with spirocheticidal drugs is instituted

**hery** *vt* -ED/-ING/-ES [ME *herien*, fr. OE *herian*; akin to OHG *harēn* to call, Goth *hazjan* to praise] *obs* : GLORIFY, PRAISE

**her·ze·go·vinian** \ˌhertsəgō'vēnēən, ˌhər-, -vin-\ *n* -s *cap* [*Herzegovina*, region in the northwestern Balkan peninsula + E *-ian*] : a native of Herzegovina

**hes** *pl of* HE

**hesh** \'hesh\ *dial var of* HUSH

**hesh·van** *also* **hes·van** *or* **chesh·van** *or* **ches·van** \'keshvən\ *n* -s *usu cap* [Heb *ḥeshwān*, short for *marḥeshwān* Marheshvan] : the 2d month of the civil year or the 8th month of the ecclesiastical year in the Jewish calendar — see MONTH table

**he·si·od·ic** \ˌhēsē'ädik *sometimes* ˌhesē- *or* ˌhēzē-\ *adj, usu cap* [*Hesiod*, 8th cent. B.C. Greek poet (fr. Gk *Hēsiodos*) + E *-ic*] : of or relating to the poet Hesiod or his simple practical maxims or theology

**he·si·o·ne** \hə'sīə(ˌ)nē\ *n, cap* [NL, after *Hesione*, Trojan princess of Greek mythology saved from a monster by Hercules, fr. L, fr. Gk *Hēsionē*] : a genus (the type of the family Hesionidae) of marine free-swimming polychaete worms having long peristomial cirri and two pairs of eyes

**hes·i·tan·cy** \'hezəd·ənsē, -zətən-, -si *also* -zət°n- *sometimes* -ztən- *or* 'hesə-\ *or* **hes·i·tance** \-n(t)s\ *n, pl* **hesitancies** *or* **hesitances** [LL *haesitantia*, fr. L, action of stammering, fr. *haesitant-, haesitans* + *-ia* -y] **1** : the quality or state of being hesitant: as **a** : INDECISION ⟨had lost that nervous ~ that had so troubled her —Elizabeth Goudge⟩ **b** : RELUCTANCE ⟨had no ~ in entering the field of composition —Fannie L. G. Cole⟩ **2** : an act or instance of hesitating : HESITATION ⟨her girlish *hesitancies*, her maidenly delays and refusals —S.H. Adams⟩

**hes·i·tant** \-nt\ *adj* [L *haesitant-, haesitans*, pres. part. of *haesitare*] : given to hesitation : tending to hold back (as from fear, indecision, or disinclination) ⟨a ~ fighter⟩ ⟨~ policies⟩
**syn** see DISINCLINED

**hes·i·tant·ly** *adv* : in a hesitant manner

**hes·i·tate** \'hezəˌtāt *sometimes* 'hezˌtāt *or* 'hesəˌtāt, *usu* -ād·+V\ *vb* -ED/-ING/-S [L *haesitatus*, past part of *haesitare* to stick fast, stammer, hesitate, fr. the stem of *haerēre* to stick; akin to Lith *gaišti* to loiter, delay] *vi* **1 a** : to hold back in doubt or indecision : avoid facing a decision, encounter, or problem ⟨the government *hesitated* before each policy⟩ **b** : to hold back from or as if from scruple ⟨~ at treason⟩ **2** : to delay usu. momentarily : PAUSE ⟨a glimpse of a deer as it *hesitated* before disappearing into the underbrush⟩ **3** : STAMMER ~ *vt* : to express in a hesitant manner ⟨choose rather to ~ my opinion than to assert it roundly —J.R.Lowell⟩

**syn** HESITATE, WAVER, VACILLATE, and FALTER agree in meaning to show irresolution or uncertainty. HESITATE implies a pause or other sign of indecision before acting ⟨no properly qualified student should *hesitate* to apply —*Official Register of Harvard Univ.*⟩ ⟨the young second officer *hesitated* to break the established rule of every ship's discipline —Joseph Conrad⟩ ⟨she *hesitated* a minute and then she said, 'Yes.' —Dorothy Baker⟩ WAVER implies hesitation after having seemed to decide and usu. suggests weakness or retreat from a decision ⟨the great man, who never *wavered* in his faith —H.S.Canby⟩ ⟨he was a good student and possessed an un*wavering* will —Nora Waln⟩ ⟨Henry was in the grip of his own master-passion and he did not *waver* —Francis Hackett⟩ VACILLATE implies prolonged hesitation from inability to reach a decision ⟨the . . . government has been *vacillating* in its policies on such emigration —*Collier's Yr. Bk.*⟩ ⟨I have *vacillated* when I should have insisted; temporized when I should have taken definite action —Ngaio Marsh⟩ FALTER suggests a hesitation or wavering evident in some physical sign of nervousness, lack of courage, or outright fear, as an uncertainty or breaking of the voice ⟨kept the bright excited look upon her face without *faltering* —F. Tennyson Jesse⟩ ⟨his steps perceptibly *falter* —*Times Lit. Supp.*⟩ ⟨his eyes did not flinch and his tongue did not *falter* —Joseph Conrad⟩

**hes·i·tat·er** *also* **hes·i·ta·tor** \-ād·ə(r), -ātə-\ *n* -s : one that hesitates

**hes·i·tat·ing·ly** \'‡‡ˌ‡‡‡, ˌ‡‡'‡‡‡\ *adv* : HESITANTLY

**hes·i·ta·tion** \ˌhezə'tāshən *sometimes* ˌhesə-\ *n* -s [L *haesitation-, haesitatio*, fr. *haesitatus* + *-ion-, -io* -ion] **1** : the act or action of hesitating (as by holding back, pausing, or faltering) ⟨~ before decisions⟩ ⟨~ in accepting an offer⟩ **2** : a faltering in speech : STAMMERING **3** *also* **hesitation waltz** : a waltz in which the dancers intersperse at pleasure a gliding movement; *also* : the gliding movement in such a waltz

**hesitation form** *n* : a sound (as \ə\, \ə̃\, or \ə̃\ usu. prolonged) or word (as er, uh, mmm, what-you-may-call-it, well) involuntarily or deliberately used while a speaker is uncertain about the fitting expression of his thought or the correct name of a person or object

**hes·i·ta·tive** \'hezəˌtā|d·|iv, -zətə|, -zəd·ə|, |t|, |ēv *sometimes* 'heztə| *or* 'hesə-\ *adj* : showing or characterized by hesitation — **hes·i·ta·tive·ly** \|əvlē, |ēv-, -li\ *adv*

**hesp** \'hesp\ *dial var of* HASP

**hes·ped** \'heˌsped\ *n, pl* **hes·pe·dim** \he'spādəm, -ˌdēm\ [Heb *hespēdh*] : an oration or eulogy at a Jewish memorial service

**hes·pe·ria** \he'spirēə, -pēr-\ *n, cap* [NL, fr. L, west, fr. Gk, fr. *hesperos* of the evening, western (fr. *hesperos, hespera* evening) + *-ia* -y — more at WEST] : a genus of skipper butterflies that is the type of the family Hesperiidae and includes many small butterflies of the northern hemisphere that are mostly tawny with dark and pale markings

¹**hes·pe·ri·an** \(')‡'‡rēən\ *adj, usu cap* [L *Hesperia* west + E *-an*] **1** : WESTERN, OCCIDENTAL **2** [NL *Hesperia* + E *-an*] : of or relating to the Hesperiidae

²**hesperian** \"\ *n* -s **1** *usu cap* : an inhabitant of the West : OCCIDENTAL **2** : a butterfly of the family Hesperiidae

¹**hes·per·id** \'hespərəd\ *or* **hes·pe·ri·id** \(')he'spirēəd\ *adj* [NL *Hesperiidae*] : of or relating to the Hesperiidae

²**hesperid** *or* **hesperiid** *n* -s : an insect of the family Hesperiidae : a skipper butterfly

**hes·per·i·date** \he'sperəˌdāt\ *or* **hes·per·id·e·ous** \ˌhespə'ridēəs\ *adj* [NL *hesperidium* + E *-ate* or *-eous*] : of, relating to, or being a hesperidium

**hes·per·id·e·an** *or* **hes·per·id·i·an** \ˌhespə'ridēən\ *adj, usu cap* [*Hesperides* mythological paradisiacal garden growing golden apples (fr. the *Hesperides*, the nymphs that guard it, fr. L, fr. Gk) + E *-an, -ian*] : of, relating to, or having the characteristics of the gardens of the Hesperides

**hes·per·i·din** \he'sperəd°n, -ˌsperə'din\ *n* -s [NL *hesperidium* + E *-in*] : a crystalline bioflavonoid glycoside $C_{28}H_{34}O_{15}$ found in most citrus fruits and esp. in orange peel that yields hesperitin, glucose, and rhamnose on hydrolysis — see CITRIN

**hes·per·id·i·um** \ˌhespə'ridēəm\ *n, pl* **hesperid·ia** \-ēə\ [NL, fr. the *Hesperides* + NL *-ium*; fr. the myth of the golden apples of the Hesperides] : a berry (as an orange or lime) having a leathery rind — see FRUIT illustration

**hes·per·i·idae** \ˌhespə'rīəˌdē\ *n pl, cap* [NL, fr. *Hesperia*, type genus + *-idae*] : a large family of skipper butterflies (superfamily Hesperioidea) comprising the typical skippers — see HESPERIA; compare MEGATHYMIDAE

**hes·per·i·nos** \ˌhespərə'nōs, -nōs\ *n* -ES [LGk, fr. Gk, adj., of the evening, fr. *hesperos, hespera* evening + *-inos* -ine — more at WEST] : the office in the Eastern Church corresponding to vespers in the Western Church

**hes·pe·ri·oi·dea** \(ˌ)heˌspirē'ȯidēə\ *n pl, cap* [NL, fr. *Hesperia* + *-oidea*] : a superfamily of Lepidoptera comprising insects often considered butterflies but usu. distinguished from the typical butterflies by the hooked tips of the widely separated antennae, peculiarities of the wing venation, and the erratic and often very swift flight — see HESPERIIDAE, MEGATHYMIDAE, SKIPPER

**hes·per·is** \'hespərəs\ *n, cap* [NL, fr. L, dame's violet, fr. Gk, fr. fem. of *hesperios* of the evening, fr. *hesperos, hespera* evening] : a genus of biennial or perennial Eurasian herbs (family Cruciferae) having large purple or white racemose flowers — see DAME'S VIOLET

**hes·per·i·tin** *also* **hes·per·e·tin** \he'sperət°n, -ˌsperə'tin\ *n* -s [prob. irreg. fr. *hesperidin*] : a crystalline compound $C_{16}H_{14}O_6$ derived from flavanone and obtained by hydrolysis of hesperidin; a monomethyl ether of eriodictyol

**hes·per·or·nis** \ˌhespə'rȯrnəs\ *n, cap* [NL, fr. Gk *hesperos* western + NL *-ornis*] : a genus of swimming birds (order Hesperornithiformes) from the Cretaceous of Kansas that resemble loons in form, that have teeth in each jaw implanted in a long groove, and that in some cases exceed five feet in length

**hes·per·or·nith·i·for·mes** \ˌhespə(ˌ)rȯrˌnithə'fȯrˌmēz\ *n pl, cap* [NL, fr. *Hesperornith-, Hesperornis* + *-iformes*] : an order of extinct aquatic birds (superorder Odontognathae) including the genus *Hesperornis* and related Cretaceous forms

**hesselbach's triangle** *n, usu cap H* : TRIANGLE OF HESSELBACH

¹**hes·sian** \'heshən, *chiefly Brit* 'hesēən\ *adj, usu cap* [*Hesse*, region or state in southwestern Germany + E *-ian*] : of or relating to Hesse in Germany or the Hessians

²**hessian** \"\ *n* -s **1** *cap* **a** : a native of Hesse, a region or state in southwestern Germany **b** : a German mercenary often a native of Hesse serving in the British forces during the American Revolution **c** : a mercenary soldier **2 a** : HESSIAN BOOT **b** : HESSIAN ANDIRON **3** *chiefly Midland* **a** : SCAMP, RASCAL — used esp. of a child **b** : a troublesome or meddlesome person — used esp. of a woman **4** *also* **hessian cloth** : BURLAP

**hessian andiron** *n, usu cap H* : an andiron with an upright shaped to represent a Hessian soldier

**hessian boot** *n, usu cap H* : a high boot with a top extending to just below the knee and commonly ornamented with a tassel that was introduced into England by the Hessians early in the 19th century

Hessian boot

**hessian crucible** *n, usu cap H* : a cheap brittle fragile but very refractory crucible composed of the finest fireclay and sand and commonly used for a single heating

**hessian fly** *n, often cap H* [so called fr. the belief it was brought to America by Hessian soldiers] : a small two-winged fly (*Mayetiola destructor*) which is destructive to wheat in America and whose larvae live between the base of the lower leaves and the stalk and suck the juices of the plant

**hess image** \'hes-\ *n, usu cap H* [after Carl von *Hess* †1923 Ger. ophthalmologist] : a third positive afterimage in a succession of visual afterimages resulting from a brief light stimulus

**hess·ite** \'heˌsīt\ *n* -s [G *hessit*, fr. Henry *Hess* †1850 Swiss chemist in Russia + G *-it* -ite] : a mineral $Ag_2Te$ consisting of a lead-gray sectile silver telluride often auriferous and usu. massive

**hessonite** *var of* ESSONITE

**hess's law** \'hesəz-\ *n, usu cap H* [after Henry *Hess*] : a statement in chemistry: the heat change in a chemical reaction is the same regardless of the number of stages in which the reaction is effected

**hest** \'hest\ *n* -s [ME *hest, heste*, alter. of *hes*, fr. OE *hǣs*; akin to OE *hātan* to command, call, be called — more at HIGHT] *archaic* : COMMAND

**hes·thog·e·nous** \(')hes'thäjənəs\ *adj* [irreg. fr. Gk *esthēs* clothing + E *-genous*] : having a covering of down when hatched : DASYPAEDIC

**hesvan** *usu cap, var of* HESHVAN

**hes·y·chasm** \'hesəˌkazəm, 'hezə-\ *n* -s *often cap* [fr. *hesychast*, after such pairs as E *enthusiast: enthusiasm*] : hesychastic belief or practice

**hes·y·chast** \-ˌkast\ *n* -s *often cap* [MGk *hēsychastēs*, fr. LGk, quietist, hermit, fr. Gk *hēsychazein* to be still, keep quiet, fr. *hēsychos* quiet; perh. akin to OE *sīd* long — more at SIDE] : one of an Eastern Orthodox ascetic sect of mystics originating among the monks of Mount Athos in the 14th century and practicing a quietistic method of contemplation for the purpose of attaining a beatific vision or similar mystical experience

**hes·y·chas·tic** \ˌ‡‡'kastik\ *adj* [Gk *hēsychastikos*, fr. (assumed) Gk *hēsychastos* (verbal of *hēsychazein*) + Gk *-ikos* -ic] **1** : SOOTHING, CALMING — used esp. of a style of ancient Greek music **2** *often cap* [*hesychast* + *-ic*] : of or relating to the hesychasts or their solitary meditative mysticism

¹**het** *var of* HETH

²**het** \'het\ *n* -s *usu cap* : CHECHEHET

³**het** \'het, *usu* -ed·+V\ *dial var of* ²HEAT

⁴**het** \"\ *chiefly Scot var of* HOT

⁵**het** \"\ *dial past of* HEAT

**he·tae·ra** \hə'tirə\ *or* **he·tai·ra** \-'tīrə\ *n, pl* **hetae·rae** \-i(ˌ)rē\ *or* **hetaeras** *or* **hetairas** \-ˌrəz\ *or* **hetai·rai** \-ˌīˌrī\ [Gk *hetaira*, lit., companion, fem. of *hetairos* comrade, companion] **1** : one of a class of highly cultivated courtesans in ancient Greece **2** : DEMIMONDAINE ⟨the lady in the canary-colored carriage was New York's first fashionable ~ —*Harper's*⟩ ⟨a hair-pulling fight between two drunken *hetaerae* over a free spender —*Amer. Mercury*⟩

**he·tae·rism** *or* **he·tai·rism** \-ˌrizəm\ *n* -s [Gk *hetairismos*, fr. *hetaira* + *-ismos* -ism] **1** : a general system of temporary or continued sexual relations outside wedlock : CONCUBINAGE **2** : a state of society conceived as existing in the past and characterized by the holding of women in common

**he·tae·ro·lite** \hə'tirəˌlīt\ *n* -s [Gk *hetairos* companion + E *-lite*] : a mineral $ZnMn_2O_4$ consisting of a zinc-manganese oxide found with chalcophanite

**hetchel** *var of* HATCHEL

**heter-** *or* **hetero-** *comb form* [MF or LL; MF, fr. LL, fr. Gk, fr. *heteros*; akin to Gk *heis, hen* one — more at SAME] **1** : other than usual : other : different ⟨*hetero*geneous⟩ ⟨*hetero*dox⟩ ⟨*Heter*anthera⟩ — opposed to *hom-, is-, orth-* **2** : for, from, or to a different species ⟨*hetero*agglutinin⟩ **3 a** : containing atoms of different kinds ⟨*hetero*cyclic⟩ **b** : isomeric with or closely related to a (specified) compound ⟨*hetero*xanthine⟩

¹**het·er·akid** \ˌhed·ə'rākəd, -rak-\ *adj* [NL *Heterakidae*] : of or relating to the family Heterakidae; *esp* : caused by worms of the genus *Heterakis* ⟨~ transmission of blackhead⟩

²**heterakid** \"\ *n* -s : a worm of the family Heterakidae

**het·er·aki·dae** \ˌ‡‡'‡kəˌdē\ *n pl, cap* [NL, fr. *Heterakis*, type genus + *-idae*] : a somewhat variably limited family comprising nematode worms with three lips, a small buccal capsule, and usu. a posterior esophageal bulb and sometimes being included in the family Ascaridae — see HETERAKIS

**het·er·a·kis** \ˌ‡‡'rākəs\ *n, cap* [NL, fr. *heter-* + Gk *akis* pointed object — more at ACIDANTHERA] : a genus (the type of the family Heterakidae) of nematode worms including the common cecal worm of chickens and turkeys

**het·er·an·drous** \ˌhed·ə'randrəs\ *adj* [*heter-* + *-androus*] : having stamens of different length or form — **het·er·an·dry** \'‡‡ˌ‡drē\ *n* -ES

**het·er·an·gi·um** \ˌ‡‡'ranjēəm\ *n, cap* [NL, fr. *heter-* + *-angium*] : a genus of Devonian seed ferns having a protostelic stem resembling that of members of the genus *Gleichenia*

**het·er·an·the·ra** \-'ran(t)thərə\ *n, cap* [NL, fr. *heter-* + *-anthera*] : a genus of aquatic or marsh herbs (family Pontederiaceae) having flowers with a salverform perianth, three stamens, and a many-seeded capsule

**het·er·atomic** \ˌhed·ər+\ *or* **het·ero·atomic** \ˌhed·ə(ˌ)rō+\ *adj* [*heter-* + *atomic*] : made up of atoms of different kinds

**het·er·auxesis** \ˌhed·ər+\ *n* [NL, fr. *heter-* + *auxesis*] : allometric growth — compare ALLOMETRY — **het·er·auxetic** \"+\ *adj*

**het·er·axial** \"+\ *adj* [*heter-* + *axial*] : having three unequal axes perpendicular to each other (as in animals having biradial or bilateral symmetry)

**heterecious** *var of* HETEROECIOUS

**het·er·ism** \'hed·əˌrizəm\ *n* -s [*heter-* + *-ism*] : variability of animals and plants

**het·er·i·za·tion** \ˌhed·ərə'zāshən, -ˌrī'z-\ *n* -s [*heter-* + *-ization*] : a changing from one form into another

**het·ero** \'hed·ə(ˌ)rō\ *adj* [*heter-*] : relating to or being an atom or element other than the predominating or significant one (as carbon) esp. in a ring of a molecule or compound ⟨~ atoms such as nitrogen or oxygen⟩

**het·ero·agglutinin** \ˌhed·ə(ˌ)rō+\ *n* [*heter-* + *agglutinin*] : a hemagglutinin found in serum and reacting with red cells of animals of other species than the one producing the serum

**het·ero·autotroph** \"+\ *n* [*heter-* + *autotroph*] : a heteroautotrophic organism

**het·ero·autotrophic** \"+\ *adj* [*heter-* + *autotrophic*] : requiring a simple organic source of carbon but utilizing inorganic nitrogen for metabolism

**het·ero·auxin** \"+\ *n* [G, fr. *heter-* + *auxin*] : INDOLEACETIC ACID

**het·ero·ba·sid·i·ae** \ˌhed·ərōbə'sidēˌē\ *n pl, cap* [NL, fr. *heter-* + *-basidiae* (fr. *basidium*)] *in some classifications* : a subclass of Basidiomycetes comprising fungi with a basidium that is transversely or vertically septate or forked or has four rounded terminal cells from each of which a sterigma and spore arise and including Tremellales and other orders or being restricted to the order Tremellales — compare EUBASIDIAE, TELIOSPOREAE

**het·ero·basidiomycetes** \ˌhed·ər(ˌ)ō+\ *n pl, cap* [NL, fr. *heter-* + *Basidiomycetes*] : a subclass of fungi (class Basidiomycetes) including the rusts, smuts, and jelly fungi that has septate or deeply divided basidia and basidiospores which often germinate to form conidia or similar spores — compare HOMOBASIDIOMYCETES — **het·ero·basidiomycetous** \"+\ *adj*

**het·ero·ba·sid·io·my·cet·i·dae** \ˌ‡‡(ˌ)‡bəˌsidē(ˌ)ōˌmī'sedəˌdē\ *n pl, cap* [NL, fr. *heter-* + *Basidiomycetes* + *-idae*] *syn of* HETEROBASIDIOMYCETES

**het·ero·basidium** \"+\ *n* [NL, fr. *heter-* + *basidium*] : a basidium that is septate or with deep divisions (as in the subclass Heterobasidiomycetes)

**het·ero·blas·tic** \ˌhed·ərō'blastik\ *adj* [*heter-* + *-blastic*] **1** : having an indirect embryonic development — opposed to *homoblastic*; compare EMBRYOGENY **2** : arising from different germ layers — used of functionally similar organs of related animals **3** : having young and adult forms different ⟨~ leaves of flowering plants⟩ — **het·ero·blas·ty** \'‡‡‡ˌblastē\ *n* -ES

**het·ero·cap·sa·les** \ˌhed·ə(ˌ)rōˌkap'sāˌlēz\ *n pl, cap* [NL] : an order of yellowish to brownish green algae (class Xanthophyceae) that form amorphous or arborescent palmelloid colonies containing an indefinite number of cells which are capable of reverting to a motile state directly or through zoospore formation — compare HETEROCOCCALES, VOLVOCALES

**het·ero·carpus** \ˌhed·ərō'kärpəs\ *n, cap* [NL, fr. *heter-* + *carpus*] : a genus of bioluminescent prawns occurring in the Indian ocean

**heterocaryon** *var of* HETEROKARYON

**heterocaryosis** *var of* HETEROKARYOSIS

**het·ero·cellular** \ˌhed·ə(ˌ)rō+\ *adj* [*heter-* + *cellular*] : composed of more than one kind of cell

**het·er·oc·era** \ˌhed·ə'räsərə\ *n pl, cap* [NL, fr. *heter-* + *-cera*] : a division of Lepidoptera consisting of the moths — compare RHOPALOCERA — **het·er·oc·er·ous** \ˌ‡‡'‡‡rəs\ *adj*

¹**het·ero·cerc** \'hed·ərōˌsərk\ *n* -s [*heter-* + *-cerc* (fr. Gk *kerkos* tail)] : a heterocercal fish

²**heterocerc** \"\ *adj* : HETEROCERCAL

**het·ero·cer·cal** \ˌ‡‡‡'sərkəl\ *adj* [*heter-* + *-cercal*] **1** : having the upper lobe larger than the lower with the end of the vertebral column prolonged and somewhat upturned in the upper lobe — used of the tail fin of various fishes (as sharks) **2** : having or relating to a heterocercal tail fin — **het·ero·cer·cal·i·ty** \ˌhed·əˌrōˌsər'kaləd·ē\ *n* -ES

**het·ero·charge** \'hed·ərō+ˌ-\ *n* [*heter-* + *charge*] : a charge on an electret that is of sign opposite to that of the electrode orig. in contact with it — compare HOMOCHARGE

**het·er·o·che·lous** \ˌhed·ərō'kēləs\ *adj* [*heter-* + *chel-* + *-ous*] *of a crustacean* : having the chelae unlike in size and form — **het·er·o·che·ly** \'‡‡‡ˌkēlē\ *n* -ES

**het·ero·chlamydeous** \ˌ‡‡(ˌ)‡+\ *adj* [ISV *heter-* + *chlamydeous*] : having a perianth whose calyx and corolla are differentiated as to color and texture — compare HOMOCHLAMYDEOUS

**het·er·o·chlo·ri·da·les** \ˌ‡‡(ˌ)ōˌklōrə'dāˌlēz\ *n pl, cap* [NL, fr. *Heterochlorid-, Heterochloris*, genus of algae + *-ales*] : an order of yellow-green algae including all members of the Xanthophyceae having flagellated vegetative cells

**het·ero·chromatic** \ˌhed·ə(ˌ)rō+\ *adj* [*heter-* + *chromatic*] **1** : of, relating to, or having different colors; *specif* : having a more or less complex pattern of colors — opposed to *homochromatic* **2** : made up of various wavelengths or frequencies : not monochromatic **3** [*heterochromatin* + *-ic*] : of or relating to heterochromatin — **het·ero·chromatism** \"+\ *n* -s

**het·ero·chromatin** \"+\ *n* [G, fr. *hetero-* heter- + *chromatin*] **:** densely staining chromatin appearing as nodules in or along chromosomes — compare EUCHROMATIN

**het·ero·chro·ma·ti·za·tion** \,hed·ərō,krōmәd·ә'zāshәn, -mә-,tī'z-\ *n* -S [*heterochromat-* (fr. *heterochromatin*) + *-ization*] **:** the state of being or becoming heterochromatic **:** the transformation of genetically active euchromatin to inactive heterochromatin — **het·ero·chromatized** \¦==¦=mә,tīzd\ *adj*

**het·ero·chrome** \'===,krōm\ *adj* [ISV *heter-* + *-chrome*] **:** HETEROCHROMATIC

**het·ero·chro·mia** \,===¦krōmēә\ *n* -S [NL, fr. *heter-* + *-chromia*] **:** a difference in coloration in two anatomical structures or two parts of the same structure which are normally alike in color ⟨~ of the iris⟩

**het·ero·chromomere** \¦hed·ә(,)rō+\ *n* [*heter-* + *chromomere*] **:** a chromomere of the heterochromatic region of a chromosome; *also* **:** a granule of heterochromatin

**het·ero·chromosome** \"+\ *n* [ISV *heter-* + *chromosome*] **:** a sex chromosome

**het·ero·chro·mous** \¦hed·әrә¦krōmәs\ *or* **het·ero·chro·mic** \-mik\ *adj* [*heter-* + *chrom-* + *-ous* or *-ic*] **:** of different colors

**het·er·och·ro·nism** \,hed·ә'räkrә,nizәm\ *also* **het·er·och·ro·ny** \-,nē\ *n, pl* **heterochronisms** *also* **heterochronies** [*heterochronism* fr. NL *heterochronus* heterochronous (fr. *heter-* + Gk *-chronos* -chronous) + E *-ism; heterochrony* fr. NL *heterochronia*, fr. *heterochronus* + L *-ia* -y] **1 :** deviation from the typical embryological sequence of formation of organs and parts as a factor in evolution — compare FETALIZATION **2 :** irregularity in time relationships; *specif* **:** the existence of differences in chronaxies among functionally related tissue elements — **het·er·och·ro·nis·tic** \¦==,==¦nistik\ *adj* — **het·er·och·ro·nous** \¦==¦räkrәnәs\ *adj*

**het·er·och·tho·nous** \¦==¦räkthәnәs\ *adj* [*heter-* + *-chthonous* (as in *autochthonous*)] **1 :** not indigenous **:** FOREIGN, NATURALIZED ⟨a ~ flora⟩ **2 a :** not formed in the place where it now occurs **:** TRANSPORTED ⟨~ rock⟩ **b :** removed from the original deposit (as by erosion) and reembedded (as certain fossils)

[1]**het·er·o·clite** \'hed·әrә,klīt\ *n* -S [MF, n. & adj.] **1** *in the grammar of various languages* **:** a word irregular in inflection; *esp* **:** a noun irregular in declension (as Latin *pecus* having case forms of both third and fourth declensions) **2 :** one that deviates from the common rule or from common forms ⟨modern poetry is not a privilege of ~s —Wallace Stevens⟩

[2]**heteroclite** \"\ *adj* [MF or LL; MF, fr. LL *heteroclitus* irregularly inflected, fr. Gk *heteroklitos*, fr. *heter-* + (assumed) Gk *klitos* (verbal of Gk *klinein* to lean, incline, inflect) — more at LEAN] **:** deviating from ordinary forms or rules **:** IRREGULAR, ANOMALOUS, ABNORMAL ⟨a confusing, dusty, ~ accretion of objects —Janet Flanner⟩

**het·er·o·clit·ic** \¦===¦klid·ik\ *adj* **:** marked by irregularity of inflection ⟨many nouns . . . are ~ in one or more cases —F.W. Householder⟩

**het·ero·coc·ca·les** \,hed·ә(,)rō,kä'kā(,)lēz\ *n pl, cap* [NL, fr. *Heterococcus*, genus of algae (fr. *heter-* + *-coccus*) + *-ales*] **:** an order of yellow-green algae including all members of the class Xanthophyceae having the immobile vegetative cells surrounded by a cell wall and incapable of returning to the motile state directly

**het·ero·coe·la** \,hed·ərō'sēlә\ *n pl* [NL, fr. *heter-* + *-coela*, neut. pl. of *-coelus* -coelous] *syn of* SYCONOSA

**het·ero·coe·lan** \¦==¦=lәn\ *adj* [NL *Heterocoela* + E *-an*] **:** of or relating to the Syconosa

**het·ero·coe·lous** \-lәs\ *adj* [*heter-* + *-coelous*] **1 :** of or relating to vertebrae having saddle-shaped articular surfaces ⟨~ birds⟩ **2** [NL *Heterocoela* + E *-ous*] **:** of or relating to the Syconosa

**het·er·o·cont** \'hed·ərō,känt\ *adj* [NL *Heterocontae*] **:** of or relating to the Heterokontae

**heterocontae** *syn of* HETEROKONTAE

**het·ero·co·tyl·ea** \,hed·ә(,)rōkә'tilēә, -,käd°l'ēә\ [NL, fr. *heter-* + *-cotylea* (fr. Gk *kotylē* cup, small vessel) — more at KETTLE] *syn of* MONOGENEA

**het·er·o·crine** \'hed·әrә,krin, -rīn,-rēn; -,krōn\ *adj* [*heter-* + *-crine* (as in *endocrine*)] *of a gland* **:** having both an endocrine and an exocrine secretion **:** MIXED

**het·ero·cy·cle** \-,sīkәl\ *n* [*heter-* + *cycle*] **:** a heterocyclic ring system or a heterocyclic compound

[1]**het·ero·cyclic** \¦===¦sīklik, -lēk *also* -sik-\ *adj* [ISV *heter-* + *cyclic*] **:** relating to, characterized by, or being a ring composed of atoms of different elements ⟨furan and quinoline are ~⟩ — distinguished from *isocyclic*

[2]**heterocyclic** \"\ *n* **:** a heterocyclic compound or a heterocyclic ring system

**het·ero·cyst** \'hed·әrә,sist\ *n* [ISV *heter-* + *cyst*] **:** one of the large transparent thick-walled cells resembling spores occurring at intervals along the filament in certain filamentous blue-green algae

**het·ero·dac·tyl** \¦hed·ərō¦dakt°l\ *adj* [ISV *heter-* + *-dactyl* (fr. Gk *daktylos* finger, toe)] **:** HETERODACTYLOUS

**het·ero·dac·ty·lism** \-tә,lizәm\ *n* -S [*heter-* + *-dactylism*] **1 :** unilateral polydactylism **2 :** a greater degree of polydactylism on one side than on the other

**het·ero·dac·ty·lous** \-tәlәs\ *adj* [*heter-* + *-dactylous*] **:** having the first and second toes turned backward ⟨trogons are ~⟩

**het·er·od·era** \,hed·ә'rädәrә\ *n, cap* [NL, fr. *heter-* + *-dera* (fr. Gk *derē* neck) — more at DER-] **:** a genus (the type of the family Heteroderidae of the superfamily Tylenchoidea) of minute nematode worms many of which attack the roots and underground stems of various cultivated plants (as sugar beets, potatoes, peas) — compare GOLDEN NEMATODE, ROOT-KNOT NEMATODE

**het·er·odon** \'hed·әrә,dän\ *n, cap* [NL, fr. *heter-* + *-odon*] **:** a genus of small stocky colubrid snakes comprising the No. American hognose snakes

[1]**het·er·odont** \-nt\ *adj* [ISV *heter-* + *-odont*] **1 :** having the teeth differentiated into incisors, canines, and molars ⟨~ mammals⟩ ⟨man is ~⟩ — opposed to *homodont* **2 :** having both cardinal and lateral teeth that fit into depressions on the opposite valve — compare HETERODONTA

[2]**heterodont** \"\ *n* -S **:** an animal with heterodont dentition

**het·er·odon·ta** \,===¦däntә\ *n pl, cap* [NL fr. *heter-* + *-odonta*] *in some classifications* **:** an order of Lamellibranchia comprising bivalve mollusks with few hinge teeth but usu. with both lateral and cardinal teeth and with unequal adductor muscles

**het·er·odon·ti·dae** \-tә,dē\ *n pl, cap* [NL, fr. *Heterodontus*, type genus + *-idae*] **:** a family of small sharks (suborder Squaloidea) having a few recent representatives in warm parts of the Pacific and Indian oceans but known since Jurassic times, bearing two dorsal fins each armed with a spine, and having the posterior teeth arranged in a dense pavement adapted for crushing the shells of mollusks — see HETERODONTUS

**het·er·odon·tus** \-tәs\ *n, cap* [NL, fr. *heter-* + *-odontus* (fr. Gk *odont-*, *odōn* tooth) — more at TOOTH] **:** the type genus of Heterodontidae including most recent representatives of the family — see PORT JACKSON SHARK

**het·er·o·dox** \'hed·әrә,däks, 'hetәr-, 'he·tr-\ *adj* [LL *heterodoxus*, fr. Gk *heterodoxos*, fr. *hetero-* heter- + *doxa* opinion — more at DOXOLOGY] **1 :** differing from an established religious point of view: **a :** contrary to acknowledged religious opinion or belief **:** differing from a religious standard or official position **:** UNORTHODOX, HERETICAL ⟨~ sermon⟩ **b :** accepting or teaching heretical or unorthodox opinions or doctrines ⟨the ~ opponent of the established religion has often much more real faith than most of its followers —M.R.Cohen⟩ **2 :** lacking the usual content, qualities, or values **:** not following traditional form or procedure **:** UNCONVENTIONAL ⟨some ~ ideas on books —H.J.Laski⟩ ⟨the societies representing the orthodox practice of medicine have generally succeeded in keeping . . . ~ practitioners out —D.D.McKean⟩ — **het·er·o·dox·ly** *adv* — **het·ero·dox·ness** *n* -ES

**het·er·o·doxy** \-sē,-si\ *n* [Gk *heterodoxia*, fr. *heterodoxos* + *-ia* -y] **1 :** the quality or state of being heterodox **:** departure from orthodoxy ⟨the unbridled ~ of the gay nineties —M.L. Bach⟩ **2 :** a heterodox opinion or doctrine ⟨revived the long-decaying . . . ~ and established it as the religion of the Persian state —H.A.R.Gibb⟩

**het·er·od·ro·mous** \¦hed·ә¦rädrәmәs\ *adj* [*heter-* + *-dromous*] **:** having the genetic spiral of the branches reversed in its direction from that of the main stem ⟨~ leaf arrangement⟩ ⟨a ~ tendril⟩ — compare HOMODROMOUS — **het·er·od·ro·my** \,==-'==mē\ *n* -ES

[1]**het·ero·dyne** \'hed·әrә,dīn, 'hetәr-,'he·tr-\ *adj* [*heter-* + *dyne*] **:** of or relating to the production of an electrical beat between two radio frequencies one of which usu. is that of a received signal-carrying current and the other that of an uninterrupted current introduced into the apparatus — compare SUPERHETERODYNE

[2]**heterodyne** \"\ *vt* -ED/-ING/-S **:** to combine (a radio frequency) with a different frequency so that a beat is produced ⟨a low value of signal frequency (generally about 100 kc), which is subsequently multiplied and *heterodyned* to produce the desired carrier frequency —*Radio Corp. of Amer. Rev.*⟩

[1]**het·er·oe·cious** *or* **het·er·e·cious** \¦hed·ә¦rēshәs\ *adj* [*heter-* + *-oecious* or *-ecious* (fr. Gk *oikia* house + E *-ous*) — more at VICINITY] **:** passing through the different stages in its life cycle on alternate and often unrelated hosts ⟨~ rusts⟩ ⟨~ insects⟩ — contrasted with *homoecious;* compare AUTOECIOUS — **het·er·oe·cious·ly** *adv* — **het·er·oe·cious·ness** *n* -ES — **het·er·oe·cism** \,==¦rē,sizәm\ *n* -S — **het·er·oe·cy** \'==,rēsē\ *n* -ES

[2]**heteroecious** *var of* HETEROICOUS

**het·er·oe·cis·mal** \,hed·ә'rē,sizmәl; ¦hed·ә¦rē¦s-, -rō¦-\ *adj* [*heteroecism* (fr. [1]*heteroecious* + *-ism*) + *-al*] **:** HETEROECIOUS

**het·ero·erotic** \¦hed·ә(,)rō+\ *adj* [*heter-* + *erotic*] **:** ALLOEROTIC

**het·ero·erotism** \"+\ *n* [*heter-* + *erotism*] **:** ALLOEROTISM

**het·ero·fermentative** \¦hed·ә(,)rō+\ *adj* [*heter-* + *fermentative*] **:** producing a fermentation resulting in a number of end products — used esp. of lactic-acid bacteria that ferment carbohydrates and produce volatile acids and carbon dioxide as well as lactic acid

**het·ero·fermenter** \"+\ *n* [*heter-* + *fermenter*] **:** a heterofermentative organism

**het·ero·fertilization** \"+\ *n* [*heter-* + *fertilization*] **:** double fertilization in a seed plant (as maize) that results in phenotypically and probably genotypically different endosperm and embryo ⟨~ is considered to result when the polar nuclei and the egg fuse with male nuclei of differing genetic constitution⟩

**het·ero·gamete** \"+\ *n* [ISV *heter-* + *gamete*] **:** either of a pair of gametes that differ in form, size, or behavior, that are characteristic of most multicellular animals and many plants, and that occur typically as large nonmotile oogametes and small motile sperms — compare ISOGAMETE

**het·ero·gametic** \"+\ *adj* [*heter-* + *gametic*] **1 :** exhibiting heterogamety **:** DIGAMETIC **2 :** of or relating to a heterogamete or to heterogamety

**het·ero·gam·e·tism** \¦==(,)=¦gamә,tizәm\ *n* -S **:** HETEROGAMETY

**het·ero·gam·e·ty** \-mәd·ē\ *n* -ES [*heter-* + *gamete* + *-y*] **:** the production by one sex of a species of two types of gametes of which one is destined to produce a male and the other a female

**het·er·og·a·mous** \¦hed·ә¦rägәmәs\ *also* **het·ero·gam·ic** \¦hed·ərō¦gamik\ *adj* [*heter-* + *-gamous* or *-gamic*] **:** exhibiting or characterized by diversity in the reproductive elements or processes: as **a** *of sexual reproduction* **:** characterized by fusion of unlike gametes; *esp* **:** OOGAMOUS 1 — often used of processes in higher organisms in contrast to *anisogamous;* compare ISOGAMOUS **b :** having heterogamous reproduction **c :** exhibiting alternation of generations in which two kinds of sexual generation (as dioecious and parthenogenetic) alternate **d :** bearing flowers of two kinds (as perfect and pistillate) — used esp. of sedges and composites and opposed to *homogamous*

**het·er·og·a·my** \,hed·ә'rägәmē\ *n* -ES [ISV *heter-* + *-gamy*] **1 :** the condition of being heterogamous — opposed to HOMOGAMY **2 :** heterogamous reproduction

**het·ero·gangliate** \¦hed·ә(,)rō+\ *adj* [*heter-* + *gangliate*] **:** having the nerve ganglia more or less widely separated and unsymmetrically situated ⟨~ mollusks⟩

**het·er·o·gen** \'hed·әrәjәn,-,jen, 'he·tr-\ *n* -S [*heter-* + *-gen*] **:** a group of heterozygous hybrid organisms

**het·er·o·gene** \-,jēn\ *adj* [Gk *heterogenēs*] *archaic* **:** HETEROGENEOUS

**het·er·o·ge·neal** \¦=(=)=¦jēnēәl, -nyәl\ *adj* [ML *heterogeneus* + E *-al*] *archaic* **:** HETEROGENEOUS

**het·er·o·ge·ne·ity** \,hed·әrәjә'nēәd·ē, ,hetәr-, ,he·tr-, -rōj-, ¦әtē, -i *sometimes* -nā¦ *or* ÷ -nī¦\ *n* -ES [ML *heterogeneitas*, fr. *heterogeneus* heterogeneous + L *-itas* -ity] **:** the quality or state of being heterogeneous ⟨speaking by radio may vastly increase the number and ~ of your hearers —H.D.Scott⟩ ⟨the cultural ~ of the area —Mary Tew⟩ ⟨order which prevents variation from becoming a disordered ~ —John Dewey⟩

**het·er·o·ge·neous** \¦=(=)=¦jēnēәs, -nyәs, *Brit sometimes* -¦jen-\ *adj* [ML *heterogeneus*, fr. Gk *heterogenēs*, fr. *hetero-* heter- + *-genēs* born — more at -GEN] **1 :** differing in kind ⟨a ~ population —L.W.Doob⟩ ⟨genetically ~⟩ **2 :** consisting of dissimilar ingredients or constituents ⟨~ substances⟩ ⟨a town may be culturally or economically ~ —*Notes & Queries on Anthropology*⟩ **:** having different values, opinions, or backgrounds ⟨the family is ~ enough to make quite a good party in itself —Rose Macaulay⟩ **3 a :** made up of parts or elements that are not unified, compatible, or proportionate ⟨no ~ hotchpotch but a book with an underlying unity —Roger Pippett⟩ **b :** incapable of comparison in respect to magnitude **:** being incommensurable ⟨volume and area are ~ quantities⟩ **4 :** having different genders in the singular and plural number ⟨Latin *locus* "place", which is masculine but has a neuter plural *loca*, is a ~ noun⟩ **5 :** possessed of unlike quality or meanings **:** DISPARATE ⟨not all the artists who painted . . . him from life were competent, and their results are ~ —J.C.Fitzpatrick⟩ **6 :** not uniform in structure or composition ⟨the ~ earth⟩ ⟨a ~ weld⟩ ⟨tumors which have a ~ composition by reason of structure and presence of necrosis —*Yr.Bk. of Endocrinology*⟩ ⟨the beam of x ray is not . . . monochromatic but ~, containing wavelengths over a large range —*Medical Physics*⟩ **7 :** relating to or occurring in or being a system that is not uniform throughout but consists of phases separated by boundaries (as solid-solid phases, solid-liquid phases, or solid-liquid-vapor phases) ⟨~ reaction⟩ — **het·er·o·ge·neous·ly** *adv* — **het·er·o·ge·neous·ness** *n* -ES

**heterogeneous ray** *n* **:** a vascular ray consisting of both upright and procumbent cells — compare HOMOGENEOUS RAY

**het·ero·gen·er·a·tae** \,hed·ә(,)rō,jenә'rād·(,)ē, -'räd·(,)ī\ *n pl, cap* [NL, fr. *heter-* + L *generatae* (fem. pl. of *generatus*, past part. of *generare* to generate) — more at GENERATE] **:** a class of brown algae including those having two alternating generations unlike in vegetative structure, the larger sporophyte being often macroscopic and the smaller gametophyte usu. microscopic — compare ISOGENERATAE

**het·ero·genesis** \¦hed·ərō+\ *n* [NL, fr. *heter-* + L *genesis*] **1 :** ABIOGENESIS **2 :** ALTERNATION OF GENERATIONS: as **a :** alternation of a dioecious and one or more parthenogenetic generations **b :** alternation of a haploid with a diploid generation

**het·ero·genetic** \¦==(,)=+\ *adj* [*heter-* + *genetic*] **1 :** relating to or characterized by heterogenesis **2 :** HETEROPHILE

**heterogenetic association** *n* **:** the pairing in synapsis of genomes from diverse ancestors in a polyploid organism

**heterogenetic induction** *n, bot* **:** the union of two or more stimuli **:** complex stimulation

**het·er·o·gen·ic** \¦hed·әrә¦jenik\ *adj* **1** [*heterogeny* + *-ic*] **:** HETEROGENETIC **2** [*heter-* + *gene* + *-ic*] **:** containing more than one allele of a gene — used of a cell or of population

**het·er·og·e·nist** \,hed·ә'räjәnәst\ *n* -S [*heterogeny* + *-ist*] **:** ABIOGENIST

**het·er·og·e·nous** \¦==¦räjәnәs\ *adj* **1** [*heter-* + *-genous*] **:** of other origin **:** not originating within the body — opposed to *autogenous* **2** [ML *heterogenus* diverse, fr. Gk *heterogenēs* — more at HETEROGENEOUS] **:** HETEROGENEOUS 2

**heterogenous graft** *n* **:** HETEROGRAFT

**het·er·og·e·ny** \,==¦räjәnē\ *n* -ES [*heterogenous* + *-y*] **1 :** a heterogenous collection or group ⟨the descendants of the ~ of Arab tribes that settled in Samaria —A.N.Williams b.1914⟩ **2** [*heter-* + *-geny*] **:** HETEROGENESIS **3 :** the application of different genders to neuter things

[1]**het·er·og·nath** \'hed·әräg,nath\ *adj* [NL *Heterognathi*] **:** of or relating to the Heterognathi

[2]**heterognath** \"\ *n* -S **:** [2]CHARACIN

**het·er·og·na·thi** \,hed·ә'rägnә,thī\ *n pl, cap* [NL, fr. *heter-* + *-gnathi* (pl. of *-gnathus* -gnathous)] *in some classifications* **:** an order of teleost fishes that resemble members of the family Cyprinidae but have an adipose fin and teeth in the jaws and that comprise Characidae and related families now usu. included in a division of the suborder Cyprinoidea — compare OSTARIOPHYSI

**het·er·o·gone** \'hed·әrә,gōn\ *n* -S [back-formation fr. *heterogony*] **:** a heterogonous plant

**het·er·o·gon·ic** \¦hed·әrә¦gänik\ *or* **het·er·og·o·nous** \¦hed·ә¦rägәnәs\ *adj* [*heterogony* + *-ic* or *-ous*] **1 :** of, relating to, or characterized by heterogony; *esp* **:** ALLOMETRIC **2 :** being that course of development in which a generation of parasites is succeeded by a free-living generation — used of certain nematode worms; distinguished from *homogonic*

**het·er·og·o·nism** \,hed·ә'rägә,nizәm\ *n* -S [*heterogonous* + *-ism*] **:** HETEROGONY

**het·er·og·o·nous·ly** *adv* **:** in a heterogonous manner

**het·er·og·o·ny** \-nē\ *n* -ES [ISV *heter-* + *-gony*] **1 :** the state of having two or more kinds of perfect flowers varying in relative length of androecium and gynoecium — opposed to *homogony;* distinguished from *heteromorphism* **2 a :** ALTERNATION OF GENERATIONS; *esp* **:** alternation of a dioecious and hermaphroditic generation **b :** heterogamous reproduction **c :** ALLOMETRY

**het·ero·graft** \'hed·ərō+,-\ *n* [ISV *heter-* + *graft*] **:** a graft of tissue taken from a donor of one species to be grafted into a recipient of another species ⟨the use of ~s has proved impracticable in cosmetic surgery⟩ — compare AUTOGRAFT, HOMOGRAFT

**het·ero·graph·ic** \¦hed·ərә¦grafik\ *adj* **:** of, relating to, or characterized by heterography — opposed to *homographic*

**het·er·og·ra·phy** \,hed·ә'rägrәfē\ *n* -ES [*heter-* + *-graphy*] **1 :** spelling differing from standard current usage **2 :** spelling in which the same letters represent different sounds in different words or syllables (as in current English orthography)

**het·er·og·y·nous** \¦hed·ә¦räjәnәs\ *or* **het·er·og·y·nal** \-n°l\ *adj* [*heterogynous* fr. *heter-* + *-gynous; heterogynal* fr. *heterogynous* + *-al*] **:** having females of more than one kind ⟨bees and ants are ~⟩

**het·er·oi·cous** \-¦rōikәs\ *also* **het·er·oe·cious** \-¦rēshәs\ *adj* [*heter-* + *-oicous*, *-oecious* (fr. Gk *oikos* dwelling + E *-ous*) — more at VICINITY] **:** having archegonia and antheridia either on the same branch or on different branches of the same plant — compare PAROICOUS, POLYOICOUS

**het·ero·karyon** *also* **het·ero·caryon** \¦hed·ərō+\ *n* -S [NL, fr. *heter-* + *karyon* or *caryon*] **:** a cell in the mycelium of a fungus that contains two or more genetically unlike nuclei — compare DIKARYON, HOMOKARYON

**het·ero·kary·o·sis** *or* **het·ero·cary·o·sis** \,===,karē'ōsәs\ *n* -ES [NL, fr. *heter-* + *kary-* or *cary-* + *-osis*] **:** the condition of having cells that are heterokaryons

**het·ero·kary·ot·ic** *or* **het·ero·cary·ot·ic** \¦hed·ә(,)rō¦karē¦äd·ik\ *adj* [*heter-* + *kary-* or *cary-* + *-otic*] **:** of, relating to, or consisting of heterokaryons ⟨a ~ division⟩ ⟨~ mycelia⟩

**het·ero·kinesis** \¦hed·ә(,)rō+\ *n* [NL, fr. *heter-* + *-kinesis*] **:** qualitative nuclear division — used of the meiotic reduction division in the heterogametic sex — **het·ero·kinetic** \"+\ *adj*

**het·ero·kon·tae** \,hed·ərō'kän,tē\ *n pl, cap* [NL, fr. *heter-* + *-kontae* (fr. Gk *kontos* punting pole, fr. *kentein* to prick, goad); fr. the unequal length of the flagella — more at CENTER] *in some classifications* **:** a class of algae equivalent to Xanthophyceae that includes all the yellow-green algae having flagella of unequal length — compare ISOKONTAE

**het·ero·lecithal** \"+\ *adj* [*heter-* + Gk *lekithos* yolk of an egg + E *-al*] **:** having the yolk unequally distributed — opposed to *homolecithal*

**het·er·ol·o·cha** \,hed·ә'rälәkә\ *n, cap* [NL, alter. of *Heteralocha*, fr. *heter-* + *-alocha* (fr. Gk *alochos* spouse, bedfellow, concubine)] *in some classifications* **:** a genus coextensive with *Neomorpha*

**het·er·o·log·i·cal** \¦hed·әrә¦läjәkәl\ *also* **het·er·o·log·ic** \-jik\ *adj* [*heterology* + *-ical* or *-ic*] **:** of or relating to or characterized by heterology **:** HETEROLOGOUS — **het·er·o·log·i·cal·ly** \-jәk(ә)lē\ *adv*

**het·er·ol·o·gous** \¦hed·ә¦rälәgәs\ *adj* [*heter-* + Gk *logos* proportion, word + E *-ous* — more at LEGEND] **1 :** characterized by heterology **:** consisting of different elements or of like elements in different proportions **:** DIFFERENT **2 :** derived from a different species ⟨~ serum⟩ — compare AUTOLOGOUS, HOMOLOGOUS — **het·er·ol·o·gous·ly** *adv*

**heterologous graft** *n* **:** HETEROGRAFT

**heterologous series** *n* **:** a series (as ethane, ethyl alcohol, acetaldehyde, acetic acid) of related derivatives not homologous

**heterologous stimulus** *n* **:** a stimulus capable of affecting any available sensory end organ and thought to be further capable of being interpreted centrally as a stimulus of the kind to which the end organ is adapted to respond ⟨a blow on the eye acts as a *heterologous stimulus* seen as a flash of light⟩ — compare HOMOLOGOUS STIMULUS

**het·er·ol·o·gy** \-'rälәjē\ *n* -ES [ISV *heter-* + *-logy*] **:** the lack of correspondence of apparently similar bodily parts due to differences in fundamental makeup or origin — compare ANALOGY, HOMOLOGY

**het·ero·lysin** \¦hed·ərō+\ *n* [ISV *heter-* + *lysin*] **:** a hemolysin from an animal of a different species

**het·er·ol·y·sis** \,hed·ә'rälәsәs\ *n* [NL, fr. *heter-* + *-lysis*] **1 :** destruction by lysins or enzymes from another source **2 :** decomposition of a compound into two oppositely charged particles or ions (as $X{:}Y \rightarrow X^{+} + {:}B^{-}$) — compare HOMOLYSIS — **het·er·o·lyt·ic** \¦hed·ərō¦lid·ik\ *adj*

**het·er·o·mal·lous** \¦hed·ərō¦malәs\ *adj* [Gk *heteromallos* woolly, fr. *hetero-* heter- + *mallos* lock of wool] **:** spreading or turning in different directions — used of leaves of various mosses; opposed to *homomallous*

**het·er·o·mas·ti·gote** \¦===¦mastә,gōt\ *or* **het·er·o·mas·ti·gate** \-,gāt\ *adj* [*heteromastigote*, alter. of *heteromastigate*, fr. *heter-* + *mastig-* + *-ate*] **:** having two unlike flagella ⟨~ dinoflagellates⟩

**het·er·o·me·les** \,===¦mē(,)lēz\ *n, cap* [NL, fr. *heter-* + *-meles* (fr. Gk *mēlon* apple)] *in some classifications* **:** a genus of plants including only the toyon — compare PHOTINIA

**het·er·om·er·ous** \¦hed·ә¦rämәrәs\ *adj* [*heter-* + Gk *meros* part + E *-ous* — more at MERIT] **1 :** unrelated in chemical composition — used of homeomorphous substances **2** *of a flower* **:** having one or more whorls the number of whose members differs from that of the remaining whorls — opposed to *isomerous* **3 :** having a thallus with one or more layers of algal cells ⟨~ lichens⟩ — opposed to *homoeomerous*

**het·ero·mesotroph** \¦hed·ərō+\ *n* -S [*heter-* + *mesotroph*] **:** a heteromesotrophic organism

**het·ero·mesotrophic** \"+\ *adj* [*heter-* + *mesotrophic*] **:** requiring a single organic source of nitrogen and carbon for metabolism

**het·ero·metabolic** \"+\ *or* **het·ero·metabolous** \"+\ *adj* [*heter-* + *metabolic* or *metabolous*] **:** of or relating to or exhibiting heterometabolism

**het·ero·metabolism** \"+\ *also* **het·ero·metaboly** \"+\ *n* [*heter-* + *metabolism* or *metaboly*] *of insects* **:** development with incomplete or direct metamorphosis in which the young nymph is fundamentally like the adult and no pupal stage precedes maturity — distinguished from *holometabolism;* compare HEMIMETABOLISM

**het·ero·metatrophic** \"+\ *adj* [*heter-* + *metatrophic*] **:** requiring complex organic sources of carbon and nitrogen for metabolism — compare HOLOZOIC

**het·ero·met·ric** \¦hed·ərō¦me·trik\ *adj* [ISV *heter-* + *-metric*] **:** characterized by diversity of meter

**het·er·o·mi** \,hed·ә'rō,mī\ *n pl, cap* [NL, fr. *heter-* + *-omi* (fr. Gk *ōmos* shoulder) — more at HUMERUS] **:** a small order of eellike deep-sea teleost fishes with a spiny dorsal fin

**het·er·o·mor·phic** \¦hed·ərō¦mȯrfik\ *or* **het·er·o·mor·phous** \-fәs\ *adj* [ISV *heter-* + *-morphic* or *-morphous*] **1 :** deviating from the usual form or exhibiting diversity of form: as **a :** having different forms at different stages of development ⟨holometabolic insects and certain plants with complex life cycles are ~⟩ **b :** having different forms in different members of a colony ⟨the polyps of many complex compound jellyfishes are highly ~ being chiefly specialized for feeding, defense, motility, or reproduction⟩ **c :** of irregular or unusual structure **:** of variable shape ⟨the leaves of emergent plants are commonly ~⟩ **d :** unlike in form or size — used specif. of synaptic chromosomes ⟨the X and Y chromosomes constitute a ~ pair⟩ ⟨~ bivalents⟩ **2 :** exhibiting or undergoing heteromorphosis

**het·er·o·mor·phism** \\,==='mȯr,fizəm\\ *n* -s [ISV *heter-* + *-morphism*] **1 :** the quality or state of being heteromorphic **2 :** dissimilarity in crystal form shown by compounds of similar composition — contrasted with *homeomorphism* and *isomorphism* **3 :** HETEROGONY 1 **4 :** POLYMORPHISM

**het·er·o·mor·phite** \\-,fīt\\ *n* -s [ISV *heter-* + *morph-* + *-ite*] **:** a mineral $Pb_7Sb_8S_{19}$ consisting of a lead antimony sulfide related closely to fülöppite, plagionite, and semseyite

**het·er·o·mor·pho·sis** \\,==='mȯrfəsə̇s\\ *n* [NL, fr. *heter-* + *-morphosis*] **1 :** the production in an organism of an abnormal or misplaced part esp. in place of one that has been lost (as the regeneration of a tail in place of a head) — compare HOMOMORPHOSIS **2 a :** the production of a malformed or malplaced tissue or organ **b :** the formation of tissue of a different type from that from which it derives

**het·er·o·mor·phy** \\'===,mȯrfē\\ *n* -ES [ISV *heter-* + *-morphy*] **:** HETEROMORPHISM

**het·ero·mya** \\,hed·ərō'mīə\\ [NL, fr. *heter-* + *-mya*] *syn of* HETEROMYARIA

**het·ero·my·ar·ia** \\-ōmī'a(a)rēə\\ *n pl, cap* [NL, fr. *heter-* + *-myaria*] *in some classifications* **:** a division of Lamellibranchia comprising bivalve mollusks having two adductor muscles the anterior one of which is very small — compare ISOMYARIA, MONOMYARIA — **het·er·o·my·ar·i·an** \\¦====¦=rēən\\ *adj*

1**het·er·o·my·id** \\¦hed·ərō¦mīə̇d\\ *adj* [NL *Heteromyidae*] **:** of or relating to the Heteromyidae

2**heteromyid** \\"\\ *n* -s **:** one of the Heteromyidae

**het·er·o·my·i·dae** \\,==='mīə,dē\\ *n pl, cap* [NL, fr. *Heteromys,* type genus + *-idae*] **:** a family of New World rodents having fur-lined external cheek pouches, large eyes, well developed ears, elongated hind limbs and tail adapted to leaping and balancing, and the ability to live on dry food and depending on metabolic water to survive under extreme desert conditions — see POCKET MOUSE 1

**het·ero·mys** \\'===,mis\\ *n, cap* [NL, fr. *heter-* + *-mys*] **:** the type genus of the family Heteromyidae

**het·ero·nemertea** \\¦hed·ərō+\\ *n pl, cap* [NL, fr. *heter-* + *Nemertea*] **:** an order of Nemertea (class Anopla) comprising long slender forms with cerebral organs and often with caudal cirri — **het·ero·nemertean** \\"+\\ *adj or n*

**het·ero·nemertini** \\"+\\ [NL, fr. *heter-* + *Nemertini*] *syn of* HETERONEMERTEA

1**het·er·o·ne·re·id** \\¦hed·ərō¦nirēə̇d\\ *adj* [NL *heteronereid-, heteronereis*] **:** of, relating to, or having the characters of a heteronereis

2**heteronereid** \\"\\ *n* -s **:** HETERONEREIS

**het·ero·nereis** \\¦hed·ərō+\\ *n* [NL, fr. *heter-* + *Nereis*] **:** a free-swimming dimorphic sexual individual of certain polychaete worms (family Nereidae) characterized by greatly enlarged eyes, enlarged and modified parapodia and other appendages, and more or less complete obliteration of the internal viscera by masses of developing germ cells

**het·er·o·neu·ra** \\,==='n(y)u̇rə\\ *n pl, cap* [NL, fr. *heter-* + *-neura*] *in some classifications* **:** a suborder of Lepidoptera including those forms in which the venation of the fore wings differs from that of the hind wings — compare HOMONEURA

**het·er·on·o·mous** \\¦hed·ə¦ränəməs\\ *adj* [G *heteronom* (fr. *heter-* + *-onom,* as in *autonom* autonomous, fr. Gk *autonomos*) + E *-ous* — more at AUTONOMOUS] **1 :** subject to or involving different laws of growth ⟨in most segmented animals . . . the segmentation is ~ —Libbie H. Hyman⟩ **2 :** subject to external controls and impositions **:** originating outside the self or one's own will ⟨nor is the Christian view ~, in the sense that the will is enslaved by the dictates of a despot alien to the self's will —W.W.Beach⟩ — **het·er·on·o·mous·ly** *adv*

**het·er·on·o·my** \\,=='==mē\\ *n* -ES [G *heteronomie,* fr. *heter-* + *-onomie* (as in *autonomie* autonomy, fr. Gk *autonomia*) — more at AUTONOMY] **1 :** a subjection to something else: as **a :** a subordination to the law or domination of another (as in political subjection) **b :** the condition of lacking moral freedom or self-determination ⟨in ~ the will . . . is obeying laws not of its own making —D.D.Runes⟩ — opposed to *autonomy* **2 :** the quality or state of being heteronomous

**het·ero·nuclear** \\¦hed·ərō+\\ *adj* [*heter-* + *nuclear*] **1 :** HETEROCYCLIC **2 :** of or relating to different rings in a chemical compound ⟨~ substitution in naphthalene⟩ **3 :** of or relating to a molecule composed of different nuclei ⟨hydrogen chloride HCl and deuterium hydride HD consist of ~ diatomic molecules⟩

**het·er·on·y·mous** \\¦hed·ə¦ränəməs\\ *adj* [LGk *heterōnymos,* fr. Gk *hetero-* heter- + *onyma, onoma* name — more at NAME] **:** having different designations ⟨parent and child are ~ relatives⟩ — opposed to *homonymous* — **het·er·on·y·mous·ly** *adv*

**het·ero·ou·sia** \\¦hed·ərō¦üzēə, -üsēə, -üzh(ē)ə, -üsh(ē)ə\\ *also* **het·er·ou·sia** \\¦hed·ə¦rü-\\ *n* [LGk, fr. Gk *hetero-, heter-* heter- + *ousia*] **:** difference in essence or substance

1**het·ero·ou·sian** *also* **het·er·ou·sian** \\-ən\\ *adj* [LGk *heteroousios, heterousios* (fr. Gk *hetero-, heter-* heter- + *ousia*) + E *-an*] **1 :** having different essential qualities **:** being of a different nature **2** *often cap* **:** of or relating to the heteroousians

2**heteroousian** \\"\\ *also* **heterousian** \\"\\ *n* -s *often cap* **:** an Arian holding that the Son was of a different substance from the Father — compare HOMOIOUSIAN, HOMOOUSIAN

**het·er·o·path·ic** \\¦hed·ərō¦pathik\\ *adj* [*heter-* + Gk *pathos* experience, suffering, emotion + E *-ic* — more at PATHOS] **1 :** different in operation or effect ⟨~ laws —J.S.Mill⟩ **2 :** identifying self with another

**het·er·o·pel·mous** \\-¦pelməs\\ *adj* [*heter-* + *-pelmous*] **:** having each of the two flexor tendons of the toes bifid with the branches of one going to the first and second toes and those of the other to the third and fourth toes

**het·er·o·pet·al·ous** \\-¦ped·ᵊləs\\ *adj* [*heter-* + *-petalous*] **:** having dissimilar petals

**het·er·oph·a·gous** \\¦hed·ə¦räfə̇gəs\\ *adj* [*heter-* + *-phagous*] **1 :** ALTRICIAL **2 :** feeding or living on two or more hosts at different stages of the life history ⟨digenetic trematodes are ~⟩

**het·er·o·phe·my** \\'hed·ərə,fēmē\\ *n* -ES [*heter-* + Gk *phēmē* voice, speech (fr. *phanai* to say) + E *-y* — more at BAN] **:** unconscious use of words other than those intended

**het·er·o·phil antibody** \\'==rə,fil-\\ *n* **:** an antibody characteristic of human blood during an attack of infectious mononucleosis that agglutinates sheep red blood cells

1**het·er·o·phile** \\'===,fīl\\ *also* **het·er·o·phil** \\-,fil\\ *or* **het·er·o·phil·ic** \\¦===¦filik\\ *adj* [*heter-* + *-phile* or *-phil* or *-philic*] **:** reacting serologically with an antigen of another species

2**heterophile** \\"\\ *or* **heterophil** \\"\\ *n* -s [*heter-* + *-phile* or *-phil*] **:** NEUTROPHIL — used esp. in veterinary medicine

**het·er·oph·o·ny** \\,hed·ə'räfənē\\ *n* -ES [Gk *heterophōnia* diversity of note, fr. *heter-* + *-phōnia* -phony] **:** a singing or sounding of the same melody by two or more voices or instruments usu. with some modifications (as in rhythm or ornamentation) by one or both of the performers

**het·er·o·pho·ria** \\,hed·ərō'fōrēə\\ *n* -s [NL, fr. *heter-* + *-phoria*] **:** latent strabismus in which one eye tends to deviate either medially or laterally — compare EXOPHORIA — **het·ero·phor·ic** \\¦===¦fȯrik\\ *adj*

**het·ero·phy·es** \\-'fī(,)ēz\\ *n, cap* [NL, fr. LGk *heterophyēs* of different nature, fr. Gk *heter-* + *phyē* growth, nature; akin to Gk *phyein* to bring forth — more at BE] **:** a genus (the type of the family Heterophyidae) of small digenetic trematode worms infesting the small intestine of dogs, cats, and man in Egypt and much of tropical Asia

1**het·er·o·phy·id** \\¦===¦fīə̇d\\ *adj* [NL *Heterophyidae,* family of trematode worms, fr. *Heterophyes,* type genus + *-idae*] **:** of or relating to the genus *Heterophyes* or family Heterophyidae

2**heterophyid** \\"\\ *n* -s **:** a heterophyid worm

**het·ero·phylesis** \\¦hed·ə(,)rō+\\ *n* [NL, fr. *heter-* + *phylesis*] **:** the quality or state of being heterophyletic

**het·ero·phyletic** \\"+\\ *adj* [*heter-* + *phyletic*] **:** of or relating to or possessing two or more lines of descent

**het·er·o·phyl·lous** \\¦hed·ərō¦filəs\\ *adj* [*heter-* + *-phyllous*] **1 :** having the foliage leaves of more than one form on the same plant or stem ⟨many eucalypts, pondweeds, and crowfoots are ~⟩ — opposed to *isophyllous* **2 :** having two or more forms of foliation of the septal margins ⟨~ ammonites⟩ — **het·er·o·phyl·ly** \\'===,filē\\ *n* -ES

**het·er·o·phyte** \\'hed·ərə,fīt\\ *n* -s [*heter-* + *-phyte*] **:** a plant that is dependent for food materials upon other living or dead plant or animal organisms or their products **:** PARASITE, SAPROPHYTE — compare AUTOPHYTE — **het·er·o·phyt·ic** \\¦===¦fid·ik\\ *adj*

**het·er·o·pi·idae** \\,hed·ərō'pīə,dē\\ *n pl, cap* [NL, fr. *Heteropia,* type genus (fr. *heter-* + *-opia*) + *-idae*] **:** a family of sponges (order Heterocoela) with a distinct dermal cortex pierced by inhalant pores and with subdermal triradiate spicules

**het·er·o·pla·sia** \\-'plāzh(ē)ə\\ *n* -s [NL, fr. *heter-* + *-plasia*] **1 :** a development of a tissue from tissue of a different kind **2 :** a formation of abnormal tissue or of normal tissue in an abnormal locality

**het·er·o·plasm** \\'hed·ərō,plazəm\\ *n* [ISV *heter-* + *-plasm*] **:** tissue formed or growing where it does not normally occur

**het·er·o·plas·tic** \\¦===¦plastik\\ *adj* [ISV *heter-* + *-plastic*] **1 :** of or relating to heteroplasm or heteroplasty or heteroplasia **2 :** HETEROLOGOUS — **het·er·o·plas·ti·cal·ly** \\-tə̇k(ə)lē\\ *adv*

**het·er·o·plas·ty** \\'===,plastē\\ *n* -ES [ISV *heter-* + *-plasty*] **1 :** HETEROPLASIA **2 :** a grafting of tissue from an individual of one species into an individual of a different species

1**het·er·o·ploid** \\-,plȯid\\ *adj* [ISV *heter-* + *-ploid*] **:** having a chromosome number that is greater or smaller usu. by one than the somatic number characteristic of the species but not a simple multiple of the haploid chromosome number — compare POLYPLOID

2**heteroploid** \\"\\ *n* -s **:** a heteroploid individual

**het·er·o·ploi·dy** \\-dē\\ *n* -ES **:** the condition of being heteroploid

**het·er·o·pod** \\-,päd\\ *n* -s [NL *Heteropoda*] **:** one of the Heteropoda

**het·er·op·o·da** \\,hed·ə'räpədə\\ *n pl, cap* [NL, fr. *heter-* + *-poda*] **:** a small division of Pectinibranchia (suborder Taenioglossa) formerly ranked as a separate order and comprising pelagic gastropod mollusks that swim at the surface with the ventral side up with a foot or a part of it forming a median fin and that have a transparent body and a transparent shell or none — **het·er·op·o·dous** \\¦==¦==dəs\\ *adj*

**het·er·op·o·dal** \\¦==¦==dᵊl\\ *adj* [*heter-* + *pod-* + *-al*] **:** of or relating to nerve cells having different kinds of branches

**het·ero·polar** \\¦hed·ərō+\\ *adj* [ISV *heter-* + *polar*] **1 :** of, relating to, or having unlike poles ⟨~ systems⟩ **2 :** POLAR 5b, IONIC — used esp. of chemical bonds or of crystals; distinguished from *homopolar* — **het·ero·polarity** \\"+\\ *n*

**het·er·o·poly** \\¦hed·ərō¦pälē\\ *adj* [ISV *heteropoly-*] **:** containing several groups or ions of different acid-forming elements

**heteropoly-** *comb form* [ISV *heter-* + *poly-*] **:** containing several groups or ions of different acid-forming elements — in names of complex inorganic acids and their salts ⟨*heteropoly*molybdates such as phosphomolybdates⟩; compare ISOPOLY-

**heteropoly acid** *n* **:** any of a large group of complex oxygen-containing acids derived from two or more different inorganic acids by elimination of water from two or more molecules of the acids; *esp* **:** an acid regarded as formed by combination of several molecules of an acid anhydride (as molybdenum trioxide or tungsten trioxide) with a second acid that furnishes the central atom (as phosphorus or silicon) of the complex — distinguished from *isopoly acid*

**het·ero·polymer** \\¦hed·ərō+\\ *n* [G, fr. *hetero-* heter- + *polymer*] **:** COPOLYMER

**het·er·op·tera** \\,hed·ə'räptərə\\ *n pl, cap* [NL, fr. *heter-* + *-ptera*] **:** a suborder of Hemiptera or sometimes a separate order comprising the true bugs — compare HOMOPTERA — **het·er·op·ter·ous** \\¦==¦==rəs\\ *adj*

**het·ero·pycnosis** \\¦hed·ərō+\\ *n* [NL, fr. *heter-* + *pycnosis*] **:** a differential degree of condensation that distinguishes various chromosomes (as sex) or parts of chromosomes in a nucleus — **het·ero·pycnotic** \\"+\\ *adj*

**het·er·o·scope** \\'hed·ərə,skōp\\ *n* [*heter-* + *-scope*] **:** an apparatus for measuring the range of vision in strabismus — **het·er·os·co·py** \\,hed·ə'räskəpē\\ *n* -ES

1**het·ero·sexual** \\¦hed·ərō+\\ *adj* [ISV *heter-* + *sexual*] **1 :** of or relating to or characterized by heterosexuality ⟨sexual relationships between individuals of opposite sexes are ~ —A.C.Kinsey⟩ — opposed to *homosexual* **2 :** of or relating to different sexes ⟨~ twins⟩ ⟨a ~ flock of chickens —*Anatomical Record*⟩ ⟨the pairing off . . . is seldom ~ —A.J.Liebling⟩

2**heterosexual** \\"\\ *n* -s **:** a heterosexual individual

**het·ero·sexuality** \\"+\\ *n* [ISV *heter-* + *sexuality*] **:** the manifestation of sexual desire toward a member of the opposite sex ⟨the achievement of a healthy ~ —F.E.Williams⟩

**het·er·o·side** \\'hed·ərō,sīd, '==(,)=,sīd\\ *n* -s [ISV *heter-* + *-oside*] **:** a glycoside that on hydrolysis yields a noncarbohydrate as well as a glycose — compare HOLOSIDE

**het·er·o·si·pho·na·les** \\¦hed·ərō,sīfə'nā(,)lēz\\ *n pl, cap* [NL, fr. *heter-* + *siphon-* + *-ales*] **:** an order of yellow-green algae comprising the siphonaceous members of the class Xanthophyceae and including the single genus *Botrydium*

**het·er·o·sis** \\,hed·ə'rōsə̇s\\ *n, pl* **hetero·ses** \\-ō,sēz\\ [NL, fr. Gk *heterōsis* alteration, alter. of *heteroiōsis,* fr. *heteroioun* to alter (fr. *heteroios* different in kind, fr. *heteros* other) + *-ōsis* -osis — more at HETER-] **:** a greater vigor or capacity for growth frequently displayed by crossbred animals or plants as compared with those resulting from inbreeding

**het·er·o·site** \\'hed·ərə,sīt\\ *n* -s [F *hétérosite,* fr. Gk *heteros* other, different + F *-ite*] **:** a mineral isomorphous with purpurite and consisting of phosphate of iron and manganese

**het·er·o·so·ma·ta** \\,hed·ərō'sōməd·ə\\ *n pl, cap* [NL, fr. *heter-* + *-somata*] **:** an order or other group of teleost fishes consisting of the flatfishes — **het·er·o·so·mate** \\¦===¦sō,māt\\ *adj* — **het·er·o·so·ma·tous** \\-_məd·əs\\ *adj*

**het·er·o·so·ma·ti** \\,==='sōməd·,ī\\ *or* **het·er·o·so·mi** \\-'sō,mī\\ [NL, fr. *heter-* + *-somati* (fr. Gk *somata*) or *-somi* (pl. of *-somus*)] *syn of* HETEROSOMATA

**het·er·o·some** \\'hed·ərə,sōm\\ *n* -s [*heter-* + *-some*] **:** HETEROCHROMOSOME

**het·er·o·spo·re·ae** \\,hed·ərō'spōrē,ē\\ *n pl, cap* [NL, fr. *heter-* + *-sporeae* (fr. Gk *spora* seed) — more at SPORE] *in some classifications* **:** a primary subdivision of Pteridophyta including the Lycopodiaceae and Equisetaceae and producing two kinds of asexual spores

**het·er·o·spo·ri·um** \\-rēəm\\ *n, cap* [NL, fr. *heter-* + *-sporium*] **:** a form genus of imperfect fungi (family Dematiaceae) with echinulate and 2-septate to several-septate brown conidia

**het·er·o·spor·ous** \\¦===¦spōrəs, ¦hed·ə¦räspərəs\\ *also* **het·er·o·spor·ic** \\¦==rō¦spōrik\\ *adj* [*heter-* + *-sporous* or *-sporic*] **:** characterized by heterospory **:** reproducing asexually by heterospory ⟨~ plants⟩; *specif* **:** producing microspores and megaspores ⟨some pteridophytes and all spermatophytes are ~⟩

**het·er·o·spo·ry** \\'==rō,spōrē, ,=='räspərē\\ *n* -ES [*heter-* + *-spory*] **1 :** the production of asexual spores of more than one kind **2 :** the development of microspores and megaspores in some ferns and fern allies and in all seed plants — opposed to *homospory*

**het·ero·static** \\¦hed·ərō+\\ *adj* [ISV *heter-* + *static*] **:** of or relating to a method of electrostatic measurement in which one potential is measured by means of a different potential — **het·ero·statically** *adv*

**het·er·os·tra·ca** \\,hed·ə'rästrə̇kə\\ [NL] *syn of* HETEROSTRACI

1**het·er·os·tra·can** \\¦==¦==kən\\ *adj* [NL *Heterostraci* + E *-an*] **:** of or relating to the Heterostraci

2**heterostracan** \\"\\ *n* -s **:** an animal or fossil of the order Heterostraci

**het·er·os·tra·ci** \\,=='=strə,sī\\ *n pl, cap* [NL, fr. *heter-* + Gk *ostrakon* shell, potsherd — more at OSTRACON] **:** a class or other division of ostracoderms with widely separated nares and eyes and with an exoskeleton which may consist of a few large plates or numerous placoid scales

**het·er·o·stroph·ic** \\¦hed·ərō¦sträfik\\ *adj* **1** [Gk *heterostrophos* + E *-ic*] **:** consisting of strophes differing in metrical form **2** [NL *heterostrophus* + E *-ic*] **:** relating to or marked by heterostrophy ⟨a shell with ~ whorls⟩

**het·er·os·tro·phous** \\¦hed·ə¦rästrəfəs\\ *adj* [NL *heterostrophus*] **:** HETEROSTROPHIC 1

**het·er·os·tro·phy** \\,=='==fē\\ *n* -ES [ISV *heter-* + *-strophy* (fr. Gk *strophē* turn)] **:** the quality or state of being coiled in a direction opposite to the usual one

**het·er·o·styled** \\'hed·ərō,stīld\\ *adj* [*heter-* + *-styled*] **:** having styles of two or more distinct forms or of different lengths ⟨~ buckwheat⟩ — compare HOMOSTYLED

**het·er·o·sty·lism** \\,==='stī,lizəm\\ *also* **het·er·o·sty·ly** \\'===,stīlē\\ *n, pl* **heterostylisms** *also* **heterostylies** [*heterostylism* fr. *heter-* + *style* + *-ism; heterostyly* fr. *heter-* + *-styly*] **:** HETEROGONY 1

**het·er·o·sty·lous** \\¦===¦stīləs\\ *adj* [*heter-* + *-stylous*] **:** HETEROSTYLED

**het·ero·suggestion** \\¦hed·ə(,)rō+\\ *n* [ISV *heter-* + *suggestion*] **:** suggestion used by one person to influence another

**het·ero·syllabic** \\"+\\ *adj* [*heter-* + *syllabic*] **:** belonging to another syllable or to different syllables

**het·ero·syllis** \\"+\\ *n, pl* **heterosylles** [NL, fr. *heter-* + *Syllis*] **:** a modified sexual form of an annelid of the family Syllidae comparable to a heteronereis

**het·er·o·tac·tic** \\¦hed·ərō¦taktik\\ *also* **het·er·o·tac·tous** \\-təs\\ *adj* [*heter-* + *-tactic* or *-tactous* (fr. Gk *taktos* ordered, fixed)] **:** characterized by or exhibiting heterotaxis

**het·er·o·tax·ic** \\-¦taksik\\ *adj* [NL *heterotaxis* + E *-ic*] **:** HETEROTACTIC

**het·er·o·tax·is** \\,==='taksə̇s\\ *also* **het·er·o·tax·ia** \\-ksēə\\ *n, pl* **heterotax·es** \\-k,sēz\\ *also* **heterotax·i·as** \\-ksēəz\\ [NL, fr. *heter-* + *-taxis* or *-taxia*] **:** abnormal arrangement (as of organs or parts of the body or of geological strata)

**het·er·o·taxy** \\'===,taksē\\ *n* -ES [NL *heterotaxia*] **:** HETEROTAXIS

**het·ero·telic** \\¦hed·ərō+\\ *adj* [*heter-* + *telic*] **:** existing for the sake of something else **:** having an extraneous end or purpose — contrasted with *autotelic*

**het·er·o·thal·lic** \\¦hed·ərō¦thalik\\ *adj* [*heter-* + *thall-* + *-ic*] **1 :** having two or more genetically incompatible but morphologically similar haploid phases which function as separate sexes or strains — used esp. of certain algae and fungi or of the unisexual spores producing these strains — compare HOMOTHALLIC, MINUS, PLUS **2 :** DIOECIOUS — **het·er·o·thal·lism** \\,==='tha,lizəm\\ *n* -s — **het·er·o·thal·ly** \\'===,thalē\\ *n* -ES

**het·er·o·therm** \\'===,thərm\\ *n* [*heter-* + *-therm*] **:** POIKILOTHERM

**het·ero·ther·mic** \\¦hed·ərō¦thərmik\\ *also* **het·ero·ther·mal** \\-mal\\ *or* **het·ero·ther·mous** \\-məs\\ *adj* [*heter-* + *thermic* or *thermal* or *-thermous*] **:** POIKILOTHERMIC

**het·er·ot·ic** \\¦hed·ə¦räd·ik\\ *adj* [fr. NL *heterosis,* after such pairs as NL *narcosis:* E *narcotic*] **:** of, relating to, or exhibiting heterosis ⟨~ tetraploids⟩ ⟨a ~ modification⟩

**het·er·o·to·pia** \\,hed·ərō'tōpēə\\ *also* **het·er·ot·o·py** \\,hed·ə'räd·əpē\\ *n, pl* **heterotopias** *also* **heterotopies** [NL *heterotopia,* fr. *heter-* + *-topia* -topy] **:** displacement in or difference of position: as **a :** deviation of an organ from the normal position **b :** an abnormal habitat **c :** the grafting of tissue into an abnormal location (as skin into the anterior chamber of the eye) — **het·er·o·top·ic** \\¦===¦täpik\\ *adj* — **het·er·ot·o·pous** \\¦==¦räd·əpəs\\ *adj*

**het·ero·transplant** \\¦hed·ərō+\\ *n* [*heter-* + *transplant*] **:** HETEROGRAFT — **het·ero·transplantation** \\"+\\ *n*

**het·er·o·trich** \\'==rō,trik\\ *n* -s [NL *Heterotricha*] **:** one of the Heterotricha

**het·er·ot·ri·cha** \\,hed·ə'rä·trə̇kə\\ *n pl, cap* [NL, fr. *heter-* + *-tricha*] **:** a suborder of Spirotricha comprising ciliate protozoans that have uniform or reduced ciliation but no cirri and containing free-living organisms (as members of the genus *Stentor*) as well as commensals and parasites of vertebrate intestines — see BALANTIDIUM

**het·er·o·tri·cha·les** \\,hed·ərō·trə'kā(,)lēz\\ *n pl, cap* [NL, fr. *heter-* + *trich-* + *-ales*] **:** an order of yellow-green algae comprising all those with cells arranged in simple or branching filaments and including the single family Tribonemaceae

**het·er·o·trich·i·da** \\-rō·'trikədə\\ [NL, fr. *heter-* + *trich-* + *-ida*] *syn of* HETEROTRICHA

**het·er·o·tri·cho·sis** \\-rō·trə'kōsə̇s\\ *n* [NL, fr. *heter-* + *trich-* + *-osis*] **:** a condition of having hair of variegated color

**het·er·ot·ri·chous** \\¦hed·ə¦rä·trə̇kəs\\ *adj* [prob. fr. NL *heterotrichus*] **:** having the thallus differentiated into a prostrate portion and an upright or projecting system ⟨many algae are ~⟩ — **het·er·ot·ri·chy** \\,=='rä·trə̇kē\\ *n* -ES

**het·er·ot·ro·pal** \\¦==¦rä·trəpəl\\ *adj* [Gk *heterotropos* of different sort, various + E *-al*] **:** AMPHITROPOUS

**het·er·o·troph** \\'hed·ərō·,träf\\ *also* **het·er·o·trophe** \\-,trōf\\ *n* -s [*heter-* + *-troph* or *-trophe* (prob. fr. Gk *trophos* one that feeds)] **:** a heterotrophic individual — **het·er·ot·ro·phism** \\,hed·ə'rä·trə,fizəm\\ *n* — **het·er·ot·ro·phy** \\-_fē\\ *n* -ES

**heterotroph hypothesis** *n* **:** a hypothesis in biology: the most primitive first life was heterotrophic — compare AUTOTROPH HYPOTHESIS

**het·er·o·troph·ic** \\¦hed·ərō·¦träfik, -¦trōf-\\ *adj* [*heter-* + *-trophic*] **:** obtaining nourishment from outside sources; *specif* **:** requiring complex organic compounds of nitrogen and carbon for metabolic synthesis ⟨most animals and those plants that do not carry on photosynthesis are ~⟩ — opposed to *autotrophic* — **het·er·o·troph·i·cal·ly** \\-fə̇k(ə)lē\\ *adv*

**het·er·o·tro·pia** \\,==='trōpēə\\ *n* -s [NL, fr. *heter-* + *-tropia*] **:** STRABISMUS

**het·er·ot·ro·pous** \\¦hed·ə¦rä·trəpəs\\ *adj* [Gk *heterotropos* of different sort, various, fr. *hetero-* heter- + *-tropos* -tropous] **:** AMPHITROPOUS

**het·ero·typic** \\¦hed·ərō+\\ *also* **het·ero·typical** \\"+\\ *adj* [*heter-* + *typic* or *typical*] **1 :** of or being the reduction division of meiosis as contrasted with typical mitotic division — compare HOMEOTYPIC **2** *usu heterotypical* **:** of or being a genus containing groups of species showing various degrees of relationship **3 :** different in kind, arrangement, or form ⟨a ~ ecological community⟩ ⟨monkeys paralyzed with one poliomyelitis virus . . . show no . . . antibody . . . to a ~ virus —Isabel M. Morgan⟩ — **het·ero·typically** \\"+\\ *adv*

**heterousia** *var of* HETEROOUSIA

**het·ero·xanthine** \\¦hed·ərō+\\ *also* **het·ero·xanthin** \\"+\\ *n* [ISV *heter-* + *xanthine* or *xanthin*] **:** a crystalline compound $C_6H_6N_4O_2$ sometimes found in urine; 7-methyl-xanthine

**het·er·ox·e·nous** \\¦hed·ə¦räksənəs\\ *adj* [*heter-* + *-xenous*] **:** infesting more than one kind of host; *esp* **:** requiring at least two kinds of host to complete the life cycle — used of various parasites (as the malaria parasites or the liver flukes)

**het·er·o·ze·te·sis** \\,hed·ərōzē'tēsə̇s\\ *n, pl* **heterozete·ses** \\-tē,sēz\\ [NL, fr. *heter-* + Gk *zētēsis* search, inquiry (fr. *zētein* to seek, inquire)] **:** IGNORATIO ELENCHI

**het·ero·zygosis** \\¦hed·ərō+\\ *n* [NL, fr. *heter-* + *zygosis*] **1 :** a union of genetically dissimilar gametes to form a heterozygote **2 :** the state of being a heterozygote — compare HOMOZYGOSIS

**het·ero·zy·gos·i·ty** \\"+zī¦gäsəd·ē\\ *n* -ES **:** HETEROZYGOSIS 2

**het·ero·zygote** \\"+\\ *n* [*heter-* + *zygote*] **:** an animal or plant that contains genes for both members of at least one pair of allelomorphic characters and that segregates according to Mendel's laws and does not breed true to type with respect to the specified character **:** a heterozygous individual — compare HOMOZYGOTE — **het·ero·zygotic** \\"+\\ *adj*

**het·er·o·zy·gous** \\¦hed·ərō¦zīgəs\\ *adj* [*heter-* + *-zygous*] **1 :** of, relating to, or derived from a heterozygote **2 :** producing two types of gametes with respect to one or more allelomorphic characters — opposed to *homozygous* — **het·er·o·zy·gous·ly** *adv*

**heth** *also* **cheth** *or* **hheth** *or* **kheth** *or* **het** \\'k̲āt, -āth, -ās, -et, -eth, -es\\ *n* -s [Heb *ḥēth*] **1 :** the eighth letter of the Hebrew alphabet — symbol ח; see ALPHABET table **2 :** the letter of the Phoenician alphabet or of various other Semitic alphabets that corresponds to Hebrew heth

**het·man** \\'hetmən\\ *n* -s [Pol, fr. G *hauptmann* headman] **:** a cossack leader

**het·man·ate** \\-ə,nāt\\ *n* -s **:** the administration of a hetman

**HETP** \\,ā,chē,tē'pē\\ *abbr or n* -s hexaethyl tetraphosphate

**Het·ra·zan** \\'he·trə,zan\\ *trademark* — used for diethylcarbamazine citrate

**hets** *pl of* HET

**het up** *adj* [ˢhet] *chiefly dial* : being in a state of excitement : worked up : ANGRY — used esp. to connote indignation or enthusiasm ⟨all *het up* over going⟩

**HEU** *abbr* hydroelectric unit

**heu·chera** \'hyükərə\ *n* [NL, after J. H. von *Heucher* †1747 Ger. botanist] **1** *cap* : a genus of No. American herbs (family Saxifragaceae) having basal cordate or orbicular leaves and small panicled flowers with petals entire or lacking **2** -s : any plant of the genus *Heuchera*

**heu gase** *or* **heu gaze** \hyü'gāz\ [origin unknown] — used as a view halloo in hunting otters

**heugh** *or* **heuch** \'kyük\ *n* -s [ME *hough, hogh, heuch,* fr. OE *hōh*] **1** *chiefly Scot* **a** : a steep crag or cliff **b** : a ravine or glen with overhanging sides **2** *chiefly Scot* **a** : a shaft of a coal mine **b** : an open coal pit

**heu·land·ite** \'hyülən,dīt\ *n* -s [Henry *Heuland* 19th cent. Eng. mineral collector + E *-ite*] : a zeolite $(Na,Ca)_{4-6}Al_6(Al,Si)_4Si_{26}O_{72}.24H_2O$ consisting of a hydrous aluminosilicate of sodium and calcium often occurring as foliated masses with pearly luster on the cleavage surfaces

**¹heu·ris·tic** \(')hyü¦ristik, -tēk\ *adj* [G *heuristisch,* fr. NL *heuristicus,* fr. Gk *heuriskein* to discover, find] : serving to guide, discover, or reveal; *specif* : valuable for stimulating or conducting empirical research but unproved or incapable of proof — often used of arguments, methods, or constructs that assume or postulate what remains to be proven or that lead a person to find out for himself ⟨even vague and dubious assertions can render good services to empirical research as a ~ stimulus —Edgar Zilsel⟩ ⟨making the hypothesis more . . . completely understood as a ~ device —J.M.Yinger⟩ ⟨some wish to avoid the term . . . not deeming it a useful ~ tool —R.W.Firth⟩ — **heu·ris·ti·cal·ly** \-tək(ə)lē, -tēk-, -li\ *adv*

**²heuristic** \"\ *n* -s [G *heuristik,* fr. NL *heuristica,* fr. fem. of *heuristicus*] **1** : the science or art of heuristic procedure **2** : heuristic argument

**heurt** *or* **heurte** *var of* HURT

**heus·ler alloy** \'hyüslə(r)-\ *n, usu cap H* [after Conrad *Heusler* 19th cent. Ger. mining engineer and chemist] **1** : a magnetic alloy composed of the nonmagnetic metals copper, manganese, and tin approximately in the proportions $Cu_2MnSn$ **2** : any similar magnetic alloy (as one in which tin is replaced by aluminum, arsenic, antimony, bismuth, or boron, or copper is replaced by silver)

**hev** *dial var of* HAVE

**he·vea** \'hēvēə\ *n* [NL, fr. Sp *jebe* rubber plant, of AmerInd origin] **1** *cap* : a small genus of So. American trees (family Euphorbiaceae) which have trifoliolate leaves, small panicled apetalous flowers, and a capsular fruit and many of which yield latex used in rubber manufacture **2** -s : any plant of the genus *Hevea*

**¹hew** \'hyü\ *vb* **hewed; hewed** *or* **hewn; hewing; hews** [ME *hewen,* fr. OE *hēawan;* akin to OHG *houwan* to hew, ON *höggva* to hew, L *cudere* to beat, Toch (A) *kot* to split] *vt* **1** : to cut with hard or rough blows of a heavy cutting instrument (as an ax, broadsword, or large chisel) ⟨the miners who ~ out the coal —G.B.Shaw⟩ **2** : to fell (as a tree) by blows of an ax : cut down **3** : to shape, form, create, or bring into being with or as if with hard rough blows or efforts ⟨my own grandparents ~*ed* their farms from the wilderness —J.T. Shotwell⟩ ⟨~ out a rock tomb⟩ ~ *vi* **1** : to make rough heavy cutting blows (as with an ax) **2** : ADHERE, CONFORM, STICK ⟨each of his . . . masterpieces ~*s* to its stanza form with meticulous accuracy —Clement Wood⟩ ⟨if he is elected . . . he will ~ to the constitutional law —*N.Y.Times*⟩ ⟨avoiding sentimentality by ~*ing* doggedly to domestic realism —Roger Pippett⟩ — often used in the phrase *hew to the line* ⟨I learned in a hard school and I know the importance of ~*ing* to the line —Archie Binns⟩ **syn** see CUT

**²hew** \"\ *now chiefly dial var of* HUE

**hew·er** \'hyüə(r), 'hyü(ə)r, 'hyüə\ *n* -s [ME, fr. *hewen,* v. + *-er*] : a person whose work is hewing ⟨these skilled island ~*s* and masons work with primitive axes, chisels and saws —J.P. O'Donnell⟩ ⟨let them be ~*s* of wood and drawers of water unto all the congregation —Josh 9:21 (AV)⟩ ⟨deserve a better future than being mere ~*s* of wood and drawers of water for the highly industrialized countries —Emilio Abello⟩

**hew·ett·ite** \'hyüə,tīt\ *n* -s [D. Foster *Hewett* b1881 Am. geologist + E *-ite*] : a mineral $CaV_6O_{16}.9H_2O$ consisting of a hydrous calcium vanadate occurring in mahogany-red silky aggregates (sp. gr. 2.5)

**hew·gag** \'hyü,gag\ *n* [origin unknown] : a toy pipe of esp. the latter part of the 19th century resembling a kazoo ⟨sound the bull-roarers, and the ~*s* —W.A.White⟩

**hew·let** \'hyülət\ *var of* HOWLET

**hewn** \'hyün\ *adj* [fr. past part. of ¹*hew*] **1** : felled, cut, or shaped by hewing (as with an ax) : roughly squared ⟨a house built of ~ logs⟩ **2** *of stone* : roughly dressed (as with a hammer)

**¹hex** \'heks\ *vb* -ED/-ING/-ES *vi* [PaG *hexe,* fr. G *hexen,* fr. *hexe,* n.] : to practice witchcraft ~ *vt* [PaG *verhexe,* fr. *ver-* for- + *hexe,* v.] **1** : to practice witchcraft upon : put a hex on ⟨he can . . . ~ him, and he knows it —J.H.Allen⟩ **2** : to affect as if by an evil spell : JINX, QUEER ⟨giving in to an unscientific fear of ~*ing* the whole project —Daniel Lang⟩ ⟨~*es* the acoustics —*Springfield (Mass.) Daily News*⟩

**²hex** \"\ *n* -ES *often attrib* **1** : SPELL, ENCHANTMENT, JINX ⟨my grandmother used to say some families had a ~ on them —Sherman Kent⟩ ⟨sung to death in a musical ~ rendered by an enemy —*Newsweek*⟩ ⟨we came to the conclusion that he had put a ~ on the cars —Linda Braidwood⟩ **2** [PaG *hex* & G *hexe,* fr. MHG *hecse, häxe;* akin to OHG *hagzissa, hagazussa* harpy, witch — more at HAG (harpy)] : a person who practices witchcraft : WITCH ⟨I couldn't talk to you without twenty old ~*es* watching —Sinclair Lewis⟩

**³hex** \"\ *adj* [short for *hexagonal*] : hexagonal in shape ⟨a bolt with a ~ head⟩

**-hex** *abbr* **1** hexachord **2** hexagon; hexagonal

**hexa-** *or* **hex-** *comb form* [Gk, fr. *hex* six — more at SIX] **1** : six ⟨*hexa*tomic⟩ **2** : containing six atoms, groups, or equivalents ⟨*hexa*oxide⟩ ⟨*hexa*cetate⟩

**hex·a·bi·ose** *or* **hex·o·bi·ose** \,heksə'bī,ōs\ *n* [*hexabiose* fr. *hexa-* + *biose; hexobiose,* ISV *hexo-* (fr. *hexa-*) + *biose*] : a disaccharide (as maltose) yielding two hexose molecules on hydrolysis

**hex·a·bromide** \¦heksə+\ *n* [*hexa-* + *bromide*] : a bromide containing six atoms of bromine in the molecule

**hex·a·canth** \'heksə,kan(t)th\ *or* **hex·a·can·thous** \¦==¦kan(t)thəs\ *adj* [NL *hexacanthus,* fr. *hexa-* + *-acanthus* (fr. Gk *akantha* thorn) — more at ACANTH-] *zool* : having six hooks; *specif* : constituting the onchosphere of a tapeworm

**hexachlor-** *or* **hexachloro-** *comb form* [*hexa-* + *chlor-*] : containing six atoms of chlorine — compare CHLOR-

**hexa·chloride** \¦heksə+\ *n* [*hexa-* + *chloride*] : a chloride containing six atoms of chlorine in the molecule

**hex·a·chlo·ro** \¦heksə¦klō(,)rō, -lō(-\ *adj* [*hexachlor-*] : containing six atoms of chlorine

**hex·a·chlo·ro·cyclohexane** \¦==¦==+\ *n* [*hexachlor-* + *cyclohexane*] : a hexachloro derivative of cyclohexane; *esp* : BENZENE HEXACHLORIDE

**hex·a·chlo·ro·ethane** \"+\ *also* **hex·a·chlor·ethane** \¦heksə,klōr, -lōr+\ *n* [ISV *hexa-* + *chlor-* + *ethane*] : a toxic crystalline compound $C_2Cl_6$ of camphoraceous odor made usu. by chlorinating tetrachloroethylene and used esp. in smoke bombs and in the control of liver flukes in ruminants

**hex·a·chlo·ro·phene** \heksə'klōrə,fēn, -lōr-\ *n* -s [*hexachlor-* + *-phene* (fr. *-phenol*)] : a crystalline phenolic antibacterial agent $CH_2(C_6HCl_3OH)_2$ made by condensing a trichlorophenol with formaldehyde and used esp. in soap

**hexa·chloroplatinate** \¦heksə+\ *n* [*hexa-* + *chloroplatinate*] : CHLOROPLATINATE

**hex·a·chord** \'heksə,kȯrd, -ō(ə)d\ *n* [*hexa-* + *-chord*] **1** : a diatonic series of six tones having a semitone between the third and fourth tones that formed the basic unit of analysis from the 11th to the 18th centuries, seven such overlapping series beginning successively on G, C, and F comprising all of the recognized tones — compare GREAT SCALE, SOLMIZATION **2** : a 6-stringed musical instrument — **hex·a·chord·ic** \¦==¦kȯrdik\ *adj*

**hex·a·con·tane** \,heksə'kän,tān\ *n* -s [ISV *hexacont-* (fr. Gk *hexēkonta* sixty) + *-ane*] : a solid paraffin hydrocarbon $C_{60}H_{122}$; *esp* : the normal hydrocarbon $CH_3(CH_2)_{58}CH_3$

**hex·a·co·ral·la** \,heksəkə'ralə\ *or* **hex·a·co·ral·lia** \-lēə\ [NL, fr. *hexa-* + L *coralla, corallia* (pl. of *corallum, corallium* coral) — more at CORAL] *syn of* ZOANTHARIA

**hex·a·co·sane** \,heksə'kō,sān\ *n* -s [ISV *hexacos-* (fr. *hexa-* + *-cos-* — fr. *eicosa-*) + *-ane*] : a solid paraffin hydrocarbon $C_{26}H_{54}$; *esp* : the normal hydrocarbon $CH_3(CH_2)_{24}CH_3$

**hex·ac·ti·nal** \¦hek(,)sak¦tīn³l, (')hek¦saktənəl\ *or* **hex·ac·tine** \(')hek¦sak,tīn, -,tən\ *adj* [*hexa-* + *-actinal* or *-actine*] : having six rays ⟨~ sponge spicules⟩

**¹hex·ac·ti·nel·lid** \¦hek(,)saktə¦neləd\ *adj* [NL *Hexactinellida*] : of, relating to, or characteristic of the Hyalospongiae

**²hexactinellid** \"\ *n* -s : one of the Hyalospongiae

**hex·ac·ti·nel·li·da** \,=(,)==¦neləda\ [NL, fr. *Hexactinella,* genus of sponges (fr. *hexa-* + *actin-* + *-ella*) + *-ida*] *syn of* HYALOSPONGIAE

**hex·ac·tin·i·an** \¦hek(,)sak¦tinēən\ *adj* [*hexa-* + *actin-* + *-an*] : having the tentacles or mesenteries in multiples of six

**hex·ad** \'hek,sad\ *or* **hex·ade** \-,sād\ *n* -s [LL *hexad-, hexas* the number six, fr. Gk, fr. *hex* six + *-ad-, -as* -ad — more at SIX] : a group or series of six

**hex·a·decane** \¦heksə+\ *n* -s [ISV *hexadec-* (fr. *hexa-* + *deca-*) + *-ane*] : any of numerous isomeric hydrocarbons $C_{16}H_{34}$; *esp* : CETANE

**hex·a·dec·a·no·ic acid** \¦heksə¦dekə¦nōik-\ *n* [*hexadecane* + *-oic*] : PALMITIC ACID

**hex·a·dec·a·nol** \,==='dekə,nȯl, -,nōl\ *n* -s [*hexadecane* + *-ol*] : any of several alcohols $C_{16}H_{33}OH$ derived from cetane; *esp* : CETYL ALCOHOL

**hex·a·dec·ene** \-'de,sēn\ *n* -s [ISV *hexadec-* (fr. *hexa-* + *deca-*) + *-ene*] : any of several straight-chain isomeric hydrocarbons $C_{16}H_{32}$ of the ethylene series; *esp* : CETENE

**hexa·decyl** \¦heksə+\ *n* [*hexadecane* + *-yl*] : an alkyl radical derived from a hexadecane; *esp* : CETYL

**hex·ad·ic** \(')hek¦sadik\ *adj* [*hexad* + *-ic*] : of or relating to a hexad

**hex·a·di·ene** \,heksə'dī,ēn\ *n* -s [ISV *hexa-* + *-diene*] : any of six straight-chain isomeric diolefins $C_6H_{10}$

**hex·a·em·er·al** \¦heksə¦emərəl\ *or* **hex·a·em·er·ic** \-rik\ *adj* [*hexaemeron* + *-al* or *-ic*] : of or relating to the hexaemeron

**hex·a·em·er·on** \,=='emə,rän\ *or* **hex·a·hem·er·on** \-'he-\ *n* -s [LL *hexaëmeron,* fr. Gk *hexaēmeron,* fr. neut. of *hexaēmeros* of six days, fr. *hexa-* + *hēmera* day — more at HEMERA] : the six days of the creation

**hexa·ethyl tetraphosphate** \¦heksə+ . . . -\ *n* [*hexa-* + *ethyl*] : an insecticide $(C_2H_5)_6P_4O_{13}$ obtained synthetically usu. as a yellow liquid mixture containing tetraethyl pyrophosphate — called also *HETP*

**hexa·fluoride** \"+\ *n* [*hexa-* + *fluoride*] : a fluoride containing six atoms of fluorine in the molecule

**hex·a·foos** \'heksə,füs\ *n, pl* **hexafoos** [PaG *hexefuss,* fr. *hex* witch + *fuss* foot (fr. OHG *fuoz*) — more at HEX, FOOT] : a three-toed or triangular mark put on some Pennsylvania barns to keep evil spirits from the cattle or for decoration

**¹hex·a·gon** \'heksə,gän *sometimes* -sēgən\ *n* -s [Gk *hexagōnon,* neut. of *hexagōnos* hexagonal, fr. *hexa-* six (fr. *hex*) + *-gōnos* -cornered, -angled (fr. *gōnia* angle, corner) — more at SIX, -GON] : a plane polygon of six angles and therefore six sides — see AREA table **2** : a hexagonal object

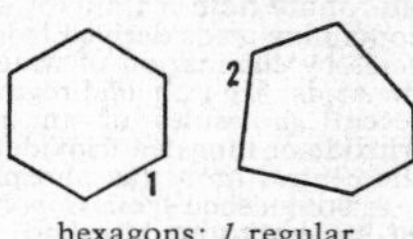

hexagons: *1* regular, *2* irregular

**²hexagon** \"\ *adj* : constituting a hexagon ⟨a ~ tower⟩

**hex·ag·o·nal** \(')hek¦sagən³l, -saig-\ *adj* **1** : having six angles and six sides : six-sided : divided into hexagons **2** : having a hexagon as section or base **3** : relating or belonging to a hexagonal system — see SCALENOHEDRON illustration — **hex·ag·o·nal·ly** \-³lē, -³li\ *adv*

**hexagonal system** *n* : a crystal system characterized by three equal lateral axes intersecting at angles of 60 degrees and a vertical axis of variable length at right angles (as in the hexagonal prism) — see CRYSTAL SYSTEM illustration

**hex·a·gram** \'heksə,gram\ *n* [ISV *hexa-* + *-gram*] : a figure formed by completing externally an equilateral triangle on each side of a regular hexagon

hexagram

**¹hex·a·gram·mid** \¦==¦gra,mid\ *adj* [NL *Hexagrammidae*] : of or relating to the Hexagrammidae

**²hexagrammid** \"\ *n* -s : a member of the family Hexagrammidae

**hex·a·gram·mi·dae** \,heksə'gramə,dē\ *n pl, cap* [NL, fr. *Hexagrammos,* type genus + *-idae*] : a family of marine carnivorous fishes (order Scleroparei) of the northern Pacific ocean that includes several food fishes — see GREENLING

**hex·a·gram·mos** \-a,mäs\ *n, cap* [NL, fr. *hexa-* + *-grammos* (fr. Gk *gramma* line) — more at GRAMMAR] : the type genus of the family Hexagrammidae

**hex·a·he·dral** \¦heksə¦hēdrəl\ *adj* [NL *hexahedron* + E *-al*] : having the form of a hexahedron

**hexahedral coordination** *n* : the state or condition of being surrounded by eight atoms whose centers lie at the corners of a hexahedron

**hex·a·he·dron** \,=='=drən\ *n, pl* **hexahedrons** \-rənz\ *also* **hexahe·dra** \-rə\ [NL, fr. LL, fr. Gk *hexaedron,* fr. neut. of *hexaedros* of six surfaces, fr. *hexa-* + *-edros* (fr. *hedra* base, seat)] **1** : a polyhedron of six faces **2** : ¹CUBE 5

**hexahemeron** *var of* HEXAEMERON

**hexahydr-** *or* **hexahydro-** *comb form* [ISV *hexa-* + *hydr-*] : combined with six atoms of hydrogen — in names of chemical compounds ⟨*hexahydro*benzene⟩

**hexa·hydrate** \¦heksə+\ *n* [*hexa-* + *hydrate*] : a chemical compound with six molecules of water — **hexa·hydrated** \"+\ *adj*

**hex·a·hy·dric** \¦heksə¦hīdrik\ *adj* [*hexa-* + *-hydric*] : HEXAHYDROXY — used esp. of alcohols and phenols

**hex·a·hy·drite** \,=='hī,drīt\ *n* -s [ISV *hexa-* + *hydr-* + *-ite*] : a mineral $MgSO_4.6H_2O$ consisting of a hydrous magnesium sulfate

**hexa·hydroxy** \¦heksə+\ *adj* [*hexahydroxy-*] : containing six hydroxyl groups in the molecule

**hexahydroxy-** *comb form* [ISV *hexa-* + *hydroxy-*] : containing six hydroxyl groups — in names of chemical compounds

**hex·a·kis·octahedron** \¦heksəkis+\ *n* [NL, fr. Gk *hexakis* six times (fr. *hex* six) + NL *octahedron* — more at SIX] : HEXOCTAHEDRON

**hex·a·kis·tetrahedron** \"+\ *n* [NL, fr. Gk *hexakis* six times + NL *tetrahedron*] : HEXTETRAHEDRON

**hex·a·mer** \'heksəmə(r)\ *n* -s [*hexa-* + *-mer*] : a polymer formed from six molecules of a monomer — **hex·a·mer·ic** \¦heksə¦merik\ *adj*

**hex·am·er·al** \(')hek¦sam(ə)rəl\ *adj* [*hexamerous* + *-al*] : HEXAMEROUS

**hex·am·er·ous** \-rəs\ *adj* [*hexa-* + *-merous*] **1** *bot* : consisting of six parts : having floral whorls composed of six members **2** *zool* : having six parts or parts in multiples of six arranged radially — used esp. of anthozoans in which the tentacles and mesenteries are in multiples of six

**hexa·metaphosphate** \¦heksə+\ *n* [*hexa-* + *metaphosphate*] : a metaphosphate glass; *esp* : SODIUM HEXAMETAPHOSPHATE — not used systematically

**¹hex·am·e·ter** \hek'samәd·ə(r), -mәtә-\ *n* [L, fr. Gk *hexametron,* fr. neut. of *hexametros*] : a line of six metrical feet or of six dipodies: as **a** : the six-foot dactylic line of Greek and Latin epic poetry in which the first four feet are dactyls or spondees, the fifth a dactyl, and the sixth a spondee (as in Vergil's "Arma virumque cano Trojae qui primus ab oris") **b** : the six-foot dactylic line of English poetry (as in Coleridge's "Strongly it bears us along on swelling and limitless billows")

**²hexameter** \(')=¦==\ *adj* [L, fr. Gk *hexametros* of six meters, fr. *hexa-* + *-metros* (akin to *metron* measure) — more at MEASURE] **1** : having six metrical feet — used esp. of dactylic or spondaic verse **2** : having six dipodies — used esp. of classical iambic, trochaic, or anapestic verse

**hex·a·me·tho·ni·um** \,heksəmә'thōnēәm\ *n* -s [NL, fr. *hexa-* + *methonium*] : the bivalent substituted ammonium ion $[(CH_3)_3N(CH_2)_6N(CH_3)_3]^{++}$ derived by methylation of hexamethylenediamine; *also* : any salt (as the chloride or bromide) containing this ion used as a ganglionic blocking agent in the treatment of hypertension

**hexa·methyl** \¦heksə+\ *adj* [ISV *hexa-* + *methyl*] : containing six methyl groups in the molecule

**hexa·methylene** \"+\ *n* [ISV *hexa-* + *methylene*] **1** : CYCLOHEXANE **2** : the bivalent radical $-CH_2(CH_2)_4CH_2-$ derived from normal hexane by removal of one hydrogen atom from each end carbon atom

**hexamethylene·diamine** \"+\ *n* [ISV *hexamethylene* + *diamine*] : a crystalline base $H_2N(CH_2)_6NH_2$ made by hydrogenation of adiponitrile and used in the manufacture of nylon; 1,6-hexane-diamine

**hexa·methylene·tetramine** \"+\ *n* [ISV *hexamethylene* + *tetramine*] : a crystalline tricyclic weak base $(CH_2)_6N_4$ made by the action of ammonia on formaldehyde and used chiefly as a source of formaldehyde (as in the manufacture of phenolic resins), as a vulcanization accelerator, and in medicine as a urinary antiseptic — called also *hexamine, methenamine*

**hex·am·e·trist** \hek'samә-trəst\ *n* -s [*hexameter* + *-ist*] : one who writes in hexameters

**hex·a·mine** \,heksə'mēn, hek'samən\ *n* [by contr.] : HEXAMETHYLENETETRAMINE

**hex·am·i·ta** \hek'samәd·ә\ *n, cap* [NL, fr. *hexa-* + *-mita* (fr. Gk *mitos* thread) — more at DIMITY] : a genus (the type of the family Hexamitidae) of binucleate zooflagellates having six anterior and two trailing flagella and including free-living forms as well as intestinal parasites of birds (as *H. meleagridis*) and of salmonid fishes (as *H. salmonis*) that are associated with enteritides — compare GIARDIA

**hex·am·i·ti·a·sis** \hek,samә'tīәsәs\ *n* -ES [NL, fr. *Hexamita* + *-iasis*] : infestation with or disease caused by flagellates of the genus *Hexamita*

**¹hex·am·i·tid** \(')hek¦samәd·әd\ *adj* [NL *Hexamitidae,* family of zooflagellates, fr. *Hexamita,* type genus + *-idae*] : of or relating to the genus *Hexamita* or family Hexamitidae

**²hexamitid** \"\ *n* -s : a member of the genus *Hexamita* or family Hexamitidae

**hex·ammine** \hek'sa,mēn, -mən, ,heksә'mēn\ *n* [*hexa-* + *ammine*] : an ammine containing six molecules of ammonia

**hex·a·nal** \'heksә,nal\ *n* -s [*hexane* + *-al*] : a volatile liquid aldehyde $CH_3(CH_2)_4CHO$ of irritating odor obtained from several volatile oils (as eucalyptus oil and peppermint oil) — called also *caproaldehyde*

**hex·an·chi·dae** \hek'saŋkә,dē\ *n pl, cap* [NL, fr. *Hexanchus,* type genus + *-idae*] : a family of sharks consisting of many fossil forms and a few living forms that have one dorsal fin and a palatoquadrate which articulates with the postorbital part of the skull

**hex·an·chus** \hek'saŋkәs\ *n, cap* [NL, fr. *hexa-* + *anchus* (prob. fr. Gk *anchein* to strangle) — more at ANGER] : the type genus of the family *Hexanchidae* sometimes considered to include all living members of the family but sometimes restricted to those with six pairs of branchial clefts

**hex·ane** \'hek,sān\ *n* -s [ISV *hexa-* + *-ane*] : any of five isomeric volatile liquid paraffin hydrocarbons $C_6H_{14}$ found in petroleum; *esp* : the normal hydrocarbon $CH_3(CH_2)_4CH_3$

**hexa·nitrate** \¦heksә+\ *n* [*hexa-* + *nitrate*] : a compound containing six nitrate groups in the molecule

**hexa·ni·tro·diphenylamine** \¦heksә¦nī-trō+\ *n* [ISV *hexa-* + *nitro-* + *diphenylamine*] : a light-yellow poisonous crystalline compound $[(NO_2)_3C_6H_2]_2NH$ made by nitrating diphenylamine and used as a high explosive — called also *dipicrylamine;* see AURANTIA

**hex·a·no·ic acid** \¦heksә¦nōik-\ *n* [ISV *hexan-* (fr. *hexane*) + *-oic*] : CAPROIC ACID — used in the system of nomenclature adopted by the International Union of Pure and Applied Chemistry

**hex·a·no·yl** \¦heksә¦nōәl; hek'sanә,wil, -,wēl\ *n* -s [ISV *hexan-* (fr. *hexanoic acid*) + *-oyl*] : CAPROYL

**hexa·partite** \¦heksә+\ *adj* [*hexa-* + *partite*] : SEXPARTITE

**hexa·petaloid** \"+\ *adj* [*hexa-* + *petaloid*] : having or being a perianth with six petaloid divisions

**hexa·petalous** \"+\ *adj* [*hexa-* + *-petalous*] : having or being a perianth with six petals

**hex·a·pla** \'heksәplә\ *n* -s *often cap* [LL, fr. Gk *hexapla,* fr. neut. pl. of *hexaplous, hexaploos* sixfold, fr. *hexa-* + *-plous, -ploos* -fold (as in *diploos* double) — more at DOUBLE] : an edition or work in six texts or versions in parallel columns — compare TETRAPLA — **hex·a·plar** \-lә(r)\ *adj, often cap*

**hex·a·plar·ic** \¦heksә¦plarik\ *also* **hex·a·plar·i·an** \¦==¦pla(a)rēәn\ *adj, often cap* : of or relating to a hexapla; *esp* : of or relating to the edition of the Old Testament compiled by Origen in the 3d century A.D. and consisting of the Hebrew text, a transliteration in Greek, and the Greek versions of Aquila, Symmachus, the Septuagint, and Theodotion

**¹hex·a·ploid** \'heksә,plȯid\ *adj* [ISV *hexa-* + *-ploid*] : sixfold in appearance or arrangement; *specif* : having or being six times the monoploid chromosome number ⟨a ~ cell⟩ — compare DIPLOID, HAPLOID, POLYPLOID

**²hexaploid** \"\ *n* -s : a hexaploid individual

**hex·a·ploidy** \-dē\ *n* -ES : the condition of being hexaploid

**¹hex·a·pod** \'heksә,päd\ *n* -s [Gk *hexapod-, hexapous,* adj., six-footed, fr. *hexa-* + *pod-, pous* foot — more at FOOT] : INSECT 1b

**²hexapod** \"\ *adj* **1** : six-footed **2** : of or relating to insects

**hex·ap·o·da** \hek'sapәdә\ *n pl, cap* [NL, fr. *hexa-* + *-poda*] *in some classifications* : a class or other division of Arthropoda coextensive with the class Insecta — used esp. when Collembola and Protura are considered with the typical insects

**hex·ap·o·dous** \-dәs\ *adj* : HEXAPOD

**hex·ap·o·dy** \-dē\ *n* -ES [ISV *hexa-* + *-pody* (as in *dipody*)] : a prosodic line or group consisting of six feet

**hex·arch** \'hek,särk\ *adj* [*hexa-* + *-arch*] *of a root* : having six radiating vascular strands ⟨the ~ roots of an onion⟩

**¹hex·a·so·mic** \¦heksә¦sōmik\ *adj* [*hexa-* + *-somic*] : having one chromosome or a few chromosomes hexaploid in otherwise diploid nuclei

**²hexasomic** \"\ *n* -s : a hexasomic individual

**hex·as·ter** \'hek,sastә(r)\ *n* [NL, fr. *hexa-* + *-aster* (star)] : a triaxon sponge spicule usu. with equal rays

**hex·as·ter·oph·o·ra** \hek,sastә'räf(ә)rә\ *n pl, cap* [NL, fr. *hexaster* + *-o-* + *-phora*] : an order of Hyalospongiae comprising sponges with hexasters but not amphidisks among the spicules

**hex·a·stich** \'heksә,stik\ *also* **hex·as·ti·chon** \hek'sastә,kän\ *n, pl* **hexastichs** *also* **hex·as·ti·cha** \=ˈ=stәkә\ [NL *hexastichon,* fr. ML, prob. fr. Gk *hexastichon,* neut. of *hexastichos* of six rows, of six lines, fr. *hexa-* + *stichos* row, line; akin to Gk *steichein* to go — more at STICH] : a group, stanza, or poem of six lines — **hex·a·stich·ic** \¦heksә¦stikik\ *adj*

**hex·a·sty·lar** \¦heksә¦stīlә(r)\ *adj* : HEXASTYLE

**¹hex·a·style** \'heksә,stīl\ *n* [L *hexastylos,* adj., of six columns] : a portico with six columns

**²hexastyle** \"\ *adj* : marked by columniation with six columns across the front — compare DISTYLE

**hex·a·sty·los** \,heksә'stī,läs\ *n* -ES [NL, fr. L, adj., of six columns, fr. Gk, fr. *hexa-* + *stylos* column, pillar — more at STOIC] : a hexastyle building

**hexa·syllabic** \¦heksә+\ *adj* [Gk *hexasyllabos* (fr. *hexa-* + *syllabē* syllable) + E *-ic* — more at SYLLABLE] : comprising six syllables

**hexa·syllable** \"+\ *n* [*hexa-* + *syllable*] : a word of six syllables

**hexatetrahedron** *var of* HEXTETRAHEDRON

**hex·a·teu·chal** \¦heksә¦tükәl, -sә-¦tyü-\ *adj, usu cap* [*Hexateuch* the first 6 books of the Bible (fr. *hexa-* + *-teuch,* as in *Pentateuch* the first 5 books of the Bible) + E *-al* — more at PENTATEUCHAL] : of or relating to the first six books of the Old Testament

**hex·atomic** \¦heks+\ *adj* [*hexa-* + *atomic*] **1** : consisting of six atoms **2** : having six replaceable atoms or radicals

**hex·a·tri·a·con·tane** \,heksә,trīә'kän,tān\ *n* [ISV *hexatriacont-* (fr. *hexa-* + *triacont-* — fr. Gk *triakonta* thirty) + *-ane*]

: a solid paraffin hydrocarbon $C_{36}H_{74}$; *esp* : the normal hydrocarbon $CH_3(CH_2)_{34}CH_3$

**hexa·valent** \¦heksə+\ *adj* [ISV *hexa-* + *valent*] : having a valence of six

**hex·ax·on** \hek'sak,sän\ *n* [NL, fr. *hexa-* + Gk *axōn* axle, axis — more at AXIS] : HEXASTER

**hexed** *past of* HEX

**hex·en·be·sen** \'heksən,bāzᵊn\ *n* -s [G, fr. *hexen* (pl. of *hexe* witch) + *besen* broom, fr. OHG *besmo* — more at HEX, BESOM] : WITCHES'-BROOM

**hex·ene** \'hek,sēn\ *n* -s [ISV *hexa-* + *-ene*] : any of the three straight-chain hexylenes

**hex·er** \'heksə(r)\ *n* -s [¹*hex* + *-er*] : a person who hexes

**hex·e·rei** \,heksə'rī\ *n* -s [PaG, fr. G, fr. *hexen* to practice witchcraft + *-erei* -ery (fr. MHG *-erīe*, fr. OF *-erie*) — more at HEX] : WITCHCRAFT

**hexes** *pres 3d sing of* HEX, *pl of* HEX

**hex·oes·trol** *also* **hex·oes·trol** \hek'se,strōl, -rōl\ *n* -s [*hexane* + NL *estrus* or *oestrus* + E *-ol*] : a crystalline estrogenic diphenol $[HOC_6H_4CH(C_2H_5)-]_2$ derived from diphenylethane; dihydro-diethylstilbestrol

**hex·ine** \'hek,sīn\ *archaic var of* HEXYNE

**hexing** *pres part of* HEX

**hex·i·tol** \'heksə,tōl, -,tōl\ *n* -s [*hexose* + *-itol*] : any of the hexahydroxy alcohols $HOCH_2(CHOH)_4CH_2OH$ obtainable by reduction of the corresponding hexoses and in some cases (as mannitol and sorbitol) occurring naturally

**hex mark** *or* **hex sign** *n* : a usu. stylized often symbolic design placed on a structure (as a building or an enclosure for animals) for the purpose of warding off evil spirits or simply for its decorative effect — compare HEXAFOOS

**hexo·barbital** \¦heksə+\ *n* [*hexo-* (fr. *hexa-*) + *barbital*] : a crystalline barbiturate $C_{12}H_{16}N_2O_3$ used as a sedative and hypnotic and in the form of its soluble sodium salt as an intravenous anesthetic of short duration

**hexo·barbitone** \"+\ *n* [*hexo-* (fr. *hexa-*) + *barbitone*] : HEXOBARBITAL

**hexobiose** *var of* HEXABIOSE

**hex·octahedral** \(ˈ)heks+\ *adj* [NL *hexoctahedron* + E *-al*] : having the shape or symmetry of a hexoctahedron

**hex·octahedron** \"+\ *n* [NL, fr. *hexa-* + *octahedron*] : an isometric crystal having 48 equal triangular faces

hexoctahedron

**hex·ode** \'hek,sōd\ *n* -s [ISV *hexa-* + *-ode*] : a vacuum tube with six electrodes consisting of a cathode, an anode, a control grid, and three additional grids or other electrodes

**hex·o·ic acid** \(ˈ)hek¦sōik-\ *n* [*hexane* + *-oic*] : any of the monocarboxylic acids $C_5H_{11}COOH$ (as caproic acid) derived from the hexanes

**hexo·kinase** \¦heksō+\ *n* [ISV *hexose* + *kinase*] : any of several enzymes that occur in living tissues (as muscle, brain, yeast) and are important in carbohydrate metabolism in which they accelerate the phosphorylation of hexoses (as the formation of glucose 6-phosphate from glucose and adenosine triphosphate in the presence of magnesium ions or similar cations)

**-hex·ol** \'hek,sōl, -,sōl\ *n suffix* -s [ISV *hexa-* + *-ol*] : containing six hydroxyl groups ⟨cyclohexane*-hexol*⟩

**hex·one** \'hek,sōn\ *n* -s [ISV *hexa-* + *-one*; orig. formed as G *hexon*] : METHYL ISOBUTYL KETONE — used esp. of the technical grade

**hex·on·ic acid** \(ˈ)hek¦sänik-\ *n* [ISV *hexa-* + *-onic*] : an aldonic acid (as gluconic acid) that contains six carbon atoms in a molecule

**hex·os·a·mine** \hek'säsə,mēn\ *n* [ISV *hexose* + *amine*] : an amine (as glucosamine) derived from a hexose by replacement of hydroxyl by the amino group

**hex·o·san** \'heksō,san\ *n* -s [*hexose* + *-an*] : any of a class of polysaccharides (as fructosans or glucosans) yielding only hexoses on hydrolysis

**hex·ose** \'hek,sōs\ *n* -s [ISV *hexa-* + *-ose*] : any of a class of monosaccharides $C_6H_{12}O_6$ (as glucose or fructose) containing six carbon atoms in the molecule

**hexose phosphate** *n* : a phosphoric derivative of a hexose (as glucose phosphate) of which two types have been found in living tissues as intermediates of carbohydrate metabolism: **a** *or* **hexose monophosphate** : a mono-phosphoric ester or acylal $C_6H_{11}O_5(OPO_3H_2)$ **b** *or* **hexose diphosphate** : a diphosphoric ester $C_6H_{10}O_4(OPO_3H_2)_2$

**hex·oxide** \(ˈ)heks+\ *n* [*hex-* + *oxide*] : an oxide containing six atoms of oxygen in the molecule

**hex·partite** \(ˈ)heks+\ *adj* [*hexa-* + *partite*] *archit* : SEXPARTITE

**hex·tetrahedral** \(ˈ)heks+\ *adj* [NL *hextetrahedron* + E *-al*] : having the shape or symmetry of a hextetrahedron

**hex·tetrahedron** \"+\ *n* [NL, fr. *hexa-* + *tetrahedron*] : a 24-faced crystalline form of the tetrahedral group of the isometric system

**hex·u·lose** \'heksyə,lōs\ *n* -s [*hexa-* + *-ulose*] : a ketose $C_6H_{12}O_6$ (as fructose or sorbose) containing six carbon atoms in the molecule; *esp* : the isomer having the carbonyl group in the beta or 2-position; compare GLUCOSE illustration

**hex·u·ron·ic acid** \¦heksyə¦ränik-\ *n* [*hexa-* + *-uronic*] **1** : ASCORBIC ACID — now little used **2** : a uronic acid (as glucuronic acid) derived from a hexose (as glucose)

**hex·yl** \'heksəl\ *n* -s [ISV *hexa-* + *-yl*] : an alkyl radical $C_6H_{13}$ derived from a hexane; *esp* : the normal radical $CH_3(CH_2)_4CH_2-$

**hex·yl·ene** \'heksə,lēn\ *n* -s [ISV *hexyl* + *-ene*] : any of several liquid isomeric hydrocarbons $C_6H_{12}$ belonging to the ethylene series and including the hexenes

**hex·yl·ic acid** \(ˈ)hek¦silik-\ *n* [ISV *hexyl* + *-ic*] : HEXOIC ACID

**hexylresorcinol** \¦==¦==,=\ *n* [*hexyl* + *resorcinol*] : a white or yellowish white crystalline phenol $C_6H_{13}C_6H_3(OH)_2$ used in medicine as an antiseptic and internally as an anthelmintic; 1,3-dihydroxy-4-*n*-hexyl-benzene

**hex·yne** \'hek,sīn\ *n* -s [*hexa-* + *-yne*] : any of three isomeric straight-chain hydrocarbons $C_6H_{10}$ of the acetylene series

¹**hey** \'hā\ *interj* [ME *hei, hey*] — used to call attention or to incite, to express interrogation, surprise, or exultation, or with indefinite meaning in the burden of a song

²**hey** *var of* HAY

**hey cockalorum** *n* : HIGH COCKALORUM 1

¹**hey·day** \'hā,dā\ *interj* [fr. earlier *heyda*, alter. of ¹*hey*] *archaic* — used to express frolicsomeness, exultation, or sometimes wonder

²**heyday** *also* **heydey** \"\ *n* **1** *archaic* : high spirits : FROLICSOMENESS, WILDNESS, JOY **2** : a time of highest strength, vigor, or prosperity : ACME ⟨in the ~ of his power⟩ ⟨Athens and Venice in their commercial ~ —David Riesman⟩ ⟨during the ~ of the fur trade —Grace L. Nute⟩

¹**hey rube** *interj* [¹*hey* + *rube*] — used traditionally as a rallying cry among circus or carnival folk in a fight with townspeople

²**hey rube** *n* : a usu. free-for-all fight between circus or carnival folk and townspeople ⟨we found ourselves with an old-fashioned *hey rube* and obliged to move the show on that night —Herbert Gold⟩

**hf** *abbr* half

**HF** *abbr* **1** *often not cap* high frequency **2** home fleet **3** home forces

**Hf** *symbol* hafnium

**HFC** *abbr* high-frequency current

**HFM** *abbr* hold for money

**hg** *abbr* **1** hectogram **2** heliogram

**HG** *abbr* **1** Her Grace; His Grace **2** High German **3** home guard

**Hg** *symbol* [NL *hydrargyrum*] mercury

**h girder** *n, cap H* : a girder like an I beam but with wider flanges

**hgm** *abbr* hectogram

**hgt** *abbr* height

**HH** *abbr* **1** Her Highness; His Highness **2** His Holiness

**hhd** *abbr* hogshead

**hheth** *var of* HETH

**HHG** *abbr* household goods

**h hinge** *n, cap 1st H* : a hinge with leaves that when open resemble the letter H

H hinge

**h hour** *n, usu cap 1st H* [*h* (abbr. for *hour*)] : the hour set for launching a specific tactical operation — compare D DAY, ZERO HOUR

**hi** \'hī(ē), -ī(i)\ *interj* [ME *hy*] — used to express greeting or to attract attention

**HI** *abbr* high intensity

**hi·a·tal** \(ˈ)hī¦ād·ᵊl\ *adj* [*hiatus* + *-al*] **1** : having a rock texture in which the sizes of the individual crystals do not vary in a continuous series but are in two or more series of marked differences **2** : HIATUS

¹**hi·a·tus** \hī'ād·əs, -ātəs\ *n* -ES [L, fr. past part. of *hiare* to gape — more at YAWN] **1 a** : a break in or as if in a material object : GAP : APERTURE ⟨the weedy ~ between the town and the railroad —Willa Cather⟩ ⟨the ~ between the theory and the practice of the party —J.G.Colton⟩ **b** : a gap or passage through an anatomical part or organ; *esp* : a gap through which another part or organ passes **2 a** : an interruption or lapse in or as if in time or continuity ⟨the programs that are to fill in during the summer ~ —Saul Carson⟩ ⟨if deposition of sediment should cease everywhere for a time, a natural . . . ~ in the stratigraphic record would result —C.O.Dunbar⟩ ⟨~*es* of thought when certain links in the association of ideas are dropped —Edmund Wilson⟩ **b** : the occurrence of or relationship between two vowel sounds without pause or intervening consonantal sound (as when *beyond* is pronounced without a \y\ sound) **syn** see BREAK

²**hiatus** \"\ *adj* **1** : involving a hiatus **2** *of a hernia* : having a part that herniates through the esophageal hiatus of the diaphragm

**hi·ba arborvitae** \'hēbə-\ *n* [Jap *hiba*] : a large Japanese evergreen tree (*Thujopsis dolobrata*) that has glossy green leaves with a broad white band on the underside and is used as an ornamental

**hi·ba·chi** \hē'bächē\ *n* -s [Jap, fr. *hi* fire + *hachi* bowl] : a charcoal brazier

**hib·ber·tia** \hi'bərd·ēə, -rsh(ē)ə\ *n* [NL, fr. George *Hibbert* †1837 Eng. merchant and botanist + NL *-ia*] **1** *cap* : a genus of Australasian shrubs (family Dilleniaceae) having showy yellow or white flowers with numerous stamens and five fugacious petals **2** -s : any plant of the genus *Hibbertia*

**hi·ber·na·cle** \'hībə(r),nakəl\ *n* -s [NL *hibernaculum*] : HIBERNACULUM 2a ⟨brought forth a frog from his ~ in the leaves —John Burroughs⟩

**hi·ber·nac·u·lum** \,hībə(r)'nakyələm\ *n, pl* **hibernacu·la** \-lə\ [NL, fr. L, winter residence, fr. *hibernus* of winter, wintry + *-culum* -cle — more at HIBERNATE] **1** : the winter resting part of a plant (as a bud or underground stem) **2 a** : a shelter that is occupied during the winter by a dormant insect or other animal and that usu. has a characteristic structure for each species — called also *hibernacle* **b** : an encysted bud in a freshwater bryozoan that survives the winter and develops into a colony in the spring **c** : the epiphragm of a snail

**hi·ber·nal** \(ˈ)hī¦bərnᵊl\ *adj* [LL *hibernalis*, fr. L *hibernus* of winter + *-alis* -al] : of or relating to winter : WINTRY

¹**hi·ber·nant** \'hībə(r)nənt\ *adj* [L *hibernant-, hibernans*, pres. part. of *hibernare*] : HIBERNATING ⟨~ animals⟩

²**hibernant** \"\ *n* -s : an animal that hibernates

**hi·ber·nate** \'hībə(r),nāt, *usu* -ād·+V\ *vi* -ED/-ING/-S [L *hibernatus*, past part. of *hibernare*, fr. *hibernus* of winter, wintry; akin to L *hiems* winter, Gk *cheimōn*, OSlav *zima*, Skt *himā*] **1 a** : to pass the winter in a torpid or lethargic state; *specif* : to pass the winter in a torpid condition in which the body temperature drops to a little above freezing and metabolic activity is reduced nearly to zero — used esp. of various mammals; compare AESTIVATE **b** : to pass the winter in a resting state — used esp. of the spores and winter buds of various plants **2 a** : to pass the winter esp. in a milder climate ⟨six million farmers lived close enough to Florida to ~ there easily —Alva Johnston⟩ **b** : to be or become inactive or dormant ⟨a few mots survive, to ~ in the mind, and come out again on an early summer day —Osbert Sitwell⟩

**hibernating gland** *n* : a tissue found beneath the skin of the back or abdomen of various mammals that consists of brownish fat cells in a network of vascular connective tissue and serves as a storage for food

**hi·ber·na·tion** \,hībə(r)'nāshən\ *n* -s **1** : the act of hibernating ⟨a new concept of the relation between food and ~ of the black bear —R.E.Trippensee⟩ **2** : the state of one that hibernates ⟨came out of his comfortable ~ to make his first political pronouncement since his retirement —*Time*⟩ — opposed to *aestivation*

**hi·ber·na·tor** \'hībə(r),nād·ə(r), -ātə-\ *n* -s : one that hibernates

¹**hi·ber·nian** \(ˈ)hī¦bərnēən, -bōn-,-bəin-, -nyən\ *adj, usu cap* [*Hibernia* Ireland (fr. L) + E *-an*] **1** : of, relating to, or characteristic of Ireland **2** : of, relating to, or characteristic of the Irish

²**hibernian** \"\ *n* -s *usu cap* : a native or inhabitant of Ireland : IRISHMAN

**hibernian green** *n, often cap H* : a dark yellowish green that is yellower and paler than holly green (sense 1), lighter and stronger than deep chrome green, and yellower, lighter, and stronger than average hunter green — called also *paradise green*

**hi·ber·nian·ism** \hī'bərnēə,nizəm, -bōn-,-bəin-, -nyə-\ *n* -s *usu cap* : HIBERNICISM

**hi·ber·ni·cism** \-nə,sizəm\ *n* -s *usu cap* [ML *Hibernicus* Irish (fr. *Hibernia* + L *-icus* -ic) + E *-ism*] : something characteristically Irish; *specif* : IRISH BULL

**hi·ber·ni·cize** \-,sīz\ *vt* -ED/-ING/-S *often cap* [ML *Hibernicus* + E *-ize*] : to make Irish : express in an Irish way

**hiberno-** *comb form, usu cap* [*Hibernia*] **1** : Irish and ⟨*Hiberno*-Celtic⟩ **2** : Ireland ⟨*Hibernology*⟩

**hi·bis·cus** \hī'biskəs, hə'-\ *n* [NL, fr. L *hibiscum, hibiscus* marshmallow] **1** *cap* : a large widely distributed genus of herbs, shrubs, or small trees (family Malvaceae) with dentate or lobed leaves and large showy flowers — see CHINA ROSE, KENAF, ROSE OF SHARON **2** -ES : any plant of the genus *Hibiscus*

**hi·bi·to** \(h)ē'bē(,)tō\ *n, pl* **hibito** *or* **hibitos** *usu cap* [Sp, of AmerInd origin] **1 a** : an extinct Cholonan people of northwestern Peru **b** : a member of such people **2** : the language of the Hibito people

**hibsch·ite** \'hip,shīt\ *n* -s [Joseph E. *Hibsch* b1882 Czech mineralogist + E *-ite*] : a mineral $Ca_3Al_2(SiO_4)_2(OH)_4$ consisting of a calcium aluminum silicate-hydroxide

**hic** *often read as* 'hik\ *interj* [imit.] — used to express the sound of a hiccup

**hicaco** *var of* ICACO

**hic·a·tee** *or* **hic·o·tee** \'hikə,tē, ¦==¦=\ *or* **hic·o·tea** \,hikə'tāə\ *n* -s [Sp *hicotea, jicotea*, prob. fr. Taino *icotea, icota*] : a West Indian freshwater tortoise (*Chrysemys palustris*)

**hic·can** *also* **hi·can** \(ˈ)hī¦kan, -kän\ *n* -s [*hickory* + *pecan*] : the nut of a tree produced by hybridizing a hickory and a pecan

**hic·cius doc·cius** \¦hiksh(ē)əs'däksh(ē)əs, ¦hiksēəs'däksēəs\ *n* [perh. modif. of L *hic est doctus* this is a learned man] *archaic* : a juggler's formula

¹**hic·cup** *or* **hic·cough** \'hi¦kəp *sometimes* 'hē¦ or ¦,kəp or ¦,kȯf or ¦,käf\ *n* -s [*hiccup* of imit. origin; *hiccough* by folk etymology (influence of *cough*) fr. *hiccup*] **1** : a spasmodic inspiratory movement of the diaphragm involuntarily checked by a sudden closure of the glottis that produces a characteristic sound **2** *or* **hiccups** *pl but sometimes sing in constr* : an attack of hiccuping ⟨severe ~*s* is sometimes seen after operation —*Lancet*⟩ ⟨intractable ~ . . . may be successfully treated —*Jour. Amer. Med. Assoc.*⟩

²**hiccup** *also* **hiccough** \"\ *vb* **hiccuped** *also* **hiccupped** *also* **hiccoughed**; **hiccuped** *also* **hiccupped** *also* **hiccoughed**; **hiccuping** *also* **hiccupping** *also* **hiccoughing**; **hiccups** *also* **hiccoughs** *vi* **1** : to have or suffer from hiccups : make a hiccup **2** : to make a sound suggestive of hiccups ⟨the locomotive ~*ed* and belched a gobbet of smoke into the air —S.H. Adams⟩ ~ *vt* : to speak with or as if with hiccups — usu. used with *out* ⟨was ~*ing* out the lines —W.M.Thackeray⟩

**hic·cup–nut** \'=(,)=,=\ *n* **1** : the seed of an ornamental southern African red-flowering shrub (*Combretum bracteosum*) **2** : the plant that bears hiccup-nuts

**hicht** \'hikt\ *Scot var of* HEIGHT

**hichu** *var of* ICHU

**hic ja·cet** \(ˈ)hik'jāsət, (ˈ)hēk'yäkət\ *n* -s [L, here lies] : an inscription on a tombstone : EPITAPH ⟨among the knightly brasses of the graves, and by the cold *hic jacets* of the dead —Alfred Tennyson⟩

¹**hick** \'hik\ *n* -s [fr. *Hick*, nickname for *Richard*] : an awkward, rude, unsophisticated, or provincial person ⟨their dullest gags, especially written down for the ~*s* —Edmund Wilson⟩ ⟨the immemorial game of luring ~*s*, tired businessmen and holidaymakers into their shows —Sheldon Cheney⟩ **syn** see BOOR

²**hick** \"\ *adj* : of, relating to, or having the characteristics of a hick : suggestive of hicks : COUNTRY ⟨a ~ town⟩

³**hick** \"\ *n* -s [imit.] : HICCUP 1

⁴**hick** \"\ *vi* -ED/-ING/-S : HICCUP 1

¹**hick·ey** *also* **hicky** \'hikē, -ki\ *n, pl* **hickeys** *also* **hickies** [origin unknown] **1 a** : a threaded coupling used to attach an electrical fixture to an outlet box **b** : a device for bending pipe and conduit **2** : a contrivance or device whose name is unknown or forgotten : GADGET ⟨that little ~ with the rubber roller on a handle —*Bagpipe*⟩

²**hickey** \"\ *n* -s [origin unknown] **1** : PIMPLE **2** : a defect in a negative or printing plate

**hick joint** *n* [perh. fr. the name *Hick*] : a joint finished flush with the surface of masonry

¹**hick·o·ry** \'hik(ə)rē, -ri\ *n* -ES [short for *pokahickory*, fr. Virginia *pawcohiccora* food prepared fr. pounded nuts and water] **1 a** : an American tree of the genus *Carya* — see HICKORY NUT; TREE illustration **b** : the valuable hard wood of various hickories **2** : a switch or cane used typically for punishing a child **3** : a rapid gait : CLIP **4 a** : any of various Australian trees (as the featherwood or various members of the genera *Acacia* and *Eucalyptus*) **b** : the wood of an Australian hickory

²**hickory** \"\ *adj* **1** : of, relating to, or made of hickory ⟨a ~ chair⟩ **2 a** : marked by firmness or toughness ⟨the old general, with all his ~ characteristics —Washington Irving⟩ **b** : marked by the absence of religious zeal or devotion : religiously indifferent or lukewarm

³**hickory** \"\ *vt* -ED/-ING/-ES : to give a whipping to : CANE, SWITCH

**hickory acacia** *n* : an Australian acacia (*Acacia leprosa*) with hard reddish brown wood

**hickory bark beetle** *also* **hickory bark borer** *n* : a small beetle (*Scolytus quadrispinosus*) that burrows beneath the bark of various hickories

**hickory borer** *n* : any of various beetles whose larvae live under the bark or in the wood of hickories

**hickory elm** *n* : ROCK ELM 1

**hickoryhead** \'=(=)=,=\ *n* : RUDDY DUCK

**hickory horned devil** *n* : a caterpillar that has a greenish body, red head, and four large curved anterior spines and is the larva of the regal moth

**hickory midge** *n* : a gallfly (*Caryomyia caryae*) that forms globular galls on the leaves of various hickories; *broadly* : a member of the genus *Caryomyia*

**hickory nut** *n* : the oblong or nearly orbicular nut or fruit of the hickory that is usu. compressed on the sides, sharp-pointed at the apex, and enclosed in a 4-valved husk

**hickory oak** *n* : CANYON LIVE OAK

**hickory pine** *n* **1** : BRISTLECONE PINE **2** : TABLE-MOUNTAIN PINE

**hickory poplar** *n* : TULIP TREE 1

**hickory shad** *n* [so called fr. the similarity of the stomachs to hickory nuts] **1** : FALL HERRING **2** : GIZZARD SHAD

**hickory shirt** *also* **hickory** *n* : a shirt made of a strong twilled cotton fabric with vertical stripes and used esp. for work clothing

**hickory shuckworm** *n* : a small white brown-headed grub that is the larva of an olethreutid moth (*Laspeyresia caryana*) and that feeds in the developing fruits of hickory and pecan

**hickory wattle** *n* : a Queensland acacia (*Acacia aulacocarpa*)

**hicks** *pl of* HICK, *pres 3d sing of* HICK

**hicks·ite** \'hik,sīt\ *n* -s *usu cap* [Elias *Hicks* †1830 Am. Quaker minister + E *-ite*] : a member of a liberal branch of Quakers who emphasize the Inner Light at the expense of historical Christianity and the Bible

**hicks yew** *or* **hicks' yew** \'hiks(əz)-\ *n, usu cap H* [fr. *Hicks* nurseries, Westbury, L.I.] : a hybrid yew (*Taxus media hicksii*) having a columnar shape and ascending branches

**hick·wall** \'hi,kwȯl\ *n* [ME *hygh-whele*, prob. of imit. origin] *dial Eng* : GREEN WOODPECKER

**hicky** *var of* HICKEY

**hi·co·ria** \hi'kōrēə\ [NL, modif. of E *hickory*] *syn of* CARYA

**hicotee** *or* **hicotea** *var of* HICATEE

**hid** \'hid\ *adj* [ME, fr. past part. of *hiden* to hide — more at HIDE] : HIDDEN ⟨like the ~ scent in an unbudded rose —John Keats⟩

**hid·abil·i·ty** \,hīdə'biləd·ē\ *n* **1** : the quality or state of being hidable **2** : ability to obscure ⟨paints of superior durability, ~, and color-holding qualities —*Amer. Builder*⟩

**hid·able** \'hīdəbəl\ *adj* : capable of being hidden ⟨jewels are such ~ trifles —*English Digest*⟩

**hid·age** \'hīdij\ *n* -s [ML *hidagium*, fr. *hida* hide (fr. ME *hyde*) + *-agium* -age] *old Eng law* **1** : a tax or tribute paid to the royal exchequer for every hide of land **2** : the value or measure assessed as a basis for hidage

**hi·dal·go** \hi'dal(,)gō, sē'thäl-\ *n* -s *often cap* [Sp, fr. OSp *fijo dalgo*, lit., son of something, son of riches or property] : a member of the lower nobility of Spain

**hid·at·ed** \'hī,dād·əd\ *adj* [NL *hidatus* (past part. of *hidare* to measure in hides, fr. ML *hida* hide) + E *-ed*] : measured in hides

**hid·a·tion** \hī'dāshən\ *n* -s [NL *hidatus* + E *-ion*] : a measuring in or assessing by hides

**hi·dat·sa** \hi'dätsə, -dat-\ *n, pl* **hidatsa** *also* **hidatsas** *usu cap* **1 a** : a Siouan people of the Missouri River valley in No. Dakota related to the Crow — compare GROS VENTRE **b** : a member of such people **2** : the language of the Hidatsa people

**hid·den** \'hidᵊn\ *adj* [fr. past part. of ²*hide*] **1** : being out of sight or off the beaten track : CONCEALED ⟨pulling a ~ switch —D.J.Ingle⟩ ⟨a ~ Broadway restaurant —Scott Fitzgerald⟩ **2** : UNEXPLAINED, UNDISCLOSED, OBSCURE, SECRET ⟨rendering . . . apparent that which is ~ —Matthew Arnold⟩ ⟨rid your mind of any ~ hates or grudges —W.J.Reilly⟩; *specif* : not shown in the accounts or not shown on the books under the usual heading ⟨~ assets⟩ **3** : obscured by something that makes recognition difficult : covered up ⟨~ vowel⟩ ⟨clouds race across the ~ moon⟩ ⟨~ transfers of dollars, the largest item being the estimated $125 million spent by U. S. troops in Germany —*Americana Annual*⟩ — **hid·den·ly** *adv* — **hid·den·ness** \-ᵊn(n)əs\ *n* -ES

**hidden fifth** *n* : an unsounded musical interval of a fifth that is implied by the similar up or down motion of two voice parts and that if sounded would produce consecutive fifths

**hidden hunger** *n* : a nutritional deficiency caused by lack of balance in an otherwise full diet ⟨*hidden hunger* is suffered by cats . . . permitted to eat only liver —Doris Bryant⟩

**hid·den·ite** \'hidᵊn,īt\ *n* -s [William E. *Hidden* †1918 Am. mineralogist + E *-ite*] : a transparent yellow to green spodumene valued as a gem — compare KUNZITE

**hidden octave** *n* : an unsounded musical interval of an octave that is implied by the similar up or down motion of two voice parts and that if sounded would produce consecutive octaves

**hidden pensioner** *n* : an employee no longer performing at peak efficiency but retained in service at a wage exceeding his value to the employer

**hidden quantity** *n, Latin prosody* : the quantity of a hidden vowel so situated that its natural quantity is not determinable by scansion (as when it comes before a double consonant or before two or more consecutive consonants other than a mute and a liquid in the same word)

**hidden reserve** *n* : SECRET RESERVE

¹**hide** \'hīd\ *n* -s [ME *hyde*, fr. OE *hīgid, hīd*; akin to OE *hīwan* members of a household — more at HOME] : any of various old English units of land area; *esp* : a unit of 120 acres used in the Domesday Book — see CARUCATE, SULUNG

**2hide** \"\ *vb* **hid** \'hid\ **hidden** \'hidᵊn\ *or* **hid; hiding** \'hīdiŋ\ **hides** \'hīdz\ [ME *hiden*, fr. OE *hȳdan;* akin to MIr *codal* skin, Gk *keuthein* to conceal, Skt *kuhara* cave, OE *hȳd* hide, skin — more at 4HIDE] *vt* **1 a :** to deposit in a place of concealment **:** put out of sight **:** SECRETE ⟨~ a key under a doormat⟩ **b :** to conceal for shelter or protection **:** SHIELD ⟨Rock of Ages, cleft for me, let me ~ myself in thee —A.M. Toplady⟩ **2 :** to withhold from someone or from public knowledge **:** keep secret ⟨fled to her room to ~ her grief —Andrew Meredith⟩ ⟨to keep a secret, you must also ~ the fact that you have one to keep —Piero Compton⟩ **3 a :** to screen from view or from detection by the senses **:** cover up ⟨a thick mantle of glacial deposits ~*s* the solid rocks —L.D. Stamp⟩ ⟨the purling water was nearly *hidden* by the birr of wings —Sacheverell Sitwell⟩ ⟨sugar coating ~*s* the taste of pills⟩ **b :** to submerge in something that makes comprehension difficult **:** BURY 3b, OBSCURE ⟨pokes fun at some of his colleagues who ~ their important messages in language only intelligible to other professors —*Word Study*⟩ ⟨facts *hidden* in folklore⟩ ~ *vi* **1 a :** to remain out of sight **:** become concealed ⟨*hid* in the island bushes is a frigate —H.S.Canby⟩ ⟨spongy bogs . . . *hiding* here and there in the woods —John Muir †1914⟩ **b :** to go into or remain in concealment to evade authority or pursuit ⟨fewer places for violators to ~ —*Newsweek*⟩ — often used with *out* or *up* ⟨people who do not wish to have any contact with the military government authorities are . . . *hiding* out on farms —Nora Waln⟩ ⟨went back to the ranch kind of slow to give me time to ~ up —C.T.Jackson⟩ **2 :** to seek protection or evade responsibility **:** take refuge — usu. used with *behind* ⟨~*s* behind dark glasses, hoping to avoid being recognized⟩ ⟨heads of companies who are not . . . gift-minded ~ behind their boards of directors —*Saturday Rev.*⟩ **syn** see CONCEAL — **hide one's face from :** to turn away from **:** IGNORE ⟨I will forsake them and *hide my face from* them, and they will be devoured —Deut 31:17 (RSV)⟩ — **hide one's head 1** *obs* **:** to take shelter or refuge ⟨alack the heavy day when such a sacred king should *hide his head* —Shak.⟩ **2 :** to keep silent for fear of reproach ⟨the pessimists *hid their heads* at the opening of the new century —Oscar Handlin⟩ — **hide one's light under a bushel :** to be excessively modest **:** conceal one's abilities **:** shrink from public notice ⟨a fine poet who *hid her light under a bushel*⟩

**3hide** \"\ *n* -s **1 :** a hiding place ⟨knew his ~ had to be very good to elude the scrutiny of the local liquor raiders —*Springfield (Mass.) Union*⟩ **2** *Brit* **:** 3BLIND 2 ⟨in shooting at driven lions it is best to wait until they have passed the ~ —James Stevenson-Hamilton⟩

**4hide** \"\ *n* -s *often attrib* [ME *hid, hide,* fr. OE *hȳd;* akin to OHG *hūt* skin, hide, ON *hūth* skin, hide, L *cutis* skin, Gk *kytos* hollow vessel, *skytos* skin, leather, OPruss *keuto* shell, covering, Skt *skunāti* he covers; basic meaning: to cover, conceal] **1 a :** the outer covering of an animal **:** COAT ⟨bald patches of rock like the ~ of a bison when it is shedding —Norman Mailer⟩ **b :** a raw or tanned pelt taken from an adult of one of the larger animals (as a cow) as distinguished from a skin of one of the smaller or younger animals (as a goat or calf) ⟨calfskins . . . produce a softer leather than cattle ~*s* —G.S. Brady⟩ **c :** a piece of dressed pelt used as material for a manufactured article **:** LEATHER ⟨ladies' luggage set, in English ~ —*advt*⟩ **2 a :** the skin of a human being ⟨he had a certain hard brownness of ~ . . . a horny quality in his face and hands —Arthur Morrison⟩ ⟨much of the industrial plant was doubtless built out of the ~*s* of the people —W.O. Douglas⟩ **b :** a covering aspect or front that gives protection against outside pressure ⟨too tough a ~ to have hurt feelings⟩ **c :** LIFE ⟨such strategy often saved the ~ of the Grand Old Party —Dixon Wecter⟩ — **hide or hair** *or* **hide nor hair :** a vestige or trace of a missing person or object ⟨a wife he hadn't seen *hide or hair* of in over 20 years —H.L.Davis⟩ ⟨turned the closet inside out but couldn't find *hide or hair* of the beach umbrella⟩ ⟨no one has seen *hide nor hair* of him since —*Time*⟩

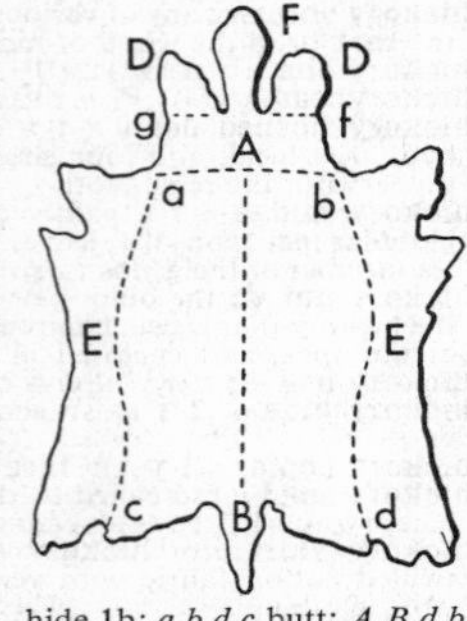

hide 1b: *a b d c* butt; *A B d b, A B c a* bends; *a b f g* shoulder; *E, E,* belly; *D, D,* cheeks; *F* head

**5hide** \"\ *vt* -ED/-ING/-S **:** to give a beating to **:** FLOG ⟨victualed him and clothed him and *hided* him for his own good when he needed it —S.H.Adams⟩

**hide and coop** *n* [*coop* fr. *coop*, interj. used by players to call out from their hiding places] **:** HIDE-AND-SEEK

**1hide–and–seek** \,==ˈ=\ *n* **1** *or* **hide–and–go–seek** \,==(,)=ˈ=\ **:** a children's game in which one player blinds his eyes and after giving the others time to hide goes looking for and tries to catch them — called also *hide-and-coop, hy spy, I spy* **2 :** a procedure resembling the game of hide-and-seek usu. by involving reciprocal deception or evasion ⟨rumrunners playing *hide-and-seek* with government agents —*Amer. Guide Series: Fla.*⟩

**2hide–and–seek** \"\ *vi* [1*hide-and-seek*] **:** to play at hide-and-seek ⟨opposing planes *hide-and-seeking* in the darkness —F.V.Drake⟩

**1hideaway** \ˈ==,=\ *n* -s [fr. *hide away*, v.] **1 :** a place of retreat or concealment **:** REFUGE ⟨intimate, private ~*s* —P.E. Deutschman⟩ ⟨a ~ . . . used to secrete slaves on the Underground Railway —*Amer. Guide Series: Md.*⟩ **2 :** a small secluded restaurant or place of entertainment ⟨dine-and-dance places, exclusive ~*s* —*Emporia (Kans.) Gazette*⟩

**2hideaway** \"\ *adj* [fr. *hide away*, v.] **:** CONCEALED, SECLUDED ⟨~ bed⟩ ⟨~ restaurant⟩

**hidebound** \ˈ=,=\ *adj* [4*hide* + *bound*] **1 a :** having a dry skin lacking in pliancy and adhering closely to the underlying flesh and usu. also a rough and lusterless coat esp. as an accompaniment to disease — used of domestic animals **b :** having scleroderma — used of human beings **c :** having the bark so close and constricting that it impedes growth — used of trees **2 a** *obs* **:** sparing in expenditure **:** MISERLY **b :** having an inflexible or ultraconservative character **:** BIGOTED, NARROW ⟨a nature sometimes ~ and selfish and narrow to the last degree —G.G.Coulton⟩ ⟨the most ~ bureaucrat could not have been more obsoletely reactionary, uninventive, and obstructive —G.B.Shaw⟩ ⟨judicial proceedings should not be ~ by arbitrary rules handed down from the past —K. W.Colgrove⟩ — **hide·bound·ness** \ˈhīd,baůndnəs *also* -ndnəs\ *n* -ES

**hideland** \ˈ=,=\ *n* [1*hide* + *land*] **:** 1HIDE

**hide·less** \ˈhīdləs\ *adj* [4*hide* + *-less*] **:** lacking a hide or skin

**hid·eos·i·ty** \,hidēˈäsəd·ē\ *n* -ES [fr. *hideous*, after such pairs as E *curious : curiosity*] **:** a hideous thing **:** HIDEOUSNESS ⟨the high-water mark of ~ —*Architectural Rev.*⟩ ⟨this vile incrustation of *hideosities* —Dan Wickenden⟩

**hid·eous** \ˈhidēəs *sometimes* ÷ˈhijəs\ *adj* [alter. (influenced by such words as *courteous*) of ME *hidous*, fr. OF *hisdos, hidous, hideus*, fr. *hisde, hide* terror] **1 a :** offensive to the sight **:** GRUESOME, UGLY ⟨one man still living in ~ squalor among the bones of his fellow travelers —Mabel R. Gillis⟩ ⟨a ~ congeries of fuming kilns —V.S.Pritchett⟩ ⟨writers concerning the warthog generally commence by enlarging upon its ~ appearance —James Stevenson-Hamilton⟩ ⟨a lampshade . . . too ~ for anyone in their senses to buy —W.H.Auden⟩ **b :** offensive to another of the senses **:** FRIGHTFUL, TERRIBLE ⟨the ~ gasping struggle the asthmatic woman was making to get her breath —Leslie Ford⟩ ⟨during the summer this southward-facing row of buildings must be ~ with heat —G.R. Stewart⟩ **c :** appallingly large **:** MONSTROUS ⟨the great scar on a mountainside left by the racing snow, and the ~ mass of snow and soil and rock . . . on the valley floor —Russell Henderson⟩ **2 a :** offensive to the mind or to the moral sense **:** HATEFUL, SHOCKING ⟨monstrous and ~ thoughts —J.C.Powys⟩ ⟨a ~ pattern of injustice —Paul Blanshard⟩ **b :** EMBARRASSING, LUDICROUS, DISMAYING ⟨I am in ~ straits about the . . . performance of a play of mine —G.B.Shaw⟩ ⟨a ~ accident attended the serving of the dessert —Jean Stafford⟩ **syn** see UGLY

**hid·eous·ly** *adv* **:** in a hideous manner ⟨~ snarling white plaster lions —Mollie Panter-Downes⟩

**hid·eous·ness** *n* -ES **:** the quality or state of being hideous

**hideout** \ˈ=,=\ *n* -s [fr. *hide out*, v.] **:** a place of refuge, retreat, or concealment ⟨spiriting his lovely client off to a little ~ that he has —Wolcott Gibbs⟩ ⟨had stopped to refuel their car while taking him to their ~ —*Fingerprint Identification*⟩

**hideout gun** *n* **:** a handgun that can be easily concealed upon the person

**hide powder** *n* **:** powdered hide usu. specially prepared and standardized for use in the analysis of tannins and tanning materials

**hid·er** \ˈhīdə(r)\ *n* -s [ME, fr. *hiden* to hide + *-er* — more at HIDE] **:** one that hides

**hide rope** *n* **1 :** a rope plaited from strips of green hide **2 :** a fiber rope used for tying baled goods (as hides)

**hides** *pl of* HIDE, *pres 3d sing of* HIDE

**hide splitter** *n* **:** one that separates the grain layer from the flesh layer of a hide

**hide spreader** *n* **:** one that spreads raw hides one on top of another to form a pack for curing

**hidey–hole** *or* **hidy–hole** \ˈhīdē,hōl\ *n* [alter. of earlier *hiding-hole*] **:** HIDEAWAY 1

**1hiding** *n* -s [ME *hidinge*, fr. *hiden* to hide + *-inge* -ing] **1 :** the act or action of hiding; *esp* **:** a withdrawal from one's usual haunts to evade authority or secure privacy ⟨having got into difficulties with the government for his press reports and cartoons, he went into ~ —*Irish Digest*⟩ **2 :** a place or means of concealment ⟨take me to that ~ in the hills —Alfred Tennyson⟩

**2hiding** *n* -s [fr. gerund of 5*hide*] **:** an infliction of physical punishment **:** BEATING ⟨a fighter . . . who had been taking ~*s* in the gymnasium —*Sporting Life*⟩ ⟨the roof of a van really takes a ~ in all weathers —Keith Winser⟩; *esp* **:** WHIPPING ⟨put her over my knee and gave her a ~ —Saul Bellow⟩

**hiding power** *n* **:** the ability of a paint or painting material to obscure the surface upon which it is applied — distinguished from *coverage*

**1hid·lings** \ˈhidlənz, -liŋz\ *or* **hid·lins** \-lənz\ *adv* [ME *hidlinges*, fr. *hid* (past part. of *hiden* to hide) + *-linges* -lings — more at HIDE] *chiefly Scot* **:** in a clandestine manner **:** SECRETLY — usu. used with *in*

**2hidlings** \"\ *or* **hidlins** \"\ *adj, chiefly Scot* **:** SECRET, CLANDESTINE

**hidr–** *or* **hidro–** *comb form* [NL, fr. Gk *hidrōs* sweat — more at SWEAT] **:** of or by means of perspiration **:** of the sweat glands ⟨*hidr*adenitis⟩ ⟨*hidro*cystoma⟩

**hidrad·e·ni·tis** \,hi,dradᵊnˈīd·əs, ,hī,-\ *n* [NL, fr. *hidr-* + *adenitis*] **:** inflammation of a sweat gland

**hi·dro·sis** \hiˈdrōsəs, hī'-\ *n, pl* **hidro·ses** \-ō,sēz\ [NL, fr. Gk *hidrōsis*, fr. *hidrōt-, hidrōs* sweat + *-sis*] **:** excretion of sweat **:** PERSPIRATION

**hi·drot·ic** \(ˈ)=ˈdräd·ik\ *adj* [Gk *hidrōtikos*, fr. *hidrōt-, hidrōs* sweat + *-ikos* -ic] **:** causing perspiration **:** DIAPHORETIC, SUDORIFIC

**1hie** \ˈhī\ *vb* **hied; hied; hying** *or* **hieing** \ˈhīiŋ\ **hies** [ME *hien*, fr. OE *hīgian* to strive, be eager, hasten; akin to OSw *hikka* to pant, Norw, to sob, Russ *sigat'* to jump, Skt *śīghra* quick] *vi* **:** to go quickly **:** HASTEN ⟨thither we advise you to ~ —*New Yorker*⟩ ~ *vt* **:** to cause (oneself) to go quickly ⟨*hied* myself to the post office —H.A.Chippendale⟩

**2hie** \ˈhē\ *chiefly Scot var of* HIGH

**hie·lan** *or* **hie·land** \ˈhēlən(d), -nt\ *Scot var of* HIGHLAND

**hield** *vi* -ED/-ING/-S, [ME *helden, heelden, hielden* — more at HEEL] *obs* **:** TILT, LEAN, HEEL ⟨let it be laid in a dish ~*ing* toward the one side —Peter Morwen⟩

**hie·le·man** *or* **hee·la·man** *or* **hei·la·man** \ˈhēləmən\ *n* -s [native name in Australia] **:** an elongated wooden shield used by Australian aborigines

**hielmite** *var of* HJELMITE

**hi·emal** \ˈhīəməl\ *adj* [L *hiemalis*, fr. *hiem-, hiems* winter + *-alis* -al — more at HIBERNATE] **:** of or relating to winter **:** WINTRY

**hieng** \hēˈeŋ\ *n, pl* **hieng** *or* **hiengs** *usu cap* **1 :** a mountain people of Cambodia **2 :** a member of the Hieng people

**hie on** *vt* **:** to rouse to quick action **:** urge on ⟨*hie on* a hound⟩

**hier–** *or* **hiero–** *comb form* [LL, fr. Gk, fr. *hieros* powerful, supernatural, holy, sacred — more at IRE] **:** sacred **:** holy ⟨*hier*archy⟩ ⟨*hiero*glyph⟩

**hiera** *pl of* HIERON

**hi·er·a·cite** \ˈhīərə,sīt, hīˈerə,s-, ,hīəˈrā,s-\ *or* **hi·er·a·cian** \,hīəˈrāshən\ *n* -s *usu cap* [*Hieracite* fr. LL *Hieracita*, fr. *Hieracas*, 4th cent. A.D. Egyptian ascetic + *-ita* -ite; *Hieracian* fr. *Hieracas* + E *-ian*] **:** a follower of the ascetic Hieracas

**hi·er·a·ci·um** \,hīəˈrāshēəm\ *n* [NL, fr. Gk *hierakion* hawkweed, fr. *hierak-, hierax* hawk, fr. *hienai* to hurry — more at VIA] **1** *cap* **:** a very large and nearly cosmopolitan genus of weedy perennial herbs (family Compositae) having simple often basal leaves and heads of yellow or reddish orange ray flowers — see ORANGE HAWKWEED **2** *pl* **hieracia** *also* **hieraciums :** any plant of the genus *Hieracium*

**hi·er·a·co·sphinx** \,hīəˈrākə+,-\ *n* [Gk *hierako-* (fr. *hierak-, hierax* hawk) + E *sphinx*] **:** a hawk-headed sphinx

**hi·era pic·ra** \,hīərəˈpikrə\ *n* [ML, lit., powerful or sacred antidote] **:** a cathartic powder made of aloes and canella bark

**hi·er·arch** \ˈhīə,rärk, -,råk *also* ˈhī,r-\ *n* -s [MF or ML; MF *hierarche*, fr. ML *hierarcha*, fr. Gk *hierarchēs*, fr. *hier-* + *-archēs* -arch] **1 :** a religious leader holding high office or vested with controlling authority **:** chief prelate **:** HIGH PRIEST ⟨the important central painting . . . shows the apostolic succession of ~*s* —W.E.Needham⟩ ⟨steps taken by the British East India Company to . . . establish relations with the Tibetan ~*s* —Beatrice D. Miller⟩ **2 :** one having authority or pontifical dignity resembling that of a hierarch ⟨former ministers, generals, blackshirt ~*s* —Janet Flanner⟩ ⟨proceed with the utmost decorum and in what the ~*s* . . . considered the best of Senate tradition —*N.Y. Times Mag.*⟩

**hi·er·ar·chal** \,hīəˈrärkəl, -ˈråk- *also* (ˈ)hī¦r-\ *or* **hi·er·ar·chi·al** \-kēəl\ *adj* **:** HIERARCHICAL — **hi·er·ar·chal·ly** \¦=ˈ=kəlē, -li\ *or* **hi·er·ar·chi·al·ly** \-kēəlē, -li\ *adv*

**hi·er·ar·chi·cal** \-kəkəl, -kēk-\ *or* **hi·er·ar·chic** \-kik,-kēk\ *adj* [MF or ML; MF *hierarchique*, fr. ML *hierarchicus*, fr. *hierarchia* + L *-icus* -ic, -ical] **1 :** of, relating to, or controlled by a religious hierarchy ⟨the liturgy of the mass presupposes . . . the ~ order of church and society corresponds to the divine hierarchy —Jacob Taubes⟩ **2 a :** of an authoritarian or aristocratic character **:** STRATIFIED ⟨although the ~ federal arrangement is typical, there are many organizations which are unitary —D.D.McKean⟩ ⟨only a ~ society with a leisure class at the top can produce works of art —*Partisan Rev.*⟩ **b :** having the power to control **:** INFLUENTIAL ⟨a denial . . . due to pressure from a political or ~ source interfering with the due course of judicial proceedings —M.R.Cohen⟩ **3 :** of or relating to a classification of people according to artistic, social, economic, or other criteria ⟨a ~ feeling has grown up in Italy about the standings of the artists —R.M.Coates⟩ ⟨the ~ status of a child in relation to other members of the family —Norman Cameron⟩ ⟨the tailor, department head, and floor supervisor were summoned, appealed to, and appalled in *hierarchic* succession —Marvin Barrett⟩ **4 :** of, relating to, or constituting a related series **:** SEQUENTIAL ⟨the ~ arrangement of cultures constructed by the 19th century anthropologists —Henry Orenstein⟩ — **hi·er·ar·chi·cal·ly** \-k(ə)lē, -kēk-, -li\ *adv*

**hi·er·ar·chism** \ˈhīə,rär,kizəm, -,rå,k- *also* ˈhī,r-\ *n* -s **:** the system or authority of a hierarchy

**hi·er·ar·chi·za·tion** \,(,)=(=),=kəˈzāshən, -,kīˈz-\ *n* -s **1 :** the act or process of establishing a hierarchy ⟨~ . . . leads to a clear-cut stratification of all members of any organized group —P.A.Sorokin⟩ **2 :** the quality or state of being a hierarchy ⟨the traditional ~ of the three orders of abstraction —F.G. Connolly⟩

**hi·er·ar·chize** \ˈhīə,rär,kīz, -,rå,k- *also* ˈhī,r-\ *vt* -ED/-ING/-S **:** to arrange hierarchically ⟨*hierarchized* systems of organization —C.H.Page⟩

**hi·er·ar·chy** \ˈhīə,rärkē, -,råk-, -ki *also* ˈhī,r\ *n* -ES [ME *ierarchie*, fr. MF *ierarchie, hierarchie*, fr. ML *hierarchia*, fr. LGk, fr. Gk *hierarchēs* + *-ia* -y] **1 :** a rank or order of holy beings — *see* CELESTIAL HIERARCHY **2 :** a form of government administered by an authoritarian group ⟨the company town implies a ~ despotically, if benevolently, guiding the lives of those beneath —W.H.Whyte⟩ ⟨the ~ relates all units in vertical levels of responsibility —J.E.Pate⟩; *esp* **:** control exercised by a priesthood ⟨unlimited centralization of ecclesiastical ~ —A.C.N.Gallenga⟩ **3 a :** an authoritarian body of religious officials organized by rank and jurisdiction ⟨the priest, with the ~ at his back, was in theory almost everything to his people —G.G.Coulton⟩ ⟨three cardinals and 65 bishops attended the annual meeting of the American ~ —*Official Catholic Yearbook*⟩ ⟨the power . . . of the great Buddhist ~ is nothing less than stupendous —Edith Hamilton⟩ **b :** a controlling group of any kind ⟨when all power is centered in the top ~ of a single party, there is none left over to serve as a check against the ruling class —A.M.Schlesinger b.1917⟩ ⟨officials at the pinnacle of the mobilization ~ —*Wall Street Jour.*⟩ ⟨the publisher who has . . . exceeded his proper function by becoming the head and dictator of the newspaper ~ —Alistair Cooke⟩ ⟨at the bottom of the ~ of managerial personnel are the foremen —Kurt Braun⟩ ⟨rising steadily in the ~ of the local Boy Scouts —Brendan Gill⟩ **4 a :** the classification of a group of people with regard to ability or economic or social standing ⟨the function of true criticism is to establish a definite ~ among the great artists of the past —C.W.Shumaker⟩ ⟨continuous waves of new immigrants, each pushing the preceding waves upward in the ethnic ~ —Richard Hofstadter⟩ ⟨the seating arrangement was an accurate index of the Hollywood ~ —Budd Schulberg⟩ **b :** a group of people so classified ⟨made his way into the ~ of business families in Montreal —Hugh MacLennan⟩ **c :** the status attaching to such a group ⟨the social ~ that may be associated with possessions —Ruth Benedict⟩; *specif* **:** a graded series of social statuses or class levels ⟨upper and lower class ~ in a community⟩ **5 a :** the arrangement of objects, elements, or values in a graduated series ⟨the ~ of occupations is based on the degree of skill and responsibility they entail⟩ ⟨government officials determine the ~ of importance of affairs of state⟩ **b :** a series of objects, elements, or values so arranged ⟨the Supreme Court is the head of a ~ of federal courts —Felix Frankfurter⟩ ⟨in the multicellular organism there is a ~ of levels — cells, tissues, organs —A.B.Novikoff⟩; *specif, logic* **:** a series the members of which are grouped in accordance with a principle (as of importance, perfection or priority) ⟨~ of values⟩ ⟨an ontological ~ in which the objects of knowledge are arranged in an ascending order of reality —George Boas⟩ **c :** the stratification so achieved ⟨a rigid ~ of clubs —R.M.Lovett⟩; *specif* **:** a table of statistical correlations having a constant proportional relationship and graded from high to low

**1hi·er·at·ic** \,hīəˈrad·ik *also* (ˈ)hī¦r-\ *adj* [L *hieraticus*, fr. Gk *hieratikos*, fr. (assumed) *hieratos* (verbal of *hierasthai* to be a priest, fr. *hieros* powerful, supernatural, holy, sacred) + *-ikos* -ic — more at IRE] **1 :** written in, constituting, or belonging to a cursive form of ancient Egyptian writing simpler and less pictorial than the hieroglyphic ⟨only those who served in the temples knew the secret of the ~ writing —W.M.James⟩ — see DEMOTIC 2 **2** *also* **hi·er·at·i·cal** \-d·əkəl\ **:** of, relating to, or associated with priestly functions **:** SACERDOTAL ⟨the gestures ~ as if from some slow and ancient ritual —Hallam Tennyson⟩ ⟨~ art of the church —Herbert Read⟩ ⟨the powerful ~ sculpture of the Aztecs —B.D. Wolfe⟩ — **hi·er·at·i·cal·ly** \-ək(ə)lē\ *adv*

**2hieratic** \"\ *n* -s **:** a cursive form of ancient Egyptian writing ⟨the oldest dated papyrus . . . is written in ~ —H.B.Van Hoesen & F.K.Walter⟩

**hi·er·a·tite** \ˈhīərə,tīt\ *n* -s [It, fr. *Hiera* (Vulcano), one of the Lipari islands, Italy + It *-ite*] **:** a mineral $K_2SiF_6$ consisting of potassium fluosilicate found as grayish concretions in the fumaroles of Vulcano

**–hi·er·ic** \hīˈ¦erik, -rēk\ *adj comb form* [Gk *hieron* (*osteon*) sacrum (fr. hieron — neut. of *hieros* powerful, sacred — + *osteon* bone) + E *-ic* — more at IRE] **:** having (such) a sacrum ⟨dolicho*hieric*⟩ ⟨platy*hieric*⟩

**hiero–** — see HIER-

**hi·er·och·loe** \,hīəˈräklə(,)wē\ *n, cap* [NL, fr. *hier-* + Gk *chloē* young grass] **:** a genus of aromatic perennial grasses native to temperate and cold regions having spikelets with a perfect terminal floret and two staminate florets — see HOLY GRASS

**hi·er·oc·ra·cy** \-kräsē\ *n* -ES [*hier-* + *-cracy*] **:** government by ecclesiastics **:** HIERARCHY

**hi·er·o·crat·ic** \,hī(ə)rə¦krad·ik\ *or* **hi·er·o·crat·i·cal** \-d·əkəl\ *adj* [fr. *hierocracy*, after such pairs as E *democracy: democratic, democratical*] **:** of or relating to government by ecclesiastics (as priests or prelates)

**hi·er·o·dule** \ˈhī(ə)rə,d(y)ül, hīˈer-\ *n* -s [LL *hierodulus*, fr. Gk *hierodoulos*, fr. *hier-* + *doulos* slave] **:** a slave attached to the service of a temple; *esp* **:** a sacred prostitute in ancient Greece

**hi·er·o·du·lic** \¦hī(ə)rə¦d(y)ülik, (¦)hī¦er-\ *adj* **:** of or relating to a hierodule

**1hi·er·o·glyph** \ˈhī(ə)rə,glif, -rō-\ *n* -s [F *hiéroglyphe*, fr. MF *hieroglyphe*, back-formation fr. *hieroglyphique*] **1 :** a character used in a system of hieroglyphic writing ⟨Maya ~*s* were sculptured or . . . incised on stone stelae —J.E.S.Thompson⟩ esp. in ancient Egypt ⟨~*s* often occur on monuments written vertically and from left to right —J.E.M.White⟩ — compare IDEOGRAM **2 :** something that resembles a hieroglyph in form or symbolism ⟨the river glistened in a ~ across the country —D.H.Lawrence⟩ ⟨at the corners of her eyes and mouth were written the decipherable ~*s* of disillusion —Helen Howe⟩ ⟨symbolic ~*s* consisting of nothing more than a few brush strokes —*Times Lit. Supp.*⟩

**2hieroglyph** \"\ *vt* -ED/-ING/-S **:** to express in or inscribe with hieroglyphics ⟨the first ~*ed* sarcophagus we had yet seen —Amelia B. Edwards⟩

**1hi·er·o·glyph·ic** \¦=(=)=¦glifik, -fēk\ *or* **hi·er·o·glyph·i·cal** \-fəkəl, -fēk-\ *adj* [*hieroglyphic* fr. MF *hieroglyphique*, fr. LL *hieroglyphicus*, fr. Gk *hieroglyphikos*, fr. *hier-* + *glyphikos* of carving; *hieroglyphical* fr. MF *hieroglyphique* + E *-al* — more at GLYPHIC] **1 a :** written in, constituting, or belonging to that form of ancient Egyptian writing in which the characters are for the most part recognizable pictures of objects — compare DEMOTIC, HIERATIC **b :** written in, constituting, or belonging to any system of writing in which the characters are to a substantial degree recognizable pictures ⟨finest of the three surviving Maya ~ books —J.E.S.Thompson⟩ **2 :** inscribed with hieroglyphic characters ⟨~ obelisk⟩ **3 :** resembling hieroglyphic in form ⟨coleus mosaic — causing . . . ~ markings on leaves —*Experiment Station Record*⟩, symbolism ⟨~ emblem⟩, or illegibility ⟨the most ~ of prescriptions —H.V. Morton⟩ ⟨*hieroglyphical* entries in thick, half-obliterated pencil —Bram Stoker⟩ — **hi·er·o·glyph·i·cal·ly** \-fək(ə)lē, -li\ *adv*

**2hieroglyphic** \"\ *n* -s **1 :** HIEROGLYPH 1 **2 :** a system of hieroglyphic writing ⟨a German philologist . . . started the decipherment of Hittite ~ —C.J.Rolo⟩; *specif* **:** the picture script of the ancient Egyptian priesthood ⟨the elaborate ~ . . . was too slow and laborious a method of writing for the needs of everyday business —J.H.Breasted⟩ — often used in pl. but sing. or pl. in constr. **3 :** something that resembles a hieroglyphic in form, symbolic content, or difficulty of decipherment ⟨the frightening ~*s* of . . . shorthand —*advt*⟩ ⟨the traditional ~ that was said to identify for tramps the houses where meals were certain —Ben Riker⟩ ⟨the *hieroglyphic*-covered blackboard —Philip Hamburger⟩

hieroglyphics (Egyptian)

**3hieroglyphic** *vt* [2*hieroglyphic*] *obs* **:** HIEROGLYPH

**hieroglyphic hittite** *n, usu cap both Hs* **:** a language related to cuneiform Hittite and known from inscriptions in the Hittite hieroglyphic writing — see INDO-EUROPEAN LANGUAGES table

**hi·er·o·glyph·ist** \,=(=)=ˈglifəst, ˈ=(=)=,=; ,hīəˈrägləf-, hīˈrä-\ *n* -s **:** a writer of hieroglyphics

**hi·er·o·gram** \ˈhī(ə)rə,gram\ *n* [*hier-* + *-gram*] **:** a sacred emblem or graphic symbol

**hi·er·o·gram·mat** \,hī(ə)rəˈgramət, -,mat\ *or* **hi·er·o·gram·mate** \-,mət, -,māt\ *n* -s [Gk *hierogrammateus*, fr. *hier-* + *grammateus* scribe, fr. *grammat-, gramma* letter, writing — more at GRAMMAR] **:** a writer of sacred records esp. in hieroglyphics

**hi·er·o·gram·mat·ic** \,hī(ə)rəgrəˈmad·ik\ *or* **hi·er·o·gram·mat·i·cal** \-d·əkəl\ *adj* [*hier-* + Gk *grammat-, gramma* letter, writing + E *-ic, -ical*] **:** of or relating to hierograms

**hi·er·o·graph** \ˈhī(ə)rə,graf, -rȧf\ *n* [*hier-* + *-graph*] **:** HIEROGRAM — **hi·er·o·graph·ic** \ˌ==(=)=ˈgrafik\ *or* **hi·er·o·graph·i·cal** \-fəkəl\ *adj*

**hi·er·og·ra·phy** \,hīəˈrägrəfē, hīˈr-\ *n* -ES [LGk *hierographia*, fr. Gk *hier-* + *-graphia* -graphy] **:** descriptive writing on sacred subjects **:** a treatise on religion

**hi·er·ol·a·try** \-ˈäləˈtrē\ *n* -ES [*hier-* + *-latry*] **:** worship of saints or sacred things

**hi·er·o·log·ic** \ˌhī(ə)rəˈläjik\ *or* **hi·er·o·log·i·cal** \-jəkəl\ *adj* **:** of or relating to hierology

**hi·er·ol·o·gist** \,hīəˈräləjəst, hīˈr-\ *n* -s **:** one skilled in hierology

**hi·er·ol·o·gy** \-jē\ *n* -ES [*hier-* + *-logy*] **1 :** a body of knowledge of sacred things **:** the literary or traditional embodiment of the religious beliefs of a people ⟨the ~ of Greece⟩ **2 :** HAGIOLOGY

**hi·er·o·mon·ach** \,hī(ə)rōˈmänək, -ä,nak; ,hīəˈrämə,nak\ *n* -s [LGk or MGk *hieromonachos*, fr. Gk *hier-* + *monachos* monk — more at MONK] **:** HIEROMONK

**hi·er·o·monk** \ˈhī(ə)rō,məŋk\ *n* [part. trans. of LGk or MGk *hieromonachos*] **:** a monk of the Eastern Church who is also a priest

**hi·er·on** \ˈhīə,rän\ *n, pl* **hi·era** \-ərə\ [Gk, fr. neut. of *hieros* holy, sacred — more at IRE] **:** a consecrated place (as a temple) in ancient Greece

**hi·er·o·nym·ic** \ˌhī(ə)rəˈnimik\ *also* **hi·er·o·nym·i·an** \-mēən\ *adj, usu cap* [Eusebius *Hieronymus* (St. Jerome) †420 church father + E *-ic* or *-ian*] **:** of, relating to, or composed by St. Jerome ⟨the *Hieronymic* version of the Bible⟩

**hi·er·on·y·mite** \,hīəˈränə,mīt, hīˈr-\ *also* **hi·er·o·nym·i·an** \,hī(ə)rəˈnimēən\ *n* -s *usu cap* [Eusebius *Hieronymus* + E *-ite* or *-ian*] **:** a member of any of various hermit orders named in honor of St. Jerome

**hi·er·o·phant** \ˈhī(ə)rə,fant; hīˈerə,fant, -,fənt\ *n* -s [LL *hierophanta, hierophantes*, fr. Gk *hierophantēs*, fr. *hier-* + *-phantēs* (fr. *phainein* to reveal, show, make known) — more at FANCY] **1 :** a priest in ancient Greece ⟨a ~ . . . dressed in a fawn skin, with a crown of poplar leaves —L.P.Smith⟩; *specif* **:** the chief priest of the Eleusinian mysteries **2 a :** a spokesman or interpreter ⟨the ~ of Beauty, the dedicated poet of the cult —F.R.Leavis⟩ ⟨the molder and ~ of the national life —Van Wyck Brooks⟩ **b :** a leading advocate ⟨sociologists have long been ~s of methodology —R.K.Merton⟩

**hi·er·o·phan·tic** \ˌhī(ə)rəˈfantik, (ˌ)hīˌer-\ *adj* [Gk *hierophantikos*, fr. *hierophantēs* + *-ikos* -ic] **:** of, relating to, or resembling a hierophant — **hi·er·o·phan·ti·cal·ly** \-tək(ə)lē\ *adv*

**hi·er·o·sol·y·mi·tan** \,hī(ə)rōˈsäləˈmītᵊn\ *adj, usu cap* [LL *Hierosolymitanus*, fr. *Hierosolyma* Jerusalem (fr. Gk *Hierosolyma*) + L *-ita* -ite + *-anus* -an] **:** of or relating to the city of Jerusalem

**hi·er·ur·gi·cal** \ˌhīəˈrərjəkəl, (ˈ)hīˈr-\ *adj* **:** of or relating to hierurgy

**hi·er·ur·gy** \ˈhīə,rərjē, -ī,rər-\ *n* -ES [Gk *hierourgia*, fr. *hierourgos* sacrificing priest (fr. *hier-* + *-ergos*, fr. *ergon* work) + *-ia* -y] **:** an act or rite of worship **:** LITURGY

**hies** *pl of* HIE, *pres 3d sing of* HIE

**hifalutin** *var of* HIGHFALUTIN

**¹hi-fi** \ˈhīˈfī\ *n* -s [*high fidelity*] **1 :** HIGH FIDELITY **2 :** the equipment needed to play high-fidelity recordings ⟨to own *hi-fi* is to join a community of music lovers —Brooks Atkinson⟩ **3 :** the practice of listening to high-fidelity recordings as a pastime ⟨up to the present, *hi-fi* has been largely . . . the hobby of the enthusiastic amateur —Thomas Heinitz⟩

**²hi-fi** \ˈ=ˌ=\ *adj* **1 :** of or relating to hi-fi ⟨*hi-fi* fan⟩ ⟨*hi-fi* range⟩ **2 :** characterized by high fidelity ⟨*hi-fi* recording⟩ **3 :** designed to reproduce hi-fi recordings ⟨*hi-fi* phonograph⟩

**hi-flash** \ˈhīˈ=\ *adj* [*high flash*] **:** having a high flash point — used esp. of solvents ⟨*hi-flash* naphtha⟩

**hig·gle** \ˈhigəl\ *vi* **higgled; higgled; higgling** \-g(ə)liŋ\ **higgles** [prob. alter. of ¹*haggle*] **:** to bargain for small advantages (as in buying and selling) **:** HAGGLE, CHAFFER ⟨the purchaser *higgling* about the cart —Walt Whitman⟩

**¹hig·gle·dy-pig·gle·dy** *also* **hig·gle·ty-pig·gle·ty** \ˌhigəld|ē-ˈpigəld|ē, -lt| . . . lt|, |ˌ . . . |i\ *adv* [origin unknown] **:** in confusion **:** without order or coherence **:** TOPSY-TURVY ⟨everything was heaped *higgledy-piggledy* on the luggage racks —Leonide Zarine⟩

**²higgledy-piggledy** *also* **higglety-pigglety** \"\ *adj* **:** CONFUSED, JUMBLED ⟨a *higgledy-piggledy* patchwork of . . . overlapping powers —F.D.Roosevelt⟩

**hig·gler** \ˈhig(ə)lə(r)\ *n* -s **:** an itinerant peddler **:** HAWKER ⟨is as a rule sold to ~s —T.D.Marsh⟩ ⟨belonged to a local ~ . . . a man that used the roads buying poultry for resale —F.M. Ford⟩

**¹high** \ˈhī\ *adj* -ER/-EST [ME *hegh, hey, high*, fr. OE *hēah*; akin to OHG *hōh* high, ON *hār*, Goth *hauhs* high, L *cacumen* top, point, OIr *cūar* bent, crooked, Skt *kucati* he contracts, bends, curves; basic meaning: bending] **1 a** (1) **:** having a relatively great upward extension **:** LOFTY ⟨a ~ tree⟩ ⟨a ~ mountain⟩ (2) **:** being at or rising to a considerable elevation above the ground or other base **:** ELEVATED ⟨a ~ leap⟩ ⟨a ~ plateau⟩ (3) **:** of, relating to, or located on highlands or a plateau ⟨*High* Asia⟩ (4) *of a person* **:** TALL (5) **:** having a specified altitude or elevation ⟨a new office building 10 stories ~⟩ — often used in combination ⟨knee-*high*⟩ ⟨sky-*high*⟩ (6) **:** articulated with some part of the tongue close to the palate ⟨\ē\, \i\, \ü\, and \u̇\ are ~ vowels⟩ (7) **:** pitched above shoulder height ⟨a ~ ball⟩ **b** (1) **:** advanced toward its acme or fullest extent ⟨it was now ~ June —Guy McCrone⟩ **:** advanced toward its most active or culminating period ⟨an Italian vacation during the ~ season —*N.Y. Times*⟩; *specif* **:** constituting the late, fully developed, or most creative stage or period (as of an artistic style or career or historical movement) ⟨*High* Baroque⟩ ⟨*High* Gothic⟩ ⟨the ~ period of William Faulkner's work —M.D.Geismar⟩ ⟨the ~ middle ages⟩ (2) none too early **:** verging on lateness — usu. used in the phrase *high time* ⟨~ time . . . that your mother came home —Isa Glenn⟩ (3) **:** acute in pitch **:** SHARP, SHRILL ⟨a ~ tone⟩ ⟨a ~ alto voice⟩ ⟨she heard the ~ giggles of the . . . young men —Louis Auchincloss⟩ **:** RAISED, LOUD ⟨"halt!" he called in a ~ voice⟩; *also* **:** of or relating to those musical notes or tones in the three-line or thrice-accented octave esp. in singing ⟨she sang a ~ C easily⟩ (4) **:** long past **:** ANCIENT, REMOTE ⟨the use of which goes back . . . to a ~ antiquity —Edward Clodd⟩ (5) **:** being far toward one of the poles with the equator as base — used chiefly in the phrase *high latitude* (6) **:** being near the wind — used of a ship or its head when pointing close to the wind (7) **:** being toward the middle or near the end of a series of compounds ⟨~*er* alcohols containing six or more carbon atoms⟩ (8) **:** having a complex organization **:** greatly differentiated or developed phylogenetically — usu. used in the comparative degree of advanced types of animals and plants ⟨the ~*er* algae⟩ ⟨the ~*er* apes⟩ (9) **:** sexually mature and active ⟨~ males of the species⟩ (10) **:** exhausted of nearly all air or gas ⟨~ vacuum⟩ **c** (1) **:** of relatively great degree, size, or amount ⟨gambling for ~ stakes⟩ ⟨unemployment was ~⟩ ⟨the ~ cost of living⟩ ⟨enjoyed a ~ standard of living⟩ ⟨moved at a ~ speed⟩ ⟨going into the market at the time of ~ business —Samuel Johnson⟩ ⟨an automobile engine having ~ compression⟩ (2) **:** dear in price **:** EXPENSIVE ⟨everything is so ~ nowadays⟩ (3) **:** VIOLENT, STRONG, VEHEMENT ⟨a ~ wind came up⟩ ⟨the ~ passions of this hour⟩ **:** marked by high waves ⟨a ~ sea⟩ (4) **:** containing a relatively great amount ⟨a food ~ in iron⟩ (5) **:** having more value than another card ⟨the queen is ~*er* than the jack⟩ **:** capable of taking a trick ⟨the nine is ~⟩ (6) **:** giving the highest ratio of propeller-shaft to engine-shaft speed and the lowest multiplication of torque ⟨a ~ transmission gear⟩ ⟨in ~ gear⟩ **d** (1) **:** INTENSE, EXTREME ⟨people of ~ anxiety —Vance Packard⟩ ⟨~ disfavor in her face —Edna Ferber⟩ ⟨the boys were in ~ glee —H.A. Chippendale⟩ ⟨the ~ brilliance of this gem⟩ ⟨my . . . uncle's ~ disapproval —Joyce Cary⟩ ⟨the ~ seriousness . . . and the sound scholarship which inform his work —C.I.Glicksberg⟩ ⟨his hopes were ~⟩ (2) **:** RICH, LUXURIOUS ⟨indulged in a brief but reckless period of ~ living —H.M.Skala⟩ (3) **:** marked by a pink or rosy glow or flush **:** FLORID ⟨a large, personable widow, with a . . . ~ complexion —Dorothy Sayers⟩ ⟨a sturdy, handsome, *high*-colored woman —Carl Van Doren⟩; *also* **:** BRIGHT, PRONOUNCED ⟨fall styles in ~ shades —*N. Y. Times*⟩ ⟨~ flesh tints play a major part in the tonal organization of the picture —Bernard Smith⟩ (4) **:** strong-scented **:** slightly tainted ⟨should cook game when it is ~⟩; *also* **:** MALODOROUS, STINKING ⟨dead . . . had been there since yesterday, and they were plenty ~ —Shelby Foote⟩ ⟨found their blankets a little ~ for civilized noses —Jackson Burgess⟩ (5) **:** INTENSIVE ⟨made their localities into symbols of ~ farming —A.W.Smith⟩ ⟨the first systematic efforts at ~ breeding —E.D. Ross⟩ **2 :** elevated or advanced in rank, quality, or character: as **a** (1) **:** of exalted social or political standing **:** ARISTOCRATIC, POWERFUL ⟨~ society consisting of the Spaniards and Creoles of property —C.L.Jones⟩ ⟨mainly concerned with Roman ~ life —William Murray⟩ ⟨a ~ official of the government⟩ (2) **:** of the first or great consequence **:** IMPORTANT, SUPREME ⟨primarily a parliament is a ~ court of justice —A.F.Pollard⟩ ⟨~ preparations were necessary for this journey —Herbert Hoover⟩ **:** GRAVE, SERIOUS ⟨a ~ insult⟩ ⟨aroused ~ displeasure⟩ **:** CRITICAL, CLIMACTIC ⟨at this ~ hour of Australia's history —W.F.Hambly⟩ ⟨the ~ moments were the start in the freshness of morning —John Buchan⟩ ⟨the ~ point of the novel is the escape⟩ ⟨the ~ spot of the Republican doings will come Friday night —*Spokane (Wash.) Spokesman-Rev.*⟩ (3) **:** relating to matters of the first importance **:** conducted on an exalted political or social level ⟨offered a fertile field for ~ intrigue —Carl Bridenbaugh⟩ ⟨born into the world of ~ politics⟩ (4) **:** rating or ranking as best, first, or most eligible ⟨the ~ man among entrants in the tryout⟩ ⟨if a bidder should be the ~ bidder on a facility —*U. S. Code*⟩ **b** (1) **:** morally or spiritually exalted **:** NOBLE, EDIFYING ⟨a man of ~ character⟩ ⟨met his death in the ~ Roman fashion —John Buchan⟩ ⟨writing is a ~ calling —Cyril Connolly⟩ ⟨good intent and ~ purpose are not enough —D.D.Eisenhower⟩ ⟨~ thinking and plain living⟩ (2) **:** intellectually or artistically of the first order **:** EXCELLENT ⟨the ~ tradition of the European fairy story and folk tale —*Brit. Book News*⟩ ⟨a theatrical production of ~ quality⟩ (3) **:** preeminent among or surpassing other civilizations or societies by some criteria ⟨the ~ civilizations of Middle America and the Andean Highlands —Holger Cahill⟩ (4) **:** characterized by sublime, heroic, or stirring events or subject matter **:** intensely moving **:** EXCITING ⟨a tale of ~ adventure⟩ ⟨~ romance and profound sympathy for the proletariat appear side by side in the poetry —*Encyc. Americana*⟩ ⟨the act in which she faces her accusers is ~ drama⟩ ⟨the ~ tragedy ends with both . . . dying but clasping each other's hands —Leslie Rees⟩ (5) **:** depending not so much on situation as on fine characterization and witty dialogue ⟨~ comedy⟩ (6) **:** conforming to some standard of correctness or excellence in speech or grammar ⟨the ~ Arabic of the Koran —J.C.Swaim⟩ (7) **:** not of the ordinary or routine sort **:** EXTRAVAGANT, BOISTEROUS ⟨an hour for ~ . . . nonsense —Elinor Wylie⟩ ⟨held ~ revelry at the castle that night⟩ ⟨along with her went excitement and ~ occasion —Nadine Gordimer⟩ **c :** difficult to comprehend or master **:** RECONDITE, ABSTRUSE ⟨when it comes to philosophy, ~ thought, and the eternal verities —Bergen Evans⟩ **3 a** (1) **:** indicating or reflecting anger **:** WRATHFUL ⟨saw there were going to be ~ words —Dodie Smith⟩ ⟨threatening them in very ~ language —George Willison⟩ (2) **:** ARROGANT, OVERBEARING, IMPERIOUS ⟨carry things with a ~ hand —John Buchan⟩ ⟨you certainly take a very ~ tone —Louis Auchincloss⟩ (3) **:** PRETENTIOUS, AMBITIOUS ⟨a ~ boast, but it is true —W.R.Inge⟩ ⟨makes ~ claims for his invention⟩ **b** (1) **:** ZEALOUS, EAGER, FAVORABLE, KEEN — usu. used with *on* ⟨is unusually ~ on her next venture —Lewis Funke⟩ ⟨has been particularly ~ on him —*Newsweek*⟩ (2) **:** extreme, devoted, or rigid in advocacy or practice esp. in matters of doctrine or ceremony ⟨hated as the leader of ~ toryism —*Brit. Book News*⟩; *specif, usu cap* **:** HIGH CHURCH **c** (1) **:** ELATED, GAY, CHEERFUL ⟨she hadn't the ~ spirits which endear grown-ups to healthy children —Joseph Conrad⟩ ⟨had a ~ old time together⟩ ⟨his heart was ~ as he entered the old homestead⟩ ⟨those were the ~ days —Sinclair Lewis⟩ (2) **:** hysterically or feverishly excited or gay **:** keyed up ⟨so ~ from nervous tension . . . they need half a dozen drinks to sober down —Alfred Bester⟩ ⟨like a ~ patient after shock treatment —Joseph Hitrec⟩ (3) **:** INTOXICATED, DRUNK ⟨getting ~*er* all the time by nipping at . . . martinis —Daniel Curley⟩ ⟨~ as a kite⟩; *also* **:** excited or stupefied by a narcotic substance (as heroin)

**syn** TALL, LOFTY: HIGH, the most general of these terms, implies marked extension upward, usu. from a base or foundation, or placement at a conspicuous height above the ground or above some lower level taken as the norm ⟨a *high* building⟩ ⟨a *high* cliff⟩ ⟨a *high* cupboard⟩ In extension it is often used to indicate a great degree of what it modifies or to stress a certain moral elevation ⟨a *high* color⟩ ⟨a *high* volume of sound⟩ ⟨a *high* purpose⟩ TALL applies to what rises or grows high by comparison with others of its kind, esp. when it is small in breadth as compared to its height ⟨a *tall* man⟩ ⟨a *tall* flagpole⟩ LOFTY, suggesting a greater, more imposing altitude than HIGH or TALL, has a much wider figurative than literal application carrying the idea of moral grandeur, dignity, or stature or of superciliousness ⟨a *lofty* mountain⟩ ⟨a *lofty* position in the church⟩ ⟨a *lofty* plane of conversation⟩ ⟨a *lofty* attitude toward servants⟩

**²high** \ˈhī\ *adv* -ER/-EST [ME *heghe, heye, highe, high*, fr. OE *hēah, hēage*, fr. *hēah*, adj.] **:** in a high manner: as **a** (1) **:** at or to a great distance or altitude ⟨after a cup of tea we walked a little ~*er* —John Seago⟩ ⟨climbed ~ on the ladder⟩ ⟨the waves dashed ~⟩ — often used in combination ⟨a *high*-climbing vine⟩ (2) **:** far up toward the source ⟨allow passage of . . . vessels as ~ as Albany —Herman Beukema⟩ — usu. used with *up* ⟨lives ~ up the river⟩ **b :** in or to a high position, amount, or degree ⟨prices have gone too ~⟩ ⟨that young man is aiming ~⟩ ⟨how ~ can one rise in this organization⟩ ⟨delay had cost ~ in bitterness —*Time*⟩ — often used in combination ⟨a *high*-ranking official⟩ **c :** RICHLY, LUXURIOUSLY ⟨has gay reunions . . . and lives ~ —J.W.Krutch⟩ — often used in the phrases *high off the hog* or *high on the hog* ⟨the new America is eating too ~ on the hog for its own good —*Newsweek*⟩

**³high** \"\ *n* -s [ME *hegh, hey, high*, fr. *hegh, hey, high*, adj.] **1 :** an elevated place or region: as **a :** HILL, KNOLL ⟨flat as a table top, without a single ~ or low —Harold Sinclair⟩ **b :** the upper region **:** the space overhead **:** SKY — usu. used with *on* ⟨each lifted on ~ his knife —A.C.Whitehead⟩ ⟨watched the birds wheeling on ~⟩ **c :** HEAVEN — used with *on* ⟨a judgment from on ~ —C.S.Kilby⟩ **d :** a region of high barometric pressure **:** ANTICYCLONE **2 a :** a high point **:** a top level **:** HEIGHT, ACME ⟨carrying snobbery to new . . . ~s —Leslie Charteris⟩ ⟨a ~ of 38 was due today . . . the weatherman forecast —*Cleveland (Ohio) Plain Dealer*⟩; *specif* **:** the highest price paid for a security during a specified period ⟨the daily ~⟩ **b :** the transmission gear giving the highest ratio of propeller-shaft to engine-shaft speed and the lowest multiplication of torque and consequently the highest speed of travel of an automotive vehicle **c** (1) **:** the highest trump that has been dealt in any game of the all-fours family (2) **:** the highest-ranking combination of upcards in stud poker **3 :** people of a class regarded as socially superior ⟨you find scoundrels among both the ~ and the low⟩ **4 :** HIGH SCHOOL ⟨she learned bookkeeping in ~ —John O'Hara⟩ **5** *slang* **:** the excited or stupefied state produced by a narcotic substance (as heroin)

**high altar** *n* [ME] **:** the principal altar in a church

**high analysis** *adj, of a fertilizer* **:** containing more than 20 percent of total plant nutrients

**high and dry** *adv* **1 :** out of the reach of the current or tide **:** out of water — used of a ship aground above water **2 :** in a helpless or abandoned position **:** without recourse ⟨millions of old people were left *high and dry* —M.A.Abrams⟩ ⟨resting *high and dry* on a bed of concrete —Dana Burnet⟩

**high and low** *adv* **:** upstairs and downstairs **:** EVERYWHERE ⟨looked for it *high and low*⟩

**high-and-mighty** \ˌ=ˌ=ˈ==\ *adj* **:** characterized by arrogance **:** IMPERIOUS ⟨rivermen . . . who had been *high-and-mighty* now were sitting on drift logs, literally, wondering what was coming next —Frederick Way⟩

**high-angle fire** *n* **:** cannon fire delivered at elevations greater than that for the maximum range

**high-back** \ˈ=ˌ=\ *adj, of a vowel* **:** high and back

**¹highball** \ˈ=ˌ=\ *n* [¹*high* + *ball*] **1 a** [so called fr. the fact that in early RR practice a metal ball was raised on a pole as a go-ahead signal to the engineer] **:** a railroad signal for a train to proceed at full speed **b :** a fast train **2 :** a drink of spirituous liquor mixed with water or more often a carbonated beverage (as seltzer or ginger ale) and served in a tall glass usu. with ice ⟨applejack ~⟩ ⟨whiskey ~⟩

**²highball** \"\ *vi* **:** to go at full or high speed ⟨see how safely they ~ with a full load —*Civil Engineering*⟩ ⟨a ~*ing* express train⟩ ~ *vt* **:** to drive at full or high speed ⟨how we ~*ed* those camions up —Christopher Morley⟩

**high·ball·er** \"ə(r)\ *n* [¹*highball* (signal) + *-er*] **:** SIGNALMAN

**high bar** *n* **:** a horizontal bar adjusted above head height and used as a support in some gymnastic exercises

**high beam** *n* **:** the focus of a vehicle headlight that sends the light forward for maximum long-range illumination of the road ahead and is intended for driving in open country — contrasted with *low beam*

**high beams** *n pl, New Eng* **:** LOFT

**high·be·lia** \hīˈbēlyə, -lēə\ *n* -s [¹*high* (in contrast to *lo-*, punningly taken as *low*) + *lobelia*] **:** any of various tall-growing American lobelias; *esp* **:** GREAT LOBELIA

**high·bind·er** \ˈhī,bīndə(r)\ *n* -s [fr. the *Highbinders*, a gang of vagabonds in New York City *ab*1806] **1 a :** THUG, GANGSTER, RUFFIAN ⟨this gang of ~s were supposed to be enforcing the law —Julien Hyer⟩ **b :** HATCHET MAN; *specif* **:** a member of an organized band of Chinese professional killers operating in the Chinese quarter of an American city **2 a :** a person who engages in fraudulent or shady activities **:** CONFIDENCE MAN, SWINDLER ⟨employ the saliva test on horses to guard against ~s injecting stimulants —C.B.Davis⟩ ⟨the ~ boys of the last Florida boom —Robert Moses⟩; *specif* **:** a corrupt or scheming politician ⟨the county payroll has 2,200 experienced vote raisers, many of them ~s of the lowest degree —*Nation*⟩

**high·bind·ing** \-diŋ\ *n* **:** SKULDUGGERY, FRAUD ⟨the techniques of larceny and ~ —R.H.Rovere⟩ ⟨the aroma of ~ will not down —R.B.McKerrow⟩

**high blood pressure** *n* **:** HYPERTENSION

**high blower** *n* **:** a horse that produces blowing esp. during exercise

**high-blown** \ˈ=ˌ=\ *adj* **:** inflated esp. with conceit **:** PRETENTIOUS ⟨*high-blown* but slightly mystifying verse —Stuart Keate⟩

**high blueberry** *n* **:** HIGHBUSH BLUEBERRY

**high-boiling** \ˈ=ˌ==\ *adj* **:** boiling at a relatively high temperature

**highborn** \ˈ=ˌ=\ *adj* **:** of noble birth

**highboy** \ˈ=ˌ=\ *n* **:** a high chest of drawers mounted on a base which has legs of considerable length and usu. several drawers esp. in style between 1690 and 1780 — compare BONNET TOP, LOWBOY

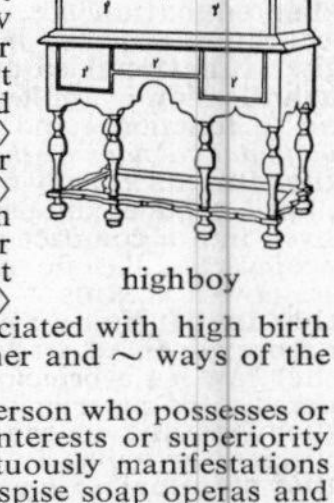
highboy

**high-braced** \ˈ=ˌ=\ *adj, archery* **:** HIGH-STRUNG

**high brass** *n* **1 :** brass containing at least 33 percent zinc — compare LOW BRASS **2 :** high-ranking officers or officials ⟨the living honorees weren't always political or military or railroad *high brass* —B.A.Botkin & A.F.Harlow⟩ ⟨doesn't know enlisted men and their opinion of *high brass* —G.W.Johnson⟩

**highbred** \ˈ=ˌ=\ *adj* **1 :** marked by high birth or breeding **:** coming from superior stock ⟨the ~ descendant of an ancient baron —Sir Walter Scott⟩ ⟨a ~ dog⟩ **2 :** having the characteristics of or associated with high birth or breeding **:** REFINED ⟨the grand manner and ~ ways of the society he frequented —J.R.Lowell⟩

**¹highbrow** \ˈ=ˌ=\ *n* [¹*high* + *brow*] **:** a person who possesses or has pretensions to strong intellectual interests or superiority **:** one who regards aloofly or contemptuously manifestations of mass culture **:** EGGHEAD ⟨~s . . . despise soap operas and are repelled by the success stories in popular magazines —W. O.Aydelotte⟩ ⟨~s who believe that . . . art is for art's sake —A.J.Toynbee⟩

**²highbrow** \"\ *adj* **:** of, relating to, or appropriate to a highbrow **:** having or giving the appearance of strong intellectual interests or superiority ⟨liking jazz or not liking jazz is almost equally ~ today —Roger Angell⟩ ⟨a Chinese scholar can be ineffably ~ —E.R.Hughes⟩ ⟨the magazine . . . will be uncompromisingly ~ —*Time*⟩

**high-browed** \ˈ=ˌ=\ *adj* **1 :** having a high brow **2 :** HIGHBROW ⟨the *high-browed* literary critics⟩

**high·brow·ism** \ˈhī,brau̇,izəm\ *n* -s **:** the state of mind associated with a highbrow **:** self-conscious intellectual superiority **:** INTELLECTUALISM

**high-brown** \ˈ=ˌ=\ *adj* **:** being a high yellow

**highbush** \ˈ=ˌ=\ *adj* **:** forming a notably tall or erect bush ⟨~ willows⟩ **:** borne on a highbush plant ⟨the ~ berries are larger and sweeter⟩

**highbush blueberry** *n* **1 :** any of several tall-growing blueberries of eastern No. America; *esp* **:** a highly variable moisture-loving shrub (*Vaccinium corymbosum*) that has deciduous ovate to broadly lanceolate leaves, whitish or pinkish flowers, and bluish to blackish edible fruit usu. with a distinct bloom and that is the source of most cultivated blueberries — compare EVERGREEN BLUEBERRY, RABBITEYE **2 :** the fruit of a highbush blueberry

**highbush cranberry** *n* **:** CRANBERRY BUSH 2

**highbush huckleberry** *n* **:** BLACK HUCKLEBERRY

**high-card pool** *n* **:** RED DOG 3

**high-central** \ˈ=ˌ==\ *adj, of a vowel* **:** high and central

**high chair** \ˈ=ˌ=\ *n* **:** a child's chair with long legs, a feeding tray, and a footrest

**high church** *adj, usu cap H&C* [back-formation fr. *high churchman*] **:** tending toward or stressing sacerdotal, liturgical, ceremonial, traditional, and Catholic elements as appropriate to the life of the Christian church — compare LOW CHURCH

**high churchman** *n, often cap H&C* **:** a person who adheres to High Church principles

**high-class** \ˈ=ˌ=\ *adj* [fr. the phrase *high class*] **:** of a class rated as superior in high degree **:** FIRST-CLASS ⟨modern *high-class* accommodations⟩ ⟨a *high-class* mechanic⟩

**high-climber** \ˈ=ˌ==\ *n* **1 :** CLIMBER 1a **2 :** HIGH RIGGER

high chair

**high cockalorum** *n* **1** *Brit* **:** a boys' game of leapfrog — used as a shout during the game **2 :** a person with pretensions to great importance **:** a high-and-mighty person **:** BIG SHOT ⟨placed himself as the *high cockalorum* of the universe —J.F.Stevens⟩

**high command** *n* **1 :** the supreme headquarters of a military force **2 :** the supreme leadership or decision-making group of any organization ⟨the Republican *high command* attempted to repair this damage —*New Yorker*⟩

**high commission** *n* **1 :** a group of persons delegated supreme authority and responsibility for the performance of some duty or the execution of some trust ⟨the Allied *High Commission* for Germany⟩ **2 :** the office or jurisdiction of a high commissioner ⟨the Western Pacific *high commission* includes the Gilbert and Ellice Islands Colony —Martin Wight⟩

**high commissioner** *n* **1 :** a representative of one country stationed in another; *esp* **:** a representative of the government of one British Commonwealth country in the capital of another with representational functions broadly similar to those of an ambassador — compare AGENT-GENERAL **2 a :** the

chief officer of a colonial territory or dependency **b :** the chief representative officer in a mandate, protectorate, or trust territory **3 :** the chief officer of an international commission or other agency ⟨the United Nations *high commissioner* for refugees⟩
**high council** *n* **:** a body of 12 high priests in the Mormon Church presided over by the stake presidency and having executive and judicial authority within the stake — compare APOSTLE
**high–count** \ˈ=ˈ=\ *adj* **:** having a large number of warp and weft yarns to the square inch ⟨a *high-count* percale sheeting⟩ — compare THREAD COUNT
**high court** *n* **:** a superior court: as **a :** SUPREME COURT **b :** an Australian court that is the highest and has power of judicial review of legislation
**high court of justice** *usu cap H&C&J* **:** the system of superior courts having the highest general criminal and civil jurisdiction in England and Wales and including divisions corresponding to the formerly independent courts now constituting it — compare ADMIRALTY 3, CHANCERY 1a, COURT OF COMMON PLEAS 1, COURT OF KING'S BENCH, EXCHEQUER 2, PROBATE COURT
**high court of justiciary** *usu cap H&C&J* **:** the supreme court having jurisdiction over criminal cases in Scotland ⟨their trial began in the *High Court of Justiciary* in Edinburgh —David Masters⟩ — compare COURT OF SESSION
**high cranberry** *n* **:** CRANBERRY BUSH 2
**high crime** *n* **1 :** a crime of an infamous nature contrary to public morality but not technically constituting a felony; *specif* **:** an offense which the U.S. Senate deems to constitute adequate grounds for removal of the president, vice-president, or any civil officer as a person unfit to hold public office and deserving of impeachment **2 :** a crime of a serious or aggravated nature
¹**high–cut** \ˈ=ˈ=\ *adj* [*high* + *cut*] **1 :** cut high up **2 :** having a high top — used of a boot
²**high–cut** \ˈ=ˌ=\ *n* **:** a laced boot reaching well up the calf of the leg
**high daddy** *n* **:** HIGHBOY
**high day** *n* [ME] **:** HOLY DAY, FEAST DAY
**highday** *interj* [by alter.] *obs* **:** HEYDAY
**high–dried** \ˈ=ˈ=\ *adj* **:** deprived of an unusually high percentage of its moisture by drying or baking
**highdried** \ˈ=ˌ=\ *n* -s [*high-dried*] **:** RED HERRING
**high dutch** *n, cap H&D* **1 :** HIGH GERMAN **2 :** the literary Dutch of the Netherlands in contrast to Afrikaans or Low Dutch
**high–duty** \ˈ=ˈ==\ *adj* [fr. the phrase *high duty*] **1** *of a machine* **:** being capable of doing a large amount of work in a specified time ⟨a *high-duty* drill⟩ **2 :** constituting products subject to a relatively high tax ⟨*high-duty* goods⟩
**high enema** *n* **:** an enema in which the injected material reaches the colon — compare LOW ENEMA
**high·er** \ˈhī(ə)r, -īə\ *comparative of* HIGH
**higher arithmetic** *n* **:** the general theory of numbers
**higher bacterium** *n* **:** any of numerous bacteria of comparatively complex organization — often contrasted with *eubacterium*
**higher certificate** *n* **:** HIGHER SCHOOL CERTIFICATE
**higher criticism** *n* **:** the literary-historical study of the Bible that seeks to determine such factors as authorship, date, place of origin, circumstances of composition, purpose of the author, and the historical credibility of each of the various biblical writings together with the meaning intended by their authors — compare LOWER CRITICISM
**higher degree** *n* **:** ADVANCED DEGREE
**higher education** *n* **:** education beyond the secondary level **:** education provided by a college or university
**higher functional calculus** *n* **:** functional calculus in which quantification is applied not only to individual variables but also to functional and propositional variables — called also *functional calculus of the second order*
**higher fungus** *n* **:** any of numerous fungi with hyphae well-developed, septate, and usu. at some stage of development interwoven into a compact tissue esp. in the fruiting body (as in Ascomycetes, Basidiomycetes and Fungi Imperfecti) — compare LOWER FUNGUS
**higher institution** *n* **:** an educational institution of collegiate or more advanced grade
**higher law** *n* **:** a principle of divine or moral law that is considered to be superior to constitutions and enacted legislation
**higher learning** *n* **:** education, learning, or scholarship on the collegiate or university level
**higher mammal** *n* **:** any of the placental or eutherian mammals; *esp* **:** a member of the Educabilia
**higher mathematics** *n pl but sing in constr* **:** mathematics of more advanced content than ordinary arithmetic and algebra, geometry, trigonometry, and beginning calculus
**higher school certificate** *n* **:** a certificate awarded on the successful completion of an examination taken by British secondary-school students who are preparing to enter a university
**higher thought** *n, usu cap H&T* **:** NEW THOUGHT
**higher–up** \ˌ==ˈ=\ *n* -s [fr. the phrase *higher up*] **:** a superior officer or official **:** a chief leader or agent in an organization ⟨brought to the attention of the *higher-ups* in the . . . State Department —Lindsay Rogers⟩
**high·est** \ˈhīəst\ *superlative of* HIGH
**highest common factor** *n* **:** the largest integer or polynomial of highest degree that is an exact divisor of each of two or more integers or polynomials respectively
**high explosive** *n* **:** a detonating explosive (as trinitrotoluene) used for its shattering effect
¹**high·fa·lu·tin** \ˌhīfəˈlütᵊn\ *also* **high·fa·lu·ting** \", -üd·|in, -üt|, |ēŋ\ *or* **hi·fa·lu·tin** *adj* [perh. fr. ¹*high* + alter. of *fluting*, pres. part. of ²*flute*] **1 :** characterized by or reflecting an attitude of self-importance or superciliousness **:** PRETENTIOUS ⟨~ people like the kind of fine ladies his wife was always playing bridge with —Nathaniel La Mar⟩ ⟨impress our correspondents by ~ letterheads —H.F.Ellis⟩ **2 :** expressed in or marked by the use of high-flown bombastic language **:** POMPOUS ⟨has written perhaps half a dozen excellent pieces . . . and a great deal of ~ bathos —H.L.Mencken⟩ ⟨a study of American adolescence done in a rather high-toned and ~ way —*Time & Tide*⟩ ⟨pretentious idealism or just ~ and pretentious talk —William Chomsky⟩
²**highfalutin** \"\ *n* -s **:** high-flown pretentious language **:** BOMBAST ⟨a medium . . . in which dramatic characters can express the purest poetry without ~ —T.S.Eliot⟩
**high fashion** *n* **:** HIGH STYLE
**high festival** *n* **:** a church festival observed in the more liturgical churches with full ceremonial
**high fidelity** *n* **:** the reproduction of sound with a high degree of faithfulness to the original (as by a radio or phonograph loudspeaker) — compare HI-FI
**high finance** *n* **:** large and complex financial operations or the major financial institutions that engage in them — sometimes used with an implication of unethical practice ⟨*high finance* is . . . Greek to most people —J.R.Aswell & E.J. Michelson⟩
**high five** *n* **:** ³CINCH
**high flanker** *n* **:** a male horse with incompletely descended testes
**highflier** *or* **highflyer** \ˈ=ˌ==\ *n* **1 :** one that flies high **2** *archaic* **:** one who is uncompromisingly orthodox or extreme in point of doctrine; *esp* **:** one who is extreme in supporting the claims to authority of the Church of England **:** HIGH CHURCHMAN **3 :** FLIER 6 ⟨took a ~ in watermelons that year —F.B.Gipson⟩
**high–flown** \ˈ=ˈ=\ *adj* **1 :** being high above the ordinary level of thought or sentiment **:** ELEVATED, EXALTED ⟨argue in terms of *high-flown* ideals —Oliver Franks⟩ **2 :** having a turgid or inflated character **:** BOMBASTIC, PRETENTIOUS ⟨*high-flown* talk of preserving the moral tone of the school —Leslie Rees⟩ ⟨the usual inflated rhetoric and *high-flown* vocabulary —James Yaffe⟩
**high–flying** \ˈ=ˈ==\ *adj* **1 :** rising to a considerable height ⟨displaying *high-flying* hoofs and thrashing tails —Court Paige⟩ **2 a :** inflated or pretentious in style, content, or ambition **:** HIGH-FLOWN ⟨a *high-flying* dissertation on the means to attain a social revolution —Wilfred Fienburgh⟩ ⟨*high-flying* proposals⟩ **b :** having an extremely lofty or metaphysical character **:** being too abstract or remote from human affairs **:** TRANSCENDENTAL ⟨directed against the intuitional, or *high-flying* school —C.N.Feidelson⟩ ⟨mocked the *high-flying* . . . Platonists —P.D.Partner⟩
**high forest** *n* [trans. of G *hochwald*] **:** a forest from seed — compare COPPICE
**high frequency** *n* **:** a frequency that is relatively high; *specif* **:** a radio frequency in the middle range of the radio spectrum — see RADIO FREQUENCY table
**high–frequency** \ˈ=ˈ===\ *adj* [*high frequency*] **1 :** occurring very frequently ⟨drills based on the repetition of *high-frequency* words⟩ **2 :** relating to high frequency: as **a :** involving a radio wave of high frequency — used esp. of sound waves and vibrations **b :** SUPERSONIC 1
**high–frequency telephony** *n* **:** an art or process of telephonic communication by means of carrier currents over electric conductors (as transmission lines) through the use of transmitting and receiving equipment like those used in radio
**high–front** \ˈ=ˈ=\ *adj, of a vowel* **:** high and front
**high gear** *n* **1 :** ³HIGH 2b **2 :** a state of intense or maximum activity ⟨the political campaign will move into *high gear* —G.C.Wright⟩ ⟨operations went into *high gear* last year —*N.Y. Times*⟩
**high german** *n, cap H&G* [trans. of G *hochdeutsch*] **1 :** German as natively used in southern and central Germany — see MIDDLE HIGH GERMAN, OLD HIGH GERMAN; compare BENRATH LINE, LOW GERMAN **2 :** ³GERMAN 2b
**high german consonant shift** *n, usu cap H&G* **:** CONSONANT SHIFT 2
**high grade** *n* **:** something that is of superior grade: as **a :** ore of high value or of relatively high value as compared with the average ore in a specific mine **b :** a grade animal that in conformation and economic qualities approximates the breed to which its known purebred ancestors belong
¹**high–grade** \ˈ=ˈ=\ *adj* [*high grade*] **:** of superior grade or quality ⟨*high-grade* writing⟩ ⟨*high-grade* manganese⟩: as **a :** being securities or other investments involving little or no risk and affording a relatively assured income ⟨*high-grade* bonds⟩ **b :** being near the upper extreme of the range in which it may occur ⟨a *high-grade* moron approaches normality⟩ ⟨a *high-grade* hydrocephalic exhibits maximum deformity⟩ — compare LOW-GRADE
²**high–grade** \"\ *vt* [*high grade*] **:** to steal (rich ore) from a mine; *also* **:** to mine only (the rich ore) — **high–grader** \ˈ=ˈ==\ *n* — **high–grading** \ˈ=ˈ==\ *n*
**high–ground willow oak** *n* **:** TURKEY OAK c
**high–grown** \ˈ=ˈ=\ *adj* **1 :** grown tall **2 :** covered with tall vegetation ⟨a *high-grown* slope⟩ **3** *of coffee* **:** grown at a high altitude
**high–handed** \ˈ=ˈ==\ *adj* **:** OVERBEARING, ARBITRARY ⟨*high-handed* behavior⟩ — **high–hand·ed·ly** *adv* — **high–hand·ed·ness** *n* -ES
**high hat** *n* **1 :** BEAVER 3 **2** *usu* **high–hat** \ˈ=ˈ=\ **:** one who assumes an attitude of superiority **:** SNOB, SWELL ⟨amid the gasps of the *high-hats* he . . . threw in his lot with the British Labor Party —*New Republic*⟩
¹**high–hat** \ˈ=ˈ=\ *adj* [*high hat*] **:** supercilious or snobbish in attitude or manner **:** ARISTOCRATIC ⟨*high-hat* over the type of job she wants —*Springfield (Mass.) Union*⟩ ⟨cold, impersonal, a trifle *high-hat* —*Nation*⟩
²**high–hat** \"\ *vt* [*high hat*] **:** to look down one's nose at **:** treat snobbishly **:** SNUB ⟨*high-hatted* her . . . when they were sober —Edmund Wilson⟩ ⟨the literati tended to *high-hat* the first issues —Jay Franklin⟩
**high heal–all** *n* **:** WOOD BETONY 2
**high–hearted** \ˈ=ˈ==\ *adj* [ME *highe herted*] **1 :** full of courage or nobility **:** HIGH-SPIRITED ⟨*high-hearted* language —Archibald MacLeish⟩ **2 :** full of gaiety **:** INSOUCIANT, LIGHTHEARTED ⟨a *high-hearted* junket —*Hunting's Monthly List*⟩ — **high–heart·ed·ly** *adv* — **high–heart·ed·ness** *n* -ES
**high–high** \ˈ=ˈ=\ *adj, of tide* **:** higher than the normal high
**high–hold·er** \ˈ=ˌhōldə(r)\ *also* **high–hole** \ˈ=ˌhōl\ *or* **high–hol·er** \ˈ=ˌhōlə(r)\ *n* [by folk etymology fr. ME *hygh-whele*, prob. of imit. origin] *dial* **:** ³FLICKER
**high holiday** *or* **high holy day** *n, usu cap both Hs & D* **:** either of the Jewish religious holidays Rosh Hashanah and Yom Kippur observed respectively on the 1st and the 10th of Tishri with particular solemnity
**high horse** *n* **1 :** an unyielding, pretentious, or arrogant mood **:** a high and mighty air or attitude ⟨when he . . . saw the desperate need for more men, he came down off his *high horse* —J.F.Dobie⟩ ⟨wanted to get on her *high horse* and treat him as if he were nothing —William Heuman⟩ **2 :** a sulky or resentful mood, air, or attitude ⟨on your *high horse* because he didn't praise your mince —Arnold Bennett⟩
**high–house** \ˈ=ˌ=\ *n* **:** a trap house on the left side of a skeet range that projects the target from a point 10 feet from the ground — called also *hi-trap*; compare LOW-HOUSE
**high hurdles** *n pl but sing or pl in constr* **:** a track event of 120 yards or 110 meters distance with ten 3 ft. 6 in. hurdles to be surmounted — compare LOW HURDLES
**high iron** *n* **:** a main-line railroad track
**high·ish** \ˈhīish\ *adj* **:** rather high ⟨with a ~ collar and a black cord necktie —*New Yorker*⟩
**high–jack** *var of* HIJACK
**high jinks** *also* **hi–jinks** *or* **high jinx** \ˈhīˈjiŋ(k)s\ *n pl* **1 :** an old Scottish game of forfeits at drinking **2 :** boisterous or noisy sport **:** HORSEPLAY ⟨the juvenile *high jinks* of a college reunion —John Mason Brown⟩ ⟨the officers and men . . . were indulging in *high jinks* ashore —H.C.Ickes⟩
**high jump** *n* **:** a jump for height in a track or field contest either from a standing position or from a running start
**high jumper** *n* **:** an athlete who participates in the high jump
**high jumping** *n, pl* **high jumpings :** the act or action of performing the high jump
**high–key** \ˈ=ˈ=\ *adj* **:** having or producing light tones only with little contrast — used of a photographic print or subject or of the lighting of a photographic subject
¹**high·land** \ˈhīlənd *sometimes* -ˌland *or* -ˌlaa(ə)nd\ *n* [ME, fr. *high* + *land*] **1 :** elevated or mountainous land **2** *usu cap* [²*Highland*] **:** WEST HIGHLAND
²**highland** \"\ *adj* **1 :** of or relating to a highland **:** inhabiting or growing in a highland **2** *usu cap* [fr. the *Highlands*, northern part of Scotland] **:** of, related to, or typical of the Highlands of Scotland ⟨typically *Highland* . . . a strange mixture of pride and tenderness, of poverty and generosity —Ian Finlay⟩
**high·land·er** \-də(r)\ *n* -s **1 :** an inhabitant of a highland **2** *usu cap* **:** an inhabitant of the Highlands of Scotland — compare LOWLANDER
**highland fling** *n, usu cap H* **:** a Scottish folk dance that is performed usu. by three or four persons, with nimble footwork and low kicks
**highland pony** *n, usu cap H* **:** a comparatively large hardy pony native to the Highlands of Scotland and some adjacent islands
**high–lead** \ˈ=ˌlēd\ *n* **:** SPAR TREE
**high–lead logging** *n* **:** HIGH-LINE LOGGING
**high–level** \ˈ=ˈ==\ *adj* **1 :** carried out or engaged in at a high altitude ⟨were ordered to take to the slit trenches if the *high-level* attack developed —*Coast Artillery Jour.*⟩ **2 a :** of, involving, or engaged in by persons of high position, rank, or achievement ⟨a *high-level* staff to set up and supervise a political and operational training center —S.K.Padover⟩ ⟨time to push the proposal for a *high-level* conference —Drew Middleton⟩ ⟨*high-level* discussions of the control of atomic energy —C.L.Sulzberger⟩ **b :** holding high position or rank ⟨*high-level* government officials will meet . . . to discuss the outlook for aluminum —T.E.Mullaney⟩
¹**highlight** \ˈ=ˌ=\ *n* [¹*high* + *light*] **1 a :** the lightest spot or area (as in a painting or engraving) **:** a spot or any of several spots in a modeled drawing or painting that receives the greatest amount of illumination **b :** a bright part of a photographic picture or subject represented by a considerable density in the negative and by nearly clear paper or other support in the print **2 :** an event, detail, topic, or accomplishment of major significance or special interest ⟨one of the ~*s* of the fashionable London season —Emily Hahn⟩ ⟨more analysis will be written . . . later but here are some ~*s* —*Kiplinger Washington Letter*⟩ ⟨these are only ~*s:* he also wrote . . . several volumes of verse, numerous short stories —E.P. Earnest⟩
²**highlight** \"\ *vt* **1 :** to illuminate with vivid distinctness **:** throw a strong light upon ⟨designed for general store lighting and to ~ featured merchandise —*Electrical World*⟩ ⟨matches flared, momentarily ~*ing* the faces —*Nat'l Geographic*⟩ **2 :** to paint out the highlight areas of (a halftone negative); *also* **:** to etch away the light dots in the corresponding areas of (a printing plate) — compare DROP OUT **3 a :** to center attention upon **:** cause to loom large in importance or urgency **:** EMPHASIZE, STRESS ⟨these publications . . . ~*ed* the deficiencies of the current freshman program —T.F.Dunn⟩ ⟨~ a major factor in the Hemisphere's aid program —*Atlantic*⟩ **b :** to constitute a highlight or distinctive feature of ⟨the slang that ~*s* his dialogue —Bennett Cerf⟩ ⟨three new talents . . . ~*ed* the year —*Britannica Bk. of the Yr.*⟩
**highlight halftone** *n* **:** DROPOUT 3
**highlighting** \ˈ=ˌ==\ *n* **1 :** the act or effect of casting a highlight upon or giving prominence to something ⟨~ is accomplished by the use of high-powered . . . spotlights —H.F.Helvenston⟩ **2 :** additional illumination for enhancing the highlights on a photographic subject
**high–line** \ˈ=ˈ=\ *adj* **:** being a fisherman or fishing boat with a large or the largest catch ⟨*high-line* vessels sometimes average 400,000 pounds per man —*Commercial Fishing*⟩
**highline** \ˈ=ˌ=\ *n* **1 :** a high-voltage electric transmission line **2 :** a line or cable strung between ships or from ship to shore (as for the transfer of cargo or crew)
**high–line logging** *n* **:** logging in which the logs with one end in the air are hauled in by a highline cable
**highliner** \ˈ=ˌ==\ *n* **:** a high-line fisherman or fishing boat
**high–lived** \ˈ=ˈlīvd\ *adj, of a horse* **:** HIGH-SPIRITED ⟨a horse of kind disposition but very *high-lived* —J.L.Hervey⟩
**high liver** *n* **:** one that lives luxuriously
**high·lone** \ˈhīˌlōn\ *adv* [by alter.] *dial* **:** ALONE ⟨the baby has just learned to stand ~⟩
**high lonesome** *n, dial* **:** DRUNK, BENDER, SPREE ⟨got on a *high lonesome* and told the barkeeper his business —J.F.Dobie⟩
**highlow** \ˈ=ˌ=\ *n, dial chiefly Eng* **:** an ankle-high laced boot
**high–low** \ˈ=ˈ=\ *n* **1 :** a come-on or echo in bridge or whist in which the play of an unnecessarily high card is later confirmed by the play of a lower card of the same suit **2 :** a game of poker in which the highest ranking and lowest ranking hands divide the pot equally
**high–low–jack** \ˌ=ˌ=ˈ=\ *n* **:** any of several card games derived from all fours (as cinch, pitch, seven-up) in each of which there are special scoring values for winning the highest trump in play, the lowest trump in play, the jack of trumps, and either the ten of trumps or the most points with ace counting 4, king 3, queen 2, and jack 1
**high·ly** *adv* [ME *heghly, heyly, highly*, fr. OE *hēalīce*, fr. *hēah* high + *-līce* -ly — more at HIGH] **1 :** in or to a high place, level, or rank ⟨only a few ~ placed persons . . . know the entire story —H.L.Stimson⟩ **2 a :** in or to a high degree, amount, or extent **:** EXTREMELY, INTENSELY ⟨a ~ interesting article⟩ ⟨a ~ successful play⟩ ⟨a ~ educated woman⟩ **b :** at a high rate or wage ⟨a ~ paid skilled worker⟩ **3 a :** in a noble or elevated manner **:** SOLEMNLY ⟨let us now and here ~ resolve to . . . march along the path of real progress —F.D. Roosevelt⟩ **b :** with high approval or favor **:** FAVORABLY ⟨does not think ~ of many of his films —*Current Biog.*⟩
**highly–strung** \ˌ==ˈ=\ *adj* **:** HIGH-STRUNG
**high mallow** *n* **:** a common biennial hirsute mallow (*Malva sylvestris*) native to Europe and naturalized in the eastern U.S. having an erect stem, long-petioled leaves and rose-purple flowers with darker veins
**high mass** *n, often cap H&M* [ME] **:** a mass that is sung and not said by a priest with the assistance of a deacon and subdeacon and characteristically with incense, music, and greater ceremonial than in a low mass
**high–melting** \ˈ=ˈ==\ *adj* **:** melting at a relatively high temperature
**high milling** *n* **:** a process of making flour from grain by several successive grindings and intermediate sorting
**high–minded** \ˈ=ˈ==\ *adj* **1** *archaic* **:** PROUD, ARROGANT **2 :** of or marked by or reflecting elevated principles and feelings ⟨a *high-minded* man⟩ ⟨*high-minded* talk⟩ — **high–mind·ed·ly** *adv* — **high–mind·ed·ness** *n* -ES
**high–mixed** \ˈ=ˈ=\ *adj, of a vowel* **:** high and central
**high moor** *n* **:** a boggy acid upland area characterized by abundant heaths and sphagnum
**high–muck–a–muck** \ˈhīˌməkēˌmək, |ə|-\ *or* **high–muckety–muck** \|əd·ē-\ *n* [by folk etymology fr. Chinook Jargon *hiu muckamuck* plenty to eat] **:** a person of high station or importance; *esp* **:** such a person marked by arrogance or conceit
**high·ness** *n* -ES [ME *heghnes, heynes, highnes*, fr. OE *hēahnes, hēanes*, fr. *hēah* high + *-nes* -ness — more at HIGH] **1 :** the quality or state of being high **:** ELEVATION, LOFTINESS ⟨the ~ of a flooded river⟩ **2 :** a person of honor — used as a title given to kings, princes, or other persons of exalted rank ⟨His Royal *Highness* the Prince of Wales⟩
**high noon** *n* **1 :** precisely noon **2 :** the most advanced, flourishing, or creative stage or period ⟨the *high noon* of his genius —John Pfeiffer⟩ ⟨the *high noon* of mid-Victorian liberalism —*Times Lit. Supp.*⟩
**high–octane** \ˈ=ˈ==\ *adj* **1 :** having a high octane number (as at least 80) and hence good antiknock properties ⟨*high-octane* aviation gasoline⟩ **2 :** of extreme degree **:** HIGH-POWERED **:** high quality ⟨aquavit, that *high-octane* Swedish liqueur —Bill Hosakawa⟩ ⟨verbs produced by back-formation are usually challenged by *high-octane* purists —H.L. Mencken⟩
**high–pass filter** *n* **:** an electric-circuit filter that transmits only frequencies above a prescribed frequency limit
**high–pitched** \ˈ=ˈ=\ *adj* **:** having a high pitch: as **a** (1) **:** being lofty in tone or thought ⟨the magazine was a little *high-pitched* intellectually —R.G.Martin⟩ (2) **:** marked by or exhibiting strong feeling or intense sensibility **:** AGITATED ⟨*high-pitched* denunciations —James Gray⟩ ⟨a *high-pitched* religiosity —Roger Fry⟩ ⟨that restless *high-pitched* life —Gertrude Atherton⟩ **b :** pitched in a high key or register ⟨the composition was too *high-pitched* for the singer⟩ ⟨spoke in a *high-pitched* voice⟩ **c :** inclining steeply ⟨a *high-pitched* roof⟩
**high place** *n* [ME] **:** a temple or altar used by the ancient Semites and built usu. on a hill or elevation
**highpockets** \ˈ=ˌ==\ *n pl but sing in constr* **:** a very tall lank man
**high polymer** *n* **:** a macromolecular substance (as polystyrene or cellulose) consisting of molecules that are large multiples of units of low molecular weight
**high port** *n* **:** a cross-body position in which a rifle is carried while a soldier is charging or jumping
**high–powered** *also* **high–power** \ˈ=ˈ==\ *adj* **:** having high power or quality: as **a :** having great drive, energy, or capacity **:** DYNAMIC ⟨import *high-powered* professional talent to help him —T.H.White b. 1915⟩ ⟨many *high-powered* executives . . . work themselves to death —Bruce Bliven b. 1889⟩ **b** *usu* *high-power* using a cartridge with a bullet heavy enough and having a muzzle velocity high enough for hunting deer and larger game ⟨a *high-power* rifle⟩
¹**high–pressure** \ˈ=ˈ==\ *adj* [fr. the phrase *high pressure*] **1 a :** having, involving, or operating at a high or comparatively high pressure ⟨a *high-pressure* automobile tire⟩ **b :** having a high barometric pressure **2 a :** using or characterized by forceful methods of selling **:** AGGRESSIVE, INSISTENT ⟨a *high-pressure* salesman⟩ ⟨*high-pressure* blurbs about toothpaste —*Amer. Guide Series: N.Y.*⟩ — compare LOW-PRESSURE **b :** imposing or involving severe strain or tension ⟨the . . . stresses of *high-pressure* occupations —*Fortune*⟩ ⟨the *high-pressure* merry-go-round of big business administration —*Current Biog.*⟩
²**high–pressure** \"\ *vt* [fr. the phrase *high pressure*] **:** to urge to a course of action with insistent, importunate, or forceful arguments **:** overcome the resistance of by such methods ⟨don't try to *high-pressure* me —Edwin Corle⟩ ⟨beware of salesmen who seek to *high-pressure* you into precipitate purchases —*Assoc. of Better Business Bureaus*⟩ ⟨*high-pressuring* the elected representatives of the people —Karl Schriftgiesser⟩

**high-pressure area** *n* : ³HIGH 1d
**high priest** *n* [ME *hege prest*] **1** : a chief priest; *esp* : the head of the Jewish priesthood in ancient times **2** : a priest of the Melchizedek priesthood in the Mormon Church **3** : a principal officer of a Masonic chapter **4** : the head of a movement or chief expounder of a doctrine ⟨the philosophical *high priests* of modern education —M.B.Smith⟩
**high priestess** *n* : a female high priest
**high priesthood** *n* : the priesthood of a high priest; *specif* : the Melchizedek priesthood of the Mormon Church
**high-priestly** \ˈ=ˌ==\ *adj* [*high priest* + *-ly*] : of, relating to, or having the characteristics of a high priest
**high-proof** \ˈ=ˈ=\ *adj* : highly rectified : very strongly alcoholic ⟨*high-proof* spirits⟩
**high relief** *n* [trans. of F *haut-relief*] : sculptural relief in which half or more than half of the natural circumference of the modeled form projects from the surrounding surface — distinguished from *bas-relief*
**high renaissance** *n*, *usu cap H&R* : the artistic style of the first half of the 16th century in western Europe esp. as manifested in Rome and Florence and characterized by heroic centralized composition, technical mastery of drawing and conception, and a mature humanistic content
**high rigger** *n* **1** : a logger who rigs spar trees — called also *high-climber* **2** : a worker who erects high ladders for acrobatic performances
**highroad** \ˈ=ˌ=\ *n* **1** *chiefly Brit* : HIGHWAY **2** : the best approach : an easy way ⟨there is no one ~ to literary appreciation —Geoffrey Bullough⟩ ⟨the direct ~ to salvation —*New Republic*⟩
**high roller** *n* **1** : one who spends freely in fast or luxurious living ⟨one wealthy cowman . . . who was always a *high roller* in town —Ross Santee⟩ **2** : one who gambles recklessly or for high stakes ⟨round up some . . . *high rollers* to fade his bets —C.B.Davis⟩
**highs** *pl of* HIGH
¹**high school** *n* **1** : a secondary school usu. public-supported and usu. organized on a 3-year or 4-year basis and comprising several divisions (as college preparatory, commercial, vocational, general) **2** *Brit* : a college preparatory school **3** : a school specializing in adult education often professional or technical but sometimes liberal — compare FOLK HIGH SCHOOL
²**high school** *n* [trans. of F *haute école*] : a system of advanced exercises in horsemanship
**high school·er** \ˈ=ˌskülə(r)\ *n* : a high school student
**high sea** *n* : the open part of the sea or ocean: as **a** : the sea or ocean lying outside the territorial waters or maritime belts of a country — usu. used in pl. **b** : the part of the sea or ocean within which transactions are subject to court of admiralty jurisdiction — usu. used in pl.
**high-sighted** *adj*, *obs* : looking upward : HAUGHTY
**high sign** *n* : SIGNAL; *esp* : a warning or informing signal given stealthily or with gestures — usu. used in the phrase *give the high sign* ⟨gave her the *high sign* when the plainclothes police . . . had gone off to supper —Ida A. R. Wylie⟩
**high-sounding** \ˈ=ˈ==\ *adj* : POMPOUS, IMPOSING ⟨*high-sounding* but barren title —J.L.Motley⟩
**high-speed** \ˈ=ˈ=\ *adj* **1** : operated or adapted for operation at high speed **2** : suitable for or relating to the production of short-exposure photographs of rapidly moving objects or events of short duration (as for analytical measurement or study) ⟨*high-speed* film⟩ ⟨*high-speed* photography⟩
**high-speed steel** *n* : an alloy tool steel which when heat-treated retains much of its hardness and toughness at red heat thus enabling tools made of it to cut at high speeds even though red-hot through friction
**high-speed turn** *n* : TEMPO TURN
**high-spirited** \ˈ=ˈ===\ *adj* : characterized by a bold, energetic, or lofty spirit : having ardor or fire : not dull or apathetic ⟨a *high-spirited* tomboy of a child —Katharine Scherman⟩ — **high-spirit·ed·ly** *adv* — **high-spirit·ed·ness** *n* -ES
**high-step** \ˈ=ˌ=\ *vi* [back-formation fr. *high-stepper*] : to move with a high step ⟨*high-stepping* across the sand —Nadine Gordimer⟩
**high-stepper** \ˈ=ˈ==\ *n* : one that steps high; *esp* : a spirited horse that moves with a high step
**high-stepping** \ˈ=ˈ==\ *adj* **1** : moving with a high step ⟨a *high-stepping* horse⟩ **2** : given to the pursuit of pleasure : living fast or wild ⟨a *high-stepping* town with plenty of fun for all —Helene Huff⟩
**high-stick·ing** \ˈ=ˈstikiŋ\ *n* : the act of carrying the blade of the stick at an illegal height in the game of ice hockey
**high street** *n* [ME *hege strete*, *heighe strete*, fr. OE *hēahstrǣt*, fr. *hēah* high + *strǣt* street — more at HIGH, STREET] *Brit* : a main or principal street
**high-strung** \ˈ=ˈ=\ *adj* **1** : being in a state of tense or extreme sensibility : highly sensitive or nervous ⟨a *high-strung* person⟩ ⟨dogs . . . are *high-strung* creatures —Joyce Cary⟩ **2** *of an archery bow* : having a distance greater than a fistmele between handle and bowstring
**high style** *n* : the newest in fashion or design often with extreme lines and usu. adopted by a limited number of people — called also *high fashion*
¹**hight** \ˈhīt, *Scot* ˈhiḵt\ *vb past* [ME *highten*, fr. *hehte*, *heet*, *highte* (past of *hoten*), fr. OE *heht*, past of *hātan* to command, promise, call, be called; akin to OHG *heizzan* to command, promise, call, ON *heita*, Goth *haitan*, and prob. to L *ciēre* to put in motion, move, Gk *kiein* to go away, travel, *kinein* to set in motion, Skt *cyavate* he moves, goes away; basic meaning: to set in motion] **1** *archaic* : CALLED, NAMED ⟨Childe Harold was he ~ —Lord Byron⟩ **2** *chiefly Scot* **a** : pledged as security **b** : PROMISED
²**hight** *var of* HEIGHT
**high table** *n* : an elevated table in the dining room of a British college for use by the master and fellows of the college and distinguished guests
**hightail** \ˈ=ˌ=\ *vi* : to move at full speed or rapidly esp. in making a getaway : clear out ⟨a young purse snatcher ~*ing* up a steep hill —Elgar Dolson⟩ — often used with *it* ⟨~*ed* it straight through town —Eudora Welty⟩ ⟨where Washington and his troops made their final stand before ~*ing* it across the Hudson —Bernard Kalb⟩ ⟨~*ed* it off with another man —Shelby Foote⟩
**high tea** *n*, *Brit* : a meal served between five and six o'clock usu. with meat, salad, stewed fruit, cakes or cookies, and with tea
**high-temperature** \ˈ=ˈ=. . .\ *adj* : operating or carried out at high temperatures ⟨*high-temperature* furnaces⟩ ⟨*high-temperature* carbonization of coal⟩
**high-temperature cement** *n* : a cement capable of resisting high temperatures without fusing, softening, or spalling and suitable for the bonding of refractory materials
**high-temperature short-time method** *n* : FLASH PASTEURIZATION
**high-tension** \ˈ=ˈ==\ *adj* : having a high voltage or relating to apparatus to be used at high voltage — used esp. to indicate thousands of volts
**high-test** \ˈ=ˈ=\ *adj* : passing a difficult test; *specif* : having a high volatility — used esp. of gasoline and naphtha
**high-test hypochlorite** *n* : CALCIUM HYPOCHLORITE b
**high tide** *n* **1** : the tide when it is high water **2** : the culminating point : CLIMAX ⟨it was, perhaps, *high tide* of the . . . movement, its greatest hour —J.B.Martin⟩
**hightoby** \ˈ=ˈ==\ *n* [short for earlier *hightobyman*, fr. thieves' argot *hightoby* highway, highway robbery (fr. ¹*high* + *toby*) + *man*] *Brit* : HIGHWAYMAN
**high-toned** \ˈ=ˈ=\ *also* **high-tone** \ˈ=ˌ=\ *adj* **1 a** : having a high moral or intellectual tone or quality : DIGNIFIED ⟨Jefferson's *high-toned* . . . and yet devastating reply —C.G. Bowers⟩ ⟨the London *Times* . . . and other *high-toned* publications —H.L.Mencken⟩ **b** : of superior social rank, manners, or breeding : ARISTOCRATIC ⟨the *highest-tone* plantation owners in this state —Lillian Hellman⟩ ⟨discreet, decorous, and *high-toned* establishments —Eugene Burr⟩ ⟨has just admitted to its *high-toned* studbook a new breed of dog —*New Yorker*⟩ **2** : marked by pretensions to superior social status : putting on airs : PRETENTIOUS, HIGH-FLOWN ⟨*high-toned* insincerity —David Gascoyne⟩
**high treason** *n* [ME *hye treasoune*] **1** : treason against the sovereign or the state being in old English law the highest offense against the state — compare PETIT TREASON **2** : TREASON
**highty-tighty** \ˌhīd-ēˈtīd-ē\ *adj* [by alter.] : HOITY-TOITY ⟨had a *highty-tighty* way that repulsed me —W.A.White⟩
¹**high-up** \ˈ=ˈ=\ *adj* [²*high* + *up*] : of high rank or status ⟨*high-up* officers on both sides —M.A.Hancock⟩
²**high-up** \"\ *n*, *pl* **high-ups** : a person of high rank or status ⟨the *high-ups* in London and America —Frederick Howard⟩
**highveld** \ˈ=ˌ=\ *n* [part trans. of Afrik *hoogveld*, fr. *hoog* high + *veld* field, veldt] *southern Africa* : plateau land with an elevation of about 4000 feet used esp. for grazing
**high-warp** \ˈ=ˈ=\ *adj* : having the warp threads hung or strung vertically ⟨*high-warp* tapestry⟩
**high water** *n* **1 a** : water at its utmost flow or greatest elevation; *specif* : the water of the sea, a lake, or river at its ordinarily highest level or flow **b** : the time of such elevation **2** : FRESHET ⟨wanted a new house after a *high water* on the river carried her old one away —Shirley A. Grau⟩
**high-water** \ˈ=ˈ==\ *adj* [*high water*] : unusually short; *esp* : having or being trousers that are unfashionably short ⟨an ancient *high-water* suit —Sinclair Lewis⟩ ⟨bought me *high-water* pants —Calder Willingham⟩
**high-water line** *or* **high-water mark** *n* **1 a** : the line of the shore of the sea or of a lake or river to which the waters usu. reach at high water: (1) : the line that marks the limit of the rise of the medium tides of the sea between the spring and neap tides (2) : the line that marks the limit of the soil so affected by the water of a lake or river as to have a nature and vegetation distinct from that of the banks **b** : a mark showing the highest level reached by a body of water **2** *usu high-water mark* : the highest point : ACME ⟨the *high-water mark* of a girl's social career —Hamilton Basso⟩
**high-water shrub** *n* : MARSH ELDER 2
**highway** \ˈ=ˌ=\ *n* -S *often attrib* [ME *heghewei*, *highway*, fr. OE *hēiweg*, *hēahweg*, fr. *hēah* high + *weg* way — more at HIGH, WAY] **1 a** : a road or way on land or water that is open to public use as a matter of right whether or not a thoroughfare : a public road or way (as a footpath, road, or waterway) including the right-of-way — compare PRIVATE WAY **b** : such a road or way established and maintained (as by a state) in accordance with law **c** : a main direct road (as between one town or city and another) — sometimes contrasted with *byway* **2** : a primary or well-known aspect or field ⟨the ~*s* and byways of literature⟩
**highway bond** *n* : a bond issued by a taxing jurisdiction the proceeds of which are for the construction of highways
**highway engineer** *n* : an engineer whose training or occupation is in highway engineering
**highway engineering** *n* : a branch of civil engineering dealing with the planning, location, design, construction, and maintenance of highways and with the regulations and control devices employed in highway traffic operations
**high·way·man** \ˈ=ˌ=mən *sometimes* (ˈ)=ˈ==\ *n*, *pl* **highwaymen** : a person who robs on the public road : a highway robber
**highway post office** *n* : a bus carrying mail which is sorted in transit
**highway robbery** *n* **1** : robbery committed on or near a public highway esp. against travelers **2** : excessive profit or advantage derived from a business transaction
**highwheeler** \ˈ=ˈ==\ *n* : a steam locomotive with large driving wheels for high-speed passenger-train service
**high wine** *n* : distilled spirits containing a high percentage of alcohol — usu. used in pl.
**high wire** *n* : a tightrope considerably higher above ground than the one ordinarily used
**high-wrought** \ˈ=ˈ=\ *adj* **1** : wrought with fine art or skill : ELABORATE ⟨the recipient of these *high-wrought* epistles —*Times Lit. Supp.*⟩ **2** : worked up or agitated to a high degree ⟨a *high-wrought* passion⟩
**high yellow** *n* : a mulatto or colored person of light-yellow color
**HIH** *abbr* Her Imperial Highness; His Imperial Highness
**hi·jack** *or* **high-jack** \ˈhīˌjak\ *vt* [origin unknown] **1 a** (1) : to steal by stopping a vehicle carrying contraband, illicit, or stolen goods ⟨~ a truckload of bootleg whiskey —*Emporia (Kans.) Gazette*⟩ (2) : to stop in transit and steal the cargo of ⟨~ a truck near the foot of the mountain⟩ (3) : to hold up and rob in the manner of one who hijacks ⟨attempted to ~ us for the jewelry right in daylight —Frank O'Leary⟩ **b** : to steal or rob as if by hijacking ⟨accused of ~*ing* half a million marks' worth of textiles —Joseph Wechsberg⟩ ⟨connives against the republic and has to flee the country in a ~*ed* airplane —Harvey Swados⟩ ⟨reputedly ~*ed* the less intrepid gentry of their ill-got booty and their slaves —*N.Y. Herald Tribune*⟩ **c** : KIDNAP ⟨about sixty thousand Kanakas were enticed or ~*ed* to Australia —Alan Moorehead⟩ **2 a** : to subject to extortion or swindling ⟨has deliberately set out to . . . ~ the American people through uncontrolled profits and inflation —Philip Murray †1952⟩ **b** : COERCE, FORCE ⟨~*ing* buyers into purchasing unwanted accessories —N.K.Teeters & J.O.Reinemann⟩
**hi·jack·er** *or* **high-jack·er** \-kə(r)\ *n* : one that hijacks ⟨repair-bill ~*s* —*Road & Track*⟩ ⟨~*s* stole . . . over $20 million worth of cargo from trucks —*Business Week*⟩
**hijinks** *var of* HIGH JINKS
**hij·ra** *or* **hij·rah** \ˈhijrə\ *n* -S [Ar *hijrah*, lit., flight] : HEGIRA
¹**hike** \ˈhīk\ *vb* -ED/-ING/-S [perh. akin to ¹*hitch*] *vt* **1 a** *dial chiefly Eng* : to raise or toss with the horns : GORE **b** *dial Brit* : to toss up and down : SWING **2** : to move, pull, or raise often with a jerk or other sudden motion ⟨*hiked* him out —Adrian Bell⟩ ⟨*hiked* himself onto my bed⟩ ⟨*hiking* their dresses above their knees —E.D.Radin⟩ ⟨sections *hiked* into place by cranes —*Newsweek*⟩ **3** : to increase in amount esp. sharply or suddenly ⟨~ taxes on luxury goods⟩ ⟨~ rents⟩ **4** : to cause to hike ⟨*hiked* himself off to work⟩ : guide or lead on a hike ⟨*hiked* them until their feet hurt⟩ ~ *vi* **1 a** : MARCH, TRAMP, WALK ⟨*hiked* 10 miles that day⟩ ⟨you have to park the car . . . and ~ in —Linda Braidwood⟩; *esp* : to go on a long walk or march for pleasure or exercise ⟨loves to ~⟩ ⟨arranged to spend the weekend *hiking*⟩ **b** *dial chiefly Eng* : to go away : DECAMP — usu. used with *off* or *out* **c** : to journey or travel by any means ⟨~ on skis through snow and dark —Carl Jonas⟩ ⟨borrowed some money and *hiked* over to Paris⟩ **2** *dial Brit* : to toss up and down : JOLT, JOUNCE, SWAY **3** : to rise or go up as if by being pulled : work upward out of place ⟨no shrinking, no sagging, no *hiking* —*N.Y.Times*⟩ —usu. used with *up* ⟨her skirt and slip had *hiked* up in back —Ralph Chapman⟩
²**hike** \"\ *n* -S **1** : TRAMP, MARCH; *esp* : a long walk undertaken for pleasure or exercise **2** : a lifting or a moving upward (as of a quantity, amount, degree) : INCREASE, RISE ⟨a 10 percent ~ in taxes⟩ ⟨called for a ~ in production⟩ ⟨wage ~*s*⟩
**hik·er** \-kə(r)\ *n* -S : one that hikes; *esp* : a person who goes on a hike for pleasure or exercise
**hi·ku·li** \(h)iˈkülē\ *n* -S [Huichol] : PEYOTE
**hila** *pl of* HILUM
**hi·lar** \ˈhīlə(r)\ *adj* [NL *hilum* + E *-ar*] : of, relating to, or located near a hilum
¹**hi·lar·ia** \həˈla(a)rēə, hīˈ-\ *n* -S *usu cap* [L, fr. neut. pl. of *hilaris*] : an imperial Roman festival of the cult of Cybele held on the vernal equinox to celebrate the renewal of life on earth in the spring symbolized by the resurrection of the god Attis
²**hilaria** \"\ *n*, *cap* [NL, irreg. fr. Auguste de Saint-*Hilaire* †1853 Fr. botanist + NL *-ia*] : a small genus of grasses of the southwestern U. S. and Mexico having a terminal spike with the spikelets in threes — see CURLY MESQUITE
**hi·lar·i·ous** \həˈla(a)rēəs, -ler-, -lār- *also* (ˈ)hīˈl-\ *adj* [modif. (influenced by E *-ious*) of L *hilarus*, *hilaris*, fr. Gk *hilaros* — more at SILLY] : marked by hilarity : affording or given to hilarity : LUDICROUS, MERRY, MIRTHFUL ⟨serious plays . . . alternated with ~ broad comedy —W.P.Eaton⟩ ⟨a joyous, lighthearted, and ~ mode of life —C.A. and Mary Beard⟩
**hi·lar·i·ous·ly** *adv* : in a hilarious manner
**hi·lar·i·ous·ness** *n* -ES : HILARITY
**hi·lar·i·ty** \həˈlarəd-ē, -ətē, -i *also* hīˈ- *or* -ler-\ *n* -ES [MF *hilarité*, fr. L *hilaritat-*, *hilaritas*, fr. *hilarus*, *hilaris* + *-itat-*, *-itas* -ity] **1** : temperate gaiety : CHEER, CHEERFULNESS ⟨wine gives not light, gay, ideal ~ but tumultuous, noisy, clamorous merriment —Samuel Johnson⟩ **2** : boisterous merriment : intense mirth or laughter ⟨in a continual gale of ~⟩
**hil·a·ry·mas** \ˈhil(ə)rēməs\ *n* -ES *usu cap* [ME *Hillarimesse*, fr. St. *Hilary* †*ab* A.D. 367 bishop of Poitiers + ME *messe* mass — more at MASS] : the feast of St. Hilary on January 13 in the Anglican calendar and January 14 in the Roman Catholic calendar
**hil·a·ry term** \ˈhilərē-\ *n*, *usu cap H* [after St. *Hilary*] **1** *chiefly Brit* **a** : the term from January 11 to 31 during which the superior courts of England were formerly open — compare EASTER TERM, MICHAELMAS TERM **b** *also* **hilary sitting** : the sitting of the High Court of Justice of England between January 11 and the Wednesday before Easter **2** *chiefly Brit* : the second academic term in a British university beginning in mid January and ending before Easter
**hilch** \ˈhilch, -lsh\ *vi* -ED/-ING/-ES [prob. alter. of Sc *hilt* to limp, alter. of ²*halt*] *chiefly Scot* : to hobble along : LIMP
**hil·de·brand·ine** \ˌhildəˈbranˌdən, -nˌdīn\ *also* **hil·de·brand·ian** \-ndēən\ *adj*, *usu cap* [*Hildebrand* (Pope Gregory VII), Ital. prelate + E *-ine* or *-ian*] **1** : of or relating to Hildebrand esp. with reference to his drastic reforms of church government and his assertion of papal supremacy over the lower clergy and civil authorities **2** : adhering to the principles of Hildebrand ⟨the *Hildebrandine* party⟩
¹**hil·ding** \ˈhildiŋ\ *adj* [perh. fr. pres. part. of *hild*, *hyld*, obs. var. of *hield*] *archaic* : lacking moral principles, convictions, or courage : BASE
²**hilding** \"\ *n* -S *archaic* : a hilding person
**hil·gard·ite** \ˈhilˌgärˌdīt, -gər-\ *n* -S [Eugene W. *Hilgard* †1916 Amer. geologist + E *-ite*] : a mineral $Ca_8(B_6O_{11})_3Cl_4.4H_2O$ consisting of hydrous chloride and borate of calcium occurring in colorless monoclinic crystals
**hili** *pl of* HILUS
**hi·lif·er·ous** \(ˈ)hīˈlif(ə)rəs\ *adj* [ISV *hili-* (fr. NL *hilum*) + *-ferous*] : bearing a hilum
**hil·i·gay·non** *also* **hil·i·gai·non** \ˌhiləˈgīnən\ *n*, *pl* **hiligaynon** *or* **hiligaynons** *also* **hiligainon** *or* **hiligainons** *usu cap* [native name on Panay] **1 a** : a Bisayan people inhabiting Panay and part of Negros, Philippines **b** : a member of the Hiligaynon people **2** : an Austronesian language of the Hiligaynon people related to but not mutually intelligible with Cebuan and frequently considered a dialect of Bisayan
¹**hill** \ˈhil\ *n* -S *often attrib* [ME *hill*, *hul*, fr. OE *hyll*; akin to OE *holm* island, OS *holm* hill, ON *holmr* island, L *collis* hill, *culmen* top, *celsus* high, Gk *kolōnos* hill, Lith *kelti* to lift up, and perh. to OE *heall* stone, rock, ON *hallr* stone, Goth *hallus* rock, cliff, and perh. to Skt *kūṭa* hammer, mallet; basic meaning: rising, raising] **1** : a natural elevation of land of local area and well-defined outline: **a** : a more or less rounded elevation as contrasted with a peaked or precipitous one — compare BUTTE, MESA **b** : a conspicuous elevation in a comparatively flat country ⟨the seven ~*s* on which Rome was built⟩ **c** (1) : any of the inferior elevations of a rugged country : an elevation higher than a rise and lower than a mountain (2) **hills** *pl* : a range or group of hills ⟨visited the Black ~*s* and the Rocky mountains⟩ **d** : hilly country ⟨a ~ district⟩ ⟨~ people⟩ — often used in pl. ⟨lives in the ~*s*⟩ **2** : a heap or mound of earth or other material reared by human or animal agency ⟨the ~*s* of a prairie dogs' town⟩ **3** : a group of several seeds or plants planted in one hole ⟨sow five seeds to each ~⟩ ⟨a ~ of beans⟩ **4** : an incline esp. in a road : SLOPE ⟨trucks laboring up the long ~⟩ **5** *dial* : dry land surrounded by swamp, marsh, or water : solid ground **6** : an elevation on any surface : RIDGE ⟨the ~*s* and hollows of the cobblestone pavement⟩ — **over the hill** : past the peak : on the downgrade ⟨I was *over the hill* as far as moneymaking was concerned —W.A.White⟩ — compare *go over the hill* at GO OVER
²**hill** \"\ *vt* -ED/-ING/-S **1** : to form into a heap ⟨~ up soil around roses⟩ **2** : to heap or draw earth around or upon ⟨~*ed* the potatoes⟩
³**hill** \"\ *vt* -ED/-ING/-S [ME *hulen*, *hilen*, *hillen*, prob. fr. ON *hylja* to hide, cover; akin to OHG *hullen* to cover, Goth *huljan* to cover, OE *helan* to hide, conceal — more at HELL] *dial Eng* : to protect by covering : HIDE
**hill-and-dale** \ˌ==ˈ=\ *adj* [fr. the phrase (*over*) *hill and dale*] *of a phonograph record* : having a groove of varying depth
¹**hill·bil·ly** \ˈhilˌbilē, -li, ˈ=ˌ==\ *n* -ES [¹*hill* + *Billy*, nickname for *William*] **1** : a person from a backwoods area (as the mountains of the southern U.S.) — often used disparagingly **2** : a hillbilly song
²**hillbilly** \"\ *adj* **1** : of or relating to a hillbilly : suggestive of hillbillies **2** : relating to or characterized by hillbilly music
**hillbilly music** *n* **1** : folk songs and folk style of singing and playing of the southern U.S. **2** : any music deriving from or imitating folk style or the style of the western cowboy esp. as exploited commercially — called also *country music*
**hillbird** \ˈ=ˌ=\ *n* **1** : UPLAND PLOVER **2** : FIELDFARE
**hill climb** *n* : a road race over a hilly course held by an automobile or motorcycle club
**hillcrest** \ˈ=ˌ=\ *n* : the top line of a hill
**hillculture** \ˈ=ˌ==\ *n* -S [trans. of D *bergcultuur*] : agriculture utilizing erosion-preventing crops that are ecologically and economically best suited for sloping or hilly land
**hill-drop** \ˈ=ˌ=\ *adj* : planting a full hill at desired intervals ⟨a *hill-drop* corn planter⟩
**hil·le·brand·ite** \ˈhiləˌbranˌdīt, -==ˈ=ˌ=\ *n* -S [William F. *Hillebrand* †1925 Amer. chemist + E *-ite*] : a mineral $Ca_2SiO_3(OH)_2$ consisting of a hydrous calcium silicate occurring in white masses
**hil·lel·ite** \ˈhiˌleˌlīt\ *n* -S *usu cap* [*Hillel* †A.D. 9 Jewish teacher + E *-ite*] : an adherent of the liberal and humanitarian principles of interpretation of the Jewish law developed by Rabbi Hillel and opposed by the Shammaites
**hill·er** \ˈhilə(r)\ *n* -S : an attachment to a cultivator or plow for hilling plants
**hill fox** *n* : a fox (*Vulpes himalaicus*) that has fur of a pale fulvous color and is found in the mountains of India
**hill grub** *n* : a larva of the antler moth (*Cerapteryx graminis*) that is often destructive to pasture grasses in England
**hill holder** *n* : a device other than a hand brake that keeps a motor vehicle from backing down an incline when the foot is removed from the brake pedal; *esp* : such a device connected to a clutch pedal to keep the brakes applied as long as the clutch pedal is depressed
**hill indexing** *n*, *pl* **hill indexings** : indexing by preplanting a potato of each hill
**hill·i·ness** \ˈhilēnəs, -lin-\ *n* -ES : the quality or state of being hilly
**hill·man** \ˈhilmən\ *also* **hills·man** \-lzm-\ *n*, *pl* **hillmen** *also* **hillsmen** : a man native to or inhabiting a hilly or mountainous often isolated area and typically differing markedly in outlook, customs, and speech from a man of the plains
**hill myna** *n* : an Asiatic starling (*Gracula religiosa*) that is black with a white spot on the wings and a pair of flat yellow wattles on the head and is often tamed and taught to pronounce words
**hil·lo** *or* **hil·loa** \həˈlō, ˈhi(ˌ)lō, ˈhiˈlō — *see* HELLO\ *archaic var of* HELLO
**hil·lock** \ˈhilək\ *n* -S [ME *hilloc*, fr. *hill* + *-oc* -ock] : a small hill : MOUND — **hill·ocked** \-kt\ *adj* — **hill·ocky** \-kē\ *adj*
**hillock tree** *n* : an Australian shrub (*Melaleuca hypericifolia*) with showy spikes of red flowers
**hill of beans** : something of negligible importance or value — used chiefly in negative constructions ⟨doesn't amount to a *hill of beans*⟩ ⟨not worth a *hill of beans*⟩
**hill partridge** *n* **1** : any of numerous partridges of southern Asia and the East Indies that constitute a genus (*Arborophila*) of the family Phasianidae — called also *tree partridge* **2** : SPUR FOWL
**hill planter** *n* : a machine that is used for planting seed (as corn) in hills
**hill reaction** \ˈhil-\ *n*, *usu cap H* [after Robin *Hill*, Brit. chemist] : a photochemical liberation of oxygen from water by cells or cell fragments containing chlorophyll that is equivalent to the photochemical phase of plant photosynthesis
**hills** *pl of* HILL, *pres 3d sing of* HILL
**hillside** \ˈ=ˌ=\ *n*, *often attrib* [ME *hulle syde*, fr. *hulle*, *hill* hill + *syde*, *side* side] : a part of a hill between the summit and the foot ⟨a green valley whose ~*s* . . . are a mass of yellow buttercups —*Amer. Guide Series: Minn.*⟩ ⟨pell-mell down the ~ streets —Sherwood Anderson⟩
**hillside plow** *n* : SWIVEL PLOW

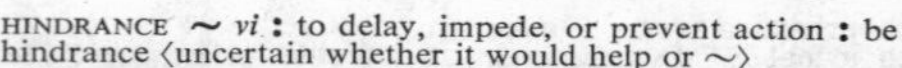

**hillslope** \'=,=\ *n* : HILLSIDE

**hills-of-snow** \',==\ *n, pl* **hills-of-snow** : a Japanese hydrangea (*Hydrangea arborescens grandiflora*) with large clusters of snow-white sterile flowers

**hill star** *n* : any of several hummingbirds comprising the genus *Oreotrochilus* and inhabiting parts of the Andes

**hill station** *n* : a village or government post (as in India) situated in the hills or low mountain ranges and serving usu. as a health resort in the hot season

**hill tit** *n* : any of numerous small Asiatic singing birds of *Siva, Leiothrix*, and related genera

**hilltop** \'=,=\ *n* : the highest part of a hill

**hil·lul ha·shem** \kə̇,lülhə'shām\ *n* -s [Heb *ḥillūl hashshēm* desecration of the name (of God)] : an act in contravention of Jewish religious or ethical principles that is regarded as an offense to God — compare KIDDUSH HASHEM

**hillwort** \'=,=\ *n* : WILD THYME

**hilly** \'hilē, -li\ *adj* -ER/-EST [ME, fr. *hill* + *-y*] **1** : abounding with hills **2** : inclining like a hill : of the character of a hill : STEEP

**hi·lo grass** \'hē(,)lō-\ *n* [Hawaiian *hilo*] : a sour grass (*Paspalum conjugatum*) that is common in the Hawaiian islands and is often a troublesome weed because of its ability to cover vast areas in a short time

**hil·sa** \'hilsə *also* -l(t)sə\ *n* -s [Hindi *hilsā*, fr. Skt *ilīśa, illiśa*] : a valuable anadromous herring (*Clupea ilisha*) of India resembling a shad

[1]**hilt** \'hilt\ *n* -s [ME, fr. OE; akin to OS *helta* oar handle, OHG *helza* hilt, ON *hjalt* hilt, W *cleddyf* sword, OE *healt* lame — more at HALT] **1** : a handle of a sword or dagger **2** : the handle of any weapon or of a tool (as a miner's pick) — **to the hilt** *or* **up to the hilt** : to the very limit : FULLY, COMPLETELY ⟨mortgaged the farm *up to the hilt*⟩ ⟨proved its importance *to the hilt*⟩

hilt

[2]**hilt** \"\ *dial past of* HOLD

[3]**hilt** \"\ *dial var of* HOLD

**hi·lum** \'hīləm\ *n, pl* **hi·la** \-lə\ [NL, fr. L, trifle] **1 a** : a scar on a seed (as a bean) marking the point of attachment of the ovule to the funiculus **b** : the nucleus of a starch grain **c** : a small lateral outgrowth on a basidiospore near the point of its attachment to the sterigma on which it was borne **2** : a mark or notch in or opening from a bodily part suggesting the hilum of a bean: as **a** : the part of a gland or of certain other organs where the blood vessels, nerves, or ducts leave and enter ⟨the ~ of the kidney⟩ ⟨the ~ of the lung⟩ **b** : a small opening in the statoblast of a sponge

**hi·lus** \-ləs\ *n, pl* **hi·li** \-,lī\ [NL, alter. of *hilum*] : HILUM 2a

[1]**him** \(h)im, ,him, ̩ēm\ *pron, objective case of* HE [ME, fr. OE, dat. of *hē* he — more at HE] **1** : [1]HE 1, 2, 3, 4: **a** — used as indirect object of a verb ⟨friends who have given ~ the most sympathy —W.M.Thackeray⟩ **b** — used as object of a preposition ⟨we may not fight a duel with Death nor engage in controversy with ~ —W.L.Sullivan⟩ **c** — used as direct object of a verb ⟨I know ~⟩ **d** — used in comparisons after *than* and *as* when the first term in the comparison is the direct or indirect object of a verb or the object of a preposition ⟨the jacket fits you as well as ~⟩ ⟨give me the book rather than ~⟩ ⟨this treatment would be more beneficial to you than ~⟩ **e** — used in absolute constructions esp. together with a prepositional phrase, adjective, or participle ⟨I met him down near the river, at the height of the first run of fish, and ~ without his rod —Alasdair Carmichael⟩ ⟨~ being such a fool, the Fool Killer heard about him —Helen Eustis⟩ **f** — used by speakers on all educational levels and by many reputable writers though disapproved by some grammarians in the predicate after forms of *be*, in comparisons after *than* and *as* when the first term in the comparison is the subject of a verb, and in other positions where it is itself neither the subject of a verb nor the object of a verb or preposition ⟨it was ~⟩ ⟨she is as tall as ~⟩ ⟨~ and his promises!⟩ **g** — used in substandard speech and formerly also by reputable writers as the subject of a verb which it does not immediately precede or as part of the compound subject of a verb ⟨damned be ~ that first cries "Hold, enough!" —Shak.⟩ ⟨~ and his wife was real old-timers —Vance Randolph⟩ **h** — used like the adjective *his* with a gerund by speakers and writers on all educational levels though disapproved by some grammarians ⟨what do you think of ~ becoming a doctor⟩ **2** : HIMSELF — used reflexively as indirect object of a verb ⟨he went to his . . . tailor . . . and got ~ a . . . gray spring suit —W.A.White⟩, object of a preposition ⟨he couldn't decide whether to have the package delivered or take it with ~⟩, or direct object of a verb ⟨a child that . . . finds ~ suddenly in his mother's arms again —Nathaniel Hawthorne⟩

[2]**him** \'him\ *n* -s : MAN, BOY ⟨four ~s and a her —Charles Dickens⟩

**HIM** *abbr* Her Imperial Majesty; His Imperial Majesty

**hi·ma** \'hēmə\ *also* **hu·ma** \'hümə\ *n, pl* **hima** *or* **himas** *also* **huma** *or* **humas** *usu cap* **1** : a Bantu-speaking pastoral people who constitute the ruling segment of the population of the Uganda kingdoms of Nyankole, Nyoro, and Toro and an inferior class among the Ganda people, are found also in Ruanda and on the western shore of Lake Albert in the Congo, and are supposed to be cognate in origin with the Tusi and perhaps the Galla and Somali **2** : a member of the Hima people

**hima·laya berry** \,himə'lāə-; hə'mäl(ə)yə-, -'mål, \|lē̤ə-; *sometimes* \himə'lāyə- *or* -'lāyə- *or* -'līə-\ *n, usu cap H* [fr. the *Himalayas*, mountain range between Nepal and Tibet] : a European blackberry (*Rubus procerus*) introduced and naturalized in the U.S. and having leaves strongly whitened beneath with dense felty tomentum

**himalaya honeysuckle** *n, usu cap H* : a Himalayan shrub honeysuckle (*Leycesteria formosa*) of the family Caprifoliaceae with drooping spikes of purplish flowers

[1]**hima·layan** *pronunc at* HIMALAYA BERRY +n\ *adj, usu cap* [*Himalayas* + E *-an*] **1** : of, relating to, or characteristic of the Himalayas **2** : extremely large ⟨was responsible for a *Himalayan* blunder⟩

[2]**himalayan** \"\ *n* **1** *or* **himalayan rabbit** *usu cap H* **a** : a breed of small white domesticated rabbits with black nose, feet, tail, and ear tips **b** -s *often cap H* : a rabbit of this breed **2** -s : total or partial restriction of pigmentation to the cooler parts of the body (as tail, paws, face, ears) occurring as one of a polygenic series of variants in mammalian coat color dominant to albinism but recessive to chinchilla and the wild type and exhibited in typical form in the Himalayan rabbit and less perfectly in the Siamese cat

**himalayan barley** *n, usu cap H* : an Asiatic barley (*Hordeum vulgare trifurcatum*) having the awns represented by short furcate branches

**himalayan black bear** *n, usu cap H* : BLACK BEAR 2

**himalayan cedar** *n, usu cap H* : DEODAR

**himalayan cypress** *n, usu cap H* : BHUTAN CYPRESS

**himalayan fir** *n, usu cap H* : a very large evergreen tree (*Abies spectabilis*) of the mountains of northern India that is cultivated for its majestic habit and luxuriant foliage

**himalayan hare** *n, usu cap H* : a large long-eared hare (*Lepus oiostolus*) that is usu. silvery brown with the tail white above and is found at high elevations in Tibet

**himalayan lilac** *n, usu cap H* : a shrub (*Syringa emodi*) of the mountains of northern India that has pale-lilac or white flowers

**himalayan pine** *n, usu cap H* : a Himalayan tree (*Pinus excelsa*) with wide-spreading branches and drooping bluish-gray leaves — called also *Asiatic white pine*

**himalayan rhubarb** *n, usu cap H* : an East Indian herb (*Rheum emodi*) that is one of the sources of emodin — called also *Indian rhubarb*

**himalayan snow cock** *n, usu cap H* : a snow cock (*Tetraogallus himalayensis*) having a chestnut pectoral band and a white chest with black bars

**himalayan spruce** *n, usu cap H* : a spruce (*Picea smithiana*) of the Himalayan region that is cultivated for ornament

**hima·lo-chinese** \,himə(,)lō, hə̇'mäl(-+ \ *adj, usu cap H&C* [*Himalo-*, fr. *Himalayas*] : BURMO-CHINESE

**hi·man·to·pus** \hə'mantəpəs\ *n, cap* [NL, fr. Gk *himantopous*, a kind of water bird, fr. *himant-, himas* thong, strap + *-o-* + *pous* foot] : a genus of wading birds comprising the stilts

**hi·mat·i·on** \hə'mad·ē,än, -ēən\ *n* -s [Gk, dim. of *himat-, hima, heimat-, heima* garment, fr. *hennynai* to clothe — more at WEAR] : a long loose outer garment of ancient Greece consisting of a rectangular cloth worn by both men and women usu. with one end pulled over the left shoulder from the rear and the remainder going round the back, under the right arm and across the front and draped over the left arm or shoulder — compare CHITON, CHLAMYS, PEPLOS, TRIBON

himation

**hi·me·ji** \hə'mājē\ *adj, usu cap* [fr. *Himeji*, Japan] : of or from the city of Himeji, Japan : of the kind or style prevalent in Himeji

**hime·ne** *also* **himi·ne** \'hēmə,nā, 'him-\ *n* -s [Tahitian, Hawaiian, & Marquesan *himene*, fr. E *hymn*] : a native song or hymn of French Oceania

**himp** \'himp\ *vi* -ED/-ING/-S [prob. akin to G dial. *hümpen, himpen* to limp] *dial Eng* : LIMP

**him·self** \(h)im'=, ēm'=\ *pron* [ME, fr. OE *him selfum*, dat., him himself, fr. *him* + *selfum*, dat. of *self* — more at SELF] **1** : that identical male one : that identical one regarded as masculine (as by personification) : that identical one whose sex is unknown or immaterial — compare [1]HE; used (1) reflexively as object of a preposition or direct or indirect object of a verb ⟨everyone must look out for ~⟩ ⟨in those days Providence was still busying ~ with everybody's affairs —Arnold Bennett⟩ ⟨he got ~ a new suit⟩; (2) for emphasis in apposition with *he, who, that*, or a noun ⟨he ~ informed me⟩ ⟨he informed me ~⟩ ⟨the composer ~ conducted the symphony⟩ ⟨the composer conducted the symphony ~⟩ ⟨criticizing the king's advisers and the king ~⟩ ⟨the judge, who had once been a lawyer ~⟩; (3) for emphasis instead of nonreflexive *him* as object of a preposition or direct or indirect object of a verb ⟨his income supports his wife and ~⟩; (4) for emphasis instead of *he* or instead of *he himself* as subject of a verb ⟨he was never influenced in art by any fashions save those ~ created —Osbert Sitwell⟩ or as predicate nominative ⟨he has only one loyal disciple and that is ~⟩ or in comparisons after *than* or *as* ⟨he associated mainly with people younger than ~⟩; (5) in absolute constructions ⟨~ simple, fair-minded, unhappy, he comes in contact with the more extravagant varieties of Americans abroad —Carl Van Doren⟩ **2** : his normal, healthy, or sane condition ⟨he came to ~⟩ : his normal, healthy, or sane self ⟨ill for some time, he is now ~ again⟩ **3** *Irish & Scot* : a man of consequence; *esp* : the master of the house ⟨she has . . . breakfast on the table before ~ is up —Cahir Healy⟩ **4** : YOURSELF — used in speaking to or as if to a baby ⟨did he hurt ~⟩; used in some English dialects in addressing a boy or a person of higher or lower social status than the speaker; compare [1]HE 4

[1]**him·yar·ite** \'himyə,rīt\ *n* -s *usu cap* [*Ḥimyar*, a legendary ancient king in Yemen + E *-ite*] **1 a** : an Arab people of antiquity dwelling in southern Arabia **b** : a member of such people **2** : an Arab of a group of related ancient peoples of southern Arabia that included besides the Himyarites proper the Sabaeans and Minaeans, that had a civilization of great antiquity, and that were completely absorbed by northern Arabs by the time of Muhammad

[2]**himyarite** \"\ *or* **him·yar·it·ic** \',==ˈrid·ik\ *adj, usu cap* : of or relating to the ancient Himyarites or their language

**himyaritic** \"\ *or* **himyarite** \"\ *n* -s *usu cap* : the language of the Himyarites occurring in inscriptions ranging from about 700 B.C. to A.D. 550

[1]**hin** \̩(h)ən, ̩(h)ēn\ *pron* [ME, fr. OE *hine*, accus. of *hē* he — more at HE] *dial chiefly Eng* : HIM

[2]**hin** \'hin, -ē̤-\ *n* -s [Heb *hīn*, fr. Egypt *hnw*] : an ancient Hebrew unit of measure for liquids equal to about a gallon and a half

**hi·na·lea** \,hēnə'lāə\ *n* -s [Hawaiian] : a brilliantly marked convict fish (*Hepatus triostegus*) of the Hawaiian islands that is often used for food

**hi·nau** \'hē,naù\ *n* -s [Maori] : a New Zealand timber tree (*Elaeocarpus dentatus*) whose bark yields a useful dye

**hi·na·ya·na** \,hēnə'yänə, -ēnē'(y)ä-\ *n* -s *cap* [Skt *hīnayāna*, lit., lesser vehicle, fr. *hīna* left behind, inferior, lesser (fr. *hīyate* he is left) + *yāna* action of going, vehicle, fr. *yāti* he goes; akin to *jahāti* he leaves — more at GO, JANITOR] : the smaller more conservative branch of Buddhism dominant in Ceylon, Burma, Thailand, and Cambodia and characterized by adherence to the Pali scriptures and to the nontheistic nonspeculative ideal of self-purification to nirvana through contemplative and moral effort esp. as an arhat — called also *Little Vehicle, Pali Buddhism, Southern Buddhism, Theravada*; compare MAHAYANA

**hi·na·ya·nist** \-nəst\ *n* -s *usu cap* : an adherent of Hinayana — **hi·na·ya·nis·tic** \',==(,)=ˈnistik\ *adj, usu cap*

[1]**hind** \'hīnd\ *n, pl* **hinds** *also* **hind** [ME *hinde*, fr. OE *hind*; akin to OHG *hinta* hind, ON *hind*, Gk *kemas* young deer, Skt *śáma* hornless; basic meaning: hornless] **1** : a female of the red deer — compare HART, STAG **2** : any of various typically spotted groupers — see RED HIND, ROCK HIND, SPECKLED HIND

[2]**hind** \"\ *n* -s [ME *hine* servant, farmhand, fr. OE *hīna*, gen. of *hīwan*, pl., members of a household — more at HOME] **1 a** : a farm laborer in northern England and Scotland; *esp* : a skilled farm worker who is provided with a cottage on the farm as a home for himself and his family **b** : an English farm manager : BAILIFF **2** : an unsophisticated countryman : HICK, RUSTIC

[3]**hind** \", *before consonants & in "hind end" often* -n\ *adj* [ME *hint*, prob. back-formation fr. OE *hinder*, adv., behind, *hindan*, adv., from behind, behind, & *hindema* last; akin to OHG *hintar*, prep., behind, *hintaro*, adj., rear, *hintana*, adv., from behind, behind, ON *hindri* last, Goth *hindana*, adv., behind, beyond, *hindar*, prep., behind, beyond, and prob. to OE *hē* he — more at HE] : of or forming the part that follows or is behind : BACK, REAR ⟨the dog's ~ legs⟩ ⟨the handkerchief in his ~ pocket⟩ — compare FORE — **on one's hind legs** : taking an indignant or determinedly independent attitude ⟨got up *on my hind legs* . . . and sounded off —Saul Bellow⟩

[4]**hind** \'hīnd\ *n* -s : HINDQUARTER ⟨a ~ of beef⟩

**hind·ber·ry** \'hīn(d)-— *see* BERRY\ *n* [fr. (assumed) ME *hindberie*, fr. OE (akin to OHG *hintberi* raspberry), fr. *hind* + *berie* berry — more at BERRY] : EUROPEAN RASPBERRY

**hindbrain** \'=,=\ *n* **1 a** : the posterior of the three primary divisions of the vertebrate brain or the parts developed from it including the cerebellum, pons, and medulla oblongata **b** : METENCEPHALON 1 — distinguished from *myelencephalon* **c** : MYELENCEPHALON **2** : the posterior segment of the brain of an invertebrate (as an insect) : TRITOCEREBRUM

**hindcast** \'=,=\ *n* : a statistical calculation determining probable past conditions (as of marine wave characteristics at a given place and time)

**hind end** *see* [3]HIND\ *n* **1** : a part that follows behind : REAR ⟨the *hind end* of a train⟩ **2** : BUTTOCKS, RUMP

[1]**hin·der** \'hində(r)\ **hindered**; **hindered**; **hindering** \-d(ə)riŋ\ **hinders** *vb* [ME *hindren, hinderen*, fr. OE *hindrian*; akin to OHG *hintarōn* to hinder, ON *hindra*, and prob. to OE *hinder* behind — more at HIND] *vt* **1** *obs* : to do harm to : IMPAIR, DAMAGE ⟨fight against Jerusalem, and to ~ it —Neh 4:3 (AV)⟩ **2** : to make slow or difficult the course or progress of : RETARD, HAMPER ⟨policies that will further or ~ the cause of independence⟩ ⟨was greatly ~*ed* in his efforts by bad weather⟩ **3** : to keep from occurring, starting, or continuing : hold back : PREVENT, CHECK — often used with *from* ⟨machines are sometimes ~*ed* by speed from delivering their best performance —Edith Diehl⟩ ⟨could not ~ himself from dwelling upon it —Stephen Crane⟩ **4** : to interfere with the activity of (a group or molecule of a compound) esp. as a result of space relationships — compare BLOCK 1g, STERIC HINDRANCE ~ *vi* : to delay, impede, or prevent action : be a hindrance ⟨uncertain whether it would help or ~⟩

**syn** IMPEDE, OBSTRUCT, BLOCK, BAR, DAM: HINDER indicates a checking or holding back from acting, moving, or starting, often with harmful or annoying delay or interference ⟨shallow water and constantly shifting sandbars at the mouth of the Mississippi impeded navigation and *hindered* the full development of New Orleans as a port —*Amer. Guide Series: La.*⟩ ⟨after the war German physicists maintained that the Nazis *hindered* research on a bomb, certainly did nothing to work toward an atomic power plant —*Current Biog.*⟩ IMPEDE suggests checking motion or progress by or as if by clogging or fettering so that forward activity is difficult ⟨he looked at her, startled, and placed his hand on hers, *impeding* the rapidity of her embroidery needle —Rose Macaulay⟩ ⟨action is *impeded* by a multitude of rules and regulations drawn up by the agency itself —E.M.Eriksson⟩ OBSTRUCT indicates hindering free and easy passage by obstacles in the way or by interference ⟨at some point below the Danish camp he *obstructed* the course of the Lea, so that the Danish ships could not be brought downstream —F.M.Stenton⟩ ⟨charged with *obstructing* the military in the execution of duty —Francis Stuart⟩ ⟨the restriction of the power of the House of Lords to *obstruct* legislation —Alfred Plummer⟩ BLOCK indicates complete obstruction to egress, passage, or exit ⟨roads *blocked* by the storm⟩ ⟨the steamer Heilo, which, having run aground, was *blocking* the entrance to Corinto harbor —*Current Biog.*⟩ ⟨a polyglot of diagnostic labels and systems, effectively *blocking* communication and the collection of medical statistics —G.N.Raines⟩ BAR is often a close synonym for BLOCK; it may indicate a purposive blocking or suggest a prohibiting that renders a physical obstacle unnecessary ⟨streetcars that, if not quite medieval, *bar* the road to the hurrying traveler —*N. Y. Times*⟩ ⟨to *bar* further immigration of aliens⟩ DAM may apply to obstructing whatever flows or may be thought of as flowing ⟨*dam* up the waters⟩ ⟨instances in which the bile ducts are blocked so that the bile is *dammed* back —Morris Fishbein⟩ ⟨the nun in her cell lost in contemplation is but inspired by a desire which, *dammed* in its earthly course, rises and rises to unimaginable heights —Francis Stuart⟩

[2]**hinder** \"\ *n* -s : accidental interference esp. by an opponent in some games (as handball and squash) that prevents a fair and unobstructed chance to return a ball

[3]**hind·er** \'hīndə(r), *dial Brit* " *or* 'hində- *or* 'hin(t)ə-\ *adj* [ME, prob. fr. OE *hinder*, adv., behind — more at HIND] **1** : situated behind or at or in the rear : BACK, HIND ⟨a long oval forward part and a taillike ~ portion —R.E.Coker⟩ **2** *dial Brit* : YONDER

[4]**hind·er** \'hīndə(r), *Brit* " *or* 'hində- *or* 'hin(t)ə-\ *n* -s *chiefly dial* : BUTTOCKS

**hindering impediment** *n* : IMPEDIENT IMPEDIMENT

**hin·der·ing·ly** *adv* : in a hindering manner

**hin·der·lands** *or* **hin·der·lings** *or* **hin·der·lins** \'hindərlənz, 'hin(t)ə-\ *n pl* [*hinderlands* alter. of *hinderlins, hinderlings*; *hinderlins, hinderlings* fr. [3]*hinder* + *-lings* or *-lins* (alter. of *-lings*)] *Scot* : BUTTOCKS

**hind·er·most** \'hīndə(r),mōst, *chiefly Brit* -,məst\ *adj* [alter. (influenced by *most*) of ME *hindermest*, fr. [3]*hinder* + *-mest* -most] *archaic* : HINDMOST

**hin·der·some** \'hində(r)səm\ *adj* [[1]*hinder* + *-some*] *now dial* : likely to hinder : TROUBLESOME

**hind-foremost** \'='=(,)=\ *adv* : with the hind part before : in reverse order

**hindgut** \'=,=\ *n* **1** : the posterior part of the alimentary canal of a vertebrate embryo **2** : the portion of the posterior intestine of an invertebrate formed by an infolding of the ectoderm

[1]**hin·di** \'hin(,)dē\ *n* -s *cap* [Hindi *hindī*, fr. *Hind* India, fr. Per] **1 a** : a literary language of northern India usu. written in the Devanagari alphabet that is the official language of several states in India and is scheduled to become the official language of the republic **b** : a complex of vernacular dialects of northern India for which Hindi is the usual literary language **2** : a member of a cultural group inhabiting the middle and upper Ganges-Jumna valley, speaking a Hindi dialect, and characterized by dark skin, tall stature, and long head

[2]**hindi** \"\ *adj, usu cap* : of or relating to northern India or its language ⟨*Hindi* troops⟩ ⟨*Hindi* dialects⟩

**hind kidney** *n* : METANEPHROS

**hind·ley's screw** \'hīn(d)lēz-, 'hi\ *n, usu cap H* [after Henry *Hindley*, 18th cent. Eng. clockmaker] : an endless screw or worm shaped like an hourglass to fit a part of the circumference of a worm wheel so as to increase the bearing area and thereby diminish the wear — called also *hourglass screw*

**hind·most** \'hīn(d),mōst, *chiefly Brit* -,məst\ *adj* [[3]*hind* + *-most*] : farthest in or toward the rear : most remote : LAST

**hindneck** \'=,=\ *n* : NAPE — used chiefly of birds

**hindquarter** \'=,==\ *n* **1** : the back half of a side of beef, veal, mutton, or lamb including a leg and usu. one or more ribs **2 hindquarters** *pl* : the hind biped of a quadruped; *broadly* : all the structures of a quadruped that lie posterior to the attachment of the hind legs to the trunk including the hind legs, rump, and posterior part of the back

**hin·drance** *also* **hin·der·ance** \'hind(ə)rən(t)s\ *n* -s [ME *hinderaunce*, fr. *hindren, hinderen* to hinder + *-aunce* -ance — more at HINDER] **1** : the state of being hindered ⟨his rebellion against . . . his tremor of knee and ~ of speech —Glenway Wescott⟩ **2** : the action of hindering ⟨~ of industry by too easily obtained patents —*Jour. of Patent Office Society*⟩ **3** : something that hinders : BLOCK, DRAWBACK ⟨sunken hulks that are a ~ to navigation⟩

**hinds** *pl of* HIND

**hindsaddle** \'=,==\ *n* : a wholesale cut of veal, lamb, or mutton consisting of undivided hindquarters and usu. including one pair of ribs — compare FORESADDLE

**hind shank** *n* : a cut of beef, veal, or mutton from the upper part of a hind leg

[1]**hindside** \'=,=\ *n* [[3]*hind* + *side*] *chiefly dial* : the back side ⟨she had her dress on ~ to⟩ ⟨put on his clothes ~ before⟩

[2]**hindside** \"\ *prep, chiefly dial* : BEHIND

**hindsight** \'=,=\ *n* **1** : a rear sight of a firearm **2** : perception of the nature and demands of an event after it has happened ⟨that ~ is better than foresight is axiomatic⟩

[1]**hin·du** *also* **hin·doo** \'hin(,)dü\ *n* -s [Per *Hindū*, fr. *Hind* India, fr. OPer *Hindu* — more at INDIA] **1** *usu cap* : an adherent of Hinduism **2** *cap* : a native or inhabitant of India

[2]**hindu** *also* **hindoo** \"\ *adj, usu cap* **1** : of, relating to, or characteristic of the Hindus ⟨a *Hindu* poet⟩ **2** : of, relating to, or characteristic of Hinduism ⟨*Hindu* gods⟩

**hin·du·ism** \-ü,izəm\ *n* -s **1** *usu cap* : a complex body of social, cultural, and religious beliefs and practices evolved in and largely confined to the Indian subcontinent and marked by a caste system, an outlook tending to view all forms and theories as aspects of one eternal being and truth, a belief in ahimsa, karma, dharma, samsara, and moksha, and the practice of the way of works, the way of knowledge, or the way of devotion as the means of release from the round of rebirths : the way of life and form of thought of a Hindu — compare AVATAR, BHAKTI, BRAHMANISM, JNANA-MARGA, KARMA-MARGA **2** *usu cap* : a religious philosophy based on Hinduism **3** *cap* : the dominant cultic religion of India marked by participation in one of the bhakti sects (as Vaishnavism, Sivaism, Shaktism)

**hin·du·ize** \-ü,īz\ *vt* -ED/-ING/-S *often cap* : to bring into conformity with Hinduism : make Hindu (as in customs, outlook, or religion)

**hindu numeral** *or* **hindu-arabic numeral** *n, usu cap H&A* : ARABIC NUMERAL

[1]**hin·du·stani** \,hindü'stanē, -də'-, -tän-,-tàn-, -ni\ *also* **hin·do·stani** \", -dō'-\ *n* -s *cap* [Hindi *Hindūstānī*, fr. Per *Hindūstān* India] **1** : Hindi, Urdu, and various vernacular dialects of northern India comprising a group of which literary Hindi and Urdu are considered diverse written forms **2** : the dialect of Delhi and the region to the northeast of Delhi **3** : a form of speech allied to Urdu but less divergent from Hindi, used in some urban areas and formerly in the British army, and commonly written in the Roman alphabet

[2]**hindustani** \',=='==\ *also* **hindostani** \',=='==\ *adj, usu cap* : of or relating to Hindustan or its people or Hindustani

**hind wing** *n* : a posterior wing of an insect

[1]**hine** *obs var of* HIND

**²hi·ne** \'hē(,)nā\ *n* -s [native name in Burma] **:** a male Indian elephant without tusks or tushes — compare TUSKER

**hi·ney** *var of* ²HEINIE

**¹hing** \'hiŋ\ *dial var of* HANG

**²hing** \"\ *dial past of* HANG

**³hing** \"\ *n* -s [Hindi *hīṅg*, fr. Skt *hiṅgu*] **:** ASAFETIDA

**¹hinge** \'hinj\ *n* -s *often attrib* [ME *heng, heeng, hyng;* akin to MD *henge, hengene* hook, handle, MLG *henge* hinge; derivatives fr. the root of E *hang*] **1 a :** a jointed or flexible device on which a door, lid, or other swinging part turns comprising typically a pair of metal leaves joined through the knuckles by a pin — see BUTT HINGE, CLEANING HINGE, H HINGE, HOOK-AND-EYE HINGE, PIANO HINGE **b :** a flexible ligamentous joint (as of a bivalve shell) **c** (1) **:** a paper or muslin joint, stub, or guard in a bound book that strengthens or permits the free flexing of a section, insert leaf, or map (2) **:** ¹JOINT 2d **d :** a small piece of thin gummed paper used in fastening a stamp in an album or on a sheet — called also *mount* **2** *obs* **a :** the earth's axis **b :** a cardinal point of the compass **3 :** something on which a development turns or depends **:** a basic issue or determining factor **:** TURNING POINT **4 :** a strategic point or line in the battle position of an army **5 :** HINGE LINE

**²hinge** \"\ *vb* -ED/-ING/-S *vt* **1 :** to attach by or furnish with hinges **2 :** to mount (a stamp) with a hinge **:** fasten a hinge to (a stamp) ~ *vi* **:** to be contingent or dependent on a single cardinal point or sole decisive consideration — used with *on* or *upon* ⟨a decision on which success or irrevocable failure *hinged* —Bernard De Voto⟩ **syn** see DEPEND

**hingecorner** \'≈,≈\ *n* **:** a hinged corner (as on a box or packing case)

**hinged–back tortoise** *n* **:** any of various grotesque tropical African tortoises that constitute a genus *Kinixys* of the family Testudinidae and have the posterior part of the carapace hinged

**hinged frame** *n* **:** a revolver frame hinged forward of the trigger to allow the forward portion of the frame to be rocked forward so as to expose the cylinder for loading and cleaning

**hinged·ly** \'hinj(ə)dlē\ *adv* **:** by means of hinging ⟨each of said inner panels being ~ connected to an end of one of the inner panels —*Modern Packaging*⟩

**hinge fault** *n* **:** a fault in the earth's surface in which displacement increases in one direction from a hinge line

**hinge joint** *n* **:** a joint that permits motion in one plane; *esp* **:** GINGLYMUS

**hinge·less** \'hinjləs\ *adj* **:** having no hinge

**hinge line** *also* **hinge** *n* **1 a :** an imaginary line on the earth's surface which can be regarded as a boundary between a stable region and one undergoing upward or downward movement **b :** a line around which one wall of a fault may appear to have rotated with respect to the other wall **2 :** the dorsal edge or border of a bivalve shell on which the hinge is situated

**hinge plate** *n* **1 :** the part of each valve that supports the hinge teeth in a bivalve mollusk **2 :** the part of a brachiopod that bears the sockets of the dorsal valve

**hing·er** \'hinjə(r)\ *n* -s **:** one that makes or puts on hinges

**hinge tooth** *n* **:** a projection of one valve of a bivalve shell that is located near the hinge line and that fits into a corresponding indentation in the other valve

**hinging post** *n* **:** GATEPOST

**hin·gle** \'hiŋgəl\ *n* -s [ME *hengle;* akin to MD *hengel* fishhook, MLG & MHG, hook, handle; derivatives fr. the root of E *hang*] *dial Eng* **:** the part (as a gate hinge or pot handle) by which something hangs

**hink** *n* -s [prob. of Scand origin; akin to ON *hinkr* hesitation, fr. *hinka* to limp, fr. MLG *hinken;* akin to OE *hincian* to limp, OHG *hinkan* to limp, ON *skakkr* crooked, askew — more at SHANK] *obs* **:** HESITATION, FALTERING

**hin·kum·boo·by** \'hiŋkəm,bübē\ *n* [fr. *hinkumbooby* (in the refrain *hinkumbooby round about*), prob. fr. Sc *hinkum* mischievous child + *booby*] *chiefly Scot* **:** a singing game similar to looby-loo

**hin·most** \'hinməst, -,mōst\ *dial Brit var of* HINDMOST

**hin·na** \'hinə\ [Sc *hin-* (fr. *hae*) + *na*] *Scot* **:** have not

**hin·ner** \'hinər\ *Scot var of* ³HINDER

**hin·ney** *or* **hin·ny** *or* **hin·nie** \'hinī\ *dial Brit var of* HONEY

**hin·ni·tes** \hi'nīd·(,)ēz\ *n, cap* [NL, fr. L *hinnus* + NL *-ites*] **:** a genus of scallops (family Pectinidae) containing forms that become attached to the substrate with consequent thickening and modification of the shell to resemble that of an oyster and including the rock oyster (*H. giganteus*) of the Pacific coast of No. America

**hin·ny** \'hinē\ *n* -ES [modif. of L *hinnus*, prob. modif. (influenced by L *hinnire* to neigh, of imit. origin) of Gk *ginnos*, *innos*, prob. of non-IE origin] **:** a hybrid between a stallion and an ass that differs from the mule in having a more bushy tail, in having a body disproportionately large in comparison with the legs, and in being of a gentler disposition

**hi·no·ki** \hə'nōkē\ *or* **hinoki cypress** *n* -s [Jap *hinoki*, lit., fire tree] **1 :** SUN TREE **2 :** the wood or fiber of the hinoki

**hins** *pl of* HIN

**hins·dal·ite** \'hinz,dā,līt, -,dȯ,l-\ *n* -s [*Hinsdale* county, Colo., its locality + E *-ite*] **:** a mineral $(Pb,Sr)Al_3(PO_4)(SO_4)(OH)_6$ consisting of a basic lead and strontium aluminum sulphate and phosphate occurring in coarse crystals and masses

**¹hint** \'hint\ *n* -s [prob. alter. of obs. *hent* act of seizing — more at HENT] **1** *archaic* **:** an occasion that can be taken advantage of **:** OPPORTUNITY ⟨look about you ere the ~ be past —Alexander Ross⟩ **2 a :** a suggestion for action given in an indirect or summary manner ⟨a list of helpful ~s for new students⟩ **b :** a statement conveying by implication what it is preferred not to say explicitly ⟨dropping ~s . . . of something mysterious and important about to happen —Sherwood Anderson⟩ ⟨his failure for some years to declare himself definitely in the struggle against the Nazis laid him open to . . . ~s of cowardice —H.J.Muller⟩ **3 :** a usu. slight indication of the approach, existence, or nature of something **:** SIGN, FOREWARNING, CLUE ⟨when the . . . beat of a tom-tom rose without ~ or introduction —William Beebe⟩ ⟨I can give only a ~ of the treasures to be found in the . . . museum —Dana Burnet⟩ **4 :** a very small amount **:** SUGGESTION ⟨friendly and cheerful with just the right ~ of respect —Margaret Kennedy⟩ **:** SUSPICION ⟨carry out this task . . . without ~ of favoritism —Peyton Boswell⟩ **:** DASH ⟨turnip greens seasoned with a ~ of vinegar⟩ ⟨a ~ of nutmeg and a suspicion of orange-flower water —Elinor Wylie⟩ **5** *Scot* **:** MOMENT, INSTANT

**²hint** \"\ *vb* -ED/-ING/-S *vt* **1 :** to seek to convey by a hint **:** to bring to mind by a slight reference or allusion rather than a full or explicit expression ⟨~ a suspicion⟩ ⟨~*ed* that he would like to be invited⟩ ⟨your father ~*ed* that the school wasn't good enough for you —Mary Austin⟩ **2 :** to indicate or reveal in the manner of a hint ⟨mighty ruins around the city ~ a better past —Curtis Dahl⟩ **:** PRESAGE, FORESHADOW, SUGGEST ⟨a cool, bright day, ~*ing* Indian summer —John Muir⟩ **3 :** to cause to go by hinting **:** send by a hint ⟨~ them along tactfully . . . toward the stuff that counts —Christopher Morley⟩ ~ *vi* **1 :** to make an indirect suggestion, allusion, or reference **:** give a hint ⟨~ broadly for the coveted invitation⟩ ⟨the face of the old retainer ~*ed* of things still untold —T.B.Costain⟩ — usu. used with *at* ⟨finally caught on to what he was ~*ing* at⟩ ⟨little gusts of wind ~*ed* at the storm to follow⟩ **2** *Scot* **:** to go about slyly or furtively esp. in order to further one's own interests **:** slink about or watch quietly **syn** see SUGGEST

**³hint** \"\ *adj* -ER/-EST [by alter.] *Scot* **:** HIND

**⁴hint** \"\ *prep, Scot* **:** BEHIND

**⁵hint** \"\ *n* -S **1** *Scot* **:** BACK, REAR **2** *Scot* **:** a furrow left between two ridges in plowing

**⁶hint** \"\ *vi* -ED/-ING/-S *Scot* **:** to plow up the furrow that is left in the last between two ridges **:** finish a ridge in plowing

**hint·er** \'hintə(r)\ *n* -s **:** one that hints

**hin·ter·hand** \'hintə(r)+,-\ *n* [G, fr. *hinter* rear, last + *hand*] **:** ENDHAND

**hin·ter·land** \'hintə(r),land, -laa(ə)nd\ *n* [G, fr. *hinter* rear + *land*] **1 a :** a region behind a coast or other usu. specified place ⟨the herdsmen have tended to avoid the immediate ~ of the coast —Walter Fitzgerald⟩; *specif* **:** the territory extending inland from a coastal colony (as along a river system or to the recognized boundary of another territory) over which the colonial power is sometimes held to possess sovereignty **b :** a region that provides supplies for the nation controlling it ⟨the vast ~ Nazi Germany has conquered in eastern and southern Europe —*New Republic*⟩ **c :** a region remote from cities and towns **:** WILDERNESS ⟨when this section, then a rough and rugged ~, was first being settled —*Amer. Guide Series: Minn.*⟩ **d :** a part of a country or region lying beyond any or all of its metropolitan or cultural centers **:** INTERIOR, STICKS ⟨by various profound thinkers in the ~ and by their counterparts in New York —G.J.Nathan⟩ ⟨steer the American out of the capital cities abroad and into the ~s, into the country pubs and . . . village taverns —Horace Sutton⟩ **2 :** the area often including satellites of which a city is the economic or cultural center **:** an urban zone of influence ⟨sometimes the ~s of different seaports overlap —W.G.Moore⟩ **3 :** a little-known sometimes contributory area of knowledge **:** FRONTIER ⟨a ~ of surgery hitherto neglected by the regular practitioner —W.T. Stead⟩ **:** BACKGROUND ⟨taught . . . to read around a subject, to understand its ~ —Hewlett Johnson⟩

**hint·ing·ly** *adv* **:** in a hinting manner

**hin·ton test** \'hint'n-, -ntən-\ *n, usu cap H* [after William A. *Hinton* b1883 Am. physician] **:** a blood-serum test for syphilis

**hin·tze·ite** \'hin(t)sə,īt\ *n* -s [G *hintzeit*, fr. Carl A. F. *Hintze* †1916 Ger. mineralogist + G *-it* -ite] **:** KALIBORITE

**hi·o·don** \'hīə,dän\ *n, cap* [NL, irreg. fr. *hy-* + *-odon*] **:** a genus (the type of the family Hiodontidae) of No. American freshwater fishes comprising the mooneyes — **hi·o·dont** \-nt\ *adj or n*

**h ion** *n, cap H* **:** HYDROGEN ION

**hiort·dahl·ite** \'yō(r)t,dä,līt, -,dəl-\ *n* -s [Norw *hiortdahlit*, fr. T. H. *Hiortdahl* †1925 Norw. chemist + Norw *-it* -ite] **:** a rare mineral $(Ca,Na)_{13}Zr_3Si_9(O,OH,F)_{33}$ consisting essentially of a sodium calcium zirconium silicate containing also fluorine and occurring as pale yellow tabular triclinic crystals

**¹hip** \'hip\ *also* **hep** \'hep\ *n* -s [ME *hepe, heppe, hipe*, fr. OE *hēope;* akin to OS *hiopo* bramble, OHG *hiafo, hiufa, hiefa* hip, bramble, Norw dial. *hjupa*, Dan *hyben*, and perh. to OPruss *kaāubri* thorn] **:** the ripened false fruit of a rosebush (as the dog rose) that consists of a fleshy receptacle enclosing numerous achenes

**²hip** \'hip\ *n* -s *often attrib* [ME *hip, hippe, hepe*, fr. OE *hype;* akin to OHG *huf* hip, Goth *hups* hip, L *cubitus, cubitum* elbow, *cubare* to lie down, Gk *kybos* cube, cubical die, vertebra, hollow before the hip (in cattle), OE *hēah* high — more at HIGH] **1 a** (1) **:** the laterally projecting region of each side of the lower or posterior part of the mammalian trunk that is formed by the lateral parts of the pelvis and upper part of the femur together with the fleshy parts covering them **:** HAUNCH (2) **:** HIP JOINT 1 **b :** COXA 2 **2 a :** the external angle formed by the meeting of two sloping sides or skirts of a roof that have their wall plates running in different directions **b** *also* **hip joint :** the junction between an inclined end post and the top chord of a truss **c :** HIP RAFTER — **on the hip** *archaic* **:** at a disadvantage ⟨feeling that she had the culprit *on the hip* —Anthony Trollope⟩

**³hip** \"\ *vt* **hipped; hipped; hipping; hips 1 :** to strain, injure, or fracture the hip of — usu. used of livestock **2 a :** to throw (an opponent) over one's hip in wrestling **:** throw by a cross-buttock **b :** to bump with one's hip (as in checking a sports opponent) ⟨I took a throw from the outfield, . . . *hipped* him, and he went sprawling to the right of the plate —G.R. Tebbetts⟩ **c :** to support or carry on the hip ⟨he loaded his small revolver and *hipped* it —Christopher Morley⟩ **3 :** to make (as a roof) with a hip

**⁴hip** \"\ *vb* **hipped; hipped; hipping; hips** [ME *hippen, huppen;* akin to OE *hoppian* to hop — more at HOP] *vi, now dial Brit* **:** to hop esp. on one foot ~ *vt, dial Brit* **:** to pass over **:** MISS, SKIP

**⁵hip** \"\ *n* -s [by shortening & alter.] *archaic* **:** HYPOCHONDRIA ⟨you have caught the ~ of your hypochondriac wife —Richard Cumberland †1811⟩

**⁶hip** \"\ *vt* **hipped; hipped; hipping; hips :** to make depressed, worried, or hypochondriac ⟨I rather would hearten than ~ thee —Elizabeth B. Browning⟩

**⁷hip** \"\ *interj* [origin unknown] — usu. used to begin a cheer ⟨~ ~ hooray⟩

**⁸hip** *var of* HEP

**hip and thigh** *adv* **:** OVERWHELMINGLY, UNSPARINGLY ⟨smote him *hip and thigh* with great slaughter —Judg 15:8 (RSV)⟩

**hip–and–valley roof** *n* **:** a roof so shaped as to have both hips and valleys — compare HIP ROOF

**hip bath** *n* **:** SITZ BATH

**hip·ber·ry** \'hip- —*see* BERRY\ *n* **:** ¹HIP

**hipbone** \'≈,≈\ *n* [ME *hipboon*, fr. *hip* + *boon* bone — more at BONE] **:** INNOMINATE BONE

**hip boot** *n* **:** a boot reaching to the hips that is worn esp. by fishermen

hip boot

**hip girdle** *n* **:** PELVIC GIRDLE

**hip joint** *n* **1 :** the articulation between the femur and the innominate bone **2 :** ²HIP 2b

**hip knob** *n* **:** a finial, ball, or other ornament at the intersection of the hip rafters and the ridge of a roof

**hiplength** \'≈,≈\ *adj* **:** extending to or over the hips ⟨a ~ coat⟩

**hip·less** \'hipləs\ *adj* **:** having or seeming to have no hips

**hipline** \'≈,≈\ *n* **:** the line formed by the lower edge of a hiplength garment or by measuring the hip at its fullest part

**hip lock** *n* **:** a cross-buttock in which a headlock is held throughout the maneuver

**hipp–** *or* **hippo–** *comb form* [L, fr. Gk, fr. *hippos* — more at EQUINE] **:** horse ⟨*hippo*gastronomy⟩ ⟨*hipp*uric acid⟩

**hip·pa** \'hipə\ [NL, alter. of L *hippus*, a sea fish, fr. Gk *hippos*, lit., horse] *syn of* EMERITA

**hip·parch** \'hi,pärk\ *n* -s [Gk *hipparchos, hipparchēs*, fr. *hipp-* + *-archos, -archēs* -arch] **:** a commander of cavalry in ancient Greece

**hip·par·i·on** \hi'pa(a)rē,än, -ēən\ *n* [NL, fr. Gk, pony, dim. of *hippos* horse] **1** *cap* **:** a genus of extinct Miocene and Pliocene three-toed mammals related to but not now considered direct ancestors of the horse **2** -s **:** any animal or fossil of the genus *Hipparion*

**hip·pe·as·trum** \,hipē'astrəm\ *n* [NL, fr. Gk *hippeus* horseman (fr. *hippos*) + *astron* star; fr. the equitant leaves and the star-shaped flowers — more at STAR] **1** *cap* **:** a genus of tropical American bulbous plants (family Amaryllidaceae) that are widely cultivated for their showy white to crimson flowers and that are sometimes included in the genus *Amaryllis* **2** -s **:** any amaryllis of the genus *Hippeastrum*

**¹hipped** \'hipt\ *adj* [²*hip* + *-ed*] **1 :** having hips ⟨a ~ roof⟩ — often used in combination ⟨a broad-*hipped* person⟩ **2 :** HIP-SHOT

**²hipped** \'hipt\ *adj* [⁵*hip* + *-ed*] **1 :** marked by worry, depression, or hypochondria ⟨with his bad habits and his domestic grievances he became completely ~ —H.W.Longfellow⟩ ⟨felt ~ because no one . . . bothered about his claret-colored ribbon —Philip Gibbs⟩ **2 :** absorbed or interested to an extreme or unreasonable degree **:** OBSESSED — usu. used with *on* ⟨married to a girl who is ~ on psychoanalysis —Bennett Cerf⟩

**hip·pe·la·tes** \,hipə'lād·(,)ēz\ *n, cap* [NL, fr. Gk *hippelatēs* horse driver (fr. *hipp-* + *elatēs* driver (fr. *elaunein* to drive); fr. the large spurs] **:** a genus of small black American eye gnats (family Chloropidae) including some that are held to be vectors of pinkeye and yaws

**hip·pen** *or* **hip·pin** \'hipən\ *n* -s [²*hip* + *-en* or *-in* (alter. of *-ing*)] *dial* **:** a baby's diaper

**hip·pe·ty–hop** *or* **hip·pi·ty–hop** \'hipəd·ē'häp\ *or* **hip·pe·ty–hop·pe·ty** *or* **hip·pi·ty–hop·pi·ty** \-äpəd·ē\ *adv (or adj)* [irreg. fr. ⁴*hip* + *hop*] **:** with a hopping rhythm or motion ⟨the rabbit went *hippety-hop* across the lawn⟩ ⟨rising and falling in their saddles, with a *hippity-hop* motion —Laura Krey⟩

**hip·peu·tis** \hi'pyüd·əs\ *n, cap* [NL, prob. fr. Gk *hippeutēs* horseman, fr. *hippos* horse — more at EQUINE] **:** a genus of freshwater snails (family Planorbidae) that are occas. the intermediate hosts of some medically important flukes

**hip·pic** \'hipik\ *adj* [Gk *hippikos*, fr. *hippos* horse + *-ikos* -ic] **:** of or relating to horses or horse racing ⟨the chief English ~ events of the season —*Punch*⟩

**hip·pid·i·on** \hi'pidē,än, -ēən\ *n, cap* [NL, fr. Gk *hippidion*, dim. of *hippos*] **:** a genus of extinct Pleistocene horses of Argentina and Brazil

**hip·pid·i·um** \-ēəm\ [NL, alter. of *Hippidion*] *syn of* HIPPIDION

**hippier** *comparative of* HIPPY

**hippiest** *superlative of* HIPPY

**hipping** *pres part of* HIP

**hip·pio·spongia** \'hipē(,)ō+\ *n, cap* [NL, alter. of *Hippospongia*] **:** a genus of sponges (family Spongiidae) containing numerous important commercial sponges

**hip·pish** \'hipish\ *adj* [⁵*hip* + *-ish*] **:** characterized by or suffering from worry, depression, or hypochondria **:** HIPPED

**hip·ple** \'hipəl\ *n* -s [ME *heepil, hypil*, dim. of *heep, hepe* heap — more at HEAP] *dial Eng* **:** a small heap; *esp* **:** a small haycock

**hip·po** \'hi(,)pō\ *n* -s [by shortening] **:** HIPPOPOTAMUS

**hippo–** — see HIPP-

**hip·po·bos·ca** \,hipə'bäskə\ *n, cap* [NL, fr. *hipp-* + *-bosca* (fr. Gk *boskein* to feed)] **:** the type genus of the family Hippoboscidae

**¹hip·po·bos·cid** \'≈≈'bäs(k)əd\ *adj* [NL *Hippoboscidae*] **:** of or relating to the Hippoboscidae

**²hippoboscid** \"\ *n* -s **:** a fly of the family Hippoboscidae

**hip·po·bos·ci·dae** \,≈≈'bäs(k)ə,dē\ *n pl, cap* [NL, fr. *Hippobosca*, type genus + *-idae*] **:** a family of winged or wingless dipterans that comprise the louse flies, are bloodsucking parasites on birds and mammals, and are larviparous bringing forth single advanced larvae from time to time which almost immediately pupate — compare SHEEP KED

**hip·po·camp** \'hipə,kamp\ *n* [Gk *hippokampos*] **:** HIPPOCAMPUS 1

**hip·po·cam·pal** \'≈≈'kampəl\ *adj* [NL *hippocampus* + E *-al*] **:** of or relating to the hippocampus

**hippocampal convolution** *or* **hippocampal gyrus** *n* **:** a convolution of the cerebral cortex that borders the hippocampus and contains elements of both archipallium and neopallium

**hippocampal fissure** *n* **:** DENTATE FISSURE

**hip·po·cam·pine** \'≈≈'kam,pīn, -,pən\ *adj* [NL *Hippocampus* + E *-ine*] **:** of or relating to sea horses

**hip·po·cam·pus** \,≈≈'kampəs\ *n* [NL, fr. Gk *hippokampos* sea horse, legendary sea monster, fr. *hippo-* hipp- + *kampos* sea monster] **1** *pl* **hippocam·pi** \-m,pī\ **:** a legendary creature with the head and forequarters of a horse and the tail of a dolphin or fish **2** *pl* **hippocampi :** a curved elongated ridge extending over the floor of the descending horn of each lateral ventricle of the brain, consisting of gray matter covered on the ventricular surface with white matter, and forming the larger part of the archipallium **3** *cap* **:** a genus of fishes (family Syngnathidae) consisting of the typical sea horses

**hip·po·cas·ta·na·ce·ae** \,hipə,kastə'nāsē,ē\ *n pl, cap* [NL, fr. *Hippocastanum*, type genus in former classifications (fr. *hipp-* + Gk *kastanon* chestnut) + *-aceae*] **:** a family of trees (order Sapindales) having opposite palmately lobed leaves, showy flowers in large clusters, and nutlike seeds encased in a leathery capsule and including the buckeyes

**hip·po·centaur** \'hipə+\ *n* [L *hippocentaurus*, fr. Gk *hippokentauros*, fr. *hippo-* hipp- + *kentauros* centaur] **:** CENTAUR

**hip·po·cras** \'hipə,kras, -,krəs\ *n* -ES [ME *ypocras*, after *Hippocras, Hypocras, Ypocras* Hippocrates †*ab*377 B.C. Greek physician, its legendary inventor; prob. fr. his name's having been falsely analyzed as Gk *hypo* under + *krasis* mixture] **:** an aromatic highly spiced wine of medieval Europe

**hip·po·crat·ea** \,hipə'krad·ēə\ *n, cap* [NL, after *Hippocrates*] **:** a genus (the type of the family Hippocrateaceae) of tropical trees or twining shrubs having a 3-lobed capsule with winged seeds — see WOOD ALMOND

**hip·po·crat·e·a·ce·ae** \,≈≈,krad·ē'āsē,ē\ *n pl, cap* [NL, fr. *Hippocratea*, type genus + *-aceae*] **:** a family of tropical shrubs or trees (order Sapindales) having opposite leaves and small 5-parted flowers — **hip·po·crat·e·a·ceous** \'≈≈≈≈'āshəs\ *adj*

**hip·po·crat·ic** \'hipə'krad·ik, -atl, ēk\ *also* **hip·po·crat·i·cal** \ə̇kəl, ēk-\ *adj, usu cap* [LL *Hippocraticus*, fr. *Hippocrates* (fr. Gk *Hippokratēs*) + *-icus* -ic, -ical] **:** of or relating to Hippocrates or to the school of medicine that took his name

**hippocratic facies** *n, usu cap H* **:** the face as it appears near death and in some debilitating conditions marked by sunken eyes and temples, pinched nose, and tense hard skin

**hippocratic finger** *n, usu cap H* **:** a clubbed finger

**hippocratic oath** *n, usu cap H* **:** an oath embodying a code of medical ethics that is usu. taken by those about to begin medical practice

**hip·poc·ra·tism** \hi'päkrə,tizəm\ *n* -s *usu cap* [*Hippocrates* + E *-ism*] **:** the medical doctrine of the Hippocratic school

**hip·po·crene** \'hipə,krēn, ,≈≈'krēnē\ *n* -s *usu cap* [fr. *Hippocrene*, a fountain in ancient Greece that was fabled to have burst forth when the ground was struck by the hoof of the winged horse Pegasus and that was supposed to be a source of poetic inspiration, fr. L, fr. Gk *Hippokrēnē*, fr. *hippo-* hipp- + *krēnē* fountain] **:** poetic inspiration ⟨we shrink from a cup of the purest *Hippocrene* after the critics' solar microscope —J.R. Lowell⟩ ⟨a loiterer by the waves of *Hippocrene* —O.W.Holmes †1894⟩

**hip·po·crep·i·form** \'hipə'krepə,fȯrm\ *adj* [*hipp-* + Gk *krēpis* boot + E *-form* — more at CREPIDULA] **:** shaped like a horseshoe

**¹hip·po·drome** \'hipə,drōm\ *n* -s [MF, fr. L *hippodromos*, fr. Gk, fr. *hippo-* hipp- + *dromos* racecourse — more at -DROME] **1 :** an oval stadium for horse and chariot races in ancient Greece **2 a :** an arena for equestrian performances **b** (1) **:** a spectacle presented in a hippodrome (2) **:** an activity suggesting such a spectacle **3 :** a sports contest with a predetermined winner

**²hippodrome** \"\ *vi* -ED/-ING/-S **1 :** to arrange or fix a sports contest whose winner is predetermined **2 :** to act as if in a hippodrome **:** attract attention by or as if by spectacular performance

**hip·po·drom·ic** \'≈≈'drämik, -rōm-\ *adj* **:** of, relating to, or having the characteristics of a hippodrome

**hip·po·glos·sus** \,hipə'gläsəs, -lȯs-\ *n, cap* [NL, fr. *hipp-* + *-glossus* (fr. Gk *glōssa* tongue) — more at GLOSS] **:** a genus of flatfishes containing the typical halibuts and sometimes being made to be the type of a separate family but usu. included in the Pleuronectidae

**hip·po·griff** \'hipə,grif\ *n* -s [F *hippogriffe*, fr. It *ippogrifo*, fr. *ippo-* (fr. L *hippo-* hipp) + *grifo* griffin, fr. L *gryphus* — more at GRIFFIN] **:** a legendary animal having the foreparts of a winged griffin and the body and hindquarters of a horse

**hip·po·griffin** \'hipə+\ *n* [by alter. (influenced by *griffin*)] **:** HIPPOGRIFF

**¹hip·poid** \'hi,pȯid\ *adj* [NL *Hippoidea*] **:** of or relating to the Hippoidea

**²hippoid** \"\ *n* -s **:** a mammal of the group Hippoidea

**hip·poi·dea** \hi'pȯidēə\ *n pl, cap* [NL, fr. *hipp-* + *-oidea*] *in some classifications* **:** a division of perissodactylous mammals comprising the Equidae and extinct related forms

**hip·po·lith** \'hipə,lith\ *or* **hip·po·lite** \-līt\ *n* -s [NL *hippolithus*, fr. *hipp-* + *-lithus* -lith, -lite] **:** a concretion from the intestines of the horse

**hip·pol·o·gy** \hi'päləjē\ *n* -ES [ISV *hipp-* + *-logy*] **:** the study of the horse

**hip·pol·y·te** \hi'pälə(,)tē\ *n, cap* [NL, after *Hippolyte*, Amazon in Greek mythology, fr. Gk *Hippolytē*] **:** a common and widely distributed genus (the type of the family Hippolytidae) of small prawns having the abdomen sharply bent at the third segment — **hip·pol·y·tid** \-,təd\ *adj or n*

**hip·pom·a·nes** \hi'pämə,nēz\ *n* -ES [L, fr. Gk, fr. *hippo-* hipp- + *-manes* (fr. *mainesthai* to rage, be furious) — more at MIND] **:** a growth found on the forehead of a newborn foal and held in antiquity to be aphrodisiac

**hip·po·mo·bile** \'hipəmō'bē(ə)l, ,≈≈'mō,b-\ *n* [*hipp-* + *-mobile* (as in *automobile*)] **:** a horse-drawn vehicle

**hip·po·mor·pha** \,hipə'mȯrfə\ *n pl, cap* [NL, fr. *hipp-* + *-morpha*] **:** a suborder of Perissodactyla comprising horses, asses, zebras, and many extinct related forms

**¹hip·po·nac·te·an** \,hipə,nak'tēən, -'nakte-\ *adj, usu cap* [L *Hipponacteus* of Hipponax (fr. *Hipponact-, Hipponax*, 6th cent. B.C. Greek poet reputed to have invented the choliamb, fr. Gk *Hippōnakt-, Hippōnax*) + E *-an*] **:** of or relating to Hipponax or to the verse forms ascribed to him; *specif* **:** CHOLIAMBIC

**²hipponactean** \"\ *n* -s *usu cap* **:** a Hipponactean verse; *specif* **:** a hypercatalectic form of glyconic

**hipponactean distich** *n, usu cap H* **:** a distich composed of a catalectic trochaic dimeter and iambic trimeter

**hip·po·pathology** \¦hi(,)pō+\ *n* [*hipp-* + *pathology*] **:** the pathology of the horse

**hip·poph·aë** \hi'päfə,ē\ *n, cap* [NL, fr. L *hippophaes*, fr. Gk, spurge] **:** a genus of thorny deciduous Old World shrubs (family Eleagnaceae) including the sea buckthorn

**hip·poph·a·gism** \hi'päfə,jizəm\ *n* -S [*hipp-* + *-phagism*] **:** HIPPOPHAGY

**hip·poph·a·gist** \-,jəst\ *n* -S [*hippophagy* + *-ist*] **:** one that eats horseflesh — **hip·poph·a·gis·ti·cal** \hi¦päfə¦jistəkəl\ *adj*

**hip·poph·a·gous** \(')hi¦päfəgəs\ *adj* [*hipp-* + *-phagous*] **:** eating horseflesh

**hip·poph·a·gy** \=ˈ==fəjē\ *n* -ES [*hipp-* + *-phagy*] **:** the act or practice of eating horseflesh

**hip·po·pod** \'hipə,päd\ *n, pl* **hippopods** \-dz\ *or* **hippop·o·des** \hi'päpə,dēz\ [*hipp-* + *-pod*] **:** a legendary creature having the body of a man and the legs of a horse

**hip·po·pot·am·ic** \¦hi(,)pōpə¦tamik, ¦hipəpə¦–; ¦hipə¦päd·ə·(,)mik\ *or* **hip·po·po·ta·mi·an** \¦hi(,)pōpə¦tāmēən, ¦hipəpə¦-\ *adj* **:** of, relating to, or resembling the hippopotamus; *specif* **:** UNWIELDY

**hip·po·pot·a·mus** \,hipə'päd·əməs, -ätəm-\ *n* [L, fr. Gk, fr. *hippo-* hipp- + *potamos* river, fr. *petesthai* to fly, dart, rush — more at FEATHER] **1** *pl* **hip·popotamus·es** \-səz\ *or* **hippopota·mi** \-,mī, -(,)mē\ **:** any of various large herbivorous four-toed chiefly aquatic mammals of the order Artiodactyla with an extremely large head and mouth, bare and very thick skin, and short legs; *esp* **:** a member of the most genus *Hippopotamus* (as *H. amphibius*) formerly common in most rivers of Africa that is except for the elephant the bulkiest existing quadruped and has long canine and incisor teeth that yield a good quality of ivory **2** *cap* [NL, fr. L] **:** a genus (the type of the family Hippopotamidae) of mammals that includes the typical hippopotamuses

hippopotamus

**hippos** *pl of* HIPPO

**hip·po·si·de·ros** \,hi(,)pōsə'dirəs, -,sī'd-\ *n, cap* [NL, fr. *hipp-* + Gk *sidēros* iron, object made of iron] **:** a large genus (the type of the family Hipposideridae) of horseshoe bats comprising some 40 species and ranging from northwest Africa to the Philippines and Australia

**hip·po·spongia** \¦hipə+\ [NL, fr. *hipp-* + *Spongia*] *syn of* SPONGIA

**hip·po·ti·grine** \,hipə¦tīgrən, -,grīn\ *adj* [NL *Hippotigris*, subgenus of *Equus* containing the zebras (fr. *hipp-* + Gk *tigris* tiger) + E *-ine* — more at TIGER] **:** of or relating to the zebra

**hip·pot·o·my** \hi'päd·əmē\ *n* -ES [ISV *hipp-* + *-tomy* (as in *anatomy*)] **:** the anatomy of the horse

**hip·pot·ra·gine** \hi'pä·trə,jīn, -ə,gīn, -əjən, -əgən\ *adj* [NL *Hippotragus* + E *-ine*] **:** of or relating to the genus *Hippotragus* or to any of the antelopes belonging to it

**hip·pot·ra·gus** \-rəgəs\ *n, cap* [NL, fr. *hipp-* + Gk *tragos* he-goat] **:** a genus of large antelopes with long annulated backwardly curved horns that includes the sable and roan antelopes and the extinct blaubok

**hip·pu·rate** \hi'pyu̇,rāt, 'hipyə,r-\ *n* -S [ISV *hippuric* + *-ate*] **:** a salt or ester of hippuric acid

**hip·pu·ric acid** \(')hi¦pyu̇rik-\ *n* [*hipp-* + *-uric*] **:** a white crystalline nitrogenous acid $C_6H_5CONHCH_2COOH$ formed in the liver as a detoxication product of benzoic acid and present in the urine of herbivorous animals and in small quantity in human urine — called also *benzoylglycine*

**hip·pu·ri·case** \hi'pyu̇rə,kās, -āz\ *n* -S [ISV *hippuric* + *-ase*] **:** HISTOZYME

**hip·pu·ris** \hi'pyu̇rəs\ *n, cap* [NL, fr. Gk *hippouris* horsetail fr. *hipp-* + *-ouris* (fr. *oura* tail)] **:** a widely distributed genus of small-flowered aquatic herbs (family Haloragaceae) with single erect stems and verticillate leaves

**hip·pu·rite** \'hipyə,rīt\ *n* -S [NL *Hippurites*] **:** a mollusk or fossil of the genus *Hippurites*

**hip·pu·ri·tes** \,hipyə'rīd·(,)ēz\ *n, cap* [NL, fr. *hipp-* + *ur-* (tail) + *-ites*] **:** a genus (the type of the family Hippuritidae) of aberrant marine bivalve mollusks that are confined to the Cretaceous and whose lower valve is conical, usu. longitudinally ribbed, and attached by its apex and whose upper valve is depressed conic with a nearly central umbo — **hip·pu·rit·ic** \¦==¦rid·ik\ *adj* — **hip·pu·ri·tid** \-¦rīd·əd\ *adj or n* — **hip·pu·ri·toid** \-¦rīd·,òid\ *adj*

**hip·pus** \'hipəs\ *n* -ES [NL, fr. Gk *hippos* horse, eye complaint — more at EQUINE] **:** a spasmodic variation in the size of the pupil of the eye caused by a tremor of the iris

**-hippus** \"\ *n comb form* [NL, fr. Gk *hippos*] **:** horse — in generic names esp. in paleontology ⟨*Eohippus*⟩

**hip·py** \'hipē\ *adj, usu* -ER/-EST **:** having or resembling large hips ⟨farthingales . . . to make the hips seem *hippier* and the waist tinier —*Britannica Bk. of the Yr.*⟩

**hip rafter** *n* **:** the rafter extending from the wall plate to the ridge and forming the angle of a hip roof

**hip roll** *n* **:** a tile or strip that covers the angle of a hip roof

**hip roof** *n* **:** a roof having sloping ends and sloping sides — compare HIP-AND-VALLEY ROOF

**hips** *pl of* HIP, *pres 3d sing of* HIP

**hip·shot** \'=,=\ *adj* **1 :** having the hip dislocated **2 :** having one hip lower than the other ⟨spun slowly toward the long mirror . . . and posed ~ like a model —Crary Moore⟩

**hipster** *var of* HEPSTER

**hip tile** *n* **:** a tile for covering the hip of a roof

**hip vertical** *n* **:** a vertical member whose upper end is at the hip of a truss

**hir·able** *or* **hire·able** \'hīrəbəl\ *adj* **:** capable of being hired **:** available for hire

hip roof

**hi·ra·do ware** \hə'rä(,)dō-\ *n, usu cap H* [fr. *Hirado*, town and island of Japan where such porcelain is manufactured] **:** a Hizen porcelain characteristically decorated in underglaze blue with a design showing children playing under a fir tree

**hi·ra·ga·na** \¦hirə¦gänə\ *n* -S [Jap, lit., flat kana] **:** the cursive script that is one of two sets of symbols in which Japanese kana is written — compare KATAKANA

**hir·car·rah** \hər'kärə\ *n* -S [Per *harkāra*, fr. *har* every, all (fr. OPer *haruva-*) + *kār* work, deed, fr. MPer, fr. OPer *kar-* to do, make] *India* **:** COURIER, SPY

**hirch** *var of* HIRTCH

**hir·cine** \'hər,sīn, -,sᵊn\ *adj* [L *hircinus*, fr. *hircus* he-goat + *-inus* -ine; perh. akin to L *horrēre* to bristle — more at HORROR] **:** of, relating to, or suggestive of a goat; *esp* **:** resembling a goat in smell

**hir·co·cer·vus** \,hərkō'sərvəs\ *n* -ES [LL, fr. L *hircus* he-goat + *cervus* stag; trans. of Gk *tragelaphos*, fr. *tragos* he-goat + *elaphos* stag] **:** a legendary creature that is half goat and half stag

**hir·die-gir·die** \¦hirdi¦girdi, ¦hərdi¦gər-\ *adv* [alter. of *hiddie-giddie*, fr. ME (Sc) *hiddy-giddy*, prob. redupl. (influenced by *hed*, head) of *giddy*] *dial Brit* **:** TOPSY-TURVY

**hir·dum-dir·dum** \¦hirdəm¦dirdəm, ¦hərdəm¦dər-\ *n* [prob. redupl. (influenced by *heard*) of *dirdum*] *dial Brit* **:** UPROAR

**¹hire** \'hī(ə)r, 'hīə\ *n* -S [ME, fr. OE *hȳr*; akin to OFris *hēre* tax, lease, rent, OS *hūra*, *hūria*, MLG & MD *hūre*] **1 a :** payment for the temporary use of something ⟨the heaviest single item of government expenditure is . . . the ~ of the money we borrowed for the war —G.B.Shaw⟩ **b :** payment for labor or personal services **:** WAGES ⟨the laborer is worthy of his ~ —Lk 10: 7 (AV)⟩ **2 a** (1) **:** the act of hiring ⟨the government office which controlled the ~ of coolies —Dillon Ripley⟩ (2) **:** an instance of such act ⟨the monthly base compensation payroll . . . is $70,000 as the result of new ~s and merit and length-of-service increases —*U.S.Code*⟩ **b :** the state of being hired **:** EMPLOYMENT ⟨men of every political leaning are in the ~ of big corporations —Robert Shaplen⟩ **syn** see WAGE — **for hire** *also* **on hire :** available for use or service in return for payment ⟨a coal lighter which plies *for hire* up and down the Meuse —H.J.Laski⟩ ⟨a thrashing machine went *on hire* from farm to farm —Flora Thompson⟩

**²hire** \"\ *vb* -ED/-ING/-S [ME *hiren*, fr. OE *hȳrian*; akin to OFris *hēra* to lease, MLG & MD *huren*; denominatives fr. the root of E ¹*hire*] *vt* **1 a :** to engage the personal services of for a fixed sum **:** employ for wages ⟨many clergy fought in person, and others *hired* substitutes —G.G.Coulton⟩ ⟨the leader . . . ~s staff people to think up the ideas —W.H.Whyte⟩ — sometimes used with *away* or *on* ⟨can ~ them away from any company . . . if you offer them a few more dollars —W.J.Reilly⟩ ⟨the crew was fully *hired* on —John Hersey⟩ **b :** to engage the temporary use of for a fixed sum ⟨came down with a hundred people in four private cars and *hired* a whole floor of the . . . hotel —Scott Fitzgerald⟩ ⟨*hired* a car for the afternoon —Elizabeth Bowen⟩ **c** *archaic* **:** BORROW ⟨she can ~ the money, and I know she will pay you —A.D.McFaul⟩ **2 a :** to grant the personal services of for a fixed sum — often used with *out* ⟨have been *hiring* themselves out as practical consultants —Vance Packard⟩ ⟨the colonel had *hired* out most of his slaves —Winston Churchill⟩ **b :** to grant the temporary use of for a fixed sum ⟨bored-looking camels which they ~ to visitors as props for exotic snapshots —Mollie Panter-Downes⟩ — often used with *out* ⟨the town council *hired* out chairs for visitors —B.L.K.Henderson⟩ **3 :** to pay for having (something done) ⟨my father . . . had to ~ all his share of the farm work done —W.A.White⟩ ~ *vi* **:** to accept employment ⟨asked me if I would ~ with him to tend shop and keep books —John Woolman⟩ — **hire one's time :** to pay one's master for the right to use one's time for one's own gain

**hired girl** *n* **:** a woman employed as a domestic; *specif* **:** one living in a farm household who helps around the house and performs light farm chores

**hired hand** *n* **:** FARMHAND

**hired man** *n* **:** a man employed to do odd jobs about a house, estate, or farm; *esp* **:** FARMHAND

**hire in** *vi* **:** to accept employment and begin to work ⟨most of the guys . . . who've *hired in* over the past fourteen years —Warner Bloomberg⟩

**hire·less** \'hī(ə)rləs, -īəl-\ *adj* **:** receiving no payment or reward ⟨preaching . . . in most of the great towns as an ~ volunteer —S.T.Coleridge⟩

**hire·ling** \-liŋ,-lēŋ\ *n* -S *often attrib* **1 :** one who is hired; *esp* **:** one whose motives and interests in serving another are chiefly gainful ⟨was murdered by ~s in the service of foreign powers —Stoyan Christowe⟩ **2 :** one whose motives are venal or mercenary ⟨baser ~s who live by lies on good men's lives —Lord Byron⟩ **3 :** a horse for hire ⟨went to a neighboring livery stable to look for ~s —Evelyn Waugh⟩

**hire on** *vi* **:** to find or accept employment ⟨doubtful that he could *hire on* as a Hollywood extra —F.B.Gipson⟩

**hire out** *vi* **:** to accept employment ⟨young Englishman who *hired out* as a photographer —Marcus Duffield⟩

**hire purchase** *n* **1** *chiefly Brit* **:** a contract of hire with an option of purchase in which a person hires goods for a specified period and at a fixed rent with the condition that if he retains the goods for the full period and pays all the installments of rent as they become due the contract shall determine and the title vest absolutely in him and that if he chooses he may at any time during the term surrender the goods and be quit of any liability for future installments upon the contract — compare CONDITIONAL SALE **2** *chiefly Brit* **:** the practice of buying by hire purchase

**hir·er** \'hīrə(r)\ *n* -S [ME, fr. *hiren* to hire + *-er*] **:** one that hires

**hiring** *n* -S [ME, fr. gerund of *hiren* to hire — more at HIRE] **:** the contract or relationship between the parties to a transaction in which one hires the services or property of the other

**hiring hall** *n* **:** a union-operated employment agency or placement office where registered applicants are referred to jobs (as in the shipping industry) on a rotation basis — compare SHAPE-UP

**hir·ling** \'hərlən, 'hir-, -liŋ\ *var of* HERLING

**hir·mos** *or* **heir·mos** \ir'mòs\ *n, pl* **hir·moi** *or* **heir·moi** \-'mė\ [LGk *heirmos*, fr. Gk, series, sequence, connection; akin to Gk *leirein* to fasten together — more at SERIES] **:** a troparion, hymn, or canticle with a fixed rhythm and melody that is used as a standard rhythmic and melodic pattern for other troparia in the canon of the Eastern Church

**hirn** \'hərn, -i-\ *var of* ¹HERN

**hir·ne·o·la** \(,)hər'nēələ\ [NL, dim. of L *hirnea* jug] *syn of* AURICULARIA

**hiro·shi·ma** \¦hirə¦shēmə, -rō¦-; hə'rōshəmə, -'räsh-,-'rōsh-; *Jap approximately* hi'rō'shē(,)mä\ *adj, usu cap* [fr. *Hiroshima*, Japan] **:** of or from the city of Hiroshima, Japan **:** of the kind or style prevalent in Hiroshima

**¹hir·ple** \'hirpəl\ *vi* -ED/-ING/-S [ME (Sc dial.) *hirplen*] *chiefly Scot* **:** to walk with a limp **:** HOBBLE

**²hirple** \"\ *n* -S *Scot* **:** LIMP

**hirsch·sprung's disease** \'hirsh,pru̇ŋz-\ *n, usu cap H* [after Harold *Hirschsprung* †1916 Dan. physician] **:** congenital megacolon

**¹hir·sel** *also* **hir·sle** \'hirsəl\ *n* -S [ME *hirsill*, fr. ON *hirzla*, *hirthsla* safekeeping, custody, fr. *hirtha* to guard sheep, fr. *hirthir* shepherd — more at HERD] **1** *Scot* **:** a flock of sheep **2** *Scot* **:** the land grazed by a flock of sheep ⟨like a poor lamb that has wandered from its own native ~ —Sir Walter Scott⟩ **3** *Scot* **:** a large number or quantity **:** MULTITUDE

**²hirsel** *also* **hirsle** \"\ *vt* **hirseled** *or* **hirselled** *also* **hirsled; hirseled** *or* **hirselled** *also* **hirsled; hirseling** *or* **hirselling** *also* **hirsling; hirsels** *also* **hirsles** *Scot* **:** to arrange in or as if in flocks

**³hirsel** *also* **hirsle** \"\ *vb* **hirseled** *or* **hirselled** *also* **hirsled; hirseled** *or* **hirselled** *also* **hirsled; hirseling** *or* **hirselling** *also* **hirsling; hirsels** *also* **hirsles** [origin unknown] *vi* **1** *Scot* **:** to move along a surface awkwardly **:** SLITHER **2** *Scot* **:** to move clumsily or with difficulty **:** SCRAMBLE **3** *Scot* **:** to move with a rustling or grating noise ~ *vt, Scot* **:** to cause to move awkwardly or with difficulty

**hirst** \'hirst\ *n* -S [ME *hirst*, *hurst* grove, knoll — more at HURST] **1** *Scot* **a :** a barren unproductive plot of ground **b :** a sandbank in a river **2** *Scot* **:** a great number or quantity **3** *Scot* **:** the part of the floor of a mill where the millstones turn in their framework

**hirst·ie** \'hirsti\ *adj* [*hirst* + *-ie* (Sc var. of *-y*)] *Scot* **:** BARE, BARREN

**hir·su·tal** \(¦)hər¦süd·ᵊl\ *adj* [L *hirsutus* + E *-al*] **:** of or relating to the hair

**hir·sute** \'hər,süt, 'hi(ə)r,s-, 'hə̄,s-, 'həi,s-, 'hiə,s-, (,)=ˈ=, *usu* -üd·+V\ *adj* [L *hirsutus*; akin to L *hirtus* rough, shaggy, *horrēre* to bristle — more at HORROR] **1 a :** rough with hair or bristles **:** HAIRY, SHAGGY ⟨the dog's master patted the ~ fellow —Horace Sutton⟩ **b** *biol* **:** pubescent with coarse stiff hairs **c :** covered with feathers that resemble hair **2 :** of, relating to, or having the characteristics of hair — **hir·sute·ness** *n* -ES

**hir·su·tel·la** \,hər(,)sü'telə, ,hir-\ *n, cap* [NL, fr. L *hirsutus* + NL *-ella*] **:** a genus of basidiomycetous fungi of uncertain taxonomic position that are associated with and believed to be parasitic upon various insects

**hir·su·ti·es** \(,)hər'süshē,ēz, hir-\ *n, pl* **hirsuties** [NL, fr. L *hirsutus*] **:** HIRSUTISM

**hir·sut·ism** *pronunc at* HIRSUTE + ,izəm\ *n* -S [ISV *hirsute* + *-ism*] **:** excessive growth of hair of normal or abnormal distribution **:** HYPERTRICHOSIS

**hir·su·tu·lous** \(¦)hər¦süchələs, ¦hir-\ *adj* [*hirsute* + *-ulous*] **:** minutely or slightly hirsute

**¹hirtch** \'hirch\ *vi* -ED/-ING/-ES [origin unknown] **1** *Scot* **:** to shudder with or as if with cold **2** *Scot* **:** to walk with a jerky hobbling motion

**²hirtch** \"\ *n* -ES *Scot* **:** HITCH

**hir·tel·la** \(,)hər'telə, hir-\ *n, cap* [NL, fr. L *hirtus* + NL *-ella*] **:** a genus of chiefly tropical American shrubs or small trees (family Rosaceae) having axillary or terminal racemes of small white or purplish flowers with numerous stamens

**hir·tel·lous** \(¦)hər¦teləs, ¦hir-\ *adj* [L *hirtus* + *-ellus* (diminutive suffix)] **:** finely hirsute ⟨thickened ~ leaves⟩

**hiru·din** \'hir(y)ədən, hə'rüdᵊn\ *n* -S [fr. *Hirudin*, a trademark] **:** a preparation of the active principles of the buccal glands of a leech used to retard or prevent the clotting of blood

**hir·u·din·ea** \,hir(y)ə'dinēə\ *n pl, cap* [NL, fr. *Hirudin-*, *Hirudo*] **:** a class of hermaphroditic aquatic, terrestrial, or parasitic annelid worms distinguished by a coelom nearly obliterated by connective tissue and reduced to a series of vascular sinuses, by modification of the hindmost segments into a sucking disk, and by the absence of parapodia and setae — compare GNATHOBDELLIDA, PHARYNGOBDELLIDA, RHYNCHOBDELLIDA — **hir·u·din·e·an** \¦==¦dinēən\ *adj or n*

**hir·u·din·ei** \,==ˈdinē,ī\ [NL, fr. *Hirudin-*, *Hirudo*] *syn of* HIRUDINEA

**hir·u·di·ni·a·sis** \,hir(y)ədə'nīəsəs, hə,rüdᵊn'ī-\ *n, pl* **hirudi·nia·ses** \-ī·ə,sēz\ [NL, fr. *Hirudin-*, *Hirudo* + *-iasis*] **:** infestation with leeches

**hir·u·din·i·dae** \,hir(y)ə'dinə,dē\ *n pl, cap* [NL, fr. *Hirudin-*, *Hirudo*, type genus + *-idae*] **:** a family of aquatic leeches that have 5-ringed segments, 5 pairs of eyes, and usu. 3-toothed jaws and that include the common medicinal leech

**hi·ru·di·nize** \hə'rüdᵊn,īz\ *vt* -ED/-ING/-S **:** to retard or prevent the coagulation of (blood) by the injection of hirudin

**hi·ru·do** \hə'rü(,)dō\ *n, cap* [NL, fr. L, leech] **:** a genus (the type of the family Hirudinidae) of the order Gnathobdellida that includes the common medicinal leech

**¹hirun·dine** \hə'rəndən, -,dīn; 'hirən,dīn\ *adj* [L *hirundo* swallow + E *-ine*] **:** of, relating to, or resembling the swallow

**²hirundine** \"\ *n* -S [NL *Hirundinidae*] **:** ¹SWALLOW 1

**hir·un·din·i·dae** \,hirən'dinə,dē\ *n pl, cap* [NL, fr. *Hirundin-*, *Hirundo*, type genus (fr. L, swallow) + *-idae*] **:** a family of passerine birds consisting of the swallows and martins — **hi·run·di·nous** \hə'rəndənəs\ *adj*

**¹his** [ME, fr. OE, gen. of *hē* he — more at HE] *obs possessive of* ¹HE

**²his** \(h)iz, ¦hiz, ¸ēz\ *adj* [ME, fr. OE, gen. of *hē*] **1 a :** of or relating to him or himself as possessor **:** due to him **:** inherent in him **:** associated or connected with him ⟨a wise man who built ~ house upon the rock —Mt 7: 24 (RSV)⟩ ⟨the western ocean in one of the very worst of ~ moods —Cicely F. Smith⟩ ⟨did he bump ~ little head⟩ — compare ¹HE **b :** of or relating to him or himself as author, doer, giver, or agent **:** effected by him **:** experienced by him as subject **:** that he is capable of ⟨reading Shakespeare's histories as well as ~ comedies and tragedies⟩ ⟨~ promise⟩ ⟨success attributed to ~ having been prompt⟩ ⟨he ran ~ fastest⟩ **c :** of or relating to him or himself as object of an action **:** experienced by him as object ⟨he awaited ~ confirmation by the senate⟩ ⟨a secret combination against a person with the object of ~ hurt or injury —H.E.Scudder⟩ **d :** that he has to do with or is supposed to possess or to have knowledge or a share of or some special interest in ⟨the boy who knows ~ baseball —David Dempsey⟩ ⟨he enthusiastically supports ~ local symphony —*Amer. Guide Series: Minn.*⟩ **e :** that is esp. significant for him **:** that brings him good fortune or prominence — used with *day* or sometimes with other words indicating a division of time ⟨this was ~ day and the treat was on him —H.A.Chippendale⟩ **2** *obs* **:** ITS — used as late as the 17th century with no implied personification ⟨if the salt have lost ~ savor, wherewith shall it be salted? —Mt 5: 13 (AV)⟩ **3** *archaic* **:** 'S — used after a noun or noun phrase in place of the possessive ending *'s* ⟨at the tide of Christ ~ birth —Thomas Fuller⟩ ⟨in George the First ~ time —W.M.Thackeray⟩ ⟨Billy Bones, ~ fancy —R.L.Stevenson⟩

**³his** \'hiz\ *pron, sing or pl in constr* [ME, fr. OE, gen. of *hē*] **1 :** his one or his ones — used without a following noun as a pronoun equivalent in meaning to the adjective *his* ⟨if my brother had my shape, and I had ~ —Shak.⟩ ⟨my dog is large and ~ is small⟩ ⟨your eyes are blue and ~ are brown⟩; often used after *of* to single out one or more members of a class belonging to or connected with a particular male person or animal ⟨a friend of ~⟩ ⟨four or five books of ~⟩ or merely to identify something or someone as belonging to or connected with a particular male person or animal without any implication of membership in a more extensive class ⟨that overbearing manner of ~⟩ ⟨those big feet of ~⟩ **2 :** something that belongs to him **:** what belongs to him ⟨all that is ~ is hers⟩

**his** *abbr* history

**hish** \'hish\ *dial var of* HISS

**his heels** *n pl but sing or pl in constr* **:** a jack that is turned up as the starter in cribbage and that scores two points for the dealer

**his·ing·er·ite** \'hisiŋə,rīt, 'hizi-\ *n* -S [G *hisingerit*, fr. Wilhelm *Hisinger* †1852 Swed. geologist + G *-it* -ite] **:** a mineral perhaps $Fe_2Si_2O_5(OH)_4.2H_2O$ consisting of a black amorphous iron ore that is a hydrous ferric silicate

**his·lop·ite** \'hizlə,pīt, 'hisl-\ *n* -S [Stephen *Hislop* †1863 Eng. missionary to India and amateur geologist + E *-ite*] **:** a bright green Indian calcite

**hisn** *or* **his'n** \'hizᵊn\ *pron* [ME *hysene*, alter. (influenced by the *-n* in *min* mine, *thin* thine) of *his*] *dial* **:** HIS

**his·pa** \'hispə\ *n* [NL, irreg. fr. L *hispidus* rough, hairy, bristly] **1** *cap* **:** a genus (often the type of the family Hispidae) of spiny Old World beetles with larvae that are leaf miners **2** -S **:** a beetle of *Hispa* or various closely related genera

**his·pan·ic** \(')hi¦spanik, -nēk\ *adj, usu cap* [L *Hispanicus*, fr. *Hispania* Spain, Iberian peninsula + L *-icus* -ic] **:** relating to, or derived from the people, speech, or culture of Spain or of Spain and Portugal; *often* **:** LATIN-AMERICAN ⟨the folklore of *Hispanic* groups⟩ — **hispanic-american** \"+\ *adj, usu cap H&A*

**his·pan·i·cism** \hi'spanə,sizəm\ *n* -S *usu cap* **:** a word, phrase, or mode of expression distinctive of Spanish esp. when it appears in an English context

**his·pan·i·cist** \-,səst\ *n* -S *usu cap* **:** HISPANIST

**his·pan·i·ci·za·tion** \(,)=,==sə'zāshən, -,sī'z-\ *n* -S *often cap* **:** the act or a process of hispanicizing

**his·pan·i·cize** \=ˈ==,sīz\ *vt* -ED/-ING/-S *often cap* **:** to make Spanish: **a :** to cause to acquire a quality, qualities, traits or outlook distinctive of Spanish culture or Spaniards ⟨to ~ the conquered Indians⟩ **b :** to modify (language or a particular word or expression) to conform to language characteristics distinctive of Spanish ⟨"beisbol" is *hispanicized* "baseball"⟩ **c :** to bring under the control of Spain or Spaniards ⟨the government was *hispanicized*⟩

**his·pa·ni·dad** \ēspänē'thä(th)\ *n* -S *often cap* [Sp, fr. *hispánico* Hispanic (fr. L *Hispanicus*) + *-dad* -ty (fr. L *-tat-*, *-tas*)] **:** hispanism esp. as adapted to fascist purposes and used for the undermining of U.S. influence in Latin America

**his·pan·io·lize** \hi'spanyə,līz, ,hispən'yō,l-\ *vt* -ED/-ING/-S *often cap* [modif. (influenced by *Hispanic*) of Sp *españolizar*, fr. *español* Spanish (fr. — assumed — VL *Hispaniolus*, fr. L *Hispania* Spain) + *-izar* -ize] **:** HISPANICIZE

**his·pa·nism** \'hispə,nizəm\ *n* -S *often cap* [Sp *hispanismo*, fr. *hispano* Spanish, Hispanic (fr. L *Hispanus*) + *-ismo* -ism] **1 :** the Spanish and Latin-American movement to reassert the spiritual and cultural unity of Spain and the Latin-American countries and promote the return to classic Spanish culture and Spanish supremacy in Latin America — compare HISPANIDAD **2 :** a linguistic feature of Spanish origin or due to Spanish influence

**his·pa·nist** \-,nəst\ *n* -S *usu cap* [Sp *hispanista*, fr. *hispano* + *-ista* -ist] **:** a scholar specially informed in the Spanish or Portuguese languages or Spanish or Portuguese literature, linguistics, or civilization

**his·pa·ni·za·tion** \,hispənə'zāshən, -,nī'z-\ *n* -S *often cap* [Sp *hispanización*, fr. *hispanizar* + *-ación* -ation] **:** HISPANICIZATION

**his·pa·nize** \'hispə,nīz\ *vt* -ED/-ING/-S *often cap* [Sp *hispanizar*, fr. *hispano* + *-izar* -ize] **:** HISPANICIZE

**his·pano** \hi'spa(,)nō, -pä(-, -pā(-; 'hispə,nō\ *n* -S *cap* [short for *Hispano-American*] **:** a native or resident of the southwestern U.S. descended from Spaniards settled there before annexation

**hispano-** *comb form, usu cap* [Sp *hispano*, fr. L *Hispanus*] **:** Spanish and ⟨*Hispano*-German⟩ **:** Spanish ⟨*hispanophile*⟩

**hispano-moresque** \=¦==, ¦==(,)=+\ *adj, usu cap H&M* **1 :** of, relating to, or produced in the era of Moorish ascendancy in Spain — used chiefly of art or cultural objects (as pottery, textiles) **2** *of a rug* **:** antique and oriental and found in Spain

**his·pan·o·phile** \hi'spanə,fīl\ *also* **his·pano·phil** \-,fil\ *n* -S often cap [*Hispano-* + *-phile, -phil*] **:** one partial to Spain or esp. fond of Spanish culture or civilization

1**his·per·ic** \(')hi¦sperik\ *adj, usu cap* [fr. *Hisperica famina*, 6th cent. Latin work written in Ireland in the Hisperic style] **:** belonging to or constituting a style of Latin writing that probably originated in Ireland in the 6th century and that is characterized by extreme obscurity intentionally produced by periphrasis, coinage of new words, and very liberal use of loanwords to express quite ordinary meanings

2**hisperic** \"\ *n* -s *cap* **:** Hisperic Latin

**his·pid** \'hispə̇d\ *adj* [L *hispidus;* prob. akin to L *horrēre* to bristle — more at HORROR] **:** rough or covered with bristles, stiff hairs, or minute spines ⟨a ~ leaf⟩ — **his·pid·i·ty** \hi'spidəd·ē\ *n* -ES

**his·pid·u·lous** \(')hi¦spijələs\ *also* **his·pid·u·late** \-lə̇t, -ˌlāt\ *adj* [*hispid* + *-ulous* or *-ulate* (fr. *-ulous* + *-ate*)] **:** minutely hispid

**his·pine** \'hiˌspīn, -ˌspə̇n\ *adj* [NL *Hispa* + E *-ine*] **:** of or related to the genus *Hispa*

1**hiss** \'his\ *vb* -ED/-ING/-ES [ME *hissen*, of imit. origin] *vi* **:** to make a sharp sibilant sound: as **a :** to make the sound by which an animal (as a goose or snake) indicates alarm, fear, or irritation ⟨the kitten ~*ed* at sight of the dog⟩ **b :** to make such a sound as an expression of hatred, passion, or disapproval ⟨the crowd booed and ~*ed*⟩ **c :** to escape or move with a hissing sound ⟨the wind ~*ed* about the caves⟩ — used esp. of substances under pressure ⟨steam ~*ing* from the kettle's spout⟩ ⟨air ~*ed* from the faulty valve⟩ **~** *vt* **1 :** to condemn or express contempt or dislike for by hissing ⟨~*ed* the speaker from the stage⟩ **2 :** to utter with a hissing sound ⟨~ dispraise⟩ ⟨sibilants should be clearly ~*ed*⟩

2**hiss** \"\ *n* -ES **1 :** a prolonged sibilant sound like that of the speech sound \s\ or \z\: as **a :** any of various animal sounds usu. indicative of alarm, fear, or irritation ⟨the ~ of an aroused gander⟩ ⟨startled by the sharp ~ of a snake⟩ **b :** the sound made by steam or other gas escaping through a narrow opening **c** (1) **:** the friction that characterizes the utterance of a voiceless fricative consonant (2) **:** a voiceless fricative; *specif* **:** \s\ — compare BUZZ **2 :** a hiss used as an expression of dislike, disapprobation, or contempt ⟨~*es* rose from all parts of the audience⟩

3**hiss** \"\ *or* **hissing** *adj* **:** being or involving the sibilant \s\ or \z\ ⟨~ sibilants of Georgian speech⟩ — compare HUSH

**hiss·able** \'hisəbəl\ *adj* **:** fit for hissing ⟨a sibilant ~ malediction⟩ **:** deserving to be hissed ⟨a thoroughly ~ villain⟩

**his·self** \(h)i(z)'=, ē(z)'=\ *also* **his·sel** \-'sel\ *pron* [ME *his self*, fr. *his* + *self*] *substand* **:** HIMSELF ⟨when he come to ~ they told him it was a Union hospital —Helen Eustis⟩

**hiss·er** \'hisə(r)\ *n* -s [ME, fr. *hissen* + *-er*] **:** one that hisses

**hissing** *n* -s [ME, fr. gerund of *hissen* to hiss] **1 :** an act or instance of emitting a hiss **2 :** an occasion of contempt **:** an object of scorn ⟨the priests, because of their breaches of the restrictions . . . made their calling a reproach and a ~ —A.M. Young⟩

**hissing adder** *or* **hissing snake** *also* **hissing viper** *n* **:** HOGNOSE SNAKE

**hiss·ing·ly** *adv* **:** in a hissing manner **:** with a sound of hissing

**hissy** \'hisē\ *n* -ES [origin unknown] *Southwest* **:** a fit of temper **:** TANTRUM

1**hist** \s *often prolonged and usu with* p *preceding and/or* t *or a glottal stop following; often read as* 'hist\ *interj* [origin unknown] — used to demand attention or quietly to attract a person's attention

2**hist** \'hīst\ *dial var of* HOIST

**hist-** *or* **histo-** *comb form* [F, fr. Gk *histos* mast, beam of a loom, loom, web, fr. *histanai* to cause to stand — more at STAND] **:** tissue ⟨*hist*amine⟩ ⟨*histo*physiology⟩

**hist** *abbr* **1** histology **2** historian; historic; historical; history

**his·tami·nase** \hi'stamə̇ˌnās, 'histəm-, -āz\ *n* -s [ISV *histamine* + *-ase*] **:** a flavoprotein enzyme occurring widely in plant and animal tissues (as in the kidney and small intestine) and capable of oxidizing histamine and various diamines (as putrescine) — called also *diamine oxidase*

**his·ta·mine** \'histəˌmēn, -ˌmə̇n\ *also* **his·ta·min** \-ˌmə̇n\ *n* -s [ISV *hist-* + *amine*] **:** a crystalline base $C_3H_3N_2CH_2CH_2NH_2$ that is found in ergot and other plants and usu. combined in animal tissues, that is formed from histidine by decarboxylation, and that is held to be responsible for the dilation and increased permeability of blood vessels which play a major role in allergic reactions; 4(or 5)-imidazole-ethylamine — see ANTIHISTAMINE, GASTRIN — **his·ta·min·ic** \¦==¦minik\ *adj*

**histamine flare** *n* **:** an allergic tissue reaction to histamine manifested by local flushing of the skin

**his·ta·min·er·gic** \¦==ˌmə̇¦nərjik\ *adj* [ISV *histamine* + *-ergy* + *-ic*] **1** *of autonomic nerve fibers* **:** liberating histamine **2** *of autonomic nerve fibers* **:** activated by histamine

**his·tamino·lyt·ic** \¦==ˌmēnə¦lid·ik, -ˌmin-; hi¦stamənō¦l-\ *adj* [ISV *histamine* + *-o-* + *-lytic*] **:** breaking down or tending to break down histamine ⟨~ action of blood plasma⟩

**histe** \'hīst\ *dial var of* HOIST

**his·ter** \'histə(r)\ *also* **hister beetle** *n* -s [NL *Hister*, genus of beetles, fr. L *hister* actor, fr. Etruscan; fr. the fact that these beetles play dead when disturbed] **:** a beetle of the family Histeridae

1**his·ter·id** \-tərə̇d\ *adj* [NL *Histeridae*] **:** of or relating to the Histeridae

2**histerid** \"\ *n* -s **:** HISTER

**his·ter·i·dae** \hi'sterəˌdē\ *n pl, cap* [NL, fr. *Hister*, type genus + *-idae*] **:** a family of rather sluggish dark-colored and often shining beetles that live chiefly in decaying organic matter and have larvae which prey on other insects and insect larvae

**histi-** *or* **histio-** *comb form* [Gk *histion* web, cloth, sail, dim. of *histos* mast, beam of a loom, loom, web — more at HIST-] **1 :** sail ⟨*Histio*pterus⟩ **2 :** tissue ⟨*histio*cyte⟩

**his·ti·dase** \'histəˌdās, -āz\ *n* -s [ISV *histid*in + *-ase*] **:** an enzyme occurring esp. in the liver of vertebrates that is capable of deaminating histidine to form urocanic acid

**his·ti·dine** \-ˌdēn, -ˌdə̇n\ *also* **his·ti·din** \-ˌdə̇n\ *n* -s [ISV *hist-* + *-idine, -idin;* orig. formed as G *histidin*] **:** a crystalline basic amino acid $C_3H_3N_2CH_2CH(NH_2)COOH$ that is essential in the nutrition of the rat, is synthesized by microorganisms and by plants, and is formed by the decomposition of most proteins (as globin); 4(or 5)-imidazole-alanine

**hist·ie** \'histi\ *var of* HIRSTIE

**his·ti·o·cyte** \'histēəˌsīt\ *n* -s [ISV *histi-* + *-cyte*] **:** a phagocytic tissue cell that may be fixed or freely motile, is derived from the reticuloendothelial system, and resembles the monocyte with which it is sometimes identified — called also *clasmatocyte, macrophage* — **his·ti·o·cyt·ic** \¦===¦sid·ik\ *adj*

**his·ti·o·cy·to·ma** \ˌ==(ˌ)=ˌsīˈtōmə\ *n, pl* **histiocytomas** \-məz\ *also* **histiocyto·ma·ta** \-məd·ə\ [NL, fr. ISV *histiocyte* + NL *-oma*] **:** a tumor consisting predominantly of histiocytes, being usu. nonmalignant, and occurring esp. in young male dogs

**his·ti·o·cy·to·sis** \-'tōsə̇s\ *n, pl* **histiocyto·ses** \-ōˌsēz\ [NL, fr. ISV *histiocyte* + NL *-osis*] **:** abnormal multiplication of histiocytes; *broadly* **:** a condition characterized by such multiplication

**his·ti·oid** \'histēˌȯid\ *adj* [ISV *histi-* + *-oid*] **:** HISTOID

**his·ti·ol·o·gy** \ˌhistē'äləjē, -ji\ *n* -ES [by alter.] **:** HISTOLOGY

**his·ti·oph·a·gous** \¦==¦äfəgəs\ *adj* [*histi-* + *-phagous*] **:** feeding on tissues ⟨~ protozoans⟩

**his·ti·o·phor·i·dae** \ˌhistēə'fȯrəˌdē\ [NL, fr. *Histiophorus*, type genus (fr. *histi-* + *-phorus*) + *-idae*] *syn of* ISTIOPHORIDAE

**his·ti·op·ter·i·dae** \ˌ==ˌäp'terəˌdē\ *n pl, cap* [NL, fr. *Histiopterus*, type genus (fr. *histi-* + *-pterus*) + *-idae*] **:** a family of deep-sea percoid fishes with compressed body, rough scales, and strong fin spines — see BOARFISH

**histo-** — see HIST-

**his·to·blast** \'histəˌblast\ *n* [ISV *hist-* + *-blast*] **:** a cell or cell group possessing broad histogenetic capacity: as **a :** HISTIOCYTE **b :** IMAGINAL DISK

**his·to·chemical** \¦hi(ˌ)stō+\ *adj* [*hist-* + *chemical*] **:** of, relating to, or by means of histochemistry — **his·to·chemical·ly** \"+\ *adv*

**his·to·chemistry** \"+\ *n* [ISV *hist-* + *chemistry*] **:** a science that deals with the chemical constitution of living cells and tissues by combining the techniques of biochemistry and histology

**his·to·chem·o·graph** \¦hi(ˌ)stōkeməˌgraf, -räf\ *n* [*hist-* + *chem-* + *-graph*] **:** a picture or pattern produced on a photographic plate by the chemical action of a histological specimen in contact with the emulsion — **his·to·che·mog·ra·phy** \-ˌke'mägrəfē, -ˌkə̇'-\ *n* -ES

**his·to·cyte** \'histəˌsīt\ *n* -s [ISV *hist-* + *-cyte*] **1 :** HISTIOCYTE **2 :** a cell (as in various lower invertebrates) with highly developed capacity to form tissues

**his·to·gen** \-təjə̇n, -ˌjen\ *n* -s [ISV *hist-* + *-gen*] **:** a zone or clearly delimited region of primary tissue in or from which the specific parts of a plant organ are believed to be produced — see DERMATOGEN, PERIBLEM, PLEROME; HISTOGEN THEORY; compare CALYPTROGEN, CORPUS, TUNICA

**his·to·genesis** \ˌhistə+\ *n* [NL, fr. *hist-* + L *genesis*] **:** the formation and differentiation of tissues ⟨the ~ of floral organs⟩ ⟨~ of a neoplasm⟩

**his·to·ge·net·ic** \¦histəjə̇¦ned·ik\ *adj* [*hist-* + *genetic*] **1 :** of or relating to histogenesis **2 :** of or relating to histogenetics — **his·to·ge·net·i·cal·ly** \-d·ə̇k(ə)lē\ *adv*

**his·to·ge·net·ics** \-d·iks\ *n pl but sing or pl in constr* **:** a branch of genetics concerned with the genetic significance and basis of somatic variation (as in the production of bud sports and graft hybrids)

**his·to·gen·ic** \¦=(ˌ)=¦jenik\ *adj* [ISV *hist-* + *-genic*] **:** producing tissue

**histogen theory** *n* **:** a theory in botany: a growing point (as of a stem or root) consists of three histogens each of which gives rise to a different tissue — see DERMATOGEN, PERIBLEM, PLEROME

**his·tog·e·ny** \hi'stäjənē\ *n* -ES [ISV *hist-* + *-geny*] **:** HISTOGENESIS

**his·to·gram** \'histəˌgram\ *n* -s [*histo*ry + *-gram*] **:** a graphical representation of a frequency distribution by means of rectangles whose widths represent the class intervals and whose heights represent the corresponding frequencies

**his·tog·ra·phy** \hi'stägrəfē\ *n* -ES [ISV *hist-* + *-graphy*] **:** description of bodily tissue

**his·toid** \'hiˌstȯid\ *adj* [ISV *hist-* + *-oid*] **1 :** resembling the normal tissues ⟨~ tumors⟩ **2 :** developed from or consisting of but one tissue

**his·to·log·i·cal** \'histə¦läjə̇kəl, -jēk-\ *also* **his·to·log·ic** \-jik, -jēk\ *adj* **:** of or relating to histology or to the microscopic structure of the tissues of organisms ⟨~ studies⟩ ⟨the ~ picture in Bright's disease⟩ — **his·to·log·i·cal·ly** \-jə̇k(ə)lē, -jēk-, -li\ *adv*

**his·tol·o·gist** \hi'stäləjə̇st\ *n* -s **:** a specialist in histology

**his·tol·o·gy** \-jē, -ji\ *n* -ES [F *histologie*, fr. *hist-* + *-logie* -logy] **1 :** a branch of anatomy that deals with the minute structure of animal and vegetable tissues as discernible with the microscope **:** microscopic anatomy — compare CYTOLOGY **2 :** a treatise on histology **3 :** tissue structure or organization (as of an organism) ⟨the ~ of a fetus⟩ ⟨the ~ of the pancreas⟩

**his·tol·y·sis** \-ləsə̇s\ *n* [NL, fr. *hist-* + *-lysis*] **1 :** the breakdown of bodily tissues **2 :** the process by which in the pupa of a holometabolous insect many or most of the larval organs dissolve into a creamy material and leave intact only various groups of cells out of which new organs for the imago are formed

**his·to·lyt·ic** \¦histə¦lid·ik\ *adj* [fr. NL *histolysis*, after such pairs as E *analysis : analytic*] **:** of, relating to, or inducing histolysis

**his·tol·y·zate** \hi'stäləˌzāt\ *n* -s [irreg. fr. NL *histolysis* + E *-ate*] **:** a product of tissue lysis

**his·to·metabasis** \¦hi(ˌ)stō+\ *n* [NL, fr. *hist-* + *metabasis*] **:** fossilization in which the minute details of texture of the organism are retained

**his·tom·o·nad** \hi'stäməˌnad\ *n* [NL *Histomonad-, Histomonas*] **:** a protozoan of the genus *Histomonas*

**his·tom·o·nal** \(')hi¦stämənᵊl\ *adj* **:** of, relating to, or caused by histomonads ⟨~ diarrhea⟩

**his·tom·o·nas** \='==ˌnəs, -ˌnas\ *n, cap* [NL, fr. *hist-* + *monas*] **:** a genus of zooflagellates (family Mastigamoebidae) that exhibit both amoeboid and flagellate phases, are parasites in the liver and intestinal mucosa of chickens, turkeys, and various other birds and are usu. considered to include a single species (*H. meleagridis*) that is the causative agent of blackhead

**his·tomo·ni·a·sis** \(ˌ)hiˌstämə'nīəsə̇s, ˌhistəmə-\ *n* -ES [NL, fr. *Histomonas* + *-iasis*] **:** infection with or disease caused by protozoans of the genus *Histomonas* **:** BLACKHEAD 3

**his·tone** \'hiˌstōn\ *n* -s [ISV *hist-* + *-one*] **:** any of various simple proteins that are soluble in water but insoluble in dilute ammonia, that yield a high proportion of basic amino acids on hydrolysis but are less strongly basic than protamines, and that are found esp. in some glandular tissues (as thymus) combined with deoxyribonucleic acid

**his·to·pathologic** *or* **his·to·pathological** \¦hi(ˌ)stō+\ *adj* **:** of or relating to histopathology ⟨a ~ process⟩ **:** involving the methods of histopathology ⟨a ~ examination⟩

**his·to·pathologist** \"+\ *n* **:** a pathologist who specializes in the detection of the effects of disease on body tissues; *esp* **:** one who identifies neoplasms by their histological characteristics

**his·to·pathology** \"+\ *n* [ISV *hist-* + *pathology*] **1 :** a branch of pathology concerned with the tissue changes characteristic of disease **2 :** the tissue changes that affect a part or accompany a disease ⟨~ of the eye⟩ ⟨~ of tuberculosis⟩

**his·to·physiology** \"+\ *n* [*hist-* + *physiology*] **1 :** a branch of physiology concerned with the function and activities of tissues **2 :** structural and functional tissue organization (as of a body part) ⟨the ~ of the thyroid gland⟩

**his·to·plas·ma** \ˌhistə'plazmə\ *n* [NL, fr. *hist-* + *plasma*] **1** *cap* **:** a genus of fungi (family Coccidioidaceae) usu. considered to consist of a single widespread species (*H. capsulatum*) of fungi that cause histoplasmosis, live parasitically as heavily encapsulated yeastlike cells in blood, lymph, or various tissues, and grow saprophytically (as on nutritive media) as a mycelium that produces both conidia and chlamydospores **2** -s **:** any fungus of the genus *Histoplasma*

**his·to·plas·min** \-mə̇n, '==ˌ==\ *n* -s [ISV *histoplasm-* (fr. NL *Histoplasma*, genus name of *Histoplasma capsulatum*) + *-in*] **:** a sterile filtrate of a culture of a fungus (*Histoplasma capsulatum*) used in a cutaneous test for histoplasmosis

**his·to·plas·mo·sis** \-ˌplaz'mōsə̇s\ *n, pl* **histoplasmo·ses** \-ōˌsēz\ [NL, fr. *Histoplasma* (genus name of *Histoplasma capsulatum*) + *-osis*] **:** a disease that is endemic in the Mississippi and Ohio river valleys of the U.S., is caused by infection with a fungus (*Histoplasma capsulatum*), and is marked by benign involvement of lymph nodes of the trachea and bronchi usu. without symptoms or by severe progressive generalized involvement of the lymph nodes and the reticuloendothelial system with fever, anemia, leukopenia and often with local lesions (as of the skin, mouth, or throat)

**his·to·ri·an** \hi'stōrēən, -tȯr- *sometimes* -tär-\ *n* -s [MF *historien*, fr. L *historia* narrative, history + MF *-en* -an — more at HISTORY] **1 :** a writer of history; *esp* **:** one that produces a work of scholarly synthesis as distinguished from a compilation or chronicle ⟨an ~ and not a mere chronicler —*Times Lit. Supp.*⟩ **2 :** CHRONICLER

**his·to·ri·at·ed** \-rēˌād·ə̇d\ *adj* [ML *historiat*us (past part. of *historiare* to tell a story in pictures, fr. LL, to relate, fr. L *historia* narrative, history) + E *-ed* — more at HISTORY] **:** adorned with figures (as flowers, animals) having significance rather than purely decorative elements (as scrolls, diapers) — used orig. of the elaborately decorated initials of books and manuscripts and now chiefly of a symbolic representational manner of presenting supplementary information on a map or chart

1**his·tor·i·cal** \hi'stȯrə̇kəl, -tär-, -rēk-\ *or* **his·tor·ic** \-rik, -rēk\ *adj* [*historical* fr. L *historicus* (fr. Gk *historikos* exact, precise, historical, fr. *historia* inquiry, information, narrative, history + *-ikos* -ic) + E *-al; historic* fr. L *historicus* — more at HISTORY] **1** *usu historical* **a :** of, relating to, or having the character of history esp. as distinguished from myth or legend ⟨an ~ event⟩ ⟨the ~ middle ages were quite unlike those of fiction⟩ **b :** based on or dealing with history ⟨~ studies⟩ **:** true to history **:** accurate in respect to history ⟨reproducing the manners of the period with ~ fidelity⟩ **c :** used in the past and reproduced in historical presentations **d :** based on, resulting from, or acknowledged to be true because of past events or experiences ⟨the ~ necessity for space of growing populations⟩ **2** *usu historic* **a :** important, famous, or decisive in history ⟨*historic* battlefields⟩ ⟨*historic* buildings⟩ **b :** having considerable importance, significance, or consequence ⟨an *historic* occasion⟩ **3 a :** SECONDARY 1e **b** *usu historical* **:** DIACHRONIC ⟨~ grammar⟩ ⟨~ linguistics⟩

2**historical** \"\ *n* -s **:** a novel, play or motion picture based upon history

**historical cost** *n* **1 :** a cost computed after production from records made concurrently with various steps of production — contrasted with *predetermined cost* and *standard cost* **2 :** the value at which a capital asset is recorded on the books representing the outlay of money or its equivalent given in exchange at the time of acquisition ⟨depreciation is based on *historical cost* rather than on replacement value⟩ **3 :** the original cost of a property in a public utility

**historical criticism** *n* **:** criticism in the light of historical evidence — compare HIGHER CRITICISM

**historical geology** *n* **:** a branch of geology that deals with the chronology of the events in the earth's history

**historical infinitive** *n* **:** the present infinitive used with a subject nominative as a finite verb in place of a past indicative

**his·tor·i·cal·ly** \-rə̇k(ə)lē, -rēk-, -li\ *adv* **1 :** in accordance with or in respect to history ⟨an ~ accurate account⟩ **:** as a matter of history ⟨popular leaders have ~ appeared when the needs and tensions were great enough⟩ **2 :** in the course of history **:** in past times or previous dealings ⟨all employees whom an employer has ~ treated together —*U.S.Code*⟩

**historical materialism** *n* **:** the part of dialectical materialism dealing with the history of society and holding that ideas and institutions develop as the superstructure of a material economic base, that the course of history is dominated by the struggle of competing classes, and that the final dialectical stages comprise the development of capitalism, the dictatorship of the proletariat, and after the withering away of the state the emergence of a classless society

**historical method** *n* **:** a technique of presenting information (as in teaching or criticism) in which a topic is considered in terms of its earliest phases and followed in an historical course through its subsequent evolution and development

**his·tor·i·cal·ness** \-kəlnə̇s\ *n* -ES **:** the quality or state of being historical

**historical novel** *n* **:** a novel having as its setting a period of history and usu. introducing some historical personages and events

**historical perfect** *n* **:** the perfect tense when used in Latin to express action completed in an indefinite past

**historical present** *n* **:** the present tense used in telling of past events

**historical school** *n* **1 :** a school of economics developed in Germany in the middle of the 19th century that emphasizes institutional factors in society and pursues a systematic investigation of the development of economic institutions — compare CLASSICAL 3b(3) **2 :** a school of legal philosophy that emphasizes the relation of the evolution of law to the historical milieu and minimizes the importance of arbitrary human action and of natural processes to its development **3 :** a school of ethnology that emphasizes empirical study of the historical continuity of a specific culture or culture area as contrasted with comparative study of diverse or related cultures or culture areas

**historical sociology** *n* **:** a branch of sociology concerned with study of the origins, stages, and laws of social life and social institutions

**his·tor·i·cism** \hi'stȯrəˌsizəm, -tär-\ *n* -s **1 a :** a theory that all sociocultural phenomena are historically determined, that all truths are relative, that there are no absolute values, categories, or standards, and that the student of the past must enter into the mind and attitudes of past periods, accept their point of view, and avoid all intrusion of his own standards or preconceptions **b :** the practice of writing or treating history in accordance with such a theory **c :** a theory of history holding that the development of human society is a process governed by inexorable laws of change operating independently of human wills or wishes **2 a :** a strong or exaggerated concern with or respect for the institutions and traditions of the past ⟨stands for ~ and empiricism in the tradition of Burke —*Times Lit. Supp.*⟩ **b :** the use of or undue reliance upon historical forms or styles in art esp. in architectural design

1**his·tor·i·cist** \-ˌsə̇st\ *n* -s [fr. *historicism*, after such pairs as E *baptism : baptist*] **:** an advocate of historicism

2**historicist** \"\ *adj* **:** of, relating to, or based on historicism

**his·to·ric·i·ty** \ˌhistə'risəd·ē, -ətē, -i\ *n* -ES [prob. fr. F *historicité*, fr. L *historicus* + F *-ité* -ity] **1 :** the quality or state of being historic esp. as distinct from the mythological or legendary **2 :** a condition of being placed in the stream of historical developments; *also* **:** a result of such placement

**his·tor·i·cize** \hi'stȯrəˌsīz, -tär-\ *vb* -ED/-ING/-S *vt* **1 :** to render historic **:** give an appearance of historical verity or significance to ⟨the traditional myth of the god's victory over the dragon . . . is *historicized* as the triumph of Yahweh over the enemies of Israel —Philip Wheelwright⟩ **2 :** to make dependent on historicism esp. as a basis for action or an explanation of occurrences ⟨various disciplines also have been nationalized and over-*historicized* —Christian Gauss⟩ **~** *vi* **:** to use historical material or depend on historicism ⟨the nationalist and *historicizing* spirit of the 19th century —G.M.J. Moser⟩

**historico-** *comb form* [NL, fr. L *historicus* — more at HISTORICAL] **:** historical **:** historical and ⟨*historico*philosophical⟩ ⟨*historico*social⟩

**his·tor·i·co·critical** \hi¦stȯrə̇(ˌ)kō, -tär-, -rē(-+\ *adj* **:** based on or involving the use of techniques of both historian and critic ⟨an ~ examination of religion⟩ — **his·tor·i·co·critical·ly** \"+\ *adv*

**his·to·ried** \'hist(ə)rēd, -rid\ *adj* **:** related in or as history **:** having a history **:** HISTORICAL

**his·to·ri·ette** \hi¦stōrē¦et, -tȯr-, ˌ=ˌ=='=\ *n* -s [F, fr. L *historia* narrative, history + F *-ette* (dim. suffix) — more at HISTORY] **:** a short history or story

**his·tor·i·fy** \hi'stȯrəˌfī, -tär-\ *vt* -ED/-ING/-S [*history* + *-fy*] **:** to record in or as history

**historio-** *comb form* [MF, fr. LL, fr. Gk, fr. *historia* inquiry, information, narrative, history — more at HISTORY] **:** history ⟨*historio*metric⟩ ⟨*historio*grapher⟩

**his·to·ri·og·ra·pher** \(ˌ)hiˌstōrē'ägrəfə(r), -tȯr- *sometimes* -tär-\ *n* -s [MF *historiographeur*, fr. LL *historiographus* (fr. Gk *historiographos*, fr. *historio-* + *-graphos* writer, fr. *graphein* to write) + MF *-eur* -or — more at CARVE] **1 :** a writer of history **:** HISTORIAN **2 :** a person appointed to write a history or to record the continuing history of a country, group, or institution **:** an official historian ⟨since 1924 has been ~ of the Protestant Episcopal Diocese of Virginia —*Christian Century*⟩

**his·to·ri·og·ra·pher·ship** \-ˌship\ *n* **:** the office of historiographer

**his·to·ri·o·graph·ic** \hi¦stōrēə¦grafik, -tȯr- *sometimes* -tär-\ *also* **his·to·ri·o·graph·i·cal** \-fə̇kəl\ *adj* **:** of or relating to historiography — **his·to·ri·o·graph·i·cal·ly** \-fə̇k(ə)lē\ *adv*

**his·to·ri·og·ra·phy** \(ˌ)hiˌstōrē'ägrəfē, -tȯr- *sometimes* -tär-\ *n* -ES [MF *historiographie*, fr. Gk *historiographia*, fr. *historio-* + *-graphia* -graphy] **1 a :** the writing of history; *esp* **:** the writing of history based on the critical examination of sources, the selection of particulars from the authentic materials, and the synthesis of particulars into a narrative that will stand the test of critical methods **b :** the principles, theory, and history of historical writing ⟨a course in ~⟩ **2 :** the product of historical writing **:** a body of historical literature ⟨no single work in our ~ has moved more Englishmen —*Times Lit. Supp.*⟩ ⟨for most of the 9th century northern ~ shrinks to a few disconnected annals —F.M.Stenton⟩

**his·to·ri·ol·o·gy** \-'äləjē\ *n* -ES [*historio-* + *-logy*] **:** the study or knowledge of history

**his·to·rism** \'histəˌrizəm\ *n* -s [G *historismus*, fr. *historie* history (fr. L *historia*) + G *-ismus* -ism] **:** HISTORICISM 1

1**his·to·ry** \'hist(ə)rē, -ri\ *n* -ES [L *historia*, fr. Gk *historia* inquiry, information, narrative, history, fr. *historein* to inquire into, examine, relate (fr. *histor-*, *histōr* judge) + *-ia* -y; akin to Gk *idein* to see — more at WIT] **1 :** a narrative of events connected with a real or imaginary object, person, or career **:** TALE, STORY; *esp* **:** such a narrative devoted to the exposition of the natural unfolding and interdependence of the events treated ⟨carefully recording the ~ of our vacation for father⟩ ⟨a ~ of passion, greed, and retribution⟩ **2 a :** a systematic written account comprising a chronological record of events (as affecting a city, state, nation, institution, science, or art) and usu. including a philosophical explanation of the cause and origin of such events — usu. distinguished from *annals* and *chronicle* **b :** a treatise presenting systematically related natural phenomena (as of geography, animals, or plants) ⟨an illustrated ~ of British birds⟩ **c :** an account of a sick person's family and personal background, his past health, and present illness **3 :** a branch of knowledge that records and explains past events as steps in the sequence of human activities **:** the study of the character and significance of events — usu. used with a qualifying adjective ⟨medieval ~⟩ ⟨European ~⟩ **4** [MF *histoire* story, history, picture, fr. L *historia*] **a** (1) *obs* **:** a pictorial representation of an historical subject (2) *or* **history painting :** painting esp. popular in the 17th and 18th centuries in which a complex of figures conveys a story or message usu. based on history or legend **b** (1) *obs* **:** DRAMA 1 (2) **:** a drama based on historical events **5 a :** the events that form the subject matter of a history **:** a series of events clustering about some center of interest (as a nation, a department of culture, a natural epoch or evolution, a living being or a species) upon the character and significance of which these events cast light **b :** the character and significance of such a center of interest — compare LIFE HISTORY **c** *broadly* **:** past events ⟨that's all ~ now⟩; *esp* **:** those events involving or concerned with mankind **d :** previous treatment, handling, or experience (as of a metal) ⟨the results of heat treating will depend in part on the previous ~ of the specimen⟩ ⟨thermal ~ may modify photoelectric reactivity of certain compounds⟩ ⟨there was a ~ of repeated exposure to near-freezing temperature that might explain the mutation⟩

2**history** \"\ *vt* -ED/-ING/-ES [ME *historien*, fr. MF *historier*, fr. LL & ML *historiare* — more at HISTORIATED] **1** *obs* **:** NARRATE, RECOUNT **2** *obs* **:** to decorate with an historical record or scenes from history

**his·to·ry·less** \-ləs\ *adj* **:** having no history or no recorded history or no history worthy of record

**historymaker** \'==(=)=,==\ *n* **:** one that by acts, ideas, or existence modifies the course of history

**history of religions :** the objective study of the origin and historical development of the religions of mankind — compare COMPARATIVE RELIGION

**history painting** *n* **1 :** HISTORY 4a(2) **2 :** the practice or techniques of painting histories

**his·to·toxic** \¦histə+\ *adj* [ISV *hist-* + *toxic*] **1 :** toxic to tissues ⟨~ agents⟩ **2 :** of, relating to, or caused by a histotoxin ⟨the development of a ~ anoxia⟩

**his·to·toxin** \"+\ *n* [*hist-* + *toxin*] **:** any of various poisonous substances formed in specific body tissues and usu. deleterious to the body in which they are formed

**his·to·troph** \'histə,träf, -rōf\ *or* **his·to·trophe** \-rōf\ *n* -s [F *histotrophe*, fr. *hist-* + *-trophe* (fr. Gk *trophos* one that feeds or rears)] **:** all materials supplied for nutrition of the embryo in viviparous animals from sources other than the maternal bloodstream — compare EMBRYOTROPH, HEMOTROPHE

**his·to·trop·ic** \¦histə¦träpik\ *adj* [*hist-* + *-tropic*] **:** exhibiting or characterized by histotropism

**his·tot·ro·pism** \hi'stä·trə,pizəm\ *n* [*hist-* + *-tropism*] **:** attraction (as of a parasite) to a particular kind of tissue

**his·to·zo·ic** \¦histə¦zōik\ *adj* [*hist-* + *-zoic*] **:** living in the tissues of a host ⟨~ parasites⟩

**his·to·zyme** \'histə,zīm\ *n* [ISV *hist-* + *-zyme*] **:** an enzyme widely distributed in mammalian tissues that is capable of splitting acyl groups from hippuric acid and other acylated amino acids or from peptides — called also *hippuricase*

**his·trio** \'histrē,ō\ *n* -s [L, alter. of *hister*, fr. Etruscan] **:** ACTOR

**his·tri·ob·del·lea** \,histrē,äb'delēə\ *n pl, cap* [NL, fr. L *histrio* actor + NL *-bdellea* (fr. Gk *bdella* leech)] **:** a small group of segmented invertebrate animals that are intermediate in some respects between the Aschelminthes and the Annelida and that are all parasitic on marine crustaceans

**his·tri·on** \'histrē,än\ *n* -s [MF, fr. L *histrion-, histrio*] **:** ACTOR

1**his·tri·on·ic** \¦histrē¦änik, -nēk\ *also* **his·tri·on·i·cal** \-nəkəl, -nēk-\ *adj* [LL *histrionicus*, fr. L *histrion-, histrio* + *-icus* -ic] **1 :** of or relating to actors, acting, or the theater ⟨an able actor ever seeking ~ perfection⟩ **2 :** deliberately affected **:** THEATRICAL, STAGED ⟨her heart attacks were as ~ as her sister's fits of temper⟩ — **his·tri·on·i·cal·ly** \-nək(ə)lē, -nēk-, -li\ *adv*

2**histrionic** \"\ *n* -s **1 :** ACTOR **2 histrionics** *pl but sometimes sing in constr* **a :** theatrical performances **b :** staged or stagy conduct or exhibition of temperament usu. intended to produce some particular effect or response in others

**his·tri·on·i·cus** \,histrē'änəkəs\ *n, cap* [NL, fr. LL, adj., histrionic; fr. their handsome plumage] **:** a genus of ducks including only the harlequin duck

**his·tri·o·nism** \'histrēə,nizəm\ *n* -s **:** THEATRICALITY

**his·trix** \'histriks\ [NL, alter. of *Hystrix*] *syn of* HYSTRIX

1**hit** \'hit, *usu* -id·+V\ *vb* **hit; hit; hitting; hits** [ME *hitten*, fr. ON *hitta* to hit upon, meet up with, hit; perh. akin to OE *hentan* to pursue, attack, seize — more at HUNT] *vt* **1 a :** to reach or get at by striking with or as if with a sudden blow ⟨~ a ball⟩ ⟨be ~ by adversity⟩ **b :** to come in quick forceful contact with ⟨the ball ~ the house and bounced off⟩ **2 a :** to cause to come into sudden forceful contact ⟨~ his hand against the wall⟩ ⟨~ the stick against the railing⟩ **b :** to deliver (a blow) usu. in a vigorous or violent manner **:** STRIKE **c :** to strike a blow at or to ⟨~ the table suddenly⟩ ⟨~ the boy in the eye⟩ **3 a :** to affect esp. strongly and to the detriment or distress of ⟨life had never ~ her very hard —Nevil Shute⟩ ⟨drought ~ the range country early that year⟩ **b :** to criticize adversely **:** CENSURE ⟨no prime minister in our history has been ~ so hard by a biographer who knew him —*Times Lit. Supp.*⟩ **4 :** to make a request of or a claim or demand upon (as for a loan or a job) ⟨~ his friend for 10 dollars⟩ — often used with *up* ⟨~ up his father's friends for work⟩ **5 a :** to come upon, find, or discover by or as if by chance or accident ⟨spent years in prospecting without ever *hitting* gold⟩ **b :** to meet with, reach, or experience by or as if by chance or accident ⟨after several weeks of travel, we ~ our first snowstorm⟩ ⟨~ a run of bad luck⟩ **6 :** to reach or attain by or as if by hitting: as **a :** to accord with usu. exactly and purposely ⟨writing that ~s the public taste precisely⟩ **b :** to act in precise accord with ⟨~s a musical cue⟩ **c :** to reach as a rate, standard, or level ⟨a car that can ~ 100 mph.⟩ ⟨prices ~ an all-time high⟩ ⟨when you ~ the middle sixties⟩ **d** *of fish* **:** to bite at or on **:** TAKE ⟨in certain times of the season fish will only ~ live bait⟩ **e :** to appear in or on (as for public sale, consumption, use) ⟨sweet corn ~s the markets in New England in midsummer⟩ ⟨a magazine that ~s the newsstands early in the month⟩ ⟨morning papers often ~ the streets in the late evening⟩ ⟨this recording will ~ the jukeboxes soon⟩ **f** *of an author* **:** to achieve publication in ⟨took him some time to ~ the better magazines⟩ **g :** to be reported in ⟨~ the front pages⟩ **h :** to impinge on or command the attention of ⟨advertising techniques designed to ~ the subconscious mind⟩ **i :** STRESS, EMPHASIZE ⟨always ~ the message-bearing words firmly⟩ ⟨inclined to ~ the wrong syllable⟩ **j :** to arrive at, in, or on usu. for a brief or transitory stay ⟨arranged to ~ town two days before his brother⟩ ⟨when the first forces ~ the beach⟩ ⟨planned on *hitting* all the new night spots⟩ **k** (1) **:** to reach or strike (as a target) for a score in a game or contest ⟨unbelievable ability to ~ the basket⟩ (2) **:** to succeed in making (a scoring play) ⟨~ three goals before their opponents were well warmed up⟩ (3) *slang* **:** to win in a lottery or game of chance or acquire as if by so winning ⟨~ first prize⟩ ⟨an act that didn't ~ the big money until he took it to New York⟩ — often used with *for* and the thing or the amount gained ⟨~ the numbers pool for $2000⟩ ⟨~ the company education fund for a year in technical school⟩ **l** *slang* (1) **:** to go, lie, or drop on or upon usu. suddenly or at once ⟨~ the deck⟩ (2) **:** to get onto and begin to move along or travel on ⟨~ the road⟩ ⟨~ the right path⟩ **7 :** to capture with precision (as a mood, an idea, a personal characteristic in a description or representation) ⟨none of these analyses seem quite to ~ the main characteristic —R.D.Ellmann⟩ **8 :** to set in operation or cause to function by or as if by striking or touching ⟨~ the lights⟩ ⟨*hitting* slow chords on a guitar⟩ ⟨had to ~ the brakes suddenly⟩ **9 :** to indulge in (as liquor) esp. excessively, habitually, or compulsively ⟨had been *hitting* the bottle for days⟩ **10 a :** to deal another card to (a player at blackjack) **b :** to have another card dealt to (a hand in blackjack) **c :** FILL *vt* 7 ~ *vi* **1 :** to strike or strike out at something with or as if with a sudden blow (as of the fist or a missile) ⟨in the third round he began *hitting* wildly⟩ ⟨*hitting* only about once in five shots⟩ **2 a :** to come into forcible contact with something ⟨when he fell, he ~ hard⟩ — often used with *against* ⟨tipped over and ~ against the wall and was damaged⟩ **b :** ATTACK ⟨guessed at where they would ~, and the date of D day —Dan Levin⟩ **c** *of a fish* **:** STRIKE *vi* 15b **d :** to arrive with a disturbing or damaging effect ⟨a heavy storm that ~ just at sundown⟩ ⟨had been still in school when the bad times ~⟩ ⟨the grippe ~ unusually severely that year⟩ **3 a :** to meet or reach something aimed at or desired **:** succeed in attaining or obtaining something often by or as if by chance — often used with *on* or *upon* ⟨~ on a solution⟩ ⟨~ upon a satisfactory explanation⟩ **b :** to draw or be dealt a valuable card in poker ⟨drew to an inside straight and ~⟩ **c :** to hit a blot **4** *of a crop, now dial* **:** to germinate, grow, or yield well **5** *obs* **:** to be in agreement **:** SUIT — used with *with* ⟨the scheme ~ so exactly with my temper —Daniel Defoe⟩ **6 :** to direct one's course **:** direct oneself ⟨~ for the nearest lunchroom⟩ ⟨in spring the peddlers ~ up the coast with packs and carts⟩ **7** *of an internal-combustion engine* **:** to fire the charge in the cylinders **8 a :** to be a winner (as in a lottery) **b :** to make a score (as in a game) **syn** see STRIKE — **hit a blot 1 :** to capture a man exposed on a point in backgammon **2 :** to find a flaw (as in a policy or argument) — **hit for six 1** *Brit* **:** to hit for six runs in cricket **2** *Brit* **:** to hit hard **:** DEFEAT, TROUNCE — **hit it off :** to associate agreeably **:** get along well **:** have a mutually congenial relationship ⟨had *hit it off* from the very start⟩ — **hit it up :** to work, play, or perform with speed, animation, or abandon ⟨the band was already *hitting it up* when we arrived⟩ — **hit one's stride :** to reach one's best speed or performance **:** exhibit maximum competence or capability — **hit the books** *or* **hit one's books :** to study esp. with intensity — **hit the bricks** *slang* **:** to go on strike **:** walk out — **hit the hay** *or* **hit the sack** *slang* **:** to go to bed — **hit the high points** *or* **hit the high spots :** to touch on or at the most important or salient points or places ⟨a lecture that *hit* only *the high points* of the subject⟩ ⟨with only three days in town the best we could do was *hit the high spots*⟩ — **hit the jackpot** *slang* **:** to be or become notably and usu. unexpectedly successful — **hit the nail on the head :** to perform effectively or be effective **:** be exactly right — **hit the roof** *also* **hit the ceiling :** to give vent to a burst of anger or angry protest — **hit the silk** *slang* **:** to parachute from an airplane — **hit the spot :** to give complete or special satisfaction — used esp. of food or drink

2**hit** \"\ *n* -s [ME *hete*, fr. *hitten*, v.] **1 a :** a blow striking an object aimed at — contrasted with *miss* ⟨scored a ~ on his first try⟩ ⟨two ~s and three misses out of five tries⟩ **b :** an impact of one thing against another **:** COLLISION **2 a :** a stroke of luck **:** a fortunate chance ⟨answered the questions correctly by a series of lucky ~s⟩ **b :** a theatrical production, book, or song that is conspicuously successful or popular; *broadly* **:** anything that is exceedingly popular, pleasing, or successful ⟨this new style is a big ~ with the high-school set⟩ **c :** a win in various gambling games ⟨a string of 20 ~s on a pinball machine⟩ **3 :** a censorious, sarcastic, or telling remark or statement ⟨took a sharp ~ at grasping politicians⟩ **4 :** a backgammon game won after the opponent has removed some of his men **5** *dial* **:** a bountiful crop — used esp. of fruit **6 :** a stroke in various games by which a ball is hit so as to result in a score, advancement of a runner, or some other advantage; *specif, in baseball* **:** BASE HIT **7** *printing* **:** IMPRESSION 6b ⟨even two ~s of white ink didn't quite seem to cover the green cloth —*Book Production*⟩

3**hit** \(')hit, *usu* -id·+V\ *obs or dial var of* IT

**hit-and-miss** \¦=¦=¦=\ *adj* **:** sometimes hitting or corresponding in position and sometimes not **:** RANDOM, HIT-OR-MISS

**hit-and-run** \¦=¦=¦=\ *adj* **1 :** being or relating to a baseball play in which a base runner starts for the next base as the pitcher starts to pitch and the batter attempts to hit the ball **2 a** (1) *of the driver of a vehicle* **:** guilty of leaving the scene of an accident without stopping to render assistance or to comply with legal requirements (2) **:** caused by, resulting from, or involving a hit-and-run driver ⟨increasing numbers of *hit-and-run* deaths⟩ ⟨a *hit-and-run* accident⟩ **b :** involving or intended for quick specific action or results rather than permanent use ⟨small *hit-and-run* units of troops⟩ ⟨*hit-and-run* merchandising⟩

**hit-and-runner** \"ə(r)\ *n* **:** one that hits and runs away; *esp* **:** a hit-and-run driver

1**hitch** \'hich\ *vb* -ED/-ING/-ES [ME *hytchen*] *vt* **1 :** to move with jerks or jerkily ⟨~*ing* his chair closer to the table⟩ **2 a :** to catch or fasten by or as if by a hook or a knot ⟨~*ed* his horse to the top rail of the fence⟩ **b :** to connect (a vehicle or implement) with a source of motive power ⟨~ a rake to a tractor⟩ or to attach (a source of motive power) to a vehicle or instrument ⟨~ the horses to the wagon⟩ **c** *slang* **:** to join in marriage **3 :** to introduce into a literary work esp. irrelevantly or by obvious straining ⟨can't avoid ~*ing* in a word or two about personal responsibility⟩ **4 :** HITCHHIKE ⟨could ~ a ride on their trucks —Dillon Ripley⟩ ~ *vi* **1 :** to move interruptedly or with halts and jerks usu. due to an obstruction or impediment **:** HOBBLE ⟨~*ed* slowly along on his cane⟩ **2 a :** to become entangled or made fast **:** become linked or yoked ⟨presumably these infinitesimal particles ~*ed* together to become matter⟩ **b** *slang* **:** to become joined in marriage — often used with *up* ⟨decided to ~ up⟩ **3 :** HITCHHIKE ⟨could not risk ~*ing* back —James Jones⟩ — **hitch horses** *archaic* **:** to act or be in agreement **:** HARMONIZE — usu. used with *together*

2**hitch** \"\ *n* -ES **1 :** a sudden movement or pull **:** JERK, TWITCH ⟨gave his trousers a ~⟩ **2 a :** HOBBLE, LIMP ⟨a ~ in his gait⟩ **b** *dial* **:** CRICK ⟨had a ~ in his back⟩ **3 :** a sudden halt or stop (as from an accident) **:** ENTANGLEMENT, OBSTRUCTION, STOPPAGE, IMPEDIMENT ⟨a ~ in the performance⟩ **4 :** the act or fact of catching hold of or on something (as a hook) **5 :** a connection between a vehicle or implement and a detachable source of motive power (as a tractor or a horse) **6** *slang* **:** a period of military service; *broadly* **:** a sharply delimited period in one's life ⟨served a three-year ~ in prison⟩ ⟨put in a ~ with the diplomatic service after leaving the army⟩ **7 :** a recess cut in rock to support the end of a timber in mining or tunneling operations **8 :** any of various knots used to form a temporary loop or noose in a line or to secure a line temporarily to an object; *sometimes* **:** HALF HITCH **9 :** HITCHHIKE, LIFT 5b ⟨get a ~ into town —Irwin Shaw⟩

3**hitch** \"\ *n* -ES [origin unknown] **:** a minnow (*Lavinia exilicauda*) with silvery sides and dark back that occurs in streams about San Francisco and Monterey and reaches a length of 12 inches

**hitch and kick** *n* **:** a standing high jump in which the jumper springs from, kicks with, and alights on the same foot

**hitch·cock chair** *also* **hitchcock** \'hich,käk\ *n, usu cap H* [after Lambert H. *Hitchcock* †1852 Am. furniture manufacturer] **:** a turned usu. rush-seated chair with legs often and back always slightly bent with a top rail and back posts above the seat, and with a finish usu. of black paint and stenciled decoration

Hitchcock chair

**hitch·er** \'hichə(r)\ *n* -s **:** one that hitches or catches (as a boat hook)

1**hitchhike** \'=,=\ *vb* [2*hitch* + *hike*] *vi* **:** to travel by securing free rides from passing vehicles or in transport available by chance ⟨boys *hitchhiking* home from school⟩ ⟨soldiers *hitchhiking* back to their base in a military plane⟩ ~ *vt* **1 :** to proceed or progress on (as a course or way) by hitchhiking ⟨*hitchhiked* his way to the Pacific coast⟩ **2 :** to obtain (a ride) as a hitchhiker ⟨*hitchhiked* a lift on the next plane out⟩

2**hitchhike** \"\ *n* **1 :** a trip made by hitchhiking **2** *or* **hitch·hik·er** \"ə(r)\ **:** a brief commercial that follows a radio or television program and usu. advertises a secondary product of the sponsor

**hitch·hik·er** \"ə(r)\ *n* **:** one that hitchhikes

**hitch·i·ly** \'hichəlē, -li\ *adv* **:** in a hitchy manner **:** JERKILY

**hitching** *pres part of* HITCH

**hitching bar** *n* **:** HITCHRACK

**hitching post** *n* **:** a fixed and often elaborate standard to which a horse or team can be fastened to prevent straying — compare HITCHRACK

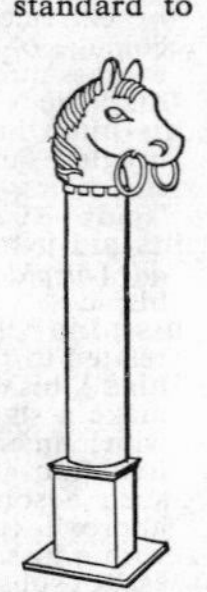

hitching post

**hitch·i·ti** \'hichəd·ē\ *n, pl* **hitchiti** *or* **hitchitis** *usu cap* **1 a :** a Muskogean people of Georgia, member of the Creek confederacy **b :** a member of such people **2 :** the language of the Hitchiti people

**hitch kick** *n* **1 :** a running motion executed by a broad jumper while in the air to increase the distance of his jump **2 :** HITCH AND KICK

**hitch pin** *n* **:** one of a row of slanting metal pins in a piano action to which the strings are attached at the ends opposite the tuning pins

**hitchrack** \'=,=\ *n* **:** a fixed horizontal rail to which a horse or team can be fastened to prevent straying — compare HITCHING POST

**hitch up** *vi* **:** to harness a draft animal or team and make it fast (as to a wagon or implement) ⟨we *hitched up* and were on our way before sunrise⟩

**hitchy** \'hichē, -chi\ *adj* -ER/-EST **:** having impeded movement **:** JERKY

**hithe** \'hīth, -th\ *n* -s [ME *hythe*, fr. OE *hȳth*; akin to OS *hūth* port] **:** a small port or harbor esp. on a river — now used chiefly in place names

1**hith·er** \'hithə(r)\ *adv* [ME *hider, hither*, fr. OE *hider*; akin to ON *hethra* here, Goth *hidre* hither, L *citro* hither, *citra* on this side — more at HE] **1 :** to this place ⟨bring ~ your sick and sorrowful⟩ ⟨~ came the children to play⟩ — compare *hence, thither* **2** *obs* **:** to this point, source, conclusion, design **:** HERETO

2**hither** \"\ *adj* [ME *hider, hither*, fr. *hider, hither*, adv.] **1 :** being on the side next or toward the person speaking **:** NEARER ⟨on the ~ side of the hill⟩ — compare FARTHER, THITHER **2** *of time* **:** EARLIER

**hither and thither** *adv* [ME *hider and thider*, fr. OE] **:** to and fro **:** backward and forward **:** in various and usu. random directions ⟨roving *hither and thither*⟩

**hither-and-thither** \¦===¦==\ *vi* -ED/-ING/-S [*hither and thither*] **:** to move confusedly or at random

**hither and yon** *also* **hither and yond** *adv* **:** HITHER AND THITHER

**hith·er·most** \'==,mōst *also chiefly Brit* -,məst\ *adj* [2*hither* + *-most*] **:** nearest on this side

1**hith·er·to** \'==,tü, ,==¦=\ *adv* [ME *hiderto*, fr. *hider* (adv.) + *to* (prep.)] **1 :** up to this time **:** as yet **:** until now ⟨~ unknown resources⟩ **2 :** to this place ⟨the appointed delegates shall come ~⟩

2**hitherto** \"\ *adj* **:** existing or done hitherto **:** PREVIOUS, PRIOR ⟨our ~ experience suggests⟩

**hith·er·ward** \'== wə(r)d\ *also* **hith·er·wards** \-dz\ *adv* [ME *hiderward, hitherwarde*, fr. OE *hiderweard*, fr. *hider* hither + *-weard* -ward] **:** toward this place **:** HITHER

**hit·le·ri·an** \(')hit¦lirēən\ *adj, usu cap* [Adolf *Hitler* †1945 dictator of Germany + E *-ian*] **:** of, relating to, or suggestive of Adolf Hitler or his regime in Germany ⟨a *Hitlerian* disregard of human rights⟩

**hit·ler·ism** \'hitlə,rizəm\ *n* -s *usu cap* [A. *Hitler* + E *-ism*] **:** the extreme nationalistic doctrines of the German National Socialist party under the leadership of Adolf Hitler, from about 1930 **:** NAZISM

1**hit·ler·ite** \-,rīt, *usu* -īd·+V\ *n* -s *usu cap* [A. *Hitler* + E *-ite*] **:** an adherent of Hitlerism

2**hitlerite** \"\ *adj, usu cap* **:** HITLERIAN

**hit·less** \'hitləs\ *adj, of a baseball player or team* **:** making no base hits

**hit off** *vt* **:** to characterize precisely and usu. satirically ⟨in a brilliant metaphor . . . hits himself *off* with terrible accuracy —V.S.Pritchett⟩ ⟨really *hits off* the contours and hierarchies of an English village with an amusing slyness —H.J.Laski⟩; *broadly* **:** IMITATE ⟨*hits off* an old turkey-gobbler to perfection⟩ ~ *vi* **:** to be in harmony or agreement **:** ACCORD ⟨soft shade that will *hit off* with anything⟩ ⟨his late arrival *hit off* perfectly with our plan⟩

**hit-off** \'=,=\ *n* -s [*hit off*] **:** a clever imitation ⟨did an amusing *hit-off* of his brother⟩

**hit or miss** *adv* **:** without regard to accuracy or precision **:** at random **:** in a happy-go-lucky fashion

**hit-or-miss** \¦=¦=¦=\ *adj* [*hit or miss*] **:** unpredictable and uncertain usu. through lack of care, forethought, system, or plan **:** marked by indifferent, ill-considered, or empirical expediency ⟨making all allowances for the *hit-or-miss* element in affirmations of a general kind —*Times Lit. Supp.*⟩; *broadly* **:** having no fixed or predetermined pattern ⟨a *hit-or-miss* carpet⟩ **syn** see RANDOM

**hit out** *vi* **:** to aim angry often random blows ⟨*hit out* and . . . caught him right between the eyes —H.A.Chippendale⟩ ⟨*hitting out* at injustice and prejudice⟩

**hit parade** *n* [fr. *Your Hit Parade*, a service mark] **:** a group or listing of transitorily most popular items of a particular kind (as popular songs)

**hi-trap** \'hī,=\ *n* [alter. of *high* + *trap*] **:** HIGH-HOUSE

**hit-run** \'=¦=\ *adj* **:** HIT-AND-RUN 2

**hits** *pres 3d sing of* HIT, *pl of* HIT

**hit-skip** \'=¦=\ *adj* **:** HIT-AND-RUN 2

**hit·ta·ble** \'hid·əbəl, -itə-\ *adj* **:** capable of being hit

**hit·ter** \'hid·ə(r), -itə-\ *n* -s **:** one that hits

**hit theory** *n* **:** a theory in genetics: the mutafacient action of mutagenically active radiations depends upon the taking up of an effective amount of the radiation by a sensitive region of the cell

**hitting** *pres part of* HIT

1**hit·tite** \'hi,tīt, 'hid·ə,|, *usu* |īd·+V\ *n* -s *usu cap* [Heb *Ḥittī* (fr. Hitt *ḫatti*) + E *-ite*] **1 :** a member of the aboriginal population of the ancient city or country of Khatti in eastern Asia Minor **2 a :** a member of a conquering people in Asia Minor and later in Syria whose origin is not certainly known, whose characteristic features, the sloping forehead and large aquiline nose, as preserved in Hittite and Egyptian reliefs, seem to have been derived from the autochthonous Hittites, and whose empire in the 2d millennium B.C. rivaled the Babylonian and Egyptian **b :** an Indo-European or Indo-Hittite language of this people known from a large body of texts in cuneiform writing largely found at Bogazköy in central Asia Minor — compare HIEROGLYPHIC HITTITE; see INDO-EUROPEAN LANGUAGES table

2**hittite** \"\ *adj, usu cap* **:** of or relating to the Hittites or their language

**hittite hieroglyph** *n, usu cap 1st H* **1 hittite hieroglyphs** *pl* **:** a system of writing known from inscriptions from Asia Minor and esp. northern Syria dating from about 1500 B.C. to about 600 B.C. and composed of pictorial symbols partly ideographic and partly phonetic in which the language Hieroglyphic Hittite was written **2 :** a character in the Hittite hieroglyphs

**hittite hieroglyphic** *n, usu cap 1st H* **:** HITTITE HIEROGLYPH

**hit·tit·ol·o·gy** \,hi,tīd·'äləjē, ,hid·,īd·'ä-, ,hi,tī'tä-\ *also* **hit·tol·o·gy** \hi'tä-\ *n* -ES *usu cap* [*Hittito-* or *Hitto-* (fr. 1*Hittite*) + *-logy*] **:** a branch of knowledge concerned with Hittite philology, archaeology, and history

**hit·ty-mis·sy** \¦hid·ē¦misē\ *adv (or adj)* [irreg. fr. *hit or miss* + *-y*] **:** HIT OR MISS

**hit wicket** *adj, of a batsman in cricket* **:** having broken the wicket with the bat or some part of the person in making a stroke at a ball — used in the phrase *out, hit wicket;* abbr *hw*

1**hive** \'hīv\ *n* -s [ME *hive, heve*, fr. OE *hȳf*; akin to ON *hūfr* hull of a ship, L *cupa* tub, cask, Gk *kypellon* cup, *kypros*, a measure for grain, Skt *kūpa* hole, cave, OE *hēah* high — more at HIGH] **1 :** a container for housing honeybees now usu. consisting of a base, a lower rectangular hive body containing removable frames for brood, one or more upper supers that provide room for the storage honey, and a weather-tight cover — called also *beehive;* compare BEE GUM, SKEP **2 :** the bees of one hive **:** a colony of bees **3 :** something resembling a hive: as **a** *obs* **:** a head covering suggesting a plaited skep **b :** a dwelling place **:** a center of family life ⟨forced out of the family ~ by the excess of hands and the deficiency of land —H.E.Scudder⟩ **c :** a center of activity or a place swarming with busy occupants ⟨the teeming ~ of a great railroad station⟩ ⟨a ~ of political unrest⟩ **d :** a source or point of origin ⟨the ~ from which these barbarians came lay far to the north⟩

**²hive** \"\ *vb* -ED/-ING/-S *vt* **1 a :** to collect into, place in, or cause to enter a hive ⟨*hived* 7 swarms of wild bees⟩ **b :** to shelter in or as if in a hive ⟨these rascals that the city ~*s*⟩ **2 a :** to store up in a hive ⟨a strong colony in a good season may ~ 100 pounds of honey⟩ **b :** to gather and accumulate for future need **:** lay up in store ⟨why did they penuriously ~ and distribute water —Norman Douglas⟩ — sometimes used with *up* or *away* ⟨*hiving* away the extra dollars⟩ ~ *vi* **1 a** *of bees* **:** to enter and take possession of a hive ⟨the swarm *hived* readily⟩ **b :** to reside or gather like bees in close association ⟨the multitudes that ~ in city apartments⟩ **2 :** to secrete oneself or shut oneself up — usu. used with *up* ⟨*hiving* up in an old camp to sit out the storm⟩

**³hive** \"\ *n* -S [back-formation fr. *hives*] **:** an urticarial wheal **:** a lesion of hives

**hive bee** *n* **:** a domestic honeybee

**hive body** *n* **:** the brood chamber of a hive

**hive·less** \'hīvləs\ *adj* **:** having no hive

**hive off** *vi* **:** to break away from a group like a swarm from a hive of bees ⟨a portion of a nation *hives off* to a new territory and builds a new nationalism of its own —R.M.MacIver⟩

**hiv·er** \'hīvə(r)\ *n* -S **:** one that hives

**hives** \'hīvz\ *n pl but sing or pl in constr* [origin unknown] **1 :** URTICARIA **2 :** an eruptive skin disease

**hive syrup** *n* **:** compound syrup of squill formerly employed as an emetic in croup and as an expectorant

**hive tool** *n* **:** a blunt metal chisel that has the end opposite the blade bent at right angles to the shaft and is used by beekeepers to separate supers and to scrape away propolis from parts of the hive

hive tool

**hive vine** *n* **:** PARTRIDGEBERRY

**hive·ward** \'hīvwə(r)d\ *or* **hive·wards** \-dz\ *adv* **:** toward a hive ⟨bees flying ~ in a straight line⟩

**hi·vite** \'hī,vīt\ *also* **hiv·vite** \'hi,v-\ *n* -S *usu cap* **:** a member of one of the ancient Canaanite peoples who were conquered by the Israelites

**hi·wi hi·wi** \,hēwē'hēwē\ *n* [Maori] **:** a small marine spiny-finned food fish (*Chironemus fergussoni*) of New Zealand

**hi·ya** \'hīyə\ *interj* [alter. of *how are you*] — used as an informal greeting

**hi·zen porcelain** \'hē,zen-, -'-\ *n, usu cap H* [fr. *Hizen,* old province of Kyushu Island, Japan] **:** any of several Japanese porcelains noted for rich decoration, delicate coloring, and fine modeling

**hizz** \'hiz\ *obs or dial var of* HISS

**hiz·zie** \'hizi\ *Scot var of* HUSSY

**HJ** *abbr* [L *hic jacet*] here lies

**hjelm·ite** *also* **hielm·ite** \'(h)yel,mīt, hē'el-\ *n* -S [Sw *hjelmit,* fr. P. J. *Hjelm* †1813 Swedish chemist + Sw *-it* -ite] **:** a black mineral that contains yttrium, iron, manganese, uranium, calcium, columbium, tantalum, tin, and tungsten oxide, is often metamict, and has uncertain affinities — compare SAMARSKITE, TAPIOLITE

**hjelm·slev·ian** \(')(h)yelmz'levēən, -eüm-,- m(p)'sl-\ *adj, usu cap* [Louis *Hjelmslev* b1899 Dan. linguist + E *-ian*] **:** belonging to or characteristic of the linguistic methods or terminology of Louis Hjelmslev

**HJR** *abbr* House joint resolution

**HJS** *abbr* [L *hic jacet sepultus*] here lies buried

**hkf** *abbr* handkerchief

**hl** *abbr* hectoliter

**HL** *abbr* **1** height-length **2** *often not cap* [L *hoc loco*] in this place; [L *hujus loci*] of this place **3** horizontal line **4** House of Lords

**h l hinge** *n, cap 1st H&L* **:** H AND L HINGE

**hm** *abbr* hectometer

**HM** *abbr* **1** half morocco **2** handmade **3** harbor master **4** harmonic mean **5** headmaster; headmistress **6** heavy mobile **7** Her Majesty; His Majesty **8** *often not cap* [L *hoc mense*] in this month; [L *hujus mensis*] of this month **9** home missions

**hmd** *abbr* humid

**HMD** *abbr* hydraulic mean depth

**HMG** *abbr* **1** heavy machine gun **2** Her Majesty's Government; His Majesty's Government

**hmlt** *abbr* hamlet

**HMP** *abbr* **1** handmade paper **2** [L *hoc monumentum posuit*] he erected this monument

**HMS** *abbr* **1** Her Majesty's Service; His Majesty's Service **2** Her Majesty's Ship; His Majesty's Ship

**hnd** *abbr* **1** hand **2** hundred

**hndbk** *abbr* handbook

**¹ho** \'hō\ *interj* [ME] — used typically to express surprise or delight or indignation or derision or to attract attention and esp. postpositively to attract attention to something specified ⟨land ~⟩; often used postpositively as a rallying cry with a specified direction or destination ⟨westward ~⟩

**²ho** \"\ *v imper* [ME, fr. OF *ho* halt, stop] — a call intended to stop a movement or an action; compare WHOA

**³ho** \"\ *vi, dial Eng* **:** ³HONE

**⁴ho** \"\ *n, pl* **ho** *or* **hos** *usu cap* **1 a :** a people of the northeastern part of the Indian subcontinent south of the Ganges plain **b :** a member of such people **2 :** the Munda language of the Ho people

**ho** *abbr* house

**HO** *abbr* **1** head office; home office **2** holy day of obligation **3** hostilities only

**Ho** *symbol* holmium

**hoactzin** *var of* HOATZIN

**¹hoar** \'hō(ə)r, 'hȯ(ə)r, -ōə, -ȯ(ə)\ *adj* [ME *hor, hoor,* fr. OE *hār;* akin to OHG *hēr* gray, old, ON *hārr* gray, old, Gk *kirros* orange yellow, Skt *śiti* white] *archaic* **:** HOARY ⟨whose beard with age is ~ —S.T.Coleridge⟩

**²hoar** \"\ *n* -S [ME *hor, hoor,* fr. *hor, hoor,* adj.] **1** *archaic* **:** HOARINESS **2 a :** a hoary coating ⟨the thick ~ of dust which had accumulated on their shoes —Thomas Hardy⟩ **b :** HOARFROST, RIME

**¹hoard** \'hō(ə)rd, 'hȯ(ə)rd, 'hōəd, 'hȯ(ə)d\ *n* -S [ME *hord,* fr. OE; akin to OHG *hort* treasure, ON *hodd,* Goth *huzd* treasure, Gk *kysthos* vulva, OE *hȳdan* to hide — more at HIDE] **1 :** a collection or accumulation or amassment of something usu. of special value or utility that is put aside for preservation or safekeeping or future use often in a greedy or miserly or otherwise unreasonable manner and that is often kept hidden or as if hidden **:** a supply or stock or fund of something that is stored up and closely and often jealously guarded ⟨a ~ of money⟩ ⟨a ~ of provisions⟩ ⟨a ~ of facts⟩; *often* **:** TREASURE ⟨dug up a ~ of gold and jewels⟩ ⟨a ~ of old coins⟩ **2** *obs* **:** the place where a hoard is kept **:** REPOSITORY; *specif, obs* **:** TREASURY

**²hoard** \"\ *vb* -ED/-ING/-S [ME *horden,* fr. OE *hordian,* fr. *hord,* n.] *vt* **1 :** to collect or accumulate or amass into a hoard **:** lay up a hoard of ⟨~*ing* their money and refusing to make even reasonable expenditures⟩ **2 :** to keep (as a desire) hidden and in reserve and allow to develop or become strengthened ⟨she ~*ed* her intention —Virginia Woolf⟩ ⟨the people outside disperse their affections, you ~ yours, you nurse them into intensity —Joseph Conrad⟩ ~ *vi* **:** to lay up a hoard; *esp* **:** to practice hoarding **syn** see ACCUMULATE

**³hoard** \"\ *n* -S [alter. of earlier *hourd,* prob. fr. F dial., scaffold, scaffolding, fr. OF *hourt* scaffold, scaffolding, platform, of Gmc origin; akin to OHG *hurt* hurdle — more at HURDLE] **:** ²HOARDING 1

**¹hoard·ing** \'hōrdiŋ, 'hȯr-, -dēŋ\ *n* -S [fr. gerund of ²*hoard*] **1 :** the greedy or miserly accumulation and storing or hiding of money or goods **2 :** something hoarded — usu. used in pl. ⟨the ~*s* of a lifetime⟩

**²hoarding** \"\ *n* -S [³*hoard* + *-ing*] **1 :** a temporary board fence put about a building being erected or repaired **2** *Brit* **:** BILLBOARD

**hoard·ing·ly** *adv* **:** in a manner marked by hoarding **:** in a greedy or miserly manner

**hoarfrost** \'⸗,⸗\ *n* [ME *horforst,* fr. *hor, hoor* hoar + *forst, frost* frost] **:** FROST 1c(1)

**hoar-green** \'⸗'⸗\ *adj* **:** grayish white with greenish cast

**hoarhead** \'⸗,⸗\ *n* [ME *horheed,* fr. *hor, hoor* hoar + *heed* head] *archaic* **:** one having a hoary head

**hoarhound** *var of* HOREHOUND

**hoar·i·ly** \'hōrəlē, 'hȯr-, -li\ *adv* **:** in a hoary manner

**hoar·i·ness** \-rēnəs, -rin-\ *n* -ES **:** the quality or state of being hoary

**hoarse** \'hō(ə)rs, 'hȯ(ə)rs, -ōəs, -ȯ(ə)s\ *adj, usu* -ER/-EST [ME *hors,* alter. (perh. influenced by *harsk* harsh) of earlier *hos,* fr. OE *hās;* akin to OHG *heis* hoarse, ON *hāss,* OE *hāt* hot — more at HOT] **1 :** marked by a relatively low harsh or husky often muffled or laboriously forced quality of sound having little or no resonance **:** not clear or smooth or musical in tone **:** rough-sounding **:** RAUCOUS, GRATING, RASPING, CROAKING ⟨the ~ voice of a person with a cold⟩ ⟨the ~ sound made by a frog⟩ ⟨the ~ cry of a crow⟩ **2 :** having a hoarse voice or cry **:** making hoarse sounds ⟨had caught a cold and was quite ~⟩ ⟨~ from too much talking⟩ ⟨~ with emotion⟩ **syn** see LOUD

**hoarse·ly** *adv* **:** in a hoarse manner **:** with a hoarse voice or cry or sound or tone

**hoars·en** \'hōrsᵊn, 'hȯr-, 'hōəs-, 'hȯ(ə)s-\ *vb* **hoarsened; hoarsened; hoarsening** \-s(ᵊ)niŋ\ **hoarsens** *vt* **:** to make hoarse ⟨it agitated their bodies and ~*ed* their voices —Walter O'Meara⟩ ~ *vi* **:** to become hoarse ⟨the deep voice ~*ed* —E.C.Marston⟩

**hoarse·ness** \-snəs\ *n* -ES [alter. (influenced by *hoarse*) of ME *hosnes,* fr. OE *hāsnys,* fr. *hās* hoarse + *-nys, -nes* -ness] **:** the quality or state of being hoarse

**hoarstone** \'⸗,⸗\ *n* [ME *horeston, harestan,* fr. OE *hār stān,* fr. *hār* hoar + *stān* stone] **1** *Brit* **:** a stone used anciently to mark boundaries **2** *Brit* **:** a stone erected anciently as a memorial (as of an event)

**hoary** \'hōrē, 'hȯr-, -ri\ *adj, usu* -ER/-EST **1 a :** gray or white; *specif* **:** gray or white with age ⟨nodded his ~ head⟩ **b** (1) **:** having hair that is gray or white with age ⟨a ~ old man⟩ (2) **:** CANESCENT 2 (3) *of a plant* **:** having grayish or whitish leaves **2 a** (1) **:** very old **:** ANCIENT ⟨~ legends⟩; *esp* **:** impressively or venerably old ⟨the ~ walls of the castle⟩ ⟨the ~ figure of the prophet⟩ (2) **:** so old or so familiar as to be without freshness and sparkle ⟨~ jokes⟩ or devoid of interest or ability to stimulate ⟨~ clichés⟩ ⟨~ half-truths⟩ **:** TRITE, STALE, HACKNEYED **b :** far removed in time past **:** REMOTE ⟨~ antiquity⟩

**hoary alder** *n* **:** SPECKLED ALDER

**hoary alyssum** *n* **:** a tall leafy perennial European plant (*Berteroa incana*) with gray-green foliage, entire leaves, and pubescent pods that is naturalized in No. America and is sometimes troublesome as a weed

**hoary bat** *n* **:** a rather large migratory bat (*Lasiurus cinereus*) having yellowish or brown hair tipped with white

**hoary cinquefoil** **:** SILVERWEED a(2)

**hoary cress** *or* **hoary peppergrass** *or* **hoary pepperwort** *n* **:** a perennial cruciferous European herb (*Cardaria draba*) with clasping stem leaves, clusters of small white flowers, and reniform or cordate depressed pods that is naturalized widely in America and often becomes a troublesome weed in the western U.S.

**hoary-haired** \'⸗⸗'⸗\ *adj* **:** having hoary hair

**hoary-headed** \'⸗⸗'⸗⸗\ *adj* **:** having a hoary head

**hoary marmot** *n* **:** a large gray marmot (*Marmota pruinosa*) of northwestern No. America — called also *mountain badger*

**hoary pea** *n* **:** a plant of the genus *Tephrosia; esp* **:** GOAT'S RUE

**hoary plantain** *n* **1 :** a widely distributed Old World perennial plantain (*Plantago media*) that is naturalized in No. America and has a flat rosette of finely hirsute leaves and a tall scape bearing inconspicuous whitish fragrant flowers **2 :** a No. American annual or biennial plantain (*P. virginica*) with long soft hairs on the leaves

**hoary puccoon** *n* **:** a No. American perennial herb (*Lithospermum canescens*) with hairy foliage

**hoary redpoll** *n* **:** HORNEMANN'S REDPOLL

**hoary vervain** *n* **:** a densely white hairy perennial herb (*Verbena stricta*) of central No. America with showy purplish blue spicate flowers

**hoary willow** *n* **:** a white-leaved No. American shrub (*Salix candida*)

**¹hoast** \'hōst\ *n* -S [ME *host, hoost,* fr. ON *hōsti;* akin to OE *hwōsta* cough, OHG *huosto* cough, Skt *kāsate* he coughs] *dial Brit* **:** COUGH

**²hoast** \"\ *vb* -ED/-ING/-S [ME *hosten,* fr. ON *hōsta;* akin to ON *hōsti,* n.] *dial Brit* **:** COUGH

**hoa·tzin** \wä(t)'sēn\ *or* **hoac·tzin** \wäk(t)'s-\ *also* **hoa·cin** \wä's-\ *n, pl* **hoatzins** \-ēnz\ *also* **hoatzi·nes** \-ē(,)näs\ *or* **hoac·tzins** \-ēnz\ *also* **hoactzi·nes** \-ē(,)näs\ [AmerSp, fr. Nahuatl *uatzin* pheasant] **:** a crested bird (*Opisthocomus hoazin*) of tropical So. America constituting the suborder Opisthocomi of the Galliformes that is somewhat smaller than a pheasant and that has olivaceous plumage marked with white above and that has a disagreeable strong musky smell and the young of which have a well-developed claw on the first and second fingers of the wing by means of which they climb about — called also *stinkbird*

**¹hoax** \'hōks\ *vt* -ED/-ING/-ES [prob. by contr. of *hocus*] **:** to trick into believing or accepting or doing something **:** play upon the credulity of so as to bring about belief in or acceptance of what is actually false and often preposterous **:** take in **:** DELUDE, DUPE, MISLEAD, VICTIMIZE ⟨~*ed* them into thinking the diamonds were genuine⟩ ⟨eager to ~ people into swallowing propaganda⟩ ⟨even the experts were ~*ed*⟩ **syn** see DUPE

**²hoax** \"\ *n* -ES **1 :** an act intended to trick or dupe **:** a piece of trickery **:** IMPOSTURE ⟨played a ~ on the miners —*New Republic*⟩ ⟨~*es* have occurred even in the present century —R.W.Murray⟩ **2 :** something accepted or believed in through trickery **:** something established by fraud or fabrication ⟨the book was once thought to be based on actual experience, but it is now recognized as a literary ~⟩ ⟨Piltdown man is one of the biggest ~*es* ever launched on the scientific world⟩

**¹hob** \'häb\ *n* -S [ME *hob, hobbe,* fr. *Hobbe,* nickname of *Robert* or *Robin*] **1** *now dial Eng* **a :** a clownish lout **b :** RUSTIC **2** *now dial Eng* **:** HOBGOBLIN, ELF **3 :** a male ferret — **play hob 1 :** to cause mischief **:** make trouble **:** cause an upset **:** cause confusion or disruption or havoc — usu. used with *with* ⟨would disorganize his life and *play hob* with his standard of living —John Lardner⟩ **2 :** to take liberties **:** make free — usu. used with *with* ⟨a biased book that *plays hob* with historical fact⟩ — **raise hob 1 :** to play hob — usu. used with *with* ⟨the war . . . *raised hob* with international trade —*Harper's*⟩ **2 a :** to show extreme irritation or wrath ⟨his . . . wife was getting on his nerves and he was *raising* unaccountable *hob* —V.B.Hass⟩ — often used with *with* ⟨*raised hob* with him for being late⟩ **b :** to be riotous (as with intoxication or glee) and cause a rumpus ⟨going to go out tonight and *raise hob*⟩

**²hob** \"\ *n* -S [origin unknown] **1 :** a level projection (as of brickwork, stone, or iron) at the back or side of an open fireplace on which something (as a kettle) can be placed to be kept warm **2** *archaic* **a :** a peg or stake used as a target in quoits and similar games **b :** a game in which such a peg or stake is used **3 :** HOBNAIL **4 a** (1) **:** a cutting tool consisting of a fluted steel worm that is used in a milling machine for cutting the teeth of worm wheels or screw chasers or other tool devices or used in a gear hobber for hobbing the teeth of gear wheels (2) **:** MASTER TAP (3) **:** SELLERS HOB (4) **:** an engraved steel block that is casehardened and used to impress an embossing die or a die-casting die — called also *hub* **b :** LEADER 1d

**³hob** \"\ *vt* **hobbed; hobbed; hobbing; hobs 1 :** to furnish with hobnails **2 a :** to cut (as the teeth of worm wheels) with a hob **b :** to impress (as an embossing die) with a hob

**¹hob and nob** \'häbə(n)'näb\ *interj* [prob. alter. of earlier *hob or nob,* alter. of *hab or nab* — more at HABNAB] *archaic* — used as an informal toast in convivial drinking

**²hob and nob** \"\ *also* **hob a nob** \"\ *adv (or adj) archaic* **:** in a close and friendly relationship **:** in a warmly companionable relationship

**³hob and nob** \"\ *or* **hob-a-nob** \"\ *archaic var of* ¹HOBNOB

**ho·bart** \'hō,bärt\ *adj, usu cap* **:** of or from Hobart, the capital of Tasmania **:** of the kind or style prevalent in Hobart

**hob·ba·de·hoy** *or* **hob·ba·dy·hoy** \,häbəde'hȯi\ *also* **hob·ber·de·hoy** \-bə(r)d-\ *archaic var of* HOBBLEDEHOY

**hob·ber** \'häbə(r)\ *n* -S **1 :** a machine used for hobbing; *also* **:** the operator of such a machine **2 :** a pitched horseshoe or quoit leaning against a stake or peg without ringing it — called also *leaner*

**¹hobbes·ian** \'häbzēən\ *adj, usu cap* [Thomas *Hobbes* †1679 Eng. philosopher + E *-ian*] **:** of or relating to Hobbes or Hobbism

**²hobbesian** \"\ *n* -S *usu cap* **:** HOBBIST

**hobbied** *past of* HOBBY

**hobbies** *pres 3d sing of* HOBBY

**hob·bil** \'häbəl\ *n* -S [alter. of obs *hoball,* prob. fr. ¹*hob*] *now dial Eng* **:** a stupid individual **:** DOLT

**hob·bism** \'hä,bizəm\ *n* -S *usu cap* **:** the philosophical system of Hobbes; *esp* **:** Hobbes' political theory maintaining that man has a natural right to self-preservation and happiness and that the clashing interests and desires of individuals must be controlled by a strong government esp. of a monarchist constitution

**¹hob·bist** \'häbəst\ *n* -S *usu cap* **:** a follower of Hobbes or advocate of Hobbism

**²hobbist** \"\ *adj, usu cap* **:** HOBBESIAN

**¹hob·ble** \'häbəl\ *vb* **hobbled; hobbled; hobbling** \-b(ə)liŋ\ **hobbles** [ME *hoblen;* akin to MD *hobbelen* to turn, roll] *vi* **1 :** to move along unsteadily or with great difficulty or uncertainty **:** advance waveringly or laboriously or painfully **:** limp along **:** move lamely **:** struggle along ⟨the crippled ship managed to ~ into port⟩ ⟨try to ~ along to the end of the school term⟩; *specif* **:** to walk with a halting labored typically up-and-down movement often marked by lurching or wobbling ⟨saw an old man *hobbling* down the street⟩ ⟨*hobbling* along on his crutches⟩ **2** *of an arrow* **:** to wobble in flight ~ *vt* **1 :** to cause to hobble **:** make lame **:** CRIPPLE ⟨was *hobbled* by an ankle injury⟩ **2** [prob. alter. of *hopple*] **a :** to tie or otherwise fasten together the legs of (as a horse) to prevent straying or to keep under control **:** FETTER ⟨*hobbled* the horses before turning them loose⟩ **b :** to interfere with the free movement or advance of **:** HAMPER, OBSTRUCT, IMPEDE ⟨felt himself *hobbled* by his parents' lack of understanding⟩ ⟨*hobbling* factory production by inefficient methods⟩

**²hobble** \"\ *n* -S **1 :** a hobbling movement or hobbling manner of walking ⟨had a bad ~ —Adrian Bell⟩ **2** *archaic* **:** an awkward or perplexing situation **3 a :** something used for tying the legs (as of a horse) esp. to prevent straying **:** FETTER **b :** something that restrains or hampers ⟨censorship and other ~*s* of free expression⟩ **4 :** HOBBLE SKIRT

**hobblebush** \'⸗⸗,⸗\ *n* [²*hobble* + *bush;* fr. the hindrance caused by its drooping branches] **:** a shrub (*Viburnum alnifolium*) of northern No. America that has long straggling branches and opposite double-toothed leaves — called also *American wayfaring tree*

**hobbled** *adj* [fr. past part. of ¹*hobble*] *West* **:** tied together beneath the belly of a horse — used of stirrups

**hob·ble·de·hoy** \,häbəldē'hȯi\ *n* -S [origin unknown] **:** a usu. awkward callow adolescent male **:** a gawky youth

**hobble out** *vt* **:** to attach hobbles to (as a horse) and allow to wander about esp. in a pasture ⟨had *hobbled out* some horses not far from his cabin —Ross Santee⟩ ⟨and *hobbled* the animals *out* to graze —Fred Gipson⟩

**¹hob·bler** \-b(ə)lə(r)\ *n* -S [¹*hobble* + *-er*] **:** one that hobbles

**²hob·bler** \'häb(ə)lə(r)\ *n* -S [alter. (perh. influenced by ¹*hobble*) of *hoveler*] **:** an unlicensed boat pilot or a freelance longshoreman in some parts of southern England

**hob·ble·shew** \'häbəl,shü\ *or* **hob·ble·show** \-,shō\ *var of* HUBBLESHEW

**hobble skirt** *n* [²*hobble*] **:** a skirt with bottom fullness constricted at the ankles by a band

**hob·ble·te·hoy** \,häbəltē'hȯi\ *or* **hob·by·de·hoy** \-bēdē'-\ *archaic var of* HOBBLEDEHOY

**hob·bling·ly** *adv* [*hobbling* (pres. part. of ¹*hobble*) + *-ly*] **:** with a hobbling movement **:** LAMELY

**hob·bly** \'häb(ə)li\ *adj* [*hobble* + *-y*] *dial Brit* **:** having a rough uneven surface

**¹hob·by** \'häbē, -bi\ *n* -ES [ME *hoby, hobyn,* perh. fr. *Hobbin,* nickname of *Robert* or *Robin*] **1** *or* **hobby horse** *archaic* **:** a small or medium-sized light horse esp. of Irish origin having a gentle ambling pace **2** *archaic* **:** HOBBYHORSE 1,3 **3 a :** HOBBYHORSE 4a **b :** a specialized pursuit (as stamp collecting, painting, woodworking, gardening) that is outside one's regular occupation and that one finds particularly interesting and enjoys doing usu. in a nonprofessional way as a source of leisure-time relaxation; *broadly* **:** any favorite pursuit or interest **4** *archaic* **:** DANDY HORSE

**²hobby** \"\ *vi* -ED/-ING/-ES **:** to follow a hobby **:** have a hobby ⟨*hobbied* in photography for many years⟩ ⟨now *hobbies* at painting⟩

**³hobby** \"\ *n* -ES [ME *hoby,* modif. of MF *hobé,* fr. OF, alter. of *hobel,* perh. fr. *hobeler* to skirmish, prob. fr. MD *hobbelen* to turn, roll — more at HOBBLE] **:** a small falcon (*Falco subbuteo*) widely distributed in the Old World and formerly trained for hawking and flown at small birds (as larks)

**hobbyhorse** \'⸗⸗,⸗\ *n* **1 a :** a figure designed to resemble a horse and made of light material (as wickerwork) that is fastened about the waist of a dancer (as in the morris dance or in Spanish or Javanese dance rituals) who dances about imitating the movements of a high-spirited horse **b :** a dancer wearing this figure and performing a dance associated with it **2** *obs* **:** BUFFOON **3 a :** a child's plaything which consists typically of a stick having an imitation horse's head at one end and sometimes wheels at the other and which the child straddles and pretends to ride — called also *stick horse* **b :** one of the horses on a merry-go-round **c :** ROCKING HORSE **4 a :** something (as a pet idea or favorite topic or special object of concern) with which one is preoccupied or to which one constantly reverts ⟨this is one of his political ~*s*⟩; *specif* **:** a cranky obsession **b** *archaic* **:** HOBBY 3b **5 :** DANDY HORSE

hobbyhorse 3a

**hob·by·ist** \'häbēəst, -biə-\ *n* -S [¹*hobby* + *-ist*] **1** *archaic* **:** one that is preoccupied with a pet idea or cranky obsession **2 :** one that has one or more hobbies; *esp* **:** one that is particularly fond of cultivating hobbies

**hobby lantern** *n* [¹*hob* + *-y*] *dial Eng* **:** WILL-O'-THE-WISP

**hob ferret** *n* **:** ¹HOB 2

**hobgoblin** \'⸗,⸗⸗\ *n* [¹*hob* + *goblin*] **1 :** a goblin esp. when conceived of as mischievous or impish **2 :** BOGEY 3 ⟨unreason has taken the place of evil as the ~ of a rational society —Albert Hubbell⟩ **:** BUGABOO ⟨a foolish consistency is the ~ of little minds —R.W.Emerson⟩

**hobnail** \'⸗,⸗\ *n, often attrib* [²*hob* + *nail*] **1 :** a short nail with a large head and a sharp point that is used esp. for studding soles of heavy shoes (as work shoes) **2** *archaic* **:** a countrified often loutish individual **:** CLODHOPPER ⟨troops of ~*s* clumping to church —W.M.Thackeray⟩ **3 a :** a pattern consisting of small tufts usu. closely spaced (as on some bedspreads) or of similarly spaced bosses often having the shape of diamonds (as in some vases and other objects made of pressed glass) **b :** one of the tufts or bosses used in such a pattern

**hobnailed** \'⸗,nāld\ *adj* **1 :** studded with or as if with hobnails ⟨~ boots⟩ **2 a :** marked by the wearing of heavy shoes or boots studded with hobnails ⟨~ laborers⟩ ⟨the ~ entry of investigating officialdom into the classroom —M.H.Bernstein⟩ **b :** countrified and often loutish ⟨too ~ to have much feeling⟩

**hobnail liver** *also* **hobnailed liver** *n* **1 :** the liver as it appears in one form of cirrhosis in which it is shrunken and hard and covered with small projecting nodules **2 :** the cirrhosis associated with hobnail liver **:** LAENNEC'S CIRRHOSIS

**¹hob·nob** \ˈhäb,näb\ *vi* **hobnobbed; hobnobbed; hobnobbing; hobnobs** [alter. of *habnab*] **1** *archaic* **:** to drink sociably or convivially — often used with *with* **2 a :** to associate familiarly **:** go about in an easy informal companionship **:** chum around — often used with *with* ⟨once *hobnobbed* with kings and princes⟩ ⟨have *hobnobbed* ever since they were boys⟩ **b :** to talk informally and freely to or with someone **:** speak familiarly — usu. used with *with* **:** CHAT ⟨officials have long enjoyed the practice of *hobnobbing* with newspapermen —Douglass Cater⟩ — **hob·nob·ber** \-näbə(r)\ *n* -s

**²hobnob** \"\ *n* -s **:** an informal sociable meeting and chat **:** GET-TOGETHER ⟨going to have a quiet little ~ with them⟩

**¹ho·bo** \ˈhō(,)bō\ *n, pl* **hoboes** *also* **hobos** [perh. alter. of

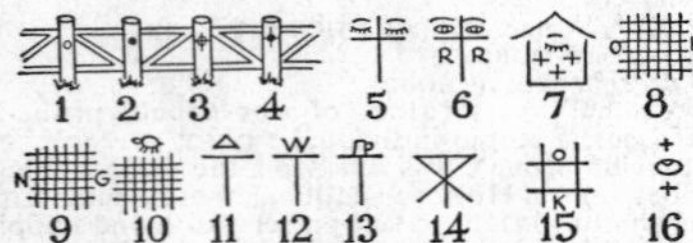


common symbols used by hoboes: *1* good for a handout, *2* cranky woman or bad dog, *3* not generous, *4* stay away, *5* police not hostile, *6* police hostile; *R R* used for railroad police, *7* jail good for a night's lodging, *8* clean jail, *9* jail food no good, *10* unclean jail, *11* jail has rock pile, *12* jail is a workhouse, *13* saloons in town, *14* town is hostile, *15* streets good for begging, *16* plainclothes detectives here

*ho, boy*, a call used in the northwestern U.S. in the 1880's by railway mail handlers when delivering mail] **1 :** a migratory worker **2 a :** one that is homeless and usu. penniless and that leads a largely vagrant life often by choice and that occas. works at odd jobs **:** TRAMP **b :** ⁷BUM 1a, 1b **syn** see VAGABOND

**²hobo** \"\ *vi* -ED/-ING/-S **:** to live or travel in the manner of a hobo ⟨spent two years ~*ing* around the country⟩

**ho·bo·he·mia** \,hō(,)bōˈhēmēə\ *n* [blend of *hobo* and *bohemia*] **1 :** a usu. run-down urban district in which hoboes congregate **2 :** a fringe group of society made up of hoboes **:** the hobo realm — **ho·bo·he·mi·an** \ˌ==(,)=ˈhēmēən\ *adj or n*

**ho·bo·ism** \ˈhō(,)bō,izəm\ *n* -s **:** the condition of being a hobo

**¹hob or nob** \ˌhäbə(r)ˈnäb\ *var of* ¹HOB AND NOB

**²hob or nob** *archaic var of* ¹HOBNOB

**hobs** *pl of* HOB, *pres 3d sing of* HOB

**hob·son–job·son** \ˈhäbsənˈjäbsən\ *n* -s *usu cap H&J* [Anglo-Indian modif. (influenced by the Eng. surnames *Hobson* and *Jobson*) of Ar *yā Ḥasan! yā Ḥusayn!* O Hasan! O Husain! (cry repeated at the Muharram festival as an expression of mourning for Hasan and Husain, grandsons of Muhammad, killed in the early struggles between the Sunni and Shi'a parties)] **:** assimilation of the sounds of a word or words foreign to a language into the sounds of a word or words coined or already existent in the language (as Spanish *cuca racha* has become English *cockroach* or as English *riding coat* has become French *redingote*) ⟨the law of Hobson-Jobson has played a great role in the evolution of surnames —R.F. Barton⟩ — compare FOLK ETYMOLOGY

**hob·son's choice** \ˌhäbsənz-\ *n, usu cap H* [after Thomas *Hobson* †1631 Eng. liveryman; fr. his practice of requiring every customer to take the horse which stood nearest the door] **1 :** an apparent freedom to take or reject something offered when in actual fact no such freedom exists **:** an apparent freedom of choice where there is no real alternative: **a :** the forced acceptance of something whether one likes it or not (as in a so-called free election where only one candidate is proposed) **b** (1) **:** the necessity of accepting something objectionable through the fact that one would otherwise get nothing at all (as an underpaid job rather than no job at all) (2) **:** the necessity of accepting one of two or more equally objectionable things (as enslavement or annihilation by a conquered people) **2 :** something that one must accept through want of any real alternative **:** the object of a Hobson's choice ⟨military unity . . . is . . . a *Hobson's choice* which all accept —V.D.Hurd⟩

**hob tap** *n* [²*hob*] **:** MASTER TAP

**hob·thrush** \ˈhäb,thrəsh\ *n* [prob. irreg. fr. ¹*hob* + obs. E *thurse* goblin, fr. ME *thirs* malevolent supernatural being, fr. OE *thyrs* demon; akin to OHG *duris* giant, ON *thurs*] *dial Eng* **:** HOBGOBLIN

**hoc** \ˈhäk\ *n* -s [F, perh. fr. L, this, neut. of *hic* this] **:** a card game in which the holder gives certain cards any value

**¹hoch** \ˈhäk, -ō-\ *chiefly Scot var of* HOCK

**²hoch** \ˈhōk\ *interj, often cap* [G, lit., high, fr. OHG *hōh* — more at HIGH] — used to express salutation and approval

**hoche·laga** \,(,)h(ä)sh(ə)ˈlagə, |ōsh-, |ōsh, -lä-\ *n, pl* **hochelaga** *or* **hochelagas** *usu cap* **1 :** an extinct Iroquoian people located on the site of present Montreal **2 :** a member of the Hochelaga people

**hoch·moor** \ˈhōk+,-\ *adj* [G *hoch* high + *moor* fen, swamp, fr. OHG *muor* — more at MOOR] **:** being or growing on various acid peats or peaty soils ⟨the ~ soils along the Baltic coast⟩ ⟨certain ~ plants⟩

**höchst** \ˈhə(r)kst, ˈhōk-, ˈhek- *Ger* ˈhœkst *or* -œk-\ *adj, often cap* [*Höchst*, former city (now part of Frankfurt am Main) in western Germany] **:** of or being a German porcelain made during the 18th century and largely influenced by the styles of Meissen porcelain

**¹hock** \ˈhäk\ *n* -s [ME *hocke*, fr. OE *hoc*] **:** any of several mallows of the genera *Althaea* and *Malva* — now used only in holly*hock*

**²hock** \"\ *vb* -ED/-ING/-S [ME *hocken* to celebrate Hocktide, fr. *hocke-, hoke-* (in *hockedai, hokeday* Hockday)] *vt, archaic* **:** to tease or harass after a manner formerly customary at Hocktide ~ *vi* **:** to behave in a brash rambunctious manner suitable to Hocktide

**³hock** \"\ *n* -s [prob. alter. of *hook*] *chiefly Brit* **:** a strong usu. handled hook used esp. for cargo handling or for hanging meat

**⁴hock** \"\ *n* -s [alter. of ME *hoch, hough*, fr. OE *hōh* heel; akin to ON *hāsin* hock, sinew, Skt *kaṅkāla* skeleton] **1 a :** the tarsal joint or its region in the hind limb of a digitigrade quadruped (as the horse) that corresponds to the ankle of man but is elevated and bends backward and that is a compound joint containing a number of small bones and having a prominence at the back caused by the calcaneum and corresponding to the heel of man — see COW illustration **b :** the corresponding joint of a fowl's leg — called also *knee;* see COCK illustration **2 :** a small cut of meat from either the front or hind leg just above the foot — used esp. of pork ⟨pork ~*s* and sauerkraut⟩ **3** *chiefly dial* **:** the hip and thigh — often used in pl. ⟨so hipless . . . his pants . . . forever slipping down around his ~*s* —F.B. Gipson⟩

**⁵hock** \"\ *vt* -ED/-ING/-S **:** to disable by cutting the tendons of the hock **:** HAMSTRING

**⁶hock** \"\ *n* -s *often cap* [modif. of *Hochheimer* fr. *Hochheim*, Germany, its locality] *chiefly Brit* **:** RHINE WINE 1

**⁷hock** \"\ *n* -s [D *hok* pen (for animals), hovel, prison] **1 a :** restraint of goods usu. as a pledge for a loan ⟨put his winter overcoat into ~⟩ ⟨had difficulty getting the technical supplies out of ~ with the customs⟩ **b** *slang* **:** PRISON ⟨will be 10 years before he gets out of ~⟩ **2** [Afrik *hok*, fr. D] *Africa* **:** a small or temporary building or enclosure ⟨a chicken ~⟩ — **in hock :** PAWNED ⟨his watch was *in hock*⟩ **:** in debt ⟨the company was heavily *in hock* to the banks⟩

**⁸hock** \"\ *vt* -ED/-ING/-S **:** to pledge as security for a loan **:** PAWN

**⁹hock** \"\ *n* -s [perh. short for *hockelty*] **:** the last card in a faro dealing box

**hock·day** \ˈhäk,dā\ *or* **hoke·day** \ˈhōk-\ *n, usu cap* [ME *hockedai, hokeday*] **1 :** the second Tuesday after Easter celebrated in England before the 18th century with rough sport and humorous play orig. for the collection of funds for community purposes — called also *Hock Tuesday* **2 :** the second Monday after Easter — called also *Hock Monday*

**hock disease** *n* [⁴*hock*] **:** perosis of the young chicken or turkey

**hock·el·ty** \ˈhäkəltē\ *n* -ES [origin unknown] **:** ⁹HOCK

**hock·er** \ˈhäkə(r)\ *n* -s **:** one that hocks

**²hocker** \"\ *vi* -ED/-ING/-S [modif. of Norw dial. *hokra* to crouch, fr. ON *hūka* to squat] *dial Eng* **:** to behave or move in an awkward flustered manner

**hock·et** *or* **ho·quet** \ˈhäkət\ *n* -s [ME *hocket* obstacle, fr. MF *hoquet*, of imit. origin] **1 :** HICCUP **2** *in medieval music* **:** an interruption of a voice part by interjected rests resulting in a broken musical line; *also* **:** a composition using such an interruption as a contrapuntal device

**¹hock·ey** \ˈhäkē, -ki\ *n* -s *often attrib* [perh. fr. MF *hoquet* shepherd's crook, dim. of *hoc* hook, of Gmc origin; akin to MD *hoec* corner — more at HOOK] **1 :** a game in which two parties of players provided with sticks curved or hooked at the end seek to drive a ball or other small object through opposite goals: as **a :** FIELD HOCKEY **b :** ICE HOCKEY **2 :** HOCKEY STICK

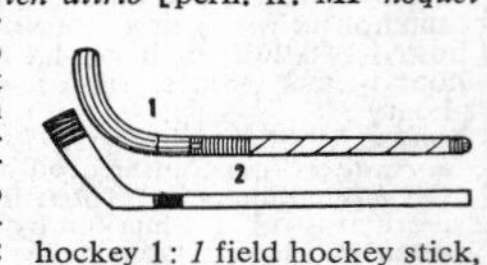


hockey 1: *1* field hockey stick, *2* ice hockey stick

**²hockey** \"\ *n* -ES [earlier *hocky*, prob. fr. LG *hokk* pile of sheaves (fr. MLG *hocke;* akin to MD *hocke*, ME *hock* pile, ON *hūka* to squat) + E *-y* — more at HAWKER] **1** *chiefly dial* **:** HARVEST HOME **2** *chiefly dial* **:** a harvest-home supper

**³hock·ey** \", ˈhōk-, ˈhīk-\ *n* -ES [origin unknown] *chiefly Midland* **:** EXCREMENT, FECES

**⁴hockey** \"\ *vi* -ED/-ING/-S *chiefly Midland* **:** DEFECATE

**hock·ey·ist** \ˈhäkēəst, -kiə-\ *also* **hock·ey·ite** \-ē,īt\ *n* -s **:** a hockey player

**hockey skate** *n* **:** a tubular skate made with a short curved blade and a shoe giving support and protection to the foot and ankle and worn esp. by ice hockey players

hockey skate

**hockey stick** *n* **:** a curved or angled stick used in playing hockey

**hocking** *pres part of* HOCK

**hock·ing ale** \ˈhäkiŋ-\ *n* [ME *hokyng*, gerund of *hoken, hocken* to celebrate Hocktide — more at HOCK] *archaic* **:** ale for the Hocktide festival

**hock leg** *n* [⁴*hock*] **:** a cabriole having a broken curve on the inner side of the knee — see LEG illustration

**hock monday** \ˈhäk-\ *n, usu cap H&M* [ME *hoc Monday*, fr. *hoc-, hocke-, hoke-* (in *hockedai, hokeday* Hockday) + *Monday*] **:** HOCKDAY 2

**hock money** \"+\ *n, usu cap H* [ME *hockemoney*, fr. *hocke-, hoke-* + *money*] *archaic* **:** money collected at Hocktide

**hocks** *pl of* HOCK, *pres 3d sing of* HOCK

**hock shop** *n* [⁷*hock*] **:** PAWNSHOP

**hocktide** \ˈ=,=\ *n, usu cap* [ME *hoketyde*, fr. *hoke-* + *tyde, tide* time, season — more at TIDE] **:** Hock Monday and Hock Tuesday

**hock tuesday** *n, usu cap H&T* [ME *hoke Tuesday*, fr. *hoc-, hocke-, hoke-* (in *hockedai, hakeday* Hockday) + *Tuesday*] **:** HOCKDAY 1

**hocs** *pl of* HOC

**¹ho·cus** \ˈhōkəs\ *n, pl* **hocuses** *or* **hocusses** [short for *hocus-pocus*] **1** *obs* **a :** CONJURER, CHEAT, DECEIVER **b :** CHEATING, TRICKERY, FRAUD **2 :** drugged liquor

**²hocus** \"\ *vt* **hocused** *or* **hocussed; hocused** *or* **hocussed; hocusing** *or* **hocussing; hocuses** *or* **hocusses 1 :** DECEIVE, CHEAT **2 a :** ADULTERATE, DRUG ⟨~*ed* liquor⟩ **b :** to ply with stupefying drugs

**¹ho·cus–po·cus** *also* **ho·kus–po·kus** \ˌhōkəsˈpōkəs\ *n* -ES [prob. invented by jugglers in imitation of Latin] **1 a** *obs* **:** JUGGLER, TRICKSTER **b** *archaic* **:** a juggler's trick or art **:** SLEIGHT OF HAND **2 :** words or a formula used (as by jugglers) in pretended incantations without regard to the usual meaning **3 :** nonsense or sham used or intended to cloak deception ⟨the *hocus-pocus* of city politics⟩; *broadly* **:** something that confuses, misleads, or is difficult to comprehend ⟨the tape recordings, through some electronic *hocus-pocus*, will retain all the visual quality of the original telecast —*Newsweek*⟩

**²hocus–pocus** \"\ *vb* **hocus-pocussed** *or* **hocus-pocused; hocus-pocussed** *or* **hocus-pocused; hocus-pocussing** *or* **hocus-pocusing; hocus-pocusses** *or* **hocus-pocuses** *vi* **:** to play the part of a conjurer; *broadly* **:** TRICK, CHEAT ~ *vt* **:** to play tricks on **:** TRICK, BEFOOL ⟨got through *hocus-pocussing* the jury —Shelby Foote⟩

**¹hod** \ˈhäd\ *n* -s [prob. fr. MD *hodde;* akin to MHG *hotte, hotze* cradle, G dial. *hotteln, hotzeln* to shake, Lith *kutėti* to shake up, ME *schuderen* to shudder — more at SHUDDER] **1 :** a tray or trough with a pole handle that is borne on the shoulder for carrying mortar, brick, or similar loads **2 :** a utensil for holding or carrying coal **:** COAL SCUTTLE

**²hod** \"\ *vi* **hodded; hodded; hodding; hods** [prob. imit.] *Scot* **:** to bob up and down **:** JOG

**³hod** \ˈhōd\ *vb* [by alter.] *Scot* **:** HIDE

**⁴hod** \ˈhäd, -ō-\ *dial Eng var of* HOLD

**ho·dag** \ˈhō,dag\ *n* -s [origin unknown] **:** a mythical animal reported chiefly from Wisconsin and Minnesota, noted for its ugliness, lateral horns, and hooked tail, and reputed to be outstanding in both ferocity and melancholy

**hod carrier** *n* **:** a laborer employed in carrying bricks, mortar, concrete, or plaster to supply bricklayers, stonemasons, cement finishers, or plasterers on the job

**hod·den** \ˈhädᵊn\ *n* -s [origin unknown] *chiefly Scot* **:** coarse cloth of undyed wool

**hodden grey** *n, dial Brit* **:** HODDEN; *esp* **:** hodden prepared from a mingling of white or light fleeces with a small proportion of natural black wool

**hod·dle** \ˈhädᵊl\ *vi* -ED/-ING/-S [prob. by alter.] *Scot* **:** WADDLE

**hoddy-doddy** \ˌhädēˈdädē\ *n, pl* **hoddy-doddies** [prob. alter. and redupl. of *dodman, hodmadod*] **1** *dial Eng* **a :** GARDEN SNAIL **b :** a snail shell **2** *archaic* **a :** a short and stout person **b :** a henpecked man **:** CUCKOLD **c :** FOOL, BLOCKHEAD, SIMPLETON

**hod·dy·poll** \ˈ==,pōl\ *n* -s [*hoddy-* (fr. *hoddy-doddy*) + *poll*] **1 :** a fumbling inept person **2** *obs* **:** CUCKOLD

**hod·ful** \ˈhäd,fu̇l\ *n, pl* **hodfuls** *also* **hodsful :** the quantity that may be carried at one time in a hod ⟨a ~ of coal⟩; *broadly* **:** a considerable quantity **:** LOTS ⟨had ~*s* of fun⟩

**hodge** \ˈhäj\ *n* -s [ME *Hoge*, nickname of *Roger*] **:** an English rustic or farm laborer

**¹hodge·podge** \ˈhäj,päj\ *n* -s [alter. of *hotchpotch*] **1 :** a heterogeneous mixture often of incongruous and ill-suited elements **:** MIXTURE, MEDLEY **2 :** HOTCHPOTCH 1

**²hodgepodge** \"\ *vt* -ED/-ING/-S **:** to make into a hodgepodge

**hodg·kin's disease** \ˈhäjkənz-\ *n, usu cap H* [after Thomas *Hodgkin* †1866 Eng. physician] **:** a disease of unknown cause that is characterized by progressive enlargement of lymph glands, spleen, and liver and by progressive anemia and that in some respects suggests an inflammatory or tumorous process

**hodg·kin·son·ite** \ˈhäjkənsə,nīt\ *n* -s [H. H. *Hodgkinson* Am. mineralogist + E *-ite*] **:** a mineral $MnZn_2SiO_5.H_2O$ consisting of a hydrous zinc manganese silicate that occurs in the form of pink to reddish brown crystals

**ho·di·er·nal** \ˌhōdēˈərnᵊl, ˌhäd-\ *adj* [obs. E *hodiern* hodiernal (fr. L *hodiernus*, fr. *hodie* today, contr. of *hoc die* this day) + E *-al*] **:** of this day

**hodja** *var of* KHOJA

**hod·ma·dod** \ˈhädmə,däd\ *n* -s [alter. and redupl. of *dodman*] **1** *dial Eng* **a :** SNAIL; *esp* **:** GARDEN SNAIL **b :** a snail shell **2** *dial Eng* **:** a deformed or clumsy person **3** *dial Eng* **:** SCARECROW

**hod·man** \ˈhädmən\ *n, pl* **hodmen** [¹*hod* + *man*] *chiefly Brit* **:** HOD CARRIER; *broadly* **:** one whose duties are mere routine assistance **:** HACK

**ho·do·graph** \ˈhädə,graf, -räf\ *n* [Gk *hodos* path + E *-graph* — more at CEDE] **:** a path described by the extremity of a vector drawn from a fixed origin and representing the linear velocity of a moving point — **ho·do·graph·ic** \ˌ==ˈgrafik\ *adj*

**ho·do·scope** \ˈ==,skōp\ *n* [Gk *hodos* path + E *-scope*] **:** an instrument for tracing the paths of cosmic-ray or other ionizing particles by means of ion counters in close array

**hods** *pl of* HOD, *pres 3d sing of* HOD

**¹hoe** \ˈhō\ *n* -s [ME *hogh*, fr. OE *hōh;* prob. akin to OE *hōh* heel — more at ⁴HOCK] *obs* **:** PROMONTORY, HILL, CLIFF — used in English place names ⟨on the *Hoe* at Plymouth⟩

**²hoe** \"\ *n* -s [ME *howe*, fr. MF *houe*, fr. OF, of Gmc origin; akin to MD *houwe* mattock, OHG *houwa;* derivative fr. the verb represented by OHG *houwan* to hew — more at HEW] **1 a :** an agricultural implement that usu. consists of a thin flat blade set transversely on a long handle and is used esp. for cultivating, weeding, or loosening the earth around plants **b :** an implement that functions like a hoe and is arranged with a wheel and one or two handles for more rapid cultivation **c :** a one-horse tillage implement for cultivating between rows (as of vines or bushes) ⟨a berry ~⟩ ⟨a grape ~⟩ **d :** any of various cultivating or weeding implements usu. for use with animal or mechanical draft — see ROTARY HOE, SPRING HOE, SPRING-TRIP HOE, WHEEL CULTIVATOR **2 :** an implement or tool felt to resemble or serving a purpose like that of a hoe: as **a :** a rake designed for stirring up a furnace fire **b :** an instrument for spreading and mixing mortar, concrete, or similar substances **c :** BACKHOE

hoe 1a

**³hoe** \"\ *vb* **hoed; hoed; hoeing; hoes** [ME *howwen*, fr. *howe*, n.] *vi* **:** to use a hoe **:** work with a hoe ⟨was ~*ing* in the field by the road⟩ ~ *vt* **:** to weed, cultivate, or thin (a crop) with a hoe ⟨~ out the strawberries⟩ **:** remove (weeds) by hoeing ⟨soon have to ~ the weeds from the corn⟩ **:** dress or cultivate (land) by hoeing ⟨*hoed* 7 acres with a spring hoe⟩

**⁴hoe** \"\ *n* -s [E dial. (Shetland) *ho*, of Scand origin; akin to ON *hār* dogfish, shark, tholepin — more at HAYE] *chiefly Scot* **:** SPINY DOGFISH

**hoecake** \ˈ=,=\ *n* [²*hoe* + *cake;* fr. its being baked on the blade of a hoe] **1** *chiefly South & Midland* **:** a small cake made of cornmeal, water, and salt usu. cooked before an open fire **2** *chiefly South & Midland* **:** a hoecake to which shortening has been added and which is usu. baked on a griddle or in an oven

**hoe culture** *also* **hoe agriculture** *or* **hoe cultivation** *n* **:** the growing of crops by hand methods including use of a hoe for stirring the soil

**hoedown** \ˈ=,=\ *n* -s [³*hoe* + *down*] **1 a :** a lively old-time dance; *esp* **:** SQUARE DANCE **b :** a lively hillbilly tune played usu. to accompany folk or square dancing **2 a :** an informal dancing party at which hoedowns are danced **b** *slang* **:** a loud or spectacular affair (as a social or theatrical event)

**hoe drill** *n* **:** a seed drill with hoeing devices for opening furrows

**hoeg·bom·ite** \ˈhōgbə,mīt, ˈhæg-\ *n* -s [Sw *högbomit*, fr. Arvid Gustaf *Högbom*, 20th cent. Swed. scientist + Sw *-it* -ite] **:** a mineral $Mg(Al,Fe,Ti)_4O_7$(?) consisting of an oxide of magnesium, aluminum, iron, and titanium

**ho·er** \ˈhōə(r), -ōr\ *n* -s **:** one that hoes

**hoer·nes·ite** \ˈhərnə,sīt, ˈhōr-\ *n* -s [G *hörnesit*, fr. Moritz *Hoernes* †1868 Austrian paleontologist + G *-it* -ite] **:** a mineral $Mg_3As_2O_8.8H_2O$ consisting of hydrous magnesium arsenate occurring as crystals resembling gypsum

**hoff·man clamp** \ˈhäfmən, ˈhȯf-\ *n, usu cap H* [prob. fr. the name *Hoffman*] **:** a pinchcock for flexible tubing controlled by a screw

**hoffmann's anodyne** *n, usu cap H* [after Friedrich *Hoffmann* †1742 Ger. physician] **:** COMPOUND SPIRIT OF ETHER

**hoffmann's drops** *n pl, usu cap H* [after Friederich *Hoffmann* †1742] **:** SPIRIT OF ETHER

**hof·mann reaction** *or* **hofmann rearrangement** \ˈhäfmən-, ˈhȯf-, ˈhōf-\ *n, usu cap H* [after August Wilhelm von *Hofmann* †1892 Ger. chemist] **:** the conversion of an acid amide $RCONH_2$ to an amine $RNH_2$ with one less carbon atom by treatment with sodium hypobromite

Hoffman clamp

**hofmann's violet** *n, usu cap H* **:** any of several violet dyes that are alkylated fuchsines made by treating rosaniline with an alkyl halide (as ethyl iodide)

**hof·meis·ter series** \ˈhäf,mīstə(r), ˈhȯf-, ˈhōf-\ *n, usu cap H* [after Franz *Hofmeister* †1922 Austro-Ger. physiological chemist] **:** an arrangement of salts, anions, or cations in descending order of their effect upon a physical phenomenon (as the swelling of gelatin) — called also *lyotropic series*

**¹hog** \ˈhȯg, -äg-\ *n, pl* **hogs** *also* **hog** *often attrib* [ME *hogge*, fr. OE *hogg*, perh. of Celt origin; akin to W *hwch* hog, Corn *hoch* — more at SOW] **1 a :** a domestic swine **:** PIG, SOW, BOAR; *esp* **:** an adult or a growing animal weighing more than 120 pounds — compare PORK **b** *Brit* **:** ²BARROW **c :** a wild boar; *broadly* **:** any of various animals of the family Suidae — usu. used in combination ⟨the wart*hogs* and river ~*s* are tropical relatives of our domestic swine⟩ **2** *usu* **hogg** *Brit* **a :** a young sheep usu. less than or about a year in age and not yet shorn; *also* **:** wool from such a sheep **b :** a young domestic animal (as a bullock) of similar age — often used in combination ⟨several good *hogg* colts⟩ **3 :** a person felt to resemble a hog esp. in selfishness, gluttony, or filthiness — often used in combination **4** *or* **hogg** *slang* **a** *Brit* **:** SHILLING **b :** DIME **5 :** a curling stone that fails to pass the hog score **6 :** a machine with revolving cutters for reducing bulk material (as waste lumber or animal carcasses) to small bits — called also *hogger* **7 :** a frame of timber or a heavy flat rough broom hauled along a ship's bottom under water to clean it **8 :** an agitator for mixing and stirring pulp in papermaking **9** *slang* **:** a railroad locomotive — **on the hog** *slang* **:** having no funds **:** BROKE

**²hog** \"\ *vb* **hogged; hogged; hogging; hogs** *vt* **1 :** to cut (a horse's mane) short **:** ROACH **2 :** to clean the bottom of (a ship) with a hog **3 a :** to cause to arch like the back of a hog **b :** to cause (as a ship or timber) to bow up in the middle and sag at the ends usu. as a result of improper loading or supporting **4 a** *Brit* **:** to winter over (young sheep) **b :** to utilize (an unharvested crop) by turning in hogs to feed — often used with *down* or *off* ⟨got a drove of gilts to ~ down the corn⟩ ⟨it would be cheaper to ~ off that piece than to harvest it⟩ **5 a :** to take, grasp, or retain selfishly or in excess of one's due or need ⟨don't ~ the light, I want to read too⟩ ⟨*hogging* everything in sight⟩ **b :** to consume voraciously — usu. used with *down* ⟨*hogged* down his dinner and rushed out⟩ ⟨finished the book next day, *hogging* it down in great gulps —Bruce Marshall⟩ **6 :** to play (a curling stone) so as not to pass the hog score **7 :** to tear up or shred (bulk material) into bits with a hog ~ *vi* **1 :** to become curved upward in the middle like a hog's back — used esp. of a ship or its bottom or keel **2 :** to act like a hog esp. in taking more than one's share

**ho gage** \ˈā,chō-\ *n, usu cap H&O* [*half o gage*] **:** a scale of ⅛ inch to one foot used in model railroading for trains and track layout with a distance between rails of ⅝ inch

**ho·gan** \ˈhō,gän, -gən, -gan\ *n* -s [Navaho *hogan*, fr. *ho-*, deictic prefix + *-gan* dwelling] **:** a conical, hexagonal, or octagonal dwelling characteristic of the Navaho Indian made with a door traditionally facing east and constructed of logs and sticks covered with mud, sods, or adobe or sometimes of stones — compare LODGE 8a

**hog and hominy** *n* **:** pork and Indian corn; *broadly* **:** meager or very plain and simple food

**hogan–mogan** *obs var of* HOGEN-MOGEN

**ho·garth chair** \ˈhō,gärth, -gäth-\ *n, usu cap H* [after William *Hogarth* †1764 Eng. painter] **:** any of certain 18th century English side chairs, usu. with hooped back and cabriole legs

**ho·garth·ian** \(ˈ)hōˈgärthēən, -gäth-\ *adj, usu cap* [William *Hogarth* + E *-ian*] **:** relating to, characteristic of, or suggesting Hogarth or his work ⟨a thoroughly *Hogarthian* attitude⟩ ⟨*Hogarthian* cartoons of the human scene —*Dial*⟩

**hogarth's line** *n, usu cap H* [after William *Hogarth*, who considered it the essence of beauty] **:** an S-shaped line used for decorative and compositional purposes esp. in painting and engraving

**hogback** \ˈ=,=\ *n* **1 :** an arched back suggesting that of a hog ⟨most of the sunfishes have ~*s*⟩ **2 :** something felt to resemble the back of a hog in outline or section: as **a :** a ridge of land formed by the outcropping edges of tilted strata; *broadly* **:** a ridge with a sharp summit and steeply sloping sides **b :** a sharp rise in the floor of a coal mine **c :** HOGFRAME

**hog-backed** \'=;=\ *or* **hogback** \'=,=\ *adj* **:** having an arched back or prominence ⟨a *hog-backed* island in the channel⟩
**hog badger** *n* **:** HOG-NOSED BADGER
**hog banana** *n* **:** a rather large coarse-textured red-skinned banana that is usu. eaten cooked
**hog bean** *n* **:** HENBANE 1
**hogbite** \'=,=\ *n* **:** GUM SUCCORY 1
**hog brace** *n* **:** HOGFRAME
**hog brake** *n* **:** BRACKEN 1b
**hog cane** *n* **:** SALT REED GRASS
**hog chain** *n* **:** a chain or a tie rod used in a ship to prevent hogging
**hogchoker** \'=,==\ *also* **hogchoke** \'=,=\ *n* **:** a small American sole (esp. *Achirus fasciatus*) of no market value
**hog cholera** *n* **:** a highly infectious often fatal virus disease of swine characterized by fever, loss of appetite, diarrhea, petechial hemorrhages esp. in the kidneys and lymph glands, and in chronic cases intestinal ulceration often complicated by secondary infection with the necrotic enteritis bacterium
**hog clover** *n* **:** BUR CLOVER
**hog constable** *n* **:** HOGREEVE
**hog corn** *n* **:** poor quality Indian corn
**hog-corn ratio** *n* **:** CORN-HOG RATIO
**hog cranberry** *n* **1 :** CROWBERRY 1a **2 :** BEARBERRY 1
**hog deer** *n* **:** a white-spotted deer (*Axis porcinus* syn. *Hyelaphus porcinus*) of India about two feet high at the withers
**hog-dressed** \'=;=\ *adj, of a meat animal* **:** bled and eviscerated but having the skin left on the carcass
[1]**hogen-mogen** \ˌhōgənˈmōgən\ *n* -s *usu cap H&M* [prob. alter. of D *hoogmogend* all-powerful] **1** *obs* **:** a person of consequence or one who affects authority **2** *archaic* **:** HOLLANDER; *collectively* **:** the people of Holland — often used disparagingly
[2]**hogen-mogen** \"\ *adj, usu cap H&M* **1** *obs* **a :** HIGH-AND-MIGHTY **b** *of liquor* **:** STRONG **2** *archaic* **:** DUTCH
**hog feeder** *n* **:** an operator who feeds bulk material into and supervises a shredding or mincing hog — called also *hogger*
**hog fennel** *n* **:** a plant of *Oxypolis* or the closely related genus *Lomatium*
**hogfish** \'=,=\ *n* see PLURAL *note* **1 :** any of various fishes felt to resemble a hog: as **a :** a large West Indian and Florida wrasse (*Lachnolaimus maximus*) often used for food **b :** a pigfish (*Orthopristis chrysopterus*) **c :** LOG PERCH **d :** a large red spiny-headed European marine scorpion fish (*Scorpaena scorfa*) **2** *obs* **a :** PORPOISE **b :** MANATEE
**hog flu** *n* **:** SWINE INFLUENZA
**hogframe** \'=,=\ *n* **:** a trussed frame extending fore and aft esp. in American river and lake steamers, being usu. above deck, and reaching to the ends to increase longitudinal strength and stiffness and prevent hogging — called also *hogback, hogging frame*
**hog fuel** *n* **:** ground up or powdered wood used for fuel
**hogg** *var of* HOG
**hog·gas·ter** \'hȯgəstə(r), 'häg-\ *n* -s [ME *hogaster*, fr. *hogge* hog + L *-aster* (dim. suffix) — more at HOG] **1** *archaic* **:** a boar in its third year **2** *archaic* **:** HOG 2a
**hogged** \'hȯgd, -ä-\ *adj* **1 :** raised in the center or falling away at the ends or sides **:** HOG-BACKED — used esp. of a ship or of a road that is sharply convex in section **2** *of a horse's mane* **:** cut short **:** ROACHED
**hoggee** *var of* HOGGY
[1]**hog·ger** \'hägər, 'hog-\ *n* -s [origin unknown] **1** *chiefly Scot* **:** a stocking made without a foot and worn as a gaiter **2** *chiefly Scot* **:** an old stocking used for keeping money
[2]**hog·ger** \'hȯgə(r), 'häg-\ *n* -s [partly fr. [1]*hog* + *-er;* partly fr. [2]*hog* + *-er*] **1 a :** a machine tool that takes heavy cuts at high speed **b :** HOG 6 **2 a** *slang* **:** a locomotive engineer — called also *hoghead* **b :** HOG FEEDER
**hog·ger·el** \'häg(ə)rəl\ *n* -s [ME (Sc dial), dim. of *hogge* hog, sheep — more at HOG] *Brit* **:** a young sheep; *usu* **:** HOG 2a
**hog·gery** \'hȯg(ə)rē, 'häg-, -ri\ *n* -ES **1 :** a place where hogs are kept **:** PIGGERY, HOG HOUSE **2 :** hoggish character or manners **:** gross animality **:** GREED
**hog·get** \'hägət\ *n* -s [ME, fr. [1]*hog* + *-et*] *chiefly Brit* **:** HOG 2a
**hog·gin** *also* **hog·ging** \'hȯgən, 'häg-, -giŋ\ *n* -s [origin unknown] **:** a material composed of screenings or siftings of gravel or of a mixture of loam, coarse sand, and fine gravel
**hogging** *pres part of* HOG
**hogging frame** *or* **hogging girder** *n* **:** HOGFRAME
**hogging line** *n* **:** a line or chain used to draw a collision mat into position over a damaged area of a ship's hull
**hog·gish** \'hȯgish, 'häg-, -gēsh\ *adj* **:** like a hog esp. in gluttony or selfishness — compare PIGGISH, SWINISH — **hog·gish·ly** *adv* — **hog·gish·ness** *n* -ES
**hoggs** *pl of* HOGG
**hog gum** *n* **1 a :** a gum resin obtained from a West Indian tree (*Moronobea coccinea*) of the family Guttiferae **b :** a similar product obtained from other trees (as *Rhus metopium*) **c :** TRAGACANTH; *also* **:** a similar gum (as bassora or kutira) **2 :** any of various tropical trees chiefly of the families Anacardiaceae and Guttiferae that produce hog gum or are associated or confused with trees producing hog gum
**hog·gy** *or* **hog·gee** \'hȯgē, 'häg-\ *n, pl* **hoggies** *or* **hoggees** [prob. fr. [1]*hog* + *-y* or *-ee* (alter. of *-y*)] **:** a towpath driver for the early 19th century barge transportation system in parts of the eastern U. S.
**hog·head** \'hȯg,hed, 'häg-\ *n, slang* **:** HOGGER 2a
**hogherd** \'=,=\ *n* [ME] **:** SWINEHERD
**hog hook** *n* **:** a hook with a transverse handle for handling a hog carcass while scalding it
**hog house** *n* **:** a building in which hogs are housed **:** PIGPEN, STY; *esp* **:** a building with facilities for housing a number of hogs under one roof
**hog in** *vi, of a cutting tool* **:** to dig in and take a bigger cut than intended with a possible stalling of the machine or breaking of the tool
**hog in armor :** one self-conscious or ill at ease in fine clothes
**hog-killing** \'=,==\ *or* **hog-killing time** *n, dial* **:** a jolly or riotous party
**hog latin** *n, usu cap L* **:** PIG LATIN
**hogleg** \'=,=\ *n, chiefly West* **:** a large single-action revolver of the type carried in the West by cowboys and frontiersmen
**hoglike** \'=,=\ *adj* **:** like or like that of a hog ⟨a heavy ~ face⟩
**hog lily** *n* **:** SPATTERDOCK
**hog line** *n* **:** HOG SCORE
**hog·ling** \'hȯgliŋ, 'häg-\ *n* -s [ME, fr. *hog* + *-ling*] **1** *obs* **:** PIGLET **2** *dial Brit* **:** LAMB
**hog lot** *n* **:** an enclosure usu. with housing in which hogs are reared or fattened for market
**hog louse** *n* **:** a large sucking louse (*Haematopinus suis*) that is parasitic on the hog and in some areas is associated with the transmission of swine pox
**hog·man** \'=mən\ *n, pl* **hogmen 1 :** a raiser of or attendant on hogs **:** a hog farmer **:** SWINEHERD **2 :** HOG FEEDER
**hog·ma·nay** *also* **hag·me·na** \ˌhägməˈnā\ *n* -s *sometimes cap* [origin unknown] **1** *Scot* **:** NEW YEAR'S EVE **2 :** a traditional Scottish celebration at New Year's Eve: **a :** the going about of children from house to house singing and asking for gifts usu. of cakes or nuts **b :** the going about from house to house with the intention of being the first visitor **3 :** a cake, gift, or treat given at New Year's Eve
**hog-maned** \'=;mānd\ *adj* **:** having a short bristly mane **:** ROACHED
**hog millet** *n* **:** MILLET 1a
**hog mol·ly** \-,mälē\ *n* **1** *or* **hog mullet :** HOG SUCKER **2 :** LOG PERCH
**hog money** *n* **:** early 17th century copper coins of Bermuda bearing the image of a hog and valued from twopence to a shilling
**hog-mouthed fry** \'=,=-\ *n* **:** a small fish (*Anchoviella choerostomus*) that resembles an anchovy and is common at Bermuda
**hognose** \'=,=\ *adj* **:** having a rounded cutting edge — used of a cutting or boring tool
**hog-nosed badger** \'=,=-\ *n* **:** a large short-legged Asiatic badger (*Arctonyx collaris*) with white fur tipped with black and white markings on face, neck, tail, and ears — called also *sand badger*
**hog-nosed skunk** *n* **:** a large stocky white-backed skunk (*Conepatus mesoleucus*) of southwestern No. America with a short white tail and a naked muzzle; *also* **:** any of several closely related So. American skunks — called also *white-backed skunk*
**hog-nosed viper** *n* **:** any of several small tropical American pit vipers (genus *Bothrops*) related to the fer-de-lance but with short fangs and venom of low toxicity
**hognose snake** *or* **hog-nosed snake** *n* **:** any of certain moderate-sized stout-bodied No. American snakes that constitute the genus *Heterodon*, are perfectly harmless though often reputed deadly prob. because of the threatening way in which they dilate the neck, flatten the head, and hiss and blow when startled, and are noted for the habit of rolling over on the back and playing dead when their threatening display is ineffective — called also *blowing adder, flatheaded adder, puffing adder, sand viper*
**hognut** \'=,=\ *n* **1 :** EARTHNUT 1a **2 :** PIGNUT 2 **3 :** JAMAICA COBNUT
**ho·go** \'hō(,)gō\ *n* -s [modif. of F *haut goût* high savor or flavor] *now dial Eng* **:** a notably strong flavor or smell
**hog oiler** *n* **:** a device that automatically applies oil or insecticide to the skin of a hog that rubs against it
**hog out** *vt* **1 :** to cut (metal) out of a piece of work at very high speeds and very fast feeds **2 :** to machine (as a part) from a billet of size and shape such that the removal of much metal is necessary in order to achieve the shape desired
**hog peanut** *n* **:** a plant of the genus *Amphicarpa* that is usu. considered to constitute a single variable species (*A. bracteata*), is widely distributed in eastern and central No. America, and produces abundant subterranean fruits, each containing a single edible seed which resembles a peanut, is much relished by hogs, and was formerly important in Amerindian dietary — called also *wild peanut*
**hogpen** \'=,=\ *n* **:** PIGPEN 1
**hog perch** *n* **:** LOG PERCH
**hog plum** *n* **1 :** a tree of the genus *Spondias; esp* **:** a tropical American tree (*S. mombin*) sometimes cultivated for its edible yellow fruits which resemble plums **2 :** POISON-WOOD 1 **3 :** the Chickasaw plum or other wild plum of the southern U. S. **4 :** FALSE SANDALWOOD 1
**hog potato** *n* **1 :** a small or inferior potato often boiled for hog feed **2 a :** MAN-OF-THE-EARTH **b :** DEATH CAMAS
**hog pox** *n* **:** SWINE POX 2
**hogreeve** \'=,=\ *n* -s **:** a former New England town officer responsible for the impounding of stray hogs
**hog ring** *n* **1 :** a split metal ring usu. with beveled points that can be pushed through the median cartilage of the nose of a pig and there locked to prevent rooting or to serve as a means of leading the animal **2 :** an upholstery fastener resembling a hog ring — **hog-ringer** \'=,==\ *n*

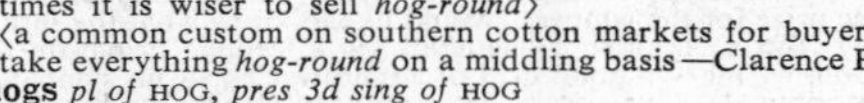
hog rings 1

**hog-round** \'=;=\ *adv (or adj)* **:** at a flat rate **:** without grading ⟨sometimes it is wiser to sell *hog-round*⟩ ⟨a common custom on southern cotton markets for buyers to take everything *hog-round* on a middling basis—Clarence Poe⟩
**hogs** *pl of* HOG, *pres 3d sing of* HOG
**hog's-back** \'=,=\ *n* **:** HOGBACK
**hog's-bean** \'=,=\ *n, pl* **hog's-beans 1 :** HENBANE **2 :** SEA STARWORT
**hog score** *n* **:** a line that is marked across a curling rink 7 yards in front of each tee and that a stone must pass or be removed from the ice — called also *hog line;* see CURLING illustration
**hog scraper** *n* **:** a circular concave metal disk with a sharp rim suitable for scraping the bristles from a hog carcass and a handle often in the form of a candle holder in the center of its convex surface; *also* **:** a candlestick with a hog-scraper base
**hog's fennel** *n* **1 :** a European sulphurweed (*Peucedanum officinale* or a closely related species) **2 :** MAYWEED 1
**hog's-haw** \'=,=\ *n, pl* **hog s-haws :** a hawthorn (*Crataegus brachyacantha*) of the southern U.S.
**hogs·head** \'hȯgz,hed, 'häg-, *sometimes* -zəd *dial* -zət\ *n* [ME *hoggeshed*, fr. *hogges* (gen. of *hogge* hog) + *hed* head — more at HOG, HEAD] **1 :** a large cask or barrel; *esp* **:** one containing from 63 to 140 gallons — abbr. *hhd* **2 :** any of various units of capacity equal to the amount a hogshead will hold: as **a :** a U.S. unit equal to 63 gallons **b :** a British unit equal to 54 imperial gallons or 64.85 U.S. gallons **3 :** something (as an unpleasant person) felt to resemble the head of a hog
**hog's head cheese** \'hȯ|gz,hed-, 'hä|, =¦=-\ *n, dial* **:** HEADCHEESE
**hog sheer** *n* **:** the deck curve of a ship in which the middle portion of the deck is higher than the ends
**hog-skin** \'=,=\ *n* **1 :** PIGSKIN 1 **2 :** an article (as a saddle or a pair of gloves) made of pigskin
**hog's-meat** \'=,=\ *n, pl* **hog's-meats 1 :** a small chiefly tropical American herb (*Boerhavia coccinea*) with sticky foliage and reddish flowers **2 :** a tropical American ornamental vine (*Aristolochia grandiflora*) with poisonous roots
**hog snake** *n* **:** HOGNOSE SNAKE
**hog's-potato** \'=;=(,)=\ *n, pl* **hog's-potatoes :** HOG POTATO 2
**hogs·teer** \'hȯgz,ti(ə)r, 'häg-, -g,st-\ *n* [alter. of *hoggaster*] **:** a wild boar in his third year
**hog sucker** *n* **:** a No. American fish (*Hypentelium nigricans*) of the family Catostomidae that is brassy olive marked with brown, is widely distributed in warm clear shallow streams, and in some areas is used as food — called also *hog molly*
**hog-tie** \'=,=\ *vt* **1 :** to make (a thrown animal) helpless by tying the hind legs together and then to one or both front legs with a short line ⟨*hog-tying* calves for branding⟩ **2 :** to make (as a person) helpless ⟨financial institutions . . . damned for *hog-tying* the region's economy —*Frontier*⟩ ⟨a police force *hog-tied* by graft and corruption⟩ **syn** see HAMPER
**hog wallow** *n* **1 a :** a depression in land made by the wallowing of swine **b :** a similar depression said to be due to heavy rains **2 :** a land surface characterized by numerous low rounded mounds — usu. used in pl.
**hogwash** \'=,=\ *n* [ME *hoggyswassh*, fr. *hoggys* (gen. of *hogge* hog) + *wassh* wash — more at HOG, WASH] **1 a :** SWILL 1a, SLOP 4a(1) **b :** poor or flavorless food or drink **2 :** something (as writing or propaganda) that is insipid, worthless, or lacking in real substance ⟨the ~ of political oratory⟩
**hogweed** \'=,=\ *n* **:** any of various weeds or coarse plants: as **a :** RAGWEED 2 **b :** KNOTWEED **c :** DOG FENNEL **d :** HORSEWEED **e** *Brit* (1) **:** COW PARSNIP (2) **:** HEDGE PARSLEY
**hog-wild** \'=;=\ *adj* **:** free from restraint and often disorderly or foolish ⟨*hog-wild* enthusiasm⟩ **:** overenthusiastic and often extravagant or intemperate ⟨legislatures gone *hog-wild* on spending⟩
**hog wire** *n* **1 :** barbed wire having 4-pointed barbs and weighing about 400 pounds per mile **2 :** heavy woven fencing with the meshes smaller at the bottom and usu. with the bottommost wire barbed
**hogwort** \'=,=\ *n* **:** an annual silvery green weed (*Croton capitatus*) of the southeastern U.S. — called also *woolly croton*
**hog-wrestle** \'=,==\ *n, slang* **:** an informal dance (as a country dance) sometimes marked by coarse vulgar conduct
**hoh** \'hō\ *n, pl* **hoh** *or* **hohs** *usu cap* **1 :** an Indian people of the Olympic Peninsula, Washington, speaking the Quileute language **2 :** a member of the Hoh people
**ho·he** \'hō(,)hā\ *n, pl* **hohe** *or* **hohes** *usu cap* **:** ASSINIBOIN

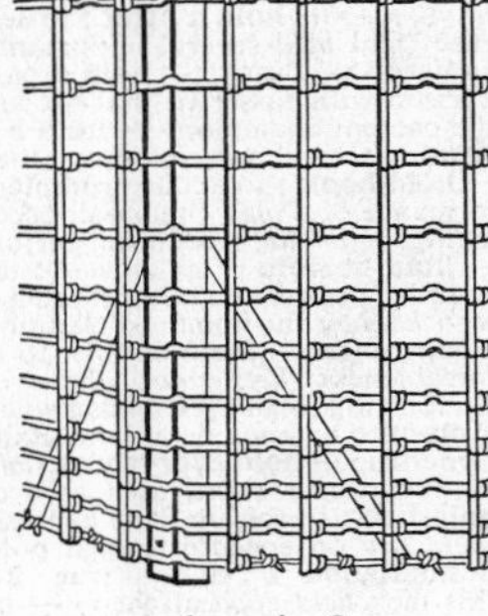
hog wire 2

[1]**ho·hen·stau·fen** \'hōən,s(h)taufən, ,==ˈ==\ *adj, usu cap* **:** of or relating to a German princely family of Swabian origin that furnished sovereigns of the Holy Roman Empire from 1138–1254 and of Sicily from 1194–1266
[2]**hohenstaufen** \"\ *n* -s *usu cap* **:** a member of the Hohenstaufen family; *esp* **:** a Hohenstaufen sovereign
[1]**ho·hen·zol·lern** \'hōən,z|älə(r)n, -ōən(t)‚s|, |ōl-, ,==ˈ==\ *adj, usu cap* **:** of or relating to a German princely family founded about the 11th century that furnished kings of Prussia from 1701–1918 and German emperors from 1871–1918
[2]**hohenzollern** \"\ *n* -s *usu cap* **:** a member of the Hohenzollern family; *esp* **:** a Hohenzollern sovereign
**ho·hen·zol·lern·ism** \-ə(r),nizəm\ *n* -s *usu cap* **:** Prussianism as developed under and exemplified by the Hohenzollern rulers of Germany
**hohl·flö·te** \'hōl,flād·ə, -lǣd·ə, *G* -lœtə\ *or* **hohl·flute** \-flüt, *usu* -üd·+V\ *n* -s [*hohlflöte* fr. G, fr. *hohl* hollow (fr. OHG *hol*) + *flöte* flute; *hohlflute* part trans. of G *hohlflöte* — more at HOLE, DOPPELFLÖTE] **:** a pipe-organ flute stop usu. in 8-foot pitch with a dull hollow quality
**hoh·mann·ite** \'hōmə,nīt\ *n* -s *usu cap* [G *hohmannit*, fr. Thomas *Hohmann*, its discoverer + G *-it* -ite] **:** a mineral $Fe_2(SO_4)_2(OH)_2·7H_2O$ consisting of a hydrated basic ferric sulfate
**ho·ho·kam** \'hōhō,käm, hōˈhōkəm\ *adj, usu cap* [Pima *húhukamJ* ancient one] **:** of or belonging to a prehistoric desert culture of southwestern U.S. centering in the Gila valley of Arizona and contemporaneous with the Anasazi culture to the north and characterized by irrigated agriculture, large pit houses, good pottery, decorative bone and shell ornaments, and use of cremation
**ho-hum** \'hō,həm\ *adj* [imit.] **:** dull and routine **:** UNINTERESTED, UNINTERESTING ⟨looked on in *ho-hum* unconcern —*Springfield (Mass.) Union*⟩ — often used interjectionally
**hoi** *var of* HOY
[1]**hoick** \'hȯik\ *vt* -ED/-ING/-S [prob. alter. of [1]*hike*] **1** *chiefly dial* **:** to yank or pull with a jerk ⟨before you could have counted ten, I was ~*ed* out of my job —Vincent Sheean⟩ **2 :** to cause (an airplane) to climb steeply
[2]**hoick** \"\ *n* -s **:** a rough or jerky movement in rowing
[3]**hoick** \"\ *vi* -ED/-ING/-S [imit.] **:** to clear the throat **:** HAWK
**hoicks** \'hȯiks\ *also* **hoick** \-k\ *interj* [origin unknown] — used chiefly to urge on hounds
**hoigh** *n* -s [prob. alter. of *hoy*] *obs* **:** a state of excitement
**hoi pol·loi** \ˌhȯipəˈlȯi, *chiefly Brit* hȯiˈpä,lȯi\ *n pl* [Gk *hoi polloi* the many] **1 :** ordinary people **:** the general populace **:** MULTITUDE, MASSES ⟨strain so hard in making their questions comprehensible to *hoi polloi* —S.L.Payne⟩ ⟨burlesque performance . . . for the *hoi polloi* —Henry Miller⟩ **2** *slang* **:** people of distinction or wealth or elevated social status **:** ELITE
**hoise** \'hȯiz\ *vt* **hoised** \-zd\ *or* **hoist** \-ȯist\ **hoised** *or* **hoist; hoising; hoises** [alter. of earlier *heise*, prob. fr. MD *hischen* or (assumed) MLG *hissen* (whence LG *hissen*), of imit. origin] **1** *dial* **:** to raise upward or into the air by means of a tackle **:** HOIST ⟨~ the mainsail⟩ **2** *dial* **:** to lift and carry off — **hoist with one's own petard** *or* **hoist by one's own petard :** blown up by one's own bomb; *usu* **:** victimized or hurt by one's own scheme
[1]**hoist** \'hȯist, *chiefly dial* 'hīst\ *vb* -ED/-ING/-S [alter. of *hoise*] *vt* **:** RAISE, LIFT, ELEVATE: as **a :** to raise into position by means of tackle ⟨~ all sails⟩ ⟨~*ed* the mate's boat aboard⟩ **b :** to raise (a flag or a hoist of flags) often as a formal indication of possession or sovereignty **c :** to move from one place to another by or as if by lifting ⟨groaned as they ~*ed* him into the ambulance⟩ ⟨~*ing* himself out of bed⟩ **d** *slang* **:** to pick up and drink ⟨decided to ~ a few with the boys⟩ **e :** to cause to be or become higher or greater ⟨the war ~*ed* prices⟩ **f** *slang* **:** STEAL ~ *vi* **1 :** to become hoisted **:** RISE ⟨the load ~*s* well with the new tackle⟩ ⟨let it ~ right up to the upper block⟩ **2 :** to pull on a rope in hoisting something ⟨~ until it's near the top⟩ — often used with *away* **syn** see LIFT
[2]**hoist** \"\ *n* -s **1 :** an act of hoisting **:** LIFT, BOOST ⟨gave him a ~ over the wall⟩ **2 :** an apparatus (as a mechanical tackle or hydraulic lift) by which things are hoisted: as **a** *chiefly Brit* **:** a freight or other service elevator **b :** CHAIN HOIST **3 a :** the extent to which something can be hoisted or its mass or dimension when hoisted ⟨a sail with a 30-foot ~⟩ ⟨a ~ of several tons⟩ **b** (1) **:** the perpendicular edge or height of a flag when viewed flying or as if flying from a staff — compare [2]FLY 6c (2) **:** the part of the field of a flag that adjoins the staff **c :** the height or depth of a square sail except a course **:** the length of a fore-and-aft sail or staysail as measured along the luff **4 a :** a string of flags hoisted or to be hoisted as a signal usu. from one ship to another **b :** a message or information conveyed by such a hoist
**hoist·er** \-tə(r)\ *n* -s **:** one that hoists; *esp* **:** a mechanical apparatus for hoisting or one who operates it
**hoisting pad** *n* [*hoisting* fr. gerund of [1]*hoist*] **:** metal fittings on a boat for attaching hoisting equipment
**hoisting tower** *n* **:** a temporary elevator shaft of scaffolding used to hoist materials on building-construction work
**hoist·man** \-tmən\ *n, pl* **hoistmen** [[2]*hoist* + *man*] **:** the operator of a hoist **:** ENGINEMAN
**hoistway** \'=,=\ *n* **:** a passage (as an elevator shaft) through or along which a thing may be hoisted
**hoit** \'hȯit\ *n* -s [E dial. *hoit*, v., to romp, play the fool] *dial Brit* **:** a lazy stupid person
[1]**hoi·ty-toi·ty** \ˌhȯid·ēˈtȯid·ē, ˌhīd·ēˈtīd·ē\ *n* -ES [redupl. of *hoity*, fr. E dial. *hoit*, v.] **1 a** *obs* **:** thoughtless or frivolous or giddy behavior **b :** affectation of superiority **:** patronizing pomposity **2 :** a hoity-toity person
[2]**hoity-toity** \"\ *adj* **1 :** THOUGHTLESS, FRIVOLOUS, GIDDY, FLIGHTY ⟨very *hoity-toity* of me not to know that royal personage—W.S.Maugham⟩ **2 :** affecting superiority **:** haughty and patronizing **:** POMPOUS ⟨*hoity-toity* airs and graces⟩ ⟨an inflated *hoity-toity* manner⟩
**ho·ja** \'ō(,)hä\ *n* -s [Sp, leaf, fr. L *folia*, pl. of *folium* leaf — more at BLADE] *Southwest* **:** a piece of corn husk formerly used for rolling cigarettes
**hok** \'häk\ *n* -s [Afrik *hak*, fr. D *hok* hutch, hovel, fr. MD *hocke* corn, grain — more at HOCK] *Africa* **:** a small enclosure (as for storage) **:** PEN
**ho·kal·tec·an** \ˌhōˌkalˈtekən, ˌhōkəl-\ *n, pl* **hokaltecan** *or* **hokaltecans** *usu cap* [by alter.] **:** HOKAN-COAHUILTECAN
**ho·kan** \'hōkən\ *also* **ho·ka** \-kə\ *n, pl* **hokan** *or* **hokans** *also* **hoka** *or* **hokas** *usu cap* [coined 1913 by Roland B. Dixon †1934 and Alfred L. Kroeber †1960 Am. anthropologists] **1 :** a language stock centering in California comprising the Chimarikan, Esselenian, Kulanapan, Quoratean, Shastan, Yuman, and Yanan families **2 :** a language phylum generally considered as comprising the Hokan stock plus Chumashan, Jicaquean, Salinan, Serian, Supanecan, Tequistlatecan, and Washoan
**hokan-coahuiltecan** \ˌhōkən+\ *n, usu cap H&C* **:** the Hokan language phylum enlarged by the inclusion of Coahuiltecan and sometimes Karankawa and Tonkawan — called also *Hokaltecan*
**hokan-siouan** \"+\ *n, usu cap H&S* **:** a language phylum comprising the Hokan, Supanecan, and Coahuiltecan language stocks
[1]**hoke** \'hōk\ *n* -s [by shortening] **:** HOKUM
[2]**hoke** \"\ *vt* -ED/-ING/-S *slang* **:** to give a false quality or value to **:** FAKE — usu. used with *up* ⟨tired of these *hoked-up* excuses⟩
**hokeday** *usu cap, var of* HOCKDAY
[1]**ho·key** \'hōkē\ *interj* [origin unknown] — used as a mild oath
[2]**hok·ey** \"\ *adj* [irreg. fr. *hokum* + *-y*] *slang* **:** marked by hokum **:** being characterized by or the product of hoking **:** hoked up ⟨a ~ version of an old favorite⟩
**hokey-pokey** \ˌhōkēˈpōkē\ *n* -s [prob. alter. of *hocus-pocus*] **1** *slang* **:** HOKUM, BUNKUM, MONKEY BUSINESS **2 :** ice cream packaged in small portions (as between sweet wafers or in a paper cup) and sold by street vendors or peddlers
**hokh·mah** *or* **hok·mah** *or* **chok·mah** \'kȯk(,)mä, =ˈ=\ *n* -s *usu cap, often attrib* [Heb *ḥokhmāh* wisdom] **:** WISDOM LITERATURE
**hok·ku** \'hō(,)kü, 'hä(-\ *n, pl* **hokku** [Jap, fr. *hok* beginning first + *ku* hemistich] **1 :** a fixed lyric form of Japanese origin having three short unrhymed lines of five, seven, and five syllables and being typically epigrammatic or suggestive — compare HAIKU **2 :** a lyric in hokku form

**hok–lo** \'hȯ(,)klō, 'hä(-\ *n, pl* **hok–lo** *or* **hok–los** *usu cap* [Chin (Cant), man from Fukien, fr. *hok* Fukien + *lo* man, person] **:** a member of a people with a distinctive dialect that inhabit sectors of northeastern Kwangtung including Swatow and parts of adjacent southern Fukien including Amoy and that have migrated in large numbers to Formosa and various countries of southeast Asia

**ho·kum** \'hōkəm\ *n* -s [prob. blend of [1]*hocus-pocus* and *bunkum*] **1 :** a device found to elicit a display of mirth or sentimental emotion from an audience and therefore deliberately used to impel persons to a desired action **2 :** something worthless or untrue **:** BUNKUM

**hokus–pokus** *var of* HOCUS-POCUS

**hol** \'häl\ *n* -s [by shortening] *Brit* **:** HOLIDAY

**hol-** *or* **holo-** *comb form* [ME *holo-*, fr. OF, fr. L *hol-*, *holo-*, fr. Gk, fr. *holos* — more at SAFE] **1 a :** complete **:** entire **:** total ⟨*holo*graph⟩ ⟨*holo*parasite⟩ **b :** completely **:** totally **:** throughout ⟨*hol*arthritic⟩ ⟨*holo*branchiate⟩ ⟨*holo*axial⟩ ⟨*holo*crystalline⟩ **c :** without division **:** forming one piece ⟨*holo*gnathous⟩ ⟨*holo*rhinal⟩ **2 a :** similar **:** homogeneous ⟨*holo*morph⟩ **b :** similarly **:** homogeneously ⟨*holo*gamous⟩ **3** *usu holo-* **:** containing the highest possible number of hydroxyl groups — in names of inorganic acids ⟨*holo*phosphoric acid $P(OH)_5$ or $H_5PO_5$⟩ ⟨*holo*quinonoid⟩

**hol** *abbr* hollow

**ho·la** \'ō(,)lä\ *interj* [Sp] — used esp. among Latin Americans to attract attention or to shout encouragement or exultation

**hol·andric** \(')häl, (')hōl+\ *adj* [ISV *hol-* + *andric*] **1 a :** inherited solely in the male line **b :** transmitted by a gene or genes in the nonhomologous portion of the Y chromosome **2 :** having the full number of testes characteristic of a group — compare METANDRIC

**hol·an·dry** \'hä,landrē, 'hō,-\ *n* -ES **:** the quality or state of being holandric

**hol·arctic** \(')häl, (')hōl+\ *adj* [*hol-* + *arctic*] **1 :** of or relating to the arctic regions **2** *usu cap* **:** of, relating to, or being the biogeographic realm or region that includes the northern parts of the Old and the New World and comprises the Palaearctic and Nearctic regions or subregions

**holard** \'hä,lärd, 'hō,-\ *n* -s [*hol-* + Gk *ardein* to water] **:** the entire water content of the soil — compare CHRESARD, ECHARD

**hol·as·pid·e·an** \¦hä,la¦spidēən, ¦hō,-\ *adj* [*hol-* + *aspid-* + *-ean*] **:** having a single series of large scutes on the posterior side of the tarsus (as in the true larks)

**hol·bein stitch** \'hō|l,bīn *sometimes* 'hä|\ *n, usu cap H* [after Hans *Holbein* †1543 Ger. artist; fr. the kind of embroidery seen in his paintings] **:** a running stitch worked twice often in different colors on the same line to make a continuous reversible pattern

Holbein stitch

**hol·boell's grebe** \'hōl,bu̇lz-\ *n, usu cap H* [after Carl P. *Holboell* †1856 Dan. civil servant] **:** a red-necked grebe (*Colymbus grisegena holboelli*) of America and eastern Asia

**hol·co·dont** \'hälkə,dänt\ *adj* [ISV *holc-* (fr. Gk *holkos* furrow) + *-odont*] **:** having the teeth set in a long continuous groove

**hol·co·no·ti** \,hälkə'nōd·,ī, -d·(,)ē\ *n pl, cap* [NL, fr. *holco-* (fr. Gk *holkos* furrow) + *-noti* (fr. Gk *nōton* back) — more at NATES] **:** the Embiotocidae regarded as an independent order of fishes

**hol·cus** \'hälkəs\ *n, cap* [NL, fr. L, wall barley (*Hordeum murinum*), fr. Gk *holkos* wall barley, furrow — more at SULCUS] **:** a genus of Old World grasses widely naturalized in America with velvety pubescence and deciduous spikelets — see VELVET GRASS

[1]**hold** \'hōld *dial sometimes* -lt\ *vb* **held** \'held\ *or dial past* **hilt** \'hilt\ **held** *or archaic* **hold·en** \'hōldən\ **holding; holds** \'hōl(d)z\ [ME *holden*, fr. OE *healdan*, *haldan;* akin to OHG *haltan* to hold, ON *halda*, Goth *haldan* to tend cattle, L *celer* rapid, Gk *kellein* to run a ship to land, Skt *kālayati* he drives, holds, carries] *vt* **1 a :** to retain in one's keeping **:** maintain possession of **:** not give up or relinquish **:** POSSESS, HAVE ⟨*held* property worth millions⟩ ⟨~ several slaves as household servants⟩ ⟨~*s* the title to the property⟩ ⟨~*s* the power to hire or fire at will⟩ **b :** to retain or occupy by force **:** defend and not retreat from ⟨the soldiers *held* the bridge against all attacks⟩ **c :** to keep control of or authority or jurisdiction over ⟨wished to ~ the territory because of the fur trade⟩ **d :** to have power over **:** affect strongly and unremittingly ⟨a pleasurable excitement *held* him —D.G.Gerahty⟩ ⟨invalidism *held* him for eight years —J.C.Archer⟩ **e :** to have possession of the privileges, benefits, or perquisites of ⟨~*s* the eastern seaboard under an authorization granted by the manufacturer of the goods⟩ **f :** to use or keep as a threat or as a means of gaining advantage **2 :** to impose restraint upon or limit in motion or action ⟨the bushing *held* the drive shaft so that it had no play whatsoever⟩: as **a :** to refrain from producing (as speech or noise) ⟨~ your talk, man⟩ **b** (1) **:** to keep back **:** not loose **:** not let go ⟨~ the dogs so the strangers can pass⟩ (2) **:** STAY, ARREST ⟨~ him with a glance⟩ ⟨a strange compunction *held* his hand as he raised it to strike⟩ ⟨tried to ~ him from an action he would always regret⟩ (3) **:** DELAY ⟨*held* the curtain for an hour until the arrival of the royal carriage at the theater⟩ (4) **:** to stop the action of usu. temporarily ⟨time must be allowed . . . for ~*ing* the press while waiting for the sheet to dry —F.W.Hoch⟩ **c** (1) **:** to keep from advancing or succeeding in attack ⟨were able to ~ the enemy⟩ (2) **:** to keep (as an opposing team) from gaining an advantage ⟨the weaker team *held* the stronger during the first half⟩ **d :** to restrict or limit (as in amount of variation, advance, gain, loss) by acting to control or oppose ⟨*held* the sound to one level of loudness⟩ ⟨*held* the army to only a few miles' gain⟩ ⟨*held* the opposing team to only two runs⟩ **e :** to bind legally or morally **:** CONSTRAIN ⟨~ a man to his word⟩ — often used with an adjective complement ⟨~ a man responsible for his actions⟩ ⟨~ the men accountable for all money spent⟩ **f** *Scot* **:** to oppress by affliction **:** keep down **:** hold down **g :** DETAIN ⟨*held* him in conversation for ten minutes before letting him go⟩ **h :** RESTRICT, LIMIT ⟨bouts have been *held* to three 1½-minute rounds —Barrett McGurn⟩ **i :** to tense muscles in order to brace (oneself) ⟨had to ~ himself against the swaying and bumping of the coach⟩ **j :** to keep (a herd of cattle) together in a unit ⟨out ~*ing* the herd while the rest were eating⟩ **3** *obs* **:** to abide by (as a promise) or keep inviolate (as a faith) **4 a :** to have or keep in the grasp ⟨~ a child's hand⟩ ⟨~ a pocketbook tightly⟩ ⟨this volume is a joy to ~ as well as to read —J.M.Chase⟩ **b** (1) **:** to keep as if in a grasp **:** cause to be or remain in a particular situation, position, or relation, within certain limits, or of a particular quality ⟨~ a person in suspense⟩ ⟨~ an emotion under rigid control⟩ ⟨~ a ladder steady⟩ ⟨~ a child in check⟩ ⟨~ himself in readiness⟩ ⟨the stern demands of necessity *held* men in their grip —V.L.Parrington⟩ ⟨the searchlight . . . caught and *held* them in its glare —Nevil Shute⟩ (2) **:** to place and usu. not allow to move ⟨~ a pad of gauze to a wound⟩ ⟨~ your hand against my cheek⟩ **:** FIX ⟨*held* his eyes steadily on the picture⟩ **c** (1) **:** SUPPORT, SUSTAIN ⟨the building was *held* by concrete underpinning⟩ ⟨roof will ~ a deadweight of 94 inches of snow —*Monsanto Mag.*⟩ ⟨~*s* his seventy-two years easily⟩ (2) **:** to keep (as a bank of dirt) from eroding, collapsing, or washing away ⟨pines and other hardy trees were planted to ~ the sand —George Farwell⟩ **d** (1) **:** RETAIN ⟨struggling to ~, or to capture, the allegiance of the British people —F.A.Ogg & Harold Zink⟩ ⟨the parents still ~ the children's affection⟩ ⟨the suit ~*s* its press well⟩ ⟨a plastic that will ~ any shape you press it into⟩ **:** to retain by not vomiting ⟨unable to take a bite of food or ~ it on his stomach when it was forced upon him —F.B.Gipson⟩ **:** retain by not discharging ⟨the metal *held* the electrical charge for a long time⟩ (2) **:** to keep in custody **:** keep as a prisoner ⟨the cops agreed that the death was accidental, and did not ~ him —*Time*⟩ **e** (1) **:** to have in one's keeping **:** STORE ⟨another consideration was the cost of storing type — we certainly could not afford to ~ it forever —B.L.Stratton⟩ **:** keep on file or record ⟨the title is *held* at the registry of deeds⟩ (2) **:** RESERVE ⟨called the hotel and asked them to ~ a room for him⟩ ⟨*held* a few seats in case some visiting celebrities turned up⟩ **f :** BEAR, CARRY, COMPORT ⟨something unbending and strong, peasantlike, in the way he ~*s* himself —Madaleine Chapsal⟩ **g** (1) **:** to maintain in being or action **:** keep up without interruption, diminution, or flagging **:** SUSTAIN, PRESERVE ⟨~ one's course due north⟩ ⟨~ silence⟩ (2) **:** to maintain in a given condition (as of temperature, pressure, or humidity) or stage of processing (3) **:** to maintain a given condition in (4) **:** to maintain the articulation of (a speech sound) or the production of (as a note in music) ⟨the vowel in *feet* is not *held* as long as the vowel in *feed*⟩ **h :** to keep the uninterrupted interest, attention, or devotion of **:** keep from other interests, attractions, or places ⟨the play *held* the audience for over three hours⟩ ⟨a community that . . . ~*s* young people and offers inducements to them to stay and help build a greater hometown —J.C.Penney⟩ ⟨newspaper editing did not ~ him long —A.H.Meneely⟩ ⟨wants to ~ her husband while resisting his domination —H.M.Parshley⟩ **i :** to keep (as a letter or package) from being delivered usu. temporarily ⟨asked the post office to ~ his mail until he returned⟩ **j :** to cover (the ears) so as to prevent hearing ⟨when I spoke she *held* her ears —Eudora Welty⟩ **k :** to constitute or provide adequate satisfaction for ⟨enough food to ~ him for a week⟩ ⟨had had enough of high causes and noble sacrifice to ~ them for a long time —F.L.Allen⟩ **l** (1) **:** not to veer or alter from ⟨the car *held* 70 miles an hour for 20 miles⟩ ⟨prices had *held* the same level for a month⟩ ⟨had trouble ~*ing* his course⟩ (2) **:** to be free of marked bouncing, swerving, or skidding on ⟨a car that ~*s* the road well at any speed⟩ **m :** to make an exhibition of or call persistently to one's consciousness ⟨trying to entertain his audience by ~*ing* his betters to ridicule⟩ **n :** to fix on and not turn away from ⟨for a few minutes the flashlight *held* the canoe, then lost it —Erle Stanley Gardner⟩ **5 a** (1) **:** to receive and retain ⟨the can ~*s* gasoline⟩ **:** have within **:** CONTAIN ⟨the cemetery which *held* the bodies of his family for seven generations back⟩ ⟨the room *held* only Victorian furniture⟩ ⟨the envelope which *held* his ticket —J.P.Marquand⟩ (2) **:** to have or retain within its limits as if in a container ⟨throw into a word every trace of meaning it can ~ —C.S.Kilby⟩ ⟨the cast *held* some noted singers⟩ ⟨could ~ large quantities of verse in his mind without effort⟩ (3) **:** to keep within moderate bounds the characteristic intoxicating effects of (an alcoholic liquor) ⟨drank heavily but *held* it well⟩ **b** (1) **:** to be able or designed to receive and retain or contain ⟨a special container to ~ flammable liquids⟩ ⟨the basket that *held* outgoing mail was empty⟩ (2) **:** ACCOMMODATE ⟨the hotel could ~ over 300 guests⟩ ⟨sleeping platforms ran the length of the side walls in two tiers, ~*ing* eight men —Meridel Le Sueur⟩ **c :** to be marked or characterized by as an essential feature ⟨the volume *held* an historical rather than a literary interest⟩ ⟨its steeply pitched gable roof ~*s* one dormer —*Amer. Guide Series: Md.*⟩ ⟨a scene that *held* many fond memories for him⟩ ⟨the famous hymn of creation . . . ~*s* an awesome vastness of mood —Emma Hawkridge⟩ **d :** to provide or have in reserve as a reward ⟨the story ~*s* a happy ending for everybody⟩ ⟨the tournament ~*s* a nice prize for the winner⟩ ⟨would like to know what the future ~*s*⟩ **6 a :** HARBOR, EXPERIENCE ⟨~ a feeling⟩ ⟨a nation for whom we all ~ a good deal of admiration⟩ ⟨~*s* no sympathy for criminals⟩ **b :** ACCEPT ⟨~ a point of view⟩ **:** BELIEVE ⟨~ a theory⟩ ⟨~ opposing opinions⟩ **:** subscribe to ⟨the aesthetic philosophy we happen to ~ —C.I.Glicksberg⟩ **c** (1) **:** CONSIDER, REGARD, THINK, JUDGE ⟨*held* that the action was dishonest⟩ ⟨*held* calculus to be too difficult for that age group⟩ ⟨*held* by many to be the greatest contemporary tennis player⟩ ⟨the expression of those truths *held* to be self-evident —F.B.Millett⟩ (2) **:** to decide in a judicial ruling ⟨the court *held* that the man was sane⟩ (3) **:** ESTEEM, VALUE ⟨the story is that he *held* it so lightly that he lost the land on one turn of the cards —*Amer. Guide Series: N.C.*⟩ **d :** to have or maintain in judgment or regard ⟨~ someone in contempt⟩ ⟨~ a parent in honor⟩ **7 a :** to engage in with someone else or with others **:** do by concerted action ⟨the student body *held* games in the afternoon⟩ **b :** CONVOKE, CONVENE ⟨the king *held* an assembly of all his courtiers⟩ ⟨the second court session was *held* in the afternoon⟩ **:** arrange for and have in a united action ⟨the company *held* a feast to celebrate victory⟩ **:** schedule and assemble or meet ⟨some classes were *held* in the evening⟩ **8 a :** to be or stand in (as a relative position) ⟨~*s* second place in the city golf tournament⟩ ⟨urban redevelopment continues to ~ an important place in planning programs —*Collier's Yr. Bk.*⟩ **b :** to have earned or been appointed, promoted, or elected to and now occupy (as an office) ⟨~*s* a captaincy in the navy⟩ ⟨~*s* a secretaryship in the club⟩ ⟨*held* the presidency for two terms⟩ **c :** to have earned or been awarded (as an academic degree) ⟨~*s* an M.D. from one of the best medical schools⟩ ⟨~*s* a German Ph.D.⟩ ⟨~*s* a medal of honor⟩ **9** *now dial Brit* **:** BET, WAGER **10 a** *obs* **:** to handle so as to guide or manage (as reins or a gun) **b :** POINT, AIM, DIRECT — used with *on* ⟨*held* a gun on the grocer while an accomplice robbed the till⟩ **11** *obs* **:** to endure or bear up under (as rough handling or invidious comparison) **~** *vi* **1 a :** to maintain position **:** not retreat **:** remain unconquered or unsubdued ⟨the troops *held* in the face of repeated attacks⟩ **b** (1) **:** to continue or remain esp. as is or of the same kind or quality **:** LAST ⟨winter *held* until the middle of March⟩ ⟨his anger *held* for several days⟩ ⟨the output of copper *held* at the level of the year before⟩ ⟨hoping that the good weather would ~⟩ **:** not change or alter ⟨we can go if the present circumstances ~⟩ ⟨our luck *held* and we won⟩ ⟨the habit of a lifetime *held* —John Buchan⟩ — often used with *up* ⟨the good weather *held* up for several days⟩ (2) **:** to endure a test or trial ⟨their courage *held* against all odds⟩ — often used with *up* ⟨if his interest ~*s* up⟩ **2 a :** to maintain a grasp on or a connection with something **:** remain fastened to something (as by a strap) **:** keep hold ⟨the anchor *held* in the rough sea⟩ **:** not slip **:** not lose a grip **:** CLING ⟨felt his rubber soles grip and ~⟩ **b** *of a female mammal* **:** to hold to service **:** CONCEIVE **3 :** to derive right or title (as to the possession of lands or as land to be held) — usu. used with *of* or *from* ⟨*held* of the crown by an outright gift⟩ **4 :** to bear or carry oneself ⟨a man who *held* aloof from strangers⟩ ⟨asked the boy to ~ still⟩ **5 :** to be or remain valid **:** APPLY ⟨the rule ~*s* only in special cases⟩ **:** prove consistent or acceptable to reason or logic ⟨the theory does not ~ under analysis⟩ **6 :** to go ahead **:** continue as one has been going ⟨the travelers *held* on their way⟩ ⟨*held* south for several miles⟩ **:** not veer or fluctuate in progress or forward movement ⟨the plane *held* steadily on its course by automatic control⟩ **7 :** to restrain or withhold oneself **:** cease or forbear an intended or threatened action **:** HALT, STOP, PAUSE ⟨wished that he might ~ a while and stop his incessant chatter⟩ **8 :** to take place ⟨went . . . to the place where the funeral service was ~*ing* —John Bennett⟩ ⟨annual show and sale of highland ponies ~*s* on Monday —*Scotsman*⟩ **9 :** to pause in archery between drawing and loosing an arrow **10 :** to hold copy (as in proofreading) **syn** see CONTAIN, HAVE, KEEP — **hold a brief :** to act as or be a counsel in a legal case ⟨had *held* several important *briefs*⟩ — **hold a brief for :** ADVOCATE, DEFEND — **hold a candle to :** to qualify for comparison with ⟨asserted that no wrestler could *hold a candle to* the current champion⟩ — **hold a close wind** *or* **hold a good wind :** to sail very close to the wind making little leeway — **hold book :** to act as prompter during a rehearsal or a performance of a play ⟨help paint scenery, carry props, do a little acting, and *hold book* during performances —Maurice Zolotow⟩ — **hold bottom** *of an anchor* **:** to hold in holding ground — **hold by :** to remain faithful to **:** hold to or be devoted to ⟨those who *hold by* the humanist tradition⟩ — **hold copy :** to work as a copyholder — **hold court :** to act with marked and courtly sociableness ⟨*held court* whenever he was in public nodding and bowing to all his friends and acquaintances⟩ — **hold down a claim :** to remain on land claimed so as to establish one's ownership — **hold everything** *slang* **:** to stop or cease an action or operation — usu. used as a command or exhortation — **hold fire :** to refrain from expressing oneself or taking action ⟨*held fire* on specific foreign policy questions —*N.Y.Times*⟩ — **hold good 1 :** to hold true **2 :** to hold up **:** ENDURE, LAST ⟨his luck *held good* all year⟩ — **hold hands :** to go hand in hand esp. as an expression of affection — **hold in demesne** *law* **:** to hold in one's own possession or power — **hold one's breath 1 :** to cease breathing momentarily (as from fear) **2 :** to be in extreme suspense ⟨*held her breath* all during the examination for fear the child would not pass⟩ — **hold one's ground :** to maintain a position ⟨the speaker calmly *held his ground* in the face of angry opposition⟩ — **hold one's horses** *slang* **:** to stop action or talk for a moment **:** wait or be patient for a minute — usu. used as a command or exhortation — **hold one's own :** to maintain one's position **:** prove at least equal to opposition ⟨proved able to *hold their own* under heavy attack⟩ ⟨the lighter boy *held his own* well against the heavier boxer⟩ — **hold one's peace :** to keep silent **:** keep one's thoughts to oneself ⟨felt it would do no good to complain so *held his peace*⟩ — **hold one's tongue :** to keep silent ⟨told the boy sharply to *hold his tongue*⟩ — **hold tack with 1** *of a boat* **:** to keep on the same tacks as and change tacks with (another boat) **2 :** to keep up with (as in activity) — **hold the bag** *also* **hold the sack 1 :** to be or be left empty-handed or with only the most undesirable items of a group of apportioned items **2 :** to bear alone and in full a responsibility that should properly have been shared by others ⟨when the police began to investigate, five of the men left the country leaving the sixth *holding the bag*⟩ — **hold the boards :** to hold the stage — **hold the field 1 :** to maintain a position in a field of play or an arena of contest **2 :** to remain dominantly before the public ⟨a doctrine which *held the field* for quite five hundred years —R.W.Southern⟩ — **hold the fort 1 :** to maintain a firm position usu. against opposition ⟨found himself *holding the fort* against a solid block of opponents of the plan⟩ **2 :** to take care of usual affairs ⟨a skeleton staff was left to *hold the fort* at the office during the Saturday morning —Dorothy Sayers⟩ — **hold the line :** to keep things as they are without undesirable alteration ⟨*holding the line* on the price of electrical appliances despite increased costs⟩ ⟨*hold the line* on present taxes⟩ — **hold the market :** to buy or sell in order to maintain prices as they are — **hold the stage :** to continue to be produced — used of a play — **hold the wind :** to sail close to the wind without making much leeway — **hold to 1 a :** to remain steadfast, attached, or faithful to **:** adhere to ⟨*hold to* an established plan⟩ ⟨*hold to* one's purpose⟩ ⟨*hold to* one's family in all circumstances⟩ **b :** to subscribe to **:** BELIEVE ⟨those who *hold to* the doctrine of spontaneous generation —J.B.Conant⟩ **2 :** to stay close to or on (as a particular course) ⟨the new ships *hold* closely *to* the major trade lanes —R.H.Brown⟩ — **hold to account :** to hold responsible ⟨*hold* all salesmen *to account* for the money spent on company business⟩ — **hold to service** *of a domestic animal* **:** to become pregnant **:** SETTLE — **hold true :** to remain true or valid esp. under changed circumstances ⟨the theory *holds true* in all applications⟩ — **hold up one's head :** to conduct oneself in a normally unashamed manner ⟨if they found out that she had cheated, she would be unable to *hold up her head* again⟩ — **hold water 1 a :** to retain water without leaking **b :** to be whole, consistent, or valid **:** stand up under criticism or analysis ⟨an accusation which would *hold water* in a court of law —Michael Howard⟩ ⟨an explanation that would not *hold water* if the true facts were known⟩ **2 :** to hold oars steady in the water usu. at right angles to the direction of movement to check headway — **hold with :** to agree with (as a principle) or approve of (as a practice) ⟨political methods that few would *hold with*⟩

[2]**hold** \'hōld, *dial often* -lt\ *n* -s [ME *hold*, *holde* hold, possession, land that is held, property, fr. OE *heald*, *hald* protection, keeping, fr. *healdan*, *haldan* to hold] **1 a :** a place of temporary shelter or refuge; *also* **:** a lair or a lurking place (as of a fish) **b :** STRONGHOLD **2 a :** CONFINEMENT, CUSTODY **b :** a place of confining **:** PRISON **3 a** (1) **:** the act or the manner of holding or grasping (as in the hands or arms) ⟨released his ~ on the man's arm⟩ ⟨has a strong ~ for a small man⟩ **:** GRASP ⟨took a firm ~ on the club⟩ **:** CLASP, GRIP ⟨in his arms his ~ was tight and reassuring⟩ — often used idiomatically without an article as object of *catch*, *get*, *have*, *seize*, *take* ⟨got ~ of the oar and was pulled out of the water⟩ ⟨seized ~ as the rope brushed his fingers⟩ ⟨held out a hand and waited until the child took ~⟩ ⟨took ~ of the knob and opened the door⟩ ⟨the boy's sneakers suddenly took ~ and stopped him from sliding off the roof⟩ ⟨saw that the climber had ~ of the rope before he began to haul on it⟩ (2) **:** a manner of grasping an opponent in wrestling ⟨knee ~*s* and body presses⟩ **b** (1) **:** a nonphysical bond, grip, or clasp which attaches, restrains, or constrains or by or through which something is affected, controlled, dominated, or possessed — often used with *on*, *upon*, or *over* ⟨afraid they might lose their ~ on the domestic market —*Sydney (Australia) Bull.*⟩ ⟨yet the ~ of the public school upon the middle-class mind has not weakened —Roy Lewis & Angus Maude⟩ ⟨the father had a strong ~ over his children⟩ and often used idiomatically without an article as object of *catch*, *get*, *have*, *seize*, *take* ⟨the newspapers got ~ of the story⟩ ⟨after a moment of panic he got ~ of himself⟩ ⟨seized ~ and stepped up production 50 percent⟩ ⟨in the confusion of contradictory ideas we did not know what philosophy he had ~ of⟩ (2) **:** an action, expedient, or device for achieving an end ⟨arguing that in . . . politics no ~*s* are barred —*New Republic*⟩ **c :** conscious grasp **:** full comprehension — used with *on* or *upon* ⟨at the point of sleep one loses his ~ on the real world⟩ ⟨how weak was his ~ upon character —Roger Fry⟩ **4 :** something that may be grasped as a support ⟨climbed up the rock using some ledges and jutting pieces as ~*s*⟩ **5 :** a pause between the completion of the draw and the release of the arrow in archery **6 a :** FERMATA **b :** a rhythmic lengthening of a word or syllable or a symbol used to indicate this **c :** the time between the onset and the release of a vocal articulation **7 :** a sudden motionless posture at the end of a dance or dance phrase **8 a :** an order or indication that something is to be reserved ⟨put a ~ on all the hotel rooms still unoccupied⟩ **b :** an order or indication that some action is to be delayed ⟨announced a ~ on all takeoffs until the weather cleared⟩ **c :** a notation on a depositor's account to indicate that the balance or a portion thereof should not be paid out

[3]**hold** \"\ *n* -s [fr. (assumed) ME *hold*, alter. (prob. influenced by ME [2]*hold*) of ME [1]*hole*] **1 a :** the interior of a ship below decks; *esp* **:** the cargo deck of a ship **b :** the interior of a plane; *esp* **:** the cargo compartment of a plane **2 a :** a division of the interior esp. the cargo deck of a ship **b :** a division of the interior of a plane esp. for cargo

[4]**hold** \"\ *n* -s [OE, fr. ON *hölthr* free landowner, man; akin to OE *hæle*, *hæleth* man, hero, OS *helith* man, hero, ON *halr* man, and perh. to Skt *kalya* healthy — more at CALLI-] **:** an officer of high rank in the Danelaw corresponding to the high reeve of the Anglo-Saxons

**hold·able** \'hōldəbəl\ *adj* **:** capable of being held **:** of a size or character that makes holding convenient or desirable

**holdall** \'=,=\ *n* -s [[1]*hold* + *all*] **:** a container for miscellaneous articles; *esp* **:** an often cloth traveling case or bag

**hold away** *vi* **1** *Scot* **:** to remain at a distance **:** hold off **2** *chiefly Scot* **:** to continue on one's way

**hold back** *vb* [[1]*hold* + *back*] *vt* **1 a :** to keep in check **:** RESTRAIN, CURB ⟨had to *hold* the children *back* from running out into the street⟩ **b :** to keep from advancing to the next stage, grade, or level ⟨followed the policy of *holding* any child *back* who could not read adequately⟩ **2 a :** to retain in one's keeping ⟨*held* a large sum *back* to cover costs of handling⟩ **b :** to keep to oneself ⟨who is at liberty to speak and *hold* nothing *back* —F.L.Paxson⟩ **3 :** to shade (a portion of an image in photography) while printing to reduce the density **~** *vi* **:** to keep oneself from doing, feeling, or indulging in something **:** hold aloof ⟨*held back* from making a complete statement about his political position⟩ ⟨were asked to *hold back* on food deliveries during the shortage⟩ ⟨when they asked the child to come in he *held back*⟩ **syn** see KEEP

**holdback** \'=,=\ *n* [*hold back*] **1 :** a device (as an iron catch on a carriage shaft with a looped strap) to enable a horse to back or hold back a vehicle **2 :** one of several devices for holding something back or open: as **a :** a device (as a specially constructed hinge) for holding a door, shutter, or casement window open **b :** TIEBACK **3 a :** the act of holding something back or of holding back on something (as work or production) ⟨ordered a ~ until negotiations looked more auspicious⟩ **b :** something held back or withheld often temporarily ⟨a ~ of a week's salary to be paid on satisfactory completion of the job⟩

**hold beam** *n* **:** a beam placed in the hold of a ship to supply usu. transverse structural strength

**hold–clear** \'=¦=\ *n* -s [fr. the phrase *hold clear*] **:** a device for holding a railroad signal in any position other than its most restrictive

**hold down** *vb* [¹*hold* + *down*] *vt* **1 a :** to keep in subjection ⟨conquered them but had no success in *holding* them *down*⟩ **b :** RESTRAIN, CURB ⟨noisy despite all efforts to *hold* them *down*⟩ **2 :** to retain continuously and handle competently (as a job) **:** hold and keep ⟨a man who had *held down* some significant political positions⟩ **3 :** to take care of ⟨some friends *held down* his grocery business while he was sick⟩ ~ *vi* **:** to limit oneself ⟨he is not stopping smoking but *holding down* to three cigarettes a day⟩ — **hold down on :** to keep down or low ⟨*held down on* the price he was willing to pay⟩

**hold–down** \ˈ=,=\ *n* -s [*hold down*] **:** a clamp or other device for holding a part down against another part (as a sheet against the bed of a press or a battery against the bottom of its container)

**holden** *archaic past part of* HOLD

**hol·den·ite** \ˈhōldə,nīt\ *n* -s [Albert F. *Holden* †1913 Am. mining engineer + E *-ite*] **:** a mineral $(Mn,Ca)_4(Zn,Mg,Fe)_2(AsO_4)(OH)_5O_2$ consisting of a basic manganese zinc arsenate with minor calcium, magnesium, and iron and occurring as red orthorhombic crystals at Franklin, New Jersey

**¹hold·er** \ˈhōldə(r)\ *n* -s [ME, fr. *holden* to hold + *-er*] **1 :** one that holds something: as **a** (1) **:** POSSESSOR, OWNER — often used in combination ⟨slave*holder*⟩ ⟨job*holder*⟩ (2) **:** one who holds any estate in land **:** a person in constructive possession of land having the right of immediate possession thereto which he can exercise without hindrance **:** a tenant in his own right or under another in actual possession of land **b :** a person in possession of and legally entitled to receive payment of a bill, note, or check **:** the payee, endorsee in possession, or the bearer of a bill, note, or check — compare HOLDER IN DUE COURSE **c :** a worker who holds articles during an industrial process **d :** one who has won or been awarded and reaps the benefits of a scholarship or fellowship **e :** one who has won, earned, or been awarded a trophy, title, or degree ⟨the ~ of a tennis championship⟩ ⟨was ~ of several swimming cups⟩ ⟨the ~ of a college degree in animal husbandry⟩ **2 :** a device or contrivance by which or a container in which something is held ⟨umbrella ~⟩ ⟨a flower ~⟩: as **a :** either of two loops attached to reins for holding a pulling horse **b :** a thick protective cloth pad for grasping hot utensils **c :** a narrow tubular device often used by smokers for holding a cigarette or cigar while smoking it **d :** a flat lightproof container in which photographic films or plates may be held for use in a camera **e :** a device that resembles a safety pin and is used in knitting for holding stitches temporarily to keep them from dropping **3 :** something (as a strap or rail) which one may grasp for support or for steadying oneself **4 :** a device by which something (as a door or shutter) is held back or open

holder 2c

**²holder** \"\ *n* -s [ME, fr. (assumed) ME *hold* + ME *-er* — more at ³HOLD] **:** a worker in the hold of a ship

**holder–forth** \ˌ==ˈ=\ *n, pl* **holders–forth :** one that holds forth **:** PREACHER, RANTER

**holder in due course :** the holder of a negotiable instrument that is complete and regular on its face who takes it in good faith and for value before it is overdue and without notice of its dishonor or of any infirmity in it or of any defect in the title of the person negotiating it

**holder–on** \ˌ==ˈ=\ *n, pl* **holders–on** *or* **holder–ons 1 :** a worker who bucks rivets **2 :** a pneumatic tool used in place of a dolly to back up rivets while they are being headed

**holder process** *n* **:** HOLDING METHOD

**holder–up** \ˌ==ˈ=\ *n, pl* **holders–up** *or* **holder–ups :** one that holds something up; *specif* **:** a man who holds up the setting punch in riveting

**holdfast** \ˈ=,=\ *n* -s *often attrib* [fr. the phrase *hold fast*] **1 :** something that secures, holds in place, or supports: as **a** (1) **:** a rhizoidal base resembling a sucker but without absorption cells by which the thallus of many algae (as seaweeds) is attached to its support (2) **:** a discoid extremity of a tendril in certain plants (as the Virginia creeper) by which the vines fix themselves to flat surfaces **b :** an organ (as the acetabulum of a trematode or the scolex of a tapeworm) by which a parasitic animal attaches itself to its host **2 :** something to which something else (as a guy line or tackle) may be secured firmly **3 :** an actinomycotic tumor of the jaw — not used technically

**hold·fast·ness** \ˈhōl(d),fas(t)nəs, -faas-,-fais-,-fȧs-\ *n* -ES **:** the tendency to keep a firm often stubborn hold (as on a position or possession) **:** TENACITY, PERSISTENCE

**hold forth** *vb* [ME *holden forth*, fr. *holden* to hold + *forth*] *vt* **:** OFFER, EXHIBIT, PROPOUND ⟨*hold forth* the hopes of better times to come⟩ ⟨*hold* it *forth* that one can cure all ailments of the spirit⟩ ~ *vi* **1 :** to speak out in public esp. at length **:** HARANGUE, PREACH — often used disparagingly **2 :** to conduct one's affairs ⟨a group of nuclear physicists now *holding forth* at their annual convention⟩ **3 :** to take place **:** undergo performance ⟨a region in which every variety of winter sports *holds forth*⟩

**hold in** *vb* [ME *holden in*, fr. *holden* to hold + *in*] *vt* **:** to keep in check **:** RESTRAIN, CURB ⟨the rider had a hard time *holding* his horse *in*⟩ ~ *vi* **:** to restrain oneself **:** keep silent ⟨wanted to speak but thought better of it and *held in*⟩

**¹holding** *n* -s [ME *holdyng*, gerund of *holden* to hold] **1 :** the act of one that holds or takes hold **:** HOLD, GRIP, CLASP **2 :** something that is held: as **a :** land held esp. by a vassal of a superior **:** TENEMENT ⟨small ~*s* of less than 5 acres —*Americana Annual*⟩ **b :** an actual judgment or ruling of a court upon any issue of law raised in a case **:** the actual final decision of a court on the particular facts of a given case as distinguished from the dictum ⟨difficult to find a recent . . . enactment that equals in impact and scope this judicial ~ —J.P.Roche & M.M.Gordon⟩ **c :** any property that is owned or possessed — usu. used in pl. ⟨record-breaking frozen fish ~*s* totaled 179 million pounds —*Americana Annual*⟩ ⟨the ~*s* of American libraries —*Current Biog.*⟩ **3 :** something that holds **:** a means of holding **:** ATTACHMENT, CONNECTION **4 :** personal contact esp. with the hands or arms that retards or interferes with the movement of an opponent in some sports (as basketball, football, soccer) **5 :** a company or enterprise owned or controlled by a holding company

**²holding** *adj* [ME *holdyng*, pres. part. of *holden* to hold] **1 :** effecting a delay **:** being a hindrance or interference ⟨a ~ action to prevent the passage of more drastic control legislation —E.P.Hutchinson⟩ **2 :** designed for usu. temporary storage or retention ⟨a ~ refrigerator at a railhead⟩ ⟨a ~ pen for the horses⟩ ⟨shunted the cars onto the ~ track⟩

**holding attack** *n* **:** a secondary attack designed to hold an enemy in position in a military envelopment

**holding company** *n* **:** a company that owns part or all of one or more other companies for purposes of control — compare INVESTMENT COMPANY

**holding fund** *n* **:** a sum of money allotted or set aside for investment usu. for noncommercial purposes (as scholarships or grants-in-aid)

**holding ground** *n* **:** bottom that an anchor can hold in

**holding method** *n* **:** a method of pasteurization in which a fluid (as milk or fruit juice) is heated to not less than 143° F for at least 30 minutes

**holding–out partner** \ˌ==ˈ=-\ *n* **:** NOMINAL PARTNER

**holding–up hammer** \ˌ==ˈ=-\ *n* **:** a riveter's dolly

**hold·man** \ˈhōl(d)mən\ *n, pl* **holdmen :** a dock worker who works in a ship's hold in loading or unloading a ship

**hold off** *vb* [ME *holden of*, fr. *holden* to hold + *of* off] *vt* **1 a :** to keep at a distance ⟨a tendency to *hold* people *off*⟩ **b :** WITHSTAND ⟨*held* all enemy attacks *off*⟩ **2 :** POSTPONE, DELAY ⟨*held off* going to see a doctor⟩ ⟨tries to *hold off* making decisions⟩ ~ *vi* **1 a :** to keep aloof ⟨a tendency to *hold off* from people⟩ **b :** ABSTAIN ⟨*held off* from smoking for a month⟩ **2 :** to hold back **:** HESITATE ⟨*held off* from answering directly⟩

**hold–off** \ˈ=,=\ *n* -s [*hold off*] **:** the act or period of holding off **:** a delay or period of delay or postponement

**hold on** *vi* [ME *holden on*, fr. *holden* to hold + *on*] **1 a :** to go on **:** maintain a course **:** CONTINUE ⟨*held on* in their route until they arrived at a river⟩ **b :** to remain unconquered or undefeated ⟨felt they could *hold on* under siege for at least two months⟩ **2 a :** to maintain one's position **:** hold on to something **:** hang on ⟨a ledge where the tree roots could *hold on*⟩ **b :** to delay action (as in making a sale) ⟨wanted to sell but *held on*, hoping for a rise in price⟩ **3 :** to wait a minute **:** STOP, CEASE — used esp. in the imperative ⟨the man became irritated at the speaker and finally cried, "*Hold on!*"⟩ — **hold on to 1 a :** to keep in the grasp esp. with persistence ⟨the child *held on to* the man's hand tightly⟩ ⟨*held on to* what he had with desperation⟩ **b :** to keep control of ⟨*held on to* his temper⟩ ⟨had a hard time *holding on to* himself⟩ **2 a :** not to relinquish **:** not give up or abandon ⟨she *held on to* a quiet plan of her own —Margaret Deland⟩ **b :** to continue to produce (as a sound) or sing (as a note) ⟨*held on to* the final chord for a long time⟩

**hold out** *vb* [¹*hold* + *out*] *vt* **1 a :** to reach or stretch out ⟨the cook *held* a plate of food *out* to him⟩ ⟨*held* his hand *out* with a smile⟩ **b :** OFFER, PROFFER ⟨a job that seemed to *hold* many more opportunities *out* to him than his old one⟩ ⟨could *hold out* no hope of advancement⟩ **2 :** to make out to be **:** REPRESENT ⟨*held* himself *out* as a trained pharmacist⟩ **3 a** *archaic* **:** to keep up **:** CONTINUE, MAINTAIN **b** *obs* **:** SUSTAIN **c** *archaic* **:** to defend against a foe **4 :** to retain possession of (a card) secretly for the purpose of cheating or deceiving in a game (as poker) ~ *vi* **1 a :** to remain unsubdued by opposing forces **:** not yield or give way **:** LAST, ENDURE ⟨the garrison under siege *held out* for almost a month⟩; *also* **:** to continue to operate **:** not fail ⟨prayed the engine would *hold out* until we got home⟩ **b :** to refuse to come to an agreement or make a settlement until certain terms are met ⟨*held out* for a shorter working day⟩ **2 :** to hang out ⟨a gang of adolescents who *hold out* at the corner drug store⟩ — **hold out on 1 :** to withhold something from ⟨she didn't tell me she was rich; she's been *holding out on* me⟩ **2 :** to withhold a part or the whole of ⟨threatened to *hold out on* his sister's dividends if she didn't pose —*Fortune*⟩

**holdout** \ˈ=,=\ *n* -s [*hold out*] **1 :** the act or an instance of holding out: as **a :** a holding out by a negotiator to try to force concessions **b :** the act of secreting one or more cards of a pack for private use in a gambling game **2 :** a mechanism designed to assist a holdout in a game of cards **3 :** something held out **4 :** one that holds out (as in negotiations or an anticipated action) ⟨there was one ~ among the negotiators⟩ ⟨expected her to go from the movies to television but she remained a ~⟩

**hold over** *vb* [¹*hold* + *over*] *vi* **1 :** to continue in occupancy of land or exercise the powers of office beyond the limits of the term set or fixed **2 :** to continue into the succeeding beat or measure — used of a note or tone **3 :** to continue to exist **:** REMAIN, LAST, ENDURE ⟨no rancor *held over* through the years —W.A.White⟩ ~ *vt* **1 a :** to keep for future action **:** POSTPONE ⟨*held* the picnic *over* until better weather came⟩ ⟨*held over* several bills until the next session⟩ **b :** to keep in one's possession or as part of one's knowledge **:** RETAIN **:** not lose ⟨a conviction *held over* from school days —Robertson Davies⟩ **2 a :** to retain in possession or occupancy esp. of a post or office from an earlier term or period **:** keep on ⟨department heads who had been *held over* from the previous administration⟩ **b :** to renew or prolong the engagement of (as a performer or an act) **:** CONTINUE ⟨*held* the acrobats *over* for a second week⟩ ⟨a smash hit *held over* by popular demand⟩ **3 :** to continue (as the production of a note) into the succeeding beat or measure

**¹holdover** \ˈ=,=\ *n* -s [*hold over*] **1 :** one that holds over or is held over: as **a :** one that remains in office after the departure of his associates **b :** CARRY-OVER 2 **c :** a tree left in cutting as a reserve for a future crop or a tree remaining after fire or wind damage **d :** HANGOVER 2a **e :** an act or a performer whose engagement is immediately continued **f :** a team member remaining on a team from a past season ⟨a backfield consisting of a new man and three ~*s*⟩ **2 :** a cell where one is held for appearance before a court

**²holdover** \"\ *adj* **1 :** of, belonging to, or being a holdover ⟨a team with four ~ players⟩ ⟨the city has a ~ mayor although almost all other officials are new⟩ **2** *plant pathol* **:** permitting survival of a pathogenic organism under unfavorable conditions ⟨a ~ canker⟩ ⟨a ~ stage⟩

**holds** *pres 3d sing of* HOLD, *pl of* HOLD

**hold together** *vt* **1 :** to preserve as a unit **:** keep from separating into component parts ⟨only rubber bands *held* the toy *together*⟩ **:** preserve from disintegrating or failing ⟨only the force of the man's will *held* the company *together* in the last five years⟩ ⟨are of different inspirations but all *held together* by a remarkable unity —*Amer. Guide Series: Conn.*⟩ **2 :** to keep from nervous or mental collapse ⟨the novelist's attempt to *hold* himself *together* —Pat Frank⟩ ~ *vi* **:** to remain loyal to each other **:** preserve a unanimity of feeling or action ⟨we have only to *hold together* to go safely through the dark valley —Sir Winston Churchill⟩

**hold up** *vb* [ME *holden up*, fr. *holden* to hold + *up*] *vt* **1 a** (1) **:** RAISE, LIFT ⟨*hold* your hand *up* if you wish the chairman to recognize you⟩ ⟨*hold up* the object so it can be seen more clearly⟩ (2) **:** SUPPORT, SUSTAIN ⟨the underpinnings were not adequate to *hold* the house *up*⟩ ⟨the confiscated money *held* the toppling regime *up* for only a short time⟩ **b :** HOLD *vt* 4m **c :** to expose or call to attention as something one subscribes to, advocates, or lives by ⟨*held* a high standard *up* for his colleagues to follow⟩ ⟨*held up* the Old Testament in opposition to 18th century rationalism —William Petersen⟩ **2 a :** to rein in **:** CHECK, HALT ⟨*hold up* a horse⟩ **b :** to prevent (a fox or cub) from leaving a covert thus assuring a find and kill in fox hunting **c :** to stop, delay, or impede the course or advance of ⟨the accident *held* the traffic *up* for an hour⟩ ⟨a storm that *held* deliveries *up* for a day⟩ ⟨felt that she was *holding* her husband *up* in his career⟩ **3 :** to refuse to play (the winning card of a suit led) **4 :** to rob at gun's point ⟨*held* a gas station *up* and got away with several thousand dollars⟩ ⟨plotting to *hold up* a bank⟩ ~ *vi* **1 a** (1) **:** to remain undismayed or unsubdued (as under attack or misfortune) ⟨was determined to *hold up* for her children's sake⟩ ⟨*hold up* under attack⟩ (2) **:** to keep from falling **:** not to collapse, crumble, or fall apart ⟨an industry that *held up* well in the depression⟩ **b :** to prove true, accurate, or valid ⟨much depends on how well the weather forecasts *hold up*⟩ ⟨wondered if the charges would *hold up* in court⟩ **c :** to prove effective **:** PREVAIL ⟨despite attempts to countermand them, the provisions of the old charter *held up*⟩ **2 a :** to keep up **:** not fall behind or lose ground **:** hold out ⟨even the smaller children *held up* pretty well until the last mile⟩ **b :** to retain interest or artistic effectiveness esp. over an extended period of time ⟨a book that *holds up* well⟩ **3 :** to stop an action or postpone an intended action ⟨planned a picnic but the rain forced us to *hold up*⟩ **4 :** to keep from raining **:** remain clear ⟨a beautiful day, if it only *holds up*⟩ — **hold up on 1 :** DELAY, POSTPONE ⟨ran out of money and had to *hold up on* all plans to travel⟩ **2 :** to hold back (sense 2a) ⟨the court *held up on* the money until the estate was totally settled⟩

**holdup** \ˈ=,=\ *n* -s [*hold up*] **1 :** the act or process of holding something up: as **a :** a robbery at the point of a gun **b :** a delay or a stopping of something ⟨a week's ~ in the completion of the plans⟩; *specif* **:** the delay or keeping back of a liquid during fractional distillation or reflex extraction with solvents or of a gas in fluidization **c :** the saving for later use of a card that could win the current trick in a bridge game **2 :** an instance of extortion **3 :** a place where livestock may be temporarily held on a range

**holdup man** *n* **:** a criminal who commits a holdup ⟨had mistaken the gendarme for a *holdup man* —H.A.Chippendale⟩

**hold yard** *n* **:** a yard for holding railroad cars or trains convenient for immediate use

**¹hole** \ˈhōl\ *n* -s [ME, hole, hollow place, hold (of a ship), fr. OE *hol* hole, hollow place (fr. neut. of *hol*, adj., hollow) & OE *holh* hole, hollow; akin to OHG *hol*, adj., hollow, ON *holr*, adj., hollow, Goth us*hulon* to hollow out, L *caulis* stalk of a plant, Gk *kaulos* stem, and perh. to Skt *kulyā* brook, ditch; basic meaning: hollow] **1 a :** an opening into or through anything **:** APERTURE, PERFORATION ⟨a ~ in a roof⟩ ⟨shot a ~ through a board⟩ ⟨entered the shed through a ~ in the side⟩ ⟨fishing through a ~ in the ice⟩ **b :** a pocket of a pool table ⟨dropped the eight ball in the corner ~⟩ **c :** an opening in a defensive football lineup (as a space between players or created by a player who is out of position or has been blocked) that offers an opportunity for an offensive player to advance the ball **2 a :** a hollow place **:** a cavity in a solid body or area ⟨a ~ in an apple⟩ ⟨a ~ in the hillside⟩: as (1) **:** a hollow in the ground **:** EXCAVATION, PIT, CAVE ⟨the steam shovel had dug a large ~⟩ (2) **:** a hollow in the ground filled with soft material (3) **:** a deep place in a body of water (4) **:** a mine, a well, or other shaft dug or drilled in the earth **b :** an unfilled or blank area (as in a page or column printed or to be printed) ⟨expand your story to fill an 18-line ~⟩ **c :** the hold of a ship **d :** a sense of loss or persistent yearning for something lost — usu. used in the phrase *to make a hole in* ⟨the loss of his daughter made quite a ~ in the man's life⟩ **e** (1) **:** a defect that exists in a crystal (as of a semiconductor) due to an electron having left its normal position in one of the crystal bonds and that is equivalent in many respects to a positively charged particle (2) **:** VACANCY 7 **f :** an air pocket as it affects an aircraft usu. causing it to drop suddenly **3 a :** an underground habitation or lurking place usu. excavated **:** DEN, BURROW ⟨the fox in his ~⟩ ⟨a rabbit ~⟩ **b :** a prison cell esp. for solitary confinement **4 a :** FLAW, FAULT ⟨looking for ~*s* in his character⟩ **b :** a weak spot or inconsistency (as in a line of reasoning) ⟨his stories are full of ~*s* since he does not explain how his characters get from one psychological state to another⟩ ⟨ingenious theory in which . . . there are many ~*s* —V.S.Pritchett⟩ **c :** an oversight or inadequate provision (as in a law, statute, treaty, or agreement) that permits significant evasions ⟨stop up the manifest ~*s* in the neutrality laws —R.M.Lovett⟩ **5 a :** a small cavity or perforation of significance in various games: as (1) **:** a small cavity into which a marble is to be played in any of various marble games (2) **:** a usu. lined cavity 4½ inches in diameter and 4 or more inches deep in a putting green into which the ball is to be played in a game of golf **b** (1) **:** the unit of play from a tee to its corresponding hole in a game of golf (2) **:** the fairway from a tee to its corresponding green on a golf course (3) **:** the score made in playing the ball from the tee into the hole in a game of golf **6 a :** a mean, dingy, or small and disreputable place esp. of lodging or habitation ⟨lived in some ~ or other across the tracks⟩ ⟨the ladies' cabin . . . is a dreadful ~ —Rachel Henning⟩ **b :** a place that one finds objectionable or offensive **7 :** a small bay **:** COVE **8 :** an awkward embarrassing position **:** FIX ⟨the loss of so competent an assistant put him in a ~ for a little while⟩ ⟨the noble heroes that got the rebels out of a ~ at the battle of Long Island —Kenneth Roberts⟩ **:** a losing position ⟨the ball team dropped the next two games which put them in the ~ by five games⟩; *esp* **:** a position of debt or financial loss ⟨in the ~ to the tune of several thousand dollars⟩ ⟨lent him some money to get him temporarily out of a ~⟩ **9** *West* **:** a level grassy mountain valley — usu. used in place names ⟨Jackson *Hole*⟩ **10 :** a side track branching from a main line of a railroad — **in the hole 1 a :** FACEDOWN — used of a hole card in stud poker **b :** having a score below zero **2 a :** next but one to bat in a ball game **b** *of a pitcher* **:** having pitched more balls than strikes to a batter **c** *of a batter* **:** having two strikes against him

**²hole** \"\ *vb* -ED/-ING/-S [ME *holen*, fr. OE *holian*; akin to OHG *holōn* to hollow out, ON *hola*, Goth us*hulon*; denominative fr. the root of OE *hol* hole] *vt* **1 :** to make a hole in (as by cutting, digging, boring, or shooting at) **:** PERFORATE, PIERCE ⟨*holing* the fence posts to take the crosspieces⟩ ⟨the ship was *holed* along the waterline by enemy fire⟩ **2 a :** to drive (as an animal or ball) into a hole ⟨the dogs *holed* the fox⟩ ⟨*holed* the ball in a single shot⟩ **b :** to place in a hole **3 :** to undercut (the coal) in a bed in coal mining ~ *vi* **1 :** to make a hole in something; *esp* **:** to excavate or undercut in coal mining **2 a :** to go or get into a hole **b** *of a train* **:** to take a side track so that an oncoming train can pass on the main track

**hole·able** \ˈhōləbəl\ *adj* **:** capable of being holed esp. in one stroke

**hole–and–corner** \ˌ=ˈ==\ *also* **hole–in–corner** \ˈ=ˌ==\ *adj* **1 :** hidden from public view esp. for reprehensible reasons **:** CLANDESTINE, UNDERHAND ⟨carrying on a *hole-and-corner* intrigue —*Times Lit. Supp.*⟩ ⟨done behind my back in a *hole-and-corner* fashion —Dorothy Sayers⟩ ⟨following a *hole-in-corner*, semiconspiratorial existence —*N. Y. Times*⟩ **2 :** belonging to the peripheral unimportant activities of life **:** INSIGNIFICANT ⟨marriage degenerated into a *hole-and-corner* existence in which spirit and intellect played no part —Olive Arden⟩ ⟨a *hole-and-corner* life in some obscure community —H.G.Wells⟩

**hole board** *n* **:** COMBER BOARD

**hole card** *n* **1 :** a card in stud poker that is properly dealt facedown and that the holder need not expose before the showdown — called also *down card* **2 :** a possession, action, or power that carries often unexpected weight in negotiations or other relationships and that is held in reserve or used as its most strategic advantage

**ho·lec·ty·pi·na** \hō,lektəˈpīnə\ *n pl, cap* [NL, fr. *Holectypus*, genus of sea urchins (fr. *hol-* + Gk *ektypos* worked in relief) + *-ina*] **:** a suborder of extinct sea urchins (order Exocycloida) having a central peristome, an excentric periproct, an Aristotle's lantern, and nonpetaloid ambulacra and found in Jurassic, Cretaceous, and Eocene strata

**¹ho·lec·ty·poid** \hōˈlektə,pȯid\ *adj* [NL *Holectypoida*] **:** of or relating to the Holectypina

**²holectypoid** \"\ *n* -s [NL *Holectypoida*] **:** a sea urchin of the suborder Holectypina

**ho·lec·ty·poi·da** \hō,lektəˈpȯidə\ [NL, fr. *Holectypus* + *-oida*] *syn of* HOLECTYPINA

**hole–high** \ˈ=ˈ=\ *adj* **:** stopping or resting on a line that is roughly even with the hole one is playing toward — used of an approach shot in golf

**hole in** *vi* **:** to take refuge or lodging **:** put up for the night ⟨stopped traveling and *holed in* at a motel⟩

**hole in one :** ¹ACE 4

**hole–in–the–wall** \ˈ===ˌ=\ *n, pl* **holes–in–the–wall :** a small and insignificant place esp. difficult to locate ⟨in the jewelry business and ran a *hole-in-the-wall* you could barely squeeze into⟩ ⟨a *hole-in-the-wall* patent-medicine manufacturer⟩

**hole·less** \ˈhōlləs\ *adj* [*hole* + *-less*] **:** having no hole or aperture

**hole out** *vt* **1 :** to play (the ball) into the cup in a game of golf **2 :** to complete a hole in golf for ⟨his second putt *holed* him *out* for a six⟩ ~ *vi* **1 :** to play one's ball into the cup in a game of golf

**holeproof** \ˈ=,=\ *adj* **1 a :** designed to be proof against holes worn in by ordinary use ⟨~ stockings⟩ **b :** having no flaws or weak points ⟨the evidence against the prisoner was ~⟩ **2 :** designed to prevent evasion or subversion — used of a law, statute, provision, or system ⟨asked them to formulate laws that were ~ and would stop graft and corruption in the city⟩

**hol·er** \ˈhōlə(r)\ *n* -s [²*hole* + *-er*] **1 :** one that digs or fashions holes **2 :** one that has a specified number of holes — used in combinations ⟨the golf course was only a nine-*holer*⟩ ⟨the outhouse was a two-*holer*⟩

**holes** *pl of* HOLE, *pres 3d sing of* HOLE

**hole saw** *n* **:** CROWN SAW

**hole through** *vi* **:** to connect two underground tunnels by removing the rock that divides them

**hole up** *vi* **1 :** to take refuge or shelter in a hole or cave or as if in one **:** seek protection ⟨gone upstate to where her people were . . . figured on *holing up* with them for a while until she got over being afraid —R.F.Mirvish⟩ ⟨*holed up* in caves until they were blasted out by tommy gun and dynamite —*Newsweek*⟩ **2 :** to go into hiding ⟨breaks jail and *holes up* in an isolated turkey ranch —*Newsweek*⟩ ⟨badmen who *holed up* in badlands where others dared not venture —*Ford Times*⟩ ~ *vt* **1 a :** to place in or as if in a refuge, a shelter, or a hiding place ⟨during the wartime absence of her husband . . . she was *holed up* with two small sons on a farm —*New Yorker*⟩ **b :** IMPRISON ⟨the gunman *holed* them *up* in the house for two days⟩ **2 :** to hold up or delay esp. for a long time ⟨housing legislation is *holed up* in a Senate committee —*Time*⟩

**holey** \ˈhōlē, -li\ *adj* [ME *holly*, fr. *hole*, *hol* hole + *-y*] **:** having a hole or being full of holes ⟨wearing a ~ bathing suit —*Time*⟩

**holey dollar** *n* **:** a Spanish piece of eight or dollar having a round hole in its center, bearing the denomination 5 shillings, and current in Australia 1813–29 — called also *colonial dollar, pierced dollar, ring dollar*

**hol·ger niel·sen method** \ˈhōlgə(r)ˈnēlsən-\ *n, usu cap H&N* [after *Holger Nielsen* †1955 Dan. army officer who originated it] : BACK PRESSURE-ARM LIFT METHOD

**hol ha·mo·ed** *or* **chol ha·mo·ed** \ˌkōlhäˈmōəd\ *n pl, sometimes cap* [Heb *ḥol ha-moed*, lit., the secular portion of the festival] : the four intermediate semiholidays between the first two and last two full festival days of Passover; *also* : the five intermediate days between the first two and last two days of Sukkoth

**ho·li** \ˈhōlē\ *n -s usu cap* [Hindi *holī*, fr. Skt *holikā*] : a Hindu spring festival characterized by boisterous and usu. ribald revelry including esp. the throwing of colored water and powder

**ho·lia** \ˈhōlēə\ *n -s* [origin unknown] : HUMPBACK SALMON

**¹hol·i·day** \ˈhäləˌdā, *chiefly Brit* -ˌdi\ *n -s* [ME, fr. OE *hāligdæg*, fr. *hālig* holy + *dæg* day — more at HOLY, DAY] **1** : HOLY DAY **2 a** : a day on which one is exempt from one's usual labor or vocational activity ⟨had a ~ on the day the boss's daughter was married⟩ **b** : a time of release from work : FESTIVITY, CELEBRATION — usu. used in the phrase *to make holiday* ⟨the people who are making ~ flock to the beaches⟩ **c** *chiefly Brit* : VACATION ⟨everybody is on ~ in August —Joy Packer⟩ ⟨went on ~ for two weeks⟩ — often used in pl. with *the* ⟨worried about how to keep the child occupied for the ~*s*⟩ **d** : a period of exemption (as from a tax or from fear) ⟨tax ~*s* up to ten years —J.P.McEvoy⟩ ⟨gave myself a ~ from sad forebodings —Mary B. Chesnut⟩ : a period of relief ⟨a ~ from periodical literature —Aldous Huxley⟩ **3 a** : a day marked by a general cessation from work as an act of public commemoration of some event and often accompanied by public ceremonies and parades — see LEGAL HOLIDAY, NATIONAL HOLIDAY **b** : a good time : a festive occasion ⟨massacring soldiers to make a despot's ~ —H.R.G.Greaves⟩ **4** : a spot accidentally left uncovered on a coated or painted surface

**²holiday** \ˈ"\ *adj* : of, belonging to, or befitting a holiday : FESTIVE, CAREFREE ⟨~ reading⟩ ⟨wearing ~ clothes⟩ ⟨a face with a ~ look⟩ ⟨~ atmosphere on the excursion boat⟩

**³holiday** \ˈ"\ *vi* : to take or spend a holiday esp. in a journey or at a resort ⟨~*ing* in the country⟩

**holiday disease** *n* [so called fr. its frequent occurrence after holidays as a result of overexertion] : azoturia of horses

**hol·i·day·er** \ˈhäləˌdāə(r)\ *n -s* [³*holiday* + *-er*] : one on a holiday : VACATIONER ⟨~*s* who want to lead the fairly simple life for their all too short two-week break —Marvin Schwartz⟩

**holiday flag** *n* : the largest size of the national flag flown (as at U.S. Navy shore installations and Marine Corps posts) on national holidays and special occasions — compare GARRISON FLAG

**holidaymaker** \ˈ==(ˌ)=ˌ==\ *n* : HOLIDAYER ⟨boatloads of ~*s* —*Nat'l Geographic*⟩

**hol·i·days** \ˈhäləˌdāz\ *adv* : on holidays : on any holiday

**holier** *comparative of* HOLY

**¹holier-than-thou** \ˈ====ˌ=\ *adj* [compar. of ¹*holy*] : marked by an objectionable air of usu. pious superiority ⟨preserved always an infuriating *holier-than-thou* attitude toward his erring younger brother⟩ ⟨loudly prayed with a *holier-than-thou* expression on his face —G.W.Benson⟩

**²holier-than-thou** \ˈ"\ *n -s* : one that is holier-than-thou ⟨his success in self-reform turned him into a *holier-than-thou* before his less successful friends⟩

**holiest** *superlative of* HOLY

**ho·li·ly** \ˈhōləlē\ *adv* [ME, fr. *holy* + *-ly*] : in a holy manner : PIOUSLY

**¹ho·li·ness** \ˈhōlēnəs, -lin-\ *n -es* [ME *holynesse*, fr. OE *hālignes*, fr. *hālig* holy + *-nes* -ness — more at HOLY] **1** : the quality or state of being holy : SANCTITY, SAINTLINESS ⟨the ~ of the saints⟩ ⟨the ~ of the consecrated place⟩ — often used as a title for various high religious dignitaries ⟨His *Holiness* Pope Pius XII⟩ ⟨His *Holiness* the Dalai Lama⟩ **2** : a state of moral and spiritual perfection : complete sanctification : SINLESSNESS; *specif* : a state of sinlessness that according to some small religious groups is bestowed as a blessing on a Christian believer following conversion and is often a prerequisite of salvation

**²holiness** \ˈ"\ *adj, often cap* : emphasizing a perfectionist doctrine of holiness as a prerequisite of salvation ⟨the group was Arminian, Pentecostal, and *Holiness*⟩

**holiness body** *or* **holiness church** *n, often cap H* : one of numerous small religious groups in America emphasizing a perfectionist doctrine of holiness

**holing** *pres part of* HOLE

**holis** *pl of* HOLI

**hol·ish·kes** \ˈkälishkəz\ *n pl* [Yiddish] : stuffed cabbage

**ho·lism** \ˈhōˌlizəm\ *n -s* [*hol-* + *-ism*] **1** : the philosophic theory first formulated by Jan C. Smuts that the determining factors in nature are wholes (as organisms) which are irreducible to the sum of their parts and that the evolution of the universe is the record of the activity and making of these wholes **2** : a theory or doctrine according to which a whole cannot be analyzed without residue into the sum of its parts or reduced to discrete elements — compare GESTALT PSYCHOLOGY, ORGANICISM

**ho·list** \ˈhōləst\ *n -s* [*hol-* + *-ist*] : an advocate of holism or holistic principles ⟨a ~ who denied that the English state, for example, is a logical construction out of individual people, and who asserted that it is an organism which develops, and responds to challenges, according to holistic laws —J.W.N. Watkins⟩

**ho·lis·tic** \(ˈ)hōˈlistik\ *adj* **1** : of, relating to, or based on holism **2 a** : in accordance with a theory of holism or conceptions advocated by holism ⟨the ~ strain in his thinking⟩ **b** : emphasizing the organic or functional relation between parts and wholes ⟨a ~ rather than an atomistic approach to the study of culture⟩ — **ho·lis·ti·cal·ly** \-tək(ə)lē\ *adv*

**holk** \ˈhōk\ *var of* ²HOWK

**¹holl** \ˈhäl\ *adj* [ME, fr. OE *hol* — more at HOLE] *dial Eng* : HOLLOW

**²holl** \ˈ"\ *n -s* [ME, fr. OE *hol*, fr. neut. of *hol*, adj., hollow] : a hollow place: as **a** : *dial Eng* : DITCH **b** *obs* : a ship's hold

**¹hol·land** \ˈhälənd\ *n -s often cap* [ME *holand*, fr. *Holand*, county in the Netherlands, fr. MD *Holland*] **1 a** : a linen shirting of former times made in the Netherlands **b** : a cotton or linen fabric in plain weave usu. heavily sized or glazed and used for window shades, bookbinding, clothing **2** : a smooth glazed or unglazed finish for cotton fabrics to make them opaque or semiopaque **3** : ²DUTCH 1b

**²holland** \ˈ"\ *adj, usu cap* [fr. *Holland* the Netherlands, kingdom in northwestern Europe] **1** : NETHERLANDS **2** : of or belonging to a landholding company organized in Holland about 1791 to sell land in western New York state to settlers ⟨*Holland* purchase⟩

**hol·lan·daise** \ˌhälənˈdāz\ *n -s* : GOULASH 2a

**hollandaise sauce** *also* **hollandaise** *n -s* [part trans. of F *sauce hollandaise*, lit., Dutch sauce, fr. *sauce* + *hollandaise*, fem. of *hollandais* Dutch, fr. *Hollande* Holland, country in northwestern Europe] : sauce made of butter, yolks of eggs, and lemon juice or vinegar

**holland blue** *n, often cap H* : a dark blue that is redder and duller than Peking blue or Flemish blue and greener and less strong than Japan blue — called also *canton, orion*

**hol·land·er** \ˈhäləndə(r)\ *n -s* **1 cap a** : a native or inhabitant of the Netherlands **b** : a Dutch ship **2** *often cap* : DUTCH CLINKER **3** *often cap* [so called fr. its invention in the Netherlands] : a paper-pulp beater typically consisting of an iron roll set with steel blades and revolving in an oval tub

**holland gin** *n, usu cap H* : HOLLANDS

**hol·land·ite** \ˈhälənˌdīt\ *n -s* [Sir Thomas H. *Holland* †1947 Brit. geologist + E *-ite*] : a mineral $MnBaMn_6O_{14}$ consisting of a crystallized manganate of barium and manganese from central India

**hol·lands** \ˈhälən(d)z\ *n, usu cap* [modif. of D *hollandsch* Dutch, fr. *hollandsch genever* Dutch gin] : gin made in the Netherlands

**hol·lan·tide** \ˈhälənˌtīd\ *n, usu cap* [by shortening & alter.] *dial Eng* : ALLHALLOWTIDE

**¹hol·ler** \ˈhälə(r)\ *vb* **hollered; hollered; hollering** \-l(ə)riŋ\ **hollers** [alter. of ²*hollo*] *vi* **1** *chiefly dial, of a bird or animal* : to utter its characteristic cry or call ⟨spring frogs were ~*ing* in the marsh last night⟩ **2 a** : to make a loud noise ⟨the children were seeing who could ~ the loudest⟩ **b** : to shout or cry out to attract attention or summon someone ⟨~ for help⟩ or in pain or fear ⟨heard his brothers ~*ing* as they were killed —G.F.Weisel⟩ or in enthusiasm or exuberance ⟨baseball fans ~*ing* for the team⟩ **3** : GRIPE, COMPLAIN, GRUMBLE ⟨people will always ~ about an increase in taxes⟩ ~ *vt* **1 a** : to express by hollering ⟨~ encouragement⟩ **b** : to call out (a word or phrase) ⟨~ uncle⟩ ⟨~ bloody murder⟩ **2** *chiefly dial* : to call or summon by hollering — often used with *out* ⟨wake up first in the morning and ~ out the ranch hands⟩

**²holler** \ˈ"\ *n -s* **1** : a shout or outcry esp. of joy or exuberance ⟨with a whoop and a ~ the winners left⟩ or to attract attention or summon aid **2** : GRIPE, COMPLAINT ⟨the new law brought a ~ from the minority⟩ **3** : an American Negro work song freely improvised usu. in terms of the particular occupation of the moment and often without words ⟨cornfield ~⟩ — compare JUBILEE 8

**³holler** \ˈ"\ *chiefly dial var of* HOLLOW

**holler guy** *n, slang* : a member of a team who unofficially but effectively assumes responsibility for the success of the team during a game by the direction of play or by constant encouraging chatter

**hollering** *adj* [fr. pres. part. of ¹*holler*] : marked by or as if by shouting ⟨~ headlines . . . were always about murder of one sort or another —William Saroyan⟩

**hollering distance** *n, dial* : HAILING DISTANCE

**hol·ler·ith machine** \ˈhälərəth-\ *also* **hollerith** *n -s usu cap H* [after Herman *Hollerith*, 19th cent. inventor] : a machine for tabulating and sorting punched cards and tabulating data from them

**hollies** *pl of* HOLLY

**hol·lin** *or* **hol·len** \ˈhälən\ *n -s* [ME *holen, holyn*, fr. OE *holen, holegn* — more at HOLLY] *dial Brit* : HOLLY

**¹hol·lo** \ˈhä(ˌ)lō, häˈlō, həˈlō\ *or* **hol·la** \ˈhälə; häˈlä, həˈl-, -ˈlȧ\ *or* **hol·loo** \ˈhä(ˌ)lü, häˈlü, həˈlü\ *also* **hol·loa** \ˈhä(ˌ)lō, häˈlō, həˈlō\ *interj* [origin unknown] **1** — used to attract attention **2** — used as a call of encouragement or jubilation

**²hollo** \ˈ"\ *or* **holla** \ˈ"\ *or* **holloo** \ˈ"\ *also* **holloa** \ˈ"\ *vb* -ED/-ING/-ES *vi* : to cry hollo : call out : HOLLER ~ *vt* **1 a** : to call or cry hollo to : attract the attention of **b** : to call encouragement to **2** : to utter loudly : HOLLER ⟨that reeling man . . . ~*ing* bawdy inanities —C.C.Morrison⟩

**³hollo** \ˈ"\ *or* **holla** \ˈ"\ *or* **holloo** \ˈ"\ *also* **holloa** \ˈ"\ *n, pl* **hollos** *or* **holloes** *or* **hollas** *or* **holloos** *also* **holloas** : an exclamation or call of hollo ⟨listening to the ~*s* of the fox hunters⟩ : HOLLOING, SHOUTING, HOLLER

**hol·long** \ˈhäˌlȯŋ\ *n -s* [Assamese *holoṅ* large] : an East Indian timber tree (*Dipterocarpus pilosus*) having resinous decay-resistant wood

**¹hol·low** \ˈhä(ˌ)lō, -lə *often* -ləw+V\ *adj, often* -ER/-EST [ME *holwe, holg, holh*, fr. *holg, holh* hole, den, fr. OE *holh* hole, hollow — more at HOLE] **1 a** : constituting a depression or a low or excavated place ⟨a ~ spot in the road⟩ ⟨the force of the meteor's fall made a ~ place in the open plain⟩ : curved or rounded inward : CONCAVE ⟨the dish was covered by a ~ piece of metal⟩ : SUNKEN ⟨~ temples⟩ **b** : marked by hollows or sunken areas ⟨his face became gaunter and more ~ with each passing year⟩ **c** *of the sea* : having deep-troughed waves **d** : having a concave face or surface — used of various tools esp. when designed for curved work ⟨~ adz⟩ ⟨~ auger⟩ ⟨~ punch⟩ **2 a** (1) : having an empty space or cavity within : not solid ⟨a ~ tree⟩ ⟨~ sphere⟩ (2) *of a two-dimensional figure* : being in outline only : not filled in : consisting partly of unfilled spaces ⟨~ letters⟩ **b** : EMPTY ⟨a ~ walnut⟩ ⟨a ~ feeling in the stomach⟩ **c** (1) : devoid of worth, value, significance, or substance ⟨a ~ victory⟩ ⟨a ~ gain⟩ ⟨the whole celebration seems strangely ~ and unreal —W.F.Hambly⟩ ⟨the ~ position taken by the opposition⟩ : lacking in qualities that give substance, worth, or moral or intellectual solidity ⟨men of social significance but essentially ~⟩ (2) : devoid of any significant ideas, principles, or purposes ⟨we are the ~ men —T.S.Eliot⟩ ⟨a ~ generation of youths⟩ **d** : having hollow spaces in the interior; *esp* : having a net area less than 75 percent of the gross area — used of a masonry unit (as a brick or building tile) **3 a** : sounding or reverberating like a sound made in a cave or large empty enclosure : muffled and sepulchral : breathy and lacking in overtones : producing confused echoes ⟨the car in the empty garage started with a ~ roar⟩ ⟨the ~ echo of the monkeys' call —M.P.O'Connor⟩ ⟨the ~ subdued sound of the wind outside —Robert Murphy⟩ **b** : making or being a sound of or as if of beating on a hollow enclosure ⟨the ~ drumming of horses' hooves on the bridge⟩ **4** : marked by insincerity or lack of good faith ⟨a ~ greeting to an enemy⟩ ⟨a ~ promise⟩ : FALSE, DECEITFUL, TREACHEROUS ⟨a ~ heart⟩ ⟨a ~ truce⟩ ⟨talk about war aims sounded ~ to them —F.L. Allen⟩ **5** : COMPLETE, THOROUGH **syn** see VAIN

**²hollow** \ˈ"\ *vb* -ED/-ING/-S [ME *holwen*, fr. *holwe*, adj.] *vt* **1 a** : to make hollow : form an indentation or concavity in — usu. used with *out* ⟨~ out half of a coconut shell⟩ ⟨~*ed* a place out in the cliffside where he could hide⟩ **b** : to make concave or cause to be curved or rounded inward ⟨the can cover must be cut in two, and each half so ~*ed* as to fit around the pipe —Emily Holt⟩ ⟨the short double woolly scarf which you could ~ into a cap —Fred Majdalany⟩ **c** (1) : to gouge, dig, or scrape the inside out of — usu. used with *out* ⟨~*ed* out a stump and filled it with concrete⟩ (2) : GUT — often used with *out* ⟨dozens of dead cities, their insides ~*ed* out by dynamite and fire —Norman Cousins⟩ **2** : to form by hollowing something out ⟨rain barrels ~*ed* out from trees —Robert Shaplen⟩ : EXCAVATE — usu. used with *out* ⟨engineers ~*ed* out a tunnel through the mountain⟩ ~ *vi* : to become hollow ⟨her cheeks ~*ed* suddenly as she sucked in her breath⟩

**³hollow** \ˈ"\ *n -s* [¹*hollow*] **1 a** : a low spot surrounded by elevations : a depressed or low part of a surface : CONCAVITY, CHANNEL, BASIN ⟨driving down through the ~ in the road⟩ ⟨the ~ of the hand⟩; *esp* : a small valley : RAVINE, NOTCH, DINGLE **2 a** : an unfilled space within anything : CAVITY, HOLE ⟨in the ~ of a tree⟩ **b** : an area marked by such a space or cavity ⟨the horse buses rumble by, dropping a note as their hooves strike the ~ of the bridge —*Times Lit. Supp.*⟩ ⟨pounding on the ~ of the wall⟩

**⁴hollow** \ˈ"\ *adv* [¹*hollow*] : HOLLOWLY ⟨the attacks on him rang ~ because he had proved his honesty and integrity⟩

**holloware** \ˈ=(ˌ)=ˌ=\ *n* [by alter.] : HOLLOW WARE

**hollow back** *n* : a book back in which the backs of the sections are affixed to the backbone of the cover only at the joints, the separation sometimes being made by a flattened tubular lining of paper or cloth; *also* : a book so bound or a style of binding featuring this construction — called also *open back, spring back;* compare TIGHT BACKBONE; see SPINE illustration

**hollow cabochon** *n* : a cabochon with a concave back

**hollow charge** *n* : an explosive which concentrates its force in one direction (as in a projectile designed to blow a hole through armor plate)

**hollow-cut** \ˈ=(ˌ)=ˈ=\ *adj* : made with a pile cut in graduated lengths for a corded effect — used of normally even-pile fabrics (as velveteen)

**hollow-faced bat** \ˈ=(ˌ)=ˌ=-\ *n* : any of various Asiatic or African bats (genus *Nycteris*) with a basin-shaped depression in the front of the skull that is margined by fleshy foliate outgrowths

**hollow-ground** \ˈ=(ˌ)=ˈ=\ *adj* : ground so as to have a concave surface behind the cutting edge ⟨a *hollow-ground* razor⟩ ⟨a *hollow-ground* blade of a skate⟩

**hollow handle** *n* : a haft of a piece of silver flatware molded of two hollow halves soldered together and fastened to the shank of the object (as a knife or a serving fork or spoon)

**hollow heart** *n* : an abnormal condition of potato tubers which is usu. the result of rapid and uneven growth and in which the central tissue ruptures and leaves a cavity

**hollow horn** *n* : debility in cattle popularly attributed to the hollowness of their horns

**hollow-horned** \ˈ=(ˌ)=ˈ=\ *adj* **1** : having permanent horns with a bony core into which the frontal sinuses often extend to form air spaces (as in cattle, sheep, goats, and true antelopes) **2** *of lumber* : HONEYCOMBED

**hollow-horning** \ˈ=(ˌ)=ˈ==\ *n, of lumber* : HONEYCOMBING

**hollow leg** *n, slang* : an unusual capacity for alcoholic drinks

**hol·low·ly** *adv* : in a hollow manner ⟨the sound echoed ~ in the cave⟩

**hollow mill** *n* : a milling cutter with three or more cutting edges enclosing and revolving around the cylindrical workpiece

**hol·low·ness** *n -es* [ME *holownesse*, fr. *holwe, holowe* hollow + *-nesse* -ness] : the quality or state of being hollow ⟨testing the wall for ~ by tapping on it lightly⟩ ⟨the ~ and trickery of these appeals —F.D.Roosevelt⟩ ⟨the ~, the sham, the silliness of the empty pageant —Oscar Wilde⟩

**hollow newel** *n* : an opening in the center of a winding staircase in place of a newel-post, the stairs being supported each step by those below, and all held in place by the wall — called also *open newel;* distinguished from *solid newel*

**hollow newel stair** *n* : OPEN-NEWEL STAIR

**hollow organ** *n* : any visceral organ that has the form of a hollow tube or pouch (as the stomach or intestine) or that includes a cavity which subserves a vital function (as the heart or bladder)

**hollow square** *n* : a formation of troops in former military tactics in the shape of a square with the sides each usu. consisting of several ranks of soldiers and the middle holding the officers and the colors

**hollow stalk** *or* **hollow stem** *n* : any plant disease characterized by degeneration or decay of the pith of the stalk (as of tobacco caused by *Erwinia aroideae* or of cauliflower caused by boron deficiency)

**hollow tail** *n* : WOLF-IN-THE-TAIL

**hollow wall** *n* : CAVITY WALL

**hollow ware** *n* : articles (as of pottery, glass, or metal) that have volume and significant depth ⟨cups, bowls, and pots are typical *hollow ware*⟩ — distinguished from *flatware*

**holls** *pl of* HOLL

**hol·lus·chick** \ˈhäləsˌchik\ *n, pl* **holluschick·ie** \-kē\ [modif. of Russ *kholostyak* bachelor] : a young male fur seal

**hol·ly** \ˈhälē, -li\ *n -es often attrib* [ME, fr. OE *holegn, holen;* akin to OHG *hulis* holly, ON *hulfr*, MIr *cuilenn*] **1 a** : a tree or shrub of the genus *Ilex* (as English holly or American holly) — see CHINESE HOLLY, INKBERRY 1; compare MATÉ **b** : the foliage or branches of this tree or shrub used for esp. Christmas decoration **2** : a tree whose leaves resemble those of holly (as *Prunus ilicifolia* and *Photinia arbutifolia* of California, members of the genus *Olearia* of New Zealand, or the holm oak) **3** : SEA HOLLY

European holly

**holly bay** *n* **1** : LOBLOLLY BAY **2** : EVERGREEN MAGNOLIA

**holly family** *n* : AQUIFOLIACEAE

**holly fern** *n* : any of certain ferns having fronds of a texture and glossy surface suggesting holly: as **a** : an evergreen fern (*Polystichum lonchitis*) of the north temperate zone **b** : a Californian fern (*Polystichum aculeatum*) that is often cultivated for ornament **c** : a tropical Old World fern (*Cyrtomium aculeatum*)

**hollygrape** \ˈ==ˌ=\ *n* : OREGON GRAPE

**holly green** *n* **1** : a dark yellowish green that is greener, stronger, and very slightly darker than average palm green, greener, lighter, and stronger than deep chrome green or average hunter green, and greener and deeper than golf green **2** : a moderate olive green that is yellower and paler than forest green and yellower, lighter, and stronger than cypress or Lincoln green

**hol·ly·hock** \ˈhälēˌhäk, -li-, -ˌhȯk\ *n -s* [ME *holihoc*, fr. *holi, holy* holy + *hoc* hock (mallow)] **1** : a tall perennial Chinese herb (*Althaea rosea*) cultivated in gardens as a biennial with large coarse rounded leaves and showy flowers in a large terminal spike **2** : a deep purplish red that is bluer and deeper than Harvard crimson (sense 2) or American beauty and redder and duller than magenta (sense 2a)

**hollyhock delphinium** *n* : any of various cultivated larkspurs with narrow flower clusters forming spires

**hollyhock tree** *n* : an Australian shrub (*Hibiscus splendens*) with showy rose-colored flowers

**holly laurel** *n* : ISLAY

**holly leaf miner** *n* : a small black fly (*Phytomyza ilicis*) having a yellowish larva that tunnels in the leaves of various hollies

**holly–leaved barberry** \ˈ=ˌ=ˌ=-\ *or* **hollyleaf barberry** \ˈ==-ˌ=ˌ=-\ *n* : OREGON GRAPE

**holly–leaved cherry** *or* **hollyleaf cherry** *n* : ISLAY

**holly oak** *n* : an oak (as the holm oak) with leaves like holly

**holly rose** *n* : a West Indian shrub (*Turnera ulmifolia*) with showy yellow flowers

**¹hol·ly·wood** \ˈhälēˌwu̇d, -li-\ *n, usu cap* [fr. *Hollywood*, district in the city of Los Angeles, California] **1 a** : the American motion-picture industry ⟨a lawyer speaking for *Hollywood* before an investigating committee⟩ **b** : a place constituting a center for a motion-picture industry ⟨there are many *Hollywoods* besides the one in California —*N.Y. Times*⟩ **2** : something produced by or befitting the American motion-picture industry or its productions ⟨pure *Hollywood* —Will Irwin & T.M.Johnson⟩

**²hollywood** \ˈ"\ *adj, usu cap* **1** : of or from Hollywood, a district of Los Angeles, Calif. : of the kind or style prevalent in Hollywood ⟨a *Hollywood* fashion⟩ **2** : of, relating to, produced by, or characteristic of the American motion-picture industry esp. as centered in Los Angeles, Calif., and vicinity ⟨a *Hollywood* film technique⟩

**hollywood bed** *n, usu cap H* **1** : a bed consisting of a mattress on a box spring supported by 4 or 6 low legs and sometimes having an upholstered headboard separately fastened to a wall **2** : any bed on a low frame and without a footboard, corner posts, and sometimes a headboard

Hollywood bed

**hollywood gin** *or* **hollywood** *n, usu cap H* [so called fr. its introduction by the motion-picture colony in Hollywood] : a method of scoring in gin rummy whereby each deal is scored as though part of three different games

**¹hol·ly·wood·ian** \ˌhälēˈwu̇dēən, -liˈ-\ *n -s cap* : a native or resident of Hollywood, Calif.; *also* : a person employed in the Hollywood motion-picture industry

**²hollywoodian** \ˈ=ˈ===\ *adj, cap* : of or befitting Hollywood or Hollywoodians

**hol·ly·wood·ish** \ˈhälēˌwu̇dish\ *adj, usu cap* : HOLLYWOODIAN ⟨*Hollywoodish* klieg lights and grinding cameras —*Newsweek*⟩ ⟨a *Hollywoodish* sort of bombast —Moses Smith⟩

**hol·ly·wood·ite** \ˈ==ˌwu̇ˌdīt\ *n -s cap* : HOLLYWOODIAN

**hol·ly·wood·ize** \-ˌdīz\ *vt* -ED/-ING/-S *often cap* : to make (as an author or his writings) conform to standards set up by the American motion-picture industry ⟨does not believe that the author can be completely *Hollywoodized* —A.A.VanDuym⟩

**hollywood palm** *n, usu cap H* : a glabrous perennial (*Kalanchoe verticillata*) of southern Africa that is used as an ornamental pot plant and that has long linear leaves mottled with violet brown and terminal clusters of salmon to scarlet flowers

**hol·ly·woody** \-ˌu̇dē\ *adj, usu cap* : characterized by the less desirable qualities attributed to motion pictures as produced by Hollywood ⟨the story was called thick and *Hollywoody* —Janet Flanner⟩

**¹holm** *or* **holme** \ˈhōm *also* -ōlm\ *n -s* [ME, fr. OE *holm*, fr. ON *hōlmr* small island; akin to OE *holm* sea, OS *holm* hill, OE *hyll* hill — more at HILL] **1** *Brit* : a small island in a river or lake or near the mainland — often used in place names **2** *chiefly Brit* : flat land near a river : BOTTOMS

**²holm** \ˈ"\ *n -s* [ME, alter. of *holen* holly, fr. OE — more at HOLLY] : HOLM OAK

**holm·berry** \ˈ=- — *see* BERRY\ *n* [²*holm* + *berry*] : the berry of the butcher's-broom

**holmes·ian** \ˈhōmzēən *also* -ōlm-\ *adj* [Sherlock *Holmes*, a detective in stories by Sir Arthur Conan Doyle †1930 Brit. writer + E *-ian*] *usu cap* : of, belonging to or suggesting the detective Sherlock Holmes

**holmes light** \ˈhōmz- *also* -ōlmz-\ *or* **holmes signal** *n, usu cap H* [prob. fr. the name *Holmes*] : a signaling device that consists of a case containing impure calcium phosphide and a float and that when thrown into water generates hydrogen phosphides that take fire spontaneously

**holm·gang** \'hō(l)m,gaŋ\ *n* [ON *hōlmganga*, fr. *hōlmr* small island + *ganga* act of going; akin to OE *gang* act of going — more at GANG] *archaic* **:** a duel esp. on an island

**holm·gren yarn test** \'hōm|grən, -,gren- *also* -ōlm|\ *also* **holm·gren test** *n, usu cap H* [after Alarik Frithiof *Holmgren* †1897 Swed. physiologist] **:** a method of testing color vision by the use of colored wool yarns

**holmi·um** \'hō(l)mēəm\ *n* -s [NL, fr. *Holmia* (latinized form of *Stockholm*, Sweden) + NL *-ium*; fr. the locality near which minerals rich in yttrium are found] **:** a trivalent metallic element of the rare-earth group that occurs with yttrium (as in gadolinite) and that forms cream-colored or yellow compounds and is among the most highly magnetic known — symbol *Ho*; see ELEMENT table

**holm oak** *n* [²*holm*] **1 :** an evergreen oak (*Quercus ilex*) of southern Europe with leaves resembling those of holly **2 :** the hard wood of the holm oak

**holm·quist·ite** \'hōm,kwi,stīt *also* -ōlm-\ *n* -s *usu cap* [Sw *hölmquistit*, fr. Per Johan *Hölmquist*, Swed. scientist + Sw *-it* -ite] **:** a mineral $(Na,K,Ca)Li(Mg,Fe)_3Al_2Si_8O_{22}(OH)_2$ consisting of an alkali and a silicate of iron, magnesium, lithium, and aluminum and related to hornblende

**holm tree** *n* [ME *holme tre*, fr. ²*holm* + *tree*] **:** HOLM OAK

**holo-** — see HOL-

**holo·axial** \¦hälō, ¦hōlō+\ *adj* [*hol-* + *axial*] *of a crystal system* **:** having all the axes of symmetry possible

**holo·baptist** \"+\ *n* [*hol-* + *Baptist*] **:** IMMERSIONIST

**holo·basidium** \"+\ *n* [NL, fr. *hol-* + *basidium*] *syn of* AUTOBASIDIUM

**holo·benthic** \"+\ *adj* [*hol-* + *benthic*] **:** inhabiting the deep sea during all stages of life

**hol·o·blas·tic** \¦hälō¦blastik, ¦hōl-\ *adj* [ISV *hol-* + *-blastic*] *of an egg* **:** undergoing complete cleavage as a result of the absence of an impeding mass of yolk material **:** having cleavage planes that divide the whole egg into distinct and separate though coherent blastomeres — opposed to *meroblastic* — **hol·o·blas·ti·cal·ly** \-tək(ə)lē\ *adv*

**hol·o·branch** \'hälə,braŋk, 'hōl-\ *n* -s [ISV *hol-* + *-branch*] **:** a fish gill in which the branchial arch has two rows of lamellae or filaments — compare HEMIBRANCH 2

**hol·o·car·pic** \¦hälō¦kärpik, ¦hōl-\ *adj* [*hol-* + *-carpic*] **1 :** having the whole thallus developed into a fruiting body or sporangium ⟨~ algae⟩ ⟨~ fungi⟩ **2 :** lacking rhizoids and haustoria — compare EUCARPIC

**hol·o·car·pous** \-pəs\ *adj* [*hol-* + *-carpous*] **:** HOLOCARPIC 1

**holo·caust** \'hälə,kȯst, 'hōl- *also* 'hȯl- *or* |,käst *sometimes* -lē| *or* -lil *or* |,kəst\ *n* -s [ME, fr. OF *holocauste*, fr. LL *holocaustum*, fr. Gk *holokauston*, neut. of *holokaustos* burnt whole, fr. *hol-* + *kaustos* burnt, fr. *kaiein* to burn — more at CAUSTIC] **1 :** a burnt sacrifice **:** a sacrificial offering wholly consumed by fire **2 :** a complete or thorough sacrifice or destruction esp. by fire ⟨burned all his books and paper in a giant ~⟩ ⟨thousands of enemy troops consumed in the ~ —Upton Sinclair⟩ ⟨an atomic global ~ —J.B.Conant⟩ — **holo·caus·tic** \¦==¦kȯstik, -tēk *also* -¦käs-\ *adj*

**holo·cellulose** \¦hälō, ¦hōlō+\ *n* [ISV *hol-* + *cellulose*; orig. formed in G] **:** the total polysaccharide fraction of wood or straw and the like that is made up of cellulose and all of the hemicelluloses and that is obtained by removing the extractives and the lignin from the original natural material

**hol·o·cene** \'hälə,sēn, 'hōl-\ *adj, usu cap* [ISV *hol-* + *-cene*] **:** RECENT 3

**hol·o·cen·trid** \,hälō'sen·trəd, ,hōl-\ *n* -s [NL *Holocentridae*] **:** a fish of the family Holocentridae

**hol·o·cen·tri·dae** \-rə,dē\ *n pl, cap* [NL, fr. *Holocentrus*, type genus + *-idae*] **:** a family of tropical marine fishes closely related to and in old classifications included in the Berycidae

**hol·o·cen·trus** \-rəs\ *n, cap* [NL, fr. *hol-* + *-centrus* (fr. Gk *kentros* sharp point, fr. *kentein* to prick, goad) — more at CENTER] **:** the type genus of the family Holocentridae containing certain typical squirrelfishes

**hol·o·ceph·a·la** \,hälō'sefələ, ,hōl-\ [NL, fr. *hol-* + *-cephala*] *syn of* HOLOCEPHALI

¹**hol·o·ceph·a·lan** \¦==¦==lən\ *or* **hol·o·ce·pha·li·an** \¦hälōsə¦fālēən, ¦hōl-\ *adj* [NL *Holocephali* + E *-an* or *-ian*] **:** of or relating to the subclass Holocephali

²**holocephalan** \"\ *or* **holocephalian** \"\ *n* -s **:** a fish of the subclass Holocephali

**hol·o·ceph·a·li** \¦hälō¦sefə,lī, ¦hōl-\ *n pl, cap* [NL, fr. *hol-* + *-cephali*] **:** a subclass of Chondrichthyes that is sometimes made a separate class, includes the recent chimaeras and certain chiefly extinct related fishes some of which date from Devonian time, and is distinguished by a cartilaginous skeleton, gill clefts covered by a fold of skin, high compressed head with small narrow mouth and the dentition reduced to broad flat plates, and a body tapering off into a long tail — **hol·o·ceph·a·lous** \¦==¦sefələs\ *adj*

**hol·o·cho·a·nite** \¦hälō¦kōə,nīt, ¦hōl-\ *n* -s [NL *Holochoanites*, suborder of nautiloids in some classifications, fr. *hol-* + Gk *choanē* funnel (fr. *chein* to pour) + NL *-ites* -ite — more at FOUND] **:** a fossil nautiloid in which the funnels about the siphuncle extend from one septum to the next — **hol·o·cho·a·nit·ic** \¦==,==¦nid·ik\ *adj*

**ho·loch·ro·al** \hə'läkrəwəl\ *adj* [*hol-* + Gk *chrōs* skin, color + E *-al* — more at GRIT] **:** having compound eyes with the visual area covered by a continuous cornea — used esp. of certain trilobites

**hol·o·clas·tic** \¦hälō¦klastik, ¦hōl-\ *adj* [ISV *hol-* + *-clastic*] **:** being or belonging to ordinary sedimentary rocks as distinguished from tuffs or pyroclastic rocks

**hol·o·coe·not·ic** \¦hälōsē¦näd·ik, ¦hōl-\ *adj* [*hol-* + *coen-* + *-otic*] **:** acting in concert — used of the impact of a complex environment on living organisms

**hol·o·crine** \'hälə̇krən, 'hōl-, -ə,krīn\ *adj* [ISV *hol-* + *-crine* (fr. Gk *krinein* to separate, decide) — more at CERTAIN] **:** producing a secretion consisting of altered secretory cells; *also* **:** produced by a holocrine gland — compare MEROCRINE

**holo·crystalline** \¦hälō, ¦hōlō+\ *adj* [ISV *hol-* + *crystalline*] **:** completely crystalline **:** made up wholly of crystals or crystalline particles — used of a rock (as granite)

**hol·o·dac·tyl·ic** \¦hälō¦,dak¦tilik, ¦hōl-\ *adj* [MGk *holodaktylos* (fr. Gk *hol-* + *daktylos* dactyl) + E *-ic*] *of a hexameter* **:** having all the feet dactyls except the last

**hol·o·dis·cus** \¦hälō'diskəs, ¦hōl-\ *n, cap* [NL, fr. *hol-* + *-discus*] **:** a small genus of shrubs (family Rosaceae) of western No. America that resemble spirea and have flowers in a pendant pyramidal panicle and achenes enclosed in the calyx

**holo·enzyme** \¦hälō, ¦hōlō+\ *n* [ISV *hol-* + *enzyme*] **:** a complete active enzyme consisting of an apoenzyme combined with its coenzyme

**holo·gamete** \"+\ *n* [*hol-* + *gamete*] **:** a hologamous gamete

**ho·log·a·mous** \hə'lägəməs\ *adj* [*hol-* + *-gamous*] **1 :** having gametes of essentially the same size and structural features as vegetative cells — used of various flagellates, ciliates, diatoms, and desmids **2 :** having the entire thallus developing into a gametangium — used of thalloid plants, esp. fungi

**ho·log·a·my** \-mē\ *n* -ES [*hol-* + *-gamy*] **:** the condition of being hologamous

**hol·o·go·nia** \,hälə'gōnēə, ,hōl-\ *n pl, cap* [NL, fr. *hol-* + *-gonia* (fr. Gk *gonos* offspring, procreation, genitals) — more at GON-] *in some classifications* **:** an order of Nematoda comprising forms in which the germinal area extends the whole length of the gonad — compare TELOGONIA — **hol·o·gon·ic** \¦==¦gänik\ *adj*

**holo·gonidium** \¦hälō, ¦hōlō+\ *n* [NL, fr. *hol-* + *gonidium*] **:** SOREDIUM

¹**hol·o·graph** \'hälə,graf, 'hōl-\ *n* [LL *holographus* written entirely in one's own hand, fr. LGk *holographos*, fr. Gk *hol-* + *-graphos* written, writing (fr. *graphein* to write) — more at CARVE] **:** a document (as a letter, deed, or will) wholly in the handwriting of the person from whom it proceeds and whose act it purports to be

²**holograph** \"\ *or* **hol·o·graph·ic** \¦==¦grafik\ *or* **hol·o·graph·i·cal** \-fəkəl\ *adj* **:** being a holograph **:** written entirely in one's own hand

**holographic will** *n* **:** a testamentary instrument that is written entirely by the testator in his own handwriting and signed by him and that even if unattested is usu. recognized as a valid will in most jurisdictions

**holo·gynic** \¦hälō, ¦hōlō+\ *adj* [ISV *hol-* + *gynic*] **:** inherited solely in the female line, presumably through transmission as a recessive factor in the nonhomologous portion of the X chromosome — **ho·log·y·ny** \hə'läjənē\ *n* -ES

**hol·o·he·dral** \¦hälō¦hēdrəl, ¦hōl-\ *adj* [*hol-* + Gk *hedra* seat + E *-al* — more at SIT] *of a crystal* **:** having all the faces required by complete symmetry — compare HEMIHEDRAL, TETARTOHEDRAL — **hol·o·he·drism** \,==¦hē,drizəm\ *n* -s — **hol·o·he·dry** \-ēdrē\ *n* -ES

**hol·o·he·dron** \,==¦hēdrən\ *n, pl* **holohedrons** *or* **holohedra** [NL, fr. *hol-* + *-hedron*] **:** a holohedral crystal form

**holo·hemihedral** \¦hälō, ¦hōlō+\ *adj* [*hol-* + *hemihedral*] **:** belonging to, presenting, or being hemihedral crystal forms

**holo·hyaline** \"+\ *adj* [*hol-* + *hyaline*] *of a rock* **:** wholly glassy

**ho·lo·ku** \hō'lōkü\ *n* -s [Hawaiian *holokū*] **:** a woman's long one-piece gown usu. made with some fitting and a train and worn esp. in Hawaii

**holo·mastigote** \¦hälō, ¦hōlō+\ *adj* [*hol-* + *mastigote*] **:** having many flagella scattered evenly over the body

**holo·metabola** \"+\ *n pl, cap* [NL, fr. *hol-* + *Metabola*] *in some classifications* **:** a group comprising all insects that have complete metamorphosis

**holo·metabolic** \"+\ *adj* [*hol-* + *metabolic*] **:** HOLOMETABOLOUS

**holo·metabolism** \"+\ *n* [*hol-* + Gk *metabolē* change + E *-ism* — more at METABOLISM] *of an insect* **:** development with complete metamorphosis — distinguished from *heterometabolism*; compare AMETABOLISM — **holo·metabolous** \"+\ *adj*

**holo·metaboly** \"+\ *n* [ISV *hol-* + *metaboly*] **:** HOLOMETABOLISM

**hol·o·mic·tic** \¦hälō¦miktik, ¦hōl-\ *adj* [*hol-* + *-mictic* (fr. Gk *miktos* mixed; akin to Gk *misgein* to mix) — more at MIX] *of a lake* **:** undergoing a complete circulation that extends to the deepest parts during overturn

**hol·o·mor·pho·sis** \,hälō'mȯrfəsəs, ,hōl- *sometimes* -ō,mȯr'fōsəs\ *n, pl* **holomorpho·ses** \-,sēz\ [NL, fr. *hol-* + *-morphosis*] **:** the complete regeneration of a lost part

**hol·o·my·ar·i·an** \¦hälō(,)mī¦a(a)rēən, ¦hōl-\ *also* **hol·o·my·ar·i·al** \-ēəl\ *adj* [NL *Holomyaria*, division of nematode worms in some classifications (fr. *hol-* + *-myaria*) + E *-an* or *-al*] *of a nematode worm* **:** having the muscle layer continuous or divided into two longitudinal zones without true muscle cells

**holo·nephros** \¦hälō, ¦hōlō+\ *n* [NL, fr. *hol-* + *-nephros*] **:** a hypothetical generalized vertebrate kidney consisting of a single nephric tubule in each trunk segment of either side of the body

**holo·parasite** \"+\ *n* [ISV *hol-* + *parasite*; orig. formed as G *holoparasit*] **:** an obligate parasite — compare HEMIPARASITE — **holo·parasitic** \"+\ *adj*

**hol·o·pho·tal** \¦hälə¦fōd·əl, ¦hōl-\ *adj* [*hol-* + *phot-* + *-al*] **:** of or relating to a holophote; *esp* **:** reflecting the whole of the light from a light source in a given direction

**hol·o·phote** \'==,fōt\ *n* -s [back-formation fr. *holophotal*] **:** an optical apparatus for collecting and throwing in a desired direction by means of lenses or reflectors a large amount of the light from a source (as a lighthouse lamp)

**holo·phrase** \'halə,frāz, 'hōl-\ *n* [*hol-* + *phrase*] **:** a single word expressing a complex of ideas; *also* **:** HOLOPHRASIS

**ho·loph·ra·sis** \hə'läfrəsəs\ *n, pl* **holophra·ses** \-,sēz\ [*hol-* + Gk *phrasis* expression, phrase] **:** the expression of a complex of ideas by a single word; *also* **:** HOLOPHRASE

**hol·o·phrasm** \'hälə,frazəm, 'hōl-\ *n* -s [fr. *holophrastic*, after such pairs as E *spasm*: *spastic*] **:** HOLOPHRASE

**hol·o·phras·tic** \¦==¦frastik\ *adj* [ISV *hol-* + *-phrastic* (fr. Gk *phrastikos* expressive, fr. *phrazein* to express) — more at PHRASE] **:** of or relating to holophrasis **:** equivalent to a whole phrase **:** expressing a complex of ideas in a single word

**hol·o·phyt·ic** \¦hälō¦fid·ik, ¦hōl-\ *adj* [*hol-* + *-phytic*] **:** obtaining food after the manner of a green plant **:** PHOTOAUTOTROPHIC — opposed to *holozoic*; compare HEMIZOIC

**hol·o·plank·ton** \¦hälō¦plaŋktən, ,hōl-\ *n* [ISV *hol-* + *plankton*] **:** plankton composed of organisms that pass their whole life floating, drifting, or swimming weakly in the water — compare HEMIPLANKTON — **hol·o·plank·ton·ic** \¦==(,)plaŋk¦tänik\ *adj*

**hol·o·plast** \'hälō,plast, 'hōl-\ *n* -s [*hol-* + *-plast*] **:** paneling made of plastic-impregnated paper tubes with a variety of surfaces

**hol·op·neus·tic** \¦häləp¦n(y)üstik, ¦hōl-\ *adj* [ISV *hol-* + *-pneustic* (fr. Gk *pneustikos* of or for breathing, fr. — assumed — Gk *pneustos* — verbal of Gk *pnein* to breathe — + Gk *-ikos* -ic) — more at SNEEZE] **:** having all the spiracles or tracheal stigmata open — distinguished from *apneustic*; used of various insects

**hol·optic** \(')häl, (')hōl+\ *adj* [*hol-* + *optic*] *of a two-winged fly* **:** having the compound eyes contiguous in front — compare DICHOPTIC

¹**hol·op·tych·i·an** \¦häləp¦tikēən, ¦hōl-\ *adj* [NL *Holoptychius* + E *-an* (adj. suffix)] **:** ¹HOLOPTYCHIID

²**holoptychian** \"\ *n* -s [NL *Holoptychius* + E *-an* (n. suffix)] **:** ²HOLOPTYCHIID

¹**hol·op·tych·i·id** \-ēəd\ *adj* [NL *Holoptychiidae*] **:** of or relating to the Holoptychiidae

²**holoptychiid** \"\ *n* -s [NL *Holoptychiidae*] **:** a fish of the family Holoptychiidae

**hol·op·ty·chi·idae** \,häləptə'kīə,dē, ,hōl-\ *n pl, cap* [NL, fr. *Holoptychius*, type genus + *-idae*] **:** a family of Devonian fishes (order Rhipidistia) having unossified vertebrae, teeth of complicated structure, and the body covered with imbricating cycloid enameled scales

**hol·op·tych·i·us** \,==¦tikēəs\ *n, cap* [NL, fr. *hol-* + *-ptychius* (fr. Gk *ptych-, ptyx* fold) — more at PTYCH-] **:** the type genus of Holoptychiidae

**holo·rhinal** \¦hälō, ¦hōlō+\ *adj* [*hol-* + *rhinal*] *of a bird* **:** having the anterior border of the nasal bones not deeply cleft — opposed to *schizorhinal*

**holo·saprophyte** \"+\ *n* [ISV *hol-* + *saprophyte*; orig. formed in G] **:** a totally saprophytic organism **:** an obligate saprophyte — compare HEMISAPROPHYTE

**holo·sericeous** \"+\ *adj* [*hol-* + *sericeous*] **:** covered with silky hair **:** entirely sericeous

**hol·o·side** \'hälə,sīd, 'hōl-\ *n* -s [ISV *hol-* + *-oside*] **:** a glycoside that yields only glycoses on hydrolysis — compare HETEROSIDE

**holo·siderite** \¦hälō, ¦hōlō+\ *n* [ISV *hol-* + *siderite*] **:** meteoric iron or a meteorite consisting of metallic iron without stony matter

**holo·siphonate** \"+\ *adj* [*hol-* + *siphonate*] **:** having a completely tubular siphon — used of the Dibranchia

**hol·o·so·ma·ta** \,hälō'sōməd·ə, ,hōl-, -'säm-\ *n pl, cap* [NL, fr. *hol-* + Gk *-somata*] *in some classifications* **:** a division of ascidians comprising compound ascidians with zooids of which the bodies are not divided into regions and sometimes including the simple ascidians — **hol·o·som·a·tous** \¦==¦sämad·əs, -¦sōm-\ *adj*

**hol·o·spondaic** \¦hälō, ¦hōlō+\ *adj* [*hol-* + *spondaic*] **:** made up wholly of spondees

¹**ho·los·te·an** \hō'lästēən\ *or* **ho·los·te·ous** \-ēəs\ *adj* [NL *Holostei* + E *-an* or *-ous*] **:** of or relating to fishes of the order Holostei

²**holostean** \"\ *n* -s **:** a fish of the order Holostei

**ho·los·tei** \-ē,ī\ *n pl, cap* [NL, fr. *hol-* + *-ostei* (fr. Gk *osteon* bone) — more at OSSEOUS] *in many classifications* **:** an order of ganoid fishes having a well-developed bony skeleton and approaching teleosts in structure now usu. restricted to the gars (family *Lepisosteidae*) and various extinct genera (as *Lepidotes* and *Semionotus*) but sometimes extended to include the bowfin and related fishes or made a superorder including the teleosts — compare CYCLOGANOIDEI, GINGLYMODI

**holo·steric** \¦hälō, ¦hōlō+\ *adj* [ISV *hol-* + *steric*] **:** wholly solid — used of a barometer (as the aneroid) constructed without the use of liquids

**ho·los·te·um** \hə'lästēəm\ *n, cap* [NL, fr. Gk *holosteon*, a plant, fr. *hol-* + *osteon* bone] **:** a Eurasian genus of plants (family Caryophyllaceae) resembling chickweed and having the flowers in cymes like umbels — see JAGGED CHICKWEED

**hol·o·sto·ma·ta** \,hälō'stōməd·ə, ,hōl-, -tām-\ *n pl, cap* [NL, fr. *hol-* + *-stomata*] *in many classifications* **:** a suborder of Digenea coextensive with the family Strigeidae

**hol·o·stom·a·tous** \¦==¦stäməd·əs, -tōm-\ *adj* [*hol-* + *-stomatous*] **:** having the margin of the aperture entire and more or less circular ⟨~ gastropod shells⟩

**hol·o·stome** \'hälə,stōm, 'hōl-\ *adj or n* [NL *Holostomata*] **:** STRIGEID

**ho·los·to·mous** \hə'lästəməs\ *adj* [*hol-* + *-stomous*] **:** HOLOSTOMATOUS

**hol·o·sty·lic** \¦hälō¦stīlik, ¦hōl-\ *adj* [*hol-* + *-stylic*] **:** having the jaws connected directly with the cranium ⟨~ chimaeras⟩ — compare AUTOSTYLIC

**holo·symmetric** \¦hälō, ¦hōlō+\ *or* **holo·symmetrical** \"+\ *adj* [*hol-* + *symmetric, symmetrical*] **:** HOLOHEDRAL — **holo·symmetry** \"+\ *n*

**holo·systematic** \"+\ *adj* [*hol-* + *systematic*] **:** HOLOHEDRAL

**holo·systolic** \"+\ *adj* [ISV *hol-* + *systolic*] **:** relating to an entire systole

**holo·thecal** \"+\ *adj* [*hol-* + *thecal*] **:** BOOTED 2

**holo·thoracic** \"\ *adj* [*hol-* + *thorac-* + *-ic*] **:** having the three parts of the thorax closely united ⟨~ insects⟩ — compare SCHIZOTHORACIC

**hol·o·thu·ria** \,hälō'thu̇rēə, ,hōl-\ *n, cap* [NL, fr. L, a water polyp, fr. Gk *holothourion*] **1 :** a Linnaean genus containing various rather wormlike aquatic animals (as some gephyreans and holothurians) originally thought to be modified mollusks **2 :** a large cosmopolitan genus of holothurians that is the type of the family Holothuriidae and is characterized by the presence of scattered more or less papillate pedicels — compare TREPANG

**hol·o·thu·ri·ae** \-ē,ē\ [NL, fr. *Holothuria*] *syn of* HOLOTHURIOIDEA

¹**hol·o·thu·ri·an** \¦==¦thu̇rēən\ *adj* [NL *Holothuria* + E *-an*] **:** belonging to the Holothurioidea

²**holothurian** \"\ *n* -s **:** one of the Holothurioidea **:** SEA CUCUMBER

**hol·o·thu·rid·ea** \,hälōthə'ridēə, ,hōl-\ *or* **hol·o·thu·roi·da** \-'rȯidə\ [NL, fr. *Holothuria* + *-idea* or *-oida*] *syn of* HOLOTHURIOIDEA

**hol·o·thu·ri·idae** \-'rīə,dē\ *n pl, cap* [NL, fr. *Holothuria*, type genus + *-idae*] **:** a large cosmopolitan family (order Aspidochirota) of holothurians that includes all those of economic importance — see HOLOTHURIA

¹**hol·o·thu·ri·oid** \¦hälō¦thu̇rē,ȯid, ¦hōl-\ *adj* [NL *Holothurioidea*] **:** ¹HOLOTHURIAN

²**holothurioid** \"\ *n* [NL *Holothurioidea*] **:** ²HOLOTHURIAN

**hol·o·thu·ri·oi·dea** \,==,==¦ȯidēə\ *n pl, cap* [NL, fr. *Holothuria* + *-oidea*] **:** a class of echinoderms comprising the sea cucumbers and having a more or less elongate form usu. with well-marked bilateral symmetry and differentiated dorsal and ventral surfaces, a flexible but tough and muscular body with the skeleton reduced to scattered ossicles or spicules, a water-vascular system with radial ambulacral vessels and tube feet for creeping, respiratory trees, Cuvierian organs, and strong branched tentacles about the mouth — compare TREPANG

**hol·o·thu·roi·dea** \,hälōthə'rȯidēə, ,hōl-\ [NL, irreg. fr. *Holothuria* + *-oidea*] *syn of* HOLOTHURIOIDEA

**hol·o·trich** \'hälə,trik, 'hōl-\ *n* -s [NL *Holotricha*] **:** a protozoan of the order Holotricha

**ho·lot·ri·cha** \hə'lä·trəkə\ *n pl, cap* [NL, fr. *hol-* + *-tricha*] **:** a large order of uniformly ciliated euciliate protozoans without adoral zone, usu. with a cytostome, and with holozoic or saprozoic nutrition — **ho·lot·ri·chal** \-kəl\ *or* **ho·lot·ri·chous** \-kəs\ *adj* — **ho·lot·ri·chous·ly** *adv*

**hol·o·trich·i·da** \,hälō'trikədə, ,hōl-\ [NL, fr. *Holotricha* + *-ida*] *syn of* HOLOTRICHA

**holo·type** \'hälə,tīp, 'hōl-\ *n* [*hol-* + *type*] **1 :** the single specimen designated by an author as the type of a species or lesser taxon at the time of establishing a group — compare LECTOTYPE **2 :** the type of a species or lesser taxon designated at a date later than that of establishing a group or by another person than the author of the taxon — compare NEOTYPE — **holo·typ·ic** \¦==¦tipik\ *adj*

**hol·o·zo·ic** \¦hälō¦zōik, ¦hōl-\ *adj* [*hol-* + *-zoic*] **:** obtaining food after the manner of most animals by ingesting complex organic matter **:** HETEROTROPHIC — opposed to *holophytic*; compare HEMIZOIC

**holp** *now chiefly dial past of* HELP

**holped** *now chiefly dial past of* HELP

**holpen** *now chiefly dial past part of* HELP

**hols** *pl of* HOL

**hol·stein-friesian** \'hōlz,tēn, -l,st- *also* -tīn *or NewEng* 'hälə-(,)stēn\ *or* **holstein** *n* [fr. *Holstein*, region of NW Germany, its later locality + *Friesian*] **1** *usu cap H&F* **:** a breed of large dairy cattle orig. from northern Holland and Friesland that produce large quantities of comparatively low-fat milk and that are usu. black and white in irregular patches **2** -s *often cap H&F* **:** any animal of the Holstein-Friesian breed

¹**hol·ster** \'hōlztə(r), -l(t)st-\ *n* -s [D; akin to OE *heolstor* darkness, cover, ON *hulstr* case, Goth *hulistr* veil, OE *helan* to conceal — more at HELL] **1 :** a usu. leather case for a pistol that is often open at the top to facilitate quick withdrawal, that often conforms to the pistol's shape, and that is usu. carried at the belt or under one arm or often at the front of a saddle **2 holsters** *pl* **:** housings or standards for a set of rolls in steel manufacturing

²**holster** \"\ *vt* **holstered; holstered; holstering** \-t(ə)riŋ\ **holsters :** to place in a holster

holster 1

**holster stock** *n* **:** a pistol holster that can be attached to the pistol to form a shoulder stock

¹**holt** \'hōlt\ *n* -s [ME, fr. OE; akin to OHG *holz* wood, ON *holt*, L *clades* destruction, Gk *klados* twig — more at GLADIATOR] **1** *now dial* **a :** a small woods **:** COPSE **b :** a wooded hill or rise **2 :** a planted grove of osiers or willows

²**holt** \"\ *n* [ME, alter. of ²*hold*] **1** ²HOLD 3 **2** *dial Brit* **:** a den or lair esp. of a burrowing animal (as an otter)

**ho·lus-bo·lus** \¦hōləs¦bōləs\ *adv* [prob. redupl. of *bolus*] **:** all at once **:** ALTOGETHER ⟨gulped it down, *holus-bolus*⟩ ⟨existing economic system was taken over *holus-bolus* —A.J.Bruwer⟩

¹**ho·ly** \'hōlē, -li\ *adj* -ER/-EST [ME *holy, hooly, haly*, fr. OE *hālig*; akin to OHG *heilag* holy, ON *heilagr*, Goth *hailags*, OE *hāl* whole — more at WHOLE] **1 a :** set apart and dedicated to the service or worship of God or a god **:** HALLOWED, SACRED ⟨~ vessels⟩ ⟨the ~ priesthood⟩ **b :** dedicated to or laying claim to being dedicated to a sacred or selfless purpose ⟨gave money to various ~ causes⟩ **2 a** (1) **:** perfect in righteousness and divine love **:** infinitely good **:** worthy of complete devotion and trust **:** commanding one's fullest powers of adoration and reverence ⟨the ~ Lord God Almighty⟩ (2) **:** of or befitting something that is perfect or worthy in this way ⟨a smile of ~ sweetness —George Meredith⟩ **b :** spiritually whole, sound, or perfect **:** of unimpaired innocence or proved virtue **:** pure in heart **:** GODLY, PIOUS — often used in mild oaths ⟨my ~ aunt⟩ **3 a :** venerated because of association with someone or something holy ⟨~ relics⟩ ⟨the ~ cross⟩ **b** *of a saint or saintly person* **:** worthy of veneration **:** worthy of veneration ⟨to him every action of the campaign was ~⟩ — **c :** to be treated with veneration or the utmost respect ⟨to him every action of the campaign was ~⟩ **d :** being awesome, frightening, or beyond belief ⟨the child was a ~ terror⟩ ⟨so frightened he had the ~ horrors⟩ **4 :** not capable of being approached with impunity **:** filled with mysterious, superhuman, and potentially fatal power **:** dangerously powerful if violated ⟨some words are considered so ~ they must never be spoken aloud —Stuart Chase⟩

²**holy** \"\ *n* -ES [ME *holi*, adj., fr. OE] **1** [trans. of LL *sanctus*] **:** a holy place **:** SANCTUARY **2** *obs* **:** SAINT **3** *cap* **:** ²GOD 1 ⟨into the presence of the *Holy*⟩

**holy ark** *n, often cap H&A* **:** ARK 3

**holy basil** *n* **:** a basil (*Ocimum sanctum*) found in the tropics of the Old World that is extensively naturalized in tropical America and that in India is held sacred to Vishnu

**holy bread** *n* [ME *holy brede*] **1 :** bread consecrated in the Eucharist **2 :** bread provided for the Communion service **3 :** ANTIDORON

**holy cats** *interj* — used as an exclamation of surprise, amazement, or bewilderment

**holy clover** *n* **:** SAINFOIN 1

**holy communion** *n, usu cap H&C* **:** COMMUNION 2

**holy cow** *interj* — used as an exclamation of surprise, amazement, or bewilderment

**holy cross day** *n, usu cap H&C&D* : HOLY-ROOD DAY 2

**holy day** *n* [ME *haly day*, fr. OE *hāligdæg* — more at HOLIDAY] **1 :** a day set aside as having special religious significance to be commemorated by religious services, feasting, or fasting; *specif* : HOLY DAY OF OBLIGATION **2** *archaic* : HOLIDAY

**holy day of obligation 1 :** one of the days on which Roman Catholics are obliged to hear mass and abstain from servile work ⟨Sunday is a common *holy day of obligation*⟩ **2 :** one of the days on which communicants of the Episcopal Church are obliged to take Communion

**holy dollar** *n* [by alter.] : HOLEY DOLLAR

**holy doors** *n pl, often cap H&D* : the doors and esp. the central doors in the iconostasis in an Eastern church that separate the bema from the main part of the church — called also *royal doors*

**holy family** *n, usu cap H&F* : a painting or piece of sculpture in which the infant Jesus and the Virgin are represented attended by sacred personages (as St. Joseph, the infant St. John Baptist, St. Elisabeth, and St. Anna or angels or fathers of the church)

**holy father** *n, usu cap H&F* : POPE 1a

**holy fire** *n* [ME *holy fuyre*, trans. of L *sacer ignis*] *archaic* : ERYSIPELAS

**holy ghost** *n, cap H&G* [ME *holi gost*, fr. OE *hālig gāst*, trans. of LL *spiritus sanctus*, trans. of Gk *pneuma hagion*, trans. of Heb *ruaḥ ha-godesh* holy spirit] : HOLY SPIRIT

**holy ghost flower** *also* **holy ghost orchid** *or* **holy ghost** *n, usu cap H&G* [so called fr. the resemblance of part of the flower to a dove, a symbol of the Holy Ghost] : DOVEFLOWER

**holy grail** *n, usu cap H&G* : ²GRAIL

**holy grass** *n* [so called fr. the custom in northern Europe of strewing it before church doors on saints' days] : any of several sweet-scented grasses of the genus *Hierochloe*; *esp* : SWEET GRASS

**holy green** *n* : TERRE VERTE 2

**holy herb** *n* [trans. of LGk *hierobotanē*] **1 :** YERBA SANTA **2 :** HOLY BASIL **3 :** VERVAIN 1

**holy innocents' day** *n, usu cap H&I&D* : the day of December 28 commemorating the children slain by Herod after he had been told by the Magi of the birth of a king of the Jews

**holy joe** *n, usu cap H&J, slang* : PARSON, CHAPLAIN

**holy jumper** *n, usu cap H&J* : JUMPER 1a

**holy kiss** *n* [trans. of LL *osculum sanctum*, trans. of Gk *philēma hagion*] : KISS OF PEACE

**holy lamb** *n, usu cap H&L* : AGNUS DEI 1

**holy mackerel** *interj* — used as an exclamation of surprise or amazement

**holy moses** *interj* — used as an exclamation of surprise or amazement

**holy mysteries** *n pl, usu cap H&M* : the liturgy in the Eastern Church

**holy of holies** [ME *holi of halowes*, trans. of LL *sanctum sanctorum*, trans. of Gk *to hagion tōn hagiōn*, trans. of Heb *qōdesh ha-qŏdōshim*] **1 a :** the innermost chamber of a Jewish temple **b :** the bema in an Eastern Orthodox church : SANCTUARY **c :** a very sacred place ⟨father's study was always considered the *holy of holies* by the children⟩ **2 :** something considered as if very sacred ⟨defeated that legislative *holy of holies*, a veterans' pension bill —*Newsweek*⟩

**holy oil** *n* [ME *holi oylle*] **1 :** CHRISM 1a **2 :** olive oil blessed by a bishop or in an Eastern church by a priest — see OIL OF CATECHUMENS, OIL OF THE SICK **3 :** the oil taken from the grave of a saint or in an Eastern church from the lamps at the altar and used for various blessings

**holy one** *n* **1** *cap H&O* : ²GOD a(1) ⟨the Lord, the *Holy One* of Israel —Isa 10:20 (RSV)⟩ **2** *often cap H&O* : ANGEL ⟨and behold, a watcher, a *holy one*, came down from heaven —Dan 4:13 (RSV)⟩ **3** *cap H&O* : CHRIST 1 ⟨the *Holy One* of God —Mk 1:24 (RSV)⟩

**holy order** *n, often cap H&O* [ME] **1 :** MAJOR ORDER **2 holy orders** *pl* : ORDINATION **3 :** ORDER 1a(2) — usu. used in pl.

**holy people** *n, usu cap H&P* : the supernatural beings of the sacred world who in the religion of the Navahos have great power to help or harm humans — contrasted with *Earth People*

**holy place** *n* **1 :** a place set apart for religious rites; *specif* : the larger chamber of the Jewish tabernacle and temple separated from the holy of holies by a veil **2 :** a place made sacred by association : SHRINE; *specif* : one of various places (as of the birth, death, resurrection, and ascension of Jesus) of religious pilgrimage

**holy pole** *n* [prob. alter. of *holey pole*; fr. its hollow stems] : ANT TREE

**holy roller** *n, usu cap H&R* **1 :** one of a minor religious sect in the U. S. and Canada whose meetings are often characterized by frenzied excitement **2 :** one of various religious groups resembling or felt to resemble the Holy Rollers

**holy-rood day** *n, usu cap H&R&D* [ME *holi rode dei*] **1 :** the 3d day of May on which occurs the feast of the Invention of the Cross **2 :** September 14 — called also *Holy Cross Day*

**holy sacrament** *n, usu cap H&S* [ME] : SACRAMENT 2

**holy saturday** *n, usu cap H&S* [ME] : the Saturday immediately preceding the festival of Easter : the vigil of Easter

**holy scripture** *n, usu cap H&S* [ME] : BIBLE 1, 5

**holy scriptures** *n pl, usu cap H&S* : BIBLE 1, 5

**holy smoke** *interj* — used to express surprise or amazement ⟨*holy smoke!* You'd think a man 26 years old . . . would have more sense —E.J.Curran⟩

**holy spear** *n* : ¹LANCE 2c

**holy spirit** *n, cap H&S* [ME *hooli spirit*, trans. of LL *spiritus sanctus*] : God as present and active in the spiritual experience of men : the third person of the Trinity — called also *Holy Ghost*

**¹holystone** \ˈ⸗⸗,⸗\ *n* [¹*holy* + *stone*; prob. fr. the fact that seamen likened it to a prayer book or bible] : a soft sandstone used to scrub a ship's decks

**²holystone** \"\ *vb* : to scrub with a holystone

**holy synod** *n* : a governing body in an autocephalous church being composed usu. of several bishops representing the whole episcopate of the particular church under the presidency of the primate

**holy table** *n, usu cap H&T* : the altar or communion table

**holy thistle** *n* **1 :** BLESSED THISTLE 1 **2 :** MILK THISTLE 1

**holy thursday** *n, usu cap H&T* [ME, fr. OE *hālig thunresdæg*] **1** ASCENSION DAY **2 :** MAUNDY THURSDAY

**holytide** \ˈ⸗⸗,⸗\ *n* [ME *halitide*, fr. *hali* holy + *tide*] : a time devoted to religion

**holy tree** *n* : CHINABERRY 2

**holy unction** *n, often cap H&U* [ME *hooly unctioun*] : a ceremonial in Eastern Orthodox and various Catholic non-Roman churches of anointing with oil the dead or those in imminent danger of dying

**holy war** *n* **1 :** a war waged for what is regarded as a holy purpose **2 :** JIHAD

**holy water** *n* [ME, fr. OE *hāligwæter*, fr. *hālig* holy + *wæter* water] : water blessed by a priest and used as a purifying sacramental in church and home

**holy-water sprinkler** *n* : MORNING STAR 2

**holy week** *n, usu cap H&W* [ME *hali wuca*] : the week before Easter in which the Passion of Christ is commemorated among Christians

**holy well** *n* : a well or spring venerated often from pagan times for reputed healing properties

**holy writ** *n* [ME, fr. OE *hālige writu* holy writings] **1** *usu cap H&W* : BIBLE 1 **2 :** a writing that is taken to be as sacred as the Bible ⟨the potpourri of special nostrums . . . became a kind of political *holy writ* —N.E.Long⟩

**holy year** *n, usu cap H&Y* : a jubilee year

**hom-** *or* **homo-** *comb form* [L, fr. Gk, fr. *homos* — more at SAME] **1 :** one and the same : similar : alike ⟨*homo*geneous⟩ ⟨*hom*onym⟩ — opposed to *heter-* **2 :** homologous with a (specified) organic compound esp. with a formula containing one carbon and two hydrogen atoms $CH_2$ more than the compound to whose name the prefix is added ⟨*homo*serine $HOCH_2CH_2CH(NH_2)COOH$⟩ **3 :** from the same species : corresponding in type of structure ⟨*homo*graft⟩ ⟨*homo*lysin⟩

**ho·ma** \ˈhōmə\ *n* -s [Av *haoma* haoma, plant that is the source of haoma and is conceived as the tree of life — more at SOMA] **1 :** HAOMA **2** *or* **hom** \ˈhōm\ [*hom* fr. Per *hōm*, fr. Av *haoma*] : a stylized tree pattern originating in Mesopotamia as a symbol of the tree of life and used esp. in Persian textiles

**¹hom·age** \ˈ(h)ämij, –mēj\ *n* -s [ME *omage*, *homage*, fr. OF *omage*, *hommage*, fr. *om*, *omme*, *homme* man, vassal (fr. L *homin-*, *homo* man) + *-age*; akin to OE *guma* man, OHG *gomo*, ON *gumi*, Goth *guma* man, OPruss *smoy* human being, Toch B *śaumo* human being, L *humus* earth — more at HUMBLE] **1 a :** a feudal solemn public ceremony by which in return for a fief (as a tenancy of land) a man acknowledges himself the man or vassal of a lord and recognizes the rights and duties inherent in this relationship — compare COMMENDATION 4, FEALTY 1, LIEGE **b :** the relationship between a feudal lord and his man **c :** an act done or payment made in meeting the obligations of vassalage **2 :** a body of persons bound under feudal law by homage; *specif* : the body of tenants attending a manorial court or those acting as jury **3 a :** reverential regard : RESPECT, DEFERENCE ⟨the ~ that matter pays to spirit —Clive Bell⟩; *esp* : respect shown by external action : OBEISANCE ⟨then the ~ of . . . peers; and again the air was lively with the trumpets and drums —Hector Bolitho⟩ **b :** flattering attention : TRIBUTE ⟨turned to look at the young woman . . . and permitted himself the ~ of a smile —Guy McCrone⟩ ⟨the present pamphlet is a modest . . . ~ to one of the leading linguists of our time —André Martinet⟩ **syn** see HONOR

**²homage** \"\ *vt* -ED/-ING/-S [MF *hommager*, fr. *hommage*] : to pay homage to

**homage blue** *n* : a dark purplish blue that is slightly less strong and very slightly darker than Scotch blue and slightly less strong and very slightly lighter than national flag blue

**hom·ag·er** \-jə(r)\ *n* -s [ME *omager*, fr. MF *omagier*, *hommagier*, fr. *omage*, *hommage* + *-ier* -er] **1 :** one that pays homage **2 :** one who holds land by fief; *specif* : one of the tenants of a manor

**homal-** *or* **homalo-** *comb form* [NL, fr. Gk, fr. *homalos*; akin to Gk *homos* same — more at SAME] **1 :** flat : even ⟨*homalo*sternal⟩ **2 :** equal ⟨*homalo*graphic⟩

**ho·mali·um** \hōˈmalēəm, -māl-\ *n, cap* [NL, fr. *homal-* + *-ium*] : a large widely distributed genus of tropical trees (family Flacourtiaceae) including several that yield hard heavy durable timber used for construction or cabinetwork — see ORANGA

**ho·mal·o·do·the·ri·um** \hō,malədōˈthirēəm\ *n, cap* [NL, irreg. fr. *homal-* + Gk *odont-*, *odōn* tooth + NL *-therium* — more at TOOTH] : a genus of extinct So. American Miocene herbivorous mammals (order Notoungulata) the size of a small ox with the teeth comparatively undifferentiated, the 5-toed feet ending in heavy blunt claws, and the forefeet adapted for digging

**homalographic** *var of* HOMOLOGRAPHIC

**hom·a·lo·no·tus** \,häməlōˈnōd·əs\ *n, cap* [NL, fr. *homal-* + *-notus*] : a genus of Silurian and Devonian trilobites having long indistinctly 3-lobed bodies

**¹hom·a·lop·sid** \,häməˈläpsəd\ *adj* [NL *Homalopsidae*] : of or relating to the Homalopsidae

**²homalopsid** \"\ *n* -s : a snake of the family Homalopsidae

**hom·a·lop·si·dae** \,⸗⸗ˈ⸗sə,dē\ *n pl, cap* [NL, fr. *Homalopsis*, type genus (fr. *homal-* + *-opsis*) + *-idae*] : a family of venomous opisthoglyphous water snakes of southeastern Asia and northern Australia that are often included as a subfamily in the family Colubridae

**ho·man's sign** \ˈhōmənz-\ *n, usu cap H* [after John *Homans* †1954 Am. surgeon] : pain in the calf of the leg or dorsiflexion of the foot with leg extended diagnostic of thrombosis in the deep veins of the area

**ho·mar·i·dae** \hōˈmarə,dē\ *n pl, cap* [NL, fr. *Homarus*, type genus + *-idae*] : a family of decapod crustaceans (tribe Astacura) comprising the large-clawed lobsters

**hom·a·rus** \ˈhämərəs\ *n, cap* [NL, fr. F *homard* lobster, fr. MF, of Scand origin; akin to ON *humarr* lobster — more at CAMBARUS] : a genus of decapod crustaceans including the common lobsters of Europe and No. America and the little Cape lobster (*H. capensis*) of southern Africa and with the related genus *Nephrops* constituting a family (Homaridae or Nephropsidae)

**hom·atomic** \,hōm, ˌhäm+\ *adj* [*hom-* + *atomic*] : consisting of like atoms

**hom·atropine** \(ˈ)hōm, (ˈ)häm+\ *n* [ISV *hom-* + *atropine*] : a poisonous crystalline ester $C_{16}H_{21}NO_3$ of tropine and mandelic acid used (as in the form of its hydrobromide) for dilating the pupil of the eye

**hom·axial** \(ˈ)hōm, (ˈ)häm+\ *or* **hom·ax·o·ni·al** \ˌ⸗ak-ˈsōnēəl\ *also* **hom·ax·on·ic** \-ˈsänik\ *adj* [*hom-* + *axial* or *-axonial*, *-axonic* (fr. Gk *axon-*, *axōn* axle, axis + E *-ial* or *-ic*) — more at AXIS] *biol* : having all the axes equal

**¹hombre** *var of* OMBRE

**²hom·bre** \ˈämbrē, ˈəm-, -m(,)brā\ *n* -s [Sp, man, fr. L *homin-*, *homo* — more at HOMAGE] : GUY ⟨that conceited ~ . . . will be riding in here —Zane Grey⟩ ⟨bad ~*s* held up the stagecoach⟩

**hom·burg** \ˈhäm,bərg, -bəg, -bəig *also* -bùrg *or* -bùəg\ *n* -s [fr. *Homburg*, town near Wiesbaden, Germany, where such hats were first made] *often cap* : a man's hat of smooth-finished felt with a stiff curled ribbon-bound brim and a high tapered crown creased lengthwise

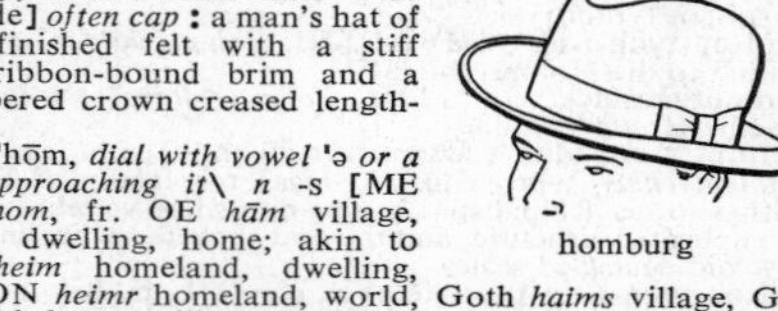
homburg

**¹home** \ˈhōm, *dial with vowel* ˈɔ *or a vowel approaching it*\ *n* -s [ME *hoom*, *hom*, fr. OE *hām* village, country, dwelling, home; akin to OHG *heim* homeland, dwelling, house, ON *heimr* homeland, world, Goth *haims* village, Gk *kōmē*, Lith *kaimas* village, OE *hīwan* members of a household, L *civis* citizen, Gk *koiman* to put to sleep — more at CEMETERY] **1 a :** the house and grounds with their appurtenances habitually occupied by a family : one's principal place of residence : DOMICILE **b :** a private dwelling : HOUSE ⟨interpret . . . history through the architecture of its stores and ~*s* —R.W. Howard⟩ **c :** the refuge or usual haunt of an animal ⟨the pool at the foot of the rapids is . . . the ~ of big trout —Alexander MacDonald⟩ **2 :** one's abode after death ⟨I'm but a stranger here, heaven is my ~ —T.R.Taylor⟩ **3 a :** the social unit formed by a family living together in one dwelling ⟨a man establishes a ~ and makes use of a specific piece of land —P.E. James⟩ **b :** the family environment to which one is emotionally attached : focus of domestic affections ⟨~ is where the heart is⟩ **4 a :** a familiar or suitable setting : congenial environment ⟨finds no spiritual ~ in the gang —John Brooks⟩ ⟨the theater would have been the proper ~ for his characters and plots —L.O.Coxe⟩ **b :** normal environment : HABITAT ⟨California is the ~ of the redwood⟩ ⟨the ~ of petroleum is in sedimentary rocks —A.M.Bateman⟩ **c :** center of cultivation : FOCAL POINT ⟨concept of a university as the ~ of learning —J.B. Conant⟩ **5 a :** the country or place of origin ⟨Britain is the ~ of railroads —Richard Joseph⟩ ⟨in the ~ of the direct primary —F.L.Paxson⟩; *specif* : MOTHER COUNTRY ⟨people . . . from the old ~*s* moved into the same pursuits because they had brought across similar skills —Oscar Handlin⟩ **b :** center or base of operations : LOCATION, HEADQUARTERS ⟨the amphitheater . . . will be the ~ of one of two festival companies —E.B.Radcliffe⟩ ⟨the four largest national broadcasting networks . . . have their ~ in the city —*Amer. Guide Series: N. Y.*⟩ ⟨the pilot . . . heads for ~ —*Newsweek*⟩ **6 :** an establishment taking the place of a home — see NURSING HOME, TOURIST HOME; compare FUNERAL HOME **7 a :** the objective toward which a player progresses in certain active sports (as baseball) or toward which he moves his pieces in various board games (as backgammon) **b :** an area in which a player is safe from attack **c :** one's original position in a square-dance set **d** (1) **:** either of two lacrosse positions nearest the opponent's goal (2) **:** a player assigned to either of these positions — compare INSIDE HOME, OUTSIDE HOME — **at home** \ət'hōm *sometimes chiefly Brit & NewEng* ət'ōm\ **1 a :** in one's own house or home ⟨generally to be found *at home* in the morning⟩ **b :** ready to receive callers ⟨the newly wed couple will be *at home* after June 15⟩ **2 a :** in the country of origin : on the domestic front ⟨totalitarianism is despotic *at home* and expansionist abroad —George Fischer⟩ **b :** in the mother country ⟨people . . . *at home* and throughout the Commonwealth —Wendell Willkie⟩ **3 a :** in a familiar or congenial relationship : relaxed and comfortable : at ease ⟨a pleasant manner that soon made me feel *at home*⟩ ⟨he is . . . *at home* among the diplomatic and fashionable circles —Peggy Durdin⟩ **b :** in harmony with the surroundings : acclimated to the environment ⟨in the universities where basic research is most *at home* —M.H.Trytten⟩ ⟨*at home* in surf, the young abound in rock pools —J.L.B.Smith⟩ **4 :** on familiar ground : COMPETENT, KNOWLEDGEABLE ⟨*at home* in Italian opera —George Jellinek⟩ ⟨the sciences of biology and psychology in which the author is masterfully *at home*⟩

**²home** \"\ *adv* [ME *hoom*, *hom*, *home*, fr. OE *hām*, acc. of *hām*, n.] **1 a :** to or at one's principal place of residence ⟨go ~ on the bus⟩ ⟨stay ~ and practice the piano⟩ **b :** to one's family ⟨writes ~ once a week⟩ **c :** to or at the focus of one's sympathies ⟨has deserted the speculative heights . . . and is back ~ among the sweet and profound bums —Paul Pickrel⟩ **2 :** to or at the country or place of origin ⟨ordering diplomats ~ from various parts of the world⟩ ⟨customs differ from those back ~⟩; *specif* : to the mother country ⟨ordinances passed in the colonies are periodically transmitted ~⟩ **3 a :** to the final or closed position : to the full or ultimate limit ⟨drive a nail ~⟩ ⟨shove ~ a bolt⟩; *specif* : into position for loosing from a bow ⟨draw an arrow ~⟩ **b** (1) **:** to or toward a ship or its interior ⟨haul an anchor ~⟩ (2) **:** from the sea onto the shore ⟨the wind is blowing ~⟩ **c :** to an ultimate objective (as the finish line) in a game or sport : to the end of a course ⟨he had 33 on the outward nine and 35 coming ~ —*N. Y. Times*⟩ **d :** to a successful, rewarding, or winning end ⟨if the long shot comes ~ —Richard Scammon⟩ ⟨when my ship comes ~⟩ **4 a :** to the center of consciousness or sensitivity ⟨insights . . . whose truth strikes ~ to any candid and reflective mind J.H.Randall⟩ ⟨the full significance of this discovery was brought ~ to him —J.B.Conant⟩ **b :** to the point of uncovering underlying facts or truths ⟨questions are asked, parried, pressed ~ —R.W.Speaight⟩

**³home** \"\ *adj* [¹*home*] **1 :** of, relating to, or adjacent to a home ⟨~ building⟩ ⟨~ cooking⟩ ⟨doctored my scratches with some of their ~ remedies —Bruce Siberto⟩ ⟨tramped with him over his ~ acres —Witmer Stone⟩ **2 a :** of or relating to the country or place of origin : DOMESTIC, NATIVE ⟨~ industry⟩ ⟨~ city⟩ ⟨~ language⟩; *specif* : of or relating to the mother country ⟨gap between the ~ and the Kenya points of view —Lionel Fleming⟩ **b :** of or relating to the vicinity of the home : LOCAL ⟨after finishing a preparatory course in the ~ academy . . . attended Yale College —F.L.Riley⟩ **c :** of or relating to a headquarters or base of operations ⟨~ territory⟩ esp. of an athletic team ⟨will close their ~ season today —*N.Y.Times*⟩ **3 a :** reaching the mark physically or emotionally : well-aimed and effective ⟨dispatched the bull with a dexterous ~ thrust⟩ ⟨this was a very ~ question —A.R. Smith⟩ **b :** being in proximity to or constituting the objective in a game or sport ⟨in Saturday's race he was forced . . . wide at the ~ turn —*Sydney (Australia) Bull.*⟩ ⟨the counter is moved around the board and up the path to the ~ space⟩ **4 :** ORIGINAL, NORMAL — used of the position of a machine or its parts ⟨the cylinder travels past the ~ position, and is then pushed back . . . against a catch —John Southward⟩

**⁴home** \"\ *vb* -ED/-ING/-S [¹*home*] *vi* **1 a :** to go or return home ⟨a plane ~*s* to its carrier⟩ ⟨when school is out a boy ~*s* to his dog and his marbles⟩; *specif, of an animal* : to return accurately to its home or natal area from a distance ⟨a pigeon ~*s* to its loft⟩ ⟨a salmon ~*s* to the stream in which it was spawned⟩ **b :** to move toward an objective by following a beam or landmark — usu. used with *on* or *in* ⟨picked up a radio beam and *homed* on it toward the fiord —Sloan Wilson⟩ ⟨mariners . . . sought the dark spires of Oakland's redwoods to ~ on —J.W.Noble⟩ ⟨with one engine out of action, the aircraft turned back and *homed* in on the . . . radio beacon —*U.N.Bull.*⟩ **c :** to become guided to a target by an emanation from it — usu. used with *on* or *in* ⟨the new long-range electric torpedo . . . ~*s* on the noise of the target ship's propellers —*N.Y.Times*⟩ ⟨keep the missile *homing* in on the source of heat —*Newsweek*⟩ **2 :** to have a home or headquarters ⟨several fine publishers have *homed* in that marvelous city —H.G.Merriam⟩ ~ *vt* **1 :** to send to or provide with a home ⟨radar installations . . . *homed* friendly aircraft to land bases —*Crowsnest*⟩ ⟨hidden pools and much wider creeks each of which *homed* its cranes —I.L.Idriess⟩ **2 :** to teach (a pigeon) to return to a loft

**home-** *or* **homeo-** *or* **homoe-** *or* **homoeo-** *also* **homoi-** *or* **homoio-** *comb form* [L & Gk; L *homoeo-*, fr. Gk *homoi-*, *homoio-*, fr. *homoios*, fr. *homos* — more at SAME] : like : similar ⟨*homeo*pathy⟩ ⟨*homoeo*graphy⟩ ⟨*homoio*thermic⟩

**home-and-home** \ˌ⸗⸗ˈ⸗\ *adj* : taking place alternately on the home grounds of competing teams or participants engaged in successive contests or contests related by being on the same schedule ⟨*home-and-home* series⟩

**home base** *n* **1 :** HOME PLATE **2 :** HOME 5b **3 :** HOME 7a

**homebody** \ˈ⸗,⸗⸗\ *n* : one whose life centers around the home and its activities : STAY-AT-HOME ⟨he and his wife are *homebodies*: they love to read and listen to records —*Time*⟩

**homeborn** \ˈ⸗ˈ⸗\ *adj* : home produced : INDIGENOUS ⟨~ hockey players breaking up the Canadian monopoly⟩

**¹homebound** \ˈ⸗,⸗\ *adj* [¹*home* + ⁴*bound*] : confined to the home ⟨~ invalid⟩

**²homebound** \ˈ⸗ˈ⸗\ *adj* [¹*home* + ¹*bound*] : going homeward ⟨~ traveler⟩ ⟨became eligible for redeployment and were shipped to ~ outfits —W.J.Statoff⟩

**homebred** \ˈ⸗ˈ⸗\ *adj* **1 :** HOMEBORN **2** *archaic* : having little experience outside the home : UNSOPHISTICATED

**home brew** *n* **1 :** an alcoholic beverage made at home or with homemade equipment usu. by trial-and-error methods **2 :** something formulated at home ⟨puritanism in rural England was never a *home brew*; it was always imported from the town —H.J.Massingham⟩

**home car** *n* : a freight car on the tracks of the railroad line to which it belongs — contrasted with *foreign car*

**homecoming** \ˈ⸗ˈ⸗⸗\ *n* -s [ME *homcomyng*, fr. *hom* home + *comyng* coming] **1 :** a return to or arrival at one's home ⟨take off for Lisbon on his last ~ —Henry La Cossitt⟩ ⟨dramatic moment of the bride's ~ —Sinclair Lewis⟩ **2 a :** the return of a group of people to a place formerly frequented or regarded as home ⟨a holiday celebrating the ~ of . . . illustrious natives —Thomas Sugrue⟩ **b :** an occasion for or celebration of such a return ⟨traveled halfway across the continent to be present at his college ~⟩

**homecraft** \ˈ⸗,⸗\ *n* : the household arts (as cooking); *esp* : handcrafts (as weaving) that may be practiced at home

**home demonstration** *n* : a demonstration of a new or useful method of performing a household task; *specif* : a demonstration given to women in rural areas by an agent of a government extension service

**home economics** *n pl but usu sing in constr* : the theory and practice of homemaking; *specif* : a field of study and research forming part of an academic curriculum of formal subjects and practical skills (as in nutrition, clothing, child care, home furnishing and decoration, household accounts, family and community relationships) necessary for good family management and family life

**home economist** *n* : a specialist in home economics

**home edition** *n* : CITY EDITION

**home factor** *n* : DOMESTIC FACTOR

**homefelt** \ˈ⸗,⸗\ *adj, archaic* : felt in one's own breast : INWARD, PRIVATE

**home folks** *n pl* : the people of one's home locality; *esp* : the members of one's immediate family

**home freezer** *n* : FREEZER 1d(2)

**home fried potatoes** *n pl* : COTTAGE FRIED POTATOES

**home front** *n* : a sphere of civilian activity directly or indirectly supporting the armed forces of a nation at war by production and supply of war materiel, civilian defense, and the preservation of public order and morale ⟨in somber contrast to the tinsel prosperity of the *home front* —Oscar Handlin⟩

**homegrown** \ˈ⸗ˈ⸗\ *adj* **1 :** grown or produced at home or in the vicinity of the home : NATIVE, LOCAL ⟨~ corn⟩ ⟨~ bacon⟩ ⟨~ wool⟩ ⟨smoked bad ~ cigarettes —Upton Sinclair⟩ ⟨put up with ~ amateur talkers during most of the season —H.W. Wind⟩ **2 :** produced or located in or characteristic of the

home country or place of origin : DOMESTIC, INDIGENOUS ⟨~ politician⟩ ⟨~ literature⟩ ⟨~ industry⟩ ⟨a delightful mixture of ~ raffishness and imported elegance —Peggy Durdin⟩
**home guard** *n* : a force organized often on a volunteer basis for local defense or home protection esp. when the regular army is in a combat area — compare HOME RESERVE
**home guardsman** *n, pl* **home guardsmen** : a member of a home guard
**home industry** *n* : a gainful employment carried on in the home
**homekeeping** \ˈ⸗,⸗⸗\ *adj* : STAY-AT-HOME
**home key** *n* : one of the eight keys for the characters *asdf* and *jkl;* on which the fingers normally rest in starting position for touch typing — called also *guide key*
**home·land** \ˈhōm,land, -aa(ə)nd *also* -ˌlənd\ *n* **1** : country of origin : native land ⟨represents his ~ in international competition⟩; *specif* : MOTHER COUNTRY ⟨urged to . . . support the ~ — although many of them never had been citizens —Oscar Handlin⟩ **2** : chief place of residence : region in which one's home is located ⟨appetizing dishes from her ~, the Pennsylvania Dutch country —V.O.Williams⟩
**home·less** \-ˌləs\ *adj* : having no home or permanent place of residence ⟨the ~, unhappy, uprooted look of a displaced person —John Mason Brown⟩ — **home·less·ly** *adv*
**home·less·ness** *n* -ES : the quality or state of being homeless
**homelife** \ˈ⸗,⸗\ *n* : the domestic routine or way of living ⟨television will change the ~ of America —L.A.Appley⟩
**homelike** \ˈ⸗,⸗\ *adj* : having the qualities associated with family living : simple and wholesome : INVITING ⟨a ~ meal⟩ ⟨the hotel tries to create a ~ atmosphere⟩ — **home·like·ness** *n*
**home·li·ness** \ˈhōmlēnəs, -lin-\ *n* -ES [ME *hoomlynesse*, fr. *hoomly* homely + *-nesse* -ness] : the quality or state of being homely: **a** : COZINESS, INTIMACY **b** : lack of elegance, beauty, or refinement **c** : SIMPLICITY ⟨voters attracted by his ~ of speech⟩
**¹home·ly** \-lē,-li\ *adj* -ER/-EST [ME *hoomly, homly,* fr. *hoom, hom* home + *-ly* (adj. suffix) — more at HOME] **1** : HOMEY **2 a** : established on a friendly footing : INTIMATE — often used with *with* ⟨asked them to . . . dinner at our house and they came and were ~ with us —*Times Lit. Supp.*⟩ **b** : frequently encountered : COMMONPLACE, FAMILIAR ⟨translates the issue into ~ terms and makes the point beyond all doubt —Robert Bendiner⟩ ⟨an English garden full of the old ~ plants —David Ewen⟩ **3** : of a sympathetic character : KINDLY ⟨nature, the ~ nurse . . . has her own ways of comforting —G.G.Coulton⟩ **4 a** : natural and unaffected : SIMPLE ⟨~ courtesy⟩ ⟨a pastorale written in ~ muted prose about life on a farm —*New Yorker*⟩ **b** : free from ornament or complexity : PLAIN ⟨~ food⟩ ⟨shrines that are simple, quaint, ~ and common —J.C.Powys⟩ ⟨so many bizarre forms of dinosaur that these are almost ~ by comparison —W.E. Swinton⟩ **c** : free from ambiguity : DIRECT ⟨~ vigor of expression⟩ **d** : lacking in elegance or sophistication ⟨a ~ audience drawn from the surrounding farms⟩ **5** : lacking in physical beauty or proportion : plain-featured : UNATTRACTIVE ⟨an awkward, lanky giant whose ~ countenance was surmounted by a shock of rough black hair —Allan Nevins & H.S.Commager⟩ ⟨make possible retirement of at least two or three of the buildings . . . downright ~ to behold —B.F.Wright⟩ **syn** see PLAIN
**²homely** *adv* [ME *hoomly, homly,* fr. *hoom, hom* + *-ly* (adv. suffix)] *obs* : in a homely way : FAMILIARLY, KINDLY : RUDELY
**home·lyn** \ˈhōmlən, ˈhäm-\ *also* **homelyn ray** *n* -S [origin unknown] : a European ray (*Raja maculata*)
**homemade** \ˈhō,mād *also* -ōm,m-\ *adj* **1 a** : made or prepared in the home or on the premises ⟨~ bread⟩ ⟨~ skis⟩ **b** : constructed, produced, or acquired by one's own efforts ⟨~ jalopy⟩ ⟨used ~ apparatus in his experiments⟩ ⟨this obviously ~ memoir —*New Yorker*⟩ ⟨a major with . . . a ~ education —Mari Sandoz⟩ **2** : of domestic origin or manufacture : NATIVE ⟨~ Saturday Reviews and Yankee Athenaeums —H.L.Mencken⟩ ⟨~ typewriters⟩
**homemaker** \ˈ⸗,⸗⸗\ *n* **1** : one that makes a home : one whose occupation is household and family management — usu. used of a wife and mother as distinguished from a paid housekeeper **2** : a welfare worker placed by a social agency to take care of a family during the absence or illness of the mother
**homemaking** \ˈ⸗,⸗⸗\ *n* : the creation and maintenance of a wholesome family environment — compare HOME ECONOMICS
**home mission** *n* : a religious mission conducted within the nation or national territories of the sponsoring church or organization — called also *national mission;* compare FOREIGN MISSION
**home missionary** *n* : a missionary appointed to a home mission
**homeo-** — see HOME-
**ho·meo·blas·tic** \ˌhōmēōˈblastik, ˌhäm-\ *adj* [ISV *home-* + *-blastic;* orig. formed as G *homöoblastisch*] : having a texture corresponding to the equigranular in igneous rock and grains of approximately equal size — used of metamorphic rock
**ho·meo·chromatic** \ˌ⸗mē(ˌ)ō+\ *adj* [*home-* + *chromatic*] : of similar color
**ho·meo·ch·ro·nous** \ˌhōmēˈäkrənəs, ˌhäm-\ *adj* [*home-* + *-chronous*] : recurring at the same period of life in succeeding generations — used of organs, traits, or other characters; compare HETEROCHRONISM 1
**ho·meo·crystalline** \ˌhōmē(ˌ)ō, ˌhäm-+\ *adj* [ISV *home-* + *crystalline;* orig. formed as G *homöokrystallinisch*] : having the crystals of the constituent minerals equally developed : GRANITIC
**home office** *n* : principal business location or base of operations : HEADQUARTERS ⟨the branch manager had a telegram from the *home office* informing him of price changes⟩ ⟨the diplomat cables the *home office* for instructions⟩
**ho·me·ol·o·gy** \ˌhōmēˈäləjē, ˌhäm-\ *n* -ES [*home-* + *-logy*] : SIMILARITY, LIKENESS
**ho·meo·morph** \ˈ⸗mēəˌmȯrf\ *n* -S [ISV *home-* + *-morph*] : an individual bearing a superficial resemblance to another; *specif* : a crystalline substance exhibiting homeomorphism
**ho·meo·mor·phic** \ˌ⸗⸗⸗ˈmȯrfik\ *adj* [*home-* + *-morphic*] **1** : characterized by homeomorphism; *specif* : topologically equivalent — used of geometric figures **2** : HOMOMORPHIC
**ho·meo·mor·phism** \-ˌfizəm\ *n* -S [ISV *homeomorphous* + *-ism*] **1** : a near similarity of crystalline forms between unlike chemical compounds — compare HETEROMORPHISM 2 **2** : topological equivalence between two geometric figures in which each can be transformed into the other by a continuous deformation
**ho·meo·mor·phous** \-ˌfəs\ *adj* [Gk *homoiomorphos* of like form, fr. *homoio-* home- + *-morphos* -morphous] **1** : manifesting homeomorphism **2** : HOMOMORPHOUS
**ho·meo·mor·phy** \ˈ⸗⸗⸗ˌfē\ *n* -ES [*home-* + *-morphy*] : HOMOMORPHY
**ho·meo·path** \-ˌpath\ *n* -S [G *homöopath,* fr. *homöo-* home- + *-path*] : a believer in or practitioner of homeopathy
**ho·meo·path·ic** \ˌ⸗⸗⸗ˈpathik\ *adj* [G *homöopathisch,* fr. *homöo-* home- + *-pathisch* -pathic] **1** : of or relating to the belief in or practice of homeopathy ⟨~ remedy⟩ **2** : of a diluted or analogous nature ⟨a ~ abolitionist, intellectually persuaded rather than emotionally —W.A.White⟩ — **ho·meo·path·i·cal·ly** \-thək(ə)lē\ *adv*
**homeopathic magic** *n* : IMITATIVE MAGIC
**ho·me·op·a·thy** \ˌhōmēˈäpəthē, ˌhäm-\ *n* -ES [G *homöopathie,* fr. *homöo-* home- + *-pathie* -pathy] : a system of medical practice that treats a disease by the administration of minute doses of a remedy that would in healthy persons produce symptoms of the disease treated — compare ALLOPATHY
**ho·meo·pla·sia** \ˌ⸗mēōˈplāzh(ē)ə\ *n* -S [NL, fr. *home-* + *-plasia*] : a growth of tissue similar to normal tissue
**ho·meo·plas·tic** \ˌ⸗⸗⸗ˈplastik\ *adj* [*home-* + *-plastic*] : formed by or related to homeoplasia
**homeosis** *var of* HOMOEOSIS
**ho·me·osmotic** \ˌhōmē, ˌhämē+\ *adj* [*home-* + *osmotic*] : having a relatively constant bodily osmotic pressure that is maintained independent of the osmotic pressure of the external environment — compare POIKILOSMOTIC
**ho·meo·sta·sis** \ˌhōmēōˈstāsəs, ˌhäm-, -ˈstasəs; -mēˈästəsəs\ *n* -ES [NL, fr. *home-* + *-stasis*] **1** : a tendency toward maintenance of a relatively stable internal environment in the bodies of higher animals through a series of interacting physiological processes (as the maintenance of a fairly constant degree of body heat in the face of widely varying external temperatures) **2** : a tendency toward maintenance of a relatively stable psychological condition of the individual with respect to contending drives, motivations, and other psychodynamic forces **3** : a tendency toward maintenance of relatively stable social conditions among groups with respect to various factors (as food supply and population among animals) and to competing tendencies and powers within the body politic, to society, or to culture among men
**ho·meo·stat·ic** \ˌ⸗mēōˈstad·ik\ *adj* [*home-* + *-static*] : related to or characterized by homeostasis
**homeothermic** *var of* HOMOIOTHERMIC
**homeotic** *var of* HOMOEOTIC
**ho·meo·transplant** \ˌhōmē(ˌ)ō, ˌhäm-+\ *or* **ho·moio·trans·plant** \hōˈmȯiō+\ *n* [*home-* + *transplant*] : HOMOGRAFT
**¹ho·meo·type** \ˈhōmēə, ˈhäm+,-\ *n* [*home-* + *type*] : a biological specimen that has been carefully compared with and identified with an original or primary type
**²homeotype** \"\ *adj* : HOMEOTYPIC
**ho·meo·typic** *also* **ho·meo·typical** \ˌ⸗⸗⸗+\ *adj* [*home-* + *typic, typical*] : being or relating to the second or equational meiotic division — compare HETEROTYPIC, MEIOSIS
**homeowner** \ˈ⸗,⸗⸗\ *n* : one that owns a home
**ho·meo·zo·ic** \ˌhōmēōˈzōik, ˌhäm-\ *adj* [ISV *home-* + *-zoic*] : of, relating to, or being one or more biogeographic regions throughout which the forms of life are the same or similar
**homeplace** \ˈ⸗,⸗\ *n* : a family home or its location
**home plate** *n* : a 5-sided slab of whitened rubber that is 17 inches wide and anchored flush with the ground at the apex of the baseball diamond, that determines the width of the strike zone, and that must be touched by a base runner in order to score a run — called also *home, home base, platter, rubber;* see BASEBALL illustration
**home port** *n* **1** : the port from which a ship hails or from which it is documented **2 a** : the port from which a man-of-war normally operates **b** : the dockyard in which a ship in the British navy is commissioned and to which she returns for refits
**home position** *n* : HOME 7c
**¹ho·mer** \ˈhōmə(r)\ *also* **cho·mer** \ˈkō-\ *n* -S [Heb *ḥōmer*] : an ancient Hebrew unit of capacity for dry or liquid measure equal to about 10½ or in later times 11½ bushels or about 100 gallons
**²hom·er** \ˈhōmə(r)\ *n* -S [¹*home* + *-er*] **1** : HOMING PIGEON **2 a** : HOME RUN **b** *slang* : a sports official who favors the home team
**³homer** \"\ *vi* **homered; homered; homering** \-m(ə)riŋ\ **homers** : to hit a home run
**home rails** *n pl* : shares of domestic railroads offered on the London Stock Exchange
**home range** *n* : the area to which an animal confines his activities — compare TERRITORY
**home reserve** *n* : a part of the organized armed forces of a country whose members live at home, carry on their usual vocations, and except for occasional calls for drill or instruction are liable to call only in emergency — called also *militia, national guard, territorial reserve;* compare HOME GUARD
**ho·me·ria** \hōˈmirēə\ *n, cap* [NL, fr. *Homer,* Greek poet + NL *-ia*] : a genus of southern African herbs (family Iridaceae) that resemble tulips and are sometimes poisonous to cattle — see CAPE TULIP
**ho·me·ri·an** \hōˈmirēən, -mer-\ *adj, usu cap* [*Homer* + E *-ian*] : HOMERIC
**ho·mer·ic** \hōˈmerik, -rēk\ *adj, usu cap* [L *Homericus,* fr. Gk *Homērikos,* fr. *Homēros* Homer, traditional Greek epic poet who prob. lived *ab* the 8th cent. B.C. + Gk *-ikos* -ic] **1** : of or relating to the Greek poet Homer, his age, or his writings ⟨classical *Homeric* conception of death —Alfred Einstein⟩ **2** : of epic proportions : HEROIC, GARGANTUAN ⟨*Homeric* feats of reporting —Stanley Walker⟩ ⟨~ laughter⟩ — **ho·mer·i·cal·ly** \-rək(ə)lē, -rēk-, -li\ *adv, often cap*
**ho·mer·i·can** \-rəkən\ *adj, usu cap* [L *Homericus* + E *-an*] *archaic* : HOMERIC
**homeric simile** *n, usu cap H* : EPIC SIMILE
**ho·mer·ist** \ˈhōmərəst\ *n* -S *usu cap* : a specialist in Homer and his epics
**home road** *n* : the railroad owning or leasing a car in freight⸗car interchange
**ho·mer·ol·o·gist** \ˌhōməˈräləjəst\ *n* -S *usu cap* : a specialist in Homerology
**ho·mer·ol·o·gy** \-jē\ *n* -ES *usu cap* [*Homer* + *-o-* + *-logy*] : a study of Homer's poems and of his life and times
**homeroom** \ˈ⸗,⸗\ *n* **1** : a schoolroom where pupils of the same class or grade but often with different academic programs report at the opening of school and meet informally under the guidance of a teacher to conduct class business, plan and organize group activities, and discuss individual and group problems **2** : a group of pupils assigned to the same homeroom
**home row** *n* : the bank of keys on a typewriter containing the home keys
**home rule** *n* **1 a** : self-government esp. with regard to local and internal legislation by the inhabitants of a dependent or federated country or territory or colony ⟨split the Liberal party over the issue of *home rule* for Ireland —C.J.Friedrich⟩; *specif, Brit* : dominion status **b** : the political theory or principle of self-government **2 a** : partial municipal autonomy granted to some cities whereby they are authorized to frame their own charters and manage their own affairs within limits set by the state esp. as to taxation, finance, police, and education **b** : limited authority granted by a state to a county esp. with regard to the determination of its organizational structure
**home ruler** *n* : one that advocates home rule; *specif, often cap H&R* : an advocate or supporter of Irish home-rule policy ⟨emphatically an Irishman . . . and a strong *home ruler* —H.H.Johnston⟩
**home run** *n* : a hit in baseball that enables the batter to make a complete circuit of the bases and score a run
**homes** *pl of* HOME, *pres 3d sing of* HOME
**home scrap** *n* : steel scrap that is utilized within the plant where it originates
**homeseeker** \ˈ⸗,⸗⸗\ *n* : one that seeks a home; *esp* : a pioneer in search of land on which to settle ⟨excitement caused by the advent of ~s from the eastern states —*Atlantic*⟩
**homesick** \ˈ⸗,⸗\ *adj* [back-formation fr. *homesickness*] **1** : longing for home and family while absent from them ⟨the boy was ~ his first week at camp⟩ **2** : yearning for a familiar or sympathetic environment ⟨that stretch of blue water was the one thing he was ~ for —Willa Cather⟩ ⟨~ for their comparatively carefree nineteenth-century past—A.J.Toynbee⟩
**home·sick·ness** *n* -ES [trans. of G *heimweh*] : the quality or state of being homesick : NOSTALGIA
**home signal** *n* : a railroad signal placed at the beginning of a block to indicate whether or not the block is clear — compare DISTANT SIGNAL
**homesite** \ˈ⸗,⸗\ *n* **1** : a location suitable for a home ⟨divided the lakefront into ~s⟩ **2** : the location of a home ⟨stayed in their bombed-out ~s —M.W.Childs⟩
**¹homespun** \ˈ⸗,⸗\ *adj* [*home* + *spun*] **1 a** : spun or made at or as if at home ⟨~ cloth⟩ ⟨turn out woven and knitted goods on hand machines that preserve the ~ quality —J.M.Mead⟩ **b** : made of homespun or of a fabric resembling homespun ⟨yeomanry . . . turned out in their working clothes and ~ country garbs —Washington Irving⟩ ⟨other popular cotton suiting choices include . . . ~ types that have weave interest —*Women's Wear Daily*⟩ **2 a** : of or relating to the common people : PLEBEIAN, UNSOPHISTICATED ⟨~ tastes⟩ ⟨~ virtues⟩ ⟨both still assume the air of ~ country boys —T.H.White b.1915⟩ : FOLKSY ⟨oozed with idiosyncrasy, naïveté and ~ humor —E.S.Turner⟩ ⟨prose which varies from the movingly lyrical to the designedly ~ —Clifton Fadiman⟩ **b** : of unaffected simplicity : UNPRETENTIOUS ⟨dresses up his thoughts in very plain ~ garments —William Clark⟩ ⟨~, kindly, shrewd men whose strength resided in their simplicity —Norman Cousins⟩ **c** : plain and direct : PRACTICAL, STRAIGHTFORWARD ⟨will make a good ~ wife —Thomas Hardy⟩ ⟨managed the affairs of local government with the same ~ skill that went to their farming —V.L.Parrington⟩ ⟨circumstances which brought forth . . . a ~ nationalism —A.G.Mazour⟩
**²homespun** \"\ *n* -S **1 a** : a loosely woven usu. woolen or linen fabric handloomed in the home from uneven hand-spun yarns **b** : a machine-made tweedy material of a plain weave and spongy texture usu. made from irregular woolen, cotton, rayon, or linen yarns and used for outer garments and upholstery **2** : a character or utterance possessing the rustic simplicity of homespun ⟨instead of the silken splendor of the upper middle classes he gives us the ~ of the poor —Grace Frank⟩
**¹home·stead** \ˈhōmˌsted, -m,st- *also* -ˌtəd *or* -ˌstəd\ *n* [¹*home* + *stead*] **1 a** : the home and land of a family; *esp* : ancestral home ⟨coming into possession . . . of the old Abbot ~ "Three Beeches" —Witmer Stone⟩ **b** : a private residence : HOUSE ⟨a seventeenth-century farm ~ with thatched roof —A.N. Whitehead⟩ **c** : the living quarters on a ranch in Australasia ⟨a good station to manage because the ~ is near the middle —Nevil Shute⟩ **2 a** : a tract of land usu. consisting of 160 acres acquired from U.S. public lands by filing a record and living on and cultivating the tract ⟨these fences marked the boundaries of the small ~s which had recently been claimed —Agnes M. Cleaveland⟩ **b** : the land and buildings on such a tract occupied as a home for the owner and his family and more or less legally protected in some jurisdictions from the claims of creditors against both the owner and his surviving spouse and minor children — see HOMESTEAD LAW
**²homestead** \"\ *vt* : to acquire or occupy as a homestead under a homestead law ⟨lacked the experience needed to ~ virgin territory —R.A.Billington⟩ ~ *vi* : to acquire or settle on land under a homestead law ⟨the original settler in the area . . . has lived there since he ~*ed* back in 1902 —Byron Fish⟩
**home·stead·er** \-də(r)\ *n* -S **1** : one who seeks or establishes a homestead under a homestead law ⟨announced that the lands ceded by the Cherokee tribes . . . would be thrown open to ~s —*Amer. Mercury*⟩ **2** : the possessor of a homestead
**homestead law** *n* **1** : a law conferring special privileges or exemptions upon owners of homesteads; *esp* : a law exempting a homestead from attachment or sale under execution for general debts **2** : any of several legislative acts authorizing the sale of public lands to settlers
**homestead lease** *or* **homestead selection** *n, Austral* : a leasehold tenure; *esp* : one created by the Crown Land Acts of 1884 and subsequent legislation
**home·ster** \ˈhōmztə(r), -mst-\ *n* -S [¹*home* + *-ster*] *Brit* **1** : a member of the home team in an athletic contest **2** : HOMEBODY
**homestretch** \ˈ⸗ˈ⸗\ *n* **1** : the part of a racecourse between the last curve and the winning post — compare BACKSTRETCH **2** : the final stage (as of a project) ⟨reached the ~ on his thesis with two weeks to spare⟩
**home study** *n* : a course of instruction administered by mail and carried on in the student's home — compare CORRESPONDENCE SCHOOL
**home table** *n* : the side of the inner table in backgammon into which a player moves his stones before bearing off
**hometown** \ˈ⸗ˈ⸗\ *n, often attrib* : the city or town of one's birth or principal residence ⟨his ~ gave the new champion a rousing welcome⟩
**home truth** *n* **1** : an unpleasant fact that jars the sensibilities ⟨*home truths* demand utterance but not in a scolding voice or a tone edged with arrogance —H.M.Wriston⟩ **2** : a statement of undisputed fact
**home visitor** *n* : a caseworker who helps children to adjust to school and community life through individual guidance based on information gathered by visits with parents, teachers, and schoolmates
**¹home·ward** \ˈhōmwə(r)d\ *or* **home·wards** \-dz\ *adv* [ME *homward, homwards,* fr. OE *hāmweard,* fr. *hām* home + *-weard* -ward — more at HOME] : in the direction of one's house or place of origin : toward home ⟨battling my way ~ one dark night against the wind and rain —L.P.Smith⟩
**²homeward** *adj* : being or going in the direction of home ⟨a few belated ~ figures were hurrying along —Michael Foster⟩
**home·ward·ly** *adv* : HOMEWARD
**homework** \ˈ⸗,⸗\ *n* **1** : work done at home; *specif* : remunerative employment carried on in the home usu. on a piecework basis ⟨the wife and mother . . . tries to eke out the scanty income by ~ —Mabel Elliott & Francis Merrill⟩ **2 a** : an assignment given to a student to be completed outside of the classroom ⟨hurried to finish his ~ so he could play ball⟩ **b** : preparatory reading or research (as for a discussion) ⟨put in . . . two days on ~ prior to each meeting —Dwight Macdonald⟩
**homeworker** \ˈ⸗ˈ⸗⸗\ *n* : one that carries on remunerative employment in the home ⟨concealed the existence of ~s who were not paid proper overtime wages —*Progressive Labor World*⟩
**hom·ey** *also* **homy** \ˈhōmē, -mi\ *adj* -ER/-EST [¹*home* + *-y*] **1** : having an air of comfortable intimacy or domesticity : COZY, FAMILIAR ⟨took a chair by the fire and looked round the ~ room with a sigh of relief —*Strand Mag.*⟩ ⟨just the right size teapot . . . in the regular old brownware, very ~ —*New Yorker*⟩ **2 a** : having an air of simple informality or hospitality usu. associated with home : FRIENDLY, UNPRETENTIOUS ⟨lends a ~ touch —*Vanity Fair*⟩ ⟨private power companies traveling under the ~ alias of "local interests" —Leland Olds⟩ **b** : of a family nature : INTIMATE ⟨like the candidate to answer a few ~ questions designed to elicit the lowdown on his wife and relatives —Claud Cockburn⟩ **c** : FOLKSY ⟨written in the excruciatingly ~ prose that is so often confused with the American vulgate —W.H.Whyte⟩ — **hom·ey·ness** *or* **hom·i·ness** \-mēnəs, -min-\ *n* -ES
**homi·ci·dal** \ˌhäməˈsīdᵊl *also* ˌhōm-\ *adj* : of, relating to, or having a tendency toward homicide : MURDEROUS — **homi·ci·dal·ly** \-dᵊlē, -dᵊli\ *adv*
**homi·cide** \ˈhäməˌsīd *also* hōm-\ *n* -S [in sense 1, fr. ME, fr. MF, fr. L *homicida,* fr. *homi-* (fr. *homo* human being, man) + *-cida* -cide (killer); in sense 2, fr. ME, fr. MF, fr. L *homicidium,* fr. *homi-* + *-cidium* -cide (killing) — more at HOMAGE] **1** : a person who kills another person : MANSLAYER ⟨the ~ must observe a rigorous taboo —J.G.Frazer⟩ **2 a** : a killing of one human being by another ⟨tabloid headlines about the latest ~⟩; *specif* : a killing of a human being through human agency ⟨charged with drunken driving and vehicle ~⟩ **b** : a squad of detectives that specializes in solving murders ⟨the boys in ~ will get all the details —Thurston Scott⟩
**homi·cid·i·ous** \ˌ⸗⸗ˈsidēəs\ *adj* [L *homicidium* + E *-ous*] *archaic* : HOMICIDAL
**homi·culture** \ˈhämə, ˈhōmə + ,-\ *n* [L *homi-* (fr. *homo* man) + E *culture*] : scientific physical improvement of mankind
**hom·i·lete** \ˈhäməˌlēt\ *n* -S [Gk *homilētēs* disciple, scholar, fr. *homilein*] : HOMILIST
**hom·i·let·ic** \ˌ⸗⸗ˈled·ik\ *adj* [LL *homileticus,* fr. Gk *homilētikos* affable, social, fr. *homilētos* (verbal of *homilein* to consort with, talk with, address, make a speech) + *-ikos* -ic — more at HOMILY] **1** : of the nature of a homily : resembling a sermon **2** : of or relating to homiletics : HORTATORY
**hom·i·let·i·cal** \-d·əkəl\ *adj* [in sense 1, fr. Gk *homilētikos* + E *-al;* in sense 2 fr. LL *homileticus* + E *-al*] **1** *obs* : of or relating to friendly companionship : SOCIAL **2** : HOMILETIC — **hom·i·let·i·cal·ly** \-k(ə)lē\ *adv*
**hom·i·let·ics** \ˌ⸗⸗ˈled·iks\ *n pl but sing in constr* [Gk *homilētikē* art of conversation, fr. fem. of *homilētikos*] **1** : the art of preaching ⟨have on occasion made ~ a substitute for statecraft —J.M.Blum⟩ **2** : a branch of theology that deals with homilies or sermons ⟨a lecturer in ~⟩
**ho·mil·i·ary** \häˈmilē,erē\ *n* -ES [ML *homiliarium,* fr. LL *homilia* homily + L *-arium* -ary] : a book of homilies
**hom·i·list** \ˈhäməl əst\ *n* -S [*homily* + *-ist*] : one who prepares or delivers a homily
**hom·i·lite** \-ˌlīt\ *n* -S [G or Sw *homilit,* fr. Gk *homilein* + G or Sw *-it* -ite] : a mineral $(Ca,Fe)_3Al_5B_2Si_2O_{16}$ consisting of a black or blackish brown iron calcium borosilicate
**hom·i·lize** \-ˌlīz\ *vi* -ED/-ING/-S [*homily* + *-ize*] : to deliver a homily : PREACH
**hom·i·ly** \ˈhäməlē, -li\ *n* -ES [alter. (influenced by LL *homilia*) of ME *omelie,* fr. MF, fr. LL *homilia,* fr. LGk, fr. Gk, conversation, discourse, fr. *homilein* to consort with, talk with, address, make a speech, fr. *homilos* crowd, assembly) + *-ia* — more at MILITATE] **1 a** : a discourse on a religious theme esp. delivered to a congregation during a church service

⟨ideas derived from *homilies* and the common teaching of the church —W.P.Ker⟩ **2 :** a lecture or discussion on a moral theme **:** ADMONITION ⟨the criminal of old was given copious drafts of exhortation and ~ administered . . . by reformers —B.N.Cardozo⟩

**homin-** *or* **homini-** *comb form* [L *homin-, homo* — more at HOMAGE] **:** man **:** human ⟨*hominine*⟩ ⟨*hominiform*⟩ ⟨*hominisection*⟩

**hom·i·nal** \ˈhämən³l\ *adj* [*homin-* + *-al*] **:** of, relating to, or constituted by man as a species **:** HUMAN ⟨the vegetable, animal, and ~ kingdoms⟩

**hominess** *var of* HOMEYNESS

¹**homing** *n* -s [fr. gerund of ⁴*home*] **1 a :** an accurate return of an animal to a known place (as a home range) **b :** a tendency to return to a known place as a facet of animal behavior ⟨~ is a well-known characteristic of salmon⟩ ⟨~ is an acquired skill operating through topographical memory —*Biol. Abstracts*⟩ **2 :** navigation toward an objective by maintaining a constant bearing on a radio beam or other point of reference ⟨for ~ a loop antenna located perpendicular to the center line of the aircraft is used —*Aircraft Navigation Manual*⟩

²**homing** *adj* [fr. pres. part. of ⁴*home*] **1 :** home-returning; *specif* **:** habitually returning to a known place ⟨shad are ~ fish⟩ **2 :** guiding or being guided to an objective ⟨~ beacon⟩ ⟨an acoustic ~ torpedo which, attracted by the submarine's noise, would follow it down and detonate on contact —R.S.Benson⟩

**homing pigeon** *n* **:** a racing pigeon sometimes used for carrying messages and trained to return to its loft from distances up to 500 miles or more by being released at gradually increased distances from home — compare CARRIER PIGEON

¹**hom·i·nid** *also* **hom·o·nid** \ˈhämənəd, -ˌnid\ *or* **ho·min·i·an** \hōˈminēən\ *n* -s [*hominid* fr. NL *Hominidae*; *homonid* alter. of *hominid*; *hominian* fr. NL *Homin-, Homo* + E *-ian*] **:** one of the Hominidae **:** a manlike creature **:** MAN ⟨fossil ~s . . . are already quite uniformly assignable to our present genus *Homo* —W.M.Krogman⟩

²**hominid** \"\ *also* **hominian** \"\ *adj* **:** of, relating to, or characterizing the Hominidae ⟨regarding man as emerging from a welter of genetically related ~ types —Weston LaBarre⟩

**ho·min·i·dae** \hōˈminəˌdē\ *n pl, cap* [NL, fr. *Homin-, Homo*, type genus + *-idae*] **:** a family of mammals (order Primates) to which man and his ancestors belong **:** a family of animals consisting of mankind — see HOMO, MAN 1b(2), PITHECANTHROPUS

**hom·i·nine** \ˈhäməˌnīn, -mən\ *adj* [*homin-* + *-ine*] **:** HUMAN

**hom·i·nism** \-ˌnizəm\ *n* -s [*homin-* + *-ism*] **:** pragmatic humanism that regards man as only a highly differentiated animal

**hom·i·niv·o·rous** \ˌ==ˈniv(ə)rəs\ *adj* [*homin-* + *-vorous*] **:** man-eating

¹**hom·i·noid** \ˈhäməˌnȯid\ *adj* [NL *Hominoidea*] **1 :** of, relating to, or characterizing the Hominoidea **2 :** resembling the Hominidae **:** MANLIKE

²**hominoid** \"\ *n* -s **:** one of the Hominoidea **:** an animal resembling man

**hom·i·noi·dea** \ˌ==ˈnȯidēə\ *n pl, cap* [NL, fr. *Homin-, Homo* + *-oidea*] **1** *in some classifications* **:** a major division of Primates segregating *Homo* and related fossil forms from the great apes **2 :** a superfamily of Anthropoidea comprising the great apes and the recent and fossil hominids as distinguished from the lower Old World monkeys — compare CERCOPITHECIDAE

**hom·i·ny** \ˈhämənē, -ni\ *n* -ES [prob. fr. a word of Algonquian origin whose 1st constituent is unknown and whose 2d constituent is akin to Natick *-minne* small fruit, grain (used in all names given to prepared corn)] **:** kernels of hulled corn (as white flint corn) with the germ removed and either whole or ground — see HOMINY GRITS; compare ¹GRIT 2a

**hominy grits** *n pl but sing or pl in constr* **:** hominy in uniform granular particles

**hom·ish** \ˈhōmish\ *adj* [¹*home* + *-ish*] **:** HOMEY — **hom·ish·ness** *n* -ES

**hommock** *var of* HUMMOCK

¹**ho·mo** \ˈhō(ˌ)mō\ *n, cap* [NL, fr. L, man, human being — more at HOMAGE] **:** the genus of man **:** a genus of mammals consisting of mankind that is the type and sole surviving member of the family Hominidae and is usu. held to include a single recent species (*H. sapiens*) comprising all surviving and various extinct men — see MAN 1b(2)

²**homo** \"\ *n* -s [by shortening] *slang* **:** HOMOSEXUAL

**homo-** *in pronunciations below*, ¦== = ¦hō(ˌ)mō *or* ¦hä(ˌ)mō *or* -ˌmə\ — see HOM-

**homo alieni juris** \ˈhō(ˌ)mō+\ *n* [L] **:** a man under the control of another — opposed to *homo sui juris*

**homo·basidiomycetes** *pronunc at* HOMO- +\ *n pl, cap* [NL, fr. *hom-* + *Basidiomycetes*] **:** a subclass of Basidiomycetes comprising fungi with nonseptate and nondivided basidia and basidiospores that usu. germinate directly to form a mycelium and including the gill fungi, pore fungi, coral fungi, and bird's-nest fungi and the puffballs and stinkhorns — compare HETEROBASIDIOMYCETES

**homo·ba·sid·io·my·cet·i·dae** \¦==(ˌ)=bəˌsidē(ˌ)ōˌmīˈsed·əˌdē\ *syn of* HOMOBASIDIOMYCETES

**homo·basidium** \"+\ *n* [NL, fr. *hom-* + *basidium*] **:** AUTOBASIDIUM

**homo·blas·tic** \¦==¦blastik\ *adj* [*hom-* + *-blastic*] **:** having a direct embryonic development **:** arising from cells of the same kind; *specif* **:** having the embryo similar in appearance to the adult plant and developing directly from the fertilized seed — **homo·blas·ty** \ˈ==ˌ=tē\ *n* -ES

**homocaryon** *var of* HOMOKARYON

¹**homo·centric** *also* **homo·centrical** *pronunc at* HOMO- +\ *adj* [NL *homocentricus*, fr. Gk *homokentros* concentric (fr. *homo-* hom- + *-kentros*, fr. *kentron* center) + L *-icus* -ic — more at CENTER] **:** having the same center ⟨~ spheres⟩; *specif* **:** diverging from or converging toward a common center — used of light rays forming a pencil

²**homocentric** \"\ *adj* [L *homo* man, human being + E *-centric* — more at HOMAGE] **:** centered on man ⟨the universe is not ~ —Junjiro Takakusu⟩ — **homo·centrically** \"+\ *adv*

**homo·cercal** *pronunc at* HOMO- +\ *adj* [*hom-* + *-cercal*] **1 :** having the upper and lower lobes approximately symmetrical and the vertebral column ending at or near the middle of the base — used of the tail fin of various fishes (as most teleosts) **2 :** having or relating to a homocercal tail fin — compare ISOCERCAL

**homo·charge** \"+ˌ\ *n* [*hom-* + *charge*] **:** a charge on an electret that is of the same sign as that of the electrode orig. in contact with it — compare HETEROCHARGE

**homo·chlamydeous** \"+\ *adj* [*hom-* + *chlamydeous*] **:** having a perianth whose inner and outer series are similar or not differentiated into calyx and corolla ⟨the lily has a typical ~ perianth⟩ — compare ACHLAMYDEAE

**homo·chromatic** \"+\ *adj* [*hom-* + *chromatic*] **1 :** of or relating to one color **2** *of an afterimage* **:** having approximately the same hues as an original image — opposed to *heterochromatic*

**homo·chromosome** \"+\ *n* [*hom-* + *chromosome*] **:** AUTOSOME

**ho·moch·ro·nous** \(ˈ)hōˈmäkrənəs, (ˈ)häˈ-\ *adj* [*hom-* + *-chronous*] **:** HOMOCHRONOUS

**homo·cline** *pronunc at* HOMO- + ˌ-\ *n* [*hom-* + *cline*] **:** a climatically similar environment; *specif* **:** a region climatically similar to another specified region ⟨New World ~*s* of certain parts of Australia⟩

**homo·cli·nal** \¦==¦klīn³l\ *adj* **:** of or relating to a homocline

**homo·cline** \ˈ==ˌklīn\ *n* -s [*hom-* + *-cline*] **:** a layer of stratified rock (as one limb of an anticline or syncline) in which the strata dip consistently in one general direction though the angle of dip may vary greatly from place to place — compare MONOCLINE

**homo·coe·la** \ˌ==ˈsēlə\ [NL, fr. *hom-* + *-coela* (fr. neut. pl. of *-coelus* -coelous)] *syn of* ASCONOSA

**homo·cyclic** \¦==+\ *adj* [*hom-* + *cyclic*] **:** ISOCYCLIC

**homo·cysteine** \"+\ *n* [*hom-* + *cysteine*] **:** a crystalline amino acid $HSCH_2CH_2CH(NH_2)COOH$ held to be formed by demethylation of methionine in the animal organism; α-amino-γ-mercapto-butyric acid

**homo·cystine** \"+\ *n* [*hom-* + *cystine*] **:** a crystalline amino acid $[-SCH_2CH_2CH(NH_2)COOH]_2$ formed by oxidation of homocysteine

**homo·dermic** \"+\ *adj* [*hom-* + *dermic*] *biol* **:** originating from the same germ layer — **homo·der·my** \ˈ==ˌdərmē\ *n* -ES

**homo·dont** \ˈ==ˌdänt\ *adj* [ISV *hom-* + *-odont*] **:** having all the teeth similar in form ⟨the porpoise is a ~ animal⟩ — opposed to *heterodont*

**ho·mod·ro·mal** \hōˈmädrəməl, häˈ-\ *adj* [NL *homodromus* + E *-al*] **:** HOMODROMOUS

**ho·mod·ro·mous** \-məs\ *or* **homo·drome** \ˈhōməˌdrōm, ˈhäm-\ *adj* [NL *homodromus*, fr. *hom-* + *-dromus* -dromous] **:** having the genetic spiral following the same direction in both stem and branches — compare HETERODROMOUS

**ho·mod·ro·my** \hōˈmädrəmē, häˈ-\ *n* -ES [ISV *homodromous* + *-y*] **:** the quality or state of being homodromous

**homo·dynamic** *pronunc at* HOMO- +\ *adj* [*hom-* + *dynamic*] **:** producing a continuous succession of generations until interrupted by adverse circumstances (as cold or lack of food) — used of an insect

**homo·dyne** \ˈ==ˌdīn\ *adj* [*hom-* + *dyne*] **:** of or relating to the process of detecting a radio wave by the aid of a locally generated current or wave of exactly the same frequency as that of the incoming wave ⟨~ reception⟩ — see ZERO BEAT

**homoe-** *or* **homoeo-** — see HOME-

**ho·moe·an** \(ˈ)hōˈmēən, (ˈ)häˈ-, ˈ=ˈmē-\ *or* **ho·moi·an** \(ˈ)=ˈmȯi(y)ən\ *n* -s *often cap* [*Homoean* fr. NL *Homoeus* (fr. Gk *homoios* like) + E *-an*; *Homoian* fr. Gk *homoios* + E *-an* — more at HOME-] **:** a member of an Arian party holding to the doctrine that the Son is like the Father though not in essence — compare ANOMOEAN, APOLLINARIAN, HOMOIOUSIAN

**ho·moe·cious** \(ˈ)hōˈmēshəs, (ˈ)häˈ-\ *adj* [*hom-* + Gk *oikia* house + E *-ous* — more at VICINITY] **:** having the same host during the entire life cycle — used esp. of a beetle parasitic in the nest of an ant — contrasted with *heteroecious*; compare AUTOECIOUS

**ho·moe·om·er·al** \ˌhōmēˈämərəl, ¦häm-\ *adj* [Gk *homoiomerēs* consisting of equal parts (fr. *homoio-* home- + *-merēs*, fr. *meros* part) + E *-al* — more at MERIT] *prosody* **:** having like or corresponding parts

**ho·moe·o·me·ria** \ˌhōˌmēəməˈrīə, häˌ-, ˌ=ˌmē(ˌ)ōm-, -ˈmirēə\ *n, pl* **homoeomeri·ae** \-rīˌē, -rēˌē\ [L] **:** HOMOEOMERY — **ho·moe·o·me·ri·an** \-rīən, -rēən\ *n* -s — **ho·moeo·me·ri·an·ism** \-əˌnizəm\ *n* -s

**ho·moeo·mer·ic** \¦==¦merik, ¦===¦-, -mir-\ *or* **ho·moeo·mer·i·cal** \-rəkəl\ *adj* [*homoeomery* + *-ic*, *-ical*] **1 :** of or relating to homoeomery **2 :** consisting of homogeneous parts or particles **3** *usu* **homoeomeric** [Gk *homoiomerēs* + E *-ic*] **:** HOMOEOMERAL

¹**homoe·om·er·ous** \¦hōmē¦ämərəs, ¦häm-\ *adj* [Gk *homoiomerēs* + E *-ous*] **1 :** having the algal cells scattered throughout the thallus ⟨~ lichens⟩ — opposed to *heteromerous* **2** [*homoeomery* + *-ous*] **:** HOMOEOMERIC 1, 2 **3 :** HOMOEOMERAL

²**homoeomerous** \"\ *adj* [*home-* + Gk *mēros* thigh + E *-ous*] **:** having the sciatic artery developed as the main artery of the thigh — used of a bird

**ho·moe·om·ery** \ˌ==ˈ==rē\ *n* -ES [L *homoeomeria*, fr. Gk *homoiomereia*, fr. *homoiomerēs* + *-eia* -y] **1 :** one of an infinite number of homogeneous ultimate particles of matter constituting through their combination and separation everything in the world **2 :** an Anaxagorean theory postulating homoeomeries

**ho·moe·o·sis** *or* **ho·me·o·sis** \ˌhōmēˈōsəs, ˌhäm-\ *n* -ES [NL, fr. Gk *homoiōsis* assimilation, resemblance, fr. *homoioun* to make like, become like (fr. *homoios* like) + *-sis* — more at HOME-] *biol* **:** an assumption by one part or structure in a series of a form characteristic of another member of the series ⟨with a wing of the fore-wing type in place of one of the normal hind wings, it provides an extreme instance of ~ —G.E.Hyde⟩ — compare HETEROMORPHOSIS

**ho·moeo·te·leu·tic** \hōˌmēətə¦lüd·ik, häˌ-; ¦hōmē(ˌ)ōtə-, ¦häm- *also* -təl¦yü-\ *adj* [Gk *homoioteleutos* having the same ending (fr. *homoio-* home- + *-teleutos*, fr. *teleutē* end) + E *-ic* — more at TELEUT-] **1 :** having the same or similar endings ⟨~ words⟩ **2** [*homoeoteleuton* + *-ic*] **:** due to homoeoteleuton ⟨~ error⟩

**ho·moeo·te·leu·ton** \=ˌ==təˈlüˌtän *also* -təlˈyü-\ *n* -s [LL, fr. Gk *homoioteleuton*, fr. neut. of *homoioteleutos*] **:** an occurrence in writing of the same or similar endings near together (as in neighboring clauses or lines) whether happening by chance or done for rhythmical effect ⟨~ is a frequent cause of omissions in copying⟩

**ho·moe·ot·ic** *also* **home·ot·ic** \¦hōmē¦äd·ik, ¦häm-\ *adj* [fr. NL *homoeosis*, *homeosis*, after such pairs as NL *hypnosis*: E *hypnotic*] **:** of or relating to homoeosis

**ho·moe·ot·o·py** \ˌ==ˈädəpē\ *n* -ES [*home-* + *-topy*] **:** HOMOEOTELEUTON

**homo·erotic** \ˌhō(ˌ)mō, ¦hä(ˌ)mō+\ *adj* [*hom-* + *erotic*] **1 :** involving or characterized by homoeroticism ⟨the ~ level of development⟩ **2 :** HOMOSEXUAL

**homo·eroticism** *also* **homo·erotism** \"+\ *n* [*hom-* + *eroticism* or *erotism*] **1 :** the tendency to obtain libidinal gratification from a member of one's own sex **2 :** HOMOSEXUALITY

**ho·mo fa·ber** \¦hō(ˌ)mōˈfābə(r), -ˌbe(ə)r; -ˈfäbə-\ *n* [NL, lit., skillful man] **1 :** man the maker or creator **2** *in Bergsonism* **:** man as engaged in transforming both himself morally and material things — contrasted with *homo sapiens*

**homo·fermentative** \ˌhō(ˌ)mō, ¦hä(- +\ *adj* [*hom-* + *fermentative*] **:** producing a fermentation resulting wholly or principally in a single end product — used esp. of economically important lactic-acid bacteria that ferment carbohydrates to lactic acid

**homo·fermenter** \"+\ *n* [*hom-* + *fermenter*] **:** a homofermentative organism

**homo·gametic** *pronunc at* HOMO- +\ *adj* [*hom-* + *gametic*] **:** forming one kind of germ cell; *esp* **:** having an X chromosome in all gametes — compare DIGAMETIC, HETEROGAMETIC

**ho·mog·a·mous** \hōˈmägəməs, häˈ-\ *or* **homo·gam·ic** *pronunc at* HOMO- +¦gamik\ *adj* [*hom-* + *-gamous*, *-gamic*] **:** characterized by or relating to homogamy

**ho·mog·a·my** \hōˈmägəmē, häˈ-\ *n* -ES [G *homogamie*, fr. *homo-* hom- + *-gamie* -gamy] **1 a :** a state of having flowers alike throughout (as in the heads of chicory and related plants or the spikes of many sedges) — opposed to *heterogamy* **b :** the maturing of the stamens and pistils at the same period — used of a perfect or monoclinous flower **2 a :** reproduction within an isolated group perpetuating qualities by which it is differentiated from the larger group of which it is a part — compare APOGAMY **b :** the mating of like with like whether selection is determined by physical or cultural similarities or both

**homo·gangliate** *pronunc at* HOMO- +\ *adj* [*hom-* + *gangliate*] **:** having symmetrically arranged nervous ganglia ⟨~ annelid worms⟩ ⟨~ arthropods⟩

**ho·mo·gen** \ˈ==jən, -ˌjen\ *n* -s [*hom-* + *-gen*] *biol* **1 :** a group having a common origin **2 :** one of two or more homogenous organs or parts

**ho·mog·e·nate** \hōˈmäjəˌnāt, hə-, -nət\ *n* -s [*homogenize* + *-ate*] **:** a substance that has been homogenized; *esp* **:** biological tissue that has been finely divided (as by a grinder) and thoroughly mixed ⟨liver ~⟩ — compare MACERATE

**homo·ge·neal** \ˌhōməˈjēnyəl, -nēəl *sometimes* ˌhäm-\ *adj* [ML *homogeneus* + E *-al*] **:** HOMOGENEOUS

**ho·mo·ge·ne·i·ty** \ˌhōməjəˈnēəd·ē, -mōj-, -ətē, -i *sometimes* ˌhäm- *or* -näə- *or* -nīə-\ *n* -ES [ML *homogeneitas*, fr. *homogeneus* + *-itas* -ity] **:** the quality or state of being homogeneous

**ho·mo·ge·neous** \¦==¦jēnēəs, -nyəs, *Brit sometimes* -¦jen-\ *adj* [ML *homogeneus*, *homogenus*, fr. Gk *homogenēs*, fr. *homo-* hom- + *-genēs* (fr. *genos* kind, race) — more at SAME, KIN] **1 a :** of a similar kind or nature **:** COMPARABLE, EQUIVALENT ⟨the three schools . . . are relatively ~ —B.F.Wright⟩ **b :** having no discordant elements **:** CONSISTENT, COMPATIBLE ⟨everything about her was ~: her looks, her possessions, the way in which she dressed —Osbert Sitwell⟩ ⟨country people . . . whose manners and morals were ~ with those of the country itself —Van Wyck Brooks⟩ **2 a :** of uniform structure or composition throughout ⟨~ granite⟩ ⟨~ sand deposits . . . laid down under steady conditions of wind —R.A.Bagnold⟩; *specif* **:** relating to, occurring in, or being a system that contains no internal physical boundaries ⟨~ system⟩ ⟨~ catalysis⟩ **b :** of a single type **:** showing no variation ⟨bituminous coal is often treated as a ~ product —G.G.Somers⟩ ⟨customary to speak of the Asian mind as though it were ~ —Iqbal Singh⟩; *specif* **:** MONOCHROMATIC 2 **c :** consisting of uniform elements (as of people or groups with similar background) ⟨~ nation⟩ ⟨~ community⟩ ⟨the sound of a full consort of viols is rich and ~ —Robert Donington⟩ **3 :** of the same mathematical degree or dimensions in every term in the symbols considered ⟨a ~ equation⟩ **4 :** HOMOGENOUS 1 — **ho·mo·ge·neous·ly** *adv* — **ho·mo·ge·neous·ness** *n* -ES

**homogeneous equilibrium** *n* **:** equilibrium in a homogeneous system

**homogeneous ray** *n* **:** a vascular ray consisting of only upright or only procumbent cells — compare HETEROGENEOUS RAY

**homogeneous reaction** *n* **:** reaction in a homogeneous system

**homogeneous reactor** *n* **:** a nuclear reactor in which the fuel is distributed (as by being dissolved in a liquid) uniformly or approximately uniformly throughout the moderator material

**homogeneous roof** *n* **:** a roof (as a concrete dome) forming a solid shell of one material

**homo·genesis** *pronunc at* HOMO- +\ *n* [NL, fr. *hom-* + *genesis*] **:** production of offspring that resemble the parents — compare HETEROGENESIS 2

**homo·genetic** *or* **homo·genetical** \"+\ *adj* [*hom-* + *genetic*, *genetical*] **:** HOMOGENOUS

**homo·gen·ic** \"+\ *adj* [*hom-* + *genic*] **1 :** HOMOGENOUS **2 :** having only one allele of a gene or genes — used of a gamete or of a population

**ho·mog·e·ni·za·tion** \hōˌmäjənəˈzāshən, hə-, hä-, -ˌnīˈz-\ *n* -s **1 :** the quality or state of being homogenized **2 :** the act or process of homogenizing

**ho·mog·e·nize** \=ˈ==ˌnīz\ *vb* -ED/-ING/-S [*homogenous* + *-ize*] *vt* **1 a :** to blend (diverse elements) into a smooth mixture ⟨after these two main ingredients . . . have been thoroughly *homogenized* —D.A.Dearle⟩ **b :** to blend as if by homogenizing **:** make homogeneous ⟨trying to legislate decency or ~ social relations by law —Malcolm Moos⟩ **c :** to anneal (an alloy) for a long time at a high temperature to make more nearly uniform in chemical composition throughout **2 a :** to reduce to particles of uniform size evenly distributed ⟨~ peanut butter⟩ ⟨a fragment of cocoon . . . was cut into small pieces and *homogenized* into tiny fragments in water —*Science*⟩; *specif* **:** to grind (tobacco leaves) into a pulp and compress into a sheet for use as binder **b :** to reduce the particles of (a liquid) to uniform size and distribute them evenly ⟨~ paint⟩ — compare EMULSIFY **c :** to break up the fat globules and other solids of (milk or cream) by means of a homogenizer ~ *vi* **:** to attain a uniform state or consistency through reduction or blending ⟨heat causes the product to ~⟩

**homogenized** *adj* **1 :** reduced to small evenly distributed particles ⟨~ baby food⟩ ⟨~ cosmetics⟩ **2 :** of unvarying uniformity **:** HOMOGENEOUS ⟨Americans are anything but a standard ~ article —David Davidson⟩

**ho·mog·e·niz·er** \-zə(r)\ *n* -s **:** one that homogenizes; *esp* **:** a machine that forces a substance through fine openings against a hard surface for the purpose of blending or emulsification — compare COLLOID MILL, EMULSIFIER

**ho·mog·e·nous** \-ˌnəs\ *adj* [ML *homogenus* of the same kind — more at HOMOGENEOUS] **1 :** of, relating to, or exhibiting homogeny **2 :** HOMOPLASTIC 2 **3 :** HOMOGENEOUS

**homo·gen·tis·ic acid** *pronunc at* HOMO- +¦jen¦tizik-\ *n* [*homogentisic* ISV *hom-* + *gentisic* (in *gentisic acid*)] **:** a crystalline acid $C_6H_3(OH)_2CH_2COOH$ formed as an intermediate in the metabolism of phenylalanine and tyrosine and found esp. in the urine in cases of alkaptonuria

**ho·mog·e·ny** \hōˈmäjənē, hə-, häˈ-\ *n* -ES [Gk *homogeneia*, fr. *homogenēs* of the same kind + *-ia* -y — more at HOMOGENEOUS] **:** correspondence between parts or organs due to descent from the same ancestral type **:** HOMOLOGY — opposed to *homoplasy*

**homo·gone** *pronunc at* HOMO- +ˌgōn\ *adj* [*hom-* + *-gone*] **:** HOMOGONOUS

**homo·gon·ic** \¦==¦gänik, -ˈgōn-\ *adj* [*hom-* + *-gonic* (fr. *-gone* + *-ic*)] **:** being that course of development in which one generation of parasites immediately succeeds another — used of various nematode worms; distinguished from *heterogonic*

**ho·mog·o·nous** \hōˈmägənəs, hə-, häˈ-\ *adj* **:** of or relating to homogony — **ho·mog·o·nous·ly** *adv*

**ho·mog·o·ny** \-nē\ *n* -ES [*hom-* + *-gony*] **:** a condition of having one kind of flowers with the androecium and gynoecium of uniform relative length — opposed to *heterogony*

**ho·mo·graft** *pronunc at* HOMO- +ˌ-\ *n* [*hom-* + *graft*] **:** a graft of tissue taken from a donor of the same species as the recipient — compare HETEROGRAFT

**homo·graph** \ˈhäməˌgraf, ˈhōm-, -raa(ə)f, -raif, -räf\ *n* [*hom-* + *-graph*] **:** one of two or more words spelled alike but differing in derivation or meaning or pronunciation (as *fair*, market and *fair*, beautiful; *lead*, to conduct and *lead*, metal) — called also *homonym*

**homo·graph·ic** \¦==¦grafik\ *adj* [*hom-* + *-graphic*] **1 :** of, relating to, or consisting of a homograph **2 :** employing a single and separate character to represent each sound **:** PHONETIC — opposed to *heterographic*

**ho·mog·ra·phy** \häˈmägrəfē, hōˈ-, -fi\ *n* -ES [*hom-* + *-graphy*] **:** homographic spelling

**homo·he·dral** *pronunc at* HOMO- +¦hēdrəl *sometimes chiefly Brit* ¦hed-\ *adj* [*hom-* + *-hedral*] **:** having equal or corresponding faces; *also* **:** HOLOHEDRAL

**homoi-** *or* **homoio-** — see HOME-

**homoian** *often cap, var of* HOMOEAN

**ho·moio·genetic** \hōˌmȯiō+\ *adj* [*home-* + *genetic*] **:** having the ability to induce the formation of a similar part when grafted into an undetermined field ⟨the ~ inducing of a new neural tube by a neural tube graft⟩ — used of a determined part of an embryo

**ho·moio·me·ria** \hōˌmȯi(y)əməˈrīə, ˌhōmēōm-, ˌhämēōm-, -ˈmirēə\ *n, pl* **homoiomeri·ae** \-rīˌē, -rēˌē\ [Gk *homoiomereia* — more at HOMOEOMERY] **:** HOMOEOMERY — **ho·moio·me·ri·an** \-rīən, -rēən\ *n* -s — **ho·moio·me·ri·an·ism** \-əˌnizəm\ *n* -s

**ho·moi·osmotic** \(¦)hō¦mȯi, (¦)hä¦- +\ *adj* [*home-* + *osmotic*] **:** having a bodily osmotic regulating mechanism and having body fluids that differ in osmotic pressure from the surrounding medium or from sea water ⟨~ animals include all the land and freshwater vertebrates⟩ — compare POIKILOSMOTIC

**ho·moio·te·leu·ton** \hōˌmȯi(y)ətəˈlüˌtän *also* -təlˈyü-\ *n* -s [Gk — more at HOMOEOTELEUTON] **:** HOMOEOTELEUTON

**ho·moio·therm** \hōˈmȯi(y)əˌthərm\ *or* **homeo·therm** \ˈhōmēə-, ˈhäm-\ *n* -s [*home-* + *-therm*] **:** a homoiothermic organism

**ho·moio·ther·mic** \hō¦mȯi(y)ə¦thərmik\ *or* **homeo·ther·mic** \¦hōmēō-, ¦häm-\ *also* **ho·moio·ther·mal** \hō¦mȯi(y)ə¦thərməl\ *adj* [*home-* + *-thermic*, *thermal*] **:** having a relatively uniform body temperature maintained nearly independent of the environmental temperature **:** WARM-BLOODED

**ho·moio·ther·my** \hōˈmȯi(y)əˌthərmē\ *or* **homeo·ther·my** \ˈhōmēō-, ˈhäm-\ *also* **ho·moio·ther·mism** \hōˈmȯi(y)əˌthərˌmizəm\ *n, pl* **homoiothermies** *or* **homeothermies** *also* **homoiothermisms** [*home-* + *-thermy* or *-thermism* (fr. *therm-* + *-ism*)] **:** the state of being homoiothermic **:** warm-blooded condition or state

**homoiotransplant** *var of* HOMEOTRANSPLANT

**ho·moi·ou·sia** \ˌhōˌmȯiˈüzēə, -ˈüsēə, -ˈüzh(ē)ə, -ˈüsh(ē)ə\ *n* -s [NL, fr. LGk *homoiousios* + L *-ia* -y] **:** similarity but not identity in essence or substance **:** essential likeness

¹**ho·moi·ou·sian** \-ən\ *n* -s *often cap* [LGk *homoiousios* of like substance (fr. Gk *homoi-* home- + *-ousios*, fr. *ousia* substance, being) + E *-an* (n. suffix)] **:** one that accepts the homoiousian doctrine

²**homoiousian** \"\ *adj* [LGk *homoiousios* + E *-an* (adj. suffix)] **1 a :** holding to the doctrine that the Son is essentially like the Father but not of the same substance **b :** of or relating to the doctrine of homoiousia — distinguished from *homoousian*; compare HETEROOUSIAN **2 :** of or relating to the homoiousians **3 :** of or relating to homoiousia

**ho·moi·ou·sian·ism** \-əˌnizəm\ *n* -s **:** the doctrines and beliefs of the homoiousians

**ho·moi·ou·sious** \-əs\ *adj* [LGk *homoiousios*] **:** HOMOIOUSIAN

**homo·karyon** *also* **homo·caryon** *pronunc at* HOMO- +\ *n* -s [NL, fr. *hom-* + *karyon*] **:** a cell in the mycelium of a fungus that contains two or more genetically identical nuclei — compare DIKARYON, HETEROKARYON

**homo·kary·osis** *or* **homo·cary·osis** \ˌ══ˌkarēˈōsə̇s\ *n* -ES [NL, fr. *homokaryon, homocaryon* + *-osis*] **:** the condition of having homokaryons

**homo·kary·ot·ic** *or* **homo·cary·ot·ic** \ˌ══ˌ══ˈäd·ik\ *adj* [irreg. fr. NL *homokaryon, homocaryon* + E *-ic*] **1 :** of, relating to, or being part of a homokaryon ⟨~ nuclei⟩ **2 :** involving or consisting of homokaryons **:** exhibiting homokaryosis ⟨a ~ mycelium⟩ ⟨~ development⟩

**homo·lateral** *pronunc at* HOMO- + \ *adj* [ISV *hom-* + *lateral*] **:** IPSILATERAL

**homo·lecithal** \"+\ *adj* [*hom-* + *lecithal*] **:** having the yolk small in amount and nearly uniformly distributed — used of an egg; opposed to *heterolecithal;* compare ALECITHAL

**ho·mo le·ga·lis** \ˌhō(ˌ)mōləˈgāləs, -gäl-,-gal-\ *n* [ML] **:** one whose status as a citizen or member of a community is recognized in law **:** a legal person

**ho·mol·o·gate** \hōˈmälə,gāt\ *vb* -ED/-ING/-S [ML *homologatus*, past part. of *homologare*, fr. Gk *homologein* to agree, fr. *homologos* agreeing — more at HOMOLOGOUS] *vt* **1 :** to agree with **:** SANCTION ⟨~ the act of an ally⟩ **2 :** APPROVE, ALLOW, CONFIRM ⟨a party to an adverse judgment ~*s* it by failure to appeal⟩ **3** *Scots law* **:** to cause (a document or transaction that is defective or informal) to be validated **:** RATIFY **4 :** to confirm officially (some aspect of the performance of an airplane, as speed, altitude, duration) ~ *vi* **:** to be or act in accord **:** AGREE, CONCUR — **ho·mol·o·ga·tion** \ˌ══ˌ══ˈgāshən\ *n* -S

**homo·log·i·cal** *pronunc at* HOMO- + ˈläjəkəl\ *also* **homo·log·ic** \-jik\ *adj* [*homology* + *-ical, -ic*] **:** relating to or characterized by homology **:** HOMOLOGOUS — **homo·log·i·cal·ly** \-jək(ə)lē\ *adv*

**ho·mol·o·gize** \hōˈmälə,jīz, hə'-\ *vb* -ED/-ING/-S [*homologous* + *-ize*] *vi* **:** to be homologous **:** CORRESPOND ⟨a man's arm ~*s* with a dog's foreleg⟩ ~ *vt* **1 :** to make homologous ⟨~ one set of rules with another⟩ **2 :** to demonstrate the homology of (as parts)

**ho·mol·o·giz·er** \-zə(r)\ *n* -S **:** one that homologizes

**homolo·gou·me·na** \ˌhäməlōˈgüməna, hō,mäl-\ *also* **homolo·gu·me·na** \-ˈg(y)ü-\ *n pl* [LGk *homologoumena*, fr. Gk, neut. pl. of *homologoumenos*, pres. passive part. of *homologein* to agree, fr. *homologos*] **:** books of the New Testament acknowledged as authoritative and canonical from the earliest time — compare ANTILEGOMENA

**ho·mol·o·gous** \hōˈmäləgəs, hə'-\ *adj* [Gk *homologos* agreeing, fr. *hom-* hom- + *-logos* (fr. *legein* to speak) — more at LEGEND] **1 :** of, relating to, or characterized by homology: as **a :** having the same relative position, proportion, value, or structure **:** CORRESPONDING ⟨~ constituents in logically equivalent . . . sentences —Arthur Pap⟩ **b** (1) **:** corresponding in structure or origin — compare ANALOGOUS 2a (2) **:** of like genic constitution — used of allelic chromosomes **c :** belonging to or consisting of a chemical series whose members exhibit homology **d :** showing geometrical homology **2 :** derived from or developed in response to organisms of the same species ⟨a ~ tissue graft⟩ ⟨bacteria suspended in a ~ serum⟩ — compare AUTOLOGOUS, HETEROLOGOUS — **ho·mol·o·gous·ly** *adv*

**homologous graft** *n* **:** HOMOGRAFT

**homologous serum hepatitis** *or* **homologous serum jaundice** *n* **:** INFECTIOUS HEPATITIS

**homologous stimulus** *n* **:** an agent (as light or sound) that is the normal stimulus of a sense organ and is able to produce its specialized stimulation only when acting on the organ adapted to receive it — compare HETEROLOGOUS STIMULUS

**homologous theory** *n* **:** a theory in botany: the sporophyte and gametophyte in plants are essentially alike, the sporophyte having developed by direct modification of the gametophyte — compare ANTITHETIC THEORY

**homologous twin** *n* **:** IDENTICAL TWIN

**homolo·graph·ic** \ˌhäməlōˈgrafik, hō,mäl- *or* **hom·a·lo·graph·ic** \ˌhäməl-\ *adj* [modif. of F *homalographique*, fr. *homalo-* homal- + *-graphique* -graphic] **:** preserving the mutual relations of parts esp. as to size and form

**homolographic projection** *n* **:** an equal-area map projection — compare MOLLWEIDE PROJECTION

**homo·logue** *or* **homo·log** \ˈhōmə,lȯg, ˈhäm- *also* -läg\ *n* -S [fr. *homologous*, after such pairs as E *analogous: analogue*] **1 :** one that exhibits homology ⟨interlingual ~⟩ ⟨~*s* of the ethylene series⟩ ⟨corresponding sides of similar polygons are ~*s* of each other⟩ ⟨pectoral fin, wing, and arm are ~*s*⟩ **2 :** a homologous chromosome or pair of chromosomes

**ho·mol·o·gy** \hōˈmäləjē, hə'-, -ji\ *n* -ES [Gk *homologia* agreement, fr. *homologos* agreeing + *-ia* -y — more at HOMOLOGOUS] **1 :** a similarity often attributable to common origin **:** AFFINITY ⟨the anthropologist is in the curious position of dealing with . . . striking *homologies* not necessarily due to historical contact —Edward Sapir⟩ **2 a :** likeness short of identity in structure or function between parts of different organisms due to evolutionary differentiation from the same or a corresponding part of a remote ancestor ⟨the structural relation between the wing of a bird and the pectoral fin of a fish is a familiar example of ~⟩ — distinguished from *analogy* **b :** correspondence in structure between different parts of the same individual **3 a :** the relation existing between chemical compounds in a series whose successive members have in composition a regular difference esp. of one carbon and two hydrogen atoms $CH_2$ (as in the series of alcohols beginning with methyl alcohol $CH_3OH$, ethyl alcohol $C_2H_5OH$, propyl alcohol $C_3H_7OH$) **b :** the relation existing among elements in the same group of the periodic table (as the elements of the halogen group) **4 :** a one-to-one correspondence of two coplanar geometrical figures whereby the junction lines of correspondent points are copunctal in the center of homology and the junction points of correspondent lines are collinear on the axis of homology

**ho·mol·o·sine projection** \hōˈmälə,sīn-\ *n* [*homolographic* + 

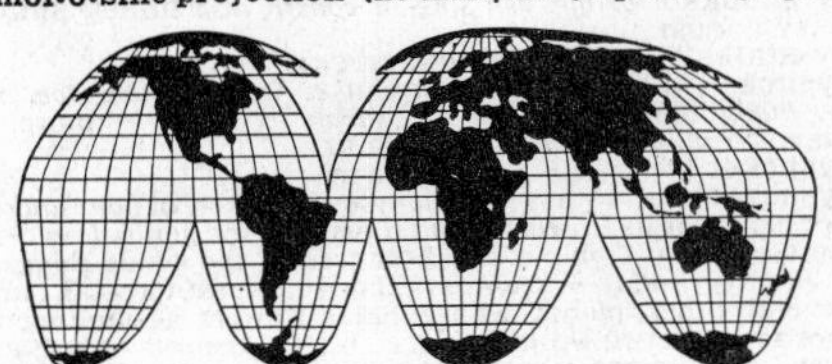

homolosine projection

*sine*] **:** an equal-area map projection that combines the sinusoidal projection for latitudes up to 40° with the homolographic for areas poleward of these latitudes

**ho·mol·y·sis** \hōˈmäləsə̇s\ *n* [NL, fr. *hom-* + *-lysis*] **:** the decomposition of a chemical compound into two neutral atoms or radicals (as X:Y → X· + Y·) — compare HETEROLYSIS — **homo·lyt·ic** \ˌhōmōˈlid·ik, ˌhäm-\ *adj*

**homo·mal·lous** *pronunc at* HOMO- + ˌmaləs\ *adj* [*hom-* + *-mallous* (as in *heteromallous*)] **:** uniformly curving to one side — used of the leaves of mosses; opposed to *heteromallous*

**ho·mo men·su·ra** \ˌhō(ˌ)mō,menˈsürə\ *n* [L, lit., man the measure] **:** a doctrine first propounded by Protagoras holding that man is the measure of all things, that everything is relative to human apprehension and evaluation, and that there is no objective truth

**homo·metrical** *pronunc at* HOMO- + \ *adj* [*hom-* + *metrical*] **:** having the same meter — **homo·metrically** \"+\ *adv*

**homo·mor·phic** \"+ˈmȯrfik\ *adj* [*hom-* + *-morphic*] **1 :** of, relating to, or characterized by homomorphism or homomorphy **2 :** alike in form or size — used specif. of synaptic chromosomes; compare HETEROMORPHIC d

**homo·mor·phism** \"+ˌfizəm\ *n* -S [ISV *hom-* + *-morphism*] **:** likeness in form: as **a :** HOMOMORPHY **b :** the state of having perfect flowers of only one type — distinguished from *heterogony* — **homo·mor·phous** \ˌ══ˈ══fəs\ *adj*

**homo·mor·pho·sis** \ˌ══ˈmȯrfəsə̇s *sometimes* -mȯrˈfōsə̇s\ *n* [NL, fr. *hom-* + *-morphosis*] **:** regeneration by an organism of a part similar to one that has been lost — compare HETEROMORPHOSIS

**homo·mor·phy** \ˈ══ˌfē\ *n* -ES [ISV *hom-* + *-morphy*] **:** similarity of form (as in external characters) with different fundamental structure **:** superficial resemblance between organisms of different groups due to convergence — opposed to *homophyly;* compare HOMOLOGY 2a

**homo·neu·ra** \ˌ══ˈn(y)ürə\ *n pl, cap* [NL, fr. *hom-* + *-neura*] **:** a suborder of primitive Lepidoptera including those forms in which the venation is alike in the two pairs of wings — compare HETERONEURA

**homonid** *var of* HOMINID

**ho·mon·o·mous** \(ˈ)hōˈmänəməs, (ˈ)häˈ-\ *adj* [Gk *homonomos* under the same laws, fr. *homo-* hom- + *-nomos* (fr. *nomos* usage, custom, law) — more at NIMBLE] **:** similar in function and structure and developed to a like degree — used of metameric parts and animals ⟨a few insects have nearly ~ legs and wings⟩ — **ho·mon·o·mous·ly** *adv*

**homo·nuclear** *pronunc at* HOMO- + \ *adj* [*hom-* + *nuclear*] **1 :** of or relating to the same ring in a chemical compound ⟨~ substitution in naphthalene⟩ **2 :** of or relating to a molecule composed of like nuclei (as hydrogen $H_2$ or nitrogen $N_2$)

**homo·nym** \ˈhämə,nim, ˈhōm-\ *n* -S [L *homonymum* the same word used to denote different things, fr. Gk *homōnymon*, fr. neut. of *homōnymos* having the same name] **1 a :** HOMOPHONE **b :** HOMOGRAPH **c :** one of two or more words spelled and pronounced alike but different in meaning (as *pool* of water and *pool* the game) **2 :** NAMESAKE **3 :** a taxonomic designation rejected because the identical term has been used to designate another group of the same rank — compare SYNONYM

**homo·nym·ic** \ˌ══ˈnimik\ *adj* **:** of, relating to, or being homonyms — **homo·nym·i·ty** \ˌ══ˈnimədē\ *n* -ES

**ho·mon·y·mous** \hōˈmänəməs, häˈ-\ *adj* [L *homonymus*, fr. Gk *homōnymos* having the same name, fr. *homo-* hom- + *-ōnymos* (fr. *onyma, onoma* name) — more at NAME] **1 a :** having two or more different significations **:** AMBIGUOUS — used chiefly of words **b :** having the same designation ⟨the state and its capital are ~⟩ — opposed to *heteronymous* **c :** HOMONYMIC **2 a :** standing in the same relation; *specif* **:** relating to or being a convergence of the eyes such that the object is beyond the fixation point resulting in double vision with the right-eye image to the right of the left-eye image ⟨~ diplopia⟩ **b :** UNILATERAL ⟨~ hemianopia⟩ — **ho·mon·y·mous·ly** *adv*

**ho·mon·y·my** \-mē\ *n* -ES [LL *homonymia* identity of name, fr. Gk *homōnymia*, fr. *homōnymos* + *-ia* -y] **:** the quality or state of being homonymous

**homo·osis** \ˌhōmōˈōsə̇s, ˌhäm-\ *n* -ES [NL, fr. *hom-* + *-osis*] **:** development in one part of an organism of a structure normally produced in another part

**homo·ou·sia** \ˌ══ˈüzēə, -üsēə, -üzh(ē)ə, -üsh(ē)ə\ *n* -S [NL, fr. LGk *homoousios* + L *-ia* -y] **:** identity in essence or substance

**[1]homo·ou·sian** \-ən\ *n* -S *often cap* [modif. (influenced by LGk *homoousios*) of LL *homousianus*, adj. & n., fr. LGk *homoousios* of the same substance (fr. Gk *homo-* hom- + *ousios*, fr. *ousia* substance) + L *-anus* -an] **:** one that accepts the homoousian doctrine of the Nicene Creed

**[2]homoousian** \"\ *adj* **1 a :** holding to the doctrine of the Nicene Creed that the Son of God is of the same essence or substance with the Father **b :** of or relating to the doctrine of homoousia — distinguished from *homoiousian;* compare HETEROOUSIAN **2 :** of or relating to the homoousians **3 :** of or relating to homoousia

**homo·ou·sian·ism** \-ə,nizəm\ *n* -S **:** the doctrines and beliefs of the homoousians

**homo·ou·si·on** \-üz(h)ē,än, -üs(h)-\ *n* -S *often cap* [Gk, acc. masc. sing. of *homoousios*] **:** a theological doctrine holding that Christ is of one substance with God ⟨the very existence of Christianity . . . was at stake over the *Homoousion* —C.H. Turner⟩

**homo·pet·al·ous** \ˌ══ˈpedᵊləs\ *adj* [ISV *hom-* + *-petalous*] **:** having petals alike

**homo·phone** \ˈhämə,fōn, ˈhōm-\ *n* [ISV *hom-* + *-phone*] **1 :** one of two or more words pronounced alike but different in meaning or derivation or spelling (as *all* and *awl; to, too,* and *two; rite, write, right,* and *wright*) — called also *homonym* **2 :** a character or group of characters pronounced the same as another character or group ⟨η, ι, υ, ει, and οι are ~*s* in modern Greek, all being pronounced \ē\⟩

**homo·phon·ic** \ˌ══ˈfänik\ *adj* [Gk *homophōnos* + E *-ic*] **1 :** sounding alike or being of the same musical pitch **:** UNISONOUS **2 :** relating to homophony **:** MONOPHONIC — compare POLYPHONIC **3 :** having all musical parts moving in the same rhythm — **homo·phon·i·cal·ly** \-nək(ə)lē\ *adv*

**ho·moph·o·nous** \hōˈmäfənəs, häˈ-, hə'-\ *adj* [Gk *homophōnos*, fr. *homo-* hom- + *-phōnos* (fr. *phōnē* sound, voice) — more at BAN] **1 :** HOMOPHONIC 1 **2** *also* **homo·phone** \ˈhämə,fōn, ˈhōm-\ **:** being a homophone

**ho·moph·o·ny** \hōˈmäfənē, häˈ-, hə'-\ *n* -ES [Gk *homophōnia*, fr. *homophōnos* + *-ia* -y] **1 :** sameness of sound **:** the quality or state of being homophonous **2 a :** UNISON **b :** MONODY 4a — compare POLYPHONY **c :** composition in which the voice or instrumental parts move in one rhythm in chordal style

**homo·phyletic** *pronunc at* HOMO- +\ *adj* [ISV *hom-* + *phyletic;* orig. formed as G *homophyl*] **:** relating to homophyly **:** belonging to the same race

**ho·moph·y·ly** \hōˈmäfəlē\ *n* -ES [ISV *hom-* + *phyl-* + *-y;* orig. formed as G *homophylie*] **:** resemblance due to common ancestry — opposed to *homomorphy*

**homo·pla·sia** \ˌ══ *at* HOMO- + ˈplāzh(ē)ə\ *or* **homo·pla·sis** \-ˈplāsə̇s\ *n, pl* **homopla·sias** \-āzh(ē)əz\ *or* **homopla·ses** \-ā,sēz\ [NL, fr. *hom-* + *-plasia, -plasis*] **:** HOMOPLASY

**homo·plas·tic** \ˌ══ˈplastik\ *adj* [ISV *hom-* + *-plastic*] **1 :** of or relating to homoplasy ⟨~ organ⟩ **2 :** of, relating to, or derived from another individual of the same species ⟨~ graft⟩ — **homo·plas·ti·cal·ly** \-tək(ə)lē\ *adv*

**homo·plasy** \ˈ══ˌplāsē, -lasē; hōˈmäplasē, häˈ-\ *n* -ES [*hom-* + *-plasy*] **:** correspondence between parts or organs acquired as the result of parallel evolution or convergence — opposed to *homogeny*

**homo·ploid** \ˈ══ˌplȯid\ *adj* [*hom-* + *-ploid*] **:** exhibiting similar degrees of ploidy

**homo·polar** \ˌ══+\ *adj* [ISV *hom-* + *polar*] **1 :** having the poles of the primary axis alike **2 :** alike in both senses (as AB and BA) with respect to physical or other property — used of a direction in crystals; compare CENTER OF SYMMETRY 2 **3 a :** relating to, characterized by, or being a union of atoms of like state as regards polarity **:** NONPOLAR, NONIONIC — distinguished from *heteropolar;* compare IONIC, POLAR **b :** UNIPOLAR ⟨~ dynamo⟩ — **homo·polarity** \"+\ *n*

**homopolar generator** *n* **:** a generator producing direct current without reversals of potential or resort to commutation

**homopolar machine** *n* **:** ACYCLIC MACHINE

**homo·polymer** *pronunc at* HOMO- +\ *n* [*homogeneous* + *polymer*] **:** a polymer (as polyethylene, polyvinyl acetate) containing only units of one single monomer

**homo·polymerization** \"+\ *n* **:** the process of homopolymerizing

**homo·polymerize** \"+\ *vi* -ED/-ING/-S [*homopolymer* + *-ize*] **:** to form a homopolymer

**ho·mop·tera** \hōˈmäptərə\ *n pl, cap* [NL, fr. *hom-* + *-ptera*] **:** a large and important suborder of Hemiptera (sometimes considered a separate order) comprising the cicadas, lantern flies, leafhoppers, spittle insects, treehoppers, aphids, psyllas, whiteflies, and scales all of which have a small prothorax and sucking mouthparts consisting of a jointed beak and undergo an incomplete metamorphosis — compare HETEROPTERA — **ho·mop·ter·an** \-rən\ *adj* — **ho·mop·ter·ous** \-rəs\ *adj*

**ho·mop·ter·ist** \-rə̇st\ *n* -S [NL *Homoptera* + *-ist*] **:** a specialist on or student of the Homoptera

**ho·mop·ter·on** \-ˌrän\ *n* -S [NL, back-formation fr. *Homoptera*] **:** one of the Homoptera

**ho·mor·elaps** \hōˈmȯrə,laps\ [NL, prob. irreg. fr. *hom-* + *Elaps*] *syn of* ELAPS

**hom·organic** \ˌhōm, ˌhäm+\ *adj* [*hom-* + *organic*] **:** sharing one or more of the articulating vocal organs **:** articulated with the same basic closure or constriction but differentiated by one or more modifications ⟨\p\, \b\, and \m\ are ~, contact of the two lips being common to all three⟩

**homos** *pl of* HOMO

**ho·mo sapi·ens** \ˌhō(ˌ)mōˈsapēənz, -sāp- *also* -ē,enz *or* -ē,en(t)s\ *n* [NL, a biological species, fr. *Homo* + *sapiens* (specific epithet), fr. L, wise — more at SAPIENT] **1** *usu cap H* **:** MANKIND 1 **2** *pl* **homo sapiens :** sentient, conscious, thinking man — contrasted with *homo faber*

**homo·sce·das·tic** *pronunc at* HOMO- + s(k)əˈdastik\ *adj* [*hom-* + LGk *skedastikos* able to scatter, fr. Gk *skedastos* capable of being scattered (fr. *skedannynai* to scatter) + *-ikos* -ic — more at SHATTER] **:** having equal standard deviations ⟨~ statistical distributions⟩ — **homo·sce·das·tic·i·ty** \ˌ══ˌ══s(k)ə,daˈstisəd·ē\ *n* -ES

**[1]ho·mo·sexual** \ˌhōmə, -mō +\ *adj* [*hom-* + *sexual*] **1 :** of, relating to, or being of the same sex ⟨~ twins⟩ **2 a :** of, relating to, or exhibiting homosexuality ⟨~ tendency⟩ ⟨~ act⟩ — opposed to *heterosexual* **b :** involving, characterized by, or based on homosexuality ⟨a child's ~ phase⟩

**[2]homosexual** \"\ *n* -S **:** one who is inclined toward or practices homosexuality

**ho·mo·sexualist** \ˌ══+\ *n* **:** HOMOSEXUAL

**ho·mo·sexuality** \"+\ *n* **1 :** atypical sexuality characterized by manifestation of sexual desire toward a member of one's own sex **2 :** erotic activity with a member of one's own sex — compare LESBIANISM **3 a :** a stage in normal psychosexual development occurring during prepuberty in the male and during early adolescence in the female during which libidinal gratification is sought with members of one's own sex **b :** the extent to which one's libido is fixated at a homoerotic level

**ho·mo sig·no·rum** \ˌhō(ˌ)mōsigˈnōrəm\ *n* [NL, lit., man of signs] **:** a conventionalized figure often found in old almanacs showing a man surrounded by signs of the zodiac from which lines point to the parts of the body thought to be subject to their influence

**ho·mo·spor·ous** *pronunc at* HOMO- + ˈspōrəs; (ˈ)hōˈmäspərəs, (ˈ)häˈ-\ *adj* [*hom-* + *-sporous*] **:** characterized by homospory — compare PROTHALLIUM

**homo·spory** \ˈ══ˌspōrē, ═ˈ═ˌspərē\ *n* -ES [*hom-* + *-spory*] **:** the production by various plants (as the club mosses and horsetails) of asexual spores of only one kind — opposed to *heterospory*

**ho·mos·te·us** \hōˈmästēəs, häˈ-\ *n, cap* [NL, fr. *hom-* + *-osteus*] **:** a genus of very large flattened Devonian fishes (subclass Arthrodira) having slender toothless jaws

**homo·styled** *pronunc at* HOMO- + ˌstīld\ *also* **homo·sty·lic** \ˌ══ˈstīlik\ *or* **homo·sty·lous** \-īləs\ *adj* [*homostyled* fr. *hom-* + *styled; homostylic* fr. *hom-* + *style* + *-ic; homostylous* fr. *hom-* + *-stylous*] **:** having styles all of one length — compare HETEROSTYLED

**homo·sty·ly** \ˈ══ˌstīlē\ *n* -ES [ISV *hom-* + *-styly;* orig. formed as G *homostylie*] **:** HOMOGONY

**ho·mo sui juris** \ˌhō(ˌ)mō+\ *n* [L] **:** a man under his own control — opposed to *homo alieni juris*

**homo·tac·tic** *pronunc at* HOMO- + ˈtaktik\ *adj* [*hom-* + *-tactic*] **:** HOMOTAXIAL

**homo·tax·e·ous** \-ˈtaksēəs\ *adj* [NL *homotaxis* + E *-eous*] **:** HOMOTAXIAL

**homo·tax·ia** \ˌ══ˈtaksēə\ *n* -S [NL, fr. *hom-* + *-taxia*] **:** HOMOTAXIS

**homo·tax·i·al** \ˌ══ˈtaksēəl\ *adj* [NL *homotaxis* + E *-al*] **:** of or relating to homotaxis — **homo·tax·i·al·ly** \-əlē\ *adv*

**homo·tax·is** \ˌ══ˈtaksə̇s\ *n* [NL, fr. *hom-* + *-taxis*] **:** similarity in arrangement; *esp* **:** similarity in fossil content and in order of arrangement of stratified deposits that are not necessarily contemporaneous

**ho·mo·taxy** \ˈ══ˌtaksē\ *n* -ES [NL *homotaxia*] **:** HOMOTAXIS

**homo·thal·lic** *pronunc at* HOMO- + ˈthalik\ *adj* [*hom-* + *thall-* + *-ic*] **1 :** having only one haploid phase producing genetically compatible gametes — used esp. of algae and fungi or of the spores producing such a phase; compare HETEROTHALLIC **2 :** MONOECIOUS

**homo·thal·lism** \ˌ══ˈtha,lizəm\ *n* -S **:** the quality or state of being homothallic

**ho·mo·therm** \ˈ══ˌthərm\ *n* -S [*hom-* + *-therm*] **:** HOMOIOTHERM

**homo·ther·mous** \ˌ══ˈthərməs\ *also* **homo·ther·mal** \-məl\ *or* **homo·ther·mic** \-mik\ *adj* [*hom-* + *-thermous, thermal, thermic*] **:** HOMOIOTHERMIC

**homo·thet·ic** \ˌ══ˈthed·ik\ *adj* [ISV *hom-* + Gk *thetikos* fit for placing; orig. formed as F *homothétique* — more at THETIC] **:** similar and similarly oriented — used of geometric figures

**homo·top·ic** \-ˈtäpik\ *adj* [*hom-* + Gk *topos* place + E *-ic*] **1 :** relating to the same or corresponding places or parts ⟨~ tumors⟩ **2 :** HOMEOMORPHIC — **ho·mot·o·py** \hōˈmäd·əpē\ *n* -ES

**homo·transplant** *pronunc at* HOMO- + \ *n* [*hom-* + *transplant*] **:** HOMOGRAFT — **homo·transplantation** \"+\ *n*

**ho·mot·ro·pous** \hōˈmä·trəpəs\ *or* **ho·mot·ro·pal** \-pəl\ *adj* [F *homotrope* (fr. *homo-* hom- + *-trope*) + E *-ous* or *-al*] **:** having the radicle directed toward the hilum ⟨~ seeds⟩

**homo·typ·al** *pronunc at* HOMO- + ˈtīpəl\ *adj* **:** of or relating to a homotype

**homo·type** \ˈ══ˌ+\ *n* [*hom-* + *type*] **1 :** a part or organ of the same fundamental structure as another **:** HOMOLOGUE ⟨the right arm is the ~ of the right leg⟩ ⟨one arm is the ~ of the other⟩ **2 :** HOMEOTYPE

**homo·typ·ic** \ˌ══ˈtipik\ *or* **homo·typ·i·cal** \-pəkəl\ *adj* **1 :** of or relating to a homotype **2 :** being the equational division of meiosis — **homo·typ·i·cal·ly** \-pək(ə)lē\ *adv*

**homo·typy** \ˈ══ˌtīpē\ *n* -ES [ISV *hom-* + *-typy*] **:** the relation existing between homotypes **:** SERIAL HOMOLOGY

**homo·zygosis** \ˌ══+\ *n* [NL, fr. *hom-* + *zygosis*] **1 :** the union of gametes identical for one or more pairs of genes **:** the act or process of becoming a homozygote **2 :** the quality or state of being a homozygote — compare HETEROZYGOSIS

**homo·zygosity** \"+\ *n* -ES **:** HOMOZYGOSIS 2

**homo·zygote** \"+\ *n* [ISV *hom-* + *zygote*] **:** an animal or plant containing either but not both members of at least one pair of allelomorphic characters **:** an individual that breeds true to type and is termed pure with respect to a specified character — compare HETEROZYGOTE, MENDEL'S LAWS — **homo·zygotic** \"+\ *adj*

**homo·zy·gous** \"+ˈzīgəs\ *adj* **1 :** possessing genes for only one member of at least one pair of allelomorphic characters **2 :** producing only one type of gamete with respect to a specified character — opposed to *heterozygous* — **homo·zy·gous·ly** *adv*

**hom·rai** \ˈhōm,rī, ˈhäm-\ *or* **homu·rai** \-mə,rī\ *n* -S [Nepali *hōgrāyo*] **:** a large hornbill (*Buceros bicornis*) of India and southeastern Asia

**homs** \ˈhōmz, -m(p)s\ *adj, usu cap* [fr. *Homs*, Syria] **:** of or from the city of Homs, Syria **:** of the kind or style prevalent in Homs

**homuncio** *n* -ES [L, dim. of *homin-, homo* man — more at HOMAGE] *obs* **:** HOMUNCULUS

**ho·mun·cu·lar** \(ˈ)hōˈməŋkyələ(r)\ *adj* [*homunculus* + *-ar*] **:** resembling or characteristic of a homunculus

**ho·mun·cu·lus** \═ˈ══ləs\ *n, pl* **homuncu·li** \-,lī\ [L, dim. of *homin-, homo* man] **:** a little man **:** DWARF **:** MANIKIN; *specif* **:** a manikin that is artificially produced in a cucurbit by an alchemist

**homy** *var of* HOMEY

**hon** \ˈhən\ *n* -S [short for *honey*] **:** SWEETHEART, DEAR ⟨you're a great old girl, ~ —Sinclair Lewis⟩

**hon** *abbr* honor; honorable; honorary; honored

**ho·nan** \ˈhōˈnan\ *n* -S [fr. *Honan*, province in China where it was originally made] **:** a lustrous lightweight silk material resembling pongee now widely imitated in other fibers

**honble** *abbr* honorable

**hon·da** \ˈhändə\ *also* **hon·do** \-n(ˌ)dō\ *n* -S [Sp *honda* sling, fr. L *funda*, perh. fr. Gk *sphendonē*] **:** a metal, knotted, or spliced eye at one end of a lariat through which the other end is passed to form a running noose or lasso

**hon·do** \ˈhän(ˌ)dō\ *n* -S [Sp, bottom, fr. L *fundus* — more at BOTTOM] **:** a broad low-lying arroyo in the southwestern U.S.

**[1]hon·du·ran** \(ˈ)hänˈd(y)ürən, -ür-\ *adj, usu cap* [*Honduras* + E *-an* (adj. suffix)] **:** of, relating to, or characteristic of Honduras

**[2]honduran** \"\ *n* -S *cap* [*Honduras* + E *-an* (n. suffix)] **:** a native or inhabitant of Honduras

**[1]hon·du·ra·ne·an** *also* **hon·du·ra·ni·an** \ˌhänd(y)əˈrānēən\

*adj, usu cap* [irreg. fr. *Honduras* + E *-ean, -ian,* vars. of *-an* (adj. suffix)] : HONDURAN

**²honduranean** *or* **honduranian** \"\ *n* -s *usu cap* [irreg. fr. *Honduras* + E *-ean, -ian,* vars. of *-an* (n. suffix)] : HONDURAN

**hon·du·ras** \(ʼ)hän¦d(y)u̇rəs, -)ür-\ *adj, usu cap* [fr. *Honduras,* republic in Central Amer.; British *Honduras,* crown colony in Central Amer.] : of or from Honduras : of the kind or style prevalent in Honduras : HONDURAN

**honduras bark** *n, usu cap H* [fr. Rep. of *Honduras,* its locality] : CASCARA AMARGA

**honduras cedar** *n, usu cap H* : SPANISH CEDAR

**honduras mahogany** *n, usu cap H* **1** : an important Central American timber tree (*Swietenia macrophylla*) closely related to true mahogany **2** : MAHOGANY 1a(2)

**honduras rosewood** *n, usu cap H* : a valuable dark streaked wood from one or more Central American trees of the genus *Dalbergia* (as *D. stevensonii* and *D. cubilquitzensis*)

**¹hone** \ˈhōn\ *n* -s [ME, fr. OE *hān* stone; akin to ON *hein* whetstone, L *cos,* Gk *kōnos* cone, Skt *sisāti* he sharpens, *sana* whetstone] **1 a** : a fine-grit stone used for sharpening a cutting implement (as a razor) — compare OILSTONE, WHETSTONE **b** : an artificial stone covered with an abrading substance and used for sharpening **2** : a tool for enlarging holes to precise tolerances and controlling finishes esp. of internal cylindrical surfaces by means of a mechanically rotated and expanded abrasive **3** : a drag for dressing and smoothing a road surface (as gravel)

**²hone** \"\ *vt* -ED/-ING/-S **1** : to sharpen with or as if with a hone : WHET ⟨learned to ~ and strop his razor correctly —G.S.Perry⟩ ⟨*honed* his antlers sharp as knives —D.C.Peattie⟩ ⟨the Yankee character was *honed* sharp right here —Bernard DeVoto⟩ **2** : to enlarge or smooth with a hone ⟨cylinder bodies are bored and then *honed* to a mirror finish —*Mechanical Engineering*⟩ ⟨the walls of the vestibule are lined with *honed* pink stone from Mankato —*Amer. Guide Series: Minn.*⟩

**³hone** \"\ *vi* -ED/-ING/-S [MF *hoigner* to murmur, grumble, perh. alter. (influenced by *groigner* to grumble, fr. L *grunnire* to grunt) of *honir, honnir* to dishonor, of Gmc origin; akin to OE *hīenan, hȳnan* to abase, OHG *hōnen* to revile, Goth *haunjan* to abase; causative-denominative fr. a Gmc adjective represented by OE *hēan* lowly, abject, Goth *hauns* humble; akin to OHG *hōna* scorn, ON *hāth* act of jeering, Gk *kauros* bad, Latvian *kauns* disgrace — more at GRUNT] **1** *now dial* : to grumble and moan **2** *now dial* : LONG, YEARN — usu. used with *for* or *after* ⟨'tis vain, 'tis vain, my dear young man, to ~ for Barbara Allen —*Barbara Allen*⟩

**hon·er** \-nə(r)\ *n* -s [²*hone* + *-er*] : one that hones

**¹hon·est** \ˈänəst\ *adj, sometimes* -ER/-EST [ME *honest, honeste,* fr. OF *honeste,* fr. L *honestus* honorable, decent, handsome, fr. *honos, honor* esteem, honor] **1 a** : free from fraud or deception : LEGITIMATE, TRUTHFUL ⟨make an ~ dollar⟩ ⟨an atmosphere still magically colored by gentility, culture and ~ wealth —Winston Brebner⟩ ⟨the first need is for ~ and candid presentation of the facts —Dean Acheson⟩ **b** : of unquestioned authenticity : GENUINE, REAL ⟨making ~ stops at stop signs —*Christian Science Monitor*⟩ ⟨when it's not making ~ rain . . . it's misting from the marshes or fogging from the sea —T.H.Fielding⟩ — often used intensively in hyphened combination with *to* and an object ⟨the first *honest*-to-God American beauty I had seen in four months —Tom O'Reilly⟩ ⟨a real *honest*-to-goodness Cape Cod lobster stew —M.F.Leonard⟩ **c** (1) : free of ostentation or pretense : HUMBLE ⟨younger sons . . . were often apprenticed to some ~ trade —Wallace Clare⟩ (2) : free of ornament or disguise : PLAIN ⟨a cafeteria which . . . serves really good ~ food —C.M.Smith⟩ **2 a** *obs* : of good repute : ESTIMABLE **b** : virtuous in the eyes of society : REPUTABLE ⟨the fortune . . . made the woman ~, as her second protector immediately married her —G.L.Phillips⟩ **c** *chiefly Brit* : GOOD, WORTHY ⟨an ~ fellow, who did his best to please⟩ ⟨I keep six ~ serving-men —Rudyard Kipling⟩ **3 a** : of a creditable nature : PRAISEWORTHY ⟨workers who would not take the trouble to turn out an ~ job —Roy Lewis & Angus Maude⟩ **b** *obs* : of good reputation : RESPECTABLE ⟨now let's go to an ~ alehouse and sing Old Rose —Izaak Walton⟩ **4 a** : characterized by integrity : adhering to principle : UPRIGHT ⟨~ merchants⟩ ⟨no ~ prostitute would have had the face to ask the prices they asked —Robert Graves⟩ **b** : frank and straightforward : SINCERE ⟨early in life I had to choose between ~ arrogance and hypocritical humility —F.L.Wright⟩ ⟨an ~ appeal to the people was the last thing desired by the Federalists —V.L.Parrington⟩ **c** : direct and uncomplicated : INNOCENT, SIMPLE ⟨the ~ sleep of any tired child —Alice Marriott⟩ ⟨the ~ average playgoer simply wants to be told what play is best worth going to—for him —C.E.Montague⟩

**syn** see UPRIGHT

**²honest** \"\ *vt* -ED/-ING/-S *obs* : to make honest or honorable : JUSTIFY

**³honest** \"\ *adv* : HONESTLY ⟨I have ever found thee ~ true —Shak.⟩ ⟨~ I won't tell⟩ — often used intensively in hyphened combination with *to* and an object ⟨knowing I was *honest*-to-goodness off and away —Helen Eustis⟩

**honest injun** *adv, usu cap I* : on my word of honor : HONESTLY

**hon·est·ly** *adv* [ME, fr. ¹*honest* + *-ly*] **1** : in an honest manner : with honesty

**hon·est·ness** *n* -ES [ME *honestnes,* fr. ¹ *honest* + *-nes* -ness] : the quality or state of being honest

**hone·stone** \ˈ=,=\ *n* : a stone suitable for making hones for sharpening; *also* : a hone made from such a stone

**hon·es·ty** \ˈänəstē, -ti\ *n* -ES [ME *honeste* estimable character, honor, fr. OF *honesté,* fr. L *honestat-, honestas,* fr. *honestus* honorable] **1** *obs* : estimable character; *esp* : CHASTITY ⟨the honor of a maid is her name; and no legacy is so rich as ~ —Shak.⟩ **2 a** : fairness and straightforwardness of conduct : INTEGRITY ⟨was not greatly pleased with Lincoln, though admitting his ~ and fair capability —W.C.Ford⟩ **b** : adherence to the facts : freedom from subterfuge or duplicity : TRUTHFULNESS, SINCERITY ⟨~ is the best policy⟩ ⟨the field worker depends on the ~ of the people for correct replies —J.M.Mogey⟩ ⟨a film of rare ~ and heart —Arthur Knight⟩ ⟨peaceable life in all godliness and ~ —1 Tim 2:2 (AV)⟩ **3** [so called fr. the semitransparent pods] : a European plant of the genus *Lunaria* (esp. *L. annua*) — called also *satinpod*

**honesty clause** *n* : FULL REPORTING CLAUSE

**hone·wort** \ˈhōn,-\ *n* [*hone-* (of unknown origin) + *wort*] : any of several plants of the family Umbelliferae: as **a** : STONE PARSLEY **b** : a perennial herb (*Cryptotaenia canadensis*) with thin three-foliolate leaves and small white flowers — called also *wild chervil*

**¹hon·ey** \ˈhənē, -ni\ *n, pl* **hon·eys** *or* **hon·ies** \-nēz,-niz\ [ME *hony,* fr. OE *hunig;* akin to OHG *honag* honey, ON *hunang,* L *canicae* bran, Gk *knēkos* tawny, and perh. to Skt *kāñcana* gold] **1 a** : a sweet viscid material that is elaborated out of the nectar of flowers in the honey sac of various kinds of bees and stored in the nest for use during the winter as food for the larvae or esp. in the case of the honeybee for the colony and that has a flavor and color depending largely on the plants from which the nectar is gathered with that of clover being esp. esteemed by man for whom as for certain wild animals honey constitutes a favorite article of food — compare HONEYCOMB, INVERT SUGAR **b** : a sweet fluid resembling honey that is collected or elaborated by various other insects — compare HONEY ANT, HONEYDEW **2 a** : SWEETHEART, DEAR — often used as a term of endearment **b** : something superlative in appearance, excellence, complexity, or degree ⟨a ~ of a full-length coat . . . in white American broadtail —Lois Long⟩ ⟨incidental romance and a ~ of an Indian battle at the end —Muriel Burns⟩ ⟨it must have been a ~ with the complicated distilling columns, the automatic controls, the valves and pressure tanks —Joseph Starobin⟩ ⟨if there is a postwar depression . . . it will be a ~ —George Soule⟩ **3** : the quality or state of being sweet : SWEETNESS : something that is sweet ⟨coaxed him with ~ in her voice⟩ ⟨seduced by the ~ of admiration⟩ **4** *pharmacy* : any of various preparations consisting of simple mixtures of medicaments with honey ⟨borax ~⟩ **5** : a sweet syrupy liquid (as maple syrup) with a flavor resembling honey — see APPLE HONEY **6** *or* **honey yellow** : a dark grayish yellow that is redder, stronger, and slightly lighter than California green, redder, stronger, and slightly lighter than olivesheen, and very slightly redder than yellowstone — called also *middle stone* **7** : HONEY LOCUST

**²honey** \"\ *vb* **hon·eyed** *also* **hon·ied** \-nēd,-nid\ **honeyed** *also* **honied; honeying; honeys** *also* **honies** [ME *honien,* fr. *hony,* n.] *vt* **1** : to sweeten with or as if with honey **2 a** : to call one "honey" as a term of endearment ⟨their husbands were ~*ing* . . . them all the time —Thomas Hart⟩ **b** : to speak ingratiatingly to : FLATTER ⟨the station master . . . ~*ed* him up the steps of the last coach —Thomas Wood †1950⟩ ~ *vi* **1** : to use blandishments or cajolery — often used with *up* ⟨by ~*ing* up to his landlady got his socks darned and his buttons sewn on⟩ **2** : to be flattering or obsequious : FAWN ⟨rough to common men but ~*ing* at the whisper of a lord —Alfred Tennyson⟩

**³honey** \"\ *adj* **hon·i·er** \-nēə(r), -niə-\ **hon·i·est** \-nēəst, -niə-\ *adj* [ME *hony,* fr. *hony,* n.] **1** : of or relating to honey or its production ⟨~ cake⟩ **2 a** : resembling honey (as in color or sweetness) ⟨among the walking shoes is one of ~ or black alligator —*New Yorker*⟩ ⟨the ~ peace in old poems —Robinson Jeffers⟩ **b** *archaic* : DEAR ⟨my good sweet ~ lord —Shak.⟩

**honey agaric** *n* : HONEY MUSHROOM

**honey ant** *n* : any of various ants some of whose workers serve as receptacles for the storage of honey which they are able to regurgitate from their greatly distended abdomens when it is needed to feed other members of the colony

**honey badger** *n* : RATEL

**honey bag** *n* : HONEY SAC

**honeyballs** \ˈ=,=,=\ *n pl* : BUTTONBUSH

**honey balm** *n* : a sweet-scented mint (*Melittis melissophyllum*) of central and southern Europe

**honey bear** *n* **1** : KINKAJOU **2** : SLOTH BEAR

**honeybee** \ˈ=,=,=\ *n* : any of certain social honey-producing bees of *Apis* and related genera; *esp* : a native European bee (*Apis mellifera*) that is kept for its honey and wax in most parts of the world, has developed into several races differing in size, color, disposition, and productivity, and has escaped to the wild wherever suitable conditions prevail — compare BLACK BEE, CARNIOLAN BEE, DRONE, HONEYCOMB, ITALIAN BEE, QUEEN BEE, WORKER

honeybees: *1* queen, *2* drone, *3* worker

**honey beige** *n* : DORADO 2

**honey bell** *n* : an African shrub (*Mahernia verticillata*) of the family Sterculiaceae having sweet honey-yellow flowers and used as an ornamental

**hon·ey·ber·ry** \ˈ=s= — *see* BERRY\ *n* **1** : the fruit of either of two trees having sweetish berries: **a** : an Old World hackberry (*Celtis australis*) **b** : GENIP 2 **2** : a tree that bears honeyberries

**honeybind** *also* **honeybine** \ˈ=,=,=\ *n* : WOODBINE 1

**honey bird** *n* **1** : HONEY GUIDE **2** : HONEY EATER

**honeyblob** \ˈ=,=,=\ *n, Brit* : GOOSEBERRY

**honey–blonde** \¦=,=¦=\ *adj* : HONEY 2a

**honeybloom** \ˈ=,=,=\ *n* : SPREADING DOGBANE

**honey bread** *n* : CAROB 1

**honeybunch** *or* **honeybun** \ˈ=,=,=\ *n* : HONEY 2a

**honey buzzard** *n* : a European hawk (*Pernis apivorus*) related to the kites and feeding on insects and small reptiles and often tearing up nests of wasps and bumblebees to eat their larvae — called also *honey kite*

**honey clover** *n* **1** : WHITE SWEET CLOVER **2** : KURA CLOVER

**¹honeycomb** \ˈ=,=,=\ *n, often attrib* [ME *hunigcamb,* fr. *hunig* honey + *camb* comb — more at ¹HONEY, COMB] **1 a** : a mass of hexagonal prismatic wax cells varying in size according to their use built by honeybees in their nest or hive to contain their brood and stores of honey — compare BEESWAX **b** : a mass of cells containing honey used as an article of food ⟨pats of butter stamped with a swan, and slabs of ~ —Mary Webb⟩ **2** : a flaw in metal due to imperfect casting, corrosion, or the abrasive action of gunpowder ⟨a scratch or spot of ~ in the grooves renders the rifle completely useless for match-shooting —W.W.Greener⟩ **3 a** : something that resembles a honeycomb in structure or appearance ⟨a ~ of pigeonholes stuffed with old letters —Berton Roueché⟩ ⟨a ~ of dark, roofed-in arcades —Mollie Panter-Downes⟩ ⟨is experimenting with metal ~ made of stainless steel —Reid Hale⟩ ⟨a red ~ of fire burning far into a great pine root —Eve Langley⟩; *specif* : a building facade having a multicellular pattern of repeated units **b** (1) : a weave with a small allover pattern of raised squares, oblongs, or diamonds with indented centers formed by long floats (2) : a reversible fabric of this weave made usu. of cotton or wool and used for clothing or towels — called also *waffle cloth* **c** *or* **honeycomb stomach** : RETICULUM 1 **d** : HONEYCOMB SPONGE

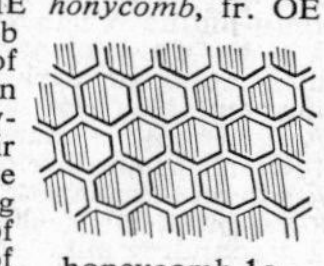
honeycomb 1a

**²honeycomb** \"\ *vt* **1 a** : to cause to be full of cavities like a honeycomb : make into a tissue of holes separated by thin walls or partitions : PIT ⟨both substances eat and ~ the pipe —Emily Holt⟩ ⟨the tunnels of the subways ~ rocks and rivers and skyscrapers —*Amer. Guide Series: N. Y. City*⟩ ⟨the limestone country hereabouts is ~*ed* with caves and grottoes —Tom Marvel⟩ **b** : to make into a checkered pattern : FRET ⟨the 650,000-odd peasant settlements which ~ the countryside —Daniel & Alice Thorner⟩ ⟨blouses are ruched and ~*ed* in alternating panels⟩ **2 a** : to penetrate into every part of : FILL, INFILTRATE ⟨a book that has been ~*ed* with classical allusions⟩ ⟨the . . . government is ~*ed* with spies —T.H.White b.1915⟩ **b** : SUBVERT, WEAKEN ⟨the gigantic edifice of prices was ~*ed* with speculative credit —F.L.Allen⟩ ~ *vi* : to become pitted, checked, or cellular in structure or appearance ⟨acids cause boiler metal to ~⟩ ⟨the cliff opened . . . before the girl, ~*ing* into archways and steep flights of stairs —Kay Boyle⟩

**honeycomb coral** *n* : a fossil coral of *Favosites* or a related genus

**honeycombing** *n* : internal cracking or checking in lumber due to imperfect seasoning and often not visible on the surface — called also *hollow-horning*

**honeycomb ringworm** *n* : FAVUS

**honeycomb sponge** *n* : a fine soft-fibered commercial sponge (*Hippospongia equina elastica*) of a massive form occurring in the Mediterranean and Red seas

**honeycomb stitch** *n* : any of various decorative stitches used in smocking, lacemaking, or knitting to form a honeycomb pattern

**honeycomb tripe** *n* : TRIPE 1a(2)

**honeycreeper** \ˈ=,=,=\ *n* : any of numerous small bright-colored oscine birds constituting the family Coerebidae found in tropical and subtropical America — see BANANA QUIT; compare CREEPER 4, HONEY EATER

**honeycup** \ˈ=,=,=\ *n* : SENSITIVE PEA

**hon·ey·dew** \ˈhənē,d(y)ü, -ni,-\ *n* **1** : a saccharine deposit found on the leaves of many plants that is secreted usu. by aphids or scales but sometimes by a fungus esp. of the genus *Claviceps* **2** : something as sweet as honeydew or as honey ⟨on ~ hath fed, and drunk the milk of paradise —S.T.Coleridge⟩ ⟨a gentle ~ of a southern girl —Raymond Walters b.1912⟩ **3** : tobacco moistened with molasses **4** : a moderate orange that is redder and paler than Persian orange, redder and paler than ocher brown, and redder, stronger, and slightly darker than average apricot **5** : HONEYDEW MELON

**hon·ey·dewed** \-üd\ *adj* : covered with honeydew ⟨~ foliage⟩

**honeydew melon** *n* : a smooth-skinned white, greenish white, or pale yellow muskmelon derived from the winter melon and having greenish very sweet flesh

**honeydrop** \ˈ=,=,=\ *n* : a drop of honey or something like a drop of honey in sweetness

**honey eater** *n* : any of several oscine birds that constitute the family Meliphagidae, are found mostly in the south Pacific, and have a long protrusible tongue adapted for extracting nectar and small insects from flowers — called also *honeysucker;* see BELLBIRD, FLYING COACHMAN, FRIARBIRD, STITCHBIRD, WATTLEBIRD; compare HONEYCREEPER

**hon·ey·ed** *also* **hon·ied** \-nēd,-nid\ *adj* [ME *honied,* fr. past part. of *honien* to honey] : sweetened with or as if with honey ⟨stilling the ~ air —Walter de la Mare⟩ ⟨many a wily rogue beguiles with ~ tongue —Peggy Bennett⟩ — **hon·ey·ed·ly** *adv* — **hon·ey·ed·ness** *n* -ES

**honey extractor** *n* : EXTRACTOR 1c

**honeyflow** \ˈ=,=,=\ *n* : a supply or period of availability of floral nectar suitable for bees to convert into honey ⟨some swarming was evident . . . due to the heavy ~ —*Canadian Bee Jour.*⟩ ⟨the ~ . . . began during the latter part of June —*Western Canada Beekeeper*⟩

**honeyflower** \ˈ=,=,=\ *n* : any of several flowers yielding nectar copiously: as **a** : a plant of the genus *Melianthus* **b** : either of two Australian shrubs (*Protea mellifera* or the related *Lambertia formosa*) **c** : BEE ORCHIS **d** : a sweet sultan (*Centaurea moschata*)

**honeyflower family** *n* : MELIANTHACEAE

**hon·ey·fug·gle** \ˈhənē,fəgəl\ *also* **hon·ey·fo·gle** \-fōg-\ *or* **hon·ey·fu·gle** \-f(y)üg-\ *vb* -ED/-ING/-S [perh. fr. ¹*honey* + E dial. *fugel* to cheat, trick] *vt* **1** *chiefly dial* **a** : DECEIVE, CHEAT, COZEN **b** : to obtain by cheating or deception : FINAGLE **2** *chiefly dial* : FLATTER, CAJOLE, BLANDISH ~ *vi, chiefly dial* : to ingratiate or seek to ingratiate oneself so as to cheat or deceive

**honey gland** *n* : NECTARY

**honey gold** *n* : a moderate yellow that is redder and deeper than colonial yellow or mustard yellow and greener and stronger than brass

**honey grass** *n* **1** : MOLASSES GRASS **2** : MELIC GRASS

**honey guide** *n* **1** : any of several small plainly colored nonpasserine birds of the family Indicatoridae esp. of the genera *Indicator* and *Prodotiscus* that inhabit Africa, the Himalayas, and the East Indies and include some that lead men or lower animals to the nests of bees — compare BARBET **2** : a spot or stripe of a different color from the rest of the corolla that is found on the petals of many flowers and is assumed to act as a guide to insects in their quest of nectar

**honeying** *pres part of* HONEY

**honey kite** *n* : HONEY BUZZARD

**hon·ey·less** \ˈhənēləs\ *adj* : lacking honey

**honey locust** *n* **1 a** (1) : a tall usu. spiny No. American tree (*Gleditsia triacanthos*) that has bipinnate leaves, small greenish flowers in drooping racemes followed by long twisted pods containing seeds resembling beans and separated by a sweet edible pulp, and very hard durable reddish or reddish brown wood (2) : LOCUST 3a(2) (3) : CLAMMY LOCUST **b** : the wood of a honey locust **2 a** : MESQUITE 1a; *esp* : any of various large arborescent tropical American mesquites with strong heavy wood **b** : the wood of such a tropical American mesquite

**honey mesquite** *n* : MESQUITE 1a

**¹hon·ey·moon** \ˈhənē,mün, -ni,-\ *n, often attrib* [¹*honey* + *moon* (month); fr. the idea that the first month of marriage is the sweetest] **1 a** : a trip or vacation taken by a newly married couple ⟨has planned ~*s* for more than 60,000 newlyweds —Walter Winchell⟩ ⟨a popular ~ resort⟩ ⟨obviously a ~ couple⟩ **b** : a period usu. of exceptional compatibility immediately following marriage ⟨made their ~ last a lifetime⟩ **2** : a period of unusual harmony following the establishment of a new relationship ⟨today . . . congress thwarts the president, after a brief ~ in each administration —Irving Brant⟩ ⟨the ~ period of war alliance —Merle Fainsod⟩

**²honeymoon** \"\ *vi* -ED/-ING/-S : to spend a honeymoon ⟨had a fashionable wedding and ~*ed* in Bermuda⟩ — **hon·ey·moon·er** \-ünə(r)\ *n* -S

**honeymoon bridge** *n* : any of several forms of auction or contract bridge for two players

**honeymouthed** *also* **honeylipped** \¦=¦=¦=\ *adj* : sweet or cajoling in speech ⟨cajoled him with ~ flattery until his suspicion was quieted —John Bennett⟩

**honey mushroom** *or* **honey fungus** *n* : an edible agaric (*Armillaria mellea*) commonly associated with the roots of trees : SHOESTRING FUNGUS — called also *honey agaric*

**honeymyrtle** \ˈ=,=,=\ *n* : an Australian tree of the genus *Melaleuca*

**honey of rose** *pharmacy* : a mixture of fluid extract of rose and purified honey

**honey palm** *n* : COQUITO PALM

**honey plant** *n* : any of numerous flowering plants that furnish nectar suitable for the making of honey by insects; *specif* : a plant of the genus *Hoya*

**honeypod** \ˈ=,=,=\ *n* **1** : MESQUITE 1a **2** : a pod of a mesquite

**honey possum** *or* **honey mouse** *n* : a small chestnut-brown long-muzzled phalanger (*Tarsipes spencerae*) of southwestern Australia that feeds upon nectar and small insects

**honeypot** \ˈ=,=,=\ *n* [ME *hony pot,* fr. *hony* honey + *pot*] **1** : a receptacle for honey: **a** : one of the isolated waxen vessels constructed by some wild bees **b** : a glass or crockery container for table use ⟨early blown ~*s* or jam pots have high lids, deep rims, and solid finials —C.W.Drepperd⟩ **2 honeypots** *pl* : a game in which a child (called the *honeypot*) with his hands clasped under his hams is swung backward and forward by his arms until his grip relaxes in order to find his weight which is reckoned at a pound for each swing **3** : a flower head of a southern African shrub (*Protea cynaroides*) which when open is shaped like a pot and consists of an involucre of showy bracts surrounding a head of small flowers **4 a** : HONEY ANT **b** : a replete of a honey ant

**honeypot ant** *n* : HONEY ANT

**honeys** *pl of* HONEY, *pres 3d sing of* HONEY

**honey sac** *or* **honey stomach** *n* : a distension of the esophagus of a bee in which the honey is elaborated : CROP 2c

**honeyscented gum** \ˈ=,=,=\ *n* : YELLOW BOX

**honey shucks** *n pl but usu sing in constr, also* **honey shuck** : HONEY LOCUST

**honey–stalks** \ˈ=,=,=\ *n pl* : HONEYSUCKLE CLOVER

**honeysuck** \ˈ=,=,=\ *n* [ME *honysouke,* fr. OE *hunisūce,* fr. *huni-, hunig* honey + *-sūce* (fr. *sūcan* to suck) — more at ¹HONEY, SUCK] *now dial* : HONEYSUCKLE

**honeysucker** \ˈ=,=,=\ *n* : HONEY EATER

**honeysuckle** \ˈ=,=,=\ *n* -S [ME *honysoukel,* alter. of *honysouke*] **1** *obs* : clover or its flowers **2 a** : a plant of the genus *Lonicera* — see WOODBINE 1 **b** : a shrub or tree of the genus *Banksia* (esp. *B. integrifolia*) — see AUSTRALIAN HONEYSUCKLE **3** : any of several other plants with tubular flowers abounding in honey: as **a** : BUSH HONEYSUCKLE **b** : COLUMBINE **c** HONEYFLOWER **d** : PINXTER FLOWER **e** : SWAMP AZALEA **4** : REWAREWA

**honeysuckle apple** *n* : SWAMP APPLE

**honeysuckle clover** *n, chiefly dial* : a clover (as red clover or white Dutch clover) that is rich in nectar

**honeysuckled** \ˈ=,=,=\ *adj* : covered with honeysuckle

**honeysuckle family** *n* : CAPRIFOLIACEAE

**honeysuckle ornament** *n* : ANTHEMION

**honey–sweet** \¦=¦=\ *adj* [ME *hony sweete,* fr. OE *hunigswēte,* fr. *hunig* honey + *swēte* sweet] : sweet with or as if with honey ⟨*honey-sweet* blossoms⟩ ⟨*honey-sweet* voice⟩

**honeysweet** \ˈ=,=\ *n* [*honey-sweet*] : a white woolly perennial herb (*Tidestromia oblongifolia*) of the desert region of the U.S. forming broad flat mats and having stems and involucral bracts that often turn reddish with age and honey-scented yellow flowers

**honey–tongued** \¦=¦=\ *adj* : SMOOTH-TONGUED

**honey tree** *n* **1** : a forest tree that harbors wild bees and honey **2** : JAPANESE RAISIN TREE

**honey tube** *n* : either of a pair of small cornicles borne on the dorsal part of one of the abdominal segments of many aphids and formerly believed to secrete honeydew

**honey vine** *n* : SAND VINE

**honeywood** \ˈ=,=,=\ *n* : a Tasmanian shrub (*Bedfordia salicina*) of the family Compositae having white foliage and heads of yellow flowers

**honeywort** \ˈ=,=,=\ *n* **1** : a European plant of the genus *Cerinthe* (esp. *C. retorta*) often cultivated for its flowers which yield much honey **2** : a sweet-scented crosswort (*Galium cruciatum*)

**honey yellow** *n* : HONEY 6

**hong** \ˈhäŋ, ˈhȯŋ\ *n* -S [Chin (Cant) *hŏng* row, mercantile firm, guild] **:** a commercial establishment or house of foreign trade in China ⟨clippers . . . known equally in Canton ~s and European countinghouses —*Nat'l Geographic*⟩

**hong kong** \ˈhäŋ,käŋ, ˈhȯŋ,kȯŋ, (ˌ)═ˈ═\ *adj, usu cap H&K* [fr. *Hong Kong*, British crown colony in southeastern China] **:** of or from the British crown colony of Hong Kong **:** of the kind or style prevalent in Hong Kong

**¹honied** *var of* HONEYED

**²honied** *past of* HONEY

**honier** *comparative of* HONEY

**honies** *pl of* HONEY, *pres 3d sing of* HONEY

**honiest** *superlative of* HONEY

**honing** *pres part of* HONE

**hon·i·ton** \ˈhänətᵊn, ˈhən-\ *or* **honiton lace** *n, usu cap H* [fr. *Honiton*, municipal borough in Devonshire, England] **:** any of various laces made orig. at Honiton, England; *esp* **:** a bobbin lace with designs of foliage, figures, or flowers, joined by brides or appliquéd to machine-made net

**¹honk** \ˈhäŋk, -ȯ- *sometimes* -ə-\ *n* -s [imit.] **1 :** the cry of a goose **2 :** a sound resembling the cry of a goose

**²honk** \"\ *vb* -ED/-ING/-S *vi* **1 :** to utter the characteristic cry of a goose ⟨northbound geese ~ overhead —Corey Ford⟩ **2 :** to make a noise resembling the cry of a goose ⟨seals ~ing and splashing in a tank⟩ ⟨a fogbound ship ~s mournfully⟩ ~ *vt* **:** to cause (as a horn) to make a honk ⟨pulled up in front of the house and ~ed his horn⟩ ⟨finished her tears and ~ed her nose into the . . . handkerchief —Peggy Bennett⟩

**honk·er** \-kə(r)\ *n* -s **:** one that honks; *specif* **:** CANADA GOOSE

**honky-tonk** \ˈhäŋkē,täŋk, ˈhȯŋkē,tȯŋk, ˈhəŋkē,təŋk, -ki-, ═ˈ═\ *n* -s *often attrib* [origin unknown] **:** a cheap nightclub or dance hall **:** DIVE 2 ⟨a row of brothels, gin mills and *honky-tonks* —Robert O'Brien⟩ ⟨a real honky-tonk joint, with hill-billy music and pinball machines going full blast —A.L.Davis⟩

**hon·ni·a·sont** \ˈhänēə,sänt\ *n, pl* **honniasont** *or* **honniasonts** *usu cap* **1 :** an Iroquoian people of the valley of the upper Ohio river and its tributaries **2 :** a member of the Honniasont people

**hono·lu·lan** \ˌhänᵊlˈülən, -nəˈlü- *also* ˌhōn-\ *n* -s *cap* [*Honolulu*, Hawaii + E *-an*] **:** a native or inhabitant of Honolulu

**hono·lu·lu** \═ˈ═(ˌ)lü *sometimes* -ˌlə\ *adj, usu cap* [fr. *Honolulu*, Hawaii] **:** of or from Honolulu, the capital of Hawaii **:** of the kind or style prevalent in Honolulu

**¹hon·or** \ˈänə(r)\ *n* -s *see -or in Explan Notes, often attrib* [ME *onour, honur, honor* fr. OF *onur, honur, honeur, honor*, fr. L *honor-, honos* or *honor*] **1 a :** good name or public esteem **:** REPUTATION, GLORY ⟨a national administration of such integrity . . . that its ~ at home will ensure respect abroad —D.D.Eisenhower⟩ ⟨a prophet is not without ~ except in his own country —Mt 13:57 (RSV)⟩ **b :** outward respect or admiration **:** RECOGNITION, DEFERENCE ⟨a dinner in ~ of the football coach⟩ ⟨treat the clergy with ~⟩ **2 :** a special prerogative **:** PRIVILEGE ⟨I have the ~ to inform you⟩ ⟨the second artist . . . to be accorded the ~ of designing the annual Christmas seal —*Phoenix Flame*⟩ **3 :** a person of superior standing or importance — now used esp. as a title for and in a mode of address to certain holders of high office (as judges and mayors of cities) ⟨if Your *Honor* please⟩ ⟨His *Honor* presided⟩ **4 a :** one that is of intrinsic value **:** ASSET ⟨he is an ~ to his profession⟩ **b** *obs* **:** one that decorates **:** ORNAMENT ⟨the woods, in scarlet ~s bright —William Cowper⟩ **5 :** an evidence or symbol of distinction **:** mark of respect or admiration: as **a :** an exalted title or rank ⟨elected United States Senator in 1794 and governor of Maryland . . . he declined both ~s — *Amer. Guide Series: Md.*⟩ **b** (1) **:** BADGE, DECORATION ⟨among his ~s is the Order of the Golden Fleece⟩ (2) a ceremonial rite or observance ⟨the general was buried with full military ~s⟩ (3) **honors** *pl* **:** drum ruffles and trumpet flourishes and the national anthem or other music played during a ceremony when troops are presented **c** *archaic* **:** a gesture of deference **:** BOW ⟨they . . . made their ~s very prettily as they passed by us —Samuel Richardson⟩ **d honors** *pl* **:** social courtesies or civilities esp. as when rendered by a host ⟨the president did the ~s and the new club member acknowledged each introduction with a gracious nod⟩ ⟨handed him the carving knife, and asked him to do the ~s of the table⟩ **e** (1) **:** an academic grade, distinction, or award conferred on a superior student by a school or college ⟨received her B.A. with first class ~s from the University of London —B.F.Wright⟩ ⟨gained a first with ~s in mathematics —Lois I. Woodville⟩ (2) *or* **honors** *pl but sing in constr* **:** a course of study either supplementing or replacing a regular course, open to students of superior ability, and usu. culminating in an examination or thesis to determine eligibility for a degree with special distinction ⟨~ study gives to seniors . . . an opportunity to do independent study and research in their major field —*Bull. of Bates College*⟩ ⟨British universities offer two types of courses in the faculties of arts and science: an ~s course . . . and an ordinary, pass, or general course —I.L.Kandel⟩ **f :** an accolade for supremacy in a contest or field of competition ⟨the debating team won regional ~s⟩ ⟨airlines vie for commercial ~s⟩ **g :** an achievement award earned by a camp fire girl ⟨Camp Fire's method of giving individual recognition is the ~ bead —*Camp Fire Girl*⟩ **6 :** CHASTITY, PURITY, VIRGINITY — used of a woman ⟨fought fiercely for her ~ and her life —Barton Black⟩ **7 a :** a holding of a large amount of land including numerous manors **b :** the seignorial franchise or jurisdiction annexed to such a holding **8 a :** adherence to high standards of justice and responsibility **:** ethical conduct **:** INTEGRITY ⟨code of ~⟩ ⟨an acute sense of ~ in private and business matters —Edith Wharton⟩ — compare BUSHIDO, NOBLESSE OBLIGE **b :** one's word given as a guarantee of performance **9 a** (1) *or* **honor-card :** an ace, king, queen, jack, or ten (2) **:** the ace, king, queen, jack, or ten of the trump suit in bridge or any ace when the contract is no-trump considered from the standpoint of its scoring value (3) **:** the ace, king, queen, or jack of the trump suit in whist (4) **:** the scoring value of honors held in bridge or whist — usu. used in pl. (5) **honors** *pl* **:** HONOR SCORE **b :** the privilege of playing first; *specif* **:** the privilege of driving a golf ball first from the tee that is granted the winner of the previous hole or the last unhalved hole **c :** one of 28 special-value tiles in the game of Mah-Jongg

**syn** HONOR, HOMAGE, REVERENCE, DEFERENCE, and OBEISANCE agree in signifying respect or esteem shown to another or claimed by him as a right. HONOR can apply to the recognition of one's title to great respect or to the expression of that respect ⟨to hold a statesman in high *honor*⟩ ⟨it was a proud day for the family there to see you get your *honor* —Agnes S. Turnbull⟩ ⟨to accept the *honor* the university proffered him⟩ HOMAGE adds the idea of accompanying praise or tribute esp. from one owing allegiance ⟨the ostentatious *homage* paid by state officials to bishops —*Times Lit. Supp.*⟩ ⟨brought up in the veneration of a man so truly worthy of *homage* —Matthew Arnold⟩ ⟨the *homage* which man owes his Creator —M.W.Baldwin⟩ REVERENCE implies profound respect usu. colored by love, devotion, or awe ⟨a *reverence* for all things sacred⟩ ⟨they rather produce in man thoughtfulness, *reverence*, a sense, confused yet precious, of the boundless importance of the unseen world —Charles Kingsley⟩ ⟨a *reverence* for government —Sherwood Anderson⟩ DEFERENCE implies a yielding or submitting to another's judgment or preference out of respect or reverence ⟨the attitude of *deference* which Elizabethan children were taught to cultivate toward their fathers —G.E.Dawson⟩ ⟨the magistrate and the clergyman . . . were conceded a *deference* which superior education, and not superior birth, compelled —H.E.Scudder⟩ OBEISANCE implies a show of honor or reverence by or as if by bowing or kneeling, often applying to a self-humbling gesture in confession of defeat or subjection ⟨the court is also showing great *obeisance* to the wishes of the executive and administrative branches —*New Republic*⟩ ⟨continually making humble *obeisance* to supercilious superiors —A.E.Wier⟩ ⟨unfortunate growing things . . . found that they were clipped, mowed, segregated, pruned, espaliered and generally bullied into *obeisance* —T.H.Robsjohn-Gibbings⟩ **syn** see in addition FAME

**²honor** \"\ *vt* **honored; honored; honoring** \-n(ə)riŋ\ **honors** *see -or in Explan Notes* [ME *onouren, honouren*, fr. OF *onurer, honurer, honeurer*, fr. L *honorare*, fr. *honor-, honos* or *honor*] **1 a :** to show high regard or appreciation for **:** pay tribute to **:** EXALT, PRAISE ⟨~ your father and your mother —Exod 20:12 (RSV)⟩ ⟨he has been ~ed at half a dozen public luncheons and banquets —J.A.Morris b. 1904⟩ **b :** to confer a distinction upon ⟨the only Englishman in all history that the world ~s with the surname of Great —Kemp Malone⟩ ⟨in addition to his French decorations, he was ~ed by the governments of Great Britain, Italy, Belgium, Serbia, and Venezuela —J.J.Senturia⟩ **2 :** to be a credit to **:** ADORN ⟨the quality of his statesmanship would ~ any country⟩ **3 a :** to treat with consideration **:** RECOGNIZE, RESPECT ⟨federal bill . . . to ~ state commitments of addicts —D.W.Maurer & V.H. Vogel⟩ ⟨truck drivers were ~ing the picket line —*Springfield (Mass.) Union*⟩ **b :** to live up to or fulfill **:** carry out ⟨~ a treaty⟩ ⟨~ a contract⟩; *specif* **:** to accept and comply with the terms of ⟨~ a check⟩ ⟨~ a requisition . . . for the surrender of a violator —P.G.Auchampaugh⟩ **4 :** to salute with a bow usu. at the beginning or at the end of a square dance ⟨~ your partner⟩

**¹hon·or·able** \ˈänər(ə)bəl, -nrəb-\ *adj, see -or in Explan Notes* [ME *honourable, honorable*, fr. MF, fr. L *honorabilis*, fr. *honorare* + *-abilis* -able] **1 a** *obs* **:** up to a standard of respectability (as in quality, size, amount) **:** DECENT, CONSIDERABLE ⟨when he plays at tables, chides the dice in ~ terms —Shak.⟩ **b :** deserving of honor **:** ADMIRABLE, DIGNIFIED ⟨judges are ~ for their high calling⟩ ⟨marriage is an ~ estate —*Bk. of Com. Prayer*⟩ **2 :** conferring honor ⟨won an ~ mention for verse⟩ **3 a :** of great renown **:** ILLUSTRIOUS ⟨comes of a family ~ for centuries⟩ **b** *usu cap* (1) **:** belonging to a family or having a rank entitled to honor — used as a courtesy title for the younger children of earls and for all children of viscounts and barons and for maids of honor and also given to the wife of any man having a courtesy title; abbr. *Hon.*; compare MOST HONORABLE, RIGHT HONORABLE (2) **:** being of high eminence or dignity — used in the U.S. as a title or in a mode of reference for members of congress and of state legislatures, cabinet officers and their assistants, commissioners of bureaus, heads of state departments, judges, mayors of cities, and various other high government officials; abbr. *Hon.* **4 a :** doing credit to the possessor ⟨~ wounds⟩ **b :** consistent with an untarnished reputation ⟨~ dismissal⟩ ⟨~ peace terms⟩ **5 :** characterized by integrity **:** ETHICAL, UPRIGHT ⟨Brutus is an ~ man —Shak.⟩ ⟨~ in all his dealings⟩ ⟨assured her that his intentions were ~⟩ **syn** see UPRIGHT

**²honorable** \"\ *n* -s *see -or in Explan Notes* [ME *honourable, honorable*, fr. *honourable, honorable*, adj.] **1 a :** any of various members of British noble families ⟨a host of little cousins, lords and ~s for playmates —*Time*⟩ **b :** any of various high British governmental officials to whom the title of Honorable is officially applied **2 :** a person of rank or distinction ⟨the guest list was studded with judges, congressmen, and other ~s⟩

**honorable discharge** *n* **:** a formal release given a member of the armed forces at the conclusion (as by expiration of his enlistment) of a period of honest and faithful service

**hon·or·able·ness** \-lnəs\ *also* **hon·or·abil·i·ty** \ˌän(ə)rəˈbilədē\ *n* -ES **:** the quality or state of being honorable

**honorable ordinary** *n, heraldry* **:** an ordinary as distinguished from a subordinary

**hon·or·ably** \ˈänər(ə)blē, -nrəb-, -li\ *adv* [ME *honourably, honorably*, fr. *honourable, honorable*, adj. + *-y*] **:** in an honorable manner **:** with honor ⟨dealt ~ with his opponent⟩ ⟨was ~ discharged from the marine corps⟩

**hon·or·and** \ˈänəˌrand, -raa(ə)nd\ *n* -s [fr. L *honorandus*, gerundive of *honorare* to honor — more at HONOR] **:** one that is awarded an honor (as an honorary degree)

**hon·or·ar·i·ly** \ˌänəˈrerəlē, -li\ *adv* **:** in an honorary manner

**hon·o·rar·i·um** \ˌänəˈrerēəm, -ˈra(a)r-, -ˈrär-\ *n, pl* **honorar·ia** \-ēə\ *also* **honorariums** [L, fr. neut. of *honorarius* honorary] **:** an honorary payment or reward usu. given as compensation for services on which custom or propriety forbids any fixed business price to be set or for which no payment can be enforced at law ⟨supplementing his income by *honoraria* from speaking engagements⟩ ⟨the medal carries an ~ of $500⟩

**¹hon·or·ary** \ˈänəˌrerē, -eri\ *adj* [L *honorarius*, fr. *honor* honor + *-arius* -ary — more at HONOR] **1 a :** having or conferring distinction ⟨~ scholar⟩ ⟨~ bridesmaid⟩ ⟨~ engineering society⟩ **b :** COMMEMORATIVE ⟨~ plaque⟩ ⟨wrote an ~ ode for the centennial⟩ **2 a :** conferred in recognition of achievement or service without the usual prerequisites, duties, or obligations **:** TITULAR ⟨does not really tell us what it is like to hold an ~, though honorable, position in a domain where once his word was law —Richard Griffith⟩ ⟨two hard-earned degrees . . . and several ~ ones —A.W.Griswold⟩ **b :** UNPAID, UNREMUNERATIVE, VOLUNTARY ⟨~ secretary⟩ ⟨in the Australian theater play-writing remains very largely an ~ task and consequently a luxury —Leslie Rees⟩ **3 :** dependent on honor for fulfillment **:** MORAL — used esp. of an obligation

**²honorary** \"\ *n* -ES [L *honorarium*] **1** *archaic* **:** HONORARIUM **2** [by shortening] **:** an honorary society ⟨elected to . . . the senior men's ~ —Neil Stueck⟩ **3** [*honorary* (degree)] **:** an honorary degree or its recipient

**honorary canon** *n* **:** a cleric appointed to assist occas. in the services of a cathedral but not residentiary and not entitled to stipend or vote in the chapter — compare MAJOR CANON

**honorary trust** *n* **:** a transfer of property for a designated noncharitable purpose that empowers the transferee to apply the property to the designated purpose or else to surrender it to the one making the transfer or to his estate and that is not enforceable as a trust because it does not benefit a specific ascertainable existing person

**honor attendant** *n* **1 :** BRIDESMAID **2 :** MAID OF HONOR 2

**honor camp** *n* **:** a work camp of trusted prisoners conducted under an honor system

**honor-card** \═ˌ═\ *n* **:** HONOR 9a(1)

**honor court** *n, Eng feudal law* **:** a court held for an honor as a whole

**honored** *adj* **1 :** held in honor **:** RESPECTED **2 :** accorded recognition

**hon·or·ee** \ˌänəˈrē\ *n* -s **:** one that receives an honor

**hon·or·er** \ˈänərə(r)\ *n* -s [ME *honurer*, fr. *onouren, honouren, honuren* to honor + *-er* — more at HONOR] **:** one that honors

**honor guard** *n* **:** GUARD OF HONOR

**hon·o·ri·al** \(ˈ)äˈnōrēəl\ *adj* [¹*honor* + *-ial*] **:** of or relating to a seignorial holding under English feudal law

**¹hon·or·if·ic** \ˌänəˈrifik, -fēk\ *also* **hon·or·if·i·cal** \-fəkəl, -fēk-\ *adj* [*honorific* fr. L *honorificus*, fr. *honorare* to honor; *honorifical* fr. L *honorificus* + E *-al*] **1 :** conferring or conveying honor ⟨~ social status commonly attaches to membership in a recognized profession —D.D.McKean⟩ ⟨a largely honorary but distinctly ~ post —*Time*⟩ ⟨the elaborate set of ~ words used to people of rank —Margaret Mead⟩ **2 :** belonging to or constituting a class of grammatical forms used in speaking to or about a social superior — **hon·or·if·i·cal·ly** \-fək(ə)lē, -fēk-, -li\ *adv*

**²honorific** \"\ *n* -s **1 :** an honorific term of address esp. when used by an Oriental to convey verbal respect ⟨a leader in the movement to abolish caste distinctions — he has officially repudiated the hereditary . . . ~ of "Pandit" before his name —Robert Trumbull⟩ **2 :** an honorific word or form

**honoring** *pres part of* HONOR

**ho·no·ris cau·sa** \(h)äˌnōrəˈskau̇sə, (h)əˌn-, (h)ōˌn-, (h)ȯˌn-, -nȯr-, -kau̇(ˌ)sä, -kau̇(ˌ)zä *sometimes* -kȯzə\ *adv (or adj)* [L] **:** as a token of respect or honor; *esp* **:** in recognition of distinctions or accomplishments not achieved in course ⟨degrees conferred *honoris causa*⟩ ⟨the degree of doctor of laws *honoris causa*⟩

**hon·or·less** \ˈänə(r)ləs\ *adj, see -or in Explan Notes* **:** lacking honor

**honor point** *n* **1 :** a point in an escutcheon of arms approximately midway between the middle chief point and the fess point — see POINT illustration **2 honor points** *pl* **:** HONOR SCORE 1

**honor price** *n* **:** a price paid by an offender or his kinsmen to the injured person or his kinsmen under ancient Irish law — compare CRO, ERIC, GALANAS

**honor roll** *n* **:** a roster of names of persons deserving honor: as **a :** a list of pupils achieving academic distinction **b :** a public memorial listing the names of local citizens who have served in the armed forces

**honors** *pl of* HONOR, *pres 3d sing of* HONOR

**honor score** *n* **1 :** a score that does not count toward game in contract bridge — called also *honor points, honors* **2 :** a space provided on a contract bridge score sheet for recording extra tricks, penalties, and bonuses

**honor society** *n* **:** a society for the recognition of scholarly achievement esp. at the undergraduate level in colleges and universities

**honors of war :** courtesies granted a vanquished enemy (as the privilege of marching out from a camp or town armed and with colors flying)

**honor system** *n* **:** a system granting freedom from customary surveillance (as to students or prisoners) with the understanding that those who are so freed will be bound by their honor to observe regulations ⟨prison farms operated under the *honor system*⟩; *specif* **:** a system of conducting examinations without faculty supervision

**honor trick** \═ˌ═\ *n* **:** a high card or combination of high cards having a specified trick-winning expectancy and used as a basis for evaluating the strength of a contract bridge hand — called also *quick trick*

**hon·our** \ˈänə(r)\ *chiefly Brit var of* HONOR

**hon·tish** \ˈhäntish\ *adj* [origin unknown] *dial Eng* **:** HAUGHTY

**hony** *abbr* honorary

**honyak** *or* **honyock** *usu cap, var of* HUNYAK

**¹hoo** *obs var of* HO

**²hoo** *dial var of* WHO

**³hoo** \ˈhü\ *interj* [origin unknown] — used chiefly to express an emotional reaction (as of surprise or triumph) or as a call

**⁴hoo** \(ˈ)hü\ *chiefly Scot var of* HOW

**⁵hoo** \"\ *var of* ⁴HOW

**¹hooch** \ˈhük\ *interj, chiefly Scot* [origin unknown] — used to express emotion (as excitement, elation)

**²hooch** \ˈhüch\ *n* -ES [short for *hoochinoo*] *slang* **:** alcoholic liquor esp. when inferior, obtained illicitly, or made surreptitiously

**hoochie-coochie** *or* **hoochy-koochy** *var of* HOOTCHY-KOOTCHY

**hoo·chi·noo** \ˈhüchəˌnü, ═ˌ═ˈ═\ *n* -s [fr. the *Hoochinoo* Indians, a Tlingit people of Alaska that made such liquor, fr. Tlingit *Hutsnuwu*, lit., grizzly bear fort] **:** a distilled liquor made by Alaska Indians

**¹hood** \ˈhu̇d\ *n* -s [ME *hood, hod*, fr. OE *hōd*; akin to OFris *hōd* head covering, *hōde* guard, protection, OHG *huot* head covering, helmet, *huota* guard, protection, ON *höttr* head covering, and perh. to L *cassis* helmet, MIr *cais* love; basic meaning: protecting, covering] **1 a** (1) **:** a covering usu. of cloth or leather for the head and neck and sometimes the shoulders that is attached to a garment or worn separately and is made with a loose or close-fitting opening for the face — see COWL 1, FRENCH HOOD (2) **:** a flexible covering of mail worn by an armored man usu. under a helmet or dependent from a steel cap esp. to protect the neck (3) **:** the head covering of an ecclesiastical garment; *esp* **:** a monk's cowl (4) **:** a protective covering for the head and face that often extends below the shoulders, is made of various resistant materials, and is used by persons exposed to special hazards (as heat, fumes, radiation) **b :** a covering for a hawk's head and eyes **c :** a covering for a horse's head; *also* **:** BLINDER **2 :** something felt to resemble a hood: as **a** (1) **:** an ornamental fold at the back of an ecclesiastical vestment (2) **:** an ornamental scarf that is worn over an academic gown so as to swathe the neck and hang loose or form a closed pouch in back and that indicates by its color the wearer's college and often his degree or field of specialization — see ACADEMIC COSTUME **b :** a color marking or crest on the head of an animal or an expansion of the head that occupies the position of or suggests a hood ⟨a cobra spreading his ~⟩ — compare HOODED **c** (1) **:** a cap of foam on water (2) **:** the upper fine-textured part of a batholith **d** (1) **:** a hood-shaped upper petal of some flowers (as of monkshood) — called also *helmet* (2) **:** a thickened structure that replaces the awn in barleys **e :** an unblocked usu. cone-shaped hat body of felt, straw, or other material **3 :** a covering that protects or obscures like a hood: as **a** *chiefly Brit* (1) **:** a covering of earth and hay or straw over a heap of produce (2) **:** a thatch or shelter of straw over a beehive (3) **:** CAPSHEAF 1 **b :** a cap over the top of a chimney; *esp* **:** a metal cap designed to secure constant draft by turning with the wind **c** (1) **:** a top cover for the body of a vehicle (as a carriage or perambulator) that is usu. flexible and designed to be folded back when desired (2) *Brit* **:** the top of an automobile; *esp* **:** a fabric top for a convertible **d** (1) **:** a projecting cover above a hearth forming the upper part of a fireplace and confining and directing smoke to its flue (2) **:** an enclosure or cover (as a canopy or booth) for exhausting by means of a draft disagreeable or noxious fumes, sprays, smoke, or dusts ⟨installed a ~ over the kitchen range⟩ (3) **:** the part of a furnace cupola shell above the charging hole (4) **:** BONNET 2e(4) **e :** a covering or porch for a companion hatch or other opening on a boat **f :** a projecting canopy on a building (as over a door or window) **g :** the endmost plank of a strake or plate of a shell strake, reaching the stem or stern of a wooden ship or both stem and stern **h** (1) **:** a protective cowl or cover for mechanical devices or parts of them (2) **:** the removable metal covering over the engine of an automobile — called also *bonnet* **i :** a covering over the front of a stirrup **j :** a covering that protects and supports the connections of a suspended electric lighting unit **k** (1) **:** an arched or rounded top on furniture (2) **:** the case enclosing the dial and works of some tall clocks **l :** a metal band that holds the reel of a fishing rod in position on the reel seat **m :** a protective cover (as of metal, paper, or plastic) fitted over the lip or top of a container and used esp. to maintain sterile or sanitary conditions of the unopened package **4 :** HOODED SEAL

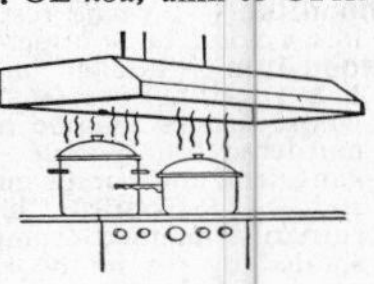
hood 3(d)2

**²hood** \"\ *vt* -ED/-ING/-S [ME *hooden, hoden*, fr. *hood, hod*, n.] **1 :** to cover or furnish with a hood ⟨one must ~ the young hawk early in his training⟩ **2 :** to cover over or obscure (as for protection or concealment) **:** HIDE ⟨~ing the flashlight with his hand⟩; *esp* **:** to partially close (the eyes or eyelids) ⟨~ed her eyes against the sun⟩

**³hood** \ˈhu̇d, -ü-\ *n* -s [short for *hoodlum*] *slang* **:** HOODLUM: as **a :** a gangster or racketeer **b :** a gunman or strong-arm man

**-hood** \ˌhu̇d, *after voiceless consonants sometimes* ˌu̇d *as in* ˈprēˌstu̇d *one pronunciation of "priesthood"*\ *n suffix* -s [ME *-hod, -hode*, fr. OE *-hād*; akin to OFris&OS *-hēd*, suffix denoting state or condition, OHG *-heit*; all fr. a prehistoric Gmc word represented by OE *hād* person, rank, state, condition, OHG *heit* person, rank, state, condition, ON *heithr* honor, Goth *haidus* manner, way; akin to OE *hādor* bright, clear, OHG *heitar*, ON *heithr*, and prob. to L *caesius* bluish gray, *caelum* sky, heaven, Skt *citra* variegated, bright, *ketu* brightness, light; basic meaning: bright] **1 :** state **:** condition **:** quality **:** character ⟨boy*hood*⟩ ⟨girl*hood*⟩ ⟨hardi*hood*⟩ ⟨unlikeli*hood*⟩ **2 :** an instance of a specified state, condition, quality, or character ⟨false*hood*⟩ **3 :** individuals sharing a specified state, condition, quality, or character ⟨brother*hood*⟩

**hoodcap** \ˈ═ˌ═\ *n* **:** HOODED SEAL

**hood clock** *also* **hooded clock** *n* **:** a wall or mantel clock having the movement enclosed in a case and the weights and pendulum if weight-driven exposed to view

**hooded** *adj* [ME *hoded, hooded*, fr. *hod, hood* + *-ed*] **1 a :** covered or furnished with a hood or something resembling a hood **b :** having the awn replaced by a trifurcate hood — used of some cereal grasses **2 a :** shaped like a hood **b :** rolled in expanded conical form with a reflexed tip **:** CUCULLATE — used of plant organs ⟨arums with ~ spathes⟩ **3 a :** having the head conspicuously different in color from the rest of the body — used chiefly of birds **b :** having a crest on the head that suggests a hood ⟨~ seals⟩ **c** *of a cobra* **:** having the skin at each side of the neck capable of expansion by movements of the ribs — **hood·ed·ness** *n* -ES

**hooded crow** *n* **1 :** a European crow (*Corvus cornix*) that is black with gray back and underparts and is closely related to the carrion crow **2** *India* **:** HOUSE CROW

**hooded gull** *n* **:** BLACK-HEADED GULL; *esp* **:** a common European gull (*Larus ridibundus*)

**hooded ladies' tresses** *n pl but sing or pl in constr* **:** a native orchid (*Spiranthes romanzoffiana*) that is widely distributed in northern No. America and occurs occas. in Ireland and eastern Asia and that has spikes of small creamy or straw-colored almond-scented flowers with sepals and petals partly fused into an upward arching hood

**hooded merganser** *or* **hooded sheldrake** *n* **:** a small No. American merganser (*Lophodytes cucullatus*) having a high vertical nearly circular crest on the head of the adult male

**hooded milfoil** *n* **:** PURPLE BLADDERWORT

**hooded oriole** *n* **:** an oriole (*Icterus cucullatus*) of the southwestern U.S. and Mexico that occurs in several races and is distinguished by the yellow head and black throat of the male

**hooded pitcher plant** *n* **:** a yellow-flowered pitcher plant (*Sarracenia minor*) of the southeastern U.S. having variegated trumpet-shaped leaves with green and purple veins and white or yellowish blotches and with the orifice closely covered by an arched hood

**hooded rat** *n* **:** a strain of the black rat developed in captivity and characterized by a white body and black head

**hooded seal** *n* **:** a large seal (*Cystophora cristata*) of the north Atlantic distinguished by a large inflatable sac upon the fore-part of the head of the male

**hooded snake** *n* **:** COBRA

**hooded tern** *n* **:** LITTLE TERN

**hooded top** *n* **:** BONNET TOP

**hooded violet** *n* **:** a usu. purple-flowered tufted violet (*Viola cucullata*) of No. America having the young leaves rolled in and the lateral petals bearded

**hooded warbler** *n* **:** an American warbler (*Wilsonia citrina*) having in the male the forehead, ear coverts, and lower parts gamboge yellow and the rest of the head, neck, and chest black

**hood·ie** *also* **hoody** \'hu̇di, 'hēdi, 'hēdi\ *n, pl* **hoodies** [¹*hood* + *-ie, -y*] **1 a** *or* **hoodie crow :** HOODED CROW 1 **b :** CARRION CROW **2** *dial Brit* **:** a hooded gull (*Larus ridibundus*)

**hooding** *pres part of* HOOD

**hooding end** *or* **hood end** *n* **:** the end of a hood of a ship that enters the rabbet in the stempost or sternpost

**hood·less** \'hu̇dləs\ *adj* **:** lacking a hood ⟨an African ~ cobra⟩

**hoodlike** \'=,=\ *adj* **:** resembling a hood ⟨a ~ crest⟩ **:** enclosing like a hood ⟨a ~ upper petal⟩

**hood·lum** \'hüdləm *also* 'hu̇d-\ *n* -s [origin unknown] **1 a :** THUG, RUFFIAN, MOBSTER; *esp* **:** a small-time criminal whose crimes include acts of violence ⟨a gang of ~s had murdered four people —J.A.Michener⟩ ⟨a ~ . . . works for gangsters, and bumps guys off after they have been put on the spot —C.R.Cooper⟩ **b :** one who behaves in an uncouth or ruffianly manner ⟨some of the tenderest scenes . . . were spoiled by ~s in the gallery —*Amer. Guide Series: Wash.*⟩ **c :** a young ruffian or street loafer **:** a rowdy or misbehaved child or adolescent ⟨that kid was a real ~, . . . shot craps and everything —*Lamp*⟩ **2** *West* **a** *or* **hoodlum wagon :** a wagon used at roundup to carry bedding and miscellaneous supplies **b :** the driver of a hoodlum, usu. serving also as cook's helper

**hood·lum·ish** \-mish\ *adj* **:** like or typical of a hoodlum ⟨~ louts⟩ ⟨~ behavior⟩

**hood·lum·ism** \-lə,mizəm\ *n* -s **:** conduct typical of a hoodlum **:** rough rowdy behavior **:** delinquency or criminality marked esp. by gross disregard for the rights of others

**hood·man-blind** \¦hu̇dmən¦=\ *n, archaic* **:** BLINDMAN'S BUFF

**hoodmold** \'=,=\ *also* **hood molding** *n* **:** a molding that projects over the head of an arch and forms the outermost member of the archivolt **:** DRIPSTONE

hoodmold

¹**hoo·doo** \'hü(,)dü\ *n* -s [of African origin; akin to Hausa *hu³'du³ba¹* to arouse resentment against someone] **1 :** VOODOO **2 a :** something that brings or is associated with the occurrence of bad luck **:** JINX, JONAH — compare MASCOT **b :** bad luck **3 a :** a natural column or pinnacle of rock common in parts of western No. America that results from weathering or erosion and occurs in varied and often fantastic forms **b :** EARTH PILLAR

²**hoodoo** \"\ *adj* **1 :** of, relating to, or being a hoodoo ⟨~ priests⟩ ⟨a ~ fetish⟩ **2 a :** persistently unlucky as if under a spell ⟨a ~ ship⟩ **:** JINXED **b :** bringing or associated with bad luck ⟨when that ~ planet crops up in a horoscope⟩

³**hoodoo** \"\ *vt* -ED/-ING/-S **:** to cast a spell on **:** bring to misfortune by occult means; *broadly* **:** be a source of misfortune to

**hoo·doo·ism** \-,izəm\ *n* -s **:** VOODOOISM

**hoods** *pl of* HOOD, *pres 3d sing of* HOOD

**-hoods** *pl of* -HOOD

**hoodsheaf** \'=,=\ *n* [¹*hood* + *sheaf*] **:** CAPSHEAF 1

¹**hood·wink** \'hu̇,dwiŋk\ *vt* [¹*hood* + *wink*] **1** *archaic* **:** to blind by covering the eyes **:** BLINDFOLD **2** *obs* **:** to hide out of sight or mind **3 :** to deceive by false appearance **:** impose upon ⟨such an easy person to ~⟩ ⟨packages designed to ~ buyers⟩ **syn** see DUPE

²**hoodwink** \"\ *n* **1 :** the act of hoodwinking **2 :** a device for concealing or dissembling (as a mask or blindfold) **:** BLIND

**hood·wink·er** \-kə(r)\ *n* **:** one that hoodwinks

**hoodwise** \'=,=\ *adv* [¹*hood* + *-wise*] **:** in the manner of or so as to serve the purpose of a hood ⟨held a newspaper ~ over her hat⟩

**hoodwort** \'=,=\ *n* **:** MAD-DOG SKULLCAP

**hoo·ey** \'hüē, -üi\ *n* -s [origin unknown] **:** something false or unacceptable **:** HOKUM, NONSENSE — often used interjectionally

¹**hoof** \'hu̇f, 'hüf\ *n, pl* **hooves** \vz\ *or* **hoofs** \fs\ [ME, fr. OE *hōf;* akin to OFris & OS *hōf* hoof, OHG *huof,* ON *hōfr* hoof, Skt *śapha* hoof, claw, Av *safa-* horse's hoof] **1 a :** a curved covering of horn that protects the front of or more or less extensively encloses the ends of the digits of an ungulate mammal and that corresponds to a nail or claw — see COW illustration **b :** a hoofed foot esp. of a horse or other equine — compare CLOVEN FOOT **c :** FOOT; *esp* **:** a large, heavy, or ill-managed human foot ⟨heard those *hooves* on the stair⟩ **2** *now chiefly dial* **:** a hoofed animal; *usu* **:** a hoofed domestic mammal ⟨hadn't a ~ fit to dress⟩ **3 :** one of the smaller and more angulate plates (as a marginal plate) of the shell of the hawksbill turtle; *also* **:** the tortoise shell composing these plates — used chiefly commercially — **on the hoof 1** *of meat animals* **:** LIVING, LIVEWEIGHT ⟨10 cents a pound *on the hoof*⟩ ⟨*on the hoof* meat is supplied —*Nat'l Geographic*⟩ **2** *of persons* **:** in ordinary condition **:** without an opportunity for any special show ⟨meeting people *on the hoof* across a sales counter⟩ ⟨executives expert at judging men *on the hoof*⟩

²**hoof** \"\ *vb* -ED/-ING/-S *vt* **1 :** WALK ⟨~*ed* a mile to school each day⟩ ⟨~*ing* it to town⟩ **2 :** KICK, TRAMPLE ⟨buffalo ~*ed* up the dust⟩ ⟨colts ~*ing* the sod⟩ **3 :** to put out by or as if by kicking **:** throw out **:** EJECT, BOOT ⟨uncle got me ~*ed* out of that —F.M.Ford⟩ ~ *vi* **:** to move on the feet (as in walking, tramping, or dancing); *esp* **:** to execute noisy rhythmic footwork (as in tap-dancing)

**hoof-and-mouth disease** *n* **:** FOOT-AND-MOUTH DISEASE

**hoofbeat** \'=,=\ *n* **:** the sound of a hoof striking the ground or other hard surface ⟨~s fading in the distance⟩

**hoofbound** \'=,=\ *adj* **:** having a dry and contracted hoof that occasions pain and lameness

**hoofed** \'hu̇ft, -üft\ *adj* **1 :** having hoofs **:** UNGULATE — often used in combination ⟨cloven-*hoofed*⟩ **2** *of a shoe* **:** having a broad rounded front

**hoofed locust** *n* [so called fr. the fact that sheep closely crop the vegetation when they graze] **:** SHEEP — usu. used disparagingly by cattlemen

**hoof·er** \'hu̇fə(r), -üf-\ *n* -s **1 :** one that travels on foot **2** *slang* **:** DANCER; *esp* **:** a professional dancer (as in vaudeville or a chorus)

**hoof foot** *n* **:** a furniture foot in the form of a usu. cloven hoof

**hoof·i·ness** \-fēnəs, -fin-\ *n* -ES **:** the quality or state of being hoofed

**hoof·less** \-fləs\ *adj* **:** lacking hooves

**hoof·let** \-lət\ *n* -s [¹*hoof* + *-let*] **:** a small hoof; *esp* **:** FALSE HOOF

hoof foot

**hooflike** \'=,=\ *adj* **:** resembling a hoof; *esp* **:** having the horny texture of a hoof ⟨~ calluses⟩

**hoof-pick** \'=,=\ *n* **:** a hooked implement used to remove foreign objects from a hoof

**hoofprint** \'=,=\ *n* **:** an impression or hollow made by a hoof

**hoofrot** \'=,=\ *n* **:** FOOT ROT 2

**hoog·aars** \'hō,gärs\ *n, pl* **hoogaars** \",-rz\ [D, fr. *hoog* high + *aars* buttocks] **:** a Dutch sloop

**hoo-ha** \'hü,hä\ *n* -s [origin unknown] **:** HULLABALOO

¹**hook** \'hu̇k\ *n* -s [ME *hok, hook,* fr. OE *hōc;* akin to OFris *hōk* corner, MD *hoec* fishhook, corner, OE *haca* bolt, OHG *hāko* hook, Icel *haki* hook, ON *haka* chin, MIr *ailcheng* rake, stand for weapons, Lith *kengė* hook, latch] **1 a** (1) **:** an implement for cutting grass or grain **:** SICKLE, SCYTHE (2) **:** an implement for cutting or lopping **:** BILLHOOK **b :** a hand fork with the tines turned nearly at right angles to the handle ⟨a potato ~⟩ ⟨manure ~s⟩ **c :** a curved metal prong attached to a leather wristband for tearing the husks from an ear of corn **2 a :** a piece of metal or other hard or tough material formed or bent into a curve or at an angle for catching, holding, sustaining, or pulling something ⟨a ~ for fastening a gate⟩ ⟨a ~ for filing papers⟩ **b :** any of various hooked objects: as (1) **:** BREASTHOOK (2) **:** an artificial replacement for the hand made in the form of a hook (3) **:** an instrument used in surgery to take hold of tissue ⟨crypt ~⟩ ⟨chordotomy ~⟩ (4) **:** the part of a hook and eye that is bent over to form a finger that fits into the eye (5) **:** a long pole with a hooked end by which one in the wings can reach out and pull a performer off the stage — often used in the phrase *get the hook* (6) **:** FIRE HOOK **3 a :** FISHHOOK; *broadly* **:** any angling device or lure capable of taking but one fish at a time **b :** something designed to attract and ensnare **4 :** a part of a hinge that is fixed to a post and on which the part that is fixed to a door or gate hangs and turns **5 :** something felt to resemble a hook: as **a :** a sharp bend or curve (as in a stream) or a spit or narrow cape of sand or gravel turned landward at the outer end ⟨wave action may build spits into ~s⟩ **b** (1) **:** an angular or recurved mark (as a written character or an element in one) (2) **:** EAR ⟨the ~ of lower-case g or q⟩ (3) **:** ⁵FLAG 3a (4) **:** PARENTHESIS 3a — used in printing; usu. in pl. **c** (1) **:** a recurved part or appendage of a plant or animal ⟨burrs clinging by their ~s⟩ (2) *or* **hook bone :** the projecting angle of the hipbone of cattle — usu. used in pl. ⟨a good covering of flesh over the ~s⟩ **d :** the angle between the face of a tooth and a line to the center of a circular saw or to a line perpendicular to the back of a band saw **e :** ANCHOR **f hooks** *pl, slang* **:** FINGERS ⟨just let me get my ~s on him⟩ **g :** a lever by which a device (as a fire-alarm box) is actuated **h :** a mobile wrecking crane; *broadly* **:** a wreck train or car mounting a crane **6 a :** an act or instance of hooking ⟨the cow gave a sudden ~ and ripped his sleeve⟩ **b :** a flight of a ball (as in golf, cricket, bowling, baseball) that deviates from a straight course in a direction opposite to the dominant hand of the player projecting it; *also* **:** a ball following such a course — compare SLICE, SPIN **c :** a short blow delivered with a circular motion by a boxer while the elbow remains bent and rigid **7 :** CROOK 2b — **by hook or by crook** *also* **by hook or crook :** by any means **:** fairly or unfairly ⟨determined to win *by hook or by crook*⟩ — **drop off the hooks** *or* **slip off the hooks** *Brit* **:** DIE — **off the hook** *adv (or adj)* **:** out of a difficulty or trouble ⟨counted on his friends to get him *off the hook*⟩ — **off the hooks** *obs* **:** disordered in mind or body **:** UNHINGED, DERANGED — **on one's own hook :** on one's own account or responsibility **:** without authorization or assistance **:** by oneself **:** INDEPENDENTLY

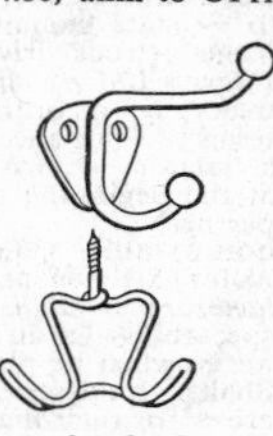
hooks 2a

²**hook** \"\ *vb* -ED/-ING/-S [ME *hoken,* fr. *hok, hook,* n.] *vt* **1 :** to give the form of a hook to **:** CROOK ⟨~*ed* an arm about the stanchion⟩ **2 a :** to make fast with or as if with a hook or hooks ⟨~ a dress⟩ **b :** to seize, capture, or hold with a hook ⟨~*ed* a large trout⟩ **c :** to secure or catch as if with a hook ⟨~*ed* herself a husband⟩: as (1) *slang* **:** to reduce to a complete loss of self-control **:** make wholly dependent — usu. used in passive ⟨~*ed* by the morphine habit⟩ (2) *slang* **:** to entrap into improper, undesirable, or foolish activity ⟨when the sucker listens he's half ~*ed*⟩ (3) **:** to hold (a dancing partner) by interlocking feet or elbows; *also* **:** to interlock (feet or elbows) in dancing **3 a :** to seize and draw with or as if with a hook ⟨~*ed* the logs out of the channel⟩ **b :** to take by stealth **:** STEAL, PILFER ⟨~*ing* apples from the tree⟩ **4 :** to strike or pierce with the points of the horns **:** GORE **5 a :** to make (as a rug) by drawing loops of thread, yarn, or cloth through a coarse fabric with a hook **b :** to so draw (as yarn) in forming a pattern ⟨~*ed* heavy woolen rags into an ombré pattern⟩ **6 a :** to strike (a boxing opponent) with a hook **b :** to strike or throw (as a golf ball or bowling ball) so that a hook results — compare FADE, SLICE **c :** to hit (a bowled cricket ball) to leg with a stroke in which the bat swings upward and in a leg direction **d** (1) **:** to intercept (the ball) in rugby and propel backward with the heel of the boot from the front line of the scrum (2) **:** to gain possession of (the ball) in soccer by reaching out, intercepting, and drawing with the foot ~ *vi* **1 :** to bend sharply so as to form a hook **:** CURVE ⟨the beak ~s strongly downward⟩ **2** *slang* **:** to make off **:** LEAVE, DEPART ⟨~*ed* for home⟩ — usu. used with formulary *it* ⟨~ it, the cops are coming⟩ **3 :** to secure or fasten by or as if by a hook ⟨a dress that ~s in back⟩ **4 a :** to make an attack with the horns ⟨the bull ~*ed* at his handler⟩ **b :** to deliver a hook in boxing ⟨~*ing* expertly but without much power⟩ **5 a** *of a ball* **:** to travel in or be a hook ⟨the ball ~*ed* badly but bounced onto the fairway⟩ **b** *of a player* **:** to hook a ball ⟨~*ed* into the rough⟩ **c :** to shoot or attempt to score in basketball with a hook shot

**hookah** *also* **hooka** \'hu̇kə, 'hükə\ *n* -s [Ar *huqqah* round box, casket, bottle of a water pipe] **:** a pipe for smoking that has a long flexible tube whereby the smoke is cooled by passing through water — compare NARGILEH

**hook-and-butt joint** *n* **:** a scarf joint formed to resist tension

**hook and eye** *n* **:** a two-part fastening device (as on a garment or a door) consisting of a wire hook that catches over a bar or into a loop of wire — see FASTENER illustration

**hook-and-eye** \¦=,=¦=\ *adj* [*hook and eye*] **:** having religious scruples against the wearing of buttons ⟨a *hook-and-eye* sect⟩

**hook-and-eye hinge** *n* **:** a hinge intended for use on a gate and consisting of an L-shaped hook secured to one member (as the gatepost) and fitted into an eye-shaped loop or screw hook secured to the other member (as the gate)

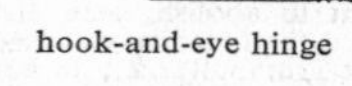
hook-and-eye hinge

**hook and ladder** *n* **1** *or* **hook-and-ladder truck :** LADDER TRUCK **2** *or* **hook-and-ladder company :** LADDER COMPANY

**hook-and-liner** \¦=,=¦==\ *n* **:** a boat (as a tuna clipper) for fishing with hook and line

**hook·a·roon** \¦hu̇kə¦rün\ *n* -s [¹*hook* + *-aroon* (as in *pick-aroon*)] **:** ²PICKAROON

**hook-bill** \'=,=\ *n* **:** a parrot or a closely related bird (as a cockatoo or parrakeet) esp. when domesticated

**hook-billed** \'=¦bild\ *adj* **:** having a strongly curved bill or jaws ⟨a *hook-billed* salmon⟩

**hook bolt** *n* **:** a bolt hooked at one end and threaded at the other to receive a nut

**hook bones** *n* **:** HOOK 5c(2)

**hook check** *n* **:** a technique of gaining possession of an ice-hockey puck or diverting it to a teammate by hooking it away from the opponent with one's stick

hook bolts

**hook climber** *n* **:** a plant (as a climbing rose) that climbs by hooks or prickles

**hooked** \'hu̇kt\ *adj* **1 :** having the form of a hook ⟨the ~ bill of a bird of prey⟩ **2 :** provided with a hook or hooks ⟨a fireman's ~ ax⟩ **3 :** made by hooking ⟨a ~ design⟩ ⟨~ carpets⟩ **4** *slang* **:** addicted to narcotics **:** having reached a state of physical dependence on narcotics — **hooked·ness** \'hu̇k(t)nəs, -kədn-\ *n* -ES

**hooked rug** *n* **:** a rug formed by hooking into a strong coarse fabric back loops (as of yarn or strips of cloth) to form a surface pile

¹**hookem-snivey** \¦hu̇kəm¦snivi\ *n* -s [fr. earlier *hook and snivey,* prob. fr. *hook* (to steal)] *dial chiefly Eng* **:** TRICKERY, DECEIT

²**hookem-snivey** *adj, dial chiefly Eng* **:** DECEITFUL, TRICKY

¹**hook·er** \'hu̇kə(r)\ *n* -s [²*hook* + *-er*] **1 a :** one that hooks esp. habitually ⟨that cow is a bad ~⟩ **b** *slang* **:** THIEF, PICKPOCKET **c** [fr. the fact that they fasten their clothes with hooks rather than buttons] *usu cap* **:** one of the Amish Mennonites **d :** a worker that uses a hook or hooking device to fasten, move, handle, or form articles with which he works: as (1) **:** a logger that fastens logs to hooks, cables, or tongs by which they may be skidded or loaded (2) **:** a steelworker that guides billets in a rolling mill (3) **:** a sponge fisher that detaches sponges with a sponge hook (4) **:** a maker of hooked rugs (5) **:** an operator of a machine for folding and measuring cloth **e :** a player in the front row of a rugby scrum who hooks the ball **2** *slang* **:** DRINK; *esp* **:** a copious drink of liquor ⟨a ~ of hard cider⟩ **3** [prob. fr. ²*hook* (to entrap) + *-er*] *slang* **:** PROSTITUTE

²**hooker** \"\ *n* -s [D *hoeker,* fr. earlier *hoeckboot,* fr. MD *hoecboot* fishing boat, fr. *hoec* fishhook + *boot* boat — more at HOOK] **1 :** a Dutch boat with two masts **2 :** a fishing boat with one mast used on the coasts of England and Ireland **3 :** an old, outmoded, or clumsy boat

**hooker cell** \"-\ *n, usu cap H* [after Albert H. *Hooker* †1936 Am. electrochemist] **:** a cell that has graphite anodes and wire-screen cathodes covered with asbestos diaphragms and that is used for making sodium hydroxide and chlorine by electrolysis of sodium chloride

**hoo·ke·ri·a·les** \(,)hu̇r,kirē'ā(,)lēz\ *n pl, cap* [NL, fr. *Hookeria,* genus of mosses (fr. Sir William J. *Hooker* †1865 Eng. botanist + NL *-ia*) + *-ales*] **:** an order of usu. pleurocarpous mosses with branched prostrate gametophores, asymmetrical leaves often with two midribs, and capsules with a double peristome

**hooker-out** \¦==¦=\ *n, pl* **hookers-out** [*hook out,* v. + *-er*] **1 :** a tonger in a wireworks **2 :** STICKMAN 1c(1)

**hooker's green** *n, usu cap H* [after William *Hooker* †1832 Eng. botanical painter] **1 :** a green pigment consisting of a mixture of Prussian blue and gamboge **2 :** a moderate to strong green that is yellower and less strong than spearmint

**hooker's orchid** *n, usu cap H* [after Sir William J. *Hooker* †1865 Eng. botanist] **:** a long-spurred orchid (*Habenaria hookeri*) having basal leaves and petals connivent under the upper sepal

**hooke's law** \'hu̇ks-\ *n, usu cap H* [after Robert *Hooke* †1703 Eng. scientist] **:** a statement of elasticity: the stress within an elastic solid up to the elastic limit is proportional to the strain responsible for it

**hookey** *var of* HOOKY

**hook gage** *n* **:** an instrument for measuring the rise or drop in elevation of a liquid (as water in a reservoir) from a previously recorded level by means of a pointed hook that is directly connected to a fixed part containing a scale (as a vernier) and is submerged and moved gradually until its point just pierces the surface of the liquid from beneath when the measurement is taken

**hook-headed spike** \'=,==-\ *n* **:** a spike with extended head to hook over the base of a railroad rail and secure it to a tie

**hookier** *comparative of* HOOKY

**hookiest** *superlative of* HOOKY

**hooking** *pres part of* HOOK

**hooking iron** *n* **:** a hand tool with a pointed metal blade for removing caulking from seams (as of a boat)

**hook·ish** \'hu̇kish\ *adj* **:** somewhat hooked ⟨a prominent ~ nose⟩

**hook ladder** *n* **:** POMPIER LADDER

**hook·less** \-kləs\ *adj* **:** having no hooks

**hook·let** \-klət\ *n* -s [¹*hook* + *-let*] **:** a small hook ⟨a circle of ~s on the tapeworm scolex⟩ — see ECHINOCOCCUS illustration

**hooklike** \'=,=\ *adj* **:** resembling a hook esp. in recurved form or in ability to grasp and hold ⟨~ thorns⟩

**hook·man** \'hu̇kmən, -,man\ *n, pl* **hookmen :** a worker that uses a gaff or a cant hook (as in handling logs or fish)

**hook money** *n* **:** Persian larin money

**hooknose** \'=,=\ *n* **:** an aquiline nose

**hook order** *n* **:** a pattern of social organization within a herd of cattle that is characterized by the right of any member to hook one of lower status without fear of retaliation and its submission to hooking by one of higher rank — compare PECK ORDER

**hook pass** *n* **:** a basketball pass executed in a manner similar to that of a hook shot

**hook rope** *n* **:** a rope with a hook on the end used esp. on shipboard for clearing and handling lines

**hook rug** *n* **:** HOOKED RUG

**hooks** *pl of* HOOK, *pres 3d sing of* HOOK

**hook screw** *n* **:** SCREW HOOK

**hookshop** \'=,=\ *n* [²*hook* (to entrap) + *shop*] *slang* **:** BROTHEL 2

**hook shot** *n* **:** a clear or bank shot in basketball in which a player shoots sideways for the basket by bringing the ball up over his head in an arc with the far hand and releasing it in a usu. flat trajectory

**hook slide** *n* **:** a foot-first slide to a base in a baseball game in which the runner with both legs extended throws his body to either side to avoid the baseman and hooks the base with the inside foot

**hook squid** *n* **:** any of certain squids (*Enoploteuthis* and related genera) in which the acetabula of the sessile arms are modified into a formidable armament of hooks

**hook strip** *n* **:** a horizontal strip or band of wood supporting a series of hooks (as for hanging hats and coats)

**hookswinging** \'=,==\ *n* **:** a voluntary ritual torture in which the individual is suspended by hooks inserted into the muscles of the back

**hook tender** *n* **:** a working foreman in charge of a crew yarding logs

**hooktip** \'=,=\ *or* **hook-tip moth** *n* **:** a moth of the family Drepanidae

**hook·um** \'hu̇kəm\ *n* -s [Hindi *hukm,* fr. Ar, decision, judgment] *India* **:** COMMAND, ORDER; *esp* **:** an official paper giving instructions

**hook·um-pake** \'hu̇kəm,pāk\ *n* -s [imit.] *Midland* **:** WOODCOCK 1a(2)

**hookum-snivey** *var of* HOOKEM-SNIVEY

**hook up** *vi* **:** to attach a horse or other source of draft to a vehicle ⟨*hooked up* and drove to the meadow⟩ ~ *vt* **1 :** to attach (as a team) to a vehicle **2 :** to install in or connect into a suitable environment to function as part of a system ⟨*hooked* the big parlor heater *up* each fall⟩ ⟨*hook* the gas *up*⟩ ⟨finished *hooking up* the new bathroom⟩ **3** *dial* **:** MARRY ⟨arranged to have the parson *hook* them *up*⟩

**hookup** \'=,=\ *n* -s [*hook up*] **1 :** a group or number of items cooperating or acting together: as **a :** an assemblage (as of apparatus or circuits) used for a specific purpose (as radio transmission or reception); *also* **:** the general scheme or plan of such an assemblage **b :** a sequence or arrangement of communicating and usu. interacting parts (as the steering gear or brake mechanism of an automobile) ⟨the stoker ~ on the furnace⟩ **2 :** the establishment of a hookup **:** a linking of two or more items into an interacting whole: as **a :** an assembling of parts into a functional whole ⟨finished the ~ of the new pump⟩ **b :** a midair recoupling of a parasite fighter airplane to the belly of the bomber from which it was previously launched **3 :** the end of a line transposed to the line above and preceded by a left-hand bracket ⟨~s are sometimes necessary in narrow-measure setting⟩ **4 :** a state of cooperation or alliance between diverse and often supposedly mutually antagonistic elements ⟨explaining the ~ between politics and crime⟩ ⟨a ~ designed to protect the sovereignty of small na-

**ho·oku·pu** \ˌhōəˈkü(ˌ)pü\ *n* -s [Hawaiian *hoʻokupu*] **:** a Hawaiian ceremonial presentation of gifts offered as tribute to a chief

**hookweed** \ˈ=,=\ *n* **:** SELF-HEAL

**hookworm** \ˈ=,=\ *n* **1 :** any of numerous parasitic nematode worms (family Ancylostomatidae) having strong buccal hooks or plates for attaching to the host's intestinal lining and including serious bloodsucking pests of man, many domestic and wild mammals, and a few birds — see ANCYLOSTOMA **2 :** *or* **hookworm disease :** disease caused by hookworms **:** ANCYLOSTOMIASIS

**hook·wormy** \ˈ"ē\ *adj* **:** infested by hookworms

**hook wrench** *or* **hook spanner** *n* **:** a wrench having a hook at the end (as for turning a bolt head or nut)

¹**hooky** \ˈhu̇kē, -ki\ *adj* -ER/-EST [¹*hook* + -*y*] **1 :** full of or covered with hooks **2 :** resembling or having the form of a hook

²**hooky** \"\ *or* **hook·ey** \"\ *n, pl* **hookies** *or* **hookeys** [prob. fr. ²*hook* (to make off) + -*y*] **:** TRUANT — used chiefly in the phrase *play hooky*

**hool** \ˈhēl, -üə-\ *Scot var of* HULL

**ho·olau·lea** \ˌhōəˌlau̇ˈlāə\ *n* -s [Hawaiian *hoʻolauleʻa*, fr. *hoʻo* to make + *lau* much + *leʻa* gaiety] **:** a Hawaiian celebration or festival

**hoo·let** \ˈhülət\ *chiefly Scot var of* HOWLET

**hoo·ley** \ˈhülē\ *n* -s [origin unknown] **:** an Irish party usu. with music

**hoo·ley-ann** \ˌhülēˈan\ *also* **hoo·li·an** \", (ˈ)hülˈyan\ *n* -s [origin unknown] *West* **:** a throw with a lariat in which the loop is well spread and settles from above on its objective

**hoo·li·gan** \ˈhüləgən, -lēg-\ *n* -s *often attrib* [perh. after an Irishman named *Hooligan fl* 1898 in Southwark, London, England] **1 :** HOODLUM 1 **2 :** a person that as a representative of some special interest (as a political or racial philosophy) attempts to override the legal and human rights of other people **3 :** a gambling game played with 10 dice in which a player attempts to throw a selected number 26 or more times in 13 throws

**hoo·li·gan·ism** \-gəˌnizəm\ *n* -s **:** lawless disorderly conduct typical of hooligans; *often* **:** VANDALISM

**hoo·li·han** \ˈhüləˌhan\ *vt* **hoolihanned; hoolihanned; hoolihanning; hoolihans** [prob. fr. the name *Hoolihan*] *West* **:** to bring down (a steer) in bulldogging by leaping well forward on the horns rather than by twisting

**hoo·lock** \ˈhüˌläk, -lək\ *n* -s [native name in Assam or Burma] **:** a small gibbon (*Hylobates hoolock*) of Assam and upper Burma; *broadly* **:** a gibbon of the genus *Hylobates*

¹**hoo·ly** \ˈhœli\ *adv* [ME *holy*, of Scand origin; akin to ON *hōfliga* fairly, with moderation, fr. *hōfligr* moderate, fr. *hōf* moderation, proportion + -*ligr* -ly; akin to ON *hefja* to lift — more at HEAVE] *chiefly Scot* **:** in a slow, careful, or gentle manner

²**hooly** \"\ *adj* [ME (Sc dial.) *huly*, of Scand origin; akin to ON *hōfligr* moderate] *chiefly Scot* **:** SLOW, CAREFUL

**ho·oma·li·ma·li** \ˌhōəˌmälēˈmälē\ *n* -s [Hawaiian *hoʻomalimali*] *Hawaii* **:** something designed primarily to attract favorable attention **:** SOFT SOAP

**hoon** \ˈhün, -ü-\ *n* -s [Hindi *hūn*, *hun*] *India* **:** PAGODA 2

**hoondee** *or* **hoondi** *var of* HUNDI

¹**hoop** \ˈhüp, -ü-\ *n* -s *often attrib* [ME *hop, hoop*, fr. OE *hōp*; akin to OFris *hōp* ring, band, MD *hoep* ring, band, hoop, Lith *kabė* hook, and perh. to OIr *camm* crooked — more at CHANGE] **1 a :** a strip of wood or metal bent in a circular form and united at the ends that is used esp. for holding together the staves of containers (as casks, tubs, barrels) — see BARREL illustration **b :** such a hoop or a substitute used as a plaything — compare HULA HOOP **2 :** something felt to resemble a hoop **:** a circular figure or object esp. when serving or viewed as a retaining band **:** RING, CIRCLET: as **a :** FINGER RING **b :** either or both members of an embroidery hoop **c :** one of the cylindrical forgings that are concentric with the tube and that are shrunk in rows upon the tube, jacket, or inner layer in the construction of a built-up gun **d :** CHEESE HOOP **e :** a large circle of light material usu. supporting a sheet of paper through which performers leap in various spectacular shows (as in a circus) **f :** a piece of cane looped at one end for handing messages to the crew of a moving railroad train **g :** the rim of a basketball basket; *broadly* **:** the entire basket **3 :** a circle or series of graduated circles of whalebone, metal, or other flexible material inserted into a petticoat or joined by tapes and used to expand a woman's skirt ⟨wore ~*s* under ruffled white mull⟩ **4 a** *dial Eng* **:** an old unit of capacity (as for grain) varying from ¼ peck to 4 pecks **b** *obs* **:** the quantity of drink contained between any two adjacent hoops of a hooped quart pot **5 hoops** *pl* **:** light strip steel folded up like a skein of wool into lengths of 14 feet **6 :** a croquet wicket **7 :** a shoulder yoke used for carrying loads

hoop 3

²**hoop** \"\ *vb* -ED/-ING/-S [ME *hoopen*, fr. *hop, hoop*, n.] *vt* **1 a :** to bind, enclose, or fasten (as a barrel) with hoops **b :** CLASP, ENCLOSE, SURROUND **2 a :** to place on or in a hoop ⟨~*ing* her embroidery⟩ ⟨~ curds in the making of cheese⟩ **b :** to score at basketball ⟨~*ed* 5 points to win the game⟩ **3 :** to give the form of a hoop or partial hoop to ⟨a measuring worm ~*ing* his back⟩ ⟨~*ed* the backs of the chairs in a graceful arch⟩ ~ *vi* **1 :** to assume the form of a hoop or partial hoop ⟨the cat's back ~*ed* under his hand⟩ **2 :** to keep a hula hoop revolving about the body

³**hoop** \ˈhüp, -ü-\ *archaic var of* WHOOP

⁴**hoop** *n* -s [MF *huppe*, fr. L *upupa*, of imit. origin like Gk *epop-, epops* hoopoe, G dial *huppupp*] *obs* **:** HOOPOE

**hoop ash** *n* **1 :** BLACK ASH 1 **2 :** HACKBERRY

**hoop back** \ˈ=,=\ *n* **:** a back (as of a Windsor chair) formed by a bent piece of wood fitted with vertical spindles

**hoop dance** *n* **:** a male exhibition dance with hoops performed among Indian peoples and imitators from New Mexico to the Great Lakes

**hoop driver** *n* **:** a tool for setting and tightening hoops (as on a barrel)

**hooped** *adj* **1 :** made with or shaped like a hoop ⟨a ~ chair back⟩; *esp* **:** having a full rounded contour ⟨a horse with well-hooped ribs⟩ **2 :** having, wearing, or enclosed by a hoop ⟨a ~ skirt⟩ ⟨graceful ~ dancers⟩ ⟨~ curds ripening into cheese⟩

hoop back

**hooped·ness** \-p(t)nəs, -pədn-\ *n* -ES **:** the quality or state of being hooped

**hoopee** *var of* WHOOPEE

¹**hoop·er** \ˈhu̇pə(r), ˈhüp-\ *n* -s **:** one that hoops: as **a :** a man or machine that makes or applies hoops (as to barrels or tubs) **b :** a worker that stretches skins (as sealskins) over a hoop-shaped frame for curing or processing **c :** HOOPSTER

²**hooper** *or* **hooper swan** *var of* WHOOPER SWAN

**hoop·erat·ing** *or* **hooper rating** \ˈhu̇pəˈrād·iŋ, ˈhüp-, -ātˌ, ]ēn\ *n* -s *usu cap H* [after Claude E. *Hooper* †1954 Am. statistician] **:** a percentage indication of the number of radios or television sets tuned to a particular program at a particular time ⟨rain on a Sunday raises *Hooperatings* —Saul Carson⟩ ⟨the most glamorous, high *Hooperating* show on the air —Frederic Wakeman⟩

**hoop fastener** *n* **:** a special nail for securing the hoops of a barrel

**hoo·pid salmon** \ˈhüpəd-, ˈhüp-\ *also* **hoopid** *n* -s [origin unknown] **:** SILVER SALMON

**hoop·ing** \ˈhu̇piŋ, ˈhüp-\ *n* -s [¹*hoop* + -*ing*] **1 :** stock for making hoops **2 :** HOOPS; *esp* **:** a set of hoops used together ⟨the ~ on this barrel is too slack⟩

**hoop iron** *n* **:** iron in thin strips used for or suitable for use as barrel hoops ⟨arrowheads of sharpened *hoop iron*⟩

**hoop·la** *also* **houp-la** \ˈhüˌplä, ˈhu̇-, -lä\ *n* -s [F *houp-là*, interj.] **1 a :** excited commotion ⟨the ~ occasioned . . . by the report —C.J.Rolo⟩; *often* **:** gay or rowdy excitement ⟨holiday ~ and parties⟩ **b :** gaudy, artificial, or pretentious show **:** TO-DO ⟨opportunities for plenty of romantic ~ in a costume drama —John McCarten⟩ ⟨launched the new promotion in a blaze of ~⟩ **c :** something (as utterances) designed to bewilder or confuse ⟨official ~ about the back of organized crime being broken —Joseph LeBaron⟩ **:** BUNKUM, BALLYHOO **2** [influenced in meaning by ¹*hoop*] **:** a game in which novelty items are won by tossing rings over them

**hoople** \ˈhüpəl, ˈhüp-\ *n* -s [D *hoepel*, dim. of *hoep* hoop, fr. MD — more at HOOP] *dial* **:** HOOP; *esp* **:** a child's hoop for play

**hoop·less** \-pləs\ *adj* **:** lacking a hoop ⟨an old ~ barrel⟩

**hooplike** \ˈ=,=\ *adj* **:** like a hoop **:** ARCHED, ROUNDED

**hoop·man** \ˈhu̇pmən, ˈhüp-\ *n, pl* **hoopmen :** a basketball player

**hoop net** *n* **:** an elongated cylindrical net supported by one or more hoops and fitted with one or more valves resembling funnels through which fishes may enter but not escape that is used esp. in rivers or other waters where fishes tend to move along regular paths

**hoo·poe** *also* **hoo·poo** \ˈhü(ˌ)pü, -pō\ *n* -s [imit. alter. of ⁴*hoop*] **:** any of certain Old World nonpasserine birds (family Upupidae) having a slender decurved bill; *esp* **:** a widely distributed bird (*Upupa epops*) of Europe, Asia, and northern Africa that is of the size of a large thrush with a handsome erectile semicircular crest and cinnamon-colored and black plumage and feeds on insects and other small invertebrates found about decaying organic matter — see WOOD HOOPOE

**hoop–petticoat daffodil** *also* **hoop–petticoat narcissus** *n* **:** a small early-flowering narcissus (*Narcissus bulbocodium*) that has yellow conical to bell-shaped flowers borne singly, is native from southern France to Morocco, and is widely grown as a rock-garden plant

**hoop pine** *n* **:** an araucaria (*Araucaria cunninghamii*) of Australia and New Guinea that yields a valuable light soft even-textured wood

**hoop pole** *n* **:** a straight slender length of green sapling wood usu. of hickory or white oak that was formerly used as stock for barrel hoops

**hoop ring** *n* **:** a finger ring in the form of a plain or ornamented band or with low-mounted stones along the band

**hoops** *pl of* HOOP, *pres 3d sing of* HOOP

**hoopskirt** \ˈ=,=\ *n* **1 :** an underskirt stiffened with or as if with hoops **2 :** a full outer skirt expanded by petticoats or hoops

**hoop snake** *n* **1** *chiefly South and Midland* **:** a fabled snake of extremely venomous character that rolls itself up with its tail in its mouth to proceed at great speed in the manner of a hoop and destroys both animal and plant life with a sting in the end of its tail **2 :** either of two harmless brightly colored burrowing colubrid snakes chiefly of the southeastern U.S.: **a :** a large snake (*Farancia abacura*) that is blue black above and largely red below and has a sharp nonvenomous spine at the end of its tail — called also *horn snake* **b :** RAINBOW SNAKE

**hoop·ster** \ˈhu̇pstə(r), ˈhüp-\ *n* -s [¹*hoop* + -*ster*] **1 :** a basketball player **2 :** one that keeps a hula hoop revolving

**hoopstick** \ˈ=,=\ *n* **1 a :** HOOP POLE **b :** a light framing member for a carriage or wagon hood **2 :** a stick for rolling a child's play hoop

**hoop withe** *or* **hoop withy** *n* **1 :** a tropical Old World shrub (*Colubrina asiatica*) the fruits of which are used as fish poison in the Philippines **2 :** a tropical American shrub of a genus (*Trichostigma*) of the family Phytolaccaceae (esp. *T. octandrum*)

**hoopwood** \ˈ=,=\ *n* **1 :** BLACK ASH 1 **2 :** a winterberry (*Ilex laevigata*)

**hoorah** *or* **hooray** *var of* HURRAH

**hoorah's nest** *or* **hooraw's nest** *var of* HURRAH'S NEST

**hoo·roosh** \həˈrüsh\ *n* -ES [imit.] **:** a wild, hurried, or excited state or situation **:** CONFUSION ⟨such a ~ as we had getting to the docks⟩

¹**hoose** \ˈhüs\ *chiefly Scot var of* HOUSE

²**hoose** *also* **hooze** \ˈhüz\ *n* -s [prob. akin to E *wheeze*] **1** *dial Eng* **:** a dry cough **:** WHEEZING, WHEEZE **2 :** verminous bronchitis of cattle, sheep, and goats caused by larval strongylid roundworms irritating the bronchial tubes and producing a dry hacking cough — called also *husk*

³**hoose** *or* **hooze** \"\ *vi* -ED/-ING/-S *dial Eng* **:** WHEEZE

**hoose·gow** *also* **hoos·gow** \ˈhüsˌgau̇\ *n* -s [Sp *juzgado* panel of judges, tribunal, courtroom, fr. past part. of *juzgar* to judge, fr. L *judicare* — more at JUDGE] *slang* **:** JAIL, LOCKUP, GUARDHOUSE, PRISON

¹**hoosh** \ˈhüsh\ *interj* [origin unknown] — used esp. in driving away animals

²**hoosh** \"\ *vt* -ED/-ING/-ES [perh. alter. of *hoise*] *chiefly Irish* **:** BOOST, LIFT

³**hoosh** \"\ *n* -ES *chiefly Irish* **:** HOIST, BOOST

⁴**hoosh** \"\ *n* -ES [origin unknown] **:** a thick soup

¹**hoo·sier** \ˈhüzhə(r)\ *n* -s [perh. alter. of E dial. *hoozer* anything large of its kind] **1 :** an awkward, unhandy, or unskilled person; *esp* **:** an ignorant rustic **2** *usu cap* **:** INDIANAN — used as a nickname

²**hoosier** \"\ *adj, usu cap* **:** of or relating to Indiana or its people ⟨the *Hoosier* state⟩

³**hoosier** \"\ *vi* -ED/-ING/-S *slang* **:** to loaf on or botch a job

**hoo·sier·ism** \-zhəˌrizəm\ *n* -s *usu cap* **:** a turn of speech typical of or peculiar to natives of a geographic area centered on Indiana

¹**hoot** \ˈhüt, *usu* -üd·+V\ *vb* -ED/-ING/-S [ME *houten, hoten*, of imit. origin] *vi* **1 :** to utter a loud shout; *usu* **:** to cry out or shout in contempt ⟨matrons and girls shall ~ at thee no more —John Dryden⟩ **2 a :** to make the natural throat noise of an owl **b :** to make a sound resembling the hoot of an owl — used esp. of other birds or mammals **3 :** to make a loud clamorous mechanical sound — used esp. of a siren and similar devices ⟨foghorns ~*ing* in the gloom⟩ ~ *vt* **1 a :** to assail with contemptuous cries or other expressions of disapproval or contempt ⟨men of goodwill ~*ed* by rowdies⟩ **b :** to check, interrupt, or drive out by hooting ⟨~*ed* down the speaker⟩ ⟨~*ing* unpopular actors off the stage⟩ **2 :** to express in or by hoots ⟨~*ed* his disapproval⟩

²**hoot** \"\ *n* -s **1 :** a loud inarticulate shout or noise; *esp* **:** a derisive cry ⟨gave a ~ of contempt⟩ **2 a :** the cry of an owl **b :** a sound (as of a motor horn) suggesting this cry **3 :** a very small amount **:** BIT, TRIFLE, WHIT — used chiefly in negative constructions and esp. with the indefinite article ⟨don't care a ~ what you decide⟩ ⟨she didn't really give two ~*s* about me —Eric Soames⟩

³**hoot** \"\ *or* **hoots** \-ts\ *interj* [origin unknown] *chiefly Scot* — used to express impatience, mild dissatisfaction, or objection and often in combination ⟨~ awa⟩ ⟨~ mon⟩

⁴**hoot** \"\ *n* -s [Maori *utu* price, requital] *slang Austral* **:** MONEY

**hoo·ta·ma·gan·zy** \ˌhüd·əməˌganzē\ *n* -ES [by alter.] **:** HOODED MERGANSER

**hootch** *var of* ²HOOCH

**hootchy-kootchy** *or* **hootchie-kootchie** \ˌhüchēˈküchē, ˌhu̇chiˈku̇chi\ *also* **hootchy-kootch** \-ˈküch\ *or* **hoochie-coochie** *or* **hoochy-koochy** *n, pl* **hootchy-kootchies** *also* **hootchy-kootches** *or* **hoochie-coochies** *or* **hoochy-koochies** [perh. alter. of *hula-hula*] **:** COOCH

**hoo·te·nan·ny** *or* **hoot·nan·ny** *also* **hoo·ta·nan·ny** \ˈhütᵊnˌanē, ˈhütˌna-, ≠(ᵊ)ˈ≠≠\ *n* -ES [origin unknown] **1 a** *chiefly dial* **:** THING, GADGET; *usu* **:** a device or piece of mechanical equipment — used esp. when the standard name is unknown ⟨the ~ that goes on top of the carburetor⟩ **b** *usu hootnanny* **:** a device for holding a crosscut saw in position while sawing a log from the under side **2** *usu hootenanny* **:** a gathering at which folk singers entertain often with the audience joining in

**hoot·er** \ˈhüd·ə(r), -ütə-\ *n* -s **1 :** one that hoots: as **a** *chiefly Brit* **:** a whistle, siren, or other device (as on an automobile or in a factory) for producing a loud hooting noise **b :** a bird (as an owl or blue grouse) that has a hooting call **2 :** ²HOOT 3

**hoot·ing·ly** *adv* **:** in the manner of a hoot ⟨sounded ~ in the empty hall⟩ **:** to the point of hooting ⟨~ astonished⟩

**hoot owl** *n* **:** OWL; *esp* **:** any of various owls (as the tawny owl of Europe or the barred owl of America) having a loud hooting call

**hooved** \ˈhu̇vd, -ü-\ *adj* **:** having or characterized by hooves ⟨the ~ mammals⟩ **:** HOOFED — often used in combination ⟨strong-*hooved*⟩

**hoo·ver apron** \ˈhüvə(r)-\ *n* [after Herbert *Hoover* †1964 31st president of the U. S.; fr. its popularity among home gardeners when Hoover was food administrator in World War I] **:** a woman's coverall in the form of a dress that closes by a tie at the waist and has an overlapping reversible front

**hoo·ver·crat** \ˈhüvə(r)ˌkrat\ *n* -s *usu cap* [Herbert *Hoover* + E *democrat*] **:** a Democrat of the southern U.S. voting for or supporting Herbert Hoover in the presidential election of 1928 — **hoo·ver·crat·ic** \ˌ≠≠ˈkrad·ik\ *adj, usu cap*

**hoo·ver·ism** \ˈhüvəˌrizəm\ *n* -s *often cap* [Herbert *Hoover* + E -*ism*] **:** a system or views formulated by or attributed to Herbert Hoover

**hoo·ver·ize** \-ˌrīz\ *vb* -ED/-ING/-S *often cap* [Herbert *Hoover* + E -*ize*; fr. his policy as U.S. food administrator 1917–19] *vi* **:** to economize esp. in the use of food ~ *vt* **:** to be saving of or sparing in the use of (food)

**hoo·ver·ville** \-və(r)ˌvil\ *n, usu cap* [Herbert *Hoover* + E -*ville* (final constituent in many names of towns); fr. the prevalence of such housing during his presidency] **:** a collection of ramshackle dwellings erected upon a dump or urban wasteland and occupied by dispossessed, unemployed, or migratory persons

**hooves** *pl of* HOOF

¹**hop** \ˈhäp\ *vb* **hopped; hopped; hopping; hops** [ME *hoppen*, fr. OE *hoppian*; akin to MLG *hüpfen, hüpfen, hopfen* to hop, ON *hoppa* to hop, OE *hype* hip — more at HIP] *vi* **1 a :** to move by a quick springy leap or in a series of leaps **:** JUMP ⟨chalked out a hopscotch game and began to ~ around its squares —Dorothy C. Fisher⟩ ⟨~ on a fast-moving train⟩; *esp* **:** to move by leaping with all feet off the ground ⟨a . . . bird came *hopping* around —Francis Birtles⟩ **b :** to jump on one foot or move about in such manner ⟨requiring the applicant to ~ on the toes of each foot —H.G.Armstrong⟩ **c :** BOUNCE, REBOUND ⟨the ball *hopped* around the playing field⟩ **2 a :** to emerge with a quick elastic movement suggestive of a leap ⟨*hopped* out of bed bright and early⟩ ⟨*hopped* out of the car and opened the door for the lady⟩ **b :** to move or go quickly **:** make a quick trip **:** RUN ⟨do you want to ~ down to the store —Oakley Hall⟩ ⟨*hopped* down to the city for the day⟩; *specif* **:** to make a flight usu. of short duration ⟨Western Airlines . . . ~*s* all over the West —Gladwin Hill⟩ ⟨~*s* to Miami for Christmas —Phil Gustafson⟩ **c** *slang chiefly Brit* **:** to go away **:** SCRAM ⟨state your business and get *hopping* —Ruth Park⟩ — usu. used with *it* ⟨no, thanks . . . got to ~ it —Richard Llewellyn⟩ **3 :** to set about doing something — usu. used in the phrase *hop to it* ⟨lots of work to be done . . . you'd better ~ to it —Gordon Webber⟩ **4 :** to make a verbal attack **:** give a tongue-lashing ⟨expect them to make . . . mistakes and don't ~ all over them when they do —W.J.Reilly⟩ ~ *vt* **1 a :** to jump over ⟨the men *hopped* the rails and were in the boats —H.A.Chippendale⟩ **b :** to give a hopping motion to ⟨*hopped* the ball up and down⟩ **c :** to get upon by or as if by hopping **:** climb aboard ⟨~ a freight⟩ ⟨*hopped* a street car —John Dos Passos⟩ **d :** HITCHHIKE ⟨~ a ride⟩ **2 a :** to transport in an airplane from one point to another ⟨the heaviest machinery can be *hopped* over the Andes —*Skyways*⟩ ⟨save . . . travel time by *hopping* them for short distances —*Time*⟩ **b :** to cross by airplane ⟨fears about air armadas *hopping* the Atlantic —S.L.A.Marshall⟩ **3** *slang* **:** to attack physically or verbally **:** JUMP ⟨~ an enemy aircraft⟩ **4 :** to wait on **:** give service to **:** TEND, SERVE ⟨you're here to ~ bells —Calder Willingham⟩ ⟨young girls and boys in uniform *hopping* cars —Horace McCoy⟩ ⟨did you think I was going to . . . ~ bar for the rest of my life —Maritta Wolff⟩

²**hop** \"\ *n* -s **1 a :** an instance of hopping **:** a short brisk leap esp. on one leg **b** (1) **:** BOUNCE, REBOUND ⟨the shortstop took it on the first ~⟩ ⟨one mortar shell hit a tree, took a freak ~ —Mack Morriss⟩ (2) **:** a slight, sudden elevation taken by a fast pitched ball in its course of flight **2 :** DANCE, BALL ⟨formal and informal ~*s* —*Career for Tomorrow*⟩ ⟨going to the junior *hop*⟩; *also* **:** a party with dancing **3 a :** a flight in an airplane usu. of short duration ⟨made his dramatic ~ to Paris last week —*New Republic*⟩ **b :** a usu. short or quick trip or excursion ⟨supplement their rations with ~*s* across the border —Richard Joseph⟩ ⟨weekend ~*s* to Paris —Sinclair Lewis⟩ ⟨required long ~*s* on bad trains —Virginia D. Dawson and Betty D. Wilson⟩ **c :** a ride given by a passing vehicle ⟨~*s* most of the way, and a little walking —J.A. Michener⟩ — **on the hop** *adv (or adj), Brit* **:** in the act **:** with the goods **:** by surprise or unawares — usu. used in the phrase *catch on the hop* ⟨would never catch him *on the hop* —*Sydney (Australia) Bull.*⟩ ⟨that flood of customers caught them *on the hop* —Fred Majdalany⟩

³**hop** \"\ *n* -s *often attrib* [ME *hoppe*, fr. MD; akin to OS feld*hoppo* hop, OHG *hopfo* hop, Norw *hupp* tassel, OE *scēaf* sheaf — more at SHEAF] **1 a :** a twining Eurasian vine (*Humulus lupulus*) with 3-lobed or 5-lobed leaves and small greenish dioecious flowers that is widely cultivated in America, occurs often as an escape, and is sometimes confused with a native hop plant (*H. Americanus*) **b hops** *pl* **:** the ripened and dried pistillate cones of hop used chiefly to impart a bitter flavor to malt liquors and also in medicine as a tonic **2** *slang* **:** a narcotic drug; *esp* **:** OPIUM

⁴**hop** \"\ *vb* **hopped; hopped; hopping; hops** *vt* **1 :** to impregnate with hops **2 a** (1) **:** to drug or stimulate with drugs **:** DOPE ⟨I'm not drunk . . . I'm *hopped* to the eyes —Ernest Hemingway⟩ — usu. used with *up* ⟨maybe he was *hopped up* on dope of some sort —Shirley A. Grau⟩ (2) **:** to administer a stimulant to (a race horse) **b :** to stimulate or excite by any means **:** ROUSE — used with *up* ⟨used those alumni banquets to ~ everybody up —Millard Lampell⟩ ⟨*hopped* up by the music —Morley Callaghan⟩ **c :** to increase the power of (an engine) or the power of the engine of (a vehicle) beyond an original rating — used with *up* ⟨~ up the motor⟩ ~ *vi* **:** to gather or grow hops

**ho·pak** \ˈhōˌpak\ *n* -s [Ukrainian — more at GOPAK] **:** GOPAK

**hop aphid** *n* **:** a widely distributed aphid (*Phorodon humuli*) that feeds on the growing shoots of hops and other cultivated plants — called also *hop fly, hop louse*

**hop back** *n* **:** a brewing vat into which the wort is run after boiling in the copper and which has a perforated false bottom for straining off the hops — called also *hop jack*

**hopbine** *or* **hopbind** \ˈ=,=\ *n* **:** BINE a

**hopbush** \ˈ=,=\ *n* **:** a shrub or tree of the genus *Dodonaea* — see AKEAKE 1

**Hop·cal·ite** \ˈhäpkəˌlīt\ *trademark* — used for a granular mixture of specially prepared manganese dioxide with other oxides used as a catalyst esp. for removing carbon monoxide from air by oxidation or for detecting carbon monoxide in gas analysis

**hop clover** *n* **1 :** any of several plants of the genus *Trifolium* with heads of yellow flowers resembling hop **2 :** BLACK MEDIC

¹**hope** \ˈhōp\ *vb* -ED/-ING/-S [ME *hopen*, fr. OE *hopian*; akin to OFris *hopia* to hope, MLG & MD *hopen*, MHG *hoffen* to hope, and perh. to OE *hoppian* to hop — more at HOP] *vi* **1 :** to cherish a desire with expectation ⟨~*s* for great things from his son⟩ **2** *archaic* **:** to place confidence or trust — usu. used with *in* ⟨I ~ in thy word —Ps 119:81 (RSV)⟩ ~ *vt* **1 a :** to desire with expectation or with belief in the possibility of obtaining **:** cherish hope of ⟨what I have been longing for, though I never *hoped* it —Rachel Henning⟩ **b :** DESIRE, TRUST ⟨~ and expect to be back in my laboratory —E.J.Simmons⟩ ⟨~ he'll let us in⟩ **2** *Midland* **:** WISH ⟨all *hoped* him well —H.E.Giles⟩ **syn** see EXPECT — **hope against hope :** to hope without any basis for expecting fulfillment

²**hope** \"\ *n* -s [ME, fr. OE *hopa*; akin to OFris, MLG, & MD *hope*, MHG *hoffe*; derivatives fr. the root of E ¹*hope*] **1 :** TRUST, RELIANCE ⟨all my ~ is in the Lord⟩ **2 a :** desire accompanied with expectation of obtaining what is desired or belief that it is obtainable ⟨wished but not with ~ —John Milton⟩ ⟨all ~ is dead⟩ ⟨are in ~*s* of an early recovery⟩ **b :** one on whom hopes are centered ⟨the team's only ~ for victory⟩ **c :** a source of hopeful expectation **:** PROMISE ⟨viewed America as the land of ~⟩ **d :** something that is hoped for **:** an object of hope ⟨the arrival of reinforcements was their last forlorn ~⟩ ⟨a healthy family is the ~ . . . of every homemaker —Mary S. Switzer⟩

³**hope** \"\ *n* -s [ME, fr. OE *hop*; akin to OE *hype* hip — more at HIP] **1** *now chiefly dial* **:** a piece of arable land surrounded by waste; *esp* **:** one surrounded by swamp or marsh **2** *dial chiefly Brit* **:** a broad upland valley sometimes rounded and often with a stream running through it **3** *now dial* **:** a small bay or inlet

**ho·pea** \'hōpēə\ *n, cap* [NL, after John *Hope* †1786 Sc. physician and botanist] **:** a genus of tropical trees (family Dipterocarpaceae) with simple leaves, usu. fragrant flowers with one-sided spikes or racemes, and often hard heavy wood — compare MERAWAN

**hope chest** *n* **1 :** a young woman's accumulation of clothes and domestic furnishings (as silver, linen) kept in or as if in a chest in anticipation of her marriage — compare BOTTOM DRAWER **2 :** a box for use as a hope chest

[1]**hope·ful** \'hōpfəl\ *adj* [[2]*hope* + *-ful*] **1 :** full of hope or agreeable expectation **:** inclined to hope **:** happily expectant **2 :** having qualities which inspire hope **:** giving promise of good or of success ⟨a ~ prospect⟩ — **hope·ful·ly** \-fəlē, -li\ *adv* — **hope·ful·ness** *n* -ES

[2]**hopeful** \"\ *n* -s **:** a person who aspires hopefully or expectantly to become or achieve something ⟨before the convention . . . meets the various presidential ~*s* have set up headquarters —D.D.McKean⟩ ⟨not all who want to write can go to universities . . . a large army of ~*s* is scattered all over the land —Edward Uhlan⟩

**hope·ite** \'hō,pīt\ *n* -s [Thomas C. *Hope* †1844 Scot. chemist + E *-ite*] **:** a mineral $Zn_3(PO_4)_2.4H_2O$ consisting of a hydrous phosphate of zinc (sp. gr. 2.76–2.85)

**hope·less** \'hōpləs\ *adj* **1 a** (1) **:** devoid of hope **:** having no expectation of good **:** DESPAIRING ⟨girls feel ~ if they haven't a marriage at least in sight —Sidonie M. Gruenberg⟩ ⟨three lonely and ~ old women —Upton Sinclair⟩ ⟨was never ~ of anybody —Margaret Deland⟩ (2) **:** reflecting or indicating lack of hope ⟨gazed with lusterless, ~ eyes —Jack London⟩ **b :** not susceptible of remedy or cure **:** INCURABLE ⟨should be aware of his responsibility if he declares a . . . patient ~ —*Jour. Amer. Med. Assoc.*⟩ **c :** being beyond redemption **:** offering no prospect of change or improvement ⟨the dream of every magazine writer who is not a ~ hack —Raymond Chandler⟩ ⟨as an actor he is really ~⟩ ⟨a ~ extrovert, giving herself completely and trustingly to everyone —*Holiday*⟩ ⟨a ~ Anglophile —Richard Joseph⟩ **2 a :** giving no ground for hope **:** promising nothing desirable **:** DESPERATE ⟨the situation looked ~ indeed —C.B.Nordhoff & J.N.Hall⟩ **b :** incapable of solution, management, or accomplishment **:** IMPOSSIBLE, INSOLUBLE ⟨a ~ task⟩ ⟨had a ~ jumble of papers on my hands —*Phoenix Flame*⟩ ⟨the defective . . . whose redemption is ~ —B.N.Cardozo⟩ ⟨worked at depths that seemed ~ fifty years ago —Waldemar Kaempffert⟩ ⟨in ~ conflict with religion —R.W.Murray⟩ ⟨lucidity ~ to find amid all the cluttering detail of advanced works —*Geog. Journal*⟩ **syn** see DESPONDENT

**hope·less·ly** *adv* **:** in a hopeless manner

**hope·less·ness** *n* -ES **:** the quality or state of being hopeless

**hop·er** \'hōpə(r)\ *n* -s [ME, fr. *hopen* to hope + *-er*] **:** one that hopes

**hopes** *pres 3d sing of* HOPE, *pl of* HOPE

**hope·well** \'hōp,wel\ *or* **hope·well·ian** \(')hōp¦welēən\ *adj, usu cap* [after Cloud *Hopewell*, 19th cent. Am. farmer on whose Ohio farm type stations were found] **:** of or belonging to the most advanced of the mound-building cultures of No. America centered in the Ohio and Illinois river valleys and characterized by large complex earthworks and burial mounds, artistic excellence in artifacts, and frequent cremation of the dead

**hop flea beetle** *n* **:** a small flea beetle (*Psylliodes punctulata*) sometimes injurious to hops

**hop flour** *or* **hop meal** *n* **:** LUPULIN

**hop fly** *n* **:** HOP APHID

**hophead** \'≈,≈\ *n* [[3]*hop* + *head*] *slang* **:** a drug addict

**hop hornbeam** *n* **:** a tree of the genus *Ostrya*; *esp* **:** an American tree (*O. virginiana*) with fruiting clusters resembling hops

**ho·pi** \'hō(,)pē, -,pi\ *n, pl* **hopi** *also* **hopis** *usu cap* [Hopi *Hópi*, lit., good, peaceful] **1 a :** a Shoshonean people of Pueblo Indians in northeastern Arizona **b :** a member of such people **2 :** the language of the Hopi people **3 :** FRENCH BEIGE

**hoping** *pres part of* HOPE

**hop·ing·ly** *adv* **:** in a hopeful manner ⟨regarded me ~⟩

**hopi way** *n, usu cap H&W* **:** the ethical and behavioral code of the Hopi people depicted dramatically in the annual ceremonial cycle and including rules for each of the roles which a person of either sex and at the various age levels is expected to assume throughout life

**hop jack** *n* **:** HOP BACK

**hop kiln** *n* **:** a kiln for drying hops

[1]**hop·kins·ian** \hä'pkinzēən\ *n* -s *usu cap* [Samuel *Hopkins* †1803 Am. clergyman + *-ian*] **:** a follower of the clergyman Samuel Hopkins who taught a rigorous form of Calvinistic theology

[2]**hopkinsian** \(')≈¦≈≈≈\ *adj, usu cap* **:** of or relating to Hopkinsians or to Hopkinsianism

**hop·kins·ian·ism** \≈'≈≈ə,nizəm\ *n* -s *usu cap* **:** the theology taught by Samuel Hopkins holding that one must submit unconditionally to the will of God and be willing to be damned if the glory of God requires it

**hop·lite** \'hä,plīt\ *n* -s [Gk *hoplitēs*, fr. *hoplon* tool, weapon, piece of armor (fr. *hepein* to care for, prepare) + *-itēs* -ite — more at SEPULCHER] **:** a heavily armed infantry soldier of ancient Greece equipped with helmet, cuirass, greaves, shield, spear, and sword

**hoplo-** *comb form* [NL, fr. Gk *hopl-, hoplo-* tool, weapon, piece of armor, fr. *hoplon*] **:** heavily armed **:** having powerful offensive members — used chiefly in zoological taxa ⟨*Hoplonemertea*⟩

**hop·lo·car·i·da** \,häplō'karədə\ *n pl, cap* [NL, fr. *hoplo-* + *-carida* (fr. Gk *karid-, karis* shrimp, prawn)] **:** a division of Malacostraca coextensive with an order Stomatopoda of tropical marine burrowing crustaceans comprising the mantis shrimps and having a reduced capelike carapace, a large powerful abdomen, five pairs of anteriorly directly thoracic maxillipeds of which the second pair form greatly enlarged raptorial arms, and enlarged swimming appendages on the abdomen with large branching gills on the exopodites

**hop·lo·ceph·a·lus** \-'sefələs\ *n, cap* [NL, fr. *hoplo-* + *-cephalus*] **:** a genus of moderately venomous Australian elapid snakes

**hop·lo·nemertea** \'häplō+\ *n pl, cap* [NL, fr. *hoplo-* + *Nemertea*] **:** an order of Nemertea (class Enopla) comprising variable forms with the proboscis armed with styles and with an intestinal cecum — **hop·lo·nemertean** \"+\ *adj*

**hop·lo·nemertini** \"+\ [NL, fr. *hoplo-* + *Nemertini*] *syn of* HOPLONEMERTEA

**hop·lo·pho·ne·us** \,häplə'fōnēəs\ *n, cap* [NL, fr. *hoplo-* + Gk *phonios* murderous] **:** a genus of primitive sabertooths from the Oligocene and Miocene of western No. America having the large heads and canines of later forms but small brains and a grasping forefoot

**hop louse** *n* **:** HOP APHID

**hop marjoram** *n* **:** CRETAN DITTANY

**hop medic** *n* **:** BLACK MEDIC

**hop merchant** *n* **:** a comma butterfly (*Polygonia comma*)

**hop mildew** *n* **1 :** either of two parasitic fungi attacking the hop: **a :** a powdery mildew (*Sphaerotheca humuli*) **b :** a downy mildew (*Peronoplasmopara humuli*) **2 :** disease of hops caused by a hop mildew

**hop oil** *also* **hops oil** *n* **:** a brownish yellow aromatic essential oil obtained from hops and used chiefly in flavoring cereal beverages

**hop-o'-my-thumb** \¦häpəmə'thəm, -,mī¦-\ *n, pl* **hop-o'-my-thumbs :** a very diminutive person **:** DWARF, PYGMY

**hopped** *adj* **:** impregnated with hops

**hopped-up** \'≈¦≈\ *adj* [fr. past part. of *hop up*, v.] **1 a :** being under the stimulating or stupefying influence of a narcotic drug **:** DOPED ⟨when . . . not *hopped-up*, she had a certain pride in her bearing —Polly Adler⟩ **b** (1) **:** full of enthusiasm **:** ENTHUSIASTIC, EXUBERANT, AROUSED, ROUSED, EXCITED ⟨all *hopped-up* over the visit —Danton Walker⟩ ⟨squeaking past an obstinate, *hopped-up* . . . team —*Official Basketball Guide*⟩ (2) **:** dressed up **:** EMBELLISHED ⟨this *hopped-up* image of plantation life —Manny Farber⟩ ⟨*hopped-up* commonplaces about abstract evil and abstract good —A.M.Mizener⟩ **2 :** having its engine power increased beyond the original rating ⟨a *hopped-up* hot rod —*Science Newsletter*⟩

[1]**hop·per** \'häpə(r)\ *n* -s [ME, fr. *hoppen* to hop + *-er* — more at HOP] **1 :** one that hops: as **a :** a leaping insect (as a leafhopper, grasshopper, or froghopper); *specif* **:** an immature hopping form usu. of an insect that is winged as an adult (as the larva of a cheese fly or a young grasshopper or locust) **b** (1) **:** a person who makes flights or trips of usu. short duration ⟨the first island-*hopper* in the Caribbean —*Newsweek*⟩ (2) **:** one who flits about from one place of a specified kind to another of the same kind — usu. used in combination ⟨a table-*hopper*⟩ ⟨a bar*hopper*⟩ **c :** a batted ball which rebounds from the ground **2 a :** a chute, box, or receptacle usu. funnel-shaped with an opening at the lower part for delivering material (as grain, fuel, or coal) **b :** something like or likened to a hopper in form or function as: (1) **:** any of the compartments of a hopper frame or the hopper frame itself (2) **:** a feeder for animals; *esp* **:** one from which food flows automatically from an enclosed reservoir to the compartment from which it is eaten **c :** a box usu. on the desk of the clerk or other official of a legislative body into which a proposed bill is dropped **d :** the process of realization or preparation — used in the phrase *in the hopper* ⟨your show is in the ~ and you might just as well . . . not worry —E.J.Kahn⟩ ⟨a plan for exempting . . . small businesses from wage controls is in the ~ —*Washington Report*⟩ **3 a :** a ship used esp. to convey mud, gravel, or sand dredged from harbors out to sea and constructed with a full midship section from which the cargo is discharged through the bottom **b :** HOPPER CAR **c** (1) **:** a tank holding water or other liquid and having a device for releasing its contents through a pipe at the bottom (2) **:** a toilet bowl

[2]**hopper** \"\ *n* -s [[3]*hop* + *-er*] **1 :** a hop picker **2 :** a brewery worker who pours dried hops into casks **3 :** an inverted pyramid or cone through which malt passes to the grinding mill in the brewing process

**hopper boy** *n* **:** a revolving rake used in flour milling to spread and stir freshly ground flour for cooling before it is bolted

**hopperburn** \'≈≈,≈\ *n* **:** a browning and shriveling of potato foliage associated with the feeding of the potato leafhopper — compare TIPBURN

**hopper car** *n* **:** a freight car with a floor sloping to one or more hinged doors or hoppers for discharging bulk contents (as coal, ore, sand) by gravity and with a permanent roof and roof hatches when used for carrying bulk commodities (as cement) which must be kept dry

hopper car

**hopper closet** *n* **:** a toilet with a hopper

**hopper crystal** *n* **:** a funnel-shaped crystal

**hop·per·doz·er** \'häpə(r),dōzə(r)\ *n* [[1]*hopper* + *-dozer* (as in *bulldozer*)] **:** a device for catching and destroying insects (as grasshoppers) that is drawn on runners across a field and has a shield against which insects jump and fall into a pan containing kerosene or oil

**hopper frame** *n* **:** a window frame that has superimposed fanlights opening inward and is used esp. in hospitals — called also *hospital light*

**hoppergrass** \'≈≈,≈\ *n* [by alter.] *dial* **:** GRASSHOPPER

**hop·per·man** \'≈≈mən\ *n, pl* **hoppermen 1 :** a member of the crew of a hopper barge **2 :** a worker who adjusts and attends hoppers

**hop·pet** \'häpət\ *n* -s [obs. E *hopper* basket, seed-basket (fr. ME, fr. *hoppen* to hop + *-er*) + *-et* — more at HOP] *dial Eng* **:** BASKET, BUCKET

[1]**hop·ping** \'häpiŋ, -pēŋ\ *adj* **1 :** journeying or flitting about from one place of a specified kind to another place of the same kind — usu. used in combination ⟨thus began a frenetic show-*hopping* existence —*N.Y.Times*⟩ **2 :** moving about busily **:** working hard **:** intensely active **:** BUSY ⟨intrigue and foul play keep the captain ~ —Andrea Parke⟩ ⟨the drivers were kept ~ to cover . . . 66 square miles —*Crowsnest*⟩ **3 :** extremely angry **:** FURIOUS

[2]**hopping** \"\ *adv* **:** EXTREMELY, VIOLENTLY — used in the phrase *hopping mad* ⟨apt to get ~ mad and bring suit —Margaret Nicholson⟩ ⟨~ mad when we discovered that barbed wire —W.A.White⟩

**hopping dick** *n, usu cap D* **:** a Jamaican thrush (*Turdus aurantius*) resembling a blackbird (*Turdus merula*)

**hop·ping·ly** *adv* **:** in a hopping manner ⟨flown ~ away —Israel Zangwill⟩

**hoppin john** \'häpən-\ *also* **hopping john** *n, usu cap J* **:** a stew made with cowpeas, rice, and bacon or salt pork esp. popular in the southern states and traditionally served on New Year's Day

[1]**hop·ple** \'häpəl\ *vt* **hoppled; hoppled; hoppling** \-p(ə)liŋ\ **hopples** [prob. fr. [1]*hop* + *-le*] **:** to fetter the feet of (as a horse or cow) **:** HOBBLE

[2]**hopple** \"\ *n* -s **:** a fetter used for grazing horses or cattle or a leg harness usu. of leather to control the gait of trotting or pacing horses — used chiefly in pl.

[1]**hop·py** \'häpē, -pi\ *adj* -ER/-EST [[3]*hop* + *-y*] **1 :** abounding in hops **2 :** having the bitter taste of hops — used esp. of ale or beer

[2]**hoppy** \"\ *n* -ES *slang* **:** a drug addict

[3]**hoppy** \"\ *adj* -ER/-EST [[2]*hop* + *-y*] **:** characterized by a hopping step or movement ⟨a restless, ~ Frenchman —Ludwig Bemelmans⟩ ⟨a lively little blue crane with a ~ leg —I.L. Idriess⟩

**hops** *pres 3d sing of* HOP, *pl of* HOP

**hopsack** \'≈,≈\ *n* [ME *hopsak* sack for hops, fr. *hoppe* hop + *sak* sack] **:** HOPSACKING 2

**hopsacking** \'≈,≈≈\ *n* [[3]*hop* + *sacking*] **1 :** material of hemp and jute used esp. as bagging by hop growers **2 :** a rough-surfaced clothing fabric loosely woven of various fibers in an open basket weave

**hopsage** \'≈,≈\ *n* [[3]*hop* + *sage*] **:** any of certain low shrubs of alkaline regions of western No. America that constitute the genus *Grayia* of the family Chenopodiaceae and are locally important native browse plants; *esp* **:** an erect much-branched shrub (*G. spinosa*) having the flowers in dense terminal spikes, the fruiting bracts broadly rounded and often tinged with red, and forming a cluster resembling the strobilus of a hopvine

[1]**hopscotch** \'≈,≈\ *n* [[1]*hop* + *scotch* (line)] **:** a child's game of many variations in which a player tosses a small flat stone or similar object consecutively into the lined and numbered areas of a figure outlined upon the ground, hops on one foot through the figure and back to the area in which the stone lies, picks up the stone, and hops on out trying to avoid errors (as stepping on a line or losing balance)

one form of hopscotch figure

[2]**hopscotch** \"\ *vi* **:** to move with or as if with the hopping step used in the game of hopscotch ⟨children ~ between the tables —Willie S. Ethridge⟩

**hops oil** *var of* HOP OIL

**hop, step, and jump** *n* **:** a field event in which the participants cover as much ground as possible by a hop, stride, and jump in succession usu. after a running start

**hop·toad** \'häp,tōd\ *also* **hop·py·toad** \-pē,-\ *n, chiefly dial* **:** TOAD

**hop tree** *n* [[3]*hop*] **:** a small American tree (*Ptelea trifoliata*) having 2-seeded samaras as fruits

**hop trefoil** *n* **:** HOP CLOVER

**hopvine** \'≈,≈\ *n* **1 :** the twining stem of the hop **:** HOPBINE **2 :** a hop plant

**hopyard** \'≈,≈\ *n* **:** a hop field

**hoquet** *var of* HOCKET

**hor** *abbr* **1** horizon; horizontal **2** horological; horology

[1]**ho·ra** *also* **hor·ra** \'hōrə, 'hȯrə\ *n* -s [NHeb & Romanian; NHeb *hōrāh*, fr. Romanian *horă*, fr. Turk *hora*] **1 :** a folk dance of Romania and Israel in which dancers form a circle, lock arms, and dance to the left or right with grapevine steps and hops **2 :** music to which the hora is danced

[2]**hora** \"\ *n* -s [native name in Ceylon] **:** a tree (*Dipterocarpus Zeylanicus*) of Ceylon with reddish brown strong heavy wood

**ho·ra·ry** \'hōrərē\ *adj* [ML *horarius*, fr. L *hora* hour + *-arius* -ary — more at HOUR] *archaic* **:** of or relating to an hour **:** noting the hours

**ho·ra·tian** \hə'rāshən, hō'-,hȯ'- *also* -shēən\ *adj, usu cap* [L *Horatianus*, fr. *Horatius* Horace (Quintus Horatius Flaccus) †8 B.C. Latin poet + L *-anus* -an] **:** of or relating to the poet Horace or resembling his poetic style (as in finish of form and aptness of diction)

**ho·ra·tio al·ger** \hə¦rā(,)shō¦alj'ə(r), -āshē,ō-\ *adj, usu cap H&A* [after *Horatio Alger* †1899 Am. clergyman and author of juvenile fiction] **:** of, relating to, or resembling the works of Horatio Alger in which success is achieved through self-reliance and hard work ⟨their own *Horatio Alger* myth of honest poor boy rises to riches —James Jones⟩

**horde** \'hō(ə)rd, 'hȯ(ə)rd, -ōəd, -ȯ(ə)d\ *n* -s [MF, G & Pol; MF & G *horde*, fr Pol *horda*, of Mongolic origin; akin to Mongolian *ordu, orda* court, camp, horde, Kalmuck *orda*] **1 a** (1) **:** a clan or tribal group of Tatar or other Mongolian nomadic tent dwellers claiming exclusive hunting or grazing rights over a defined area (2) **:** a people or tribe of nomadic life **b :** a usu. small and typically nomadic social group composed of allied or related family groups occupying a common territory; *esp* **:** such a group among the Australian aborigines **c :** a hypothetical primordial social unit comprised of a number of families ⟨the primitive ~ posited by evolutionists⟩ **2 :** an unorganized or loosely organized mass of individuals **:** a vast number **:** CROWD, SWARM, AGGLOMERATION ⟨circling ~*s* of mixed insects —B.J.Haimes⟩ ⟨unpolluted . . . by their brief contact with the touristic ~ —Arnold Bennett⟩ ⟨~*s* of Irish . . . came to the American shore —*Amer. Guide Series: N.Y.*⟩ ⟨most companies today take ~*s* of pictures —W.B.Eidson⟩ **syn** see CROWD

**hor·de·in** \'hȯ(r)dēən\ *n* -s [F *hordéine*, fr. L *hordeum* barley + F *-ine*] **:** a prolamin found in the seeds of barley

**hor·de·nine** \-də,nēn, -,nən\ *n* -s [ISV *horden-* (fr. L *hordeum*) + *-ine*; orig. formed in F] **:** a crystalline alkaloid $HOC_6H_4CH_2CH_2N(CN_3)_2$ found in germinating barley and in mescal

**hor·de·o·lum** \hȯ(r)'dēələm\ *n, pl* **hordeo·la** \-lə\ [NL, alter. of LL *hordeolus*, dim. of L *hordeum* barley] **:** [4]STY

**hor·de·um** \'hȯ(r)dēəm\ *n* [NL, fr. L, barley; akin to OHG *gersta* barley, Gk *kri*, Alb *drith*, and prob. to L *horrēre* to bristle — more at HORROR] **1** *cap* **:** a widely distributed genus of grasses having the flowers in dense spikes often with long-awned glumes and the one-flowered spikelets in clusters of two or three at each joint of the rachis — see BARLEY **2** -s **:** any grass of the genus *Hordeum*

**hore·hound** *or* **hoar·hound** \'hō(ə)r,haund, 'hȯ(ə)r-, 'hōə,h-, 'hȯ(ə),h-\ *n* [by folk etymology fr. ME *horhoune*, fr. OE *hārhūne*, fr. *hār* hoary + *hūne* horehound — more at HOAR] **1 a :** a European aromatic mint (*Marrubium vulgare*) that is naturalized in the U.S., has pubescent leaves and small axillary flowers, has a very bitter taste, and is used as a tonic and anthelmintic — called also *white horehound* **b :** an extract or confection made from this plant and used as a remedy for coughs and colds **2 :** any of several labiates resembling horehound in appearance — used with an attributive or qualifying adjective ⟨black ~⟩ ⟨water ~⟩

**horehound bug** *n* **:** a widespread orange and black Australian bug (*Agonoscelis rutila*) destructive to the foliage of horehound and other crop plants

**ho·rite** \'hōr,īt\ *n* -s *usu cap* **1 :** a cave-dwelling people of the biblical period prior to the time of Abraham that inhabited the Dead sea region of the eastern Mediterranean **2 :** a member of the Horite people

[1]**ho·ri·zon** \hə'rīzᵊn\ *n* -s [alter. (influenced by LL *horizon*) of ME *orisonte, orizon*, fr. LL *horizont-, horizon*, fr. Gk *horizont-, horizōn*, fr. pres. part. of *horizein* to separate, part, bound, define, fr. *horos* boundary, limit + *-izein* -ize; akin to L *urvus* circumference of a city, Oscan *uruvú* boundary] **1 a :** a circle that bounds the part of the earth's surface visible from a given point **:** an apparent junction of earth and sky **b** (1) **:** a great circle 90 degrees from the zenith and constituting the equator of the horizon system of coordinates (2) **:** the circle in which a plane perpendicular to the direction of gravity intersects the celestial sphere (3) **:** the plane tangent to the earth's surface at the observer's position (4) **:** a level mirror (as the surface of mercury in a shallow vessel or a plane reflector adjusted to the true level artificially) used esp. in observing altitudes — called also *artificial horizon, false horizon* **c** *or* **horizon line :** an imaginary line in a picture on which is projected the point of sight or station point of the spectator and which in a landscape replaces the natural horizon — compare PERSPECTIVE **d** (1) **:** the fullest range or widest limit of perception, interest, appreciation, knowledge, or experience ⟨the ~ of the human intellect has widened wonderfully during the past hundred years —C.W.Eliot⟩ ⟨your ~ contracts, your mind's eye is focused upon a small circle of . . . details —Jan Struther⟩ (2) **:** the range or limit of hope or expectation or a visible and seemingly attainable end or object lying within or upon it **:** GOAL, PROSPECT ⟨youth . . . demands of life some hope and ~ —John Buchan⟩ ⟨China with its ~*s* of industrialization and trade —M.W.Straight⟩ **2 a :** the geological deposit of a particular time, usu. identified by distinctive fossils **:** a stratigraphic level or position in the geologic column **:** a natural soil layer; *also* **:** ZONE **b :** any of the reasonably distinct layers of soil or its underlying material seen in a vertical section or profile of land and gradually developed as a result of natural soil-forming processes (as the incorporation of organic matter with disintegrated rock material) — see A-HORIZON, B-HORIZON, C-HORIZON, D-HORIZON **c** (1) **:** a cultural area or level of development indicated by widely separated groups of artifacts showing cultural similarities (as in specific styles or objects) (2) **:** a period of time indicated by a particular level of development in an excavated site **3 :** HORIZON BLUE 2 **syn** see RANGE

[2]**horizon** \"\ *vt* -ED/-ING/-S **:** to limit by a horizon

**ho·ri·zon·al** \-z(ᵊ)nəl\ *adj* **:** of or relating to a horizon **:** having a horizon ⟨the functional significance of a ~ diffusion —*Amer. Antiquity*⟩ ⟨never has the opportunity for the individual career been so exalted . . . so ~ —S.N.Behrman⟩

**horizon blue** *n* **1 :** a variable color averaging a light greenish blue to blue **2** *also* **horizon :** a greenish white

**horizon clubber** *n* [*Horizon Club* + *-er*] **:** a member of Horizon Club, the senior program of the Camp Fire Girls for girls in the ninth grade through high school or about 15 through 18

**horizon coordinate** *n* **:** any member of a system of celestial coordinates based on the horizon of the observer with azimuth being the primary coordinate and altitude the secondary coordinate

**ho·ri·zon·less** \-z°nləs\ *adj* **:** devoid of a horizon **:** HOPELESS ⟨it was a ~ grind —Philip Hamburger⟩

**horizon system of coordinates :** a system of celestial coordinates based on the observer's horizon with its coordinates being altitude and azimuth

[1]**hor·i·zon·tal** \,hȯrə¦zäntᵊl, ,här-\ *adj* [LL *horizont-, horizon* + E *-al*] **1 a :** of, relating to, or situated near the horizon **b :** parallel to the horizon **:** being on a level **:** FLAT ⟨a ~ line⟩ ⟨a ~ surface⟩ **c :** measured or contained in a plane of the horizon ⟨~ distance⟩ **d :** placed or operating chiefly along a plane parallel to the horizon — used esp. of machines and mechanical devices ⟨a ~ escapement⟩ **e** *bot* **:** situated in a plane at a right angle to the plane of the primary axis ⟨~ branches⟩ **f** *of a stamp* **:** having a rectangular shape with the longer sides forming the top and bottom **2 a :** applied equally or uniformly to all individuals in a group **:** OVERALL, GENERAL ⟨~ rate increases⟩ ⟨demands for ~ slashing of local government costs —O.K.Armstrong⟩ ⟨the increased ~ spread of buying power —Bud Wilson⟩ **b :** relating to, uniting, or consisting of individuals of similar type or on the same level: as (1) **:** consisting of two or more economic units on the same level of production or distribution ⟨his gigantic ~ and vertical combination of business ventures is efficiently run —Claire Sterling⟩ ⟨a ~ merger⟩ (2) **:** of, relating to, or comprising persons of similar status ⟨a union made up of meat cutters or railroad engineers . . . would be considered ~ —J.F.Cuber⟩ ⟨it must be . . . ~, in the sense of uniting students of similar ages —*General Education in a Free Society*⟩ ⟨~ strata . . . based upon the social values that are attached to occupation, education, place of residence in the community, and associations —August Hollingshead⟩ (3) **:** relating to the

motion of a succession of musical notes or tones forming a melodic line or part — **hor·i·zon·tal·ly** \-ᵊlē, -ᵊli\ *adv*

2**horizontal** \"\ *n* -s **:** something that is horizontal; *esp* **:** a horizontal line ⟨the mood of quiet is emphasized by the ~s of the lake —S.M.Green⟩

**horizontal bar** *n* **1 :** a bar fixed in horizontal position for gymnastic exercise **2 :** an event in gymnastic competition

**horizontal engine** *n* **:** an engine with horizontal line of stroke

**horizontal fault** *n* **:** a fault in the earth's crust with no vertical displacement

**horizontal intensity** *n* **:** the horizontal component of the intensity of the earth's magnetic field

**hor·i·zon·tal·i·ty** \ˌhȯrəˌzänˈtaləd·ē, ˌhär-\ *n* -ES **:** the quality or state of being horizontal ⟨his houses have a pronounced ~ —J.M.Richards⟩

**hor·i·zon·tal·ize** \ˌhȯrəˈzäntᵊlˌīz, ˌhär-\ *vt* -ED/-ING/-S **:** to arrange horizontally ⟨information with which to scale and ~ the model —*U.S. Army Tech. Manual*⟩

**horizontal kiln** *n* **:** a kiln that has its axis in a horizontal as opposed to a vertical position with the materials being processed moved through by the slight slope and rotation of the kiln itself or carried through on conveyors

**horizontal ladder** *n* **:** a ladder of wood or metal held in a horizontal position usu. by upright supports and used in a gymnasium or on a playground for suspension exercises esp. for the development of arm and shoulder-girdle strength

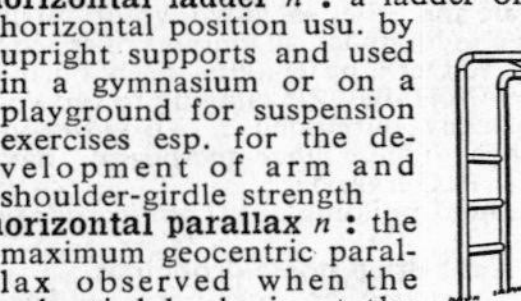
horizontal ladder

**horizontal parallax** *n* **:** the maximum geocentric parallax observed when the celestial body is at the horizon

**horizontal pendulum** *n* **:** a pendulum that oscillates in a horizontal plane (as a compass needle on its pivot)

**horizontal section** *n* **:** a section representing an object as cut horizontally through its center

**horizontal structure** *n* **:** POLYPHONY 1 — compare VERTICAL STRUCTURE

**horizontal training** *n* **:** the operation of training fruit trees or grapevines so that the branches will spread out laterally in a horizontal direction — compare ESPALIER

horizontal training of a tree

**hor·key** \ˈhȯrkē\ *var of* 2HOCKEY

**horloge** *var of* HOROLOGE

**hor·me** \ˈhȯr(ˌ)mē\ *n* -s [G, fr. Gk *hormē* impulse, attack, assault — more at SERUM] **:** vital energy as an urge to purposive activity

**hor·mic** \-ˌmik\ *adj* **:** of or relating to horme; *specif* **:** purposively directed toward a goal ⟨~ activities of the organism⟩

**hormic psychology** *n* **:** psychology concerned with the purposive factor or force in behavior

**hor·mi·go** \(h)ȯ(r)ˈmē(ˌ)gō\ *n* -s [AmerSp, fr. Sp *hormiga* ant, fr. L *formica* — more at PISMIRE] **1 :** ANT TREE **2 :** QUIRA

**hor·mism** \ˈhȯ(r)ˌmizəm\ *n* -s [*horme* + *-ism*] **:** HORMIC PSYCHOLOGY

**hor·mo·den·dron** \ˌhȯ(r)məˈdendrən\ *syn of* HORMODENDRUM

**hor·mo·den·drum** \-rəm\ *n, cap* [NL, fr. Gk *hormos* chain, necklace (fr. *eirein* to fasten) + *dendron* tree — more at SERIES, DENDR-] **:** a form genus of imperfect fungi (family Dematiaceae) having dull brownish to black spores produced in chains resembling trees

**hor·mo·gon** \ˈhȯ(r)məˌgän\ *or* **hor·mo·gone** \-ˌgōn\ *n* -s [NL *hormogonium*] **:** HORMOGONIUM

**hor·mo·go·na·les** \ˌhȯ(r)məgōˈnā(ˌ)lēz\ *n pl, cap* [NL, fr. *hormogonium* + *-ales*] **:** an order of filamentous blue-green algae having the capacity to form hormogonia

**hor·mo·go·ni·um** \ˌhȯ(r)məˈgōnēəm\ *n, pl* **hormogo·nia** \-ēə\ [NL, fr. Gk *hormos* + *gonium*] **:** a portion of a filament between two heterocysts in many blue-green algae that becomes detached as a reproductive body — **hor·mog·o·nous** \(ˈ)hȯ(r)ˈmägənəs\ *adj*

**hor·mo·nal** \(ˈ)hȯ(r)ˈmōnᵊl\ *adj* [ISV *hormone* + *-al*] **:** of, relating to, or effected by hormones — **hor·mo·nal·ly** \-ᵊlē\ *adv*

**hor·mone** \ˈhȯrˌmōn, ˈhȯ(ə)-,\ *n* -s [Gk *hormōn*, pres. part. of *horman* to stir up, set in motion, fr. *hormē* impulse, attack, assault — more at SERUM] **1 :** a specific organic product of living cells that, transported by body fluids or sap, produces a specific effect on the activity of cells remote from its point of origin **:** internal secretion **:** AUTACOID; *esp* **:** such a product exerting a stimulatory or excitatory effect on a cellular activity — compare AUXIN, CHALONE, PLANT HORMONE **2 :** a synthetic substance that resembles a naturally occurring hormone in producing a specific biological effect — compare GROWTH REGULATOR

**hormonelike** \ˈ=,=,=\ *adj* **:** resembling a hormone esp. in physiological action

**hor·monic** \(ˈ)hȯ(r)ˈmänik, -mōn-\ *adj* **:** HORMONAL

**hor·mon·iza·tion** \ˌhȯ(r)ˌmōnəˈzāshən\ *n* -s **:** the process of hormonizing

**hor·mon·ize** \ˈhȯ(r)ˌmōˌnīz\ *vt* -ED/-ING/-S [*hormone* + *-ize*] **:** to treat with a hormone; *specif* **:** to castrate chemically — compare CAPONETTE

**hor·mo·noid** \ˈhȯ(r)məˌnȯid, -ˌmōn-\ *adj* **:** resembling that of a hormone

**hor·mo·spore** \ˈhȯrməˌspō(ə)r\ *n* [NL *hormogonium* + E *spore*] **:** a terminally borne hormogonium in some blue-green algae with cells modified in shape and having exceptionally thick walls

1**horn** \ˈhȯ(ə)rn, ˈhȯ(ə)n\ *n* -s [ME, fr. OE; akin to OHG & ON *horn*, Goth *haurn*, L *cornu* horn, *cerebrum* brain, Gk *keras* horn, Skt *śṛṅga*] **1 a** (1) **:** one of the paired bony processes that arise from the upper part of the head of many ungulate mammals, that function chiefly as weapons, and that in cattle and related forms are usu. present in both sexes and are unbranched and permanent with a bony core anchored to the skull and a sheath of horn and in deer are solid deciduous bony outgrowths usu. branching and usu. present only in the male — see ANTLER; COW illustration (2) **:** a horned animal (3) **:** a part like an animal's horn attributed to a divine or supernatural being and esp. to the devil **b :** a natural projection or excrescence from an animal that resembles or suggests a horn: as (1) **:** a projection (as the casque of a hornbill) from the beak of a bird (2) **:** a tuft of feathers on the head of a bird (as a horned owl) (3) **:** a projection from the head or thorax of an insect or from the head of a reptile or fish (4) **:** a sharp spine in front of the fins of a fish (as a horned pout) (5) **:** one of the tentacles of a snail **c** (1) **:** the tough fibrous material derived from epithelial tissue and consisting chiefly of keratin with which the horns of cattle and related animals are covered (2) **:** any similar substance (as that which forms the hoof crust of horses, sheep, cattle) (3) **:** a manufactured product (as a plastic resembling horn) (4) **:** a bow tip made of horn into which the bowstring nock is cut (5) **:** HORN SPOON **2 d :** the hollow horn of an animal used as a drinking cup ⟨handed him a ~ filled with red Chilean wine —*Time*⟩ or for holding other liquid or substance (as ink or powder); *also* **:** DRINK ⟨did sometimes take a ~ when he thought it would do him good —*Atlantic*⟩ **e :** CORNUCOPIA **2 :** something resembling or suggestive of a horn: as **a :** one of the curved ends of a crescent; *esp* **:** a cusp of the moon when crescent-shaped **b** (1) **:** a body of land or water shaped like a horn (2) **:** a sharp peak in a rugged mountain region **c** (1) **:** a horn-shaped part of a device or mechanism (as a blacksmith's anvil or a horning press); *specif* **:** a part of a shoemaking machine over which a shoe is placed when being tacked, nailed, pegged, and in some instances sewed (2) **:** one of the outer ends of a ship's crosstrees; *also* **:** one of the points of the jaws of a gaff or boom (3) **:** a high pommel of a saddle; *also* **:** either of the projections on a lady's saddle for supporting the leg — see STOCK SADDLE illustration (4) **:** a short lever attached to a control surface of an airplane by means of which it is operated (5) *or* **horn antenna :** a radio antenna in which a metallic envelope that is usu. a rectangular cross-section wave guide flares out to project a signal into space (6) **:** a tube of varying sectional area used in some types of loudspeaker **d :** an erect penis — usu. considered vulgar **e :** CORNU **3 a :** a musical wind instrument formed from the horn of an animal (as an ox or ram); *specif* **:** SHOFAR **b** (1) **:** a brass wind instrument employing the lips as the vibrating medium (as the trumpet, saxhorn, tuba) or a plastic, wood, or metal imitation used as a children's toy (2) **:** FRENCH HORN (3) **:** a wind instrument (as the saxophone, clarinet, trombone) used in a jazz band **c** (1) **:** a usu. electrically operated device (as on an automobile or a diesel locomotive or in a factory) that makes a noise like that of a horn and is used for sounding a warning signal (2) **:** AIR HORN **4 a :** a means of defense **:** source of strength **:** POWER, GLORY, PRIDE ⟨The Lord is . . . the ~ of my salvation —Ps 18:2 (RSV)⟩ ⟨the election of a prominent layman . . . will help to elevate the ~ of the church —A.W.Long⟩ **b** [so called fr. the old custom of cutting the spurs from cockerels when they were castrated and implanting them in the comb, where they would grow into hornlike members that made it easy to pick out the capons, capons being frequent symbols of cuckoldry] **:** an imaginary horn supposedly growing upon the head of a cuckold and regarded as an emblem of his state — usu. used in pl. **c :** one of the equally disadvantageous alternatives presented by a dilemma ⟨to get off the ~s of this dilemma will not be easy —*Atlantic*⟩

2**horn** \"\ *adj* [ME, fr. *horn*, n.] **:** of or resembling horn or a horn; *esp* **:** composed or made of horn or a similar substance (as a plastic) ⟨~ spectacles⟩

3**horn** \"\ *vb* -ED/-ING/-S [1*horn*] *vt* **1 :** CUCKOLD **2 a :** to butt or gore with the horns **b :** to drive with the horns — used with *out* or *off* ⟨the young bull who had come to ~ the old one out of the herd —*Omnibook*⟩ **3 a** (1) **:** to wedge or fasten (as a boom or spar of a ship) as if between horns ⟨~ the boom in a crotch⟩ (2) **:** to install (the frame of a ship) square to the keel after allowing for the keel's declivity **b :** to press or hammer (a piece of metal) on the horn of an anvil **4** *dial Eng* **:** to proclaim or spread the news of ~ *vi*, *dial Eng* **:** to talk in a gossipy manner

**horn alligator** *n* **:** leather from an alligator's back

**horn angle** *n* **:** a figure formed by two plane curves tangent to each other on the same side of their mutual tangent line

**hornbeam** \ˈ=,=\ *n* [1*horn* + *beam*; fr. its hard, smooth, close-grained wood — more at BEAM] **1 :** a tree of the genus *Carpinus*: as **a :** an Old World tree (*C. betulus*) with smooth gray bark, hardy white wood, and leaves resembling those of the beech **b :** a similar tree (*C. caroliniana*) of America **2 :** HOP HORNBEAM **3 :** PLANER TREE

**hornbill** \ˈ=,=\ *n* **:** any of various large bulky omnivorous chiefly arboreal birds of Africa, southern Asia, and the East Indies constituting the suborder Bucerotes and having plumage that is predominantly black and white and an enormous bill that is usu. surmounted by a horny casque

**horn·blende** \ˈhȯrnˌblend, ˈhȯ(ə)n-\ *n* [G, fr. *horn* horn (fr. OHG) + *blende* blende — more at HORN, BLENDE] **1 :** a mineral approximately $Ca_2Na(Mg,Fe)_4(Al,Fe,Ti)_3Si_6O_{22}(O,OH)_2$ consisting of the common black, dark green, or brown variety of aluminous amphibole, containing considerable iron, and occurring as distinct crystals and in columnar, fibrous, and granular form **2 :** AMPHIBOLE

**horn·blen·dic** \(ˈ)hȯ(r)nˈblendik\ *adj* **:** containing hornblende in quantity **:** resembling or relating to hornblende

**horn·blend·ite** \ˈ=ˌblenˌdīt\ *n* -s [*hornblende* + *-ite*] **:** a granular igneous rock composed almost entirely of hornblende

**horn·blend·iza·tion** \ˌhȯ(r)nˌblendəˈzāshən\ *n* -s **:** the transformation of a rock into hornblende by replacement processes

**horn block** *n* **:** PEDESTAL 3a

**hornbook** \ˈ=,=\ *n* **1 :** a child's primer formerly in use consisting typically of a sheet of parchment or later of paper mounted on a thin wooden board and protected by a sheet of transparent horn and having on it the alphabet and other rudiments such as the digits and often the Lord's Prayer — compare BATTLEDORE 3 **2 :** a rudimentary treatise ⟨~s of political theory —V.O.Key⟩

**horn cell** *n* **:** a nerve cell lying in one of the gray columns of the spinal cord

**horn chestnut** *n* **:** WATER CHESTNUT

**horn·church** \ˈhȯrnˌchərch\ *adj, usu cap* [fr. *Hornchurch*, urban district, England] **:** of or from the urban district of Hornchurch, England **:** of the kind or style prevalent in Hornchurch

**horn–core** \ˈ=,=\ *n* **:** the bony inner shaft of a typical horn (as that of a cow)

**horn dance** *n* **:** a dance of Abbots Bromley, Staffordshire, England, with characters and patterns similar to those of the morris and distinguished by men carrying antlers

**horned** \ˈhȯ(ə)rnd, ˈhȯ(ə)nd *sometimes when not in combination* -nəd\ *adj* [ME, fr. OE *horn* + *-ed*] **1 :** having horns ⟨a mythical ~ beast, the unicorn⟩ — often used in combination ⟨long-*horned*⟩ **2 :** having a process or appendage resembling a horn **3 :** having a part shaped like a horn ⟨the ~ moon —S.T.Coleridge⟩

**horned adder** *n* **:** HORNED VIPER

**horned bladderwort** *n* **:** a No. American bog or aquatic herb (*Stomoisia cornuta*) with stems and minute linear leaves underground and solitary or few yellow showy irregular flowers on a slender naked scape

**horned cattle** *n* **:** cattle with horns; *specif* **:** bovine animals (as cows, bulls, steers)

**horned crab** *n* **:** a decorator crab (*Stenocionops furcata*)

**horned dace** *n* **:** a common No. American cyprinid fish (*Semotilus atromaculatus*)

**horned frog** *n* **1 :** any of various So. American frogs constituting a genus (*Ceratophrys*) of the family Leptodactylidae and usu. having triangular processes on the eyelids **2 :** HORNED TOAD

**horned grebe** *n* **:** a grebe (*Colymbus auritus*) that is widely distributed in northern parts of the northern hemisphere, is chiefly dark above and silky white below, and is distinguished when in breeding plumage by a glossy black head banded on either side with gold which encloses the eye and terminates in a brief ear tuft

**horned hazel** *n* **:** BEAKED HAZEL

**horned hog** *n* **:** BABIRUSA

**horned hummer** *n* **:** SUN GEM

**horned iguana** *n* **:** a Haitian iguana (*Metopoceras cornutus*) having three hornlike scales on the head

**horned lark** *n* **:** a small lark (*Eremophila alpestris*) and its subspecies widely distributed in the northern hemisphere

**horned lizard** *n* **:** HORNED TOAD

**horned milfoil** *n* **:** PURPLE BLADDERWORT

**horned·ness** \ˈhȯrnədnəs, -n(d)nəs, ˈhȯ(ə)n-\ *n* -ES **:** the quality or state of being horned

**horned owl** *n* **:** any of various owls (as the American great horned owl) having conspicuous tufts of feathers on the head

**horned pheasant** *n* **:** CRIMSON TRAGOPAN

**horned pondweed** *n* **:** a submerged aquatic weed (*Zannichellia palustris*)

**horned poppy** *n* **:** a yellow-flowered Eurasian herb (*Glaucium flavum*) adventive in the U. S.

**horned pout** *n* **:** BULLHEAD 1b; *esp* **:** a common bullhead (*Ameiurus nebulosus*) of the eastern U. S. which has been introduced into streams of the Pacific coast — called also *Sacramento cat*

**horned puffin** *n* **:** a puffin of the north Pacific having a small fleshy appendage resembling a horn on the eyelid

**horned rattlesnake** *n* **:** SIDEWINDER

**horned ray** *n* [so called fr. its cephalic fins or processes] **:** a ray of the family Mobulidae **:** DEVILFISH, MANTA

**horned rush** *n* **:** any of various sedges of the genus *Rhynchospora*; *esp* **:** a tall sedge (*R. corniculata*) of the eastern U. S. with a long-beaked achene

**horned screamer** *n* **:** a screamer (*Anhima cornuta*) of northern So. America with a long slender yellowish white process resembling a horn on the forehead — compare CRESTED SCREAMER

**horned shark** *n* **:** a small California shark (*Heterodontus francisci*) related to the bullhead of Australia

**horned snake** *n* **1 :** HORNED VIPER **2 :** HOOP SNAKE

**horned toad** *n* **:** any of various small harmless insectivorous lizards constituting the genus *Phrynosoma* (family Iguanidae) of the dry sandy plains of the western U. S. and Mexico and having several hornlike spines on the head and a broad flat body covered with spiny scales

**horned violet** *n* [so called fr. the elongated spur of the corolla] **:** TUFTED PANSY

**horned viper** *n* **:** a common desert-dwelling viper (*Aspis cornutus*) of Egypt and Asia Minor distinguished by a horny scale resembling a spike above each eye — compare ASP

**horned wavey** *n* **:** ROSS'S GOOSE

**hor·ne·mann's redpoll** \ˈhȯ(r)nəˌmänz-\ *n, usu cap H* [after Friedrich K. *Hornemann* †1801 Ger. explorer] **:** a redpoll (*Carduelis hornemanni*) of Europe with a small and pale breast and rump

**hor·ne·oph·y·ton** \ˌhȯ(r)nēˈäfəˌtän\ *n, cap* [NL, fr. *horneo-* (fr. E *horn*) + *phyton*] **:** a genus of Devonian fossil plants (family Rhyniaceae) similar to those of the genus *Rhynia* but smaller and lacking vascular tissue in the rhizome and considered to be one of the earliest forms of vascular land plants

**horn·er** \ˈhȯrnər\ *n* -s [ME, fr. 1*horn* + *-er*] **1 :** one who works or deals in horn **2 :** one who blows a horn **3** *obs* **:** one who cuckolds another man **4** *slang* **:** one who inhales heroin

**hor·ne·ro** \(h)ȯ(r)ˈne(ˌ)rō\ *n* -s [AmerSp, fr. Sp, baker, fr. *horno* oven (fr. L *furnus*) + *-ero* -er; fr. the fact that its nest resembles an oven — more at FURNACE] **:** BAKER BIRD

**hor·ner's method** \ˈhȯrnərz-\ *n, usu cap H* [after William G. *Horner* †1837 Eng. mathematician] **:** a numerical method of successive approximations used for computing to any number of decimal places an approximate value of any real root of an algebraic equation with real coefficients

**horner's syndrome** *n, usu cap H* [after Johann F. *Horner* †1886 Swiss ophthalmologist] **:** a syndrome marked by sinking in of the eyeball, contraction of the pupil, drooping of the upper eyelid, and vasodilation and anhidrosis of the face, and caused by injury to the cervical sympathetic innervation

**hor·net** \ˈhȯrnət, ˈhȯ(ə)n-, *usu* -əd·+V\ *n* -s [ME *hernet*, *harnette*, fr. OE *hyrnet*; akin to OS *hornut* hornet, OHG *hurnuz*, *hornaz*, MD *horsel*, L *crabro* hornet, Lith *širšė* wasp, and prob. to OE *horn* — more at HORN] **:** any of the larger social wasps of the family Vespidae that are vigorous strong-flying insects with powerful stings, usu. construct nests of macerated wood pulp resembling paper, and feed on both animal and vegetable matter — see GIANT HORNET, WHITE-FACED HORNET; compare YELLOW JACKET

white-faced hornet

**hornet's nest** *n* **:** a troublesome situation **:** angry reaction ⟨must have known that his frank comments . . . would stir up a *hornet's nest* —*U. S. Investor*⟩

**horn·fels** \ˈhȯrnˌfels\ *n, pl* **hornfels** [G, fr. *horn* horn (fr. OHG) + *fels* cliff, rock, fr. OHG *felis*, *felisa* — more at HORN, FELL] **:** a fine-grained silicate rock produced by contact metamorphism

**hornfish** \ˈ=,=\ *n* **:** a fish of the family Triacanthidae

**horn fly** *n* **:** a small black European blood-sucking two-winged fly (*Haematobia irritans*) introduced into No. America and other cattle-raising areas that clusters about the horns of cattle or hovers about their backs and causes great irritation by its bites

**horn gap** *n* **:** an arc gap formed by two horn-shaped electrodes that diverge so that the arc extinguishes itself

**hornier** *comparative of* HORNY

**horniest** *superlative of* HORNY

**horn·i·fy** \ˈhȯ(r)nəˌfī\ *vt* -ED/-ING/-ES [1*horn* + *-ify*] **:** to make hard like horn; *specif* **:** to make keratotic ⟨*hornified* skin⟩

**horn·i·ly** \ˈhȯ(r)nəlē\ *adv* **:** in a horny manner

**horn in** *vi* **:** to participate without invitation or often consent **:** butt in **:** INTRUDE ⟨*horned in* with advice⟩ ⟨*horn in* on a deal⟩

1**horning** *pres part of* HORN

2**horn·ing** \ˈhȯrniŋ\ *n* -s *chiefly North* **:** SHIVAREE

**horning press** *or* **horn press** *n* **:** a punch press with a horn by means of which the seams on hollow tinware are closed

**horn·ist** \ˈhȯrnəst\ *n* -s **:** a performer on a French horn

**hor·ni·to** \(h)ȯ(r)ˈnēd·(ˌ)ō\ *n* -s [Sp, dim. of *horno* oven — more at HORNERO] **:** a low oven-shaped mound in volcanic regions that emits smoke and vapors

**horn knot** *n* **:** SPIKE KNOT

**horn·less** \ˈ=ləs\ *adj* **:** having no horn

**horn·less·ness** *n* -ES **:** the condition of being hornless

**horn lightning arrester** *n* **:** a lightning arrester in which the spark gap is formed by two wires that diverge like a pair of horns — see LIGHTNING ARRESTER illustration

**hornlike** \ˈ=,=\ *adj* **1 :** having the form of a horn esp. in being elongated, pointed, and protruding ⟨a ~ process⟩ **2 :** resembling horn **:** CORNEOUS, HORNY, KERATINOUS

**horn mercury** *n* [so called fr. its horny appearance when fused] **:** CALOMEL

**horn of plenty :** CORNUCOPIA

**horn owl** *n* **:** HORNED OWL

**hornpie** \ˈ=,=\ *n* [1*horn* + *pie*; fr. the tufted feathers on its head] *dial Eng* **:** LAPWING

**hornpipe** \ˈ=,=\ *n* [ME fr. *horn* + *pipe*] **1 a :** a single reed wind instrument popular in England and thought to be of Celtic origin consisting of a wooden or bone pipe with holes at intervals along its length and with the bell and mouthpiece usu. made of horn — compare PIBGORN, STOCKHORN **b :** a lively country dance tune in 3/2, 3/4, or 4/4 time orig. played on this instrument **2 :** a lively folk dance of the British Isles usu. performed by a single person and orig. accompanied by hornpipe playing **3 :** a tune in the rhythm of a hornpipe

**horn poppy** *n* **:** HORNED POPPY

**hornpout** \ˈ=,=\ *n* **:** HORNED POUT

**horn quicksilver** *n* [so called fr. its horny appearance when fused] **:** native calomel

**horn–rimmed** \ˈ=ˈ=\ *adj* **:** having rims of horn

**horn–rims** \ˈ=,=\ *n pl* **:** spectacles with horn rims ⟨a stocky girl with *horn-rims* —William DuBois⟩

**horns** *pl of* HORN, *pres 3d sing of* HORN

**horn shark** *n* **:** HORNED SHARK

**horn shell** *n* **:** a snail of the genus *Cerithidea*

**horn silver** *n* [trans. of G *hornsilber*] **:** CERARGYRITE

**horn snake** *n* **:** HOOP SNAKE

**horn socket** *n* **:** a fishing tool consisting of a cone which seizes broken rods or tools in bored wells

**horn spoon** *n* **1 :** a spoon made of horn — used chiefly interjectionally in the phrase *by the great horn spoon* ⟨cookies, by the great *horn spoon* —Hamlin Garland⟩ **2** *also* **horn :** a small receptacle like a trough made from a section of cow horn and used for careful washing tests in gold mining

**hornstone** \ˈ=,=\ *n* [trans. of G *hornstein*] **:** a mineral consisting of a variety of quartz much like flint but more brittle

**horn·swog·gle** *also* **horn·swag·gle** \ˈhȯ(r)nˌswägəl\ *vt* -ED/-ING/-S [origin unknown] **:** BAMBOOZLE, HOAX ⟨continued to ~ the trading public right and left —F.L.Allen⟩

**horn·swog·gled** *also* **horn·swag·gled** \-ld\ *adj* **:** DAMNED 2a ⟨I'll be ~ if they didn't owe him $400 then —*N.Y. Sun*⟩

**horntail** \ˈ=,=\ *n* **:** any of various insects constituting a family (Siricidae) of Hymenoptera related to the typical sawflies but having larvae that burrow in woody plants and on the females a stout hornlike ovipositor for depositing the egg within the plant

**horn timber** *n* **:** a timber extending aft from the sternpost to the transom of a ship and forming the central support of the stern

**hornweed** \ˈ=,=\ *n* **:** HORNWORT

**hornworm** \ˈ=,=\ *n* **:** a larva of various hawkmoths (as a tobacco worm) having a hornlike tail process

**hornwort** \ˈ=,=\ *n* **1 :** a plant of the genus *Ceratophyllum* **2 :** a plant of the order Anthocerotales

**horn wrack** *n* **:** a bryozoan of the genus *Flustra*

**horny** \ˈhȯrnē, ˈhȯ(ə)nē, -ni\ *adj* -ER/-EST [ME, fr. 1*horn* + *-y*] **1 a :** of or made of horn or of a hornlike substance ⟨after the ~ material has been cut away —Morris Fishbein⟩ **b :** HARD, CALLOUS ⟨his feet were ~ and scarred —W.S.Maugham⟩ — often used in combination ⟨*horny*-handed⟩ **c :** compact and homogeneous with a dull luster like that of flint or of an animal's horn — used of the texture of a mineral **2 :** having horns or hornlike projections **3** [¹*horn* (erect penis) + *-y*] **:** easily excited sexually **:** LASCIVIOUS — usu. considered vulgar

**horny coral** *n* **:** GORGONIAN

**hornyhead chub** *also* **hornyhead** \ˈ=,=\ *n* **:** a common chub (*Nocomis biguttatus*) of the larger streams from Pennsylvania to Wyoming and south to Alabama distinguished by the males having the head covered with conical hornlike processes during the breeding season

**horny laminae** *n pl* **:** laminae on the inside of the wall of an animal's hoof

**horny sponge** *n* **:** a sponge lacking spicules but having a spongin skeleton that is more or less horny

**ho·ro·ka·ka** \,hōrəˈkäkə\ *n* -s [Maori] **:** a prostrate woody Australasian herb (*Mesembryanthemum australe*)

**ho·ro·loge** \ˈhōrə,lōj, ˈhär-, -läj\ *or* **hor·loge** \ˈhȯr,l-\ *n* -s [ME *orloge, oriloge, horologe*, fr. MF, fr. L *horologium*, fr. Gk *hōrologion*, fr. *hōro-* (fr. *hōra* period of time, time of day) + *-logion* (fr. *legein* to gather, speak, tell) — more at HOUR, LEGEND] **:** a timekeeping device; *esp* **:** an early or primitive one (as a sundial or an early clock using a foliot)

**ho·rol·o·ger** \həˈräləjə(r)\ *n* -s [*horology* + *-er*] **:** HOROLOGIST

**hor·o·log·ic** \ˌhȯrəˈläjik, ˌhär-, -jēk\ *also* **hor·o·log·i·cal** \-jəkəl, -jēk-\ *adj* [ML *horologicus*, fr. MGk *hōrologikos*, fr. Gk *hōrologion* + *-ikos* -ic, -ical] **:** of or relating to a horologe or horology — **hor·o·log·i·cal·ly** \-jək(ə)lē, -jēk-, -li\ *adv*

**ho·ro·lo·gion** \,ȯrəˈlō,yȯn\ *n* [MGk *hōrologion*, fr. Gk, timepiece] **:** a liturgical book in the Eastern Church containing the daily offices corresponding to the Western breviary

**ho·rol·o·gist** \həˈräləjəst\ *n* -s **:** a person skilled in the practice or theory of horology **:** a maker of clocks or watches

**hor·o·lo·gium** \,hȯrəˈlōj(ē)əm\ *n, pl* **horolo·gia** \-jə\ [L] **1 :** TIMEPIECE **2** [ML, fr. MGk *hōrologion*] **:** HOROLOGION

**¹ho·rol·o·gy** \həˈräləjē\ *n* -ES [ME *horologie*, fr. L *horologium*] **:** TIMEPIECE

**²horology** \"\ *n* -ES [Gk *hōro-* + E *-logy*] **1 :** the science of measuring time **2 :** the principles and art of constructing instruments for indicating time

**ho·rom·e·try** \həˈrämə·trē\ *n* -ES [Gk *hōro-* + E *-metry*] **:** HOROLOGY 1

**ho·ro·pi·to** \,hōrəˈpēd·(,)ō\ *n* -s [Maori] **:** NEW ZEALAND PEPPER TREE

**ho·rop·ter** \həˈräptə(r), ˈhō,r-\ *n* -s [F *horoptère*, fr. Gk *horos* boundary + *optēr* one that looks] **:** the locus of points in external space whose images are formed on corresponding places of the two retinas and which are therefore seen single — **hor·op·ter·ic** \ˌhō,räpˈterik\ *adj*

**¹hor·o·scope** \ˈhȯrə,skōp, ˈhär-\ *n* [MF, fr. L *horoscopus*, fr. Gk *hōroskopos*, fr. *hōro-* + *skopos* observer, fr. *skopein* to view, watch — more at SPY] **:** a diagram representing the twelve mundane houses and showing the relative positions of planets and signs of the zodiac at a particular time used by astrologers to foretell the events of a person's life or to answer horary questions ⟨cast a ~ in order to determine the exact day and hour at which a vessel should weigh anchor —G.L. Kittredge⟩; *specif* **:** NATIVITY

horoscope

**²horoscope** \"\ *vb* -ED/-ING/-S *vi* **:** to make horoscopes ~ *vt* **:** to cast the horoscope of — **hor·o·scop·er** \-pə(r)\ *n* -s

**hor·o·scop·ic** \ˌ==ˈskäpik, -kōp-, -pēk\ *adj* [L *horoscopicus*, fr. Gk *hōroskopikos*, fr. *hōroskopos* + *-ikos* -ic] **:** of or relating to a horoscope

**hor·o·tel·ic** \ˌhȯrəˈtelik\ *adj* **:** of or relating to horotely

**hor·o·tely** \ˈ==,=lē\ *n* -ES [Gk *horos* boundary, limit + *telos* end, consummation, degree of completion, state of maturity + E *-y*] **:** biological evolution at rates within the range or rate distribution usual for a given group of plants or animals — compare BRADYTELY, TACHYTELY

**horra** *var of* HORA

**hor·ren·dous** \hȯˈrendəs, hä'-, hə'-\ *adj* [L *horrendus*, fr. gerundive of *horrēre* to bristle, tremble — more at HORROR] **:** being such as to inspire horror **:** DREADFUL, FEARFUL, FRIGHTFUL, HORRIBLE ⟨began slapping some ~ taxes on these huge estates —A.C.Spectorsky⟩ ⟨a . . . ~ blending of Hollywood and history —Charles Lee⟩ — **hor·ren·dous·ly** *adv*

**hor·rent** \ˈhȯrənt, ˈhär-\ *adj* [L *horrent-, horrens*, pres. part. of *horrēre*] *archaic* **:** standing up like bristles **:** covered with bristling points **:** BRISTLED, BRISTLING ⟨~ with figures in strong relief —Thomas De Quincey⟩

**hor·ri·bi·le dic·tu** \hō,ribə(,)lēˈdik(,)tü, hä,-, hə,-\ [L] **:** horrible to say ⟨there is, *horribile dictu*, no mention of the fact that he was president of Harvard —*Times Lit. Supp.*⟩

**¹hor·ri·ble** \ˈhȯrəbəl, ˈhär-\ *adj* [ME *orrible, horrible*, fr. MF, fr. L *horribilis*, fr. *horrēre* to bristle, tremble, shudder + *-ibilis* -ible — more at HORROR] **1 :** marked by or conducive to horror **:** likely to arouse fear, dread, or abhorrence ⟨coconuts in the ~ likeness of a head shrunken by headhunters —Sinclair Lewis⟩ ⟨her hearers derived a ~ enjoyment from . . . her wrath —Charles Dickens⟩ **2 :** extremely unpleasant or disagreeable **:** conducive to feelings of acute dislike, disgust, or repulsion ⟨of all horrors in this blessed town, snow is the most ~ —W.M.Thackeray⟩ ⟨the weather is always ~ when I travel —Aldous Huxley⟩ **syn** see FEARFUL

**²horrible** \"\ *adv* [ME *orrible, horrible*, fr. orrible, horrible, adj.] **:** to an extreme degree **:** HORRIBLY, EXCEEDINGLY ⟨she was ~ mad⟩

**³horrible** \"\ *n* -s [¹*horrible*] **:** a horrible person or thing; *specif* **:** a person fantastically garbed (as for a masquerade or holiday parade) — usu. used in pl. ⟨the ~*s*, grotesquely costumed children, will parade along a few . . . streets —*Time*⟩ — see ANTIQUES AND HORRIBLES

**hor·ri·ble·ness** *n* -ES [ME *orriblenesse, horriblenesse*, fr. *orrible, horrible* + *-nesse* -ness] **:** the quality or state of being horrible

**hor·ri·bly** \-blē,-bli\ *adv* **:** in a horrible manner

**hor·rid** \ˈhȯrəd, ˈhär-\ *adj, sometimes* -ER/-EST [L *horridus*, fr. *horrēre*] **1** *archaic* **:** ROUGH, RUGGED, BRISTLING **2 a :** being such as to inspire horror **:** DREADFUL, HIDEOUS, SHOCKING ⟨performed a ~ . . . rite of that strange magic —Emma Hawkridge⟩ ⟨over the island a ~ stillness tarried —Jean Stafford⟩ **b :** inspiring disgust or repulsion **:** very offensive **:** NASTY ⟨gave her a loud . . . smack on the back, with ~ familiarity —Liam O'Flaherty⟩ ⟨he's a ~ person⟩ — **hor·rid·ly** *adv* — **hor·rid·ness** *n* -ES

**hor·rif·ic** \hȯˈrifik, hä'-, hə'-\ *adj* [MF *horrifique*, fr. L *horrificus*, fr. *horrēre* to bristle, tremble, shudder + *-ificus* -ific — more at HORROR] **:** dreadful to behold or contemplate **:** inspiring horror or fear **:** HORRIFYING, HORRIBLE ⟨this ~ picture of conditions in the mining industry —*Brit. Book News*⟩ ⟨~ black headlines in our daily papers —Charles Jackson⟩ **syn** see FEARFUL

**hor·rif·i·cal·ly** \-fək(ə)lē\ *adv* **:** in a horrific manner

**hor·ri·fi·ca·tion** \,hȯrəfəˈkāshən, ,här-\ *n* -s [L *horrificare* to horrify + E *-tion* — more at HORRIFY] **1 :** the act of horrifying or condition of being horrified **2 :** something that horrifies ⟨his two overcoats making him look like a mountain of ~ —Arthur Miller⟩

**hor·ri·fied** \ˈ==,fīd\ *adj* **:** filled with or marked or attended by a sensation, appearance, or attitude of horror **:** expressing or reflecting horror ⟨we were ~, frightened, and angry at the same time —W.A.White⟩ ⟨strained his eyeballs in a ~ stare at vacancy —G.D.Brown⟩ ⟨grip the reader with a . . . ~ fascination —Norman Birkett⟩ — **hor·ri·fied·ly** \-f(ə)dlē, -li\ *adv*

**hor·ri·fy** \ˈhȯrə,fī, ˈhär-\ *vt* -ED/-ING/-ES [L *horrificare*, fr. *horrificus* horrific — more at HORRIFIC] **:** to cause to feel horror **:** strike with horror ⟨smoking right through soup, fish, meat, salad, and dessert in a way to ~ the epicure —Frances Perkins⟩ ⟨may ~ some employers who are still living in the nineteenth century —Roy Lewis & Angus Maude⟩ **syn** see DISMAY

**hor·ri·fy·ing·ly** *adv* **:** in a horrifying manner **:** so as to horrify

**hor·rip·i·late** \hȯˈripə,lāt\ *vt* -ED/-ING/-S [back-formation fr. *horripilation*] **:** to produce horripilation in (as by sudden fear) ⟨a strange, wild, *horripilating* tale —R.C.Lewis⟩

**hor·rip·i·la·tion** \(,)=,==ˈlāshən\ *n* -s [LL *horripilation-, horripilatio*, fr. L *horripilatus* (past part. of *horripilare* to bristle, be shaggy, fr. *horrēre* + *pilus* hair) + *-ion-, -io* -ion — more at PILE] **:** a bristling of the hair of the head or body (as from disease, terror, or chilliness) **:** GOOSEFLESH

**¹hor·ror** \ˈhȯrə(r), ˈhär-\ *n* -s [ME *orrour, horrour*, fr. MF *orror, horror, horreur*, fr. L *horror* action of trembling or shuddering, terror, horror, fr. *horrēre* to bristle, tremble, shudder + *-or*; akin to OE *gorst* gorse, Gk *chēr* hedgehog, *chersos* dry land, mainland, OIr *garb* rough, Skt *harṣate* he becomes stiff, resists, shudders; basic meaning: stiffening] **1 a :** a painful emotion of intense fear, dread, or dismay **:** CONSTERNATION ⟨I saw astonishment giving place to ~ on the faces of the people about me —H.G.Wells⟩ ⟨only to find to my ~ that the dealer knew its value as well as I —H.J.Laski⟩ **b :** intense aversion or repugnance ⟨shrank from the task with all the ~ of a well-bred English gentleman —Virginia Woolf⟩ ⟨the Spanish ~ of any taint of Moorish blood —A.H.Quinn⟩ **2 a :** the quality of inspiring horror **:** repulsive, horrible, or dismal quality or character ⟨statements emphasizing the ~ of this disclosure —Elmer Davis⟩ ⟨sat in silence . . . contemplating the ~ of their lives —Liam O'Flaherty⟩ **b :** something (as an experience, event, or object) that inspires horror **:** something that is horrible ⟨for him the reef was not a beautiful thing but a ~ —Alan Moorehead⟩ ⟨I know that this Nazi ~ has to be destroyed —Upton Sinclair⟩ ⟨made speeches, and hired lawyers, but was unable to avert the ~ —Alva Johnston⟩ **c horrors** *pl* (1) **:** a state of extreme nervous depression or apprehension **:** BLUES, NERVES ⟨smells and . . . sounds which could give one the ~*s* —Marcia Davenport⟩ ⟨his nervous breakdowns, the attacks of the ~*s* he is known to have suffered from —V.S.Pritchett⟩ ⟨one of their best batsmen was in the ~*s* —Ray Robinson⟩ (2) **:** DELIRIUM TREMENS ⟨came home roaring drunk and that night had the ~*s*⟩ **syn** see FEAR

**²horror** \"\ *adj* **:** specializing in or marked by themes or incidents of extreme violence, cruelty, or weird or macabre quality **:** calculated to inspire feelings of dread or horror **:** BLOODCURDLING ⟨some ~ stories from the Old Testament —J.C.Swaim⟩ ⟨an Elizabethan ~ play —Geoffrey Grigson⟩ ⟨has the strange fascination of a ~ novel —Alfred Frankfurter⟩ ⟨~ comics⟩

**horror–struck** \ˈ==,=\ *adj* **:** struck with horror ⟨stood *horror-struck* as they watched . . . their own city destroyed —*Nashville Tennessean*⟩

**horror va·cui** \ˌ==ˈvakyə,wī\ *n* [NL, horror of a vacuum] **:** horror of empty spaces; *esp* **:** an aversion to empty spaces in artistic designs ⟨the Germans share this *horror vacui*, but there is always a marked spatial curiosity in their ornament —Nikolaus Pevsner⟩

**hor·ry** \ˈhäri\ *adj* [ME *hory*, fr. OE *horig*, fr. *horh* filth, phlegm; akin to OFris *hore* mud, filth, OS *horu, horo* dirt, filth, OHG *horo* dirt, filth, ON *horr* nasal mucus — more at CORYZA] *now dial Eng* **:** disgustingly dirty **:** FOUL

**¹hors con·cours** \,ȯr,kōⁿˈkü(ə)r\ *adv* [F, outside of competition] **:** in the manner of one that does not compete ⟨finished too late to enter competition . . . and was shown *hors concours* —R.F.Hawkins⟩

**²hors concours** \"\ *adj* [F, outside of competition] **1 :** excluded from competition ⟨artists . . . who had already received a medal . . . were *hors concours* —John Rewald⟩ **2 :** being without equal or rival **:** SUPREME ⟨these practitioners of the art . . . salute her as *hors concours* —J.M.Murry⟩

**hors de com·bat** \,ȯrdəˌkōⁿˈbä\ *adv (or adj)* [F] **:** out of the combat **:** in a disabled condition ⟨the master of that art is able . . . to put an untrained antagonist completely *hors de combat* —Lafcadio Hearn⟩ ⟨with the president *hors de combat* and . . . on the verge of complete retirement —R.H.Rovere⟩

**hors d'oeuvre** \ȯrˈdərv, ȯ(ə)ˈdərv, ȯ(ə)ˈdēv, -dəiv; *sometimes* ȯrˈdəv\ *n, pl* **hors d'oeuvres** *also* **hors d'oeuvre** \-v(z)\ [F *hors-d'œuvre* something nonessential, sidedish, hors d'oeuvre, fr. the phrase *hors d'œuvre*, nonessential, lit., outside of work] **:** an appetizer usu. one of an assortment served on plates, shells, or compartmented dishes with crackers or toast bits on the side — usu. used in pl.; compare CANAPÉ 1

**¹horse** *R* ˈhȯ(ə)rs, *–R* ˈhȯ(ə)s, *dial R* ˈhōs *or* ˈhä(r)s *–R* ˈhäs\

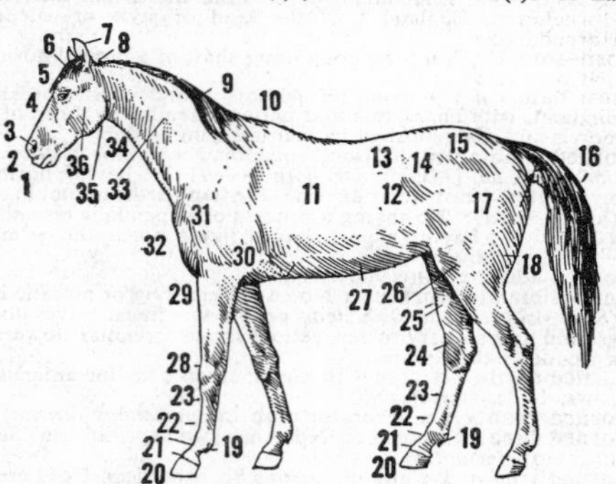

parts of the horse: *1* mouth, *2* nose, *3* nostril, *4* face, *5* forehead, *6* forelock, *7* ear, *8* poll, *9* mane, *10* withers, *11* ribs, *12* flank, *13* loin, *14* haunch, *15* croup, *16* tail, *17* thigh, *18* buttock, *19, 19* fetlocks, *20, 20* hooves, *21, 21* coronets, *22, 22* pasterns, *23, 23* cannons, *24* hock, *25* gaskin, *26* stifle, *27* belly, *28* knee, *29* forearm, *30* elbow, *31* shoulder, *32* breast, *33* neck, *34* throatlatch, *35* lower jaw, *36* cheek

*n, pl* **horses** *also* **horse** [ME *hors*, fr. OE; akin to OFris *hors, hars* horse, OS *hros, hers*, OHG *hros*, ON *hross*, and perh. to ON *hrata* to stagger, fall — more at CARDINAL] **1 a** (1) **:** a large solid-hoofed herbivorous mammal (*Equus caballus*) domesticated by man since a prehistoric period and used as a beast of burden, a draft animal, or for riding, and distinguished from the other existing members of the genus *Equus* and family Equidae by the long hair of the mane and tail, the usual presence of a callosity on the inside of the hind leg below the hock, and other less constant characters (as the larger size, larger hooves, more arched neck, small head, short ears) (2) **:** a horse over 14.2 hands tall — compare COLT, PONY (3) **:** RACEHORSE ⟨play the ~*s*⟩ **b** (1) **:** the male of the horse **:** STALLION; *sometimes* **:** a gelding as distinguished from an entire male (2) **:** a stallion four years old or older — used in the terminology of the U.S. Trotting Association **c** (1) **:** any of various extinct animals closely related to the horse (2) **:** any member of the family Equidae **2 :** any of several devices: as **a :** a hook-shaped tool used in making embossed or hammered work **b** (1) **:** FOOTROPE (2) **:** a breastband or similar protection for a sailor in an exposed position (3) **:** TRAVELER 3b (4) **:** JACKSTAY 1 **c :** a frame usu. with legs used for supporting something (as planks, a staging, clothing) **:** TRESTLE; *specif* **:** a sloping frame used in printing for holding paper about to be printed **d :** a notched board to support the steps of a staircase **e** (1) **:** SIDE HORSE (2) **:** LONG HORSE **3** *horse pl* **:** HORSEMEN ⟨the whole party of 1500 ~ —H.A.Shield⟩; *esp* **:** CAVALRY ⟨a regiment of ~⟩ **4 a :** a mass of the same geological character as the wall rock occurring within a vein; *esp* **:** a body of useless rock within an ore deposit **b :** a mass of rock enclosed between two branches of a fault or vein **5 a :** HORSEPOWER **b** *slang* **:** HEROIN ⟨went back on the ~ —*Police Dragnet*⟩ — **from the horse's mouth :** from the original source **:** from an unimpeachable source ⟨information he had just obtained . . . *from the horse's mouth* —*Newsweek*⟩

**²horse** \"\ *vb* -ED/-ING/-S [ME *horsen*, fr. *hors*, n.] *vt* **1 a :** to provide with a horse; *specif* **:** to provide horses for (a vehicle) **b :** to place on a horse **2 a :** to lift, pull, or push roughly or by main force ⟨*horsing* him around in the snow —Theodore Morrison⟩ ⟨sweating gunners *horsed* their pieces into action —Bruce Catton⟩ **b :** to hang (leather) on a horse to drain — often used with *up* **3 :** to subject to horseplay **:** play a joke on **:** KID ⟨if there was nothing else to do, you could ~ the . . . newspaper vendor —Wallace Stegner⟩ ~ *vi* **1** *of a mare* **:** to be in heat **:** be willing to take a stallion **2 :** to engage in horseplay **:** PLAY, FOOL — usu. used with *around* ⟨I ~ around quite a lot, just to keep from getting bored —J.D.Salinger⟩ ⟨I never ~ around much with the women —Norman Mailer⟩ **3 :** to read a proof by comparing it directly with copy

**³horse** \"\ *adj* [¹*horse*] **1 a :** relating to a horse **:** of or for a horse **b :** hauled or powered by a horse ⟨a ~ barge⟩ **2 :** large or coarse of its kind ⟨~ corn⟩ **3 :** mounted on horse ⟨~ dragoons⟩ **:** for mounted troops ⟨~ barracks⟩

**horse aloes** *n* **:** CABALLINE ALOES

**horse–and–buggy** \ˌ==ˈ==\ *adj* **1 :** of or relating to the era before the advent of the automobile and other socially revolutionizing major inventions ⟨devotes a lovingly lavish amount of space to *horse-and-buggy* days —A.W.Derleth⟩ ⟨having been born in the *horse-and-buggy* era —J.N.Hall⟩ **2 :** clinging to outworn attitudes or ideas **:** hopelessly outmoded **:** OLD-FASHIONED ⟨*horse-and-buggy* thinking⟩ ⟨the *horse-and-buggy* naval strategists of yesterday —F.H.Gervasi⟩

**horse ant** *n* **:** a large red mound-building ant (*Formica rufa*) of Europe and No. America

**horse apples** *n pl, chiefly dial* **:** dried horse droppings

**¹horseback** \ˈ=,=\ *n* [ME *horsback*, fr. *hors* horse + *back*] **1 :** the back of a horse **2 a :** a natural ridge of sand, gravel, or rock **:** HOGBACK **b :** a mound, ridge, bank, or parting of barren rock in a coal seam

**²horseback** \"\ *adv* **:** on horseback

**horse·back·er** \"ə(r)\ *n* **:** a person on horseback

**horse balm** *n* **1 :** an erect smooth perennial strong-scented herb (*Collinsonia canadensis*) of eastern No. America with serrate pointed leaves and a loose panicle of yellowish flowers — called also *horseweed* **2 :** a plant of the genus *Monarda*

**horsebane** \ˈ=,=\ *n* **:** a European water dropwort (*Oenanthe phellandrium*)

**horsebean** \ˈ=,=\ *n* **1 :** BROAD BEAN 1 **2 :** a West Indian bean of the genus *Canavalia* **3 :** JERUSALEM THORN 2

**horse block** *n* **:** a block or platform for use in mounting or dismounting from a horse or entering or leaving a vehicle

**horse boat** *n* **:** a boat for conveying horses and cattle

**horse bot** *also* **horse bee** *n* **:** HORSE BOTFLY; *specif* **:** the larval stage of a horse botfly

**horse botfly** *n* **:** any of several botflies chiefly attacking horses; *esp* **:** a cosmopolitan cloudy-winged form (*Gasterophilus intestinalis*) that glues its eggs to the hairs esp. of the forelegs whence they are taken into the mouth where they hatch into young bots and pass into the stomach and become attached to the lining

**horse box** *n* **:** a railroad car or trailer for transporting horses (as racers)

**horseboy** \ˈ=,=\ *n, Brit* **:** HOSTLER

**horse brass** *n* **:** a brass ornament fastened to a martingale

**horsebreaker** \ˈ=,==\ *n* **:** one who breaks or trains horses

**horse brier** *n* **:** GREENBRIER

**horsebrush** \ˈ=,=\ *n* **:** any of several plants of the genus *Tetradymia* (family Compositae) that occur on rangelands in the western U.S. and are a major cause of bighead of American sheep

**horsebush** \ˈ=,=\ *n, in the Bahama islands* **:** any of several plants: as **a :** a West Indian tree (*Peltophorum adnatum*) of the family Leguminosae with densely brown-tomentose foliage and racemose yellow flowers **b :** an annual weedy herb (*Heliotropium parviflorum*) with spicate white flowers **c :** a West Indian sticky shrub (*Gundlachia corymbosa*) of the family Compositae with alternate leaves and many small white flowers in corymbose heads

**horse cane** *n* **:** GREAT RAGWEED

**horsecar** \ˈ=,=\ *n* **1 :** a railroad car or streetcar drawn by horses **2 :** a car fitted for transporting horses

**horse cassia** *n* **1 :** an East Indian cassia (*Cassia marginata*) with long pods containing a black cathartic pulp used as a horse medicine **2 :** CANAFISTULA 2

**horse cavalry** *n* **:** cavalry mounted on horses as distinct from mechanized cavalry

**horse chestnut** *n* [so called fr. its having been used to treat respiratory ailments in horses] **1 a :** a large Asiatic tree (*Aesculus hippocastanum*) that was introduced into Europe in the 16th century and is widely cultivated as an ornamental and shade tree and naturalized as an escape in much of the temperate zone and that has a rough bark, coarse branches, opposite palmately compound leaves, and predominantly white flowers in showy terminal clusters which are followed by large glossy brown seeds enclosed in a coarsely prickly bur; *broadly* **:** any of several trees of the genus *Aesculus* — see BUCKEYE, TREE illustration **b :** the seed of a horse chestnut **2 :** a dark grayish brown that is deeper and very slightly redder than average chocolate brown and deeper and very slightly yellower than African brown

**horse–chestnut family** *n* **:** HIPPOCASTANACEAE

**horsecloth** \ˈ=,=\ *n* **:** a cloth for a covering or trapping of a horse

**horse conch** *n* **:** a massive conch (*Fasciolaria gigantea*) of the warm western Atlantic, the animal being bright red and enclosed in a yellowish spired shell as much as two feet in length

**horse coper** *n, Brit* **:** a horse dealer; *esp* **:** a dishonest one ⟨a timber buyer was thought to hold the same kind of reputation as a *horse coper* —F.D.Smith & Barbara Wilcox⟩

**horse·cors·er** *or* **horse·cours·er** \ˈ=,kȯrsər, -,kōr-\ *n* [¹*horse* + obs. *corser, courser* horsedealer, fr. *corse* (to barter) or *course* (var. of *corse*) + *-er*] *archaic* **:** a dealer in horses; *esp* **:** a tricky dealer

**horse crab** *n* **1 :** KING CRAB **2 :** either of two very large crabs (*Telmessus cheiragonus* and *Erimacrus isenbeckii*) widely distributed in waters of moderate depths along the coasts of the northern Pacific ocean

**horse crevalle** *n* **:** BLUE RUNNER

**horsed** *past of* HORSE

**horse daisy** *n* **1 :** DAISY 1b **2 :** MAYWEED 1

**horse dance** *n* **1 :** a dance of No. American Indians imitating the rearing of a horse **2 :** a dance executed on either a hobby-horse or a live horse

**horse devil** *n* **:** a wild indigo (*Baptisia lanceolata*) of the southern U.S. that when dried and withered is rolled about by the wind sometimes frightening horses

**horse doctor** *n* **1 :** one who doctors horses **:** VETERINARIAN **2 :** an inadequately trained or incompetent doctor

**horse elder** *n* **:** ELECAMPANE

**horse–eye** \ˈ=,=\ *or* **horse–eye bean** *n* **1 :** a seed of the cowhage (*Mucuna pruriens*); *also* **:** the plant itself **2 :** OXEYE BEAN **3 :** a seed of the hyacinth bean

**horse–eye jack** *also* **horse–eyed jack** \ˈ=,=-\ *n* **:** any of several carangid food fishes: as **a :** a blue and silver carangid fish (*Caranx latus*) of the tropical western Atlantic **b :** BIG-EYED SCAD

**horseface** \ˈ=,=\ *n* **:** a long homely face

**horse family** *n* **:** EQUIDAE

**horsefeathers** \ˈ=,==\ *n pl, slang* **:** NONSENSE, BALDERDASH — often used interjectionally

**horse fiddle** *n, chiefly dial* **:** a noisemaking device based on the principle of a rosined bow drawn across a string

**horsefish** \ˈ=,=\ *n, pl* **horsefish** *or* **horsefishes 1 a :** MOONFISH a **b :** SAUGER **c :** a sea horse (genus *Hippocampus*) **d :** a dusky rough-skinned southern African scorpaenid fish (*Congiopodus torvus*) **2 :** KING CRAB 1

**horseflesh** \ˈ=,=\ *n* **1 :** the flesh of a horse esp. when slaughtered for food **2 :** horses considered esp. with reference to riding, driving, or racing **3 :** any of several hard often reddish West Indian timbers: as **a :** SABICU **b :** the wood of a bully tree (*Manilkara bidentata*) **c :** the wood of black mangrove

**horseflesh mahogany** *n* **1 :** any of several hard mottled tropical American woods that somewhat resemble mahogany

**2 :** a tree (as *Peltophorum adnatum* or *Hieronyma caribaea*) that yields horseflesh mahogany
**horseflesh ore** *n* [so called fr. its reddish color when newly fractured] *dial Eng* **:** BORNITE
**horsefly** \'ˌ≈ˌ≈\ *n* **1 :** any of numerous rather large stocky swift-flying two-winged flies constituting the family Tabanidae having in the female a piercing proboscis with which they suck the blood of animals (as horses and cattle) inflicting painful bites — compare CHRYSOPS, GREENHEAD **2 :** any of several other flies annoying to horses (as the horse tick *Hippobosca equina*)
**horsefly weed** *n* [so called fr. its supposed ability to drive away horseflies] **:** INDIGO BROOM
**horse gentian** *n* **:** a plant of the genus *Triosteum*; *esp* **:** FEVERROOT
**horse gowan** *n* **1 :** DAISY 1b **2 :** CHAMOMILE **3 :** DANDELION **4 :** any of several plants of the genera *Crepis* and *Hypochaeris*
**horse gram** *or* **horse grain** *n* **:** a twining herb (*Dolichos biflorus*) of the tropics of the Old World that is cultivated in India for fodder with the seeds being used as food
**horsehair** \'ˌ≈ˌ≈\ *n*, *often attrib* [ME *hors her*, fr. *hors* horse + *her* hair — more at HAIR] **1 a :** a hair of a horse esp. from the mane or tail **b :** a quantity of such hairs **2 :** HAIRCLOTH
**horsehair blight** *n* **:** a disease of tea and other tropical plants caused by a fungus (*Marasmius equicrinis*) the mycelium of which hangs in black festoons from the branches
**horsehair lichen** *n* **:** any of several lichens esp. of the genus *Alectoria* with a thallus consisting of filaments resembling hair — called also *horsetail lichen*
**horsehair snake** *or* **horsehair worm** *n* **:** a free-living adult gordioid worm
**horsehead** \'ˌ≈ˌ≈\ *n* **:** MOONFISH a
**horse•heal** *or* **horse•heel** \'ˌ≈ˌhē(ə)l\ *n* [by folk etymology fr. ME *horselne*, *horshelne*, *horshelyn*, fr. OE *horselene*, *horshelene*, fr. *hors* horse + *elene*, *eolone* elecampane, fr. ML *elena* (*campana*) — more at HORSE, ELECAMPANE] **:** ELECAMPANE
**horsehide** \'ˌ≈ˌ≈\ *n* **1 :** the hide of a horse or colt or leather made from either — compare CORDOVAN **2 :** BASEBALL 2
**horse hoe** *n* **:** a horse-drawn surface cultivator
**horsehoof** \'ˌ≈ˌ≈\ *n*, *pl* **horsehoofs** [ME *horshoof*, fr. *hors* horse + *hoof*] **:** COLTSFOOT
**horsehoof clam** *n* **:** a large tropical clam (*Hippopus hippopus*) related to and much resembling the giant clam (*Tridacna derasi*) — called also *horseshoe clam*
**horsekeeper** \'ˌ≈ˌ≈≈\ *n* [ME *horskepare*, fr. *hors* horse + *kepare*, *keper* keeper] **:** one who has charge of horses **:** GROOM
**horse knacker** *n* **:** KNACKER
**horse knob** *or* **horse knop** *n* **:** KNAPWEED
**horse latitudes** *n pl* **:** either of two belts or regions in the neighborhood of 30° N. and 30° S. latitude characterized by high pressure, calms, and light baffling winds; *esp* **:** that part of the northern belt which is over the Atlantic ocean
**horselaugh** \'ˌ≈ˌ≈\ *n* **:** a loud boisterous laugh **:** GUFFAW
**horseleech** \'ˌ≈ˌ≈\ *n* [ME *horsleche*, fr. *hors* horse + *leche* leech — more at LEECH] **:** a common European leech (*Haemopis gulo*) that feeds chiefly on worms; *also* **:** any of several related No. American leeches
**horse•less carriage** \'≈ləs-\ *n* **:** AUTOMOBILE — used esp. of early models
**horselike** \'ˌ≈ˌ≈\ *adj* **:** resembling a horse
**horse louse** *n* **1 :** a sucking louse (*Haematopinus asini*) found on horses and other equines **2 :** any of several biting lice infesting horses
**horse mackerel** *n* **1 :** any of several large scombroid fishes: as **a :** BLUEFIN TUNA **b :** CHILE BONITO **2 :** any of various large fishes of the family Carangidae; *esp* **:** a large Atlantic food fish (*Trachurus trachurus*)
**horse•man** \'≈mən\ *n*, *pl* **horsemen** [ME *horsman*, fr. *hors* horse + *man*] **1 a :** a rider on horseback **b :** one skilled in managing horses **2 :** a breeder or raiser of horses
**horse•man•ship** \-ˌship\ *n* **:** the art of riding horseback **:** equestrian skill **:** MANEGE
**horsemeat** \'ˌ≈ˌ≈\ *n* **:** the flesh of the horse esp. for use as food ⟨a ~ butcher⟩ ⟨~ is important in the diet of mink⟩
**horsemint** \'ˌ≈ˌ≈\ *n* [ME *horsminte* fr. *hors* + *minte* mint] **:** any of various coarse mints: as **a :** WATER MINT **b :** a plant of the genus *Monarda*; *esp* **:** a tall erect perennial herb (*M. punctata*) with petioled lanceolate leaves somewhat hairy beneath and heads of purple-spotted creamy flowers subtended by purplish or whitish bracts
**horse–mule** \'ˌ≈ˌ≈\ *n* **:** a male mule
**horse mushroom** *n* **:** a rather coarse edible mushroom (*Agaricus arvensis*) with a hollow stem, pale gills, and a broad white cap — compare MEADOW MUSHROOM
**horse mussel** *n* **:** a large coarse marine mussel (*Modiolus modiolus*) found on the shores of northern Europe and America; *also* **:** any similar closely related species
**horse nettle** *n* **:** a coarse prickly weed (*Solanum carolinense*) common in eastern and southern U.S., having white or pale-purple flowers and bright-yellow fruit resembling berries — called also *ball nettle*, *bull nettle*
**horse opera** *n* **:** a motion picture or radio or television play having its scene laid in the western U.S. and usu. having cowboys as its principal characters
**horse parlor** *n* **:** a place where betting on horses is carried on
**horse piece** *n* **:** one of the large pieces into which blubber is cut before mincing
**horse pistol** *n* **:** a large pistol formerly carried by horsemen
**¹horseplay** \'ˌ≈ˌ≈\ *n* [¹*horse* + *play*] **:** rough or boisterous play
**²horseplay** \"\ *vi* **:** to engage in horseplay ⟨~*ed* around with the boys —Betty Smith⟩
**horseplayer** \'ˌ≈ˌ≈≈\ *n* [¹*horse* + *player*] **:** one who habitually bets on horse races
**horseplaying** \'ˌ≈ˌ≈≈\ *n* [¹*horse* + *playing*] **:** betting on horse races
**horse plum** *n* **1 :** AMERICAN PLUM **2 :** CANADA PLUM
**horsepond** \'ˌ≈ˌ≈\ *n* **:** a pond for watering horses
**horse post** *n* **1 :** a hitching post **2 a :** a mail carrier who makes his deliveries on horseback **b :** a mail service performed by such carriers
**horsepower** \'ˌ≈ˌ≈≈\ *n* **1 a :** the power that a horse exerts in pulling **b :** a machine worked by a horse **2 :** a standard unit of power equal in the U.S. to 746 watts and nearly equivalent to the English gravitational unit of the same name that equals 550 foot-pounds of work per second — compare BRAKE HORSEPOWER, INDICATED HORSEPOWER
**horsepower–hour** \'ˌ≈ˌ≈ˌ≈\ *n* **:** the work performed or energy consumed by working at the rate of one horsepower for one hour, being equal to 1,980,000 foot-pounds
**horsepox** \'ˌ≈ˌ≈\ *n* **:** a virus disease of horses related to cowpox and marked by a vesiculopustular eruption of the skin esp. on the pasterns and sometimes by a vesiculopapular inflammation of the buccal mucosa — called also *equine variola*
**horse purslane** *n* **:** a coarse tropical American fleshy weed (*Trianthema portulacastrum*) of the family Aizoaceae
**horse racer** *n* **1 :** one who keeps horses for racing **2 :** JOCKEY **3 :** a devotee of horse racing
**horse racing** *n* **:** the racing of horses as a sport
**horseradish** \'ˌ≈ˌ≈≈\ *n* **1 a :** a tall coarse white-flowered herb (*Armoracia lapathifolia*) native to Europe and widely cultivated **b :** the pungent root of horseradish **c :** KERGUELEN CABBAGE **2 :** a condiment made of the grated root of the horseradish plant often moistened with vinegar or a similar substance
**horseradish tree** *n* **1 :** an East Indian tree (*Moringa oleifera*) that has a horseradish-flavored root and is cultivated throughout the tropics for its elongated capsular fruit which when young is pickled or cooked as a vegetable and for its seeds which yield ben oil **2 :** any Australian tree of the genus *Codonocarpus* (family Phytolaccaceae) having pungent leaves suggesting the flavor of horseradish or mustard
**horse rake** *n* **:** a horse-drawn rake
**horse room** *n* **:** a bookmaker's establishment which provides information on horse races and opportunity to bet on them
**horses** *pl of* HORSE, *pres 3d sing of* HORSE
**horse savin** *n* **:** COMMON JUNIPER
**horse sense** *n* **:** plain shrewd unsophisticated common sense ⟨juries seldom accept purely scientific evidence if it seems in conflict with everyday *horse sense* —E.M.Lustgarten⟩ **syn** see SENSE

**horseshit** \'ˌ≈ˌ≈\ *n* **1 :** horse droppings — usu. considered vulgar **2 :** BUNK, NONSENSE — usu. considered vulgar
**¹horseshoe** \'ˌ≈ˌ≈\ *n* [ME *hors sho*, fr. *hors* + *sho* shoe] **1 :** a shoe for horses usu. consisting of a narrow plate of iron conformed to the rim of a horse's hoof **2 :** something (as a valley or other physical feature) shaped like a horseshoe ⟨the town . . . stood in the mouth of a ~ —John Buchan⟩ ⟨the vast ~ of hills surrounding the central plains —D.G.E.Hall⟩ **3 horseshoes** *pl* **:** a game like quoits played with horseshoes or with horseshoe-shaped pieces of metal which are thrown from one peg in the ground toward another 40 feet away with the object of ringing or coming close to the peg

underside of typical horseshoes: *1* plain shoe, *2* shoe with toe and heel calks

**²horseshoe** \"\ *vt* **1 :** to furnish with horseshoes **:** put shoes on (a horse) **2 :** to put in the shape of a horseshoe; *specif* **:** to make (an architectural arch) like a horseshoe
**³horseshoe** \"\ *adj* **1 :** shaped like a horseshoe ⟨a ~ curve⟩ ⟨the ~ bend of a river⟩ **2** *of an arch* **:** having an intrados that widens above the springing before narrowing to a rounded or pointed crown — see ARCH illustration
**horseshoe bat** *n* **:** any of several bats of the Old World (families Rhinolophidae and Hipposideridae) having a more or less horseshoe-shaped leaf on the nose
**horseshoe clam** *n* **:** HORSEHOOF CLAM
**horseshoe crab** *n* **:** KING CRAB
**horseshoe kidney** *n* **:** congenital partial fusion of the kidneys resulting in a horseshoe shape
**horseshoe nail** *n* **:** a thin pointed nail with heavy flaring head that is used to fix a horseshoe to the hoof
**horseshoe plate** *n* **:** a plate around a ship's rudder stock that is shaped like a horseshoe and designed to prevent water from entering the rudder trunk
**horseshoer** \'ˌ≈ˌ≈≈\ *n* **:** one who makes horseshoes or shoes horses; *specif* **:** BLACKSMITH 1b
**horseshoe snake** *n* **:** a harmless colubrid snake (*Zamenis hippocrepis*) of Spain and Africa
**horseshoe vetch** *n* **:** a European herb (*Hippocrepis comosa*) of the family Leguminosae with yellow umbellate flowers succeeded by flattened pods that separate into horseshoe-shaped joints
**horseshoe violet** *n* **:** BIRD'S-FOOT VIOLET
**horse show** *n* **:** a competitive exhibition of horses and vehicles esp. as an annual fashionable event
**horsesickness** \'ˌ≈ˌ≈≈\ *n* **:** AFRICAN HORSE SICKNESS
**horse's neck** *n* **:** a tall drink consisting of ginger ale or ginger ale and a liquor served iced in a large tumbler with a spiral of lemon peel hanging over the rim
**horse sorrel** *n* **1 :** a European water dock (*Rumex hydrolapathum*) **2 :** SHEEP SORREL 1
**horse sponge** *n* **:** a sponge of ᵗhe genus *Hippiospongia*
**horse stinger** *n*, *dial Eng* **:** DRAGONFLY
**horse sugar** *n* **:** SWEETLEAF
**horse syphilis** *n* **:** DOURINE
**horsetail** \'ˌ≈ˌ≈\ *n* [ME *horse tayle* fr. *horse*, *hors* + *tayle*, *tail*] **1 :** the tail of a horse **2 :** a plant of the genus *Equisetum*
**horsetail agaric** *or* **horsetail fungus** *n* **:** SHAGGYMANE
**horsetail corn** *n* **:** INDIAN CORN
**horsetail family** *n* **:** EQUISETACEAE
**horsetail lichen** *n* **:** HORSEHAIR LICHEN
**horsetaillike** \'ˌ≈ˌ≈ˌ≈\ *adj* **:** resembling a plant of the genus *Equisetum*
**horsetail milkweed** *n* **:** WHORLED MILKWEED
**horsetail tree** *n* **:** a tree of the genus *Casuarina*; *esp* **:** a tree (*C. equisetifolia*) planted in the southern and southwestern U.S. that is used for windbreaks and planting on sand dunes and also as an ornamental
**horse thistle** *n* [ME *hors thistel*, fr. *hors* + *thistel* thistle] **:** PRICKLY LETTUCE
**horse thyme** *n*, *dial Eng* **:** WILD BASIL
**horse tick** *n* **1 :** a louse fly attacking horses — compare HIPPOBOSCIDAE **2 :** any tick attacking horses
**horse trade** *n* **1 :** a swap of horses usu. accompanied by bargaining and compromise **2 :** negotiation accompanied by shrewd bargaining and usu. by reciprocal concessions **:** practical compromise ⟨a political *horse trade*⟩ ⟨his *horse trades* with foreign governments have been masterpieces of commercial diplomacy —J.D.Ratcliff⟩
**horse–trade** \'ˌ≈ˌ≈\ *vi* [back-formation fr. *horse trading* & *horse trader*] **:** to engage in a horse trade
**horse trader** *n* **:** one who engages in horse trading
**horse trading** *n* **:** the act or practice or an instance of making a horse trade ⟨the . . . foreign ministers had finally gotten down to *horse trading* —*Newsweek*⟩ ⟨lively *horse trading* in . . . smoke-filled back rooms —*N. Y. Herald Tribune*⟩
**horse•tree** \'≈(ˌ)trē, -ˌtri\ *n*, *dial Eng* **:** WHIFFLETREE
**horse violet** *n* **:** BIRD'S-FOOT VIOLET
**horseweed** \'ˌ≈ˌ≈\ *n* **1 :** a common No. American weed (*Erigeron canadense*) with linear leaves and small discoid heads of yellowish flowers **2 :** HORSE BALM **3 :** GREAT RAGWEED **4 :** WILD LETTUCE 1b(3)
**¹horsewhip** \'ˌ≈ˌ≈\ *n* [¹*horse* + *whip*] **:** a whip for horses
**²horsewhip** \"\ *vt* **:** to flog with a horsewhip
**horsewoman** \'ˌ≈ˌ≈≈\ *n*, *pl* **horsewomen 1 :** a woman horseback rider **2 :** a woman skilled in riding horseback or in caring for or managing horses
**horsewood** \'ˌ≈ˌ≈\ *n* **:** SEA GRAPE 1b
**horse wrangler** *n* **:** a ranch hand who takes care of the saddle horses
**hors•ey** *also* **horsy** *pronunc at* ¹HORSE + ē *or* i\ *adj* **horsier**; **horsiest 1 :** relating to, resembling, or suggestive of a horse ⟨bounced the boy on his knee in a ~ manner —Wright Morris⟩ ⟨not ~ or masculine, but a woman of whom one could be proud —Kathleen Freeman⟩ **2 :** addicted to or having to do with horses or horse racing or characteristic of the manners, dress, or tastes of horsemen ⟨the ~ set⟩ ⟨a ~, flashy, tweedy sort of man —Lewis Mumford⟩
**hors•ford•ite** \'hȯ(r)sfə(r)ˌdīt\ *n* -s [Eben N. *Horsford* †1893 Am. chemist + E *-ite*] **:** a mineral $Cu_5Sb$ consisting of a massive silver-white copper antimony alloy (sp. gr. 8.8)
**hors•i•ly** *pronunc at* ¹HORSE + əlē *or* əli\ *adv* **:** in a horsey manner
**hors•i•ness** \-sēnəs, -sin-\ *n* -ES **:** the quality or state of being horsey
**horsing** *adj* [fr. pres. part. of ²*horse*] *of a mare* **:** being in heat
**horst** \'hȯ(ə)rst\ *n* -s [G, thicket, eyrie, horst, fr. OHG *hurst* thicket — more at HURST] **:** a tract or block of the earth's crust separated by faults from adjacent tracts or blocks that have been relatively depressed — compare GRABEN
**hort** *abbr* horticultural; horticulture
**hor•ta•tion** \hȯ(r)'tāshən\ *n* -s [L *hortation-*, *hortatio*, fr. *hortatus* (past part. of *hortari* to urge, exhort) + *-ion-*, *-io* -ion — more at YEARN] **:** EXHORTATION
**hor•ta•tive** \'hȯ(r)d·əd·iv\ *adj* [LL *hortativus*, fr. L *hortatus* + *-ivus* -ive] **:** giving exhortation **:** ADVISORY, EXHORTATIVE — **hor•ta•tive•ly** \-ə̇vlē\ *adv*
**hor•ta•to•ri•ly** \ˌ≈≈'tōrəlē\ *adv* **:** in a hortatory manner
**hor•ta•to•ry** \-d·əˌtōrē\ *adj* [LL *hortatorius*, fr. L *hortatus* + *-orius* -ory] **:** giving or characterized by exhortation **:** EXHORTATORY, HORTATIVE
**hor•tense blue** \'hȯrˌten(t)s-, ≈'≈-\ *n*, *often cap H* [prob. fr. the name *Hortense*] **:** PRUSSIAN BLUE 2
**hortense violet** *n*, *often cap H* [prob. fr. the name *Hortense*] **:** a moderate purple that is bluer and duller than heliotrope (sense 4a), bluer, lighter, and stronger than average amethyst, and bluer, stronger, and slightly lighter than manganese violet
**hor•ti•cul•tur•al** \ˌhȯ(r)d·əˌkəlch(ə)rəl, -)tə'-\ *adj* **1 :** relating to horticulture **2 :** produced under cultivation (as by breeding) — compare BOTANICAL — **hor•ti•cul•tur•al•ly** \-rəlē, -li\ *adv*
**horticultural bean** *n* **:** a shell bean characterized by pods splashed with carmine or red and white and by white or buff-colored seeds marked with red
**horticultural variety** *n* **:** a variety of plant that has originated under cultivation as distinct from a botanical variety
**hor•ti•cul•ture** \'hȯ(r)d·əˌkəlchə(r), -)tə,- *also* ˌ≈≈'≈≈\ *n* [L

*hortus* garden + E *-i-* + *culture* — more at YARD] **:** the cultivation of an orchard, garden, or nursery on a small or large scale **:** the science and art of growing fruits, vegetables, flowers, or ornamental plants — compare FLORICULTURE, OLERICULTURE, POMOLOGY
**hor•ti•cul•tur•ist** \ˌ≈≈'≈kəlch(ə)rəst\ *n* **:** a specialist in horticulture
**hor•ton•o•lite** \hȯ(r)'tänᵊlˌīt, 'hȯ(r)tᵊn-\ *n* -s [Silas R. *Horton*, 19th cent. Am. mineralogist + E *-o-* + *-lite*] **:** a mineral $(Fe,Mg,Mn)_2SiO_4$ of the olivine series consisting of a dark silicate of iron, magnesium, and manganese
**hor•to•ri•um** \hȯ(r)'tōrēəm, -tȯr-\ *n*, *pl* **hortoriums** \-ēəmz\ *or* **horto•ria** \-ēə\ [NL, fr. L *hortus* + *-orium* -ory] **:** an institution or museum for the collection, preservation, and study of horticultural specimens
**hor•tu•lan** \'hȯ(r)chələn\ *adj* [L *hortulanus*, fr. *hortulus* small garden (dim. of *hortus* garden) + *-anus* -an] **:** of or relating to a garden
**hortulan plum** *n* [NL *hortulana* (specific epithet of *Prunus hortulana*), fr. L, fem. of *hortulanus*] **:** a wild-goose plum (*Prunus hortulana*)
**hor•tus sic•cus** \ˌhȯ(r)d·ə(s)'sikəs\ *n* [NL, lit., dry garden] **:** a collection of dried botanical specimens **:** HERBARIUM
**hos** *pl of* HO
**ho•sack•ia** \hō'sakēə, -'za-\ *n*, *cap* [NL, fr. David *Hosack* †1835 Am. botanist + NL *-ia*] **:** a large genus of mostly western No. American herbs (family Leguminosae) having pinnate leaves, yellow or red flowers, and linear flat pods
**¹ho•san•na** \hō'zanə *sometimes* -zä- *or* -zȧ-\ *n* -s [ME *osanna*, fr. LL, fr. Gk *hōsanna*, fr. Heb *hōshīʿāh nnā* save now, we pray] **:** an expression of enthusiastic praise **:** ACCLAMATION ⟨the law was passed with a considerable fanfare of editorial ~*s* —Herbert Asbury⟩ ⟨men with loud ~*s* will confess her greatness —John Milton⟩ — used interjectionally as a cry of acclamation and adoration ⟨*hosanna!* Blessed be he who comes in the name of the Lord —Mk 11: 9 (RSV)⟩
**²hosanna** \"\ *vt* -ED/-ING/-S **:** to acclaim with or as if with shouts of "hosanna" **:** APPLAUD ⟨the act of him who has been ~*ed* as if he were a savior —Henry Angus⟩
**¹hose** \'hōz\ *n*, *pl* **hose** *or* **hoses** [ME, fr. OE *hosa* stocking, husk; akin to OS, OHG, & ON *hosa* leg covering, Gk *kystis* bladder, OE *hȳd* hide — more at HIDE] **1** *pl* **hose a** (1) **:** a cloth leg covering that reaches down to the ankle and sometimes covers the foot ⟨footless athletic ~ worn over socks are part of a baseball uniform⟩ (2) **:** STOCKING, SOCK ⟨a pair of ~⟩ — usu. used in pl. **b** (1) **:** a close-fitting garment similar to tights that covers the body from the waist to and sometimes including the feet and is usu. attached to a doublet by points ⟨eight times thrust through the doublet, four through the ~ —Shak.⟩ (2) **:** short breeches often reaching to the knee — see TRUNK HOSE **2** *now dial Brit* **:** a sheath enclosing an inflorescence (as a spathe or the ensheathing leaves about the developing spike of a cereal grass) **3** *pl sometimes* **hoses a :** a flexible tube (as of rubber, plastic, or fabric) for conveying fluids (as air, steam, powdered coal, or water from a faucet or hydrant) **b :** such a tube with nozzle and attachments **c :** the tubing as material **4 :** HOSEL

hose 3a

**²hose** \"\ *vt* -ED/-ING/-S [ME *hosen*, fr. *hose*, n.] **1** *archaic* **:** to provide with hose for the legs **2 a :** to spray or water with a hose ⟨~ the garden⟩ **b :** to wash or drench with water from a hose — usu. used with *down* ⟨the bridge . . . had been *hosed* down by the fire department —*N.Y.Times*⟩
**hose•bird** \'hōzˌbərd\ *n* [prob. alter. of *whore's brood*] *dial Eng* **:** RASCAL, RAPSCALLION
**hose bridge** *or* **hose jumper** *n* **:** a contrivance that permits traffic to pass over or under lines of fire hose
**hose cart** *or* **hose wagon** *also* **hose truck** *or* **hose carriage** *n* **:** a wheeled vehicle for carrying fire hose
**hose clip** *n* **:** a device for clamping or supporting a hose
**hose cock** *or* **hose bib** *n* **1 :** SILL COCK **2 :** PINCHCOCK
**hose company** *n* **:** a company of men who bring and manage hose in fire fighting
**hose–in–hose** \ˌ≈≈'≈\ *n* **:** a double flower in which one corolla appears to be within another (as in various daturas and primulas)
**ho•sel** \'hōzəl\ *n* -s [¹*hose* + *-el*] **:** a socket in the head of a golf club into which the shaft is inserted — see GOLF illustration
**hose•less** \'hōzləs\ *adj* **:** having no hose to wear
**hose•man** \-mən, -ˌman\ *n*, *pl* **hosemen :** one who uses, tends, or repairs hose; *esp* **:** a fireman who belongs to a hose company
**hos•en** \'hōzᵊn\ *now dial pl of* HOSE
**hose net** *n*, *chiefly Scot* **:** a fishnet shaped like a stocking
**hosepipe** \'ˌ≈ˌ≈\ *n* **:** HOSE 3
**ho•sha•na** *or* **ho•sha•nah** \hō'shä(ˌ)nä, -nə\ *n*, *pl* **hoshanoth** *or* **hosha•not** \-ˌnōt(h), -ōs\ [Heb *hōshīʿāh nnā*, lit., save now, we pray] **1 :** a cry of entreaty in the liturgical litany chanted in the synagogue on Sukkoth esp. during the processional circuits around the altar on Hoshana Rabbah **2 :** the prayer chanted on Hoshana Rabbah
**hoshana rab•bah** *or* **hoshanah rab•ba** \-'rä(ˌ)bä, -ˌbə\ *n*, *usu cap H&R* [Aram *hōshaʿnā rabbā*] **:** the 7th day of the Festival of Sukkoth observed on the 21st day of Tishri with special prayers and ceremonies in the synagogue by Orthodox and Conservative Jews
**ho•sier** \'hōzhə(r)\ *n* -s [ME *hosyere*, fr. *hose* + *-yere* -ier] **:** one who deals in hosiery
**ho•siery** \'hōzh(ə)rē, -ri, ÷ -z(ə)-\ *n* -ES *often attrib* [*hosier* + *-y*] **1 :** HOSE 1a **2** *chiefly Brit* **:** KNITWEAR
**hos•pice** \'häspəs\ *n* -s [F, fr. L *hospitium* hospitality, lodging, inn, fr. *hospit-*, *hospes* host, stranger, guest — more at HOST] **1 :** an establishment providing rest or entertainment for travelers; *esp* **:** one kept by a religious order **2 :** a lodging for students, young workers, or the underprivileged often maintained by a religious order — compare HOSTEL
**hos•pi•ta•ble** \hä'spid·əbəl, 'häˌspi|, |tə-, *also* 'häspə| *sometimes* hȯ's- *or* 'hȯ(ˌ)s- *or* hə'spi|\ *adj* [NL *hospitabilis*, fr. L *hospitare* to be a guest, lodge + *-abilis* -able] **1 a :** marked by or given to generous and cordial reception and entertainment of guests or strangers ⟨they are ~ . . . : give a guest everything, and leave him free to do as he likes —Bram Stoker⟩ ⟨this ~, talkative man who was everywhere bustling about, trying to be of service —O.E.Rölvaag⟩ **b :** promising or suggesting generous and cordial welcome and entertainment ⟨wrote off immediately on his return to his inn the most ~ of invitations —W.M.Thackeray⟩ ⟨small incommunicable mysteries . . . chambered in their inner hearts and guarded by their ~ faces —A.T.Quiller-Couch⟩ **c :** offering a pleasant or sustaining environment **:** not hostile ⟨hard sandstone ridges carry a soil sufficiently ~ for forest growth —*Amer. Guide Series: N.J.*⟩ ⟨the British Isles enjoy a ~ climate, but the British gardener does not have life too easy —Emily Hahn⟩ **2 :** marked by ready or willing receptivity (as of new ideas) **:** favorably disposed esp. to the new or strange ⟨keep the mind open and ~ to new evidence on any side of the question —W.J.Reilly⟩ ⟨freedom to inquire and teach . . . provides a climate more ~ to fresh vision —Sidney Hook⟩ **syn** see SOCIAL
**hos•pi•ta•ble•ness** *n* -ES *archaic* **:** the quality or state of being hospitable
**hos•pi•ta•bly** \-blē, -bli\ *adv* **:** in a hospitable manner
**¹hos•pi•tal** \'häl,spid·ᵊl\ |tᵊl *also* |ˌspə̇| *sometimes* 'hȯ|\ *n* -s *often attrib* [ME, fr. OF, fr. LL *hospitale*, fr. L, bedroom, fr. neut. of *hospitalis* of a guest, hospitable, fr. *hospit-*, *hospes* host, stranger, guest + *-alis* -al — more at HOST] **1** *archaic* **:** HOSPICE 1 ⟨an adjacent ~ founded by the princess . . . for the reception of pilgrims —Horace Walpole⟩ **2 :** a charitable institution for the needy, aged, infirm, or young; *specif* **:** one institution for the education of the young ⟨received his formal education at Christ's *Hospital* in London⟩ **3 a :** an institution or place where sick or injured persons are given medical or surgical care — usu. used Brit. without an article when the object of a preposition ⟨so badly wounded that he died in ~ —*Manchester Guardian Weekly*⟩ ⟨diagnosed frostbitten toes and removed him immediately to ~ —Alexander Tewnion⟩; compare CLINIC, MEDICAL CENTER, SANATORIUM **b :** a place for the care and treatment of sick or injured animals **4 :** a

workshop for the repair of any of various small objects ⟨a doll ~⟩ ⟨a fountain-pen ~⟩

**2hospital** *adj* [L *hospitalis*] *obs* **:** HOSPITABLE

**hospital apprentice** *n* **:** an enlisted man in the U. S. Navy training to be a hospitalman

**hospital bed** *n* **:** a bed with a frame in three sections equipped with mechanical spring parts that permit raising the head end, foot end, or middle as required

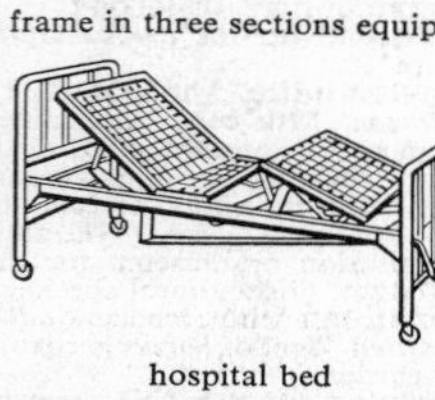

hospital bed

**hospital corpsman** *n* **:** a petty officer of the U.S. Navy performing general medical duties, giving first aid, and serving as a technician and assistant to the medical officer

**hos·pi·tal·er** *or* **hos·pi·tal·ler** *pronunc at* HOSPITAL + ə(r), ⸗'⸗⸗⸗\ *n* -s [ME *hospitalier, hospiteler*, fr. MF *hospitalier*, fr. ML *hospitalarius*, fr. LL *hospitale* hospice + L *-arius* -ary — more at HOSPITAL] **1** *usu cap* **:** a member of a religious military order established in Jerusalem in the 12th century and revived as an honorary society in 1879 by Leo XIII — called also *Knight of Malta, Knight of Rhodes, Knight of St. John of Jerusalem* **2 :** a member of any of numerous religious orders chiefly concerned with the care of the sick or needy **3 :** a chaplain of a London hospital

**hospital fever** *n* **:** typhus fever or fever associated with hospital gangrene prevalent in hospitals before the development of modern sanitation

**hospital gangrene** *n* **:** gangrene prevalent in crowded hospitals before the development of modern sanitation

**hos·pi·tal·ism** \-,lizəm\ *n* -s **1 a :** the factors and influences (as of system or custom) that adversely affect the health of hospitalized persons **b :** the effect of such factors on mental or physical health **2 :** the physical and mental effects on infants and children resulting from their living in foundling homes

**hos·pi·tal·i·ty** \,häspə'taləd·ē, -ətē, -i *sometimes* ,hȯs-\ *n* -ES [ME *hospitalite*, fr. MF *hospitalité*, fr L *hospitalitat-, hospitalitas*, fr. *hospitalis* of a guest, hospitable + *-itat-, -itas* -ity — more at HOSPITAL] **1 a :** the cordial and generous reception and entertainment of guests or strangers socially or commercially ⟨built a house, and later a tavern . . . whose ~ was known to thousands —*Amer. Guide Series: Vt.*⟩ ⟨the meaning of country ~ . . . extends far beyond threshold and board —Louise D. Rich⟩ **b :** an instance of hospitality — usu. used in pl. ⟨convivial and domestic *hospitalities* —R.W. Emerson⟩ **2 :** ready receptivity esp. to new ideas and interests ⟨hope to give ~ on my walls to new and promising American talent —Bennett Cerf⟩ ⟨the great tradition in poetry has always offered ungrudging ~ to ideas —J.L.Lowes⟩

**hos·pi·tal·iza·tion** \,⸗(,)⸗⸗ə'zāshən, -,ī'z-\ *n* -s **1 :** the act or process of being hospitalized ⟨pain persisted constantly through a two-day period, finally necessitating ~ —*Jour. Amer. Med. Assoc.*⟩ **2 :** the period of stay in a hospital ⟨drug treatment shortened the length of ~ —*Today's Health*⟩ ⟨entitled to ~ for two weeks —*Newsweek*⟩

**hospitalization insurance** *n* **:** insurance that provides benefits to cover or partly cover hospital expenses — see HOSPITAL SERVICE CONTRACT

**hos·pi·tal·ize** \'⸗(,)⸗⸗,īz\ *vt* -ED/-ING/-S **:** to place in a hospital as a patient — compare INSTITUTIONALIZE ⟨the child was *hospitalized* at once for diagnosis and treatment —*Jour. Amer. Med. Assoc.*⟩

**hospital light** *n* **:** HOPPER FRAME

**hos·pi·tal·man** \'⸗(,)⸗⸗ mən\ *n, pl* **hospitalmen :** an enlisted man in the U.S. Navy performing general medical duties

**hospital service contract** *n* **:** hospitalization insurance that provides for payment of actual hospital charges within specified limits as contrasted with cash benefits

**hospital ship** *n* **:** a ship equipped as a hospital; *esp* **:** one constructed or assigned specif. to assist the wounded, sick, and shipwrecked in time of war in accordance with international law

**hospital train** *n* **:** a railway train equipped for the transport of sick and wounded military personnel

**hos·pi·tious** \(')hä¦spishəs\ *adj* [L *hospiti*um hospitality, lodging, inn + E *-ous* — more at HOSPICE] *archaic* **:** HOSPITABLE

**hos·pi·ti·um** \hä'spishēəm, -id·ē-\ *n, pl* **hospi·tia** \-ēə\ [L] **1 :** HOSPICE 1 **2** *chiefly Brit* **:** HOSTEL 2a (1)

**hos·po·dar** \'häspə,där\ *n* -s [Romanian, fr. Ukrainian, fr. *hospod'* lord, master; akin to OSlav *gospodĭ, gospodinŭ* lord, master — more at GOSPODIN] **:** a governor of Moldavia and Walachia under Turkish rule

**1host** \'hōst\ *n* -s [ME *ost, oost, host, hoost*, fr. OF *ost, host*, fr. LL *hostis*, fr. L, stranger, enemy — more at GUEST] **1 :** a large number of men gathered for war **:** ARMY ⟨the destruction of Pharaoh's ~ in that sea —W.L.Sperry⟩ ⟨walls that must be directly stormed by the ~*s* of courage —A.E.Stevenson b.1900⟩ **2 a :** ANGELS ⟨a multitude of the heavenly ~ praising God —Lk 2:13 (RSV)⟩ **b :** the sun, moon, and stars ⟨all the ~ of heaven —Deut 4:19 (RSV)⟩ **3 :** a very large number **:** a great quantity **:** MULTITUDE, MYRIAD ⟨a whole ~ of children began to push at the door —Ernest Beaglehole⟩ ⟨hotel with its long lobbies filled with . . . ~*s* of rocking chairs —Marjory S. Douglas⟩ ⟨writing a ~ of accumulated book reviews —H.J.Laski⟩ ⟨a whole ~ of national monuments, military parks, memorials, and cemeteries —C.L.Wirth⟩

**2host** \"\ *vi* -ED/-ING/-S **:** to gather in a host **:** assemble usu. for a hostile purpose

**3host** \"\ *n* -s [ME *oste, hoste* host, guest, fr. OF, fr. L *hospit-, hospes* host, stranger, guest, fr. *hostis* stranger, enemy] **1 a :** INNKEEPER **b :** one who receives or entertains guests or strangers socially or commercially ⟨ourself will mingle with society and play the humble ~ —Shak.⟩ **2 a :** a living animal or plant affording subsistence or lodgment to a parasite — see ALTERNATE HOST, DEFINITIVE HOST, INTERMEDIATE HOST **b :** the larger, stronger, or dominant one of a commensal or symbiotic pair **c** (1) **:** an individual into which a tissue or part is transplanted from another (2) **:** an individual in whom an abnormal growth (as a cancer) is proliferating **3 :** a mineral or rock that is older than other minerals or rocks introduced into it or formed within or adjacent to it

**4host** \"\ *vb* -ED/-ING/-S [ME *osten, hosten*, fr *oste, hoste*, n.] *vi, obs* **:** LODGE ⟨go bear it to the Centaur, where we ~, and stay there —Shak.⟩ ~ *vt* **1 :** to receive or entertain socially **:** serve as host to ⟨will ~ the cadets during their visit —*Springfield (Mass.) Daily News*⟩ **2 a :** to receive or entertain guests at **:** serve as host at ⟨the garden party he had ~*ed* last spring —*Saturday Rev.*⟩ ⟨~*ed* the shower, at which 70 relatives were present to meet the bride —*Sacramento (Calif.) Bee*⟩ **b :** EMCEE ⟨successfully ~*ed* a series of television programs⟩

**5host** \"\ *n* -s [ME *oste, hoste*, fr. MF *osté, hosté*, back-formation fr. *ostez, hostez*, pl. of *ostel, hostel* — more at HOSTEL] *obs* **:** LODGING — used in the phrase *at host* ⟨lay at ~ . . . in the Centaur —Shak.⟩

**6host** \"\ *n* -s *usu cap* [ME *oste, hoste*, fr. MF *oiste, hoiste*, fr. LL & L; LL *hostia* Eucharist, fr. L, sacrifice] **1 :** the eucharistic wafer or bread before or after consecration **2** *obs* **:** SACRIFICE

**hos·ta** \'hōstə, 'häs-\ *n* [NL, after Nicolaus T. *Host* †1834 Austrian botanist] **1** *cap* **:** a genus of Asiatic perennial herbs (family Liliaceae) that have ribbed basal leaves often blotched or bordered with white and scapes of white, blue, or lilac flowers and that are widely cultivated as ornamentals **2** -s **:** any plant of the genus *Hosta*

**hos·tage** \'hästij, -tēj *sometimes* 'hȯs-\ *n* -s [ME *ostage, hostage*, fr. OF, fr. *oste, hoste* host, guest + *-age* — more at HOST] **1 a** *obs* **:** the state of a person given or kept as a pledge pending the fulfillment of an agreement, demand, or treaty ⟨if he stand in ~ for his safety —Shak.⟩ **b :** a person in such a state ⟨two boys . . . had been held as ~*s* for seven years —*N.Y. Times*⟩ **c :** a pledge, security, or guarantee usu. of good faith or intentions ⟨you know now your ~*s:* your uncle's word and my firm faith —Shak.⟩ **2** *archaic* **:** HOSTEL, INN **syn** see PLEDGE

**hos·tage·ship** \-,ship\ *n* -s **:** the quality or state of a hostage

**host·al** \'hōstᵊl\ *adj* [*3host* + *-al*] **:** relating to hosts ⟨a parasite with wide ~ range⟩

**1hos·tel** \'hästᵊl\ *n* -s [ME *ostel, hostel*, fr. OF, fr. LL *hospitale* hospice — more at HOSPITAL] **1 :** a public house for entertaining or lodging travelers **:** INN ⟨folks used to ride up the bumpy road . . . to dine at the little ~ —Hodding Carter⟩ **2 a** *chiefly Brit* **:** housing maintained by a public or private organization or institution: (1) **:** DORMITORY 2 (2) **:** a rest home or rehabilitation center for the chronically ill, the aged, or the physically handicapped (3) **:** living quarters for newly arrived immigrants **b :** one of a system of supervised inexpensive lodgings or shelters for use by youth esp. on hiking or bicycling trips — called also *youth hostel* **3** *obs* **:** TOWN HOUSE

**2hos·tel** \", *dial* -səl\ *vi* -ED/-ING/-S [ME *hostelen*, fr. *hostel*, n.] **: 1** *dial Eng* **:** LODGE **2 :** to travel usu. by foot or by bicycle staying at hostels overnight ⟨hundreds of outdoor-minded vacationers will ~ alone or in independent groups of two or three this summer —Phil Spelman⟩

**hos·tel·er** \-stələ(r), *in sense 1* " *or* -slə-\ *n* -s [ME *osteler, hosteler*, fr. OF *ostelier, hostelier*, fr. *ostel, hostel* + *-ier*] **1 :** one that lodges or entertains guests or strangers: **a :** the officer in charge of guests in a religious house **b** *archaic* **:** INNKEEPER **2 a :** one residing in a hostel **b :** one that goes hosteling

**hos·tel·ry** \'hästᵊlrē *sometimes* 'häsəl-\ *n* -ES [ME *ostelrie, hostelrie*, fr. MF *ostelerie, hostelerie*, fr. *ostel, hostel* + *-erie* -ery] **:** a place where food and lodging are available to the traveler **:** INN, HOTEL ⟨a large wooden-porched building with mansard roof is a typical ~ of the Civil War period —*Amer. Guide Series: Vt.*⟩

**1host·ess** \'hōstəs\ *n* -ES [ME *ostesse, hostesse*, fr. OF, fr. *oste, hoste* host, guest + *-esse* -ess — more at HOST] **1 :** a female innkeeper ⟨had a good understanding with the brother of mine ~ —Washington Irving⟩ **2 :** a woman who receives and entertains guests socially ⟨successful party giving amounts to little more than the friendly enthusiasm of the host and ~ —Emily Post⟩ **3 :** one whose job is to serve patrons: as **a :** a woman in charge of a public dining room who seats diners and ensures pleasant and efficient service **b :** a woman who directs social activities at a hotel or resort **c** (1) **:** a woman employed by a railroad or bus line to give personal service to passengers (2) **:** AIR HOSTESS **d :** a woman who acts as social partner in a dance hall or nightclub

**2hostess** \"\ *vb* -ED/-ING/-ES *vi* **:** to act as hostess ⟨had to arrange for the afternoon she was ~*ing* —W.L.George⟩ ~ *vt* **:** to serve as hostess at ⟨enjoyed ~*ing* the party⟩

**hostess cart** *n* **:** DINNER WAGON, TEA CART

**hostess gown** *n* **:** a dressy negligee or housecoat worn esp. for informal entertainment at home

**hostess house** *n* **:** an establishment at military installations for the lodging and entertainment of visitors

**host·ess–ship** \'hōstə(sh),ship, -təs,sh-\ *n* **:** the position or role of hostess

**1hos·tile** \'hä\|stᵊl *also* \|,stīl *or* \|(,)stil *sometimes* 'hȯ\|\ *adj* [MF or L; MF, fr. L *hostilis*, fr. *hostis* stranger, enemy + *-ilis* -ile — more at GUEST] **1 a :** of or relating to an enemy ⟨a ~ army⟩ ⟨~ territory⟩ ⟨turned the guns toward a ~ position⟩ **b :** marked by malevolence and a desire to injure ⟨might commit some ~ act, attempt to strike me or choke me —Jack London⟩ **c :** marked by antagonism or unfriendliness ⟨the instinct of Americans has always been ~ to the alignment of classes in political parties —H.S.Commager⟩ **d :** marked by resistance esp. to new ideas **:** unfavorable esp. to the new or strange ⟨are ~ to the idea of literature for the sake of enjoyment —M.R.Cohen⟩ **e :** offering an unpleasant or forbidding environment **:** not hospitable ⟨searching the ~ glaring desert for gold —*Amer. Guide Series: Ariz.*⟩ ⟨maps of the area indicated the ~ character of the land —C.L. Walker⟩ **2 a :** of or relating to an opposing party in a legal controversy ⟨~ claim⟩ **b :** adverse to the interests of an owner or possessor of property ⟨~ use⟩ ⟨~ title⟩ **c** *of a witness* **:** subject to cross-examination because of evident hostility shown during direct examination

**2hostile** \"\ *n* -s **:** one that is hostile; *esp* **:** an American Indian unfriendly to whites ⟨ought to have guessed the ~*s* would try to come in here —Alan LeMay⟩

**hostile embargo** *n* **:** a government's embargo on the movement of enemy ships — compare CIVIL EMBARGO

**hostile fire** *n* **:** a fire that is not confined in a receptacle specif. made to contain fire — used in fire-insurance contracts; compare FRIENDLY FIRE

**hos·tile·ly** \-tᵊl(l)\|ē, -tīll\|, -til(l)\|, \|i\ *adv* **:** in a hostile manner

**hos·tile·ness** \-ᵊlnəs, -īln-, -iln-\ *n* -ES **:** the quality or state of being hostile

**hostile possession** *n* **:** ADVERSE POSSESSION

**hos·til·i·ty** \hä'stiləd·ē, -ətē, -i *sometimes* hȯ'-\ *n* -ES [MF or LL; MF *hostilité*, fr. LL *hostilitat-, hostilitas*, fr. L *hostilis* + *-itat-, -itas* -ity] **1 a :** a hostile or antagonistic state ⟨the civilized south and the barbarous north stood in perpetual ~ —Kemp Malone⟩ **b** (1) **:** hostile action ⟨the Spanish expedition encountered ~ . . . and was forced to flee —R.W.Murray⟩ (2) **hostilities** *pl* **:** overt acts of warfare **:** WAR ⟨the outbreak of *hostilities*⟩ **2 :** antagonism, opposition, or resistance in thought or principle **:** ANIMOSITY ⟨there was tension, there was ~ and envy in the air —Theodor Reik⟩ ⟨~ to annexation has different grounds in different places —B.K.Sandwell⟩ **syn** see ENMITY

**hos·ti·mel·la** \,hästə'melə\ *n, cap* [NL, fr. *Hostim*, Czechoslovakia, its locality + NL *-ella*] **:** a form genus of fossil plants based on naked sporangia that are now commonly believed to be the fruiting structures of plants of the genus *Asteroxylon*

**host·ing** \'hōstiŋ\ *n* -s [ME, fr. *1host* + *-ing*] **1 a :** the mustering of armed men **b :** a hostile incursion or encounter ⟨strange to us it seemed . . . that angel should with angel war, and in fierce ~ meet —John Milton⟩ **2 :** GATHERING ⟨the good people who come out about this time of night to hold their ~ on the hills —O.S.J.Gogarty⟩

**hos·tler** \'(h)äslə(r) *sometimes* 'həs-\ *n* -s [ME *osteler, hosteler, hostler* innkeeper, hostler — more at HOSTELER] **1 a** *also* **os·tler** \'äs-\ **:** one who takes care of horses at an inn or stable **:** GROOM **b :** one who is in charge of the horses or mules used in an industry **:** STABLEMAN **2 a :** one who takes charge of a railroad locomotive after a run **:** one who moves and services locomotives in enginehouse or roundhouse territory **b :** one employed in the storage garage of a transportation company to assist with the moving about and servicing of trucks or buses **c :** a worker who cleans, oils, or otherwise services machines (as cranes, dinkeys, boilers) that are in almost constant use

**hostler's control** *n* **:** a simplified throttle provided to move the unit of a diesel locomotive not equipped with a regular engineer's control

**host·less** \'hōstləs\ *adj* [*3host* + *-less*] **:** having no host

**hos·tling** \'(h)äsliŋ *sometimes* 'həs-\ *n* -s [perh. alter. of *hosteling*, gerund of *2hostel*] **:** the act or process of handling a locomotive between runs that includes taking it to the enginehouse and delivering it to the road crew

**host·ly** \'hōstlē\ *adj* [*3host* + *-ly*] **:** of or appropriate to a host ⟨still so young-looking that people did not instinctively lay upon him ~ duties —John Updike⟩

**hos·try** \'hōstrē\ *n* -ES [ME *ostrie, hostrie*, fr. MF *osterie, hosterie*, fr. *oste, hoste* host, guest + *-erie* -ery — more at HOST] *archaic* **:** HOSTELRY

**hosts** *pl of* HOST, *pres 3d sing of* HOST

**1hot** \'hät, *usu* -äd·+V\ *adj* **hotter; hottest** [ME *hoot, hot*, fr. OE *hāt;* akin to OFris & OS *hēt* hot, OHG *heiz*, ON *heitr* hot, Goth *heito* fever, Lith *kaĩsti* to get hot] **1 :** having heat in a degree exceeding normal body heat **:** having a relatively high temperature **:** giving or capable of giving a sensation of heat **:** capable of burning, searing, or scalding ⟨~ stove⟩ ⟨~ forehead⟩ **2 a :** ARDENT, FIERY ⟨~ blood of youth⟩ ⟨~ tempers⟩ **:** VEHEMENT ⟨~ words were exchanged⟩ **b :** VIOLENT, RAGING ⟨~ battle⟩ **c :** URGENT, FEVERISH ⟨messengers sent in ~ haste⟩ **d** (1) *of an animal* **:** being in heat (2) **:** LUSTFUL, LECHEROUS **e :** ZEALOUS, EAGER ⟨~ for reform⟩ ⟨~ patriot⟩ ⟨~ baseball fan⟩ ⟨~ fisherman⟩ **f** (1) *of jazz* **:** ecstatic and emotionally exciting and usu. marked by complex rhythms and free contrapuntal improvisations on the melody — often contrasted with *sweet* (2) *of a jazz performer* **:** stimulated and inspired to complete rhythmic and melodic freedom **3 a :** having the sensation of an uncomfortable degree of body heat **:** too warm for comfort ⟨~ and tired⟩ ⟨I'm too ~ in this sweater⟩ **b :** causing discomfort or distress through excessive warmth or humidity ⟨~ climate⟩ ⟨this room is ~ and stuffy⟩ ⟨~ sunshine⟩ **c** (1) **:** naturally or constitutionally possessing heat — used in medieval physiology, natural philosophy, and astrology to name one of the qualities of the four elements (2) *of a sign of the zodiac* **:** having a hot complexion **4 a :** having or retaining the heat of cooking ⟨this pudding is best when served ~⟩ ⟨will you have ~ or iced coffee⟩ **b :** not yet grown cool or stale **:** newly made or received **:** FRESH ⟨news ~ from the press⟩ ⟨following a ~ scent⟩; *also* **:** close to something pursued or sought ⟨~ on the trail of the murderer⟩ ⟨guess again, you're getting *hotter*⟩ **c :** suggestive of heat ⟨~ smell of burning rubber⟩ ⟨~ sound of buzzing flies⟩ or of burning or glowing objects ⟨I like ~ colors . . . hot orange and red and shocking pink —Mitzi Gaynor⟩ **d** (1) *of type* **:** made by the casting of hot metal into a mold (2) **:** using type so made ⟨~ composition⟩ — compare COLD **e :** uncomfortable to an intolerable or dangerous degree **:** UNSAFE ⟨the police were making the town too ~ for him⟩ **5 :** PUNGENT, PEPPERY, BITING ⟨~ sauce⟩ ⟨~ pickles⟩ **6 :** showing energy or activity in an unusual degree: as **a :** of intense and immediate interest ⟨~ news story⟩ ⟨~ scandal⟩ **b :** unusually lucky or successful ⟨~ streak at poker⟩ or favorable ⟨the dice are ~ for me tonight⟩ **c :** temporarily capable of unusual performance (as in a sport) ⟨any one of half a dozen golfers might get ~ and win this tournament⟩ ⟨~ favorite in the race⟩ **d** *of merchandise or securities* **:** readily salable **:** enjoying current popularity ⟨~ items in women's wear⟩ **e** (1) **:** very good — used as a generalized term of approval ⟨a real ~ lawyer⟩ ⟨he's ~ in math⟩ (2) *slang* **:** ABSURD, UNBELIEVABLE ⟨wants to fight the champion? that's a ~ one⟩ **7 :** having or charged with high energy: as **a :** electrically charged; *esp* **:** charged with high voltage **b** *of a cartridge* **:** having a powder load which gives a high muzzle velocity and corresponding high chamber pressure and flat trajectory — used esp. of hand-loaded ammunition **c :** RADIOACTIVE ⟨~ material⟩; *also* **:** dealing with radioactive material ⟨~ laboratory⟩ **d** *of an airplane* **:** FAST; *esp* **:** characterized by a high landing speed **8 a :** stolen or otherwise illegally obtained ⟨~ jewels⟩ ⟨~ bonds⟩; *also* **:** CONTRABAND **b :** wanted by the police **:** fugitive from justice **c** *of a commodity* **:** prohibited by law or agreement from being shipped or handled ⟨~ oil⟩

**2hot** \"\ *adv* [ME *hoote, hote*, fr. OE *hāte*, fr. *hāt*, adj.] **:** HOTLY ⟨the sun shines ~ —Shak.⟩ ⟨*hot*-glowing coals⟩ ⟨took a club and gave it to him ~ and heavy⟩

**3hot** \"\ *n* -s [ME *hoot, hot*, fr. *hoot, hot*, adj.] **1** *dial* **:** HEAT **2 :** HOT DOG

**4hot** \"\ *vb* **hotted; hotted; hotting; hots** [*1hot*] *vi, chiefly Brit* **:** to become warm or heated — usu. used with *up* ⟨fresh air ~*s* up quickly⟩ ⟨the argument had *hotted* up considerably⟩ ~ *vt, chiefly Brit* **:** WARM, HEAT; *specif* **:** to warm over (food) — usu. used with *up* ⟨there's some stew and dumplings left I can ~ up in a minute —Victoria Lincoln⟩

**5hot** \"\ *n* -s [ME *hott*, fr. OF *hotte, hote*, of Gmc origin; akin to G dial. *hutte, hotte* basket, pannier, MHG *hotte, hotze* cradle — more at HOD] **1** *now dial Eng* **:** a basket for carrying earth or manure **2** *dial Brit* **:** a little heap or pile (as of manure) **3** *obs* **:** a padded sheath for the spur of a gamecock

**hot air** *n* **:** empty talk **:** unsubstantiated and often boastful statements ⟨used to talk a lot of *hot air* about medicine —A.J. Cronin⟩ ⟨threats both ways are just *hot air*, big talk and face saving —*Kiplinger Washington Letter*⟩

**hot–air engine** *n* **:** an engine using heated air as the working substance

**hot–air furnace** *n* **:** a heating unit enclosed in a casing from which warm air is circulated through the building in ducts by gravity convection or by fans

**hotbed** \'⸗,⸗\ *n* **1 :** a bed of soil enclosed in a low glass frame heated by fermenting manure or by other means and used for forcing or for raising early seedlings — compare COLD FRAME **2 :** a place or environment which favors rapid growth or development ⟨~ of crime⟩ **3 :** a frame or area in a rolling mill on which hot bars or rails are laid to cool

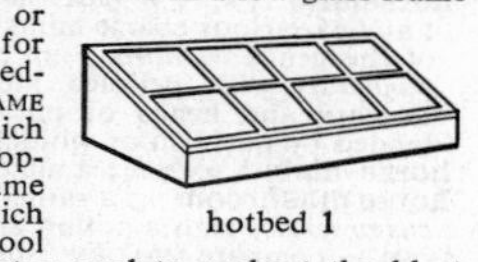

hotbed 1

**hot–blast stove** *n* **:** an apparatus used to preheat the blast for an iron blast furnace and consisting of firebrick passages which alternately receive heat from burning gas and then give up this heat to the incoming blast

**hotblood** \'⸗,⸗\ *n* **:** one that is hotblooded: as **a :** one having strong passions or a quick temper **b :** THOROUGHBRED 1b

**hot–blooded** \'⸗¦⸗⸗\ *adj* **1 :** having hot blood **:** EXCITABLE, HIGH-SPIRITED, ARDENT, PASSIONATE **2 a** *of a horse* **:** having Arab or Thoroughbred ancestors **b** *of a horse and other livestock* **:** of pure or superior breeding — **hot–blood·ed·ness** *n* -ES

**hotbox** \'⸗,⸗\ *n* **1 :** a journal bearing (as of a railroad car) overheated by friction **2 :** SWEATBOX 2

**hot–brain** \'⸗,⸗\ *n, archaic* **:** HOTHEAD

**hot–brained** \'⸗¦⸗\ *adj, archaic* **:** HOTHEADED

**hot bread** *n* **:** bread, rolls, biscuits, or muffins served still hot from baking — usu. used in pl.

**hot–bulb** \'⸗¦⸗\ *adj* **:** having an ignition system in which the charge is ignited by spraying it into a separate chamber kept above the ignition temperature of the charge by the heat of compression — used of a semidiesel engine

**hot buttered rum** *n* **:** a hot drink consisting of rum and water spiced and sweetened and served with a lump of butter floating on the surface

**hot cake** *n* **:** GRIDDLE CAKE

**hot cap** *n* **:** a paper or plastic cap set over growing plants in early spring for protection from frost

**hot–cathode** \'⸗¦⸗,⸗\ *adj* **:** operated by thermionic emission from a heated cathode ⟨*hot-cathode* tube⟩

**hotch** \'häch\ *vb* -ED/-ING/-ES [prob. fr. MF *hocher* to shake, fr. OF *hochier*, of Gmc origin; akin to MHG *hotteln, hotzeln* to shake — more at HOD] *vi* **1** *dial Brit* **:** to shake, jog, and wiggle **:** FIDGET **2** *dial Brit* **:** to change position or shift weight to make room **:** HITCH ~ *vt, chiefly Scot* **:** to cause to shake or shift

**hot·cha** \'hä(,)chä, -,chə\ *n* -s [prob. irreg. fr. *1hot*] *slang* **:** hot jazz ⟨band began to play the blatant ~ —John Fante⟩

**hot chisel** *n* **:** a chisel used in cutting hot metal

**hotch·pot** \'häch,pät\ *n* [ME *hochepot*, fr. MF, fr. OF, fr. *hochier* to shake + *pot* — more at HOTCH, POTAGE] **1 :** HOTCHPOTCH 1 **2 :** HODGEPODGE 1 **3** [AF *hochepot*, fr. OF, hotchpotch] **:** a throwing into a common lot of property for equality of division which requires that advancements to a child be made up to the estate by contribution or by an accounting **:** COLLATION 5

**hotch·potch** \-,päch\ *n* -ES [alter. of *hotchpot*] **1 a :** a thick soup of barley, peas, and other vegetables, and often also meat **b :** a stew of meat and vegetables **2** *chiefly Brit* **:** HODGEPODGE 1 **3 :** HOTCHPOT 3

**hot cockles** *n pl but sing in constr* **:** a game in which one player covers his eyes and tries to guess who strikes him

**hot corner** *n* **:** the fielding position of the third baseman in baseball

**hot cross bun** *n* **:** a raisin bun marked with a cross made of sugar frosting traditionally served on Good Friday

**hot deck** *n* **:** a pile of logs from which logs are hauled to the mill as soon as they are cut and yarded — compare COLD DECK

**hot dish** *n* **:** CASSEROLE 3 ⟨had a *hot dish* and salad for lunch⟩

**1hot dog** *n* [prob. so called fr. the fancied resemblance of a frankfurter to a dachshund] **:** a cooked frankfurter usu. served in a long split roll and garnished with mustard, onion, or other savory substance

**2hot dog** *interj* — used to express approval or gratification

**hot–draw** \'⸗,⸗\ *vt* **:** to draw (as metal or nylon) while hot or with application of heat

**1ho·tel** \(')hō¦tel\ *n* -s [F *hôtel*, fr. OF *ostel, hostel* — more at

HOSTEL] 1 *obs* : a city mansion of a person of rank or wealth 2 a : a house licensed to provide lodging and usu. meals, entertainment, and various personal services for the public : INN b : a building of many rooms chiefly for overnight accommodation of transients and several floors served by elevators, usu. with a large open street-level lobby containing easy chairs, with a variety of compartments for eating, drinking, dancing, exhibitions, and group meetings (as of salesmen or convention attendants), with shops having both inside and street-side entrances and offering for sale items (as clothes, gifts, candy, theater tickets, travel tickets) of particular interest to a traveler, or providing personal services (as hairdressing, shoe shining), and with telephone booths, writing tables, and washrooms freely available

²**hotel** \"\ *vt* **hotelled; hotelled; hotelling; hotels** : to lodge at a hotel

³**hotel** \"\ *usu cap* — a communications code word for the letter *h*

**hotel car** *n* : a railroad car with facilities for preparing and serving food and for sleeping

**hô·tel de ville** \(,)(h)ō,teldə'vēl\ *n, pl* **hôtels de ville** \-l(z)d-\ [F] : a town hall in France and other European countries

**ho·tel dieu** \l'dyə(r), -yō\ *n, pl* **hotels dieu** \-l(z)'d-\ *cap D* [F *hôtel-Dieu*, fr. OF *ostel Dieu*, fr. *ostel, hostel* hostel, hospice + *Dieu* God, fr. L *deus* — more at HOSTEL, DEITY] : a medieval hospital

**ho·tel·dom** \hō'teldəm\ *n* -s : hotels and hotel workers ⟨you can't talk connectedly to anybody except . . . to a minor part of ~ and of officialdom —Laura Z. Hobson⟩

**ho·tel·ier** \,ōtel'yā\ *n* -s [F *hôtelier*, fr. OF *ostelier, hostelier* — more at HOSTELER] : HOTELKEEPER

**hotelkeeper** \(')≈'≈,≈≈\ *n* : a proprietor or manager of a hotel

**ho·tel·less** \hō'tel\|əs\ *adj* : lacking a hotel ⟨some parts of the country are nearly ~⟩

**hotel lock** *n* : a knob lock that can be operated by a master key

**ho·tel·man** \(')≈'≈mən, -,man\ *n, pl* **hotelmen** : HOTELKEEPER

**hotel rack** *n* : the unsplit rib section of a foresaddle of lamb

**hot flash** *or* **hot flush** *n* : a sudden usu. brief sensation of heat and reddening of the skin accompanying sudden dilation of skin capillaries usu. associated with endocrine imbalance esp. that accompanying menopause

¹**hotfoot** \'hät,fu̇t, *usu* -üd-+V\ *adv* [ME *hot fot*] : in haste : without delay : HASTILY ⟨sent ambassadors ~ to the Turk —Francis Hackett⟩ ⟨drove his vessel ~ for the Boston pier —Mary H. Vorse⟩

²**hotfoot** \"\ *vi* : to go hotfoot : HASTEN, HURRY — used with *it* ⟨~*ing it* north . . . with a Texas posse on its heels —W.F. Harris⟩ ~ *vt* : to give (someone) a hotfoot : ANNOY, GOAD

³**hotfoot** \"\ *n* -s [¹*hot* + *foot*] 1 : a practical joke in which a match is surreptitiously inserted in the side of a victim's shoe and lighted 2 a : a stinging rebuke : INSULT, TAUNT ⟨administers one intellectual ~ after another to the Philistine public —Edgar Johnson⟩ b : GOAD, SPUR ⟨has given tradition-bound Baltimore a ~ —*Newsweek*⟩

**hot-galvanize** \'≈'≈,≈\ *vt* : to galvanize by dipping in molten zinc

**hot-gospeler** \'≈'≈≈≈\ *n* : an evangelical preacher : REVIVALIST

**hothead** \'≈,≈\ *n* : a hotheaded person

**hotheaded** \'≈'≈≈\ *adj* 1 : having a hot head (as from drinking) 2 : FIERY, HASTY, IMPETUOUS — **hot·head·ed·ly** *adv* — **hot·head·ed·ness** *n* -ES

**hothearted** \'≈'≈≈\ *adj* : HOTHEADED

¹**hothouse** \'≈,≈\ *n* [¹*hot* + *house*] 1 *obs* : TURKISH BATH 2 *obs* : BROTHEL 3 : a room or building kept heated for drying something (as green pottery) 4 : a greenhouse maintained at a high temperature for the culture of tender or tropical plants and other plants (as cucumbers and tomatoes) requiring such a temperature 5 : SWEAT HOUSE 1 6 : HOTBED 2 ⟨the prose is a ~ of clichés —*New Yorker*⟩ ⟨the great city is . . . a ~ of decadence and of every perversion —François Bondy⟩

²**hothouse** \"\ *adj* 1 : grown in a hothouse : artificially cultivated ⟨~ grapes⟩ 2 : having the qualities of a plant raised in a hothouse : lacking normal resistance to cold or adversity : SOFT, DELICATE, DECADENT ⟨~ voluptuousness⟩ ⟨her father . . . was a brittle, ~ sort of creature —Frederick Prokosch⟩

**hothouse lamb** *n* : the meat of a lamb born out of the normal lambing season and usu. marketed during the period from January to March

**ho·tis test** \'hōd·əs-\ *n, usu cap H* [after R. P. *Hotis* †1935 Amer. agricultural marketing specialist] : a test for the presence of the common streptococcus of bovine mastitis in milk made by incubating a sample of milk with the aniline dye bromcresol purple, the appearance of yellow patches or coloration being indicative of the presence of the organism

**hot lead** *n* : fired bullets : GUNFIRE ⟨settled arguments with *hot lead*⟩

**hot logging** *n* : logging in which the logs are taken from stump directly to stream landing or mill — compare COLD DECK

**hot·ly** *adv* : in a hot or fiery manner : ARDENTLY, EAGERLY, PUNGENTLY, VIOLENTLY, HASTILY, LUSTFULLY

**hotmelt** \'≈,≈\ *n* : a fast-drying nonvolatile adhesive made of synthetic resins and plasticizers and applied hot in the molten state

**hot money** *n* : money of foreign ownership deposited or invested to avoid depreciation and constituting a threat to national currency and credit by being liable to sudden withdrawal — called also *funk money*

**hot·ness** *n* -ES 1 : the quality or state of being hot : the sensation of heat 2 : TEMPERATURE ⟨a thermometer measures the ~ of an object⟩

**hot-not** \'hät,nät\ *n* -s *usu cap* [Afrik] *Africa* : HOTTENTOT

**hot oven** *n* : a baking oven heated to a temperature between 400° and 450° F

**hot pack** *n* : absorbent material (as a blanket or squares of gauze) wrung out in hot water, wrapped around the body or a portion of the body, and covered with dry material to hold in the moist heat ⟨*hot pack* for an infected arm⟩

**hot-pack method** *n* : a method of canning in which food is partly cooked in an open kettle before being put in containers and then sterilized as in the cold-pack method

**hot pants** *n pl* : EAGERNESS, IMPETUOSITY; *esp* : impatient sexual desire ⟨still got *hot pants* for her, if you want to call that love —Mary McCarthy⟩

**hot papa** *n, slang* : HOT SUITMAN

**hot pepper** *n* 1 : any of various capsicum fruits (as cayenne) that contain significant amounts of capsaicin, are characterized by marked pungency, usu. have rather thin walls, and vary in form from spherical to greatly elongated — compare SWEET PEPPER 2 : a plant (as a bird pepper or cone pepper) that bears hot peppers

**hot plate** *n* 1 : a heated iron plate (as on a cooking range) for cooking or for keeping food warm 2 : a simple portable gas or electric heater for heating liquids or laboratory materials or for cooking in limited spaces 3 : a food plate with a hot-water jacket for keeping food warm (as for infants or invalids)

**hot pond** *n* : a log pond kept open by means of hot water and steam

**hot pot** *n* : a stew of meat and vegetables

**hot potato** *n* : a question or issue that involves unpleasant or dangerous consequences for anyone dealing with it ⟨bingo parties and church raffles have . . . developed into such a *hot potato* that everyone concerned now is seeking some easy solution —*N.Y. Times*⟩

hot plates: electric, *A*; gas, *B*

¹**hot-press** \'≈'≈\ *n* 1 : a calendering machine in which paper or cloth is glossed by being pressed between glazed boards and hot metal plates 2 : a hydraulic oil press in which the contents are kept hot by steam radiators

²**hot-press** \'≈'≈\ *vt* 1 : to gloss (paper or cloth) or to express (oil) by combined heat and pressure 2 : to press (wood or metal) while hot

**hot press** *n, Brit* : a small heated room for drying laundry

**hot-presser** \'≈,≈≈\ *n* : one that operates a hot-press

**hot pursuit** *n* : fresh pursuit esp. across state or territorial lines

**hot-quench** \'≈'≈\ *vt* : to quench (a metal) in a hot bath (as of molten salt, lead, or oil)

**hot rock** *n* : a highly skilled or daredevil airplane pilot

**hot rod** *n* : an automobile rebuilt or modified for high speed and fast acceleration

**hot rod·der** \-'rädə(r)\ *n* 1 : a hot-rod driver, builder, or enthusiast 2 : one who drives a car in a showy or reckless manner

**hot roll** *n, West* : BEDROLL

**hot-roll** \'≈'≈\ *vt* : to roll (metal) while hot or with the application of heat — compare COLD-ROLL

**hots** *pl of* HOT, *pres 3d sing of* HOT

**hot saw** *n* : a power saw for cutting hot metal — distinguished from *cold saw*

**hot seat** *n* 1 *slang* : ELECTRIC CHAIR 2 : a position of uneasiness or embarrassment or anxiety : a position involving oppressive responsibility ⟨on the *hot seat*, directing a half-million dollar gamble —Mark Stroock & Percy Knauth⟩ ⟨kept Iran on a political *hot seat* —*Armed Forces Talk*⟩ 3 *slang* : an ejection seat in an airplane

**hot-short** \'≈'≈\ *adj, of metal* : short or brittle when heated beyond a red heat — compare COLD-SHORT, RED-SHORT — **hot-short·ness** *n*

**hot shot** *n* : shot heated to redness in order to set fire to buildings or ships

¹**hotshot** \'≈,≈\ *n* [¹*hot* + *shot*] 1 a : a fast freight usu. hauling merchandise or perishables in scheduled service b : a very fast airplane or vehicle 2 *slang* : a skillful, showy, and aggressive person; *esp* : one holding a position of importance by exercise of skill, showiness, and aggression 3 a : a skilled workman b : a skilled performer in a sport (as golf, basketball, baseball) that involves shooting or aiming 4 : FIRE FIGHTER

²**hotshot** \"\ *adj* 1 *slang* : highly skilled, fast-working, or showy; *also* : important or successful by exercise of skill, adroitness, or showiness ⟨a ~ surgeon with more business than he can handle⟩ 2 *of a freight carrier* : NONSTOP, THROUGH, FAST ⟨a ~ freight train⟩

**hot slaw** *n* : coleslaw prepared with a cooked dressing

**hot spot** *n* 1 : a place that is hotter than the surrounding surface: as a : a spot in the intake manifold of an internal-combustion engine which is heated by the exhaust gases to aid in the vaporization of the fuel b : an overheated spot in the combustion chamber tending to cause preignition c : a place in the shell of a furnace hotter than the rest d : an uncooled portion of a combustion chamber against which a charge is sprayed for ignition in a semidiesel engine 2 : a region of high forest-fire frequency 3 a : an area in a plastered wall containing alkaline salts that cause paper and paints to discolor b : an area on a negative or print representing excessive illumination of a part of the subject c : an area of excessive illumination (as on a subject or on the easel of an enlarger) in a pictorial reproduction 4 : a center of night life : NIGHTCLUB

**hot-spot** \'≈,≈\ *vt* [*hot spot*] : to check a forest fire at hot spots

**hot spring** *n* : THERMAL SPRING; *esp* : a spring with water above 98° F

**hotspur** \'≈,≈\ *n* [ME *hatspore*, fr. *hat, hoot, hot* hot + *spore* spur — more at HOT, SPUR] : a rash hotheaded impetuous man

**hot stove league** *n* : sports followers (as of baseball) gathering for off-season discussion ⟨first place a baseball fan might look for some good, between-seasons, *hot stove league* reading —J.K.Hutchens⟩

**hot stuff** *n, slang* : something or someone unusually good or extraordinary or formidable ⟨in surf casting . . . the man who can average one hundred yards is *hot stuff* —*Fisherman's Encyc.*⟩

**hot stuff man** *n* : a bakery worker who removes baked goods from pans

**hot suit·man** \-'sütmən\ *n, pl* **hot suitmen** : a man esp. equipped to rescue the crew of a burning airplane

**hot-swage** \'≈'≈\ *vt* : to swage (metal) while hot

**hot-sy-tot-sy** \,hätsē'tätsē\ *adj* [coined *ab*1926 by Billie De Beck †1942 Am. cartoonist] *slang* : comfortably stable or secure : PERFECT, OK ⟨had a quarrel, but everything is *hotsy-totsy* now⟩

**hott** \'hät\ *var of* ⁵HOT

**hotted** *past of* HOT

**hot-tempered** \'≈'≈≈\ *adj* : having a quick or violent temper

**hot·ten** \'hät³n\ *vb* -ED/-ING/-S [¹*hot* + *-en*] *vt, dial* : HEAT ⟨~ the soup, ma⟩ ~ *vi, dial* : to grow hot : become angry or lively ⟨warmed and then ~*ed* to his subject —Adria Langley⟩

**hot·ten·tot** \'hät³n,tät, *usu* -äd-+V\ *n* -s [Afrik *Hottentot, Hotnot*] 1 *usu cap* a : a people of southern Africa apparently akin to both the Bushmen and the Bantus and having moderately negroid features, typically very long heads, and prominent buttocks — see GRIQUA, NAMA b : a member of such people 2 *usu cap* : the Khoisan language of the Hottentot people 3 : a common So. African marine sparid food fish (*Pachymetopon blochii*)

**hottentot apron** *n, usu cap H* : an excessive development of the labia minora occurring in Hottentot women

**hottentot bread** *or* **hottentot's bread** *n, usu cap H* 1 : ELEPHANT'S-FOOT 1 2 : the thick edible rootstock of elephant's-foot

**hottentot bustle** *n, usu cap H* : STEATOPYGIA

**hottentot fig** *or* **hottentot's fig** *n, usu cap H* : a low-growing woody southern African perennial (*Carpobrotus edulis*) of the family Aizoaceae that has angular stems, opposite succulent leaves united at the base, and large yellow or purplish rose flowers, that is cultivated as a ground cover, and that sometimes occurs as an escape in the southwestern U.S.

¹**hotter** *comparative of* HOT

²**hot·ter** \'hätə(r\ *vi* -ED/-ING/-S [perh. fr. Flem *hotteren* to shake; akin to MHG *hotteln, hotzeln* to shake — more at HOD] 1 *dial Brit* a : to shake esp. with rage or laughter b : to move shakily : JOLT c : to crowd together in confusion 2 *dial Brit* a : RUMBLE ⟨~*ing* thunder⟩ b : to talk incoherently : MUTTER, MUMBLE, STAMMER

³**hotter** \"\ *n* -s 1 *dial Brit* : the act or motion of hottering 2 *dial Brit* : a swarm or heap of things

**hottest** *superlative of* HOT

**hotting** *pres part of* HOT

**hot·tish** \'häd·ish\ *adj* : somewhat hot

**hot·to·nia** \hä'tōnēə\ *n, cap* [NL, fr. Peter *Hotton* †1709 Dutch botanist + NL *-ia*] : a genus of aquatic herbs (family Primulaceae) with submerged crowded leaves and small white or purplish racemose flowers — see FEATHERFOIL

**hot top** *n* : a feedhead for an ingot mold

**hot-trod** \'≈,≈\ *n* 1 *Scot* : the pursuit with hounds and horn in old border forays 2 *Scot* : the signal for such pursuit

**hot up** *vi* 1 : to grow hot, lively, or exciting ⟨the gossip began to *hot up* —*Life*⟩ 2 : to speed up ⟨the air raids began to *hot up* about the beginning of February —George Orwell⟩ ~ *vt* 1 : AROUSE, ANNOY ⟨getting him all *hotted up* —Lord Beaverbrook⟩ 2 : to make livelier or speedier ⟨a protest against . . . the genteel *hotting up* of Shakespearean productions robbed of all poetry —Stephen Spender⟩

**hot-walker** \'≈,≈≈\ *n* : one employed to cool out horses ⟨got odd jobs as a *hot-walker* and exercise boy —*Time*⟩

**hot wall** *n* : a wall provided with heating flues for hastening the growth or ripening of fruit

**hot war** *n* : an armed conflict : a shooting war — compare COLD WAR

**hot water** *n* : a dangerous or distressing predicament : TROUBLE, DIFFICULTY ⟨primitive people take exception to a camera . . . so that indiscriminate snap shooting has landed more than one explorer in *hot water* —W.W.Howells⟩

**hot-water bag** *or* **hot-water bottle** *n* 1 : a stoppered rubber bag or earthenware bottle filled with hot water to provide warmth 2 *Brit* : HEATING PAD ⟨electric *hot-water bottles*⟩

**hot-water heating** *n* : central heating by means of hot water circulated through pipes or radiators

**hot-water treatment** *n* : a treatment of plants or plant parts for the eradication of parasites (as loose smut of wheat) involving immersion in water at a temperature above the thermal death point of the parasite but below that of the host

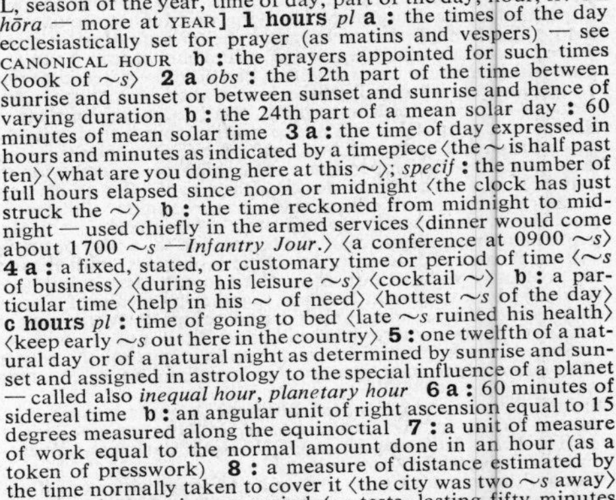

hot-water bag

**hot wave** *n* : a period of relatively high temperatures; *specif* : one caused by the southerly winds in front of an advancing cyclone or by the accumulating heat in a stagnant anticyclone — called also *heat wave*

**hot well** *n* 1 : HOT SPRING 2 : a reservoir in a condensing steam-engine or turbine installation for receiving the warm condensed steam drawn from the condenser

**hot-wire** \'≈'≈\ *adj* : operated by the thermal expansion of a wire through which an electric current is passed or by the convective cooling (as by air) of a wire heated by passage through it of an electric current, the expansion or contraction of the wire usu. deflecting a pointer ⟨*hot-wire* ammeter⟩ ⟨*hot-wire* anemometer⟩

**hot-work** \'≈'≈\ *vt* : to roll, forge, press, or shape (metal) while hot

**hou·ba·ra** \hü'bärə\ *n* -s [Ar *ḥubārā* bustard] : a bustard (*Chlamydotis undulata* syn. *Houbara undulata*) of northern Africa or its eastern form (*C. u. macqueenii*) found in Persia, India, and sometimes in England — called also *ruffed bustard*

**houdah** *var of* HOWDAH

**hou·dan** \'hü,dan, ü'dä"\ *n* -s *usu cap* [F, fr. *Houdan*, village in northern France where it was developed] : a domestic fowl of a French breed of medium size with a V-shaped leaf comb, mottled black-and-white or pure-white plumage and crest, and five toes

**hou·die** \'hau̇di\ *var of* HOWDIE

**hou·dry process** \'hüdrē-\ *n, usu cap H* [after Eugene *Houdry* b1892 Am. engineer] : a cracking process for making high-octane gasoline by passing oil vapors through a fixed bed of an aluminum silicate catalyst in the form of pellets

**houf** \'hau̇f\ *var of* HOWF

¹**hough** \'häk, 'hōk\ *n* -s [ME *hoch, hough* — more at HOCK] *chiefly Scot* : ⁴HOCK

²**hough** \"\ *vt* -ED/-ING/-S [ME *houghen*, fr. *hough*, n.] *now chiefly Scot* : HAMSTRING ⟨thou shalt ~ their horses, and burn their chariots —Josh 11:6 (AV)⟩

**hough·er** \'häkə(r)\ *n* -s : one that hamstrings cattle; *specif* : one of a band of lawbreakers in Ireland that hamstrung cattle

**hough·ma·gan·dy** \,häkmə'gandi\ *n* -ES [perh. irreg. fr. ¹*hough* + *canty*] *Scot* : FORNICATION

**hou·here** \hō'herə\ *n* -s [Maori] 1 *NewZeal* : RIBBONWOOD 1 2 *NewZeal* : RIBBON TREE

**hounce** \'hau̇n(t)s\ *n* -s [origin unknown] *dial Eng* : an ornament on the collar of a cart horse

¹**hound** \'hau̇nd\ *n* -s [ME, fr. OE *hund*; akin to OHG *hunt* dog, ON *hundr*, Goth *hunds*, L *canis*, Gk *kyōn*, Skt *śvā*] 1 a : DOG b : a dog of any of various breeds used in the chase that have typically large drooping ears and a deep voice and follow their prey by scent c *Brit* : FOXHOUND 2 : a mean or despicable person ⟨that low-down, sneaking ~⟩ 3 a : DOGFISH 1 b *Newfoundland* : OLD-SQUAW 4 : one of the chasers in the game hare and hounds 5 : one closely attached to a habit or pursuit : ADDICT ⟨autograph ~⟩ ⟨an expert lens ~ —H.H.Miller⟩ — often used in combinations ⟨booze*hound*⟩ ⟨chow*hound*⟩

²**hound** \"\ *vt* -ED/-ING/-S [ME (Sc dial.) *hounden*, fr. *hound*, n.] 1 a : to hunt, chase, or track with hounds or as if with hounds b : to pursue unrelentingly ⟨was ~*ed* by his creditors⟩ : heckle or harass unceasingly ⟨~*ed* from office by the press⟩ 2 : to set on the chase : incite to pursuit ⟨~ a dog at a hare⟩ — often used with *on* ⟨~ on pursuers⟩ **syn** see BAIT

³**hound** \"\ *n* -s [ME *hune, hownde*, of Scand origin; akin to ON *hūnn* cube, knob at the top of a masthead, young of an animal, bear cub — more at CAVE] 1 **hounds** *pl* : the framing at the masthead of a ship for supporting the heel of the topmast and the upper parts of the lower rigging 2 : a sidebar connecting the tongue of a wagon with the forecarriage or the reach with the hind carriage in order to give additional rigidity to those parts

**hound band** *n* : an iron band at the mast hounds of a ship for attaching the shrouds

**hound color** *n* : a color pattern typical of hound breeds and consisting of black and tan distributed in clearly defined patches on a white ground

**hound dog** *n, chiefly South* : HOUND

**hound·er** \'hau̇ndə(r)\ *n* -s : one that hounds

**houndfish** \'≈,≈\ *n* [ME, fr. *hound* + *fish*] 1 : DOGFISH 1 2 : NEEDLEFISH

**hound·ing** \'hau̇ndiŋ\ *n* -s [³*hound* + *-ing*] : the portion of a mast between the hounds and deck or of a bowsprit between the cap and gammon iron

**hound·ish** \'hau̇ndish\ *adj* : of, relating to, or having the characteristics of a hound ⟨a mongrel with a vaguely ~ look⟩

**houndman** \'hau̇n(d)mən\ *n, pl* **houndmen** : a keeper of hounds

**hound-marked** \'≈'≈\ *adj* : marked with hound color

**hound music** *n* : the baying of hounds on a scent

**houndsbane** \'hau̇n(d)z,≈\ *n* -s : HOREHOUND

**houndsberry** *n* [ME *houndesberye*, fr. *hound* + *berye* berry — more at BERRY] 1 *obs* : BLACK BRYONY 2 *obs* : BLACK NIGHTSHADE

**houndsfoot** \'≈,≈\ *n* -s [¹*hound* + *foot*; intended as trans. of G *hundsfott* or D *hondsvot*, lit., dog's vulva] *archaic* : a worthless rascal

**houndshark** \'≈,≈\ *n* : DOGFISH 1

**hound's-tongue** \'≈,≈\ *n, pl* **hound's-tongues** [ME *hundestunge*, fr. OE, fr. *hund* dog + *tunge* tongue — more at HOUND, TONGUE] 1 : any of various coarse plants of the genus *Cynoglossum* (esp. *C. officinale*) having tongue-shaped leaves and reddish flowers succeeded by nutlets covered with barbed prickles 2 : YELLOW CLINTONIA

**houndstooth check** *or* **hound's-tooth check** \'≈,≈-\ *n* : a small broken-check pattern; *also* : a fabric woven in this pattern

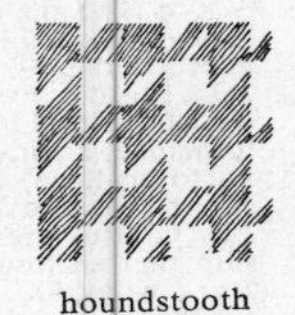

houndstooth check

**houndy** \'hau̇ndē\ *adj* : HOUNDISH

**houpe** *var of* ⁴HOOP

**houp-la** *var of* HOOPLA

**houppe·lande** \'hü,pländ, ≈'≈\ *n* -s [F, fr. OF *hoppelande*] : a loose belted overgown of the 14th and 15th centuries usu. with long wide sleeves, dagged edges, a fur lining, and full-length skirt often with slits in it

**hour** \'au̇(ə)r, 'au̇ə, *esp in the South* 'au̇wə(r\ *n* -s [ME *our, hour*, fr. OF *ore, ure, hore, hure, heure*, fr. L & L; LL *hora* canonical hour, fr. L, season of the year, time of day, part of the day, hour, fr. Gk *hōra* — more at YEAR] 1 **hours** *pl* a : the times of the day ecclesiastically set for prayer (as matins and vespers) — see CANONICAL HOUR b : the prayers appointed for such times ⟨book of ~s⟩ 2 a *obs* : the 12th part of the time between sunrise and sunset or between sunset and sunrise and hence of varying duration b : the 24th part of a mean solar day : 60 minutes of mean solar time 3 a : the time of day expressed in hours and minutes as indicated by a timepiece ⟨the ~ is half past ten⟩ ⟨what are you doing here at this ~⟩; *specif* : the number of full hours elapsed since noon or midnight ⟨the clock has just struck the ~⟩ b : the time reckoned from midnight to midnight — used chiefly in the armed services ⟨dinner would come about 1700 ~s —*Infantry Jour.*⟩ ⟨a conference at 0900 ~s⟩ 4 a : a fixed, stated, or customary time or period of time ⟨~ of business⟩ ⟨during his leisure ~s⟩ ⟨cocktail ~⟩ b : a particular time ⟨help in his ~ of need⟩ ⟨hottest ~s of the day⟩ c **hours** *pl* : time of going to bed ⟨late ~s ruined his health⟩ ⟨keep early ~s out here in the country⟩ 5 : one twelfth of a natural day or of a natural night as determined by sunrise and sunset and assigned in astrology to the special influence of a planet — called also *inequal hour, planetary hour* 6 a : 60 minutes of sidereal time b : an angular unit of right ascension equal to 15 degrees measured along the equinoctial 7 : a unit of measure of work equal to the normal amount done in an hour (as a token of presswork) 8 : a measure of distance estimated by the time normally taken to cover it ⟨the city was two ~s away⟩ 9 a : a class session or period ⟨~ tests, lasting fifty minutes each, are given several times during the semester⟩ b : CREDIT HOUR, SEMESTER HOUR ⟨three-*hour* course⟩ — **after hours** *adv* 1 a : after the close of the regular working day ⟨worked on his invention at home *after hours*⟩ b : after classroom hours 2 : after the legal closing time set for a public place (as a saloon) — **on the hour** *adv* : at exactly the full hour ⟨from 8 a.m. to 10 p.m. trains leave every hour *on the hour*⟩

**hour·age** \'au̇(ə)rij\ *n* -s **:** aggregate working or traveling time in hours

**hour angle** *n* **:** the angle between the celestial meridian of an observer and the hour circle of a celestial object measured westward from the meridian — compare MERIDIAN ANGLE

**hour circle** *n* **1 :** a circle of the celestial sphere passing through the two poles **2 :** the circle upon an equatorial telescope mounted perpendicular to the polar axis and graduated in hours and subdivisions of hours of right ascension **3 :** a small metal circle attached to the pole of an artificial globe and divided into 24 parts to mark differences of time at different places

**¹hourglass** \'ˌ=\ *n* [*hour* + *glass*] **1 :** an instrument for measuring time consisting of a glass vessel having two symmetrical compartments from the uppermost of which a quantity of sand, water, or mercury occupies an hour in running through a small aperture into the lower one and an hour returning when the instrument is turned upside down **2 :** the space of time measured by an hourglass

hourglass

**²hourglass** \"\ *adj* **:** shaped like an hourglass ⟨~ waistline⟩ ⟨~ contraction of the stomach⟩ ⟨~ tumor⟩

**hourglass screw** *or* **hourglass worm** *n* **:** HINDLEY'S SCREW

**hourglass spider** *n* **:** a black widow or a closely related spider

**hourglass stomach** *n* **:** a stomach divided into two communicating cavities by a circular constriction usu. caused by the scar tissue around an ulcer

**hour hand** *n* **:** the index showing the hour on a timepiece

**hou·ri** *or* **hu·ri** \'hu̇rē, 'hu̇rē, 'hau̇rē, -rī\ *n* -s [F *houri*, fr. Per *hūri*, fr. Ar *ḥūrīyah*, sing. of *ḥūr* (in *ḥūr al-'ayn* fair black-eyed women)] **1 :** one of the dark-eyed virgins of perfect beauty that in Muslim belief live with the blessed in paradise **2 :** a voluptuously beautiful young woman

**hour·less** \'=ləs\ *adj* **:** being outside of time **:** TIMELESS

**hour line** *n* **:** a dial line for indicating the hour

**hour–long** \'=ˈ=\ *adj* **:** lasting for an hour ⟨*hour-long* radio program⟩

**¹hour·ly** *pronunc at* HOUR + lē *or* li\ *adv* [ME, fr. *hour* + *-ly* (adv. suffix)] **:** at or during every hour **:** FREQUENTLY **:** CONTINUALLY ⟨strife, which ~ was renewed —John Dryden⟩

**²hourly** \"\ *adj* [*hour* + *-ly* (adj. suffix)] **1** *obs* **:** happening within an hour **:** BRIEF, RECENT **2 :** happening or done every hour **:** occurring hour by hour **:** renewed hour by hour **:** FREQUENT, CONTINUAL ⟨~ train service⟩ ⟨in ~ expectation of the rain's stopping⟩ **3 :** using an hour as the unit for determining an amount (as for reckoning wages) ⟨engaged and paid on an ~ basis⟩

**hourly–rated** \ˈ==ˌ==\ *adj* **:** receiving a fixed wage of a certain amount per hour — contrasted with *salaried*

**hours** *pl of* HOUR

**hour wheel** *n* **:** the wheel in a timepiece that carries the hour hand

**hou·sa·ton·ic** \ˌhüsə'tänik, -üzə-\ *n* -s *usu cap* [fr. the *Housatonic* river, Mass. & Conn.] **:** STOCKBRIDGE

**¹house** \'hau̇s; *sing. possessive* -au̇səz, -au̇zəz\ *n, pl* **hous·es** \-au̇zəz *chiefly substand* -au̇səz\ *often attrib* [ME *hous*, fr. OE *hūs*; akin to OHG & ON *hūs* house, Goth *gudhūs* temple, and prob. to OE *hȳd* hide — more at HIDE] **1 a :** a structure intended or used for human habitation **:** a building that serves as one's residence or domicile esp. as contrasted with a place of business **:** a building containing living quarters for one or a few families — sometimes used at law of a room or other part of such a building; see BUNGALOW, COTTAGE, MANSION; APARTMENT BUILDING, BOARDINGHOUSE, DWELLING HOUSE, LODGING HOUSE, ROOMING HOUSE, TENEMENT HOUSE; compare APARTMENT, HOME, HOMESTEAD, HOTEL, INN, TENEMENT **b :** regular existence in or as if in a house ⟨left home to set up ~ in another town⟩ ⟨children imitating their elders by playing ~⟩ **c :** a place of habitation, rest, or abode ⟨~ of death⟩ ⟨fleshly ~ of the soul⟩ **d** *dial Eng* **:** the chief living room (as the kitchen) of a farmhouse or cottage **2 a :** something (as a shell, nest, den) that serves an animal for shelter or habitation ⟨muskrat ~⟩ **b :** a building in which something is kept or stored ⟨carriage ~⟩ ⟨reptile ~⟩ ⟨a ~ for hens⟩ **3 a :** MUNDANE HOUSE **b :** a zodiacal sign regarded as the seat of a planet's greatest influence — called also *mansion, planetary house* **c** *obs* **:** a square on a chessboard **d :** the circular area 12 feet in diameter surrounding the tee within which a curling stone must rest in order to count **4 a** *archaic* **:** those who dwell in the same house **:** HOUSEHOLD ⟨himself believed and his whole ~ —Jn 4:53 (AV)⟩ **b :** a family of ancestors, descendants, and kindred **:** a race of persons from the same stock; *esp* **:** a noble family ⟨the great ~s of England⟩ **5 a :** the residence of a religious community **b :** the members of a religious community **6 a :** a college in a university **b :** a hall or dormitory in a college or school ⟨~ dinner⟩; *also* **:** the students in a hall or dormitory ⟨~ team⟩ **7 a :** one of the estates of a kingdom or other government assembled in parliament or legislature **:** a body of men united in a legislative capacity ⟨the *House* of Lords⟩ *also* **:** a quorum of such a body — see HOUSE OF ASSEMBLY, HOUSE OF COMMONS, HOUSE OF DELEGATES, HOUSE OF REPRESENTATIVES **b :** the building or the chamber in which such a body holds its sessions **8 :** a body of men forming a deliberative or consultative assembly esp. of an ecclesiastical or a collegiate character ⟨~ of bishops⟩ ⟨~ of convocation⟩ **9 a :** a business organization **:** FIRM, PARTNERSHIP ⟨banking ~⟩ ⟨~ of tea importers⟩ ⟨printing ~⟩ ⟨publishing ~⟩ **b** (1) **:** the operators of a gambling game **:** the management of a gambling establishment ⟨a percentage of each pot goes to the ~⟩ (2) **:** a gambling establishment **:** CASINO **10 a :** HOTEL, RESTAURANT, BARROOM ⟨have a drink on the ~⟩ **b :** BROTHEL **11 a :** a building for dramatic or musical performances **:** THEATER **b :** an audience esp. in a theater ⟨playing to small ~s⟩ ⟨a good ~ at the opening⟩ ⟨I'll concentrate on acting, because I don't have to count the ~ —*Newsweek*⟩ **12 :** a structure rising above the deck of a tanker or cargo ship that encloses living quarters or the bridge **13** *archaic Brit* **:** WORKHOUSE — used with *the* **14 :** a clump of trees or shrubs growing on a slight elevation in a Florida prairie **15** *Brit* **:** any of several lotto or keno games

**²house** \'hau̇z, *chiefly substand* -au̇s\ *vb* -ED/-ING/-S [ME *housen*, fr. OE *hūsian*, fr. *hūs* house] *vt* **1 a :** to provide with a permanent dwelling place or living quarters ⟨trying to feed and ~ his family⟩ **b :** to lodge or shelter temporarily ⟨guests were *housed* in a separate cottage⟩ **:** find shelter for **c :** to confine within a house ⟨*housed* with a bad cold⟩ — often used with *up* ⟨*housed* up all day in these four walls⟩ **d :** to store in a house ⟨~ garden tools in a shed⟩ **2 a :** to encase, enclose, or shelter as if by putting in a house ⟨so timorous a soul *housed* in so impressive a body —A.W.Long⟩ **b :** to stow or secure in a safe place ⟨~ the upper spars of a ship⟩ ⟨~ a yacht for the winter⟩ **c :** to cover (a deck) with a roof **3 :** to serve as shelter for **:** CONTAIN ⟨those caves may ~ snakes⟩ ⟨library ~s thousands of volumes⟩ ⟨former stately homes now ~ professional and business offices⟩ **4 :** to provide (as a play or opera) with a theater **5 :** to fit (as machinery or gears) with shrouds or protective walls or housings **6 a :** to cut a housing in (as a timber) **b :** to insert into or put together by means of a housing ~ *vi* **1 :** to take shelter **:** find refuge **:** LODGE, DWELL, HARBOR ⟨graze where you will, you shall not ~ with me —Shak.⟩ — used often with *up* ⟨~ up in a cave for the winter⟩ **2** *of a planet* **:** to have position in a mundane house or a mansion

**³house** \'hau̇s, -au̇z\ *n, pl* **hous·es** \-au̇zəz, -au̇səz\ [ME *houce, house*, fr. MF *houce, housse*, of Gmc origin; akin to MHG *hulst, hulft* covering, OE *heolstor* darkness, cover — more at HOLSTER] **:** ²HOUSING

**⁴house** \'hau̇z, -au̇s\ *vt* -ED/-ING/-S **:** to cover with or as if with a housing **:** CAPARISON ⟨a gaily *housed* horse⟩

**house agent** *n, chiefly Brit* **:** a real-estate broker or agent

**house amish** *n, usu cap A* **:** Amish Mennonites who have no churches, who purposely avoid owning church property, and who worship in the various homes of members on a rotating basis

**house ant** *n* **:** any of various ants common in human dwellings — compare PHARAOH ANT

**house arrest** *n* **:** confinement often under guard to one's house or quarters or a hospital instead of in a jail or prison

**house bill** *n* **:** a bill originating in the U.S. House of Representatives

**house board** *n* **:** a display board on the front of a theater

**¹houseboat** \'ˌ=\ *n* [¹*house* + *boat*] **1 :** a barge fitted up with cabins and designed for use as a dwelling or for leisurely cruising in quiet waters **2 :** a yacht having sleeping accommodations for several people

houseboat

**²houseboat** \"\ *vi* **:** to live or cruise in a houseboat

**housebote** \'ˌ=\ *n* -s [part. trans. of (assumed) ME *housbote* (whence ML *husbota* & AF *ousbote*), fr. ME *hous* house + *bote* repair, deliverance — more at BOOT] **:** wood allowed to a tenant for repairing a house — compare ESTOVERS

**housebound** \'ˌ=\ *adj* **:** confined to the house ⟨bad weather kept us ~ for days⟩ ⟨~ with a severe cold⟩

**houseboy** \'ˌ=\ *n* **:** HOUSEMAN 1

**¹house-break** \'hau̇s,brāk\ *vi* [back-formation fr. *housebreaker* & *housebreaking*] **:** to commit housebreaking

**²housebreak** \"\ *vt* [back-formation fr. *housebroken*] **1 :** to train (an animal or a baby) to live in a domestic environment with respect to sanitary habits **2 a :** to teach acceptable social manners to **:** accustom to indoor living **:** make tractable or polite **b :** to break the spirit of **:** TAME, SUBDUE

**house·break·er** \-kə(r)\ *n* [ME *housbreker*, fr. *hous* house + *breker* breaker] **1 :** one that commits housebreaking **2** *chiefly Brit* **:** one that pulls down old buildings **:** WRECKER

**housebreaking** \'ˌ=ˌ=\ *n* [¹*house* + *breaking*] **1 :** an act of breaking open and entering with a felonious purpose the dwelling house of another by day or night — compare BURGLARY **2 :** an act of pulling down old buildings

**housebroken** \'ˌ=ˌ=\ *or* **housebroke** \'ˌ=\ *adj* **:** trained to live in a house **:** adjusted to indoor conditions ⟨~ dog⟩ ⟨~ plant⟩

**housebuilder** \'ˌ=ˌ=\ *n* **:** one whose business is to build houses

**house–building rat** \'ˌ=ˌ=-\ *n* **:** a large Australian rat (*Leporillus conditor*) that builds a large nest of sticks

**houseburn** \'ˌ=\ *n* **:** an injury to tobacco leaves in the curing barn resulting from fungus activity caused by excess moisture — compare POLE ROT

**house car** *n* **1 :** an enclosed freight car (as a boxcar, refrigerator car, stockcar) **2 :** a railroad car for handling goods to be loaded or unloaded at a freight house

**housecarl** \'ˌ=\ *also* **hus·carl** \'hüs,-\ *n* [OE *hūscarl*, fr. ON *hūskarl*, fr. *hūs* house + *karl* carl — more at HOUSE, CARL] **:** a member of the small standing army or bodyguard of a Danish or early English king or noble

**house cat** *n* **:** CAT 1a

**house centipede** *n* **:** a widespread long-legged centipede (*Scutigera coleoptrata*) common in damp sheltered places (as the cellars of buildings) and believed to be valuable as a destroyer of flies, roaches, and other noxious insects

**house·clean** \'hau̇s,klēn\ *vb* [back-formation fr. *housecleaning*] *vi* **1 :** to remove dirt and accumulated rubbish from a house, room, or building **:** clean a house and its furniture **2 :** to get rid of unwanted or useless or obnoxious items or people **:** clean house ~ *vt* **1 :** to set (a house or room) in order by thorough cleaning of surfaces and furnishings **2 :** to improve or reform (as an administrative department) by ridding of undesirable people or inefficient practices

**housecleaner** \'ˌ=ˌ=\ *n* [*house* + *cleaner*] **:** one that housecleans

**housecleaning** \'ˌ=ˌ=\ *n* [*house* + *cleaning*] **1 :** the removal of dirt and rubbish from a house esp. after long accumulation ⟨spring ~⟩ **2 :** the act of improving or reforming by removal of undesirable, inefficient, or corrupt elements ⟨a thorough ~ which will sweep away the cobwebs of learning and clear our attics of academic lumber —Marjorie Nicolson⟩ ⟨urged that a thorough ~ was needed to rid the business of sharp practices —*Advertising Age*⟩

**housecoat** \'ˌ=\ *n* **:** an informal garment for wear around the house: as **a :** a woman's one-piece usu. long-skirted garment that has a front closing and is similar in cut to a dressing gown or negligee ⟨wearing . . . an emerald-green taffeta ~ —Edmund Wilson⟩ **b :** a man's lounging coat or jacket usu. of fine material (as silk or velvet) — compare SMOKING JACKET

**housecraft** \'hau̇s,kraft\ *n, Brit* **:** HOUSEHOLD ART

**house cricket** *n* **:** any of various crickets living in or about dwellings; *esp* **:** a widely distributed American cricket (*Acheta domesticus*)

**house crow** *n* **:** a common crow (*Corvus splendens*) of India familiar as a scavenger and resembling the hooded crow of Europe

**housed** *past of* HOUSE

**house detective** *or* **house dick** *n* **:** one who is employed by a department store, hotel, or place of entertainment to prevent disorderly or improper conduct of patrons

**housedoor** \'ˌ=\ *n* **:** the front or main door of a house

**house drain** *n* **:** the horizontal drain in a basement that receives the waste discharge from stacks and extends a few feet outside the foundation — called also *building drain, collection line*

**house dramatist** *n* **:** a writer of plays for a particular theater

**housedress** \'ˌ=\ *n* **:** a dress with simple lines suitable for work about the house and made usu. of a washable printed fabric

**house dust** *n* **:** an airborne respiratory allergen of uncertain origin found about houses and held to be the chief cause of nonseasonal hay fever

**house-fast** \'hüs,fast\ *adj, chiefly Scot* **:** HOUSEBOUND

**housefather** \'ˌ=ˌ=\ *n* **:** the father or male head of any collection of persons living together as a family; *specif* **:** a man in charge of a dormitory, hall, or hostel for young people or children

**house finch** *n* **:** a small redheaded finch (*Carpodacus mexicanus*) closely related to the purple finch and represented by several races in the western U.S. and Mexico including the common familiar house finch (*C. m. frontalis*) that often nests about houses and is a good singer

**house flag** *n* **1 :** a flag with an emblem denoting a commercial house or line to which a merchant ship belongs **2 :** the personal flag of a yacht owner

**housefly** \'ˌ=\ *n* **1 :** a two-winged fly (*Musca domestica*) with mouthparts adapted for lapping or sipping that is found in all habitable parts of the world, being often a most abundant and familiar insect about human habitations during the warm part of the year and acting as a mechanical agent in transmitting diseases (as typhoid fever) by alighting on infected substances and then on food **2 :** any of various flies of similar appearance or habitat (as the lesser housefly or the stable fly)

**housefront** \'ˌ=\ *n* **:** the facade of a house

**house·ful** \'hau̇,sfu̇l\ *n* -s **:** as much or as many as a house will accommodate ⟨~ of guests⟩

**house fungus** *n* **:** any of several saprophytic fungi (as *Coniophora cerebella* and *Merulius lacrymans*) developing upon and rotting wood exposed to moisture in houses

**housefurnishings** \'ˌ=ˌ=ˌ=\ *n pl* **:** furnishings for a house; *esp* **:** small articles of household equipment (as kitchen utensils)

**house girl** *n* **:** HOUSEMAID

**house god** *n* **:** HOUSEHOLD GOD

**houseguest** \'ˌ=\ *n* **:** a guest staying overnight or longer

**househeating** \'ˌ=ˌ=\ *n* **1 :** HOUSEWARMING **2 :** central heating of a dwelling

**¹house·hold** \'hau̇,sōld, -au̇s,hō-\ *n* [ME *houshold*, fr. *hous* house + *hold*] **1** *obs* **a :** the maintaining of a house **:** HOUSEKEEPING **b :** household goods and chattels **2 :** those who dwell under the same roof and compose a family **:** a domestic establishment; *specif* **:** a social unit comprised of those living together in the same dwelling place **3 households** *pl* **:** ALL-PURPOSE FLOUR

**²household** \"\ *adj* [ME *houshold*, fr. *houshold*, n.] **1 :** of or relating to a household **:** DOMESTIC ⟨~ tasks⟩ **2 :** FAMILIAR **:** COMMON ⟨~ remedy⟩ ⟨~ legend⟩

**household ammonia** *n* **:** dilute ammonia water for household use often containing small amounts of detergents

**household art** *n* **:** one of the arts or techniques (as cooking, sewing, baby care) concerned with the maintenance and care of a household — usu. used in pl.

**household economics** *n pl but usu sing in constr* **:** HOME ECONOMICS

**house·hold·er** \-də(r)\ *n* [ME *housholder*, fr. *hous* + *holder*] **1 :** the master or head of a family **:** one who occupies a house or separate tenement with his family or alone **2 :** FREEHOLDER

**house·hold·er·ship** \-(r),ship\ *n* **:** the position or status of a householder

**household franchise** *n* **:** the right of voting in parliamentary and other elections in Great Britain restricted before 1918 to householders

**household god** *n* **1 household gods** *pl* **:** LARES AND PENATES **2 :** a deeply respected or revered person, thing, idea, or custom ⟨the Victorian *household gods* Respectability, Prudery and Humbug squat smugly on their pedestals —*N.Y.Herald Tribune*⟩

**house·hold·ing** \-diŋ\ *n* [ME *housholding*, fr. *hous* + *holding*, gerund of *holden* to hold — more at HOLD] **:** the management or occupation of a house or tenement

**house·hold·ry** \-drē\ *n* -ES **:** HOUSEHOLDING, DOMESTIC ECONOMY, HOUSEKEEPING

**household stuff** *n, archaic* **:** housefurnishings and furniture

**household troops** *n pl* **:** troops appointed to attend and guard a sovereign or his residence

**household word** *n* **:** a common word or phrase **:** BYWORD ⟨*penicillin* has become a new *household word* —W.E.Swinton⟩

**house-keep** \'hau̇,skēp\ *vi* [back-formation fr. *housekeeping* & *housekeeper*] **:** to keep house **:** act as housekeeper; *esp* **:** to prepare meals regularly for oneself and family ⟨a large cafeteria for those who do not wish to ~ —Diana Rice⟩

**house·keep·er** \-pə(r)\ *n* [ME *howskepare*, fr. *hows, hous* house + *kepare, keper* keeper — more at KEEPER] **1** *archaic* **:** HOUSEHOLDER **2** *obs* **:** one who exercises hospitality **3 a :** a woman who is employed on a permanent basis to do the work in a private home either supervised by or taking the place of a housewife ⟨she came as a general domestic but we gave her the status of ~ —Margo Fischer⟩ **b :** a woman who is employed in a hotel or an institution to supervise the cleaning personnel **4 :** one in charge of a house **:** CARETAKER, JANITOR

**housekeeping** \'ˌ=ˌ=\ *n* [*house* + *keeping*] **1** *archaic* **:** the state of occupying a dwelling house as a householder **2 :** the care or management of domestic concerns **:** the management of a house and home affairs **3 :** the physical care and control of industrial or state property to ensure maintenance, proper and full utilization, and disposition

**¹housel** *n* -s [ME, fr. OE *hūsel* sacrifice, Eucharist; akin to Goth *hunsl* sacrifice, and prob. to Av *spənta-* holy, Lith *šventas*] *archaic* **:** the Eucharist or the act of administering or receiving it

**²housel** *vt* -ED/-ING/-S [ME *houselen*, fr. OE *hūslian*, fr. *hūsel*, n.] *archaic* **:** to administer the Eucharist to

**houseleek** \'ˌ=\ *n* [ME *howsleke*, fr. *hows, hous* house + *leke, lek* leek — more at HOUSE, LEEK] **:** a plant of the genus *Sempervivum*: as **a :** a common European succulent (*S. tectorum*) found on old walls and roofs and having pink flowers and leaves clustered in a basal rosette which produces numerous offsets **b :** a plant (*S. soboliferum*) having the offsets produced high among the leaves of the rosette

**house·less** \'hau̇sləs\ *adj* [ME *housles*, fr. *hous* + *-les* -less] **1 :** destitute of the shelter of a house **:** SHELTERLESS, HOMELESS ⟨~ wanderer⟩ **2 :** destitute of houses ⟨~ desert⟩ — **house·less·ness** *n* -ES

**house·let** *n* -s \-lət\ **:** a very small house

**houselights** \'ˌ=\ *n pl* **:** the lights that illuminate the spaces in a theater occupied by an audience before and after performance on the stage ⟨the ~ went down and the footlights came up —W.L.White⟩ ⟨the ~ darkened and the curtain rose —Thyra S. Winslow⟩

**houseline** \'ˌ=\ *n* [so called fr. the use of small tarred lines to wrap around large ropes] **:** a light rope made of three strands left-laid and used for seizing

**house machine** *n* **:** a mechanical device for laying and forming rope

**house magazine** *n* **:** HOUSE ORGAN

**house·maid** \'hau̇s,mād\ *n* **:** a female servant employed to do housework

**house·maid·ing** \-diŋ\ *n* -s **:** the work of a housemaid

**housemaid's knee** *n* [so called fr. its frequent occurrence among servant girls who work a great deal on their knees] **:** a swelling over the knee due to an enlargement of the bursa in the front of the patella

**house·man** \'hau̇smən\ *n, pl* **housemen 1 :** one hired to perform general work or the heavy duties about a house, hotel, or similar establishment — called also *houseboy* **2 :** an attendant in a gambling house who sells and cashes in chips, collects house fees from players, explains rules, or plays games for the house **3 a :** HOUSE DETECTIVE **b :** BOUNCER 3 **4** *chiefly Brit* **:** ⁴INTERN 1b

**house martin** *n* **:** ²MARTIN 1

**housemaster** \'ˌ=ˌ=\ *n* **:** a master in charge of a house in a boys' boarding school

**housemastership** \'ˌ=ˌ=ˌ=\ *n* **:** the position of a housemaster

**housemate** \'ˌ=\ *n* **:** one that lives in the same house with another

**housemistress** \'ˌ=ˌ=\ *n* **1 :** a mistress of a house **2 :** a woman in charge of a house in a girls' boarding school

**house mite** *n* **:** CLOVER MITE

**house money** *n* **:** money used or set aside for household expenses

**house mosquito** *n* **:** any of various mosquitoes frequenting houses; *esp* **:** a widespread mosquito (*Culex pipiens*) of Europe and No. America

**house moss** *n, dial* **:** rolls of soft dust that commonly collect on floors and under furniture

**housemother** \'ˌ=ˌ=\ *n* **:** a mother of a family **:** a woman living at the head of a household or small community; *specif* **:** a woman acting as hostess, chaperon, and often as housekeeper in a dormitory, hall, or hostel where young people or children reside

**house mouse** *n* **:** a mouse that frequents houses; *esp* **:** a common nearly cosmopolitan usu. gray mouse (*Mus musculus*) that lives and breeds about buildings and is important as a consumer of human food, as a vector of diseases, and as an experimental animal

**hous·en** \'hau̇zᵊn\ *dial pl of* HOUSE

**house of assembly :** a legislative body or the lower house of a legislature (as in the American colonies and various British colonies, protectorates, and countries of the Commonwealth)

**house of assignation :** a house maintained and used for illicit sexual intercourse **:** BROTHEL

**house of cards :** CARDHOUSE

**house of commons :** the lower house of a legislative body in some countries (as Great Britain, Canada)

**house of correction :** an institution where persons are confined who have committed a minor offense and are considered capable of reformation — compare REFORMATORY

**house of delegates :** the lower house of the legislature of some states (as Virginia, Maryland)

**house of detention 1 :** a place where prisoners and occasionally witnesses are detained pending a criminal trial **2 :** DETENTION HOME

**house officer** *n, Brit* **:** ⁴INTERN 1b

**house of god** *cap G* [trans. of LL *domus Dei*] **:** TEMPLE, CHURCH — called also *house of prayer, house of worship*

**house of ill fame** *or* **house of ill repute :** BROTHEL

**house of issue :** an investment bank that originates new security offerings for public distribution or joins with other houses in purchase groups that underwrite such offerings

**house of life :** HOUSE OF THE ASCENDANT

**house of mercy 1 :** a charitable institution for lodging, relieving, or reclaiming those in distress or disgrace **2 :** HOSPITAL

**house of office** [ME *hous of offyce*] *obs* **:** a building or room (as a kitchen or pantry) used for domestic purposes; *esp* **:** PRIVY

**house of refuge :** a charitable institution for giving shelter and protection to the homeless or destitute

**house of representatives :** the lower house of the legislature of many countries and states

**house of the ascendant** [ME *hous of the ascendent*] **:** the first mundane house
**house of worship** *or* **house of prayer :** HOUSE OF GOD
**house organ** *n* **1 :** a publication typically in magazine format issued periodically by a business concern to further its interest among employees and sales personnel or among agents and customers **2 :** a publication put out by or for a professional group with relevant matter of special interest
**house painter** \ˈ=,==\ *n* **:** one whose business or occupation is painting houses
**houseparent** \ˈ=,==\ *n* **:** one of a married couple in charge of a dormitory, hall, or hostel where children or young people reside **:** HOUSEFATHER, HOUSEMOTHER
**house party** *n* **:** a gathering and entertainment lasting over one or more nights of a party of guests usu. in a house in the country; *also* **:** the guests in a house
**housephone** \ˈ=,=\ *n* **:** a telephone that is connected to the switchboard of a building (as a hotel or apartment house) but not directly to the exchange
**house physician** *n* **:** a physician who is employed by and lives in a hospital — compare ⁴INTERN 1b, RESIDENT
**house place** *n, dial* **:** ¹HOUSE 1d
**houseplant** \ˈ=,=\ *n* **:** a plant grown or kept indoors
**housepride** \ˈ=,=\ *n* **:** pride in one's house or housekeeping
**house-proud** \ˈ=,=\ *adj* **:** proud of one's house or housekeeping
**hous·er** \ˈhau̇zə(r)\ *n* -s [²*house* + *-er*] **1 :** one that promotes or administers housing projects **2 :** HOUSEBOAT
**house-raising** \ˈ=,==\ *n* **:** the joint erection of a house or its framework by a gathering of neighbors
**house rat** *n* **:** any of several rats (as the black rat) common about dwellings
**houseroom** \ˈ=,=\ *n* **:** space for accommodation in a house **:** LODGING ⟨getting food, raiment, and ~ for three people ashore —Joseph Conrad⟩
**house rule** *n* **:** a rule applying to a game only among a certain group or in a certain place (as a gambling house)
**houses** *pl of* HOUSE, *pres 3d sing of* HOUSE
**house seat** *n* **:** a seat (as in a theater) reserved by the management for special guests
**house sewer** *n* **:** a prolongation of a house drain extending from a few feet outside a foundation to a connection with a public sewer in the street or alley — called also *building sewer*
**house shrew** *n* **:** a common European shrew (*Crocidura russula*) sometimes found in barns and other outbuildings
**house slipper** *n* **:** a slipper for indoor wear — compare BEDROOM SLIPPER
**housesmith** \ˈ=,=\ *n* **:** an ironworker who assists in erecting a steel skeleton or other steelwork used in buildings
**house snake** *n* **1 :** MILK SNAKE **2 :** any of several harmless African colubrid snakes (genus *Boaedon*) that live chiefly on mice and rats
**house sparrow** *n* **:** a sparrow (*Passer domesticus*) native to most of Europe and parts of Asia that has been intentionally introduced into America, Australia, New Zealand, and elsewhere to destroy insects and caterpillars although it feeds largely upon grain seeds — called also *English sparrow*
**house spider** *n* **:** any of various spiders (as members of the genus *Tegenaria*) that habitually live in buildings
**house staff** *n* **:** the resident physicians and surgeons in a hospital
**house steward** *n* **:** one employed to manage the domestic affairs of a large household or a club
**house surgeon** *n* **:** a surgeon fully qualified in his specialty and resident in a hospital
**house-to-house** \ˈ=,=ˈ=\ *adj* **:** made or applying successively to all the residences in an area ⟨a *house-to-house* canvass for signatures⟩
**housetop** \ˈ=,=\ *n* **:** the roof of a house; *esp* **:** the level surface of a flat roof — **from the housetops** *adv* **:** for all to hear **:** PUBLICLY, OPENLY ⟨shouted *from the housetops* that our defenses were fully adequate —F.D.Roosevelt⟩
**house track** *n* **:** a railroad track alongside or inside a freight house for loading and unloading cars **:** STATION TRACK
**house trailer** *n* **:** a trailer that can be used as living quarters
**house-train** \ˈ=,=\ *vt, chiefly Brit* **:** ²HOUSEBREAK
**house trap** *n* **:** a trap in the house drain for preventing the entrance of gases from a sewer

house trailer

**house·ward** \ˈhau̇swə(r)d\ *adv* **:** toward the house **:** HOMEWARD
**housewares** \ˈ=,=\ *n pl* **:** HOUSEFURNISHINGS
**housewarming** \ˈ=,==\ *n* **:** a party to celebrate the taking possession of a house or premises
¹**house·wife** \ˈhau̇,swīf *or esp in sense 2* ˈhəzəf *or* ˈhəsə̇f\ *n, pl* **house·wives** \-īvz,-ə̇fs\ [ME *houswif,* fr. *hous* house + *wif* woman, wife — more at HOUSE, WIFE] **1 :** a married woman in charge of a household; *specif* **:** a married woman who occupies herself with the domestic affairs of her household and who engages in no employment for pay or profit **2 :** a pocket-size container (as a bag or roll of cloth) for carrying small articles (as thread, needles, scissors) — called also *hussy*
²**house·wife** \ˈhau̇,swīf\ *vb* -ED/-ING/-S *vt, archaic* **:** to manage with skill and economy **:** HUSBAND ~ *vi, archaic* **:** ECONOMIZE
**house·wife·li·ness** \-īflēnə̇s -lin-\ *n* -ES **:** the quality or state of being housewifely
**house·wife·ly** \-īflē, -li\ *adj* **:** relating, belonging, or appropriate to a housewife ⟨~ virtues⟩ ⟨~ indignation over high prices⟩ **:** DOMESTIC, THRIFTY
**house·wife·ry** \ˈhau̇,swīf(ə)rē, -ri, *chiefly Brit* -,swə̇f-\ *n* -ES [ME *houswiferie,* fr. *houswif* + *-erie* -ery] **:** the business of a housewife **:** HOUSEKEEPING
**house·wif·ish** \-,swīfish\ *adj* **:** belonging or appropriate to a housewife **:** DOMESTIC, PETTY
**housework** \ˈ=,=\ *n* **:** the work of housekeeping (as kitchen work, sweeping, scrubbing)
**houseworker** \ˈ=,==\ *n* **:** one that does general housework for wages **:** HOUSEMAID
**housewrecker** \ˈ=,==\ *n* **:** WRECKER 1b
**house wren** *n* **:** a common wren (*Troglodytes aedon*) that nests about houses and walls throughout the U.S. and migrates south in winter
**housewright** \ˈ=,=\ *n* **:** a builder of wooden houses **:** a house carpenter
**housey-housey** *or* **housie-housie** \ˈhau̇si,ˈhau̇si\ *n* -s [¹*house* + *-ie* or *-ey* (var. of *-ie*)] *Brit* **:** HOUSE 15
¹**hous·ing** \ˈhau̇ziŋ, -zēŋ\ *n* -s [ME; partly fr. *hous,* n., house + *-ing;* partly fr. gerund of *housen* to house — more at HOUSE] **1 :** SHELTER, LODGING **2 a :** the act of placing under shelter **b :** the act of living in a house **3 :** dwellings provided for numbers of people or for a community ⟨~ for the aged⟩ **4 a :** something that covers or protects (as of boards over a ship's deck) **b :** a case or enclosure esp. for a machine or part, an instrument, a lamp ⟨the differential ~ on an automobile⟩ **c :** a tube or cylindrical sleeve or casing (as an enclosed bearing) in which a shaft revolves **5 :** a portion of a mast that is beneath the deck or of a bowsprit that is inboard **6 a :** the space taken out of a structural member (as a timber) to admit the insertion of part of another — compare MORTISE **b :** a hollowed space (as a niche) for holding a piece of sculpture **7** [perh. fr. D *huizing* (fr. *huis* house + *-ing*) or LG *hüsing,* fr. *hus* house + *-ing*)] **:** HOUSELINE
²**housing** \ˈ"\ *n* -s [ME, fr. *house* housing + *-ing* — more at HOUSE] **1 :** an ornamental cover for a horse's saddle **2 housings** *pl* **:** TRAPPINGS, ORNAMENTATION
**housing development** *n* **:** a group of individual dwellings or of apartment houses commonly of similar design and built and leased under one management — compare COLONY 4c
**housing estate** *n, Brit* **:** HOUSING DEVELOPMENT
**housing project** *n* **:** a publicly supported and administered housing development planned usu. for low-income families
**hous·ton** \ˈ(h)yüstən\ *adj, usu cap* [fr. *Houston,* Tex.] **:** of or from the city of Houston, Texas ⟨a *Houston* shopping center⟩ **:** of the kind or style prevalent in Houston
**hous·to·nia** \(h)yüˈstōnēə, hüˈ-,hau̇ˈ-\ *n* [NL, fr. William *Houston* †1733 Scot. botanist + NL *-ia*] **1** *cap* **:** a genus of No. American herbs (family Rubiaceae) with entire leaves and small blue, lilac, or white tubular lobed flowers — see BLUET **2** -s **:** any plant of the genus *Houstonia*
**hous·to·ni·an** \(h)yüˈstōnēən\ *n* -s *cap* [*Houston,* Tex. + E *-ian*] **:** a native or resident of Houston, Texas
**hous·ton's fold** *or* **houston's valve** \ˈ(h)yü|stənz-, ˈhü|, ˈhau̇|\ *n, usu cap H* [after John *Houston* †1845 Irish surgeon] **:** any of the valvular folds in the lining of the rectum
**hout·ing** \ˈhau̇d·iŋ\ *n* -s [D, fr. MD *houtic,* perh. fr. *hout* wood; akin to OHG *holz* wood — more at HOLT] **:** an anadromous fish (*Coregonus oxyrhynchus*) of the North sea that ascends rivers and estuaries of northwestern Europe to spawn
**hou·tou** \ˈhü(,)tü\ *n* -s [modif. of Arawak *hotoli,* of imit. origin] **:** a So. American motmot (*Momotus momota*)
**hou·va·ri** \ˌ(h)üvəˈrē\ *n* -s [AmerSp *huvari, hurivari*] **:** a severe thunderstorm with strong land breezes in the West Indies
**ho·va** \ˈhōvə, ˈhüv\ *n, pl* **hova** *or* **hovas** *usu cap* **1 a :** the dominant native people of central Madagascar **b :** a member of such people — compare MALAGASY **2 :** the language of the Hova people
¹**hove** *past of* HEAVE
²**hove** *vb* -ED/-ING/-S [fr. *hove,* past of *heave*] *vi, archaic* **:** RISE, HEAVE ~ *vt, archaic* **:** to lift or swell up **:** RAISE
³**hove** \ˈhōv\ *dial Eng var of* HALF
⁴**hove** *vi* -ED/-ING/-S [ME *hoven*] *obs* **:** HOVER 1, 4
**hoved** *dial past of* HEAVE
¹**hov·el** \ˈhəvəl *sometimes* ˈhäv-\ *n* -s [ME] **1** *chiefly dial* **:** an open shed or canopy for sheltering livestock or protecting produce **2 a :** TABERNACLE **b :** a niche like those that replace pinnacles on some Gothic churches and shelter statues **3 a :** a shed or open-roofed shelter for human beings **b :** a poor cottage **:** a small mean house **:** HUT **4 :** a large conical or conoidal brick structure within which a firing kiln is built
²**hovel** \ˈ"\ *vt* **hoveled** *or* **hovelled; hoveled** *or* **hovelled; hoveling** *or* **hovelling** \-v(ə)liŋ\ **hovels 1 :** to put in a hovel **:** provide with a roof ⟨~ thee with swine, and rogues forlorn —Shak.⟩ **2 :** to shape (as a chimney) like a hovel or hut
³**hov·el** \ˈhävəl *also* ˈhəv-\ *vb* **hoveled** *or* **hovelled; hoveled** *or* **hovelled; hoveling** *or* **hovelling; hovels** [back-formation fr. *hoveler*] *vt, Brit* **:** to aid (a ship) by pilotage, unloading, or landing passengers ~ *vi, Brit* **:** to aid ships in the capacity of a hoveler
**hov·el·er** *or* **hov·el·ler** \-v(ə)lə(r\ *also* **huf·fler** \ˈhəflə(r\ *n* -s [origin unknown] **1 :** a usu. unlicensed coast boatman who does odd jobs in assisting ships or goes out to wrecks to land passengers or secure salvage **2 :** a boat that is used by a hoveler
¹**ho·ven** \ˈhōvən\ *archaic & dial past part of* HEAVE
²**hoven** \ˈ"\ *adj* [fr. archaic past part. of *heave*] **:** afflicted with bloat
³**hoven** \ˈ"\ *n* -s **:** BLOAT 2
**ho·ve·nia** \hōˈvēnēə\ *n, cap* [NL, fr. David ten *Hove* †1787 Dutch senator + connective *-n-* + NL *-ia*] **:** a genus of Asiatic trees or shrubs (family Rhamnaceae) having alternate serrate leaves, small greenish flowers, and indehiscent fruit
¹**hov·er** \ˈhəvə(r) *also* ˈhäv-\ *vb* **hovered; hovered; hovering** \-v(ə)riŋ\ **hovers** [ME *hoveren,* freq. of *hoven* to hover] *vi* **1 a :** to hang fluttering in the air or on the wing ⟨the hawk ~*ed* searching the ground below⟩ **:** remain floating or suspended about or over a place or object ⟨clouds of smoke ~*ed* over the building⟩ **b** *of an airplane* **:** to maintain altitude without forward motion **2 a :** to hang about **:** move to and fro near a place threateningly, watchfully, uncertainly, irresolutely ⟨doormen annoy me . . . ~*ing* anxiously over people —Evelyn Barkins⟩ ⟨the shark was still ~*ing* about —Francis Birtles⟩ ⟨the thermometer ~*ed* around 90⟩ ⟨the boat ~*ed* outside the three-mile limit⟩ **b :** to be in a state of uncertainty, irresolution, or suspense ⟨when he was hesitating or ~*ing* over a word —David Abercrombie⟩ ⟨~*ing* uncomfortably behind a cigar —Tennessee Williams⟩ ⟨the country ~*ed* on the brink of famine⟩ **3 :** to crouch in hiding **:** COWER ⟨as if a gash had been torn in the web of restraint behind which she forced him to ~ —Marcia Davenport⟩ ⟨the bathtub fell . . . and crushed the woman ~*ing* in the cellar —*Springfield (Mass.) Union*⟩ **4** *dial Brit* **:** WAIT, LINGER ~ *vt* **1** *obs* **:** to flutter (the wings) so as to remain suspended in air **2 :** to brood over ⟨a hen ~*s* her chicks⟩
²**hover** \ˈ"\ *n* -s **1 :** the act or state of hovering ⟨the sweep and ~ of the pale birds —Mary H. Vorse⟩ ⟨the smoke from the croft house rises, a ~ of peat-scented blue —Naomi Mitchison⟩ **2 :** a group of trout **3 a** *dial* **:** a shelter (as an overhanging bank or hedge) for an animal or fish **b :** a floating island of vegetation **4 :** a canopy or other device for holding the heat of a brooder near the floor or ground so that it is available to young birds or animals cared for in the brooder
**hov·er·er** \-vərə(r)\ *n* -s **:** one that hovers
**hover fly** *n* **:** a syrphus fly or other fly that hovers in air
**hover hawk** *n* **:** a kestrel (*Falco tinnunculus*)
**hovering** *adj* **:** SUSPENDED, UNCERTAIN, WAVERING, POISED — **hov·er·ing·ly** *adv*
**hovering accent** *or* **hovering stress** *n* **:** distribution of energy, pitch, or duration in two adjacent syllables in some utterance of verse when a heavy syllable occurs next to a syllable bearing the metrical ictus so that for perception the stress seems to be divided or diffused nearly equally over both (as *cornfield* in the line "that o'er/the green'/cornfield/did pass'")
**hovering act** *n* [fr. gerund of ¹*hover*] **:** an act prohibiting or regulating the roving or hovering of domestic or foreign ships within certain limits; *esp* **:** an act providing for the boarding of foreign ships and inspection of cargo manifests outside the three-mile limit (as within four leagues of the coast) in order to enforce revenue or security laws esp. for protection of the commerce of a coastal nation
**hoverplane** \ˈ==,=\ *n, Brit* **:** HELICOPTER
**hove to** *adv (or adj)* [fr. past part. of *heave to*] **:** in a stationary position with head to wind **:** at a standstill ⟨ore freighters *hove to* in the fog —Richard Bissell⟩ ⟨lying *hove to* on the fishing bank⟩
**Ho·vis** \ˈhōvə̇s\ *trademark* — used for a wheat flour or bread made from it that includes wheat germ made inactive by heating
¹**how** \(ˈ)hau̇\ *adv* [ME *hou, how,* adv & conj., fr. OE *hū;* akin to OFris *hū, hō* how, OS *hū, hwō,* OHG *hwuo* how, OE *hwā* who — more at WHO] **1 a :** in what manner or way ⟨~ explain behavior so contrary to the principles of good authorship —G.M.Fess⟩ ⟨the continuing problems of . . . ~ to say what we mean —Stuart Chase⟩ ⟨learn ~ to enter a room properly⟩ ⟨tell him ~ to do it⟩ — often used as an intensive ⟨~ they laughed⟩ **b :** by what means or process ⟨at his wit's end regarding ~ to support himself —C.S.Forester⟩ ⟨question of ~ to increase the benefits under the . . . Retirement System —W.J.Kennedy⟩ **c** *obs* **:** SOMEHOW, ANYHOW ⟨by ransom or ~ else —John Milton⟩ **2 a :** to what extent, degree, number, or amount ⟨~ little we know of human motives⟩ ⟨~ far can he be trusted⟩ **b :** by what measure or quantity ⟨concerned with ~ much to eat⟩ ⟨decided ~ deep to cut⟩ ⟨~ hard do you plan to make it⟩ **3 a :** in what state, condition, or plight ⟨~ are things at home⟩ ⟨~ are you⟩ ⟨~ are you off for money⟩ **b :** at what price ⟨~ is the market today⟩ **4 a :** for what reason or excuse ⟨in the face of his own knowledge, ~ can he make such a statement —Weston LaBarre⟩ **:** for what possible or plausible reason ⟨~ could he have said that⟩ — often used with *ever* ⟨~ can I ever leave you⟩ **b :** from what cause **:** WHY ⟨~ did you come to sell your house⟩ **5 a** *archaic* **:** by what name or designation ⟨~ art thou called —Shak.⟩ **b :** with what meaning **:** to what effect ⟨~ are we to interpret such behavior⟩ **6 a :** what in that case **:** what then ⟨~ if, when I am laid into the tomb, I awake before the time —Shak.⟩ ⟨~ if I had denounced you when you forced your way in there —Max Peacock⟩ **b :** WHAT — used to introduce or imply a question ⟨~ about the other one, do you want it too⟩ ⟨~ say you, maiden, will you wed —W.S.Gilbert⟩ or in requests to repeat what has not been understood ⟨~ is that again⟩ **c** *dial* **:** what did you say **7** — used to express surprise or admiration ⟨~ do you like that⟩ — **and how** — used as an intensive ⟨prices are going up, *and how*⟩ — **how about :** what do you say to or think of ⟨*how about* a game of tennis⟩ **:** would you like to have ⟨*how about* some more pie⟩ or agree to ⟨well, *how about it,* are you coming⟩ — **how come :** how does it happen that **:** WHY ⟨*how come* you're here so early⟩ — **how do you do :** HELLO — used to express a polite greeting or formal salutation face-to-face — **how so :** how is that so **:** what do you mean **:** WHY ⟨it won't work? *how so*⟩
²**how** \ˈ"\ *conj* [ME *hou, how*] **1 a** (1) **:** the way or manner in which ⟨it was odd ~ writers never seemed to have anything to do except write —Martha Gellhorn⟩; *also* **:** the state or condition in which (2) **:** to what degree or extent ⟨knows ~ small the town is⟩ (3) **:** of the way or manner in which ⟨be careful ~ you talk⟩ **b :** THAT ⟨told them ~ he had a situation —Charles Dickens⟩ **2 :** in whatever way or manner **:** AS ⟨a reader can shift his attention ~ he likes —William Empson⟩
³**how** \ˈhau̇\ *n* -s [¹*how*] **1 :** the manner or method in which something is done or comes about ⟨most of the film is devoted to the grim ~*s* and not the difficult whys of battle —John McCarten⟩ **2 :** a question concerning manner or method ⟨the eternal whys and ~*s* of small children —Jeanne Massey⟩
⁴**how** \ˈhü\ *n* -s [ME *houwe, how,* fr. OE *hūfe* — more at CYPHELLA] **1** *Scot* **:** COIF, HOOD; *esp* **:** NIGHTCAP **2** *Scot* **:** an infant's caul
⁵**how** \ˈhau̇\ *n* -s [ME, fr. ON *haugr* hill; akin to OHG *houg* hill, ON *hār* high — more at HIGH] *now dial Eng* **:** a low hill **:** MOUND, HILLOCK — used chiefly in place names
⁶**how** \ˈ"\ *interj* [ME] **1** *now chiefly dial* — used to attract attention or express greeting ⟨~ now, my masters!⟩ or to urge on (as a sheep dog) ⟨~ sheep!⟩ **2** *chiefly Scot* — used to express pain or grief
⁷**how** \ˈhau̇\ *var of* HOWE
⁸**how** \ˈhau̇\ *interj* [of Siouan origin; akin to Dakota *hâo,* Omaha *hau*] — used as a greeting esp. in imitation of American Indian speech
⁹**how** \ˈ"\ *usu cap* — a communications code word for the letter *h*
**how** *abbr* howitzer
**how·ard·ite** \ˈhau̇ə(r),dīt\ *n* -s [Luke *Howard* †1864 Eng. meteorologist + E *-ite*] **:** a stony meteorite composed essentially of anorthite, olivine, and bronzite
¹**how·be·it** \(ˈ)hau̇ˈbēə̇t\ *adv* [ME *how be it*] **:** be it as it may **:** NEVERTHELESS ⟨~, the whole problem . . . cannot be solved —G.A.Llano⟩
²**howbeit** \ˈ"\ *conj* **:** ALTHOUGH ⟨are highly ingenious . . . and pleasantly diverting, ~ in certain passages of somewhat lowbrow content —Ben Crisler⟩
¹**howd** \ˈhau̇d\ *vi* -ED/-ING/-S [origin unknown] *chiefly Scot* **:** to move from side to side or up and down
²**howd** \ˈ"\ *n* -s **:** a lurching rocking movement
**how·dah** *or* **hou·dah** \ˈhau̇də\ *n* -s [Hindi *hauda,* fr. Ar *haudaj*] **:** a seat or covered pavilion on the back of an elephant or camel
**how·der** \ˈhau̇dər\ *vt* -ED/-ING/-S [freq. of *howd*] *chiefly Scot* **:** to heap or crowd together **:** HUDDLE
**how·die** *or* **how·dy** \ˈhau̇di\ *n, pl* **howdies** [origin unknown] *chiefly Scot* **:** MIDWIFE
**how do** \(ˈ)hau̇ˈdü\ *interj* [short for *how do you do*] *dial* — used to express greeting

howdah

**how-do-you-do** *also* **how-d'ye-do** *or* **how-de-do** \ˌhau̇dəyəˈdü, -dəyēˈdü, ˌhau̇dēˈdü, -au̇diˈdü, (ˈ)hau̇dˈdü\ *n* [fr. the phrase *how do you do?* or *how d'ye do?*] **:** an embarrassing situation **:** a troublesome fix ⟨this is a pretty *how-do-you-do*⟩
¹**how·dy** \ˈhau̇dē, -di\ *interj* [alter. of *how do*] — used to express greeting
²**howdy** \ˈ"\ *vb* -ED/-ING/-ES *vt, dial* **:** to say the words *how do you do* to ~ *vi, dial* **:** to exchange greetings
¹**howe** \ˈhau̇\ *n* -s [ME (northern dial.) *how,* alter. of *holl* — more at HOLL] **1** *chiefly Scot* **:** HOLLOW, DEPRESSION; *esp* **:** VALLEY **2** *Scot* **:** the middle part of a night or of winter
²**howe** \ˈ"\ *adj* [ME (northern dial.) *how,* alter. of *holl* — more at HOLL] *Scot* **:** HOLLOW, DEEP
³**howe** \ˈ"\ *adv, Scot* **:** in a hollow voice ⟨it spak right ~, my name is Death —Robert Burns⟩
⁴**howe** \ˈhō, ˈhau̇\ *dial Eng var of* HOE
**how·ea** \ˈhau̇ēə\ *n, cap* [NL, fr. Lord *Howe* island, in the southwestern Pacific] **:** a genus of feather palms having papery spathes and flowers each with 30 to 40 stamens and sunken in pits on the spadix that are succeeded by fruits resembling pecans
**ho·wei·tat** \(,)hōˌwāˈtat\ *n, pl* **howeitat** *or* **howeitats** *usu cap* **1 :** a Bedouin people of northern Arabia **2 :** a member of the Howeitat people
¹**how·el** \ˈhau̇(ə)l\ *n* -s [prob. fr. LG *höwel* plane, fr. MLG *hövel;* akin to OHG *hubil* hill, OE *hȳf* beehive — more at HIVE] **1 :** a cooper's plane having a convex sole for smoothing the insides of casks and for chamfering, crozing, and chiming **2 :** a rounded cut above and below the croze in a barrel stave
²**howel** \ˈ"\ *vt* **howeled** *or* **howelled; howeled** *or* **howelled; howeling** *or* **howelling; howels :** to smooth with a howel
**how·ell** \ˈhau̇(ə)l\ *n* -s *usu cap* [after E. C. *Howell* †1907 Am. journalist and whist expert] **1 :** HOWELL SYSTEM **2 a :** a duplicate game conducted by the Howell system **b :** a game of duplicate bridge in which match-point scoring is used
**howell-jol·ly body** \-zhōˈlē, -ˈjälē-\ *n, usu cap H&J* [after William H. *Howell* †1945 Am. physiologist and Justin M. J. *Jolly* †1953 Fr. physician] **:** one of the basophilic granules that are probably nuclear fragments, that sometimes occur in red blood cells, and that indicate by their appearance in circulating blood that red cells are leaving the marrow while incompletely mature (as in certain anemias)
**howell settlement** *n, usu cap H* [after E. C. *Howell*] **:** a method of scoring in the game of hearts whereby after the play of each deal each player puts into a pot for every heart he has taken as many chips as there are other players in the game and withdraws from the pot the number of chips representing the difference between 13 and the number of hearts he has taken
**howell system** *or* **howell movement** *n, usu cap H* [after E. C. *Howell*] **:** a method of conducting a game of duplicate bridge or whist so that each pair plays one set of boards against each other pair — compare MITCHELL MOVEMENT
**howe truss** \ˈhau̇-\ *n, usu cap H* [after William *Howe* †1852 Am. inventor] **:** a truss having vertical and diagonal members between the upper and lower horizontal members

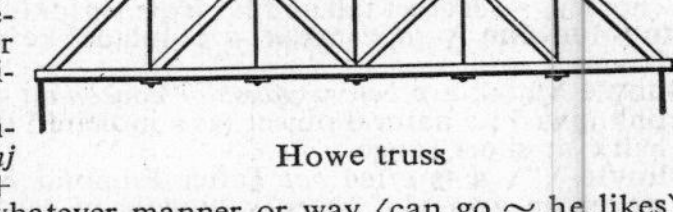

Howe truss

¹**how·ev·er** \hau̇ˈ(w)evə(r)\ *conj* [ME, fr. *how* + *ever*] **1a :** in whatever manner or way ⟨can go ~ he likes⟩ **b :** no matter to what degree or extent ⟨~ much he gives her, she wants more⟩ **2** *archaic* **:** ALTHOUGH ⟨*howe'er* thou art a fiend, a woman's shape doth shield thee —Shak.⟩
²**however** *adv* **1a :** to whatever degree or extent ⟨has done this for ~ many thousands of years —Emma Hawkridge⟩ ⟨every device, ~ paltry, was resorted to —W.H. Prescott⟩ **b :** in whatever manner or way ⟨shall serve you, sir, truly, ~ else —Shak.⟩ **2 :** in spite of that **:** on the other hand **:** BUT ⟨it still seems possible, ~, that conditions will improve⟩ ⟨I would like to go; ~, I think I'd better not⟩ **3** *archaic* **:** at all events **:** at least **:** in any case **4 :** how in the world ⟨~ did you manage it⟩
¹**howf** *or* **howff** \ˈhau̇f\ *n* -s [D *hof* enclosure, burial ground, garden, resort; akin to OE *hof* enclosure, court, dwelling, temple, OHG, court, garden, landed property, ON, enclosure, roofed temple, OE *hȳf* beehive — more at HIVE] **1** *chiefly Scot* **:** a dwelling place **2** *chiefly Scot* **:** an accustomed haunt or resort; *specif* **:** a favorite tavern
²**howf** *or* **howff** \ˈ"\ *vi* -ED/-ING/-S **1** *Scot* **a :** to take up one's abode **:** LODGE **b :** to make frequent visits **2** *Scot* **:** to take shelter
**how·go·zit curve** \hau̇ˈgōzə̇t-\ *n* [alter. of the phrase *how goes it?*] **:** a running graph of the progress of an airplane flight involving the distance covered, fuel consumed, and time elapsed and enabling the pilot to determine the equitime point
**how·ish** \ˈhau̇ish\ *adj* [short for *I don't know howish,* fr. the phrase *I don't know how* + *-ish*] *archaic* **:** feeling vaguely ill
**how·it·zer** \ˈhau̇ə̇tsə(r)\ *n* -s [D *houwitser,* fr. G *haubitze,* fr.

MHG *haufnitz* ballista, fr. Czech *houfnice*] **:** a cannon shorter than a gun of the same caliber employed to fire projectiles at medium muzzle velocities at relatively high angles of elevation at a target (as enemy artillery behind a ridge) which cannot be reached by flat-trajectory weapons

**¹howk** \ˈhōk\ *dial Brit var of* HAWK

**²howk** \ˈ"\ *vb* -ED/-ING/-S [ME *holken;* akin to MLG *holken* to hollow out; derivatives fr. the root of OE *hol* hollow — more at HOLE] *vt, dial Brit* **:** to hollow out **:** EXCAVATE, DIG — often used with a preposition ⟨lobsters had got at it . . . and ~*ed* pieces out of it —E.F.Benson⟩ ~ *vi, dial Brit* **:** DIG ⟨the dog was ~*ing* in the yard⟩

**howk·it** \ˈhau̇kət\ *adj* [fr. Sc past part. of *²howk*] *Scot* **:** dug up **:** hollowed out

**¹howl** \ˈhau̇l, *esp before pause or consonant* -au̇əl\ *vb* -ED/-ING/-S [ME *houlen;* akin to MD *hūlen* to howl, MHG *hiulen, hiuweln* to howl, OHG *hūwila* owl, Gk *kōkyein* to shriek, wail, lament, Skt *kauti* he cries out] *vi* **1 :** to utter or emit a loud sustained doleful sound or outcry characteristic of dogs and wolves ⟨wolves ~*ing* in the arctic night⟩ ⟨the only sound is a melancholy wind ~*ing* —John Buchan⟩ **2 :** to cry out or exclaim with lack of restraint and prolonged loudness through strong impulse, feeling, or emotion ⟨the scalded men ~*ing* in agony⟩ ⟨the hungry mob ~*ed* about the Senate house, threatening fire and massacre —J.A.Froude⟩ ⟨proctors ~*ing* at the blunder⟩ **3 :** to go on a spree or rampage ⟨this is my night to ~⟩ ~ *vt* **1 :** to utter or announce noisily with unrestrained demonstrative outcry ⟨newsboys ~*ing* the news⟩ **2 :** to affect, effect, or drive by adverse outcry — used esp. with *down* ⟨supporters of the Administration . . . ready to ~ down any suggestion of criticism —*Wall Street Jour.*⟩ **syn** see ROAR

**²howl** \ˈ"\ *n* -S **1 :** a loud protracted mournful rising and falling cry characteristic of a dog or a wolf **2 a :** a prolonged cry of distress **:** WAIL **b :** a yell or outcry of disappointment, rage, or protest **3 :** PROTEST, COMPLAINT ⟨raise a ~ over high taxes⟩ ⟨set up a ~ that he was being cheated⟩ **4 :** something that provokes laughter ⟨his act was a ~⟩ **5 :** a noise produced in an electronic amplifier usu. by undesired regeneration of alternating currents of audio frequency **:** OSCILLATION — called also *squeal*

**howl·er** \ˈhau̇lə(r)\ *n* -S **1 :** one that howls; *specif* **:** a professional wailer for the dead **2 :** HOWLER MONKEY **3 :** a glaringly stupid and ridiculous blunder esp. in the use of words ⟨his autobiography is spotted with ~*s* such as his description of the winter of 1938–39 as one of "peaceful preparation for war" —Geoffrey Parsons †1956⟩ **4 :** an electric buzzer **syn** see ERROR

**howler monkey** *or* **howling monkey** *n* **:** any of various So. and Central American monkeys having a long prehensile tail and a peculiar enlargement of the hyoid and laryngeal apparatus enabling them to make remarkable howling noises and constituting the genus *Alouatta*

**howl·et** \ˈhau̇lət, *dial Brit* ˈhül-\ *n* -S [ME *howlat, howlott,* prob. fr. *oule, owle, howle* owl + *-at, -ott* (vars. of *-et*) — more at OWL] **1** *now dial* **:** OWL, OWLET **2** *dial Brit* **:** a noisy dirty person

**howling** *adj* **1 :** producing, filled with, or marked by howling ⟨a ~ storm⟩ **2 :** WILD, SAVAGE, DESOLATE ⟨~ wilderness⟩ **3 :** very great **:** EXTREME, PRONOUNCED ⟨~ success⟩ — **howl·ing·ly** *adv*

**how·lite** \ˈhau̇,līt\ *n* -S [Henry *How* †1879 Canadian mineralogist + E *-ite*] **:** a mineral $Ca_2SiB_5O_9(OH)_5$ consisting of a white nodular or earthy calcium borosilicate

**howm** \ˈhəu̇m\ *chiefly Scot var of* HOLM

**how·rah** \ˈhau̇rə\ *adj, usu cap* [fr. *Howrah,* India] **:** of or from the city of Howrah, India **:** of the kind or style prevalent in Howrah

**hows** *pl of* HOW

**how's about** [by alter.] *substand* **:** how about

**how·ship's lacuna** \ˈhau̇,ships-\ *n, usu cap H* [after John *Howship* †1841 Eng. anatomist] **:** a groove or cavity containing osteoclasts in bone that is undergoing absorption

**how·so** \ˈhau̇(,)sō\ *adv* [ME, fr. *how* + *so*] *archaic* **:** HOWEVER

**how·so·ev·er** \ˌhau̇sə'wevə(r), -(,)sō;ev-\ *adv* [ME, fr. *how* + *so* + *ever*] **1 :** in what manner soever **:** to whatever degree or extent ⟨I am glad he's come, ~ he comes —Shak.⟩ **2** *archaic* **:** HOWEVER

**how·som·ev·er** \ˌhau̇sə'mevə(r)\ *adv* [alter. of *howsoever*] *chiefly dial* **:** HOWSOEVER, NEVERTHELESS, HOWEVER

**how-to** \ˈ=,tü\ *adj* [fr. *how to* in phrases like *how to make a birdhouse*] **:** giving practical instruction and advice (as on a craft, trade, hobby) ⟨publishing paperbound books, mostly of a *how-to* nature —*Publishers' Weekly*⟩ ⟨the magazine has a regular *how-to* section⟩

**hox** \ˈhäks\ *vt* -ED/-ING/-ES [ME *hoxen,* fr. *hox* hock sinew, fr. OE *hōhsinu,* fr. *hōh* heel + *sinu, seonu* sinew — more at HOCK, SINEW] **1 :** HAMSTRING **2 :** to pester by following **:** HARASS, ANNOY

**¹hoy** *or* **hoi** \ˈhȯi\ *interj* [ME] — used in greeting or in calling attention or in driving animals or to express surprise or alarm

**²hoy** \ˈ"\ *n* -S **:** HAIL, SHOUT, CALL ⟨better give that boat a ~⟩

**³hoy** \ˈ"\ *n* -S [ME *hoy, hoye,* fr. MD *hoei*] **1 :** a small usu. sloop-rigged coasting ship formerly used in conveying passengers and goods from place to place or as a tender to larger ships in port **2 :** a heavy barge used for weighty or bulky cargo

**¹hoya** \ˈhȯi(y)ə\ *n* [NL, after Thomas *Hoy* †1821 Eng. gardener] **1** *cap* **:** a large genus of climbing Australasian shrubs (family Asclepiadaceae) having fleshy leaves and nectariferous flowers with a rotate corolla and a star-shaped crown — see WAX PLANT, HONEY PLANT **2** -S **:** any plant of the genus *Hoya*

**²hoya** \ˈ"\ *n* -S [AmerSp, fr. Sp, large hole, pit, ditch, valley, fr. L *fovea* small pit] **:** a valley or basin high in rugged mountains (as the Andes)

**¹hoy·den** \ˈhȯidᵊn\ *n* -S [perh. fr. obs. D *heiden* country lout, fr. MD *heidijn, heiden* heathen, one that lives on a heath; akin to OE *hǣthen* heathen — more at HEATHEN] **1** *obs* **:** a rude clownish youth **2 :** a girl or woman of loud, boisterous, or carefree behavior **:** TOMBOY ⟨dancing in public with a troop of country ~*s* —Thomas Hardy⟩

**²hoyden** \ˈ"\ *vi* -ED/-ING/-S **:** to act like a hoyden

**³hoyden** \ˈ"\ *adj, of a girl* **:** RUDE, ILL-BRED, ROISTERING

**hoy·den·ish** \-ᵊnish\ *adj* **:** LIVELY, TOMBOYISH, UNLADYLIKE ⟨horsey, ~, six feet tall and far from shrinking —Sara H. Hay⟩

**hoy·den·ism** \-ᵊn,izəm\ *n* -S **:** unladylike or tomboyish behavior

**¹hoyle** \ˈhȯil, *esp before pause or consonant* -ȯiəl\ *n* -S [origin unknown] **:** a natural object (as a molehill) used as an archery mark at short range

**²hoyle** \ˈ"\ *n* -S *often cap* [after Edmond *Hoyle* †1769 Eng. writer on games] **:** an encyclopedia of card games and usu. other indoor games; *esp* **:** a book of rules accepted as standard or authoritative

**hoyle shooting** *n* [*¹hoyle*] **:** an archery pastime like roving except that the marks are always at short range

**hoy·man** \ˈhȯimən\ *n, pl* **hoymen :** one who owns or navigates a hoy

**HP** *abbr* **1** half pay **2** handmade paper **3** high-pass **4** high power **5** high pressure **6** high priest **7** hire purchase **8** horizontal parallax **9** *often not cap* horsepower **10** house physician **11** House of Parliament

**HPH** *abbr, often not cap* horsepower-hour

**h-pile** \ˈ=,=\ *n, cap H* **:** a steel pile having an H-shaped cross section

**HPO** *abbr* highway post office

**h pole** *n, cap H* **:** a telegraph pole built up of two parallel poles braced together

**hps** *abbr* harpsichord

**HQ** *abbr* **1** headquarters **2** *often not cap* [L *hoc quaere*] look for this; see this

**hr** *abbr* hour

**HR** *abbr* **1** high resistance **2** high run **3** home rule **4** home run **5** House of Representatives

**hrd** *abbr* hard

**hr factor** \(ˈ)āˈchär-\ *n, usu cap H* **:** an agglutinogen present in Rh-negative blood and apparently reciprocally related to the Rh factor

**HRH** *abbr* Her Royal Highness; His Royal Highness

**HRIP** *abbr* [L *hic requiescit in pace*] here rests in peace

**hrt** *abbr* heart

**hrtwd** *abbr* heartwood

**HS** *abbr* **1** hemstitched **2** [L *hic sepultus; hic situs*] here is buried **3** high school **4** high speed **5** *often not cap* [L *hoc sensu*] in this sense **6** honorary secretary **7** house surgeon

**h's** *or* **hs** *pl of* H

**h-scope** \ˈ=,=\ *n, usu cap H* **:** a radarscope on which signals appear as two dots joined by a line whose slope indicates the angle of elevation — compare B-SCOPE

**hse** *abbr* house

**HSE** *abbr* [L *hic sepultus est; hic situs est*] here is buried

**h section** *n, cap H* **:** a rolled structural metal section with an H-shaped cross section and wide flanges

**hsg** *abbr* housing

**HSH** *abbr* Her Serene Highness; His Serene Highness

**h-shaped** \ˈ=,=\ *adj, cap H* **:** having the shape of a capital H

**hsia** \ˈshēˈä\ *n, usu cap H* [Chin (Pek) *hsia⁴*] **1 :** the first dynasty of China said to have been founded by the legendary emperor Yu **2** -S **:** the people of the Hsia dynasty

**hsi-fan** \ˈshēˈfän\ *n, pl* **hsi-fan** *usu cap H&F* [Chin (Pek) *hsi¹ fan¹* fr. *hsi¹* west, western + *fan¹* foreign, barbarous] **:** any of several east Tibetan peoples on the western border of China

**hsin** \ˈshin\ *n* -S [Chin (Pek) *hsin⁴*] *Confucianism* **:** the cardinal virtue faithfulness or veracity

**hsiung-nu** \shēˈu̇ŋˈnü\ *n, pl* **hsiung-nu** *usu cap H&N* [Chin (Pek) *hsiung¹ nu²,* fr. *hsiung¹* cruel, fierce + *nu²* slave, servant] **:** an ancient horse-using people related to or identical with the Huns, including the Jung and Ti peoples of Chinese history, and recorded in Chinese annals as being a powerful nation and in the 3d century B.C. occupying all the country between the Caspian sea and the Great Wall and dominating much of Mongolia

**HSM** *abbr* Her Serene Majesty; His Serene Majesty

**h-stretcher** \ˈ=,==\ *n, cap H* **:** a common leg brace for furniture consisting of two stretchers from front to back joined by a central crossbar

H-stretcher

**ht** *abbr* **1** heat **2** height

**HT** *abbr* **1** half time **2** herd test **3** high-tension **4** high tide **5** *often not cap* [L *hoc tempore*] at this time **6** *often not cap* [L *hoc titulo*] under this title

**HTA** *abbr* heavier than air

**htg** *abbr* heating

**HTH** *abbr* high-test hypochlorite

**hu** \ˈhü\ *n, pl* **hu** *or* **hus** *usu cap* [Chin (Pek) *hu²,* lit., dewlap of an ox] **:** an ancient Tatar people of northwest China related to the Hsiung-Nu

**hua** \ˈhyüə\ *n, cap* [NL] **:** a genus of freshwater snails of eastern Asia (family Thiaridae) including important intermediate hosts of the Chinese liver fluke and the human lung fluke

**huabi** *usu cap, var of* HUAVE

**hua·ca** \ˈwäkə\ *or* **gua·ca** \ˈgw-\ *n* -S [Sp *guaca, huaca,* fr. Quechua *wáka*] **:** an ancient Peruvian sacred object: **a :** GOD, SPIRIT **b :** any object (as a mountain, animal, shrine, or artifact) inhabited by a god or spirit **:** FETISH — compare MANITOU, NAGUAL, ZEMI **c :** a pre-Columbian ruin (as a tomb or burial mound)

**hua·co** \-(,)kō\ *n* -S [Sp *guaco, huaco,* fr. Quechua *wáko, wáku,* fr. *wáka*] **:** a pre-Columbian relic of Peru (as an object discovered in a tomb)

**hua·ji·llo** \wäˈhē(,)(y)ō\ *also* **hua·ji·lla** \-ē(y)ə\ *n* -S [MexSp *guajillo, huajillo, guajilla, huajilla,* dim. of *guaje* gourd, fr. Nahuatl *huaxin*] **:** either of two honey plants from Texas and adjacent Mexico: **a :** a spiny shrub (*Pithecolobium brevifolium*) **b :** a sweet-scented shrub (*Acacia berlandieri*)

**hualapai** *or* **hualpai** *usu cap, var of* WALAPAI

**hualpi** *usu cap, var of* WALPI

**hua·mu·chil** \wäˈmü,chēl\ *or* **gua·mu·chil** \gw-\ *also* **cua·mu·chil** \kw-\ *n* -S [MexSp *guamúchil, huamúchil, cuamúchil* — more at CAMACHILE] **:** CAMACHILE

**huanaco** *var of* GUANACO

**huan·ca·pam·pa** \ˌwäŋkəˈpämpə\ *n, pl* **huancapampa** *or* **huancapampas** *usu cap* [Sp, fr. *Huancapampa* (now *Huancabamba*), region of Peru] **:** CHINCHAISUYU

**hua·nu·co coca** \ˈwänə,kō-\ *n, usu cap H* [AmerSp (Peru) *huánuco,* prob. fr. *Huánuco,* town and department in Peru] **:** COCA 2a

**hua·pan·go** \wäˈpäŋ(,)gō\ *n* -S [MexSp, a festival celebrated in the state of Veracruz, dance typical of this festival, *huapango,* fr. *Huapango,* town in Veracruz, Mexico] **:** a fast and complicated Mexican couple dance that is usu. performed on a wooden platform to accentuate the rhythmic beating of heels and toes

**hua·ra·che** \wəˈrächē\ *also* **gua·ra·che** \ˈ"\ *or* **hua·ra·cho** \-(,)chō\ *n* -S [MexSp *guarache, huarache*] **:** a low-heeled sandal; *esp* **:** a sling-backed sandal having an upper made of interwoven leather thongs

huarache

**hua·ri** \ˈwä(,)rē\ *n, pl* **huari** *or* **huaris** *usu cap* [Pg, of AmerInd origin] **1 a :** an Indian people of western Mato Grosso, Brazil **b :** a member of such people **2 :** the language of the Huari people

**hua·ri·zo** \wäˈrē(,)zō, -ē(,)sō\ *n* -S [AmerSp] **:** the offspring of a male llama and a female alpaca

**huar·pe** \ˈwär(,)pā\ *n, pl* **huarpe** *or* **huarpes** *usu cap* [Sp, of AmerInd origin] **1 a :** a group of Indian peoples of western Argentina including the Allentiac of the San Juan province **b :** a member of such peoples **2 :** a language family consisting of the languages spoken by the Huarpe peoples — **huar·pe·an** \-pēən\ *adj or n, usu cap*

**huasima** *var of* GUACIMO

**huas·tec** *or* **huax·tec** \ˈwä,stek\ *also* **huas·teca** \wäˈstäkə, -tekə\ *or* **huas·te·co** \-(,)kō\ *n, pl* **huastec** *or* **huastecs** *or* **huaxtec** *or* **huaxtecs** *usu cap* [Sp *guasteco, guaxteco, huasteco, huaxteco,* of AmerInd origin] **1 a :** an Indian people of the states of San Luis Potosi, Veracruz, and Tamaulipas, Mexico **b :** a member of such people **2 :** the Mayan language of the Huastec people — **huas·tecan** \(ˈ)wäˈstekən, -tek-\ *adj, usu cap*

**hua·ve** \ˈwävē\ *or* **hua·bi** \ˈ", -äbē\ *n, pl* **huave** *or* **huaves** *or* **huabi** *or* **huabis** *usu cap* [Sp, of AmerInd origin] **1 a :** an Indian people of the region between the lagoons and the Gulf of Tehuantepec, Oaxaca, Mexico **b :** a member of such people **2 :** the language of the Huave people that is without proven affinities — **hua·ve·an** \-vēən\ *adj, usu cap*

**huayule** *var of* GUAYULE

**¹hub** \ˈhəb\ *n* -S [prob. alter. of *²hob*] **1 a :** the usu. cylindrical central part of a wheel **:** NAVE — compare AXLE BOX **b :** the central part of a propeller or motor-driven fan to which the blades are attached ⟨raising the propeller ~ above water so that we could get the prop off —K.M.Dodson⟩ **2 a :** a chief center of activity **:** FOCAL POINT ⟨heart, ~, and pivot of this new Virginia Metropolis is the Pentagon —A.W.Atwood⟩ ⟨Indianapolis . . . became the ~ of a rail center with lines running in all directions —R.H.Brown⟩ ⟨this fact must serve as the ~ of the analysis —*Political Science Quarterly*⟩ ⟨the ~ of every hemoglobin molecule is one atom of iron —D.C. Peattie⟩ ⟨Boston Statehouse is the ~ of the solar system —O.W.Holmes †1894⟩; *specif* **:** a center of circulation in architectural planning ⟨the dwelling has a novel ~ floor plan, permitting easy access between rooms —*N.Y. Herald Tribune*⟩ **b :** a durable marker placed at an important point of a survey for use (as in triangulation) **3 a :** a steel punch from which a working die for a coin or medal is made and which in modern processes bears the design as cut by a reducing machine copying the engraver's model **b :** ²HOB 4a(4) **c :** MASTER TAP **d** (1) **:** a boss that resembles the hub of a wheel (2) **:** BARREL 3d **e :** a piece in a lock that is turned by the knob spindle passing through it and that moves the bolt **4 :** a ridge on the backbone of a book (as a leather-bound book) formed by a covering cord or a strip of cardboard **:** ¹BAND 5b(1) **5 :** a connection or point of confluence: as **a** (1) **:** a short coupling used to join pipes in plumbing (2) *also* **hubb :** BELL 5i **b :** a hole on the panelboard of a piece of electrical equipment into which a wire is plugged **:** electrical contact **c :** the enlarged base by which a hollow needle (as for a hypodermic) may be attached to a syringe or other device **syn** see CENTER

**²hub** \ˈ"\ *vt* **hubbed; hubbed; hubbing; hubs :** ³HOB 2b

**³hub** \ˈ"\ *adj, usu cap* [fr. the *Hub,* nickname for Boston, Mass.] *chiefly NewEng* **:** of or relating to the city of Boston, Mass. ⟨*Hub* officials⟩

**hu·ba·bo** \(h)üˈbä(,)bō\ *n, pl* **hubabo** *or* **hubabos** *usu cap* [Sp, of AmerInd origin] **1 :** an Indian people of the northern part of the Dominican Republic **2 :** a member of the Hubabo people

**hu·bam clover** \ˈhyü,bam-\ *also* **hubam** *n* -S *often cap H* [Harold DeMott *Hughes* b1882 Am. agronomist, its discoverer + *Alabama,* state in the U.S., source of the seed for the experimental plot in which it was discovered] **:** an annual variety (*Melilotus alba annua*) of sweet clover

**hub-and-spigot joint** \ˌ=='==-\ *n* **:** BELL-AND-SPIGOT JOINT

**hubba-hubba** \ˌhəbəˈhəbə\ *interj* [origin unknown] — used to express approval, excitement, or enthusiasm

**hub·bard squash** \ˈhəbə(r)d-\ *also* **hubbard** *n* -S *usu cap H* [prob. fr. the name *Hubbard*] **:** any of various winter squashes having the fruit generally ovoid and pointed at the end away from the stem, the skin smooth to strongly warted, and ranging in color from dark green to orange

**hub·bell·ite** \ˈhəbə,līt\ *n* -S [fr. *Hubbellite,* a trademark] **:** an oxychloride cement that contains finely powdered copper, is fungicidal and germicidal, possesses high tensile strength and adhesive properties, and is resistant to abrasion

**hub·ber** \ˈhəbə(r)\ *n* -S [*¹hub* + *-er*] **:** one that sinks hobs into steel for die stamping

**hub·bite** \ˈhə,bīt\ *n* -S *usu cap* [the *Hub,* nickname for Boston + E *-ite*] **:** BOSTONIAN

**hub·ble** \ˈhəbəl\ *n* -S [prob. short for *hubbleshew*] *dial Brit* **:** HUBBUB, UPROAR

**hubble-bubble** \ˌhəbəlˈbəbəl\ *n* -S [redupl. of *bubble*] **1 :** WATER PIPE 2; *esp* **:** a rudimentary water pipe sometimes consisting merely of a bowl mounted on a coconut in which there is a hole that serves as a mouthpiece — compare HOOKAH, NARGILEH **2 :** a burble of sound or flurry of activity **:** COMMOTION ⟨for hours a merry but rather tedious *hubble-bubble,* suggesting liquor, was heard ascending from the cabin skylight —R.A.W.Hughes⟩ ⟨the *hubble-bubble* of spring-cleaning —*Manchester Guardian Weekly*⟩

**hub·ble·shew** *or* **hub·ble·show** \ˈhəbəl,shō, -shü\ *n* -S [perh. fr. obs. Flem *hobbel-sjobbel, hobbel-sobbel* in an uproar, confusedly] *chiefly Scot* **:** UPROAR, TUMULT, COMMOTION

**hub·bly** \ˈhəb(ə)lē\ *adj* [alter. of *hobbly*] **:** having an uneven surface **:** ROUGH ⟨a ~ road⟩ ⟨a ~ sea⟩

**hub·bub** \ˈhə,bəb\ *n* -S [prob. of Celt origin; akin to ScGael *ub ub, ubub,* an interj. of contempt] **1 :** a noisy confusion of sound **:** DIN, UPROAR ⟨a ~ of cocks crowing and children shouting —Alan Moorehead⟩ ⟨~ of an orchestra tuning up⟩ **2 :** a state of tumultuous confusion or excitement **:** TURMOIL ⟨swarmed onto the field in a wild ~ after winning the game⟩ ⟨the animated excitement and ~ that gives the . . . institution its friendly vitality —Aline B. Saarinen⟩ ⟨it behooves culture to . . . save the individual in the midst of this industrial ~ —J.C. Powys⟩ **3 :** an Indian game resembling dice played with bones and a tray — used by New England settlers **syn** see DIN

**hub·bu·boo** *or* **hub·ba·boo** \ˌhəbəˈbü\ *n* -S [prob. of Celt origin like *hubbub*] **:** HUBBUB 1, 2

**hub·by** \ˈhəbē, -bi\ *n* -ES [by alter.] **:** HUSBAND — not often in formal use

**hubcap** \ˈ=,=\ *n* **:** a removable metal cap screwed or clamped over the end of an axle; *esp* **:** such a cap used on the wheel of a motor vehicle

hubcap on an automobile wheel

**hu·bris** \ˈh(y)übrəs\ *also* **hy·bris** \ˈhīb-\ *n* -ES [Gk *hybris* — more at OUT] **:** overweening pride or self-confidence **:** ARROGANCE ⟨the very best critics of the past have made so many blunders . . . that our own critics today should be careful to avoid ~ —*Times Lit. Supp.*⟩ — contrasted with *sophrosyne*

**hu·bris·tic** \hyüˈbristik\ *adj* [Gk *hybristikos,* fr. *hybristēs* violent, wanton, insolent man (fr. *hybris*) + *-ikos* -ic] **:** INSOLENT, VAIN, ARROGANT — **hu·bris·ti·cal·ly** \-tək(ə)lē\ *adv*

**hubs** *pl of* HUB, *pres 3d sing of* HUB

**hu·chen** \ˈhükən, -k-\ *also* **huch** \-k,-k\ *n* -S [G] **:** a large elongate predacious game fish (*Hucho hucho*) of the Danube that resembles the Atlantic salmon but may attain a weight of 130 pounds

**huch·nom** \ˈhüchnəm\ *n, pl* **huchnom** *or* **huchnoms** *usu cap* [Yuki] **1 a :** an Indian people of the Eel river valley in northwestern California **b :** a member of such people **2 :** the Yuki dialect of the Huchnom people

**hu·cho** \ˈh(y)ü(,)kō\ *n* [NL, fr. G *huchen, huch*] **1** *cap* **:** a European genus of large riverine fishes (family Salmonidae) that are closely related to the salmons and trouts of the genus *Salmo* from which they are distinguished esp. by the absence of teeth along the median line of the hyoid bone **2** -S **:** any fish of the genus *Hucho; esp* **:** HUCHEN

**¹huck** \ˈhək\ *vi* -ED/-ING/-S [ME *hukken,* prob. back-formation fr. *hukster, hokster* huckster — more at HUCKSTER] *now dial Eng* **:** HIGGLE, BARGAIN

**²huck** \ˈ"\ *n* -S [ME *hokebone* — more at HUCKLE] *chiefly dial* **:** HIP, HAUNCH

**³huck** \ˈ"\ *n* -S [by shortening] **:** HUCKABACK

**⁴huck** \ˈ"\ *n* -S [by alter.] *dial* **:** HUSK

**huck·a·back** \ˈhəkə,bak, -,bək\ *n* [origin unknown] **1 :** a textured weave in which yarns are floated on a plain ground to form small allover patterns **2 :** an absorbent durable cotton, linen, or cotton and linen fabric with a huckaback weave used chiefly for towels

**huck·le** \ˈhəkəl\ *n* -S [akin to ME *hokebone* hip, haunch, and perh. to ON *hūka* to squat — more at HAWKER] **:** HIP, HAUNCH

**huckleback** \ˈ==,=\ *n* **:** HUMPBACK

**¹huck·le·ber·ry** \ˈhəkəl— *see* BERRY\ *n* [perh. alter. of *hurtleberry*] **1 a :** an edible dark-blue to black berry with 10 hard bony nutlets that is typically smaller and more acid than a blueberry **b :** any of several No. American shrubs of the genus *Gaylussacia* (esp. *G. baccata*) whose fruit is a huckleberry — see BOX HUCKLEBERRY **2 :** BLUEBERRY 1: as **a :** a dark-fruited as distinguished from a blue-fruited blueberry **b :** WHORTLEBERRY 1 **c :** a stiff evergreen shrub (*Vaccinium ovatum*) with edible garnet to black berries and glossy foliage much used as greenery in floral arrangements and decorations

**²huckleberry** \ˈ"\ *vi* **:** to pick or look for huckleberries ⟨go ~*ing*⟩

**huckleberry family** *n* **:** ERICACEAE

**huckleberry oak** *n* **:** a low, spreading, often prostrate shrub (*Quercus vaccinifolia*) of southwestern U.S. with slender branches and green leaves that resemble those of the huckleberry

**hucklebone** \ˈ==,=\ *n* **1 :** HIPBONE, HOOK 5c(2) **2 :** TALUS **3** *archaic* **:** KNUCKLEBONE 2

**¹huck·ster** \ˈhəkstə(r)\ *n* -S [ME *hukster, hokster,* fr. MD *hokester, hoekster,* fr. *hoken, hoeken* to peddle, bear on the back, squat + *-ster* — more at HAWKER] **1 :** one that sells goods along the street or from door to door **:** HAWKER, PEDDLER **2 a** *archaic* **:** one that buys to resell at a profit **:** MIDDLEMAN **b :** one that acts primarily from mercenary motives **3 a :** one that produces advertising material for commercial clients **:** ADMAN ⟨home is not the plastic chromium dream . . . the ~*s* promised to them —R.W.Kenny⟩; *specif* **:** one that prepares or delivers commercials for radio or television ⟨~*s* speak only to sponsors; and sponsors don't speak at all, they read sales charts —Walter Goodman⟩ ⟨a syrupy-voiced ~ proclaiming the virtues of Dinkelspiel's Deodorant —Bennett Cerf⟩ **b :** one that employs persuasive showmanship to make a sale or attain an objective ⟨the most adroit ~ of $1000 trinkets in our time —Maurice Zolotow⟩ ⟨minds taught to respond without reflection to the slogans of our political ~*s* —*New Republic*⟩

**²huckster** \ˈ"\ *vb* **huckstered; huckstered; huckstering** \-t(ə)riŋ\ **hucksters** *vi* **:** HAGGLE ⟨~ over prices on the

black market⟩ ~ *vt* **1 :** to deal in or bargain over **:** retail for profit ⟨~ fresh eggs⟩ ⟨~ real estate⟩ ⟨~ his services⟩ **2 :** to promote by showmanship ⟨a store where cheap stuff is ballyhooed and ~*ed* into seeming richness —C.W.Drepperd⟩
**huck·ster·er** \-t(ə)rə(r)\ *n* -s *archaic* **:** HUCKSTER
**huckstering** *n* -s [fr. gerund of ²*huckster*] **:** the activities or occupation of a huckster
**huck·ster·ism** \-tə,rizəm\ *n* -s **:** persuasive showmanship in advertising or selling **:** COMMERCIALISM 2 ⟨sponsoring the Metropolitan Opera broadcasts . . . without the faintest trace of bad taste or ~ —Howard Taubman⟩ ⟨the unashamed ~ practiced by our present government —R.L.Riggs⟩
**hud** \ˈhəd\ *n* -s [ME *hudde*] *dial Eng* **:** a husk or hull esp. of a berry
**hud·ders·field** \ˈhədə(r)z,fēld\ *adj, usu cap* [fr. *Huddersfield,* England] **:** of or from the county borough of Huddersfield, England **:** of the kind or style prevalent in Huddersfield
**¹hud·dle** \ˈhədᵊl\ *vb* **huddled; huddled; huddling** \-d(ᵊ)liŋ\ **huddles** [prob. fr. or akin to ME *hoderen* to huddle together, wrap up; prob. akin to ME *hiden* to hide — more at HIDE] *vt* **1** *Brit* **:** to throw together or complete carelessly or hurriedly ⟨things happened as in a badly directed moving picture, all *huddled*, all hurried —Donn Byrne⟩ — often followed by a directional adverb ⟨the solemnities had to be *huddled* through at express speed —*Manchester Examiner*⟩ ⟨weakness . . . to ~ up his stories rather than to wind them off to an orderly conclusion —George Saintsbury⟩ **2 :** to conceal from view **:** cover up ⟨political deaths are *huddled* and secret —*Time & Tide*⟩ **3 a :** to mass together **:** CROWD ⟨give me your tired, your poor, your *huddled* masses yearning to breathe free —Emma Lazarus⟩ ⟨ours is a nation in which military and civilian targets are *huddled* together —D. H. McLachlan⟩ ⟨all over the country people are *huddled* round their radios —F.L.Allen⟩ **b :** to draw (oneself) together **:** CROUCH ⟨the men *huddled* themselves low against the wind —A.J.Cronin⟩ ⟨he was *huddled* in his cot, trying to keep warm —Gertrude Atherton⟩ **4** *dial chiefly Eng* **:** HUG, EMBRACE **5 a** *archaic* **:** to herd into or out of a place in a disorderly mass ⟨we were *huddled* out like a flock of sheep, by a file of soldiers —Frederick Marryat⟩ **b :** to pull on unceremoniously or wrap oneself closely in (clothes) ⟨she *huddled* her purple woolen coat round her —Rumer Godden⟩ — often used with *on* ⟨I *huddled* on my clothes —A.T.Quiller-Couch⟩ ~ *vi* **1 a :** to gather in a group **:** press close together **:** ASSEMBLE, BUNCH ⟨passengers . . . ~ like sheep at entrance gates —Bennett Cerf⟩ ⟨an opera chorus ~*s* round a few haughty soloists —G.B. Shaw⟩ ⟨little printers' cafés . . . ~ near the thundering presses —Francis Aldor⟩ **b :** to curl up **:** CROUCH ⟨*huddled* in the lee of a rock, trying to get a little protection from the wind —H.D. Quillin⟩ ⟨a long gray cat *huddled* watchfully in the window —Katherine A. Porter⟩ — often used with *up* ⟨*huddled* up, closed his eyes, and went quite . . . peacefully to sleep —James Hilton⟩ **c :** to dress oneself hurriedly or wrap something around oneself ⟨hip-length coat, with a big collar to ~ —Lois Long⟩ **2** *obs* **:** to act in a precipitate manner ⟨fools ~ on, and always are in haste —Nicholas Rowe⟩ **3 a :** to hold a consultation **:** CONFER ⟨worried financiers *huddled* to discuss the possible effects of the blow on California's economy —*Newsweek*⟩ ⟨the gang . . . ~*s* around a table in a small upstairs room —John Mason Brown⟩; *specif* **:** to gather behind the scrimmage line in a football game and agree on team strategy **b :** to pause for thought in a bridge game
**²huddle** \"\ *n* -s **1 a :** a close-packed group **:** JUMBLE, BUNCH ⟨~*s* of cows and sheep⟩ ⟨the ugly ~ of weather-beaten shacks and wharves where the fishermen kept their tackle —L.C. Douglas⟩ ⟨~ of meaningless words —Edith Sitwell⟩ ⟨the four harpooners, the cooper, and myself were sitting in a ~ in the steerage —H.A.Chippendale⟩ **b :** a shapeless mass **:** LUMP ⟨a ~ of black against the starlight —Marjory S. Douglas⟩ **2 :** CONFUSION, DISARRAY, MUDDLE ⟨equally free from the dullness of slow or the hurry and ~ of quick time —Earl of Chesterfield⟩ **3 a :** MEETING, DISCUSSION, CONFERENCE ⟨spent some eight hours in a ~ with a dozen laymen and priests —M.E.Bennett⟩ ⟨secret ~*s* were held by five leading Republicans —*Newsweek*⟩ ⟨a ~ of social scientists put the finishing touches on a massive study of American life —F.L.Allen⟩ — often used in the phrase *go into a huddle* ⟨at the end of the bout the judges go into a ~ to determine the winner⟩ ⟨she went into a series of ~*s* with cheese experts —Harry Thompson⟩ ⟨go into a ~ with yourself about it —Mary D. Gillies⟩ **b :** a strategy conference of football players behind the line of scrimmage **c :** a long pause for thought by a bridge player before he bids or plays ⟨went into a ~ before making his first discard —Oswald Jacoby⟩
**hud·dler** \ˈhəd(ᵊ)lə(r)\ *n* -s **:** one that huddles
**huddling** *adj* **:** in a huddle or hurry **:** JUMBLED, RUSHING ⟨horsemen charged the ~ crowd⟩ ⟨the ~ and tumultuous brook —Sir Walter Scott⟩ — **hud·dling·ly** *adv*
**hud·up** \(,)həˈdəp, -dap; həˈrəp, hᵊˈrəp\ *v imper* [perh. alter. of *get up*] — used as a command to horses or oxen to go ahead or go faster
**¹hu·di·bras·tic** \ˌhyüdəˈbrastik\ *adj, usu cap* [*Hudibras,* mock-heroic satirical poem in octosyllabic couplets by Samuel Butler †1680 Eng. poet + E *-tic* (as in *fantastic*)] **1 :** written in humorous octosyllabic couplets **2 :** smartly and sportively burlesque **:** MOCK-HEROIC — **hu·di·bras·ti·cal·ly** \-tək(ə)lē\ *adv, usu cap*
**²hudibrastic** \"\ *n* -s **:** an octosyllabic couplet used in humorous verse
**hud·son bay pine** \ˈhədsən,bā-\ *n, usu cap H&B* [fr. *Hudson bay* or *Hudson's bay,* inland sea in northern Canada] **:** JACK PINE 1
**hudson bay sable** *n, usu cap H&B* **:** AMERICAN SABLE
**hud·so·nia** \ˌhədˈsōnēə\ *n* [NL, fr. William *Hudson* †1793 Eng. botanist + NL *-ia*] **1** *cap* **:** a genus of low heathlike No. American herbs (family Cistaceae) with hoary or villous foliage and usu. bright yellow flowers **2 :** any plant of the genus *Hudsonia*
**hud·so·ni·an** \ˌhədˈsōnēən\ *adj, usu cap* [*Hudson* (*bay*) + E *-ian*] **1 :** of or relating to Hudson bay **2 :** of, relating to, or being a subdivision of the biogeographic Boreal zone extending across No. America from Labrador to Alaska, being bounded to the south and in certain high mountain regions by the isotherm indicating a mean temperature of 57.2° Fahrenheit during the 6 hottest weeks of the year, and marking the northern extent of the coniferous forest belt
**hudsonian chickadee** *n, usu cap H* **:** CHICKADEE
**hudsonian curlew** *n, usu cap H* **:** the No. American variety (*Numenius phaeopus hudsonicus*) of the whimbrel
**hudsonian godwit** *n, usu cap H* **:** an American godwit (*Limosa haemastica*) with a long slightly upturned bill and underparts that are finely black barred during the spring
**hudson's bay blanket** *n, usu cap H&B* **:** a heavy woolen blanket with one or more broad stripes usu. black on a red ground or varicolored on a white ground at each end to indicate its weight
**¹hue** \ˈhyü\ *n* -s [ME *hewe* appearance, shape, kind, color, fr. OE *hīw, hēow;* akin to ON *hȳ* fine hair, down, Goth *hiwi* form, appearance, OE *hār* hoary — more at HOAR] **1 :** SHAPE, COMPLEXION, ASPECT ⟨a ghost town in modern ~ —*Springfield* (*Mass.*) *Union*⟩ ⟨songs . . . of a sad and somber ~ —William Black⟩ ⟨political parties of every ~ —Louis Wasserman⟩ **2 a :** COLOR 1; *esp* **:** gradation of color ⟨the work of an inspired painter can reveal to us the ~*s* and shades of twilight —Colin Clark⟩ **b :** the attribute of colors that permits them to be classed as red, yellow, green, blue, or an intermediate between any contiguous pair of these — used in psychology; see COLOR 1b **c :** hue in the Munsell color system — used in psychophysics; see the Color Charts explanation at COLOR **syn** see COLOR
**²hue** \"\ *vb* -ED/-ING/-S [ME *hewen* to form, fashion, color, fr. OE *hīwian,* fr. *hīw,* n.] *vt* **:** TINGE ⟨*hued* their sight with rainbow beauty —Peggy Bennett⟩ ~ *vi* **:** to take on color **:** become colored ⟨in highlights it *hued* to dull silver gray —William Beebe⟩
**³hue** \"\ *vb* -ED/-ING/-S [ME *huwen,* fr. OF *huer* to shout, hoot, fr. *hu,* interj. used esp. to apprise of danger] *vi, now dial* **:** to make outcry **:** SHOUT ~ *vt, obs* **:** to shout at **:** drive with shouts
**⁴hue** \"\ *n* -s [ME *hew, hu,* fr. OF *hue,* outcry, noise, fr *huer*] **:** SHOUT, OUTCRY

**hue and cry** *n* [⁴*hue*] **1 a :** a loud outcry used in the pursuit of felons and joined and taken up by all who heard it in the pursuit **b :** the pursuit of a felon or a written proclamation for the capture of a felon or the finding of stolen goods **2 :** a clamor of pursuit or protest ⟨had visions of sheriffs . . . posses and *hue and cry* —Esther Forbes⟩ ⟨conservative politicians joined in the *hue and cry* against the school and its doctrines —Hunter Mead⟩ **3 :** HUBBUB ⟨the unloading . . . was being conducted with a *hue and cry,* with raucous bangs and crashes —Jean Stafford⟩
**hueb·ner·ite** \ˈhēbnə,rīt, ˈhyüb-\ *n* -s [G *hübnerit,* fr. Adolf *Hübner,* 19th cent. Ger. foundry superintendent + G *-it* -ite] **:** a mineral $MnWO_4$ consisting of manganese tungstate, having a brownish red to nearly black color, occurring in columnar or foliated masses, and being isomorphous with wolframite
**hue circle** *or* **hue circuit** *also* **hue cycle** *n* **:** COLOR CIRCLE
**hued** \ˈhyüd\ *adj* [ME *hewed* formed, fashioned, colored, fr. OE *gehīwod, hīwod,* past part. of *gehīwian, hīwian* to hue — more at HUE] **:** COLORED — usu. used in combination ⟨green-hued⟩ ⟨rich, many-*hued* prose —Ray Corsini⟩
**hue·ful** \ˈhyüfəl\ *adj* **:** having hue and saturation **:** CHROMATIC
**hue·huetl** \(ˈ)wāˈ(h)wātᵊl\ *n* -s [MexSp, fr. Nahuatl] **:** an ancient vertically cylindrical Mexican Indian drum usu. hollowed from a tree trunk and fitted with a skin head
**hue·less** \ˈhyüləs\ *adj* [ME *heweles* shapeless, colorless, fr. OE *hīwlēas,* fr. *hīw* appearance, shape, kind, color + *-lēas* -less — more at HUE] **1 :** COLORLESS **2 :** having no hue **:** GRAY — **hue·less·ness** *n* -ES
**huemul** *var of* GUEMAL
**huer·ta** \ˈwer(,)tä\ *n* -s [Sp, large vegetable garden or orchard, fr. *huerto* small vegetable garden or orchard, fr. L *hortus* garden — more at YARD] **:** a piece of highly cultivated land (as for an orchard) in Spain
**¹huff** \ˈhəf\ *vb* -ED/-ING/-S [imit.] *vi* **1 a :** to emit puffs (as of air or steam) **:** BLOW, PANT ⟨he ~*ed* and he puffed and he blew the house down —*Three Little Pigs*⟩ ⟨another tug ~*s* quietly somewhere down below —W.V.Anderson⟩ **b :** to progress with puffing ⟨the first cyclists ~*ed* into sight —*Time*⟩ **2 a :** to speak in a threatening and bombastic manner **:** make empty threats **:** BLUSTER, RANT ⟨faced with new wage demands, management ~*s* about spiraling costs and the dangers of inflation⟩ ⟨children will soon discover that this is only ~*ing* and puffing on your part —H.R.Litchfield & L.H.Dembo⟩ **b** (1) **:** to react indignantly **:** speak resentfully **:** SNAP, STORM ⟨the father ~*s* and puffs and says, "Do you think I'm made of money" —Peter DeVries⟩ (2) **:** to behave indignantly **:** FLOUNCE ⟨resigned in pique and ~*ed* off to London —Janet Flanner⟩ **3** *archaic* **:** to become angry **:** take offense ⟨the woman has ~*ed* and won't trust me —Frederick Marryat⟩ **4** *now dial* **:** to expand in size **:** ENLARGE ⟨the bread ~*s*⟩ **5 :** to remove an opponent's checker from the board for failure to make a possible jump ~ *vt* **1 a :** to blow into **:** INFLATE, PUFF ⟨it ~*s* air steadily . . . through its hollow shaft —*Newsweek*⟩ ⟨their buying ~*ed* low-priced motor shares —*Time*⟩ **b :** to accomplish with puffing ⟨~*ed* himself up and stumped out of the room —Jackson Burgess⟩ **2** *archaic* **:** to treat with contempt **:** BULLY ⟨quarreling with his bread and butter and ~*ing* the waiter —Washington Irving⟩ ⟨the beast in scorn ~*ed* the uplifted club —J.C.Fairbairn⟩ **3 :** to make angry or petulant **:** PROVOKE, ANNOY ⟨this astounding rigidity of custom ~*ed* the king —Francis Hackett⟩ **4 :** to remove (an opponent's checker) from the board for failure to make a possible jump
**²huff** \"\ *n* -s **1 :** ²PUFF 1a ⟨at the moment of firing he might actually turn his face away from his sights to avoid the ~ from the pan —Odell & Willard Shepard⟩ **2 :** a fit of anger or pique ⟨in an . . . unprecedented display of parliamentary ~, refused to join the traditional procession —Mollie Panter-Downes⟩ — usu. used in the phrase *in a huff* ⟨the dissenting experts will secede in a ~ —Ernst Pulgram⟩ ⟨if you encounter a person who's in a ~ about something, you'd better wait until he cools off —W.J.Reilly⟩ **3** *obs* **a :** an attitude or display of arrogance ⟨quell . . . the ~ of the proud —Randle Cotgrave⟩ **b :** an arrogant or conceited person ⟨this young ~ commanded a sergeant to pay him respect —William Darrell⟩ **4** *dial Eng* **a :** light leavened pastry **b :** HUFF CAP 1 **5 :** an act of huffing in checkers **syn** see OFFENSE
**³huff** \"\ *adj, dial* **:** HUFFED, OFFENDED
**¹huffcap** \ˈ=,=\ *n* -s [¹*huff* + *cap*] **1** *obs* **:** strong ale **2** *obs* **:** SWAGGERER, BULLY
**²huffcap** \"\ *adj* **1** *obs* **:** INTOXICATING **2** *archaic* **:** SWAGGERING ⟨a ~ hero . . . mouthed and strutted out his hour on the stage —A.C.Swinburne⟩
**huff·i·ly** \ˈhəfəlē, -li\ *adv* **:** in a huffy manner
**huff·i·ness** \-fēnəs, -fin-\ *n* -ES **:** the quality or state of being huffy
**huff·ing·ly** *adv, archaic* **:** in an arrogant or sulky manner
**huff·ish** \ˈhəfish\ *adj* **:** ARROGANT, SULKY **syn** see IRRITABLE
**¹huf·fle** \ˈhəfəl\ *vi* -ED/-ING/-S [¹*huff* + *-le*] *now dial Eng* **:** to blow in gusts ⟨the winds do ~ queerer tonight than ever afore —Thomas Hardy⟩
**²huffle** \"\ *n* -s **:** GUST ⟨five haggard pines . . . knuckle together against the ~*s* of wind —Leah B. Drake⟩
**huffler** *var of* HOVELER
**huff-snuff** *n* -s [¹*huff* + *snuff*] *obs* **:** SWASHBUCKLER
**huffy** \ˈhəfē, -fi\ *adj* -ER/-EST [²*huff* + *-y*] **1 :** HAUGHTY, ARROGANT ⟨relapsed into . . . ~ complacency —*Harper's*⟩ **2 a :** roused to indignation **:** IRRITATED, SULKY ⟨stayed ~ a good while —Mark Twain⟩ — usu. used with *get* ⟨now don't get ~ if I offer a frank criticism⟩ **b :** easily offended **:** TOUCHY ⟨not ~ and crabbed like yourself —Augusta Gregory⟩ **syn** see IRRITABLE
**¹hug** \ˈhəg\ *vb* **hugged; hugged; hugging; hugs** [perh. of Scand origin; akin to ON *hugga* to comfort, soothe; akin to OE *hycgan* to think, consider, understand, OHG *huggen* to think, ON *huga* & *hyggja,* Goth *hugjan,* and perh. to Gk *kyknos* swan — more at CYGNET] *vt* **1 a :** to press tightly **:** CLUTCH ⟨the grip of her knees *hugging* Saidi's hot, rippling withers —L.C.Douglas⟩; *specif* **:** to clasp within the arms ⟨hurries down the gangplank to ~ his waiting wife⟩ ⟨she sat up in bed and *hugged* her knees —Louis Auchincloss⟩ **b :** to squeeze between the forelegs ⟨discounting the chances of being . . . *hugged* to death in the claws of a 9-foot anteater —George Weller⟩ **2 a** *archaic* **:** to show fondness for ⟨*hugged* the authors as his bosom friends —John Arbuthnot⟩; *specif* **:** to curry favor with ⟨refused to fight, on the ground that his opponent had been guilty of *hugging* attorneys —T.B.Macaulay⟩ **b :** CONGRATULATE, FELICITATE ⟨*hugged* ourselves that we hadn't had to be told —A.N.Whitehead⟩ **c :** to cling to or hold fast **:** CHERISH, KEEP ⟨~ our half belief in ghosts —W.W. Howells⟩ ⟨*hugged* his miseries like a sulky child —John Buchan⟩ ⟨an effort to ~ all credit to himself —Jonathan Daniels⟩ **3 :** to stay close or adhere to ⟨the road ~*s* the river⟩ ⟨this blast . . . helps the normal airflow ~ the contour of the flap —Richard Witkin⟩ ⟨collars either ~ the neck or stand away —*Women's Wear Daily*⟩ ⟨berries ~ the stem⟩ ⟨skaters ~ the bonfire⟩ ⟨a sailboat ~*s* the wind⟩ ⟨the faint aroma . . . *hugged* them like smog —Sally Benson⟩ **4** *dial Eng* **:** to carry with difficulty **:** LUG ~ *vi* **1 :** to press together **:** CROWD ⟨in groups that *hugged* together —Francis Hackett⟩ **2 a :** to embrace or adhere closely ⟨they *hugged* and kissed⟩ ⟨the revolving part is *hugging* closely against one side —Terrell Croft⟩ **b :** to crush a victim by squeezing with the forelegs ⟨'tis a bear's talent not to kick but ~ —Alexander Pope⟩ — **hug one's chains :** to be glad of servitude
**²hug** \"\ *n* -s **1 :** an affectionate embrace ⟨gave him a motherly ~⟩ **2 :** a crushing or restraining grasp ⟨bitter ~ of mortality —Walt Whitman⟩
**¹huge** \ˈhyüj *also* ˈyüj\ *adj* -ER/-EST [ME *huge, hoge,* modif. of OF *ahuge, ahoge*] **:** very large or extensive: as **a :** of great size or area **:** GIGANTIC, VAST ⟨the two ships settled . . . to the bottom, each with a ~ hole in her hull —T.E.Cooney⟩ ⟨~ organizations like the American Express Company —Richard Joseph⟩ ⟨a ~ country estate⟩ ⟨~ number of stories —G.B. Saul⟩ **b :** of sizable scale or degree **:** ENORMOUS ⟨the days of the NRA when there was ~ government spending —T.W. Arnold⟩ ⟨~ popular demand for higher education —V.S. Pritchett⟩ ⟨gleeful . . . from under his heavy brows with a ~ disgust —G.D.Brown⟩ ⟨turns . . . a dismal failure into a ~ success —Jeanne Massey⟩ **c :** of limitless scope or character **:** UNBOUNDED ⟨his ~ personal talent —Virgil Thomson⟩ ⟨go through rubbish heaps and find rings and scissors and broken noses buried in the ~ past —Virginia Woolf⟩ ⟨~ sense of destiny —Henry Wallace⟩
**syn** VAST, IMMENSE, ENORMOUS, ELEPHANTINE, MAMMOTH, GIANT, GIGANTIC, GIGANTEAN, COLOSSAL, GARGANTUAN, HERCULEAN, CYCLOPEAN, TITANIC, BROBDINGNAGIAN: HUGE is a rather general term indicating extreme largeness, usu. in size, bulk, or capacity ⟨an enormous volume of heavy, inky vapor, coiling and pouring upward in a *huge* and ebony cumulus cloud —H.G.Wells⟩ ⟨the Texan question and Mexican War made *huge* annexations of Southwestern territory certain —Allan Nevins & H.S.Commager⟩ VAST denotes extreme largeness or broadness, esp. of extent or range ⟨the Great Valley of California, a *vast* elliptical bowl averaging 50 miles in width and more than 400 miles long —*Amer. Guide Series: Calif.*⟩ ⟨consider the *vast* varieties of religions ancient and modern —M.R.Cohen⟩ IMMENSE suggests size far in excess of ordinary measurements or accustomed concepts ⟨an *immense* quill, plucked from a distended albatross' wing —Herman Melville⟩ ⟨found the balloon at an *immense* height indeed, and the earth's convexity had now become strikingly manifest —E.A. Poe⟩ ⟨the *immense* waste of war —D.W.Brogan⟩ ENORMOUS also indicates a size or degree exceeding accustomed bounds or norms ⟨heavy wagons, *enormous* loads, scarcely any less than three tons —*Amer. Guide Series: Calif.*⟩ ⟨the princes of the Renascence lavished upon private luxury and display *enormous* amounts of money —Lewis Mumford⟩ ELEPHANTINE suggests the cumbersome or ponderous largeness of the elephant ⟨similar *elephantine* bones were being displayed . . . as relics of the "giants" mentioned in the Bible —R.W.Murray⟩ ⟨*elephantine* grain elevators —*Amer. Guide Series: N.Y.*⟩ MAMMOTH is similar to ELEPHANTINE ⟨her parties were . . . *mammoth* — she rarely invited fewer than 100 people —*Time*⟩ ⟨a *mammoth* cyclotron —G.F.Whicher⟩ GIANT indicates unusual size or scope ⟨loaded with a typical unit of *giant* industrial equipment, the new car weighs more than a million pounds —*Pa. Railroad Annual Report*⟩ ⟨his *giant* intellect⟩ GIGANTIC and the less common GIGANTEAN are close synonyms of GIANT, perhaps more likely to be used in metaphorical extensions ⟨*gigantic* jewels that a hundred negroes could not carry —G.K.Chesterton⟩ ⟨a justice of the Supreme Court . . . however *gigantic* his learning and his juridic rectitude —H.L.Mencken⟩ COLOSSAL may suggest vast proportion ⟨three sets of *colossal* figures of men and animals . . . the largest man is 167 feet long —*Amer. Guide Series: Calif.*⟩ ⟨the sun blazed down . . . the heat was *colossal* —C.S.Forester⟩ GARGANTUAN suggests the hugeness of Rabelais's Gargantua and is often used in reference to appetites and similar physical matters ⟨*gargantuan* breakfasts . . . pigs' knuckles and sauerkraut, liver and bacon, ham and eggs, beef stew —Edna Ferber⟩ HERCULEAN suggests the superhuman power of the Greek hero Hercules or the superhuman difficulties of his famous labors ⟨a *Herculean* task confronted them. Some 1700 miles of track had to be laid through a wilderness —Allan Nevins and H.S.Commager⟩ CYCLOPEAN suggests the superhuman size and strength of the Cyclops of Greek mythology ⟨of *cyclopean* masonry, consisting of very large blocks of stone —*Scientific American*⟩ TITANIC suggests colossal size and, often, primitive earth-shaking strength ⟨*titanic* water fronds speedily choked both these rivers —H.G. Wells⟩ ⟨it was his *titanic* energy that broke the fetters of medievalism —M.R.Cohen⟩ BROBDINGNAGIAN suggests the hugeness of the inhabitants of the Brobdingnag of *Gulliver's Travels* ⟨a brand-new *Brobdingnagian* hotel —Isaac D'Israeli⟩
**²huge** \"\ *adv* [ME, fr. *huge, hoge,* adj.] **:** HUGELY ⟨the sky was swelling ~ with the last dusk —John Dos Passos⟩
**huge·ly** *adv* [ME, fr. *huge, hoge* + *-ly*] **:** in a huge manner **:** EXTREMELY, IMMENSELY ⟨a ~ interesting account —Bernard De Voto⟩ ⟨~ successful work —Roger Shattuck⟩ ⟨children enjoyed themselves ~ in games —Rex Ingamells⟩ ⟨business gained ~ at the expense of government —Herbert Agar⟩
**huge·ness** *n* -ES [ME *hugenes,* fr. *huge, hoge* huge + *-nes* -ness] **:** the quality or state of being huge **:** IMMENSITY
**huge·ous** \-jəs\ *adj* [¹*huge* + *-ous*] **:** HUGE — **huge·ous·ly** *adv*
**hug·ga·ble** \ˈhəgəbəl\ *adj* **:** of a kind that invites hugging **:** CUDDLESOME ⟨a ~ teddy bear⟩
**hugged** *past of* HUG
**hug·ger** \ˈhəgə(r)\ *n* -s **:** one that hugs
**¹hugger-mugger** \ˈhəgə(r),məgə(r), ,==ˈ==\ *n* [origin unknown] **1 :** the act or practice of concealment **:** SECRECY ⟨had always had the impression that sex was sin . . . here it was treated without any *hugger-mugger* or snickering —A.W.Long⟩ **2 :** a disorderly jumble **:** CONFUSION, MUMBO JUMBO ⟨engage in the *hugger-mugger* of international politics and moneymaking —H.R.Isaacs⟩ ⟨apart from the effect of all this unwholesome *hugger-mugger* on their minds, there was the greater tragedy that they were being shortchanged educationally —Victor Boesen⟩
**²hugger-mugger** \"\ *adv* **:** in secrecy or confusion
**³hugger-mugger** \"\ *adj* **1 :** of a clandestine nature **:** SECRET ⟨an eventual *hugger-mugger* hanging —P.H.Newby⟩ **2 :** of a confused or disorderly nature **:** JUMBLED ⟨readers will be puzzled by what at first appears a completely *hugger-mugger* haphazard arrangement — Ralph Abercrombie⟩
**⁴hugger-mugger** \"\ *vb* **hugger-muggered; hugger-muggered; hugger-muggering** \-g(ə)riŋ\ **hugger-muggers** *vt* **:** to keep secret **:** hush up ~ *vi* **1 :** to act or confer stealthily **2 :** to muddle around
**hugger-muggery** \-g(ə)rē, -ri\ *n* -ES **:** HUGGER-MUGGER 1
**hugging** *adj* **:** tending to hug **:** CLINGING — **hug·ging·ly** *adv*
**hug·gle** \ˈhəgəl, ˈhüg-\ *vt* **huggled; huggled; huggling** \-g(ə)liŋ\ **huggles** [freq. of ¹*hug*] *dial Eng* **:** HUG, CUDDLE
**hug-me-tight** \ˈ===,=\ *n* -s **1 :** a woman's short close-fitting bed jacket or undergarment usu. knitted of wool and sleeveless **2 :** a woman's short wraparound jacket

hug-me-tight 1

**hu·go·esque** \ˌ(h)yü(ˌ)gōˈesk\ *adj, usu cap* [Victor *Hugo* †1885 Fr. writer + E *-esque*] **:** of, relating to, or characteristic of Victor Hugo or his works
**hu·go·nis** \(h)yüˈgōnəs\ *n* -ES [NL (specif. epithet of *Rosa hugonis*), after Father *Hugo* — more at FATHER HUGO'S ROSE] **:** FATHER HUGO'S ROSE
**hugo rose** *n, usu cap H* [after Father *Hugo*] **:** FATHER HUGO'S ROSE
**hugs** *pres 3d sing of* HUG, *pl of* HUG
**hu·gue·not** \ˈhyügə,nät *sometimes* -nōt, + V *usu* -ād· *or* -ōd·; *sometimes* -nō\ *n, pl* **huguenots** \-äts, -ōts, -ō(z)\ *usu cap* [MF, fr. (Geneva dial.) *huguenot* Genevan partisan of an alliance with Fribourg and Bern as a means of preventing annexation by Savoy, alter. (after Besançon *Hugues* †1532 leader of the movement in Geneva to prevent annexation by Savoy) of *eidgnot,* fr. G (Swiss dial.) *eidgnoss* confederate, fr. MHG *eitgenōz,* fr. *eit* oath (fr. OHG *eid*) + *genōz* comrade, fr. OHG *ginōz;* akin to OHG *niozzan* to use, enjoy — more at OATH, NEAT] **:** a French Protestant in the 16th and 17th centuries **:** a member of the Reformed or Calvinistic communion — **hu·gue·not·ic** \ˌ==ˈnäd·ik, -nōt, ǀēkǀ *adj, usu cap* — **hu·gue·not·ism** \ˈ===,izəm, -,nōt, ǀ,tiz-, -,nō,iz-\ *n* -s *usu cap* **:** the doctrines and practices of the French Huguenots
**huh** *typically a snort or a strong* h-*sound followed by an* ᵊ *sound or by the vowel* ˈə *usu nasalized, the last part varying in intonation; often read as* ˈhə\ *interj* [origin unknown] — used typically to express surprise, disbelief, or disgust
**hüh·ner·ko·bel·ite** \ˈh(y)ünə(r)ˈkōbə,līt\ *n* -s [*Hühnerkobel,* region in Bavaria, Germany, its locality + E *-ite*] **:** a mineral $(Na,Ca)(Fe,Mn)_2(PO_4)_2$ consisting of phosphate of sodium, calcium, iron, and manganese and being isomorphous with varulite
**huh·ner test** \ˈh(y)ünə(r)-\ *n, usu cap H* [after Max *Huhner* †1947 Am. surgeon] **:** a test used in sterility studies that involves postcoital examination of aspirated vaginal and intracervical fluid to determine the presence or survival of spermatozoa in these areas
**hu·hu** \ˈhü(,)hü\ *n* -s [Maori] **:** a large creamy white roundheaded grub that is the larva of a yellowish brown New Zealand beetle (*Prionoplus reticularis*), bores in dead trees and timber, and was formerly much used as food by the Maori
**hui** \ˈhü(,)ē\ *n* -s [Hawaiian] **1** *Hawaii* **a :** PARTNERSHIP, SYNDICATE ⟨efforts by mainland capital to gain control of

Hawaiian Airlines are believed to have been thwarted by a local ~ that has secretly bought close to 70,000 shares —*Honolulu Advertiser*⟩ **b** : CLUB, ASSOCIATION ⟨the ~ is an organization of civic-minded . . . women who cooperate in furthering the interests of the Y.W.C.A. —*Honolulu Star-Bull.*⟩ **2** [Hawaiian & Maori] : community gathering : ASSEMBLY ⟨when the ~ broke up at 4 p.m. the issue was still in doubt —*New Zealand Jour. of Agric.*⟩

**hu·ia** \'hüyə\ *also* **huia bird** *n* -S [Maori *huia*] : a bird (*Neomorpha acutirostris* or *Heteralocha acutirostris*) related to the starlings, confined to a small region in the mountains of New Zealand, and having black white-tipped tail feathers prized by Maori chiefs and worn as insignia of rank

**hui·chol** \wē'chōl\ *n, pl* **huichol** \"\ *or* **huicho·les** \-ōlēz, -ō(,)lās\ *usu cap* [Sp, of AmerInd origin] **1 a** : a Nahuatlan people of the mountains between Zacatecas and Nayarit, Mexico **b** : a member of such people **2** : the language of the Huichol people

**huid** \'hœd, -ïe-\ *Scot var of* HOOD

**huil** \'hœl, -ïe-\ *Scot var of* HULL

**hui·lie** \'hœli\ *var of* HOOLY

**hui·pil** \wē'pēl\ *n, pl* **huipils** \-lz\ *or* **huipi·les** \-(,)lās\ [MexSp, fr. Nahuatl *huipilli*] : a straight slipover one-piece garment that is made by folding a rectangle of material end to end, sewing up the straight sides but leaving openings near the folded top for the arms, and cutting a slit or a square in the center of the fold to furnish an opening for the head, is often decorated with embroidery, and is worn as a blouse or dress by women chiefly in Mexico and Central America

**hui·pi·lla** \wē'pē(y)ə\ *n* -S [MexSp] : PINGUIN

**hui·sa·che** \wē'sächē\ *n* -S [MexSp, fr. Nahuatl *huixachi*, fr. *huitztli* thorn + *izachi* abundant] : a thorny shrub or small tree (*Acacia farnesiana*) found abundantly in the southern U.S. and throughout tropical regions and having fragrant yellow flowers used in making perfumery — called also CASSIE

**huis·co·yol** \wēskə'yōl\ *n* -S [MexSp, fr. Nahuatl *huitzcoyolli*, fr. *huitztli* thorn + *coyolli, coyulli*, a nut-bearing palm] : a shrubby Central American palm (*Bactris subglobosa*) that forms impenetrable thickets

**huis·quil** \'wē,skēl\ *or* **guis·quil** \'gw-\ *n* -S [AmerSp *huisquil, güisquil*] : CHAYOTE

**hui·tain** \wē'tān, *F* wētaⁿ\ *n, pl* **huitains** \-ānz, -aⁿ(z)\ [MF, fr. *huit* eight (fr. L *octo*) + *-ain*, fr. L *-anus* -an — more at EIGHT] **1** : OCTASTICH **2** : OCTAVE 2b

**hukama** *pl of* HAKIM

**huke** \'hyük\ *n* -S [ME *huyke, huke*, fr. MD *huik*] **1** : a medieval hooded cloak worn orig. by women but later by both sexes **2** : a late medieval close-fitting gown for either sex

**hu·ki·lau** \,hükē,laü\ *n* -S [Hawaiian, fr. *huki* pull + *lau* net] *Hawaii* : a seine-fishing party often involving large numbers of people and much revelry

**1hu·la** \'hülə\ *also* **hula-hula** \'==,==\ *n* -S [Hawaiian] **1** : a sinuous mimetic Polynesian dance of conventional form and topical adaptation performed by men and women singly or together and usu. accompanied by chants and rhythmic drumming ⟨the ~ was in essence a magical ritual designed to bring rain and cause fertility —E.S.C.Handy⟩ ⟨a lovely brown maiden performed a ~ in the aisle of the cabin to entertain the passengers —Horace Sutton⟩ **2** : the music to which a hula is performed ⟨snatches of ~s being sung —Armine von Tempski⟩

**2hula** \"\ *vi* -ED/-ING/-S : to dance a hula

**3hula** \"\ *n, pl* **hula** *or* **hulas** *usu cap* **1 a** : a people of the Territory of Papua **b** : a member of such people **2** : the Austronesian language of the Hula people

**Hula–Hoop** *trademark* — used for a hoop made usu. of plastic or rubber for twirling about the body by movements like those of the hula

**hula–hoop** \'==,=\ *vi* [*Hula-Hoop*] : to twirl a Hula-Hoop hoop about one's body

**hula skirt** *n* : a grass skirt worn by a hula dancer or an imitation of such a skirt ⟨a young girl, wearing a *hula skirt* of cellophane, came to the car and took their order —Speed Lamkin⟩

hula skirt

**hulch** *adj* [origin unknown] *obs* : HUMPED ⟨a man with a ~ back —Charles Cotton⟩

**hule** *var of* ULE

**hul gul** *var of* HULL-GULL

**1hulk** \'həlk\ *n* -S [ME *hulke*, fr. OE *hulc*, fr. ML *holcas, hulca*, fr. Gk *holkas* barge, trading vessel, fr. *helkein* to pull, drag, tow — more at SULCUS] **1** : SHIP; *specif* : a heavy ship of clumsy build ⟨the colossal ~ was the Great Eastern, the forerunner of today's ocean liners —James Dugan⟩ **2** : one that is bulky or unwieldy ⟨faced by a ~ of a man, well over six feet tall and professionally broad-shouldered —William Phillips b. 1878⟩ ⟨towering ~s of two vast apartment houses —Lewis Mumford⟩ ⟨the black ~s of the mountains across the bay —H.T.DeSa⟩ **3** *obs* : HULL ⟨her ~ painted over with sparkling vermilion —James Hayward⟩ **4 a** : the body of an old wrecked or dismantled ship unfit for sea service ⟨for a clubhouse the boys used an abandoned ~ they found on the waterfront⟩ **b** : an abandoned wreck or shell ⟨the ~s of British tanks rusting in the fields —J.A.Phillips⟩ ⟨once-glittering halls were left empty ~s —*Foreign Affairs*⟩ ⟨the moribund ~ of the Spanish Empire —J.H.Plumb⟩ **c** : a ship used as a prison ⟨a celebrated lock picker . . . serving time in a prison ~ —Rufus Jarman⟩ — usu. used in pl. ⟨every prisoner sent to the ~s —Kenneth Roberts⟩

**2hulk** \"\ *vb* -ED/-ING/-S *vi* **1** *dial Eng* : to move lazily or ponderously ⟨~s up from his chair by the hearth —Emmett Gowen⟩ **2** : to appear impressively large or massive : BULK, LOOM ⟨the smoking port and Vesuvius ~*ing* beyond —William Sansom⟩ ⟨a horned owl coasted into a perch on a dead tree stub, and it ~*ed* there against the sky —Hugh Fosburgh⟩ ~ *vt* : to condemn to or lodge in a hulk

**3hulk** \"\ *vt* -ED/-ING/-S [alter. of *holk* to hollow out — more at HOWK] *dial* : DISEMBOWEL

**hulking** *adj* [1*hulk* + *-ing*] : of great size or powerful build : HUSKY, MASSIVE ⟨a big ~ figure of a man with thick shoulders and no neck worth mentioning —Claudia Cassidy⟩ ⟨three ~ battleships —Norris Houghton⟩

**hulky** \'həlkē, -ki\ *adj* -ER/-EST [1*hulk* + *-y*] : HULKING

**1hull** \'həl\ *n* -S [ME *hul, hull, hole*, fr. OE *hulu*; akin to OHG *helawa* oat chaff, *hala* hull, OE *helan* to conceal — more at HELL] **1 a** : the outer covering of a fruit or seed (as the husk of a grain or nut or the pod of the pea) **b** : the persistent calyx or involucre that subtends some fruits (as the strawberry) **2** *dial Eng* : HUT, HOVEL, SHED **3 a** (1) : the frame or body of a ship exclusive of masts, yards, sails, and rigging — see SHIP illustration (2) *obs* : HULK 4a **b** (1) : the portion of a flying boat which furnishes buoyancy when in contact with the water and to which the main supporting surfaces and other parts are attached (2) : the main structure of a rigid airship consisting of a covered elongated framework which encloses the gasbags and supports the cars and equipment **c** : the armored body of a vehicle ⟨casting . . . huge steel tank ~s in a single piece —G.H.Johnston⟩ ⟨the ~ of an armored car is . . . of lighter-weight plate —*Principles of Automotive Vehicles*⟩ **4** : COVERING, CASING: as **a** : the shell of a crustacean ⟨shrimp ~s and heads are used as fertilizer⟩ **b** : a film of water encasing a soil particle **c** (1) : an empty ammunition shell case ⟨hot, spent cartridge ~s would be showering all over —Thomas Anderson⟩ (2) : CARTRIDGE ⟨won the national crown for the second time with a variety of . . . .22 ~s —Charles Askins b.1907⟩

**2hull** \"\ *vb* -ED/-ING/-S [ME *holen, hullen*, fr. *hole, hul, hull*, n.] *vt* **1 a** : to remove the husks or shells of : SHUCK ⟨~ ears of corn⟩ ⟨~ peas⟩ ⟨~ pecans⟩ ⟨~ oysters⟩ **b** : to remove the outer skin of : DECORTICATE ⟨~ kernels of corn⟩ ⟨~ coffee beans⟩ ⟨~ barley⟩ **c** : to remove the calyx of ⟨~ strawberries⟩ **2** : to pierce or strike the hull of (as a ship) ~ *vi* **1** : to float or drift with sails furled : lie ahull **2** *archaic* : IDLE ⟨I am to ~ here a little longer —Shak.⟩

**3hull** \"\ *adj, usu cap* [fr. *Hull*, England] : of or from the county borough of Hull, or Kingston upon Hull, England : of the kind or style prevalent in Hull

**1hul·la·ba·loo** *also* **hul·la·bal·loo** \'hələbə,lü, ,==='=\ *sometimes* -lēb- *or* -lib-\ *or* **hel·la·bal·loo** \'hel-, ,hel-\ *n* -S [perh. irreg. fr. *hallo* + Sc *baloo*, interj. used to hush children] **1** : a babel of noise and confusion : HUBBUB ⟨didn't whisper because there was such a ~ down in the cut that nobody could hear him anyhow —J.B.Benefield⟩ **2** : an excited clamor or controversy : UPROAR ⟨this attempt was accompanied by a big propaganda ~ —*Cavalry Jour.*⟩ ⟨a terrific ~ at the Met this season over the merits of three rival supersopranos —Winthrop Sargeant⟩ **syn** see DIN

**2hullabaloo** \"\ *vb* -ED/-ING/-S *vi* : to make a hullabaloo ~ *vt* : BALLYHOO 2

**hull down** *adv (or adj)* **1** *of a ship* **a** : at such a distance that only the superstructure is visible ⟨had cleared with a leading wind . . . and was *hull down* long before dark —Raymond McFarland⟩ **b** : with main deck awash ⟨one ship . . . after another went *hull down* into the sucking tide —D.C.Peattie⟩ **2** *of a tank or other armored vehicle* : in a place of concealment but in position to observe the enemy and deliver fire ⟨were standing *hull down* behind a hillock and on each of their turrets was a figure staring forward through field glasses —Peter Rainier⟩

**hulled barley** *n* : barley in which the husks adhere to the kernel — called also *Scotch barley*

**hulled corn** *n* : whole grain corn from which the hulls have been removed by soaking or boiling in lye water — see HOMINY

**hull·er** \'hələ(r)\ *n* -S : one that hulls: as **a** : a machine that removes the hulls from grain, nuts, or castor beans **b** : a machine that threshes clover and separates the seeds from the hulls **c** : a small hand tool for removing hulls from strawberries

huller c

**hul·let** \'hələt, 'hùl-\ *var of* HOWLET

**hull–gull** *or* **hul gul** \'həl,gəl\ *n* [origin unknown] : a children's game in which one player guesses how many beans or other small objects are in another's handful and gives up or receives beans according as his guess is high, low, or exact

**hull insurance** *n* : insurance protecting the owners against loss caused by damage or destruction of waterborne craft or aircraft

**hul·lion** \'həlyən\ *var of* HALLION

**hull–less** *or* **hul·less** \'hələs\ *adj* **1** : having no hull **2 a** *of barley* : having the kernels free within the husk **b** *of popcorn* : having short thick ears and pointed kernels with a white tender seed coat

**hul·lo** \(,)hə'lō, 'hə(,)lō, 'hə'lō\ *chiefly Brit var of* HELLO

**hullock** *n* -S [origin unknown] *obs* : a small piece of sail kept standing to hold a ship's head to the wind in a storm

**hul·loo** \(,)hə'lü, 'hə(,)lü, 'hə'lü\ *var of* HALLO

**hu·lock** \'hü-\ *also* **hulock gibbon** *or* **hulock monkey** *n* -S [*hulock* fr. native name in Assam or Burma] : HOOLOCK

**hul·site** \'həl(t),sīt\ *n* -S [Alfred *Hulse* Brooks †1924 Am. scientist + E *-ite*] : a mineral $(Fe,Ca,Mg)_4(Fe,Sn)_2B_2O_{10}$(?) consisting of a hydrous iron calcium magnesium tin borate

**hul·ver** \'həlvə(r)\ *n* -S [ME *hulver, holver*, fr. ON *hulfr* — more at HOLLY] *dial Eng* : HOLLY

**1hum** \'həm\ *vb* **hummed; hummed; humming; hums** [ME *hummen*; akin to MHG *hummen* to hum, D *hommelen* to hum, *hommel* bumblebee, OHG *humbal*] *vi* **1 a** : to utter a sound like or suggestive of that of the speech sound \m\ prolonged : continue voicing a nasal on one pitch or on varying pitches ⟨~ in time to the music⟩; *esp* : to utter such a sound to express dissent, approval, surprise, or embarrassment ⟨*hummed* and hawed and finally blurted out his views⟩ **b** : to make the natural noise of an insect (as a bumblebee) in motion ⟨a bee *hummed* by —Zane Grey⟩ ⟨mosquitoes *humming* —R.A.W. Hughes⟩ **c** : to make a low prolonged sound like that of an insect : DRONE, BUZZ ⟨the top ~s⟩ ⟨the snoring of his grandfather *hummed* like the coming of wasps —Elizabeth Enright⟩ ⟨a kettle was *humming* on a small gas stove —Ellen Glasgow⟩ ⟨electric power lines ~ —*Lamp*⟩ **d** : to give forth a low murmuring indistinct sound from the blending of many voices ⟨the sound of children's voices with which the house was always *humming* —J.M.Brinnin⟩ **e** : to produce a continuous blend of nonvocal sounds ⟨all night the printing plants *hummed* —Bill Davidson⟩ ⟨shrapnel and bullets *hummed* through the brush —Dave Richardson⟩ ⟨once, this place had *hummed* with noise: the ring of hammer upon anvil, the rasping of the saws that hewed the oak logs —Elizabeth Goudge⟩ **f** : to have an internal humming ⟨my head ~s⟩ **2** : to be very active as if noisily ⟨steel and other industries are *humming* along at much higher rates of operation —R.M.Blough⟩ ⟨the business started to ~ —Isabelle M. Hoover⟩ ⟨to make the free world ~ with full productive activity —Max Ascoli⟩ ~ *vt* **1** : to sing with the lips closed and without articulation ⟨~ a tune⟩ **2** : to affect by humming ⟨*hummed* me to sleep⟩ ⟨~ herself to rest⟩ : express by humming ⟨*hummed* his displeasure⟩

**2hum** \"\ *n* -S [ME, fr. *hummen*, v.] : the act of humming or the sound made by humming ⟨a ~ of approbation⟩: as **a** : a low monotonous noise (as of bees in flight or a whirling wheel) : DRONE, BUZZ **b** : the confused noise (as of a crowd or machinery) heard at a distance ⟨the ~ of industry⟩ ⟨the high-pitched ~ of swift power belts —*Amer. Guide Series: Ark.*⟩ **c** : the humming of a melody; *also* : MELODY **d** : an undesired audio signal in the output of a piece of electronic equipment usu. of low frequency resulting from direct pickup of a power signal or the residual power signal in a power supply

**3hum** \"\ *n* -S [imit.] : an inarticulate nasal sound or murmur (as from embarrassment or hesitation) ⟨after some evasive ~s he gave his answer⟩ — often used interjectionally to express hesitation or doubt, dissent, deliberation, or embarrassment; compare 4HEM

**4hum** \"\ *n* -S [short for 1*humbug*] : HUMBUG

**5hum** \"\ *vt* **hummed; hummed; humming; hums** [short for 2*humbug*] : HUMBUG

**6hum** \'hüm\ *n* -S [Serbo-Croatian, hill] : an isolated residual hill or mass of limestone (as in a region of karst topography)

**hum** *abbr* **1** [NL *humaniora*] the humanities **2** humor; humorous

**hu·ma** \'hümə\ *usu cap, var of* HIMA

**1hu·man** \'hyümən *also* 'yü-\ *adj, sometimes* -ER/-EST [ME *humayne, humain*, fr. MF *humain*, fr. L *humanus*, fr. *hum-* (akin to L *homo* man, human being) + *-anus* -an — more at HOMAGE] **1 a** : of or relating to man : characteristic of man ⟨~ voices⟩ ⟨vulnerability of the ~ body⟩ **b** : primarily or usu. harbored by, affecting, or attacking man ⟨~ appendicitis⟩ ⟨the common ~ flea⟩ **2 a** : being a man : consisting of men ⟨contrived for the destruction of the ~ species —Tobias Smollett⟩ ⟨the ~ race⟩ ⟨some special quality in the ~ beings who have made this particular transition —A.J.Toynbee⟩ **b** : of or relating to the social life or collective relations of mankind ⟨~ progress⟩ ⟨~ history and evolution⟩ ⟨in the course of ~ events —*U.S. Declaration of Independence*⟩ **3** : characteristic of or relating to man in his essential nature: as **a** : of, relating to, or resembling man or his attributes in distinction from the lower animals ⟨to be ~ is to understand, to evaluate, to choose, to accept responsibility —Lewis Mumford⟩ ⟨the gregarious impulses of ~ beings —J.B.Conant⟩ **b** : of or relating to man as distinguished from the superhuman, from the divine, or from nature : belonging to finite intelligence and powers ⟨to err is ~; to forgive, divine —Alexander Pope⟩ ⟨there are no absolutes and man must content himself with being ~ —H.E.Clurman⟩ **c** : susceptible to, representative of, or exemplifying the range of feelings, strengths, or weaknesses of which man is capable ⟨a very ~ world, filled with joy and sorrow, innocence and evil⟩ ⟨for all his stiff outward bearing, he is very ~⟩ ⟨the story of the ascent is a great ~ document⟩ ⟨far too ~ a creature to care much for art —Max Beerbohm⟩ **d** : having to do with, portraying, or arising from the small or large joys, sorrows, passions, struggles, or other interest-provoking experiences or situations of individual persons ⟨~ comedy⟩ ⟨full of the milk of ~ kindness —Shak.⟩ ⟨those *human*-interest yarns —Erle Stanley Gardner⟩ ⟨no business like book retailing for ~ interest —Allan McMahan⟩ ⟨a careful history of the ~ side of the whole case —M.R.Cohen⟩ ⟨nearly all these books contain the same ~ stories about the Queen —*N.Y. Times Book Rev.*⟩ **4** : symbolized in a representation of the zodiac or in a configuration of the stars by a man (as Aquarius), woman (as Virgo), or child (as Gemini) **5** : HUMANE ⟨balance her sharp tongue and uncertain moods against her warmly ~ disposition —Havelock Ellis⟩ **6** : having some of the characteristics of a living person : like a human ⟨the nearest of blood to me a d the ~*est* was not a person nor a villager —H.D.Thoreau⟩ ⟨the woods began to open up, and the country looked more ~ —Willa Cather⟩ ⟨the statue is more ~ than the beings at his feet —Clifton Fadiman⟩ ⟨the humbler aspects of our cities are more ~ than the skyscrapers —Walter Pach⟩ **7** : consisting of members of the family Hominidae : HOMINID ⟨the several fossil ~ genera⟩ **8** : unpredictably fallible or erratic : not behaving by known law : ENIGMATIC ⟨must always consider the ~ element⟩ ⟨Americans like other human beings are bewilderingly ~ —Max Lerner⟩ ⟨such an inconsistency is very ~ —P.E.More⟩

**2human** \"\ *n* -S : a human being ⟨sprung of ~s that inhabit earth —George Chapman⟩ ⟨incomprehensible to us ~s —William James⟩ ⟨no ~ since Adam —G.W.Cable⟩ ⟨the least developed of all ancestral ~s —A.L.Kroeber⟩ ⟨what has been found true about rats may be applied to ~s —E.E.Slosson⟩ ⟨like most of us lazy and indecisive ~s —T.H.Fielding⟩ ⟨as completely scientific and objective an approach as a ~ is capable of —R.A.Hall b. 1911⟩ ⟨two thousand million ~s —G.H.T.Kimble⟩

**human botfly** *n* : a large fly (*Dermatobia hominis*) of the family Cuterebridae that has brown wings and bluish body, is widely distributed in tropical America, and undergoes its larval development subcutaneously in man and other mammals

**hu·mane** \(')hyü'mān *also* (')yü-\ *adj, sometimes* -ER/-EST [ME *humayne, humain* — more at HUMAN] **1** *obs* : HUMAN **2** : marked by compassion, sympathy, or consideration for other human beings or animals ⟨a ~ warden⟩ ⟨~ treatment⟩ ⟨a ~ attitude⟩ **3** : characterized by or tending to broad humanistic culture : HUMANISTIC ⟨~ studies⟩

**human ecology** *n* : a branch of sociology that studies the relationship between a human community and its environment; *specif* : the study of the spatial and temporal interrelationships between men and their economic, social, and political organization

**hu·mane·ly** *adv* : in a humane manner

**hu·mane·ness** \-ānnəs\ *n* -ES : the quality or state of being humane

**human engineering** *n* **1** : management of human beings and affairs esp. in industry with a view to securing satisfactory adjustment esp. in terms of maximum work efficiency and job satisfaction **2** : a science drawing upon various other sciences (as physiology, anatomy, physical anthropology, applied psychology) that deals with the design and positioning of machines, instruments, and controls (as in flying) so that they may be used with maximum efficiency by human beings

**human equation** *n* : the factor of human strength or weakness that needs to be considered in predicting the outcome of any social, political, economic, or mechanical process operated by human agency

**humaner** *comparative of* HUMAN *or of* HUMANE

**humane society** *n, often cap H&S* **1** *chiefly Brit* : a lifesaving society **2** : a society concerned with the promotion of humane conduct or ideals or having charitable or philanthropic ends ⟨the *Humane Society* is a child-caring agency —A.E.Fink⟩; *specif* : a society for the prevention of cruelty to animals

**humanest** *superlative of* HUMAN *or of* HUMANE

**human geography** *n* : ANTHROPOGEOGRAPHY

**hu·man·ics** \hyü'maniks *also* yü-\ *n pl but sing in constr* : a subject that treats of human nature or human affairs

**hu·man·i·o·ra** \(,)(h)yü,manē'ōrə\ *n pl* [NL *humaniora* (*studia*), lit., more humane studies] : humanistic studies : HUMANITIES ⟨on the borderland between science and the ~ —*Chronica Botanica*⟩

**hu·man·ism** \'(h)yümə,nizəm\ *n* -S [1*human* + *-ism*; in some senses prob. fr. F *humanisme* or G *humanismus*] **1 a** : devotion to the humanities : literary culture **b** *often cap* : the learning or cultural impulse that is characterized by a revival of classical letters, an individualistic and critical spirit, and a shift of emphasis from religious to secular concerns and that flowered during the Renaissance **2** : devotion to human welfare : interest in or concern for man : HUMANITY, HUMANITARIANISM ⟨born in a city tenement, he early acquired the kind of ~ that is humanitarian —Donald Davidson⟩ ⟨wrote that medicine was a social science and urged doctors to participate in the battles of ~ —B.J.Stern⟩ **3** : a doctrine, set of attitudes, or way of life centered upon human interests or values: as **a** : a philosophy that rejects supernaturalism, regards man as a natural object, and asserts the essential dignity and worth of man and his capacity to achieve self-realization through the use of reason and scientific method — called also *naturalistic humanism, scientific humanism*; compare INSTRUMENTALISM, PRAGMATISM **b** *often cap* : a religion subscribing to these beliefs : RELIGIOUS HUMANISM **c** : a philosophy advocating the self-fulfillment of man within the framework of Christian principles — called also *Christian humanism*; see INTEGRAL HUMANISM **4** : NEW HUMANISM

**1hu·man·ist** \-nəst\ *n* -S [prob. fr. MF *humaniste*, fr. L *humanus* + MF *-iste* -ist] **1 a** : a person who pursues the study of the humanities ⟨accused by ~s of having an exclusive interest in social sciences —*Publ's Mod. Lang. Assoc. of Amer.*⟩ ⟨called for a greater understanding betweed scientists and ~s —*Science*⟩ **b** : an adherent or practitioner of Renaissance humanism; *specif* : a Renaissance scholar devoting himself to the study of classical letters **2** : a person who is devoted to human welfare : one who is marked by a strong interest in or concern for man : HUMANITARIAN ⟨a ~, a lover of all sorts of people —*Yale Rev.*⟩ ⟨a ~, who felt deeply about inequality . . . wherever he saw it —Max Lerner⟩ **3 a** *often cap* : a person who subscribes to the doctrines of scientific humanism; *specif* : a member of a religious society or cult subscribing to such doctrines **b** : a person who subscribes to a form of philosophical humanism **c** : NEW HUMANIST

**2humanist** \"\ *or* **hu·man·is·tic** \'==;nistik, -tēk\ *adj* **1 a** : of or relating to Renaissance humanism or humanists ⟨the *humanistic* revival of learning⟩ **b** : of, relating to, or concerned with the humanities : CULTURAL ⟨the fact that *humanistic* subjects . . . have a part in the development of the students —*Science*⟩ ⟨Greek . . . the most exacting *humanist* study —Robert Birley⟩ **2** : of or relating to philosophical or religious humanism in any of its forms ⟨what we need is a *humanistic* religion . . . man-centered and comfortable —R.C. Hartnett⟩ ⟨supernaturalist and *humanist* strategies of motivation —K.D.Burke⟩ ⟨the *humanist* belief in continuous emergent evolution —Wendell Thomas⟩ **3** : marked by or expressive of devotion to human welfare or strong interest in or concern for man : HUMANITARIAN ⟨the liberal approach has been a *humanist* approach —M.W.Straight⟩ ⟨incorporate the socialist idealism of Russia with the *humanist* individualism of America —Cyril Connolly⟩ ⟨respect and *humanistic* regard for all other members of our species —Weston La Barre⟩

**hu·man·is·ti·cal·ly** \'==;nistək(ə)lē, -tēk-, -li\ *adv* : in a humanistic manner

**1hu·man·i·tar·i·an** \(,)hyü,manə'terēən, (,)yü-, -taar-,-tār-\ *n* -S [*humanity* + *-arian*] : a person actively concerned in promoting human welfare and esp. social reform : PHILANTHROPIST

**2humanitarian** \(,)=;==;===\ *adj* : of, relating to, or characteristic of humanitarians or humanitarianism : zealously concerned for or active in the promotion of human welfare and esp. of social reform : PHILANTHROPIC, HUMANE ⟨to use the A-bomb was wrong on ~ grounds —E.M.Zacharias⟩ ⟨a refreshing example of . . . ~ zeal —Benjamin Farrington⟩ ⟨a hard, stern race . . . little responsive to ~ appeal —V.L. Parrington⟩

**hu·man·i·tar·i·an·ism** \-ēə,nizəm\ *n* -S : concern for human welfare esp. as expressed through philanthropic activities and interest in social reforms : the practice or display of humanitarian principles ⟨extended their ~ to include the Indian tribes —H.M.Hyman⟩

**hu·man·i·ty** \hyü'manəd·ē, -ətē, -i *also* yü-\ *n* -ES [ME *humanite*, fr. MF *humanité*, fr. L *humanitat-, humanitas*, fr. *humanus* human, humane + *-itat-, -itas* -ity — more at HUMAN] **1** : the quality or state of being humane : kind or generous behavior or disposition : COMPASSION, BENEVOLENCE ⟨which she had intended to do with beautiful mercy, a lovely ~ —Elizabeth Taylor⟩ ⟨bespeaking ~ for the enemy in the midst of a bloody struggle —C.G.Bowers⟩ **2 a** : the totality of attributes which distinguish man from other beings : the condition of being human : essential human quality or character ⟨very ape-looking, but with many marks of an incipient ~ —J.S.Weiner⟩ ⟨man's ~ consists of his . . . labor power —Hannah Arendt⟩ ⟨seem coldly to deny him a common ~ —Philip Woodruff⟩ ⟨committed to a belief in the ~ of all men and women —Brendan Sexton⟩ **b humanities** *pl* (1) : human attributes or qualities ⟨his work has the ripeness of the 18th century, and its rough *humanities* —Pamela H. Johnson⟩ (2) : things pleasing to human tastes or sensibilities ⟨it has *humanities:* many mirrors, for example, which augment the numbers of the guests —Philip Wylie⟩ **3** [ML *humanitas,* fr. L] **a** *archaic* : the study of classical language and literature **b** *in Scottish universities* : Latin language and literature **c humanities** *pl* : the branches of learning regarded as having primarily a cultural character and usu. including languages, literature, history, mathematics, and philosophy **4 a** : the totality of human beings : the human race : MANKIND ⟨a fierce compassion for the woes of ~ —Maurice Bowra⟩ **b** : PEOPLE, MEN ⟨the packed mass of ~ below would swing . . . with the movement of the ship —C.S.Forester⟩

**hu·man·ization** \ˌhyümənə'zāshən, -ˌnī'z- *also* ˌyü-\ *n* -s : the act or process of humanizing : the fact or condition of being humanized ⟨an increasing ~ of the industrial process —E.M.Erikson⟩ ⟨the changes in the carved figures well illustrate the growing ~ of the divine and the saintly —G.C. Sellery⟩

**hu·man·ize** \'==,nīz\ *vb* -ED/-ING/-s [F *humaniser,* fr. MF, fr. L *humanus* + MF *-iser* -ize] *vt* **1 a** : to give a human character or aspect to : treat or regard as human : represent in human form ⟨there is no worship here, . . . but nevertheless they ~ the crocodiles —W.W.Howells⟩ **b** : to adapt or make congenial to human nature, sensibilities, or use : make more sympathetic or responsive to human needs or desires ⟨dedicated himself . . . to the *humanizing* of business and finance —George Wolf⟩ **2** : to make humane : make gentle : SOFTEN, REFINE, CIVILIZE ⟨nations have feebly tried to ~ and regulate war —Vera M. Dean⟩ ⟨New England was appointed to guide the nation, to . . . ~ it —Van Wyck Brooks⟩ ~ *vi* **1** : to become human **2** : to have or spread a civilizing influence ⟨it is the function of women to ~ —M.F.A.Montagu⟩

**humankind** \'==,=\ *n sing but sing or pl in constr* : the human race : MANKIND

**humanlike** \'==,=\ *adj* : like or resembling humans : like or resembling that of humans ⟨salmon . . . live a ~ existence —June Collins⟩ ⟨very ~ gods inhabit a . . . delightful heaven —Edith Hamilton⟩

**hu·man·ly** *adv* **1 a** : from the viewpoint of man : as concerns the human aspect ⟨lesser known but more ~ and historically interesting phase of his character —*Publ's Mod. Lang. Assoc. of Amer.*⟩ ⟨dramatic action that is at once ingenious, ~ illuminating, and true —Leslie Rees⟩ ⟨operate a successful organization both economically and ~ —*Current Biog.*⟩ **b** : within the range of human capacity ⟨policy that will insure, so far as it is ~ possible to do so, high employment —A.E.Stevenson b.1900⟩ **2** : in a human manner : after the manner of man ⟨what . . . children need most sorely is to be made ~ articulate —George Sampson⟩ ⟨men want more than merely to live . . . they want to live ~ —Ludwig Von Mises⟩

**human nature** *n* [ME *nature humayne,* fr. MF *nature humaine*] : the nature of man: **a** : the complex of behavioral patterns, attitudes, and ideas which man has acquired socially — called also *cultural nature* ⟨socially conditioned *human nature* . . . the qualities of the personality that make it like other personalities within the same society —A.L.Kroeber⟩ **b** : the complex of fundamental dispositions and traits of man sometimes considered innate ⟨belief that "you can't change *human nature*" —A.A.Van Duym⟩

**hu·man·ness** \-mən(n)əs\ *n* -ES : the quality or state of being human ⟨we miss the humanity, or ~, that would inspire us to love or to hate his people —*New Yorker*⟩ ⟨the public image of you lacks warmth, and depth, and ~ —Stewart Alsop⟩

**¹hu·man·oid** \-mə,nȯid\ *adj* [¹*human* + *-oid*] : having human characters esp. as opposed to anthropoid

**²humanoid** \"\ *n* -s : a humanoid being ⟨the ~s and the anthropoids part company between a million and two million years ago —J.A.Thomson⟩

**human relations** *n pl but usu sing in constr* **1** : the social relations between human beings esp. when being investigated **2** : a study of the human problems arising from organizational and interpersonal relations in industry esp. with reference to the employer-employee relationship and the interaction between personal traits, group membership, and productive efficiency **3** : a course, study, or program designed to develop better interpersonal and intergroup adjustments

**humans** *pl of* HUMAN

**hu·mate** \'hyü,māt\ *n* -s [*humic* + *-ate*] : a salt or ester of a humic acid

**humbird** \'=,=\ *n* : HUMMINGBIRD

**¹hum·ble** \'həmbəl *also* 'əm-\ *adj* -ER/-EST [ME *umble, humble,* fr. OF, fr. L *humilis* low, slight, humble, fr. *humus* earth, ground + *-ilis* -ile; akin to Gk *chthōn* earth, *chamai* on the ground, Skt *kṣam* earth, ground] **1 a** : having a low opinion of one's own importance or merits : modest or meek in spirit, manner, or appearance : not proud or haughty ⟨essentially ~ . . . and self-effacing, he achieved the highest formal honors and distinctions —B.K.Malinowski⟩ ⟨to them even the president was ~ —Sinclair Lewis⟩ ⟨a spot where a man feels his own insignificance and may well learn to be ~ —Samuel Butler †1902⟩ **b** : reflecting, expressing, or offered in a humble spirit ⟨my *humblest* apologies for the long wait —T.B. Costain⟩ ⟨beg to submit my ~ notion —Vicki Baum⟩ ⟨hear my ~ cry —Fanny J. Crosby⟩ ⟨loathed his cringing look and ~ smile⟩ **2 a** : ranking low in the social or political scale ⟨a man of ~ origin⟩ ⟨all civil servants, no matter how ~, should be disenfranchised —J.H.Plumb⟩ ⟨a ~ fisherman⟩ **b** : ranking low in some hierarchy or scale : INSIGNIFICANT ⟨in the study of the life of animals, however ~, we are studying . . . our own complex human life —W.E.Swinton⟩ ⟨the ~ weeds of the field⟩ ⟨the giant stellar family of which our sun is a ~ member —George Gamow⟩ **c** : of inferior value or worth : not costly or luxurious : MEAN, BASE, UNPRETENTIOUS ⟨chief clerks have mahogany desks; to the others is relegated the *humbler* walnut —H.J.Laski⟩ ⟨artisans . . . who work by hand with gold, silver, and the *humbler* metals —*New Yorker*⟩ ⟨the ~ fare of any Mexican peon —Green Peyton⟩ : of modest dimensions or proportions ⟨freighters using the same slips as the ~ powerboats of small fishermen —*Amer. Guide Series: Mass.*⟩ ⟨equally ~ were the beginnings of . . . the important State Department of Agriculture —*Amer. Guide Series: N.Y.*⟩ **syn** MEEK, MODEST, LOWLY: HUMBLE suggests absence of vanity and pride, feeling of weakness or lack of worth, self-depreciation, or an abject attitude and demeanor ⟨love hath made her *humble,* and her race doth she forget, and her noble and mighty heart —William Morris⟩ ⟨she prays there as the light goes out, prays with an *humble* heart, and walks home shrinking and silent —W.M.Thackeray⟩ ⟨the cook drew himself up in a smugly *humble* fashion, a deprecating smirk on his face —Jack London⟩ MEEK may suggest patient, subdued, retiring mildness and gentleness, sometimes even a spiritless, cowed submissiveness ⟨the most modest, silent, sheep-faced and *meek* of little men —W.M.Thackeray⟩ ⟨her father, of course, was the lion of the party, but seeing that we were all *meek* and quite willing to be eaten, he roared to us rather than at us —Samuel Butler †1902⟩ MODEST may contrast with *brash* or *self-assertive;* without any implication of abjectness or submissiveness, it may imply unobtrusive lack of boastfulness or conceit or jealous demand for recognition ⟨a simple, *modest,* retiring man —F.D.Roosevelt⟩ ⟨the anthropologist is entirely proper and *modest* in refusing as an anthropologist to make judgments on other cultural beliefs with respect to their epistemological truth —Weston La Barre⟩ LOWLY, close to *humble,* may stress complete lack of worldly pretentiousness ⟨a monk of Lindisfarne, so simple and *lowly* in temper that he traveled on foot —J.R.Green⟩ ⟨you hold aloof from me because you are rich and lofty — and I poor and *lowly* —W.S. Gilbert⟩

**²humble** \"\ *vt* **humbled; humbled; humbling** \-b(ə)liŋ\ **humbles** [ME *humblen,* fr. *humble,* adj.] **1** : to make humble in spirit or manner : bring down the pride or arrogance of ⟨having *humbled* your heart . . . you may find him —Francis Yeats-Brown⟩ ⟨*humbled* himself before the rich and great⟩ **2** : to destroy the power, independence, or prestige of : defeat decisively : DEGRADE, ABASE ⟨the great marshal *humbled* his enemies in a swift, brilliantly conducted campaign⟩ ⟨it was now the turn of the Church to be *humbled*⟩

**humble-bee** \'həmbəl,bē\ *n* [ME *humbylbee,* fr. *humbyll-* (akin to MD *hommel* bumblebee) + *bee* — more at HUM, BEE] : BUMBLEBEE

**hum·ble·ness** *n* -ES [ME *humblenesse,* fr. *humble* + *-nesse* -ness] : the quality or state of being humble : HUMILITY

**humble pie** *n* [*humbles*] **1 a** : a meat pie formerly made of the inferior parts of a deer and served to the huntsman and other servants **b** : a meat pie made of the humbles of a hog **2** [influenced in meaning by ¹*humble*] : submission, apology, or retraction esp. made under pressure or in humiliating circumstances : HUMILIATION ⟨would it mean such a deal of *humble pie?* —Margery Sharp⟩ — often used in the phrase *eat humble pie* ⟨forced to eat *humble pie* —H.W.Van Loon⟩ ⟨before I'd go and eat *humble pie* to the sergeant . . . he might break my neck —Henry Lapham⟩

**humble plant** *n* : SENSITIVE PLANT 1

**humbler** *comparative of* HUMBLE

**hum·bles** \'həmbəlz\ *n pl* [by folk etymology fr. *umbles*] : the heart, liver, kidneys, and other small pieces of a deer or of a hog — compare HUMBLE PIE 1

**humblest** *superlative of* HUMBLE

**humbling** *adj* : tending to humble : causing humbleness ⟨a ~ sense of our power —A.E.Stevenson b.1900⟩ — **hum·bling·ly** *adv*

**hum·bly** \'həmblē, -li *also* 'əm-\ *adv* [ME *umbly, humbly, humblely,* fr. *umble, humble* + *-ly*] : in a humble manner: as **a** : with humility : with a humble aspect or bearing ⟨must say ~ to the haughty dealers —Pearl Buck⟩ **b** : in a humble position or condition ⟨strategically, though ~ placed, he holds the job of official translator —Ralph de Toledano⟩

**hum·boldt·ine** \'həm,bōl,tēn, -ltᵊn\ *n* -s [F *humboldtine,* fr. Baron Alexander von *Humboldt* †1859 Ger. naturalist and traveler + F *-ine*] : a mineral $FeC_2O_4.2H_2O$ consisting of ferrous oxalate

**hum·boldt·ite** \-l,tīt\ *n* -s [in sense 1, fr. Alex. von *Humboldt* + E *-ite;* in sense 2, fr. G *humboldtit,* modif. of F *humboldtine*] **1** : DATOLITE **2** : HUMBOLDTINE

**hum·boldt's lily** \'həm,bōlts-\ *n, usu cap H* [after Alex. von *Humboldt*] : a Californian bulbous herb (*Lilium humboldtii*) with showy orange-red purple-spotted flowers

**¹hum·bug** \'həm,bəg\ *n* -s [origin unknown] **1 a** : something designed to deceive and mislead : QUACKERY, HOAX, FRAUD, IMPOSTURE ⟨contrived so many delicious ~s to foist on the gullible public —R.L.Taylor⟩ **b** : a person who usu. willfully deceives or misleads others as to his true condition, qualities, or attitudes : one who passes himself off as something that he is not : SHAM, HYPOCRITE, IMPOSTOR ⟨denounced as ~s the playwrights who magnify the difficulties of their craft —*Times Lit. Supp.*⟩ ⟨he's no doctor; he's a ~⟩ **c** : an attitude or spirit of pretense and deception or self-deception ⟨in all his ~, in all his malice and hollowness —Mary Lindsay⟩ **d** : something empty of sense or meaning : DRIVEL, NONSENSE ⟨a frightful lot of ~ talked about glasses —L.B.Somerville-Large⟩ ⟨academic ~⟩ **2** *Brit* : a peppermint candy **syn** see IMPOSTURE

**²humbug** \"\ *vt* : impose on : DECEIVE, CAJOLE, HOAX ⟨*humbugged* me into buying his worthless stock⟩ ⟨*humbugged* by their doctors, pillaged by their tradesmen —G.B.Shaw⟩ ~ *vi* : to play the part of a humbug

**hum·bug·gery** \-,bəg(ə)rē, -ri\ *n* -ES : HUMBUG

**hum·ding·er** \ˌhəm'diŋə(r)\ *n* -s [prob. alter. of ¹*hummer*] : something extraordinary or of striking excellence ⟨a ~ in the . . . tradition of fantastic humor —Sarah C. Gross⟩ ⟨a sandstorm roared in, a real ~ —Shine Philips⟩

**¹hum·drum** \'həm,drəm\ *adj* [irreg. redupl. of ¹*hum*] : having a routine or commonplace character : lacking interest, excitement, or sparkle : MONOTONOUS, WORKADAY, PROSAIC ⟨makes rather ~ use of a good idea —Eric Keown⟩ ⟨the more ~ aspects of military life, like drill, neatness, and organization —Blair Clark⟩ ⟨the ~ problem of making ends meet —*Amer. Guide Series: Mass.*⟩

**²humdrum** \"\ *n* : the quality or state of being humdrum ⟨the ordinary, average day, with its good human ~ —C.E.Montague⟩ ⟨give him that very experience of the ~ of clerical life —Compton Mackenzie⟩

**hum·dud·geon** \ˌhəm'dəjən\ *or* **hum·dur·geon** \-dərjən\ *n* -s [prob. fr. ⁴*hum* + *dudgeon*] **1** *Scot* : a loud complaint or noise ⟨the auld carline went . . . on top of her head, making such a *humdudgeon* —Hugh McCrae⟩ **2** *Scot* : an imaginary illness or pain

**¹hum·ean** *or* **hum·ian** \'hyümēən\ *adj, usu cap* [David *Hume* †1776 Scot. philosopher + E *-an* or *-ian*] : of, like, or relating to the philosophical system or methods of the philosopher Hume esp. his philosophical skepticism

**²humean** *or* **humian** \"\ *n* -s *usu cap* : a follower of the philosophy of Hume

**hu·mect** \hyü'mekt\ *vb* -ED/-ING/-s [L *humectare, umectare,* fr. *humectus, umectus* moist, fr. *humēre, umēre* to be moist — more at HUMOR] *archaic* : MOISTEN

**¹hu·mec·tant** \-ktənt\ *adj* [L *humectant-, humectans, umectant-, umectans,* pres. part. of *humectare, umectare*] : MOISTENING ⟨~ properties⟩

**²humectant** \"\ *n* -s : a substance that promotes retention of moisture (as glycerol, various glycols, sorbitol)

**hu·mec·tate** \-k,tāt\ *vb* -ED/-ING/-s [L *humectatus, umectatus,* past part. of *humectare, umectare*] *archaic* : MOISTEN

**hu·mec·ta·tion** \ˌhyü,mek'tāshən\ *n* -s [LL *humectation-, humectatio, umectation-, umectatio,* fr. L *humectatus, umectatus* + *-ion-, -io* -ion] **1** *archaic* : the action or process of moistening **2** *archaic* : the quality or state of being moist

**¹hu·mer·al** \'hyümərəl\ *adj* [prob. fr. F *huméral,* fr. MF *humeral,* fr. NL *humerus* + MF *-al*] **1** : of, relating to, or situated in the region of the humerus : BRACHIAL **2** [LL *humeralis, umeralis,* fr. L *humerus, umerus* + *-alis* -al] : of or belonging to the shoulder ⟨the ~ horny plates or any of several scales on the plastron of turtles⟩ **3** : of, relating to, or being any of several body parts that are analogous in structure, function, or location to the humerus or shoulder ⟨the ~ anterior basal angle of an insect's wing⟩ ⟨the ~ anterior corner of the thorax of a two-winged fly⟩

**²humeral** \"\ *n* -s **1** : a large bone that forms part of the shoulder girdle of certain fishes not homologous with the humerus **2** : a humeral part (as a scale or plate)

**humeral veil** *n* [trans. of ML *velum humerale*] : an oblong veil or scarf of the same material as the vestments that is worn around the shoulders at high mass by a subdeacon when he holds the paten between the offertory and pater noster and by a priest when he carries the monstrance in a procession or raises it to give the benediction

**humero-** *comb form* [ISV, fr. NL *humerus*] : humeral and ⟨*humero*dorsal⟩

**hu·mer·us** \'hyümərəs\ *n, pl* **humeri** \-ə,rī\ [NL, fr. L *humerus, umerus* upper arm, shoulder; akin to ON *āss* mountain ridge, Goth *ams* shoulder, Gk *ōmos,* Toch A *es,* Skt *aṁsa*] **1** : the long bone of the upper arm or forelimb : the longest bone of the upper extremity articulating above by a rounded head with the glenoid fossa, having below a broad articular surface divided by a ridge into a medial pulley-shaped portion and a lateral rounded eminence that articulate with the ulna and radius respectively, and providing various processes and modified surfaces for the attachment of muscles **2** : the shoulder region of an insect; *also* : any of various structures located in this region (as the coxa of a foreleg or the lateral angle of the prothorax)

**hu·met** \hyü'met\ *n* -s [origin unknown] : a heraldic bar or a fess couped at its ends

**hu·met·ty** \hyü'med·ē\ *also* **hu·met·tée** \", ˌhyümə'tā\ *adj* [*humet* + *-y* or *-ée* (fr. MF *-é,* past part. ending of some verbs) — more at -EE] *heraldry* : couped at the extremities

**hum·hum** \'həm,həm\ *n* -s [Ar *ḥammām* bath; fr. its use as toweling] : a coarse cotton cloth formerly imported from India

**humian** *usu cap, var of* HUMEAN

**hu·mic** \'hyümik\ *adj* [prob. fr. F *humique,* fr. NL *humus* + F *-ique* -ic] : relating to or composed at least in part of organic matter : relating to or derived from humus

**humic acid** *n* : any of various organic acids that are insoluble in alcohol and organic solvents and are obtained from humus

**hu·mid** \'hyüməd *also* 'yü-\ *adj* [F or L; MF *humide,* fr. L *humidus, umidus,* fr. *humēre, umēre* to be moist or damp — more at HUMOR] : containing or characterized by perceptible moisture : DAMP, MOIST, VAPOROUS ⟨~ air⟩ ⟨a hot ~ climate⟩ **syn** see WET

**hu·mid·i·fi·ca·tion** \(h)yü,midəfə'kāshən\ *n* -s [fr. *humidify,* after such pairs as E *identify: identification*] : the process of making humid

**hu·mid·i·fi·er** \='=ə,fī(ə)r, -īə\ *n* -s **1** : a device for supplying or maintaining humidity **2** : a textile or tobacco worker who tends a humidifying system to keep the moisture content of rooms at the desired level

**hu·mid·i·fy** \-fī\ *vt* -ED/-ING/-ES [prob. fr. F *humidifier,* fr. *humide* humid + *-ifier* -ify] : to make humid (as the atmosphere) : MOISTEN

**hu·mid·i·stat** \-də,stat\ *n* -s [*humidity* + *-stat*] : an instrument for regulating or maintaining the degree of humidity — called also *hygrostat*

**hu·mid·i·ty** \hyü'midəd·ē, -ətē, -i *also* yü-\ *n* -ES [ME *humidite,* fr. MF *humidité,* fr. LL *humiditas, umiditas,* fr. L *humidus, umidus* moist, damp + *-itat-, -itas* -ity — more at HUMID] : a moderate degree of wetness (as of a solid surface or the air) perceptible to the eye or to touch : MOISTURE, DAMPNESS — see ABSOLUTE HUMIDITY, RELATIVE HUMIDITY

**hu·mid·ly** *adv* : in a humid manner : WETLY ⟨eyes . . . beaming ~ through their dark lashes —*Dublin Bk. of Irish Verse*⟩

**hu·mi·dor** \'hyümə,dȯ(ə)r, -ō(ə) *also* 'yü-\ *n* -s [*humid* + *-or*] : a case or enclosure (as for storing cigars) in which the air is kept properly humidified : *also* : a contrivance (as a tube containing moistened sponges) placed in a case to keep the air moist

**hu·mi·fi·ca·tion** \ˌhyüməfə'kāshən\ *n* -s [NL *humus* + E *-i-* + *-fication*] : the process of the formation of humus

**hu·mi·fied** \'hyümə,fīd\ *adj* [NL *humus* + E *-ified* (fr. *-ify* + *-ed*)] : converted into humus ⟨~ organic matter⟩

**hu·mi·fuse** \-,fyüs\ *adj* [ISV *humi-* (fr. L *humus* earth, ground) + L *fusus,* past part. of *fundere* to pour — more at FOUND] : spread over the surface of the ground : PROCUMBENT ⟨~ plant stems⟩

**hu·mil·i·ate** \hyü'milē,āt, *also* yü-, *usu* -ād·+V\ *vt* -ED/-ING/-S [LL *humiliatus,* past part. of *humiliare,* fr. L *humilis* low, humble — more at HUMBLE] : to reduce to a lower position in one's own eyes or the eyes of others : injure the self-respect of : HUMBLE, MORTIFY ⟨insulted and *humiliated* his darling niece —Hilaire Belloc⟩

**humiliating** *adj* : lowering one's position or dignity : HUMBLING, MORTIFYING ⟨a ~ peace⟩ — **hu·mil·i·at·ing·ly** *adv*

**hu·mil·i·a·tion** \(ˌ)=,=lē'āshən\ *n* -s [ME *humiliacioun,* fr. MF *humiliation,* fr. LL *humiliation-, humiliatio,* fr. *humiliatus* + L *-ion-, -io* -ion] **1 a** : the act of humiliating ⟨His incarnation was the ~ of His godhead —R.J.Wilberforce⟩ **b** : the state of being humiliated ⟨what submission, what cringing and fawning, what servility, what abject ~ —Charles Dickens⟩ **2** : an instance of humiliation ⟨watched China undergo one ~ after another —E.P.Snow⟩

**hu·mil·i·a·tive** \='=lē,ād·iv, -lēəd·-\ *adj* : tending to humiliate : causing humiliation

**hu·mil·i·ty** \hyü'miləd·ē, -ətē, -i *also* yü-\ *n* -ES [ME *humilite,* fr. MF *humilité,* fr. L *humilitat-, humilitas,* fr. *humilis* low, humble + *-itat-, -itas* -ity — more at HUMBLE] **1** : the quality or state of being humble in spirit : freedom from pride or arrogance ⟨we all need . . . ~ in the face of what we do not understand —Nicola Chiaromonte⟩ **2** *New Eng* : any of several snipes

**hu·min** \'hyümən\ *n* -s [G, fr. NL *humus* + G *-in*] : any of various dark-colored insoluble usu. amorphous substances formed in many reactions: as **a** : a substance obtained from humus (as the residue from treatment with cold alkali) **b** : a pigment formed in the acid hydrolysis of protein containing tryptophan — compare MELANOIDIN

**hu·mir·ia** \hyü'mirēə\ *n, cap* [NL, modif. of Pg *umiri* umiri — more at UMIRI] : a genus (the type of the family Humiriaceae) of So. American balsam-yielding trees with small cymose flowers

**hu·mir·i·a·ce·ae** \=,=='āsē,ē\ *n pl, cap* [NL, fr. *Humiria,* type genus + *-aceae*] : a family of tropical American and African trees or shrubs (order Geraniales) by some treated as a subfamily of the Linaceae but having bilocular anthers and numerous stamens — **hu·mir·i·a·ceous** \(ˌ)=,=='āshəs\ *adj*

**hum·ism** \'hyü,mizəm\ *n* -s *usu cap* [David *Hume* + E *-ism* — more at HUMEAN] : the philosophical system or methods of Hume; *esp* : philosophical skepticism according to which it is impossible to demonstrate any necessary connection between occurrences

**hu·mit** \'hyümət\ *n* -s [short for *humiture*] : the unit used in expressing humiture ⟨a humiture of 68 ~s⟩

**hum·ite** \'hyü,mīt\ *n* -s [Sir Abraham *Hume* †1838 Eng. mineral collector + E *-ite*] : a white, yellow, brown, or red mineral $Mg_7Si_3O_{12}(F,OH)_2$ consisting of a basic magnesium silicate containing fluorine that is brittle and of vitreous to resinous luster, that is found in the masses ejected from Vesuvius and elsewhere, and is related to chondrodite, norbergite, and olivine (hardness 6.-6.5.; sp. gr. 3.1-3.2)

**humite group** *n* : a group of isomorphous minerals consisting of olivine, chondrodite, humite, and clinohumite and closely resembling one another in chemical composition, physical properties, and crystallization

**hu·mi·ture** \'hyümə,chü(ə)r\ *n* -s [blend of *humidity* and *temperature*] : a combined measurement of temperature and humidity computed in integers by adding the temperature in degrees Fahrenheit to the relative humidity and dividing by two and choosing the next integer if a fraction of ½ is left over ⟨when the temperature is 75° F and the relative humidity is 60 percent the ~ is 68⟩

**hum·lie** \'həmli\ *n* -s [*hummel* + *-ie*] *Scot* : a polled domestic bovine : DODDIE

**hum·ma·ble** \'həməbəl\ *adj* : capable of or lending itself to being hummed ⟨a ~ melody, a catchy tune —John Mason Brown⟩

**hummed** *past of* HUM

**¹hum·mel** *also* **hum·ble** \'həməl\ *adj* [ME *hommyll;* akin to LG *hummel* polled animal] **1** *Scot* : AWNLESS — used of grain **2** *Scot* : HORNLESS — used of cattle or stags

**²hummel** *also* **humble** \"\ *vt* **hummeled** *or* **hummelled** *also* **humbled; hummeled** *or* **hummelled** *also* **humbled; hummeling** *or* **hummelling** *also* **humbling** \-m(ə)liŋ\ **hummels** *also* **humbles** *chiefly Scot* : to separate (barley or oats) from the awns and tips of hull

**³hummel** \"\ *n* -s **1** *chiefly Scot* : HUMLIE **2** *chiefly Scot* : a hornless stag

**hum·mel·er** *or* **hum·mel·ler** \-m(ə)lə(r)\ *n* -s : one that hummels

**¹hum·mer** \'həmə(r)\ *n* -s [¹*hum* + *-er* (n. suffix)] **1** : one that hums; *specif* : HUMMINGBIRD **2** : HUMDINGER ⟨the early pace was certainly a ~ —G.F.T.Ryall⟩ — **on the hummer** **1** *dial* : not in working order **2** *dial* : not well : under the weather

**²hum·mer** \'həmə(r), 'hu̇m-\ *vb* [freq. of ¹*hum*] *dial Brit* : MURMUR, MUMBLE

**humming** *adj* [ME, fr. pres. part. of *hummen* to hum — more at HUM] **1** : DRONING, BUZZING ⟨the ~ sound of telephone wires⟩ **2** : extremely busy : BOOMING, BRISK ⟨the tobacco warehouses . . . are ~ centers of activity —*Amer. Guide Series: N.C.*⟩ — **hum·ming·ly** *adv*

**hummingbird** \'==,=\ *n* : any of numerous nonpasserine birds constituting a family (Trochilidae) that is noted for the small size of most species and the brilliant iridescent plumage of the males which in some forms have remarkable crests, neck tufts, or elongated tail feathers, and being anatomically related to the swifts and like them having narrow wings with long primaries but a slender bill and a very extensile tongue

**hummingbird moth** *n* : HAWKMOTH

**hummingbird sage** *n* : CRIMSON SAGE

**hummingbird's trumpet** *n* : CALIFORNIA FUCHSIA

**¹hum·mock** \'həmək\ *or* **hom·mock** \'häm-\ *n* -s [alter. of ³*hammock*] **1 a** : a rounded or conical knoll or hillock : a slight rise of ground above a level surface **2** : a ridge or pile of ice (as in an ice field or floe) **3** : HAMMOCK 2

**2hummock** \"\ *vb* -ED/-ING/-S : to form into hummocks esp. on an ice field

**hum·mocky** \-kē,-ki\ *adj* : abounding in hummocks : resembling a hummock : UNEVEN ⟨a ~ road⟩ ⟨~ fields⟩ ⟨stopped by ~ ice —T.H.Manning⟩

**hum·mum** \ˈhə(,)məm\ *also* **hum·mums** \-məmz\ *n, pl* **hummums** *usu cap* [fr. the *Hummums*, a 17th cent. bathhouse in Covent Garden, London, England, fr. Turk *hamam*, fr. Ar *hammām* bath] : TURKISH BATH

**hum note** *n* : the humming tone given by the whole mass of a vibrating bell sounding an octave below its fundamental note — called also *hum tone*

**1hu·mor** \ˈ(h)yümə(r)\ *n* -s *see -or in Explan Notes* [ME *humour*, fr. MF *humeur*, fr. ML & L; ML *humor* humor of the body, fr. L *humor*, *umor* moisture, fluid; akin to MD *wac* damp, wet, ON *vökr* damp, L *humēre*, *umēre* to be moist or damp, *uvidus* damp, moist, Gk *hygros* wet, Skt *ukṣati* he sprinkles, he moistens] **1 a** (1) : a normal functioning fluid or semifluid of the body (as the blood, lymph, or bile) esp. of vertebrates (2) : a secretion that is itself an excitant of activity (as certain hormones) — see NEUROHUMOR **b** (1) *in medieval physiology* : a fluid or juice of an animal or plant; *specif* : one of the four fluids entering into the constitution of the body and determining by their relative proportions a person's health and temperament — see BLACK BILE, BLOOD, PHLEGM, YELLOW BILE (2) : constitutional or habitual disposition, character, or bent : TEMPERAMENT ⟨are you an agreeable person? Have you a pleasant ~? —Alfred Buchanan⟩ ⟨every word they spoke . . . attested to their mutual love, the combining of their ~s —Djuna Barnes⟩ ⟨the women were horrified or admiring, as their ~ moved them —Edith Wharton⟩ (3) : temporary state of mind : TEMPER, MOOD ⟨not in a ~ to hear you further —Thomas Hardy⟩ ⟨in excellent ~⟩ ⟨after the execution . . . the ~ of the court involuntarily changed —Francis Hackett⟩ (4) : a sudden, unpredictable, or unreasoning inclination : CAPRICE, WHIM, FANCY ⟨a very frolicsome and tricky creature . . . full of wild fantastic ~s —W.H.Hudson †1922⟩ ⟨conceived the ~ of impeaching casual passersby . . . and wreaking vengeance on them —Charles Dickens⟩ ⟨victims of nature's cataclysmic ~s, dust storms and drought —Julian Dana⟩ (5) **humors** *pl* : actions revealing the oddities or quirks of human temperament : whimsical or fantastic actions : VAGARIES ⟨the ~s and small details of ordinary life —John Erskine †1951⟩ **c** *obs* : MOISTURE, VAPOR ⟨the ~s of the dank morning —Shak.⟩ **2 a** : that quality in a happening, an action, a situation, or an expression of ideas which appeals to a sense of the ludicrous or absurdly incongruous : comic or amusing quality ⟨the ~ of his plight⟩ ⟨the delightful ~ of a book⟩ **b** : the mental faculty of discovering, expressing, or appreciating ludicrous or absurdly incongruous elements in ideas, situations, happenings, or acts : droll imagination or its expressions ⟨the man is completely without ~⟩ — compare WIT **c** : the act of or effort at being humorous : something (as an action, saying, or writing) that is or is designed to be humorous ⟨his heavy ~ fell completely flat⟩ ⟨never read any ~ above the so-called comics —Ellie Tucker⟩ ⟨a ~ magazine⟩ **syn** see MOOD, WIT — **out of humor** *adv* : in a bad humor : out of sorts

**2humor** \"\ *vt* **humored**; **humored**; **humoring** \-m(ə)riŋ\ **humors** *see -or in Explan Notes* **1** : to comply with the humor of : soothe or content by indulgence or compliance : INDULGE ⟨one must discover and ~ his weaknesses —H.M. Parshley⟩ **2** : to comply with the nature of : adjust matters to the peculiarities or exigencies of : adapt oneself to ⟨yielding to, and ~*ing* the motion of the limbs and twigs —William Bartram⟩ **syn** see INDULGE

**hu·mor·al** \-mərəl\ *adj* [MF, fr. ML *humoralis*, fr. *humor* + L *-alis* -al — more at HUMOR] : of, relating to, proceeding from, or involving a bodily humor — now often used of endocrine factors as opposed to neural or somatic ⟨~ control of sugar metabolism⟩

**hu·mored** \ˈ(h)yümə(r)d\ *adj* : having a specified humor — now used only in combination ⟨a good-*humored* child⟩ ⟨a bad-*humored* man⟩ — **hu·mored·ly** *adv*

**hu·mor·esque** \ˌ(h)yüməˈresk\ *n* -s [G *humoreske*, fr. *humor* (fr. E) + *-eske* -esque] : a musical composition typically whimsical or fanciful in character : CAPRICCIO

**hu·mor·ist** \ˈ(h)yümərəst\ *n* -s [MF *humoriste*, fr. *humeur* humor + *-iste* -ist] **1** *archaic* : a person subject to humors or whims : one who has some peculiarity or eccentricity of character which he indulges in odd or whimsical ways **2 a** : a person given to the display or enjoyment of humor: as **a** : a person with a strong sense of humor : a facetious person : JOKER, WAG ⟨two local ~s go in . . . to make a goat of the doctor —*Sydney (Australia) Bull.*⟩ **b** : a writer specializing in or noted for the quality of his humor ⟨a great and powerful ~⟩

**hu·mor·is·tic** \ˌ==ˈristik\ *adj* : HUMOROUS ⟨that book was to be ~ and undoubtedly . . . would have amused many people —Felix Reichmann⟩

**hu·mor·less** \ˈ(h)yümə(r)ləs\ *adj* **1** : lacking in humor ⟨heavy, ~, slow-moving, methodical —T.H.Fielding⟩ **2** : offered, said, or done in dead seriousness : reflecting the lack of a sense of humor ⟨~ memorizing of 500 dates . . . for a three-hour third-degree oral examination —L. Ruth Middlebrook⟩ ⟨his ~ proposal aroused covert snickers⟩ — **hu·mor·less·ness** *n* -ES

**hu·mor·ous** \ˈ(h)yüm(ə)rəs\ *adj* [MF *humereux*, fr. *humeur* + *-eux* -ous] **1** *archaic* : subject to or governed by humor or caprice : CAPRICIOUS, WHIMSICAL **2** *obs* : MOIST, HUMID, WATERY **3 a** : full of or characterized by humor : FUNNY, JOCULAR ⟨a ~ poem⟩ ⟨earned part of his way through college by selling ~ drawings —*Current Biog.*⟩ ⟨stories in a ~ vein⟩ **b** : possessing, indicating, or expressive of a sense of humor : given to the display or appreciative of humor ⟨short, rotund, with . . . ~ brown eyes —R.M.Lovett⟩ ⟨a very kindly and rather ~ man —O.W.Holmes †1935⟩ ⟨vented a low ~ laugh —Thomas Hardy⟩ ⟨studied his own life . . . with a shrewd and ~ eye —Harrison Smith⟩ **syn** see WITTY

**hu·mor·ous·ly** *adv* : in a humorous manner

**hu·mor·ous·ness** *n* -ES : the quality or state of being humorous

**hu·mor·some** \-mə(r)səm\ *adj* : full of humors : WHIMSICAL

**humour** *Brit var of* HUMOR

**hu·mous** \ˈ(h)yüməs\ *adj* [NL *humus* + E *-ous*] : of or relating to humus : containing a relatively large amount of humus ⟨~ soils⟩

**1hump** \ˈhəmp\ *n* -s [akin to Fris *hompe* lump, chunk, D *homp* lump, chunk, MLG *hump* bump, ON *aptrhuppr* flank of an animal, Norw dial. *hupp*, *hump* flank of an animal, L *incumbere* to lie down, Gk *kymbē* drinking cup, bowl, boat, Skt *kumbha* pot, OE *hype* hip — more at HIP] **1** : a rounded protuberance: as **a** : the protuberance formed by a crooked back in human beings **b** : a fleshy protuberance on the back of an animal (as a camel, bison, or whale) **2** *Brit* : a fit of depression or sulking ⟨enough to give anyone the ~ to see him now —Samuel Butler †1902⟩ **3 a** (1) : MOUND, HUMMOCK (2) : a conspicuous bulge or protruding section of coastline ⟨the ~ of Brazil⟩ (3) : a mountain range or mountain that has to be crossed — used chiefly in aeronautics ⟨over the ~ from Chile to Buenos Aires⟩ ⟨the Himalayan ~⟩ **b** : an elevation in a railroad switch yard up one side of which the cars are pushed by an engine and down the other side of which they are switched by gravity to their proper tracks **4 a** : a difficult, trying, or critical phase (as of an undertaking) — often used in the phrase *over the hump* ⟨in the production of machine tools the Soviet Union is over the ~ —P.E.Mosely⟩ **b** : strenuous exertion or effort : GO, HUSTLE — often used in the phrases *on the hump* ⟨my duties keep me pretty much on the ~ —*New Yorker*⟩ and *get a hump on* ⟨nowadays even ministers of the gospel know how to get a ~ on —J.W.Krutch⟩

**2hump** \"\ *vb* -ED/-ING/-S *vt* **1** : to exert (oneself) ⟨last year he had to ~ himself and make over a million —*Fortune*⟩ **2** : to make humpbacked : HUNCH ⟨stood ~*ed* with pain —F.B. Gipson⟩ **3** *chiefly Brit* : to put or carry on the back or shoulder ⟨we ~*ed* our barracks bags, piled in the wet trucks —H.D. Skidmore⟩ ⟨rose at six in the morning to ~ coal . . . to the neighbors' homes —*Books of the Month*⟩; *also* : to carry in any way ⟨helped . . . ~ in the crates of beer —Audrey Barker⟩ **4** : to sort (freight cars) in a classification yard and assemble in trains by means of a hump **5** : to copulate with — usu. considered vulgar ~ *vi* **1 a** : to exert oneself : HUSTLE, HURRY ⟨will have to ~ to get through . . . tomorrow —Richard Bissell⟩ ⟨keeps me ~*ing* even with three assistants —C.E. Lovejoy⟩ ⟨~ along and do your chores —Howard Troyer⟩ **b** : to move swiftly or at top speed : RACE ⟨it's moving southeast and ~*ing* toward the north —*Springfield (Mass.) Daily News*⟩ ⟨really ~*ing* along ahead of that tail wind —Norman Carlisle⟩ **2** : to rise in a hump : form a hump ⟨the . . . highway ~*s* and dips in a manner which discourages fast driving —*Amer. Guide Series: Conn.*⟩ ⟨~*s* up to 11,600 feet —A.H. Brown⟩

**humpback** \ˈ=,=\ *n* **1** : a crooked back : a humped back : KYPHOSIS **2** : a humpbacked person : HUNCHBACK **3 a** *also* **humpback whale** : a whalebone whale of the genus *Megaptera* related to the rorquals but having very long flippers, being black above and white below, attaining large size, but yielding inferior whalebone and oil **b** (1) : HUMPBACK SALMON (2) : the black sea bass (*Centropristes striatus*)

**humpbacked** \ˈ=,=\ *adj* : having a humped back

**humpbacked whitefish** *n* : an Alaskan whitefish (*Coregonus nelsoni*)

**humpback grunt** *n* : YELLOW GRUNT

**humpback salmon** *also* **humpbacked salmon** *n* : a small salmon (*Oncorhynchus gorbuscha*) which ascends Pacific coast rivers of Asia and of America from California to Alaska

**humpback sucker** *n* : a large sucker (*Xyrauchen texanus*) of the Colorado basin reputed to attain a weight of 7 pounds

**humped** \ˈhəm(p)t\ *adj* : having a hump : HUMPBACKED

**humped cattle** *n* : domestic cattle developed from an Indian species (*Bos indicus*) and characterized by a hump of fat and muscle above the shoulders : Brahman cattle : domestic zebus

**1humph** *typically a snort or a strong* h-*sound followed by a contemptuously intoned* m-*sound or vowel* ˈə *the* ˈə *usu nasalized; often read as* ˈhəm(p)f\ *n* -s [imit. of a grunt] : a sound expressive of doubt or contempt ⟨voiced many a skeptical ~ —*Time*⟩ — often used as an interjection

**2humph** \ˈhəm(p)f\ *vb* -ED/-ING/-s *vi* : to utter a humph ⟨~*ed* and shagged upstairs —Feike Feikema⟩ ~ *vt* : to utter in a tone suggestive of a humph ⟨might as well give one to the Queen of England, ~*ed* a correspondent —Horace Sutton⟩

**humping track** *n* : a yard track for sorting freight cars by humping

**hump·less** \ˈhəmpləs\ *adj* : having no hump

**hump rider** *n* : a yardman who rides and brakes cars in hump yards not equipped with car retarders

**humps** *pl of* HUMP, *pres 3d sing of* HUMP

**hump-shouldered** \ˈ=ˌ==\ *adj* : having a humped shoulder ⟨their life preservers making them appear *hump-shouldered* —H.D.Skidmore⟩

**hump sore** *n* : infestation of the skin of Indian cattle by a filarial worm (*Stephanofilaria assamensis*); *also* : the hide-damaging lesions it causes esp. about the hump and neck

**hump speed** *n* : the speed of a seaplane during takeoff at which the water resistance reaches a maximum

**hump·ty** \ˈhəm(p)ti\ *n* -ES [perh. after *Humpty-Dumpty*] *Brit* : a low soft cushioned seat ⟨the dean, curled on a ~, was frankly listening —Dorothy Sayers⟩

**hump·ty-dump·ty** \ˌhəm(p)tēˈdəm(p)tē, -ti . . . ti\ *n* -ES *often cap H&D* [after *Humpty-Dumpty*, egg-shaped nursery-rhyme character who fell from a wall and broke into bits] : something that once damaged can never be repaired or made operative again ⟨the exchange crisis . . . that brought the *Humpty-Dumpty* of currency stabilization tumbling —*Atlantic*⟩ ⟨people fled into their suddenly *Humpty-Dumpty* world —Robert O'Brien⟩

**1humpy** \ˈhəmpē, -pi\ *adj* -ER/-EST [1*hump* + *-y*] : full of humps or bunches : covered with protuberances : HUMPED

**2hum·py** \"\ *n* -ES [native name in Australia] *Austral* : a small, primitive, or ramshackle dwelling : SHANTY, SHACK, HUT

**hump yard** *n* : a railroad switch yard having a hump

**hums** *pres 3d sing of* HUM, *pl of* HUM

**humstrum** \ˈ=,=\ *n* -s [1*hum* + *strum*] **1** : a crude fiddle; *broadly* : any out-of-tune musical instrument **2** : HURDY-GURDY

**hum tone** *n* : HUM NOTE

**hu·mu·hu·mu·nu·ku·nu·ku·a·pu·aa** \ˌhüməˈhüməˌnükəˈnükəˌäpəˈwäˌä\ *n* -s [Hawaiian] : a small Hawaiian triggerfish

**hu·mu·lene** \ˈhyümyəˌlēn\ *n* -s [ISV *humul-* (fr. NL *Humulus*) + *-ene*] : a liquid sesquiterpene $C_{15}H_{24}$ in hop oil and clove oil — called also *alpha-caryophyllene*

**hu·mu·lone** \-ˌlōn\ *or* **hu·mu·lon** \-ˌlän\ *n* -s [ISV *humul-* (fr. NL *Humulus*) + *-one*] : a bitter crystalline antibiotic $C_{21}H_{30}O_5$ obtained from lupulin

**hu·mu·lus** \-ləs\ *n, cap* [NL, fr. ML, hop (plant), prob. of Gmc origin; akin to OE *hymele* hop, MLG *homele*, ON *humli*] : a genus of herbaceous vines (family Urticaceae) with palmate leaves and pistillate flowers in clusters resembling catkins or cones — see 3HOP

**hu·mus** \ˈ(h)yüməs\ *n* -ES [NL, fr. L, earth, ground — more at HUMBLE] : a brown or black complex and varying material formed by the partial decomposition of vegetable or animal matter : the organic portion of soil

**1hun** \ˈhən\ *n* -s [LL *Hunni*, pl.] **1** *cap* : a member of a nomadic Mongolian people who were driven westward from Mongolia about A.D.200 and obtaining control of a large portion of central and eastern Europe under Attila about the middle of the 5th century forced even Rome to pay tribute until their power was terminated by their defeat at Châlons in 451 and the death of Attila in 453 — compare EPHTHALITE **2 a** *often cap* : a person who is wantonly destructive : VANDAL **b** *usu cap* : GERMAN; *esp* : a German soldier in World War I or World War II ⟨the recoiling Hitlerites and *Huns* are redoubling their ruthless cruelties —*Britannica Bk. of the Yr.*⟩ — usu. used disparagingly

**2hun** \"\ *n* -s [by shortening] *usu cap* : HUNGARIAN PARTRIDGE

**hun** *abbr* hundred

**hu·na·nese** \ˌhünəˈnēz, -ēs\ *adj, usu cap* [*Hunan*, province in China + E *-ese*] : of or relating to the province of Hunan

**2hunanese** \"\ *n, pl* **hunanese** *cap* : a native or inhabitant of Hunan

**1hunch** \ˈhənch\ *vb* -ED/-ING/-ES [origin unknown] *vi* **1** : to push, thrust, or move oneself forward ⟨~*ed* along for a short spell of safe steps —T.B.Costain⟩ ⟨heavy shoulders . . . ~*ed* through the open door —S.H.Adams⟩ **2 a** : to assume a bent or crooked posture esp. in sitting : bend one's body into an arch or hump ⟨a technical sergeant ~*es* in a tiny cubicle —*Fortune*⟩ ⟨gripped the wheel, ~*ing* over it —Gregor Felsen⟩ ⟨folded his hands on the table and ~*ed* forward —Hugh MacLennan⟩ **b** : to draw or compress oneself into a ball : curl up ⟨~*ed* up on the rug —Margery Allingham⟩ ⟨~ beneath the covers, in my curled red ball of darkness —Randall Jarrell⟩ **c** : HUDDLE, SQUAT ⟨we ~*ed* close to the damp earth —H.D.Skidmore⟩ ⟨the home ~*es* on a one-acre point of land —*Springfield (Mass.) Union*⟩ ⟨the mountains ~*ed* around the valley —Helen Rich⟩ **d** : to rise so as to form a hump or arch : REAR ⟨the sea ~*ed* up and hurled itself on the . . . land —H.E.Rieseberg⟩ ⟨his shoulder ~*ed* convulsively —Bernard DeVoto⟩ **3** : FUDGE 2a ~ *vt* **1** : PUSH, JOSTLE, SHOVE ⟨I would ~ my chair . . . closer to my dear and only cronies —Mary Nash⟩ ⟨tugboats . . . ~*ed* their ocean-going charges to the quayside —Newman Bumstead⟩ **2** : to thrust or bend so as to form a hump or arch : CROOK, ARCH ⟨the crow ~*ed* its shoulders, like an old woman seeking comfort in her moldy coat —Edita Morris⟩ ⟨kept his . . . body ~*ed* slightly forward —Tennessee Williams⟩ ⟨if you ~ yourself up . . . it is probably due to self-consciousness or fatigue —*Farmer's Weekly (So. Africa)*⟩ : HUDDLE ⟨~*ed* ourselves into a little group in the corner⟩

**2hunch** \"\ *n* -ES **1** : the act or an instance of hunching : PUSH ⟨give him a good ~ with your foot —Abraham Tucker⟩ **2** [prob. back-formation fr. *hunchbacked*] **a** : a rounded protuberance : HUMP ⟨his back carried a huge ~ —William Scoresby †1857⟩ **b** : a thick piece : LUMP ⟨barter it for a ~ of cake —Flora Thompson⟩ **3** : a strong intuitive feeling ⟨expressed her ~ that the photograph had slid off the desk —*Saturday Rev.*⟩; *esp* : a strong intuitive feeling as to how something (as a course of action) will turn out ⟨on a ~, resolved to establish a rail and shipping terminus here —*Amer. Guide Series: Texas*⟩

**hunchback** \ˈ=,=\ *n* [back-formation fr. *hunchbacked*] **1** : a back with a hunch or hump : KYPHOSIS **2** : a hunchbacked person

**hunchbacked** \ˈ=,=\ *adj* [perh. fr. 1*hunch* + *-backed* (fr. 1*back* + *-ed*)] : HUMPBACKED

**hund** \ˈhən(d), -ü-,-ü-\ *dial var of* HOUND

**hund** *abbr* hundred

**hun·der** \ˈhən(d)ə(r)\ *or* **hun·dert** \-(d)ə(r)t\ *dial var of* HUNDRED

**hun·di** *also* **hoon·dee** *or* **hoon·di** \ˈhündē\ *n* -s [Hindi *huṇḍī*] : a negotiable instrument, bill of exchange, or promissory note of India used esp. in the internal finance of trade

**1hun·dred** \ˈhəndrəd, ÷ -ndə(r)d, *rapid* -nə(r)d, *dial or substand* -nə(r)t\ *n, pl* **hundreds** *or* **hundred** [ME, fr. OE; akin to OFris *hundred*, *hunderd* hundred, OS *hunderod*, ON *hundrath*; all fr. a prehistoric WGmc-NGmc compound whose constituents are akin respectively to OE *hund* hundred and Goth *garathjan* to count; akin to OHG *hunt* hundred, OS & Goth *hund*, L *centum*, Gk *hekaton*, Skt *śatam*; all fr. a prehistoric word derived fr. the root of E *ten* — more at TEN, REASON] **1** : 10 tens : twice 50 : five twenties : five score : the square of ten — see NUMBER table **2 a** : 100 units or objects ⟨a total of a ~⟩ **b** : a group or set of 100 ⟨arranged by ~*s*⟩ **3 a** : the numerable quantity symbolized by the arabic numerals 100 **b** : the letter C **4** : the number occupying the position three to the left of the decimal point in the Arabic notation (as 9 in the number 2968) — usu. used in pl. **5 a** : any of various British units of quantity for commercial items (as for 120 boards, 120 nails, or 140 pecks or 35 bushels of lime) **b** : HUNDREDWEIGHT **6 a** : a hundred-pound note **b** : a hundred-dollar bill **7 a** : a division of a county orig. English but later established also in certain British possessions and formerly having its own local court **b** : the body of landholders and residents of a hundred **8** : **hundreds** *pl* — used in combination to designate a specified century ⟨the early fifteen-*hundreds*⟩ — **by the hundred** *or* **by the hundreds** : in great numbers ⟨examples can be found *by the hundreds* —H.S. Morrison⟩

**2hundred** \"\ *adj* [ME, fr. OE, fr. *hundred*, n.] : being 100 in number ⟨a ~ years⟩ — usu. preceded by *a*, *an*, or a numeral (as *one*, *four*)

**1hun·dred·fold** \ˈ==ˌfōld\ *adv* [ME, fr. 2*hundred* + *-fold*] : by 100 times ⟨increased a ~⟩ ⟨increased one ~⟩ — usu. preceded by *a*, *an*, or a numeral (as *one*, *four*)

**2hundredfold** \"\ *adj* [ME, fr. 2*hundred* + *-fold*] : being 100 times as large, as great, or as many as some understood size, degree, or amount : very great — usu. preceded by *a*, *an*, or a numeral (as *one*, *four*)

**hundred-legs** \ˈ==,=\ *n pl but sing or pl in constr* : CENTIPEDE

**1hundred-percent** \ˌ===ˈ=\ *adj* **1** : PERFECT, UNALLOYED, GENUINE **2** : THOROUGHGOING, UNQUESTIONABLE ⟨the resources of the *hundred-percent* American —*The Bookman*⟩

**2hundred-percent** \"\ *adv* : without qualification or reservation : ENTIRELY, COMPLETELY ⟨a *hundred-percent* pure wool⟩

**hundred-percent·er** \"ə(r)\ *n* -s [*hundred-percent (American)* + *-er*] : a thoroughgoing, unqualified, and often blatant nationalist; *esp* : a self-proclaimed opponent of foreign alliances, influences, and interests ⟨the vociferous nationalism of the *hundred-percenters* . . . is about to be most rowdy —Walter Lippmann⟩ ⟨could never be a *hundred-percenter* as long as he did not possess an American birth certificate —*Amer. Mercury*⟩

**hundred-percent·ism** \-ˌizəm\ *n* -s : the beliefs and practices of a hundred-percenter ⟨laws . . . passed under the stress of antialien phobia and *hundred-percentism* —*Christian Century*⟩

**1hun·dredth** \ˈhəndrədth, ˈhən(d)ə(r)|, |tth\ *adj* [ME *hundreth*, fr. *hundred* + *-th*] **1** : being number 100 in a countable series ⟨the ~ day⟩ — see NUMBER table **2** : being one of a hundred equal parts into which anything is divisible ⟨a ~ share of the money⟩

**2hun·dredth** \"\ *n, pl* **hundredths** \-dths, -t(th)s\ **1** : number 100 in a countable series **2** : the quotient of a unit divided by 100 : one of 100 equal parts of anything

**hundredweight** \ˈ==,=\ *n, pl* **hundredweight** *or* **hundredweights** : any of various units of weight ranging from 100 to about 120 pounds: as **a** : a unit equal to 100 pounds — called also *short hundredweight* **b** *Brit* : a unit equal to 112 pounds — called also *long hundredweight*; see MEASURE table **c** : METRIC HUNDREDWEIGHT

**hung** *past of* HANG

**1hun·gar·i·an** \ˌhəŋˈga(a)rēən, -ger-,-gār-\ *n* -s *cap* [*Hungary*, country in central Europe + E *-an*] **1 a** : a native or inhabitant of Hungary : MAGYAR **b** : one that is of Hungarian descent **2** : the language of the Magyars : MAGYAR 2

**2hungarian** \ˌ=ˈ===\ *adj, usu cap* **1** : of, relating to, or characteristic of Hungary **2** : of, relating to, or characteristic of the people of Hungary

**hungarian balsam** *n, usu cap H* : a resin from the Swiss mountain pine

**hungarian blue** *n, often cap H* : AZURITE BLUE

**hungarian brome** *or* **hungarian forage grass** *n, usu cap H* : AWNLESS BROMEGRASS

**hungarian goulash** *n, usu cap H* : GOULASH

**hungarian grass** *or* **hungarian millet** *n, usu cap H* : FOXTAIL MILLET

**hungarian green** *n, often cap H* : MALACHITE GREEN 3

**hungarian gypsy scale** *n, usu cap H* : a musical scale having a whole step between steps 1 and 2, half steps between 2 and 3, 4 and 5, 5 and 6, 7 and 8, and augmented seconds between 3 and 4, and 6 and 7 — compare HARMONIC MINOR SCALE

c d e♭ f♯ g a♭ b c
1 2 3 4 5 6 7 8

Hungarian gypsy scale

**hungarian lilac** *n, usu cap H* : a central European shrub (*Syringa josikaea*) having lilac-violet flowers in upright clusters and with the lobes of the corolla nearly upright

**hungarian paprika** *also* **hungarian pepper** *n, usu cap H* **1** : a paprika produced in Hungary from peppers of slight pungency and distinctive flavor; *esp* : one produced from the fleshy fruit freed from seeds and stalk — see KING'S PAPRIKA **2** : a plant producing peppers suitable for making Hungarian paprika

**hungarian partridge** *n, usu cap H* : a common European partridge (*Perdix perdix*)

**hungarian vetch** *or* **hungarian clover** *n, usu cap H* : a European vetch (*Vicia cannonica*) introduced into the Pacific Northwest as a hay, forage, and silage crop esp. on heavy clay soils and having stems and leaves with hair which give the plants a gray color

**hun·ga·ry** \ˈhəŋgərē, -ri\ *adj, usu cap* [fr. *Hungary*, country in central Europe] : of or from Hungary : of the kind or style prevalent in Hungary : HUNGARIAN

**hungary blue** *n, often cap H* : COBALT BLUE 2

**1hun·ger** \ˈhəŋgə(r)\ *n* -s [ME, fr. OE *hungor*; akin to OHG *hungar* hunger, ON *hungr*, Goth *hūhrus* hunger, Gk *kenkei* he is hungry, Skt *kāṅkṣati* he desires, Lith *kanka* pain; basic meaning: burning, hurting] **1 a** : a craving, desire, or urgent need for food **b** : an uneasy sensation occasioned normally by the lack of food and resulting directly from stimulation of the sensory nerves of the stomach by the contraction and churning movement of the empty stomach **c** : a weakened disordered condition brought about by prolonged lack of food ⟨die of ~⟩ **2** : FAMINE ⟨the great ~*s* and . . . pestilences of the past —*Times Lit. Supp.*⟩ **3** : a strong desire or craving ⟨a ~ for knowledge⟩ ⟨land ~⟩ **4** : a craving for or deterioration from lack of a specified substance ⟨potash ~⟩ — used esp. of plants

**2hunger** \"\ *vb* **hungered**; **hungered**; **hungering** \-g(ə)riŋ\ **hungers** [ME *hungrin*, *hungeren*, fr. OE *hyngran*; akin to OHG *hungaren* to hunger, ON *hungra*, Goth *huggrjan* to hunger, OE *hungor*, n., hunger] *vi* **1** : to feel or be oppressed by hunger ⟨the poor ~, yet are not fed⟩ **2** : to have an eager desire : LONG ⟨the world today ~*s* for ideals⟩ ~ *vt* : to make hungry : force by hunger ⟨the besiegers ~*ed* the garrison into surrender⟩ **syn** see LONG

**hunger flower** *n* : a whitlow grass (*Draba incana*) growing in dry soil

**hunger grass** *n* : SLENDER FOXTAIL

**hungering** *adj* : having the sensation of hunger ⟨a ~ man⟩ — **hun·ger·ing·ly** *adv*

**hun·ger·ly** \ˈhəŋgə(r)lē\ *adj, archaic* : having a hungry look

**hunger strike** *n* **:** the action of one esp. a prisoner who refuses to eat anything or enough to sustain life so as to obtain compliance with his demands

**hun·ger–strike** \'ˌ=,=\ *vi* [hunger strike] **:** to engage in a hunger strike

**hungerweed** \'=,=\ *n* **1 :** CORN CROWFOOT **2 :** SLENDER FOXTAIL

**hung over** *adj* [fr. *hangover*, n., after *hung*, past part. of *hang*, v.] **:** suffering from a hangover ⟨the next morning after the party everybody was *hung over*⟩

**hun·gri·ly** \'həŋgrəlē, -li\ *adv* [ME, fr. *hungry* + *-ly*] **:** in a hungry manner **:** with avidity **:** LONGINGLY, EAGERLY ⟨looking ~ to the day of cheaper power —Gordon Dean⟩ ⟨I read ~ —Jan Valtin⟩

**hun·gri·ness** \-grēnəs, -grin-\ *n* -ES **:** the quality or state of being hungry

**hun·gry** \'həŋgrē, -gri, *chiefly in substand speech* -ŋr-, *dial* 'hōŋ-\ *adj* -ER/-EST [ME, fr. OE *hungrig*, fr. *hungor* hunger + *-ig* -y — more at HUNGER] **1 a :** feeling hunger **:** feeling distress from lack of food **:** having a keen appetite ⟨the ~ children trooped into the house⟩ **b :** marked by famine or lack of food ⟨gloom reigned in the ~ countryside⟩ ⟨the ~ days of the great famine⟩ ⟨listen, Captain, this town is ~ —John Hersey⟩ **c :** reflecting or indicating hunger or keen appetite ⟨stand at the row of pastries with a ~ look⟩ **2 :** having, reflecting, or characterized by an ardent desire or craving **:** longing eagerly **:** AVID ⟨~ for affection⟩ ⟨with a kind of ~ fervor —Robertson Davies⟩ ⟨~ for jobs and patronage —H.F.Wilkins⟩ — often used in combination ⟨a land-*hungry* people⟩ ⟨the fuel-*hungry* East⟩ ⟨a trade-*hungry* nation⟩ **3 :** not rich or fertile **:** POOR, BARREN ⟨a ~ soil⟩ ⟨~ ore⟩

**hungry rice** *n* **:** FUNDI

**hungryroot** \'=,=\ *n* **:** the root of the spikenard (sense 2a)

**hung up** *adj* [fr. past part. of *hang up*] **:** DELAYED, DETAINED ⟨was *hung up* at the office and missed his train⟩

**hunia** \'hünēə\ *n* -S [prob. native name in India] **:** a tall long-legged sheep used in southern Asia as a fighting and pack animal

**¹hunk** \'həŋk\ *n* -S [Flem *hunke*; perh. akin to D *homp* lump, chunk — more at HUMP] **:** a large lump or piece ⟨a ~ of bread⟩ ⟨~s of iron⟩

**²hunk** \"\ *also* **hunky** \'həŋkē, -ki\ *adj* [fr. obs. E dial. (New York) *hunk* goal, home (in games), fr. D *honk*, fr. MD *honc* corner, hiding place; akin to WFris *honck*, *honcke* house, hiding place] **1** *slang* **:** ALL RIGHT **:** HUNKY-DORY, OK **2** *slang* **:** EVEN — usu. used with *get* ⟨getting ~ on him —J.B.Benefield⟩ ⟨we'll get ~ with him good —S.F.Eckfeld⟩ ⟨"I'll get ~," I whispered —Harold Robbins⟩

**¹hun·ker** \'həŋkə(r)\ *vi* **hunkered; hunkered; hunkering** \-k(ə)riŋ\ **hunkers** [perh. of Scand origin; akin to ON *hokra* to crouch, creep, *hūka* to squat — more at HAWKER] **:** CROUCH, SQUAT — usu. used with *down* ⟨~*ed* down around the deerskin which they were scraping —Kenneth Roberts⟩ ⟨~*ed* down on his heels —Luke Short⟩

**²hunker** \"\ *n* -S [origin unknown] **1** *usu cap* **:** a member of the conservative section of the Democratic party in New York, 1845–1848 **2 :** a conservative in any respect **:** a person opposed to change or innovation ⟨to this day there are ~*s* . . . who object to it —H.L.Mencken⟩

**hun·kers** \-kə(r)z\ *n pl* [¹*hunker* + *-s*] **:** HAUNCHES ⟨perched there on his ~ —Gerard Perry⟩

**hunks** \'həŋks\ *n pl but sing or pl in constr* [origin unknown] **:** a surly ill-natured person **:** a covetous sordid man **:** MISER ⟨some old ~ of a sea captain —Herman Melville⟩ ⟨all the prudence and selfishness of an old ~ —Thomas Gray⟩

**hun·ky** *also* **hun·kie** \'həŋkē, -ki\ *n, pl* **hunkies** *often cap* [prob. shortening & alter. of *Hungarian* + *-y*, *-ie*] **:** a person of central or east European birth or descent; *esp* **:** an industrial worker of such birth or descent — usu. used disparagingly

**hunky–dory** \ˌhəŋkē¦dōrē, -kə¦d-, -ki..ri, -dȯr-\ *adj* [*hunky* (var. of ²*hunk*) + *-dory* (origin unknown)] **:** quite satisfactory **:** FINE ⟨everything was *hunky-dory*⟩

**hun·nic** \'hənik, -nēk\ *adj, usu cap* [ML *Hunnicus*, fr. LL *Hunni* Huns + L *-icus* -ic] **:** HUNNISH

**hun·nish** \-nish, -nēsh\ *adj, usu cap* [*Hun* + *-ish*] **:** of, like, or relating to the Huns **:** BARBAROUS — **hun·nish·ness** *n* -ES *usu cap*

**huns** *pl of* HUN

**¹hunt** \'hənt\ *vb* -ED/-ING/-S [ME *hunten*, fr. OE *huntian*; akin to OE *hentan* to attack, seize, OHG *herihunda* battle spoils, ON *henda* to grasp, OSw *hinna* to attain, reach, Goth *frahinthan* to take captive] *vt* **1 a :** to follow or search for (game or prey) for the purpose and with the means of capturing or killing **:** pursue (game or prey) for food or in sport ⟨~ buffalo⟩ ⟨wolves ~ large prey only in packs⟩; *esp* **:** to pursue with weapons and often with trained animals **b :** to use or manage in the search for game ⟨~*s* a pack of dogs⟩ **2 a :** to pursue, follow, or track (a person) esp. with the object of capture — often used with *down* ⟨surviving patriots . . . were ~*ed* down in legal manner and put to death —J.A.Froude⟩ **b :** to try to find, locate, or obtain esp. by sustained or careful search or effort ⟨missing persons are ~*ed* by the police⟩ ⟨he's ~*ing* a job⟩ **c :** to find, uncover, or obtain after diligent search — used with *up*, *out*, or *down* ⟨~*ing* out recondite meanings in poems —Howard M. Jones⟩ ⟨~*ed* up a lot of valuable new evidence⟩ **3 :** to drive or chase esp. by hounding, harrying, or persecuting ⟨members of the colonial council . . . were ~*ed* from their homes —J.T.Adams⟩ **4 :** to traverse or go over in quest of game or quarry ⟨~*s* the swamp for moths —J.D. Hart⟩ ~ *vi* **1 :** to take part in a hunt **:** pursue game **2 :** to attempt to find, uncover, or obtain something esp. by diligent search — used with *for* or *after* ⟨~ for a lost wallet⟩ ⟨~*ing* for a street address⟩ ⟨ideas would not come to me if I went out to ~ for them —Ellen Glasgow⟩ **3 :** to oscillate alternately to each side of a neutral point or to run alternately faster and slower instead of steadily because of insufficient stability controls — used esp. of a device or machine ⟨sudden changes of load frequently cause the governor to ~, i.e., to open too wide, then close too far, and so on —S.H.Mortensen & Sterling Beckwith⟩ ⟨~*ing*, in electrical engineering, is a periodic increase or decrease in the speed of synchronous machinery operating in parallel, such as generators or motors —F.D.Jones⟩ ⟨a magnetic compass . . . must be damped to prevent lengthy oscillation or ~*ing* —Benjamin Dutton⟩ **4** *of a bell* **:** to shift continuously up or down in the order of striking in change ringing **syn** see SEEK

**²hunt** \"\ *n* -S [ME *hunte*, fr. *hunten*, v.] **1 :** the act, practice, or an instance of hunting **:** CHASE ⟨the ~ is up; the morn is bright and gray —Shak.⟩ **2 :** an association of huntsmen **:** a number of persons with horses and dogs engaged in hunting or riding to hounds ⟨a gate was being held open . . . and the ~ was streaming through —Adrian Bell⟩ **3 :** an instance of hunting (as in a mechanical device) **4 :** a regular course followed by each bell up or down the striking order in change ringing

**hunt·able** \'həntəbəl\ *adj* **:** capable of being hunted

**hunt and peck** *n* **:** a mode of typing in which one looks at the keyboard and uses random fingering ⟨types fast and accurately, by *hunt and peck* —Brendan Gill⟩ — compare TOUCH SYSTEM

**huntaway** \'=,=\ *adj* [fr. *hunt away*, v.] *NewZeal, of a dog* **:** trained to follow after and drive on a flock of sheep

**hunted** *adj* **1 :** being the object of a search, pursuit, or persecution ⟨a ~ man⟩ ⟨a ~ minority⟩ **2 :** reflecting or expressing the terror or fears of one who is hunted ⟨the prisoner's face lost its ~, hopeless look —Julian Dana⟩ ⟨a glitter of apprehension in her ~ eyes —Edith Wharton⟩ — **hunt·ed·ly** *adv*

**hunt·er** \'həntə(r)\ *n* -S [ME, fr. *hunten* + *-er*] **1 a :** a person who hunts game **:** HUNTSMAN **b :** a dog used or trained for hunting **c :** a horse used or adapted for use in hunting; *esp* **:** one exhibiting endurance, speed, and ability to carry weight and trained for facility in cross-country work and jumping **2 :** a person who hunts or searches diligently or systematically for something ⟨~*s* with camera —S.H.Holbrook⟩ ⟨~*s* after the philosopher's stone —M.R.Cohen⟩ — often used in combination ⟨sensation-*hunters*⟩ **3 a :** a large Jamaican cuckoo (*Hyetornis pluvialis*) **b :** HUNTING SPIDER **4 :** a pocket watch having a hunting case **5 :** HUNTER GREEN

**hunter green** *or* **hunter's green** *n* **:** a variable color averaging a dark yellowish green that is yellower and duller than holly green (sense 1), greener and stronger than deep chrome green, and greener and duller than golf green — called also *elephant green*

**hunter–killer** \¦=·=¦=·=\ *adj* **:** of or relating to a coordinated air-sea operation against enemy submarines ⟨a *hunter-killer* group⟩

**hun·ter's canal** \'həntə(r)z-\ *n, usu cap H* [after John *Hunter* †1793 Scot. surgeon] **:** an aponeurotic canal in the middle third of the thigh through which the femoral artery passes

**hunter's moon** *n* **:** the full moon after the harvest moon

**hunter's pink** *n* **:** any of several vivid or strong reds used for hunting jackets

**hunth** *abbr* hundred thousand

**¹hunting** *n* -S [ME, fr. OE *huntung*, fr. *huntian* to hunt + *-ung* -ing] **1 :** the act, practice, or an instance of chasing, taking, or killing game or wild animals **:** CHASE, SHOOTING **2 :** the act, practice, or an instance of trying to find or obtain esp. by diligent search or effort ⟨the bibliographical ~ that lies behind any research work —H.N.Southern⟩ ⟨have had little time for book-*hunting* —H.J.Laski⟩

**²hunting** *adj* [fr. pres. part. of ²*hunt*] **1 :** given to or interested in hunting ⟨a ~ man⟩; *also* **:** PREDACIOUS ⟨a ~ wasp⟩ **2 :** of, relating to, or used or adapted for use in hunting ⟨a ~ saddle⟩

**hunting boot** *n* **:** a heavy strong boot often extending to the knee and commonly laced from the instep to the top

**hunting box** *n, chiefly Brit* **:** a hunting lodge

**hunting case** *n* **:** a watchcase with a hinged cover to protect the crystal from accidents (as on the hunting field)

**hunting cat** *or* **hunting leopard** *n* **:** CHEETAH

**hunting crow** *n* **:** any of several tropical Asiatic long-tailed crested birds (genus *Kitta*) that resemble jays and have predominantly pale green, red, or sometimes yellow plumage and red bill and feet

**hunting dog** *n* **1 :** a dog used in hunting game **2 a :** AFRICAN HUNTING DOG **b :** DHOLE

**hun·ting·don elm** \'həntiŋdən-\ *n, usu cap H* **:** an erect vigorous hybrid ornamental tree (*Ulmus hollandica vegetata*) with usu. forked stems and pubescent branches

**hun·ting·don·shire** \-,shi(ə)r, -iə, -,shə(r)\ *or* **hun·ting·don** *adj, usu cap* [fr. *Huntingdonshire* or *Huntingdon* county, England] **:** of or from the county of Huntingdon, England **:** of the kind or style prevalent in Huntingdon

**huntingdon willow** *n, usu cap H* **:** WHITE WILLOW 1

**hunting ground** *n* **:** a place or area used for hunting; *specif* **:** a region in which game is hunted ⟨the planting of waterfowl food in the public *hunting grounds* —J.B.Robson⟩ ⟨the *hunting ground* of a peaceful tribe⟩ — compare HAPPY HUNTING GROUND

**hunting horn** *n* **:** a signal horn used in the chase; *specif* **:** a long conical tube coiled in a large circle and having a large flaring end and a trumpet mouthpiece — compare FRENCH HORN

**hunting knife** *n* **:** a large stout knife used to skin and cut up and sometimes to dispatch game

hunting knife

**hunting seat** *n, chiefly Brit* **:** a hunting lodge of some pretensions

**hunting shirt** *n* **:** a shirt worn for hunting; *esp* **:** a long jacket resembling a shirt and usu. of fringed deerskin worn by frontiersmen

hunting shirt

**hunting spider** *n* **:** any of several spiders that hunt their prey instead of catching it in a web **:** WOLF SPIDER

**hun·ting·ton's chorea** \'həntiŋtənz-\ *n, usu cap H* [after George *Huntington* †1916 Am. neurologist] **:** hereditary chorea developing in adult life and ending in dementia

**hunting tooth** *n* **:** a tooth in the larger of two geared wheels which makes its number of teeth prime to the number in the smaller wheel with the object of equalizing wear

**hunting watch** *n* **:** HUNTER 4

**hunt·ress** \'hən·trəs\ *n* -ES [ME *hunteresse*, fr. *hunter* + *-esse* -ess] **:** a female hunter; *specif* **:** one who follows the chase

**hunts** *pres 3d sing of* HUNT, *pl of* HUNT

**hunts·man** \'hən(t)smən\ *n, pl* **huntsmen 1 :** HUNTER 1a **2 :** a person who manages a hunt and looks after the hounds esp. in fox hunting

**huntsman's–cup** \¦==¦=\ *n, pl* **huntsman's–cups :** PITCHER PLANT a

**huntsman's–horn** \¦==¦=\ *n, pl* **huntsman's–horns :** a pitcher plant (*Sarracenia flava*) of the southern U.S.

**hunt's–up** \ˌhən(t)¦səp\ *n, pl* **hunt's–ups 1 :** a tune played on a hunting horn to call out the hunters; *also* **:** a rousing song or tune **2 :** a pipers' tune used by Christmas wait

**hunt table** *n* **:** a low table usu. semicircular in shape

**hunt the slipper :** a circle game in which players attempt to pass a slipper from one to another without being discovered by the player who is it

**hun·yak** \'hən,yäk, 'hün-,'hún-, -yak\ *or* **hun·yock** \-yäk\ *also* **hon·yak** \'hän-\ *or* **hon·yock** \-yäk\ *n* -S *usu cap* [by alter. (influence of *Polack*)] **:** HUNKY —usu. used disparagingly

**hu·on pine** \'hyüən-\ *n, usu cap H* [fr. *Huon* river, Tasmania] **:** a large Tasmanian timber tree (*Dacrydium franklinii*) with light yellow aromatic wavy-grained wood used for carving and shipbuilding

**¹hup** \'həp\ *interj* [origin unknown] **1** — used to urge on a horse **2** — used as a command (1) to a horse to turn to the right or (2) to a dog to down

**²hup** \"\ *vb* **hupped; hupped; hupping; hups** *vt, chiefly dial* **:** to turn (a horse) to the right ~ *vi, of a dog* **:** DOWN ⟨promptly *hupped* . . . at a handler's command —*Amer. Field*⟩

**hu·pa** \'hüpə\ *n, pl* **hupa** *or* **hupas** *usu cap* **1 a :** an Athapaskan people of the Trinity river valley, California **b :** a member of such people **2 :** a language of the Hupa and Chilula peoples

**hup·pah** *or* **chup·pah** \'ku̇pə, -(,)pä, ku̇'pä\ *n, pl* **hup·poth** *or* **hup·pot** \'ku̇,pōt(h), -ōs, ,=¦=\ *also* **huppahs** [Heb *ḥuppāh* cover, canopy] **:** a canopy under which bride and groom stand during a Jewish wedding ceremony

**hu·ra** \'hyu̇rə\ *n, cap* [NL, prob. modif. of Carib *urari* sandbox tree] **:** a genus of tropical American trees (family Euphorbiaceae) having milky juice, monoecious flowers, and capsular fruit

**hur·cheon** \'hərchən\ *n* -S [ME *hirchoun*, *hurcheoun* — more at URCHIN] **1** *chiefly Scot* **:** HEDGEHOG **2** *chiefly Scot* **:** URCHIN

**hurcn** *abbr* hurricane

**hurd·en** \'hərdən\ *var of* HARDEN

**hur·dies** \'hərdiz\ *n pl* [origin unknown] *dial Brit* **:** BUTTOCKS, RUMP

**¹hur·dle** \'hərdᵊl, 'hə̄d-, 'həid-\ *n* -S [ME *hirdel*, *hurdel*, fr. OE *hyrdel*; akin to OHG *hurd* hurdle, ON *hurth* door, Goth *haurds* door, L *cratis* wickerwork, hurdle, Gk *kartalos* basket, Skt *kṛnatti* he spins, *cṛtati* he ties, and perh. to L *crassus* thick; basic meaning: to twist] **1 a :** a portable panel of wattled twigs, osiers, or withes and stakes, or sometimes of iron or rails, used for fencing in land or livestock, reinforcing a wall or breastwork, or spanning a bog or ditch **b :** a frame or sled formerly used in England for dragging traitors to a place of execution **c :** an artificial barrier over which men or horses leap in a race **2 :** something that acts as a barrier **:** OBSTACLE ⟨once you have passed the final ~ — an interview with a selection board —E.O.Hauser⟩ ⟨one of the worst ~*s* a staff man faces is the valley of distrust that exists between echelons of command —W.H.Whyte⟩ ⟨a session of the foreign ministers . . . removed the final ~*s* in the way of a peace conference —A.H.Vandenberg †1951⟩ **3 a hurdles** *pl* **:** HURDLE RACE **b :** a jump made after the last approach step and carrying a diver to the end of the board in a running dive

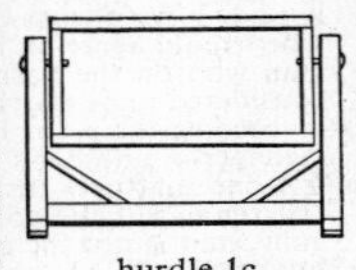

hurdle 1c

**²hurdle** \"\ *vb* **hurdled; hurdled; hurdling** \-d(ᵊ)liŋ\ **hurdles** *vt* **1 :** to fence in or reinforce with hurdles **2 :** to leap over (an obstacle) while running **3 :** to get across or past **:** OVERCOME, SURMOUNT ⟨only the boldest pioneers would ~ a pathless wilderness —R.A.Billington⟩ ⟨student performers . . . had to ~ a series of competitive auditions —*Collier's*⟩ ⟨engineers . . . wrestle with the multitude of problems to be *hurdled* in the construction of thruway spurs —*N.Y.Times*⟩ ~ *vi* **:** to leap over an obstacle while running; *specif* **:** to run a hurdle race

**hurdle gate** *n* **:** the crosspiece of a track hurdle that swings up to form a high hurdle or down to form a low hurdle

**hur·dler** \-d(ᵊ)lə(r)\ *n* -S [¹*hurdle* + *-er*] **1 :** one that makes hurdles ⟨authoritative minds in postwar Britain are recognizing the value of the . . . thatcher, ~, and kindred craftsmen in the total national economy —Mary E. Jones⟩ **2 :** one that runs in hurdle races ⟨the ~ is actually a sprinter until he reaches the first hurdle —W.H.O'Connor⟩

**hurdle race** *n* **1 :** a track event in which artificial barriers must be leaped — called also *hurdles;* compare HIGH HURDLES, LOW HURDLES **2 :** a horse race over a flat course equipped with movable hurdles — compare STEEPLECHASE

**hurdle racer** *n* **:** a horse trained for hurdle racing

**hurdlework** \'=,=\ *n* **:** work made of hurdles **:** WICKERWORK

**hurds** \'hərdz\ *n pl* [ME *herdes*, *hurdes* (pl.), fr. OE *heordan* (pl.); akin to OE *-heord* hair of a woman's head, ON *haddr* hair of a woman's head, Gk *keskeon* tow, Russ *kosa* braid] **:** the coarse parts of flax or hemp that adhere to the fiber after it is separated — called also *hards*

**hurdy–gurdist** \ˌhərdē¦gərdəst\ *or* **hurdy–gurdy·ist** \¦=·=¦=·=dēəst\ *n* -S **:** a hurdy-gurdy player

**hur·dy–gur·dy** \ˌhərdē¦gərdē, ¦hə̄dē¦gə̄dē, ¦həidē¦gəidē, -di¦...di\ *n* -ES [prob. imit.] **1 :** a stringed musical instrument resembling a lute in which the sound is produced by the friction of a rosined wheel turned by a crank against the strings and the pitches are varied by a set of mechanical keys **2 a :** BARREL ORGAN 1 **b :** STREET PIANO **3 :** a crank or windlass used to haul in heavy trawls or lines in deep-sea fishing

hurdy-gurdy 1

**hure** \'hyu̇(ə)r\ *n* -S [ME, fr. OF, cap, head of a wild animal] **1 :** a close-fitting cap **2** [F, fr. OF] **:** the head of a boar, wolf, or bear

**hu·reau·lite** \'hyu̇(,)rō,līt, hyə'r-\ *n* -S [F, fr. *Hureaux*, north of Limoges, France + F *-lite*] **:** a mineral $H_2Mn_5(PO_4)_4.4H_2O$ consisting of a hydrous manganese phosphate having a yellowish, orange-red, rose, or grayish color, and occurring in prismatic monoclinic crystals or massive

**hur·gi·la** \(,)hər'gēlə\ *n* -S [Hindi *hargīlā*, *hargilā*, lit., bone swallower, fr. *haṛ*, *hāṛ* bone + *gīlā* swallower, fr. Skt *gilati*, *girati* he swallows — more at VORACIOUS] **:** ADJUTANT BIRD

**huri** *var of* HOURI

**hur·kle** \'hərkəl\ *vi* -ED/-ING/-S [ME *hurkelen*, *hurklen*; akin to D *hurken* to squat, MLG *hurken*, MHG *hūren*] *now dial Brit* **:** to draw up the limbs and crouch or squat

**¹hurl** \'hərl *esp before pause or consonant* 'hər·əl; 'hə̄l,'həil\ *vb* -ED/-ING/-S [ME *hurlen*, prob. of imit. origin] *vi* **1 a :** to move rapidly or violently **:** RUSH, HURTLE ⟨sent the car ~*ing* over the roads —Sherwood Anderson⟩ ⟨a myriad senseless atoms . . . go ~*ing* forever through the infinite inane —P.E.More⟩ **b :** WHIRL ⟨now I've plenty money I'll make the tavern ~, a bottle of good brandy and on each arm a girl —Carl Sandburg⟩ **2** *chiefly Scot* **:** to wheel or drive in a vehicle esp. with a heavy or clumsy movement ⟨now and then we'll ~ in a coach —Robert Tannahill⟩ **3 a :** to play the game of hurling **b** *baseball* **:** PITCH ~ *vt* **1 a :** to impel with great vigor **:** DRIVE, THRUST ⟨could ~ his great strength into the ax head —Irving Bacheller⟩ ⟨~*ing* its mighty breakers upon the rocky ramparts —*Amer. Guide Series: Mich.*⟩ ⟨the forces that were to be ~*ed* against the Turks —N.T.Gilroy⟩ **b :** to impel (oneself) violently or impetuously ⟨he ~*ed* himself around the corner against the squall . . . with almost drunken violence —Liam O'Flaherty⟩ ⟨the characteristic wholeheartedness with which he continued to ~ himself at life —John Mason Brown⟩ **2 :** to throw down or out with violence ⟨~ the tyrant from his throne⟩ **3 a :** to throw or cast forcefully **:** FLING ⟨for forty-five minutes a battleship and lesser ships ~*ed* salvo after salvo at the field —H.L.Merillat⟩ ⟨a jet of gas . . . ~*s* strings of drill pipe and massive tools upwards —*Irish Digest*⟩ ⟨literally ~*ing* the ring I had given her in my face —Rex Ingamells⟩ **b** *obs* **:** to throw in wrestling **c** *baseball* **:** PITCH ⟨both ~*ed* scoreless ball for five innings —*Los Angeles (Calif.) Examiner*⟩ **4 :** to send or utter with vehemence ⟨~*ed* crisp piercing shrieks at the train —William Beebe⟩ ⟨publishers . . . took a delight in ~*ing* back at the tyro any copy he was venturesome enough to offer —A.W.Long⟩ ⟨he suddenly began to ~ reproaches down on her where she sat a little below him —Josephine Pinckney⟩ **5** *chiefly Scot* **:** to wheel or drive (a vehicle) **:** TRUNDLE **syn** see THROW

**²hurl** \"\ *n* -S [ME *hurl*, *hurle* swirl of water, strife, fr. *hurlen*, v.] **1 a :** a forceful throw or thrust; *specif* **:** a rushing swirl of water ⟨the halt and ~ of an angry, crashing, tempestuous seaway —C.C.Shaw⟩ **b** *Scot* **:** a downward rush (as of stones on a hill) **2 :** the stick used in the Irish game of hurling

**³hurl** \'hərl\ *dial Brit var of* WHIRL

**hurl·bar·row** \'hərl,bärə\ *n* [¹*hurl* + *barrow*] *chiefly Scot* **:** WHEELBARROW

**hurlbat** \'=,=\ *n* [ME *hurlebat*, fr. *hurlen* to hurl + *bat*] **1** *obs* **:** either of two ancient Roman weapons: **a :** ³CESTUS **b :** a short javelin having a thong by which it could be recovered after it was hurled **2 a :** a game resembling hurling and popular in Tudor England **b :** ²HURL 2

**hurlement** *n* -S [¹*hurl* + *-ment*] *obs* **:** TUMULT, CONFUSION

**hurl·er** \'hərlər; 'hə̄lə(r, 'həil-\ *n* -S **:** one that hurls: as **a :** one that takes part in a game of hurling **b :** a baseball pitcher

**hurl·ey** *also* **hurly** \-lē\ *n, pl* **hurleys** *also* **hurlies** [¹*hurl* + *-y*] **1 :** HURLING **2 :** the stick or the ball used in the game of hurling

**hur·ley·house** \'hərli,hüs\ *n* [*hurley-* (prob. fr. ²*hurl* + *-y*) + *house*] *Scot* **:** a large dilapidated house

**hurling** *n* -S [fr. gerund of ¹*hurl*] **1 :** an early form of football popular esp. in Cornwall in which each side tries to throw or carry the ball to its own goal or to get it beyond the parish boundary **2 :** an Irish game resembling field hockey in which teams of 15 players use a broad-bladed stick to catch, balance and run with, or hurl a 9″ to 10″ ball in an effort to score by hurling the ball over or under a crossbar between goalposts

**hur·ly** \'hərlē\ *n* -ES [prob. short for ¹*hurly-burly*] **:** CONFUSION, UPROAR, TUMULT

**¹hurly–burly** \ˌhərlē¦bərlē, ¦hə̄lē¦bə̄lē, ¦həilē¦bəilē, -li¦...li\ *n* -ES [prob. alter. & redupl. of *hurling* (gerund of ¹*hurl*)] **1 :** CONFUSION, TURMOIL, TUMULT, UPROAR ⟨through all the *hurly-burly* of the days immediately preceding election —A.D.H. Smith⟩ ⟨men and women relaxing after a hard day in the *hurly-burly* of the garment district —Al Hine⟩ ⟨delighted in the *hurly-burly* of her uninhibited conversation —Ellery Sedgwick⟩ **2 :** an act or instance of tumult **:** MELEE ⟨in the *hurly-burly* the poet is seized by the enemy —Donald Davidson⟩

**²hurly–burly** \"\ *adj* **:** TUMULTUOUS, CONFUSED ⟨outrageous clothes and *hurly-burly* antics —G.E.Fox⟩

**³hurly–burly** *adv, obs* **:** in a hurly-burly manner

**hu·ro** \'hyu̇(,)rō\ *n, cap* [NL *Huron-*, *Huro*, fr. Lake *Huron*, lake partly in Michigan and partly in Ontario, Canada] *in some classifications* **:** a genus of sunfishes containing solely the largemouth black bass which is now usu. included in *Micropterus*

**¹hu·ron** \'hyu̇rən, -yür-, -,rän\ *n, pl* **huron** *or* **hurons** *usu cap* [F, lit., boor, fr. MF, fr. *hure* disheveled head of hair, head of a wild animal] **1 a :** an Iroquoian people orig. of the St. Lawrence valley and Ontario and later of the midwestern U.S. **b :** a member of such people **2 :** the language of the Huron people

**²huron** \"\ *n* -S [NL *Huron-*, *Huro*] **:** LARGEMOUTH BLACK BASS

**³hu·ron** \ü'rōn, -rȯn\ *n* -S [AmerSp *hurón*, fr. Sp, ferret, fr. ML *furon-*, *furo*, fr. LL, cat, thief, fr. L *fur* thief — more at FURTIVE] **:** a grison (*Grison vittatus*) or related animal of So. America

**hu·ro·ni·an** \hyü'rōnēən\ *adj, usu cap* [Lake *Huron* (north of which the system was first differentiated)] **:** of or relating to a division of the Proterozoic — see GEOLOGIC TIME table

**hur·ple** *var of* HIRPLE

**¹hur·rah** \hə'rō, (')hu̇'r-, hü'r-, -rä,-rȧ\ *or* **hoo·ray** *also* **hur·ray** \-rā\ *interj* [perh. fr. G *hurra*, prob. fr. MHG *hurrā*, fr.

*hurre* (imper. of *hurren* to move quickly, of imit. origin) + *ā*, interj.] — used to express joy, approbation, or encouragement

**2hurrah** \"\ *or* **hoorah** \"\ *also* **hooray** \-rā\ *n* -s **1 a :** a display of excitement or acclamation : FANFARE ⟨many institutions were just being founded with the ~ of circuses coming to town —Ernestine Evans⟩ ⟨the everyday business of war as opposed to its ~ and heroism —*New Republic*⟩ **b :** ENTHUSIASM ⟨whose tireless ~ occasionally lifts the . . . book into some sort of magic while he is on the stage —Kappo Phelan⟩ **2 a :** FUSS, CONTROVERSY ⟨raised a big ~ over her reckless extravagance⟩ **b :** RAILLERY ⟨the crew rode them hard, but it was the sort of good-humored ~ that made a kid feel he was one of the bunch —F.B.Gipson⟩ **3 :** SPREE

**3hurrah** \"\ *also* **hoorah** \"\ *or* **hooray** \"\ *vb* -ED/-ING/-S *vi* **1 :** to shout hurrah : CHEER **2 :** to behave in a lively or boisterous way : ROMP **3 :** TEASE ~ *vt* **:** to harass, SCOLD

**hurrah bush** *n* **:** FETTERBUSH 1

**hurrah's nest** \-rōz-,-räz-,-ráz-\ *also* **hoorah's nest** \"\ *or* **hoo·raw's nest** \"\ *n* **:** an untidy heap : MESS ⟨in spite of all efforts, the lockers generally become a *hurrah's nest* . . . a place for everything and nothing in its place —S.S.Rabl⟩; *specif* **:** a tangle of debris blocking a trail or stream

**hurr-bur** \'hər,bər\ *n* -s [prob. redupl. of *¹burr*] **:** BURDOCK

**hur·ri** \'hu̇rē\ *also* **har·ri** \'härē\ *n, pl* **hurri** *or* **hurris** *usu cap* [Akkadian *hurri*] **:** HURRIAN

**hur·ria** \'hərēə\ *n pl, cap* [NL] **:** a small genus of East Asian broad-snouted water snakes (family Homalopsidae)

**hur·ri·an** \'hu̇rēən\ *n* -s *usu cap* **1 a :** an ancient non-Semitic people prominent in northern Mesopotamia, Syria, and eastern Asia Minor about 1500 B.C. and regarded by some scholars as identical with the Horites **b :** a member of such people **2 :** the language of the Hurrian people

**hur·ri·cane** \'hər·ə,kān, 'hə·r|, |ē,k-, |i,k- *also* |ēkən *or* |əkən *or* |ikən\ *n* -s *often attrib* [Sp *huracán*, fr. Taino *hurakán*, fr. *hura* wind, to blow away] **1 a :** a tropical cyclone with winds of 73 miles per hour or greater but rarely exceeding 150 miles per hour, usu. accompanied by rain, thunder, and lightning, and esp. prevalent from August to October in the tropical No. Atlantic and tropical Western Pacific but occas. moving into temperate latitudes — see BEAUFORT SCALE table; compare TYPHOON **b :** something resembling a hurricane esp. in violence : STORM ⟨the noise rose to a ~ —Dorothy C. Fisher⟩ ⟨a rushing ~ of blows struck him as he stood up —Donn Byrne⟩ ⟨the damage done by emotional ~*s* is not confined to the object of wrath —J.A.O'Brien⟩ **2** *dial* **:** an area where trees have been blown down by a hurricane or tornado ⟨there was a place about eight miles east of Bloomington which was known for many years as the ~ —J.A.Woodburn⟩ **syn** see WIND

**hurricane bird** *n* **:** FRIGATE BIRD

**hurricane deck** *or* **hurricane roof** *n* **:** AWNING DECK, PROMENADE DECK

**hurricane globe** *or* **hurricane glass** *also* **hurricane shade** *n* **:** a glass chimney placed over a candle to keep it from being blown out by the wind — see HURRICANE LAMP

**hurricane lamp** *n* **1** *or* **hurricane lantern :** an oil lantern having a glass chimney with a perforated metal lid that permits the egress of air but protects the flame from high winds and used usu. on shipboard and to mark outdoor construction projects — called also *tornado lantern* **2 :** a candlestick equipped with a hurricane globe **3 :** an electric lamp equipped with a hurricane globe instead of a shade

hurricane lamp 2

**hurricane–proof** \'═(,)═¦═\ *adj* **:** able to withstand a hurricane

**hurricano** *n* -ES [modif. of Sp *huracán* hurricane] *obs* **1 :** WATERSPOUT **2 :** HURRICANE

**hurried** *adj* [fr. past part. of *¹hurry*] **1 a :** characterized by speed : FAST ⟨~ rush of a locomotive⟩ **b :** characterized by commotion : TUMULTUOUS ⟨~ life of a city⟩ **2 a :** done or working under pressure ⟨gave ~ last-minute instructions to the crew⟩ ⟨a shorter version for the ~ reader⟩ **b :** done with excessive haste : HASTY ⟨the ~ funeral was a shocking indignity —A.M.Young⟩; *specif* **:** executed so hastily as to be perfunctory ⟨it is a short book, but never spare or ~ —D.C.DeJong⟩ — **hur·ried·ness** *n* -ES

**hur·ried·ly** \'hər·ēdlē, 'hə·r|, |ēd-, -li\ *adv* **:** in a hurried manner : QUICKLY, HASTILY

**hur·ri·er** \|ēə(r)\ *n* -s **:** one that hurries or causes to hurry

**hur·ri·some** \'hərisəm\ *adj (or adv)* [*¹hurry* + *-some*] *dial Eng* **:** HASTY, RUSHED

**hur·rite** \'hu̇,rīt\ *n* -s *usu cap* [*Hurri* + *-ite*] **:** HURRIAN

**hur·rock** \'hərək\ *n* [perh. of Scand origin; akin to ON *hörgr* pile of stones, shrine; akin to OE *hearg* shrine, OHG *harug* sacred grove, shrine, and perh. to OE *heard* hard — more at HARD] *dial Eng* **:** a heap of stones or rubbish

**1hur·ry** \'hər·|ē, 'hə·r|, |i\ *vb* -ED/-ING/-ES [perh. fr. ME *horyen*; prob. of imit. origin like MHG *hurren* to move quickly] *vt* **1 a :** to carry or cause to go fast : SPEED ⟨an ambulance *hurried* him to the hospital⟩ ⟨the quest to discover whither modern science is ~*ing* us —Howard M. Jones⟩ ⟨fishing for either species don't ~ your lure —L.S.Marceau⟩ **b** *archaic* **:** to impel to rash or precipitate action ⟨that hard-to-be-governed passion of youth *hurried* me frequently into intrigues with low women —Benjamin Franklin⟩ **2** *dial Eng* **:** to cause distress to : HARASS ⟨I've been very much *hurried* this morning; for I've just learned of the death of my old friend —A.B.Evans⟩ **3 a :** to impel to greater speed : QUICKEN, PROD ⟨heard the train coming and *hurried* his pace⟩ ⟨used his spurs to ~ the horse⟩ ⟨hates to be *hurried* at mealtime⟩ **b :** to speed up the progress or completion of : EXPEDITE ⟨~ dinner by doing the meat in the pressure cooker⟩ ⟨electronic machines ~ the sorting of data⟩ ⟨cultural exchange can ~ the development of world understanding⟩; *specif* **:** to perform with undue haste ⟨some of the most perfect passages are *hurried* over as if they were a mistake on the composer's part —Warwick Braithwaite⟩ ~ *vi* **:** to move or act with haste : go fast : RUSH ⟨we'll have to ~ if we want to see the curtain go up⟩ ⟨sheep . . . stared at her through the ~*ing* snowflakes —Ellen Glasgow⟩ — often used with an adverb to lend emphasis or indicate direction ⟨~ up or you'll miss the train⟩ ⟨small launches ~*ing* back and forth —Tom Marvel⟩ ⟨a stiff northwest wind was blowing and patches of clouds *hurried* by —H.H.Arnold & I.C.Eaker⟩ ⟨the nation *hurried* forward along the path of . . . consolidation —V.L.Parrington⟩ **syn** see SPEED

**2hurry** \"\ *n* -ES **1 a :** DISTURBANCE, TUMULT, COMMOTION ⟨the incessant ~ and trivial activity of daily life . . . seem to prevent, or at least discourage, quiet and intense thinking —C.W.Eliot⟩; **b** *dial Brit* **:** DISPUTE, RUCTION **2 a** *obs* **:** disturbance of mind : mental turmoil ⟨there is nothing like hurrying the body, to divert the ~ of the mind —Francis Fuller⟩ **b** *now dial* **:** a minor illness **3 :** a recurrent agitation of sound ⟨the ~ of water or languor of sand —Michael Sayers⟩ **4 a :** excessive haste : PRECIPITANCE ⟨the blind ~ of the universe —Bertrand Russell⟩ **b :** a state of eagerness or urgency : RUSH ⟨it was going to be a wonderful party and she was in a ~ to get there⟩ ⟨they were all good reporters; but they were all in too big a ~, for fear somebody else would beat them to it —Elmer Davis⟩ **5 :** a tremolo in the strings or a roll on the drum accompanying an exciting situation in dramatic music **syn** see HASTE — **in a hurry** *adv* **:** in a short time or at a fast rate : HURRIEDLY, SPEEDILY ⟨they are not translations to be read *in a hurry*; they do not yield their charm easily —T.S. Eliot⟩ ⟨the new grammar can be taught *in a hurry* by a nonlinguist —MacCurdy Burnet⟩

**1hurry–burry** \¦həri¦bəri\ *n* -ES [redupl. (influenced by *hurly-burly*) of *²hurry*] *Scot* **:** HURLY-BURLY

**2hurry–burry** \"\ *adv, Scot* **:** in a hurly-burly manner

**hurry call** *n* **:** an emergency summons

**hurry–durry** *adj* [redupl. of *²hurry*] *obs, of weather* **:** windy and rainy

**hurrying** *adj* [fr. pres. part. of *¹hurry*] **:** swiftly moving : HASTENING — **hur·ry·ing·ly** *adv*

**1hurry–scurry** *or* **hurry–skurry** \¦hər·|ē¦skər·|ē, |hə·r| . . . ə·r|ē, |i¦, . . . |i\ *adv (or adj)* [redupl. (prob. influenced by *¹helter-skelter*) of *²hurry*] **:** in or with disorderly haste : HELTER-SKELTER

**2hurry–scurry** *or* **hurry–skurry** \"\ *n* -ES **:** a confused rush : TURMOIL

**hurry–up** \'══¦═\ *adj* [fr. *hurry up*, v.] **1 a :** of an emergency nature : RUSH ⟨*hurry-up* call⟩ ⟨*hurry-up* job⟩ **b :** equipped to respond to an emergency ⟨*hurry-up* wagon⟩ **2 :** speeded up : completed in a hurry : HASTY ⟨*hurry-up* breakfast⟩ ⟨*hurry-up* briefing⟩

**hur·sin·ghar** \¦hərsin¦gär\ *n* -s [Hindi *harsingār, hārsingār, hārsinghār*] **:** an East Indian tree (*Nyctanthes arbortristis*) of the family Oleaceae with flowers that yield a dye used as a substitute for saffron

**hurst** *also* **hyrst** \'hərst\ *n* -s [ME *hurst*, fr. OE *hyrst*; akin to OS & OHG *hurst* thicket, OIr *crann* tree, and perh. to Gk *prinos* holm oak] **1 a :** a grove or wooded knoll — often used in combination in place names ⟨Elm*hurst*⟩ **b** *heraldry* **:** a clump of trees **2 :** a bank or piece of rising ground; *esp* **:** a sandbank in a river

**1hurt** \'hər|t, 'hə̄|, 'həi|, *usu* |d.+V\ *vb* **hurt** *or dial* **hurted**; **hurt** *or dial* **hurted**; **hurting**; **hurts** [ME *hurten, hirten* to cause or allow to strike, injure, prob. fr. OF *hurter* to collide with, prob. of Gmc origin; akin to ON *hrūtr* ram (male sheep); akin to ON *hjörtr* hart — more at HART] *vt* **1 a :** to afflict with bodily pain : INJURE, WOUND ⟨the hot sand ~*s* my feet⟩ ⟨was badly ~ in the wreck⟩ ⟨got ~ in a bombing raid⟩ **b :** to do physical or material harm to : DAMAGE, IMPAIR ⟨the submarine is ~ by heavy depth charges⟩ ⟨the walkout is not ~*ing* service as much as the strikers hoped⟩ **c :** to do substantial or fundamental harm to : WEAKEN ⟨the story is ~ but not ruined by too many long descriptive passages⟩ **2 a :** to cause pain or anguish to : DISTRESS, OFFEND ⟨disillusions of the mind ~ less than disillusions of the heart —W.L.Sullivan⟩ ⟨was ~ by their lack of confidence in him⟩ ⟨it ~*s* me to think of all that land wasted —Ellen Glasgow⟩ **b :** to be detrimental to : CHECK, HAMPER ⟨the charges of graft will ~ his chances in the fall election⟩ ⟨a good wife can't help a husband as much as a bad wife can ~ one —W.H.Whyte⟩ ~ *vi* **1 a :** to feel pain or frustration : ACHE, SUFFER ⟨her hand . . . ~ from lugging the suitcase —John Dos Passos⟩ ⟨knocked a young heifer in the head because he . . . figured she had ~ long enough —Caroline Miller⟩ ⟨atomic-energy programs are ~*ing* from lack of enough scientific help —*Newsweek*⟩ **b** *chiefly Midland* **:** to be in need : WANT **2 :** to cause damage or distress : do harm ⟨hit the aggressor . . . where it will ~ most —D.H.McLachlan⟩ ⟨essential needs abroad must be met even if it ~*s* at home —J.S.Carson⟩ ⟨the rain may hold off but it won't ~ to take your umbrella⟩ **syn** see INJURE

**2hurt** \"\ *n* -s [ME *hurte, hurt, hirt*, prob. fr. OF *hurte* shock of a collision, stroke, blow, fr. *hurter* to collide with] **1 :** a wounding blow or stroke : cause of injury or damage ⟨the superiority . . . of the United States was a ~ to British prestige —Bernard Brodie⟩ ⟨this tower of granite, weathering the ~*s* of so many ages —R.W.Emerson⟩ **2 a :** a bodily injury or wound ⟨rattleweed, made into a tincture, is better than arnica for ~*s* of every sort —Emily Holt⟩ **b :** mental distress or anguish : RESENTMENT, SUFFERING ⟨are apt to be exasperated, and say things in immediate ~ which a little later they realize they do not wholly mean —A.E.Sutherland⟩ ⟨her sympathy eased his ~⟩ **3 :** WRONG, HARM, DISADVANTAGE, DETRIMENT ⟨his soul-stuff, by working on which a sorcerer may do the man himself grievous ~ —J.G.Frazer⟩ ⟨subordinating cosmic to moral considerations, to the ~ of both —M.R.Cohen⟩ **syn** see INJURY

**3hurt** \"\ *adj* [ME, fr. past part. of *hurten*, v.] **1 :** injured in body or spirit : WOUNDED, RESENTFUL ⟨ambulances . . . quickly dispose of ~ men and women —J.C.Powys⟩ ⟨an air of ~ innocence⟩ ⟨hoped to avoid ~ feelings over rejection of the plan⟩ **2 :** physically impaired : DAMAGED ⟨~ book sale⟩ ⟨restore ~ land with woods, game cover, and water —Russell Lord⟩

**4hurt** *also* **heurt** *or* **heurte** \'hərt\ *n* -s [MF *heurte*, prob. fr. *heurter* to collide with, knock, fr. OF *hurter* to collide with; perh. fr. the idea that it represents the mark of a blow] *heraldry* **:** a roundel azure

**hurt·able** \'hərd·əbəl\ *adj* **:** capable of being hurt

**1hur·ter** \'hərd·ər\ *n* -s [ME *hurtur, hurtour* metal reinforcement for the shoulder of an axle, fr. AF *hurteuer*, fr. OF *hurter* to collide with] *archaic* **:** BUFFER, REINFORCEMENT; *esp* **:** a bumper that stops the wheels of a gun carriage as the piece is run into battery

**2hurt·er** \"\ *n* -s [*¹hurt* + *-er*] *archaic* **:** one that injures

**hurt·ful** \'hərtfəl, 'hə̄t-, 'həit-\ *adj* **:** causing injury or suffering : DAMAGING, PAINFUL ⟨regarded as ~ to the profession —H.A. Wagner⟩ ⟨~ to low-income classes —*Dun's Rev.*⟩ ⟨the crippled child hobbling to catch up was a ~ sight⟩ — **hurt·ful·ly** \-fəlē, -li\ *adv* — **hurt·ful·ness** *n* -ES

**1hurt·ing** \'hərd·iŋ\ *n* -s [ME *hurtinge, hirtinge* injury, hurt, gerund of *hurten, hirten* to cause or allow to strike, injure] *chiefly dial* **:** PAIN, DISTRESS

**2hurting** *adj* [fr. pres. part. of *¹hurt*] **:** PAINFUL, DISTRESSING ⟨his breath came in ~ gasps⟩

**1hur·tle** \'hərd·ᵊl, 'hə̄|, 'həi|, |tᵊl\ *vb* **hurtled**; **hurtled**; **hurtling** \|d·ᵊliŋ, |t(ᵊ)liŋ\ **hurtles** [ME *hurtlen* to collide, cause or allow to strike, freq. of *hurten* to cause or allow to strike] *vi* **1** *archaic* **:** to meet violently : hit with impact : COLLIDE ⟨together *hurtled* both their steeds —Edward Fairfax⟩ **2 :** to progress with the sound or suddenness of violent motion : CLATTER, CRASH ⟨boulders *hurtled* down the cliffs⟩ ⟨the morning gun . . . sent its echoes *hurtling* through the coco palms —G.P.Insh⟩ ⟨stubbed his foot against the doorjamb and *hurtled* into the hall —Liam O'Flaherty⟩ **3 :** to move rapidly : dash headlong : RUSH, SHOOT ⟨you can ~ along at supersonic speeds —Irwin Edman⟩ ⟨somehow he had *hurtled* past the propellers' blades —*Time*⟩ ⟨the country was *hurtling* toward disaster —Sidney Warren⟩ ~ *vt* **1 :** to propel violently : CATAPULT, FLING ⟨the subway ~*s* hordes of workers daily into lower Manhattan⟩ ⟨Indians ~ flaming arrows over the stockade wall⟩ ⟨when he ~*s* himself into a dance —John Mason Brown⟩ **2** *dial Eng* **:** CROUCH

**2hurtle** \"\ *n* -s **:** an act of hurtling : THROW, COLLISION

**hur·tle·ber·ry** \'hərd·ᵊl- — *see* BERRY\ *n* [ME *hurtilberye*, fr. *hurtil-* (irreg. fr. OE *horte* whortleberry) + *berye* berry] **1** *archaic* **:** BLUEBERRY 1; *esp* **:** WHORTLEBERRY 1 **2** *archaic* **:** HUCKLEBERRY 1

**hurt·less** \'hərtləs\ *adj* [ME *hurtles*, fr. *hurte, hurt, hirt* wounding blow + *-les* -less] **1 :** free from harm : UNHURT **2 :** incapable of inflicting injury : HARMLESS — **hurt·less·ly** *adv* — **hurt·less·ness** *n* -ES

**hurtling** *adj* [fr. pres. part. of *¹hurtle*] **:** characterized by rushing violence : SPEEDING, TUMULTUOUS — **hurt·ling·ly** *adv*

**hurts** *pres 3d sing of* HURT, *pl of* HURT

**hus** *pl of* HU

**1hus·band** \'həzbənd\ *n* -s [ME *housbonde, husbonde* husbandman, married man, master of a house, fr. OE *hūsbonda* master of a house, fr. ON *hūsbōndi*, fr. *hūs* house + *bōndi* householder, peasant owning his own land — more at HOUSE, BOND] **1** *obs* **:** HUSBANDMAN 1 **2 a :** a married man ⟨~ and wife should agree on how to budget the family income⟩ **b :** a man who on the basis of his tribal or societal institutions is considered to be married ⟨under the levirate a man was obliged to become the ~ of his brother's widow⟩ **3 a** *archaic* **:** the manager of another's property : STEWARD **b :** SHIP'S HUSBAND **4 :** one that uses thriftily or saves for future use : HOARDER ⟨a glean ~*s* of the gold —S.V.Benét⟩ ⟨speaks his whole mind gaily, and is not the cautious ~ of a part —W.B.Yeats⟩

**2husband** \"\ *vt* -ED/-ING/-S [ME *husbonden*, fr. *housbonde, husbonde*, n.] **1** *archaic* **:** to plow and grow crops on (land) : CULTIVATE **2 a :** to take care of : utilize to advantage : MANAGE ⟨the ancient Nile is controlled at its source . . . and its waters are to be ~*ed* for the benefit of the farmers —Elizabeth II⟩; *specif* **:** to equip, supply, and maintain (a ship) **b :** to use sparingly or hold back for future use : CONSERVE, SAVE ⟨~ one's strength or resources⟩ ⟨~ their air strength . . . for the best nights, rather than risk losses from the weather —A.A.Michie⟩ ⟨toys . . . ~*ed* for the benefit of baby —Robert Grant †1940⟩ **3** *archaic* **:** to marry or find a husband for

**hus·band·age** \-dij\ *n* -s **:** a commission paid to a ship's husband by the owners for managing its affairs

**hus·band·er** \-də(r)\ *n* -s **:** one that husbands

**hus·band·land** \'həzbən(d)lənd\ *n* [ME *husbondeland*, fr. *housbonde, husbonde* + *land*] **1 a :** the holding of a manorial tenant **b :** a quantity of arable land equal to two bovates : VIRGATE **2 :** the land occupied and tilled by the tenants of a manor as distinguished from the demesne lands

**hus·band·less** \'həzbən(d)ləs\ *adj* **:** having no husband

**hus·band·like** \-(d),līk\ *adj* **:** HUSBANDLY 1b

**1husbandly** *adv* [ME, fr. *¹husband* + *-ly* (adv. suffix)] *obs* **:** in a thrifty manner : ECONOMICALLY

**2hus·band·ly** \'həzbən(d)lē, -li\ *adj* [*¹husband* + *-ly* (adj. suffix)] **1 a** *obs* **:** of or relating to a farmer or farming **b :** consistent with good farm management practice **2 :** of, relating to, or befitting a husband : MARITAL **3** *obs* **:** THRIFTY, FRUGAL

**hus·band·man** \'həzbən(d)mən\ *n, pl* **husbandmen** [ME *housbondeman*, fr. *housbonde* + *man*] **1 :** one that plows and cultivates land : FARMER ⟨where the menace of erosion has become most manifest . . . both landlords and tenants have become *husbandmen* under grave handicaps —Russell Lord⟩ ⟨the parable of the *husbandmen* in St. Mark's Gospel —Leonardo Olschki⟩ **2** *Brit* **:** a rural laborer : FARMHAND **3 :** a specialist in a branch of farm husbandry ⟨dairy ~⟩ ⟨poultry ~⟩

**hus·band·ry** \'həzbəndrē, -ri\ *n* -ES [ME *housbondrie*, fr. *housbonde* + *-rie* -ry] **1** *obs* **:** the care of a household : domestic management ⟨I commit into your hands the ~ and manage of my house until my lord's return —Shak.⟩ **2 a :** the judicious use of resources : CONSERVATION, THRIFT ⟨this careful ~ of his remaining powers —W.V.T.Clark⟩ ⟨borrowing dulls the edge of ~ —Shak.⟩ **b :** the control or use of resources : MANAGEMENT ⟨problems of soil conservation and ~ of water resources —*Brit. Book News*⟩ **3 :** the cultivation or production of plants and animals : AGRICULTURE, FARMING ⟨some dealt in corn, others in sheep and wool, others in a mixed ~ —G.M. Trevelyan⟩ ⟨commercial farming has not displaced subsistence ~ —J.M.Mogey⟩ **4** *obs* **:** the tenantry or husbandland of a manor **5 :** the scientific control and management of a specified branch of farming ⟨more limited experimental work is also being carried out in . . . animal ~ —C.J.Bishop⟩

**hus·band·ry·man** \'═══mən\ *n, pl* **husbandrymen :** HUSBANDMAN 3

**huscarl** *var of* HOUSECARL

**1hush** \'həsh, *when imperative* " *or* sh *often prolonged*\ *vb* -ED/-ING/-ES [back-formation fr. *²husht*, taken as a past participle] *vt* **1 :** to repress the agitation or clamor of : LULL, SILENCE, CALM, QUIET ⟨sleep . . . ~*ed* by solemn-sounding waterfalls —John Muir †1914⟩ ⟨his movement ~*ed* the courtroom —B.A.Williams⟩ **2 :** to gloss over or put at rest : MOLLIFY, QUELL ⟨their protests are mild and . . . can be easily ~*ed* —Paul Blanshard⟩ ⟨brings her flowers to ~ his conscience⟩ ⟨his wife . . . serves him quickly and silently, ~*ing* signs of disorder in the children —H.A.Overstreet⟩ — often used with *up* ⟨this contradiction is ~*ed* up —L.A.Fiedler⟩ **3 :** to keep from public knowledge : treat confidentially : SUPPRESS ⟨police attempt to ~ the crime —*Books of the Month*⟩ — usu. used with *up* ⟨the story of her disgrace was ~*ed* up —Edith Sitwell⟩ ⟨trying to ~ it up, but it was plain suicide —Vicki Baum⟩ ~ *vi* **:** to become quiet : grow still ⟨the crowd ~*ed*, and she sang —Franc Shor⟩ — used in the imperative to enjoin silence or urge moderation of sound ⟨~, baby, go to sleep⟩ ⟨~, boys, the party's getting noisy⟩

**2hush** \'həsh\ *adj* **1 :** devoid of sound : SILENT, STILL ⟨everything was . . . ~ as midnight about the house —Laurence Sterne⟩ **2 :** designed to prevent the dissemination of certain information ⟨~ money⟩ ⟨a ~ policy concerning any faults . . . in the American economy —Jerome Frank⟩ **3** *or* **hushing** [fr. the use of a prolonged \sh\ sound in hushing (enjoining silence)] **:** being the sibilants \sh\ and \zh\ — compare HISS

**3hush** \"\ *n* -ES **1 a :** silence or freedom from agitation : STILLNESS, CALM ⟨sickroom ~⟩ ⟨cathedral ~ of the deep woods⟩ ⟨a ~ and a solemnity about the proceedings —Hugh Walpole⟩ **b :** a suspension of noise or activity : CESSATION, LULL ⟨after a time there came a profound ~ and out of the stillness a woman's voice rose —Lyle Saxon⟩ **2 :** restriction of information : SECRECY ⟨prompted the policy of ~ in regard to the presence of the disease on their properties —*Australasian*⟩

**4hush** \'hu̇sh, 'həsh\ *vb* -ED/-ING/-ES [imit.] *vi, dial Brit* **:** to gush forth in a rapid stream : RUSH ~ *vt, dial Eng* **:** to expose (ore) by washing a hillside with water under pressure : FLUSH — **hush·ing** \-shən, -shiŋ\ *n* -s

**5hush** \"\ *n* -ES *dial Brit* **:** a rushing sound as of wind or water; *specif* **:** a swell of the sea

**hush·a·by** *or* **hush–a–bye** \'həshə,bī\ *v imper* [*¹hush* + connective *-a-* + *²bye*] **:** be still and go to sleep — used to soothe a child to sleep

**hushed** \'həsht\ *adj* [fr. past part. of *¹hush*] **1 a :** free of noise or agitation : CALM, STILL ⟨~ silence of the reading room⟩ **b :** marked by suspension of noise or activity : reduced to silence ⟨~ attention of the spectators —L.P.Stryker⟩ ⟨an atmosphere of ~ suspense⟩ **2 :** marked by secrecy or caution : CONFIDENTIAL, DISCREET ⟨~ meeting of political strategists⟩ ⟨counseled his clients in ~ tones⟩ — **hushed·ly** \-shədlē, -shtlē, -li\ *adv*

**hush·ful** \'həshfəl\ *adj* [*³hush* + *-ful*] **:** full of silence : QUIET — **hush·ful·ly** \-fəlē\ *adv*

**1hush–hush** \'═¦═\ *vt* [fr. *hush! hush!*, repeated imperative use of *¹hush*] **1 :** to enjoin to silence ⟨was *hush-hushed* by army censors when he started to report soldier opinion on the issue⟩ **2 :** HUSH *vt* 3

**2hush–hush** \"\ *adj* **:** marked by secrecy or concealment : kept from public knowledge : SECRET, CONFIDENTIAL ⟨a specific cure for one of the *hush-hush* diseases, gonorrhea —*Science News Letter*⟩ ⟨decreed an end to the . . *hush-hush* atmosphere that has shielded major presidential policies —Ray Tucker⟩; *specif* **:** subject to official censorship ⟨military intelligence, cryptography, secret chemical corps projects and other *hush-hush* assignments —Sidney Shalett⟩ ⟨of all air corps planes, this is the most *hush-hush* —D.C.Cooke⟩

**3hush–hush** \"\ *n* **:** a policy or atmosphere of concealment : SECRECY, SUPPRESSION ⟨the *hush-hush* surrounding new car design⟩ ⟨after decades of *hush-hush*, the problem of mental illness is now being openly discussed⟩; *specif* **:** CENSORSHIP ⟨wartime *hush-hush* concerning plane losses⟩

**hush puppy** *n* [*¹hush* + *puppy*; fr. its occasional use as food for dogs] *chiefly South* **:** a cornmeal bread shaped into small cakes and fried in deep fat — usu. used in pl.; compare CORN DODGER

**1husht** \'həsht\ *interj* [ME *huissht*] *archaic* — used to enjoin silence

**2husht** \"\ *adj* [ME *hussht*, fr. *huissht*, interj.] *archaic* **:** HUSHED

**hush tube** *n* **:** a tube for conducting the inflow beneath the surface of the water in a flush tank to reduce noise

**husi** *var of* JUSI

**1husk** \'həsk\ *n* -s [ME *husk, huske*, prob. modif. of MD *huuskijn, huusken* small house, small cover, fr. *huus* house, cover + *-kijn, -ken* -kin; akin to OE *hūs* house — more at HOUSE] **1 a :** the outer covering of a kernel or seed esp. when dry and membranous : the chaff of grain : HULL, POD; *specif* **:** CAROB 1b ⟨with the ~*s* that the swine did eat —Lk 15:16 (AV)⟩ **b :** one of the leaves enveloping an ear of corn : BRACT ⟨corn roasted in the ~*s*⟩ **2 a :** something that resembles a husk : an outer layer or empty framework : SHELL ⟨much of the remote past is conserved in the ~ of convention —Norman Lewis⟩ ⟨the wind . . . blew through that eerie ~ of a room —Edita Morris⟩ **b** *slang* **:** GUY, FELLOW ⟨you're some ~ —Sinclair Lewis⟩ **c :** a classic drop ornament made of whorls of conventionalized foliage usu. in diminishing series and used esp. in an 18th century style of furniture introduced by Robert Adam **3 a :** the outer skin or shell of an animal ⟨the sea floor is littered with the discarded ~*s* of small crustaceans⟩ **b :** a supporting framework: as (1) **:** the decorative covering around the holder that supports the socket and bulb of an electric lamp (2) **:** a frame supporting the arbor of a large circular saw

husk 2c

**2husk** \"\ *vt* -ED/-ING/-S **:** to remove the outer skin or covering of : PEEL, STRIP ⟨~ rice⟩ ⟨~ corn⟩ ⟨~ a coconut⟩ ⟨would ~ it of its religious and political bias —S.E.Hyman⟩

**3husk** \"\ *n* -s [prob. fr. obs. *husk*, v., to have a dry cough, of imit. origin] **1 :** HOOSE ⟨an outbreak of ~ was observed in a flock of 200 sheep —*Veterinary Bull.*⟩ **2 :** HUSKINESS

**4husk** \"\ *vb* -ED/-ING/-S *vi* **:** to become husky ⟨tried to keep

his voice from ~*ing* with emotion⟩ ~ *vt* **:** to utter in a husky voice ⟨the sultry singer in the cabaret ~*s* out the latest ballad⟩

**¹hus·ka·naw** \'həskə,nȯ\ *or* **hus·ka·naw·ing** \-ȯiŋ\ *n* -s [of Algonquian origin; akin to Natick *wuskenoo* he is young] **:** an initiation rite for youths at puberty practiced by various Indians of Virginia and including fasting and the use of narcotics

**²huskanaw** \"\ *vt* -ED/-ING/-S **:** to subject to a huskanaw

**husk corn** *n* **:** POD CORN

**husked** *adj* [¹*husk* + *-ed*] **1 :** covered with a husk **2** [fr. past part. of ²*husk*] **:** stripped or deprived of the husk

**husk·ened** \'həskənd\ *adj* [prob. irreg. fr. ²*husky* + *-en* + *-ed*] **:** HUSKY

**husk·er** \'həskə(r)\ *n* -s **:** one that husks: as **a :** a participant in a cornhusking **b :** HUSKING GLOVE **c :** HUSKER-SHREDDER

**husker-shredder** \'==,==\ *n* **:** a power machine that husks corn ears and cuts up the husks and stalks for fodder

**husk·i·ly** \'həskəlē, -li\ *adv* **:** in a husky manner

**husk·i·ness** \-kēnəs, -kin-\ *n* -ES **:** the quality or state of being husky

**husking** *n* -s [fr. gerund of ²*husk*] **1 :** an act or process of peeling or stripping off an outer layer ⟨the ~ of coffee beans⟩ ⟨corn ready for ~⟩ **2** *also* **husking bee :** a neighborly gathering of farm families to husk corn ⟨~*s*, berry-pickings and winter sleigh rides —Van Wyck Brooks⟩

**husking glove** *n* **:** a glove with metal plates and hooks on the palm and palm side of the fingers that is used in husking corn

**husking peg** *or* **husking pin** *n* **:** a peg of wood or metal strapped or tied to the hand as an aid in husking corn

**husk-tomato** *n* **:** GROUND-CHERRY

**¹husky** \'həskē, -ki\ *adj* -ER/-EST [¹*husk* + *-y*] **1 :** containing or full of husks ⟨the kernels are plump and not very ~ —*Farmers Weekly (So. Africa)*⟩ **2 :** of the nature of a husk **:** MEMBRANOUS, RATTLING, EMPTY ⟨the nut is contained in a ~ shell —S.J.Watson⟩ ⟨his footfalls were ~ in cinders —Richard Llewellyn⟩ ⟨repeated that ~ phrase so often —Willa Cather⟩

**²husky** \"\ *adj* -ER/-EST [prob. fr. ³*husk* + *-y*] **:** dry or roughened as with emotion **:** HOARSE ⟨the voices of the chief women mourners had become worn and ~ —J.A.Lomax⟩ ⟨~ voices bawled at the yokes of steers —Carl Sandburg⟩ ⟨makes all the instruments sound powerful but ~ —Virgil Thomson⟩

**³husky** \"\ *adj* -ER/-EST [prob. fr. ¹*husk* + *-y*; prob. fr. the toughness and harsh texture of a corn husk] **1 :** big and muscular **:** BURLY, ROBUST ⟨a crew of ~ lumberjacks⟩ **2 a :** of sizable proportions or vigorous potential **:** LARGE, POWERFUL ⟨a ~ $19 million in the like period last year —Mitchell Gordon⟩ ⟨a big, ~, honestly built . . . power cruiser —*Yankee*⟩ ⟨there still was a ~ United Nations army left in Korea —A.J. Liebling⟩ **b :** having or producing strength **:** STURDY ⟨a ~ beef stew⟩

**⁴husky** \"\ *n* -ES **:** one that is husky or powerful ⟨foremen looked over the *huskies* crowded in these rooms to pick their crews —*Amer. Guide Series: Minn.*⟩ ⟨these four breeds of engines are *huskies* —R.M.Neal⟩

**⁵husky** \"\ *n* -ES *sometimes cap* [prob. by shortening & alter. fr. *Eskimo*] **1** *dial* **:** an Eskimo of Labrador and northeastern Canada or his language ⟨a huge whale . . . which the old-time *huskies* had killed with harpoons and lances —D.B.Putnam⟩ — sometimes taken to be offensive **2 a :** a heavy-coated working dog (as an Eskimo dog or malamute) of the New World arctic region used esp. as a sled dog **b :** SIBERIAN HUSKY

**hu·so** \'hyü(,)sō, -)zō\ *n* -s [ML, fr. OHG *hūso*; akin to Norw dial. *huse* fish skull, ON *hauss* skull, OE *hȳd* hide, skin; prob. fr. the armored head — more at HIDE] **1 :** BELUGA 1 **2 :** HUCHEN

**huss** \'həs\ *n* -ES [alter. of ME *husk, huske*] *dial* **:** DOGFISH

**hus·sar** \(,)hə'zär, |ä(r *sometimes* -'s|\ *n* -s [Hung *huszár* hussar, (obs.) highway robber, fr. Serb *husar, gusar* pirate, fr. ML *cursarius* — more at CORSAIR] **1 a** *often cap* **:** a horseman of the Hungarian light cavalry organized in the 15th century **b :** a member of the light cavalry of various European armies usu. distinguished by a brilliant much-decorated uniform often featuring the dolman and the busby **c :** a member of certain now mechanized European cavalry units **2 :** any of several brilliantly colored snappers (family Lutjanidae) — see YELLOW-BANDED HUSSAR

**hussar monkey** *n* **:** PATAS

**hus·ser·li·an** \(')hu̇'sərlēən, -ser-\ *adj, usu cap* [Edmund *Husserl* †1938 Ger. philosopher + E *-ian*] **:** of or relating to the German philosopher Husserl or his theories ⟨*Husserlian* phenomenology⟩

**¹huss·ite** \'hə,sīt, 'hu̇,-\ *n* -s *usu cap* [NL *hussita*, fr. John *Huss* †1415 Bohemian religious reformer + L *-ita* -ite] **:** a member of the Bohemian religious and nationalist movement originating with John Huss, marked by advocacy of the Wycliffite doctrines of clerical purity and poverty and the supremacy of the Bible and by insistence upon communion in both bread and wine for the laity, and split after the death of Huss into the Calixtin and Taborite parties — compare LOLLARD 2

**²hussite** \"\ *adj, usu cap* **:** of, relating to, or characteristic of John Huss or the Hussites

**huss·it·ism** \-īd-,izəm\ *also* **huss·ism** \-,izəm\ *n* -s *usu cap* [*hussitism* fr. ¹*hussite* + *-ism*; *hussism* fr. John *Huss* + E *-ism*] **:** the beliefs and practices of the Hussites

**hus·sy** *also* **hus·sey** \'həz|ē, 'həs|, |i\ *or* **huz·zy** \'həz|\ *n* -ES [alter. of *housewife*] **1** *obs* **:** the female head of a house **:** HOUSEWIFE **2 :** a lewd or brazen woman **:** JADE **3 :** a saucy or mischievous girl **:** MINX **4** *dial* **:** HOUSEWIFE 2

**hus·ting** \'həstiŋ, -tēŋ\ *n* -s [ME, fr. OE *hūsting*, fr. ON *hūsthing*, fr. *hūs* house + *thing* assembly — more at HOUSE, THING] **1 :** a deliberative assembly or council in early medieval England; *esp* **:** one called by a king or other leader **2 a** *or* **hustings** *pl but sing in constr* **:** a court held in London before the lord mayor, recorder, and sheriffs or aldermen **b hustings** *pl but sing in constr or* **hustings court :** a local court in some cities in Virginia **3** *or* **hustings** *pl but sing in constr* **:** the upper end or dais of the guildhall where the London husting sits **4 a** *or* **hustings** *pl but sing in constr* **:** a raised platform from which candidates for the British Parliament were formerly nominated and from which they addressed their constituency **b :** the proceedings at a parliamentary election **5 hustings** *pl but sing or pl in constr* **a :** an election platform **:** STUMP ⟨the charge . . . is expected to resound from political ~*s* throughout the land —*Foreign Policy Bull.*⟩ **b :** an act or process of electioneering ⟨an election which has generated far more excitement than the usual off-year ~*s* —*Saturday Rev.*⟩ ⟨the rough give-and-take of the ~*s* —*Yale Rev.*⟩

**¹hus·tle** \'həsəl\ *vb* **hustled; hustled; hustling** \-s(ə)liŋ\ **hustles** [D *husselen, hutselen* to shake, toss, fr. MD *hutselen*, freq. of *hutsen* to shake; akin to G dial. *hotteln, hotzeln* to shake — more at HOD] *vt* **1 :** to shake or jar together in confusion **:** JOSTLE ⟨~ pennies in a hat⟩ **2 a :** to crowd or push roughly **:** SHOVE ⟨in the cell into which we were *hustled* were forty or fifty Negroes —R.M.Lovett⟩; *specif* **:** to jostle with intent to rob ⟨they ~ old gentlemen; the old gentleman glances down, his watch is gone —E.M.Forster⟩ **b :** to convey forcibly or hurriedly ⟨grabbed him by the arm and *hustled* him out the door —John Dos Passos⟩ ⟨~ freight aboard the scow —N.C.McDonald⟩ ⟨allow himself to be *hustled* across the frontier —F.A.Ogg & Harold Zink⟩ **c :** to urge forward precipitately ⟨~ the tourist from one museum to the next⟩ ⟨~ your horse and don't say die —W.S.Gilbert⟩ ⟨trying to ~ history along —N.E.Nelson⟩ **3 a :** to obtain by energetic activity **:** GATHER, EARN ⟨*hustled* new customers —*Time*⟩ ⟨*hustled* himself a job as a section hand —Pearl Puckett⟩ **b :** to exert pressure on **:** sell or promote business with **:** WORK ⟨a waiter has to learn . . . that he must not ~ the customers —Robert Sylvester⟩ ⟨they ~ them for drinks —A.J.Liebling⟩ ⟨played it safe by *hustling* both sides of the street —Nelson Algren⟩ **c :** to deprive of one's possessions by force or fraud **:** ROB, CHEAT ⟨made the rounds of lovers' lanes . . . *hustling* the occupants of parked cars —C.L.Lamson⟩ ⟨~*s* schoolboys out of their lunch money with phony dice —Nelson Algren⟩; *specif* **:** to lure into a gambling game ~ *vi* **1 :** PUSH, SHOVE, PRESS ⟨curious throngs ~ to the scene of the crime⟩ ⟨someone *hustled* against him in the crowd⟩ **2 :** to move or act with vigorous speed **:** bestir oneself energetically **:** HURRY ⟨urged her to ~ across the street before the light changed⟩ ⟨ten miles of track a day were laid by *hustling* crews —R.A. Billington⟩ **3 a :** to make strenuous efforts to secure money or business ⟨our quartet was out *hustling* . . . and we knew we stood good to take in a lot of change before the night was over —Louis Armstrong⟩ ⟨diesel boats ~ at the docks —H.G. Nickels⟩ **b :** to solicit for prostitution ⟨there are fewer girls working in houses than there are *hustling* on the streets —Polly Adler⟩ **4 :** to obtain money by fraud or deception **:** SWINDLE; *specif* **:** to lure a victim into a crooked gambling game

**²hustle** \"\ *n* -s **1 :** an act of jostling or shoving **2 a :** energetic activity ⟨increase of leisure, diminution of ~, are the ends to be sought —Bertrand Russell⟩ ⟨the ~ and bustle in construction of motels —A.L.Himbert⟩ **b :** a hurried motion **:** MOVE ⟨get a ~ on to stockpile these essential materials —*Congressional Record*⟩ **3** *slang* **a :** an income-producing activity **:** JOB **b (1) :** an act or instance of fraud **:** SWINDLE, RACKET **(2) :** HUSTLER

**hustle-bustle** \'==;==\ *n* **:** energetic confusion

**hustle-cap** \'==,=\ *n* [¹*hustle* + *cap*] **:** a game of pitch and toss in which coins are shaken in a cap

**hus·tle·ment** \'həsəlmənt\ *n* -s [ME *ostelement, hustilment* article of furniture, fr. MF *ostillement, oustillement*, fr. OF *ustillement*, fr. *ustil* article of furniture, tool, utensil, prob. fr. (assumed) VL *usitilia* (pl.) utensils, alter. of L *utensilia* — more at UTENSIL] *now dial* **:** household goods **:** FURNITURE, KNICKKNACKS — often used in pl.

**hus·tler** \'həs(ə)lə(r)\ *n* -s **1 a :** a pickpocket's accomplice **b :** one who obtains money by fraudulent means **:** petty racketeer; *specif* **:** a professional gambler **c :** PROSTITUTE **2 :** an active, enterprising, sometimes unscrupulous individual **:** GO-GETTER, LIVE WIRE **3 a :** VENDOR **b :** one that delivers or transports **c :** a pottery worker who carries greenware to the kiln shed or other place of processing **4** *New Zeal* **:** a tillage implement with tines used to stir the soil

**hustling** *adj* [fr. pres. part. of ¹*hustle*] **1 :** characterized by hustling activity **:** ENERGETIC **2 :** soliciting or productive of illicit gain; *specif* **:** WHORING

**¹hut** \'hət, *usu* -əd·+V\ *n* -s [MF *hutte* temporary dwelling of simple construction, of Gmc origin; akin to OHG *hutta* temporary dwelling of simple construction; akin to OE *hȳd* hide, skin — more at HIDE] **1 a :** a temporary structure used as living quarters for troops esp. in a theater of operations **b :** a rudimentary structure erected by the army for a special purpose (as a field aid station) **c :** a room or building used as a recreation center for troops in World War I **2 a :** an often small and temporary dwelling of simple construction **:** COTTAGE, SHACK ⟨sod ~⟩ ⟨the simplest of the primitive dwellings of the colonists were conical ~*s* of branches, rushes, and turf —Fiske Kimball⟩ **b** *Austral* **:** a house for shearers or other laborers on a ranch **c :** a simple shelter from the elements ⟨bathing ~⟩ ⟨round a winding road you come to a small ~ and a turnstile —Fred Streeter⟩ ⟨small wooden ~*s* inside which fishermen . . . can sit in comparative comfort with a portable stove while waiting for a nibble from far below the frozen surface —James Montagnes⟩; *specif* **:** overnight cabin ⟨hostel ~s⟩ ⟨mountain ~*s*⟩

**²hut** \"\ *vb* **hutted; hutted; hutting; huts** *vt* **:** to provide with usu. temporary living quarters **:** HOUSE, BILLET ⟨were no sooner *hutted* than we were on the march —S.W.Mitchell⟩ ~ *vi* **:** to become housed or quartered **:** LODGE ⟨his troops *hutted* among the heights —Washington Irving⟩

**¹hutch** \'həch\ *n* -ES [ME *hucche, huche*, fr. OF *huche*] **1 a :** a chest or compartment for storage **:** BIN, LOCKER **b :** a low cupboard with doors usu. surmounted by two open shelves **2 a :** a pen or coop for an animal **:** CAGE ⟨provided a ~ for them in the garden —T.E.Donne⟩ **b :** a cageful of animals ⟨kept . . . a ~ or two of hare —Joyce Warren⟩ **3 :** a cramped or flimsy shelter for a man **:** SHACK, SHANTY **4 a :** a car on low wheels in which coal is drawn and hoisted out of a mine pit **b (1) :** the bottom compartment of an ore-dressing jig **(2) :** the mineral product that collects there

hutch 1b

**²hutch** \"\ *vt* -ED/-ING/-ES **1** *archaic* **:** to put away or store in a hutch **:** HOARD **2 :** to wash (ore) in a box or jig

**³hutch** *adj* [perh. alter. of *hulch*] *obs* **:** HUMPED

**hutch burn** *n* **:** an inflammation of the skin of rabbits esp. on the hind feet and adjacent parts associated with unclean urine-soiled cages

**hutch·e·so·ni·an** \,həchə'sōnēən\ *adj, usu cap* [Francis *Hutcheson* †1746 Scot. philosopher + E *-ian*] **:** of or relating to the theories of the Scottish philosopher Francis Hutcheson

**hutch·et** \'həchət\ *n* -s [MF *huchet*, fr. *hucher* to cry out, fr. OF *huchier*, prob. of imit. origin] **:** a hunter's horn **:** BUGLE 2

**hutch·in·so·ni·an teeth** *or* **hutchinsonian incisors** \'həchən-'sōnēən-\ *n pl, often cap H* [*hutchinsonian* fr. Sir Jonathan *Hutchinson* + E *-ian*] **:** HUTCHINSON'S TEETH

**hutch·in·son·ite** \'həchənsə,nīt\ *n* -s [Arthur *Hutchinson* †1937 Eng. mineralogist + E *-ite*] **:** a mineral $(Pb,Tl)_2(Cu,Ag)As_5S_{10}$ consisting of sulfide of lead, copper, and arsenic, with thallium and silver replacing variable amounts of lead and copper, and occurring in small red orthorhombic crystals

**hutch·in·son's teeth** \'həchənsənz-\ *also* **hutchinson teeth** *n pl but sing or pl in constr, usu cap H* [after Sir Jonathan *Hutchinson* †1913 Eng. surgeon] **:** peg-shaped teeth having a crescentic notch in the cutting edge and occurring esp. in children with congenital syphilis

**hutchinson's triad** *n, usu cap H* **:** a triad of symptoms comprising Hutchinson's teeth, interstitial keratitis, and deafness and occurring in children with congenital syphilis

**hutch·ins's goose** \'həchənz(əz)-\ *n, usu cap H* [after Thomas *Hutchins* †1790 Eng. attaché of the Hudson's Bay Company] **:** a variety (*Branta canadensis hutchinsii*) of the Canada goose closely resembling but smaller than the typical form, breeding in arctic America and migrating south through the U.S., but being rare east of the Mississippi

**hutch table** *n* **:** a combination table and chest whose top can be tilted back to convert the unit into a chair or settee

**hut circle** *n* **:** a ring of stones or earth marking the site of a prehistoric dwelling

**hu·tia** *also* **ju·tia** \(h)ü'tēə\ *n* -s [Sp *hutia* & AmerSp *jutia*, fr. Taino *hutia*] **:** any of several large edible hystricomorph rodents that constitute two West Indian genera (*Capromys* and *Geocapromys*) and a related So. American genus (*Procapromys*), are closely related to the coypus, and are now extinct over much of their range

**hutkeeper** \'=,==\ *n*, *Austral* **:** the man in charge of a hut on a ranch

**hut·man** \'hətmən\ *n, pl* **hutmen :** a member of the staff of an overnight hut for hikers

**hutmaster** \'=,==\ *n* **:** the manager of an overnight hut for hikers

**hut·ment** \'hətmənt\ *n* -s [²*hut* + *-ment*] **1 a :** a collection of huts **:** ENCAMPMENT **b :** the act or process of housing people in huts **2 :** HUT; *specif* **:** a prefabricated portable army housing unit usu. made of plywood and accommodating 16 to 20 men

**huts** *pl of* HUT, *pres 3d sing of* HUT

**hutted** *adj* [fr. past part. of ²*hut*] **:** consisting of or supplied with huts ⟨single-story ~ wards —*Lancet*⟩ ⟨a ~ camp⟩

**hut·te·ri·an brethren** \,hə|'tirēən-, hü|, hu̇|\ *n, cap H&B* [*hutterian* fr. Jakob *Hutter* (or *Huter*) †1536 Moravian Anabaptist + E *-ian*] **:** a Mennonite sect of northwestern U.S. and Canada living in communities and holding property in common

**hut·ter·ite** *also* **hu·ter·ite** \'həd·ə,rīt, 'hü|, 'hu̇|\ *n* -s *usu cap* **:** a member of the Hutterian Brethren

**hutting** *pres part of* HUT

**¹hut·to·ni·an** \,hə'tōnēən\ *adj, usu cap* [James *Hutton* †1797 Scot. geologist + E *-ian*] **:** of or relating to the views of the Scottish geologist James Hutton

**²huttonian** \"\ *n* -s *usu cap* **:** an adherent of Huttonian theories (as uniformitarianism) of geology — **hut·to·ni·an·ism** \-ēə,nizəm\ *n* -s *usu cap*

**hut·ton·ite** \'hət°n,īt\ *n* -s [Colin O. *Hutton* b1910 Am. geologist born in New Zealand + E *-ite*] **:** a mineral $ThSiO_4$ consisting of monoclinic silicate of thorium dimorphous with thorite

**hut·ton's vireo** \'hət°nz-\ *n, usu cap H* [prob. fr. the name *Hutton*] **:** a vireo (*Vireo huttoni*) of western No. America having a dull olive back and dingy white underparts

**hut·ton·weed** \-°n,wēd\ *n* [prob. fr. the name *Hutton*] **:** WILD TEASEL

**hu·tu** \'hü(,)tü\ *n, pl* **hutu** *or* **hutus** *usu cap* **:** RUNDI

**hu·tukh·tu** *or* **hu·tuk·tu** \hü'tu̇k(,)tü\ *n* -s *often cap* [Mongolian *khutuktu* eminent, fr. *khutuk* eminence] **:** a Lamaist dignitary believed to be an incarnation of Buddha; *specif* **:** the spiritual ruler of Mongolia

**hut urn** *n* **:** a prehistoric cinerary urn made in the form of a round hut with a conical roof and found esp. in southern Italy

**hu·tzul** *also* **hu·zul** \hüt'sül\ *n, pl* **hutzul** *or* **hutzuls** *usu cap* **1 :** a mountain people of the high Carpathians in Slovakia, Ruthenia, and Poland speaking a Ruthenian dialect **2 :** a member of the Hutzul people

**hux·le·ian** *also* **hux·ley·an** \'həkslēən, ,=='==\ *adj, usu cap* [Thomas H. *Huxley* †1895 Eng. biologist or Aldous L. *Huxley* b1894 Eng. novelist and critic + E *-an*] **:** of or relating to the English biologist Thomas H. Huxley or his novelist grandson Aldous Huxley

**huy·gens eyepiece** \'hīgənz-, 'hȯi|\ *also* **huy·ghe·ni·an eyepiece** \(')=¦gēnēən-\ *n, usu cap H* [*huyghenian* irreg. fr. Christian *Huygens* (or *Huyghens*) †1695 Du. physicist + E *-ian*] **:** a compound eyepiece so designed and placed that its field lens intercepts converging rays from an objective and forms a real image within the eyepiece

**huy·gens' principle** *also* **huy·ghens' principle** \'=,ganz(əz)-\ *n, usu cap H* **:** a principle in physics: every point of an advancing wave front is a new center of disturbance from which emanate independent wavelets whose envelope constitutes a new wave front at each successive stage of the process

**huz** \(¦)(h)əz, (¦)(h)üz\ *pron* [by alter.] *dial Brit* **:** US

**huzz** \'həz\ *vi* -ED/-ING/-ES [imit.] **:** BUZZ

**¹huz·zah** *or* **huz·za** \(,)hə'zä, -zȧ\ *n* -s [origin unknown] **:** a cheer or shout of applause **:** HURRAH — often used interjectionally to express joy or approbation

**²huzzah** *or* **huzza** \"\ *vb* -ED/-ING/-S *vi* **:** to shout huzzah **:** HURRAH ~ *vt* **:** APPLAUD, CHEER

**huzzy** *var of* HUSSY

**HV** *abbr* **1** high velocity **2** high voltage

**hvy** *abbr* heavy

**HW** *abbr* **1** high water **2** highway **3** hit wicket **4** hot water

**hwan** \'(h)wän\ *n, pl* **hwan** [Korean] **:** a former monetary unit of So. Korea established in 1953 and replaced in 1962 by the won

**HWL** *abbr* high-water line

**HWM** *abbr* high-water mark

**hwy** *abbr* highway

**hy-** *or* **hyo-** *comb form* [NL, fr. Gk *hyo-* upsilon (Υ, υ), fr. *y, hy* upsilon] **1 :** connecting with the hyoid arch ⟨*hyo*glossus⟩ **2 :** hyoid and ⟨*hyo*thyroid⟩

**hy** *abbr* **1** heavy **2** henry

**hy·a·cinth** \'hīə,sin(t)th, -,sən-\ *n, pl* **hyacinths** \-n(t)s, -n(t)ths\ [L *hyacinthus*, a precious stone, a flowering plant, fr. Gk *hyakinthos*] **1 a :** a precious stone of the ancients sometimes held to be the sapphire **b (1) :** a transparent red or brownish zircon sometimes used as a gem **(2) :** a red or brownish essonite used as a gem **2 a :** a plant of the ancients held to be the Turk's-cap lily, iris, larkspur, or gladiolus **b (1) :** a plant of the genus *Hyacinthus*; *esp* **:** the common garden hyacinth (*H. orientalis*) widely grown for the beauty and fragrance of its flowers — see ROMAN HYACINTH **(2) :** any of several other plants of the family Liliaceae — usu. used with preceding qualifier; see SUMMER HYACINTH, WATER HYACINTH **3 :** a light violet to moderate purple **4 :** PURPLE GALLINULE

hyacinth 2b(1)

**hyacinth bacteriosis** *n* **:** a destructive bacterial disease of the hyacinth caused by a bacterium (*Xanthomonas hyacinthi*) that attacks both dry bulbs and growing plants

**hyacinth bean** *n* **:** a large twining vine (*Dolichos lablab*) that is native to the Old World tropics, has dark purple racemes of pealike flowers, and is widely grown as an ornamental, less often as a source of fodder, and sometimes for its edible pods and seeds

**hyacinth blue** *n* **:** a deep purplish blue that is slightly bluer than mazarine blue, redder and paler than average sapphire (sense 2a), and redder, lighter, and stronger than cyanine blue (sense 1b)

**hy·a·cin·thi·an** \,hīə'sin(t)thēən\ *adj* **:** HYACINTHINE

**hy·a·cin·thine** \,hīə¦sin(t)thən, -n,thīn\ *adj* [L *hyacinthinus*, fr. Gk *hyakinthinos*, fr. *hyakinthos* hyacinth + *-inos* -ine] **1 :** having any one of the four colors hyacinth, hyacinth blue, hyacinth violet, or hyacinth red **2 a :** of, relating to, or resembling the hyacinth ⟨his ~ locks descend in wavy curls —Alexander Pope⟩ **b :** adorned or decorated with hyacinths ⟨with ~ chaplet crowned —Francis Fawkes⟩

**hyacinth red** *n* **:** a grayish reddish orange that is slightly lighter than Etruscan red and yellower and darker than Persian melon

**hyacinth squill** *n* **:** an ornamental bulbous Mediterranean plant (*Scilla hyacinthoides*) with lilac-purple flowers

**hy·a·cin·thus** \,hīə'sin(t)thəs\ *n, cap* [NL, fr. L, a flowering plant] **:** a genus of Old World bulbous and scapose herbs (family Liliaceae) having flowers in terminal mostly compact racemes and a bell-shaped corolla with a prominent tube and short limb — see HYACINTH

**hyacinth violet** *n* **:** a deep purple that is bluer and slightly darker than petunia violet, redder than pontiff, bluer, lighter, and stronger than imperial purple (sense 2), and bluer and paler than dahlia purple (sense 2)

**¹hy·ae·na** \hī'ēnə\ *var of* HYENA

**²hyaena** \"\ *n, cap* [NL, fr. L, hyena — more at HYENA] **:** the type genus of the family Hyaenidae

**hy·ae·nan·che** \,hīə'naŋkē\ *n, cap* [NL, fr. L *hyaena* hyena + NL *-anche* (fr. Gk *anchein* to strangle); fr. the use of the fruit in poisoning hyenas — more at HYENA, ANGER] **:** a genus of trees (family Euphorbiaceae) of southern Africa with coriaceous whorled leaves, cymose staminate flowers, and solitary pistillate flowers

**hy·ae·narc·tos** \-'närk,täs\ *n, cap* [NL, fr. L *hyaena* hyena + Gk *arktos* bear — more at ARCTIC] **:** a genus of large Old World Pliocene and Pleistocene bears

**hy·ae·nid** \hī'ēnəd, -'en-\ *n* -s [NL *Hyaenidae*] **:** one of the Hyaenidae

**hy·aeni·dae** \hī'ēnə,dē, -'en-\ *n pl, cap* [NL, fr. *Hyaena*, type genus + *-idae*] **:** a family of carnivorous mammals comprising the hyenas and usu. the aardwolf

**hy·aeno·don** \hī'ēnə,dän, -'en-\ *n* [NL *Hyaenodont-, Hyaenodon*, fr. *Hyaena* + *-odont-, -odon* -odon] **1** *cap* **:** the type genus of Hyaenodontidae comprising extinct carnivorous mammals from Eocene, Oligocene, and possibly Miocene deposits of Eurasia, Africa, and No. America **2** -s **:** a mammal of the genus *Hyaenodon*

**¹hy·aeno·dont** \-änt\ *adj* [NL *Hyaenodontidae*] **:** of or relating to the Hyaenodontidae

**²hyaenodont** \"\ *n* -s [NL *Hyaenodontidae*] **:** an animal of the family Hyaenodontidae

**hy·aeno·don·ti·dae** \(,)hī,ēnə'däntə,dē, -,en-\ *n pl, cap* [NL, fr. *Hyaenodont-, Hyaenodon*, type genus + *-idae*] **:** a family of typically rather slender long-skulled, more or less digitigrade clawed extinct carnivores of the suborder Creodonta varying from a few inches in length to the size of some of the recent large cats (as the leopard)

**hy·aeno·don·toid** \(¦)=¦==¦dän,tȯid\ *adj* [NL *Hyaenodontidae* + E *-oid*] **:** of, relating to, or resembling the Hyaenodontidae

**hyal-** *or* **hyalo-** *comb form* [LL, glass, fr. Gk, fr. *hyalos* transparent stone, glass] **1 :** glass **:** glassy ⟨*hyal*escent⟩ ⟨*hyalo*crystalline⟩ **2 :** transparent or translucent substance ⟨*hyal*ogen⟩

**hy·a·les·cence** \ˌhīəˈlesᵊn(t)s\ *n* -s [*hyal-* + *-escence*] **:** the quality or state of being hyalescent

**hy·a·les·cent** \¦==¦lesᵊnt\ *adj* [*hyal-* + *-escent*] **:** becoming or appearing hyaline

**¹hy·a·line** \ˈhīələn, -əˌlīn\ *adj* [LL *hyalinus*, fr. Gk *hyalinos*, fr. *hyalos* transparent stone, glass + *-inos* -ine] **1 :** of, resembling, or consisting of glass ⟨a glimpse of bay below, a rock-set ~ circlet —Sybille Bedford⟩ **2 a** *biol* **:** transparent or nearly so ⟨a ~ membrane⟩ **b** *mineralogy* (1) **:** GLASSY (2) **:** lacking crystallinity **:** AMORPHOUS

**²hy·a·line** \"\, *in sense 2* -əˌlēn *or* -ələn\ *n* -s **1 :** something transparent (as the smooth sea or the clear atmosphere) ⟨the morning is as clear as diamond or as ~ —Sacheverell Sitwell⟩ **2** *or* **hy·a·lin** \-ələn\ [prob. ISV *hyal-* + *-ine* or *-in*] **a :** a nitrogenous substance closely related to chitin that forms the main constituent of the walls of hydatid cysts and yields a sugar on decomposition **b :** any of several similar translucent substances collecting around cells, capable of being stained by eosin, and yielding a carbohydrate as a cleavage product

**hyaline cartilage** *n* [¹*hyaline*] **:** translucent bluish white cartilage that has the cartilage cells embedded in an apparently homogeneous matrix, is the commonest type of cartilage present in joints and in respiratory passages, and forms most of the fetal skeleton

**hyaline cast** *n* [¹*hyaline*] **:** a renal cast characterized by homogeneity of structure

**hyaline degeneration** *n* [¹*hyaline*] **:** tissue degeneration chiefly of connective tissues in which structural elements of affected cells are replaced by homogeneous translucent material that stains intensely with acid dyes

**hy·a·lin·iza·tion** \ˌhīələnəˈzāshən\ *n* -s **:** the process of becoming hyalinized or the state of being hyaline

**hy·a·lin·ize** \ˈhīələˌnīz\ *vi* -ED/-ING/-S [¹*hyaline* + *-ize*] **:** to become hyaline; *esp* **:** to undergo hyaline degeneration

**hy·al·i·no·crystalline** \hīˈalə(ˌ)nō+\ *adj* [ISV ¹*hyaline* + *-o-* + *crystalline*; orig. formed as G *hyalinokristallin*] *of rock* **:** having a texture partly glassy and partly crystalline

**hy·a·li·no·sis** \ˌhīələˈnōsəs\ *n, pl* **hyalino·ses** \-ōˌsēz\ [NL, fr. LL *hyalinus* hyaline + NL *-osis*] **1 :** HYALINE DEGENERATION **2 :** a condition characterized by hyaline degeneration

**hy·a·lite** \ˈhīəˌlīt\ *n* -s [G *hyalit*, fr. Gk *hyalos* transparent stone, glass + G *-it* -ite] **:** a colorless opal that is sometimes clear as glass and sometimes translucent or whitish and that occurs as globules or crusts lining cavities or cracks in rocks

**hy·a·lithe** \ˈhīəˌlith, -līth\ *n* -s [prob. modif. (influenced by E *-lith*) of F *hyalite* hyalithe, hyalite, fr. G *hyalit* hyalite] **:** an opaque glass that resembles porcelain and is sometimes used as a gemstone

**hyalo-** — see HYAL-

**hy·a·lo·basalt** \ˌhīə(ˌ)lō+\ *n* [ISV *hyal-* + *basalt*; orig. formed in G] **:** BASALT GLASS

**hy·a·lo·crystalline** \"+\ *adj* [*hyal-* + *crystalline*] **:** HYALINOCRYSTALLINE

**hy·al·o·gen** \hīˈaləjən, -ˌjen\ *n* -s [ISV *hyal-* + *-gen*; prob. orig. formed in G] **:** any of several insoluble substances related to mucoids that are found in many animal structures (as hydatid cysts or sponges) and that yield hyalines on hydrolysis

**hy·a·loid** \ˈhīəˌlȯid\ *adj* [Gk *hyaloeidēs*, fr. *hyalos* glass + *-eidēs* -oid] *anat* **:** GLASSY, TRANSPARENT

**hyaloid membrane** *n* **:** a very delicate membrane enclosing the vitreous humor of the eye

**hy·al·o·mere** \hīˈaləˌmi(ə)r\ *n* -s [*hyal-* + *-mere*] **:** the pale nonrefractile portion of a blood platelet — compare CHROMOMERE

**hy·a·lom·ma** \ˌhīəˈlämə\ *n, cap* [NL, fr. *hyal-* + *-omma*] **:** an Old World genus of ticks that attack wild and domestic mammals and sometimes man, produce severe lesions by their bites, and often serve as vectors of viral and protozoal diseases

**hy·a·lo·mucoid** \ˌhīə(ˌ)lō+\ *n* [*hyal-* + *mucoid*] **:** a mucoprotein in the vitreous humor

**hy·a·lo·ne·ma** \ˌhīəlōˈnēmə\ *n, cap* [NL, fr. *hyal-* + *-nema*] **:** a genus of hyalosponges having a long stem composed of very long slender transparent siliceous fibers twisted together like the strands of a cord

**hy·al·o·phane** \hīˈaləˌfān\ *n* -s [G *hyalophan*, fr. *hyal-* + *-phan* -phane] **:** a mineral $BaAl_2Si_2O_8$ consisting of a monoclinic feldspar isomorphous with and resembling adularia

**hy·a·lo·pi·lit·ic** \ˌhīə(ˌ)lōˌpīˈlid·ik\ *adj* [ISV *hyalopilit-* (fr. G *hyalopilitisch* hyalopilitic, fr. *hyal-* + Gk *pilos* felt + G *-it* -ite + *-isch* -ish, fr. OHG *-isc*) + *-ic* — more at PILE (hair)] **:** composed of or characterized by innumerable slender microlites embedded in glass ⟨a ~ structure is frequently found in basic lavas⟩

**hy·alo·plasm** \hīˈaləˌplazəm, ˈhīəlō,-\ *n* -s [prob. fr. G *hyaloplasma*, fr. *hyal-* + *-plasma* -plasm] **:** the clear apparently homogeneous ground substance of cytoplasm that is essentially the continuous phase of a multiple-phase colloidal system

**hy·a·lo·plas·ma** \ˌhīəlōˈplazmə\ *n* [prob. fr. G] **:** HYALOPLASM

**hy·a·lo·sid·er·ite** \ˌhīəlōˈsidəˌrīt\ *n* [G *hyalosiderit*, fr. *hyal-* + Gk *sidēros* iron + G *-it* -ite] **:** an olivine containing much iron

**hy·alo·sponge** \hīˈalōˌspənj, ˈhīəl-\ *n* [NL *Hyalospongiae*] **:** one of the Hyalospongiae

**hy·a·lo·spon·gea** \ˌhīəlōˈspənjēə, -pän-\ [NL, fr. *hyal-* + *-spongea* (irreg. fr. L *spongia* sponge) — more at SPONGE] *syn of* HYALOSPONGIAE

**hy·a·lo·spon·gia** \"\ [NL, fr. *hyal-* + *-spongia*] *syn of* HYALOSPONGIAE

**hy·a·lo·spon·gi·ae** \-ēˌē\ *n pl, cap* [NL, fr. *hyal-* + *-spongiae*] **:** a class of Porifera comprising sponges with 6-rayed siliceous spicules, no surface epithelium, and the choanocytes restricted to finger-shaped chambers — see GLASS SPONGE

**hy·a·lo·te·kite** \ˌhīəlōˈtēˌkīt\ *n* -s [Sw *hyalotekit*, fr. *hyal-* + Gk *tēkein* to melt + Sw *-it* -ite; fr. the fact that it fuses to a clear glass — more at THAW] **:** a mineral approximately $(Pb,Ca,Ba)_4BSi_6O_{17}(OH,F)$ consisting of a borosilicate and fluoride of lead, barium, and calcium found in crystalline masses

**hy·al·uro·nate** \ˌhīəˈlu̇rəˌnāt\ *n* -s [ISV *hyaluronic* + *-ate*] **:** a salt or ester of hyaluronic acid

**hy·al·uron·ic acid** \¦hīəlu̇¦ränik-\ *n* [*hyaluronic* ISV *hyal-* + *-uronic*] **:** a viscous mucopolysaccharide acid that occurs chiefly in connective tissues or their derivatives — compare MUCOITINSULFURIC ACID

**hy·al·uron·i·dase** \ˌ===ˈränəˌdās, -āz\ *n* -s [ISV *hyaluronid-* (fr. *hyaluronic acid*) + *-ase*] **:** an enzyme that splits hyaluronic acid and thus lowers the viscosity of the acid and facilitates the spreading of fluids through tissues either advantageously (as in the absorption of drugs) or disadvantageously (as in the dissemination of infection), that occurs in many normal tissues, in malignant growths, in invasive bacteria, and in certain venoms but is usu. prepared from mammalian testes, and that is used esp. to aid in the dispersion of fluids (as local anesthetics) injected subcutaneously for therapeutic purposes — called also *spreading factor*

**hyb** *abbr* hybrid

**hy·blae·an** \(ˈ)hīˈblēən\ *adj, usu cap* [L *hyblae*us of Hybla (fr. Gk *hyblaios*, fr. *Hybla*, ancient town in Sicily famous for the excellence of its honey) + E *-an*] **:** MELLIFLUOUS, HONEYED ⟨golden and *Hyblaean* eloquence —A.C.Swinburne⟩

**¹hyb·o·dont** \ˈhibəˌdänt\ *adj* [NL *Hybodont-*, *Hybodus*] **:** of or relating to the genus *Hybodus* or family Hybodontidae

**²hybodont** \"\ *n* -s [NL *Hybodont-*, *Hybodus*] **:** a hybodont shark

**hyb·o·dus** \-ədəs\ *n, cap* [NL *Hybodont-*, *Hybodus*, fr. Gk *hybos* hump + NL *-odont*, *-odus*] **:** a large genus (the type of the family Hybodontidae) of extinct sharks existing from the Trias to the Lower Cretaceous that are usu. included among the Squaloidea but are sometimes placed with related extinct forms in a separate suborder of the order Pleurotremata

**hy·bo·sis** \hīˈbōsəs, hə'-\ *n, pl* **hybo·ses** \-ōˌsēz\ *also* **hybo·sises** [NL, fr. Gk *hybos* hump + NL *-osis*] **:** a virus disease of cotton in which the leaves are reduced and distorted

**¹hy·brid** \ˈhībrəd, *substand* -ˌbred\ *n* -s [L *hybrida* animal whose parents belong to different varieties or to different species, person whose parents belong to different ethnic groups, prob. of non-IE origin; akin to the source of L *imbr-*, *imber* offspring of a tame sheep and a wild sheep] **1 :** an offspring of two animals or plants of different races, breeds, varieties, species, or genera; *specif* **:** an individual produced by union of gametes from parents of different genotype — compare CROSSBREED, MENDEL'S LAW, MULE **2 :** a person or group produced by the blending of two diverse cultures or traditions ⟨the cultural ~ occupies a marginal position between two cultures⟩ ⟨every civilized group . . . has been a ~ —H.J.Muller⟩ **3 a :** one that is heterogeneous in origin or composition **:** COMPOSITE ⟨most of the tools are original designs or ~*s* evolved from established forms —Victor Boesen⟩ ⟨the vice-president is a ~ in the government, being both an executive and legislative officer —Arthur Krock⟩ **b :** LOANBLEND

**²hybrid** \"\ *adj* **1 a :** marked by heterogeneity in origin, composition, or appearance **:** COMPOSITE ⟨difficulties with normal English are . . . its ~ vocabulary and the irregularities of English spelling —G.A.Miller⟩ **b :** being a linguistic hybrid ⟨a ~ term⟩ **2 :** of, relating to, or resulting from the union of gametes from parents of different genotype ⟨the high percentage of intermarriage, however, has made the population . . racially ~ —*Current Biog.*⟩ **3 :** having characteristics resulting from the blending of two diverse cultures or traditions ⟨a remarkable ~ culture in which Norse and Irish elements are inextricably combined —F.M.Stenton⟩

**hy·bri·da** \ˈhībrədə\ *n, pl* **hybri·dae** \-rəˌdē\ [NL, fr. L] **:** an interspecific hybrid

**hybrid clover** *n* **:** ALSIKE CLOVER

**hybrid coil** *n* **:** a transformer having three windings two of which are in series to facilitate maintenance of voltage balance to ground

**hybrid corn** *n* **1 :** a corn resulting from crossbreeding; *specif* **:** the grain of Indian corn developed by hybridizing two or more inbred strains **2 :** the plant that is grown from the grain of hybrid corn and that conforms to a standard of desirable characteristics including increased size, yield, or disease resistance but whose own grain produces an inferior progeny

**hy·brid·ism** \ˈhībrəˌdizəm\ *n* -s [ISV *hybrid* + *-ism*] **1 :** HYBRIDITY **2 :** the fusion of diverse cultures or traditions ⟨the ~ of Puerto Rico combines both No. American and Spanish culture⟩

**hy·brid·ist** \-dəst\ *n* -s [*hybrid* + *-ist*] **:** HYBRIDIZER

**hy·brid·i·ty** \hīˈbridəd·ē, -ətē, -i\ *n* -ES [ISV *hybrid* + *-ity*] **:** the quality or state of being hybrid

**hy·brid·iz·able** \ˈhībrəˌdīzəbəl, ˌ==ˈ===\ *adj* **1 :** capable of producing a hybrid by crossing with another species or form **2 :** reproducible by hybridization

**hy·brid·iza·tion** \ˌhībrədəˈzāshən, -ˌdīˈz-\ *n* -s **:** the act or process of hybridizing or the state of being hybridized

**hy·brid·ize** \ˈhībrəˌdīz\ *vb* -ED/-ING/-S [*hybrid* + *-ize*] *vt* **:** to cause to produce hybrids **:** CROSS, INTERBREED ⟨laid out ranches . . . where they could fatten and ~ their stock —R.A.Billington⟩ ~ *vi* **:** to produce hybrids ⟨the possibility . . . that Homo sapiens and Neanderthal were *hybridizing* in northwest India or central Asia prior to the third interglacial —J.E.Weckler⟩

**hy·brid·iz·er** \-zə(r)\ *n* -s **:** one that hybridizes ⟨is a noted botanist and ~ of native iris —*Wild Flower*⟩

**hy·brid·ous** \ˈhībrədəs\ *adj* **:** HYBRID

**hybrid perpetual** *or* **hybrid perpetual rose** *n* **:** any of certain cultivated bush roses derived chiefly from the bourbon and characterized by vigorous hardy growth, a tendency to recurrent blooming, and good-sized often fragrant flowers borne singly or in groups of two to five — see HYBRID TEA

**hybrid polyantha** *n* **:** FLORIBUNDA

**hybrid rock** *n* **:** a rock formed by the mixing of two magmas or by the assimilation of the intruded by the intruding rock

**hybrids** *pl of* HYBRID

**hybrid swarm** *n* **:** a variable local population at the junction of the range of two interfertile species or subspecies resulting from extensive interbreeding and hybridization

**hybrid tea** *or* **hybrid tea rose** *n* **:** any of numerous cultivated bush roses derived chiefly from crosses of tea roses and hybrid perpetuals and characterized by intermediate hardiness and vigor, strongly recurrent bloom, and long pointed buds followed by large usu. scentless flowers borne singly or in groups of two to five

**hybrid vigor** *n* **:** unusual vigor associated with hybridity **:** HETEROSIS

**hybris** *var of* HUBRIS

**hyd** *abbr* **1** hydraulic; hydraulics **2** hydrographic; hydrography **3** hydrostatic; hydrostatics

**hy·dan·to·ic acid** \ˌhīˌdan¦tōik-\ *n* [*hydantoic* ISV *hydrogen* + *allantoic*] **:** a white crystalline acid $NH_2CONHCH_2COOH$ obtained esp. by boiling hydantoin with alkalies

**hy·dan·to·in** \hīˈdantəwən\ *n* -s [ISV *hydrogen* + *allantoin*; prob. orig. formed in G] **1 :** a crystalline weakly acidic compound $C_3H_4N_2O_2$ that is a di-oxo derivative of imidazole with a sweetish taste, that is found in beet juice and made synthetically (as by the action of hydriodic acid on allantoin), and that is used in organic synthesis **2 :** a derivative of the hydantoin compound (as diphenylhydantoin)

**hy·dan·to·in·ate** \-əˌnāt\ *n* -s [*hydantoin* + *-ate*] **:** a salt of hydantoin or one of its derivatives

**hydat-** *or* **hydato-** *comb form* [prob. fr. NL, fr. Gk, fr. *hydat-*, *hydōr* — more at WATER] **:** water ⟨*Hydat*ina⟩ ⟨*hydato*genesis⟩

**hy·da·thode** \ˈhīdəˌthōd\ *n* -s [ISV *hydat-* + *-hode* (fr. Gk *hodos* way, road); prob. orig. formed in G — more at CEDE] **:** an epidermal structure in higher plants functioning in the exudation of water; *specif* **:** an opening in the epidermis resembling a stoma below which is a chamber usu. filled or bordered by thin-walled loosely arranged cells — called also *water pore, water stoma*; see GUTTATION, WATER GLAND

**hy·da·tid** \ˈhīdəd·əd, -īdətəd\ *n* [prob. fr. (assumed) NL *hydatid-*, *hydatis*, fr. Gk, watery vesicle, fr. *hydat-*, *hydōr* water] **1** *also* **hydatid cyst :** a larval tapeworm typically comprising a fluid-filled sac from the inner walls of which develop daughter cysts and scolices but occas. forming an uncircumscribed proliferating spongy mass that actively invades and metastasizes in the host's tissues — see ECHINOCOCCUS; compare COENURUS, CYSTICERCOID, CYSTICERCUS **2 a :** an abnormal cyst or cystic structure; *esp* **:** HYDATIDIFORM MOLE **b :** HYDATID DISEASE

**hydatid disease** *n* **:** a form of echinococcosis caused by the development of hydatids of a tapeworm (*Echinococcus granulosus*) in the tissues esp. of the liver or lungs of man and certain animals

**hy·da·tid·i·form** \ˌhīdəˈtidəˌfȯrm\ *also* **hy·dat·i·form** \(ˈ)hīˈdad·əˌfȯrm\ *adj* [*hydatidiform* prob. alter. (influenced by *hydatid*) of *hydatiform*; *hydatiform* ISV *hydat-* (fr. *hydatid*) + *-iform*; prob. orig. formed as F *hydatiforme*] **:** resembling a hydatid **:** CYSTIC

**hydatidiform mole** *n* **:** a mass in the uterus consisting of enlarged edematous degenerated placental villi growing in clusters resembling grapes and usu. associated with death of the fetus

**hy·da·tid·o·cele** \ˌhīdəˈtidəˌsēl\ *n* -s [NL, prob. fr. (assumed) NL *hydatid-*, *hydatis* + NL *-o-* + *-cele*] **:** a tumorous condition of the scrotum caused by local infestation with echinococcus larvae

**hydatid of mor·ga·gni** \-mȯ(r)ˈgänyē\ *usu cap M* [after Giovanni B. *Morgagni* †1771 Ital. physician] **1 :** a small stalked or pedunculated body found between the testicle and the head of the epididymis in the male or attached to the fimbriae of the fallopian tube or the broad ligament in the female and considered to be a remnant of the duct of the pronephros or of the upper end of the müllerian duct **2 :** a small unstalked or sessile body found in the same situation in the male only and considered to be a remnant of the müllerian duct

**hy·da·tid·o·sis** \ˌhīdəˌtiˈdōsəs\ *n, pl* **hydatid·oses** \-ōˌsēz\ [NL, prob. fr. (assumed) NL *hydatid-*, *hydatis* + NL *-osis*] **:** ECHINOCOCCOSIS; *specif* **:** HYDATID DISEASE

**hy·dat·i·na** \hīˈdatᵊnə\ *n, cap* [NL, fr. *hydat-* + *-ina*] **:** a genus of stout-bodied naked rotifers (order Monogononta)

**hy·da·to·genesis** \ˌhīdə(ˌ)tō+\ *n* [*hydat-* + *genesis*] **1 :** the crystallization of minerals in certain rocks by the water present in a magma; *esp* **:** the process of depositing minerals in veins from aqueous solutions **2 :** the crystallization of salt or gypsum from normal aqueous solutions

**hy·da·to·genetic** \"+\ *adj* [fr. *hydatogenesis*, after E *genesis*: *genetic*] **:** HYDATOGENIC

**hy·da·to·gen·ic** \¦hīdətō¦jenik\ *or* **hy·da·tog·e·nous** \ˌhīdəˈtäjənəs\ *adj* [G *hydatogen* hydatogenic (fr. *hydat-* + *-gen* -genic, -genous, fr. Gk *-genēs* born) + E *-ic* or *-ous* — more at -GEN] **1 :** crystallized from or deposited by aqueous solutions **2 :** of or relating to hydatogenesis

**hy·da·to·mor·phic** \¦hīdətō¦mȯrfik\ *adj* [G *hydatomorphose* crystallization from aqueous solutions (fr. *hydat-* + *-morphose* -morphosis) + E *-ic*] **:** of, relating to, or produced by crystallization from aqueous solutions — **hy·da·to·mor·phism** \ˌ===ˈmȯrˌfizəm\ *n* -s

**hy·da·to·pneumatolytic** \¦hīdə(ˌ)tō +\ *or* **hy·da·to·pneumatic** \"+\ *adj* [*hydatopneumatolytic* fr. *hydat-* + *pneumatolytic*; *hydatopneumatic* fr. *hydat-* + *pneumatic*] *of ore deposits* **:** formed by the joint agency of water and vapor

**hy·der·a·bad** \ˈhīd(ə)rəˌbad, -ˌbäd, ˌ=(=)=ˈ=\ *adj, usu cap* **1** [fr. *Hyderabad*, city in south central India] **:** of or from the city of Hyderabad, India **:** of the kind or style prevalent in Hyderabad **2** [fr. *Hyderabad*, city in southwest Pakistan] **:** of or from the city of Hyderabad, Pakistan **:** of the kind or style prevalent in Hyderabad

**hyd·na·ce·ae** \hidˈnāsēˌē\ *n pl, cap* [NL, fr. *Hydnum*, type genus + *-aceae*] **:** a family of fungi (order Agaricales) that are distinguished by a hymenium spread out over teeth, spines, or warty emergences or a fleshy, woody, or leathery fruiting body and that include several which cause rot in timbers and a few which are edible

**hyd·no·car·pic acid** \¦hidnə¦kärpik-\ *n* [*hydnocarpic*, ISV *hydnocarp-* (fr. NL *Hydnocarpus*) + *-ic*] **:** a low-melting unsaturated acid $C_5H_7(CH_2)_{10}COOH$ occurring as the glyceride in chaulmoogra oil and hydnocarpus oil; 11-(2-cyclopenten-1-yl)-undecanoic acid

**hyd·no·car·pus** \ˌ==ˈkärpəs\ *n* [NL, fr. *hydno-* (fr. Gk *hydnon* truffle) + *-carpus*] **1** *cap* **:** a genus of Indo-Malayan trees (family Flacourtiaceae) with alternate leaves, small dioecious racemose flowers, and capsular fruits — compare CHAULMOOGRA **2** -ES **:** any tree of the genus *Hydnocarpus*

**hydnocarpus oil** \¦==¦==-\ *n* **:** a fatty oil obtained from seeds of trees of the genus *Hydnocarpus* (esp. *H. wightiana*) — compare CHAULMOOGRA OIL

**hyd·noid** \ˈhidˌnȯid\ *adj* [NL *Hydnum* + E *-oid*] **:** of, relating to, or characteristic of the genus *Hydnum*

**hyd·no·ra** \hidˈnōrə, ˈhidnərə\ *n, cap* [NL, irreg. fr. Gk *hydnon* truffle] **:** a genus (the type of the family Hydnoraceae) of African root parasites having soft spines on the inner surface of the perianth lobes resembling those of the hymenium of a fungus of the genus *Hydnum*

**hyd·no·ra·ce·ae** \ˌhidnəˈrāsēˌē\ *n pl, cap* [NL, fr. *Hydnora*, type genus + *-aceae*] **:** a family of African and Argentinian highly modified flowering plants (order Aristolochiales) that are parasitic on the roots of other plants and consist of a branched subterranean system of leafless rhizoid shoots from which large succulent solitary flowers are sent up to the surface of the ground — compare RAFFLESIACEAE — **hyd·no·ra·ceous** \¦==¦rāshəs\ *adj*

**hyd·num** \ˈhidnəm\ *n, cap* [NL, fr. Gk *hydnon* truffle] **:** the type genus of the family Hydnaceae

**hydr-** *or* **hydro-** *comb form* [alter. (influenced by L *hydr-*, *hydro-*) of ME *ydr-*, *ydro-*, fr. OF *ydr-* & MF *ydro-*, fr. L *hydr-*, *hydro-*, fr. Gk, fr. *hydōr* — more at WATER] **1 a :** water ⟨*hydro*gel⟩ ⟨*hydro*electricity⟩ **b :** hydraulic ⟨*hydro*press⟩ **2 :** water-loving organism — chiefly in generic names ⟨*Hydr*acarina⟩ ⟨*Hydro*dictyon⟩ **3 a :** hydrogen **:** containing hydrogen ⟨*hydr*iodic acid⟩ ⟨*hydro*borate⟩ **b** *now usu* **hydro- :** combined with hydrogen — esp. in names of organic compounds ⟨*hydro*quinidine⟩ **c :** combined with water by hydration ⟨*hydr*acrylic acid⟩ or by hydrolysis ⟨*hydro*cellulose⟩ **4 :** characterized by an accumulation of fluid in a (specified) bodily part ⟨*hydro*nephrosis⟩ **5 a :** combined with water — in names of minerals ⟨*hydro*hetaerolite⟩ **b :** characterized by addition of water or its constituents — in names of varieties of minerals ⟨*hydro*mica⟩ **6** [NL, fr. *Hydra* (genus of polyps)] **:** hydroid ⟨*hydro*medusa⟩ ⟨*hydro*rhiza⟩

**hy·dra** \ˈhīdrə\ *n* [alter. (influenced by L *Hydra*) of earlier *idre* complicated evil thing, fr. ME *Ydre*, *Ydra* Hydra (mythical many-headed serpent slain by Hercules that grew two heads in place of each one that was cut off unless the wound was cauterized), fr. MF & L; MF *Ydre* Hydra, fr. L *Hydra*, fr. Gk; akin to Gk *hydros* water snake — more at OTTER] **1** -s **:** a many-sided problem or obstacle that presents new difficulties each time one aspect of it is solved or overcome **2** [NL, fr. L *Hydra* (mythical serpent)] **a** -s **:** any of a number of small freshwater hydrozoan polyps constituting *Hydra* and related genera, usu. living attached to sticks, leaves, or other submerged objects, and consisting of a simple tube with a mouth at one extremity surrounded by a circle of tentacles with which to capture food, the young developing either from eggs or as buds that become detached from the side of the parent after differentiating **b** *cap* **:** a common genus of hydras

**hy·dra·car·i·an** \ˌhīdrəˈka(a)rēən\ *n* -s [ISV *hydracar-* (fr. NL *Hydracarina*) + *-ian*] **:** one of the Hydrachnellae

**hy·drac·a·ri·na** \ˌhīˌdrakəˈrīnə, -ˈrēnə\ [NL, fr. *hydr-* + *Acarina*] *syn of* HYDRACHNELLAE

**hy·drac·a·rine** \(ˈ)hīˈdrakəˌrīn, -ˌrēn, -ˌrən\ *adj* [NL *Hydracarina*] **:** of or relating to the Hydrachnellae

**hy·drach·nel·lae** \ˌhīˌdrakˈneˌ(ˌ)lē\ *n pl, cap* [NL, fr. *Hydrachna* + *-ellae* (pl. of *-ella*)] **:** a superfamily or higher group of Acarina comprising freshwater and marine mites that are usu. rather large and often bright red, that have two pairs of eyes, tarsi usu. with two claws and without an empodium, and chelicerae with a sickle-shaped movable digit, and that with few exceptions breathe by means of a well-developed tracheal system — see HALACARIDAE, HYDRACHNIDAE

**hy·drach·nid** \hīˈdraknəd\ *n* -s [NL *Hydrachnidae*] **:** one of the Hydrachnellae

**hy·drach·ni·dae** \-nəˌdē\ *n pl, cap* [NL, fr. *Hydrachna*, type genus (fr. *hydr-* + Gk *achna*, *achnē* foam, chaff) + *-idae* — more at EAR] *in some classifications* **:** a large family of water mites (group Hydrachnellae) that includes all the common free-living mites of fresh water and a few parasites of the gills of mollusks and that is now usu. broken up into numerous separate families

**hy·drach·noi·dea** \ˌhīˌdrakˈnȯidēə\ [NL, fr. *Hydrachna* + *-oidea*] *syn of* HYDRACHNELLAE

**hy·dra·coral** \¦hīdrə+\ *n* [perh. irreg. fr. NL *Hydrocorallinae*] **:** HYDROCORAL

**hy·drac·ry·late** \hīˈdrakrəˌlāt, ˌhīdrəˈkriˌl-\ *n* -s [ISV *hydracrylic* + *-ate*] **:** a salt or ester of hydracrylic acid

**hy·dracryl·ic acid** \¦hīdrə¦krilik-\ *n* [*hydracrylic* ISV *hydr-* + *acrylic*] **:** a syrupy acid $HOCH_2CH_2COOH$ that is isomeric with lactic acid and decomposes easily on heating into acrylic acid

**hy·drac·ry·lo·ni·trile** \hīˈdrakrə(ˌ)lōˈnīˌtrəl, -ˌtrēl, -īl\ *n* [*hydr-* + *acrylonitrile*] **:** ETHYLENE CYANOHYDRIN

**hy·drac·tin·ia** \ˌhīˌdrakˈtinēə\ *n, cap* [NL, fr. *hydr-* + *Actinia*] **:** a genus of marine hydroids that have separate and distinctive polyps for nutritive, reproductive, and defensive functions borne on a dense encrusting coenosarc and that are commonly associated with shells containing hermit crabs — **hy·drac·tin·i·an** \¦=¦=¦tinēən\ *adj or n*

**hydraemia** *var of* HYDREMIA

**hy·dra·gogue** *also* **hydragog** \ˈhīdrəˌgäg\ *n* -s [obs. *hydragogue*, adj., causing a watery discharge from the bowels, fr. LL *hydragogus*, fr. Gk *hydragōgos*, fr. *hydr-* + *agōgos* leading, drawing forth — more at -AGOGUE] **:** a cathartic that causes copious watery discharges from the bowels

**hydra-headed** \¦==¦==\ *adj* [*Hydra*, mythical many-headed serpent + *headed* — more at HYDRA] **:** having many centers or branches ⟨a *hydra-headed* organization⟩ ⟨passive but *hydra-headed* resistance —Edward Crankshaw⟩

**hy·dral·a·zine** \hīˈdraləˌzēn, -ˌzən\ *n* -s [prob. fr. *hydr-* + phth*alazine*] **:** a crystalline base $C_8H_5N_2NHNH_2$ used in the treatment of hypertension; 1-hydrazino-phthalazine

**Hydra-Matic** \¦hīdrə¦mad·ik\ *trademark* — used for an automobile transmission having a fluid coupling and automatic gear-shifting controls

**hy·dram·ni·os** \hīˈdramnēˌäs\ *also* **hy·dram·ni·on** \-ˌän\ *n*

[NL, fr. *hydr-* + *amnios* or *amnion*] **:** excessive accumulation of the amniotic fluid

**hy·dran·gea** \hī'drānjə *sometimes* -ran- *or* -raan-, *chiefly in substand speech* ˌhīdə'r-\ *n* [NL, fr. *hydr-* + *-angea* (fr. Gk *angeion* vessel); prob. fr. the shape of the seed capsule — more at ANGI-] **1** *cap* **:** a large genus of widely distributed shrubs and one woody vine (family Saxifragaceae) with opposite leaves and corymbose clusters of usu. showy flowers — compare HYDRANGEACEAE **2** -s **:** a plant of the genus *Hydrangea* having ample white or tinted flower clusters in which all or most of the flowers are sterile: as **a :** a shrub (*H. macrophylla*) commonly grown in greenhouses **b :** a hardy fall-blooming shrub (*H. paniculata* or its variety *H. paniculata grandiflora*) **3 :** the dried rhizome and roots of the wild hydrangea (*Hydrangea arborescens*) formerly used in pharmacy as a diuretic

**hydrangea blue** *n* **:** a pale purplish blue that is deeper and slightly redder than starlight blue and bluer and deeper than haze blue, moonstone blue, or Ontario violet

**hy·dran·ge·a·ce·ae** \(ˌ)hīˌdrānjē'āsēˌē, -ran-,-raan-\ *n pl, cap* [NL, fr. *Hydrangea*, type genus + *-aceae*] *in some classifications* **:** a family of shrubs and trees (order Rosales) that are now usu. included in Saxifragaceae

**hydrangea family** *n* **:** SAXIFRAGACEAE

**hydrangea pink** *n* **:** a moderate pink that is yellower and less strong than arbutus pink, yellower and paler than blossom pink, and paler than chalk pink — called also *aurore*

**hydrangea red** *n* **:** a grayish red that is bluer and duller than Pompeian red or bois de rose, yellower and less strong than blush rose, and yellower and duller than appleblossom

**hy·drant** \'hīdrənt\ *n* -s [*hydr-* + *-ant* (n. suffix)] **1 :** a discharge pipe with a valve and spout at which water may be drawn from the mains of waterworks — called also *fireplug* **2 :** FAUCET

hydrant

**hy·dranth** \'hīˌdran(t)th\ *n* -s [ISV *hydr-* + *-anth* (fr. Gk *anthos* flower) — more at ANTHOLOGY] **:** one of the nutritive zooids of a hydroid colony, each having a mouth, digestive cavity, and tentacles

**hy·drarch** \'hīˌdrärk\ *adj* [*hydr-* + *-arch* (adj. comb. form)] **:** originating in water — used of an ecological succession; compare HYDROSERE, MESARCH, XERARCH

**hy·drar·gil·lite** \hī'drärjəˌlīt\ *n* [*hydr-* + *argillite*] **1** *obs* **:** WAVELLITE **2 :** GIBBSITE

**hy·drar·gyr·ia** \ˌhī(ˌ)drär'jirēə\ *also* **hy·drar·gy·ri·a·sis** \hīˌdrärjə'rīəsəs\ *n, pl* **hydrargyrias** *also* **hydrargyriases** [NL, fr. *hydrargyrum* + *-ia* or *-iasis*] **:** MERCURIALISM

**hy·drar·gy·rism** \hī'drärjəˌrizəm\ *n* -s [ISV *hydrargyr-* (fr. NL *hydrargyrum*) + *-ism*] **:** MERCURIALISM

**hy·drar·gy·rum** \-ˌrəm\ *n* -s [NL, alter. of L *hydrargyrus*, fr. Gk *hydrargyros*, fr. *hydr-* + *argyros* silver — more at ARGENT] **:** MERCURY — symbol *Hg*

**hy·drar·thro·sis** \ˌhī(ˌ)drär'thrōsəs\ *n, pl* **hydrarthro·ses** \-ōˌsēz\ [NL, fr. *hydr-* + *arthr-* + *-osis*] **:** a watery effusion into a joint cavity

**hydras** *pl of* HYDRA

**hy·drase** \'hīˌdrās, -āz\ *n* -s [*hydr-* + *-ase*] **:** an enzyme that promotes addition of water to its substrate or removal of water therefrom

**hy·dras·tine** \hī'draˌstēn, -stən\ *also* **hy·dras·tin** \-stən\ *n* -s [ISV *hydrast-* (fr. NL *Hydrastis*) + *-ine* or *-in*] **:** a bitter crystalline alkaloid $C_{21}H_{21}NO_6$ derived from isoquinoline that is an active constituent of hydrastis and berberis preparations and is the parent compound of narcotine

**hy·dras·ti·nine** \hī'drastəˌnēn, -nən\ *n* -s [ISV *hydrastine* + *-ine*; prob. orig. formed as G *hydrastinin*] **:** a crystalline base $C_{11}H_{13}NO_3$ formed by the oxidation of hydrastine and useful in controlling uterine hemorrhage; 5-(methylamino-ethyl)-piperonal

**hy·dras·tis** \hī'drastəs\ *n* [NL, prob. irreg. fr. *hydr-*] **1** *cap* **:** a genus of herbs (family Ranunculaceae) having palmately lobed leaves and small greenish apetalous flowers — see GOLDENSEAL **2** -es **:** the dried rhizome and roots of the goldenseal (*Hydrastis canadensis*) formerly used in pharmacy as a bitter tonic

**¹hy·drate** \'hīˌdrāt, -drət, *usu* -d·+V\ *n* -s [ISV *hydr-* + *-ate* (n. suffix)] **:** a product of hydration: as **a :** a compound or complex ion formed by the union of water with some other substance and represented as actually containing water **:** a solvate containing molecules of water — compare WATER OF CRYSTALLIZATION, WATER OF HYDRATION ⟨Glauber's salt is a ∼⟩ ⟨the aluminum ion forms a ∼ $[Al(H_2O)_6]^{+++}$⟩ **b :** a compound containing hydroxyl ⟨camphene ∼ $C_{10}H_{17}OH$⟩ **:** HYDROXIDE ⟨calcium ∼⟩ — used chiefly commercially

**²hy·drate** \-ˌdrāt\ *vb* -ED/-ING/-S [ISV *hydr-* + *-ate* (v. suffix)] *vt* **1 :** to cause to take up or combine with water or with hydrogen and hydroxyl in the proportion in which they form water (as by chemical reaction or by adsorption) **:** subject to hydration — compare AQUATE **2 :** to maintain or restore the normal proportion of fluid in the body of esp. by oral or intravenous administration **3 :** to subject (paper pulp) to prolonged beating esp. in making glassine and greaseproof papers in order to increase moisture resistance ∼ *vi* **:** to take up or combine with water or with hydrogen and hydroxyl **:** undergo hydration

**hydrated** *adj* [fr. past part. of ²*hydrate*] **1 :** containing combined water (as in a hydrate) **:** HYDROUS **2** *of paper pulp* **:** subjected to prolonged beating to make moisture-resistant paper

**hydrated alumina** *n* **:** ALUMINUM HYDROXIDE

**hydrated lime** *n* **:** a dry white powder consisting essentially of calcium hydroxide obtained by treating lime with water — called also *slaked lime*

**hy·dra·tion** \hī'drāshən\ *n* -s [²*hydrate* + *-ion*] **1 :** the act or process of combining with water: as **a :** the introduction of additional fluid into the body (∼ sometimes helps to reduce the concentration of toxic substances in the tissues) **b :** a chemical reaction in which water takes part with the formation of only one product ⟨∼ of ethylene to ethyl alcohol⟩; *esp* **:** a reaction in which water takes part in the form of intact molecules ⟨∼ of sodium sulfate to the decahydrate⟩ — compare HYDROLYSIS, SOLVATION **c :** the addition of water to a calcium aluminate powder to produce cement **2 :** the quality or state of being hydrated: as **a :** the condition of having adequate fluid in the body tissues **b :** a physical change in paper fibers due to adsorption and imbibition of water caused by prolonged beating

**hy·dra·tor** \'hīˌdrād·ə(r)\ *n* -s [²*hydrate* + *-or*] **:** one that hydrates

**hy·dra·trop·ic acid** \ˌhīdrəˌträpik-\ *n* [*hydratropic* ISV *hydr-* + *atropic* being an alpha-phenyl-acrylic acid $CH_2{:}C(C_6H_5)COOH$ obtainable by the decomposition of atropine (ISV *atrop-* — fr. *atropine* — + *-ic*)] **:** a colorless liquid acid $C_6H_5CH(CH_3)COOH$ obtained by reduction of alpha-phenyl-acrylic acid; α-phenyl-propionic acid

**hydra–tuba** \'ˌ=ˌ=\ *n* [*hydra* (polyp) + *tuba* (horn); fr. the similarity in shape to a trumpet] **:** SCYPHISTOMA

**hy·drau·cone** \'hīdrōˌkōn\ *n* [*hydraulic* + *cone*] **:** a draft tube symmetrical with the axis of a water turbine and enlarging in diameter at the lower end where the water impinges upon a horizontal slab as it enters the tailrace

**hydrauli** *pl of* HYDRAULUS

**¹hy·drau·lic** \hī'drólik, -lēk *also* -räl-\ *n* -s [L *hydraulicus*, adj.] **:** a hydraulic machine or device ⟨brakes are four-wheel ∼s —*Motor Life*⟩; *specif* **:** HYDRAULIC ORGAN

**²hy·drau·lic** \(')=ˌ=\ *adj* [L *hydraulicus* being a hydraulic organ, fr. Gk *hydraulikos*, fr. *hydraulis* hydraulic organ (fr. *hydr-* + *-aulis*, fr. *aulos* reed instrument like an oboe) + *-ikos* -ic — more at ALVEOLUS] **1 :** operated, moved, or effected by means of water **2 a :** of or relating to hydraulics ⟨∼ engineer⟩ **b :** of or relating to water or other liquid in motion ⟨∼ erosion . . . of shore reef fronts —*Scientific Monthly*⟩ **3 :** operated by the resistance offered or the pressure transmitted when a quantity of water, oil, or other liquid is forced through a comparatively small orifice or through a tube — used of a mechanism ⟨∼ buffer⟩ ⟨∼ brake⟩ ⟨∼ equipment⟩ ⟨∼ system⟩; *also* **:** relating to a device operated in this way ⟨∼ pressure⟩ ⟨∼ action⟩ **4 :** hardening or setting under water ⟨∼ cement⟩ ⟨∼ lime⟩ — **hy·drau·li·cal·ly** \-lək(ə)lē, -lēk-, -li\ *adv*

**³hydraulic** \"\ *vt* **hydraulicked; hydraulicked; hydraulicking; hydraulics :** to subject to the action of a powerful stream or jet of water or excavate in this manner **:** SLUICE

**hydraulic brake** *n* **:** a brake (as for a motor vehicle) in which

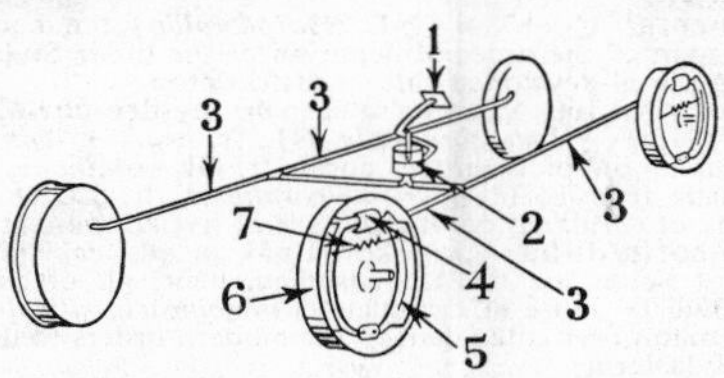

four-wheeled hydraulic brake system· *1* pedal; *2* master cylinder containing piston; *3, 3, 3, 3,* lines to each wheel; *4* wheel cylinder containing opposed pistons; *5* shoe; *6* drum; *7* return spring

the braking force is applied through a mechanism operated like a small hydraulic press

**hydraulic cement** *n* **:** a cement that is capable of hardening under water — see PORTLAND CEMENT, POZZOLANA

**hydraulic classification** *n* **:** the sorting of small particles (as of ground ore) by allowing them to settle against rising currents of fresh water of different velocities

**hydraulic coupling** *n* **:** FLUID COUPLING

**hydraulic dredge** *n* **:** a floating dredge using a centrifugal pump to draw mud or saturated sand (as from a river channel) and discharge it elsewhere

**hydraulic elevator** *n* **:** an elevator operated by the weight or pressure of water — see HYDRAULIC PLUNGER ELEVATOR, HYDRAULIC ROPE-GEARED ELEVATOR

**hydraulic engineering** *n* **:** a branch of civil engineering that deals with the use and control of flowing water (as for power or in placer mining)

**hydraulic–fill dam** *n* **:** a dam constructed by washing earthy materials into place

**hydraulic fluid** *n* **:** a fluid usu. of low viscosity (as oil or glycerol but seldom water) used in a hydraulically operated mechanism ⟨*hydraulic fluid* in a brake cylinder⟩

**hydraulic gradient** *or* **hydraulic grade line** *n* **:** a line joining the points of highest elevation of water in a series of vertical open pipes rising from a pipeline in which water flows under pressure

**hy·drau·lic·i·ty** \ˌhī(ˌ)drō'lisəd·ē\ *n* -ES [ISV ²*hydraulic* + *-ity*] **:** the capacity which hydraulic cements or their ingredients have for hardening under water

**hydraulic jack** *n* **:** a jack designed on the principle of the hydraulic press

**hydraulic jump** *n* **:** a sudden usu. turbulent rise of water flowing rapidly in an open channel where it encounters an obstruction or change in the channel slope

**hy·drau·lick·er** \hī'drólikə(r)\ *n* -s [¹*hydraulic* + *-er*] **:** one that operates a hydraulic mechanism; *specif* **:** a worker who shapes hats in a hydraulic press

**hydraulic lift** *n* **:** HYDRAULIC ELEVATOR; *esp* **:** one used for lifting motor vehicles (as for servicing in a garage)

**hydraulic lime** *n* **:** a hydraulic cementitious product made by burning hydraulic limestone

**hydraulic limestone** *n* **:** a limestone containing silica and alumina and yielding a lime that will harden under water

**hydraulic mean depth** *n* **:** HYDRAULIC RADIUS

**hydraulic mining** *n* **:** mining by the action of powerful jets of water — compare PLACER MINING

**hydraulic oil** *n* **:** an oil used as a hydraulic fluid

**hy·drau·li·con** \hī'drōləˌkän\ *n* -s [Gk *hydraulikon organon*] **:** HYDRAULUS

**hydraulic organ** *n* [trans. of Gk *hydraulikon organon*, fr. *hydraulikon* (neut. of *hydraulikos* being a hydraulic organ) + *organon* organ — more at HYDRAULIC] **:** HYDRAULUS

**hydraulic packing** *n* **:** packing made of a material that is highly resistant to the action of water esp. under high pressure

**hydraulic plunger elevator** *n* **:** a hydraulic elevator having a steel-tube plunger several feet longer than the travel of the car encased in a cylinder sunk into the ground and actuated by water pressure assisted by a counterweight and controlled by valves operated from the car, the water being forced out as the car descends

**hydraulic press** *n* **:** a machine in which great force with slow motion is communicated to a large plunger by means of liquid forced into the cylinder in which it moves by a piston pump of small diameter to which the power is applied — called also *Bramah press, hydrostatic press*

**hydraulic radius** *n* **:** the ratio of the cross-sectional area of a channel or pipe in which a fluid is flowing to the wetted perimeter of the conduit

**hydraulic ram** *n* **1 :** a pump that forces running water to a higher level by utilizing the kinetic energy of flow, only a small portion of the water being so lifted by the velocity head of a much larger portion when the latter is suddenly checked by the closing of a valve **2 :** the larger output piston of a hydraulic press or similar machine

**hydraulic rope–geared elevator** \-'=ˌ=-\ *n* **:** a hydraulic elevator in which one end of a system of ropes and sheaves is attached to the elevator car and the other end to a piston operating in a cylinder

hydraulic ram: *1* original flow, *2* output pipe, *3* air chamber, *4* check valve

**hy·drau·lics** \hī'dróliks, -lēks *also* -räl-\ *n pl but usu sing in constr* **:** a branch of science that deals with practical applications (as the transmission of energy or the effects of flow) of water or other liquid in motion

**hydraulic sprayer** *n* **:** a machine for the large-scale application of insecticides or fungicides to crops in the form of a spray — compare MIST BLOWER

**hy·drau·lus** \hī'dróləs\ *n, pl* **hydrauli** *or* **hydrauluses** [L, fr. Gk *hydraulos* hydraulic organ, fr. *hydr-* + *aulos* reed instrument like an oboe — more at ALVEOLUS] **:** an ancient Roman pipe organ using water pressure as a means of compressing the air

**hydraz–** *or* **hydrazo–** *comb form* [ISV, fr. *hydrazine*] **1 :** related to hydrazine ⟨*hydraz*ide⟩ **2** *usu* **hydrazo– :** containing the bivalent radical –NHNH– derived from hydrazine by removal of one hydrogen atom from each nitrogen atom — esp. in names of compounds in which the radical is united to two hydrocarbon radicals ⟨*hydrazo*toluene⟩

**hy·dra·zide** \'hīdrəˌzīd, -zəd\ *n* -s [ISV *hydraz-* + *-ide*] **:** any of a class of chemical compounds $RCONHNH_2$ resulting from the replacement by an acid radical of hydrogen in hydrazine or in one of its derivatives ⟨acetic ∼⟩ — compare PHENYLHYDRAZIDE

**hy·draz·i·dine** \hī'drazəˌdēn, -dən\ *n* -s [ISV *hydrazine* + *-idin*] **:** an organic base of the general formula $RC(=NH)NHNH_2$ or $RC(=NNH_2)NH_2$ formed by the action of hydrazine on an imido ester — compare AMIDINE

**hy·dra·zine** \'hīdrəˌzēn, -zən\ *n* -s [ISV *hydr-* + *az-* + *-ine*; orig. formed as G *hydrazin*] **:** a colorless fuming corrosive strongly reducing liquid compound $NH_2NH_2$ that is a weaker base than ammonia, that is usu. made by dehydration of hydrazine hydrate, and that is used chiefly as a component of fuels for rocket and jet engines and in making salts (as the sulfate) and organic derivatives; *also* **:** an organic base (as phenylhydrazine) derived from this compound

**hydrazine hydrate** *n* **:** a colorless liquid base $N_2H_4.H_2O$ made usu. by reaction of sodium hypochlorite and ammonia or urea and used for the same purposes as hydrazine

**hy·dra·zin·i·um** \ˌhīdrə'zinēəm\ *n* -s [ISV *hydrazine* + *-ium*] **:** either of two cations derived from hydrazine; *esp* **:** the univalent cation $NH_2NH_3^+$ ⟨∼ chloride $NH_2NH_3Cl$ or hydrazine hydrochloride $NH_2NH_2.HCl$⟩

**hydrazino–** *comb form* [ISV, fr. *hydrazine*] **:** containing the univalent radical $NH_2NH–$ derived from hydrazine by removal of one hydrogen atom ⟨1-*hydrazino*phthalazine⟩

**hy·dra·zo·ate** \ˌhīdrə'zōˌāt\ *n* -s [*hydrazoic* + *-ate*] **:** a salt of hydrazoic acid **:** AZIDE

**hy·draz·o·benzene** \hī'drazō, ¦hīdrəzō+\ *n* [ISV *hydraz-* + *benzene*] **:** a crystalline compound $C_6H_5NHNHC_6H_5$ obtained by alkaline reduction of nitrobenzene or azobenzene and capable of being converted into aniline by reduction, into azobenzene by oxidation, and into benzidine by rearrangement in the presence of hydrochloric acid

**hy·dra·zo·ic acid** \¦hīdrə¦zōik-\ *n* [*hydrazoic* fr. *hydr-* + *az-* + *-ic*] **:** a colorless volatile poisonous explosive liquid $HN_3$ when pure that has an unbearable odor, is made usu. by reaction of nitrous oxide with fused sodium amide or of hydrazine hydrate with ethyl nitrite in alkaline alcoholic solution, and yields explosive salts of heavy metals (as lead azide) — called also *azoimide*

**hy·dra·zone** \'hīdrəˌzōn\ *n* -s [ISV *hydraz-* + *ketone*; orig. formed as G *hydrazon*] **:** any of a class of compounds containing the grouping $>C{=}NNHR$ formed by the action of hydrazine or a substituted hydrazine (as phenylhydrazine) on a compound containing the carbonyl group (as an aldehyde or ketone) ⟨acetone ∼ $(CH_3)_2C{:}NNH_2$⟩ — see OSAZONE; compare AZINE 2

**hy·dra·zo·ni·um** \ˌhīdrə'zōnēəm\ *n* -s [ISV *hydraz-* + *-onium*] **:** HYDRAZINIUM

**hy·dre·mia** *also* **hy·drae·mia** \hī'drēmēə\ *n* -s [NL, fr. *hydr-* + *-emia*] **:** an abnormally watery state of the blood — **hy·dre·mic** *also* **hy·drae·mic** \(')hī¦drēmik\ *adj*

**hy·dren·ceph·a·lus** \ˌhī(ˌ)dren'sefələs\ *also* **hy·dren·ceph·a·ly** \-lē\ *n* -ES [*hydrencephalus* fr. NL, fr. *hydr-* + *-encephalus*; *hydrencephaly* ISV *hydr-* + *-encephaly*] **:** HYDROCEPHALUS

**hy·dria** \'hīdrēə\ *n, pl* **hydri·ae** \-ēˌē\ [L, fr. Gk, fr. *hydōr* water — more at WATER] **:** an ancient Greek or Roman water jar characterized by horizontal side handles and a vertical back handle and in the earlier form an angular and abrupt shoulder — compare KALPIS

hydriae

**¹hy·dric** \'hīdrik\ *adj* [ISV *hydr-* + *-ic*] **:** relating to or containing hydrogen

**²hydric** \"\ *adj* [*hydr-* + *-ic*] **:** characterized by, relating to, or requiring an abundance of moisture ⟨a ∼ habitat⟩ ⟨∼ plants⟩ — compare MESIC, XERIC — **hy·dri·cal·ly** \-rək(ə)lē\ *adv*

**-hy·dric** \¦hīdrik, -rēk\ *adj suffix* [ISV *hydr-* + *-ic*] **1** *archaic* **:** containing acid hydrogen ⟨di*hydric*⟩ **2 :** containing hydroxyl — esp. in terms relating to classes of alcohols and phenols ⟨hexa*hydric* alcohols⟩

**hy·drich·thys** \hī'drikthəs\ *n, cap* [NL, fr. *hydr-* + *-ichthys*] **:** a genus of colonial hydrozoans parasitic on the skin and tissues of fish

**hy·dri·dae** \'hīdrəˌdē\ [NL, fr. *hydr-* + *-idae*] *syn of* HYDROPHIDAE

**hy·dride** \'hīˌdrīd, -drəd\ *n* -s [ISV *hydr-* + *-ide*] **1** *archaic* **:** HYDROXIDE **2 :** a binary of hydrogen usu. with a more electropositive element or radical

**hy·dri·do·borate** \¦hīdrədō+\ *n* [short for *tetrahydridoborate*] **:** BOROHYDRIDE

**hy·dri·form** \'hīdrəˌfórm\ *adj* [prob. fr. (assumed) NL *hydriformis*, fr. NL *Hydra* + *-iformis* -iform] **:** resembling a polyp of the genus *Hydra*

**-hy·drin** \'hīdrən\ *n comb form* -s [ISV *hydr-* + *-in*] **:** chemical compound containing halogen or cyanogen in place of alcoholic hydroxyl esp. of only part of the hydroxyl ⟨iodo*hydrin*⟩

**hy·drin·dene** \hī'drinˌdēn\ *n* [ISV *hydr-* + *indene*] **:** INDAN

**hy·dri·od·ic acid** \¦hīdrē¦ädik-\ *n* [*hydriodic* ISV *hydr-* + *iodic*] **:** a strong liquid acid HI that resembles hydrochloric acid chemically but in addition is a strong reducing agent and that is formed by solution of hydrogen iodide in water

**hy·dri·o·dide** \hī'drīəˌdīd, -dəd\ *n* [ISV *hydriodic* + *-ide*] **:** a compound of hydriodic acid ⟨pyridine ∼⟩ — distinguished from *iodide*; compare HYDROCHLORIDE

**hy·dri·on** \'hīdrēˌīən\ *n* [*hydr-* + *ion*] **:** HYDROGEN ION

**hy·dri·o·taph·ia** \ˌhīdrēō'tafēə\ *n* -s [NL, fr. *hydrio-* (fr. Gk *hydria* water jar, cinerary urn) + *-taphia* (fr. Gk *taphē* burial); akin to Gk *thaptein* to bury — more at HYDRIA, EPITAPH] **:** URN BURIAL

**hydri·ote** \'hidrēˌōt, 'hīd-\ *n, usu cap* [*Hydra*, Greek island in the Aegean sea + E *-i-* + *-ote*] **:** a native or inhabitant of the Greek island of Hydra

**¹hy·dro** \'hī(ˌ)drō\ *n* -s **1** [short for ¹*hydropathic*] *Brit* **a :** a hotel that caters to people taking a water cure **b :** an establishment that furnishes water cures **:** SPA **2** [short for *hydroelectric*] **a** *chiefly Canada* **:** hydroelectric power **b :** a hydroelectric power plant

**²hydro** \"\ *adj* [by shortening] **:** HYDROELECTRIC ⟨∼ power⟩

**³hydro** \"\ *adj* [*hydr-*] **:** HYDROGEN **:** combined with hydrogen ⟨∼ derivatives⟩

**hydro–** *in pronunciations below* ¦==ˌ=ˌhī(ˌ)drō *or* -ˌdrə\ — see HYDR-

**hy·droa** \hī'drōə\ *n* -s [F, prob. alter. (influenced by F *hydr-*, fr. L) of Gk *hidrōa* (pl.) prickly heat, fr. *hidrōs* sweat — more at SWEAT] **:** an itching usu. vesicular eruption of the skin; *esp* **:** one induced by exposure to light

**hy·dro·ab·i·et·yl alcohol** \ˌ== *at* HYDRO- + ə'bīəlˌtēl- *or* 'abēə|\ *n* [*hydroabietyl* fr. *hydr-* + *abiet-* (fr. *abietic acid*) + *-yl*] **:** a soft viscous resinous substance obtained by hydrogenation of the methyl ester of rosin and used esp. as a plasticizer

**hy·dro–airplane** \¦hī(ˌ)drō+\ *n* **:** SEAPLANE

**hy·dro·alcoholic** \"+\ *adj* [*hydr-* + *alcohol* + *-ic*] **:** of or relating to water and alcohol ⟨∼ solutions⟩

**hy·dro·aromatic** \"+\ *adj* [ISV *hydr-* + *aromatic*] **:** derived from the aromatic compounds by adding hydrogen to the ring **:** ALICYCLIC ⟨cyclohexane is a ∼ compound formed by hydrogenating benzene⟩

**hy·dro·atmospheric** \"+\ *adj* [*hydr-* + *atmosphere* + *-ic*] **:** of or relating to both water and air

**hy·dro·basaluminite** \"+\ *n* [*hydr-* + *basaluminite*] **:** a mineral $Al_4(SO_4)(OH)_{10}.36H_2O$ consisting of hydrous sulfate and hydroxide of aluminum

**hy·dro·bat·i·dae** \ˌ==+'badˌəˌdē\ *n pl, cap* [NL, fr. *Hydrobates*, type genus (fr. *hydr-* + *-bates*) + *-idae*] **:** a family of birds consisting of the storm petrels

**hy·dro·benzoin** \¦== *at* HYDRO- +\ *n* [ISV *hydr-* + *benzoin*; orig. formed in G] **:** a crystalline compound $(C_6H_5CHOH)_2$ formed by action of sodium amalgam on benzaldehyde and yielding benzoin on oxidation

**hy·dro·biological** \"+\ *adj* [*hydrobiology* + *-ical*] **:** of or relating to hydrobiology

**hy·dro·biology** \"+\ *n* [ISV *hydr-* + *biology*; prob. orig. formed as G *hydrobiologie*] **:** the biology of bodies or units of water; *esp* **:** LIMNOLOGY

**hy·dro·bomb** \'==+ˌ-\ *n* [*hydr-* + *bomb*] **:** an aerial torpedo propelled by a rocket engine after entering the water

**hy·dro·boracite** \ˌ==+'-\ *n* [obs. G *hydroboracit* (now *hydroborazit*), fr. G *hydr-* + ML *borac-*, *borax* borax + G *-it* -ite] **:** a mineral $CaMgB_6O_{11}.6H_2O$ consisting of a white hydrous calcium magnesium borate and occurring in fibrous and foliated masses

**hy·dro·borate** \"+'-\ *n* [short for *tetrahydroborate*] **:** BOROHYDRIDE

**hy·dro·bromic acid** \¦== *at* HYDRO- + . . . -\ *n* [*hydrobromic* ISV *hydr-* + *bromic*] **:** a strong liquid acid HBr that is formed by solution of hydrogen bromide in water, that resembles hydrochloric acid chemically but in addition is a weak reducing agent, and that is used chiefly in making bromides and as a catalyst

**hy·dro·bromide** \ˌ==+'-\ *n* [ISV *hydrobromic* + *-ide*] **:** a compound of hydrobromic acid — distinguished from *bromide* ⟨pyridine ∼ $C_5H_5N.HBr$⟩; compare HYDROCHLORIDE

**hy·dro·cal·u·mite** \“+'kalyə,mīt\ *n* [*hydr-* + *c-* (fr. *calcium*) + *alum-* (fr. *aluminum*) + *-ite*] **:** a colorless to light green mineral $Ca_2Al(OH)_7.3H_2O$ consisting of hydrous hydroxide of calcium and aluminum

**hy·dro·car·bon** \¦== *at* HYDRO- +\ *n* [*hydr-* + *carbon*] **:** any of a large class of organic compounds containing only carbon and hydrogen, comprising paraffins, olefins, members of the acetylene series, alicyclic hydrocarbons (as cyclic terpenes and steroid hydrocarbons), and aromatic hydrocarbons (as benzene, naphthalene, biphenyl), and occurring in many cases in petroleum, natural gas, coal, and bitumens — **hy·dro·car·bonaceous** \“+\ *adj*

**hy·dro·carbonate** \“+\ *n* [ISV *hydr-* + *carbonate*] **:** BICARBONATE

**hydrocarbon cement** *n* **:** a cement containing bitumen

**hy·dro·carbonic** \“+\ *or* **hy·dro·carbonous** \“+\ *adj* **:** of, relating to, or of the nature of a hydrocarbon

**hydrocarbon oil** *n* **:** any of various oily liquids consisting chiefly or wholly of mixtures of hydrocarbons (as petroleum or many of its products) — compare MINERAL OIL

**hy·dro·car·y·a·ce·ae** \,==+,karē'āsē,ē\ *n pl, cap* [NL, fr. *hydr-* + *cary-* + *-aceae*] *in some classifications* **:** a family coextensive with the Trapaceae — **hy·dro·car·y·a·ceous** \¦==,==¦āshəs\ *adj*

**hy·dro·cauline** \¦== *at* HYDRO- +¦kȯ,līn, -,lən\ *adj* [*hydrocaulus* + *-ine*] **:** resembling a hydrocaulus

**hy·dro·cau·lus** \,==+'kȯləs\ *n, pl* **hydrocau·li** \-ȯ,lī\ [NL, fr. *hydr-* + Gk *kaulos* stem — more at HOLE] **:** the simple or branched stem of a hydroid

**hy·dro·cele** \'==+,sēl\ *n* -S [L, fr. Gk *hydrokēlē*, fr. *hydr-* + *kēlē* tumor — more at -CELE] **:** an accumulation of serous fluid in a sacculated cavity esp. the scrotum

**hy·dro·cellulose** \¦== *at* HYDRO- +\ *n* [ISV *hydr-* + *cellulose;* prob. orig. formed in F] **:** a substance obtained as a gelatinous mass or a fine powder by the partial hydrolysis of cellulose usu. by means of acids

[1]**hy·dro·ce·phal·ic** \¦==+sə¦falik\ *adj* [*hydrocephalus* + *-ic*] **:** relating to, characterized by, or exhibiting hydrocephalus

[2]**hydrocephalic** \“\ *n* -S **:** one that is afflicted with hydrocephalus

**hy·dro·ceph·a·loid** \“+¦sefə,lȯid\ *adj* [*hydrocephalus* + *-oid*] **:** resembling hydrocephalus

**hy·dro·ceph·a·lous** \-,ləs\ *adj* [*hydrocephalus* + *-ous*] **:** having hydrocephalus

**hy·dro·ceph·a·lus** \,==+'sefələs\ *also* **hy·dro·ceph·a·ly** \-lē\ *n* -ES [*hydrocephalus* fr. LL, hydrocephalus, hydrocephalous, fr. Gk *hydrokephalos* characterized by hydrocephalus, fr. *hydr-* + *-kephalos* -cephalous; *hydrocephaly* prob. fr. F *hydrocéphalie*, fr. *hydrocéphale* hydrocephalous (fr. LL *hydrocephalus*) + *-ie* -y] **1 :** an abnormal increase in the amount of cerebrospinal fluid within the cranial cavity, with expansion of the cerebral ventricles, enlargement of the skull esp. the forehead, and atrophy of the brain **2 :** a condition resulting from or an individual affected with such an increase in the cerebrospinal fluid

**hy·dro·ce·ram·ic** \¦==+sə¦ramik\ *adj* [prob. fr. F *hydrocéramique*, fr. *hydrocérame* pottery vessel employed for cooling liquid by evaporation of what exudes (fr. *hydr-* + Gk *keramos* pottery, jar) + *-ique* -ic] **:** made of clay that remains porous after firing — used of pottery vessels employed for cooling liquid by evaporation of what exudes; compare GOGLET

**hy·dro·ce·rus·site** \,==+sə'rə,sīt\ *n* [Sw *hydrocerussit*, fr. *hydr-* + *cerussit* cerussite, fr. G *zerussit*] **:** a mineral $Pb_3(OH)_2(CO_3)_2$ consisting of a basic lead carbonate that crystallizes in thin colorless hexagonal plates

**hy·dro·char·i·da·ce·ae** \,==+,karə'dāsē,ē\ [NL, irreg fr. *Hydrocharis* + *-aceae*] *syn of* HYDROCHARITACEAE

**hy·dro·char·i·da·ceous** \¦==,==¦dāshəs\ *adj* [NL *Hydrocharidaceae* + E *-ous*] **:** HYDROCHARITACEOUS

**hy·droch·a·ris** \hī'dräkərə̇s\ *n, cap* [NL, fr. *hydr-* + Gk *charit-*, *charis* grace, beauty; akin to Gk *chairein* to rejoice — more at YEARN] **:** a small genus (the type of the family Hydrocharitaceae) of Old World aquatic herbs with petioled floating leaves — see FROGBIT

**hy·dro·char·i·ta·ce·ae** \,== *at* HYDRO- +,karə'tāsē,ē\ *n pl, cap* [NL, fr. *Hydrocharit-*, *Hydrocharis*, type genus + *-aceae*] **:** a family of very simple widely distributed nearly stemless aquatic herbs (order Naiadales) with a 6-parted perianth and somewhat fleshy fruit — see ELODEA, VALLISNERIACEAE — **hy·dro·char·i·ta·ceous** \¦==,==¦tāshəs\ *adj*

**hydrochinone** *or* **hydrochinon** *var of* HYDROQUINONE

**hy·dro·chloric acid** \¦== *at* HYDRO- + . . . -\ *n* [*hydrochloric* ISV *hydr-* + *chloric*] **:** a strong corrosive irritating liquid acid HCl that is formed by solution of hydrogen chloride in water and is normally present in dilute form in gastric juice, that is usu. made by the action of sulfuric acid on salt, and that is widely used in industry (as for pickling metals) and in the laboratory — called also *muriatic acid*

**hy·dro·chloride** \,==+'-\ *n* [ISV *hydrochloric* + *-ide*] **:** a compound of hydrochloric acid — used esp. with the names of organic bases for convenience in naming salts; distinguished from *chloride* ⟨pyridine ~, $C_5H_5N.HCl$ is the same as pyridinium chloride, $C_5H_6NCl$⟩

**hy·dro·chlorinate** \¦== *at* HYDRO- +\ *vt* [*hydr-* + *chlorinate*] **:** to treat or combine with hydrochloric acid or hydrogen chloride ⟨~ rubber⟩ — **hy·dro·chlorination** \“+\ *n*

**hy·dro·choe·rus** \,==+'kirəs, -'kēr-\ *n, cap* [NL, fr. *hydr-* + *-choerus*] **:** a genus consisting of the capybara

**hy·dro·choleresis** \¦== *at* HYDRO- +\ *n* [NL, fr. *hydr-* + *choleresis*] **:** increased production of watery liver bile without necessarily increased secretion of bile solids — compare CHOLERESIS

[1]**hy·dro·choleretic** \“+\ *adj* [fr. *hydrocholeresis*, after such pairs as E *diuresis: diuretic*] **:** of, relating to, or characterized by hydrocholeresis

[2]**hydrocholeretic** \“\ *n* **:** an agent that produces hydrocholeresis

**hy·dro·chore** \'==+,kō(ə)r\ *n* -S [*hydr-* + *-chore*] **:** a plant that depends primarily on water for the distribution of its seeds or spores — compare ANEMOCHORE

**hy·dro·cho·ry** \-ōrē\ *n* -ES [*hydrochore* + *-y*] **:** dissemination of seeds or plants by water

**hy·dro·cinchonine** \¦== *at* HYDRO- +\ *n* [ISV *hydr-* + *cinchonine*] **:** CINCHOTINE

**hy·dro·cin·na·mal·de·hyde** \,==+,sinə'maldə,hīd\ *n* [*hydrocinnamic* + *aldehyde*] **:** an oily liquid compound $C_6H_5CH_2CH_2CHO$ that has a floral odor, occurs in species of cinnamon, and is used in perfumes

**hy·dro·cinnamic acid** \¦== *at* HYDRO- + . . . -\ *n* [*hydrocinnamic* ISV *hydr-* + *cinnamic*] **:** a white crystalline acid $C_6H_5CH_2CH_2COOH$ obtained from cinnamic acid by hydrogenation; β-phenyl-propionic acid

**hy·dro·cla·di·um** \,==+'klādēəm\ *n, pl* **hydrocla·dia** \-ēə\ [NL, fr. *hydr-* + Gk *kladion* twig, dim. of *klados* branch — more at GLADIATOR] **:** one of the small branchlets bearing the hydrothecae in a colony of plumularian hydroids

**hy·dro·clas·tic** \¦== *at* HYDRO- +¦klastik\ *adj* [*hydr-* + *-clastic*] **:** clastic through the agency of water — used of fragmental rocks deposited by the agency of water; compare PYROCLASTIC

**hy·dro·cleis** \'==+,klīs *or* -,klās\ *n, cap* [NL, fr. *hydr-* + Gk *kleis* key — more at CLOSE] **:** a small genus of Brazilian aquatic herbs (family Butomaceae) with broad leaves and solitary showy yellow flowers — see WATER POPPY

**hy·dro·cleys** \“\ *syn of* HYDROCLEIS

**hy·dro·climate** \¦== *at* HYDRO- +\ *n* [*hydr-* + *climate*] **:** the varied physical factors (as temperature, pH, density, turbidity) and often associated chemical factors (as concentration of certain ions) that characterize a particular aquatic habitat

**hy·dro·codimer** \“+\ *n* [*hydr-* + *codimer*] **:** hydrogenated codimer containing octanes

**hy·dro·coele** *or* **hy·dro·coel** \'==+,sēl\ *n* -S [*hydr-* + *-coele*] **:** the water-vascular system of an echinoderm or the pouch or cavity in the embryo from which it develops

**hy·dro·colloid** \¦== *at* HYDRO- +\ *n* [*hydr-* + *colloid*] **:** any of several substances that yield gels with water (as alginic acid salts, agar, carrageenin, and related polysaccharide gums) and that are used esp. as protective colloids and as impression materials in dentistry — **hy·dro·colloidal** \“+\ *adj*

**hy·dro·col process** \'hīdrə,kȯl-\ *n, usu cap H* [prob irreg. fr. *hydr-* (hydrogen)] **:** a modified Fischer-Tropsch process for producing chiefly high-octane gasoline from natural gas

**hy·dro·cooler** \'== *at* HYDRO- + ,-\ *n* **:** an apparatus used in hydrocooling

**hy·dro·cooling** \“+,-\ *n* **:** the process of removing heat from freshly harvested fruits and vegetables by bathing them in ice water

**hy·dro·coral** \¦==+\ *n* [NL *Hydrocorallia*] **:** a compound hydrozoan of the order Milleporina or the order Stylasterina having a well-developed calcareous skeleton

**hy·dro·co·ral·lia** \,==+kə'ralēə\ *or* **hy·dro·cor·al·li·nae** \-,kȯrə'lī,nē\ [*Hydrocorallia* fr. NL, fr. *hydr-* + *-corallia* (fr. L *corallia*, pl. of *corallium* coral, fr. Gk *korallion*); *Hydrocorallinae* fr. NL, fr. *hydr-* + *-corallinae* (fr. LL *corallinae*, fem. pl. of *corallinus* coral red)] *syn of* HYDROCORALLINA

**hy·dro·cor·al·li·na** \,==+,kȯrə'līnə\ *n pl, cap* [NL, fr. *hydr-* + *-corallina* (fr. LL *corallina*, neut. pl. of *corallinus* coral red) — more at CORALLINE] *in some classifications* **:** a hydrozoan order equivalent to the modern orders Milleporina and Stylasterina

[1]**hy·dro·cor·al·line** \¦== *at* HYDRO- + ¦kȯrə,līn, -,lən\ *adj* [NL *Hydrocorallina*] **:** of or relating to the Hydrocorallina

[2]**hydrocoralline** \“\ *n* -S [NL *Hydrocorallina*] **:** a hydrozoan of the order Hydrocorallina **:** MILLEPORE, STYLASTER

**hy·dro·cortisone** \“+\ *n* [*hydr-* + *cortisone*] **:** a crystalline hormone $C_{21}H_{30}O_5$ occurring in the adrenal cortex and also prepared synthetically that is a dihydro derivative of cortisone and is used similarly; 17-hydroxycorticosterone — called also *cortisol*

**hy·dro·cotarnine** \“+\ *n* [ISV *hydr-* + *cotarnine;* prob. orig. formed as G *hydrokotarnin*] **:** a crystalline alkaloid $C_{12}H_{15}NO_3$ obtained from opium and also formed by the reduction of cotarnine

**hy·dro·cot·y·le** \,==+'käd·ᵊlē\ *n, cap* [NL, fr. *hydr-* + Gk *kotylē* cup; prob. fr. the watery habitat and the cuplike shape of the leaves — more at KETTLE] **:** a genus of low creeping widely distributed herbs (family Umbelliferae) with crenate peltate leaves and umbellate flowers — see MARSH PENNYWORT

**hy·dro·cracking** \'==+,-\ *n* **:** the cracking of hydrocarbons in the presence of hydrogen

**hy·droc·te·na** \hī'dräktənə\ *n, cap* [NL, fr. *hydr-* + *-ctena* (fr. Gk *kten-*, *kteis* comb) — more at PECTINATE] **:** a genus of trachyline medusae resembling ctenophores

**hy·dro·cyanic acid** \¦== *at* HYDRO- + . . . -\ *n* [*hydrocyanic* ISV *hydr-* + *cyanic*] **:** a very weak poisonous liquid acid HCN or HNC that is formed by solution of hydrogen cyanide in water, is readily made by the action of an acid on a cyanide, and is used chiefly in fumigating against insects, rats, and mice and in organic synthesis — called also *prussic acid*

**hy·dro·cyanide** \,==+'-\ *n* [ISV *hydrocyanic* + *-ide*] **:** a compound of hydrocyanic acid — distinguished from *cyanide;* compare HYDROCHLORIDE

**hy·dro·cycle** \'==+,-\ *n* [*hydr-* + *cycle*] **:** a cycle for riding on water

**hy·dro·cyclist** \“+,-\ *n* [*hydrocycle* + *-ist*] **:** one that rides a hydrocycle

**hy·droc·y·on** \hī'dräsē,än\ *n, cap* [NL, fr. *hydr-* + Gk *kyōn* dog — more at HOUND] **:** a genus of large African carnivorous freshwater fishes of the family Characidae — compare TIGER FISH

**hy·dro·dam·a·lis** \,== *at* HYDRO- + 'damələ̇s\ *n, cap* [NL, fr. *hydr-* + Gk *damalis* heifer; akin to Gk *damalēs* young bull — more at DAMA] **:** a genus of aquatic mammals that includes only the Steller's sea cow and is now usu. placed in the family Dugongidae but was formerly made type of a separate family

**hy·dro·dic·ty·on** \-'diktē,än\ *n, cap* [NL, fr. *hydr-* + Gk *diktyon* net, fr. *dikein* to throw — more at DISH] **:** a genus (the type of the family Hydrodictyaceae) of unicellular freshwater green algae of the order Chlorococcales that associate in colonies of cylindrical multinucleate cells joined by their ends into pentagonal meshes which are linked in a continuous elongate saccular network often reaching a length of 20 centimeters

**hy·dro·dynamic** \¦== *at* HYDRO- +\ *also* **hy·dro·dynamical** \“+\ *adj* [*hydrodynamic* fr. NL *hydrodynamicus*, fr. *hydr-* + *dynamicus* of or relating to power, fr. Gk *dynamikos* powerful; *hydrodynamical* fr. NL *hydrodynamicus* + E *-al* — more at DYNAMIC] **:** of or relating to hydrodynamics — **hy·dro·dynamically** \“+\ *adv*

**hy·dro·dy·nam·ics** \,==+dī'namiks\ *n pl but usu sing in constr* [NL *hydrodynamica*, fr. neut. pl. of *hydrodynamicus* hydrodynamic] **:** a branch of hydromechanics that deals with the motion of fluids and the forces acting on solid bodies immersed in fluids and in motion relative to them — compare HYDROSTATICS

**hy·dro·electric** \¦== *at* HYDRO-+\ *adj* [ISV *hydr-* + *electric*] **:** of, relating to, or employed in the production of electricity by waterpower

**hy·dro·electricity** \“+\ *n* [*hydr-* + *electricity*] **:** electricity produced by water power

**hy·dro·ex·tract** \,==+ik'strakt, -ek-\ *vt* [back-formation fr. *hydroextractor*] **:** to treat with a hydroextractor — **hy·dro·ex·trac·tion** \-akshən\ *n*

**hy·dro·extractor** \¦== *at* HYDRO-+\ *n* [*hydr-* + *extractor*] **:** a usu. centrifugal machine for extracting water (as from yarn or cloth)

**hy·dro·ferrocyanic acid** \“+ . . . -\ *n* [*hydroferrocyanic* ISV *hydr-* + *ferrocyanic* (as in *ferrocyanic acid*)] **:** FERROCYANIC ACID

**hy·dro·fin·ing** \'==+,fīniŋ\ *n* [*hydr-* + *-fining* (fr. *refining*)] **:** a process for improving the quality of gasoline and other petroleum products by treating with hydrogen in the presence of a catalyst at a temperature below that at which decomposition takes place — compare HYDROFORMING

**hy·dro·flap** \'==+,-\ *n* [*hydr-* + *flap*] **:** an adjustable planing surface on a fuselage or seaplane hull used to provide a pitching moment to counteract the tendency of an aircraft to dive on its first contact with the water

**hy·dro·fluoric acid** \¦== *at* HYDRO- + . . .-\ *n* [*hydrofluoric* ISV *hydr-* + *fluoric;* prob. orig. formed as F *hydrofluorique*] **:** a weak poisonous liquid acid HF that is formed by solution of hydrogen fluoride in water, that resembles hydrochloric acid chemically but attacks silica and silicates (as glass or porcelain) forming gaseous silicon tetrafluoride and must therefore be handled and stored in equipment of steel, lead, rubber, wax, or other nonsilicate materials, and that is used chiefly in making other fluorine compounds, in polishing and etching glass, and in pickling metals

**hy·dro·flu·or·ide** \,=='-\ *n* [ISV *hydrofluoric* + *-ide*] **:** a compound of hydrofluoric acid — distinguished from *fluoride;* compare HYDROCHLORIDE

**hy·dro·fluosilicic acid** \¦== *at* HYDRO-+ . . .-\ *n* [*hydrofluosilicic* ISV *hydr-* + *fluosilicic*] **:** FLUOSILICIC ACID

**hy·dro·foil** \'==+,-\ *n* [*hydr-* + *foil*] **1 :** a flat or curved plane surface designed to obtain reaction upon its surfaces from the water through which it moves ⟨ships of all sizes may be effectively stabilized against rolling . . . by the use of controlled ~*s* —F.D.Braddon⟩ — compare AIRFOIL, HYDROPLANE **2 :** an underwater plate or fin attached by struts to a seaplane (where it is retractable) or to a speedboat for lifting the hull clear of the water as speed is increased

**hy·dro·form·ate** \,==+'fȯr,māt\ *n* [*hydroforming* + *-ate*] **:** a product obtained by hydroforming

**hy·dro·form·er** \¦==+,fȯrmər\ *n* [*hydroforming* + *-er*] **:** the unit in a petroleum refinery in which hydroforming is carried out

**hy·dro·form·ing** \-miŋ\ *n* -S [*hydr-* + *-forming* (fr. *reforming*)] **:** a process for producing high-octane gasoline or aromatic hydrocarbons (as toluene, xylenes) by dehydrogenation and aromatization of petroleum naphthas usu. containing a high ratio of naphthenes in a stream of added hydrogen and in the presence of a catalyst at elevated temperature

**hy·dro·for·myl·a·tion** \,==+,fȯ(r)mə̇'lāshən\ *n* -S [*hydr-* + *formyl* + *-ation*] **:** the addition of a hydrogen atom and a formyl group to the molecule of a compound containing a double bond by reaction with hydrogen and carbon monoxide, the chief product being one or more aldehydes — compare OXO PROCESS

**hy·dro·fuge** \'==+,fyüj\ *adj* [ISV *hydr-* + *-fuge;* prob. orig. formed in F] **:** shedding water — used of the pubescent coating of many aquatic insects

**hy·dro·garnet** \¦== *at* HYDRO- +\ *n* [*hydr-* + *garnet*] **:** one of a group of minerals of the general formula $A''_3B'''_2(SiO_4)_{3-x}(OH)_{4x}$ that are isomorphous with various garnets — compare HIBSCHITE

**hy·dro·gel** \'==+,jel\ *n* [*hydr-* + *-gel* (fr. *gelatin*)] *chem* **:** a gel in which the liquid is water

**hy·dro·gen** \'hīdrə̇jə̇n, -rēj-\ *n* -S [F *hydrogène*, fr. *hydr-* (water) + *-gène* -gen; fr. the fact that water is generated by its combustion] **:** a nonmetallic univalent element that is the simplest and lightest of the elements, that is normally a colorless odorless highly flammable diatomic gas, that occurs in the free state only sparsely on the earth and in its atmosphere though abundantly in the sun, many stars, and nebulae, and in combination as a constituent of innumerable compounds from many of which it can be readily prepared (as from water by electrolysis, from natural gas or other hydrocarbons by reaction with steam or by pyrolysis, from acids by reaction with active metals), and that is used chiefly in synthesis (as of ammonia and methanol), in reducing or hydrogenating a variety of compounds (as in hardening oils to fats), as a mixture with oxygen or as atomic hydrogen in producing very high temperatures (as in welding), as liquid hydrogen for rocket fuel and in producing very low temperatures, and in filling balloons — symbol *H;* see DEUTERIUM, ELEMENT table, ORTHO-HYDROGEN, PARA-HYDROGEN, SYNTHESIS GAS, TRITIUM

**hydrogen arsenide** *n* **:** ARSINE

**hy·dro·gen·ase** \-jə̇,nās, hī'dräjə,-\ *n* -S [ISV *hydrogen* + *-ase*] *biochem* **:** an enzyme that promotes the formation and utilization of gaseous hydrogen and occurs esp. in bacteria

**hy·dro·gen·ate** \-āt, *usu* -ād·+V\ *vt* -ED/-ING/-S [*hydrogen* + *-ate*] **1 :** to combine with hydrogen ⟨~ a vegetable oil to a fat⟩ **2 :** to treat with or expose to hydrogen ⟨~ rosin⟩ — compare HARDEN *vt* 1a — **hy·dro·gen·a·tor** \-ād·ə(r)\ *n* -S

**hy·dro·gen·a·tion** \,hīdrə̇jə̇'nāshən, hī,dräjə̇'-\ *n* -S [ISV *hydrogen* + *-ation*] **:** the process of hydrogenating: as **a :** the addition of hydrogen to the molecule of an unsaturated organic compound usu. in the presence of a catalyst (as nickel) and often at elevated temperature and pressure ⟨~ of benzene to cyclohexane⟩ **b :** a decomposition (as of hydrocarbons) at high temperature and pressure with addition of hydrogen to the molecules formed **:** HYDROGENOLYSIS ⟨~ of coal to gasoline and oils⟩ — called also *destructive hydrogenation*

**hydrogen bomb** \'===-\ *n* **:** a bomb whose violent explosive power is due to the sudden release of atomic energy resulting from the union of light nuclei (as of hydrogen atoms) at very high temperature and pressure to form helium nuclei — called also *fusion bomb*

**hydrogen bond** *n* **:** a linkage through hydrogen of two electronegative atoms esp. fluorine, oxygen, or nitrogen with one side of the linkage usu. being a conventional covalent bond (as the –O–H bond in water H–O–H or alcohol R–O–H) and the other side being primarily electrostatic in character ⟨the stable hydrogen fluoride ion $HF_2^-$ or $[F^-H^+F^-]^-$ is held together by a *hydrogen bond*⟩ — see ASSOCIATION 7

**hydrogen bromide** *n* **:** a colorless irritating gas HBr that fumes in moist air and yields hydrobromic acid when dissolved in water and that is formed as a by-product in the bromination of organic compounds but is usu. made by the direct union of hydrogen and bromine vapor or by the reaction of bromine, red phosphorus, and water

**hydrogen chloride** *n* **:** a colorless pungent nonflammable poisonous gas HCl that fumes strongly in moist air and yields hydrochloric acid when dissolved in water and that is obtained primarily as a by-product of the chlorination of organic compounds or by burning hydrogen in chlorine

**hydrogen cyanide** *n* **:** a very poisonous mobile volatile liquid or gas HCN or HNC that has an odor of bitter almonds, that occurs in many plants usu. combined as glycosides (as amygdalin) and also in coke-oven gas, that can be synthesized from ammonia and carbon monoxide or from ammonia, oxygen or air, and natural gas, and that yields hydrocyanic acid when dissolved in water

**hydrogen dioxide** *n* **:** HYDROGEN PEROXIDE

**hydrogen electrode** *n* **:** an electrode composed typically of platinum black on platinum over which a stream of hydrogen is bubbled and that under specified conditions serves as the standard electrode with an assigned potential of zero to which all other electrode potentials are referred for purposes of comparison

**hydrogen fluoride** *n* **:** a colorless mobile fuming corrosive poisonous liquid or gas HF or (HF)*n* that yields hydrofluoric acid when dissolved in water, is made usu. by the action of sulfuric acid on fluorite, and is used chiefly in the manufacture of fluorine and fluorides and as a catalyst esp. in the alkylation of branched-chain paraffins with olefins to produce superior motor fuels — called also *anhydrous hydrofluoric acid*

[1]**hy·dro·gen·ic** \¦== *at* HYDRO- +¦jenik\ *adj* [*hydr-* + *-genic*] **1 :** formed by the agency of water ⟨dinosaur footprints in ~ rock⟩ **2 :** developed under the dominant influence of water (as in a cold humid region) ⟨~ soil⟩

[2]**hydrogenic** \“\ *adj* [ISV *hydrogen* + *-ic*] **:** resembling hydrogen in nuclear composition

**hy·dro·gen·ide** \'hīdrə̇jə̇,nīd, hī¦dräjə,-\ *n* -S [*hydrogen* + *-ide*] **:** HYDRIDE

**hydrogen iodide** *n* **:** a heavy colorless gas HI that fumes in moist air and yields hydriodic acid when dissolved in water and that is usu. made by the direct catalytic union of hydrogen and iodine vapor or by the reaction of iodine, red phosphorus, and water

**hydrogen ion** *n* **1 :** the cation $H^+$ of acids consisting of a hydrogen atom whose electron has been transferred to the anion of the acid and existing in aqueous solution as a hydronium ion **:** PROTON **2 :** HYDRONIUM

**hydrogen–ion concentration** *n* **:** the concentration of hydrogen ions in a solution expressed usu. in moles per liter or in pH units and used as a measure of the acidity of the solution ⟨indicator dyes for narrow ranges of *hydrogen-ion concentration*⟩

**hy·dro·ge·ni·um** \,hīdrə'jēnēəm\ *n* -S [NL, fr. E *hydrogen* + NL *-ium*] **:** HYDROGEN

**hy·dro·gen·ize** \'hī'dräjə,nīz, 'hīdrə̇jə̇,-\ *vt* -ED/-ING\-S **:** HYDROGENATE

**hy·dro·gen·ol·y·sis** \,hīdrə̇jə̇'näləsə̇s\ *n* [*hydrogen* + *-o-* + *-lysis*] **:** a chemical reaction analogous to hydrolysis in which hydrogen plays a role similar to that of water **:** destructive hydrogenation ⟨~ of hydrazine to ammonia⟩

**hy·dro·gen·om·o·nas** \,hīdrə̇jə̇'nämə,nas\ *n, cap* [NL, fr. ISV *hydrogen* + NL *-o-* + *-monas*] **:** a genus of short rod-shaped soil bacteria (family Methanomonadaceae) that are facultative autotrophs capable of oxidizing hydrogen to form water and using carbon dioxide as a source of carbon for growth

**hy·drog·e·nous** \(')hī¦dräjənəs\ *adj* **:** of, relating to, or containing hydrogen

**hydrogen oxide** *n* **:** WATER

**hydrogen peroxide** *n* **:** a colorless syrupy explosive corrosive compound $H_2O_2$ that has a bitter metallic taste and causes blisters on the skin, that is prepared in aqueous solutions in various ways (as by the electrolysis of sulfuric acid and hydrolysis of the persulfuric acid formed, by the action of acid on barium peroxide, or by the autoxidation of anthraquinone derivatives) and can be concentrated usu. by distillation, and that is used chiefly in dilute form as a bleach and antiseptic and in more concentrated forms as an oxidizing agent and propellant (as for rockets)

**hydrogen selenide** *n* **:** a colorless flammable poisonous gas $H_2Se$ that has a disagreeable odor, resembles hydrogen sulfide, and is usu. formed by the action of acids on selenides

**hydrogen sulfide** *n* **:** a colorless flammable very poisonous gas $H_2S$ that has a disagreeable odor suggestive of rotten eggs and is slightly soluble in water to give a weakly acidic solution, that is formed by putrefaction esp. of animal matter, that is found also in many mineral waters, in most volcanic gases, and in most natural gas and petroleum deposits and is formed in many industrial processes (as coking of coal) usu. as an objectionable impurity, that is recovered as a by-product from many of these sources or is prepared by the action of an acid on a metallic sulfide or by synthesis from hydrogen and sulfur vapor, and that is used chiefly in making elemental sulfur, sulfuric acid, and other sulfur compounds and in analysis as a precipitant for metallic ions

**hy·dro·geology** \¦==  *at* HYDRO- +\ *n* [F *hydrogéologie*, fr. *hydr-* + *géologie* geology] **1 :** a branch of geology concerned with the occurrence and utilization of surface and ground water and with the functions of water in modifying the earth esp. by erosion and deposition **2 :** the phenomena with which hydrogeology deals

**hy·dro·glider** \'==+,-\ *n* **:** a glider equipped with floats

**hy·drog·no·sy** \hī'drägnəsē\ *n* -ES [ISV *hydr-* + *-gnosy*] **:** the history and description of the waters of the earth

**hy·dro·graph** \'== *at* HYDRO- +,graf\ *n* [*hydr-* + *-graph*] **1 :** a mechanism for recording on a chart the changing level of water (as in a well, reservoir, stream) **2 :** a chart produced by this mechanism

**hy·drog·ra·pher** \hī'drägrəfə(r)\ *n* -S [*hydrography* + *-er*] **:** a specialist in hydrography

**hy·dro·graph·ic** \¦== *at* HYDRO- +¦grafik\ *also* **hy·dro·graph·i·cal** \-fəkəl\ *adj* [*hydrographic* fr. F *hydrographique*, fr. MF, fr. *hydr-* + *-graphique* -graphic (fr. LL *-graphicus*); *hydrographical* fr. MF *hydrographique* + E *-al*] **:** of or relating to hydrography — **hy·dro·graph·i·cal·ly** \-fək(ə)lē\ *adv*

**hydrographic basin** *n* **:** the drainage area of a stream

**hydrographic surveying** *n* **:** surveying of coastlines, bays, harbors, and of the ocean bed

**hy·drog·ra·phy** \hī'drägrəfē\ *n* -ES [MF *hydrographie*, fr. *hydr-* + *-graphie* -graphy (fr. L *-graphia*)] **1 :** the description and study of seas, lakes, rivers, and other waters: as **a :** the measurement of flow and investigation of the behavior of streams esp. with reference to the control or utilization of their waters **b :** the measurement of tides and currents esp. as an aid in navigation **c :** the surveying, sounding, and charting of bodies of water **2 :** bodies of water or a representation of them on a map

**hy·dro·grossularite** \¦== *at* HYDRO- +\ *n* [*hydr-* + *grossularite*] **:** a mineral $Ca_3Al_2(SiO_4)_{3-x}(OH)_{4x}$, consisting of silicate of calcium and aluminum in which silicon is partly replaced by hydrogen with *x* near ½ **:** one of the hydrogarnets intermediate between grossularite (*x*=0) and hibschite (*x*=1)

**hy·dro·halide** \"+\ *n* [*hydr-* + *halide*] **:** a compound (as a hydrochloride) with one of the halogen acids **:** a hydrogen halide

**hy·dro·halite** \"+\ *n* [G *hydrohalit*, fr. *hydr-* + *halit* halite, fr. NL *halites*] **:** a mineral $NaCl.2H_2O$ consisting of a hydrated chloride of sodium formed only from salty water below the freezing temperature of pure water

**hy·dro·hetaerolite** \"+\ *n* [*hydr-* + *hetaerolite*] **:** a mineral of uncertain composition approximately $Zn_2Mn_4O_8.H_2O$ consisting of a hydrous oxide of zinc and manganese

**hy·dro-hotel** \¦hī(,)drō+\ *n* [¹*hydro* + *hotel*] *Brit* **:** HYDRO 1a

¹**hy·droid** \'hī,drȯid\ *also* **hy·droidean** \(')hī¦drȯidēən\ *adj* [*hydroid* fr. NL *Hydroida; hydroidean* fr. NL *Hydroidea* + E *-an* (adj. suffix)] **:** of or relating to the Hydroida or Hydrozoa **:** resembling a polyp of the genus *Hydra*

²**hydroid** \"\ *also* **hydroidean** \"\ *n* -S [*hydroid* fr. NL *Hydroida; hydroidean* fr. NL *Hydroidea* + E *-an* (n. suffix)] **1 :** one of the Hydroida **:** HYDROZOAN **2 :** the polyp form of a hydrozoan as distinguished from the medusa form — see HYDROMEDUSA

¹**hy·droi·da** \hī'drȯidə\ *n pl, cap* [NL, fr. *Hydra*, included genus + *-oida*] **:** an order of Hydrozoa comprising forms alternating a well-developed asexual polyp generation with a generation of free medusae or of abortive medusoid reproductive structures on the polyps — *see* LEPTOMEDUSAE

²**hydroida** \"\ [NL, fr. *Hydra*, included genus + *-oida*] *syn of* HYDROZOA

**hydroid coral** *n* **:** HYDROCORAL

**hy·droi·dea** \hī'drȯidēə\ [NL, fr. *Hydra* + *-oidea*] *syn of* HYDROIDA

**hy·droi·des** \hī'drȯi(,)dēz\ *n, cap* [NL, prob. fr. *Hydra* (genus of polyps) + *-oides* (fr. L *-oides* -oid)] **:** a genus of tube-dwelling marine polychaete worms frequently present in the fouling of ship bottoms

**hydroid polyp** *n* **:** HYDROPOLYP

**hy·dro·kinetic** \"+\ *adj* [*hydr-* + *kinetic*] **:** of or relating to the motions of fluids or the forces which produce or affect such motions — opposed to *hydrostatic*

**hy·dro·kinetics** \"+\ *n pl but usu sing in constr* [*hydr-* + *kinetics*] **:** a branch of kinetics that deals with liquids — compare HYDRAULICS

**hy·drol** \'hī,drōl, -rōl\ *n* -S [*hydr-* + *-ol*] **1 a :** the simple water molecule $H_2O$ **b :** a polymer $(H_2O)_n$ of this molecule **2 :** a secondary alcohol (as benzhydrol) esp. of the aromatic series **3** [prob. irreg. fr. *hydr-*] *also* **hydrol syrup :** a light brown syrupy mother liquor from the manufacture of dextrose used in the fermentation industries

**hy·dro·lase** \'hīdrə,lās\ *n* -S [ISV *hydrol* (fr. E) + *-ase*] **:** a hydrolytic enzyme (as an esterase)

**hy·drol·a·try** \hī'drälə·trē\ *n* -ES [*hydr-* + *-latry*] **:** the worship of water

**hy·dro·lea** \hī'drōlēə\ *n, cap* [NL, fr. *hydr-* + L *olea* olive; fr. the watery habitat and the resemblance of the leaves to those of the olive — more at OLEA] **:** a genus of blue-flowered perennial herbs (family Hydrophyllaceae) of warm regions having entire leaves and flowers with two distinct styles and bilocular ovaries and capsules

**hy·dro·lith** \'== *at* HYDRO- +,lith\ *n* -S [ISV *hydr-* + *-lith*; prob. orig. formed as F *hydrolithe*] **:** CALCIUM HYDRIDE

**hy·dro·log·ic** \¦hīdrə¦läjik\ *or* **hy·dro·log·i·cal** \-jəkəl\ *adj* [*hydrologic* ISV *hydrology* + *-ic*; *hydrological* fr. NL *hydrologia* hydrology + E *-ical*] **:** of or relating to hydrology — **hy·dro·log·i·cal·ly** \-jək(ə)lē\ *adv*

**hydrologic cycle** *n* **:** a complex sequence of conditions through which water naturally passes from water vapor in the atmosphere through precipitation upon land or water surfaces and ultimately back into the atmosphere as a result of evaporation and transpiration

**hy·drol·o·gist** \hī'dräləjəst\ *n* -S [*hydrology* + *-ist*] **:** a specialist in hydrology

**hy·drol·o·gy** \-jē\ *n* -ES [NL *hydrologia*, fr. L *hydr-* + *-logia* -logy] **1 :** a science dealing with the properties, distribution, and circulation of water; *specif* **:** the study of water on the surface of the land, in the soil and underlying rocks, and in the atmosphere, particularly with respect to evaporation and precipitation **2 :** the physical factors studied by hydrologists (as precipitation, stream flow, snow melt, groundwater storage, and evaporation) ⟨the ~ of Mexico⟩

**hy·dro·lube** \'== *at* HYDRO- +,-\ *n* [*hydr-* + *lube*] **:** any of various nonflammable hydraulic fluids having a water-glycol base

**hy·dro·lymph** \"+,-\ *n* [*hydr-* + *lymph*] **:** a watery circulatory fluid that substitutes for blood or hemolymph in some of the lower invertebrates (as jellyfishes)

**hy·drol·y·sate** \hī'dräl ə,sāt\ *also* **hy·drol·y·zate** \-,zāt\ *n* -S [*hydrolysis* or *hydrolyze* + *-ate*] **:** a product of hydrolysis

**hy·drol·y·sis** \hī'dräləsəs\ *n* [ISV *hydr-* + *-lysis*] **:** a chemical reaction of water in which a bond in the reactant other than water is split and hydrogen and hydroxyl are added with the formation usu. of two or more new compounds, some types of hydration however often being included ⟨~ of a salt to an acid and a base⟩ ⟨~ of an ester to an acid and an alcohol⟩ — compare SAPONIFICATION, SOLVOLYSIS

**hy·dro·lyte** \'== *at* HYDRO- +,līt\ *n* -S [*hydr-* + *-lyte*] **:** a substance subjected to hydrolysis

**hy·dro·lyt·ic** \¦==+¦lid·ik\ *adj* [ISV *hydr-* + *-lytic*] **:** of, relating to, or causing hydrolysis

**hy·dro·lyz·able** \'hīdrə,līzəbəl\ *adj* [ISV *hydrolyze* + *-able*] **:** capable of hydrolyzing or of being hydrolyzed ⟨compounds containing ~ groups⟩

**hy·dro·lyze** *also* **hy·dro·lyse** \'hīdrə,līz\ *vb* -ED/-ING/-S [ISV, fr. *hydrolysis*, after such pairs as E *analysis: analyze*] *vt* **:** to subject to hydrolysis ~ *vi* **:** to undergo hydrolysis

**hy·dro·lyz·er** \-zə(r)\ *n* -S **:** a piece of equipment in which hydrolysis is carried out ⟨starch ~s⟩

**hy·dro·magnesite** \¦== *at* HYDRO- +\ *n* [G *hydromagnesit*, fr. *hydr-* + *magnesit* magnesite, fr. F *magnésite*] **:** a mineral $Mg_4(OH)_2(CO_3)_3.3H_2O$ consisting of a basic magnesium carbonate occurring in the form of small white crystals or chalky crusts

**hy·dro·man·cer** \'hīdrə,man(t)sə(r)\ *n* -S [alter. (influenced by *hydromancy*) of ME *idromauncer*, fr. *ydromancye* hydromancy + *-er*] **:** one that engages in hydromancy

**hy·dro·man·cy** \-sē, -si\ *n* -ES [alter. (influenced by L *hydromantia*) of ME *ydromancye*, fr. MF *ydromancie*, fr. L *hydromantia*, fr. (assumed) Gk *hydromanteia*, fr. Gk *hydr-* + *manteia* divination — more at -MANCY] **:** divination by water or other liquid (as by visions seen therein or the ebb and flow of tides)

**hy·dro·mechanics** \¦== *at* HYDRO- +\ *n pl but usu sing in constr* [ISV *hydr-* + *mechanics*] **:** a branch of mechanics that deals with the equilibrium and motion of fluids and of solid bodies immersed in them

**hy·dro·medusa** \"+\ *n, pl* **hydromedusae** [NL, fr. *hydr-* + *medusa*] **:** a medusa that is produced as a bud from a hydroid (as of the orders Anthomedusae and Leptomedusae) and that constitutes the sexual generation of this hydroid and produces new asexual polyps from eggs and sperm

**hy·dro·medusae** \"+\ *n pl, cap* [NL, fr. *hydr-* + *medusae* (pl. of *medusa*)] **:** a formerly recognized subclass of Hydrozoa nearly coextensive with Hydrozoa as now restricted

¹**hy·dro·medusan** \"+\ *or* **hy·dro·medusoid** \"+\ *adj* [NL *hydromedusa* or *Hydromedusae* + E *-an* (adj. suffix) or *-oid*] **:** of or relating to a hydromedusa or the Hydromedusae

²**hydromedusan** \"\ *n* -S [NL *Hydromedusae* + E *-an* (n. suffix)] **:** one of the Hydromedusae

³**hydromedusan** \"\ *n* -S [NL *hydromedusa* + E *-an* (n. suffix)] **:** HYDROMEDUSA

**hy·dro·mel** \'hīdrə,mel\ *n* -S [alter. (influenced by LL *hydromel*) of ME *ydromel*, fr. MF & LL; MF *ydromel*, fr. LL *hydromel*, fr. L *hydromeli*, fr. Gk, fr. *hydr-* + *meli* honey — more at MELLIFLUOUS] **1 :** a liquor consisting of honey diluted in water which upon fermentation becomes mead **2** *pharmacy* **:** a laxative containing honey and water

**hy·dro·meningitis** \¦== *at* HYDRO- +\ *n* [NL, fr. *hydr-* + *meningitis*] **:** meningitis with serous effusion

**hy·dro·metallurgical** \"+\ *adj* [*hydrometallurgy* + *-ical*] **:** of or relating to hydrometallurgy — **hy·dro·metallurgically** \"+\ *adv*

**hy·dro·metallurgy** \"+\ *n* [ISV *hydr-* + *metallurgy*] **:** treatment of ores by wet processes (as leaching and accompanying operations)

**hy·dro·metamorphism** \"+\ *n* [*hydr-* + *metamorphism*] **:** the alteration of rock by the addition, subtraction, or exchange of material brought or carried in solution by water and without the influence of high temperature or pressure — compare DYNAMOMETAMORPHISM

**hy·dro·meteor** \"+\ *n* [ISV *hydr-* + *meteor*] **:** a product of the condensation of atmospheric water vapor (as fog, rain, hail)

**hy·dro·meteorological** \"+\ *adj* [*hydrometeorology* + *-ical*] **:** of or relating to hydrometeorology

**hy·dro·meteorology** \"+\ *n* [*hydr-* + *meteorology*] **:** a branch of meteorology having to do with water in the atmosphere esp. as precipitation

**hy·drom·e·ter** \hī'drämәd·ə(r)\ *n* [*hydr-* + *-meter*] **:** an instrument for measuring the specific gravity of a liquid commonly consisting of a thin glass or metal tube graduated to indicate either specific gravities or percentages of solution constituents and weighted so that it floats upright — compare ALCOHOLOMETER, NICHOLSON'S HYDROMETER

**hy·dro·me·tra** \¦== *at* HYDRO- +'mē·trə\ *n* -S [NL, fr. *hydr-* + *-metra*] **:** an accumulation of watery fluid in the uterus

**hy·dro·met·ric** \¦hīdrə¦me·trik\ *or* **hy·dro·met·ri·cal** \-rəkəl\ *adj* [*hydrometric* ISV *hydrometr-* (fr. NL *hydrometria* hydrometry) + *-ic*; *hydrometrical* fr. NL *hydrometria* + E *-ical*] **:** of or relating to hydrometry

**hy·drom·e·trid** \hī'drämə·trəd\ *adj* [NL *Hydrometridae*] **:** of or relating to the Hydrometridae

**hy·dro·met·ri·dae** \¦== *at* HYDRO- +'me·trə,dē\ *n pl, cap* [NL, fr. *Hydrometra*, type genus (fr. *hydr-* + *-metra*, fr. Gk *metrein* to measure, traverse, fr. *metron* measure) + *-idae* — more at MEASURE] **:** a family of small slender long-legged semiaquatic bugs closely related to the water striders

**hy·drom·e·try** \hī'drämə·trē\ *n* -ES [NL *hydrometria*, fr. *hydr-* + *-metria* -metry] **:** the measurement of specific gravity esp. of a liquid

**hy·dro·mica** \¦== *at* HYDRO- +\ *n* [*hydr-* + *mica*] **:** any of several varieties of muscovite that are less elastic and more unctuous than mica and have a pearly luster and some of which contain more water and less potash than ordinary muscovite — **hy·dro·micaceous** \"+\ *adj*

**hy·dro·morphic** \¦==+¦mȯrfik\ *adj* [*hydr-* + *-morphic*] **:** of or relating to an intrazonal soil (as the waterlogged soil of a bog area) characterized by an excess of moisture — compare CALOMORPHIC, HALOMORPHIC

**hy·dro·mys** \'==+,mis\ *n, cap* [NL, fr. *hydr-* + *-mys*] **:** a genus of myomorph rodents comprising the Australian beaver rats

**hy·dro·negative** \¦== *at* HYDRO- +\ *adj* [*hydr-* + *negative*] **:** characterized by negative hydrotaxis or hydrotropism

**hy·dro·ne·phro·sis** \¦==+nə'frōsəs\ *n* [NL, fr. *hydr-* + *nephrosis*] **:** cystic distension of the kidney caused by the accumulation of urine in the kidney pelvis as a result of obstruction to outflow and accompanied by atrophy of the kidney structure and cyst formation

**hy·dro·ne·phrot·ic** \¦===¦fräd·ik\ *adj* [fr. NL *hydronephrosis*, after such pairs as NL *hypnosis*: E *hypnotic*] **:** affected with hydronephrosis

**hy·dro·nitrogen** \¦== *at* HYDRO- +\ *n* [*hydr-* + *nitrogen*] **:** a compound of hydrogen and nitrogen (as ammonia, hydrazine, hydrazoic acid)

**hy·dro·ni·um** \hī'drōnēəm\ *n* -S [ISV *hydr-* + *-onium*] **:** a hydrated hydrogen ion; *esp* **:** OXONIUM — used chiefly in inorganic chemistry ⟨~ perchlorate $[H_3O]^+[ClO_4]^-$⟩; called also *hydrogen ion*

**hy·dron·y·my** \hī'dränəmē\ *n* -ES [ISV *hydr-* + *-onymy*] **:** names of bodies of water

¹**hy·dro·path·ic** \¦hīdrə¦pathik, -thēk\ *adj* [ISV *hydropathy* + *-ic*] **:** of or relating to hydropathy or to an establishment where it is obtainable ⟨advocating and using a ~ system for the cure of fevers —*Amer. Guide Series: Vt.*⟩ — **hy·dro·path·i·cal·ly** \-thək(ə)lē, -thēk-, -li\ *adv*

²**hydropathic** \"\ *n* -S *Brit* **:** a water-cure resort or establishment

**hy·drop·a·thy** \hī'dräpəthē, -thi\ *n* -ES [ISV *hydr-* + *-pathy*; prob. orig. formed as G *hydropathie*] **:** a method of treating disease by copious and frequent use of water both externally and internally — compare HYDROTHERAPY

**hy·dro·pericardium** \¦== *at* HYDRO- +\ *n* [NL, fr. *hydr-* + *pericardium*] **:** an excess of watery fluid in the pericardial cavity

**hy·dro·period** \"+\ *n* **:** the period during which a soil area is waterlogged ⟨upland swamps with a 5-month ~⟩

**hy·dro·peritoneum** \"+\ *n* [NL, fr. *hydr-* + *peritoneum*] **:** ASCITES

**hy·dro·peroxide** \"+\ *n* [ISV *hydr-* + *peroxide*] **:** a compound of an element or radical with the univalent group —OOH ⟨sodium ~ NaOOH⟩

**hy·dro·phane** \'==+,fān\ *n* -S [*hydr-* + *-phane*] **:** a semitranslucent variety of opal that becomes translucent or transparent on immersion in water

**hy·droph·a·nous** \hī'dräfənəs\ *adj* [*hydrophane* + *-ous*] **:** made transparent by immersion in water

**hy·droph·i·dae** \hī'dräfə,dē\ *n pl, cap* [NL, fr. *Hydrophis*, type genus + *-idae*] **:** a family of aquatic snakes that comprises the sea snakes and was formerly considered to constitute a subfamily of the family Colubridae

**hy·dro·phi·idae** \,hīdrə'fīə,dē\ [NL, fr. *Hydrophis* + *-idae*] *syn of* HYDROPHIDAE

**hy·dro·phil** \'hīdrə,fil\ *n* -S [obs. *hydrophil*, adj., hydrophytic, fr. NL *hydrophilus* water-loving] **:** HYDROPHYTE

**hy·dro·phil·ic** \¦==¦filik\ *also* **hy·dro·phile** \'==,fīl\ *adj* [*hydrophilic* fr. NL *hydrophilus* water-loving + E *-ic*; *hydrophile* fr. NL *hydrophilus*] **:** of, relating to, or having a strong affinity for water ⟨~ colloids swell in water and are relatively stable⟩ **:** readily wet by water ⟨cotton is a ~ fiber⟩ — opposed to *hydrophobic*; compare HYGROSCOPIC, LIPOPHILIC, LYOPHILIC, ORGANOPHILIC

**hydrophilic ointment** *n*, *pharmacy* **:** an ointment base easily removable with water

**hy·droph·i·lid** \hī'dräfələd\ *adj* [NL *Hydrophilidae*] **:** of or relating to the Hydrophilidae

**hy·dro·phil·i·dae** \,hīdrə'filə,dē\ *n pl, cap* [NL fr. *Hydrophilus*, type genus (fr. *hydr-* + *-philus*) + *-idae*] **:** a large family of diving beetles that are mostly of scavenging or predaceous habits and of elliptical form and black color and that live chiefly in quiet pools and carry with them a film of air for respiration

**hy·droph·i·lism** \hī'dräfə,lizəm\ *n* -S [*hydrophilous* + *-ism*] **:** HYDROPHILY

**hy·droph·i·lite** \hī'dräfə,līt\ *n* -S [G *hydrophilit*, fr. *hydr-* + Gk *philos* loving + G *-it* -ite; fr. the fact that it is very hygroscopic] **:** a mineral $CaCl_2$ of very rare occurrence consisting of native calcium chloride

**hy·droph·i·lous** \hī'dräfələs\ *adj* [NL *hydrophilus* water-loving, fr. *hydr-* + *-philus* -philous, fr. Gk *philos* loving — more at -PHILOUS] **1 :** pollinated by the agency of water **2 :** HYDROPHYTIC

**hy·droph·i·ly** \-lē\ *n* -ES [*hydrophilous* + *-y*] **:** the quality or state of being hydrophilous

**hy·dro·phis** \'hīdrəfəs\ *n, cap* [NL, fr. *hydr-* + *-ophis*] **:** the type genus of the family Hydrophidae comprising sea snakes of the western and southern Pacific ocean

**hy·dro·phobe** \'hīdrə,fōb\ *n* -S [LL *hydrophobus* one that has hydrophobia, fr. *hydrophobus*, adj., having hydrophobia, fr. Gk *hydrophobos*, fr. *hydr-* + *-phobos* -phobous] **:** one that is averse to or sheds water

**hy·dro·pho·bia** \¦==¦fōbēə\ *n* [LL, fr. Gk, fr. *hydr-* + *-phobia*] **1 :** a morbid dread of water **2 :** RABIES

**hydrophobia skunk** *also* **hydrophobia cat** *n, Southwest* **:** LITTLE SPOTTED SKUNK

**hy·dro·pho·bic** \¦==¦fōbik *also* -¦fäb-\ *adj* [LL *hydrophobicus* characterized by hydrophobia, fr. Gk *hydrophobikos*, fr. *hydrophobia* + *-ikos* -ic] **1 :** of, relating to, or suffering from hydrophobia **2 :** resistant to or avoiding wetting ⟨most insects have ~ cuticle⟩ **3** *also* **hydrophobe** [*hydrophobe* fr. LL *hydrophobus* having hydrophobia, fr. Gk *hydrophobos*] **a :** of, relating to, or having a lack of affinity for water ⟨~ colloids are relatively unstable⟩ **b :** not readily wet by water ⟨nylon is a ~ fiber⟩ — opposed to *hydrophilic*; compare LIPOPHILIC, LYOPHOBIC — **hy·dro·pho·bic·i·ty** \,hīdrəfō'bisəd·ē\ *n* -ES

**hydrophobous** *adj* [LL *hydrophobus* having hydrophobia] *obs* **:** HYDROPHOBIC

**hy·dro·phone** \'== *at* HYDRO- +,fōn\ *n* [*hydr-* + *-phone*] **:** an electroacoustic transducer for listening to sound transmitted through water ⟨detection of submarines by ~⟩ ⟨underwater seismic surveying by ~⟩

**hy·dro·phore** \"+,fō(ə)r\ *n* -S [*hydr-* + *-phore*] **:** an instrument for obtaining specimens of water (as in a river, lake, or ocean) from any desired depth

**hy·dro·pho·ria** \,==+'fōrēə, -'fȯr-\ *n* -S [Gk, fr. *hydr-* + *-phoria* act of carrying — more at -PHORIA] **:** an act of carrying water; *specif* **:** a scene on a Greek water jar showing women carrying water from a fountain

**hy·dro·phyl·la·ce·ae** \,==+fə'lāsē,ē\ *n pl, cap* [NL, fr. *Hydrophyllum*, type genus + *-aceae*] **:** a family of chiefly No. American herbs or undershrubs (order Polemoniales) having a cymose often helicoid inflorescence and usu. numerous ovules in each cell of a capsular fruit — see HYDROPHYLLUM, PHACELIA — **hy·dro·phyl·la·ceous** \¦===¦lāshəs\ *adj*

**hy·dro·phyl·li·um** \,==+'filēəm\ *n, pl* **hydrophyl·lia** \-ēə\ [NL, fr. *hydr-* + *-phyllium* (fr. Gk *phyllion* small leaf, dim. of *phyllon* leaf) — more at BLOW (to blossom)] **:** one of the leaflike organs regarded as greatly modified zooids that cover other zooids of many siphonophores

**hy·dro·phyl·lum** \,==+'filəm\ *n, cap* [NL, fr. *hydr-* + *-phyllum*] **:** a genus of No. American herbs (family Hydrophyllaceae) having lobed or pinnate deeply and sharply toothed leaves and bell-shaped cymose flowers

**hy·dro·phyte** \'==,+,fīt\ *n* -S [ISV *hydr-* + *-phyte*] **:** a plant growing in water: **a :** a vascular plant growing wholly or partly in water; *esp* **:** a perennial aquatic plant having its overwintering buds under water — compare HELOPHYTE **b :** a plant requiring an abundance of water for growth and growing in water or in soil too waterlogged for most other plants to survive — compare MESOPHYTE, XEROPHYTE — **hy·dro·phyt·ic** \¦==¦fid·ik\ *adj*

**hy·droph·y·ton** \hī'dräfə,tän\ *n, pl* **hydrophy·ta** \-fəd·ə\ [NL, fr. *hydr-* + Gk *phyton* plant — more at PHYT-] **:** a common support connecting the zooids of a hydroid colony usu. including a hydrorhiza and a hydrocaulus — **hy·droph·y·tous** \-fəd·əs\ *adj*

**hy·drop·ic** \hī'dräpik\ *also* **hy·drop·i·cal** \-pəkəl\ *adj* [*hydropic* alter. (influenced by L *hydropicus*) of ME *ydropike*, *idropik*, fr. MF *ydropique*, fr. L *hydropicus*, fr Gk *hydrōpikos*, fr. *hydrōp-*, *hydrōps* hydrops + *-ikos* -ic; *hydropical* fr. L *hydropicus* + E *-al*] **1 :** of, relating to, or exhibiting hydrops; *esp* **:** EDEMATOUS **2 :** characterized by swelling and imbibition of fluid — used of a type of cellular degeneration — **hy·drop·i·cal·ly** \-pək(ə)lē\ *adv*

¹**hy·dro·plane** \'== *at* HYDRO- +,-\ *n* [*hydr-* + *plane*] **1 :** a hydrofoil or any surface (as of an airplane pontoon) having a similar shape and tendency **2 a :** a speedboat equipped with hydrofoils or having a stepped bottom that provides more than one lifting surface so that the hull is raised wholly or partially out of the water as the boat attains forward speed **b :** DIVING PLANE **3 :** SEAPLANE — not used technically

²**hydroplane** \"\ *vi* **1 :** to skim over the water with the hull either clear of the surface or barely immersed **2 :** to drive or ride in a hydroplane

**hy·dro·planula** \¦==+\ *n* [NL, fr. *hydr-* + *planula*] **:** a larval stage of a coelenterate intermediate between the planula and actinula stages

**hy·dro·pneumatic** \"+\ *adj* [ISV *hydr-* + *pneumatic*] **:** of, relating to, or operating by means of both water and air or other gas ⟨a ~ elevator⟩

**hy·dro·pneumothorax** \"+\ *n* [NL, fr. *hydr-* + *pneumothorax*] **:** the presence of gas and serous fluid in the pleural cavity

**hy·dro·polyp** \"+\ *n* [ISV *hydr-* + *polyp*] **1 :** a polyp of a hydrozoan **2 :** HYDRULA 2

**hy·dro·pon·ic** \¦hīdrə¦pänik\ *adj* [fr. *hydroponics*, after such pairs as E *geoponics*: *geoponic*] **:** of or relating to hydroponics — **hy·dro·pon·i·cal·ly** \-nək(ə)lē\ *adv*

**hy·dro·pon·i·cist** \,=='pänəsəst\ *n* -S **:** a specialist in hydroponics

**hy·dro·pon·ics** \¦==¦päniks\ *n pl but usu sing in constr* [*hydr-* + *-ponics* (as in *geoponics*)] **:** the growing of plants in nutrient solutions with or without sand, gravel, or other inert medium to provide mechanical support

**hy·dro·positive** \¦== *at* HYDRO- +\ *adj* [*hydr-* + *positive*] *biol* **:** characterized by positive hydrotaxis or hydrotropism

**hy·drop·o·tes** \hī'dräpə,tēz\ *n, cap* [NL, fr. Gk *hydropotēs* water drinker, fr. *hydr-* + *potēs* drinker; akin to Gk *pinein* to drink — more at POTABLE] **:** a genus of deer consisting of a few small Chinese species (*H. inermis*) having no antlers

**hydropower** \'==,=\ *n* [²*hydro* + *power*] **:** hydroelectric power

**hy·dro·press** \'== *at* HYDRO- +,-\ *n* **:** HYDRAULIC PRESS

**hy·drops** \'hī,dräps\ *also* **hy·drop·sy** \-sē, -si\ *n* -ES [*hydrops* fr. L, fr. Gk *hydrōps*; *hydropsy* alter. (influenced by L *hydropisis*) of earlier *idropesie*, fr. ME *ydropesie*, fr. OF *idropisie*, fr. L *hydropisis*, modif. of Gk *hydrōps* — more at DROPSY] **1 :** EDEMA **2 :** distention of a hollow organ with fluid ⟨~ of the gall bladder⟩ **3** *or* **hydrops fetalis :** congenital erythroblastosis

**hy·dro·quinine** \¦== *at* HYDRO- +\ *n* [ISV *hydr-* + *quinine*] **:** a bitter crystalline antipyretic alkaloid $C_{20}H_{26}N_2O_2$ found with quinine in cinchona bark and usu. present in commercial quinine; dihydro-quinine

**hy·dro·quinone** \"+\ *also* **hy·dro·chinone** \"+\ *or* **hy·dro·chi·non** \,==+'kī,nän\ *n* [ISV *hydr-* + *quinone*; orig. formed as G *hydrochinon*] **:** a white crystalline strongly reducing phenol $C_6H_4(OH)_2$ occurring naturally in the form of the glucoside arbutin, made usu. by reduction of quinone, and used chiefly as a photographic developer, as an antioxidant esp. for fats and oils, and as a stabilizer and inhibitor (as in the polymerization of vinyl compounds); *para*-dihydroxy-benzene — see QUINHYDRONE

**hy·dro·rhi·za** \,==+'rīzə\ *n, pl* **hydrorhi·zae** \-ī(,)zē\ [NL, fr. *hydr-* + *-rhiza*] **:** a rootstock or decumbent stem by which a hydroid is attached to other objects — **hy·dro·rhi·zal** \¦==¦rīzəl\ *adj*

**hy·dro·rrhea** \‚==+'rēə\ *n* -s [NL, fr. *hydr-* + *-rrhea*] **:** a profuse watery discharge (as from the nose)

**hy·dro·rubber** \¦== *at* HYDRO- +\ *n* [*hydr-* + *rubber*] *chem* **:** a substance $(C_5H_{10})_x$ obtained as an elastic or tough inelastic mass by catalytic hydrogenation of rubber

**hydros** *pl of* HYDRO

**hy·dro·salpinx** \"+\ *n* [NL, fr. *hydr-* + *salpinx*] **:** abnormal distension of one or both fallopian tubes with fluid usu. due to inflammation

**hy·dro·scope** \'==+‚skōp\ *n* [ISV *hydr-* + *-scope*; prob. orig. formed as It *idroscopio*] **:** a device for enabling a person to see an object at a considerable distance below the surface of water by means of a series of mirrors enclosed in a steel tube — compare WATER GLASS — **hy·dro·scop·ic** \¦==¦skäpik\ *also* **hy·dro·scop·i·cal** \-pəkəl\ *adj*

**hy·dro·separator** \¦== *at* HYDRO- +\ *n* [*hydr-* + *separator*] **:** a settling tank (as for an industrial process) in which solids in suspension are separated from the suspending liquid

**hy·dro·sere** \'==+‚-\ *n* **:** an ecological sere originating in an aquatic habitat

**hy·dro·silicate** \¦== *at* HYDRO- +\ *n* [ISV *hydr-* + *silicate*] **:** a hydrous silicate

**hy·dro·ski** \'==+‚-\ *n* **:** a sometimes retractable hydrofoil attached below the fuselage of a seaplane to accelerate take-offs and simplify landings

**hy·dro·sol** \"+‚sól, -‚sōl\ *n* [*hydr-* + *-sol* (fr. *solution*)] *chem* **:** a sol in which the liquid is water

**hy·dro·some** \"+‚sōm\ *also* **hy·dro·so·ma** \‚==+'sōmə\ *n* -s [NL *hydrosoma*, fr. *hydr-* + *-soma*] **:** the entire colony of a compound hydrozoan **:** HYDROID

**hy·dro·sphere** \'==+‚-\ *n* [ISV *hydr-* + *sphere*] **1 :** the aqueous vapor of the entire atmosphere **2 :** the aqueous envelope of the earth including oceans, lakes, streams, and underground waters and the aqueous vapor in the atmosphere

**hy·dro·spire** \"+‚-\ *n* [*hydr-* + *spire* (coil)] **:** a flattened calcareous pouch or tube on either side of the middle line of the inner surface of the ambulacra of a blastoid, located within the cavity of the calyx, opening on the exterior by a small aperture, and presumed to form part of the respiratory system — **hy·dro·spi·ric** \¦==¦spīrik\ *adj*

**hy·dro·stat·ic** \¦==+¦stad·|ik, -at|, |ēk\ *also* **hy·dro·stat·i·cal** \-|əkəl, |ēk-\ *adj* [*hydrostatic* prob. fr. NL *hydrostaticus*, fr. *hydr-* + *staticus* static; *hydrostatical* prob. fr. NL *hydrostaticus* + E *-al* — more at STATIC] **:** of or relating to liquids at rest or to the pressures they exert or transmit — opposed to *hydrokinetic* — **hy·dro·stat·i·cal·ly** \|ək(ə)lē, |ēk-, -li\ *adv*

**hydrostatic arch** *n* **:** an arch designed to bear at each point a pressure proportional to the depth below a datum line

**hydrostatic balance** *n* **:** a balance for weighing a substance in water to ascertain its specific gravity

**hydrostatic bed** *n* **:** WATER BED

**hydrostatic head** *n* **:** a measure of pressure at a given point in a liquid in terms of the vertical height of a column of the liquid which would produce the same pressure

**hydrostatic press** *n* **:** HYDRAULIC PRESS

**hydrostatic pressure** *n* **:** pressure exerted by or existing within a liquid at rest with respect to adjacent bodies

**hy·dro·stat·ics** \¦== *at* HYDRO- + 'stad·iks\ *n pl but usu sing in constr* [prob. fr. NL *hydrostatica*, fr. neut. pl. of *hydrostaticus* hydrostatic] **:** a branch of physics that deals with the characteristics of liquids at rest and esp. with the pressure in a liquid or exerted by a liquid on an immersed body — compare HYDRODYNAMICS

**hy·dro·stome** \'==+‚stōm\ *n* -s [*hydr-* + *-stome*] **:** the mouth of a hydroid

**hy·dro·sulfide** \¦== *at* HYDRO- +\ *n* [ISV *hydr-* + *sulfide*] **:** a compound derived from hydrogen sulfide by the replacement of half its hydrogen by an element or radical ⟨potassium ~ KSH⟩ — compare MERCAPTAN

**hy·dro·sul·fite** \‚==+'səl‚fīt\ *n* [ISV *hydrosulfurous* + *-ite*] **:** a salt of hydrosulfurous acid; *esp* **:** SODIUM HYDROSULFITE — not used scientifically; called also *dithionite, hyposulfite*

**hy·dro·sulfureted** \¦== *at* HYDRO- +\ *or* **hy·dro·sulfuretted** \"+\ *adj* [*hydr-* + *sulfureted, sulfuretted*, past part. of *sulfuret*] **:** combined or impregnated with hydrogen sulfide

**hy·dro·sulfuric acid** \" + . . . -\ *n* [*hydrosulfuric* ISV *hydr-* + *sulfuric*] **:** HYDROGEN SULFIDE

**hy·dro·sulfurous acid** \" + . . . -\ *n* [*hydrosulfurous* ISV *hydr-* + *sulfurous*] **:** an unstable acid $H_2S_2O_4$ known only in aqueous solution formed by reducing sulfurous acid or in the form of salts — not used scientifically; called also *dithionous acid, hyposulfurous acid*

**hy·dro·tac·tic** \¦==+¦taktik\ *adj* [fr. NL *hydrotaxis*, after such pairs as NL *chemotaxis*: E *chemotactic*] **:** of or relating to hydrotaxis

**hy·dro·tal·cite** \‚==+'tal‚sīt\ *n* -s [G *hydrotalkit*, fr. *hydr-* + *talk* talc (prob. fr. MF *talc*) + G *-it* -ite] **:** a pearly-white mineral $Mg_6Al_2(OH)_{16}(CO_3).4H_2O$ consisting of hydrous aluminum and magnesium hydroxide and carbonate

**hy·dro·taxis** \¦==*at* HYDRO- +\ *n* [NL, fr. *hydr-* + *-taxis*] **:** a taxis in which moisture is the directive factor

**hy·dro·the·ca** \‚==+'thēkə\ *n* [NL, fr. *hydr-* + L *theca* sheath, case — more at TICK] **:** a cup-shaped extension of the perisarc in hydroids of the group Leptomedusae that surrounds and protects the hydranths when they are contracted — **hy·dro·the·cal** \¦==¦thēkəl\ *adj*

**hy·dro·therapeutic** \¦== *at* HYDRO- +\ *or* **hy·dro·thera·peutical** \"+\ *adj* [*hydr-* + *therapeutic, therapeutical*] **:** of, relating to, or involving the methods of hydrotherapy

**hy·dro·therapeutics** \"+\ *n pl but usu sing in constr* [*hydr-* + *therapeutics*] **:** HYDROTHERAPY

**hy·dro·therapist** \"+\ *n* [*hydrotherapy* + *-ist*] **:** a specialist in hydrotherapy

**hy·dro·therapy** \"+\ *n* [ISV *hydr-* + *therapy*] **:** the treatment of disease or disability by the external application of water ⟨~ by cold compresses to reduce fever⟩ ⟨~ of crippled limbs in a whirlpool bath⟩

**hy·dro·thermal** \"+\ *adj* [ISV *hydr-* + *thermal*; orig. formed in G] **:** of or relating to hot water — used esp. of the formation or metamorphism of minerals by the action of hot solutions rising up through the earth's crust from a cooling magma

**hy·dro·tho·rax** \¦==+'thōr‚aks, -'thò‚ra-\ *n* [NL, fr. *hydr-* + L *thorax*] **:** an excess of serous fluid in the pleural cavity; *esp* **:** an effusion resulting from a failing circulation (as in heart disease or from lung infection)

**hy·dro·trop·ic** \¦==+¦träpik\ *adj* [ISV *hydr-* + *-tropic*] **1 :** exhibiting or characterized by hydrotropism **2** *chem* **:** relating to or causing hydrotropy ⟨~ solvents⟩ — **hy·dro·trop·i·cal·ly** \-pək(ə)lē\ *adv*

**hy·drot·ro·pism** \hī'drä·trə‚pizəm\ *n* [ISV *hydr-* + *-tropism*] **:** a tropism (as in many plant roots) in which water or water vapor constitutes the orienting factor

**hy·drot·ro·py** \-rəpē\ *n* -ES [ISV *hydr-* + *-tropy*] *chem* **:** solubilization of a sparingly soluble substance in water brought about by an added agent

**hy·dro·tungstite** \¦== *at* HYDRO- +\ *n* [*hydr-* + *tungstite*] **:** a mineral $H_2WO_4.H_2O$ consisting of hydrous tungstic acid

**hy·dro·turbine** \‚==+'-\ *n* **:** a hydraulic turbine

**hy·dro·type** \'==+‚tīp\ *n* [ISV *hydr-* + *type*] **:** a positive printing process in photography that uses a gelatin-coated plate containing dichromate on which appears after the plate has been exposed to light under a positive and then soaked in a dye solution a positive image of dye that is transferred to a sheet of paper coated with soft gelatin

**hy·dro·ureter** \¦== *at* HYDRO-+\ *n* [NL, fr. *hydr-* + *ureter*] **:** abnormal distension of the ureter with urine

**hy·drous** \'hīdrəs\ *adj* [*hydr-* + *-ous*] **:** containing water **:** WATERY; *specif* **:** HYDRATED

**hydrous wool fat** *n* **:** LANOLIN a

**hy·dro·vane** \'== *at* HYDRO-+‚vān\ *n* [*hydr-* + *vane*] **1 :** HYDROFOIL **2 :** DIVING PLANE

**hy·drox·am·ic acid** \¦hī‚dräk¦samik-\ *n* [*hydroxamic* ISV *hydroxy-* + *am-* (fr. *amide*) + *-ic*] **:** any of a class of weak acids (as RCONHOH) that are acylated derivatives of hydroxylamine

**hy·drox·ide** \hī'dräk‚sīd\ *n* [ISV *hydr-* + *oxide*] **1 :** a compound of hydroxyl with an element or radical — used esp. of bases containing a metal (as lithium hydroxide LiOH) or a quaternary ammonium radical (as tetramethylammonium hydroxide $(CH_3)_4NOH$) **2 :** any of various hydrated oxides (as aluminum hydroxide) regarded as containing hydroxyl

**hydroxide ion** *or* **hydroxyl ion** *n* **:** the anion $OH^-$ of basic hydroxides

**hydroximino-** *comb form* [*hydroxy-* + *imin-*] **:** isonitroso-

**hydroxo-** *comb form* [*hydroxyl* + *-o-*] **:** containing hydroxyl as a coordinated group ⟨potassium *hydroxo*stannate $K_2Sn(OH)_6$⟩ ⟨*hydroxo*cobalamin⟩ — compare HYDROXY-

**hy·drox·o·ni·um** \‚hī‚dräk'sōnēəm\ *n* -s [*hydroxy-* + *-onium*] **:** HYDRONIUM

**hy·droxy** \(')hī¦dräksē\ *adj* [*hydroxy-*] **:** relating to or containing hydroxyl ⟨~ molecule⟩ — compare -HYDRIC 2, HYDROXY-

**hydroxy-** *or* **hydrox-** *comb form* [ISV, fr. *hydroxyl*, fr. E] **:** hydroxyl **:** containing hydroxyl esp. in place of hydrogen — in names of chemical compounds or radicals ⟨*hydroxy*alkyl⟩ ⟨*hydroxa*mic acids⟩ — compare HYDROXO-

**hy·droxy·acetic acid** \(¦)hī¦dräksē+ . . .-\ *n* **:** GLYCOLIC ACID

**hydroxy acid** *n* **:** an acid (as lactic acid, tartaric acid, salicylic acid) having one or more hydroxyl groups in the molecule in addition to that present in the acid group itself

**hydroxy amine** *n* **:** AMINO ALCOHOL

**hydroxyamino-** *or* **hydroxamino-** *comb form* [*hydroxy-* + *amin-*] **:** containing the univalent radical –NHOH of hydroxylamine

**hy·droxy·benzoic acid** \(¦)hī¦dräksē+ . . .-\ *n* [*hydroxybenzoic* ISV *hydroxy-* + *benzoic*] **:** any of three crystalline monohydroxy derivatives $HOC_6H_4COOH$ of benzoic acid: as **a :** the colorless para-substituted acid used in making several of its esters that are effective preservatives — called also *para-hydroxybenzoic acid, p-hydroxybenzoic acid* **b :** SALICYLIC ACID

**hy·droxy·butyric acid** \"+ . . .-\ *n* **:** a hydroxy derivative $C_3H_6(OH)COOH$ of butyric acid; *esp* **:** the beta derivative $CH_3CHOHCH_2COOH$ found in the blood and urine esp. in conditions of impaired metabolism — see KETONE BODY

**hy·droxy·citronellal** \"+\ *n* **:** a liquid hydroxy aldehyde $(CH_3)_2C(OH)(CH_2)_3CH(CH_3)CH_2CHO$ obtained by hydration of citronellal and used in perfumery to impart an odor of lily of the valley

**hy·droxy·corticosterone** \"+\ *n* **:** a hydroxy derivative of corticosterone; *esp* **:** HYDROCORTISONE

**hy·droxy·de·oxy·corticosterone** \'hī‚dräksē'dē‚äksē +\ *or* **hy·droxy·des·oxy·corticosterone** \-'de‚zäksē, -'de‚sä-+\ *n* [*hydroxy-* + *deoxy-* or *desoxy-* + *corticosterone*] **:** a crystalline steroid hormone $C_{21}H_{30}O_4$ occurring in the adrenal cortex

**hy·droxy·ethyl** \(¦)hī¦dräksē+\ *n* **:** a hydroxy derivative of ethyl; *esp* **:** the beta or 2-derivative $HOCH_2CH_2$–

**hy·droxy·eth·yl·a·tion** \(‚)hī‚dräksē‚ethə'lāshən\ *n* -s [*hydroxyethyl* + *-ation*] **:** the introduction of a hydroxyethyl group into a compound usu. by reaction with ethylene oxide

**hydroxy ketone** *n* **:** a hydroxy derivative of a ketone

**hy·drox·yl** \hī'dräksəl\ *n* -s [*hydr-* + *ox-* + *-yl*] **:** the univalent group or radical OH consisting of one atom of hydrogen and one of oxygen that is characteristic esp. of hydroxides, oxygen acids, alcohols, glycols, phenols, and hemiacetals

**hy·drox·yl·amine** \hī¦dräksələ¦mēn; ‚hī‚dräk'silə‚mēn, -‚mən\ *n* [ISV *hydroxyl* (fr. E) + *amine*] **:** a colorless low-melting crystalline unstable compound $NH_2OH$ that is a weaker base than ammonia and forms stable crystalline salts with acids, that is made by reaction of its salts with alkali, and that is used chiefly as a reducing agent and as an intermediate — see OXIME

**hy·drox·yl·ammonium** \(¦)hī¦dräksəl+\ *n* [ISV *hydroxyl* (fr. E) + *ammonium*] **:** the univalent cation $HONH_3^+$ derived from hydroxylamine and present in its salts which are obtainable by hydrolysis of a primary nitroparaffin (as nitromethane) with water and a strong acid ⟨~ chloride $HONH_3Cl$ or hydroxylamine hydrochloride $NH_2OH.HCl$⟩

**hy·drox·yl·apatite** \"+\ *or* **hy·droxy·apatite** \(¦)hī¦dräksē+\ *n* [*hydroxylapatite* fr. G *hydroxylapatit*, fr. *hydroxyl* (fr. E) + *apatit* apatite; *hydroxyapatite* fr. *hydroxy-* + *apatite*] **:** apatite containing hydroxyl: as **a :** apatite in which hydroxyl predominates over fluorine, chlorine, and carbonate **b :** calcium phosphate hydroxide $Ca_5(OH)(PO_4)_3$ — see CALCIUM PHOSPHATE 1b(2)

**hy·drox·yl·ate** \hī'dräksə‚lāt\ *vt* -ED/-ING/-S [*hydroxyl* + *-ate*] **:** to introduce hydroxyl into (a compound or radical) usu. by replacement of hydrogen — **hy·drox·yl·ation** \hī‚dräksə'lāshən\ *n* -s

**hydroxyl-herderite** \¦==¦==‚=\ *n* [*hydroxyl* + *herderite*] **:** a mineral $CaBe(PO_4)(OH)$ consisting of phosphate and hydroxide of calcium and beryllium and being isomorphous with herderite

**hy·drox·yl·ic** \‚hī‚dräk¦silik\ *adj* [ISV *hydroxyl* (fr. E) + *-ic*] **:** of or relating to hydroxyl

**hy·droxy·methyl** \(¦)hī¦dräksē+\ *n* **:** the univalent radical $HOCH_2$– derived from methanol by removal of one hydrogen atom attached to carbon — called also *methylol*

**hy·droxy·meth·yl·ation** \(‚)hī‚dräksē‚methə'lāshən\ *n* -s [*hydroxymethyl* + *-ation*] **:** the introduction of a hydroxymethyl group into a compound

**hy·droxy·naphthoic acid** \(¦)hī¦dräksē+ . . .-\ *n* **:** any of several crystalline acids $C_{10}H_6(OH)COOH$ derived from the naphthols: as **a :** a yellow acid derived from beta-naphthol and used as an intermediate for azo dyes and pigments — called also *beta-hydroxynaphthoic acid, 3-hydroxy-2-naphthoic acid*; see DYE table I (under *Developer 8*), NAPHTHOL AS **b :** a white to reddish acid derived from alpha-naphthol and used as an analytical reagent — called also *1-hydroxy-2-naphthoic acid*

**hy·droxy·proline** \"+\ *n* **:** a crystalline amino acid $HOC_4H_7NCOOH$ obtained in the levorotatory L-form esp. by hydrolysis of gelatin or collagen — called also *4-hydroxyproline*

**hy·droxy·quinoline** \"+\ *n* **:** any of seven hydroxy derivatives of quinoline; *esp* **:** OXINE

**hy·droxy·tryptamine** \"+\ *n* -s [ISV *hydroxy-* + *tryptamine*] **:** SEROTONIN

**hy·drox·y·zine** \hī'dräksə‚zēn\ *n* -s [*hydroxy-* + pipera*zine*] **:** a tranquilizer and antihistamine $C_{21}H_{27}ClN_2O_2$ that is an ether alcohol derived from piperazine

**hy·dro·zinc·ite** \hīdrō'ziŋ‚kīt\ *n* [G *hydrozinkit*, fr. *hydr-* + *zink* zinc + *-it* -ite] **:** a mineral $Zn_5(OH)_6(CO_3)_2$ consisting of a basic zinc carbonate occurring as white, grayish, or yellowish masses or crusts (sp. gr. 3.58–3.8)

**hy·dro·zoa** \‚hīdrə'zōə\ *n pl, cap* [NL, fr. *hydr-* (hydroid) + *-zoa*] **:** a class of coelenterates that includes various simple and compound polyps and jellyfishes having no stomodaeum or gastric tentacles and differing widely in appearance, structure, and habits, some being attached polyps which have no free-swimming stage, others being always free-swimming and the majority having an alternation of a free-swimming sexual generation with an attached asexual generation — see HYDROIDA, MILLEPORINA, SIPHONOPHORA, STYLASTERINA, TRACHYLINA

[1]**hydrozoan** \¦==¦zōən\ *or* **hydrozoal** \-ōəl\ *adj* [NL *Hydrozoa* + E *-an* (adj. suffix) or *-al* (adj. suffix)] **:** of or relating to the Hydrozoa

[2]**hydrozoan** \"\ *n* -s [NL *Hydrozoa* + E *-an* (n. suffix)] **:** one of the Hydrozoa

**hy·dro·zo·on** \‚==+'zō‚än\ *n, pl* **hydro·zoa** \-ōə\ *or* **hydro·zoons** [NL, fr. *hydr-* + *-zoon*] **:** HYDROZOAN

**hy·dru·la** \'hīdrələ\ *n* -s [NL, dim. of *hydra* (hydrozoan polyp)] **1 :** a hypothetical primitive polyp of simple type **2 :** a developmental phase of many coelenterates (as hydroids) in which they have the form of a simple polyp

**hy·dru·ra·ce·ae** \‚hī‚drü'rāsē‚ē\ *n pl, cap* [NL, fr. *Hydrurus*, type genus + *-aceae*] **:** a family of algae (order Chrysocapsales) that includes the genus *Hydrurus* and related forms when these are considered to be algae rather than protozoans

**hy·drur·ga** \hī'drŭrgə\ *n, cap* [NL, irreg. fr. *hydr-*] **:** a genus of mammals (family Phocidae) comprising the leopard seal

**hy·dru·rus** \hī'drŭrəs\ *n, cap* [NL, fr. *hydr-* + *-urus*] **:** a genus of colonial plantlike flagellates (order Chrysomonadina) occurring as sticky foul-smelling branched feathery greenish brown tufts in cold flowing water — see HYDRURACEAE

**hydt** *abbr* hydrant

**hy·e·na** *or* **hy·ae·na** \hī'ēnə\ *n* -s [L *hyaena*, fr. Gk *hyaina*, fr. *hys* hog — more at sow] **1 :** any of several large strong nocturnal carnivorous Old World mammals constituting the family Hyaenidae, having a long thick neck, large head, powerful jaws, rough coat, and four-toed feet with nonretractile claws, and feeding largely on carrion — compare CAVE HYENA **2** *Austral* **:** TASMANIAN WOLF

striped hyena

**hyena dog** *n* **:** AFRICAN HUNTING DOG

**hy·e·nia** \hī'ēnēə\ *n, cap* [NL, fr. *Hyen*, locality near Nord Fjord, western Norway, near which the fossils on which the genus is based were discovered + NL *-ia*] **:** a genus of small Devonian fossil plants (order Hyeniales) having horizontal rhizomes bearing aerial shoots with small bifurcated leaves in whorls and pendulous terminal sporangia

**hy·e·ni·a·les** \(‚)hī‚ēnē'ā(‚)lēz\ *n pl, cap* [NL, fr. *Hyenia* + *-ales*] **:** an order of Devonian sphenopsid plants known only in the fossil state — see CALAMOPHYTON, HYENIA

**hy·enic** *or* **hy·aenic** \(')hī¦ēnik, -¦en-\ *adj* [*hyena, hyaena* + *-ic*] **:** of, relating to, or like a hyena

**hy·e·ni·form** \(')hī¦ēnə‚fôrm\ *adj* [*hyena* + *-iform*] **:** HYENOID

**hy·e·noid** \hī'ē‚nóid\ *adj* [*hyena* + *-oid*] **:** resembling a hyena

**hyenoid dog** *n* **:** any of several No. American Miocene and Pliocene carnivorous mammals constituting *Borophagus* and related genera of the family Canidae and being intermediate in character between the true dogs and the hyenas

**hyet-** *or* **hyeto-** *comb form* [Gk, fr. *hyetos*; akin to Gk *hyei* it is raining — more at SUCK] **:** rain ⟨*hyet*al⟩ ⟨*hyeto*meter⟩ ⟨*hyeto*graphy⟩

**hy·e·tal** \'hīəd·ᵊl\ *adj* **:** of or relating to rain, rainfall, or rainy regions

**hy·et·o·graph** \hī'ed·ə‚graf, -rȧf\ *n* [ISV *hyet-* + *-graph*] **1 :** a chart showing average annual rainfall **2 :** HYETOMETROGRAPH

**hy·et·o·graph·ic** \(‚)hī¦ed·ə¦grafik\ *also* **hy·et·o·graph·i·cal** \-fəkəl\ *adj* [*hyetography* + *-ic, -ical*] **:** of or relating to hyetography — **hy·et·o·graph·i·cal·ly** \-fək(ə)lē\ *adv*

**hy·e·tog·ra·phy** \‚hīə'tägrəfē\ *n* -ES [ISV *hyet-* + *-graphy*] **:** scientific description of the geographical distribution of rain

**hy·et·o·log·i·cal** \(‚)hī¦ed·ᵊl¦äjəkəl\ *adj* [*hyet-* + *-logy* + *-ical*] **:** of or relating to hyetology

**hy·e·tol·o·gy** \‚hīə'täləjē\ *n* -ES [*hyet-* + *-logy*] **:** a branch of meteorology that deals with precipitation (as of rain and snow)

**hy·e·tom·e·ter** \-ämad·ə(r)\ *n* [*hyet-* + *-meter*] **:** RAIN GAGE

**hy·e·to·met·ro·graph** \‚hīətō'me·trə‚graf, -rȧf\ *n* [*hyet-* + *metr-* (measure) + *-graph*] **:** a self-registering rain gage

**hyg** *abbr* hygiene

**hy·ge·ian** \(')hī¦jēən\ *adj* [*Hygeia*, ancient Greek goddess of health (fr. L *Hygea*, fr. Gk *Hygieia*, fr. *hygieia* health, fr. *hygiēs* sound, healthy) + E *-an*] **1** *usu cap* **:** of or relating to Hygeia, the ancient Greek goddess of health **2 :** of or relating to health or to medical practice

**hy·ge·ist** \'hījēəst\ *n* -s [Gk *hygeia* health (alter. of *hygieia*) + E *-ist*] **:** HYGIENIST

**hy·giene** \'hī‚jēn *sometimes* ='=\ *n* -s [F *hygiène* & NL *hygiena*, *hygieina*, fr. Gk *hygieinē*, fem. of *hygieinos* healthful, relating to health, fr. *hygiēs* sound, healthy, fr. a prehistoric compound whose first and second constituents respectively are akin to OIr *so-* good, well, OSlav *sŭdravŭ* healthy, Av *hu-* good, well, Skt *su* and to Lith *gyvas* living — more at QUICK] **1 :** the science which deals with the establishment and maintenance of health in the individual and the group ⟨took a course in municipal ~⟩ **2 :** conditions or practices conducive to health ⟨infant mortality was very high because of bad ~ and the lack of nourishing foods —P.E.James⟩

**hy·gien·ic** \¦hī¦jenik, (')hī¦jen-, -nēk *also* (')hī¦jēn-\ *also* **hy·gien·i·cal** \-nəkəl, -nēk-\ *adj* [prob. fr. F *hygiénique*, fr. *hygiène* hygiene + *-ique* -ic, -ical] **:** of, relating to, or conducive to health or hygiene **syn** see HEALTHFUL

**hy·gien·i·cal·ly** \-nək(ə)lē, -nēk-, -li\ *adv* **:** in a hygienic manner

**hy·gien·ics** \‚hījē'eniks, hī'jen- -nēks *also* hī'jēn-\ *n pl but sing in constr* **:** HYGIENE 1

**hy·gien·ist** \(')hī¦jēnəst, (')hī¦jen-, *also* ¦hījē¦en- *or* 'hījən-\ *n* -s [ISV *hygiene* + *-ist*] **:** a specialist in hygiene; *esp* **:** one skilled in a specified branch of hygiene ⟨dental ~⟩ ⟨mental ~⟩

**hygr-** *also* **hygro-** *comb form* [Gk, fr. *hygros* moist, wet — more at HUMOR] **1 :** humidity **:** moisture **:** moist ⟨*hygr*ic⟩ ⟨*hygro*stat⟩ ⟨*hygro*phobia⟩ ⟨*hygro*phyte⟩ **2 :** moisture and and **:** of or relating to moisture and ⟨*hygro*thermal⟩

**hy·gric** \'hīgrik\ *adj* [ISV *hygr-* + *-ic*] **:** of, relating to, or containing moisture

**hy·grine** \'hī‚grēn, -grən\ *n* -s [ISV *hygr-* + *-ine*; orig. formed as G *hygrin*] **:** a colorless liquid ketonic alkaloid $C_8H_{15}NO$ derived from pyrrolidine and obtained from coca leaves

**hy·gro·deik** \'hīgrə‚dīk\ *n* -s [*hygr-* + *-deik* (fr. Gk *deiknynai* to show) — more at DICTION] **:** a hygrometer having wet-bulb and dry-bulb thermometers and an adjustable index for determining relative humidity

**hy·gro·expansivity** \¦hī(‚)grō+\ *n* **:** expansivity due to moisture or humidity

**hy·gro·graph** \'hīgrə‚graf, -rȧf\ *n* [ISV *hygr-* + *-graph*] **:** an instrument for recording automatically variations in the humidity of the atmosphere

**hy·grol·o·gy** \hī'gräləjē\ *n* -ES [ISV *hygr-* + *-logy*] **:** a branch of physics that deals with the phenomena of humidity

**hy·gro·ma** \hī'grōmə\ *n, pl* **hygromas** \-məz\ *or* **hygro·ma·ta** \-məd·ə\ [NL, fr. *hygr-* + *-oma*] **1 :** a cystic tumor of lymphatic origin **2 :** a cyst esp. of the knee of cattle caused by injury or infection

**hy·grom·e·ter** \hī'grämad·ə(r)\ *n* [prob. fr. F *hygromètre*, fr. *hygr-* + *-mètre* -meter] **:** any of several instruments for measuring the humidity of the atmosphere — see DEW-POINT HYGROMETER, HAIR HYGROMETER, PSYCHROMETER

**hy·gro·met·ric** \¦hīgrə¦me·trik\ *also* **hy·gro·met·ri·cal** \-rəkəl\ *adj* [prob. fr. F *hygrométrique*, fr. *hygrométrie* hygrometry + *-ique* -ic, -ical] **1 :** of or relating to hygrometry or to humidity **2 :** HYGROSCOPIC — **hy·gro·met·ri·cal·ly** \-rək(ə)lē\ *adv*

**hygrometric water** *n* **:** water in a mineral that can be released by raising its temperature to 110° C

**hy·grom·e·try** \hī'grämə·trē\ *n* -ES [F *hygrométrie*, fr. *hygr-* + *-métrie* -metry] **:** a branch of physics that deals with the measurement of humidity esp. of the atmosphere

**hy·groph·i·la** \hī'gräfələ\ *n* [NL, fr. *hygr-* + *-phila*] **1** *cap* **:** a genus of aquatic herbaceous or woody plants (family Acanthaceae) having leaves resembling those of the willow **2** -s **:** any plant of the genus *Hygrophila*

**hy·gro·phile** \'hīgrə‚fīl\ *or* **hy·gro·phil·ic** \¦==¦filik\ *adj* [*hygrophile* fr. F, fr. *hygr-* + *-phile*; *hygrophilic* prob. fr. F *hygrophile* + E *-ic*] **:** HYGROPHILOUS

**hy·groph·i·lous** \(')hī¦gräfələs\ *adj* [prob. fr. F *hygrophile* + E *-ous*] **:** living or growing in moist places

**hy·gro·phyte** \'hīgrə‚fīt\ *n* -s [ISV *hygr-* + *-phyte*] **1 :** a plant living under conditions of plentiful moisture **2 :** HYDROPHYTE — **hy·gro·phyt·ic** \¦==¦fid·ik\ *adj*

**hy·gro·scope** \'hīgrə‚skōp\ *n* [*hygr-* + *-scope*] **:** an instrument that shows changes in humidity (as of the atmosphere) — compare HYGROMETER

**hy·gro·scop·ic** \¦==¦skäpik\ *adj* [*hygroscope* + *-ic*] **1 a :** readily taking up and retaining moisture ⟨glycerol is ~⟩ ⟨~ soils⟩ ⟨common salt is slightly ~⟩ — compare DELIQUESCENT, HYDROPHILIC **b :** taken up and retained under certain conditions of humidity and temperature — used of moisture ⟨~ water is not removed from clay by drying at 110° C⟩ **2 a** *bot* **:** sensitive to moisture ⟨~ tissues⟩ ⟨~ organs⟩ **b :** induced by moisture ⟨turgor movements are ~⟩ — **hy·gro·scop·i·cal·ly**

\-pȯk(ə)lē\ *adv* — **hy·gro·sco·pic·i·ty** \ˌhīgrəˌskōˈpisəd·ē\ *n* -ES

**hygroscopic cell** *n* : BULLIFORM CELL

**hygroscopic coefficient** *n* : the percentage of water that is absorbed and held in equilibrium by a soil in a saturated atmosphere

**hygroscopic moisture** *or* **hygroscopic water** *n* : moisture held firmly as a film on soil particles and not responding to capillary action

**hy·gro·stat** \ˈhīgrəˌstat\ *n* -s [*hygr-* + *-stat*] : HUMIDISTAT

**hy·gro·thermal** \ˈhīgrə+\ *adj* [*hygr-* + *thermal*] : of or relating to a combination of moisture and heat

**hy·gro·ther·mo·graph** \ˌhīgrəˈthərməˌgraf\ *n* [*hygr-* + *therm-* + *-graph*] : an instrument that records both humidity and temperature on the same chart

**hying** *pres part of* HIE

**hyk·sos** \ˈhikˌsōs, -sās, -sōs, -səs\ *adj, usu cap* [Gk *Hyksōs*, dynasty ruling Egypt, fr. Egypt *ḥq3 ḫ3swt* ruler of the countries of the nomads] : of or relating to a Semite dynasty ruling Egypt from about 1650 to 1580 B.C. and known as the Shepherd kings

**hyl-** *or* **hylo-** *comb form* [Gk, wood, matter, fr. *hylē* wood, forest, material, matter] **1** : matter : material ⟨*hylo*morphism⟩ ⟨*hylo*morphous⟩ **2** : wood ⟨*hylo*phagous⟩ : forest ⟨*Hylo*cichla⟩

**hy·la** \ˈhīlə\ *n* [NL, fr. Gk *hylē* wood, forest] **1** *cap* : a large genus (the type of the family Hylidae) of arciferous amphibians comprising the typical toads that have swollen terminal phalanges resembling claws and forming adhesive pads adapted to an arboreal habitat **2** -s : any amphibian of the genus *Hyla; broadly* : TREE TOAD

**hy·lam** \(ˈ)hīˈläm\ *n, pl* **hylam** *or* **hylams** *usu cap* **1 a** : a people of southeastern China derived from intermarriage between the Chinese and the Li tribesmen of the island of Hainan **b** : a member of such people **2** : the language of the Hylam people

**hy·le** \ˈhī(ˌ)lē\ *n* -s [LL, matter, fr. Gk *hylē* wood, matter; perh. akin to OE *syll* sill — more at SILL] *philos* : whatever receives form or determination from outside itself : MATTER; *esp* : CHAOS 2

**hy·le·an** \(ˈ)hīˈlēən\ *adj* [prob. fr. G *Hyläa*, region of tropical rain forest in the basin of the Amazon river in So. America (fr. Gk *Hylaia*, forested region on what is now the Dnieper river in the Ukraine, fr. *hylaia*, fem. of *hylaios* of the forest, wild, fr. *hylē* wood, forest) + E *-an*] : covered with forest : WOODED

**hy·leg** \ˈhīˌleg\ *n* -s [modif. of Per *hailāj* material body] : the astrological position of the planets at the time of birth

**hy·le·gi·a·cal** \ˌhīləˈjīəkəl\ *adj* [irreg. fr. *hyleg*] : of or relating to a hyleg

**hy·le·mya** \ˌhīləˈmīə\ *n, cap* [NL, fr. Gk *hylē* wood, forest + *mya, myia* fly — more at MIDGE] : a genus of two-winged flies (family Anthomyiidae) including numerous species having larvae that are maggots (as the onion maggot) boring in economically important plants

**hy·lic** \ˈhīlik\ *adj* [LL *hylicus*, fr. Gk *hylikos*, fr. *hylē* wood, matter + *-ikos* -ic] **1** : of or relating to matter : MATERIAL, CORPOREAL ⟨~ wants⟩ **2** : of or relating to the lowest of the three Gnostic divisions of mankind — compare ²PSYCHIC 3, ²PNEUMATIC 1

**hy·lid** \ˈhīləd\ *n* -s [NL *Hylidae*] : a tree toad of the family Hylidae

**hy·li·dae** \ˈhīləˌdē\ *n pl, cap* [NL, fr. *Hyla*, type genus + *-idae*] : a large family of predominantly arboreal rather slender-bodied frogs with elongated hind limbs, rounded adhesive disks on the digits, and the thumbs not enlarged in the male — see TREE TOAD

**hy·lob·a·tes** \hīˈläbəˌtēz\ *n, cap* [NL, fr. *hyl-* + *-bates*] : a genus of primates comprising the typical gibbons that with the siamang and extinct related forms make up a subfamily of Pongidae or in some classifications a separate family

**hy·lo·cereus** \ˈhīlō+\ *n, cap* [NL, fr. *hyl-* + *Cereus*] : a genus of climbing sometimes epiphytic tropical American cacti with angular stems and mostly white very showy fragrant flowers — see NIGHT-BLOOMING CEREUS

**hy·lo·cich·la** \ˌhīlōˈsiklə\ *n, cap* [NL, fr. *hyl-* + Gk *kichlē* thrush; akin to Gk *chelidōn* swallow — more at CELANDINE] : a genus of thrushes containing the wood thrush, hermit thrush, veery, and other American species

**hy·lo·co·mi·um** \-ˈkōmēəm\ *n, cap* [NL, fr. *hyl-* + Gk *komē* hair + NL *-ium*] : a small genus of mostly feathery mosses of the family Hypnaceae

**hy·lo·des** \hīˈlō(ˌ)dēz\ [NL, fr. *Hyla* + *-odes*] *syn of* ELEUTHERODACTYLUS

**hy·loid** \ˈhīˌlȯid\ *adj* [NL *Hyla* + E *-oid*] : resembling or belonging to the family Hylidae

**hy·lo·mor·phic** *also* **hy·le·mor·phic** \ˌhīləˈmȯrfik\ *adj* [*hylomorphism, hylemorphism* + *-ic*] : of, relating to, or based on hylomorphism

**hy·lo·mor·phism** *also* **hy·le·mor·phism** \ˌ==ˈmȯ(r)ˌfizəm\ *n* -s [*hylomorphism* fr. *hyl-* + *morph-* + *-ism*; *hylemorphism* alter. (influenced by Gk *hylē* matter) of *hylomorphism*] *Aristotelianism* : a doctrine that corporeal beings consist of a combination of Aristotelian forms and primordial matter

**hy·lo·mor·phous** \ˌ==ˈmȯrfəs\ *adj* [*hyl-* + *-morphous*] : having a material form

**hy·lo·mys** \ˈhīləˌmis\ [NL, fr. *hyl-* + *-mys*] *syn of* ECHINOSOREX

**hy·loph·a·gous** \(ˈ)hīˈläfəgəs\ *adj* [*hyl-* + *-phagous*] *zool* : eating wood ⟨~ insects⟩

**hy·lo·theism** \ˈhīlō+\ *n* [*hyl-* + *theism*] : a doctrine equating God with matter — compare MATERIALISM

**hy·lo·the·ist** \"+\ *n* [*hyl-* + *theist*] : an advocate of hylotheism — **hy·lo·the·istic** \"+\ *adj*

**hy·lot·o·mous** \(ˈ)hīˈläd·əməs\ *adj* [Gk *hylotomos*, fr. *hyl-* + *tomos* cutting, sharp, fr. *temnein* to cut — more at TOME] *zool* : cutting wood ⟨~ insects⟩

**hy·lo·zo·ic** \ˌhīləˈzōik\ *adj* [*hyl-* + *zo-* + *-ic*] : of or relating to hylozoism

**hy·lo·zo·ism** \ˌ==ˈzōˌizəm\ *n* [*hyl-* + *zo-* + *-ism*] : a doctrine that all matter is animated — used esp. of the theories of early Greek philosophers

**hy·lo·zo·ist** \ˌhīləˈzōəst\ *n* -s [*hyl-* + *zo-* + *-ist*] : an advocate of hylozoism

**hy·lo·zo·is·tic** \ˈhīləzōˈistik\ *adj* [*hyl-* + *zo-* + *-istic*] : of, relating to, or having the characteristics of hylozoism or the hylozoists

**¹hy·men** \ˈhīmən\ *n* -s [L, fr. Gk *hymēn* wedding song, fr. *Hymēn* Hymen, god of marriage (lit., a wedding cry); perh. akin to Gk *hymnos* hymn, song of praise] **1** *archaic* : MARRIAGE **2** *archaic* : a wedding song

**²hymen** \"\ *n* -s [LL, fr. Gk *hymēn* membrane, caul; prob. akin to Skt *syūman* band, thong, L *suere* to sew — more at SEW] : a fold of mucous membrane partly closing the orifice of the vagina — called also *maidenhead*

**hymen-** *or* **hymeno-** *comb form* [NL, fr. Gk, fr. *hymen-*, *hymēn* membrane, caul] : hymen : membrane ⟨*hymeno*tomy⟩ ⟨*Hymeno*ptera⟩

**hy·me·naea** \ˌhēməˈnēə\ *n, cap* [NL, prob. fr. L *hymenaeus* wedding song, marriage] : a genus of tropical American timber trees (family Leguminosae) having large white or purplish flowers in panicles and pinnate leaves consisting of a single pair of large thick glossy leaflets — see COURBARIL

**hy·me·na·ic meter** \ˌ==ˈnāik-\ *n* [LL *hymenaicum metrum*] : a dactylic dimeter — symbol ‒◡◡|‒◡◡

**hy·men·al** \ˈhīmənᵊl\ *adj* [²*hymen* + *-al*] : of, relating to, or affecting the hymen

**¹hy·me·ne·al** \ˌhīməˈnēəl\ *adj* [L *hymenaeus* marriage, wedding song (fr. Gk *hymenaios*, fr. *Hymen-*, *Hymēn* Hymen) + E *-al*] : of or relating to marriage : NUPTIAL — **hy·me·ne·al·ly** \-ēəlē, -lī\ *adv*

**²hymeneal** \"\ *n* -s **1 hymeneals** *pl, archaic* : NUPTIALS **2** *archaic* : a wedding hymn

**hymenean** *n* -s [L *hymenaeus* wedding, wedding song + E *-an*] *obs* : ¹HYMEN

**hy·me·ni·al** \(ˈ)hīˈmēnēəl\ *adj* [NL *hymenium* + E *-al*] : of or relating to the hymenium

**hymenial layer** *n* : HYMENIUM

**hy·me·nif·er·ous** \ˌhīməˈnif(ə)rəs\ *adj* [NL *hymenium* + E *-ferous*] : having a hymenium

**hy·me·ni·um** \hīˈmēnēəm\ *n, pl* **hyme·nia** \-nēə\ *or* **hymeniums** [NL, fr. *hymen-* + *-ium*] : a spore-bearing layer in fungi or their fruiting bodies (as apothecia or the sporophores of agarics) consisting of a group of asci or basidia often interspersed with paraphyses, setae, and other sterile structures

**hy·me·no·cal·lis** \ˌhīmənōˈkaləs\ *n, cap* [NL, fr. *hymen-* + *-callis* (fr. Gk *kallos* beauty); fr. the delicate texture of the perianth — more at CALLI-] : a genus of tropical and subtropical American bulbous plants (family Amaryllidaceae) with linear basal leaves and umbels of usu. white or pink but sometimes yellow tubular flowers — compare PERUVIAN DAFFODIL

**hy·me·no·chae·te** \-ˈkēd·(ˌ)ē\ *n, cap* [NL fr. *hymen-* + Gk *chaitē* long flowing hair — more at CHAETA] : a genus of fungi (family Thelephoraceae) having a corky or leathery sporophore and a hymenium which appears downy because of the many simple cystidia projecting from it — see BROWN ROOT DISEASE

**hy·me·no·gas·tra·ce·ae** \-(ˌ)nōˌgaˈstrāsēˌē\ *n pl, cap* [NL, fr. *Hymenogastr-*, *Hymenogaster*, type genus (fr. *hymen-* + *-gaster*) + *-aceae*] : a family of basidiomycetous fungi of the order Hymenogastrales forming subterranean irregularly globose sporophores — see FALSE TRUFFLE, RHIZOPOGON

**hy·me·no·gas·tra·les** \-āˈ(ˌ)lēz\ *n pl, cap* [NL, fr. *Hymenogastr-*, *Hymenogaster*, genus of fungi + *-ales*] : an order of gasteromycetous fungi (subclass Homobasidiomycetes) having a distinct basidiocarp with a usu. fleshy or waxy gleba which remains closed at least until after the basidia have discharged the basidiospores

**hy·men·oid** \ˈhīməˌnȯid\ *adj* [Gk *hymenoeidēs*, fr. *hymeno-* hymen- + *-eidēs* -oid] : MEMBRANOUS

**hy·me·no·le·pi·did** \ˌhīmənōˈlepəˌdid\ *adj* [NL *Hymenolepididae*, family of tapeworms, fr. *Hymenolepid-*, *Hymenolepis*, type genus + *-idae*] : of or relating to the genus *Hymenolepis* or family Hymenolepididae

**hy·me·nol·e·pis** \ˌ==ˈnäləpəs\ *n, cap* [NL, fr. *hymen-* + *-lepis*] : a genus of small taenioid tapeworms (type of the family Hymenolepididae) including numerous comparatively innocuous parasites (as the dwarf tapeworm of man) of birds and mammals that usu. require insect intermediate hosts but may be able in some cases (as the dwarf tapeworm) to complete the life cycle in a single host by means of a hexacanth which hatches in the intestine, invades a villus, and there develops into a cysticercoid which ultimately escapes and develops into an adult tapeworm in the lumen of the intestine

**hy·me·no·lichenes** \ˈhīmənō+\ *n pl, cap* [NL, fr. *hymen-* + *Lichenes*] : a subgroup of Lichenes comprising lichens in which the fungal component is a hymenomycete and being coextensive with the group Basidiolichenes

**hy·me·no·my·cete** \-ˌmīˌsēt, -ˌmīˈsēt\ *n* -s [NL *Hymenomycetes*] **1** : a fungus of the order Agaricales **2** : a fungus having a fruiting body with a definite hymenium

**hy·me·no·my·ce·tes** \-ˌmīˈsēd·(ˌ)ēz\ *n pl, cap* [NL, fr. *hymen-* + *-mycetes*] *in some classifications* : a subclass of Basidiomycetes coextensive with the order Agaricales

**hy·me·no·my·ce·tous** \-ˈsēd·əs\ *adj* [*hymen-* + *-mycetous*] : of, relating to, or being a hymenomycete : having a hymenium

**hy·meno·phore** \hīˈmenəˌfō(ə)r, ˈhīmənō-\ *also* **hy·me·noph·o·rum** \ˌhīməˈnäfərəm\ *n, pl* **hymenophores** \-ˌfō(ə)rz\ *also* **hymenopho·ra** \-äf(ə)rə\ [NL *hymenophorum*, fr. *hymeno-* (irreg. fr. *hymenium*) + *-phorum*] **1** : the hymenium-bearing portion of the sporophore in fungi **2** : SPOROPHORE

**hy·me·no·phyl·la·ce·ae** \ˌhīmə(ˌ)nōfəˈlāsēˌē\ *n pl, cap* [NL, fr. *Hymenophyllum*, type genus + *-aceae*] : a family of ferns having delicate fronds with sessile sporangia on a receptacle resembling a bristle and surrounded by a cup-shaped, tubular, or 2-valved involucre — **hy·me·no·phyl·la·ceous** \ˌ==(ˌ)==ˈlāshəs\ *adj*

**hy·me·no·phyl·li·tes** \ˌ==(ˌ)=fəˈlīd·(ˌ)ēz\ *n pl, cap* [NL, fr. *Hymenophyllum*, genus of ferns + *-ites* -ite] : a genus of fossil ferns of the Carboniferous and perhaps of more recent age bearing a superficial resemblance to the existing genus *Hymenophyllum*

**hy·me·no·phyl·lum** \ˌ===ˈfiləm\ *n, cap* [NL, fr. *hymen-* + *-phyllum*] : a genus (the type of the family Hymenophyllaceae) of tropical hygrophytic and usu. epiphytic ferns distinguished from *Trichomanes* by having the valves of the involucre bearing the sporangia separate

**hy·me·nop·ter** \ˌhīməˈnäptə(r)\ *n* -s [NL *Hymenoptera*] : HYMENOPTERON

**hy·me·nop·tera** \-ˈnäptərə\ *n pl, cap* [NL, fr. Gk, neut. pl. of *hymenopteros* membrane-winged, fr. *hymeno-* (fr. *hymen-*, *hymēn* membrane, caul) + *-pteros* -pterous — more at HYMEN] : an extensive order of highly specialized insects that include the bees, wasps, ants, ichneumons, sawflies, gall wasps, and related forms, that often associate in large colonies with complex social organization, that have usu. four membranous wings typically with a thickened dark spot near the anterior edge of the forewings, the abdomen generally borne on a slender pedicel, and in the female complex ovipositors at the posterior end of the body which may be modified into sawing, boring, or piercing organs or in one group converted into a sting, and that undergo complete metamorphosis, the larva being usu. a footless grub — **hy·me·nop·ter·ous** \ˌ==ˈ=t(ə)rəs\ *adj*

**hy·me·nop·ter·ist** \ˌ==ˈtərəst\ *or* **hy·me·nop·ter·ol·o·gist** \ˌ==ˌ==ˈräləjəst\ *n* -s : a specialist in the Hymenoptera

**hy·me·nop·ter·ol·o·gy** \ˌ==ˌ==ˈräləjē\ *n* -ES [ISV *hymenoptero-* (fr. NL *Hymenoptera*) + *-logy*; prob. orig. formed as F *hyménoptérologie*] : a branch of entomology concerned with Hymenoptera

**hy·me·nop·ter·on** \ˌ==ˈtəˌrän, -rən\ *also* **hy·me·nop·ter·an** \-tərən\ *n, pl* **hymenop·tera** \-tərə\ [*hymenopteron* fr. NL *Hymenopteron*, sing. of *Hymenoptera*; *hymenopteran* fr. NL *Hymenoptera* + E *-an*] : one of the Hymenoptera

**hy·men·ot·o·my** \ˌhīməˈnäd·əmē\ *n* -ES [ISV *hymen-* + *-tomy*; prob. orig. formed as F *hyménotomie*] : surgical incision of the hymen

**hymens** *pl of* HYMEN

**hy·met·ti·an** \(ˈ)hīˈmed·ēən\ *also* **hy·met·tic** \-d·ik\ *adj, usu cap* [L *Hymettius* (fr. *Hymettus*, mountain near Athens, Greece fr. Gk *Hymēttos*) + E *-an* or *-ic*] : of or relating to Mount Hymettus ⟨*Hymettian* marble⟩ ⟨*Hymettian* honey⟩

**¹hymn** \ˈhim\ *n* -s *often attrib* [ME *ymne*, *hympne*, partly fr. OE *ymen*, *hymen*, fr. L *hymnus* and partly fr. MF *himpne*, fr. ML *hympnus*, fr. L *hymnus* and partly fr. OF *ymne*, fr. ML *ymnus*, fr. L *hymnus*; L *hymnus* fr. Gk *hymnos* song of praise] **1 a** : a song of praise to God ⟨grows into the chorus . . . with its triumphal ~: Lift up your heads, O ye gates —J.P.Larsen⟩ **b** : a metrical composition adapted for singing in a religious service ⟨collection of ~s, carols, anthems, gospel songs —*Saturday Rev.*⟩ **2** : a song of praise or joy ⟨in jolly ~s they praise the god of wine —John Dryden⟩ **3** : something resembling a hymn esp. in expressing praise : PAEAN ⟨this prose ~ of contentment in simple and external things —Douglas Bush⟩ ⟨the plot of this ~ to American domesticity —Jack Weeks⟩ ⟨painted a ~ to the wonder of light —Lewis Mumford⟩

**²hymn** \"\ *vb* **hymned**; **hymned**; **hymning** \ˈhimiŋ *sometimes* -mniŋ\ **hymns** *vt* : to sing the praises of : EXTOL ⟨still ~s his love of the earth and proclaims his faith in the race that inhabits it —B.R.Redman⟩; *specif* : to worship in song ~ *vi* : SING ⟨the lark ~s on high⟩; *specif* : to sing a hymn ⟨the choir ~s softly in the chancel⟩

**¹hym·nal** \ˈhimnəl\ *n* -s [ME *hymnale*, fr. ML *hymnale*, *hymnare*, fr. L *hymnus* hymn + *-ale* (neut. of *-alis* -al) or *-are* (neut. of *-aris* -ar)] : a collection of church hymns : HYMNBOOK

**²hymnal** \"\ *adj* [L *hymnus* hymn + E *-al*] : of or relating to a hymn ⟨a ~ rite⟩

**hym·na·ry** \ˈhimnərē\ *also* **hym·nar·i·um** \him'na(a)rēəm\ *n, pl* **hymnaries** \-nərēz\ *also* **hymnar·ia** \-na(a)rēə\ [ML *hymnarium*, fr. L *hymnus* hymn + *-arium* -ary] : ¹HYMNAL

**hymn board** *also* **hymn tablet** *n* : a usu. wooden tablet that holds removable numerals and is hung on a wall or pillar of a church to inform the congregation of the numbers of the hymns and responsive readings for a service of worship

HYMNS
29
132
SEL84
PSALM
23

hymn board

**hymnbook** \ˈ=ˌ=\ *n* : ¹HYMNAL

**hymner** \ˈhimə(r), -mnə-\ *n* -s : one that sings hymns

**hym·nic** \ˈhimnik\ *adj* : of, relating to, or having the characteristics of a hymn ⟨~ praise⟩ ⟨~ prose⟩

**hym·nist** \-nəst\ *n* -s : a writer of hymns

**hymn·less** \ˈhimləs\ *adj* : lacking a hymn

**hymnlike** \ˈ=ˌ=\ *adj* : resembling or suggesting a hymn

**hym·no·dist** \ˈhimnədəst\ *n* -s [LL *hymnodia* hymnody + E *-ist*] : HYMNIST

**hym·no·dy** \-dē\ *n* -ES [LL *hymnodia*, fr. Gk *hymnōidia*, fr. *hymnōidein* to sing a hymn or song of praise (fr. *hymnos* hymn, song of praise + *aeidein* to sing) + *-ia* -y — more at ODE] **1** : the singing of hymns **2** : the writing of hymns ⟨a pioneer in Byzantine ~, whose compositions were to come into extensive use —K.S.Latourette⟩ **3 a** : a study of hymns and their composition ⟨an authority on ~⟩ **b** : a body of hymns of a specified kind or period ⟨~ of the early church⟩

**hym·nog·ra·pher** \him'nägrəfə(r)\ *n* -s [Gk *hymnographos* (fr. *hymnos* hymn + *-graphos* -graph) + E *-er*] **1** : a writer on hymnography **2** : HYMNIST

**hym·nog·ra·phy** \-fē\ *n* -ES [*hymnographer* + *-y*] **1** : an exposition and bibliography of hymns **2** : HYMNODY

**hym·no·log·ic** \ˈhimnəˈläjik\ *or* **hym·no·log·i·cal** \-jəkəl\ *adj* : of or relating to hymnology — **hym·no·log·i·cal·ly** \-jək(ə)lē\ *adv*

**hym·nol·o·gist** \him'näləjəst\ *n* -s : HYMNIST

**hym·nol·o·gy** \-jē\ *n* -ES [Gk *hymnologia* singing of hymns, fr. *hymnos* song of praise, hymn + *-logia* -logy] : HYMNODY

**hymns** *pl of* HYMN, *pres 3d sing of* HYMN

**hyne** \ˈhīn\ *adv* [ME, prob. alter. of ME (northern dial.) *hethen*, fr. ON *hethan* hence; akin to OE *heonan* hence — more at HENCE] *now dial Eng* : HENCE

**hy·no·bi·idae** \ˌhīnōˈbīəˌdē\ *n pl, cap* [NL, fr. *Hynobius*, type genus (fr. *hyno-* — perh. fr. Gk *hynis* plowshare — + NL *-bius*) + *-idae*] : a small family of primitive Asiatic salamanders (suborder Cryptobranchoidea) sometimes included in the Ambystomidae from which they can be distinguished by more adult skull characters, smaller size, and short saccular egg pouches

**¹hyo-** — see HY-

**²hyo-** *comb form* [L&Gk; L, fr. Gk, fr. *hys* swine — more at SOW (swine)] : derived from or related to swine ⟨*hyo*deoxycholic⟩

**hyo·branchial** \ˈhīō+\ *adj* [*hy-* + *branchial*] : of, relating to, or joining the hyoid and branchial arches

**hyo·bran·chi·um** \ˌhīōˈbraŋkēəm\ *n, pl* **hyobran·chia** \-ēə\ [NL, fr. *hy-* + *-branchium* (fr. Gk *branchion* gill) — more at BRANCHIA] : a typically somewhat Y-shaped bone that serves to support the tongue and tongue muscles in a snake and is considered to result from fusion of the hyoid and remnants of the branchial arches

**hyo·deoxycholic acid** *or* **hyo·desoxycholic acid** \ˈhī(ˌ)ō+ . . . -\ *n* [ISV ²*hyo-* + *deoxy-* or *desoxy-* + *cholic*] : a crystalline bile acid $C_{22}H_{37}(OH)_2COOH$ found in the bile of the pig and wild boar; 3,6-dihydroxy-cholanic acid

**hy·o·don** [NL, fr. *hy-* + *-odon*] *syn of* HIODON

**hyo·epiglottic** *also* **hyo·epiglottidean** \ˈhī(ˌ)ō+\ *adj* [*hy-* + *epiglottic* or *epiglottidean*] : connecting the hyoid bone and epiglottis

**hyo·glossal** \ˈhīō+\ *adj* [*hy-* + *glossal*] **1** : of or relating to the tongue and hyoid arch **2** [NL *hyoglossus* + E *-al*] : of or relating to the hyoglossus

**hyo·glos·sus** \-ˈgläsəs, -lȯs-\ *n, pl* **hyoglos·si** \-ˌsī\ [NL, fr. *hy-* + *-glossus* (fr. Gk *glōssa* tongue) — more at GLOSS] : a flat muscle on each side of the tongue connecting it with the body and greater cornu of the hyoid

**hy·oid** \ˈhīˌȯid\ *also* **hy·oi·dal** \(ˈ)hīˈȯidᵊl\ *or* **hy·oi·de·an** \-dēən\ *adj* [*hyoid* fr. NL *hyoides* hyoid bone; *hyoidal* fr. *hyoid* + *-al*; *hyoidean* fr. NL *hyoides* + E *-an*] **1** : of, relating to, or being the hyoid bone **2** : of, relating to, or being the second postoral visceral arch from which the hyoid bone of the higher vertebrates is in part formed

**hyoid bone** *also* **hyoid** *n* -s [NL *hyoides*, fr. Gk *hyoeidēs*, adj., shaped like the letter upsilon (Υ, υ), being the hyoid bone, fr. *hyo-* (fr. *y*, *hy* upsilon) + *-eidēs* -oid] : a bone or complex of bones situated at the base of the tongue and developed from the second and third visceral arches, supporting the tongue and its muscles, and being in man a U-shaped structure placed horizontally with the convexity forward, two large cornua directed backward, and two lesser cornua directed upward and backward

**hy·ol·i·thes** \hīˈäləˌthēz\ *n, cap* [NL, prob. fr. *hy-* + *-lithes* (fr. Gk *lithos* stone)] : a genus of Paleozoic swimming pteropod mollusks esp. common in the Cambrian — **hy·ol·i·thid** \-thəd\ *adj or n*

**hyo·mandibula** \ˈhī(ˌ)ō+\ *n* -s [NL, fr. *hy-* + LL *mandibula*] **1** : the hyomandibular arch **2** : a bone or cartilage derived from the hyomandibular arch

**¹hyo·mandibular** \"+\ *adj* [*hy-* + *mandibular*] : of or derived from the hyoid arch and mandible; *specif* : being or relating to the dorsal segment of the hyoid arch

**²hyomandibular** \"\ *n* -s : a bone or cartilage derived from the dorsal hyoid arch, being part of the articulating mechanism of the lower jaw in fishes, and forming the columella or stapes of the ear of higher vertebrates

**hyo·mental** \ˈhīō+\ *adj* [*hy-* + *mental* (of the chin)] : of or relating to the hyoid bone and chin

**hyo·plastron** \"+\ *n, pl* **hyoplastra** [*hy-* + *plastron*] : the second lateral bony plate in the plastron of most turtles — called also *hyosternum*

**hyo·scapular** \"+\ *adj* [*hy-* + *scapular*] : of or relating to the hyoid bone and scapula

**hy·o·scine** \ˈhīəˌsēn, -sən\ *n* -s [ISV *hyosc-* (fr. NL *Hyoscyamus*, genus that produces it) + *-ine*; orig. formed as G *hyoscin*] : SCOPOLAMINE; *esp* : the levorotatory form of scopolamine

**hy·o·scy·a·mine** \ˌhīəˈsīəˌmēn, -mən\ *n* -s [G *hyoscyamin*, fr. NL *Hyoscyamus* (genus that produces it) + G *-in* -ine] : a poisonous crystalline alkaloid $C_{17}H_{23}NO_3$ known in three optically isomeric forms : the ester of tropine and tropic acid; *esp* : the levorotatory form of this alkaloid that readily yields the racemic form atropine (as by treatment with alkali), that occurs in henbane, belladonna, and various other plants of the family Solanaceae (as species of *Datura*), and that is more active than atropine in most pharmacological effects and is used similarly (as in sedation and in relieving spasms)

**hy·o·scy·a·mus** \-məs\ *n* [NL, fr. L, henbane, fr. Gk *hyoskyamos*, lit., swine's bean, fr. *hyos* (gen. of *hys* swine) + *kyamos* bean — more at SOW (swine)] **1** *cap* : a genus of poisonous Eurasian herbs (family Solanaceae) having simple leaves, somewhat irregular flowers, and circumscissile capsular fruit — see HENBANE **2** -ES : the dried leaves of the henbane containing the alkaloids hyoscyamine and scopolamine and used as an antispasmodic and sedative

**hyo·sternal** \ˈhīō+\ *adj* [*hy-* + *sternal*] **1** : of or relating to the hyoid bone and sternum **2** [NL *hyosternum* + E *-al*] : of or relating to the hyosternum

**hyo·sternum** \"+\ *n, pl* **hyosterna** [NL, fr. *hy-* + *sternum*] : HYOPLASTRON

**hyo·strongylus** \"+\ *n, cap* [NL, fr. ²*hyo-* + *Strongylus* (genus of parasitic nematode worms)] : a genus of nematode worms (family Trichostrongylidae) including the common small red stomach worm (*H. rubidus*) of swine

**hy·o·sty·lic** \ˈhīōˈstīlik\ *adj* [*hy-* + *-stylic*] : having the jaws connected with the cranium by the hyomandibular ⟨a large majority of fishes are ~⟩ — **hyo·sty·ly** \ˈ==ˌ=lē\ *n* -ES

**hy·o·there** \ˈhīōˌthi(ə)r\ *n* -s [NL *Hyotherium*] : a member of the genus *Hyotherium*

**hy·o·the·ri·um** \ˌhīōˈthirēəm\ *n, cap* [NL, fr. ²*hyo-* + *-therium*] : a genus of swine of the Miocene and lower Pliocene on the direct ancestral line of the modern wild boar and domestic swine

**hyo·thyreoid** \ˈhīō+\ *adj* [*hy-* + *thyreoid*] : THYROHYOID

**hyo·thyroid** \"+\ *adj* [*hy-* + *thyroid*] : THYROHYOID

**hyp** *n* -s [by shortening] *obs* : HYPOCHONDRIA

**hyp-** — see HYPO-

**hyp** *abbr* hypothesis; hypothetical

**hyp·abyssal** \¦hip+\ *adj* [ISV *hypo-* + *abyssal;* orig. formed as G *hypabyssisch*] **:** of or relating to a fine-grained igneous rock intermediate in texture between the plutonites and extrusive rocks and usu. formed at a moderate distance below the surface

**hyp·acu·sic** \¦hipə¦kyüsik, -kü-\ *or* **hyp·acou·sic** \-kü-\ *adj* [NL *hypacusia, hypacousia* defective hearing (fr. *hypo-* + *-acusia, -acousia*) + E *-ic*] **:** slightly deaf — used esp. of partial deafness associated with lessened irritability of the auditory nerve

**hy·pae·thral** \hī'pēthrəl, hə'-\ *adj* [L *hypaethrus* in the open air, uncovered (fr. Gk *hypaithros*, fr. *hypo-* + *-aithros* — fr. *aithēr* ether, heaven, air) + E *-al* — more at ETHER] **1** *of an ancient temple* **:** having a roofless central space — opposed to *cleithral* **2 :** open to the sky **3 :** OUTDOOR

**hyp·algesia** \¦hip, ¦hīp+\ *also* **hyp·al·gia** \hi'palj(ē)ə, hī'-\ *n* [NL, fr. *hypo-* + *algesia* or *-algia*] **:** diminished sensitivity to pain

**hyp·al·lac·tic** \¦hipə¦laktik, ¦hīp-\ *adj* [Gk *hypallaktikos*, fr. (assumed) Gk *hypallaktos* (verbal of Gk *hypallassein* to interchange, exchange) + Gk *-icos* -ic] **:** of, relating to, or of the nature of hypallage

**hy·pal·la·ge** \hi'palə(,)jē, hī'-\ *n* -S [LL, fr. Gk *hypallagē*, lit., interchange, fr. *hypallassein* to interchange, fr. *hypo-* + *allassein* to change (fr. *allos* other) — more at ELSE] **:** interchange in syntactic relationship between two terms (as in "you are lost to joy" for "joy is lost to you")

**hy·pan·dri·um** \hi'pandrēəm, hī'-\ *n, pl* **hypan·dria** \-ēə\ [NL, fr. *hypo-* + *andr-* + *-ium*] **:** a plate or modified area underlying the genitalia of a male insect; *esp* **:** the fused coxites of the ninth abdominal segment when these form a ventral covering plate for the genitalia

**hy·pan·thi·al** \(')hi¦pan(t)thēəl, (')hī'-\ *adj* **:** of, relating to, or of the nature of a hypanthium

**hy·pan·thi·um** \˸ˌ˸thēəm\ *n, pl* **hypan·thia** \-ēə\ [NL, fr. *hypo-* + *anth-* + *-ium*] **:** an enlargement of the usu. cup-shaped receptacle bearing on its rim the stamens, petals, and sepals of a flower and often enlarging and surrounding the fruits (as in the rose hip) — called also *calyx tube*

**hy·pan·trum** \hi'pan·trəm, hī'-\ *n, pl* **hypan·tra** \-rə\ [NL, fr. *hypo-* + LL *antrum* cavity in the body — more at ANTRUM] **:** a notch on the neural arch at the anterior ends of the vertebrae of various reptiles that articulates with the hyposphene — compare ZYGANTRUM

**hy·pa·pan·te** \ˌēpə,pän'dē\ *n* -S *cap* [LL or LGk; LL *hypapante*, fr. LGk *hypapantē*, lit., meeting, fr. Gk *hypapantan* to meet, fr. *hypo-* + *apantan* to meet — more at APANTESIS] **:** a feast celebrated by the Eastern Orthodox Church on February 2 commemorating primarily the presentation of Jesus and his meeting Simeon and Anna in the temple and secondarily the purification of the Virgin Mary — compare CANDLEMAS

**hyp·apophysis** \¦hip, ¦hīp+\ *n, pl* **hypapophyses** [NL, fr. *hypo-* + *apophysis*] **:** a ventral process or element of a vertebra: as **a :** a hemal spine **b :** HYPOCENTRUM

**hyp·ar·chic** \(')hi¦pärkik, (')hī¦-\ *adj* [*hypo-* + *-archic* (as in *autarchic*)] **:** affected by adjacent genes — used of genes in mosaic tissues that do not manifest their effect if epistatic genes are present in adjacent tissues: compare AUTARCHIC

**hyp·arterial** \¦hip, ¦hīp+\ *adj* [*hypo-* + *arterial*] **:** situated below an artery — used of branches of the bronchi given off below the pulmonary artery; compare EPARTERIAL

**hy·pas·pist** \hi'paspəst\ *n* -S [Gk *hypaspistēs*, fr. *hypaspizein* to serve as shield bearer, fr. *hypo-* + *aspis* shield + *-izein* -ize — more at ASPID-] **:** SHIELD BEARER; *esp* **:** a Macedonian shield bearer

**hyp·automorphic** \¦hip, ¦hīp+\ *adj* [*hypo-* + *automorphic*] **1 :** HYPIDIOMORPHIC **2 :** SUBHEDRAL

**hyp·axial** \(')hip, (')hīp+\ *also* **hyp·axonic** \(¦)hip, (¦)hīp+\ *adj* [*hypaxial* fr. *hypo-* + *axial; hypaxonic* fr. *hypo-* + Gk *axon-, axōn* axle, axis + E *-ic* — more at AXIS] **:** beneath the axis of the vertebral column

**hype** \'hīp\ *n* -S [short for *hypodermic*] **1** *slang* **:** HYPODERMIC **2** *slang* **:** a narcotics addict

**hy·per** \'hīpə(r)\ *vi* -ED/-ING/-S [origin unknown] *chiefly NewEng* **:** BUSTLE, HURRY ⟨must ~ about —J.R.Lowell⟩

**hyper-** *prefix* [alter. (influenced by L *hyper-*) of ME *iper-*, fr. LL *hyper-*, fr. L, fr. Gk, fr. *hyper* — more at OVER] **1 :** over **:** above **:** beyond **:** SUPER- ⟨*hyper*barbarous⟩ ⟨*hyper*emphasis⟩ **2 :** overmuch **:** excessively **:** EXTRA- ⟨*hyper*critical⟩ ⟨*hyper*sensitive⟩ **3 a :** excessive in extent or quality ⟨*hyper*esthesia⟩ ⟨*hyper*emesis⟩ **b :** located above ⟨*hyper*apophysis⟩ **4** *in ancient Greek music* **a :** being the upper octave in a disdiapason ⟨*hyper*lydian⟩ **b** *of an interval* **:** measured upward ⟨*hyper*diapason⟩

**hy·pera** \'hīpərə\ *n, cap* [NL, fr. Gk *hypera* upper rope, brace (of a ship), fr. *hyper* above, over] **:** a large genus of small often mottled or hairy weevils whose legless larvae feed destructively on numerous crop plants (as legumes) and have ventral ridges that function as legs — compare ALFALFA WEEVIL, CLOVER LEAF WEEVIL

**hy·per·acid** \¦hīpə(r)+\ *adj* [*hyper-* + *acid*] **:** excessively acid **:** containing more than the normal amount of acid ⟨a ~ secretion⟩ — **hy·per·acidity** \"+\ *n* -ES

**hy·per·active** \"+\ *adj* [*hyper-* + *active*] **:** excessively or pathologically active

**hy·per·adre·no·cor·ti·cism** \ˌ˸˸ə,drēnō'kȯ(r)d·ə,sizəm, -,dren-\ *n* -S [*hyper-* + *adrenocortical* + *-ism*] **1 :** the presence of excess adrenocortical products in the body **2 :** the syndrome resulting from hyperadrenocorticism that is often a complication of medication with adrenal hormones, fractions, or stimulants

**hyperaemia** *var of* HYPEREMIA

**hyperaesthesia** *var of* HYPERESTHESIA

**hy·per·algesia** \¦hīpə(r)+\ *n* [NL, fr. *hyper-* + *algesia*] **:** increased sensitivity to pain or enhanced intensity of pain sensation — **hy·per·algesic** \"+\ *adj*

**hy·per·apophysis** \"+\ *n, pl* **hyperapophyses** [NL, fr. *hyper-* + *apophysis*] **:** a process on the dorsal side of a vertebra that projects laterally and backward

**hy·per·azotemia** \"+\ *n* [NL, fr. *hyper-* + *azotemia*] **:** the presence of abnormal amounts of nitrogenous substances in the blood

**hy·per·bar·ic** \¦hīpə(r)¦barik\ *adj* [*hyper-* + Gk *baros* weight + E *-ic* — more at GRIEVE] **:** having a specific gravity greater than that of cerebrospinal fluid — used of solutions for spinal anesthesia; opposed to *hypobaric*

**hy·per·ba·ton** \hī'pərbə,tän\ *n, pl* **hyperbatons** \-nz\ *or* **hyperba·ta** \-bəd·ə\ [L, fr. Gk, fr. neut. of *hyperbatos* transposed, inverted, fr. *hyperbainein* to step over, scale, fr. *hyper-* + *bainein* to step, walk — more at COME] **:** a transposition or inversion of idiomatic word order (as "echoed the hills" for "the hills echoed")

**hy·per·bilirubinemia** \¦hīpə(r)+\ *n* [NL, fr. *hyper-* + *bilirubinemia*] **:** BILIRUBINEMIA

**hy·per·bo·la** \hī'pərbələ, -pəb-,-pəib-\ *n, pl* **hyperbolas** \-ləz\ *or* **hyperbo·lae** \-,lē, -,lī\ [NL, fr. Gk *hyperbolē* hyperbola, excess] **:** a plane curve generated by a point so moving that its distance from a fixed point divided by its distance from a fixed line is a positive constant greater than 1 **:** a curve formed by a section of a right circular cone when the cutting plane makes a greater angle with the base than the cone's side makes

hyperbola

**hy·per·bo·le** \-(,)lē\ *n* -S [L, fr. Gk *hyperbolē* hyperbole, excess, extravagance, fr. *hyperballein* to exceed, fr. *hyper-* + *ballein* to cast, throw — more at DEVIL] **:** extravagant exaggeration that represents something as much greater or less, better or worse, or more intense than it really is or that depicts the impossible as actual (as "mile-high ice-cream cones") — opposed to *litotes*

**¹hy·per·bol·ic** \¦hīpə(r)¦bälik, -lēk\ *also* **hy·per·bol·i·cal** \-lәkəl, -lēk-\ *adj* [*hyperbolic* fr. LL *hyperbolicus*, fr. Gk *hyperbolikos* excessive, fr. *hyperbolē* hyperbole, excess + *-ikos* -ic; *hyperbolical*, alter. (influenced by L *hyper-*) of ME *iperbolicalle*, fr. LL *hyperbolicus* + ME *-alle, -al* -al] **:** of, characterized by, or given to hyperbole ⟨a ~ style⟩ — **hy·per·bol·i·cal·ly** \-lәk(ə)lē, -lēk-, -li\ *adv*

**²hyperbolic** \"\ *also* **hyperbolical** \"\ *adj* [*hyperbolic* fr. NL *hyperbola* + E *-ic; hyperbolical* fr. Gk *hyperbolē* hyperbola, excess + E *-ical*] **:** of, relating to, or analogous to a hyperbola

**hyperbolic cosecant** *n* **:** the hyperbolic function that is analogous to the cosecant and defined by the equation $\operatorname{csch} x = \frac{1}{\sinh x}$ — abbr. *csch*

**hyperbolic cosine** *n* **:** the hyperbolic function that is analogous to the cosine and defined by the equation $\cosh x = \frac{e^x + e^{-x}}{2}$ — abbr. *cosh*

**hyperbolic cotangent** *n* **:** the hyperbolic function that is analogous to the cotangent and defined by the equation $\coth x = \frac{\cosh x}{\sinh x}$ — abbr. *coth*

**hyperbolic function** *n* **:** any of a set of six functions analogous to the trigonometric functions but related to the hyperbola in a way similar to that in which trigonometric functions are related to a circle

**hyperbolic geometry** *n* **:** geometry that adopts all of Euclid's axioms except the parallel axiom, this being replaced by the axiom that through any point in a plane there pass more lines than one that do not intersect a given line in the plane

**hyperbolic navigation** *n* **:** a system of radio navigation (as loran) in which the time difference between receipt of signals from two stations of known position determines a line of position in the form of a hyperbola

**hyperbolic paraboloid** *n* **:** a saddle-shaped quadric surface whose sections by planes parallel to one coordinate plane are hyperbolas while those sections by planes parallel to the other two are parabolas if proper orientation of the coordinate axes is assumed

**hyperbolic secant** *n* **:** the hyperbolic function that is analogous to the secant and defined by the equation $\operatorname{sech} x = \frac{1}{\cosh x}$ — abbr. *sech*

**hyperbolic sine** *n* **:** the hyperbolic function that is analogous to the sine and defined by the equation $\sinh x = \frac{e^x - e^{-x}}{2}$ — abbr. *sinh*

**hyperbolic tangent** *n* **:** the hyperbolic function that is analogous to the tangent and defined by the equation $\tanh x = \frac{\sinh x}{\cosh x}$ — abbr. *tanh*

**hy·per·bo·lism** \hī'pərbə,lizəm, -pəb-,-pəib-\ *n* -S [*hyperbole* + *-ism*] **:** HYPERBOLE

**hy·per·bo·list** \-ləst\ *n* -S **:** a user of hyperbole ⟨humorists and ~s —John Hersey⟩

**hy·per·bo·lize** \-,līz\ *vb* -ED/-ING/-S *vi* **:** to indulge in hyperbole ~ *vt* **:** to exaggerate to a hyperbolic degree ⟨~ the esthetic modes of the moment —*Times Lit. Supp.*⟩

**hy·per·bo·loid** \-,lȯid\ *n* -S [NL *hyperbola* + E *-oid*] **:** a quadric surface whose sections by planes parallel to one coordinate plane are ellipses while those sections by planes parallel to the other two are hyperbolas if proper orientation of the coordinate axes is assumed — **hy·per·bo·loi·dal** \˸˸¦˸lȯidᵊl\ *adj*

**hyperboloid of revolution :** the surface generated by a hyperbola rotating about one of its axes

**hy·per·bo·re·al** \¦hīpə(r)¦bōrēəl, -bȯr-\ *adj* [L *Hyperborei* + E *-al*] *archaic* **:** HYPERBOREAN

**¹hy·per·bo·re·an** \-ēən, -,bə¦rē-\ *adj* [L *Hyperborei*, ancient legendary people living in the far north (fr. Gk *Hyperboreoi, Hyperboreioi*, fr. *hyper-* + *boreioi*, masc. pl. of *boreios* northern, of the north wind, fr. *Boreas* north, northwind) + E *-an* — more at BOREAS] **1 :** of, relating to, or inhabiting an extreme northern region **:** FRIGID, FROZEN ⟨drags us out of our ~ gloom into the South —John Davenport⟩ **2 :** of or relating to any of the arctic peoples of Asia or No. America

**²hyperborean** \"\ *n* -S *often cap* **1 :** a member of an arctic people (as the Chukchi and Koryak of northeastern Asia and the Eskimo of No. America) **2 :** one who lives in a cool northern climate ⟨we are *Hyperboreans* — we know well enough how far off we live —W.A.Kaufmann⟩

**hy·per·brachycephal** \¦hīpə(r)+\ *n* [*hyper-* + *brachycephal*] **:** a hyperbrachycephalic person

**hy·per·brachycephalic** \"+\ *adj* [*hyper-* + *brachycephalic*] **:** having a very round or broad head with a cephalic index of over 85

**hy·per·brachycephaly** \"+\ *n* **:** the quality or state of being hyperbrachycephalic

**hy·per·brachycranial** *or* **hy·per·brachycranic** \"+\ *adj* [*hyper-* + *brachycranial* or *brachycranic*] **:** having a very round or broad skull with a cranial index of 85 to 90

**hy·per·brachycrany** \"+\ *n* [ISV *hyper-* + *brachycrany*] **:** the quality or state of being hyperbrachycranial

**hy·per·brachyskelic** \"+\ *adj* [*hyper-* + *brachyskelic*] **:** having the length of the legs less than three-fourths that of the trunk with a skelic index below 75

**hy·per·cal·ce·mia** *also* **hy·per·cal·cae·mia** \,hīpə(r),kal'sēmēə\ *n* [NL, fr. *hyper-* + *calcemia, calcaemia* calcium in the blood (fr. *calc-* + *-emia, -aemia*)] **:** an excess of calcium in the blood — **hy·per·cal·ce·mic** \¦˸˸¦˸sēmik\ *adj*

**hy·per·cap·nia** \,hīpə(r)'kapnēə\ *n* [NL, fr. *hyper-* + *-capnia*] **:** the presence of excessive amounts of carbon dioxide in the blood — **hy·per·cap·nic** \¦˸˸¦˸nik\ *adj*

**hy·per·catalectic** \¦˸˸+\ *adj* [LL *hypercatalecticus*, fr. *hypercatalectus* (fr. Gk *hyperkatalēktos*, fr. *hyper-* + *katalēktos* catalectic) + *-icus* -ic — more at CATALECTIC] **:** of, relating to, or exhibiting hypercatalexis

**hy·per·catalexis** \"+\ *n* [NL, fr. *hyper-* + *catalexis*] **:** occurrence of an additional syllable at the end of a line of verse after the line is metrically complete; *esp* **:** occurrence of a syllable after the last complete dipody in verse measured by dipodies

**hy·per·cathexis** \"+\ *n* [NL, fr. *hyper-* + *cathexis*] **:** excessive concentration of desire upon a particular object

**hy·per·ce·men·to·sis** \,hīpə(r),sē,men·¦tōsəs\ *n, pl* **hypercemento·ses** \-ō,sēz\ [NL, fr. *hyper-* + *cementum* + *-osis*] **:** excessive formation of cementum at the root of a tooth

**hy·per·chamaerrhine** \¦hīpə(r)+\ *adj* [ISV *hyper-* + *chamaerrhine;* orig. formed as G *hyperchamärrhin*] **:** having a very short broad nose with a nasal index of 58 or above

**hy·per·chamaerrhiny** \"+\ *n* [ISV *hyper-* + *chamaerrhiny*] **:** the quality or state of being hyperchamaerrhine

**hy·per·chlor·hy·dria** \¦˸˸,klōr'hīdrēə\ *n* -S [NL, fr. *hyper-* + *-chlorhydria* hydrochloric acid in the gastric juice (fr. *chlor-* + *hydr-* + *-ia*)] **:** the presence of a greater than typical proportion of hydrochloric acid in gastric juice that occurs in many normal individuals but is esp. characteristic of various pathologic states (as ulceration) — compare ACHLORHYDRIA, HYPOCHLORHYDRIA

**hy·per·cholesterolemia** *or* **hy·per·cholesteremia** \¦˸˸+\ *also* **hy·per·cho·les·ter·in·emia** \"+kə,lestərə¦nēmēə\ *n* [NL, fr. *hyper-* + *cholesterolemia*, or *cholesteremia*, or *-cholesterinemia*, (fr. E *cholesterin* + NL *-emia*)] **:** the presence of excess cholesterol in the blood — **hy·per·cho·les·ter·e·mic** \-tə¦rēmik\ *adj*

**hy·per·chro·ma·tism** \,˸˸'krōmə,tizəm\ *n* -S [*hyper-* + *chromatin* + *-ism*] **:** the development of excess chromatin or of excessive nuclear staining esp. as a part of a pathologic process

**hy·per·chromatosis** \¦hīpə(r)+\ *n* [NL, fr. *hyper-* + *chromatosis*] **1 :** HYPERCHROMIA **2 :** HYPERCHROMATISM

**hy·per·chro·mia** \,˸˸'krōmēə\ *n* -S [NL, fr. *hyper-* + *-chromia*] **1 :** excessive pigmentation (as of the skin) **2 :** a state of the red blood cells marked by increase in the hemoglobin content — **hy·per·chro·mic** \¦˸˸¦˸mik\ *adj*

**hyperchromic anemia** *n* **:** any of various anemias (as pernicious anemia) that are characterized by abnormally high color index, increase of hemoglobin in individual red blood cells, and marked reduction in the number of red blood cells and alteration and irregularity in their form and that are associated with deficiency or unavailability of an antianemic factor — compare HYPOCHROMIC ANEMIA

**hy·per·conjugation** \¦˸˸+\ *n* [*hyper-* + *conjugation*] **:** resonance in an organic chemical structure that involves as part of the resonance hybrid the separation of a proton from a methyl or other alkyl group situated next to an electron-deficient unit (as a double bond or carbonium ion), the electrons released by the proton tending to move toward the electron-deficient function with resultant stabilization of the entire structure (as in a trisubstituted propylene $H{-}CH_2CR{=}CR_2 \longleftrightarrow H^+ CH_2{=}CR{-}CR_2^-$) — called also *no-bond resonance*

**hy·per·conscious** \"+\ *adj* [*hyper-* + *conscious*] **:** excessively aware **:** acutely conscious ⟨~ of strain or falsity —Elizabeth Bowen⟩ ⟨a politically ~ country —J.E.Burchard⟩

**¹hy·per·coracoid** \"+\ *n* [*hyper-* + *coracoid*] **:** a hypercoracoid bone

**²hypercoracoid** \"\ *adj* **:** of, relating to, or being the upper of two bones at the base of the pectoral fin of teleost fishes sometimes regarded as homologous with the scapula of the higher vertebrates

**hy·per·correct** \"+\ *adj* [*hyper-* + *correct*] **1 :** excessively proper **:** FINICKY ⟨fastidious and ~ to the point of prissiness⟩ **2 :** of, characterized by, or constituting hypercorrection

**hy·per·correction** \"+\ *n* **:** an alteration of a speech habit on the basis of a false analogy (as when *between you and I* is used by one who is substituting *it is I* for *it is me* or when \'fiŋə(r)\ is used for *finger* by one who is attempting to rid himself of pronunciations like \'siŋə(r)\ for *singer*)

**hy·per·critic** \"+\ *n* [*hyper-* + Gk *kritikē* criticism — more at CRITIC] **1** *obs* **:** HYPERCRITICISM **2** [NL *hypercriticus*, n. or adj., fr. *hyper-* + L *criticus*, n. or adj., critic — more at CRITIC] **:** a carping or unduly censorious critic

**hy·per·critical** \"+\ *also* **hy·per·critic** \"+\ *adj* [*hypercritical* fr. NL *hypercriticus* + E *-al; hypercritic* fr. NL *hypercriticus*] **:** meticulously or excessively critical esp. of small and trivial matters **:** overnice in judgment **:** CAPTIOUS, FAULTFINDING ⟨only the critical or ~ grammarian . . . discovers anything wrong in it —Otto Jespersen⟩ ⟨constant ~ belittling of the efforts of others —Harold Rosen & H.E.Kiene⟩ **syn** see CRITICAL

**hy·per·critically** \"+\ *adv* **:** in a hypercritical manner **:** CAPTIOUSLY, CARPINGLY

**hy·per·criticism** \"+\ *n* [*hyper-* + *criticism*] **:** captious or carping criticism

**hy·per·criticize** \"+\ *vt* **:** to criticize excessively ~ *vi* **:** to be hypercritical

**hy·per·cry·algesia** \,hīpə(r),krī+\ *n* -S [NL, fr. *hyper-* + *cry-* + *algesia*] **:** excessive pain due to cold

**hy·per·di·a·lect·ism** \,hīpə(r)'dīə,lek,tizəm\ *n* -S [*hyper-* + *dialect* + *-ism*] **:** an attempted dialectical form or pronunciation that overreaches dialectical authenticity — compare HYPERURBANISM

**hy·per·dimensional** \¦˸˸+\ *adj* [*hyper-* + *dimensional*] **:** of or relating to space of more than three dimensions — **hy·per·dimensionality** \"+\ *n* -ES

**hy·per·dolichocephal** \"+\ *n* [*hyper-* + *dolichocephal*] **:** a hyperdolichocephalic person

**hy·per·dolichocephalic** \"+\ *adj* [*hyper-* + *dolichocephalic*] **:** having a very long narrow head with a cephalic index of less than 70

**hy·per·dolichocephaly** \"+\ *n* **:** the quality or state of being hyperdolichocephalic

**hy·per·dolichocranial** \"+\ *adj* [ISV *hyper-* + *dolichocranial*] **:** having a very long narrow skull with a cranial index of 65 to 70

**hy·per·dolichocrany** \"+\ *n* [ISV *hyper-* + *dolichocrany*] **:** the quality or state of being hyperdolichocranial

**hy·per·dulia** \"+\ *n* [ML, fr. L *hyper-* + ML *dulia*] *Roman Catholicism* **:** veneration of the Virgin Mary as the holiest of creatures — compare LATRIA

**hypered** *past of* HYPER

**hy·per·emesis** \¦hīpə(r)+\ *n* [NL, fr. *hyper-* + Gk *emesis* vomiting — more at EMESIS] **:** excessive vomiting

**hyperemesis grav·i·dar·um** \-,gravə'da(a)rəm\ *n* [NL, lit., excessive vomiting in pregnant women] **:** excessive vomiting during pregnancy

**hy·per·e·mia** *or* **hy·per·ae·mia** \,hīpə'rēmēə\ *n* -S [NL, fr. *hyper-* + *-emia, -aemia*] **:** excess of blood in a body part (as from active dilation of blood vessels or from obstruction of blood flow) — **hy·per·e·mic** \¦˸˸¦rēmik\ *adj*

**hy·per·endemic** \¦hīpə(r)+\ *adj* [*hyper-* + *endemic*] **1 :** exhibiting a high and continued incidence — used chiefly of human diseases ⟨~ malaria⟩ **2 :** marked by hyperendemic disease — used of geographic areas ⟨a ~ focus of plague⟩ — **hy·per·endemicity** \"+\ *n* -ES

**hy·per·er·gic** \¦hīpə¦rərjik\ *adj* **:** having a degree of sensitivity toward an allergen greater than that typical of age group and community — compare NORMERGIC

**hy·per·gy** \˸˸,jē\ *n* [ISV *hyper-* + *allergy;* prob. orig. formed as G *hyperergie*] **:** the quality or state of being hyperergic

**hy·per·essence** \¦hīpə(r)+\ *n* [*hyper-* + *essence*] **:** a concentrated essence (as of flowers)

**hy·per·es·the·sia** *or* **hyperaesthesia** \,hīpərəs'thēzhə\ *n* [NL, fr. *hyper-* + *-esthesia, -aesthesia* (as in *anesthesia, anaesthesia*)] **1 :** excessive or pathological sensitivity of the skin or of a particular sense **2 :** heightened perceptiveness of or response to the environment

**hy·per·esthetic** \¦˸˸+\ *adj* **:** of, relating to, or affected with hyperesthesia

**hy·per·es·trin·ism** \,hīpə'(r)estrə,nizəm\ *n* -S [*hyper-* + *estrin* + *-ism*] **:** a condition marked by the presence of excess estrins in the body and often accompanied by functional uterine bleeding — compare HYPERESTROGENISM

**hy·per·es·tro·gen·ism** \-trəjə,nizəm\ *n* -S [*hyper-* + *estrogen* + *-ism*] **:** a condition marked by the presence of excess estrogens in the body

**hy·per·euryene** \¦hīpə(r)+\ *adj* [*hyper-* + *euryene*] **:** having a very high wide forehead with an upper facial index of less than 45

**hy·per·euryeny** \"+\ *n* **:** the quality or state of being hypereuryene

**hy·per·euryprosopic** \"+\ *adj* [G *hypereuryprosop* hypereuryprosopic (fr. *hyper-* + *euryprosop* euryprosopic) + E *-ic*] **:** having a very short broad face with a facial index below 80

**hy·per·euryprosopy** \"+\ *n* [ISV *hyper-* + *euryprosopy;* prob. orig. formed as G *hypereuryprosopie*] **:** the quality or state of being hypereuryprosopic

**hy·per·eutectic** \"+\ *adj* [*hyper-* + *eutectic*] **:** containing the minor component in an amount in excess of that contained in the eutectic mixture

**hy·per·eutectoid** \"+\ *adj* [*hyper-* + *eutectoid*] **1 :** containing the minor component in an amount in excess of that contained in the eutectoid **2** *of steel* **:** containing more than 0.80 percent carbon

**hy·per·fo·cal distance** \¦hīpə(r)¦fōkəl-\ *n* [ISV *hyper-* + *focal*] **:** the nearest distance upon which a photographic lens may be focused to produce satisfactory definition at infinity

**hy·per·form** \'hīpə(r)+,-\ *n* [*hyper-* + *form*] **:** a speech form resulting from hypercorrection

**hy·per·ga·mous** \(')hī¦pərgəməs\ *adj* **:** of, relating to, or constituting hypergamy

**hy·per·ga·my** \˸'˸˸mē\ *n* -ES [*hyper-* + *-gamy*] **:** marriage into an equal or higher caste or social group — used of Hindu laws forbidding women to marry men of inferior caste

**hy·per·geometric** *also* **hy·per·geometrical** \¦hīpə(r)+\ *adj* [*hyper-* + *geometric* or *geometrical*] **:** involving, related to, or analogous to operations or series that transcend ordinary geometrical operations or series

**hy·per·glob·u·lin·emia** \,˸˸,gläbyələ'nēmēə\ *n* -S [NL, fr. *hyper-* + ISV *globulin* + NL *-emia*] **:** the presence of excess globulins in the blood

**hy·per·glu·ce·mia** \¦hīpə(r)¦glü¦sēmēə\ *n* -S [NL fr. *hyper-* + *gluc-* + *-emia*] **:** HYPERGLYCEMIA

**hy·per·glycemia** \¦˸˸+\ *n* [NL, fr. *hyper-* + *glycemia*] **:** excess of sugar in the blood — compare HYPERINSULINISM — **hy·per·glycemic** \"+\ *adj*

**hyperglycemic-glycogenolytic factor** *n* **:** GLUCAGON

**hy·per·gol** \'hīpə(r),gȯl, -gōl\ *n* -S [G, fr. *hyp-* (fr. *hyper-*) + *erg-* + *-ol* (fr. L *oleum* oil) — more at OIL] **:** a hypergolic fluid propellant

**hy·per·golic** \¦˸˸¦gȯlik, -gäl-,-gōl-\ *adj* [*hypergol* + *-ic*] **:** self-igniting upon contact of components without a spark or other external aid — used esp. of a fluid rocket propellant

**hy·per·hep·a·rin·emia** \ˌ⸗⸗ˌhepərə'nēmēə\ *n* -s [NL, fr. *hyper-* + ISV *heparin* + NL *-emia*] : the presence of excess heparin in the blood (as from ionizing radiation) usu. resulting in hemorrhage — **hy·per·hep·a·rin·emic** \¦⸗⸗¦⸗⸗⸗¦⸗mik\ *adj*

**hy·per·hidrosis** \¦⸗⸗+\ *also* **hy·per·idro·sis** \+ə'drōsəs, -ˌī¦d-\ *n* [NL, fr. *hyper-* + *hidrosis* or *-idrosis*] : generalized or localized excessive sweating — opposed to *hypohidrosis*

**hy·per·i·ca·ce·ae** \hīˌperə'kāsēˌē\ *n pl, cap* [NL, fr. *Hypericum*, type genus + *-aceae*] *in some classifications* : a family of dicotyledonous plants of warm and temperate regions that are distinguished by opposite resinous-dotted leaves, regular flowers with numerous fascicled stamens, and a 3- to 5⸗ loculed ovary and that are often included among the Guttiferae

**hy·per·i·ca·les** \-ā(ˌ)lēz\ [NL, fr. *Hypericum* + *-ales*] *syn of* PARIETALES

**hy·per·i·cin** \hī'perəsən\ *n* -s [ISV *hyperic-* (fr. NL *Hypericum*, genus that produces it) + *-in*] : a violet crystalline pigment $C_{30}H_{16}O_8$ from St.-John's-wort that has a red fluorescence and causes hypericism

**hy·per·i·cism** \-ˌsizəm\ *n* -s [NL *Hypericum*, genus that causes it + E *-ism*] : a severe dermatitis of domestic herbivorous animals due to photosensitivity resulting from eating St.-John's-wort — compare FAGOPYRISM

**hy·per·i·cum** \-rəkəm\ *n, cap* [NL, fr. L *hypericum*, *hypericon* a plant, St.-John's-wort, ground pine, fr. Gk *hyperikon*, *hypereikos*, a plant, St.-John's-wort, prob. fr. *hypo-* + *ereikē* heath, heather — more at BRIER] : a large and widely distributed genus of herbs or shrubs (family Guttiferae) that are characterized chiefly by their pentamerous and often showy yellow flowers

**hy·per·immune** \¦hīpə(r)+\ *adj* [*hyper-* + *immune*] : exhibiting an unusual degree of immunization ⟨~ swine⟩: **a** *of a serum* : containing exceptional quantities of antibody **b** *of an antibody* : having the characteristics of a blocking antibody

**hy·per·immunization** \"+\ *n* : the quality or state of being hyperimmunized

**hy·per·immunize** \"+\ *vt* [*hyper-* + *immunize*] : to induce a high level of immunity or of circulating antibodies in (as by a long course of injections of antigen, repeated increasing doses of antigen, or the use of adjuvants along with the antigen)

**hy·per·in** \'hīpərən\ *n* -s [*hyper-* (fr. NL *Hypericum*, genus that produces it) + *-in*] : a glycoside $C_{21}H_{20}O_{12}$ found in various plants (as St.-John's-wort and apples); quercetin 3⸗ galactoside

**hy·per·infection** \¦hīpə(r)+\ *n* [*hyper-* + *infection*] : repeated reinfection with larvae produced by parasitic worms already in the body due to the ability of various parasites to complete the life cycle within a single host — compare AUTO-INFECTION

**hypering** *pres part of* HYPER

**hy·per·in·su·lin·ism** \ˌ⸗⸗'⸗(⸗)⸗ˌizəm\ *n* -s [ISV *hyper-* + *insulin* + *-ism*] : the presence of excess insulin in the body resulting in hypoglycemia and often accompanied by weakness, susceptibility to fatigue, tremor, sweating, and other evidences of debility

**hy·per·irritability** \¦hīpə(r)+\ *n* [*hyper-* + *irritability*] : excessive irritability : abnormally great or uninhibited response to stimuli

**hy·per·irritable** \"+\ *adj* [*hyper-* + *irritable*] : marked by hyperirritability

**hy·per·keratinization** \"+\ *n* [*hyper-* + *keratinization*] : HYPERKERATOSIS

**hy·per·keratosis** \"+\ *n, pl* **hyperkeratoses** [NL, fr. *hyper-* + *keratosis*] **1** : hypertrophy of the corneous layer of the skin **2 a** : any of various conditions marked by hyperkeratosis **b** : a disease of cattle marked by thickening and wrinkling of the hide and formation of papillary outgrowths on the buccal mucous membranes, often accompanied by watery discharge from eyes and nose, diarrhea, loss of condition, and abortion of pregnant animals, and now believed to result from ingestion of the chlorinated naphthalene of various lubricating oils — called also *X-disease*, *XX-disease*

**hy·per·keratotic** \"+\ *adj* [*hyper-* + *keratotic*] : of, relating to, or marked by hyperkeratosis

**hy·per·kinesia** *also* **hy·per·kinesis** \"+\ *n, pl* **hyperkinesias** *also* **hyperkinesises** [NL, fr. *hyper-* + *-kinesia* or *-kinesis*] : abnormally increased and usu. purposeless and uncontrollable muscular movement

**hy·per·kinetic** \"+\ *adj* [*hyper-* + *kinetic*] : of, relating to, or marked by hyperkinesia

**hy·per·leptene** \"+\ *adj* [*hyper-* + *leptene*] : having a very high narrow forehead with an upper facial index of 60 or over

**hy·per·lepteny** \"+\ *n* [*hyper-* + *lepteny*] : the quality or state of being hyperleptene

**hy·per·leptoprosopic** \"+\ *adj* [G *hyperleptoprosop* hyperleptoprosopic (fr. *hyper-* + *leptoprosop*) + E *-ic*] : having a very long narrow face with a facial index of 93 and over on the living and of 95 and over on the skull

**hy·per·leptoprosopy** \"+\ *n* [ISV *hyper-* + *leptoprosopy*; orig. formed as G *hyperleptoprosopie*] : the quality or state of being hyperleptoprosopic

**hy·per·leptorrhine** \¦hīpə(r)+\ *adj* [*hyper-* + *leptorrhine*] : having a very long narrow nose with a nasal index of 40 to 55

**hy·per·leptorrhiny** \"+\ *n* [*hyper-* + *leptorrhiny*] : the quality or state of being hyperleptorrhine

**hy·per·leptosome** \"+\ *adj* [*hyper-* + *leptosome*] : very tall and slender

**hy·per·lipemia** \"+\ *n* [NL, fr. *hyper-* + *lipemia*] : the presence of excess fat or lipids in the blood — **hy·per·lipemic** \"+\ *adj*

**hy·per·makroskelic** \"+\ *adj* [*hyper-* + *makroskelic*] : having extremely long legs in proportion to the trunk with a skelic index of 100 or over

**hy·per·mas·tig·i·da** \ˌhīpə(r)ˌma'stijədə\ [NL, fr. *hyper-* + *mastig-* + *-ida*] *syn of* HYPERMASTIGINA

**hy·per·mas·tig·i·na** \-jənə\ *n pl, cap* [NL, fr. *hyper-* + *mastig-* + *-ina*] : an order (subclass Zoomastigina) of complex cellulose-producing flagellates that have numerous flagella and are symbiotic in the intestine of termites and other wood⸗ consuming insects

**¹hy·per·mastigote** \¦hīpə(r)+\ *adj* [*hyper-* + *mastigote*] : of or relating to the Hypermastigina

**²hypermastigote** \"\ *n* -s : a flagellate of the order Hypermastigina

**hy·per·mature** \"+\ *adj* [*hyper-* + *mature*] : having passed the stage of full development or differentiation ⟨a ~ cataract⟩

**hy·per·metabolism** \"+\ *n* [*hyper-* + *metabolism*] : metabolism at an increased or excessive rate

**hy·per·metamorphic** \"+\ *adj* [*hyper-* + *metamorphic*] : exhibiting or involving hypermetamorphosis

**hy·per·metamorphosis** \"+\ *n* [NL, fr. *hyper-* + *metamorphosis*] : a method of development in an insect (as the blister beetle) in which the larva passes through numerous instars each markedly diverse from the rest in structure

**hy·per·me·ter** \hī'pərmədˌər\ *n* [LL *hypermeter*, *hypermetrus* hypercatalectic, fr. Gk *hypermetros* beyond measure, beyond the meter, fr. *hyper-* + *-metros* (akin to *metron* measure, meter) — more at MEASURE] **1** : a hypercatalectic verse **2** : a period comprising more than two or three cola — called also *hypermetron*

**hy·per·metric** *or* **hy·per·metrical** \¦hīpə(r)+\ *adj* [Gk *hypermetros* beyond measure, beyond the meter + E *-ic* or *-ical*] : exceeding the normal measure; *specif* : having a redundant syllable ⟨a poem with numerous ~ lines⟩

**hy·per·me·tron** \hī'pərməˌträn\ *n* -s [NL, fr. Gk, neut. of. *hypermetros* beyond the meter, beyond measure] : HYPERMETER 2

**hy·per·met·rope** \ˌhīpə(r)'meˌtrōp\ *n* -s [ISV *hypermetr-* (fr. Gk *hypermetros*) + *-ope*] : HYPEROPE

**hy·per·me·tro·pia** \-mə'trōpēə\ *n* -s [NL, fr. Gk *hypermetros* + NL *-opia*] : HYPEROPIA — **hy·per·me·tropic** \¦⸗⸗mə-¦träpik, -rōp-\ *adj* — **hy·per·me·tropi·cal** \-pəkəl\ *adj* — **hy·per·met·ro·py** \ˌ⸗⸗'me·trəpē\ *n* -ES

**hy·per·me·try** \hī'pərmə·trē\ *n* -ES [*hyper-* + *-metry*] : the addition of one or more syllables beyond the required measure at the end of a line or other metrical unit

**hy·perm·ne·sia** \ˌhī(ˌ)pərm'nēzh(ē)ə\ *n* -s [NL, fr. *hyper-* + *-mnesia*] : abnormally vivid or complete memory or the reawakening of impressions long seemingly forgotten (as at a moment of extreme danger) — **hy·perm·ne·sic** \-ēzik, -ēsik\ *adj*

**hy·per·morph** \'hīpərˌmȯrf\ *n* -s [*hyper-* + *-morph*] **1** : a long-limbed and long-headed person : ECTOMORPH — opposed to *hypomorph* **2** : a mutant gene having a similar but greater effect than the corresponding wild-type gene — compare HYPOMORPH — **hy·per·mor·phic** \¦⸗⸗¦mȯrfik\ *adj* — **hy·per·mor·phism** \-ˌfizəm\ *n* -s

**hy·per·mor·pho·sis** \ˌ⸗⸗'mȯrfəsəs *sometimes* -ˌmȯr'fōsəs\ *n* [NL, fr. *hyper-* + *-morphosis*] : excessive growth of some member of a body

**hy·per·motility** \¦hīpə(r)+\ *n* [ISV *hyper-* + *motility*] : abnormal or excessive movement; *specif* : excessive motility of all or part of the gastrointestinal tract — compare HYPOMOTILITY

**hy·per·myotonia** \"+\ *n* [NL, fr. *hyper-* + *myotonia*] : muscular hypertonicity

**hy·per·ne·phro·ma** \ˌ⸗⸗nə'frōmə, -ne'-\ *n, pl* **hypernephromas** \-ōməz\ *or* **hypernephroma·ta** \-mədə\ [NL, fr. Gk *hyper-* + *nephr-* + *-oma*] : a tumor of the kidney resembling the adrenal cortex in its histological structure

**hy·per·nic** \¦⸗⸗¦nik\ *n* -s [*hyper-* + *Nicaragua*, country of Central America] **1** : any of several tropical American dyewoods (as various brazilwoods or logwood) **2** : a dye or an extract used in dyeing that is obtained from a hypernic

**hy·pero·ar·tia** \ˌhīpərō'ärsh(ē)ə, -ärd-ēə\ *n pl, cap* [NL, fr. Gk *hyperōia* palate (fr. fem. of *hyperōios* upper, fr. *hyper* over, above) + NL *-artia* (fr. Gk *artios* complete, perfect); akin to Gk *arti* just, exactly, *arariskein* to fit — more at OVER, ARM] : an order of cyclostomi consisting of the lampreys as distinguished from the hagfishes — compare HYPEROTRETA

**¹hy·pero·ar·tian** \¦⸗⸗⸗¦ärsh(ē)ən, -ärd-ēən\ *adj* [NL *Hyperoartia* + E *-an*] : of or relating to the Hyperoartia

**²hyperoartian** \"\ *n* -s : one of the Hyperoartia

**hy·pero·ar·tii** \ˌ⸗⸗⸗'ärshēˌī, -ärd-ēˌī\ [NL, fr. Gk *hyperōia* palate + NL *-artii* (fr. Gk *artios* complete, perfect)] *syn of* HYPEROARTIA

**hy·per·on** \'hīpəˌrän\ *n* -s [prob. fr. *hyper-* + *-on*] : an elementary particle that obeys Fermi-Dirac statistics but differs from nucleons in one or more intrinsic quantum properties

**hy·per·on·to·morph** \¦hīpə¦räntəˌmȯrf\ *n* -s [*hyper-* + *ont-* + *-morph*] : an ectomorphic body type or individual — opposed to *meso-ontomorph*

**hy·pero·odon** \ˌhīpə'rōəˌdän\ *n, cap* [NL, fr. Gk *hyperōios* upper + NL *-odon*] : a genus of beaked whales distinguished esp. by prominent crests on the maxillary bones

**hy·per·ope** \'hīpəˌrōp\ *n* -s [*hyper-* + *-ope*] : one affected with hyperopia

**hy·per·opia** \ˌ⸗⸗'rōpēə\ *n* -s [NL, fr. *hyper-* + *-opia*] : a condition in which visual images come to a focus behind the retina of the eye because of defects in the refractive media of the eye or because of abnormal shortness of the eyeball — called also *farsightedness* — **hy·per·opic** \¦⸗⸗¦rōpik, -räp-\ *adj*

**hy·per·orthognathous** \¦hīpə(r)+\ *adj* [*hyper-* + *orthognathous*] : having a very flat facial profile with a facial angle of 93 degrees or above

**hy·per·os·mia** \ˌhīpə'räzmēə\ *n* -s [NL, fr. *hyper-* + *-osmia* (as in *anosmia*)] : extreme acuteness of the sense of smell — **hy·per·os·mic** \¦⸗⸗¦mik\ *adj*

**hy·per·os·to·sis** \ˌhīpəˌrä'stōsəs\ *n, pl* **hyperosto·ses** \-ōˌsēz\ [NL, fr. *hyper-* + *-ostosis*] **1** : excessive formation of bone tissue esp. in the skull **2 a** : the condition resulting from hyperostosis **b** : one of the bony outgrowths produced by hyperostosis

**hy·per·os·tot·ic** \¦⸗⸗¦⸗¦städ·ik\ *adj* [fr. NL *hyperostosis*, after such pairs as NL *exostosis*: E *exostotic*] : of, relating to, or affected with hyperostosis

**hy·per·o·tre·ta** \ˌhīpərō'trēdə\ *n pl, cap* [NL, fr. Gk *hyperōia* palate (fr. fem. of *hyperōios* upper) + NL *-treta* (fr. Gk *trētos* perforated, fr. *tetrainein* to perforate, pierce) — more at THROW] : an order of Cyclostomi including the hagfishes as distinguished from the lampreys — compare HYPEROARTIA

**¹hy·per·o·tre·tan** \¦⸗⸗⸗¦trētᵊn\ *or* **hy·per·o·tre·tous** \-ēd·əs\ *adj* [NL *Hyperotreta* + E *-an* or *-ous*] : of or relating to the Hyperotreta

**²hyperotretan** \"\ *n* -s : one of the Hyperotreta

**hy·per·o·tre·ti** \ˌ⸗⸗⸗'trēdˌī\ [NL, fr. Gk *hyperōia* palate + NL *-treti* (fr. Gk *trētos* perforated)] *syn of* HYPEROTRETA

**hy·per·oxide** \¦hīpə(r)+\ *n* [ISV *hyper-* + *oxide*] : a compound containing a relatively large proportion of oxygen; *esp* : SUPEROXIDE

**hy·per·panchromatic** \"+\ *adj* [*hyper-* + *panchromatic*] : sensitive to blue and green and highly sensitive to red — used of a photographic film or plate

**hy·per·parasite** \"+\ *n* [*hyper-* + *parasite*] : a parasite that is parasitic upon another parasite : a secondary parasite — used esp. of fungi and of hymenopterous insects that attack the primary parasites of other insects — **hy·per·parasitic** \"+\ *adj*

**hy·per·parasitism** \"+\ *n* [*hyper-* + *parasitism*] **1** : the quality or state of being hyperparasitic **2** : parasitism involving excessive numbers of parasites

**hy·per·parasitize** \"+\ *vt* : to live on or in as a hyperparasite

**hy·per·par·a·thy·roid·ism** \ˌ⸗⸗ˌ⸗⸗'⸗ˌ⸗+ˌizəm\ *n* [ISV *hyper-* + *parathyroid* + *-ism*] : the presence of excess parathyroid hormone in the body resulting in disturbance of calcium metabolism with increase in serum calcium and decrease in inorganic phosphorus, loss of calcium from bone, and renal damage with frequent kidney-stone formation

**hy·per·path·ia** \-'pathēə\ *n* -s [NL, fr. *hyper-* + *-pathia*] **1** : disagreeable or painful sensation in response to a normally innocuous stimulus (as touch) **2** : a condition in which the sensations of hyperpathia occur — **hy·per·path·ic** \¦⸗⸗¦pathik\ *adj*

**hy·per·peristalsis** \¦⸗⸗+\ *n* [NL, fr. *hyper-* + *peristalsis*] : excessive or excessively vigorous peristalsis — compare HYPERMOTILITY

**hy·per·pha·gia** \ˌ⸗⸗'fāj(ē)ə\ *n* -s [NL, fr. *hyper-* + *-phagia*] : abnormally increased desire for food frequently resulting from injury to the hypothalamus — compare POLYPHAGIA

**hy·per·pha·lan·gism** \-fə'lanˌjizəm, -fā'-\ *n* -s [ISV *hyper-* + *phalang-* (fr. NL *phalang-*, *phalanx*) + *-ism*] : the presence of supernumerary phalanges in fingers or toes

**hy·per·pharyngeal** \¦⸗⸗+\ *adj* [*hyper-* + *pharyngeal*] : EPIPHARYNGEAL 2

**hy·per·physical** \"+\ *adj* [*hyper-* + *physical*] **1** : being beyond or more than the physical **2** : independent of the physical or not being within its confines — **hy·per·physically** \"+\ *adv*

**hy·per·pi·e·sia** \ˌ⸗⸗ˌpī'ēzh(ē)ə\ *also* **hy·per·pi·e·sis** \-ˌpī'ēsəs, -'pīəsəs\ *n, pl* **hyperpiesias** *also* **hyperpieses** [*hyperpiesia*, NL, fr. *hyper-* + *-piesia* (fr. Gk *piesis* pressure — fr. *piezein* to press — + NL *-ia*); *hyperpiesis*, NL, fr. *hyper-* + Gk *piesis*] : HYPERTENSION; *esp* : ESSENTIAL HYPERTENSION

**¹hy·per·pi·et·ic** \¦⸗⸗¦pī¦ed·ik\ *adj* [fr. NL *hyperpiesia*, after such pairs as NL *anesthesia*: E *anesthetic*] : marked by hyperpiesia

**²hyperpietic** \"\ *n* -s : a person having hyperpiesia

**hy·per·pi·tu·i·ta·rism** \ˌ⸗⸗pə'tüəˌtaˌrizəm, -pə·'tyü-\ *n* -s [ISV *hyper-* + *pituitar-* (fr. *pituitary*) + *-ism*] **1** : excessive activity of the pituitary body esp. in the production of growth⸗ regulating hormones — compare HYPOPITUITARISM **2** : a growth abnormality dependent on hyperpituitarism (as acromegaly and various gigantisms)

**hy·per·pituitary** \¦⸗⸗+\ *adj* [*hyper-* + *pituitary*] : marked by hyperpituitarism ⟨giant ferns, banana leaves, creepers, and ~ trees —Michael Rosene⟩

**hy·per·plane** \¦⸗⸗+\ *n* [*hyper-* + *plane*] : a figure in hyperspace corresponding to a plane in ordinary space

**hy·per·pla·sia** \¦⸗⸗¦plāzh(ē)ə\ *n* -s [NL, fr. *hyper-* + *-plasia*] : an abnormal or unusual increase in the elements composing a part (as of the cells of a tissue) — compare HYPERTROPHY, HYPOPLASIA — **hy·per·plas·tic** \¦⸗⸗¦plastik\ *adj*

**hy·per·platycnemic** \¦⸗⸗+\ *adj* [*hyper-* + *platycnemic*] *of a shinbone* : much flattened laterally with a platycnemic index of less than 55

**hy·per·platymeric** \"+\ *adj* [*hyper-* + *platymeric*] *of a thigh-bone* : much flattened laterally with a platymeric index of less than 75

**¹hy·per·ploid** \'hīpə(r)ˌplȯid\ *adj* [ISV *hyper-* + *-ploid*] : having or being a chromosome number slightly greater than an exact multiple of the monoploid number

**²hyperploid** \"\ *n* -s : a hyperploid organism

**hy·per·ploidy** \-dē\ *n* -ES [ISV *hyperploid* + *-y*] : the quality or state of being hyperploid

**hy·per·pnea** *also* **hy·per·pnoea** \ˌhīpərp'nēə, -ˌpərp'nēə\ *n* -s [NL, fr. *hyper-* + *-pnea* or *-pnoea*] : abnormally rapid or deep breathing : HYPERVENTILATION — compare DYSPNEA, EUPNEA — **hy·per·pne·ic** \¦⸗(ˌ)¦nēik\ *adj*

**hy·per·predator** \¦hīpə(r)+\ *n* [*hyper-* + *predator*] : a predator that preys chiefly on another predatory animal

**hy·per·prognathous** \"+\ *adj* [*hyper-* + *prognathous*] : having exceedingly prominent jaws with a facial profile angle below 70 degrees

**hy·per·pro·sex·ia** \ˌ⸗⸗prə'seksēə\ *n* -s [NL, fr. *hyper-* + Gk *prosexis* attention (fr. *prosechein* to pay attention to, fr. *pros* toward + *echein* to hold) + NL *-ia* — more at PROS-, SCHEME] : excessive fixity of attention on a stimulus object

**hy·per·pro·throm·bin·emia** *or* **hy·per·pro·throm·bin·ae·mia** \-prōˌthrämbə'nēmēə\ *n* -s [NL, fr. *hyper-* + ISV *prothrombin* + NL *-emia* or *-aemia*] : excess of prothrombin in the blood

**hy·per·pyretic** \¦⸗⸗+\ *adj* [ISV *hyper-* + *pyretic*] : of, relating to, or affected with hyperpyrexia

**hy·per·pyrexia** \"+\ *n* [NL, fr. *hyper-* + *pyrexia*] : exceptionally high fever either in comparison to the fever usu. accompanying a particular disease or absolutely (as in heat stroke)

**hy·per·re·flex·ia** \ˌhīpə(r)rə'fleksēə\ *n* -s [NL, fr. *hyper-* + E *reflex* + NL *-ia*] : overactivity of physiological reflexes

**hy·per·resonance** \¦hīpə(r)+\ *n* [*hyper-* + *resonance*] : an exaggerated chest resonance heard in various abnormal pulmonary conditions — **hy·per·resonant** \"+\ *adj*

**hypers** *pres 3d sing of* HYPER

**hy·per·secretion** \"+\ *n* [ISV *hyper-* + *secretion*] : excessive production of a bodily secretion — **hy·per·secretory** \"+\ *adj*

**hy·per·sensibility** \"+\ *n* [ISV *hyper-* + *sensibility*] : HYPERESTHESIA

**hy·per·sensitive** \"+\ *adj* [*hyper-* + *sensitive*] **1** : excessively sensitive ⟨extracultivated, ~, delicate manhood —*Saturday Rev.*⟩ **2 a** : abnormally susceptible to an antigen, drug, or other agent — compare ALLERGY 2, ANAPHYLAXIS **b** : reacting violently to attack by a parasite so that sudden death of invaded tissues provides a barrier against further invasion **3** : of or relating to a photographic emulsion whose speed and sensitivity are increased before the image-forming exposure (as by treatment with ammonia or by exposure to heat or light) — **hy·per·sensitiveness** \"+\ *n* — **hy·per·sensitivity** \"+\ *n*

**hy·per·sensitization** \"+\ *n* : an act or process of hypersensitizing

**hy·per·sensitize** \"+\ *vt* [*hypersensitive* + *-ize*] : to make hypersensitive

**hy·per·solid** \"+\ *n* [*hyper-* + *solid*] : a figure (as a hypersphere) in hyperspace that corresponds to a solid in ordinary three-dimensional space

**hy·per·som·nia** \ˌhīpə(r)'sämnēə\ *n* -s [NL, fr. *hyper-* + *-somnia* (as in L *insomnia*)] **1** : sleep of excessive depth or duration **2** : the condition of sleeping for excessive periods at intervals with intervening periods of normal duration of sleeping and waking — compare NARCOLEPSY, SOMNOLENCE

**hy·per·sonic** \¦⸗⸗+\ *adj* [ISV *hyper-* + *sonic*] **1** : of, relating to, or being speed five times or more that of sound in air — compare SONIC **2** : moving, capable of moving, or utilizing air currents that move at hypersonic speed ⟨~ wind tunnel⟩

**hy·per·sorp·tion** \¦⸗⸗¦sȯrpshən\ *n* [*hyper-* + *adsorption*] : the selective adsorption of various hydrocarbons from gaseous mixtures on activated carbon (as propane from natural gas or ethylene from gases produced in the refining of petroleum)

**hy·per·space** \¦⸗⸗+\ *n* [ISV *hyper-* + *space*] **1** : space of more than three dimensions **2** : space other than ordinary euclidean space

**hy·per·spatial** \¦⸗⸗+\ *adj* [*hyper-* + *spatial*] : of or relating to hyperspace

**hy·per·sphere** \'⸗⸗+ˌ-\ *n* [*hyper-* + *sphere*] : a sphere that is the analogue in hyperspace of the sphere in ordinary space

**hy·per·splenic** \¦⸗⸗+\ *adj* : marked by hypersplenism

**hy·per·splenism** \ˌ⸗⸗'spléˌnizəm, -leˌn-\ *n* -s [ISV *hyper-* + *splen-* + *-ism*] : a condition marked by excessive destruction of one or more kinds of blood cells in the spleen

**hy·per·stereoscopic** \¦⸗⸗+\ *adj* [*hyper-* + *stereoscopic*] : having an enhanced three-dimensional appearance due to an abnormally large separation between the binocular points of view (as with some prism binoculars or in stereoscopic photographs) — **hy·per·stereoscopy** \"+\ *n*

**hy·per·sthene** \'hīpə(r)ˌsthēn\ *n* -s [F *hypersthène*, fr. *hyper-* + Gk *sthenos* strength — more at ASTHEN-] : a mineral $(Mg,Fe)SiO_3$ consisting of an orthorhombic grayish or greenish black or dark brown pyroxene that is a silicate of magnesium and iron isomorphous with enstatite and often has a bronze luster on the cleavage surface — **hy·per·sthenic** \¦⸗⸗¦sthenik, -thēn-\ *adj*

**hy·per·sthe·nite** \ˌ⸗⸗'sthēˌnīt\ *n* -s [G *hypersthenit*, fr. *hypersthen* hypersthene (fr. F *hypersthène*) + *-it* -ite] **1** : a rock composed of hypersthene and labradorite **2** : pyroxenite composed essentially of hypersthene

**hy·per·sthen·iza·tion** \-ˌsthenə'zāshən, -ˌnī'z-\ *n* -s : development of hypersthene by metamorphic processes

**hy·per·strophic** \¦⸗⸗¦sträfik *also* -rōf-\ *adj* [*hyper-* + Gk *strophos* twisted band, cord + E *-ic* — more at STROPHE] : characterized by a coiling of the shell to the left combined with an asymmetric arrangement of the organs like that of an individual of the same or related species with a shell coiled to the right

**hy·per·surface** \"+\ *n* [*hyper-* + *surface*] : a surface that is the analogue in hyperspace of a surface in three-dimensional space

**hy·per·susceptibility** \"+\ *n* [*hyper-* + *susceptibility*] : the quality or state of being hypersensitive

**hy·per·susceptible** \"+\ *adj* [*hyper-* + *susceptible*] : HYPERSENSITIVE

**hy·per·tel·ic** \¦hīpə(r)¦telik\ *adj* : of, relating to, or exhibiting hypertely

**hy·per·tely** \hī'pərd·ᵊlē; 'hīpərˌtelē, ˌ⸗⸗'⸗⸗\ *n* -ES [ISV *hyper-* + *tel-* (end) + *-y*] : an extreme degree of imitative coloration or ornamentation not explainable on the ground of utility

**hy·per·tense** \¦hīpə(r)+\ *adj* [*hyper-* + *tense*] : excessively tense ⟨a furiously ambitious young ~ instructor —Christopher Morley⟩

**hy·per·ten·sin** \ˌ⸗⸗'ten(t)sən\ *n* -s [ISV *hypertension* + *-in*] : any of several vasoconstrictor pressor polypeptides formed by partial hydrolysis of hypertensinogen — called also *angiotonin*

**hy·per·ten·sin·ase** \-səˌnās, -āz\ *n* -s [ISV *hypertensin* + *-ase*] : an enzyme found esp. in the kidney and intestine that inactivates hypertensin

**hy·per·ten·sin·o·gen** \-ˌten'sinəjən, -ˌjen\ *n* -s [ISV *hypertensino-* (fr. *hypertensin*) + *-gen*] : a globulin of blood plasma and serum that is produced by the liver and when acted on by renin forms hypertensin

**hy·per·tension** \¦⸗⸗+\ *n* [ISV *hyper-* + *tension*] **1** : abnormally high arterial blood pressure: **a** : such blood pressure occurring without apparent or determinable prior organic changes in the tissues possibly because of hereditary tendency, emotional tensions, faulty nutrition, or hormonal influence **b** : such blood pressure with demonstrable organic changes (as in nephritis, diabetes, and hyperthyroidism) **2** : a systemic condition resulting from hypertension that is either symptomless or is accompanied by nervousness, dizziness, or headache ⟨a morass of ~ and domestic misery —C.J.Rolo⟩

**¹hy·per·ten·sive** \-'ten(t)siv, -sēv *also* -səv\ *adj* [ISV *hypertension* + *-ive*] : marked by a rise in blood pressure : suffering or caused by hypertension

**²hypertensive** \"\ *n* -s : an individual affected with hypertension

**Hy·per·therm** \'⸗⸗ˌthərm\ *trademark* — used for an apparatus using hot humid air to produce artificial fever for remedial purposes

**hy·per·ther·mia** \ˌ⸗⸗ˈthərmēə\ *n* -s [NL, fr. *hyper-* + *therm-* + *-ia*] **:** hyperpyrexia esp. when induced artificially for therapeutic purposes — **hy·per·ther·mic** \ˌ⸗⸗ˈthərmik\ *adj*

**hy·per·thyroid** \ˌ⸗⸗+\ *adj* [ISV *hyper-* + *thyroid*] **:** of, relating to, or having hyperthyroidism

**hy·per·thyroidism** \ˈ"+\ *n* [ISV *hyper-* + *thyroid* + *-ism*] **1 :** excessive functional activity of the thyroid gland **2 :** the abnormal condition resulting from hyperthyroidism marked by increased metabolic rate, enlargement of the thyroid gland, rapid heart rate, high blood pressure, and various secondary symptoms — see EXOPHTHALMIC GOITER, GOITER

**hy·per·thy·ro·sis** \ˌ⸗⸗ˌthīˈrōsəs\ *also* **hy·per·thy·re·o·sis** \-ˌthīrēˈōsəs\ *n, pl* **hyperthyro·ses** *also* **hyperthyreo·ses** \-ō̇ˌsēz\ [NL, fr. *hyper-* + *thyr-* or *thyreo-* + *-osis*] **:** HYPERTHYROIDISM

**hy·per·to·nia** \ˌ⸗⸗ˈtōnēə\ *or* **hy·per·tony** \ˈ⸗⸗ˌtōnē, hīˈpərtᵊnē\ *n, pl* **hypertonias** *or* **hypertonies** [NL *hypertonia*, fr. *hyper-* + *-tonia* -tony] **:** HYPERTONICITY

**hy·per·tonic** \ˌhīpə(r)+\ *adj* [ISV *hyper-* + *tonic*] **1** *of living tissue* **:** having excessive tone **2** *of a fluid* **:** having a higher osmotic pressure than a fluid under comparison or used as a standard — compare ISOTONIC

**hy·per·tonicity** \ˈ"+\ *n* **:** the quality or state of being hypertonic

**hy·per·tonus** \ˈ"+\ *n* [NL, fr. *hyper-* + *tonus*] **:** HYPERTONICITY

**hy·per·trichosis** \ˈ"+\ *n, pl* **hypertrichoses** [NL, fr. *hyper-* + Gk *trichōsis* growth of hair (fr. *trich-* + *-ōsis* -osis)] **:** excessive growth of hair

**hy·per·trophic** \hīˈpərtrə(ˌ)fik; ˌhīpərˈtrāfik, -rōf-\ *or* **hy·per·tro·phous** \(ˈ)hīˌpərtrəfəs\ *adj* [*hyper-* + *-trophic* or *-trophous*] **:** of or relating to hypertrophy **:** affected with or tending to hypertrophy

**hypertrophic arthritis** *n* **:** DEGENERATIVE ARTHRITIS

**hy·per·tro·phied** \(ˈ)hīˌpərtrəfēd\ *adj* **:** marked by hypertrophy **:** excessively or abnormally developed **:** OVERGROWN ⟨~ tonsils⟩ ⟨a ~ carnival —Janet Flanner⟩ ⟨~ capitalists —G.B.Shaw⟩

**¹hy·per·tro·phy** \ˈ⸗ˈ⸗fē\ *n* [prob. fr. NL *hypertrophia*, fr. *hyper-* + *-trophia* -trophy] **1 :** overgrowth or excessive development of an organ or part (as that resulting from unusually steady or severe use or in compensation for an organic deficiency); *specif* **:** increase in bulk without increase in the number of constituent elements that is produced by thickening of the muscle fibers ⟨cardiac ~⟩ — compare HYPERPLASIA, HYPOTROPHY **2 :** exaggerated growth in size or complexity **:** excessive enlargement ⟨economic concentration increasing at a parallel rate with business ~ —Paul Johnson⟩ ⟨a certain ~ in the contrapuntal writing making for very complicated listening —K.H.Wörner⟩

**²hypertrophy** \ˈ"\ *vb* -ED/-ING/-ES *vt* **:** to affect with hypertrophy ~ *vi* **:** to increase or grow in size beyond the normal ⟨a healthy kidney *hypertrophies* when the other fails⟩ ⟨orthodoxies ~ as inspiration declines⟩

**hy·per·urbanism** \ˌhīpər+\ *n* -s [*hyper-* + *urban* + *-ism*] **:** a form, pronunciation, or usage that overreaches correctness in an effort to avoid provincial speech

**hy·per·uricemia** \ˌhīpə(r)+\ *n* -s [NL, fr *hyper-* + *uric-* + *-emia*] **:** excess uric acid in the blood (as in gout)

**hy·per·ventilation** \ˈ"+\ *n* [ISV *hyper-* + *ventilation*] **:** excessive ventilation; *specif* **:** excessive rate and depth of respiration leading to abnormal loss of carbon dioxide from the blood

**hy·per·vi·ta·min·osis** \ˌ⸗⸗ˌvīdəməˈnōsəs\ *n, pl* **hypervitamino·ses** \-ō̇ˌsēz\ [NL, fr *hyper-* + ISV *vitamin* + NL *-osis*] **:** an abnormal state resulting from excessive intake of one or more vitamins esp. over a long period of time

**hy·per·vol·emia** \ˌhīpə(r)väˈlēmēə\ *n* -s [NL, fr. *hyper-* + *vol-* (fr. E *volume*) + *-emia*] **:** an excessive volume of blood in the body

**hyp·es·the·sia** \ˌhipəsˈthēzh(ē)ə, ˌhīp-, -ˌpes-\ *n* [NL, fr. *hypo-* + *-esthesia* (as in *anesthesia*)] **:** impaired or lessened tactile sensibility

**hy·pha** \ˈhīfə\ *n, pl* **hy·phae** \-ī(ˌ)ē\ [NL, fr. Gk *hyphē* web; akin to Gk *hyphos* web — more at WEAVE] **1 :** one of the individual threads that make up the mycelium of a fungus, increase by apical growth, and are coenocytic in the Phycomycetes but transversely septate in the Ascomycetes and Basidiomycetes **2 :** a simple or branched filamentous outgrowth from the cortex or other inner tissues of various large seaweeds esp. of the order Fucales

**hy·phae·ne** \hīˈfēnē\ *n, cap* [NL, fr. Gk *hyphainein* to weave — more at WEAVE] **:** a genus of tropical African fan palms having branching trunks, dioecious flowers, and one-seeded fruits with thick rinds — see DOOM PALM

**hy·phaer·e·sis** \hīˈferəsəs, *esp Brit* -ˈfi(ə)r-\ *n, pl* **hyphaere·ses** \-əˌsēz\ [Gk *hyphairesis*, fr. *hyphairein* to take from under, subtract, fr. *hypo-* + *hairein* to take — more at HERESY] **:** the omission of a sound, letter, or syllable from the body of a word — compare SYNCOPE 2a

**hy·phal** \ˈhīfəl\ *adj* [NL *hypha* + E ¹*-al*] **:** of, relating to, or constituting a hypha

**hyphal body** *n* **:** an irregularly shaped often thickened fragment formed (as in members of the genus *Entomophthora*) by segmentation of a hypha and sometimes multiplying by fission or budding

**hy·phan·tria** \hīˈfan·trēə\ *n, cap* [NL, fr. Gk, female weaver, fem. of *hyphantēs* weaver, fr. *hyphainein* to weave] **:** a genus of arctiid moths including some No. American species having hairy social larvae that are serious pests of trees — see FALL WEBWORM

**¹hy·phen** \ˈhīfən\ *n* -s [LL & Gk; LL, a diacritical mark (-) used to indicate that two words are to be read as a compound, fr. Gk, *hyph' hen* under one, fr. *hypo* under + *hen* (neut. of *heis* one) — more at UP, SAME] **1 :** the punctuation mark - used to divide or to compound words or word elements: **a :** a mark used for division esp. at the end of a line terminating with a syllable of a word that is completed in the next line, between letters or syllables repeated to give the effect of stuttering, sobbing, or halting expression (as in *s-s-sorry*), or between the letters of a word spelled out letter by letter (as in *p-r-o-b-a-t-i-o-n-a-r-y*) **b :** a mark used for compounding esp. in a compound containing a prepositional phrase (as in *mother-in-law*), in a compound adjective (as in *first-rate*), in a compound whose first element is *self* (as in *self-pity* ), in a compound whose second element is capitalized (as in *pro-British*), in a compound containing reduplication (as in *bang-bang*), in a spelled-out compound numeral (as in *twenty-five*), in a compound whose meaning differs from that of an otherwise identical word (as in *re-formation*), in a compound containing a vowel otherwise confusingly doubled (as in *co-opt*), or in a compound containing the same letter three successive times (as in *bell-less*) **2 :** something resembling a hyphen ⟨the lady whose odd smile is the merest ~ —Karl Shapiro⟩

**²hyphen** \ˈ"\ *vt* **hyphened; hyphened; hyphening** \-f(ə)niŋ\ **hyphens :** to connect (as two words or the parts of a word) with a hyphen **:** mark with a hyphen

**¹hy·phen·ate** \ˈhīfəˌnāt, *usu* -ād·+V\ *vt* -ED/-ING/-S [¹*hyphen* + *-ate*] **:** HYPHEN — **hy·phen·ation** \ˌhīfəˈnāshən\ *n* -s

**²hy·phen·ate** \-ˌnə̇t, ˌnāt, *usu* \d·+V\ *n* -s [back-formation fr. *hyphenated* (adj.)] **:** a hyphenated person; *specif* **:** a resident or citizen of the U.S. whose recent foreign national origin divides or is believed to divide his patriotic loyalties ⟨the effect of war hysteria upon a household of so-called ~s —*N.Y. Times*⟩ ⟨denounced ~s and called for national preparedness —*Current History*⟩

**hyphenated** *adj* [fr. past part. of ¹*hyphenate*; fr. the use of hyphenated words (as German-American, Irish-American) to designate foreign-born citizens of the U.S.] **:** of, relating to, or constituting a person or unit of mixed or diverse composition or origin ⟨~ Canadians —*N.Y. Herald*⟩ ⟨~ activity as both commercial florists and horticultural journalists —Richard Thruelsen⟩

**hy·phen·ic** \(ˈ)hīˌfenik\ *adj* **:** of or relating to hyphens

**hy·phen·ism** \ˈhīfəˌnizəm\ *n* -s [¹*hyphen* + *-ism*; fr. the use of hyphenated words (as German-American, Irish-American) to designate foreign-born citizens of the U.S.] **:** the quality or state of being a hyphenate **:** the conduct that marks or is ascribed to hyphenates ⟨~ in the United States is almost extinct —E.A.Mowrer⟩

**hy·phen·iza·tion** \ˌhīfənəˈzāshən, -ˌnīˈz-\ *n* -s **:** the joining of syllables or words with hyphens

**hy·phen·ize** \ˈhīfəˌnīz\ *vt* -ED/-ING/-S **:** HYPHEN

**hy·phes·so·bry·con** \hīˌfesəˈbrīˌkän\ *n, cap* [NL, fr. *hyphesso-* (fr. Gk *hyphēssōn* of lesser stature, fr. *hypo-* + *hēssōn* inferior, less) + *Brycon*, genus of fishes (fr. Gk *brykein* to eat greedily, bite, devour)] **:** a genus of small brilliantly colored So. American characin fishes including several that are often kept in the tropical aquarium

**hypho-** *comb form* [NL, fr. Gk *hyphē*, *hyphos* web — more at WEAVE] **:** web **:** tissue ⟨*hypho*drome⟩

**hy·pho·chyt·ri·a·les** \ˌhīfōˌkiˌtrēˈā(ˌ)lēz\ *n pl, cap* [NL, fr. *Hyphochytrium* genus of fungi (fr. *hypho-* + Gk *chytrion* small pot, cup, dim. of *chytris* small pot, dim. of *chytra* earthen pot) + *-ales* — more at CHYTRA] **:** a small order of lower fungi (subclass Oomycetes) that in general resemble members of the order Chytridiales but have anteriorly uniflagellate zoospores

**hy·pho·mi·cro·bi·a·les** \-ā(ˌ)lēz\ *n pl, cap* [NL, fr. *Hyphomicrobium* + *-ales*] **:** a small order of solitary or colonial chiefly free-living and aquatic sometimes stalked bacteria that reproduce by budding or by budding and longitudinal fission

**hy·pho·mi·cro·bi·a·ce·ae** \ˌhī(ˌ)fōˌmīˌkrōbēˈāsēˌē\ *n pl, cap* [NL, fr. *Hyphomicrobium*, type genus (fr. *hypho-* + *microbium*) + *-aceae*] **:** a small family of heterotrophic soil or water bacteria (order Hyphomicrobiales) that often have the individual cells linked by fine filaments

**hy·pho·my·ce·ta·les** \ˌhī(ˌ)fōˌmīsəˈtā(ˌ)lēz\ [NL, fr. *hypho-* + *mycet-* + *-ales*] *syn of* MONILIALES

**hy·pho·my·cete** \ˌhīfōˈmīˌsēt, ˌ⸗⸗ˌ⸗ˈ⸗\ *n* -s [NL *Hyphomycetes*] **:** a fungus of the subclass Hyphomycetes

**hy·pho·my·ce·tes** \ˌhīfōˌmīˈsēd·ēz\ *n pl, cap* [NL, fr. *hypho-* + *-mycetes*] *in some classifications* **:** a subclass of fungi coextensive with the order Moniliales or including both the Moniliales and the Mycelia Sterilia — **hy·pho·my·ce·tic** \ˌ⸗⸗ˌ⸗ˈsēd·ik\ *adj* — **hy·pho·my·ce·tous** \-d·əs\ *adj*

**hy·pho·my·co·sis** \ˌhīfōˌmīˈkōsəs\ *n* [NL, fr. *Hyphomycetes* + *-osis*] **1 :** infection with a hyphomycete **2 :** BURSATI 1

**hy·pho·po·di·ate** \ˌhīfōˈpōdēət, -ēˌāt\ *adj* [NL *hyphopodium* + E *-ate*] **:** having a hyphopodium

**hy·pho·po·di·um** \ˌ⸗⸗ˈpōdēəm\ *n, pl* **hyphopo·dia** \-ēə\ [NL, fr. *hypho-* + *-podium*] **:** a short 1-celled or 2-celled often lobed outgrowth from the mycelium of various ectoparasitic fungi that serves to attach the fungus to the host (as in the sooty molds)

**hy·pid·i·o·mor·phic** \hīˌpidēōˈmȯrfik\ *adj* [ISV *hypo-* + *idiomorphic*] **:** partly idiomorphic — used of a rock only some of whose constituents have a distinct crystalline form — **hy·pid·i·o·mor·phi·cal·ly** \-fə̇k(ə)lē\ *adv*

**hypn-** *or* **hypno-** *comb form* [F *hypn-*, fr. LL, fr. Gk, fr. *hypnos* — more at SOMNOLENT] **1 :** sleep ⟨*hypn*agogic⟩ **2 :** hypnotism ⟨*hypno*genesis⟩

**hyp·na·ce·ae** \hipˈnāsēˌē\ *n pl, cap* [NL, fr. *Hypnum*, type genus + *-aceae*] **:** a family of mosses (order Hypnobryales) that usu. grow in dense mats and have asymmetrical capsules — see HYPNUM — **hyp·na·ceous** \(ˈ)hipˌnāshəs\ *adj*

**hyp·na·gog·ic** *or* **hyp·no·gog·ic** \ˌhipnəˌgäjik\ *adj* [*hypnagogic* fr. F *hypnagogique*, fr. *hypn-* + *-agogique* (fr. Gk *-agōgikos* as in *paidagōgikos* pedagogic); *hypnogogic*, alter. of *hypnagogic*] **:** of, relating to, or associated with the drowsiness preceding sleep ⟨~ hallucinations⟩ — opposed to *hypnopompic*

**hyp·nea** \ˈhipnēə\ *n, cap* [NL, fr. *Hypnum*, genus of mosses] **:** a genus (the type of the family Hypneaceae) comprising red algae of the order Gigartinales that have a thallus of terete fleshy branches with the tips curving inward like tendrils and that include one (*H. musciformis*) which is occas. used as a source of agar

**hyp·no·analysis** \ˌhipnō+\ *n* [NL, fr. *hypnosis* + psychoanalysis] **:** psychoanalytic psychotherapy that uses hypnosis to facilitate transference by helping to dissolve resistance, assimilate interpretation, and recover repressed memories — compare HYPNOTHERAPY

**hyp·no·bryales** \ˈ"+\ *n pl, cap* [NL, fr. *hypno-* (fr. *Hypnum*, genus of mosses) + *Bryales*] **:** an order of Musci comprising mosses with a pleurocarpous sporophyte and a capsule usu. inclined at the end of a long seta and with an entire endostome

**hyp·no·cyst** \ˈhipnəˌsist\ *n* [*hypn-* + *-cyst*] **1 :** HYPNOSPORE **2 :** an encysted form by which various protozoans resist adverse conditions (as cold or drought)

**hyp·no·gen·e·sis** \ˌhipnōˈjenəsəs\ *n* [NL, fr. *hypn-* + L *genesis*] **:** the production of a hypnotic state

**hyp·no·ge·net·ic** \ˌhipnōjəˌned·ik\ *adj* [*hypn-* + *-genetic*] **1 :** inducing a hypnotic state **2 :** inducing sleep — **hyp·no·ge·net·i·cal·ly** \-d·ə̇k(ə)lē\ *adv*

**hyp·nog·e·nous** \(ˈ)hipˌnäjənəs\ *adj* [*hypn-* + *-genous*] **:** HYPNOGENETIC

**¹hyp·noid** \ˈhipˌnȯid\ *adj* [NL *Hypnum* + E *-oid*] **:** of, relating to, or resembling mosses of the genus *Hypnum* or related forms

**²hypnoid** \ˈ"\ *or* **hyp·noi·dal** \(ˈ)hipˌnȯidᵊl\ *adj* [*hypnoid* fr. NL *hypnosis* + E *-oid*; *hypnoidal* fr. *hypnoid* + *-al*] **:** of, relating to, or resembling sleep or hypnosis

**hyp·nol·o·gy** \hipˈnäləjē\ *n* -ES [*hypn-* + *-logy*] **:** the scientific study of sleep and hypnotic phenomena

**hyp·none** \ˈhipˌnōn\ *n* -s [ISV *hypn-* + *-one*; orig. formed in F] **:** ACETOPHENONE

**hyp·no·pho·bia** \ˌhipnəˈfōbēə\ *or* **hyp·no·pho·by** \ˈ⸗⸗ˌbē\ *n, pl* **hypnophobias** *or* **hypnophobies** [NL *hypnophobia*, fr. *hypn-* + *-phobia*] **:** morbid fear of sleep — **hy·pno·pho·bic** \ˌ⸗⸗ˈfōbik *also* -ˈfäb-\ *adj*

**hyp·no·pom·pic** \ˌhipnəˌpämpik\ *adj* [*hypn-* + *pomp-* (fr. Gk *pompē* act of sending, escort, procession) + *-ic* — more at POMP] **:** dispelling sleep **:** of, relating to, or associated with the semiconsciousness preceding waking ⟨~ dreams⟩ — opposed to *hypnagogic*

**hyp·no·sis** \hipˈnōsəs\ *n, pl* **hypno·ses** \-ōˌsēz\ [NL, fr. *hypn-* + *-osis*] **1 :** a state that resembles normal sleep but differs in being induced by the suggestions and operations of the hypnotizer with whom the hypnotized subject remains in rapport and responsive to his suggestions which may induce anesthesia, blindness, hallucinations, and paralysis while suggestions of curative value may also be accepted — compare POSTHYPNOTIC **2 :** any of various conditions that resemble sleep — compare CATAPLEXY **3 :** HYPNOTISM 1

**hyp·no·sperm** \ˈhipnə+ˌ-\ *n* [*hypn-* + *sperm*] **:** HYPNOSPORE

**hyp·no·sporangium** \ˌhipnō+\ *n* [NL, blend of E *hypnospore* and NL *sporangium*] **:** a sporangium containing hypnospores

**hyp·no·spore** \ˈhipnə+ˌ-\ *n* [*hypn-* + *spore*] **:** a very thick-walled asexual resting spore (as of various green algae) — **hyp·no·spor·ic** \ˌ⸗⸗ˌspōrik, -pȯr-\ *adj*

**hyp·no·therapeutic** \ˌhipnō+\ *adj* [fr. *hypnotherapy*, after E *therapy: therapeutic*] **:** of, relating to, or promoting hypnotherapy

**hyp·no·therapy** \ˈ"+\ *n* [*hypn-* + *therapy*] **1 :** the treatment of disease by hypnotism **2 :** psychotherapy that facilitates suggestion, reeducation, or analysis by means of hypnosis — compare HYPNOANALYSIS

**¹hyp·not·ic** \(ˈ)hipˌnäd·ik, -ät|, |ēk\ *adj* [F or LL; F *hypnotique*, fr. MF, fr. LL *hypnoticus*, fr. Gk *hypnōtikos* inclined to sleep, putting to sleep, soporific, fr. (assumed) Gk *hypnōtos* (verbal of Gk *hypnoun* to put to sleep, sleep, fr. *hypnos* sleep) + Gk *-ikos* -ic — more at SOMNOLENT] **1 :** tending to produce sleep **:** SOPORIFIC **2** [short for *neurohypnotic*] **:** of or relating to hypnosis or hypnotism **:** being under, susceptible to, or tending to induce hypnosis ⟨his noble brow and ~ stare —Julian Maclaren-Ross⟩ ⟨the mother's ~ will —Leslie Rees⟩ ⟨~ suspension of all his faculties —Mary Austin⟩

**²hypnotic** \ˈ"\ *n* -s **1 :** a drug or other agent that produces or tends to produce sleep **:** SOPORIFIC **2 :** one that is or is capable of being hypnotized

**hyp·not·i·cal·ly** \|ə̇k(ə)lē, |ēk-, -li\ *adv* **:** in a hypnotic manner ⟨~ interesting from beginning to end —*Harper's*⟩ **:** by means of hypnotism ⟨a fictitious meal ~ suggested —P.S.deQ.Cabot⟩

**hyp·no·tism** \ˈhipnəˌtizəm\ *n* -s [short for *neurohypnotism*] **1 :** the study of or the act or practice of inducing hypnosis — compare MESMERISM **2 :** HYPNOSIS 1

**hyp·no·tist** \ˈhipnətə̇st, -əd·ə̇st\ *n* -s **:** one that practices hypnotism

**hyp·no·tiz·abil·i·ty** \ˌhipnəˌtīzəˈbilid·ē\ *n* **:** susceptibility to hypnotism

**hyp·no·tiz·able** \ˈhipnəˌtīzəbəl, ˌ⸗⸗ˈ⸗⸗⸗\ *adj* **:** that can be hypnotized

**hyp·no·tize** *or* **hyp·no·tise** \ˈhipnəˌtīz\ *vb* -ED/-ING/-S [*hypnotism* + *-ize* or *-ise*] *vt* **1 :** to induce hypnosis in **2 :** to deaden (judgment or resistance) by or as if by hypnotic suggestion ⟨gave a passion to his oratory which *hypnotized* criticism —J.H.Plumb⟩ ~ *vi* **:** to practice hypnosis **:** use hypnotic art or suggestion

**hyp·no·toxin** \ˌhipnə+\ *n* [ISV *hypn-* + *toxin*] **:** a hypothetical hormonal product of brain tissue that is held to induce sleep

**hyp·num** \ˈhipnəm\ *n* [NL, fr. LGk *hypnon*, a lichen] **1** *cap* **:** the type genus of the family Hypnaceae comprising mosses with the leaves arranged in three rows — see PLUME MOSS **2** -s **:** any moss of the genus *Hypnum*

**¹hy·po** \ˈhī(ˌ)pō\ *n* -s [by shortening] **:** HYPOCHONDRIA ⟨nor is his spirit drooping with the ~s —*Amer. Mercury*⟩

**²hypo** \ˈ"\ *n* -s [short for *hyposulfite*] **:** sodium thiosulfate used as a fixing agent in photography

**³hypo** \ˈ"\ *n* -s [short for *hypodermic*] **1 :** HYPODERMIC SYRINGE **2 :** HYPODERMIC INJECTION **3 :** STIMULUS ⟨a sure ~ for car sales —*Hartford (Conn.) Times*⟩

**⁴hypo** \ˈ"\ *vt* -ED/-ING/-S **1 :** to administer a hypodermic injection to ⟨purged the calf with laxative, ~*ed* it with penicillin —*Time*⟩ **2 :** to stimulate as if with a hypodermic injection **:** EXCITE, ACCELERATE ⟨tried to ~ her interest —*Saturday Rev.*⟩ ⟨giant giveaways to ~ their sales figures —Bennett Cerf⟩ ⟨prefer their parties ~*ed* occasionally with a new face or figure —Maureen Daly⟩

**hypo-** *in pronunciations below* ˌ⸗⸗ = ˌhī(ˌ)pō *or* -ˌpə\ *or* **hyp-** *prefix* [alter. (influenced by LL *hypo-*, *hyp-*) of ME *ypo-*, fr. OF, fr. LL *hypo-*, *hyp-*, fr. Gk, fr. *hypo* — more at UP] **1 :** under **:** beneath **:** down ⟨*hypo*blast⟩ ⟨*hypo*dermic⟩ **2 :** less than normal or normally ⟨*hypo*calcemia⟩ ⟨*hypo*chromia⟩ ⟨*hypo*chlorhydric⟩ ⟨*hypo*sensitive⟩ **3 :** in a lower state of oxidation **:** in a low usu. the lowest position in a series of compounds ⟨*hypo*vanadous⟩ ⟨*hyp*oxanthine⟩ **4 a** *in ancient Greek music* (1) **:** being the lower octave in a disdiapason ⟨*hypo*lydian⟩ (2) *of an interval* **:** measured downward ⟨*hypo*diapason⟩ **b** *in medieval music* **:** being in a plagal mode ⟨*hypo*dorian⟩

**hy·po·adre·nia** \ˌ⸗⸗ *at* HYPO- + əˈdrēnēə\ *also* **hy·po·adre·nal·ism** \-nəˌlizəm\ *n* -s [*hypoadrenia* fr. NL, fr. *hypo-* + *adren-* + *-ia*; *hypoadrenalism* fr. *hypo-* + *adrenal* + *-ism*] **:** decreased activity of the adrenal glands; *specif* **:** adrenocortical insufficiency

**hy·po·aeolian mode** \ˌ⸗⸗+. . .-\ *n* [LL *hypoaeolius* hypoaeolian (fr. — assumed — Gk *hypoaiolios*, fr. Gk *hypo-* + *Aiolios* Aeolian, fr. *Aiolis* Aeolis, ancient country in Asia Minor) + E *-an*] **:** a plagal ecclesiastical mode consisting of a tetrachord and an upper conjunct pentachord represented on the white keys of the piano by an ascending diatonic scale from E to E — see MODE illustration

**hy·po·aesthesia** \ˈ"+\ *chiefly Brit var of* HYPESTHESIA

**hy·po·al·bu·min·emia** \ˌ⸗⸗+(ˌ)alˌbyümə̇ˈnēmēə\ *n* -s [NL, fr. *hypo-* + *albumin-* + *-emia*] **:** hypoproteinemia marked by reduction in serum albumins

**hy·po·allergenic** \ˌ⸗⸗+\ *adj* [*hypo-* + *allergenic*] **:** having a relatively low capacity to induce hypersensitivity

**hypo-alum toning process** *n* [²*hypo* + *alum*] **:** a method of altering a developed silver photographic image to a sepia color by means of a warm solution containing essentially hypo and alum

**hy·po·bar·ic** \ˌ⸗⸗+ˌbarik\ *adj* [*hypo-* + Gk *baros* weight + E *-ic* — more at GRIEVE] **:** having a specific gravity less than that of cerebrospinal fluid — used of solutions for spinal anesthesia; opposed to *hyperbaric*

**hy·po·basal** \ˈ"+\ *adj* [ISV *hypo-* + *basal*] *bot* **:** situated posterior to the basal wall ⟨the ~ lower segment of a developing embryo⟩ — compare EPIBASAL

**hy·po·basidium** \ˈ"+\ *n* [NL, fr. *hypo-* + *basidium*] **:** a special cell constituting the base of the basidium in various fungi of the orders Auriculariales and Tremellales in which haploid nuclei fuse and from which the epibasidium arises

**hy·po·batholithic** \ˈ"+\ *adj* [*hypo-* + *batholithic*] **:** of, relating to, or constituting ore deposits that occur in deeply eroded batholiths

**hy·po·benthos** \ˈ"+\ *n* [NL, fr. *hypo-* + *benthos*] **:** the fauna of the deep sea

**hy·po·blast** \ˈ⸗⸗+ˌblast\ *n* [*hypo-* + *-blast*] **:** the endoderm of an embryo

**hy·po·blas·tic** \ˌ⸗⸗ˈblastik\ *adj* **:** of, relating to, or derived from hypoblast **:** ENDODERMAL

**¹hy·po·branchial** \ˌ⸗⸗+\ *adj* [*hypo-* + *branchial*] **1 :** situated below the gills **:** of or relating to the ventral wall of the pharynx; *specif* **:** of or relating to the endostyle **2 :** of, relating to, or being the segment of a branchial arch between the basibranchial and the ceratobranchial

**²hypobranchial** \ˈ"\ *n* -s **:** a hypobranchial bone or cartilage

**hy·po·bro·mite** \ˌ⸗⸗+ˈbrōˌmīt\ *n* -s [ISV *hypobrom-* (fr. *hypobromous acid*) + *-ite*] **:** a salt or ester of hypobromous acid

**hy·po·bro·mous acid** \ˌ⸗⸗ˌbrōməs. . .-\ *n* [ISV *hypo-* + *bromine* + *-ous*] **:** an unstable acid HBrO that resembles hypochlorous acid and is obtained in solution by reaction of bromine water with silver nitrate or in the form of unstable salts by reaction of bromine with alkaline solutions

**hy·po·bu·lia** \ˌ⸗⸗+ˈbyülēə\ *n* -s [NL, fr. *hypo-* + *-bulia*] **:** lowered ability to make decisions or to act — **hy·po·bu·lic** \ˌ⸗⸗ˌ⸗lik\ *adj*

**hy·po·cal·ce·mia** *also* **hy·po·cal·cae·mia** \ˌ⸗⸗+kalˈsēmēə\ *n* -s [NL, fr. *hypo-* + *calcemia*, *calcaemia* calcium in the blood (fr. *calc-* + *-emia*, *-aemia*)] **:** a deficiency of calcium in the blood — **hy·po·cal·ce·mic** *also* **hy·po·cal·cae·mic** \ˌ⸗⸗ˌ⸗ˈmik\ *adj*

**hy·po·cap·nia** \ˌ⸗⸗+ˈkapnēə\ *n* -s [NL, fr. *hypo-* + *-capnia*] **:** deficiency of carbon dioxide in the blood

**hy·po·carp** \ˈ⸗⸗+ˌkärp\ *or* **hy·po·car·pi·um** \ˌ⸗⸗+ˈkärpēəm\ *n, pl* **hypocarps** \-ps\ *or* **hypocar·pia** \-ēə\ [NL *hypocarpium*, fr. *hypo-* + *-carpium* -carp] **:** an enlarged sometimes edible peduncle beneath some fruits (as the cashew apple)

**hy·po·caust** \ˈ⸗⸗+ˌkȯst\ *n* -s [L *hypocaustum*, *hypocauston*, fr. Gk *hypokauston*, fr. neut. of *hypokaustos* heated by a hypocaust, fr. (assumed) Gk *hypokaustos*, verbal of Gk *hypokaiein* to light (a fire) under, fr. *hypo-* + *kaiein* to burn — more at CAUSTIC] **:** a central heating system of an ancient Roman dwelling, public bath, or other building consisting of an underground furnace or fire chamber and a series of tile flues for distribution of the heat

**hy·po·cellular** \ˌ⸗⸗ *at* HYPO-+\ *adj* [*hypo-* + *cellular*] **:** containing less than the normal number of cells ⟨~ bone marrow in chronic lead poisoning⟩

**hy·po·center** \ˈ"+\ *n* [*hypo-* + *center*] **:** the point on the earth's surface directly below the center of a nuclear bomb explosion

**hy·po·centrum** \ˈ"+\ *n, pl* **hypocentra** [NL, fr. *hypo-* + *centrum*] **:** a ventral part of the body of a vertebra that is usu. wedge-shaped or horseshoe-shaped, consists of the fused lower arcualia of the anterior of the two arches from which each vertebra is formed, and is characteristic of some fishes, stegocephalians, and primitive reptiles — called also *intercentrum*

**hy·po·ceph·a·lus** \ˌ⸗⸗+ˈsefələs\ *n, pl* **hypocepha·li** \-fəˌlī\ [NL, fr. *hypo-* + *-cephalus* (fr. Gk *kephalē* head) — more at CEPHALIC] **:** a circular sheet of papyrus containing extracts from the 162d chapter of the Book of the Dead stiffened with plastered linen and placed as an amulet under the head of an ancient Egyptian mummy in the coffin

**hy·po·chae·ris** \ˈ"+ˈkirəs\ *n, cap* [NL, alter. of L *hypochoeris*, a plant, fr. Gk *hypochoiris* succory plant, fr. *hypo-* + *-choiris* (fr. *choiros* young pig, pig) — more at CHAEROPUS] **:** a large widely distributed genus of milky-juiced herbs (family Compositae) that have basal leaves and scapose yellow flower heads and include some (as the cat's-ear) that are cosmopolitan weeds of open lands

**hy·po·chil** \ˈ⸗⸗+ˌkil\ *or* **hy·po·chil·i·um** \ˌ⸗⸗+ˈkilēəm\ *n* -s [NL *hypochilium*, fr. *hypo-* + Gk *cheilos* lip + NL *-ium* — more at GILL] **:** the lower part of the labellum in orchids

**hy·po·chil·o·morph** \¦==+¦kilə,mȯrf\ *adj* [NL *Hypochilomorphae*] **:** of or relating to the Hypochilomorphae

**hy·po·chil·o·mor·phae** \,==,=='mȯr(,)fē\ *n pl, cap* [NL, fr. *hypo-* + *chil-* + *-morphae*] **:** a suborder of Araneida comprising arachnomorph spiders with two pairs of book lungs

**hy·po·chloremia** \¦== *at* HYPO- +\ *n* [NL, fr. *hypo-* + *chloremia*] **:** abnormal decrease of chlorides in the blood — **hy·po·chlor·e·mic** \"+,klōr¦ēmik\ *adj*

**hy·po·chlor·hy·dria** \,==+,klōr'hīdrēə\ *n* -S [NL, fr. *hypo-* + *chlorhydria* hydrochloric acid in the gastric juice (fr. *chlor-* + *hydr-* + *-ia*)] **:** deficiency of hydrochloric acid in the gastric juice — compare HYPERCHLORHYDRIA — **hy·po·chlor·hy·dric** \¦==,=¦=drik\ *adj*

**hy·po·chlorite** \¦== *at* HYPO- +\ *n* [ISV *hypochlor-* (fr. *hypochlorous acid*) + *-ite*] **:** a salt or ester of hypochlorous acid: as **a :** SODIUM HYPOCHLORITE **b :** CALCIUM HYPOCHLORITE

**hy·po·chlorous acid** \¦==+...-\ *n* [ISV *hypo-* + *chlorous*; orig. formed as F *hypochloreux*] **:** an unstable strongly oxidizing but weak acid HClO that is obtained in solution along with hydrochloric acid by reaction of chlorine with water or in the form of salts by reaction of chlorine with alkaline solutions and that is used chiefly in the form of salts as an oxidizing agent, bleaching agent, disinfectant, and chlorinating agent

**hy·poch·na·ce·ae** \,hī(,)päk'nāsē,ē\ [NL, fr. *Hypochnus* + *-aceae*] *syn of* THELEPHORACEAE

**hy·poch·nus** \hī'päknəs\ [NL, fr. *hypo-* + Gk *chnoos, chnous* dust, fine down; akin to Gk *chnauein* to gnaw, nibble, OE *gnagan* to gnaw — more at GNAW] *syn of* TOMENTELLA

**hy·po·choeris** \,== *at* HYPO- +'kirə̇s\ [NL, fr. L, a plant — more at HYPOCHAERIS] *syn of* HYPOCHAERIS

**hy·po·chon·der** *or* **hy·po·chon·dre** \"+'kändə(r)\ *n* -S [LL *hypochondria*, pl., abdomen] *archaic* **:** HYPOCHONDRIUM

**hy·po·chon·dria** \,hīpə'kändrēə, -pō'- *sometimes* ,hip-\ *n* -S [NL, fr. LL, pl., abdomen, belly (formerly supposed to be the seat of hypochondria), fr. Gk, fr. *hypochondria*, neut. pl. of *hypochondrios* under the cartilage of the breastbone, fr. *hypo-* + *-chondrios* (fr. *chondros* cartilage, cartilage of the breastbone, granule, grain) — more at GRIND] **:** extreme depression of mind or spirits often centered on imaginary physical ailments ⟨her ~, her insecurity, her staunch integrity, and loneliness —Bosley Crowther⟩ ⟨the present philosophical and political ~ about moral skepticism —Charles Frankel⟩; *specif* **:** HYPOCHONDRIASIS

[1]**hy·po·chon·dri·ac** \¦==¦=drē,ak\ *adj* [F *hypochondriaque*, adj. & n., fr. MF, fr. Gk *hypochondriakos*, adj., of the abdomen, fr. *hypochondrion*, sing., *hypochondria*, pl., abdomen + *-akos* (adj. suffix)] **1** *also* **hy·po·chon·dri·al** \-ēəl\ **a :** situated below the costal cartilages **b :** of, relating to, or being the two regions of the abdomen lying on either side of the epigastric region and above the lumbar regions — see ABDOMINAL REGION illustration **2** *or* **hy·po·chon·dri·a·cal** \¦hīpə¦kən¦drīəkəl, -pō¦, ¦,kän- *sometimes* ¦hip-\ **:** affected, characterized, or produced by hypochondria

[2]**hypochondriac** \"\ *n* -S [F *hypochondriaque*] **:** one affected by hypochondria or hypochondriasis ⟨a ~ . . . lives in a world of sick imagination —J.W.Krutch⟩ ⟨some miserable ~ whose interests are bounded by his own ailments —Bertrand Russell⟩

**hy·po·chon·dri·a·sis** \,hīpəkən'drīəsə̇s\ *n, pl* **hypochondria·ses** \-īə,sēz\ [NL, fr. *hypochondria* + *-iasis*] **:** hypochondria of pathological proportions **:** morbid concern about one's health esp. when accompanied by delusions of physical disease

**hy·po·chon·dri·ast** \,hīpə'kändrē,ast\ *n* -S [NL *hypochondria* + E *-ast* (as in *enthusiast*)] **:** HYPOCHONDRIAC

**hy·po·chon·dri·um** \-ēəm\ *n, pl* **hypochon·dria** \-ēə\ [NL, fr. Gk *hypochondrion* abdomen, belly, fr. neut. sing. of *hypochondrios*] **:** either hypochondriac region of the body

**hy·po·chordal** \¦== *at* HYPO- +\ *adj* [*hypo-* + *chordal*] **:** ventral to the spinal cord

**hy·po·chro·mia** \,==+'krōmēə\ *n* [NL, fr. *hypo-* + *-chromia*] **1 :** deficiency of color or pigmentation **2 :** deficiency of hemoglobin in the red blood cells (as in nutritional anemia)

**hy·po·chro·mic** \¦==¦=mik\ *adj* [NL *hypochromia* + E *-ic*] **:** exhibiting hypochromia

**hypochromic anemia** *n* **:** any of various anemias that are characterized by abnormally low blood color index, deficiency of hemoglobin, and usu. microcytic red blood cells and are associated with lack of available iron, whether by reason of excessive loss (as in hemorrhage), inadequate intake, or faulty assimilation — compare HYPERCHROMIC ANEMIA

**hy·po·clei·di·an** \¦==+¦klīdēən\ *adj* [NL *hypocleidium* + E *-an*] **:** of or relating to a hypocleidium

**hy·po·clei·di·um** \,=='==əm\ *n, pl* **hypoclei·dia** \-ēə\ [NL, fr. *hypo-* + Gk *kleidion* small key, dim. of *kleid-, kleis* key, hook, clavicle — more at CLEID-] **:** a median process on the wishbone of many birds often connected with the sternum by a ligament or ossified with it

**hy·po·condylar** \¦== *at* HYPO- +\ *adj* [*hypo-* + *condylar*] **:** located under or below a condyle

**hy·po·cone** \'==+,-\ *n* [*hypo-* + *cone*] **:** the principal rear inner cusp of a mammalian upper molar

**hy·po·con·id** \,==+'känə̇d\ *n* -S [*hypo-* + [2]*con-* + *-id*] **:** the principal rear outer cusp of a mammalian lower molar

[1]**hy·po·coracoid** \¦== *at* HYPO- +\ *n* [*hypo-* + *coracoid*] **:** a hypocoracoid bone

[2]**hypocoracoid** \"\ *adj* **:** of, relating to, or being the lower of two bones at the base of the pectoral fin attached behind the clavicle and sometimes regarded as homologous with the coracoid of the higher vertebrates

**hypoco·rism** \hī'päkə,rizəm, hə̇'-; ,hīpə'kōr,izəm, ,hip-\ *n* -S [LL *hypocorisma* diminutive (n.), fr. Gk *hypokorisma* endearing name, fr. *hypokorizesthai* to call by endearing names, fr. *hypo-* + *korizesthai* to caress (fr. *koros* boy, *korē* girl) — more at CRESCENT] **1 :** a pet name or term of endearment **2 :** the formation or use of pet names ⟨~ is the frequent practice of fond parents⟩ **3 :** BABY TALK 1b ⟨~ is hardly in keeping with human dignity —A.W.Read⟩

[1]**hypo·co·ris·tic** \¦hīpəkə¦ristik, ¦hip-; hī¦päk-, hi¦-\ *adj* [Gk *hypokoristikos* diminutive, fr. (assumed) Gk *hypokoristos* (verbal of Gk *hypokorizesthai*) + Gk *-ikos* -ic] **1 :** of, relating to, or used as a pet name or form of baby talk **2 :** forming a hypocoristic word — used of a suffix, abbreviation, or other modification

[2]**hypocoristic** \"\ *n* **:** a hypocoristic term

**hy·po·cot·yl** \'== *at* HYPO- +,käd·ᵊl, ,=='==\ *n* -S [ISV *hypo-* + *-cotyl*] **:** the part of the axis of a plant embryo or seedling below the cotyledon — compare EPICOTYL, RADICLE

**hypocotyl arch** *n* **:** the part of the stem that is normally below the cotyledons but in various seedlings (as of the bean) grows at a differential rate and curves so as to be the first structure to appear above the ground

**hy·po·cotyledonary** \"+\ *adj* [*hypocotyledonary*, ISV *hypo-* + *cotyledonary*] **:** located below the cotyledons

**hy·po·cre·a·ce·ae** \,==+krē'āsē,ē\ *n pl, cap* [NL, fr. *Hypocrea*, type genus (fr. *hypo-* + Gk *kreas* flesh) + *-aceae* — more at RAW] **:** a family of fungi that have brightly colored fleshy or membranous ascocarps, include parasites of economic plants, and are usu. included in Hypocreales but sometimes placed in Sphaeriales and then held to include the Nectriaceae

**hy·po·cre·a·les** \-'ā(,)lēz\ *n pl, cap* [NL, fr. *Hypocrea*, genus of fungi + *-ales*] **:** an order of fungi (subclass Euascomycetes) closely related to and probably derived from the Sphaeriales — see HYPOCREACEAE

**hyp·o·crise** *or* **hyp·o·crize** \'hipə,krīz\ *vi* -ED/-ING/-S [F *hypocriser*, fr. MF, fr. OF *ypocrisie* hypocrisy] **:** to act hypocritically

**hy·poc·ri·sy** \hə̇'päkrəsē, -si *sometimes* hī'-\ *n* -ES [ME *ipocrisie*, fr. OF *ypocrisie*, fr. LL *hypocrisis*, fr. Gk *hypokrisis* act of playing a part on the stage, hypocrisy, outward show, fr. *hypokrinesthai* to answer, play a part on the stage, act, pretend, fr. *hypo-* + *krinesthai* to dispute, *krinein* to decide, judge — more at CERTAIN] **1 :** the act or practice of pretending to be what one is not or to have principles or beliefs that one does not have ⟨the passing stranger who took such a vitriolic joy in exposing their pretensions and their ~ —Van Wyck Brooks⟩; *esp* **:** the false assumption of an appearance of virtue or religion ⟨may admit that our conventional morality often serves as a cover for ~ and selfishness —Lucius Garvin⟩ **2 :** an act or instance of hypocrisy ⟨the little *hypocrisies* which are so frequently the rule rather than the exception in human contacts —Erle Stanley Gardner⟩

**hy·poc·ri·tal** \hə̇'päkrəd·ᵊl, ¦hipə¦krid·ᵊl\ *adj* **:** HYPOCRITICAL

[1]**hyp·o·crite** \'hipə,krit, *usu* -id·+V\ *n* -S [ME *ipocrite*, fr. OF *ypocrite*, fr. LL *hypocrita*, fr. Gk *hypokritēs* actor on the stage, pretender, hypocrite, fr. *hypokrinesthai*] **:** one who pretends to be what he is not or to have principles or beliefs that he does not have; *esp* **:** one who falsely assumes an appearance of virtue or religion ⟨I dare swear he is no ~, but prays from his heart —Shak.⟩

[2]**hypocrite** \"\ *adj* [ME *ypocrite*, fr. *ypocrite*, *ipocrite*, n.] **:** HYPOCRITICAL ⟨our ~ century —Wyndham Lewis⟩

**hypocrite plant** *n* **:** MEXICAN FIRE PLANT 1

**hyp·o·crit·i·cal** \¦hipə¦krid·|ə̇kəl, -it|, |ēk-\ *or* **hyp·o·crit·ic** \|ik, |ēk\ *adj* [[1]*hypocrite* + *-ical* or *-ic*] **:** of or relating to a hypocrite or hypocrisy **:** DISSEMBLING, FALSE, SPECIOUS ⟨a ~ gesture of modesty and virtue —Robert Graves⟩ — **hyp·o·crit·i·cal·ly** \|ə̇k(ə)lē, |ēk-, -li\ *adv*

**hy·po·crystalline** \¦== *at* HYPO- +\ *adj* [ISV *hypo-* + *crystalline*] **:** HEMICRYSTALLINE

**hy·po·cu·pre·mia** *or* **hy·po·cu·prae·mia** \,==+,k(y)ü'prēmēə\ *also* **hy·po·cu·pro·sis** \-rōsə̇s\ *n, pl* **hypocupremias** *or* **hypocupraemias** *also* **hypocuproses** [NL, fr. *hypo-* + *cupr-* + *-emia* or *-aemia* or *-osis*] **1 :** a deficiency in blood copper esp. of a domestic animal **2 :** a diseased condition resulting from a blood-copper deficiency — **hy·po·cu·pre·mic** \¦==,=¦prēmik\ *adj*

**hy·po·cycloid** \¦== *at* HYPO- +\ *n* [*hypo-* + *cycloid*] **:** a curve traced by a point on the circumference of a circle rolling internally on another circle — compare EPICYCLOID

hypocycloid *H* traced by point *P* on circle *R* rolling within fixed circle *F*

**hy·po·derm** \'==+,dərm\ *n* [NL *hypoderma* (tissue)] **1 a :** HYPODERMIS 2b **b :** HYPOBLAST **2 :** HYPODERMIS 1

[1]**hy·po·der·ma** \,==+'dərmə, -'dōmə, -'dəimə\ *n* [NL, fr. *hypo-* + Gk *derma* skin, fr. *derein* to skin — more at TEAR] **1** *cap* **:** a cosmopolitan genus (the type of the family Hypodermatidae) of two-winged flies that have larvae parasitic in the tissues of vertebrates **2** -S **:** an insect or maggot of the genus *Hypoderma*

[2]**hypoderma** \"\ *n* [NL, fr. *hypo-* + Gk *derma* skin] **1 :** HYPODERMIS 2b **2 :** HYPODERMIS 1

**hy·po·der·mal** \¦==¦=məl\ *adj* [NL *hypoderma* + E *-al*] **:** of or relating to a hypodermis ⟨~ tissues⟩ **:** lying beneath an outer skin or epidermis ⟨~ glands⟩

**hy·po·dermatic** \¦==(,)dər¦mad·ik\ *adj* [*hypo-* + *dermatic* dermal (fr. Gk *dermatikos*, fr. *dermat-* + *-ikos* -ic] **:** HYPODERMIC — **hy·po·der·mat·i·cal·ly** \-d·ə̇k(ə)lē\ *adv*

[1]**hy·po·der·mic** \¦hīpə¦dərmik, -¦dōm-, -¦dəim-, -mēk\ *adj* [ISV *hypo-* + *dermic*] **1 :** of or relating to the parts beneath the skin **2 a :** adapted for use in injecting medication or drugs beneath the skin **b :** administered by injection beneath the skin **3 :** resembling a hypodermic injection in effect **:** ROUSING, STIMULATING ⟨one of the most ~ personalities he had ever known —Robert Rice⟩

[2]**hypodermic** \"\ *n* -S **1 :** HYPODERMIC INJECTION **2 :** HYPODERMIC SYRINGE

**hy·po·der·mi·cal·ly** \-mə̇k(ə)lē, -mēk-, -li\ *adv* **:** in a hypodermic location or manner; *specif* **:** by means of a hypodermic

**hypodermic injection** *n* **:** an injection made into the subcutaneous tissues

**hypodermic medication** *n* **:** application of medicaments by injection under the skin

**hypodermic needle** *n* **1 :** NEEDLE 1c(2) **2 :** a hypodermic syringe complete with needle

**hypodermic syringe** *n* **:** a small syringe used with a hollow needle for injection of material into or beneath the skin

hypodermic syringe

**hypodermic tablet** *n* **:** a water-soluble tablet that contains a specified amount of medication and is intended for hypodermic administration

**hy·po·der·mis** \,=='=mə̇s\ *n* [NL, fr. *hypo-* + *-dermis*] **1 :** the tissue immediately beneath the epidermis of a plant esp. when lignified, suberized, or otherwise modified to serve as a supporting and protecting layer **2 a :** HYPOBLAST **b :** the cellular layer that underlies and secretes the chitinous cuticle of arthropods and some other invertebrates

**hy·po·der·moc·ly·sis** \,==(,)dər'mäkləsə̇s\ *n, pl* **hypoder·mocly·ses** \-lə,sēz\ [NL, fr. *hypo-* + *derm-* + *clysis*] **:** subcutaneous injection of fluids (as saline or glucose solution)

**hy·po·der·mo·sis** \-'mōsə̇s\ *n* -ES [NL, fr. *hypo-* + *derm-* + *-osis*] **:** infestation with warbles

**hy·po·der·mous** \¦==¦dərməs\ *adj* [NL *hypodermis* + E *-ous*] **:** HYPODERMAL

**hy·po·dochmius** \¦== *at* HYPO- +\ *n* [NL, fr. *hypo-* + L *dochmius*] **:** a metrical line of three trochees the last of which lacks a final unstressed syllable

**hy·po·dorian mode** \¦==+...-\ *n* [LL *hypodorius* hypodorian (fr. Gk *hypodōrios*, fr. *hypo-* + *Dōrios* Dorian) + E *-an*; *hypodorian mode*, trans. of Gk *hypodōria harmonia* — more at DORIAN] **1 :** a Greek mode consisting of two disjunct tetrachords represented on the white keys of the piano by a descending diatonic scale from A to A — see GREEK MODE illustration **2 :** a plagal ecclesiastical mode consisting of a tetrachord and an upper conjunct pentachord represented on the white keys of the piano by an ascending diatonic scale from A to A — see MODE illustration

**hy·po·dy·namia** \,==+,dī'namēə, -,də̇'-, -nām-\ *n* -S [NL, fr. *hypo-* + *-dynamia*] **:** decrease in strength or power

**hy·po·dynamic** \¦== *at* HYPO- +\ *adj* [*hypo-* + *dynamic*] **:** marked by or exhibiting hypodynamia

**hypoed** *past of* HYPO

**hy·po·er·gic** \¦==+¦ərjik\ *adj* **:** having a degree of sensitivity toward an allergen less than that typical of age group and community — compare NORMERGIC

**hy·po·ergy** \'==,ərjē\ *n* -ES [ISV *hypo-* + all*ergy*] **:** the quality or state of being hypoergic

**hy·po·eutectic** \¦==+\ *adj* [*hypo-* + *eutectic*] **:** containing the minor component in an amount less than in the eutectic mixture

**hy·po·eutectoid** \"+\ *adj* [*hypo-* + *eutectoid*] **1 :** containing the minor component in an amount less than that contained in the eutectoid **2** *of steel* **:** containing less than 0.80 percent carbon

**hy·po·fer·re·mia** *also* **hy·po·fer·rae·mia** \,==+,fe'rēmēə\ *n* -S [NL, fr *hypo-* + L *ferrum* iron + NL *-emia* or *-aemia* — more at FARRIER] **1 :** deficiency in blood iron esp of a domestic animal **2 :** a diseased condition resulting from a blood iron deficiency

**hy·po·function** \¦== *at* HYPO-+\ *n* [*hypo-* + *function*] **:** decreased or insufficient function esp. of an endocrine gland

**hypogaeum** *var of* HYPOGEUM

**hy·pog·a·my** \hī'pägəmē, hə̇'-\ *n* -ES [*hypo-* + *-gamy*] **:** marriage into a lower caste, class, or social group

**hy·po·gas·tric** \¦== *at* HYPO- + ¦gastrik\ *adj* [F *hypogastrique*, fr. MF, fr. *hypogastre* hypogastrium (fr. Gk *hypogastrion*) + *-ique* -ic] **:** of or relating to the lower median region of the abdomen — see ABDOMINAL REGION illustration

**hypogastric artery** *n* **:** ILIAC ARTERY 3

**hypogastric plexus** *n* **:** the sympathetic nerve plexus that supplies the pelvic viscera, lies in front of the promontory of the sacrum, and extends down into two lateral portions

**hypogastric vein** *n* **:** a vein that accompanies the hypogastric artery, drains the pelvis and the gluteal and perineal regions, and unites with the external iliac vein to form the common iliac vein

**hy·po·gas·tri·um** \,==+'gastrēəm\ *n, pl* **hypogas·tria** \-ēə\ [NL, fr. Gk *hypogastrion*, fr. *hypo-* + *gastr-* + *-ion* -ium] **:** the hypogastric region

**hy·po·ge·al** \¦==+¦jēəl\ *or* **hy·po·ge·ous** \-əs\ *also* **hy·po·ge·an** *or* **hy·po·gae·an** \-ən\ *or* **hy·po·ge·ic** \-ēik\ *adj* [LL *hypogeus* subterranean (fr. Gk *hypogeios, hypogaios*) + E *-al* or *-ous* or *-an* or *-ic*] **1 a** *of a plant or plant part* **:** growing below the surface of the ground; *esp, of a cotyledon* **:** remaining below the ground while the epicotyl elongates **b** *of plant germination* **:** producing hypogeal cotyledons **2 :** living below the surface of the ground — used esp. of an insect; distinguished from *aerial* and *epigeal* **3** *geol* **:** occurring below the surface or within the interior of the earth ⟨~ forces⟩ — **hy·po·ge·al·ly** \-əlē\ *adv*

**hy·po·gee** \'==+jē\ *n* -S [F or L; F *hypogée*, fr. MF, fr. L *hypogeum*] **:** HYPOGEUM

**hyp·o·gene** \"+,jēn\ *adj* [*hypo-* + *-gene* (as in *epigene*)] **1 :** formed, crystallized, or lying at depths below the earth's surface **:** PLUTONIC — used of various rocks; opposed to *epigene* **2 :** formed by generally ascending solutions — used of ore deposits; opposed to *supergene*

**hy·po·gen·e·sis** \¦== *at* HYPO-+¦jenəsə̇s\ *n* [NL, fr. *hypo-* + L *genesis*] **1 :** direct development without alternation of generations **2 :** underdevelopment esp. of an organ or function

**hy·po·ge·net·ic** \"+jə̇¦ned·ik\ *adj* **:** of, relating to, or exhibiting hypogenesis

**hy·po·gen·ic** \"+¦jenik\ *adj* [*hypogene* + *-ic*] **:** of, relating to, or constituting hypogene action or crystallization ⟨a district under the influence of ~ activities reaches a condition of seismic strain —*Encyclopedia Britannica*⟩

**hy·po·gen·i·tal·ism** \,==+'jenəd·ᵊl,izəm\ *n* -S [ISV *hypo-* + *genital* + *-ism*] **:** subnormal development of genital organs **:** genital infantilism

**hy·pog·e·nous** \(')hī¦päjənəs, hə̇'p-\ *adj* [ISV *hypo-* + *-genous*] **1 :** growing on the lower side (as of a leaf) — used esp. of a fungus **2 :** HYPOGENIC

**hy·po·ge·um** *or* **hy·po·gae·um** \,== *at* HYPO- + 'jēəm\ *n, pl* **hypo·gea** *or* **hypo·gaea** \-ēə\ [L, fr. Gk *hypogeion, hypogaion*, fr. neut. of *hypogeios, hypogaios* subterranean, fr. *hypo-* + *gē, gaia* earth, ground] **1 a :** the subterranean part of an ancient building **:** CELLAR **b :** the underground service galleries of an ancient amphitheater **2 :** an ancient underground burial chamber or series of such rooms **:** CATACOMB

**hy·po·glos·sal** \¦==+¦gläsəl, -lȯs-\ *adj* [NL *hypoglossus* + E *-al*] **:** of, relating to, or constituting the hypoglossal nerve ⟨~ fissure⟩

**hypoglossal nerve** *also* **hypoglossal** *n* -S **:** either of the 12th and final pair of cranial nerves being a motor nerve arising usu. from three roots in the medulla oblongata and supplying muscles of the tongue and hyoid apparatus in higher vertebrates but being absent in lower forms

**hy·po·glos·sus** \,=='=səs\ *n, pl* **hypoglos·si** \-ä,sī, -ȯ,sī\ [NL, fr. *hypo-* + *-glossus* (fr. Gk *glōssa* tongue) — more at GLOSS] **:** HYPOGLOSSAL NERVE

**hy·po·glot·tis** \,==+'gläd·ə̇s\ *n* [Gk *hypoglōttis*, fr. *hypo-* + *glōtta, glōssa* tongue] **1 :** the underpart of the tongue **2 :** a sclerite adjoining the labium of various beetles

**hy·po·glu·ce·mia** *also* **hy·po·glu·cae·mia** \,==+,glü'sēmēə\ *n* -S [NL, fr. *hypo-* + *gluc-* + *-emia* or *-aemia*] **:** HYPOGLYCEMIA

**hy·po·glycemia** \¦==+\ *n* [NL, fr. *hypo-* + *glycemia*] **:** abnormal decrease of sugar in the blood — see HYPERINSULINISM — **hy·po·glycemic** \"+\ *adj*

**hy·pog·na·thous** \(')hī¦pägnəthəs\ *adj* [*hypo-* + *-gnathous*] **1 :** having the lower jaw longer than the upper **2 :** having the mouthparts ventrally directed — used esp. of certain insects with biting mouthparts directed downward and often somewhat backward; compare PROGNATHOUS

**hy·po·gonadal** \¦== *at* HYPO-+\ *adj* **1 :** suffering from or marked by hypogonadism **2 :** marked by or exhibiting deficient development of secondary sexual characteristics

**hy·po·gonad·ism** \,==+'gō,na,dizəm *or* 'gä,n-\ *n* -S [ISV *hypo-* + *gonad* + *-ism*] **1 :** functional incompetence of the gonads esp. in the male with subnormal or impaired production of both hormonal and reproductive elements **2 :** an abnormal state involving gonadal incompetence **:** EUNUCHOIDISM

**hy·pog·y·nous** \(')hī¦päjənəs\ *adj* [*hypo-* + *-gynous*] **1 :** inserted upon the receptacle or axis below the gynoecium and free from it — used of sepals, petals, and stamens; compare EPIGYNOUS **2** *of a flower* **:** having sepals, petals, or stamens inserted as hypogynous parts — **hy·pog·y·ny** \='==nē\ *n* -ES

**hy·po·hal·ite** \,== *at* HYPO- + 'ha,līt\ *n* [*hypohalous* acid + *-ite*] **:** a salt or ester of a hypohalous acid

**hy·po·hal·ous acid** \¦==¦haləs-\ *n* [*hypo-* + *hal-* + *-ous*] **:** an acid HXO derived from the halogens and including hypochlorous acid, hypobromous acid, and hypoiodous acid

**hy·po·hidrosis** \¦==+\ *n* [NL, fr. *hypo-* + *hidrosis*] **:** abnormally diminished sweating — opposed to *hyperhidrosis*

**hy·po·hip·pine** \,==+'hi,pīn, -,pə̇n\ *n* -S [NL *Hypohippus* + E *-ine* (fr. *-ine*, adj. suffix)] **:** an animal or fossil of the genus *Hypohippus*

**hy·po·hip·pus** \-,pəs\ *n, cap* [NL, fr. *hypo-* + *-hippus*] **:** a genus of extinct long-necked long-bodied short-limbed horses showing adaptations for life in forests and known from remains found in the Miocene of America and the Pliocene of China

**hy·po·hy·al** \¦==+¦hīəl\ *adj* [*hypo-* + *hyoid* + *-al*] **:** of, relating to, or constituting one or two small elements of each side of the hyoid arch of most fishes between the ceratohyal and the median basihyal

**hy·po·hyaline** \"+\ *adj* [*hypo-* + *hyaline*] **:** partly glassy — used of rocks

**hy·poid** \'hī,pȯid\ *adj* [short for *hyperboloidal*] **:** utilizing, used for, or relating to hypoid gears ⟨~ rear axle⟩ ⟨~ grease⟩

**hypoid gear** *also* **hypoid** *n* -S **:** one of a pair of bevel gears that are used esp. in automotive transmissions, are designed so that the axis of the pinion does not intersect the axis of the gear, and have the teeth on the pinion cut spirally and the teeth on the gear cut nonradially

hypoid gears

**hypoing** *pres part of* HYPO

**hy·po·io·dite** \,== *at* HYPO- + 'īə,dīt\ *n* -S [ISV *hypo-* + *iod-* + *-ite*] **:** a salt or ester of hypoiodous acid

**hy·po·iodous acid** \¦==+...-\ *n* [ISV *hypo-* + *iodous*] **:** a very unstable very weak acid HIO that resembles hypochlorous acid and is obtained in solution by treating mercury oxide (sense b) with iodine in water or in the form of unstable salts in solution by reaction of iodine with alkali

**hy·po·ionian mode** \"+...-\ *n* [*hypo-* + L *ionius* Ionian + E *-an* — more at IONIAN] **:** a plagal ecclesiastical mode consisting of a tetrachord and an upper conjunct pentachord represented on the white keys of the piano by an ascending diatonic scale from G to G — see MODE illustration

**hy·po·ischium** \"+\ *n* [NL, fr. *hypo-* + *ischium*] **:** a small median bony rod passing backward from the ischial symphysis and supporting the ventral wall of the cloaca in most lizards

**hy·po·ka·le·mia** \,==+,kā'lēmēə\ *n* -S [NL, fr. *hypo-* + *kalium* + *-emia*] **:** a deficiency of potassium in the blood — **hy·po·ka·le·mic** \¦==,=¦=mik\ *adj*

**hy·po·limnetic** \¦== *at* HYPO- +\ *or* **hy·po·lim·ni·al** \"+¦limnēəl\ *adj* [NL *hypolimnion* + E *-etic* or *-ial*] **:** of or relating to a hypolimnion

**hy·po·lim·ni·on** \,=='limnē,än, -ēən\ *n, pl* **hypolim·nia** \-ēə\ [NL, fr. *hypo-* + Gk *limnion* small lake, dim. of *limnē* lake, sea] **:** the part of a lake below the thermocline made up of water that is stagnant and of essentially uniform temperature except during the period of overturn — compare EPILIMNION

**hy·po·lithic** \¦==+\ *adj* [*hypo-* + Gk *lithos* stone + E *-ic*] *of plants* **:** growing beneath rocks

**hy·po·locrian mode** \"+...-\ *n* [*hypo-* + *locrian*] **:** a plagal ecclesiastical mode consisting of a tetrachord and an upper conjunct pentachord represented on the white keys of the piano by an ascending diatonic scale from F to F but rarely used because its tetrachord and pentachord comprise respectively the forbidden augmented fourth and diminished fifth — see MODE illustration

**hy·po·lydian mode** \"+...-\ *n* [LL *hypolydius* hypolydian (fr. Gk *hypolydios*, fr. *hypo-* + *lydios* Lydian) + E *-an*; *hypolydian mode*, trans. of Gk *hypolydios tonos*] **1 :** a Greek mode consisting of two disjunct tetrachords represented on the white keys of the piano by a descending diatonic scale from F to F — see GREEK MODE illustration **2 :** a plagal ecclesiastical mode consisting of a tetrachord and an upper conjunct pentachord represented on the white keys of the piano by an ascending diatonic scale from C to C — see MODE illustration

**hy·po·mag·ne·se·mia** \ˌ⸗⸗+ˌmagnəˈsēmēə\ *n* -s [NL, fr. *hypo-* + *magnes*ium + *-emia*] **:** deficiency of magnesium in the blood constituting a prime factor in grass tetany or milk fever in cattle — **hy·po·mag·ne·se·mic** \¦⸗⸗¦⸗⸗¦sēmik\ *adj*

**hy·po·ma·nia** \ˌ⸗⸗+ˈmānēə\ *n* [NL, fr. *hypo-* + LL *mania*] **:** a mild mania — **hy·po·man·ic** \¦⸗⸗¦manik\ *adj*

**hy·po·menorrhea** \¦⸗⸗ *at* HYPO- +\ *n* [NL, fr. *hypo-* + *menorrhea*] **:** decreased menstrual flow

**hy·po·metabolism** \"+\ *n* [*hypo-* + *metabolism*] **:** a state (as in myxedema or hypothyroidism) marked by an abnormally low metabolic rate

**hy·po·mixolydian mode** \"+...-\ *n* [*hypo-* + *mixolydian* (*mode*)] **:** a plagal ecclesiastical mode consisting of a tetrachord and an upper conjunct pentachord represented on the white keys of the piano by an ascending diatonic scale from D to D — see MODE illustration

**hy·po·moch·li·on** \ˌ⸗⸗+ˈmäklēˌän\ *n* -s [L, fr. Gk, fr. *hypo-* + *mochlion* small lever, dim. of *mochlos* lever; akin to Gk *mogos* exertion, labor — more at MOGI-] *archaic* **:** FULCRUM

**hy·po·morph** \ˈ⸗⸗+ˌmȯrf\ *n* -s [*hypo-* + *-morph*] **1 :** a short-limbed and round-headed person **:** ENDOMORPH — opposed to *hypermorph* **2 :** a mutant gene having a similar but weaker effect than the corresponding wild-type gene — compare HYPERMORPH — **hy·po·mor·phic** \¦⸗⸗¦mȯrfik\ *adj*

**hy·po·mor·pho·sis** \ˌ⸗⸗+ˈmȯ(r)fəsə̇s *sometimes* -ˌmȯ(r)ˈfōs-\ *n* [NL, fr. *hypo-* + *-morphosis*] **1 :** DEDIFFERENTIATION 1 **2 :** inhibition of differentiation (as in an embryo)

**hy·po·motility** \¦⸗⸗ *at* HYPO- +\ *n* [ISV *hypo-* + *motility*] **:** abnormal deficiency of movement; *specif* **:** decreased motility of the stomach or intestine — compare HYPERMOTILITY

**hy·po·nas·tic** \"+¦nastik\ *adj* [ISV *hyponasty* + *-ic*] **:** of, relating to, or caused by hyponasty — **hy·po·nas·ti·cal·ly** \-tə̇k(ə)lē\ *adv*

**hy·po·nas·ty** \ˈ⸗⸗ˌnastē\ *n* -ES [ISV *hypo-* + *-nasty;* orig. formed as G *hyponastie*] **:** a nastic movement in which a plant part is bent inward and upward

**hy·po·na·tre·mia** \ˌ⸗⸗+nəˈtrēmēə\ *n* -s [NL, fr. *hypo-* + *natr*ium + *-emia*] **:** deficiency of sodium in the blood

**hy·po·nitrite** \¦⸗⸗ *at* HYPO- +\ *n* [ISV *hyponitr-* (fr. *hyponitrous acid*) + *-ite*] **:** a salt or ester of hyponitrous acid

**hy·po·nitrous acid** \" + . . . -\ *n* [*hypo-* + *nitrous* (*acid*)] **:** an explosive crystalline weak acid $H_2N_2O_2$ or HON=NOH obtained usu. in the form of its salts by oxidation of hydroxylamine or by reduction of nitrites

**hy·po·nome** \ˈ⸗⸗+ˌnōm\ *n* -s [Gk *hyponomē* underground passage, *hyponomos* underground passage, water pipe, conduit, fr. *hyponemesthai* to undermine, fr. *hypo-* + *nemesthai* to inhabit, spread over, be situated upon, middle of *nemein* to distribute, pasture — more at NIMBLE] **:** the swimming funnel of a cephalopod — **hy·po·nom·ic** \¦⸗⸗¦nämik\ *adj*

**hy·po·nutrition** \¦⸗⸗+\ *n* [*hypo-* + *nutrition*] **:** UNDERNUTRITION

**hy·po·nych·i·al** \¦⸗⸗+¦nikēəl\ *adj* [NL *hyponychi*um + E *-al*] **1 :** of or relating to the hyponychium **2 :** located under a nail

**hy·po·nych·i·um** \ˌ⸗⸗ˈ⸗⸗əm\ *n* -s [NL, fr. *hypo-* + *-onychium*] **1 :** the thickened layer of epidermis beneath the free end of a nail **2 :** MATRIX 1c

**hy·po·nym** \ˈ⸗⸗+ˌnim\ *n* -s [*hypo-* + *-onym*] **:** NOMEN NUDUM; *specif* **:** a generic name not based on a recognizable species — **hy·po·nym·ic** \¦⸗⸗¦nimik\ *adj* — **hy·pon·y·mous** \(ˈ)hī¦pänəməs, hə̇ˈp-\ *adj*

**hy·po-on·to·morph** \ˌ⸗⸗+ˈäntōˌmȯrf\ *n* -s [*hypo-* + *ont-* + *-morph*] **:** an endomorphic individual

**hy·po·ovar·i·an·ism** \ˌ⸗⸗+ˌōˈva(a)rēəˌnizəm\ *n* -s [*hypo-* + *ovarian* + *-ism*] **:** a condition marked by a deficiency of ovarian function **:** female hypogonadism — compare INFANTILISM

**hy·po·parathyroid** \¦⸗⸗ *at* HYPO- +\ *adj* [prob. back-formation from *hypoparathyroidism*] **:** of or affected by hypoparathyroidism

**hy·po·par·a·thy·roid·ism** \ˌ⸗⸗+ˌparəˈthīˌrȯiˌdizəm\ *n* -s [ISV *hypo-* + *parathyroid* + *-ism*] **:** deficiency of parathyroid hormone in the body; *also* **:** the resultant abnormal state marked by low serum calcium and a tendency to chronic tetany

**hy·po·par·ia** \ˌ⸗⸗+ˈpa(a)rēə\ *n pl, cap* [NL, fr. *hypo-* + *-paria* (fr. Gk *pareia* cheek)] **:** an order of trilobites with marginal facial suture and small pygidium known from the Lower Ordivician through the Cambrian — **hy·po·par·i·an** \¦⸗⸗¦⸗⸗ən\ *adj or n*

**hy·po·pha·lan·gism** \ˌ⸗⸗+fəˈlanˌjizəm\ *n* -s [*hypo-* + *phalange* + *-ism*] **:** a condition in which the number of phalanges of fingers or toes is less than normal

**hy·poph·a·mine** \hīˈpäfəˌmēn, -ˌmə̇n\ *n* [NL *hypoph*ysis + E *amine*] **:** either of two hormones obtained from the posterior lobe of the pituitary gland: **a :** OXYTOCIN **b :** VASOPRESSIN

1**hy·po·pharyngeal** \¦⸗⸗ *at* HYPO- +\ *adj* [*hypo-* + *pharyngeal*] **1 :** located below or in the lower part of the pharynx **2** [fr. NL *hypopharynx*, after NL *pharynx:* E *pharyngeal*] **:** of or relating to the hypopharynx **3 :** of or relating to a bone behind the last functional gill arch in teleost fishes that represents the ceratobranchial of the fifth branchial arch

2**hypopharyngeal** \"\ *n* **:** a hypopharyngeal element esp. of bone

**hy·po·pharynx** \"+\ *n* [NL, fr. *hypo-* + *pharynx*] **1 :** an appendage or thickened fold on the floor of the mouth of many insects that resembles a tongue, is very conspicuous in Orthoptera, and is believed to be sensory in function although sometimes modified into a piercing organ **2 :** the pharyngeal end of the esophagus

**hy·po·phloe·o·dal** \"+¦flēədᵊl\ *or* **hy·po·phloe·od·ic** \"+flē¦ädik\ *or* **hy·po·phloe·ous** \"+¦flēəs\ *adj* [*hypophloeodal*, *hypophloeodic* fr. *hypo-* + Gk *phloiōdēs* resembling rind or bark (fr. *phloios* bark + *-ōdēs* -ode) + E *-al* or *-ic; hypophloeous* fr. *hypo-* + Gk *phloios* + E *-ous*] **:** living just beneath the bark ⟨~ lichens⟩

**hy·po·phosphate** \"+\ *n* [ISV *hypophosph-* (fr. *hypophosphoric acid*) + *-ate*] **:** a salt or ester of hypophosphoric acid

**hy·po·phos·pha·te·mia** \ˌ⸗⸗+ˌfäsfəˈtēmēə\ *n* -s [NL, fr. *hypo-* + ISV *phosphate* + NL *-emia*] **:** deficiency of phosphates in the blood that is due to inadequate intake, excessive excretion, or defective absorption and that results in bone defects and other disturbances

**hy·po·phosphite** \¦⸗⸗+\ *n* [*hypophosph*orous (acid) + *-ite*] **:** a salt of hypophosphorous acid

**hy·po·phosphoric acid** \" + . . . -\ *n* [ISV *hypo-* + *phosphoric*] **:** an unstable tetrabasic acid $H_4P_2O_6$ usu. obtained in the form of its salts (as by oxidation of red phosphorus in alkaline solution)

**hy·po·phosphorous acid** \" + . . . -\ *n* [F *hypophosphoreux*, fr. *hypo-* + *phosphoreux* phosphorous] **:** a low-melting deliquescent crystalline strong monobasic acid $H_3PO_2$ usu. obtained by acidifying one of its salts and used as a reducing agent

**hy·po·phre·nia** \ˌ⸗⸗+ˈfrēnēə\ *or* **hy·po·phre·no·sis** \"+frəˈnōsə̇s\ *n, pl* **hypophrenias** \-əz\ *or* **hypophreno·ses** \-ōˌsēz\ [NL, fr. *hypo-* + *-phrenia* or *-phrenosis* (fr. Gk *phren-*, *phrēn* mind, heart + NL *-osis*)] **:** MENTAL DEFICIENCY — **hy·po·phren·ic** \¦⸗⸗¦frenik *also* -rēn-\ *adj*

**hy·po·phrygian mode** \¦⸗⸗ + . . . -\ *n* [*hypophrygian* (fr. LL *hypophrygius* hypophrygian — fr. Gk *hypophrygios*, fr. *hypo-* + *phrygios* Phrygian, fr. *Phrygia*, ancient country in west central Asia Minor — + E *-an*) + *mode;* trans. of Gk *hypophrygia harmonia*] **1 :** a Greek mode consisting of two disjunct tetrachords represented on the white keys of the piano by a descending diatonic scale from G to G — see GREEK MODE illustration **2 :** a plagal ecclesiastical mode consisting of a tetrachord and an upper conjunct pentachord represented on the white keys of the piano by an ascending diatonic scale from B to B — see MODE illustration

**hy·poph·y·ge** \hīˈpäfə(ˌ)jē, hə̇ˈ-\ *n* -s [NL, fr. Gk *hypophygē* refuge, recess, fr. *hypo-* + *phygē* flight, fr. *pheugein* to flee — more at FUGITIVE] **:** a hollow curvature esp. under a Doric capital in some Greek buildings — compare APOPHYGE

**hy·po·phyl·lous** \¦⸗⸗ *at* HYPO- +¦filəs\ *adj* [*hypo-* + *-phyllous*] **:** located on the under side of a leaf — compare EPIGENOUS

**hy·poph·y·se·al** \(¦)hī¦päfə¦sēəl, -¦zē- *also* ¦hīpə¦fizē-\ *also* **hy·po·phys·i·al** \¦hīpə¦fizēəl\ *adj* [*hypophyseal*, alter. of *hypophysial; hypophysial* fr. NL *hypophysi*s + E *-al*] **:** of or relating to the hypophysis

**hy·poph·y·sec·to·mize** \(ˌ)hīˌpäfəˈsektəˌmīz\ *vt* -ED/-ING/-S **:** to remove the pituitary body from ⟨defects in *hypophysectomized* animals⟩

**hy·poph·y·sec·to·my** \-təmē\ *n* -ES [ISV *hypophys-* (fr. NL *hypophysis*) + *-ectomy*] **:** surgical removal of the pituitary body

**hy·poph·y·sis** \hīˈpäfəsə̇s\ *n, pl* **hypophyses** \-əˌsēz\ [NL, outgrowth, pituitary body (esp. in *hypophysis cerebri*, lit., outgrowth of the brain), fr. Gk, outgrowth, attachment underneath, process of a bone, fr. *hypophyein* to grow up below, fr. *hypo-* + *phyein* to grow, produce, bring forth — more at BE] **1** *also* **hypophysis ce·re·bri** \-səˈrēˌbrī, -ˈserəˌ-\ **:** PITUITARY BODY **2 a :** a cell or cells in a seed plant resulting from the transverse division of the next adjoining suspensor cell and giving rise to the tip of the root **b :** APOPHYSIS 2

**hypopi** *pl of* HYPOPUS

**hy·po·pi·al** \(ˈ)hī¦pōpēəl, hə̇ˈp-\ *adj* [NL *hypop*us + E *-ial*] **:** of, relating to, or consisting of a hypopus

**hy·po·pi·tu·i·ta·rism** \ˌ⸗⸗ *at* HYPO- + pə̇ˈtüətəˌrizəm, -pə̇ˈtyü-\ *n* -s [ISV *hypo-* + *pituitar-* (fr. *pituitary*) + *-ism*] **:** deficient activity of the pituitary body esp. in the production of growth-regulating hormones or of those fractions (as the gonadotrophic or thyrotrophic hormones) that regulate the secretory activity of other endocrine organs — compare HYPERPITUITARISM

**hy·po·pituitary** \¦⸗⸗+\ *adj* [*hypo-* + *pituitary*] **:** of or relating to pituitary deficiency

**hy·pop·i·tys** \hīˈpäpəd·ə̇s, hə̇ˈ-\ *n, cap* [NL, fr. *hypo-* + Gk *pitys* pine — more at PINE (tree)] *in some classifications* **:** a genus of plants comprising the pinesaps and including leafless saprophytic herbs with erect stems and racemose flowers that are commonly placed in the genus *Monotropa*

**hy·po·plankton** \¦⸗⸗ *at* HYPO- +\ *n* [*hypo-* + *plankton*] **:** the plankton inhabiting the greatest depths esp. immediately over the bottom but sometimes throughout the whole abyssal zone — **hy·po·planktonic** \"+\ *adj*

**hy·po·pla·sia** \ˌ⸗⸗+ˈplāzh(ē)ə\ *n* -s [NL, fr. *hypo-* + *-plasia*] **:** a condition of arrested development in which an organ or part remains below the normal size or in an immature state — compare HYPERPLASIA

**hy·po·plas·tic** \¦⸗⸗¦plastik\ *adj* [*hypo-* + *plastic*] **:** of, relating to, or marked by hypoplasia

**hypoplastic anemia** *n* **:** APLASTIC ANEMIA

**hy·po·plastral** \¦⸗⸗+\ *adj* **:** of or relating to the hypoplastron

**hy·po·plastron** \"+\ *n* [*hypo-* + *plastron*] **:** either of the third lateral pair of bony plates in the plastron of most turtles

**hy·po·ploid** \ˈ⸗⸗+ˌplȯid\ *adj* [*hypo-* + *-ploid*] **:** having a chromosome number a little smaller than an exact multiple of the monoploid number

**hy·po·pneus·tic** \¦⸗⸗+¦n(y)üstik, ¦hīˌpäp¦-\ *adj* [*hypo-* + *-pneustic*] **:** having some of the respiratory spiracles lacking or nonfunctional — used chiefly of larval insects

**hy·po·po·tas·se·mia** \ˌ⸗⸗+pəˌtaˈsēmēə\ *n* -s [NL, fr. *hypo-* + *potass*ium + *-emia*] **:** HYPOKALEMIA — **hy·po·po·tas·se·mic** \¦⸗⸗⸗ˌ⸗¦sēmik\ *adj*

**hy·po·pro·sex·ia** \ˌ⸗⸗+prəˈseksēə\ *n* -s [NL, fr. *hypo-* + Gk *prosexis* attention (fr. *prosechein* to pay attention to, fr. *pros* toward + *echein* to hold) + NL *-ia*] *psychol* **:** defective fixity of attention on a stimulus object

**hy·po·pro·tein·emia** \"+ˌprōˌtēˈnēmēə, ˌprōd·ēəˈn-\ *n* -s [NL, fr. *hypo-* + ISV *protein* + NL *-emia*] **:** abnormal decrease of protein in the blood — **hy·po·pro·te·in·e·mic** \¦⸗⸗ˌ⸗⸗⸗¦nēmik\ *adj*

**hy·po·pro·throm·bin·e·mia** \ˌ⸗⸗+(ˌ)prōˌthrämbəˈnēmēə\ *n* -s [NL, fr. *hypo-* + ISV *prothrombin* + NL *-emia*] **:** deficiency of prothrombin in the blood usu. due to vitamin K deficiency or liver disease (esp. obstructive jaundice) and resulting in delayed clotting of blood or spontaneous bleeding (as from the nose or into the skin) — **hy·po·pro·throm·bin·e·mic** \¦⸗⸗(ˌ)⸗¦⸗⸗¦nēmik\ *adj*

**hy·pop·ter·on** \hīˈpäptəˌrän, hə̇ˈ-\ *n, pl* **hypop·tera** \-ərə\ [NL, fr. *hypo-* + Gk *pteron* feather, wing — more at FEATHER] **:** the tuft of feathers of a bird's wing comprising the axillars

**hy·pop·ti·lum** \hīˈpäptələm, hə̇ˈ-\ *n, pl* **hypopti·la** \-lə\ [NL, fr. *hypo-* + Gk *ptilon* wing, feather, down; akin to Gk *petesthai* to fly — more at FEATHER] **:** AFTERSHAFT

**hyp·o·pus** \ˈhipəpəs\ *n, pl* **hypo·pi** \-ˌpī\ [NL, fr. Gk *hypopous* furnished with feet, fr. *hypo-* + *pous* foot — more at FOOT] **:** a nonfeeding migratory larva of some mites that is passively distributed by an animal to which it has attached itself

**hy·po·pyg·i·al** \¦⸗⸗ *at* HYPO- + ¦pijēəl\ *adj* [NL *hypopygi*um + E *-al*] **:** of or relating to a hypopygium

**hy·po·pyg·i·um** \ˌ⸗⸗+ˈpijēəm\ *also* **hy·po·py·gid·i·um** \"+pəˈjidēəm\ *n, pl* **hypopyg·ia** *also* **hypopygid·ia** \-ēə\ [NL, fr. *hypo-* + *-pygium* (fr. *pyg-* + *-ium*) or *-pygidium* (fr. Gk *pygidion* small rump) — more at PYGIDIUM] **:** a modified 9th abdominal segment of many insects with which the copulatory apparatus is associated; *esp* **:** such a modified segment together with the copulatory apparatus of a dipterous insect

**hy·po·py·on** \hīˈpōpēˌän, hə̇ˈ-\ *n* -s [NL, fr. Gk, ulcer, fr. *hypopyon*, neut. of *hypopyos* suppurative, fr. *hypo-* + *pyon* pus — more at FOUL] **:** a collection of pus in the anterior chamber of the eye

**hyp·or·che·ma** \ˌhīpə(r)ˈkēmə\ *or* **hyp·or·cheme** \ˈhīpə(r)ˌkēm\ *n, pl* **hyporchema·ta** \-məd·ə\ *or* **hyporchemes** [Gk *hyporchēma*, fr. *hyporcheisthai* to dance to music, fr. *hypo-* + *orcheisthai* to dance — more at ORCHESTRA] **:** an ancient Greek choral song and dance usu. in honor of Apollo or Dionysus — **hy·por·che·mat·ic** \¦⸗⸗kē¦mad·ik\ *adj*

**hy·po·rhined** \ˈ⸗⸗ *at* HYPO- +ˌrīnd\ *adj* [*hypo-* + *rhin-* + *-ed*] **:** having small nostrils

**hy·po·ri·bo·fla·vin·o·sis** \ˌ⸗⸗+ˌrībəˌflāvə̇ˈnōsə̇s *also* -rib- *or* -lav-\ *n, pl* **hyporiboflavino·ses** \-ōˌsēz\ [NL, fr. *hypo-* + ISV *riboflavin* + NL *-osis*] **:** ARIBOFLAVINOSIS

**hy·por·rhyth·mic** \¦⸗⸗+¦rit͟hmik *sometimes* -ithm-\ *adj* [Gk *hyporrhythmos* hyporrhythmic (fr. *hypo-* + *rhythmos* measure, rhythm) + E *-ic* — more at RHYTHM] *in Greek and Latin prosody* **:** deficient as to rhythm — used of a hexameter in which the end of a word coincides with the end of each foot and which accordingly has no true caesura

**hypos** *pl of* HYPO, *pres 3d sing of* HYPO

**hy·po·scleral** \"+\ *adj* [*hypo-* + *scleral*] **:** located beneath the sclera of the eye

**hy·po·scope** \ˈ⸗⸗+ˌskōp\ *n* [*hypo-* + *-scope*] **:** a military periscope designed for use as a hand instrument or for attachment to a rifle

**hy·po·secretion** \¦⸗⸗ *at* HYPO- +\ *n* [*hypo-* + *secretion*] **:** production of a body secretion at an abnormally slow rate or in abnormally small quantities

**hy·po·sensitive** \"+\ *adj* [*hypo-* + *sensitive*] **:** exhibiting or marked by deficient response to stimulation — **hy·po·sensitivity** \"+\ *n*

**hy·po·sensitization** \"+\ *n* [*hypo-* + *sensitization*] **:** the state or process of being hyposensitized

**hy·po·sensitize** \"+\ *vt* [*hypo-* + *sensitize*] **:** to reduce the sensitivity of (an individual) esp. to an allergen **:** DESENSITIZE

**hy·po·spa·dia** \ˌ⸗⸗+ˈspādēə\ *or* **hy·po·spa·dy** \ˈ⸗⸗ˌspādē\ *n, pl* **hypospadias** *or* **hypospadies** [NL *hypospadia*, fr. Gk *hypospadias* man with hypospadias] **:** HYPOSPADIAS

**hy·po·spa·di·ac** \¦⸗⸗¦spādēˌak\ *adj* [Gk *hypospadias* man with hypospadias + E *-ac* (as in *elegiac*)] **:** of or affected with hypospadias

**hy·po·spa·di·as** \ˌ⸗⸗ˈspādēəs\ *n* -ES [NL, fr. Gk, man with hypospadias, fr. *hypo-* + *-spadias* (prob. fr. *spadōn* eunuch, fr. *span* to tear, pluck off, pull, draw) — more at SPAN] **:** an abnormality of the penis in which the urethra opens on the under surface

**hy·po·sphene** \ˈ⸗⸗+ˌsfēn\ *n* [*hypo-* + Gk *sphēn* wedge] **:** a median wedge-shaped posterior process on the neural arch of the vertebrae of certain extinct reptiles — compare HYPANTRUM

**hypospray** \ˈ⸗(ˌ)⸗ˌ⸗\ *n* [3*hypo* + *spray*] **:** a device with a spring and plunger for administering a medicated solution by forcing it in extremely fine jets through the unbroken skin

**hy·po·stase** \ˈ⸗⸗ *at* HYPO-+ˌstās\ *n* -s [NL *hypostasis*] **:** a disk of lignified tissue formed at the base of the ovule in certain orders of plants

**hy·pos·ta·sis** \hīˈpästəsə̇s\ *n, pl* **hyposta·ses** \-əˌsēz\ [LL, substance, sediment, fr. Gk, support, sediment, foundation, substance, fr. *hyphistasthai* to support, stand under, fr. *hypo-* + *histasthai* to stand, middle of *histanai* to cause to stand — more at STAND] **1 a :** something that settles at the bottom of a fluid **:** SEDIMENT, DEPOSIT **b :** the settling of blood in the dependent parts of an organ or body **2 a** *in the original Nicene use* **:** the essence or substance of the triune Godhead — called also *ousia* **b** *in later use* (1) one of the persons of the Godhead or Trinity (2) **:** the individual as subject or substance **c :** the whole personality of Christ as distinguished from his human and divine natures **3** *obs* **:** basis of support **:** FOUNDATION **4** *philos* **a** *Plotinism* **:** any of the three aspects or essential principles constituting the Godhead: (1) **:** the transcendent one (2) **:** NOUS, SPIRIT (3) **:** LOGOS, WORLD SOUL **b** *Thomism* **:** the substance or rational nature of an individual or person; *also* **:** PERSON, INDIVIDUAL **c :** substance as an ontological entity or category **:** a self-subsistent reality or mode of being **d :** a hypothetical or conceptual entity **:** a reified abstraction **:** HYPOSTATIZATION ⟨as far as the Buddhist ~ of the law is concerned, we should search in vain for a Christian equivalent —Joachim Wach⟩ ⟨for legal purposes a right is only the ~ of a prophecy —Alfred Lief⟩ **5** [NL, fr. LL] **:** failure of a gene to produce its usual effect when coupled with another gene that is epistatic toward it **6** [NL, fr. LL] **:** HYPOSTASE **7 a :** the mention of a word, grammatical form, or word group (as *in*, *un-*, *in the dark*) as a linguistic element **b :** a linguistic element so referred to — called also *citation form*, *quotation noun*

**hy·pos·ta·size** \hīˈpästəˌsīz\ *vt* -ED/-ING/-S [LL *hypostas*is + E *-ize*] **:** HYPOSTATIZE

**hy·po·stat·ic** \¦⸗⸗ *at* HYPO-+¦stad·ik\ *adj* [Gk *hypostatikos*, fr. *hypostatos* substantially existing (verbal of *hyphistasthai* to support, stand under) + *-ikos* -ic] **1** *or* **hy·po·stat·i·cal** \-d·ə̇kəl\ **:** of or relating to substance **:** ELEMENTAL **2** *or* **hypostatical** [F *hypostatique*, fr. MF, fr. ML *hypostaticus*, fr. Gk *hypostatikos*] **:** of or relating to theological hypostasis **3** [fr. NL *hypostasis*, after NL *-stasis:* E *-static*] **a** *of a gene* **:** exhibiting hypostasis in the presence of a corresponding epistatic gene **b** *of a hereditary character* **:** suppressed by epistasis **:** appearing recessive to another character due to mediation by a hypostatic gene **4** [fr. LL *hypostasis*, after such pairs as E *emphasis: emphatic*] **:** depending on or due to hypostasis ⟨~ congestion⟩ ⟨~ pneumonia⟩ — **hy·po·stat·i·cal·ly** \-d·ə̇k(ə)lē\ *adv*

**hypostatic union** *n* [part trans. of F *union hypostatique*, fr. MF] **:** union in one hypostasis; *esp* **:** the union of the divine and human natures of Christ in one hypostasis

**hy·pos·ta·ti·za·tion** \hīˌpästəd·ə̇ˈzāshən\ *n* -s **1 :** an act or instance of hypostatizing **:** REIFICATION ⟨realism is built on the fallacy of ~, the supposition that an abstract term must somehow have a denotation —T.T.Lafferty⟩ **2 :** something that is hypostatized

**hy·pos·ta·tize** *or* **hy·pos·ta·tise** \hīˈpästəˌtīz\ *vt* -ED/-ING/-S [Gk *hypostat*os substantially existing + E *-ize* or *-ise*] **:** to make into or regard as a hypostasis: **a :** to transform (a conceptual entity) into or construe as a self-subsistent substance ⟨we are told that the conception of God, or the Sacred, or the Mana, or the Totem, is nothing but *hypostatized* society itself —P.A.Sorokin⟩ **b :** to assume as concrete **:** REIFY ⟨our ingrained habit of *hypostatizing* impressions, of seeing things and not sense-data —Susanne K. Langer⟩

**hy·po·sthenia** \¦⸗⸗ *at* HYPO-+\ *n* [NL, fr. *hypo-* + Gk *sthenos* strength + NL *-ia* — more at STHENIC] **:** lack of strength **:** bodily weakness — **hy·po·sthenic** \"+\ *adj*

**hy·pos·the·nu·ria** \hīˌpästhəˈn(y)u̇rēə\ *n* -s [NL, fr. *hypo-* + Gk *sthenos* strength + NL *-uria*] **:** the secretion of urine of low specific gravity due to inability of the kidney to concentrate the urine normally — **hy·pos·the·nu·ric** \⸗¦⸗⸗¦n(y)u̇rik\ *adj*

**hy·pos·to·ma** \hīˈpästəmə, hə̇ˈ-\ *n, pl* **hypostomas** \-məz\ *or* **hy·po·sto·ma·ta** \ˌ⸗⸗ *at* HYPO-+ˈstōməd·ə\ [NL, fr. *hypo-* + *-stoma*] **:** HYPOSTOME

**hy·po·sto·ma·ta** \ˌ⸗⸗ *at* HYPO-+ˈstōməd·ə\ [NL, fr. *hypo-* + *-stomata*] *syn of* HYPOSTOMIDES

**hy·po·sto·mat·ic** \¦⸗⸗+ˌstō¦mad·ik\ *adj* [*hypo-* + *stomatic*] *of a leaf* **:** having stomata only on the underside

**hy·po·stom·a·tous** \"+¦stäməd·əs, -tōm-\ *adj* [*hypo-* + *-stomatous*] **1** *of a fish* **:** having the mouth on the lower side **2 :** HYPOSTOMATIC

1**hy·po·stome** \ˈ⸗⸗+ˌstōm\ *n* -s [ISV *hypo-* + *-stome*] **:** any of several structures associated with the mouth: as **a :** the labrum of a trilobite or crustacean **b :** the manubrium of a hydrozoan **c :** an organ like a rod that arises at the base of the beak in various mites and in ticks

2**hypostome** \"\ *n* -s [NL *Hypostoma*, genus of fishes, fr. *hypo-* + *-stoma*] **:** a fish of the order Hypostomides

**hy·po·stom·i·des** \ˌ⸗⸗+ˈstäməˌdēz\ *n pl, cap* [NL, fr. *Hypostoma*, genus of fishes] **:** an order or suborder of teleost fishes coextensive with the family Pegasidae

**hy·pos·to·mous** \(ˈ)hī¦pästəməs, hə̇ˈp-\ *adj* [*hypo-* + *-stomous*] **:** HYPOSTOMATOUS

**hy·po·stroma** \¦⸗⸗ *at* HYPO- +\ *n* [NL, fr. *hypo-* + *stroma*] **:** a compact mass of hyphae below the true stroma and beneath the host epidermis of a fungus — **hy·po·stromal** \"+\ *adj*

1**hy·po·style** \ˈ⸗⸗+ˌstīl\ *adj* [Gk *hypostylos* resting upon pillars, fr. *hypo-* + *stylos* pillar] **:** having the roof resting upon rows of columns **:** constructed by means of columns ⟨~ halls of antiquity⟩

2**hypostyle** \"\ *n* [1*hypostyle*] **:** a hypostyle hall

3**hypostyle** \"\ *n* [*hypo-* + *style* (cusp)] **:** a small cusp between the hypocone and metacone of a molar tooth

**hy·po·stypsis** \¦⸗⸗ *at* HYPO-+\ *n* [NL, fr. *hypo-* + *stypsis*] **:** mild or moderate astringency

**hy·po·styptic** \"+\ *adj* [*hypo-* + *styptic*] **:** mildly or moderately styptic

**hy·po·sulfite** \"+\ *n* [*hyposulf-* (fr. *hyposulfurous acid*) + *-ite*] **1 :** THIOSULFATE — used chiefly in photography **2 :** HYDROSULFITE

**hy·po·sulfurous acid** \"+. . .-\ *n* [ISV *hypo-* + *sulfurous* (*acid*)] **1** *archaic* **:** THIOSULFURIC ACID **2 :** HYDROSULFUROUS ACID

**hy·po·syllogistic** \"+\ *adj* [*hypo-* + *syllogistic*] **:** having syllogistic value or purpose without the form

**hy·po·synergia** \"+\ *n* [NL, fr. *hypo-* + *synergia*] **:** imperfect coordination

**hy·po·tac·tic** \"+¦taktik\ *adj* [Gk *hypotaktikos*, fr. (assumed) Gk *hypotaktos* (verbal of Gk *hypotassein* to arrange under) + Gk *-ikos* -ic] **:** of, relating to, or exhibiting hypotaxis

**hy·po·tarsus** \"+\ *n* [NL, fr. *hypo-* + *tarsus*] **:** CALCANEUM 2

**hy·po·tax·is** \ˌ⸗⸗+ˈtaksə̇s\ *n* [Gk, subjection, submission, fr. *hypotassein* to arrange under, subject, put after, fr. *hypo-* + *tassein* to arrange — more at TACTICS] **:** syntactic subordination (as by a conjunction) — opposed to *parataxis*

**hy·po·tension** \¦⸗⸗ *at* HYPO-+\ *n* [ISV *hypo-* + *tension*] **:** abnormally low tension esp. of blood vessels — called also *low blood pressure*

1**hy·po·tensive** \"+\ *adj* [ISV *hypotens*ion + *-ive*] **1 :** characterized by or due to hypotension **2 :** causing low blood pressure or a lowering of blood pressure ⟨~ anesthesia⟩ ⟨~ drugs⟩

2**hypotensive** \"\ *n* -s **:** a person with hypotension

**hy·pot·e·nuse** \hīˈpätᵊnˌ(y)üs *also* -üz\ *also* **hy·poth·e·nuse** \-äthəˌn(y)-\ *n* -s [L *hypotenusa*, fr. Gk *hypoteinousa*, fr. fem. of *hypoteinōn*, pres. part. of *hypoteinein* to subtend, fr. *hypo-* + *teinein* to stretch] **:** the side of a right-angled triangle that is opposite the right angle

**hy·po·thalamic** \¦⸗⸗ *at* HYPO-+\ *adj* [*hypo-* + *thalamic*] **1 :** located below the thalamus **2** [NL *hypothalam*us + E *-ic*] **:** of, relating to, or involving the hypothalamus

**hypothalamico-** *or* **hypothalamo-** *comb form* [*hypothalamico-* fr. *hypothalamic* + *-o-; hypothalamo-* fr. NL *hypothalamus*] **:** hypothalamic and ⟨*hypothalamico*hypophyseal⟩ ⟨*hypothalamo*cortical⟩

**hy·po·thalamus** \¦==+\ *n* [NL, fr. *hypo-* + *thalamus*] **:** a basal part of the diencephalon that lies beneath the thalamus on each side, forms the floor of the third ventricle, and is usu. considered to include vital autonomic regulatory centers and sometimes the posterior pituitary lobe

**hy·po·thallus** \"+\ *n* [NL, fr. *hypo-* + *thallus*] **1 :** a marginal outgrowth of hyphae from the thallus in crustose lichens **2 :** a residue like a film that remains after the formation of sporangia in slime molds of the class Myxomycetes

**hy·poth·ec** \hə'päthik, hī'-\ *n* -s [F&LL; F *hypothèque,* fr. MF, fr. LL *hypotheca,* fr. Gk *hypothēkē* deposit, pledge, mortgage, fr. *hypotithenai* to deposit as a pledge, put under, propose — more at HYPOTHESIS] *1 Roman & civil law* **:** an obligation, right, or security given by contract or by operation of law to a creditor over property of the debtor without transfer of possession or title to the creditor — compare PIGNUS, PLEDGE **2** *Scot* **:** AFFAIR, CONCERN

**hy·po·theca** \¦== *at* HYPO- +\ *n* [NL, fr. *hypo-* + *-theca*] **:** the inner or bottom half or valve of the diatom frustule — compare EPITHECA — **hy·po·thecal** \"+\ *adj*

**hy·poth·e·cary** \hə'päthə,kerē, hī'-\ *adj* [LL *hypothecarius,* fr. *hypotheca* hypothec + L *-arius* -ary] **:** of, relating to, or created or secured by a hypothec ⟨~ right⟩

**¹hy·poth·e·cate** \hə'päthə,kāt, hī'-, *usu* -ād.+V\ *vt* -ED/-ING/-S [ML *hypothecatus,* past part. of *hypothecare* to pledge, fr. LL *hypotheca* pledge, hypothec] **:** to subject to a hypothec **:** to pledge without delivery of title or possession; *specif* **:** to pledge (a ship) by a bottomry bond

**²hy·poth·e·cate** \hī'-\ *vb* -ED/-ING/-S [Gk *hypothēkē* suggestion, counsel, pledge, mortgage + E *-ate*] **:** HYPOTHESIZE

**hy·poth·e·ca·tion** \hə,päthə'kāshən, (,)hī,-\ *n* -s [ML *hypothecation-, hypothecatio,* fr. *hypothecatus* (past part.) + L *-ion-, -io* -ion] **1** *Roman, civil, & maritime law* **:** the act or contract by which property (as real property) is hypothecated **2** *Roman, civil, & maritime law* **:** the right or power of a creditor or claimant over property owned by his debtor or another who has pledged it for the debt to cause the property to be sold to satisfy his claim if payment is defaulted

**hypothecation certificate** *n* **:** a certificate attached to a bill of exchange empowering the holder to dispose of merchandise if payment or acceptance is refused — called also *letter of hypothecation*

**hy·poth·e·ca·tor** \=ˈ==,kād·ə(r)\ *n* [¹*hypothecate* + *-or*] **:** one that hypothecates

**hy·poth·e·ca·tory** \=ˈ==,kə,tōrē\ *adj* [¹*hypothecate* + *-ory*] **:** HYPOTHECARY

**hy·po·thecium** \¦== *at* HYPO- +\ *n* [NL, fr. *hypo-* + *thecium*] **:** a layer of dense hyphal tissue just below the hymenium of lichens and fungi — compare EPITHECIUM

**¹hy·pothe·nar** \hī'päthə,när, |_nər, ¦hīpə¦thē|\ *n* [NL, fr. Gk, hypothenar of the hand, fr. *hypo-* + *thenar*] **:** the hypothenar eminence

**²hypothenar** \(')=¦===\ *also* **hy·pothe·nal** \-thən°l,-thēn-\ *adj* **:** of, relating to, or constituting the prominent part of the palm of the hand above the base of the little finger or a corresponding part in the forefoot of an animal

**hypothenuse** *var of* HYPOTENUSE

**hy·po·the·ria** \,== *at* HYPO- +'thirēə\ *n pl, cap* [NL, fr. *hypo-* + *-theria*] **:** a hypothetical order including the as yet undiscovered ancestors of the mammals

**hy·po·thermal** \¦==+\ *adj* [*hypo-* + *thermal*] **:** of or relating to a hydrothermal metalliferous ore vein deposited at high temperature — compare EPITHERMAL, MESOTHERMAL

**hy·po·ther·mia** \,==+'thərmēə\ *n* -s [NL, fr. *hypo-* + *-thermia*] **:** subnormal temperature of the body often induced artificially to facilitate cardiac surgery — compare REFRIGERATION

**hy·poth·e·sis** \hī'päthəsəs\ *n, pl* **hypothe·ses** \-ə,sēz\ [L, fr. Gk, fr. *hypotithenai* to suppose, propose, put under, fr. *hypo-* + *tithenai* to place, put — more at DO] **1 :** a proposition tentatively assumed in order to draw out its logical or empirical consequences and so test its accord with facts that are known or may be determined ⟨it appears, then, to be a condition of the most genuinely scientific ~ that it be . . . of such a nature as to be either proved or disproved by comparison with observed facts —J.S.Mill⟩ ⟨most of the great unifying conceptions of modern science are working *hypotheses* —Bernard Bosanquet⟩ **2 a :** an assumption or concession made for the sake of argument **b :** an interpretation of a practical situation or condition taken as the ground for action **3 :** the antecedent clause in a conditional statement **4 :** a hypothetical relation **:** the conditioning of one thing by another

**hy·poth·e·size** \-ə,sīz\ *vb* -ED/-ING/-S *vi* **:** to make a hypothesis ~ *vt* **:** to adopt as a hypothesis **:** ASSUME ⟨we can ~ any value as truth . . . but there are varying probabilities for each hypothesis we make —Lester Guest⟩

**¹hy·po·thet·i·cal** \¦hīpə¦thed·ə̇kəl, -et|, |ēk-\ *also* **hy·po·thet·ic** \|ik, |ēk\ *adj* [*hypothetical* fr. LL *hypotheticus* (fr. Gk *hypothetikos*) + E *-al; hypothetic* fr. F *hypothétique,* fr. LL *hypotheticus*] **1 :** involving logical hypothesis **:** ASSUMED, CONDITIONAL — distinguished from *categorical* **2 :** of or depending on supposition **:** CONJECTURAL — contrasted with *actual* — **hy·po·thet·i·cal·ly** \|ək(ə)lē, |ēk-, -li\ *adv*

**²hypothetical** \"\ *n* -s **:** a hypothetical statement or proposition **:** IMPLICATION 2b

**hypothetical imperative** *n* [trans. of G *hypothetischer imperativ*] **:** an imperative of conduct that springs from expediency or practical necessity rather than from moral law — contrasted with *categorical imperative*

**hypothetical question** *n* **:** a question based on hypothetical facts concerning which a witness in court is asked for an opinion

**hypothetical syllogism** *n* [trans. of LL *hypotheticus syllogismus*] **1 :** a syllogism consisting wholly of hypothetical propositions — called also *pure hypothetical syllogism* **2 :** a syllogism consisting partly of hypothetical propositions — called also *mixed hypothetical syllogism;* compare MODUS PONENS, MODUS TOLLENS

**hy·po·thet·i·co-deductive** \|əkō-\ *adj* [*hypothetic* + *-o-*] **:** of or relating to scientific method in which hypotheses suggested by the facts of observation are proposed and consequences deduced from them so as to test the hypotheses and evaluate the consequences **:** AXIOMATIC

**hypothetico-disjunctive** *adj* **:** of, relating to, or constituting a logical proposition that combines hypothesis and disjunction

**hy·po·thyroid** \¦== *at* HYPO- +\ *adj* [*hypo-* + *thyroid*] **:** of, relating to, or affected by hypothyroidism

**hy·po·thyroidism** \"+\ *n* -s [ISV *hypo-* + *thyroid* + *-ism*] **:** deficient activity of the thyroid gland; *also* **:** a resultant abnormal state marked by lowered metabolic rate and general loss of vigor — compare CRETINISM, MYXEDEMA

**hy·po·to·nia** \,==+'tōnēə\ *or* **hy·pot·o·ny** \hī'pät°nē, hə'-\ *n, pl* **hypotonias** *or* **hypotonies** [NL *hypotonia,* fr. *hypo-* + *-tonia*] **:** HYPOTONICITY

**hy·po·tonic** \¦== *at* HYPO- +\ *adj* [ISV *hypo-* + *tonic*] **1** *of living tissue* **:** having less than the normal tone **2** *of a fluid* **:** having a lower osmotic pressure than a fluid under comparison or used as a standard — compare ISOTONIC

**hy·po·tonicity** \"+\ *n* **:** the quality or state of being hypotonic

**hy·po·tonus** \"+\ *n* -ES [NL, fr. *hypo-* + *tonus*] **:** HYPOTONICITY

**hy·po·tra·che·li·um** \,==+trə'kēlēəm\ *n* [L, fr. Gk *hypotrachēlion,* fr. *hypo-* + *trachēlos* neck] **:** GORGERIN

**hy·po·trem·a·ta** \"+'tremədˑə, -rēm-\ *n pl, cap* [NL, fr. *hypo-* + *-tremata*] **:** an order of Chondrichthyes comprising the rays — compare PLEUROTREMATA

**hy·po·trich** \'==+,trik\ *n* -s [NL *Hypotricha*] **:** one of the Hypotricha

**hy·pot·ri·cha** \hī'pä·trəkə\ *n pl, cap* [NL, fr. *hypo-* + *-tricha*] **:** a suborder of Spirotricha comprising ciliates that have cilia only on the ventral surface and usu. fused to cirri and that often have tactile bristles on the dorsum — compare EUPLOTES, OXYTRICHA, STYLONYCHIA — **hy·pot·ri·chous** \(')=¦==kəs\ *adj*

**hy·po·trich·ia** \,== *at* HYPO- +'trikēə\ *n* -s [NL, fr. *hypo-* + *-trichia*] **:** HYPOTRICHOSIS

**hy·po·trich·i·da** \-kədə\ [NL, fr. *hypo-* + *trich-* + *-ida*] *syn of* HYPOTRICHA

**hy·po·tri·cho·sis** \,==+trə'kōsəs\ *n* [NL, fr. *hypo-* + Gk *trichōsis* growth of hair (fr. *trich-* + *-ōsis* -osis)] **:** congenital deficiency of hair — **hy·po·tri·chot·ic** \¦===¦käd·ik\ *adj*

**hy·po·trochanteric** \¦== *at* HYPO- +\ *adj* [*hypo-* + *trochanteric*] **:** situated beneath a trochanter

**hy·po·trochoid** \"+\ *n* [*hypo-* + *trochoid*] **:** a plane curve traced by a point on the radius or extended radius but not on the circumference of a circle rolling on the inside of a fixed circle — compare EPITROCHOID — **hy·po·trochoidal** \"+\ *adj*

**hy·pot·ro·phy** \hī'pä·trəfē, hə'-\ *n* [ISV *hypo-* + *-trophy*] **1 :** subnormal growth — compare HYPERTROPHY **2 :** greater growth of the lower than of the upper side of horizontal or ascending branches or roots — opposed to *epitrophy*

**hy·po·tympanic** \¦== *at* HYPO- +\ *adj* [in sense 1, fr. *hypo-* + *tympanic;* in sense 2, fr. NL *hypotympanum* + E *-ic*] **1 :** located below the tympanum **2 :** of or relating to the hypotympanum

**hy·po·tympanum** \"+\ *n* [NL, fr. *hypo-* + *tympanum*] **:** the lower part of the middle ear — compare EPITYMPANUM

**hy·po·type** \'==+,-\ *n* [*hypo-* + *type*] **:** a specimen of a species not of the original type series but known by published description, figure, or listing

**hy·po·typic** \¦==+\ *or* **hy·po·typical** \"+\ *adj* [in sense 1, fr. *hypo-* + *typic* or *typical;* in sense 2, fr. *hypotype* + *-ic* or *-ical*] **1 :** imperfectly typical **2 :** of or relating to a hypotype

**hy·po·ty·po·sis** \,==+,tī'pōsəs\ *n, pl* **hypotypo·ses** \-ō,sēz\ [Gk *hypotypōsis,* fr. *hypotypoun* to sketch, outline, fr. *hypo-* + *typoun* to stamp, form (fr. *typos* impression, cast)] **:** vivid picturesque description

**hy·po·valve** \'==+,-\ *n* [*hypo-* + *valve*] **1 :** one half of the shell of a dinoflagellate **2 :** the hypotheca of a diatom

**hy·po·vanadate** \¦==+\ *n* [ISV *hypo-* + *vanadate*] **:** a salt (as potassium hypovanadate $K_2V_4O_9$) containing tetravalent vanadium in the anion — called also *vanadite*

**hy·po·vi·ta·min·osis** \,==+,vīd·əmə'nōsəs\ *n* -ES [NL, fr. *hypo-* + ISV *vitamin* + NL *-osis*] **:** AVITAMINOSIS

**hy·po·vi·ta·min·ot·ic** \¦==¦===¦näd·ik\ *adj* **:** AVITAMINOTIC

**hy·po·vo·le·mia** \,==+,vä'lēmēə\ *n* -s [NL, fr. *hypo-* + *vol-* (fr. E *volume*) + *-emia*] **:** decrease in the volume of the circulating blood — **hy·po·vo·le·mic** \¦==,=¦lēmik\ *adj*

**hy·po·xanthine** \¦==+\ *n* [ISV *hypo-* + *xanthine*] **:** a purine base $C_5H_4N_4O$ found in plant and animal tissues, formed by hydrolysis of adenine and inosinic acid, and yielding xanthine on oxidation; 6-hydroxy-purine

**hy·pox·e·mia** \,hī,päk'sēmēə\ *n* -s [NL, fr. *hypo-* + ¹*ox-* + *-emia*] **:** deficient oxygenation of the blood

**hy·pox·ia** \hī'päksēə\ *n* -s [NL, fr. *hypo-* + ¹*ox-* + *-ia*] **:** a deficiency of oxygen reaching the tissues of the body whether due to environmental deficiency or impaired respiratory and circulatory organs — **hy·pox·ic** \(')=¦=sik\ *adj*

**hy·pox·is** \hī'päksəs, hə'-\ *n, cap* [NL, irreg. fr. *hypo-* + Gk *oxys* sharp — more at OXY-] **:** a genus of small scapose herbs (family Amaryllidaceae) having numerous hairy linear leaves from a corm or short rootstock and umbellate yellow flowers with 6-parted perianth — see STAR GRASS 1

**hy·pox·y·lon** \hī'päksə,län\ *n, cap* [NL, fr. *hypo-* + *-xylon*] **:** a genus of fungi (family Xylariaceae) having effuse to hemispherical stromata and including a species (*H. pruinatum*) that causes a canker of poplars — compare XYLARIA

**hy·po·zeug·ma** \,== *at* HYPO- +'zügmə\ *n* [LL, fr. *hypo-* + L *zeugma*] **:** the joining of several subjects with a single verb

**hy·po·zeux·is** \"+'züksəs\ *n* -ES [LL, fr. LGk, fr. Gk *hypozeugnynai* to subjugate, yoke under, fr. *hypo-* + *zeugnynai* to yoke — more at YOKE] **:** the use in a parallel construction of successive clauses each complete with subject and verb

**hy·po·zoic** \¦==+¦zōik\ *adj* [ISV *hypo-* + *-zoic*] **:** lying under the fossiliferous systems

**hypped** \'hipt\ *archaic var of* HIPPED

**hyp·pish** \'hipish\ *adj* [*hyp* + *-ish*] **:** affected with hypochondria **:** BLUE, DEPRESSED, MELANCHOLIC

**hyps** *pl of* HYP

**hyps-** *or* **hypsi-** *or* **hypso-** *comb form* [in sense 1, fr. Gk, fr. *hypsos;* in sense 2, fr. Gk, fr. *hypsi;* Gk *hypsos* & Gk *hypsi* akin to Gk *hypo* under — more at UP] **1 :** height ⟨*hypso*graphy⟩ **2 :** on high **:** aloft ⟨*hypsi*cephalic⟩ ⟨*hyps*odont⟩

**hyp·si·brachycephalic** \¦hipsə̇, -sē+\ *adj* [*hyps-* + *brachycephalic*] **:** having a high broad head

**hyp·si·brachycephalism** \"+\ *n* [*hyps-* + *brachycephalism*] **:** the quality or state of being hypsibrachycephalic

**hyp·si·brachycephaly** \"+\ *n* [*hypsibrachycephalic* + *-y*] **:** HYPSIBRACHYCEPHALISM

**hyp·si·ceph·al** \,hipsə'sefəl\ *n* -s [ISV *hyps-* + *-cephal* (as in *dolichocephal*)] **:** a person having a high forehead

**hyp·si·ce·phal·ic** \¦hipsəsə̇¦falik\ *also* **hyp·si·ceph·a·lous** \¦hipsə¦sefələs\ *adj* [*hyps-* + *-cephalic* or *-cephalous*] **:** having a high forehead with a length-height index of 62.6 or higher — compare HYPSICRANIC

**hyp·si·conch** \'hipsə,käŋk, -änch\ *adj* [*hyps-* + *-conch* (fr. L *concha* conch, shell) — more at CONCH] *anthropol* **:** having high orbits with an orbital index of 89 or over — **hyp·si·con·chy** \-äŋkē, -änchē\ *n* -ES

**hyp·si·cra·ni·al** \¦hipsə¦krānēəl\ *or* **hyp·si·cra·nic** \-nik\ *adj* [G *hypsikran* hypsicranial (fr. *hyps-* + Gk *kranion* cranium) + E *-ial* or *-ic* — more at CRANIUM] **:** having a high skull with a length-height index of 75 or over — **hyp·si·cra·ny** \¦==¦krānē\ *n* -ES

**hyp·si·dolichocephalic** \¦hipsə̇, -sē+\ *adj* [*hyps-* + *dolichocephalic*] **:** having a head that is high and narrow or high and long or high, long, and narrow

**hyp·si·dolichocephalism** \"+\ *n* [*hyps-* + *dolichocephalism*] **:** the quality or state of being hypsidolichocephalic

**hyp·si·dolichocephaly** \"+\ *n* [*hyps-* + *dolichocephaly*] **:** HYPSIDOLICHOCEPHALISM

**hyp·si·dont** \'hipsə,dänt\ *adj* [*hyps-* + *-dont* (fr. *-odont*)] **:** HYPSODONT

**hyp·sil·i·form** \(')hip¦silə,fȯrm\ *adj* [*hypsil-* (fr. MGk *hy psilon* upsilon) + *-iform*] **:** HYPSILOID

**hyp·si·loid** \'hipsə,lȯid\ *adj* [MGk *hypsiloeidēs,* fr. *hy psilon* upsilon, lit., simple y + *-oeidēs* -oid] *anat* **:** resembling a Greek capital letter upsilon in form

**hyp·si·loph·o·don** \,hipsə'läfə,dän\ *n, cap* [NL, fr. Gk *hypsilophos* high-crested (fr. *hyps-* + *lophos* crest) + NL *-odon*] **:** a genus (the type of the family Hypsilophodontidae) of small primitive ornithopod dinosaurs of the Wealden of the Isle of Wight

**hyp·si·loph·o·dont** \¦==¦==,dänt\ *adj* [NL *Hypsilophodontidae,* family of dinosaurs, fr. *Hypsilophodont-, Hypsilophodon,* type genus + *-idae*] **:** of or relating to the genus *Hypsilophodon* or family Hypsilophodontidae

**hyp·si·prym·no·don** \,hipsə'primnə,dän\ *n, cap* [NL, fr. *hyps-* + Gk *prymnos* endmost, hindmost + NL *-odon*] **:** a genus of marsupial mammals comprising the musk kangaroos

**hyp·sis·tar·i·an** \¦hipsə¦sta(a)rēən\ *n* -s *usu cap* [LGk *Hypsistarioi,* pl., fr. *hypsistarioi,* pl. of *hypsistarios* worshiping the highest (fr. Gk *hypsistos* highest, fr. *hypsi* on high) + E *-an*] **:** a member of a sect of the 4th to the 9th century in Asia Minor combining heathen, Jewish, and Christian tenets

**hyp·si·stenocephalic** \¦hipsə̇, -sē+\ *adj* [*hyps-* + *stenocephalic*] **:** having an extremely high narrow head

**hyp·si·sten·o·ceph·a·lism** \,==+,stenə'sefə,lizəm\ *n* [*hypsistenocephalic* + *-ism*] **:** the quality or state of being hypsistenocephalic

**hyp·si·stenocephaly** \¦==+\ *n* [*hyps-* + *stenocephaly*] **:** HYPSISTENOCEPHALISM

**hypso-** — see HYPS-

**hyp·so·chrome** \'hipsə,krōm\ *n* [ISV *hyps-* + *-chrome*] **:** an atom or group that when introduced into a compound causes a visible lightening of color (as from green toward yellow) — contrasted with *bathochrome* — **hyp·so·chro·mic** \¦==¦krōmik\ *adj*

**hyp·so·dont** \'hipsə,dänt\ *adj* [*hyps-* + *-odont*] **1** *of teeth* **:** having high or deep crowns and short roots (as the molar teeth of a horse) — compare BRACHYDONT **2 :** having hypsodont teeth

**hyp·so·dont·ism** \-n,tizəm\ *n* -s [*hypsodont* + *-ism*] **:** the quality or state of being hypsodont

**hyp·so·donty** \-nē\ *n* -ES [*hypsodont* + *-y*] **:** HYPSODONTISM

**hyp·sog·ra·phy** \hip'sägrəfē\ *n* -ES [ISV *hyps-* + *-graphy*] **1 :** a branch of geography that deals with the measurement and mapping of the varying elevations of the earth's surface with reference to sea level **2 :** topographic relief or the devices (as color shadings) by which it is indicated on maps

**hyp·so·isotherm** \¦hip(,)sō+\ *n* [*hyps-* + *isotherm;* trans. of G *höhenisotherme*] **:** an isotherm that is drawn on a vertical section of the atmosphere and sometimes also of the ground to show the distribution of temperature in the vertical

**hyp·som·e·ter** \hip'sämədˑə(r)\ *n* [ISV *hyps-* + *-meter*] **1 :** an apparatus for estimating elevations in mountainous regions from the boiling points of liquids **2 :** any of various instruments used to determine the height of trees by triangulation

**hyp·so·met·ric** \¦hipsə¦me·trik\ *or* **hyp·so·met·ri·cal** \-rə̇kəl\ *adj* **:** of or relating to hypsometry

**hyp·som·e·try** \hip'sämə·trē\ *n* -ES [Gk *hypsos* height + E *-metry*] **:** the science of measuring heights (as with reference to sea level)

**hyp·so·phyll** \'hipsə,fil\ *n* -s [NL *hypsophyllum* trans. of G *hochblatt,* lit., high leaf), fr. *hyps-* + *-phyllum* -phyll] **:** a floral leaf beneath the sporophylls **:** BRACT, SCALE LEAF — **hyp·so·phyl·lar** \¦==¦filə(r)\ *or* **hyp·so·phyl·lary** \-lərē\ *or* **hyp·so·phyl·lous** \-ləs\ *adj*

**¹hy·pu·ral** \(')hī¦pyu̇rəl\ *adj* [*hypo-* + *ur-* (tail) + *-al*] **:** of, relating to, or constituting the bony structure chiefly formed of the expanded and more or less fused hemal spines of the last few vertebrae that supports the caudal fin rays in most teleost fishes

**²hypural** \"\ *n* -s **:** a hypural bone

**hy·ra·ce·um** \hī'rāsēəm\ *n* -s [NL, fr. *hyrac-, hyrax* + *-eum* (as in *castoreum*)] **:** a southern African product somewhat like castoreum said to be excreted by the hyrax and formerly much used as a folk remedy and as a fixative for perfumes

**hy·rach·y·us** \hī'rakēəs\ *n, cap* [NL, fr. *Hyrac-, Hyrax,* genus of ungulates + *-hyus* (fr. Gk *hy-, hys* hog, swine) — more at SOW (female hog)] **:** a genus (the type of the family Hyrachyidae) of primitive perissodactyl ungulates related to the rhinoceroses and common in the No. American Eocene

**¹hy·rac·id** \(')hī¦rasəd\ *adj* [NL *Hyracidae*] **:** of or relating to the Procaviidae

**²hyracid** \"\ *n* -s **:** a member of the family Procaviidae **:** CONEY

**hy·rac·i·dae** \hī'rasə,dē\ [NL, fr. *Hyrac-, Hyrax* + *-idae*] *syn of* PROCAVIIDAE

**hy·rac·i·form** \(')=¦=ə,fȯrm\ *adj* [NL *hyrac-, hyrax* + E *-iform*] **:** resembling a hyrax

**hy·ra·ci·na** \,hīrə'sīnə\ [NL, fr. *Hyrac-, Hyrax* + *-ina*] *syn of* HYRACOIDEA

**hy·rac·o·don** \hī'rakə,dän\ *n, cap* [NL, fr. *Hyrac-, Hyrax* + *-odon*] **:** a genus (the type of the family Hyracodontidae) of Eocene and Oligocene perissodactyls related to the rhinoceroses but hornless and of light agile build with all feet three-toed

**¹hy·rac·o·dont** \(')=¦=ə,dänt\ *adj* [NL *Hyracodont-, Hyracodon*] **:** of or relating to the genus *Hyracodon* or family Hyracodontidae

**²hyracodont** \"\ *n* -s **:** a mammal of the genus *Hyracodon* or family Hyracodontidae

**hy·ra·coid** \'hīrə,kȯid\ *n* -s [NL *Hyracoidea*] **:** one of the Hyracoidea

**hy·ra·coi·dea** \,==¦kȯidēə\ *n pl, cap* [NL, fr. *Hyrac-, Hyrax* + *-oidea*] **:** an order of Old World ungulate mammals that is now restricted to Africa and southwestern Asia and that comprises various extinct animals and the surviving hyraxes which find their nearest living relatives in the elephants and sirenians but in many respects resemble rabbits

**hy·ra·co·there** \'hīrəkō,thir\ *n* -s [NL *Hyracotherium*] **:** an animal or fossil of the genus *Hyracotherium*

**hy·ra·co·the·ri·um** \,==='thirēəm\ *n, cap* [NL *Hyrac-, Hyrax* + *-o-* + *-therium*] **:** a genus of lower Eocene perissodactylous mammals about the size of a fox having four-toed forelimbs and three-toed hind limbs and regarded as among the earliest ancestors of the modern horse — see EQUIDAE illustration

**¹hy·rax** \'hī,raks\ [NL, fr. Gk, mouse, shrewmouse; akin to L *susurrus* hum, murmur — more at SWARM] *syn of* PROCAVIA

**²hyrax** \"\ *n, pl* **hyraxes** \-ksəz\ *also* **hyra·ces** \-īrə,sēz\ [NL, fr. ¹*Hyrax*] **:** any of certain small mammals that constitute the order Hyracoidea and are characterized by thickset body with short legs and ears and rudimentary tail, feet with soft pads and broad nails, and teeth of which the molars resemble those of the rhinoceros and the incisors those of rodents — called also *coney*

**³hyrax** \"\ *n* -ES [origin unknown] **:** a microscopic mounting medium of high refractive index that consists of a naphthalene derivative dissolved in benzene or xylol, is used esp. for mounting semiopaque structures (as diatom frustules), and tends to darken but not crystallize with age

**hyr·ca·ni·an** \¦hər¦kānēən\ *also* **hyr·can** \'hərkən\ *adj, usu cap* [*hyrcanian* fr. L *Hyrcanius* Hyrcanian (fr. *Hyrcania,* ancient country or province of Asia) + E *-an; hyrcan* fr. L *Hyrcanus* Hyrcanian, fr. Gk *Hyrkanos,* n., Hyrcanian, inhabitant of Hyrcania] **:** of or relating to the ancient land of Hyrcania southeast of the Caspian sea

**hyrst** *var of* HURST

**hy·son** \'hīs°n\ *n* -s [Chin (Peking) *hsi¹ ch'un¹,* lit., flourishing spring] **:** a Chinese green tea made from thinly rolled and twisted leaves

**hyson skin** *n* **:** the light and inferior leaves separated from hyson by a winnowing machine

**hy spy** \'hī-\ *n* [prob. fr. *hi, spy!* (call used by the hiders in the game as a signal to the searchers to start looking for them), fr. *hi* + *spy,* n.] **:** HIDE-AND-SEEK

**hys·sop** \'hisəp\ *n* -s [ME *ysop,* partly fr. OE *ysopan* and partly fr. OF *ysope;* OE & OF, fr. L *hyssopum, hyssopum, hyssopus,* fr. Gk *hyssōpon, hyssōpos,* of Sem origin; akin to Heb *ēzōbh* hyssop, Assyr-Bab *zūpu,* Syriac *zōfā*] **1 a :** a plant used in bunches for purificatory sprinkling rites by the ancient Hebrews **b :** a European mint (*Hyssopus officinalis*) that has highly aromatic and pungent leaves and is often cultivated in gardens as a remedy for bruises **2 a** [prob. fr. ML *hyssopus* (also, the plant), fr. L] **:** ASPERGILLUM **b :** the holy water sprinkled in the asperges

**hyssop loosestrife** *n* **:** GRASS POLY

**hyssop oil** *n* **:** an essential oil obtained from hyssop and used chiefly in liqueurs

**hyssop skullcap** *n* **:** a perennial herb (*Scutellaria integrifolia*) of the eastern U.S. with showy blue flowers

**hys·so·pus** \'hisəpəs, hə'sōp-\ *n, cap* [NL, fr. L, hyssop] **:** a Eurasian genus of perennial herbs or subshrubs (family Labiatae) having floral whorls in bracted spikes — see HYSSOP 1

**hyssop violet** *n* **:** a grayish purple that is redder and stronger than telegraph blue, bluer and deeper than mauve gray, and bluer, lighter, and stronger than average rose mauve

**hys·taz·a·rin** \hə'stazərən\ *n* -s [ISV *hyst-* (fr. Gk *hysteros* latter, later) + *alizarin;* orig. formed in G] **:** a yellow crystalline compound $C_{14}H_6O_2(OH)_2$ produced along with its isomer alizarin by condensation of phthalic anhydride and pyrocatechol; 2,3-dihydroxy-anthraquinone

**hyster-** *or* **hystero-** *comb form* [F or L; F *hystér-,* fr. MF, fr. L *hyster-,* fr. Gk, fr. *hystera* womb] **1 :** womb ⟨*hyster*ectomy⟩ ⟨*hystero*myoma⟩ **2** [NL, fr. *hysteria*] **:** hysteria ⟨*hystero*genic⟩ **:** hysteria and ⟨*hystero*neurasthenia⟩

**hys·ter·ec·to·mize** \,histə'rektə,mīz\ *vt* -ED/-ING/-S **:** to remove the uterus by surgery

**hys·ter·ec·to·my** \-,mē\ *n* -ES [ISV *hyster-* + *-ectomy*] **:** surgical removal of the uterus

**hys·ter·e·sis** \,histə'rēsəs\ *n, pl* **hystere·ses** \-ē,sēz\ [NL, fr. Gk *hysterēsis* shortcoming, deficiency, need, fr. *hysterein* to come late, be behind (fr. *hysteros* later, latter) + *-ēsis* -esis] **1 a :** the lagging of a physical effect on a body behind its cause (as behind changed forces and conditions) ⟨there is a good deal of ~, that is, a time lag between the cooling and the setting to be expected of the jelly —J.W.McBain⟩ ⟨all manometers must be tested for ~ as well as for sensitivity and natural frequency —H.D.Green⟩ **b :** a lagging of elongation behind tensile stress and of contraction behind release from stress in an elastic solid due to internal friction **c :** a lagging of magnetization and hence of magnetic induction behind magnetic intensity and of demagnetization behind reduction of intensity in a ferromagnetic substance (as iron) **d :** a lagging of electric polarization behind electric intensity and of depolarization behind reduction of intensity in a dielectric **2 a :** the influence of the previous history or treatment of a body on its subsequent response to a given force or changed condition ⟨the influence of the previous treatment of a gel upon its behavior is known as ~ —B.S.Meyer & D.B.Anderson⟩ ⟨a study has been made of the phenomenon of rennet ~, in which the time of coagulation of heated milk is progressively greater with increase in the time interval between heating and addition of rennet —J.S.Fruton⟩ **b :** the changed response of a body that results from this influence ⟨the permeability depends on the past history (magnetically speaking) of the iron, a phenomenon known as ~ —F.W.Sears⟩ **3 :** HYSTERESIS LOSS

**hysteresis coefficient** *n* **:** the constant in a formula for hysteresis loss that is characteristic of the substance under test

**hysteresis loop** *n* **:** a cycle of alternating changes involving elastic, magnetic, or dielectric hysteresis; *also* **:** the loop-shaped graph representing such a cycle

**hysteresis loss** *n* **:** loss of energy in the form of heat due to hysteresis (as in an alternating-current core)

**hysteresis motor** *n* **:** a synchronous motor that utilizes the hysteresis effect in a solid rotor of permanent-magnet material to achieve synchronism and that is used esp. in sound recording and reproducing machines

**hys·ter·et·ic** \ˌhistəˈred·ˌik, -et|, |ēk\ *adj* [fr. NL *hysteresis*, after such pairs as NL *exegesis:* E *exegetic*] **:** of, relating to, or marked by hysteresis — **hys·ter·et·i·cal·ly** \|ək(ə)lē, |ēk-, -li\ *adv*

**hys·te·ria** \həˈsterēə, -tir-\ *n* -s [NL, fr. E *hysteric* + NL *-ia*] **1 a :** a psychoneurosis that is marked by emotional excitability involving disturbances of the psychic, sensory, vasomotor, and visceral functions **b :** a similar disease of domesticated animals; *specif* **:** CANINE HYSTERIA **2 :** conduct or an outbreak of conduct exhibiting unmanageable fear or emotional excess in individuals or groups ⟨could not fail to destroy his system, never very strong and pitched to ~ from the first —H.M. Ledig-Rowohlt⟩ ⟨weeping generously . . . and wildly giggling, in a ~ which she could not control —Arnold Bennett⟩ ⟨swept up into the systematized ~ of the war —Scott Fitzgerald⟩ ⟨the ghost dance was the religious expression of a social ~ —W.W. Howells⟩ **syn** see MANIA

**hys·te·ri·a·ce·ae** \həˌstirēˈāsēˌē\ *n pl, cap* [NL, fr. *Hysterium*, type genus (fr. Gk *hystera* womb + NL *-ium*) + *-aceae*] **:** a family of ascomycetous fungi (order Hysteriales) that is often considered to be derived from the family Sphaeriaceae from which it is distinguished chiefly by the form and method of opening of the ascomata of its members

**hys·te·ri·a·gen·ic** \həˈsterēəˈjenik, -tir-\ *adj* [NL *hysteria* + E *-genic*] **:** HYSTEROGENIC

**hys·te·ri·a·les** \həˌstirēˈā(ˌ)lēz\ *n pl, cap* [NL, fr. *Hysterium*, genus of fungi + *-ales*] **:** an order of fungi of the subclass Euascomycetes that is characterized by elongated ascomata opening by a longitudinal slit and includes various fungi which cause leaf cast of conifers — see HYSTERIACEAE

**¹hys·ter·ic** \həˈsterik, (ˈ)hiˈs-, -rēk\ *adj* [L *hystericus* of the womb] **:** HYSTERICAL ⟨raved and ran hither and thither in ~ insanity —W.M.Thackeray⟩

**²hysteric** \"\ *n* -s **1 :** one subject to or suffering from hysteria **2 :** an overemotional or unstable person ⟨Bohemia, which has always been (along with better things) the refuge of fakers, self-deceivers, and ~s —C.J.Rolo⟩ ⟨a charlatan, a lucky ~, and a lying demagogue —John Gunther⟩

**hys·ter·i·cal** \həˈsterəkəl, (ˈ)hiˈs-, -rēk-\ *adj* [L *hystericus* hysterical (fr. Gk *hysterikos*, fr. *hystera* womb + *-ikos* -ic) + E *-al;* fr. its being orig. applied to women thought to be suffering from disturbances of the womb] **1 :** of, relating to, or marked by hysteria ⟨during ~ conditions various functions of the human body are disordered —Morris Fishbein⟩ — compare PSYCHOGENIC **2 :** exhibiting unrestrained emotionalism ⟨had absorbed all the serenity of America, and left none for his restless, rickety, ~ countrymen —R.W.Emerson⟩ — **hys·ter·i·cal·ly** \-rək(ə)lē, -rēk-, -li\ *adv*

**hys·ter·icky** \-rəkē\ *adj* **:** HYSTERICAL ⟨up I went with all the courage I could muster, but a sort of ~ feeling —W.G. Hammond⟩

**hys·ter·ics** \həˈsteriks, -rēks\ *n pl but usu sing in constr, also* **hys·ter·ic** \-k\ **:** a fit of uncontrollable laughter or crying **:** HYSTERIA ⟨she'll go all to pieces and start bawling and having ~ —Erle Stanley Gardner⟩

**¹hys·ter·i·form** \həˈsterəˌfȯrm\ *adj* [ISV *hyster-* + *-iform*] **:** resembling hysteria

**²hysteriform** \"\ *adj* [NL *Hysterium*, genus of fungi + E *-form*] **:** HYSTERIOID

**hys·te·ri·oid** \həˈstirēˌȯid\ *adj* [NL *Hysterium*, genus of fungi + E *-oid* — more at HYSTERIACEAE] **:** BOAT-SHAPED ⟨the ~ apothecia of fungi of the order Hysteriales⟩

**hystero-** — see HYSTER-

**hys·tero·crystalline** \ˌhistə(ˌ)rō+\ *n* -s [ISV *hystero-* (fr. Gk *hysteros* latter, later) + *crystalline;* orig. formed as G *hysterokrystallin*] **:** a secondary crystallization in igneous rock

**hys·tero–epilepsy** \"+\ *n* [ISV *hyster-* + *epilepsy*] **:** a hysteria characterized by motor convulsions resembling those of epilepsy — **hys·tero–epileptic** \"+\ *adj*

**hys·ter·o·gen·ic** \ˌhistərōˈjenik\ *adj* [*hyster-* + *-genic*] **:** inducing hysteria

**hys·ter·o·gram** \ˈhistərōˌgram\ *n* [*hyster-* + *-gram*] **:** a roentgenogram made by hysterography

**hys·ter·o·graph** \-raf,-rȧf\ *n* [*hyster-* + *-graph*] **:** HYSTEROGRAM — **hys·ter·o·graph·ic** \ˌ===ˈgrafik\ *adj*

**hys·ter·og·ra·phy** \ˌhistəˈrägrəfē\ *n* -ES [*hyster-* + *-graphy*] **:** examination of the uterus by roentgenography after the injection of an opaque medium

**hys·ter·oid** \ˈhistəˌrȯid\ *also* **hys·ter·oi·dal** \ˌ=ˈ=ˈrȯidᵊl\ *adj* [*hysteroid*, ISV *hyster-* + *-oid; hysteroidal* fr. *hysteroid* + *-al*] **:** resembling hysteria

**hys·ter·ol·o·gy** \ˌhistəˈräləjē\ *n* -ES [LL *hysterologia*, fr. LGk, fr. Gk *hysteros* latter, later + *-logia* -logy] *archaic* **:** HYSTERON PROTERON

**hys·ter·o·mor·phous** \ˌhistərōˈmȯrfəs\ *adj* [Gk *hysteros* later, latter + E *-morphous*] **:** of, relating to, or constituting mineral deposits formed on the earth's surface by mechanical or chemical concentration

**hys·ter·on pro·ter·on** \ˈhistəˌränˈprōd·əˌrän\ *n* [LL, fr. Gk, lit., later earlier, the latter earlier] **1 :** a figure of speech consisting of reversal of a natural or rational order (as in "then came the thunder and the lightning") **2 :** a logical fallacy consisting in assuming as a premise something that follows from what is to be proved

**hys·tero–oophorectomy** \ˌhistə(ˌ)rō+\ *n* [*hyster-* + *oophor-* + *-ectomy*] **:** surgical removal of the uterus and ovaries

**hys·ter·o·pexy** \ˈhistərōˌpeksē\ *n* -ES [ISV *hyster-* + *-pexy*] **:** surgical fixation of a displaced uterus

**hys·ter·o·phyte** \ˈhistərōˌfīt\ *n* -S [NL *hysterophytum*, fr. *hyster-* + *-phytum* -phyte] **:** HETEROPHYTE

**hys·ter·or·rha·phy** \ˌhistəˈrärəfē\ *n* -ES [ISV *hyster-* + *-rrhaphy*] **1 :** a suturing of an incised or ruptured uterus **2 :** HYSTEROPEXY

**hys·ter·or·rhex·is** \ˌhistərōˈreksəs\ *n, pl* **hysterorrhex·es** \-kˌsēz\ [NL, fr. *hyster-* + *-rrhexis*] **:** rupture of the uterus

**hys·ter·o·sal·pin·gog·ra·phy** \ˌhistərōˌsalˌpiŋˈgägrəfē\ *n* -ES [ISV *hyster-* + *salping-* + *-graphy*] **:** examination of the uterus and fallopian tubes by roentgenography after injection of an opaque medium

**hys·tero–salpingo–oophorectomy** \ˌhistə(ˌ)rō+\ *n* [*hyster-* + *salping-* + *oophorectomy*] **:** surgical removal of uterus, oviducts, and ovaries

**hys·ter·o·scope** \ˈhistərōˌskōp\ *n* [ISV *hyster-* + *-scope*] **:** an instrument used in inspection of the uterus — **hys·ter·o·scop·ic** \ˌ===ˈskäpik\ *adj* — **hys·ter·os·co·py** \ˌhistəˈräskəpē\ *n* -ES

**hys·ter·o·sto·mat·o·my** \ˌhistərōˌstōˈmad·əmē\ *n* -ES [F *hystérostomatomie*, fr. *hystér-* hyster- + *stoma-* + *-tomie* -tomy] **:** surgical incision of the uterine cervix

**hys·ter·o·tely** \ˈhistərōˌtelē\ *n* -ES [Gk *hysteros* latter, later + *telos* end, completion, maturity + E *-y* — more at WHEEL] **:** relatively retarded differentiation of a structure or organ so that it shows a form usu. associated with a stage of development earlier than that shown by the individual plant or animal as a whole — compare PROTHETELY

**hys·ter·o·the·ci·um** \ˌhistərōˈthēs(h)ēəm\ *n* [NL, fr. *hyster-* + *-thecium*] **:** a narrow elongated ascocarp opening at maturity by a narrow lengthwise slit

**hys·ter·ot·o·my** \ˌhistəˈräd·əmē\ *n* -ES [NL *hysterotomia*, fr. *hyster-* + *-tomia* -tomy] **:** surgical incision of the uterus **:** CESAREAN, HYSTEROSTOMATOMY

**hys·tric·i·dae** \həˈstrisəˌdē\ *n pl, cap* [NL, fr. *Hystric-*, *Hystrix*, type genus + *-idae*] **:** a family of Old World hystricomorph rodents comprising the terrestrial porcupines that was formerly extended to include the New World arboreal porcupines — compare ERETHIZONTIDAE

**¹hys·tri·coid** \ˈhistrəˌkȯid\ *adj* [NL *Hystricoidea*] **:** of or relating to the Hystricoidea

**²hystricoid** \"\ *n* -s **:** a rodent of the superfamily Hystricoidea

**hys·tri·coi·dea** \ˌ==ˈkȯidēə\ *n pl, cap* [NL, fr. *Hystric-*, *Hystrix* + *-oidea*] **1** *in some classifications* **:** a major division of hystricomorph rodents equivalent to the Hystricidae **2** *in some classifications* **:** HYSTRICOMORPHA

**¹hys·tri·co·morph** \ˈhistrəkōˌmȯrf\ *adj* [NL *Hystricomorpha*] **:** of or relating to the Hystricomorpha

**²hystricomorph** \"\ *n* -s **:** a rodent of the suborder Hystricomorpha

**hys·tri·co·mor·pha** \ˌ===ˈmȯrfə\ *n pl, cap* [NL, fr. *Hystric-*, *Hystrix* + *-morpha*] **:** a suborder of Rodentia comprising forms distinguished by a zygomatic arch in which the jugal bone forms the center block and including porcupines, guinea pigs, chinchillas, and many others — **hys·tri·co·mor·phic** \ˌ===ˈmȯrfik\ *or* **hys·tri·co·mor·phous** \-fəs\ *adj*

**¹hys·trix** \ˈhistriks\ *n, cap* [NL, fr. L, porcupine, fr. Gk] **:** a genus of terrestrial porcupines that is the type of the family Hystricidae

**²hystrix** \"\ *n, cap* [NL] **:** a genus of perennial grasses (family Gramineae) of No. America, Asia, and New Zealand having loosely flowered spikes with spikelets becoming widely divergent — see BOTTLE BRUSH GRASS

**hyte** \ˈhīt\ *adj* [origin unknown] *Scot* **:** stark raving mad

**hy·ther·graph** \ˈhīthə(r)ˌgraf, -rȧf\ *also* **hy·ther·o·graph** \-ərō,-\ *n* [*hyther-* or *hythero-* (fr. Gk *hydōr* water + *thermē* heat) + *-graph*] **:** a climograph that records temperature and rainfall

**Hz** *abbr* hertz

**hzy** *abbr* hazy

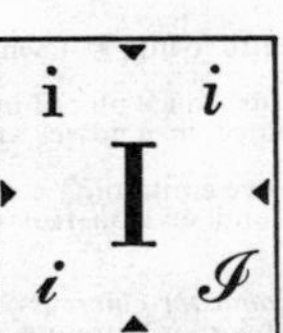

**¹i** \'ī\ *n, pl* **i's** *or* **is** \'īz\ *often cap, often attrib* **1 a :** the ninth letter of the English alphabet **b :** an instance of this letter printed, written, or otherwise represented **c :** a speech counterpart of orthographic *i* (as long *i* in *side*, short *i* in *sit*, or *i* in French *élite*) **2 :** ONE — see NUMBER table **3 :** a printer's type, a stamp, or some other instrument for reproducing the letter *i* **4 :** someone or something arbitrarily or conveniently designated *i* esp. as the ninth in order or class **5 :** something having the shape of the capital letter I **6 :** a unit vector parallel to the x-axis

**²i** \(¦)ī, ·ə, *often* ·ä *or* ·à *when unemphatic esp in contracted forms as* "I'm" & "I'll"\ *pron, cap* [ME *ich, i*, fr. OE *ic*; akin to OHG *ih* I, ON *ek*, Goth *ik*, L *ego*, Gk *egō, egōn*, Skt *aham*] **1 :** the one who is speaking or writing ⟨*I* shall not want —Ps 23:1 (AV)⟩ — used as a nominative pronoun of the first person singular by one speaking or writing to refer to himself as the doer of an action ⟨*I* will not hurt you⟩ ⟨whither thou goest, *I* will go —Ruth 1:16 (AV)⟩ or the subject of a predicated condition ⟨*I* don't feel very well today⟩ or sometimes in the predicate after forms of *be* ⟨it will not be *I* —D.D.Eisenhower⟩ ⟨it is *I* —Mk 6:50 (AV)⟩ or in comparisons after *than* or *as* when the first term in the comparison is the subject of a verb ⟨you can do it just as well as *I*⟩ ⟨he writes much better than *I*⟩ ⟨thou art stronger than *I* —Jer 20:7 (AV)⟩ or in some absolute or elliptical constructions esp. when not used with a prepositional phrase or an adjective or a participle ⟨who, *I*? You're foolish to say that anyone would do it⟩ or after *but* in a compound subject ⟨no one but *I* could have known —H. G.Wells⟩ — see ME, MINE, MY; compare WE **2 a** *now chiefly substand* **:** ME — used in a compound object ⟨belongs to my mother and *I*⟩ ⟨between you and *I*⟩ ⟨he saw my brother and *I*⟩ **b** *now dial Eng* **:** ME — used emphatically as object of a verb ⟨give the ball to *I*⟩ or preposition ⟨give poor *I* another chance⟩ ⟨my father hath no child but *I* —Shak.⟩ **3 :** the one who acts as authorized spokesman of a social or military system (as an army) ⟨*I* order you to report for duty⟩ ⟨*I* arrest you in the name of the law⟩

**³i** \'ī\ *n, pl* **i's** *or* **is** *cap* **1 :** someone possessing and aware of possessing a distinct and personal individuality **:** SELF, EGO ⟨there is but one *I* —Mary B. Eddy⟩ ⟨society has been atomized down to its elemental particles each of which is an *I* —W.P. Webb⟩; *also* **:** the quality or state of possessing such individuality ⟨the crowd is like a community in that it can be any size, the difference being that the We precedes the *I* —Howard Griffin⟩ **2 :** an excessively egotistic person **:** one that uses the first person pronoun excessively ⟨just a big *I*⟩ **3 :** a dichotomous part of one's self ⟨the other *I*⟩

**⁴i** *or* **i'** _i\ *now chiefly dial var of* IN

**⁵i** *obs var of* AYE

**⁶i** *abbr, often cap* **1** [L *id*] that **2** [L *imperator; imperatrix*] emperor; empress **3** imperial **4** incendiary **5** incomplete **6** independent **7** indicated; indicative **8** industrial **9** infantry **10** infield **11** inhibitory **12** initial **13** inner **14** inside **15** inspector **16** instantaneous **17** institute; institution **18** instrumental **19** intelligence **20** interceptor **21** interest **22** international **23** intransitive **24** Iraqi **25** iron **26** island; isle **27** Israeli

**⁷i** *symbol, cap* **1** iodine **2** candlepower **3** electric current **4** moment of inertia **5** imaginary unit

**¹i-** *comb form* [*inactive*] **:** inactive (sense c) ⟨*i*-inositol⟩ — usu. joined to second element with a hyphen

**²i-** *comb form* [by shortening] **:** IS- 2b ⟨*i*-butyl⟩ — usu. joined to second element with a hyphen

**-i-** [ME, fr. OF, fr. L, thematic vowel of most nouns and adjectives in combination] — used as a connective vowel to join two elements of usu. Latin origin, being either identical with ⟨aur*i*form⟩ or representative of ⟨Herb*i*vora⟩ an original Latin stem vowel or simply inserted ⟨cant*i*lever⟩; compare -O-

**¹-ia** \ēə, yə, iə\ *n suffix* [NL, fr. L & Gk, suffix forming feminine abstract nouns] **1** -s **:** pathological condition ⟨pneumon*ia*⟩ ⟨hyster*ia*⟩ ⟨diphther*ia*⟩ **2 :** genus consisting of (specified plants or animals) ⟨Wistar*ia*⟩ ⟨Osm*ia*⟩

**²-ia** \"\ *n pl suffix* [NL, fr. L (neut. pl. of *-ius*, adj. ending) & Gk, neut. pl. of *-ios*, adj. ending] **1 :** taxonomic division (as class, order) consisting of (specified plants or animals) ⟨Cryptogam*ia*⟩ ⟨Mammal*ia*⟩ **2 :** things belonging to or derived from or relating to (something specified) ⟨Maryland*ia*⟩ ⟨tabloid*ia*⟩

**³-ia** *pl of* -IUM

**IA** *abbr* **1** incorporated accountant **2** infected area **3** *often not cap* [L *inter alia*] among other things **4** international angstrom

**IAA** *abbr* indoleacetic acid

**IAC** *abbr* **1** industry advisory committee **2** interview-after-combat

**-ial** \ēəl, yəl, iəl, əl\ *adj suffix* [ME, fr. MF *-iel, -ial*, fr. L *-ialis*, fr. *-i-* + *-alis* -al] **:** -AL ⟨gerund*ial*⟩

**iamb** \'ī,am, -,aa(ə)m *also* -mb\ *n, pl* **iambs** \-mz\ [L *iambus*, fr. Gk *iambos*] **1 :** a metrical foot of two syllables unstressed and stressed respectively (as in *above, invent*, and Tennyson's 4-foot line "he watches from his mountain walls") or short and long respectively (as in classical prosody) **:** a disyllabic rising cadence — symbol ◡ –; compare TROCHEE **2 :** verses written in iambs

**iam·bel·e·gus** \,ī,am'beləgəs\ *n* -ES [LL, fr. Gk *iambelegos*, fr. *iambos* + *elegos* song of mourning or lamentation, prob. of non-IE origin] **:** a verse used in classical prosody consisting of an iambic dimeter and half an elegiac pentameter

**¹iam·bic** \ī'ambik, -bēk\ *n* -s [L *iambicus*, adj.] **1 :** IAMB **2 :** a piece of usu. satiric verse written in iambs (as that developed by the Ionian Greeks in the period succeeding the epic) **:** a lampoon written in iambs

**²iambic** \(')⸗¦⸗⸗\ *adj* [L *iambicus*, fr. Gk *iambikos*, fr. *iambos* + *-ikos* -ic] **:** relating to or consisting of iambs or iambics ⟨~ verse⟩ — **iam·bi·cal·ly** \-bək(ə)lē, -bēk-, -li\ *adv*

**iam·bist** \⸗'⸗bəst, '⸗,⸗-\ *n* -s [Gk *iambistēs*, fr. *iambizein* to write iambs, fr. *iambos* + *-izein* -ize] **:** one who writes iambic verse

**iam·bog·ra·pher** \,ī,am'bägrəfə(r)\ *n* -s [MGk *iambographos* writer of iambs (fr. Gk *iambos* + *-graphos*, fr. *graphein* to write) + E *-er* — more at CARVE] **:** IAMBIST; *esp* **:** one given to or noted for writing iambic lampoons

**iam·bus** \ī'ambəs\ *n, pl* **iambus·es** \-bəsəz\ *also* **iam·bi** \-,bī\ [L, fr. Gk *iambos*] **:** IAMB

**-ian** \ēən, yən, iən, ən\ — see -AN

**-iana** — see -ANA

**I and E** *abbr* information and education

**I and P** *abbr* indexed and paged

**I and R** *abbr* **1** initiative and referendum **2** intelligence and reconnaissance

**I and S** *abbr* **1** inspection and security **2** inspection and survey

**¹ian·thi·na** \ē'an(t)thənə, ī'-\ [NL, by alter.] *syn of* JANTHINA

**²ianthina** \"\ *n* -s **:** JANTHINA 2

**ian·thine** \ē'an(t)thən, (')ī¦a-\ *adj* [L *ianthinus* — more at JANTHINA] **:** having a violet color

**ian·thin·i·dae** \,ī,an'thinə,dē\ [NL, fr. *Ianthina*, type genus + *-idae*] *syn of* JANTHINIDAE

**ian·thi·nite** \ē'an(t)thə,nīt, ī'-\ *n* -s [G *ianthinit*, fr. L *ianthinus* + G *-it* -ite] **:** a mineral $2UO_2.7H_2O$ consisting of a hydrous uranium dioxide and occurring as violet orthorhombic crystals

**¹iao** \(')ē¦aù\ *n* -s [Samoan] **:** WATTLEBIRD 1a

**²iao** \"\ *n* -s [native name in Hawaii] **:** a small silversides often used as bait in fishing

**ia·pyg·i·an** \,īə'pij(ē)ən\ *n* -s *usu cap* [*Iapygia*, ancient region in southeastern Italy (fr. L, fr. Gk) + E *-an*] **1 :** a member of one of several peoples anciently inhabiting the peninsula of Apulia in southeastern Italy **2 :** the language of the Iapygians

**²iapygian** \¦⸗¦⸗(⸗)⸗\ *adj, usu cap* **:** of or relating to the Iapygians

**ia·pyg·i·dae** \,īə'pijə,dē\ [NL, fr. *Iapyg-, Iapyx*, type genus (of *Japyg-, Japyx*) + *-idae*] *syn of* JAPYGIDAE

**iarovize** *var of* JAROVIZE

**IAS** *abbr* indicated airspeed

**-ias** *pl of* -IA

**ia·si** \'yäsh(ē)\ *or* **ias·sy** \'yäsē\ *adj, usu cap* [fr. *Iaşi* (*Jassy*), Romania] **:** of or from the city of Iasi, Romania **:** of the kind or style prevalent in Iasi

**-i·a·sis** \'īəsəs\ *n suffix, pl* **-i·a·ses** \-,sēz\ [NL, fr. L, fr. Gk, suffix of action, fr. verbs in *-ian, -iazein* (fr. nouns in *-ia* -y) + *-sis*] **:** morbid state or condition **:** disease having characteristics of (something specified) ⟨elephant*iasis*⟩ ⟨satyr*iasis*⟩ **:** disease produced by (something specified) ⟨ancylostom*iasis*⟩ ⟨habronem*iasis*⟩

**ias·us** \ē'asəs, ī'-\ [NL, fr. *Iasus, Iassus*, ancient city of Asia Minor] *syn of* JASUS

**iat·mul** \'yät,mül\ *n, pl* **iatmul** *or* **iatmuls** *usu cap* **1 :** a Papuan people of the Sepik district, Territory of New Guinea **2 :** a member of the Iatmul people

**iat·ric** \(')ī¦a·trik, -rēk\ *also* **iat·ri·cal** \-rəkəl, -rēk-\ *adj* [Gk *iatrikos*, fr. *iatros* healer, physician (fr. *iasthai* to heal) + *-ikos* -ic, -ical; perh. akin to L *ira* anger — more at IRE] **1 :** of or relating to a physician or medical treatment **:** MEDICAL ⟨outstanding ~ ability⟩ **2 :** MEDICINAL, HEALING, CURATIVE ⟨an extract with a remarkable ~ quality⟩

**-i·at·ric** \ē¦a·trik, -rēk\ *also* **-i·at·ri·cal** \-rəkəl, -rēk-\ *adj comb form* [*-iatric* fr. NL *-iatria* -iatry + E *-ic*; *-iatrical* fr. *-iatric* + *-al*] **:** of or relating to medical treatment **:** of or relating to healing ⟨hydr*iatric*⟩ ⟨psych*iatric*⟩

**-i·at·rics** \-ks\ *n pl comb form usu sing in constr* [*-iatric* + *-s*] **:** medical treatment **:** healing ⟨gyn*iatrics*⟩ ⟨ped*iatrics*⟩

**-iatrist** \'īə·trəst, ē¦a·trəst\ *n comb form* -s [*-iatry* + *-ist*] **:** physician **:** healer ⟨psych*iatrist*⟩ ⟨pod*iatrist*⟩

**iatro-** *comb form* [NL, fr. Gk, fr. *iatros* physician] **1 :** physician **:** medicine **:** healing ⟨*iatro*logy⟩ ⟨*iatro*genic⟩ **2 :** physician and ⟨*iatro*chemist⟩ **:** medicine or healing and ⟨*iatro*physics⟩ ⟨*iatro*-astrological⟩

**iat·ro·chemical** \ī¦a·trō, ē¦-+\ *adj* [*iatro-* + *chemical*] **:** of or relating to iatrochemistry **:** ¹CHEMICAL 1b

**iat·ro·chemist** \"+\ *n* [*iatro-* + *chemist*] **:** one believing in or practicing iatrochemistry

**iat·ro·chemistry** \"+\ *n* [*iatro-* + *chemistry*] **:** chemistry combined with medicine — used of the chemistry of the period about 1525–1660 dominated by the teachings of Paracelsus; compare IATROPHYSICS

**iat·ro·gen·ic** \"+¦jenik\ *adj* [*iatro-* + *-genic*] **:** induced by a physician — used chiefly of imagined ailments induced in a patient by autosuggestion based on a physician's words or actions during examination — **iat·ro·ge·nic·i·ty** \⸗,⸗⸗jə-'nisəd·ē\ *n* -ES

**iat·ro·mathematics** \ī¦a·trō, ē¦-+\ *n pl but usu sing in constr* [NL *iatromathematica*, fr. *iatro-* + L *mathematica* mathematics, astrology; after Gk *iatromathēmatikos* one that practices medicine in conjunction with astrology — more at MATHEMATICS] **:** IATROPHYSICS

**iat·ro·physicist** \"+\ *n, archaic* **:** one who specializes in iatrophysics

**iat·ro·physics** \"+\ *n pl but usu sing in constr* [ISV *iatro-* + *physics*] **:** physics combined with medicine — used of a school of medicine of the 17th century that explained disease and the activities of the body in terms of physics rather than of chemistry; compare IATROCHEMISTRY

**-i·atry** \'īə·trē, ē¦a·t-, -ri\ *n comb form* -ES [F *-iatrie*, fr. NL *-iatria*, fr. Gk *iatreia* art or action of healing, fr. *iatros* physician + *-eia* -y — more at IATRIC] **:** medical treatment **:** healing ⟨pod*iatry*⟩ ⟨gyn*iatry*⟩ ⟨psych*iatry*⟩

**IAZ** *abbr* inner artillery zone

**ib** *abbr* [L *ibidem*] in the same place

**IB** *abbr* **1** in bond **2** inbound **3** incendiary bomb **4** intelligence branch **5** invoice book

**iba** \'ēbə\ *n* -s [Tag] **:** a medium-sized Philippine tree (*Cicca acida*) sometimes cultivated for its edible roundish greenish white fruit

**IBA** *abbr* indolebutyric acid

**ibad** \'ē,bäd\ *n, pl* **ibad** *or* **ibads** *usu cap* **1 :** an Arab people in Hira between the Euphrates and the Arabian desert **2 :** a member of the Ibad people

**iba·dan** \'ēbäd^ən, -bad-\ *adj, usu cap* [fr. *Ibadan*, Nigeria] **:** of or from the city of Ibadan, Nigeria **:** of the kind or style prevalent in Ibadan

**iba·dhi** \ə'bädē\ *n, pl* **ibadhi** *or* **ibadhis** *usu cap* [after 'Abdallah ibn-*Ibād*] **:** ¹IBADITE

**¹iba·dite** *also* **aba·dite** \ə'bä,dīt\ *n* -s *usu cap* ['Abdallah ibn-*Ibād* (*Abād*), 7th cent. Arab religious leader + E *-ite*] **:** a member of an austere Muslim sect found chiefly in the northern part of Africa

**²ibadite** \"\ *n* -s *usu cap* [*Ibad* + *-ite*] **:** IBAD

**iba·loi** \¦ēbə¦lói\ *n, pl* **ibaloi** *or* **ibalois** *usu cap* **:** NABALOI

**iban** \(')ē¦bän\ *n, pl* **iban** *or* **ibans** *usu cap* [Iban] **1 a :** a Dayak people of Sarawak, Borneo — called also *Sea Dayak* **b :** a member of such people **2 :** the Austronesian language of the Iban people

**iba·nag** \¦ēbə¦näg\ *n, pl* **ibanag** *or* **ibanags** *usu cap* **1 a :** a people of northern Luzon inhabiting chiefly the Cagayan valley **b :** a member of such people **2 :** the Austronesian language of the Ibanag people

**i bar** *n, cap I* **:** a rolled iron or steel bar of I section used in construction work

**i beam** *n, cap I* **:** a rolled iron or steel beam or a cast steel beam of I section; *also* **:** a built-up beam of I section used esp. in structural ironwork (as in steel-framed buildings) — called also *I girder*

**¹ibe·ri·an** \ī'birēən\ *n* -s *cap* [*Iberia*, ancient region of the Caucasus approximately equivalent to modern Georgia (fr. L *Iberia, Hiberia*, fr. Gk *Ibēria*) + E *-an*] **:** a member of one or more peoples anciently inhabiting the Caucasus in Asia between the Black and Caspian seas in the approximate region of the Soviet republic of Georgia and prob. being the ancestors of the Kartvelians

**²iberian** \(')⸗¦⸗⸗⸗\ *adj, usu cap* **:** of, relating to, or characteristic of Asiatic Iberia, its inhabitants, or their language **:** GEORGIAN

**³iberian** \⸗'⸗⸗⸗\ *n* -s *cap* [*Iberia*, peninsula in southwestern Europe that contains Spain and Portugal (fr. L *Iberia, Hiberia*, fr. Gk *Ibēria*) + E *-an*] **1 a :** a member of one or more Caucasoid peoples anciently inhabiting the peninsula comprising Spain and Portugal and the Basque region about the Pyrenees, prob. being related in origin to the Mauretanians and other peoples of the northern part of Africa and early known to the Greeks and later conquered by the Romans, being short and dark and dolichocephalic, and being prob. the builders of the neolithic stone structures (as cairns, dolmens) found esp. in Spain and in the northern part of Africa and in France and Great Britain **b :** a native or inhabitant of Spain or Portugal or the Basque region about the Pyrenees **2 :** one or more of the languages natively spoken by the ancient Iberians

**⁴iberian** \(')⸗¦⸗⸗⸗\ *adj, usu cap* **:** of, relating to, or characteristic of the Iberian peninsula, its inhabitants, or their language ⟨tragedy and death are indeed recurrent themes in *Iberian* art —George Woodcock⟩

**iberian tortoise** *or* **iberian turtle** *n, usu cap I* **:** a common tortoise (*Clemmys leprosa* syn. *Testudo ibera*) of southwestern Europe and northern Africa

**ibe·ric** \(')ī¦birik, -ber-\ *adj, usu cap* [L *Ibericus, Hibericus*, fr. *Iberia, Hiberia* Iberia + *-icus* -ic] **:** IBERIAN

**ibe·ris** \ī'birəs\ *n, cap* [NL, fr. L, peppergrass, fr. Gk *ibēris*, perh. fr. *Ibēria* (in Europe)] **:** a genus of Old World mostly glabrous plants (family Cruciferae) having entire or pinnatifid sometimes fleshy leaves and flowers with two long and two short petals succeeded by a broad ovate pod, the herbaceous members being often cultivated for their flat-topped clusters of white or purplish flowers — see CANDYTUFT

**ibe·rite** \'ībə,rīt, ī'bi,r-\ *n* -s [Sw or G *iberit*, fr. *Iberia* (in Europe), its locality + Sw or G *-it* -ite] **:** an alteration product of cordierite

**ibero-** *comb form, usu cap* [L *Iberus, Hiberus*] **:** Iberian **:** Iberian and ⟨*Ibero*-American⟩

**ibero-romance** \ī¦birō+\ *n, cap I&R* [*Ibero-* + *Romance*] **1 :** the Romance language of the Iberian peninsula prior to the emergence of Spanish, Portuguese, and Catalan as national languages **2 :** a language group of the Romance division consisting of Spanish, Portuguese, and Catalan

**ibex** \'ī,beks\ *n* [L] **1** *pl* **ibex** *or* **ibex·es a :** one of several wild goats living chiefly in high mountain areas (as the Alps) of the Old World and having large recurved horns transversely ridged in front **b :** a wild goat (*Capra aegagrus*) now found in Asia Minor and supposed to be the progenitor of the domestic goat **c** (1) **:** MOUNTAIN GOAT (2) **:** MOUNTAIN SHEEP **2** *cap* [NL, fr. L] *in some classifications* **:** a genus that comprises the ibex and that is often considered a subgenus of *Capra*

**IBI** *abbr* invoice book, inwards

**ibi·bio** \,ibə'bē(,)ō\ *n, pl* **ibibio** *or* **ibibios** *usu cap* **1 a :** a people of southeastern Nigeria **b :** a member of such people **2 :** the language of the Ibibio people, belonging to the Central branch of the Niger-Congo language family

**ibid** \'ibəd\ *abbr* [L *ibidem*] in the same place

**ibi·dem** \'ibə,dem, -,dəm; ə'bīdəm, ə'bēd-, -,dem\ *adv* [L] **:** in the same place — usu. abbreviated and used (as in a footnote) to avoid repetition of source data (as author, title) in a reference immediately preceding; abbr. *ibid., ib.*

**ibid·i·dae** \ī'bidə,dē\ [NL, fr. *Ibid-, Ibis*, genus of birds (fr. L *ibid-, ibis*) + *-idae*] *syn of* THRESKIORNITHIDAE

**ibid·i·um** \ī'bidēəm\ [NL, fr. L *ibid-, ibis* ibis + NL *-ium*; fr. the shape of the anthers] *syn of* SPIRANTHES

**-ibility** — see -ABILITY

**ibis** \'ībəs *sometimes* 'ēb-\ *n, pl* **ibis** *or* **ibis·es** [L *ibid-, ibis*, fr. Gk *ibis*, fr. Egypt *hby*] **:** any of several wading birds related to the herons and constituting the family Threskiornithidae that inhabit warm regions in both hemispheres and feed on aquatic and amphibious animals and are distinguished by a long slender downwardly curved bill resembling a curlew's bill

**ibisbill** \'⸗⸗,⸗\ *n* **:** a bluish gray bird (*Ibidorhyncha struthersii*) of central Asia having a long downcurved red bill and resembling a lapwing

**-ible** — see -ABLE

**IBM** *abbr or n* -s **:** an intercontinental ballistic missile

**ibo** \'ē(,)bō\ *or* **ig·bo** \'ig,bō\ *n, pl* **ibo** *or* **ibos** *or* **igbo** *or* **igbos** *usu cap* **1 a :** a Negro people of the country about the lower Niger **b :** a member of such people **2 :** a Kwa language of the Igbo people used as a language of trade and education in a large area of southern Nigeria

**IBO** *abbr* invoice book, outwards

**ibo·ga·ine** \ə'bōgə,ēn\ *n* -s [ISV *iboga* (fr. NL, specific epithet of *Tabernanthe iboga*, fr. a native name in central Africa) + *-ine*] **:** a crystalline alkaloid $C_{20}H_{26}N_2O$ obtained from the roots, bark, and leaves of a plant (*Tabernanthe iboga*) of equatorial Africa

**ibo·li·um privet** \ī'bōlēəm-\ *or* **ibo·ta privet** \ī'bōd·ə-\ *n* [*ibolium*, NL (specific epithet of *Ligustrum ibolium*), irreg. fr. Jap *ibota* wax tree + L *oleum* oil — more at OIL] **:** a privet (*Ligustrum ibolium*) produced by hybridizing two privets (*L. obtusifolium* and *L. ovalifolium*) that has pubescent branches and midribs of the under surfaces of the leaves and a glabrous calyx

**ib·seni·an** \(')ib¦sēnēən, (')ip¦-, -sen-\ *adj, usu cap* [Henrik *Ibsen* †1906 Norw. poet and dramatist + E *-ian*] **:** of, relating to, or having the characteristics of the playwright Ibsen or his plays

**ib·sen·ism** \'ibsə,nizəm, 'ips-\ *n* -s *usu cap* [Henrik *Ibsen* + E *-ism*] **1 :** dramatic invention or construction characteristic of Ibsen whose plays attack conventional hypocrisies **2 :** adherence to or championship of Ibsen's plays and ideas

**¹ib·sen·ite** \-,nīt\ *n* -s *usu cap* [Henrik *Ibsen* + E *-ite*] **1 :** an admirer or devotee of Ibsen **2 :** a dramatist who imitates Ibsen's manner or technique

**²ibsenite** \"\ *adj, usu cap* **:** IBSENIAN

**¹-ic** \ik, ēk; ,ik *in a few words that have a heavy stress on a syllable preceding the penult, as* "politic"\ *adj suffix* [ME *-ik, -ic*, fr. OF & L; OF *-ique*, fr. L *-icus* — more at -Y] **1 :** having the character or form of **:** being ⟨panoram*ic*⟩ ⟨rhomb*ic*⟩ ⟨Samoyed*ic*⟩ **:** consisting of ⟨run*ic*⟩ **2 a :** of or relating to ⟨alderman*ic*⟩ ⟨datur*ic*⟩ ⟨Koran*ic*⟩ **b :** related to, derived from, or containing ⟨alcohol*ic*⟩ — esp. in names of acids and related compounds ⟨bor*ic*⟩ ⟨cinnam*ic*⟩ ⟨ole*ic*⟩ **3 :** in the manner of **:** like that of **:** characteristic of ⟨Byron*ic*⟩ ⟨quixot*ic*⟩ ⟨Puritan*ic*⟩ **4 :** associated or dealing with ⟨Ved*ic*⟩ **:** utilizing ⟨electron*ic*⟩ ⟨atom*ic*⟩ **5 :** characterized by **:** exhibiting ⟨nostalg*ic*⟩ **:** affected with ⟨allerg*ic*⟩ ⟨parapleg*ic*⟩ **6 :** caused by ⟨amoeb*ic*⟩ **7 :** tending to produce ⟨analges*ic*⟩ **8 :** having the highest valence of a (specified) element or a valence relatively higher than in compounds or ions named with an adjective ending in *-ous* ⟨ferr*ic* iron⟩ ⟨sulfur*ic* acid⟩ — compare -ATE 2

**²-ic** \"\ *n suffix* -s [ME *-ik, -ic*, fr. OF & L; OF *-ique*, fr. L *-icus*, fr. *-icus* (adj. suffix)] **:** one having the character or nature of **:** one belonging to or associated with **:** one exhibiting or affected by ⟨glycon*ic*⟩ **:** one that produces ⟨ecbol*ic*⟩

**IC** *abbr* **1** immediate constituent **2** *often not cap* in charge **3** index correction **4** information center **5** information circular **6** inspected and condemned **7** interior communications **8** internal combustion **9** internal connection

**ica** \'ēkə\ *n, pl* **ica** *or* **icas** *usu cap* [Sp, of AmerInd origin] **1 a :** a Chibchan people of northern Colombia **b :** a member of such people **2 :** the language of the Ica people

**icac·i·na·ce·ae** \i,kasə'nāsē,ē\ *n pl, cap* [NL, fr. *Icacina*, type genus (fr. ISV *icaco* + NL *-ina*) + *-aceae*] **:** a family of tropical chiefly woody plants of the order Sapindales with alternate leaves, panicled flowers, and drupaceous fruit — **icac·i·na·ceous** \¦⸗¦⸗⸗¦nāshəs\ *adj*

**icaco** \i'kä,kō, ī'kä,-\ *or* **icaco plum** *also* **hi·caco** \(h)i-\ *n* -s [Sp *icaco, hicaco*, fr. Arawak] **:** COCO PLUM

**-i·cal** \əkəl, ēk-\ *adj suffix* [ME, fr. LL *-icalis* (as in *clericalis* clerical, *grammaticalis* grammatical, *radicalis* radical) — more at CLERICAL, GRAMMATICAL, RADICAL] **:** -IC ⟨cosm*ical*⟩ ⟨fantast*ical*⟩ — sometimes differing from *-ic* in that adjectives formed with *-ical* have a wider or more transferred semantic range than corresponding adjectives in *-ic* ⟨economic*al*: economic⟩ ⟨prophetical: prophetic⟩

**¹icar·i·an** \i'ka(a)rēən, (')ī¦k-\ *adj, usu cap* [L *Icarius* of Icarus, fr. Gk *Ikarios*, fr. *Ikaros* Icarus, Greek mythological character who flew so high on man-made wings that the sun melted them and sent him to destruction) + E *-an*] **:** of, relating to, or characteristic of Icarus: **a :** soaring too high for safety ⟨*Icarian* flight⟩ **b :** inadequate for or incapable of bringing about an ambitious project ⟨*Icarian* methods⟩

**²icarian** \"\ *adj, usu cap* [F *Icarien*, fr. *Icarie*, communistic utopia in *Voyage en Icarie* (1842), novel by Étienne Cabet †1857 Fr. political radical (fr. *Icarie* Icaria, island in the Aegean sea) + F *-en* -an] **:** of, relating to, or constituting a communistic settlement established in the U.S. during the latter half of the 19th century by a group of French immigrants ⟨the last *Icarian* utopia . . . fizzled out in 1895 —*Time*⟩

**³icarian** \"\ *n* -s *usu cap* [F *Icarien*, fr. *Icarien*, adj.] **:** a member of an Icarian community

**ICAS** *abbr* intermittent commercial and amateur service

**ICBM** *abbr or n* -s **:** an intercontinental ballistic missile ⟨the ~ era —Clay Blair⟩

**¹ice** \'īs\ *n* -s *often attrib* [ME *is*, fr. OE *īs*; akin to OFris, OS, & OHG *īs* ice, ON *īss*, Av *isu-* icy, *aexa-* cold, and perh. to Russ *ineĭ* frost, Lith *ynis*] **1 a :** water reduced to the solid state by cooling and when pure constituting a nearly colorless brittle substance that in freezing expands about one eleventh in volume, that has a specific gravity of 0.9166 as compared with 1.0 for water at 4°C, that under normal atmospheric pressure is formed at and has a melting point of 0°C or 32°F, that occurs in the common form as hexagonal crystals, and that in large masses is classed as a rock — compare BLUE ICE, FROST, SNOW; HEAT OF FUSION **b :** the layer of frozen water covering a surface (as of a road, rink, or body of water) ⟨broke through the ~⟩ **:** the surface of a sheet of ice ⟨slipped on the ~⟩ ⟨skated down the ~⟩ ⟨an ~ carnival⟩ **2 :** the quality or state of being emotionally cold (as from formality, reserve, embarrassment, or hostility) ⟨perceptibly chilled by the ~ in his voice⟩ ⟨thawed a little of the ~ that held his lady's heart —Robert Murphy⟩ — compare BREAK THE ICE **3 :** a substance resembling ice in appearance or solid form ⟨these hydrogen ~s might well be retained in meteoritic particles —P.M.Millman⟩; *specif* **:** ICING **4 a :** a sweet frozen food containing a fruit juice or other flavoring and usu. served as a dessert or refreshment; *specif* **:** one containing no milk or cream (as a fruit ice or water ice) **b** *Brit* **:** a serving of ice cream; *specif* **:** ICE-CREAM CONE **5** *slang* **:** DIAMONDS ⟨fenced the ~ for the gang⟩; *broadly* **:** JEWELRY

**6** *slang* : protection money paid by an operator of illicit business ⟨a $20,000,000-a-year bookmaking syndicate that paid out $1,000,000 in ~ to the police —*N.Y. Times*⟩ **7** : allowance made in directing a curling stone for its deviation from a straight course ⟨make the shot . . . by using the ~ and weight suggested by his skip —Ken Watson⟩ — **on ice** *adv* **1 a** : with every likelihood of being won ⟨with their lead they had the game *on ice*⟩ **b** : with every likelihood of being fulfilled — used of a contract in a card game **2** : in reserve ⟨put the project *on ice* until funds were sent⟩ ⟨kept the invention *on ice* for 10 years⟩ **3** *slang* : in safekeeping ⟨put you *on ice* quietly till they've had time to settle up their affairs —Dorothy Sayers⟩; *specif* : in jail or prison ⟨*on ice* pending his appearance in court —*Front Page Detective*⟩ — **on thin ice** : in a situation involving great risk ⟨in opposing mob passions he was *on thin ice*⟩

**²ice** \"\ *vb* -ED/-ING/-S [ME *isen*, fr. *is*, n.] *vt* **1 a** : to coat with or convert into ice ⟨sleet *iced* the turnpike⟩ ⟨weather that *iced* his breath⟩ **b** : to chill esp. by surface contact with ice ⟨~ the champagne before serving⟩ ⟨an *iced* melon⟩ ⟨a frown that *iced* his enthusiasm⟩ **c** : to load or supply with ice ⟨a portable cooler *iced* with cubes from the refrigerator⟩ ⟨stations for *icing* refrigerator cars containing perishables⟩ **2** : to cover with or as if with icing ⟨~ a cake⟩ ⟨houses *iced* over with multicolored stuccoes —Norman Lewis⟩ **3** : to put in a secure place or state or in reserve : put on ice ⟨sank a free throw . . . to ~ the victory —*Spokane Spokesman-Rev.*⟩ ⟨has frozen all major route applications . . would probably ~ a merger too —*Time*⟩ ~ *vi* **1** : to become ice cold : FREEZE ⟨the two bottles were *icing* in a bucket —Lionel Trilling⟩ **2 a** : to become covered with ice ⟨at the first sign of snow or *icing*, equipment is deployed along the turnpike —*Roads & Streets*⟩ — often used with *up* ⟨the airplane propeller and wings may ~ up⟩ **b** : to have ice form inside — usu. used with *up* ⟨the airplane carburetor *iced up*⟩

**-ice** \əs\ *n suffix* -S [ME *-ice*, *-ise*, fr. OF, fr. L *-itius* (masc.), *-itia* (fem.), *-itium* (neut.), suffixes forming adjectives and nouns; akin to Gk *-sios*, Skt *-tya*] : act ⟨service⟩ : quality ⟨justice⟩ : condition ⟨cowardice⟩

**ice age** *n* **1** : a time of widespread glaciation **2** *usu cap I&A* : the Pleistocene glacial epoch

**ice anchor** *n* : a small anchor usu. having one fluke and used for mooring a boat to ice

**ice apron** *n* : a wedge-shaped structure for protecting a bridge pier from floating ice

**ice ax** *n* : a mountain-climbing tool that has a pick and adze at one end of a shaft and a spike or a ferrule at the other end and that is used esp. for cutting steps, belaying, and glissading

**ice bag** *n* : a waterproof bag designed to hold cracked ice and used for local application of cold to the body — see ICE CAP, ICE COLLAR

**ice banner** *n* : SNOW BANNER

**ice barrier** *n* : the outer margin of the antarctic ice sheet

ice bag

**ice bear** *n* : POLAR BEAR

**ice belt** *n* : ICE FOOT 1

**ice·berg** \ˈīs,bərg, -bōg,-bəig\ *n* [prob. part trans. of Dan or Norw *isberg*, fr. *is* ice + *berg* mountain, fr. ON, rock — more at BARROW] **1 a** *archaic* : GLACIER **b** : a large mass of land ice broken from a glacier at the edge of a body of water that when afloat has only a small part above the surface and that in the ocean floats with subsurface currents often to great distances — called also *berg*; compare GROWLER, ICE ISLAND **2** : an emotionally cold person **3** : something of which only a fraction is observed or explicit ⟨the seven-eighths of the ~ of personality that is submerged and never seen —W.E.Allen⟩

**iceberg lettuce** *also* **iceberg** *n* : any of various crisp freely blanching head lettuces

**ice bird** *n* **1** : any of several sea birds that frequent ice floes: as **a** : DOVEKIE 2 **b** : PRION **2** : an Indian goatsucker (*Caprimulgus asiaticus*)

**iceblink** \ˈ=,=\ *n* **1** : a yellowish or whitish glare in the sky over an ice field (as in polar regions) — called also *ice sky*; compare SNOWBLINK, WATER SKY **2** : a cliff of ice on a coast (as of Greenland)

**ice bloom** *n* : a brownish purple color imparted to ice in some regions by the growth of desmids of the genus *Ancyclonema*

**ice-blue** \ˈ=ˈ=\ *adj* : very pale greenish blue like the color seen in a cake of clear ice

**iceboat** \ˈ=,=\ *n* **1** : a vehicle similar to a boat that has runners, is propelled on ice by sails or sometimes a propeller or jet propulsion, and is used chiefly for sport; *esp* : one having a center timber or long slender hull rigged fore-and-aft with a mainsail and sometimes also a jib and resting on a pivoted steering runner at the stern or bow and two other runners outrigged at each end of a running plank **2** : ICEBREAKER

iceboat 1

**iceboating** \ˈ=,==\ *n* : the sport of sailing in iceboats

**ice·bone** \ˈīs,=\ *n* [prob. trans. of D *ijsbeen* (fr. MD *isebeen*, *ijsbeen*) or LG *isbeen*, fr. MLG *isbēn*; both prob. by folk etymology fr. L *ischium* + MD *been* bone or MLG *bēn* — more at ISCHIUM] : AITCHBONE

**icebound** \ˈ=ˈ=\ *adj* **1** : surrounded with ice so as to be incapable of advancing ⟨an ~ ship⟩ **2** : surrounded or obstructed with ice so as to hinder access : iced in ⟨an ~ coast⟩ **3** : constricted by inhibitions or taboos ⟨sweet young things whose ~ virtue excited them to . . . sighing and languishing whenever a man was about —Max Peacock⟩

**icebox** \ˈ=,=\ *n* : an insulated cabinet or box having a compartment for ice and used for refrigeration (as of food); *broadly* : REFRIGERATOR ⟨an electric ~⟩

**icebreaker** \ˈ=,==\ *n* **1** : an ice apron or other structure that protects a bridge pier from floating ice **2** : a ship designed or equipped (as with a reinforced bow) to make and maintain a channel through the ice **3** : the right whale of the arctic **4** : something that breaks the ice on a project or social occasion ⟨pictures of girls . . . intended as an ~ between us and the French officers —Nathaniel Benchley⟩; *specif* : MIXER 1c

**ice candle** *n*, *dial* : ICICLE

**ice cap** *n* **1** : an ice bag shaped to be fitted to the head **2** : a cover of perennial ice and snow (as in the polar regions or on a mountain peak above the snow line); *specif* : a glacier forming on an extensive area of relatively level land (as a plateau, or a large part of a continent) and flowing outward from its center ⟨the endless polar *ice cap* was running between eight and eighty feet thick —W.R.Anderson⟩

**ice car** *n* : a railway car that is specially insulated for transporting ice

**ice cave** *n* **1** : a cave so protected from the summer heat that ice remains in it throughout all or most of the year **2** : a cave or tunnel in ice; *esp* : one formed in a glacier by meltwater streams

**ice cellar** *n* : an underground room where foods and drinks are kept cool by ice

**ice chest** *n* : ICEBOX

**ice chisel** *n* : a long-handled chisel for cutting holes in ice (as for fishing) or splitting blocks of ice

**ice-cold** \ˈ=ˈ=\ *adj* : extremely cold or impassive ⟨plunged into the *ice-cold* water⟩ ⟨planning all his battles . . . with an *ice-cold* brain —Brian Horrocks⟩

**ice collar** *n* : an ice bag shaped to fit around the neck

**ice color** *n* [so called fr. its being treated with a diazo solution in the presence of ice] : AZOIC DYE

**icecraft** \ˈ=,=\ *n* : skill in traveling on an ice surface or through waters containing floating ice

**ice cream** \(ˈ)=ˈ=, ˈ=,=\ *n* **1** : a frozen food containing cream or butter fat, flavoring, sweetening, and usu. eggs; *specif* : such a food made smooth by stirring during freezing — distinguished from *mousse* and *parfait* **2** : a serving of ice cream

**ice-cream** *adj* [*ice cream*] : of a color similar to that of vanilla ice cream — usu. used of clothing ⟨a gentleman in a blue serge coat and *ice-cream* pants —Conrad Richter⟩

**ice-cream cone** *n* : a crisp conical wafer usu. about five inches long holding ice cream

ice-cream cone

**ice-cream fork** *n* : a fork of medium size that has a bowl-shaped or blade-shaped end terminating usu. in three short tines and is used for eating ice cream or sherbets

**ice-cream freezer** *n* : a hand or power operated machine for freezing and stirring ice cream; *specif* : a can rotated by a crank within a tub of ice and salt so that the ice-cream mixture in it is stirred by a dasher

**ice-cream soda** *n* : a sweet food drink of soda water, flavored syrup, and ice cream

**ice crusher** *n* : a device for crushing ice; *specif* : a kitchen grinder having a hopper, a crank, blades, and a cup and used for crushing ice cubes

**ice crystal** *n* : ICE NEEDLE

**ice cube** *n* : a small block of artificial ice formed in a mold or cut from a larger block and commonly used for icing drinks

**iced** *adj* : containing cracked ice or ice cubes ⟨~ coffee⟩

**iced firn** *n* : a mixture of ice and firn

**ice dike** *n* : a formation of secondary ice in a glacier along a crevice

**iced-tea spoon** *n* : a teaspoon with a very long handle

**ice duck** *n* : any of various ducks found in icy seas; *esp* : OLDSQUAW 1

**icefall** \ˈ=,=\ *n* **1** : a frozen waterfall or similar mass of ice **2** : a falling of ice (as from an iceberg or glacier) **3** : the mass of jumbled and usu. jagged blocks of ice into which a glacier may break when it moves down a steep declivity

**ice feathers** *n pl* : ¹RIME 2

**ice field** *n* **1** : an extensive sheet of sea ice larger than an ice floe **2** : a large body of glacial ice : ICE CAP

**icefish** \ˈ=,=\ *n* : any of several small, shining, more or less translucent fishes: as **a** : a fish of the family Salangidae **b** : CAPELIN **c** : a common No. American smelt (*Osmerus mordax*)

**ice fishing** *n* : fishing through a hole in the ice

**ice floe** *n* : a flat free mass of floating sea ice of usu. visible extent larger than a pan and smaller than an ice field; *broadly* : a large floating fragment of sheet ice

**ice flower** *n* : FROST FLOWER 2

**ice fog** *n* : a fog composed of ice particles

**ice foot** *n* **1** : a wall or belt of ice frozen to the shore in arctic regions having a base at or below the low-water mark and formed as a result of the rise and fall of the tides, freezing spray, or stranded ice **2** : the ice at the front of a glacier

**ice fork** *n* : a fork or serrated chisel for splitting or chopping up ice

**ice fox** *n* : ARCTIC FOX

**ice-free** \ˈ=ˈ=\ *adj* : free from ice; *esp* : not frozen over in winter ⟨an *ice-free* port⟩

**ice front** *n* : the lower or outer margin of a glacier

**ice gland** *n* : a roughly cylindrical and more or less vertical column of ice in névé

**ice green** *n* : a variable color averaging a very light bluish green that is lighter, stronger, and slightly bluer than spray

**ice gull** *n* : any of several northern gulls; *esp* : IVORY GULL

**ice hockey** *n* : a goal game played on an ice rink by two teams of six players on skates whose object is to direct a puck into the opponents' goal with a hockey stick

200 ft. 85 ft.

ice hockey rink: *A,A*, penalty shot lines; *B,B*, goal creases; *C,C*, goal cages; *D,D*, end zones; *E* neutral zone

**icehouse** \ˈ=,=\ *n* : a building for storing ice

**ice in** *vt* : to cause to be icebound ⟨a port that is *iced in* during the winter⟩

**ice island** *n* : a mass of floating ice resembling an island; *specif* : one discharged from arctic shelf ice that may extend several hundred square miles in area and several hundred feet in depth and floats with a subsurface current around the north pole — compare BARRIER BERG

**ice-laid** \ˈ=ˈ=\ *adj* : deposited by ice ⟨an *ice-laid* boulder till⟩

**ice lance** *n* : an ice tester used by the Eskimo for determining the thickness and therefore the safety of ice

**ice·land** \ˈīslənd, -,sland, -laa(ə)nd\ *adj*, *usu cap* [fr. *Iceland*, island between the No. Atlantic and the Arctic oceans, fr. ME *Island*, fr. ON *Īsland*, fr. *īss* ice + *land* — more at ICE, LAND] : of or from Iceland : of the kind or style prevalent in Iceland : ICELANDIC

**iceland dog** *or* **iceland cur** *n*, *usu cap I* : a breed of small shaggy-haired dogs supposed to have originated in Iceland and kept in England as pets during the 16th and 17th centuries

**ice·land·er** \ˈī,slandə(r), -slən-, -,slaan-\ *n* -S *cap* [Dan *Islænder*, fr. *Island* Iceland + *-er*] : a native or inhabitant of Iceland

**iceland gull** *n*, *usu cap I* : a large white-winged gull (*Larus leucopterus*) that is similar to but smaller than the glaucous gull and that breeds in the arctic regions and migrates south to northern France and the northern U.S.

**¹ice·lan·dic** \(ˈ)ī;slandik, -laan-\ *adj*, *usu cap* [*Iceland* + E *-ic*] **1 a** : of, relating to, or characteristic of Iceland **b** : of, relating to, or characteristic of the Icelanders **2** : of, relating to, or characteristic of the Icelandic language

**²icelandic** \"\ *n* -S *cap* : a Scandinavian language of the Icelandic people — compare OLD ICELANDIC, OLD NORSE; see INDO-EUROPEAN LANGUAGES table

**iceland moss** *also* **iceland lichen** *n*, *usu cap I* : a lichen (*Cetraria islandica*) with branched flattened partly erect thallus that grows in mountainous and arctic regions and is used (as in Scandinavia) as a medicine or as food for humans and livestock and as a source of glycerol

**iceland pony** *n*, *usu cap I* : a short stocky hardy usu. chestnut-colored pony developed in Iceland by interbreeding ponies of European origin

**iceland poppy** *n*, *usu cap I* **1** : either of two nearly stemless perennial poppies that tend to grow in a firm close turf: **a** : a subarctic poppy (*Papaver nudicaule*) of both hemispheres that is hairy and somewhat glaucous with pinnately lobed or cleft petioled leaves and fragrant typically yellow and white flowers borne on slender wiry scapes **b** : a similar Old World alpine poppy (*Papaver alpinum*) with white and yellow or often pink or orange flowers and glabrous foliage **2** : any of various cultivated poppies that are prob. derived from one or the other of the wild Iceland poppies, are commonly grown as biennials or short-lived perennials, and have small or medium-sized single or double flowers chiefly of pastel color — compare SHIRLEY POPPY

**iceland sea grass** *n*, *usu cap I* **1** : a sea lettuce (*Ulva latissima*) **2** : any of various green algae of the genus *Enteromorpha*

**iceland spar** *also* **iceland crystal** *n*, *usu cap I* : a transparent calcite the best of which is obtained in Iceland, which easily cleaves into rhombohedrons, and which is used for polariscope prisms because of its strong double refraction

**ice·less** \ˈīsləs\ *adj* : having or using no ice

**icelike** \ˈ=,=\ *adj* : resembling ice

**ice line** *n* : the graph on a phase diagram of the state of equilibrium between ice and water

**ice machine** *n* : a machine for making ice artificially

**ice-man** \ˈī,sman, -maa(ə)n *also* -smən\ *n*, *pl* **icemen** **1** : a man who is skilled in traveling upon ice (as among glaciers) **2** : one who retails or delivers ice : an ice dealer **3** : one who prepares and cares for an ice rink

**ice·man·ship** \ˈīsmən,ship\ *n* : ICECRAFT

**ice milk** *n* : a frozen food that is soft in texture and is made of skim milk : frozen custard

**ice needle** *n* : one of a number of slender ice particles that float in the air in clear cold weather — called also *ice crystal*

**ice·ni** \īˈsē,nī\ *n pl*, *usu cap* [L] : an ancient British people that under its queen Boadicea revolted against the Romans in A.D. 61 — **ice·ni·an** \(ˈ)ī;sēnēən\ *or* **icenic** \-nik, (ˈ)ī;sen-\ *adj*, *usu cap*

**ice pack** *n* **1** : an expanse of pack ice **2** : crushed ice placed in a suitable container (as an ice bag) or folded in a towel and applied to the body

**ice paper** *n* : a paper coated with an adhesive containing a salt that crystallizes when the coating dries and gives a frosted appearance

**ice partridge** *n* : IVORY GULL

**ice petrel** *n* : an antarctic shearwater (*Adamastor cinereus*)

**ice pick** *n* : a hand tool with a needlelike spike for chipping ice

**ice pillar** *n* : a pedestal of glacial ice covered with a stone or debris that has given protection from solar heat and caused the ice to melt less rapidly than that around it

ice pick

**ice pilot** *or* **ice master** *n* : a pilot trained in navigating amid ice

**ice pink** *n* : a European alpine dwarf herb (*Dianthus glacialis*) with bright red flowers

**¹ice plant** *n* : an Old World annual herb (*Mesembryanthemum crystallinum*) that is widely naturalized in warm regions and that has fleshy foliage covered with glistening papillate dots or vesicles; *broadly* : FIG MARIGOLD

**²ice plant** *n* : a plant where artificial ice is manufactured

**ice plow** *n* : a grooving device resembling a plow that is used in cutting ice (as on a river or pond) into cakes

**ice point** *n* : the temperature at which ice is in equilibrium with air-saturated water at standard atmospheric pressure and which is commonly used as a fixed point in calibrating thermometers and is represented by 0° C or 32° F

**icequake** \ˈ=,=\ *n* : the concussion attending the breaking up of masses of ice

**ic·er** \ˈīsə(r)\ *n* -S : one that ices: as **a** : a worker who covers food (as fresh produce or cases of milk) with ice before shipment **b** : a worker who mixes icing or ices baked goods

**ice raft** *n* : ICE FLOE

**ice-raft** \ˈ=,=\ *vt* [*ice raft*] : to transport on or in an iceberg or other floating ice ⟨a granitic boulder . . . might have reached its present location by *ice-rafting* —*Jour. of Geol.*⟩ ⟨*ice-rafted* sediment⟩

**ice river** *or* **ice stream** *n* : a valley glacier

**iceroot** \ˈ=,=\ *n* : GOLDENSEAL 1

**ices** *pl of* ICE, *pres 3d sing of* ICE

**-ices** *pl of* -ICE

**ice shed** *n* : a glacial divide from which ice moves in opposite directions

**ice sheet** *n* : a glacial ice cover : ICE CAP ⟨the *ice sheets* on some Greenland promontories⟩; *esp* : one (as a continental glacier) spreading outward over a large land area and concealing all or most surface features ⟨the great *ice sheets* covering much of Europe during the ice age⟩

**ice shelf** *n* : SHELF ICE

**ice·shock·le** \ˈī,shäkəl\ *dial Brit var of* ICICLE

**ice show** *n* : an ice-skating entertainment consisting of various exhibitions (as solo figure skating, group spectacles) often with musical accompaniment

**ice skate** *n* **1** : a metal runner or blade attached by a frame to the sole of a shoe for skating on ice **2 a** : SKATE 1a(1) **b** : DOUBLE-RUNNER 2

**ice-skate** \ˈ=,=\ *vi* : to glide on ice skates — **ice skater** *n*

**ice sky** *n* : ICEBLINK

**ice storm** *n* : a storm in which falling rain freezes as soon as it touches any object

**ice structure** *n* : an imperfection consisting usu. of a group of cracks about an included foreign body in a diamond or other gem

**ice table** *n* : GLACIER TABLE

**ice tea** *n* : iced tea

**ice tint** *n* : a very pale green that is yellower and paler than tourmaline, emerald tint, or microcline green

**ice tongs** *n pl* **1** : tongs having usu. two handles and hooked points for lifting large blocks of ice **2** : small tongs often with claw-shaped ends for handling ice in an ice tub

**ice tub** *n* : a container (as of silver or glass) shaped like a tub or bowl to hold ice ready for use

**ice water** *n* : chilled or iced water esp. for drinking

**ice well** *n* : a cold storage pit containing a solid cake of ice built up during freezing weather

**ice whale** *n* : the right whale of the arctic

**ice yacht** *n* : ICEBOAT

ice tongs 1

**icg** *abbr* icing

**¹ich** \(ˌ)ich, ˌ(ə)ch\ *pron* [ME — more at I] *archaic & dial Brit* : I

**²ich** *also* **ick** \ˈik\ *n* -S [by shortening & modif. fr. NL *ichthyophthirius* or *ichthyophthiriasis*] : a severe dermatitis of freshwater fish that results from invasion of the skin by a ciliated protozoan (*Ichthyophthirius multifiliis*) and is esp. destructive in the aquarium and hatchery — called also *ichthyophthiriasis*, *ichthyophthirius*

**ich** *abbr* ichthyology

**ich·a·bod** \ˈikə,bäd\ *interj*, *usu cap* [Heb *ī-khābhōdh* inglorious] — used to express regret for departed glory ⟨a refreshingly cheerful note in the thundering chorus whose burden is "*Ichabod*" —G.W.Johnson⟩

**ich-laut** \ˈik,lau̇t\ *n* -S *sometimes cap I* [G, fr. *ich* I + *laut* sound] : the voiceless palatal fricative sound represented by the *ch* of German *ich* that is phonemically often allophonic with the ach-laut

**ichn-** *or* **ichno-** *comb form* [Gk, fr. *ichnos*] : footprint : track ⟨*ichnology*⟩

**ich·neu·mia** \ikˈn(y)ümēə\ *n*, *cap* [NL, fr. L *ichneumon* + NL *-ia*] : a genus of African carnivorous mammals (family Viverridae) containing the white-tailed mongooses

**ich·neu·mon** \-mən\ *n* -S [L, fr. Gk *ichneumōn*, mongoose, small wasp, lit., tracker, fr. *ichneuein* to track, fr. *ichnos* track, footstep; the mongoose so called fr. the ancient belief that it hunted out the eggs of the crocodile; the wasp so called fr. its hunting of spiders] **1** : MONGOOSE; *esp* : the No. African mongoose (*Herpestes ichneumon*) that was highly regarded in ancient times for being supposed to devour crocodiles' eggs **2** : ICHNEUMON FLY

**ich·neu·mo·nes** \-məˌnēz\ *n pl*, *cap* [NL, fr. L, pl. of *ichneumon*] : ICHNEUMONOIDEA

**ichneumon fly** *n* : any of a large superfamily (Ichneumonoidea) of hymenopterous insects that have many-jointed antennae, fore wings with a usu. triangular stigma, petiolate abdomen, and in the female a commonly long sheathed ovipositor for use on other insect larvae (as caterpillars) which the larval ichneumon fly burrows in and feeds on and ultimately kills thereby constituting an important natural check on many destructive insects

**¹ich·neu·mo·nid** \(ˈ)=;=mənəd\ *adj* [NL *Ichneumonidae*] : of or relating to the Ichneumonidae

**²ichneumonid** \"\ *n* -S : an insect of the family Ichneumonidae

**ich·neu·mon·i·dae** \,==ˈmänə,dē\ *n pl*, *cap* [NL, fr. *Ichneumon*, type genus (fr. L) + *-idae*] : a family including the typical ichneumon flies that have no costal cell and two recurrent veins in the fore wing

**ich·neu·mo·noi·dea** \(,)=,=məˈnȯidēə\ *n pl*, *cap* [NL, fr. *Ichneumon*, genus of ichneumon flies + *-oidea*] : a superfamily of Hymenoptera consisting of the ichneumon flies

**ich·nite** \ˈik,nīt\ *n* -S [*ichn-* + *-ite*] : a fossil footprint

**ich·no·graph·ic** \ˌiknəˈgrafik\ *or* **ich·no·graph·i·cal** \-fəkəl\ *adj* : of or having the form of an ichnography

**ich·nog·ra·phy** \ikˈnägrəfē\ *n* -ES [L *ichnographia*, fr. Gk, fr. *ichno-* ichn- + *-graphia* -graphy] : a horizontal section (as of a building) showing true dimensions according to a geometric scale : GROUND PLAN, MAP

**ich·no·lite** \ˈiknə,līt\ *n* -S [*ichn-* + *-lite*] : a fossil footprint

**ich·nol·o·gy** \ikˈnäləjē\ *n* -ES [*ichn-* + *-logy*] : the study of fossil footprints

**icho** \ˈē(,)chō\ *n* -S [Jap *ichō*] : GINKGO

**ichor** \ˈī,kȯ(ə)r, -ō(ə), -kə(r)\ *n* -S [LL & Gk; LL, sanies, fr. Gk *ichōr* fluid in the veins of the gods, sanies, prob. of non-IE origin] **1** *Greek mythol* : an ethereal fluid taking the place of blood in the veins of the gods **2 :** a thin watery or blood-tinged discharge (as from an ulcer) — compare SANIES **3 :** a concentrated magma rich in mineralizers

**ichor·ous** \ˈīkərəs\ *adj* **:** of, resembling, or characterized by ichor **:** THIN, WATERY, SEROUS, SANIOUS

**ichs** *pl of* ICH

**ich·tham·mol** \ikˈtha,mōl, ˈikthə,-, -mōl\ *n* -s [ISV *ichthyo*-sulfonate + *ammonium* + *-ol*] **:** a brownish black viscous liquid prepared from a distillate of bituminous schists by sulfonation followed by neutralization with ammonia and used as an antiseptic and emollient

**ich·thus** \ˈikthəs\ *also* **ich·thys** \-thəs\ *n* -ES [Gk *ichthys* fish; akin to Arm *jukn* fish, Lith *žuvis*, OPruss *suckis*] **:** a representation of a fish used in ancient times as a pagan fertility talisman or amulet or as a Christian symbol for the Greek word *ichthys* interpreted as an acrostic in which the Greek letters are the initials of the words *Iēsous Christos theou hyios sōtēr* meaning Jesus Christ Son of God Savior

**ichthy-** *or* **ichthyo-** *comb form* [L, fr. Gk, fr. *ichthys*] **:** fish ⟨*ichthyic*⟩ ⟨*ichthyology*⟩

**ich·thy·ic** \ˈikthē(,)ik, (ˈ)ikˈthīik\ *adj* [*ichthy-* + *-ic*] **:** of or relating to fishes or having the form of a fish

**ich·thy·ism** \ˈikthē,izəm\ *or* **ich·thy·is·mus** \,==ˈizməs\ *n*, *pl* **ichthyisms** *or* **ichthyismuses** [NL *ichthyismus*, fr. *ichthy-* + *-ismus* -ism] **:** poisoning from fish — compare ICHTHYOSARCOTOXISM

**ich·thy·ob·del·la** \,==,äbˈdelə\ *n*, *cap* [NL, fr. *ichthy-* + *-bdella*] **:** a genus (the type of the family Ichthyobdellidae) of elongated freshwater and marine leeches (order Rhynchobdellida) parasitic on fishes and other vertebrates

**¹ich·thy·ob·del·lid** \,==,=ˈdeləd\ *adj* [NL *Ichthyobdellidae* family of leeches, fr. *Ichthyobdella*, type genus + *-idae*] **:** of or relating to the genus *Ichthyobdella* or family Ichthyobdellidae

**²ichthyobdellid** \"\ *n* -s **:** a leech of the genus *Ichthyobdella* or family Ichthyobdellidae

**ich·thyo·ceph·a·li** \,ikthēōˈsefə,lī\ [NL, fr. *ichthy-* + *-cephali*] *syn of* SYNBRANCHOIDEA

**ich·thy·o·col** *or* **ich·thy·o·coll** \ˈikthēə,käl\ *or* **ich·thy·o·col·la** \,==ˈkälə\ *n* -s [L *ichthyocolla*, fr. Gk *ichthyokolla*, fr. *ichthy-* + *kolla* glue — more at PROTOCOL] **:** ISINGLASS 1

**ich·thy·o·dea** \,==ˈōdēə\ *n pl*, *cap* [NL, fr. *ichthy-* + *-odea*] *in some former classifications* **:** a suborder of Amphibia comprising forms having the gills or gill clefts usu. persistent (as the siren, the congo snake, and members of the genera *Proteus* and *Necturus*) — compare MUTABILIA — **ich·thy·o·di·an** \,==ˈōdēən\ *adj*

**ich·thy·o·dont** \ˈikthēə,dänt\ *n* -s [*ichthy-* + *-odont*] **:** a fossil fish tooth

**ich·thyo·dor·u·lite** \,==ōˈdȯr(y)ə,līt\ *also* **ich·thyo·dor·y·lite** \-rə,-\ *n* -s [*ichthy-* + *dory-* or *doru-* (alter. of *dory-*) + *-lite*] **:** a fossil fin spine, dermal spine, or tubercle of a fish or ichthyoid vertebrate

**ich·thyo·fauna** \ˈ===+\ *also* **ich·thy·fauna** \ˈikthē+\ *n* [NL, fr. *ichthy-* + *fauna*] **:** the fish life of a region

**¹ich·thy·oid** \ˈikthē,ȯid\ *adj* [Gk *ichthyoeidēs*, fr. *ichthy-* + *-oeidēs* -oid] **:** resembling a fish — **ich·thy·oi·dal** \ˈ==ˈȯidᵊl\ *adj*

**²ichthyoid** \"\ *n* -s **:** an animal that resembles a fish; *specif* **:** one of the Ichthyopsida

**ichthyoid blood cell** *n* **:** MEGALOBLAST

**Ich·thy·ol** \ˈikthē,ōl, -,ōl\ *trademark* — used for ichthammol

**ich·thy·o·lite** \ˈikthēə,līt\ *n* -s [F *ichtyolithe*, fr. *ichty-* ichthy- + *-lithe* -lite] **:** a fossil fish or fragment of a fish — **ich·thy·o·lit·ic** \ˈ===ˈlid·ik\ *adj*

**ich·thy·o·log·i·cal** \ˈ===ˈläjəkəl\ *adj* **1 :** of or relating to ichthyology **2 :** PISCINE — **ich·thy·o·log·i·cal·ly** \-jək(ə)lē\ *adv*

**ich·thy·ol·o·gist** \,==ˈäləjəst\ *n* -s **:** a specialist in ichthyology

**ich·thy·ol·o·gy** \-jē\ *n* -ES [*ichthy-* + *-logy*] **1 :** a branch of zoology that deals with fishes **2 :** a treatise on fishes

**ich·thyo·mor·pha** \,ikthēəˈmȯrfə\ [NL, fr. *ichthy-* + *-morpha*] *syn of* CAUDATA

**ich·thyo·mor·phic** \ˈ===ˈfik\ *also* **ich·thyo·mor·phous** \-fəs\ *adj* [*ichthy-* + *-morphic*, *-morphous*] **:** having the shape or some other feature of a fish ⟨~ idols⟩

**ich·thy·oph·a·gi** \,ikthēˈäfə,jī\ *n pl* [L, pl., fr. Gk *ichthyophagoi*, pl. of *ichthyophagos* fish-eating, fr. *ichthyophagein* to eat fish, fr. *ichthy-* + *phagein* to eat — more at BAKSHEESH] **:** a people (as in ancient times on the African coast of the Red sea) living largely on sea food **:** fish eaters

**ich·thy·oph·a·gist** \-jəst\ *n* -s **:** one that eats or subsists on fish

**ich·thy·oph·a·gous** \ˈ==ˈ=gəs\ *adj* [Gk *ichthyophagos*] **:** eating or subsisting on fish **:** PISCIVOROUS

**ich·thy·oph·thi·ri·a·sis** \,ikthē,äfthəˈrīəsəs\ *n* [NL, fr. *Ichthyophthirius* + *-iasis*] **:** ICH

**ich·thy·oph·thir·i·us** \,ikthēäfˈthirēəs\ *n* [NL, fr. *ichthy-* + *-phthirius* (fr. *Phthirius*)] **1** *cap* **:** a genus of oval holotrichous ciliates comprising a single species (*I. multifiliis*) that are parasitic in the skin of various freshwater fishes where they encyst and multiply causing a severe and sometimes fatal inflammation **2** -ES **:** ICH

**¹ich·thy·op·sid** \ˈ==ˈäpsəd\ *adj* [NL *Ichthyopsida*] **:** of or relating to the Ichthyopsida

**²ichthyopsid** \"\ *n* -s **:** a vertebrate of the group Ichthyopsida

**ich·thy·op·si·da** \,==ˈ=sədə\ *n pl*, *cap* [NL, fr. *ichthy-* + Gk *opsis* appearance + NL *-ida* — more at OPTIC] *in some esp former classifications* **:** a group of vertebrates comprising the agnathous vertebrates, fishes, and amphibians — compare MAMMALIA, SAUROPSIDA — **ich·thy·op·si·dan** \ˈ==ˈ=sədən, -dᵊn\ *adj or n*

**¹ich·thy·op·te·ryg·ia** \,==,=təˈrijēə\ *n pl*, *cap* [NL, fr. *ichthy-* + Gk *pterygia*, pl. of *pterygion* fin] *in some classifications* **:** a subclass of fossil aquatic reptiles occurring from the late Carboniferous through the Jurassic and including the small freshwater Mesosauria and the extremely ichthyoid Ichthyosauria

**²ichthyopterygia** \"\ [NL, fr. *ichthy-* + Gk *pterygia*] *syn of* ICHTHYOSAURIA

**ich·thy·op·te·ryg·i·um** \-jēəm\ *n*, *pl* **ichthyopteryg·ia** \-jēə\ [NL, fr. *ichthy-* + Gk *pterygion* small wing, fin, dim. of *pteryg-*, *pteryx* wing — more at PTERYG-] **:** the vertebrate limb when having the form of a fin whether as a definitive organ or in the course of individual or evolutionary development; *esp* **:** any of the paired fins that are the typical limbs of fishes — compare CHIROPTERYGIUM

**ich·thy·or·nis** \,==ˈȯrnəs\ *n*, *cap* [NL, fr. *ichthy-* + *-ornis*] **:** the type genus of Ichthyornithidae comprising extinct birds of the Upper Cretaceous that have biconcave vertebrae, articulated quadrate bones, sharp conical teeth set in sockets, well-developed wings, and a keeled sternum and that are similar in size and probably in habits to a tern

**ich·thy·or·ni·thes** \,==ˈȯrnə,thēz, -,ȯrˈnī(,)thēz\ *n pl*, *cap* [NL, fr. pl. of *Ichthyornis*] *in some classifications* **:** a superorder of extinct birds coextensive with the order Ichthyornithiformes

**ich·thy·or·nith·i·dae** \-,ȯrˈnithə,dē\ *n pl*, *cap* [NL, fr. *Ichthyornith-*, *Ichthyornis*, type genus + *-idae*] **:** a family of extinct birds (order Ichthyornithiformes) from the Upper Cretaceous of No. America that comprises the genus *Ichthyornis* and in some classifications *Apatornis* and possibly one other genus

**ich·thy·or·nithi·for·mes** \-,ȯrnəthəˈfȯr,mēz, -,ȯr,nith-\ *n pl*, *cap* [NL, fr. *Ichthyornith-*, *Ichthyornis* + *-iformes*] **:** an order of extinct toothed birds (superorder Odontognathae) coextensive with the family Ichthyornithidae in its broadest scope

**ich·thyo·sar·co·tox·ism** \,ikthēō,särkəˈtäk,sizəm\ *n* -s [*ichthy-* + *sarc-* + *tox-* + *-ism*] **:** poisoning from eating the flesh of poisonous fishes — compare ICHTHYISM

**ich·thyo·saur** \ˈ===,sȯ(ə)r\ *n* -s [NL *Ichthyosaurus*] **:** a reptile of the order Ichthyosauria

**ich·thyo·sau·ria** \,==ˈsȯrēə\ *n pl*, *cap* [NL, fr. *ichthy-* + *-sauria*] **:** an order of Mesozoic marine reptiles most abundant in the Lias having an ichthyoid body, elongated snout, short neck, dorsal and caudal fins, limbs modified into paddles by the flattening of the bones, multiplication of the phalanges and addition of from one to four digits, eyes very large and protected by a ring of bony sclerotic plates, and numerous conical teeth set in grooves and adapted for catching fish — **ich·thyo·sau·ri·an** \ˈ===ˈ=rēən\ *adj or n* — **ich·thyo·sau·roid** \-,rȯid\ *adj*

**¹ich·thyo·sau·rid** \ˈ===ˈ=rəd\ *adj* [NL *Ichthyosauridae*] **:** of or relating to the Ichthyosauridae

**²ichthyosaurid** \"\ *n* -s **:** a reptile of the family Ichthyosauridae

**ich·thyo·sau·ri·dae** \,===ˈ=rə,dē\ *n pl*, *cap* [NL, fr. *Ichthyosaurus*, type genus + *-idae*] **:** a family of ichthyosaurs widely distributed in Jurassic and Cretaceous rocks of both hemispheres — see ICHTHYOSAURUS

**ich·thyo·sau·rus** \-rəs\ *n* [NL, fr. *ichthy-* + *-saurus*] **1** *cap* **:** the type genus of Ichthyosauridae comprising highly variable Jurassic ichthyosaurs and orig. including most of the later ichthyosaurs most of which are now placed in other genera **2** -ES **:** any reptile of the genus *Ichthyosaurus*

**ich·thy·o·si·form** \ˈ==ˈōsə,fȯrm\ *adj* [NL *ichthyosis* + E *-iform*] **:** resembling ichthyosis or that of ichthyosis

**ich·thy·o·sis** \,==ˈōsəs\ *n*, *pl* **ichthyo·ses** \-ō,sēz\ [NL, fr. *ichthy-* + *-osis*] **:** a congenital disease usu. of hereditary origin characterized by skin that is rough, thick, and scaly and resembles that of a fish — called also *fishskin disease*

**ich·thy·ot·ic** \ˈ==ˈäd·ik\ *adj* **:** of or relating to ichthyosis

**ich·thy·ot·o·mi** \,==ˈäd·ə,mī\ *n pl*, *cap* [NL, fr. *ichthy-* + *-tomi* (fr. Gk *temnein* to cut) — more at TOME] **:** a subclass or order of Chondrichthyes comprising chiefly Carboniferous and early Permian sharks having a slender and elongated body with diphycercal tail and archipterygial fins — compare PLEURACANTHUS — **ich·thy·ot·o·mous** \ˈ==ˈäd·əməs\ *adj*

**ich·thyo·tox·ism** \,==ōˈtäk,sizəm\ *n* -s [*ichthy-* + *tox-* + *-ism*] **:** ICHTHYISM

**ichthys** *var of* ICHTHUS

**-ich·thys** \ˈikthəs\ *n comb form* [NL, fr. Gk *ichthys* — more at ICHTHUS] **:** fish — in generic names chiefly in ichthyology ⟨*Dinichthys*⟩ ⟨*Nemichthys*⟩

**ichu** \ˈē(,)chü\ *or* **ichu grass** *or* **hi·chu** \ˈ(h)ē-\ *n* -s [Quechua *ichu*] **:** a valuable grass (*Stipa ichu*) of the upper Andes that is used as forage and for thatching

**-i·cian** \ˈishən\ *n suffix* -s [ME *-icien*, *-ician*, fr. OF *-icien*, fr. L *-ica* (as in *rhetorica* rhetoric) + OF *-ien* -ian — more at RHETORIC] **:** a specialist or practitioner in a (specified) field ⟨*beautician*⟩ ⟨*technician*⟩

**ici·ca** \əˈsēkə\ *n* -s [Pg, fr. Tupi] **1 :** a tropical American timber tree of the genus *Protium* **2 :** any of several Brazilian gum-producing trees; *esp* **:** BALATA

**ici·cle** \ˈī,sikəl, -,sək-, -,sēk-\ *n* -s [ME *isikel*, fr. *is* ice + *ikel* icicle, fr. OE *gicel*; akin to OHG *ihilla* icicle, ON *jökull* icicle, glacier, *jaki* piece of ice, MIr *aig* ice, W *iâ*] **1 :** a pendent usu. conical mass of ice formed by the freezing of dripping water **2 :** an emotionally unresponsive person **3 :** a long hanging Christmas tree ornament (as a thin strip of lead foil) **4 :** a metal projection forming on the upper inside of a pipe joint during welding

**icier** *comparative of* ICY

**iciest** *superlative of* ICY

**ic·i·ly** \ˈīsəlē, -li\ *adv* **:** in an icy manner ⟨an ~ unenthusiastic audience of . . . bankers —Mollie Panter-Downes⟩

**ic·i·ness** \ˈīsēnəs, -sin-\ *n* -ES **:** the quality or state of being icy ⟨her voice carried . . . a quality of ~ —Louis Bromfield⟩

**¹ic·ing** \ˈīsiŋ, -sēŋ\ *n* -s [fr. gerund of ²*ice*] **:** a sweet coating for baked goods usu. made from sugar and butter combined with water, milk, or egg white, flavored, often colored, and often cooked — called also *frosting*

**²icing** *n* -s [fr. the phrase *icing the puck*] **:** the act or an instance of an ice-hockey player's shooting the puck from within his own defensive zone through the neutral zone and beyond the opponents' goal line

**icing station** *n* **:** railway facilities for icing refrigerator cars

**icing sugar** *n*, *chiefly Brit* **:** CONFECTIONERS' SUGAR

**ick** *var of* ICH

**ick·er** \ˈikər\ *n* -s [fr. (assumed) ME (Sc dial.), fr. OE *eher*, var. of *ēar* — more at EAR] *Scot* **:** a head of grain

**ick·i·ness** \ˈikēnəs\ *n* -ES **:** the quality or state of being icky

**ick·le** \ˈikəl\ *n* -s [ME *ikel* — more at ICICLE] *dial Eng* **:** ICICLE

**icky** \ˈikē\ *adj* -ER/-EST [perh. baby-talk alter. of *sticky*] **1 :** STICKY ⟨cooing baby talk at him in an ~ way —Kathleen O'Malley⟩ — often used as a generalized expression of disapproval **2 :** lacking sophistication **:** not hep ⟨music you want to dance to — not wild and not ~ —Ralph Flanagan⟩

**icon** \ˈī,kän *sometimes* -,kən\ *n* -s [L, fr. Gk *eikōn*, fr. *eikenai* to resemble; perh. akin to Lith *paveikslas* example, *įvykti* to occur, come about] **1 :** a usu. pictorial representation **:** IMAGE **2** [LGk *eikōn*, fr. Gk] **a** *also* **ikon** *or* **ei·kon** \"\ **:** a sacred image venerated in churches and homes of Eastern Christianity depicting Christ, the Virgin Mary, a saint, or some other religious subject in the conventional manner of Byzantine art and typically painted on a small wooden panel often with a repoussé metal cover but also enameled on metal or made of mosaic **b :** an object of uncritical devotion **:** IDOL; *esp* **:** a traditional belief or ideal ⟨the ridiculous drudgery of the Ph.D. and the devotion of university administration to the ~ of that degree —*Times Lit. Supp.*⟩ **3** *in philosophy of language and semiotic* **:** a sign (as a straight line on a map) that signifies by virtue of sharing a property with what it represents (as a straight road) — contrasted with *index* and *symbol* ⟨a photograph, a star chart, a model, a chemical diagram are ~s, while the word 'photograph', the names of the stars and of chemical elements are symbols —C.W.Morris⟩

**icon-** *or* **icono-** *also* **eikon-** *or* **eikono-** *or* **ikon-** *or* **ikono-** *comb form* [Gk *eikon-*, *eikono-*, fr. *eikon-*, *eikōn*] **:** image ⟨*iconism*⟩ ⟨*iconomania*⟩ ⟨*iconometry*⟩

**icon** *abbr* iconography

**¹ico·ni·an** \(ˈ)īˈkōnēən\ *adj*, *usu cap* [*Iconi*um (now Konya, Turkey), ancient city of Asia Minor (fr. L) + E *-an*] **:** of or relating to Iconium

**²iconian** \"\ *n* -s *cap* **:** a native or inhabitant of Iconium

**icon·ic** \(ˈ)īˈkänik\ *adj* [L *iconicus*, fr. Gk *eikonikos*, fr. *eikon-*, *eikōn* image + *-ikos* -ic — more at ICON] **1 :** of, relating to, or having the character of an icon ⟨~ veneration⟩ ⟨~ theories⟩ ⟨~ signs or conventional signs⟩ **2 :** resembling an icon — **icon·i·cal·ly** \-nək(ə)lē\ *adv* — **ico·nic·i·ty** \,īkəˈnisəd·ē\ *n* -ES

**icon·o·clasm** \īˈkänə,klazəm\ *n* -s [fr. *iconoclast*, after such pairs as E *baptist*: *baptism*] **:** the doctrine, practice, or attitude of an iconoclast **:** image breaking

**icon·o·clast** \-,klast, -aa(ə)st,-aist\ *n* -s [ML *iconoclastes*, fr. MGk *eikonoklastēs*, lit., image destroyer, fr. Gk *eikono-* icon- + MGk *-klastēs* -clast] **1 a :** one who destroys religious images or opposes their veneration **b** *usu cap* **:** one of a religious party in the Eastern Empire in the 8th and 9th centuries that opposed the use of icons **2 :** one who attacks established beliefs, ideals, customs, or institutions ⟨the blundering cruelty of the tough-minded ~ —Lucius Garvin⟩

**icon·o·clas·tic** \(ˈ)ˈ==ˈklastik, -laas-,-lais-, -tēk\ *adj* **1 :** of or relating to iconoclasm or iconoclasts ⟨~ outbursts associated with the Reformation⟩ ⟨the Byzantine ~ controversy⟩ **2 :** being or befitting an iconoclast **:** marked by or having the character of iconoclasm ⟨an ~ critic of the monarchy⟩ ⟨an ~ article opposing the prevailing educational philosophy⟩ **3 :** tending to produce iconoclasm or overthrow what is established ⟨the ~ influence of modern science⟩ — **icon·o·clas·ti·cal·ly** \-tək(ə)lē, -tēk-, -li\ *adv*

**icon·o·dule** \īˈkänə,d(y)ül\ *n* -s [*icon-* + Gk *doulos* slave] **:** one who venerates icons and defends their devotional use

**icon·o·du·list** \ˈ=ˈ==,d(y)üləst, (,)=,==ˈ==\ *n* -s [*iconoduly* + *-ist*] **:** ICONODULE

**icon·o·du·ly** \=ˈ==,=lē\ *n* -ES [*icon-* + ML *dulia* veneration — more at DULIA] **:** the veneration of images

**ico·nog·ra·pher** \,īkəˈnägrəfə(r)\ *n* -s [*iconography* + *-er*] **:** a maker or designer of figures or drawings esp. of a conventional or mechanical type

**icon·o·graph·ic** \(ˈ)īˈ==ˈgrafik\ *or* **icon·o·graph·i·cal** \-fəkəl\ *adj* **1 :** of or relating to iconography ⟨experimenting in ~ forms⟩ ⟨~ studies⟩ ⟨analyze . . . his use of *iconographical* types, for the art of the Middle Ages and the Renaissance is rich in symbolism —K.M.Setton⟩ **2 :** representing something by pictures or diagrams ⟨cartographic and ~ items illustrative of colonial history⟩ — **icon·o·graph·i·cal·ly** \-fək(ə)lē\ *adv*

**ico·nog·ra·phy** \,īkəˈnägrəfē\ *n* -ES [Gk *eikonographia* sketch, description, fr. *eikonographein* to describe (fr. *eikon-* icon- + *graphein* to draw, write) + *-ia* -y — more at CARVE] **1 a :** illustration of a subject by pictures or other visual representations ⟨figures . . . to be placed alongside the work of such masters of crustacean ~ —*Nature*⟩ **b :** pictures and other visual representations illustrating or relating to a subject ⟨a discovery adding another portrait to the ~ of Columbus⟩; *specif* **:** art representing religious or legendary subjects by conventional images and symbols ⟨sculptures . . . of the highest importance for the history of both Indian art and Buddhist ~ —V.A.Smith⟩ **c** (1) **:** the imagery selected to convey the meaning of a work of art or the identity of its figures and setting and comprising figures or objects or features often fixed (as in medieval religious art) by convention **:** a set of symbolic forms ⟨the guitar, the wine glass, the playing cards together form an ~ suggestive of pleasant, carefree moments —Aline B. Saarinen⟩ (2) **:** the set of conventions or principles governing such imagery ⟨the types of the Muses in art . . . must wait until the Roman period before their ~ and their roles are definitively codified —J.J.Seznec⟩ **2 :** ICONOLOGY **3 :** a book, list, or other record featuring or dealing with iconography

**ico·nol·a·ter** \-ˈnäləd·ə(r)\ *n* -s [*icon-* + *-later*] **:** a worshiper of images or icons

**ico·nol·a·try** \-lətrē\ *n* -ES [Gk *eikono-* icon- + *-latry*] **:** IMAGE WORSHIP

**icono·log·i·cal** \(ˌ)ī,känᵊlˈäjəkəl, ˌīkən-\ *adj* **:** of, relating to, or constituting iconology ⟨~ elaboration of abstract painting⟩

**ico·nol·o·gist** \,īkəˈnäləjəst\ *n* -s **:** a specialist in iconology

**ico·nol·o·gy** \-jē\ *n* -ES [F *iconologie*, fr. *icono-* icon- + *-logie* -logy] **:** the description, history, or analysis of symbolic art (as in the medieval church) or of artistic symbolism **:** the study of icons or iconography

**icono·mat·ic** *or* **ikono·mat·ic** \(ˌ)ī,känəˈmad·ik, ˌīkən-\ *adj* [*icon-* + *onomat-*, *onoma* name + E *-ic* — more at NAME] **:** of or relating to a form of writing believed to be intermediate between picture writing and phonetic writing in which pictures or signs stand not for objects themselves but for their names considered as phonetic elements only — **icono·mat·i·cal·ly** \-d·ək(ə)lē\ *adv*

**icono·mat·i·cism** \(,)ī,känəˈmad·ə,sizəm, ,īkən-\ *n* -s **:** iconomatic writing

**icon·o·ma·tog·ra·phy** *also* **ikon·o·ma·tog·ra·phy** \(,)ī-,känəməˈtägrəfē\ *n* -ES [*iconomatic*, *ikonomatic* + *-o-* + *-graphy*] **:** iconomatic writing

**ico·nom·e·ter** \,īkəˈnäməd·ə(r)\ *n* [ISV *icon-* + *-meter*] **1 :** an instrument for determining the distance of an object of known size or the size of an object at known distance by measuring the image of it produced by a lens of known focal length **2 a :** an instrument that determines the proper objective to be used in taking a picture of given size from a given standpoint and that consists of a diopter and an open rectangular frame sliding on a graduated rod **b :** a direct viewfinder having a metal frame

**icono·met·ric** \(ˌ)ī,känəˈme·trik, ˌīkən-\ *adj* **:** of, relating to, or ascertained by iconometry

**ico·nom·e·try** \,īkəˈnämə·trē\ *n* -ES [ISV *icon-* + *-metry*] **:** the art of estimating the distance or size of an object by the use of an iconometer

**icon·o·scope** \īˈkänə,skōp\ *n* [fr. *Iconoscope*, a trademark] **:** a camera tube containing an electron gun and a photoemissive mosaic screen each cell of which produces a charge proportional to the varying light intensity of the optical image focused on the screen by the camera lenses, these charges being transformed as the beam of electrons from the gun scans the screen into voltages that are subsequently amplified and transmitted as television picture signals — called also *ike*

**ico·nos·ta·sis** \,īkəˈnästəsəs\ *also* **ico·no·stas** \ēˈkōnəˈstäs\ *n*, *pl* **ico·nostases** \,īkəˈnästə,sēz, ēˈkōnəˈstäsəz\ [*iconostasis* modif. of MGk *eikonostasi*, *eikonostasion*, fr. LGk *eikonostasion* shrine, fr. *eikono-* icon- + *-stasion* (fr. Gk *histanai* to stand); *iconostas* fr. Russ *ikonostas*, fr. MGk *eikonostasi*, *eikonostasion* — more at STAND] **:** a screen or partition with doors and tiers of icons that separates the bema from the nave in Eastern churches

**icons** *pl of* ICON

**icosa-** *also* **icosi-** *or* **icos-** *comb form* [Gk *eikosa-*, *eikosi-*, *eikos-*, fr. *eikosi* — more at VICENARY] **:** twenty ⟨*icosahedron*⟩

**icosa·he·dral** \(ˌ)īˈkōsəˈhēdrəl, -käs- *sometimes chiefly Brit* -hed-\ *adj* **:** of or having the form of an icosahedron

**icosa·he·dron** \-drən *sometimes* -,drän\ *n* -s [Gk *eikosaedron*, fr. *eikosa-* icosa- + *-edron* -hedron] **1 :** a polyhedron having 20 faces **2 :** an imaginary polyhedron in the Laban system of dance notation representing the 20 principal movement directions of a dancer in its center

regular icosahedron

**icosa·se·mic** \-ˈsēmik\ *adj* [*icosa-* + *-semic*] *in ancient prosody* **:** having or equal to 20 morae

**icosa·sphere** \=ˈ==+,-\ *n* [*icosa-* + *sphere*] **:** a spherical tank for volatile liquids built of twenty steel plates corresponding to the faces of a regular icosahedron

**icosi·tetrahedron** \īˈkōsə, -käsə +\ *n* [*icosi-* + *tetrahedron*] **:** an isometric crystal form with 24 faces; *specif* **:** TRAPEZOHEDRON

**icos·te·idae** \,ī,käˈstēə,dē\ *n pl*, *cap* [NL, fr. *Icosteus*, type genus + *-idae*] **:** a family of deepwater fishes (order Malacichthyes) comprising the ragfishes and having a soft skeleton and skin loose and naked or with small prickles or scales

**icos·te·us** \īˈkästēəs\ *n*, *cap* [NL, fr. Gk *eikein* to yield, give way + NL *-osteus* — more at WEAK] **:** the type genus of the family Icosteidae comprising two various typical ragfishes of the Pacific ocean

**ico·type** \ˈīkə,tīp\ *n* [Gk *eikōs* like (part. of *eikenai* to resemble) + E *type* — more at ICON] **:** a typical specimen of a species accurately identified but not serving as the basis for a published description

**-ics** \(,)iks, ,ēks\ *n pl suffix but sing or pl in constr* [*-ic* (as in arithmetic) + *-s*; after Gk pl. nouns ending in *-ika*, as *mathēmatika* mathematics] **1** *usu sing in constr* **:** study **:** knowledge **:** skill **:** practice ⟨*optics*⟩ ⟨*linguistics*⟩ ⟨*pediatrics*⟩ ⟨*homiletics*⟩ **2** *usu sing in constr* **:** systematic formulation **:** treatise ⟨*economics*⟩ ⟨*politics*⟩ **3** *usu pl in constr* **:** characteristic actions or activities ⟨*heroics*⟩ ⟨*hysterics*⟩ ⟨*gymnastics*⟩ **4** *usu pl in constr* **:** characteristic qualities, operations, or phenomena ⟨*acoustics*⟩ ⟨*mechanics*⟩ ⟨*phonetics*⟩

**ICSH** *abbr* interstitial-cell-stimulating hormone

**ic·tal** \ˈiktᵊl\ *adj*, *med* **:** of, relating to, or caused by ictus

**ic·ta·lu·rus** \,iktəˈlürəs, -təlˈyü-\ *n*, *cap* [NL, irreg. fr. *ichthy-* + Gk *ailouros* cat] **:** a genus of large catfishes (family Ameiuridae) of the fresh waters of No. America

**icter-** *or* **ictero-** [MF or L *icter-*, fr. Gk *ikter-*, fr. *ikteros*] *comb form* **1 :** jaundice ⟨*icterogen*⟩ ⟨*icterohemorrhagic*⟩ ⟨*icteroid*⟩ **2 :** jaundice and ⟨*icteroanemia*⟩

**ic·ter·ic** \(ˈ)ikˈterik\ *adj* [MF or L; MF *icterique*, fr. L *ictericus*, fr. Gk *ikterikos*, fr. *ikteros* jaundice + *-ikos* -ic; akin to Gk *iktinos* kite, *iktis* yellow-breasted marten] **:** of, relating to, or affected with jaundice

**icteric index** *var of* ICTERUS INDEX

**ic·ter·i·dae** \ikˈterə,dē\ *n pl*, *cap* [NL, fr. *Icterus*, type genus + *-idae*] **:** a large family of American oscine birds comprising the orioles, the American blackbirds, the bobolinks, and the meadowlarks and having nine primaries, a sharp conical bill, and no rictal bristles

**ic·ter·ine** \ˈiktə,rīn, -,rən\ *adj* [NL *Icterus* + E *-ine*] **:** resembling or relating to the family Icteridae

**icterine warbler** *n* **:** a small greenish warbler (*Hippolais icterina*) common in central Europe

**ic·ter·i·tious** \ˈiktəˈrishəs\ *or* **ic·ter·i·tous** \(ˈ)=ˈterəd·əs\ *adj* [*icterus* + *-itious* or *-itous*] **:** of a jaundiced color **:** YELLOW

**ic·tero·anemia** \ˈiktə(,)rō+\ *n* [NL, fr. *icter-* + *anemia*] **:** a disease characterized by jaundice, anemia, and marked destruction of red blood cells and seen esp. in swine

**ic·ter·o·gen·ic** \ˈiktərōˈjenik, (ˈ)ikˈterəˈj-\ *also* **ic·ter·og·e·nous** \ˈiktəˈräjənəs\ *adj* [*icter-* + *-genic*, *-genous*] **:** causing or tending to cause jaundice

**ic·tero·hematuria** \ˈiktə(,)rō+\ *n* -s [NL, fr. *icter-* + *hematuria*] **:** an infectious disease of sheep that is marked by jaundice and caused by a parasitic protozoan (*Babesia ovis*) which destroys red blood cells — compare TEXAS FEVER

**ic·ter·oid** \'iktə,rȯid\ *adj* [ISV *icter-* + *-oid*] **:** resembling jaundice **:** of a yellow tint like that produced by jaundice

**ic·ter·us** \'iktərəs\ *n* [NL, fr. Gk *ikteros* jaundice, a yellow bird] **1** -ES **:** JAUNDICE **2** *cap* **:** the type genus of the family Icteridae comprising the American orioles

**icterus gravis** \-'gravəs, -räv-, -rāv-\ *n* [NL, lit., severe jaundice] **1 :** a condition marked by severe jaundice; *specif* **:** ERYTHROBLASTOSIS **2** *or* **icterus ne·o·na·to·rum** \-,nē-ənə'tōrəm\ **:** a common fatal disease of newborn mules related to erythroblastosis fetalis in the human and due to sensitization of the horse dam to blood elements derived from the ass sire

**icterus index** *or* **icteric index** *n* **:** a figure representing the amount of bilirubin in the blood as determined by comparing the color of a sample of test serum with a set of color standards ⟨an *icterus index* of 15 or above indicates active jaundice⟩

**ic·tic** \'iktik\ *adj* **:** of or relating to an ictus

**ic·tid·o·saur** \ik'tidə,sȯ(ə)r\ *n* -S [NL *Ictidosauria*] **:** a reptile of the Ictidosauria

**ic·tido·sau·ria** \(,)ik,tidə'sȯrēə, ,iktədō's-\ *n pl, cap* [NL, fr. Gk *iktid-, iktis* yellow-breasted marten + NL *-o-* + *-sauria*] **:** an order of Reptilia comprising a number of imperfectly known Upper Triassic forms intermediate in character between the therapsids and the most primitive true mammals — compare MICROCONODON

**ic·ti·o·bus** \ik'tīəbəs\ *n, cap* [NL, irreg. fr. *ichthy-* + Gk *bous* ox, cow (also, a kind of fish) — more at COW] **:** a common genus of buffalo fishes

**ic·to·gen·ic** \'iktə¦jenik\ *adj* [*ictus* + *-o-* + *-genic*] *med* **:** giving rise to ictus

**ic·to·nyx** \'iktə,niks\ *n, cap* [NL, fr. Gk *iktis* yellow-breasted marten + NL *-onyx*] **:** a genus of African mustelid mammals comprising the zorils

**ic·tus** \'iktəs\ *n* -ES [L, fr. *ictus*, past part. of *icere* to strike; akin to Gk *aichmē* lance, *iktea* wounded, Lith *iēšmas* spit, OPruss *aysmis* and perh. to ON *eigin* newly-sprouted seed, MLG *ine* awn] **1 a** (1) **:** recurring stress or beat in a rhythmic usu. metrical series of sounds **:** metrical accent (2) **:** the place of the stress or beat in a metrical foot — compare ARSIS, THESIS **b :** ACCENT 6b **2 a :** a beat or pulsation esp. of the heart **b :** a sudden attack or seizure esp. of apoplexy **:** STROKE

**ICW** *abbr* interrupted continuous waves

**icy** \'īsē, -si\ *adj* **icier**; **iciest**; [¹*ice* + *-y*] **1 a :** covered with, abounding in, or consisting of ice ⟨skidded on the ~ street⟩ ⟨exploring the ~ polar wastes⟩ ⟨the ~ cliffs at the glacier's edge⟩ **b :** intensely cold ⟨~ weather⟩ ⟨an ~ room⟩ **2 :** characterized by coldness (as of manner, influence) **:** CHILLING, FRIGID, COLD ⟨got an ~ stare from the stranger⟩ **3 :** sure to be fulfilled — used of a contract in a card game

**¹id** \'id\ *n* -S [G, short for *idioplasma* idioplasm — more at IDIOPLASM] **:** a hypothetical structural unit of living matter resulting from the successive aggregation of biophores and determinants

**²id** \"\ *n* -S [NL, fr. L, it; trans. of G *es*] **:** the primitive undifferentiated part of the psychic apparatus that reacts blindly on a pleasure-pain level, is the seat of psychic energy, and is the ultimate source of higher psychic components (as ego and superego)

**³id** \"\ *n* -S *often attrib* [¹*-id*] **:** a skin rash that is secondary to a primary infection elsewhere and is considered to be an allergic reaction of the skin to the circulating antigen ⟨a syphilitic ~⟩

**¹-id** \əd, (,)id\ *n suffix* -S [in sense 1, fr. L *-ides*, masc. patronymic suffix, fr. Gk *-idēs*; in sense 2, fr. It *-ide*, fr. L *-id-, -is*, fem. patronymic suffix, fr. Gk; in sense 3, fr. F *-ide*, fr. L *-id-, -is*, fem. patronymic suffix] **1 a :** one belonging to a (specified) natural group or line of descent ⟨Melanes*id*⟩ ⟨Austral*id*⟩ **b :** one belonging to a (specified) dynastic line ⟨Fatim*id*⟩ **2 a :** meteor associated with or radiating from a (specified) constellation or comet ⟨Perse*id*⟩ ⟨Biel*id*⟩ **b :** variable star of a (specified) source or type ⟨Cephe*id*⟩ **3** *also* **-ide** \,īd, ,əd, (,)id\ **:** skin rash caused by (something specified) ⟨bacter*id*⟩ ⟨syphil*id*⟩

**²-id** \"\ *adj suffix* **:** of, relating to, or characteristic of a (specified) natural group or line of descent ⟨pre-Mongol*id* artifacts⟩

**³-id** \"\ — see -IDE

**⁴-id** \"\ *n suffix* -S [prob. fr. L *-id-, -is*, formative element of some nouns, fr. Gk] **1 :** structural element of a lower molar or premolar ⟨protocon*id*⟩ **2 :** structure, body, or particle of a (specified) kind ⟨chromat*id*⟩

**id** *abbr* **1** [L *idem*] the same **2** island

**ID** *abbr* **1** identification **2** inside diameter; internal diameter **3** inside dimensions **4** intelligence department **5** intradermal

**-i·da** \ədə\ *n pl suffix* [NL (neut. pl. in form), fr. L- *ides*, patronymic suffix] **:** animals that are or have the form of — in names of higher taxa (as orders and classes) ⟨Scorpion*ida*⟩ ⟨Acar*ida*⟩ ⟨Bero*ida*⟩ — **-i·dan** \ədən, əd°n\ *n or adj suffix*

**-i·dae** \ə,dē\ *n pl suffix* [NL, fr. L (pl. of *-ides*, masc. patronymic suffix), fr. Gk *-idai*, pl. of *-idēs*, masc. patronymic suffix] **:** members of the family of — in patronymic group names ⟨Alcmaeon*idae*⟩ ⟨Homer*idae*⟩ ⟨Seleuc*idae*⟩; in names of families of animals substituted for the last syllable of the genitive case of the name of the type genus ⟨Aphid*idae* from *Aphis*⟩ ⟨Equ*idae* from *Equus*⟩

**¹idae·an** *or* **ide·an** \(')ī¦dēən\ *adj, usu cap* [L *idaeus* Idaean (fr. Gk *idaios*, fr. *Idē* Mt. Ida in Crete) + E *-an*] **1 :** of, relating to, or dwelling on Mt. Ida in Crete **2 :** of, relating to, or characteristic of the ancient Greek goddess Rhea with whom Mt. Ida was associated

**²idaean** \"\ *adj, usu cap* [L *idaeus* Idaean (fr. Gk *idaios*, fr. *Idē* Mt. Ida in Asia Minor) + E *-an*] **1 :** of, relating to, or dwelling on Mt. Ida in Asia Minor **2 :** of, relating to, or characteristic of the ancient Greek goddess Cybele with whom Mt. Ida was associated

**idae·in** *also* **ide·in** \ī'dēən\ *n* -S [ISV *idae-, ide-* (fr. NL *vitis-idaea* — specific epithet of the mountain cranberry *Vaccinium vitis-idaea minus* —, fr. L *vitis* vine + *idaea*, fem. of *idaeus*) + *-in*] **:** an anthocyanin pigment obtained in the form of the greenish brown crystalline chloride $C_{21}H_{21}ClO_{11}$ from the skin of red apples and from cranberries and similar fruit; a galactoside of cyanidin

**¹ida·ho** \'īdə,hō\ *adj, usu cap* [*Idaho*, state in the northwestern U.S., prob. of AmerInd origin] **:** of or from the state of Idaho **:** of the kind or style prevalent in Idaho **:** IDAHOAN

**²idaho** \"\ *n, pl* **idahoes** *also* **idahos** *usu cap* **:** an elongated potato rich in starch and suitable for baking that is grown esp. in Idaho

**¹ida·ho·an** \¦īdə¦hōən\ *adj, usu cap* [*Idaho* + E *-an*] **:** of, relating to, or characteristic of Idaho or Idahoans

**²idahoan** \"\ *n* -S *cap* **:** a native or resident of Idaho

**idaho fescue** *n, usu cap I* **:** a tall meadow grass (*Festuca idahoensis*) of central and western No. America with smooth filiform leaves, an open inflorescence, and awns about half as long as the lemmas

**idaho white pine** *n, usu cap I* **1 :** WESTERN WHITE PINE 1 **2 :** the wood of western white pine

**ida·lian** \(')ī¦dālēən, lyən\ *adj, usu cap* [*Idalium*, ancient town in Cyprus + E *-an*] **:** of or relating to the ancient town Idalium that was a center of the worship of Aphrodite

**idant** \'i¦d°nt, 'ī¦, |,dant\ *n* -S [ISV ¹*id* + *-ant;* orig. formed in G] **:** a hypothetical structural unit arising from an aggregation of ids and forming a basic element of the germ plasm in the Weismannian theory of heredity

**id·dings·ite** \'idiŋ,zīt\ *n* -S [Joseph P. *Iddings* †1920 Am. geologist + E *-ite*] **:** a mineral consisting of a silicate of calcium, magnesium, and iron of doubtful composition and forming pseudomorphs after olivine

**¹ide** \'īd\ *n* -S [back-formation fr. *ides*] **:** one of the ides

**²ide** \"\ *n* -S [Sw *id* — more at EDIFY] **:** a European freshwater cyprinid food fish (*Idus idus*) — see ORFE

**¹-ide** \,īd, əd, (,)id\ *also* **-id** \əd, (,)id\ *n suffix* -S [G & F; G *-id*, fr. F *-ide* (as in *oxide*) — more at OXIDE] **1 :** binary chemical compound or compound regarded as binary — added to contracted name of the nonmetallic or more electronegative element ⟨iron ox*ide*⟩ ⟨hydrogen sulf*ide*⟩ or radical ⟨am*ide*⟩ ⟨ethox*ide*⟩ **2 a :** chemical compound derived from or related to another (usu. specified) compound ⟨anhydr*ide*⟩ ⟨glycol*ide*⟩ ⟨phthal*ide*⟩ **b :** acetal derivative of a sugar — in names of glycosides replacing final *-e* of the name of the sugar ⟨arabin*oside*⟩ ⟨cerebr*oside*⟩ — compare -OSIDE **3 :** one of a class of organic esp. naturally occurring compounds ⟨lip*ide*⟩ ⟨phosphat*ide*⟩ ⟨pept*ide*⟩ ⟨sacchar*ide*⟩ **4 :** chemical element of a series of metallic elements of increasing atomic numbers ⟨actin*ide*⟩ ⟨lanthan*ide*⟩

**²-ide** — see -ID

**idea** \(')ī¦dēə, (')ī¦diə; *chiefly in southern US* 'ī,dē(ə) *or* 'ī,di(ə); *dial or archaic* (')ī¦dē; *in NewEng extremely frequent with intrusive* r —(')ī¦dēər *or* (')ī¦di(ə)r\ *n* -S [L, fr. Gk, fr. *idein* to see — more at WIT] **1 a :** a presentation of sense, concept, or representation: as (1) *Platonism* **:** an archetype or subsistent form **:** a transcendent universal (2) *Aristotelianism* **:** the form-giving cause **:** FORM (3) *Lockeanism* **:** an immediate object or a compound of immediate objects of sensation or reflection — see COMPLEX IDEA, SIMPLE IDEA (4) *Berkeleianism* **:** an impression of sense or imagination; *esp* **:** PERCEPT (5) *Humism* **:** a representation or construct of memory and association as distinguished from direct impression of sense (6) *Kantianism* **:** a transcendent but nonempirical concept of reason **:** NOUMENON (7) *Hegelianism* **:** the highest category **:** the complete and final product of reason; *also* **:** its realization or embodiment — compare ABSOLUTE **b :** an object of a concept **2 a :** a conception or standard of any perfection **:** IDEAL **b :** a preliminary plan **:** CONCEPTION, DESIGN; *usu* **:** a plan or purpose of action **:** PROJECT ⟨his ~ of going in for law⟩ ⟨a new ~ for decorating the house⟩ **3** *archaic* **:** a visible representation of a conception (as an abstract perfection) or of a design **:** a replica of a pattern or archetype **:** a realized ideal **4 a** *obs* **:** an image or picture recalled by memory **b :** an indefinite or fanciful conception or notion **:** a figment of the imagination **:** FANCY, SUPPOSITION, OPINION ⟨that is a mere ~ of yours⟩ ⟨a head full of absurd ~s⟩ ⟨I've an ~ we'll win⟩ **5 :** an object of the mind existing in apprehension, conception, or thought **:** NOTION, THOUGHT, IMPRESSION ⟨a clear ~ of his responsibility⟩ **6 :** a product of reflection or mental concentration **:** a formulated thought or opinion ⟨~s on a subject⟩ ⟨clearly defined ~s⟩ **7 :** whatever is known, believed, or supposed regarding any object ⟨the child's ~ of air⟩ **8 :** the central or key meaning or the chief end of a particular action or situation ⟨get the ~⟩ — see BIG IDEA **9 :** a musical figure or theme **10** *Christian Science* **:** an image in Mind

**syn** IDEA, CONCEPT, CONCEPTION, THOUGHT, NOTION, IMPRESSION: IDEA may apply to an image or formulation of something seen or known, of something imagined and visualized, of something vaguely assumed, guessed at, or sensed ⟨practically every American boy who is not tied to his mother's apron strings is going to encounter other boys whose *ideas* of fighting are very different from his own —Margaret Mead⟩ ⟨success with the steamboat inspired Colonel John Stevens to work on the *idea* of a steam railroad —*Amer. Guide Series: N.J.*⟩ ⟨an earlier paper has reviewed the development during the Middle Ages of the *idea* that the Kingdom of France had natural frontiers which it was her right, even her duty, to attain —N.J.G.Pounds⟩ CONCEPT may indicate a fairly definite mental formulation determined by consideration of instances, although the word readily admits of suggesting foundations differing with individuals ⟨thus the popular *concept* of what news was came more and more to be formed upon what news was printed —F.L.Mott⟩ ⟨if his *concept* of the national security he has sworn to defend impels him to dispatch troops into foreign regions and in situations that may involve the United States in war, the sole responsibility is his —Arthur Krock⟩ ⟨the emerging of a fresh *concept* of architecture needed to produce new forms and revitalize tradition —*Amer. Guide Series: Mich.*⟩ CONCEPTION, often interchangeable with CONCEPT, may stress the idea of the mental action of imagining and formulating rather than the notion of its result ⟨the *conception*, building, and profitable sale of the New York, Chicago & St. Louis Railway, commonly known as the Nickel Plate, was in great measure due to him —K.F.Geiser⟩ ⟨the Malays have a whole system of tabooed and substituted words, based as usual on the *conception* of all Nature as animate and sensitive —J.G. Frazer⟩ THOUGHT is a general term but is likely to imply the result of ratiocination, of thinking, reasoning, or meditating, rather than fancying or imagining ⟨the next 10 years Abbot devoted to the final elaboration of his *thought* in abstruse technical form in *The Syllogistic Philosophy* —F.A.Christie⟩ ⟨Adams' first *thought* was that Palmerston wished a quarrel; his second, that it might be connected with a desire for mediation —W.C.Ford⟩ ⟨there are insights which are spoiled by *thought* —Lewis Leary b.1906⟩ NOTION may suggest a vague half-formed idea not resolved by much thought and analysis ⟨the *notion* that primitive languages lack the power of abstraction —A.A.Hill⟩ ⟨the *notion* that history shows a continual progress and especially a progress in the liberation of the individual is amply refuted by many examples —M.R.Cohen⟩ ⟨the British have some queer and quaint *notions* about Americans — some almost as peculiar as our preconceived ideas about them —Richard Joseph⟩ IMPRESSION applies to a first notion frankly lacking in analysis, consideration, and thought ⟨when he steps out on the street his first *impression* is of broad radiating avenues —*Amer. Guide Series: Minn.*⟩ ⟨the additional real difficulty of eliminating all possibility of adding subjective *impressions* to objective findings —W.C.Allee⟩

**-id·ea** \'idēə\ *n pl suffix* [NL (neut. pl. in form), fr. Gk *-ideus*, n. suffix with quasi-patronymic value] **:** animals that are or have the form of — in names of higher taxa ⟨Car*idea*⟩ ⟨Phoron*idea*⟩

**ideaed** *also* **idea'd** *pronunc at* IDEA + d\ *adj* **:** having a specified kind of idea or a specified number of ideas ⟨a one-*ideaed* man⟩ ⟨eager bright-*ideaed* students⟩ **:** characterized by ideas ⟨alert ~ men are priceless treasures⟩

**idea·is·tic** \(,)ī¦dēə¦istik, ¦īdē¦i-\ *adj* **:** relating to, concerned with, or based on ideas esp. as abstract or symbolic matters of mind

**¹ide·al** \(')ī¦dē(ə)l, -diəl\ *adj* [F or LL; F *idéal*, fr. LL *idealis*, fr. L *idea* + *-alis* -al] **1 a :** existing as a mere mental image **:** existing in fancy or imagination only **:** IMAGINARY, HYPOTHETICAL ⟨confusing ~ and concrete things⟩; *broadly* **:** lacking practicality **:** VISIONARY ⟨a purely ~ concept of society⟩ **b :** relating to or constituting mental images, ideas, or conceptions **:** IDEATIONAL, CONCEPTUAL ⟨life and death appeared to me ~ bounds —Mary W. Shelley⟩ **c :** embodying or symbolizing an idea **2 :** of or relating to an ideal or to perfection of kind **:** existing as a perfect exemplar **:** embodying or symbolizing an ideal ⟨~ beauty⟩ ⟨an ~ moral character⟩ **3 :** existing as a patterning or archetypal idea; *usu* **:** of or relating to Platonic ideas **4 :** of or relating to philosophical idealism

**²ideal** \"\ *n* -S [F or G; F *idéal*, fr. G *ideal*, fr. *ideal-* (as in *idealform* ideal form), fr. LL *idealis*, adj.] **1 a :** a conception of something in its highest perfection ⟨a perfect circle is an ~ impossible to construct⟩ **b :** a standard of perfection, beauty, or excellence believed to be capable of realization or attainment ⟨the ~s of our civilization⟩ **2 :** one regarded as exemplifying an ideal and often taken as a model for imitation ⟨considered the older man his ~⟩ **3 :** an ultimate object or aim of endeavor **:** GOAL ⟨their ~ was a quiet unhurried life⟩ **4 :** a subset of a ring that contains as an element the sum or difference of any two elements and the product of any element with an element of the ring ⟨the integers ending in 0 are an ~ in the ring of all integers⟩ **syn** see MODEL

**ideal engine** *n* **:** a heat engine operating on a reversible cycle (as a Carnot cycle)

**idea·less** *pronunc at* IDEA + ləs\ *adj* **:** lacking an idea or ideas

**ideal gas** *n* **:** a gas in which there is no attraction between the molecules; *usu* **:** a gas conforming exactly to the ideal-gas law

**ideal–gas law** *n* **:** GAS LAW C

**ide·al·ism** \(')ī¦dē(ə),lizəm, -diə,l- *sometimes* 'ī,dē,- *or* 'ī,diə-\ *n* -S [prob. fr. G or F; G *idealismus*, fr. F *idéalisme*, fr. *idéal* + *-isme* -ism] **1 :** a theory that affirms that mind or the spiritual and ideal is of central importance in reality: as **a :** a theory that regards reality as essentially spiritual or the embodiment of mind or reason esp. by asserting either that the ideal element in reality is dominant (as in Platonism) or that the intrinsic nature and essence of reality is consciousness or reason (as in Hegelianism) — called also *metaphysical idealism* **b :** a theory that identifies reality with perceptibility or denies the possibility of knowing anything except psychical reality and proceeds from the affirmation that the mental life alone is knowable to a dogmatic dualism (as in Cartesianism and Lockeanism) which in metaphysics results in realism, to a subjective idealism in metaphysics (as in Berkeleianism), or to solipsism or skepticism (as in Humism) — called also *epistemological idealism;* see ABSOLUTE IDEALISM, MONISTIC IDEALISM, OBJECTIVE IDEALISM, PERSONAL IDEALISM, PLURALISTIC IDEALISM, SUBJECTIVE IDEALISM, TRANSCENDENTAL IDEALISM **2 a :** the practice of forming ideals or living under their influence **:** tendency to idealize **b :** something that is idealized **:** an ideal representation or experience **3 :** literary or artistic theory or practice that values ideal or subjective types or aspects of beauty more than formal or sensible qualities or that affirms the preeminent value of imagination as compared with faithful copying of nature — opposed to *realism*

**¹ide·al·ist** \- ləst\ *n* -S [¹*ideal* + *-ist*] **1 a :** an adherent of a philosophical theory of idealism **b :** an artist or author who advocates or practices idealism in art or writing **2 :** one whose conduct is influenced or guided by ideals; *usu* **:** one that places ideals before practical considerations **:** VISIONARY, DREAMER

**²idealist** \"\ *adj* **:** IDEALISTIC

**ide·al·is·tic** \(')ī¦dē(ə)¦listik, (,)ī¦diə¦l-, -tēk *sometimes* 'ī,dēə¦l- *or* 'ī,diə¦l-\ *adj* **1 :** of, relating to, or advocated by idealists or idealism ⟨~ theories⟩ **2 :** exhibiting, practicing, or characterized by idealism ⟨an ~ man⟩ ⟨an ~ view of life⟩ — **ide·al·is·ti·cal·ly** \-tək(ə)lē, -tēk-, -li\ *adv*

**ide·al·i·ty** \,īdē'alәd·ə, -di'a-, -ətē, -i\ *n* -ES [¹*ideal* + *-ity*] **1 a :** the quality or state of being ideal **b :** existence only in idea **2 :** something imaginary or idealized **:** an unreal or unrealistic thing or concept **3 :** the poetic or creative faculty — used orig. in phrenology

**ide·al·iza·tion** \(,)ī,dē(ə)lə'zāshən, -diəl-, -,lī'z- *sometimes* ,ī,deə(,)l- *or* ,īdiə(,)l-\ *n* -S **1 a :** an act or the process of idealizing **b :** a product of idealizing **2 :** the employment of idealistic methods

**ide·al·ize** \(')ī¦dē(ə),līz, -diə,l- *sometimes* 'ī,dēə,l- *or* 'ī,diə,l-\ *vb* -ED/-ING/-S *see -ize in Explan Notes* [prob. fr. G *idealisieren*, fr. *ideal* + *-isieren* -ize] *vt* **1 :** to make ideal **:** give an ideal form or value to **:** attribute ideal characteristics and excellences to ⟨tended to ~ her friends⟩ **2 :** to treat (an artistic subject) idealistically ~ *vi* **1 :** to form ideals **2 :** to work idealistically — **ide·al·iz·er** \-zə(r)\ *n* -S

**ideal·less** *pronunc at* IDEAL + ləs\ *adj* **:** lacking ideals **:** basing conduct and judgments on the everyday realities of life; *broadly* **:** MATERIALISTIC

**ide·al·ly** *pronunc at* IDEAL + (l)ē *or* (l)i\ *adv* **1 :** in idea or imagination **:** by means of ideas **:** MENTALLY **2 :** in relation to or in the manner of an exemplar, archetype, or pattern **3 a :** conformably to or in respect to an ideal **:** PERFECTLY **b :** for best results or greatest enjoyment, efficiency, or value ⟨~ each meal should be planned in relation both to activity and to other meals of the day⟩ **c :** in accordance with an ideal or typical standard **:** CLASSICALLY

**ide·al·ness** *n* -ES **:** the quality or state of being ideal ⟨~ of his prose⟩ ⟨the ~ of such aspirations⟩

**idealogue** *var of* IDEOLOGUE

**idealogy** *var of* IDEOLOGY

**ideal point** *n* **:** a point at infinity that in projective geometry is the assumed intersection of any two parallel lines

**ideal realism** *n* **:** any of various philosophical theories combining idealistic and realistic elements; *specif* **:** a theory combining idealistic epistemology with realistic metaphysics — called also *real idealism*

**ideals** *pl of* IDEAL

**ideal solution** *n* **:** a solution in which the interaction between molecules of the components does not differ from the interactions between the molecules of each component; *usu* **:** a solution that conforms exactly to Raoult's law — compare ACTIVITY 6b, ACTIVITY COEFFICIENT, FUGACITY 2b

**ideal truth** *n* **:** NORMATIVE TRUTH

**ideal type** *n* **:** an abstraction of features from empirical reality and their embodiment into a unified conceptual scheme of hypothetical validity ⟨sees the *ideal type* of monogamy in Christian marriage —Rodney Needham⟩ ⟨analysis of social situations by the use of *ideal types*⟩

**ideal utilitarianism** *n* **:** UTILITARIANISM 1b

**idea man** *n* **:** a person with an unusual capacity for visualizing and formulating new techniques, approaches, products

**ideamonger** *pronunc at* IDEA +,-\ *n* **:** one that deals in ideas **:** IDEA MAN

**i·de·an** *usu cap, var of* IDAEAN

**idea·pho·ria** \(,)ī,dēə'fōrēə, ,ī,deə-\ *n* -S [NL, fr. L *idea* + NL *-phoria*] **:** capacity for creative thought or imagination

**ideas** *pl of* IDEA

**ideas of reference :** a delusion that accompanies certain abnormal mental states in which remarks overheard and people seen seem to be concerned with and usu. inimical to oneself

**¹ide·ate** \'īdē,āt, ī'd-\ *vb* -ED/-ING/-S [*idea* + *-ate*] *vt* **:** to form in idea **:** CONCEIVE, PRECONCEIVE, PREFIGURE; *usu* **:** to have ideas, thoughts, or impressions of **:** remember, imagine, or think of when not in the actual presence of ~ *vi* **1 :** to form an idea **2 :** to invent by working through ideas

**²ide·ate** \'īdē,āt, ī'dēət\ *n* -S [NL *ideatum*] **:** IDEATUM

**ide·a·tion** \,īdē'āshən\ *n* -S **:** the capacity of the mind to form or entertain ideas; *broadly* **:** the process of entertaining and relating ideas

**ide·a·tion·al** \¦==¦āshən°l, -āshnəl\ *adj* **:** of, relating to, or produced by ideation; *broadly* **:** consisting of or referring to ideas or thoughts of objects not immediately present to the senses — compare IDEALISTIC, PERCEPTUAL — **ide·a·tion·al·ly** \-n°lē, -nəlē, ¦li\ *adv*

**ide·a·tive** \ī'dēəd·iv, 'īdē,ād·-\ *adj* [¹*ideate* + *-ive*] **:** IDEATIONAL

**ide·atum** \,īdē'ād·əm\ *n, pl* **ide·ata** \-d·ə\ [NL, fr. L *idea* + *-atum*, neut. of *-atus* -ate — more at IDEA] *philos* **:** the actual existence supposed to correspond with an idea

**idée fixe** \(,)ē,dā'fēks\ *n, pl* **idées fixes** \-ks(əz)\ [F] **:** FIXED IDEA

**idée-force** \-'fō(ə)rs\ *n, pl* **idées-forces** \-rs(əz)\ [F, fr. *idée* idea + *force*] **:** an idea considered as a real factor in the behavior of an individual or social group and thus in the course of events

**idein** *var of* IDAEIN

**ide·ist** \(')ī¦dēəst, 'ī,dēə-\ *n* -S [*idea* + *-ist*] **:** an adherent of an idealistic philosophy; *specif* **:** an advocate of epistemological idealism

**idem** *with reference to a person* 'ī,dem *or* 'ē,dem, *with reference to a thing* 'ī,dem *or* 'i,dem, *the masculine Latin form having a long i & the neuter form a short i*\ *pron* [L, same — more at IDENTITY] **:** something previously mentioned **:** SAME — used chiefly in bibliographies to avoid repetition of author's name and title when a reference to an item immediately follows another to the same item ⟨~ page 30⟩; abbr. *id.*

**idem so·nans** \¦ī,dem'sō,nanz, ¦i,dem'sō,nän(t)s\ [L] **:** having the same sound — used of a rule in law that the occurrence in a document of a spelling of a material word that is wrong but has the sound of the word intended (as *Lawrance* for *Lawrence* or *Kean* for *Keen*) does not vitiate the instrument

**-i·dene** \ə,dēn\ *n suffix* -S [ISV *-ide* + *-ene*] **:** radical having two valence bonds at the point of attachment ⟨ethyl*idene* $CH_3CH<$⟩ ⟨eth*idene*⟩ — compare -YLIDENE

**¹ident** \ī'dent\ *n* -S [by shortening] **:** IDENTIFICATION

**²ident** \"\ *vb* -ED/-ING/-S [by shortening] **:** IDENTIFY

**iden·ta.code** \ī'dentə,kōd, ə'd-\ *n* [*identification* + connective *-a-* + *code*] **:** a means of identification of a pedigreed animal consisting of a tattoo mark that is recorded on both pedigree and certificate of ownership

**iden·tic** \ī¦dentik, ə'd-\ *adj* [prob. fr. ML *identicus*] **:** IDENTICAL ⟨recognition of ~ themes in the apparently incongruous —R.P.Blackmur⟩: as **a :** constituting an action or expression in which two or more governments follow precisely the same course or employ an identical form — compare JOINT 2a(3) **b :** constituting an action or expression in which a government follows precisely the same course or employs identical forms with reference to two or more other governments **syn** see SAME

**iden·ti·cal** \-tәkəl, -tēk-\ *adj* [prob. fr. ML *identicus* (fr. LL *identitas* identity + L *-icus* -ic) + E *-al*] **1 :** expressing or effecting identity — used chiefly of propositions in logic and of equations and operations in mathematics **2 :** being the same **:** having complete identity ⟨the ~ place where we stopped before⟩ — often used with *same* or *very* for emphasis ⟨the same ~ menu⟩ ⟨the very ~ house⟩ **3 a :** showing exact likeness **:** characterized by such entire agreement in qualities and attributes that identity may be assumed — often used with *with* and sometimes with *to* ⟨a replica that is ~ with the original⟩ **b :** very similar **:** having such close resemblance and such minor difference as to be essentially the same **:** appearing or seeming exactly alike ⟨saw the ~ dress on sale for three dollars⟩ ⟨the two plants were ~⟩ — often used with *with* or *to* ⟨his examination paper was ~ to his brother's⟩ ⟨political issues are seldom ~ with religious⟩ **4 :** having the same cause or origin ⟨~ infections⟩ **syn** see LIKE, SAME

**identical equation** *n* **:** an equation that is satisfied for all values of the literal symbols

**iden·ti·cal·i·ty** \(,)ī,dentə'kaləd·ē, ə,den-, -lətē, -i\ *n* -ES **:** IDENTICALNESS

**iden·ti·cal·ly** \-'dentək(ə)lē, -tēk-, -li\ *adv* **:** in an identical manner **:** with complete identity ⟨shoes ~ alike⟩; *specif* **:** for all values of the mathematical symbols involved

**iden·ti·cal·ness** \-kəlnəs\ *n* -ES **:** the quality or state of being identical

**identical points** *n pl* **:** points on the retinas of the two eyes that occupy corresponding positions in respect to the retinal centers

**identical proposition** *n* **:** a proposition in logic whose subject and predicate are identical in meaning and whose affirmation is therefore superfluous ⟨"nothing inconceivable can be conceived" is an *identical proposition*⟩

**identical rhyme** *n* **:** RIME RICHE

**identical twin** *n* **:** either member of a pair of twins produced from a single zygote

**iden·ti·fi·a·bil·i·ty** \(,)ī,dentə,fīə'biləd·ē, ə,d-, -lətē, -i\ *n* **:** the quality or state of being identifiable

**iden·ti·fi·a·ble** \ˌ=ˈ==,=əbəl, (,)=,==ˈ=əbəl\ *adj* **:** subject to identification **:** capable of being identified — **iden·ti·fi·a·bly** \-blē,-bli\ *adv*

**iden·ti·fi·ca·tion** \(,)=,==,fə'kāshən\ *n* -S *often attrib* [prob. fr. F, fr. *identité* identity + *-fication* — more at IDENTITY] **1 a :** an act or the action of identifying or the state of being identified **b :** a means of identifying **:** evidence of identity ⟨experienced travelers always carry some ~⟩ ⟨a driver's license is sufficient ~⟩ **2 a :** a mental mechanism wherein the individual gains gratification, emotional support, or relief from anxiety by attributing to himself consciously or unconsciously the characteristics of another person or group **b :** orientation of the self in regard to something (as a familial or ethnic group, class, nation, ideology) with a resulting feeling of close emotional association ⟨the immigrant's ~ with his new country⟩ **3 :** CONDENSATION 5

**identification bracelet** *n* **:** a bracelet with a narrow plaque for the owner's name

**identification tag** *n* **:** either of two metal tags worn suspended around the neck by a member of the armed forces and stamped with his name, serial number, and other information

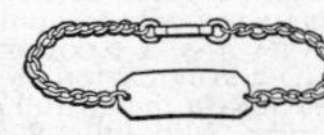

identification bracelet

**iden·ti·fi·ca·to·ry** \ī'dentəfəkə,tōrē, ə'd-, ,ī,den-'tif-, *chiefly Brit* =ˌdentifiˈkāt(ə)ri *or* -ā·tri\ *adj* [*identification* + *-ory*] **:** concerned with or serving for identification ⟨~ thinking⟩ ⟨~ traits⟩

**iden·ti·fi·er** \ī'dentə,fī(ə)r, ə'd-, -fīə\ *n* -S **:** one that identifies

**iden·ti·fy** \-fī\ *vb* -ED/-ING/-S [prob. fr. F *identifier*, fr. *identité* identity + *-fier* -fy — more at IDENTITY] *vt* **1 a :** to cause to be or become identical **:** regard as identical ⟨*identified* their own interests with those of the rulers⟩ **b :** to link in an inseparable fashion **:** make correlative with something ⟨may not rationally ~ itself with any one church⟩ **c :** to conceive as united in spirit, principle, outlook, or interest ⟨*identified* himself with the middle classes⟩; *broadly* **:** to associate or join (as oneself) with some interest (as a business or political party) **2 a :** to establish the identity of ⟨soon *identified* the child⟩ **:** show or prove the sameness of (as with something known, stated, or possessed) ⟨tried to ~ the stolen property as his own⟩ ⟨could not immediately ~ the quotation⟩ **b :** to determine the taxonomic position of (a biological specimen) ⟨*identified* it as a member of the genus *Salix* but could not determine the species⟩ ~ *vi* **:** to be or become the same **:** associate in such a way as to have unity (as of interests, purpose, effect) ⟨our tastes do not always ~⟩ ⟨people long in association tend to ~ with one another⟩ **:** practice identification ⟨to ~ is to share the interests and acts of another person until identification results —C.R.Adams⟩

**identifying pronoun** *n* **:** a pronoun referring to something as identical with what has been mentioned ⟨*same* is an *identifying pronoun*⟩

**iden·tism** \-n-,tizəm\ *n* -S [*identity* + *-ism*] **:** IDENTITY PHILOSOPHY

**iden·ti·ty** \ī'den(t)əd·ē, ə'den-, -ətē, -i\ *n* -ES [MF *identité*, fr. LL *identitat-, identitas*, irreg. fr. L *idem* same (fr. *is* he) + *-itat-, -itas* -ity — more at ITERATE] **1 a :** sameness of essential or generic character in different examples or instances **:** the limit approached by increasing similarity ⟨the ~ of the red in the rug with the red of a brick⟩ **b :** sameness in all that constitutes the objective reality of a thing **:** SELFSAMENESS, ONENESS **:** sameness of that which is distinguishable only in some accidental fashion (as being designated by different names, or the object of different perceptions, or different in time and place) ⟨the ~ of Scott with the author of Waverley⟩ ⟨the sense of ~ arising in shared experience⟩ **c :** an instance of such sameness **2 :** unity and persistence of personality **:** unity or individual comprehensiveness of a life or character ⟨lost consciousness of his own ~⟩ **3 :** the condition of being the same with something described, claimed, or asserted or of possessing a character claimed ⟨establish the ~ of stolen goods⟩ **4** *archaic* **:** individual or real existence **5** *Schellingian philos* **:** reality at its deepest level at which subject and object are one **6 a :** IDENTICAL PROPOSITION **b :** IDENTICAL EQUATION **7** *Austral* **:** CHARACTER 8a **8** *or* **identity element :** an operator that leaves unchanged an element on which it operates ⟨since if zero is added to any integer, the sum is the same integer, zero is an additive ~⟩

**identity card** *n* **:** a usu. official card bearing identifying data about the individual to whom it pertains

**identity philosophy** *n* **:** a monistic philosophical theory (as the philosophy of Schelling) that rejects any ultimate bifurcation into spirit and nature or subject and object and finds fundamental unity in the Absolute

**identity principle** *n* **:** LAW OF IDENTITY

**ideo-** *comb form* [F *idéo-*, fr. Gk *idea* — more at IDEA] **:** idea ⟨*ideo*crat⟩ ⟨*ideo*genetic⟩ ⟨*ideo*logy⟩

**ide·oc·ra·cy** \,īdē'äkrəsē, ,id-\ *n* -ES [*ideo-* + *-cracy*] **:** government or social management based on abstract ideas

**ideo·ge·net·ic** \,īdē(,)ōjə¦ned·ik, ¦id-\ *adj* [*ideo-* + *-genetic*] **:** originating ideas

**ideo·gram** \'īdēə,gram, 'id-, -raa(ə)m *sometimes* ī'dēə- *or* ī'diə-\ *n* [*ideo-* + *-gram*] **1 a :** a picture, a conventionalized picture, or a symbol that symbolizes a thing or an idea but not a particular word or phrase for it **b :** a picture, a conventionalized picture, or a symbol that symbolizes a thing or an idea but not a particular word or phrase for it and that if pictorial symbolizes not the object pictured but some thing or idea that the object pictured is supposed to suggest or emblematize — distinguished from *pictogram* **2 :** a symbol or group of symbols that as used in the writing of a particular language represents usu. a particular morpheme, word, or phrase but without providing separate phonetic representation of the individual phonemes or syllables composing the morpheme, word, or phrase **:** LOGOGRAM a; *specif* **:** a symbol or group of symbols used for convenience in writing an alphabetic language and directly representing a word or phrase or in some instances an idea expressible by any of two or more different words or phrases (as in English *3* read as *three*, + read as *plus*, & read as *and*, $ read as *dollar* or *dollars*, *1960* read as *one thousand nine hundred and sixty* or *nineteen hundred and sixty* or *nineteen sixty*) **3 :** a composite character in Chinese writing made by combining two or more other characters for words of related meaning

**ideo·gram·ic** *or* **ideo·gram·mic** \ˌ===¦gramik, =ˈ==-\ *adj* **:** of, relating to, or characterized by the use of ideograms

**ideo·gram·mat·ic** \-,grə'mad·|ik, -at|, |ēk\ *adj* [*ideogram* + *-atic* (as in *epigrammatic*)] **1 :** being an ideogram **2 :** IDEOGRAMIC

**ideo·graph** \'===,graf, ='==-, -raa(ə)f,-raif,-rȧf\ *n* [*ideo-* + *-graph*] **:** IDEOGRAM

**ideo·graph·ic** \ˌ===¦grafik, =¦==-, -fēk\ *adj* [*ideo-* + *-graphic*] **1 :** consisting of or characterized by the use of ideograms ⟨an ~ script⟩ ⟨the ~ stage in the development of writing⟩ **2 :** being an ideogram ⟨an ~ sign⟩ **3 :** of or relating to an ideogram ⟨these characters had sometimes an ~, and sometimes a phonetic value —David Diringer⟩ — **ideo·graph·i·cal·ly** \-fək(ə)lē, -fēk-, -li\ *adv*

**ide·og·ra·phy** \,īdē'ägrəfē, id-, -fi\ *n* -ES [*ideo-* + *-graphy*] **1 :** the use of ideograms **2 :** the representation of ideas by graphic symbols

**ideo·log·i·cal** \,īdēə¦läjəkəl, ¦id-, -jēk- *sometimes* ¦ēd-\ *or* **ideo·log·ic** \-jik,-jēk\ *also* **idea·log·i·cal** \-dēə¦l-\ *adj* **1 :** of, relating to, or based on ideology ⟨~ conflict⟩ **2 :** relating to or concerned with ideas ⟨an ~ application of a theory⟩ **3 :** symbolically suggestive of an idea or mood ⟨~ drama⟩ — **ideo·log·i·cal·ly** \-jək(ə)lē, -jēk-, -li\ *adv*

**ide·ol·o·gist** \,īdē'äləjəst, ,id- *sometimes* ,ēd-\ *n* -S [F *idéologiste*, fr. *idéologie* + *-iste* -ist] **1 a :** a specialist in the science of ideas **:** a student of the origin and nature of ideas **b :** an advocate or adherent of a particular system or doctrine of ideology **2 :** IDEOLOGUE 1

**ide·ol·o·gize** \-,jīz\ *vt* -ED/-ING/-S [*ideology* + *-ize*] **1 :** to interpret or formulate ideologically ⟨the dogged tendency of our time to ~ all things into grayness —Lionel Trilling⟩ **2 :** to cause (as an individual or a social institution) to accept or conform to a particular ideology ⟨planners who attempt to alter and ~ the fundamental character of our culture⟩

**ideo·logue** *also* **idea·logue** \'īdēə,lóg, 'id-, ī'dē- also -läg\ *n* -S [F *idéologue*, back-formation fr. *idéologie*] **1 :** THEORIST, DREAMER, VISIONARY **2 :** IDEOLOGIST 1b

**ide·ol·o·gy** \,īdē'äləjē, ,id-, -ji *sometimes* ,ēd-\ *also* **ide·al·o·gy** \",-ē'al-\ *n* -ES [F *idéologie*, fr. *idéo-* ideo- + *-logie* -logy] **1 a :** a branch of knowledge concerned with the origin and nature of ideas **b :** a theory in philosophy advocated by Destutt de Tracy (1754–1836): ideas originate from sensation **2 :** visionary speculation **:** idle theorizing; *often* **:** an impractical theory or system of theories **3 a :** a systematic scheme or coordinated body of ideas or concepts esp. about human life or culture **b :** a manner or the content of thinking characteristic of an individual, group, or culture ⟨bourgeois ~⟩ ⟨medical, legal, and other professional *ideologies*⟩ ⟨kept his ~ inviolate⟩ **c** (1) **:** the integrated assertions, theories, and aims that constitute a sociopolitical program ⟨a national ~ that was not static but altered with altering circumstances⟩ (2) **:** an extremist sociopolitical program or philosophy constructed wholly or in part on factitious or hypothetical ideational bases

**ideo·motor** \,īdēə, ¦id- +-\ *adj* [ISV *ideo-* + *motor*] **1** *of movement or action* **:** resulting from the impingement of ideas on the system **:** not reflex **2 :** of, relating to, or concerned with ideomotor activity ⟨~ theory⟩ ⟨~ suggestions⟩

**ideo·pho·bia** \ˌ==='fōbēə\ *n* [NL, fr. *ideo-* + *-phobia*] **:** fear or distrust of ideas or of reason

**ideo·plas·tic** \ˌ===¦plastik\ *adj* [ISV *ideo-* + *-plastic*; orig. formed as F *idéoplastique*] **1 :** modified by mental activity ⟨~ factors in digestion⟩ **2** *of an art form* **:** rendered symbolic or conventional through the mental remodeling of natural subjects — **ideo·plas·tic·i·ty** \-,pla¦stisəd·ē\ *n*

**ideo·type** \'===+,-\ *n* [*ideo-* + *type*] **:** a specimen collected from other than the type locality but identified as belonging to a particular taxon by the author of that taxon

**ides** \'īdz\ *n pl but sing or pl in constr* [MF, fr. L *idus*, prob. of non-IE origin] **:** the 15th day of March, May, July, or October or the 13th day of any other month in the ancient Roman calendar; *broadly* **:** this day and the seven days preceding it counting backward toward the nones — compare CALENDS

**-ides** *pl of* -IDE

**ide·sia** \ī'dēzh(ē)ə\ *n* [NL, fr. Evert I. *Ides*, 17th cent. German-born Dutch statesman and traveler in the service of Russia + NL *-ia*] **1** *cap* **:** a monotypic genus (family Flacourtiaceae) comprising a single Asiatic tree (*I. polycarpa*) that has a broad spreading head, large alternate long-petioled cordate leaves, and large terminal panicles of apetalous flowers followed by fleshy orange red berries and that is widely grown as an ornamental where the climate is relatively mild **2** -S **:** any plant of the genus *Idesia*

**id·gah** \'id(,)gä\ *n* -S [Per *ʽīdgāh*, fr. *ʽīd* feast (fr. Ar) + Per *-gāh* place, fr. MPer *gās*, fr. OPer *gāthu-*; akin to Av *gātavplace*, Skt *gātu* going, way, course] **:** a place set apart for public prayers on the two chief Muslim feasts

**-idia** *pl of* -IDIUM

**idi·acan·thus** \,idēə'kan(t)thəs\ *n*, *cap* [NL, fr. Gk *idios* + NL *-acanthus*] **:** a genus (the type of the family Idiacanthidae) of black deep-sea stomiatoid fishes that include a number of typical dragonfish

**id·i·asm** \'idē,azəm\ *n* -S [Gk *idiasmos* peculiarity, fr. *idiazein* to be peculiar, fr. *idios* one's own, private, peculiar — more at IDIOT] **:** an individual mannerism (as in literary style)

**id·ic** \'idik\ *adj* [*¹id* + *-ic*] **:** relating to or consisting of ids ⟨~ constituents of germ plasm⟩

**idig·bo** \ə'dig,bō, 'ēdig,bō\ *n* -S [native name in Africa] **1 :** an African tree (*Terminalia worensis*) valued for its light yellow wood **2 :** the wood of the idigbo

**-i·din** \ədən, əd°n\ *or* **-i·dine** \ə,dēn, ədən, əd°n\ *n suffix* -S [ISV *¹-ide* + *-in*, *-ine*] **:** chemical compound related in origin or structure to another compound: as **a** *usu -idin* **:** aglycon of a glycoside ⟨pelargon*idin* from pelargonin⟩ **b** *usu -idine* **:** completely hydrogenated form of a cyclic base ⟨pyrrol*idine* from pyrrole⟩ ⟨thiazol*idine* from thiazole⟩ **c** *usu -idine* **:** base obtained otherwise than by hydrogenation ⟨tolu*idine* or tol*idine* from toluene⟩ ⟨guan*idine* from guanine⟩

**idio-** *comb form* [Gk, fr. *idios* — more at IDIOT] **1 :** one's own **:** personal **:** separate **:** distinct ⟨*idio*type⟩ ⟨*idio*syncrasy⟩ **2 :** self-produced **:** arising within ⟨*idio*lysin⟩ ⟨*idio*reflex⟩ ⟨*idio*pathic⟩ ⟨*idio*ventricular rhythm⟩

**id·io·adaptation** \¦idē(,)ō\ *n* [*idio-* + *adaptation*] **:** evolutionary modification involving progressive specialization that results in more perfect adaptation of an organism to a particular environment with corresponding loss of adaptability to new or changing environment

**id·io·an·drospo·rous** \¦idē(,)ō¦andrə¦spōrəs, -¦an¦drǎspər-\ *adj* [*idio-* + *androspore* + *-ous*] *of an alga* **:** bearing androspores and oogonia on separate filaments — compare GYNANDROSPOROUS

**id·io·biology** \,idē(,)ō+\ *n* [ISV *idio-* + *biology*; orig. formed as G *idiobiologie*] **:** a branch of biology concerned with the study of organisms as individuals

**id·io·blap·sis** \,idēō'blapsəs\ *n* -ES [NL, fr. *idio-* + Gk *blapsis* damage, fr. *blaptein* to damage] **:** a hypothetical familial allergy presumably manifested in alteration of pulse rate following the ingestion of an allergenic food

**id·io·blap·tic** \ˌ==='tik\ *adj* [*idio-* + Gk *blaptikos* hurtful, fr. *blaptein* + *-ikos* -ic] **:** of or relating to idioblapsis

**id·io·blast** \'idēə,blast\ *n* [ISV *idio-* + *-blast*; orig. formed in G] **1 a :** an isolated plant cell (as a sclereid) that differs markedly in form, contents, or wall structure from neighboring cells **b :** a hypothetical structural unit of a living cell — compare BIOPHORE **2 :** a crystal in a metamorphic rock that is bounded by its own faces, looks like a phenocryst, but is of later growth — **id·io·blas·tic** \¦idēə¦blastik\ *adj*

**id·io·chromatic** \¦idē(,)ō+\ *adj* [ISV *idio-* + *chromatic*] **:** colored inherently and characteristically **:** having a distinctive and constant coloration ⟨copper sulfate is an ~ substance⟩ — used esp. of minerals; compare ALLOCHROMATIC 1

**id·io·chromatin** \"+\ *n* [ISV *idio-* + *chromatin*] **:** the part of the chromatin of a cell that is thought to transmit genes and function in reproduction — compare TROPHOCHROMATIN

**id·io·chromosome** \"+\ *n* [ISV *idio-* + *chromosome*] **:** SEX CHROMOSOME

**id·i·oc·ra·sy** \,idē'äkrəsē\ *n* -ES [LGk *idiokrasia*, prob. MS var. of Gk *idiosynkrasia* idiosyncrasy — more at IDIOSYNCRASY] **:** peculiarity of constitution **:** IDIOSYNCRASY

**id·i·o·crat·ic** \¦idēə¦krad·ik\ *or* **id·i·o·crat·i·cal** \d·əkəl *also* |ək\ *adj* [fr. *idiocrasy*, after such pairs as E *apostasy: apostatic, apostatical*] **:** IDIOSYNCRATIC — **id·i·o·crat·i·cal·ly** \-d·ək(ə)lē\ *adv*

**id·i·o·cy** \'idēəsē, -si\ *n* -ES [fr. *idiot*, after such pairs as E *accurate: accuracy*] **1 :** extreme mental deficiency commonly due to incomplete or abnormal development of the brain and usu. congenital or due to arrest of development following disease or injury in early childhood **2 a :** something notably stupid or foolish ⟨the usual bureaucratic *idiocies* —W.M. Hitzig⟩ **b :** something so light, frothy, and trivial that it is usu. considered silly ⟨amused by his amiable *idiocies*⟩

**id·io·cy·cloph·a·nous** \¦idē(,)ō¦sī¦kläfənəs\ *adj* [ISV *idio-* + *cycl-* + *phan-* (fr. Gk *phainein* to show) + *-ous* — more at FANCY] **:** IDIOPHANOUS

**id·io·genesis** \¦idēə+\ *n* [NL, fr. *idio-* + *genesis*] **:** spontaneous origin (as of disease)

**id·io·genetic** \"+\ *adj* [*idio-* + *-genetic*] **:** originating spontaneously ⟨an apparently ~ disorder⟩

**id·io·glos·sia** \,idēə'gläsēə, -lós-\ *n* -S [NL, fr. *idio-* + *-glossia*] **:** a condition in which the affected person pronounces his words so badly as to seem to speak a language of his own

**id·io·gram** \'idēə,gram\ *n* [ISV *idio-* + *-gram*] **:** a diagrammatic representation of a chromosome complement or karyotype

**id·io·graph** \-,graf, -rȧf\ *n* [LGk *idiographon* autograph, fr. neut. of Gk *idiographos* specially written, in the author's handwriting, fr. *idio-* + *-graphos* (fr. *graphein* to write) — more at CARVE] **:** a mark or signature peculiar to an individual

**id·io·graph·ic** \ˌ===¦grafik\ *adj* [ISV *idio-* + *-graphic*; orig. formed as G *idiographisch*] **:** relating to, involving, or dealing with the concrete, individual, or unique ⟨considering history an ~ discipline⟩ — contrasted with *nomothetic*

**id·io·kinetic** \¦idē(,)ō+\ *adj* [*idio-* + *kinetic*] *of movement* **:** induced by activity of the pyramidal tracts of the brain

**id·io·lalia** \,idēō'lālēə, -lal-\ *n* -S [NL, fr. *idio-* + *-lalia*] **:** IDIOGLOSSIA

**id·i·o·lect** \'idēə,lekt\ *n* -S [*idio-* + *-lect* (as in *dialect*)] **:** the language or speech pattern of one individual at a particular period of his life

**id·i·om** \'idēəm\ *n* -S [MF & LL; MF *idiome*, fr. LL *idioma*, fr. Gk *idiōma* peculiarity, peculiarity of style, idiom, fr. *idiousthai* to appropriate, fr. *idios* one's own, private, peculiar — more at IDIOT] **1 a :** the language proper or peculiar to a people or to a district, community, or class **:** TONGUE, DIALECT **b :** the syntactical, grammatical, or structural form peculiar to a language **:** the genius, habit, or cast of a language **2 :** an expression established in the usage of a language that is peculiar to itself either in grammatical construction (as *no, it wasn't me*) or in having a meaning that cannot be derived as a whole from the conjoined meanings of its elements (as *Monday week* for "the Monday a week after next Monday"; *many a* for "many taken distributively"; *had better* for "might better"; *how are you?* for "what is the state of your health or feelings?") **3 :** a style or form of artistic expression (as in painting, writing, composing) that is characteristic esp. of an individual, a period or movement, or a medium or instrument ⟨an interesting orchestral ~⟩ ⟨surrealist ~⟩ ⟨imagination has its specific hereditary ~s —George Santayana⟩ **syn** see LANGUAGE

**id·i·om·at·ic** \¦idēə¦mad·|ik, -at|, |ēk\ *also* **id·i·om·at·i·cal** \|əkəl, |ēk-\ *adj* [LGk *idiōmatikos* peculiar, characteristic, fr. Gk *idiōmat-, idiōma* + *-ikos* -ic, -ical] **1 :** of, relating to, or conforming to idiom ⟨~ fluency in speech and writing⟩ ⟨a highly ~ concerto⟩ ⟨~ English⟩ **2 :** peculiar to a particular group or individual **:** INDIVIDUAL ⟨one person acting in his ~ purposeful fashion to evoke a response from another —John Dewey⟩ ⟨grows to value the physical sex life per se rather than as a symbol of ~ relationships —F.S.Chapin⟩ ⟨how vigorous and ~ was the native life —John Buchan⟩ — **id·i·o·mat·i·cal·ly** \|ək(ə)lē, |ēk-, -li\ *adv* — **id·i·o·mat·ic·ness** \|iknəs, |ēk-\ *n* -ES

**id·i·om·e·ter** \,idē'ämədə(r)\ *n* [*idio-* + *-meter*] **:** an instrument for ascertaining the personal equation of an astronomical observer

**idiom neutral** *n*, *usu cap I&N* **:** an artificial language partially derived from Volapük and having a vocabulary consistently selected on the basis of the maximum internationality of the roots

**id·i·om·og·ra·phy** \,idēə'mägrəfē\ *n* -ES [F *idiomographie*, fr. *idiome* idiom + *-o-* + *-graphie* -graphy — more at IDIOM] **:** the description of idiom

**id·i·om·ol·o·gy** \-'mäləjē\ *n* -ES [*idiom* + *-o-* + *-logy*] **:** the study of idiom

**id·io·morph** \'idēə,mórf\ *n* -S [*idio-* + *-morph*] **:** a pattern of repeated letters in cryptography ⟨the ~ PXLXAP fits the probable word STATES⟩ — compare ISOMORPH c

**id·io·mor·phic** \ˌ==¦mórfik\ *adj* [Gk *idiomorphos* + E *-ic*] **1 :** having the proper form or shape **:** AUTOMORPHIC — used of minerals the growth of whose crystals in a rock has not been interfered with; contrasted with *allotriomorphic* **2 :** of, relating to, or being an idiomorph — **id·io·mor·phi·cal·ly** \-fək(ə)lē\ *adv*

**id·io·mor·phism** \,==='fizəm\ *n* -S [*idiomorphic* + *-ism*] **:** the condition of being idiomorphic (sense 1)

**id·io·mor·phous** \¦==¦=fəs\ *adj* [Gk *idiomorphos* having a form of its own, fr. *idio-* + *-morphos* -morphous] **:** IDIOMORPHIC 1

**id·io·muscular** \¦idē(,)ō+\ *adj* [ISV *idio-* + *muscular*] **:** relating to muscular tissue exclusively; *esp* **:** originating in muscle ⟨~ contraction⟩

**-idion** — see -IDIUM

**id·i·o·path·ic** \¦idēə¦pathik\ *adj* **1 :** peculiar to the individual **:** INNATE ⟨~ sensitivity⟩ **2 :** arising spontaneously or from an obscure or unknown cause **:** PRIMARY ⟨~ epilepsy⟩ — **id·i·o·path·i·cal·ly** \-thək(ə)lē\ *adv*

**id·i·op·a·thy** \,idē'äpəthē\ *n* -ES [Gk *idiopatheia*, fr. *idio-* + *-patheia* -pathy] **:** an idiopathic anomaly or disease

**id·i·oph·a·nous** \,idē¦äfənəs\ *adj* [*idio-* + *phan-* (fr. Gk *phainein* to show) + *-ous* — more at FANCY] *of a crystal* **:** exhibiting interference figures without the aid of a polariscope

**id·io·phone** \'idēə,fōn\ *n* [G *idiophon*, fr. *idio-* + *-phon* -phone] **:** a musical instrument (as a bell, gong, rattle) the source of whose sound is the vibration of its elastic constituent material unmodified by any special tension (as in a drum) — **id·io·phon·ic** \ˌ===¦fänik\ *adj*

**id·io·plasm** \'idēə,plazəm\ *n* [ISV *idio-* + *-plasm*; orig. formed as G *idioplasma*] **:** the part of protoplasm held to function specif. in transmission of hereditary properties and commonly equated with chromatin — opposed to *trophoplasm* — **id·io·plas·mat·ic** \ˌ===¦plaz¦mad·ik\ *or* **id·io·plas·mic** \-zmik\ *adj*

**id·io·retinal** \¦idē(,)ō+\ *adj* [*idio-* + *retinal*] **:** peculiar to the retina; *specif* **:** originating subjectively in the retina ⟨~ light⟩

**id·i·or·rhythmic** \¦idēə+\ *adj* [LGk *idiorrhythmos* (fr. Gk *idio-* + *rhythmos* measured motion, measure, proportion) + E *-ic* — more at RHYTHM] *Eastern Church* **:** SELF-REGULATING — used of (1) monks that live separately, hold property, work individually in supporting themselves, and though members of a monastery supervised by an elected council are not under direct daily supervision or (2) of monasteries so organized

**id·i·or·rhyth·mism** \,==='rith,mizəm\ *n* -S **:** a system of monastic self-regulation in the Eastern Church — compare IDIORRHYTHMIC

**id·i·o·se·pi·idae** \,idē(,)ōsə'pīə,dē\ *n pl*, *cap* [NL, fr. *Idiosepion* or *Idiosepius*, type genus (fr. *idio-* + Gk *sēpion* cuttlefish bone) + *-idae* — more at SEPIA] **:** a family of squids that includes a single tiny squid (*Idiosepius pygmaeus* or *Idiosepion pygmaeum*) of the Indian ocean which lacks an internal shell and is considerably less than an inch in length

**id·io·some** \'idēə,sōm\ *n* -S [*idio-* + *-some*] **:** any of several specialized cellular organelles: as **a :** IDIOBLAST 1b **b :** ACROSOME **c :** an area of modified cytoplasm surrounding a centrosome **d :** SEX CHROMOSOME

**id·i·o·syn·cra·sy** *also* **id·i·o·syn·cra·cy** \,idēə'siŋkrəsē, -dēō-, -sink-, -rəsi\ *n* [Gk *idiosynkrasia*, fr. *idio-* + *-synkrasia* (fr. *synkrasis* action of commingling or blending — fr. *synkerannynai* to commingle, blend, fr. *syn-* + *kerannynai* to mingle, mix — + *-ia* -y) — more at CRATER] **1 :** characteristic peculiarity of habit or structure **2 a :** a peculiarity of physical or mental constitution or temperament **:** a characteristic distinguishing an individual; *broadly* **:** ECCENTRICITY **b :** individual hypersensitiveness (as to a drug or food) ⟨anemia accompanying the use of a sulfa drug is usually considered to be due to ~⟩

**¹id·i·o·syn·crat·ic** \ˌidēōˌsinˈkradˌik, -dē(ˌ)ōˈs-, -siŋˈ-, -at|, |ēk\ *adj* [fr. *idiosyncrasy*, after such pairs as E *apostasy*: *apostatic*] **1 :** peculiar to the individual ⟨an ~ gesture⟩ : of, relating to, or resulting from idiosyncrasy ⟨~ response to a drug⟩ ⟨~ disease⟩ **2 :** marked by idiosyncrasy : ECCENTRIC ⟨is so ~ in his literary judgments that it is impossible to think of him as a sound critic —*Saturday Rev.*⟩ — **id·i·o·syn·crat·i·cal·ly** \|ək(ə)lē, |ēk-, -li\ *adv*

**²idiosyncratic** \"\ *n* -s : one that is idiosyncratic

**¹id·i·ot** \ˈidēət, *chiefly dial* ˈijə| *or* ˈējə|; *usu* |d·+V\ *n* -s [ME, fr. MF *idiote*, fr. L *idiota*, fr. Gk *idiōtēs* person in a private station, person without professional knowledge, ignorant person, common man, fr. *idios* one's own, private, peculiar; akin to L *sed*, *se* without, *sui* of oneself — more at SUICIDE] **1** *obs* : an ignorant or unschooled person : a simple unlearned person : CLOWN 1 **2 :** a person afflicted with idiocy; *specif* : a feebleminded person that has a mental age not exceeding two years and accordingly requires complete custodial care **3 a :** a silly simple person : SIMPLETON, BLOCKHEAD ⟨he means well but he is such an ~⟩ **b :** a person who fails to exhibit normal or usual sense, discrimination, or judgment esp. at a particular time or in respect to a particular subject ⟨I don't know why I was such an ~⟩ ⟨a perfect ~ about budgeting⟩ **c :** a professional fool : JESTER **4** [Gk *idiōtēs*] *obs* : a person in private station or one not schooled in a trade or profession — *usu* **syn** see FOOL

**²idiot** \"\ *adj* [ME, fr. *idiot* (n.)] **1 :** IDIOTIC **2 :** fit for, typical of, or suitable to idiots : being such as an idiot might be expected to have, engage in, display ⟨~ terror⟩ ⟨those ~ hats⟩ ⟨such ~ war⟩

**idiot board** *n* : a device (as a projection of a script) used to prompt a television speaker and placed out of range of the camera

**id·i·ot·cy** \ˈidēətsē, -si\ *n* -ES [¹*idiot* + -*cy*] **1 :** IDIOCY 1 **2 :** something worthy of an idiot : utter folly

**id·i·ot·ic** \ˌidēˈäd·ik, -ät|, |ēk\ *adj* [LL *idioticus* unskilled, rude, simple, fr. Gk *idiōtikos* private, unprofessional, ordinary, fr. *idiōtēs* + -*ikos* -ic] **1 :** relating to or like an idiot **2 :** characterized by idiocy : FOOLISH, SENSELESS

**id·i·ot·i·cal** \|əkəl, |ēk-\ *adj* [LL *idioticus* + E -*al*] **1** *obs* : lacking education : IGNORANT, UNSCHOOLED **2 :** IDIOTIC 2

**id·i·ot·i·cal·ly** \|ək(ə)lē, |ēk-, -li\ *adv* **1 :** like an idiot : in an idiot or idiotic way ⟨behaved ~⟩ **2 :** ABSURDLY, RIDICULOUSLY ⟨~ cheap⟩

**id·i·ot·i·cal·ness** \-kəlnəs\ *n* -ES : extreme stupidity or foolishness

**id·i·ot·ism** \ˈidēəd·ˌizəm, -ēəˌti-\ *n* -s [in sense 1, fr. MF *idiotisme*, fr. L *idiotismus* common or vulgar manner of speaking, fr. Gk *idiōtismos* way of a common man, manner of speech of a common man, fr. *idiōtēs* common man + -*ismos* -ism; in sense 2, fr. ¹*idiot* + -*ism* — more at IDIOT] **1 a** *obs* : IDIOM 1 **b :** IDIOM 2 **2** *archaic* : IDIOCY

**id·i·ot·ize** \-əd·ˌīz, -əˌtīz\ *vt* -ED/-ING/-s [¹*idiot* + -*ize*] : to make a fool of : cause to become or behave like an idiot

**id·i·ot·ry** \-ətrē, -ri\ *n* -ES [¹*idiot* + -*ry*] *chiefly Scots law* : IDIOCY

**idiot savant** *pronunc at* IDIOT + *pronunc at* SAVANT, *or* ēˌdyōsəˈväⁿ\ *n, pl* **idiots savants** \-n(t)s, -äⁿ(z)\ [F, lit., skilled idiot] : a person that is in general mentally defective but that displays unusual aptitude or brilliance in some special field

**idiot's delight** *n* : any of various solitaire card games

**idiot sheet** *also* **idiot card** *n* : a large card bearing usu. hand-lettered words or phrases for prompting a speaker or actor during a telecast — compare IDIOT BOARD

**id·i·o·zome** \ˈidēəˌzōm\ *n* -s [ISV *idio-* + Gk *zōma* girdle — more at ZONE] : ACROSOME

**id·i·tol** \ˈidəˌtȯl, -tōl\ *n* -s [ISV *idose* + -*itol*] : a sweet crystalline hexahydroxy alcohol $C_6H_{14}O_6C_6H_8(OH)_6$ obtained by a reduction of idose or sorbose

**-id·i·um** \ˈidēəm\ *also* **-id·i·on** \-ēˌän, -ēən\ *n suffix, pl* **-idi·ums** \-ēəmz\ *or* **-id·ia** \-ēə\ *also* **idions** [NL, fr. Gk -*idion*, dim. suffix] : small one : lesser one ⟨anther*idium*⟩ ⟨chrom*idium*⟩

**¹idle** \ˈīdᵊl\ *adj* **idler** \-d(ᵊ)lə(r)\ **idlest** \-d(ᵊ)ləst\ [ME *idel* (also, empty, void), fr. OE *īdel*; akin to OFris *īdel* empty, worthless, vain, OS *īdal*, OHG *ītal*] **1 a :** lacking worth or basis : leading to nothing : GROUNDLESS, USELESS ⟨~ theorizing⟩ ⟨an ~ rumor⟩ ⟨it would be ~ to argue further⟩ **b :** having no particular reason for existing or occurring : light, casual, and superficial ⟨~ chatter⟩ ⟨took an ~ glance about⟩ ⟨asked out of ~ curiosity⟩ **2 a :** not occupied or employed: as (1) *of a person* : having no employment or business : UNEMPLOYED ⟨closed factories and ~ workmen⟩ (2) *of a period of time* : marked by want of activity esp. of a useful or constructive nature : WASTED ⟨passed his ~ days in sloth⟩ ⟨that ~ hour just before dusk⟩ (3) *of a thing* : not turned to normal or appropriate use ⟨~ tenements⟩ : not called into active service ⟨~ capital⟩ **b** (1) : given to rest or ease : seeking to avoid labor or employment : TRIFLING, LAZY, SLOTHFUL ⟨a careless ~ worker⟩ ⟨~ boys playing in the streets⟩ (2) : having no regular occupation or evident lawful means of support ⟨answer to the charge of being an ~ person⟩ (3) : IDLING ⟨an engine running at fast ~ speed⟩ **3** *now dial Eng* **a :** LIGHTHEADED, FOOLISH **b :** MISCHIEVOUS **syn** see INACTIVE, VAIN

**²idle** \"\ *vb* **idled; idled; idling** \-d(ᵊ)liŋ\ **idles** *vi* **1 :** to lose or spend time in idleness ⟨*idling* in the garden⟩; *esp* : to move idly ⟨*idled* along the stream bank⟩ **2 :** to run disconnected or unloaded so that power is not used for external or useful work — used esp. of a motor, engine, pulley wheel ~ *vt* **1 :** to spend (as time) in idleness — often used with *away* ⟨*idling* away a pleasant summer day⟩ **2 :** to make or leave idle ⟨cutbacks in orders that *idled* thousands of workers⟩ ⟨the common cold ~s more people than any other disease⟩ **3 :** to cause to idle ⟨~ a motor⟩

**³idle** \"\ *n* -s [²*idle*] : an act or instance or the state of idling ⟨an engine running at ~⟩

**idleby** *n* -s [¹*idle* + -*by* (as in the name *Crosby*)] *obs* : IDLER

**idleheaded** \ˈ=ˌ=ˈ=\ *adj* **1 :** FOOLISH, STUPID, SILLY **2** *obs* : out of one's head : DELIRIOUS, CRAZY

**idle·hood** \ˈīdᵊlˌhu̇d\ *n, archaic* : IDLENESS

**idle·man** \-ˌmən\ *n, pl* **idlemen** *archaic* : a man of substance who does not need to work for a living

**idle·ness** *n* -ES [ME *idelnesse* (also, vanity) fr. OE *īdelnes*, fr. *īdel* + -*nes* -ness] : the quality or state of being idle (as through lack of worth, occupation, employment, industry) ⟨the ~ of our search⟩ ⟨increasing ~ in the auto industry⟩ ⟨a person of unbelievable ~⟩; *also* : an instance of such idleness ⟨our yesterday's ~ forgotten⟩

**idler** \ˈīd(ᵊ)lə(r)\ *n* -s **1 :** one that idles or is unoccupied : one that spends his time in inaction : a lazy person **2 a :** IDLER GEAR **b :** IDLER PULLEY **c :** IDLER WHEEL **3 :** a member of a ship's crew that has constant day duties and keeps no night watch **4 :** an empty railroad car placed between two cars that support a load; *also* : an empty flatcar placed at either end of a loaded flatcar to take the overhang but not the weight of a projecting load **5 :** a member of a fish-dressing gang who washes gutted fish or a wharf laborer who carries fish and supplies to the cleaners and removes scrap

**idler gear** *n* **1 :** a gear placed between a driving and a driven gear to transfer motion without change of direction or gear ratio **2 :** a gear for support or guidance instead of power transmission

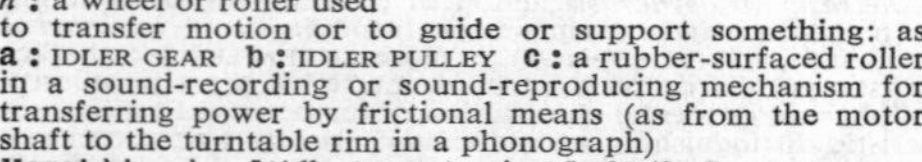

idler gear

**idler pulley** *n* : a guide or tightening pulley for a belt or chain (as in a conveyor system)

**idler wheel** *also* **idle wheel** *n* : a wheel or roller used to transfer motion or to guide or support something: as **a :** IDLER GEAR **b :** IDLER PULLEY **c :** a rubber-surfaced roller in a sound-recording or sound-reproducing mechanism for transferring power by frictional means (as from the motor shaft to the turntable rim in a phonograph)

**idleset** \ˈ=ˌ=\ *n* [¹*idle* + *set* (setting)] *chiefly Scot* : IDLENESS

**idlesse** \ˈīdləs\ *n* -s [¹*idle* + ME -*esse* -ess] : IDLENESS

**idling** *n* -s : the act of one that idles

**idly** \ˈīd(ᵊ)lē, -li\ *adv* [ME *idilly*, fr. OE *īdellīce*, fr. *īdel* idle + -*līce* -ly — more at IDLE] : in an idle manner: as **a :** INEFFECTUALLY, VAINLY **b :** LAZILY, INDOLENTLY; *broadly* : without especial interest or effort : CASUALLY **c** *obs* : FOOLISHLY, INCOHERENTLY

**ido** \ˈē(ˌ)dō\ *n* -s *cap* [Esperanto, offspring, fr. Gk -*idēs*, patronymic suffix] : an international artificial language produced by modification of Esperanto

**ido-** — see ID-

**ido·crase** \ˈīdōˌkrās, ˈid-, -āz\ *n* -s [F, fr. Gk *eidos* form, shape + *krasis* mixture fr. *kerannynai* to mix — more at IDYLL, CRATER] : a mineral $Ca_{10}(Mg,Fe)_2Al_4Si_9O_{34}(OH)_4$ that is a complex silicate of calcium, magnesium, iron, and aluminum — called also *vesuvianite*

**idol** \ˈīdᵊl\ *n* -s *often attrib* [ME *idel*, *idol*, fr. OF *idele*, *idle*, *idole*, fr. LL *idolum*, fr. Gk *eidōlon* phantom, image, image of a god; akin to Gk *eidos* shape, form — more at WISE] **1 a :** an image of a divinity : a representation or symbol of a deity or any other being or thing made or used as an object of worship; *broadly* : a false god : a heathen deity **b :** an image (as of a saint) used in Christian worship **2 a :** an appearance, aspect, or likeness of something ⟨sense perception is explained, after the manner of Democritus, by ~s or images or thin filmlike forms, which emanate from the objects around us —Frank Thilly⟩ **b** *obs* : EFFIGY, STATUE **c** *obs* : PRETENDER, IMPOSTOR **3 :** a form or appearance visible but without substance : an incorporeal image or phantom **4 :** something or someone on which the affections are strongly and often excessively set : an object of passionate devotion : a person or thing greatly loved or adored **5 :** a false notion or conception : FALLACY, IDOLUM 2

**idol·a·ter** \īˈdäləd·ə(r), -ətə- *sometimes* əˈd-\ *n* -s [alter. (influenced by MF *idolatre*) of ME *idolatrer*, *idolatrour*, fr. MF *idolatre* (fr. LL *idololatres*, fr. Gk *eidōlolatrēs*, fr. *eidōlon* idol + -*latrēs* -later) + ME -*er* or -*our* -or — more at IDOL] **1 :** a worshiper of idols : one that pays divine honors to an image, statue, or natural object as a representation of deity **2 :** a person that devotes intense or excessive and often blind affection, adoration, or admiration to an object not normally or usu. a subject of worship ⟨no indiscriminating ~ of Great Britain —B.J.Hendrick⟩

**idol·a·tress** \-lətrəs\ *n* -ES : a female idolater

**idol·a·tric** \(ˈ)īˈdälə(ˌ)trik, ¦īdəˈla·tr-\ *also* **ido·lat·ri·cal** \¦īdəˈla·trəkəl\ *adj* [ML *idolatricus*, fr. *idolatria* idolatry + L -*icus* -ic, -ical] : IDOLATROUS

**idol·a·trize** \īˈdäləˌtrīz *sometimes* əˈd-\ *vb* -ED/-ING/-s [*idolatry* + -*ize*] *vi* : to worship idols : pay idolatrous worship ~ *vt* : to make an idol of : IDOLIZE — **idol·a·triz·er** \-zə(r)\ *n* -s

**idol·a·trous** \(ˈ)īˈdälətrəs *sometimes* əˈd-\ *adj* : of or relating to idolatry: as **a :** being or resembling idolatry ⟨~ veneration for antiquity⟩ **b :** given to or practicing idolatry ⟨an ~ worshiper⟩ — **idol·a·trous·ly** *adv* — **idol·a·trous·ness** *n* -ES

**idol·a·try** \-ˈ=lə·trē, -ri\ *n* -ES [ME *idolatrie*, fr. OF, fr. ML *idolatria*, alter. of LL *idololatria*, fr. Gk *eidōlolatreia*, fr. *eidōlon* + *latreia* -latry] **1 a :** the worship of a physical object as a god; *esp* : such worship of a made image **b :** the giving of absolute religious devotion and ultimate trust to something that is not God **2 :** immoderate attachment or devotion to or veneration for something : respect or love that approaches that due a divine power **3** *obs* : an object of idolatry

**idol·ism** \ˈīdᵊlˌizəm\ *n* -s **1 a :** the worship of idols **b :** IDOLIZATION **2 :** IDOLUM 2

**idol·ist** \-əst\ *n* -s *archaic* : IDOLATER 1

**idol·i·za·tion** \ˌīdᵊləˈzāshən, -ˌlīˈz-\ *n* -s : the act of idolizing or state of being idolized ⟨the ~ to which they were subjected⟩

**idol·ize** \ˈīdᵊlˌīz\ *vb* -ED/-ING/-s *see -ize in Explan Notes vt* : to make an idol of : worship idolatrously; *broadly* : to love to excess : reverence to adoration ⟨~ gold⟩ ⟨boys at just the right age for *idolizing* military or sports heroes⟩ ~ *vi* : to practice idolatry — **idol·iz·er** \-zə(r)\ *n* -s

**idolo-** *also* **eidolo-** *comb form* [LL & Gk; LL *idolo-*, fr. Gk *eidōlo-*, fr. *eidōlon* — more at idol] : idol : image ⟨*idolo*cracy⟩ ⟨*idolo*mania⟩ ⟨*idolo*clastic⟩

**idololatry** *n* -ES [LL *idololatria* — more at IDOLATRY] *obs* : IDOLATRY

**idol shepherd** *n* : a counterfeit or worthless shepherd ⟨woe to the *idol shepherd* that leaveth the flock —Zech 11:17 (AV)⟩ — compare SHEPHERD 2

**idols of the cave** [trans. of NL *idola specus*] : idola due to individual peculiarities or prejudices — compare IDOLUM 2

**idols of the forum** *or* **idols of the market** [trans. of NL *idola fori*] : idola due to human factors (as language) — compare IDOLUM 2

**idols of the theater** [trans. of NL *idola theatri*] : idola due to traditional doctrines and methods — compare IDOLUM 2

**idols of the tribe** [trans. of NL *idola tribus*] : idola due to human nature itself or to the tribe or race of man (as anthropomorphic projections) — compare IDOLUM 2

**ido·lum** \īˈdōləm\ *n, pl* **ido·la** \-lə\ [in sense 1, fr. L & Gk; L, phantom, image, fr. Gk *eidōlon* phantom, image, idol; in sense 2, NL, fr. LL, idol, fr. Gk *eidōlon* — more at IDOL] **1 :** EIDOLON **2 :** a form of false thinking : FALLACY, IDOL 5; *specif* : one of the four varieties of fallacy distinguished by Francis Bacon in his *Novum Organum* (1620) — compare IDOLS OF THE CAVE, IDOLS OF THE FORUM, IDOLS OF THE THEATER, IDOLS OF THE TRIBE

**-i·done** \əˌdōn\ *n suffix* -s [ISV ¹-*ide* + -*one*] : oxo derivative of a compound whose name ends in -*idine* ⟨pyrrol*idone*⟩

**ido·ne·i·ty** \ˌīdəˈnēəd·ē\ *n* -ES [ML *idoneitas*, fr. L *idoneus* + -*itas* -ity] *archaic* : the quality or state of being idoneous : SUITABILITY, FITNESS

**ido·ne·ous** \(ˈ)īˈdōnēəs\ *adj* [L *idoneus*] *archaic* : FIT, APPROPRIATE, SUITABLE, PROPER

**idos** *pl of* IDO

**idose** \ˈīˌdōs, ˈiˌd- *also* -ōz\ *n* -s [ISV *id-* (fr. ISV *idonic* — *acid* — $C_6H_{12}O_7$, fr. L *idem* same + ISV *gulonic*) + -*ose* — more at IDENTITY] : a sugar $C_6H_{12}O_6$ epimeric with gulose and obtainable along with gulose by synthesis from xylose

**ido·tea** \īˈdōdēə\ [NL, irreg. fr. Gk *Eidothea*, a sea goddess] *syn of* IDOTHEA

**idothea** \īˈdōthēə, -däth-\ *n, cap* [NL, alter. of *Idotea*] : a large and widely distributed genus (the type of the family Idotheidae) of small marine cursorial isopods

**i doubt it** \ˈ=ˈ=\ *n, cap first I* : a card game in which each player tries to be first to empty his hand by laying down a number of cards and calling them the rank it is his turn to play (as two, ten, ace), discarding them if no one says "I doubt it" or if his claim is proved correct, but having to take up all discards on the table if it is shown that he included cards not called for

**IDR** *abbr* infantry drill regulations

**id·ri·a·lite** \ˈidrēəˌlīt\ *n* -s [F *idrialite*, fr. *Idria* (Idrija), Yugoslavia + F -*lite*] : a mineral prob. $C_{43}H_{32}O$ occurring as a crystalline hydrocarbon and melting at 205° C

**-i·dro·sis** \əˈdrōsəs\ *n comb form, pl* **-idro·ses** \-ōˌsēz\ [NL, fr. Gk -*idrōsis*, fr. *hidrōsis* act of sweating, fr. *hidroun* to sweat (fr. *hidrōs* sweat) + -*sis* — more at SWEAT] : a specified form of sweating ⟨chrom*idrosis*⟩ ⟨brom*idrosis*⟩ ⟨hyper*idrosis*⟩

**ids** *pl of* ID

**-ids** *pl of* -ID

**¹id·u·mae·an** *or* **id·u·me·an** \ˌidyəˈmēən, ˌijə-, ¦idə¦-\ *n* -s *usu cap* [*Idumaea* or *Idumea*, ancient region south of the Dead sea in Palestine (fr. L *Idumaea*, fr. Gk *Idoumaia*) + E -*an*] : EDOMITE

**²idumaean** \"\ *adj, usu cap* : of or relating to the Edomites : EDOMITIC

**idun·it** \(ˈ)īˈdənət\ *n* -s [alter. of *I done it*] : an autobiographical or confessional account usu. of a sensational character

**idyll** *or* **idyl** \ˈīdᵊl, *chiefly Brit* ˈid-\ *n* -s [L *idyllion*, *idyllium*, fr. Gk *eidyllion*, dim. of *eidos* shape, form, literary form; akin to Gk *idein* to see — more at WIT] **1 a :** a short descriptive poem usu. dealing with pastoral or rural life : ECLOGUE **b :** a simple descriptive work either in poetry or prose that deals with rustic life or pastoral scenes or suggests a mood of peace and contentment **c :** a narrative poem (as Tennyson's *Idylls of the King*) treating more or less fully an epic, romantic, or tragic theme **2 a :** a lighthearted carefree episode or one of such pastoral charm and simplicity as to be a fit subject for a poetic idyll **b :** a romantic or amorous interlude **3 :** a pastoral or romantic musical composition

**idyl·lic** \(ˈ)īˈdilik, -lēk *sometimes* əˈd-\ *adj* **1 :** of, relating to, or being an idyll **2 :** pleasing or picturesque in its natural simplicity ⟨romantic memories of a lost cause threw an ~ haze over earlier times —V.L.Parrington⟩ — **idyl·li·cal·ly** \-lək(ə)lē, -lēk-, -li\ *adv*

**idyll·ist** \ˈīdᵊləst, *chiefly Brit* ˈid-\ *n* -s : a composer of idylls : an idyllic writer

**idyl·li·um** \īˈdilēəm, əˈd-\ *also* **idyl·li·on** \-ēˌän, -ēən\ *n, pl* **idyl·lia** \-ēə\ [L — more at IDYLL] *archaic* : IDYLL

**ie** \ˈē(ˌ)ā\ *or* **ieie** \ˈē(ˌ)āˈē(ˌ)ā\ *n* -s [Hawaiian] **1 :** a Pacific Islands screw pine (*Freycinetia arborea*) having prop roots which yield a fiber **2 :** a mat or basket made of the fiber of the ie

**-ie** *also* **-y** *or* **-ey** \ē, i\ *n suffix, pl* **-ies** *or* **-eys** [ME (Sc) -*ie*] **1 a :** little one : dear little one ⟨bird*ie*⟩ ⟨boot*ie*⟩ ⟨Jean*ie*⟩ **b —** in names of articles of feminine apparel ⟨night*ie*⟩ ⟨pant*ie*⟩ **2 :** one belonging to : one having to do with ⟨book*ie*⟩ ⟨deck*ie*⟩ ⟨hack*ie*⟩ ⟨town*ie*⟩ **3 :** one of (such) a kind or quality ⟨bigg*ie*⟩ ⟨cut*ie*⟩ ⟨smart*ie*⟩ ⟨tough*ie*⟩ ⟨dark*ey*⟩

**ie** \ˌthad·ˈiz, -aˈtız; (ˈ)īˈē\ *abbr* [L *id est*] that is

**IE** *abbr or n* -s : industrial engineer

**IE** *abbr* **1** Indo-European **2** initial equipment **3** inside edge

**¹-ier** — see ²-ER

**²-ier** \ˌi(ə)r, ¦iə\ *n suffix* -s [MF — more at -EER] : person belonging to, connected with, or engaged in ⟨cash*ier*⟩ ⟨gondol*ier*⟩

**ier·oe** \ˌēəˈrōi\ *n* -s [ScGael *iarogh*] *Scot* : a great-grandchild

**¹if** \(ˌ)if, əf, f, *chiefly dial* (¦)ef\ *conj* [ME *yif*, *if*, fr. OE *gif*; akin to OFris *jef*, *ef* if, OS *ef* if, whether, OHG *ibu*, *oba* if, whether, Goth *ibai* whether, and perh. to L *is* he,that — more at ITERATE] **1 a :** in the event that : in case ⟨~ the train is on time, we'll meet him⟩ ⟨the news ~ false will prove distressing⟩ **b :** allowing, conceding, or granting that ⟨~ he actually did commit the crime⟩ **c :** SUPPOSING ⟨~ the money were right here on the table, you couldn't count it⟩ **d :** so long as : on condition that ⟨~ any part of the plan succeeds, you will get the credit⟩ ⟨~ you can keep your head when all about are losing theirs —Rudyard Kipling⟩ **2 :** WHETHER ⟨not knowing ~ the candidate had the necessary qualifications⟩ ⟨asked ~ the mail had come⟩ ⟨doubts ~ two and two make four —Matthew Prior⟩ **3 —** used to introduce an exclamation expressing a wish ⟨~ it would only rain⟩ **4 :** even though : although perhaps ⟨an interesting ~ untenable argument⟩ ⟨~ we are broke, still we got our money's worth⟩ — **if anything** *adv* : on the contrary even : perhaps even : possibly even ⟨despite reports, conditions had *if anything* worsened⟩ ⟨*if anything* you ought to apologize⟩

**²if** \ˈif\ *n* -s **1 :** CONDITION ⟨an argument with too many ~s in it⟩ : STIPULATION ⟨a contract weakened by ~s⟩ **2 :** SUPPOSITION ⟨a theory full of ~s⟩

**IF** *abbr* **1** in full **2** *often not cap* intermediate frequency **3** *often not cap* [L *ipse fecit*] he did it himself

**ifa·fa lily** \əˈfäfə-\ *n, usu cap I* [*ifafa* fr. native name in southern Africa] : a bulbous scapose southern African herb (*Cyrtanthus mackenii*) of the family Amaryllidaceae used as an ornamental and having linear leaves and drooping waxy whitish or yellowish flowers in a terminal umbel

**if-bet** \ˈ=ˌ=\ *n* : a bet placed with a bookmaker whereby a bettor has money on a horse in a subsequent race provided his horse in an earlier race wins

**if–clause** \ˈ=ˌ=\ *n* : a conditional clause — compare THEN-CLAUSE

**ife** \ˈēfə\ *n* -s [Pg, fr. native name in Angola] : a tropical African bowstring hemp (*Sansevieria cylindrica*) the cylindrical leaves of which yield a strong cordage fiber

**-if·er·ous** \ˈif(ə)rəs\ *adj comb form* [ME, fr. L -*ifer* (fr. -*i-* + -*fer*) & MF -*ifere* (fr. L -*ifer*) + ME -*ous* — more at -FER] : -FEROUS

**IFF** *abbr or n* -s [abbr. of *identification, friend or foe*] : the electronic equipment or the system used to identify approaching craft as friendly or hostile ⟨was identified by his *IFF*⟩

**if·fen** \ˈifən\ *conj* [by alter.] *dial* : IF

**if·fy** \ˈifē, -fi\ *adj, sometimes* -ER/-EST [¹*if* + -*y*] : abounding in contingencies or unknown qualities or conditions : PROVISORY ⟨an ~ question⟩ ⟨some very ~ political steps —*New Republic*⟩

**ifil** *var of* IPIL

**if money** \ˈ=ˌ=ˌ=\ *n, pl* **if moneys** *or* **if monies** : money from earnings on one race automatically applied to a subsequent race when an if-bet is placed

**-i·form** \əˌfȯrm, -ō(ə)m\ *adj comb form* [MF & L; MF -*iforme*, fr. L -*iformis*, fr. -*i-* + -*formis* -form] : -FORM

**i formation** *n, cap I* : an offensive football formation in which the quarterback, left and right halfbacks, and fullback line up behind the center and perpendicular to the line

**-i·for·mes** \əˈfȯrˌmēz, -ō(ə)-, -\ *n pl comb form* [NL, fr. L, masc. & fem. pl. of -*iformis* -iform] : ones having (such a) form — in taxonomic names of animals ⟨Anser*iformes*⟩

**IFR** *abbr* instrument flight rules

**ifrit** \ˈiˌfrēt, əˈf-\ *n* -s [Ar *'ifrīt* — more at AFREET] : AFREET

**ifs** *pl of* IF

**if–then** \ˈ=ˈ=\ *adj* : CONDITIONAL, HYPOTHETICAL ⟨an *if-then* proposition⟩

**ifu·gao** \ˌēfüˈgau̇\ *n, pl* **ifugao** *or* **ifugaos** *usu cap* [Sp, fr. a native name in the Philippines] **1 a :** a people inhabiting northern Luzon, Philippines **b :** a member of such people **2 :** the Austronesian language of the Ifugao people

**-i·fy** \əˌfī\ *vb suffix* -ED/-ING/-ES [ME -*ifien*, fr. OF -*ifier*, fr. L -*ificare*, fr. -*i-* + -*ficare* -fy] : -FY

**IG** *abbr* **1** inspector general **2** intendant-general

**iga·la** \ēˈgälə\ *also* **iga·ra** \-ärə\ *n, pl* **igala** *or* **igalas** *also* **igara** *or* **igaras** *usu cap* **1 :** a Yoruba-speaking people on the Niger at its confluence with the Benue in Nigeria **2 :** a member of the Igala people

**ig·bira** *or* **ig·ba·ra** \ˈigbərə\ *n, pl* **igbira** *or* **igbiras** *or* **igbara** *or* **igbaras** *usu cap* **1 :** a Negro people of the Benue river region **2 :** a member of the Igbira people

**igbo** *usu cap, var of* IBO

**ig·dyr** \igˈdi(ə)r\ *n, pl* **igdyr** *or* **igdyrs** *usu cap* **1 :** a nomadic Turkoman people in Turkmenistan by the Caspian sea **2 :** a member of the Igdyr people

**-ig·er·ous** \ˈij(ə)rəs\ *adj comb form* [L -*iger* (fr. -*i-* + -*ger* -gerous) + E -*ous*] : -GEROUS

**igi·gi** \ēˈjējē\ *n pl* [Assyr-Bab, fr. Sumerian] : a group of heavenly spirits under the god Anu in Babylonian religion

**i girder** *n, cap I* : I BEAM

**ig·loo** *also* **ig·lu** \ˈi(ˌ)glü\ *n* -s [Eskimo *iglu*, *igdlu* house] **1 a :** an Eskimo house usu. made of sod, wood, or stone when permanent or of snow blocks in the shape of a dome when built for temporary purposes **b :** a building shaped like a dome: as (1) : a magazine for storing munitions (2) : a hut for housing poultry **2 :** a cavity in the snow shaped like a dome and made by a seal over its breathing hole in the ice

igloo 1a

**ign** *abbr* **1** ignition **2** [L *ignotus*] unknown

**ignaro** *n* -s *often cap* [after *Ignaro*, character in *The Faerie Queene* by Edmund Spenser †1599 Eng. poet] *obs* : IGNORAMUS

**ig·na·tia** \igˈnāsh(ē)ə\ *n* -s [NL, fr. *ignatii* (specific epithet of *Strychnos ignatii*), after Saint *Ignatius*, 1st–2d cent. Christian prelate, bishop of Antioch] : the dried ripe seeds of the St.-Ignatius's-bean used like nux vomica

**¹ig·na·tian** \(ˈ)igˈnāsh(ē)ən\ *adj, usu cap* **1** [St. *Ignatius* of Loyola (Íñigo de Oñez y Loyola) †1556 Span. soldier & ecclesiastic + E -*an*] **a :** of or relating to St. Ignatius of Loyola **b :** of or relating to the Society of Jesus founded by St. Ignatius of Loyola **2** [St. *Ignatius*, bishop of Antioch + E -*an*] : of, relating to, or characteristic of St. Ignatius, bishop of Antioch

**²ignatian** \"\ *n* -s *usu cap* **1 :** a follower of St. Ignatius, bishop of Antioch **2 :** a follower of St. Ignatius of Loyola

**ig·na·tius bean** \igˈnāsh(ē)əs-\ *n, usu cap I* : SAINT-IGNATIUS'S-BEAN

**ig·ne·ous** \ˈignēəs\ *adj* [L *igneus*, fr. *ignis* fire; akin to Skt *agni* fire, Lith *ugnis*, OSlav *ognĭ*] **1 :** of, relating to, resembling, or suggestive of fire : containing fire : FIERY ⟨an ~ desert atmosphere⟩ **2 :** relating to, resulting from, or suggestive of the intrusion or extrusion of magma or the activity of volcanoes

**igneous fusion** *n* **:** fusion by heat alone unassisted by solution in the water of crystallization

**igneous rock** *n* **:** rock formed by solidification of a molten magma — compare PLUTONIC ROCK, VOLCANIC ROCK

**ig·ne·ri** \ig'nerē\ *or* **ine·ri** \ə'-\ *n, pl* **igneri** *or* **igneris** *or* **ineri** *or* **ineris** *usu cap* [F, fr. Carib] **1 a :** an aboriginal Arawakan people of the Lesser Antilles **b :** a member of such people **2 :** the language of the Igneri people

**ig·nes·cent** \(')ig¦nes³nt\ *adj* [L *ignescent-, ignescens,* pres. part. of *ignescere* to catch fire, fr. *ignis* fire] **1 :** capable of emitting sparks ⟨~ stone⟩ **2 :** INFLAMMATORY, VOLATILE ⟨an ~ personality⟩

**igni-** *comb form* [L, fr. *ignis* — more at IGNEOUS] **:** fire **:** burning ⟨*igni*ferous⟩ ⟨*igni*puncture⟩

**ig·nis fat·u·us** \¦ignəs'fachəwəs\ *n, pl* **ig·nes fat·ui** \-,nēz-'fachə,wī\ [ML, lit., foolish fire] **1 :** a light that sometimes appears in the night usu. over marshy ground and that is often attributable to the combustion of marsh gas — called also *jack-o'-lantern, will-o'-the wisp* **2 :** a deceptive or false goal **:** a misleading ideal ⟨the *ignis fatuus* of a world without wars⟩

**ig·nit·abil·i·ty** *also* **ig·nit·ibil·i·ty** \(,)ig,nīd·ə'biləd·ē\ *n* -ES **:** the quality or state of being ignitable ⟨the ~ of coal⟩

**ig·nit·able** *also* **ig·nit·ible** \(')ig¦nīd·əbəl\ *adj* **:** capable of being ignited

**¹ignite** *adj* [L *ignitus*] *obs* **:** intensely hot **:** FIERY, ARDENT

**²ig·nite** \ig'nīt, *usu* -īd·+V\ *vb* -ED/-ING/-S [L *ignitus,* past part. of *ignire* to ignite, fr. *ignis* fire] *vt* **1 :** to subject to fire or intense heat; *specif* **:** to render luminous by heat **2 a :** to set aflame ⟨~ paper⟩; *also* **:** KINDLE ⟨~ a fire⟩ **b :** to cause (a fuel mixture) to burn ⟨a rocket . . . ~*ed* by remote control —Milton Bracker⟩ **3 :** to heat up **:** EXCITE, INFLAME ⟨oppression that *ignited* the hatred of the people⟩ ~ *vi* **1 :** to catch fire **:** begin to burn ⟨slowly the fire *ignited*⟩ **2 :** to begin to glow **:** become luminescent

**ig·nit·er** *or* **ig·ni·tor** \-īd·ə(r)\ *n* -S **:** one that ignites: as **a :** a charge usu. of black gunpowder used to facilitate the ignition of a propelling charge and sometimes of a bursting charge **b :** a device for igniting fuel mixture (as in an internal-combustion engine, a jet engine, or a rocket engine) **c :** a separately energized electrode used for restriking the arc in an ignitron

**ig·ni·tion** \ig'nishən\ *n* -S **1 :** the act or action of igniting: as **a** (1) **:** subjection to the action of fire or intense heat **:** setting fire **:** KINDLING (2) **:** an analytical procedure of heating an inorganic substance with free access to air — compare INCINERATION **b :** the setting fire to a single point of the charge in the explosion of a charge of powder for ballistic purposes **2 :** the process or means of igniting a fuel mixture (as in an internal-combustion engine, a rocket engine, or an oil-burning furnace)

**ignition charge** *n* **:** a small charge usu. of black powder used to facilitate the ignition of the main charge

**ignition temperature** *or* **ignition point** *n* **:** the lowest temperature at which a combustible substance when heated (as in a bath of molten metal) takes fire in air and continues to burn — called also *autogenous ignition temperature;* compare FIRE POINT

**ignition tube** *n* **:** a heavy-walled test tube of hard glass for examining the behavior of heated substances

**ig·ni·tron** \ig'nī·,trän\ *n* -S [*igni-* + *-tron*] **:** a mercury-containing half-wave-rectifier tube in which the arc is restruck at the beginning of each cycle by a special electrode separately energized by an auxiliary circuit

**ig·no·bil·i·ty** \,ignō'biləd·ē\ *n* [L *ignobilitas,* fr. *ignobilis* + *-itas* -ity] **:** the quality or state of being ignoble

**ig·no·ble** \(')ig¦nōbəl\ *adj* [L *ignobilis,* fr. *i-* (fr. *in-* ¹in-) + *gnobilis, nobilis* noble — more at NOBLE] **1 :** of low birth or common origin **:** PLEBEIAN ⟨an ~ mob⟩ **2 :** displaying, motivated by, or characterized by baseness or meanness **:** DESPICABLE ⟨~ laws⟩ ⟨~ purposes⟩

**ignoble hawk** *n* **:** a short-winged hawk that rakes for its prey **:** ACCIPITER — used chiefly in the technical language of falconry

**ig·no·ble·ness** *n* **:** IGNOBILITY

**ig·no·bly** \-blē,-bli\ *adv* **:** in an ignoble manner

**ig·no·min·i·ous** \¦ignə¦minēəs\ *adj* [MF or L; MF *ignominieux,* fr. L *ignominiosus,* fr. *ignominia* + *-osus* -ous] **1 :** marked by, full of, or characterized by disgrace or shame **:** DISHONORABLE ⟨an ~ fate⟩ ⟨an ~ peace treaty⟩ **2 :** deserving of shame or infamy **:** DESPICABLE ⟨~ language⟩ **3 :** HUMILIATING, DEGRADING ⟨~ labor⟩

**ig·no·min·i·ous·ly** *adv* **:** in an ignominious manner

**ig·no·min·i·ous·ness** *n* -ES **:** the quality or state of being ignominious

**ig·nomi·ny** \'ignə,minē, -mini *also* -,mən- *or* əg'nämən-\ *n* -ES [MF or L; MF *ignominie,* fr. L *ignominia,* fr. *ig-* (as in *ignorare* to be ignorant of, ignore) + *nomin-, nomen* name + *-ia* -y — more at IGNORE, NAME] **1 :** deep personal disgrace ⟨the ~ of prison⟩ **2 :** disgraceful or dishonorable conduct, quality, or action ⟨~ of abandoning his comrades⟩ **syn** see DISHONOR

**ig·no·my** \'ignəmē\ *n* -ES [modif. of MF *ignominie* or L *ignominia*] *archaic* **:** IGNOMINY

**ig·nor·able** \(')ig¦nōrəbəl, -nȯr-\ *adj* **:** capable of being ignored

**ig·no·ra·mus** \,ignə'rāməs *sometimes* -ram-\ *n* -ES [NL, fr. L, we do not know, 1st pl. pres. indic. of *ignorare* to be ignorant of — more at IGNORE] **1 :** an endorsement formerly written on a bill of indictment by a grand jury when it considered the evidence insufficient to warrant the finding of a true bill; *also* **:** a bill returned with such an endorsement **2** [after *Ignoramus,* an ignorant lawyer in *Ignoramus* (1615), play by George Ruggle †1622, Eng. playwright] **:** an utterly ignorant person **:** DUNCE

**ignoramus waltz** *n* **:** an easy two-step waltz

**ig·no·rance** \'ignərən(t)s\ *n* -S [ME *ignoraunce,* fr. OF *ignorance,* fr. L *ignorantia,* fr. *ignorant-, ignorans* + *-ia* -y] **:** the quality or state of being ignorant ⟨~ of facts⟩

**ig·no·rant** \-nt\ *adj* [ME *ignoraunt,* fr. MF *ignorant,* fr. L *ignorant-, ignorans,* pres. part. of *ignorare* to be ignorant of, ignore — more at IGNORE] **1 a :** destitute of knowledge **:** UNINSTRUCTED, UNLEARNED ⟨an ~ society⟩ **b :** resulting from or exhibiting lack of perception, knowledge, or intelligence ⟨~ errors⟩ ⟨~ public spokesmen⟩ **2 a :** UNAWARE, UNINFORMED ⟨frauds palmed off on an ~ public⟩ — often used with *of* or *in* ⟨~ of the true significance of the news⟩ **b :** INNOCENT, GUILELESS ⟨~ hope⟩ **3 a :** UNCIVILIZED, BACKWARD, UNENLIGHTENED ⟨~ absolutism⟩ **b :** PRIMITIVE, CRUDE ⟨~ devices⟩

**syn** ILLITERATE, UNLETTERED, UNEDUCATED, UNTAUGHT, UNTUTORED, UNLEARNED, NESCIENT: IGNORANT indicates a lack of knowledge, either in general or of a particular point ⟨a population of uncivilized peasants, *ignorant,* illiterate, superstitious, cruel, and land hungry —G.B.Shaw⟩ ⟨the disputants on both sides were *ignorant* of the matter they were disputing about —Havelock Ellis⟩ ILLITERATE is now most commonly used in reference to inability to read and write or to gross unfamiliarity with the written language and the world of learning ⟨*illiterate* in the sense that they could not read or write, or . . . functionally *illiterate* in the sense that they were unable to understand what they read —I.L.Kandel⟩ ⟨as near *illiterate* as one can be who can read and write, her grammar and spelling being equally uncertain —H.S.Canby⟩ UNLETTERED stresses the fact of unfamiliarity with reading and writing or with written learning, often without any implication of condemnation ⟨even written in English, a paper like this would answer every purpose; for the *unlettered* natives, standing in great awe of the document, would not dare to molest us —Herman Melville⟩ ⟨*unlettered* provincials who knew their nets, or trades, or farms, but could hardly be expected to follow the Emperor's physician in his theories of Greek science —J.R. Perkins⟩ UNEDUCATED and UNTAUGHT simply indicate lack of formal schooling; the latter is sometimes used to describe natural spontaneity ⟨*untaught* graces⟩ UNTUTORED is sometimes used to refer to the unschooled condition of primitives ⟨the poor Indian, whose *untutored* mind —Alexander Pope⟩ ⟨taught so many flat lies that their false knowledge is more dangerous than the *untutored* natural wit of savages —G.B. Shaw⟩ UNLEARNED may suggest lack of much learning or ignorance of advanced subjects ⟨such generosity becomes, in effect, a cruel sentimentality, when it crowds the profession with thousands of unwanted persons, most of them relatively unskilled and *unlearned* —Robert Evett⟩ NESCIENT may apply to a deep, determined, or invincible ignorance of what is outside one's immediate ken ⟨most men are not intended to be any wiser than their cocks and bulls — duly scientific of their yard and pasture, peacefully *nescient* of all beyond —John Ruskin⟩

**ig·no·rant·ism** \-nt·,izəm, -n·,ti-\ *n* -S [F *ignorantisme,* fr. *ignorant* + *-isme* -ism] **:** OBSCURANTISM ⟨fascism . . . founding its educational policy on basic ~ —D.F.Fleming⟩

**ig·no·rant·ly** *adv* [ME *ignorauntly,* fr. *ignoraunt* + *-ly*] **:** in an ignorant manner

**ig·no·rant·ness** *n* -ES **:** the quality or state of being ignorant

**ig·no·ra·tio elen·chi** \,ignə'rād·ē,ōō'leŋ,kē\ *n* [NL, lit., ignorance of proof; trans. of Gk *elenchou agnoia*] **:** a fallacy in logic of supposing that the point at issue is proved or disproved by an argument which proves or disproves something not at issue; *also* **:** an argument based on such a fallacy

**ig·no·ra·tion** \,ignə'rāshən\ *n* -S [L *ignoration-, ignoratio,* fr. *ignoratus* (past part. of *ignorare*) + *-ion-, -io* -ion] **1 :** complete or utter ignorance ⟨the ~ of the true relation of each organism to its environment —A.N.Whitehead⟩ **2** [*ignore* + *-ation*] **:** an act or action of ignoring ⟨changed from complete ~ of my presence to an almost pathetic agreement with every word I said —H.J.Laski⟩

**ig·nore** \ig'nō(ə)r, -'nȯ(ə)r, -ōə, -ȯ(ə)\ *vt* -ED/-ING/-S [F *ignorer,* fr. L *ignorare,* fr. *ignarus* ignorant, unknown, fr. *i-* (fr. *in-* ¹in-) + *gnarus* knowing, known; akin to L *gnoscere, noscere* to know — more at KNOW] **1** *archaic* **:** to be ignorant of **2 :** to refuse to take notice of ⟨~ a friendly gesture⟩ **:** shut the eyes to ⟨~ public abuses⟩ **:** disregard willfully ⟨~ evidence⟩ **3 :** to reject or throw out (a bill of indictment) as false or ungrounded — compare IGNORAMUS 1 **syn** see NEGLECT

**ig·nor·er** \ig'nōrə(r), -nȯr-\ *n* -S **:** one that ignores

**ignote** *adj* [L *ignotus,* fr. *i-* (fr. *in-* ¹in-) + *gnotus, notus* known, past part. of *gnoscere, noscere* to know] *obs* **:** UNKNOWN

**ig·o·rot** \,ēgə'rōt, '==,=\ *n, pl* **igorot** *or* **igorots** *usu cap* **1 a :** any of several related peoples inhabiting the mountains of northwestern Luzon, Philippines: (1) **:** a people inhabiting the Mountain Province south of Kalinga (2) **:** KANKANAI (3) **:** NABALOI (4) **:** BONTOK **b :** a member of any of these peoples **2 :** any of the Austronesian languages of the Igorot peoples

**IGS** *abbr* imperial general staff

**igua·na** \ə'gwänə, ē'-\ *n* [Sp, fr. Arawak *iwana*] **1 a** *also* **gua·na** \'gwänə\ -S **:** any of a number of large herbivorous tropical American lizards (family Iguanidae) being typically dark-colored with a serrated dorsal crest and a gular pouch, attaining a length of several feet, and serving as an important article of human food in their native habitat **b** *cap* [NL, fr. Sp] **:** the type genus of Iguanidae **2** *also* **gua·na** \'gwänə\ *or* **gua·no** \-ä(,)nō\ -S **:** any of various large lizards: as **a :** LACE LIZARD **b :** TUATARA

**¹igua·nid** \ə'gwänəd, ē'-\ *adj* [NL *Iguanidae*] **:** of or relating to the Iguanidae

**²iguanid** \"\ *n* -S **:** a lizard of the family Iguanidae

**igua·ni·dae** \-nə,dē\ *n pl, cap* [NL, fr. *Iguana,* type genus + *-idae*] **:** a large family of chiefly New World lizards including the iguanas and many of the small inoffensive lizards (as the pine lizard and horned toads) of the U. S. and being distinguished from the related Agamidae by possession of pleurodont dentition

**igua·no·don** \-,dän\ *n, cap* [NL, fr. Sp *iguana* + NL *-odon*] **:** a genus of large herbivorous ornithischian dinosaurs (type of a family Iguanodontidae) from the early Cretaceous of Belgium and England having the head compressed, the jaws probably provided with a horny covering in front like that of a turtle but with numerous spatulate serrated teeth farther back, and the forelimbs comparatively small and provided with large three-toed hind limbs used chiefly in walking and a large heavy tail which doubtless assisted in standing upright — **igua·no·dont** \-nt\ *adj or n*

**igua·no·don·toi·dea** \=,==,dän·'tȯidēə\ *or* **igua·no·don·tia** \=,==,'dänch(ē)ə\ [NL, fr. *Iguanodont-, Iguanodon* + *-oidea* or *-ia*] *syn of* ORNITHOPODA

**¹igua·noid** \ə'gwä,nȯid, ē'-\ *adj* [*iguana* + *-oid*] **:** of or relating to an iguana or the iguanas

**²iguanoid** \"\ *n* -S **1 :** a lizard like an iguana **2 :** a lizard of the family Iguanidae

**igua·pe** \ē'gwä(,)pā\ *n* -S [fr. *Iguape,* fishing port and river in Brazil] **:** CANDLENUT 1

**IGY** *abbr* international geophysical year

**IH** *abbr, often not cap* inside height

**i-head** \'=,=\ *adj, cap I* **:** having valves in the cylinder head ⟨an *I-head* gasoline engine⟩

**¹ihi** \'ē(,)hē\ *n* -S [Maori *hihi*] **:** STITCHBIRD

**²ihi** \"\ *n* -S [Maori *ihe*] **:** either of two important New Zealand food fishes (order Synentognathi): **a :** a halfbeak (*Hemiramphus intermedius*) **b :** a skipper (*Scombresox forsteri*)

**ih·lat** \ē'lät\ *n, pl* **ihlat** *or* **ihlats** *usu cap* **1 :** an orig. nomadic Sunnite people of Persia **2 :** a member of the Ihlat people

**ih·le·ite** \'ēlə,īt, -lē,-\ *n* -S [G *ihleit,* fr. M. *Ihle,* 19th cent. Bohemian superintendent of mines + G *-it* -ite] **:** COPIAPITE

**IHP** *abbr, often not cap* indicated horsepower

**ih·ram** \ē'räm\ *n* -S [Ar *iḥrām*] **1 :** a state of consecration assumed by Muslims on pilgrimage to Mecca **2 :** the ceremonially plain clothing worn by Muslims on pilgrimage

**IHS** *or* **IHC** *or* **JHS** *or* **YHS** *symbol* [LL IHS, IHC, fr. Gk IHC, IHΣ (the capitalized forms of the Greek letters iota, eta, and sigma), short for *Iēsous* Jesus] — used as a Christian symbol and monogram for *Jesus*

**IHVH** *var of* YHWH

**II** *abbr* **1** indorsement irregular **2** inventory and inspection

**i iron** *n, cap 1st I* **:** I BAR

**ii·wi** \ē'ēwē\ *n* -S [Hawaiian *'i'iwi*] **:** an Hawaiian honeycreeper (*Vestiaria coccinea*) with chiefly bright vermilion plumage formerly used in making feather cloaks

**ijo** \'ē(,)jō\ *also* **ijaw** \-jȯ\ *n, pl* **ijo** *or* **ijos** *also* **ijaw** *or* **ijaws** *usu cap* **1 a :** a Negro people of the Niger delta **b :** a member of such people **2 :** the language of the Ijo people **3 :** a branch of the Niger-Congo language family containing only the Ijo language

**ijo·lite** \'ē(y)ə,līt, 'iyə,-\ *n* -S [*Ijo,* river and village in Finland + E *-lite*] **:** a granular igneous rock consisting chiefly of nephelite and augite typically with calcite, apatite, and titanite accessories

**ik·a·ry** \'ikərē\ *n* -ES [Russ *ikra*] *archaic* **:** CAVIAR

**ikat** \'ē,kät\ *n* -S [Malay, tying-up, fastening, binding (as yarns prior to dyeing)] **1 :** a technique of fabric decoration common in Malaya, Indonesia, and Latin America in which warp and sometimes also weft yarns are tied-and-dyed before weaving **2 :** a fabric of tied-and-dyed design **:** CHINÉ

**ike** \'īk\ *n* -S [by alter. and shortening] **:** ICONOSCOPE

**ikh·wan** \ik'wän\ *n pl, usu cap* [Ar *ikhwān,* lit. brethren] **:** Muslim brethren united by the ties of common membership in the Wahhabi sect of central Arabia

**ikmo** *var of* ITMO

**ikon** *var of* ICON

**ikon-** *or* **ikono-** — see ICON-

**il** *abbr* illustrated; illustration; illustrator

**IL** *abbr* **1** including loading **2** inside left **3** *often not cap* inside length **4** interline

**il-** — see IN-

**-il** \əl, ³l, (¦)il\ *also* **-ile** \", ¦ēl, ¦īl\ *n suffix* -S [G *-il* & F *-ile,* prob. fr. F *-ile* & L *-ilis* -ile, adj. suffix] **:** substance related to (something specified) ⟨benzil⟩

**ila** \'ēlə\ *n, pl* **ila** *or* **ilas** *usu cap* **1 a :** a Bantu-speaking people of northern Rhodesia **b :** a member of such people **2 :** a Bantu language of the Ila people

**ila·ma** \ə'lämə\ *n* -S [MexSp, fr. Nahuatl *ilamatzapotl,* fr. *ilamatl* old woman + *tzapotl* sapodilla; fr. the fancied resemblance of the fruit to an old woman's head] **1 :** a tropical American tree (*Annona diversifolia*) grown in the southern U.S. that has a whitish fruit with pinkish tinge **2 :** the fruit of the ilama

**ilang-ilang** *or* **ylang-ylang** \'ē,läŋ'ē,läŋ\ *n* -S [Tag] **1 :** a tree (*Canangium odoratum*) of the Malay archipelago, the Philippines, and adjacent areas that has very fragrant greenish yellow flowers **2 :** a perfume distilled from the flowers of the ilang-ilang tree

**ilang-ilang oil** *n* **:** a yellowish essential oil that has a fine floral odor, is obtained chiefly in the Philippines and on Réunion Island from the flowers of the ilang-ilang tree, and is used in perfumes, cosmetics, and soaps — compare CANANGA OIL

**ila·va** \ə'lävə\ *or* **ila·van** \-vən\ *n* -S *usu cap* [Tamil & Malayalam *iravan*] **1 :** a large caste of cultivators in southern India **2 :** a member of the Ilava caste

**ile-** *also* **ileo-** *comb form* [NL *ileum*] **1 :** ileum ⟨*ileo*stomy⟩ **2 :** ileal and ⟨*ileo*cecal⟩

**¹-ile** \əl, ³l, ¸īl, (,)il\ *adj suffix* [ME, fr. MF, fr. L *-ilis*] **:** of, relating to, suited for, or capable of ⟨contract*ile*⟩ ⟨expans*ile*⟩

**²-ile** \"\ *n suffix* -S [prob. fr. *-ile* (as in *quartile,* n. — quartile aspect — and *sextile,* n.)] **:** segment of a (specified) size in a frequency distribution ⟨cent*ile*⟩ ⟨dec*ile*⟩

**³-ile** — see -IL

**il·e·al** \'ilēəl\ *also* **il·e·ac** \-ē,ak\ *adj* [*ile-* + *-al* or *-ac*] **:** of, relating to, or involving the ileum

**il·e·i·tis** \,ilē'īd·əs\ *n, pl* **il·e·it·i·des** \-'id·ə,dēz\ [NL, fr. *ile-* + *-itis*] **:** inflammation of the ileum — see REGIONAL ILEITIS

**il·eo·cecal** \¦ilē(,)ō+\ *adj* [*ile-* + *cecal*] **:** of, related to, or involving both ileum and cecum ⟨the ~ region⟩

**ileocecal valve** *n* **:** the valve formed by two folds of mucous membrane at the opening of the ileum into the large intestine

**il·eo·colic artery** \"+. . .-\ *n* [*ile-* + *colic*] **:** a branch of the superior mesenteric supplying the terminal part of the ileum and the beginning of the colon

**ileocolic valve** *n* **1 :** ILEOCECAL VALVE **2 :** a circular valvular ridge between small intestine and colon in animals (as amphibians) that lack a cecum

**ileon** *n* -S [ME, modif. of L *ile, ilium, ileum* groin] *obs* **:** ILEUM

**il·e·os·to·my** \,ilē'ästəmē\ *n* -ES [ISV *ile-* + *-stomy*] **1 :** an operation to create an artificial anus by making an opening from the ileum through the abdominal wall **2 :** the orifice made by ileostomy

**ileostomy bag** *n* **:** a container designed to receive feces discharged through an ileostomy

**iles·ite** \'īl,zīt\ *n* -S [M.W.*Iles* †1890 Am. mineralogist + E *-ite*] **:** a mineral $(Mn,Zn,Fe)SO_4.4H_2O$ consisting of a green hydrous manganese zinc iron sulfate

**il·e·um** \'ilēəm\ *n, pl* **il·ea** \-ēə\ [NL, fr. L *ile, ilium, ileum* groin, viscera; prob. akin to Gk *ilia* female genitals, *ilion* female pubes, and perh. to Pol *jelito* intestine, sausage, Russ *liton'ya* third stomach of ruminants] **:** the last division of the small intestine constituting the part between the jejunum and large intestine, in man forming the last three fifths of the part of the small intestine beyond the end of the duodenum, and being smaller and thinner-walled than the jejunum with fewer circular folds but more numerous Peyer's patches

**il·e·us** \'ilēəs\ *n* -ES [L, fr. Gk *eileos, ileos,* from *eilein, illein* to roll] **:** obstruction of the bowel; *specif* **:** a condition that is commonly marked by painful distended abdomen, vomiting of dark or fecal matter, toxemia, and dehydration and that results when the intestinal contents back up because peristalsis fails although the lumen is not occluded — called also *paralytic ileus*

**ilex** \'ī,leks\ *n* [ME, fr. L, prob. of non-IE origin like Gk (Macedonian dial.) *ilax* holm oak] **1** -ES **:** HOLM OAK **2** [NL, fr. L] **a** *cap* **:** a large genus of widely distributed trees and shrubs (family Aquifoliaceae) having small flowers and berries — see HOLLY **b** -ES **:** any plant of this genus

**il·ford** \'ilfə(r)d\ *adj, usu cap* [fr. *Ilford,* Eng.] **:** of or from the municipal borough of Ilford, England **:** of the kind or style prevalent in Ilford

**ilia** *pl of* ILIUM

**il·i·ac** \'ilē,ak\ *adj* [NL *ilium* + E *-ac* (fr. L *-acus,* adj. suffix, fr. Gk *-akos*)] **1** *archaic* **:** ILEAL **2 :** of or relating to the ilium **:** located in the region of the ilium ⟨~ bone⟩ ⟨~ graft⟩ — see ABDOMINAL REGION illustration

**iliac artery** *n* **1 :** either of the large arteries supplying blood to the lower trunk and hind limbs and arising by bifurcation of the aorta which in man occurs at the level of the fourth lumbar vertebra to form one vessel for each side of the body — called also *common iliac artery* **2 :** the outer branch of either iliac artery that passes beneath Poupart's ligament to become the femoral artery — called also *external iliac artery* **3 :** the inner branch of either common iliac artery that soon breaks into several branches and supplies blood chiefly to the pelvic and gluteal areas — called also *hypogastric artery, internal iliac artery*

**iliac crest** *n* **:** the thick curved upper border of the ilium

**iliac fascia** *n* **:** an aponeurotic layer lining the back part of the abdominal cavity and covering the psoas and iliacus muscles

**iliac fossa** *n* **:** the inner concavity of the ilium

**iliac index** *n* **:** the anthropometric ratio of the distance between the iliac spines and that between the topmost margin of the crest of the ilium and the lower margin of the acetabulum multiplied by 100

**ili·a·cus** \ə'līəkəs\ *n, pl* **ilia·ci** \-ə,sī\ [NL, fr. *ilium*] **:** a muscle that flexes the thigh or bends the pelvis and lumbar region forward, has its origin from the iliac fossa, iliac crest, the base of the sacrum, and adjoining parts, and is inserted into the outer side of the tendon of the psoas major, the capsule of the hip joint, and the lesser trochanter of the femur

**iliac vein** *n* **:** any of three veins on each side of the body corresponding to and accompanying the iliac arteries

**il·i·ad** \'ilēəd *also* -ē,ad\ *n* -S *often cap* [fr. the *Iliad,* ancient Greek epic poem dealing with the siege of Troy and attributed to Homer, fr. L *Iliad-, Ilias,* fr. Gk *Iliad-, Ilias,* lit., of Ilium, fr. *Ilion* Troy] **1 :** a long narrative; *esp* **:** an epic in the Homeric tradition ⟨the farmer has inspired no ringing saga or ~ —*Scribner's*⟩ **2 a :** a series of martial exploits regarded as suitable for epic commemoration ⟨who leaving his glad school days . . . joined England's bitter *Iliad* —Margaret Wilson⟩ **b :** a series of miseries or disasters ⟨opens another *Iliad* of woes to Europe —Edmund Burke⟩

**il·i·ad·ic** \¦ilē¦adik\ *adj* **1** *usu cap* **:** of or relating to the *Iliad* of Homer **2** *often cap* **:** of, relating to, or being an iliad ⟨*iliadic* adventures during wartime⟩

**ili·a·hi** \,ēlē'ähē\ *n* -S [Hawaiian] **:** an Hawaiian sandalwood tree (*Santalum freycinetianum*) yielding an aromatic wood

**il·i·al** \'ilēəl\ *adj* [NL *ilium* + E *-al*] **:** ILIAC

**¹il·i·an** \'ilēən\ *adj, usu cap* [*Ilium* (Troy), ancient city in northwestern Asia Minor + E *-an*] **:** of or relating to ancient Troy

**²ilian** \"\ *n* -S *cap* **:** an inhabitant of ancient Troy

**ili·au** \,ēlē'aü\ *n* -S [Hawaiian, lit., hidebound] **:** a destructive disease of young sugarcane endemic in Hawaii caused by a fungus (*Gnomonia iliau*) and characterized by binding of the leaf bases tightly about the stem

**ili·ca·ce·ae** \,ilə'kāsē,ē\ [NL, fr. *Ilic-, Ilex,* type genus + *-aceae*] *syn of* AQUIFOLIACEAE

**ili·ma** \ə'lēmə\ *n* -S [Hawaiian *'ilima*] **:** a small shrub of the genus *Sida* (esp. *S. fallax*) commonly bearing tiny yellow or orange flowers that are often used in Hawaiian leis

**ilio-** *comb form* [NL *ilium*] **:** iliac and ⟨*ilio*costal⟩ ⟨*ilio*pelvic⟩

**il·i·o·cos·ta·lis** \,ilēō,kä'stāləs, -täl-, -tal-\ *n* -ES [NL, fr. *ilio-* + LL *costalis* rib, fr. L *costa* rib + *-alis* -al, adj. suffix)] **:** the lateral division of the sacrospinalis muscle that helps to keep the trunk erect and consists of a part from the ilium to the lower ribs which draws the trunk to the same side or depresses the ribs, a part from the lower to the upper ribs which draws the trunk to the same side and approximates the ribs, and a part from the ribs to the cervical transverse processes which draws the neck to the same side and elevates the ribs — called also respectively *iliocostalis lumborum, iliocostalis dorsi, iliocostalis cervicis*

**il·io·femoral ligament** \¦ilē(,)ō+. . .-\ *n* [ISV *ilio-* + *femoral*] **:** a ligament that extends from the anterior inferior spine of the ilium to the intertrochanteric line of the femur and divides below into two branches

**il·io·hypogastric nerve** \"+. . .-\ *n* [ISV *ilio-* + *hypogastric*] **:** a branch of the first lumbar nerve distributed to the iliohypogastric regions

**ilioinguinal nerve** \"+. . .-\ *n* [*ilio-* + *inguinal*] **:** a branch of the first lumbar nerve distributed to the ilioinguinal regions

**il·io·lumbar artery** \"+...-\ *n* [*ilio-* + *lumbar*] **:** a branch of the posterior trunk of the iliac artery (sense 3)

**iliolumbar ligament** *n* **:** a ligament connecting the transverse process of the last lumbar vertebra with the iliac crest

**il·io·pectineal eminence** \"+...-\ *n* [*ilio-* + *pectineal*] **:** an eminence indicating the junction of the ilium and the pubis

**iliopectineal line** *n* **:** a line or ridge on the inner surface of the innominate bone marking the border between the true and false pelvis

**il·io·psoas** \,ilēō'sōəs, -ē'äpsəwəs\ *n* [NL, fr. *ilio-* + *psoas*] **:** a muscle consisting of the iliacus and psoas major muscles

**il·io·pso·at·ic** \¦ilē(,)ōsō¦ad·ik, -ē¦äpsə¦wa-\ *adj* **:** of or relating to the iliopsoas

**il·io·tibial band** \¦ilē(,)ō+...-\ *n* [*ilio-* + *tibial*] **:** a downward continuation of the fascia lata that resembles a tendon and is inserted into the lateral tuberosity of the tibia

**il·i·um** \'ilēəm\ *n, pl* **il·ia** \-ēə\ [NL, fr. L *ilium, ileum, ile* groin, viscera — more at ILEUM] **1 :** the dorsal and upper one of the three bones composing either lateral half of the pelvis being in man broad and expanded above and narrower below where it joins with the ischium and pubis to form part of the acetabulum **2** *archaic* **:** ILEUM

[1]**ilk** \'ilk, 'ik\ *pron* [ME *ilk, ilke*, fr. OE *ilca* same, fr. a prehistoric compound whose constituents are akin respectively to Goth *is* he and OE *gelīc* like — more at ITERATE, LIKE] *now chiefly Scot* **:** SAME — used with preceding *that* esp. in the names of landed families ⟨Grant of that ~ means Grant of Grant⟩

[2]**ilk** \"\ *n* -s **:** FAMILY, SORT, KIND — often used disparagingly ⟨determinists, materialists, agnostics, behaviorists and their ~ —John Dewey⟩ **syn** see TYPE

[3]**ilk** \"\ *adj* [ME, adj. & pron., fr. OE *ylc, ǣlc* — more at EACH] *chiefly Scot* **:** EACH, EVERY

[4]**ilk** \"\ *pron* [ME] *chiefly Scot* **:** EACH

**il·ka** \'ilkə\ *adj* [ME *ilka, ilkan*, fr. *ilk* each + *a, an* (indef. art.)] *chiefly Scot* **:** EACH, EVERY ⟨and ~ bird sang o' its luve —Robert Burns⟩

**ilka day** *n, Scot* **:** WEEKDAY

[1]**ill** \'il\ *adj* **worse** \'wərs, -ōs, -əis\ *also sometimes and in sense 2c often* **ill·er** \'ilə(r)\ *or substand* **wors·er** \'wərsə(r), -ōs-,-əis-\ **worst** \'wərst, -ōst, -əist\ *also sometimes and in sense 2c often* **ill·est** \'iləst\ [ME *ill, ille*, fr. ON *illr*] **1 a** *now chiefly Scot* **:** immoral or vicious or corrupt or otherwise morally reprehensible **b :** resulting from or accompanied by or evidencing an evil, malicious, or malevolent intention ⟨~ deeds that wrecked their lives⟩ **c :** that imputes evil to or implies evil in something referred to **:** that ascribes evil to or assumes evil in something referred to ⟨an ~ opinion of everything they did⟩ ⟨attaching an ~ significance to what was said⟩ ⟨in ~ repute⟩ **2 a :** that causes or is accompanied by pain or discomfort or inconvenience or that is otherwise disagreeable ⟨died an ~ death⟩ ⟨the ~ smells of a fish market⟩ ⟨had an ~ taste⟩ **b :** that causes or tends to result in harm **:** HURTFUL, INJURIOUS, PERNICIOUS ⟨its ~ effects were felt for many generations —Gilbert Highet⟩ ⟨a decision that can have only ~ results⟩ ⟨did them an ~ service⟩ **c** (1) **:** affected with some ailment **:** INDISPOSED **:** not being in good health **:** AILING, UNWELL, SICK ⟨is ~ with a fever⟩ ⟨incurably ~ with cancer —*Time*⟩ **:** UNSOUND, FAILING ⟨suffers from chronically ~ health⟩ **:** UPSET, DISORDERED ⟨emotionally ~⟩ ⟨mentally ~⟩ (2) **:** affected by nausea often to the point of vomiting **:** NAUSEATED, SICK ⟨thought she would be ~ after the ride on the roller coaster⟩ **3 a :** that is not suited to circumstances or that is not to one's advantage **:** UNPROPITIOUS, UNTOWARD, UNLUCKY ⟨its leaders were choosing an ~ moment for a revolution —J.A.Froude⟩ **:** not promising well **:** INAUSPICIOUS ⟨an ~ omen⟩ **:** marked by unfavorable events **:** contrary to one's hopes and expectations ⟨had a discouraging run of ~ luck⟩ **b :** that involves difficulties with regard to the accomplishment of an objective **:** HARD, TROUBLESOME ⟨beauty is intangible, vague, ~ to be defined —M.F.Tupper⟩ **:** so difficult as to make effort useless **:** POINTLESS ⟨it is ~ prophesying; but one has hope of a regeneration of our literature —*Yale Rev.*⟩ **4 a :** that is not up to an accepted standard of worth or ability **:** notably imperfect or unsatisfactory **:** quite faulty **:** INFERIOR, DEFECTIVE ⟨a period of ~ management⟩ ⟨an ~ specimen of humanity⟩ **b :** that is not up to an accepted standard of propriety **:** UNPOLISHED, CRUDE, BOORISH ⟨~ manners⟩ ⟨~ behavior⟩ **c** *archaic* **:** notably unskillful or inexpert or inefficient **:** MALADROIT ⟨I am ~ at describing female apparel —Charles Lamb⟩ **5 a :** UNFRIENDLY, HOSTILE ⟨~ feeling that culminated in bloody feuds⟩ **b :** HARSH, CRUEL ⟨~ treatment of minorities⟩ **c** *now chiefly dial* (1) *of an animal* **:** dangerously fierce **:** FEROCIOUS, SAVAGE (2) *of a person* **:** cantankerous and irritable **:** CROSS, SURLY, GRUMPY **syn** see BAD

[2]**ill** \"\ *adv* **worse** \"\ **worst** \"\ [ME *ille*, fr. ON *illa*, fr. *illr*, adj.] **1 a :** with displeasure or offense ⟨the remark was ~ received⟩ **b :** in an unfriendly or harsh or malevolent manner ⟨were ~ treated during their stay⟩ **c :** in such a way as to reflect unfavorable estimation of something referred to or to cast aspersion or blame on something referred to ⟨spoke very ~ of them⟩ ⟨however ~ he might think of that general —John Buchan⟩ **2 :** in a reprehensible manner ⟨an *ill*-spent youth⟩ **3** *now dial Eng* **:** to a grave extent **:** SERIOUSLY ⟨was ~ hurt⟩ **4 a :** not to any real extent **:** not really **:** HARDLY, SCARCELY **:** by the narrowest margin or none at all ⟨can ~ afford further expense⟩ ⟨they were soon ~ content —A.M. Young⟩ **b :** only with great trouble or difficulty ⟨except in matters of doctrine Pilgrim and Puritan consorted ~ together —V.L.Parrington⟩ **5 a :** UNADVANTAGEOUSLY, UNPROPITIOUSLY, UNLUCKILY ⟨warned them that it would go ~ with them if they insisted⟩ ⟨the whole affair turned out ~⟩ **b :** in a faulty or inefficient or otherwise defective manner **:** IMPERFECTLY, INEFFECTIVELY ⟨the economic irresponsibility of prison life left me ~ equipped to live up to my good intentions —Frank O'Leary⟩ ⟨has been bad propaganda, ~ calculated to achieve its objects —G.E.G.Catlin⟩ — often used in combination ⟨*ill*-smelling⟩ esp. with adjectives in *-ed* ⟨*ill*-prepared⟩

[3]**ill** \"\ *n* -s [ME, fr. *ill, ille* (adj.)] **1 a** (1) **:** the reverse of good **:** EVIL ⟨not knowing whether the outcome would be for good or for ~⟩ ⟨if ~ should befall her —E.T.Thurston⟩ (2) *archaic* **:** the reverse of virtue **:** WICKEDNESS **b** *archaic* **:** the reverse of a good act **:** a wicked deed **2 a** *archaic* **:** CALAMITY, DISASTER **b :** MISFORTUNE, DISTRESS ⟨a morbid fear of some future ~⟩ **c** (1) **:** AILMENT, SICKNESS ⟨measles and other ~*s* of childhood⟩ (2) **:** something that bothers or disturbs or afflicts ⟨once again society is asking the papers to remedy a social ~ by suppressing the facts —Herbert Brucker⟩ **:** DIFFICULTY, TROUBLE, DISORDER ⟨political and economic ~*s*⟩ **3 :** something (as an opinion, a remark) that reflects unfavorable estimation or casts aspersion or blame ⟨spoke no ~ of them⟩ **syn** see EVIL

**ill** *abbr* **1** illuminated; illumination **2** illustrated; illustration; illustrator **3** [L *illustrissimus*] most illustrious

**-il·la** \'ilə\ *n suffix, pl* **-illae** *or* **-illas** [NL, alter. of L *-ella*] **:** -ELLA ⟨*Spongilla*⟩

**illaborate** *adj* [L *illaboratus*, fr. *in-* [1]in- + *laboratus*, past part. of *laborare* to labor — more at LABOR] *obs* **:** carelessly done **:** ROUGH

**ill-advised** \¦=¦=\ *adj* **:** not well counseled **:** IMPRUDENT, RASH **: a :** acting without wise and sufficient counsel or deliberation ⟨would be *ill-advised* to accept the offer⟩ **b :** following upon or resulting from or showing a lack of wise and sufficient counsel or deliberation ⟨*ill-advised* efforts⟩ ⟨tactics that were *ill-advised*⟩ ⟨*ill-advised* laws⟩ — **ill-advisedly** \¦=¦==\ *adv*

**il·lae·nus** \ə'lēnəs\ *n, cap* [NL, fr. Gk *illaenein* to squint] **:** a genus of Ordovician and Silurian trilobites

**ill-affected** \¦=¦==\ *adj* **1** *archaic* **:** not well disposed **:** alienated in disposition **2** *obs* **:** not healthy **:** AILING, DISEASED

**il·la·nun** \ēl'yä(,)nün\ *n, pl* **illanun** *or* **illanuns** *usu cap* [Maranao *Ilanun*, fr. *i-* from + *lanaw* lake + *-n* suffix denoting a people or language] **1 :** the Maranao people of northern Borneo and of the southwest coastal area of the island of Mindanao in the Philippines **2 :** a member of the Illanun people

[1]**il·lapse** \ə'laps\ *n* -s [L *illapsus* infusion, influx, fr. *illapsus*, past part. of *illabi* to fall into, flow into, fr. *in-* [2]in- + *labi* to fall, slide — more at SLEEP] **:** INFLUX, ACCESSION ⟨the ~ of the Spirit at Pentecost —B.J.Kidd⟩

[2]**illapse** \"\ *vi* -ED/-ING/-S [L *illapsus*, past part.] *archaic* **:** FLOW, GLIDE, SLIP

**il·laq·ue·ate** \ə'lakwē,āt\ *vt* -ED/-ING/-S [L *illaqueatus*, past part. of *illaqueare* to trick, enmesh, ensnare, fr. *in-* [2]in- + *laqueare* to ensnare, fr. *laqueus* noose, snare — more at DELIGHT] *archaic* **:** SNARE

**ill at ease** *adj* **:** not feeling easy **:** UNCOMFORTABLE, ANXIOUS ⟨back of all our lives is the somber setting of a world *ill at ease* and beset by perils —Agnes Repplier⟩ ⟨and wandered around rather *ill at ease* among swirls and eddies of people I didn't know —Scott Fitzgerald⟩

**il·la·tion** \ə'lāshən\ *n* -s [LL *illation-, illatio*, fr. L, action of bringing in, fr. *illatus* (suppletive past part. of *inferre* to bring in, infer, fr. *in-* [2]in- + *latus*, suppletive past part. of *ferre* to carry) + *-ion-, -io* -ion — more at TOLERATE, BEAR] **1 :** the action of inferring **:** INFERENCE **2 :** something inferred

[1]**il·la·tive** \'ilәd·iv, ə'lād·iv\ *n* -s [L *illativum* conclusion, fr. neut. of *illativus*] **1 a :** a word (as *therefore*) or phrase (as *as a consequence*) expressing the formation of or introducing an inference **b :** ILLATION 2 **2** [L *illatus* + E *-ive*] **a :** a grammatical case used in some languages (as Hungarian) that expresses a relationship of motion into or direction toward **b :** a word having the inflection of this case

[2]**illative** \"\ *adj* [LL *illativus*, fr. L *illatus* + *-ivus* -ive] **1 a :** expressing the formation of or introducing an inference ⟨an ~ conjunction⟩ **b :** having the nature of, dependent on the use of, or arrived at by inference ⟨an ~ conclusion⟩ ⟨~ reasoning⟩ ⟨the ~ relation between what is asserted in two or more propositions —M.R.Cohen⟩ **c :** of or relating to inference marked by the use of or by ability in drawing an inference ⟨the ~ faculty of the human mind⟩ **2** [L *illatus* + E *-ive*] **:** of, relating to, or having the nature of an illative ⟨an ~ case ending⟩ — **il·la·tive·ly** \-d·əvlē\ *adv*

**illaudable** \(')i(l), ə +\ *adj* [L *illaudabilis*, fr. *in-* [1]in- + *laudabilis* laudable — more at LAUDABLE] **:** deserving no praise or commendation ⟨an ~ way of acting⟩ — **il·laudably** \"+\ *adv*

**il·la·war·ra ash** \¦ilә¦wärә-\ *n, usu cap I* [fr. *Illawarra* district, New South Wales, Australia] **:** an Australian timber tree (*Elaeocarpus cyaneus*) with racemose flowers and blue globular fruit

**illawarra mountain pine** *n, usu cap I* **:** an Australian cypress pine (*Callitris cupressiformis*)

**ill-being** \'=¦==\ *n* **:** the condition of being unprosperous or otherwise below a desirable standard of living — opposed to *well-being*

**ill blood** *n* **:** BAD BLOOD

**ill-boding** \'=¦==\ *adj* **:** boding evil **:** INAUSPICIOUS

**ill-bred** \'=¦=\ *adj* **1 :** showing (as by rudeness, boorishness) the results of poor upbringing **:** lacking good manners **:** IMPOLITE, UNCIVIL, RUDE, LOUTISH ⟨*ill-bred* remarks⟩ ⟨*ill-bred* behavior⟩ **2 :** inferior (as in physical characteristics) by reason of being the offspring of mismatched parents ⟨an *ill-bred* animal⟩

**ill-come** \'il(,)kəm\ *adj* **:** UNWELCOME ⟨wondered what this *ill-come* visitor might be seeking —Rafael Sabatini⟩

**ill-conditioned** \¦=¦==\ *adj* **:** having a bad temper or mean disposition **:** SURLY, IRRITABLE ⟨three hours after shaving he developed a dark smear about the lips which made him look . . . treacherous and *ill-conditioned* —John Wain⟩ ⟨some *ill-conditioned*, growling fellow —Charles Dickens⟩

**ill-contrived** \¦=¦=\ *adj, chiefly Scot* **:** ILL-CONDITIONED

**ill convenience** *n, archaic* **:** INCONVENIENCE

**ill convenient** *adj, archaic* **:** INCONVENIENT

**ill-deed·ie** \¦=¦dēdi\ *adj* [ME *ille-dedy*, fr. *ille ded* ill deed + *-y*] *Scot* **:** given to evil deeds or to making trouble

**ill-disposed** \¦=¦=\ *adj* **:** not well disposed **:** UNSYMPATHETIC **:** alienated in disposition

**ill-doer** \'=¦==\ *n* **:** one that does evil

**ill-doing** \'=¦==\ *n* **:** the action of perpetrating evil **:** the action of doing or furthering wrong

**ill ease** *n* **:** UNEASINESS

**il·lec·e·bra·ce·ae** \ə,lesə'brāsē,ē\ [NL, fr. *Illecebrum*, type genus (fr. L *illecebra* attraction, fr. *illicere* to entice, fr. *in-* [2]in- + *-licere*, fr. *lacere* to entice) + *-aceae* — more at DELIGHT] *syn of* CORRIGIOLACEAE

**il·legal** \(')i(l), ə+\ *adj* [F or ML; F *illégal*, fr. ML *illegalis*, fr. L *in-* [1]in- + *legalis* legal — more at LEGAL] **:** contrary to or violating a law or rule or regulation or something else (as an established custom) having the force of law **:** UNLAWFUL, ILLICIT ⟨the ~ use of taxpayers' money⟩ ⟨~ trade restrictions⟩ ⟨an ~ trial⟩ ⟨an ~ pitching technique in baseball⟩ ⟨an ~ chess move⟩ — compare NONLEGAL — **il·legally** \"+\ *adv*

**illegal abortion** *n* **:** abortion artificially induced for reasons other than medical

**il·legality** \¦i(l)+\ *n* [F or ML; F *illégalité*, fr. ML *illegalitat-, illegalitas*, fr. *illegalis* + L *-itat-, -itas* -ity] **1 :** the quality or state of being illegal ⟨the ~ of the contract was evident⟩ **2 :** an illegal action or procedure ⟨the right to resist ~⟩

**il·legalization** \(¦)i(l), ə+\ *n* **:** the action of illegalizing ⟨~ of gambling, drinking, and prostitution did not destroy the demand —H.D.Lasswell⟩

**il·legalize** \(')i(l), ə+\ *vt, see -ize in Explan Notes* **:** to make or declare illegal ⟨~*s* excessive or discriminatory initiation fees —*Newsweek*⟩

**il·legibility** \(¦)i(l), ə+\ *n* **:** the quality or state of being illegible

**il·legible** \(')i(l), ə+\ *adj* [[1]in- + *legible*] **1 :** incapable of being read or deciphered **:** not legible ⟨injured his right hand in football, making his handwriting almost ~ —E.S.Bates⟩ ⟨no way of knowing by his ~ face whether he told the truth or not —Jean Stafford⟩ **2 :** not readable because of language or content ⟨a mediaeval jargon that is now but little less ~ than Coptic —J.B.Cabell⟩ — **il·legibly** \"+\ *adv*

**il·legitimacy** \¦i(l)+\ *n* **1 :** the quality or state of being illegitimate **2 :** BASTARDY 2

[1]**il·legitimate** \"+\ *adj* [[1]in- + *legitimate*] **1 a :** not recognized by law as lawful offspring **:** BASTARD; *usu* **:** born of parents not married to each other **b :** conceived in fornication or adultery **2 :** not rightly deduced or inferred **:** ILLOGICAL ⟨an ~ inference⟩ ⟨an ~ supposition⟩ **3 :** departing in some way from the regular or expected **:** IRREGULAR, ERRATIC ⟨~ unions between broken chromosomes —*Encyc. Britannica*⟩ ⟨~ pollination⟩ **4 a :** contrary to or violating a law or regulation **:** ILLEGAL **:** not sanctioned by law **:** UNWARRANTED ⟨an ~ seizure of power⟩ ⟨an ~ government⟩ **b :** not authorized by good usage **:** not widely accepted **:** not reputable ⟨an ~ phrase⟩ **c** *of a taxon* **:** published either validly or invalidly but not according with the rules of the relevant international code — **il·legitimately** \"+\ *adv*

[2]**il·legitimate** \"+\ *vt* **:** to make or declare or prove to be illegitimate **:** BASTARDIZE ⟨testimony that would certainly ~ her older son⟩

[3]**illegitimate** *like* [1]ILLEGITIMATE\ *n* -s **:** a person that is in some way illegitimate or that is regarded as illegitimate; *esp* **:** BASTARD

**il·legitimation** \¦i(l)+\ *n* **1 :** the action of illegitimating **2** *obs* **:** the state of being illegitimate **:** ILLEGITIMACY

**il·legitimatize** \"+\ *vt* **:** ILLEGITIMATE

**il·le·ism** \'ilē,izəm\ *n* -s [L *ille* he, that one, that + E *-ism* — more at LARIAT] **:** excessive use of the pronoun *he* esp. in reference to oneself

**il·le·ist** \-ēəst\ *n* -s [L *ille* + E *-ist*] **:** one who makes excessive use of the pronoun *he* esp. in reference to himself

**iller** *comparative of* ILL

**illest** *superlative of* ILL

**ill fame** *n* [ME] **:** bad repute; *esp* **:** reputation for immorality or vice ⟨a house of *ill fame*⟩ — **ill-famed** \'=¦=\ *adj*

**illfare** \'=,=\ *n* **:** the condition of faring badly or of not being well off ⟨no regard for the ~ of the workers —W.J.H.Sprott⟩ — opposed to *welfare*

**ill-fared** \'=¦=\ *adj* **:** that has fared badly **:** UNSUCCESSFUL, INAUSPICIOUS ⟨it is surely going too far to assume that the *ill-fared* arrangement was wholeheartedly supported —G.A. Craig⟩

**ill-faring** \'=¦==\ *adj* **:** faring badly

**ill-fated** \'=¦==\ *adj* **1 :** having or destined to an evil fate **:** UNFORTUNATE, HAPLESS ⟨an *ill-fated* army⟩ ⟨an *ill-fated* ship⟩ ⟨started out on the *ill-fated* expedition⟩ **2 :** that causes or marks the beginning of misfortune or bad luck ⟨an *ill-fated* suggestion⟩ ⟨met them in an *ill-fated* hour⟩ **syn** see UNLUCKY

**ill-favored** \'=¦==\ *adj* **1 :** unattractive or disagreeable in physical appearance **:** unpleasant to look at ⟨an *ill-favored* old man⟩ ⟨her *ill-favored* features⟩; *esp* **:** having an unattractive or ugly face **2 :** that gives offense or arouses resentment **:** OBJECTIONABLE ⟨an *ill-favored* word that no one likes⟩ ⟨*ill-favored* behavior⟩ **syn** see UGLY

**ill-given** \'=¦==\ *adj, chiefly Scot* **:** ILL-DISPOSED

**ill-gotten** \'=¦==\ *also* **ill-got** \'=¦=\ *adj* **:** obtained dishonestly or otherwise unlawfully or unjustly ⟨*ill-gotten* wealth⟩ ⟨*ill-gotten* gains⟩

**illguide** \'=¦=\ *vt, Scot* **:** to treat or handle badly **:** MISMANAGE

**ill humor** *n* **:** a disagreeable mood marked by surliness and irritability **:** CROSSNESS ⟨was in an *ill humor* and sulked⟩ — **ill-humored** \'=¦==\ *adj* — **ill-hu·mored·ly** \'=¦==\ *adv*

[1]**il·liberal** \(')i(l), ə+\ *adj* [MF or L; MF, fr. L *illiberalis* unworthy of a freeman, ignoble, stingy, fr. *in-* [1]in- + *liberalis* worthy of a freeman, noble, generous — more at LIBERAL] **:** not liberal: as **a** *archaic* (1) **:** lacking a liberal education **:** UNSCHOOLED (2) **:** lacking culture and refinement **:** marked by rude manners or behavior **:** COARSE, VULGAR **b :** requiring or emphasizing physical dexterity rather than intellectual ability **:** not belonging to or having the qualities of the liberal arts ⟨trades and other ~ occupations⟩ ⟨an ~ education⟩ **c** *archaic* **:** not generous **:** STINGY **d** (1) **:** not broad-minded **:** having a constricted narrow viewpoint or outlook so as often to be small-minded or pettily prejudiced or bigoted **:** INTOLERANT ⟨the ~ or fanatically intolerant spirit which war psychology always engenders —M.R.Cohen⟩ ⟨~ thinking⟩ (2) **:** opposed to liberalism ⟨~ tendencies⟩ — **il·liberally** \"+\ *adv*

[2]**illiberal** \"+\ *n* **:** one that is illiberal; *esp* **:** one that is opposed to liberalism

**il·liberalism** \"+\ *n* **:** opposition to liberalism

**il·liberality** \(¦)i(l), ə+\ *n* [MF or L; MF *illiberalité*, fr. L *illiberalitat-, illiberalitas* conduct unworthy of a freeman, ignobility, stinginess, fr. *illiberalis* + *-itat-, -itas* -ity] **:** the quality or state of being illiberal

**il·liberalize** \(')i(l), ə+\ *vt* **:** to make illiberal

**il·licit** \(')i(l), ə+\ *adj* [L *illicitus*, fr. *in-* [1]in- + *licitus* lawful — more at LICIT] **:** not permitted **:** not allowed **:** UNLAWFUL ⟨~ trade⟩ — **il·lic·it·ly** \"+\ *adv*

**illicit process** *n* **:** a fallacy of distribution in which a term is distributed in a conclusion that has not been distributed in the premises

**il·lici·um** \ə'lis(h)ēəm, -likē-\ *n* [NL, fr. L, allurement] **1** *cap* **:** a small genus of evergreen trees (family Magnoliaceae) with aromatic persistent leaves and nodding yellow or purplish flowers — see CHINESE ANISE, STAR ANISE **2** *pl* **il·licia** \-ēə\ *or* **illiciums :** the first spine of the dorsal fin of a pediculate fish migrated to the upper lip and transformed into a complex tentacle that serves as a lure to attract other fish within range of the capacious jaws

**illighten** *vt* [by alter. (influence of [2]in-)] *obs* **:** ENLIGHTEN

**il·limitability** \(¦)i(l), ə+\ *n* **:** the quality or state of being illimitable

[1]**il·limitable** \(')i(l), ə+\ *adj* [[1]in- + *limitable*] **:** incapable of being limited or bounded **:** MEASURELESS ⟨the ~ reaches of space and time⟩ — **il·limitableness** \"+\ *n* — **il·limit·ably** \"+\ *adv*

[2]**illimitable** \"\ *n* -s **:** something illimitable ⟨the ~*s* that are the past and the future⟩

**illimitate** *adj* [LL *illimitatus*, fr. L *in-* [1]in- + *limitatus*, past part. of *limitare* to limit — more at LIMIT] *obs* **:** UNLIMITED

**il·limitation** \(¦)i(l), ə+\ *n* [[1]in- + *limitation*] **:** the quality or state of being unlimited **:** freedom from limitation

**il·limited** \(')i(l), ə+\ *adj* [[1]in- + *limited*] *archaic* **:** free from limitation or restraint **:** UNBOUNDED ⟨in a fullhearted evensong of joy ~ —Thomas Hardy⟩ — **il·limitedly** \"+\ *adv, archaic* — **il·limitedness** \"+\ *n, archaic*

**il·lin·i·um** \ə'linēəm\ *n* -s [NL, fr. *Illinois* + NL *-ium*] **:** chemical element 61 — a name now superseded by *promethium*

**il·li·noi·an** \¦ilə¦nȯi(y)ən\ *adj, usu cap* [*Illinois* (state) + E *-an*] **:** belonging to the third glacial stage during the glacial epoch in No. America

[1]**il·li·nois** \¦ilə¦nȯi *sometimes* ¦el- *or esp in southern Illinois & in the southern US* -ȯiz\ *n, pl* **illinois** \-ȯi(z)\ *usu cap* [F, of Algonquian origin; akin to Miami *alänia* man, Shawnee *hilenawe*] **1 a :** a confederacy of Indian peoples of Illinois and Iowa and Wisconsin **b :** a member of such peoples **2 :** an Algonquian language of the Illinois and Miami peoples

[2]**illinois** \"\ *adj, usu cap* [*Illinois*, state in the north central U.S., fr. [1]*illinois*] **:** of or from the state of Illinois **:** of the kind or style prevalent in Illinois **:** ILLINOISAN

[1]**il·li·nois·an** \¦=¦nȯi(y)ən, -ȯiz°n\ *also* **il·li·nois·ian** \-ȯizhən, -zēən\ *or* **il·li·noi·an** \-ȯi(y)ən\ *adj, usu cap* [*Illinois* + E *-an, -ian*] **1 :** of, relating to, or characteristic of the state of Illinois **2 :** of, relating to, or characteristic of the people of Illinois

[2]**illinoisan** \"\ *also* **illinoisian** \"\ *or* **illinoian** \"\ *n* -s *cap* **:** a native or resident of Illinois

**illinois gooseberry** *n, usu cap I* **:** MISSOURI GOOSEBERRY

**illinois nut** *n, usu cap I* **:** PECAN

[1]**il·li·pe** \'ilə(,)pē\ [NL, fr. Malayalam *ilippa* — more at ILLUPI] *syn of* MADHUCA

[2]**illipe** *or* **illipi** *var of* ILLUPI

**illipe butter** *n* **:** any of various vegetable fats: as **a :** MOWRAH BUTTER **b** *or* **illipe tallow :** BORNEO TALLOW — used esp. in the chocolate industry

**il·liquid** \(')i(l), ə+\ *adj* [[1]in- + *liquid*] **1 :** not being cash or readily convertible into cash ⟨~ holdings⟩ **2 :** deficient in liquid assets ⟨an ~ bank⟩ — **il·liquidity** \¦i(l)+\ *n*

**il·lite** \'i,līt\ *n* -s [*Illinois* (state) + E *-ite*] **1 :** a group of minerals found in clays and having essentially the crystal structure of muscovite **2 :** one of the minerals of the illite group; *esp* **:** the mineral having the composition of muscovite or of a hydrated muscovite but giving a line-poor X-ray powder pattern — **il·lit·ic** \(')i¦lid·ik, -lit-\ *adj*

**il·literacy** \(')i(l), ə+\ *n* **1 :** the quality or state of being illiterate; *esp* **:** inability to read or write **2 :** a mistake or crudity (as in reading, writing, or speaking) made by or typical of one who is illiterate

[1]**il·literate** \"+\ *adj* [L *illiteratus*, fr. *in-* [1]in- + *litteratus* lettered, learned — more at LITERATE] **1 :** having little or no education **:** UNLETTERED, IGNORANT; *esp* **:** unable to read or write ⟨a largely ~ population⟩ **2 a :** showing or marked by a lack of familiarity with language and literature **:** deficient in literary background **:** UNCULTURED ⟨an ~ speaker⟩ ⟨an ~ magazine⟩ ⟨an ~ style of writing⟩ **b :** violating generally accepted usage patterns of speaking or writing in such a way as to indicate ignorance or lack of culture ⟨~ words and phrases⟩ ⟨~ pronunciations⟩ **3 :** showing or marked by a lack of acquaintance with the fundamentals or background of a particular field of knowledge ⟨musically ~⟩ ⟨politically ~⟩ **syn** see IGNORANT

[2]**illiterate** \"+\ *n* **:** an illiterate person; *esp* **:** a person unable to read or write

**il·literately** \"+\ *adv* **:** in an illiterate manner

**il·literateness** \"+\ *n* -ES **:** ILLITERACY

**ill-judged** \'=¦=\ *adj* **:** UNWISE, INJUDICIOUS ⟨ponderous and *ill-judged* irony —E.M.Forster⟩

**ill-judging** \'=¦==\ *adj* **1** *archaic* **:** judging faultily or uncritically **2** *archaic* **:** judging hostilely or malevolently

**ill-kempt** \'=¦kem(p)t\ *adj* [[2]*ill* + *-kempt* (as in *unkempt*)] **:** UNKEMPT ⟨untidy and *ill-kempt*, he looked perfectly at home —W.S.Maugham⟩

**ill-looked** \'=¦lükt\ *adj, archaic* **:** not pleasant in appearance

**ill-looking** \'=¦==\ *adj* **:** not pleasant in appearance

**ill-mannered** \'=¦==\ *adj* **:** marked by bad manners **:** UNCIVIL ⟨an *ill-mannered* guest⟩ **syn** see RUDE

**illmo** *abbr* [It *illustrissimo*] most illustrious

**ill-natured** \'=¦==\ *adj* **1 :** having or showing a malevolent or spiteful disposition ⟨*ill-natured* people say . . . that his hair . . . is a wig —W.M.Thackeray⟩ **2 :** having or showing a bad temper or peevish disposition **:** CROSS, SURLY ⟨is pretty *ill-natured* until he's had his coffee⟩ — **ill-natured·ly** \"lē, -li\ *adv*

**ill·ness** \'ilnəs\ *n* -ES **1** *obs* **a** : WICKEDNESS, DEPRAVITY **b** : DISAGREEABLENESS, UNPLEASANTNESS **2** : an unhealthy condition of the body or mind : MALADY ⟨a severe ~⟩

**il·local** \(ˈ)i(l), ə+\ *adj* [LL *illocalis*, fr. L *in-* ¹in- + LL *localis* local — more at LOCAL] : not confined to a particular place ⟨the doctrine that God is ~⟩ — **il·locality** \ˌi(l)+\ *n*

**ill off** *adv* (*or adj*) : BADLY OFF ⟨were not so *ill off* by the modest standards of that day —G.M.Trevelyan⟩

**il·logic** \(ˈ)i(l), ə+\ *n* [¹*in-* + *logic*] : the quality or state of being illogical : lack of logic ⟨an argument that was full of ~⟩

**il·logical** \"+\ *adj* [¹*in-* + *logical*] **1** : not observing the principles of logic : reasoning unsoundly through ignorance or negligence of logic ⟨the speaker seemed most ~ as he developed his argument⟩ **2** : contrary to or devoid of logic ⟨this policy was extremely ~ —Aidan Mulloy⟩ ⟨~ resentment against a group of his friends —W. F. de Morgan⟩ — **il·logically** \"+\ *adv* — **il·logicalness** \"+\ *n*

**il·logicality** \(ˌ)i(l), ə+\ *n* **1** : ILLOGIC ⟨the scientist rebels against the ~ of such reasoning —J.M.Grant⟩ **2** : an instance of illogic : a piece of illogic ⟨the book is full of *illogicalities*⟩

**ill–omened** \ˈ=ˈ==\ *adj* : having or marked by bad omens : INAUSPICIOUS, UNLUCKY ⟨it was to be an *ill-omened* day for them⟩

**il·loricate** *or* **il·loricated** \(ˈ)i(l), ə+\ *adj* [¹*in-* + *loricate, loricated*] : having no lorica ⟨~ rotifers⟩

**ills** *pl of* ILL

**ill–seen** \ˈ=ˈ=\ *adj, archaic* : not well regarded or thought of

**ill–set** \ˈ=ˈ=\ *adj* **1** : not well set : poorly set or placed **2** *chiefly Scot* : SPITEFUL

**ill–sorted** \ˈ=ˈ==\ *adj* **1** : not well matched : badly suited ⟨an *ill-sorted* couple⟩ **2** *Scot* : DISPLEASED

**ill–starred** \ˈ=ˈ=\ *adj* : ILL-FATED ⟨an *ill-starred* romance⟩ ⟨the holiday was *ill-starred* from the outset —Bennett Cerf⟩ **syn** see UNLUCKY

**ill–tempered** \ˈ=ˈ==\ *adj* : having a bad temper : SURLY, IRRITABLE ⟨*ill-tempered* and tyrannical to his sister —Catherine M. Brown⟩ — **ill–temperedly** *adv* — **ill–temperedness** *n* -ES

**illth** \'ilth *also* -ltth\ *n* -S [¹*ill* + *-th* (as in *wealth*)] **1** : the condition of being economically unprosperous or miserable ⟨the glaring disparity between the state's natural wealth and its human ~ —*Christian Century*⟩ **2** : something that produces or is symptomatic of illth ⟨much of the goods on our shelves is wealth rather than ~ —*Nation*⟩

**ill–treat** \ˈ=ˈ=\ *vt* : to treat cruelly or improperly : MALTREAT ⟨they do not *ill-treat* the butlers —C.G.Harper⟩ — **ill–treatment** \ˈ=ˈ==\ *n*

**il·lu·ci·date** \ə'lüsəˌdāt *also* əl'yü-\ *vt* -ED/-ING/-S [²*in-* + L *lucidus* clear + E *-ate* — more at LUCID] *archaic* : ELUCIDATE

**il·lude** \ə'lüd *also* əl'yüd\ *vt* -ED/-ING/-S [ME *illuden*, fr. MF or ML; MF *illuder*, fr. ML *illudere*, fr. L, to mock or jeer at — more at ILLUSION] **1 a** : DELUDE, DECEIVE ⟨in order to ~ him regarding the paternity of the child —R.F.Hawkins⟩ **b** : to subject to an illusion ⟨at the cinema I am . . . completely *illuded* —J.E.Agate⟩ **2** [L *illudere*] *obs* : MOCK, DERIDE **3** *archaic* : to escape from : ELUDE ⟨glad to ~ the burdens of the day —George Crabbe †1832⟩

**il·luk** \'iləkˌ -ˌlük\ *or* **illuk grass** *n* -S [prob. native name in Malaya] : COGON

**il·lume** \ə'lüm *also* əl'yüm\ *vt* -ED/-ING/-S [short for *illumine*] **1** *archaic* **a** : to make bright with or as if with light : light up ⟨the beams yet filter through, *illuming* the wide spaces beneath —W.H.Hudson †1922⟩ **b** : ENLIGHTEN ⟨calculated . . . to ~ the minds of all classes of mankind —George Borrow⟩ **2** *obs* : IGNITE, KINDLE

**il·lu·mi·na·bil·i·ty** \=ˌ===ˈbiləd·ē, -ətē, -i\ *n* : the capability of being illuminated

**il·lu·mi·na·ble** \-mənəbəl\ *adj* [LL *illuminabilis*, fr. L *illuminare* to illuminate + *-abilis* -able — more at ILLUMINATE] : capable of being illuminated

**il·lu·mi·na·graph·ic** \=ˌ===ˈgrafik\ *adj* [*illumination* + *-graphic*] *of a camera* : designed for photographing the image formed by a convex mirror for recording the sources and intensities of light affecting a specific area

**il·lu·mi·nance** \=ˈ==nən(t)s\ *n* -S [*illuminate* + *-ance*] : ILLUMINATION 2

**¹il·lu·mi·nant** \-nənt\ *n* -S [L *illuminant-, illuminans*, pres. part. of *illuminare*] : something that illuminates; *esp* : something (as gas, petroleum, an electric lamp) that gives physical light

**²illuminant** \"\ *adj* [L *illuminant-, illuminans*] : that illuminates : ILLUMINATING, ENLIGHTENING

**¹il·lu·mi·nate** \-nət, *usu* -nəd·+V\ *adj* [ME, fr. L *illuminatus*, past part.] **1** *archaic* : made bright with light ⟨leaves ~ with autumnal hues —H.W.Longfellow⟩ **2** *archaic* : being or claiming to be intellectually or culturally or spiritually enlightened to a superior extent

**²il·lu·mi·nate** \ə'lüməˌnāt *also* əl'yü-; *usu* -ād·+V\ *vt* [L *illuminatus*, past part. of *illuminare*, fr. *in-* ²in + *luminare* to light up, fr. L *lumin-, lumen* light — more at LUMINARY] **1 a** (1) : to give physical light to : supply with light : light up ⟨*illuminated* a picture that hung on the wall —G.B.Shaw⟩ : make bright with light : bathe in light ⟨destroyers ~ the little boats with their searchlights —H.W.Baldwin⟩ (2) : to light up artificially with usu. brilliant lights or decorative lighting effects ⟨the city was *illuminated* in celebration of the victory⟩ ⟨the fountains are beautifully *illuminated* at night⟩ (3) : to make luminous or shining ⟨the beautiful smile that slowly ~s her face —Vernon Jarratt⟩ **b** : to give spiritual or intellectual light to : enlighten spiritually or intellectually ⟨bought a couple of books for the train to Edinburgh, but I can't say I was greatly *illuminated* —H.J.Laski⟩ **c** *archaic* : to set alight : KINDLE ⟨the butler . . . *illuminated* the antique Gothic chandelier —W.M.Thackeray⟩ **2** : to make clear : clear up : remove obscurity from : ELUCIDATE ⟨worked out and *illuminated* broad principles of constitutional interpretation —W.P.M.Kennedy⟩ ⟨historical insight clarifies and *illuminates* the critical activity of a period —C.I.Glicksberg⟩ **3** : to make illustrious or glorious ⟨brilliant achievements that ~ that era⟩ : make resplendent ⟨splendid tapestries and paintings *illuminated* the walls⟩ **4** : to decorate (as a letter or part of a page) with gold or silver or brilliant colors or with often elaborate designs or miniature pictures ⟨beautiful *illuminated* manuscripts of the middle ages⟩

**³il·lu·mi·nate** \-ˌnət, *usu* -nəd·+V\ *n* -S [NL *illuminati*, pl.] *archaic* : a person possessing or claiming to possess unusual enlightenment

**il·lu·mi·na·ti** \=ˌ==ˈnä|d·(ˌ)ē, -ˈnä|, |(ˌ)t|, |i *also* -ˈnaˌtī\ *n pl* [It & NL; It, fr. NL, masc. pl. of *illuminatus*, past part. of *illuminare*] **1** *usu cap* **a** : ALUMBRADOS **b** : members of an 18th century German secret society professing deistic and republican principles **2** : persons who are or who claim to be unusually enlightened ⟨make the enjoyment of poetry primarily an affair of the ~ —J.L.Lowes⟩

**illuminating** *adj* : that illuminates; *esp* : highly informative ⟨an ~ lecture⟩ ⟨an ~ remark⟩ ⟨an ~ illustration⟩ — **il·lu·mi·nat·ing·ly** *adv*

**illuminating engineer** *n* : an engineer specializing in illuminating engineering

**illuminating engineering** *n* : a branch of engineering that deals with planning the lighting systems of new buildings and outdoor areas (as streets, parking lots) and the study and correction of old lighting installations

**illuminating gas** *n* : a gas (as coal gas or carbureted water gas) used for lighting

**illuminating projectile** *n* : a projectile that bursts by the action of a time fuze so as to eject a pyrotechnic element that is usu. held suspended by a parachute after ejection and that lights up terrain — compare STAR SHELL

**il·lu·mi·na·tion** \əˌlüməˈnāshən *also* əlˌyü-\ *n* -S [ME *illuminacioun*, fr. MF or LL; MF *illumination*, fr. LL *illumination-, illuminatio*, fr. L *illuminatus* (past part. of *illuminare* to illuminate) + *-ion-, -io* -ion — more at ILLUMINATE] **1** : the action of illuminating or condition of being illuminated: as **a** : spiritual or cultural or intellectual enlightenment ⟨claimed she had received divine ~⟩ ⟨found great ~ in the lecture⟩ **b** (1) : a giving of physical light or the state of being lighted up ⟨the brilliant ~ of the room⟩ (2) : decorative lighting or lighting effects ⟨~ of the city in celebration of the victory⟩ **c** : decoration (as of an initial letter, a text) by the art of illuminating ⟨was much interested in the ~ of manuscripts⟩ **2** : the luminous flux per unit area on an intercepting surface at any given point — called also *illuminance* **3** : one of the decorative features used in the art of illuminating or in decorative lighting ⟨marveled at the intricate designs and other ~s of the manuscript⟩ ⟨the city was resplendent in its many ~s⟩

**il·lu·mi·na·tism** \=ˈ==ˌnäˌtizəm\ *n* -S [NL *illuminati* + E *-ism*] : ILLUMINISM

**il·lu·mi·na·tist** \=ˌ==ˈnä|d·əst, -ˈnä|, |tə- *also* -ˈnā|· =ˈ==ˌnətə-\ *n* -S [NL *illuminati* + E *-ist*] : ILLUMINIST

**il·lu·mi·na·tive** \=ˈ==ˌnā|d·|iv, -ˌnə|, |t|, |ēv *also* |əv\ *adj* : of, relating to, or producing illumination ⟨had arrived at what is called the ~ stage of mysticism⟩ : ILLUMINATING ⟨had an ~ talk with the scientist⟩

**il·lu·mi·na·to** \=ˌ==ˈnä|d·(ˌ)ō, -ˈnä|, |(ˌ)tō\ *sing of* ILLUMINATI

**il·lu·mi·na·tor** \=ˈ==ˌnād·ə(r), -ātə-\ *also* =ˌ==ˈnäˌtō(ə)r *or* -ō(ə)\ *n* -S [LL, fr. L *illuminatus* (past part. of *illuminare* to illuminate) + *-or*] : one that illuminates: as **a** : one that enlightens intellectually or culturally or spiritually **b** : a device that gives physical light or that is used to direct light to a specific area or that is used to concentrate or reflect light **c** : one that practices the art of illuminating esp. manuscripts

**il·lu·mine** \=ˈ=mən\ *vt* -ED/-ING/-S [ME *illuminen*, fr. MF or L; MF *illuminer*, fr. L *illuminare* — more at ILLUMINATE] : ILLUMINATE

**il·lu·min·er** \-mənə(r)\ *n* -S [alter. of ME *illuminour*, fr. *illuminen* + *-our* -or] : ILLUMINATOR

**il·lu·mi·nism** \-məˌnizəm\ *n* -S [NL *illuminati* + E *-ism*] **1** : belief in or claim to a personal intellectual or cultural or spiritual superiority not accessible to mankind in general **2** *usu cap* : beliefs or claims viewed as forming the doctrine or principles of the Illuminati

**il·lu·mi·nist** \-ˌnəst\ *n* -S *often attrib* [NL *illuminati* + E *-ist*] **1** : one that professes illuminism **2** *usu cap* : one of the Illuminati

**il·lu·mi·nom·e·ter** \=ˌ==ˈnäməd·ə(r)\ *n* [*illumination* + *-o-* + *-meter*] : a photometer for measuring illumination usu. by the brightness of an illuminated surface

**il·lu·pi** \'iləˌpī, -(ˌ)pē\ *also* **il·li·pe** \-(ˌ)pē\ *or* **il·li·pi** *or* **il·lu·pie** \-ˌpī, -(ˌ)pē\ *n* -S [Tamil *iluppai* & Malayalam *ilippa*] : an important East Indian tree (*Madhuca malabrorum*) whose leaves and juice and bark are used medicinally and whose nuts yield oil and whose very sweet flowers are eaten dried or cooked with other foods — compare MAHUA

**illus** *abbr* illustrated; illustration; illustrator

**ill–usage** \ˈ=ˈ==\ *n* : harsh, unkind, or abusive treatment : MALTREATMENT ⟨my wits sharpened by hunger and *ill-usage* —W.J.Locke⟩

**ill–use** \ˈ=ˈ=\ *vt* : MALTREAT, ABUSE ⟨those who he thought had stolen his ideas or otherwise *ill-used* him —*William & Mary Quarterly*⟩

**il·lu·sion** \ə'lüzhən *also* əl'yü-\ *n* -S [ME *illusioun*, fr. MF *illusion*, fr. LL *illusion-, illusio*, fr. L, action of mocking, jeering, fr. *illusus* (past part. of *illudere* to mock or jeer at, fr. *in-* ²in- + *ludere* to play, mock, jeer) + *-ion-, -io* -ion — more at LUDICROUS] **1 a** *obs* : the action of deceiving or attempting to deceive **b** (1) : the state or fact of being intellectually deceived or deluded or misled by others or by oneself either intentionally or unintentionally in such a way as to have false impressions or ideas marked by the attribution of more to something or less to something than is actually the case : MISAPPREHENSION, MISCONCEPTION, DELUSION, FANCY ⟨the happy ~s of youth⟩ (2) : an instance of such deception or delusion ⟨a dreamy life that was filled with one ~ after another⟩ **2 a** (1) : a misleading image presented to the vision : false show; *specif* : APPARITION ⟨these were all an ~ and a phantasma, a thing that appeared, but did not really exist —F.W.Robertson⟩ (2) : something that deceives or deludes or misleads intellectually in such a way as to produce false impressions or ideas that exaggerate or minimize reality or that attribute existence to what does not exist or nonexistence to what does exist ⟨most modern great men are mere ~s sprung out of a national hunger for greatness —Sherwood Anderson⟩ **b** (1) : perception of something objectively existing in such a way as to cause or permit misinterpretation of its actual nature either because of the ambiguous qualities of the thing perceived or because of the personal characteristics of the one perceiving or because of both factors ⟨heat rays shimmering on the road produced the ~ of pools of water⟩ ⟨the horizontal lines cause an optical ~, making the object appear in a different position from what it really is in —Richard Jefferies⟩ (2) : HALLUCINATION 1a (3) : a pattern capable of reversible perspective **3** : a fine plain transparent bobbinet or tulle usu. of silk and used for veils, trimmings, dresses



optical illusions: figure *A*: *a* is actually equal to *b*; figure *B*: either side *a* or side *b* may appear nearer the observer; figure *C*: *o* may be regarded as either the near or the far corner of the block

**il·lu·sion·al** \-zhənᵊl, -zhnəl\ *adj* : ILLUSIONARY

**il·lu·sion·ary** \-zhəˌnerē, -ri\ *adj* : of, relating to, marked by, or producing illusion ⟨~ stage effects⟩

**il·lu·sioned** \-zhənd\ *adj* : having illusions ⟨~ lovers⟩

**il·lu·sion·ism** \-zhəˌnizəm\ *n* -S **1** : a theory or doctrine affirming that the phenomenal world is wholly or nearly wholly illusory **2** : the use of or propensity for the use of often extreme illusionary effects esp. in art and decoration (as in the use of a technique in painting whereby an object represented appears nearer an observer than the surface on which it is painted)

**il·lu·sion·ist** \-ˌnəst\ *n* -S *often attrib* **1** : an adherent of the theory or doctrine of illusionism **2** : one that produces illusionary effects: as **a** : a painter or sculptor or architect whose work is marked by illusionism **b** : a ventriloquist or sleight-of-hand performer or magician

**il·lu·sion·is·tic** \=ˌ=zhəˈnistik\ *adj* : of, relating to, or marked by illusionism ⟨~ devices have been abundant in sculpture —P.A.Sorokin⟩

**il·lu·sion·less** \=ˈ=zhənləs\ *adj* : free from illusion ⟨the cold neon light of a modern novelist's ~ imagination —*N.Y. Herald Tribune Bk. Rev.*⟩

**il·lu·sive** \=ˈ=s|iv, |ēv *also* -z| *or* |əv\ *adj* [*illusion* + *-ive*] : ILLUSORY — **il·lu·sive·ly** \|əvlē, -li\ *adv* — **il·lu·sive·ness** \|ivnəs, |ēv- *also* |əv-\ *n* -ES

**il·lu·so·ri·ly** \ə'lüs(ə)rəlē, -üz(-, -li *also* əl'yü-\ *adv* : in an illusory manner

**il·lu·so·ri·ness** \-rēnəs, -rin-\ *n* -ES : the quality or state of being illusory

**il·lu·so·ry** \-rē, -ri\ *adj* [LL *illusorius* mocking, deceptive, fr. L *illusus* (past part. of *illudere* to mock or jeer at) + *-orius* -ory — more at ILLUSION] : of, relating to, or marked by illusion : based on or producing illusion : DECEPTIVE, UNREAL ⟨a tense period of ~ peace⟩ ⟨filled with ~ hopes⟩ **syn** see APPARENT

**illusory appointment** *n* : an appointment of a nominal or disproportionately small share of property to one of a class (as to one among several brothers) regarded as void in courts of equity because fraudulently defeating the intent of the original donor (as a violation of the power of appointment

**il·lus·trat·able** \'iləˌstrād·əbəl, -ātəb- *also* ə'ləˌs-\ *adj* : capable of being illustrated

**¹il·lus·trate** \'iləˌstrāt *also* ə'ləˌs-; *usu* -ād·+V\ *vb* -ED/-ING/-S [L *illustratus*, past part. of *illustrare*, fr. *in-* ²in + *lustrare* to purify, make bright, fr. *lustrum* — more at LUSTRUM] *vt* **1** *obs* **a** : to enlighten intellectually or culturally or spiritually **b** : to give physical light to : light up **2 a** *archaic* : to make illustrious : confer honor or distinction on **b** *obs* (1) : to make luminous or bright (2) : ADORN **3 a** : to make clear : remove obscurity from : make intelligible : CLARIFY, ELUCIDATE ⟨*illustrated* the new theory by careful references to what was already known⟩ **b** (1) : to make clear by giving examples or instances ⟨used many examples to ~ his lecture on what had been accomplished⟩ (2) : to make clear by reason of being an example or instance : serve as an example or instance of ⟨a national hero who embodies and ~s the nation's passionate love of freedom⟩ **c** (1) : to make clear or more helpful or attractive by furnishing or combining with apt visual features (as photographs, charts, slides) or other sensory aids (as recordings of music, speech) ⟨the author has *illustrated* the book with some excellent pictures⟩ ⟨*illustrated* the lecture on the history of art with a couple of short films and some color slides⟩ ⟨discussed some aspects of jazz and *illustrated* the talk with tape recordings⟩ (2) : to make clear or more helpful or attractive by reason of being an apt visual feature or other sensory aid ⟨a wealth of photographs ~ the book⟩ **d** : to provide with visual features (as photographs) or other sensory aids (as recordings) ⟨the book is very well *illustrated*⟩ ⟨a beautifully *illustrated* magazine⟩ **4** : to show to advantage : set in a clear light : clearly exhibit : DEMONSTRATE ⟨the gaiety we too often associate with levity of character is, as the French ~ it, a necessity of mental health —W.C.Brownell⟩ ⟨honoring and *illustrating* the supreme worth of freedom —Agnes Repplier⟩ ⟨a situation that ~s the need for tolerance⟩ ~ *vi* : to make something clear by furnishing an example or instance ⟨the speaker hesitated and then said he would endeavor to ~⟩

**²illustrate** *adj* [L *illustratus*] **1** *obs* : RESPLENDENT **2** *obs* : ILLUSTRIOUS

**illustrated** *n* -S *chiefly Brit* : a newspaper or magazine or other periodical marked by the inclusion of much pictorial material

**il·lus·tra·tion** \ˌiləˈstrāshən *sometimes* əˌləˈs-\ *n* -S [ME *illustracione*, fr. MF *illustration*, fr. L *illustration-, illustratio*, fr. *illustratus* + *-ion-, -io* -ion] **1 a** : the action of illustrating or condition of being illustrated **b** *obs* (1) : intellectual or cultural or spiritual enlightenment (2) : physical illumination **c** *archaic* : the action of making or condition of being made illustrious or honored or distinguished ⟨admirably translated by himself in ~ of Shelley —T.L.Peacock⟩ **2** : something that serves to illustrate: as **a** : an example or instance that helps make something clear ⟨gave an ~ of what he meant⟩ **b** : a picture or drawing or diagram or some other sensory aid that helps make something (as a book, a lecture) clear or more helpful or attractive **syn** see INSTANCE

**il·lus·tra·tion·al** \ˌ=ˌ=ˈstrāshənᵊl, -shnəl *sometimes* əˌləˈs-\ *adj* : of, relating to, or having the character of illustration : serving to illustrate : ILLUSTRATIVE ⟨~ technique⟩ ⟨a purely ~ drawing⟩

**il·lus·tra·tive** \ə'ləstrəˌd·|iv, |t| *sometimes* ə'ləˌstrā| *or* 'iləˌstrā| *or* |ēv *or* |əv\ *adj* : that illustrates : serving to illustrate ⟨plenty of ~ material is to be found in the book⟩ ⟨an ~ anecdote⟩ ⟨a remark that was ~ of his attitude toward life⟩ — **il·lus·tra·tive·ly** \|əvlē, |ēv-, -li\ *adv*

**il·lus·tra·tor** \'iləˌstrād·ə(r), -ātə- *also* ə'ləˌs-\ *n* -S [LL, fr. *illustratus* (past part. of *illustrare* to illustrate) + *-or* — more at ILLUSTRATE] : one that illustrates; *specif* : an artist that makes illustrations (as for books, magazines, advertising copy)

**il·lus·tra·to·ry** \ə'ləstrəˌtōrē, -tór-, -ri\ *n* -ES : ILLUSTRATIVE

**il·lus·tri·ous** \ə'ləstrēəs\ *adj* [L *illustris* (prob. back-formation fr. *illustrare* to illustrate) + E *-ous* — more at ILLUSTRATE] **1** : notably or brilliantly outstanding because of dignity (as of birth, rank, position) or because of achievements or actions or because of qualities possessed : very distinguished : greatly respected : EMINENT, FAMOUS ⟨a man who comes of an ~ family⟩ ⟨the ~ heroes of antiquity⟩ ⟨~ accomplishments⟩ **2** *obs* **a** : shining brightly with light **b** : clearly evident — **il·lus·tri·ous·ly** *adv* — **il·lus·tri·ous·ness** *n* -ES

**il·lu·vial** \(ˈ)i'lüvēəl, -vyəl *also* (ˈ)il'yü-\ *adj* [²*in-* + *-luvial* (as in *alluvial*)] : of, relating to, or marked by illuviation or illuviated materials or areas ⟨~ soil⟩

**il·lu·vi·ate** \i'lüvēˌāt *also* il'yü-\ *vi* -ED/-ING/-S [²*in-* + *-luviate* (as in *alluviate*)] : to undergo illuviation

**il·lu·vi·a·tion** \(ˌ)=ˌ==ˈāshən\ *n* -S [²*in-* + *-luviation* (as in *alluviation*)] : accumulation of dissolved or suspended soil materials in one area or horizon as a result of eluviation from another

**il·lu·vi·um** \=ˈ=vēəm\ *n, pl* **illuviums** \-ēəmz\ *or* **illu·via** \-ēə\ [NL, fr. ²*in-* + *-luvium* (as in *alluvium*)] : material leached from one soil horizon and deposited in another — compare ALLUVIUM, COLLUVIUM

**ill will** *n* [ME, part trans. of ON *illvili*, fr. *illr* ill + *vili* will — more at ILL] : unfriendly feeling : ANIMOSITY, HOSTILITY ⟨a growing *ill will* between the two countries⟩ ⟨bore them no *ill will*⟩ **syn** see MALICE

**ill–willer** \ˈ=ˈ==\ *n, archaic* : one that has an unfriendly disposition toward something specified ⟨an *ill-willer* to the human race —Thomas Hood †1845⟩

**ill–will·ie** \ˈ=ˈwili\ *adj* [ME (Sc dial.), fr. *ill will* + *-ie*] *chiefly Scot* : having an unfriendly disposition

**ill–wish** \ˈ=ˈ=\ *vt* **1** *dial Eng* : to wish evil or ill to **2** *dial Brit* : to put an evil spell on : BEWITCH, HEX

**il·ly** \'il(l)ē, -i\ *adv* [¹*ill* + *-ly*] : BADLY, ILL ⟨never were two beings more ~ assorted —Washington Irving⟩ ⟨his ~ concealed pride —Della Lutes⟩

**il·lyr·i·an** \ə'lirēən\ *adj, usu cap* [*Illyria*, ancient country on the eastern shore of the Adriatic sea (fr. L, fr. Gk) + E *-an*] **1 a** : of, relating to, or characteristic of ancient Illyria **b** : of, relating to, or characteristic of the Illyrians **2** : of, relating to, or characteristic of the Illyrian languages

**²illyrian** \"\ *n* -S *cap* **1** : a native or inhabitant of ancient Illyria **2 a** : the Indo-European languages of the Illyrians poorly attested and hence not certainly classified — see INDO-EUROPEAN LANGUAGES table **b** *obs* : SERBOCROATIAN

**il·lyr·ic** \-rik\ *adj, usu cap* [L *illyricus*, fr. Gk *illyrikos*, fr. *Illyria* + Gk *-ikos* -ic] : ILLYRIAN

**il·men·ite** \'ilməˌnīt\ *n* -S [G *ilmenit*, fr. *Ilmen* range, Ural Mts., U.S.S.R. + G *-it* -ite] : a usu. massive iron-black mineral $FeTiO_3$ of submetallic luster that is an important ore of titanium and is a compound of iron and titanium and oxygen and may sometimes occur in rhombohedral crystals with very close crystal-structural relations to hematite

**il·meno·rutile** \ˌilmə(ˌ)nō+\ *n* [G *ilmenorutil*, fr. *Ilmen* range + G *-o-* + *rutil* rutile] : black rutile containing niobium

**ilmo** *abbr* [It *illustrissimo*] most illustrious

**ILO** *abbr. often not cap* in lieu of

**ilo·ca·no** *or* **ilo·ka·no** \ˌēlōˈkä(ˌ)nō\ *n, pl* **ilocano** *or* **ilocanos** *or* **ilokano** *or* **ilokanos** *usu cap* [Sp *ilocano*, fr. *iloko* (native name in the Philippines) + Sp *-ano* -an] **1 a** : a major people inhabiting northern Luzon in the Philippines **b** : a member of such people **2** : the Austronesian language of the Ilocano people

**ilo·ilo** \ˌēlōˈē(ˌ)lō\ *adj, usu cap* [fr. *Iloilo*, Philippines] : of or from the city of Iloilo in the Philippines : of the kind or style prevalent in Iloilo

**ilo·ko** \ē'lō(ˌ)kō\ *n, pl* **iloko** *or* **ilokos** *usu cap* [native name in the Philippines] : ILOCANO

**i lon·ga** \'ī'lȯŋgə\ *n* [L, long i] : a taller variety of the letter *i* used occas. in writing Latin in classical times to indicate the sound \ē\ as contrasted with \i\

**ilon·got** \(ˌ)ēˌlȯŋˈgōt\ *n, pl* **ilongot** *or* **ilongots** *usu cap* [native name in the Philippines] **1 a** : a people inhabiting northern Luzon in the Philippines **b** : a member of such people **2** : the Austronesian language of the Ilongot people

**ilot** \'īlət\ *var of* ISLOT

**il più forte** \ēl'pyü+\ *adj* (*or adv*) [It] : very loud : as loud as possible — used as a direction in music

**il più piano** \"+\ *adj* (*or adv*) [It] : very soft : as soft as possible — used as a direction in music

**ILS** *abbr* instrument landing system

**il·se·mann·ite** \'il(t)səməˌnīt, 'ilzə-\ *n* -S [G *ilsemannit*, fr. J. C. *Ilsemann* †1822 Ger. mining commissioner + G *-it* -ite] : a mineral $Mo_3O_8.nH_2O$(?) consisting of black, blue-black, or blue earthy massive hydrous oxide or perhaps sulfate of molybdenum

**il·va·ite** \'ilvəˌīt\ *n* -S [G *ilvait*, fr. *Ilva* (Elba), Ital. island in the Mediterranean + G *-it* -ite] : a silicate $CaFe_3Si_2O_8(OH)$ of iron and calcium and sometimes manganese related to epidote and occurring in black prismatic crystals and columnar masses (hardness 5.5–6, sp. gr. 4.0)

**il·y·san·thes** \ˌiləˈsan(t)(ˌ)thēz\ *n, cap* [NL, fr. Gk *ilys* mud + NL *-anthes*] : a genus of low herbs (family Scrophulariaceae) with opposite leaves and small solitary usu. purplish flowers — see FALSE HEDGE HYSSOP

**il·y·si·idae** \ˌiləˈsīəˌdē\ [NL, fr. *Ilysia*, genus of burrowing snakes (fr. Gk *ilys* mud + NL *-ia*) + *-idae;* akin to OSlav *ilŭ* mud] + *-idae*] *syn of* ANILIIDAE

**im-** — see IN

**im** *abbr* immature

**IM** *abbr* **1** imperial measure **2** inner marker **3** intramuscular

**[1]im·age** \ˈimij, -mēj\ *n* -s [ME, fr. OF, short for *imagene*, fr. L *imagin-*, *imago;* akin to L *imitari* to imitate] **1 :** a reproduction of a person or thing: as **a :** STATUE **b** (1) **:** DEVICE, EMBLEM (2) **:** a figure used as a talisman or amulet esp. in conjurations (as by sorcerers in casting spells) **c** (1) **:** PICTURE, PORTRAIT (2) **:** a sculptured or fabricated object of symbolic value **:** IDOL; *specif* **:** a holy picture (as an ikon) **2 :** a thing actually or seemingly reproducing another: as **a** (1) **:** the optical counterpart of an object produced by a lens, mirror, or other optical system and being the geometric figure made up of the foci corresponding to the points of the object — see REAL IMAGE, VIRTUAL IMAGE (2) **:** an analogous phenomenon in some field other than optics ⟨an acoustic ~⟩ ⟨an electric ~⟩ **b :** any likeness of an object produced on a photographic material **3 :** exact likeness **:** SEMBLANCE **4 a :** a tangible or visible representation **:** INCARNATION ⟨a civil servant who is the ~ of conscientiousness⟩ **b** *archaic* **:** an illusory appearance **:** APPARITION **5 a** (1) **:** a mental picture **:** IMPRESSION ⟨a soldier haunted by ~*s* of battle⟩ ⟨~*s*, as contrasted with sensations, are the responses during a narrative —Bertrand Russell⟩ (2) **:** a mental conception held in common by members of a group and being symbolic of a basic attitude and orientation toward something (as a person, class, racial type, political philosophy, or nationality) ⟨the Frenchman's ~ of America⟩ **b :** the memory of a perception in psychology that is modified by subsequent experience and that contains both intellectual and emotional elements elicited by intrapsychic and extrapsychic stimuli; *also* **:** the representation of a stimulus object on a receptor mechanism **c :** IDEA, CONCEPT ⟨conflicting ~*s* of good and evil⟩ **6 :** a markedly vivid, effective, or graphic representation or description ⟨the set for the play being the ~ of a New England village⟩ **7 a :** something concrete or abstract introduced (as in a poem or speech) to represent something else which it strikingly resembles or suggests (as the use of *sleep* for *death*) — compare EMBLEM, SYMBOL **b :** a figure of speech (as a metaphor or simile) **:** TROPE **8 :** a person who is strikingly like another person in appearance, manner, or thought ⟨a son who is the ~ of his father⟩

**[2]image** \", *chiefly in pres part* -məj\ *vt* -ED/-ING/-S **1 :** to describe or portray in language esp. in an effective or vivid manner **2 :** to call up a mental picture of **:** IMAGINE ⟨we no longer ~ the native landscape in the terms beloved of Rossetti and Tennyson —Vincent Buckley⟩ **3 a :** REFLECT, MIRROR ⟨a face *imaged* in a mirror⟩ **b :** to make appear (as in desired form) **:** PROJECT ⟨film *imaged* on a screen⟩ **4 a :** to create a representation of **:** DEPICT, PORTRAY ⟨a national hero *imaged* in bronze on a village green⟩ **b** (1) **:** to create or produce a suggestion of **:** ADUMBRATE ⟨a symphony *imaging* the beauty of nature⟩ (2) **:** to represent symbolically **:** stand as a symbol of ⟨acres of headstones *imaging* the losses of war⟩

**image dissector** *n* **:** a camera tube resembling the iconoscope and having the electronic image focused electromagnetically through an aperture and voltages that are subsequently amplified and transmitted as television-picture signals being produced by electron multiplication

**im·age·less** \-ləs\ *adj* **:** characterized by absence of mental images ⟨an ~ thought⟩

**image orthicon** *n* **:** a camera tube that is similar to the iconoscope or the orthicon and uses secondary emission and electron multiplication to produce the voltages that are subsequently amplified and transmitted as television-picture signals

**im·ag·er** \ˈimijə(r), -mēj-\ *n* -s **:** one that images **:** a vivid describer or portrayer

**im·ag·ery** \-j(ə)rē, -ri\ *n* -ES [ME *imagerie*, fr. MF, fr. *image* + *-erie* -ery] **1 :** the product of image makers (as a statue, emblem, or idol) **:** IMAGES; *also* **:** the art of making images **2** *obs* **:** IMAGE WORSHIP **3 :** ornate or heightened description or figures of speech; *specif* **:** the often peculiarly individual concrete or figurative diction used by a writer in those portions of his texts where he wishes to produce a particular effect (as a special emotional appeal or a train of intellectual associations) ⟨Shakespeare's ~⟩ **4 :** mental images; *esp* **:** the products of imagination ⟨psychotic ~⟩

**images** *pl of* IMAGE, *pres 3d sing of* IMAGE

**image slicer** *n* **:** an attachment for a stellar spectrograph comprised of a system of very small mirrors that direct strips of light from various portions of the star-image disk so that they pass through the narrow slit of the spectrograph thereby increasing the intensity of the star's spectrum several times

**image space** *n* **:** a space in connection with an optical system each of whose points is an image of a corresponding point in the object space

**image tube** *n* **:** CAMERA TUBE

**image worship** *n* **:** the worship of images as the special residence of a divine spirit or supernatural power **:** IDOLATRY

**imag·in·able** \əˈmaj(ə)nəbəl\ *adj* [ME, fr. LL *imaginabilis*, fr. L *imaginari* to imagine + *-abilis* -able — more at IMAGINE] **:** capable of being imagined **:** CONCEIVABLE ⟨the biggest lies ~⟩ ⟨any ~ situation⟩ — **imag·in·able·ness** \-nəs\ *n* -ES — **imag·in·ably** \-blē, -bli\ *adv*

**imagi·nal** \əˈmajənᵊl, *in sense 4* -māgən- *or* -mägən- *or* -mågən- *or* -mājən- *or* -majən-\ *adj* [*imagine* + *-al*] **1 :** of or relating to imagination ⟨~ objects⟩ **2** [LL *imaginalis*, fr. L *imagin-*, *imago* image + *-alis* -al — more at IMAGE] **:** of or relating to an image ⟨the idea of weeping can be translated into its ~ equivalent, as rain —K.D.Burke⟩ **3** [NL *imagin-*, *imago* + E *-al*] **:** relating to mental images **4** [NL *imagin-*, *imago* + E *-al*] **:** of or relating to the insect imago

**imaginal disk** *also* **imaginal bud** *n* **:** one of the clusters of undifferentiated cells in the larvae and pupae of some insects from which the wings, legs, and other organs of the adult are formed

**imaginal type** *n* **:** a tendency of an individual to have images arising predominantly from one or another sense (as from vision, hearing, or taste)

**imaginant** *n* -s [L *imaginant-*, *imaginans*, pres. part. of *imaginari* to imagine — more at IMAGINE] *obs* **:** IMAGINER

**imag·i·nar·i·ly** \əˌmajəˈnerəlē, -li, ˌiˌ==ˈ===\ *adv* **:** in an imaginary manner

**imag·i·nar·i·ness** \əˈ==ˌnerēnəs, -rin-\ *n* -ES **:** the quality or state of being imaginary

**[1]imag·i·nary** \əˈmajəˌnerē, -ri\ *adj* [ME, fr. L *imaginarius*, fr. *imaginari* to imagine + *-arius* -ary] **1 a :** having no real existence **:** existing only in imagination or fancy **:** UNREAL, FANCIED, FICTITIOUS, HYPOTHETICAL ⟨to guard the cattle against their real and their ~ foes, the wolves and the witches —J.G. Frazer⟩ **b :** formed, characterized, or ascribed outside the evidence of reality **:** shaped, endowed, or attributed imaginatively or arbitrarily ⟨the statue of John Harvard . . . is an ~ likeness; no portrait of Harvard is known to exist —*Amer. Guide Series: Mass.*⟩ **2** *obs* **:** of the nature of or suggesting an image **3** *obs* **:** IMAGINATIVE **4 :** containing or related to the imaginary unit

**syn** FANCIFUL, VISIONARY, FANTASTIC, CHIMERICAL, QUIXOTIC: IMAGINARY stresses lack of reality; it indicates an existence, formation, or ascription by imagination, not fact ⟨those nervous persons who may be terrified by *imaginary* dangers are often courageous in the face of real danger —Havelock Ellis⟩ In relation to things, FANCIFUL indicates formation or conditioning by free, unrestrained fancy or imagination; in relation to people, it indicates a tendency to give free rein to the imagination ⟨*fanciful* tale of his own exploits tells how he was carried, wounded, down the mountainside in a big buckskin bag tied to the back of a wrinkled squaw —*Amer. Guide Series: Calif.*⟩ ⟨one may perhaps without being too *fanciful* see in his art something of the magic of the Celt —Irving Babbitt⟩ VISIONARY applies to a person given to seeing visions or to the ideas and notions from visions rather than real facts and hence impractical, wild, and impossible of fulfillment or fruition ⟨planning, as his *visionary* father might have done, to go to Brazil to pick up a fortune —Carl Van Doren⟩ ⟨unless, therefore, our philosophic vision receives technical development . . . it may rightly be condemned as unsubstantial and *visionary* —M.R.Cohen⟩ FANTASTIC and its variant FANTASTICAL heighten the notion of extravagant fancy far transcending the usual, ordinary, or real ⟨one of those eoan errors to which we are subject before the clear commonplace of daylight orders and moderates our tenebrous and *fantastical* imaginations —Rose Macaulay⟩ ⟨a *fantastic* world inhabited by monsters of iron and steel —Louis Bromfield⟩ ⟨two heroes may mangle each other in every impossible and *fantastic* way, beyond the bounds of the faintest shadow of verisimilitude —H.O.Taylor⟩ CHIMERICAL suggests the wild, utterly unreal, and extravagantly imaginary characteristics of creations of classical mythology ⟨the defeat was more complete, more humiliating . . . the hopes of revival more *chimerical* —*Times Lit. Supp.*⟩ ⟨as *chimerical* as a specter —Bernard Smith⟩ QUIXOTIC describes completely unrealistic and impractical devotion to romantic or chivalric ideals ⟨was *quixotic*, and would not permit a secret service and spies —G.K.Chesterton⟩ ⟨among the last *quixotic* acts of his life was an attempt to set up a Greek academy for aspiring authors —Alfred Kreymborg⟩ ⟨be so *quixotic* as to stand upon principles at the risk of losing the business —R.M.Cunningham⟩

**[2]imaginary** \"\ *n* -ES **1** *obs* **:** a figment of imagination **2 :** a complex number (as $2+3i$) whose imaginary part is not zero

**imaginary number** *n* **:** IMAGINARY 2

**imaginary part** *n* **:** the part of a complex number (as "3i" in $2+3i$) that has the imaginary unit as a factor

**imaginary unit** *n* **:** the positive square root of minus 1 **:** $+\sqrt{-1}$ — symbol *i*

**imag·i·na·tion** \əˌmajəˈnāshən\ *n* -s [ME *imaginacioun*, fr. MF *imagination*, fr. L *imagination-*, *imaginatio*, fr. *imaginatus* (past part. of *imaginari* to imagine) + *-ion-*, *-io* -ion — more at IMAGINE] **1 :** an act or process of forming a conscious idea or mental image of something never before wholly perceived in reality by the imaginer (as through a synthesis of remembered elements of previous sensory experiences or ideas as modified by unconscious mechanisms of defense); *also* **:** the ability or gift of forming such conscious ideas or mental images esp. for the purposes of artistic or intellectual creation ⟨our simple apprehension of corporeal objects, if present, is sense; if absent, is ~ —Joseph Glanvill⟩ **2 a :** creative ability **:** GENIUS ⟨the great ~*s* of literature⟩ **b :** ability to confront and deal with a problem **:** RESOURCEFULNESS ⟨the attempt shows suggestions of the ~ that the situation demands⟩ **3** *obs* **:** a plotting or scheming esp. of evil **:** PLOT ⟨all their vengeance and all their ~*s* against me —Lam 3:60 (AV)⟩ **4 a :** a mental image, conception, or notion formed by the action of imagination **b :** a creation of the mind; *esp* **:** an idealized or poetic creation ⟨the gory ~*s* of folk poetry⟩ **c :** fanciful or empty assumption ⟨idle ~*s*⟩ **5 :** popular or traditional belief **:** usual or accepted conception ⟨the Magna Charta . . . has operated in the meaning given it in ~ rather than by its literal contents —John Dewey⟩

**syn** FANCY, FANTASY, PHANTASY: IMAGINATION, freer of derogatory connotations than the other terms, is the most comprehensive, applying to the power of creating, in the mind or in an outward form as in a literary work, images of things once known but absent, of things never seen or never seen in their entirety, of things actually nonexistent, of things created new from diverse old elements, or of things perfected or idealized; it may carry the implication of mere tricky concoction, as of things unreal or odd, but is more frequently nearer the other extreme in suggesting the genuine artist's gift of perceiving more deeply or essentially and creating the interestingly and the significantly new and vital ⟨all youth lives much in reverie; thereby the stronger minds anticipate and rehearse themselves for life in a thousand *imaginations* —H.G.Wells⟩ ⟨*imagination* being little else than another name for illusion —Samuel Butler⟩ ⟨the *imagination* is able to manipulate nature as by creating three legs and five arms but it is not able to create a totally new nature —Wallace Stevens⟩ ⟨the production of vivid images, usually visual images . . . is the commonest and the least interesting thing which is referred to by *imagination* —I.A.Richards⟩ ⟨a product of fancy rather than imagination — if one accepts fancy as decorative and *imagination* as creative —Pamela L. Travers⟩ ⟨*imagination*, in his opinion, gets at relationships that are true at the deepest level of experience —F.A.Pottle⟩ ⟨*imagination* is something akin to what it was in Wordsworth, a means of deepest insight and sympathy —Roy Pascal⟩ ⟨it is only through *imagination* that men become aware of what the world might be —Bertrand Russell⟩ FANCY now usu. suggests the power to conceive and give expression to images of things removed from reality, usu. of things purely, sometimes frivolously though often delightfully, imaginary, often contrasting with IMAGINATION in suggesting a more superficial often factitious power of inventing the novel or unreal by recombining existing elements as opposed to the imagination's gift of grasping a deeper, more organic reality ⟨like all weak men of a vivid *fancy*, he was constantly framing dramas of which he was the towering lord —G.D.Brown⟩ ⟨the associative faculty performs, to a varying extent in individual cases, constantly shifting arrangements and rearrangements of the data of observation, thought, feeling . . . which Coleridge distinguishes from imagination by the word *fancy* —George Whalley⟩ ⟨in a creative artist the imagination functions . . . in three ways. It is partly mere *fancy*, which moves happily into make-believe —K.P.Kempton⟩ FANTASY or PHANTASY suggests the power of unrestrained, often extravagant or delusive, fancy, stressing the unreal more than *fancy;* PHANTASY is used more frequently than FANTASY in the technical sense of image-making power in general ⟨hard to say where the actuality ends and the *fantasy* begins in these sketches of life —B.C.L.Keelan⟩ ⟨fairy stories and *fantasy* are phenomenally popular —Lavinia R. Davis⟩ ⟨an appealing *fantasy*, though its appeal does not lie in what is fantastic about it. It lies in what is realistic and homely —*Time*⟩ ⟨a *fantasy* . . . may be distinguished from the representation of something that actually exists, but it is not opposed to "reality" and not an "escape" from reality. Thus, the idea of a rational society, or the image of a good house to be built, or the story of something that never happened, is a fantasy —Lionel Trilling⟩ ⟨this mechanical man or robot idea has been decidedly overdone in the writings of *fantasy* —C.C. Furnas⟩ ⟨a mixture . . . of comic *phantasy*, improbable adventure and rainbow colors —G.E.Fox⟩ ⟨a novelist is a person who has a highly developed gift of *phantasy* —Bernard De Voto⟩ ⟨its invention is based on the extinction of a wish *phantasy* belonging to the period of puberty —D.F.Tait⟩

**imag·i·na·tion·al** \-shənᵊl, -shnəl\ *adj* **:** of, relating to, involving, caused by, or suggestive of the imagination

**imag·i·na·tive** \əˈmaj(ə)nə|d·|iv, -jəˌnā|, |t|, |ēv *also* |əv\ *adj* [ME, fr. MF *imaginatif*, fr. *imagination* + *-if* -ive] **1 :** of or relating to the imagination: as **a :** created, inspired, guided, or drawn from the imagination and not from known facts or sources ⟨an ~ biography⟩ **b :** tending to provoke, excite, or enliven the imagination ⟨a few ~ comments⟩ **c** (1) **:** able to handle new or difficult problems **:** RESOURCEFUL ⟨a young and ~ general⟩ (2) **:** imbued with or showing an ability to draw conclusions, suggest hypotheses, make comparisons, or create systems ⟨an ~ interpretation of a poem⟩ ⟨an ~ critic⟩ ⟨~ research⟩ (3) **:** full of freshness, originality, or vividness ⟨~ patterns⟩ **d :** devoid of truth **:** FALSE ⟨the report of his death was wholly ~⟩ **2 :** of or relating to images; *esp* **:** showing a distinctive or fine command of artistic images ⟨~ diction⟩

**imag·i·na·tive·ly** \|əvlē, -li\ *adv* **:** in an imaginative manner ⟨a play produced ~⟩ ⟨an ~ planned garden⟩

**imag·i·na·tive·ness** \|ivnəs, |ēv- *also* |əv-\ *n* -ES **:** the quality or state of being imaginative

**imag·i·na·tor** \əˈmajəˌnād·ə(r)\ *n* -s [L *imaginatus* (past part. of *imaginari*) + E *-or*] **:** one that imagines; *esp* **:** a person who creates (as an artistic or intellectual work)

**imag·ine** \əˈmajən *sometimes* -maaj-; *when "I" precedes or when imperative & sentence-initial often* ˈm-\ *vb* **imagined; imagined; imagining** \-j(ə)niŋ\ **imagines** [ME *imaginen*, fr. MF *imaginer*, fr. L *imaginari*, fr. *imagin-*, *imago* image — more at IMAGE] *vt* **1 :** to form an idea of **:** create a mental image of ⟨~ accidents at every turn⟩ **2 :** to create by or as if by the imagination **:** FABRICATE ⟨*imagining* stories to fool the public⟩ **3 :** THINK, SUPPOSE, GUESS ⟨I ~ it will rain⟩ ~ *vi* **1** *obs* **:** PONDER, MEDITATE **2 :** to use the imagination; *specif* **:** to form images or conceptions **3 :** SUPPOSE, THINK

**syn** see THINK

**imag·in·er** \-j(ə)nə(r)\ *n* -s [ME, fr. *imaginen* + *-er*] **:** one that imagines

**imaging** *pres part of* IMAGE

**im·ag·ism** \ˈimiˌjizəm, -mēˌ-, -məˌ-\ *n* -s **:** a movement in poetry (as in America and England before World War I) advocating concrete language and figures of speech, modern subject matter, freedom in the use of meter, and avoidance of romantic or mystic themes — compare SYMBOLISM

**[1]im·ag·ist** \-ˌjəst\ *n* -s [[1]*image* + *-ist*] **:** one that follows the precepts of imagism

**[2]im·ag·ist** \"\ *or* **im·ag·is·tic** \ˌ==ˈjistik, -tēk\ *adj* **:** of or relating to imagism — **im·ag·is·ti·cal·ly** \-tək(ə)lē, -tēk-, -li\ *adv*

**ima·go** \əˈmā(ˌ)gō, -mä(-, -må(-\ *n, pl* **imagoes** *or* **imag·i·nes** \-māgəˌnēz; -mägəˌnēz, -måg-, -ˌnās; -mājəˌnēz, -maj-\ [NL, fr. L, image — more at IMAGE] **1 :** an insect in its final adult sexually mature usu. winged state — compare LARVA, NYMPH, PUPA **2 :** a conception of the parent that is retained in the unconscious, elaborated by infantile phantasies, and bound with the affect pertaining to the infantile period; *also* **:** an idealized mental image of any person including the self

**imam** \əˈmäm, (ˈ)ēˈ-, -mam\ *n* -s [Ar *imām*] **1 :** the prayer leader of a mosque **2 :** the caliph who is the spiritual and secular head of Islam **3 :** one of the twelve divinely inspired leaders of the Shiʻa appointed to guide men; *also* **:** one of their earthly representatives descended from Muhammad and appointed head of the Muslim community **4 :** one of the founders of the four orthodox schools of Muslim jurisprudence; *also* **:** any authoritative Muslim scholar who founds a school of interpretation or is followed as an authority in theology and law **5 :** any of various sovereign princes that claim descent from Muhammad and that exercise spiritual and temporal leadership over a Muslim region

**imam·ate** \-ˌāt\ *n* -s *often cap* **1 :** the office of an imam **2 :** the region or country ruled over by an imam ⟨the ~ of Yemen⟩

**imami** \-ē\ *n* -s [Ar *imāmī*, fr. *imām*] *usu cap* **:** TWELVER

**iman·to·phyl·lum** \(ˌ)īˌmantəˈfiləm\ [NL, irreg. fr. Gk *himanto-* (fr. *himant-*, *himas* thong) + NL *-phyllum*] *syn of* CLIVIA

**ima·ret** \əˈmärət\ *n* -s [Turk, fr. Ar ʻ*imārah* building] **:** an inn or hospice in Turkey

**ima·ri ware** \əˈmärē-\ *n, usu cap I* [fr. *Imari*, Japan, where it is made] **:** a Hizen porcelain characteristically decorated in red, green, and blue with a design of bamboo and cherry blossoms or hedges of brushwood growing out of stylized rocks

**im·balance** \(ˈ)im+\ *n* [[1]*in-* + *balance*] **:** absence of balance: as **a** (1) **:** loss of parallel relation between the optical axes of the eyes caused by faulty action of the extrinsic muscles and often resulting in diplopia (2) **:** absence of biological equilibrium (as in a gland) **b :** lack of balance between segments of a nation's economy (as between debit and credit in international payments or between costs and prices) **c :** a disproportion between the number of males and females in a population

**imbarn** *vt* -ED/-ING/-S [[2]*in-* + *barn* (n.)] *obs* **:** to gather into or store in a barn **:** GARNER

**im·base** \əm+\ *var of* EMBASE

**im·bat** \(ˈ)imˈbät\ *n* -s [Turk] **:** a cooling etesian wind in the Levant (as in Cyprus)

**im·ba·uba** \ˌimbəˈübə\ *also* **im·ba·ubao** \-üˌbau̇\ *n* -s [Pg *ambaúba*, *imbaúba*, *umbaúba*, fr. Tupi *ambauba*, *umbauba*] **:** TRUMPETWOOD

**im·be** \(ˈ)imˈbā\ *n* -s [Pg *imbé*, fr. Tupi] **1 :** a cordage fiber derived from the stems of an epiphytic Brazilian plant (*Philodendron imbe*) **2 :** the plant that yields imbe fiber

**[1]im·be·cile** \ˈimbəsəl *also* -(ˌ)sil *or* -ˌsīl, *chiefly Brit* -ˌsēl\ *adj* [MF *imbecille*, fr. L *imbecillus* weak, weak-minded, fr. *in-* [1]in- + *-becillus* (perh. fr. *bacillus*, *bacillum* small staff) — more at BACILLUS] **1** *archaic* **:** WEAK, FEEBLE **2** [F *imbécile*, fr. L *imbecillus*] **a :** of, relating to, or befitting an imbecile **b :** markedly inane, idiotic, foolish, or stupid — used as a generalized term of contempt

**[2]imbecile** \"\ *n* -s [F *imbécile*, fr. *imbécile*, adj] **1 :** one marked by mental deficiency: as **a :** one who has a less-than-normal average intelligence and intellectual capacity that is usu. above that of an idiot but below that of a moron **b :** a feebleminded person who has a mental age of approximately three to seven years and who requires special care and supervision in the performance of routine daily tasks of self-care (as feeding and clothing himself) **2 :** FOOL, IDIOT — used as a generalized term of contempt **syn** see FOOL

**im·be·cile·ly** \-əl(l)|ē, -il(l)|, -īll|, -ēll|, |i\ *adv* **:** in an imbecile manner

**im·be·cil·ic** \ˌimbəˈsilik, -ilēk\ *adj* **:** characteristic or suggestive of an imbecile ⟨an ~ grin⟩ ⟨~ conclusions⟩

**im·be·cil·i·ty** \ˌimbəˈsiləd·ē, -lətē, -i\ *n* -ES [MF *imbecillité*, fr. L *imbecillitat-*, *imbecillitas* weakness, weak-mindedness, fr. *imbecillus* + *-itat-*, *-itas* -ity] **1 a :** the quality or state of being weak **b :** INCAPACITY, INABILITY ⟨~ of judgment⟩ **2** [F *imbécillité*, fr. L *imbecillitat-*, *imbecillitas*] **:** the quality or state of being mentally weak — compare MENTAL DEFICIENCY **3 a :** complete nonsense **:** utter foolishness ⟨the ~ of trying to live without food⟩; *also* **:** FUTILITY **b :** something that is foolish or nonsensical

**imbed** *var of* EMBED

**imbellious** *also* **imbellic** *adj* [L *imbellis* (fr. *in-* [1]in- + *-bellis*, fr. *bellum* war) + E *-ous* or *-ic* — more at BELLICOSE] *obs* **:** not warlike

**im·bibe** \əmˈbīb\ *vb* -ED/-ING/-S [in sense 1, fr. ME *enbiben*, fr. MF *embiber*, fr. L *imbibere* to drink in, conceive, fr. *in-* [2]in- + *bibere* to drink; in other senses, fr. L *imbibere* — more at POTABLE] *vt* **1** *archaic* **:** to cause to absorb liquid **:** SOAK **2 a :** to receive into the mind and retain **:** ASSIMILATE ⟨~ moral principles⟩ **b :** to assimilate (as gas, light, or heat) or take into solution **3 a :** to consume by drinking ⟨~*s* vast quantities of strong coffee⟩ **b :** to drink in **:** ABSORB ⟨plants can ~ as much nourishment through their leaves as via their roots —F.J.Taylor⟩ ⟨a sponge *imbibing* moisture⟩ ~ *vi* **1 :** DRINK 2 **2 a :** to take in or up liquid **b :** to absorb or assimilate moisture, gas, light, or heat

**im·bib·er** \-ībə(r)\ *n* -s **:** one that imbibes

**im·bi·bi·tion** \ˌimbəˈbishən, -mˌbīˈbi-\ *n* -s [in sense 1, fr. ME *imbybycyon*, fr. MF *imbibition*, fr. L *imbibitus* (past part. of *imbibere*) + MF *-ion;* in other senses, fr. L *imbibitus* + E *-ion*] **1** *obs* **a :** saturation with or solution in liquid **b :** mixture of solid and liquid by such imbibition **2 :** the act or action of imbibing: as **a :** the taking up and sorption of fluid by a colloidal system resulting in swelling and offering a possible explanation of certain biological phenomena (as the retention of water by desert plants) — compare OSMOSIS 1, SYNERESIS 2 **b :** IMBIBITION PROCESS

**im·bi·bi·tion·al** \ˌ=(ˌ)=ˈbishənᵊl, -shnəl\ *adj* **:** of, relating to, or characterized by imbibition

**imbibition process** *n* **:** a process by which a photographic print is produced by absorption of a water-soluble dye by a relief image or a differentially absorbing image in gelatin or a similar medium or in which a previously formed dye image is transferred by absorption from one layer into another layer

**im·bi·rus·sú** \ˌimbərəˈsü, -rüˈsü\ *n* -s [Pg *embiruçú*, *embirussú*, fr. Tupi *embirussú*, *imbirussú*, fr. *embira*, *imbira* embira + *-ussú* big] **:** a timber tree of So. and Central America that is an undetermined species of the genus *Bombax* and that bears pods yielding a brownish fiber similar to kapok

**imbitter** *var of* EMBITTER

**imbosom** *var of* EMBOSOM

**imbound** *var of* EMBOUND

**imbrace** *obs var of* EMBRACE

**imbreviate** *vt* -ED/-ING/-S [ML *imbreviatus*, past part. of *imbreviare*, fr. L *in-* [2]in- + ML *brevis*, *breve* brief — more at BRIEF (n.)] *obs* **:** to write or enter in the form of a brief **:** ENROLL, REGISTER

**im·brex** \ˈimˌbreks, -ˌbriks\ *n, pl* **imbri·ces** \-ˌbrəˌsēz, -əˌkās\ [L] **1 :** a curved roof tile used esp. by the ancient Romans **:** PANTILE **2** [NL, fr. L] **:** one of the scales or subdivisions of imbricated ornament

**[1]im·bri·cate** \ˈimbrəkə|t, -rēk-, -rəˌkā|, *usu* |d·+V\ *adj* [LL *imbricatus*, past part. of *imbricare* to cover with imbrices, fr. L *imbric-*, *imbrex* (fr. *imbr-*, *imber* rain) + *-atus* -ate; akin to

Gk *ombros* rain, Skt *abhra* cloud, Arm *amb*, and perh. to L *nebula* mist, vapor, cloud — more at NEBULA] **1 :** lying lapped over each other in regular order in the manner of tiles or shingles on a roof — used esp. of bud scales, involucral bracts, fish scales **2 :** overlapping at the margins — used esp. of leaves in the bud — **im·bri·cate·ly** *adv*

**²im·bri·cate** \-rə,kāt, *usu* -ād·+V\ *vb* -ED/-ING/-S [LL *imbricatus*, past part.] *vt* **:** to cause (as tiles or layers of tissue in closing a wound) to overlap ~ *vi* **:** OVERLAP

**imbricated snout beetle** *n* **:** a small light-colored weevil (*Epicaerus imbricatus*) destructive to many vegetables and fruits

**imbricated texture** *n* **:** a texture in certain minerals (as tridymite) resembling overlapping plates

**im·bri·ca·tion** \,imbrə'kāshən\ *n* -S **1 :** an overlapping esp. of tiles or shingles or of successive layers of tissue in the closure of a wound **2 :** a decoration or pattern showing imbrication

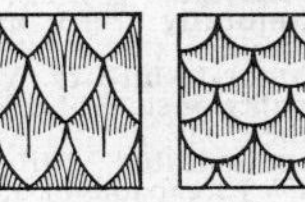
imbrication 1

**im·bro·glio** \əm'brōl(,)yō, -rōl-\ *or* **em·bro·glio** \", em-\ *n* -S [It *imbroglio*, fr. *imbrogliare* to entangle, confuse, embroil, fr. OIt, fr. MF *embrouiller* — more at EMBROIL] **1 :** a confused mass **:** CONGLOMERATION ⟨an ~ of papers and books⟩ **2 a :** an intricate or complicated situation (as in a drama or novel) **b :** an acutely painful or embarrassing misunderstanding ⟨an ~ between foreign ministers⟩ **c :** a violently confused or bitterly complicated altercation **:** EMBROILMENT ⟨an ~ over misuses of public funds⟩ **3 :** a musical passage designed to effect confusion by sharply contrasting the rhythm and meter (as between the voice parts in an opera)

**im·brue** \əm'brü\ *or* **em·brue** \", em-\ *vt* -ED/-ING/-S [ME *enbrewen, embrowen*, prob. fr. MF *abrevrer, abreuver, embevrer* to soak, drench, fr. (assumed) VL *abbiberare*, fr. L *ad-* + (assumed) VL *biberare* to give to drink, fr. L *bibere* to drink — more at POTABLE] **:** DRENCH ⟨a nation *imbrued* with the blood of executed men⟩

**imbrued** *adj* **:** stained with blood

**im·brute** \əm+\ *also* **em·brute** \əm, em+\ *vb* -ED/-ING/-S [²*in-* or ¹*en-* + *brute* (n.)] *vi* **:** to sink to the level of a brute **:** become bestial ~ *vt* **:** to degrade to the level of a brute **:** BRUTALIZE

**im·bue** \əm'byü\ *also* **em·bue** \", em-\ *vt* -ED/-ING/-S [L *imbuere* to dye, wet, moisten, prob. fr. *in-* ²in- + *-buere* (of unknown origin)] **1 :** to tinge or dye deeply ⟨a landscape deeply *imbued* with shadow⟩ **2 :** to cause to become penetrated **:** IMPREGNATE, PERMEATE ⟨a statesman *imbued* with a deep sense of national pride⟩ **syn** see INFUSE

**im·bu·ia** *or* **em·bu·ia** *also* **im·bu·ya** \əm'büyə\ *n* -S [Pg] **1 :** any of several Brazilian timber trees of the genera *Nectandra* and *Phoebe* (family Lauraceae) **2 :** the light to dark brown lustrous durable often strikingly figured wood of the imbuias that is readily polished and much used for fine cabinetwork — called also *Brazilian walnut*

**im·er·i·na** \,imə'rēnə\ *n, pl* **imerina** *or* **imerinas** *usu cap* **:** HOVA

**im·er·i·nite** \,imə'rē,nīt\ *n* -S [F *imerinite*, fr. *Imerina*, province of Madagascar, its locality + F *-ite*] **:** a monoclinic amphibole $Na_2(Mg,Fe)_6Si_8O_{22}(O,OH)_2$ that is related to richterite and occurs in colorless to blue acicular crystals **:** a basic silicate of sodium, iron, and magnesium

**im·er·i·tian** \,imə'rishən\ *also* **im·er·e·tian** \-rēsh-\ *n* -S *cap* [*Imeritia* or *Imeretia*, district of Georgian S.S.R. in the southern Caucasus + E *-an*] **1 :** a Georgian-speaking people of Imeritia **2 :** a member of the Imeritian people

**im·hoff tank** \'im,hȯf-, -hōf-\ *n, usu cap I* [after Karl *Imhoff* b1876 Ger. engineer] **:** a tank for sewage clarification consisting of an upper or sedimentation chamber with sloping floor leading to slots through which the solids settle to the lower sludge-digestion chamber

**imid-** *or* **imido-** *comb form* [ISV, fr. *imide*] **1** *now usu* **imido-** **:** containing the bivalent group =NH characteristic of imides united to or in one or two radicals of acid character ⟨*imido*carbonic acid $HN{=}C(OH)_2$⟩ ⟨*imido*disulfuric acid $HN(SO_2OH)_2$⟩ ⟨*imid*ate⟩ — distinguished from *imin-* **2 :** IMIN- — now less used than formerly

**imidaz-** *or* **imidazo-** *comb form* [ISV, fr. *imidazole*] **:** imidazole ⟨7-*imidazo* [4.5-*d*] pyrimidine⟩

**im·id·azole** \,imə'da,zōl -,da'z-\ *n* [ISV *imid-* + *azole*] **1 :** a white crystalline heterocyclic base $C_3H_4N_2$ made by the action of ammonia and formaldehyde on glyoxal and isomeric with pyrazole; 1,3-diazole — called also *glyoxaline*; compare STRUCTURAL FORMULA **2 :** any of a large class of derivatives of imidazole including histidine and histamine

[structural formula: imidazole 1]

**im·id·az·o·line** \,imə'dazə,lēn\ *n* -S [*imidazole* + *-ine*] **:** any of three dihydro derivatives $C_3H_6N_2$ of imidazole; *also* **:** a derivative of these — called also *glyoxalidine*

**im·id·az·o·lyl** \-zə,lil\ *n* -S [ISV *imidazole* + *-yl*] **:** any of four univalent radicals $C_3H_3N_2$ derived from imidazole by removal of one hydrogen atom

**im·ide** \'i,mīd, -,məd\ *n* -S [ISV, alter. of *amide*] **1 :** any of a class of compounds derived from ammonia by replacement of two hydrogen atoms by a metal ⟨calcium ~ CaNH⟩ ⟨lithium ~ $Li_2NH$⟩ — called also *metallic imide* **2 :** any of a class of compounds derived from ammonia by replacement of two hydrogen atoms by one bivalent acid radical or by two univalent acid radicals; *esp* **:** a cyclic compound (as phthalimide, saccharin) containing a bivalent acyl radical — called also *acid imide*; compare AMIDE — **imid·ic** \(')i¦midik\ *adj*

**imidic acid** *n* [ISV *imide* + *-ic*] **:** any of various acids characterized by the presence of the imido group; *esp* **:** one of a class of organic acids containing a carboxyl group in which the carbonyl oxygen atom is replaced by an imido group and having the general formula RC(=NH)OH but known only in the form of derivatives (as esters or acid chlorides)

**im·i·do** \'imə,dō\ *adj* [*imid-*] **1 :** relating to or containing the group =NH or a substituted group =NR united to one or two radicals of acid character — distinguished from *imino* **2 :** IMINO

**imido ester** *n* **:** an ester of an imidic acid

**imid·o·gen** \ə'midəjən, -,jen\ *n* -S [F *imidogène*, fr. *imid-* + *-gène* -gen] **:** a bivalent radical =NH derived from ammonia esp. as detected in the free state — compare IMIDO, IMINO

**imin-** *or* **imino-** *comb form* [ISV, fr. *imine*] **:** containing the bivalent group =NH characteristic of imines united to or in a nonacid bivalent radical ⟨*imino*porphyrins⟩ — distinguished from *imid-*

**im·in·az·ole** \,imə'na,zōl, -,na'z-\ *n* [*imin-* + *azole*] **:** IMIDAZOLE

**im·ine** \'i,mēn, -,mən\ *n* -S [ISV, alter. of *amine*] **:** any of a class of compounds (as ethylenimine) derived from ammonia by replacement of two hydrogen atoms by a bivalent hydrocarbon radical or other nonacid organic radical — distinguished from *amine*

**im·i·no** \'imə,nō\ *adj* [*imin-*] **:** relating to or containing the group =NH or a substituted group =NR united to a radical other than an acid radical — distinguished from *imido*

**imino ether** *n* **:** IMIDO ESTER

**imit** *abbr* imitation; imitative

**im·i·ta·bil·i·ty** \,imədə'biləd·ē, -mətə-, -lətē, -i\ *n* **1 :** the quality or state of being imitable **2 :** the power of exhibiting Platonic imitation

**im·i·ta·ble** \-əbəl\ *adj* [MF, fr. L *imitabilis*, fr. *imitari* + *-abilis* -able] **1 :** capable of being imitated or copied ⟨the music is curiously devoid of those analyzable — and ~ — features —Winthrop Sargeant⟩ **2 :** worthy of imitation — **im·i·ta·ble·ness** *n* -ES

**im·i·tan·cy** \'imədənsē, -mətə-, -si\ *n* -ES [*imitate* + *-ancy*] **:** tendency to imitation **:** IMITATIVENESS

**im·i·tant** \-nt\ *n* -S [L *imitant-, imitans*, pres. part. of *imitari*] **:** something that imitates **:** a counterfeit or substitute article or product

**im·i·tate** \'imə,tāt, *usu* -ād·+V\ *vt* -ED/-ING/-S [L *imitatus*, past part. of *imitari* — more at IMAGE] **1 :** to follow as a pattern, model, or example **:** copy or strive to copy (as in acts, manners, conduct) **:** assume the form or likeness of ⟨drama that ~s life⟩ **2 :** to produce a likeness of (as in form, character, color, qualities, conduct, manners) **:** REPRODUCE, COPY **3 :** to be or appear like **:** resemble in external appearance ⟨paper finished to ~ leather⟩ **4 a :** MIMIC, MOCK ⟨~ another's intonations⟩ ⟨*imitating* his father's halting walk⟩ **b :** to exhibit or assume mimicry of **:** MIMIC 4 ⟨chameleons *imitating* their background⟩ ⟨the viceroy butterfly is said to ~ the monarch⟩ **5** *dial Eng* **:** ATTEMPT, ENDEAVOR — usu. followed by an infinitive ⟨that colt will ~ to throw you, give him a chance⟩ **syn** see COPY

**im·i·tat·ee** \,imə,tād·'ē, -ā¦tē\ *n* -S [*imitate* + *-ee*] **:** one that is imitated

**im·i·ta·tion** \,imə'tāshən, *attrib* ¦==¦==\ *n* -S *often attrib* [L *imitation-, imitatio*, fr. *imitatus* + *-ion-, -io* -ion] **1 :** an act or instance of imitating **:** an assumption of or mimicking of the form of something that serves or is regarded as a model ⟨~ is the sincerest form of flattery⟩ ⟨the ~ of leaves by certain butterflies is unbelievably perfect⟩ ⟨a style developed in ~ of classic models⟩ **2 :** something that is made or produced as a copy **:** an artificial likeness **:** COUNTERFEIT ⟨risible ~s of his schoolfellows⟩ ⟨a convincing ~ of colonial architecture⟩ **3 a :** a literary work or composition designed to reproduce the style or manner of another author **b :** a free translation or an adaptation or parody esp. when involving transformation of cultural, social, or temporal situation **4 :** the repetition in a voice part of the melodic theme, phrase, or motive previously found in another part **5 a** *in Platonism* **:** the process through which a sensible object is informed by or participates in a subsistent idea or transcendent archetype — compare PARTICIPATION **b** *in Aristotelianism* (1) **:** the artistic simulation of anything as it is actually (2) **:** its representation as it is ideally or as it ought to be **6 a :** the execution of an act supposedly as a direct response to the perception of another person performing the act **b :** the assumption of the modes of behavior observed in other individuals

**im·i·ta·tion·al** \¦imə¦tāshən°l, -shnəl\ *adj* **:** relating to, marked by, or employed in imitation ⟨~ propensities⟩

**imitation art paper** *n* **:** a paper that is heavily filled with clay and given a high finish on the calenders

**imitation brick** *n* **:** brick made of material other than clay or shale but having the same appearance

**imitation leather** *n* **:** a material (as a coated fabric, rubber or plastic composition, or paper) made and finished to resemble genuine leather

**im·i·ta·tive** \'imə,tād·iv, -məd·əl, |t|, |ēv *also* |əv\ *adj* [LL *imitativus*, fr. L *imitatus* + *-ivus* -ive] **1 a :** marked by imitation **:** exhibiting some of the qualities of or formed after a model, pattern, or original ⟨acting is an ~ art⟩ **b :** ONOMATOPOEIC ⟨~ words intended to reproduce or represent a natural sound⟩ **c :** exhibiting mimicry **2 :** inclined to imitate **:** given to imitation ⟨man is an ~ being⟩ **3 :** imitating something superior **:** COUNTERFEIT — **im·i·ta·tive·ly** \|əvlē, |li\ *adv* — **im·i·ta·tive·ness** \|ivnəs, |ēv- *also* |əv-\ *n* -ES

**imitative magic** *n* **:** magic based on the assumption that a desired result (as rain, the death of an enemy) can be brought about or assured by mimicking it — called also *homeopathic magic*; compare SYMPATHETIC MAGIC

**im·i·ta·tor** \'imə,tād·ə(r), -ātə-\ *n* -S [L, fr. *imitatus* (past part. of *imitari* to imitate) + *-or* — more at IMAGE] **:** one that imitates **:** one that gives or produces imitations

**im·i·ta·tress** \'imə¦tā·trəs\ *also* **im·i·ta·trix** \-riks\ *n, pl* **imitatress·es** \-rəsəz\ *also* **imitatri·ces** \,==¦tā·trə,sēz, -,tə'trī(,)sēz\ *or* **imitatrix·es** \-==¦tā·triksəz\ **:** a female imitator

**im·mac·u·la·cy** \ə'makyələsē, -si\ *n* -ES **:** the quality or state of being immaculate

**im·mac·u·late** \-lət, *usu* -ləd·+V\ *adj* [ME *immaculat*, fr. L *immaculatus*, fr. *in-* ¹in- + *maculatus*, past part. of *maculare* to spot, stain — more at MACULATE] **1 :** having no stain or blemish **:** SPOTLESS, UNDEFILED, PURE ⟨an ~ heart⟩ **2 :** containing no flaw, fault, or error ⟨an ~ book⟩ **3 a :** lacking any spot, soil, or smirch **:** spotlessly clean ⟨his linen was ~⟩ **b** *biol* **:** having no colored spots or marks — **im·mac·u·late·ly** *adv* — **im·mac·u·late·ness** *n* -ES

**immaculate conception** *n* [trans. of ML *immaculata conceptio*] **1** *usu cap I & C* **:** a conception in which the offspring is immediately and constantly preserved free from original sin by divine grace — used of the conception of the Virgin Mary in the womb of Saint Anne and made an article of faith of the Roman Catholic Church by Pius IX; distinguished from *virgin birth* **2 :** conception not preceded by sexual intercourse; *broadly* **:** production of something without evident source or origin ⟨the naturalist must insist that reason is not of *immaculate conception* —H.J.Muller⟩

**im·malleable** \(')i(m), ə+\ *adj* [¹*in-* + *malleable*] **:** lacking malleability **:** UNYIELDING, RIGID

**im·manacle** \ə+\ *vt* [²*in-* + *manacle* (n.)] *archaic* **:** MANACLE, FETTER

**im·mane** \(')i¦mān, ə'm-\ *adj* [L *immanis*, fr. *in-* ¹in- + *manis, manus* good — more at MATURE] **1** *archaic* **:** vast in size or extent **:** HUGE **2** *archaic* **:** extremely cruel **:** INHUMAN

**im·ma·nence** \'imənən(t)s\ *n* -S **1 :** the state or quality of being indwelling or inward or of not going beyond a particular domain **:** INHERENCE: as **a :** the condition of being in the mind or experientially given **b** *in Kantianism* **:** the condition of being within the limits of possible experience — contrasted with *transcendence* **2 :** the indwelling presence of God in the world

**im·ma·nen·cy** \-nənsē, -si\ *n* -ES **1 :** IMMANENCE **2 :** the doctrine of immanence; *esp* **:** the principle that God is immanent in the world — distinguished from *transcendence*

**im·ma·nent** \-nənt\ *adj* [LL *immanent-, immanens*, pres. part. of *immanēre* to remain in place, inhabit, fr. *in-* ²in- + L *manēre* to remain — more at MANSION] **1 a :** remaining or operating within the subject considered **:** INDWELLING, INHERENT, INTRINSIC ⟨considering both ~ and external factors in social evolution⟩ ⟨in many cults . . . objects of cult are the temporary abodes of spirits; when the spirits are ~ the objects receive ceremonial treatment —*Notes & Queries on Anthropology*⟩ **b** *of a mental event* **:** confined to consciousness or to the mind **:** SUBJECTIVE ⟨a cognition is an ~ act of mind —William Hamilton †1856⟩ — contrasted with *transcendent* **2 :** being or characterizing the relation of the world to mind according to various philosophies — **im·ma·nent·ly** *adv*

**im·ma·nen·tal** \¦imə¦nent°l\ *adj* **:** relating to the doctrine of immanence **:** affirming and emphasizing the indwelling presence of God in the world ⟨an ~ religion⟩

**immanent cause** *n, Spinozism* **:** a cause originating and evolving within an entity ⟨God is the *immanent cause* of all things rather than the transient cause —*transl*⟩ — contrasted with *transient cause*

**im·ma·nent·ism** \'imənənt·,izəm, -nən-,ti-\ *n* -S **1 :** an epistemological theory according to which the relation of the world to the mind of an individual is one of immanence **2 :** any of several theories according to which the relation of God, mind, or spirit to the world including individuals is one of immanence ⟨the high ~ or near pantheism of Emerson and of the whole transcendentalist school owed not a little to oriental thought —C.S.Braden⟩

**im·ma·nent·ist** \-nəntəst, -,nen-\ *n* -S **:** an advocate of immanentism

**im·ma·nen·tis·tic** \¦imənən·¦tistik\ *or* **im·ma·nent·ist** \'imənəntəst, -,nen-\ *adj* **:** relating to or characteristic of immanentism

**im·ma·nent·iza·tion** \,imənəntə'zāshən, -,nentə'z-, -,nənt-,ī'z-\ *n* -S **:** the process of rendering immanent

**im·manifest** \(')i(m), ə+\ *adj* [¹*in-* + *manifest*] **:** not manifest

**im·manity** *n* -ES [L *immanitas*, fr. *immanis* immane + *-itas* -ity — more at IMMANE] *obs* **:** MONSTROSITY

**im·mantle** \ə+\ *vt* [²*in-* + *mantle* (n.)] **:** to cover or encircle with or as if with a mantle

**im·marble** *var of* EMMARBLE

**im·mar·ces·ci·ble** *or* **im·mar·ces·si·ble** \¦i(m),mär¦sesəbəl\ *adj* [LL *immarcescibilis*, fr. L *in-* ¹in- + LL *marcescibilis* withering, fr. L *marcescere* to wither, fade away + *-ibilis* -ible — more at MARCESCENT] **:** IMPERISHABLE, INDESTRUCTIBLE — **im·mar·ces·ci·bly** *or* **im·mar·ces·si·bly** \-blē\ *adv*

**im·marginate** \(')i(m), ə+\ *adj* [¹*in-* + *marginate*] **:** lacking a definite margin

**immask** *vt* [²*in-* + *mask* (n.)] *obs* **:** to cover with or as if with a mask **:** DISGUISE

**im·material** \¦i(m)+\ *adj* [ME *immateriel*, fr. MF, fr. LL *immaterialis*, fr. L *in-* ¹in- + LL *materialis* material — more at MATERIAL] **1 :** not consisting of matter **:** INCORPOREAL, SPIRITUAL, DISEMBODIED ⟨in making mind purely ~ . . . the body ceases to be living —John Dewey⟩ ⟨ghosts and other ~ entities⟩ **2** *obs* **:** having little body or substance **:** FLIMSY **3 a :** of no substantial consequence **:** UNIMPORTANT ⟨wholly ~ whether he stays or not⟩ ⟨the exact form of government appears ~ —Aidan Mulloy⟩ **b :** not material or essential to a legal matter or case — **im·materially** \"+\ *adv* — **im·materialness** \"+\ *n*

**im·materialism** \"+\ *n* **1 :** immaterial state or being **2 :** a philosophical theory that views external bodies as being of the essence of mind; *specif* **:** BERKELEIANISM

**im·materialist** \"+\ *n* **:** an advocate of philosophical immaterialism

**im·materiality** \"+\ *n* **:** the quality or state of being immaterial; *also* **:** something immaterial

**im·materialize** \"+\ *vt* **:** to render immaterial or incorporeal

**im·ma·te·ri·als** \,i+\ *n pl* **:** immaterial or incorporeal things

**im·matriculate** \,i+\ *vt* [ML *immatriculatus*, past part. of *immatriculare* to join, fr. L *in-* ²in- + ML *matricula* — more at MATRICULA] *archaic* **:** MATRICULATE, ENROLL

**im·matriculation** \,i+\ *n* [prob. fr. G *immatrikulation*, fr. ML *immatriculatus* + G *-ion*] **:** an act, state, or process of being enrolled (as in an official register) ⟨lands on which a native title can be shown are put through a process of ~; a tax is then levied —F.M.Keesing⟩

**¹im·mature** \¦i(m)+\ *adj* [L *immaturus*, fr. *in-* ¹in- + *maturus* mature — more at MATURE] **1** *archaic* **:** PREMATURE, UNTIMELY **2 a :** lacking complete growth, differentiation, or development ⟨poor thin ~ soils⟩ ⟨~ animals⟩ **:** UNRIPE ⟨~ fruit⟩ **b** (1) **:** having capacities or potentialities for attaining but not yet having attained a definitive form or state ⟨~ talents⟩ ⟨a vigorous but ~ school of art⟩ **:** CRUDE, UNFINISHED (2) *of a topographic feature* **:** predictably due to undergo further changes **:** not having attained maturity — used esp. of valleys and drainages while most of the area is well above baselevel **c :** exhibiting less than a normal or expected degree of maturity ⟨emotionally ~ adults⟩ ⟨the alcoholic is an ~, maladjusted individual —W.L.Wilkins⟩ — **im·maturely** \"+\ *adv* — **im·matureness** \"+\ *n*

**²im·mature** \"+\ *n* -S **:** an immature individual; *esp* **:** a young bird that has molted the juvenal plumage but has not yet acquired complete adult plumage

**im·matured** \"+\ *adj* [¹*in-* + *matured*, past part. of *mature*] **:** IMMATURE

**im·maturity** \"+\ *n* [L *immaturitas*, fr. *immaturus* + *-itas* -ity] **1 :** the state or quality of being immature ⟨emotional and cultural ~⟩ ⟨the ~ of such coarse mineral soils⟩ **2 :** something immature ⟨childish *immaturities*⟩ ⟨always within his *immaturities* is the saving grace of his willingness . . . to accept responsibility —*Times Lit. Supp.*⟩

**im·measurability** \(¦)i+\ *n* **:** the quality or state of being immeasurable

**im·measurable** \(')i(m)+\ *adj* [ME *ynmesurable*, fr. *yn-* ¹in- + *mesurable* measurable — more at MEASURABLE] **:** incapable of being measured **:** IMMENSURABLE; *broadly* **:** indefinitely extensive **:** ILLIMITABLE — **im·measurableness** \"+\ *n* — **im·measurably** \"+\ *adv*

**im·measured** \"+\ *adj* [¹*in-* + *measured*] **:** IMMEASURABLE, VAST

**im·mechanical** \¦i(m)+\ *adj* [¹*in-* + *mechanical*] *archaic* **:** not mechanical **:** UNTECHNICAL

**im·me·di·a·cy** \ə'mēdēəsē, -si, *chiefly Brit* -mējəs- *or* -mēdyəs-\ *n* **1 :** the quality or state of being immediate; *usu* **:** freedom from or absence of an intervening medium **:** direct presence **:** DIRECTNESS, CONTIGUITY ⟨the ~ of personal experience —*London Calling*⟩ ⟨television has on occasion furnished a startling ~ . . . to news reports —F.L.Mott⟩ — opposed to *mediacy* **2 :** something that is immediate ⟨the ~ of our need⟩ — usu. used in pl. ⟨the *immediacies* of life⟩ **3 :** the state or relation under feudal law of being immediate lord or vassal **4 a :** the direct content of consciousness or consciousness itself as distinguished from what consciousness represents or mediates a knowledge of **b :** direct awareness or presentations of sense as contrasted with what is added by memory and association or thought **c :** the quality of something that is self-evident or intuited as contrasted with something that is arrived at by thought or reason

**im·me·di·ate** \ə'mēdē|ət, *usu* |d·+V; *chiefly Brit* -mējət *or* -mēdyət\ *adj* [LL *immediatus*, fr. L *in-* ¹in- + *mediatus* mediate — more at MEDIATE] **1 a :** acting or being without the intervention of another object, cause, or agency **:** DIRECT, PROXIMATE ⟨the ~ cause of death⟩ **b :** of or relating to psychic immediacy **:** being or occurring without reference to other states or factors **:** INTUITIVE ⟨~ knowledge⟩ **2** *of relations between persons* **a :** having no individual intervening **:** being next in line or relation **:** not secondary or remote ⟨the ~ parties to the quarrel⟩ ⟨only the ~ family was present⟩ ⟨you are most ~ to our throne —Shak.⟩ **b :** standing in or being the relation of vassal and lord when the one holds directly of the other **3 a :** occurring, acting, or accomplished without loss of time **:** made or done at once **:** INSTANT ⟨an ~ need for help⟩ ⟨~ expenses⟩ ⟨agreed to an ~ marriage⟩ **b** *of time* **:** near to or related to the present ⟨sometime in the ~ past⟩ ⟨the ~ future is uncertain⟩ **4 :** characterized by contiguity **:** existing without intervening space or substance ⟨bring the chemicals into ~ contact very cautiously⟩; *broadly* **:** being near at hand **:** not far apart or distant ⟨hid the money in the ~ neighborhood⟩

**immediate annuity** *n* **:** an annuity which is purchased with a single premium and on which the initial payment is made to the annuitant within the first year

**immediate constituent** *n* **:** any of the two or three meaningful parts directly forming a larger expression

**immediate inference** *n* **1 :** an inference drawn from a single premise **2 :** the operation of drawing an inference from a single premise

**¹im·me·di·ate·ly** *pronunc at* IMMEDIATE +lē *or* li; *or* ÷-mēdət-\ *adv* [ME *immediatly*, fr. LL *immediatus* + ME *-ly*] **1 :** without intermediary **:** in direct connection or relation **:** CLOSELY ⟨~ contiguous⟩ ⟨~ away from the shore⟩ **2 :** without interval of time **:** without delay **:** STRAIGHTWAY ⟨~ after the meeting⟩ ⟨come home ~⟩

**²immediately** \"\ *conj* **:** as soon as ⟨~ his intentions are understood, he may leave⟩

**im·me·di·ate·ness** *pronunc at* IMMEDIATE +nəs\ *n* -ES **:** the quality or state of being immediate **:** IMMEDIACY ⟨the ~ of their relationship⟩

**im·me·di·a·tism** \-ə,tizəm\ *n* -S **1 :** IMMEDIATENESS **2 :** a policy or practice of gaining a desired end by immediate action; *specif* **:** a policy advocating the immediate abolition of slavery **3 :** an epistemological theory that views the object of perception as directly knowable

**im·me·di·a·tist** \-əd·əst, -ətə-\ *n* -S **:** one that advocates or believes in immediatism

**im·medicable** \(')i(m)+\ *adj* [L *immedicabilis*, fr. *in-* ¹in- + *medicabilis* medicable — more at MEDICABLE] **:** being such as cannot be healed or remedied **:** INCURABLE ⟨this ~ evil⟩ — **im·medicably** \"+\ *adv*

**im·mel·mann** \'imalmən, -l,män\ *vi* -ED/-ING/-S *often cap* [*Immelmann (turn)*] **:** to execute an Immelmann turn

**immelmann turn** *also* **immelmann** *n, usu cap I* [after Max *Immelmann* †1916 Ger. aviator] **:** a maneuver in which an airplane is first made to complete half of a loop and is then rolled half of a complete turn — called also *reverse turn*

**im·melodious** \¦i(m)+\ *adj* [¹*in-* + *melodious*] **:** not melodious

**im·memorable** \(')i(m)+\ *adj* [L *immemorabilis*, fr. *in-* ¹in- + *memorabilis* memorable — more at MEMORABLE] **1 :** not memorable **2 :** IMMEMORIAL — **im·memorably** \"+\ *adv*

**im·memorial** \¦i(m)+\ *adj* [prob. fr. F *immémorial*, fr. MF *immemorial*, fr. L *in-* ¹in- + *memorial* — more at MEMORIAL] **:** extending beyond the reach of memory, record, or tradition **:** indefinitely ancient ⟨existing from time ~⟩ ⟨a chapel of ~ age —Andrew Lang⟩ ⟨~ elms —Alfred Tennyson⟩ — **im·memorially** \"\ *adv*

**¹im·mense** \ə'men(t)s\ *adj, sometimes* -ER/-EST [MF, fr. L *immensus* immeasurable, boundlesss, vast, fr. *in-* ¹in- + *mensus*, past part. of *metiri* to measure — more at MEASURE] **1 :** marked by greatness in size, amount, number, degree, force, significance; *often* **:** transcending usual procedures of measuring and estimating ⟨the Los Angeles Aqueduct . . . like an ~ snake along the base of the mountains —*Amer. Guide Series: Calif.*⟩ ⟨thousands of lakes and ponds afford congenial haunts for ~ numbers of water birds —*Amer. Guide Series: Minn.*⟩ ⟨the ~ relief of the armistice —Mary Austin⟩ **2 :** supremely good **:** EXCELLENT, FINE ⟨the reading has been ~ . . . started on the *Odyssey* and read six books with uncritical joy —H.J.Laski⟩ **syn** see HUGE

**²immense** \"\ *n* -s **:** immense space, extent, or number **:** IMMENSITY ⟨the dark ~ of air —Alfred Tennyson⟩

**im·mense·ly** *adv* **:** to an immense degree **:** VERY, EXCEEDINGLY

**im·mense·ness** *n* -ES **:** the quality or state of being immense **:** IMMENSITY

**im·men·si·ty** \-n(t)sәd·ē, -әtē, -i\ *n* -ES [ME *inmensitee*, fr. MF or L; MF *immensité*, fr. L *immensitat-, immensitas*, fr. *immensus* + *-itat-, -itas* -ity] **1 a :** immeasurable or boundless size, quantity, or degree **:** vastness in extent or bulk **:** unlimited extension ⟨the starry ~ of the heavens⟩ **b :** greatness of scope ⟨the ~ of this concept⟩ ⟨undertook a task of grave ~⟩ **2 :** something that is immense **:** vast or infinite being, existence, or space ⟨the gigantic temples of Egypt, those massive *immensities* of granite —Edith Hamilton⟩ ⟨the mountain reared its white ~ before us⟩

**im·mensurability** \(ˌ)i(m)+\ *n* [ML *immensurabilitas*, fr. LL *immensurabilis* + L *-itas* -ity] **:** the quality or state of being immensurable

**im·mensurable** \(')i(m)+\ *adj* [LL *immensurabilis*, fr. L *in-* ¹in- + LL *mensurabilis* measurable — more at MEASURABLE] **:** not capable of being measured; *esp* **:** vastly large — **im·mensurableness** \"+\ *n* -ES

**im·mensurate** \(')i(m)¦men(t)s(ə)rət, -mench(ə)-\ *adj* [LL *immensuratus*, fr. L *in-* ¹in- + LL *mensuratus*, past part. of *mensurare* to measure — more at MENSURABLE] **:** UNMEASURED, UNLIMITED

**im·merd** \i'mərd\ *vt* -ED/-ING/-S [²in- + L *merda* dung; akin to Gk *smordoun* to copulate, OSlav *smrŭděti* to stink, and prob. to L *mordēre* to bite — more at SMART] *archaic* **:** to cover with ordure

**im·merge** \(')i(m)¦mərj\ *vb* [L *immergere* — more at IMMERSE] *vt, archaic* **:** to plunge (something) into, under, or within a fluid or other medium **:** IMMERSE ~ *vi* **1 a** *obs* **:** to plunge into a fluid **b :** to plunge into or immerse oneself in something ⟨no need to ~ further into this topic⟩ **2** *obs, of a celestial body* **:** to disappear by passing behind some obscuring agent (as a horizon or another celestial body)

**im·mer·gence** \-jən(t)s\ *n* **:** act of immerging

**immerit** *n* [¹in- + *merit*] *obs* **:** lack of worth **:** DEMERIT

**immerited** *adj* [¹in- + *merited*] *obs* **:** UNDESERVED

**im·mer·sal** \ə'mərsəl, -məs-, -məis-\ *n* -s [*immerse* + *-al*] **:** the state of being immersed ⟨his complete ~ in affairs of state⟩

**im·merse** \ə'mərs, -məs, -məis\ *vb* -ED/-ING/-S [L *immersus*, past part. of *immergere*, fr. *in-* ²in- + *mergere* to dip, merge — more at MERGE] *vt* **1 a** (1) **:** to plunge or dip into a liquid ⟨~ the cut beans in boiling water to blanch⟩ ⟨test the temperature before *immersing* yourself in the pool⟩ (2) **:** to baptize by immersion **b :** to enclose in something **:** EMBED, INCLUDE, SINK, BURY ⟨fossils *immersed* in sandstone⟩ ⟨the lower half of the cuttings should be *immersed* in moist sand⟩ **2 :** to engross the attention of **:** engage deeply **:** ABSORB ⟨~s himself completely in his work⟩ ⟨has been *immersed* almost all his life in the business of the law —M.R.Cohen⟩ ~ *vi* **:** to become absorbed **:** PLUNGE, SINK **syn** see DIP

**immersed** *adj* **:** submerged in or as if in a fluid: as **a :** completely engrossed **b** (1) *of a bodily structure* **:** completely embedded in or sunk below the surface of another part or organ (2) *of the capsule of a moss* **:** covered by the perichaetium **c** *of a plant* **:** growing wholly under water

**immersed wedge** *n* **:** the wedge-shaped portion of a ship that becomes immersed when the ship rolls

**im·mers·ible** \-səbəl\ *adj* **:** capable of being immersed

**im·mer·sion** \-mər|zhən, -mə|, -məi|, |sh-\ *n* -s [LL *immersion-, immersio*, fr. L *immersus* + *-ion-, -io* -ion] **:** an act of immersing or a state of being immersed: as **a** (1) **:** a sinking or plunging usu. into or within a fluid **:** DIPPING ⟨the sense of chill that follows ~ of the hand in a volatile liquid⟩ (2) **:** submersion in water for the purpose of Christian baptism **:** baptism by complete submersion of the person in water — compare AFFUSION, ASPERSION **b :** disappearance of a celestial body either by passing behind another (as in the occultation of a star by the moon) or by passing into its shadow (as in the eclipse of a satellite) — compare EMERSION **c :** SIMPLE IMMERSION

**im·mer·sion·al** \-zhənᵊl, -zhnəl, -sh-\ *adj* **:** of, relating to, or occurring through immersion ⟨~ baptism⟩

**immersion cup** *n* **:** a cup used for examining a gem immersed in a liquid of high refractive index

**immersion foot** *n* **:** a painful condition of the feet marked by inflammation and stabbing pain and followed by discoloration, swelling, ulcers, and numbness due to prolonged exposure to moist cold usu. without actual freezing — compare TRENCH FOOT

**immersion heater** *n* **:** a usu. electric unit for heating a liquid by immersion

**im·mer·sion·ism** \-zhə,nizəm, -sh-\ *n* -s **:** a doctrine that immersion is essential to Christian baptism **:** the practice of baptism by immersion

**im·mer·sion·ist** \-‚nəst\ *n* -s **:** one that advocates or practices immersionism

**immersion lens** *or* **immersion objective** *n* **:** an objective of short focal distance designed to work with a drop of liquid (as oil or water) between front lens and cover glass

**immersion liquid** *n* **:** a liquid of known refractive index used by gemmologists to reduce refraction of light at the surfaces of a gem and facilitate examination of the interior

immersion heater

**immesh** *var of* ENMESH

**im·methodical** *also* **im·methodic** \¦i(m)+\ *adj* [¹in- + *methodical, methodic*] **:** lacking method or order **:** not methodical ⟨a careless ~ program⟩ — **im·methodically** \"+\ *adv*

**im·metrical** \(')i(m)+\ *adj* [¹in- + *metrical*] **:** lacking meter **:** UNMETRICAL ⟨a harsh ~ line of verse⟩ — **im·metrically** \"+\ *adv*

**im·meu·bles** \ēmœbl(ᵊ), -b(lə)\ *n pl* [F, pl. of *immeuble* piece of fixed property, fr. MF, fr. *immeuble* immovable (in *biens immeubles* immovable property), fr. OF *immoble*, fr. L *immobilis* — more at IMMOBILE] **:** a class of property under French law that consists essentially of immovables — compare MEUBLES

**im·mie** \'imē\ *n* -s [*imm-* (fr. *imitation agate*) + *-ie*] **:** MARBLE 2a; *esp* **:** a glass marble streaked with colors

**¹im·mi·grant** \'imәgrәnt, -mēg- *sometimes* -‚grant *or* -‚graa(ә)nt\ *n* -s [L *immigrant-, immigrans*, pres. part. of *immigrare*] **:** one that immigrates: **a :** a person that comes to a country for the purpose of permanent residence — compare EMIGRANT **b :** a plant or animal that appears and becomes established in an area in which it was previously unknown

**²immigrant** \"\ *adj* **:** of, relating to, or composed of immigrants ⟨an ~ fauna⟩ ⟨department concerned with ~ affairs⟩ **:** IMMIGRATING ⟨~ birds⟩

**im·mi·grate** \'imә‚grāt\ *vb* [L *immigratus*, past part. of *immigrare* to remove, go in, fr. *in-* ²in- + *migrare* to migrate — more at MIGRATE] *vi* **:** to come to dwell or settle **:** to enter and usu. become established ⟨white blood cells ~ to the site of the injury⟩; *esp* **:** to come into a country of which one is not a native for the purpose of permanent residence ~ *vt* **:** to bring in or send as immigrants

**im·mi·gra·tion** \‚imә'grāshәn\ *n* -s *often attrib* **1 :** an act or instance of immigrating; *specif* **:** a going into a country for the purpose of permanent residence **2 :** a party of immigrants; *broadly* **:** the number of immigrants arriving during a given period

**im·mi·gra·tion·al** \¦imә¦grāshәnᵊl, -shnәl\ *adj* **:** relating to or concerned with immigration

**immigration pressure** *n* **:** the effect on the makeup of a natural population of recurrent immigrations of individuals capable of interbreeding with the original stock

**im·mi·gra·to·ry** \'imәgrә‚tōrē, -mēg-, -ōr-, -ri\ *adj* **:** of, relating to, or constituting immigration ⟨~ movements of populations⟩

**immind** *vt* [²in- + *mind* (n.)] *obs* **:** REMIND

**im·mi·nence** \'imәnәn(t)s\ *n* -s [L *imminentia*, fr. *imminent-, imminens* + *-ia* -y] **1** *also* **im·mi·nen·cy** \-nәnsē, -si\ -ES **:** the quality or state of being imminent **2 :** something that is imminent; *usu* **:** impending evil or danger

**im·mi·nent** \-nәnt\ *adj* [L *imminent-, imminens*, pres. part. of *imminēre* to project, threaten, fr. *in-* ²in- + *-minēre* (akin to L *mont-, mons* mountain) — more at MOUNT] **1 :** ready to take place **:** near at hand **:** IMPENDING ⟨our ~ departure⟩; *usu* **:** hanging threateningly over one's head **:** menacingly near ⟨in ~ jeopardy⟩ ⟨this ~ danger⟩ **2 :** IMMANENT — **im·mi·nent·ly** *adv* — **im·mi·nent·ness** *n* -ES

**im·min·gle** \i+\ *vb* [²in- + *mingle*] **:** BLEND, INTERMINGLE

**im·mi·nu·tion** \‚imә'n(y)üshәn\ *n* -s [L *imminution-, imminutio*, fr. *imminutus* (past part. of *imminuere* to lessen, fr. *in-* ²in- + *minuere* to lessen) + *-ion-, -io* -ion — more at MINOR] *archaic* **:** DIMINUTION

**im·miscibility** \(ˌ)i(m)+\ *n* **:** inability to mix or become homogeneous

**im·miscible** \(')i(m)+\ *adj* [¹in- + *miscible*] **:** incapable of mixing or being mixed **:** unable to blend or attain homogeneity ⟨makes separate polyphonic lines more ~ by writing them sometimes in different keys —Joseph Kerman⟩ — used esp. of liquids ⟨~ solvents⟩; compare INCOMPATIBLE — **im·miscibly** \"+\ *adv*

**im·mis·er·i·za·tion** \i‚mizәrә'zāshәn, -‚rī'z-\ *n* -s [²in- + *miserable* + *-ization*; intended as trans. of G *verelendung*] **:** act of making or state of becoming miserable; *esp* **:** IMPOVERISHMENT ⟨the ~ of the proletariat⟩

**im·mis·sion** \(')i¦mishәn\ *n* [L *immission-, immissio*, fr. *immissus* past part. of *immittere* to send in (fr. *in-* ²in- + *mittere* to send) + *-ion-, -io* -ion — more at SMITE] **1 a** *archaic* **:** an act of sending or letting in **:** INJECTION, ADMISSION, INTRODUCTION **b** *obs* **:** something introduced **2 :** COMMIXTURE 2

**im·mit** \i'mit\ *vt* **immitted; immitted; immitting; immits** [L *immittere*] *archaic* **:** to send or let in **:** INJECT, ADMIT, INTRODUCE

**im·mitigable** \(')i(m)+\ *adj* [LL *immitigabilis*, fr. L *in-* ¹in- + *mitigare* to mitigate + *-abilis* -able — more at MITIGATE] **:** not capable of being mitigated, softened, lessened, or appeased ⟨such ~ evil⟩ — **im·mitigableness** \"+\ *n* -ES — **im·mitigably** \"+\ *adv*

**im·mix** \i'miks\ *vt* [back-formation fr. *immixed* mixed in, fr. ME *immixte*, fr. L *immixtus*, past part. of *immiscēre* to mix in, fr. *in-* ²in- + *miscēre* to mix — more at MIX] **:** to mix intimately **:** mix in or up **:** COMMINGLE

**im·mix·able** \(')i(m)¦miksәbәl\ *adj* [¹in- + *mixable*] **:** IMMISCIBLE

**im·mixture** \i+\ *n* [L *immixtus* + E *-ure*] **:** the act of immixing **:** the quality or state of being immixed **:** an intimate mixture

**im·mobile** \(')i(m), ә+\ *adj* [ME *in-mobill*, fr. L *immobilis*, fr. *in-* ¹in- + *mobilis* movable — more at MOBILE] **:** incapable of being moved **:** IMMOVABLE, FIXED, STABLE; *broadly* **:** UNMOVING, MOTIONLESS

**im·mo·bi·lism** \ә'mōbә‚lizәm\ *n* -s [F *immobilisme*, fr. *immobile* (fr. L *immobilis*) + *-isme* -ism] **:** a governmental policy characterized by compromise and moderation often to the point of ignoring basic issues and stagnation of progressive trends

**im·mo·bi·list** \-‚lәst\ *n* -s **:** one who advocates immobilism

**im·mobility** \¦i(m)+\ *n* [MF *immobilité*, fr. LL *immobilitat-, immobilitas*, fr. L *immobilis* + *-itat-, -itas* -ity] **:** the quality or state of being immobile **:** FIXEDNESS; *broadly* **:** MOTIONLESSNESS

**im·mobilization** \(ˌ)i(m), ә+\ *n* [F *immobilisation*, fr. *immobiliser* + *-ation*] **:** the act of immobilizing or state of being immobilized: as **a** (1) **:** quiet rest in bed for a prolonged period used in the treatment of disease (as tuberculosis) (2) **:** fixation (as by a plaster cast) of a body part usu. to promote healing in normal structural relation **b :** loss of evolutionary plasticity due to existence in a relatively constant environment resulting in elimination of mutations and variability

**im·mobilize** \(')i(m), ә+\ *vt, see -ize in Explan Notes* [F *immobiliser*, fr. *immobile* + *-iser* -ize] **:** to make immobile **:** fix in place or position **:** render incapable of movement: as **a :** to interfere with or prevent freedom of movement or effective use of (as military forces or equipment) ⟨our planes were *immobilized* by bad weather⟩ ⟨the enemy was *immobilized* by lack of transport⟩ **b :** to fix (as a body part) so as to reduce or eliminate motion usu. by means of a cast or splint, by strapping, or by strict bed rest ⟨*immobilizing* a fractured bone by a cast and continuous traction⟩ ⟨~ an injury⟩ ⟨the patient was *immobilized* for three months⟩ **c** (1) **:** to withhold (specie) from circulation to serve as security for other money (2) **:** to convert (circulating capital) into fixed capital

**im·mo·bi·liz·er** \"ә(r)\ *n* **:** one that immobilizes

**im·moderacy** \(')i(m), ә+\ *n* -ES **:** IMMODERATENESS

**im·moderate** \"+\ *adj* [ME *immoderat*, fr. L *immoderatus*, fr. *in-* ¹in- + *moderatus*, past part. of *moderare* to moderate — more at MODERATE] **1 :** lacking in moderation **:** exceeding just, usual, or suitable bounds **:** EXTRAVAGANT, UNREASONABLE ⟨~ demands⟩ ⟨an ~ speed⟩ ⟨~ appetites⟩ ⟨an ~ theorist⟩ **2** *obs* **a :** characterized by excess **:** INTEMPERATE **b :** having no limits **:** BOUNDLESS **syn** see EXCESSIVE

**im·moderately** \"+\ *adv* [ME, fr. *immoderat* + *-ly*] **:** without moderation **:** to an immoderate degree

**im·moderateness** \"+\ *n* **:** the quality or state of being immoderate

**im·moderation** \(ˌ)i(m), ә+\ *n* [MF *immoderacion*, fr. L *immoderation-, immoderatio*, fr. *in-* ¹in- + *moderation-, moderatio* moderation — more at MODERATION] **:** lack of moderation

**im·modest** \(')i(m), ә\ *adj* [L *immodestus*, fr. *in-* ¹in- + *modestus* modest — more at MODEST] **:** lacking or deficient in modesty: as **a :** failing in the reserve or restraint that decorum or custom requires ⟨brash ~ boasting⟩ ⟨the ~ claims of the billboards⟩ **b :** deficient in sexual modesty **:** not conforming to the sexual mores of a particular time or place **:** BRAZEN, INDECENT ⟨a thoroughly ~ costume⟩ ⟨~ conduct⟩ — **im·modestly** \"\ *adv*

**im·modesty** \"+\ *n* [L *immodestia*, fr. *immodestus* + *-ia* -y] **1 :** lack of modesty, delicacy, or decent reserve **:** FORWARDNESS, BOLDNESS **2 :** lack of decency **:** IMPROPRIETY, UNCHASTITY

**im·modulated** \"+\ *adj* [¹in- + *modulated*] **:** lacking modulation

**im·mo·late** \'imә‚lāt, *usu* -ād·+V\ *vt* -ED/-ING/-S [L *immolatus*, past part. of *immolare*, fr. *in-* ²in- + *mola* spelt grits; fr. the ancient custom of sprinkling victims with sacrificial salted meal; akin to *molere* to grind — more at MILL] **1 :** to offer in sacrifice (as to a deity); *esp* **:** to kill as a sacrificial victim **2 :** to sacrifice or abnegate (as oneself) usu. in the interests of some cause or objective ⟨the end to which she has *immolated* all her affections —T.L.Peacock⟩ ⟨*immolating* himself for his family's sake⟩ **3 :** KILL, DESTROY ⟨the millions *immolated* in war⟩ ⟨a party of [African] hunting dogs would assuredly chase and ~ any single domestic canine —James Stevenson-Hamilton⟩

**im·mo·la·tion** \‚imә'lāshәn\ *n* -s [L *immolation-, immolatio*, fr. *immolatus* + *-ion-, -io* -ion] **1 :** the act of immolating or state of being immolated **2 :** something that is immolated

**im·mo·la·tor** \'imә‚lād·ә(r), -ātә-\ *n* -s [L, fr. *immolatus* + *-or*] **:** one that immolates

**im·mo·ment** \i+\ *or* **im·momentous** \¦i(m)+\ *adj* [¹in- + *moment* (n.) *or momentous*] **:** TRIFLING, UNIMPORTANT

**im·moral** \(')i(m), ә+\ *adj* [¹in- + *moral*] **:** not moral **:** inconsistent with purity or good morals **:** contrary to conscience or moral law **:** WICKED, LICENTIOUS ⟨an ~ man⟩ ⟨such ~ acts⟩; *broadly* **:** opposed to, critical of, or in conflict with generally or traditionally held moral principles ⟨refusal to acknowledge the boundaries set by convention is the source of frequent denunciations of art as ~ —John Dewey⟩ — compare UNMORAL

**im·moralism** \"+\ *n* [G *immoralismus*, fr. *immoral* (fr. F or E) + *-ismus* -ism] **:** an ethical viewpoint (as that of Nietzsche) that would institute a new scale of values in opposition to the traditional

**im·moralist** \"+\ *n* **1 :** an advocate or practicer of immorality **2 :** an advocate of immoralism

**im·morality** \¦i(m)+\ *n* [¹in- + *morality*] **1 :** the quality or state of being immoral **:** VICE, WICKEDNESS; *esp* **:** UNCHASTITY **2 :** an immoral act or practice

**im·moralize** \(')i(m), ә+\ *vt* **:** to make immoral **:** DEMORALIZE

**im·morally** \"+\ *adv* **:** in an immoral manner **:** with immorality

**im·mor·ta·bil·i·ty** \(‚)i‚mȯ(r)d·ә'bilәd·ē, ә‚m-\ *n* **:** the quality or state of being capable of attaining or fit for immortality

**im·mor·ta·ble** \(')i(m)¦mȯ(r)d·әbәl, ә'm-\ *adj* [*immortal* + *-able*] **:** capable of attaining immortality

**¹im·mortal** \(')i(m), ә+\ *adj* [ME, fr. L *immortalis*, fr. *in-* ¹in- + *mortalis* mortal — more at MORTAL] **1 :** not mortal **:** exempt from liability to die ⟨the ~ gods⟩ **2 :** connected with or relating to immortality ⟨I have ~ longings in me —Shak.⟩ **3 :** destined to persist through the ages **:** exempt from oblivion **:** IMPERISHABLE, ABIDING ⟨those ~ words⟩ ⟨his fame ~⟩

**²immortal** \"\ *n* **1 a :** an immortal being **:** one exempt from death **b immortals** *pl, often cap* **:** the gods of the Greek and Roman pantheon **2 a immortals** *pl, often cap* **:** a body of troops immortal in some way: as (1) **:** the royal bodyguard of ancient Persia whose number was always kept full (2) **:** troops famous for gallant behavior in war (3) **:** troops that never see war **b :** a person (as an author) whose fame is lasting **c** *usu cap* **:** any of the 40 members of the Académie française **3 a** *in Confucianism* **:** an ideal human being of antiquity **b** *in Taoism* **:** one that has reached a divine state that is the highest to which man can attain **c :** a Chinese saint **4** *also* **immortal hand :** a stud-poker hand that is sure to win

**im·mortalism** \"+\ *n* **:** a doctrine of or belief in the soul's immortality

**im·mortalist** \"+\ *n* **:** one that affirms a belief in immortalism

**im·mor·tal·i·ty** \¦i(m‚)mȯ(r)¦talәd·ē, -lәtē, -i *sometimes* ә‚mȯ(r)- *or* ‚imә(r)-\ *n* [ME *immortalite*, fr. MF *immortalité*, fr. L *immortalitat-, immortalitas*, fr. *immortalis* + *-itat-, -itas* -ity] **:** the quality or state of being immortal: as **a :** exemption from death or annihilation **:** unending existence **:** everlasting life ⟨the ~ of the soul⟩ ⟨human ~⟩ **b :** exemption from oblivion **:** lasting fame ⟨the ~ of these stirring words⟩ ⟨his deeds have earned him a place in the hearts of men⟩

**im·mor·tal·iz·able** \i(m)'mȯ(r)d·ᵊl‚īzәbәl, ә'm-, -)tᵊl-, (‚)=-‚==¦===\ *adj* **:** capable of being immortalized

**im·mor·tal·iza·tion** \=‚===ә'zāshәn, -‚ī'z-\ *n* -s [F *immortalisation*, fr. *immortaliser* to immortalize + *-ation*] **:** the act or process of making immortal; *also* **:** the state of being made immortal

**im·mor·tal·ize** \='==‚īz\ *vt* -ED/-ING/-S *see -ize in Explan Notes* [MF *immortaliser*, fr. *immortal* (fr. L *immortalis*) + *-iser* -ize — more at IMMORTAL] **:** to make immortal: **a :** to cause to live or exist forever **:** endow with everlasting life **b :** to exempt from oblivion **:** perpetuate in fame

**im·mor·tal·iz·er** \"ә(r)\ *n* -s **:** one that immortalizes something; *esp* **:** a writer who preserves in his work something of the present for posterity

**im·mortally** \(')i(m), ә+\ *adv* **1 :** ETERNALLY, EVERLASTINGLY, FOREVER, PERPETUALLY **2 :** to a superhuman or excessive degree **:** INFINITELY

**im·mor·telle** \¦i‚mȯ(r)¦tel, ә‚=¦=\ *n* -s [F, fr. fem. of *immortel* immortal, fr. L *immortalis* — more at IMMORTAL] **1 :** EVERLASTING 3 **2** *or* **immortelle tree :** any of various coral trees; *esp* **:** a large red-flowered tree (*Erythrina micropteryx*) widely used in tropical America as an ornamental and as a shade tree in cacao plantations

**im·mortification** \(ˌ)i(m)+\ *n* [F, fr. MF, fr. ML *immortificatus* disciplined, fr. L *in-* ²in- + LL *mortificatus*, past part. of *mortificare* to mortify — more at MORTIFY] *archaic* **:** a lack of discipline (as of bodily appetites and desires)

**im·motile** \(')i(m), ә+\ *adj* [¹in- + *motile*] **:** lacking motility **:** incapable of movement — **im·motility** \¦i(m)\ *n*

**im·motive** \(')i(m)+\ *adj* [¹in- + *motive*] **:** UNMOVING, IMMOVABLE

**im·movability** \(ˌ)i(m), ә+\ *n* **:** the quality or state of being immovable

**¹im·movable** *also* **im·moveable** \(')i(m), ә+\ *adj* [ME *immovable*, fr. ¹in- + *movable*] **1 :** incapable of being moved **:** firmly fixed **:** FAST ⟨the ~ hills⟩; *broadly* **:** not moving or not intended to be moved **:** STATIONARY **2 a :** STEADFAST, UNALTERABLE, UNYIELDING ⟨an ~ purpose⟩ **b :** not capable of being moved in feeling or sympathies **:** UNIMPRESSIBLE, IMPASSIVE ⟨a stern ~ man⟩ **3 :** not liable to be removed **:** permanent in place or tenure **:** FIXED ⟨an ~ estate⟩ — **im·movableness** \"+\ *n*

**²immovable** *also* **immoveable** \"\ *n* **1 :** one that cannot be moved **2 immovables** *pl, Roman & civil law* **a :** lands, houses thereon, and all things adhering or belonging there by nature (as trees, minerals) or by act of man (as planted crops, fertilizer) — compare ACCESSION 2c **b :** all personal property permanently attached to immovable property that cannot be removed without injury to the latter — see FIXTURE 2c **c :** all personal property placed on immovable property by the owner for its service, improvement, or exploitation **d :** an interest or estate in immovable property **3** *Scots law* **:** heritable property as opposed to movable property

**immovable feast** *n* **:** an ecclesiastical feast that always occurs on the same day of the year

**immovable fixture** *n* **:** FIXTURE 2c(1)

**im·movably** \(')i(m), ә+\ *adv* [ME, fr. *immovable* + *-ly*] **:** so as to be incapable of movement or of being moved ⟨hills brooding ~ over the town⟩

**im·mund** \ә'mәnd\ *adj* [L *immundus*, fr. *in-* ¹in- + *mundus* clean — more at MOTHER (dregs)] **:** UNCLEAN, FILTHY — **im·mun·di·ty** \-dәd·ē\ *n* -ES

**¹im·mune** \ә'myün\ *adj* [L *immunis* exempt from public service, exempt, fr. *in-* ¹in- + *-munis* (fr. *munia* services, obligations) — more at MEAN (common)] **1 a :** FREE, EXEMPT ⟨~ from further taxation⟩ ⟨a book is a tool . . . and should be as ~, almost, from decoration as a crowbar or a cartridge —Holbrook Jackson⟩ **b :** PROTECTED, GUARDED — usu. used with *from* or *against* ⟨~ from political pressures by reason of his office⟩ ⟨a full life is ~ against boredom⟩ **2** [F *immun*, fr. L *immunis*] **:** not susceptible or responsive — usu. used with *to* ⟨~ to all pleas⟩ ⟨the Soviet Union has not been ~ to the pressures of coexistence —L.S.Feuer⟩ ⟨a streptococcus ~ to antibiotics⟩; *esp* **:** having a high degree of natural or acquired resistance to a disease ⟨~ to diphtheria⟩ **3 a :** having or producing antibodies to a corresponding antigen or hapten ⟨an ~ serum⟩ **b :** produced in response to the presence of a corresponding antigen ⟨~ agglutinins⟩ **4** *of cotton yarn* **:** treated so as to repel the usual dyes for cotton

**²immune** \"\ *n* -s **:** an immune individual

**immune body** *n* **:** ANTIBODY

**im·muned** \-nd\ *adj* [¹*immune* + *-ed*] **:** IMMUNIZED — used chiefly of domestic animals

**immune globulin** *or* **immune serum globulin** *n* **:** globulin from the blood of a person or animal immune to a particular disease

**immune serum** *n* **:** ANTISERUM

**im·mun·ist** \ә'myünәst, 'imyәn-\ *n* -s [F *immuniste*, fr. *immun* + *-iste* -ist] **:** one that enjoys an immunity (as from service or payment of some due)

**im·mu·ni·ty** \ә'myünәd·ē, -әtē, -i\ *n* -ES [L *immunitas*, fr. *immunis* + *-itas* -ity] **1 a :** freedom or exemption from a charge, duty, obligation, office, tax, imposition, penalty, or service esp. as granted by law to a person or class of persons **b :** a freedom granted to a special category of persons from the normal burdens and duties arising out of a legal relationship with other persons ⟨legislative ~⟩ ⟨judicial ~⟩ **2** *obs* **:** unrestrained license or an instance of it **3 a :** lack of susceptibility (as to a natural hazard) ⟨this alloy has complete ~ to rust⟩ ⟨no one has assured ~ from error⟩ **b :** freedom from or security against something noxious or injurious ⟨the long ~ of America from outside threats or dangers —D.W. Brogan⟩ **4** [F *immunité*, fr. *immun* + *-ité* -ity] **:** a condition of being able or the capacity to resist a particular disease esp. through preventing development of a pathogenic microorganism or by counteracting the effects of its products — see ACTIVE IMMUNITY, ACQUIRED IMMUNITY, NATURAL IMMUNITY, PASSIVE IMMUNITY

**im·mu·ni·za·tion** \ˌimyənə'zāshən, ˌnī'z- *also* əˌmyü\ *n* -s **:** the creation of immunity usu. against a particular disease ⟨~ against smallpox⟩; *esp* **:** treatment of an organism for the purpose of making it immune to subsequent attack by a particular pathogen

**im·mu·nize** \'imyəˌnīz\ *vt* -ED/-ING/-S *see -ize in Explan Notes* [G *immunisieren*, fr. *immun* immune (fr. F) + *-isieren* -ize — more at IMMUNE] **:** to make immune ⟨the best known examples . . . are in semiarid regions, a circumstance that has *immunized* the scarps from attack by vigorous consequent rivers —C.A.Cotton⟩; *esp* **:** to cause to produce antibodies against an antigen or hapten

**immuno-** *comb form* [ISV, fr. *immune*] **:** immune and immunity ⟨*immuno*compatible⟩ ⟨*immuno*diagnosis⟩ ⟨*immuno*body⟩

**im·mu·no·biologic** *also* **immunobiological** \ˌimyə(ˌ)nō, əˌmyü(ˌ)nō+\ *adj* [*immuno-* + *biologic, biological*] **:** of or relating to the physiological reactions characteristic of the immune state ⟨~ anomalies in leprosy —*Biol. Abstracts*⟩ — **im·mu·no·biology** \"+\ *n*

**im·mu·no·chemical** \"+\ *adj* [*immuno-* + *chemical*] **:** of or relating to immunochemistry — **im·mu·no·chemically** \"+\ *adv*

**im·mu·no·chemist** \"+\ *n* [*immuno-* + *chemist*] **:** a specialist in immunochemistry

**im·mu·no·chemistry** \"+\ *n* [ISV *immuno-* + *chemistry*] **:** a branch of chemistry that deals with substances (as antibodies, antigens, or haptens) and reactions (as concerned in the phenomena of immunity-antibody production)

**im·mu·no·gen** \ə'myünəjən, -ˌjen\ *n* -s [fr. *Immunogen*, a trademark] **:** an antigen that is prepared by extracting fresh living organisms and is usu. highly specific in antigenic action and low in protein of the organism

**im·mu·no·genesis** \ˌimyə(ˌ)nō, əˌmyü(ˌ)nō+\ *n* [NL, fr. *immuno-* + *genesis*] **:** immunity production

**im·mu·no·genetic** *also* **immunogenetical** \"+\ *adj* [*immuno-* + *genetic, genetical*] **:** of or relating to immunogenetics

**im·mu·no·genetics** \"+\ *n pl but sing or pl in constr* [*immuno-* + *genetics*] **1 :** a branch of immunology that deals with the interrelation of immunity to disease and genetic makeup **2 :** a study of biological interrelationships by serological means

**im·mu·no·gen·ic** \"+¦jenik\ *adj* [*immuno-* + *-genic*] **:** producing immunity — compare ANTIGENIC — **im·mu·no·gen·i·cal·ly** \-nək(ə)lē\ *adv* — **im·mu·no·ge·nic·i·ty** \-jə'nisəd·ē\ *n* -ES

**im·mu·no·log·ic** \"+¦läjik\ *also* **im·mu·no·log·i·cal** \-jəkəl\ *adj* **:** of or relating to immunology — **im·mu·no·log·i·cal·ly** \-jək(ə)lē\ *adv*

**im·mu·nol·o·gist** \ˌimyə'näləjəst\ *n* -s **:** a specialist in immunology

**im·mu·nol·o·gy** \-jē\ *n* -ES [ISV *immuno-* + *-logy*] **1 :** a science that deals with the phenomena and causes of immunity **2 :** a treatise on immunology

**im·mu·no·therapy** \ˌimyə(ˌ)nō, əˌmyü(ˌ)nō+\ *n* [ISV *immuno-* + *therapy*] **:** treatment of or prophylaxis against disease that is based on the production of antibodies and induction of immunity and that chiefly employs antigens or antigenic preparations (as antisera, toxoids, vaccines)

**im·mu·no·transfusion** \"+\ *n* [ISV *immuno-* + *transfusion*] **:** transfusion of blood from a donor in whom there has been stimulated the production of antibodies for an infectious agent affecting the recipient

**im·mu·ra·tion** \ˌimyə'rāshən\ *n* -s **:** act of immuring or state of being immured

**im·mure** \ə'myů(ə)r, -üə\ *vt* -ED/-ING/-S [ML *immurare*, fr. L *in-* ²in- + *murus* wall — more at MURAL] **1** *obs* **:** to enclose or fortify with a wall **2 a :** to enclose within or as if within walls ⟨*immured* in an isolated outpost⟩ ⟨scientists who ~ themselves in special research⟩ **b :** to shut up **:** IMPRISON, INCARCERATE ⟨a fairy princess *immured* in a tower⟩ **3 :** to build into a wall ⟨an ancient altar half-*immured*⟩; *esp* **:** to punish by entombing within a wall or between walls ⟨a nun who broke her vow might be *immured*⟩ ⟨*immuring* these heretics⟩

**im·mure·ment** \-ü(ə)rmənt, -üəm-\ *n* -s **:** the quality or state of being immured ⟨the ~ within colleges of the artist, the poet in residence —Marcus Cunliffe⟩

**im·musical** \(')i(m), ə+\ *adj* [¹*in-* + *musical*] **:** INHARMONIOUS, UNMUSICAL, DISCORDANT — **im·musically** \"+\ *adv*

**im·mutability** \(ˌ)i(m), ə+\ *n* [L *immutabilitas*, fr. *immutabilis* immutable + *-itas* -ity] **:** the quality or state of being immutable

**im·mutable** \(')i(m), ə+\ *adj* [ME, fr. L *immutabilis*, fr. *in-* ¹in + *mutabilis* mutable — more at MUTABLE] **:** not capable or susceptible of change **:** UNCHANGEABLE, UNCHANGING, INVARIABLE, UNALTERABLE ⟨~ laws⟩ — **im·mutableness** \"+\ *n* — **im·mutably** \"+\ *adv*

**immutation** *n* [L *immutation-*, *immutatio*, fr. *immutatus* (past part. of *immutare* to change, alter, fr. *in-* ²in- + *mutare* to change) + *-ion-*, *-io* -ion — more at MUTABLE] *obs* **:** CHANGE, ALTERATION, MUTATION

**immy** *abbr* immediately

**imo·chagh** *also* **imo·shagh** \ˌēmō'shăg\ *n* -s *usu cap* **:** a member of the southern branch of the Tuareg people

**imo·hagh** \ˌēmō'häg\ *n* -s *usu cap* **:** a member of the northern branch of the Tuareg people

**imo·ni·um** \(')i¦mōnēəm, (')i¦m-\ *n* -s [*imine* + *ammonium*] **:** ammonium in which a bivalent radical is a substituent

**imou pine** \'ēˌmü-\ *n* [prob. native name in New Zealand] *NewZeal* **:** RIMU

¹**imp** \'imp\ *n* -s [ME *impe*, fr. OE *impa*, fr. *impian* — more at ²IMP] **1 a** *obs* **:** SHOOT, BUD, SLIP; *also* **:** GRAFT **b** *archaic* **:** OFFSPRING, PROGENY, CHILD, SCION **2 a** *archaic* **:** an evil or malicious child **b :** a small demon, devil, or wicked spirit ⟨~s released from a sorcerer's bottle —William Peden⟩ **c :** a mischievous child **:** URCHIN ⟨as disagreeable a young ~ as you'd ask to see —G.B.Shaw⟩

²**imp** \"\ *vt* -ED/-ING/-S [ME *impen*, fr. OE *impian*; akin to OHG *impfōn* to graft; both fr. a prehistoric OHG-OE word derived fr. (assumed) VL *imputare* (whence OF *enter* to graft), fr. L *in-* ²in- + *putare* to cut, prune — more at PAVE] **1** *archaic* **:** to graft into or on **:** IMPLANT **2 a :** to graft or repair (a wing, tail, or feather) with a feather to improve a falcon's flying capacity **b** *archaic* **:** to fasten wings on or to **:** equip with wings **c** *archaic* **:** eke out **:** REPAIR, INCREASE, STRENGTHEN, EQUIP

**imp** *abbr* **1** imperative **2** [L *imperator; imperatrix*] emperor; empress **3** imperfect **4** imperial **5** impersonal **6** import; imported; importer **7** imprimatur **8** impression **9** imprimatur **10** [L *imprimis*] in the first place **11** imprint **12** improved; improvement

¹**im·pact** \(ˌ)im¦pakt\ *vb* -ED/-ING/-S [L *impactus*, past part. of *impingere* to strike or push at or against — more at IMPINGE] *vt* **1 a :** to fix firmly by or as if by packing or wedging ⟨a substance ~*ed* in the upper intestine⟩ ⟨the mule lay . . . ~*ed* in the loam —Ben Johnson⟩ **b :** to press together or mix into a clotted, wedged, or tightly bound mass ⟨goblets of clay and drops of sweat ~*ed* into a hot mulch —*Time*⟩ ⟨puns that can ~ the scabrous with the sublime in a word —Eleanor Clark⟩ **c :** to press down and wedge or force in or under ⟨the golden nuggets of wisdom being ~*ed* in tons of verbosity —Dwight MacDonald⟩ **d :** to fill up **:** CROWD, CONGEST ⟨~*s* the area with military and defense workers and their families —Tait Trussell⟩ **2 a :** to have an impact upon **:** make contact with **:** impinge upon ⟨the images ~*ing* the human retina —T.H. Benton b. 1889⟩ **b :** to drive or transmit with a forceful impact ⟨the critic who . . . is supposed to ~ his messianic visions of jazz perfection to musicians struggling at his feet —*Saturday Rev.*⟩ ~ *vi* **:** to have an impact ⟨the world did not ~ upon me until I got to the post office —Christopher Morley⟩ **:** impinge or make contact esp. forcefully ⟨image the ~*ing* ball splashing into the loose mass of surface balls —R.A.Bagnold⟩ ⟨how will total war ~ on such a poet —*Times Lit. Supp.*⟩

²**im·pact** \'imˌpakt\ *n* -s **1 a :** the act of impinging or striking (as of one body against another or of a stream squarely against a fixed or moving surface) **b :** a forceful contact, collision, or onset **:** the degree or concentration of force in a collision **:** the impetus communicated in or as if in a collision ⟨felt the terrific ~ of the blow⟩ ⟨air rendered incandescent by the vehemence of the ~*s* of the electrons against its molecules —K.K.Darrow⟩ **2 :** the force of impression of one thing on another **: a :** the notable ability to arouse and hold attention and interest **:** the power of impressing ⟨a way of securing a maximum of dramatic ~ on the reader —W.M.Frohock⟩ **b :** a concentrated force producing change **:** an esp. forceful effect checking or forcing change **:** an impelling or compelling effect ⟨the ~ of modern science and technology upon society as a whole —Harrison Brown⟩ ⟨the ~ of terror⟩ ⟨loses the ~ of the basic story in a maze of philosophies —Whitney Betts⟩; *also* **:** the degree of such force ⟨American youth in the early 1930s felt spiritually paralyzed by the ~ of confusing events —J.W.Chase⟩

**syn** BRUNT, COLLISION, CLASH, SHOCK, BUMP, JOLT, JAR, IMPINGEMENT, PERCUSSION, CONCUSSION: IMPACT now commonly suggests the driving impetus or momentum in or as if in a collision or the dynamic force in impressing or compelling change ⟨the aunt's home shook at the *impact* and the windows were smashed —Norman Cousins⟩ ⟨the *impact* of world war on the lives of countless millions —R.H.Jackson⟩ BRUNT now indicates the major part of the force of an onset, collision, jar, stress, or strain ⟨a number of the leaders had . . . fled from the persecution, leaving the little people to bear its *brunt* —Maurice Samuel⟩ ⟨the national financial panic was felt throughout the state, but it was Duluth that bore the *brunt* of the disaster . . . it was rendered almost totally bankrupt —*Amer. Guide Series: Minn.*⟩ COLLISION implies a forceful running together of more or less complex things through accident and with resulting harm, or a sharp opposition or conflict ⟨the *collision* between two ships in a fog⟩ ⟨the buyers and sellers of capital could do almost as they pleased with it, no matter how much damage a *collision* between them might bring about —F.L.Allen⟩ CLASH suggests a noisy, metallic striking together, a sharp skirmish or brawl, or a sharp direct variance, opposition, or contrast ⟨roll of cannon and *clash* of arms —Alfred Tennyson⟩ ⟨fishermen from the Michigan mainland . . . violently opposed further settlement by the Mormons. *Clashes* occurred at several places —*Amer. Guide Series: Mich.*⟩ ⟨a *clash* or conflict between his demands and the strict limitations upon the supply⟩ SHOCK may refer to a very forcible onslaught or violent collision literally or figuratively ⟨the *shock* of the cavalry charge⟩ ⟨the discoveries of physical science came as a *shock* to the general mind of Europe —Laurence Binyon⟩ ⟨the *shock* of physical dislocation effected a very considerable modification of old attitudes —John Dewey⟩ BUMP indicates a sudden thudding blow, esp. one checking forward progress with some force ⟨a *bump* on the head⟩ ⟨the springs were broken by the bad *bump* during the detour⟩ JOLT refers to an abrupt violent blow or movement tending to shake, agitate, or unsettle, or, figuratively, to a shock or major surprise ⟨newly picked fruit being bruised by the *jolts* of shipment⟩ ⟨we have no offensive naval policy . . . I fear there will be some horrible *jolts* in the future —F.D. Roosevelt⟩ JAR usu. refers to some wrenching dislodgment or break in continuity ⟨the bottles were cracked by the *jars* they underwent in shipment⟩; it may refer to an agitation or shaking up ⟨the fall gave him a *jar*⟩ IMPINGEMENT now is less likely to indicate violent collision than lighter overlaying or more subtle infringement or penetration ⟨each little *impingement* of sound struck on her consciousness —Adria Langley⟩ PERCUSSION, more common in technical than in general language, may suggest a sharp, purposive tapping or knocking ⟨musical instruments that sound by *percussion*, as the drum⟩ CONCUSSION, which may mean a blow or collision, is now more likely to suggest the shattering effects, including noise, of a collision or explosion, or the stunning, weakening effect of a heavy blow ⟨from the shelter survivors heard the *concussions* of the bombing raid⟩ ⟨suffered a *concussion* in the collision⟩

**impact bomb** *n* **:** a bomb that detonates on striking an object

**impacted** *adj* **1 :** driven together (as the broken ends of a fractured bone) **2 a :** wedged into a passage (as a fetus in the birth canal, a calculus in a duct, a foreign body in the larynx) **b** *of a tooth* **:** wedged between the jawbone and another tooth ⟨~ and unerupted normal teeth are excised —K.H. Thoma⟩

**impacted crop** *n* **:** crop-bound of poultry

**impact extrusion** *n* **:** a process in which metal is forced by a quick blow to flow around a punch; *also* **:** the product so formed

**im·pact·ful** \'ˌ=ˌfəl, ='=-\ *adj* **:** having a forceful impact **:** producing a marked impression ⟨some of the most ~ heroines of current films —Martha Wolfenstein & Nathan Leites⟩

**im·pac·tion** \im'pakshən\ *n* -s [LL *impaction-*, *impactio*, fr. L *impactus* + *-ion-*, *-io* -ion] **:** the act of becoming or the state of being impacted; *specif* **:** lodgment or an instance of lodgment of something (as a tooth or feces or calculi) in a body passage or cavity ⟨fecal ~⟩ ⟨~ of the rumen⟩

**im·pact·ite** \'imˌpakˌtīt\ *n* -s [²*impact* + *-ite*] **:** a glassy object produced by fusion of rock or meteoritic fragments by the heat developed from the impact of a meteorite on the earth's surface

**im·pac·tive** \(')im¦paktiv\ *adj* **1 :** having an impact or marked effect ⟨the ~ wonder that is in natural things —R.L.Cook⟩ ⟨the ~ scrutiny of strange faces —Scott Fitzgerald⟩ **2 :** resulting from impact ⟨~ shocks —G.L.Riddell⟩

**im·pac·tor** *or* **im·pact·er** \-tə(r)\ *n* -s **:** a machine (as a steam hammer or a pile driver) or part that operates by striking blows

**impact parameter** *n* **:** the perpendicular distance from the center of the force field to the initial path of the particle deflected by the field in nuclear scattering

**impact pressure** *n* **:** DYNAMIC PRESSURE

**impact strength** *n* **:** the resistance of a material (as metal or ceramic ware) to fracture by a blow, expressed in terms of the amount of energy absorbed before fracture

**impact test** *n* **:** a test for determining the impact strength of a material ⟨the *impact test* of the pottery was made with a dropping metal ball⟩

**impact tube** *n* **:** a Pitot tube having its orifice headed directly into an oncoming stream of fluid

**impact wrench** *n* **:** an electrically or pneumatically operated wrench that gives a rapid succession of sudden torques

**impaint** *vt* [²*in-* + *paint* (n.)] *obs* **:** PAINT, DEPICT

¹**im·pair** \im'pa(a)(ə)r, -pe|, |ə\ *vb* -ED/-ING/-S [ME *empeiren*, *empairen*, *impairen*, fr. MF *empeirer*, *emperer*, *empirer*, fr. OF *empeirier*, *empirier*, fr. (assumed) VL *impejorare*, fr. L *in-* ²in- + LL *pejorare* to make worse — more at PEJORATIVE] *vt* **:** to make worse **:** diminish in quantity, value, excellence, or strength **:** do harm to **:** DAMAGE, LESSEN ⟨the output of produce was ~*ed* by the cold weather⟩ ⟨~ their health by wild living⟩ ⟨had to teach so many pupils it ~*ed* his own musical career⟩ ⟨his pleasure was ~*ed* by worry about money⟩ ~ *vi*, *obs* **:** DETERIORATE **syn** see INJURE

²**impair** \"\ *n* -s *archaic* **:** IMPAIRMENT, DETERIORATION, INJURY

³**im·pair** \'imˌpa(a)(ə)r, -pə|, |ə\ *n* -s [F, fr. *impair* odd, fr. L *impar* — more at IMPAR] **:** the odd numbers in roulette when a bet is made on them ⟨made a large bet on ~⟩

**im·pair·able** \im'pa(a)rəbəl, -per-\ *adj* **:** capable of being impaired

**impaired life** *or* **impaired risk** *n* **:** a person whose physical condition according to insurance ratings is below that required for life insurance at standard rates

**im·pair·er** \-rə(r)\ *n* -s **:** one that impairs ⟨lack of confidence is often an ~ of efficiency⟩

**im·pair·ment** \-a(a)|(ə)rmənt, -e|, |əm-\ *n* -s [ME *empeirement*, fr. MF *empeirement*, fr. OF, fr. *empeirier*, fr. to impair + *-ment* — more at IMPAIR] **:** the act of impairing or the state of being impaired **:** INJURY ⟨physical and mental diseases and ~*s* of man —*Current Biog.*⟩ **:** DETERIORATION ⟨any ~ . . . of his bodily vigor through sickness or age —J.G.Frazer⟩ **:** LESSENING ⟨an ~ of the pain⟩

**im·pala** *also* **im·pal·la** \im'palə, -päla\ *n*, *pl* **impalas** *or* **impala** *also* **impallas** *or* **impalla** [Zulu] **:** a large African antelope (*Aepyceros melampus*) of a brownish bay color, white below, with a black crescentic stripe on the haunch, the male being distinguished by slender annulated lyrate horns

**impala lily** *n* **:** a succulent-stemmed shrub (*Adenium multiflorum*) of the family Apocynaceae of southern Africa with showy pink and white flowers borne after the leaves fall

**im·palatable** \(')im+\ *adj* [¹*in-* + *palatable*] **:** UNPALATABLE

**im·pale** \əm'pāl, *esp before pause or consonant* -āəl\ *also* **em·pale** \əm,em-\ *vt* [MF & ML; MF *empaler*, fr. ML *impalare*, fr. L *in-* ²in- + *palus* stake, pole — more at POLE] **1** *archaic* **a :** to enclose with poles, stakes, or a palisade **b :** to hem in **:** ENCLOSE, SURROUND, CONFINE, ENCIRCLE **2 a :** to pierce or pierce through with a pole or with something pointed; *esp* **:** torture or kill by fixing on a sharp stake **b :** to fix in a position by piercing or piercing through with something pointed or to cause to be so fixed ⟨the head . . . *impaled* upon the bowsprit of his sloop —Nike Anderson⟩ ⟨having some man rush at you so that he *impaled* his chest upon the ice pick —Erle Stanley Gardner⟩ ⟨a butterfly *impaled* by a pin —Louis Bromfield⟩ **c :** to fix in a position as if by piercing or piercing through in such a manner **:** fix in a position of defeat or helplessness or one from which there is no escape or retreat ⟨*impaled* itself on a dilemma —S.W.Chapman⟩ ⟨a question on which . . . he had always been insecurely *impaled* —Marcia Davenport⟩ ⟨*impaled* his victim neatly with his logic —V.L.Parrington⟩ **d :** to deflate by telling logic or biting wit **3 :** to join or conjoin in heraldry by impalement

**im·pale·ment** \-mənt\ *n* -s [MF *empalement*, fr. *empaler* + *-ment*] **1 :** the act of impaling or the state of being impaled: as **a** (1) *archaic* **:** ENCLOSING, ENCIRCLING, CONFINING (2) **:** the union of two or more coats of arms side by side on a heraldic shield divided palewise **b :** a piercing or piercing through with a pale, spike, or other pointed thing (as for fixing in a position or by an accidental fall) **c** (1) **:** a placing or a being placed in an inescapable and awkward position (as of defeat or helplessness) (2) **:** a deflating or a being deflated by telling logic or biting wit **2 :** an enclosing fence or palisade

**im·palpability** \(ˌ)im+\ *n* **:** the quality or state of being impalpable

¹**im·palpable** \(')im+\ *adj* [¹*in-* + *palpable*] **1 a :** incapable of being felt by the touch ⟨an ~ pulse⟩ **:** not palpable **:** INTANGIBLE ⟨as ~ as a dream —Nathaniel Hawthorne⟩ ⟨the ~ aura of power that emanated from him —Osbert Sitwell⟩ **b :** extremely fine so that no grains or grit can be felt ⟨an ~ cloud⟩ ⟨an ~ powder⟩ ⟨the ~ mud —*Encyc. Britannica*⟩ **2 :** not readily apprehended by the mind ⟨an ~ beauty of style⟩ — **im·palpably** \"+\ *adv*

²**impalpable** \"\ *n* -s **:** something impalpable ⟨an intellectual, dealing eternally in ~*s*⟩

**im·panate** \im'panət, 'impəˌnāt\ *or* **im·pa·nat·ed** \'impəˌnād·əd\ *adj* [*impanate* fr. ML *impanatus*, fr. L *in-* ²in- + L *panis* bread + *-atus* -ate; *impanated* fr. ML *impanatus* + E *-ed* — more at FOOD] **:** embodied in bread in impanation

**im·pa·na·tion** \ˌimpə'nāshən\ *n* -s [ML *impanation-*, *impanatio*, fr. *impanatus* impanate + L *-ion-*, *-io* -ion] **1 :** the inclusion of the body of Christ in the eucharistic bread in a hypostatic union without change in either substance — compare INVINATION **2 :** the Christian theological doctrine affirming the real presence of Christ in the Eucharist by impanation and invination — compare CONSUBSTANTIATION, TRANSUBSTANTIATION

**im·pa·na·tor** \'impəˌnād·ə(r)\ *n* -s [ML, fr. *impanatus* + L *-or*] **:** one holding the doctrine of impanation

**im·panel** \əm+\ *also* **em·panel** \əm, em+\ *vt* [²*in-* or ¹*en-* + *panel* (n.)] **:** to enter in or on a panel **:** enroll (as a list of jurors) in a court of justice

**im·papy·rat·ed** \ˌimpə'pīˌrād·əd, im'papəˌr-\ *adj* [²*in-* + *papyrus* + *-ate* + *-ed*] **:** recorded on or as if on papyrus

**im·par** \'imˌpär\ *adj* [NL, fr. L, unequal, uneven, fr. *in-* ¹in- + *par* equal — more at PAIR] *anat* **:** UNPAIRED, AZYGOUS

**im·paradise** \əm+\ *or* **em·paradise** \əm,em+\ *vt* [²*in-* or ¹*en-* + *paradise* (n.)] **1 a :** to put in paradise ⟨an *imparadised* saint⟩ **b :** to make supremely happy **:** transport with delight or joy ⟨*imparadised* in her lover's arms⟩ **2 :** to convert into a paradise

**imparalleled** *adj* [¹*in-* + *paralled*] *obs* **:** UNPARALLELED

**im·paripinnate** \(ˌ)im+\ *adj* [NL *imparipinnatus*, fr. L *impar* + NL *-i-* + *pinnatus* pinnate — more at PINNATE] **:** ODD-PINNATE

**im·parisyllabic** \(ˌ)im+\ *adj* [*impar* + E *-i-* + *-syllabic*] **:** not having the same number of syllables in all declensional cases ⟨the Latin words *lapis, lapidis* and *mens, mentis* are ~⟩

**im·parity** \(')im+\ *n* [LL *imparitas*, fr. L *impar* + *-itas* -ity] **:** difference esp. of degree, rank, excellence, number **:** INEQUALITY, DISPARITY

**impark** *vt* [ME *imparken*, fr. AF *emparker*, fr. OF *en-* ¹en- + *park, parc* — more at PARK] **1** *obs* **a :** to enclose or confine in a park **b :** ENCLOSE **2** *obs* **:** to enclose (as woods) for a park

**im·parl** \əm'pärl\ *or* **em·parl** \əm,em-\ *vi* -ED/-ING/-S [ME *enparlen*, fr. MF *emparler*, fr. *en-* ¹en- + *parler* to speak — more at PARLEY] **:** to have an imparlance **:** confer esp. regarding settlement of a dispute

**im·par·lance** \-lən(t)s\ *n* [AF *emparlance*, fr. MF *emparler* + *-ance*] **1** *obs* **:** mutual discourse **:** CONFERENCE, DISCUSSION **2 a :** time formerly given to a party before pleading in a lawsuit for making an amicable settlement **b :** the delay or continuance of a suit **c :** a petition or leave for such a delay

**im·part** \əm'pär|t, -pä|, *usu* |d·+V\ *vb* [MF&L; MF *impartir*, fr. L *impartire*, *impertire*, fr. *in-* ²in- + *partire* to divide, part — more at PART] *vt* **1 :** to give or grant (what one has or of what one has) or give rise to (in another) by contact, association, or influence ⟨~*ed* his fortune to the needy⟩ ⟨his manner of speaking ~*ed* authority to a mediocre plan⟩ ⟨the chief hope of ~*ing* a new direction and purpose to the lives of prisoners —*Times Lit. Supp.*⟩ **:** COMMUNICATE, TRANSMIT ⟨his very position ~*ed* a political significance to whatever he did⟩ ⟨their elegance was ~*ed* to the passengers . . . who were forced to sit ramrod straight —*Fortnight*⟩ ⟨a sudden motion ~*ed* to the air —*Encyc. Americana*⟩ ⟨the musician ~*ed* a lyric quality to the piece⟩ ⟨~ knowledge to students⟩ **2 :** to communicate the knowledge of **:** DISCLOSE ⟨told to ~ what he knew to the police⟩; *esp* **:** to give utterance to **:** reveal in writing or speaking ⟨~*ed* her plans to him in their talk⟩ ⟨~*ed* the events in a letter⟩ ~ *vi* **:** GIVE, BESTOW ⟨the aspect of receiving, and the aspect of ~*ing* —S.W.Rowland & Brian Magee⟩

**im·par·ta·tion** \ˌimˌpär'tāshən, -pä't-\ *n* -s **:** the act of imparting or the state of being imparted

**im·partial** \(')im, əm+\ *adj* [¹*in-* + *partial*] **:** not partial; *esp* **:** not favoring one more than another **:** treating all alike **:** UNBIASED, EQUITABLE ⟨in any criminal trial . . . the jury may be ~ but it is never neutral —M.C.Bernays⟩ ⟨law shall be uniform and ~ —B.N.Cardozo⟩ **syn** see FAIR

**impartial chairman** *n* **:** an arbitrator, referee, or umpire jointly employed by union and management to interpret or to resolve differences arising out of the terms of a labor agreement

**im·partiality** \(ˌ)im, əm+\ *n* **:** the quality or state of being impartial **:** freedom from bias or favoritism **:** DISINTERESTEDNESS, FAIRNESS ⟨the ~ of the scientific spirit —John Dewey⟩ ⟨with wonderful ~, the play admits shenanigans and sentiment —*Time*⟩

**im·partially** \(')im, əm+\ *adv* **:** in an impartial manner **:** without bias or special favor ⟨smiled at them both ~ —T.B. Costain⟩

**im·par·tial·ness** *n* -ES **:** the quality or state of being impartial

**im·partibility** \(ˌ)im+\ *n* **:** the quality or state of being impartible

**im·partible** \(')im+\ *adj* [LL *impartibilis*, fr. L *in-* ¹in- + *partibilis* partible — more at PARTIBLE] **:** not partible **:** not subject to partition ⟨decided that the office should be held jointly by his two sisters, an absurd decision which ignored the historic principle that great offices of state were ~ —G.H. White⟩ ⟨an ~ inheritance⟩ — **im·partibly** \"+\ *adv*

**im·participable** \ˈim+\ *adj* [1in- + *participable*] **:** not participable **:** incapable of being shared ⟨an ~ office⟩
**im·par·tite** \(ˈ)imˈpärˌtīt\ *adj* [LL *impartitus*, fr. L *in-* 1in- + *partitus*, past part. of *partire* to divide — more at PART] **:** UNDIVIDED
**im·part·ment** \imˈpärtmənt\ *n* -s **:** the act of imparting or something that is imparted **:** COMMUNICATION, TRANSMISSION
**im·passability** \(ˌ)im+\ *n* **:** the quality or state of being impassable ⟨stopped by the complete ~ of the road⟩
**im·passable** \(ˈ)im+\ *adj* [1in- + *passable*] **:** incapable of being passed: as **a :** incapable of being traveled, traveled through, or crossed ⟨an ~ road⟩ ⟨an ~ jungle⟩ ⟨an ~ river⟩ **b :** incapable of being put into circulation ⟨counterfeit bills so crude they were ~⟩ **c :** INSURMOUNTABLE ⟨an ~ obstacle to discussion⟩ — **im·passableness** \"+\ *n* — **im·passably** \"+\ *adv*
**im·passe** \ˈim,pas, -paa(ə)s, -pais, -päs *also* imˈp- *or* ˈam,p- *or* amˈp-\ *n* -s [F, fr. *in-* 1in- + *-passe* (fr. *passer* to pass — more at PASS] **1 :** an impassable road or way **:** BLIND ALLEY, CUL-DE-SAC **2 a :** a predicament affording no obvious escape ⟨placed himself in an impossible ~ by at one and the same time attacking the heads of the party and recognizing its supreme authority —*Times Lit. Supp.*⟩ **b :** DEADLOCK ⟨negotiations between the two parties had reached an ~ since neither side would compromise in any way⟩
**im·passibility** \(ˌ)im, əm+\ *n* -ES [ME *impassibilite*, fr. MF or LL; MF *impassibilité*, fr. LL *impassibilitat-, impassibilitas*, fr. *impassibilis* + *-itat-, -itas* -ity] **:** the quality or state of being impassible ⟨the ~ or aloofness she showed sometimes toward me —Mary McCarthy⟩
**im·passible** \əm, (ˈ)im+\ *adj* [ME, fr. MF or LL; MF, fr. LL *impassibilis*, fr. L *in-* 1in- + *passibilis* passible — more at PASSIBLE] **1 a :** incapable of suffering or of experiencing pain ⟨the Godhead is ~, for where there is perfection and unity, there can be no suffering —Aldous Huxley⟩ **b :** incapable of being harmed **:** inaccessible to injury ⟨as ~ as a ghost —Walker Percy⟩ **2 :** incapable of feeling **:** IMPASSIVE, UNFEELING, COLD ⟨the murderer stood ~ gazing down at his victim⟩ — **im·pas·si·bly** \-əblē, -li\ *adv*
**im·pas·sion** \əmˈpashən, -paash-,-paish-\ *vt* **impassioned; impassioned; impassioning** \-sh(ə)niŋ\ **impassions** [prob. fr. It *impassionare*, fr. *in-* 2in- (fr. L) + *passione* passion, fr. LL *passion-, passio* — more at PASSION] **:** to move or affect strongly **:** arouse the feelings or passions of ⟨dampens the ardor of the most ~*ed* newcomer —*Amer. Guide Series: Tenn.*⟩ ⟨the ideal of an elected emperor that ~*ed* the revolutionaries —Norbert Mühlen⟩ **:** fill with passion or mark by evidence of strong feeling ⟨public speaking is more ~*ed* than private speaking —A.T. Weaver⟩
**1im·pas·sion·ate** \-sh(ə)nət, *usu* -əd·+V\ *adj* [It *impassionato*, past part. of *impassionare*] **:** IMPASSIONED — **im·pas·sion·ate·ly** *adv*
**2im·pas·sion·ate** \-shə,nāt, *usu* -ād·+V\ *vt, archaic* **:** IMPASSION
**3im·passionate** \(ˈ)im+\ *adj* [1in- + *passionate*] *archaic* **:** without passion or feeling **:** DISPASSIONATE
**im·pas·sioned** \əmˈpashənd, -paash-, -paish-\ *adj* **:** actuated or characterized by or filled with passion or zeal **:** showing great warmth of feeling **:** ARDENT ⟨an ~ oration⟩ ⟨the expression of ~ love of ideal beauty —Richard Garnett †1906⟩
**syn** PASSIONATE, ARDENT, FERVENT, FERVID, PERFERVID: IMPASSIONED indicates intense, strong, and fiery feeling demanding expression ⟨much would I have given to have understood some of his *impassioned* bursts; when he tossed his arms overhead, stamped, scowled, and glared, till he looked like the very Angel of Vengeance —Herman Melville⟩ ⟨as his *impassioned* language did its work the multitude rose into fury —J.A.Froude⟩ PASSIONATE applies to vehemence or violence of emotion sometimes extinguishing rationality ⟨he heard for the first time mamma's *passionate* appeal to him never to let Judy forget mamma —Rudyard Kipling⟩ ⟨may profess Socialism or Communism in *passionate* harangues from one end of the country to the other, and even suffer martyrdom for it —G.B. Shaw⟩ ⟨it had not been condemned in the court of human reason, but lynched outside of it by the *passionate* and uncompromisingly ruthless war spirit, common to Communists and Fascists —M.R.Cohen⟩ ARDENT is almost always complimentary and may apply to the fiery or warm expression of lasting intense zeal and militancy ⟨an *ardent* Jeffersonian, vigorously partisan in the pulpit —H.E.Starr⟩ ⟨a man of violent temper, strong prejudices and an *ardent* Tory had left Virginia because of the unpopularity he had stirred up there against himself —*Amer. Guide Series: Md.*⟩ FERVENT may connote a depth and intensity of glowing feeling, often sustained and steady ⟨a strong and popular preacher, *fervent*, sometimes fiery, inclined to speak everywhere as though addressing a congregation —J.A.Faulkner⟩ ⟨a *fervent* loyalty such as soldiers feel for a general who leads them in some cause dear to all —Rebecca West⟩ FERVID may apply to a warmly or even feverishly expressed emotion, often spontaneous and always intense ⟨because his *fervid* manner of lovemaking offended her English phlegm —Arnold Bennett⟩ ⟨the most *fervid* and momentous oratory of Revolutionary days —*Amer. Guide Series: Mass.*⟩ PERFERVID may suggest extreme emotional excitement, sometimes overwrought or factitious ⟨in his *perfervid* flag-waving moments —S.H.Adams⟩
**im·pas·sioned·ly** \-n(d)lē, -li\ *adj* **:** in an impassioned manner
**im·pas·sioned·ness** \-n(d)nəs\ *n* -ES **:** the quality or state of being impassioned ⟨the ~ of his plea for mercy⟩
**im·passive** \əm, (ˈ)im+\ *adj* [1in- + *passive*] **1 :** devoid of passion, feeling, or receptivity to impression: **a** *archaic* **:** unsusceptible to pain, suffering, injury, or harm **:** INVULNERABLE **b :** unsusceptible to physical feeling **:** INSENSIBLE, INANIMATE ⟨a dial cut in ~ stone —Virginia Woolf⟩ **c :** unsusceptible to or destitute of emotion **:** UNIMPRESSIONABLE ⟨the violet pallor of death . . . enveloped her in an ~ remoteness —Ellen Glasgow⟩ ⟨a large dull ~ man⟩ **2 :** giving no sign of feeling or emotion **:** EXPRESSIONLESS ⟨beneath a reserved and ~ surface, a highly nervous and sensitive person —Havelock Ellis⟩ ⟨a cold ~ stare —Charles Dickens⟩ **3 :** not moving in any way **:** MOTIONLESS ⟨we can load up a piece of amber . . . with the greatest possible excess of negative charge, and still it remains absolutely ~ in the presence of a magnet —K.K.Darrow⟩
**syn** STOIC, APATHETIC, PHLEGMATIC, STOLID: IMPASSIVE applies to one who shows no passion, emotion, sensation, or noticeable interest in situations in which such a reaction might be expected ⟨the veil of *impassive* reserve with which I concealed the whole of my intimate personal life —Havelock Ellis⟩ ⟨I watched the man's face while Nelson was relating the story, but he remained *impassive*, showing neither interest in nor concern for our plight —C.B.Nordhoff & J.N.Hall⟩ STOIC may suggest an indifference to pain or pleasure, perhaps through a conscious schooling of oneself in fortitude ⟨it sums up not only the cataclysm of a world, but also the *stoic* and indomitable temper that endures it —J.L.Lowes⟩ ⟨a *stoic* atmosphere of fortitude in adversity —Orville Prescott⟩ APATHETIC may describe a puzzling, remiss, or blameworthy indifference or a preoccupation with something else that precludes normal interest and reactions ⟨enforcement of the liquor laws was lax, and sentiment was *apathetic* to the evils of excessive drinking —C.A.Dinsmore⟩ ⟨the row of stolid, dull, vacant plowboys, ungainly in build, uncomely in face, lifeless, *apathetic* —Samuel Butler †1902⟩ PHLEGMATIC describes a temperament or disposition not given to ready emotional reaction or similar response ⟨the religious mysticism that lurked in the heart of primitive Puritanism found no response in his *phlegmatic* soul —V.L.Parrington⟩ STOLID implies an accustomed heavy or cloddish obtuse imperceptive and incurious lack of interest, emotion, or other response ⟨an agricultural parish, peopled by *stolid* Saxon rustics, in whom the temperature of religious zeal was little, if at all, above absolute zero —Aldous Huxley⟩ ⟨watched for an expression of hatred, or pity, or horror, on the faces of the multitude. No emotion whatsoever was displayed —nothing but *stolid* indifference —V.G.Heiser⟩
**im·passively** \"+\ *adv* **:** in an impassive manner ⟨submitted ~ to arrest —*Time*⟩
**im·passiveness** \"+\ *n* **:** IMPASSIVITY
**im·passivity** \ˌim+\ *n* **:** the quality or state of being impassive **:** a lack or absence of feeling or expression ⟨behind her ~ lay passionate growing anxiety —Marcia Davenport⟩ ⟨his majestic ~ contrasting with the overt astonishment with which a row of savagely ugly attendant chiefs grinned —G.B.Shaw⟩
**im·paste** \imˈpāst\ *vt* [It *impastare*, fr. *in-* 2in- (fr. L) + *pasta* dough, paste, fr. LL — more at PASTE] **1 :** to make into a paste **2 :** to decorate by impasto
**im·pas·to** \imˈpa(,)stō, -pä-,-paa-,-pá-\ *n* -s *often attrib* [It, fr. *impastare*] **:** the thick application of a pigment to a canvas or panel in painting ⟨~ tempera —Ralph Mayer⟩ ⟨~ effects —*Yankee*⟩; *also* **:** the body of pigment so applied ⟨paint laid on in so thick an ~ that it appears almost in bas-relief —R.M. Coates⟩
**im·pa·ter·nate** \ˌimpəˈtərnət\ *adj* [1in- + *paternal* + *-ate*] **:** fatherless as a result of parthenogenetic development
**im·patience** \(ˈ)im, əm+\ *n* [ME *impacience*, fr. OF & L; OF *impacience, impatience*, fr. L *impatientia*, fr. *impatient-, impatiens* + *-ia* -y] **:** the quality or state of being impatient: as **a :** restlessness or chafing of spirit (as under irritation, delay, or opposition) ⟨~ of restraint⟩ **b :** manifest disapproval or intolerance ⟨~ of delay or incompetence⟩ **:** manifest unwillingness to be tolerant ⟨~ with red tape and outworn procedure —R.M.Dawson⟩ **c :** restless or eager desire or longing ⟨~ to get his mark completed on time⟩
**im·patiency** \"+\ *n* [L *impatientia*] *archaic* **:** IMPATIENCE
**im·pa·tiens** \əmˈpāshənz, -shē,enz, -shən(t)s\ *n* [NL, fr. L, adj., impatient; fr. the fact that the ripe pods burst open and scatter their seeds when slight pressure is applied] **1** *cap* **:** a large genus of widely distributed annual plants (family Balsaminaceae) with watery juice, irregular spurred or saccate flowers, and dehiscent capsules — see BALSAM 4, JEWELWEED **2** *or* **impatience**, *pl* **impatiens** *or* **impatiences :** any plant of the genus *Impatiens*
**1im·patient** \(ˈ)im, əm+\ *adj* [ME *impacient*, fr. MF *impacient, impatient*, fr. L *impatient-, impatiens*, fr. *in-* 1in- + *patient-, patiens* patient — more at PATIENT] **1 a :** not patient **:** restless or short of temper esp. under irritation, delay, opposition **:** FRETFUL ⟨an ~ mood⟩ ⟨an ~ disposition⟩ ⟨the temper of the youth of his country is violent, ~, and revolutionary —Louis Fischer⟩ **b :** not bearing with composure **:** INTOLERANT ⟨~ of poverty or delay⟩ ⟨~ of this prolonged parting from their pets —F.D.Smith & Barbara Wilcox⟩ ⟨~ of preaching without practice —A.J.Russell⟩ **:** showing quickly an unwillingness to be unconcerned or tolerant (as with something one dislikes or disapproves of) ⟨~ with anything like dishonesty —W.L.Frierson⟩ **2 :** prompted by or giving evidence of impatience ⟨an ~ speech⟩ ⟨~ restlessness⟩ ⟨an ~ honesty —S.H.Adams⟩ **3 a :** restlessly or eagerly desirous **:** ANXIOUS ⟨~ to see his sweetheart⟩ ⟨quite ~ for the concert evening —Jane Austen⟩ ⟨~ to know what did occur —E.K. Brown⟩ ⟨~ for home —E.A.Weeks⟩ **b :** marked by intolerance of delay ⟨an ~ wait⟩ ⟨~ hours⟩ **4** *obs* **:** UNENDURABLE — **im·patiently** \"+\ *adv* — **im·patientness** \"+\ *n*
**2impatient** \"\ *n* **:** one that is impatient
**impatronize** *vt* [MF *impatroniser*, fr. *in-* 2in- + *patron* patron, master + *-iser* -ize — more at PATRON] *obs* **:** to give or take possession of
**im·pavid** \(ˈ)im+\ *adj* [L *impavidus*, fr. *in-* 1in- + *pavidus* fearful — more at PAVID] *archaic* **:** FEARLESS — **im·pavidly** \"+\ *adv*
**im·pawn** \im+\ *vt* [2in- + *pawn* (n.)] *archaic* **:** to put in pawn
**im·pay·able** \aⁿpāyäbl(ᵊ), -b(lə)\ *adj* [F, fr. MF, incapable of being paid, fr. *in-* 1in- + *payable* — more at PAYABLE] **:** PRICELESS, INVALUABLE
**1im·peach** \əmˈpēch\ *vt* -ED/-ING/-ES [ME *empechen*, fr. MF *empecher*, fr. OF *empeechier*, fr. LL *impedicare* to entangle, fetter, fr. L *in-* 2in- + *pedica* fetter, fr. *ped-, pes* foot — more at FOOT] **1** *obs* **:** HINDER, PREVENT, IMPEDE **2 a :** to bring an accusation (as of wrongdoing or impropriety) against **:** charge with a crime or misdemeanor; *specif* **:** to charge (a public official) before a competent tribunal with misbehavior in office **:** arraign or cite for official misconduct ⟨~ the president⟩ ⟨~ a circuit-court judge⟩ **b :** to inform against or give incriminating evidence against **:** accuse or aid in accusing **:** peach on **c :** to challenge, impugn, or charge as having some fault esp. as biased, venal, not credible, or invalid ⟨the testimony of the 1850 federal census . . . ~*es* the accuracy of his memory —Dixon Wecter⟩ ⟨in a state of mind to ~ the justice of the republic —Charles Dickens⟩ ⟨~ the testimony of a witness⟩ **3 :** to convict of impropriety, misdemeanor, misconduct in office, or bias, venality, or invalidity; *also* **:** to cause (an official) to be removed from office because of such a conviction **syn** see ACCUSE
**2impeach** *n, obs* **:** IMPEACHMENT
**im·peach·able** \-chəbəl\ *adj* **1 :** capable of being impeached **:** chargeable with misconduct, inadequacy, or other fault which might lead to being impeached **2 :** capable of being used as the charge in an impeachment ⟨an ~ offense⟩
**im·peach·ment** \-chmənt\ *n* -s [ME *empechement*, fr. MF, fr. *empecher* + *-ment*] **:** the act or result of impeaching: **a** *obs* **:** HINDRANCE, OBSTRUCTION, IMPEDIMENT **b** *obs* **:** INJURY, HARM, DAMAGE **c :** a calling into question or discrediting (as the purity of one's motives or one's honesty) ⟨the ~ of his character⟩ ⟨the ~ of the witness's testimony⟩ **d :** a calling to account for some high crime or offense before a competent tribunal **:** ARRAIGNMENT; *esp* **:** the arraignment (as of a public official) for misconduct while in office **e** (1) **:** conviction of bias, venality, invalidity, or other fault (2) **:** conviction of misconduct and usu. removal from office — **without impeachment of waste** *of a tenant* **:** exempt from suit for waste committed — used in a real estate lease
**im·pearl** \əm+\ *or* **em·pearl** \əm,em+\ *vt* [prob. fr. MF *emperler*, fr. *en-* 1en- + *perle* pearl — more at PEARL] **:** to form into pearls or into the likeness of pearls; *also* **:** to form of or adorn with or as if with pearls
**im·pec·ca·bil·i·ty** \(ˌ)im,pekəˈbiləd·ē, əm-, -lətē, -i\ *n* **:** the quality or state of being impeccable ⟨have never pretended to ~ —George Meredith⟩
**im·pec·ca·ble** \(ˈ)imˈpekəbəl, əmˈp-\ *adj* [L *impeccabilis*, fr. *in-* 1in- + *peccare* to sin + *-abilis* -able — more at PECCANT] **1 :** not capable of sinning or liable to sin **:** exempt from the possibility of wrongdoing ⟨no soul is absolutely ~ —F.W. Robertson⟩ **2 :** free from fault or blame **:** FLAWLESS, IRREPROACHABLE ⟨women of ~ character and honorable life —Herbert Mitgang⟩ ⟨this masterly record . . . written with ~ discretion and understanding —John Hayward b.1905⟩ ⟨an ~ figure in trim dinner jacket and starched shirt —Truman Capote⟩ — **im·pec·ca·ble·ness** \-bəlnəs\ *n* -ES — **im·pec·ca·bly** \-blē, bli\ *adv*
**im·pec·can·cy** \-kənsē, -si\ *n* [LL *impeccantia*, fr. L *in-* 1in- + LL *peccantia* sinfulness — more at PECCANCY] **:** the quality or state of being impeccant **:** SINLESSNESS
**im·pec·cant** \-nt\ *adj* [1in- + *peccant*] **:** free from error or fault **:** SINLESS
**im·pectinate** \(ˈ)im+\ *adj* [1in- + *pectinate*] **:** not pectinate
**im·pecuniary** \ˌim+\ *adj* [1in- + *pecuniary*] *archaic* **:** IMPECUNIOUS
**im·pe·cu·nios·i·ty** \ˌimpə,kyünēˈäsəd·ē, -pē,-, -nˈyü-, -sətē, -i\ *n* -ES **:** IMPECUNIOUSNESS
**im·pe·cu·nious** \ˌimpəˈkyünyəs, -pē-, -nēəs\ *adj* [1in- + obs. E *pecunious* rich, fr. ME *pecunyous*, fr. L *pecuniosus*, fr. *pecunia* money + *-osus* -ose — more at FEE] **:** having very little or no money usu. habitually **:** INDIGENT, PENNILESS ⟨this eager ~ young man who has fared so richly in his poverty —Edith Wharton⟩ **syn** see POOR
**im·pe·cu·nious·ly** *adv* **:** in an impecunious manner ⟨an ~ situated family⟩ ⟨plodding his way ~ through life⟩
**im·pe·cu·nious·ness** *n* -ES **:** the quality or state of being impecunious **:** INDIGENCE, POVERTY
**im·pe·cu·ni·ty** \ˌimpəˈkyünəd·ē, -pēˈ-, -nətē, -i\ *n* -ES [*impecunious* + *-ty*] **:** IMPECUNIOUSNESS
**imped** *past of* IMP
**im·ped·ance** \əmˈpēdᵊn(t)s\ *n* -s [*impede* + *-ance*] **1 a :** the apparent opposition in an electrical circuit to the flow of an alternating current that is analogous to the actual electrical resistance to a direct current and that is the ratio of effective electromotive force to the effective current **b :** the resistance to passage of a substance (as water or water vapor) through a film **2 :** the ratio of the pressure to the volume displacement at a given surface in a sound-transmitting medium
**impedance bond** *n* **:** an iron-core coil of low resistance and relatively high reactance used on electrified railroads to provide a continuous path around insulated joints for the return propulsion current and to confine the alternating-current signaling energy to its own track circuit
**impedance bridge** *n* **:** BRIDGE
**im·pede** \əmˈpēd\ *vt* -ED/-ING/-S [L *impedire*, fr. *in-* 2in- + *-pedire* (fr. *ped-, pes* foot) — more at FOOT] **:** to interfere with or get in the way of the progress of ⟨storms *impeded* the vessels —*Amer. Guide Series: N.C.*⟩ ⟨are further *impeded* in our work by financial stringency —C.A.Robinson⟩ **:** hold up **:** BLOCK ⟨the departure was *impeded* by heavy rain⟩ ⟨his progress was *impeded* by sickness and poverty⟩ **:** detract from ⟨no heavy weight of fable *impedes* the reader's enjoyment —Elizabeth Janeway⟩ **syn** see HINDER
**im·pe·di·ent impediment** \əmˈpēdēənt-\ *n* [*impedient* fr. L *impedient-*, impediens, pres. part. of *impedire*] **:** a bar to marriage that is an obstacle to the marriage if known but that does not make the marriage void after it has been solemnized — called also *hindering impediment*
**im·ped·i·ment** \əmˈpedəmənt\ *n* -s [L *impedimentum*, fr. *impedire* + *-mentum* -ment] **1 a :** the act or state of being impeded **:** OBSTRUCTION ⟨trying to determine where the ~*s* of growth lay in the life cycle⟩ **b :** something that impedes **:** HINDRANCE, BLOCK ⟨some ~ lay between him and advancement⟩ ⟨the destruction of all ~*s* to love —C.D.Lewis⟩ ⟨strove to get ahead despite all ~*s* in his path⟩; *esp* **:** an organic obstruction to speech ⟨some small ~ slowed his conversation⟩ **2 impediments** *pl, archaic* **:** IMPEDIMENTA **3 a :** a bar to the formation of a contract arising out of the lack of capacity of one of the parties (as from minority or want of sufficient mental capacity) **b :** a bar or hindrance (as lack of sufficient age, lack of genuine consent) to a lawful marriage sometimes resulting in complete nullity of marriage without any decree or declaration or in the marriage being voidable by the injured party — see ABSOLUTE IMPEDIMENT, DIRIMENT IMPEDIMENT, IMPEDIENT IMPEDIMENT, PROHIBITIVE IMPEDIMENT, RELATIVE IMPEDIMENT **syn** see OBSTACLE
**im·ped·i·men·ta** \əm,pedəˈmentə, ,im-\ *n pl* [L, pl. of *impedimentum* impediment] **:** things that impede or hinder progress or movement; *esp* **:** baggage, equipment, or supplies ⟨the photographer left all his ~ in the hall⟩ ⟨the supply trains dropped the ~ at convenient stopping places on the army's route⟩ ⟨clubs, bag, cart, umbrella, spiked shoes and all the other ~ of the golfer⟩
**im·ped·i·men·tal** \(ˌ)im¦pedəˈmentᵊl, əm¦-\ *adj, archaic* **:** being an impediment **:** HINDERING, OBSTRUCTIVE
**im·ped·i·tive** \(ˈ)im¦pedəd·iv, əmˈp-\ *adj* [F *impéditif*, fr. MF *impeditif*, fr. L *impeditus* (past part. of *impedire* to impede) + MF *-if* -ive — more at IMPEDE] **:** tending to impede **:** hindering or being a hindrance **:** OBSTRUCTIVE
**im·pe·dor** \əmˈpēdə(r)\ *n* -s [*impede* + *-or*] **:** an electric-circuit element that introduces impedance
**im·pel** \əmˈpel\ *vt* **impelled; impelled; impelling; impels** [L *impellere*, fr. *in-* 2in- + *pellere* to drive — more at FELT] **1 a :** to urge or drive by force or constraint ⟨*impelled* out of England . . . by religious dissension —Evelyn Wrench⟩ **:** exert strong moral pressure on or affect with marked moral compulsion in a particular direction ⟨*impelled* to resist oppressive laws⟩ ⟨felt *impelled* to tolerate what he intensely disliked⟩ ⟨continued to write, *impelled* by profit instead of vision and recollection —*Saturday Rev.*⟩ **b :** to create or generate by force or constraint ⟨land hunger *impelled* the deceit, trickery, bribery which whites practiced upon the red man —H.M. Hyman⟩ ⟨his symphonies and symphonic poems are *impelled* by picturesque Celtic folklore —Norman Demuth⟩ **2 :** to impart motion to **:** give a physical impulse to **:** PROPEL ⟨*impelling* a wheelbarrow along the street —Nathaniel Hawthorne⟩ **syn** see MOVE
**1im·pel·lent** \(ˈ)imˈpelənt, əmˈp-\ *adj* [L *impellent-, impellens*, pres. part. of *impellere*] **:** IMPELLING
**2impellent** \"\ *n* -s **:** something that impels
**im·pel·ler** *also* **im·pel·lor** \əmˈpelə(r)\ *n* -s **1 :** one that impels **2 :** ROTOR 1a, 1b; *also* **:** a blade of a rotor — see JET ENGINE illustration
**impelling** *adj* **:** markedly effective **:** FORCEFUL ⟨an ~ personality⟩ ⟨an ~ skill as a teller of tales⟩ — **im·pel·ling·ly** *adv*
**im·pend** \əmˈpend\ *vi* -ED/-ING/-S [L *impendēre*, fr. *in-* 2in- + *pendēre* to hang — more at PENDANT] **1** *archaic* **:** to hang suspended (as over one's head) ⟨a profuse crop of hair ~*ing* over the top of his face —Thomas Hardy⟩ **:** jut out and seem to hang suspended ⟨the crags . . . now begin to ~ terribly over your way —Thomas Gray⟩ **2 a :** to threaten from near at hand or as in the immediate future **:** MENACE ⟨trouble ~*ed* over the entire enterprise⟩ **b :** to be imminent **:** give promise of occurring in the immediate future ⟨went indoors because rain ~*ed*⟩ **:** be about to occur ⟨the most critical contests ~ —Cabell Phillips⟩
**impendence** *or* **impendency** *n, pl* **impendences** *or* **impendencies** *obs* **:** the quality or state of being impending
**im·pend·ent** \-dənt\ *adj* [L *impendent-, impendens*, pres. part. of *impendēre*] **:** IMPENDING
**impending** *adj* **:** that is about to occur **:** IMMINENT ⟨an ~ crisis⟩ ⟨an ~ storm⟩ ⟨~ danger⟩
**im·penetrability** \(ˌ)im, əm+\ *n* **1 :** the quality or state of being impenetrable **2 :** the property of matter from which two portions of matter cannot occupy the same space at the same time
**im·penetrable** \(ˈ)im, əm+\ *adj* [ME *impenetrabel*, fr. MF *impenetrable*, fr. L *impenetrabilis*, fr. *in-* 1in- + *penetrabilis* penetrable — more at PENETRABLE] **1 a :** incapable of being penetrated or pierced **:** not admitting the passage of other bodies **:** not to be entered **:** IMPERVIOUS ⟨an ~ shield⟩ ⟨an ~ forest⟩ ⟨an ~ barrier⟩ **b :** inaccessible to knowledge, reason, sympathy **:** not to be moved by logic or other method of persuasion **:** UNIMPRESSIBLE ⟨an ~ heart⟩ ⟨an ~ stupidity⟩ **c :** incapable of being dealt with in a way that brings a usu. warm, cordial, or unguarded response ⟨an ~ reserve⟩ ⟨an ~ gloom⟩ **2 :** incapable of being comprehended **:** INSCRUTABLE, UNFATHOMABLE ⟨an ~ mystery⟩ ⟨a child speaking in an ~ language of its own⟩ **3 :** having the property of impenetrability ⟨~ matter⟩ — **im·penetrableness** \"+\ *n* — **im·penetrably** \"+\ *adv*
**im·penetrate** \əm+\ *vt* [2in- + *penetrate*] **:** to penetrate thoroughly ⟨power to isolate and ~ Poland and the Balkan States —John Gunther⟩ **syn** see PERMEATE
**im·penetration** \(ˌ)im, əm+\ *n* **:** the act of impenetrating or the state of being impenetrated
**im·penitence** *also* **im·penitency** \(ˈ)im, əm+\ *n* [LL *impaenitentia*, fr. *impaenitent-, impaenitens* + L *-ia* -y] **:** the quality or state of being impenitent **:** failure or refusal to repent
**1im·penitent** \"+\ *adj* [LL *impaenitent-, impaenitens*, fr. L *in-* 1in- + *paenitent-, paenitens* penitent — more at PENITENT] **:** not penitent **:** not repenting of sin **:** not contrite — **im·penitently** \"+\ *adv* — **im·penitentness** \"+\ *n* -ES
**2impenitent** \"\ *n* **:** one that is impenitent
**imper** *abbr* imperative
**im·pe·ra·ta** \ˌimpəˈräd·ə\ *n, cap* [NL, after Ferrante *Imperato* †1625 It. apothecary] **:** a genus of tropical grasses having slender erect culms and a narrow panicle with spikelets surrounded by long silky hairs — see COGON
**1im·per·ate** \ˈimpə,rāt\ *vt* -ED/-ING/-S [L *imperatus*, past part. of *imperare* to command — more at EMPEROR] **:** COMMAND, GOVERN — **im·per·a·tion** \ˌimpəˈrāshən\ *n* -s
**2imperate** *adj* [L *imperatus*] *obs, of an act* **:** COMMANDED — contrasted with *elicit*
**im·per·a·ti·val** \(ˌ)im¦perəˈtīvəl, əm-\ *adj* **:** of or relating to the grammatical imperative **:** expressing an imperative meaning **:** having an imperative function — **im·per·a·ti·val·ly** \-vəlē\ *adv*
**1im·per·a·tive** \əmˈperəd·iv, -rət|\ *adj* [LL *imperativus*, fr. L *imperatus* (past part. of *imperare* to command) + *-ivus* -ive — more at EMPEROR] **1 a :** of, relating to, or being the grammatical mood that expresses the will to influence the behavior of another (as in a command, entreaty, or exhortation) — compare INDICATIVE **b :** expressive of or being a command, entreaty, or exhortation **:** having a rule of conduct ⟨an ~ tone of voice⟩ **:** commanding often imperiously ⟨an ~ manner⟩ ⟨~ persons rush about giving orders⟩ ⟨"you must let me speak,"

said the woman, in an ~ voice —A. Conan Doyle⟩ **c :** restraining, controlling, and directing ⟨the democratic instinct is in France too ~ —W.C.Brownell⟩ **2 :** not to be avoided or evaded **:** URGENT, OBLIGATORY, BINDING, COMPULSORY ⟨an ~ duty⟩ ⟨an ~ engagement⟩ **syn** see MASTERFUL, PRESSING

**²imperative** \"\ *n* -s **1 :** the imperative mood or a verb form or verbal phrase expressing it ⟨an ~ of the verb⟩ **2 :** COMMAND, ORDER ⟨a sheep dog emits ~*s* to his flock hardly distinguishable from those that the shepherd employs toward him —Bertrand Russell⟩; *also* **:** RULE, GUIDE ⟨lived by certain simple ~*s*⟩ **3 a :** an obligatory act or duty ⟨the social ~*s* of our time —M.J.Rosenberg⟩ ⟨it is an ~ that we try again before giving up⟩ **b :** an imperative judgment, proposition, or statement — see CATEGORICAL IMPERATIVE, HYPOTHETICAL IMPERATIVE **c :** NECESSITY, NEED ⟨the terrible ~ of reaching the springs —D.L.Morgan⟩ ⟨the sheer ~ of survival —*New Republic*⟩ **d :** an unavoidable fact compelling or insistently calling for action ⟨the ~*s* of physical battle —*N.Y. Herald Tribune Bk. Rev.*⟩ ⟨economic ~*s*⟩ **e :** a quality or aspect that gives authority or obligatoriness or that demands action ⟨the ~ of law is not simply the ~ of grammatical form —Glenn Negley⟩ ⟨by the conscious direction of the people quite apart from the ~ of events —T.K.Finletter⟩

**im·per·a·tive·ly** \|ə̇vlē, -li\ *adv* **:** in an imperative manner

**im·per·a·tive·ness** \|ivnə̇s\ *n* -ES **:** the quality or state of being imperative

**im·pe·ra·tor** \ˌimpəˈrädə̇r, ˌ==ˈrāˌtȯ(ə)r\ *n* -s [L — more at EMPEROR] **:** supreme leader esp. of the ancient Romans **:** COMMANDER, EMPEROR — **im·per·a·to·ri·al** \(ˌ)imˌperəˈtōrēəl\ *adj*

**imperatorious** *adj* [L *imperatorius*, fr. *imperator* + *-orius* -ory] *obs* **:** IMPERATORIAL

**im·pe·ra·tor·ship** \ˌimpəˈrädə̇rˌship\ *n* **:** the position of imperator

**im·per·ceiv·able** \ˌim+\ *adj* [¹*in-* + *perceivable*] *archaic* **:** IMPERCEPTIBLE

**im·per·cep·ti·bil·i·ty** \ˌim+\ *n* **:** the quality or state of being imperceptible

**¹im·per·cep·ti·ble** \ˌim+\ *adj* [MF, fr. ML *imperceptibilis*, fr. L *in-* ¹in- + LL *perceptibilis* perceptible — more at PERCEPTIBLE] **:** not perceptible: **a :** not capable of being perceived by a sense or of affecting a sense ⟨color is ~ to the touch⟩ ⟨made an almost ~ gesture of assent⟩ **b :** not capable of being perceived or discriminated mentally ⟨the difference between the two propositions was ~ to him⟩ **c :** extremely slight, gradual, or subtle ⟨saw him grow up by ~ gradations⟩ — **im·per·cep·ti·ble·ness** \"+\ *n* -ES — **im·per·cep·ti·bly** \"+\ *adv*

**²imperceptible** \"\ *n* -s **:** something that is imperceptible

**im·per·cep·tion** \ˌim+\ *n* [¹*in-* + *perception*] **:** a lack of perception

**im·per·cep·tive** \"+\ *adj* [¹*in-* + *perceptive*] **:** not perceptive **:** UNPERCEIVING **:** lacking perception ⟨~ persons have been intolerably bored by masterpieces —*N.Y.Herald Tribune*⟩ ⟨stupid and ~ of even the grossest differences between foods⟩ — **im·per·cep·tive·ness** \"+\ *n* — **im·per·cep·tiv·i·ty** \"+\ *n*

**im·per·cip·i·ence** \ˌim+\ *n* **:** the quality or state of being unperceptive **:** lack of perception

**im·per·cip·i·ent** \"+\ *adj* [¹*in-* + *percipient*] **:** UNPERCEPTIVE ⟨agitated by the strangely ~ criticisms of his work —Hesketh Pearson⟩

**im·per·ence** \ˈimpərən(t)s\ *n* -s [by alter.] *substand Brit* **:** IMPUDENCE

**imperf** *abbr* **1** imperfect **2** imperforate

**¹im·per·fect** \(ˈ)im, əm+\ *adj* [alter. (influenced by L *imperfectus*) of ME *imperfit, imparfit*, fr. MF *imparfait*, fr. L *imperfectus*, fr. *in-* ¹in- + *perfectus* perfect — more at PERFECT] **1 a :** falling short of perfection **:** not perfect (as in form, development, or function) **:** not complete in parts or attributes **:** not satisfying the standard or ideal **:** DEFECTIVE, INADEQUATE, INCOMPLETE ⟨had only an ~ understanding of his task⟩ ⟨in the ~ light of the moon —Anthony Trollope⟩ ⟨what an ~ husband he had always been —H.G.Wells⟩ ⟨~ mortals⟩ ⟨drainage of the region is ~ —*Jour. of Geol.*⟩ **b :** DICLINOUS **2 :** of, relating to, or being a verb tense used to designate a continuing state or an incomplete action esp. in the past **3 a** *in medieval church music* (1) **:** twofold rather than threefold in time value — used of notation; compare PERFECT (2) **:** having a duple rather than triple rhythm — used of a rhythmic mode **b :** DIMINISHED 2 **4 :** not enforceable at law **:** lacking some essential element required by law **:** depending for fulfillment upon moral rather than legal duty ⟨an ~ obligation⟩ **:** enforceable only under certain conditions **:** DEFEASIBLE ⟨an ~ mortgage⟩ ⟨an ~ grant avoidable by the government⟩ — **im·per·fect·ly** \"+\ *adv* — **im·per·fect·ness** \"+\ *n* -ES

**²imperfect** *vt, obs* **:** to make imperfect

**³im·per·fect** \(ˈ)im, əm+\ *n* **:** an imperfect tense; *also* **:** the verb form expressing it

**imperfect cadence** *n* **1 :** an authentic or plagal cadence in which the third or the fifth of the final chord appears in the soprano part or in which one or both of the cadential chords are inverted — compare PERFECT CADENCE; see CADENCE illustration **2 :** HALF CADENCE

**imperfect competition** *n* **:** competition among sellers of inhomogeneous products in which the sellers are sufficiently few in number so that each exerts an influence upon the market **:** limited competition

**imperfect diphthong** *n* **:** PARTIAL DIPHTHONG

**im·per·fect·ed** \(ˌ)im, əm+\ *adj* [¹*in-* + *perfected*] **:** not perfected **:** IMPERFECT — **im·per·fect·ed·ly** \"+\ *adv*

**imperfect flower** *n* **:** a diclinous flower

**imperfect fungus** *n* **:** a fungus of which only the conidial stage is known **:** one of the Fungi Imperfecti

**im·per·fect·i·bil·i·ty** \(ˌ)im, əm+\ *n* [¹*in-* + *perfectibility*] **:** the quality or state of being imperfectible

**im·per·fect·i·ble** \(ˌ)im, əm+\ *adj* [¹*in-* + *perfectible*] **:** incapable of being made perfect

**im·per·fec·tion** \ˌim+\ *n* [ME *imperfeccioun*, fr. MF or LL; MF *imperfection* fr. LL *imperfection-, imperfectio*, fr. L *imperfectus* + *-ion-, -io* -ion — more at IMPERFECT] **1 a :** the quality or state of being imperfect **:** lack of perfection **:** INCOMPLETENESS ⟨dissatisfied with the ~ of man⟩ ⟨saw the ~ of the dress⟩ **b :** the quality or aspect in which something is incomplete **:** DEFICIENCY, FAULT, BLEMISH ⟨tried to cover up the ~*s* in the cloth⟩ **2** *in medieval church music* **a :** duple time **b :** the occasional division of a triple measure into two equal parts **3 a :** a sheet that is rejected because of faulty printing; *also* **:** a replacement for such a sheet **b :** a printed or folded book section or a complete gathered or sewed but unbound book that has been rejected for any reason **4 :** a piece of type cast to fill a deficiency in a type font

**¹im·per·fec·tive** \(ˌ)im, əm+\ *adj* [¹*in-* + *perfective*] *of a verb form or aspect* **:** expressing action as incomplete or without reference to completion **:** expressing action as continuing **:** expressing action as reiterated **:** DURATIVE — opposed to *perfective* — **im·per·fec·tiv·i·ty** \"+\ *n*

**²imperfective** \"\ *n* **:** the imperfective aspect or form of a verb

**imperfect number** *n* **:** a number (as 15) that is not equal to the sum of its divisors — compare PERFECT NUMBER; see ABUNDANT NUMBER, DEFICIENT NUMBER

**imperfect stage** *n* **:** any of various conidial or asexual stages in the life history of a fungus

**imperfect usufruct** *n* **:** the right of usufruct allowed in a thing consumed in the using — called also *quasi usufruct*

**im·per·fo·ra·ta** \(ˌ)im, əm+\ *n pl, cap* [NL, fr. ¹*in-* + *Perforata*] *in some classifications* **:** a division of the Foraminifera having imperforate shells

**¹im·per·fo·rate** \(ˈ)im, əm+\ *adj* [¹*in-* + *perforate*] **1 :** not perforated **:** having no opening or aperture; *specif* **:** lacking the normal opening ⟨an ~ anus⟩ **2** *of a stamp or a sheet of stamps* **:** lacking perforations or rouletting **3 :** having the umbilicus obliterated by the later whorls — used of various spiral shells

**²imperforate** \"\ *n* -s **:** an imperforate stamp

**im·per·fo·rat·ed** \(ˈ)im, əm+\ *adj* [¹*in-* + *perforated*] **:** IMPERFORATE

**im·per·fo·ra·tion** \(ˌ)im, əm+\ *n* [F, fr. *in-* ¹in- + *perforation* — more at PERFORATION] **:** the quality or state of being without perforation

**¹im·pe·ri·al** \(ˌ)imˈpirēəl, əmˈp-, -pēr-\ *adj* [ME *emperial, imperial*, fr. MF, fr. LL *imperialis*, fr. L *imperium* command, supreme authority, empire + *-alis* -al — more at EMPIRE] **1 a :** of or relating to an empire or an emperor esp. of a particular or implicit empire ⟨the national poet of the empire, in whom ~ patriotism found its highest expression —James Bryce⟩ ⟨~ Caesar⟩ ⟨his view was ~ rather than provincial —Carl Bridenbaugh⟩ **b :** of, relating to, or befitting supreme authority or one that exercises it **:** of the rank of or suitable to an emperor or supreme ruler **:** ROYAL, SOVEREIGN **c :** of or relating to a state as governing or being supreme over colonies, dependencies, or many subdivisions; *specif, usu cap* **:** of or relating to Britain as such a state ⟨make an essential contribution . . . to New Zealand and *Imperial* history —*Notes & Queries*⟩ ⟨British *Imperial* communications —*Brit. Book News*⟩ **d :** HAUGHTY, REGAL, COMMANDING, IMPERIOUS ⟨stood there, tall, broad, ~ —Donn Byrne⟩ ⟨the rigid, ~ hyacinth —Rebecca West⟩ ⟨humoring us with her fatigued ~ smiles —Arnold Bennett⟩ **2 a :** of superior or unusual size or excellence ⟨a rich man living on an ~ diet⟩ ⟨grow from the little old town of the nineties to the ~ city that stands there now —W.A.White⟩ ⟨a homicidal mania on an ~ scale —Ellery Sedgwick⟩ **b :** of fancy quality — used as a designation for various commercial products **c :** SELF-AGGRANDIZING, GRANDIOSE ⟨thoughts that were partly dreams . . . ~, childish dreams —Audrey L. Barker⟩ **3** *of a measure or weight* **:** being the British legal standard **:** belonging to the official British series of weights and measures ⟨the ~ gallon⟩ — **im·pe·ri·al·ly** \-ēəlē, -li\ *adv* — **im·pe·ri·al·ness** \-ēəlnə̇s\ *n* -ES

**²imperial** \"\ *n* -s **1 :** a medieval silk and gold fabric of oriental origin **2** *usu cap* [Russ, prob. fr. Pol *imperjał*, a kind of coin, fr. ML *imperialis*, a medieval coin, fr. LL *imperialis*, adj., imperial] **:** an adherent of the Holy Roman emperor or a soldier of his troops **:** IMPERIALIST **3 :** a person of imperial rank **:** EMPEROR, EMPRESS **4 :** a size of paper usu. 23 x 31, 22½ x 29, or 22 x 30 inches **5 :** a game similar to piquet but having a trump; *also* **:** any of several scoring combinations in the game **6 a :** a luggage case for the top of a coach **b :** the top, roof, or second-story compartment of a coach or carriage, esp. a diligence **7 :** a gold coin of imperial Russia worth 10 rubles when first issued in 1745 and 15 rubles from 1897–1917 **8** [F *impériale*, fr. fem. of *impérial* imperial, fr. LL *imperialis*; fr. the beard worn as a young man by Napoleon III †1873 emperor of France] **:** a pointed beard growing below the lower lip **9 :** something of unusual size or excellence **10 :** a dark reddish purple that is lighter and stronger than average plum (sense 6a), bluer and stronger than violet carmine or average grape wine, and bluer and deeper than royal purple (sense 1) — called also *Cotinga purple*

imperial 8

**imperial blue** *n* **:** a deep blue that is greener and deeper than Yale blue, greener, lighter, and stronger than royal (sense 8b), and greener and stronger than Napoleon blue

**imperial bushel** *n* **:** BUSHEL 1b

**imperial city** *n* **1 :** a city (as Rome) that is the seat of empire **2 :** a city that is an immediate vassal of the emperor of the Holy Roman Empire

**imperial crown** *n, often cap I, sometimes cap C* **1 :** a crown emblematic of independent sovereignty: as **a :** the crown in the royal regalia of England that is used for the crowning in the coronation ceremony, that consists of a circlet of gold heightened with four crosses formée alternately with four fleurs-de-lis and has two arches rising from the crosses and surmounted by a mound and a cross formée, and that is ornamented with precious stones — called also *St. Edward's crown* **b :** the crown of an emperor or of an empire **2 :** a conventionalized representation of an imperial crown; *esp* **:** a figure of a crown in the style of the imperial crown of England often used as an emblem of the sovereignty of the British monarch or as a heraldic bearing **3 :** IMPERIAL STATE CROWN

**imperial crown of state** *often cap I&C&S* **:** IMPERIAL STATE CROWN

**imperial dome** *or* **imperial roof** *n* **:** a pointed dome or roof the vertical section of which is an ogee

**imperial eagle** *n* **:** an eagle (*Aquila heliaca*) of southern Europe and Asia the adult of which is dark brown with white shoulder patches — called also *king eagle*

**imperial gallon** *n* **:** GALLON 1b

**imperial green** *n* **1 :** PARIS GREEN 2b **2 :** EMERALD GREEN

**im·pe·ri·al·ism** \əmˈpirēəˌlizəm, -pēr-\ *n* -s **1 a :** the power or the government of an emperor **:** imperial authority **:** an imperial system ⟨the ~ of Caesar⟩ ⟨educational ~ —*Current Biog.*⟩ **b :** an imperial quality ⟨with dramatic ~ and disarming gentility . . . the epitome of mysterious womanhood —Louise Mace⟩ **2 a :** the policy, practice, or advocacy of seeking or the acquiescing in the extension of the control or empire of a nation by the acquirement of new territory or dependencies esp. when lying outside the nation's natural boundaries, by the extension of its rule over other races of mankind (as where commerce demands the protection of the flag), or by the closer union of more or less independent parts (as for war, copyright, or internal commerce) **b :** any extension of power or authority or an advocacy of such extension ⟨union ~ —S.H.Slichter⟩ ⟨cultural ~⟩

**¹im·pe·ri·al·ist** \-ləst\ *n* -s [¹*imperial* + *-ist*] **1 :** one that adheres to an emperor or to his party; *esp* **:** one loyal to the Holy Roman Empire **2 :** one who favors or practices imperialism

**²imperialist** \"\ *or* **im·pe·ri·al·is·tic** \(ˌ)imˌ===ˈlistik, əm-, -tēk\ *adj* **:** of, relating to, practicing, or favoring imperialism ⟨the great faiths . . . are *imperialistic*, going out to bring into the fold others than those people among whom they grew up —W.W.Howells⟩ ⟨an ~ war⟩ ⟨*imperialistic* in seeking to convert almost the whole of political science to his own interests —David Easton⟩ ⟨autocratic control and *imperialistic* expansion —Sigmund Neumann⟩ ⟨*imperialistic* policies of aggression among the weaker races —Lewis Mumford⟩ — **im·pe·ri·al·is·ti·cal·ly** \-tə̇k(ə)lē, -tēk-, -li\ *adv*

**im·pe·ri·al·iza·tion** \=ˌ===lə̇ˈzāshən, -ˌlīˈz-\ *n* -s **:** the act of imperializing or the state of being imperialized

**im·pe·ri·al·ize** \=ˈ===ˌlīz\ *vt* -ED/-ING/-S **:** to make imperial **:** invest with an imperial quality or character **:** bring to the form of an empire

**imperial jade** *n, usu cap I* **:** ³JADE 1a

**imperially crowned** *adj, of a heraldic bearing* **:** crowned with an imperial crown

**imperial mammoth** *also* **imperial elephant** *n* **:** the largest known mammoth (*Archidiskidon imperator*) of the American Pleistocene reaching a height of 14 feet

**imperial moth** *n* **:** a large American saturniid moth (*Eacles imperialis*) marked with yellow, lilac, or purplish brown whose rough hairy larva feeds esp. on maple, sumach, and pine trees

**imperial pigeon** *n* **:** any of various very large Asiatic and Australasian pigeons that constitute a distinct subfamily of Columbidae — compare NUTMEG PIGEON

**imperial preference** *n* **:** the preferential lowering of tariff rates accorded in the British Commonwealth to its members

**imperial purple** *n* **1 :** a grayish violet **2** *of textiles* **:** a deep purple that is redder and duller than hyacinth violet or petunia violet and redder and less strong than dahlia purple (sense 2)

**imperial red** *also* **imperial scarlet** *n* **:** vermilion or a color resembling it

**imperials** *pl of* IMPERIAL

**imperial state crown** *n, usu cap I&S&C* **:** an English royal crown worn on various state occasions that is more richly jeweled than the imperial crown but lighter in weight and usu. remade for successive sovereigns — called also *state crown*

**imperial stone** *n* **:** a light olive brown that is deeper than drab or sponge and deeper and slightly redder than average mustard tan

**imperial tea** *n* **:** a high-grade Chinese green tea made usu. from older leaves

**imperial woodpecker** *n* **:** a woodpecker (*Campephilus imperialis*) of northern Mexico that has black plumage with white markings on the wings and neck, a red crest in the male, and a white bill and that is the largest woodpecker known, the male being about two feet in length

**imperial yellow** *n* **:** YELLOW OCHER

**im·per·il** \əm+\ *vt* **imperiled** *or* **imperilled**; **imperiled** *or* **imperilled**; **imperiling** *or* **imperilling**; **imperils** [²*in-* + *peril* (n.)] **:** to bring into peril **:** expose to danger of imminent harm or loss **:** endanger or threaten danger to ⟨a jungle of aggressive power politics which ~*s* . . . the healing of the wounds of war —Mark Starr⟩ ⟨people whose investments were ~*ed* —G.W.Johnson⟩ ⟨stray mines . . . began to turn up off the Pacific coast, ~*ing* commercial shipping —Alan Hynd⟩ **syn** see VENTURE

**im·per·il·ment** \-mənt\ *n* -s **:** the act of imperiling or the state of being imperiled ⟨cut down on the convoy escort to the ~ of shipping everywhere⟩

**im·pe·ri·ous** \(ˈ)imˈpirēəs, əmˈp-, -pēr-\ *adj* [L *imperiosus*, fr. *imperium* command, supreme authority, empire + *-osus* -ous — more at EMPIRE] **1 a** *obs* **:** IMPERIAL 1 a, 1b **b :** COMMANDING, DOMINANT, LORDLY ⟨sweeps through her social duties with ~ kindness —Margaret Landon⟩ **c** *obs* **:** MAJESTIC, STATELY **2 :** ARROGANT, OVERBEARING, DOMINEERING **3 :** IMPERATIVE, URGENT, COMPELLING ⟨at the mercy of the most ~ of instincts, of passions, and of intoxications —Arthur Symons⟩ ⟨so ~ became the commercial demand —Lewis Mumford⟩ **syn** see MASTERFUL

**im·pe·ri·ous·ly** *adv* **:** in an imperious manner ⟨drew him ~ apart from the others —George Meredith⟩ ⟨clung to authority as ~ as a king who refuses to abdicate —Ellen Glasgow⟩

**im·pe·ri·ous·ness** *n* -ES **:** the quality or state of being imperious

**im·per·ish·abil·i·ty** \(ˌ)im, əm+\ *n* **:** the quality or state of being imperishable

**¹im·per·ish·able** \(ˈ)im, əm+\ *adj* [¹*in-* + *perishable*] **:** not perishable **:** not subject to decay **:** enduring permanently **:** INDESTRUCTIBLE ⟨an ~ monument⟩ ⟨~ fame⟩ ⟨peace is not ~ —M.W.Straight⟩ ⟨an ~ memory⟩ — **im·per·ish·able·ness** \"+\ *n* — **im·per·ish·ably** \"+\ *adv*

**²imperishable** \"\ *n* **:** something imperishable ⟨a classic to take its place among the ~*s*⟩

**im·pe·ri·um** \əmˈpirēəm, -per-, -pēr-\ *n* -s [L, command, supreme authority, empire — more at EMPIRE] **1 a** (1) **:** supreme power or absolute dominion esp. over a large area ⟨surrender the showy shadow of ~ to secure the solid substance of colonial loyalty and cooperation —Oliver Benson⟩ (2) **:** regulatory powers or control ⟨had relinquished all ~ . . . over the land in question —*U.S. Code*⟩ ⟨existing governments had exhausted their ~ —Walter Lippmann⟩ **b :** an area over which such power or dominion is exercised **:** TERRITORY, EMPIRE ⟨the portentous ~ of the cartels —R.M.MacIver⟩ **2 a :** the right to command **:** the right of jurisdiction which includes the right to employ the force of the state to enforce the laws **:** executive power **:** SOVEREIGNTY **b** *Roman law* **:** the power to hear and determine cases and to give judgments — compare DOMINIUM, JURISDICTION

**imperium in im·pe·rio** \-ˌinəmˈpirēˌō, -per-,-pēr-\ *n* [NL] **:** a government, power, or sovereignty within a government, power, or sovereignty

**im·per·ma·nence** *or* **im·per·ma·nen·cy** \(ˈ)im+\ *n* [¹*in-* + *permanence, permanency*] **:** the quality or state of being impermanent ⟨the ~ . . . of all the dear world of beauty —C.E.Montague⟩ ⟨the sense of the ~ of things, the transitoriness of life —Laurence Binyon⟩ ⟨the foolishness of love and the *impermanency* of all human relationships —Lafcadio Hearn⟩

**im·per·ma·nent** \"+\ *adj* [¹*in-* + *permanent*] **:** not permanent **:** not lasting **:** TRANSIENT ⟨politics is an ~ factor of life —James Thurber⟩ **:** UNSTABLE ⟨broken homes, ~ family life —Bingham Dai⟩ **:** soon destroyed ⟨~ log and palm cottages raised on stilts above the bayous —*Amer. Guide Series: La.*⟩ — **im·per·ma·nent·ly** \"+\ *adv*

**im·per·me·abil·i·ty** \(ˌ)im, əm+\ *n* **:** the quality or state of being impermeable

**im·per·me·a·bi·li·za·tion** \(ˌ)imˌpərmēəˌbiləˈzāshən; -ˌbələ̇ˈz-, -bəˌlīˈz-\ *n* -s [F *imperméabilisation*, fr. *imperméabiliser* + *-ation*] **:** the act of impermeabilizing something

**im·per·me·a·bi·lize** \=ˈ===ˌbəˌlīz\ *vt* -ED/-ING/-S [F *imperméabiliser*, fr. LL *impermeabilis* + F *-iser* -ize] **:** to make impermeable esp. to liquids

**im·per·me·able** \(ˈ)im, əm+\ *adj* [LL *impermeabilis*, fr. L *in-* ¹in- + LL *permeabilis* permeable — more at PERMEABLE] **:** not permeable **:** not permitting passage (as of a fluid) through its substance **:** IMPASSABLE, IMPERVIOUS ⟨an ~ stone⟩ ⟨a coat ~ to rain⟩ ⟨an ~ layer of scum⟩ — **im·per·me·able·ness** \"+\ *n* — **im·per·me·ably** \"+\ *adv*

**im·per·mis·si·bil·i·ty** \ˌim+\ *n* **:** the quality or state of being impermissible

**im·per·mis·si·ble** \"+\ *adj* [¹*in-* + *permissible*] **:** not permissible ⟨his secret and legally ~ objective —B.N.Meltzer⟩ ⟨has taken ~ liberties —J.D.Clarkson⟩ — **im·per·mis·si·bly** \"+\ *adv*

**impers** *abbr* impersonal

**im·per·son·able** \(ˈ)im, əm+\ *adj* [¹*in-* + *personable*] **:** not personable **:** UNATTRACTIVE

**¹im·per·son·al** \"+\ *adj* [LL *impersonalis*, fr. L *in-* ¹in- + LL *personalis* personal — more at PERSONAL] **1 a** (1) *of a verb* **:** not predicated of a personal or determinate subject **:** denoting the action of an unspecified agent and hence used with no expressed subject (as *methinks*) or with a merely formal subject (as *is raining* in *it is raining*) (2) **:** consisting of either an indefinite pronoun and an impersonal verb (as *it is raining* or French *on dit*) or the expletive *there* and such a verb (as *there is* in *there is fog ahead*) **b** *of a pronoun* **:** INDEFINITE **c** *of a proposition* **:** having an indeterminate subject **2 a** (1) **:** having no personal reference or connection **:** not referring or belonging to any particular person ⟨when I say that a belief is ~ I mean that those desires which enter into its causation are universal human desires, and not such as are peculiar to the person in question —Bertrand Russell⟩ ⟨the brightly ~ sunshine —K.M.Dodson⟩ ⟨an ~ coat of arms⟩ (2) **:** not engaging the human personality or person ⟨the machine as compared with the hand tool is an ~ agency —John Dewey⟩ **b :** not representing or existing as a person **:** not having personality ⟨nature becomes an ~ slave —W.H.Auden⟩ **c :** not primarily affecting or involving the emotions of the person who has it ⟨an ~ interest in law⟩ ⟨the ~ attitude of a doctor⟩ — **im·per·son·al·ly** \"+\ *adv*

**²impersonal** \"\ *n* **:** something impersonal; *specif* **:** an impersonal verb

**im·per·son·al·ism** \(ˈ)im, əm+\ *n* **1 :** IMPERSONALITY ⟨the ~ of research in the sciences⟩ ⟨the trend toward ~ in office relations⟩ **2 :** the policy of being impersonal in relations with other persons or of maintaining impersonal relations among a group

**im·per·son·al·i·ty** \(ˌ)im, əm+\ *n* [¹*impersonal* + *-ity*] **1 :** the lack or absence of a personal or human character ⟨the ~ of natural law⟩ **2 :** the quality or state of not involving personal feelings or the emotions or of being unemotional and disinterested ⟨marveled at the ~ of the thinking of so passionate a man⟩ ⟨the emotional detachment and ~ required of a good playwright —Leslie Rees⟩ ⟨so much ~, so much coldness and emphasis on technique —Manny Farber⟩ **3 a :** the quality or state of not involving, not being activated by, or not tracing to a personal agent ⟨the ~ of the popular ballad⟩ ⟨the ~ of the machine⟩ **b :** a quality or state marked by an absence or suppression of human expression or a minimizing of the significance of personality ⟨the ~ of society⟩ ⟨the ~ of the world money market⟩ **c :** the quality of not bearing on only a single or a particular person ⟨the ~, the universality of his remarks⟩ **4 :** something impersonal ⟨forced to deal with *impersonalities* such as the state or the law⟩

**im·per·son·al·iza·tion** \(ˌ)im, əm+\ *n* **:** the act of impersonalizing or the state of being impersonalized ⟨the growing ~ of higher civilizations —A.L.Kroeber⟩

**im·per·son·al·ize** \(ˈ)im, əm+\ *vt* [¹*impersonal* + *-ize*] **:** to make impersonal ⟨one cannot ~ entirely a cosmic human drama like that war —W.A.White⟩

**¹im·per·son·ate** \əmˈpərsᵊnˌāt, -pəs-, -pəis-, *usu* -ād+V\ *vt* [²*in-* + *person* + *-ate* (v. suffix)] **1 a** *obs* **:** to give or ascribe the qualities of a person to **:** PERSONIFY **b** *archaic* **:** TYPIFY, EXEMPLIFY **2 :** to assume the character of **:** pretend to be in actuality or personality, appearance, or behavior **:** PERSONATE ⟨caught trying to ~ an officer⟩ ⟨do not have the correct intonation for the character they are trying to ~ —Samuel Selden⟩ ⟨the dancers *impersonated* animals⟩ **3 a :** to give personal expression to ⟨an actor who could ~ any emotion⟩

b : to give expression to the person of ⟨music to ~ the hero of the opera⟩

**²im·per·son·ate** \-sᵊnət, usu -əd.+V\ adj [²in- + person + -ate (adj. suffix)] : invested with personality ⟨in the dictator all the forces of evil found an ~ expression⟩

**im·per·son·a·tion** \əm,⸗⸗ˈāshən, ,im-\ n : the act of impersonating or the state of being impersonated ⟨arrested for his ~ of an army major⟩ ⟨a man noted for his ~ of women⟩ ⟨the musical ~ of the hero himself —Eric Blom⟩

**im·per·son·a·tor** \⸗ˈ⸗⸗,ād·ə(r), -ātə-\ n : one that impersonates; esp : an entertainer who impersonates an individual, a type of person, an animal, or an inanimate object

**im·personification** \,im+\ n [²in- + personification] : EMBODIMENT

**im·personify** \"+\ vt [²in- + personify] archaic : to give a personal form or expression to : PERSONIFY

**im·pertinence** also **impertinency** \im+, əm+, or in senses 1a & 2a ˈim+;-\ n [impertinence fr. F, fr. ML impertinentia, fr. LL impertinent-, impertinens + L -ia -y; impertinency fr. F impertinence + E -y] **1** : the quality or state of being impertinent: as **a** : lack of relevance or appropriateness : IRRELEVANCE, UNFITNESS **b** : lack of due respect for others in conduct : INCIVILITY, INSOLENCE ⟨the ~, the brashness had gone forever —Katharine F. Gerould⟩ **2** : something impertinent or an instance of impertinence: **a** : an irrelevant thing or matter ⟨at the climax of high tragedy all scenic adjuncts become an ~ —W.B.Adams⟩ **b** : an impertinent or uncivil act or person ⟨irritated by the man's social faults and ~s⟩ ⟨unwilling to scold the young ~ that was his son⟩

**¹im·pertinent** \(ˈ)im, əm+\ adj [ME, fr. MF, fr. LL impertinent-, impertinens, fr. L in- ¹in- + pertinent-, pertinens, pres. part. of pertinēre to reach out, extend, pertain — more at PERTAIN] **1 a** : not pertinent : not significantly belonging or related to the matter in hand : IRRELEVANT, INAPPLICABLE ⟨should rigidly exclude courses of study ~ to their central purposes —H.W.Sams⟩ **b** obs : not suitable or congruous : INAPPROPRIATE **c** archaic : FRIVOLOUS, FOOLISH **2** : not restrained within the due or proper bounds esp. of propriety or good breeding in words or actions : guilty of or prone to rudeness or incivility ⟨a child taught not to make ~ remarks to his elders⟩ ⟨approach complete strangers, ask them a battery of ~ questions —S.L.Payne⟩

**syn** IMPERTINENT, OFFICIOUS, MEDDLESOME, INTRUSIVE, OBTRUSIVE: IMPERTINENT implies a concerning of oneself offensively with what is another's business ⟨all that had occurred to make my former interference in his affairs absurd and *impertinent* —Jane Austen⟩ ⟨we were secure from all *impertinent* interference in our concerns —Herman Melville⟩ ⟨something so extremely *impertinent* in entering upon a man's premises, and using them without paying —William Cowper⟩ OFFICIOUS implies an offering of unwelcome or offensive services, attentions, or assistance ⟨cannot walk home from office, but some *officious* friend offers his unwelcome courtesies to accompany me —Charles Lamb⟩ ⟨had no desire to call in a detective for fear the man might become an *officious* nuisance⟩ MEDDLESOME stresses an annoying and usu. prying interference in others' business ⟨turns with scorn upon the Abolitionists and their *meddlesome* interference with the beneficent ways of Providence —V.L.Parrington⟩ ⟨a vain, *meddlesome* vagabond, and must needs pry into a secret which certainly did not concern him —Charles Kingsley⟩ INTRUSIVE applies to one who has or something that reveals a disposition to be unduly curious about another's business ⟨made an inconspicuous fourth in their small world, always at hand yet never *intrusive* —B.A.Williams⟩ ⟨to protect oneself by silence from well-meaning but *intrusive* friends⟩ OBTRUSIVE is like INTRUSIVE but usu. stresses more objectionable actions than a disposition, suggesting an undue, improper, or offensive conspicuousness of interference ⟨she knelt and watched, quietly, without expressing any *obtrusive* concern for his safety —Floyd Dell⟩ ⟨the *obtrusive* attentions of sycophants and henchmen⟩

**²impertinent** \"\ n : an impertinent person : one that is presumptuous, meddlesome, or insolent

**im·per·ti·nent·ly** adv [ME, fr. impertinent + -ly] : in an impertinent manner ⟨prying ~ into my affairs⟩

**im·per·ti·nent·ness** n -ES : IMPERTINENCE

**im·per·turb·abil·i·ty** \,impər,tərbəˈbiləd·ē\ n : the quality or state of being imperturbable ⟨no excitement or depression ever disturbed his extraordinary ~⟩

**im·per·turb·able** \-ˈtərbəbəl\ adj [ME, fr. LL imperturbabilis, fr. L in- ¹in- + perturbare to perturb + -abilis -able — more at PERTURB] : marked by extreme calm, impassivity, assurance, and steadiness : unlikely to be disconcerted, agitated, or alarmed ⟨hitherto ~, he now showed signs of alarm⟩ ⟨an ~ self-possession —Albert Dasnoy⟩ **syn** see COOL

**im·per·turb·able·ness** n -ES : IMPERTURBABILITY ⟨a certain calm indifference, a certain ~ —J.C.Powys⟩

**im·per·turb·ably** \-blē\ adv : in an imperturbable manner ⟨stalked ~ about the streets . . . or stood impassively in doorways —Green Peyton⟩

**im·perturbation** \(ˌ)im+\ n [LL imperturbation-, imperturbatio, fr. L in- ¹in- + perturbation-, perturbatio perturbation — more at PERTURBATION] : freedom from agitation : CALMNESS, QUIETUDE

**im·perturbed** \ˌim+\ adj [¹in- + perturbed] : not perturbed : CALM

**im·per·vi·a·ble** \(ˈ)imˈpərvēəbəl\ adj [alter. (influenced by impermeable) of impervious] : IMPERVIOUS, IMPERMEABLE

**im·pervious** \(ˈ)im+\ adj [L impervius, fr. in- ¹in- + pervius pervious — more at PERVIOUS] **1 a** : not allowing entrance or passage through : IMPENETRABLE ⟨waterproofed so that the coat was ~ to rain⟩ ⟨a steel ~ to bullets⟩ **b** : not capable of being damaged or harmed ⟨a carpet material ~ to most rough treatment⟩ **2** : not capable of being affected or disturbed ⟨a man ~ to criticism⟩ ⟨looked at her, ~ to her tears —Jean Stafford⟩ : not open ⟨~ to arguments or facts⟩ — **im·perviously** \"+\ adv — **im·perviousness** \"+\ n

**im·pest** \əmˈpest\ archaic var of EMPEST

**impester** vt [MF empestrer — more at PESTER] obs : ENTANGLE, EMBARRASS

**im·pe·tig·i·nized** \ˌimpəˈtijə,nīzd\ adj [L impetigin-, impetigo + E -ize + -ed] : secondarily covered with crusts — used of skin diseases or lesions ⟨~ dermatitis⟩

**im·pe·tig·i·nous** \-nəs\ adj [LL impetiginosus, fr. L impetigin-, impetigo + -osus -ous] : of, relating to, or like impetigo — **im·pe·tig·i·nous·ly** adv

**im·pe·ti·go** \ˌimpəˈtē(ˌ)gō, -tī(-\ n -s [L, fr. impetere to attack — more at IMPETUS] : an acute contagious skin disease characterized by the formation of vesicles, pustules, and yellowish crusts and caused by staphylococci or streptococci transmitted by contact between persons or between healthy and infected skin

**im·pe·trate** \ˈimpə,trāt\ vt -ED/-ING/-S [L impetratus, past part. of impetrare, fr. in- ²in- + -petrare (fr. patrare to accomplish) — more at PERPETRATE] **1** : to obtain by request or entreaty : PROCURE **2** : to ask for : ENTREAT

**im·pe·tra·tion** \ˌimpəˈtrāshən\ n -S [L impetration-, impetratio, fr. impetratus + -ion-, -io -ion] **1** : the act of impetrating : petition or a procuring by petition **2** Old Eng law : the act of obtaining from Rome by solicitation a benefice which belonged to the disposal of the king or other lay patron of the realm

**im·pe·tra·tive** \ˈimpə,trād·iv\ adj [LL impetrativus, fr. L impetratus + -ivus -ive] : of, relating to, or being impetration : consisting of, getting, or tending to get by entreaty

**im·pe·tra·to·ry** \ˈimpə·trə,tōrē\ adj [L impetratus + E -ory] archaic : IMPETRATIVE

**im·pet·u·os·i·ty** \(ˌ)im,pechəˈwäsəd·ē, əm-, -sətē, -i\ n -ES [MF impetuosité, fr. OF, fr. LL impetuosus + OF -ité -ity] **1** : the quality or state of being impetuous ⟨the ~ of his proposal —Louis Auchincloss⟩ **2** : an impetuous action or impulse ⟨a man driven by *impetuosities* and whims⟩

**im·pet·u·o·so** \(ˌ)im,pechəˈwō(ˌ)sō, -)zō\ adj (or adv) [It, fr. LL impetuosus] : IMPETUOUS — used as a direction in music

**im·pet·u·ous** \(ˈ)imˈpechəwəs, əmˈp-\ adj [ME, fr. MF impetueux, fr. LL impetuosus, fr. L impetus + -osus -ous] **1** : marked by force and violence of movement or action : FURIOUS ⟨an ~ wind⟩ ⟨with ~ speed⟩ ⟨match his more ~ neighbors working furiously at their hobbies —G.B.Shaw⟩ **2** : impulsively vehement in feeling ⟨of a very warm and ~ nature, responded to their affection with quite a tropical ardor —W.M.Thackeray⟩ : hastily or rashly energetic or passionate ⟨~ in his habits . . . lost his temper and punched another officer in the nose —J.G.Cozzens⟩ ⟨restless, energetic, ~, temperamental, and at times a little irascible —A.W.Long⟩ **syn** see PRECIPITATE

**im·pet·u·ous·ly** adv : in an impetuous manner ⟨a stream rushing ~ over rocks⟩

**im·pet·u·ous·ness** n -ES [ME impetuousnes, fr. impetuous + -nes -ness] : the quality or state of being impetuous

**im·pe·tus** \ˈimpəd·əs, -pətəs\ n -ES [L, attack, assault, impetus, fr. impetere to attack, fr. in- ²in- + petere to go to or toward, rush at, attack, seek — more at FEATHER] **1 a** (1) : a driving or impelling force ⟨trying to discover the ~ behind all this activity⟩ : IMPULSE ⟨an intermittent force, each ~ being of only the shortest duration⟩ (2) : INCENTIVE, STIMULUS ⟨felt no ~ to do well in school⟩ **b** : stimulation or encouragement resulting in increased activity ⟨gave a good deal of ~ to the musical activity of the city⟩ **2** : the property possessed by a moving body in virtue of its mass and its motion — used of bodies moving suddenly or violently to indicate the origin and intensity of the motion rather than the quantity or effectiveness

**im·pey·an pheasant** \ˈimpēən-\ n [Sir Elijah Impey †1809 Eng. jurist, and Lady Impey †1818 his wife, who introduced the bird into England + E -an] : a monal (*Lophophorus impejanus*) ranging from Afghanistan to Assam

**impf** abbr imperfect

**im·phee** \ˈim(p)fē\ n -s [Zulu imfe] : any of several African sorghums

**im·pi** \ˈimpē\ n -s [Zulu] : a body of Kaffir warriors or other southern African native armed men

**im·picture** \əm+\ vt [²in- + picture (n.)] archaic : to represent as if in a picture : PORTRAY

**im·piety** \(ˈ)im, əm+\ n [MF impieté, fr. L impietat-, impietas, fr. impius impious + -tat-, -tas -ty — more at IMPIOUS] **1 a** : the quality or state of being impious : lack of piety : IRREVERENCE, UNGODLINESS ⟨~, in denying the gods recognized by the state —J.S.Mill⟩ **b** : UNDUTIFULNESS ⟨guilty of filial ~ in showing no respect for his father's advice⟩ **2** : an impious act ⟨his sins turned into his *impieties* —William Empson⟩

**im·pig·no·rate** \əmˈpignə,rāt\ vt [LL or ML impignoratus, impigneratus, past part. of impignorare, impignerare, fr. L in- ²in- + pignorare, pignerare to pledge — more at PIGNORATE] : PLEDGE, PAWN, MORTGAGE — **im·pig·no·ra·tion** \⸗,⸗⸗ˈrāshən\ n

**imp·ing** \ˈimpiŋ\ n -s [ME, fr. gerund of impen to graft — more at IMP] : the process in falconry of mending a broken pinion by inserting one end of a specially prepared needle into the stub of the feather and the other into the shaft of the original feather or a replacement feather

**im·pinge** \əmˈpinj\ vb -ED/-ING/-S [L impingere to strike or push at or against, fr. in- ²in- + -pingere (fr. pangere to fasten, drive in) — more at PACT] vi **1** : to strike or dash esp. with a sharp collision : come into sharp contact — usu. used with *on, upon*, or *against* ⟨when an elastic ball ~s on another —K.K.Darrow⟩ ⟨I heard the rain ~ upon the earth —James Joyce⟩ ⟨the creak of oarlocks *impinged* on his ear⟩ ⟨something ~s violently on your senses —Peggy Durdin⟩ ⟨a strong light *impinging* on the eyes and causing a sudden pain⟩ **2** : to come into a relationship as if impinging : make an impression : touch closely or bear directly — usu. used with *on* or *upon* ⟨waiting for the germ of a new idea to ~ upon my mind —Phyllis Bentley⟩ ⟨the objects that *impinged* upon his imagination with the greatest impact —*Times Lit. Supp.*⟩ ⟨in that line of reasoning we ~ upon an abstruse metaphysical problem⟩ ⟨political forces that ~ on everyone's daily life⟩ **3** : ENCROACH, INFRINGE — usu. used with *on* ⟨*impinging* on other people's rights⟩ ⟨not that I want to ~ on any man's recreation —Ezra Pound⟩ ~ vt : to cause (as a gas or a flame) to strike ⟨*impinging* live steam on the printed surface —*Chem. & Engineering News*⟩

**im·pinge·ment** \-mənt\ n -s : the act of impinging or the state of being impinged upon: as **a** : a sharp collision : a striking or dashing against **b** : INFLUENCE, EFFECT, ENCROACHMENT, INFRINGEMENT ⟨the ~ of American power upon Asiatic life without adequate comprehension of the vast complexities of Asiatic politics —Reinhold Niebuhr⟩ ⟨the ~ of Russia's security aims upon interests of Britain or the U.S. —Allan Taylor⟩ **syn** see IMPACT

**impingement black** n : CHANNEL BLACK

**im·pin·gent** \-jənt\ adj [L impingent-, impingens, pres. part. of impingere] : IMPINGING ⟨ecological factors ~ upon the production and use of foods —Theodore Stern⟩

**im·ping·er** \-jə(r)\ n -s : an instrument for collecting samples of dust or other suspended particles esp. in air by impinging a stream of the suspension on a surface or in a liquid (as water)

**impinguate** vt -ED/-ING/-S [LL impinguatus, past part. of impinguare, fr. L in- ²in- + pinguis fat — more at PINGUID] obs : FATTEN

**im·pi·ous** \ˈimpēəs, (ˈ)imˈpīəs\ adj [L impius, fr. in- ¹in- + pius pious — more at PIOUS] : not pious : IRREVERENT: **a** : lacking reverence for God, a deity, or for what is sacred : PROFANE, IRRELIGIOUS ⟨an ~ life⟩ **b** : lacking in proper respect (as for parents or for something usu. held in general respect) ⟨an ~ son⟩ ⟨an ~ flouting of experience —Donagh MacDonagh⟩ ⟨any alteration in the ceremonies that surrounded Thanksgiving would have been considered ~ and heartbreaking by my mother —John Cheever⟩

**syn** PROFANE, BLASPHEMOUS, SACRILEGIOUS: IMPIOUS usu. implies extreme disrespect for a divinity or his attributes and manifestations ⟨the *impious* challenge of power divine —William Cowper⟩ ⟨who is there more *impious* than a backsliding priest? —John Steinbeck⟩ PROFANE in this sense may suggest not only the disrespect involved in IMPIOUS but also desecration, intentional or not, of something to be held inviolate ⟨hitherto no liberal statesman has been so audacious as to "imagine the king's death" and lay *profane* hands on the divine right of nations to seek their own advantage at the cost of the rest by such means as the rule of reason shall decide to be permissible —Thorstein Veblen⟩ ⟨I collected bones from charnel houses; and disturbed, with *profane* fingers, the tremendous secrets of the human frame —Mary W. Shelley⟩ BLASPHEMOUS may apply to strong and intentional impiety or profanation fervently expressed or performed or to the harboring and abetting of ideas calculated to lower the awesome dignity of a deity ⟨*blasphemous* conversation⟩ ⟨it is *blasphemous* because it attributes to God purposes which we would not respect even in an earthly parent —J.A.Pike⟩ SACRILEGIOUS commonly may describe any flagrant depredation, disrespect, or contempt ⟨*sacrilegious* in his scandalous burlesques of the gods⟩ All of these words lend themselves to broad and inexact uses.

**im·pi·ous·ly** adv : in an impious manner

**im·pi·ous·ness** n : IMPIETY

**imp·ish** \ˈimpish, -pēsh\ adj : of, relating to, or befitting an imp; esp : MISCHIEVOUS ⟨the spectacle is weird and grotesque, and suggests something ~ and uncanny —John Burroughs⟩ ⟨took ~ delight in pestering his parents⟩ ⟨the child's ~ face⟩ — **imp·ish·ly** adv — **imp·ish·ness** n -ES

**im·pit·e·ous** \(ˈ)imˈpid·ēəs\ adj [¹in- + piteous] : PITILESS, CRUEL

**impl** abbr **1** imperial **2** implement

**im·placa·bil·i·ty** \(ˌ)im,plakəˈbiləd·ē, əm-, -lətē, -i also -plāk-\ n [LL implacabilitas, fr. L implacabilis + -itas -ity] : the quality or state of being implacable ⟨the ~ of his resentments —Jane Austen⟩ ⟨the ~ of a Greek tragedy —Arthur Schlesinger b. 1917⟩

**im·placa·ble** \(ˈ)imˈplakəbəl, əmˈp- also -plāk-\ adj [MF or L; MF, fr. L implacabilis, fr. in- ¹in- + placabilis placable — more at PLACABLE] **1 a** : not placable : not capable of being appeased or pacified : INEXORABLE ⟨an ~ enemy⟩ ⟨an ~ resentment⟩ ⟨single-minded and ~, even unmerciful, in his servitude to the law —M.S.Mayer⟩ **b** : incapable of being significantly changed or modified : following a due unalterable course ⟨the ~ lives of plants —Clifford Gessler⟩ ⟨the ~ logic of his career⟩ ⟨the measured, arranged, ~ movement of the universe —A.J.Cronin⟩ **2** : incapable of being relieved or mitigated ⟨an ~ disease⟩ ⟨the horns of an ~ dilemma —J.C.Powys⟩ ⟨his ~ interest in love —William McFee⟩ ⟨watched that ~ blaze of space as far as the mountainous horizon —D.C.Peattie⟩ — **im·placa·ble·ness** \-bəlnəs\ n — **im·placa·bly** \-blē, -bli\ adv

**im·place·ment** \əmˈplāsmənt\ n [modif. (influenced by ²in-) of F emplacement] — more at EMPLACEMENT] : EMPLACEMENT

**im·placentalia** \(ˌ)im+\ n pl, cap [NL, fr. ¹in- + Placentalia] in former classifications : the monotremes and marsupials regarded as a systematic unit characterized by the absence or rudimentary development of a placenta

**¹im·plant** \əm+\ also **em·plant** \əm,em+\ vt [²in- or ¹en- + plant] **1 a** : to fix or set securely or deeply ⟨a ruby ~ed in a gold ring⟩ **b** : to set or fix as permanent in the consciousness, the psyche, or habit patterns : INSTILL, INCULCATE ⟨~ good habits in children⟩ ⟨~ in a person the idea that the end of the world is near⟩ ⟨such a taste . . . simply cannot be ~ed —H.L.Mencken⟩ **2** archaic : PLANT **3 a** : to insert in a living site for growth, formation of an organic union, or absorption **b** : to insert an implant in ⟨100 patients have been ~ed with nylon ribbons without complications —U.K.Henschke⟩

**syn** IMPLANT, INCULCATE, INSTILL can mean, in common, to introduce into the mind. IMPLANT implies teaching and stresses a fixing firmly in the mind of what is taught or advocated ⟨the duty of Congress to see that educational institutions *implant* only sound ideas in the minds of students —Elmer Davis⟩ ⟨the teacher, the parent, or the friend can often do much to *implant* this conviction —C.W.Eliot⟩ ⟨in me especially, she *implanted* a respect for pioneering tradition —Rex Ingamells⟩ ⟨sea voyagers . . . may remain to *implant* their knowledge and practices in the new territory —C.D. Forde⟩ INCULCATE lays stress on repeated persistent efforts to impress on or fix in the mind ⟨it is no part of the duty of a university to *inculcate* any particular philosophy of life —Walter Moberly⟩ ⟨a means of *inculcating* in the conscripts intense patriotism and religious devotion to the state —Chitoshi Yanaga⟩ ⟨the seriousness *inculcated* in men by two cataclysmic world wars —S.P.Lamprecht⟩ INSTILL implies a gradual usu. gentle method of imparting knowledge usu. over a long period of time ⟨the principles which had been *instilled* in her soul from the time she began to speak —Ruth Park⟩ ⟨schools must plan to *instill* not only knowledge, but more of permanent refined interests; not only scholarship, but more of character and social purpose —A.C.Ellis⟩ ⟨a profound sense of public duty will be *instilled* into boys and girls of the governing class as soon as they are able to understand such an idea —Bertrand Russell⟩

**²im·plant** \ˈim+,-\ n : something implanted esp. in tissue (as a graft, a small container of radioactive material for treatment of cancer, or a pellet containing hormones to be gradually absorbed)

**im·plan·ta·tion** \ˌim,planˈtāshən, -laan-,-lān-\ n **1** : the act or process of implanting or the state of being implanted: as **a** : the placement of the root of a tooth in an artificially prepared socket in the jawbone **b** *in placental mammals* : the process of attachment of the embryo to the maternal uterine wall **c** : experimental addition of tissue or other material to an intact embryo **d** : medical treatment by the insertion of an implant **2** : the spontaneous passage of cells esp. of tumors to a new site with subsequent growth — compare METASTASIS

**im·plastic** \(ˈ)im+\ adj [¹in- + plastic] : not plastic : not readily molded : STIFF — **im·plasticity** \ˌim+\ n

**im·plausibility** \(ˌ)im, əm+\ n **1** : the quality or state of being implausible ⟨put on his guard by the ~ of the man's explanation⟩ **2** : something implausible

**im·plausible** \(ˈ)im, əm+\ adj [¹in- + plausible] : not plausible : having a quality that provokes disbelief ⟨experienced a number of ~ adventures⟩ ⟨gave the teacher an ~ explanation of his absence from school⟩ — **im·plausibleness** \"+\ n — **im·plausibly** \"+\ adv

**im·pleach** \əm+\ vt [²in- + pleach] : PLEACH, INTERWEAVE

**im·plead** \əmˈplēd\ vb [ME empleden, impleden, fr. MF empleider, emplaider, fr. OF empleidier, emplaidier, fr. en- ¹en- + pleidier, plaidier to plead — more at PLEAD] vt **1 a** : to institute and prosecute a suit against in a court : sue or prosecute at law ⟨the government, as a general rule, claims an exemption from being sued in its own courts . . . will not permit itself to be ~ed therein —H.M.Hart⟩ **b** archaic : ACCUSE, IMPEACH **2** archaic : PLEAD **3** : to include or incorporate as part of or party to a legal suit or action ⟨modern procedure permits a defendant to ~ . . . a third person —Herbert Peterfreund⟩ ⟨the bond . . . was ~ed as a part of the motion for judgment —*Southeastern Reporter*⟩ ~ vi, archaic : PLEAD

**im·plead·able** \-dəbəl\ adj, archaic : capable of being sued or prosecuted at law

**im·plead·er** \-də(r)\ n **1** : one that impleads **2** : INTERPLEADER

**im·pledge** \əm+\ vt [²in- + pledge (n.)] archaic : PLEDGE

**¹im·ple·ment** \ˈimpləmənt\ n -s [ME, fr. LL implementum action of filling up, fr. L implēre to fill up, finish (fr. in- ²in- + plēre to fill) + -mentum -ment — more at FULL] **1 a** : an article (as of apparel or furniture) serving to equip ⟨the ~s of religious worship⟩ **b** : a tool or utensil forming part of equipment for work ⟨a farm ~⟩ ⟨an ~ of war⟩ ⟨the ~s of his trade⟩ ⟨useful ~s such as axes, chisels, gouges, arrowheads, pestles and mortars, and ornamented pipes —*Amer. Guide Series: R.I.*⟩ ⟨the need for an ~ to help roll the heavy logs —*McGill News*⟩ **c** : one that serves as an instrument or tool ⟨judges striving to be efficient ~s of justice⟩ ⟨the most stringent ~ that could be employed . . . would be withdrawal of safe conduct for Swedish ships plying the Atlantic —*Newsweek*⟩ **2** Scots law : FULFILLMENT, PERFORMANCE

**syn** IMPLEMENT, TOOL, INSTRUMENT, APPLIANCE, UTENSIL apply in common to any device usu. relatively simple for performing a mechanical or manual operation. IMPLEMENT applies to anything, usu. a contrivance, necessary to effect an end or perform a task ⟨spades and other gardener's *implements*⟩ ⟨swords, guns, and *implements* of war⟩ ⟨propaganda as an *implement* of cold war⟩ ⟨the quill pen was an early *implement* of communication⟩ TOOL suggests an implement adapted to facilitate a given work, esp. the work of a craftsman or artisan ⟨carpenter's *tools*⟩ ⟨a pipe wrench and other plumber's *tools*⟩ ⟨a new research *tool*, in the form of a bibliography of all the literature on the arctic put out in the last 75 years —*Science*⟩ ⟨reference *tools* like the dictionary and the encyclopedia —*English Language Arts*⟩ ⟨the breeder uses three basic *tools* to bring about the genetic improvement of animals . . . selection, inbreeding, and crossing —*Science in Farming*⟩ INSTRUMENT suggests delicate construction or precision work as in dentistry, surgery, or surveying and may extend beyond mechanical or manual operation as in instruments for recording temperatures or rates of speed or musical instruments or in any more or less precise device for achieving any end ⟨the laboratory *instruments* necessary to careful scientific research⟩ ⟨an oscilloscope and other radio-testing *instruments*⟩ ⟨language is the essential *instrument* for the acquirement and communication of ideas —L.J.Shehan⟩ ⟨in a day when novels were considered *instruments* of Satan —*Amer. Guide Series: N.Y.*⟩ APPLIANCE is used usu. for a device which effects work but which is moved by some power other than or in addition to guidance or control by hand ⟨washing machines, vacuum cleaners, and other household *appliances*⟩ ⟨*appliance* means current-consuming equipment, fixed or portable; for example, heating, cooking, and small motor-operated equipment —*Nat'l Electric Safety Code*⟩ ⟨the clutch cleats for the sheet lines, reefing gears, and many other *appliances* used with the enormous sails —E.J.Schoettle⟩ UTENSIL suggests something useful in accomplishing work, esp. domestic work or work similar to it, and usu. manageable by hand ⟨pipe, pipe cleaners, and other smoking *utensils*⟩ ⟨a rolling pin, a fork, a frying pan and an oven are the *utensils* with which she makes her pie —Gilbert Ryle⟩ ⟨kitchen *utensils*⟩ ⟨fingers were the only eating *utensils* —H.A.Chippendale⟩

**²im·ple·ment** \-,ment, -mənt — see ²-MENT\ vt -ED/-ING/-S **1 a** : to carry out : ACCOMPLISH, FULFILL ⟨wondering how he might best ~ his purpose⟩ ⟨continued to clamor for action to ~ the promise —*N.Y.Times*⟩ ⟨a committee to ~ the plans so well formulated⟩; esp : to give practical effect to and ensure of actual fulfillment by concrete measures ⟨failure to carry out and ~ the will of the majority —Clement Attlee⟩ ⟨an agency created to ~ the recommendation of the committee⟩ ⟨programs to ~ our foreign policy⟩ **b :** to provide instruments or means of practical expression for ⟨survey the problem as a whole and ~ the joint interest in an expanding economy —George Soule⟩ **2 :** SUPPLEMENT **syn** see ENFORCE

**im·ple·men·tal** \¦==¦ment°l\ *adj* **:** of, relating to, or being an implement or relating to or providing implementation

**im·ple·men·ta·ry** \-ntərē, -n·trē, -ri\ *adj* **:** providing implementation ⟨~ legislation⟩

**im·ple·men·ta·tion** \,==mən·'tāshən, -(,)men-\ *n* -s **:** the act of implementing or the state of being implemented

**im·ple·ment·er** *or* **im·ple·men·tor** \'==,mentə(r)\ *n* -s **:** one that implements

**im·ple·men·tif·er·ous** \¦==(,)=·¦tif(ə)rəs\ *adj* **:** bearing or containing implements ⟨~ strata at an archaeological site⟩

**im·ple·tion** \əm'plēshən\ *n* -s [LL *impletion-, impletio,* fr. L *impletus* (past part. of *implēre* to fill up) + *-ion-, -io* -ion — more at IMPLEMENT] *archaic* **:** the act of filling or the state of being full

**im·pli·able** \(,)im¦plīəbəl, əm'p-\ *adj* [¹*in-* + *pliable*] **:** not pliable **:** INFLEXIBLE

**im·pli·cant** \'impləkənt, -lēk-\ *n* -s [L *implicant-, implicans,* pres. part. of *implicare*] **:** something that implies (as a proposition)

¹**im·pli·cate** \-kə|t, -,kā|, *usu* |d.+V\ *adj* [L *implicatus*] **1** *obs* **:** INTERTWINED, ENTANGLED, INVOLVED **2 :** IMPLIED, IMPLICIT ⟨content to let this accusation remain ~ in her questions —Osbert Sitwell⟩

²**im·pli·cate** \-,kāt, *usu* -ād.+V\ *vt* [L *implicatus,* past part. of *implicare* to infold, involve, implicate, engage — more at EMPLOY] **1** *archaic* **:** to fold or twist together **:** INTERWEAVE, ENTWINE ⟨the meeting boughs and *implicated* leaves —P.B. Shelley⟩ **2 :** to involve as a consequence, corollary, or natural inference **:** IMPLY **3 a :** to bring into intimate or incriminating connection **:** involve deeply or unfavorably ⟨evidence *implicating* many high officials in the conspiracy⟩ ⟨an innocent person *implicated* by circumstances in a crime⟩ ⟨all men, even the most virtuous and wise, are *implicated* in historic evil —Reinhold Niebuhr⟩ **b :** to involve in the nature or operation of something **:** connect intimately **:** require or entail as a natural or necessary cause, concomitant, or consequence ⟨local diseases often ~ a general derangement of the system⟩ ⟨each element in life forms part of a cultural mesh: one part *implicates* . . . the other —Lewis Mumford⟩ **syn** see INCLUDE

³**im·pli·cate** *same as adj*\ *n* -s [¹*implicate*] **:** something (as a proposition) implied or involved ⟨made ethics independent of theology and theology a series of ~*s* from the moral life —E.E. Aubrey⟩

**im·pli·ca·tion** \,==¦kāshən\ *n* -s [ME *implicacioun,* fr. L *implication-, implicatio,* fr. *implicatus,* + *-ion-, -io* -ion] **1 :** the act of implicating or the state of being implicated: **a** *archaic* **:** a twisting together **:** ENTWINEMENT, INTERWEAVING **b :** close connection, relationship, or involvement (as from long association, logical inevitability, intimate accompaniment) ⟨in the arts, in literature, and in science . . . all these activities were freeing themselves from their religious ~*s* —Stringfellow Barr⟩ ⟨looked upon railroad operation purely in its engineering ~*s* —O.S.Nock⟩; *esp* **:** an incriminating involvement ⟨suspected of ~ in a number of robberies⟩ **2 a :** the act of implying or the state of being implied ⟨no concept that by ~ views a functional bureaucracy as the ruling class can be tolerated —K.A.Wittfogel⟩ ⟨speak of their own language with at least an ~ of disparagement —George Sampson⟩ ⟨whether in words or by ~ —O.W.Holmes †1935⟩ **b :** one of several formal logical relationships or a statement containing propositions in such a relationship: (1) **:** a logical relationship of the form symbolically rendered "if *p* then *q*" in which *p* and *q* are propositions and in which *p* is false or *q* is true or both; *also* **:** a statement in this form — called also *material implication* (2) **:** a logical relationship of the form symbolically rendered "if *p* then strictly *q*" in which *q* is deducible from *p; also* **:** a statement in this form — called also *logical implication, strict implication* **c :** the symbol used to indicate one of these two formal relationships and rendered "if . . . then" or the logical operation implicit in one of them **3 :** something implied ⟨two propositions with a clear ~⟩ **:** INFERENCE ⟨was aware of the ~ to be found in his remarks⟩ **:** SUGGESTION, CONNOTATION ⟨tea is very important in British life, and a spectacular rise in its price does have political ~*s* —Michael Davie⟩ ⟨a book is a bulwark against the ~ of lack of culture —Allan McMahan⟩

**im·pli·ca·tion·al** \¦==¦kāshən°l, -shnəl\ *adj* **:** IMPLICATIVE — **im·pli·ca·tion·al·ly** \-°l|ē, -əl|, |i\ *adv*

**im·plica·tive** \'impləˌkād·iv, im'plikəd·-\ *adj* **:** of, relating to, or being implication or an implication **:** involving implication ⟨an ~ statement⟩ ⟨an ~ function⟩; *also* **:** tending to implicate — **im·plica·tive·ly** \-d·əvlē\ *adv* — **im·plica·tive·ness** \-d·ivnəs\ *n* -ES

**im·plica·to·ry** \'impləkə,tōrē, im'plik-, *chiefly Brit* ¦impləˈkātəri *or* -ˈa·tri\ *adj* **:** IMPLICATIVE

**im·plic·it** \(')im¦plisət, əm'p-, *usu* -sǝd.+V\ *adj* [L *implicitus,* past part. of *implicare* to infold, involve, implicate, engage — more at EMPLOY] **1** *obs* **:** tangled or twisted together **:** INTERWOVEN **2 a** (1) **:** tacitly involved in something else **:** capable of being understood from something else though unexpressed **:** capable of being inferred **:** IMPLIED — compare EXPLICIT ⟨draws no social conclusions of his own, but they are ~ —Robert Lasch⟩ ⟨the artistic standards of our time are . . . ~ rather than codified —Michael Kitson⟩ (2) **:** involved in the nature or essence of something though not revealed, expressed, or developed **:** POTENTIAL ⟨the oak is ~ in the acorn⟩ ⟨a sculptor may see different figures ~ in a block of stone —John Dewey⟩ ⟨the drama ~ in an idea becomes explicit when it is shown as a point of view which a person holds and upon which he acts —F.J.Hoffman⟩ **b** (1) **:** not appearing overtly **:** confined in the organism ⟨~ behavior⟩ ⟨~ speech⟩ (2) *of a culture* **:** capable of being derived only as an implication from behavior **:** not apparent or overt to the people it characterizes **:** tacit and underlying **3 a :** lacking doubt or reserve **:** UNQUESTIONING, WHOLEHEARTED ⟨~ obedience⟩ ⟨an ~ trust⟩ **b** *obs* **:** UNQUALIFIED, ABSOLUTE ⟨~ ignorance —Francis Bacon⟩ **4** *archaic* **:** marked by an implicit faith, credulity, or obedience — **im·plic·it·ly** *adv* — **im·plic·it·ness** *n* -ES

**implicit definition** *n* **:** CONTEXTUAL DEFINITION

**implicit function** *n* **:** a mathematical function defined by means of a relation that is not solved for the function in terms of the independent variable or variables — opposed to *explicit function*

**im·plic·i·ty** \əm'plisəd·ē\ *n* -ES [prob. fr. F *implicité,* fr. *implicite* implicit (fr. L *implicitus*) + *-té* -ty] **:** the quality or state of being implicit ⟨the strangeness of a man's life and the ~ with which he accepts it —Albert Camus⟩

**implied** *past of* IMPLY

**implied authority** *or* **implied agency** *n* **:** authority that is not proved expressly but by inferences and reasonable deductions and that arises out of the language and course of conduct of the principal toward his agent and the agency

**implied contract** *n* **1 :** a contract inferred to have been entered into by the parties to it from their conduct or from a special relationship existing between them **2 :** QUASI CONTRACT

**im·plied·ly** \əm'plī(ə)dlē\ *adv* [ME, fr. *implied* (past part. of *implien* to imply) + *-ly* — more at IMPLY] **:** by implication ⟨uncataloged situations will arise and, not being specifically prohibited, will be taken as ~ permitted —W.E.Jackson b. 1919⟩

**implied malice** *n* **:** malice proved indirectly from all the attendant circumstances when it is impossible to prove the actual state of mind as evincing it — called also *constructive malice;* distinguished from *malice in fact*

**implied power** *n* **:** a power that is reasonably necessary and appropriate to carry out the purposes of a power expressly granted — usu. used in pl.

**implied trust** *n* **1 :** a trust created by operation of law for reasons based on considerations of morality, justice, conscience, and fair dealing, or to prevent unjust enrichment **2 :** a trust found by judicial construction to have been intended by the settlor notwithstanding the intent was not clearly manifested in express terms

**implied warranty** *n* **:** a warranty raised in the operation of law though not expressly made and arising out of a particular transaction for reasons of public policy (as, that a ship chartered is seaworthy, that food sold to people is fit for human consumption, that goods sold are merchantable)

**im·plode** \əm'plōd\ *vi* -ED/-ING/-S [²*in-* + *-plode* (as in *explode*)] **:** to burst inward ⟨when a vacuum tube breaks it ~*s*⟩

**im·plo·ra·tion** \,implə'rāshən -lō'r-, -lȯ'r-\ *n* -s [MF or L; MF, fr. L *imploration-, imploratio,* fr. *imploratus* (past part. of *implorare* to implore) + *-ion-, -io* -ion] **:** earnest supplication **:** IMPLORING

**im·plore** \əm'plō(ə)r, -ō(ə)r, -ōə, -ȯ(ə)\ *vb* -ED/-ING/-S [MF or L; MF *implorer,* fr. L *implorare,* fr. *in-* ²in- + *plorare* to cry out, wail, lament, prob. of imit. origin] *vt* **1 :** to call upon in supplication **:** urgently petition **:** BESEECH ⟨*implored* his Maker for help out of his trouble⟩ ⟨but don't, I ~ you, let the metropolis monopolize your attention or your time —Richard Joseph⟩ **2 :** to call for or pray for earnestly or in supplication ⟨~ someone else's help in a crisis⟩ ⟨~ another chance to prove his innocence⟩ ⟨asked in a voice that *implored* a favorable answer —Aldous Huxley⟩ ~ *vi* **:** ENTREAT, PRAY ⟨wished he would stop begging and *imploring*⟩ **syn** see BEG

**im·plor·ing·ly** *adv* **:** in the manner of one that implores **:** BESEECHINGLY

**im·plor·ing·ness** *n* -ES **:** the quality or state of one that implores

**im·plo·sion** \əm'plōzhən\ *n* -s [²*in-* + *-plosion* (as in *explosion*)] **1 :** the action of imploding — contrasted with *explosion* **2 a :** APPLOSION **b :** the inrush of air in forming a suction stop

¹**im·plo·sive** \-ōs|iv, |ēv *also* -ōz| *or* |əv\ *adj* [²*in-* + *-plosive* (as in *explosive*)] **:** of, relating to, or being an implosion **:** formed or uttered with implosion — **im·plo·sive·ly** \|əvlē, -li\ *adv*

²**implosive** \"\ *n* -s **:** an implosive consonant **:** SUCTION STOP

**im·ploy** \əm'plȯi\ *archaic var of* EMPLOY

**im·plume** \əm+\ *or* **em·plume** \əm,em+\ *vt* [²*in-* or ¹*en-* + *plume* (n.)] **:** to furnish with or as if with plumes

**im·plumed** \(')im, əm+\ *adj* [¹*in-* + *plumed*] *archaic* **:** having no feathers

**implunge** *vb* [²*in-* + *plunge*] *obs* **:** PLUNGE

**im·plu·vi·um** \(')im¦plüvēəm, əm'p-\ *n, pl* **implu·via** \-ēə\ [L, fr. *in-* ²in- + *-pluvium* (fr. *pluere* to rain) — more at FLOW] **:** a cistern or tank in the atrium or peristyle of a house of ancient Rome to receive the water falling through the compluvium

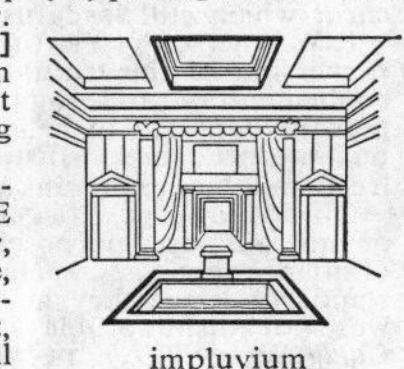

impluvium

**im·ply** \əm'plī\ *vt* **implied; implied; implying; implies** [ME *emplien, implien,* fr. MF *emplier,* fr. L *implicare* to infold, involve, implicate, engage — more at EMPLOY] **1** *obs* **:** ENFOLD, ENTWINE, ENWRAP **2 a :** to indicate or call for recognition of as existent, present, or related not by express statement but by logical inference or association or necessary consequence ⟨enrollment in the college *implies* willingness on the part of the student to comply with the requirements and regulations of the college —*Bull. of Mt. Saint Mary's College*⟩ ⟨the philosophy of nature which is *implied* in Chinese art —Lawrence Binyon⟩ ⟨democracy *implies* a number of freedoms⟩ ⟨emergency and crisis ~ conflict —H.S.Langfeld⟩ **b :** to involve as a necessary concomitant (as by general or logical implication, by signification, or by very nature or essence) ⟨two propositions may ~ a third⟩ ⟨war *implies* fighting⟩ ⟨an acorn *implies* an oak⟩ **3 :** to convey or communicate not by direct forthright statement but by allusion or reference likely to lead to natural inference **:** suggest or hint at ⟨the girl's evasive answer and burning brow seemed to ~ that her suitor had changed his mind —Edith Wharton⟩ ⟨made me sick to hear him ~ that somebody would make a report against him —Joseph Conrad⟩ ⟨the tone of the book was *implied* by shrewd advertisements —J.D.Hart⟩ **syn** see INCLUDE, SUGGEST

**im·pocket** \əm+\ *vt* [²*in-* + *pocket* (n.)] *archaic* **:** to keep or put in a pocket

**im·po·fo** \əm'pō(,)fō\ *n* -s [Zulu *im-pofu*] **:** ELAND

**impolder** *var of* EMPOLDER

**im·policy** \əm+\ *n* [¹*in-* + *policy*] **:** the quality or state of being impolitic **:** unsuitableness to the end in view **:** INEXPEDIENCY; *also* **:** an impolitic act

**impolished** *adj* [¹*in-* + *polished*] *obs* **:** not polished

**im·polite** \¦im+\ *adj* [L *impolitus* unpolished, unrefined, fr. *in-* ¹in- + *politus* polished, refined — more at POLITE] **:** not polite: **a** *obs* **:** lacking culture, cultivation, polish **b :** lacking in politeness, in etiquette, or in consideration of others **syn** see RUDE

**im·po·lite·ly** *adv* **:** in an impolite manner **:** RUDELY ⟨~ turning his back on her⟩

**im·po·lite·ness** *n* **:** the quality or state of being impolite **:** RUDENESS; *also* **:** an impolite act or remark

**im·politic** \(')im, əm+\ *also* **im·political** \¦im+\ *adj* [¹*in-* + *politic, political*] **:** not politic **:** contrary to or lacking in policy **:** UNWISE, INEXPEDIENT ⟨unjust and ~ discriminations between racial and other classes of citizens —E.P.Hutchinson⟩ ⟨would be manifestly ~ to start a brawl —Max Peacock⟩ — **im·politically** \¦im+\ *adv* — **im·politicalness** \"+\ *n* -ES — **im·politicly** \(')im, əm+\ *adv* — **im·politicness** \"+\ *n* -ES

**im·pon·der·a·bil·ia** \(,)im,pändərə'bilēə, əm-, -lyə\ *n pl* [NL, fr. neut. pl. of ML *imponderabilis*] **:** IMPONDERABLES ⟨it ignores these ~ without which life is no life, history no history, and a people no people —*Amer. Quarterly*⟩

**im·ponderability** \(')im, əm+\ *n* **:** the quality or state of being imponderable

¹**im·ponderable** \(')im, əm+\ *adj* [ML *imponderabilis,* fr. L *in-* ¹in- + LL *ponderabilis* ponderable — more at PONDERABLE] **:** not ponderable **:** incapable of being weighed, measured, or evaluated with exactness ⟨supposed that there was an ~ electrical fluid which pervaded all space —S.F.Mason⟩ ⟨such ~ human factors as an aesthetic sensitivity —Hunter Mead⟩ — **im·ponderableness** \"+\ *n* -ES — **im·ponderably** \"+\ *adv*

²**imponderable** \"\ *n* **:** an imponderable thing, element, or agency ⟨spiritual ~*s*⟩ ⟨that huge ~ which enters the courtroom: public opinion —Catherine Bowen⟩ ⟨the overriding importance of ~*s* in determining human conduct —John Russell b. 1872⟩

**im·ponderous** \(')im, əm+\ *adj* [¹*in-* + *ponderous*] **:** having no weight or insignificant weight **:** very light

**impone** *vt* -ED/-ING/-S [L *imponere* to put upon, impose, fr. *in-* ²in- + *ponere* to put, place — more at POSITION] *obs* **:** STAKE, WAGER

**im·po·nent** \əm'pōnənt, 'im,p-\ *n* -s [L *imponent-, imponens,* pres. part. of *imponere*] **:** one that imposes

**imporous** *adj* [¹*in-* + *porous*] *obs* **:** not porous

¹**im·port** \(')im¦pō(ə)rt, əm'p-, -ō(ə)r|, -ōə|, -ȯ(ə)|, *usu* |d.+V\ *vb* -ED/-ING/-S [ME *importen,* fr. L *importare* to bring or carry into, introduce, cause, fr. *in-* ²in- + *portare* to carry — more at PORT] *vt* **1 a :** to bear or convey as purport, meaning, information, or portent **:** MEAN, SIGNIFY ⟨his words ~*ed* that some change in plans had to be made⟩ ⟨the verse then would ~ that the riders have let their freedom . . . get out of hand —Warren Carrier⟩ **b** *archaic* **:** EXPRESS, STATE **c :** to involve as a consequence or inevitable concomitant **:** IMPLY ⟨honor ~*s* justice⟩ **2 :** to bring from a foreign or external source **:** introduce from without ⟨food ~*ed* into the city from surrounding farms⟩ ⟨another murder case . . . distinguished by the local animosities sought to be ~*ed* into the trial —H.W. H.Knott⟩ ⟨~*ed* some college boys for the dance⟩; *esp* **:** to bring (as wares or merchandise) into a place or country from another country ⟨a business that ~*ed* toys from Japan⟩ ⟨~*ed* wheat during the grain shortage⟩ ⟨Icelanders . . . ~*ed* the literature of the Continent, translating it into their own tongue —Charlton Laird⟩ ⟨Canada also ~*s* a great many leading scientists —*Report: (Canadian) Royal Commission on Nat'l Development*⟩ — opposed to *export* **3** [MF *importer,* fr. OIt *importare,* fr. L] *archaic* **:** to be of importance or consequence to **:** have to do with **:** have a bearing on **:** CONCERN ~ *vi* [MF *importer*] **:** to be of moment or consequence **:** MATTER ⟨it ~*s* little that we are early or late⟩ **syn** see MEAN

²**im·port** \'im,p-\ *n* -s **1 :** something contained as signification or intention **:** PURPORT, MEANING ⟨trying vainly to fathom the ~ of the speaker's words⟩ ⟨a gesture whose ~ he knew immediately⟩ **2 :** WEIGHT, CONSEQUENCE, SIGNIFICANCE ⟨less concerned about the literary value of his books than about their social ~⟩ ⟨a man of great ~⟩ **3 :** something (as an article of merchandise) brought in from an outside source (as a foreign country) ⟨the car was a British ~ —Frances G. Patton⟩ ⟨chief ~*s* were machinery and vehicles, raw wool and cotton —*Americana Annual*⟩ **4 :** IMPORTATION ⟨a proclamation allowing the ~ of an additional 51 million pounds of peanuts —*Time*⟩ **syn** see IMPORTANCE

¹**importable** *adj* [ME, fr. MF, fr. LL *importabilis,* fr. L *in-* ¹in- + *portare* to carry, bear + *-abilis* -able — more at PORT] *obs* **:** UNENDURABLE, INTOLERABLE

²**im·port·able** \(')im¦pōr|d·əbəl, əm'p-, -pō(r)|, -pōə|, |tə-\ *adj* [¹*import* + *-able*] **:** capable of being imported ⟨an ~ article of merchandise⟩

**im·por·tance** \əm'pōr|t°n(t)s, -ō(ə)|, *chiefly in NewEng & the South* |d·ən- *or* |tən-\ *n* -s [MF, fr. OIt *importanza,* fr. *importante*] **1 a :** the quality or state of being important **:** WEIGHT, SIGNIFICANCE ⟨an event of ~ in the history of the country⟩ ⟨a natural resource of great ~ to industry⟩ **b :** an important aspect or bearing ⟨this feat has several ~*s* —*Time*⟩ **2** *obs* **:** IMPORT, MEANING, SIGNIFICATION **3** *obs* **:** IMPORTUNITY, SOLICITATION **4** *obs* **:** a matter of importance

**syn** CONSEQUENCE, SIGNIFICANCE, IMPORT, MOMENT, WEIGHT: IMPORTANCE, the most general of these nouns, signifies a quality or state that is of value or influence, often with the implication that this is in someone's opinion ⟨issues which, whilst not the major significance, have some *importance* —*Current History*⟩ ⟨the *importance* of taking a wide, strategic view has prevailed —A.P.Ryan⟩ ⟨her sense of *importance* will help her —H.M.Parshley⟩ ⟨a position of some *importance* in the industry⟩ ⟨clusters of huge inverted pleats that add *importance* to the skirt —Lois Long⟩ When used interchangeably with IMPORTANCE, CONSEQUENCE often applies to social rank, public position, or reputation but more generally implies an importance by reason of effects, results, or interrelationships ⟨a man of some *consequence*⟩ ⟨a subscription library in every town of *consequence* in the country —*Amer. Guide Series: Pa.*⟩ ⟨the newspapers have been demanding these things for years, and nothing of any real and lasting *consequence* ever seems to happen —Herman Kogan⟩ SIGNIFICANCE can be used interchangeably with IMPORTANCE or CONSEQUENCE, although in meaning basically *that which is signified (to anyone)* it usu. stresses strongly the mere fact of having value or worth and sometimes the relativity of that value or worth ⟨a person of some *significance*⟩ ⟨here, in 1864, occurred a battle of some strategic *significance* —*Amer. Guide Series: Ark.*⟩ ⟨a temper tantrum once in a while should be overlooked for it has little *significance* —H.R.Litchfield & L.H.Dembo⟩ ⟨such trivia take on *significance* only if the reader is able to catch the subtle hints of impending disaster —Leland Miles⟩ ⟨a generation of boys and girls who understand the social *significance* of the family —*Current Biog.*⟩ IMPORT usu. stresses, even more than SIGNIFICANCE, the relativity of the value or worth, bringing out the idea of a significance bearing upon or in relation to person or thing specified or strongly implied ⟨the Contemporary Theater, concentrating on plays of sociological *import* —*Amer. Guide Series: Mich.*⟩ ⟨when we allow our mind to dwell upon such considerations as these, the entire *import* of the illustration changes —John Dewey⟩ ⟨the differences between one variety of man and another, points of negligible *import* in medicine —A.L.Kroeber⟩ ⟨other measures of international *import* upon which he voted —*Current Biog.*⟩ MOMENT, very like SIGNIFICANCE or IMPORT though less frequent in oral communication, usu. suggests worthiness of consideration, often stressing the conspicuousness or self-evidence of the significance or worthiness ⟨some excerpts describe matters of greater *moment* than do others —*Times Lit. Supp.*⟩ ⟨the questions before the Department of State were many and of grave *moment* —W.C.Ford⟩ ⟨the material inequalities of our worldly life will be found to be of no *moment* in the hereafter —P.G.Waris⟩ WEIGHT tends to stress largeness of possible consequence or import as of something that must be taken into account or whose presence does or may seriously alter an outcome ⟨men who take the lead, and whose opinions and wishes have great *weight* with the others —J.G.Frazer⟩ ⟨the author's expertness in the field lends *weight* to his conclusions —H.M.Hyman⟩ ⟨a gap between their appreciation of a man's value at any moment and his real *weight* —Hilaire Belloc⟩ ⟨diplomatic questions remained, but they had no such *weight* as those of the wartime —W.C.Ford⟩

**im·por·tan·cy** \-nsē,-nsi\ *n* -ES *archaic* **:** IMPORTANCE

**im·por·tant** \-nt\ *adj* [MF, fr. OIt *importante* (verbal of *importare* to be important), fr. L *important-, importans,* pres. part. of *importare* to bring or carry in, convey, cause — more at IMPORT] **1 a :** marked by or possessing weight or consequence **:** valuable in content or relationship **:** SIGNIFICANT ⟨an ~ day in one's life⟩ ⟨an ~ consideration⟩ ⟨a country producing petroleum in ~ quantities⟩ **b :** significant or large in amount or size ⟨spent ~ money on a small gem for his wife⟩ ⟨an ~ part of the architect's time was devoted to department-store design —*Current Biog.*⟩ **2 a :** giving evidence of or seeming to relate to something of consequence ⟨holding the attorney's letter in his hand, and with so solemn and ~ an air that his wife . . . thought the worst was about to befall —W.M.Thackeray⟩ ⟨took long ~ strides in the direction of the courthouse⟩ **b :** giving evidence of a feeling of personal importance **:** marked by self-complacency, ostentation, or pompousness ⟨an ~ manner⟩ **3** *obs* **:** IMPORTUNATE, URGENT — **im·por·tant·ly** *adv* — **im·por·tant·ness** *n* -ES

**im·por·ta·tion** \,im,pōr'tāshən, -pō(r)'-, -pōə'- *also* -,pə(r)'-\ *n* -s [¹*import* + *-ation*] **1 :** the act or practice of bringing in (as merchandise) from an outside or foreign source ⟨the ~ of goods from Holland⟩ ⟨the ~ of foreign labor⟩ **2 :** IMPORT 3 ⟨the car was an ~ from Italy⟩

**import credit** *n* **:** a credit which is opened by an importer with a bank in his own country and upon which the exporter he deals with may draw bills of exchange — compare EXPORT CREDIT

**imported** *past of* IMPORT

**imported cabbageworm** *n* **:** the larva of the common white cabbage butterfly that is a serious pest of cabbage and related plants

**imported currantworm** *n* **:** a larval sawfly (*Nematus ribesii*) that is native to Europe but now widespread in No. America and that is very destructive to the foliage of currants, gooseberries, and related plants

**im·por·tee** \,im,pōr¦tē, -,pər-\ *n* -s [¹*import* + *-ee*] **:** one that has been imported ⟨~*s* brought in to harvest the cherry crop⟩

**im·port·er** *pronunc at* ¹IMPORT + ə(r)\ *n* **:** one that imports; *esp* **:** one whose business is the importation and sale of goods from a foreign country

**importing** *pres part of* IMPORT

**imports** *pres 3d sing of* IMPORT, *pl of* IMPORT

**im·por·tu·na·cy** \əm'pȯrchənəsē; ¦impər'tün-, -r·'tyün-\ *n* -ES **:** IMPORTUNATENESS

**im·por·tu·nate** \əm'pȯrchənət; ¦impər¦tünət, -r·¦tyü-\ *adj* [prob. fr. ¹*importune* + *-ate*] **1 :** BURDENSOME, TROUBLESOME **2 :** troublesomely urgent **:** unreasonably solicitous **:** overly persistent in request or demand ⟨an ~ petitioner⟩ ⟨an ~ curiosity⟩ ⟨~ requests for assistance⟩ **syn** see PRESSING

**im·por·tu·nate·ly** *adv* **:** in an importunate manner

**im·por·tu·nate·ness** *n* -ES **:** the quality or state of being importunate

¹**im·por·tune** \¦impər¦tün, -,pər-, -r·¦tyün; əm'pȯrchən, -(,)chün\ *adj* [ME, fr. MF & L; MF *importun,* fr. L *importunus* unfit, troublesome, rude, fr. *in-* ¹in- + *-portunus* (as in *opportunus* fit, convenient) — more at OPPORTUNE] **:** IMPORTUNATE — **im·por·tune·ly** *adv*

²**importune** \"\ *vb* -ED/-ING/-S [MF or ML; MF *importuner,* fr. ML *importunare,* fr. L *importunus*] *vt* **1 a :** to press or urge with frequent or unreasonable requests or troublesome persistence ⟨were being *importuned* to try their luck with the play —Claudia Cassidy⟩ ⟨*importuned* many businessmen to come to Washington —John McDonald⟩ **b** *archaic* **:** to request or beg for urgently **2 a :** ANNOY, WORRY, TROUBLE **b :** to make immoral or lewd advances toward ⟨arrested for

*importuning* a male person in the park⟩ ~ *vi* **1** : to beg, urge, or solicit persistently or troublesomely **2** : to make immoral or lewd advances toward another ⟨fined for *importuning* in a public convenience —T.A.Cullen⟩ **syn** see BEG

**im·por·tun·er** \-nər\ *n* -s : one that importunes

**im·por·tu·ni·ty** \ˌimpər'tünəd·ē, -ˌpȯr-, -r'tyü-\ *n* -ES [ME *importunite*, fr. MF *importunité*, fr. L *importunitat-, importunitas*, fr. *importunus* + *-itat-, -itas* -ity] : the quality or state of being importunate : pressing or pertinacious solicitation : troublesome pertinacity

**im·pose** \əm'pōz\ *vb* -ED/-ING/-S [MF *imposer*, modif. (influenced by *poser* to put, place) of L *imponere* to put upon, impose, deceive, cheat, fr. *in-* ²in- + *ponere* to put, place — more at POSE, POSITION] *vt* **1** *obs* : CHARGE, IMPUTE **2** : to give or bestow (as a name or title) authoritatively or officially **3 a** *obs* : to cause to be burdened : SUBJECT — used with *to* **b** (1) : to make, frame, or apply (as a charge, tax, obligation, rule, penalty) as compulsory, obligatory, or enforcible ⟨~ a duty on a city official⟩ ⟨the obligations *imposed* by international law —*Encyc. Americana*⟩ : LEVY ⟨~ a tax on all unmarried men⟩ : INFLICT ⟨~ punishment upon a traitor⟩ ⟨flying ~s a heavy nervous strain on the individual —H.G. Armstrong⟩ : force one to submit to or come into accord with — usu. used with *on* or *upon* ⟨moved the newspapers to ~ a uniformity upon the written language —Oscar Handlin⟩ ⟨~ their dictates on the smaller nations —Vera M. Dean⟩ ⟨~ restraints upon the children⟩ (2) : to establish forcibly ⟨he *imposed* himself as leader⟩ ⟨~ law and order on a primitive people⟩ ⟨*imposed* a uniform organization over the whole of Lowland Britain —L.D.Stamp⟩ (3) : to make to prevail as a basic pattern, order, or quality ⟨neoclassic styles were *imposed* on the landscape —*Amer. Guide Series: Ariz.*⟩ **c** *archaic* : to lay (as a charge) upon a person **d** : to bring into being : CREATE, GENERATE ⟨the dangers and irritations *imposed* by many railroad grade crossings —*Amer. Guide Series: Minn.*⟩ **4 a** *obs* : to lay (the hands) on in an ecclesiastical rite (as blessing or confirmation) **b** *archaic* : SET, PLACE, PUT, DEPOSIT **c** (1) : to arrange (type or plated pages) on an imposing stone preparatory to locking up in a chase; *sometimes* : to arrange and lock up (pages) (2) : to arrange (the component parts of a nonletterpress printing surface) in a similar manner **5 a** : to force into the company or upon the attention of another ⟨~ oneself upon others⟩ **b** : to inflict by deception or fraud : pass off ⟨~ fake documents upon a gullible public⟩ ⟨so long as imaginary events are not *imposed* upon the reader as historical evidence —J.L. Clifford⟩ ~ *vi* : to take usu. unwarranted advantage of something ⟨I was not formally invited to my friend's party and I would not wish to ~ by going uninvited⟩ **syn** see DICTATE — **impose on** *or* **impose upon 1 a** : to force oneself esp. obnoxiously on (others) **b** *obs* : to encroach or infringe on : INFRINGE **2** : to take unwarranted advantage of : exploit a personal relationship with ⟨got a reputation for *imposing on* friends for their time and money⟩ : ABUSE ⟨did not wish to *impose upon* what privileges he had⟩ **3** : to practice deception on : DECEIVE, DEFRAUD, CHEAT ⟨an attempt to *impose on* the good-natured tolerance of the public —Roger Fry⟩ ⟨succeed in deceiving, and *imposing upon*, others —George Meredith⟩

**imposed load** *n* : the part of the total load sustained by a structure or member thereof that is applied to it after erection — compare DEAD LOAD

**im·pos·er** \-zə(r)\ *n* : one that imposes; *esp* : STONEMAN 1

**imposing** *adj* **1** *archaic* : insistent and exacting **2** *archaic* : DECEPTIVE, TREACHEROUS **3** : impressive because of size, scope, bearing, dignity, or grandeur : COMMANDING ⟨an ~ building⟩ ⟨an ~ appearance⟩ **syn** see GRAND

**im·pos·ing·ly** *adv* : in an imposing manner; *esp* : IMPRESSIVELY

**im·pos·ing·ness** *n* -ES : the quality or state of being imposing

**imposing stone** *or* **imposing table** *or* **imposing surface** *n* : a slab of stone or metal on which matter to be printed is imposed

**im·po·si·tion** \ˌimpə'zishən\ *n* [ME *imposicioun*, fr. MF & LL; MF *imposition*, fr. LL *imposition-, impositio*, fr. L *impositus* (past part. of *imponere*) + *-ion-, -io* -ion] **1** : the act of imposing: as **a** : the laying on of the hands as a religious ceremony (as in ordination or confirmation) **b** : a putting, placing, or laying on ⟨the ~ of color on the clear wood⟩ ⟨the ~ of a second layer on the first⟩ **c** : an applying by compelling means ⟨the ~ of rigid censorship⟩ ⟨the ~ of a foreign form on a domestic product⟩ **d** : a levying or assessment (as of a tax or a fine) ⟨the ~ of extra charges for extra services⟩ ⟨the ~ of a high tariff⟩ **e** : the arranging on an imposing stone of matter to be printed **2** : something imposed: as **a** : LEVY, TAX ⟨an ~ of 5000 francs on a coat⟩ **b** *obs* : COMMAND, CHARGE **c** : an excessive, unwarranted, or uncalled-for requirement or burden ⟨severe ~s on her children —John Dollard⟩ **d** : an exercise imposed as punishment on a student (as at an English public school) **3** : the act of imposing upon another or the condition of being imposed upon : DECEPTION ⟨know that their tricks are ~s —W.W.Howells⟩ **4** : the order of arrangement of imposed pages or other matter ⟨the standard ~s are simple multiples of 16 pages —*Plan for a Good Book*⟩

**im·pos·i·tor** \əm'päzəd·ə(r), -z(ə)t(r)\ *n* -s [*impose* + *-itor* (as in *compositor*)] : STONEMAN 1

**im·possibilism** \(')im, əm+\ *n* [L *impossibilis* + E *-ism*] **1** : a political purpose or plan felt to be impossible of achievement **2** : the advocacy of an impossible purpose or plan

¹**im·possibilist** \"+\ *n* [L *impossibilis* + E *-ist*] : an advocate of impossibilism

²**impossibilist** \"\ *adj* : of or relating to impossibilism

**im·possibility** \(ˌ)im, əm+\ *n* [ME *impossibilite*, fr. MF & LL; MF *impossibilité*, fr. LL *impossibilitat-, impossibilitas*, fr. L *impossibilis* + *-itat-, -itas* -ity] **1** : the quality or state of being impossible: as **a** : IMPRACTICABILITY ⟨never deterred by the seeming ~ of any task⟩ **b** : incapability of being dealt with by reasonable or acceptable means ⟨his cool cheek, his frightful temper, his sheer ~ —James Cameron⟩ ⟨the ~ of the political setup for an honest man⟩ **2** *obs* : INABILITY **3** : something impossible of attainment ⟨a child who always goes after *impossibilities*⟩

¹**im·possible** \(')im, əm+\ *adj* [ME, fr. MF & L; MF, fr. L *impossibilis*, fr. *in-* ¹in- + *possibilis* possible — more at POSSIBLE] **1 a** : incapable of being or of occurring : not within the realm of the possible : contrary to the nature of reality ⟨an ~ motion⟩ ⟨an ~ creature⟩ **b** (1) : felt to be incapable of being done, attained, or fulfilled : felt to be utterly impracticable ⟨a land ~ of conquest⟩ (2) : extremely and almost insuperably difficult under the circumstances : having little likelihood of accomplishment or completion ⟨spent his time indefatigably doing ~ tasks for the committee⟩ **c** *of a statement* : SELF-CONTRADICTORY **2 a** : out of the question : UNACCEPTABLE ⟨~ coloring in a picture⟩ ⟨an ~ political candidate⟩ : extremely undesirable ⟨relieving ~ and unfair economic conditions —F.D.Roosevelt⟩ ⟨his claret was ~ —Elinor Wylie⟩ : marked by very undesirable qualities ⟨his wife is simply ~ . . . uses perfumery, and has an awful voice —Margaret Deland⟩ **b** : difficult or extremely awkward to deal with or so markedly odd as to be unpleasant or objectionable ⟨a positive genius for collecting ~ people —Ngaio Marsh⟩ ⟨an almost ~ man to have for an enemy —Bruce Catton⟩ — **im·possibleness** \"+\ *n*

²**impossible** \"\ *n* [ME, fr. *impossible*, adj.] : something impossible : IMPOSSIBILITY

**im·possibly** \"+\ *adv* **1** : in an impossible manner or to an impossible degree ⟨an ~ idealistic young man⟩ **2** : to a degree that causes hardship or prevents a remedy ⟨food and clothing are ~ expensive⟩ ⟨~ far away from all sources of supply —June Platt⟩

¹**im·post** \'im,pōst\ *n* [MF, fr. ML *impositum*, fr. neut. of L *impositus*, past part. of *imponere* to put upon, impose — more at IMPOSE] **1** : something imposed or levied : TAX, TRIBUTE, DUTY **2** : the weight carried by a horse in a handicap race

²**impost** \"\ *vt* : to classify (imports) in order to fix import duties

³**impost** \"\ *n* [F *imposte*, fr. MF, fr. OIt *imposta*, fr. fem. of *imposto* (past part. of *imporre* to put upon, impose), fr. L *impositus*] : a block, capital, or molding (as of a pillar, pier, or wall) from which an arch springs — see ARCH illustration

**imposterous** *adj, obs* : IMPOSTROUS

**im·pos·tor** *or* **im·pos·ter** \əm'pästə(r)\ *n* -s [MF & LL; MF *imposteur*, fr. LL *impostor*, fr. L *impostus, impositus* (past part. of *imponere* to put upon, impose, deceive, cheat) + *-or* — more at IMPOSE] : one that practices imposture : one that assumes an identity, character, or title not his own for the purpose of deception : PRETENDER, FRAUD, HUMBUG

**im·pos·trous** \(')im¦pästrəs, əm'p-\ *adj* : of, relating to, or being an imposture : DECEITFUL, FRAUDULENT

**impostumate** *or* **imposthumate** *vb* -ED/-ING/-S [¹*impostume, imposthume* + *-ate*] *vt, obs* : to affect with an impostume : to cause to have an impostume ~ *vi, obs* : to form an impostume

¹**im·pos·tume** \əm'päs(ˌ)chüm, -s(ˌ)t(y)üm, -stəm\ *or* **im·pos·thume** \", -s(ˌ)thüm, -s·thəm\ *n* -s [ME *emposteme, empostyme, imposteme*, fr. MF *apostume, empostume*, fr. L *apostema* — more at APOSTEME] **1** *archaic* : ABSCESS, CYST **2** *archaic* : an instance or source of moral corruption

²**impostume** *vb* [ME *empostemen*, fr. *emposteme*, n.] *obs* : IMPOSTUMATE

¹**im·pos·ture** \əm'päschə(r)\ *n* [LL *impostura*, fr. L *impostus, impositus* (past part. of *imponere* to put upon, impose, deceive, cheat) + *-ura* -ure — more at IMPOSE] **1** : the act or practice of imposing on or deceiving someone by means of an assumed character or name : the act or conduct of an impostor ⟨careful not to detect cases of malingering . . . and thus placed a premium on ~ —G.E.Fussell⟩ **2** : an instance of imposture ⟨admitted under oath that the whole defense of insanity was an ~ and a sham —B.N.Cardozo⟩

**syn** CHEAT, FRAUD, DECEIT, DECEPTION, COUNTERFEIT, SHAM, FAKE, HUMBUG, SIMULACRUM: IMPOSTURE applies to any situation in which a spurious object or action is passed off as genuine and bona fide ⟨its values . . . are an *imposture*: pretending to honor and distinction it accepts all that is vulgar and base —Edmund Wilson⟩ CHEAT applies to any abuse of credence and faith by misleading or trickery and also to delusion induced by the victim's credulousness ⟨though the counts allowed the *cheat* for fact . . . and let the tale o' the feigned birth pass for true —Robert Browning⟩ ⟨the *cheat* which still leads us to work and live for appearances —R.W.Emerson⟩ FRAUD is likely to indicate a calculated perversion of the truth; applied to a person it may be less condemnatory and suggest pretence and hypocrisy ⟨many persons persisted in believing that his supposed suicide was but another *fraud* —Justin M'Carthy⟩ ⟨the pious *fraud* who freely indulges in the sins against which he eloquently preaches —Oliver La Farge⟩ DECEIT indicates anything that deceives or misleads, usu. purposefully, and is strongly condemnatory ⟨Indians were . . . treacherous according to the white man's standards, since they held that the basest trickery or *deceit* was not dishonorable if directed against a foe —*Amer. Guide Series: R.I.*⟩ DECEPTION is often interchangeable with DECEIT but is used without condemnation in reference to sleights and feints and to innocent or natural characteristics likely to mislead ⟨practice gross *deception* on the public with all the earnestness of a moral "crusade" —K.S.Davis⟩ ⟨a fast backfield trained in *deception*⟩ COUNTERFEIT refers to a close imitation or copy of a thing, usu. one made or circulated for dishonest gain ⟨this bill's a *counterfeit*⟩; in reference to persons or ideas or qualities it suggests spurious although close imitation without culpable intent to deceive ⟨not really a married woman and a housemistress but only a kind of *counterfeit* —Arnold Bennett⟩ SHAM is severe in censuring what fraudulently imitates or purports to be a genuine reality ⟨perhaps her devotion to Marcellus was a *sham* and her real intention was that Agrippa should be goaded into putting him out of the way —Robert Graves⟩ ⟨if people would only build on facts, not on *shams* —Ellen Glasgow⟩ FAKE refers to something factitious or assumed with plausible closeness to the original, genuine, or true; it may or may not condemn, depending on culpable intent to deceive ⟨Gaston B. Means's volume, *The Strange Death of President Harding*, . . . bears every imprint of being a thoroughgoing *fake* —S.H.Adams⟩ ⟨he pretends everything is what it is not, he is a *fake* —Katherine A. Porter⟩ HUMBUG indicates elaborate pretense, esp. so flagrant that it approaches transparency ⟨you're a *humbug*, sir . . . will speak plainer, if you wish it. An imposter, sir —Charles Dickens⟩ ⟨these liars warn't no kings nor dukes, at all, but just low-down *humbugs* and frauds —Mark Twain⟩ SIMULACRUM indicates an image or imitation but usu. lacks the suggestion that it is made to defraud; it may indicate an image utterly wanting in essential substance or reality ⟨nothing but a coat and a wig and a mask smiling below it — nothing but a great *simulacrum* —W.M.Thackeray⟩ ⟨something whose essence was not there at all, a stiff lifeless *simulacrum* —J.C. Powys⟩

²**imposture** *vi, obs* : to practice imposture ~ *vt* **1** *obs* : to show to be an imposture **2** *obs* : DECEIVE

**im·pos·tur·ing** \-chəriŋ\ *n* : IMPOSTURE 2 ⟨think . . . these concealments and ~s can be exaggerated —John Cheever⟩

**im·pos·tur·ous** \(')im¦päschərəs, əm'p-\ *adj* : IMPOSTROUS

**im·potable** \(')im+\ *adj* [LL *impotabilis*, fr. L *in-* ¹in- + LL *potabilis* potable — more at POTABLE] : not suited for drinking : UNDRINKABLE

**im·po·tence** \'impəd·ən(t)s, ¦tən- *also* ¦t°n- *sometimes except in sense b* (')im¦pō¦ *or* əm'pō\ *also* **im·po·ten·cy** \-nsē,-nsi\ *n, pl* **impotenc·es** *also* **impoten·cies** [ME *impotence, impotencie*, fr. MF & ML; MF *impotence*, fr. ML *impotentia*, fr. L, lack of self-control, fr. *impotent-, impotens* + *-ia* -y] **1** : the quality or state of being impotent: as **a** : lack of strength : WEAKNESS, FEEBLENESS ⟨the very ~ of the government, the impossibility of doing anything —Upton Sinclair⟩ : HELPLESSNESS ⟨reduce them to intellectual ~ —H.J.Laski⟩ ⟨a small force . . . reduced to ~ a fortress that had been expected to withstand attack for at least 2 weeks —*Military Rev.*⟩ **b** (1) : a physical or psychological abnormal state usu. of a male characterized by inability to copulate — compare STERILITY (2) : STERILITY — not used technically **2** [L *impotentia*] *obs* : lack of self-restraint or self-control

¹**im·po·tent** \-nt\ *adj* [ME, fr. MF & L; MF, fr. L *impotent-, impotens*, fr. *in-* ¹in- + *potent-, potens* potent — more at POTENT] **1 a** : not potent : lacking in power, strength, or vigor : deficient in capacity : WEAK, POWERLESS ⟨he liked to be bad and see them all ~ to correct him —Stuart Cloete⟩ ⟨its ~ ruling classes —Edward Shils⟩ ⟨a relatively ~ preparation of penicillin⟩ ⟨a lame and ~, and a trite, conclusion —Howard M. Jones⟩ **b** : unable to copulate : wanting in procreative power; *broadly* : STERILE — usu. used of males **2** [L *impotent-, impotens*] *obs* : incapable of self-restraint : UNGOVERNABLE, VIOLENT **syn** see STERILE

²**impotent** \"\ *n* : one that is impotent

**im·po·tent·ly** *adv* : in an impotent manner : FEEBLY, WEAKLY, HELPLESSLY

**im·po·tent·ness** *n* : IMPOTENCE

¹**im·pound** \əm'paund\ *vt* -ED/-ING/-S [²*in-* + *pound* (enclosure)] **1 a** : to shut up in or as if in a pound : CONFINE, ENCLOSE ⟨to catch and ~ stray dogs⟩ ⟨explosive release of the breath which had been ~*ed* in the mouth cavity —A.L. Kroeber⟩ **b** : to seize and hold in the custody of the law ⟨~ stray cattle⟩ ⟨~ the files of a court⟩ ⟨all slave ships that put into Bahama ports were ~*ed* and their cargoes freed —Marjory S. Douglas⟩ **c** : to take possession of : APPROPRIATE **2** : to collect (water) for irrigation, hydroelectric use, flood control, or similar purpose : confine and store (water) in an impoundment

²**im·pound** \'im,p-\ *n* : a reservoir for impounding

**im·pound·able** \(')im¦paundəbəl, əm'p-\ *adj* : capable of or liable to impoundment

**im·pound·ment** \əm'paun(d)mənt\ *also* **im·pound·age** \-ndij\ *n* -s **1** : the act of impounding or the state of being impounded **2** : a body of water formed by impounding (as by a dam); *also* : the quantity of water in such a body

**im·pov·er·ish** \əm'päv(ə)rish, -rēsh, *esp in pres part* -rəsh\ *vt* -ED/-ING/-ES [ME *enpoverisen*, fr. MF *empoveriss-*, stem of *empovrir*, fr. *en-* ¹en- + *povre* poor — more at POOR] **1** : to make poor : reduce to poverty or indigence ⟨a family ~*ed* by misfortune and sickness⟩ ⟨a foolish effort to ~ life by robbing men of sustaining vision —M.R.Cohen⟩ ⟨the provinces were ~*ed* of their scientific talent —S.F.Mason⟩ **2** : to exhaust the strength, richness, or fertility of : make sterile ⟨worked the land year after year until it was ~*ed*⟩ **syn** see DEPLETE

**impoverished** *adj, of a fauna or flora* : represented by few species or individuals : SCANTY

**im·pov·er·ish·ment** \-mənt\ *n* -s [AF *empoverissement*, fr. MF *empoveriss-* + *-ment*] : the act of impoverishing or the state of being impoverished ⟨soil ~⟩ ⟨spiritual ~⟩

**impower** *obs var of* EMPOWER

**impr** *abbr* improved; improvement

**im·practicability** \(ˌ)im, əm+\ *n* **1** : the quality or state of being impracticable **2** : something impracticable

**im·practicable** \(')im, əm+\ *adj* [¹*in-* + *practicable*] **1 a** : not practicable : incapable of being performed or accomplished by the means employed or at command : INFEASIBLE ⟨economically ~ to maintain an air force which will provide absolute security —*Nat'l Aviation Policy*⟩ ⟨regretted that his appointment as chaplain . . . was at present ~ —Rose Macaulay⟩ **b** : incapable of being passed, scaled, or conveniently negotiated ⟨an ~ road⟩ ⟨an ~ cliff⟩ **2** *archaic* : UNMANAGEABLE, INTRACTABLE **3** : IMPRACTICAL, UNWISE, IMPRUDENT ⟨the tear is apt to go clear across the sail, making it ~ for you to continue —H.A.Calahan⟩ : lacking common sense in practical matters ⟨given him up for many years as ~ and hopeless —George Meredith⟩ — **im·practicableness** \"+\ *n* — **im·practicably** \"+\ *adv*

**im·practical** \(')im, əm+\ *adj* [¹*in-* + *practical*] : not practical: as **a** (1) : not wise to put into or keep in practice or effect : not pleasing to common sense or prudence ⟨slavery, we have been taught, was economically ~ —Carol L. Thompson⟩ (2) : IDEALISTIC ⟨an ~ pipe dream —James Laughlin⟩ : THEORETICAL ⟨an anchorite living austerely and owning little, but rich in ~ and priceless honor —W.L.Sullivan⟩ **b** : incapable of dealing sensibly or prudently with practical esp. economic matters ⟨a totally ~ man who would have starved but for his wife's common sense⟩ **c** : IMPRACTICABLE : incapable of being put into use or effect or of being accomplished or done successfully or without extreme trouble, hardship, or expense ⟨all of the aircraft-engine mufflers . . . have been found ~ —H.G.Armstrong⟩ ⟨feels that any . . . plan might prove so expensive — and so ~ — that he does not intend to try a new one —*Time*⟩ ⟨a totally ~ scheme for making a quick million⟩ ⟨led him to write music that is vocally ~ —A.T.Davison⟩ — **im·practicality** \(ˌ)im, əm+\ *n* — **im·practicalness** \(')im, əm+\ *n*

**im·pre·cate** \'imprəˌkāt, -rē,-, *usu* -ād.+V\ *vb* -ED/-ING/-S [L *imprecatus*, past part. of *imprecari*, fr. *in-* ²in- + *precari* to ask, entreat, pray — more at PRAY] *vt* **1 a** *archaic* : to call down by prayer : INVOKE **b** : to invoke evil upon : CURSE ⟨*imprecated* the weather when the ink froze in his fountain pen —Stanley Snaith⟩ **2** *archaic* : to beg or pray for ~ *vi* **1** *obs* : to invoke evil **2** : to utter imprecations : CURSE

**im·pre·cat·ing·ly** \'==,===,,=='=== \ *adv* : in the manner of one cursing : with curses

**im·pre·ca·tion** \ˌ==ˈkāshən\ *n* -s [L *imprecation-, imprecatio*, fr. *imprecatus* + *-ion-, -io* -ion] **1** : the act of imprecating esp. by invoking evil : CURSING **2 a** : PLEA, SUPPLICATION ⟨the ~s to the Lord for forgiveness —W.A.White⟩ **b** : CURSE, MALEDICTION ⟨uttered ~s under his breath⟩

**im·preca·to·ry** \'imprəkəˌtōrē, 'imprēk-, əm'prek-, -tȯr-, -ri, *chiefly Brit* ¦impri¦kātəri *or* -ä·tri\ *adj* : of, relating to, or being imprecation : invoking evil : CURSING

**im·precise** \¦im+\ *adj* [¹*in-* + *precise*] : not precise: as **a** : not exact ⟨~ astronomical observation⟩ **b** : vague or indefinite in nature, form, or outline ⟨~ dawn changes to photographic clearness —Han Suyin⟩ ⟨made him a rather ~ offer⟩ — **im·precisely** \"+\ *adv* — **im·preciseness** \"+\ *n*

**im·precision** \¦im+\ *n* [¹*in-* + *precision*] : the quality or state of being imprecise : lack of precision ⟨it is the indefiniteness, the ~ of the process that is baffling —Herbert Read⟩ ⟨an ~ of language⟩ : INACCURACY ⟨trying to mark as accurately as possible with tools calibrated with great ~⟩

**im·predicable** \(')im, əm+\ *adj* [¹*in-* + *predicable*] : not predicable

**im·preg** \'im,preg\ *n* -s [*impregnated* (*wood*)] : wood impregnated with a resin so that face checking is reduced and compressional strength and hardness, electrical resistance, and resistance to moisture, acid, and decay are increased

**im·pregn** \im'prēn\ *vt* -ED/-ING/-S [LL *impraegnare* — more at IMPREGNATE] *archaic* : IMPREGNATE

**im·preg·na·bil·i·ty** \(ˌ)im,pregnə'biləd·ē, əm-, -lətē, -i\ *n* -ES : the quality or state of being impregnable

¹**im·preg·na·ble** \(')im¦pregnəbəl, əm'p-\ *adj* [alter. (influenced by *impregnate*) of earlier *impreignable*, alter. (influenced by such words as *reign, deign*, with silent *g*) of earlier *imprenable*, fr. ME, fr. MF, fr. *in-* ¹in- + *prenable* capable of being captured, fr. *pren-* (stem of *prendre* to take, capture, fr. L *prehendere* to grasp, seize) + *-able* — more at GET] **1** : incapable of being taken by assault : able to resist attack : UNCONQUERABLE, UNASSAILABLE ⟨an ~ fortress⟩ ⟨~ virtue⟩; *also* : incapable of being broken into or escaped from ⟨an ~ cell⟩ **2** : being beyond criticism or question : not subject to higher authority ⟨an ~ social position⟩ ⟨of ~ financial standing⟩ ⟨an ~ reputation for honesty⟩ — **im·pregnableness** \"+\ *n* -ES — **im·pregnably** \"+\ *adv*

²**im·preg·na·ble** \əm'pregnəbəl\ *adj* [²*impregnate* + *-able*] : capable of being impregnated (as an egg)

¹**im·preg·nant** \əm'pregnənt\ *adj* [LL *impraegnant-, impraegnans*, pres. part. of *impraegnare*] **1** *obs* : IMPREGNATED, SATURATED, PERMEATED, IMBUED **2** *archaic* : IMPREGNATING

²**impregnant** \"\ *n* -s : an agent (as an oil, plastic, insecticide, resin) used to penetrate another substance (as cloth, paper, plaster, concrete, pulp, wood)

¹**im·preg·nate** \əm'pregnət, *usu* -nəd.+V\ *adj* [LL *impraegnatus*, past part.] : IMPREGNATED

²**im·preg·nate** \əm'preg,nāt, 'im,p-, *usu* -ād.+V\ *vt* -ED/-ING/-S [LL *impraegnatus*, past part. of *impraegnare*, fr. L *in-* ²in- + *praegnas* pregnant — more at PREGNANT] **1 a** (1) : to make pregnant : cause to conceive : get with child or young (2) : to introduce sperm cells into : INSEMINATE **b** : to infuse an active principle into : make fruitful or fertile : FERTILIZE, IMBUE **2 a** : to cause to be filled, imbued, mixed, furnished, or saturated (as with particles of another substance) ⟨~ wood with creosote⟩ ⟨gauze *impregnated* with medicament⟩ ⟨a cake strongly *impregnated* with brandy⟩ ⟨the chamber . . . *impregnated* with the odor of furniture paste —Arnold Bennett⟩ **b** (1) : to mix with : INTERPENETRATE ⟨quicksilver ore ~s sandstone in California —A.M.Bateman⟩ (2) : to have a marked permeating or coloring effect upon ⟨a very notable poem *impregnated* with the pessimism of a time —R.M.Lovett⟩ ⟨criticism . . . richly *impregnated* with history —C.W.Shumaker⟩ **c** : to force by impregnation ⟨plastics *impregnated* into cloth —Jack DeMent⟩ **3** : to influence markedly : INDOCTRINATE ⟨*impregnated* with socialistic ideas⟩ **syn** see PERMEATE

**im·preg·na·tion** \ˌim,preg'nāshən\ *n* -s [F or L; F *imprégnation*, fr. MF *impregnation*, fr. ML *impraegnation-, impraegnatio*, fr. LL *impraegnatus* + L *-ion-, -io* -ion] **1** : the act of impregnating or the state of being impregnated: as **a** : a causing to conceive : FECUNDATION, FERTILIZATION **b** : INFUSION, SATURATION **c** : INDOCTRINATION **2** : something with which something else is impregnated: as **a** : a mineral concentration consisting of small scattered grains in a rock matrix **b** : IMPREGNANT

**im·preg·na·tor** \əm'preg,nād·ə(r), 'im,p-, -ātə-\ *n* -s [ML *impraegnator*, fr. LL *impraegnatus* + L *-or*] : one that impregnates: as **a** : an operator of a machine that impregnates (as a fabric with a chemical compound) **b** : an instrument used for artificial insemination

**impresa** *n* -s [It, undertaking, chivalric deed, heraldic device, motto, fr. fem. of *impreso*, past part. of *imprendere* to undertake, fr. (assumed) VL *imprehendere* — more at EMPRISE] **1** *obs* : DEVICE, EMBLEM **2** *obs* : a sentence usu. accompanying an impresa **b** : MOTTO, PROVERB, MAXIM

**im·pre·sar·i·al** \¦imprə¦särēəl, -sa(a)r-, -ser-, -sär-\ *adj* : of or belonging to an impresario

**im·pre·sar·io** \ˌ==ˈsrē,ō\ *n* -s *see sense 1* [It, manager, impresario, fr. *impresa* + *-ario* -ary (fr. L *-arius*)] **1** *pl also* **im·pre·sa·ri** \-ˌrē\ : the projector, manager, or conductor of an opera or concert company **2 :** one who puts on or sponsors an entertainment (as a concert, television show, art exhibition, or sports contest) **3 :** MANAGER, PRODUCER, DIRECTOR ⟨a former beerhall ~ —Upton Sinclair⟩ ⟨an egregious ~ of letters, who kept a squad of writers churning out copy marketed under his signature —C.J.Rolo⟩ ⟨the ~ of the best intelligent conversation to be heard in his time —*Times Lit. Supp.*⟩

**im·prescribable** \ˌim+\ *adj* [¹in- + *prescribe* + *-able*] **:** IMPRESCRIPTIBLE

**im·prescriptibility** \ˌim+\ *n* **:** the quality or state of being imprescriptible

**im·prescriptible** \ˌim+\ *adj* [MF; fr. *in-* ¹in- + *prescriptible* — more at PRESCRIPTIBLE] **:** not subject to prescription **:** INALIENABLE ⟨the ~ rights of man⟩; *also* **:** ABSOLUTE — **im·prescriptibly** \"+\ *adv*

**imprese** *n* -s [MF, fr. OIt *impresa* — more at IMPRESA] *obs* **:** IMPRESA

**¹im·press** \əmˈpres\ *vb* [ME *impressen*, fr. L *impressus*, past part. of *imprimere*, fr. *in-* ²in- + *-primere* (fr. *premere* to press) — more at PRESS] *vt* **1 a :** to apply with pressure so as to press or imprint ⟨~ a signet ring on wax⟩ ⟨the fingerprint file . . . in which all 10 fingers are ~*ed* on the card —*FBI Bull.*⟩ **b :** to produce (as a mark or image) by pressure ⟨a perfect spiral ~*ed* on such a cylinder —S.F. Mason⟩ **:** IMPRINT ⟨~ one's name on a metal strip by machine⟩ ⟨~ an odd design on the wood⟩ **c :** to press, stamp, or print in or upon ⟨~*ed* the wax with his seal⟩ **:** mark by or as if by pressure ⟨~ his children with the right attitudes⟩ **2 a :** to produce or imprint an esp. vivid impression of (as on the mind or memory) ⟨~ an idea on the mind⟩ ⟨the general custom for boys to be whipped on certain days to ~ things on their memories —T.B.Costain⟩ ⟨beliefs which have been ~*ed* upon us in our childhood —Frank Thilby⟩ **:** cause to have a strong effect (as of compulsion) ⟨~*ing* his will upon others by sheer force of character —V.L.Parrington⟩ **b :** to produce an impression on **:** affect esp. forcibly or deeply ⟨~ a friend with the sincerity of one's intentions⟩ ⟨~ one favorably⟩ **:** arouse strong feeling (as concern, admiration, dislike) in ⟨the altered manner of his son ~*ed* him strangely —George Meredith⟩ ⟨the bigness of it awed them, the resources ~*ed* them —Joseph Baily⟩ **c :** to mark with an imposed quality or characteristic ⟨~ the poem with the cynicism of his outlook⟩ **3 a** *obs* **:** PRINT ⟨~ the Bible⟩ **b :** to print (a stamp) directly on (a postcard, envelope) ⟨~*ed* with a 2 cent stamp⟩ **4 a :** EXERT ⟨~ a force upon a sail⟩ **b :** to transfer or transmit (as a movement) by communication ⟨~ a motion upon a ball⟩ **c :** to apply (an electromotive force or voltage) to a circuit from an outside source (as a generator) **~** *vi* **:** to produce an impression **:** arouse the strong interest or admiration of another ⟨did not wish to make friends at parties but only to ~ with his sense of personal destiny⟩ ⟨a small child acting up before company in an effort to ~⟩ **syn** see AFFECT

**²im·press** \ˈim,p- *sometimes* əmˈp-\ *n* **1 :** the act of impressing or stamping ⟨sealing by the old-time process of ~ —L.F.Middlebrook⟩ **2 a :** a mark made by pressure that produces indentation or embossment **:** IMPRINT ⟨noting the ~ of wheels in lava —Richard Llewellyn⟩ ⟨a matrix in fairly durable metal to receive the ~ of the punch —G.C.Sellery⟩ **b :** an image or figure of something formed by or as if by pressure; *esp* **:** SEAL ⟨the most beautiful seal cuttings are shown on the ~*es* of the old Salem documents —L.F.Middlebrook⟩ **c :** a product of pressure or influence **3 :** a characteristic mark of distinction **:** STAMP ⟨the picture bore the ~ of the artist⟩ **:** distinctive quality ⟨his soft mind had . . . taken an ~ from the society which surrounded him —T.B.Macaulay⟩ ⟨the ~ of a fresh and vital intelligence is stamped unmistakably upon all that is best in his work —Lytton Strachey⟩ **4** *archaic* **:** IMPRESA **5 :** IMPRESSION ⟨his work has made a decided ~ upon our time —W.R.Benét⟩ **:** EFFECT ⟨words are but symbols and, like all symbols, have a varying ~ —Philip Wittenberg⟩ ⟨made his strongest ~ upon the country by his . . . two speeches —G.H.Haynes⟩ ⟨left an enduring ~ on my life, although our relations were always impersonal —A.J. Liebling⟩

**³im·press** \əmˈp-\ *vt* [²in- + *press* (take by force)] **1 :** to levy or take by force for public service; *esp* **:** to take or force by impressment (as into naval service) ⟨in searching for British sailors upon our ships, she ~*ed* our own —Owen Wister⟩ **2 a :** to enlist or procure the services or aid of by forcible argument or persuasion ⟨all able-bodied survivors were ~*ed* for the task of finding and caring for the injured —*Amer. Guide Series: Texas*⟩ **b :** to force or forcibly persuade ⟨~*ed* him into a white coat for the Christmas festivities —Nancy Hale⟩

**⁴im·press** \ˈim,p-, əmˈp-\ *n* **:** IMPRESSMENT

**⁵impress** *n* [alter. of ²*imprest*] *obs* **:** pay in advance

**⁶im·press** \əmˈpres\ *vt* [alter. of ¹*imprest*] *archaic* **:** to make an advance payment of (money)

**⁷im·press** \ˈim,p-, əmˈp-\ *n* [alter. of *imprese*] **:** EMBLEM, DEVICE ⟨their shields broken, their ~*es* defaced —Edmund Burke⟩

**im·press·able** \əmˈpresəbəl\ *adj* **:** capable of being impressed

**im·pressed** \əmˈprest\ *adj* [ME, fr. past part. of *impressen*] **1 :** deeply or markedly affected by impression **2 a :** lying below the general surface as if stamped into it ⟨~ dots⟩ **b :** having markings lying below the surface ⟨an ~ skin⟩ — **im·pressed·ly** \-sədlē,-stlē, -li\ *adv*

**impressed species** *n* **:** SENSIBLE SPECIES

**impressed stamp** *n* **:** a stamp (as for postage or revenue) printed directly on a cover, document, or other paper bearing it — compare EMBOSSED STAMP

**impressed watermark** *n* **:** an imitation watermark made by pressing rubber letters or a design on the paper web before drying

**im·press·ibil·i·ty** \(,)im,presəˈbiləd·ē, əm-, -lətē, -i\ *n* -ES **:** the quality or state of being impressible

**im·press·ible** \əmˈpresəbəl\ *adj* [¹*impress* + *-ible*] **:** capable of being impressed **:** SUSCEPTIBLE, SENSITIVE — **im·press·ible·ness** \-bəlnəs\ *n* -ES — **im·press·i·bly** \-blē, -bli\ *adv*

**im·pres·sion** \əmˈpreshən\ *n* -S [ME *impressioun*, fr. MF *impression*, fr. L *impression-*, *impressio*, fr. *impressus* (past part of *imprimere* to impress) + *-ion-*, *-io* -ion — more at IMPRESS] **1 :** the act or process of impressing: as **a** (1) **:** an affecting by stamping, bearing upon, pressing, pressing into, or otherwise exerting a physical force that marks, grooves, embosses, or prints in some way ⟨the worker held the metal firm during the ~ by the die⟩ ⟨a firm ~ of the seal on the wax⟩ (2) *archaic* **:** the printing process **b :** a communicating or giving of a mold, style, trait, or character by an external force or influence ⟨a parent concerned with the ~ of good traits on the mind and personality of his children⟩ **2 :** the effect or product of an impression: as **a** (1) **:** an indentation, stamp, embossment, form, or figure resulting from physical contact usu. with pressure ⟨the strokes became wedge-shaped ~*s* which gave cuneiform its name —Peter Lawrence⟩ ⟨a banking system whose principal features would be a circulation of notes bearing a common ~ —*Encyc. Americana*⟩ ⟨a well-printed book has a sharp, clean ~ —Joseph Blumenthal⟩ (2) *obs* **:** a telling mark or trace (3) **:** a negative imprint in plastic material of the surfaces of the teeth and adjacent portions of the jaw from which a positive likeness may be produced in dentistry (4) **:** METER IMPRESSION **b :** an esp. marked influence or effect on feeling, sense, or mind ⟨the bad dream made a terrible ~ on the child⟩ ⟨the ~ of the ocean was vivid in his mind⟩ ⟨made a favorable ~ on the audience⟩ ⟨the more emotion the reading arouses, the deeper the ~ on the learner —W.F.Mackey⟩ ⟨square chimneys thrusting upward add to the ~ of weight —*Amer. Guide Series: Ark.*⟩ **c** (1) **:** a characteristic trait or feature resulting from influence ⟨the ~ produced by an environment on a person's habits⟩ (2) **:** an effect of alteration or improvement ⟨the fur traders . . . made little permanent ~ on the wilderness —R.A.Billington⟩ ⟨a candle or lamp struggled feebly from a window but made no ~ on the darkness —S.H.Holbrook⟩ **d :** a telling image impressed on the senses or the mind ⟨looking over the steep hills, the first ~ is of an immense void like the sea —Richard Jefferies⟩ ⟨drank in all the new ~*s* eagerly —Havelock Ellis⟩ **3 :** a stamp of wax, metal, or other substance on which a seal has been impressed **4** *archaic* **a :** CHARGE, ATTACK **b :** strong effect **:** IMPACT, SHOCK **5** *obs* **:** an atmospheric condition or phenomenon **6 a :** the amount of pressure with which an inked printing surface deposits its ink on the paper in the printing process ⟨each form should be made ready with as light an ~ as practicable —John Southward⟩ **b :** one instance of the meeting of a printing surface and the material being printed ⟨plates badly worn after a million ~*s*⟩; *also* **:** a single print or copy so made **c :** all the copies of a book or other publication printed in one continuous operation from a single makeready ⟨first published in 1939 and now available in a third ~ —*Times Lit. Supp.*⟩ — called also *printing;* compare EDITION **7 :** a usu. indistinct or imprecise notion, remembrance, belief, or opinion ⟨an ~ of familiarity with a face⟩ ⟨the mistaken ~ that they were out of enemy territory⟩ ⟨cold, and mysterious, and ghostly — that is my first and lasting ~ of Mycenae—Mary Chubb⟩ **8 a :** the first coat of color in painting **b :** a coat of paint for ornament or preservation **9 :** an imitation or representation of salient features in an artistic or theatrical medium (as a ballet, painting, or theatrical monologue) ⟨the novel was an ~ of the battle from the point of view of the common soldier⟩; *esp* **:** an imitation in caricature of a noted personality as a form of theatrical entertainment ⟨the comedian gave several ~*s* of famous movie and television stars⟩ **syn** see IDEA

**im·pres·sion·abil·i·ty** \əmˌpresh(ə)nəˈbiləd·ē, -lətē, -i\ *n* **:** the quality or state of being impressionable **:** susceptibility to impressions ⟨that flabby ~ which is dignified under the name of creative temperament —John O'Hara⟩

**im·pres·sion·able** \əmˈpresh(ə)nəbəl\ *adj* [F *impressionnable*, fr. *impression* + *-able*] **:** capable of being easily impressed: **a :** easily influenced or affected ⟨the ~ years of a child's life⟩ ⟨an ~ heart⟩ **b :** capable of being molded or printed on ⟨an ~ plastic material⟩ ⟨paper that was very ~⟩ — **im·pres·sion·able·ness** \-bəlnəs\ *n* -ES — **im·pres·sion·a·bly** \-blē,-bli\ *adv*

**im·pres·sion·al** \-shənᵊl,-shnəl\ *adj* **:** of, relating to, or being impressions — **im·pres·sion·al·ly** \-ᵊlē,-əlē\ *adv*

**im·pres·sion·ary** \-shəˌnerē\ *adj* **:** IMPRESSIONISTIC

**impression cylinder** *n* **:** the cylinder of a rotary printing press that carries the paper and impresses it by counterrotation against the inked printing surface on the plate cylinder; *also* **:** the cylinder of a cylinder press

**im·pres·sion·ism** \əmˈpreshəˌnizəm\ *n* -S [F *impressionnisme*, fr. *impression* + *-isme* -ism] **1 a** *often cap* **:** a theory or practice in painting esp. among French painters of about 1870 of depicting the natural appearances of objects by means of dabs or strokes of primary unmixed colors in order to simulate actual reflected light, the subject matter being generally outdoor scenes painted directly — often contrasted with *expressionism;* compare LUMINISM, NEO-IMPRESSIONISM, PLEIN AIR, POSTIMPRESSIONISM **b :** a rough modeling or texturing of a surface in sculpture to produce a shimmering or scintillating effect **2 a :** the depiction of scene, emotion, or character (as in literature) by the use of detail that is sometimes brief and essential but often of great intricacy and elaborateness and that is intended to achieve a vividness, colorfulness, or effectiveness more by evoking subjective and sensory impressions (as of mood and atmosphere) than by re-creating or representing an objective reality **b :** a style of musical composition designed to create vague impressions and moods through rich and varied harmonies and timbres — often contrasted with *expressionism* **c :** the creation of the impression of a scene or its mood or atmosphere in a drama by the use of undramatic dialogue or nonobjective or symbolic scenery **d :** the creating of a general impression in a movie by the use of a series of shots that have no immediate logical or narrative connection **3 a** (1) **:** a practice in esp. literary criticism of presenting and elaborating one's subjective reactions to a work of art (2) **:** a critical theory that advocates or defends such a practice as the only valid one in criticism **b :** a vague and subjective response (as to a work of art) ⟨her attack is almost always human, rather critical, highly personal, degenerating occasionally into vague ~ —Mark Schorer⟩

**im·pres·sion·ist** \-sh(ə)nəst\ *n* -S [F *impressionniste*, fr. *impression* + *-iste* -ist] **:** an adherent or follower of impressionism; *specif, usu cap* **:** a member of a group of artists in France who exhibited together between 1874 and 1886 and many of whom practiced impressionism in their painting

**im·pres·sion·is·tic** \(ˌ)imˌpreshəˈnistik, əm-, -tēk\ *or* **im·pres·sion·ist** \əmˈpresh(ə)nəst\ *adj* **:** of, belonging to, or being impressionism; *specif, usu cap* **:** of or belonging to the French Impressionists — **im·pres·sion·is·ti·cal·ly** \(ˌ)imˌpreshəˈnistək(ə)lē, əm-, -tēk-, -li\ *adv*

**impressions** *pl of* IMPRESSION

**im·pres·sive** \əmˈpresiv, ˈim,p-, -sēv *also* -səv\ *adj* [¹*impress* + *-ive*] **1** *obs* **:** IMPRESSIBLE **2 :** making or tending to make a marked impression (as because of size, eminence, dignity of bearing, or achievement) **:** having the power to impress **:** notably exciting attention or feeling or arousing awe or admiration ⟨the Grand Canyon of the Colorado, one of the world's most ~ natural wonders —*Amer. Guide Series: Ariz.*⟩ ⟨an ~ speech⟩ ⟨an ~ list of titles to a man's name⟩ ⟨a very ~ play⟩ ⟨the country is ~ for the immensity of the barren reaches and the vast horizons —*Amer. Guide Series: Oregon*⟩ **syn** see MOVING

**im·pres·sive·ly** \-səvlē, -li\ *adv* **:** in an impressive manner ⟨a garrulous young man with ~ complete information on all strata of shipboard life —T.O.Heggen⟩

**im·pres·sive·ness** \-sivnəs, -sēv- *also* -səv-\ *n* -ES **:** the quality or state of being impressive ⟨the man's ~ was due to his enormous size and thunderous voice⟩

**im·press·ment** \əmˈpresmənt\ *n* -S [³*impress* + *-ment*] **:** the act of seizing for public use or of impressing into public service ⟨the ~ of sailors⟩ ⟨opposed such measures as the conscription of state officials and ~ of private property —Hallie Farmer⟩

**im·pres·sure** \-eshə(r)\ *n* [¹*impress* + *-ure*] **1** *archaic* **:** the act of pressing or impressing **2** *archaic* **a :** an impressed mark **b :** a mental or sensory impression

**¹im·prest** \əmˈprest\ *vt* -ED/-ING/-S [prob. fr. It *imprestare*, fr. *in-* ²in- (fr. L) + *prestare* to lend, fr. L *praestare* to stand before, go surety for, furnish, present — more at PREST] **1** *archaic* **:** to make an advance or loan of (money) **2** *obs* **a :** to make an advance of money to **b :** to draw (as money) by way of advance

**²im·prest** \ˈim,p-\ *n* -S **:** a loan or advance of money: **a :** pay advanced to a soldier or sailor **b :** money advanced from government funds to enable a person to discharge his duties

**³imprest** \"\ *adj* **:** advanced or lent esp. as an imprest

**⁴imprest** *n* -S [prob. alter. (influenced by ²*imprest*) of ⁴*impress*] *obs* **:** IMPRESSMENT

**⁵imprest** *vt* -ED/-ING/-S [prob. alter. (influenced by ¹*imprest*) of ³*impress*] *obs* **:** to impress into army or naval service

**imprest accountant** *n, Eng law* **:** a person to whom an advance of public money is legally made

**imprest fund** *n* **:** a sum kept on hand, periodically replenished, and used for small expenditures

**im·pri·ma·tur** \ˌimprəˈmäd·ə(r), |tə- *also* -mā|\ *n* -S [NL, let it be printed, 3d sing. pres. subj. passive of *imprimere* to print, fr. L, to impress — more at IMPRESS] **1 a :** a license to print or publish (as a book or paper) **b :** approval of that which is published under the circumstances that censorship of the press exists **c :** IMPRINT b(1) **2 a :** SANCTION, APPROVAL ⟨gives its ~ to the shameless attack —Eugene Lyons⟩ **b :** a sign or mark of approval ⟨puts the ~ of approval on the morals and decency of wholesale, universal betting —T.E. Dewey⟩

**im·pri·ma·tu·ra** \(,)im,prēməˈtůrə\ *or* **im·prim·a·ture** \imˈprimə,chů(ə)r\ *n* -S [modif. of It *imprimitura*, fr. *imprimito* (past part. of *imprimere* to impress, print, stamp, mark, fr. L, to impress) + *-ura* -ure — more at IMPRESS] **:** a thin preliminary glaze applied to the ground in painting

**imprime** *vt* [prob. fr. ²*in-* + *prime* (first)] *obs* **:** to separate (as a deer) from the herd

**imprimery** *n* -ES [F *imprimerie*, fr. MF, fr. *imprimer* to print (fr. NL *imprimare*) + *-erie* -ery — more at IMPRIMATUR] *obs* **:** a printing office

**im·pri·mis** \imˈprīməs, -rēm-\ *adv* [ME *inprimis*, fr. L *in primis* among the first (things)] **:** in the first place — used to introduce a list of items or considerations

**¹im·print** \əmˈprint\ *vt* [ME *emprenten*, *imprenten*, fr. MF *empreinter*, fr. OF, fr. *empreinte* imprint (n.)] **1 a :** to mark by pressure (as a figure on an object or as the object itself with the figure) **:** IMPRESS ⟨a machine to ~ code numbers on metal merchandise⟩ **b** *archaic* **:** PRINT **c :** to add an imprint to ⟨~*ed* statement enclosures⟩ ⟨a ~ missing letter⟩ **2 :** to fix indelibly or permanently (as on the memory) ⟨~*ing* her features, her look, her smile, her voice, upon his memory —Edith Sitwell⟩ **3 :** to stamp the characteristics of ⟨~*ing* his own personality on his productions —E.Bentley⟩ **4 :** to establish a response in by imprinting ⟨ducklings of five species were ~*ed* on human beings as their parent-companions at hatching —Margaret M. Nice⟩

**²im·print** \ˈim,p-\ *n* [modif. (influenced by ²*in-*) of MF *empreinte*, fr. OF, fr. fem. of *empreint*, past part. of *empreindre* to imprint, impress, fr. L *imprimere* to impress, imprint — more at IMPRESS] **:** something imprinted or printed: as **a :** a mark (as a figure or symbol) made by pressure ⟨the footstep left its ~ in the mud⟩ ⟨bore the ~ of a circle and dot in the center —Zane Grey⟩ ⟨an ~ of the town seal on each bond —*Springfield (Mass.) Union*⟩ **b** (1) **:** a publisher's name often with address and date of publication usu. placed in a book at the foot of a title page (2) **:** a printer's name or identifying device usu. placed in a book on the copyright page (3) **:** a dealer's or retailer's name and address printed on matter (as a blotter, catalog, or promotional piece) put out by a wholesaler or supplier (4) **:** a correction (as of a letter that shows imperfectly in a run of printed sheets) struck in by running the printed sheets through the press a second time (5) **:** the name of the manufacturer of a stamp printed in the margin of a sheet or of a single stamp **c :** an indelible distinguishing effect or influence ⟨the teacher left her ~ on several generations of students⟩ ⟨the raw western settlements . . . so strongly marked by the ~ of the industrial process —Sinclair Lewis⟩ ⟨their work bears a sort of regional ~ —Malcolm Cowley⟩

**imprinted stamp** *n* **:** a postage or revenue stamp printed directly on the piece of paper on which it is to be used as distinguished from an adhesive stamp

**imprinting** *n* **:** a speedy and usu. stable learning pattern appearing early in the life of a member of a social species and involving recognition of identification characters for its own kind or for a surrogate ⟨the young of many precocial birds establish family relations by ~ that involves attraction to the first moving object seen⟩

**im·pris·on** \əmˈprizᵊn\ *vt* **imprisoned; imprisoned; imprisoning** \-z(ᵊ)niŋ\ **imprisons** [ME *enprisonen*, *imprisonen*, fr. OF *emprisoner*, fr. *en-* ¹en- + *prison* — more at PRISON] **1 :** to put in prison **:** confine in a jail **2 :** to limit, restrain, or confine as if by imprisoning ⟨have ~*ed* its turbulent water between granite walls —Arnold Bennett⟩ ⟨~*s* him with her possessiveness —*Newsweek*⟩ ⟨deftly and with one arm only, he ~*ed* her —Susan Ertz⟩ ⟨~*ed* little sausages in pastry and baked them —Robertson Davies⟩

**im·pris·on·able** \-z(ᵊ)nəbəl\ *adj* **1 :** capable of being imprisoned **2 :** legally entailing imprisonment as a penalty ⟨an ~ offense⟩

**im·pris·on·ment** \-zᵊnmənt\ *n* -S [ME *enprisonement*, *inprisonment*, fr. MF *emprisonnement*, fr. OF, fr. *emprisoner* + *-ment*] **1 :** the act of imprisoning or the state of being imprisoned **:** CONFINEMENT, RESTRAINT **2 :** constraint of a person either by force or by such other coercion as restrains him within limits against his will

**im·probability** \(ˌ)im, əm+\ *n* **1 :** the quality or state of being improbable **2 :** something improbable

**im·probable** \(ˈ)im,əm+\ *adj* [MF or L; MF, fr. L *improbabilis*, fr. *in-* ¹in- + *probabilis* probable — more at PROBABLE] **:** not probable **:** unlikely to be true or to occur **:** not easily believable ⟨an ~ story⟩ ⟨an ~ event⟩ ⟨characters unreal, dialogue artificial, plots highly ~ —C.J.Rolo⟩ — **im·probably** \"+\ *adv*

**im·pro·ba·tion** \ˌimprōˈbāshən\ *n* [MF, fr. L *improbation-*, *improbatio* disapprobation, fr. *improbatus* (past part. of *improbare* to disapprove, fr. *in-* ¹in- + *probare* to examine, approve, prove) + *-ion-*, *-io* -ion — more at PROVE] **1** *archaic* **:** DISAPPROVAL **2** [L *improbation-*, *improbatio*] *Scots law* **:** an act by which falsehood and forgery are proved **:** an action brought for the purpose of having some instrument declared false or forged

**im·probative** *also* **im·probatory** \əm+\ *adj* **:** of or belonging to improbation

**im·probity** \(ˈ)im,əm+\ *n* [MF or L; MF *improbité*, fr. L *improbitat-*, *improbitas*, fr. *improbus* bad, dishonest (fr. *in-* ¹in- + *probus* good, honest) + *-itat-*, *-itas* -ity — more at PROVE] **:** lack of probity **:** lack of integrity or rectitude **:** DISHONESTY

**im·proficiency** \ˌim+\ *n* [¹*in-* + *proficiency*] *archaic* **:** lack of proficiency

**im·profitable** \(ˈ)im,əm+\ *adj* [ME, fr. MF, fr. *in-* ¹in- + *profitable* — more at PROFITABLE] **:** UNPROFITABLE

**im·progressive** \ˌim+\ *adj* [¹*in-* + *progressive*] *archaic* **:** UNPROGRESSIVE — **im·progressively** \"+\ *adv, archaic* — **im·progressiveness** \"+\ *n, archaic*

**¹im·promp·tu** \əmˈpräm(p)(ˌ)t(y)ü, -(ˌ)chü\ *adv* [F, fr. L *in promptu* in readiness, at hand] **:** without previous study, preparation, or consideration **:** on the spur of the moment **:** EXTEMPORANEOUSLY ⟨being able to speak ~ and at length on any given subject —Bryan MacMahon⟩ ⟨any cry of contrition that ever came ~ from a human being —C.E.Montague⟩

**²impromptu** \"\ *n* -S [F, fr. *impromptu*, adv.] **1 :** something made or done impromptu **:** an extemporaneous composition, address, or remark ⟨the witty ~ must not smack of the midnight oil —Cecil Lavery⟩ **2 a :** a piece of music composed or played impromptu **b :** a musical composition suggesting improvisation

**³impromptu** \"\ *adj* [F, fr. *impromptu*, adv.] **1 :** made, done, or formed on or as if on the spur of the moment **:** IMPROVISED, MAKESHIFT ⟨postponements or changes of plan were always ~ —Marcia Davenport⟩ ⟨delegates . . . formed for an ~ parade through the aisle —C.E.Egan⟩ ⟨an ~ bench was made of a long board placed on two chairs and covered with quilts —B.A.Botkin⟩ **2 :** composed or uttered without previous study, preparation, or consideration **:** EXTEMPORANEOUS, UNREHEARSED ⟨an ~ addition to his prepared text —Foster Hailey⟩ ⟨a short ~ speech⟩

**⁴impromptu** \"\ *vb* -ED/-ING/-S [¹*impromptu*] **:** EXTEMPORIZE, IMPROVISE

**im·proper** \(ˈ)im,əm+\ *adj* [MF *impropre*, fr. L *improprius*, fr. *in-* ²in- + *proprius* own, proper — more at PROPER] **:** not proper: as **a :** not accordant with fact, truth, or right procedure **:** INCORRECT, INACCURATE ⟨arrived at an ~ conclusion from the premises⟩ ⟨charges of bribery, falsification of records, acceptance of ~ fees —*Current Biog.*⟩ **b :** not regularly or normally formed or not properly so called ⟨~ fractions⟩ **c :** not suited to the circumstances, design, or end ⟨an ~ medicine⟩ ⟨wore an ~ dress to the tea⟩ **d :** not in accord with propriety, modesty, good taste, or good manners **:** INDECOROUS ⟨most ~ to intrude a dog into the houses of the people they were calling on —Joseph Conrad⟩ ⟨highly ~ to dress ship at any time with college banners —C.D.Lane⟩ **:** INDECENT ⟨guilty of using ~ language⟩ ⟨dressing a scandalously ~ dress⟩ — **im·properly** \"+\ *adv* — **im·properness** \"+\ *n*

**improper diphthong** *n* **1 :** a vowel digraph **2 :** PARTIAL DIPHTHONG **3 :** an alpha, eta, or omega with an iota subscript

**improper fraction** *n* **:** a fraction in which the numerator is greater than or equal to the denominator or is of higher or equal degree

**improper integral** *n* **:** a definite integral whose region of integration includes a point at which the integrand is undefined or tends to infinity or whose region of integration does not have all limits finite

**improportion** *n, obs* **:** DISPROPORTION — **improportionate** *adj, obs*

**improportionable** *adj* [¹*in-* + *proportionable*] *obs* **:** DISPROPORTIONATE

**¹im·pro·pri·ate** \əmˈprōprē,āt\ *vt* -ED/-ING/-S [ML or NL *impropriatus*, past part. of *impropriare*, fr. L *in-* ²in- + *propriare* to appropriate — more at APPROPRIATE] **1** *obs* **:** APPROPRIATE **2 a :** to take over (a benefice or ecclesiastical property) and make one's own ⟨the town which had *impropriated* the revenues of the church —T.D.Atkinson⟩ **b** : to transfer (monastic property) to lay control or ownership — distinguished from *appropriate*

**²im·pro·pri·ate** \-ət\ *adj* [NL or ML *impropriatus*] : IMPROPRIATED : lay as distinguished from clerical

**im·pro·pri·a·tion** \(,)im,prōprē'āshən, əm-\ *n* -s **1** : the act of impropriating or state of being impropriated **2** : something impropriated : APPROPRIATION

**im·pro·pri·a·tor** \əm'prōprē,ād·ə(r)\ *n* -s : one to or by whom something is impropriated

**im·propriety** \,im+\ *n* [F or LL; F *impropriété*, fr. LL *improprietat-, improprietas*, fr. L *improprius* improper + *-tat-, -tas* -ty — more at IMPROPER] **1** : the quality or state of being improper ⟨shocked by the ~ of the young man's action⟩ ⟨guilty of ~ of speech and indecency of dress⟩ ⟨saw no ~ in giving preference to personal friends and relatives —W.E. Stevens⟩ **2** : something improper : an unsuitable or improper act or remark ⟨puns and jokes and pungent *improprieties* —*Times Lit. Supp.*⟩; *specif* : an unacceptable use of a word or of language

**im·prosperous** \(')im,əm+\ *adj* [¹*in-* + *prosperous*] *archaic* : not prosperous : POOR, UNSUCCESSFUL

**im·prov·abil·i·ty** \(,)im,prüvə'biləd·ē, əm-, -lətē, -i\ *n* : the quality or state of being improvable : capability of improving or of being improved

**im·prov·able** \əm'prüvəbəl\ *adj* [²*improve* + *-able*] **1** *archaic* : capable of being profited from or turned to good account **2** : capable of improving or of being improved : susceptible of improvement — **im·prov·able·ness** \-bəlnəs\ *n* — **im·prov·a·bly** \-blē, -bli\ *adv*

**¹im·prove** \əm'prüv\ *vt* [ME *improven*, fr. MF *improver*, fr. L *improbare* to disapprove, blame, reject — more at IMPROBATION] **1 a** *obs* : to show to be wrong : CONFUTE **b** *Scots law* : to prove false or forged : DISPROVE, INVALIDATE **2** *obs* : REPROVE, CENSURE

**²improve** \"\ *vb* [alter. (influenced by *approve*) of earlier *emprou, emprow*, fr. AF *emprouer* to invest profitably, to cultivate profitably, fr. OF *en-* ¹en- + *prou* profit — more at PROW] *vt* **1 a** : to make greater in amount or degree : INCREASE, AUGMENT, ENLARGE, INTENSIFY ⟨*improved* the chance that the committee could reach agreement⟩ **b** *obs* : to raise the price of **c** *obs* : to make (an evil) worse **2 a** : to enhance in value or quality : make more profitable, excellent, or desirable ⟨~ the appearance of a display⟩ ⟨~ one's health by exercise⟩ ⟨exhibited an *improved* optical viewfinder —*Americana Annual*⟩ **b** *archaic* : to speak on in order to make more generally profitable or turn to better spiritual account **c** : to increase the value of (land or property) by bringing under cultivation, reclaiming for agriculture or stock raising, erecting buildings or other structures, laying out streets, or installing utilities (as sewers) ⟨*improved* farmland⟩ **d** *Scots law* : to grant (a lease) for a long term to encourage a tenant in good husbandry **e** : to grade and drain (a road) and apply surfacing material (as gravel, crushed rock, or oil) other than pavement **3** *archaic* **a** : to avail oneself of : EMPLOY, USE **b** : OCCUPY **4 a** : to turn to profit or to good account : employ to good purpose : use to advantage ⟨~ an opportunity to make friends⟩ ⟨~ one's time by studying⟩ **b** *archaic* : to cause (money or capital) to yield a profit by investment **5 a** : to turn or convert by improving ⟨~ a nag into a racehorse⟩ **b** : to spend, remove, or dissipate by improvements ⟨a tribe *improved* out of existence⟩ ~ *vi* **1 a** : INCREASE, AUGMENT ⟨the price of cotton is *improving*⟩ ⟨the demand for more commodities *improved*⟩ **b** : to rise in value : enhance in price ⟨stocks are *improving*⟩ **2** : to advance or make progress in what is desirable : grow better ⟨the invalid's health *improved* daily⟩

**syn** IMPROVE, BETTER, AMELIORATE, and HELP mean to correct, make more acceptable, or bring nearer to a higher standard of goodness in part or in some degree. IMPROVE and BETTER are general and interchangeable and are often used of things that are orig. bad or unacceptable ⟨famed for his quick wit and his ability to *improve* a script during a performance —G.S. Perry⟩ ⟨increase his powers of field observation and notation while he *improves* his knowledge of the area —J.F.Hart & Eugene Mather⟩ ⟨*bettering* the general conditions of tenant farmers —*Current Biog.*⟩ ⟨has invariably *bettered* the tunes and often transformed a doggerel text into excellent poetry —*Amer. Guide Series: Tenn.*⟩ AMELIORATE is applied chiefly to things that are unacceptable, esp. conditions difficult to endure or causing suffering, and implies partial relief or alterations that make the conditions more tolerable ⟨*ameliorate* the lot of thousands of victimized human beings —Arnold Bennett⟩ ⟨abolish feudalism or *ameliorate* its vices —W.O. Douglas⟩ ⟨his care in *ameliorating* personality conflicts —Harold Koontz & Cyril O'Donnell⟩ HELP implies a bettering that still leaves room for improvement ⟨*help* farmers meet the fertilizer shortage⟩ ⟨exercises to *help* overcome a speech defect⟩

— **improve on** *or* **improve upon** : to improve or make useful additions or amendments to ⟨an inventor who *improved on* the carburetor system of the automobile⟩ ⟨remembered all the backwoods stories his customers told him — and doubtlessly *improved on* them a little —G.S.Perry⟩

**improved cylinder** *n* : a gun barrel with a choke

**improved wood** *n* : wood that has been strengthened by the filling in or closing of the voids in the cellular structure and by compression under heat

**im·prove·ment** \-vmənt\ *n* -s [alter. of ME *emprowment* profitable investment, profitable cultivation of land, fr. AF *emprouement*, fr. *emprouer* + OF *-ment*] **1** : the act or process of improving: as **a** : profitable employment or use ⟨the ~ of one's time in reading⟩ **b** : BETTERMENT ⟨went to college not for a degree but for professional ~⟩ : AMELIORATION ⟨the ~ of the patient's state of health⟩ **c** : the enhancement or augmentation of value or quality : an increasing of profitableness, excellence, or desirability ⟨an ~ of farm stock⟩ ⟨an ~ of the property by building several outbuildings and a new barn⟩ ⟨an ~ in living standards⟩ **2 a** : the state of being improved; *esp* : enhanced value or excellence ⟨saw a great ~ in the man's health and frame of mind⟩ ⟨pleased by the ~ of the transportation system⟩ **b** : an instance of such improvement : something that improves in this way: as (1) : a permanent addition to or betterment of real property that enhances its capital value and that involves the expenditure of labor or money and is designed to make the property more useful or valuable as distinguished from ordinary repairs — see BENEFICIAL IMPROVEMENT, NECESSARY IMPROVEMENT, VOLUNTARY IMPROVEMENT (2) : an alteration or addition to an existing subject of invention or discovery that does not destroy its identity or essential character but accomplishes greater efficiency or economy : a modification improving and making more valuable an existing discovery or invention

**improvement factor** *n* : an annual increase in compensation that enables workers to share in the benefits from increased productivity — usu. used in labor negotiations

**improvements and betterments insurance** *n* : insurance for the benefit of a tenant covering improvements made by the tenant to property which he occupies under lease

**im·prov·er** \əm'prüvə(r)\ *n* : one that improves: as **a** *chiefly Brit* (1) : an employee who accepts instruction or the opportunity to work in place of wages (2) : a worker who has completed an apprenticeship but is not yet qualified as a full-fledged member of a trade or occupation **b** : a device for giving shape to a dress; *esp* : BUSTLE **c** : an agent added to improve a substance ⟨potassium bromate is used as a flour ~⟩

**im·providence** \(')im,əm+\ *n* [MF or LL; MF, fr. LL *improvidentia*, fr. *improvident-, improvidens* + L *-ia* -y] : the quality or state of being improvident ⟨unemployment compensation and pensions against ~ in old age —C.O.Gregory⟩

**im·provident** \(')im, əm+\ *adj* [LL *improvident-, improvidens*, fr. L *in-* ¹in- + *provident-, providens* provident — more at PROVIDENT] : not provident : lacking foresight or forethought : not foreseeing or providing for the future : NEGLIGENT, THRIFTLESS ⟨~ throughout his brilliant career . . . in later years became penniless —*Amer. Guide Series: Md.*⟩ ⟨I'm ~: I live in the moment when I'm happy —Edith Wharton⟩ — **im·providently** \"+\ *adv*

**im·providentially** \(')im, əm+\ *adv* : IMPROVIDENTLY

**improving** *adj* [fr. pres. part. of ²*improve*] : morally or intellectually uplifting or designed to be so often to the detriment of any intrinsic excellence ⟨urged his children to read only ~ literature⟩ — **im·prov·ing·ly** *adv*

**im·provi·sate** \əm'prävə,zāt *sometimes* 'imprəvə,z- *or* əm'prävə,sāt\ *vb* -ED/-ING/-S [back-formation fr. *improvisation*] : IMPROVISE

**im·provi·sa·tion** \(,)im,prävə'zāshən, əm- *also* ,imprəvə'z- *sometimes* (,)=,prävə'sā- *or* ,imprə,vī'zā- *or* (,)=,prōvə'zā- *or* -ōvə'sā-\ *n* -s [F, fr. *improviser* + *-ation*] **1** : the act of improvising or the quality or state of being improvised: as **a** (1) : extemporaneous composition (as of music or poetry) (2) : the extemporaneousness of such composition **b** (1) : a course pursued in accordance with no previously devised plan, policy, or consideration ⟨his conduct at the time was merely an ~⟩ ⟨the policy of a democracy thus becomes an eternal ~ —H.L.Mencken⟩ ⟨the flight into the East was not an ~, a sudden, last-minute, desperate measure —A.R. Williams⟩ (2) : the extemporaneous quality of such a course ⟨the ~ of the country's relation with foreign powers⟩ **2** : something improvised or designed to seem improvised : IMPROMPTU — **im·provi·sa·tion·al** \-āshən°l, -āshnəl\ *adj*

**im·provi·sa·tor** *pronunc at* IMPROVISATE + ə(r)\ *n* -s [F or It; F *improvisateur*, fr. It *improvvisatore*, fr. *improvvisato* (past part. of *improvvisare*) + *-ore* -or] : IMPROVISER, IMPROVISATORE ⟨he has been a great ~, and that his improvisation is not without merit is proved by his spectacular career —O.D. Tolischus⟩

**im·prov·i·sa·to·re** \əm,prävəzə'tōrē\ *n, pl* **improvisato·ri** \"\ *or* **improvisatores** \-ēz\ [It *improvvisatore*] : IMPROVISER; *esp* : one who composes and recites verse extempore

**im·prov·i·sa·to·ri·al** \əm'prävəzə'tōrēəl\ *adj* : of or relating to improvisation — **im·prov·i·sa·to·ri·al·ly** \-ēəlē\ *adv*

**im·provi·sa·to·ry** \əm'prävəzə,tōrē, ,imprə'vīz-, *chiefly Brit* ,imprə,vīzātəri *or* -ā·tri\ *adj* : IMPROVISATORIAL

**im·provi·sa·tri·ce** \əm,prävəzə'trēchē\ *n, pl* **improvisa·tri·ci** \"\ *or* **improvisatrices** \-chēz\ [It *improvvisatrice*, fr. *improvvisatore*] : a female improvisatore

**im·pro·vise** \'imprə,vīz *also* ,=='=\ *vb* -ED/-ING/-S [F *improviser*, fr. It *improvvisare*, fr. *improvviso* unprovided, sudden, extempore, fr. L *improvisus* unforeseen, unexpected, fr. *in-* ¹in- + *provisus* foreseen — more at PROVISO] *vt* **1** : to compose, recite, or sing esp. in verse or to play on an instrument or act extemporaneously ⟨his cast, who ~ dialogue, gags, and situations as they go along —*Current Biog.*⟩ **2 a** : to bring about, arrange, or make on the spur of the moment or without preparation ⟨the cook . . . hastily *improvised* a supper —Willa Cather⟩ ⟨housed in *improvised* temporary quarters —*Report: (Canadian) Royal Commission on Nat'l Development*⟩ ⟨had to ~ policy always —James Cameron⟩ **b** : to construct or fabricate out of what is conveniently at hand ⟨an *improvised* laboratory —*Current Biog.*⟩ ⟨fish . . . with *improvised* hooks and lines —*Amer. Guide Series: N.Y. City*⟩ ~ *vi* : to improvise something esp. in verse or music : EXTEMPORIZE

**im·pro·vis·er** *or* **im·pro·vi·sor** \-zə(r)\ *n* -s : one that improvises

**¹im·provision** \,im+\ *n* [¹*in-* + *provision*] : lack of forethought : IMPROVIDENCE

**²im·pro·vi·sion** \,imprə'vizhən\ *n* [*improvise* + *-ion*] : IMPROVISATION

**im·pro·vi·so** \,imprə'vē(,)zō\ *adv (or adj)* [It *improvviso* — more at IMPROVISE] : EXTEMPORE

**im·prudence** \(')im, əm+\ *n* [MF or L; MF, fr. L *imprudentia*, fr. *imprudent-, imprudens* + *-ia* -y] **1** : the quality or state of being imprudent : lack of caution, circumspection, or due regard to consequences **2** : an imprudent act

**im·prudency** \"+\ *n* -ES [L *imprudentia*] *archaic* : IMPRUDENCE

**im·prudent** \(')im, əm+\ *adj* [ME, fr. L *imprudent-, imprudens*, fr. *in-* ¹in- + *prudent-, prudens* prudent — more at PRUDENT] : not prudent : lacking discretion : INJUDICIOUS ⟨very ~ in her parent to encourage her . . . in such idolatry and silly romantic ideas —W.M.Thackeray⟩ ⟨the deep ulcer on my leg . . . renders it ~ to take passage at this time —C.B. Nordhoff & J.N.Hall⟩ ⟨would be ~ for a noneconomist to talk about the details of economic policy —A.M.Schlesinger b.1917⟩ — **im·prudently** \"+\ *adv* — **im·prudentness** \"+\ *n* -ES

**imps** *pl of* IMP, *pres 3d sing of* IMP

**imp·son·ite** \'im(p)sə,nīt\ *n* -s [*Impson* valley, Oklahoma + E *-ite*] : a mineral consisting of an asphalt much like albertite but almost insoluble in turpentine

**impt** *abbr* important

**imptr** *abbr* importer

**im·puberty** \(')im, əm+\ *n* [ML *impubertas*, fr. L *in-* ¹in- + *pubertas* puberty — more at PUBERTY] : the quality or state of not having reached puberty

**im·pubic** \"+\ *adj* [L *impubes* (fr. *in-* ¹in- + *pubes* adult) + E *-ic* — more at PUBES] : not arrived at puberty : IMMATURE ⟨toiled in the fields with her ~ children —Thomas Beer⟩

**im·pu·dence** \'impyədən(t)s *also* -d°n-\ *also* **im·pu·den·cy** \-nsē, -si\ *n, pl* **impudences** *also* **impudencies** [*impudence* fr. ME, fr. L *impudentia*, fr. *impudent-, impudens* impudent + *-ia* -y; *impudency* fr. L *impudentia*] **1** : the quality or state of being impudent: as **a** *obs* : SHAMELESSNESS, INDECENCY **b** : an attitude marked by disrespect or insolence : cocky self-assurance **c** *archaic* : cool self-possession or self-reliance **2** : an impudent remark or act ⟨the mother would not endure her son's ~s⟩

**im·pu·dent** \-nt\ *adj* [ME, fr. L *impudent-, impudens*, fr. *in-* ¹in- + *pudent-, pudens*, pres. part. of *pudēre* to feel shame — more at PUDIC] **1** *obs* : lacking modesty **2** : marked by contemptuous or cocky boldness or disregard of others ⟨an arrogant and ~ boy given to insulting strangers⟩ : INSOLENT ⟨stood there . . . in an ~ swaggering posture —Helen T. Lowe⟩ : FORWARD, DISRESPECTFUL ⟨entertainingly ~ stories —Gerald Bullett⟩ : bold and brazen ⟨one of the most ~ miscarriages of justice⟩ **syn** see SHAMELESS

**im·pu·dent·ly** *adv* : in an impudent manner

**im·pu·dent·ness** *n* -ES : IMPUDENCE

**im·pu·dic·i·ty** \,impyə'disəd·ē, -yü'-\ *n* [MF *impudicité*, fr. L *impudicus* immodest, shameless (fr. *in-* ¹in- + *pudicus* bashful, modest, chaste) + MF *-ité* -ity — more at PUDIC] : IMMODESTY, SHAMELESSNESS

**im·pugn** \əm'pyün\ *vt* -ED/-ING/-S [ME *impugnen, impungnen*, fr. MF *impugner*, fr. L *impugnare*, fr. *in-* ²in- + *pugnare* to fight — more at PUGNACIOUS] **1** *obs* **a** : to assail physically : FIGHT **b** : OPPOSE, RESIST **2** : to assail by words or arguments : call into question : make insinuations against : GAINSAY ⟨~ one's honesty⟩ ⟨~ one's claim to property⟩ ⟨frequent recourse to sword or pistol, whenever honor was ~*ed* —*Amer. Guide Series: La.*⟩ **syn** see DENY

**im·pugn·able** \-nəbəl\ *adj* : capable of being impugned : subject to question

**im·pugna·tion** *n* -s [ME *impugnacioun, impungnacioun*, fr. MF or L; MF *impugnation*, fr. L *impugnation-, impugnatio*, fr. *impugnatus* (past part. of *impugnare* to impugn) + *-ion-, -io* -ion] **1** \,im,pəg'nāshən\ *obs* : ATTACK, OPPOSITION **2** \,im,pyü'n-\ *archaic* : IMPUGNMENT

**im·pugn·ment** \əm'pyünmənt\ *n* -s : the act of bringing into question or gainsaying or the state of being brought into question or gainsaid

**im·puissance** \(')im, əm+\ *n* [MF, fr. *in-* ¹in- + *puissance* — more at PUISSANCE] : POWERLESSNESS, WEAKNESS

**im·puissant** \"+\ *adj* [F, fr. MF, fr. *in-* ¹in- + *puissant* — more at PUISSANT] : POWERLESS, FEEBLE

**¹im·pulse** \'im,pəls *also* -lts\ *n* [L *impulsus*, fr. *impulsus*, past part. of *impellere* to impel — more at IMPEL] **1 a** : the act of driving onward with sudden force : IMPULSION, THRUST, DRIVE, PUSH **b** : the effect of an impelling force : motion produced by a sudden or momentary force : IMPETUS ⟨the ~ of the pumping by the heart is carried down so that a finger applied to the artery anywhere near the surface permits a counting of the pulse rate —Morris Fishbein⟩ **c** : a wave of excitation transmitted through certain tissues and esp. nerve fibers and muscles that results in physiological activity or inhibition **d** : an electrical or mechanical action or force usu. of brief duration ⟨the ~s received by the radio set are . . . unimaginably small —A.C.Morrison⟩; *specif* : such an action or force actuating an operation (as in a computer) ⟨can be started either by hand or by an air ~ —*Swiss Industry & Trade*⟩ **2 a** : a force so communicated as to produce motion suddenly or immediately ⟨an ~ of the wind⟩: (1) : the motive force given by the escape wheel in the driving train of a timepiece to the pendulum or balance (2) : the muscular effort initiating a rhythmic dance movement (3) : a short directed motion ⟨written with one ~ of the pen —J.R.Gregg⟩ **b** : INCENTIVE ⟨under the ~ of transportation profits —*Amer. Guide Series: Mich.*⟩ **c** : an inspiration or motivation esp. giving a usu. new form or tendency ⟨those who give the religious life a new ~ need disciples to organize the impulse before it runs to seed —Hallam Tennyson⟩ ⟨his more successful stories derive from the same kind of ~ as his poetry —F.R.Leavis⟩ ⟨he received from America fresh artistic ~s —Anatole Chujoy⟩ **3 a** : a sudden spontaneous inclination or an incitement of the mind or spirit arising either directly from feeling or from some outer influence and prompting some usu. unpremeditated action ⟨constitutionally inclined to resist ~ and to take long views —George Santayana⟩ ⟨some uncontrollable ~ . . . may have driven the defendant to the commission of the murderous act —B.N.Cardozo⟩ ⟨act on ~⟩; *also* : the force actuated by such a motive or propensity ⟨a man who is driven chiefly by ~⟩ ⟨~s of greed —Bertrand Russell⟩ **b** : a propensity or natural tendency usu. other than rational ⟨a man of good ~s⟩ ⟨the sexual ~⟩ ⟨the fundamental ~ of self-expression —Havelock Ellis⟩ ⟨the systematizing ~, the restless passion for order of the Greeks —John Buchan⟩ ⟨never approaches a new task save with the ~ to postpone it —H.A.Overstreet⟩ **4 a** : the product of the average value of a force and the time during which it acts being a quantity equal to the change in momentum produced by the force if the body acted on is free **b** : PULSE 4a **syn** see MOTIVE

**²im·pulse** \", əm'p-\ *vt* [L *impulsus*, past part.] **1** : to give an impulse to **2** : to initiate an impulse in (a counter of a computer)

**impulse buying** *n* : the buying of merchandise on impulse rather than from premeditation

**impulse charge** *n* : an explosive used to provide an initial impetus (as to a torpedo)

**impulse excitation** *n* : a method of producing damped alternating current in which the duration of the impressed voltage is short compared with the duration of the current produced — compare QUENCHED GAP

**impulse face** *n* : the lifting plane of one of the club teeth of the escape wheel in a lever-escapement watch or the surface of the pallet stone which is engaged thereby

**impulse goods** *n* : merchandise (as inexpensive or luxury items) likely to be bought on impulse or without significant forethought as opposed to staple or essential goods

**impulse movement** *n* : a clock movement (as of a turret clock) in which the hands are driven by means of energy received by its pendulum in the form of electromagnetic impulses

**impulse pallet** *n* : a pallet stone in a roller of a chronometer balance that receives the driving impulse of the teeth of the escape wheel

**impulse pin** *n* : ROLLER JEWEL

**impulse turbine** *n* : a turbine in which the rotor is driven by fluid jets impinging directly against the blades — compare REACTION TURBINE

**im·pul·sion** \əm'pəlshən\ *n* -s [ME, fr. MF or L; MF, fr. L *impulsion-, impulsio*, fr. *impulsus* (past part. of *impellere* to impel) + *-ion-, -io* -ion — more at IMPEL] **1 a** : the act of impelling or the state of being impelled : the sudden or momentary action of a body in motion impinging on another body **b** : the impelling force or impulse **c** : an onward tendency derived from an impulsion : IMPETUS; *specif* : a marked or vigorous forward drive of a horse in a gait **2 a** : an influence acting usu. unexpectedly or temporarily on the mind or will and urging to action; *also* : an action provoked by such an influence **b** : drive to motor activity or creative effort **c** : IMPULSE 2c **3** : COMPULSION 2

**im·pul·sive** \(')im'pəls|iv, əm'p-, |ēv *also* -l(t)s| *or* |əv\ *adj* [prob. fr. MF *impulsif*, fr. *impulsion* + *-if* -ive] **1** : having the power of or actually driving or impelling ⟨an ~ force⟩ ⟨an ~ influence⟩ **2 a** : actuated by or esp. prone to act on impulse ⟨a houseful of ~ children⟩ ⟨the ~ buying of luxury items⟩ ⟨~, capricious and touchy —D.C.Buchanan⟩ ⟨men's thoughtless or ~ acts —M.R.Cohen⟩ **b** : COMPULSIVE 3 **3** : acting momentarily ⟨a mechanism giving the mechanism ~ thrusts⟩ **syn** see SPONTANEOUS

**im·pul·sive·ly** \|əvlē, -li\ *adv* : in an impulsive manner ⟨so happy she flung her arms ~ around his neck and kissed him⟩

**im·pul·sive·ness** \|ivnəs, |ēv- *also* |əv-\ *n* -ES : the quality or state of being impulsive ⟨the ~ with which he took up attractive theories —H.E.Scudder⟩

**im·pul·siv·i·ty** \,im,pəl'sivəd·ē, -vətē, -i *also* -lt's-\ *n* -ES : IMPULSIVENESS

**impulsor** *n* -s [L, fr. *impulsus* (past part.) + *-or*] *obs* : one that impels

**im·punctate** \(')im, əm+\ *adj* [¹*in-* + *punctate*] : lacking pores ⟨an ~ brachiopod shell⟩ or impressed punctate markings ⟨a beetle with elytra ~⟩

**impunely** *adv* [obs. E *impune* unpunished (fr. L *impunis*) + *-ly*] *obs* : with impunity

**im·pu·ni·bly** \(')im'pyünəblē, əm'p-\ *adv* [L *impunis* + E *-ible* + *-ly*] *archaic* : with impunity

**im·pu·ni·ty** \əm'pyünəd·ē, -nətē, -i\ *n* -ES [MF or L; MF *impunité*, fr. L *impunitat-, impunitas*, fr. *impunis* unpunished (back-formation fr. *impune*, adv., without punishment, fr. *in-* ¹in- + *-pune*, irreg. fr. *poena* punishment, pain) + *-itat-, -itas* -ity — more at PAIN] : exemption or freedom from punishment, harm, or loss ⟨trespassing with ~⟩ ⟨many individuals can with apparent ~ remain essentially infants forever, intellectually —Weston La Barre⟩

**¹im·pure** \(')im, əm+\ *adj* [F & L; F, fr. L *impurus*, fr. *in-* ¹in- + *purus* pure — more at PURE] **1** : not pure: as **a** : UNCHASTE, LEWD, OBSCENE ⟨~ language⟩ ⟨given to ~ ideas⟩ **b** : containing something unclean : DIRTY, FOUL, FILTHY, UNWHOLESOME ⟨~ water⟩ ⟨~ air⟩ **c** : unclean for ceremonial or religious purposes or not purified or hallowed by rites : DEFILED, UNHOLY, UNHALLOWED **d** : not accurate : not idiomatic ⟨~ Latin⟩ : marked by an intermixture of foreign elements ⟨an ~ dialect⟩ or by substandard, incongruous, or objectionable locutions ⟨an ~ style⟩ **e** : mixed or impregnated with an extraneous esp. inferior substance : ADULTERATED, UNRECTIFIED ⟨an ~ chemical⟩ ⟨~ food⟩ ⟨an ~ diamond⟩ **f** *of art or decoration* : MIXED, BASTARD ⟨an ~ style of ornamentation⟩ **g** : designed to serve a purpose chiefly other than artistic — used of art or an art form (as a poem or painting) ⟨there is ~ poetry, social and political poetry —Jacob Isaacs⟩ **2** : HETEROZYGOUS — **im·purely** \"+\ *adv* — **im·pureness** \"+\ *n*

**²impure** *vt, obs* : to make impure

**im·pu·ri·fy** \əm'pyu̇rə,fī\ *vt* [¹*impure* + *-ify*] : to make impure : ADULTERATE ⟨a source that is being continually *impurified* by alien additions —Walter de la Mare⟩

**im·puritan** \(')im, əm+\ *n* [¹*in-* + *puritan*] : one who is not a puritan or who is opposed to puritanism

**im·purity** \(')im, əm+\ *n* [ME *impurite*, fr. L *impuritas*, fr. *impurus* + *-itas* -ity] **1** : the quality or state of being impure **2** : something impure (as foul matter or obscene language) or something that makes impure (as a foreign ingredient)

**impurple** *obs var of* EMPURPLE

**input** *var of* INPUT

**im·put·abil·i·ty** \(,)im,pyüd·ə'bilad·ē, əm-, -üt'-, -lətē, -i\ *n* : the quality or state of being imputable

**im·put·able** \əm'pyüd·əbəl, -ütə-\ *adj* [F or ML; F, fr. MF, fr. ML *imputabilis*, fr. L *imputare* to impute + *-abilis* -able — more at IMPUTE] **1** : capable of being imputed : ASCRIBABLE, ATTRIBUTABLE, REFERABLE ⟨insofar as he was only acting as an agent the oversight was not ~ to him⟩ ⟨an occasional blurring of outline . . . is ~ to the music rather than the words —*Times Lit. Supp.*⟩ **2** *archaic* : capable of being accused or blamed : CULPABLE — **im·put·able·ness** \-bəlnəs\ *n* -ES — **im·put·a·bly** \-blē, -bli\ *adv*

**im·pu·ta·tion** \,impyə'tāshən\ *n* -s [MF or LL; MF, fr. LL *imputation-, imputatio*, fr. L *imputatus* (past part. of *imputare* to impute) + *-ion-, -io* -ion] **1** : the act of imputing: as **a** : ATTRIBUTION, ASCRIPTION ⟨the ~ of emotions, attitudes, and purposes as an explanation of overt behavior —Ernest Nagel⟩ **b** : ACCUSATION ⟨if . . . told that we are wrong we resent the ~ —J.H.Robinson †1936⟩ : INSINUATION ⟨resented the

~ that he had any direct responsibility for what she wrote —Millicent Bell⟩ **c** : the theological attribution of sin or righteousness to one on account of another's sin or righteousness **2** : something imputed **3** : the determining of the significance usu. to final profit of an element or factor or of each element or factor in a total industrial or merchandising process

**im·pu·ta·tion·al** \ˌimpyəˈtāshənᵊl, -shnəl\ *adj* : of or relating to imputation

**im·pu·ta·tive** \əmˈpyüd·əd·|iv, -ütət|\ *adj* [LL *imputativus*, fr. L *imputatus* + *-ivus* -ive] : transferred by imputation ⟨the ~ sin of Adam⟩ — **im·pu·ta·tive·ly** \|əvlē, -li\ *adv* — **im·pu·ta·tive·ness** \|ivnəs\ *n* -ES

**im·pute** \əmˈpyüt, *usu* -üd.+V\ *vt* -ED/-ING/-S [ME *inputen*, fr. L *imputare*, fr. *in-* ²in- + *putare* to consider, think — more at PAVE] **1 a** : to attribute accusingly : lay the responsibility or blame for sometimes falsely or unjustly ⟨accused him of her own fault, in *imputing* to him the wreck of her project —George Meredith⟩ **b** : to credit or ascribe to a person or a cause ⟨*imputing* to me better qualities than I possess⟩ ⟨our vices as well as our virtues have been *imputed* to bodily derangement —B.N.Cardozo⟩ ⟨*imputing* his visit to a wish of hearing that she was better —Jane Austen⟩ often falsely, accusingly, or unjustly ⟨soon began to believe in the opulence *imputed* to me —L.P.Smith⟩ ⟨*imputing* to him a guilt of which he was innocent —Edith Sitwell⟩ ⟨how dare you . . . ~ such monstrous intentions to me —G.B.Shaw⟩ **c** : to make a legal imposition of (as a charge against someone) **d** : to credit by transferal (a virtue or the benefit of a good work) to the account of someone other than the initiating agent **2** *obs* : RECKON, CONSIDER, REGARD **3** : IMPART, GIVE ⟨with his hand he ~s life to clay —Samuel Alexander⟩ **4** *obs* : to charge someone with a wrongdoing or crime **syn** see ASCRIBE

**imputed** *adj* : being the value in terms of money or hypothetical income receivable from something one has or owns that would yield real income if one wished (as a house one owns and uses but might rent) ⟨~ rent⟩ ⟨~ income⟩

**im·put·ed·ly** *adv* : by imputation

**imputed value** *n* : the value of a thing determined from its utility rather than by adding the cost of its constituent elements

**im·putrescibility** \ˌim+\ *n* : the quality or state of being imputrescible

**im·putrescible** \ˌim+\ *adj* [LL *imputrescibilis*, fr. L *in-* ¹in- + LL *putrescibilis* putrescible — more at PUTRESCIBLE] : not subject to putrescence : not capable of putrefaction

**impv** *abbr* imperative

**impx** *abbr* [L *imperatrix*] empress

¹**in** \(ˌ)in, ən; *usu* ᵊn *after* t, d, s, *or* z *as in "split in two", often* ᵊm *after* p *or* b *as in "up in front", often* ᵊŋ *after* k *or* g *as in "sick in bed", often* n *before* ə *as in "he's in a hurry"*\ *prep* [ME, fr. OE; akin to OHG *in*, prep., in, ON *ī*, Goth *in*, L *in*, Gk *en*, OPruss *en*, Russ *v*, *vo*, *vn-*] **1 a** (1) — used as a function word to indicate location or position in space or in some materially bounded object ⟨put the key ~ the lock⟩ ⟨travel ~ Italy⟩ ⟨play ~ the street⟩ ⟨wounded ~ the leg⟩ ⟨read ~ bed⟩ ⟨look up a quotation ~ a book⟩ (2) *chiefly Brit* : ON ⟨squatting down ~ his heels —R.M.Daw⟩ ⟨tramcars which run ~ tracks—*Manual of Firemanship (Gt. Brit.)*⟩ ⟨best dwelling house ~ the island —Padraic Fallon⟩ (3) : INTO ⟨broke ~ pieces⟩ ⟨called ~ council on many occasions —*U.S.Investor*⟩ ⟨threw it ~ the fire⟩ ⟨wouldn't let her ~ the house —*Springfield (Mass.) Daily News*⟩ **b** (1) — used as a function word to indicate position or location in something immaterial or intangible ⟨saw him ~ my dreams⟩ ⟨the position of the artist ~ society⟩ or the fact of belonging to a group or association ⟨you're ~ the army now⟩ ⟨are you ~ the orchestra⟩ (2) — used as a function word to indicate activity, occupation, or purpose ⟨advanced ~ hot pursuit⟩ ⟨~ search of lost treasure⟩ ⟨~ honor of this event⟩ ⟨what is all this ~ aid of . . . —*Sydney (Australia) Bull.*⟩ (3) — used as a function word to indicate a position or relationship of authority or responsibility ⟨~ charge of the company's affairs⟩ ⟨~ command of the garrison⟩ (4) : in the course of ⟨~ cooling this material hardens⟩ ⟨drowned ~ crossing the river⟩ (5) — used as a function word to indicate close connection by way of implication or active participation ⟨~ the plot⟩ ⟨~ an amateur play⟩ (6) — used as a function word to indicate engagement in a business identified with a particular commodity ⟨he's ~ oil, he's ~ rice —Ethel Merman⟩ ⟨her mother's family were . . . ~ butter —Mary Manning⟩ ⟨was ~ buttons but had started to expand into novelties —Mary Barrett⟩ **c** (1) — used as a function word to indicate a material, mental, or moral situation or condition ⟨a house ~ ruins⟩ ⟨a boy ~ love⟩ ⟨he's ~ luck⟩ ⟨~ great pain⟩ ⟨up to his waist ~ water⟩ or an environing condition ⟨the city lay ~ darkness⟩ ⟨basking ~ sunshine⟩ (2) — used as a function word to indicate something that envelops or covers ⟨a book bound ~ buckram⟩ ⟨covered ~ mud —Nevil Shute⟩ ⟨covered ~ . . . cotton plaid —*Spiegel's Catalog*⟩ (3) — used as a function word to indicate a cultivated or natural plant cover ⟨valley bottom is ~ grass —P.E. James⟩ ⟨75 percent of all the cropped land is ~ cereals —Samuel Van Valkenburg & Ellsworth Huntington⟩ ⟨most of the surface is ~ woods or brush —L.E.Klimm⟩ (4) — used as a function word to indicate something that is being worn ⟨a tall man ~ a bowler hat —Christopher Isherwood⟩ ⟨racing the horse ~ blinders⟩; often used to indicate a salient characteristic of what is being worn ⟨a lady ~ black⟩ **d** — used as a function word with an accompanying concrete word to indicate a physiological condition or process (as pregnancy or the condition of producing or yielding) ⟨~ lamb⟩ ⟨a cow ~ milk⟩ **e** (1) — used as a function word with an accompanying concrete word to indicate affluence or easy financial circumstances ⟨the Madrileño ~ the money loves to make a splash —E.D.Hauser⟩ ⟨I am generally ~ cash —Lord Byron⟩ (2) — used as a function word to indicate possession or display of some trait or attribute ⟨a gentleman ~ a gray goatee —Al Hine⟩ ⟨the sheep are ~ wool⟩ ⟨the corn's ~ silk and tassel —G.S.Perry⟩ ⟨~ figure slim —W.H.Hudson †1922⟩ **f** : under the influence of (an alcoholic drink) ⟨when ~ liquor, he would scutter up a tree like a squirrel —S.H.Adams⟩ ⟨~ drink⟩ ⟨~ one's cups⟩ **2 a** (1) : within the limits of a space of time expressed or implied ⟨early ~ April⟩ ⟨come ~ time⟩ ⟨~ the days of my childhood⟩ ⟨~ a few minutes he was there⟩ (2) : during the course of : DURING ⟨~ his long journeys throughout the country —Darcy Ribeiro⟩ ⟨~ all that time I never saw him⟩ (3) : during the space of : at any time during : FOR ⟨the coldest day ~ twenty years⟩ ⟨have not seen him ~ months⟩ **b** : AT ⟨united ~ this time of peril⟩ ⟨vested in the governor acting ~ his discretion —*Achievement in the Gold Coast*⟩ **c** — used as a function word to indicate a proportion or rate ⟨the mix was one ~ twenty —F.W.Crofts⟩ **3 a** (1) — used as a function word to indicate means or instrumentality ⟨scribbled and scratched over . . . ~ pencil or nail —William Faulkner⟩ ⟨caught his coat ~ the gate latch —L.Y.Erskine⟩ ⟨treated ~ moist heat —F.D.Smith & Barbara Wilcox⟩ (2) : by virtue of : on account of : for the reason that ⟨it is also complex, ~ being an integral part of a rich and many-sided mind —E.R.Bentley⟩ ⟨resemble the . . . Uplands ~ the fact that generally they provide an environment unfriendly to human occupancy —Samuel Van Valkenburg & Ellsworth Huntington⟩ — often used in the phrase *in that* ⟨a fallacious argument ~ that it is based on false premises⟩ (3) — used as a function word to indicate material or constituents ⟨a memorial ~ Vermont granite —Bernard De Voto⟩ ⟨tell the court . . . ~ what her cargo consisted —F.W.Crofts⟩ ⟨an artist ~ oils⟩ (4) — used as a function word to indicate degree, extent, or measure ⟨flock to his exhibitions ~ thousands —Herbert Read⟩ ⟨~ the main, we are in agreement⟩ ⟨not discouraged ~ the least⟩ (5) — used as a function word to indicate a class of objects ⟨something ~ a vacuum cleaner —John Steinbeck⟩ ⟨the latest thing ~ cars⟩ **b** — used as a function word to indicate manner, form, or arrangement ⟨buying a pig ~ installments —Dodie Smith⟩ ⟨told ~ confidence⟩ ⟨written ~ French⟩ ⟨carry all your funds ~ traveler's checks —Richard Joseph⟩ **c** : with reference to : as concerns ⟨wonder if actors of other countries are as happy ~ their audiences as we are —Phyllis Robbins⟩ ⟨great pains must be exercised ~ the amount of tannic acid used —C.M.Whittaker & C.C. Wilcock⟩ ⟨~ fall color they have few peers —Laurence Lowry⟩ ⟨Greek ~ language, culture, and religion —Franc Shor⟩ ⟨six feet ~ height⟩ ⟨a library rich ~ manuscripts⟩ ⟨~ the matter of your account⟩ **4 a** — used as a function word to indicate consideration of a thing strictly limited to its own essence, nature, or merits, apart from its relations to others ⟨~ itself, the matter has no importance⟩ ⟨nothing is beautiful ~ itself⟩; compare THING-IN-ITSELF **b** — used as a function word to indicate the specific object, sphere, or aspect to which a qualification is restricted ⟨~ him you have a fine leader⟩ ⟨much remains to be done ~ this field⟩ ⟨a very worthy gentleman, ~ truth⟩ ⟨that we expect ~ persons of your station —W.S. Gilbert⟩ ⟨my trust is ~ the Lord⟩ ⟨believe ~ his good faith⟩ ⟨rich ~ hope —Shak.⟩ **c** (1) : WITHIN — used of an inherent quality, attribute, or significance ⟨has no pity ~ him⟩ ⟨there is nothing ~ that story⟩ (2) : within the capacity or powers of ⟨if I . . . had anything like that ~ me, it would have made itself felt before now —Hamilton Basso⟩ **d** : in spiritual union with ⟨love one's brothers ~ Christ⟩ **e** : within the grant of : in the power or control of ⟨the scholarship is ~ the trustees of the fund⟩ **5** : in the key of ⟨~ F⟩ — **not in it** *slang* : not in the same class : hopelessly outclassed ⟨simply is *not in it* as far as skill and brains are concerned⟩

²**in** \ˈin\ *adv* [ME, fr. OE *in*, *inn*; akin to OHG *in*, adv., in, ON & Goth *inn*, OE *in*, prep.] **1 a** (1) : to or toward the inside esp. of a house or other building : into a certain space : INSIDE ⟨the door is locked, I can't get ~⟩ ⟨opened the window and climbed ~⟩ ⟨broke ~ and made the arrest⟩ (2) : in a particular direction : to or toward some destination ⟨drove 20 miles ~ and walked the rest of the way⟩ ⟨flew ~ on the first plane⟩ ⟨it was shank's mare from there ~ —Shelby Foote⟩ (3) : into a position of proximity : so as to be near some point : NEAR ⟨trackless trolleys able to swing ~ to the curb —*Springfield (Mass.) Union*⟩ ⟨the enemy closed ~⟩ : at close quarters ⟨advised the infielders to play ~⟩ (4) : so as to envelop gradually with something intangible or nebulous ⟨darkness closed ~⟩ ⟨the fog moved ~⟩ **b** : into the midst or into the surface of something so as to form a part ⟨put ~ some sugar⟩ ⟨mix ~ the flour⟩ ⟨paint ~ another figure⟩ — often used in combination ⟨built-*in* stabilizers⟩ **c** (1) : to its place ⟨fit a piece ~⟩ (2) : so as to conform, agree, or submit : into line ⟨fell ~ with our plans⟩ ⟨will he fit ~⟩ **d** (1) : to or into a particular place ⟨get your orders ~ early⟩ ⟨called us ~ for a conference⟩ (2) : to one's house ⟨had some friends ~ for dinner⟩ ⟨had a girl ~ to serve⟩ **2 a** (1) : within a particular place; *esp* : within the customary place of residence, practice, or business ⟨is your mother ~⟩ ⟨the doctor will be ~ at 2⟩ (2) : in a place that is the goal of a journey or course : at one's destination or terminus ⟨the whole whaling fleet was ~ —H.A.Chippendale⟩ ⟨wild riders of the High Plains, ~ from the ranches —*Amer. Guide Series: Texas*⟩ ⟨is the train ~⟩ ⟨two runs ~ last inning⟩ (3) : in place or position ⟨is the key ~⟩ ⟨had to climb a ladder because the stairs were not yet ~ —*Current Biog.*⟩ ⟨the footings are already ~ —*Building Estimating & Contracting*⟩ **b** (1) : on the interior or inner side : WITHIN ⟨shut a person ~⟩ (2) : so as to confine or surround ⟨snowed ~⟩ ⟨fence cattle ~⟩ (3) : in jail or prison ⟨what offense is he ~ for⟩ (4) *of a ship's sails* : in a furled or stowed condition **c** (1) : in the position of a participant, accomplice, insider, or observer — usu. used with *on* ⟨it's exciting to be ~ on that —May Sarton⟩ ⟨was ~ on the scheme —E.S.Morgan⟩ ⟨let some members of the diplomatic corps ~ on the government's intention —Sydney Gruson⟩ ⟨bankers who are ~ on current . . . thinking —*Wall Street Jour.*⟩ ⟨time his visit so that he might sit ~ on the Civil War —*Theatre Arts*⟩ (2) : in or into participation in a pot by betting as required by the rules ⟨come ~ for three chips⟩ ⟨count me ~⟩ ⟨stay ~ the pot⟩ **d** (1) : in office or power ⟨the Tories were ~ again —John Strachey⟩; *also* : in the position of having won an election ⟨~ by a landslide⟩ (2) : with legal privilege or title : in possession — used of a holding, possession, or seisin ⟨~ by descent⟩ (3) : in someone's good graces : on good terms — usu. used with *with* ⟨~ with the courthouse gang —D.D.McKean⟩ ⟨~ strong with the white folks —Ralph Ellison⟩ (4) : in a specified relation as regards favor, esteem, or terms of association ⟨~ bad with the boss⟩ (5) : in a position of assured or definitive success ⟨by the end of the performance I was ~ —Emmett Kelly⟩ ⟨why, you're ~, fellow —*Amateur Athlete*⟩; *also* : in vogue or style ⟨jewelry is ~ this year —G.A.Wagner⟩ **e** (1) *chiefly Brit* : in or into a burning or lighted condition ⟨blow ~ a fire⟩ ⟨the streetlights . . . were ~ —E.M.Lustgarten⟩ (2) : in season ⟨strawberries are ~⟩ : in cultivation ⟨had some two hundred acres ~ —Eve Langley⟩ : in condition to be harvested : in mature condition ⟨when cotton is ~ their devotion to the crop alters them completely —*Amer. Guide Series: Ark.*⟩ (3) : at bat (as in cricket) ⟨the last man ~⟩ (4) *of an oil well* : in or into production ⟨the well has come ~⟩ (5) : in effect ⟨rationing by points is over and rationing by the purse is ~ —*Economist*⟩ **f** (1) : in one's possession or control : at one's disposal : at hand ⟨the evidence is not all ~ —W.C.Allee⟩ ⟨the answers aren't ~ —Roscoe Drummond⟩ (2) : in a completed or terminated state ⟨when our own crops were ~ —A.W.Barkley⟩ ⟨after harvests are ~⟩ (3) : in evidence : on hand ⟨October was ~, mild and languorous —Maurice Hewlett⟩ (4) : in a specified service or employment ⟨had ~ enough time as mate —H.A.Chippendale⟩ ⟨put ~ a lot of time on that job⟩ **3** : to the end : INDEFINITELY — used as an intensive with *on* ⟨every feeding time from there on ~ —Land Kaderli⟩ — **in for** : certain to experience something, pleasant or unpleasant ⟨*in for* a whale of one hour's entertainment —Goodman Ace⟩ ⟨*in for* a storm⟩ — **in for it 1** : committed to a course **2** : certain to suffer punishment or other unpleasant experience ⟨sees us as ineluctably *in for it* —J.W.Krutch⟩ ⟨will be *in for it* if he doesn't get home on time⟩

³**in** \"\ *vt* **inned**; **inned**; **inning**; **ins** [ME *innen*, fr. OE *innian* to include, go in, fr. *in*, *inn*, adv.] *now dial chiefly Eng* : ENCLOSE, RECLAIM; *also* : HARVEST

⁴**in** \"\ *adj* [²in] **1 a** : that is located inside or within ⟨the ~ part⟩ **b** : that is in position, connection, operation, or power ⟨the ~ party⟩ **c** : having its inning ⟨the ~ team⟩ **2** : that is directed inward : proceeding or bound toward the interior or inner side : INCOMING ⟨the ~ train⟩

⁵**in** \"\ *n* -S [²in] **1** : one who is in office or power or on the inside ⟨wanted to be an ~ —W.A.White⟩ — usu. used in pl. ⟨a matter of ~s versus outs —L.K.Caldwell⟩ **2** : INFLUENCE, PULL ⟨enjoyed some sort of ~ with the commandant —Henriette Roosenburg⟩ ⟨must have an ~ someplace —W.R. Burnett⟩ **3** : a ball hit in bounds in tennis or squash

¹**in-** *or* **il-** *or* **im-** *or* **ir-** *prefix* [ME, fr. MF, OF, & L; ME *in-* fr. OF, fr. L; ME *il-* fr. MF, fr. L, fr. *in-*; ME *im-* fr. OF, fr. L, fr. *in-*; ME *ir-* fr. OF, fr. L, fr. *in-*; akin to OE *un-* — more at UN-] : not : NON-, UN- — usu. *il-* before *l* ⟨illogical⟩ and *im-* before *b*, *m*, or *p* ⟨imbalance⟩ ⟨immoral⟩ ⟨improvident⟩ and *ir-* before *r* ⟨irreducible⟩ and *in-* before other sounds ⟨inactive⟩ ⟨inapt⟩ ⟨inconclusive⟩

²**in-** *or* **il-** *or* **im-** *or* **ir-** *prefix* [ME, fr. OF, MF, & L; ME *in-* fr. OF *in-*, *en-*, fr. L *in-*, fr. *in* in, into; ME *il-* fr. MF, fr. L, fr. *in*; ME *im-* fr. MF *im-*, *em-*, fr. L *im-*, fr. *in*; ME *ir-* fr. L, fr. *in* — more at ¹IN] **1** : in : within : inward : into : toward : on ⟨implode⟩ ⟨irradicate⟩ **2** : ¹EN- ⟨illucidate⟩ ⟨imbarn⟩ ⟨immarble⟩ ⟨impanel⟩ ⟨imperil⟩ ⟨inspirit⟩ — in both senses usu. *il-* before *l*, *im-* before *b*, *m*, or *p*, *ir-* before *r*, and *in-* before other sounds

³**in-** *or* **ino-** *comb form* [NL *in-*, fr. Gk *in-*, tendon, fr. *in-*, *is*; prob. akin to L *viēre* to plait — more at WITHY] : fiber : fibrous tissue ⟨initis⟩ ⟨inogen⟩

**-in** \ən, ᵊn, ˌin\ *n suffix* -S [F *-ine*, fr. L *-ina* (with long *ī*), fem. of *-inus* (with long *ī*) of or belonging to — more at -INE] **1 a** : neutral chemical compound or compound not distinctly basic or acidic ⟨picrotoxin⟩ ⟨hematoporphyrin⟩ — esp. in names of glycerides ⟨acetin⟩ ⟨stearin⟩, glycosides ⟨amygdalin⟩ ⟨quercitrin⟩, proteins ⟨gelatin⟩ ⟨insulin⟩, and 6-membered heterocyclic compounds ⟨dioxin⟩; usu. distinguished from *-ine* **b** : enzyme ⟨emulsin⟩ ⟨myrosin⟩ — compare -ASE **c** : antibiotic ⟨penicillin⟩ ⟨streptomycin⟩ **2** : ²-INE 2a, 2b — not used systematically **3** : pharmaceutical product ⟨niacin⟩ ⟨aspirin⟩

**in** *abbr* **1** inch **2** inlet

**In** *symbol* indium

**INA** *abbr* international normal atmosphere

¹**-i·na** \ˈīnə, ˈēnə\ *n suffix, pl* **-ina** [NL, fr. L, fem. sing. and neut. pl. of *-inus* (with long *ī*) ¹-ine] : one or ones related to, resembling, or characterized by — in taxonomic names in biology ⟨Acarina⟩ ⟨Clathrina⟩ ⟨Fistulina⟩

²**-i·na** \ˈēnə *sometimes* ˈīnə\ *also* **-ine** \ˌēn *sometimes* ˌīn\ *n suffix* -S [prob. fr. It *-ina* (dim. suffix), fr. L *-ina* (with long *ī*), fem. of *-inus* (with long *ī*) ¹-ine] **1** : musical instrument ⟨concertina⟩ ⟨seraphine⟩ **2** : musical device ⟨aeoline⟩

**in·ability** \ˌin+\ *n* [ME *inabilite*, fr. MF *inhabilité*, fr. *in-* ¹in- + *habilité* ability — more at ABILITY] : the quality or state of being unable : lack of ability : lack of sufficient power, strength, resources, or capacity ⟨plead an ~ in mathematics —John Dollard⟩

**in ab·sen·tia** \ˌinabˈsench(ē)ə, ˌinəb-, -sentēə\ *adv* [L] : in absence (as of the accused person or of a person receiving a degree) ⟨awarded a degree in absentia⟩ ⟨condemned *in absentia*⟩

**in·absorbability** \ˌin+\ *n* : the quality or state of being inabsorbable

**in·absorbable** \"+\ *adj* [¹*in-* + *absorbable*] : not capable of being absorbed

**in ab·strac·to** \ˌinəbzˈtrak(ˌ)tō, -bˈst-\ *adv* [L, in the abstract] : in or from an abstract point of view : in the abstract ⟨the question could not be settled *in abstracto* —Yuen-li Liang⟩ ⟨discovering the problem purely theoretically, *in abstracto* —*Mathematical Biophysics*⟩

**in·acceptable** \ˌin+\ *adj* [¹*in-* + *acceptable*] : not acceptable

**in·accessibility** \ˌin+\ *n* [prob. fr. MF *inaccessibilité*, fr. *inaccessible* + *-ité* -ity] : the quality or state of being inaccessible

**in·accessible** \ˌin+\ *adj* [MF or LL; MF, fr. LL *inaccessibilis*, fr. L *in-* ¹in- + LL *accessibilis* accessible — more at ACCESSIBLE] **1** : not accessible: as **a** : not capable of being reached, entered, or approached ⟨~ except by heavy two-wheeled carts —C.L.Jones⟩ **b** : not capable of being obtained ⟨a rare work, today almost ~⟩ **c** : not easy to form friendly or close relations with : not susceptible to advances or influence : UNAPPROACHABLE ⟨peculiarly ~ to such questioning —Christine Weston⟩ ⟨a cold ~ figure⟩ **d** : difficult or impossible to comprehend or enter into : ABSTRUSE, ESOTERIC ⟨poetry . . . ~ to contemporary criticism —Frederick Morgan⟩ ⟨the novel . . . seems to me among the most ~ —C.J.Rolo⟩ **2** : reflecting or evidencing inaccessibility ⟨a look which was austere, ~ —Ellen Glasgow⟩ ⟨an air of ~ respectability —John Buchan⟩ — **inaccessibleness** \"+\ *n* — **in·accessibly** \"+\ *adv*

**in·accuracy** \(ˈ)in, ən+\ *n* [¹*in-* + *accuracy*] **1** : the condition of being inaccurate ⟨avoiding muddle and ~ —W.H. Dowdeswell⟩ **2** : an instance of being inaccurate : MISTAKE, ERROR ⟨when all his *inaccuracies* . . . have been acknowledged —D.C.Peattie & Eleanor R. Dobson⟩

**in·accurate** \(ˈ)in, ən+\ *adj* [¹*in-* + *accurate*] : not accurate: as **a** : containing a mistake or error : INCORRECT, ERRONEOUS ⟨an ~ account⟩ **b** : not functioning with accuracy or precision : FAULTY, DEFECTIVE ⟨the limbs are useless and sense organs are ~ —Abram Kardiner⟩ ⟨this thermometer is ~⟩ — **in·accurately** \"+\ *adv* — **in·accurateness** \"+\ *n*

**in·action** \(ˈ)in, ən+\ *n* [¹*in-* + *action*] : lack of action or activity : abstention from labor : IDLENESS, LETHARGY ⟨impatience with hypocrisy and ~ —Lillian Smith⟩

**in·activate** \(ˈ)in, ən+\ *vt* [*inactive* + *-ate*] : to make inactive: as **a** (1) : to destroy certain biological activities of ⟨~ the complement of normal serum by heat⟩ — compare REACTIVATE (2) : to cause (as an infective agent) to lose disease-producing capacity ⟨~ bacteria⟩ **b** : to remove (a unit) from the active list of a military service without disbanding — **in·activation** \(ˌ)in, ən+\ *n*

**in·active** \(ˈ)in, ən+\ *adj* [¹*in-* + *active*] : not active: as **a** (1) : marked by deliberate or enforced absence of activity or effort : SEDENTARY ⟨forced by illness to lead an ~ life⟩ (2) : not given to action or effort : not diligent, energetic, or industrious : INDOLENT, SLUGGISH ⟨dreamy and ~ by nature⟩ ⟨a very ~ police chief⟩ ⟨the rentier class, an ~ class in the economy —L.R.Klein⟩ **b** (1) : being unused or out of use : lying idle : not functioning ⟨an ~ mine⟩ ⟨an ~ machine⟩ (2) : relating to or consisting of officers and enlisted personnel of the armed forces who are not performing or available for military duties ⟨~ list⟩ ⟨~ reserve⟩ ⟨~ status⟩ (3) : being a commodity for which there is relatively little demand or in which relatively little trading occurs ⟨active, ~ and obsolete sterling patterns —*Christian Science Monitor*⟩ ⟨~ stocks⟩ (4) *of a disease* : not progressing or fulminating : QUIESCENT **c** (1) : chemically inert : UNREACTIVE ⟨~ charcoal⟩ (2) : not exhibiting any action on polarized light : optically neutral — used of stereoisomeric forms of various substances ⟨~ fructose⟩ ⟨~ camphor⟩; compare MES- 4b, RACEMIC

**syn** IDLE, INERT, PASSIVE, SUPINE: INACTIVE applies to anyone or anything not in action or not usu. in action (as in operation or use) or at work ⟨*inactive* machines⟩ ⟨an *inactive* child⟩ ⟨an *inactive* charge account⟩ IDLE applies chiefly to persons without occupation at the moment but usu. without occupation as a general or habitual thing, or to their powers, organs, or implements ⟨give work to an *idle* laborer⟩ ⟨an *idle* lathe⟩ ⟨an *idle* mind⟩ ⟨an *idle* pen⟩ INERT implies lack of power in a thing to set it in motion or by itself to produce a given effect, or suggests in a person a general indisposition to activity ⟨aimless accumulation of precise knowledge, *inert* and unutilized —A.N. Whitehead⟩ ⟨this amorphous spreading of responsibility will result in a sort of *inert*, ponderous bureaucracy —Stanley Walker⟩ ⟨would lie for hours on a chaise longue, so *inert* that the folds of chiffon which dripped from her body to the floor hung as steady as if they were stone —Rebecca West⟩ ⟨the greatest menace to freedom is an *inert* people —L.D.Brandeis⟩ PASSIVE implies immobility or a lack of positive reaction when acted upon by an external force or agent, often implying a submissiveness consisting of failure to be provoked to resistance or of a planned avoidance of any action that will give aid to the dominating force or agent ⟨some of those hours were spent in intensive cerebration, some in *passive* listening to lectures —H.M.Wriston⟩ ⟨*passive* obedience to authority⟩ ⟨*passive* resistance to oppression⟩ SUPINE implies abject inertia or passivity, often from indolence ⟨he is *supine*; he accepts his mother's truculence on his behalf with an indolence of temper which distinguishes him in this, as in all matters —Edward Hyams⟩ ⟨political and religious dissension . . . had split a weary and *supine* people into a dozen factions —P.J. Searles⟩

**in·actively** \"+\ *adv* : in an inactive manner

**inactiveness** \"+\ *n* : the quality or state of being inactive

**in·activity** \ˌin+\ *n* : the quality or state of being inactive : IDLENESS, SLUGGISHNESS

**in·adaptability** \ˌin+\ *n* : the quality or state of being inadaptable

**in·adaptable** \ˌin+\ *adj* [¹*in-* + *adaptable*] : incapable of adaptation : belonging to a fixed type

**in·adaptive** \ˌin+\ *adj* [¹*in-* + *adaptive*] : not adaptive

**in·adequacy** \(ˈ)in, ən+\ *n* [fr. *inadequate*, after *adequate*: *adequacy*] : the quality or state of being inadequate : INSUFFICIENCY ⟨~ of unemployment benefits —*Collier's Yr. Bk.*⟩

**in·adequate** \(ˈ)in, ən+\ *adj* [¹*in-* + *adequate*] : not adequate : INSUFFICIENT, DEFICIENT ⟨~ equipment⟩ ⟨~ leadership⟩ *specif* : lacking the capacity for psychological maturity ⟨the ~ individual⟩ : unable to make adequate social adjustment ⟨an offender coming from an ~ family⟩ ⟨~ parents⟩ — **in·adequately** \"+\ *adv* — **in·adequateness** \"+\ *n* -ES

**in·admissibility** *also* **in·admissability** \ˌin+\ *n* : the quality or state of being inadmissible

**in·admissible** *also* **in·admissable** \ˌin+\ *adj* [¹*in-* + *admissible*] : not proper to be allowed or received : not admissible ⟨~ behavior⟩ — **in·admissibly** \"+\ *adv*

**in-a-door bed** \ˈ==ˌ=-\ *also* **in-a-door** *n* [fr. *In-a-Dor-Bed*, a trademark] : MURPHY BED

¹**in·ad·u·nate** \ˌinəˈd(y)ünət, (ˈ)inˈajən-\ *adj* [¹*in-* + L *adunatus*, past part. of *adunare* to unite, fr. *ad-* + *unus* one — more at ONE] : not united; *specif* : having the arms completely free from the calyx — used of a crinoid

²**inadunate** \"\ *n* -S : an inadunate crinoid

**in·ad·ver·tence** \ˌinədˈvərtᵊn(t)s, ˌiˌnad-, -vət-, -vəit-\ *n* [ML *inadvertentia*, fr. L *in-* ¹in- + *advertent-*, *advertens* (pres. part. of *advertere* to advert) + *-ia* -y — more at ADVERT] **1** : the fact or action of being inadvertent; lack of care or attentiveness : INATTENTION ⟨mistakes proceed from ~⟩ **2** : an effect of inattention : a result of carelessness : an oversight, mistake, or fault from negligence ⟨annoying misprints and ~s —Tor Ulving⟩

**in·ad·ver·ten·cy** \-tᵊnsē, -si\ *n* [ML *inadvertentia*] : INADVERTENCE ⟨wars sometimes start through . . . sheer ~ —*Reporter*⟩

**in·ad·ver·tent** \¦;(,)=ˈ=ᵊnt\ *adj* [back-formation fr. *inadvertence, inadvertency*] **1** : not turning the mind to a matter : HEEDLESS, NEGLIGENT, INATTENTIVE ⟨an ~ remark⟩ **2** : UNINTENTIONAL ⟨~ violations of trade laws —*Current Biog.*⟩ — **in·ad·ver·tent·ly** *adv*

**in·advisability** \¦in+\ *n* : the quality or state of being inadvisable

**in·advisable** \¦in+\ *adj* [¹*in-* + *advisable*] : not advisable : INEXPEDIENT

**-i·nae** \ˈī(,)nē\ *n pl suffix* [NL, fr. L, fem. pl. of *-inus* -ine] : members of the subfamily of — in recent classifications substituted for the last syllable of the genitive case of the name of the type genus in all names of zoological subfamilies ⟨*Meliponinae*⟩

**in·aesthetic** \¦in+\ *adj* [¹*in-* + *aesthetic*] **1** : violating aesthetic canons or requirements : deficient in tastefulness or beauty : offensive from lack of beauty ⟨peered through those ~ spectacles —Maurice Cranston⟩ **2** : lacking aesthetic sensibility ⟨~ and quite unintellectual —A.L.Rowse⟩

**in·agglutinability** \¦in+\ *n* : the quality or state of being inagglutinable

**in·agglutinable** \"+\ *adj* [¹*in-* + *agglutinable*] : not subject to agglutination : not agglutinable

**in·a·ja** \,inəˈzhä\ *n* -s [Pg *inajá*, fr. Tupi] : a tall pinnate-leaved Brazilian palm (*Maximiliana regia*) with immense prickle-tipped spathes used for baskets, tubs, and other containers

**in·alienability** \(ˈ)in, ən+\ *n* : the quality or state of being inalienable

**in·alienable** \(ˈ)in, ən+\ *adj* [prob. fr. F *inaliénable*, fr. *in-* ¹in- + *aliénable* alienable — more at ALIENABLE] : incapable of being alienated, surrendered, or transferred ⟨~ human rights⟩ — compare INDEFEASIBLE — **in·alienableness** \"+\ *n* -ES — **in·alienably** \"+\ *adv*

**in all** *adv* : all told : ALTOGETHER ⟨some 70 ships *in all*⟩ ⟨*in all* we drove more than 40,000 miles⟩

**in alt** *adv (or adj)* : in the octave beginning with the second G above middle C ⟨ranging up to E *in alt*⟩ — see PITCH illustration

**in·alterability** \(ˈ)in, ən+\ *n* : the quality or state of being inalterable

**in·alterable** \(ˈ)in, ən+\ *adj* [ˈ*in-* + *alterable*, fr. F *altérable*, fr. *altérer* to alter + *-able* -able] : not alterable : UNALTERABLE — **in·alterably** \"+\ *adv*

**in altissimo** *adv (or adj)* [It, lit., in the highest] : in the octave beginning with the third G above middle C — see PITCH illustration

**in·amissible** \¦in+\ *adj* [F or LL; F, fr. LL *inamissibilis*, fr. L *in-* ¹in- + LL *amissibilis* amissible — more at AMISSIBLE] : incapable of being lost

**in·am·o·ra·ta** \(,)i,naməˈräd·ə, ə,n-\ *n* -s [It *innamorata*, fr. fem. of *innamorato*, past part. of *innamorare* to inspire with love, fr. *in-* ²in- + *amore* love, fr. L *amor* — more at AMOROUS] : a woman with whom one is in love or has intimate relations; *specif* : MISTRESS

**in·am·o·ra·to** \-äd·(,)ō\ *n* -s [It *innamorato*, fr. past part. of *innamorare*] : a male lover

**in-and-in** \¦=;=¦=\ *adv (or adj)* : in repeated generations of the same or closely related stock ⟨families . . . of one blood through mating or marrying *in-and-in* —F.H.Giddings⟩ ⟨this freak of color in range-bred horses is the result of *in-and-in* breeding —Andy Adams⟩

**¹in and out** *adv* **1** : alternately in and out ⟨he's been *in and out* all day⟩ **2** : to the last detail : EXHAUSTIVELY, THOROUGHLY ⟨understands his business *in and out*⟩ ⟨knew each other *in and out* —Virginia Woolf⟩

**²in and out** *n* : an obstacle found in fox hunting and steeplechasing consisting of two fences in close proximity but impossible to clear in the same jump

**in-and-out** \¦=;=¦=\ *adj* [¹*in and out*] : now good and now bad in performance ⟨an *in-and-out* showing —*Williams Alumni Rev.*⟩

**in-and-out bolt** *n* : a bolt running through from outside to inside of a ship's framing

**in-and-out bond** *n* : a masonry bond formed by headers and stretchers alternating vertically esp. at a corner

**in-and-out plating** *or* **in-and-out system** *n* : a system of construction for steel ships in which each alternate strake of plating laps over the edge of each adjoining strake

**¹inane** \(ˈ)i¦nān, əˈnān\ *adj, sometimes* -ER/-EST [L *inanis*] **1** : EMPTY, INSUBSTANTIAL ⟨azure of *inanest* space —Walter de la Mare⟩ **2** : lacking significance, meaning or profundity : SHALLOW, VACANT, FATUOUS, SILLY ⟨made some ~ remark on the weather —Joseph Conrad⟩; *also* : reflecting or indicating such condition ⟨an ~ face⟩ **syn** see INSIPID

**²inane** \"\ *n* -s : something that is empty : the emptiness of space ⟨a voyage into the limitless ~ —V.G.Childe⟩

**inane·ly** *adv* : in an inane manner

**inan·ga** \ˈē,näŋgä\ *n, pl* **inangas** *or* **inanga** [Maori] : any of several freshwater fishes (family Galaxiidae) of New Zealand and Tasmania

**¹in·animate** \(ˈ)in, ən+\ *adj* [LL *inanimatus*, fr. L *in-* ¹in- + *animatus*, past part. of *animare* to quicken, enliven, endow with breath or soul — more at ANIMATE] **1 a** : not animate : not endowed with life or spirit ⟨the inorganic world is ~⟩ : not endowed with consciousness or animal life ⟨trees are ~⟩ **b** : deprived of consciousness or of life ⟨an ~ body⟩ **c** *of a grammatical gender* : referring typically to dead things or things considered as dead — opposed to *animate* **2** : not animated or lively : DULL, SPIRITLESS ⟨her ~ movement when on the stage —W.B.Yeats⟩ — **in·animately** \"+\ *adv* — **in·animateness** \"+\ *n*

**²inanimate** *vt* [LL *inanimatus*, past part. of *inanimare*, fr. L *in-* ²in- + *animare*] *obs* : ANIMATE

**in·a·ni·tion** \,inəˈnishən\ *n* -s [ME *in-anisioun*, fr. ML *inanition-, inanitio*, fr. *inanitus* (past part. of *inanire* to make empty, fr. *inanis* empty, inane) + L *-ion-, -io* -ion] : the condition or result of being empty: **a** : the exhausted condition which results from a complete lack of food and water : MARASMUS **b** : absence or loss of social, moral, or intellectual vitality or vigor : LETHARGY ⟨an old society protects itself from ~ by expanding —Lovell Thompson⟩

**inan·i·ty** \əˈnanəd·ē, -ətē, -i\ *n* -ES [F or L; F *inanité*, fr. L *inanitat-, inanitas*, fr. *inanis* inane + *-itat-, -itas* -ity] **1** : the quality or state of being inane: as **a** : the condition of lacking all substance or content : EMPTINESS, HOLLOWNESS ⟨the present situation in the North is political ~ —J.V.Kelleher⟩ **b** : vapid, pointless, or fatuous character : lack of profundity : meaningless quality : SHALLOWNESS ⟨the ~ and dullness of most conversations —Hunter Mead⟩ ⟨a master who has suffered . . . from the ~ of his interpreters —A.E.Wier⟩ **2** : something that is foolish, trivial, or pointless ⟨fulsome *inanities* —Walker Evans⟩ ⟨the statement was a downright ~⟩

**in an·tis** \ənˈantəs\ *adv* [L, in antae] : between two antas ⟨a Greek Doric entrance *in antis* —Nikolaus Pevsner⟩

**in·apparent** \¦in+\ *adj* [¹*in-* + *apparent*] : not apparent; *specif* : not apparent clinically — used of subclinical infections

**in·appeasable** \¦in+\ *adj* [¹*in-* + *appeasable*] : UNAPPEASABLE

**in·appetence** \(ˈ)in, ən+\ *n* [¹*in-* + *appetence*] : lack of appetite ⟨complained of ~ and slight nausea —*Jour. Amer. Med. Assoc.*⟩ — **in·appetent** \"+\ *adj*

**in·applicability** \(ˈ)in, ən+\ *n* : the condition of being inapplicable

**in·applicable** \"+\ *adj* [¹*in-* + *applicable*] : not applicable : incapable of being applied : not adapted : not suitable — **in·applicableness** \"+\ *n* -ES — **in·applicably** \"+\ *adv*

**in·apposite** \(ˈ)in, ən+\ *adj* [¹*in-* + *apposite*] : not apposite : not pertinent ⟨so ~, so incongruous as to sound extremely bizarre —*Times Lit. Supp.*⟩ — **in·appositely** \"+\ *adv* — **in·appositeness** \"+\ *n*

**in·appreciable** \¦in+\ *adj* [prob. fr. F *inappréciable*, fr. MF *inappreciable*, fr. *in-* ¹in- + *appreciable* — more at APPRECIABLE] **1** *archaic* : INVALUABLE **2** : not appreciable : too small to be perceived ⟨became ~ at 615° C. —E.B.Shaud⟩ — **in·appreciably** \"+\ *adv*

**in·appreciation** \¦in+\ *n* [¹*in-* + *appreciation*] : lack of appreciation ⟨~ of his most vital criticism —F.R.Leavis⟩

**in·appreciative** \¦in+\ *adj* [¹*in-* + *appreciative*] : not appreciative — **in·appreciatively** \"+\ *adv* — **in·appreciativeness** \"+\ *n* -ES

**in·approachable** \¦in+\ *adj* [¹*in-* + *approachable*] : not approachable : INACCESSIBLE

**in·appropriate** \¦in+\ *adj* [¹*in-* + *appropriate*] : not appropriate : UNBECOMING, UNSUITABLE ⟨noise seems ~ in a place of sadness —Franz Boas⟩ — **in·appropriately** \"+\ *adv* — **in·appropriateness** \"+\ *n*

**in·apt** \(ˈ)in, ən+\ *adj* [¹*in-* + *apt*] : not apt: **a** : not suitable or appropriate ⟨a very ~ analogy⟩ **b** : not qualified or skilled : INEPT, INADEQUATE ⟨unstable, queer, ~ individuals —*Psychological Abstracts*⟩ — **in·apt·ly** *adv* — **in·apt·ness** *n* -ES

**in·aptitude** \(ˈ)in, ən+\ *n* [¹*in-* + *aptitude*] : lack of aptitude

**¹in·arch** \ən+\ *vt* [²*in* + *arch*] : to form an approach graft of or with ⟨successfully ~*ed* water sprouts to bridge rabbit damage on the apple trees⟩

**²in·arch** \ˈin+,-\ *n* -ES : APPROACH GRAFT; *also* : the plant resulting from a successful approach graft

**in·arguable** \(ˈ)in, ən+\ *adj* [¹*in-* + *arguable*] : not arguable — **in·arguably** \"+\ *adv*

**in·articulata** \¦in+\ *n pl, cap* [NL, fr. neut. pl. of *inarticulatus*] : a class of Brachiopoda comprising forms with unhinged usu. chitinophosphatic valves without teeth or sockets and including the orders Atremata and Neotremata

**in·articulate** \¦in+\ *adj* [LL *inarticulatus*, fr. L *in-* ¹in- + *articulatus*, past part. of *articulare* to utter distinctly — more at ARTICULATE] **1 a** *of a sound* : uttered or formed without the definite articulations which produce intelligible speech ⟨gave a little ~ grunt —Edith Wharton⟩ : indistinctly articulated or pronounced ⟨speech so ~ it resembled a growl⟩ **b** (1) : incapable of speech esp. under stress of emotion : MUTE ⟨almost ~ with excitement —Kenneth Roberts⟩ ⟨almost pathologically shy, he at times became totally ~ —C.B. Forcey⟩ (2) : intense or compelling to the point of preventing speech : not accompanied or attended by speech : incapable of being expressed by speech ⟨dazed with ~ pain —Edith Wharton⟩ ⟨~ misery⟩ (3) : not voiced or expressed : UNSPOKEN ⟨~ judicial notions of rightfulness or wrongfulness of motive —C.O.Gregory⟩ ⟨their ~ major premises —*Times Lit. Supp.*⟩ ⟨expressed the ~ feelings of many scientists —Harrison Brown⟩ **c** (1) : unable to speak coherently, forcefully, or purposefully ⟨remained stupidly ~, saying something noncommittal —Victoria Sackville-West⟩ ⟨~ as most of their class, they could do no more than utter bald phrases —Ruth Park⟩ (2) : having an incoherent or disjointed character ⟨the stumbling, almost ~, speech of the boy —G.W.Russell⟩ **d** : incapable of giving clear and effective expression to one's feelings, ideas, or aspirations in any way ⟨the vast majority of the natives are politically ~ —A.F.Macdonald⟩ **2** [NL *inarticulatus*, fr. ¹*in-* + *articulatus* jointed — more at ARTICULATA] **a** : not jointed : having no distinct body segments ⟨an ~ worm⟩ **b** : lacking a hinge — used esp. of certain brachiopod shells **c** [NL *Inarticulata*] : of, resembling, or relating to the Inarticulata **syn** see DUMB

**in·articulately** \"+\ *adv* : in an inarticulate manner

**in·articulateness** \"+\ *n* -ES : the quality or state of being inarticulate

**in ar·tic·u·lo mor·tis** \,i,närˈtikyə,lōˈmȯrd·əs\ *adv (or adj)* [L] : at the point of death ⟨the king appeared to be *in articulo mortis* —M.A.S.Hume⟩

**in·artificial** \(ˈ)in, ən+\ *adj* [L *inartificialis*, fr. *in-* ¹in- + *artificialis* artificial — more at ARTIFICIAL] **1** *archaic* : not characterized by art or skill : CLUMSY, INARTISTIC **2** : not characterized by affectation : ARTLESS, UNAFFECTED, PLAIN — **in·artificially** \"+\ *adv*

**in·artistic** \¦in+\ *adj* [¹*in-* + *artistic*] : not artistic : not conforming to the principles of art : lacking in taste or appreciation for art — **in·artistically** \"+\ *adv*

**-inas** *pl of* -INA

**in·as·much as** \¦inəzˈməchəz\ *conj* [ME *in as muche as*] **1** : in the degree that : insofar as ⟨everything else that is desired is desired *inasmuch as* it leads to pleasure —*Times Lit. Supp.*⟩ **2** : in view of the fact that : for the reason that : SINCE, BECAUSE ⟨should not be used for the relief of pain *inasmuch as* its analgesic value is slight —D.W.Maurer & V.H. Vogel⟩

**in·attention** \¦in+\ *n* [¹*in-* + *attention*] : failure to pay attention : DISREGARD

**in·attentive** \¦in+\ *adj* [¹*in-* + *attentive*] : not attentive : HEEDLESS, NEGLIGENT ⟨an ~ student⟩ — **in·attentively** \"+\ *adv* — **in·attentiveness** \"+\ *n*

**in·audibility** \(ˈ)in, ən+\ *n* : the quality or state of being inaudible

**in·audible** \(ˈ)in, ən+\ *adj* [LL *inaudibilis*, fr. L *in-* ¹in- + LL *audibilis* audible — more at AUDIBLE] : not audible : incapable of being heard ⟨his voice was hushed, almost ~ —E. K.Gann⟩ — **in·audibleness** \"+\ *n* -ES — **in·audibly** \"+\ *adv*

**¹in·au·gu·ral** \əˈnȯgyərəl, ÷ -g(ə)rəl\ *adj* [L *inaugurare* + E *-al*] **1** : relating to or performed or pronounced at a formal induction or investiture ⟨new recruits . . . are given an ~ address by their chief superintendent —*Times Lit. Supp.*⟩ ⟨the president's ~ address⟩ : held in connection with such an investiture ⟨an ~ ball⟩ — opposed to *exaugural* **2** : marking the commencement : being the first in a projected series ⟨an ~ meeting of a new historical society⟩ ⟨the ~ performance of a dramatic group⟩ ⟨the ~ run of the new luxury train —*Americas*⟩ ⟨the new association's ~ venture —W.F.Brown b. 1903⟩

**²inaugural** \"\ *n* -s **1** : an inaugural address **2** : the process or ceremony of inaugurating or of being inaugurated ⟨the president's ~ was held inside due to inclement weather⟩ ⟨will continue in that capacity until after the ~ —*N.Y. Times*⟩

**in·au·gu·rate** \əˈnȯgyə,rāt, ÷ -gə,r-, *usu* -ād·+V\ *vt* [L *inauguratus*, past part. of *inaugurare* to practice augury, to inaugurate, fr. *in-* ²in- + *augurare* to prophesy, augur; fr. the ceremonies connected with the telling of auguries — more at AUGUR] **1** : to introduce or induct into an office with suitable ceremonies or solemnities : invest with power or authority in a formal manner : INSTALL ⟨~ a president⟩ **2** : to begin, introduce, or mark a start or opening of: **a** : to dedicate, consecrate, or observe the opening or beginning of formally, auspiciously, and publicly ⟨a temple *inaugurated* by the emperor⟩ ⟨national assemblies and military expeditions were *inaugurated* by public prayers —G.L.Dickinson⟩ **b** : to start, commence, or institute sometimes publicly, ceremoniously, or formally with the prospect of continuing as a public service or beneficial agency or force ⟨passenger and freight service on the river was *inaugurated* in 1832 —*Amer. Guide Series: Maine*⟩ ⟨various conservation projects in the state have been *inaugurated* —*Amer. Guide Series: Del.*⟩ ⟨compulsory school attendance was not *inaugurated* . . . until 1919 —*Amer. Guide Series: Fla.*⟩ ⟨*inaugurated* the study of Greek —H.O. Taylor⟩ **c** : to begin or bring about the beginning of ⟨turning from the hero to the common man, we *inaugurated* the era of realism —J.W.Krutch⟩ ⟨until the Civil War *inaugurated* a new chapter in Kansas-Missouri relations —W.H.Stephenson⟩ **syn** see BEGIN

**in·au·gu·ra·tion** \=,==ˈrāshən\ *n* -s [L *inauguration-, inauguratio*, fr. *inauguratus* + *-ion-, -io* -ion] : the act or an instance of inaugurating: as **a** : investiture by appropriate ceremonies ⟨knighted by the king of Scotland on his ~ —L. G.Pine⟩ **b** : formal initiation, opening, or introduction ⟨~ of a new museum⟩ ⟨~ of a conference on educational problems⟩ **c** : beginning of the operation, use, or practice of something : START, INSTITUTION ⟨~ of a giant calculating machine . . . was announced —*Current Biog.*⟩ ⟨decided to postpone the ~ of fluoridation —J.M.Burns⟩ ⟨~ of scientific systems of tillage —Samuel Van Valkenburg & Ellsworth Huntington⟩

**inauguration day** *n, usu cap I & D* : a day set for the inauguration of the president of the U. S. now the January 20 but before 1934 the March 4 following the presidential election

**in·au·gu·ra·tor** \=ˈ==,rād·ə(r), -ātə-\ *n* -s : a person who inaugurates

**in·auspicious** \¦in+\ *adj* [¹*in-* + *auspicious*] : not auspicious : ILL-OMENED, UNLUCKY, UNPROPITIOUS ⟨you come at a singularly ~ moment —Rafael Sabatini⟩ **syn** see OMINOUS

**in·auspiciously** \¦in+\ *adv* : in an inauspicious manner

**in·authentic** \¦in+\ *adj* [¹*in-* + *authentic*] : not authentic — **in·authenticity** \(ˈ)in, ən+\ *n*

**in·balance** \(ˈ)in+\ *n* [¹*in-* + *balance*] : IMBALANCE ⟨physiological ~ in hyperthyroidism⟩

**inbd** *abbr* inboard

**in·bearing** \ˈ=,==\ *adj* [²*in* + *bearing*] *chiefly Scot* : OFFICIOUS

**¹in between** *adv* [²*in* + *between* (adv.)] : BETWEEN ⟨*in between* are the groves of banana trees —Henry Swanzy⟩

**²in between** *prep* [²*in* + *between* (prep.)] : BETWEEN ⟨came *in between* us⟩ ⟨*in between* the houses⟩

**¹in-between** \¦=;=ˈ=\ *n* -s [ *in between*] : INTERMEDIATE, INTERMEDIARY ⟨no *in-betweens*, no compromises —Richard Watts⟩ ⟨for the novice, the expert, or the *in-between* —Johannes Mattern⟩

**²in-between** \"\ *adj* [¹*in between*] : INTERMEDIATE ⟨his *in-between* stand on civil rights —*Newsweek*⟩ ⟨planning to carry *in-between* styles into spring —*N.Y. Times*⟩ ⟨this *in-between* status of the gibbon —Weston La Barre⟩

**inblowing** \ˈ=;==\ *adj* [⁴*in* + *blowing* (after *blow in*, v.)] : blowing inward or centripetally ⟨~ winds⟩

**¹inboard** \ˈ=,=\ *adv* [ˈ*in* + *board*] **1** : inside the line of a ship's bulwarks or hull : toward the center line of a ship — contrasted with *outboard* **2** : from without inward : toward the inside ⟨pull the throttle ~ —Clay Blair⟩ **3** : in a position closer or closest to the longitudinal axis of an aircraft ⟨flaps located ~ on a wing⟩

**²inboard** \"\ *adj* : located, moving, or being inboard ⟨~ engine⟩ ⟨~ section of a wing⟩

**inbond** \ˈ=;=\ *adj* [⁴*in* + *bond* (connection)] : laid across a wall : having bricks or stones laid as headers — opposed to *outbond*

**inborn** \ˈ=;=\ *adj* [²*in* + *born*] **1** : born in or with one : implanted by nature : NATURAL ⟨man's ~ desire to fly —H.G. Armstrong⟩ ⟨the ~ conservatism of man⟩ **2** : INHERITED, HEREDITARY ⟨the tendency toward schizophrenia was ~ —*N.Y. Times*⟩ **syn** see INNATE

**inbound** \ˈ=;=\ *adj* [²*in* + *bound*] **1** : inward bound ⟨an ~ ship⟩ ⟨~ baggage⟩ — contrasted with *outbound* **2** : relating to inward or inbound traffic ⟨~ station⟩

**inbounds line** \ˈ=,=\ *n* [fr. the phrase *in bounds*] : either of the broken lines running at right angles to the yard lines and dividing the field of play of a football field into three equal parts — see FOOTBALL illustration

**inbreak** \ˈ=;=\ *n* [⁴*in* + *break* (after *break in*, v.)] : a breaking in : INROAD, INVASION, INCURSION

**inbreathe** \ˈ=;=\ *vt* [²*in* + *breathe*] : to breathe (something) in : INHALE

**¹inbred** \ˈ=;=\ *adj* [²*in* + *bred*] **1** : bred within ⟨~ worth⟩ ⟨there was in him an ~ goodness —J.A.Froude⟩ **2** : subjected to or produced by inbreeding **syn** see INNATE

**²inbred** \ˈ=,=\ *n* -s : an individual resulting from the mating of closely related parents : a product of inbreeding

**in·breed** \ˈ=;=\ *vb* [²*in* + *breed*] *vt* **1** *archaic* : PRODUCE, GENERATE ⟨~ and cherish in a great people the seeds of virtue —John Milton⟩ **2** : to subject to inbreeding — compare CROSSBREED, OUTBREED ~ *vi, of closely related individuals* : to breed together

**inbreeding** \ˈ=,==\ *n* [fr. gerund of *inbreed*] **1** : the interbreeding of closely related individuals occurring naturally (as in a closed population), as a result of social or religious custom (as in some royal families), or as a deliberately chosen system of breeding (as of cattle or poultry) and serving esp. to preserve and fix desirable characters of and to eliminate unfavorable characters from a suitably selected stock but tending to effect an unwanted decline (as in size, vigor, or fertility) through the fixation of undesirable and often recessive characters when the initial stock is in any way defective — distinguished from *outbreeding*; compare LINEBREEDING **2 a** : confinement to a narrow range of intellectual and cultural resources issuing chiefly from a limited field of specialization ⟨the ~ of ideas —Joseph Pelej⟩ ⟨the ~ of continental philosophy —Max Rieser⟩ ⟨must avoid nationalist ~ —Mark Starr⟩ **b** : employment in an institution or locality of an excessive number of people who received their training there ⟨academic ~ is marked —Dallas Finn⟩

**inbring** \ˈ=;=\ *vt* [ME *inbringen*, fr. OE *inbringan* (prob. trans. of L *inferre* to bring in), fr. *in, inn* in (adv.) + *bringan* to bring — more at INFER, BRING] : to bring in; *esp* : to bring into court or to confiscate by legal process in Scots law

**inbuilt** \ˈ=;=\ *adj* [²*in* + *built*] : BUILT-IN ⟨the machine has no ~ knowledge of prime numbers —D.R.Hartree⟩

**¹in·bye** *also* **in·by** \(ˈ)in¦bī\ *adv* [²*in* + *bye* (var. of *by*), *by*, adv.] *chiefly Scot* : in an inward direction : INSIDE, WITHIN; *specif* : toward the workings of a mine

**²inbye** *also* **inby** \"\ *adj, chiefly Scot* : situated close by esp. near to the house ⟨the ~ land⟩

**³inbye** *also* **inby** \"\ *n, pl* **inbyes** *Scot* : land situated close by ⟨80 acres of ~⟩

**inc** *abbr* **1** [L *incisus*] engraved **2** inclosure **3** included; including; inclusive **4** income; incoming **5** incorporated; incorporation **6** increase **7** incumbent

**¹in·ca** \ˈiŋkə\ *n, pl* **incas** *also* **inca** *usu cap* [Sp, fr. Quechua *inka* king, prince, male of royal blood] **1 a** : a ruler of the Incaic Empire prior to the Spanish conquest **b** : a member of this empire's royal house; *broadly* : a person of high rank or exalted position under this empire **2 a** : a small Quechuan people of the valley of Cuzco in Peru that established hegemony over surrounding peoples to form the Incaic Empire from about 1100 until the Spanish conquest in 1531–35 **b** : any of the constituent Quechuan peoples of the Incaic Empire **3** : a member of an Inca people

**²inca** \"\ *adj, usu cap* : INCAIC

**In·ca·bloc** \-,bläk\ *trademark* — used for a shock-resistant balance jewel mounting and balance staff design in watches

**inca bone** *n, usu cap I* : the interparietal when developed as a separate bone in the skull (as frequently found in Peruvian mummies)

**inca dove** *n, usu cap I* : a small dove (*Scardafella inca*) found from Arizona to Central America

**in·ca·ic** \(ˈ)iŋ¦kāik, (ˈ)in¦-\ *adj, usu cap* [Sp *incaico*, fr. *inca* + *-ico* -ic (fr. L *-icus*)] : of or relating to the Incas or their empire

**in·calculability** \(ˈ)in, ən+\ *n* : the quality or state of being incalculable ⟨her alleged ~ turns out to be unscrupulousness which defies all morals —J.C.Blankenagel⟩

**in·calculable** \(ˈ)in, ən+\ *adj* [¹*in-* + *calculable*] : not capable of being calculated : UNPREDICTABLE ⟨the influence of environment on character is ~ and far-reaching —S.P.B.Mais⟩: as **a** : being beyond calculation : very great ⟨during the last few thousands of years, ~ quantities of hortatory literature have been produced —Aldous Huxley⟩ **b** : not foreseeable or foreseen ⟨justified in the most ~ way —Havelock Ellis⟩ : UNCERTAIN ⟨an ~ temper⟩ — **in·calculableness** \"+\ *n* -ES — **in·calculably** \"+\ *adv*

**in·ca·les·cence** \,inkəˈlesᵊn(t)s, ,iŋk-\ *n* -s [L *incalescere* + E *-ence*] : incalescent state : a growing warm or ardent

**in·ca·les·cent** \¦=;=ˈlesᵊnt\ *adj* [L *incalescent-, incalescens*, pres. part. of *incalescere* to become warm, fr. *in-* ²in- + *calescere* to become warm, incho. of *calēre* to be warm — more at LEE] : growing warm : increasing in ardor

**in-calf** \¦=;=\ *adj* [²*in* + *calf*] *of a cow, chiefly Brit* : PREGNANT

**in·caliculate** \¦in+\ *adj* [¹*in-* + *caliculate*] : having no calycle ⟨~ corals⟩

**inca magic flower** *n, usu cap I* : CANTUTA

**incamp** *obs var of* ENCAMP

**¹in·can** \ˈiŋkən\ *adj, usu cap* [¹*Inca* + *-an*] : INCAIC

**²incan** \"\ *n* -s *usu cap* **1** : an inhabitant or subject of the Incaic Empire **2** : QUECHUA 3a

**in·can·desce** \¦inkən¦des, -,kan-, -kaan-\ *vb* -ED/-ING/-S [L *incandescere*] *vi* : to be or become incandescent ~ *vt* : to cause to become incandescent

**in·can·des·cence** \,=(,)=ˈdesᵊn(t)s\ *n* -s [prob. fr. F, fr. *incandescent*] : the quality or state of being incandescent ⟨a single white flame, an ~ of the passion of avarice —Van Wyck Brooks⟩; *usu* : the glowing of a body due to its high temperature : emission by a hot body of radiation that renders it visible

**in·can·des·cent** \¦=(,)=ˈdesᵊnt\ *adj* [prob. fr. F, fr. L *incandescent-, incandescens*, pres. part of *incandescere* to become white, to become hot, fr. *in-* ²in- + *candescere* to become white, to become hot, incho. of *candēre* to shine, be white — more at CANDID] **1 a** : white, glowing, or luminous with intense heat ⟨~ carbon⟩ **b** : strikingly bright, radiant, or clear ⟨all those flowers ~ — the lilies, the roses, and clumps of white flowers and bushes of burning green —Virginia Woolf⟩ **c :** BRILLIANT, LAMBENT, LUCID ⟨set thoughts aglowing in ~ language —Antonio Iglesias⟩ ⟨wit⟩ ⟨one of his ~ masterpieces, the Symphony No. 99 —B.H.Haggin⟩ **d :** GLOWING, HOT, ARDENT ⟨a . . . youth ~ with martial ardor —*Times Lit. Supp.*⟩ **2 :** of, relating to, or being light produced by incandescence **:** producing light by incandescence ⟨the most common artificial light source is the ~ bulb —*This Is Glass*⟩ — compare INCANDESCENT LAMP, MANTLE 7a **syn** see BRIGHT

**incandescent lamp** *also* **incandescent** *n* -s **:** an electric lamp consisting essentially of a glass or quartz bulb evacuated or filled with an inert gas in which a filament commonly of tungsten gives off light when it is heated to incandescence by an electric current

3 2 4 1

incandescent lamp: *1* base, *2* lead-in wire, *3* filament, *4* bulb

**incandescent light** *n* **:** light from a source of incandescence

**in·can·des·cent·ly** *adv* **:** in an incandescent manner **:** with incandescence

**incandescent mantle** *n* **:** MANTLE 7a

**in·ca·ne·stra·to** \ˌēŋˌkänəˈsträ(ˌ)dō\ *n* -s [It *incanestrato, incannestrato*, fr. past part. of *incanestrare, incannestrare* to put into a basket, fr. *in-* (fr. L *in-* ²in-) + *canestro, cannestro* basket, fr. L *canistrum*; fr. its being poured into baskets and sold in this form — more at CANISTER] **:** a sharp white Sicilian cheese that is made of cow's milk often together with goat's milk, seasoned with salt and various spices, and used chiefly grated as a seasoning or garnish

**in·ca·nous** \ənˈkānəs\ *adj* [L *incanus*, back-formation fr. *incanescere* to become white, fr. *in-* ²in- + *canescere* to become white, incho. of *canēre* to be gray, white — more at CANESCENT] **:** hoary with white pubescence

**in·cant** \ənˈkant, -aa(ə)nt\ *vt* [L *incantare*] **1 :** ENCHANT, CHARM **2 :** to utter by way of incantation ⟨~*ing* garbled ritual to cast a spell⟩

**in·can·ta·tion** \ˌinˌkanˈtāshən, -kaan-\ *n* -s [ME *incantacioun*, fr. MF *incantation*, fr. LL *incantation-, incantatio*, fr. L *incantatus* (past part. of *incantare* to enchant) + *-ion-, -io* -ion — more at ENCHANT] **1 a :** a use of spells or verbal charms spoken or sung as a part of a ritual of magic **b :** a ceremonial chanting or reciting of incantations (as for curing disease) **c :** a use of words to obscure rather than illuminate **:** OBFUSCATION ⟨their habit of hypnotizing and magnetizing a subject by the ~*s* of repetitive argument —V.S.Pritchett⟩ **2 a :** a formula of words chanted or recited in a magic ritual for their special virtues or particular effects **b :** words used in the manner of a formula without conscious concern as to their aptness or relevance to a particular situation ⟨the ~*s* of the propagandists⟩ **c :** an expression (as of music or poetry) designed to move rather than amuse or convince ⟨uses repetition as it is used in spell and litany, as an ~ to heighten emotion, and perhaps to bypass reason —*Times Lit. Supp.*⟩ **3 :** MAGIC, SORCERY, ENCHANTMENT — **in·can·ta·tion·al** \ˌ≈ˌ≈ˈtāshənᵊl, -shnəl\ *adj*

**in·can·ta·to·ry** \ənˈkantəˌtōrē\ *adj* [L *incantatus* + E *-ory*] **:** constituting, employing, dealing with, or suitable for use in incantation ⟨mystic words with ~ power⟩ ⟨an ~ vocal style⟩

**in·capability** \(ˈ)in, ən+\ *n* **:** the quality or state of being incapable

**¹in·capable** \(ˈ)in, ən+\ *adj* [MF, fr. *in-* ¹in- + *capable* — more at CAPABLE] **1 :** lacking capacity, ability, or qualification for the purpose or end in view: as **a** *obs* **:** not able (as because of smallness) to take in, contain, hold, or keep **b** *obs* **:** not able to receive or endure **:** INTOLERANT **c** *archaic* **:** not being in a state to receive so as to be affected or moved or so as to be sensible **:** not receptive **:** not susceptible **d :** not in a state or of a kind to admit **:** not able to admit **:** INSUSCEPTIBLE — now used only with *of* **e :** not able or fit for the doing or performance **:** INCOMPETENT ⟨an ~ helper⟩ ⟨~ of understanding the matter⟩ ⟨~ of doing the work⟩ **2 a :** lacking legal qualification or power esp. because of some fundamental legal disqualification **b :** lacking the personal ability, power, or understanding required in some legal matter; *esp* **:** suffering from such a degree of mental or physical weakness as to require supervision of one's affairs by a court (as through a conservator) — compare INCOMPETENT, INSANE **c :** legally incompetent from any cause — not used technically — **in·capableness** \"+\ *n* -ES

**²incapable** \"\ *n* -s **:** one that is incapable or inefficient; *esp* **:** a person (as an imbecile or a simpleton) that is so by reason of defective mentality

**in·capably** \"+\ *adv* **:** in an incapable manner **:** without competence or capability; *esp* **:** to a degree that renders incapable ⟨~ drunk⟩

**in·capacious** \ˌin+\ *adj* [LL *incapac-, incapax* (fr. L *in-* ¹in- + *capac-, capax* capacious) + E *-ious* — more at CAPACIOUS] **1** *obs* **:** having little or insufficient size or capacity **:** CRAMPED, NARROW, STRAIT **2** *archaic* **:** mentally weak **:** lacking perception, insight, or understanding

**in·ca·pac·i·tate** \ˌinkəˈpasəˌtāt, -paas-, *usu* -ād.+V\ *vt* [*incapacity* + *-ate*] **1 :** to deprive of capacity or natural power **:** render incapable or unfit **:** DISABLE, DISQUALIFY ⟨age *incapacitated* him for war⟩ **2 :** to deprive of legal requisites or qualification **:** make legally incapable or ineligible ⟨in some states the appointment of a guardian ~*s* the ward from carrying on his business or from marriage⟩

**in·ca·pac·i·ta·tion** \ˌ≈ˌ≈≈ˈtāshən\ *n* **:** the act of incapacitating or state of being incapacitated **:** INCAPACITY

**in·capacity** \ˌin+\ *n* [F *incapacité*, fr. MF, fr. *in-* ¹in- + *capacité* capacity — more at CAPACITY] **:** the quality or state of being incapable **:** INABILITY, INCAPABILITY; *esp* **:** lack of physical or intellectual power or of natural or legal qualification

**in ca·pi·te** \(ˈ)inˈkäpəˌtā\ *adj* [L, in chief] *of a feudal tenant* **:** holding immediately of one's lord; *esp* **:** holding directly of the crown

**¹incapsulate** *var of* ENCAPSULATE

**²in·cap·su·late** \ənˈkapsələt, -ˌlāt\ *adj* [²in- + *capsule* + *-ate* (adj. suffix)] **:** ENCAPSULATED

**¹in·car·cer·ate** \ənˈkärs(ə)rət, -kȧs-, *usu* -əd.+V\ *adj* [L *incarceratus*] **:** IMPRISONED

**²in·car·cer·ate** \-səˌrāt, *usu* -ād.+V\ *vt* -ED/-ING/-S [L *incarceratus*, past part. of *incarcerare*, fr. *in-* ²in- + *carcer* prison] **1 :** to put in prison **:** IMPRISON **2 :** to shut up or away **:** CONFINE, ENCLOSE ⟨*incarcerated* in his own sensibility —J.P. Bishop⟩

**incarcerated** *adj, of a hernia* **:** IMPRISONED, CONFINED; *esp* **:** constricted but not strangulated

**in·car·cer·a·tion** \(ˌ)inˌ≈≈ˈrāshən, ən-\ *n* -s [LL *incarceration-, incarceratio*, fr. L *incarceratus* + *-ion-, -io* -ion] **1 :** a confining or state of being confined **:** IMPRISONMENT **2 :** abnormal retention or confinement of a body part; *specif* **:** a constriction of the neck of a hernial sac so that the hernial contents become irreducible

**in·car·cer·a·tor** \≈ˈ≈≈ˌrād·ə(r), -ātə-\ *n* -s **:** one that incarcerates

**in·car·di·nate** \ənˈkärdᵊnˌāt\ *vt* -ED/-ING/-S [LL *incardinatus*, past part. of *incardinare* to ordain as chief priest, fr. L *in-* ²in- + LL *cardinalis*, adj., principal — more at CARDINAL] **1 :** to adopt canonically or to receive formally (a cleric from another diocese) **2 :** to elevate to the cardinalate

**in·car·di·na·tion** \(ˌ)inˌ≈dᵊnˈāshən, ənˌ-\ *n* -s [LL *incardination-, incardinatio* appointment of a priest, fr. *incardinatus* + L *-ion-, -io* -ion] **:** the act of incardinating a cleric within the enrolled clergy of a diocese

**in·car·mined** \ənˈkärmənd, -kȧm-, -ˌmīnd *also* -ˌmēnd\ *adj* [²in- + *carmine* + *-ed*] **:** RED, REDDENED

**in·carn** \ənˈkärn\ *vb* -ED/-ING/-S [ME *incarnen*, fr. MF *incarner*, fr. LL *incarnare* to make flesh, make fleshy, incarnate — more at INCARNATE] *vt, archaic* **:** to cause to heal **:** cover with flesh ~ *vi, archaic* **:** to cause healing **:** become healed **:** heal over

**¹in·car·na·dine** \ənˈkärnəˌdīn, -ˌdən, -ˌdēn\ *adj* [MF *incarnadin*, fr. OIt *incarnadino, incarnatino*, fr. *incarnato* flesh-colored (fr. LL *incarnatus*, past part.) + *-ino* -ine (fr. L *inus*)] **1 :** of the color flesh or flesh pink **2 :** of a color of red hue

**²incarnadine** *also* **en·car·na·dine** \ənˈ-,enˈ-\ *vt* -ED/-ING/-S **:** to make incarnadine **:** REDDEN; *esp* **:** to dye flesh-colored, pink, red, or crimson

**³incarnadine** \"\ *n* -s **:** an incarnadine color

**¹in·car·nate** \(ˈ)inˈkärnət, ənˈk-, -kȧn-, -ˌnāt, *usu* \d.+V\ *adj* [ME *incarnat*, fr. LL *incarnatus*, past part. of *incarnare*] **1 a :** invested with flesh or bodily nature and form, esp. with human nature and form ⟨a monarch . . . regarded as a god ~ —D.L.Oliver⟩ ⟨an ~ spirit⟩ **b :** that is the very type or essence of ⟨purity ~⟩ ⟨that remote valley was peace ~⟩ ⟨confusion ~⟩; *broadly* **:** UTTER, UNSPEAKABLE ⟨a fiend ~⟩ **c :** made manifest or comprehensible **:** EMBODIED ⟨in the . . . United Nations there is now ~ the hope of people everywhere that this world may become one in spirit as it is in fact —H.L.Stimson⟩ **2 :** INCARNADINE — used chiefly of floral colors ⟨~ clover⟩

**²in·car·nate** \ənˈkärˌnāt, ˈinˌk-, -kȧˌn-, *usu* -ād.+V\ *vb* -ED/-ING/-S [LL *incarnatus*, past part. of *incarnare* to make flesh, make fleshy, incarnate, fr. L *in-* ²in- + *carn-, caro* flesh — more at CARNAL] *vt* **1 :** to make incarnate: as **a :** to give bodily form and substance to ⟨*incarnating* the devil as a serpent⟩ ⟨most peoples have some tradition of spiritual powers that ~ themselves as man⟩ **b :** to give a concrete or actual form to **:** embody in reality or in a more definite ideal form **:** ACTUALIZE ⟨~ a political theory in institutions⟩ ⟨*incarnating* ideals by helping others⟩ **c :** to constitute an embodiment or type of ⟨an international organization that ~*s* all our hopes for lasting peace⟩ ⟨in this man the spirit of the times is *incarnated*⟩ **2** *obs* **:** INCARN ~ *vi, obs* **:** INCARN

**in·car·na·tion** \ˌinˌkärˈnāshən, -kȧˈn-\ *n* -s [ME *incarnacioun*, fr. OF *incarnation*, fr. LL *incarnation-, incarnatio*, fr. *incarnatus* + L *-ion-, -io* -ion] **1 :** a clothing or state of being clothed with flesh **:** a taking on of or being manifested in a fleshly body **2 :** an incarnated being or idea: as **a** (1) **:** the embodiment of a deity or spirit in some form of earthly existence (as a person, an animal, or a plant) (2) *usu cap* **:** the union of divinity with humanity in Jesus Christ **b :** a concrete or actual form incorporating or exemplifying a principle, ideal, or other quality or concept **:** EMBODIMENT ⟨this busy grimy port, the very ~ of commerce and industry⟩; *esp* **:** a person showing a trait or typical character to a marked degree ⟨the very ~ of deceit⟩ **3** *archaic* **:** a rosy or red color **:** FLESH 6, CARNATION **4** *archaic* **:** a process or product of healing **5 :** a period of incarnation **:** time passed in a particular bodily form or state ⟨each ~ leading to a higher⟩ ⟨the old building had passed through several ~*s* as church, workshop, stable, and finally tearoom⟩

**in·car·na·tion·al** \ˌ≈ˌ≈ˈnāshənᵊl, -shnəl\ *adj* **:** of, relating to, or emphasizing incarnation or a doctrine of incarnation ⟨an ~ religion⟩

**in·car·na·tion·ist** \ˌ≈ˌ≈ˈnāsh(ə)nəst\ *n* -s **:** one that believes in the union of divinity with humanity in the person of Jesus Christ

**in·car·vil·lea** \ˌinˌkärˈvilēə\ *n* [NL, after Pierre d'*Incarville* †1757 Fr. Jesuit missionary] **1** *cap* **:** a genus of Asiatic herbs (family Bignoniaceae) with racemose trumpet-shaped flowers **2** -s **:** any plant of the genus *Incarvillea*

**incas** *pl of* INCA

**incase** *var of* ENCASE

**incast** \ˈ≈ˌ≈\ *n* [⁴in + *cast* (after *cast in*, v.)] *dial Eng* **:** something added for good measure

**incautelous** *adj* [¹in- + *cautelous*] *obs* **:** INCAUTIOUS

**in·caution** \(ˈ)in, ən-\ *n* [¹in- + *caution*] **:** lack of caution **:** CARELESSNESS, HEEDLESSNESS

**in·cautious** \"+\ *adj* [¹in- + *cautious*] **:** lacking in caution **:** INJUDICIOUS, HEEDLESS, CARELESS, RASH ⟨an ~ step⟩ ⟨~ talk⟩ ⟨an ~ reader⟩ — **in·cautiously** \"+\ *adv* — **in·cautiousness** \"+\ *n*

**in·ca·va·tion** \ˌinkəˈvāshən\ *n* -s [L *incavatus* (past part. of *incavare* to hollow out, fr. *in-* ²in- + *cavare* to hollow out, fr. *cavus* hollow) + *-ion-, -io* -ion — more at CAVE] **:** a hollow thing or place

**incave** *obs var of* ENCAVE

**in·ca·vo** \ēŋˈkä(ˌ)vō, ənˈkā(-\ *n* -s [It, lit., cavity, hollow, fr. *incavare* to make hollow, fr. L] **:** the part of an intaglio that is incised

**ince** *abbr* insurance

**in·celebrity** \ˌin+\ *n* [¹in- + *celebrity*] **:** lack of celebrity

**in·cend** \ənˈsend\ *vt* -ED/-ING/-S [L *incendere* to kindle, set on fire — more at INCENSE] *archaic* **:** INFLAME, EXCITE

**in·cen·di·a·rism** \ənˈsendēəˌrizəm\ *n* -s **1 :** a deliberate and unjustifiable setting of fire to property — compare ARSON, PYROMANIA **2 :** incendiary behavior ⟨party ~⟩

**in·cen·di·a·rist** \-ˌrəst\ *n* -s **:** INCENDIARY 1

**¹in·cen·di·ary** \-dēˌerē, -ri\ *n* -ES [L *incendiarius*, adj. & n., fr. *incendium* conflagration (fr. *incendere* to kindle, set afire) + *-arius* -ary — more at INCENSE] **1 a :** a person who deliberately sets fire to a building or other property **b :** an incendiary agent (as a bomb) **2 :** a person who excites or inflames factions and promotes quarrels or sedition **:** AGITATOR, EXCITER **3** *obs* **:** an exciting or causative factor esp. of something bad or unpleasant

**²incendiary** \"\ *adj* [L *incendiarius*] **1 :** of, relating to, or involving a deliberate burning of property ⟨~ fires⟩ ⟨an ~ crime⟩ **2 a :** tending to excite or inflame factions, sedition, or quarrels **:** INFLAMMATORY, SEDITIOUS ⟨an ~ speech⟩ ⟨~ literature⟩ **b :** sexually stimulating ⟨an ~ blonde⟩ **3 a :** igniting combustible materials spontaneously ⟨an ~ agent⟩ **b :** relating to, being, or involving the use of an explosive missile containing chemicals that ignite on bursting ⟨~ grenade⟩ ⟨~ warfare⟩ — see INCENDIARY BOMB

**incendiary bomb** *n* **:** a bomb that contains an incendiary agent (as jellied gasoline) and is designed to kindle fires at its objective — called also *fire bomb*

**in·cen·di·um** \ənˈsendēəm\ *n, pl* **incen·dia** \-ēə\ [ML, fr. L, conflagration] *Roman law & Roman Dutch law* **:** a crime corresponding to but of wider scope than arson in the English common law

**in·cen·sa·tion** \ˌinˌsenˈsāshən, ˌin(t)sənˈ-\ *n* -s [LL *incensatus* (past part. of *incensare*) + E *-ion*] **:** the action of censing

**¹in·cense** \ˈinˌsen(t)s *sometimes* -ˌsən-\ *n* -s [ME *encens*, *incense*, fr. OF *encens*, fr. LL *incensum* incense, fr. L, neut. of *incensus*, past part. of *incendere* to kindle, set on fire, irritate, fr. *in-* ²in- + *-cendere* to burn (akin to L *candēre* to shine, be glowing hot, be white) — more at CANDID] **1 :** material (as gums or woods) used to produce a fragrant odor when burned **2 :** the perfume or the smoke exhaled from spices and gums when burned in celebrating religious rites or as an offering to a deity; *broadly* **:** a pleasing scent or fragrance **3 :** pleasing attention **:** HOMAGE, FLATTERY **syn** see FRAGRANCE

**²in·cense** \" *sometimes* ənˈsen-\ *vb* -ED/-ING/-S [ME *encensen*, *incensen*, fr. MF *encenser*, fr. LL *incensare*, fr. *incensum*] *vt* **1 a :** to apply or offer incense to **:** burn incense before **b :** to burn or offer as an incense offering **2 a :** to perfume with or as if with incense **:** SCENT **b** *archaic* **:** FLATTER ~ *vi* **:** to burn or offer incense

**³in·cense** \(ˈ)inˈsen(t)s, ənˈs-\ *vt* -ED/-ING/-S [ME *encensen*, fr. MF *incenser*, fr. L *incensus*, past part. of *incendere* to kindle, set on fire, irritate — more at ¹INCENSE] **1** *obs* **a :** to set fire to **:** KINDLE **b :** to consume with fire **:** BURN **2 a** *archaic* **:** to excite (a passion or an emotion) into activity **:** cause to become aroused **b** *obs* **:** to inflame (a person) with a passion or emotion **c :** to cause to be extremely angry **:** arouse the wrath or indignation of ⟨such careless waste *incensed* her⟩ **3** *obs* **:** to urge to some course or action

**⁴incense** *obs var of* INSENSE

**incense burner** *n* **:** one that burns incense; *specif* **:** a vessel (as a stationary vase) for holding burning incense — compare CENSER

**incense cedar** *n* **:** any of various trees of the genus *Libocedrus*; *esp* **:** a tall tree (*L. decurrens*) of the No. American Pacific coast with a light soft straight-grained wood that is highly resistant to moisture, foliage suggesting that of a cypress, and cinnamon red bark — called also *pencil cedar, red cedar, white cedar*

**incensed** *adj* [fr. past part. of ³*incense*] **1 :** ANGERED, ENRAGED, INDIGNANT **2** *of a heraldic figure* **:** represented as enraged usu. by means of fire issuing from mouth and eyes

**incense juniper** *n* **:** a European juniper (*Juniperus thurifera*) with paired awl-shaped leaves whitened on the upper surface and fragrant wood that is sometimes burned as incense

**in·cense·less** \ˈ≈(ˌ)≈ləs\ *adj* **:** employing no incense ⟨~ churches⟩

**in·cense·ment** \ənˈsen(t)smənt\ *n* -s **:** the state of being incensed **:** intense anger or indignation

**incense shrub** *n* **:** INDIAN CURRANT 2

**incense tree** *n* **:** any of various chiefly tropical trees (as members of the genera *Commiphora, Boswellia*, and *Protium*) that produce fragrant gums or resins

**incense wood** *n* **:** the fragrant wood of either of two tropical American trees (*Protium heptaphyllum* and *P. guianense*)

**in·cen·so·ry** \ˈinˌsen(t)s(ə)rē, ənˈs-; ˈinsənˌsōrē\ *n* -ES [ML *incensorium*, fr. neut. of LL *incensorius* having burning power, fr. L *incensus* (past part. of *incendere* to kindle) + *-orius* -ory — more at INCENSE] **:** CENSER, THURIBLE

**incenter** \ˈ≈ˌ≈≈\ *n* [⁴*in* + *center*] **:** the center of a circle inscribed in a triangle or of a sphere inscribed in a tetrahedron

**¹in·cen·tive** \ənˈsentiv, -tēv *also* -t·əv\ *n* -s [ME, fr. LL *incentivum*, fr. neut. of L *incentivus*] **:** something that incites or has a tendency to incite to determination or action **:** something (as fear or hope of reward) that constitutes a motive or spur **:** INDUCEMENT ⟨money is still a major ~ in most occupations⟩ ⟨his father's promise of a bicycle was a real ~ to harder study⟩ **syn** see MOTIVE

**²in·cen·tive** \(ˈ)inˌs-, ənˈs-\ *adj* [LL *incentivus*, fr. L, setting the tune, fr. *incentus* (past part. of *incinere* to set the tune, fr. *in-* ²in- + *-cinere*, fr. *canere* to sing) + *-ivus* -ive — more at CHANT] **1 a :** serving to encourage, rouse, or move to action **:** STIMULATIVE **:** motivative in a particular direction or course ⟨increasing needs are often ~ to invention⟩ ⟨this charming book is ~ to further study⟩ **b** (1) **:** designed to enhance or improve production esp. in industry ⟨~ pay⟩ ⟨disadvantages of an ~ system⟩ (2) **:** concerned with, based on, or employing incentive measures or techniques in business or industry ⟨~ management⟩ ⟨long-term ~ experience⟩ ⟨~ studies⟩ **2** *obs* **:** serving to set on fire **:** KINDLING — **in·cen·tive·ly** \-təvlē, -li\ *adv*

**incentive wage** *n* **:** a wage based on the number of units produced by a factory pieceworker — compare BONUS SYSTEM

**¹in·cept** \ənˈsept\ *vb* -ED/-ING/-S [L *inceptus*, past part. of *incipere* — more at INCEPTION] *vt* **1** *archaic* **:** BEGIN, COMMENCE, UNDERTAKE **2** [influenced in meaning by L *capere* to take] **:** to take in: as **a :** INGEST ⟨phagocytes ~*ing* foreign particles⟩ **b :** to receive as a member ~ *vi* **:** to obtain an advanced degree and therewith the right to teach or practice a learned profession — now used only at Cambridge University

**²in·cept** \ˈinˌsept\ *n* -s **:** ANLAGE

**in·cep·tion** \ənˈsepshən\ *n* -s [L *inception-, inceptio*, fr. *inceptus* (past part. of *incipere* to begin, fr. *in-* ²in- + *-cipere*, fr. *capere* to take) + *-ion-, -io* -ion — more at HEAVE] **1 :** an act, process, or instance of beginning (as of an institution, organization, or concept) **:** COMMENCEMENT, INITIATION **2 :** an act of incepting: as **a :** a public lecture in which the candidate for a master's degree in a medieval university demonstrated his learning and competence to teach **b :** INGESTION **syn** see ORIGIN

**¹in·cep·tive** \-tiv\ *n* -s [LL *inceptivus*, adj.] **:** INCHOATIVE

**²in·cep·tive** \(ˈ)inˌs-, ənˈs-\ *adj* [LL *inceptivus*, fr. L *inceptus* (past part. of *incipere* to begin) + *-ivus* -ive — more at INCEPTION] **1 a :** BEGINNING **b :** relating to a beginning **2 :** INCHOATIVE 2 — **in·cep·tive·ly** \-təvlē\ *adv*

**in·cep·tor** \ənˈseptə(r), ˈinˌs-\ *n* -s [ME, fr. L, beginner, fr. *inceptus* + *-or*] **1** *Brit* **:** one that incepts at a university **2 :** one that begins or introduces

**in·cer·tae se·dis** \inˌkerˌtīˈsādəs, inˌsərdˌēˈsēdəs\ *adv* [L, of uncertain place] **:** in an uncertain position **:** without assurance of relationship — used of taxa ⟨the Acanthocephala have often been placed *incertae sedis* among the Nemathelminthes⟩

**incertain** *adj* [MF, fr. *in-* ¹in- + *certain*] *obs* **:** UNCERTAIN — **incertainly** *adv, obs* — **incertainty** *n, obs*

**in·certitude** \(ˈ)in, ən+\ *n* [MF, fr. LL *incertitudo*, fr. L *in-* ¹in- + LL *certitudo* certitude — more at CERTITUDE] **:** UNCERTAINTY: **a :** absence of assurance or confidence **:** DOUBT, INDECISION **b :** uncertain or insecure condition

**in·ces·san·cy** \ənˈsesᵊnsē, -nsi\ *n* -ES **:** the quality or state of being incessant

**in·ces·sant** \(ˈ)inˈsesᵊnt, ənˈs-\ *adj* [ME *incessaunt*, fr. LL *incessant-, incessans*, fr. L *in-* ¹in- + *cessant-, cessans*, pres. part. of *cessare* to delay — more at CEASE] **1 :** continuing or following without interruption **:** UNCEASING ⟨~ rains⟩ ⟨this ~ chatter⟩ **2** *obs* **:** EVERLASTING **syn** see CONTINUAL

**in·ces·sant·ly** *adv* [ME *incessauntly*, fr. *incessaunt* + *-ly*] **1 :** in an unceasing manner or course **:** without intermission or relief **:** CONTINUALLY ⟨the question ran ~ through his mind —Arnold Bennett⟩ ⟨poor and uncomfortable persons toiling ~ to create riches —G.B.Shaw⟩ **2** *archaic* **:** at once **:** IMMEDIATELY

**in·ces·sant·ness** *n* -ES **:** the quality or state of being incessant

**in·ces·sion** \ənˈseshən\ *n* [LL *incession-, incessio* pace, gait, fr. L *incessus* (past part. of *incedere* to go along, move forward, fr. *in-* ²in- + *cedere* to go, proceed) + *-ion-, -io* -ion — more at CEDE] *archaic* **:** movement onward or forward

**in·cest** \ˈinˌsest\ *n* -s [ME, fr. L *incestus* unchastity, incest (fr. *incestus* impure, unchaste, fr. *in-* ¹in- + *-cestus*, fr. *castus* pure, chaste) & *incestum*, fr. neut. of *incestus* — more at CASTE] **1 :** sexual intercourse or interbreeding between closely related individuals esp. when they are related or regarded as related (as by reason of affinity or membership in a tribal kinship, group, or clan) within degrees wherein marriage is prohibited by law or custom — compare ENDOGAMY, EXOGAMY, INBREEDING **2 :** the statutory crime of cohabitation, marriage, or sexual intercourse without marriage of parties related to each other within the degrees of consanguinity or often of affinity within which marriage is prohibited by law

**in·ces·tu·ous** \(ˈ)inˈses(h)chəwəs, ənˈs-, -)chəs\ *adj* [LL *incestuosus*, fr. L *incestus* incest + *-osus* -ous] **1 a :** constituting or involving incest ⟨an ~ relation⟩ ⟨~ unions⟩ **b :** of, relating to, or guilty of incest ⟨these ~ beasts⟩ **c :** begotten by incest ⟨~ offspring⟩ **2 :** INGROWN, DERIVATIVE, IMITATIVE — **in·ces·tu·ous·ly** *adv* — **in·ces·tu·ous·ness** *n* -ES

**¹inch** \ˈinch\ *n* -ES *often attrib* [ME *inch, inche*, fr. OE *ince, ynce*, fr. L *uncia* twelfth part, ounce, inch — more at OUNCE] **1 :** a unit of length equal to 1/36 yard or formerly to the length of 3 grains of barley placed end to end ⟨a 6-*inch* rule⟩ ⟨a width of six ~*es*⟩ — see MEASURE table **2 :** a small amount, distance, or degree (as of time or space) **:** a narrow margin or little bit ⟨escaped death by an ~⟩ ⟨couldn't see an ~ before them in the storm⟩ **3 inches** *pl* **:** STATURE, HEIGHT ⟨wore raised heels to make the most of his ~*es*⟩ ⟨a man of his ~*es* would be noticeable in any crowd⟩ **4 a :** a fall (as of rain or snow) sufficient to cover a surface or to fill a gage to the depth of one inch ⟨two ~*es* of rain⟩ **b :** a degree of atmospheric or other pressure sufficient to balance the weight of a column of mercury or other specified liquid one inch high in a barometer or manometer ⟨an atmospheric pressure of 30 ~*es*⟩ **c :** WATER-INCH **d** *chiefly Midland* **:** one twelfth of the light period of a day ⟨worked a full 12 ~*es* getting in the hay⟩ **e :** COLUMN INCH — **by inches** *also* **inch by inch** *adv* **:** very gradually or slowly — **by inch of candle :** by auction in which bidding is open only while a small piece of candle burns — **every inch** *adv* **:** to the utmost degree **:** ENTIRELY ⟨looks *every inch* a winner⟩ — **within an inch of :** almost to the point of **:** nearly to **:** very near ⟨broke down when we were *within an inch of* our destination⟩ ⟨came *within an inch of* death⟩

**²inch** \"\ *vb* -ED/-ING/-ES *vi* **:** to advance or retire by small degrees ⟨~*ed* back from the lip of the crevasse⟩; *broadly* **:** to move slowly or in little increments ⟨~*ing* along the slippery ridge⟩ ⟨Canada and the U.S. are ~*ing* back to the unity of action achieved 10 years ago —M.W.Straight⟩ ⟨prices are ~*ing* down⟩ ~ *vt* **1 :** to cause to advance or retire by small degrees ⟨~*ed* himself nearer⟩; *broadly* **:** to cause to move slowly or in little increments ⟨~*ing* their feet slowly over the ice⟩ ⟨~*ing* not only the U.S. but the United Nations forward into a war that did not have to be fought —H.L.Ickes⟩ **2** *obs* **:** to give sparingly **:** deal out in small amounts

**³inch** \"\ *n* -ES [ME *inch, ynche*, fr. ScGael *innis*; akin to OIr *inis* island, W *ynys*, Bret *enez*] **1** *now dial* **:** ISLAND — often used in the names of small islands off the coast of Scotland ⟨*Inchcolm*⟩ ⟨*Inchkeith*⟩ **2** *now dial* **:** low grassy ground by a river

**inch** *abbr* inchoative

**inchant** *obs var of* ENCHANT

**incharitable** *adj* [ME, fr. ¹*in-* + *charitable*] *obs* **:** UNCHARITABLE

**incharity** *n* [¹*in-* + *charity*] *obs* **:** lack of charity

**inchase** *archaic var of* ENCHASE

**inched** \ˈincht\ *adj* [¹*inch* + *-ed*] **:** having or measuring a specified number of inches ⟨a 4-*inched* hook⟩

**inch·er** \ˈinchə(r)\ *n* -s [¹*inch* + *-er*] **:** something having a dimension of a specified number of inches; *specif* **:** a gun having a bore of a specified number of inches — usu. used in combination with a numeral ⟨heard the 14-*inchers* firing on the coast⟩

**in chief** *adj* **1 :** heading a staff **:** LEADING — often used in combination ⟨editor-*in-chief*⟩ **2 :** PRIMARY, BASIC, INITIAL ⟨evidence *in chief*⟩ ⟨a fabric dutiable on its *in chief* value of wool⟩

**inch·ling** \ˈinchliŋ\ *n* -s [¹*inch* + *-ling*] **:** a small being of a kind likely to grow larger ⟨drew in a netful of ~*s*⟩

**inch·ma·ree clause** \ˈinchmə,rē-\ *n, usu cap I* [after *Inchmaree*, Brit. steamer; fr. its formulation as a result of the sinking of the Inchmaree in Liverpool harbor March, 1884] **:** a clause in a marine insurance policy on the hull of a ship that assuming the owners and managers of the ship have exercised due diligence makes the underwriter liable for loss or damage to hull or machinery arising from the negligence of the master, charterers, mariners, engineers or pilots from explosions, bursting of boilers, breakage of shafts, or any latent defect in hull and machinery, from contact with aircraft or land conveyances, or from any accident at docking facilities (as when loading or unloading or entering a dry dock)

**inch·meal** \ˈ⸗,mē(ə)l\ *adv* [¹*inch* + *-meal* (as in *piecemeal*)] **:** little by little **:** GRADUALLY — often used with *by*

**¹in·cho·ate** \(ˈ)inˈkōət, ənˈkō-, ˈinkə,wāt\ *adj* [L *inchoatus*, *incohatus*, past part. of *inchoare*, *incohare* to begin (lit., to hitch up), fr. *in-* ²in- + *cohum* strap fastening a plow beam to the yoke; perh. akin to Bret *morgo* hame, W *mynci* hame, OE *haga* hedge — more at HEDGE] **:** being recently begun or under-taken **:** INCIPIENT **:** being partly but not fully in existence or operation **:** INCOMPLETE: as **a :** imperfectly formed or formulated **:** DISORDERED, INCOHERENT, UNORGANIZED ⟨the general plan is ~ and incoherent, and the particular treatments disconnected —Hilary Corke⟩ ⟨the solar system . . . far out from the hub of this great wheel of stars and ~ dust and gas —L.C. Eiseley⟩ ⟨vague consumer longings and ~ needs —J.S.Gambs⟩ **b** *of a legal right or instrument or interest* **:** not yet perfected **:** not yet made certain or specific **:** not yet vested **:** INCIPIENT, EXPECTANT, POTENTIAL, CONTINGENT, IMPERFECTED ⟨an ~ right of dower⟩ ⟨an ~ equity⟩ ⟨an instrument that the law requires to be recorded is an ~ instrument until it is recorded —Besse May Miller⟩ — **in·cho·ate·ly** *adv* — **in·cho·ate·ness** *n* -ES

**²in·cho·ate** \ˈinkə,wāt, ənˈkō,āt\ *vb* -ED/-ING/-S [L *inchoatus*, *incohatus*, past part. of *inchoare*, *incohare*] *vt, archaic* **:** to cause to begin ~ *vi, archaic* **:** to make a beginning **:** START

**in·cho·a·tion** \,inkəˈwāshən\ *n* -s [LL *inchoation-*, *inchoatio*, *incohation-*, *incohatio*, fr. L *inchoatus*, *incohatus* + *-ion-*, *-io* -ion] **:** an act of beginning **:** COMMENCEMENT, INCEPTION

**¹in·cho·a·tive** \(ˈ)inˈkōəd·iv, ənˈk-\ *n* -s [LL *inchoativum*, *incohativum*, fr. neut. of *inchoativus*, *incohativus*] **:** an inchoative verb

**²inchoative** \"\ *adj* [LL *inchoativus*, *incohativus*, fr. L *inchoatus*, *incohatus* + *-ivus* -ive] **1 :** INITIAL, FORMATIVE ⟨~ stages⟩ **2 :** denoting the beginning of an action, state, or occurrence — used of certain verbs (as *begin*, *set out*, *get*, *awake*) or of certain verb forms (as *tremesco* "I fall to trembling" and some other Latin verbs in *-sco*) — **in·cho·a·tive·ly** \-d·əvlē\ *adv*

**in·chon** \(ˈ)inˈchän\ *adj, usu cap* [fr. *Inchon*, Korea] **:** of or from the city of Inchon, Korea **:** of the kind or style prevalent in Inchon

**inch–ounce** *n* **1 :** a unit of work equal to the work done in raising one ounce against the force of gravity through a distance of one inch **2 :** a unit of moment equal to the moment of a force of one ounce acting at a distance of one inch from a center of moments

**inch plant** *n* **:** a wandering Jew (*Tradescantia fluminensis*) that is often grown as a house plant

**inch–pound** \ˈ⸗ˈ⸗\ *n* **:** one twelfth of a foot-pound

**inch–ton** \ˈ⸗ˈ⸗\ *n* **:** a unit of energy or work that is equal to the work done in raising one ton against the force of gravity the height of one inch

**¹inchworm** \ˈ⸗,⸗\ *n* [¹*inch* + *worm*] **:** LOOPER 1

**²inchworm** \"\ *vb* **:** CRAWL

**in·cide** \ənˈsīd\ *vb* -ED/-ING/-S [L *incidere* — more at INCISE] *vi* **1** *archaic* **:** CUT, INCISE **2** *obs* **:** to cause loosening or resolution ~ *vt* **1** *archaic* **:** to cut into (as a lesion or tissue) **2** *archaic* **:** to cause loosening or resolution of (as phlegm)

**in·ci·dence** \ˈin(t)səd·ən(t)s *also* -dᵊn- *or* -,den-\ *n* -s [ME, fr. MF, fr. LL *incidentia*, fr. L *incident-*, *incidens* + *-ia* -y] **1** *now chiefly dial* **:** INCIDENT **2 a :** an act or the fact or manner of falling upon or affecting **:** OCCURRENCE ⟨diseases of domestic ~ —*Science*⟩ ⟨control of both the ~ of expense and the meeting of expense must lie primarily in the hands of management⟩ **b :** rate, range, or amount of occurrence or influence ⟨a rising ~ of poverty⟩; *sometimes* **:** the rate of occurrence of new cases of a particular disease in a population being studied — compare PREVALENCE **3 :** the falling of a tax upon a person who is unable to shift it onto someone else and who therefore bears the money burden of the tax ⟨the ultimate ~ of most corporation taxes is on the consumer⟩ — compare DIRECT TAX **4 a :** the arrival of something (as a projectile or a ray of light) at a surface **b :** ANGLE OF INCIDENCE 2

**incidence wire** *n* **:** STAGGER WIRE

**incidency** *obs var of* INCIDENCE

**¹in·ci·dent** \-nt\ *n* -s [ME, fr. MF, fr. ML *incident-*, *incidens*, fr. L, pres. part. of *incidere* to fall into, fall on, meet up with, occur, happen, fr. *in-* ²in- + *-cidere* (fr. *cadere* to fall) — more at CHANCE] **1 a :** an occurrence of an action or situation felt as a separate unit of experience **:** an occurrence or sometimes a situation or thing taking place as part of a larger continuum but unimportant or nonessential **:** HAPPENING ⟨conflict is an inevitable ~ in any active system of cooperation —Lewis Mumford⟩ **b :** an accompanying minor occurrence or condition **:** CONCOMITANT ⟨Madison's view . . . that taxation is a necessary ~ anyway to the exercise of any power —C.P.Curtis⟩ **c :** an occurrence noticeably varying a set or accustomed course or routine **:** an uncommon happening ⟨to remain at variance with his wife seemed to him a considerable ~ —Joseph Conrad⟩ **d :** an occurrence calling forth a sequel **:** a motivating event or situation **:** FACTOR ⟨the ~ of that conflict was slavery, but it was not its true cause —*Congressional Record*⟩ **e :** a happening or related group of happenings subordinate to a main narrative plot ⟨the melodrama and the romance . . . must be made up of swift successions of startling ~ —E.G.Sutcliffe⟩ **f :** a frequent, accustomed, or routine occurrence unworthy of note or comment ⟨a quite ordinary ~ of daily life —Arnold Bennett⟩ **2 a :** a contretemps, fracas, disturbance, or other action likely to lead to grave consequences esp. in matters diplomatic ⟨repeated minor ~*s* led finally to the danger of open combat at the boundary —*Amer. Guide Series: Maine*⟩ **b :** a military situation marked by fighting without formally declared war ⟨the Korea ~⟩ **c** *chiefly Brit* **:** a bomb explosion or other sudden violent disturbance ⟨air-raid wardens checking on ~*s*⟩ **3 a :** something dependent upon, appertaining or subordinate to, or accompanying something else of greater or principal importance ⟨an alimony agreement may be an ~ of a divorce proceeding⟩ **b :** something arising or resulting from something else of greater or principal importance ⟨a power to employ a broker may be an ~ of an express power to sell real estate⟩ **syn** see OCCURRENCE

**²incident** \"\ *adj* [ME, fr. L *incident-*, *incidens*, pres. part.] **1 a :** occurring or likely to occur esp. as a minor consequence or accompaniment ⟨confusion ~ to a quick change⟩ **:** associated or naturally related or attaching ⟨the privileges ~ to increased rank⟩ **b** *obs* **:** PERTINENT, APPOSITE, LIABLE, SUBJECT **2** *archaic* **:** occurring accidentally and without essential relationship **:** INCIDENTAL **3** *law* **:** dependent on or appertaining to another thing **:** directly and immediately relating to or involved in something else though not an essential part of it **4 a :** falling or striking on something — used esp. of light rays on a plane **b :** acting from without **:** EXTERNAL ⟨attacks by ~ forces⟩ **syn** see LIABLE

**¹in·ci·den·tal** \ˌ⸗⸗ˈdentᵊl\ *adj* [¹*incident* + *-al*; prob. influenced in meaning by ML *incidenter* incidentally, adv., fr. L *incident-*, *incidens*] **1 :** subordinate, nonessential, or attendant in position or significance: as **a :** occurring merely by chance or without intention or calculation **:** occurring as a minor concomitant ⟨allowing a few dollars extra for ~ expenses⟩ ⟨the ~ gain which such a policy may win —J.A.Hobson⟩ ⟨man may be an ~ host of the sheep liver fluke⟩ **b :** being likely to ensue as a chance or minor consequence — usu. used with *to* ⟨labor problems ~ to rapidly expanding factories —*Amer. Guide Series: Mass.*⟩ **c :** lacking effect, force, or consequence **:** not receiving much consideration or calculation ⟨a cool, purely ~, and passive contempt —Herman Melville⟩ **d :** presented purposefully but as though without consideration or intention; *often* **:** DIGRESSIVE ⟨an ~ allusion, purposely thrown out, to the day of the week —Charles Dickens⟩ **2 :** met or encountered casually or by accident **:** CHANCE ⟨~ traveling companions⟩ ⟨an ~ shipboard acquaintance⟩ **syn** see ACCIDENTAL

**²incidental** \"\ *n* -s **1 :** something that is incidental **:** a subordinate or incidental item ⟨no such ~ as personal sensibilities can be allowed to interfere with the overall plan of the survey⟩ **2 incidentals** *pl* **:** minor items (as of expense) that are not particularized ⟨a bill for tuition and ~*s*⟩

**in·ci·den·tal·ist** \ˌ⸗⸗ˈdentᵊləst\ *n* -s **:** one that is more concerned with the minutiae of incident than with broad overall views or concepts

**in·ci·den·tal·ly** \ˌ⸗⸗ˈdentlē, -tᵊlē, -li\ *adv* **1 :** by chance **:** as a matter of minor import **:** CASUALLY ⟨in this discussion grave questions were ~ brought up⟩ **2 :** by way of interjection or digression **:** in passing **:** PARENTHETICALLY ⟨touching ~ on the waterpower values⟩ ⟨another leading industry, ~, has quadrupled its business in five years⟩

**incidental music** *n* **:** descriptive music played or to be played during the action of a play to heighten a situation or project a mood (as of a battle, a storm, a death scene) or to relate directly to stage action (as a song or a dance); *broadly* **:** any music related to a play (as an overture or entr'acte) — compare BACKGROUND MUSIC

**in·ci·den·tal·ness** \ˌ⸗⸗ˈdentᵊlnəs\ *n* -ES **:** the quality or state of being incidental **:** CONCOMITANCE

**in·ci·dent·less** \ˈin(t)sədəntləs, -dᵊn-, -,den-\ *adj* **:** free from incident **:** UNEVENTFUL

**in·ci·dent·ly** \ˈin(t)sədəntlē, -dᵊn-, -li, ˌ⸗⸗ˈdent- — *in sense 2 always the last*\ *adv* **1 :** so as to be incident **2 :** INCIDENTALLY

**inciding** *pres part of* INCIDE

**in·ci·en·so** \,in(t)sēˈen(t)(,)sō\ *n* -s [AmerSp, fr. Sp, incense, fr. L *incensum* — more at INCENSE] **:** a shrubby encelia (*Encelia farinosa*) of rocky desert uplands of the southwestern U. S. and adjacent Mexico that has grayish green to almost white tomentose foliage and showy cymes of yellow flowers and that produces a resin that has been used as incense, in folk medicine, and in varnish

**in·cin·er·ate** \ənˈsinə,rāt, *usu* -ād.+V\ *vb* -ED/-ING/-S [ML *incineratus*, past part. of *incinerare*, fr. L *in-* ²in- + *ciner-*, *cinis* ashes; akin to Gk *konis*, *konia* ashes, dust; basic meaning: to rub, scratch, tickle] *vt* **:** to cause to burn to ashes **:** consume by or as if by fire ⟨*incinerating* the trash⟩ ~ *vi* **:** to be or become completely burned ⟨paper and dry leaves ~ easily⟩

**in·cin·er·a·tion** \(,)in,sinəˈrāshən, ən,-\ *n* -s [ML *incineration-*, *incineratio*, fr. L *incineratus* (past part. of *incinerare* to incinerate) + *-ion-*, *-io* -ion] **:** the act of incinerating or the state of being incinerated **:** CREMATION; *esp* **:** an analytical procedure of heating an organic substance with free access to air until only its ash remains — compare IGNITION

**in·cin·er·a·tor** \ˈ⸗ˈ⸗,rād·ə(r), -ātə-\ *n* -s **:** one that incinerates; *esp* **:** a furnace or a container for incinerating waste materials

incinerators

**¹in·cip·i·a·tive** \ənˈsipē,ād·iv, -ēəd-\ *adj* [*incipient* + *-ative*] *of a verb form or aspect* **:** expressing action about to begin or just beginning — compare HABITUATIVE

**²incipiative** \"\ *n* -s **:** an incipiative form of a verb

**in·cip·i·en·cy** \ənˈsipēənsē, -si\ *also* **in·cip·i·ence** \-ēən(t)s\ *n, pl* **incipiencies** *also* **incipiences** **:** the state or fact of being incipient **:** BEGINNING, COMMENCEMENT

**in·cip·i·ent** \(ˈ)inˈsipēənt, ənˈs-\ *adj* [L *incipient-*, *incipiens*, pres. part. of *incipere* to begin, fr. *in-* ²in- + *-cipere* (fr. *capere* to take) — more at HEAVE] **:** beginning to be or become apparent **:** COMMENCING, INITIAL ⟨the ~ stage of a fever⟩ ⟨~ light of day⟩ ⟨~ civil disorders⟩ — **in·cip·i·ent·ly** *adv*

**incipient species** *n* **:** a natural population that is more or less interfertile with another related population but is inhibited from interbreeding in nature by some specific barrier — compare ECOSPECIES

**incipient wilting** *n* **:** partial and temporary loss of turgor in a plant that occurs in the presence of adequate soil moisture and is associated with excessive water loss through transpiration

**in·ci·pit** \ˈin(t)səpət, ˈiŋkə-, *esp in senses b & c* ˈinchə-\ *n* -s [L, it begins, 3d pers. sing. pres. indic. of *incipere*] **:** BEGINNING: as **a :** the introductory words or part of a medieval manuscript or early printed book ⟨reproducing two ~*s* with superb miniatures —Raphael Levy⟩ — compare EXPLICIT **b :** the opening words of the text in a Gregorian chant or psalm tone sung usu. by the cantor **c :** the word given at the beginning of the tenor in a cantus-firmus motet that serves as a reference to the tenor's origin in the liturgy

**in·circumscription** \ˈin+\ *n* [LL *incircumscription-*, *incircumscriptio*, fr. *incircumscriptus* not circumscribed (fr. L *in-* ¹in- + *circumscriptus*, past part. of *circumscribere* to circumscribe) + L *-ion-*, *-io* -ion — more at CIRCUMSCRIBE] *archaic* **:** the quality or state of being free from bounds or limits

**incircumspect** *adj* [LL *incircumspectus*, fr. L *in-* ¹in- + *circumspectus*, past part. of *circumspicere* to look around, be cautious — more at CIRCUMSPECT] *obs* **:** IMPRUDENT, INDISCREET — **incircumspection** *n, obs* — **incircumspectly** *adv, obs*

**incis** *abbr* [L *incisus*] engraved

**in·ci·sal** \(ˈ)inˈsīzəl\ *adj* [L *incisus* + E *-al*] **:** CUTTING ⟨the ~ edge of a tooth⟩

**in·cise** \(ˈ)inˈsīz, -īs\ *vb* -ED/-ING/-S [MF or L; MF *inciser*, fr. L *incisus*, past part. of *incidere*, fr. *in-* ²in- + *-cidere* (fr. *caedere* to cut) — more at CONCISE] *vi, obs* **:** to make an incision ~ *vt* **1 :** to cut into **:** make an incision in ⟨*incised* the swollen tissue⟩ **2 a :** to carve figures, letters, or devices into **:** ENGRAVE ⟨~ a tablet with an inscription⟩ **b :** to produce (as letters, figures, or devices) by carving into a surface ⟨~ an inscription on a monument⟩ **3 a :** to produce (a narrow steep-walled valley) by downward erosion ⟨caused the streams to ~ their valleys —C.O.Dunbar⟩ **b :** to lower (itself) by eroding a deeper channel ⟨the streams then *incised* themselves to the new baselevel —C.O.Dunbar⟩ **c :** to intersect as a deep narrow cut ⟨more than twenty different submarine canyon systems ~ the continental border —J.C.Crowell⟩

**incised** *adj* **1 a :** CUT-IN, CARVED, ENGRAVED ⟨~ ornamentation⟩; *esp* **:** decorated with incised figures ⟨~ pottery⟩ **b** *of a cut or wound* **:** made with or as if with a sharp knife or scalpel **:** clean and well defined **2 :** having a margin that is deeply and sharply and more or less irregularly notched ⟨an ~ leaf⟩

**incised meander** *n* **:** the curve of a winding river with steep slopes on both sides rising to a former floodplain and usu. interpreted as due to rejuvenation of a meandering stream but prob. also formed by a combination of vertical and lateral erosion in a single cycle of valley development — compare ENTRENCHED MEANDER

**in·ci·si·form** \inˈsīzə,fȯrm, -īsə-\ *adj* [*incisor* + *-iform*] **:** having the form of or resembling a typical incisor tooth **:** shaped for cutting

**in·ci·sion** \ənˈsizhən\ *n* -s [ME *inscicioun*, fr. MF & L; MF *incision*, fr. L *incision-*, *incisio*, fr. *incisus* + *-ion-*, *-io* -ion] **1 a :** a separation of parts made or such as might be made by a cutting or pointed instrument (as a notch in the margin of a leaf or of an insect's wing) **b :** CLEFT, CUT, GASH; *specif* **:** an incised wound made by a surgeon into the tissues or an organ (as in reaching a site of injury or establishing drainage) ⟨an abdominal ~⟩ **2 :** an act or action of incising (as into a substance) ⟨a Pliocene uplift which caused valley ~ —A.M. Bateman⟩ ⟨the surgeon's skillful ~ of the tissues⟩ **3 :** the quality or state of being incisive (as in comprehension or action) **:** ACUTENESS, PENETRATION

**in·ci·sive** \(ˈ)inˈsīsiv, ənˈsī-, |ēv *also* |əv *sometimes* -īz\ *adj* [ML *incisivus*, fr. L *incisus* + *-ivus* -ive] **1 :** having a cutting edge or piercing point **:** facilitating cutting or piercing ⟨as sharp and ~ as the stroke of a fang —T.B.Costain⟩ **2 :** marked by sharpness and penetration esp. in keen clear unmistakable resolution of matter at issue or in pointed decisive effectiveness of presentation ⟨the clear, ~ genius which could state in a flash the exact point at issue —A.N.Whitehead⟩ ⟨the . . . ~ irony . . . serves to put the literary crackpots in their proper place —S.C.Chew⟩ **3 :** of, relating to, or situated near the incisors

**syn** CLEAR-CUT, CRISP, TRENCHANT, CUTTING, BITING: INCISIVE indicates a keen penetration and sharp presentation that is effective or decisive ⟨Bismarck's will had not that *incisive*, rapier quality, that quality of highly tempered steel — flexible, unbreakable, of mortal effect, decisive, a sword — which had Richelieu's —Hilaire Belloc⟩ CLEAR-CUT indicates either unmistakably clear and lucid outlining, analysis, or presentation, or finite certainty defying disbelief or question ⟨this *clear-cut* and consistent political creed is set forth throughout with the lucidity and brevity that makes a first-class popular orator —*Times Lit. Supp.*⟩ ⟨the current decision . . . was neither *clear-cut* nor definite . . . it appeared to be an attempted compromise —*N.Y. Times*⟩ CRISP in this series has a variety of suggestions: keenness, freshness, clarity, animation, terseness, vigor, sureness, effectiveness ⟨a languorous work . . . with occasional interludes of *crisp* brilliance —Anthony West⟩ ⟨*crisp* epigrams —George Santayana⟩ TRENCHANT suggests sharp penetrating acuteness often in criticism or detraction and may suggest sarcastic asperity ⟨a *trenchant* critic of the rising capitalism, delighting in exposing the fallacies of the new economics and in pricking the bladders of political reputations —V.L.Parrington⟩ CUTTING and BITING apply to sharp sarcasm, ridicule, or detraction; the former may suggest a tendency to wound by penetrating acuteness, the latter a mordant, implacable harshness ⟨the *cutting* sarcasm . . . the cruel epigrams and occasional harsh witticisms —Jack London⟩ ⟨domineering and censorious of any that stood in his way, with a *biting* wit, although he mellowed somewhat as he grew older —T.D.Bacon⟩

**incisive bone** *n* **:** PREMAXILLA

**incisive foramen** *n* **:** a pit or in some animals two pits just behind the incisor teeth transmitting the nasopalatine nerves and the greater palatine artery

**incisive fossa** *n* **:** a depression on the front of the maxillary bone above the incisor teeth

**in·ci·sive·ly** \|əvlē, -li\ *adv* **:** in an incisive manner: as **a :** CUTTINGLY ⟨outspokenly and ~ critical —W.A.Taylor⟩ **b :** with exactitude and precision ⟨high-court judges of long experience cannot ~ say how many laws are still in force —Mark Priestley⟩ ⟨enabled him to prove ~ that the concept of a Jewish race was erroneous —W.D.Wallis⟩

**in·ci·sive·ness** \|ivnəs, |ēv- *also* |əv-\ *n* -ES **:** the quality or state of being incisive; *esp* **:** concise precision of utterance or action

**in·ci·sor** \ənˈsīzə(r), ˈin,s- *sometimes* -īsə-\ *n* -s *often attrib* [NL, fr. LL, one that cuts, fr. L *incisus* + *-or*] **:** a tooth adapted for cutting; *esp* **:** one of the cutting teeth in mammals arising from the premaxillary bone of the upper jaw in front of the canines when canines are present or one of the corresponding teeth of the lower jaw — see DENTITION illustration

**in·ci·su·ra** \,in,sīˈzhu̇rə, ,in(t)sə'zh-\ *or* **in·ci·sure** \ənˈsīzhə(r)\ *n, pl* **incisu·rae** \-ü,rē\ *or* **incisures** [L *incisura*, fr. *incisus* + *-ura* -ure] **:** a notch, cleft, or fissure esp. of a body part or organ — **in·ci·su·ral** \ˌin,sīˈzhu̇rəl, ˌin(t)səˈzh-; (ˈ)inˈsīzhərəl\ *adj*

**¹in·cit·ant** \ənˈsītᵊnt\ *adj* [L *incitant-*, *incitans*, pres. part. of *incitare* to incite] **:** INCITING, CAUSATIVE, STIMULATING ⟨~ of infection⟩ ⟨an ~ factor⟩

**²incitant** \"\ *n* -s **:** an inciting agent; *esp* **:** a factor (as an infective agent) that is the essential causative agent of a particular disease ⟨where the fungal ~ is present mildew is likely to damage foliage in cold wet weather⟩

**in·ci·ta·tion** \,in,sīˈtāshən, ,in(t)sə'-\ *n* -s [MF, fr. L *incitation-*, *incitatio*, fr. *incitatus* (past part. of *incitare* to incite) + *-ion-*, *-io* -ion] **1 :** an act of inciting **:** STIMULATION **2 :** something that incites to action **:** INCITEMENT, INCENTIVE ⟨provocative statements that were an open ~ to violence⟩

**in·cite** \ənˈsīt, *usu* -īd.+V\ *vt* -ED/-ING/-S [MF *inciter*, fr. L *incitare*, fr. *in-* ²in- + *citare* to put in movement, summon — more at CITE] **1 :** to move to a course of action **:** stir up **:** spur on **:** urge on ⟨*inciting* the people to rebel⟩ ⟨*incited* to further effects by his mother's enthusiasm⟩ **2 :** to bring into being **:** induce to exist or occur ⟨such behavior is likely to ~ retaliation⟩ ⟨organisms that readily *incited* antibody formation⟩

**syn** INSTIGATE, FOMENT, ABET: INCITE may indicate both an initiating, a calling into being or action, and also a degree of prompting, furthering, encouraging, or nurturing of activity ⟨his projects for *inciting* war between the two countries⟩ ⟨posters scattered by the thousands throughout the eastern states and Europe to *incite* immigration —*Amer. Guide Series: Minn.*⟩ ⟨their tutors had *incited* them to dig deeply in the older sources of learning⟩ ⟨did I see a young lady in want of a partner, gallantry would *incite* me to offer myself as her devoted knight —T.L.Peacock⟩ INSTIGATE implies initiating or encouraging others to initiate actions or feelings, often questionable actions initiated with dubious intention ⟨pogroms *instigated* or connived at by the government as a safety valve for popular discontent —W.R.Inge⟩ ⟨a comparative study, *instigated* by the director of the investigation, which classifies a series of nonliterate cultures⟩ FOMENT indicates persistent inciting, esp. of something thought of as seething or boiling ⟨radicals *fomenting* a rebellion⟩ ⟨race theories are indeed not only a modern invention to explain such group conflicts, but also a means for *fomenting* them —M.R.Cohen⟩ ABET is likely to indicate seconding, encouraging, or aiding some action already begun, esp. a questionable activity ⟨aiding and *abetting* a friend in obtaining money under false pretenses⟩ ⟨the general, *abetted* by the excited aide-de-camp, made a fatal error⟩ ⟨the will to achieve perfection, though not so rare as it sounds, is all too rarely *abetted* by leisure —Harry Levin⟩

**in·cite·ment** \-ītmənt\ *n* -s **1 :** the act of inciting or the state of being incited ⟨through emotional ~ of each other . . . they discover paths they need to know —Kathleen Sproul⟩ **2 :** something that incites **:** INCENTIVE ⟨an ~ to further progress⟩

**in·cit·er** \-īd·ə(r), -ītə-\ *n* -s **:** one that incites

**in·cit·ing·ly** *adv* **:** so as to incite **:** in an inciting manner

**in·ci·tive** \(ˈ)inˈsīd·iv, ənˈs-\ *adj* **:** tending to incite **:** expressive of incitement

**in·ci·to·ry** \-d·ərē\ *adj* **:** serving to excite **:** STIMULATORY

**incity** \(ˈ)⸗ˈ⸗, ˈ⸗,⸗⸗\ *adj* [fr. the phase *in city*] **:** lying wholly within or serving the area within a city ⟨~ and suburban bus lines⟩ ⟨the ~ edition of the paper⟩

**in·civic** \(ˈ)⸗+\ *adj* [¹*in-* + *civic*] **:** lacking civic responsibility

**in·civil** \"+\ *adj* [MF, fr. LL *incivilis*, fr. L *in-* ¹in- + *civilis* civil — more at CIVIL] **:** not civil **:** RUDE, BARBAROUS

**in·civility** \ˈin+\ *n* [MF *incivilité*, fr. LL *incivilitat-*, *incivilitas*, fr. *incivilis* + L *-itat-*, *-itas* -ity] **1** *obs* **:** INCIVILIZATION **2 :** the quality or state of being uncivil **:** ill-bred behavior **:** DISCOURTESY, RUDENESS ⟨is it ~ to refuse to answer when spoken to⟩ ⟨never before met with such ~⟩ **3 :** a rude or ill-bred act ⟨tired of his constant *incivilities*⟩

**in·civilization** \(ˌ)in+\ *n* [¹*in-* + *civilization*] **:** the state of being uncivilized

**in·civism** \(ˈ)in+\ *n* [F *incivisme*, fr. *in-* ¹in- + *civisme* civism — more at CIVISM] **:** lack of civic-mindedness or of patriotism

**incl** *abbr* **1** inclosure **2** included; including; inclusive

**inclasp** *var of* ENCLASP

**incld** *abbr* included

**incle** *var of* INKLE

**in–clearing** \ˈ⸗,⸗⸗\ *n* [⁴*in*] *Brit* **:** the checks received for payment by a bank during the process of clearing

**in·clem·en·cy** \(ˈ)in, ən+\ *n* [L *inclementia*, fr. *inclement-*, *inclemens* + *-ia* -y] **:** the quality or state of being inclement: as **a :** severity of weather **:** STORMINESS ⟨the ~ of the exposed slope⟩ **b :** harshness or cruelty of action or disposition ⟨an honest man but with great ~ of spirit⟩

**in·clem·ent** \(ˈ)in¦klemənt, ən'k- *sometimes* 'inklәmənt\ *adj* [L *inclement-, inclemens*, fr. *in-* ¹in- + *clement-, clemens* clement — more at CLEMENT] **:** lacking clemency: as **a** *of the elements or weather* **:** physically severe **:** HARSH, ROUGH, STORMY ⟨~ weather⟩; *also* **:** marked by such weather ⟨an ~ day⟩ **b :** severe in temper or action **:** UNMERCIFUL, RIGOROUS ⟨the harsh sentence of an ~ judge⟩ — **in·clem·ent·ly** *adv* — **in·clem·ent·ness** *n* -ES

**in·clin·able** \ən'klīnəbəl\ *adj* [ME, fr. MF *enclinable, inclinable*, fr. *encliner, incliner* to incline + *-able* — more at INCLINE] **1 a :** having an inclination toward something **:** DISPOSED ⟨had formerly been very ~ to dissipation⟩ **b :** disposed to favor or think well of **:** FAVORABLE ⟨~ to our pleas⟩ **2 :** having a tendency **:** tending to or toward ⟨somewhat ~ to corpulence⟩ ⟨a heavy soil but ~ to bake and dry out⟩ **3 :** capable of being inclined ⟨an ~ punch press⟩

**in·cli·na·tion** \ˌinklə'nāshən, ˌiŋk-\ *n* -S [ME *inclinacioun*, fr. MF *inclination*, fr. L *inclination-, inclinatio*, fr. *inclinatus* (past part. of *inclinare*) + *-ion-, -io* -ion] **1 :** an act or the action of bending or inclining: as **a :** a bending forward of the head or body (as in respect, greeting, or acknowledgment) **:** BOW, NOD ⟨acknowledged his greeting with a slight ~⟩ **b :** a tilting of something **2 a** *obs* **:** natural disposition **:** NATURE, CHARACTER **b** *obs* **:** a turning of the mind in a particular direction **:** ATTENTION **c :** a particular disposition of mind or character **:** PROPENSITY, BENT ⟨a man of fixed ~s⟩; *usu* **:** favorable disposition esp. toward a particular thing, activity, or end **:** LIKING, DESIRE ⟨a strong ~ toward study⟩ ⟨an ~ to make the best of things⟩ **3 a :** direction or trend out of the true vertical or horizontal ⟨the ~ of a column⟩ ⟨the roadbed had considerable ~⟩ **b :** amount of deviation from the vertical or horizontal **:** degree or rate of slope or slant **:** GRADE ⟨an ~ of 20 degrees⟩ **c :** an inclined surface **:** SLOPE, INCLINE ⟨worked their way down the steep ~⟩ **d** (1) **:** the angle determined by two lines or planes ⟨the ~ of two rays of light⟩ (2) *in plane analytic geometry* **:** the angle made by a line with the x-axis measured counterclockwise from the positive direction of that axis **4 a :** a tendency to a particular aspect, state, character, or action ⟨men judge by the complexion of the sky the state and ~ of the day —Shak.⟩ ⟨some ~ to snow⟩ ⟨the clutch had an ~ to slip⟩ **b :** something to which one is inclined **:** an object of habit or favor **:** LIKING **5 :** DIP 3b **6 :** ENCLISIS — **in·cli·na·tion·al** \¦==¦nāshənᵊl, -shnəl\ *adj*

**inclination of an orbit :** the angle between the plane of the orbit and the plane of the ecliptic

**in·cli·na·tor** \'==ˌnād·ə(r)\ *n* -S [*inclination* + *-or*] **:** a stand with rockers for inclining a carboy to the required angle for pouring

**in·cli·na·to·ry** \ən'klīnəˌtōrē\ *adj* [L *inclinatus* + E *-ory*] **:** tending to incline or capable of inclining ⟨the ~ power of a dowsing rod⟩

**¹in·cline** \ən'klīn\ *vb* -ED/-ING/-S [ME *inclinen, enclinen*, fr. MF *encliner, incliner*, fr. L *inclinare*, fr. *in-* ²in- + *-clinare* to bend — more at LEAN] *vi* **1 :** to bend the head or body forward **:** BOW ⟨*inclining* toward the speaker to hear more clearly⟩ **2 :** to lean, tend, or become drawn esp. toward an opinion or course of conduct **:** favor an opinion, a course of conduct, or a person ⟨~ as we grow older more and more to traditional ways⟩ ⟨his heart *inclined* to the child⟩ **3 :** to deviate from a line, direction, or course **:** LEAN ⟨converging lines ~ toward each other⟩; *specif* **:** to deviate from the vertical or horizontal ⟨the shaft ~s almost 30 degrees⟩ ⟨snow-laden birches *inclining* over the road⟩ **4** *of a military formation* **:** to march or move obliquely to the front so as to gain ground on the flank as well as forward ~ *vt* **1 :** to cause to stoop or bow **:** BEND ⟨*inclining* her head in greeting⟩ **2 :** to orient in the direction of **:** impart a trend toward, liking for, or interest in **:** influence in favor of something (as a course, interest, view) ⟨increasing knowledge ~s one to further study⟩ ⟨tried to ~ him to help⟩ **3 :** to cause to deviate physically esp. from the horizontal or vertical **:** arrange in a slanting position **:** give a bend, slope, or slant to ⟨rays of light are *inclined* in passing through a medium of high refractive index⟩ ⟨*inclining* the rake against the fence⟩ **4 :** to heel (a ship) experimentally to determine stability or center of gravity — **incline one's ear :** to listen with favor **:** hear and approve

**²in·cline** \'inˌklīn, ən'k-\ *n* -S **:** an ascending or descending inclined plane **:** GRADE, GRADIENT, SLOPE: as **a :** an inclined mine shaft or inclined portion of an otherwise vertical shaft — compare ADIT **b** (1) **:** a railway track and supporting structure on a grade extending from an adjustable apron or bridge at a transfer slip (2) **:** a railway built on a slope on which cars are raised and lowered by means of a mechanically operated cable

**in·clined** \ən'klīnd *or esp in sense 2* 'inˌk-\ *adj* [ME *enclined, inclined*, fr. past part. of *enclinen, inclinen*] **1 :** having inclination, disposition, or tendency **:** well disposed **2 a :** having a leaning or slope usu. from the vertical or horizontal ⟨an ~ roadway⟩ ⟨an ~ stem⟩ **b :** making an angle with a line or plane

**inclined plane** *n* **1 :** a plane surface that makes an oblique angle with the plane of the horizon **:** a sloping plane **2 :** an inclined track on which trains or boats are raised or lowered from one level to another

**incline man** *n* **:** DILLYMAN

**in·clin·er** \ən'klīnə(r), 'inˌk-\ *n* -S **:** one that inclines

**¹inclining** *n* -S [ME *enclining, inclining*, fr. gerund of *enclinen, inclinen*] **1 :** INCLINATION, DISPOSITION **2** *archaic* **:** those who incline toward (as a person or a cause) **:** PARTY, FOLLOWING

**²in·clin·ing** \ən'klīniŋ, 'inˌk-, -nēŋ\ *adj* [fr. pres. part. of ¹*incline*] **:** LEANING, BENT: as **a** *of a plant part* **:** bent out of a perpendicular position ⟨an ~ stem⟩ **b :** ENCLITIC 1

**in·cli·nom·e·ter** \ˌinklə'nämәd·ə(r), -ˌklī'n-\ *n* [²*incline* + *-o-* + *-meter*] **1 :** an apparatus for determining the direction of the earth's magnetic field with reference to the plane of the horizon — see DIP CIRCLE, EARTH INDUCTOR **2 :** a machinist's clinometer **3 a :** an instrument for indicating the inclination to the horizontal of an esp. longitudinal axis of a ship or an airplane; *broadly* **:** any of various instruments for indicating inclination (as of the base of an oil well) **b :** an instrument giving the attitude of an airplane with reference to true gravity — called also *absolute inclinometer*

**in·clip** \ən+\ *vt* [²*in* + *clip*] *archaic* **:** CLASP, ENCLOSE

**incln** *abbr* inclusion

**incloister** *obs var of* ENCLOISTER

**inclose** *var of* ENCLOSE

**in·clud·able** *or* **in·clud·ible** \ən'klüdəbəl\ *adj* **:** capable of being included **:** proper or suitable for inclusion

**in·clude** \ən'klüd\ *vt* -ED/-ING/-S [ME *includen, encluden*, fr. L *includere*, fr. *in-* ²in- + *-cludere* (fr. *claudere* to close) — more at CLOSE] **1 :** to shut up **:** CONFINE, ENCLOSE, BOUND ⟨the nutshell ~s the kernel⟩ ⟨that divine spark *included* in every human being⟩ **2 a :** to place, list, or rate as a part or component of a whole or of a larger group, class, or aggregate ⟨*included* a sum for tips in his estimate of expenses⟩ **b :** to take in, enfold, or comprise as a discrete or subordinate part or item of a larger aggregate, group, or principle ⟨in search of a formula which should cover everything . . . even if it *included* more than I wished —T.S.Eliot⟩ **3** *obs* **:** to bring to an end **:** TERMINATE

**syn** SUBSUME, EMBRACE, COMPREHEND, IMPLY, INVOLVE, IMPLICATE: INCLUDE and SUBSUME agree in indicating the enclosure or containment by a larger class or whole of a smaller class or specific item or part. INCLUDE, the more common term, may call more attention to the single item or smaller class by stressing the fact of its existence or the fact of its not having been overlooked ⟨it would not be argued today that the power to regulate does not *include* the power to prohibit —O.W. Holmes †1935⟩ ⟨numerous pretty things, or things supposed to be pretty . . . *including* such absurdities as paper knives with fretwork handles —Herbert Spencer⟩ SUBSUME, orig. a technical term in logic and still an erudite term, may call more attention to the larger class or more comprehensive principle, may stress the fact of its existence ⟨free verse . . . is a larger rhythmic movement which *subsumes* other rhythms —J.L. Lowes⟩ ⟨I suggest that in every beautiful building its uses, its representative elements, are indeed *subsumed* into the form —Samuel Alexander⟩ EMBRACE may sometimes suggest marked effort at enclosing; it may be used with that which is vast or is quite varied in designation or classification ⟨Virginia . . . *embraced* in its possessions the present states of West Virginia, Kentucky, Ohio, Illinois, Indiana, Michigan, and Wisconsin —C.G.Bowers⟩ ⟨freedom of speech . . . *embraces* all discussion which enriches human life and helps it to be more wisely led —Zechariah Chafee⟩ COMPREHEND may suggest a noteworthy range or scope in which something is enclosed or held ⟨to find universal law, to *comprehend* all experience in a closed system —W.R.Inge⟩ ⟨to *comprehend* in a single view polities of the most varied and discrepant character —G.L. Dickinson⟩ IMPLY, INVOLVE, and IMPLICATE indicate somewhat similar relationships. IMPLY suggests drawing attention by inference to a certain existence or relationship, not by direct statement ⟨ordinarily imitation is enough to *imply* that the matter imitated is important at least to the sale of the goods —O.W.Holmes †1935⟩ It is applicable to what is logically inferential but not absolutely certain ⟨it would be argued that culture *implies* a certain freedom from parochialism —Bertrand Russell⟩ INVOLVE, on the other hand, may apply to more certain relationship and connection since it may postulate a necessary effect or consequence ⟨in every genuine metaphysical debate some practical issue, however conjectural or remote, is *involved* —William James⟩ ⟨faith *involves* an act of the will —W.R.Inge⟩ IMPLICATE postulates through one actuality or existence the fact of another but fails to suggest an effect or consequence ⟨purpose *implicates* in the most organic way an individual self —John Dewey⟩ ⟨colors are sumptuous and rich just because a total organic resonance is deeply *implicated* in them —John Dewey⟩ ⟨a catalyzing agent has been compared to a parson, who marries others without participating in the event himself. He is *implicated*, but not *involved* —L.K.Anspacher⟩

**in·clud·ed** \ən'klüdəd, 'inˌk-\ *adj* **:** ENCLOSED, CONFINED, EMBRACED ⟨an ~ angle⟩: as **a :** not projecting beyond the mouth of the corolla — used of a stamen and pistil; opposed to *exserted* **b** *of a lower jaw* **:** overlapped by the upper jaw — **in·clud·ed·ness** *n* -ES

**included phloem** *n* **:** phloem tissue lying within the secondary xylem (as in the wood of some dicotyledons)

**included sapwood** *n* **:** masses or streaks of tissue in heartwood that have the appearance and characteristics of sapwood

**in·clud·er** \ən'klüdə(r)\ *n* -S **:** one that includes

**in·clud·ing** \ən'klüdiŋ, 'inˌk-, -dēŋ\ *adj* **:** serving to enclose or cover ⟨an ~ membrane⟩

**in·cluse** \'inˌklüs, ən'k-, -üz\ *n* -S [ME, fr. L *inclusus*, fr. past part. of *includere* to enclose, include — more at INCLUDE] **:** a recluse who is voluntarily immured (as in a cave, hut, or isolated cell)

**in·clu·sion** \ən'klüzhən\ *n* -S [L *inclusion-, inclusio*, fr. *inclusus* + *-ion-, -io* -ion] **1 :** the act of including or the state of being included ⟨the ~ of domestic . . . reforms in the social program of the government —H.C.Atyeo⟩ **2 :** something that is included: as **a :** a gaseous, liquid, or solid and usu. minute foreign body enclosed in the mass of a mineral **b :** a passive product of cell activity (as a starch grain) visible within the protoplasm **c :** solid and usu. minute foreign particles (as of slag) enclosed in a solid metal **3 :** a relation between two classes that obtains when all members of the first are also members of the second — contrasted with *membership*

**inclusion body** *n* **:** a rounded or oval intracellular body that consists of elementary bodies in a matrix, is characteristic of certain virus diseases, and is believed to represent a stage in the multiplication of the virus

**inclusion disease** *n* **:** a virus disease of infants marked by the presence of inclusion bodies in the nucleus and cytoplasm of cells in the organs most affected (as lungs, liver, brain)

**in·clu·sive** \ən'klüs|iv, 'inˌk-, |ēv *also* -üz| *or* |əv\ *adj* [ML *inclusivus*, fr. L *inclusus* + *-ivus* -ive] **1 :** ENCLOSING, ENCOMPASSING ⟨~ walls⟩: as **a :** broad in orientation or scope ⟨the concept of history adopted . . . is modern and ~ —C.V.Woodward⟩ ⟨dance is not as ~ an art as literature —George Balanchine⟩ **b :** covering or intended to cover all items, costs, or services ⟨an ~ fee⟩ **c** *of a Protestant Christian church* **:** extending fellowship to Protestant Christians without regard to rigidly sectarian barriers **d** *in grammar* **:** referring to the speaker and another or some others including the hearer **2 :** comprehending the stated limits or extremes ⟨from Monday to Friday ~⟩ — opposed to *exclusive* — **in·clu·sive·ly** \|əvlē, -li\ *adv* — **in·clu·sive·ness** \|ivnəs, |ēv- *also* |əv-\ *n* -ES

**inclusive of** *prep* **:** containing as an integral part ⟨the whole cost *inclusive of* materials⟩

**in·coagulable** \¦in+\ *adj* [¹*in-* + *coagulable*] **:** incapable of coagulating

**in·coercible** \"+\ *adj* [¹*in-* + *coercible*] **1 :** incapable of being controlled, checked, or confined ⟨the ~ power of the ballot⟩ **2 a :** not reducible to a liquid by pressure — compare PERMANENT GAS **b** *archaic* **:** incapable of being confined in or excluded from vessels — used of a so-called imponderable fluid (as heat, light, electricity)

**in·cog** \'inˌkäg, ən'k-\ *adv or adj or n* [by shortening] **:** INCOGNITO

**in·cog·i·ta·bil·i·ty** \(ˌ)inˌkäjəd·ə'bilәd·ē, ən,==='===\ *n* **:** the quality or state of being incogitable

**in·cogitable** \(ˈ)in, ən+\ *adj* [L *incogitabilis* unthinking, unthinkable, fr. *in-* ¹in- + *cogitabilis* cogitable — more at COGITABLE] **:** impossible to accept or believe **:** UNTHINKABLE, INCONCEIVABLE

**incogitancy** *n* -ES [L *incogitantia*, fr. *incogitant-, incogitans* + *-ia* -y] *obs* **:** lack of thought or of the power of thinking **:** THOUGHTLESSNESS

**in·cog·i·tant** \(ˈ)in¦käjəd·ənt, ən'k-\ *adj* [L *incogitant-, incogitans*, fr. *in-* ¹in- + *cogitant-, cogitans*, pres. part. of *cogitare* to cogitate — more at COGITATE] **1 :** failing in due consideration of proper or relevant factors **:** inattentive and heedless **:** THOUGHTLESS, INCONSIDERATE **2 :** INCOGITATIVE

**in·cogitative** \(ˈ)in, ən+\ *adj* [¹*in-* + *cogitative*] **:** lacking the ability to think

**¹in·cog·ni·ta** \÷ˌinˌkäg'nēd·ə, ÷-ētə *also* ən'kägnəd·ə *or* -nətə\ *adv (or adj)* [It, fem. of *incognito*] **:** INCOGNITO — used only of a woman

**²incognita** \"\ *n* -S [It, fr. *incognita*, adj.] **:** a woman in disguise; *esp* **:** one concealing her real quality or state under some unobtrusive appearance

**¹in·cog·ni·to** \÷ˌinˌkäg'nēd·(ˌ)ō, ÷-ē(ˌ)tō *also* ən'kägnəˌtō\ *adv (or adj)* [It, fr. L *incognitus* unknown, fr. *in-* ¹in- + *cognitus*, past part. of *cognoscere* to know — more at COGNITION] **1 :** with one's identity concealed or assumed to be concealed; *esp* **:** in a capacity other than one's official capacity or under a name or title not calling for special recognition — used esp. of a personage of note ⟨the baron turned out to be a king ~⟩ **2 :** without recognition **:** UNKNOWN, UNIDENTIFIED ⟨the Neanderthal skull from Gibraltar, which had lain ~ since its discovery —Jacquetta and Christopher Hawkes⟩

**²incognito** \"\ *n* -S [It, fr. *incognito*, adj.] **1 :** one who is appearing or living incognito **2 :** the state or disguise of an incognito or incognita **3 :** the character assumed by an incognito or incognita

**in·cognizable** \(¦)in, ən+\ *adj* [¹*in-* + *cognizable*] **:** incapable of being recognized, known, or distinguished

**in·cognizance** \(ˈ)in, ən+\ *n* **:** lack of awareness, recognition, or knowledge

**in·cognizant** \"+\ *adj* [¹*in-* + *cognizant*] **:** lacking awareness or consciousness — used with *of* ⟨not ~ of the impression he was creating⟩

**in·cog·nos·ci·bil·i·ty** \ˌinˌkägˌnäsə'bilәd·ē\ *n* -ES **:** the quality or state of being incognoscible

**in·cognoscible** \(¦)in, ən+\ *adj* [LL *incognoscibilis*, fr. L *in-* ¹in- + LL *cognoscibilis* cognoscible — more at COGNOSCIBLE] **:** INCOGNIZABLE

**in·coherence** *or* **in·coherency** \¦in+\ *n* [¹*in-* + *coherence, coherency*] **1 :** the quality or state of being incoherent: as **a :** lack of cohesion or adherence **b :** lack of continuity or relevance **:** INCONGRUITY, INCONSISTENCY **2 :** something that is incoherent ⟨tearful *incoherencies*⟩

**in·coherent** \¦in+\ *adj* [¹*in-* + *coherent*] **:** lacking coherence: as **a :** lacking physical coherence or adhesiveness **:** consisting of discrete elements **:** LOOSE ⟨a dangerous slope covered with ~ shale⟩ **b :** lacking orderly continuity or relevance **:** INCONGRUOUS, INCONSISTENT ⟨a turgid ~ presentation⟩ **c :** lacking clarity or intelligibility usu. by reason of some emotional stress ⟨a voice ~ with rage⟩ ⟨a man ~ from sorrow⟩ **d :** lacking normal coordination **:** clumsy and fumbling ⟨a halting ~ gait⟩ **e :** occurring in mixed series or differing from normal patterns of language — used in cryptology of a key or an alphabet — **in·coherently** \"+\ *adv* — **in·coherentness** \"+\ *n* -ES

**in·cohering** \"+\ *adj* [¹*in-* + *cohering*, pres. part. of *cohere*] **:** lacking physical coherence

**in·cohesion** \¦in+\ *n* [¹*in-* + *cohesion*] **:** INCOHERENCE; *esp* **:** lack of orderly effective interaction between human groups ⟨difficulties resulting from the ~ of the desert nomads⟩

**in·cohesive** \¦in+\ *adj* [¹*in-* + *cohesive*] **1 :** INCOHERENT **:** lacking integration **2 :** tending to disrupt ⟨certain ~ social forces⟩

**in·coincidence** \¦in+\ *n* [¹*in-* + *coincidence*] **:** failure to conform or agree

**in·coincident** \"+\ *adj* [¹*in-* + *coincident*] **:** not coinciding

**in·combustible** \¦in+\ *adj or n* [ME, prob. fr. MF, fr. *in-* ¹in- + *combustible* — more at COMBUSTIBLE] **:** NONCOMBUSTIBLE — not used technically

**¹in·come** \'inˌkəm, *chiefly attrib also* 'inˌk- *sometimes* 'iŋˌk-\ *n* -S *often attrib* [ME, entry, arrival, fr. *in* + *come, cume* action of coming (after *comen in* to come in) — more at DOWNCOME, COME] **1** *archaic* **:** an act or an instance of coming in **:** ENTRANCE, ADVENT, INFLUX **2** *dial Brit* **a :** a place of entry **b :** INCOMER **3 :** something that comes in as an increment or addition usu. by chance **4 a :** a gain or recurrent benefit that is usu. measured in money and for a given period of time, derives from capital, labor, or a combination of both, includes gains from transactions in capital assets, but excludes unrealized advances in value **:** commercial revenue or receipts of any kind except receipts or returns of capital — see EARNED INCOME, GROSS INCOME, NET INCOME, UNEARNED INCOME; compare PROFIT, WAGE **b :** the value of goods and services received by an individual in a given period of time — compare WEALTH

**²income** \"\ *n* -S [⁴*in* + *come* (as in *oncome*)] *dial Brit* **:** TUMOR, ABSCESS

**income account** *n* **1 :** an account in which items of income or revenue are recorded **2** *or* **income statement :** a financial statement of a business showing the details of revenues, costs, expenses, losses, and profits for a given period grouped under appropriate headings — called also *profit and loss statement*

**income basis** *n* **:** a basis of reckoning income (as from investments, profits) according to the percentage that the interest or revenue bears to the actual cost with no allowance being made for the fact that payment at maturity is to be at par ⟨a bond yielding 3-percent interest on its par value and bought at 60 is on an *income basis* of 5 percent⟩

**income bond** *n* **:** a bond that is entitled to receive interest only if earned and declared by the board of directors in accordance with its indenture provisions

**in·come·less** \-ləs\ *adj* **:** having no income

**incomer** \'inˌkəmə(r)\ *n* **:** one that comes in: as **a** *dia chiefly Brit* **:** one that comes from another place **:** IMMIGRANT, STRANGER; *esp* **:** a new tenant **b :** a game bird or a trapshooting target that comes toward the shooter

**income splitting** *n* **:** an assigning of income for purposes of taxation in equal shares to two or more persons (as husband and wife) irrespective of which one actually received the income

**income tax** *n* **1 :** a tax on the net income of an individual or business concern (as a corporation) **2 a :** a tax on gross income often levied as a payroll tax by a city **b :** a tax on gross operating revenue (as of a public utility)

**¹in·com·ing** \'inˌkəmiŋ, -mēŋ\ *n* [ME, fr. *in-* + *coming* (after *comen in* to come in)] **1 :** the act of coming in **:** ARRIVAL ⟨all these ~s and outgoings disturbed our daily routine⟩ **2 :** money or other gains received **:** REVENUE, INCOME — usu. used in pl.

**²incoming** \"\ *adj* [²*in* + *coming* (after *come in*, v.)] **:** coming in: as **a :** taking or coming to occupy a place, position, or status formerly held by another ⟨his ~ tenant⟩ ⟨see what the ~ Congress will do⟩ **b :** arriving at a usual, proper, or normal destination ⟨~ waves⟩ **:** ACCRUING ⟨~ orders⟩ **c :** STARTING, BEGINNING, ENTERING ⟨high hopes for the ~ year⟩ ⟨all ~ freshmen⟩

**in·commensurability** \¦in+\ *n* [prob. fr. MF *incommensurableté*, fr. ML *incommensurabilitat-, incommensurabilitas*, fr. LL *incommensurabilis* + L *-itat-, -itas* -ity] **:** the quality or state of being incommensurable ⟨a genuine ~ between the individual and the universal —M.R.Cohen⟩

**¹in·commensurable** \¦in+\ *adj* [prob. fr. MF, fr. LL *incommensurabilis*, fr. L *in-* ¹in- + LL *commensurabilis* commensurable — more at COMMENSURABLE] **:** not commensurable **:** having no common measure ⟨quantities are ~ when no third quantity can be found that is an aliquot part of each⟩; *broadly* **:** lacking a common basis of comparison in respect to a quality (as value, size, excellence) normally subject to comparison — **in·com·men·su·ra·bly** \-əblē, -li\ *adv*

**²incommensurable** \"\ *n* -S **:** something that is incommensurable; *esp* **:** any of two or more quantities having no common measure

**in·commensurate** \¦in+\ *adj* [¹*in-* + *commensurate*] **:** not commensurate: as **a :** INCOMMENSURABLE **b :** INADEQUATE ⟨means ~ to our wants⟩ ⟨~ attention⟩

**in com·mer·cio** \ˌinkə'mərshēˌō\ *adj* [L, lit., inside of commerce] *Roman & civil law* **:** subject to private ownership — opposed to *extra commercium*

**in·com·mis·ci·ble** \¦inkə¦misəbəl\ *adj* [LL *incommiscibilis*, fr. L *in-* ¹in- + LL *commiscibilis* able to be mixed together, fr. L *commiscēre* to mix together + *-ibilis* -ible — more at COMMIX] **:** IMMISCIBLE

**incommodate** *vt* -ED/-ING/-S [L *incommodatus*, past part. of *incommodare*] *obs* **:** INCOMMODE

**in·commodation** \(¦)in, ən+\ *n* **:** DISCOMFORT, INCONVENIENCE, ANNOYANCE

**¹in·com·mode** \¦inkə¦mōd\ *vt* -ED/-ING/-S [MF *incommoder*, fr. L *incommodare*, fr. *incommodus* inconvenient, disagreeable, fr. *in-* ¹in- + *commodus* convenient — more at COMMODE] **1 a :** to give inconvenience or distress to **:** put out **:** DISCOMMODE ⟨such delays often *incommoded* passengers⟩ **b :** DISTURB, MOLEST ⟨should any player of the fielding side ~ the striker by any noise or motion —*Laws of Cricket*⟩ **2** *archaic* **:** IMPEDE, HANDICAP, OBSTRUCT

**²incommode** *adj* [F, fr. L *incommodus*] *obs* **:** INCONVENIENT

**in·commodious** \¦in+\ *adj* [¹*in-* + *commodious*] **:** tending to inconvenience: as **a** *archaic* **:** UNPLEASANT, DISAGREEABLE **b** *archaic* **:** UNCOMFORTABLE, HAMPERING **c** *obs* **:** HARMFUL, DAMAGING **d** *obs* **:** UNSUITABLE, IMPROPER **e :** offering inadequate accommodation **:** unpleasantly small and cramped ⟨an ~ little hall bedroom⟩ — **in·com·mo·di·ous·ly** *adv* — **in·com·mo·di·ous·ness** *n* -ES

**in·commodity** \¦in+\ *n* [ME *incommodite*, fr. MF *incommodité*, fr. L *incommoditat-, incommoditas*, fr. *incommodus* + *-itat-, -itas* -ity] **1 obs :** the quality or state of being incommodious **2 :** something that causes inconvenience, annoyance, or discomfort — usu. used in pl. ⟨an inconvenient, ill-balanced house . . . its unsuitability as a public building is intensified by such *incommodities* —Claud Phillimore⟩

**in·communicability** \"+\ *n* **:** the quality or state of being incommunicable

**in·communicable** \"+\ *adj* [MF or LL; MF, fr. LL *incommunicabilis*, fr. L *in-* ¹in- + LL *communicabilis* communicable — more at COMMUNICABLE] **1 :** incapable of being communicated: as **a :** not subject to sharing or division ⟨the ~ authority of the crown⟩ **b :** impossible to recount or utter **:** INEFFABLE ⟨an ~ vision⟩ ⟨into the unspeakable and ~ prison of this earth —Thomas Wolfe⟩ **2 :** unwilling or unable to communicate **:** TACITURN, RESERVED, WITHDRAWN ⟨a troubled man, ~ and abstracted⟩ **3 :** lacking means of communication ⟨his nature is ~ — he resembles neither dog nor man —Pamela L. Travers⟩ — **in·com·mu·ni·ca·ble·ness** \-nəs\ *n* -ES — **in·communicably** \¦in+\ *adv*

**in·com·mu·ni·ca·do** *also* **in·co·mu·ni·ca·do** \ˌinkəˌmyünə'kä(ˌ)dō, -kä(-\ *adv (or adj)* [Sp *incomunicado*, fr. past part. of *incomunicar* to deprive of communication, fr. *in-* ¹in- (fr. L) + *comunicar* to communicate, fr. L *communicare* to share,

impart, partake — more at COMMUNICATE] : without means of communication ⟨it had sometimes brought good luck for people to be politically ~ —A.N.Whitehead⟩; *esp* : in solitary confinement ⟨held ~ for 10 days⟩
**in·communicated** *or* **in·communicating** \¦in+\ *adj* [¹*in-* + *communicated* or *communicating*] *archaic* : lacking communication
**in·communicative** \"+\ *adj* [¹*in-* + *communicative*] : UNCOMMUNICATIVE 2
**in·com·mut·abil·i·ty** \¦inkə,myüd·ə'biləd·ē\ *n* -ES [LL *incommutabilitas*, fr. L *incommutabilis* + *-itas* -ity] : the quality or state of being incommutable
**in·commutable** \¦in+\ *adj* [ME, fr. L *incommutabilis*, fr. *in-* ¹in- + *commutabilis* commutable — more at COMMUTABLE] : not commutable: **a** : not subject or liable to alteration : UNCHANGEABLE **b** : not able to substitute one for another : UNEXCHANGEABLE ⟨these ~ skills⟩ : not interchangeable ⟨when two sounds are ~ their phonetic difference prevents their being classed under one phoneme —C.E.Bazell⟩ — **in·com·mut·a·bly** \-blē,-bli\ *adv*
**in·compact** \(¦)in, ən+\ *adj* [¹*in-* + *compact*] : loosely ordered or organized : lacking coherence or firm integration
**in·comparability** \(¦)in, ən+\ *n* : the quality or state of being incomparable
**in·comparable** \(¦)in, ən+\ *adj* [ME, fr. MF, fr. L *incomparabilis*, fr. *in-* ¹in- + *comparabilis* comparable — more at COMPARABLE] **1** : of such quality as to be beyond comparison : having no equal : eminent beyond comparison : MATCHLESS, PEERLESS, TRANSCENDENT ⟨this ~ scholar⟩ ⟨a heavenly, an ~ week of rest and pleasure⟩ **2** : not suitable for comparison : lacking such common bases or points of reference as make comparison useful, informative, or valid — usu. used with *with* or *to* ⟨this report is ~ with the earlier reports because of the use of different breakdowns of data⟩
**in·com·pa·ra·ble·ness** *n* -ES : INCOMPARABILITY
**in·comparably** \(¦)in, ən+\ *adv* [ME, fr. *incomparable* + *-ly*] : to an incomparable degree : beyond comparison : EXCEPTIONALLY
**incompass** *obs var of* ENCOMPASS
**in·compassionate** \¦in+\ *adj* [¹*in-* + *compassionate*] : lacking compassion — **in·compassionately** \"+\ *adv*
**in·compatibility** \¦in+\ *n* [F *incompatibilité*, fr. MF, fr. *incompatible*] **1** : the quality or state of being incompatible : inability to function or exist in the presence of something else: as **a** : inability to exist in peaceful harmony; *esp* : lack of adjustment in marriage **b** : a relation between dignities or public offices such that proper and faithful performance of the duties and exercise of the powers of one is inconsistent with such performance and exercise in another on the part of the same individual **c** (1) : lack of interfertility between two plants following pollination (as from characteristics of the pollen) (2) : inability of stock and scion to unite successfully in a graft **d** : the exclusion in igneous rock crystallization under conditions of equilibrium of one member of a pair of minerals by the presence of the other member **2 incompatibilities** *pl* : mutually antagonistic things or qualities : INCOMPATIBLES ⟨the inherent *incompatibilities* of dog and cat⟩
**¹in·compatible** \"+\ *adj* [MF & ML; MF, fr. ML *incompatibilis*, fr. L *in-* ¹in- + ML *compatibilis* compatible — more at COMPATIBLE] **1** : incapable of being held by one person at one time — used of offices, dignities, or benefices that would make mutually conflicting demands on a holder **2 a** : incapable of appearing or of being thought together or of entering into the same system, theory, or practice ⟨~ ideas⟩ : incapable of harmonious combination : INCONGRUOUS ⟨~ colors⟩ : incapable of harmonious association or of acting in accord : DISAGREEING ⟨~ persons⟩ **b** (1) *of drugs or medicaments* : unsuitable for use together because of chemical interaction or antagonistic physiological effects — compare SYNERGISTIC (2) *of blood or serum* : unsuitable for use in a particular transfusion because of the presence of agglutinins against the recipient's red blood cells **c** *in logic* (1) *of two propositions* : not both true — compare STROKE 14 (2) *of terms* : not consistently predicable of the same subject — compare ALTERNATIVE DENIAL **d** *of mathematical equations* : incapable of being satisfied by the same set of values for the unknowns **e** : incapable of blending into a stable homogeneous mixture — used esp. of solids or solutions ⟨ester gum is ~ with cellulose acetate when formulated into a lacquer —*Glossary of Industrial Coating Terms*⟩ — compare IMMISCIBLE **3** *obs* : INTOLERANT — **in·com·pat·i·ble·ness** \-nəs\ *n* -ES — **in·compatibly** \¦in+\ *adv*
**²incompatible** *n* -S : one that is incompatible — usu. used in pl.
**in·compensated** \(ˈ)in+\ *adj* [¹*in-* + past part. of *compensate*] : lacking compensation; *esp* : lacking physiological compensation
**in·compensation** \(¦)in, ən+\ *n* [¹*in-* + *compensation*] : lack of physiological compensation ⟨cardiac ~⟩ — **in·compensatory** \¦in+\ *adj*
**in·competence** \(ˈ)in, ən+\ *n* [F *incompétence*, fr. MF, fr. *in-* ¹in- + *compétence* — more at COMPETENCE] : the state or fact of being incompetent: as **a** : lack of physical, intellectual, or moral ability : INSUFFICIENCY, INADEQUACY ⟨his ~ was absolute⟩ **b** : lack of legal qualification or fitness ⟨the ~ of an intoxicated man to drive an automobile⟩ **c** : the inability of an organ to perform its function adequately ⟨aortic ~ may lead to enlargement of the heart⟩
**in·competency** \"+\ *n* [MF *incompétence* + E *-y*] **1 a** : the quality of being incompetent ⟨the ~ typical of idiots⟩ **b incompetencies** *pl* : incompetent acts or behavior ⟨the *incompetencies* of such immature executives⟩ **2** : INCOMPETENCE **3** : the absence of jurisdiction of a court or judge to determine a civil law case
**¹in·competent** \"+\ *adj* [MF, *incompétent*, fr. *in-* ¹in- + *compétent* — more at COMPETENT] **1 a** : lacking the qualities (as maturity, capacity, initiative, intelligence) necessary to effective independent action **b** (1) : lacking specific qualifications to perform a legal function or duty or exercise a legal right — often used without implication of any kind with respect to personal fitness; distinguished from *incapable* ⟨a wife is usually considered ~ to testify against her husband in a criminal case⟩ (2) : not acceptable in court because obtained from a legally incompetent source ⟨~ testimony⟩ ⟨~ evidence⟩ : INADMISSIBLE **c** : exhibiting or characterized by organic incompetence ⟨an ~ mitral valve⟩ **d** : inadequate to or unsuitable for a particular purpose expressed or implied ⟨certain genotypes are phenotypically ~⟩ ⟨an ~ system of government⟩ ⟨pipes ~ to carry a full head of steam⟩ **2** : being or forming strata and rock structures that have not the rigidity or strength to transmit particular stresses but that crush or flow under them — **in·competently** \"+\ *adv*
**²incompetent** \"\ *n* -S : one that is incompetent: as **a** : a person incapable of managing his affairs because of mental deficiency or immaturity ⟨children and idiots are ~s in the eyes of the law⟩ **b** : one incapable of doing properly what is required (as in a particular position) ⟨~s in public office⟩
**incompetible** *adj* [¹*in-* + *competible*] *obs* : UNSUITABLE
**in·com·plet·abil·i·ty** \¦inkəm,plēd·ə'biləd·ē\ *n* -ES : the quality or state of being incompletable
**in·com·plet·able** \¦inkəm¦plēd·əbəl\ *adj* [¹*in-* + *completable* capable of being completed, fr. *complete* + *-able*] : impossible to finish or bring to completion — **in·com·plet·able·ness** *n* -ES
**in·complete** \¦in+\ *adj* [ME *incompleet*, fr. LL *incompletus*, fr. *in-* ¹in- + L *completus* complete — more at COMPLETE] : lacking a part or parts or not having all parts arranged in final or functional order : UNFINISHED, IMPERFECTED: as **a** *of a flower* : lacking one or more sets of floral organs — compare COMPLETE, DICLINOUS **b** : SYNCATEGOREMATIC **c** *of a fertilizer* : containing two but not all three of the fertilizing agents nitrogen, phosphorus, and potassium **d** *of a football pass* : not legally caught
**incomplete antibody** *n* : BLOCKING ANTIBODY
**in·completed** \¦in+\ *adj* [¹*in-* + *completed*] : INCOMPLETE
**in·com·plete·ly** *adv* : in an incomplete manner or to an incomplete degree : not wholly, perfectly, or fully ⟨~ grown crops⟩ ⟨~ understood⟩
**in·com·plete·ness** *n* : the quality or state of being incomplete
**incomplete pupa** *n* : PUPA LIBERA
**incomplete symbol** *n* : a sign, word, or expression (as the quotation sign or the word *or*) that systematically contributes to the meaning of expressions in which it occurs but has no independent or separable meaning
**in·completion** \¦in+\ *n* [¹*in-* + *completion*] **1** : lack of completion **2** : an incomplete pass in football
**in·complex** \(¦)in, ən+\ *adj* [ML *incomplexus*, fr. L *in-* ¹in- + *complexus*, past part. of *complecti* to entwine around, embrace — more at COMPLEX] : lacking complexity : SIMPLE
**incompliable** *adj* [¹*in-* + *compliable*] *obs* : UNCOMPLIANT
**in·compliance** *or* **in·compliancy** \¦in+\ *n* [¹*in-* + *compliance*, *compliancy*] : the quality or state of being incompliant : OBSTINACY
**in·compliant** \"+\ *adj* [¹*in-* + *compliant*] **1** : lacking compliance : not cooperative and yielding **2** *of a material thing* : lacking pliability : STIFF, RESISTANT — **in·compliantly** \"+\ *adv*
**in·complicate** \(ˈ)in, ən+\ *adj* [¹*in-* + *complicate*] : SIMPLE, UNCOMPLICATED
**incomplying** *adj* [¹*in-* + pres. part. of *comply*] *obs* : free from compliance or yielding
**incomposed** *adj* [¹*in-* + *composed*] **1** *obs* : lacking calmness and composure : DISTURBED, DISORDERED **2** *obs* : not made up of diverse elements : SIMPLE
**in·composite** \(¦)in, ən+\ *adj* [L *incompositus*, fr. *in-* ¹in- + *compositus*, past part. of *componere* to put together — more at COMPOSE] **1** : lacking separable or distinguishable parts **2** *of a number* : PRIME
**in·compossibility** \¦in+\ *n* : the quality or state of being incompossible
**in·compossible** \¦in+\ *adj* [ML *incompossibilis*, fr. L *in-* ¹in- + ML *compossibilis* compossible — more at COMPOSSIBLE] : not mutually possible : INCONSISTENT, INCOMPATIBLE
**in·comprehending** \(¦)in, ən+\ *adj* [¹*in-* + *comprehending*] : lacking comprehension or lacking in comprehension — **in·comprehendingly** \"+\ *adv*
**in·comprehensibility** \(¦)in, ən+\ *n* : the quality or state of being incomprehensible
**¹in·comprehensible** \(¦)in, ən+\ *adj* [ME, fr. L *incomprehensibilis*, fr. *in-* ¹in- + *comprehensibilis* comprehensible — more at COMPREHENSIBLE] **1** *archaic* : having or subject to no limits : ILLIMITABLE ⟨an infinite and ~ substance —Richard Hooker⟩ **2 a** : impossible to comprehend : lying above or beyond the reach of the human mind ⟨the ~ mysteries of creation⟩ **b** : being beyond the powers of comprehension of a particular mind : UNINTELLIGIBLE ⟨an ~ subject to him⟩ **c** : being beyond ordinary comprehension : UNFATHOMABLE ⟨~ moods⟩ ⟨a whimsical ~ person⟩ **3** *obs* : impossible to catch or hold — **in·com·pre·hen·si·ble·ness** \-nəs\ *n* -ES — **in·comprehensibly** \¦in+\ *adv*
**²incomprehensible** \"\ *n* -S : something incomprehensible
**in·comprehension** \(¦)in, ən+\ *n* [¹*in-* + *comprehension*] : lack of comprehension or understanding ⟨their ~ of violence, their terror of social upheaval —A.M.Schlesinger b.1917⟩
**in·comprehensive** \"+\ *adj* [¹*in-* + *comprehensive*] **1** : lacking comprehensiveness; *esp* : deficient in mental grasp **2** *obs* : INCOMPREHENSIBLE — **in·comprehensively** \"+\ *adv*
**in·compressibility** \¦in+\ *n* : the quality or state of being incompressible
**in·compressible** \"+\ *adj* [¹*in-* + *compressible*] : incapable of being compressed; *broadly* : resisting compression — **in·com·press·ible·ness** \-nəs\ *n* -ES — **in·com·press·ibly** \-əblē, -li\ *adv*
**incompt** *adj* [L *incomptus*, fr. *in-* ¹in- + *comptus*, past part. of *comere* to adorn — more at COMPT] *obs* : UNKEMPT, UNPOLISHED
**in·computable** \¦in+\ *adj* [¹*in-* + *computable*] : greater than can be computed or enumerated : very great — **in·com·put·ably** \-əblē, -li\ *adv*
**incomunicado** *var of* INCOMMUNICADO
**in·concealable** \¦in+\ *adj* [¹*in-* + *concealable*] : impossible to hide
**in·conceivability** \¦in+\ *n* **1** : the quality or state of being inconceivable **2** : something inconceivable
**in·conceivable** \¦in+\ *adj* [¹*in-* + *conceivable*] **1** : falling outside the limit of what can be comprehended, accepted as true or real, or tolerated: as **a** : impossible to comprehend in the absence of actual experience or knowledge : UNIMAGINABLE ⟨color is ~ to those born blind⟩ **b** : impossible to entertain in the mind : UNTHINKABLE ⟨it is ~ that a thing can both be and not be⟩ **c** : impossible to accept as an article of faith : INCREDIBLE, UNBELIEVABLE ⟨it is ~ that God should wantonly inflict suffering⟩ **2** : hard to believe or believe in ⟨it is ~ that such losses should continue⟩ ⟨~ losses of revenue⟩ — **in·conceivableness** \"+\ *n* — **in·conceivably** \"+\ *adv*
**inconciliable** *adj* [¹*in-* + *conciliable*] *obs* : IRRECONCILABLE
**in·concinnity** \¦in+\ *n* [L *inconcinnitas*, fr. *in-* ¹in- + *concinnitas* concinnity — more at CONCINNITY] : lack of suitability or congruity : awkward or unsuitable form or character
**in·concinnous** \"+\ *adj* [L *inconcinnus*, fr. *in-* ¹in- + *concinnus* concinnous — more at CONCINNITY] *archaic* : marked by inconcinnity
**inconcludent** *adj* [¹*in-* + *concludent*] *obs* : INCONCLUSIVE
**in·con·clu·si·ble** \¦inkən¦klüzəbəl\ *adj* [¹*in-* + obs. *conclusible*, fr. L *conclusus* (past part. of *concludere* to conclude) + E *-ible* — more at CONCLUDE] : impossible to bring to an end ⟨an ~ argument⟩
**in·conclusive** \¦in+\ *adj* [¹*in-* + *conclusive*] : leading to no conclusion or to no definite result, decision, or end ⟨such ~ arguments⟩ ⟨a long and ~ war⟩ — **in·conclusively** \"+\ *adv* — **in·conclusiveness** \"+\ *n*
**inconcoct** *or* **inconcocted** *adj* [*inconcoct* fr. ¹*in-* + obs. *concoct* digested, matured, fr. L *concoctus*, past part. of *concoquere* to boil together; *inconcocted* fr. ¹*in-* + *concocted*, past part. of *concoct* — more at CONCOCT] *obs* : not matured : UNDIGESTED — **inconcoction** *n*, *obs*
**in·concrete** \(¦)in, ən+\ *adj* [LL *inconcretus*, fr. L *in-* ¹in- + *concretus*, past part. of *concrescere* to grow together — more at CONCRETE] : vague and diffuse : ABSTRACT
**in·condensable** \¦in+\ *adj* [¹*in-* + *condensable*] : incapable of being condensed
**in·con·dite** \ən'kändət, -,dīt\ *adj* [L *inconditus*, fr. *in-* ¹in- + *conditus*, past part. of *condere* to put together, fr. *com-* + *-dere* to put — more at DO] **1** : badly organized or put together : lacking finish or polished form — used chiefly of an utterance ⟨valuable factual information obscured by turgid ~ prose⟩ **2** : lacking in manners : CRUDE, UNPOLISHED
**in·conducive** \¦in+\ *adj* [¹*in-* + *conducive*] : not conducive : having no tendency toward
**In·co·nel** \'iŋkə,nel\ *trademark* — used for an alloy of approximately 80 percent nickel, 14 percent chromium, and 6 percent iron
**in·conformable** \¦in+\ *adj* [¹*in-* + *conformable*] : failing or unwilling to conform ⟨the rebels were ~ to all compromise⟩ ⟨conduct wholly ~ to our principles⟩ — **in·conformably** \"+\ *adv*
**in·conformity** \"+\ *n* [¹*in-* + *conformity*] : lack of conformity : NONCONFORMITY
**in·confused** \¦in+\ *adj* [¹*in-* + *confused*] : free from confusion : having the elements distinct : CLEAR-CUT — **in·confusedly** \"+\ *adv*
**in·congenerous** \"+\ *adj* [¹*in-* + *congenerous*] *archaic* : not belonging to the same group or kind
**in·congruence** \(¦)in, ən+\ *n* [LL *incongruentia*, fr. L *incongruent-*, *incongruens* + *-ia* -y] : INCONGRUITY
**in·congruent** \"+\ *adj* [L *incongruent-*, *incongruens*, fr. *in-* ¹in- + *congruent-*, *congruens*, pres. part. of *congruere* to come together, coincide, agree — more at CONGRUOUS] **1** : lacking congruity : INCONGRUOUS, UNSUITABLE **2** : not corresponding in shape and curvature — used of opposed articular surfaces in joints **3** : relating to the melting point of a molecular compound at which it decomposes into a new solid phase and a liquid of different composition — compare CONGRUENT 3
**in·congruently** \"+\ *adv* : in an incongruent manner
**in·congruity** \¦in+\ *n* [MF or LL; MF *incongruité*, fr. LL *incongruitat-*, *incongruitas*, fr. *incongruus* + L *-itat-*, *-itas* -ity] **1** : the quality or state of being incongruous : lack of congruity : INCONSISTENCY, INHARMONY, DISAGREEMENT **2** : something that is incongruous : a thing that lacks harmonious or rational relation to its environment ⟨Victorian *incongruities* in a typically mid-20th-century setting⟩
**in·congruous** \(ˈ)in, ən+\ *adj* [LL *incongruus*, fr. L *in-* ¹in- + *congruus* congruous — more at CONGRUOUS] : lacking congruity: as **a** : characterized by lack of harmony, consistency, or compatibility with one another ⟨~ colors⟩ ⟨~ desires⟩ **b** : characterized by disagreement or lack of conformity with something ⟨conduct ~ with avowed principles⟩ **c** : characterized by inconsistency or inharmony of its own parts or qualities ⟨an ~ story⟩ **d** : characterized by lack of propriety or suitableness ⟨~ manners⟩ — **in·congruously** \"+\ *adv* — **in·congruousness** \"+\ *n*
**in·conjunct** \(¦)in, ən+\ *adj* [LL *inconjunctus* unconnected, fr. L *in-* ¹in- + *conjunctus*, past part. of *conjungere* to join together — more at CONJOIN] *archaic*, *of celestial bodies or zodiacal signs* : lacking conjunction
**in·connected** \¦in+\ *adj* [¹*in-* + *connected*] : DISCONNECTED ⟨halting ~ ideas⟩
**in·connection** \"+\ *n* [¹*in-* + *connection*] *archaic* : DISCONNECTION
**in·con·nu** \¦inkə¦n(y)ü, ¦iŋk-; ¦aⁿkə¦nüE\ *n* -S [F, fr. *in-* ¹in- + *connu*, past part. of *connaître* to know, fr. L *cognoscere* — more at COGNITION] **1** : an unknown person : STRANGER **2** : a large oily soft-fleshed food fish (*Stenodus mackenzii*) related to the whitefish and found in Alaska, northwestern Canada, and adjoining Siberian waters
**in·conquerable** \(ˈ)in, ən+\ *adj* [¹*in-* + *conquerable*] : UNCONQUERABLE
**in·conscience** \(ˈ)in, ən+\ *n* : the quality or state of being inconscient
**in·conscient** \"+\ *adj* [prob. fr. F, fr. *in-* ¹in- + *conscient*, fr. L *conscient-*, *consciens*, pres. part. of *conscire* to know, be conscious — more at CONSCIENCE] **1 a** : lacking consciousness : MINDLESS ⟨inanimate ~ things —Percy Winner⟩ **b** : lacking full awareness : ABSTRACTED ⟨he had passed, ~, full gaze the wide-banded irises —Ezra Pound⟩ **2** : not involving or based on the action of consciousness ⟨holding creation to be the outcome of ~ natural laws⟩ — **in·consciently** \"+\ *adv*
**in·con·scio·na·ble** \(ˈ)in¦känch(ə)nəbəl, ən'k-\ *adj* [¹*in-* + *conscionable*] : UNCONSCIONABLE
**in·conscious** \(ˈ)in+\ *adj* [LL *inconscius*, fr. L *in-* ¹in- + *conscius* conscious — more at CONSCIOUS] : UNCONSCIOUS
**in·consecutive** \¦in+\ *adj* [¹*in-* + *consecutive*] : lacking in sequence and order ⟨formless ~ essays he produced by grouping . . . a miscellany of scattered reflections —*New Yorker*⟩ : not arranged in order of occurrence ⟨the entries in the Chronicle are ~ and some of them must have been written appreciably later than the events which they relate —F.M.Stenton⟩ — **in·consecutively** \"+\ *adv* — **in·con·sec·u·tive·ness** \-ivnəs\ *n*
**in·consequence** \(ˈ)in, ən+\ *n* [L *inconsequentia*, fr. *in-* ¹in- + *consequentia* consequence — more at CONSEQUENCE] **1** : the quality or state of being inconsequent: as **a** : lack of just or logical inference or argument : ILLOGICALITY **b** : lack of sequence : INCONSECUTIVENESS, IRRELEVANCE **2** : character or mood marked by inconsequence ⟨Sterne propagates his ~, while his suavity and ease of style die with him —J.L.Lowes⟩ ⟨the ~s of the Boston mind —Henry Adams⟩
**in·consequent** \"+\ *adj* [LL *inconsequent-*, *inconsequens*, fr. L *in-* ¹in- + *consequent-*, *consequens* consequent — more at CONSEQUENT] **1 a** : lacking logical order or ordered sequence of thought or reasoning ⟨it is unfortunate that such a significant book should be so slipshod and ~ —*Saturday Rev.*⟩ : ILLOGICAL, INCONSISTENT ⟨a premise based on ~ reasoning⟩ **b** : following no natural sequence : INCONSECUTIVE ⟨the string of ~ statements to which she had treated them —Ngaio Marsh⟩ **2** : marked or characterized by a lack of logic or relevancy ⟨these ~ fellows who would lower taxes but increase public expenditure⟩ **3** : of no consequence : lacking worth, significance, or importance ⟨the gay, debauched, quite ~ lad was managed like a puppet —Hilaire Belloc⟩ ⟨futile ~ dreams⟩ — **in·consequently** \"+\ *adv*
**in·con·se·quen·tia** \,in,kän(t)sə'kwench(ē)ə\ *n pl* [LL, neut. pl. of *inconsequens*] : matters of no grave moment or significance : TRIVIA ⟨the ~ of daily life⟩
**in·consequential** \(¦)in, ən+\ *adj* **1** : not regularly following from the premises; *broadly* : IRRELEVANT **2** : INCONSEQUENT 3 — **in·consequentiality** \"+\ *n* — **in·consequentially** \"+\ *adv*
**in·considerable** \¦in+\ *adj* [MF, fr. *in-* ¹in- + *considerable*, fr. ML *considerabilis* — more at CONSIDERABLE] **1** *obs* : too great to be considered or reckoned **2 a** : unworthy of consideration : TRIVIAL ⟨their duties were ~⟩ ⟨earned and spent a not ~ amount of money⟩ ⟨exercised no ~ influence⟩ **b** : SMALL, PETTY ⟨passed his life in an ~ village⟩ ⟨~ size⟩ **3** *obs* : INCONSIDERATE, CARELESS — **in·con·sid·er·a·ble·ness** \-nəs\ *n* -ES — **in·considerably** \¦in+\ *adv*
**in·con·sid·er·a·cy** \,inkən'sid(ə)rəsē\ *n* -ES [fr. *inconsiderate*, after such pairs as E *accurate*: *accuracy*] *archaic* : INCONSIDERATENESS
**¹in·considerate** \¦in+\ *adj* [L *inconsideratus*, fr. *in-* ¹in- + *consideratus*, past part. of *considerare* to consider — more at CONSIDER] **1** : not adequately considered : ILL-ADVISED, RASH, PRECIPITATE ⟨hasty and ~ conclusions⟩ **2 a** : acting or tending to act without due or reasonable deliberation : HEEDLESS, THOUGHTLESS, CARELESS ⟨some ~ person repeats like a parrot that if you gave everybody the same amount of money —G.B.Shaw⟩ ⟨that ~, wandering, featherheaded race —L.P.Smith⟩ ⟨exploring the carving with ~ fingers⟩ **b** : failing in regard for the rights or feelings of others : indifferent to propriety or courtesy ⟨a gross ~ man⟩ ⟨shockingly ~ behavior⟩ **3** *obs* : not held in consideration or esteem — **in·considerately** \"+\ *adv* — **in·con·sid·er·ate·ness** *n* -ES
**²inconsiderate** \"\ *n* -S : an inconsiderate person
**in·consideration** \¦in+\ *n* [LL *inconsideration-*, *inconsideratio*, fr. L *inconsideratus* + *-ion-*, *-io* -ion] : the quality or state of being inconsiderate : INCONSIDERATENESS
**in·considered** \¦in+\ *adj* [¹*in-* + *considered*] : INCONSIDERATE 1
**in·consistency** *also* **in·consistence** \¦in+\ *n* [¹*in-* + *consistency*, *consistence*] **1** : the quality or state of being inconsistent; as **a** : lack of agreement, consonance, harmony, or compatibility **b** : lack of stability, uniformity, or steadiness **2 a** : something that is inconsistent **b** : an instance of inconsistent character or condition
**in·consistent** \¦in+\ *adj* [¹*in-* + *consistent*] **1** : lacking consistency : INCOMPATIBLE, INCONGRUOUS, INHARMONIOUS: as **a** *of propositions, ideas, beliefs* : so related that both or all cannot be true or containing parts so related ⟨~ statements⟩ **b** : so related to something premised or understood that it cannot be true if what is thus assumed is true ⟨an ~ conclusion⟩ **2** *of a person* **a** : incoherent or illogical in thought or actions : believing incompatibles or acting in incongruous ways **b** : logically inconsequent : lacking in continuity of belief or purpose; *broadly* : INCONSTANT, CHANGEABLE, FICKLE **3** *of aesthetic relations* : not handled or developed so as to form a harmonious whole : INCONSONANT ⟨~ composition⟩ **4** : INCONGRUOUS, INCOMPATIBLE, IRRECONCILABLE — used of immaterial qualities ⟨wisdom is not ~ with mirth⟩ **5** : INCOMPATIBLE 2d — **in·consistently** \"+\ *adv* — **in·con·sist·ent·ness** *n* -ES
**in·consolable** \¦in+\ *adj* [L *inconsolabilis*, fr. *in-* ¹in- + *consolabilis* able to be comforted, fr. *consolari* to console + *-abilis* -able — more at CONSOLE] : incapable of being consoled : grieved beyond comfort : utterly disconsolate — **in·con·sol·able·ness** \-nəs\ *n* -ES — **in·con·sol·ably** \-əblē, -li\ *adv*
**in·consonance** \(ˈ)in+\ *n* : lack of consonance or harmony of sound, action, or thought : DISAGREEMENT
**in·consonant** \"+\ *adj* [¹*in-* + *consonant*] : not consonant or agreeing : INCONSISTENT, DISCORDANT
**in·conspicuous** \¦in+\ *adj* [L *inconspicuus*, fr. *in-* ¹in- + *conspicuus* conspicuous — more at CONSPICUOUS] **1** *obs* : INVISIBLE **2** *obs* : not obvious to the mental eye : INDISCERNIBLE, IMPERCEPTIBLE **3** : not readily noticeable : hardly discernible : not prominent or striking — **in·conspicuously** \"+\ *adv* — **in·conspicuousness** \"+\ *n*
**inconstance** *n* [ME *inconstaunce*, fr. MF *inconstance*, fr. L *inconstantia*] *obs* : INCONSTANCY
**in·constancy** \(ˈ)in+\ *n* [L *inconstantia*, fr. *inconstant-*,

inconstans + -ia -y] **1** : the quality or state of being inconstant : lack of constancy: as **a** : CHANGEABLENESS, FICKLENESS **b** : lack of uniformity : VARIABILITY **c** *obs* : INCONSISTENCY **2** : an instance of changeableness or of variability

1**in·constant** \"+\ *adj* [ME, fr. MF, fr. L *inconstant-, inconstans*, fr. *in-* 1in- + *constant-, constans* constant — more at CONSTANT] **1** : marked by lack of constancy : likely to change frequently often without apparent or cogent reason : given to change of character, inclination, purpose, or location ⟨unjust I may have been . . . but never ~ —Jane Austen⟩ **2** *obs* : INCONSISTENT

**syn** FICKLE, CAPRICIOUS, MERCURIAL, UNSTABLE: INCONSTANT suggests a tendency to frequent change, often without good reason ⟨for people seldom knew what they would be, young men especially, they are so amazingly changeable and *inconstant* —Jane Austen⟩; it is often used in reference to persons incapable of steadfastness in love or in reference to changeable climatic and meteorological developments ⟨supposing now . . . this lover of yours was not the sort of man we all take him to be, and that he was to turn out false, or *inconstant* —Anthony Trollope⟩ ⟨places where the soil was fertile but the rainfall uncertain and the rivers shallow and *inconstant* —A.M. Schlesinger b.1888⟩ FICKLE intensifies notions of pointless, even perverse, changeability and incapacity for steadfastness ⟨she is *fickle!* How she turns from one face to another face — and smiles into them all —Edna S. V. Millay⟩ ⟨but bitter experience soon taught him that lordly patrons are *fickle* and their favor not to be relied on —Aldous Huxley⟩ ⟨the next morning was gay with *fickle* sun-showers; it was a harlequin day, a strayed reveler from April —Elinor Wylie⟩ CAPRICIOUS is less derogatory than FICKLE but suggests motivation by caprice, whim, or fancy making for unexpected change ⟨he seemed heartless and *capricious*, as ready to drop you as he had been to take you up —George du Maurier⟩ ⟨the more *capricious* incidence of sexual passion —Lewis Mumford⟩ ⟨the *capricious* severity of a mere despot —J.R.Green⟩ ⟨a *capricious* and malevolent race of savages —Bernard De Voto⟩ MERCURIAL in this sense is likely to suggest changeability in mood, esp. rapid rise from discouragement to mirth or elation, or to suggest a versatility of gifts ⟨Allnutt's *mercurial* spirits could hardly help rising under the influence of Rose's persistent optimism —C.S. Forester⟩ ⟨*mercurial*, euphoric, he could blaze into hectic social events and become a rather too brash and boyish "life and soul of the party" —*Times Lit. Supp.*⟩ UNSTABLE, a less colorful word, indicates an incapacity to remain stable or steady, with many changes and fluctuations ⟨of some meddling, bold fanatic, mind *unstable*, weird, erratic —Sophia A. Jamieson⟩ ⟨the occupation [of mining] in general is an *unstable* one —Lewis Mumford⟩ ⟨the blots of shade and flakes of light upon the countenances of the group changed shape and position endlessly. All was *unstable*, quivering as leaves, evanescent as lightning —Thomas Hardy⟩

2**inconstant** \"\ *n* : one that is inconstant

**in·con·stant·ly** *adv* : in an inconstant manner : without constancy

**in·con·stant·ness** *n* -ES : the quality or state of being inconstant

**in·consumable** \¦in+\ *adj* [1in- + *consumable*] **1** : not capable of being consumed or destroyed (as by fire) **2** : satisfying human wants without being directly consumed in so doing ⟨machinery is commonly thought of as ~⟩ — **in·con·sum·ably** \-blē, -bli\ *adv*

**inconsumptible** *adj* [1in- + *consumptible* capable of being consumed, fr. L *consumptus* (past part. of *consumere* to consume) + E *-ible* — more at CONSUME] *obs* : INCONSUMABLE

**in-contact** \(ˈ)=ˌ=ˌ=\ *n* [fr. the phrase *in contact*] : an individual that has lived in close association with another and has thereby been exposed to infection with a disease with which that other is affected

**in·con·tam·i·na·ble** \ˌinkən¦tam(ə)nəbəl\ *adj* [LL *incontaminabilis*, fr. L *in-* 1in- + LL *contaminabilis* capable of contamination, fr. L *contaminare* to contaminate + *-abilis* -able — more at CONTAMINATE] : impossible to contaminate

**in·con·tam·i·nate** \-mənət\ *adj* [L *incontaminatus*, fr. *in-* 1in- + *contaminatus*, past part. of *contaminare* to contaminate] : free from contamination : PURE, UNDEFILED

**in·con·test·abil·i·ty** \ˌinkən,testəˈbiləd·ē\ *n* -ES : the quality or state of being incontestable

**in·con·test·able** *or* **in·con·test·ible** \ˌinkən¦testəbəl\ *adj* [*incontestable* fr. F, fr. *in-* 1in- + *contestable* capable of being contested, fr. *contester* to contest + *-able*; *incontestible*, alter. of *incontestable* — more at CONTEST] **1** : not subject to being disputed, called in question, or controverted ⟨~ evidence⟩ : offering no grounds for doubt : INDUBITABLE, UNDOUBTED ⟨an ~ genius⟩ **2** : being such that payment of claims cannot be disputed by a life insurance company for any cause except nonpayment of premiums or other reason specifically stated in the contract when the contract has been in force for a stipulated period (as one or two years) and when an insurable interest existed at its inception — **in·con·test·able·ness** *n* -ES

**incontestable clause** *n* : a clause in a life insurance policy providing the conditions under which the policy is incontestable

**in·con·test·a·bly** \-blē, -bli\ *adv* : in an incontestable manner or to an incontestable degree or level : CERTAINLY, INDUBITABLY

**incontested** *adj* [1in- + past part. of *contest*] *obs* : UNDISPUTED

**in·continence** \(ˈ)in, ən+\ *n* [ME, fr. MF or L; MF, fr. L *incontinentia*, fr. *incontinent-, incontinens* + *-ia* -y] **1** : lack of restraint : inability or disinclination to resist desire or impulse; *esp* : SALACIOUSNESS, DISSOLUTENESS ⟨fell into a life of sexual and alcoholic ~⟩ **2** : inability to retain a bodily discharge (as urine) voluntarily

**in·continency** \"+\ *n* [ME, fr. L *incontinentia*] **1** : INCONTINENCE **2** : an act of incontinence; *esp* : illicit sexual intercourse — usu. used in pl. ⟨the record of his manifold *incontinencies*⟩

**in·continent** \"+\ *adj* [ME, fr. MF or L; MF, fr. L *incontinent-, incontinens*, fr. *in-* 1in- + *continent-, continens* continent — more at CONTINENT] **1** : marked by incontinence : lacking control : UNRESTRAINED ⟨the thunderous drumming ~ downpour —Gertrude Diamant⟩; *esp* : sexually dissolute ⟨the ~ man's evil appetite —J.E.Hankins⟩ **2** : unable to retain a bodily discharge (as urine) voluntarily

1**in·continently** \"+\ *also* **incontinent** *adv* [*incontinently* fr. MF *incontinent* + E *-ly*; *incontinent* fr. ME, fr. MF, fr. LL *in continenti*] **1** : at once : without delay : IMMEDIATELY ⟨~ turned and fled⟩ **2** : with unceremonious haste : PELL-MELL ⟨fled ~ until I reached a herd's cottage —John Buchan⟩

2**incontinently** \"\ *adv* [*incontinent* (adj.) + *-ly*] : in an incontinent or unrestrained manner: as **a** : LEWDLY, LOOSELY **b** : without due or reasonable consideration ⟨making the speech he had ~ promised⟩

**in·continuous** \¦in+\ *adj* [1in- + *continuous*] : not continuous

**in·controllable** \¦in+\ *adj* [1in- + *controllable*] : UNCONTROLLABLE

**in·controllably** \"+\ *adv* : UNCONTROLLABLY

**in·controvertible** \(ˌ)in, ən+\ *adj* [1in- + *controvertible*] : not open to question : INDISPUTABLE, CERTAIN ⟨~ evidence⟩ ⟨it seemed ~ that he had deceived his friend⟩ — **in·contro·vertibly** \"+\ *adv*

**in con·tu·ma·ci·am** \¦in,käntəˈmākē,äm\ *adv* [L, lit., in contumacy] : in contempt of or in disobedience to an order or summons of a court — used chiefly in ecclesiastical law of one who has refused to submit to or appear in a court and who is thereupon convicted or condemned in his absence

1**in·convenience** \¦in+\ *n* [ME, fr. LL *inconvenientia*, fr. L *inconvenient-, inconveniens* + *-ia* -y] **1** : the quality or state of being inconvenient: as **a** *obs* : INCONGRUITY, UNSUITABLENESS, IMPROPRIETY **b** *obs* : HARM, MISCHIEF, MISFORTUNE, TROUBLE; *also* : an injury esp. when general or public as distinguished from an injury to one or a few **c** : the quality or state of being unsuited or unadapted to personal needs or comfort : DISADVANTAGE, DISCOMFORT ⟨the ~ of his quarters⟩ **2** : something that is inconvenient : something that gives trouble, embarrassment, or uneasiness : something that disturbs or impedes : DISADVANTAGE, HANDICAP ⟨loss of this extra income was a serious ~⟩ ⟨found the daily trip an ~⟩

2**inconvenience** \"\ *vt* : to subject to inconvenience : INCOMMODE

**in·conveniency** \¦in+\ *n* [LL *inconvenientia*] : INCONVENIENCE

1**in·convenient** \"+\ *adj* [ME, fr. MF, fr. L *inconvenient-, inconveniens*, fr. *in-* 1in + *convenient-, conveniens*, prp. of *convenire* to come together, be suitable — more at CONVENIENT] **1** *obs* **a** : not agreeing : INCONGRUOUS, IRRATIONAL **b** : not suitable : UNFIT **c** : morally unbecoming : IMPROPER **2** : not convenient : giving trouble, uneasiness, or annoyance : DISADVANTAGEOUS, INOPPORTUNE ⟨an ~ house⟩ ⟨a most ~ arrangement⟩ — **in·conveniently** \"+\ *adv* — **in·con·ve·nient·ness** *n* -ES

2**inconvenient** *n* -S [ME, fr. *inconvenient*, adj.] *obs* : something inconvenient: as **a** : INCONGRUITY, INCONSISTENCY, ABSURDITY **b** : an unbecoming or improper act **c** : INCONVENIENCE

**in·conversable** \¦in+\ *adj* [1in- + *conversable*] : UNCOMMUNICATIVE, RESERVED

**in·conversant** \(ˌ)in, ən+\ *adj* [1in- + *conversant*] : lacking experience in or familiarity with

**in·convertibility** \¦in+\ *n* : the quality or state of being inconvertible — used chiefly of foreign exchange

**in·convertible** \"+\ *adj* [prob. fr. LL *inconvertibilis*, fr. L *in-* 1in- + *convertibilis* changeable — more at CONVERTIBLE] : not capable of being changed into or exchanged for something else ⟨the alchemists were unwilling to accept the ~ nature of elemental metals⟩: **a** *of paper money* : not exchangeable on demand for specie **b** *of a currency* : not exchangeable for a foreign currency — **in·con·vert·ibly** \-əblē, -li\ *adv*

**in·convincible** \¦in+\ *adj* [prob. fr. LL *inconvincibilis*, fr. L *in-* 1in- + *convincibilis* able to be convinced, fr. L *convincere* to convince + *-ibilis* -ible — more at CONVINCE] : incapable of being convinced

**incony** *adj* [origin unknown] *obs* : PRETTY

**in·cooperative** \¦in+\ *adj* [1in- + *cooperative*] : lacking in cooperation or in ability or will to cooperate ⟨the patient's family was wholly ~⟩ : UNCOOPERATIVE

**in·coordinate** *also* **in·coordinated** \"+\ *adj* [1in- + *coordinate, coordinated*] : lacking coordination : not coordinate

**in·coordination** \¦in+\ *n* [ISV 1in- + *coordination*] : lack of coordination; *esp* : lack of coordination of muscular movements resulting from loss of voluntary control and usu. associated with disease — compare ATAXIA

**in·coronate** *also* **in·coronated** \ən+\ *adj* [*incoronate* fr. ML *incoronatus*, past part. of *incoronare* to crown, fr. L *in-* 2in- + *coronare* to crown; *incoronated* fr. 2in- + *coronated* — more at CROWN] : CROWNED, CORONATED

**in·coronation** \"+\ *n* [ML *incoronation-, incoronatio*, fr. *incoronatus* + L *-ion-, -io* -ion] : CORONATION

**in·corporable** \ən'kȯ(r)p(ə)rəbəl\ *adj* [L *incorporare* + E *-able*] : capable of being incorporated

**in·corporal** \(ˈ)in, ən+\ *adj* [L *incorporalis*, fr. *in-* 1in- + *corporalis* corporal — more at CORPORAL] : INCORPOREAL

1**in·cor·po·rate** \ən'kȯ(r)pə,rāt, *usu* -ād·+V\ *vb* -ED/-ING/-S [ME *incorporaten*, fr. LL *incorporatus*, past part. of *incorporare*, fr. L *in-* 2in- + *corpor-, corpus* body — more at MIDRIFF] *vt* **1 a** : to unite with or introduce into something already existent usu. so as to form an indistinguishable whole that cannot be restored to the previously separate elements without damage ⟨the complex processes by which food is *incorporated* with living tissues⟩ ⟨the committee recommended that we ~ several new rules into the bylaws⟩ **b** : to admit to membership in a corporation; *esp* : to admit (a person) to the rank, status, and privileges of an advanced degree at a British university on the basis of possession of a like degree earned at another institution **2 a** : to combine (ingredients) into one consistent whole : unite intimately (as into a new substance or presentation) ⟨*incorporated* his ideas in a monograph on classical philology⟩ : blend, combine, or mingle thoroughly to form a homogeneous product ⟨mechanically *incorporating* the materials into a smooth uniform paste⟩ **b** : to bring together in an association; *specif* : to form into a corporation recognized by law as an entity and having particular functions, rights, duties, and liabilities **3** : to give material form to : EMBODY ~ *vi* **1** : to become unified with something into a composite whole ⟨these ideas gradually *incorporated* with existing religious beliefs to form a new philosophy⟩ **2 a** *archaic* : to mingle together so as to form a new whole **b** : to form or become a corporation ⟨they will ~ as soon as they have a little more capital⟩

2**in·cor·po·rate** \ən'kȯrp(ə)rət, -ȯ(ə)p-, *usu* -əd·+V\ *adj* [ME *incorporat*, fr. LL *incorporatus*, past part.] **1** : made one body or united in one body : intimately united or blended : EMBODIED ⟨the doctrines ~ in scriptural writings⟩ **2 a** : formed into a corporation : INCORPORATED ⟨an ~ municipality⟩ **b** *obs*, *of people* : associated as members of a corporation

3**in·cor·po·rate** \(ˈ)in¦kȯrp(ə)rət, ən'k-\ *adj* [LL *incorporatus*, fr. L *in-* 1in- + *corporatus*, past part. of *corporare* to make into a body — more at CORPORATE] *archaic* : INCORPOREAL, SPIRITUAL

**incorporated** *adj* : united in one body : formed into a corporation : made a legal entity

**in·cor·po·rat·ed·ness** *n* -ES : the quality or state of being incorporated : INCORPORATION

**incorporated territory** *n* : a portion of the domain of the U.S. that does not constitute and is not a part of any state but that is considered a part of the U.S. proper and is entitled to all the benefits of the Constitution that are not specifically reserved to the states ⟨Arizona, Oklahoma, and New Mexico were all *incorporated territories* before attaining statehood⟩

**incorporating** *adj* **1** : serving to incorporate : uniting in one body **2** *of language or grammar* : POLYSYNTHETIC

**incorporating union** *n* : a union of two or more states into one political whole ⟨the association of the several sovereign states of Germany into the German Empire can be considered an *incorporating union*⟩

**in·cor·po·ra·tion** \(ˌ)in,kȯ(r)pəˈrāshən, ən-\ *n* [ME *incorporacioun, incorperacioun*, fr. LL *incorporation-, incorporatio*, fr. *incorporatus* (past part. of *incorporare* to incorporate) + L *-ion-, -io* -ion — more at INCORPORATE] **1** : an act of incorporating or the state of being incorporated: as **a** : a union of something with an existing whole into a new intimate and usu. permanent new whole ⟨~ of plasticizer with a resin⟩ ⟨~ of the conquered territory into the empire⟩ **b** : a union of diverse things into a whole : intimate mingling : COMBINATION, SYNTHESIS ⟨the ~ of these rough notes into a coherent report⟩ **c** : a creation of a corporation or esp. of a legal corporate entity **d** : INCARNATION, EMBODIMENT **2 a** *obs* : a charter of incorporation **b** : an incorporated association or entity : CORPORATION **3** : the process of word and sentence formation characteristic of incorporating languages

**incorporation by reference** : a doctrine in law: the terms of a contemporaneous or earlier writing, instrument, or document capable of being identified can be made an actual part of another writing, instrument, or document by referring to, identifying, and adopting the former as part of the latter

**in·cor·po·ra·tive** \ən'kȯ(r)pə,rād·|iv, -p(ə)rə|, |t|, |ēv *also* |əv\ *adj* : incorporating or tending to incorporate: as **a** *of language* : AGGLUTINATIVE, POLYSYNTHETIC **b** *of a state* : growing by taking over and incorporating adjacent territories ⟨the Russian Empire was a typical ~ state⟩

**in·cor·po·ra·tor** \-pə,rād·ə(r), -ātə-\ *n* : one that incorporates: as **a** : any of the persons who join as original members in incorporating a company : a member at any time of a corporation aggregate : a corporator in a corporation having no capital stock : a promoter of a corporation named as an original member **b** : a member of one British university who is incorporated in another

**in·cor·po·ra·tor·ship** \-,ship\ *n* -S : membership in a corporation

1**in·corporeal** \¦in+,=¦==\ *adj* [L *incorporeus* (fr. *in-* 1in- + *corporeus* of the body) + E *-al* — more at CORPOREAL] **1** : not corporeal : having no material body or form : not consisting of matter : IMMATERIAL **2** : of, relating to, or characteristic of beings who lack material substance ⟨~ speed⟩ ⟨that ~ music⟩ **3** : of, relating to, or constituting a right that has no physical existence but that issues out of corporate property which has a physical existence and that concerns or is annexed to or exercisable in relation to such property (as stocks, bonds, mineral rights, patents) : existing only in contemplation of law ⟨an ~ hereditament⟩ — **in·corporeality** \¦in+\ *n* — **incorporeally** \"+,=¦===\ *adv*

2**incorporeal** \"\ *n* : something that is incorporeal : an immaterial or spiritual being

**incorporeal chattel** *n* : CHOSE IN ACTION

**in·cor·po·re·i·ty** \,in,kȯ(r)pəˈrēəd·ē\ *n* [*incorporeal* + *-ity*] : the quality or state of being incorporeal : IMMATERIALITY; *also* : an incorporeal attribute or entity

**incorporeous** *adj* [L *incorporeus*] *obs* : INCORPOREAL

**in·corpsed** \ən'kȯ(ə)rpst\ *adj* [2in- + *corpse* + *-ed*] : made one with : incorporated into

**in·correct** \¦in+\ *adj* [ME, fr. MF or L; MF, fr. L *incorrectus*, fr. *in-* 1in- + *correctus*, past part. of *corrigere* to correct — more at CORRECT] **1** *obs* : not corrected or chastened ⟨it shows a will most ~ to heaven —Shak.⟩ **2** : failing to agree with a copy or model or with established rules : INACCURATE, FAULTY ⟨a careless ~ transcription⟩ ⟨an ~ edition⟩ **3 a** : failing to agree with the requirements of duty, morality, or propriety : UNBECOMING, IMPROPER ⟨~ behavior⟩ ⟨this neglect was most ~⟩ **b** : not acceptable to the best taste ⟨gray flannels are ~ for tennis⟩ **4** : failing to coincide with the truth : INACCURATE, IMPRECISE ⟨your answers are all ~⟩ **5** *of a word or expression* : formed or used in violation of grammatical principles

**in·correctly** \"+\ *adv* : in an incorrect manner

**in·correctness** \"+\ *n* : the quality or state of being incorrect

**in·correspondence** *or* **in·correspondency** \(ˌ)in+\ *n* [1in- + *correspondence, correspondency*] : lack of correspondence or harmony

**in·corrigibility** \(ˌ)in, ən+\ *n* : the quality or state of being incorrigible

1**in·corrigible** \"+\ *adj* [ME, fr. LL *incorrigibilis*, fr. L *in-* 1in- + *corrigere* to correct + *-ibilis* -ible — more at CORRECT] : incapable of being corrected or amended: as **a** (1) : bad beyond the possibility of correction or rehabilitation : utterly bad or depraved ⟨an ~ criminal⟩ ⟨such ~ conduct⟩ (2) : *of a child* : persistently bad : DELINQUENT ⟨a training school for ~ boys⟩ **b** *archaic* : INCURABLE, IRREMEDIABLE **c** : requiring no improvement or alteration : being perfect as formed or formulated ⟨his judgment is not infallible or ~ —T.D.Weldon⟩ ⟨~ truth⟩ **d** : UNMANAGEABLE, UNRULY ⟨~ hair⟩ **e** (1) : unwilling to change or to give something up ⟨an ~ traveler⟩ ⟨an ~ amateur mechanic⟩ (2) : not readily altered : STRONG, INTENSE ⟨felt an ~ optimism⟩ ⟨irritating ~ self-assurance⟩

2**incorrigible** \"\ *n* -S : something incorrigible; *esp* : an incorrigible person

**in·cor·ri·gi·ble·ness** \-nəs\ *n* -ES : the quality or state of being incorrigible

**in·corrigibly** \(ˈ)in, ən+\ *adv* : in an incorrigible manner

**in·corrodable** *also* **in·corrodible** \¦in+\ *adj* [*incorrodable* alter. of *incorrodible*; *incorrodible* fr. 1in- + *corrodible*] : impervious to corrosion

**in·corrupt** *also* **in·corrupted** \"+\ *adj* [*incorrupt* fr. ME, fr. L *incorruptus*, fr. *in-* 1in- + *corruptus* past part. of *corrumpere* to corrupt; *incorrupted* fr. 1in- + past part. of *corrupt* — more at CORRUPT] : free from corruption: as **a** *obs* : not affected with decay : not putrefied or rotten : SOUND **b** : INCORRUPTIBLE **c** : not defiled or depraved : PURE, SOUND, UNTAINTED, UPRIGHT, HONEST **d** : free from error ⟨an ~ edition prepared from the original text⟩ — **in·corruptly** \"+\ *adv* — **in·corruptness** \"+\ *n*

**in·corruptibility** \¦in+\ *n* [ME *incorrumptibiletee*, fr. LL *incorruptibilitas*, fr. *incorruptibilis* incorruptible + L *-itas* -ity] : the quality or state of being incorruptible

1**in·corruptible** \"+\ *adj* [ME, fr. MF or LL; MF, fr. LL *incorruptibilis*, fr. L *in-* 1in- + LL *corruptibilis* corruptible — more at CORRUPTIBLE] : incapable of corruption: as **a** : not subject to decay or dissolution ⟨gold is ~ by most chemical agents⟩ **b** : incapable of being bribed or morally corrupted : inflexibly just and upright

2**incorruptible** \"\ *n* -S : something that is not subject to corruption; *esp* : something of spiritual nature

**in·cor·rupt·ible·ness** \-nəs\ *n* : INCORRUPTIBILITY

**in·cor·rupt·ibly** \-əblē, -li\ *adv* : in an incorruptible manner

**in·corruption** \¦in+\ *n* [LL *incorruption-, incorruptio*, fr. L *in-* 1in- + *corruption-, corruptio* corruption — more at CORRUPTION] **1** *archaic* : the quality or state of being free from physical decay **2** : freedom from corrupt practices : UPRIGHTNESS, HONESTY

**incounter** *obs var of* ENCOUNTER

**incourage** *obs var of* ENCOURAGE

**incr** *abbr* increase; increased; increasing

1**incrassate** *vb* -ED/-ING/-S [LL *incrassatus*, past part. of *incrassare*, fr. L *in-* 2in- + *crassare* to thicken, fr. *crassus* thick — more at HURDLE] *obs* : THICKEN, INSPISSATE — **incrassation** *n* -S

2**in·cras·sate** \ən'kra,sāt\ *also* **in·cras·sat·ed** \-ād·əd\ *adj* [LL *incrassatus*] **1** : THICKENED **2** *of a plant or animal structure* : SWOLLEN, INFLATED ⟨an ~ cell wall⟩

**in·creas·able** \(ˈ)in¦krēsəbəl, ən'k-\ *adj* : capable of being increased ⟨his income was no way ~⟩

1**in·crease** \(ˈ)in¦krēs, ən'k-\ *vb* -ED/-ING/-S [ME *encresen, incresen*, fr. MF *encreiss-*, stem of *encreistre, encroistre*, fr. L *increscere*, fr. *in-* 2in- + *crescere* to grow — more at CRESCENT] *vi* **1** : to become greater in some respect (as in size, quantity, number, degree, value, intensity, power, authority, reputation, wealth) : GROW, ADVANCE, WAX — opposed to *decrease* ⟨his wealth *increased* over the years⟩ ⟨*increasing* in knowledge through study⟩ **2** : to multiply by the production of young : be prolific ⟨the herd ~*s* yearly⟩ **3** *of a Latin noun or adjective* : to have a syllable more in the genitive than in the nominative (as in *rex, regis*) ~ *vt* **1** : to make greater in some respect (as in bulk, quantity, extent, value, or amount) : add to : ENHANCE ⟨~ his possessions⟩ **2** *archaic* : to cause to be richer, more prosperous, or more powerful : ENRICH, PROMOTE **3** : to add (a stitch) to knitting by knitting twice in the same stitch (as in the front and the back of the stitch)

**syn** ENLARGE, AUGMENT, MULTIPLY: INCREASE intransitively may carry the idea of progressive growth in numbers, size, amount, quantity or intensity ⟨our population is *increasing*⟩ ⟨prices *increased* on all necessities —*Collier's Yr. Bk.*⟩ ⟨the rice yield to the acre *increased* with improved methods —*Amer. Guide Series: Texas*⟩; transitively this notion is not so prominent ⟨the trustees *increased* salaries⟩ ENLARGE suggests expansion or extension of any sort ⟨to *enlarge* a building⟩ ⟨*enlarging* the farm⟩ ⟨*enlarging* the personnel of the department⟩ ⟨the abundant opportunities which the aesthetic realm provides to *enlarge* our experience —Hunter Mead⟩ ⟨early New England life when strong men enjoyed religion and *enlarged* their minds by profound metaphysical discussion —C.A.Dinsmore⟩ AUGMENT intransitively may suggest further growth, development, or increase of something already grown or developed ⟨the literature of cryptography, both in the form of secret government manuals and openly published books, had *augmented* enormously since 1880 —Fletcher Pratt⟩; transitively it may suggest addition to sufficiency or ampleness ⟨the city police, *augmented* by special deputies, were also called out —*Amer. Guide Series: Tenn.*⟩ ⟨by their weight, which was *augmented* by laying a number of old rails on the top, these slabs have the effect of preventing any tendency for the clay to work up —O.S.Nock⟩ MULTIPLY intransitively may suggest increase by natural generation ⟨in those days the Anglo-American stock, a very fine one, *multiplied* like rabbits —W.R. Inge⟩ ⟨mosquitoes *multiply* rapidly⟩; in all uses it is likely to indicate increasing manifold ⟨skins which would *multiply* Mr. Astor's wealth —Meridel Le Sueur⟩ ⟨those ships had *multiplied* until their very numbers were menacing —Kenneth Roberts⟩

2**in·crease** \ˈin,krēs *also* ən'k-\ *n* -S [ME *encres, incres*, fr. *encresen, incresen*, v.] **1** : act of increasing: as **a** : addition or enlargement in size, extent, quantity, number, intensity, value, substance : AUGMENTATION, GROWTH, MULTIPLICATION ⟨an ~ of knowledge⟩ **b** *obs* : production of young : PROPAGATION **c** *obs* (1) : growth in wealth, dignity, or influence : ADVANCEMENT (2) : the rising of flood or tidal waters **2** : something that results from or is produced by increasing : an addition or increment : something that is added to the original stock by augmentation or growth (as progeny, issue, offspring, produce, profit, interest)

**increased** *adj* : subjected to augmentation : made or become greater ⟨~ time for study⟩ ⟨the ~ wealth of the nation⟩ — **in·creased·ly** \(ˈ)in¦krēsədlē, ən'k-, -stl-, -li\ *adv*

**increaseful** *adj*, *obs* : full of increase : PRODUCTIVE

**in·crease·ment** \(ˈ)in¦krēsmənt, ən'k-\ *n* -S [ME *encresement*, fr. *encresen* to increase + *-ment*] *archaic* : INCREASE

**in·creas·er** \-sə(r)\ *n* -s **:** one that increases: as **a :** an agent that causes something to increase ⟨these ~s of public turmoil⟩ **b** *archaic* **:** one that promotes or furthers something (as a cause, a group) **c :** a plant or animal that tends to multiply freely ⟨several of the new glads proved to be excellent ~s⟩ **d :** a coupling for joining a pipe to another of larger diameter

increaser d: *1* smaller pipe, *2* increaser, *3* larger pipe

**increasing** *adj* **:** becoming progressively greater ⟨to an ~ degree⟩ ⟨settlers came in in ~ numbers⟩

**increasing function** *n* **:** a mathematical function whose value algebraically increases as the independent variable algebraically increases over a given range

**in·creas·ing·ly** *adv* **:** to an increasing degree **:** more and more ⟨became ~ apparent⟩ ⟨~ of the opinion —W.H.Camp⟩

**in·cre·ate** \ˈinkrē,āt, ən'krēət\ *adj* [ME *increat*, fr. LL *increatus*, fr. L *in-* ¹in- + *creatus*, past part. of *creare* to create — more at CRESCENT] **:** UNCREATED, SELF-EXISTENT — **in·cre·ate·ly** *adv*

**in·creative** \(ˈ)in, ən+\ *adj* [¹*in-* + *creative*] **:** incapable of creating

**in·credibility** \(ˈ)in, ən+\ *n* **1 :** the quality or state of being incredible ⟨the sheer ~ of this situation⟩ **2 :** something that is incredible ⟨all these tales and *incredibilities*⟩

**in·credible** \(ˈ)in, ən+\ *adj* [ME, fr. L *incredibilis*, fr. *in-* ¹in- + *credibilis* credible — more at CREDIBLE] **1 a :** surpassing belief **:** too extraordinary and improbable to admit of belief ⟨an ~ cost⟩ **b :** hard to believe real or true **:** UNLIKELY, IMPROBABLE ⟨the children's appetite was ~⟩ **2** *obs* **:** INCREDULOUS, UNBELIEVING — **in·credibleness** \"+\ *n* — **in·credibly** \"+\ *adv*

**in·creditable** \"+\ *adj* [¹*in-* + *creditable*] *archaic* **:** not creditable

**in·credulity** \ˌin+\ *n* [ME *incredulite*, fr. L *incredulitas*, fr. *incredulus* + *-itas* -ity] **:** the quality or state of being incredulous **:** a withholding or refusal of belief **:** DISBELIEF

**in·credulous** \(ˈ)in, ən+\ *adj* [L *incredulus*, fr. *in-* ¹in- + *credulus* credulous — more at CREDULOUS] **1 :** indisposed to admit or accept what is related as true ⟨~ of such statements⟩ **2 :** caused by disbelief or incredulity ⟨an ~ stare⟩ **3** *obs* **:** not to be believed **:** INCREDIBLE — **in·credulously** \"+\ *adv* — **in·credulousness** \"+\ *n*

**in·creep** \ˈ=,=\ *vi* [ME *increpen*, fr. ²*in* + *crepen* to creep — more at CREEP] **:** to enter bit by bit or by slow degrees **:** creep in ⟨the ~*ing* frost⟩

**in·cremation** \ˌin+=ˈ==\ *n* [²*in* + *cremation*] **:** CREMATION

**in·cre·ment** \ˈiŋkrəmənt, ˈink-\ *n* -s [ME, fr. L *incrementum*, fr. *increscere* to increase + *-mentum* -ment — more at INCREASE] **1 :** an increasing or growth in bulk, quantity, number, or value **:** ENLARGEMENT, INCREASE **2 a :** something that is gained or added **:** an added quantity or character **b :** one of a series of regular consecutive additions of like or proportional size or value — compare UNEARNED INCREMENT **c :** one of a series of minute additions **:** a slight or imperceptible augmentation **3 :** increase in volume or value of a forest or its products during a given period **4 a :** a positive or negative change in the value of one or more of a set of variables **b :** an amount of powder packed in a bag that may be added to or removed from the propelling charge of semifixed or separate loading ammunition to permit fire at varying ranges and with varying angles of impact

**in·cre·men·tal** \ˌ==ˈment°l\ *adj* **:** of, relating to, constituting, or resulting from increments, increase, or growth

**incremental repetition** *n* **:** repetition in each stanza after the first of part of the preceding stanza — used esp. of popular ballads

**increment borer** *n* **:** ACCRETION BORER

**in·cre·pa·tion** \ˌinkrəˈpāshən\ *n* -s [MF or LL; MF, fr. LL *increpation-, increpatio*, fr. L *increpatus* (past part. of *increpare* to make a noise, upbraid, fr. *in-* ²in- + *crepare* to crack, creak, break) + *-ion-, -io* -ion — more at RAVEN] *archaic* **:** CHIDING, REBUKE, REPROOF

¹**in·crescent** \(ˈ)in, ən+\ *n* [L *increscent-, increscens*, pres. part.] **:** an increscent representation of the moon

²**increscent** \"+\ *adj* [L *increscent-, increscens*, pres. part. of *increscere* to increase — more at INCREASE] **1 :** becoming greater by gradual augmentation **:** INCREASING **2** *of the moon* **:** WAXING; *specif* **:** having the horns pointing to the dexter side

increscent

**in·cre·tion** \(ˈ)inˈkrēshən, ən-\ *n* -s [ISV ²*in-* + *secretion*] **1 :** internal secretion **:** secretion into the blood or tissues rather than into a cavity or outlet of the body **2 :** a product of internal secretion **:** AUTACOID, HORMONE — **in·cre·tion·ary** \-shə,nerē\ *adj*

**in·cre·to·ry** \(ˈ)inˈkrēd·ərē, ən'k-\ *adj* [²*in-* + *secretory*] **:** ENDOCRINE ⟨~ organs⟩

**in·crim·i·nate** \ən'krimə,nāt, *usu* -ād·+V\ *vt* [LL *incriminatus*, past part. of *incriminare*, fr. L *in-* ²in- + *crimin-, crimen* crime — more at CRIME] **1 a :** to charge with a crime or fault ⟨he *incriminated* the other boys to the teacher⟩ **b :** to furnish evidence or proof of circumstances tending to show the guilt of ⟨the testimony certainly ~s the brother⟩ ⟨those feathers under the cage are enough to ~ the cat⟩ **c :** to involve (as oneself) in a criminal prosecution or the risk of one ⟨unwilling to testify for fear of *incriminating* himself⟩ **2 :** to charge with involvement in or establish as sharing responsibility for some undesirable effect or result ⟨eye gnats have been *incriminated* in some outbreaks of pinkeye⟩ ⟨poor lighting is often *incriminated* in eyestrain⟩ **syn** see ACCUSE

**in·crim·i·na·tion** \(,)in,krimə'nāshən, ən,k-\ *n* [LL *incrimination-, incriminatio*, fr. *incriminatus* + L *-ion-, -io* -ion] **:** the act of incriminating or the state of being incriminated

**in·crim·i·na·tor** \=ˈ==,nād·ə(r), -ātə-\ *n* **:** one that incriminates

**in·crim·i·na·to·ry** \-,nə,tōrē, -tōrē, -ri\ *adj* **:** tending to incriminate

**incroach** *obs var of* ENCROACH

¹**incross** \ˈ=,=\ *n* [⁴*in* + *cross* (n.)] **1 :** an individual produced by crossing inbred lines of the same breed or strain — compare INCROSSBRED **2 :** an instance or act of crossing inbred lines of the same breed or strain

²**incross** \ˈ=,=\ *vt* [²*in* + *cross* (v.)] **:** to interbreed (inbred lines of a breed or strain)

**incrossbred** \ˈ=ˈ=,=\ *n* [⁴*in* + *crossbred*] **:** an individual produced by crossing inbred lines of separate breeds or strains — compare INCROSS

**incrossbreed** \ˌ=ˈ=,ˈ=, ˈ=ˈ=,=\ *vt* [²*in* + *crossbreed*] **:** to cause (inbred lines of different breeds or strains) to interbreed

**in·crotchet** \ən+\ *vt* [²*in-* + *crotchet* (n.)] *archaic* **:** to enclose in brackets

**in·croy·a·ble** \aⁿkrwäˈyäbl(ᵊ), -b(lə)\ *n* -s [F, fr. *incroyable*, adj., incredible, fr. MF, fr. *in-* ¹in- + *croyable* credible, fr. *croire* to believe (fr. L *credere*) + *-able*; fr. their extravagant dress and speech — more at CREED] **:** a French dandy of the late 18th century **:** DANDY, FOP

**incruent** *also* **incruental** *or* **incruentous** [*incruent, incruentous* fr. L *incruentus*, fr. *in-* ¹in- + *cruentus* bloody; *incruental* fr. L *incruentus* + E *-al*] *adj, obs* **:** UNBLOODY

**incrust** *var of* ENCRUST

**incrustant** *var of* ENCRUSTANT

¹**in·crus·tate** \ən'krə,stāt, ˈin,k\ *vt* -ED/-ING/-S [L *incrustatus*, past part. of *incrustare* — more at ENCRUST] **:** ENCRUST

²**in·crus·tate** \ən'k-\ *adj* [L *incrustatus*] **1 :** formed into or like a crust **2 :** having a crust

**in·crus·ta·tion** \ˌin,krəˈstāshən\ *or* **en·crus·ta·tion** \ˌen,-\ *n* [L *incrustation-, incrustatio*, fr. *incrustatus* + *-ion-, -io* -ion] **1 :** the act of encrusting or state of being encrusted **:** formation of a crust **2 a :** a crust or hard coating of something upon or within a body **b :** a growth or accumulation (as of habits, opinions, customs) resembling an encrusting layer **3 :** a covering or inlaying (as of marble or mosaic) attached to masonry by cramp irons or cement **4 :** something applied as an overlay or inlay ⟨~ of diamonds⟩

**in·cu·bate** \ˈiŋkyə,bāt, ˈink-, *usu* -ād·+V\ *vb* -ED/-ING/-S [L *incubatus*, past part. of *incubare* to lie upon, hatch, fr. *in-* ²in- + *cubare* to lie down, lie upon — more at HIP] *vt* **1 :** to sit upon (eggs) so as to hatch by the warmth of the body in the manner of most birds **:** BROOD **2 :** to maintain (as eggs, embryos of animals, or bacteria) under prescribed and usu. controlled conditions (as of temperature and moisture) favorable for hatching or development esp. in an incubator **3 :** to maintain (a chemically active system) under controlled conditions for the development of a reaction **4 :** to cause to develop **:** give form and substance to ⟨*incubated* the new idea for a while before giving it to his supervisor⟩ ~ *vi* **1 :** to sit on eggs **:** BROOD **2 :** to undergo incubation ⟨the cultures must ~ for five more days⟩ **3 :** to acquire form and substance **:** DEVELOP ⟨the plan *incubated* slowly on his nightly walks from work⟩

**in·cu·ba·tion** \ˌ==ˈbāshən\ *n* -s [L *incubation-, incubatio*, fr. *incubatus* + *-ion-, -io* -ion] **1 :** the act or process of incubating (as eggs, bacteria, or milk) ⟨during the ~ of the culture⟩ **2 :** the act or an instance of brooding over something in order to give it form and substance ⟨definitely named the four stages of creative thought as preparation, ~, illumination, and verification —R.S.Woodworth⟩ **3 :** the period between the infection of a plant or animal by a pathogen and the manifestation of the disease it causes **4 :** a rite among the ancient Greeks and Romans of sleeping on a skin or on the ground in order to enter into communion with the chthonic gods through dreams

**in·cu·ba·tion·al** \ˌ==ˈbāshən°l, -shnəl\ *adj* **:** of or relating to incubation

**incubation period** *n* **:** the period of brooding or incubating required to bring an egg to hatching; *broadly* **:** the length of incubating required to attain a desired or expected result ⟨many children's diseases have an *incubation period* of less than one week⟩

INCUBATION PERIODS

| BIRD | DAYS | BIRD | DAYS |
|---|---|---|---|
| canary | 14 | ostrich | 42 |
| common fowl | 21 | peafowl | 28 |
| duck | 28 | pheasant | 21–24 |
| goose | 28–32 | pigeon | 17–18 |
| guinea fowl | 26–28 | swan | 42 |
| muscovy duck | 35–37 | turkey | 28 |

**in·cu·ba·tist** \ˈ==,bātəst\ *n* -s *Brit* **:** a poultry hatcheryman

**in·cu·ba·tive** \-ād·iv\ *adj* **:** of or relating to incubation ⟨~ technique⟩ **:** characteristic of or marked by incubation ⟨~ period⟩

**in·cu·ba·tor** \-ād·ə(r), -ātə-\ *n* -s **:** one that incubates: as **a :** an apparatus by which eggs are hatched artificially consisting essentially of an insulated cabinet containing the eggs in trays or drawers, a source of artificial heat and of moisture, and controls to maintain a desired level of heat and moisture **b :** an apparatus for the maintenance of controlled conditions of heat and usu. moisture (as for the cultivation of microorganisms) **c :** an apparatus for housing premature or sick babies in an environment of controlled humidity, oxygen supply, and temperature

**incubator bird** *n* **:** MEGAPODE

**in·cu·ba·to·ri·um** \ˌ==,bäˈtōrēəm, (,)in,kyübəˈt-\ *n, pl* **incubato·ria** \-rēə\ *also* **incubatoriums** [NL, fr. L *incubatus* (past part. of *incubare* to lie upon, hatch) + *-orium* -ory — more at INCUBATE] **1 :** the ventral brooding pouch of a monotreme **2 :** MARSUPIUM 1a(1)

**in·cu·ba·to·ry** \ˈiŋkyəbə,tōrē, ˈink-, ˌ==ˈbād·ərē, ən'kyübə,tōrē\ *adj* **:** relating to or serving for incubation

**in·cu·bous** \ˈiŋkyəbəs, ˈink-\ *adj* [L *incubare* to lie upon + E *-ous* — more at INCUBATE] **1** *of leaves* **:** being so arranged that the anterior margin of each overlaps the posterior margin of the next younger **2 :** having incubous leaves ⟨~ liverworts⟩ — compare SUCCUBOUS

**in·cu·bus** \-bəs\ *n, pl* **incu·bi** \-,bī\ *also* **incubuses** [ME, fr. LL, fr. L *incubare* to lie upon, hatch] **1 :** an evil spirit believed to lie upon persons in their sleep and esp. to have sexual intercourse with women by night — compare SUCCUBUS **2 :** NIGHTMARE 2 **3 :** a person or thing that oppresses or burdens like a nightmare ⟨the security council — free for once from the ~ of the veto — was able to act swiftly and decisively —C.P.Romulo⟩

**incud-** *or* **incudo-** *comb form* [NL *incud-, incus*] **:** incus **:** incus and ⟨*incud*ectomy⟩ ⟨*incudo*malleal⟩

**in·cu·date** \ˈi[ŋ]kyə,dāt, |n|, (ˈ)=ˈkyüdət\ *also* **in·cu·dal** \-,d°l\ *adj* [*incud-* + *-ate* or *-al*] **1 :** of or relating to the incus **2 :** having an incus

**incudes** *pl of* INCUS

**in cuerpo** *adv (or adj)* [modif. of Sp *en cuerpo*, lit., in body] **1** *obs* **a :** in clothing that exposes the shape of the body **b :** in dishabille **2** *obs* **:** without clothing **:** in a naked or uncovered state

**in·cul·cate** \ən'kəl,kāt, ˈin(,)kə-, *usu* -ād·+V\ *vt* -ED/-ING/-S [L *inculcatus*, past part. of *inculcare*, lit., to tread on, fr. *in-* ²in- + *-culcare* (fr. *calcare* to tread on, trample, fr. *calc-, calx* heel) — more at CALK] **1 :** to teach and impress by frequent repetitions or admonitions **:** urge on or fix in the mind ⟨they *inculcated* these principles at every opportunity⟩ ⟨the current emotional religious revivals *inculcated* an enthusiasm for its strong feelings and vivid scenes —J.D.Hart⟩ — often used with *in* or *into*, sometimes with *upon* ⟨social pressures ~ behavior patterns in the young⟩ ⟨the techniques of plumbing were gradually *inculcated* upon his mind⟩ **2 :** to cause (as a person) to become impressed or instilled with something ⟨teachers who fail to ~ students with love of knowledge⟩ ⟨*inculcated* with every virtue⟩ — **in·cul·ca·tive** \ˈin(,)kəl,kād·iv, ən'kə-\ *adj* — **in·cul·ca·to·ry** \ən'kəlkə,tōrē, ˈin(,)kəlˈkād·ərē\ *adj* **syn** see IMPLANT

**in·cul·ca·tion** \ˌin(,)kəlˈkāshən\ *n* -s [LL *inculcation-, inculcatio*, fr. L *inculcatus* + *-ion-, -io* -ion] **:** an act of inculcating **:** teaching and impressing by frequent repetitions or admonitions

**in·cul·ca·tor** \ən'kəl,kād·ə(r), ˈin(,)kə-, -ātə-\ *n* -s [LL, fr. L *inculcatus* + *-or*] **:** one that inculcates

**in·culpability** \(ˈ)in, ən+\ *n* **:** the quality or state of being free from blame **:** INNOCENCE

**in·culpable** \(ˈ)in, ən+\ *adj* [LL *inculpabilis*, fr. L *in-* ¹in- + *culpabilis* culpable — more at CULPABLE] **:** free from guilt **:** BLAMELESS, INNOCENT — **in·culpably** \"+\ *adv*

**in·cul·pate** \ən'kəl,pāt, ˈin(,)kə-, *usu* -ād·+V\ *vt* -ED/-ING/-S [LL *inculpatus*, past part. of *inculpare*, fr. L *in-* ²in- + *culpatus*, past part. of *culpare* to blame — more at CULPABLE] **:** to impute guilt to **:** involve or implicate in a charge of misconduct **:** BLAME, INCRIMINATE ⟨his whole behavior tended to ~ him⟩ ⟨*inculpating* his brother to escape punishment himself⟩ — **in·cul·pa·tion** \ˌin(,)kəlˈpāshən\ *n* -s — **in·cul·pa·tive** \ˈin(,)kəl,pād·iv; (ˈ)inˈkəlpəd-, ən'k-\ *adj* — **in·cul·pa·to·ry** \ən'kəlpə,tōrē, *chiefly Brit* ˈin(,)kəlˈpātəri, -ā·tri\ *adj*

**in·cult** \(ˈ)inˈkəlt, ən'k-\ *adj* [L *incultus*, fr. *in-* ¹in- + *cultus*, past part. of *colere* to cultivate — more at WHEEL] **1** *archaic* **:** lacking the order that depends on tillage and cultivation **2 :** lacking finish or polish **:** CRUDE, DISORDERED — used esp. of literary style or its products or producers **3 :** lacking ease or smoothness of manner **:** UNCULTURED, RUDE, COARSE ⟨had not been an ~ sort of man ... he was quiet and sensitive —F.M. Ford⟩

**in·cul·ti·vate** \(ˈ)inˈkəltə,vāt\ *also* **in·cul·ti·vat·ed** \-ād·əd\ *adj* [*incultivate*, fr. ¹*in-* + ML *cultivatus*, past part. of *cultivare* to cultivate; *incultivated*, fr. ¹*in-* + *cultivated* — more at CULTIVATE] *archaic* **:** UNCULTIVATED

**in·culture** \(ˈ)in+\ *n* [¹*in-* + *culture*] *archaic* **:** lack of culture

**in·cum·bence** \ən'kəmbən(t)s\ *archaic var of* INCUMBENCY

**in·cum·ben·cy** \-bənsē, -si\ *n* -ES **1 :** the quality or state of being incumbent: as **a** *archaic* **:** a condition of bearing upon or overshadowing **b** *archaic* **:** the quality of being morally incumbent or incumbent as a correlate of something else **c :** the state of occupying a particular position (as a benefice or office) ⟨the mere ~ of the Labour party in the seats of authority —Edward Shils⟩ **2 :** something that is incumbent: as **a** *archaic* **:** a burdening or oppressive weight **b :** a duty, obligation, or responsibility incumbent usu. as a correlate of some position or relationship held ⟨felt it an ~ as his older brother to rebuke him⟩ ⟨these varied *incumbencies* of the father of a family⟩ **3 :** the sphere of action or period of office of an incumbent ⟨during an ~ of over 30 years⟩ ⟨six years of senatorial ~ —S.H.Adams⟩

¹**in·cum·bent** \-bənt\ *n* -s [ME, fr. L *incumbent-, incumbens*, pres. part. of *incumbere* to lie down on, give attention to, fr. *in-* ²in- + *-cumbere* to lie down (akin to L *cubare* to lie down) — more at HIP] **1 a :** the holder of an ecclesiastical benefice ⟨an archdiocese of which he was the first ~ —R.P.Casey⟩ **b :** the holder of an office esp. a public or academic office ⟨the holdover Republican ~s⟩ ⟨the last ~ of the professorship⟩ **2 :** one that occupies **:** OCCUPANT ⟨the previous ~s insisted that the house was haunted⟩ ⟨the modified bloomer ... [makes] the lower part stay put, no matter how the ~ sprawls —Lois Long⟩

²**incumbent** \"\ *adj* [L *incumbent-, incumbens*] **1 a :** lying or resting on something else esp. so as to exert a downward pressure **:** bearing down **b :** lying upon or apposed to — used either of cotyledons folded so that the hypocotyl is applied to the back of one of them or of an anther lying against the side of a filament but attached at only one point; compare ACCUMBENT 2 **c** *of a geologic stratum* **:** SUPERIMPOSED, OVERLYING **d** *of a bird's hind toe* **:** so placed that its whole length rests on the ground when the bird is standing — opposed to *insistent* **2** *obs* **:** busily engaged **:** ASSIDUOUS **3 :** falling or imposed as a duty, responsibility, or obligation — usu. used with *on* or *upon* ⟨~ on us to help⟩ ⟨demands ~ upon his position⟩ **4 :** having the status of an incumbent ⟨his duties while ~ of the secretaryship⟩; *esp* **:** occupying a specified office or position at a time expressed or implied ⟨defeated the ~ governor by a large plurality⟩ **5 a** *archaic* **:** bending over **:** OVERHANGING **b** *obs* **:** IMPENDING, THREATENING **c :** bent over so as to rest on or touch an underlying surface ⟨~ hairs on the body of an insect⟩

**in·cum·bent·ly** *adv* **:** in the manner of a duty, responsibility, or obligation

**in·cum·ber** \ən'kəmbə(r)\ *var of* ENCUMBER

**in·cu·na·ble** \ən'kyünəbəl\ *n* -s [F, fr. NL *incunabulum*] **:** INCUNABULUM

**in·cu·nab·u·lar** \ˌinkyəˈnabyələ(r)\ *adj* **:** relating to or typical of incunabula ⟨an ~ form of musical expression⟩

**in·cu·nab·u·list** \ˌ==ˈ==ləst\ *n* -s **:** one that makes a special study of incunabula

**in·cu·nab·u·lum** \-ləm\ *n, pl* **incunabu·la** \-lə\ [in sense 1, L *incunabula* swaddling clothes, cradle, origin, birthplace, fr. *in-* ²in- + *cunae* cradle + *-bulum* (n. suffix); in other senses, fr. NL, back-formation fr. L *incunabula* — more at CEMETERY] **1** *incunabula, pl* **:** earliest stages **:** BEGINNINGS, INFANCY ⟨the resulting symposium . . . outgrew its *incunabula* —*Times Lit. Supp.*⟩ **2 a :** a book printed before 1501 — called also *cradle book, fifteener* **b :** a work of art or of human industry of an early epoch **c :** a record, example, or memento of the early period of an art or human activity ⟨old record catalogs . . . any of the *incunabula* of . . . jazz —Ralph de Toledano⟩ **3 :** the cocoon of an insect

**in·cur** *R* ən'kər, + *vowel* -kər·; –*R* -kə̄, + *suffixal vowel* -kər· *also* -kə̄r, + *vowel in a following word* -kər· *or* -kə̄ *also* -kə̄r\ *vb* **incurred; incurred; incurring; incurs** [L *incurrere*, lit., to run into, fr. *in-* ²in- + *currere* to run — more at CURRENT] *vt* **1 :** to meet or fall in with (as an inconvenience) **:** become liable or subject to **:** bring down upon oneself ⟨*incurred* large debts to educate his children⟩ ⟨fully deserving the penalty he *incurred*⟩ **2** *obs* **:** to render liable or subject to **:** BRING, ENTAIL ~ *vi* **1 :** to fall as a part or lot, within a scope, or during or at a time **2** *archaic* **:** to occur as a result **:** become involved **:** ACCRUE

**in·curability** \(ˈ)in, ən+\ *n* **:** the quality or state of being incurable **:** INCURABLENESS

¹**in·curable** \(ˈ)in, ən+\ *adj* [ME, fr. MF or LL; MF, fr. LL *incurabilis*, fr. L *in-* ¹in- + *curabilis* curable — more at CURABLE] **1 :** impossible to cure ⟨an ~ disease⟩ **2 :** admitting of no remedy or correction ⟨~ optimism⟩ **:** being a thing specified beyond any possibility of alteration or control ⟨these ~ busybodies⟩

²**incurable** \"\ *n* -s **:** a person diseased beyond cure

**in·cur·able·ness** *n* -ES **:** the quality or state of being incurable

**in·cur·ably** \-blē, -bli\ *adv* **:** in an incurable manner **:** to an incurable degree ⟨an ~ social nature⟩

**in·curiosity** \(ˈ)in, ən+\ *n* [prob. fr. F *incuriosité*, fr. LL *incuriositat-, incuriositas*, fr. L *incuriosus* + *-itat-, -itas* -ity] **:** the quality or state of being incurious **:** INCURIOUSNESS

**in·curious** \(ˈ)in, ən+\ *adj* [L *incuriosus*, fr. *in-* ¹in- + *curiosus* curious — more at CURIOUS] **1 :** not curious or inquisitive **:** having no care or interest **:** INATTENTIVE, CARELESS ⟨a dull ~ gaze⟩ **2 a** *archaic* **:** done without care or nicety **:** HOMELY, COARSE **b** *obs* **:** not particular, fastidious, or critical **3** *archaic* **:** devoid of interest **:** dull and unappealing **:** not remarkable or attractive of attention **syn** see INDIFFERENT

**in·curiously** \"+\ *adv* **:** in an incurious manner **:** without curiosity or interest

**in·cu·ri·ous·ness** *n* **:** the quality or state of being incurious **:** lack of curiosity or interest

**in·cur·ment** \ən'kərmənt, -kə̄m-\ *n* -s **:** the act of incurring or state of being incurred ⟨prevented the ~ of further debts⟩ ⟨~ of guilt⟩

**in·cur·ra·ble** \-ˈkərəbəl *also* -ˈkə̄rə-\ *adj* **:** capable of being incurred

**in·cur·rence** \-ˈkər·ən(t)s *also* -ˈkə̄rə-\ *n* -s **:** the act or process of incurring ⟨~ of new responsibilities⟩

**in·cur·rent** \-nt\ *adj* [L *incurrent-, incurrens*, pres. part. of *incurrere* to run into, incur — more at INCUR] **:** running in: as **a :** occurring within a given time **b :** giving passage to a current that flows inward ⟨the ~ siphon of a bivalve mollusk⟩ ⟨an ~ pore on a sponge⟩ — see CLAM illustration

**in·cur·sion** \ən'kər|zhən, -kə̄|, -kəi|, *chiefly Brit* |shən\ *n* -s [ME, invasion, fr. MF or L; MF, fr. L *incursion-, incursio*, fr. *incursus* (past part. of *incurrere* to run into, attack, incur) + *-ion-, -io* -ion — more at INCUR] **1 :** an entering into a territory with hostile intention **:** a sudden invasion **:** a predatory or harassing inroad **:** RAID ⟨partners in the Suez ~ —*Newsweek*⟩ **2 a :** a running, bringing, or entering in or into ⟨~ of water through a weakened seam⟩ ⟨his only ~ into the arts⟩ ⟨the inevitable ~ of new techniques⟩ **b :** such action involving vigorous, forceful, or determined effort ⟨the barrier should have been sufficient to protect the adjoining owner against the ~s, not of all pigs, but of pigs of average vigor and obstinacy —B.N.Cardozo⟩ ⟨a very sudden ~ of "ah" into London speech between 1780 and 1790 —C.H.Grandgent⟩

**in·cur·sion·ary** \-zhə,nerē, -sh-, -ri\ *adj* **:** entering by or engaging in incursion **:** INVADING ⟨~ clays⟩ ⟨traces of this ~ nomad people⟩

**in·cur·sion·ist** \-zh(ə)nəst, -sh-\ *n* -s **:** a maker of an incursion **:** INVADER

**in·cur·sive** \(ˈ)inˈkərsiv, ən'k-\ *adj* [L *incursus* + E *-ive*] **:** making incursions **:** INVASIVE, AGGRESSIVE

¹**in·cur·var·i·id** \ˌin,kərˈva(a)rēəd\ *adj* [NL *Incurvariidae*] **:** of or relating to the family Incurvariidae

²**incurvariid** \"\ *n* -s **:** a moth of the family Incurvariidae

**in·cur·va·ri·idae** \ˌin,kərvəˈrīə,dē\ *n pl, cap* [NL, fr. *Incurvaria*, type genus (fr. L *incurvus* curved in — fr. *in-* ²in- + *curvus* curved — + NL *-aria*) + *-idae*] **:** a small family of minute inconspicuous moths usu. having larvae that are initially leaf miners and later casebearers

¹**in·cur·vate** \ˈin(,)kər,vāt, ən'k-\ *vb* -ED/-ING/-S [L *incurvatus*, past part. of *incurvare*, fr. *in-* ²in- + *curvare* to curve (fr. *curvus* curved) — more at CROWN] *vt* **1 :** to turn from a straight line or course **:** BEND, CROOK **:** cause to curve inward — used chiefly as past participle ⟨the gracefully *incurvated* column⟩ ~ *vi, obs* **:** to curve inward **:** BOW

²**in·cur·vate** \ˈin(,)kər,vāt, (ˈ)inˈkərvət\ *adj* [L *incurvatus*] **:** having an inward curvature **:** INCURVED

**in·curvation** \ˌin+\ *n* [L *incurvation-, incurvatio*, fr. *incurvatus* + *-ion-, -io* -ion] **1 :** the act, fact, or process of incurving or state of being incurved **:** CURVATURE, INCURVATURE **2** *obs* **:** GENUFLECTION, BOW

**in·curvature** \(ˈ)in+\ *n* [L *incurvatus* + E *-ure*] **:** the act, fact, or process of curving inward or state of being curved inward

¹**in·curve** \(ˈ)in+\ *vb* [L *incurvare*] *vt* **:** to bend so as to curve

: CURVE, CROOK; *esp* : to bend so that the resulting curve projects inward ~ *vi* : to bend or curve inward ⟨the corners ~ gracefully⟩

**²incurve** \'=,=\ *n* [⁴*in* + *curve*] **1** : a curving in ⟨clasped the jewel with a graceful ~ of the hands⟩ **2** : something that curves in ⟨the ~ at the head of the bay⟩; *esp* : DROP 2a(3)

**in·cus** \'iŋkəs, -,küs\ *n, pl* **in·cu·des** \iŋ'k(y)ü(,)dēz\ [NL, fr. L, anvil, fr. *incudere* to incuse, stamp, strike] **1 a** : the middle of a chain of three small bones in the ear of mammals — called also *anvil;* see EAR illustration **b** : the median Y-shaped structure in the mastax of a rotifer upon which the mallei work **2** : an anvil-shaped top of a thundercloud

**¹in·cuse** \(')in¦kyüz, -üs\ *adj* [L *incusus,* past part. of *incudere* to incuse, stamp, fr. *in-* ²in- + *cudere* to beat, stamp — more at HEW] : formed by stamping or punching in — used chiefly of old coins or features of their design

**²incuse** \"\ *n* -s : an incuse space, design, or lettering on a coin

**³in·cuse** \-üz\ *vt* -ED/-ING/-S [L *incusus*] : to punch or stamp in (as lettering or a design on a coin) : impress by striking

**in·cuse·ly** *adv* : in the form of an incuse or an incuse square

**incuse square** *n* : a sunken square on various ancient Greek coins with or without a raised design inside it

**in cus·to·dia le·gis** \¦in,kü'stōdēə'lāgəs\ *adv* [L] : in the custody of the law

**¹ind-** *or* **indo-** *comb form, usu cap* [Gk, India, of or connected with India, fr. *indos* of or connected with India, fr. *Indos* India (subcontinent in southern Asia), Indus (river in the northwestern part of the Indian subcontinent) — more at INDIA] **1** : India or the East Indies ⟨*Indophile*⟩ : of or connected with India or the East Indies ⟨*indaconitine*⟩ ⟨*Indo-Briton*⟩ ⟨*Indo-African*⟩ **2** : of or connected with the Indus river ⟨*Indo-Gangetic*⟩ **3** : Indo-European ⟨*Indo-Hittite*⟩

**²ind-** *or* **indi-** *or* **indo-** *comb form* [ISV, fr. L *indicum* — more at INDIGO] **1** : indigo ⟨*indole*⟩ ⟨*indirubin*⟩ ⟨*indophenin*⟩ **2** : resembling indigo (as in color) ⟨*indamine*⟩ ⟨*indophenol*⟩

**ind** *abbr* **1** independence; independent **2** index; indexed **3** indicated; indicative; indicator **4** indigo **5** indirect **6** induction **7** industrial; industry

**in·da·ba** \in'däbə\ *n* -s [Zulu *in-daba* matter, affair] **1** *southern Africa* : a conference esp. among representatives of native tribes : PARLEY, TALK **2** *Brit* : a gathering for camping or conference

**in·da·con·i·tine** \,ində'känə,tēn, -,tən\ *n* [¹*ind-* + *aconitine*] : a crystalline alkaloid $C_{34}H_{47}NO_{10}$ found in an herb (*Aconitum chasmanthum*) native to India

**in·da·gate** \'ində,gāt\ *vt* -ED/-ING/-S [L *indagatus,* past part. of *indagare,* fr. *indagin-, indago* examination, investigation, act of enclosing or surrounding, fr. OL *indu* in, within + L *agere* to drive — more at INDIGENOUS, AGENT] *archaic* : to search into : INVESTIGATE — **in·da·ga·tion** \,=='gāshən\ *n* -s *archaic* — **in·da·ga·tor** \'==,gād·ə(r)\ *n* -s *archaic*

**In·da·lone** \'ində,lōn\ *trademark* — used for butopyronoxyl

**in dam** *adv* (*or adj*), *of a domestic animal* : in the fetal state ⟨pigs sold *in dam*⟩

**in·da·mine** \'ində,mēn, -,mən\ *n* [ISV ²*ind-* + *amine;* orig. formed as G *indamin*] : any of a class of organic bases that are amino-phenyl derivatives of quinone diimine, that in the form of salts are unstable blue and green dyes, and that are used chiefly as intermediates for azine dyes (as safranines); *esp* : the simplest base $NH_2C_6H_4N{=}C_6H_4{=}NH$ that is the parent compound of the class

**in·dan** \'in,dan\ *also* **in·dane** \-dān\ *n* -s [ISV *indene* + *-an* or *-ane*] : an oily cyclic hydrocarbon $C_9H_{10}$ obtained by reducing indene — called also *hydrindene*

**indanger** *obs var of* ENDANGER

**in·dan·throne** \ən'dan,thrōn\ *n* -s [obs. E *indanthrene* indanthrone (ISV ²*ind-* + *-anthrene;* prob. orig. formed as G *indanthren*) + E *-one*] : a blue anthraquinone-azine dye that is the parent compound of several halogenated dyes — see DYE table I (under *Vat Blue 4*)

**in·dart** \ən+\ *vt* [²*in* + *dart,* v.] *archaic* : to cause (as a dart) to be thrust or thrown into something

**in·da·zole** \'ində,zōl\ *n* [ISV *indole* + *azole;* orig. formed as G *indazol*] **1** : a feebly basic crystalline bicyclic compound $C_7H_6N_2$ made by pyrolysis of *ortho*-hydrazino-cinnamic acid; benzo-pyrazole **2** : a derivative of indazole

**indear** *obs var of* ENDEAR

**in·de·bi·ta·tus assumpsit** \ən,debə'tād·əs-\ *n* [NL, lit., being indebted he undertook] : COMMON ASSUMPSIT

**inde blue** \'ind-\ *n* [ME *inde,* n., indigo blue, fr. OF *inde,* adj., indigo-blue, fr. L *indicum,* n., indigo — more at INDIGO] : INDIGO 3

**in·debt** \ən'det\ *vt* -ED/-ING/-S [back-formation fr. *indebted*] *archaic* : to place (as oneself) under an obligation (as of returning something borrowed)

**in·debt·ed** \ən'ded·əd, -etəd\ *adj* [alter. (influenced by ²*in-* and *debt*) of ME *endetted,* modif. (influenced by ME *-ed,* adj. suffix forming past participles) of OF *endeté,* past part. of *endeter* to involve in debt, fr. *en-* ¹en- + *dette, dete* debt — more at DEBT] **1** : being under the obligation of paying or repaying money : owing money : held to payment or repayment ⟨was heavily ~ to the bank for loans extended to him —A.C.Cole⟩ **2** : owing gratitude (as for a favor received or kind act done) or recognition (as of a useful service) to another ⟨felt deeply ~ to her for having given him a home⟩ ⟨was ~ to the book for most of his information⟩

**in·debt·ed·ness** *n* -ES **1 a** : the condition of being indebted ⟨should provide for the refinancing of mortgage and other ~ —F.D.Roosevelt⟩ ⟨the ~ was canceled —P.N.Garber⟩ **b** : the extent to which one is indebted ⟨admitted his deep ~ to the accomplishments of those who preceded him⟩ **2** : something (as a sum of money) that is owed ⟨Hawthorne's literary ~*es* are . . . chiefly to English writers —*Publ's Mod. Lang. Assoc. of Amer.*⟩ **syn** see DEBT

**in·debt·ment** \-'detmənt\ *n* -s *archaic* : INDEBTEDNESS

**indecence** *n* -s [prob. fr. F *indécence,* fr. L *indecentia*] *obs* : INDECENCY

**in·de·cen·cy** \ən'dēs³nsē, (')in-, -nsi\ *n* [L *indecentia,* fr. *indecent-, indecens* indecent + *-ia* -y] **1** : the quality or state of being indecent **2** : something (as a word or an action or a manner of behavior) that is indecent : an offense against decency ⟨innocent and shameless like a child's *indecencies* —W.A.White⟩

**in·de·cent** \-³nt\ *adj, sometimes* -ER/-EST [MF or L; MF *indécent,* fr. L *indecent-, indecens,* fr. *in-* ¹in- + *decent-, decens* decent] **1** : not decent: as **a** : altogether unbecoming : contrary to what the nature of things or what circumstances would dictate as right or expected or appropriate : hardly suitable : UNSEEMLY ⟨hurried away with ~ haste⟩ **b** : not conforming to generally accepted standards of morality : tending toward or being in fact something generally viewed as morally indelicate or improper or offensive : being or tending to be obscene ⟨an ~ gesture⟩ ⟨~ language⟩ ⟨an ~ costume⟩ **2** *archaic* : unpleasant to look at : UNSIGHTLY, UNCOMELY — **in·de·cent·ly** *adv*

**indecent assault** *n* : an immoral act or series of acts exclusive of rape or an attempt to commit rape committed by a male against the person of a female without her consent

**indecent exposure** *n* : intentional exposure of part of one's body (as the genitals) in a place where such exposure is likely to be an offense against the generally accepted standards of decency in a community

**in·de·cid·ua** \,ində'sijəwə\ *n pl, cap* [NL, fr. ¹*in-* + L *decidua,* neut. pl. of *deciduus* deciduous] : NONDECIDUATA

**in·de·cid·u·ate** \¦=='==wət\ *adj* [NL *indeciduatus,* fr. ¹*in-* + *deciduatus* deciduate] *of a placenta* : having the maternal and fetal elements associated but not fused so that no maternal tissue is carried off in the placenta at parturition

**in·de·cid·u·ous** \-wəs\ *adj* [¹*in-* + *deciduous*] : not deciduous ⟨~ leaves⟩ : EVERGREEN ⟨~ trees⟩

**in·de·ci·pher·able** \¦ində¦sif(ə)rəbəl, -dē¦-\ *adj* [¹*in-* + *decipherable*] : that cannot be deciphered ⟨an ~ inscription⟩ ⟨making people whose inner life has seemed to us ~ emerge as human and understandable —C.J.Rolo⟩ — **indecipherableness** *n* -ES — **in·de·ci·pher·ably** \-blē, -li\ *adv*

**in·de·ci·sion** \¦ində¦sizhən, -dē¦-\ *n* [F *indécision,* fr. *indécis* irresolute, undecided (fr. MF *indecis* not yet settled, fr. LL *indecisus,* fr. L *in-* ¹in- + *decisus,* past part. of *decidere* to decide, settle) + *-ion*] : a wavering between two or more possible courses of action : VACILLATION, IRRESOLUTION : inability or failure to arrive at a decision ⟨in a constant state of ~⟩ ⟨halted before the door in ~ —James Joyce⟩

**in·decisive** \¦in+\ *adj* : not decisive: as **a** : not being of such a sort as would definitely settle something or make something final : INCONCLUSIVE ⟨a drawn-out ~ war⟩ **b** : marked by or prone to indecision : WAVERING, VACILLATING, IRRESOLUTE : unable or failing to arrive at a decision ⟨an ~ state of mind⟩ ⟨a timid ~ sort of individual⟩ **c** : not clearly marked out : not definite : INDISTINCT, UNFIXED, VAGUE ⟨~ boundaries between right and wrong⟩ ⟨an outline that was blurred and ~⟩ — **in·de·ci·sive·ly** *adv* — **in·de·ci·sive·ness** *n*

**¹in·de·clin·able** \¦ində¦klīnəbəl, -dē¦-\ *adj* [MF, fr. LL *indeclinabilis,* fr. L *in-* ¹in- + LL *declinabilis* capable of being inflected, fr. L *declinare* to inflect grammatically + *-abilis* -able — more at DECLINE] : having no grammatical inflections : used without case endings ⟨some Latin nouns are ~⟩

**²indeclinable** \"\ *n* -s : an indeclinable word

**in·de·com·po·ni·ble** \¦in,dēkəm¦pōnəbəl\ *adj* [¹*in-* + *decompon-* (fr. L *de* from, down, away + *componere* to compose, put together) + *-ible* — more at DE-, COMPOUND] *archaic* : INDECOMPOSABLE

**in·de·com·pos·able** \-¦pōzəbəl\ *adj* [¹*in-* + *decomposable*] : not capable of being broken up into component parts ⟨a substance that resists analysis and is apparently ~⟩

**in·dec·or·ous** \ən'dekərəs, (')in¦d- *also* -krəs ¦ində¦kōr-, -dē¦-, -kȯr-\ *adj* [L *indecorus,* fr. *in-* ¹in- + *decorus* decorous] : not decorous : not proper : conflicting with accepted standards of propriety or good taste or good breeding ⟨an ~ remark⟩ ⟨~ behavior⟩ — **in·dec·or·ous·ly** *adv* — **in·dec·or·ous·ness** *n*

**in·de·co·rum** \¦ində¦kōrəm, -dē¦k-, -kȯr-\ *n* [L, neut. of *indecorus* indecorous] **1** : something (as an action) that is indecorous : an offense against decorum ⟨an ~ for which she refused to forgive him⟩ **2** : the quality or state of being indecorous : lack of decorum : IMPROPRIETY ⟨the general ~ of their lives —Lionel Trilling⟩

**in·deed** \ən'dēd\ *adv* [ME *in dede,* fr. ¹*in* + *dede* deed] **1 a** : in very fact : without any question : in truth : TRULY, CERTAINLY, ASSUREDLY, POSITIVELY ⟨was ~ glad to see her⟩ — used as an intensive often postpositively ⟨was glad ~⟩ ⟨was a king ~⟩ ⟨found themselves in real trouble ~⟩ and sometimes to reiterate a remark of another speaker ⟨you may well ask who knows how it will end; who knows, ~⟩; often used as an interjection to express irony or disbelief or surprise **b** : by all means : by any means — used to emphasize a reply or remark made in answer to an actual or implied question ⟨yes ~ I intend to go⟩ ⟨no ~ they aren't away⟩ **c** : REALLY, HONESTLY — used interrogatively to indicate that one seeks confirmation from a speaker that a statement just made by the speaker is really true ⟨~? You would like to go home?⟩ **2** : in reality : so far as the truth of the matter is concerned : in actual fact — used to indicate or emphasize that something stated or about to be stated is true and is at the same time opposed to something stated or implied or about to be stated or implied that is either untrue or merely external or apparent ⟨what seems to be cause for grief is ~ a reason for joy⟩ ⟨they were ~ heroes, though the world failed to recognize them as such⟩ **3** : all things considered : as a matter of fact : so far as that goes — used to confirm or amplify something stated ⟨he likes to have things his own way; ~, he can be quite a tyrant⟩ ⟨she is quite stupid, ~ a simpleton⟩ **4** : ADMITTEDLY, UNDENIABLY ⟨the problems involved are ~ serious ones, but I am convinced they can be solved⟩

**in·deedy** \-'dēdē, -di\ *adv* [by alter.] : INDEED 1b — not in formal use

**indef** *abbr* indefinite

**in·de·fat·i·ga·bil·i·ty** \¦ində,fad·i̇gə¦bilədē, -dē¦-, -at|, |ēg-, -ətē, -i\ *n* -ES : the quality or state of being indefatigable

**in·de·fat·i·ga·ble** \¦=='==gəbəl\ *adj* [MF, fr. L *indefatigabilis,* fr. *in-* ¹in- + *defatigare* to fatigue, tire (fr. *de* from, down, away + *fatigare* to tire) + *-abilis* -able — more at FATIGUE] : incapable of being fatigued : that continues or proceeds unremittingly and without becoming wearied : UNTIRING, UNWEARYING ⟨an ~ worker⟩ ⟨has ~ patience⟩ — **in·de·fat·i·ga·ble·ness** *n* -ES — **in·de·fat·i·ga·bly** \-blē, -li\ *adv*

**in·de·fea·si·bil·i·ty** \¦ində,fēzə¦bilədē, -dē,f-, -ətē, -i\ *n* -ES : the quality or state of being indefeasible

**in·de·fea·si·ble** \¦=='fēzəbəl\ *adj* [¹*in-* + *defeasible*] : not defeasible : not capable of or not liable to being annulled or voided or undone : that cannot be forfeited ⟨an ~ right to freedom⟩ ⟨an ~ claim to the title⟩ — compare INALIENABLE — **in·de·fea·si·bly** \-blē, -li\ *adv*

**in·de·fec·ti·bil·i·ty** \¦ində,fektə¦bilədē, -(,)dē,-, -ətē, -i\ *n* : the quality or state of being indefectible

**in·de·fec·ti·ble** \¦=='fektəbəl\ *adj* [¹*in-* + *defectible*] **1** : not subject to failure or decay : LASTING : that will not and cannot collapse or be done away with ⟨an ~ friendship⟩ ⟨maintained that the church is ~⟩ **2** : free from and incapable of defects or error : having no shortcomings : free of faults : FLAWLESS ⟨possessed what appeared to be a sort of ~ wisdom⟩ ⟨a spokesman who could hardly be considered ~⟩ — **in·de·fec·ti·bly** \-blē, -li\ *adv*

**in·defective** \¦in+\ *adj* [¹*in-* + *defective*] **1** *archaic* : free from defects : FAULTLESS, FLAWLESS **2** *archaic* : INDEFECTIBLE 1 — **in·de·fec·tive·ly** *adv, archaic*

**in·de·fen·si·bil·i·ty** \¦ində,fen(t)sə¦bilədē, -(,)dē-, -ətē, -i\ *n* : the quality or state of being indefensible

**in·de·fen·si·ble** \¦=='fen(t)səbəl\ *adj* [¹*in-* + *defensible*] : not defensible: **a** (1) : incapable of being maintained as right or valid : UNTENABLE ⟨an ~ viewpoint⟩ ⟨an ~ argument⟩ (2) : incapable of being justified or excused : UNJUSTIFIABLE, INEXCUSABLE ⟨~ error⟩ ⟨~ behavior⟩ ⟨an ~ waste of public funds⟩ **b** : incapable of being secured or protected against physical force or attack ⟨a totally ~ city⟩ — **in·de·fen·si·bly** \-blē, -li\ *adv*

**indeficiency** *n* [*indeficient* + *-cy*] *obs* : the quality or state of being unceasing or unfailing

**indeficient** *adj* [MF, fr. LL *indeficient-, indeficiens,* fr. L *in-* ¹in- + *deficient-, deficiens,* pres. part. of *deficere* to be lacking — more at DEFICIENT] *obs* : UNCEASING, UNFAILING

**in·definability** \¦in+\ *n* : the quality or state of being indefinable

**¹in·definable** \¦in+\ *adj* [¹*in-* + *definable*] : not definable: **a** : incapable of being precisely or readily described : not easily put into words ⟨an ~ feeling of terror⟩ **b** : incapable of being precisely or readily given a logical analysis ⟨an abstract concept that seems ~⟩ **c** : incapable of being precisely or readily given a semantic analysis ⟨prepositions often have a relationship to words with which they are used that is purely functional and ~⟩ **d** (1) : not clearly recognizable or ascertainable : UNCERTAIN ⟨a bent, dignified peasant of ~ age —Marcia Davenport⟩ (2) : lacking a clear outline or definitely set limits : not precisely or readily located or fixed or marked off : INDETERMINATE, VAGUE ⟨an area with ~ boundaries⟩ ⟨the lights of the December evening bathing his face with little splashes that left his eyes and mouth almost ~ —E.L.Wallant⟩ — **in·de·fin·able·ness** *n* -ES — **in·definably** \"+\ *adv*

**²indefinable** \"\ *n* -s : something (as a word or concept) that is indefinable

**¹in·definite** \(')in+, ən, (')in+\ *adj* [L *indefinitus,* fr. *in-* ¹in- + *definitus,* past part. of *definire* to limit, determine — more at DEFINITE] : not definite: as **a** (1) *of a grammatical modifier* : typically designating an unidentified or not immediately identifiable person or thing ⟨*some* in "some books", *someone's* in "someone's house" are ~ modifiers⟩ ⟨the ~ articles *a* and *an*⟩ (2) *of an adjective form or set of adjective forms* : STRONG 16b (3) *of a verb form or set of verb forms in French* : typically denoting completed occurrence of an action — usu. used in the phrase *past indefinite* ⟨*j'ai dit* "I said" contains a past ~ verb⟩ (4) *of a verb form or set of verb forms in English* : denoting an action as neither completed nor continuing ⟨*saw* in "I saw the show" is the past ~ of *see*⟩ — compare PERFECT 5, PROGRESSIVE 7 **b** : being of a nature that is not or cannot be clearly determined : not precise : VAGUE, OBSCURE, UNCERTAIN, AMBIGUOUS ⟨what he really meant to say remains ~⟩ **c** (1) : having no exact limits : indeterminate in extent or amount : not clearly fixed ⟨sentenced to an ~ prison term⟩ ⟨an area with ~ boundaries⟩ ⟨an ~ number of people⟩ (2) : not narrowly confined or restricted ⟨~ extent⟩ : continuing with no immediate end being fixed : UNLIMITED ⟨planned to spend an ~ period in Europe⟩ **d** *of floral organs* (1) : numerous and not easy to determine by reason of being neither constant in number nor in multiples of the petal number (2) : RACEMOSE — **in·def·i·nite·ly** *adv* — **in·def·i·nite·ness** *n*

**²indefinite** \"\ *n* : something that is indefinite; *esp* : a word that is grammatically indefinite ⟨*a, some,* and other ~*s*⟩

**indefinite failure of issue** : a failure of issue which determines an estate and for which no time or period is fixed in the devise — called also *general failure of issue*

**indefinite integral** *n, of a function of a variable* : a function containing an arbitrary additive and having a derivative of a function that is the given function

**indefinite proposition** *n* : a statement in logic whose subject is a common term with nothing to indicate distribution or nondistribution (as "the Chinese eat rice")

**indefinite sentence** *n* : INDETERMINATE SENTENCE

**indefinite term** *n* : an unlimited negative term in logic

**in·definitive** \¦in+\ *adj* [¹*in-* + *definitive*] : not definitive : not clearly fixed : INDETERMINATE — **in·de·fin·i·tive·ly** *adv* — **in·de·fin·i·tive·ness** *n*

**in·de·fin·i·tude** \,ində'finə,tüd, -dē'-, -ə-,tyüd\ *n* -s [fr. *indefinite,* prob. after E *infinite: infinitude*] : INDEFINITENESS

**in·de·flec·ti·ble** \¦ində¦flektəbəl\ *adj* [¹*in-* + *deflect* + *-ible*] : that cannot be deflected ⟨~ courage⟩ — **in·de·flec·ti·bly** \-blē\ *adv*

**in·dehiscence** \¦in+\ *n* [fr. *indehiscent,* after E *dehiscent: dehiscence*] : the quality or state of being indehiscent

**in·dehiscent** \"+\ *adj* [¹*in-* + *dehiscent*] : not dehiscent : remaining closed at maturity ⟨~ fruits⟩ — see FRUIT illustration

**in·deliberate** \¦in+\ *adj* [¹*in-* + *deliberate*] : not deliberate : marked by lack of forethought or intention ⟨an ~ remark⟩ — **in·de·lib·er·ate·ly** *adv* — **in·de·lib·er·ate·ness** *n* — **in·deliberation** \"+\ *n*

**in·del·i·bil·i·ty** \(,)in,delə'bilədē, -ətē, -i\ *n* -ES : the quality or state of being indelible

**in·del·i·ble** \ən'deləbəl, (')in¦d-, (')in¦deləbəl\ *adj* [ML *indelibilis,* alter. (influenced by L *-ibilis* -ible) of L *indelebilis,* fr. *in-* ¹in- + *delebilis* delible] **1** : that cannot be removed, washed away, or erased ⟨an ~ stain⟩ ⟨an ~ mark⟩ : that cannot be effaced or obliterated : PERMANENT, LASTING ⟨made an ~ impression on his mind⟩ **2** : that makes marks that cannot easily be removed (as by erasing) ⟨an ~ pencil⟩; *specif* : not attacked by strong acids or alkalies and so not easily removed by washing ⟨india ink is ~⟩ ⟨bought some ~ ink⟩ — **in·del·i·bly** \-blē, -li\ *adv*

**in·delicacy** \ən, (')in+\ *n* [¹*in-* + *delicacy*] **1** : the quality or state of being indelicate ⟨~ of speech⟩ ⟨~ of behavior⟩ **2** : something (as a coarse expression) that is indelicate ⟨a rollicking tale full of *indelicacies*⟩

**in·delicate** \"+\ *adj* [¹*in-* + *delicate*] : not delicate: **a** (1) : lacking in or offending against propriety : IMPROPER, RUDE, UNREFINED ⟨~ behavior⟩ (2) : verging on the indecent : COARSE, GROSS ⟨an ~ anecdote⟩ **b** : marked by or showing a lack of feeling for the sensibilities of others : TACTLESS ⟨an ~ allusion to her family's poverty⟩ — **in·del·i·cate·ly** *adv* — **in·del·i·cate·ness** *n*

**in·dem·ni·fi·ca·tion** \ən,demnəfə'kāshən\ *n* -s [fr. *indemnify,* after such pairs as E *amplify: amplification*] **1 a** : the action of indemnifying ⟨~ of the countries that had suffered the worst damage⟩ **b** : the condition of being indemnified ⟨did not lose hope of ~⟩ **2** : INDEMNITY 2b ⟨paid an enormous ~⟩

**in·dem·ni·fi·ca·tor** \'===,kād·ə(r)\ *n* -s [fr. *indemnification,* after such pairs as E *creation: creator*] : INDEMNIFIER

**in·dem·nif·i·ca·to·ry** \ən,dem'nifəkə,tōrē\ *adj* [fr. *indemnification,* after such pairs as E *explanation: explanatory*] : of, relating to, or designed for indemnification ⟨~ court action⟩

**in·dem·ni·fi·er** \ən'demnə,fī(ə)r\ *n* -s : one that indemnifies or that is under obligation to indemnify

**in·dem·ni·fy** \-,fī\ *vt* -ED/-ING/-ES [L *indemnis* unharmed + E *-fy*] **1 a** : to secure or protect against hurt or loss or damage : give indemnity to ⟨a plan for ~*ing* workers against time lost through illness⟩ **b** : to exempt from incurred penalties or liabilities ⟨was made a partner and *indemnified* against his previously overdrawn accounts⟩ **2** : to make compensation to for incurred hurt or loss or damage ⟨*indemnified* the town for the buildings that had been bombed⟩ **syn** see PAY

**in·dem·ni·tee** \=¦=nə¦tē\ *n* -s [*indemnity* + *-ee* (person furnished with a specified thing)] : one that is indemnified or that is entitled to be indemnified

**in·dem·ni·tor** \='=nəd·ə(r), -ətə(r)\ *n* -s [*indemnity* + *-or*] : INDEMNIFIER

**in·dem·ni·ty** \ən'demnəd·ē, -ətē, -i\ *n* -ES [ME *indempnyte,* fr. MF *indemnité,* fr. L *indemnitat-, indemnitas,* fr. *indemnis* unharmed (fr. *in-* ¹in- + *damnum* damage, harm) + *-tat-, -tas* -ty — more at DAMN] **1 a** : security or protection against hurt or loss or damage ⟨a plan that offered ~ against further financial loss⟩ **b** : exemption from incurred penalties or liabilities ⟨received ~ for his overdrawn accounts⟩ **2 a** : INDEMNIFICATION 1 **b** : something (as a sum of money paid in compensation) that indemnifies ⟨had to pay a large ~⟩

**in·dem·ni·za·tion** \=,=nə'zāshən\ *n* -s [F *indemnisation,* fr. *indemniser* to indemnify (fr. MF, fr. *indemne* unharmed — fr. L *indemnis* — + *-iser* -ize) + *-ation*] : INDEMNIFICATION

**in·demonstrability** \¦in+\ *n* : the quality or state of being indemonstrable

**in·demonstrable** \¦in+\ *adj* [¹*in-* + *demonstrable*] : incapable of being demonstrated : not subject to proof ⟨a theory that seems valid but is ~⟩ — **in·demonstrably** \"+\ *adv*

**indemny** *abbr* indemnity

**in·dene** \'in,dēn\ *n* -s [ISV *indole* + *-ene;* prob. orig. formed as G *inden*] : a liquid readily polymerizable hydrocarbon $C_9H_8$ obtained from coal tar by distillation or from petroleum by cracking and used chiefly in making resins — compare COUMARONE-INDENE RESIN

**indenize** *vt* [alter. (influenced by ²*in-*) of *endenize*] *obs* : ENDENIZEN

**¹in·dent** \ən'dent\ *vb* -ED/-ING/-S [ME *indenten, endenten,* fr. MF *endenter,* fr. OF, fr. *en-* ¹en- + *dent* tooth, fr. L *dent-, dens* — more at TOOTH] *vt* **1 a** : to cut or otherwise divide (a sheet of parchment or paper carrying two or more copies esp. of a deed or contract) so that sections having one or more edges with angular projections or a scalloped or curved outline are produced, each section being later fitted if necessary to the section having an exactly tallying edge as proof that the sections are parts of an original authentic document ⟨an ~*ed* deed⟩ **b** : to draw up (as a deed or contract) in two or more exactly corresponding copies ⟨~*ing* the agreement⟩ **2 a** (1) : to cut into or notch the edge of in such a way as to produce a scalloped outline or one with angular projections ⟨an ~*ed* stick⟩ (2) : to cut into (as a board) for the purpose of mortising or dovetailing **b** : to penetrate the edge of in such a way as to produce an outline marked by one or more recesses ⟨the coastline is ~*ed* by the sea into a succession of small bays —Han Suyin⟩ **3 a** *obs* : to come to a formal or express agreement about **b** : INDENTURE ⟨~*ed* servants⟩ **4** : to space in (as a line of a paragraph) from a left-hand margin or sometimes from a right-hand margin ⟨~*ing* the first word of a paragraph⟩ ⟨~*ed* the column of figures one inch from the right-hand margin⟩ **5** : to join together (as two boards) by or as if by mortises or dovetails **6** *chiefly Brit* : to order by an indent ⟨~*ed* guns and ammunition⟩ ⟨~*ing* books⟩ ~ *vi* **1** *obs* : to make a formal and express agreement ⟨thus would I have ecclesiastical and civil historians ~ about the bounds and limits of their subjects —Thomas Fuller⟩ **2** *obs* : to wind in and out : ZIGZAG **3** : to form an indentation ⟨the long line of coast with its series of ~*ing* bays —*Amer. Guide Series: N.J.*⟩ **4** *chiefly Brit* : to make out an indent for something ⟨~*ing* for books⟩ — **indent on** *or* **indent upon 1** *chiefly Brit* : to make an official requisition on ⟨*indented on* the governor for food⟩ **2** *chiefly Brit* : to draw on ⟨*indenting on* reserves to cover the deficit⟩

**²in·dent** \ən'dent, 'in,dent\ *n* -s **1 a** : INDENTURE 1 **b** : a certificate of indebtedness (as of interest on the public debt) issued by the federal or a state government in the late 18th or early 19th century **2** *chiefly Brit* **a** : an official requisition (as for supplies) **b** : a purchase order for goods esp. when sent from a foreign country **3** : INDENTION

**³indent** \"\ *vb* -ED/-ING/-S [ME *endenten,* fr. ¹*en-* + *denten* to dent — more at DENT] *vt* **1** : to force inward (as by striking or pressing) so as to form a depression (as a dent or hollow) ⟨~*ing* a pattern in a metal surface⟩ **2 :** to form a depression (as a dent or hollow) in the surface of by or as if by striking or pressing ⟨~*ing* the pillow with his head⟩ **:** make an indentation in ⟨wore tight-fitting pince-nez which ~*ed* the sides of his nose in two red grooves —O.S.J.Gogarty⟩ **~** *vi* **:** DENT ⟨this asphalt ~*s* easily⟩

**⁴indent** \"\ *n* -s **:** INDENTATION ⟨the damp grass was everywhere marked with the ~*s* of his sharp hooves —Llewelyn Powys⟩

**in·den·ta·tion** \ˌin,den-ˈtāshən\ *n* -s [¹*indent* + *-ation*] **1 a :** an angular cut (as a notch) or something resembling such a cut in an edge ⟨~*s* along the edge of a leaf⟩ **b :** a usu. deep recess (as in a coastline) ⟨many bays pockmark the coast with ~*s*⟩ **2 :** the action of indenting or condition of being indented **3** [³*indent* + *-ation*] **:** a usu. small surface depression (as a dent or hollow) made by or as if by striking or pressing ⟨noticed that the metal was covered with ~*s*⟩ **4 :** INDENTION 2

**in·dent·ed·ly** \ənˈdentədlē\ *adv* [*indented* (past part. of ³*indent*) + *-ly*] **:** by indentation **:** in intaglio ⟨a design made ~ in the surface of the stone⟩

**in·dent·er** *or* **in·den·tor** \-ˈdentə(r)\ *n* -s [partly fr. ¹*indent* + *-er* or *-or*, partly fr. ³*indent* + *-er* or *-or*] **:** one that indents: **a** *usu* *indentor* **:** one that orders by an indent (sense 2) **b :** an object (as of diamond, carbide, hard steel) having a pointed or rounded tip that is forcibly pressed against the surface of a metal so as to test for hardness and resistance to indentation

**in·den·tion** \-ˈdenchən\ *n* -s [¹*indent* + *-ion*] **1** *archaic* **:** INDENTATION 1 **2 a :** the action of indenting (as a line of a paragraph) or condition of being indented **b :** the blank space produced by indenting

**¹in·den·ture** \ənˈdenchə(r)\ *n* -s [ME *endenture, indenture*, fr. MF *endenture*, fr. OF, fr. *endenter* to indent (a document) + *-ure* — more at ¹INDENT] **1 a** (1) **:** a document (as a deed or contract) or a section of a document that is indented (sense 1a) (2) **:** a document (as a deed or contract) or a copy of a document that is not indented (sense 1a) but that is usu. formal and under seal and executed in two or more copies (3) **:** a contract binding one person to work for another for a given period of time (as an apprentice for a master craftsman or a new immigrant for an established colonist) — usu. used in pl. **b :** a document (as an inventory, voucher) that is not indented (sense 1a) and that may or may not be executed in two or more copies and that is formal or official and authenticated and prepared for purposes of control **2** *obs* **:** a zigzag course (as of one running) **3 :** INDENTATION 1 **4** [³*indent* + *-ure*] **:** INDENTATION 3

**²indenture** \"\ *vt* -ED/-ING/-S **1 :** to bind (as an apprentice) by indentures **2** *archaic* **:** to make an indentation (sense 3) in

**indentured labor** *n* [*indentured* fr. past part. of ²*indenture*] **:** CONTRACT LABOR 2

**in·den·ture·ship** \-ˈ==,ship\ *n* [¹*indenture* + *-ship*] **:** the condition of being indentured ⟨completed the three years of his ~⟩

**in·dependable** \ˌin+\ *adj* [¹*in-* + *dependable*] **:** UNDEPENDABLE

**in·de·pen·dence** \ˌindəˈpendən(t)s, -dēˈ-\ *n* [fr. *independent*, after such pairs as E *competent: competence*] **1 :** the quality or state of being independent **:** FREEDOM, LIBERTY ⟨their declaration of ~⟩ ⟨national ~⟩ ⟨political ~⟩ ⟨intellectual ~⟩ ⟨~ from the mother country⟩ ⟨enjoyed ~ of outside control⟩ **2** *archaic* **:** COMPETENCE 2 ⟨had a considerable ~, besides two good livings —Jane Austen⟩ **3 :** a grayish to dark purplish blue that is redder and stronger than flag blue

**independence day** *n, usu cap I&D* **:** a day set aside for public celebration of an anniversary connected with the beginnings of national independence; *specif* **:** July 4 observed as a legal holiday in the U.S. commemorating the adoption of the Declaration of Independence in 1776

**in·de·pen·den·cy** \-dənsē, -si\ *n* [*independent* + *-cy*] **1 :** INDEPENDENCE 1 **2** *usu cap* **a :** a religious movement originated in England by Robert Browne (1550?–?1633) who taught that a church consists of a body of believers bound by a covenant to God and each other and that it is independent of any higher ecclesiastical authority **b :** CONGREGATIONALISM 2 **3** *archaic* **:** COMPETENCE 2 **4 :** an independent political state (as a country, a nation)

**¹in·de·pen·dent** \ˌ==ˈ==dənt\ *adj* [¹*in-* + *dependent*] **1 :** not dependent: as **a** (1) **:** not subject to control by others **:** not subordinate **:** SELF-GOVERNING, AUTONOMOUS, FREE ⟨an ~ nation⟩ ⟨was ~ of outside control⟩ (2) **:** not affiliated with or integrated into a larger controlling unit (as a business unit) ⟨an ~ retail store⟩ (3) **:** originating from outside a given unit (as a business unit) ⟨the corporation hired ~ auditors to check its books⟩ or made by individuals from outside a given unit ⟨an ~ audit⟩ **b** (1) **:** not requiring or relying on something else (as for existence, operation, efficiency) **:** not contingent **:** not conditioned ⟨an ~ conclusion⟩ ⟨~ action⟩ ⟨two effects that are quite ~ of each other⟩ (2) **:** being or acting free of the influence of something else ⟨an ~ witness⟩ ⟨conducting an ~ investigation⟩ (3) **:** not looking to others for one's opinions or for the guidance of one's conduct **:** not biased by others **:** acting or thinking freely or disposed to act or think freely ⟨an ~ mind⟩ ⟨leading an ~ life⟩ ⟨an ~ journal of opinion⟩ (4) **:** not bound by or committed definitively to a political party **:** exercising a totally free political choice ⟨an ~ voter⟩ **c** (1) **:** not requiring or relying on others (as for support, supplies, a livelihood) ⟨was altogether ~ of the praise or condemnation of others⟩ ⟨an ~ source of revenue⟩ ⟨the job made him ~ of his parents⟩ (2) **:** not needing to work for a living **:** having a competence ⟨spent most of his time traveling idly about, having been ~ for years⟩ (3) **:** that is enough to free from the necessity of working for a living **:** making up a competence ⟨a gentleman of ~ means⟩ **d** (1) **:** refusing to look to others for help **:** disliking or refusing to accept assistance or to be under obligation to others ⟨too ~ to accept charity⟩ (2) **:** showing a desire for or love of freedom and absence of constraint **:** marked by impatience with or annoyance at restriction ⟨a bold and ~ manner of acting⟩ ⟨had an ~ air about her⟩ **2** *usu cap* **:** of, relating to, or holding the doctrines of the Independents ⟨an *Independent* church⟩ **3 a :** MAIN 6 ⟨an ~ clause⟩ **b :** ISOLATIVE — used of sound change **c :** that is neither derivable from nor incompatible with another statement ⟨an ~ proposition in logic⟩ **syn** see FREE

**²independent** \"\ *n* **1** *usu cap* **:** an adherent of Independency **2 :** one that is independent ⟨free-lance artists and other ~*s*⟩ ⟨large corporations and the smaller ~*s*⟩; *esp* **:** one that is not bound by or definitively committed to a political party ⟨one third of the voters classify themselves as ~*s* —E.S.Griffith⟩

**independent audit** *n* **:** an audit made by usu. professional auditors who are wholly independent of the company where the audit is being made — contrasted with *internal audit*

**independent baptist** *n, usu cap I&B* **:** a member of a pacifist Baptist sect organized in 1927

**independent chuck** *n* **:** a chuck for holding work by means of four jaws that may be moved separately

**independent component** *n* **:** a component in a physical-chemical system that may be varied without fixing the condition of the system

**independent contractor** *n* **:** one that contracts to do work or perform a service for another and that retains total and free control over the means or methods used in doing the work or performing the service

independent chuck

**in·de·pen·dent·ly** *adv* **:** in an independent manner **:** without dependence on another **:** FREELY ⟨living ~⟩ ⟨thinking and acting ~⟩

**independently of** *prep* **:** without regard to **:** apart from **:** aside from **:** irrespective of ⟨*independently of* what you may think, I have my own convictions⟩ ⟨it aims rather at persuading the people, *independently of* what the state may or may not want —M.R.Masani⟩

**independent of** *prep* **:** independently of ⟨*independent of* how others felt, they were sure they were right⟩ ⟨obligation . . . to obey a law, *independent of* those resources which the law provides for its own enforcement —R.P.Ward⟩

**independent variable** *n* **:** a mathematical variable not dependent on other variables

**independing** *adj* [¹*in-* + *depending* (pres. part. of *depend*)] *obs* **:** INDEPENDENT

**in·deprivable** \ˌin+\ *adj* [¹*in-* + *deprivable*] *archaic* **:** INALIENABLE

**in·der·bo·rite** \ˌindərˈbō,rīt, -bȯ,-\ *n* -s [Russ *inderborit*, fr. Lake *Inder*, Kazakhstan, U.S.S.R., its locality + Russ *bor-* + *-it* -ite] **:** a mineral $CaMgB_6O_{11}.11H_2O$ consisting of a hydrous borate of calcium and magnesium

**in·der·ite** \ˈində,rīt\ *n* -s [Russ *inderit*, fr. Lake *Inder*, Kazakhstan, U.S.S.R., its locality + Russ *-it* -ite] **:** a mineral $Mg_2B_6O_{11}.15H_2O$ consisting of a hydrous borate of magnesium

**in·describability** \ˌin+\ *n* **1 :** the quality or state of being indescribable **2 :** something indescribable

**¹in·describable** \"+\ *adj* [¹*in-* + *describable*] **:** that cannot be described: **a :** that cannot be described with precision **:** too vague or indefinite or intangible or complex to be described ⟨a strange ~ feeling —J.C.Powys⟩ **b :** that is beyond description **:** that surpasses description **:** too extreme or too much beyond experience to be adequately described ⟨filled with ~ joy⟩ ⟨scenes of ~ horror⟩ — **in·de·scrib·able·ness** *n* -ES — **in·describably** \"+\ *adv*

**²indescribable** \"\ *n* -s **1 :** something indescribable ⟨a box full of curious trinkets and other ~*s*⟩ **2 indescribables** *pl, archaic slang* **:** TROUSERS

**indesert** *n* [¹*in-* + ³*desert*] *obs* **:** the quality or state of being undeserving **:** lack of merit

**¹in·designate** \ən, (ˈ)in+\ *adj* [¹*in-* + L *designatus*, past part. of *designare* to point out, designate] **:** not quantified ⟨an ~ proposition in logic⟩

**²indesignate** \"\ *n* -s **:** an indesignate term or proposition in logic

**indesinent** *adj* [LL *indesinent-, indesinens*, fr. L *in-* ¹in- + *desinent-, desinens*, pres. part. of *desinere* to leave off, cease — more at DESINENT] *obs* **:** UNCEASING

**in·destructibility** \ˌin+\ *n* **:** the quality or state of being indestructible ⟨the ~ of matter⟩

**in·de·struc·ti·ble** \ˌindəˈstrəktəbəl, -dē'-\ *adj* [prob. fr. LL *indestructibilis*, fr. L *in-* ¹in- + *destructus* (past part. of *destruere* to tear down, destroy) + *-ibilis* -ible — more at DESTROY] **:** not destructible **:** incapable of being destroyed ⟨any belief more ~ than the belief in the ultimate triumph of justice —Robert Lynd⟩ — **in·de·struc·ti·ble·ness** *n* -ES — **in·de·struc·ti·bly** \-blē, -li\ *adv*

**in·detectable** \ˌin+\ *adj* [¹*in-* + *detectable*] **:** not detectable

**in·determinable** \ˌin+\ *adj* [¹*in-* + *determinable*] **:** not determinable: **a** *obs* **:** not subject to limitation **b :** incapable of being definitely decided or settled ⟨would have raised a host of delicate and ~ questions —Leslie Stephen⟩ **c :** incapable of being definitely fixed ⟨handed out free shoes and clothes to ~ thousands —Dwight Macdonald⟩ or ascertained ⟨a questionable and ~ relationship —Jacob Viner⟩ — **in·de·ter·min·able·ness** *n* — **in·determinably** \"+\ *adv*

**in·determinacy** \ˌin+\ *n* [*indeterminate* + *-cy*] **:** INDETERMINATION

**indeterminacy principle** *n* **:** UNCERTAINTY PRINCIPLE

**in·determinate** \ˌin+\ *adj* [ME *indeterminat*, fr. LL *indeterminatus*, fr. L *in-* ¹in- + *determinatus*, past part. of *determinare* to limit, determine — more at DETERMINE] **:** not determinate **:** not definitely determined **:** not clearly established **:** not fixed **:** not settled **:** INDEFINITE, UNCERTAIN, VAGUE, INDISTINCT: as **a** (1) **:** not precisely fixed in extent or size or number or nature ⟨a material used in an ~ number of varieties⟩ ⟨a huge container of ~ volume⟩ ⟨an insect of ~ sex⟩ (2) **:** lacking precision of meaning **:** semantically vague or unfixed ⟨an ~ and obscure phrase⟩ **b :** not fixed beforehand **:** not known in advance ⟨their future remains ~⟩ ⟨when the rebellion will occur is ~⟩ **c :** not leading to a definite end or result ⟨an ~ debate⟩ **:** remaining doubtful and unclear ⟨an ~ point of law⟩ **d** (1) **:** not limited as to the number of possible solutions ⟨an ~ problem in mathematics⟩ (2) *of a number* **:** not limited to one fixed value or to a series of fixed values — opposed to *determinate* **e :** not predetermined by some external force **:** not constrained **:** acting freely **:** SPONTANEOUS ⟨maintaining that moral choice is ~⟩ **f** (1) **:** having a capacity for indefinite elongation **:** not exhibiting determinate growth ⟨~ plants⟩ ⟨an ~ stem⟩; *esp* **:** RACEMOSE ⟨an ~ inflorescence⟩ (2) **:** having no critical photoperiod **g :** phonetically neutral ⟨an ~ vowel⟩ — **in·de·ter·mi·nate·ly** *adv* — **in·de·ter·mi·nate·ness** *n*

**indeterminate cleavage** *n* **:** cleavage in which all the early cleavage cells possess the potencies of the entire zygote — compare DETERMINATE CLEAVAGE

**indeterminate equation** *n* **:** an equation in which the unknown quantities admit of an infinite number of values or sets of values

**indeterminate form** *n* **:** any of the seven undefined expressions

$$\frac{0}{0}, \frac{\infty}{\infty}, 0 \cdot \infty, \infty - \infty, 0^0, \infty^0, \text{ and } 1^\infty$$

that a mathematical function may assume by formal substitution

**indeterminate growth** *n* **:** growth in which a plant axis is not limited by development of a terminal flower bud or other reproductive structure and so continues to elongate indefinitely (as in racemose inflorescence) — compare DETERMINATE GROWTH

**indeterminate sentence** *n* **:** a punitive sentence that fixes the term or amount of punishment only within certain limits and leaves the exact term or amount of punishment to be determined by administrative authorities

**in·determination** \ˌin+\ *n* [*indeterminate* + *-ion*] **:** the quality or state of being indeterminate

**in·determined** \ˌin+\ *adj* [¹*in-* + *determined* (past part. of *determine*)] *archaic* **:** INDETERMINATE

**in·determinism** \ˌin+\ *n* [¹*in-* + *determinism*] **1 :** a theory that the will is free and that deliberate choice and the action following such choice are not completely or not at all determined by or predictable from antecedent causes — compare DETERMINISM **2 :** the quality or state of being indeterminate; *esp* **:** UNPREDICTABILITY

**in·determinist** \"+\ *n* [fr. *indeterminism*, after such pairs as E *determinism: determinist*] **:** one that holds the theory of indeterminism

**in·deterministic** \"+\ *adj* **:** of or relating to indeterminism ⟨a mere ~ account of the moral life —Alexander Darroch⟩

**in·devotion** \ˌin+\ *n* [¹*in-* + *devotion*] *archaic* **:** lack of devotion

**in·devout** \ˌin+\ *adj* [ME *indevout* (trans. of LL *indevotus*), fr. ¹*in-* + *devout*] **:** not devout — **in·de·vout·ly** *adv*

**¹in·dex** \ˈin,deks\ *n, pl* **indexes** \-ksəz\ *or* **in·di·ces** \-ˌdə-,sēz\ *see sense 8* [L *indic-, index*, fr. *indicare* to point out, indicate — more at INDICATE] **1 :** INDEX FINGER 1, FOREFINGER **2 :** ALIDADE c **3 a :** a usu. alphabetical list that includes all or nearly all items (as topics, names of people and places) considered of special pertinence and fully or partially covered or merely mentioned in a printed or written work (as a book, catalog, or dissertation), that gives with each item the place (as by page number) where it may be found in the work, and that is usu. put at or near the end of the work **b** (1) **:** CARD INDEX (2) **:** STEP INDEX (3) **:** TAB INDEX (4) **:** THUMB INDEX **c :** a computer-processed usu. alphabetical list esp. of bibliographical information; *esp* **:** a bibliographical analysis of groups of publications that is usu. published periodically ⟨*Index Medicus*⟩ **4 :** something that serves as a pointer or indicator: as **a :** a pointer (as of metal, plastic, wood) that moves along a graduated scale (as of a weighing machine) or that remains fixed while the scale moves past its tip **b :** one of the hands on a timepiece **c :** the gnomon of a sundial **5** *obs* **:** DIRECT 1 **6 a :** something (as a manner of speaking or acting, a distinctive physical feature) in another person or thing that leads an observer to surmise a particular fact or draw a particular conclusion **:** SIGN, TOKEN, INDICATION ⟨her fatuous laugh is an ~ of her pygmy intelligence⟩ ⟨the fertility of the land is an ~ of the country's wealth⟩ **b :** a sign whose specific character is causally dependent on the object to which it refers but independent of an interpretant ⟨a bullet hole in a fence is an ~ that a shot has been fired⟩ — contrasted with *icon* and *symbol* **7 a :** a list of restricted or prohibited or otherwise proscribed material ⟨an ~ of forbidden books⟩ **b** *usu cap* **:** INDEX LIBRORUM PROHIBITORUM **8** *pl usu indices* **:** a number or symbol or expression written to the left or right of and above or below or otherwise associated with another number or symbol or expression to indicate use or position in an arrangement or expansion or to indicate a mathematical operation to be performed ⟨the *indices* 2 and 3 used to locate the element $a_{23}$ in the second row and third column of a determinant⟩ ⟨3 is the ~ in the expression $\sqrt[3]{5}$ to specify a cube root of 5⟩ **9** *or* **index mark :** a character ☞ used to direct particular attention (as to a note or paragraph) and as the seventh in series of the reference marks — called also *fist, hand* **10 a :** a ratio or other number derived from a series of observations and used as an indicator or measure (as of a condition, property, or phenomenon) ⟨a discrepancy ~ based on the differences between the students' predicted and attained honor-point ratios —*Educational & Psychological Measurement*⟩ ⟨the ~ of variation . . . is obtained by considering the positive differences between every pair of incomes in the group and averaging these differences —*Economica*⟩ ⟨an ~ is a measurable aspect of society which indicates the extent to which certain more complex aspects are present —Mabel Elliott & Francis Merrill⟩; *specif* **:** INDEX NUMBER ⟨the ~ of industrial production increased from 113.2 in December 1950 to 122.0 by November 1951 (1946 = 100) —*Americana Annual*⟩ — see CONSUMER PRICE INDEX, DOW-JONES INDEX; INDEX OF REFRACTION **b :** the ratio of one dimension of a thing (as an anatomical structure) to another dimension — see CEPHALIC INDEX **11 :** a miniature indication of denomination and value often printed on the corners of playing cards to make it unnecessary to view the full face of each card

index 11

**²index** \"\ *vb* -ED/-ING/-ES *vt* **1 a :** to provide (as a book) with an index ⟨the book will be ~*ed* in its next edition so as to make it more useful⟩ **b :** to list (as the contents of a book) in an index ⟨all persons and places mentioned are carefully ~*ed*⟩ **2 a :** to serve as an index of ⟨wrinkles ~ advancing age⟩ **b :** to point to **:** INDICATE ⟨a compass needle that ~*es* true north⟩ **3 :** to move (a machine or a piece of work held in a machine tool) so that a specific operation (as the cutting of gear teeth) will be repeated at definite intervals of space **4 :** to determine the fertility or yielding ability or disease resistance or some other character of (a plant or seed) by planting and testing a sample in advance of release for general use — used esp. of potatoes ⟨~*ing* potato eyes⟩ ⟨~*ing* a potato of each hill⟩ **~** *vi* **:** to index something

**index bar** *n* **:** the movable arm of a sextant

**index center** *n* **:** one of a pair of machine-tool centers or jaws provided with means of rotating a piece of work by predetermined equal amounts (as in cutting gear teeth)

**index crank** *n* **:** the crank of an index head whose turning a specified amount transmits through gearing a definite angular movement to the index-head spindle

**in·dex·er** \-sə(r)\ *n* -s **1 :** one that makes an index or works at indexing **2 a :** one who operates a machine for cutting index indentations into pages (as of reference books) **b :** one who prepares material (as reference books) for a machine that cuts index indentations or who prepares material for the insertion of index tabs

**index ex·pur·ga·to·ri·us** \-ik,spərgəˈtōrēəs, -ek-, -ȯr-\ *n, pl* **indices expurgato·rii** \-rē,ī, -rē,ē\ [NL, expurgatory index] **1** *sometimes cap I&E* **:** a list of proscribed material (as books) **2** *usu cap I&E* **:** a list of books once separately published and now included in the Index Librorum Prohibitorum that gives titles of works forbidden by church authority to Roman Catholics pending revision or deletion of some sections

**index finger** *n* **1 :** the digit next to the thumb **:** FOREFINGER **2 :** INDEX 9

**index forest** *n* **:** a forest that in density, volume, and increment reaches the highest average in a given locality

index finger 1

**index fossil** *n* **:** a fossil that is usu. of narrow time range and wide spatial distribution and that is used in the identification of related geologic formations (as in locating new petroleum reserves)

**index glass** *n* **:** the mirror on the index bar of a sextant or similar instrument

**index hand** *n* **:** a pointer or hand for indicating something (as a reading on a dial) **:** INDICATOR

**index head** *or* **indexing head** *n* **:** a headstock attachable to the table of a milling machine, planer, or shaper on which work may be mounted by a chuck or centers for indexing

**in·dex·i·cal** \ənˈdeksəkəl, (ˈ)in¦d-,\ *adj* [¹*index* + *-ical*] **:** of, relating to, or resembling an index ⟨~ errors⟩ ⟨~ lists⟩

**in·dex·i·cal·ly** \-sək(ə)lē\ *adv* [¹*index* + *-ical* + *-ly*] **:** by way of an index **:** in the manner of an index ⟨what is ~ referred to —C.W.Morris⟩

**in·dex·less** \ˈin,deksləs\ *adj* **:** having no index ⟨an ~ book⟩

**index li·bro·rum pro·hib·i·to·rum** \-līˈbrōrəmprō,hibəˈtōrəm, -ȯr-\ *n, pl* **indices librorum prohibitorum** [NL, index of prohibited books] **1** *sometimes cap I&L&P* **:** a list of proscribed books **2** *usu cap I&L&P* **:** a list of books condemned in whole or in part as dangerous to faith or morals by church authority and forbidden to Roman Catholics — compare INDEX EXPURGATORIUS

**index liquid** *n* **:** a liquid of known refractive index used (as in crystallography) in the determination of the refractive index of powdered substances with a microscope

**index map** *n* **:** a map that shows (as by enclosing a small area in a rectangle on a large map) the location of one or more small areas in relation to a larger area and that typically points up special features in the small areas about which information is desired

**index mark** *n* **:** INDEX 9

**index number** *n* **:** a number used to indicate change in magnitude (as of cost, price, or volume of production) as compared with the magnitude at some specified time usu. taken as 100 ⟨if the cost of an item in 1930 was one and one half as much as its cost in 1913, its *index number*, relative to 1913, was 150⟩ ⟨relative *index numbers* representing changes in price level of the particular type of asset being considered would be used for the purpose of converting fixed assets to current dollar values —*Accountants Digest*⟩ — used esp. in statistics

**index of refraction :** the ratio of the velocity of light or other radiation in the first of two media to its velocity in the second as it passes from one into the other, the first medium being usu. taken to be a vacuum — called also *refractive index*

**index percent** *n* **:** the increase in value of a tree or of a forest due to the combined volume, quality, and price increments and expressed as an annual percent of its present value

**index plane** *also* **index horizon** *n* **:** a surface (as the top of a sedimentary bed) used in working out geological structure

**index plate** *n* **:** a graduated circular plate or one with circular rows of holes differently spaced that is used in machines (as for graduating circles or cutting gear teeth)

**index re·rum** \-ˈrērəm\ *n, pl* **indices rerum** [NL, index of things] **:** an index of topics covered (as in a book)

**index species** *n* **:** a plant or animal species so highly adapted to a particular kind of environment that its presence is sufficient indication that a habitat under investigation belongs to the kind to which the species is adapted

**index table** *n* **:** a horizontal index head

**in·dexterity** \ˌin+\ *n* [¹*in-* + *dexterity*] **:** lack of dexterity

**index ver·bo·rum** \-(ˌ)vərˈbōrəm, -bȯr-\ *n, pl* **indices verborum** [NL, index of words] **:** an index of words or terms (as those discussed in a book)

**indi-** — see INDI-

**¹in·dia** \ˈindēə *chiefly Brit* -dyə\ *adj, usu cap* [fr. *India*, republic and subcontinent (including the Republic of India and Pakistan) in southern Asia, fr. L *India*, subcontinent in southern Asia, fr. Gk, fr. *Indos* India (subcontinent in southern Asia), Indus (river in the northwestern part of the Indian subcontinent), fr. OPer *Hindu* India; akin to Skt *sindhu* river, Indus, region of the Indus] **1 :** of or from the subcontinent of India **:** of the kind or style prevalent in the subcontinent of India **:** INDIAN **2 :** of or from the Republic of India **:** of the kind or style prevalent in the Republic of India

**[2]india** \"\ *usu cap* — a communications code word for the letter *i*

**india buff** *n, often cap I* : a light yellowish brown that is redder, lighter, and stronger than khaki, yellower than walnut brown, and yellower and paler than cinnamon

**india drugget** *n, usu cap I* : DRUGGET 3

**india gum** *usu cap I, var of* INDIAN GUM

**india ink** *n, often cap 1st I* [so called fr. a belief that it was made in India] **1** : a black pigment (as specially prepared lampblack mixed with a glutinous binder and sometimes perfume) in the form of sticks or cakes and used in drawing and lettering **2** : a fluid ink consisting usu. of a fine suspension of india-ink pigment in a liquid medium (as water containing a gum) — called also *China ink, Chinese ink*

**india malacca** *n, usu cap I* : any of several rattan palms of the genus *Calamus* used for making walking sticks

**in·dia·man** \-mən\ *n, pl* **indiamen** *usu cap* : a merchant ship formerly used in trade with India; *esp* : a large sailing ship used in this trade

**[1]in·di·an** \'indēən *chiefly Brit* -dyən, *in sense 2 chiefly dial* 'injən *or sometimes* 'in(,)din\ *n* -s *cap* [prob. fr. (assumed) ML *Indianus*, fr. ML *indianus*, adj.] **1 a** : a native or inhabitant of the subcontinent of India or of the East Indies — compare PAKISTANI **b** : one of the native languages of the subcontinent of India or of the East Indies **2 a** [so called fr. the belief on the part of Columbus that the lands discovered by him in 1492 and later were part of Asia] : AMERICAN INDIAN **b** : one of the native languages of American Indians

**[2]indian** \"\ *adj, usu cap* [prob. fr. ML *indianus*, fr. L *India*, subcontinent in southern Asia + *-anus* -an (adj. suffix)] **1 a** (1) : of, relating to, or characteristic of the subcontinent of India or the East Indies (2) : of, relating to, or characteristic of one of the peoples of the subcontinent of India or the East Indies **b** : of, relating to, or characteristic of one of the native languages of the subcontinent of India or the East Indies **c** (1) : ORIENTAL 4 (2) : of, relating to, or constituting the subregion of the biogeographical region that includes Ceylon and the subcontinent of India north to the Himalayas and west to the Persian gulf or sometimes these areas excepting Ceylon and the adjacent part of the subcontinent of India **2 a** [after [1]*indian* 2a] : of, relating to, or characteristic of the American Indians **b** : of, relating to, or characteristic of one of the native languages of American Indians **3** : of, relating to, or characteristic of the West Indies

**[1]in·di·ana** \,indē'anə\ *adj, usu cap* [fr. *Indiana*, state in the north central U. S., fr. NL *indiana*, fem. of *indianus*, adj., Indian (sense 2a), fr. ML, Indian (sense 1a)] : of or from the state of Indiana ⟨*Indiana* writers⟩ : of the kind or style prevalent in Indiana : INDIANAN

**[2]indiana** \"\ *n, often cap* [fr. *Indiana*, state in the north central U. S.] : a vivid purplish red that is redder, lighter, and stronger than rubellite and bluer and deeper than malmaison rose

**indiana ballot** *n, usu cap I* [so called fr. its adoption by Indiana in 1889] : an Australian ballot upon which the names of candidates are placed in separate columns according to their party affiliations with the party name and sometimes emblem at the top of each column — called also *party-column ballot;* compare MASSACHUSETTS BALLOT, OFFICE-BLOCK BALLOT

**indian agent** *n, usu cap I* : an official representative of the U. S. federal government to American Indian tribes esp. on reservations

**in·di·an·a·ite** \,indē'anə,īt\ *n* -s [*Indiana*, state in the north central U. S., its locality + E *-ite*] : a variety of halloysite

**indiana limestone** *n, usu cap I* [so called fr. its quarrying site in southern Indiana] : a usu. gray or buff oolitic Mississippian limestone of the lower Carboniferous that is uniform and easily worked and widely used for building

**indian almond** *n, usu cap I* [[2]*indian* 1] : MALABAR ALMOND

**[1]in·di·an·an** \,indē'anən\ *or* **in·di·an·i·an** \-'anēən, -nyən\ *adj, usu cap* [*Indiana* + E *-an, -ian* (adj. suffix)] **1** : of, relating to, or characteristic of the state of Indiana **2** : of, relating to, or characteristic of the people of Indiana

**[2]indianan** \"\ *or* **indianian** \"\ *n* -s *cap* [*Indiana* + E *-an, -ian* (n. suffix)] : a native or resident of Indiana

**indian antelope** *n, usu cap I* [[2]*indian* 1] : BLACK BUCK 1

**in·di·an·ap·o·lis** \,indēə'nap(ə)ləs *sometimes* -di,-\ *adj, usu cap* : of or from Indianapolis, the capital of Indiana ⟨an *Indianapolis* lawyer⟩ : of the kind or style prevalent in Indianapolis

**in·di·ana·pol·i·tan** \,indē,anə'pälət°n\ *n* -s *cap* [fr. *Indianapolis*, after such pairs as E *metropolis: metropolitan*] : a native or resident of Indianapolis, Indiana

**indian apple** *n, usu cap I* [[2]*indian* 2] : MAYAPPLE

**indian arrow** *n, usu cap I* [[2]*indian* 2] : [2]WAHOO a

**indian arrowroot** *n, usu cap I* [[2]*indian* 2] **1 a** : a tropical American arrowroot (*Maranta arundinacea*) **b** : starch from this arrowroot — called also *West Indian arrowroot* **2** [[2]*indian* 1] **a** : a stemless perennial herb (*Tacca leontopetaloides*) widely cultivated in the tropics for its starchy tuberous rootstock **b** : starch from this plant — called also *East Indian arrowroot*

**indian arrowwood** *n, usu cap I* [[2]*indian* 2] **1** : FLOWERING DOGWOOD **2** : [2]WAHOO a

**indian azalea** *n, usu cap I* [[2]*indian* 1] **1 a** : a somewhat bristly evergreen Japanese azalea (*Rhododendron indicum*) with paired or solitary bright red or rosy red flowers containing 5 stamens **b** : a hairy or bristly evergreen Chinese azalea (*Rhododendron simsii*) with large clustered rosy red to dark red flowers containing 10 stamens **2** : any of numerous usu. tender cultivated azaleas that have single or double flowers in many colors and color combinations and that have been developed by selection from and hybridization of the Chinese Indian azalea and other evergreen azaleas

**indian balm** *n, usu cap I* [[2]*indian* 2] : PURPLE TRILLIUM

**indian barberry** *n, usu cap I* [[2]*indian* 1] : any of several deciduous barberries of southern Asia including some (as *Berberis aristata*) that are occas. cultivated — see DYER'S BARBERRY

**indian bark** *n, usu cap I* [[2]*indian* 2] : EVERGREEN MAGNOLIA

**indian bean** *n, usu cap I* **1 a** : a No. American catalpa (*Catalpa bignonioides*) with flat pods resembling beans **b** : a pod of this catalpa **2** : the fruit of the groundnut **3** : HYACINTH BEAN

**indian beech** *n, usu cap I* : an Asiatic tree (*Pongamia glabra*) of the family Leguminosae that has glossy pinnate leaves and racemose creamy-white scented flowers and that is used as a shade tree and as the source of an oil used for illumination

**indian beet** *n, usu cap I* [[2]*indian* 2] : WILD LUPINE

**indian berry** *n, usu cap I* [[2]*indian* 1] : COCCULUS INDICUS

**indian birch** *n, usu cap I* : a Himalayan tree (*Betula utilis*) with bark resembling that of the common paper birch

**indian bison** *n, usu cap I* [[2]*indian* 1] : GAUR

**indian bitters** *n, usu cap I* : an American magnolia (*Magnolia fraseri*) having a bitter bark formerly used as a tonic

**indian blanket** *n, usu cap I* **1** : a blanket made by American Indians or made in imitation of Indian designs — compare NAVAHO BLANKET **2** : an annual herb (*Gaillardia pulchella*) of the central U. S. that has showy yellow flower heads marked with scarlet or purple in the center

**indian block** *n, usu cap I* : a close-quarter block used in lacrosse in which the stick is directed across the opponent's stick

**indian blue** *n, usu cap I* [[2]*indian* 1] : INDIGO 3

**indian blue pine** *n, usu cap I* [[2]*indian* 1] : BHOTAN PINE

**indian boys and girls** *n pl, usu cap I* [[2]*indian* 2] : DUTCHMAN'S-BREECHES

**indian bread** *n, usu cap I* [[2]*indian* 2] **1** : CORN BREAD **2** : TUCKAHOE 2

**indian breadroot** *n, usu cap I* [[2]*indian* 2] : BREADROOT 1

**indian bridle** *n, usu cap I* [[2]*indian* 2] : a rope bridle in which the cord passes from the animal's mouth through a loop about its throat

**indian brown** *n, usu cap I* [prob. fr. [2]*indian* 1] : OLD ENGLISH BROWN

**indian buffalo** *n, usu cap I* : an upland buffalo of eastern Asia kept for draft and milk production esp. in areas where the true water buffalo does not thrive

**indian bullfrog** *n, usu cap I* : a large loud-voiced frog (*Rana tigrina*) of India and Malaysia

**indian butter** *n, usu cap I* : butter derived from the Himalayan butter tree — called also *phulwa butter*

**indian cane** *n, usu cap I* [[2]*indian* 1] **1** : INDIAN SHOT **2** : the stem of the turmeric **3** : BAMBOO

**indian cedar** *n, usu cap I* [[2]*indian* 1] **1** : DEODAR **2** [[2]*indian* 2] : HOP HORNBEAM **3** [[2]*indian* 2] : SPANISH CEDAR **4** : TOON

**indian cherry** *n, usu cap I* [[2]*indian* 2] **1** : YELLOW BUCKTHORN **2** : JUNEBERRY

**indian chickweed** *n, usu cap I* [[2]*indian* 2] : CARPETWEED

**indian chief** *n, usu cap I* [[2]*indian* 2] : SHOOTING STAR 2

**indian cigar tree** *n, usu cap I* [[2]*indian* 2] : INDIAN BEAN 1

**indian civet** *n, usu cap I* [[2]*indian* 1] : ZIBET

**indian clover** *n, usu cap I* [[2]*indian* 2] : a plant of the genus *Trifolium* (esp. *T. dichotomum*)

**indian club** *n, usu cap I* [[2]*indian* 1] : a fairly heavy club (as of wood or metal) shaped like a large bottle or tenpin and swung about usu. with one in each hand to strengthen the muscles of the arms

Indian club

**indian cobra** *n, usu cap I* : a very venomous cobra (*Naja naja*) that is found esp. about settled areas and dwellings in southern and eastern Asia and eastward to the Philippines, that is yellowish to dark brown usu. with spectacle-shaped black and white markings on the expansible hood, and that sometimes reaches a length of 6 feet — called also *spectacled cobra*

**indian cockle** *n, usu cap I* [[2]*indian* 1] : COCCULUS INDICUS

**indian cork tree** *n, usu cap I* : an East Indian timber tree (*Millingtonia hortensis*) of the family Bignoniaceae that yields an inferior cork and is used for decoration

**indian corn** *n, usu cap I* [[2]*indian* 2] **1** : a tall cereal grass (*Zea mays*) bearing kernels on typically large ears and long cultivated in America **2 a** : the ripened ears of Indian corn **b** : the kernels of Indian corn widely used as food for human beings and livestock

**indian couch grass** *n, usu cap I* [[2]*indian* 1] : BERMUDA GRASS

**indian creeper** *n, usu cap I* [[2]*indian* 2] : TRUMPET CREEPER

**indian cucumber** *or* **indian cucumber root** *n, usu cap I* : a small American herb (*Medeola virginiana*) of the lily family with a white succulent rootstock and with leaves in two whorls of which the upper whorl subtends an umbel of small greenish yellow flowers

**indian cup** *n, usu cap I* [[2]*indian* 2] **1** : a plant of the genus *Sarracenia; esp* : PITCHER PLANT a **2** : CUP PLANT

**indian currant** *n, usu cap I* **1 a** : a No. American shrub (*Symphoricarpos orbiculatus*) **b** : the red fruit of this shrub resembling a berry **2** : a shrub (*Ribes glutinosum*) of the Pacific coast of No. America with showy racemose red flowers and black fragrant fruit

**indian devil** *n, usu cap I* [[2]*indian* 2] : WOLVERINE 1a

**indian doctor** *n, usu cap I* [[2]*indian* 2] **1** : MEDICINE MAN **2** : a white man professing himself a medical practitioner and resorting chiefly to the use of medicinal herbs

**indian dye** *n, usu cap I* [[2]*indian* 2] : GOLDENSEAL

**indian ebony** *n, usu cap I* [[2]*indian* 1] : a tree of the genus *Diospyros; esp* : a green ebony (*Diospyros melanoxylon*)

**indian elm** *n, usu cap I* [[2]*indian* 2] : SLIPPERY ELM 1

**indian fiber** *n, usu cap I* [[2]*indian* 2] : PIASSAVA 1

**indian fig** *n, usu cap I* [[2]*indian* 1] **1** : BANYAN **2** [[2]*indian* 2] **a** : any of several plants of the genus *Opuntia:* as (1) : a tropical American prickly pear (*Opuntia fidus-indica*) (2) : an eastern No. American prickly pear (*Opuntia compressa*) **b** : the edible acid fruit of one of these plants

**[1]indian file** *n, usu cap I* [[2]*indian* 2; fr. the Indian practice of going through woods in single file] : SINGLE FILE ⟨along this road the inhabitants slowly moved in *Indian file* —*Newsweek*⟩

**[2]indian file** *adv, usu cap I* : in single file ⟨where two people have to walk *Indian file* —Elizabeth Montizambert⟩

**indian fire** *n, usu cap I* [[2]*indian* 1] : BENGAL LIGHT 1

**indianfish** \'==,=\ *n* [[2]*indian* 2] **1** : an angelfish (*Pomacanthus paru*) of the western Atlantic from Florida to Brazil **2** : WARMOUTH

**indian fog** *n, usu cap I* [[2]*indian* 2] : DWARF HOUSELEEK

**indian frankincense** *n, usu cap I* [[2]*indian* 1] : FRANKINCENSE 1

**indian game** *n, usu cap I&G* [[2]*indian* 1; fr. its having been produced by crossing English game fowl with Indian and Sumatran game fowl] : CORNISH 2

**indian gift** *n, usu cap I* : something given by an Indian giver

**indian giver** *n, usu cap I* [[2]*indian* 2] : one who gives something to another and then takes it back or expects an equivalent in return

**indian giving** *n, usu cap I* : the type of giving typical of an Indian giver

**indian gooseberry** *n, usu cap I* [[2]*indian* 1] : EMBLIC

**indian gram** *n, usu cap I* [[2]*indian* 1] : CHICK-PEA

**indian grass** *n, usu cap I* [[2]*indian* 2] : WOOD GRASS 1

**indian gravelroot** *n, usu cap I* [[2]*indian* 2] : JOE-PYE WEED

**indian gum** *also* **india gum** *n, usu cap I* [[2]*indian* 1 or *india* + *gum*] **1** : GHATTI GUM **2** : STERCULIA GUM; *esp* : the common karaya gum of India

**indian harvest** *n, usu cap I* [[2]*indian* 2] *obs* : a harvest of Indian corn

**indian hawthorn** *n, usu cap I* [[2]*indian* 1] : an ornamental evergreen shrub (*Raphiolepis indica*) with sharp-serrate leaves and racemes of pink-tinged white flowers

**indian hemp** *n, usu cap I* [[2]*indian* 2] **1** : a No. American dogbane (*Apocynum cannabinum*) that yields a tough fiber formerly used in cordage; *broadly* : DOGBANE 1 — compare RHEUMATISM WEED **2** [[2]*indian* 1] : HEMP 1 **3** [[2]*indian* 1] : an Indian mallow (*Abutilon theophrasti*) **4** [[2]*indian* 1] : SUNN **5** : SWAMP MILKWEED

**indian–hemp resin** *n, usu cap I* [*indian hemp* (sense 2) + *resin*] : CHARAS

**indian hen** *n, usu cap I* [[2]*indian* 2] **1** : AMERICAN BITTERN **2** : PILEATED WOODPECKER

**indian hippo** *n, usu cap I* [[2]*indian* 2 + *hippo* (perh. alter. of [1]*hypo*)] **1** : INDIAN PHYSIC 1 **2** : the rhizome and roots of Indian hippo used as a mild emetic

**indianian** *usu cap, var of* INDIANAN

**indian ink** *n, usu cap I* [[2]*indian* 1; fr. a belief that it was made in India] *Brit* : INDIA INK

**indian ipecac** *n, usu cap I* [[2]*indian* 1] **1 a** : an Asiatic vine (*Tylophora asthmatica*) resembling milkweed **b** : the root of this vine **2** [[2]*indian* 2] : INDIAN PHYSIC **3** [[2]*indian* 2] : IPECAC 1

**in·di·an·ism** \'indēə,nizəm, -dyə,n-\ *n* -s *usu cap* **1** : the qualities or culture distinctive or felt to be distinctive of Indians, esp. of American Indians **2 a** : action or policy directed toward furthering the interests and culture of Indians, esp. of American Indians **b** : specialized interest in or emulation or glorification of the arts and crafts and other achievements of Indians, esp. of American Indians **3** : a word or phrase distinctive or felt to be distinctive of the speech of Indians, esp. of American Indians

**in·di·an·ist** \-_nəst\ *n* -s *usu cap* : a specialist in or advocate of Indianism

**in·di·an·iza·tion** \,indēənə'zāshən\ *n* -s *usu cap* : the act or process of indianizing or the state of being indianized

**in·di·an·ize** \'indēə,nīz\ *vt* -ED/-ING/-S *see -ize in Explan Notes, often cap* [[2]*indian* 1&2 + *-ize*] **1** : to make Indian (as in manner of behavior or in culture or appearance) : cause to have Indian characteristics : adapt to Indian conditions or practices ⟨contact with Indians gradually *indianized* some of the settlers⟩ **2** : to cause (as the staff of a government agency) to be made up largely or wholly of Indians

**indian jacana** *n, usu cap I* [[2]*indian* 1] : PHEASANT-TAILED JACANA

**indian jalap** *n, usu cap I* [[2]*indian* 1] : TURPETH 1

**indian jujube** *n, usu cap I* [[2]*indian* 1] **1** : a shrub or small tree (*Ziziphus mauritiana*) of southeastern Asia cultivated in the southeastern U.S. **2** : the globose dark red fruit of the Indian jujube

**indian kale** *n, usu cap I* [[2]*indian* 2] : any of several large-leaved arums (family Araceae) with edible farinaceous rootstocks: as **a** : TARO **b** : YAUTIA

**indian laburnum** *n, usu cap I* [[2]*indian* 1] : DRUMSTICK TREE

**indian lacquer** *n, usu cap I* : a natural black varnish obtained in Ceylon and the subcontinent of India as an exudation from the marking nut or a related tree (*Holigarna longifolia*)

**indian ladder** *n, usu cap I* [[2]*indian* 2] : a ladder made of or as if of a small tree so trimmed that several inches of each branch are left as a support for the foot

**indian lake** *n, usu cap I* [prob. fr. [2]*indian* 1] **1** : a red lake prepared from lac dye and formerly used by painters **2** *often cap I* : a dark to deep purplish red that is bluer and slightly lighter than magenta (sense 2c)

**indian lamb** *n, usu cap I* [[2]*indian* 1] : the pelt of the young of an Indian sheep of Persian type usu. white with a looser curl to the hair than Persian lamb and usu. dyed gray before use

**indian laurel** *also* **indian laurelwood** *n, usu cap I* **1** : an Asiatic tree (*Persea indica*) that produces canary wood **2** : any of various trees of the genus *Terminalia* (esp. *T. alata* and *T. tomentosa*)

**indian lettuce** *n, usu cap I* [[2]*indian* 2] **1** : ROUND-LEAVED WINTERGREEN **2** : AMERICAN COLUMBO **3** : a succulent herb (*Montia perfoliata*) of the Pacific coast of No. America; *broadly* : a plant of the genus *Montia* (as blinks)

**indian licorice** *n, usu cap I* : an East Indian twining herb (*Abrus precatorius*) with pinnate leaves and axillary clusters of small purple flowers and a root that is used as a substitute for licorice — see JEQUIRITY

**indian lilac** *n, usu cap I* [[2]*indian* 1] **1** : CHINABERRY 2 **2** : CRAPE MYRTLE

**indian lotus** *n, usu cap I* : an aquatic plant (*Nelumbo nucifera*) native to eastern Asia and widely cultivated for its foliage and large pink flowers — compare LOTUS 3

**indian madder** *n, usu cap I* **1** : an East Indian plant (*Rubia cordifolia*) used for dyeing in the Orient — called also *munjeet* **2** : CHAY

**indian mahogany** *n, usu cap I* [[2]*indian* 1] **1** : TOON **2 a** : ROHUN **b** : the wood of rohun

**indian maize** *n, usu cap I* [[2]*indian* 2] : INDIAN CORN

**indian mallow** *n, usu cap I* [[2]*indian* 1] **1** : any of several abutilons; *esp* : a tall annual herb (*Abutilon theophrasti*) that has velvety cordate leaves and yellow flowers, yields a long strong fiber for which it is sometimes cultivated, and is native to India but widely naturalized as an escape in warm and temperate regions — called also *velvetleaf* **2** [[2]*indian* 2] : a tropical American weed (*Sida spinosa*) with pale yellow or orange flowers that has been introduced into the U.S. and is found esp. in the southern U.S.

**indian maple** *n, usu cap I* : a Himalayan maple (*Acer caesium*) with large palmate leaves

**indian meal** *n, usu cap I* [[2]*indian* 2] : CORNMEAL

**indian meal moth** *n, usu cap I* [*indian meal* + *moth*] : a small variably marked pyralid moth (*Plodia interpunctella*) having an equally variably colored larva that feeds on cereal products and other dried foods and by its extensive webbing destroys more than it consumes

**indian melon** *n, usu cap I* [[2]*indian* 2] : BARREL CACTUS

**indian millet** *n, usu cap I* [[2]*indian* 1] **1** : DURRA **2** : PEARL MILLET 1 **3** [[2]*indian* 2] : SILKGRASS 2

**indian moccasin** *n, usu cap I* [[2]*indian* 2] : STEMLESS LADY'S-SLIPPER

**indian mound** *n, usu cap I* [[2]*indian* 2] : one of the mounds of the Mound Builders

**indian mulberry** *n, usu cap I* **1** : an East Indian shrub or small tree (*Morinda citrifolia*) with axillary heads of flowers and pulpy fruit **2 a** : WHITE MULBERRY **b** : a related mulberry (*Morus indica*)

**indian mustard** *n, usu cap I* : an Asiatic mustard (*Brassica juncea*) that has pods growing at an angle with their stems and that is used as a potherb and is widely naturalized as a weed — called also *leaf mustard*

**indian nut** *n, usu cap I* [[2]*indian* 1] **1** : BETEL NUT **2** [[2]*indian* 2] : PINE NUT 2

**indian oak** *n, usu cap I* [[2]*indian* 1] **1** : TEAK **2** : any of several oaks (esp. *Quercus dilatata*) of India

**indian ocher** *n, usu cap I* [[2]*indian* 1] : INDIAN RED 1a

**indian orange** *n, often cap I* [prob. fr. [2]*indian* 1] : a vivid reddish orange that is paler than international orange and redder and darker than golden poppy or chrome orange

**indian ox** *n, usu cap I* [[2]*indian* 1] : ZEBU

**indian paint** *n, usu cap I* [[2]*indian* 2] **1** : BLOODROOT 1 **2** : STRAWBERRY BLITE **3** : HOARY PUCCOON

**indian paintbrush** *n, usu cap I* [[2]*indian* 2] **1** : any of various American plants of the genus *Castilleja; esp* : a widely distributed annual or biennial (*C. coccinea*) of the eastern U.S. that usu. has bright scarlet floral bracts — called also *painted cup* **2** : ORANGE HAWKWEED

**indian paint fungus** *n, usu cap I* [[2]*indian* 2] : a tooth fungus (*Echinodontium tinctorum*) that causes heartrot in fir or spruce or western hemlock

**indian pangolin** *n, usu cap I* [[2]*indian* 1] : a scaly anteater (*Manis crassicaudata* syn. *Phatages crassicaudata*) with heavily scaled tail and feet and small ears

**indian pea** *n, usu cap I* [[2]*indian* 1] **1** : PIGEON PEA **2** : GRASS PEA

**indian peacock** *or* **indian peafowl** *n, usu cap I* [[2]*indian* 1] : the common domesticated peafowl (*Pavo cristatus*) which is native to India and Siam and in which the wings of the male are largely barred in black and buff — compare JAPANNED PEACOCK

**indian pear** *n, usu cap I* [[2]*indian* 2] : JUNEBERRY

**indian physic** *n, usu cap I* **1** : either of two American herbs (*Gillenia trifoliata* and *G. stipulata*) with emetic roots **2** : INDIAN BITTERS **3** : INDIAN HEMP 1

**indian pine** *n, usu cap I* [[2]*indian* 2] : LOBLOLLY PINE 1

**indian pink** *n* [[2]*indian* 1] **1** *usu cap I* **a** : CHINA PINK **b** *or* **indian pinkroot** [[2]*indian* 2] : PINKROOT a **c** [[2]*indian* 2] *West Indies* : CYPRESS VINE **d** [[2]*indian* 2] : GAYWINGS **e** [[2]*indian* 2] : INDIAN PAINTBRUSH 1 **f** [[2]*indian* 2] : any of several wild pinks of the genera *Silene* and *Lychnis* **g** [[2]*indian* 2] : CARDINAL FLOWER **2** *often cap I* : a light reddish brown that is redder, lighter, and stronger than copper tan or monkey skin and redder and duller than peach tan

**indian pipe** *n, usu cap I* [[2]*indian* 2; perh. fr. the use of its pithy stems by American Indians for the stems of tobacco pipes] : a leafless saprophytic herb (*Monotropa uniflora*) native to Asia and the U.S. that is waxy white and turns black in drying and has a solitary nodding flower that becomes erect in fruit; *broadly* : SWEET PINESAP

**indian–pipe family** *n, usu cap I* : PYROLACEAE

**indian pitcher** *n, usu cap I* [[2]*indian* 2] : PITCHER PLANT a

**indian plantain** *n, usu cap I* : any of various plants of the genus *Cacalia* that have leaves resembling those of plantains

**indian plum** *n, usu cap I* [[2]*indian* 1] **1 a** : any of several tropical trees of the genus *Flacourtia* (esp. *F. indica*) — compare GOVERNOR'S PLUM **b** : the edible rather acid plum-shaped fruit of one of these trees **2** [[2]*indian* 2] : OSOBERRY

**indian plume** *n, usu cap I* [[2]*indian* 2] : BUTTERFLY WEED 1

**indian–plum family** *n, usu cap I* : FLACOURTIACEAE

**indian poke** *n, usu cap I* : AMERICAN HELLEBORE 1

**indian pony** *n, usu cap I* **1** : an unimproved typically small hardy vigorous not esp. graceful horse of western No. America descended from stock introduced by Spaniards and redomesticated by Indians that is valuable as a utility range horse and for crossbreeding — compare MUSTANG, QUARTER HORSE **2** : [1]PINTO

**indian posy** *n, usu cap I* **1** : any of several American everlastings (as *Anaphalis margaritacea* and *Gnaphalium obtusifolium*) **2** : BUTTERFLY WEED 1

**indian potato** *n, usu cap I* : any of several American plants with edible tuberous roots: as **a** : GROUNDNUT 2a **b** : GIANT SUNFLOWER **c** : BREADROOT 1 **d** : a yamp (*Carum gairdneri*)

**indian puccoon** *n, usu cap I* [[2]*indian* 2] : HOARY PUCCOON

**indian pudding** *n, usu cap I* [[2]*indian* 2] : a pudding usu. made of cornmeal, milk, sugar, butter, molasses, and spices and baked and served as a dessert

**indian purple** *n, often cap I* [prob. fr. [2]*indian* 1] : a dark purplish red that is paler and slightly redder than pansy purple, redder and paler than raisin, bluer and paler than Bokhara, and redder and less strong than Schoenfeld's purple

**indian python** *n, usu cap I* : a very large python (*Python molurus*) of southeastern Asia that is mottled with dark blotches on an olive to pinkish tan ground

**indian red** *n* [[2]*indian* 1] **1** *usu cap I* **a** : a yellowish red ferruginous earth containing hematite and used as a pigment — called also *Persian red* **b** : any of various light red to purplish brown iron oxide pigments made by calcining iron salts (as copperas) **2** *often cap I* **a** : a strong reddish brown that is redder and slightly darker than Venetian red — called also *Japanese red, Prussian red* **b** : a moderate reddish

brown — called also *Chinese red, Majolica earth, Persian earth, Persian red, scarlet ocher, Spanish brown*
**indian redroot** *n, usu cap I* [²*indian* 2] **:** REDROOT
**indian redwood** *n, usu cap I* [²*indian* 1] **1 :** INDIAN MAHOGANY **2 :** SAPPANWOOD
**indian reed** *n, usu cap I* [²*indian* 1] **1 :** INDIAN SHOT **2** [²*indian* 2] **:** a tall American grass (*Cinna arundinacea*) resembling reed **3** [²*indian* 2] **:** WOOD GRASS 1
**indian rhubarb** *n, usu cap I* [²*indian* 1] **1 :** HIMALAYAN RHUBARB **2** [²*indian* 2] **:** a stout herb (*Peltiphyllum peltatum*) of the family Saxifragaceae of the Pacific coast of No. America with leaves that have edible petioles
**indian rice** *n, usu cap I* [²*indian* 2] **:** WILD RICE 1a
**indian ricegrass** *n, usu cap I* [²*indian* 2] **:** SILK GRASS 2
**indian robin** *n, usu cap I* **:** any of various songbirds of India resembling or related to the English robin
**indian root** *n, usu cap I* [²*indian* 2] **1 :** INDIAN PHYSIC **2 :** SPIKENARD 2a
**indian rosewood** *n, usu cap I* [²*indian* 1] **1 :** BLACKWOOD b **2 :** SISSOO
**indian runner** *n, usu cap I&R* [²*indian* 1; fr. a belief that it originated in India] **:** a breed of small upright domestic ducks noted for their egg production and known in fawn and white or pure white or penciled varieties
**indians** *pl of* INDIAN
**indian saffron** *n, usu cap I* [²*indian* 1] **1 :** SAFFLOWER 1 **2 :** ZEDOARY
**indian sage** *n, usu cap I* [²*indian* 2] **:** BONESET 1
**indian sago palm** *n, usu cap I* [²*indian* 1] **:** JAGGERY PALM
**indian salad** *n, usu cap I* **:** a waterleaf (*Hydrophyllum virginianum*) of the eastern U.S. with divided leaves and cymose bell-shaped flowers that are white or violet
**indian sandalwood** *n, usu cap I* [²*indian* 1] **:** SANDALWOOD 1a
**indian sanicle** *n, usu cap I* [²*indian* 2] **:** WHITE SNAKEROOT
**indian sarsaparilla** *n, usu cap I* **1 :** an East Indian shrub (*Hemidesmus indicus*) of the family Asclepiadaceae **2 :** the root of Indian sarsaparilla used as a substitute for sarsaparilla
**indian's-dream** \ˈ==ˌ=\ *n, pl* **indian's-dreams** *usu cap I* [*indian's* (gen. of ¹*indian* 2)] **1 :** CLIFF BRAKE **2 :** OREGON CLIFF BRAKE
**indian senna** *n, usu cap I* [²*indian* 1] **:** TINNEVELLY SENNA
**indian shamrock** *n, usu cap I* [²*indian* 2] **:** PURPLE TRILLIUM
**indian shoe** *n, usu cap I* [²*indian* 2] **1 :** STEMLESS LADY'S-SLIPPER **2 :** YELLOW LADY'S-SLIPPER
**indian shot** *n, usu cap I* [²*indian* 1] **:** a plant of the genus *Canna* (esp. *C. indica*) that has hard black seeds about the size of buckshot
**indian sign** *n, usu cap I* [prob. fr. ²*indian* 2] **1 :** a magic spell for immobilizing or making powerless an opponent or rival ⟨have put the *Indian sign* on that team and beaten them nearly every game⟩ or for subjecting another to one's full control or slightest whims or desires ⟨she's put the *Indian sign* on every bachelor in town⟩ — usu. used with *the* **2 :** HEX, JINX ⟨thought the cow had got the *Indian sign* when it wouldn't give any more milk⟩
**indian slipper** *n, usu cap I* [²*indian* 2] **:** STEMLESS LADY'S-SLIPPER
**indian soap** *or* **indian soap-plant** *n, usu cap I* [²*indian* 2] **:** SOAPBERRY TREE 1
**indian squill** *n, usu cap I* [²*indian* 1] **:** squill from an herb of the genus *Urginea* (esp. *Urginea indica*) that is the official source of the drug in Great Britain
**indian strawberry** *n, usu cap I* [prob. fr. ²*indian* 1] **1 :** a low East Indian herb (*Duchesnea indica*) naturalized in eastern No. America and resembling the true strawberry but having yellow flowers and tasteless involucrate fruit **2** [prob. fr. ²*indian* 2] **:** STRAWBERRY BLITE
**indian summer** *n, usu cap I* [²*indian* 2] **1 :** a period of warm or mild weather late in autumn or in early winter usu. characterized by a clear or cloudless sky and by a hazy or smoky appearance of the atmosphere esp. near the horizon **2 :** a period of tranquillity or happiness or prosperity or other generally favorable conditions occurring for the first time or more usu. anew toward the latter part or end of something ⟨if the nineteen-twenties constituted a sort of *Indian summer* of the old order —F.L.Allen⟩ ⟨life in the *Indian summer* of Czarist Russia —John Davenport⟩ ⟨an *Indian summer* of wartime literature —*Blackwood's*⟩ ⟨the *Indian summer* of her widowhood —Dixon Wecter⟩
**indian tan** *n, often cap I* [²*indian* 3] **:** AZTEC 3
**indian tapir** *n, usu cap I* **:** a tapir (*Tapirus indicus*) that is blackish with a broad white area on the body and that is found in Sumatra and the Malay peninsula
**indian tea** *n, usu cap I* [²*indian* 2] **1 :** a yaupon (*Ilex vomitoria*) **2 :** NEW JERSEY TEA **3 :** LABRADOR TEA a
**indian teakettle** *n, usu cap I* [²*indian* 2] **:** PITCHER PLANT
**indian thistle** *n, usu cap I* [²*indian* 2] **:** WILD TEASEL
**indian tobacco** *n, usu cap I* [²*indian* 2] **1 :** an American wild lobelia (*Lobelia inflata*) with small blue flowers and inflated capsules formerly used as an antispasmodic **2** [prob. fr. ²*indian* 1] **:** HEMP **3 :** a wild tobacco (*Nicotiana rustica*) **4 :** a plant of the genus *Antennaria; esp* **:** a common cat's-foot (*A. plantaginifolia*) of eastern No. America
**indian turmeric** *n, usu cap I* [²*indian* 2] **:** GOLDENSEAL
**indian turnip** *n, usu cap I* [²*indian* 2] **1 a :** JACK-IN-THE-PULPIT **1 b :** the acrid root of the jack-in-the-pulpit **2 :** BREADROOT
**indian warrior** *n, usu cap I* [²*indian* 2; fr. its brilliant red crest] **:** a lousewort (esp. *Pedicularis densiflora* and *P. bracteosa*) of the western U.S.
**indian wayfaring tree** *n, usu cap I* **:** a Himalayan shrub (*Viburnum cotinifolium*) with roundish leaves and showy flowers
**indian wheat** *n, usu cap I* [²*indian* 2] **1 :** INDIAN CORN **2** [prob. fr. ²*indian* 1] **:** TARTARIAN BUCKWHEAT **3 :** any of several plants of the genus *Plantago* (esp. *P. fastigiata*)
**indian whort** *n, usu cap I* [²*indian* 2] **:** BEARBERRY 1
**indian wick·a·pe** \-ˈwikəpē\ *n, usu cap I* [²*indian* 2] **:** LEATHERWOOD
**indian wickup** *or* **indian wicopy** *n, usu cap I* [²*indian* 2] **:** FIREWEED b
**indian wild dog** *n, usu cap I* [²*indian* 1] **:** DHOLE
**indian wolf** *n, usu cap I* **:** a light-colored wolf (*Canis pallipes*) that is widely distributed in desert and upland areas from the northern part of the subcontinent of India westward to northern Arabia and Iran and that is often considered to constitute an Asian variety of the common wolf of Europe
**indian-wrestle** \ˈ===ˌ==\ *vb, usu cap I* [back-formation fr. *indian wrestling*] **:** to engage in Indian wrestling
**indian wrestling** *n, usu cap I* [²*indian* 2] **1 :** wrestling in which two wrestlers lie side by side on their backs in reversed position locking their near arms and raising and locking the corresponding legs and attempt to force each other's leg down and turn the other wrestler on his face **2 a :** wrestling in which two wrestlers stand face to face gripping usu. their right hands and setting the outsides of the corresponding feet tightly against each other and attempt to force each other off balance **b :** wrestling in which two wrestlers sit face to face gripping usu. their right hands, setting corresponding elbows firmly on a surface (as the top of a table), and holding the length of the arm from the elbow to the hand tightly against each other and attempt to force each other's arm down
**indian yellow** *n* [²*indian* 1] **1** *usu cap I* **:** a yellow coloring matter: as **a :** a pigment made from the evaporated urine of cows fed on mango leaves — called also *piuri* **b :** COBALT YELLOW 1 **c :** a brilliant yellow pigment made from Naphthol Yellow S and used in coatings for paper and in distemper colors **2** *often cap I* **:** a moderate to strong orange yellow that is slightly lighter than Dutch orange — called also *purree, snowshoe*
**india oilstone** *n, usu cap I* **1 :** a manufactured abrasive material **2 :** a grinding wheel or whetstone or similar tool made of India oilstone
**india paper** *n, usu cap I* [so called fr. a belief that it originally came fr. India] **1** *also* **india proof paper :** a smooth thin delicate but not glossy paper esp. suitable for taking full-bodied impressions (as proofs of engravings, woodcuts) **2 :** a smooth thin tough opaque printing paper — called also *Bible paper*
**india print** *n, usu cap I* **:** a plain lightweight cotton cloth that usu. has hand-blocked Indian designs in rich colors on a natural ground and is used esp. for bedspreads, drapes, or skirts
**india red** *n, often cap I* **:** a deep reddish brown — called also *Arabian red, red robin*
**india rubber** *n, often cap I* **1 :** RUBBER 2a **2 a :** RUBBER 3a **b :** RUBBER 1b(3)
**india-rubber tree** *or* **india-rubber plant** *also* **india-rubber fig** *n, often cap I* **:** a rubber plant (*Ficus elastica*)
**india-rubber vine** *n, often cap I* **:** a woody vine (*Cryptostegia grandiflora*) sometimes cultivated as a source of rubber
**india tan** *n, often cap I* **:** RUSSIAN CALF
**india tint** *n, usu cap I* **:** a light shade of buff often used in coated paper and ordinary book paper
**india wheat** *n, usu cap I* **:** TARTARIAN BUCKWHEAT
¹**in·dic** \ˈindik\ *adj, usu cap* [L *indicus*, fr. Gk *indikos*, fr. *Indos* India (subcontinent in southern Asia), Indus (river in the northwestern part of the Indian subcontinent) + *-ikos* -ic — more at INDIA] **1 :** of or relating to the subcontinent of India **:** INDIAN **2 :** of, relating to, or constituting Indic
²**indic** \"\ *n, cap* **:** a branch of the Indo-European language family containing Sanskrit, Pali, the Prakrits, and related modern languages of India, Pakistan, and Ceylon (as Hindi, Urdu, Sinhalese) — see INDO-EUROPEAN LANGUAGES table
³**indic** \"\ *adj* [*indium* + *-ic*] **:** of or relating to indium
**indic** *abbr* indicated; indicative; indicator
**in·di·can** \ˈindəˌkan\ *n* -s [L *indicum* indigo + E *-an*] **1 :** a colorless crystalline glucoside $C_{14}H_{17}NO_6$ occurring esp. in indigo plants and in woad and yielding indoxyl and glucose on hydrolysis — see INDIGO 1a **2 :** the sulfuric acid ester $C_8H_6NOSO_3H$ of indoxyl or the crystalline potassium salt of this ester occurring in urine and other animal fluids as a derivative of the indole formed in the alimentary canal and yielding indigo on oxidation
**in·di·cant** \-dəkənt\ *n* -s [obs. *indicant*, adj., serving to indicate, fr. L *indicant-, indicans*, pres. part. of *indicare* to indicate] **:** something that serves to indicate ⟨a paragraph printed with a directional arrow before it as an ~⟩
**in·di·cat·able** \ˈindəˌkād·əbəl, -dē;-, -ātə-, ˌ==ˈ===\ *adj* **:** capable of being indicated
**in·di·cate** \ˈindəˌkāt, -dē,-, *usu* -ād·+V\ *vt* -ED/-ING/-S [L *indicatus*, past part. of *indicare*, fr. *in-* ²in- + *dicare* to proclaim, dedicate — more at DICTION] **:** to point out or point to or toward with more or less exactness **:** show or make known with a fair degree of certainty: as **a** (1) **:** to show the probable presence or existence or nature or course of **:** give fair evidence of **:** be a fairly certain sign or symptom of **:** reveal in a fairly clear way ⟨their laughter *indicated* their happiness⟩ ⟨his reply *indicated* total disagreement⟩ ⟨*indicated* his impatience by shrugging⟩ ⟨an anecdote that ~s the kind of people they were⟩ ⟨a fever that ~s severe illness⟩ (2) **:** to demonstrate or suggest the probable necessity or advisability of ⟨conflicting findings ~ further neurological research —*Collier's Yr. Bk.*⟩ ⟨increased luggage space is *indicated* for the family car —R.F.Loewy⟩ ⟨radical surgery is *indicated* in advanced cancer⟩ (3) **:** to show the general outlines of in advance **:** sketch beforehand **:** PRESAGE ⟨his enthusiasm ~s a bright future for him⟩ **b :** to act as a more or less exact index of **:** show or suggest the probable extent or degree of ⟨their records must ~ ability to do successful academic work —*Bull. of Bates Coll.*⟩ ⟨their popularity is *indicated* by the warm welcome they receive everywhere⟩ **c :** to state or express in a brief or cursory way **:** state or express without going into great detail **:** SUGGEST, INTIMATE, HINT ⟨the commission also *indicated* it might take action —*Wall Street Jour.*⟩ ⟨*indicated* a willingness to negotiate —*World*⟩ ⟨the general outlines of it can be *indicated* —R.L.Duffus⟩ **d :** to show the general position or direction of ⟨a map ~s where the ship was sunk⟩ **:** direct attention to with more or less preciseness (as by pointing with the finger or making a gesture) ⟨*indicated* the tray of sandwiches —Kay Boyle⟩ **:** point at ⟨the hands of the clock *indicated* noon⟩
**syn** INDICATE, BETOKEN, ATTEST, BESPEAK, ARGUE, PROVE can mean, in common, to give evidence of, or serve as a ground for, a valid or reasonable inference or an action validated by the inference. INDICATE signifies to serve as a sign or symptom pointing to (the inference or action), stressing only a general, usu. unspecified, connection between subject and object ⟨to assume that Ginger's invitation *indicated* something serious —Clarissa F. Cushman⟩ ⟨the results thus obtained are believed to be the first to *indicate* a possible magnetic effect directly attributable to a solar eclipse —H.D. Harradon⟩ ⟨the results of the physical examination *indicated* some sort of antibiotic medication⟩ BETOKEN stresses the idea of visible or otherwise perceivable evidence or portent ⟨the air with which she looked at the heathmen *betokened* a certain unconcern at their presence —Thomas Hardy⟩ ⟨towering business buildings, great warehouses, and numerous factories *betoken* its importance —*Amer. Guide Series: N.C.*⟩ ATTEST usu. implies the more or less indisputable nature of the evidence ⟨Washington's strong, natural love of children, nowhere *attested* better than in his expense accounts —J.C. Fitzpatrick⟩ ⟨the skill with which they executed these tasks *attested* to their considerable executive talents —R.A.Billington⟩ ⟨the fighting had been hard and continuous, that was *attested* by all the senses —Ambrose Bierce⟩ BESPEAK is interchangeable with *indicate* though it stresses possibly a little more the role of the subject as evidence or token ⟨a freshness and an originality that *bespeak* the intellectual vigor and intuition that he possessed —D.G.Mandelbaum⟩ ⟨a glint of pride in her eyes that *bespoke* her new dignity —Mary Lasswell⟩ ARGUE usu. stresses a reasonable or logical connection between subject and object ⟨his evasion, of course, was the height of insolence, but it *argued* unlimited resource and nerve —Rudyard Kipling⟩ ⟨a becoming deference *argues* deficiency in self-respect —A.N.Whitehead⟩ ⟨what a mistake to say that complexity *argues* culture —Norman Douglas⟩ PROVE is to demonstrate or make manifest the truth of (a conclusion), suggesting the inferential validity of the relationship between subject and object ⟨to become a writer was, however, in Thoreau's mind; his verses *prove* it, his journal proves it —H.S.Canby⟩ ⟨to them, faith is a belief in something which cannot be *proven* and understood rationally —Erich Fromm⟩ ⟨many studies have *proved* that the failure of an employee is seldom due to his lack of ability —W.J.Reilly⟩
**indicated airspeed** *n* **:** the airspeed of an airplane as indicated on an airspeed indicator **:** the airspeed in an atmosphere of standard sea-level density that would give rise to a dynamic pressure equal to that encountered
**indicated altitude** *n* **:** the height above sea level as read on an altimeter
**indicated horsepower** *n* **:** the power developed in the cylinders of an engine as calculated from the average pressure of the working fluid, the piston area, the stroke, and the number of working strokes per minute
**in·di·ca·tion** \ˌindəˈkāshən, -dē'-\ *n* -s [MF, fr. ML *indication-, indicatio* action of pointing out, fr. L, valuation, price, fr. *indicatus* (past part. of *indicare* to indicate) + *-ion-, -io* -ion] **1 :** the action of indicating **2 a :** something (as a signal, sign, suggestion) that serves to indicate ⟨refusal to accept the gift was an ~ of her displeasure⟩ ⟨gave no ~ that he heard me⟩ ⟨an ~ of what they could expect⟩; *specif* **:** a symptom or particular circumstance that indicates the advisability or necessity of (as a specific medical treatment or procedure) ⟨postpartum hemorrhage is the chief ~ for the use of ergot preparations and derivatives —C.H.Thienes⟩ **b :** something that is indicated as advisable or necessary ⟨in case of collapse the immediate ~ is artificial respiration —*Jour. Amer. Med. Assoc.*⟩ **3 :** the degree indicated in a specific instance or at a specific time on a graduated physical instrument (as a thermometer) **:** READING **4 :** suggestion (as by the use of conventionalized techniques or symbols) of architectural features (as in a drawing) rather than detailed representation of such features ⟨cross-hatching is used as an ~ of brick⟩
¹**in·dic·a·tive** \ənˈdikəd·iv, -kətiv\ *adj* [MF *indicatif*, fr. LL *indicativus*, fr. L *indicatus* (past part. of *indicare* to indicate) + *-ivus* -ive] **1 :** of, relating to, or constituting a verb form or set of verb forms that represents an attitude toward or concern with a denoted act or state as an objective fact **:** of, relating to, or constituting a verb form or set of verb forms used invariably in simple declarative sentences and in questions that can be answered by simple declarative sentences and often also in a great variety of other situations ⟨the ~ mood⟩ ⟨*is writing* in "is he writing now" is an ~ verb form⟩ — compare IMPERATIVE, SUBJUNCTIVE **2 :** that indicates **:** that points out more or less exactly **:** that reveals fairly clearly or suggests or intimates ⟨the situation was ~ of the fear, bordering on panic, which had seized the people —F.D.Roosevelt⟩ — **in·dic·a·tive·ly** *adv*
²**indicative** *n* -s **:** the indicative mood of a language ⟨*writes* is in the ~⟩ **:** a form in the indicative mood ⟨*writes* is an ~⟩
**in·di·ca·tor** \ˈindəˌkād·ə(r), -dē,k-, -ātə-\ *n* [LL, fr. L *indicatus* (past part. of *indicare* to indicate) + *-or*] **1** -s **:** one that indicates: as **a :** an index hand (as on a dial) **:** POINTER **b** (1) **:** a pressure gauge (2) **:** an instrument for automatically making a diagram that indicates the pressure in and volume of the working fluid of an engine throughout the cycle so that the horsepower and other characteristics may be deduced **c :** a speed counter for an engine **d :** a registering dial (as on a dial telegraph) **e :** ANNUNCIATOR 2a **2** -s **a :** a substance (as a dye) used to show visually usu. by its capacity for color change the condition of a solution with respect to the presence of free acid or alkali or some other substance (as in detecting the end point of a titration) ⟨litmus and phenolphthalein are acid-base ~s⟩ ⟨oxidation-reduction ~s⟩ **b :** TRACER ⟨radioactive ~s⟩ **3 a** *cap* [NL, fr. LL] **:** the type genus of the family Indicatoridae — see HONEY GUIDE **b** -s **:** any bird of the genus *Indicator* **:** HONEY GUIDE **4** -s [so called fr. a belief that its occurrence indicates that there is ginseng nearby] **:** VIRGINIA GRAPE FERN **5** -s **:** an organism or a kind of organism (as a species) or an ecological community that is so strictly associated with particular environmental conditions that its presence is indicative of the existence of these conditions in a particular environment **6** -s **:** a narrow pyritiferous seam the intersections of which with auriferous quartz veins are usu. accompanied by an ore shoot in the vein **7** -s **:** a deciphering instruction accompanying a message: as **a :** a code or cipher designation of the key **b :** INTERRUPTER b
**indicator card** *or* **indicator diagram** *n* **:** the diagram made by an indicator (sense 1b(2))
**in·di·ca·tor·i·dae** \ˌindəkəˈtōrəˌdē\ *n pl, cap* [NL, fr. *Indicator*, type genus + *-idae*] **:** a family of birds (order Piciformes) that comprises the honey guides and is sometimes considered a subfamily of Capitonidae
**indicator telegraph** *n* **:** NEEDLE TELEGRAPH
**in·di·ca·to·ry** \ənˈdikəˌtōrē, *chiefly Brit* ˈindiˈkātəri *or* -ā·tri\ *adj* [LL *indicatorius*, fr. L *indicatus* (past part. of *indicare*) + *-orius* -ory] **:** INDICATIVE 2
**in·di·ca·trix** \ˌindəˈkā·triks, ənˈdikə·(ˌ)t-\ *n* -ES [NL, fem. of LL *indicator* — more at -TRIX] **:** an ellipsoid whose axes are proportional to the principal refractive indices of a crystal and from which various optical properties of the crystal may be deduced
**in·di·ca·vit** \ˌindəˈkāvət\ *n* -s [L, he has indicated, 3d pers. sing. perf. indic. act. of *indicare* to indicate — more at INDICATE] **:** a writ of prohibition from a common-law court commanding the removal to that court of a case pending in an ecclesiastical court and prohibiting the ecclesiastical court from exercising any further jurisdiction
**indices** *pl of* INDEX
**in·di·cia** \ənˈdish(ē)ə\ *n, pl* **indicia** *or* **indicias** [L, pl. of *indicium* sign, mark, fr. *indicare* to point out, indicate] **1 a :** a distinctive mark that indicates or that is felt to indicate the nature or quality or existence or reality of something **:** INDICATION, SIGN, TOKEN, CRITERION ⟨he had in fact all the ~ of divinity —Wallace Stevens⟩ ⟨many ~ of truth —J.E.Davies⟩ ⟨the real ~ of civilization —H.J.Laski⟩ ⟨press opinion and other ~ of public sentiment —H.H.Sprout⟩ **b :** a significant or apparently significant fact or piece of evidence connected with or deduced from a set of circumstances and giving rise to conjectures having some probability of accord with the truth ⟨studied her belongings carefully but could discover no ~ as to what had become of her⟩ **2 a** (1) **:** a postal marking (as on bulk mail or business reply envelopes) often imprinted on mail or on labels to be affixed to mail and used in place of postage stamps to indicate prepayment of postage (as by use of a postage meter or by receipt of a special permit) (2) **:** a postal marking or verbal statement often imprinted on mail or on labels to be affixed to mail and used to indicate the class or type of a piece of mail or to give directives (as with regard to the proper place for an address) or some other information (as that a piece of mail may be opened for inspection by a postmaster) **b :** an identifying marking or verbal statement used to single out one thing from another ⟨each object had a tag carrying its ~⟩ or to serve as directional guides ⟨each card in the file has ~ that show the location of each book on the shelf⟩
**in·di·cial** \(ˈ)inˈdishəl, ənˈd-\ *adj* [*indicia* + *-al*] **1 :** of, relating to, or having the nature of an indication **:** INDICATIVE ⟨a remark ~ of their pride⟩ **2** [L *indic-, index* index finger, index + E *-ial*] **a :** of, relating to, or having the nature of an index ⟨an ~ glossary⟩ **b :** of or relating to the index finger — **in·di·cial·ly** \-shəlē\ *adv*
**in·dic·i·ble** \-isəbəl\ *adj* [MF, fr. LL *indicibilis*, fr. L *in-* ¹in- + *dicere* to say + *-ibilis* -ible — more at DICTION] **:** UNSPEAKABLE, INEXPRESSIBLE
**in·di·ci·um** \ənˈdishēəm\ *n, pl* **indicia** *or* **indiciums** [L, sign, mark] **:** INDICIA 1
**indico** *obs var of* INDIGO
**in·dic·o·lite** \ənˈdikəˌlīt\ *n* -s [F, fr. *indico-* (fr. L *indicum* indigo) + *-lite* — more at INDIGO] **:** an indigo-blue variety of tourmaline
¹**in·dict** \ənˈdīt, *usu* -īd·+V\ *vt* -ED/-ING/-S [alter. (influenced by ML *indictare* to indict, fr. AF *enditer*) of earlier *indite, endite*, fr. ME *inditen, enditen*, fr. AF *enditer*, fr. OF, to write down, compose — more at INDITE] **1 :** to charge with some wrong or fault or inadequacy usu. formally and after carefully weighing the matter and as if summoning for trial **:** bring a charge against **:** formally accuse; *esp* **:** to attack by accusation and condemn ⟨I ~ those citizens whose easy consciences condone such wrongdoings —F.D.Roosevelt⟩ **2 :** to charge with a crime by the finding or presentment of a jury (as a grand jury) in due form of law ⟨was ~ed for murder⟩ ⟨were ~ed with conspiracy to defraud⟩ **syn** see ACCUSE
²**indict** *vt* -ED/-ING/-S [MF *indicter*, fr. L *indictus*, past part. of *indicere*, fr. *in-* ²in- + *dicere* to say — more at DICTION] *obs* **:** PROCLAIM, DECREE
**in·dict·able** \-əbəl\ *adj* [¹*indict* + *-able*] **1 :** subject to being indicted **:** liable to indictment ⟨~ as he might be for bad taste —Oscar Cargill⟩ **2 :** that makes one liable to indictment ⟨an ~ offense⟩ — **in·dict·ably** \-blē,-bli\ *adv*
**in·dict·ee** \(ˌ)inˌdīˈdē, ən-, =ˌ=(ˌ)=\ *n* -s [alter. (influenced by ¹*indict*) of *enditee*, fr. *endite* (earlier form of ¹*indict*) + *-ee*] **:** one that is indicted
**in·dic·tion** \ənˈdikshən\ *n* -s [ME *indiccioun*, fr. LL *indiction-, indictio*, fr. L, proclamation, fr. *indictus* (past part. of *indicere* to proclaim) + *-ion-, -io* -ion] **1 a :** a 15-year cycle used as a chronological unit in several ancient and medieval systems — see ROMAN INDICTION **b** (1) **:** the edict of a Roman emperor establishing the valuation for assessing a property tax at the beginning of each 15-year cycle (2) **:** the tax or subsidy levied by this edict **2** [L *indiction-, indictio*] *archaic* **:** PROCLAMATION — **in·dic·tion·al** \-shənᵊl,-shnəl\ *adj*
**in·dict·ment** \ənˈdītmənt\ *n* -s [alter. (influenced by ML *indictare* to indict, fr. AF *enditer*) of earlier *indytement, enditement*, fr. ME *inditement, enditement*, fr. AF *enditement*, fr. *enditer* to indict + OF *-ment* — more at INDICT] **1 a :** the action of indicting; *specif* **:** the legal process by which a bill of indictment is preferred to and presented by a jury (as a grand jury) **b :** the state of being indicted **2 :** a formal written statement framed by the prosecuting authority of a state and found by a jury (as a grand jury) charging a person with an offense — compare BILL OF INDICTMENT **3** *Scots law* **:** a process of bringing a person to trial for a crime at the instance of the lord advocate
**in·dict·or** *or* **in·dict·er** \ənˈdīd·ə(r), -ītə-\ *n* -s [*indictor* alter. (influenced by ML *indictare* to indict) of earlier *endightour*, fr. ME *enditour*, fr. AF, fr. *enditer* to indict + OF *-our* -or; *indicter* alter. (influenced by ML *indictare* to indict) of earlier *inditer*, fr. ME *inditer, enditer*, alter. (influenced by ME *-er*) of *enditour*] **:** one that indicts

**in·die** \'indē\ *n* -s [by shortening & alter. fr. *independent*] *slang* : something (as a motion-picture company, a radio or television station) that is independent

**[1]in·dienne** \ˌandēˈen\ *n* -s [F, fr. fem. of *indien* Indian, fr. ML *indianus* — more at INDIAN] : a light cotton fabric with designs painted or printed in imitation of designs used orig. in subcontinental India

**[2]indienne** \"\ *adj, often cap* [F, fem. of *indien* Indian] : seasoned (as with curry) in East Indian style ⟨rice ~⟩

**in·dif·er·ous** \(ˈ)inˈdif(ə)rəs\ *adj* [*indium* + *-ferous*] : containing indium

**in·dif·fer·ence** \ənˈdifərn(t)s, -f(ə)rən-, -R *sometimes* -fən-\ *n* [MF, fr. L *indifferentia* lack of difference, fr. *indifferent-, indifferens* indifferent + *-ia* -y] **1 a** : the quality or state of being indifferent ⟨an age of ~ to religion⟩ **b** : a manifestation or instance of this quality ⟨was much distressed by his ~ toward her⟩ **2 a** *archaic* : lack of difference or distinction between two or more things ⟨journeys discover to us the ~ of places —R.W.Emerson⟩ **b** : absence of compulsion to or toward one thing or another ⟨maintaining the freedom of the will and its ~⟩

**indifference curve** *n* : a curve used in economics to indicate all possible comparative quantities of goods or services equally demanded by or of equal use to a consumer

**in·dif·fer·en·cy** \-nsē\ *n* [L *indifferentia*] *archaic* : INDIFFERENCE

**[1]in·dif·fer·ent** \(ˈ)inˈdifərnt, ənˈd-, -f(ə)rənt, -R *sometimes* -fənt\ *adj* [ME, fr. MF or L; MF, that is looked upon as not mattering one way or another, fr. L *indifferent-, indifferens* neither good nor bad, unconcerned, fr. *in-* [1]in- + *different-, differens*, pres. part. of *differre* to carry apart, be different — more at DIFFERENT] **1** : marked by impartiality : UNBIASED, UNPREJUDICED ⟨an ~ judge in a trial⟩ ⟨the jurors remained ~⟩ ⟨a remarkably ~ critic⟩ **2 a** (1) : that is looked upon as not mattering one way or another : that is regarded as being of no significant importance or value : that is viewed with neutrality ⟨what others think is altogether ~ to him⟩ (2) : that actually does not matter one way or the other : that actually lacks significant importance or value : that is of little consequence : that is unimportant or immaterial ⟨whether you choose to do it or not is a matter that is quite ~⟩ **b** : that has nothing that calls for sanction or condemnation in either observance or neglect : that may be done or not done or observed or not observed with no importance or value one way or the other ⟨ceremonies that are considered essential in some religious sects and ~ in others⟩ ⟨revived an ~ custom⟩ **3 a** (1) : marked by no special liking for or dislike of something ⟨she always seemed ~ to the arrival of visitors⟩ (2) : marked by no special preference for one thing over another : not inclined to one thing more than another ⟨was ~ to their acceptance or rejection of her invitation⟩ ⟨were ~ about which book you would decide to give them⟩ **b** : marked by a total or nearly total lack of interest in or concern about something : dully unconcerned or unfeeling : UNMOVED, LISTLESS, APATHETIC ⟨was ~ to suffering and poverty⟩ ⟨remained ~ to her pleas⟩ ⟨seemed unaffected and quite ~ in the presence of beauty⟩ **4** : neither excessive nor defective (as in size, extent, intensity) : MODERATE, AVERAGE ⟨had a couple of hills of ~ height to climb⟩ ⟨the wind was blowing with a negligible ~ strength⟩ ⟨inherited an ~ fortune⟩ **5 a** (1) : neither good nor bad : deserving neither praise nor censure : PASSABLE, MEDIOCRE, UNIMPRESSIVE ⟨does ~ work at the office⟩ ⟨turned in an ~ performance of the role⟩ (2) : that has a morally neutral nature : that is neither right nor wrong ⟨many human acts are viewed as ~⟩ **b** : not very good : rather bad : fairly poor : INFERIOR ⟨with an ~ voice like hers she shouldn't even attempt singing⟩ ⟨has ~ qualifications for the job⟩ **6** *now chiefly dial* : marked by poor general health : SICKLY **7** : characterized by lack of active quality : NEUTRAL ⟨an ~ chemical⟩ ⟨the ~ part of a magnet⟩ **8 a** : UNDIFFERENTIATED ⟨~ tissues of the human body⟩ **b** : capable of development in more than one direction ⟨~ blastema cells⟩; *esp* : not yet embryologically determined

**syn** UNCONCERNED, INCURIOUS, ALOOF, DETACHED, UNINTERESTED, DISINTERESTED: INDIFFERENT, often interchangeable with others of this group, may imply uninterested neutrality of attitude or marked lack of feeling, inclination, preference, or prejudice ⟨a soldier rigidly bound by his oath to the state and *indifferent* to the political ends to which his services might be put —Gordon Harrison⟩ ⟨nature had no sympathy with our hopes and fears, and was completely *indifferent* to our fate —L.P.Smith⟩ ⟨to be *indifferent* to any circumstances — to be quite thoughtless as to drafts and chills, careless of heat —Richard Jefferies⟩ UNCONCERNED suggests personal lack of interest, feeling, or being moved or worried or otherwise affected, perhaps arising from insensitiveness, selfishness, or stoicism ⟨how could one, knowing the warmth and beauty of living bodies, of all the glory and tenderness the world might show, go plodding *unconcerned* through life; go plodding unconcerned yoked to a life and a companionship unvarying, savorless, and without hope of gusto —James Boyd⟩ INCURIOUS may suggest lack of normal curiosity or of intellectual capacity for interest ⟨indifferent to technique, abnormally *incurious*, in fact, of all the means of the literary art —Van Wyck Brooks⟩ ⟨the faintly pained, heavy, *incurious* unamazement of cattle —R.P.Warren⟩ ALOOF applies to a show of indifference arising from great temperamental reserve, a cold, forbidding character, or a sense of superiority or disdain ⟨with a glassily *aloof* expression as though afraid he might be subjected to some unwelcome, impertinent advance by strangers —Claud Cockburn⟩ ⟨always quite *aloof* from the ordinary social life of the town —Arnold Bennett⟩ DETACHED may indicate a calm objective lack of feeling coming from absence of prejudice or selfishness ⟨Iceland, which cool island remained a little *detached* about the war —Rose Macaulay⟩ ⟨looking at him with a peculiarly *detached* and interested air —Sherwood Anderson⟩ ⟨from the cool and *detached* point of view she had attained, life appeared to her to be essentially comic —Ellen Glasgow⟩ UNINTERESTED simply indicates the fact of lack of interest ⟨*uninterested* in the election⟩ DISINTERESTED is often used with this general meaning despite efforts to restrict its application to objectivity, freedom from personal interests, especially financial, and impartiality ⟨teaching the letters of the alphabet to her wiggling and supremely *disinterested* little daughter —C.L.Sulzberger⟩ ⟨the *disinterested* advice of a parting friend, who can possibly have no personal motive to bias his counsels —J.C.Fitzpatrick⟩

**[2]indifferent** \"\ *n* -s **1 a** : one that is indifferent (as in religion or politics) **b** : a morally indifferent act **2** : a plant or a kind of plant (as a species) that has relatively unspecialized requirements and may occur more or less by chance in a variety of habitats or ecological communities — compare INDICATOR 5

**[3]indifferent** \"\ *adv, archaic* : INDIFFERENTLY

**in·dif·fer·ent·ism** \-nt·ˌizəm, -n·ˌti-\ *n* -s [F *indifférentisme*, fr. *indifférent* that is looked upon as not mattering one way or another (fr. MF *indifferent*) + *-isme* -ism] **1 a** : INDIFFERENCE; *esp* : a consciously nurtured spirit or attitude or philosophy of indifference (as toward religion) **b** : the principle or conviction that differences in religious beliefs are essentially unimportant : ADIAPHORISM; *specif* : the principle or conviction that one religion is as good as another **2** : IDENTITY PHILOSOPHY

**in·dif·fer·ent·ist** \-ntəst\ *n* -s [F *indifférentiste*, fr. *indifférent* + *-iste* -ist] : one that is marked by or adheres to indifferentism

**in·dif·fer·ent·ly** *adv* : in an indifferent manner

**in·di·gen** \'indəjən, -ˌjen\ *also* **in·di·gene** \-ˌjēn\ *n* -s [L *indigena*] **1** *usu indigene* : NATIVE 8a **2** : a biological species that is known from both wild and cultivated forms — compare CULTIGEN

**in·di·gence** \'indəjən(t)s, -dēj-\ *n* -s [ME, fr. MF, fr. L *indigentia*, fr. *indigent-, indigens* + *-ia* -y] **1** *archaic* : DEFICIENCY **2** : poverty that is usu. not severe or total : NEEDINESS

**in·di·gen·cy** \-jənsē, -si\ *n* -ES [L *indigentia*] : INDIGENCE

**in·dig·e·nist** \ənˈdijənəst\ *n* -s [Sp *indigenista*, fr. *indígena* native (fr. L *indigena*) + *-ista* -ist (fr. L)] : an advocate of Indianism esp. in Latin America

**in·dig·e·ni·za·tion** \=ˌ==nəˈzāshən, -ˌnīˈz-\ *n* -s : the action or process of indigenizing

**in·dig·e·nize** \='==ˌnīz\ *vt* -ED/-ING/-S [*indigenous* + *-ize*] **1** : to cause to have indigenous characteristics : adapt to indigenous conditions or practices ⟨an excellent way of *indigenizing* what would otherwise remain a foreign system —F.M.Keesing⟩ **2** : to cause to be made up chiefly of an indigenous personnel ⟨*indigenizing* the teaching staff of a school⟩

**in·dig·e·nous** \ənˈdijənəs\ *adj* [LL *indigenus*, fr. L *indigena*, n., native, fr. OL *indu, endo* in, within (akin to Gk *endina* entrails, Hitt *anda* within, into) + L *-gena* (akin to L *gignere* to beget); OL *indu, endo* and its cognates all fr. a prehistoric IE or Indo-Hittite compound whose first constituent is represented by L *in* and whose second constituent is akin to L *de* from, down, away — more at IN, DE-, KIN] : NATIVE: **a** (1) : not introduced directly or indirectly according to historical record or scientific analysis into a particular land or region or environment from the outside ⟨Indians were the ~ inhabitants of America⟩ ⟨species of plants that are ~ to that country⟩ (2) : originating or developing or produced naturally in a particular land or region or environment ⟨an interesting example of ~ architecture⟩ ⟨a people with a rich ~ culture⟩ (3) : of, relating to, or designed for natives ⟨the establishment of ~ schools⟩ **b** : INBORN, INNATE, INHERENT ⟨a type of behavior that is ~ to human beings⟩ **syn** see NATIVE

**in·dig·e·nous·ly** *adv* : in an indigenous manner

**[1]in·di·gent** \'indəjənt, -dēj-\ *adj* [ME, fr. MF, fr. L *indigent-, indigens*, pres. part. of *indigēre* to need, lack, fr. OL *indu, endo* in + *egēre* to need, be needy, lack; akin to OHG *ekrōdi* thin, weak, ON *ekla* scarcity] **1** : being in a condition of indigence : being poor usu. without being destitute : IMPOVERISHED, NEEDY ⟨helping the ~ by means of medical insurance⟩ **2 a** *archaic* : DEFICIENT **b** *archaic* : totally lacking in something specified ⟨tangible parts ~ of moisture —Francis Bacon⟩ **c** *obs* : being in need of something specified ⟨naturally ~ of protection —Richard Steele⟩ **syn** see POOR

**[2]indigent** \"\ *n* -s : one that is indigent

**in·di·gest** \ˌindəˈjest, -ˌdīˈ-, ənˈdīˌj-\ *adj* [ME, immature, fr. L *indigestus* confused, not arranged, fr. *in-* [1]in- + *digestus*, past part. of *digerere* to digest] **1** *archaic* : not carefully thought out or arranged **2** *archaic* : FORMLESS

**in·digested** \ˌin+(ˌ)=ˈ==\ *adj* [[1]*in-* + *digested*, past part. of *digest*] **1** *archaic* **a** : not carefully thought out or arranged **b** : FORMLESS **2** *archaic* : not having undergone digestion

**in·digestibility** \ˌin+\ *n* : the quality of being indigestible

**[1]in·digestible** \"+\ *adj* [LL *indigestibilis*, fr. L *in-* [1]in- + LL *digestibilis* digestible] : that cannot be digested or that is not easily digested: **a** : not capable of being assimilated as food or not easily or comfortably assimilated as food ⟨green bananas are ~⟩ **b** (1) : not capable of being assimilated by the mind or not easily or comfortably assimilated by the mind : incomprehensible or nearly incomprehensible ⟨an ~ mass of facts⟩ (2) : that is repugnant to the mind or sensibilities : intellectually or aesthetically unendurable or nearly unendurable ⟨a book full of ~ pedantry⟩ ⟨clashing colors that make the painting quite ~⟩ — **in·di·gest·ibly** \-blē, -bli\ *adv*

**[2]indigestible** \"\ *n* -s : something indigestible

**in·di·ges·tion** \ˌindəˈjes(h)chən, -ˌdīˈ-\ *n* [ME *indygestyon*, fr. MF *indigestion*, fr. LL *indigestion-, indigestio*, fr. L *in-* [1]in- + *digestion-, digestio* digestion — more at DIGESTION] **1** : inability to digest something or difficulty in digesting something: **a** : inability to assimilate or difficulty in assimilating food : incomplete or imperfect assimilation of food : DYSPEPSIA ⟨troubled with chronic ~⟩ **b** : inability to assimilate or difficulty in assimilating something other than food : incomplete or imperfect assimilation of something other than food ⟨the uniform impression created everywhere . . . was staleness on the part of the teachers, ~ on the part of the students —Benjamin Fine⟩ **2** : a case or attack of indigestion ⟨spoke of various ~s she had suffered —Booth Tarkington⟩ ⟨a comment that I would get an ~ from so much mental nourishment —Rafael Sabatini⟩

**in·digestive** \ˌin+\ *adj* [[1]*in-* + *digestive*] : DYSPEPTIC ⟨an ~ single woman —Charles Dickens⟩

**indigitate** *vb* -ED/-ING/-S [ML *indigitatus*, past part. of *indigitare* (influenced in meaning by L *digitus* finger), fr. L *indigitare, indigetare* to invoke (a deity), fr. *indiget-, indiges* native deity, fr. OL *indu, endo* in, within + *-iget-, -iges* (perh. fr. L *agere* to drive, lead, act) — more at INDIGENOUS, AGENT, TOE] *obs* : INDICATE

**in·dign** \(ˈ)inˈdīn, ənˈd-\ *adj* [ME *indigne*, fr. MF, fr. L *indignus*] **1** *archaic* : UNWORTHY, UNDESERVING **2** *obs* **a** : UNBECOMING, DISGRACEFUL **b** : not merited : UNDESERVED

**in·dig·nance** \ənˈdignən(t)s\ *n* -s *archaic* [fr. *indignant*, after such pairs as E *abundant: abundance*] : INDIGNATION

**in·dig·nan·cy** \-gnənsē, -si\ *n* -ES [*indignant* + *-cy*] *archaic* : INDIGNATION

**in·dig·nant** \ənˈdignənt\ *adj* [L *indignant-, indignans*, pres. part. of *indignari* to be indignant, be offended, fr. *indignus* unworthy, fr. *in-* [1]in- + *dignus* worthy — more at DECENT] **1** : filled with or marked by indignation ⟨grew suddenly quite ~ about the matter —James Hilton⟩ ⟨~ at the injustice —W.M.Thackeray⟩ ⟨were ~ over their mistreatment⟩ ⟨felt quite ~ with them⟩ **2** : arising from or prompted by or indicative of indignation ⟨wrote an ~ letter⟩ ⟨looked at her with an ~ frown⟩ **syn** see ANGRY

**in·dig·nant·ly** *adv* : with indignation : in a manner indicative of indignation ⟨~ denied the accusation⟩

**in·dig·na·tion** \ˌin(ˌ)digˈnāshən, -ˌdēg-\ *n* -s [ME *indignacioun*, fr. MF & L; MF *indignation*, fr. L *indignation-, indignatio*, fr. *indignatus* (past part. of *indignari* to be indignant) + *-ion-, -io* -ion] : typically intense deep-felt resentment or anger aroused by annoyance at or displeasure with or scorn over something that actually is or is felt to be unjust or unworthy or mean ⟨aroused public ~⟩ ⟨~ at the injustice⟩ ⟨~ over the wrong they had suffered⟩ ⟨could feel only ~ with his children⟩ ⟨~ against the ill-treatment of human beings —Leslie Rees⟩ **syn** see ANGER

**indignation meeting** *n* : a meeting held for the purpose of expressing and discussing grievances ⟨the new law was objectionable to nearly everyone and there were numerous *indignation meetings*⟩

**indignify** *vt* [[1]*in-* + *dignify*] *obs* : DISHONOR

**indignities to the person** : misconduct (as habitual incivility or ridicule or neglect) by a spouse constituting grounds for divorce in some states that makes the life of an offended spouse intolerable and burdensome, subverts the family relationship, and evidences the settled hatred of the offending spouse

**in·dig·ni·ty** \ənˈdignəd·ē, -ətē, -i\ *n* [L *indignitat-, indignitas*, fr. *indignus* unworthy + *-itat-, -itas* -ity] **1** *obs* : lack or loss of dignity or honor **2 a** : something that offends against one's personal dignity or self-respect : something humiliating or injurious to one's self-esteem : INSULT, OUTRAGE ⟨forced to suffer one ~ after another⟩ **b** : treatment that offends against or is humiliating or injurious to one's personal dignity or self-respect ⟨treated them with ~⟩ **3** *obs* : INDIGNATION **syn** see AFFRONT

**[1]in·di·go** \'indəˌgō, -dēˌ-\ *n, pl* **indigos** *or* **indigoes** [It *indaco* & It dial. (northern) *indigo, endego*, fr. L *indicum*, fr. Gk *indikon*, fr. neut. of *indikos* Indic — more at INDIC] **1 a** : a blue vat dye that was obtained orig. from plants (as indigo plants or woad) by hydrolysis of the indican present and oxidation by air of the resulting indoxyl and that unless specially purified contained other substances (as indirubin) besides the principal coloring matter — called also *natural indigo* **b** *or* **indigo blue** : the principal coloring matter $C_{16}H_{10}N_2O_2$ of natural indigo that is synthesized as a blue crystalline powder with a coppery luster usu. by oxidation of synthetic indoxyl with air in the presence of alkali and that is used chiefly as a vat dye for cotton and wool — called also *indigotin, synthetic indigo;* see DYE table I (under *Vat Blue 1*); compare INDIGO WHITE, STRUCTURAL FORMULA **c** : any of several blue vat dyes derived from or closely related to indigo **2 a** : INDIGO PLANT **b** : any of various plants resembling the indigo plant **3** *or* **indigo blue** : a variable color averaging a dark grayish blue that is redder and deeper than night blue — called also *inde blue, Indian blue*

indigo 1b

**[2]indigo** \"\ *or* **indigo–blue** \ˈ==(ˌ)=ˈ=\ *adj* : being of the color indigo

**indigo bird** *n* : INDIGO BUNTING

**indigo blue B** *or* **indigo blue R** *n, usu cap I & B* : a vat dye — see DYE table I (under *Vat Blue 35*)

**indigo broom** *n* : a wild indigo (*Baptisia tinctoria*) having bright yellow flowers and trifoliolate leaves with cuneate leaflets

**indigo brown** *n* : a brown substance found in crude natural indigo

**indigo bunting** *n* : a common small finch (*Passerina cyanea*) of the eastern U. S. marked by indigo-blue coloration in the male

**indigobush** \'==(ˌ)=ˌ=\ *n* **1** : FALSE INDIGO 1 **2** : SMOKE TREE 2 **3** : MOCK LOCUST

**indigo carmine** *n* **1** : a soluble blue dye that is the sodium salt of indigodisulfonic acid and is used chiefly as a biological stain and food color but is no longer used to any extent as a textile dye — called also *Indigotine IA* **2** : a strong greenish blue that is bluer and duller than grotto, greener and duller than cobalt blue, and greener and darker than average cerulean blue (sense 1a) — called also *chemic blue, duck blue*

**indigo copper** *n* : COVELLITE

**in·di·go·disulfonic acid** \ˌ==(ˌ)=+ . . . -\ *n* [*indigodisulfonic* ISV *indigo* + *disulfonic*] : a water-soluble disulfonic acid $C_{16}H_8N_2O_2(SO_3H)_2$ obtained by treating indigo with concentrated sulfuric acid — called also *indigo extract, 5,5′-indigotindisulfonic acid*

**indigo extract** *n* **1** : INDIGODISULFONIC ACID **2** : INDIGO CARMINE

**in·di·gof·era** \ˌindəˈgäf(ə)rə\ *n, cap* [NL, fr. ISV *indigo* + NL *-fera* (fr. L, fem. of *-fer*, adj. comb. form) — more at -FER] : a genus of tropical herbs and shrubs (family Leguminosae) having odd-pinnate leaves and flowers with keel petals laterally spurred — see INDIGO PLANT

**in·di·gof·er·ous** \ˌ==ˈgäf(ə)rəs\ *adj* [[1]*indigo* + *-ferous*] : yielding indigo

**in·di·goid** \'==ˌgȯid\ *adj* [ISV [1]*indigo* + *-oid*] : related to or resembling indigo esp. in chemical structure and dyeing properties ⟨the ~ character of a blue pigment⟩

**indigoid dye** *or* **indigoid vat dye** *also* **indigoid** *n* -s : any of a class of vat dyes characterized by the same chromophore as indigo (sense 1b) — compare THIOINDIGOID DYE

**in·dig·o·lite** \ənˈdigəˌlīt\ *n* -s [by alter. (influenced by [1]*indigo*)] : INDICOLITE

**indigo plant** *n* **1** : a plant that yields indigo: as **a** : any of several plants of the genus *Indigofera* (as *I. tinctoria* of Africa and India, *I. anil* of So. America, *I. auriculata* of Arabia and Egypt) **b** : an East Indian woody vine (*Marsdenia tinctoria*) that yields rank indigo **c** : an Asiatic herb (*Polygonum tinctorium*) **2 a** : an Australian plant (as the Darling pea) of the genus *Swainsona* **b** : BOX BRIER

**indigos** *pl of* INDIGO

**indigo snake** *n* : a large blue-black colubrid snake (*Drymarchon corais couperi*) of the southern U. S. sometimes reaching a length of almost eight feet — called also *gopher snake*

**in·di·go·sol** \'==ˌ=ˌsäl\ *n* -s [fr. *Indigosol*, a trademark] : any of various solubilized vat dyes (as that derived from indigo white)

**indigo thorn** *n* : SMOKE TREE 2

**in·di·got·ic** \ˌindəˈgäd·ik\ *adj* [ISV [1]*indigo* + connective *-t-* + *-ic*] : of, relating to, or being of the color of indigo

**in·digo·tin** \ənˈdigətən, -gəd·ən, -gətᵊn, ˌindəˈgōtᵊn\ *n* -s [ISV [1]*indigo* + connective *-t-* + *-in*] **1** : INDIGO 1b **2** *or* **indigotine IA** \"+ˌīˈā\ *usu cap* : INDIGO CARMINE — see DYE table I (under *Acid Blue 74*)

**indigotindisulfonic acid** \"+ . . . -\ *n* [*indigotindisulfonic* fr. *indigotin* + *disulfonic*] : INDIGODISULFONIC ACID

**indigo weed** *n* : INDIGO BROOM

**indigo white** *n, sometimes cap I & W* : a pale yellow crystalline compound $C_{16}H_{12}N_2O_2$ obtained by reduction of indigo and easily changed back to it by oxidation — called also *leucoindigo;* see DYE table I (under *Vat Blue 1*)

**indiligent** *adj* [L *indiligent-, indiligens*, fr. *in-* [1]in- + *diligent-, diligens*, pres. part. of *diligere* to esteem highly, love — more at DILIGENT] **1** *obs* : INATTENTIVE, HEEDLESS **2** *obs* : LAZY, IDLE

**in·direct** \ˌin+\ *adj* [ME, fr. ML *indirectus*, fr. L *in-* [1]in- + *directus* direct] : not direct: as **a** (1) : deviating from a direct line or course : not proceeding straight from one point to another : proceeding obliquely or circuitously : ROUNDABOUT ⟨following an ~ route across the continent⟩ (2) : not going straight to the point : not proceeding to an intended end by the most direct course or method ⟨making ~ but perfectly legitimate inquiries into his prospects —Mary Austin⟩ **b** : not straightforward and open : tending to mislead : DECEITFUL, DISHONEST ⟨seemed to me to be an untrustworthy ~ individual⟩ **c** : not directly aimed at or achieved ⟨doubtless they had some not clearly recognized ~ purpose in mind⟩ : not resulting directly from an action or cause ⟨there will be many ~ consequences of their stupidity⟩ **d** (1) : stating what a real or supposed original speaker said without directly quoting the actual words and marked by changes that conform the statement grammatically to the words of the one making the statement ⟨the words *he could come* in the sentence "he said that he could come" are an ~ quotation⟩ ⟨~ discourse⟩ ⟨an example of an ~ question is *how she was* in the statement "he asked her how she was"⟩ (2) *of the object of a verb* : being the secondary goal of an action ⟨*borrower* in "I gave the borrower the book" is an ~ object⟩ (3) *of a passive verb or verb form* (a) : having a subject that becomes an indirect object when the verb is made active (as *he* in the statement "he was given a book by them" becomes *him* in "they gave him a book") ⟨*was given* in "he was given a book" is an ~ passive⟩ (b) : constituting a passive verb phrase made up of a verb and prepositional adverb of such a kind that when the verb phrase is made active the prepositional adverb is necessarily retained as a preposition having an object that is the word that had been used as subject of the passive verb phrase ⟨the passive verb phrase *was shot at* in the statement "the fugitive was shot at by the police" is an ~ passive that is made active in the statement "the police shot at the fugitive"⟩ **e** : HETEROXENOUS — **in·directly** \"+\ *adv* — **in·directness** \"+\ *n*

**indirect contempt** *n* : CONSTRUCTIVE CONTEMPT

**indirect cost** *also* **indirect charge** *n* : a cost that is not identifiable with a specific product, function, or activity — contrasted with *direct cost*

**indirect development** *n* : biologic development accompanied by a metamorphosis

**indirect evidence** *n* : evidence that establishes immediately collateral facts from which the main fact may be inferred : CIRCUMSTANTIAL EVIDENCE

**indirect exchange** *n* **1** : exchange (as of checks, drafts) between three or more places **2** : exchange in which rates give the value of the unit of home currency in terms of foreign currencies — compare FIXED EXCHANGE

**indirect fire** *n* : gunfire by indirect aiming at a target not visible from the gun

**indirect initiative** *n* : the legislative initiative where a proposed measure is considered by the legislature and goes to the people by referendum if the legislature rejects it — distinguished from *direct initiative*

**in·di·rec·tion** \ˌindəˈrekshən *also* -ˌdīˈ-\ *n* [*indirect* + *-ion*] **1 a** : lack of straightforwardness and openness : DECEITFULNESS, DISHONESTY ⟨unable to tolerate their double-dealing and ~⟩ **b** : something (as an act, a statement) marked by lack of straightforwardness or by deceitfulness ⟨hated diplomatic ~s —*Rev. of Reviews*⟩ **2 a** (1) : indirect action or movement or procedure : a roundabout course or means or method ⟨free from moralizing even by ~ —Lavinia R. Davis⟩ ⟨usurp the executive power by ~ —R.W.Ginnane⟩ (2) : an action or procedure or method marked by suggestion and free of direct obvious expression ⟨creative experiments in ~ —Louis Untermeyer⟩ **b** : lack of clear-cut action or movement toward a definite objective : lack of direction : aimless wandering about ⟨a piece of writing ruined by its ~⟩ ⟨a bizarre and pathetic ~ —St. Clair McKelway⟩ ⟨a querulous old woman who seemed to be always in a dither of ~⟩ **c** : something (as an act, a statement, a method) marked by indirection ⟨a suave and elegant little comedy of ~s —*Time*⟩

**indirect labor** *n* **1 :** labor (as clerks, repair men, maintenance men) applied indirectly to a product in the manufacturing process so that the cost is not computable in, identifiable with, or chargeable directly to the specific product — compare DIRECT LABOR **2 :** the wages paid to workers who are classed as indirect labor

**indirect laying** *n* **:** the laying of an artillery piece with the line of sighting indirectly upon a target not visible from the gun

**indirect lighting** *n* **:** lighting in which the source of light is concealed and the light emitted is diffusely reflected (as by the ceiling or a wall panel)

**indirect material** *n* **:** material (as tools, cleaning supplies, lubricating oil) used in manufacturing processes which does not become an integral part of the product and the cost of which is not identifiable with or directly chargeable to it — compare DIRECT MATERIAL

**indirect method of difference :** a method of scientific induction devised by J. S. Mill according to which if two or more instances in which a phenomenon occurs have only a single circumstance in common and two or more instances in which it does not occur have nothing in common except the absence of the circumstance, the circumstance in which the two sets of instances differ is the effect, cause, or necessary part of the cause of the phenomenon

**indirect process** *n* **:** a process involving production of pig iron from which metal is then made — compare DIRECT PROCESS

**indirect reduction** *n* **1 :** the process of reducing a syllogistic argument to the first figure by taking the contradictory of the conclusion as a premise and getting the contradictory of one premise as the new conclusion — contrasted with *direct reduction* **2** *also* **indirect proof :** a reductio ad absurdum

**indirect rein** *n* **:** the use of a rein that can be pressed against a horse's neck on the side opposite the direction in which it is required to move — compare DIRECT REIN

**indirect selling** *n* **:** a selling through middlemen

**indirect syllogism** *n* **:** a syllogism that results from another by indirect reduction

**indirect tax** *n* **:** a tax exacted indirectly from a person other than the one on whom the ultimate burden of the tax is expected to fall ⟨excise and customs duties are generally included under *indirect taxes*⟩

**indirect vision** *n* **:** vision resulting from rays of light falling upon peripheral parts of the retina

**in·di·ru·bin** \ˌində'rübən\ *n* -s [²*ind-* + *rub-* (fr. L *ruber* red) + *-in* — more at RED] **:** a dark red crystalline compound $C_{16}H_{10}N_2O_2$ isomeric with indigo (sense 1b) found in natural indigo but usu. made by reaction of indoxyl with isatin

**in·dis·cern·ibil·i·ty** \ˌində,sərnə'biləd-ē, |ən-, |əin-, -lətē, -i *also* -,z|\ *n* -ES **:** the quality or state of being indiscernible

¹**in·discernible** \ˌin+\ *adj* [¹*in-* + *discernible*] **:** incapable of being discerned: **a :** not visible or perceptible ⟨his features were ~ —G.B.Shaw⟩ **b :** incapable of being recognized as distinct ⟨thought that good was ~ from evil⟩ — **in·discern·ible·ness** \"+\ *n* — **in·discernibly** \"+\ *adv*

²**indiscernible** \"\ *n* -s **:** something indiscernible; *specif* **:** something that cannot be recognized as distinct

**in·discerpible** \ˌin+\ *adj* [¹*in-* + *discerpible*] *archaic* **:** INDISCERPTIBLE

**in·dis·cerp·ti·bil·i·ty** \ˌində,sərptə'biləd-ē, -də,zər-\ *n* -ES **:** the quality or state of being indiscerptible

**in·discerptible** \ˌin+\ *adj* [¹*in-* + *discerptible*] **:** not discerptible **:** not subject to being separated into parts ⟨simple and ~ entities —James Ward⟩

**in·disciplinable** \(ˈ)in, ən+\ *adj* [¹*in-* + *disciplinable*] **:** not subject to or capable of being disciplined ⟨full of ~ energy⟩

**in·discipline** \(ˈ)in, ən+\ *n* [¹*in* + *discipline*] **:** lack of discipline ⟨coping with ~ and laxity —Cecil Sprigge⟩

**in·disciplined** \"+\ *adj* [¹*in-* + *disciplined* (past part. of *discipline*)] **:** UNDISCIPLINED ⟨~ imagination —Joseph Conrad⟩

**in·discoverable** \ˌin+\ *adj* [¹*in-* + *discoverable*] **:** UNDISCOVERABLE

**in·discreet** \"+\ *adj* [ME *indiscrete*, fr. MF & LL; MF *indiscret*, fr. LL *indiscretus*, indistinguishable, not separated, fr. *in-* ¹in- + *discretus*, past part. of *discernere* to separate, distinguish between — more at DISCERN] **1 :** not discreet: as **a :** IMPRUDENT, INJUDICIOUS, UNTACTFUL, INCONSIDERATE ⟨an ~ question⟩ ⟨~ behavior⟩ **b :** not carefully restrained **:** UNWARY, INCAUTIOUS ⟨an ~ display of interest⟩ **2** *Scot* **:** UNCIVIL, IMPOLITE — **in·discreetly** \"+\ *adv* — **in·dis·creetness** \"+\ *n*

**in·discrete** \"+\ *adj* [L *indiscretus*] **:** not discrete **:** not separated into distinct parts ⟨an ~ mass of material⟩

**in·dis·cre·tion** \ˌində'skreshən *sometimes* ÷ -rēsh-\ *n* [ME *indiscrecioun*, fr. MF *indiscretion*, fr. LL *indiscretion-, indiscretio*, fr. *indiscretus* indiscreet + L *-ion-, -io* -ion] **1 :** lack of discretion: as **a :** IMPRUDENCE, INJUDICIOUSNESS, UNTACTFULNESS, INCONSIDERATENESS ⟨warned him against ~ in his conversation⟩ **b :** lack of careful restraint **:** UNWARINESS, INCAUTION ⟨spoke calmly to her and without ~⟩ **2 :** something (as an act, procedure, remark) marked by lack of discretion ⟨had destroyed his political career by an ~ —Gamaliel Bradford⟩; *specif* **:** an act at variance with the accepted morality of a society ⟨careful not to mention the ~s of her earlier life⟩ **3** *Scot* **:** INCIVILITY, IMPOLITENESS

**in·discriminate** \ˌin+\ *adj* [¹*in-* + *discriminate*] **1 a** (1) **:** not marked by discrimination **:** not marked by careful distinction **:** not evidencing discernment ⟨~ reading habits⟩ ⟨~ viewing of television programs⟩ ⟨launched ~ destruction⟩ (2) **:** HAPHAZARD, RANDOM, HIT-AND-MISS, SWEEPING ⟨~ application of a law⟩ ⟨~ censure⟩ (3) **:** UNRESTRAINED, PROMISCUOUS ⟨~ sexual intercourse⟩ **b** (1) **:** not separated into distinct parts **:** JUMBLED, CONFUSED ⟨the babble of the crowd was an ~ mixture of several languages⟩ (2) **:** MOTLEY, HETEROGENEOUS ⟨a book filled with an ~ assortment of pictures⟩ **2 :** not exercising discrimination or discernment **:** not making careful distinctions **:** not carefully choosing **:** UNDISCRIMINATING ⟨a hospitable but not ~ host —Sarah G. Bowerman⟩ — **in·dis·criminately** \"+\ *adv* — **in·discriminateness** \"+\ *n*

**in·discriminating** \"+\ *adj* [¹*in-* + *discriminating*] **:** UNDISCRIMINATING — **in·discriminatingly** \"+\ *adv*

**in·discrimination** \ˌin+\ *n* [¹*in-* + *discrimination*] **1 :** an act or instance of not discriminating or discerning ⟨greater ~s than were possibly his —Marguerite Young⟩ **2 :** the quality of not discriminating or the condition of not being discriminated **:** lack of discrimination ⟨show habitual ~ in the choice of their friends⟩ ⟨the various parts of the book are marked by ~⟩

**in·discriminative** \ˌin+\ *adj* [¹*in-* + *discriminative*] **:** UNDISCRIMINATING — **in·discriminatively** \"+\ *adv*

**in·discriminatory** \"+\ *adj* [¹*in-* + *discriminatory*] **:** not discriminatory

**in·discussible** \"+\ *adj* [¹*in-* + *discussible*] **:** not capable of being discussed ⟨the problem has now become ~⟩

**in·dis·pens·abil·i·ty** \ˌində,spen(t)sə'biləd-ē, -lətē, -i\ *n* **:** the quality or state of being indispensable

¹**in·dis·pens·able** \ˌin+\ *also* **in·dis·pens·ible** \"\ *adj* [¹*in-* + *dispensable*] **1 :** that cannot be set aside or neglected or disregarded ⟨his ~ duty to help them⟩ ⟨an ~ obligation⟩ **2 :** that cannot be dispensed with **:** that is absolutely necessary or requisite or essential **:** that cannot be done without ⟨their assistance was ~⟩ ⟨an ~ book in this field⟩ ⟨was an ~ worker⟩ ⟨freedom to read is one of the ~ conditions of a democratic society —W.S.Dix⟩ **syn** see NEEDFUL

²**indispensable** \"\ *n* -s **1 :** something indispensable ⟨needed clothing and food and other ~s⟩ **2 indispensables** *pl*, *archaic* **:** TROUSERS

**in·dispensableness** \ˌin+\ *n* **:** INDISPENSABILITY

**in·dis·pens·ably** \ˌində'spen(t)səblē, -li\ *adv* **:** without the possibility of being dispensed with **:** to an absolutely necessary extent ⟨help that is ~ required⟩

**in·dis·pose** \ˌində'spōz\ *vt* [prob. back-formation fr. *indisposed*] **1 a :** to put out of the proper condition for something **:** make unfit ⟨not to get one's sleep . . . ~s one more or less for the day —Edward FitzGerald⟩ **b :** to cause to be disinclined **:** make averse ⟨felt the science of mathematics to ~ the mind to religious belief —J.H.Newman⟩ **2** *archaic* **:** to cause to be in poor physical health **3** *archaic* **:** to cause to be hostile **:** make unfriendly

**in·dis·posed** \-zd\ *adj* [ME, not prepared for, unfitted, malevolently inclined, fr. ¹*in-* + *disposed*] **1 :** being usu. temporarily in poor physical health; *esp* **:** somewhat unwell usu. temporarily ⟨refused to see him because, she said, she felt ~⟩ **2 :** not being in the proper disposition for something **:** AVERSE ⟨you know how ~ tenant farmers are to doing their share of work —Ellen Glasgow⟩ **3** *archaic* **:** having an unsympathetic or unfriendly or hostile attitude toward something **syn** see DISINCLINED

**in·dis·posed·ness** \ˌində'spōzədnəs, -z(d)n-\ *n* -ES **:** INDISPOSITION

**in·disposition** \(ˈ)in, ən+\ *n* [ME *indisposicioun* unfitness, prob. fr. *indisposed* unfitted, after ME *disposed*: *disposicioun* disposition] **:** the condition of being indisposed: **a** (1) **:** DISINCLINATION ⟨a certain ~ to face reality⟩ (2) *archaic* **:** lack of sympathy **:** UNFRIENDLINESS, HOSTILITY **b :** a usu. temporary condition of poor health; *esp* **:** a usu. temporary condition of being somewhat unwell ⟨has fully recovered from her recent ~⟩

**in·disputability** \(ˈ)in, ən+\ *n* **:** the quality or state of being indisputable

**in·disputable** \(ˈ)in, ən+\ *adj* [LL *indisputabilis*, fr. L *in-* ¹in- + *disputabilis* disputable] **1 :** that cannot be disputed or called into question **:** that is beyond argument **:** UNQUESTIONABLE, INCONTESTABLE, UNDENIABLE, INDUBITABLE ⟨gave ~ proof that he had been there⟩ ⟨these are facts that are clearly ~⟩ **2 :** truly existing **:** existing beyond the possibility of doubt or denial **:** REAL, ACTUAL ⟨the first ~ author I ever met —W.T.Scott⟩ ⟨secured against aggression by ~ law —Sir Winston Churchill⟩ — **in·disputableness** \"+\ *n* — **in·disputably** \"+\ *adv*

**in·disputed** \ˌin+\ *adj* [¹*in-* + *disputed*, past part. of *dispute*] *archaic* **:** UNDISPUTED

**in·dissociable** \"+\ *adj* [¹*in-* + *dissociable*] **:** that cannot be dissociated ⟨a problem that parallels the other one and is ~ from it⟩ — **in·dis·so·cia·bly** \-blē,-bli\ *adv*

**in·dissolubility** \(ˈ)in, ən+\ *n* **:** the quality or state of being indissoluble ⟨maintaining the ~ of marriage⟩

**in·dissoluble** \"+\ *adj* [¹*in-* + *dissoluble*] **:** not dissoluble: as **a :** incapable of being annulled or undone or broken **:** perpetually binding or obligatory **:** perpetually lasting **:** PERMANENT ⟨an ~ contract⟩ ⟨bound by ~ vows⟩ **b** (1) **:** incapable of being dissolved into separate elements or particles **:** incapable of being decomposed or disintegrated ⟨a hard ~ mass of material⟩ (2) **:** incapable of being dissolved in a liquid **:** INSOLUBLE ⟨a substance that is ~ in water⟩ (3) *archaic* **:** incapable of being melted or liquefied **:** INFUSIBLE — **in·dis·sol·u·ble·ness** \-nəs\ *n* -ES — **in·dis·sol·u·bly** \-blē,-bli\ *adv*

**in·dissolvable** \ˌin+\ *adj* [¹*in-* + *dissolvable*] *archaic* **:** INDISSOLUBLE

**in·distinct** \"+\ *adj* [L *indistinctus*, fr. *in-* ¹in- + *distinctus* distinct] **1 :** not distinct: as **a :** not sharply outlined or separable **:** BLURRED, CONFUSED ⟨buildings that were ~ in the fog⟩ **b :** FAINT, DIM ⟨far away he saw the ~ light of a lantern⟩ **c :** not clearly perceived **:** not clearly recognizable or understandable **:** UNCERTAIN ⟨a peculiar ~ thumping sound⟩ ⟨could hear the ~ murmur of the crowd outside her window⟩ **2** *archaic* **:** UNDISCRIMINATING — **in·distinctly** \"+\ *adv* — **in·distinctness** \"+\ *n*

**in·distinction** \ˌin+\ *n* [¹*in-* + *distinction*] **1** *archaic* **:** failure to make distinctions **2 :** absence of identifying or individualizing qualities **:** INDISTINGUISHABLENESS ⟨the leaves' shadows had a curious grayness and ~ —P.D.Boles⟩

**in·distinctive** \"+\ *adj* [¹*in-* + *distinctive*] **1 :** UNDISCRIMINATING **2 :** marked by a lack of individualizing qualities ⟨an ~ group of weather-beaten shacks —Fred Beck⟩ — **in·distinctively** \"+\ *adv* — **in·distinctiveness** \"+\ *n*

**in·distinguishability** \ˌin+\ *n* **:** the quality or state of being indistinguishable

**in·distinguishable** \"+\ *adj* [¹*in-* + *distinguishable*] **:** not distinguishable: as **a :** lacking clearly distinguishable parts or a clearly distinguishable outline **:** indeterminate in shape or structure ⟨an ~ mass of material⟩ ⟨~ forms seen in the mist⟩ **b :** not capable of being clearly perceived **:** not clearly recognizable or understandable **:** not discernible ⟨the two specimens are actually different from each other, but the differences are almost ~⟩ **c** (1) **:** not capable of being discriminated **:** lacking identifying or individualizing qualities ⟨a colorless person quite ~ from the colorless mass of humanity⟩ (2) **:** not capable of being analyzed into clearly separate and distinct parts ⟨an ~ blend of happiness and sorrow⟩ — **in·distinguishableness** \"+\ *n* — **in·distinguishably** \"+\ *adv*

**in·distinguished** \"+\ *adj* [¹*in-* + *distinguished*] **:** UNDISTINGUISHED

**in·distributable** \"+\ *adj* [¹*in-* + *distributable*] **:** not capable of being distributed

**in·disturbance** \"+\ *n* [¹*in-* + *disturbance*] *archaic* **:** freedom from disturbance **:** TRANQUILLITY

¹**in·dite** \ən'dīt, *usu* -īd·+V\ *vb* -ED/-ING/-S [ME *enditen*, fr. OF *enditer* to write down, compose, tell, make known, fr. (assumed) VL *indictare* to make known, proclaim, fr. L *indictus*, past part. of *indicere* to proclaim, fr. *in-* ²in- + *dicere* to say — more at DICTION] *vt* **1 a :** to make up or compose (as a poem or story) ⟨~ four lines of verse⟩ ⟨~ an epistle⟩ **b :** to give literary or formal expression to **c :** to put down in writing ⟨~ a message to a friend⟩ **2** *obs* **:** to dictate or prescribe esp. the exact verbal form for (something to be repeated or copied) **3** *obs* **:** INVITE ~ *vi* **:** COMPOSE, WRITE — **in·dit·er** \-īd·ə(r), -ītə-\ *n* -s

²**indite** \"\ *archaic var of* ¹INDICT

**in·dite·ment** \-mənt\ *n* -s **:** the act of inditing or the process of being indited **:** COMPOSITION

**in·di·um** \'indēəm\ *n* -s [NL, fr. ISV ²*ind-* + NL *-ium*; fr. the two indigo-blue lines in its spectrum] **:** a soft malleable easily fusible silvery white metallic element that is resistant to tarnishing and resembles aluminum and gallium in being chiefly trivalent, that occurs in very small quantities in sphalerite and other ores, and that is used chiefly as a plating for lead-coated silver bearings for airplanes — symbol *In*; see ELEMENT table

**in·divertible** \ˌin+\ *adj* [¹*in-* + *divert* + *-ible*] **:** not to be diverted or turned aside — **in·di·vert·ibly** \-blē,-bli\ *adv*

**individable** *adj* [¹*in-* + *dividable*] *obs* **:** INDIVISIBLE

**individua** *pl of* INDIVIDUUM

¹**in·di·vid·u·al** \ˌində'vij(ə)wəl, -jəl\ *adj* [ME *indyvyduall*, fr. ML *individualis* indivisible, individual, fr. L *individuus* indivisible (fr. *in-* ¹in- + *dividuus* divided, divisible, fr. *dividere* to divide) + *-alis* -al — more at DIVIDE] **1** *obs* **a :** not divisible **:** of one essence or nature **b :** not to be parted **:** INSEPARABLE **2 a :** of, belonging to, arising from, or possessed or used by an individual ⟨~ traits⟩ ⟨~ possessions⟩ ⟨the secular, modern . . . belief in ~ human rights —A.J.Toynbee⟩ ⟨~ self-reliance⟩ ⟨no private adventures, no purely ~ experiences —J.W.Krutch⟩ **b :** being an individual **:** marked by a distinctness and a complexity within a unity that characterizes organized things, concepts, organic beings, and persons **c :** intended for one person ⟨served the pudding in ~ portions⟩ **:** designed to accommodate enough for one person ⟨a small ~ baking dish⟩ **:** applying to one person ⟨an ~ policy in life insurance⟩ **3 :** existing as a separate and distinct entity **:** SINGLE, SINGULAR, PARTICULAR ⟨dolls, with movable legs and arms, glass eyes, and ~ teeth —Green Peyton⟩ ⟨a bookseller . . . handling ~ copies of net books —James Britton⟩ ⟨consists of 96 island units (comprising some 2,141 ~ islands and coral atolls) —*Americana Annual*⟩ **4** *archaic* **:** SELFSAME, IDENTICAL **5 a :** having marked individuality **:** being peculiar, striking, or uncommon enough in character to be easily identified or distinguished ⟨an ~ style of writing⟩ ⟨the odor from the dump was so putrid in so ~ a way that it was quite impossible to describe —Jean Stafford⟩ **b :** serving to distinguish or identify **c :** DISTINCTIVE, PECULIAR ⟨a threshold of susceptibility which is ~ to each system —G.W.Gray b. 1886⟩ **syn** see CHARACTERISTIC, SPECIAL

²**individual** \"\ *n* -s **1 :** a single or particular being or thing or group of beings or things: as **a :** a particular being or thing as distinguished from a class, species, or collection ⟨the primary subject matter of literature is precisely all that science leaves out: the ~, the particular, the concrete —H.J.Muller⟩ (1) **:** a single human being as contrasted with a social group or institution ⟨the rights of the ~⟩ ⟨countries in distress, like ~s in ill health, are inclined to be quarrelsome —Samuel Van Valkenburg & Ellsworth Huntington⟩ (2) **:** a single organism as distinguished from a group **b :** a particular person ⟨a rather odd ~⟩ ⟨attempting to capture rather than kill their enemies, in order that the supply of ~s for human sacrifice might be augmented —R.W.Murray⟩ **c :** the product of a single fertilization — called also *genetic individual* **d :** all the vegetative progeny of an organism exhibiting alternation of generations — called also *genetic individual*; compare CLONE **e :** a single chemical substance — compare MIXTURE 2a **2 :** an indivisible entity or a totality which cannot be separated into parts without altering the character or significance of these parts **3** *archaic* **:** SELF, PERSONALITY **4** *logic* **a :** something that cannot have instances **:** PARTICULAR **b :** something referred to by a proper name; *specif* **:** something referred to by a name or variable of the lowest logical type in a formalized language or calculus **5 :** a tournament in contract bridge in which each player changes partners after each round so that one person rather than a pair or team may be determined as winner

**individual bond** *n* **:** a fidelity bond specifying a single person as principal — compare BLANKET BOND

**in·di·vid·u·al·ism** \ˌində'vij(ə)wə,lizəm, -jə,l-\ *n* -s [F *individualisme*, fr. ML *individualis* individual + F *-isme* -ism] **1 a** (1) **:** the ethical doctrine or principle that the interests of the individual himself are or ought to be paramount in the determination of conduct **:** ethical egoism; *also* **:** conduct guided by the principle (2) **:** the conception that all values, rights, and duties originate in individuals and that the community or social whole has no value or ethical significance not derived from its constituent individuals **b** (1) **:** the doctrine which holds that the chief end of society is the promotion of individual welfare and the chief end of moral law is the development of individual character; *also* **:** conduct or practice guided by such a doctrine (2) **:** a theory or policy having primary regard for individual rights and esp. maintaining the political and economic independence of the individual or maintaining the independence of individual initiative, action, and interests (as in industrial organization or in government); *also* **:** conduct or practice guided by such a theory or policy — compare COLLECTIVISM, PATERNALISM, SOCIALISM **c :** any vigorous and independent striving toward an individual goal or any markedly independent assertion of individual opinions esp. without regard for others or in defiance of an institution or larger authority **2 a :** INDIVIDUALITY ⟨the ~ of the backwoodsman —Theodore Roosevelt⟩ **b :** an individual peculiarity **:** IDIOSYNCRASY **3 :** the philosophical doctrine that reality is constituted of individual entities (as the monads of Leibniz) **4 :** an association of two nutritionally interdependent organisms which produces a distinct individual unlike either of the components in form and conditions of life (as in lichens)

**in·di·vid·u·al·ist** \-ləst\ *n* -s [F *individualiste*, fr. ML *individualis* + F *-iste* -ist] **1 :** one that pursues a markedly independent course in thought or action **:** one that speaks or acts with marked individuality ⟨he is apt to be an ~ who has never mastered the important arts of political cooperation and teamwork —R.E.Fitch⟩ ⟨an ~, independent to excess, in conflict with . . . society —H.S.Canby⟩ ⟨a race of ~s acknowledging no authority save that of their flintlocks —Deneys Reitz⟩ **2 :** one that advocates or practices individualism ⟨the ~ . . . was soon transformed into a collectivist —Alexander Brady⟩

**in·di·vid·u·al·is·tic** \¦==¦=(=)='listik, -tēk\ *or* **individualist** *adj* **:** of, belonging to, or being individualism or an individualist: as **a :** favoring or allowing individualism ⟨the ~ polity of churches congregationally organized enables any single company of Christians to call and to ordain their own minister —W.L.Sperry⟩ **b :** consisting of individualism ⟨Spinoza's ethics is ~ in the sense that its fundamental motive is the desire for individual perfection or happiness —Frank Thilly⟩ ⟨~ theory . . . that the state, being a necessary evil, should be strictly limited to the preservation of order and the protection of the rights of the individual —W.S.Sayre⟩ **c :** arising from individualism in theory or practice ⟨transferring the democratic tradition from ~ to collectivist economic foundations —Paul Woodring⟩ **d :** characterized by marked individuality ⟨erratic and strongly ~ personalities —*Book-of-the-Month Club News*⟩ ⟨peculiarly ~ interior paintings —*Time*⟩ — **in·di·vid·u·al·is·ti·cal·ly** \¦==¦=(=)='listək(ə)lē, -tēk-, -li\ *adv*

**in·di·vid·u·al·i·ty** \ˌ===,vijə'waləd-ē, -lətē, -i\ *n* -ES **1 a :** the total character peculiar to and distinguishing an individual from others **:** the complex of characteristics serving to individualize or set off a person or a thing from others **:** distinctive character ⟨believed that one was born with a particular biochemical ~ just as one was born with a certain physical and psychological personality —*Lancet*⟩ ⟨only slowly does the child become aware of his ~⟩; *esp* **:** a markedly individual or distinctive quality ⟨though he had no great . . . originality, there was a delicate ~ in his gracious and homely pictures —Havelock Ellis⟩ **b :** an individual or individualizing quality ⟨managed to give the borrowed product a distinctive national ~ —A.L.Kroeber⟩ ⟨white wines, which have considerable ~ —*N.Y. Times*⟩ ⟨they were strikingly alike in gifts and tastes, but each had marked ~ of character —H.E.Starr⟩ ⟨the ~ or, better, the personality of each instrument of the orchestra —Nicolas Nabokov⟩ **c :** PERSONALITY ⟨quietened her by sheer force of ~ —Arnold Bennett⟩ ⟨not only is the author unknown, but in the pure ballad there is no trace of his ~ —*Encyc. Americana*⟩ **2** *archaic* **:** INDIVISIBILITY, INSEPARABILITY **3 a :** an individual characteristic ⟨the effort . . . of getting the *individualities* of a fresh group of people into one's head, is becoming every year harder for me —A.C.Benson⟩ **b :** an individual thing; *esp* **:** an individual person **4 :** the quality or state of existing as an individual or of constituting an individual **:** separate or distinct existence ⟨the great artist can transcend his own ~ —Harold Nicolson⟩ **5 :** the tendency to pursue one's course with marked independence or self-reliance **:** INDIVIDUALISM ⟨distinguished by a strong streak of ~ and independence, the counterpart probably of the same pioneer spirit which originally marked the commerce and industry of the New World —W.T. & Barbara Fitts⟩ **syn** see DISPOSITION

**in·di·vid·u·al·iza·tion** \-,vij(ə)wələ'zāshən, -jəl-, -,lī'z-\ *n* -s **1 :** the act of individualizing or the state of being individualized **2 :** a program of correctional or penal treatment for a delinquent or adult offender which is coordinated with expert information regarding his personal history and rehabilitative needs

**in·di·vid·u·al·ize** \-'vij(ə)wə,līz, -jə,l-\ *vt* -ED/-ING/-S [¹*individual* + *-ize*] **1 a :** to make individual in character **:** invest with individuality ⟨the trace of huskiness in her voice . . . proved to be an asset, helping to ~ her screen personality —*Current Biog.*⟩ ⟨the city is further *individualized* by the many university buildings —*Amer. Guide Series: Mich.*⟩ ⟨the population . . . inevitably becomes depersonalized on the one hand, *individualized* on the other —A.L.Kroeber⟩ **b :** to treat or notice individually **:** PARTICULARIZE, SPECIFY **c :** DISTINGUISH ⟨the sounds were *individualized* by sharpness of tone, incisiveness of utterance —William Beebe⟩ **2 :** to put into the hands or management of an individual ⟨more and more of our savings are institutionalized rather than *individualized* —R.R.Nathan⟩ **3 :** to adjust or adapt (as a treatment or justice) to the needs or the special circumstances of an individual — **in·di·vid·u·al·iz·er** \-īzə(r)\ *n* -s

**individual key** *n* **:** CHANGE KEY

**individual liberty** *n* **:** the liberty of those persons who are free from external restraint in the exercise of those rights which are considered to be outside the province of a government to control — compare CIVIL LIBERTY, POLITICAL LIBERTY

**in·di·vid·u·al·ly** \-'vijəlē, -j(ə)wəlē, -li\ *adv* **:** in an individual manner: as **a** *obs* **:** INDIVISIBLY, INSEPARABLY **b** *obs* **:** in respect to individual identity **c :** one by one, SINGLY, SEPARATELY ⟨the students went in ~ to consult about their programs⟩ ⟨~ constructed houses⟩ **d :** with markedly individual qualities or characteristics ⟨each of the artists paints ~⟩ **e :** as an individual **:** PERSONALLY ⟨whatever action the state takes will affect me ~⟩

**individual medley** *n* **:** a swimming race in which each competitor swims one third of the total course with the backstroke, one third with the breaststroke, and one third freestyle

**individual psychology** *n* [trans. of G *individualpsychologie*] **:** a modification of psychoanalysis developed by the Austrian psychologist Alfred Adler emphasizing feelings of inferiority and a will to power as the primary motivating forces in human behavior

**individual variable** *n, logic* **:** a variable which may be replaced by a name or a description of an individual

[1]**in·di·vid·u·ate** \ˌində'vij(ə)wə̇|t, -jəˌwā|, *usu* |d·+V\ *adj* [ML *individuatus*, past part. of *individuare* to individuate] **1 :** UNDIVIDED, INSEPARABLE **2** *obs* **:** INDIVIDUALIZED

[2]**in·di·vid·u·ate** \-jəˌwāt, *usu* -ād·+V\ *vt* -ED/-ING/-S [ML *individuatus*, past part. of *individuare*, fr. L *individuus* indivisible — more at INDIVIDUAL] **1 :** to give individuality to **:** distinguish from others of the same species ⟨the characters that . . . ~ him from all other writers —George Saintsbury⟩ **2 :** to form into a distinct entity **:** give individual form to ⟨symbolism of language which ~*s* a man's private memories —D.G.Mitchell⟩

**in·di·vid·u·a·tion** \-ˌvijə'wāshən\ *n* -s [ML *individuation-*, *individuatio*, fr. *individuatus* (past part. of *individuare*) + L *-ion-*, *-io* -ion] **:** the act or process of individuating or the state of being individuated: as **a** (1) **:** the development of the individual from the universal or the determination of the individual in the general ⟨in scholastic philosophy the principle of ~ was variously held to be matter, form, and particularity of the subject in time and space⟩ (2) **:** the process by which individuals in society become differentiated from one another, come to occupy different statuses and roles, and tend to lose group or class identity (3) **:** regional differentiation along a primary embryonic axis **:** field formation — contrasted with *evocation;* compare INDUCTOR **b :** existence as a person or individual **:** INDIVIDUALITY

**individuity** *n* -ES [LL *individuitat-*, *individuitas*, fr. L *individuus* indivisible + *-itat-*, *-itas* -ity] **1** *obs* **:** INDIVISIBILITY **2** [ML *individuitat-*, *individuitas*, fr. LL, indivisibility] *obs* **:** INDIVIDUALITY

**in·di·vid·u·um** \ˌində'vijəwəm\ *n, pl* **individ·ua** \-wə\ *or* **individuums** [LL, fr. L, indivisible entity, atom, fr. neut. of *individuus* indivisible] **1 :** an individual instance or an individual being as distinguished from a group of similar instances or beings **2** [L] **:** an indivisible entity; *specif* **:** ATOM 1a

**in·divisibility** \ˈ¦in+\ *n* **:** the quality or state of being indivisible

[1]**in·divisible** \"+\ *adj* [ME *indyvysible*, fr. LL *indivisibilis*, fr. L *in-* [1]in- + LL *divisibilis* divisible] **:** not divisible **:** not separable into parts ⟨the ~ responsibility of school and college in matters of general education —A.W.Griswold⟩ ⟨one nation, ~ —Francis Bellamy⟩ ⟨reality is one and ~ —C.D.Lewis⟩ — **in·divisibleness** \"+\ *n* — **in·di·vis·i·bly** \-blē,-bli\ *adv*

[2]**indivisible** \¦in+\ *n* -s **:** something indivisible; *specif* **:** a mathematical quantity that is assumed to admit of no further division

**in·division** \"+\ *n* [ML *indivision-*, *indivisio*, fr. L *in-* [1]in- + *division-*, *divisio-* division] **:** the state of being undivided **:** ONENESS

**indm** *abbr* indemnity

**in·do** \'in(ˌ)dō\ *n* -s *usu cap* [D, short for *Indo-Europeaan*, fr. *ind-* [1]ind- + *Europeaan* European, fr. L *europaeus* European (adj.) + D *-aan* -an (n. suffix) — more at EUROPEAN] **:** a native or inhabitant of Indonesia who has a Western education and is of mixed European usu. Dutch and Indonesian descent

**indo-** — see IND-

**in·do-african** \¦in(ˌ)dō+\ *adj, usu cap I&A* **:** of, relating to, or constituting a terrestrial biogeographic realm that includes intertropical Asia and intertropical Africa

[1]**indo-aryan** \"+\ *adj, usu cap I&A* **1 :** of, relating to, or characteristic of Indo-Aryans **2 :** of, relating to, or characteristic of one of the Aryan languages of India

[2]**indo-aryan** \"\ *n, cap I&A* **1 :** a member of one of the peoples of India of Aryan speech and physique characterized by tall stature, dolichocephaly, fair complexion with dark hair and eyes, plentiful beard, and narrow and prominent nose — compare INDIAN 1a **2 :** one of the early Indo-European invaders of Persia, Afghanistan, and India **3 :** the Indo-European languages of India and Pakistan as a group

**in·do-briton** \¦in(ˌ)dō+\ *n, cap I&B* **:** a person born in India of mixed Indian and British descent

**indo-burmese** \"+\ *adj, usu cap I&B* **:** BURMO-CHINESE

[1]**in·do-chinese** \"+\ *adj, usu cap I&C* [*Indochina*, region in southeastern Asia + E *-ese*] **1 a :** of, relating to, or characteristic of Indochina — usu. used of the countries Cambodia, Laos, and Vietnam comprised in the former French Indochina but sometimes of the region comprising all the countries of southeastern Asia: Burma, Malaya, Thailand, Cambodia, Laos, and Vietnam **b :** of, relating to, or characteristic of the Indo-Chinese esp. of Cambodia, Laos, and Vietnam **2** [[1]*ind-* + *chinese*] **:** of, relating to, characteristic of, or constituting the Tibeto-Burman, Thai, Chinese, and various neighboring languages **3** [[1]*ind-* + *chinese*] **:** BURMO-CHINESE

[2]**indo-chinese** \"\ *n, cap I&C* **1 :** a native or inhabitant of Indochina — usu. used of the people of the countries Cambodia, Laos, and Vietnam comprised in the former French Indochina but sometimes of the peoples of southeastern Asia including also those of Burma, Malaya, and Thailand **2 :** an assumed family of languages comprehending Tibeto-Burman, Thai, Chinese, and various neighboring groups

**indocibility** *n* **:** the quality or state of being indocible

**indocible** *adj* [LL *indocibilis*, fr. L *in-* [1]in- + LL *docibilis* docible] **:** UNTEACHABLE

**in·docile** \(')in, ən+\ *adj* [MF, fr. L *indocilis*, fr. *in-* [1]in- + *docilis* docile] **:** unwilling or indisposed to be taught, trained, or disciplined **:** not easily instructed or controlled **:** UNRULY ⟨a large, ~, irresponsible, domineering man —G.P.Elliott⟩

**in·docility** \¦in+\ *n* [*indocile* + *-ity*] **:** the quality or state of being indocile **:** UNTEACHABLENESS, INTRACTABLENESS

**in·doc·tri·nate** \ə̇n'däktrə̇ˌnāt, *usu* -ād·+V\ *vt* -ED/-ING/-S [prob. fr. *indoctrine* + *-ate*, v. suffix] **1 a :** to give instructions esp. in fundamentals or rudiments **:** TEACH ⟨the function of *indoctrinating* youth was given to and accepted by . . . the family and the priesthood —L.O.Garber & W.B.Castetter⟩ ⟨the recruits were *indoctrinated* for a month and then sent to specialist schools⟩ **b :** to imbue or make markedly familiar (as with a skill) ⟨*indoctrinated* themselves with the teamwork of attack —Ira Wolfert⟩ **2 :** to cause to be impressed and usu. ultimately imbued (as with a usu. partisan or sectarian opinion, point of view, or principle) ⟨had to be *indoctrinated* with the will to win —J.P.Baxter b.1893⟩ ⟨*indoctrinating* young people with alien ideologies⟩ **:** cause to be drilled or otherwise trained (as in a sectarian doctrine) and usu. persuaded ⟨~ the immigrants in a new way of life⟩ — **in·doc·tri·na·tor** \-ād·ə(r), -atə-\ *n* -s

**in·doc·tri·na·tion** \(ˌ)inˌdäktrə̇'nāshən, ənˌd-\ *n* -s [*indoctrinate* + *-ion*] **1 :** the act or process of indoctrinating or the state of being indoctrinated ⟨the proper and adequate ~ of a newly received prisoner is one of the most important points of the rehabilitation program —W.H.Maglin⟩ ⟨evidence of attempts at subversive ~ or disloyal teaching —B.F.Wright⟩ ⟨~ can be smuggled in . . . in the name of democratic education —F.C.Neft⟩ **2 :** something with or in which one is indoctrinated ⟨freedom of minds, the maxims of logic and experimental proof, of intellectual honesty, of tolerance and persuasion . . . constitute a body of ~ to which no objection can consistently be raised —R.B.Perry⟩ — **in·doc·tri·na·tion·al** \(¦)=¦==¦nāshənᵊl, -shnəl\ *adj*

**indoctrine** *vt* -ED/-ING/-S [alter. (influenced by E [2]*in-*) of ME *endoctrinen*, fr. MF *endoctriner*, fr. OF, fr. *en-* [1]en- + *doctrine* (n.)] *archaic* **:** INDOCTRINATE

**in·doc·tri·ni·za·tion** \ə̇nˌdäktrə̇nə̇'zāshən, -ˌnī'z-\ *n* -s **:** INDOCTRINATION

**in·doc·tri·nize** \ə̇n'däktrə̇ˌnīz\ *vt* -ED/-ING/-S [*indoctrin*ate + *-ize*] **:** INDOCTRINATE

[1]**in·do-dravidian** \¦in(ˌ)dō+\ *adj, usu cap I&D* **:** of, relating to, or characteristic of Indo-Dravidians

[2]**indo-dravidian** \"\ *n, cap I&D* **:** a member of a composite people resulting from intermixture between the native Dravidians of India and the Aryan invaders but having some elements of the Munda-speaking racial group

[1]**indo-european** \¦in(ˌ)dō+\ *adj, usu cap I&E* [Gk *ind-*, *indo-* India, of or connected with India + E *european* — more at IND-] **:** of, relating to, characteristic of, or constituting the Indo-European languages

[2]**indo-european** \"\ *n, cap I&E* **1 a :** the Indo-European languages **b :** the unrecorded prehistoric language from which the Indo-European languages are descended **2 a :** a speaker of Indo-European (sense 1b) **b :** a member of a people whose original tongue is one of the Indo-European languages **3 :** one who is a native or inhabitant of a country of southeastern Asia and esp. Indochina and who is of European or part-European origin or descent **:** EURASIAN

**indo-euro·pe·an·ist** \¦=(ˌ)=ˌ=='==ə̇st\ *n* -s *cap I&E* **:** a specialist in Indo-European linguistics

**indo-european languages** *n pl, usu cap I&E* **:** a family of languages comprising those spoken in most of Europe and in the parts of the world colonized by Europeans since 1500 and also in Persia, the subcontinent of India, and some other parts of Asia

INDO-EUROPEAN LANGUAGES

| BRANCH | GROUP | LANGUAGES AND MAJOR DIALECTS[1] ANCIENT | MEDIEVAL | MODERN | PROVENIENCE |
|---|---|---|---|---|---|
| GERMANIC | East | | *Gothic* | | eastern Europe |
| | North | | *Old Norse* | Icelandic<br>Faeroese<br>Norwegian<br>Swedish<br>Danish | Iceland<br>Faeroe islands<br>Norway<br>Sweden<br>Denmark |
| | West | | *Old High German*<br>*Middle High German* | German | Germany, Switzerland, Austria |
| | | | | Yiddish | Germany, eastern Europe |
| | | | *Old Saxon*<br>*Middle Low German* | | Northern Germany |
| | | | *Middle Dutch* | Dutch | Netherlands |
| | | | | Afrikaans | So. Africa |
| | | | *Middle Flemish* | Flemish | Belgium |
| | | | *Old Frisian* | Frisian | Netherlands, Germany |
| | | | *Old English*<br>*Middle English* | English | England |
| CELTIC | Continental | *Gaulish* | | | Gaul |
| | Brythonic | | *Old Welsh*<br>*Middle Welsh* | Welsh | Wales |
| | | | *Old Cornish* | *Cornish* | Cornwall |
| | | | *Middle Breton* | Breton | Brittany |
| | Goidelic | | *Old Irish*<br>*Middle Irish* | Irish Gaelic | Ireland |
| | | | | Scottish Gaelic | Scotland |
| | | | | *Manx* | Isle of Man |
| ITALIC | Osco-Umbrian | *Oscan*<br>*Umbrian*<br>*Sabellian* | | | ancient Italy |
| | Latinian or Romance[2] | *Venetic*<br>*Lanuvian*<br>*Faliscan*<br>*Praenestine*<br>Latin | | | ancient Italy |
| | | | | Portuguese | Portugal |
| | | | | Spanish | Spain |
| | | | | Judeo-Spanish | Mediterranean lands |
| | | | | Catalan | Spain (Catalonia) |
| | | | *Old Provençal* | Provençal | southern France |
| | | | *Old French*<br>*Middle French* | French | France, Belgium, Switzerland |
| | | | | Haitian Creole | Haiti |
| | | | | Italian | Italy, Switzerland |
| | | | | Rhaeto-Romanic | Switzerland, Italy |
| | | | | Sardinian | Sardinia |
| | | | | *Dalmatian* | Adriatic coast |
| | | | | Romanian | Romania, Balkans |
| Poorly preserved and of uncertain affinities within Indo-European, "Thraco-Phrygian", "Illyrian", etc. | | *Ligurian*<br>*Messapian*<br>*Illyrian*<br>*Thracian*<br>*Phrygian* | | | ancient Italy<br>ancient Italy<br>Balkans<br>Balkans<br>Asia Minor |
| Albanian | | | | Albanian | Albania, southern Italy |
| Greek | | Greek ("Ancient Greek") | Greek ("Byzantine Greek", "Middle Greek") | Greek ("Modern Greek", "New Greek") | Greece, the eastern Mediterranean |
| Baltic | | | *Old Prussian* | | East Prussia |
| | | | | Lithuanian | Lithuania |
| | | | | Latvian | Latvia |
| SLAVIC | South | | Old Church Slavonic | | |
| | | | | Slovene | Yugoslavia |
| | | | | Serbo-Croatian (Serbian, Croatian) | Yugoslavia |
| | | | | Macedonian | Macedonia |
| | | | | Bulgarian | Bulgaria |
| | West | | *Old Czech* | Czech | Czechoslovakia |
| | | | | Slovak | Czechoslovakia |
| | | | | Polish | Poland |
| | | | | Kashubian | Poland |
| | | | | Wendish | Germany |
| | | | | *Polabian* | Germany |
| | East | | *Old Russian* | Russian | Russia |
| | | | | Ukrainian | Ukraine |
| | | | | Belorussian | White Russia |
| Armenian | | | Armenian ("Old Armenian") | Armenian ("Modern Armenian") | Asia Minor, Caucasus |
| IRANIAN | West | *Old Persian* | | | ancient Persia |
| | | | *Pahlavi*<br>Persian ("Classical Persian") | Persian ("Modern Persian") | Persia (Iran) |
| | | | | Kurdish | Persia, Iraq, Turkey |
| | | | | Baluchi | West Pakistan |
| | | | | Tajiki | central Asia |
| | East | Avestan | | | ancient Persia |
| | | | *Sogdian* | | central Asia |
| | | | *Khotanese* | | central Asia |
| | | | | Pashto | Afghanistan, West Pakistan |
| | | | | Ossetic | Caucasus |
| INDIC | Dard | | | Shina<br>Khowar<br>Kafiri | upper Indus valley |
| | | | | Kashmiri | Kashmir |
| | Sanskritic | Sanskrit<br>Pali<br>*Prakrits* | *Prakrits* | | India |
| | | | | Lahnda | western Punjab |
| | | | | Sindhi | Sind |
| | | | | Panjabi | Panjab |
| | | | | Rajasthani | Rajasthan |
| | | | | Gujarati | Gujarat |
| | | | | Marathi | western India |
| | | | | Konkani | western India |
| | | | | Oriya | Orissa |
| | | | | Bengali | Bengal |
| | | | | Assamese | Assam |
| | | | | Bihari | Bihar |
| | | | | Hindi | northern India |
| | | | | Urdu | Pakistan, India |
| | | | | Nepali | Nepal |
| | | | | Sinhalese | Ceylon |
| | | | | Romany | uncertain |
| Tocharian | | | *Tocharian A*<br>*Tocharian B* | | central Asia |
| The following is sometimes considered as another branch of Indo-European, and sometimes as coordinate with Indo-European, the two together constituting Indo-Hittite | | | | | |
| Anatolian | | *Hittite*<br>*Luwian*<br>*Palaic*<br>*Hieroglyphic Hittite*<br>*Lydian*<br>*Lycian* | | | ancient Asia Minor |

[1]Italics denote dead languages. Listing of a language only in the ancient or medieval column but in roman type indicates that it survives only in some special use, as in literary composition or liturgy

[2]Romance is normally applied only to medieval and modern languages; Latinian is normally applied only to ancient languages

**in·do·gae·an** *or* **in·do·ge·an** \¦indō¦jēən\ *adj, usu cap* [NL *Indogaea,* Oriental biogeographic realm or region (fr. [1]*ind-* + *-gaea*) + E *-an*] **:** ORIENTAL

**indo-gangetic** \¦in(ˌ)dō+\ *adj, usu cap I&G* **:** of or relating to the area drained by the Indus and Ganges rivers esp. the lowland plain south of the Himalayas

**in·dogen·ide** \'indəjə,nīd; ən'däjə,n-, -nəd\ *n* -s [ISV *indogen* bivalent nitrogen-containing radical $C_8H_5NO$ (ISV [2]*ind-* + *-gen*) + *-ide*] **:** a compound that is an alkylidene substitution product of indoxyl formed by reaction of indoxyl with an aldehyde or ketone

[1]**indo-germanic** \¦in(ˌ)dō+\ *adj, usu cap I&G* [trans. of G *indogermanisch*] **:** INDO-EUROPEAN

[2]**indo-germanic** \"\ *n, cap I&G* **:** INDO-EUROPEAN 1

**in·do-hittite** \¦in(ˌ)dō+\ *n, cap I&H, often attrib* [[1]*ind-* + *hittite*] **1 :** a language family comprehending Indo-European and Anatolian — see INDO-EUROPEAN LANGUAGES table **2 :** a hypothetical parent language of Indo-European and Anatolian

[1]**indo-iranian** \"+\ *adj, usu cap both Is* **:** of, relating to, characteristic of, or constituting a subfamily of the Indo-European languages that consists of the Indic and the Iranian branches

[2]**indo-iranian** \"\ *n, cap both Is* **1 a :** the Indo-Iranian languages **b :** the unrecorded prehistoric language from which the Indo-Iranian languages are descended **2 a :** a speaker of Indo-Iranian (sense 1b) **b :** a member of a people whose original tongue is one of the Indo-Iranian languages

**indol-** *or* **indolo-** *comb form* [ISV, fr. *indole*] **1 :** indole ‹*indoloid*› **2 :** containing an indole ring fused on one side to one side of another ring ‹*indolo*quinoline›

**in·dole** \'in,dōl\ *n* -s [ISV [2]*ind-* + *-ole;* orig. formed as G *indol*] **1 :** a crystalline compound $C_8H_7N$ that is found esp. in jasmine oil, civet, and coal tar and along with skatole in the intestines and feces as a decomposition product of proteins containing tryptophan, that may be formed by reductive distillation of indigo with zinc, and that in spite of its unpleasant odor when concentrated is used as a trace component of floral perfumes (as jasmine, gardenia, or lilac) — compare STRUCTURAL FORMULA **2 :** a derivative of indole

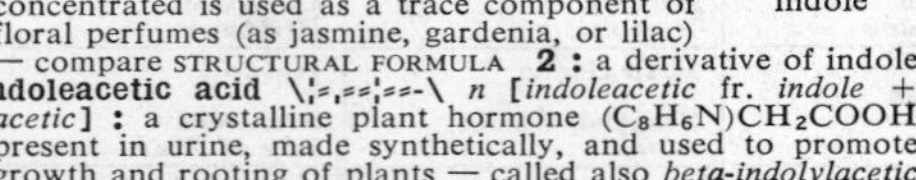
indole

**indoleacetic acid** \¦=,==¦==-\ *n* [*indoleacetic* fr. *indole* + *acetic*] **:** a crystalline plant hormone $(C_8H_6N)CH_2COOH$ present in urine, made synthetically, and used to promote growth and rooting of plants — called also *beta-indolylacetic acid, 3-indoleacetic acid, heteroauxin;* see AUXIN

**indolebutyric acid** \¦=,==¦==-\ *n* [*indolebutyric* fr. *indole* + *butyric*] **:** a crystalline acid $(C_8H_6N)CH_2CH_2CH_2COOH$ similar to indoleacetic acid in its effects on plants

**in·do·lence** \'indələn(t)s\ *n* -s [F, fr. L *indolentia* freedom from pain, fr. *in-* [1]in- + *dolentia* pain, fr. *dolent-, dolens* (pres. part. of *dolēre* to feel pain, grieve) + *-ia* -y — more at CONDOLE] **1** *or* **indolency** -ES *obs* **a :** insensibility or indifference to pain **b :** freedom from pain or a tranquillity of mind marked by neither pain nor pleasure **:** apathetic ease **2** *med* **a :** a condition of causing little or no pain ‹deceptive ~ of the tumor› **b :** a condition of growing or progressing slowly **c :** slowness in healing **3 :** laziness or inactivity arising from a love of ease or aversion to work **:** indisposition to labor **:** SLOTH ‹the hot moist air of the tropics spreads a feeling of lethargy and ~ over everything that moves —G.H.Reed b.1887› ‹~, tardiness or even downright opposition to improvements —*Farmer's Weekly (So. Africa)*› ‹literary ~, mere unwillingness to take the necessary pains —Brand Blanshard›

[1]**in·do·lent** \-nt\ *adj* [LL *indolent-, indolens* insensitive to pain, fr. L *in-* [1]in- + *dolent-, dolens* (pres. part. of *dolēre*)] **1** *med* **a :** causing little or no pain ‹an ~ tumor› **b** (1) **:** growing or progressing slowly ‹leprosy is an ~ infectious disease› (2) **:** slow to heal ‹an ~ ulcer› **2 a :** constantly indulging in ease **:** chronically averse to labor and exertion ‹a goad for an ~ writer —Van Wyck Brooks› ‹old and fat and ~ —A.E.Stevenson b.1900› **b :** conducing to or encouraging laziness or avoidance of exertion ‹the ~ heat of the afternoon› **c :** giving evidence of or exhibiting indolence ‹an ~ sigh —Willard Robertson› ‹an ~ amiability› **syn** see LAZY

[2]**indolent** \"\ *n* -s **:** one that is indolent ‹thousands of scoundrelly ~s lived there despising any honest toil —P.I.Wellman›

**in·do·lent·ly** *adv* **:** in an indolent manner

**in·do·line** \'ində,lēn, -lən\ *n* -s [ISV *indol-* + *-ine;* prob. orig. formed as G *indolin*] **:** a liquid base $C_8H_9N$ that is a stronger base than indole and is obtained from indole by reduction; 2,3-dihydro-indole

**in·do·log·i·cal** \¦ində¦läjəkəl\ *adj, often cap* **:** of or relating to Indology

**in·dol·o·gist** \ən'däləjəst\ *n* -s *often cap* **:** a specialist in Indology

**in·dol·o·gy** \-jē\ *n* -ES *usu cap* [[1]*ind-* + *-logy*] **:** the study of India and its people (as through its languages, literature, history, philosophy, customs, antiquities)

**in·do·lyl** \'ində,lil, -lēl\ *n* -s [ISV *indol-* + *-yl*] **:** the univalent radical $C_8H_6N$ derived from indole by removal of one hydrogen atom

**indolylacetic acid** \¦==,==¦==-\ *n* [*indolylacetic* fr. *indolyl* + *acetic*] **:** INDOLEACETIC ACID

**in·do-malay** \¦in(ˌ)dō+\ *adj, usu cap I&M* **:** INDO-MALAYAN 1

[1]**indo-malayan** \"+\ *adj, usu cap I&M* **1 :** of or relating to the insular and mainland areas of southeastern Asia **2 :** of or relating to the Malayan biogeographic subdivision **:** MALAYAN

[2]**indo-malayan** \"\ *n, cap I&M* **:** a member of one of the major ethnic groups that embrace the inhabitants of mainland and insular southeastern Asia including the island chains from Indonesia through the Ryukyus

**in·dom·i·ta·bil·i·ty** \(ˌ)in,dämәd·ə'bilәd·ē, ən-, -mətə-, -lətē, -i\ *n* -ES **:** the quality or state of being indomitable

**in·dom·i·ta·ble** \ən'dämәd·əbəl, -mətə-\ *adj* [LL *indomitabilis,* fr. L *in-* [1]in- + *domitare* to tame + *-abilis* -able — more at DAUNT] **:** incapable of being subdued **:** INTRACTABLE ‹~ courage› ‹an ~ will› — **in·dom·i·ta·ble·ness** \-nəs\ *n* -ES — **in·dom·i·ta·bly** \-blē, -bli\ *adv*

**in·do·ne·sia** \¦ində¦nēzh|ə *also* -ēsh| *or* -ēzē|\ *adj, usu cap* [fr. *Indonesia,* country (also called the Republic of Indonesia) and archipelago (also called the Malay Archipelago or Malaysia) off the southeast coast of Asia] **:** of or from Indonesia **:** of the kind or style prevalent in Indonesia **:** INDONESIAN

[1]**in·do·ne·sian** \|ən\ *n* -s *cap* [*Indonesia* + E *-an* (n. suffix)] **1 :** MALAYSIAN 1 **2 :** PROTO-MALAY **3 a :** a native or inhabitant of the Republic of Indonesia **b :** the Malay dialect that is the national language of the Republic of Indonesia

[2]**indonesian** \"\ *adj, usu cap* [*Indonesia* + E *-an* (adj. suffix)] **1 :** of or relating to the Republic of Indonesia, the Malay archipelago, or Indonesians **2 :** of, relating to, or constituting the subfamily of Austronesian languages spoken chiefly in the Malay peninsula and archipelago

**in·door** \'in,=, ən'=\ *adj* [alter. (influenced by E [1]*in*) of obs. E *within-door,* adj., fr. the phrase *within door* in a building] **:** of or relating to the interior of a building ‹an ~ scene› ‹an ~ swimming pool›: as **a :** of or relating to something done inside a building ‹an ~ job› ‹an ~ sport› **b :** designed for use indoors ‹an ~ dress› ‹an ~ flag› **c :** living inside an institution ‹~ paupers› **:** given within an institution ‹~ relief› **d :** inclined to stay indoors ‹Americans have become an ~ people —J.M.Fitch›

**indoor baseball** *n* **:** softball played indoors

**in·doors** \(')in¦=, ən'=\ *adv* [alter. (influenced by E [1]*in*) of *withindoors*] **1 :** in a building ‹worked ~ all afternoon› ‹stayed ~ during the storm› **2 :** into a building ‹went ~ as soon as it began to rain›

**in·do-pacific** \¦in(ˌ)dō+\ *adj, usu cap I&P* **:** of or relating to the Indo-Malayan areas of the Pacific ocean ‹an *Indo-Pacific* fish› ‹*Indo-Pacific* coral reefs›

**in·do·phe·nin** \,indō'fēnən, ən'däfənən\ *n* [ISV [2]*ind-* + *phene* + *-in;* fr. a belief that it was a derivative of benzene; orig. formed in G] **:** a blue crystalline compound $C_{24}H_{14}N_2O_2S_2$ formed by reaction of thiophene with isatin and sulfuric acid and used as a color test for the presence of thiophene in technical benzene

**in·do·phenol** \,indō+\ *n* [ISV [2]*ind-* + *phenol;* prob. orig. formed in G] **:** any of a class of blue or green dyes derived from quinone imines and used chiefly as intermediates for sulfur dyes and as dyes formed in color photography; *esp* **:** the simplest phenol $HOC_6H_4N{=}C_6H_4{=}O$

**in·do·planorbis** \¦in(ˌ)dō+\ *n, cap* [NL, fr. [1]*ind-* + *Planorbis*] **:** an Asiatic genus of freshwater snails (family Planorbidae) of veterinary importance as an intermediate host of the bovine blood fluke and other trematode worms

**in·dore** \(')in¦dō(ə)r, ən'd-\ *adj, usu cap* [fr. *Indore,* city in central India] **:** of or from the city of Indore, India **:** of the kind or style prevalent in Indore

**in·do red MV-6632** \'in(ˌ)dō-\ *n, usu cap I&R* [perh. fr. [2]*ind-*] **:** an organic pigment — see DYE table I (under *Pigment Red 87*)

**indorse** *var of* ENDORSE

**indos** *pl of* INDO

**indow** *obs var of* ENDOW

**in·dox·yl** \ən'däksəl, 'in,d-\ *n* -s [ISV [2]*ind-* + hydr*oxyl;* prob. orig. formed in G] **:** a yellow crystalline phenolic compound $(C_8H_6N)OH$ that has a strong fecal odor, that occurs combined in plants and animals but is usu. made from phenylglycine by heating with sodamide, and that on oxidation yields indigo; 3-hydroxy-indole — see INDICAN

**in·draft** \'in,=\ *n* [[4]*in* + *draft*] **1** *obs* **:** an opening into land from the sea **:** INLET **2 a :** a drawing or pulling in **:** an inward attraction **b :** an inward flow or current (as of air or water)

**in·drape** \ən'=\ *vt* [[2]*in-* + *drape*] *archaic* **:** to make into cloth **:** WEAVE

[1]**indrawing** \'=¦==\ *n* [ME *indrawinge,* fr. *in* + *drawinge,* gerund of *drawen* to draw (after ME *drawen in,* v., to draw in)] **:** the act of drawing in or inward ‹a sharp ~ of her breath —W.G.Hardy›

[2]**indrawing** \"\ *adj* [[2]*in* + *drawing,* pres. part. of *draw* (after *draw in,* v.)] **:** drawing in or inward

**indrawn** \'=,=\ *adj* [[2]*in* + *drawn,* past part. of *draw* (after *draw in,* v.)] **1 :** drawn in ‹an ~ breath› **2 :** tending to reserve, taciturnity, or egocentricity ‹an aloof, aristocratic, ~ man —W.S.White› ‹seen as selfish, ~ —*Times Lit. Supp.*›

**indre** *abbr* indenture

**indrench** *vt* [[2]*in-* + *drench*] *obs* **:** DRENCH, DROWN

**in·dri** \'indrē\ *n* [F, fr. Malagasy *indry* look!; prob. fr. an erroneous belief by the French naturalist Pierre Sonnerat (†1814), who observed the animal in its native habitat about 1780, that the natives were uttering its name when in fact they were only calling attention to its presence] **1** -s **:** the largest of the lemurs of Madagascar (*Indris brevicaudatus*) about two feet long with a rudimentary tail and brightly marked in black and white **2** [NL, fr. F] *cap* **:** a genus containing the indri and being the type of the family Indridae

[1]**in·drid** \-drəd\ *adj* [NL *Indridae*] **:** of or relating to the indris

[2]**indrid** \"\ *n* -s [NL *Indridae*] **:** INDRI

**in·dri·dae** \-drə,dē\ *n pl, cap* [NL, fr. *Indri,* type genus + *-idae*] **:** a family of lemurs comprising the indri, avahi, sifaka, and various related extinct forms

**indsl** *abbr* industrial

**in·dubious** \(')in, ən+\ *adj* [perh. fr. L *indubius,* fr. *in-* [1]in- + *dubius* dubious] *archaic* **:** INDUBITABLE, CERTAIN

**in·du·bi·ta·bil·i·ty** \(ˌ)in,d(y)übəd·ə'biləd·ē, ən-, -bətə-, -lətē, -i\ *n* -ES **:** the quality or state of being unquestionable **:** CERTAINTY ‹the English empiricists tended to lean on the ~ of the facts given —S.C.Pepper›

[1]**in·du·bi·ta·ble** \ə'===bəl\ *adj* [F or L; F, fr. L *indubitabilis,* fr. *in-* [1]in- + *dubitabilis* dubitable] **:** not dubitable **:** not open to question or doubt **:** too evident to be doubted **:** UNQUESTIONABLE ‹there is a core of ~ knowledge in education, but most of the teacher's task consists in imparting methods for understanding what is still unknown —Zechariah Chafee› — **in·du·bi·ta·ble·ness** *n* -ES

[2]**indubitable** \"\ *n* -s **:** something that is indubitable

**in·du·bi·ta·bly** \-blē, -bli\ *adv* **:** without any doubt **:** UNQUESTIONABLY ‹it is ~ true that the civilization of the West . . . has been evolving for centuries —G.C.Sellery›

**in·duce** \ən'd(y)üs\ *vt* -ED/-ING/-S [ME *enducen, inducen,* fr. L *inducere,* fr. *in-* [2]in- + *ducere* to lead — more at TOW] **1 a :** to move and lead (as by persuasion or influence) ‹powers of persuasion that would have *induced* the atheist to religion› **:** prevail upon **:** INFLUENCE, PERSUADE ‹was unable to ~ his customers to try the product› ‹condition which had *induced* many persons to emigrate from the old country —John Dewey› **b :** to inspire, call forth, or bring about by influence or stimulation ‹the gift had been solicited or *induced* by the plaintiff —R.N.Wilkin› ‹the menace of *induced* immigration —H.M.Diamond› **2** *archaic* **a :** to bring in (as a practice, condition, custom) **:** INTRODUCE **b :** ADDUCE **3 a :** to bring on or bring about **:** EFFECT, CAUSE ‹anesthesia *induced* by drugs› ‹prices that will cover the costs and ~ the production —*Defense Against Recession*› ‹an antivitamin . . . was shown to ~ gross malformation in the young —*Americana Annual*› ‹believed the Christianity . . . *induced* kindliness in men —H.J.Laski›: as (1) *embryol* **:** to cause the formation of ‹the optic cup *induces* lens in the adjacent ectoderm› (2) **:** to produce (as an electric current, an electric charge, or magnetic polarity) by induction (3) *psychol* **:** to arouse by indirect stimulation ‹~ a contrast color› **b :** AROUSE ‹music *induces* in us concepts that are vague —H.A.Overstreet› ‹*induced* a nostalgia for New England in persons who never saw the place —Mark Van Doren› **4 :** to conclude or infer from particulars or by induction — contrasted with *deduce* **5** *obs* **:** to draw on **:** OVERSPREAD

**syn** PERSUADE, PREVAIL: INDUCE may indicate overcoming indifference, hesitation, or opposition, usu. by offering for consideration persuasive advantages or gains that bring about a desired decision ‹well-meaning but misguided professors and teachers felt they were fulfilling their vocations by *inducing* brilliant boys and girls to flee the drudgery of the country and enter the elite professions —*Irish Digest*› ‹Burt, aided by his father and friends, *induced* Congress to aid his state in building such a canal —C.W.Mitman› PERSUADE may suggest a winning over by an appeal, entreaty, or expostulation addressed as much to feelings as to reason ‹*persuade* management to recognize collective bargaining —*Current Biog.*› ‹deputed by the firm of lawyers to *persuade* her to resume her married life —Anthony Powell› PREVAIL may be used in situations in which strong opposition or reluctance is overcome by sustained argument and entreaty ‹a group of citizens of all parties had *prevailed* on him to enter the race —*Current Biog.*› ‹I will go now and try to *prevail* on my mother to let me stay with you —G.B.Shaw› ‹*prevailed* upon the men in the sloop to sail up the river again, to rescue any survivors —Marjory S. Douglas›

**induced development** *n* [*induced* fr. past part. of *induce*] **:** EPIGENESIS 1

**induced draft** *n* **:** a draft produced by a suction steam jet or fan on the stack side of a furnace

**induced drag** *n* **:** the portion of the wing drag induced by or resulting from the generation of the lift

**induced investment** *n* **:** investment in inventories and equipment which is derived from and varies with changes in final output — distinguished from *autonomous investment*

**induced radioactivity** *n* **:** ARTIFICIAL RADIOACTIVITY

**induced reaction** *n* **:** a chemical reaction that proceeds more rapidly than it ordinarily would because of the influence of a second and faster reaction in the same system

**in·duce·ment** \-mənt\ *n* -s **1 a :** the act or process of inducing ‹put into effect a system of ~ to encourage workers to turn out more work› **b :** a quality or state which induces (as to action) or lures or entices ‹the ~ of philosophy was that it freed one from a sense of enslavement to circumstance› **2 a :** something that induces **:** a motive or consideration that leads one to action ‹reward is an ~ to effort› ‹offer larger ~s to students to do good work› **b** *in Roman, Scots, and civil law* **:** the consideration, reason, or motive for entering into a contract or the benefit or advantage furnished in a contractual bargain **3 a** *obs* **:** INTRODUCTION, PREFACE **b :** matter presented by way of introduction or background to explain the principal allegations of a legal cause, plea, or defense — distinguished from *surplusage* **4 :** COLLOQUIUM 2 **syn** see MOTIVE

**in·duc·er** \-sə(r)\ *n* -s **:** one that induces; *specif* **:** the part of a centrifugal blower or compressor that feeds air into the axial region of the impeller

**in·du·ci·ae** \ən'd(y)üshē,ē\ *n pl* [L *induciae, indutiae* truce, pause] **1 :** a delay allowed for the performance of a legal obligation: as **a** *in Roman, civil, English, or Scots law* (1) *or* **induciae le·ga·les** \-lə'gā(ˌ)lēz\ **:** time granted to a party to appear in answer to a summons or citation (2) **:** time granted for the preparation of a case for trial **b** *in old maritime law* **:** a period of 20 days after the safe arrival of a vessel under bottomry allowed for the sale of the cargo and the payment of the creditor's claim **2** *in international law* **:** a truce or cessation of hostilities **:** ARMISTICE

**in·duc·ible** \ən'd(y)üsəbəl\ *adj* **:** capable of being induced

**inducing** *pres part of* INDUCE

**in·du·cive** \-siv\ *adj, archaic* **:** tending to induce

**in·duct** \ən'dəkt\ *vt* -ED/-ING/-S [ME *inducten,* fr. ML *inductus,* past part. of *inducere,* fr. L, to lead in, introduce, induce — more at INDUCE] **1 a :** to put in formal possession of a benefice or living ‹has taken orders and been ~*ed* to a small country living —Nathaniel Hawthorne› **b :** to put in office with appropriate ceremonies **:** INSTALL ‹was ~*ed* as president of the college› **c :** to admit as a member ‹~ three men into a scholastic society› **d :** to introduce or initiate esp. into something secret or demanding special knowledge ‹~*ing* neophytes into the mysteries of a cult› ‹important that teachers be properly ~*ed* into the profession› ‹~ a youngster into the use of his language —Stuart Chase› **e** (1) **:** to enroll for training or service under a selective-service act (2) **:** to bring into federal service as part of the National Guard of the U.S. **2 :** LEAD, CONDUCT ‹swung the leaves of the door at just the right angle that ~*ed* you to the café —Mary Austin›

**in·duc·tance** \-ən(t)s\ *n* -s [*induct* + *-ance*] **1 :** a property of an electric circuit by which an electromotive force is induced in it by a variation of current either (1) in the circuit itself or (2) in a neighboring circuit, which is expressed in henrys and is dependent upon the size, shape, and relative positions of the circuits and upon the proximity of magnetic materials, and which in electrical theory plays a role analogous to that of inertia in mechanics — called also respectively (1) *self-inductance* and (2) *mutual inductance* **2 :** a circuit or a device possessing inductance

**inductance coil** *n* **:** REACTOR 3

**in·duct·ee** \(ˌ)in,dək'tē, ən,-, =¦=¦=\ *n* -s **:** a person brought up for induction esp. into one of the armed forces or one who is to be or has been so inducted

**in·ductile** \(')in, ən+\ *adj* [[1]*in-* + *ductile*] **:** not ductile **:** INFLEXIBLE, UNYIELDING

**in·duc·tion** \ən'dəkshən\ *n* -s [ME *induccioun,* fr. AF or ML; AF *induccion,* fr. ML *induction-, inductio,* fr. *inductus* (past part. of *inducere* to induct) + L *-ion-, -io* -ion] **1 :** the act or process of inducting, the state of being inducted, or an instance or product of induction: as **a** (1) **:** a formal or symbolic and ceremonial bringing into or introducing to actual possession (as of an office) ‹my ~ into the presidency —F.D.Roosevelt› (2) *Eng. eccl. law* **:** the ceremony of giving the actual possession of an ecclesiastical living or its temporalities to a clergyman already presented and instituted **b :** an initial experience **:** an exposure that introduces one to something previously mysterious or unknown **:** INITIATION ‹six weeks of hard physical effort was his ~ into the arts of war› ‹this grade of exercise supplies easy ~ to the technique for learners —J.M. Mitchell› **c :** an official usu. formal and ceremonial admittance (as to membership in a club) ‹awaiting his acceptance by and ~ into the secret order› **d :** the formality by which a civilian is inducted into military service under the provisions of a draft law **2** [ME *induccioun,* fr. MF or L; MF *induction* reasoning from a part to a whole, fr. L *induction-, inductio* (trans. of Gk *epagōgē*), fr. *inductus* (past part. of *inducere* to lead in, introduce, induce) + *-ion-, -io* -ion] **a :** an instance of reasoning from a part to a whole, from particulars to generals, or from the individual to the universal **:** a conclusion arrived at by reasoning from a part to a whole, from particulars to generals, or from the individual to the universal **:** INFERENCE **2 b** (1) **:** reasoning from a part to a whole, from particulars to generals, or from the individual to the universal — compare BACONIAN INDUCTION, ENUMERATIVE INDUCTION, EPAGOGE (2) **:** a process of mathematical demonstration in which the general validity of a law is inferred from its observed validity in particular cases by proving that if the law holds in a certain case it must hold in the next and therefore in succeeding cases **3** [L *induction-, inductio* action of introducing, fr. *inductus* (past part. of *inducere* to lead in, introduce, induce) + *-ion-, -io* -ion] **a :** a preface, prologue, or introductory scene esp. of an early English play **b** *obs* **:** something that leads into something else **c** *obs* **:** an initial step or action **4** [L *induction-, inductio* action of introducing] **:** the act or process of introducing, the state of being introduced, or an instance or product of introducing: as **a :** the act of bringing forward or adducing (as facts or particulars) **b :** the act of causing, initiating, or bringing on or about esp. at an early time or to a preliminary degree ‹~ of labor›; *specif* **:** the establishment of an initial state of anesthesia often with an agent other than that used subsequently to maintain the anesthetic state **c :** the production of an electric charge, magnetism, or electromotive force in an object (as an electric conductor, a magnetizable body, an electric circuit) by the proximity without contact of a similarly energized body or by the variation of a magnetic flux — see ELECTROMAGNETIC INDUCTION, ELECTROSTATIC INDUCTION, MAGNETIC INDUCTION, MUTUAL INDUCTION, SELF-INDUCTION **d :** arousal by indirect stimulation (as contrast colors from parts of the retina adjacent to a directly stimulated area) **e :** the inspiration of the fuel-air charge from the carburetor into the combustion chamber of an internal-combustion engine **f :** the sum of the processes by which the fate of embryonic cells is determined and morphogenetic differentiation brought about

**induction accelerator** *n* **:** BETATRON

**induction coil** *n* **:** an apparatus for obtaining intermittent high voltage often used to produce spark discharges and consisting of a primary coil through which the direct current flows, a mechanical or electrical interrupter, and a secondary coil of a larger number of turns in which the high voltage is induced

**induction compass** *n* **:** a compass the indications of which depend on the current generated in a coil revolving in the earth's magnetic field

**induction furnace** *n* **:** an electric furnace heated by a current which is caused to flow through the charge by electromagnetic induction — compare ARC FURNACE

**induction-harden** \=¦==¦==\ *vt* **:** to harden (a ferrous alloy) by heating above the transformation temperature by means of electromagnetic induction and then cooling as rapidly as necessary

**induction heating** *n* **:** a process of heating by means of an electric current that is caused to flow through the material to be heated or through its container (as a crucible) by electromagnetic induction — compare DIELECTRIC HEATING

**induction machine** *n* **1 :** an electric machine operating by electrostatic induction **2 :** an alternating-current machine (as an induction motor or induction generator) in which primary and secondary windings rotate with respect to each other and in which energy is transferred from one circuit to the other circuit by electromagnetic induction

**induction motor** *n* **:** any of several alternating-current motors in which the torque is produced by the reaction between a varying or rotating magnetic field that is generated in stationary field magnets and the current that is induced in the coils or circuits of the rotor

**induction period** *n* **1 :** the time that elapses between the immersion of an exposed photographic emulsion in a developer and the appearance of the photographed image **2 :** a period at the beginning of some chemical reactions during which little or no action takes place (as in the oxidation of fats by air because of the presence of antioxidants)

**inductions** *pl of* INDUCTION

**in·duc·tive** \(')in¦dəktiv, ən'd-, -tēv *also* -təv\ *adj* [in sense 1, fr. ML *inductivus,* fr. L *inductus* (past part. of *inducere* to induce) + *-ivus* -ive; in other senses, fr. *induction,* after such pairs as E *deduction: deductive* — more at INDUCE] **1 :** leading on **:** drawing on **:** INDUCING, TEMPTING ‹~ to the sin of Eve —John Milton› **2 :** of or relating to logical induction ‹the ~ method› ‹~ reasoning› **:** employing the methods of induction ‹~ science› **3 a :** of, relating to, or produced or operated by electrical induction **b :** of, relating to, or having inductance esp. mutual inductance **4 :** INTRODUCTORY, PREFATORY **5 :** involving the action of an inductor ‹~ effect of chordamesoderm⟩ : tending to produce induction ⟨~ reactions in the embryo⟩ — **in·duc·tive·ly** \-tәvlē, -li\ *adv* — **in·duc·tive·ness** \-tivnәs, -tēv- *also* -tәv-\ *n* -ES

**inductive coupler** *n* : a mutual inductor used in radio apparatus to provide coupling between two circuits

**inductive coupling** *n* : electrical coupling in which the influence is that of mutual induction usu. between two coils close together or wound on a common core

**inductive inference** *n* : INDUCTION 2b(1)

**inductive logic** *n* : a branch of logic that deals with induction; *esp* : the logic or theory of the methods and reasonings of empirical science

**inductive reactance** *n* : the part of the reactance of an alternating-current circuit that is due to inductance

**in·duc·tiv·ism** \әn'dәktә,vizәm\ *n* -S : a policy or the practice of using an inductive method or of stressing induction in one's methods

**in·duc·tiv·ist** \-,vәst\ *n* -S : one that is characterized by or advocates inductivism

**in·duc·tom·e·ter** \,in,dәk'tämәd·ә(r)\ *n* [*induction* + *-o-* + *-meter*] : a variocoupler calibrated in units of inductance

**in·duc·tor** \әn'dәktә(r)\ *n* -S [partly fr. *induct* + *-or;* partly prob. fr. *induction,* after such pairs as E *conduction: conductor*] **1** : one that inducts; *esp* : a person who inducts another into an office or benefice **2 a** : an inductance coil or reactor **b** : a mass of iron used in certain magnetic train-control devices **3** : a substance that increases the rate of a chemical reaction and that is used up during the reaction — distinguished from *catalyst* **4** : a substance capable under certain circumstances of inducing a specific type of development in embryonic or other undifferentiated tissue ⟨chordamesoderm acts on embryonic ectoderm as an ~ of neural tissue⟩ — compare COMPETENCE 5

**inductor compass** *n* : INDUCTION COMPASS

**inductor generator** *n* : a generator that induces voltage in a fixed armature by rotation of a rotor magnetized by current through a fixed field coil

**in·duc·to·ri·um** \,in,dәk'tōrēәm\ *n* -S [NL, fr. *induct-* (fr. ISV *induction*) + *-orium*] : a battery-operated apparatus containing induction coils used for producing a continuous pulsing electric current or a single pulse of current (as for physiological or pharmacological experiments)

**in·duc·to·ther·my** \әn'dәktә,thәrmē\ *n* -ES [blend of *Inductotherm* (a trademark) and E *-thermy*] : fever therapy by means of an electromagnetic induction field with the body or a part of it acting as a resistance

**inducts** *pres 3d sing of* INDUCT

**indue** *var of* ENDUE

**in·dulge** \әn'dәlj\ *vb* -ED/-ING/-S [L *indulgēre* to grant as a favor, be courteous, be kind, fr. *in-* ²in- + *-dulgēre* (prob. akin to OE *tulge* firmly, well, OS *tulgo* very, Goth *tulgus* firm, steadfast, Gk *dolichos* long, Skt *dīrgha*); basic meaning: long, enduring] *vt* **1** *archaic* : to grant as a favor : BESTOW in concession or in compliance with a wish or request — usu. used in the passive ⟨a privilege seldom *indulged* to ordinary men⟩ **2 a** : to give free rein to ⟨*indulging* idle conjectures as to what might be the news —Rafael Sabatini⟩ ⟨likes to ~ a taste for the difficult —*Current Biog.*⟩ ⟨an excellent place to ~ a normal curiosity about clocks and watches —Ellwood Kirby⟩ : take unrestrained pleasure in : yield to : GRATIFY ⟨~ a taste for exotic dishes⟩ **b** : to allow (oneself) unrestrained pleasure (as in the gratification of a normally restrained habit or desire) or unrestrained freedom (as in the expression of a normally restrained feeling) ⟨*indulged* himself in the delights of leisure⟩ ⟨~ oneself in eating and drinking⟩ ⟨*indulging* herself in histrionics⟩ **3 a** : to yield to the desire of or be forbearing in respect to out of favor or kindness under circumstances where one would not usually yield : gratify by unusual compliance : allow to proceed or act free from the restraints one would ordinarily impose : HUMOR ⟨~ a convalescing child in whatever he wishes to eat⟩ ⟨*indulged* her husband until he would not lift a finger around the house⟩ : favor in a way that pampers or treats with undue liberality ⟨a time when schoolboys were less *indulged* with pocket money than they seem to be nowadays —Archibald Marshall⟩ **b** : to grant an indulgence to or on ~ *vi* : to indulge in something ⟨offered him a drink but he protested that he did not ~⟩ — **indulge in 1** : to gratify one's taste or desire for ⟨prone to *indulge in* too many evenings of pleasure⟩ ⟨*indulging in* candy and ice cream⟩ ⟨*indulging in* the bad habit of swearing⟩ **2** : to give free rein to ⟨*indulge in* heated argument and violent language⟩ **3** : to engage in ⟨all birds *indulge in* some seasonal movement —W.H.Dowdeswell⟩ ⟨*indulging in* the curious hobby of raising tropical fish —*Times Lit. Supp.*⟩ : UNDERTAKE ⟨those who *indulge in* high-altitude flights and suffer from a mild degree of oxygen want —H.G.Armstrong⟩

**syn** INDULGE, PAMPER, HUMOR, SPOIL, BABY, and MOLLYCODDLE can mean, in common, to treat a person or his desires or feelings with unusual or special usu. undue favor or attention. INDULGE with a personal object implies extreme compliance and often weakness in gratifying another's wishes or desires which have little claim to fulfillment ⟨I wanted to *indulge* him in all his particular food fancies and very soon the air in the apartment became almost visible with the reek of garlic sausage, smoked kippers and cheeses of strong character —Virginia D. Dawson & Betty D. Wilson⟩ ⟨grandmamma is always wanting to see them, for she humors and *indulges* them to such a degree, and gives them so much trash and sweet things, that they are sure to come back sick —Jane Austen⟩ PAMPER implies inordinate gratification of an appetite or taste esp. for luxuries or for what is softening in its physical or moral effects ⟨he preserved without an effort the supremacy of character and mind over the flesh he neither starved nor *pampered* —G.L.Dickinson⟩ ⟨no country can afford to *pamper* snobbery —G.B.Shaw⟩ ⟨*pamper* a child with rich foods and constant solicitude⟩ HUMOR implies an unusual attention to or a voluntary yielding to what are regarded as another's whims or caprices, often suggesting a purposeful sometimes patronizing accommodation to another's moods ⟨*humoring* a pet fawn which had a predilection for soap and cigarette butts —Ray Corsini⟩ ⟨the tone of your voice, when you speak, is too gentle, as if you were *humoring* the vagaries of a blind man's mind —Ben Hecht⟩ ⟨*humor* a customer for the sake of making a sale⟩ SPOIL implies a foolish or excessive indulging or pampering and throws strong stress upon its injurious effects upon the character or disposition ⟨the new queen played with and *spoiled* the little stepdaughter —Edith Sitwell⟩ ⟨he had been a noisy boastful youth and had been *spoiled* by his father —Sherwood Anderson⟩ BABY implies excessive attentions, as to one unable to care for himself and needing the assistance of a mother or nurse; when applied to one presumably capable, it carries the idea of treating with excessive usu. foolish care or carefulness ⟨if he thinks I'm going to spend my days catering to his whims, *babying* him and watching over him like a child, he's mistaken —Helen S. Rush & Mary Sherkanowski⟩ ⟨your old records will last longer with this new device to *baby* them —*Coronet*⟩ MOLLYCODDLE is the strongest of this group in implying inordinate attention and suggesting a ridiculously undue care for another's health or physical comfort or for the relieving of the strain or hardship he presumably, usu. fictitiously, suffers or may suffer ⟨a mother who *mollycoddles* her children by constantly dosing them, keeping them in when it's at all cold or damp and away from other children for fear of germs⟩ ⟨protests against the policy of *mollycoddling* prisoners —J.F.Steiner & R.M.Brown⟩

**indulged** *past of* INDULGE

¹**in·dul·gence** \-jәn(t)s\ *also* **in·dul·gen·cy** \-nsē,-nsi\ *n, pl* **indulgences** *also* **indulgencies** [*indulgence* in sense 1 fr. ME, fr. MF, fr. ML *indulgentia,* fr. L, quality or state of being indulgent, kindness, complaisance, fr. *indulgent-, indulgens* indulgent + *-ia -y; indulgence* in other senses fr. ME, fr. L *indulgentia; indulgency* in sense 2a fr. ME, fr. L *indulgentia; indulgency* in sense 1 fr. ML *indulgentia; indulgency* in other senses fr. L *indulgentia*] **1** : remission of the temporal punishment including canonical penances and esp. purgatorial atonement that according to Roman Catholicism is due by divine justice for sins whose eternal punishment has been remitted and whose guilt has been pardoned by the reception of the sacrament of penance **2** : the act of indulging or the state of being indulgent: as **a** : a special often excessive leniency (as toward a sick child) : HUMORING ⟨had learned to treat his moody child with ~⟩ : any treatment marked by forbearance ⟨a crotchety old man who expected more ~ than he deserved⟩ **b** : FONDNESS, LIKING ⟨his ~ for the government of England —H.J. Laski⟩ **c** : benign tolerance ⟨mocking elegance that has little respect but much ~ for the foibles of man —Claudia Cassidy⟩ **3 a** : an indulgent act : a favor granted or an instance of forbearance ⟨sorry she allowed the children all the ~s she had in the past⟩ **b** (1) *sometimes cap* : a grant or offer of certain religious liberties as special favors made by Charles II and James II to Protestant dissenters and Roman Catholics (2) : the permission given during the same reigns to Scotch Presbyterian ministers to hold services **c** : an extension of time for payment or performance granted as a favor — compare MORATORIUM **4** : the act of indulging in something or the thing indulged in ⟨a commendable degree of ~ in outdoor sports⟩ ⟨excessive ~ in daydreaming⟩ ⟨acquired that habit of romantic reading which was to be a lifetime ~ —H.S.Canby⟩ ⟨his trips abroad were almost the only ~s he had ever allowed himself⟩ ⟨had to be content with the weekly ~ of an ice-cream soda⟩ : gratification of a kind usu. forbidden or frowned on or to a degree usu. considered excessive; *esp* : SELF-GRATIFICATION, SELF-INDULGENCE

²**indulgence** \"\ *vt* -ED/-ING/-S *Roman Catholicism* : to attach an indulgence to (as an act or an object's use) ⟨*indulgenced* prayers⟩

**in·dul·gent** \-nt\ *adj* [L *indulgent-, indulgens,* pres. part. of *indulgēre* to indulge] : indulging, prone to indulge, or characterized by indulgence ⟨a smile of ~ pity such as one might grant to a mistaken child —Jane Addams⟩ : benignly tolerant : FORBEARING : markedly permissive ⟨indictments and civil pleadings are viewed with ~ eyes —B.N.Cardozo⟩ ⟨more appreciative of his success, more ~ of his shortcomings —Nathaniel Hawthorne⟩ **syn** see FORBEARING

**in·dul·gent·ly** *adv* : in an indulgent manner ⟨very often the young girl who goes wrong is dishonored, whereas the misconduct of the wife is viewed ~ —H.M.Parshley⟩

**in·dulg·er** \-jә(r)\ *n* -S : one that indulges

**indulges** *pres 3d sing of* INDULGE

**indulging** *pres part of* INDULGE

**in·du·line** \'ind(y)ә,lēn, -,lәn\ *n* -S *usu cap* [ISV *ind-* + *-ule* + *-ine*] : any of a class of blue or violet dyes related to the safranines: as **a** : a reddish to greenish blue dye derived from phenosafranine and made by heating amino-azobenzene and aniline in the presence of hydrochloric acid — called also *Induline Spirit Soluble;* see DYE table I (under *Solvent Blue 7*) **b** : a water-soluble acid dye made by sulfonating the free base obtained by treating Induline Spirit Soluble with alkali — see DYE table I (under *Acid Blue 20*)

**in·dult** \'in,dәlt, әn'd-\ *n* -S [ME (Sc), fr. ML *indultum,* fr. LL, grant, privilege, fr. L, neut. of *indultus,* past part. of *indulgēre* to grant as a favor — more at INDULGE] : a special privilege granted by ecclesiastical authority for a definite or indefinite period of time; *specif,* **indults** *pl* : general faculties granted in the Roman Catholic Church by the pope to bishops and others to act in cases not otherwise permitted

**in·dul·to** \әn'dül(,)tō\ *n* -S [Sp, license, exemption, fr. ML *indultum* indult] *archaic* : INDULT

**in·du·ment** \'ind(y)әmәnt\ *n* -S [L *indumentum* garment, fr. *induere* to put on, don (fr. *ind-* — fr. OL *indu, endo* in — + *-uere* — as in *exuere* to take off) + *-mentum* -ment — more at INDIGENOUS, EXUVIAE] **1** *archaic* : CLOTHING, GARMENT, INVESTITURE **2** [NL *indumentum,* fr. L] : INDUMENTUM

**in·du·men·tum** \,==ˈmentәm\ *n, pl* **indumen·ta** \-tә\ *or* **indumentums** [NL, fr. L] **1** : the entire feathery covering of a bird **2** : a dense woolly pubescence (as on a leaf or an insect)

**in·du·na** \әn'dünә\ *n* -S [Zulu *in-duna* government officer] : a headman or councilor of an African people esp. the Zulus

**in·duplicate** \әn +\ *adj* [prob. fr. (assumed) NL *induplicatus,* fr. L *in-* ²in- + *duplicatus* bent, doubled up, doubled, past part. of *duplicare* to double — more at DUPLICATE] **1** : having the edges bent abruptly toward the axis — used of the parts of the calyx or corolla in a bud **2** : having the edges rolled inward and then arranged about the axis without overlapping — used of leaves in a bud

**indurance** *obs var of* ENDURANCE

¹**in·du·rate** \'ind(y)әrәt, әn'd(y)u̇r-\ *adj* [ME *indurat,* fr. L *induratus,* past part. of *indurare*] : physically or morally hardened ⟨this man whom enemies describe as cold-blooded and ~ to public opinion —M.L.Bach⟩

²**in·du·rate** \'ind(y)ә,rāt, *usu* -ād.+V\ *vb* -ED/-ING/-S [L *induratus,* past part. of *indurare,* fr. *in-* ²in- + *durare* to harden, fr. *durus* hard — more at DURE] *vt* **1** : to make unfeeling, stubborn, or obdurate ⟨the instability of many religionists . . . ~s secular men in their impiety —Isaac Taylor⟩ **2** : to make hardy : INURE ⟨had been *indurated* to want, exposure and toil —A.W.Tourgee⟩ **3** : to make hard: as **a** : to make into a compact hard rock mass by the action of heat, pressure, or cementation ⟨conglomerates are the *indurated* equivalents of gravel —F.J.Pettijohn⟩ **b** : to increase the fibrous elements of : make sclerosed ⟨*indurated* tissue⟩ **4** : to establish firmly : make deep-rooted : CONFIRM ⟨the *indurated* goat habit . . . every family keeps a goat —Ellery Sedgwick⟩ ~ *vi* **1** : to grow hard : HARDEN **2** : to become established or deep rooted

**in·du·ra·tion** \,ind(y)ә'rāshәn\ *n* -S [ME *induracion,* fr. MF or LL; MF *induration,* fr. LL *induration-, induratio,* fr. L *induratus* + *-ion-, -io* -ion] **1** : the act or process of growing hard or the state of having grown hard: as **a** : hardness or inflexibility of character, manner, or feeling : OBSTINACY, OBDURATENESS, CALLOUSNESS **b** : the act of becoming inured (as to drudgery) ⟨~ to hackwork —*Saturday Rev.*⟩ **c** : the process by which a rock or rock material is indurated **d** : an increase in the fibrous elements in tissue commonly associated with inflammation and marked by loss of elasticity and pliability : SCLEROSIS **2** : a hardened mass or formation

**in·du·ra·tive** \'ind(y)ә,rād·iv, әn'd(y)u̇rәd·-\ *adj* : of, relating to, or producing induration

**in·du·rite** \'ind(y)ә,rīt\ *n* -S [²*indurate* + *-ite*] : a smokeless powder made by treating guncotton with nitrobenzene

**indus** *abbr* industrial; industry

**in·du·sial** \әn'd(y)üzēәl, -zh(ē)әl\ *adj* [*indusium* + *-al*] : of, relating to, or being an indusium

**in·du·si·um** \-z(h)ēәm\ *n, pl* **indu·sia** \-zēә, -zh(ē)ә\ [NL, fr. L, woman's undergarment, tunic, perh. fr. *induere* to put on — more at INDUMENT] **1 a** : an outgrowth of the leaf which covers or invests the sori in many ferns **b** : a cuplike fringe of collecting hairs surrounding the stigma in the Goodeniaceae **c** : the annulus in some fungi esp. when skirtlike (as in members of the genus *Dictyophora*) **2** : a membrane serving as a covering; *esp* : AMNION

¹**in·dus·tri·al** \әn'dәstrēәl\ *adj* [partly fr. MF, produced by systematic labor, fr. *industrie* employment involving skill (fr. L *industria* diligence) + *-al;* partly fr. F *industriel* of or belonging to industry (esp. manufacturing), fr. *industrie* industry (fr. L *industria* diligence) + *-el* -al, fr. L *-alis* — more at INDUSTRY] **1** : of or belonging to industry: as **a** : being in or part of industry ⟨~ work⟩ ⟨an ~ employment⟩ **b** : being or constituting an industry ⟨an ~ enterprise⟩ **c** : characterized by highly developed industries or being chiefly dependent economically upon industry ⟨an ~ nation⟩ **d** : engaged in industry or in industries esp. at manual labor ⟨the ~ classes⟩ **e** : derived from human industry rather than from natural advantages only or from profit only ⟨~ wealth⟩ ⟨an ~ crop⟩ **f** : belonging to or aiding those engaged in industry ⟨~ wages⟩ ⟨~ safety⟩ ⟨~ training⟩ **g** : produced by an organized industry ⟨~ products⟩ **h** : used or designed or developed for use in industry ⟨~ fabrics⟩ ⟨an ~ diamond⟩ ⟨wrapping, building, and other ~ papers⟩ **2** : belonging to industrial life or accident and health insurance

²**industrial** \"\ *n* -S **1 a** : one that is employed in a manufacturing industry **b** : a company engaged in industrial production or service **2 industrials** *pl* : stocks or bonds of industrial companies **3** : something industrial (as an industrial diamond) as opposed to something else that is of the same class of things but used or designed for use for a nonindustrial purpose

**industrial accession** *n, Roman, civil, & Scots law* : accession brought about by human industry as opposed to some natural process

**industrial accident** *n* : an accident occurring during the course of employment

**industrial accident and health insurance** *n* : accident and health insurance usu. written in small amounts and subject to frequent premium payments and covering persons exposed to the hazard of occupational injury

**industrial alcohol** *n* : alcohol for industrial use; *usu* : ethyl alcohol either mixed only with water or denatured — see DENATURED ALCOHOL

**industrial art** *n* : a subject taught in elementary and secondary schools that aims at developing a manual skill, a familiarity with tools and machines, or an acquaintance with industrial processes and design

**industrial bank** *n* : a financial institution deriving funds from the sale of investment certificates and from deposits made by individual savers and investing such funds in personal loans often secured by a comaker note or chattel mortgage

**industrial carrier** *n* : a means of transportation owned, controlled, or operated by one or more industries as a private, exclusive, or common carrier

**industrial center** *n* : a Salvationist institution that provides work (as the salvaging of waste materials) and an opportunity for rehabilitation for homeless or handicapped men

**industrial chemistry** *n* : chemistry in its industrial applications esp. to processes in manufacturing and the arts and to commercial production of chemicals

**industrial democracy** *n* : the determination of a company's policies affecting the welfare of its workers by joint action of management and worker representatives

**industrial design** *n* : design concerned with the appearance of three-dimensional machine-made products; *also* : the study of the principles of such design

**industrial designer** *n* : one that works at industrial design

**industrial disease** *n* : OCCUPATIONAL DISEASE

**industrial engineer** *n* : a specialist in industrial engineering

**industrial engineering** *n* : the application of engineering principles and training and the techniques of scientific management to the maintenance of a high level of productivity at optimum cost in industrial enterprises (as by analytical study, improvement, and installation of methods and systems, operating procedures, quantity and quality measurements and controls, safety measures, and personnel administration)

**industrial geography** *n* : a branch of geography that deals with the location of industries, the geographic factors that influence their location and development, the raw materials used in them, and the distribution of their finished products

**industrial hygiene** *n* : a science devoted to the protection and improvement of the health and well-being of workers in their vocational environment

**industrial insurance** *n* **1 a** : INDUSTRIAL LIFE INSURANCE **b** : INDUSTRIAL ACCIDENT AND HEALTH INSURANCE **2** : WORKMEN'S COMPENSATION INSURANCE

**in·dus·tri·al·ism** \-ēә,lizәm\ *n* -S [F *industrialisme,* fr. *industrial-* (fr. *industriel* industrial) + *-isme* -ism — more at INDUSTRIAL] : social organization in which industries and esp. large-scale industries are dominant — compare CAPITALISM, COMMERCIALISM, MILITARISM

¹**in·dus·tri·al·ist** \-,lәst\ *n* -S [F *industrialiste* advocate of industrialism, fr. *industrial-* (fr. *industriel*) + *-iste* -ist] : one owning or engaged in the management of an esp. large-scale industry; *esp* : MANUFACTURER

²**industrialist** \"\ *adj* [F *industrialiste,* fr. *industrialiste,* n.] : of, relating to, or characterized by industrialism

**in·dus·tri·al·iza·tion** \=,===lә'zāshәn, -,lī'z-\ *n* -S : the act or process of industrializing or the state of being industrialized

**in·dus·tri·al·ize** \='===,līz\ *vb* -ED/-ING/-S — see *-ize* in *Explan Notes* [F *industrialiser,* fr. *industrial-* (fr. *industriel*) + *-iser* -ize] *vt* : to make industrial : convert to industrialism ~ *vi* : to become industrial : become converted to industrialism ⟨country has been steadily *industrializing* —Eric Goldman⟩

**industrial life insurance** *n* : life insurance which is written upon individual lives in small amounts and for which the premiums are collected weekly or monthly by agents

**in·dus·tri·al·ly** \-ēәlē, -li\ *adv* : in or by means of industry

**in·dus·tri·al·ness** \-ēәlnәs\ *n* -ES : the quality or state of being industrial

**industrial park** *n* : an area that is at a distance from the center of a city and that is designed (as by homogeneous architecture) esp. for a community of industries and businesses

**industrial property** *n* : intangible property rights (as ownership of a trademark or patent) connected with agriculture, commerce, and industry

**industrial psychology** *n* : the application of the findings and methods of experimental, clinical, and social psychology to industrial problems (as personnel selection and training) — compare PSYCHOTECHNOLOGY

**industrial railroad** *n* : a short railroad feeder owned or controlled and operated by an industrial concern — called also *tap line*

**industrial relations** *n pl* : the dealings or relationships of a usu. large business or industrial enterprise with its own workers, with labor in general, with governmental agencies, or with the public or the relationships between industries or large businesses

**industrial revolution** *n* [prob. trans. of F *révolution industrielle*] **1** : an economic revolution (as in England beginning in 1760) characterized by a marked acceleration in the output of industrial goods correlative with the introduction of power-driven machinery into industry and consequent decline of handwork and domestic production **2** : a marked general alteration in industrial or production methods in the direction of machine production and away from manual labor or personal control

**industrial school** *n* : a school specializing in the teaching of the industrial arts; *specif* : a public institution of this kind for juvenile delinquents

**industrial sociology** *n* : sociological analysis directed at institutions and social relationships within and largely controlled or affected by industry

**industrial store** *n* : COMPANY STORE

**industrial union** *n* : a labor union that admits to membership workmen in an industry irrespective of their occupation or craft — called also *vertical union*

**in·dus·tri·ous** \әn'dәstrēәs\ *adj* [MF *industrieux,* fr. L *industriosus* diligent, fr. *industria* diligence + *-osus* -ose] **1** *obs* : SKILLFUL, CLEVER, INGENIOUS **2** : perseveringly active : ZEALOUS ⟨~ in seeking out and questioning new arrivals —Gilbert Armitage⟩ **3** : characterized by industry: as **a** : marked by steady dependable energetic work : not lazy : DILIGENT ⟨an ~ worker⟩ ⟨an ~ group of campaigners⟩ **b** : constantly, regularly, or habitually occupied : BUSY ⟨an ~ housewife whose tasks seemed never-ending⟩ **c** : conducive to purposeful work or enterprise ⟨an ~ home environment⟩ **4** *obs* : characterized by design or purpose : INTENTIONAL **syn** see BUSY

**in·dus·tri·ous·ly** *adv* : in an industrious manner

**in·dus·tri·ous·ness** *n* -ES : the quality or state of being industrious ⟨a prosperity credited largely to the ~ of the people⟩

**in·dus·try** \'in(,)dәstrē, -ri *sometimes* әn'd-\ *n* -ES [ME *industrie,* fr. MF, skill, employment involving skill, fr. L *industria* diligence, fr. *industrius* diligent, fr. OL *indostruus,* fr. *indu, endo* in, within + *-struus* (akin to L *struere* to arrange, build) — more at INDIGENOUS, STRUCTURE] **1** *obs* **a** : SKILL, CLEVERNESS **b** : a use or application of skill or cleverness **2 a** : diligence in an employment or pursuit : steady attention to business ⟨all his long years of service gone . . . all his ~ and diligence thrown away —James Joyce⟩ ⟨sewing with no great amount of ~ on pieces of white material —Lillian Hellman⟩ **b** : habitual or constant work or effort ⟨a man of fine mental powers . . . unceasing ~, and simple charm —C.B.Fisher⟩ ⟨he had immense ~ but he didn't know how to think —Archibald Marshall⟩ **3 a** : systematic labor esp. for the creation of value ⟨had left the country . . . to live by his own ~ in England —Charles Dickens⟩ **b** : a department or branch of a craft, art, business, or manufacture : a division of productive or profit-making labor; *esp* : one that employs a large personnel and capital esp. in manufacturing ⟨put his money into an ~ that sold its goods on an international scale⟩ ⟨all the large *industries* in the city⟩ **c** : a group of productive or profit-making enterprises or organizations that have a similar technological structure of production and that produce or supply technically substitutable goods, services, or sources of income ⟨the automobile ~⟩ ⟨the air transport ~⟩ ⟨the poultry ~⟩ ⟨the smuggling of gold, liquor, and other contraband has become a secondary ~ —James Reach⟩ ⟨the tourist ~⟩ **d** : manufacturing activity as a whole ⟨conditions that were auspicious for the nation's ~⟩ ⟨an energetic promoter of New England ~ —*Current Biog.*⟩ **4 a** : a well-developed technique of a people esp. as evidenced in archaeological discoveries **b** : an assemblage of prehistoric implements giving clear evidence that they were used by one group of men

**in·dwell** \(ˈ)in, ən+\ *vb* [ME *indwellen* to inhabit, fr. ²*in* + *dwellen* to dwell] *vi* : to exist as an inner activating spirit, force, or principle ⟨a creative power ~*ing* in the world —Lawrence Binyon⟩ ⟨a divinity ~*ing* in nature —V.L. Parrington⟩ ~ *vt* : to exist within or inhabit as an activating spirit, force, or principle ⟨a life of God ~*s* the universe —J.H.Randall⟩ ⟨endowed with or *indwelt* by some supernatural power —E.A.Nida⟩

**in·dwell·er** \"ə(r)\ *n* [ME, fr. *indwellen* + *-er*] **1 a** : INHABITANT **b** : SOJOURNER **2** : an inner spirit, force, or principle

**indwelling** *adj* **1** : existing or residing as an inner activating spirit, force, or principle ⟨an ~ divinity —B.B.Cohen⟩ ⟨an ~ goodness⟩ **2** : left for a period of time within an organ or passage to maintain drainage, prevent obstruction, or provide a route for administration of food or drugs — used of a catheter or similar tube

**in·dyl** \ˈindᵊl, -,dil\ *n* -s [by shortening] : INDOLYL

**¹-ine** \,īn, ,ən, (,)in, ,ēn\ *adj suffix* [ME *-ine, -in*, fr. MF *-in* & L *-inus* (with long *ī*), *-inus* (with short *ĭ*); MF *-in* partly fr. L *-inus* (with long *ī*) of or belonging to; MF *-in* partly fr. L *-inus* (with short *ĭ*) made of, of or belonging to, fr. Gk *-inos* — more at -EN] **1** : of, belonging to, or relating to ⟨estuar*ine*⟩ **2** : made of : like ⟨opal*ine*⟩

**²-ine** \,ēn, ,ən\ *n suffix* -s [ME *-ine, -in*, fr. MF & L; MF *-ine*, fr. L *-ina* (with long *ī*), fem. of *-inus* (with long *ī*) of or belonging to] **1** : ¹-ITE 4 ⟨hatchett*ine*⟩ **2** : chemical substance: as **a** : chemical element — in names of the halogens ⟨astat*ine*⟩ ⟨chlor*ine*⟩ **b** (1) : basic carbon compound — in names of alkaloids ⟨quin*ine*⟩ or other organic nitrogenous bases ⟨anil*ine*⟩ ⟨guanid*ine*⟩ including six-membered ring compounds ⟨pyrid*ine*⟩ and intermediate hydrogenated forms of cyclic compounds ⟨pyrrol*ine*⟩ ⟨thiazol*ine*⟩ — usu. distinguished from *-in* (2) : carbon compound containing a basic group — in names of amino acids ⟨glyc*ine*⟩ ⟨cyst*ine*⟩ **c** : mixture of chemical compounds — esp. in commercial names (as of mixtures of hydrocarbons) ⟨gasol*ine*⟩ ⟨keros*ine*⟩ **d** : -YNE **e** : hydride ⟨ars*ine*⟩ **3** : -IN 1a — not used systematically **4** : commercial product or material ⟨glass*ine*⟩

**³-ine** — see ²-INA

**⁴-ine** \,ēn\ *n suffix* -s [ME *-ina, -ine, -in* (in feminine given names), fr. OE *-ina* (in feminine given names), fr. L *-ina* (with long *ī*, in feminine names such as *Agrippina*), fr. fem. of *-inus* (with long *ī*) of or belonging to] : female person ⟨chor*ine*⟩ ⟨dud*ine*⟩

**-in·e·ae** \ˈinē,ē\ *n pl suffix* [NL, fr. L, fem. pl. of *-ineus* (as in *gramineus* gramineous)] : plants including those of (such) a genus ⟨Abiet*ineae*⟩ : plants characterized by (such) a feature ⟨Dinocaps*ineae*⟩ — in names of botanical suborders

**in·earth** \ən+\ *vt* [²*in-* + *earth* (n.)] *archaic* : BURY, INTER

**¹in·ebri·ant** \əˈnēbrēənt\ *n* -s [L *inebriant-, inebrians*, pres. part. of *inebriare* to make drunk] : INTOXICANT

**²inebriant** \"\ *adj* [L *inebriant-, inebrians*, pres. part. of *inebriare*] : INTOXICATING

**¹in·ebri·ate** \-brē,āt, *usu* -ād.+V\ *vt* -ED/-ING/-S [L *inebriatus*, past part. of *inebriare*, fr. *in-* ²in- + *ebriare* to intoxicate, fr. *ebrius* drunk — more at SOBER] **1** : to make drunk : INTOXICATE **2** : to disorder the senses of : exhilarate as if by liquor : deprive of sense and judgment ⟨*inebriated* by his own verbosity —N.A.Jones⟩

**²in·ebri·ate** \-brēə̇t, -ē,āt, *usu* |d.+V\ *adj* [L *inebriatus*] **1** : INTOXICATED, DRUNK **2** : addicted to drinking to excess

**³inebriate** \"\ *n* -s : one who is drunk or intoxicated; *esp* : an habitual drunkard ⟨an asylum for ~*s*⟩

**inebriated** *adj* : exhilarated or confused by or as if by alcohol : TIPSY, INTOXICATED ⟨drinking steadily ... getting neither more nor less ~ —Herman Melville⟩ ⟨~ with the exuberance of his own verbosity —Benjamin Disraeli⟩ **syn** see DRUNK

**in·ebri·a·tion** \ə,nēbrēˈāshən\ *n* -s [LL *inebriation-, inebriatio*, fr. *inebriatus* + *-ion-, -io* -ion] **1** : the action of inebriating or the condition of being inebriated **2** : habitual intoxication : DRUNKENNESS

**in·ebri·ety** \,inəˈbrīəd.|ē, -īət|, |i\ *n* [prob. blend of *inebriation* and *ebriety*] : INEBRIATION, INTOXICATION ⟨the only opportunities for ~ were the visits to town —P.A. Rollins⟩ : DRUNKENNESS ⟨public facilities for dealing with ~ —Robert Straus & R.G.McCarthy⟩

**in·ebri·ous** \əˈnēbrēəs\ *adj* [perh. blend of *inebriation* and obs. E *ebrious* addicted to drink, drunk, fr. L *ebrius* drunk] **1** *obs* : INEBRIATING **2** : INEBRIATED, INTOXICATED **3** : addicted to drink

**ined** *abbr* [L *ineditus*] unpublished

**in·edible** \(ˈ)in, ən+\ *adj* [¹*in-* + *edible*] : not edible : not fit for food

**in·ed·i·ta** \(ˈ)iˈnedəd·ə, -ətə\ *n pl* [NL, fr. L, neut. pl. of *ineditus* not made known, fr. *in-* ¹in- + *editus*, past part. of *edere* to proclaim, publish — more at EDITION] : unpublished literary material

**in·edited** \(ˈ)in, ən +\ *adj* [NL *ineditus* + E *-ed*] : UNPUBLISHED ⟨~ document⟩ ⟨~ letters⟩

**in·educabilia** \(,)in, ən+\ *n pl, cap* [NL, fr. ¹*in-* + *Educabilia*] *in former classifications* : a superorder of placental mammals including the bats, rodents, edentates, and insectivores in which the brain is less developed than in the Educabilia

**in·educability** \"+\ *n* : the quality or state of being ineducable

**in·educable** \(ˈ)in, ən+\ *adj* [¹*in-* + *educable*] : incapable of being educated; *esp* : mentally retarded or psychologically disturbed so as to be unable to benefit from education provided for the normal majority

**in·education** \(,)in, ən+\ *n* [¹*in-* + *education*] : lack of education

**in·ef·fa·bil·i·ty** \(,)i,nefəˈbiləd·ē, ə,n-, -lətē, -i\ *n* -ES : the quality or state of being ineffable

**¹in·effable** \(ˈ)in, ən+\ *adj* [ME, fr. MF, fr. L *ineffabilis*, fr. *in-* ¹in- + *effabilis* effable — more at EFFABLE] **1** : incapable of being expressed in words : UNUTTERABLE, INDESCRIBABLE ⟨~ joy⟩ ⟨~ torture⟩ : UNSPEAKABLE ⟨~ disgust⟩ ⟨~ bungler⟩ **2** : not to be uttered : TABOO ⟨the ~ name of Jehovah⟩ — **in·ef·fa·ble·ness** \-nə̇s\ *n* -ES — **in·ef·fa·bly** \-blē,-bli\ *adv*

**²ineffable** \"\ *n* -s : something that is ineffable

**in·ef·face·abil·i·ty** \,inə,fāsəˈbiləd·ē\ *n* -ES : the quality or state of being ineffaceable : INDELIBILITY

**in·effaceable** \,in+\ *adj* [prob. fr. F *ineffaçable*, fr. MF, fr. *in-* ¹in- + *effaçable* effaceable (fr. *effacer* to efface + *-able*) — more at EFFACE] : not effaceable : INDELIBLE, INERADICABLE — **in·ef·face·ably** \-blē,-bli\ *adv*

**¹in·effective** \,in+\ *adj* [¹*in-* + *effective*] **1** : not producing or incapable of producing an intended effect ⟨~ remedy⟩ **2** : not capable of performing the required work or duties : INCAPABLE ⟨~ figurehead⟩ ⟨~ troops⟩ **3** : lacking in aesthetic merit ⟨~ design⟩ — **in·effectively** \"+\ *adv* — **in·effectiveness** \"+\ *n*

**²ineffective** \"\ *n* : an ineffective person or thing : one unfit for service (as in an army)

**¹in·effectual** \,in+\ *adj* [ME, fr. ¹*in-* + *effectual*] : not effectual : not producing the proper or usual effect : INEFFECTIVE, FUTILE, UNAVAILING ⟨~ attempt⟩ ⟨~ expedient⟩ ⟨~ protests⟩ — **in·effectually** \"+\ *adv* — **in·effectualness** \"+\ *n*

**²ineffectual** \"\ *n* -s : INEFFECTIVE ⟨a program of training for the ~*s* —Eugene Davidoff⟩

**in·effectuality** \,in+\ *n* : the quality or state of being ineffectual

**in·efficacious** \(,)in, ən+\ *adj* [¹*in-* + *efficacious*] : not efficacious : lacking the power to produce a desired effect : INADEQUATE — **in·efficaciously** \"+\ *adv* — **in·efficaciousness** \"+\ *n*

**in·efficacity** \"+\ *n* [¹*in-* + *efficacity*] : INEFFICACY

**in·efficacy** \(ˈ)in, ən+\ *n* [LL *inefficacia*, fr. L *inefficac-, inefficax* inefficacious (fr. *in-* ¹in- + *efficac-, efficax* efficacious) + *-ia* -y — more at EFFICACIOUS] : lack of power to produce a desired or the proper effect : INEFFECTUALNESS ⟨~ of laws in preventing crime⟩

**in·efficiency** \,in+\ *n* [¹*in-* + *efficiency*] : the quality, state, or fact of being inefficient : lack of power or energy sufficient for a desired effect : INCAPACITY ⟨the ugliness and ~ of legal prose —Malcolm Muggeridge⟩ ⟨operations ... common to all printing processes have hidden in them great *inefficiencies* and enormous waste —P.R.Russell⟩

**¹in·efficient** \"+\ *adj* [¹*in-* + *efficient*] : not efficient: **a** : not producing the effect intended or desired : INEFFICACIOUS, INSUFFICIENT ⟨~ measures⟩ **b** : wasteful of time or energy in performing work ⟨statistics show that retailing ... is ~ —*Wall Street Jour.*⟩ **c** : incapable of or indisposed to the effective performance of duties ⟨~ workman⟩ — **in·efficiently** \"+\ *adv*

**²inefficient** \"\ *n* -s : an inefficient person

**in·egalitarian** \,in+\ *adj* [¹*in-* + *egalitarian*] : marked by disparity in economic and social standing ⟨assumed that society would be aristocratic and ~ ... that there would be a sufficiently large class of persons with independent incomes —Christopher Hollis⟩

**in·elaborate** \,in+\ *adj* [¹*in-* + *elaborate*] : not elaborate : SIMPLE

**in·elastic** \"+\ *adj* [¹*in-* + *elastic*] **1** : not elastic : slow to react or respond to changing conditions ⟨~ price structure⟩ ⟨~ demand for a commodity⟩ **2** : INFLEXIBLE, RIGID, UNYIELDING — **in·elasticity** \"+\ *n*

**inelastic collision** *n, physics* : a collision in which part of the kinetic energy of the colliding particles changes into another kind of energy (as radiation)

**inelastic scattering** *n, physics* : scattering of material particles due to collisions in which the total kinetic energy of the colliding particles increases or decreases

**in·elegance** \(ˈ)in, ən+\ *n* : the quality or state of being inelegant : lack of elegance : lack of refinement, beauty, or polish (as in language, manners)

**in·elegancy** \"+\ *n* **1** *archaic* : INELEGANCE **2** : something that is inelegant ⟨*inelegancies* of prose style⟩

**in·elegant** \"+\ *adj* [MF *inelegant*, fr. L *inelegant-, inelegans*, fr. *in-* ¹in- + *elegant-, elegans* elegant — more at ELEGANT] : not elegant : deficient in beauty, polish, refinement, grace, or ornament : lacking in something that correct taste requires — **in·elegantly** \"+\ *adv*

**in·eligibility** \(,)in, ən+\ *n* : the condition or fact of being ineligible

**¹in·eligible** \(ˈ)in, ən+\ *adj* [F *inéligible*, fr. *in-* ¹in- + *éligible* — more at ELIGIBLE] **1** : not eligible : not qualified to be chosen for an office : not worthy to be chosen or preferred ⟨~ for marriage⟩ ⟨~ for the football team⟩ **2** : not expedient or desirable ⟨shawls will be brought by injudicious mothers at precisely the most ~ moments —W.L.Alden⟩

**²ineligible** \"\ *n* : one that is ineligible

**ineligible paper** *n* : notes and bills that do not meet the requirements for discount or rediscount by the Federal Reserve banks

**in·eliminable** \,in+\ *adj* [¹*in-* + *eliminable*] : incapable of being eliminated or excluded

**in·eloquent** \(ˈ)in, ən+\ *adj* [¹*in-* + *eloquent*] : not eloquent : lacking in eloquence — **in·eloquently** \"+\ *adv*

**in·eluc·ta·bil·i·ty** \,inə,ləktəˈbiləd·ē\ *n* -ES : the quality or state of being ineluctable ⟨~ of fate⟩

**in·eluc·ta·ble** \,inəˈləktəbəl\ *adj* [L *ineluctabilis*, fr. *in-* ¹in- + *eluctari* to struggle out + *-abilis* -able — more at ELUCTATION] : not to be avoided, changed, or resisted : INESCAPABLE, INEVITABLE ⟨~ facts of human existence⟩ ⟨~ conclusions of logical deduction⟩ — **in·eluc·ta·bly** \-blē,-bli\ *adv*

**in·elud·ible** \,inēˈlüdəbəl\ *adj* [¹*in-* + *elude* + *-ible*] : INESCAPABLE — **in·elud·ibly** \-blē,-bli\ *adv*

**in·enar·ra·ble** \,inēˈnarəbəl\ *adj* [ME, fr. MF *inenarrable*, fr. L *inenarrabilis*, fr. *in-* ¹in- + *enarrabilis* capable of being explained, fr. *enarrare* to explain in detail + *-abilis* -able — more at ENARRATION] : incapable of being narrated : INDESCRIBABLE, INEFFABLE ⟨~ mystery of artistic creation —N.E.Nelson⟩

**in·ept** \(ˈ)iˈnept, əˈn-\ *adj* [F *inepte*, fr. L *ineptus*, fr. *in-* ¹in- + *aptus* apt — more at APT] **1** *archaic* : not apt or fit — often used with *to* or *for* **2** : not apt for the occasion : likely to fail in its purpose : out of place : INAPPROPRIATE ⟨an ~ and highly artificial comparison —Donald Wayne⟩ ⟨the square is one of those anomalous, shabby-ornate, ~, and pitifully pretentious places —Thomas Wolfe⟩ **3** : lacking sense or reason : FOOLISH, PREPOSTEROUS ⟨it is ~, absurd, downright silly, to argue that in a world torn by ... convulsions ... literature can hide away in a hothouse —J.T.Farrell⟩ **4 a** : lacking in skill or aptitude for a particular role or task ⟨an ~ farmer ... too easily distracted by contemplation —H.V.Gregory⟩ ⟨often a little ~, clumsy about the practical things of life —Rumer Godden⟩ **b** : generally incompetent : INADEQUATE, BUNGLING ⟨they found many English officers blundering ... the brave but ~ Braddock would have done well to take ... Washington's advice —Allan Nevins & H.S.Commager⟩ **5** *Scots law* : NULL, VOID **syn** see AWKWARD

**in·ep·ti·tude** \əˈneptə,tüd, -ptə,tyüd\ *n* -s [L *ineptitudo*, fr. *ineptus* inept + *-i-* + *-tudo* -tude] **1** : UNFITNESS, UNSUITABLENESS ⟨~ of a comparison⟩ ⟨~ that ought to have kept him out of business —Van Wyck Brooks⟩ **2** : a foolish action or utterance : ABSURDITY

**in·ept·ly** \-ptlē, -li\ *adv* : in an inept manner

**in·ept·ness** \-p(t)nə̇s\ *n* -ES : the quality or state of being inept

**in·equable** \(ˈ)in, ən+\ *adj* [L *inaequabilis*, fr. *in-* ¹in- + *aequabilis* equable — more at EQUABLE] : not evenly distributed : not uniform : UNFAIR

**in·equal** \"+\ *adj* [ME, fr. L *inaequalis*, fr. *in-* ¹in- + *aequalis* equal, fr. *aequus* even, equal] **1** *archaic* : UNEQUAL **2** : uneven in quality ⟨library of several ~ books —Holbrook Jackson⟩

**inequal hour** *n* [ME] : HOUR 5

**in·equalitarian** \,in+\ *adj* [fr. *inequality* + *-arian* (as in *equalitarian*)] : INEGALITARIAN ⟨privileged and leisured class, the product of a thoroughly ~ order of society —Walter Moberly⟩

**in·equality** \"+\ *n* [MF *inequalité*, fr. L *inaequalitat-, inaequalitas*, fr. *inaequalis* + *-itat-, -itas* -ity] **1** : the quality of being unequal or uneven : lack of equality: as **a** : UNEVENNESS ⟨hampered by the ~ of the ground⟩ **b** : social disparity ⟨combination of democracy with ~ —H.S.Commager⟩ **c** : disparity of distribution ⟨~ of income⟩ or opportunity ⟨educational ~⟩ **d** : VARIABLENESS, CHANGEABLENESS ⟨~ of temperament⟩ ⟨~ of the climate⟩ **2** : an instance of being unequal (as in position, proportion, evenness, regularity) ⟨*inequalities* of a surface⟩ **3** : an irregularity or a deviation in the motion of a planet or satellite; *also* : the amount of such deviation **4** : a statement of inequality between two quantities usu. with a sign of inequality (as $<$ or $>$ or $\neq$ signifying respectively *is less than, is greater than, is not equal to*) between them ($2<3$, $4>1$, and $a+b \neq$ are *inequalities*) **5** : difference in height of successive high or low tides due chiefly to the moon's declination — called also *diurnal inequality*

**in·equigranular** \(,)in, ən+\ *adj* [¹*in-* + *equigranular*] : having or characterized by crystals of different sizes ⟨a rock of ~ texture⟩

**in·equilateral** \"+\ *adj* [¹*in-* + *equilateral*] **1** : having the two ends unequal ⟨~ bivalve mollusk⟩ **2** : having the convolutions of the shell wound obliquely around an axis

**in·equitable** \(ˈ)in, ən+\ *adj* [¹*in-* + *equitable*] : not equitable : not just : contrary to principles of equity : UNFAIR ⟨~ taxation⟩ ⟨~ division of an estate among the heirs⟩ — **in·equitableness** \"+\ *n* — **in·equitably** \"+\ *adv*

**in·equity** \"+\ *n* [¹*in-* + *equity*] **1** : lack of equity : INJUSTICE, UNFAIRNESS **2** : an instance of injustice or unfairness ⟨adequate authority to correct maladjustments and *inequities* in wage rates —H.S.Truman⟩

**in·equivalve** \"+\ *also* **in·equi·valved** \-lvd\ *adj* [¹*in-* *equi-* + *valve* or *valved* (fr. *valve* + *-ed*)] *of a bivalve mollusk or its shell* : having the valves unequal in size and form

**in·eradicable** \,in+\ *adj* [¹*in-* + *eradicate* + *-able*] : incapable of being eradicated ⟨~ superstitions⟩ — **in·eradicableness** \"+\ *n* -ES — **in·eradicably** \"+\ *adv*

**in·erasable** \"+\ *adj* [¹*in-* + *erase* + *-able*] : incapable of being erased — **in·eras·able·ness** \-nə̇s\ *n* -ES — **in·eras·ably** \-blē,-bli\ *adv*

**in·er·get·ic** \,in(,)ərˈjed·ik\ *also* **in·er·get·i·cal** \-d·ə̇kəl\ *adj* [¹*in-* + *energetic*] *archaic* : lacking energy

**ineri** *usu cap, var of* IGNERI

**in·er·mia** \əˈnərmēə\ [NL, fr. L, neut. pl. of *inermis* unarmed, defenseless, fr. *in-* ¹in- + *-ermis* (fr. *arma* arms) — more at ARM] *syn of* SIPUNCULOIDEA

**in·er·mi·cap·si·fer** \ə,nərməˈkapsəfər\ *n, cap* [NL, fr. L *inermis* + *capsi-* (fr. L *capsa* chest, case) + *-fer* — more at CASE] : a genus of tapeworms (family Anoplocephalidae) parasitic in African and Central American rodents and occas. in man

**in·errability** \(,)in, ən+\ *n* : INFALLIBILITY

**in·errable** \(ˈ)in, ən+\ *adj* [L *inerrabilis*, fr. *in-* ¹in- + *errabilis* errable, fr. *errare* to err + *-abilis* -able — more at ERR] : incapable of erring : UNERRING **syn** see INFALLIBLE

**in·errancy** \"+\ *n* : exemption from error : INFALLIBILITY ⟨doctrine of the ~ of scripture writings —*Interpreter's Bible*⟩

**in·errant** \"+\ *adj* [L *inerrant-, inerrans* inerrant, fr. *in-* ¹in- + *errant-, errans*, pres. part. of *errare* to err — more at ERR] **1** *obs* : INERRATIC **2** : free from error or mistake : UNERRING **syn** see INFALLIBLE

**in·errantly** \"+\ *adv* : INFALLIBLY, UNERRINGLY

**in·erratic** \,in+\ *adj* [¹*in-* + *erratic*] : not erratic or wandering : following a set course : FIXED ⟨~ star⟩

**inerring** *adj* [¹*in-* + *erring*] *obs* : UNERRING

**¹in·ert** \(ˈ)iˈnər|t, əˈn-, -nə̄|, -nəi|, *usu* |d.+V\ *adj* [L *inert-, iners* unskilled, idle, motionless, fr. *in-* ¹in- + *art-, ars* skill, art — more at ARM] **1** : not having the power to move itself ⟨the Newtonian world which was composed of units, or atoms, that were material, ~, and all alike —S.F.Mason⟩ ⟨~ ammunition⟩ **2** : not having or manifesting active properties : not affecting other substances when in contact with them : chemically unreactive : powerless for an expected or desired biological effect ⟨~ drug⟩ : NEUTRAL **3** : very slow to move or act : LIFELESS, SLUGGISH, INDOLENT ⟨~ bureaucrats⟩ ⟨~ contemplation of television programs⟩ ⟨politically ~ citizenry⟩ **4** *of a paint pigment* : possessing little or no hiding power when ground in oil **syn** see INACTIVE

**²inert** \"\ *n* -s : an inert person, constituent, or material: as **a** : a noncombustible gas (as nitrogen or carbon dioxide) present in a gaseous fuel **b** : EXTENDER 1a (1)

**in·ert·ance** \|tᵊn(t)s\ *n* -s : ACOUSTIC INERTANCE

**inert gas** *n* **1** : a gas (as nitrogen or carbon dioxide) that is normally chemically inactive esp. in not burning or supporting combustion **2 a** : one of the group of gases comprising helium, neon, argon, krypton, xenon, and sometimes radon **b** : a member of the helium group — called also *noble gas, rare gas*

**in·er·tia** \əˈnərshə, -nə̄sh-, -nəish- *also* -shēə\ *n, pl* **iner·tias** \-əz\ *also* **iner·ti·ae** \-shē,ē\ [NL, fr. L, lack of skill, idleness, laziness, fr. *inert-, iners* + *-ia* -y] **1 a** : a property of matter by which it remains at rest or in uniform motion in the same straight line unless acted upon by some external force, any change in the motion being measured by the acceleration of the center of mass ⟨~ carried the train past the station⟩ **b** : an analogous property of other physical quantities (as electricity) ⟨electromagnetic ~⟩ **2** : indisposition to motion, exertion, or action : INERTNESS ⟨the Soviets had to overcome the deep-rooted conservatism and ~ of the peasants —A.R. Williams⟩ : resistance to change ⟨social ~, the tendency of animals to continue repeating the same action in the same place —W.C.Allee⟩ **3** : lack of activity : SLUGGISHNESS — used esp. of the uterus in labor when its contractions are weak or irregular **4** : the period of exposure before there is a detectable effect upon a photographic emulsion

**in·er·tial** \-sh(ē)əl\ *adj* [NL *inertia* + E *-al*] : of, relating to, or of the nature of inertia ⟨~ resistance to change of direction⟩

**inertial force** *n* : a force opposite in direction to an accelerating force acting on a body and equal to the product of the accelerating force and the mass of the body

**inertial guidance** *or* **inertial navigation** *n* : guidance (as of a missile or aircraft) by means of self-contained automatically controlling devices that respond to inertial forces

**inertial mass** *n* : mass as determined by impact experiments in accordance with the law that the masses of bodies are inversely proportional to the velocities which a given force will impart to them in a given time

**inertial system** *n* : a frame of reference with respect to which Newton's laws of motion are valid

**inertia starter** *n* : an internal-combustion engine starter that utilizes the energy of a spinning flywheel set in motion by means of a hand crank or electric motor

**in·er·tion** \-shən\ *n* -s [¹*inert* + *-ion* (as in *exertion*)] *archaic* : INERTNESS, QUIETUDE

**in·ert·ly** *adv* : in an inert manner : PASSIVELY, LIFELESSLY

**in·ert·ness** *n* -ES : the quality or state of being inert : lack of activity : PASSIVITY ⟨chemical ~ makes glass a good food container⟩

**in·erudite** \(ˈ)in, ən+\ *adj* [L *ineruditus*, fr. *in-* ¹in- + *eruditus* learned, skilled, experienced — more at ERUDITE] : not erudite : IGNORANT

**-ines** *pl of* -INE

**in·escapable** \,in+\ *adj* [¹*in-* + *escape* + *-able*] : incapable of being avoided, ignored, or denied ⟨the ~ mark of his genius —F.R.Leavis⟩ : UNAVOIDABLE : necessarily present or to be reckoned with : following of strict logical necessity or moral compulsion : INEVITABLE ⟨~ that a man must owe economic obligations to his wife and to his children —Weston La Barre⟩ ⟨continuity in design appears to be ~ —J.E.Gloag⟩ — **in·es·cap·able·ness** \-nə̇s\ *n* -ES — **in·es·cap·ably** \-blē,-bli\ *adv*

**in·esculent** \(ˈ)in, ən+\ *adj* [¹*in-* + *esculent*] : not esculent : INEDIBLE

**in·escutcheon** *also* **in·escucheon** \,in+\ *n* [⁴*in* + *escutcheon, escucheon*] : a small escutcheon borne within a shield

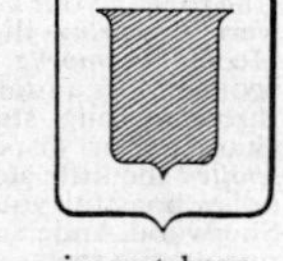

inescutcheon

**ines·ite** \ˈīnə,sīt, ˈin-, -,zīt\ *n* -s [G *inesit*, fr. Gk *ines* (pl. of *is* sinew, tendon) + G *-it* -ite — more at WITHY] : a mineral $Ca_2Mn_7Si_{10}O_{28}(OH)_2.5H_2O$ consisting of a pale red hydrous manganese calcium silicate, in small prismatic crystals or massive (hardness 6, sp. gr. 3.03)

**in es·se** \ə̇nˈesē\ *adv (or adj)* [ML] : in actual existence — contrasted with *in posse*

**¹in·essential** \,in+\ *adj* [¹*in-* + *essential*] **1** : having no essence or being **2** : not essential : UNESSENTIAL, NONESSENTIAL

**²inessential** \"\ *n* : something that is not essential : UNESSENTIAL

**in·essentiality** \,in+\ *n* : the quality or state of being inessential

**¹in·es·sive** \əˈnesiv\ *adj* [L *inesse* to be in (fr. *in-* ²in- + *esse* to be) + E *-ive* — more at IS] *of a grammatical case* : denoting position or location within

**²inessive** \"\ *n* : the inessive case of a substantive

**in·es·ti·ma·bil·i·ty** \(,)i,nestəməˈbiləd·ē, ə,n-\ *n* -ES : INESTIMABLENESS

**in·estimable** \(ˈ)in, ən+\ *adj* [ME, fr. MF, fr. L *inaestimabilis*, fr. *in-* ¹in- + *aestimabilis* estimable — more at ESTIMABLE] **1** : incapable of being estimated or computed ⟨~ errors⟩ **2** : too valuable or excellent to be measured or appreciated : above all price ⟨has performed an ~ service for his country⟩ — **in·estimable·ness** \"+\ *n* — **in·es·ti·ma·bly** \-blē,-bli\ *adv*

**in·euphonious** \,in+\ *adj* [¹*in-* + *euphonious*] : not euphonious : harsh in sound

**in·evaporable** \,in+\ *adj* [¹*in-* + *evaporable*] : incapable of being reduced in volume by evaporation

**in·eva·si·ble** \,inəˈvāzəbəl, -āsə-\ *adj* [¹*in-* + L *evasus* (past part. of *evadere* to evade) + E *-ible* — more at EVADE] : INEVITABLE

**in·evidence** \(ˈ)in, ən+\ *n* **1** *obs* : lack of evidence or manifestation **2** : the state or fact of being inevident

**in·evident** \"+\ *adj* [LL *inevident-, inevidens*, fr. L *in-* ¹in-

+ *evident-, evidens* evident — more at EVIDENT] **:** not evident **:** not clear or obvious

**in·ev·i·ta·bil·i·ty** \(,)i,nevəd·ə'biləd·ē, ə,n-, -v(ə)tə'-, -lətē, -i\ *n* -ES **:** the quality or state of being inevitable ⟨habits . . . seem to have all of the ~ that belongs to the movement of the fixed stars —John Dewey⟩ ⟨less inclined to accept the ~ of servitude —Ray Lewis & Angus Maude⟩

**¹in·ev·i·ta·ble** \ə'nevəd·əbəl, -v(ə)təb-\ *adj* [ME, fr. L *inevitabilis*, fr. *in-* ¹in- + *evitabilis* evitable — more at EVITABLE] **1 :** incapable of being avoided or evaded ⟨~ result⟩ ⟨~ day of reckoning⟩ **:** being or seeming to be in the natural order of things or foreordained ⟨~ phrase⟩ ⟨landscape, as an ~ expression of the Romantic spirit —F.J.Mather⟩ ⟨once we admit . . . that war is natural and ~ —Vera M. Dean⟩ **2 :** certain to occur or to confront one ⟨allowing for the ~ delays of such a journey⟩ ⟨the ~ gas stations at every crossroad⟩ ⟨over the pine mantel . . . were the ~ antlers —Gertrude Atherton⟩ — **in·ev·i·ta·ble·ness** \-nəs\ *n* -ES — **in·ev·i·ta·bly** \-blē, -bli\ *adv*

**²inevitable** \"\ *n* -s **:** something that is inevitable ⟨should the symptoms of aging be studied as the natural ~s of a cyclic process —Louis Berman⟩

**inevitable accident** *n, law* **:** an accident that could not have been foreseen or prevented by the due care and diligence of any human being involved in it **:** an accident caused by forces beyond the power of any human being involved to foresee or overcome by the exercise of ordinary prudence — compare ACT OF GOD

**in·exact** \¦in+\ *adj* [F, fr. *in-* ¹in- + *exact* — more at EXACT] **1 :** not exact **:** not precisely correct or true **:** INACCURATE ⟨~ translation⟩ **2 :** not rigorous and careful ⟨~ reasoner⟩ — **in·exactly** \"+\ *adv* — **in·exactness** \"+\ *n*

**in·exactitude** \"+\ *n* [F, fr. *in-* ¹in- + *exactitude* — more at EXACTITUDE] **1 :** lack of exactitude or precision **:** the quality of being inexact or inaccurate **2 :** an instance of inexactness

**in ex·cel·sis** \,in,ək'selsəs, ,i(,)nek-, -ks'kel-,-ks'chel-,-k'shel-\ *adv* [L] **:** in the highest degree **:** SUPERLATIVELY ⟨he had *in excelsis* what some people term . . . the legal mind —*Blackwood's*⟩

**in·excitability** \¦in+\ *n* **:** calmness of temper

**in·excitable** \"+\ *adj* [¹*in-* + *excitable*] **1 :** not readily excited or aroused **2** *of a nerve* **:** not subject to excitation **:** not responsive to stimulation

**in·excusability** \"+\ *n* -ES **1 :** the quality of being inexcusable **2 :** something that is inexcusable

**in·excusable** \"+\ *adj* [L *inexcusabilis*, fr. *in-* ¹in- + *excusabilis* excusable — more at EXCUSABLE] **:** not excusable **:** being without excuse or justification ⟨~ carelessness⟩ — **in·excusableness** \"+\ *n* — **in·excusably** \"+\ *adv*

**in·executable** \(¦)in, ən+\ *adj* [¹*in-* + *executable*] **:** impossible of execution or performance **:** IMPRACTICABLE

**in·execution** \"+\ *n* [prob. fr. F *inexécution*, fr. MF *inexecution*, fr. *in-* ¹in- + *execution* — more at EXECUTION] **:** failure to carry out (as an order) or enforce (as a law) **:** NONPERFORMANCE

**in·exertion** \¦in+\ *n* [¹*in-* + *exertion*] **:** lack of exertion or effort **:** INDOLENCE, LAZINESS

**in·exhausted** \"+\ *adj* [¹*in-* + *exhausted*] *archaic* **:** that is not exhausted

**in·exhaustibility** \"+\ *n* **:** the quality or state of being inexhaustible **:** UNFAILINGNESS

**in·exhaustible** \"+\ *adj* [¹*in-* + *exhaust* + *-ible*] **:** not exhaustible: as **a :** incapable of being used up **:** UNFAILING ⟨~ supplies of coal⟩ ⟨an ~ spring⟩ **b :** incapable of being wearied or worn out ⟨~ fertility of invention⟩ ⟨~ patience⟩ — **in·ex·haust·ible·ness** \-nəs\ *n* -ES — **in·ex·haust·ibly** \-blē, -bli\ *adv*

**in·exhaustive** \¦in+\ *adj* [¹*in-* + *exhaustive*] **1** *archaic* **:** INEXHAUSTIBLE **2 :** not exhaustive — **in·exhaustively** \"+\ *adv*

**in·exhaustless** \"+\ *adj* [¹*in-* + *exhaustless*] *archaic* **:** EXHAUSTLESS

**in·exigible** \(')in, ən+\ *adj* [¹*in-* + *exigible*] **:** not exigible

**in·exist** \¦in+\ *vi* [²*in-* + *exist*] *archaic* **:** to exist in something else **:** INHERE

**¹in·existence** \"+\ *n* [¹*in-* + *existence*] **:** NONEXISTENCE

**²inexistence** \"+\ *n* [²*in-* + *existence*] *archaic* **:** INHERENCE

**¹in·existent** \¦in+\ *adj* [LL *inexsistent-, inexistent-, inexsistens, inexistens*, fr. L *in-* ²in- + *exsistent-, existent-, exsistens, existens*, pres. part. of *exsistere, existere* to exist — more at EXIST] *archaic* **:** INHERENT

**²inexistent** \"\ *adj* [LL *inexistent-, inexsistent-, inexistens, inexsistens*, fr. L *in-* + *existent-, exsistent-, existens, exsistens*] **:** not having being **:** NONEXISTENT

**in·ex·o·ra·bil·i·ty** \(,)i,neks(ə)rə'biləd·ē, ə,n-, -lətē, -i *also* -negz(- *sometimes* ,inig,zȯr- *or* ,i(,)neg,zȯr- *or* ¦zȯr-\ *n* -ES [L *inexorabilitas*, fr. *inexorabilis* + *-itas* -ity] **:** the quality of being inexorable ⟨moral world of humans does not behave with the same rigor and ~ as the physical world —Weston La Barre⟩

**in·ex·o·ra·ble** \(')i¦neks(ə)rəbəl, ə'n- *also* -negz(- *sometimes* ¦inig¦zȯr- *or* ¦i(,)neg¦zȯr- *or* -¦zȯr-\ *adj* [L *inexorabilis*, fr. *in-* ¹in- + *exorabilis* exorable, fr. *exorare* to prevail upon, persuade (fr. *ex-* ¹ex- + *orare* to speak, plead, pray) + *-abilis* -able — more at ORATION] **:** not to be persuaded or moved by entreaty or prayer **:** UNYIELDING, INFLEXIBLE, RELENTLESS ⟨~ doom⟩ ⟨~ logic⟩ ⟨~ necessity⟩ ⟨~ opponent⟩ — **in·ex·o·ra·ble·ness** \-nəs\ *n* -ES — **in·ex·o·ra·bly** \-blē,-bli\ *adv*

**in·expansible** \¦in+\ *adj* [¹*in-* + *expansible*] **:** not expansible

**in·expectancy** \"+\ *n* [¹*in-* + *expectancy*] **:** lack of expectancy ⟨it isn't surfeit alone but ~ which makes entertainment so feeble —J.M.Barzun⟩

**in·expectant** \"+\ *adj* [¹*in-* + *expectant*] **:** lacking expectation ⟨small ~ audience⟩

**in·expediency** *or* **in·expedience** \"+\ *n* [¹*in-* + *expediency, expedience*] **:** the quality or fact of being inexpedient

**in·expedient** \"+\ *adj* [¹*in-* + *expedient*] **1 :** not expedient **:** not likely to achieve a purpose or bring success **:** INADVISABLE, UNPROFITABLE ⟨to rely on a deterrent that will bring the maximum of suffering to all mankind is immoral as well as ~ —Denis Healey⟩ **2 :** INCONVENIENT ⟨it was occasionally ~ to carry about measuring chains —Rudyard Kipling⟩ — **in·expediently** \"+\ *adv*

**in·expensive** \"+\ *adj* [¹*in-* + *expensive*] **:** not expensive **:** reasonable in price **:** CHEAP — **in·expensively** \"+\ *adv* — **in·expensiveness** \"+\ *n*

**in·experience** \"+\ *n* [MF, fr. LL *inexperientia*, fr. L *in-* ¹in- + *experientia* experience — more at EXPERIENCE] **:** lack of experience **:** lack of knowledge of the ways of the world or of a particular kind of work or activity

**in·experienced** \"+\ *adj* **:** lacking practical experience **:** UNTRAINED, UNTRIED, GREEN

**¹in·expert** \(¦)in, ən+\ *adj* [ME *inexperte*, fr. MF *inexpert*, fr. L *inexpertus*, fr. *in-* ¹in- + *expertus*, past part. of *experiri* to try — more at EXPERIENCE] **1 :** INEXPERIENCED **2 :** not expert **:** not skilled or dexterous — **in·expertly** \"+\ *adv* — **in·expertness** \"+\ *n*

**²in·expert** \ən+\ *n* **:** an inexpert person **:** NOVICE

**in·expiable** \(')in, ən+\ *adj* [L *inexpiabilis*, fr. *in-* ¹in- + *expiare* to expiate + *-abilis* -able — more at EXPIATE] **1 :** not capable of being expiated or atoned for **:** UNFORGIVABLE ⟨~ offense⟩ **2** *obs* **:** IMPLACABLE, UNAPPEASABLE — **in·ex·pi·a·ble·ness** \-nəs\ *n* -ES — **in·ex·pi·a·bly** \-blē,-bli\ *adv*

**in·expiate** \"+\ *adj* [LL *inexpiatus*, fr. L *in-* ¹in- + *expiatus*, past part. of *expiare*] **1 :** not expiated **2** *obs* **:** not appeased

**in·explainable** \¦in+\ *adj* [¹*in-* + *explainable*] **:** INEXPLICABLE

**in·explicability** \(¦)in, ən+\ *n* -ES **:** the quality of being inexplicable

**in·explicable** \"+\ *adj* [MF, fr. L *inexplicabilis*, fr. *in-* ¹in- + *explicabilis* explicable — more at EXPLICABLE] **1** *obs* **:** incapable of being unfolded or unraveled **:** INEXTRICABLE **2 :** not explicable **:** incapable of being explained, interpreted, or accounted for ⟨~ action⟩ ⟨~ mystery⟩ — **in·ex·plica·ble·ness** \-nəs\ *n* -ES — **in·ex·plica·bly** \-blē,-bli\ *adv*

**in·explicit** \¦in+ (,)=¦=+\ *adj* [¹*in-* + *explicit*] **:** not explicit — **in·ex·plic·it·ly** *adv* — **in·ex·plic·it·ness** *n*

**in·explosive** \¦in+\ *adj* [¹*in-* + *explosive*] **:** not liable to explode

**in·exportable** \(¦)in, ən+\ *adj* [¹*in-* + *exportable*] **:** not capable of being exported **:** not suitable for export

**in·expressibility** \¦in+\ *n* -ES **:** the quality of being inexpressible

**in·expressible** \"+\ *adj* [¹*in-* + *expressible*] **:** not capable of being expressed **:** INDESCRIBABLE, INEFFABLE ⟨~ delight⟩ **:** UNUTTERABLE, UNSPEAKABLE ⟨~ villainy⟩ — **in·ex·press·ible·ness** \-nəs\ *n* -ES — **in·ex·press·ibly** \-blē,-bli\ *adv*

**in·ex·press·ibles** \¦=,=='==bəlz\ *n pl, archaic* **:** TROUSERS

**in·expressive** \¦in+\ *adj* [¹*in-* + *expressive*] **1** *obs* **:** INEXPRESSIBLE **2 :** lacking expression **:** not expressive **:** DULL, WOODEN ⟨~ face⟩ **3 :** lacking meaning ⟨~ music⟩ ⟨~ gestures⟩ — **in·expressively** \"+\ *adv* — **in·expressiveness** \"+\ *n*

**in·ex·pugna·bil·i·ty** \,inik,spyünə'biləd·ē, ,i(,)nek-,-,spəgnə-\ *n* -ES **:** IMPREGNABILITY

**in·expugnable** \¦in+\ *adj* [MF, fr. L *inexpugnabilis*, fr. *in-* ¹in- + *expugnabilis* expugnable — more at EXPUGNABLE] **1 :** incapable of being taken by assault or subdued by force **:** IMPREGNABLE ⟨his position though strong was not ~ —G.B. Sansom⟩ **2 :** incapable of being overthrown or driven out ⟨most common and ~ error of criticism —Meyer Schapiro⟩ **:** STABLE, FIXED ⟨~ hatred⟩ — **in·ex·pugna·ble·ness** \-nəs\ *n* -ES — **in·ex·pugna·bly** \-blē,-bli\ *adv*

**in·ex·pung·ibil·i·ty** \¦=(,)=,=='biləd·ē\ *n* -ES **:** the quality or state of being inexpungible **:** INERADICABLENESS, INDELIBILITY ⟨~ of popular myths⟩

**in·ex·pung·ible** *also* **in·ex·punge·able** \¦inik¦spənjəbəl, ¦i(,)nek-\ *adj* [¹*in-* + *expunge* + *-ible, -able*] **:** incapable of being obliterated or got rid of ⟨~ scent of a bottle of perfume he had . . . broken —Louis Auchincloss⟩

**in·extended** \¦in+\ *adj* [¹*in-* + *extended*] **:** lacking extension **:** not occupying space

**in·extensibility** \"+\ *n* [¹*in-* + *extensibility*] **:** incapability of being drawn out or stretched ⟨~ of a rope⟩

**in·extensible** \"+\ *adj* [¹*in-* + *extensible*] **:** not extensible **:** incapable of being stretched

**in·extensile** \"+\ *adj* [¹*in-* + *extensile*] **:** not extensible

**in·extension** \"+\ *n* [¹*in-* + *extension*] **:** lack of extension

**in·extensional** \"+\ *adj* **:** marked by or relating to absence of stretching out

**inextensional deformation** *n* **:** a bending of a surface that preserves unchanged the length of each line element and the measure of curvature at every point

**in·extensive** \¦in+\ *adj* [¹*in-* + *extensive*] **:** not extensive

**in ex·ten·so** \,inik'sten(t)(,)sō, ,i(,)nek-\ *adv* [L] **:** at length rather than in summary ⟨the details of all the observations will be reported *in extenso* elsewhere —*Science*⟩

**in·exterminable** \¦in+\ *adj* [LL *inexterminabilis*, fr. L *in-* ¹in- + LL *exterminabilis* capable of being exterminated, exterminable, fr. L *exterminare* to exterminate + *-abilis* -able — more at EXTERMINATE] **1** *obs* **:** INTERMINABLE **2 :** incapable of extermination

**in·extinct** \"+(,)=¦=\ *adj* [L *inexstinctus, inextinctus*, fr. *in-* ¹in- + *exstinctus, extinctus*, past part. of *exstinguere, extinguere* to extinguish — more at EXTINGUISH] **:** UNEXTINGUISHED

**in·extinguishable** \¦in+\ *adj* [¹*in-* + *extinguishable*] **:** not extinguishable ⟨~ flame⟩ **:** UNQUENCHABLE, IRREPRESSIBLE ⟨~ hope⟩ ⟨~ laughter⟩ — **in·extinguishably** \"+\ *adv*

**in·ex·tir·pa·ble** \(¦)i¦nekstərpəbəl, ə'n-; ¦i(,)nek¦s-\ *adj* [F or L; F, fr. L *inexstirpabilis, inextirpabilis*, fr. *in-* ¹in- + *exstirpare, extirpare* to extirpate + *-abilis* -able — more at EXTIRPATE] **:** not capable of being extirpated **:** INERADICABLE — **in·ex·tir·pa·ble·ness** \-nəs\ *n* -ES

**in ex·tre·mis** \,inik'strāməs, ,i(,)nek-, -rēm-\ *adv* [L] **:** in extreme circumstances **:** in desperate case; *esp* **:** at the point of death

**in·extricability** \(¦)in, ən+\ *n* -ES **:** the quality or state of being inextricable ⟨~ of form and content —Peter Viereck⟩

**in·extricable** \"+\ *adj* [MF or L; MF, fr. L *inextricabilis*, fr. *in-* ¹in- + *extricabilis* extricable — more at EXTRICABLE] **1 :** not permitting extrication **:** forming a maze or tangle from which it is impossible to get free **2 a :** incapable of being disentangled or untied ⟨~ knot⟩ ⟨~ unity⟩ **b :** UNSOLVABLE ⟨~ confusion⟩ **3 :** INTRICATE, INVOLVED **:** highly elaborated ⟨~ design⟩ — **in·ex·trica·ble·ness** \-nəs\ *n* -ES — **in·ex·trica·bly** \-blē,-bli\ *adv*

**inf** *abbr* **1** infantry **2** inferior **3** infield; infielder **4** infinitive **5** infinity **6** infirmary **7** information **8** infra **9** infused; infusion

**inface** \'=,=\ *n* [⁴*in* + *face*] **:** the steeper of the two slopes of a cuesta

**in fa·cie cu·ri·ae** \-'fāshē,ē'kyu̇rē,ē\ *adv* [ML] **:** before or in the presence of the court

**infall** \'=,=\ *n* [⁴*in* + *fall*] **1 :** INCURSION ⟨~ of pirates⟩ **2 :** INLET, CONFLUENCE, JUNCTION **3 :** a falling into or on ⟨~ of meteorites⟩ ⟨~ of a cavern roof⟩

**in·fallibilism** \(¦)in+\ *n* **1 :** support of or adherence to the dogma of papal infallibility **2 :** a belief that scientific laws are not subject to change — opposed to *fallibilism*

**in·fallibilist** \"+\ *n* **1 :** one who believes in infallibility; *esp* **:** a supporter of the dogma of papal infallibility **2 :** one who believes that scientific laws are not subject to change

**in·fallibility** \(¦)in+\ *n* [ML *infallibilitas*, fr. *infallibilis* infallible + L *-itas* -ity] **:** the quality or state of being infallible

**in·fallible** \(')in, ən+\ *adj* [ML *infallibilis*, fr. L *in-* ¹in- + LL *fallibilis* fallible — more at FALLIBLE] **1 :** not fallible **:** incapable of error **:** UNERRING ⟨~ marksman⟩ ⟨~ ear for pitch in music⟩ ⟨~ memory⟩ **2 :** not liable to mislead, deceive, or disappoint **:** SURE, CERTAIN, INDUBITABLE ⟨~ remedy⟩ ⟨his accent is an almost ~ index of his family background and education —Richard Joseph⟩ ⟨~ scheme for making money⟩ **3 :** incapable of error in defining doctrines touching faith or morals

**syn** INERRABLE, INERRANT, UNERRING: INFALLIBLE describes that which is exempt from possibility of error or mistake or that which has been errorless ⟨no mathematician is *infallible;* he may make mistakes —A.S.Eddington⟩ ⟨believed in an *infallible* Bible —W.W.Sweet⟩ INERRABLE and INERRANT are erudite synonyms for INFALLIBLE sometimes used in its stead to escape connotations arising from the discussion of papal infallibility; the latter may imply that whatever is described has not so far erred ⟨the Church was ubiquitous, omniscient, theoretically *inerrant* and omnicompetent —G.G.Coulton⟩ ⟨at the moment we lack, in all English-speaking countries, the *inerrant* literary sense which gave us the Prayer Book Collects, often quite as beautiful in translation as in the original Latin —W.L.Sperry⟩ UNERRING may imply freedom from error coupled with sureness, reliability, and exactness ⟨an *unerring* marksman⟩ ⟨a man's language is an *unerring* index of his nature —Laurence Binyon⟩ ⟨the *unerring* scent of the hounds in pursuit —George Meredith⟩

**in·fal·li·ble·ness** *n* **:** INFALLIBILITY

**in·fallibly** \"+\ *adj* **:** without fail **:** SURELY, CERTAINLY ⟨must make the proper use of his opportunities or he will ~ perish —A.C.McGiffert⟩

**in·fam·a·tory** \ən'famə,tōrē, -tȯr-\ *adj* [ML *infamatorius*, fr. L *infamatus* (past part. of *infamare*) + *-orius* -ory] *archaic* **:** DEFAMATORY

**in·fame** \ən'fām\ *vt* -ED/-ING/-S [ME *enfamen*, fr. MF *enfamer, infamer*, fr. L *infamare*, fr. *infamis*] *archaic* **:** DEFAME

**in·fa·mize** \'infə,mīz\ *vt* -ED/-ING/-S [*infamous* + *-ize*] *archaic* **:** to make infamous **:** DEFAME

**in·fa·mous** \'infəməs\ *adj* [ME *infamis, infamous*, fr. L *infamis*, fr. *in-* ¹in- + *-famis* (fr. *fama* fame) — more at FAME] **1 :** having a reputation of the worst kind **:** notorious as being of vicious, contemptible, or criminal character **:** DETESTABLE, ABHORRENT ⟨one of the most ~ spies and bullies of all time —*Time*⟩ ⟨~ outlaw⟩ ⟨~ traitor⟩ ⟨~ dog has got every vice except hypocrisy —W.M.Thackeray⟩ **2 :** causing or bringing infamy **:** deserving hatred or detestation ⟨~ conduct⟩ ⟨~ vices⟩ ⟨~ treatment of prisoners⟩ ⟨men to whom totalitarianism is ~ —Jerome Frank⟩ ⟨most ~ of quack nostrums —*Time*⟩ **3 :** having a bad name as being associated with something disgraceful or detestable ⟨the street outside Newgate had not obtained one ~ notoriety that has since attached to it —Charles Dickens⟩ **4 :** convicted of an offense judged infamous ⟨~ person⟩ **syn** see VICIOUS

**infamous crime** *n* **:** a crime judged infamous because it constitutes treason or a felony, because it involves moral turpitude of a nature that creates a strong presumption that the one guilty is unworthy of belief in a court of law, or because it subjects the one guilty to infamy ⟨no person shall be held to answer for a capital or otherwise *infamous crime*, unless on a presentment or indictment of a grand jury, except in cases arising in the land or naval forces, or in the militia, when in actual service in time of war or public danger —*U.S.Constitution*⟩

**infamous crime against nature :** SODOMY

**in·fa·mous·ly** *adv* **:** in an infamous manner **:** in a manner deserving infamy ⟨how ~ he treats his wife —George Meredith⟩ **:** ATROCIOUSLY ⟨just as the work was nearly completed, being ~ done, it fell down again —L.H.Chambers⟩

**in·fa·my** \'infəmē, -mi\ *n* -ES [ME *infamye*, fr. MF *infamie*, fr. L *infamia*, fr. *infamis* + *-ia* -y] **1 a :** a lasting, widespread, and deep-rooted evil reputation brought about by something criminal, shocking, or brutal **:** the highest degree of dishonor ⟨a series of treacherous murders added to his ~⟩ **b :** an indication of such notoriety **:** strong condemnatory utterance **2 a :** an extreme and publicly known criminal, shocking, or brutal act ⟨an ~ greater than any mutiny⟩ **b :** the state or condition of being rightly and widely known for such an act ⟨his name will live in ~ for this night's work⟩ **3 :** the public disgrace or loss of character and honor or loss of civil or political rights incurred by a person convicted of an infamous crime **syn** see DISHONOR

**in·fan·cy** \'infənsē, -si\ *n* -ES [ME, fr. L *infantia*, fr. *infant-, infans* infant + *-ia* -y] **1 :** the state or period of being an infant **:** the first part of life **:** early childhood — called also *babyhood* **2 :** the beginning or early period of existence ⟨mechanical engineering was then in its ~ —O.S.Nock⟩ ⟨~ of a city⟩ **3 :** the legal status of an infant or one under age or under the age of twenty-one years **:** NONAGE, MINORITY **4 :** the initial or very early stage (as of a river) in a cycle of erosion

**infang** *n* -S [by shortening] *obs* **:** INFANGTHIEF

**in·fang·thief** \'infaŋ,thēf\ *n* [ME *infangenthef, infangthef*, fr. OE *infangenthēof, infangenthēof*, fr. *in, inn* in + *fangen* (past part. of *fōn* to seize, capture) + *thēof* thief — more at IN, PACT, THIEF] **:** a medieval franchise of exercising jurisdiction over a thief caught within the limits to which the franchise was attached **:** the right of the lord of a manor to judge a thief taken within the seigniory of such lord — distinguished from *outfangthief*

**in·fans** \'in,fanz\ *n, pl* **infan·tes** \ən'fan,,tēz\ [L] *civil law* **:** a child under seven years of age **:** a child not having the ability to speak

**¹in·fant** \'infənt\ *n* -S [ME *enfaunt, infaunt*, fr. MF *enfant*, fr. L *infant-, infans*, fr. *infant-, infans*, adj., incapable of speech, young, fr. *in-* ¹in- + *fant-, fans*, pres. part. of *fari* to speak — more at BAN] **1 a :** a child in the first year of life **:** BABY **b :** a child several years of age **2 a :** a person who is not of full age **:** MINOR **b** *common law* **:** a person under the age of 21 — see AGE 3 **3** *Brit* **:** a pupil in an infant school

**²infant** \"\ *adj* **1 :** of, relating to, exemplifying, or being in infancy or young childhood ⟨~ king⟩ ⟨~ martyr⟩ **2 :** being in an early stage of development **:** not matured or fully developed ⟨~ fruit⟩ ⟨~ navy⟩; *esp* **:** needing protection and care ⟨~ animals⟩ ⟨our ~ steel industry⟩

**¹in·fan·ta** \ən'fantə\ *n* -S [Sp & Pg, fem. of *infante*] **1 :** a daughter of the king and queen of Spain or Portugal **2 :** the wife of an infante

**²infanta** \"\ *adj, of a fashion in dress* **:** derived from Velasquez's portraits of 17th century Spanish princesses and usu. having wide skirts with side extensions

**in·fan·te** \ən'fan,tā\ *n* -S [Sp & Pg, lit., infant, fr. L *infant-, infans*] **:** a son of the king and queen of Spain or Portugal who is not the eldest — compare PRINCIPE

**in·fant·hood** \'infənt,hu̇d\ *n* **:** INFANCY

**in·fan·ti·ci·dal** \ən¦fantə¦sīdᵊl\ *adj* **:** relating to the killing of infants

**¹in·fanticide** \ən'fantə,sīd\ *n* -S [LL *infanticidium*, fr. L *infant-, infans* infant + *-i-* + *-cidium* -cide (killing) — more at INFANT] **1 :** a killing of a newly or recently born child **2 :** a practice of killing infants — compare ABORTION 1, FETICIDE

**²infanticide** \"\ *n* -S [LL *infanticida*, fr. L *infant-, infans* + *-i-* + *-cida* -cide (killer)] **:** one that kills an infant

**in·fan·tile** \'infən,tīl *also* -n·təl *sometimes* -n,tēl *or* -n·(,)til\ *adj* [prob. fr. F, fr. L *infantilis*, fr. *infant-, infans* infant + *-ilis* -ile] **1 :** of or relating to infants or infancy ⟨~ disease⟩ ⟨~ state⟩ **2 :** suitable to an infant **:** characteristic of an infant **:** very immature **:** CHILDISH ⟨~ level of entertainment⟩ ⟨~ tantrum⟩ **3 :** affected with infantilism **4** *of topography* **:** being in a very early stage of development presumably following an uplift or equivalent change with respect to base level ⟨~ stream⟩ ⟨~ drainage⟩

**infantile myxedema** *n* **:** CRETINISM

**infantile paralysis** *n* **:** POLIOMYELITIS

**infantile sexuality** *n* **:** needs and strivings in early childhood for libidinal gratification **:** pregenital eroticism

**in·fan·ti·lism** \'infən·tə,lizəm *sometimes* ən'fantᵊl,i-\ *n* -S [ISV *infantile* + *-ism*] **1 :** a condition of being abnormally childlike **:** a retention of childish physical, mental, or emotional qualities in adult life; *esp* **:** failure to attain sexual maturity **2 :** an act or expression characteristic of lack of maturity **:** PUERILITY ⟨~s of thought⟩ ⟨the ~ of selfishness —Agnes E. Meyer⟩

**in·fan·ti·lis·tic** \¦infəntə'listik\ *adj* **:** abnormally immature **:** showing infantile behavior

**in·fan·til·i·ty** \,infən·'tiləd·ē\ *n* -ES [ML *infantilitas*, fr. L *infantilis* infantile + *-itas* -ity] **:** the quality or state of being infantile **:** CHILDISHNESS

**in·fan·tine** \'infən,tīn, -tēn\ *adj* [F *infantin*, fr. MF, alter. (influenced by L *infant-, infans* infant) of *enfantin*, fr. OF, fr. *enfant* infant + *-in* -ine — more at INFANT] **:** INFANTILE ⟨~ wailing⟩ **:** CHILDISH

**infant mortality** *n* **:** the rate of deaths occurring in the first year of life

**in·fan·try** \'infən·trē, -ri\ *n* -ES [MF & OIt; MF *infanterie*, fr. OIt *infanteria*, fr. *infante* infant, boy, footman, foot soldier (fr. L *infant-, infans* infant) + *-eria* -ry — more at INFANT] **1 a :** soldiers trained, armed, and equipped to fight on foot **b :** a branch of an army composed of such soldiers **c :** an infantry regiment ⟨the 8th *Infantry*⟩ **d :** MOONLIGHT BLUE **2** [influenced in meaning by ¹*infant*] **:** a body of children

**in·fan·try·man** \-mən\ *n, pl* **infantrymen :** an infantry soldier **:** FOOT SOLDIER

**infant's breath** \'=='=\ *n* **1 :** WILD MADDER 2a **2 :** MONEYWORT

**infant school** *n, Brit* **:** PRESCHOOL, KINDERGARTEN

**in·farct** \'in,färkt, ən'f-\ *n* -S [L *infarctus*, past part. of *infarcire, infercire* to stuff, stuff full, fr. *in-* ²in- + *farcire* to stuff, fill — more at FARCE] **:** an area of coagulation necrosis in a tissue (as of the heart) resulting from obstruction of the local circulation by a thrombus or embolus

**in·farct·ed** \ən'färktəd\ *adj* **:** affected with infarction ⟨~ kidney⟩

**in·farc·tion** \-kshən\ *n* -S **:** the producing of an infarct

**in·fare** \'in,fa(a)r, -fe(ə)r\ *n* [ME *infer, infair* entrance, infare, fr. OE *infær* entrance, fr. *in, inn* in + *fær* way, journey, fr. *faran* to go, travel — more at IN, FARE] *chiefly dial* **:** a feast and reception for a newly married couple usu. at the home of the groom's family a day or two after the wedding

**infatigable** *adj* [L *infatigabilis*, fr. *in-* ¹in- + *fatigare* to fatigue + *-abilis* -able] *obs* **:** INDEFATIGABLE

**¹in·fat·u·ate** \ən'fachəwət\ *adj* [ME, fr. L *infatuatus*, past part.] **:** marked by infatuation **:** INFATUATED ⟨knowing the inwardness of that grand, ~ gabble —R.P.Warren⟩

**²in·fat·u·ate** \-chə,wāt, *usu* -ād·+V\ *vt* -ED/-ING/-S [L *infatuatus*, past part. of *infatuare*, fr. *in-* ²in- + *fatuus* foolish, fatuous — more at FATUOUS] **1** *obs* **:** to turn (as counsel) into foolishness or show to be foolish **:** FRUSTRATE **2 :** to make foolish **:** affect with folly **:** weaken the intellectual powers of or deprive of sound judgment ⟨the toys that ~ men —R.W. Emerson⟩ **3 :** to inspire with a foolish and extravagant love or desire ⟨you have *infatuated* this boy to such an extent that he would agree with you in anything —W.J.Locke⟩

**³in·fat·u·ate** \-wət\ *n* -S [¹*infatuate*] **:** an infatuated person

**in·fat·u·at·ed** \ən'fachə,wād·əd\ *adj* **:** possessed with or marked by a strong attachment or foolish or unreasoning love or desire ⟨a man absolutely ~ and delivered over to certain destruction —F.R.Leavis) ⟨how ~ she was with her lover, and how regardless of what anyone could say to her on the subject —Anthony Trollope⟩

**in·fat·u·at·ed·ly** *adv* **:** in an infatuated manner

**in·fat·u·a·tion** \ən,fachəˈwāshən\ *n* -s [LL *infatuation-, infatuatio*, fr. L *infatuatus* + *-ion-, -io* -ion] **1 :** the act of infatuating or state of being infatuated **:** strong and unreasoning attachment esp. to something unworthy of attachment ⟨an ~ with the rare that is the mark of a limited understanding —D.C.Peattie⟩ ⟨a sentimentalizing and transitory ~ for India —Paul Potts⟩ ⟨American ~ with big cars and big engines —Eugene Jaderquist⟩ ⟨the victim of a ridiculous ~ —John Morrison⟩ **2 :** something that infatuates **:** the object of an unreasoning or foolish attachment ⟨the heady ~ of speed —Ray Hare⟩ ⟨if they would turn aside from their cinquecento ~ —Norman Douglas⟩

**in·fat·u·a·tor** \-ˈ=,=,wād·ə(r)\ *n* -s **:** one that infatuates

**in·faust** \ənˈfau̇st, -ˈfȯst\ *adj* [F or L; F *infauste*, fr. L *infaustus*, fr. *in-* ¹in- + *faustus* lucky; akin to L *favēre* to be favorable — more at FAVOR] **:** not favorable **:** UNLUCKY, UNPROPITIOUS

**in·feasibility** \(ˌ)in+\ *n* **:** IMPRACTICABILITY

**in·feasible** \(ˈ)in+\ *adj* [¹*in-* + *feasible*] **:** not feasible **:** IMPRACTICABLE — **in·fea·si·ble·ness** *n*

**¹infect** *adj* [ME, fr. MF or L; MF, fr. L *infectus*, past part. of *inficere*] *obs* **:** INFECTED

**²in·fect** \ənˈfekt\ *vb* -ED/-ING/-S [ME *infecten*, fr. L *infectus*, past part. of *inficere* to stain, dye, taint, infect, fr. *in-* ²in- + *-ficere* (fr. *facere* to do, make) — more at DO] *vt* **1 :** to taint with decaying matter **:** contaminate with a disease-producing substance, germs, or bacteria ⟨~ a lancet⟩ **2 a :** to communicate a pathogen or a disease to (an individual or organ) ⟨clouds of mosquitoes ~*ed* the unprotected troops with malaria parasites⟩ ⟨condemned liver ~*ed* with flukes⟩ **b** *of a pathogenic organism* **:** to invade (an individual or organ) usu. by penetration — often used only of the actual penetration of the pathogen as distinguished from its subsequent growth in the host ⟨the polio virus probably usually ~*s* man through the nasal mucous membrane⟩; compare INFECTION 2 **3 :** to communicate or affect as if by some subtle contact: as **a :** to taint by communication of something noxious or pernicious ⟨he is deeply upset and manages to ~ her with a sense of guilt —*London Calling*⟩ ⟨intellectuals . . . become agents of discontent who ~ rich and poor, high and low —Irving Howe⟩ **b :** to work upon or seize upon so as to induce sympathy, belief, or support ⟨~*ed* everyone with his zeal for nature —Van Wyck Brooks⟩ ⟨an exuberance that tends to ~ the whole enterprise —E.J.Kahn⟩ **4** *obs* **:** DYE, STAIN **5** [by alter.] **:** INFEST ⟨fish ~*ed* with parasites⟩ **6 :** to subject (a whole cargo of an owner) to forfeiture because a part is contraband **7 :** to induce a change in quality in (the sound of a neighboring syllable) ~ *vi* **:** to become infected ⟨didn't pay any attention to it because I never ~ —Ernest Hemingway⟩

**¹in·fect·ant** \ənˈfektənt\ *adj* [²*infect* + *-ant*] **:** producing infection **:** INFECTING ⟨~ power⟩

**²infectant** *n* -s **:** an agent of infection (as a bacterium or virus)

**infected** *adj* **1 :** having undergone infection ⟨~ wound⟩ **2 :** CONTAMINATED ⟨obliged to go into ~ rooms—Jane Austen⟩ — **in·fect·ed·ness** *n* -ES

**in·fect·ibil·i·ty** \ən,fektəˈbiləd·ē\ *n* -ES **:** susceptibility to infection

**in·fect·ible** \ənˈfektəbəl\ *adj* [*infect* + *-ible*] **:** capable of being infected

**in·fec·tion** \ənˈfekshən\ *n* -s [ME *infeccioun*, fr. MF & LL; MF *infection*, fr. LL *infection-, infectio*, fr. L *infectus* + *-ion-, -io* -ion] **1 :** the act or result of affecting or infecting injuriously: **a :** contamination or pollution of matter (as air or water) **b :** corruption of character, morals, faith, loyalty ⟨focal point of moral and political ~⟩ **2 :** an act or process of infecting ⟨syphilis ~ is chiefly venereal⟩; *also* **:** the establishment of a pathogen in its host after invasion **3 :** the state produced by the establishment of an infective agent in or on a suitable host ⟨hampered by an ~ in his foot⟩ **:** a contagious or infectious disease ⟨among the more serious ~*s* of childhood are scarlet fever and meningitis⟩ **4 :** an infective agent (as a fungus, bacterium, or virus) **:** material contaminated with an infective agent and capable of causing disease **5 :** the communication of emotions or qualities through example or contact ⟨from such people . . . goes forth the ~ of goodwill —W.F.Hambly⟩ ⟨always open to the ~ of the holiday mood —Mary Austin⟩ **6 :** the subjecting of an entire cargo to forfeiture because of the contraband nature of part of it **7 :** the influence on a speech sound of a vowel sound next following or preceding **8 :** the acquisition of inductive power by embryonic cells through diffusion from adjacent organizer

**infection–exhaustion psychosis** *n* **:** any one of a group of mental disorders characterized esp. by delirium and mental confusion and occurring in connection with infections, fevers, and exhausted states

**infection hypha** *or* **infection thread** *n* **:** the hypha of a parasitic fungus that penetrates the host and establishes an infection

**infection period** *also* **infection stage** *n* **:** the period from the first evident manifestation of an infectious disease to the final host reaction — used chiefly in plant pathology

**in·fec·tious** \ənˈfekshəs\ *adj* [*infection* + *-ous*] **1 a :** capable of causing infection **:** INFECTIVE ⟨a carrier remains ~ without himself showing signs of disease⟩ ⟨viruses and other ~ agents⟩ **b :** communicable by infection ⟨an ~ disease⟩ — compare CONTAGIOUS **2 :** CORRUPTING, CONTAMINATING, VITIATING, DEMORALIZING ⟨fear is exceedingly ~ : children catch it from their elders —Bertrand Russell⟩ ⟨they say cowardice is ~ —R.L.Stevenson⟩ **3 :** capable of being easily diffused or spread **:** readily communicated **:** CATCHING, SYMPATHETIC ⟨his own delight in his great theme is ~ —Ernest Newman⟩ ⟨~ excitement⟩ ⟨~ good humor⟩ **4** *obs* **:** INFECTED **5** *of contraband goods* **:** having the effect of subjecting the entire cargo to forfeiture — **in·fec·tious·ly** *adv* — **in·fec·tious·ness** *n* -ES

**infectious abortion** *n* **:** CONTAGIOUS ABORTION

**infectious anemia** *n* **:** a serious often fatal virus disease of horses and mules marked by intermittent fever, depression, weakness, jaundice, and mucosal hemorrhages and frequently by anemia — called also *swamp fever*

**infectious bronchitis** *n* **1 :** a virus disease of chickens marked by inflammation of the bronchial tubes and abundant secretion of mucus interfering with respiration and causing gasping and choking that is often fatal in young birds and in adults seriously interferes with egg production — compare INFECTIOUS LARYNGOTRACHEITIS **2 :** any of various infective diseases of the bronchial tubes (as in horses or cows)

**infectious bulbar paralysis** *n* **:** PSEUDORABIES

**infectious chlorosis** *n* **:** a general chlorosis or a variegation due to a virus that can be transmitted from chlorotic to normal green plants by budding, grafting, or insect vectors

**infectious disease** *n* **:** a disease caused by the entrance into and growth and multiplication in the body of bacteria, protozoans, fungi, or analogous organisms (as filterable viruses) — compare CONTAGIOUS DISEASE

**infectious ectromelia** *n* **:** MOUSEPOX

**infectious equine encephalomyelitis** *n* **:** ENCEPHALOMYELITIS

**infectious hepatitis** *n* **1 :** an acute virus inflammation of the liver characterized by jaundice, fever, nausea, vomiting, and abdominal discomfort — called also *catarrhal jaundice, homologous serum hepatitis, serum hepatitis* **2 :** WEIL'S DISEASE **3 :** BLACKHEAD 3

**infectious jaundice** *n* **1 :** INFECTIOUS HEPATITIS 1 **2 :** WEIL'S DISEASE

**infectious laryngotracheitis** *n* **:** a severe highly contagious and often fatal virus disease of chickens affecting chiefly adult birds and taking the form of an inflammation of the trachea and larynx often marked by local necrosis and hemorrhage and by the formation of purulent or cheesy exudate interfering with breathing — compare INFECTIOUS BRONCHITIS, NEWCASTLE DISEASE

**infectious mastitis** *n* **:** BOVINE MASTITIS

**infectious mononucleosis** *n* **:** an acute infectious disease of unknown cause characterized by fever, malaise and prostration, swelling of lymph glands, and lymphocytosis and seen chiefly in children and young adults — called also *glandular fever, lymphadenosis*

**infectious necrotic hepatitis** *n* **:** BLACK DISEASE

**infectious sinusitis** *n* **:** a virus disease of turkeys marked by inflammation of the lining of the infraorbital sinuses resulting in great distention of the sinuses and by exudate that interferes with vision and indirectly with nutrition

**infectious vaginitis** *n* **:** EPIVAGINITIS

**in·fec·tive** \ənˈfektiv\ *adj* [ME, fr. ML *infectivus*, fr. L *infectus* (past part. of *inficere* to stain, dye, taint, infect) + *-ivus* -ive — more at INFECT] **1 :** producing infection **:** able to produce infection **:** INFECTING **2 :** affecting others **:** INFECTIOUS — **in·fec·tive·ness** *n* -ES

**in·fec·tiv·i·ty** \,in,fekˈtivəd·ē\ *n* -ES **:** the quality of being infective **:** the ability to produce infection; *specif* **:** a tendency to spread rapidly from host to host — distinguished from *virulence*

**in·fec·tor** \ənˈfektə(r)\ *n* -s **:** one that infects

**infects** *pres 3d sing of* INFECT

**in·fec·tum** \ənˈfektəm\ *n* -s [NL, fr. L, neut. of *infectus* undone, unfinished, fr. *in-* ¹in- + *-fectus* (fr. *factus*, past part. of *facere* to do, make) — more at DO] **:** an aspectual category of tenses in Latin which includes all that indicate that action or state is in progress in contrast with those tenses which indicate that action or state is completed — compare PERFECTUM

**infectuous** *adj* [ME, fr. L *infectus* + ME *-ous*] *obs* **:** INFECTIOUS

**in·fecund** \(ˈ)in+\ *adj* [ME *infecounde*, fr. L *infecundus*, fr. *in-* ¹in- + *fecundus* fruitful — more at FEMININE] **:** not fecund **:** UNFRUITFUL

**in·fecundity** \ˌin+\ *n* [L *infecunditas*, fr. *infecundus* + *-itas* -ity] **:** lack of fecundity

**infeeble** *obs var of* ENFEEBLE

**¹infeed** \ˈ=,=\ *n* [⁴*in* + *feed* (n.)] **1 a :** a feed for infeeding a tool or wheel **b :** a mechanism for feeding material into a machine ⟨bottles go into the ~ of washing machine —*Manila Times*⟩ **2 :** the process of infeeding

**²infeed** \"\ *vt* [²*in* + *feed* (v.)] **:** to feed (a tool or wheel) into work (as on a lathe) in a direction normal to that of the axis about which the work revolves

**in·feft** \inˈfeft\ *vt* **infeft** *also* **infefted; infeft** *also* **infefted; infefting; infefts** [ME (Sc dial.) *infeften*, alter. of *enfeffen* to enfeoff — more at ENFEOFF] *Scots law* **:** to invest with or give symbolical possession of inheritable property — **infeftment** *n* -s

**in·felicific** \(ˌ)in+\ *adj* [¹*in-* + *felicific*] **:** not productive of happiness **:** productive of unhappiness

**in·felicitous** \ˌin+\ *adj* [¹*in-* + *felicitous*] **:** not felicitous: **a :** UNFORTUNATE ⟨~ remark⟩ **b :** not appropriate in application **:** AWKWARD ⟨~ phrase⟩ **c :** DEFECTIVE, IMPERFECT ⟨~ typesetting due to illegible copy⟩ — **in·fe·lic·i·tous·ly** *adv* — **in·fe·lic·i·tous·ness** *n*

**in·felicity** \ˌin+\ *n* [ME *infelicite*, fr. L *infelicitas*, fr. *infelic-, infelix* unfortunate, unhappy (fr. *in-* ¹in- + *felic-, felix* fruitful, happy) + *-itas* -ity — more at FEMININE] **1 :** the quality or state of being infelicitous: **a :** UNHAPPINESS, WRETCHEDNESS, MISFORTUNE ⟨confusion and ~ of her emotions —Elinor Wylie⟩ **b :** lack of suitableness or appropriateness **2 :** something (as an act or word) that is infelicitous ⟨examined for *infelicities* before printing —E.P.Cheyney⟩

**infelt** \ˈ=,=\ *adj* [²*in* + *felt*] *archaic* **:** felt inwardly **:** HEARTFELT

**in·feminine** \(ˈ)in+\ *adj* [¹*in-* + *feminine*] **:** UNFEMININE

**infeodation** *var of* INFEUDATION

**infeoff** *obs var of* ENFEOFF

**in·fer** \R ənˈfər, + *vowel* -fər·; -R -fə̄, + *suffixal vowel* -fər· *also* -fər, + *vowel in a following word* -fər· *or* -fə̄ *also* -fər\ *vb* **inferred; inferred; inferring; infers** [MF or L; MF *inferer*, fr. L *inferre* to carry or bring into, attack, enter, introduce, cause, deduce, fr. *in* ²in- + *ferre* to carry, bring — more at BEAR] *vt* **1** *obs* **a :** to bring about **:** PROCURE **b :** to bring upon **:** INFLICT **c :** CONFER, BESTOW **2 :** to derive by reasoning or implication **:** conclude from facts or premises ⟨we see smoke and ~ fire —L.A.White⟩ **:** accept or derive as a consequence, conclusion, or probability ⟨task of physical science is to ~ knowledge of external objects from a set of signals passing along our nerves —A.S.Eddington⟩ ⟨the child ~*s* the existence of an environment which is not part of itself —James Jeans⟩ — compare IMPLY **3 :** GUESS, SURMISE ⟨given some utterance, a person may ~ from it all sorts of things which neither the utterance nor the utterer implied —I.A. Richards⟩ ⟨as may be *inferred* from the picture, travel through this type of forest was comparatively easy —C.B.Hitchcock⟩ **4 a :** to lead to as a conclusion or consequence **:** involve as a normal outcome of thought ⟨democracy ~*s* such loving comradeship —Oscar Cargill⟩ **b :** to point out **:** INDICATE ⟨this doth ~ the zeal I had to see him —Shak.⟩ — compare IMPLY **5 :** to give reason to draw an inference concerning **:** HINT ⟨did not take part in the debate except to ask a question *inferring* that the constitution must be changed —*Manchester Guardian Weekly*⟩ ⟨complain of the American accent, *inferring* that American culture is unworthy of notice —W.C.Greet⟩ **6** *obs* **:** to bring in **:** INTRODUCE ~ *vi* **:** to draw inferences ⟨men have been thinking for ages . . . have observed, *inferred*, and reasoned in all sorts of ways and to all kinds of results —John Dewey⟩

**syn** DEDUCE, CONCLUDE, JUDGE, GATHER: INFER indicates arriving at an opinion or coming to accept a probability on the basis of available evidence, which may be slight ⟨the population of Gloucester may readily be *inferred* from the number of houses which King found in the returns of hearth money —T.B.Macaulay⟩ ⟨your letter has just arrived and allows me to *infer* that you are as well as ever —O.W. Holmes †1935⟩ ⟨most of the material in this book was spoken before it was printed, as may perhaps be *inferred* from the style —Elmer Davis⟩ DEDUCE adds to INFER implications of ordered logical thought processes used in the study of logic to draw a specific inference from a general principle, in popular use to infer a truth from analysis of evidence ⟨for the apprehension of new elements requires a sensitive perception and familiarity with new details and cannot be *deduced* from established principles —M.R.Cohen⟩ ⟨a register at the head of the stairs on a wooden shelf. The last entry was in pencil, three weeks previous as to date, and had been written by someone with a very unsteady hand. I *deduced* from this that the management was not overparticular —Raymond Chandler⟩ CONCLUDE may indicate attaining to a fact, truth, or belief after ordered consideration following through with necessary consequences of evidence weighed or facts observed ⟨do not *conclude* that all state activities will be state monopolies —G.B.Shaw⟩ ⟨*concluded* that all of the senses were of equal value in obtaining knowledge of the world, and that with one sense alone "the understanding has as many faculties as with the five joined together" —S.F. Mason⟩ JUDGE stresses careful, critical examination of evidence in attempting to arrive at a wise or fit conclusion ⟨there is a unifying as well as a discriminating phase of judgment — technically known as synthesis in distinction from analysis. This unifying phase, even more than the analytic, is a function of the creative response of the individual who *judges* —John Dewey⟩ ⟨the lawfulness or unlawfulness of taking part in deeds of violence must be *judged* on the merits of each particular case —W.R.Inge⟩ GATHER implies conclusion by reflection, but not pondering on impressions formed from cumulative evidence ⟨piecing together classical tradition and references in Egyptian and Hebrew records, we *gather* that for some three centuries onwards from 1600 B.C. Phoenicia was a dependency of the Pharaohs —Edward Clodd⟩ ⟨that I myself believe there may be more than one kind of good poetry might, I think, have been *gathered* from that paragraph of mine which Professor Grierson then quotes —F.R.Leavis⟩

**in·fer·able** *also* **in·fer·ible** *or* **in·fer·ri·ble** \-ˈfərəbəl *also* ˈinf(ə)rə- *or* ənˈfərə-\ *adj* **:** capable of being inferred ⟨portion most used by travelers . . . for reasons ~ from the map —R.H.Brown⟩ — **in·fer·ably** \-blē\ *adv*

**in·fer·ence** \ˈinf(ə)rən(t)s *also* -fərn-\ *n* -s [ML *inferentia*, fr. L *inferent-, inferens* (pres. part. of *inferre*) + *-ia* -y] **1 :** the act or process of inferring **:** the act of passing from one or more propositions, statements, or judgments considered as true to another the truth of which is believed to follow from that of the former ⟨this reasoning . . . is . . . stronger than some modern ~*s* of science —Henry Adams⟩ ⟨~*s* are made, but implications are discovered⟩ — see IMMEDIATE INFERENCE, MEDIATE INFERENCE; compare DEDUCTION 1, INDUCTION 2b, TRANSFORMATION RULE **2 :** something that is inferred **:** DEDUCTION 2; *esp* **:** a proposition or conclusion arrived at by inferring ⟨the following ~*s* may be fairly drawn from these facts⟩ **3 :** the premises and conclusion that represent a process of inferring or that form the determinants of a belief ⟨the conviction that action should be based not on shadowy ~ . . . but on solid fact —C.W.Eliot⟩

**in·fer·en·tial** \ˌinfəˈrenchəl\ *adj* [ML *inferentia* + E *-al*] **1 :** relating to, involving, or resembling inference ⟨~ judgment⟩ ⟨~ procedure⟩ **2 :** deduced or deducible by inference ⟨~ evidence of his departure⟩

**in·fer·en·tial·ly** \-chəlē, -li\ *adv* **:** by way of inference **:** through inference ⟨answers to these questions are only ~ contained in this latest biography —Bosley Crowther⟩

**¹in·ferior** \ənˈfirēə(r), -ˈfēr-, (ˈ)in¦f-\ *adj* [ME, fr. L, comp. of *inferus* low, situated beneath — more at UNDER] **1 :** situated lower down or nearer what is regarded as the bottom or base **:** LOWER, NETHER ⟨~ latitudes⟩ ⟨~ rock strata⟩ **2 a :** of lower degree or rank ⟨was a member of an ~ caste⟩ ⟨a major is ~ to a colonel⟩ **b :** of low degree or rank ⟨~ classes of society⟩ **3 a :** of less importance, value, or merit **:** of poorer quality ⟨the child . . . considers himself ~ to the adult figures —G.S.Blum⟩ ⟨declined to an ~ position among the world powers⟩ ⟨~ chess move⟩ ⟨easily beat his ~ opponent⟩ **b** *of a railroad train* **:** required to yield right of way in the absence of specific orders **c :** of poor quality **:** MEDIOCRE **:** SECOND-RATE ⟨furniture of ~ workmanship⟩ ⟨~ pupil⟩ ⟨~ violinist⟩ **4 a** *of a part of the upright body* **:** situated below another and esp. another similar part — compare SUPERIOR 6a ⟨~ vena cava⟩ ⟨~ meatus of the nose⟩ ⟨~ rectus muscle of the eye⟩ **b** *of a part of the quadrupedal body* (1) **:** situated in a more posterior position (2) **:** situated more ventrad than another and esp. another similar part **:** VENTRAL **5** *of a part of a plant* **a :** situated below another organ: (1) *of a calyx* **:** free from the ovary (2) *of an ovary* **:** adnate to the calyx or other floral envelope **b :** ABAXIAL **c :** situated low on the stipe **6 :** SUBSCRIPT ⟨~ letter⟩ ⟨~ number⟩ — used usu. postpositionally ⟨for "$H_2O$" read "H, 2 ~, O"⟩; contrasted with *superior*

**²inferior** \"\ *n* -s **1 :** a person or thing inferior to another (as in worth, status, or importance) ⟨disdainful of his social ~*s*⟩ **2 :** a subscript character (as in printing)

**inferior alveolar artery** *n* **:** a branch of the internal maxillary artery that is distributed to the mucous membrane of the mouth and through the mandibular canal to the teeth of the lower jaw

**inferior alveolar canal** *n* **:** MANDIBULAR CANAL

**inferior alveolar nerve** *n* **:** a branch of the mandibular division of the fifth cranial nerve that passes into the mandibular canal to the teeth of the lower jaw

**inferior alveolar vein** *n* **:** the vein accompanying the inferior alveolar artery

**inferior colliculus** *n* **:** either member of the posterior and lower pair of quadrigeminate bodies together constituting one of the lower coordinating centers for hearing

**inferior conjunction** *n* **:** a conjunction in which a lesser or secondary celestial body passes nearer the observer than the primary body around which it revolves ⟨*inferior conjunction* of Venus to the sun⟩ — see CONFIGURATION illustration

**inferior court** *n* **:** a court having limited and specified rather than general jurisdiction — compare SUPERIOR COURT

**inferior good** *n* **:** a commodity the consumption of which decreases as its price declines or as the income of consumers rises because of the increased income available to buy preferred though more expensive commodities

**in·fe·ri·or·i·ty** \(ˌ)in,firēˈȯrəd·ē, -fēr-, -ˈär-, -ətē, -i\ *n* -ES [MF or ML; MF *inferiorité*, fr. ML *inferioritat-, inferioritas*, fr. L *inferior* + *-itat-, -itas* -ity — more at INFERIOR] **1 :** the state of being inferior **:** a lower state or condition ⟨making you feel her superiority, your ~; how poor she was; how rich you were —Virginia Woolf⟩ **2 :** sense of being inferior ⟨adolescence's indecisive shames and *inferiorities* —Ruth Park⟩

**inferiority complex** *n* [prob. trans. of G *minderwertigkeitskomplex*] **:** an acute sense of personal inferiority resulting either in timidity or through overcompensation in exaggerated aggressiveness; *broadly* **:** sense of being inferior or at a disadvantage **:** lack of assurance

**inferior laryngeal** *n* **:** a branch of the vagus nerve that supplies most of the muscles of the larynx

**in·fe·ri·or·ly** *adv* **1 :** in an inferior manner or to an inferior degree **2 :** in a lower position

**inferior maxillary nerve** *n* **:** MANDIBULAR NERVE

**inferior oblique** *n* **:** OBLIQUE 2b(2)

**inferior olive** *n* **:** a large gray nucleus that forms a lateral eminence on the medulla oblongata and has connections with the thalamus, cerebellum, and spinal cord

**inferior planet** *n* **:** a planet whose orbit lies within that of the earth

**inferior tide** *n* **:** the tide corresponding to the moon's transit of the lower meridian

**inferior valve** *n* **:** the valve by which certain bivalve mollusks become attached to an object or surface

**¹in·fer·nal** \ənˈfərnᵊl, -ˈfən-, -ˈfəin-\ *adj* [ME, fr. OF, fr. LL *infernalis*, fr. *infernus* hell (fr. L *infernus* lower, lying beneath, of the lower regions) + L *-alis* -al; akin to L *inferus* low, situated beneath — more at UNDER] **1 :** relating or belonging to a nether world of the dead and of earth deities **:** CHTHONIC — compare HADES **2 a :** relating to or inhabiting hell ⟨~ fires⟩ ⟨~ spirit⟩ **b :** resembling or suitable to hell or the character of its inhabitants **:** HELLISH, DIABOLICAL, FIENDISH ⟨~ scheme⟩ ⟨~ wickedness⟩ **3 :** DAMNABLE, DAMNED ⟨~ nuisance⟩ ⟨~ gadget⟩ ⟨~ racket⟩ — **in·fer·nal·ly** \-ᵊlē, -ᵊli\ *adv*

**²infernal** \"\ *n* -s **1** *archaic* **:** an infernal person or thing — usu. used in pl. **2 infernals** *pl, obs* **:** the infernal regions **:** HELL

**infernal blue** *n* **:** SCOTCH BLUE

**infernal machine** *n* **:** a machine or apparatus maliciously designed to explode and destroy life or property **:** a concealed or disguised bomb

**in·fer·no** \ənˈfər(ˌ)nō, -ˈfə̄(ˌ)-, -ˈfəi(ˌ)-\ *n* -s [It, hell (esp. as the title of one of the books of the *Divina Commedia*, long allegorical & philosophical poem by Dante Alighieri †1321 Ital. poet), fr. LL *infernus* — more at INFERNAL] **1 :** a place or a state of torment and suffering ⟨the ~ of the passions —Edmund Wilson⟩ ⟨~ of war⟩ ⟨~ of seething misery and poverty —G.B.Shaw⟩ **2 :** a place that resembles or suggests hell in being dark, noisy, chaotic, lawless ⟨the factory seemed an ~ of dirt and noise⟩ ⟨plunge into the ~ of the engine room —Joseph Whitehill⟩ **3 :** intense heat ⟨roaring ~ of the blast furnace⟩ **:** CONFLAGRATION ⟨girders melted in the ~⟩

**infero-** *comb form* [L *inferus* low, situated beneath — more at UNDER] **1 :** on the underside ⟨*infero*branchiate⟩ **2 :** below and ⟨*infero*lateral⟩

**in·fe·ro·branchiate** \ˌinfə(ˌ)rō+\ *adj* [*infero-* + *branchiate*] **:** having the gills on the sides under the mantle margin ⟨~ mollusk⟩

**inferred** *past of* INFER

**in·fer·rer** \ənˈfərə(r) *also* -ˈfərə(r\ *n* -s **:** one that infers

**inferrible** *var of* INFERABLE

**inferring** *pres part of* INFER

**infers** *pres 3d sing of* INFER

**in·fertile** \(ˈ)in, fərt+\ *adj* [MF, fr. LL *infertilis*, fr. L *in-* ¹in- + *fertilis* fertile — more at FERTILE] **:** not fertile or productive **:** BARREN ⟨~ egg⟩ ⟨~ soil⟩ **syn** see STERILE

**in·fertility** \ˌin+\ *n* [F *infertilité*, fr. LL *infertilitat-, infertilitas*, fr. *infertilis* infertile + *-itat-, -itas* -ity] **:** the quality or state of being infertile **:** BARRENNESS, STERILITY

**in·fest** \ənˈfest\ *vt* -ED/-ING/-S [MF *infester*, fr. L *infestare*, fr. *infestus* hostile — more at DARE] **1** *archaic* **:** to attack or harass persistently **:** WORRY, ANNOY **2 a :** to visit persistently or in large numbers **:** OVERRUN, HAUNT ⟨street ~*ed* with children⟩ ⟨lawn ~*ed* with weeds⟩ ⟨~*ed* with ghosts and poltergeists⟩ **b :** to live in or on as a parasite — used esp. of metazoan parasites of animals ⟨the flea that ~*s* cats⟩ ⟨horses ~*ed* with worms⟩

**in·fes·tant** \-tənt\ *n* -s **:** one that infests: as **a :** a visible parasite **b :** any of the smaller organisms (as clothes moth, flour beetle, vinegar eel) that attack fabrics or processed foods or liquids

**in·fes·ta·tion** \ˌin(ˌ)feˈstāshən\ *n* -s [MF, fr. LL *infestation-, infestatio*, fr. *infestatus* (past part. of *infestare* to infest) + *-ion-, -io* -ion] **1 :** the act of infesting ⟨protecting grain against ~⟩ **:** PLAGUE, ANNOYANCE **2 :** something that infests **:** SWARM ⟨~ of grasshoppers⟩ **3 :** the state of being infested esp. with metazoan parasites in or on an animal or plant body

**1infester** *vt* [2in- + fester (v.)] *obs* **:** to cause to fester

**2in·fest·er** \ənˈfestə(r)\ *n* -s [*infest* + *-er*] **:** one that infests

**in·fes·tious** \ənˈfes(h)chəs\ *adj* [*infest* + *-ious* (as in *infectious*)] **:** INFESTING ⟨to certain ~ bipeds any graft is legitimate —H.L.Ickes⟩

**1in·fes·tive** \ənˈfestiv\ *adj* [*infest* + *-ive*] **:** likely to infest **:** TROUBLESOME ⟨~ weeds⟩

**2in·festive** \(ˈ)in+\ *adj* [1in- + L *festivus* festive — more at FESTIVE] **:** not festive **:** MIRTHLESS

**in·festivity** \ˌin+\ *n* [1in- + *festivity*] **:** lack of festivity **:** MIRTHLESSNESS, DULLNESS

**in·fest·ment** \ənˈfestmənt\ *n* -s *archaic* **:** INFESTATION

**infestuous** *adj* [*infest* + *-uous* (as in *infectuous*)] *obs* **:** MISCHIEVOUS, HARMFUL

**in·feu·da·tion** *also* **in·feo·da·tion** \ˌinfyüˈdāshən\ *n* -s [ME *infeodacioun*, fr. ML *infeudation-, infeudatio, infeodation-, infeodatio*, fr. *infeudatus, infeodatus* (past part. of *infeudare, infeodare* to enfeoff), fr. *in-* 2in- + *feudum, feodum* feoff) + L *-ion-, -io* -ion — more at FEUD] **1 :** ENFEOFFMENT **2 :** a granting of tithes to laymen

**in·fib·u·late** \ənˈfibyəˌlāt\ *vt* -ED/-ING/-S [L *infibulatus*, past part. of *infibulare* to infibulate, practice infibulation upon, fr. *in-* 2in- + *fibulare* to pin, buckle together, fr. *fibula* — more at FIBULA] **:** to fasten with or as if with a buckle or clasp

**in·fib·u·la·tion** \(ˌ)inˌfibyəˈlāshən\ *n* -s [L *infibulatus* + E *-ion*] **:** an act or practice of fastening by ring, clasp, or stitches the labia majora in girls and the prepuce in boys in order to prevent sexual intercourse

**in·fi·cete** \ˈinfəˌsēt\ *adj* [L *inficetus, infacetus*, fr. *in-* 1in- + *facetus* courteous, elegant, witty, facetious] **:** not witty **:** HEAVY-FOOTED

**1in·fi·del** \ˈinfədᵊl, -əˌdel\ *n* -s [MF *infidele*, adj. & n., fr. LL *infidelis*, fr. L, untrustworthy, unfaithful, fr. *in-* 1in- + *fidelis* faithful — more at FEAL] **1 :** one that is not a Christian or opposes Christianity **2 a :** an unbeliever in respect to a particular religion **b :** one that acknowledges no religious belief — distinguished from *heretic* **3 :** one that does not believe (as in something specified or understood) **:** SKEPTIC, DISBELIEVER

**2infidel** \"\ *adj* [MF *infidele*] **1 a :** not holding the faith of a given religion; *esp* **:** non-Christian ⟨the ~ nations⟩ ⟨an ~ Saracen⟩ **b :** opposing or traitorous to Christianity ⟨~ writers⟩ ⟨an ~ sect⟩ **2 :** relating to or characteristic of unbelief or unbelievers ⟨~ tract⟩

**in·fi·del·ic** \ˌinfəˈdelik\ *or* **in·fi·del·i·cal** \-lə̇kəl\ *adj* **:** INFIDEL 2

**in·fi·del·i·ty** \ˌinfəˈdeləd·ē, -ətē, -i *sometimes* -ˌfī-\ *n* [MF *infidelité*, fr. LL & L; LL *infidelitat-, infidelitas* disbelief in Christianity, heathenism, fr. L, unfaithfulness, fr. *infidelis* + *-itat-, -itas* -ity] **1 :** lack of faith or belief in a religion **:** state or character of being infidel **2** *archaic* **:** SKEPTICISM, INCREDULITY **3 a :** breach of trust **:** unfaithfulness to a charge or a moral obligation **:** DISLOYALTY, PERFIDY **b :** marital unfaithfulness or an instance of it ⟨made no secret of his many *infidelities*⟩ **4 :** failure to reproduce (as a text or a model) exactly; *also* **:** an instance of such failure ⟨numerous *infidelities* in the translation⟩ ⟨~ in size also made printing from . . . plastic plates a hazard —*Graphic Arts Rev.*⟩

**infield** \ˈ=ˌ=\ *n* [4in + *field*] **1 a :** a field near a farmhouse **b :** land regularly manured and used year after year for the same crop (as hay or fruit) **2 a (1) :** the area of a cricket field relatively near the wickets **(2) :** a fieldsman stationed there — contrasted with *outfield* **b (1) :** the area of a baseball or softball field enclosed by the three bases and home plate **:** DIAMOND **(2) :** the defensive positions comprising first base, second base, shortstop, and third base ⟨a strong ~⟩ — contrasted with *outfield* **3 :** the area enclosed by a racetrack or running track

**in·field·er** \-də(r)\ *n* **1 :** a fielder stationed in the infield in cricket **2 :** a baseball player who covers a position in the infield

**infield fly** *n* **:** a fair fly ball other than a line drive or an attempted bunt that can be handled by an infielder and that is declared an automatic out if it occurs at a time when there are less than two outs and when runners are occupying first and second or first, second, and third bases

**in·fields·man** \-l(d)zmən\ *n* **:** INFIELDER 1

**in fi·eri** \(ˈ)inˈfēərē\ *adj* [ML] **1 :** being in process of accomplishment **:** PENDING **2 :** beginning to have existence **:** not yet completely formed

**infighter** \ˈ=ˌ==\ *n* [4in + *fighter*] **:** one that practices or is skilled at infighting ⟨able political ~⟩

**infighting** \ˈ=ˌ==\ *n* -s [4in + *fighting*] **1 a :** fighting or boxing at close range ⟨his bowie . . . was the unexcelled weapon for ~ —*Amer. Guide Series: Ark.*⟩ **b :** fighting (as between rivals) that is not openly acknowledged or conducted **2 :** fighting without rules **:** rough-and-tumble fighting

**infill** \ˈ=ˌ=\ *vt* [2in- + *fill*] **:** to fill in ⟨fractures . . . broadened by ice growth within them . . . and then ~*ed* from above as the ice melted —*Jour. of Geol.*⟩

**infilling** \ˈ=ˌ==\ *n* **:** material used (as in building) to fill in space between structural members ⟨steel skeleton with an ~ of brickwork⟩

**infilter** \=ˈ==\ *vi* [2in + *filter*] **:** to filter or sift in

**1in·fil·trate** \ənˈfilˌtrāt *also* ˈin(ˌ)fil- *sometimes* -ˌfəl-, *usu* -ād·+V\ *vb* [2in- + *filtrate*] *vt* **1 :** to cause something, (as a liquid) to enter by penetrating the pores of ⟨~ tissue with a local anesthetic⟩ **2 :** to pass into or through (a substance) by filtering or permeating **3 :** to advance (troops) by sending single men or small groups through gaps or weak points in the enemy line **4 :** to enter or become established in (as an organization) gradually or unobtrusively and in large numbers ⟨parties which labor leaders accused of being . . . infiltrated by extreme nationalists —Clifton Daniel⟩ ~ *vi* **1 :** to enter, permeate, or pass through a substance by filtering ⟨many Hebrew idioms have *infiltrated*, in translated forms, into various Jewish dialects —William Chomsky⟩ **2** *of troops* **:** to advance or to enter a hostile area by proceeding singly or in small dispersed groups ⟨tend rather to ~ to supply lines and rear installations —*Cavalry Jour.*⟩

**2infiltrate** \"\ *n* **:** something that infiltrates; *specif* **:** a substance that passes into the bodily tissues and forms an abnormal accumulation

**in·fil·tra·tion** \ˌin(ˌ)filˈtrāshən *sometimes* -fəl-\ *n* **1 :** the act or process of infiltrating ⟨~ of water through a gravel bed⟩ ⟨~ of air into a building⟩ **2 :** something that infiltrates ⟨fatty ~⟩ ⟨anesthetic drug ~⟩ **3 :** a gradual penetration by scattered units ⟨socialist ~ into a labor union⟩ ⟨~ of settlers into new territory⟩

**infiltration anesthesia** *n* **:** anesthesia of an operative site accomplished by injection of anesthetics under the skin

**infiltration capacity** *n* **:** the rate at which a soil can absorb water

**infiltration vein** *n* **:** a vein formed in country rock by interstitial deposition from percolating waters — compare IMPREGNATION 2a

**in·fil·tra·tive** \ˈinfəlˌtrād·iv, ənˈfiltrəd·-\ *adj* **:** relating to or characterized by infiltration

**in·fil·tra·tor** \ənˈfilˌtrād·ə(r), ˈinfəl-\ *n* -s **:** one that infiltrates ⟨if the first human agents that come into contact with a given culture . . . are traders, then economic values are the first ~*s* —P.A.Sorokin⟩

**in·fil·tree** \ˌinfəlˈtrē, ənˈfilˌtrē\ *n* -s [1*infiltrate* + *-ee*] **:** one who has entered another country or territory in a manner resembling military infiltration ⟨American policy to provide temporary food and housing to all ~*s* —Samuel Lubell⟩

**in·fil·trom·e·ter** \ˌin(ˌ)filˈträməd·ə(r)\ *n* -s [*infiltration* + *-o-* + *-meter*] **:** an apparatus for measuring the rate at which a soil can absorb water

**in·fi·ma species** \ˈinfəmə-\ *n* [L] **:** the lowest species in a classification or logical division — compare TREE OF PORPHYRY

**infin** *abbr* infinitive

**1in·fi·nite** \ˈinfənə̇t *sometimes* -fəˌnīt *sometimes as opposed to "finite"* (ˈ)inˈfīˌnīt *or* ənˈfīˌnīt; *usu* \|d·+V\ *adj* [ME *infinit*, fr. MF or L; MF *infinit*, fr. L *infinitus*, fr. *in-* 1in- + *finitus* limited, finite — more at FINITE] **1 :** being without limits of any kind **:** subject to no limitation or external determination ⟨philosophy compels faith in real personality, finite and relative in man, ~ and absolute in nature —F.A.Christie⟩ **2 a :** having no end **:** extending indefinitely ⟨speculate and wonder as to the structure of the universe, whether it is bounded or ~ —W.V.Houston⟩ ⟨~ duration⟩ **b :** having innumerable parts **:** capable of endless division or distinction within itself ⟨electrophones capable of ~ gradations of pitch —Robert Domington⟩ **3 :** having no limit in power, capacity, knowledge, or excellence **:** immeasurably or inconceivably great **:** BOUNDLESS ⟨~ mercy⟩ ⟨~ wisdom⟩ ⟨~ patience⟩ ⟨~ discretion⟩ **4 a :** indefinitely large or extensive **:** indefinite in number **:** IMMEASURABLE **b :** VAST, IMMENSE **c :** ENDLESS, INEXHAUSTIBLE ⟨~ ingenuity of man —Mary Webb⟩ **5** *pre-Socratic philosophy* **:** constituting the matrix or an ingredient of formed and determined reality **6** *of a verb form* **:** having neither person, number, nor mood **7 a :** not finite **:** extending or lying beyond any preassigned value however large ⟨the number of positive numbers is ~⟩ **b :** extending to infinity ⟨~ plane surface⟩ ⟨~ branch of a curve⟩ **c :** having the same power as a proper subset of itself **:** capable of being put into a one-to-one correspondence with a subset of itself — used of a mathematical aggregate — **in·fi·nite·ly** *adv* — **in·fi·nite·ness** *n*

**2infinite** \"\ *n* **:** something that is infinite **a :** boundless space or duration **:** INFINITY **b :** an incalculable or very great number ⟨an ~ of possibilities⟩ **c :** an infinite quantity or magnitude

**infinite canon** *n* **:** CIRCULAR CANON 1

**infinite integral** *n* **:** an improper integral having one or both of its limits infinite

**infinite proposition** *n* **:** a logical proposition that has an indefinite negative predicate

**infinite regress** *n* **:** an endless chain of reasoning leading backward by interpolating a third entity between any two entities — compare THIRD MAN

**infinite series** *n* **:** an endless succession of terms or of factors proceeding according to some mathematical law

**1in·fin·i·tes·i·mal** \ˌin,finəˈtesəməl, -tezə- *sometimes* -sm- *or* -zm-\ *n* -s [NL *infinitesimus* infinite in rank (fr. L *infinitus* infinite + *-esimus*, ordinal suffix + E *-al* — more at INFINITE] **1 :** a function that can be made arbitrarily close to zero **2 :** an infinitesimal quantity

**2infinitesimal** \ˌ=ˌ==ˈ=(=)=\ *adj* **1 :** capable of being made arbitrarily close to zero **2 :** immeasurably or incalculably small **:** very minute — **in·fin·i·tes·i·mal·ly** \-səmәlē, -zəmə-ˌli *sometimes* -sməl- *or* -zməl- *or* -səml- *or* -zəml-\ *adv* — **in·fin·i·tes·i·mal·ness** \-səməlnə̇s, -zəm- *sometimes* -sm- *or* -zm-\ *n* -ES

**infinitesimal calculus** *n* **:** either differential calculus or integral calculus

**in·fin·i·tes·i·mal·ism** \ˌ=ˌ==ˈ=(=)məˌlizəm\ *n* -s **:** a doctrine that the more a drug is diluted the more potent it becomes

**in·fin·i·tes·i·mal·i·ty** \-ˌtesəˈmaləd·ē\ *n* -ES **:** the quality or state of being infinitesimal

**infinite term** *n* **:** an indefinite term in a logical proposition

**in·fin·i·ti·val** \(ˌ)inˌfinəˈtīvəl, ənˌ-\ *adj* **:** relating to the infinitive — **in·fin·i·ti·val·ly** \-əlē\ *adv*

**1in·fin·i·tive** \ənˈfinəd·iv, -ətiv\ *adj* [LL *infinitivus*, fr. L *infinitus* infinite + *-ivus* -ive — more at INFINITE] **:** formed with the infinitive ⟨~ phrase⟩ — **in·fin·i·tive·ly** \-ə̇vlē, -li\ *adv*

**2infinitive** \"\ *n* -s **:** an infinite verb form normally identical in English with the first person singular that performs certain functions of a noun and at the same time displays certain characteristics (as association with objects and adverbial modifiers) of a verb and is used with *to* (as "*to err* is human"; "I asked him *to go*") except with auxiliary and certain other verbs (as "he *can see*"; "let me *go*"; "no one *saw* him *leave*")

**in·fin·i·tize** \ənˈfinəˌtīz\ *vt* -ED/-ING/-S [1*infinite* + *-ize*] **:** to make infinite **:** make free of finite limitations ⟨man's anxious effort to deny his finitude and to ~ himself by the perverse use of his freedom in pride —Will Herberg⟩

**in·fin·i·tude** \ənˈfinəˌtüd, -əˌtyüd\ *n* [prob. fr. F, fr. MF, fr. *infinit* infinite] **1 :** the quality or state of being infinite **:** INFINITENESS **2 :** something that is infinite; *esp* **:** a real as distinct from an ideal or theoretical infinity ⟨~ of outer space⟩ ⟨~ of time⟩ **3 :** an infinite number **:** an innumerable quantity

**in·fin·i·ty** \ənˈfinəd·ē, -ətē, -i\ *n* -ES [ME *infinite*, fr. MF *infinité*, fr. L *infinitat-, infinitas*, fr. *infinitus* infinite + *-itas* -ity] **1 a :** the quality of being infinite **b :** that which is infinite **:** unlimited extent of time, space, or quantity **:** BOUNDLESSNESS ⟨there cannot be more *infinities* than one; for one of them would limit the other —Walter Raleigh⟩ **2 :** unlimited capacity, energy, excellence, or knowledge ⟨~ of God's power⟩ **3 :** an indefinitely great number or amount ⟨~ of stars⟩ **4 a :** a nonexistent limit of a function that can be made to become and remain numerically larger than any preassigned value — symbol ∞ **b :** a nonexistent part of a magnitude that lies beyond any part whose distance from a given reference position is finite — symbol ∞ **c :** a transfinite number **5 :** a distance so great that the rays of light from a point source at that distance may be regarded as parallel

**1in·firm** \(ˈ)inˈfərm, ənˈf-, -ˈfə̄m, -ˈfəim\ *adj* [ME *infirme*, fr. L *infirmus, infirmis*, fr. *in-* 1in- + *firmus* strong, firm — more at FIRM] **1 :** not strong or sound physically **:** of poor or deteriorated vitality esp. as a result of age **:** FEEBLE ⟨~ body⟩ ⟨support of the poor, the insane, and the ~ —Calvin Coolidge⟩ **2 :** weak of mind, will, or character **:** FRAIL, IRRESOLUTE, VACILLATING ⟨~ judgment⟩ ⟨~ of purpose: give me the daggers —Shak.⟩ **3 :** not solid or stable **:** INSECURE, PRECARIOUS ⟨rendered this agreeable assumption . . . permanently ~ —Berton Roueché⟩ **syn** see WEAK

**2in·firm** \ənˈf-\ *vt* -ED/-ING/-S [ME *infirmen*, fr. L *infirmare*, fr. *infirmus* infirm] **1** *obs* **:** to make infirm **:** deprive of strength **:** WEAKEN **2 a :** to make doubtful or challenge the validity of **b :** INVALIDATE ⟨either to confirm or to ~ allegations of fact⟩ — **in·firm·able** \-məbəl\ *adj*

**in·fir·ma·rer** \ənˈfərmərər\ *n* -s [ME, prob. fr. ML *infirmaria, infirmarium* + ME *-er*] **:** INFIRMARIAN

**in·fir·ma·ress** \-mərə̇s\ *n* -ES **:** a female infirmarian

**in·fir·mar·i·an** \ˌinfə(r)ˈma(a)rēən\ *n* -s **:** a person having charge of an infirmary (as in a monastic institution)

**in·fir·ma·ry** \ənˈfərm(ə)rē, -ˈfə̄m-, -ˈfəim-, -ri\ *n* -ES [ML *infirmarium, infirmaria*, fr. L *infirmus* infirm + *-arium, -aria* -ary] **:** a hospital or place where the infirm or sick are lodged for treatment; *esp* **:** a building or part of a building for the sick or injured members of an institution ⟨convent ~⟩

**in·fir·ma·tion** \ˌinfə(r)ˈmāshən\ *n* -s [L *infirmation-, infirmatio*, fr. *infirmatus* (past part. of *infirmare* to infirm) + *-ion-, -io* -ion] **:** the process of infirming or making invalid — opposed to *confirmation*

**in·fir·mi·ty** \ənˈfərməd·ē, -ˈfə̄m-, -ˈfəim-, -ətē, -i\ *n* -ES [ME *infirmite*, fr. L *infirmitas*, fr. *infirmus* infirm + *-itas* -ity — more at INFIRM] **1 :** the quality or state of being infirm **:** FEEBLENESS, FRAILTY **2 a :** an unsound, unhealthy, or debilitated state **:** DISEASE, MALADY ⟨~ of body⟩ ⟨~ of mind⟩ **b :** a defect of personality or weakness of the will **:** FAILING, FOIBLE ⟨a friend should bear his friend's *infirmities* —Shak.⟩ ⟨fame . . . that last ~ of noble mind —John Milton⟩

**in·firm·ly** *adv* **:** in an infirm manner **:** FEEBLY, INSECURELY

**in·firm·ness** *n* **:** the quality or state of being infirm

**1in·fix** \(ˈ)inˈfiks, ənˈ-\ *vt* [L *infixus*, past part. of *infigere* to drive in, fasten in, fr. *in-* 2in- + *figere* to fasten, pierce — more at DIKE] **1 :** to fasten or fix by piercing or thrusting in ⟨and deep within her heart ~*ed* the wound —John Dryden⟩ **2 :** INSTILL, INCULCATE, IMPRESS ⟨~ an idea in a pupil's mind⟩ **3 :** to insert (a sound or letter) as an infix **syn** see IMPLANT

**2in·fix** \ˈinˌfiks\ *n* -ES **:** a derivational or inflectional affix appearing in the body of a word or base rather than at its beginning or end (as Sanskrit *-n-* in *vindami* "I know" as contrasted with *vid* "to know"; English *stand* as contrasted with *stood*) ⟨~*es* are sometimes inserted in the Hebrew word in order to lend it a different shade of meaning —William Chomsky⟩ — compare PREFIX

**in·fix·a·tion** \ˌin(ˌ)fikˈsāshən\ *also* **in·fix·ion** \ənˈfikshən\ *n* -s **1 :** the process of infixing **2 :** the state of being infixed

**infl** *abbr* **1** inflammable **2** inflorescence **3** influence; influenced

**in·flame** \ənˈflām\ *also* **en·flame** \en-\ *vb* [ME *enflamen, inflamen*, fr. MF *enflamer, enflammer*, fr. L *inflammare*, fr. *in-* 2in- + *flamma* flame — more at FLAME] *vt* **1 :** to set on fire **:** cause to burn, flame, or glow **:** KINDLE **2 :** to excite (as passion or appetite) to an excessive or unnatural action or heat **:** INTENSIFY, ROUSE ⟨*inflamed* mob of religious partisans —Robert Trumbull⟩ **3 a :** to provoke to anger or rage **:** EXASPERATE, IRRITATE, INCENSE, ENRAGE **b :** to cause to redden or grow hot from anger or excitement ⟨events had combined to irritate and then to ~ him —Ngaio Marsh⟩ ⟨face *inflamed* with passion⟩ **4 :** to cause inflammation in (bodily tissue) **:** produce abnormal heat in or swelling of ⟨~ the eyes⟩ ~ *vi* **1 :** to burst into flame **2 :** to become excited or angered **3 :** to become affected with inflammation

**inflamed** *adj* [fr. past part. of *inflame*] *heraldry* **:** represented as burning or as adorned with tongues of flame

**in·flam·er** \-mə(r)\ *n* **:** one that inflames

**in·flam·ing·ly** *adv* **:** in an inflaming manner

**in·flam·ma·bil·i·ty** \(ˌ)inˌflaməˈbiləd·ē, ənˌ-, -ətē, -i\ *n* **:** the quality or state of being inflammable **:** tendency to ignite readily

**1in·flam·ma·ble** \ənˈflaməbəl\ *adj* [F or ML; F, fr. ML *inflammabilis*, fr. L *inflammare* to inflame + *-abilis* -able] **1 :** capable of being easily set on fire and burning violently **:** FLAMMABLE **2 :** easily inflamed, excited, or angered **:** IRASCIBLE ⟨~ temper⟩ — **in·flam·ma·ble·ness** *n* -ES — **in·flam·ma·bly** \-blē, -li\ *adv*

**2inflammable** \"\ *n* **:** an inflammable substance **:** FLAMMABLE

**inflammable air** *n, archaic* **:** HYDROGEN

**inflammable cinnabar** *n* **:** IDRIALITE

**in·flam·ma·tion** \ˌinfləˈmāshən\ *n* [L *inflammation-, inflammatio*, fr. *inflammatus* (past part. of *inflammare* to inflame) + *-ion-, -io* -ion — more at INFLAME] **1 :** the act of inflaming or the state of being inflamed ⟨impossible to distinguish an ~ from an explosion by the amount of violence produced —*Gaseous Fuels*⟩ ⟨~ of nationalism precipitated the next great war —Hans Kohn⟩ **2 :** a local response to cellular injury (as by infection or trauma) characterized by capillary dilatation, leukocytic infiltration, heat, and commonly pain and serving as a primary mechanism for control of noxious agents and elimination of damaged tissue

**in·flam·ma·tive** \ənˈflaməd·iv\ *adj* [L *inflammatus* + E *-ive*] **:** INFLAMMATORY

**in·flam·ma·to·ri·ly** \(ˌ)inˌflaməˈtōrəlē, ənˌ-, -tȯr-, -li\ *adv* **:** in an inflammatory manner **:** so as to inflame

**in·flam·ma·to·ry** \ənˈflaməˌtōrē, -tȯr-, -ri\ *adj* [L *inflammatus* + E *-ory*] **1 :** tending to inflame or excite the senses **2 :** tending to excite anger, animosity, disorder, or tumult **:** SEDITIOUS ⟨~ speech⟩ **3 :** of, relating to, or marked by inflammation ⟨an ~ response⟩ ⟨an ~ process⟩

**1in·flat·able** \ənˈflād·əbəl\ *adj* [2*inflate* + *-able*] **:** capable of being inflated

**2inflatable** \"\ *n* -s **:** a toy or plaything capable of being inflated

**1in·flate** \ənˈflāt, *usu* -ād·+V\ *adj* [ME *inflat*, fr. L *inflatus*, past part.] *archaic* **:** INFLATED

**2inflate** \"\ *vb* -ED/-ING/-S [L *inflatus*, past part. of *inflare*, fr. *in-* 2in- + *flare* to blow — more at BLOW] *vt* **1 :** to swell or distend with air or gas ⟨~ a balloon⟩ — opposed to *deflate* **2 :** to puff up **:** ELATE ⟨~ one with pride⟩ **3 :** to expand or increase abnormally or improperly **:** extend imprudently; *esp* **:** to increase (the volume of money and credit) so that a general rise in the price level occurs ⟨deliberately *inflating* the currency⟩ ~ *vi* **:** to undergo inflation **:** fill with or as if with air **:** DISTEND **syn** see EXPAND

**inflated** *adj* **1 :** distended with air or gas **2 :** TURGID, BOMBASTIC, POMPOUS ⟨~ style⟩ **:** EXAGGERATED ⟨~ statements are made without anyone being able to check them —G.A. Craig⟩ **3 :** expanded abnormally or unjustifiably in volume ⟨~ currency⟩ or level ⟨~ prices⟩ **4 :** hollow and distended ⟨~ stem⟩ ⟨~ capsule⟩ **:** open and swelled out or enlarged ⟨~ perianth⟩ **:** BLADDERY

**syn** INFLATED, FLATULENT, TUMID, and TURGID all mean filled with something insubstantial, as air or gas, or something that causes usu. abnormal swelling or distention. INFLATED implies a blowing up to the point of tautness of surface or empty distention ⟨an *inflated* balloon⟩ or, figuratively, a stretching, expanding, heightening, or puffing up by artificial or empty means ⟨*inflated* rhetoric⟩ ⟨an *inflated* speech⟩ ⟨an *inflated* opinion of oneself⟩ FLATULENT, applying chiefly to persons affected by excessive distention by gas of the stomach or bowels, can be extended to apply to anything that is empty or lacking substance but that gives the transparent impression of fullness or substantiality ⟨enthusiasts who read into him all sorts of *flatulent* bombast —H.L.Mencken⟩ ⟨he was an overornate speaker; at his worst he was a purveyor of *flatulent* claptrap —S.H.Adams⟩ TUMID stresses noticeable esp. morbid or abnormal enlargement as by swelling or bloating or, figuratively, an empty but marked pretentiousness ⟨his face looked damp, pale under the tan, and slightly *tumid* —J. G.Cozzens⟩ ⟨the genuine scientist would never employ *tumid* phrases or half-baked simplifications —J.E.Gloag⟩ TURGID is similar to TUMID without suggesting morbidity but often adds the idea of disorder or esp. emotional unrestraint as in the use of bombast, rant, or rhapsody ⟨the book is so *turgid*, so repetitive, so full of nearly meaningless tables —Geoffrey Gorer⟩ ⟨much too much of it dwells on the *turgid* adventures of a man who marries the less attractive of a pair of sisters and indulges a yen for the other —Henry Hewes⟩ ⟨the contrast between the vivid dialogue and the *turgid* narrative passages —David Greene⟩ ⟨a *turgid* speech praising the political boss⟩

**in·flat·ed·ly** *adv* **:** in an inflated manner

**in·flat·ed·ness** *n* -ES **:** the quality or state of being inflated **:** POMPOSITY, TURGIDITY

**in·fla·tion** \ənˈflāshən\ *n* -s [ME *inflacioun*, fr. L *inflation-, inflatio*, fr. *inflatus* + *-ion-, -io* -ion] **1 :** an act of inflating or a state of being inflated: as **a :** DISTENTION **b :** empty pretentiousness **:** POMPOSITY ⟨~ either of language or imagination —Cyril Connolly⟩ **2 :** an increase in the volume of money and credit relative to available goods resulting in a substantial and continuing rise in the general price level — contrasted with *deflation*

**in·fla·tion·ary** \-shəˌnerē, -ri\ *adj* **:** of, relating to, or productive of inflation ⟨~ signs⟩ ⟨~ policies⟩

**inflationary gap** *n* **:** an excess of total disposable income over the value of the available supply of goods at a specified price level sufficient to cause an inflation of prices — compare DEFLATIONARY GAP

**inflationary spiral** *n* **:** a continuous rise in prices that is sustained by the tendency of wage increases and cost increases to react on each other

**in·fla·tion·ism** \-ˌnizəm\ *n* -s **:** the advocacy of economic inflation

**in·fla·tion·ist** \-sh(ə)nə̇st\ *n* -s *often attrib* **:** one who favors economic inflation

**in·fla·tor** *or* **in·flat·er** \ənˈflād·ə(r), -ātə-\ *n* -s **:** one that inflates; *esp* **:** a hand air pump ⟨tire ~⟩

**in·fla·tus** \ənˈflād·əs\ *n* -ES [L, fr. *inflatus*, past part. of *inflare* to inflate — more at INFLATE] **:** AFFLATUS, INSPIRATION

**in·flect** \ənˈflekt\ *vt* -ED/-ING/-S [ME *inflecten*, fr. L *inflectere*, fr. *in-* 2in- + *flectere* to bend, turn] **1 :** to turn from a direct line or course **:** BEND, CURVE ⟨in him . . . snobbery reappeared . . . as the refusal of reality unless it was highly ~*ed* —V.S. Pritchett⟩ ⟨profound feeling for music has ~*ed* all his major works —Irving Kolodin⟩ **2 :** to give inflection to (a word) **:** vary (a word) by inflection **:** DECLINE ⟨~ a noun⟩ **:** CONJUGATE ⟨~ a verb⟩ **3 :** to change or vary the pitch of (as the voice or an utterance) **:** MODULATE **4 :** to bend (part of a plant) inward toward the main axis of the part or body ~ *vi* **:** to become modified by inflection ⟨languages in which adjectives ~ like nouns⟩

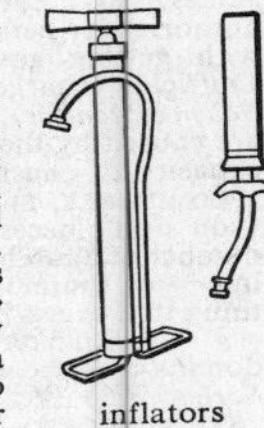

inflators

**inflected** *adj* **1 :** subjected to or characterized by inflection ⟨~ words⟩ ⟨an ~ language⟩ **2 :** INFLEXED 2 — **in·flect·ed·ness** *n* -ES

**in·flect·ible** \-təbəl\ *adj* **:** capable of being inflected

**in·flec·tion** \ən'flekshən\ *n* -S [LL *inflection-, inflectio*, L *inflexion-, inflexio*, fr. *inflectus, inflexus* (past part. of *inflectere* to inflect) + *-ion-, -io* -ion — more at INFLECT] **1 :** the act or result of curving or bending ⟨excel in movements and ~*s* of the hands —Sacheverell Sitwell⟩ **:** BEND, CURVE ⟨enclosed by ~*s* of the river —Anthony Powell⟩ **2 :** change or variation of pitch or loudness **:** modulation of the voice in speaking or singing ⟨questions end on a rising ~⟩ ⟨~*s* of humor, irony, and sentiment which are obvious to a native speaker —Geoffrey Bullough⟩ **3 a :** a modification in pitch or dynamics in a musical line **b :** a change from the monotone in liturgical chanting **4 a :** the variation or change of form that words undergo to mark distinctions of case, gender, number, tense, person, mood, voice, comparison **b :** a form, suffix, or element involved in such variation **c :** ACCIDENCE **5 a :** change of curvature from concave to convex or conversely **b** *or* **inflection point :** the point where such a change takes place

**in·flec·tion·al** \-shən°l, -shnəl\ *adj* **1 :** of, relating to, or characterized by inflection ⟨*-ed* in *played* is an ~ suffix⟩ — distinguished from *derivational* **2** *of a language* **:** characterized by the expression of grammatical relations by means of formal modification through internal change (as in *sing, sang, sung*) or fusional affixation of modifying elements (as in *walk, walked, walking, walks*) — distinguished from *agglutinative* and *isolating* — **in·flec·tion·al·ly** \-°lē, -əlē, lī\ *adv*

**in·flec·tion·less** \-shənləs\ *adj* **:** having no inflections

**in·flec·tive** \ən'flektiv, -tēv\ *adj* **1 :** capable of, relating to, or tending to inflection **:** DEFLECTING **2 :** INFLECTIONAL ⟨~ language⟩

**in·flexed** \(')in¦flekst, ən'f-\ *adj* [L *inflexus* (past part. of *inflectere* to inflect) + E *-ed* — more at INFLECT] **1 :** TURNED, BENT **2 :** bent or turned abruptly inward or downward or toward the axis ⟨~ petals of a flower⟩ ⟨~ tentacles⟩

**in·flexibility** \(¦)in, ən+\ *n* **:** the quality or state of being inflexible **:** UNYIELDINGNESS

**in·flexible** \(')in, ən+\ *adj* [ME, fr. L *inflexibilis*, fr. *in-* ¹in- + *flexibilis* flexible — more at FLEXIBLE] **1 :** not capable of being bent **:** RIGID **2 :** firm in will or purpose **:** UNYIELDING, INEXORABLE ⟨a man of upright and ~ temper —Joseph Addison⟩ ⟨~ purpose⟩ **3 :** incapable of change **:** UNALTERABLE, IMMUTABLE ⟨arbitrary and ~ rulings of bureaucracy —Edward Shils⟩ **syn** see STIFF

**in·flex·i·ble·ness** *n* **:** INFLEXIBILITY

**in·flexibly** \(')in, ən+\ *adv* **:** RIGIDLY, UNALTERABLY, STUBBORNLY, INEXORABLY

**in·flex·ion** \ən'flekshən\ *chiefly Brit var of* INFLECTION

**in·flex·ive** \ən'fleksiv\ *adj* [L *inflexus* (past part. of *inflectere* to inflect) + E *-ive*] *chiefly Brit* **:** INFLECTIVE

**in·flict** \ən'flikt\ *vt* -ED/-ING/-S [L *inflictus*, past part. of *infligere*, fr. *in-* ²in- + *fligere* to strike — more at PROFLIGATE] **1 :** to lay (a blow) on **:** cause (something damaging or painful) to be endured **:** IMPOSE ⟨threaten punishments you do not mean to ~—Bertrand Russell⟩ ⟨nor cruel and unusual punishments ~*ed* —*U. S. Constitution*⟩ ⟨~ defeat⟩ ⟨~ a beating⟩ **2 :** AFFLICT ⟨miners are still out, and industry . . . is ~*ed* with a kind of creeping paralysis —H.J.Laski⟩

**in·flict·able** \-təbəl\ *adj* **:** capable of being inflicted ⟨the largest ~ fine for this offense⟩

**in·flict·er** *or* **in·flic·tor** \-tə(r)\ *n* -S **:** one that inflicts ⟨death with his comrade, the ~ of wounds, roamed the darkened streets —Sean O'Casey⟩

**in·flic·tion** \ən'flikshən\ *n* -S [MF or LL; MF, fr. LL *infliction-, inflictio*, fr. L *inflictus* + *-ion-, -io* -ion] **1 :** the act of inflicting ⟨if the reader will bear one further ~ of statistics and formal description —Ernest Barker⟩ ⟨~ of damage by an economic association —C.A.Cooke⟩ **2 :** something inflicted ⟨I do not call these people visitors at all . . . they are ~*s* —F.A. Swinnerton⟩

**in·flic·tive** \-ktiv\ *adj* **:** causing infliction **:** acting as an infliction ⟨*The Raven* . . . delighted the ~ instincts of thousands of reciters for so long —*Times Lit. Supp.*⟩

**in·flood** \ən+\ *vb* [²in- + *flood*] *vi* **:** to flow in ~ *vt* **:** to overwhelm by flowing in upon ⟨unexpectedly in a gust of wind the scent of a plowed field . . . we are caught up, ~*ed* and informed —Alan Devoe⟩

**in·florescence** \ˌin+\ *n* [NL *inflorescentia*, fr. LL *inflorescent-, inflorescens* (pres. part. of *inflorescere* to begin to bloom, fr. *in-* ²in- + *florescere* to begin to bloom) + *-ia* -y — more at FLORESCENCE] **1 a** (1) **:** the mode of development and arrangement of flowers on an axis (2) **:** a floral axis with its appendages **:** a flower cluster or sometimes a solitary flower **b :** a cluster of reproductive organs on a moss usu. subtended by a bract ⟨many mosses have separate male ~*s*⟩ **2 :** the budding and unfolding of blossoms **:** FLOWERING

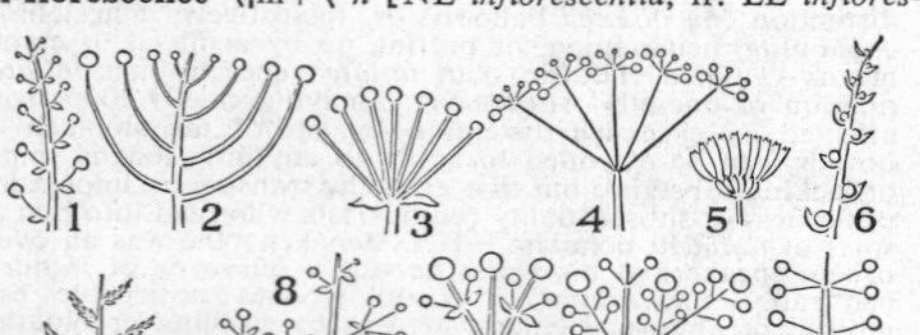

1 2 3 4 5 6 7 8 9 10 11

types of inflorescence diagrammatically illustrated: *1* raceme, *2* corymb, *3* umbel, *4* compound umbel, *5* capitulum, *6* spike, *7* compound spike, *8* panicle, *9* cyme, *10* thyrse, *11* verticillaster

**in·florescent** \ˌin+\ *adj* [LL *inflorescent-, inflorescens*, pres. part.] **:** BLOSSOMING, FLOWERING

**¹inflow** \(')=¦=\ *vi* [²in- + *flow*] **1 :** to flow in **2** *obs, of a celestial body* **:** INFLUENCE

**²inflow** \'=,=\ *n* **1 :** the act of inflowing **2 :** something that flows in **:** INFLUX ⟨~ of air⟩ ⟨~ of water⟩ ⟨~ of bank deposits⟩ ⟨~ of imports⟩

**¹in·flu·ence** \'in,flüən(t)s *sometimes* ən'f-\ *n* -S [ME, fr. MF, fr. ML *influentia*, fr. L *influent-, influens*, pres. part. of *influere* to flow in, fr. *in-* ²in- + *fluere* to flow + *-ia* -y — more at FLUID] **1 a :** an ethereal fluid thought to flow from the stars and to affect the actions of men **b :** a supposed emanation of occult power from stars **c** *obs* **:** character or temperament due to such power **2 :** the exercise of a power like the supposed power of the stars **:** an emanation of spiritual or moral force **3** *obs* **:** INFLOW, INFLUX **4 a :** the act, process, or power of producing an effect without apparent exertion of tangible force or direct exercise of command and often without deliberate effort or intent ⟨primitive men thinking that almost everything is significant and can exert ~ of some sort —William James⟩ **b :** corrupt interference with or manipulation of authority for personal gain ⟨~ may have had something to do with getting government money for the hotels —Marcus Duffield⟩ ⟨charges of corruption and ~ peddling —*Christian Science Monitor*⟩ **c :** the exertion of force at a distance ⟨tides are caused by the ~ of the moon and sun⟩ **5 :** the power or capacity of causing an effect in indirect or intangible ways **:** DOMINANCE, SWAY, ASCENDANCY ⟨under the ~ of liquor⟩ ⟨you don't necessarily measure the ~ of a religion by the number of churches it puts up —Green Peyton⟩ ⟨the intoxicating ~ of the mountain air —W.S.Gilbert⟩ **6 :** a person or thing that exerts influence ⟨open water affected by continental ~*s* —R.E.Coker⟩ ⟨Scotch-Irish, who still constitute the dominant ~, began to flow into the settlement —*Amer. Guide Series: Pa.*⟩ **7 :** INDUCTION 4c

**syn** AUTHORITY, PRESTIGE, WEIGHT, CREDIT: INFLUENCE refers to power exerted over others, often through high position, strength of intellect, force of character, or degree of accomplishment, sometimes exercised unconsciously and felt insensibly, sometimes consciously or calculatedly brought to bear ⟨as provost of the Swedish clergymen he exercised a quickening *influence* over all the Swedish congregations —G. H.Genzmer⟩ ⟨swept aside by the *influence* of the special interests bent on maintaining price levels against deflation —T. W.Arnold⟩ AUTHORITY signifies power resident in a person to command belief, acceptance, or allegiance, often through learning or wisdom ⟨Aristotle's *authority* was so great, and the homocentric system which he had espoused became so enmeshed in literature, that his system had its followers throughout the Middle Ages —G.C.Sellery⟩ ⟨the personal *authority* [of Augustus] which, far more than any legal or constitutional device, was the true secret of his later power —John Buchan⟩ ⟨to face a good orchestra with inward and outward *authority* and assurance —J.N.Burk⟩ PRESTIGE refers to the force of conspicuous excellence or of continued repute as superior, with resultant ability to command deference ⟨the almost magical *prestige* that had belonged to the original humanists —Aldous Huxley⟩ ⟨Napoleon insisted on a strict etiquette. He was right. It was only by keeping up the fiction of grandeur that he could maintain his *prestige* —André Maurois⟩ WEIGHT applies to power over or influence over others, often measurable and undeniable, and sometimes decisive ⟨Mrs. Hawthorne's authoritative air was beginning to have some *weight* with him —Archibald Marshall⟩ ⟨men who take the lead, and whose opinions and wishes have great *weight* with the others —J.G.Frazer⟩ CREDIT applies to ability to influence arising from merit or favorable reputation ⟨his position was distinctly stronger and once more he had shown his ability to handle a delicate situation to the *credit* of his government and himself —W.C.Ford⟩ ⟨the film was a success, with much of the *credit* going to the newcomer —*Current Biog.*⟩ — **under the influence :** in an intoxicated condition ⟨charged with driving *under the influence*⟩

**²influence** \"\ *vb* -ED/-ING/-S *vt* **1 :** to affect or alter the conduct, thought, or character of by indirect or intangible means **:** SWAY ⟨pilots . . . by listening to passengers who have *influenced* better judgment —*Skyways*⟩ ⟨economic and political factors that ~ decisions by managers of European zones —R.S.Thoman⟩ **2 :** to have an effect on the condition or development of **:** determine partially **:** MODIFY ⟨output was strongly *influenced* by the feelings of the worker about the job —Stuart Chase⟩ ⟨outdoor living has *influenced* the design . . . of furniture —N.C.Brown⟩ **3** *obs* **:** INDUCE, INFUSE ~ *vi, archaic* **:** to exert influence **syn** see AFFECT

**in·flu·ence·abil·i·ty** \ˌin,flüənsə'bilədē *sometimes* ən,f-\ *n* -ES **:** liability to influence

**in·flu·ence·able** \'=,==səbəl *sometimes* ='==-\ *adj* [¹*influence* + *-able*] **:** liable to be influenced **:** readily subject to influence

**influence fuse** *n* **:** PROXIMITY FUSE

**influence line** *n, often cap I* **1 :** LINE OF INFLUENCE **2 :** a graph showing the variation of the longitudinal stress, shear, bending moment, or other effect upon a structural member due to a moving load as a function of the position of that load

**influence machine** *n* **:** INDUCTION MACHINE

**in·flu·enc·er** \-sə(r)\ *n* -S **:** one that influences

**in·flu·en·cive** \'in,flüənsiv\ *adj, archaic* **:** INFLUENTIAL

**¹in·flu·ent** \'in,flüənt\ *adj* [ME, fr. L *influent-, influens*, pres. part. of *influere* to flow in — more at INFLUENCE] **1 :** flowing in; *esp* **:** contributing water to the zone of saturation and thereby sustaining or raising the water table ⟨~ seepage⟩ **2** *archaic* **:** exercising influence ⟨beneath the ~ heavens —Elizabeth B. Browning⟩

**²influent** \"\ *n* -S **1 :** a tributary stream **:** AFFLUENT; *also* **:** a stream or part of a stream that contributes water to the zone of saturation underground **2 a :** an animal or rarely a plant that has an important effect on the balance and stability of an ecological community ⟨rabbits and prairie dogs are important ~*s* in some rangelands⟩ **b :** a determining factor in the ecological balance of a human community ⟨location of home in relation to job is an ~ in city growth⟩

**in·flu·en·tial** \ˌin,flü¦enchəl\ *adj* [ML *influentia* influence + E *-al* — more at INFLUENCE] **1 :** exerting or possessing influence **:** POTENT, EFFECTIVE ⟨as ~ as any newspaper in the country —Morley Callaghan⟩ **2 :** having authority or ascendancy **:** IMPORTANT ⟨exert ~ leadership for peace —D.D. Eisenhower⟩ **3** *obs* **:** of the nature of or relating to occult influence — **in·flu·en·tial·ly** \-ch(ə)lē, -lī\ *adv*

**in·flu·en·za** \ˌin,flü'enzə\ *n* -S [It, influence, epidemic, influenza, fr. ML *influentia* influence; fr. the fact that epidemics were formerly attributed to the influence of the stars — more at INFLUENCE] **1 :** an acute highly contagious infectious virus disease that occurs in endemic, epidemic, or pandemic forms, is characterized by sudden onset, fever, prostration, severe aches and pains, and progressive inflammation of the respiratory mucous membrane, and is frequently complicated by secondary infections (as pneumonia); *broadly* **:** a human respiratory infection of undetermined cause **2 :** any of numerous febrile usu. virus diseases (as shipping fever of horses, swine influenza, infectious laryngotracheitis of poultry) marked by respiratory symptoms, inflammation of mucous membranes, and varying degrees of systemic involvement **3 :** a respiratory disease of dogs and cats that is perhaps identical with human influenza

**influenza vaccine** *n* **:** a vaccine against influenza; *specif* **:** a mixture of strains of formaldehyde-inactivated influenza virus from chick embryo culture

**in·flux** \'in,fləks\ *n* [LL *influxus*, fr. L *influxus*, past part. of *influere* to flow in — more at INFLUENCE] **1** *obs* **:** INFLUENCE **2 :** a flowing in **:** INFLOW ⟨~ of light⟩ ⟨~ of air⟩ **3 :** a continuous coming esp. of individuals in large numbers ⟨the city expected an ~ of holiday visitors⟩ **4 :** the mouth or debouchment of a river

**in·flux·ion** \ən'fləkshən, 'in,f-\ *n* [LL *influxion-, influxio*, fr. L *influxus* (past part.) + *-ion-, -io* -ion] **:** INFLUX ⟨continual ~s of new blood —John Galsworthy⟩

**in·fo** \'in(,)fō\ *abbr or n* -S information

**in·fold** \ən'fōld\ *vb* [ME *ynfoldeyn*, fr. *yn-, in-* ²in- + *foldeyn, folden* to fold — more at FOLD] *vt* **:** ENFOLD ~ *vi* **:** to fold inward or toward one another ⟨the neural crests ~ and fuse⟩ ⟨an ~*ed* leaf margin⟩ ⟨~*ing* of the hindgut walls⟩

**¹in·form** \ən'fō(ə)rm, -ō(ə)m\ *vb* [ME *enfourmen, informen*, fr. MF *enformer, enfourmer*, fr. L *informare*, fr. *in-* ²in- + *formare* to form — more at FORM] *vt* **1** *obs* **a :** to give material form to **:** mold or shape physically **b :** to set in order **:** ARRANGE **2 a :** to give character or essence to ⟨to what extent can the practice of science ~, render more significant the objects of common sense —Gail Kennedy⟩ ⟨a piety . . . quietly ~*ing* the outlook of men in politics as elsewhere —W.L. Miller⟩ **b :** to be the formative principle of ⟨eternal objects ~ actual occasions with hierarchic patterns —A.N.Whitehead⟩ ⟨everything that is made from without and by dead rules, and does not spring from within through some spirit ~*ing* it —Oscar Wilde⟩ **c :** to permeate or impregnate so as to become the characteristic quality of **:** ANIMATE, INSPIRE, INFUSE ⟨these poems are ~*ed* with sincerity —Richard Eberhart⟩ ⟨sentimental, Protestant ethos that has always ~*ed* his writing —L.A.Fiedler⟩ **3** *obs* **:** to form (the mind) in respect to character, disposition, or ability **:** TRAIN, DISCIPLINE, INSTRUCT **4** *obs* **:** GUIDE, DIRECT ⟨if old respect hither hath ~*ed* your younger feet —John Milton⟩ **5** *obs* **:** to make known **:** give instruction in (as a doctrine) **6 :** to communicate knowledge to **:** make acquainted **:** TELL, ADVISE, ENLIGHTEN ⟨accused shall enjoy the right . . . to be ~*ed* of the nature and cause of the accusation —*U.S.Constitution*⟩ ⟨obligation as a citizen is to ~ himself . . . regarding the controversial issues —Clifford Houston⟩ ⟨program of ~*ing* the rest of the world about our way of life —H.H.Davis⟩ ~ *vi* **1 :** to give information **:** impart knowledge ⟨in theory news ~*s* while advertising sells —*Banking*⟩ **2 :** to give information or intelligence to a civil authority **:** lay information **:** act as a common informer ⟨I shall not ~ upon you —Oscar Wilde⟩

**syn** ACQUAINT, APPRISE, ADVISE, NOTIFY, ADVERTISE: These verbs signify to make aware or cognizant (of something). INFORM implies the imparting of knowledge, esp. of facts or events necessary to the understanding of a pertinent matter ⟨to *inform* the students there would be no classes on Saturday⟩ ⟨kept the staff *informed* of Chinese public opinion concerning the American military action there —*Current Biog.*⟩ ACQUAINT usu. lays stress upon less centrally significant matter than INFORM does or suggests a process of introducing to or familiarizing with rather than informing of ⟨these writings were of the nature of travel books, and served . . . to *acquain* the world with a new country —*Amer. Guide Series: Minn.*⟩ ⟨*acquainting* students with political practices —F.A.Ogg & Harold Zink⟩ To APPRISE someone of something is to communicate something usu. of interest or importance to him ⟨this church, so he had been *apprised*, was founded by St. James the Less —T.G.Henderson⟩ ⟨Tristram's cutting the hazel and writing upon it with his knife in order to *apprise* the queen of his presence —Grace Frank⟩ ⟨to touch him on the sleeve and *apprise* him that I was there —Mary Austin⟩ To ADVISE someone of something is to inform him of something that may make a significant difference to him in an action, policy, or plan; it often suggests a forewarning or counseling ⟨consulted the wine card and *advised* me that the wine I had chosen had no special merit —R.M.Lovett⟩ ⟨I *advised* him strongly of the danger of switching professions without acquiring new professional qualifications —R.G.G.Price⟩ To NOTIFY is to send a notice or make a usu. formal communication generally about something requiring or worthy of attention ⟨the court clerk *notified* the witnesses when to appear⟩ ⟨*notify* a man of his acceptance in a club⟩ To ADVERTISE, rare in current use in this sense, is to inform or notify by way of warning ⟨the translators, good Protestants, were careful to *advertise* the reader that what they offered was Le Clerc's Moreri —*Times Lit. Supp.*⟩

**²inform** *adj* [MF *informe*, fr. L *informis*, fr. *in-* ¹in- + *forma* form — more at FORM] **1** *obs* **:** lacking regular form **:** SHAPELESS, DEFORMED **2** *obs* **:** lacking created form **:** UNFORMED

**in·formal** \(')in, ən+\ *adj* [¹in- + *formal*] **1 :** not formal **:** conducted or carried out without formal, regularly prescribed, or ceremonious procedure **:** UNOFFICIAL ⟨~ hearing⟩ ⟨~ discussion⟩ ⟨~ contract⟩ ⟨~ inquiries⟩ ⟨~ gathering of friends⟩ **2 :** characteristic of or appropriate to ordinary, casual, or familiar use ⟨~ English⟩ ⟨genial, ~ manner⟩ ⟨~ essay⟩ **3** *obs* **:** DERANGED, MAD ⟨poor ~ women are no more but instruments —Shak.⟩ **4** *of a design* **:** having an asymmetrical composition or arrangement made from unequal shapes and distances ⟨~ balance in a stage set⟩

**in·formality** \¦in+\ *n* [¹in- + *formality*] **1 :** the quality or state of being informal **:** lack of regular, prescribed, or customary form ⟨wayside camps, where the ~ of hardships loosened tongues —Mabel R. Gillis⟩ ⟨everyday speech in all its ~ and ease —R.A.Hall b. 1911⟩ **2 :** an informal act or proceeding ⟨the wedding ceremony was enlivened by several unexpected *informalities*⟩

**in·for·ma·lize** \ən'fȯ(r)mə,līz\ *vt* [*informal* + *-ize*] **:** to make informal or less formal ⟨college education of the future must . . . be greatly simplified and *informalized* —*Nation*⟩

**in·formally** \(')in, ən+\ *adv* **:** in an informal manner **:** without ceremony or formality ⟨addressed the gathering ~⟩ ⟨~ dressed in flannels and jacket⟩ **:** UNOFFICIALLY ⟨fast train . . . began to be called, more or less ~, the Cannonball —A.F. Harlow⟩

**informal planning** *n* **:** architectural planning in which dominant axes and strong visual climaxes are avoided in favor of freer circulation patterns and more subtle dramatic effects

**in·for·mant** \ən'fȯrmənt, -ō(ə)m-\ *n* -S [L *informant-, informans*, pres. part. of *informare* to inform — more at INFORM] **:** one that informs **:** one who gives information: as **a :** INFORMER **b :** one who supplies cultural or linguistic data in response to interrogation by an investigator ⟨findings . . . based on . . . statements of ~*s* from among both the educated and the uneducated —B.B.Ashcom⟩ ⟨analysis of great civilizations by the use of living ~*s* —Gregory Bateson⟩

**in for·ma pau·pe·ris** \-ˌfȯrmə'pȯpərəs, -'paüp-\ *adj (or adv)* [L, in the form of a pauper] **:** as a poor man **:** relieved of fees and costs in a legal action because of inability to pay ⟨permission was granted to file an appeal *in forma pauperis*⟩

**in·for·ma·tion** \ˌinfə(r)'māshən\ *n* -S *often attrib* [ME *informacioun*, fr. *enfourmen, informen* to inform + *-acioun* -ation — more at INFORM] **1 a** *obs* **:** an endowing with form **b** *obs* **:** the act of animating or inspiring **c** *obs* **:** TRAINING, DISCIPLINE, INSTRUCTION **d :** the communication or reception of knowledge or intelligence ⟨the function of a public library is ~⟩ ⟨we enclose a price list for your ~⟩ **2 :** something received or obtained through informing: as **a :** knowledge communicated by others or obtained from investigation, study, or instruction **b :** knowledge of a particular event or situation **:** INTELLIGENCE, NEWS, ADVICES ⟨latest ~ from the battle front⟩ ⟨securing ~ about conditions in the upper atmosphere⟩ ⟨~ bureau⟩ **c :** facts or figures ready for communication or use as distinguished from those incorporated in a formally organized branch of knowledge **:** DATA ⟨reliable source of ~⟩ **d :** a signal (as one of the digits in dialing a telephone number) purposely impressed upon the input of a communication system or a calculating machine **3 :** the act of informing against a person or party **4 a :** a formal accusation of a crime made by a prosecuting officer on information brought to his attention as distinguished from an indictment presented by a grand jury **:** COMPLAINT **b :** a pleading by an attorney general or other public officer setting forth a civil case or relief in which some public right of the state is asserted **c :** the document containing the depositions of the witnesses against one accused of crime **5 :** the process by which the form of an object of knowledge is impressed upon the apprehending mind so as to bring about the state of knowing **6 :** a logical quantity belonging to propositions and arguments as well as terms and comprising the sum of the synthetical propositions in which the term, proposition, or argument taken enters as subject or predicate, antecedent or consequent — see QUANTITY 5c **7 :** a numerical quantity that measures the uncertainty in the outcome of an experiment to be performed ⟨when an event occurs whose probability was *p*, the event is said to communicate an amount of ~ log (1/*p*) —W.F.Brown b. 1904⟩ ⟨the amount of ~ is defined, in the simplest cases, to be measured by the logarithm of the number of available choices —C.E. Shannon & Warren Weaver⟩ **syn** see KNOWLEDGE

**in·for·ma·tion·al** \¦==¦māshən°l, -shnəl\ *adj* **:** relating to or giving information **:** INFORMING ⟨~ service of a library⟩

**information girl** *n* **1 :** a telephone operator who gives information from the central office switchboard **2 :** a clerk at an information desk

**information theory** *n* **:** a theory that utilizes statistical techniques in dealing with the effect of encoding on the efficiency of processes of signal transmission and of communication between men (as in telecommunication or the printed word) or between men and machines or between machines and machines (as in computing machines)

**in·form·a·tive** \ən'fō(r)məd·iv, -ətiv\ *adj* [¹*inform* + *-ative*] **1** *obs* **:** having power to inform, animate, or vivify **2 :** imparting knowledge **:** INSTRUCTIVE ⟨~ lecture⟩ ⟨~ brochure⟩ **3 :** INFORMATORY — **in·form·a·tive·ly** \-əvlē, -lī\ *adv* — **in·form·a·tive·ness** \-ivnəs\ *n*

**in·form·ato·ry** \-mə,tōrē, -tȯr-, -ri\ *adj* [*information* + *-ory*] **:** INFORMING, INSTRUCTIVE ⟨a witty and ~ book⟩; *specif* **:** devised or intended to convey information ⟨~ bid in contract bridge⟩

**informatory double** *n* **:** a double made in bridge to convey information to one's partner and to invite a bid from him — called also *takeout double*

**informed** *adj* [fr. past part. of ¹*inform*] **1 :** having information ⟨an ~ citizenry⟩ ⟨a well-*informed* man⟩ **:** based on possession of information ⟨~ estimate of next year's tax receipts⟩ **2 :** EDUCATED, INTELLIGENT, CULTIVATED ⟨~ taste⟩ ⟨~ opinion⟩ ⟨transition . . . from blind habit to ~ works of art —Ernest Nagel⟩

**in·form·er** \ən'fȯrmər, -ō(ə)mə(r)\ *n* [ME *enfourmer*, fr. *enfourmen* to inform + *-er* — more at INFORM] **1** *obs* **:** one that informs, animates, or inspires ⟨nature, ~ of the poet's art —Alexander Pope⟩ **2 :** one that informs or imparts knowledge or news **3 :** one that informs against another: **a :** one that informs a magistrate of a violation of law **:** one that lays an information; *esp* **:** one that makes a practice of informing against others for violations of penal laws particularly when the informer may receive as a reward a share of the money penalty imposed — called also *common informer*; compare QUI TAM **b :** one secretly in the service of the police or of a diplomatic agency (as an embassy) that supplies information ⟨a nest of spies and ~*s*⟩

**informidable** adj [¹in- + formidable] obs : not formidable ⟨foe not ~ —John Milton⟩
**informing** adj [fr. pres. part. of ¹inform] **1** : ANIMATING, INSPIRING ⟨the concrete and the external are . . . the medium through which the ~ spirit is expressed —J.L.Lowes⟩ **2** : INFORMATIVE, INSTRUCTIVE
**in·form·ing·ly** adv : INFORMATIVELY, INSTRUCTIVELY
**informs** pres 3d sing of INFORM
**in fo·ro** \-ˈfō(ˌ)rō\ adv [L, in the forum] : before the court : within the jurisdiction
**in foro con·sci·en·ti·ae** \-ˌkänchēˈenchēˌē\ adv [L, in the forum of conscience] : privately or morally rather than legally ⟨an extrajudicial oath is binding only *in foro conscientiae*⟩
**in·for·tu·nate** \ənˈfō(r)chənət\ adj [ME *infortunat*, fr. L *infortunatus*, fr. *in-* ¹in- + *fortunatus* fortunate — more at FORTUNATE] **1** obs : UNFORTUNATE **2** : causing or presaging misfortune : UNPROPITIOUS
**in·for·tune** \(ˈ)inˈfȯrchən, ənˈ-\ n [ME, fr. MF, fr. L *infortunium*, fr. *in-* ¹in- + *-fortunium* (fr. *fortuna* fortune) — more at FORTUNE] : one of the malevolent planets (Saturn, Mars, or sometimes Mercury) in an unfavorable aspect
**infortunity** n -ES [MF *infortunité*, fr. L *infortunitat-, infortunitas*, fr. *in-* ¹in- + *fortuna* fortune + *-itat-, -itas* -ity] obs : MISFORTUNE
**infos** pl of INFO
**in·fra** \ˈinfrə, -n(ˌ)frä, -n(ˌ)frȧ\ adv [L] **1** : UNDER, BELOW **2** : LATER
**infra-** prefix [L *infra* below, underneath — more at UNDER] **1 a** : below : lower in status than — esp. in adjectives formed from adjectives ⟨*infra*human⟩ **b** : after : later than ⟨*infra*lapsarian⟩ **2** : within — esp. in adjectives formed from adjectives ⟨*infra*territorial⟩ **3** : below in a scale or series — esp. in adjectives formed from adjectives ⟨*infra*red⟩ **4** : below or beneath (a designated part of the anatomy) — esp. in adjectives formed from adjectives ⟨*infra*costal⟩
**in·fra-angelic** \ˈinfrə+\ adj [*infra-* + *angelic*] : less than angelic : HUMAN
**in·fra·basal** \"+\ adj [*infra-* + *basal*] zool : lying below a basal structure ⟨~ skeletal plate of a crinoid⟩
**in·fra·branchial** \"+\ adj [*infra-* + *branchial*] : lying below the gills — used esp. of the ventral part of the pallial chamber in the lamellibranchs
**in·fra·central** \"+\ adj [*infra-* + *central*] anat : lying below the centrum
**in·fra·class** \ˈinfrə+,-\ n [*infra-* + *class*] : a subdivision of a subclass that is more or less exactly equivalent to a superorder
**in·fra·clavicle** \ˈinfrə+\ n [*infra-* + *clavicle*] : a bony element in the shoulder girdle lying below the cleithrum in some ganoid and crossopterygian fishes and supposed to be the true homologue of the clavicle of higher animals
**in·fra·clavicular** \"+\ adj [*infra-* + *clavicular*] : relating or belonging to the infraclavicle
**in·fra·cos·ta·lis** \ˌinfrə(ˌ)käˈstaləs, -tal-, -täl-\ n, pl **infra·costa·les** \-a(ˌ)lēz, -ā(ˌ)lēz, -ä(ˌ)lās\ [NL, fr. *infra-* + L *costa* rib + *-alis* -al — more at COAST] : SUBCOSTALIS
**in·fract** \ənˈfrakt\ vt -ED/-ING/-S [L *infractus*, past part. of *infringere* to break, break off, destroy — more at INFRINGE] : BREAK, INFRINGE, VIOLATE ⟨~ the Constitution⟩
**in·fract·ible** \-təbəl\ adj [LL *infractus* unbroken (fr. L *in-* ¹in- + *fractus*, past part. of *frangere* to break) + E *-ible* — more at BREAK] : INVIOLABLE ⟨a thorough and ~ eight hours devoted to his work in Wall Street —Scott Fitzgerald⟩
**in·frac·tion** \ənˈfrakshən\ n -S [L *infraction-, infractio*, fr. *infractus* (past part. of *infringere*) + *-ion-, -io* -ion] **1** : the act of breaking or violating : BREACH, VIOLATION, INFRINGEMENT ⟨~ of a treaty⟩ ⟨minor ~s of the rules⟩ ⟨~ of code⟩ ⟨~ of discipline⟩ **2** : an incomplete fracture without displacement of the bone **syn** see BREACH
**in·frac·tor** \-ktə(r)\ n -S [prob. fr. MF *infracteur*, fr. LL *infractor*, fr. L *infractus* (past part. of *infringere*) + *-or*] : one that infracts or infringes : VIOLATOR, BREAKER
**in·fra dig** \ˈinfrəˈdig\ adj [modif. of L *infra dignitatem* beneath dignity] : being beneath one's dignity : UNDIGNIFIED ⟨it was clear . . . that off-season cruising was rather *infra dig* —Richard Gordon⟩ ⟨considered helping with the dishes to be *infra dig*⟩
**in·fra·foliar** \ˈinfrə+\ adj [*infra-* + *foliar*] : situated below the leaves ⟨~ flower clusters⟩
**in·fra·glacial** \"+\ adj [*infra-* + *glacial*] : SUBGLACIAL
**in·fra·glenoid** \"+\ adj [*infra-* + *glenoid*] : situated below the glenoid cavity of the scapula
**infraglenoid tubercle** n : a tubercle on the scapula for the attachment of the long head of the triceps muscle
**in·fra·gular** \"+\ adj [*infra-* + *gular*] : SUBESOPHAGEAL
**in·fra·human** \"+\ adj [*infra-* + *human*] : less or lower than human ⟨~ attributes⟩; *specif* : ANTHROPOID — compare SUPERHUMAN
**¹in·fra·labial** \"+\ adj [*infra-* + *labial*] : lying below the lip : SUBLABIAL
**²infralabial** \"\ n : a scale or plate bordering the lower jaw on either side of the mental of various reptiles
**¹in·fra·lap·sar·i·an** \ˌinfrəˌlapˈserēən, -sa(a)r-\ n -S [*infra-* + L *lapsus* lapse, fall + E *-arian* — more at LAPSE] : one that adheres to the doctrine of infralapsarianism — compare SUPRALAPSARIAN
**²infralapsarian** \ˌ==ˌ=ˈ===\ adj : of or relating to the doctrine of infralapsarianism
**in·fra·lap·sar·i·an·ism** \ˌ==ˌ=ˈ==əˌnizəm\ n -S : the doctrine that God foresaw and permitted the fall of man and that after the fall he then decreed election as a means of saving some of the human race — compare SUPRALAPSARIANISM
**in·fra·linear** \ˈinfrə+\ adj [*infra-* + *linear*] : placed below the line of writing : SUBLINEAR ⟨an ~ system of vocalization for Hebrew⟩
**in·fra·littoral** \"+\ adj [*infra-* + *littoral*] : situated to seaward of the region of littoral deposits ⟨~ zone⟩
**¹in·fra·marginal** \"+\ adj [*infra-* + *marginal*] **1** : situated below a margin : SUBMARGINAL ⟨~ convolution of the brain⟩ **2** : situated below the marginal cell of an insect's wing
**²inframarginal** \"\ n : an inframarginal element
**in·fra·natant** \"+\ adj [*infra-* + *natant*] : lying below a supernatant body ⟨unfiltered ~ solution from a growing culture —*Science*⟩
**in·fra·neritic** \"+\ adj [*infra-* + *neritic*] : lying at a depth greater than 120 feet below the ocean surface ⟨~ environment of sedimentation⟩ — opposed to *epineritic*
**in·frangibility** \(ˌ)in, ən+\ n : INVIOLABILITY ⟨the ~ of the given word is the first rule of politics —H.D.Scott⟩
**in·fran·gi·ble** \(ˈ)inˈfranjəbəl, ənˈf-, -raan-\ adj [MF, fr. LL *infrangibilis*, fr. L *in-* ¹in- + *frangere* to break + *-ibilis* -ible — more at BREAK] **1** : not capable of being broken ⟨~ resolution of character⟩ or separated into parts ⟨~ series⟩ **2** : not to be infringed or violated ⟨~ law⟩ — **in·fran·gi·ble·ness** n — **in·fran·gi·bly** \-blē, -bli\ adv
**in·fra·orbital** \ˈinfrə+\ adj [*infra-* + *orbital*] : situated beneath the orbit ⟨~ bone⟩
**in·fra·pose** \ˌinfrəˈpōz\ vt [*infra-* + *-pose* (as in *superpose*)] : to place under or beneath — **in·fra·position** \ˈinfrə+\ n
**in fra prae·si·dia** \ˌinfrəprēˈzidēə\ adv [L, under the protection] *of captured property* : in safe custody : completely under control
**¹in·fra·red** \ˈinfrəˈred, -frȧˈ-, -fräˈ- *sometimes* ˈinfoˈr- *by r-dissimilation*\ adj [*infra-* + *red*] **1** : lying outside the visible spectrum at its red end — used of thermal radiation of wavelengths longer than those of visible light **2** : relating to, producing, or employing infrared radiation ⟨~ therapy⟩ ⟨~ photography⟩ **3** : sensitive to infrared radiation and capable of photographing in darkness or through haze ⟨~ film⟩
**²infrared** \"\ n : infrared radiation
**infrared lamp** n : a high-power incandescent lamp operating at a lower filament temperature than a lamp used for illumination and yielding a large percentage of infrared radiation that is useful for heating purposes
**in·fra·roentgen ray** \"+...-\ n [*infra-* + *roentgen*] : GRENZ RAY
**in·fra·scap·u·la·ris** \ˌinfrəˌskapyəˈla(a)rəs\ n, pl **infra·scapula·res** \-a(a)(ˌ)rēz\ [NL, fr. *infra-* + *scapula* + *-aris* -ar] : the teres minor
**In·fra·si·zer** \ˈinfrəˌsīzə(r)\ trademark — used for an apparatus for determining the degree of fineness to which a material (as a mineral or rock) has been ground
**in·fra·social** \ˈinfrə+\ adj [*infra-* + *social*] *of insects* : lacking social organization : SOLITARY
**in·fra·sonic** \"+\ adj [*infra-* + *sonic*] **1** : having a frequency lower than about 16 cycles per second and therefore below the audibility range of the human ear and producing only a fluttering sensation with no sense of pitch — compare SONIC, SUPERSONIC **2** : utilizing or produced by infrasonic waves or vibrations
**in·fra·specific** \"+\ adj [*infra-* + *specific*] : included within a species ⟨~ categories⟩
**in·fra·spinal** \"+\ adj [*infra-* + *spinal*] : INFRASPINOUS
**in·fra·spi·na·tus** \ˌinfrə(ˌ)spīˈnādəs\ n, pl **infraspinati** [NL, fr. *infra-* + L *spina* spine + *-atus* -ate — more at SPINE] : a muscle that occupies the chief part of the infraspinous fossa of the scapula and is inserted into the greater tuberosity of the humerus
**in·fra·spinous** \ˈinfrə+\ adj [*infra-* + *spinous*] : lying below a spine; *esp* : lying below the spine of the scapula
**infraspinous fossa** n : the part of the dorsal surface of the scapula below the spine of the scapula
**in·fra·structure** \ˈinfrə+,-\ n [*infra-* + *structure*] : the underlying foundation or basic framework (as of an organization or a system) : SUBSTRUCTURE; *esp* : the permanent installations required for military purposes
**in·fra·temporal** \ˈinfrə+\ adj [*infra-* + *temporal*] : situated below the temple or temporal bone — used esp. of the lower or more lateral of the two divisions of the temporal fossae of various reptiles
**infratemporal fossa** n : a fossa in man and some other vertebrates bounded above by the plane of zygomatic arch, laterally by the ramus of the mandible, and medially by the pterygoid plate, and lodging the masseter and pterygoid muscles and the mandibular nerve
**in frau·dem le·gis** \-ˈfrȯdəm ˈlējəs\ adv [L] : in circumvention of the rules of law
**in·frequency** \(ˈ)in, ən+\ or **in·frequence** \"+\ n [L *infrequentia*, fr. *infrequent-, infrequens* infrequent + *-ia* -y] **1** obs : the quality or state of not being frequented : SOLITUDE, ISOLATION **2** : the state of rarely occurring : UNCOMMONNESS, RARENESS ⟨comparative ~ of typhoid fever⟩
**in·frequent** \"+\ adj [L *infrequent-, infrequens*, fr. *in-* ¹in- + *frequent-, frequens* frequent — more at FREQUENT] **1** obs : UNFREQUENTED **2** : seldom happening or occurring : RARE, UNCOMMON ⟨far from being ~, the crystalline state is almost universal among solids —K.K.Darrow⟩ **3** : placed or occurring at considerable distances or intervals : OCCASIONAL, SPARSE ⟨~ openings in a wall⟩ — **in·fre·quent·ly** adv
**in·frig·i·date** \ənˈfrijəˌdāt\ vt -ED/-ING/-S [LL *infrigidatus*, past part. of *infrigidare*, fr. L *in-* ²in- + LL *frigidare* to make cold, fr. L *frigidus* cold — more at FRIGID] : to make cold : CHILL
**in·fringe** \ənˈfrinj\ vb -ED/-ING/-S [L *infringere* to break, break off, weaken, destroy, fr. *in-* ²in- + *-fringere* (fr. *frangere* to break) — more at BREAK] vt **1** obs **a** : to break down : DESTROY **b** : DEFEAT, FRUSTRATE **c** : CONFUTE, REFUTE **d** : IMPAIR, WEAKEN **2** : to commit a breach of ⟨~ the peace⟩ : neglect to fulfill or obey : VIOLATE, TRANSGRESS ⟨~ a treaty⟩ ⟨~ an edict⟩ ⟨~ a contract⟩ ⟨~ a patent⟩ ⟨~ a copyright⟩ ⟨both these limits of gradient and curve must be *infringed* to reach the plateau —James Bird⟩ ⟨the statute . . . would ~ fundamental principles —O.W.Holmes †1935⟩ ~ vi : ENCROACH, TRESPASS — used with *on* or *upon* ⟨where the siesta is no catnap and a ten-o'clock dinner practically ~s on tea time —Claudia Cassidy⟩ **syn** see TRESPASS
**in·fringe·ment** \-jmənt\ n -S **1** : the act of infringing : BREACH, VIOLATION, NONFULFILLMENT ⟨~ of a treaty⟩ ⟨~ of the constitution⟩ **2** : an encroachment or trespass on a right or privilege : TRESPASS: **a** : the unlawful manufacture, use, or sale of a patented or copyrighted article, such as constitutes a tort in law **b** : the unlawful use of a trademark or trade name **syn** see BREACH
**in·fring·er** \-jə(r)\ n -S : one that infringes ⟨~ of a patent⟩
**in·fruc·tes·cence** \ˌinˌfrəkˈtesən(t)s\ n [F, fr. *in-* ²in- + L *fructus* fruit + F *-escence* (as in *inflorescence*) — more at FRUIT] : the fruiting stage of an inflorescence
**in·fructuous** \(ˈ)in, ən+\ adj [L *infructuosus*, fr. *in-* ¹in- + *fructuosus* fruitful — more at FRUCTUOUS] **1** : UNFRUITFUL **2** : FRUITLESS, UNPROFITABLE — **in·fruc·tu·ous·ly** adv
**in·fu·la** \ˈinfyələ\ n, pl **infu·lae** \-əˌlē\ [L; perh. akin to L *redimire* to tie, wreathe, *geminus* twin — more at GEMINATE] **1** : a fillet of red and white wool worn in ancient Rome as a token of religious consecration or inviolability **2** [ML, fr. L] **a** : one of two lappets that hang from the back of a bishop's miter **b** : a chasuble used principally in France and England from the 11th to the 16th century

infulae

**in·fu·mate** \ˈinfyəˌmāt, ənˈfyümət\ or **in·fu·mat·ed** \-ˌmād·əd\ adj [*infumate* fr. L *infumatus*, past part. of *infumare* to dry by smoking, fr. *in-* ²in- + *fumare* to smoke, fr. *fumus* smoke; *infumated* fr. L *infumatus* + E *-ed* — more at FUME] : clouded with blackish color ⟨~ insect wing⟩
**in·fu·ma·tion** \ˌinfyəˈmāshən\ n -S [L *infumatus* + E *-ion*] : the act or process of drying in smoke
**in·fun·dib·u·lar** \ˈin(ˌ)fənˈdibyələ(r)\ adj [NL *infundibulum* + E *-ar*] **1** : resembling a funnel **2 a** : of or relating to an infundibulum **b** : INFUNDIBULATE
**in·fun·dib·u·la·ta** \ˌ=(ˌ)=ˌdibyəˈläd·ə, -lād·ə\ [NL, fr. *infundibulum* + *-ata*] syn of GYMNOLAEMATA
**in·fun·dib·u·late** \ˈ=(ˌ)=ˈdibyəˌlāt, -lət\ adj [NL *infundibulum* + E *-ate*] **1** : having an infundibulum **2** : INFUNDIBULIFORM
**in·fun·dib·u·li·form** \-yələˌfȯrm\ adj [NL *infundibulum* + *-iform*] : having the form of a funnel or cone ⟨~ calyx⟩
**in·fun·dib·u·lum** \ˌ=(ˌ)=ˈdibyələm\ n, pl **infundibu·la** \-lə\ [NL, fr. L, funnel, fr. *infundere* to pour in — more at INFUSE] : any of various conical or dilated organs or parts: as **a** : the hollow conical process of gray matter that is borne on the tuber cinereum and constitutes the stalk of the neurohypophysis by which the pituitary body is continuous with the brain **b** : any of the small spaces having walls beset with air sacs in which the bronchial tubes terminate in the lungs **c** : the enlarged process of the right ventricle from which the pulmonary artery arises **d** : the passage by which the anterior ethmoid cells and the frontal sinuses communicate with the nose **e** : the calyx of a kidney **f** : the abdominal opening of a fallopian tube **g** : a central cavity in the Ctenophora into which the gastric sac leads
**¹in·fu·ri·ate** \ənˈfyu̇rēˌāt, *usu* -ād.+V\ vt -ED/-ING/-S [ML *infuriatus*, past part. of *infuriare*, fr. L *in-* ²in- + *furiare* to madden, fr. *furia* fury — more at FURY] : to make furious : ENRAGE, MADDEN ⟨his book will . . . ~, enlighten, and rejoice different types of readers —D.W.Brogan⟩
**²in·fu·ri·ate** \", -ēət\ adj [ML *infuriatus*, past part.] : furiously angry : INFURIATED ⟨the hunchback weak, but ~, buffeting, biting, and whimpering —Arthur Morrison⟩ — **in·fu·ri·ate·ly** adv
**in·fu·ri·at·ing·ly** adv : to a maddening degree ⟨his sorely tried and ~ trying wife —Charles Lee⟩ : so as to infuriate ⟨~ indifferent⟩
**in·fu·ri·a·tion** \ənˌfyu̇rēˈāshən\ n -S : the act of infuriating or state of being infuriated
**in·fus·cate** \ənˈfəˌskāt, -ˌskət\ or **in·fus·cat·ed** \-ˌskād·əd\ adj [*infuscate* fr. L *infuscatus*, past part. of *infuscare* to obscure, fr. *in-* ²in- + *fuscare* to darken, fr. *fuscus* dark brown, blackish; *infuscated* fr. L *infuscatus* + E *-ed* — more at DUSK] : OBSCURED ⟨~ minds⟩; *specif* : darkened with a brownish tinge ⟨~ wing of an insect⟩ — **in·fus·ca·tion** \ˌin(ˌ)fəˈskāshən\ n -S
**in·fuse** \ənˈfyüz\ vb -ED/-ING/-S [ME *infusen, enfusen*, fr. MF & L; MF *infuser*, fr. L *infusus*, past part. of *infundere* to pour in, fr. *in-* ²in- + *fundere* to pour — more at FOUND] vt **1** obs : to pour (a liquid) into something **2 a** : to instill or inculcate a principle or quality in ⟨attributes the fine spirit of the whole project to the self-respect with which men had been *infused* —Dixon Wecter⟩ **b** : INTRODUCE, INSINUATE, SUGGEST ⟨~ an idea⟩ ⟨~ a belief⟩ ⟨*infused* an aviation curriculum into some forty university departments —Phil Gustafson⟩ **3** : INSPIRE, IMBUE, ANIMATE, FILL ⟨brought together the main ideas . . . and *infused* them with the conception that the universe was the product of a historical development —S.F. Mason⟩ ⟨*infused* only with her passion for her child —Ethel Wilson⟩ **4** : to steep in water or other fluid without boiling for the purpose of extracting useful qualities : DRENCH ⟨~ tea leaves⟩ ~ vi : to undergo the process of infusion ⟨letting the tea stand a few minutes to ~ —Flora Thompson⟩
**syn** SUFFUSE, IMBUE, INGRAIN, INOCULATE, LEAVEN: INFUSE implies the introducing into one thing of a second that gives life, vigor, or new significance ⟨*infusing* life into an inanimate body —Mary W. Shelley⟩ ⟨the extraordinary force which Lawrence's imagination *infused* into his prose —*Times Lit. Supp.*⟩ ⟨whose work is for the most part *infused* with the spirit of scientific materialism —L.A.White⟩ ⟨it *infused* into them the feeling that they were not at the mercy of blind economic forces —A.R.Williams⟩ SUFFUSE implies the spreading over or through one thing of a second that gives the first thing an unusual color, aspect, texture, or quality ⟨I felt a large, healthy blush *suffuse* my features —L.P.Smith⟩ ⟨the western sky was *suffused* with the transparent yellow-green of August evenings —Ellen Glasgow⟩ ⟨an exalted feeling of martyrdom well earned *suffused* the exiles —E.J.Simmons⟩ ⟨the novel was *suffused* with a feeling for water and air, with sunlight hot and shifting —Leo Gurko⟩ IMBUE implies the introduction into a person or thing of something that completely permeates ⟨*imbued* so strongly with a sense of duty and obedience — Hanama Tasaki⟩ ⟨*imbued* with a dynamic faith —*Amer. Guide Series: Minn.*⟩ ⟨*imbue* the army with a national spirit —Hajo Holborn⟩ ⟨the mind becomes *imbued* with the scientific method —J.B.Conant⟩ INGRAIN implies a pervading of something with an irremovable dye or something suggesting such a dye ⟨morality *ingrained* in the national character —J.A.Froude⟩ ⟨the principle of serfdom was *ingrained* in medieval society — G.G.Coulton⟩ ⟨her instinctive humility and good manners were too deeply *ingrained* —Helen Howe⟩ ⟨this idea of equality was *ingrained* in the New York cabdriver —D.F.Karaka⟩ INOCULATE, in this extended sense, implies an imbuing of a person with something resembling a disease germ, often suggesting a surreptitious means ⟨those who believe that the great mass of the people are unreasoning beasts that must be controlled by *inoculating* them with myths or fictions —M.R. Cohen⟩ ⟨the democratic leveling had helped to *inoculate* the public with the idea of free schools disassociated from charity —*Amer. Guide Series: Va.*⟩ ⟨third-rate southerners *inoculated* with all the worst traits of the Yankee sharper —H.L.Mencken⟩ LEAVEN implies a transforming of something by introducing into it something else which enlivens, elevates, tempers, or markedly alters the total quality, usu. for the better ⟨*leaven* the dense mass of facts and events with the elastic force of reason —J.H.Newman⟩ ⟨there was need of idealism to *leaven* the materialistic realism of the times —V.L.Parrington⟩ ⟨knowledge . . . must be *leavened* with magnanimity before it becomes wisdom —A.E.Stevenson b. 1900⟩
**in·fus·er** \-zə(r)\ n -S : one that infuses; *esp* : a device for infusing tea leaves
**in·fusibility** \ˈin+\ n : the quality or state of being infusible
**in·fusible** \(ˈ)in, ən+\ adj [¹in- + *fusible*] : not fusible : incapable or very difficult of fusion; *specif, of a mineral* : having a melting point higher than the temperature (about 1500°C) of the ordinary blowpipe flame — **in·fu·si·ble·ness** n -ES
**infusible white precipitate** n : AMMONIATED MERCURY
**in·fusion** \ənˈfyüzhən\ n -S [ME, fr. MF & L; MF, fr. L *infusion-, infusio*, fr. *infusus* (past part. of *infundere* to pour in) + *-ion-, -io* -ion — more at INFUSE] **1 a** : the act or process of infusing ⟨an ~ of ordinary men and women would lessen the alleged remoteness of the higher civil servants from the life of the people —Ray Lewis & Angus Maude⟩ **b** : something that is infused ⟨horses of this type carry some ~ of . . . Thoroughbred blood —C.F.Rooks⟩ **2 a** : the introducing of a solution (as of glucose or salt) into a vein; *also* : the solution so used **b** (1) : the steeping or soaking usu. in water of a substance (as a plant drug) in order to extract its virtues (2) : the liquid extract obtained by this process **3** : a watery suspension of decaying organic material ⟨culturing soil amoebas in lettuce ~⟩
**in·fu·sion·ism** \-zhəˌnizəm\ n -S : the doctrine that the soul is preexistent to the body and is infused into it at conception or birth — compare CREATIONISM, TRADUCIANISM
**in·fu·sion·ist** \-nəst\ n : one who adheres to the doctrine of infusionism
**infusion process** n : a mashing process in which the whole mash is kept at about 70°C — compare DECOCTION PROCESS
**in·fu·sive** \ənˈfyüsiv, -üziv\ adj : INSPIRING, INFLUENCING ⟨the ~ force of Spring on man —James Thomson †1748⟩
**in·fu·so·ria** \ˌinfyəˈzōrēə, -ˈs-, -ȯr-\ n pl [NL, fr. neut. pl. of *infusorius*, fr. L *infusus* (past part. of *infundere* to pour in) + *-orius* -ory] **1** cap : a group of minute organisms typically found in infusions of decaying organic matter: **a** *in early classifications* : a heterogeneous group comprising various plant and animal organisms (as bacteria, algae, fungi, protozoans, and small metazoans) **b** *in later classifications* : a heterogeneous group of animals comprising protozoans and small metazoans **c** *in early modern classifications* : a major division of Protozoa comprising protozoans with differentiated locomotor organelles and including the ciliates **d** *in some recent classifications* : a class of Protozoa coextensive with the subphylum Ciliophora **2** *often cap* : microscopic animal life — not used technically
**in·fu·so·ri·al** \ˌ=ˈ==əl\ adj [NL *Infusoria* + E *-al*] : relating to, containing, or having Infusoria
**infusorial earth** n : KIESELGUHR
**¹in·fu·so·ri·an** \-ēən\ adj [NL *Infusoria* + E *-an*] : INFUSORIAL
**²infusorian** \"\ n -S : one of the Infusoria
**¹in·fu·so·ri·form** \ˌ=ˈ=ˈ=rəˌfȯrm\ adj [NL *Infusoria* + E *-form*] : resembling an infusorian
**²infusoriform** \"\ or **infusoriform larva** n -S : the minute ciliated infective larva of the Dicyemida
**in·fu·so·ri·gen** \ˌ=ˈ=rəjən, -rəˌjen\ also **in·fu·so·ri·gene** \-rəˌjēn\ n -S [²infusoriform + *-gen, -gene*] : a reduced individual of certain mesozoans that is formed within the rhombogen and that gives rise to the infusoriform larva
**in·fu·so·ri·oid** \ˌ=ˈ=rēˌȯid\ adj [NL *Infusoria* + E *-oid*] : like an infusorian
**in·fu·so·ri·um** \ˌ=ˈ=rēəm\ n, pl **infuso·ria** \-ēə\ [NL, back-formation fr. *Infusoria*] : INFUSORIAN
**in·fu·so·ry** \ənˈfyüzərē, -üsə-\ n -ES [NL *Infusoria*] archaic : INFUSORIAN — usu. used in pl.
**ing** \ˈiŋ\ n -S [ME *enge, ynge*, of Scand origin; akin to ON *eng, engi* meadow, Norw & Dan *eng*; akin to MLG *enge* meadowland, OS & OHG *angar* meadow, pasture, OE *anga* hook — more at ANGLE] *dial Eng* : a low-lying pasture or meadow
**¹-ing** \iŋ, ēŋ, ən, ēn *after any sound; after* t *(but usu not when* f, k, p, *or* s *precedes) & after* d *(but usu not when* l *or* n *precedes)*, ᵊn; *after* k *(but usu not when* s *precedes) or* g, *sometimes* ᵊŋ; *after* p, b, *or* v *(the* v *assimilating to* b), *sometimes* ᵊm *as in* ˈräbᵊm *for "robbing" or* ˈmübᵊm *for "moving"; in rapid speech, often* ŋ *or* n *after* ē, ā, ī, *or* ȯi *as in* ˈsāŋ *or* ˈsān *for "saying"; in NewEng often with intrusive* r *preceding when* ȯ *is the last sound in the infinitive form as in* ˈdrȯriŋ *or* ˈdrȯrin *for "drawing"; some have* ŋ *as their only consonant in this suffix & regard any other consonant as inelegant or substandard; some use consonants other than* ŋ *chiefly in informal speech; some use consonants other than* ŋ *for all styles of speech & of these some regard* ŋ *as artificial; for economy of space,* ŋ *is usu the only consonant shown for the suffix -ing in entries in this dictionary*\ vb suffix *or* adj suffix [ME *-inge, -ing*, alter. (influenced by *-inge* ³-ing) of *-inde, -ende*, fr. OE *-ende*, fr. *-e-* (vowel historically belonging to the verb stem) + *-nde*, pres. part. suffix — more at -ANT] — used to form the present participle ⟨*going*⟩ ⟨*sailing*⟩ and sometimes to form an adjective resembling a present participle but not derived from a verb ⟨*hulking*⟩ ⟨*swashbuckling*⟩; regularly accompanied by omission of final postconsonantal *e* of the base word ⟨*hoping*⟩ ⟨*loving*⟩, change of final *ie* of the base word to *y* ⟨*tying*⟩, or doubling of the final consonant of the base word immediately after a short stressed vowel ⟨*hopping*⟩ ⟨*planning*⟩

**²-ing** \"\ *n suffix* -s [ME, fr. OE *-ing, -ung* one of a (specified) kind, one belonging to, one descended from; akin to OHG *-ing* one of a (specified) kind, one belonging to, one descended from, ON *-ingr, -ungr,* Goth *-ings* one of a (specified) kind] **:** one of a (specified) kind ⟨sweet*ing*⟩ ⟨wild*ing*⟩

**³-ing** \"\ *n suffix* -s [ME *-inge, -ing* (in early ME a suffix forming nouns from verbs, in later ME becoming also a gerundial suffix), fr. OE *-ung, -ing,* suffix forming nouns from verbs; akin to OHG *-unga, -ung,* suffix forming nouns from verbs, ON *-ing,* suffix forming nouns from verbs, *-ung,* suffix forming nouns from nouns] **1 :** action or process ⟨becom*ing*⟩ ⟨draw*ing*⟩ ⟨runn*ing*⟩ ⟨sleep*ing*⟩ ⟨wash*ing*⟩ **:** instance of an action or process ⟨a bless*ing*⟩ ⟨a meet*ing*⟩ ⟨my com*ings* and go*ings*⟩ — in nouns formed from any fully inflected verb and functioning either as gerunds capable of being modified by an adverb and capable of having an object if the base verb is transitive ⟨after casually read*ing* the letter twice⟩ or as ordinary nouns ⟨after two casual read*ings* of the letter⟩ **2 :** something connected with an action or process: **a :** product, accompaniment, or result of an action or process ⟨an engrav*ing*⟩ ⟨a paint*ing*⟩ — in nouns formed from verbs; often in plural ⟨earn*ings*⟩ ⟨leav*ings*⟩ ⟨shav*ings*⟩ **b :** something used in an action or process ⟨a bed cover*ing*⟩ ⟨the lin*ing* of a coat⟩ — in nouns, esp. collectives ⟨carpet*ing*⟩ ⟨hous*ing*⟩ ⟨rigg*ing*⟩ ⟨shipp*ing*⟩, formed from verbs **3 :** action or process connected with (a specified thing) ⟨blackberry*ing*⟩ ⟨capital*ing*⟩ — in nouns formed from nouns **4 :** something connected with, consisting of, or used in making (a specified thing) ⟨sack*ing*⟩ ⟨scaffold*ing*⟩ ⟨shirt*ing*⟩ — in nouns, esp. collectives, formed from nouns **5 :** something related to (a specified concept) ⟨off*ing*⟩ — in nouns formed from parts of speech other than verbs and nouns; regularly accompanied by omission of final postconsonantal *e* of the base word, change of final *ie* of the base word to *y,* or doubling of the final consonant of the base word immediately after a short stressed vowel

**in·ga** *in sense 1* ˈiŋgə, *in senses 2 & 3* iŋˈgä *or* ˈiŋgə\ *n* [NL, fr. Pg *ingá* huamuchil, fr. Tupi *ingá, engá*] **1** *cap* **:** a genus of tropical shrubs and trees (family Leguminosae) having white or red flowers and large pods that contain an edible pulp and yielding an inferior timber of little durability — see GUAMA **2** -s **:** any plant of the genus *Inga* **3** [Pg *ingá*] -s **:** CAMACHILE

**in·gae·vo·nes** \ˌinjəˈvō(ˌ)nēz\ *n pl, usu cap* [L] **:** a group of Teutonic peoples inhabiting the northern coast of Europe in ancient times

**in·gae·von·ic** \ˌ≈≈ˈvänik, -ˈvōn-\ *adj, often cap* **:** of or relating to the Ingaevones

**in·ga·lik** \ˈiŋgəˌlik\ *n, pl* **ingalik** *or* **ingaliks** *usu cap* **1 a :** an Athapaskan people of the lower Yukon and Kuskokwim river valleys of Alaska **b :** a member of such people **2 :** the language of the Ingalik people

**¹in·gate** \ˈinˌgāt\ *n* [ME, fr. *in* + *gate* way, street — more at GATE] **1** *dial Eng* **:** ENTRANCE **2** *obs* **a :** a thing that enters **:** IMPORT **b :** import duty

**²ingate** \"\ *n* [⁴*in* + *gate* (channel in a mold)] **:** a gate through which the metal is poured into a foundry mold

**ingather** \ˈ≈ˌ≈\ *vb* [²*in* + *gather*] *vt* **:** to gather in; *esp* **:** HARVEST ~ *vi* **:** to gather together **:** ASSEMBLE

**ingatherer** \ˈ≈ˌ≈≈\ *n* **:** one that gathers in **:** HARVESTER

**ingathering** \ˈ≈ˌ≈(≈)≈\ *n* [⁴*in* + *gathering*] **1 :** the act of gathering **:** COLLECTION, HARVEST ⟨~ of lenten boxes⟩ ⟨members of the needlework guild turn in their finished garments at the annual ~⟩ **2 :** ASSEMBLY ⟨revivalist ~⟩

**ing·ber·lach** \ˈiŋbərlək\ *n* -s [Yiddish, pl. of *ingberl* piece of ginger candy, dim. of *ingber* ginger, fr. MHG *ingeber, ingewer,* fr. OF *gingebre* — more at GINGER] **:** a candy made chiefly of ginger and honey

**in·geminate** \ən+\ *vt* [L *ingeminatus,* past part. of *ingeminare,* fr. *in-* ²in- + *geminare* to geminate — more at GEMINATE] **:** REDOUBLE, REITERATE **syn** see REPEAT

**in·gemination** \(ˌ)in, ən+\ *n* **:** REPETITION, DUPLICATION

**ingender** *obs var of* ENGENDER

**in·gen·er·a·ble** \ənˈjen(ə)rəbəl\ *adj* [ME, fr. LL *ingenerabilis,* fr. L *in-* ¹in- + *generabilis* generable — more at GENERABLE] **:** incapable of being engendered or produced **:** ORIGINAL — **in·gen·er·a·bly** \-blē\ *adv*

**¹in·gen·er·ate** \ənˈjenəˌrāt\ *vt* [L *ingeneratus,* past part. of *ingenerare,* fr. *in-* ²in- + *generare* to beget, create — more at GENERATE] **:** to bring about the generation of **:** BEGET, CAUSE

**²in·gen·er·ate** \-en(ə)rət\ *adj* [L *ingeneratus*] **1 :** INBORN, INNATE **2** *obs* **:** GENERATED, PRODUCED — **in·gen·er·ate·ly** *adv*

**³in·generate** \(ˈ)inˈjen(ə)rət, ənˈj-\ *adj* [LL *ingeneratus,* fr. L *in-* ¹in- + *generatus,* past part. of *generare*] **:** not generated ⟨God is ~⟩

**ingenies** *pl of* INGENY

**in·ge·nios·i·ty** \(ˌ)inˌjēnēˈäsəd-ē, ənˌj-, -jēnˈyä-\ *n* -ES [F *ingéniosité,* fr. *ingénieux* ingenious + *-ité* -ity] **:** INGENUITY, SKILL, CLEVERNESS

**in·ge·nious** \ənˈjēnyəs *sometimes* -nēəs\ *adj* [MF *ingenieux,* fr. L *ingeniosus,* fr. *ingenium* natural capacity, natural disposition + *-osus* -ous — more at ENGINE] **1** *obs* **:** showing or calling for intelligence **:** marked by mental power ⟨~ studies —Shak.⟩ **2 :** marked by especial aptitude at clever discovering, inventing, or contriving ⟨the invention of the knitting frame by another ~ English clergyman —Lewis Mumford⟩ **3 :** marked by originality, resourcefulness, and cleverness in conception or execution ⟨the iron safe built into the wall . . . made by an ~ locksmith —Thomas Hardy⟩ **4** [by alter. (influence of L *ingenuus* ingenuous)] *obs* **:** INGENUOUS **syn** see CLEVER

**in·ge·nious·ly** *adv* **:** in an ingenious manner

**in·ge·nious·ness** *n* -ES **:** INGENUITY

**in·genital** \ən+\ *adj* [L *ingenitus* inborn (fr. *in-* ²in- + *genitus,* past part. of *gignere* to beget, bring forth) + E *-al* — more at KIN] **:** INNATE, INHERENT

**¹in·ge·nue** \ˈanjəˌnü, ˈaⁿzhə-, ÷ˈäⁿzhə-, ÷ˈänjə-, ˌ≈≈ˈ≈\ *n* -s [F *ingénue,* fr. fem. of *ingénu* ingenuous, fr. L *ingenuus*] **1 a :** an ingenuous unsophisticated girl or young woman **:** a girl just entering society **:** DEBUTANTE ⟨suitable dress for an ~⟩; *esp* **:** a stage part representing a character that is youthful, innocent, appealing, sweet, sympathetic ⟨musical comedy ~⟩ — compare SOUBRETTE **b :** a naive or inexperienced person ⟨this is no time to have a political ~ as secretary of state —H.L.Ickes⟩ **2 :** a pale to grayish yellow green that is greener and less strong than water green

**²ingenue** \"\ *adj* **:** of, related, or appropriate to an ingenue ⟨artless ~ air about her⟩ ⟨~ party dress⟩

**in·ge·nu·i·ty** \ˌinjəˈn(y)üəd-ē, -ətē, -i\ *n* -ES [L *ingenuitas* ingenuousness, fr. *ingenuus* ingenuous + *-itas* -ity; in sense 2 & 3, influenced in meaning by *ingenious*] **1** *obs* **:** INGENUOUSNESS, CANDOR **2 a** *obs* **:** GENIUS, TALENT **b :** the power or quality of ready invention **:** skill or cleverness in devising or combining ⟨infinite ~ of man . . . in finding new methods of torture for his fellows —Mary Webb⟩ **c :** cleverness or aptness of design or contrivance ⟨despite the ~ of this etymological contention, the origin of the name is still disputed —*Amer. Guide Series: Minn.*⟩ ⟨all the perverted ~ of propaganda —Dean Acheson⟩ **3 :** an ingenious device or contrivance ⟨sophistication in the *ingenuities* of language —T.S.Eliot⟩ ⟨explore our stateroom, and scan eagerly the *ingenuities* by which we are to be surrounded for the journey —Frank A. Swinnerton⟩

**in·gen·u·ous** \ənˈjenyəwəs\ *adj* [L *ingenuus,* fr. *in-* ²in- + *-genus* (akin to L *gignere* to beget, bring forth) — more at KIN] **1 :** FREEBORN ⟨~ Roman subjects⟩ **2** *obs* **:** of a superior character **:** NOBLE, HONORABLE ⟨symptoms of an ~ mind rather unfrequent in this age of brass —William Cowper⟩ **3 :** marked by lack of reserve, dissimulation, or guile: **a :** showing innocent or childlike simplicity, straightforwardness, frankness ⟨the Earl of Kildare's ~ explanation that he would not have burned a church if he had not thought the bishop was in it —Douglas Bush⟩ **b :** marked by lack of subtle analysis or consideration **:** SIMPLE, UNWARY, UNAWARE, OPEN ⟨a new invention (the telephone) in which it would seem ~ to believe too soon —Edith Wharton⟩ ⟨at times he was astoundingly ~, and then his dodges would not deceive the dullest —Arnold Bennett⟩ **4** [by alter. (influence of L *ingeniosus* ingenious)] *obs* **:** INGENIOUS **syn** see NATURAL

**in·gen·u·ous·ly** *adv* **:** in an ingenuous manner

**in·gen·u·ous·ness** *n* -ES **:** the quality of being ingenuous **:** absence of guile, reserve, or disguise **:** CANDOR, SIMPLICITY ⟨his airs of importance were comical in their ~ —Arnold Bennett⟩

**ingeny** *n* -ES [L *ingenium* natural character, natural disposition — more at ENGINE] *obs* **:** INTELLIGENCE, GENIUS, INGENUITY

**inger** \ˈiŋ(g)ə(r)\ *n* -s *cap* **:** INGRIAN

**in·ger·ence** \ˈinjərən(t)s, aⁿzhārääⁿs\ *n, pl* **inger·ences** \-rən(t)səz, -räāⁿs\ [F *ingérence,* fr. *ingérer* to intrude (fr. L *ingerere*) + *-ence*] **:** INTERFERENCE, INTRUSION ⟨~ in the domestic affairs of a neighboring country⟩

**inger·man** \ˈiŋ(g)ə(r)mən\ *n* -s *cap* **:** INGRIAN

**in·gest** \ənˈjest\ *vt* -ED/-ING/-s [L *ingestus,* past part. of *ingerere* to carry in, press upon, fr. *in-* ²in- + *gerere* to bear, wage, cherish — more at CAST] **1 :** to take in for digestion (as into the stomach) **2 :** to take in **:** SWALLOW, ABSORB ⟨for a country of forty-seven million, ~*ing* twelve million visitors . . . is a big swallow —Robert Shaplen⟩ ⟨trying to ~ the ideas of philosophers⟩ **syn** see EAT

**in·ges·ta** \ənˈjestə\ *n pl* [NL, fr. L, neut. pl. of *ingestus*] **:** food and other materials taken into the body by way of the digestive tract — compare EGESTA

**in·ges·tant** \-tənt\ *n* -s **:** something taken into the body by ingestion; *esp* **:** an allergen so taken

**in·gest·ible** \-təbəl\ *adj* **:** capable of being ingested

**in·ges·tion** \-jes(h)chən\ *n* -s [LL *ingestion-, ingestio* action of pouring in, fr. L *ingestus* + *-ion-, -io* -ion] **1 :** the taking of material (as food) into the digestive system **2 :** the taking of air, gas, or liquid into an engine

**in·ges·tive** \-stiv\ *adj* **:** of or relating to ingestion

**in·gine** \ənˈjīn\ *n* -s [L *ingenium* natural character, natural disposition — more at ENGINE] *Scot* **:** GENIUS, INGENUITY

**ingiver** \ˈ≈ˌ≈≈\ *n* [⁴*in* + *giver*] *Brit* **:** HANDER-IN

**ingiving** \ˈ≈ˌ≈≈\ *n* [⁴*in* + *giving* (after *give in,* v.)] **:** the act of handing in thread to a loom

**¹ingle** \ˈiŋ(g)əl\ *n* -s [ScGael *aingeal* light, fire] **1 :** FLAME, BLAZE **2 :** FIREPLACE **3 :** CORNER, ANGLE ⟨cabin . . . with its one large room and small ~*s,* or sleeping closets —H.C. Forman⟩

**²ingle** *n* -s [origin unknown] *obs* **:** CATAMITE

**³ingle** *vt* -ED/-ING/-s **1** *obs* **:** FONDLE, CARESS **2** *obs* **:** CAJOLE, WHEEDLE

**ingle cheek** *n* [¹*ingle*] *chiefly Scot* **:** FIRESIDE

**inglenook** \ˈ≈≈ˌ≈\ *n* [¹*ingle* + *nook*] **1 :** CHIMNEY CORNER **2 :** a high-backed wooden settle placed close to a fireplace

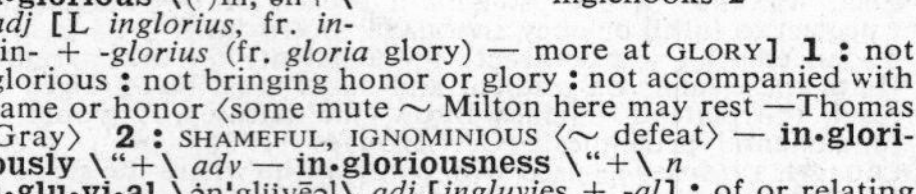

inglenooks 2

**ingle recess** *n* [¹*ingle*] **:** a recessed seating area at a fireplace **:** INGLENOOK

**ingleside** \ˈ≈≈ˌ≈\ *n* [¹*ingle* + *side*] **:** FIRESIDE

**ingliding** \ˈ≈ˌ≈≈\ *adj* [⁴*in* + *gliding* (after *glide in,* v.)] *of a diphthong or triphthong* **:** CENTERING — compare OUTGLIDING

**in·glorious** \(ˈ)in, ən+\ *adj* [L *inglorius,* fr. *in-* ¹in- + *-glorius* (fr. *gloria* glory) — more at GLORY] **1 :** not glorious **:** not bringing honor or glory **:** not accompanied with fame or honor ⟨some mute ~ Milton here may rest —Thomas Gray⟩ **2 :** SHAMEFUL, IGNOMINIOUS ⟨~ defeat⟩ — **in·gloriously** \"+\ *adv* — **in·gloriousness** \"+\ *n*

**in·glu·vi·al** \ənˈglüvēəl\ *adj* [*ingluvies* + *-al*] **:** of or relating to a crop ⟨~ membrane⟩ ⟨crop-milk is an ~ secretion⟩

**in·glu·vi·es** \-vēˌēz\ *n, pl* **ingluvies** [L, fr. *in-* ²in- + *-gluvies* (akin to *gluttire* to swallow) — more at GLUTTON] **:** the crop of a bird or insect

**in·glu·vi·itis** \(ˌ)inˌglüvēˈīd-əs, ən-\ *or* **in·glu·vi·tis** \ˌinˌglüˈvīd-əs\ *n* -ES [NL, fr. L *ingluvies* + NL *-itis*] **:** catarrhal inflammation of the crop in fowls

**in-goal** \ˈ≈ˌ≈\ *n* [⁴*in*] **:** either of the two areas of a rugby field bounded by the goal line, the dead-ball line, and the touch-in-goal lines — see RUGBY illustration

**¹ingoing** \ˈ≈ˌ≈≈\ *n* [ME, fr. *in* + *going*] **1 :** the act of going in **:** ENTRANCE **2** *Brit* **:** a sum paid when taking over a business

**²ingoing** \ˈ≈ˌ≈≈\ *adj* [²*in* + *going*] **1 :** going in ⟨~ tide⟩ **:** ENTERING ⟨~ administration⟩ **2 :** PENETRATING, THOROUGH ⟨~ mind⟩

**in·golds·by car** \ˈiŋgəl(d)zbē-\ *n* [fr. *Ingoldsby,* a trademark] **:** a dump car used to transport certain ores and concentrates

**in·got** \ˈiŋgət *also* -ˌgät; *usu* |d·+V\ *n* -s [ME, prob. modif. (resulting from incorrect division of MF *lingot* as *l'ingot,* understood as containing *l'* the, contr. of *le,* def. art., the, fr. L *ille* that one, that) of MF *lingot* mass of metal cast into a convenient shape — more at LINGOT, LARIAT] **1 :** a mold in which metal is cast **2 :** a mass of metal cast into a convenient shape for storage or transportation and to be later remelted for casting or finished (as by rolling or forging) — compare PIG

**ingot iron** *n* **:** iron containing usu. less than 0.05 percent carbon and similarly small proportions of manganese and other impurities

**in-grade** \ˈ≈ˌ≈, ≈ˈ≈\ *adj* [fr. the phrase *in grade*] **:** occurring within a specified labor grade or rate range or occupational classification ⟨*in-grade* wage increase⟩

**ingraft** *var of* ENGRAFT

**¹in·grain** \ənˈgrān, ˈinˈ≈\ *vt* -ED/-ING/-s [²*in-* + *grain* (n.)] **1** *obs* **:** ENGRAIN 1 **2 :** to work into the natural texture or mental or moral constitution **:** infix deeply **:** SATURATE, IMBUE **syn** see INFUSE

**²in·grain** \ˈ≈ˌ≈\ *adj* [fr. the phrase (dyed) *in grain*] **1** *obs* **:** dyed with kermes **2 a :** made of fiber (as wool) that is dyed before being spun into yarn **b :** made of yarn that is dyed before being knitted ⟨~ hose⟩ **3 :** of or relating to the formation of a dye or color by chemical reaction on the fiber **4 :** thoroughly worked in **:** INNATE, NATIVE ⟨~ stubbornness of character⟩

**³ingrain** \"\ *n* -s **1 :** an article made with ingrain yarns; *specif* **:** INGRAIN CARPET **2 :** innate quality or character

**ingrain carpet** *n* **:** a reversible carpet made of ingrain wool and having a similar design with the colors reversed appearing on each side

**ingrain dye** *or* **ingrain color** *n* **:** a dye or color formed on the fiber; *esp* **:** AZOIC DYE — see DYE table I

**ingrained** \ˈ≈ˌ≈, ≈ˈ≈\ *adj* [fr. past part. of ¹*ingrain*] **:** worked into the grain or fiber **:** forming a part of the essence or inmost being **:** DEEP-SEATED ⟨~ prejudice⟩ — **in·grained·ly** \-ān(ə)dlē, -li\ *adv* — **in·grained·ness** \-āndnəs, -ān(d)nəs\ *n*

**ingrandize** *var of* ENGRANDIZE

**¹in·grate** \ˈinˌgrāt *sometimes* ənˈg-, *usu* -ād·+V\ *adj* [ME *ingrat,* fr. L *ingratus,* fr. *in-* ¹in- + *gratus* pleasing, grateful — more at GRACE] **1 a** *obs* **:** DISAGREEABLE, UNPLEASANT, UNCONGENIAL **b** *obs* **:** UNFRIENDLY **2** *archaic* **:** showing ingratitude **:** UNGRATEFUL — **in·grate·ly** *adv*

**²ingrate** \"\ *n* -s **:** an ungrateful person

**ingrateful** *adj* [¹*in-* + *grateful*] *obs* **:** not grateful

**in·gra·ti·ate** \ənˈgrāshēˌāt, *usu* -ād·+V\ *vt* -ED/-ING/-s [²*in-* + L *gratia* favor, grace + E *-ate* — more at GRACE] **:** to commend to favor **:** find favor or favorable acceptance for **:** make agreeable to someone ⟨show that Newman's imagery . . . helps to ~ the view that education is a good thing in itself —Geoffrey Tillotson⟩ — usu. used with *with* ⟨where, he flattered himself, his manners would ~ him with the housewives of the district —James Joyce⟩ ⟨with what unwearying politeness he kept on trying to ~ himself with all —R.L. Stevenson⟩

**ingratiating** *adj* **1 :** capable of winning favor **:** PLEASING ⟨~ smile⟩ ⟨we are prone to respond to art works . . . in terms of their ~ effect —H.E.Clurman⟩ **2 :** intended or adopted in order to gain favor **:** pleasantly persuasive **:** FLATTERING ⟨her manner is quiet and ~ and a little too agreeable —Gordon Bottomley⟩ ⟨~ manner . . . one does not think compatible with deep spiritual experience —W.B.Yeats⟩ ⟨some of his superiors were even younger than he, but it's possible that they were also more ~ and discreet —L.M.Hughes⟩

**in·gra·ti·at·ing·ly** *adv* **:** in an ingratiating manner **:** PLEASINGLY, FLATTERINGLY

**in·gra·ti·a·tion** \-ˌgrāshēˈāshən\ *n* -s **1 :** the act of ingratiating **:** process of getting oneself in favor ⟨practice the various arts of ~⟩ **2 :** something that ingratiates ⟨American art . . . had no native conviction with which to resist this wealth of ~ —C.D.Maginnis⟩

**in·gra·tia·to·ry** \-ˈgrāsh(ē)əˌtōrē\ *adj* **:** tending to ingratiate **:** INGRATIATING

**in·gratitude** \(ˈ)in, ən+\ *n* [ME, fr. MF, fr. ML *ingratitudo,* fr. L *in-* ¹in- + LL *gratitudo* gratitude — more at GRATITUDE] **:** lack of gratitude **:** forgetfulness of or poor return for kindness received **:** UNGRATEFULNESS ⟨blow, thou winter wind! thou art not so unkind as man's ~ —Shak.⟩

**in·gra·ves·cence** \ˌingrəˈvesᵊn(t)s\ *n* -s **:** the state of becoming progressively severe ⟨persistence and ~ of behavior disorders in spite of improved circumstances —Norman Cameron⟩

**in·gra·ves·cent** \ˌ≈≈ˈvesᵊnt\ *adj* [L *ingravescent-, ingravescens,* pres. part. of *ingravescere* to become heavier, to become worse, fr. *in-* ²in- + *gravescere* to become heavy, fr. *gravis* heavy, severe — more at GRIEVE] **:** gradually increasing in severity ⟨~ disease⟩ ⟨~ abnormality of function⟩

**in·grav·i·date** \ənˈgravəˌdāt\ *vt* -ED/-ING/-s [LL *ingravidatus,* past part. of *ingravidare,* fr. L *in-* ²in- + LL *gravidare* to make pregnant, fr. L *gravidus* pregnant — more at GRAVID] *archaic* **:** IMPREGNATE

**in·gre·di·ence** \ənˈgrēdēən(t)s\ *n* -s [in sense 1, alter. of *ingredients,* pl. of ¹*ingredient;* in sense 2, fr. L *ingredi* + E *-ence*] **1 a** *archaic* **:** an ingredient or a mixture of ingredients ⟨later, the gold lost its purity and contained up to ⅓ other ~*s* —H.M.F.Schulman and H.W.Holzer⟩ **b :** the fact of entering as an ingredient ⟨this complete ~ in an occasion, so as to yield . . . fusion of individual essence with other eternal objects —A.N.Whitehead⟩ **2** *obs* **:** ENTRANCE, INGRESS

**¹in·gre·di·ent** \-nt\ *n* -s [ME, fr. L *ingredient-, ingrediens,* pres. part. of *ingredi* to go into, enter, fr. *in-* ²in- + *-gredi* (fr. *gradi* to step, go) — more at GRADE] **1 :** something that enters into a compound or is a component part of any combination or mixture **:** CONSTITUENT ⟨formula which will have just about the same ~*s* as mother's milk —Morris Fishbein⟩ ⟨fashionable books that one must read, because they are ~*s* of the talk of the day —T.L.Peacock⟩ ⟨understanding is one of the most important ~*s* of a successful marriage —Grace Nagel⟩ **2** *obs* **:** something that moves into or penetrates **syn** see ELEMENT

**²ingredient** \"\ *adj* [L *ingredient-, ingrediens,* pres. part.] **1** *obs* **:** entering in **:** PENETRATING **2 :** present as or forming an ingredient **:** COMPONENT ⟨can be used as an ~ product in breads, pies, cakes—*Shareholder*⟩ ⟨when a sequence of words has not yet congealed into phrase, while we can ask whether he knows how to use the ~ words —Gilbert Ryle⟩

**in gre·mio** \(ˈ)inˈgrēmēˌō, -rēm-\ *adv* [L, in the bosom, in the lap] **:** in abeyance

**¹in·gress** \ˈinˌgres\ *n* -ES [ME *ingresse,* fr. L *ingressus,* fr. *ingressus,* past part. of *ingredi* to go into, enter — more at INGREDIENT] **1 :** the act of entering **:** ENTRANCE ⟨~ of air into the lungs⟩ ⟨~ of immigrants⟩ ⟨~ of summer tourists⟩ **2 :** the power or liberty of entrance or access ⟨~ visa⟩ **:** means of entering ⟨gate providing ~ to the meadow⟩ **3 :** a point in an astrological direction where a significator transits the place of any other planet, the ascendant, or midheaven **4 :** an entrance of the moon into the shadow of the earth in an eclipse or of an inferior planet upon the sun's disk in transit or of a satellite or its shadow on a planet **:** the sun's entrance (as into a sign)

**²in·gress** \(ˈ)inˈgres, ənˈg-\ *vi* -ED/-ING/-ES [L *ingressus,* past part.] **1 :** to go in **:** ENTER **2 :** to mark an ingress — said of an astrological significator

**in·gres·sion** \ənˈgreshən\ *n* -s [ME, fr. L *ingression-, ingressio,* fr. *ingressus* (past part.) + *-ion-, -io* -ion] **1 :** the action of entering **:** ENTRANCE **2 :** the process whereby potentialities or eternal objects enter into or become complex actual occasions or events ⟨the ~ of an object into an event is the way the character of the event shapes itself in virtue of the being of the object —A.N.Whitehead⟩ **3 :** inward migration in gastrulation of large yolk-laden macromeres formed by holoblastic but markedly unequal cleavage

**¹in·gres·sive** \(ˈ)inˈgresiv, ənˈg-\ *adj* [L *ingressus* (past part.) + E *-ive*] **:** of or relating to ingress **:** ENTERING; *specif* **:** INCHOATIVE ⟨~ aspect⟩ — **in·gres·sive·ness** *n* -ES

**²ingressive** \"\ *n* -s **:** an ingressive verb

**ingri·an** \ˈiŋ(g)rēən\ *n* -s *cap* [*Ingria,* district of early Russia on the eastern end of the Gulf of Finland + E *-an*] **:** a member of a western division of the Finns native to the old Baltic province in which St. Petersburg was built — called also *Inger, Ingerman*

**ingross** *obs var of* ENGROSS

**ingroup** \ˈ≈ˌ≈\ *n, often attrib* [⁴*in* + *group*] **:** a social group possessing a sense of solidarity or community of interests as opposed to other social groups — compare OUTGROUP

**ingrowing** \ˈ≈ˌ≈≈\ *adj* [²*in* + *growing* (after *grow in,* v.)] **:** growing or tending inwards ⟨~ emotions⟩ **:** developing within confining limits ⟨~ toenail⟩ ⟨French playwriting was ~ and was becoming provincial —Sheldon Cheney⟩

**ingrown** \ˈ≈ˌ≈\ *adj* [²*in* + *grown*] **1 :** grown in **:** ENCLOSED; *esp, of a hair or nail* **:** having the free tip or edge embedded in the flesh **2 :** having the direction of growth or activity or interest inward rather than outward **:** WITHDRAWN, CONTRACTED ⟨the contrast between an outgoing, cultural, vibrant, liberal-aristocratic Athens and an ~, inbred, militaristic, oligarchic Sparta —Norman Cousins⟩ **3** *of a stream* **:** having enlarged the original course by undercutting the banks of the outer curves — **in·grown·ness** \-nnəs\ *n* -ES

**ingrown meander** *n* **:** an incised meander (as of a river) with a steep undercut slope on one side and a gentle slip-off slope on the other side

**ingrowth** \ˈ≈ˌ≈\ *n* [⁴*in* + *growth*] **:** a growth or development inward ⟨~ of cells⟩; *also* **:** something that grows inward

**ings** *pl of* ING

**-ings** *pl of* -ING

**in·guen** \ˈiŋgwən, -ˌgwen\ *n, pl* **ingui·na** \-ˌgwənə\ [L] **:** GROIN

**inguin-** *or* **inguino-** *comb form* [NL, fr. L *inguin-, inguen*] **:** inguinal ⟨*inguino*dynia⟩ **:** inguinal and ⟨*inguino*scrotal⟩

**¹in·gui·nal** \ˈ≈gwənᵊl\ *adj* [L *inguinalis,* fr. *inguin-, inguen* groin + *-alis* -al — more at ADEN-] **1 :** of, relating to, or in the region of the groin **2 :** of or relating to either of the lowest lateral regions of the abdomen — compare ABDOMINAL REGION

**²inguinal** \"\ *n* -s **:** one of the plates on the posterior surface of the bridge of a turtle

**inguinal canal** *n* **:** a passage about one and one half inches long that lies parallel to and a half inch above Poupart's ligament: as **a :** a passage in the male through which the testis descends into the scrotum and in which lies the spermatic cord **b :** a passage in the female accommodating the round ligament

**inguinal gland** *n* **:** any of the superficial lymphatic glands of the groin made up of two more or less distinct groups of which one is disposed along Poupart's ligament and the other about the saphenous opening

**inguinal ligament** *n* **:** POUPART'S LIGAMENT

**inguinal ring** *n* **:** ABDOMINAL RING

**ingulph** *obs var of* ENGULF

**in·gurgitate** \ən+\ *vb* -ED/-ING/-s [L *ingurgitatus,* past part. of *ingurgitare,* fr. *in-* ²in- + *gurgit-, gurges* whirlpool, abyss — more at VORACIOUS] *vt* **1 :** to swallow, devour, or drink greedily or in large quantity **:** GUZZLE ⟨produces cocktails . . . and ~s them absentmindedly without reflection —Aldous Huxley⟩ **2** *obs* **:** to overload by eating or drinking **:** CRAM ~ *vi* **:** GUZZLE, GORMANDIZE, SWILL

**in·gurgitation** \(ˌ)in, ən+\ *n* [LL *ingurgitation-, ingurgitatio,* fr. L *ingurgitatus* + *-ion-, -io* -ion] **:** the act of devouring or swallowing ⟨basically Puritan foundations were undermined by the ~ of German transcendentalism —Oskar Seidlin⟩

**in·gush** \ˈinˌgüsh, ≈ˈ≈\ *n, pl* **ingush** *or* **ingushes** *usu cap* **1 :** a Muhammadan people living north of the Caucasian mountains and related to the Chechen **2 :** a member of the Ingush people

**in·habile** \(ˈ)in+\ *adj* [F, fr. L *inhabilis,* fr. *in-* ¹in- + *habilis* easily managed, apt, skillful — more at ABLE] *archaic* **:** not fit or qualified

**in·hab·it** \ən'habət, *usu* -əd.+V\ *vb* -ED/-ING/-S [ME *enhabiten, inhabiten*, fr. MF & L; MF *enhabiter*, fr. L *inhabitare*, fr. *in-* 2in- + *habitare* to dwell — more at HABIT] *vt* **1 :** to occupy as a place of settled residence or habitat **:** live or dwell in ⟨~*ed* by a rich fauna and flora —W.H.Dowdeswell⟩ ⟨~*ed* a small apartment —Alfred Hayes⟩ **2 a :** to be at home in (a particular sphere of activity or thought) **:** OCCUPY ⟨endlessly varied characters who ~ the world of medicine —*N.Y.Times*⟩ ⟨the intellectual world we ~ —Cyril Connolly⟩ **b :** to occupy, be present in, or be inside of in any manner or form ⟨the human beings who ~ this tale —Al Newman⟩ ⟨the individual is ~*ed* by multiple wills, persons, or spirits —Weston La Barre⟩ ⟨a sculptural quality that ~*s* many of his most successful prints —Vincent Garofalo⟩ **~** *vi, archaic* **:** to have residence in a place **:** DWELL, LIVE

**in·hab·it·abil·i·ty** \ən,habəd·ə'biləd·ē, -bətə-, -lətē, -i\ *n* **:** the condition of being inhabitable

**1inhabitable** *adj* [ME, fr. MF, fr. L *inhabitabilis*, fr. *in-* 1in- + *habitabilis* habitable — more at HABITABLE] *obs* **:** not habitable; *also* **:** UNINHABITED

**2in·hab·it·able** \ən'habəd·əbəl, -bətə-\ *adj* [LL *inhabitabilis*, fr. L *inhabitare* + *-abilis* -able] **:** capable of being inhabited **:** HABITABLE

**in·hab·i·tance** \-bəd·ən(t)s, -bətən- *also* -bət°n-\ *n*-s [*inhabit* + *-ance*] **:** RESIDENCE ⟨grateful for his almost solitary ~ of the city —William Saroyan⟩

**in·hab·i·tan·cy** \-nsē, -nsi\ *n* **1 :** the act of inhabiting or the state of being inhabited **:** the state, rights, or privileges of one who is an inhabitant **:** RESIDENCE, OCCUPANCY **2 :** the site of the principal office or place of business of a corporation or association; *sometimes* **:** a fixed place of abode

**1in·hab·i·tant** \-nt\ *n* [ME *inhabitaunt*, fr. AF *enhabitant*, fr. MF (pres. part. of *enhabiter*), fr. L *inhabitant-, inhabitans*, pres. part. of *inhabitare* to inhabit] **1 :** a person who dwells or resides permanently in a place as distinguished from a transient lodger or visitor ⟨an ~ of a house⟩ ⟨an ~ of a state⟩ — compare CITIZEN, DOMICILE, RESIDENT **2 :** one that makes its habitat or is commonly found in a place ⟨with respect to its insect ~*s* —*Am Guide Series: N.H.*⟩ ⟨a normal ~ of the intestines of both man and animals —*Farmer's Weekly (So. Africa)*⟩

**2inhabitant** \"\ *adj* [L *inhabitant-, inhabitans*, pres. part.] *archaic* **:** RESIDENT, DWELLING

**inhabitate** *vt* -ED/-ING/-S [L *inhabitatus*, past part.] *obs* **:** INHABIT

**in·hab·i·ta·tion** \ən,habə'tāshən\ *n* [ME *inhabitacioun*, fr. LL *inhabitation-, inhabitatio*, fr. L *inhabitatus* (past part. of *inhabitare* to inhabit) + *-ion-, -io* -ion — more at INHABIT] **:** the act or an instance of inhabiting **:** the state of being inhabited ⟨space flight and space ~ —J.N.Leonard⟩

**inhabited** *adj* **:** having inhabitants ⟨an ~ area⟩

**in·hab·it·er** \ən'habəd·ə(r), -ətə-\ *n* -s [ME *enhabiter, inhabiter*, fr. *enhabiten, inhabiten* to inhabit + *-er* — more at INHABIT] *archaic* **:** one that inhabits

**inhabiting** *n* -s [ME *enhabiting, inhabiting*, fr. gerund of *enhabiten, inhabiten*] *archaic* **:** a dwelling place

**in·hab·i·tive·ness** \-bəd·ivnəs, -bətiv-\ *n* -ES [*inhabit* + *-ive* + *-ness*] **:** a propensity to remain permanently in the same place or residence ⟨you know my (what the phrenologists call) ~ —J.R.Lowell⟩

**in·hab·i·tress** \-bə·trəs\ *n* -ES [*inhabiter* + *-ess*] *archaic* **:** a female inhabitant

**1in·hal·ant** \(')in'hālənt, ən'h-\ *n* -s [1*inhale* + *-ant* (n. suffix)] **:** something (as an allergen, an anesthetic vapor, or a medicated nasal spray) that is inhaled

**2inhalant** \"\ *also* **in·hal·ent** \"\ *adj* [1*inhale* + *-ant* or *-ent* (adj. suffixes)] **1 :** used for inhaling or constituting an inhalant ⟨~ allergens⟩ **2 :** INCURRENT ⟨~ pores⟩

**in·ha·la·tion** \,in(h)ə'lāshən\ *n* -s *often attrib* [1*inhale* + *-ation*] **:** the act or an instance of inhaling; *specif* **:** the action of drawing air into the lungs by means of a complex of essentially reflex actions that involve changes in the diaphragm and in muscles of the abdomen and thorax which cause enlargement of the chest cavity and lungs resulting in production of relatively negative pressure within the lungs so that air flows in until the pressure is restored to equality with that of the atmosphere

**in·ha·la·tion·al** \,==;lāshən°l,-shnəl\ *adj* **:** by or involving inhalation ⟨~ therapy⟩

**in·ha·la·tor** \'==,lād·ə(r), -ātə-\ *n* -s [1*inhale* + *-ator*] **:** a device designed to provide a suitable mixture of oxygen and carbon dioxide for inhalation and used esp. in conjunction with manual artificial respiration

**1in·hale** \ən'hāl, *chiefly before pause or consonant* -āəl\ *vb* -ED/-ING/-S [2*in-* + *-hale* (as in *exhale*)] *vt* **1 :** to draw in by breathing ⟨~ air⟩ **2 :** to consume or swallow esp. eagerly or greedily ⟨*inhaled* about four meals at once —Ring Lardner⟩ ⟨*inhaling* it from their cupped fingers until their cheeks bulged —R.D.Bowen⟩ ⟨*inhaled* a strong love decoction —Abram Kardiner⟩ **~** *vi* **:** to breathe in **:** inhale air, gas, smoke, or other vapor — opposed to *exhale*

**2in·hale** \", 'in,=\ *n* -s **:** the act or an instance of inhaling ⟨kept taking deep ~*s* —J.W.Ellison b. 1891⟩

**in·hal·er** \ən'hālə(r)\ *n* -s **1 :** one that inhales **2 :** a device by means of which vapors, volatilized remedies, medicinal dusts, or anesthetics can be inhaled — compare INHALATOR **3 :** SNIFTER ⟨pouring a liberal amount of brandy into an ~ —Caroline Slade⟩

**in·harmonic** \;in+\ *adj* [1*in-* + *harmonic*] **:** not harmonic **:** DISCORDANT

**inharmonic theory** *n* **:** a postulate in phonetics: the reinforcing vibrations produced in the superglottic cavities in vowel articulation need not be multiples of the fundamental vocal-cord note — compare FORMANT, HARMONIC THEORY

**in·harmonious** \;in+\ *adj* [1*in-* + *harmonious*] **1 :** UNMUSICAL, DISCORDANT ⟨~ sounds⟩ **2 :** being not in harmony **:** CONFLICTING, JARRING, UNCONGENIAL ⟨~ surroundings⟩ — **in·harmoniously** \"+\ *adv* — **in·harmoniousness** \"+\ *n*

**in·harmony** \(')in, ən+\ *n* [1*in-* + *harmony*] **:** lack of harmony **:** DISCORD

**inhaul** \'=,=\ *n* [4*in* + *haul* (after *haul in*, v.)] **:** a rope used to draw in a ship's sail (as a spanker on its gaff)

**in·haust** \ən'hȯst\ *vt* -ED/-ING/-S [2*in-* + *-haust* (as in *exhaust*)] **:** INHALE, IMBIBE ⟨~*ing* mint juleps —Virginius Dabney⟩

**in·hell** \ən+\ *vt* [2*in-* + *hell*] *archaic* **:** to put or fix in hell

**in·here** \ən'hi(ə)r, -iə\ *vi* -ED/-ING/-S [L *inhaerēre*, fr. *in-* 2in- + *haerēre* to stick, adhere — more at HESITATE] **:** to be inherent **:** be a fixed element or attribute **:** BELONG ⟨thought all virtue *inhered* in the farmer —H.S.Commager⟩ ⟨the excellence *inhering* in the democratic faith —V.L.Parrington⟩

**in·her·ence** \ən'hirən(t)s, -her-,-hēr-\ *n* -s [ML *inhaerentia*, fr. L *inhaerent-, inhaerens* + *-ia* -y] **1 :** the quality, state, or fact of inhering or of being inherent **:** permanent existence as an attribute ⟨the ~ of multiple meanings and allusions in the particulars of a literary work —B.T.Spencer⟩ **2 :** the relation of a quality to a substance or subject ⟨~ rather than existence is said of accidents —James Albertson⟩

**in·her·en·cy** \-nsē, -nsi\ *n* -ES [ML *inhaerentia*] **1 :** INHERENCE **2 :** an inherent character or attribute ⟨culture classifications with purely taxonomic *inherencies* —W.W.Taylor⟩

**in·her·ent** \-nt\ *adj* [L *inhaerent-, inhaerens*, pres. part. of *inhaerēre*] **:** structural or involved in the constitution or essential character of something **:** belonging by nature or settled habit **:** INTRINSIC, ESSENTIAL ⟨~ rights⟩ ⟨shortcomings ~ in our approach —David Cherin⟩ ⟨an ~ laziness⟩ — **in·her·ent·ly** *adv*

**in·her·it** \ən'herət, *usu* -əd.+V\ *vb* -ED/-ING/-S [ME *enheriten* to make heir, inherit (influenced in meaning by MF *heriter* & L *hereditare* to inherit), fr. MF *enheriter* to make heir, fr. LL *inhereditare*, fr. L *in-* 2in- + LL *hereditare* to inherit — more at HERITAGE] *vt* **1 :** to come into possession of **:** POSSESS, RECEIVE ⟨power . . . which he ~*s* from the Creator himself —Eric Linklater⟩ **2 a :** to take by descent from an ancestor **:** take by inheritance **:** receive as a right or title descendible by law from an ancestor at his decease **b :** to be heir to **:** SUCCEED ⟨a son ~*s* his father⟩ **3 a :** to receive by genetic transmission **:** derive or acquire from ancestors ⟨~ a strong constitution⟩ **b :** to have in turn or receive as if from an ancestor ⟨much of the girl's clothing had been ~*ed* from the more fortunate children —Grace Metalious⟩ ⟨~*ed* from antiquity two rather contradictory views of the organic world —S.F.Mason⟩ **~** *vi* **:** to take or hold a possession, property, estate, or rights by inheritance

**in·her·it·abil·i·ty** \-,herəd·ə'biləd·ē, -rətə-, -lətē, -i\ *n* **:** the quality of being inheritable or descendible to heirs

**in·her·it·able** \-'herəd·əbəl, -rətə-\ *adj* [ME *enheritable*, fr. AF, fr. MF *enheriter* + *-able*] **1 a :** capable of being inherited **:** TRANSMISSIBLE, DESCENDIBLE ⟨an ~ title⟩ **b** (1) **:** capable of taking by inheritance (2) **:** entitled to as a birthright **2 :** capable of being transmitted from parent to child ⟨~ qualities⟩ — **in·her·it·able·ness** \-nəs\ *n* -ES — **in·her·it·ably** \-blē,-bli\ *adv*

**in·her·i·tage** \-'herəd·ij\ *n* [*inherit* + *-age*] *archaic* **:** INHERITANCE

**in·her·i·tance** \ən'herəd·ən(t)s, -rətən-,-rət°n-\ *n* -s [ME *enheritaunce*, fr. AF *enheritance*, fr. MF *enheriter* + *-ance*] **1 a :** the act of inheriting property: as (1) **:** the acquisition of real or personal property as heir to another **:** the perpetual or continuing right which a person and his heirs have to an estate or property (2) *common, feudal, & Scots law* **:** the acquisition of an ancestor's real estate upon his death by the heir under the Statute of Descent as distinguished from the successsion to his personal property by the next of kin under the Statute of Distribution (3) *Roman & Civil law* **:** the succession upon the death of an owner either by testament or by operation of law by the heir to all the estate, rights, and liabilities of the decedent, the liabilities being restricted to the value of the estate when the heir was given the benefit of inventory **b :** the reception or acquisition of genetic characters or qualities by transmission from parent to offspring **c :** the acquisition of a material or immaterial possession, condition, or trait by transmission from the past or from past generations ⟨resented his children's ~ of slavery from their mothers —Anne K. Gregorie⟩ ⟨hard-won freedoms that are ours by just ~⟩ **2 :** something that is or may be inherited: as **a** (1) **:** something that is derived by an heir from an ancestor or other person or that may be transmitted to an heir by a person (2) *common, feudal, & Scots law* **:** an estate of inheritance (as a fee simple or a fee tail) **b :** the sum total of genetic characters or qualities transmitted from parent to offspring ⟨on the maternal side his ~ was a happy one⟩ **c :** something material or immaterial that is derived or acquired from the past or from past generations ⟨the random brutality that is the ~ of centuries of blackness —Irving Howe⟩; *esp* **:** a permanent or valuable possession that is a common heritage or that is received from God or nature ⟨our great ~ of water and land —A.E.Stevenson b.1900⟩ ⟨their most precious ~, that thin layer of topsoil —K.D. White⟩ ⟨books are the major channel by which the intellectual ~ is handed down —*New Republic*⟩ **3** *obs* **:** right of possession **:** POSSESSION, OWNERSHIP

**inheritance tax** *n* **1 :** an excise tax levied upon the privilege of receiving property as heir or next of kin under the law governing intestate succession, measured by the value of the interest each successor receives, and usu. increased in rate as kinship with the deceased becomes more remote — compare LEGACY TAX **2 :** ESTATE TAX

**inherited** *adj* **:** constituting something received by inheritance ⟨~ characteristics⟩ ⟨shackled by a mass of ~ conventions —J.L.Lowes⟩ ⟨a city which follows an ~ type of industry —Samuel Van Valkenburg & Ellsworth Huntington⟩ **syn** see INNATE

**in·her·i·tor** \ən'herəd·ə(r), -rətə-\ *n* [ME *enheritour, enheriter*, fr. *enheriten* to inherit + *-our* -or or *-er* — more at INHERIT] **:** one that inherits **:** HEIR ⟨~*s* of an ancient culture⟩

**in·her·i·tress** \-rə·trəs\ *also* **in·her·i·trix** \-rə,(,)triks\ *n* -ES [*inheritress* fr. *inheritor* + *-ess*; *inheritrix* fr. *inheritor*, after such pairs as E *mediator: mediatrix*] **:** a female inheritor

**inherits** *pres 3d sing of* INHERIT

**in·he·sion** \ən'hēzhən\ *n* -s [L *inhaesus* (past part. of *inhaerēre* to inhere) + E *-ion* — more at INHERE] **:** the condition of being inherent in something **:** INHERENCE

**in·hib·it** \ən'hibət, *usu* -bəd.+V\ *vb* -ED/-ING/-S [ME *inhibiten*, fr. L *inhibitus*, past part. of *inhibēre*, fr. *in-* 2in- + *-hibēre* (fr. *habēre* to have, hold) — more at HABIT] *vt* **1 :** to prohibit from doing something **:** FORBID, INTERDICT ⟨~*s* the legislature from levying an income tax —*Britannica Bk. of the Yr.*⟩ **2 a** (1) **:** to repress, restrain, or discourage from free or spontaneous activity esp. through the operation of inner psychological impediments or conflicts or of social and cultural controls ⟨~*ed* from bold speculation by his personal loyalties and interests —V.L.Parrington⟩ ⟨a people long ~*ed* by the prevailing taboos —R.S.Ellery⟩ (2) **:** to operate against the full development or activity of **:** check, restrain, or diminish the force, intensity, or vitality of ⟨~*ed* the creative process at its sources —Harry Sylvester⟩ ⟨the heavy tax load that ~*s* investment in capital goods —*Time*⟩ **b** (1) **:** to reduce or suppress the activity of ⟨many of the iron or copper enzymes are ~*ed* by cyanides —Felix Haurowitz⟩ ⟨lubricating oil ~*ed* against rust, corrosion, and oxidation⟩ (2) **:** to retard or prevent the formation of ⟨~ rust⟩ (3) **:** to retard, interfere with, or prevent (a chemical process or reaction) ⟨~ oxidation⟩ **~** *vi* **:** to cause inhibition ⟨something that entraps and ~*s* —John Portz⟩ **syn** see FORBID, RESTRAIN

**in·hib·it·able** \-əbəl\ *adj* **:** capable of being inhibited

**inhibited** *adj* **:** being repressed, discouraged, reduced, or retarded: as **a :** characterized by, displaying, or reflecting inhibition ⟨a shy and ~ boy —Alan Harrington⟩ ⟨~ respectability —H.C.Webster⟩ **b :** having its activity reduced or suppressed ⟨~ oils⟩

**inhibiting** *adj* **:** tending to inhibit or causing inhibition ⟨an overly strict or ~ discipline —H.V.Gregory⟩

**in·hi·bi·tion** \,inə'bishən, ,inhə'-, ,in(,)(h)i'-\ *n* -s [ME *inhibicioun*, fr. MF *inhibition*, fr. L *inhibition-, inhibitio*, fr. *inhibitus* + *-ion-, -io* -ion] **:** the act or an instance of inhibiting or the state of being inhibited: as **a :** the act or an instance of formally forbidding or barring something from being done **:** PROHIBITION ⟨plain ~*s* to the exercise of that power in a particular way —John Marshall⟩; *also* **:** something that formally forbids or debars **:** IMPEDIMENT ⟨the constitutional ~ of his alien birth —F.L.Paxson⟩ **b** (1) **:** a writ from a higher court (as an ecclesiastical court) staying an inferior judge from further proceedings (2) *Eng eccl law* **:** a command of an ecclesiastical authority (as a bishop) to a minister not to perform ministerial duties (3) *Scots law* **:** a personal order prohibiting a party from contracting debts to the prejudice of the rights of others in his heritable property or realty; *also* **:** an order procured by a husband prohibiting the giving of credit to his wife **c** (1) **:** a stopping or checking of a bodily action **:** a restraining of the function of an organ or an agent (as a digestive fluid or enzyme) ⟨~ of the heartbeat by stimulation of the vagus nerve⟩ ⟨~ of plantar reflexes⟩ (2) **:** interference with or retardation or prevention of a chemical process or activity ⟨~ of a catalyst⟩ ⟨~ of rust⟩ **d** (1) **:** a desirable restraint or check upon the free or spontaneous instincts or impulses of an individual effected through the operation of the human will guided or directed by the social and cultural forces of the environment ⟨the self-control so developed is called ~ —C.W.Russell⟩ ⟨creating ~*s*, socializing the child, obviously should be one of the goals of a training school —Erwin Schepses⟩ (2) **:** a neurotic restraint upon a normal or beneficial impulse or activity caused by psychological inner conflicts or by sociocultural forces of the environment ⟨other outspoken neurotic manifestations are general ~*s* such as inability to think, to concentrate —Muriel Ivimey⟩ ⟨~*s*, phobias, compulsions, and other neurotic patterns —*Psychological Abstracts*⟩ (3) **:** repression of or restraint upon an urge, impulse, or activity of any kind ⟨locked in Puritan ~*s* —H.S.Canby⟩ ⟨obstacles and ~*s* to rural reading —C.M.Wieting⟩ ⟨throwing all her moral teachings and ~*s* overboard —Ruth Park⟩ ⟨laughed without ~ —Jean Stafford⟩

**in·hib·i·tive** \ən'hibəd·iv, -bətiv\ *adj* **:** INHIBITORY

**in·hib·i·tor** *or* **in·hib·it·er** \-bəd·ə(r), -bətə-\ *n* -s **:** one that inhibits: as **a** (1) **:** a substance for reducing corrosion or rust formation (as in an antifreeze) (2) **:** a substance for delaying gum formation (as in gasoline) (3) **:** ANTIOXIDANT **b :** a substance that interferes with a chemical process or reaction ⟨polymerization ~*s*⟩ **:** NEGATIVE CATALYST **c :** a substance that reduces the activity of another substance (as an enzyme) — compare ANTIMETABOLITE **d :** a gene that checks the normal effect of another nonallelic gene when both are present

**in·hib·i·to·ry** \-bə,tōrē, -tȯr-, -ri\ *adj* [ML *inhibitorius*, fr. L *inhibitus* (past part. of *inhibēre* to inhibit) + *-orius* -ory — more at INHIBIT] **:** of, relating to, or producing inhibition **:** tending or serving to inhibit **:** PROHIBITORY ⟨~ nervous action⟩ ⟨the ~ action of fluorides —*Americana Annual*⟩

**inholding** \'=,==\ *n* [4*in* + *holding*] **:** privately owned land inside the boundary of a national park

**in home** *n* **:** INSIDE HOME

**in·homogeneity** \(;)in, ən+\ *n* [1*in-* + *homogeneity*] **1 :** lack of homogeneity **:** the condition of not being homogeneous ⟨the degree of microscopic ~ in an alloy⟩ **2 :** a part that is not homogeneous with the larger homogeneous mass in which it is incorporated

**in·homogeneous** \"+\ *adj* [1*in-* + *homogeneous*] **:** not homogeneous **:** lacking homogeneity — **in·homogeneously** \"+\ *adv*

**inhoop** *vt* [2*in-* + *hoop* (n.)] *obs* **:** to enclose in a hoop

**in·hospitable** \(;)in, ən+\ *adj* [1*in-* + *hospitable*] **1 a :** not hospitable **:** not disposed to show hospitality ⟨an ~ person⟩ **b :** reflecting or evidencing inhospitality **:** UNFRIENDLY ⟨gave me a brief, ~ look —Louis Auchincloss⟩ **2 :** providing no shelter or sustenance **:** BARREN, DESERT ⟨~ mountain areas⟩ — **in·hospitableness** \"+\ *n* -ES — **in·hospitably** \"+\ *adv*

**inhospital** *adj* [prob. fr. MF, fr. L *inhospitalis*, fr. *in-* 1in- + *hospitalis* hospitable — more at HOSPITAL] *obs* **:** INHOSPITABLE

**in·hospitality** \(;)in, ən+\ *n* [prob. fr. MF *inhospitalité*, fr. L *inhospitalitat-, inhospitalitas*, fr. *inhospitalis* + *-itat-, -itas* -ity] **:** the quality or state of being inhospitable **:** a cold or unfriendly reception or treatment of a guest or visitor

**in·human** \(')in, ən+\ *adj* [MF & L; MF *inhumain*, fr. L *inhumanus*, fr. *in-* 1in- + *humanus* human — more at HUMAN] **1 a :** lacking the qualities of mercy, pity, kindness, or tenderness **:** CRUEL, BARBAROUS, SAVAGE ⟨an ~ tyrant⟩ ⟨what ~ rogues there are in the world —A. Conan Doyle⟩ **b :** lacking warmth or geniality **:** COLD, IMPERSONAL, MECHANICAL ⟨his usual quiet, almost ~ courtesy —F. Tennyson Jesse⟩ **c :** not worthy of or conforming to the needs of human beings ⟨living in conditions that are ~ —*Collier's Yr. Bk.*⟩ ⟨has the world's most ~ subways —*Time*⟩ ⟨one large block which would tend to be ~ and monotonous —*Architect & Building News*⟩ **2 a :** belonging to, resembling, or suggesting a nonhuman species or class of beings ⟨there is something a little ~ about them —Lewis Mumford⟩ ⟨a momentary glimpse . . . of something I didn't understand: something dark and ~ —Kenneth Roberts⟩ **b :** SUPERHUMAN ⟨models of ~ perfection —H.B. Parkes⟩ **syn** see FIERCE

**in·humane** \(;)in, ən+\ *adj* [MF *inhumain* & L *inhumanus*] **:** not humane **:** INHUMAN 1 — **in·humanely** \"+\ *adv*

**in·humanity** \;in+\ *n* [MF *inhumanité*, fr. L *inhumanitat-, inhumanitas*, fr. *inhumanus* + *-itat-, -itas* -ity] **1 :** the quality or state of being cruel or barbarous **:** CRUELTY ⟨abhorrence of its sickening ~ —G.B.Shaw⟩; *also* **:** a cruel or barbarous act **2 :** absence of warmth or geniality **:** IMPERSONALITY ⟨a professional ~ toward their job —Nicholas Monsarrat⟩

**in·hu·man·ly** *adv* **:** in an inhuman manner

**in·hu·man·ness** \-n(n)əs\ *n* **:** the quality or state of being inhuman

**in·hu·ma·tion** \,inhyü'māshən\ *n* -s [F *inhumation*, fr. *inhumer* to inhume (fr. L *inhumare*) + *-ation*] **:** BURIAL, INTERMENT

**in·hume** \ən'hyüm\ *vt* -ED/-ING/-S [prob. fr. F *inhumer*, fr. L *inhumare*, fr. *in-* 2in- + *humus* earth — more at HUMBLE] **:** to deposit in the earth **:** BURY, INTER

**-i·ni** \ə,nī, °n,ī, 'ē(,)nē, 'ēni, 'ī,nī\ *n pl suffix* [NL, fr. L, masc. pl. of *-inus* -ine] **:** animals that are or have the form of — in names of higher taxa esp. of tribes and orders ⟨*Anacanthini*⟩

**in·i·ac** \'inē,ak\ *also* **in·i·al** \-ēəl\ *adj* [NL *inion* + E *-ac* (as in *iliac*) or *-al*] **:** relating to the inion

**in·im·i·ca·ble** \ə'nimәkəbəl\ *adj* [L *inimicus* + E *-able* (as in *amicable*)] **:** INIMICAL, HOSTILE ⟨~ to the public peace or safety —*U.S. Code*⟩

**in·im·i·cal** \ə'nimәkəl, -mēk-\ *adj* [LL *inimicalis*, fr. L *inimicus* enemy + *-alis* -al — more at ENEMY] **1 a :** having the disposition or temper of an enemy **:** viewing with disfavor **:** HOSTILE ⟨mutually ~ blocs —*Wall Street Jour.*⟩ ⟨~ to that heresy —George Meredith⟩ **b :** reflecting or indicating hostility **:** UNFRIENDLY ⟨a voice apparently cold and ~ —Arnold Bennett⟩ ⟨under the ~ gaze of his father —Marguerite Steen⟩ **2 :** prejudicial in tendency, influence, or effects **:** HARMFUL, ADVERSE ⟨~ to the interests of the consumer —*Current Biog.*⟩ ⟨~ to the best interests of the company —L.M.Hughes⟩ **syn** see ADVERSE

**in·im·i·cal·ly** \-mәk(ə)lē, -mēk-, -li\ *adv* **:** in an inimical manner

**in·im·i·cal·ness** \-kəlnəs\ *n* -ES **:** the quality or state of being inimical

**in·im·i·ci·tious** \ə;nimə'sishəs\ *adj* [L *inimicitia* hostility (fr. *inimicus* enemy + *-tia*, suffix used to form abstract nouns) + E *-ous*] *archaic* **:** INIMICAL

**inimicous** *adj* [L *inimicus*, fr. *inimicus*, n., enemy] *obs* **:** INIMICAL

**in·im·i·ta·bil·i·ty** \(;)i,nimәd·ə'biləd·ē, ə,n-, -mәtə-, -lәtē, -i\ *n* **:** the quality or state of being inimitable **:** INIMITABLENESS

**in·im·i·ta·ble** \(')i;nimәd·əbəl, ə'n-, -mәtə-\ *adj* [MF or L; MF, fr. L *inimitabilis*, fr. *in-* 1in- + *imitabilis* imitable — more at IMITABLE] **:** not capable of being imitated **:** being beyond imitation **:** MATCHLESS ⟨an ~ style⟩ **:** not worthy of imitation — **in·im·i·ta·ble·ness** \-nəs\ *n* — **in·im·i·ta·bly** \-blē, -bli\ *adv*

**in in·vi·tum** \,inən'wē,tüm, -'vīd·əm\ *adv* [L, against an unwilling person] **:** against a person's will or consent **:** by force of law irrespective of assent

**in·i·o·mi** \,inē'ō,mī\ *n pl, cap* [NL, fr. *inion* + *-omi* (fr. Gk *ōmos* shoulder) — more at HUMERUS] **:** an order of mostly deep-sea teleost fishes lacking fin spines and air bladder and usu. having a dorsal adipose fin and including the lantern fishes, the lizard fishes, and related forms — **in·i·o·mous** \;==;ōməs\ *adj*

**in·i·on** \'inē,än, -ēən\ *n* -s [NL, fr. Gk, back of the head, dim. of *in-, is* sinew, tendon — more at WITHY] **:** the external occipital protuberance of the skull — see CRANIOMETRY illustration

**in·iq·ui·tous** \ə'nikwəd·əs, -wətəs\ *adj* [*iniquity* + *-ous*] **:** characterized by iniquity **:** UNJUST, WICKED ⟨~ deeds⟩ **syn** see VICIOUS

**in·iq·ui·tous·ly** *adv* **:** in an iniquitous manner

**in·iq·ui·tous·ness** *n* -ES **:** the quality or state of being iniquitous

**in·iq·ui·ty** \ə'nikwəd·ē, -wətē, -i\ *n* -ES [ME *iniquite*, fr. MF *iniquité*, fr. L *iniquitat-, iniquitas*, fr. *iniquus* uneven, unjust (fr. *in-* 1in- + *-iquus*, fr. *aequus* level, equal) + *-itat-, -itas* -ity] **1 :** absence of or deviation from just dealing **:** gross injustice **:** WICKEDNESS ⟨the ~ of bribery⟩ **2 :** an iniquitous act or thing **:** SIN ⟨whose *iniquities* are forgiven —Ps 31:1 (DV)⟩ **3** *Scots law* **:** INEQUITY, INJUSTICE — used of a decision contrary to law

**iniquous** *adj* [L *iniquus*] *obs* **:** INIQUITOUS

**in·irritability** \(;)in, ən+\ *n* **:** the quality or state of not being irritable

**in·irritable** \"+\ *adj* [1*in-* + *irritable*] **:** not irritable

**in·isle** \ən+\ *archaic var of* ENISLE

**1ini·tial** \ə'nishəl\ *adj* [MF & L; MF, fr. L *initialis*, fr. *initium* beginning (fr. *initus* — past part. of *inire* to go into, begin, fr. *in-* 2in- + *ire* to go — + *-ium*, suffix used to form abstract nouns) + *-alis* -al — more at ISSUE] **1 :** of or relating to the beginning **:** marking the commencement **:** INCIPIENT, FIRST ⟨~ symptoms of a disease⟩ ⟨this ~ series of outbreaks —Thomas Cadett⟩ **2 :** placed or standing at the beginning ⟨the ~ word of a verse⟩ **3 :** of that form regularly employed only at the beginning of a word — used of a letter in an alphabet that has two or more positional forms

**2initial** \"\ *n* -s **1 a** (1) **:** the first letter of a proper name (2) **initials** *pl* **:** the initial letters of an individual's name and surname; *also* **:** the initial letters of the name of an organization, state, or other entity (as U.S.A. for "United States of America" or C.I.O. for "Congress of Industrial Organizations") or of any group of words ⟨the ~*s* "PE" (meaning

"Previous Experience") —*U.S. Code*⟩ **b** (1) **:** a form of an alphabetical letter that regularly is used only at the beginning of a word (2) **:** a large letter beginning a text or a division or paragraph usu. capital and extending over two or more text lines and sometimes ornate and in more than one color **2 :** ANLAGE, PRECURSOR; *specif* **:** a meristematic cell

**³initial** \"\ *vt* **initialed** *or* **initialled; initialed** *or* **initialled; initialing** *or* **initialling** \-sh(ə)liŋ\ **initials** [²*initial*] **1 :** to affix an initial to ⟨~ a memorandum⟩ **:** to mark (as a handkerchief) with an initial **2 :** to authenticate and approve (as the draft of an international agreement) in a preliminary manner by the affixing of the initials of an authorized representative

**initial condition** *n* **:** any of a set of starting-point values belonging to or imposed upon the variables in an equation that has one or more arbitrary constants

**ini·tial·er** \-sh(ə)lə(r)\ *n* -s **:** a person who initials ⟨the ~s of a memorandum⟩

**initial letter** *n* **:** INITIAL 1b

**initial line** *n* **:** a ray that is rotated about the vertex to make an angle

**ini·tial·ly** \-sh(ə)lē, -li\ *adv* [¹*initial* + *-ly*] **:** in the first place **:** at the beginning

**initial reserve** *n* **:** the terminal reserve for a life-insurance policy as of the close of the preceding year plus the net premium for the current year

**initial rhyme** *n* **1 :** ALLITERATION **2 :** BEGINNING RHYME

**initial series** *n, cap I&S* **:** a Maya carved or written dating usu. at the start of a text including the date according to the long count and the date according to the positions reached in the 260-day and 365-day periods

**initial side** *n* **:** the stationary straight line that contains the point about which another straight line is revolved in forming a trigonometric figure

**initial stress** *n* **:** stress existing in a structure or mass not subjected to the action of external forces except gravity

**¹ini·ti·ate** \ə'nishē,āt *sometimes* -isē-; *usu* -ād·+V\ *vt* -ED/-ING/-S [L *initiatus*, past part. of *initiare*, fr. *initium* beginning — more at INITIAL] **1 a :** to begin or get going **:** make a beginning of **:** perform or facilitate the first actions, steps, or stages of **:** establish as an institution, custom, or trend ⟨~ a change in fashions⟩ ⟨*initiated* a new road-building program⟩ ⟨~ progressive education⟩ ⟨special powers which actively ~ and actively promote progress —W.H.Mallock⟩ ⟨~ a chain reaction⟩ **b :** to bring about the initial formation of **:** ORIGINATE ⟨polymerization chains so *initiated* —Otto Reinmuth⟩ **c :** to mark the beginning of ⟨the wholesale confiscation of property which *initiated* the Nazi regime —R.H.Jackson⟩ **2 :** to begin the instruction of in some field **:** lead to knowledge of elements or rudiments **:** foster the first steps or beginning progress of **:** aid in becoming familiar or knowing ⟨*initiated* into this tradition by his residence in Italy —Irving Babbitt⟩ ⟨felt that he was finally *initiated* —D.H.Lawrence⟩ **3 :** to receive or induct into membership of a society, club, or group, or into a certain status by or as if by special rites or formalities ⟨*initiated* into a social fraternity⟩ ⟨the club will ~ new members Tuesday⟩ **syn** see BEGIN

**²ini·tiate** \-sh(ē)ə̇t, -shē,ā\ *sometimes* -sē-; *usu* |d·+V\ *adj* [L *initiatus*] **1 :** initiated or properly admitted (as to an office, secret society, or secret learning) **2** *obs* **:** relating to an initiate ⟨my strange and self-abuse is the ~ fear —Shak.⟩

**³initiate** \"\ *n* -s **1 a :** a person who is undergoing an initiation (as into a secret order) ⟨the relationship between ~s and initiated —*Notes & Queries on Anthropology*⟩ **b :** one who has passed such an initiation or has been properly admitted (as to a fraternal organization) **2 a :** a person who is instructed or adept in some esoteric learning or mode of expression ⟨abstruse and erudite papers intelligible only to the ~ —H.C. Dent⟩ **b :** one who has been previously exposed to some experience **:** one who is at home in some area of experience or activity ⟨the ~ knows that dinner is nearing an end when the rice and tea appear —V.G.Heiser⟩

**ini·ti·a·tion** \ə̇,nishē'āshən *sometimes* -isē-\ *n* -s **1 a :** the act or an instance of formally initiating (as into an office, sect, or society) **:** the process of being formally initiated ⟨the practice of anointing with oil . . . became attached to the ~ of a king —*Brit. Book News*⟩ ⟨~ is regarded as a great occasion —A.A.Trouwborst⟩ **b** (1) **:** the rites, ceremonies, ordeals, or instructions with which one is made a member of a sect or society or is invested with a particular function or status ⟨the college fraternity has a scheme of ruthless mock ~s —C.W.Ferguson⟩ (2) **:** the ceremonies and ordeals with which a youth is formally invested with adult status in a primitive community ⟨attended some of the girls' ~, and took part in many functions of native life —Margaret C. Hubbard⟩ **c** (1) **:** the process or an instance of being initiated into some experience or sphere of activity **:** INTRODUCTION ⟨while still in high school, the youth received his ~ into his lifework —*Current Biog.*⟩ ⟨part of the child's ~ into the life of man —George Sampson⟩ ⟨his ~ to venal love is sordid —Henri Peyre⟩ ⟨had already had her ~ into court . . . and is now on probation —Beatrice Griffith⟩ (2) **:** the condition of being initiated or an initiate **:** KNOWLEDGEABLENESS ⟨clear to a reader of any degree of ~ —J.W.Beach⟩ ⟨that dullness which perhaps was due simply to lack of ~ —George Santayana⟩ **2 :** the act, process, or an instance of beginning, setting on foot, or originating **:** the condition of being begun **:** ORIGINATION, BEGINNING ⟨~ of a program to produce and test a vaccine —*Americana Annual*⟩ ⟨does not give them much power of ~ —R.H.Rovere⟩ ⟨the ~ of a leaf⟩

**¹ini·tia·tive** \ə'nishə̇d·iv, |tiv *sometimes* -shē,ā| *or* -shēə| *or* -shtiv *or* -shtēv\ *adj* [*initiate* + *-ive*] **:** of or relating to initiation **:** serving to initiate **:** INTRODUCTORY, PRELIMINARY

**²initiative** \"\ *n* -s **1 :** an introductory step or movement **:** an act designed to originate or set on foot (as a process or train of events) ⟨a new Russian ~ must now be anticipated —Frank Gorrell⟩ — often used in the phrase *on one's own initiative* ⟨don't blame me, he acted on his own ~⟩ **2 :** energy or aptitude displayed in initiation esp. of action that pioneers in some field **:** self-reliant enterprise ⟨a man of great ~⟩ ⟨unable to control the product of his ~, science —Norman Kelman⟩ **3 a :** the right or power to introduce a new measure or course of action ⟨the ~ in respect to revenue bills is in the House of Representatives⟩ **b :** a procedure or device which enables a specified number of voters by petition to propose a law and secure its submission to the electorate for approval — compare DIRECT INITIATIVE, INDIRECT INITIATIVE, REFERENDUM

**ini·ti·a·tor** \ə'nishē,ād·ə(r), -ātə- *sometimes* -isē-\ *n* -s [LL, fr. L *initiatus* (past part. of *initiare* to initiate) + *-or* — more at INITIATE] **:** one that initiates: as **a :** a person who originates or sets on foot some process or movement ⟨a great ~ in art⟩ **b :** DETONATOR c **c :** a substance that initiates a reaction ⟨benzoyl peroxide is used as an ~ in polymerization⟩ — compare CATALYST 1

**ini·tia·to·ry** \ə'nish(ē)ə,tōrē, -tȯrē, -ri *sometimes* -isēə-\ *adj* [*initiate* + *-ory*] **1 :** constituting an introduction or beginning **:** INTRODUCTORY, OPENING, FIRST ⟨abolished as soon as its ~ horrors were known —J.L.Motley⟩ **2 :** tending or serving to initiate **:** introducing by instruction or by the use and application of symbols or ceremonies **:** ELEMENTARY, RUDIMENTARY ⟨~ rites⟩

**inj** *abbr* inject; injection

**in·ject** \ə̇n'jekt\ *vt* -ED/-ING/-S [L *injectus*, past part. of *inicere, injicere*, fr. ²*in-* + *-icere, -jicere* (fr. *jacere* to throw) — more at JET] **1 a :** to throw, drive, or force in ⟨~ cold water into a condenser⟩ **b** (1) **:** to force a fluid into (a vessel, cavity, or tissue of man, animal, or plant) for preserving, hardening, or coloring structures (2) **:** to introduce (as by injection or gravity flow) a fluid into (a living body) esp. for the purpose of restoring fluid balance, treating nutritional deficiencies or disease, or relieving pain; *also* **:** to treat (an individual) with injections **c :** INTRUDE **2 :** to introduce as an element or factor in or into some situation or subject ⟨able to ~ both color and humor into this rather formidable subject —C.B.Palmer b. 1910⟩ ⟨~*ed* a disruptive element into the situation —Oscar Handlin⟩ ⟨the twists of raw emotion which she ~s into her portrayal —Roger Manvell⟩

**in·ject·able** \-təbəl\ *adj* **:** capable of being injected

**injected** *adj* **1 :** forced in or introduced esp. in the form of a fluid **2 :** CONGESTED 1

**in·jec·tion** \ə̇n'jekshən\ *n* -s [MF or L; MF, fr. L *injection-*, *injectio*, fr. *injectus* + *-ion-, -io* -ion] **1 a** (1) **:** the act or an instance of injecting a drug or other substance into the body (2) **:** a solution of a drug, nutrient, or other substance injected (as by catheter or needle) into the tissues, a vein, or a body cavity (3) **:** a solution or suspension of a drug intended for administration under or through the skin or mucous membranes by means of a hypodermic syringe (4) **:** an act or process of injecting vessels or tissues; *also* **:** a specimen prepared by injection — compare CORROSION (5) **:** the state of being injected **:** CONGESTION **b :** the intrusion of molten magma between rocks **c :** the introduction under pressure of one substance (as fuel oil, combustion air, or water spray) into a working space (as a diesel cylinder, a gas-turbine combustor, or a steam desuperheater) **2 :** the act or an instance of introducing some element or factor into a situation or subject ⟨~ into news reports of the editor's political prejudices —Martin Gardner⟩

**injection gneiss** *n* **:** MIGMATITE

**injection molding** *n* **:** a method of forming articles of plastic or rubber by heating the molding material until it is able to flow and injecting it into a mold

**injection well** *n* **:** a well into which gas, air, or water is pumped in order to increase the yield of adjacent wells

**in·jec·tor** \ə̇n'jektə(r)\ *n* -s **:** one that injects; *specif* **:** a jet pump for injecting feedwater into a boiler or fuel into a combustion chamber

**injoint** *vt* [²*in-* + *joint* (n.)] *obs* **:** JOIN

**in·ju·cun·di·ty** \,injü'kəndəd·ē\ *n* -ES [L *injucunditas*, fr. *injucundus* unpleasant, fr. *in-* ¹*in-* + *jucundus* pleasant — more at JOCUND] *archaic* **:** UNPLEASANTNESS

**in·judicial** \¦in+\ *adj* [¹*in-* + *judicial*] **:** INJUDICIOUS — **in·judicially** \"+\ *adv*

**in·judicious** \"+\ *adj* [¹*in-* + *judicious*] **1 :** not judicious **:** lacking in sound judgment **:** INDISCREET ⟨brought by ~ mothers at precisely the most ineligible moments —W.L. Alden⟩ **2 :** not according to sound judgment or discretion **:** UNWISE ⟨an ~ measure⟩ — **in·judiciously** \"+\ *adv* — **in·judiciousness** \"+\ *n*

**in·jun** \'injən\ *n* -s *cap, often attrib* [alter. of ¹*indian*] **:** AMERICAN INDIAN ⟨he'd tell tales — of *Injuns*, or folks he'd known, or things that was plumb impossible to of happened anywheres —Helen Eustis⟩

**in·junct** \ə̇n'jəŋ(k)t\ *vt* -ED/-ING/-S [*back-formation* fr. *injunction*] **:** to restrain by injunction

**in·junc·tion** \ə̇n'jəŋ(k)shən\ *n* -s [MF & LL; MF *injonction*, fr. LL *injunction-, injunctio*, fr. L *injunctus* (past part. of *injungere* to enjoin) + *-ion-, -io* -ion — more at ENJOIN] **1 :** the act or an instance of enjoining **:** an earnest admonition **:** ORDER, PROHIBITION ⟨the Hindu religion has no ~s against birth control —Mildred Gilman⟩ ⟨laid an ~ of secrecy on me⟩ ⟨delivered stern ~s —Gilbert Millstein⟩ ⟨his father's dying ~s⟩ **2 :** an equitable writ granted by a court of equity whereby one is required to do or to refrain from doing a specified act — compare INTERDICT

**¹in·junc·tive** \-ŋ(k)tiv\ *adj* [L *injunctus* + E *-ive*] **1 a :** constituting an order, prohibition, or admonition **:** ENJOINING ⟨this ~ maxim —C.H.Hamburg⟩ **b :** constituting a mood or set of verb forms usu. with imperative, optative, or subjunctive meaning **2 :** of or relating to a legal injunction ⟨~ relief was not available to the state —*New Republic*⟩ ⟨an ~ order⟩

**²injunctive** \"\ *n* -s **:** the injunctive grammatical mood or a verbal form expressing it

**in·jur·ant** \'inj(ə)rənt\ *n* -s [*injure* + *-ant*] **:** an injurious agent or substance ⟨some poison gases are lung ~s⟩

**in ju·re** \(')in'jürē, -'yü-\ *adv* [L] **:** in right, law, or justice **:** in court

**in·jure** \'injə(r)\ *vt* **injured; injured; injuring** \-j(ə)riŋ\ **injures** [back-formation fr. ¹*injury*] **1 a :** to do an injustice to **:** WRONG, OFFEND ⟨the *injured* husband sued for divorce⟩ **b :** to harm, impair, or tarnish the standing of (as a reputation or other intangible quality or asset) ⟨~ his authority —H.J. Laski⟩ ⟨~ your prospects —Thomas Hardy⟩ **c :** to give pain to (the sensibilities or feelings) ⟨~ a man's pride⟩ **2 a :** to inflict bodily hurt on ⟨*injured* by a falling brick⟩ **b :** to impair the soundness of ⟨~ your health⟩ **c :** to inflict material damage or loss on ⟨many houses were *injured* by the storm⟩ ⟨this tax will ~ all business⟩

**syn** HARM, HURT, DAMAGE, IMPAIR, MAR, SPOIL: INJURE implies the doing of an injustice to, or a wronging of, someone, esp. intentionally; it implies also an inflicting upon someone of anything detrimental to looks, health, comfort, success ⟨*injure* a man's reputation by slander⟩ ⟨*injure* a shoulder in a football game⟩ ⟨*injure* a friendship by resentment⟩ HARM stresses the inflicting of pain, suffering, or loss ⟨*harm* a dog by overfeeding it⟩ ⟨bitterness among the elders must not be permitted to *harm* or wound the innocent children of either race —Beverly Smith⟩ ⟨*harm* one's country by careless talk in wartime⟩ HURT implies the inflicting of a wound upon something (as the body, the feelings, or the commonwealth) capable of sustaining an injury ⟨seriously *hurt* in a landing under shore fire⟩ ⟨*hurt* a man's pride by belittling his accomplishments⟩ ⟨*hurt* the state by publicizing its rare and petty political feuds⟩ DAMAGE implies injury resulting in loss of value, completeness, efficiency, function ⟨furniture *damaged* by careless handling by movers⟩ ⟨an eye *damaged* by strain under bad light⟩ ⟨*damage* a motor by overheating it⟩ IMPAIR suggests a making less complete or efficient as by deterioration or diminution ⟨her excitement *impaired* her power of listening —Willa Cather⟩ ⟨beauty *impaired* by age⟩ ⟨labor with the hands or at the desk distorts or *impairs* the body —G.L.Dickinson⟩ ⟨individual rights should not be *impaired* without good reason⟩ MAR implies an injury that makes less perfect ⟨a case of smallpox which *marred* his face for life —*Time*⟩ ⟨his intellect, which was amazingly spotty, *marred* by great gaps —Norman Mailer⟩ ⟨a life of drudgery disfigures the body and *mars* and enervates the soul —G.L. Dickinson⟩ SPOIL in this connection suggests not only impairment or marring but usu. destruction or ruin ⟨they had the long Carroll upper lip that *spoiled* their looks a bit —Mary Deasy⟩ ⟨few streams and lakes which were clear and unspoiled by the works of man —Alexander MacDonald⟩ ⟨a great novel *spoiled* by hasty (and lazy) composition —H.J.Laski⟩

**in ju·re ces·sio** \-¦jürē'ses(h)ē,ō, -¦yürē'kesē,ō\ *n* [L, lit., surrender in law] **:** a procedure in Roman law whereby a defendant formally admits or concedes before the praetor the justice of the plaintiff's claim to specific property and the praetor then adjudges it to belong to the plaintiff

**injured** *adj* **1 a :** WRONGED, OFFENDED ⟨clearing the reputation of the ~ youth —J.A.Froude⟩ ⟨an air of ~ innocence⟩ ⟨~ vanity⟩ **b :** reflecting or indicating a sense of injury ⟨talking in an ~ way —William Black⟩ ⟨gave her a suspicious, ~ expression —Willa Cather⟩ ⟨relapsed into ~ gloom —Athene Seyler⟩ **2 :** physically damaged or hurt ⟨held up his ~ finger⟩ — **in·jured·ly** *adv*

**in·jur·er** \-jərə(r), -j(ə)rə\ *n* -s **:** one that injures

**in·ju·ria** \ə̇n'jürēə, -'yü-\ *n, pl* **injuri·ae** \-jürē,ē, -yürē,ī\ [L, injury] **:** invasion of another's rights **:** actionable wrong **:** INJUSTICE

**injuria abs·que dam·no** \-¦abz(,)kwē'dam(,)nō, -¦äps(,)kwä'däm(,)nō\ [L, injury without damage] — used in reference to the rule that a wrong that causes no damage will not sustain an action; compare DAMNUM ABSQUE INJURIA

**in·ju·ri·ous** \ə̇n'jürēəs\ *adj* [ME, fr. MF *injurieux*, fr. L *injuriosus*, fr. *injuria* + *-osus* -ous] **1 :** inflicting or tending to inflict injury **:** HURTFUL, HARMFUL, DETRIMENTAL ⟨inaccurate news stories ~ of national dignity —*Quill*⟩ ⟨routine detection of ~ defects —*Steel*⟩ ⟨~ to health⟩ **2 :** ABUSIVE, OFFENSIVE, DEFAMATORY ⟨speak not ~ words —George Washington⟩ — **in·ju·ri·ous·ly** *adv* — **in·ju·ri·ous·ness** *n* -ES

**¹in·ju·ry** \'inj(ə)rē, -ri\ *n* -ES [ME *injurie*, fr. L *injuria*, fr. *injurus, injurius* injurious, unjust, wrong (fr. *in-* ¹*in-* + *-jurus, -jurius*, fr. *jur-, jus* right, law) + *-ia* -y — more at JUST] **1 a :** an act that damages, harms, or hurts **:** an unjust or undeserved infliction of suffering or harm **:** WRONG ⟨take it as a personal ~ —W.R.Inge⟩ ⟨his tone was one of mingled admiration and ~ —R.H.Davis⟩ ⟨adding insult to ~⟩ **b :** a violation of another's rights for which the law allows an action to recover damages or specific property or both **:** an actionable wrong — distinguished from *harm*; compare TORT **c** *obs* **:** offensive or defamatory speech **:** INSULT **2 :** hurt, damage, or loss sustained ⟨with consequent ~ to morale and efficiency —Adam Yarmolinsky⟩ ⟨*injuries* to health⟩ ⟨without ~ to the concrete —J.R.Dalzell⟩ ⟨suffered severe *injuries* in the accident⟩

**syn** INJURY, HURT, DAMAGE, HARM, and MISCHIEF mean in common the act or result of inflicting on a person or thing something that causes loss, pain, distress, or impairment. INJURY is the most comprehensive, applying to an act or result involving an impairment or destruction of right, health, freedom, soundness, or loss of something of value ⟨sustain a leg *injury* in a fall⟩ ⟨mental or emotional upset is just as truly an *injury* to the body as a bone fracture, a burn, or a bacterial infection —G.W.Gray b. 1886⟩ ⟨the fundamental skepticism . . . inflicts the most serious *injury* on both science and religion —W.R.Inge⟩ ⟨such change is . . . a great *injury* to the child's independence and freedom from responsibility —Abram Kardiner⟩ HURT applies chiefly to physical injury but in any application it stresses pain or suffering whether injury is involved or not ⟨a would-be fighter . . . that gross, brutal frame was still capable of doing a great deal of *hurt* —Hamilton Basso⟩ ⟨wrongfully withholding from him something which is his due . . . inflicting on him a positive *hurt*, either in the form of direct suffering, or of the privation of some good which he had reasonable ground, either of a physical or of a social kind, for counting upon —J.S.Mill⟩ ⟨leaving forever to the aggressor the choice of time and place and means to cause greatest *hurt* to us at least cost to himself —D.D.Eisenhower⟩ ⟨the dentist's drill may cause quite a *hurt* though it does no injury⟩ DAMAGE applies to injury involving loss, as of property, value, or usefulness ⟨the collision inflicted great *damage* on the car⟩ ⟨realize the immense *damage* his action has done to the good name of America —H.J.Laski⟩ ⟨enough *damage* to a watch so that it no longer keeps accurate time⟩ HARM applies to any evil that injures or may injure ⟨the men were terrified of Yusuf's cruelty, and wanted to retreat out of *harm's* way —C.S. Forester⟩ ⟨a well-founded apprehension of bodily *harm* is sufficient to justify the taking of life —H.W.H.Knott⟩ ⟨a scandal may prove of great *harm* to a man's political career⟩ MISCHIEF is used to avoid the suggestion or image of particular harm or injury, designating generally any misdoing or injury, esp. irresponsible, and stressing the role of an agent, usu. personal ⟨the nearest policeman, who most likely won't turn up until the worst of the *mischief* is done —G.B.Shaw⟩ ⟨he was most violent; if Captain Downing had not been there to restrain him, I vow he'd have done me a *mischief* —Max Peacock⟩ ⟨a fence was defective, and the pigs straying did *mischief* to a trolley car —B.N.Cardozo⟩

**²injury** *vt* -ED/-ING/-ES [ME *injurien*, fr. MF *injurier*, fr. L *injuriari*, fr. *injuria*] *obs* **:** INJURE

**injust** *adj* [ME *injuste*, fr. MF *injuste*, fr. L *injustus*] *obs* **:** UNJUST

**in·justice** \(')in, ən+\ *n* [ME, fr. MF, fr. L *injustitia*, fr. *injustus* unjust (fr. *in-* ¹*in-* + *justus* just) + *-ia* -y — more at JUST] **1 :** absence of justice **:** violation of right or of the rights of another **:** INIQUITY, UNFAIRNESS ⟨flamed out against ~ —John Galsworthy⟩ **2 :** an unjust act or deed **:** WRONG ⟨the ~s that angered him were never genuine —Norman Mailer⟩

**¹ink** \'iŋk\ *n* -s *often attrib* [ME *enke, inke*, fr. OF *enke, enque*, fr. LL *encaustum* ink (orig. the purplish ink used by the late Roman emperors to sign their edicts), fr. neut. of L *encaustus* burned in, painted in encaustic, fr. Gk *enkaustos* — more at ENCAUSTIC] **1 a :** a fluid or viscous material of various colors but commonly black or blue-black that is composed essentially of a pigment or dye in a suitable vehicle and is used for writing and printing — see INDELIBLE INK, PRINTING INK, WRITING INK **b :** a similar solid preparation (as india ink) **2 :** the black protective secretion of a cephalopod

**²ink** \"\ *vt* -ED/-ING/-S **1 :** to cover or smear with ink **:** apply ink to or touch up with ink **2 a :** to go over in ink — usu. used with *in* or *over* **b :** to obliterate with ink — usu. used with *out* ⟨~*ed* out many lines⟩ **c :** to write or draw in ink ⟨~*ed* their crosses to documents they had not the skill to read —G.M.Trevelyan⟩ ⟨pointed out the neatly ~*ed* entry on the bill —Irwin Shaw⟩ **3 a :** to affix one's signature to ⟨the baseball player was offered a raise and readily ~*ed* his contract⟩ **b :** to sign to a contract ⟨~*ed* the players with little difficulty⟩

**ink ball** *also* **inking ball** *n* **:** a ball-shaped inking pad formerly used by printers

**inkberry** \'iŋk — *see* BERRY\ *n* **1 :** a holly (*Ilex glabra*) of eastern No. America with evergreen oblong leathery leaves and small black berries — called also *gallberry* **2 :** BOX BRIER **3 :** POKEWEED **4 :** the fruit of an inkberry

**ink black** *n* **:** the color of dried blue-black ink **:** a dark grayish blue to bluish black — called also *inky black*

**inkblot** \'=,=\ *n* **1 :** a blot of ink **2 :** any of several plates showing blots of ink for use in psychological testing

**inkblot test** *n* **:** RORSCHACH TEST

**inkbush** \'=,=\ *n* **:** INKWEED 1

**ink cap** *n* **:** INKY CAP

**ink disease** *n* **1 :** a destructive disease of the chestnut in Europe that is caused by a fungus (*Phytophthora cambivora*) and that produces dark cankers and a black exudate on the trunk — called also *black canker* **2 :** a destructive disease of walnuts caused by a fungus (*Phytophthora citrophthora*)

**ink·er** \'iŋkə(r)\ *n* -s **:** one that inks: as **a :** INKWRITER **b :** a worker who applies ink or stain to goods (as shoe parts or cloth); *specif* **:** a worker who touches up imperfectly dyed cloth or hosiery

**inkfish** \'=,=\ *n* **:** CUTTLEFISH, SQUID

**ink fountain** *n* **:** the mechanism in a printing press that contains the ink and releases it to the rollers

**¹ink·horn** \'iŋk,hȯrn, 'iŋ,kȯrn\ *n* [ME *enkehorn, inkehorn*, fr. *enke, inke* ink + *horn* horn] **:** a small portable bottle of horn or other material for holding ink

**²inkhorn** \"\ *adj* **:** affectedly learned or pedantic ⟨~ terms and crude Latinisms —J.W.H.Atkins⟩

**in·kie** *or* **in·ky** \'iŋkē, -ki\ *n, pl* **inkies** [by shortening & alter.] *slang* **:** INCANDESCENT LAMP

**inkier** *comparative of* INKY

**inkiest** *superlative of* INKY

**ink·i·ness** \'iŋkēnə̇s, -kin-\ *n* -ES **:** the quality or state of being inky

**ink knife** *n* **:** a spatula for mixing printing ink

**¹in·kle** *also* **in·cle** \'iŋkəl\ *vt* -ED/-ING/-S [back-formation fr. *inkling*] *chiefly dial Eng* **:** to have an inkling of ⟨began to ~ what a silly combat weapon it is —E.V.Westrate⟩

**²inkle** *also* **incle** \"\ *n* -s [origin unknown] **:** a colored linen tape or braid woven on a very narrow loom and used for trimming; *also* **:** the thread used

**ink·less** \'iŋklə̇s\ *adj* [¹*ink* + *-less*] **:** devoid of ink

**in·kling** \'iŋkliŋ, -lēŋ, *esp in sense 1* -lən\ *n* -s [ME *yngkiling*, prob. fr. gerund of *inclen* to hint at, indicate; akin to OE *inca* suspicion, doubt, quarrel, OFris *jink* angry, ON *ekki* pain, Lith *ingis* sluggard, OSlav *jędza* illness] **1** *dial chiefly Eng* **a :** a faintly perceptible sound **:** UNDERTONE ⟨could not hear an ~ of his breathing —Elizabeth Enright⟩ **b :** RUMOR **2 a :** a faint or slight suggestion **:** HINT, INTIMATION ⟨there was no path — no ~ even of a track —*New Yorker*⟩ ⟨give only a dim ~ of its native intelligence —H.J.Morgenthau⟩ **b :** a slight knowledge or vague notion ⟨had not the faintest ~ of what it was all about —H.W.Carter⟩ ⟨got his first ~s as to the roles of natural selection —E.H.Colbert⟩

**ink·man** \'iŋk,man, -,mən\ *n, pl* **inkmen :** a worker who blends inks, powders, or pastes to obtain printing inks of desired colors

**ink mushroom** *n* **:** INKY CAP

**ink plant** *n* **1 :** a plant of the genus *Coriaria*: as **a :** a plant (*C. thymifolia*) of tropical America and New Zealand the fruits of which yield a red dye used as ink in Ecuador **b :** a European plant (*C. myrtifolia*) the leaves of which yield a black dye **2 :** POKEWEED

**inkpot** \'=,=\ *n* **:** a container for ink

**ink print** *n* **:** matter printed from inked type as distinguished from embossed matter for reading by the blind

**in·kra** \iŋ'krä, iŋ'k-\ *n, pl* **inkra** *or* **inkras** *usu cap* **:** GA

**inks** *pl of* INK, *pres 3d sing of* INK

**ink sac** *n* **:** an organ in most cephalopods (as the squid) secreting an inky fluid that can be ejected from a duct opening into the terminal part of the rectum

**inkshed** \'=,=\ *n* -s [¹*ink* + *-shed* (as in *bloodshed*)] *archaic* **:** profuse use or unnecessary waste of ink in writing ⟨to spare mine own pains and prevent ~ —Andrew Marvell⟩

**inkslinger** \ˈ=,==\ *n* **1 :** WRITER, SCRIBBLER **2 :** a timekeeper in a logging camp

**ink spot** *n* **:** a plant disease characterized by black blemishes; *specif* **:** a disease of the aspen caused by fungi of the genus *Sclerotinia*

**inkstand** \ˈ=,=\ *n* **:** a small vessel for holding ink into which a pen can be dipped **:** INKWELL; *also* **:** a stand with fittings for holding ink and pens

**inkstandish** \ˈ=,=(,)=\ *n* [¹*ink* + *standish*] *archaic* **:** INKSTAND ⟨desired me to hand him the paper and ~ —Frederick Marryat⟩

**inkweed** \ˈ=,=\ *n* **1 :** any of several western No. American shrubby plants of the genus *Suaeda* used by the Indians for dyeing — called also *inkbush* **2 :** POKEWEED

**inkwell** \ˈ=,=\ *n* **:** a container for writing ink

**inkwood** \ˈ=,=\ *n* **:** a small tree (*Exothea paniculata*) of the family Sapindaceae of Florida and the West Indies having dark-colored wood and purple fruits

**inkwriter** \ˈ=,==\ *n* **:** a telegraph receiver in which the message is recorded in ink (as in dots and dashes)

inkwell

**¹inky** \ˈiŋkē, -ki\ *adj* -ER/-EST **:** consisting of, using, or resembling ink ⟨the ~ blackness of the ocean —F.G.Kay⟩ **:** soiled with or as if with ink **:** BLACK ⟨~ collars and dirty fingernails —Angela Thirkell⟩

**²inky** *var of* INKIE

**inky black** *n* **:** INK BLACK

**inky cap** *n* **:** a mushroom of the genus *Coprinus* (esp. *C. atramentarius*) having a pileus that melts into an inky fluid after the spores have matured

**inlaid** \(ˈ)=¦=\ *adj* [fr. past part. of ¹*inlay*] **:** set into a surface so as to form a decorative design or decorated with a design so formed; *specif* **:** CHAMPLEVÉ

**inlaid binding** *n* **:** MOSAIC BINDING

**in·laik** \ˈin,lāk, -lak\ *n* -S [ME (Sc), alter. of ME (Sc) *inlake*, fr. ME *in* + *lake*, *lak*, *lac* lack] *Scot* **:** LACK, DEFICIENCY

**in–lamb** \=ˈ=\ *adj, of ewes* **:** PREGNANT

**¹in·land** \ˈin,land, -lənd, -,laa(ə)nd\ *n* [ME, fr. OE, fr. *in* + *land* — more at LAND] **1** *Old Eng & feudal law* **:** the demesne land of the lord of a manor **2 :** the interior part of a country or the part remote from the centers of population ⟨the far ~ of Australia —T.C.Roughley⟩

**²inland** \"\ *adj* **1** *chiefly Brit* **:** confined to a country or state **:** not foreign **:** DOMESTIC, INTERNAL ⟨the consolidated foreign and ~ debt —*Statesman's Yr. Bk.*⟩ ⟨~ revenue⟩ **2 a :** of or relating to the inlands or interior parts of a country **:** lying in the interior **:** INTERIOR ⟨any college town, however ~ and ivory-towered —Nell G. Ahern⟩ **b :** being within the land **:** not bordering on the sea ⟨maritime and ~ provinces⟩ **3 :** limited to the inland or interior or to inland routes ⟨~ transportation⟩ ⟨~ commerce⟩

**³inland** \"\ *adv* **:** into or toward the interior **:** away from the frontier **:** away from the coast ⟨live ~⟩

**inland bill** *n* **:** a bill of exchange that is or on its face purports to be both drawn and payable within the jurisdiction (as country or state) where it is presented — compare FOREIGN BILL

**in·land·er** \-də(r)\ *n* -S [¹*inland* + *-er*] **:** one that lives inland

**inland marine insurance** *n* **:** insurance against loss of or damage to property transported in domestic commerce, instruments of transport and communication, and personal property — compare FLOATER 8, MARINE INSURANCE, OCEAN MARINE INSURANCE

**inland water** *n* **1 :** any of the waters (as lakes, canals, rivers, watercourses, inlets, and bays) within the territory of a state as contrasted with the open seas or marginal waters bordering another state subject to various sovereign rights of the bordering state — usu. used in pl. **2 :** water of the interior that does not border upon marginal or high seas or is above the rise and fall of the tides — usu. used in pl.; compare MARGINAL SEA, TERRITORIAL SEA, TERRITORIAL WATER

**inland waterway** *n* **1 :** a navigable river, canal, or sound **2 :** a system of navigable inland bodies of water — usu. used in pl.

**in–large** \ən+\ *archaic var of* ENLARGE

**in·laut** \ˈin,laůt\ *n, pl* **inlau·te** \-aůdə\ *also* **inlauts** [G, fr. *in* (fr. OHG) + *laut* sound, fr. MHG *lūt*; akin to OE *hlūd* loud — more at IN, LOUD] **:** a medial sound or position in a word or syllable — compare ANLAUT, AUSLAUT

**in–law** \(ˈ)in¦lȯ, ən'lȯ\ *vt* -ED/-ING/-S [ME *inlawen*, fr. OE *inlagian*, fr. *in* ²in + *-lagian* (fr. *lagu* law) — more at LAW] *Old Eng law* **:** to clear of outlawry or attainder **:** place under the protection of the law

**in–law** \ˈin,lȯ\ *n, pl* **in–laws** [back-formation fr. *mother-in-law*, etc.] **:** a relative by marriage — usu. used in pl. ⟨how to get along with parents and *in-laws* —Emily H. Mudd⟩

**¹in·lay** \(ˈ)in¦lā, ən'lā\ *vt* **inlaid; inlaid; inlaying; inlays** [²*in* + *lay*] **1 a** (1) **:** to set into the body of a surface or ground material ⟨~ arabesques⟩ (2) **:** to pattern or adorn (a surface or ground) by the insertion of other material ⟨~ a panel with contrasting wood⟩ **:** adorn by inlaying ⟨~ wood with mother-of-pearl⟩ (3) **:** to ornament (a leather book cover) by fitting leather or other material into cut-in areas (4) **:** to ornament (a book cover) by affixing printed paper or other decorative material into depressed areas **b** (1) **:** to insert (as a color plate) into a heavier or stouter sheet serving as a mat, frame, or support (2) **:** to provide (a book) with inlaid illustrations **c :** to reinforce (silver-plated ware) at points of wear with an additional coating of silver or piece of silver embedded before electroplating **2 :** to burnish, beat, or fuse (as wire) into an incised cavity in metal, wood, stone, or other material

**²in·lay** \ˈin,lā\ *n* -S **1 :** the process or art of inlaying **2 a :** material inlaid or prepared for inlaying; *also* **:** the ornament or pattern formed by inlaying **b** (1) **:** a tooth filling of metal or porcelain shaped to fit a cavity and then cemented into place (2) **:** a piece of tissue (as bone) laid into the site of missing tissue to bridge a defect **3 a :** an allowance (as an extra-wide seam) for clothing alteration **b :** a set-in section on a garment usu. decorative or contrasting

**¹in·lay·er** \(ˈ)in¦lāər, ən'l-, -le(ə)r\ *n* -S [¹*inlay* + *-er*] **:** one that inlays

**²in·lay·er** \ˈin,l-\ *n* [⁴*in* + *layer*] **:** an inner layer or sheathing

**inlay graft** *n* **:** a plant graft made by inserting, fastening, and sealing an accurately cut scion in a V-shaped notch in the end of a truncated stock

**inlaying** *n* -S **1 :** INLAY 1,2a **2 :** the burnishing, beating, or fusing of material (as wire) in an incised cavity in metal, wood, stone, or other material

**inleakage** \ˈ=,==\ *n* [⁴*in* + *leakage*] **:** the quantity that leaks in ⟨an actual ~ of 20,150 cubic feet per hour —*Lumber and its Utilization*⟩

**¹in·let** \ˈin,le|t, -lə|, *usu* |d·+V\ *n* -S *often attrib* [⁴*in* + *let*, n. (after *let in*, v.)] **1 :** the act or an instance of letting in **2 a** (1) **:** a bay or recess in the shore of a sea, lake, or river (2) **:** a waterway into a sea, lake, or river **:** CREEK (3) **:** a narrow strip of water running into the land or between islands; *specif* **:** a passage through a barrier island or barrier reef leading to a bay or lagoon ⟨Barnegat *Inlet*⟩ **b :** a place of entrance **:** an opening by which entrance is made **:** ORIFICE ⟨oil ~s⟩ ⟨air ~⟩ ⟨~ and outlet valves⟩ **3 :** something that is let in or inlaid **:** an inserted material **4 :** the upper opening of the cavity of the true pelvis bounded by the brim

**²in·let** \ˈin,let, *usu* -ed·+V\ *vt* **inlet; inlet; inletting; inlets** [²*in* + *let* (v.)] **1 :** to let in **:** INSERT, INLAY ⟨~ the trigger mechanism down into the stock —*Amer. Rifleman*⟩

**in·li·er** \ˈin,lī(ə)r\ *n* [⁴*in* + *-lier* (as in *outlier*)] **1 :** a mass of rock whose outcrop is wholly surrounded by rock of younger age **2 :** a distinct area or formation that is completely surrounded by another ⟨~s of an older, wilder landscape surrounded by improvement —H.C.Darby⟩; *also* **:** ENCLAVE ⟨abolish the numerous outliers and ~s of territory —R.E. Dickinson⟩

**in–line engine** \ən'līn, ˈin,l-\ *n* **:** an internal-combustion engine in which the cylinders are arranged in one or more straight lines — compare RADIAL ENGINE

**in–list** \ən'list\ *archaic var of* ENLIST

**in lo·co pa·ren·tis** \ən¦lō(,)kōpə'rentəs\ *adv* [L] **:** in the place of a parent ⟨parents or persons standing *in loco parentis* —*U.S.House Bill*⟩

**in–lot** \ˈ=,=\ *n* [⁴*in* + *lot*] **1 :** a lot of land within a larger plot **:** INTERIOR LOT ⟨in a retail district, the corner is more desirable than the *in-lots* —H.E.Hoagland⟩ **2 :** a homestead lot on a townsite granted or sold to an early settler in No. America

**in·ly** \ˈinlē, -li\ *adv* [ME *inliche*, *inly*, fr. OE *inlīce*, fr. *inlīc*, adj., inward, interior, fr. *in*, *inn* in + *-līc* -ly — more at IN] **1 :** INWARDLY, WITHIN ⟨~ excited about her —Vance Palmer⟩ **2 :** INTIMATELY, THOROUGHLY ⟨~ know all wisdom —John Masefield⟩

**¹inlying** \ˈ=,==\ *n* -S [⁴*in* + *lying*, gerund of *lie* (after *lie in*, v.)] *chiefly Scot* **:** CONFINEMENT

**²inlying** \"\ *adj* [²*in* + *lying*, pres. part. of *lie*] **:** placed or situated inside or in the interior

**inmarriage** \ˈ=,==\ *n* [⁴*in* + *marriage*] **:** marriage within one's own family, race, or other grouping **:** ENDOGAMY — contrasted with *outmarriage*

**inmarry** \ˈ=,==\ *vi* [²*in* + *marry*] **:** to marry within one's own family, race, profession, or other grouping

**¹in·mate** \ˈin,māt, *usu* -ād·+V\ *n* [⁴*in* + *mate*] **1 a** *obs* **:** LODGER, TENANT **b** *archaic* **:** one who lives in the same house or apartment with another ⟨inquired whether he was a pleasant ~ and a kind neighbor —Harriet Martineau⟩ **2 :** one of a family, community, or other group occupying a single dwelling, home, or other place of residence ⟨rush the enemy settlement when all its ~s are asleep —C.D.Forde⟩ ⟨lifted the door of a pen, stirred up its ~s with his hand —Adrian Bell⟩ ⟨entered the house and seized all its ~s⟩; *esp* **:** a person confined or kept in an institution (as an asylum, prison, or poorhouse)

**²inmate** \"\ *adj, archaic* **:** living in the house of another **:** dwelling with another

**inmeats** \ˈ=,=\ *n pl* [⁴*in* + *meats*] *dial Eng* **:** the inner parts of an animal that are used for food

**in me·di·as res** \ən¦mādē,äs'rās, -med-\ *adv* [L, lit., into the midst of things] **:** in or into the heart or substance of a matter; *esp* **:** in or into the middle of a narrative or plot without the formality of an introduction or other preliminary ⟨plunges the reader . . . *in medias res* —J.W.Aldridge⟩

**in me·mo·ri·am** \,inmə'mōrēəm, -'mȯr-, -ē,am, -ē,aa(ə)m, -ē,äm\ *adv* [L] **:** in memory of — used esp. in epitaphs and inscriptions and on floral pieces for the dead

**inmesh** *var of* ENMESH

**in–migrant** \ˈ=,==\ *n* [⁴*in* + *migrant*] **:** a person who in-migrates

**in–migrate** \(¦)in+\ *vi* [²*in* + *migrate*] **:** to come to live in a community esp. for work in an expanding industry and often as part of a large-scale movement of workers — compare OUT-MIGRATE — **in–migration** \¦in+\ *n*

**in·most** \ˈin,mōst *also chiefly Brit* -məst\ *adj* [ME *inmast*, *inmost*, alter. (influenced by *mast*, *most* most) of *inmest*, fr. OE *innemest*, superl. of *inne*, adv., in, inside, within, fr. *in*, *inn*, adv., in — more at IN] **:** deepest within **:** farthest from the surface or external part **:** INNERMOST ⟨one's ~ self —J.B.Noss⟩

**¹inn** \ˈin\ *n* -S *often attrib* [ME *inn*, *in*, fr. OE *inn* (akin to ON *inni* dwelling, refuge, inn), fr. *inn*, *in*, adv. — more at IN] **1 a :** a public house for the lodging of travelers for compensation and until capacity is reached **:** HOTEL, HOSTELRY **b :** a place of public entertainment that does not provide lodging **:** TAVERN **2 :** a residence or hostel for students — formerly used of such a residence at a British university and of various houses connected with the study and admission to the practice of law in London — compare INN OF CHANCERY, INN OF COURT

**²inn** \"\ *vi* -ED/-ING/-S [ME *innen*, *innien*, fr. OE *innian*, fr. *inn*, n.] **:** to lodge, stop, or put up at an inn

**inn** *abbr* inning

**in·nards** \ˈinə(r)dz\ *n pl* [alter. of *inwards*] **1 :** the internal organs of a man or animal ⟨treating their ~ at state expense —Mollie Panter-Downes⟩; *esp* **:** VISCERA ⟨his ~ were rumbling⟩ **2 :** the internal parts or interior of something ⟨churned up from the earth's ~ —*Time*⟩ ⟨the insidious ~ of the women's magazines —Hugh Mulligan⟩; *esp* **:** the internal parts of a structure or mechanism ⟨the iron ~ of a great four-faced clock —*New Yorker*⟩

**in·nate** \(ˈ)i¦nāt, ə'n- *sometimes* (ˈ)in¦n-; *usu* -ād· +V\ *adj* [ME *innat*, fr. L *innatus*, past part. of *innasci* to be born, be a native, be naturally suitable, fr. *in-* ²in- + *nasci* to be born — more at NATION] **1 a :** existing in or belonging to some person or other living organism from birth **:** NATIVE, NATURAL ⟨~ vigor⟩ **b :** belonging to the essential nature of something **:** INHERENT ⟨the ~ defect in a plan⟩ **c :** originating in, derived from, or inherent in the mind or the constitution of the intellect rather than derived from experience ⟨~ ideas of God, immortality, right and wrong⟩ — compare A PRIORI, INTUITIVE **2** *obs* **:** formed internally **:** hidden within **:** INTERNAL **3 a :** attached to the apex of the support of a plant (as an anther to the tip of a filament) — compare ADNATE 2 **b :** ENDOGENOUS **c :** immersed or embedded in (as the fruiting bodies in the thallus of a fungus)

**syn** INBORN, INBRED, CONGENITAL, HEREDITARY, INHERITED: INNATE applies to qualities or characteristics belonging to something as part of its inner essential nature. INNATE designates that which is part of lasting essential character, sometimes present or potential at birth ⟨simple ideas should be kept simple, and their *innate* strength should not be undermined by the use of big words and by periphrases —E.S.McCartney⟩ ⟨because of her ability to sense the *innate* talent of young and untried actors —*Amer. Guide Series: Mich.*⟩ ⟨this stubbornness has been explained as being *innate* in the Germans, as a natural racial cussedness —R.C.Wood⟩ INBORN may describe a natural native distinctive characteristic so deep-seated as to have been born in one, often present at birth ⟨there was in him a rush of *inborn* vitality like an Alpine torrent —Agnes Repplier⟩ ⟨the psychopathic personality is held to be an *inborn* (though not hereditary) deficit and is of the nature of a functional alteration —*Yr. Bk. of Neurology, Psychiatry & Neurosurgery*⟩ INBRED describes that which becomes deeply ingrained into one's nature by early environmental influences without being part of one's nature at birth ⟨those *inbred* sentiments which are . . . the true supporters of all liberal and manly morals —Edmund Burke⟩ ⟨a methodical man, an *inbred* Yankee —W.A.White⟩ CONGENITAL applies to a characteristic present at the birth of a person or inception of a thing or notion, whatever the provenience of that characteristic ⟨the newborn child's chances of survival and healthy development depend in part on his *congenital* equipment —*Times Lit. Supp.*⟩ ⟨yet art for art's sake suffers from a *congenital* disease; it professes to create substance out of form, which is physically impossible —George Santayana⟩ HEREDITARY and INHERITED describe characteristics and conditions not only present at birth but definitely coming from heredity, that is, brought about by transmission from parents and ancestors ⟨an *hereditary* propensity to kill men and eat them. True, he came from a race of cannibals —Herman Melville⟩ ⟨most of us, of course, held fast to the Republican party, for political beliefs were *hereditary*, transmissible in the male line —Ben Riker⟩ ⟨a tendency in the past to confuse *congenital* with *inherited*. It is a commonplace now that conditions present at birth are not necessarily inherited in the biological sense of the word, to quote only congenital syphilis as an example. It is also generally known that many inherited conditions first manifest themselves long after birth —Hans Grüneberg⟩

**innated** *adj* [L *innatus* + E *-ed*] *obs* **:** INNATE

**in·nate·ly** *adv* **:** in an innate manner

**in·nate·ness** *n* -ES **:** the quality or state of being innate

**in·nat·ism** \ə'nād·,izəm\ *n* -S [*innate* + *-ism*] **:** a belief in innate ideas

**in·na·tive** \(ˈ)i(n)¦nād·iv\ *adj* [L *innatus* + E *-ive*] **:** INNATE, NATURAL ⟨some ~ weakness . . . in him who condescends to victory —J.R.Lowell⟩

**in·navigable** \(ˈ)i(n), ə+\ *adj* [L *innavigabilis*, fr. *in-* ¹in- + *navigabilis* navigable — more at NAVIGABLE] **:** not navigable

**inned** *past of* IN *or of* INN

**¹in·ner** \ˈinə(r)\ *adj* [ME *inner*, *inre*, fr. OE *innera*, *inra*, compar. of *inne* in — more at INMOST] **1 a :** situated farther in ⟨an ~ chamber⟩ ⟨the ~ bark⟩ **b :** near to a center esp. of influence ⟨the ~ circles of the administration⟩ **c :** INTRAMOLECULAR — used esp. of compounds ⟨~ esters⟩ **2 :** of or relating to the mind or spirit or its phenomena ⟨the ~ life of man⟩

**syn** INWARD, INSIDE, INTERIOR, INTERNAL, INTESTINE, INTESTINAL are often interchangeable. INNER may apply to something far within or near a center; consequently it may apply to something deeply intimate or inaccessible ⟨an *inner* room⟩ ⟨no wish to write anything but a spiritual biography, and outer events only interest me here insofar as they affected my *inner* life —Havelock Ellis⟩ ⟨he had not chosen his course. It had sprung from a necessity of his nature, an *inner* logic that he scarcely questioned —Van Wyck Brooks⟩ INWARD is close in suggestion to INNER; it may apply to direction within ⟨an *inward* curve⟩ ⟨the little houses splashed in the thousands across the countryside sheltered the men turning *inward* in the quest for peace of mind —Oscar Handlin⟩ ⟨that *inward* eye which is the bliss of solitude —William Wordsworth⟩ INSIDE, used often of space relationships, may suggest the restricted, secret, or confidential not shared by those outside ⟨an *inside* room⟩ ⟨*inside* work⟩ ⟨speculating on *inside* information⟩ ⟨even the bare outline was sufficient to gratify the public's craving for the abnormal and the spectacular. But the *inside* story of the catastrophe surpassed even the wildest flights of public fancy —W.H.Wright⟩ INTERIOR may contrast with *exterior* and stress the fact of being within ⟨*interior* decorating⟩ ⟨not to be found in institutionalism, nor in the Scriptures, but in the *interior* life and spirit of man —W.R.Inge⟩ ⟨frightened by an *interior* quietness and by the thought that she had for once in her life stopped thinking —Elizabeth Bowen⟩ INTERNAL, contrasted with *external*, may apply to inner activity, force, development, or effect ⟨interested more in *internal* affairs than foreign⟩ ⟨the slavery which would be imposed upon her by her external enemies and her *internal* traitors —F.D.Roosevelt⟩ ⟨a more general process of *internal* migration that involved both regional shifts and a drift to the cities —Oscar Handlin⟩ INTESTINE and, more rarely, INTESTINAL are occas. used as synonyms for *civil* and *domestic*, in contrast to *foreign*, to describe wars and disturbances ⟨the common people fused, not without considerable *intestine* struggle, to form an Etrusco-Latin blend —R.A.Hall b.1911⟩

**²inner** \"\ *n* -S **:** a forward line player in various team sports (as soccer and field hockey) stationed between the left or right wing and the center forward

**inner anhydride** *n* **:** an anhydride formed by elimination of water from a single molecule

**inner bar** *n, Eng law* **:** the queen's or king's counsel who are permitted to plead within the bar of the court — compare OUTER BAR

**inner barrister** *n, Eng law* **:** a barrister ranking lowest among the barristers belonging to an Inn of Court

**inner bottom** *n* **:** the plating in a ship that is laid over the frames and longitudinals and that with the shell plating forms a double bottom — called also *tank top*

**inner cell mass** *n* **:** the portion of the blastodermic vesicle of a primate embryo that is destined to become the embryo proper

**inner closure** *n* **:** the inner of the two ends of the chamber formed by a stop articulation ⟨the bottom of the lungs, the glottis, or the tongue and velum may be the *inner closure*⟩ — compare OUTER CLOSURE

**inner–directed** \¦==(,)=¦==\ *adj* **:** directed in thought and action by one's own scale of values as opposed to external norms **:** NONCONFORMIST ⟨the American is undergoing a basic change from *inner-directed* to other-directed —H.S.Commager⟩

**inner–direction** \¦==(,)=¦==\ *n* **:** a sense of direction based on one's own scale of values or standards as opposed to external norms

**inner ear** *n* **:** the essential part of the vertebrate ear consisting typically of a bony labyrinth in the temporal bone enclosing a fluid-filled membranous labyrinth innervated by the auditory nerve and made up of a vestibular apparatus and three semicircular canals primarily concerned with the labyrinthine sense and a cochlea which is the seat of the actual sound receptor

**inner endodermis** *n* **:** the endodermal layer separating the stele from the pith (as in a stem where two endodermal layers are present)

**inner form** *n* **:** a form that prints the side of a sheet on which the second page appears — contrasted with *outer form*; compare SHEET IMPOSITION

**inner jib** *n* **:** a jib immediately forward of the forestaysail on a ship where several jibs are carried — see SAIL illustration

**inner keel** *n* [³*keel*] **:** KEELSON

**inner light** *n, cap I&L* **:** the divine presence in the soul of every man held in Quaker doctrine to give spiritual enlightenment, moral guidance, and religious assurance to all who seek such through faith — called also *Christ Within*, *Light Within*

**¹in·ner·ly** \ˈinə(r)lē, -li\ *adv* [ME, fr. *inner* + *-ly* (adv. suffix)] **:** INWARDLY, INLY ⟨a world that was ~ divided —Dorothy Thompson⟩

**²innerly** \"\ *adj* [ME, fr. *inner* + *-ly* (adj. suffix)] **1** *Scot* **:** INWARD, INLYING **2 :** pleasantly familiar and sociable

**inner man** *n* **1 :** the spiritual or intellectual part of man **2 :** STOMACH ⟨the *inner man* will consume the largest part of your bankroll —T.H.Fielding⟩

**inner mission** *n* [trans. of G *innere mission*] **:** a movement originating in the 19th century within the Evangelical Church of Germany that sought partly through sisterhoods and lay brotherhoods to serve neglected and unfortunate members of society and that founded Christian lodging houses, Sunday schools, orphanages, and hospitals

**innermore** \ˈ==,=\ *adj* [ME, fr. ¹*inner* + *more*] *now dial Eng* **:** located farther within **:** INNER

**¹in·ner·most** \ˈ==,mōst *also chiefly Brit* -məst\ *adj* [ME, fr. *inner* + *-most*] **:** farthest inward **:** INMOST ⟨it is his ~ being that is judged —D.C.Hodges⟩ ⟨the ~ part of the nation —F.D.Roosevelt⟩ — **inner·most·ly** *adv*

**²innermost** \"\ *n* **:** the inmost part **:** inmost being

**in·ner·ness** *n* -ES **:** the quality or state of being inner **:** inner character ⟨its superior moral sense and its more intense ~ —W.K.Ferguson⟩

**inner part** *or* **inner voice** *n* **:** a line or part intermediate between the highest and lowest (as the alto or tenor in four-part vocal music)

**inner phase** *n* **:** DISPERSED PHASE

**inner planet** *n* **:** one of the four principal planets whose orbits are innermost in the solar system ⟨Mercury, Venus, Earth, and Mars are the *inner planets*⟩

**inner post** *n* **:** a timber on the forward side of the sternpost to receive the hooding ends of the planking and in square-stern ships to support the transoms

**inner product** *n* **:** SCALAR PRODUCT

**inner proscenium** *n* **:** an inner frame (as a wooden framework) built esp. for a stage production to mask lighting equipment or narrow the stage opening or by means of special shape to give a desired design-quality to the production

**inner quantum number** *n* **:** a vector quantum number denoting the total angular momentum of an atom exclusive of nuclear spin — symbol *J* or *j*

**inner salt** *n* **:** a salt formed by reaction within the molecule of a compound having both acid and basic properties — compare DIPOLAR ION

**inner sanctum** *n* **:** SANCTUM

**innersole** \ˈ==,=\ *n* **:** INSOLE

**inner speech** *n* **:** use of words or word images in thinking without audible or visible speaking

**innerspring** \ˈ==,=\ *adj* **:** having coil springs inside a padded casing ⟨~ mattress⟩ ⟨~ cushion⟩

**inner table** *n* **:** either half of a backgammon board as determined by the players but usu. the half nearer the source of light

**inner tube** *n* **:** an airtight tube of rubber placed inside the casing of a pneumatic tire to hold air under pressure

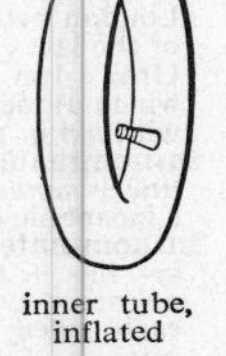

inner tube, inflated

**in·ner·vate** \i'nər,vāt ˈi(,)nər-\ *vt* -ED/-ING/-S [²*in-* + *nerve* + *-ate*] **1 :** to supply with nerves **2 :** to arouse or stimulate (a nerve or an organ) to activity

**in·ner·va·tion** \,i(,)nər'vāshən\ *n* [²*in-* + *nerve* + *-ation*] **1 :** the act, process, or an instance of innervating **:** the state of being innervated; *specif* **:** the nervous excitation necessary for the maintenance of the life and functions of the various organs **2 :** the distribution of nerves to or in a part **:** the nerve supply (as of a part or organ) — **in·ner·va·tion·al** \¦=(,)=¦vāshənᵊl, -shnəl\ *adj*

**in·nerve** \i+\ *vt* -ED/-ING/-S [²*in-* + *nerve* (n.)] **:** to give nervous energy or power to : give increased energy, force, or courage to : INVIGORATE, STIMULATE

**in·ness** \'innəs\ *n* -ES [[2]*in* + *-ness*] : inner nature : INWARDNESS

**innholder** \'=,==\ *n* [ME *inhalder*, fr. *in, inn* inn + *halder, holder* holder — more at INN, HOLDER] : INNKEEPER

**[1]inn·ing** \'iniŋ, -nēŋ\ *pres part of* INN

**[2]in·ning** \"\ *n* -s [in sense 1, fr. gerund of [3]*in;* in sense 2, fr. [2]*in* + *-ing*] **1 a :** the act of taking in, gathering, or enclosing; *specif* : the act of reclaiming land esp. from the sea or a marsh **b innings** *pl* : reclaimed lands **2 a innings** *pl but sing or pl in constr* : a division of a cricket match in which one side continues batting until ten players are retired or the side declares; *also* : the time a player stays as a batsman until he is out, until ten teammates are out, or until his side declares **b :** a team's turn at bat in baseball ending with the third out; *also* : a division consisting of a turn at bat for each team **c :** a division of a contest in other sports (as a turn at serving in badminton, two throws by one player or two throws by each contestant in horseshoes, or a player's turn in croquet) **d :** a chance or turn for action or accomplishment (as to display one's prowess, caliber, or ability) ⟨the factual . . . romance has had its ~ —Parker Tyler⟩ ⟨the young conductor who is currently having his ~*s* —Douglas Watt⟩ ⟨the opposition party now had its ~*s*⟩ ⟨keep silent in order to give the adversary his ~ —Edmond Taylor⟩

**innkeeper** \'=,==\ *n* : the landlord of an inn

**inn·less** \'inləs\ *adj* : being without an inn

**in·no·cence** \'inəsən(t)s\ *n* -s [ME, fr. MF, fr. L *innocentia*, fr. *innocent-, innocens* innocent + *-ia* -y] **1 a** (1) : freedom from guilt or sin esp. through being unacquainted with evil : purity of heart : BLAMELESSNESS ⟨postulates a state of primitive ~⟩ (2) : CHASTITY ⟨supposed to have not yet lost her ~ —T.B.Macaulay⟩ (3) : the state of being not chargeable for or guilty of a particular crime or offense **b** (1) : freedom from guile or cunning : ARTLESSNESS, SIMPLICITY ⟨the ~ of childhood⟩ (2) : lack of understanding or penetration : SILLINESS, NAÏVETÉ ⟨the ~ . . . to propose remaking the world and human nature —L.O.Coxe⟩ (3) : lack of knowledge : IGNORANCE ⟨written in entire ~ of the Italian language —E.R.Bentley⟩ ⟨full of a chuckling mirth at the ~ of our detractors —Warwick Braithwaite⟩ ⟨~ of the craft of writing —J.W.Aldridge⟩ **2 :** one that is innocent; *esp* : an innocent person **3 a :** BLUET 1c(1) **b :** either of two plants: (1) : a small herb (*Collinsia verna*) of the central U.S. (2) : a Californian herb (*C. bicolor*)

**in·no·cen·cy** \-sənsē, -nsi\ *n* -ES [ME *innocencie*, fr. L *innocentia*] : INNOCENCE; *also* : an innocent action, quality, or thing ⟨associated in my mind with milk and rice and similar *innocencies* of childhood —Elinor Wylie⟩

**[1]in·no·cent** \-sənt\ *n* -s [ME, fr. MF] **1 :** an innocent one: as **a :** a person free from or unacquainted with sin; *esp* : a young child **b** *obs* : a person guiltless of a crime charged **c :** a naïve, artless, or unsophisticated person ⟨an ~ and a novice in the ways of the world —Fred Whishaw⟩ **d :** a person who lacks the requisite experience, training, or knowledge : TENDERFOOT ⟨lending a wrench to some ~ who forgot to bring his own —W.L.Worden⟩ **2** [F, short for *herbe de Saint Innocent* Saint Innocent's herb] : BLUET 1c(1) — usu. used in pl.

**[2]innocent** \"\ *adj, sometimes* -ER/-EST [ME, fr. MF, adj. & n., fr. L *innocent- innocens*, fr. *in-* [1]in- + *nocent-, nocens* bad, wicked, fr. pres. part. of *nocēre* to harm, hurt — more at NOXIOUS] **1 a** (1) : free from guilt or sin esp. through lack of knowledge of evil : BLAMELESS, PURE, UNTAINTED ⟨an ~ child⟩ (2) : being without evil influence or effect : not arising from evil intention ⟨~ deception⟩ ⟨~ sport⟩ ⟨searching for a hidden motive in even the most ~ conversation —Leonard Wibberley⟩ (3) : reflecting or indicating freedom from guilt or sin : CANDID ⟨a child's trusting ~ eye⟩ ⟨turned on me her ~ gaze⟩ **b** (1) : free from legal guilt or fault ⟨a person ~ of a particular crime⟩ ⟨an ~ agent⟩ : free from an illegality : being without knowledge of circumstances giving notice of a defect in title or of rights existing in third persons ⟨an ~ holder or purchaser for value⟩ : being without intention of evading or circumventing the law (2) : having a lawful character : PERMITTED ⟨a wholly ~ transaction⟩; *specif* : not being contraband ⟨an ~ trade⟩ (3) : lacking or devoid of something : DESTITUTE ⟨~ of any linguistic training —A.F.Hubbell⟩ ⟨her face ~ of cosmetics —Marcia Davenport⟩ ⟨glass still ~ of water and soap —William Faulkner⟩ **2 a** (1) : lacking or reflecting lack of sophistication, guile, or self-consciousness : ARTLESS, INGENUOUS, NAÏVE ⟨a disappointing figure to ~ persons who seek his acquaintance —C.E.Montague⟩ ⟨~ vanity⟩ ⟨what an ~ notion —F.L.Allen⟩ ⟨not ~ . . . but academic and a little self-conscious —Philip Toynbee⟩ (2) : foolishly ignorant or trusting : subject to being duped : SIMPLEMINDED ⟨when it comes to a trade, he is not as ~ as he looks⟩ **b** (1) : not adept in or conversant with something : IGNORANT ⟨almost entirely ~ of Latin —C.L.Wrenn⟩ ⟨the curious but ~ explorer will find himself hopelessly lost —B.R. Redman⟩ (2) : UNSUSPECTING, UNAWARE ⟨perfectly ~ of the confusion he had created —B.R.Haydon⟩ **3 :** lacking capacity to injure : INNOCUOUS, HARMLESS ⟨unarmed hands or feet are relatively ~ —Lewis Mumford⟩ ⟨fine ~ weather —John Muir †1914⟩; *specif* : BENIGN 3c ⟨an ~ heart murmur —*Lancet*⟩ — **in·no·cent·ly** *adv* — **in·no·cent·ness** *n* -ES

**innocent converter** *n* : a person who in good faith believes himself entitled to take and possess a chattel that in fact belongs to another but is nevertheless liable for conversion of the chattel

**innocent conveyance** *n, early English & American law* : a conveyance of a greater estate than the grantor has that does not produce a forfeiture of an estate in reversion or in remainder

**innocent misrepresentation** *n* : a representation in good faith reasonably believed true by the one making it but in fact untrue

**innocent party** *n* : one who has no notice of a fact tainting a litigated transaction with illegality : one not responsible or to blame for a situation which is the basis for relief in court

**innocent passage** *n* : the right of a foreign ship in grave distress or when overcome by a force majeure to anchor in or stop at a port within the territorial waters of another state without being subject to the general jurisdiction of the latter

**innocents' day** *n, usu cap I&D* : HOLY INNOCENTS' DAY

**in·no·cu·i·ty** \,i,nä'kyüəd·ē\ *n* -ES [prob. fr. F *innocuité*, fr. L *innocuus* + F *-ité* -ity] : the quality or state of being innocuous; *also* : something that is innocuous ⟨conversation will lag and digress politely to *innocuities* —*Plain Talk*⟩

**in·noc·u·ous** \(')i¦näkyəwəs, ə'n-\ *adj* [L *innocuus*, fr. *in-* [1]in- + *-nocuus* (fr. *nocēre* to harm, hurt) — more at NOXIOUS] **1 :** producing no ill effect : working no injury : HARMLESS ⟨preliminary tests have proved it to be ~ —*Jour. of Chem. Education*⟩ **2 a :** not likely to arouse animus or give offense : INOFFENSIVE ⟨confined himself to ~ generalities⟩ **b :** not likely to arouse strong feelings : lacking the capacity to excite ⟨elaborate concealment of ~ regions —P.M.Gregory⟩ or move : PALLID, INSIPID, INSIGNIFICANT ⟨a pleasant but ~ suite —Arthur Berger⟩ — **in·noc·u·ous·ly** *adv* — **in·noc·u·ous·ness** *n* -ES

**inn of chancery** *usu cap I&C* **1 :** a house or group of buildings in London formerly used by law students for residence and study but now occupied chiefly by attorneys and solicitors — usu. used with *inn* in pl. **2 :** a society occupying an Inn of Chancery — usu. used with *inn* in pl.

**inn of court** *usu cap I&C* **1 :** one of four sets of buildings in London belonging to four societies of students and practicers of the law ⟨Inner Temple, Middle Temple, Lincoln's Inn, and Gray's Inn are the *Inns of Court*⟩ **2 :** one of four societies which alone admit to practice at the English bar — usu. used with *inn* in pl.

**in·nominable** \(')i, ə+\ *adj* [ME, fr. L *innominabilis*, fr. *in-* [1]in- + *nominare* to name + *-abilis* -able — more at NOMINATE] : incapable of being named

**in·nominate** \(')i¦nämənət, ə'nä-\ *adj* [LL *innominatus*, fr. L *in-* [1]in- + *nominatus*, past part. of *nominare*] **1 a :** having no name : UNNAMED ⟨there were no fields, as in England, each called by an ancient name; the slender tributaries were often ~ —John Buchan⟩ **b :** having an unknown or unrevealed name : ANONYMOUS ⟨progress . . . made by the accumulated activities of large groups of ~ people —*Times Lit. Supp.*⟩ **2** *Roman & civil law* **a :** of, relating to, or being any of certain classes of contracts that are real but have no special name **b :** of, relating to, or being a commutative contract in any of several categories

**innominate artery** *n* [trans. of NL *arteria innominata*] : a large artery arising from the arch of the aorta and dividing into the right common carotid and the right subclavian arteries

**innominate bone** *n* [trans. of NL *os innominatum*] : the large flaring bone that makes a lateral half of the pelvis in mammals and is composed of the ilium, ischium, and pubis which are consolidated into one bone in the adult — called also *hipbone*

**innominate vein** *n* [trans. of NL *vena innominata*] : a large vein on each side of the lower part of the neck formed by the union of the internal jugular and subclavian veins and in man uniting to form the superior vena cava

**in·nom·i·ne** \(')in'nämə,nā, -,nē, -'nōmə,nā\ *n* -s [L *in nomine* (in *in nomine Jesu* in the name of Jesus, the opening words of an introit for which such compositions were orig. written)] : an English polyphonic composition of the 16th and 17th centuries written for an instrumental ensemble (as for viols and keyboard) and using as a cantus firmus a fragment of plainsong from the antiphon for Trinity Sunday

**in·no·vant** \'inəvənt, 'inōv-\ *adj* [L *innovant-, innovans*, pres. part. of *innovare*] : having innovations (sense 3)

**in·no·vate** \'inə,vāt, 'inōv-, *usu* -ād·+V\ *vb* -ED/-ING/-s [L *innovatus*, past part. of *innovare*, fr. *in-* [2]in- + *novare* renew, modify, fr. *novus* new — more at NEW] *vt* **1 :** to introduce as or as if new ⟨~ a design⟩ **2** *archaic* : to make innovations in : CHANGE ~ *vi* : to introduce novelties : make changes ⟨he is not to ~ at pleasure —B.N.Cardozo⟩

**in·no·va·tion** \,==ˈvāshən\ *n* -s [prob. fr. MF, fr. LL *innovation-, innovatio*, fr. L *innovatus* + *-ion-, -io* -ion] **1 :** the act or an instance of innovating : the introduction of something new ⟨~ as the driving force in practical economic advance —*Times Lit. Supp.*⟩ **2 :** something that deviates from established doctrine or practice : something that differs from existing forms : CHANGE, NOVELTY ⟨the technical ~*s* of the agrarian revolution —S.F.Mason⟩ ⟨another ~ is a new straight mile course —*London Calling*⟩ ⟨his most important ~ . . . was the introduction of the seminary method of instruction for advanced students —C.F.Smith⟩ **3 a :** a shoot that arises at or near the apex of the stem of a moss plant usu. after the reproductive organs have completed their development **b :** the formation of such a shoot **4** *Scots law* : an exchange of one obligation for another, the obligor and obligee remaining the same

**in·no·va·tion·al** \¦==¦vāshənᵊl, -shnəl\ *adj* : of or relating to innovation : tending to innovate ⟨a mind so ~ —John Mason Brown⟩

**in·no·va·tive** \'==,vād·iv\ *adj* : characterized by, tending to, or introducing innovations ⟨~ behavior⟩

**in·no·va·tor** \-,vād·ə(r), -ātə-\ *n* -s [prob. fr. MF *innovateur*, fr. LL *innovator*, fr. L *innovatus* + *-or*] : one that innovates ⟨a theological ~⟩ ⟨~ of a new technique⟩

**in·no·va·to·ry** \-_və,tōrē, -,vād·ərē\ *adj* : INNOVATIVE

**in·noxious** \(')i(n), ə+\ *adj* [L *innoxius*, fr. *in-* [1]in- + *noxius* harmful — more at NOXIOUS] : INNOCUOUS ⟨an ~ substance⟩ — **in·noxiously** \"+\ *adv* — **in·noxiousness** \"+\ *n*

**inns** *pl of* INN, *pres 3d sing of* INN

**inns·bruck** \'inz,brůk, 'in(t)s,b-\ *adj, usu cap* [fr. *Innsbruck*, Austria] : of or from the city of Innsbruck, Austria : of the kind or style prevalent in Innsbruck

**in nu·ce** \(')in'nü(,)kā\ *adv* [L, in a nut] : in a nutshell ⟨the opening act contains the tragedy *in nuce* —Karl Polanyi⟩

**[1]in·nu·en·do** \,inyə'wen(,)dō\ *adv* [L, by hinting, abl. of *innuendum*, gerund of *innuere* to hint, intimate, fr. *in-* [2]in- + *nuere* to nod — more at NUMEN] : in other words : NAMELY — formerly used in legal documents to introduce matter explanatory of the text

**[2]innuendo** *also* **inuendo** \"\ *n, pl* **innuendos** *or* **innuendoes** **1 :** veiled, oblique, or covert allusion to something not directly named : HINT, INSINUATION ⟨glossy fantasy, stylishness, naughty ~ —*Time*⟩ ⟨a talk punctuated with ~*s* on both sides —J.T.Farrell⟩; *esp* : veiled or equivocal allusion reflecting upon the character, ability, or other trait of the person referred to ⟨try to undermine him by ~ —*Kiplinger Washington Letter*⟩ ⟨how difficult it is to set up a proper defense against ~ —M.S.Watson⟩ ⟨anonymous accusations, rumors, ~*s* —Nathan Schachner⟩ **2 :** a parenthetical explanation of the text of a legal document; *esp* : an interpretation in a pleading of expressions alleged to be injurious or libelous

**[3]innuendo** *also* **inuendo** \"\ *vb* -ED/-ING/-s [[2]*innuendo*] *vi* : to make innuendo ~ *vt* : to give effect to by innuendo

**in·nu·it** *also* **in·u·it** \'inyəwət, 'i,nyüət\ *n, pl* **innuit** *or* **innuits** *also* **inuit** *or* **inuits** *usu cap* [Esk, men, people, Eskimo people, pl. of *innuk, inuk* person, man, Eskimo] **1 a** (1) : the Eskimo people of America as distinguished from the Eskimo people of Asia — compare YUIT (2) : the arctic Eskimo as distinguished from the Aleuts **b :** a member of the Innuit people **2 :** the language of the Innuit people

**in·nu·mer·a·bil·i·ty** \ə,n(y)üm(ə)rə'biləd·ē\ *n* -ES [L *innumerabilitas*, fr. *innumerabilis* + *-itas* -ity] : innumerable quality ⟨without any sense of the ~ of the human race —Thornton Wilder⟩

**in·nu·mer·a·ble** \ə'n(y)üm(ə)rəbəl\ *adj* [ME, fr. L *innumerabilis*, fr. *in-* [1]in- + *numerabilis* numerable — more at NUMERABLE] **1 :** too many to be numbered or counted : indefinitely numerous : NUMBERLESS ⟨~ coral reefs and islets —*Americana Annual*⟩ **2 :** characterized by vast or countless number ⟨an ~ throng of people⟩ — **in·nu·mer·a·ble·ness** \-nəs\ *n* -ES — **in·nu·mer·a·bly** \-blē,-bli\ *adv*

**in·numerous** \(')i(n), ə+\ *adj* [L *innumerus*, fr. *in-* [1]in- + *numerus* number — more at NIMBLE] : NUMBERLESS, INNUMERABLE

**in·nutrition** \¦i(n)+\ *n* [[1]*in-* + *nutrition*] : lack of nutrition : failure of nourishment

**in·nutritious** \"+\ *adj* [[1]*in-* + *nutritious*] : not nutritious ⟨harsh and ~ fare —*Experiment Station Record*⟩

**innyard** \'=,=\ *n* : the yard of an inn

**ino-** — see [3]IN-

**inobedience** *n* [ME, fr. OF & LL; OF, fr. LL *inoboedientia*, fr. *inoboedient-, inoboediens* + L *-ia* -y] *obs* : DISOBEDIENCE

**inobedient** *adj* [ME, fr. MF & LL; MF, fr. LL *inoboedient-, inoboediens*, fr. L *in-* [1]in- + *oboedient-, oboediens* obedient — more at OBEDIENT] *obs* : DISOBEDIENT

**in·obnoxious** \¦in+\ *adj* [[1]*in-* + *obnoxious*] : INOFFENSIVE

**inobservable** *adj* [L *inobservabilis*, fr. *in-* [1]in- + *observabilis* observable — more at OBSERVABLE] *obs* : incapable of being observed

**in·observance** \¦in+\ *or* **in·observancy** \"+\ *n* [F & L; F *inobservance*, fr. L *inobservantia*, fr. *in-* [1]in- + *observantia* observance — more at OBSERVANCE] **1 :** lack of attention : HEEDLESSNESS **2 :** failure to observe : NONOBSERVANCE

**in·observant** \¦in+\ *adj* [LL *inobservant-, inobservans*, fr. L *in-* [1]in- + *observant-, observans* observant — more at OBSERVANT] : UNOBSERVANT

**in·obtrusive** \¦in+\ *adj* [[1]*in-* + *obtrusive*] : UNOBTRUSIVE ⟨tried hard to be ~ —L.S.Feuer⟩

**in·obvious** \(')in+\ *adj* [[1]*in-* + *obvious*] : not obvious

**in·occupation** \¦in+\ *n* [[1]*in-* + *occupation*] : lack of occupation

**ino·cer·a·mus** \,inō'serəməs, ,ī̄n-\ *n, cap* [NL, fr. [3]*in-* + Gk *keramos* potter's clay, pottery] : a genus of large filibranchiate bivalve mollusks (suborder Mytilacea) esp. characteristic of the Cretaceous

**in·oc·u·la·ble** \ə'näkyələbəl\ *adj* [*inoculate* + *-able*] : susceptible to inoculation : not immune; *also* : transmissible by inoculation

**in·oc·u·lant** \-lənt\ *n* -s [*inoculate* + *-ant*] : INOCULUM

**in·ocular** \(')in, ən+\ *adj* [[2]*in-* + *ocular*] : inserted in a notch in the corner of the eye ⟨~ antennae⟩

**in·oc·u·late** \ə'näkyə,lāt, *usu* -ād·+V\ *vb* -ED/-ING/-s [ME *inoculaten*, fr. L *inoculare*, fr. *in-* [2]in- + *oculus* eye, bud — more at EYE] *vt* **1 a** *archaic* : to insert a bud into or graft (as a tree) by budding **b :** to treat (seeds) with bacteria esp. for the promotion of nitrogen fixation (as in root nodules on legumes) **2 a** (1) : to communicate a disease to (an organism) by inserting its causative agent into the body ⟨12 mice *inoculated* with anthrax⟩ (2) : to introduce microorganisms or viruses onto or into (an organism or substrate) ⟨~ the culture with one loopful of spore suspension⟩ ⟨*inoculated* a rat with bacteria⟩ (3) : to introduce (as microorganisms or immune sera) into or onto a culture medium ⟨~ the spirochetes into blood agar⟩ **b :** SEED 1d **3 :** to introduce something into the mind of : IMBUE ⟨*inoculated* them with their own ideas of revolution —Raymond Schuessler⟩ ⟨~ the few who influence the many —*Current Biog.*⟩ ~ *vi* **1** *obs* : to graft by inserting buds **2 :** to introduce microorganisms, vaccines, or sera by inoculation **syn** see INFUSE

**in·oc·u·la·tion** \=,==ˈlāshən\ *n* -s [L *inoculation-, inoculatio*, fr. *inoculatus* + *-ion-, -io* -ion] : the act, process, or an instance of inoculating: as **a** (1) : the introduction of a microorganism into a suitable medium for its growth ⟨~ of mosaic virus into stocks by aphids⟩; *specif* : the communication of an infective agent (as smallpox virus) to a healthy individual to induce a mild case of disease under optimum conditions and establish lasting immunity (2) : the introduction of a serum or vaccine into a living body to establish immunity to a disease ⟨travelers in the tropics should have typhoid ~*s*⟩ **b :** the introduction of organisms into soil, seed, or water to promote nitrogen fixation or control insect pests or for other purposes **c :** the introduction of a substance into a metallic melt for the purpose of providing additional centers for crystallization **d :** the act or process of imbuing or familiarizing : the fact or an instance of being so imbued or familiarized ⟨getting a weekly or monthly ~ in ways of living and of thinking that were middle-class —F.L.Allen⟩ ⟨~ with alien attitudes and tastes⟩

**in·oc·u·la·tive** \='==,lād·iv\ *adj* : of, relating to, or characterized by inoculation

**in·oc·u·la·tor** \-d·ə(r)\ *n* -s [L, one that engrafts, fr. *inoculatus* + *-or*] : one that inoculates

**in·oc·u·lum** \ə'näkyələm\ *n, pl* **inocu·la** \-lə\ *or* **inoculums** [NL, fr. L *inoculare*] : material (as spores, bacteria, or contaminated fluids) used in or suitable for use in inoculating or inoculation

**ino·des** \ə'nō(,)dēz, ī'-\ *n, cap* [NL, fr. Gk *inōdēs* fibrous, fr. *in-* [3]in- + *-ōdēs* -ode] *in some classifications* : a genus of fan palms comprising various arborescent palmettos of the southern U.S., the West Indies, and Mexico that are now usu. included in the genus *Sabal*

**inodiate** *vt* -ED/-ING/-s [LL *inodiatus*, past part. of *inodiare* — more at ANNOY] *obs* : to make odious or hateful

**in·odorous** \(')in, ən+\ *adj* [L *inodorus*, fr. *in-* [1]in- + *odorus* odorous — more at ODOROUS] : emitting no smell : SCENTLESS, ODORLESS

**in–off** \'=,=\ *n* [fr. the phrase *in off* (*the red ball* or *the white ball*)] : a losing hazard in English billiards

**in·offensive** \¦in+\ *adj* [[1]*in-* + *offensive*] **1 :** causing no harm or injury : UNOFFENDING ⟨an ~ animal⟩ **2 a :** giving no offense or provocation : causing no disturbance : not quarrelsome : PEACEABLE ⟨a quiet, ~ man —Herman Melville⟩ **b :** giving no offense to the senses : not objectionable ⟨a refreshing, ~ . . . stimulant —*Americas*⟩ — **in·of·fen·sive·ly** *adv* — **in·of·fen·sive·ness** *n*

**in·official** \¦in+\ *adj* [[1]*in-* + *official*] : UNOFFICIAL

**in·officious** \¦in+\ *adj* [L *inofficiosus*, fr. *in-* [1]in- + *officiosus* dutiful — more at OFFICIOUS] **1** *obs* : indifferent to obligation or duty **2 :** regardless of or contrary to natural duty

**inofficious testament** *or* **inofficious will** *n* : a will made in violation of natural duty and affection and without just legal cause and depriving children and parents and sometimes others of their legitim of the testator's estate

**ino·gen** \'inəjən, 'īn-, -,jen\ *n* -s [G, fr. *ino-* [3]in- + *-gen*] : a hypothetical substance supposed to be continually decomposed and reproduced in the muscles and to serve as an oxygen reserve

**in·op·er·a·bil·i·ty** \¦i,näp(ə)rə¦biləd·ē\ *n* : the quality or state of being inoperable

**in·operable** \(')in, ən+\ *adj* [prob. fr. F *inopérable*, fr. *in-* [1]in- + *opérable* operable — more at OPERABLE] **1 :** not suitable for surgical operation ⟨an advanced and ~ cancer⟩ ⟨a developing cataract still ~⟩ **2 :** not operable

**in·operative** \(')in, ən+\ *adj* [[1]*in-* + *operative*] : not operative or not in operation : not active : producing no effect ⟨the law has become ~⟩ ⟨the quarry has been ~ for some time —L.N.Yedlin⟩ — **inoperativeness** *n*

**in·opercular** \¦in+\ *adj* [[1]*in-* + *opercular*] : INOPERCULATE

**[1]in·operculate** \¦in+\ *adj* [[1]*in-* + *operculate*] : having no operculum ⟨~ gastropod shells⟩ ⟨~ mosses⟩

**[2]inoperculate** \"\ *n* : an inoperculate animal or shell

**in·opportune** \(¦)in, ən+\ *adj* [L *inopportunus*, fr. *in-* [1]in- + *opportunus* opportune — more at OPPORTUNE] : not opportune : UNSEASONABLE, INCONVENIENT ⟨arrive at the most ~ hours —D.R.Murphy⟩ — **in·op·por·tune·ly** \-ünlē\ *adv* — **in·op·por·tune·ness** \-ünnəs\ *n*

**in·orb** \ən+\ *vt* [[2]*in-* + *orb* (n.)] : ENSPHERE, ENCIRCLE

**in·or·di·na·cy** \ə'nȯ(r)dᵊnəsē\ *n* -ES [*inordinate* + *-cy*] *archaic* : the quality, state, or an instance of being inordinate : EXCESSIVENESS

**in·or·di·nance** \-ᵊnən(t)s\ *also* **in·or·di·nan·cy** \-ᵊnənsē\ *n, pl* **inordinances** *also* **inordinancies** : the quality, state, or an instance of being inordinate

**in·ordinary** \(')in, ən+\ *adj* [[1]*in-* + *ordinary*] : not ordinary : EXTRAORDINARY

**in·or·di·nate** \ə'nȯ(r)dᵊnət, *usu* -əd·+V\ *adj* [ME *inordinat*, fr. L *inordinatus*, fr. *in-* [1]in- + *ordinatus*, past part. of *ordinare* to order, arrange — more at ORDAIN] **1 :** lacking order : not regulated : DISORDERLY **2 :** exceeding in amount, quantity, force, intensity, or scope the ordinary, reasonable, or prescribed limits : EXTRAORDINARY ⟨his ~ desire for approval —Van Wyck Brooks⟩ ⟨~ joviality can atone for an entire lack of ideas —Oscar Wilde⟩ ⟨a book of ~ length⟩ ⟨burns an ~ quantity of gasoline —H.W.Baldwin⟩ **syn** see EXCESSIVE

**in·or·di·nate·ly** *adv* [ME *inordinatly*, fr. *inordinat* + *-ly*] : in an inordinate manner : to an excessive or unreasonable degree : EXTRAORDINARILY ⟨~ ambitious⟩ ⟨the symphony is ~ long⟩ ⟨~ fond of grasshoppers —C.H.Grandgent⟩

**in·or·di·nate·ness** *n* -ES : the quality or state of being inordinate : lack of moderation : EXCESS

**in·or·di·na·tion** \ə,nȯ(r)dᵊn'āshən\ *n* -s [LL *inordination-, inordinatio*, fr. L *inordinatus* + *-ion-, -io* -ion] *archaic* : INORDINATENESS

**[1]in·organic** \¦in+(,)=¦==\ *adj* [[1]*in-* + *organic*] **1 a** (1) : being or composed of matter other than plant or animal : MINERAL ⟨the ~ world⟩ (2) : forming or belonging to the inanimate world **b :** being, containing, or relating to a chemical substance or substances not usu. classed as organic ⟨hydrochloric, sulfuric, nitric, and chlorosulfonic acids are called ~ acids —R.E.Kirk⟩ ⟨~ fertilizers⟩ **c :** being in the form of such a substance ⟨~ selenium as in sodium selenite⟩ **2 :** not arising from a process of natural or inevitable growth : ARTIFICIAL ⟨an ~ and unnatural lingo never spoken by man —Kenneth Rexroth⟩ : lacking organic structure, character, or vitality ⟨dull ~ things, without individuality or prestige —John Buchan⟩ **3** *of a sound or letter* : lacking an etymological justification — **in·organically** \"+\ *adv*

**[2]inorganic** \"\ *n* : an inorganic substance

**inorganical** *adj* [[1]*in-* + *organical*] *obs* : INORGANIC

**inorganic chemistry** *n* : a branch of chemistry that deals with chemical elements and their compounds excluding hydrocarbons and their derivatives but usu. or often including carbides and other relatively simple carbon compounds esp. some carbon-oxygen and carbon-sulfur compounds (as the oxides of carbon, metallic carbonates, and carbon disulfide) and some carbon-nitrogen compounds (as hydrogen cyanide and metallic cyanides) — compare ORGANIC CHEMISTRY

**in·organization** \¦in+\ *n* [[1]*in-* + *organization*] : lack of organization

**in·organized** \(')in, ən+\ *adj* [[1]*in-* + *organized*] : lacking organization

**in·ornate** \¦in+(,)=¦=\ *adj* [L *inornatus*, fr. *in-* [1]in- + *ornatus* adorned — more at ORNATE] : lacking adornment : UNADORNED ⟨the scrupulously ~ clergyman than which nothing could be less liable to suspicion —E.A.Poe⟩

**in·osculate** \ən+\ *vb* -ED/-ING/-s [[2]*in-* + *osculate*] : to unite by apposition or contact : unite or join so as to become or make as if one : BLEND ⟨efforts to ~ past and present —R.M. Wendlinger⟩

**in·osculation** \ən+\ *n* [²*in-* + *osculation*] **:** the act, process, or an instance of inosculating; *specif* **:** ANASTOMOSIS
**ino·silicate** \ˈinō, ˈīnō+\ *n* [³*in-* + *silicate*] **:** a class of polymeric silicates in which the silicon-oxygen tetrahedral groups share half of their oxygen atoms so as to form straight chains of indefinite length; *also* **:** a member of this class — called also *metasilicate;* compare CYCLOSILICATE, NESOSILICATE, PHYLLOSILICATE, SOROSILICATE, TECTOSILICATE
**ino·sine** \ˈinə,sēn, ˈīn-, -sən\ *n* -s [ISV *inos-* (fr. Gk *inos*, gen. of *is* sinew, tendon) + *-ine* — more at WITHY] **:** a crystalline nucleoside $C_{10}H_{12}N_4O_5$ formed by partial hydrolysis of inosinic acid or by deamination of adenosine and yielding hypoxanthine and ribose on hydrolysis
**ino·sin·ic acid** \¦==¦sinik-\ *n* [part trans. of G *inosinsäure*, fr. *inosin* inosine + *säure* acid] **:** an amorphous nucleotide $C_{10}H_{13}N_4O_8P$ that is found in muscle and is formed by deamination of adenylic acid and that yields hypoxanthine, ribose, and phosphoric acid on hydrolysis
**ino·si·tol** \əˈnōsə,tōl, ī-, -,tōl\ *n* -s [ISV *inosite* inositol (fr. Gk *inos* + ISV *-ite*) + *-ol*] **:** any of nine crystalline stereoisomeric cyclic hexahydroxy alcohols $C_6H_6(OH)_6$; cyclohexane-hexol: as **a :** an optically inactive alcohol that is a component of the vitamin B complex and a lipotropic agent, that occurs widely in plants usu. combined in the form of phytic acid, in microorganisms, and in higher animals and man esp. in vital organs and tissues (as the heart and brain) and often combined in the form of phosphatides, that is obtained chiefly from corn steepwater, and that is used in medicine — called also *i-inositol, meso-inositol, myoinositol* **b :** a sweet dextrorotatory alcohol occurring esp. in the form of its methyl ether pinitol — called also *dextro-inositol* **c :** a sweet levorotatory alcohol occurring esp. in the form of its methyl ether quebrachitol — called also *levo-inositol* **d :** SCYLLITOL
**ino·trop·ic** \¦inə¦träpik, ¦īn-\ *adj* [ISV ³*in-* + *-tropic*] **:** influencing muscular contractility — **inot·ro·pism** \əˈnä·trə,pizəm, ī'-\ *n* -s
**in ovo** \iˈnō(,)vō\ *adv* [L] **:** in the egg **:** in embryo
**in·oxidizable** \(¦)in+\ *adj* [¹*in-* + *oxidizable*] **:** not capable of being oxidized
**in·paint** \ən+\ *vt* [²*in* + *paint*] **:** to repair or restore (a painting) by repainting obliterated areas
**in pais** \-ˈpā\ *adv* [*pais* fr. MF *pais, pays* country — more at PAYSAGE] **:** in the country as distinguished from in court
**in pa·ri causa** \-ˈpärē-\ *adv* [LL, in a like case] **:** in a case where all parties stand equal in right according to law
**in pari de·lic·to** \-dəˈlik(,)tō\ *adv* [L, in a like offense] **:** in equal fault or wrong — used of parties in a legal case
**in pari ma·te·ria** \-məˈtirēə\ *adv* [LL, in a like matter] **:** on the same subject or matter **:** in a similar case ⟨there is virtually nothing of known date *in pari materia* with which it can be compared —*Times Lit. Supp.*⟩
**in par·ti·bus in·fi·de·li·um** \(,)inˈpärd·əbə,sinfəˈdālēəm\ *also* **in partibus** *adv* [ML, lit., in the regions of infidels] **:** in ideologically hostile or unsympathetic surroundings ⟨made himself missionary *in partibus infidelium* for American philosophic naturalism —J.H.Randall⟩
**in par·vo** \-ˈpär(,)vō\ *adv* [L] **:** in little **:** in miniature ⟨the reflection, *in parvo*, of the defects of the larger whole —Sonya Forthal⟩
**inpatient** \ˈ=,==\ *n* [⁴*in* + *patient*] **:** a patient in a hospital or infirmary who receives lodging and food as well as treatment — distinguished from *outpatient*
**in pa·tri·mo·nio** \-,pa·trəˈmōnē,ō\ *adv* [L, lit., within inheritance] **:** IN COMMERCIO
**inpayment** \ˈ=,==\ *n* [⁴*in* + *payment*] **1 :** the act or an instance of paying in **2 :** a payment to — contrasted with *outpayment*
**in pec·to·re** \-ˈpektərē\ *adv* [L, lit., in the breast] **:** in secret ⟨must hold their names *in pectore* —Thomas Barbour⟩
**in per·pe·tu·um** \-pə(r)ˈpechəwəm\ *adv* [L] **:** in perpetuity **:** FOREVER ⟨left certain royalties to the home *in perpetuum* —Joseph Wechsberg⟩
**in per·so·nam** \-pə(r)ˈsō,nam\ *adv (or adj)* [L, against a person] **:** against a particular person for the purpose of imposing upon him a personal liability, debt, or obligation to do or not to do a designated act ⟨proceedings and judgments are *in personam* where the court or tribunal has jurisdiction over the defendant and power to enforce obedience against him personally⟩ — compare IN REM
**in pet·to** \-ˈped·(,)ō\ *adv (or adj)* [It, lit., in breast; prob. trans. of L *in pectore*] **1 :** in private **:** SECRETLY — used esp. of a cardinal appointed by the pope but not named in consistory **2** [influenced in meaning by E *petty*] **:** in miniature **:** on a small scale ⟨an epic *in petto* —*Saturday Rev.*⟩
**inphase** \ˈ=,=\ *adj* [fr. the phrase *in phase*] **:** being of the same electrical phase
**inphase component** *n* **:** the active component of an alternating current in a reactive circuit
**in-pig** \ˈ=ˈ=\ *adj* [fr. the phrase *in pig*] *of a sow* **:** PREGNANT
**in-plant** \ˈ=,=\ *adj* [fr. the phrase *in plant*] **:** carried on, occurring within, or restricted to the confines of a manufacturing establishment or factory ⟨*in-plant* training programs⟩ ⟨the *in-plant* medical director⟩
**in·polygon** \ˈin+,-\ *n* [⁴*in* + *polygon*] **:** an inscribed polygon
**in·polyhedron** \"+,-\ *n* [⁴*in* + *polyhedron*] **:** an inscribed polyhedron

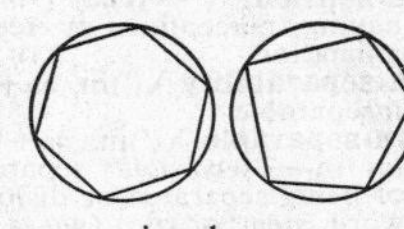
inpolygons

**in pos·se** \-ˈpäsē\ *adv (or adj)* [ML] **:** in possibility or capacity **:** not in actuality ⟨contains within itself, *in posse*, implicitly, ideally, the entire logico-dialectical process —Frank Thilly⟩ **:** POTENTIALLY — contrasted with *in esse*
¹**inpour** \ˈ=,=\ *n* [⁴*in* + *pour* (after *pour in*, v.)] **:** a pouring in **:** INRUSH ⟨the ~ of tumultuous Irish immigrants —Helen Sullivan⟩
²**in·pour** \(ˈ)=ˈ=\ *vb* **:** to pour in ⟨goods and money *inpoured* —J.J.Mallon⟩
**inpouring** \ˈ=,==\ *n* -s [⁴*in* + *pouring* (after *pour in*, v.)] **:** INPOUR ⟨viewed the ~ of bedraggled foreigners with alarm —A.D.Graeff⟩
**in-print** \ˈ=,=\ *n* [fr. the phrase *in print*] **:** a title that is in print
**in-process** \ən+\ *adj* [fr. the phrase *in process*] **:** being worked on in manufacture in distinction from raw materials and from finished products
**in pro·pria per·so·na** \ənˈprōprēəpə(r)ˈsōnə\ *adv* [L] **:** in one's own person **:** without the assistance of an attorney **:** PERSONALLY
**in·put** \ˈin,pu̇t, *usu* -ùd·+V\ *also* **im·put** \ˈim,-\ *n* [*input* fr. ⁴*in* + *put* (after *put in*, v.); *imput* alter. of *input*] **1 :** something that is put in: as **a** *chiefly Scot* **:** a contribution of money **b :** an amount put in ⟨increase the ~ of fertilizer⟩ **c (1) :** power or energy put into a machine or system for storage (as into a storage battery) or for conversion in kind (as into a mechanically driven electric generator or a radio receiver) or conversion of characteristics (as into a transformer or electronic amplifier) usu. with the intent of sizable recovery in the form of output **(2)** *on an electrical device* **:** the terminal for the input **d :** a component of production (as land, labor, or materials) ⟨~s such as seed, twine, ginning fees, and containers —D.G. Johnson⟩ **e :** data or similar information fed into a computer or accounting machine **2 :** the act, process, or an instance of putting in ⟨requires a continuous ~ of energy both for maintenance and for propagation —G.A.Bartholomew & J.B. Birdsell⟩
**input well** *n* **:** INJECTION WELL
**in querpo** *var of* IN CUERPO
**in·quest** \ˈin,kwest\ *n* [ME *enquest, inquest*, fr. OF *enqueste*, fr. fem. of (assumed) *enquest*, fr. (assumed) VL *inquaestus*, past part. of *inquaerere* to inquire — more at INQUIRE] **1 a :** a judicial or official inquiry or examination esp. before a jury ⟨a coroner's ~⟩ ⟨an ~ to fix damages⟩ **b :** a body of men esp. a jury assembled to hold such an inquiry **c :** the finding of the jury upon such inquiry or the document recording it **2 :** INQUIRY, INVESTIGATION ⟨a two-year ~ into the conduct of the executive —W.E.Binkley⟩ **syn** see INQUIRY
**inquest of office :** an inquiry made by authority or direction of the proper officer into matters (as escheat of lands) affecting the rights and interests of the crown or of the state
**in·quiet** \ən+\ *vt* [ME *inquieten*, fr. MF *inquieter*, fr. L *inquietare*, fr. *inquietus* restless, unquiet, fr. *in-* ¹in- + *quietus* quiet — more at QUIET] *archaic* **:** to disturb the peace of **:** DISQUIET
**in·qui·e·ta·tion** \(,)in,kwīəˈtāshən\ *n* -s [ME, fr. MF, fr. L *inquietation-, inquietatio*, fr. *inquietatus* (past part. of *inquietare*) + *-ion-, -io* -ion] *archaic* **:** DISTURBANCE
**in·quietude** \(ˈ)in, ən+\ *n* [ME, fr. MF or LL; MF, fr. LL *inquietudo*, fr. L *inquietus* (fr. *in-* ¹in- + *quietus* quiet) + *-tudo* -tude — more at QUIET] **1 :** disturbed state **:** UNEASINESS, RESTLESSNESS, DISQUIETUDE ⟨the dreadful ~ that comes before a surgical operation —Arnold Bennett⟩ **2 :** a disquieting or anxious thought ⟨occupied by a thousand ~s —Sir Walter Scott⟩
¹**in·qui·line** \ˈinkwə,līn, ˈiŋk-, -,lən\ *n* -s [L *inquilinus* tenant, lodger, fr. *in-* ²in- + *-quilinus* (fr. the stem of *colere* to cultivate, dwell) — more at WHEEL] **:** an animal that lives habitually in the nest or abode of some other species (as the burrowing owl in prairie dog colonies or any of several beetles and flies that live with social insects) — **in·qui·lin·ism** \-,lə,nizəm\ *n* -s — **in·qui·lin·i·ty** \,==ˈlinəd·ē\ *n* -ES — **in·qui·li·nous** \¦==¦līnəs\ *adj*
²**inquiline** \"\ *adj* **:** having the character of an inquiline
**in·qui·li·no** \,ēŋkēˈlē(,)nō\ *n* -s [AmerSp, fr. Sp, tenant, lodger, fr. L *inquilinus*] **:** a worker on a Chilean landed estate who is usu. given the use of a small plot of land, implements, seed, and a small wage in return for his labor
**in·qui·nate** \ˈinkwə,nāt\ *vt* -ED/-ING/-S [L *inquinatus*, past part. of *inquinare*, fr. *in-* ²in- + *-quinare* (akin to L *caenum* filth, ordure) — more at OBSCENE] **:** DEFILE, CORRUPT — **in·qui·na·tion** \,==ˈnāshən\ *n* -s
**in·quir·able** \ənˈkwīrəbəl\ *adj* [ME *enquirable*, fr. *enquiren* + *-able*] *archaic* **:** capable of being inquired into **:** subject or liable to inquiry
**in·quire** *also* **en·quire** \ənˈkwī(ə)r, -īə\ *vb* -ED/-ING/-S [ME *enquiren, inqueren, inquiren*, alter. (influenced by L *inquirere* to inquire) of *enqueren*, fr. OF *enquerre*, fr. (assumed) VL *inquaerere*, alter. (influenced by L *quaerere* to seek, ask) of L *inquirere*, fr. *in-* ²in- + *-quirere* (fr. *quaerere*)] *vt* **1 :** to ask about or ask **:** seek to know by asking or questioning ⟨some kindred spirit shall ~ thy fate —Thomas Gray⟩ ⟨*inquired* the way to the station⟩ ⟨*inquired* what the weather was likely to be⟩ **2 a :** to search or search into **:** INVESTIGATE, EXAMINE ⟨failed to ~ the limits of what can be said —Allen Tate⟩ **b** *archaic* **:** to search or ask for — often used with *out* **c** *obs* **:** INTERROGATE, QUESTION **~** *vi* **1 :** to put a question **:** seek for truth or information by questioning **:** ASK ⟨*inquired* about the horses —*Amer. Guide Series: La.*⟩ **2 :** to make investigation or inquiry **:** engage in study or scrutiny — often used with *into* ⟨their right to ~ into the activities of the teachers⟩ ⟨~ briefly into the effect that comes from the combination of phrases —E.K.Brown⟩ **syn** see ASK — **inquire after :** to ask about the health or well-being of ⟨the parents of the boys he played with always *inquired after* his father and mother —Scott Fitzgerald⟩
**in·qui·ren·do** \,inkwəˈren(,)dō\ *n* -s [L, by inquiring, ablative of *inquirendum*, gerund of *inquirere* to inquire] **:** an inquiry or an authority to conduct an inquiry
**in·quir·er** \ənˈkwīrə(r)\ *n* -s **:** one that inquires **:** QUESTIONER
**inquiring** *adj* **1 :** given to inquiry **:** INVESTIGATIVE ⟨an ~ mind⟩ **2 :** appearing to inquire **:** INQUISITIVE ⟨rolled ~ eyes toward my father —Kenneth Roberts⟩ ⟨~ looks⟩ — **in·quir·ing·ly** *adv*
**in·quiry** *also* **en·quiry** \ˈin,kwī(ə)rē, ənˈkwī(ə)-, ˈinkwə-, -ri *sometimes* iŋkwə/ *or* ˈin,kwi(\ *n* -ES [alter. of ME *enquery*, fr. *enqueren* + *-y*] **1 :** the act or an instance of seeking truth, information, or knowledge about something **:** examination into facts or principles **:** RESEARCH, INVESTIGATION ⟨complete freedom of ~⟩ ⟨the scientific method of ~ —C.W.Eliot⟩ ⟨that most modern of *inquiries*, the study of the cosmic rays —K.K.Darrow⟩ ⟨an ~ into the nature of truth⟩; *specif* **:** a formal or official investigation of a matter of public interest by a body (as a legislative committee) with power to compel testimony ⟨witnesses convicted of contempt of congressional *inquiries* —*Current Biog.*⟩ **2 :** the act or an instance of asking for information **:** a request for information **:** QUERY, QUESTION ⟨upon ~, I learned that he was out⟩ ⟨the information desk receives many *inquiries*⟩ ⟨would not answer my ~⟩
**syn** INQUISITION, INVESTIGATION, INQUEST, PROBE, RESEARCH: INQUIRY is a general term applicable to any quest for truth, knowledge, or information ⟨make *inquiries* about a prospective employee⟩ ⟨they made *inquiries*, and learned that Wild Bill was then in the Mint saloon —S.H.Holbrook⟩ ⟨a letter of *inquiry* to the authorities⟩ ⟨the True, which is the goal of all scientific and all philosophical *inquiry* —W.R.Inge⟩ INQUISITION suggests a sustained search, thorough and often unrelenting, for hidden facts; it may apply to merciless unremitting volleys of questions ⟨an *inquisition* into the bankruptcy proceedings⟩ ⟨the investigating committee subjecting him to a long *inquisition*⟩ INVESTIGATION may apply to a sustained and systematic inquiry, esp. of some specific proceeding ⟨an auditor *investigation* of the reported shortages⟩ ⟨the conduct of men in important areas may often be very legitimately subject to properly conducted Congressional *investigation* —Norman Thomas⟩ ⟨by their bullying tactics, by their having turned needed *investigations* into regrettable *inquisitions* —John Mason Brown⟩ INQUEST, once in more general use as a close synonym for INQUIRY, now usu. applies to an investigation, often by a coroner and his jury, into a cause of death or to a similar investigation into something disastrous or troubling ⟨it turned out on a final *inquest* that the learned lecturer had translated his piece into English —H.J.Laski⟩ ⟨it was decided at the *inquest* that the deceased had committed suicide⟩ ⟨an *inquest* on the fall of Singapore and the sinking of H.M.S. *Repulse* and H.M.S. *Prince of Wales* —*New Yorker*⟩ PROBE, in this sense, may apply to any deep, painstaking inquiry to discover something wrong or improper ⟨a *probe* resulting in the disbarring of several attorneys⟩ ⟨a *probe* into improper tax refunds⟩ RESEARCH applies to careful, prolonged study, esp. to uncover new knowledge ⟨*research* has shown and practice has established the futility of the charge that it was a usurpation when this Court undertook to declare an Act of Congress unconstitutional —O.W.Holmes †1935⟩ ⟨the *researches* . . . in the 17th century into the theory of probabilities greatly advanced the accuracy of calculations —*Encyc. Americana*⟩
**inquiry agent** *n, Brit* **:** a private detective
**in·quis·ite** \ənˈkwizət\ *vb* -ED/-ING/-S [L *inquisitus*, past part. of *inquirere* to inquire — more at INQUIRE] **1 :** to subject to inquisition; inquire into **:** INVESTIGATE, QUESTION ⟨people can stand only a short amount of *inquisiting* —G.P.Wilson⟩ **2** *obs* **:** INQUISITION
¹**in·qui·si·tion** \,inkwəˈzishən\ *n* -s [ME *inquisicioun*, fr. MF *inquisition*, fr. L *inquisition-, inquisitio*, fr. *inquisitus* (past part. of *inquirere* to inquire) + *-ion-, -io* -ion] **1 :** the act or instance of inquiring **:** INQUIRY, SEARCH, EXAMINATION, INVESTIGATION ⟨nominated himself for this delicate ~ —S.H. Adams⟩ ⟨proposed a brief ~ into the politics of the place —John Buchan⟩ **2 :** a judicial or official inquiry or examination usu. before a jury (as for ascertaining taxable property or for fixing the guilt of nuisances); *also* **:** the finding of such a jury or the document on which it is recorded **3** [ML *inquisition-, inquisitio*, fr. L] **a** *usu cap* **:** a Roman Catholic ecclesiastical tribunal esp. of medieval times and the early modern period having as its primary objective the discovery, punishment, and prevention of heresy; *specif* **:** an ecclesiastical tribunal set up in Spain under state control in 1478–80 with the object of proceeding against lapsed converts from Judaism, crypto-Jews, and other apostates that was marked by the extreme severity of its proceedings **b :** an official inquiry or investigation conducted with little or no regard for individual rights or characterized by undue harshness, bias, or hostility on the examiner's part ⟨his ~s were backed by the authority of the United States government —Elmer Davis⟩ ⟨the whole notion of loyalty ~s is a natural characteristic of the police state —*New Republic*⟩ **c :** a severe or searching questioning **:** the ordeal of such a questioning **:** GRILLING ⟨pushed toward the edge by the ~s of the psychiatrists —*Time*⟩ ⟨mumbled my way . . . through these ~s —*Adrian Bell*⟩ **syn** see INQUIRY
²**inquisition** \"\ *vb* -ED/-ING/-S *vi* **:** to make inquisition or inquiry **~** *vt* **:** to subject to inquisitorial examination
**in·qui·si·tion·al** \¦==¦zishənᵊl, -shnəl\ *adj* **:** relating to, characteristic of, or resembling an inquisition ⟨the ~ system that seeks a confession, by physical or moral torture —Janet Flanner⟩ ⟨an ~ tribunal⟩
¹**in·quis·i·tive** \ənˈkwizəd·|iv, -ət|\ *adj* [ME *inquisitif*, fr. MF, fr. LL *inquisitivus*, fr. L *inquisitus* + *-ivus* -ive] **1 :** given to examination, investigation, or research ⟨be curious, attentive, ~ as to everything —Earl of Chesterfield⟩ **2 a :** disposed to ask questions out of curiosity ⟨if somebody saw a citizen climbing a street sign they might get ~ —Bant Singer⟩; *esp* **:** inordinately or improperly curious about the affairs of another **:** PRYING ⟨I mustn't be ~ and ask questions —W.F.de Morgan⟩ ⟨she was a bit ~, as girls are —Dorothy Sayers⟩ **b :** reflecting or indicating curiosity esp. about the affairs of another ⟨his ~ face beamed with mischief —Dorothy Sayers⟩ ⟨with bright, ~ eyes —Claudia Cassidy⟩ **syn** see CURIOUS
²**inquisitive** \"\ *n* -s **:** an inquisitive person ⟨visible to such ~s as myself —William Sansom⟩
**in·quis·i·tive·ly** \|əvlē, -li\ *adv* **:** in an inquisitive manner
**in·quis·i·tive·ness** \|ivnəs\ *n* -ES **:** the quality or state of being inquisitive
**in·quis·i·tor** \ənˈkwizəd·ə(r), -ətə-\ *n* -s [MF & L; MF *inquisiteur*, fr. L *inquisitor*, fr. *inquisitus* + *-or*] **1 a :** INQUIRER, INVESTIGATOR, QUESTIONER ⟨I am come as an ~ . . . to ask you certain questions —Max Peacock⟩ **b :** a person (as a coroner or sheriff) whose official duty it is to examine and inquire **2** [ML, fr. L] **a :** a member or officer of an Inquisition **b :** a person who conducts an official inquiry or investigation with little or no regard for individual rights or with undue harshness, bias, or severity ⟨bare his entire life and personality to official ~s under pain of dismissal —E.A. Mowrer⟩
**in·quis·i·to·ri·al** \(,)in¦kwizə¦tōrēəl, -¦tȯr-\ *adj* **1 a :** of or relating to an ecclesiastical inquisitor **:** having the functions of such an inquisitor ⟨with royal and ~ authorities on the watch for him —G.C.Boyce⟩ **b :** like or typical of an ecclesiastical inquisitor **:** heedless of or flouting individual rights in seeking information or enforcing conformity **:** marked by extreme harshness or cruelty ⟨a practical police force with true ~ talents —Waldo Frank⟩ ⟨beyond discovery by the most ~ and powerful methods —J.M.Keynes⟩ **c :** offensively searching or importunate in inquiry **:** PRYING ⟨felt the press ~ to the point of antagonism —*N.Y. Times*⟩ ⟨questioned them in his ~ way —Carleton Beals⟩ **2 :** constituting or relating to a system of criminal procedure in which the judge also acts as prosecutor or in which the proceedings are secretly conducted and the accused must answer questions **3 :** relating to or having the authority to conduct official investigations ⟨the ~ power of the Senate is . . . of the highest importance —Lindsay Rogers⟩ ⟨an ~ agency⟩ — contrasted with *accusatorial* — **in·quis·i·to·ri·al·ly** \-əlē, -li\ *adv* — **in·quis·i·to·ri·al·ness** *n* -ES
**in·quis·i·tory** \ənˈkwizə,tōrē\ *adj* [ML *inquisitorius*, fr. *inquisitor*] **:** INQUISITORIAL, SEARCHING ⟨held to a high, persistent, ~ note —Scott Fitzgerald⟩
**inquisitous** *adj* [L *inquisitus*, past part.] *obs* **:** INQUISITIVE
**in·quis·i·tress** \-zə·trəs\ *n* -ES [*inquisitor* + *-ess*] **:** a female inquisitor
**inradius** \ˈ=,===\ *n* [⁴*in* + *radius*] **:** a radius of an inscribed circle or sphere — opposed to *exradius*
¹**in re** \-ˈrā, -ˈrē\ *or* **in re·bus** \-ˈrābəs, -ˈrēb-\ *adv* [*in re* fr. L, in the thing; *in rebus* fr. L, in the things] **:** in the thing or individual **:** in something existing outside the mind **:** in reality ⟨traits or relations of the properties *in re* —Alan Gewirth⟩ — compare REALISM
²**in re** *prep* [L] **:** in the matter of **:** CONCERNING, RE — often used in the title or name of a law case where the proceeding is in rem or quasi in rem and not in personam or in an ex parte proceeding (as a matter involving a probate or bankrupt estate, a guardianship, an application for laying out a public highway)
**in rem** \-ˈrem\ *adv (or adj)* [L, against a thing] **:** against a thing (as a right, status, property) ⟨proceedings and judgments are *in rem* when they adjudicate a right or a status or a title to property within the jurisdiction of a court or tribunal without having power over the person of the parties affected thereby and without power to compel personal obedience of the parties affected⟩ — compare IN PERSONAM, QUASI IN REM
**in req** *abbr* information requested
**in re·rum na·tu·ra** \-ˈrārəmnəˈtu̇rə, -ˈrēr-\ *adv* [L] **:** in the nature of things in the world of nature as distinguished from the world of human beings **:** in the realm of material things ⟨they do not signify anything *in rerum natura* —R.F.McRae⟩
¹**inring** \ˈ=,=\ *n* [⁴*in* + *ring*] **:** INWICK
²**in·ring** \ən+\ *vi* **:** INWICK
¹**inroad** \ˈ=,=\ *n* [⁴*in* + *road*] **1 :** a sudden hostile incursion or forcible entrance **:** RAID, FORAY ⟨protecting their crops of barley from the ~s of sparrows —J.G.Frazer⟩ ⟨their new homes would be reserved to them against future ~s by whites —P.W.Gates⟩ **2 :** an advance or penetration esp. at the expense of something or someone **:** a serious encroachment ⟨another sharp ~ on the principle of free speech —*Civil Liberties*⟩ ⟨the ~s of the conformist spirit on American literary life —C.J.Rolo⟩ ⟨make ~s on the domestic markets of their local competitors —Patrick McMahon⟩ ⟨synthetic materials made deep ~s into the use of leather —J.F.W. Anderson⟩
²**in·road** \ən+\ *vb* -ED/-ING/-S *vt* **:** to make an inroad into **~** *vi* **:** to make inroads
**in·roll** \ənˈrōl\ *archaic var of* ENROLL
**inrooted** \ˈ=,==\ *adj* [²*in* + *rooted*] **:** deeply rooted ⟨the ~ American philosophy of competition —William Best⟩
**inrun** \ˈ=,=\ *n* [⁴*in* + *run*] **:** an inclined trestle down which a ski jumper moves prior to the takeoff
**in·rup·tion** \ənˈrəpshən\ *n* -s [by alter.] **:** IRRUPTION
**inrush** \ˈ=,=\ *n* [⁴*in* + *rush* (after *rush in*, v.)] **:** the action or an instance of rushing or pouring in **:** INFLUX ⟨an ~ of cool maritime air —*Farmer's Weekly (So. Africa)*⟩
**inrushing** \ˈ=,==\ *adj* [⁴*in* + *rushing* (after *rush in*, v.)] **:** rushing in ⟨the ~ immigrant masses —D.W.Brogan⟩
**ins** *pl of* IN, *pres 3d sing of* IN
**-ins** *pl of* -IN
**ins** *abbr* **1** inscribed **2** inside **3** inspected; inspector **4** insular **5** insulated; insulation **6** insurance
**in·salivate** \ən+\ *vt* [²*in-* + *salivate*] **:** to mix (food) with saliva by mastication — **in·salivation** \"+\ *n*
**in·salubrious** \¦in+\ *adj* [L *insalubris*, fr. *in-* ¹in- + *salubris* healthful + E *-ous* — more at SALUBRIOUS] **:** tending to impair health **:** UNWHOLESOME, NOXIOUS ⟨an ~ environment⟩
**in·salubrity** \¦in+\ *n* [F *insalubrité*, fr. MF, fr. *insalubre* insalubrious (fr. L *insalubris*) + *-ité* -ity] **:** unhealthfulness or unwholesomeness esp. of climate
**in·salutary** \(ˈ)in, ən+\ *adj* [LL *insalutaris*, fr. L *in-* ¹in- + *salutaris* salutary] **:** not healthful or wholesome ⟨a thoroughly ~ outlook on life⟩
**in·san·able** \(ˈ)in¦sanəbəl, ən'sa-\ *adj* [L *insanabilis*, fr. *in-* ¹in- + *sanabilis* curable — more at SANABLE] **:** INCURABLE, IRREMEDIABLE
**ins and outs** *n pl* **1 :** physical twists and turns or windings and uncertainties (as of a road) ⟨knows all the *ins and outs* of the short way to the camp⟩ **2 :** characteristic peculiarities or technicalities ⟨had to learn the *ins and outs* of the new plane⟩ **:** RAMIFICATIONS ⟨the *ins and outs* of a mathematical theory⟩
**in·sane** \(ˈ)in¦sān, ən'sā-\ *adj, sometimes* -ER/-EST [L *insanus*, fr. *in-* ¹in- + *sanus* sane] **1 a** *obs, of the mind* **:** UNSOUND, DISORDERED **b** *of a person* **:** exhibiting unsoundness or disorder of mind **:** affected with insanity **:** MAD; *esp* **:** disordered in mind to such a degree as to be unable to function safely and competently in ordinary human relations — compare PSYCHOTIC **2** *obs* **:** causing insanity **3 :** used by, typical of, or for insane persons ⟨an ~ hospital⟩ ⟨~ ravings⟩ **4 :** utterly foolish or ridiculous **:** lacking any logical or practical basis **:** wildly visionary ⟨a perfectly ~ idea⟩ ⟨such ~ extravagance⟩ ⟨the *insanest* thing you ever saw⟩ — **in·sane·ness** \-ānnəs\ *n*
**in·sane·ly** *adv* **:** in an insane manner ⟨behaved ~⟩ **:** to an

insane degree : beyond the bounds of reason ⟨~ jealous⟩ : ABSURDLY, RIDICULOUSLY ⟨~ extravagant⟩
**insane root** *n* **1** : a root believed in medieval times to cause madness in those eating it and usu. identified with either henbane or hemlock **2** : HENBANE 1a
**in·san·i·tar·i·ness** \(ˈ)in¦sanə,terēnəs, ən's-, -rin-\ *n* -ES : the quality or state of being insanitary
**in·sanitary** \(ˈ)in, ən+\ *adj* [¹*in-* + *sanitary*] : deficient in sanitation : unclean to such a degree as to be injurious to health : CONTAMINATED, FILTHY, UNHEALTHY ⟨working in ~ surroundings⟩ ⟨~ storage of food⟩
**in·sanitation** \(ˈ)in, ən+\ *n* [¹*in-* + *sanitation*] : lack of sanitation : careless or dangerous hygienic conditions
**in·san·i·ty** \ən'sanəd·ē, -ətē, -i\ *n* [L *insanitas*, fr. *insanus* insane + *-itas* -ity] **1 a** : the state of being insane : unsoundness or derangement of the mind usu. occurring as a specific disorder (as schizophrenia or dementia praecox) and usu. excluding such states as mental deficiency, the psychoneuroses, and various character disorders **b** : a mental disorder ⟨dementia praecox is one of the commoner *insanities*⟩ **2** : such unsoundness of mind or lack of understanding as prevents one from having the mental capacity required by law to enter into a particular relationship, status, or transaction or as excuses one from criminal or civil responsibility **3 a** : extreme folly or unreasonableness ⟨the ~ of war⟩ **b** : something utterly foolish or unreasonable ⟨the *insanities* of daily life⟩
**syn** LUNACY, PSYCHOSIS, MANIA, DEMENTIA: INSANITY, more commonly used in law than in medicine, applies to any mental disorder of such severity as to render the person unfit to manage his own affairs or to enjoy his liberty because of the unreliability of his behavior that makes him a danger to himself and to others. LUNACY, a term legally interchangeable with insanity, popularly implies periodic mental disorder or alternating madness and lucidity. PSYCHOSIS is the technical psychiatric term for any far-reaching and prolonged behavior disorder (as dementia praecox or manic-depressive psychosis). MANIA is a phase of a mental disorder (as manic-depressive psychosis) marked by a mood of sustained and exaggerated elation, emotional expansiveness, overtalkativeness, excessive physical activity, or delusions of greatness, that characterizes any of several psychoses. DEMENTIA is the technical psychiatric term that denotes mental deterioration that is psychogenic in origin (as dementia praecox) or that results from disease that damages the brain substance (as neurosyphilis or arteriosclerosis)
**in·sa·tia·bil·i·ty** \(ˌ)in,sāshə'biləd·ē, ən,=='===, -lətē, -i *sometimes* -shēə-\ *n* [prob. fr. F or LL; F *insatiabilité*, fr. MF, fr. LL *insatiabilitas*, fr. L *insatiabilis* insatiable + *-itas* -ity] : the quality or state of being insatiable
**in·sa·tia·ble** \(ˈ)in¦sāshəbəl, ən's-, *sometimes* -shēə-\ *adj* [ME *insaciable*, *inessiabyll*, fr. MF or L; MF *insaciable*, fr. OF, fr. L *insatiabilis*, fr. *in-* ¹in- + *satiare* to satisfy + *-abilis* -able — more at SATIATE] : incapable of being satisfied or appeased ⟨an ~ desire for knowledge⟩ — **in·sa·tia·ble·ness** *n* -ES
**in·sa·tia·bly** \-blē, -bli\ *adv* : in an insatiable way : without being satisfied ⟨clawing ~ at the framework of tradition⟩ : in an insatiable degree; *broadly* : EXTREMELY, VERY ⟨~ hungry⟩
**in·sa·tiate** \(ˈ)in¦sāsh(ē)ət, ən's-\ *also* **in·sa·ti·at·ed** \-shē,ād·əd\ *adj* [*insatiate* fr. L *insatiatus*, fr. *in-* ¹in- + *satiatus* satiate, satiated; *insatiated* fr. ¹*in-* + *satiated*] : not satiated : not satisfied : INSATIABLE ⟨~ thirst⟩ ⟨such ~ cruelty⟩ — **in·sa·tiate·ly** *adv* — **in·sa·tiate·ness** *n* -ES
**in·satiety** \¦in+\ *n* [MF *insacieté*, *insatieté*, fr. L *insatietas*, fr. *in-* ¹in- + *satietas* satiety — more at SATIETY] : lack of satiety; *esp* : unsatisfied desire ⟨clothes they can never hope to own, changes they cannot afford to keep up with — must set up a tremendous store of ~ in the poor and the modest-income groups —P.M.Gregory⟩
**insatisfaction** *n* [¹*in-* + *satisfaction*] *obs* : DISSATISFACTION
**in·saturation** \¦in+\ *n* [¹*in-* + *saturation*] : the quality or state of being unsaturated
**insc** *abbr* inscribed
**in·scape** \'inz,kāp, 'in(t),sk-\ *n* [²*in-* + *-scape*] : inward significant character or quality belonging uniquely to objects or events in nature and human experience esp. as perceived by the blended observation and introspection of the poet and in turn embodied in patterns of such specif. poetic elements as imagery, rhythm, rhyme, assonance, sound symbolism, and allusion : INWARDNESS — compare HAECCEITY
**insce** *abbr* insurance
**in·sce·na·tion** \,in,sē'nāshən, ,in(t)sē'-, ,in(t)sə'-\ *n* -S [²*in-* + *scene* + *-ation*; intended as trans. of G *inszenierung*] : MISE EN SCÈNE
**in·science** \'insh(ē)ən(t)s, 'in(t)sēə-\ *n* [L *inscientia*, fr. *inscient-*, *insciens* inscient + *-ia*] : lack of knowledge : NESCIENCE
**in·scient** \-nt\ *adj* [L *inscient-*, *insciens*, fr. *in-* ¹in- + *scient-*, *sciens*, pres. part. of *scire* to know — more at SCIENCE] : exhibiting or based on inscience
**in·scrib·able** \ən'zkrībəbəl, ən'sk-\ *adj* : capable of being inscribed
**in·scribe** \ən'zkrīb, ən'sk-\ *vt* [L *inscribere*, fr. *in-* ²in- + *scribere* to write — more at SCRIBE] **1 a** : to write, engrave, print, or otherwise set down (as characters, symbols, words, or a text) esp. so as to form a lasting or public record **b** : to enter the name of esp. on a list : ENROLL **c** : to write (letters or other characters) in a particular format in cryptology; *esp* : to write (letters or other characters of a plaintext message) according to an agreed-upon route in an agreed-upon geometrical pattern preparatory to transcribing in another manner **2 a** : to write, engrave, print, or otherwise mark characters upon esp. so as to create a lasting or public record **b** : to autograph (a copy of a work of which one is the author) — often used with *to* or *for* ⟨~ one's book to an old friend⟩ **c** : to stamp deeply or impress esp. on the memory **3** : to assign or address (as a work of literature) in a style less formal than that of a dedication **4** : to draw (a figure) within a figure so as to touch in as many places as possible ⟨~ a polygon in a circle⟩ **5** *Brit* : to register the name of the holder of (a stock or other security)
**inscribed** *adj* [fr. past part. of *inscribe*] **1** : having lines or other markings deeply impressed or having the appearance of written letters (as certain insects) **2** *of a holding of stock or other security*, *Brit* : having the owner's name entered in a list kept by the issuing company or at a bank authorized to keep it and usu. transferable only by personal attendance of the owner or one entitled to act as his attorney **3** : bearing the author's signature often accompanied by an inscription — used in the book trade of a copy of a book ⟨an ~ copy⟩
¹**in·scrib·er** \-bə(r)\ *n* : one that inscribes
²**in·scrib·er** \'inz,krībə(r), 'in,sk-\ *n* [prob. fr. *in-* (fr. *input*) + *-scriber* (fr. *transcriber*)] : a device for transferring data from a punched tape onto a medium (as magnetic wire) for use in an electronic computer — compare OUTSCRIBER
**in·script** \'inz,kript, 'in,sk-\ *n* [L *inscriptum*, fr. neut. of *inscriptus* (past part.)] : INSCRIPTION
**in·scrip·tion** \ən'zkripshən, ən'sk-\ *n* [ME *inscripcioun* superscription, heading, fr. L *inscription-*, *inscriptio* act of writing upon, inscription on a monument, title, fr. *inscriptus* (past part. of *inscribere* to inscribe) + *-ion-*, *-io* -ion] **1** : something that is inscribed: as **a** : a text inscribed in order to form a lasting or public record (as on a monument, tablet, pillar, wall) **b** : a brief description of the character, contents, authorship, or occasion of a book or other composition placed at its beginning : TITLE, SUPERSCRIPTION, HEADING **c** (1) : a name and often a message prefixed to a work of literature addressing it to someone in a style or manner less formal than that of a dedication (2) : EPIGRAPH 2 **d** : the wording on a coin, medal, seal, stamp, or currency note : LEGEND **2** *archaic* : a tendinous line intersecting a muscle **3 a** : the act or process of inscribing **b** : the writing of characters in a particular format in cryptology; *esp* : the writing of the characters of a plaintext message along an agreed-upon route in an agreed-upon geometrical pattern before copying them off in another order to make a transposition cipher **c** : the entering of a name on or as if on a list : ENROLLMENT **4** *Brit* **a** : the act of inscribing securities **b inscriptions** *pl* : inscribed securities **5** : the part of a medical prescription that contains the names and quantities of the drugs to be compounded

**in·scrip·tion·al** \-shən°l,-shnəl\ *adj* **1** *archaic* : bearing an inscription **2** : of or relating to an inscription **3** : characteristic of inscriptions ⟨the revival of classical ~ capitals —*Times Lit. Supp.*⟩
**in·scrip·tion·less** \-shənləs\ *adj* : lacking any inscription ⟨buried beneath an ~ stone⟩
**in·scrip·tive** \-ptiv\ *adj* [L *inscriptus* (past part. of *inscribere* to inscribe) + E *-ive*] **1** *obs* : INSCRIBED **2** : relating to or constituting an inscription ⟨traced out the ~ lines⟩ — **in·scrip·tive·ly** \-ptəvlē\ *adv*
**inscroll** *var of* ENSCROLL
**in·scrutability** \(,)inz,krüd·ə'biləd·ē, ən-, -n,sk-, -ütə-, -lətē, -i\ *n* : the quality or state of being inscrutable
**in·scru·ta·ble** \(ˈ)inz¦krüd·əbəl, ənz'k-, -n¦sk-, -ütə-\ *adj* [ME, fr. LL *inscrutabilis*, fr. L *in-* ¹in- + LL *scrutabilis* scrutable] **1** : incapable of being investigated and understood ⟨attempting to look into the ~ future⟩ ⟨obeying ancient and ~ laws⟩; *broadly* : not readily comprehensible : MYSTERIOUS ⟨an ~ smile⟩ ⟨many fathers feel that, if they are to maintain their authority, they must be a little distant and ~ —A.C. Benson⟩ **2** : impossible to see or see through physically ⟨an ~ fog⟩ ⟨~ deeps⟩
**in·scru·ta·ble·ness** *n* -ES : INSCRUTABILITY
**in·scru·ta·bly** \-blē, -bli\ *adv* : in an inscrutable manner
**in·sculp** \ənz'kəlp, ən'sk-\ *vt* [ME *insculpen*, fr. L *insculpere*, fr. *in-* ²in- + *sculpere*, *scalpere* to cut, carve — more at SHELF] *archaic* : ENGRAVE, SCULPTURE
**in·sculpture** \ənz'k-,ən'sk-\ *n* [prob. fr. obs. F, fr. MF, fr. *in-* ²in- + *sculpture*, fr. L *sculptura* sculpture] : CARVING, INSCRIPTION
**in·sculptured** \ənz'k-,ən'sk-\ *adj* [²*in-* + *sculptured*] : CUT IN, SCULPTURED ⟨~ epitaphs⟩ ⟨an ~ border⟩
**in·seam** \'in,sēm\ *n* [²*in-* + *seam*] : an inner seam: as **a** : the seam from the crotch to the leg bottom of trousers **b** : a seam showing on the inside only used for articles (as gloves) often made with outside seams **c** : a hidden seam in a welt shoe fastening the welt, lining, and shoe upper to the insole
**in·seam·er** \-mə(r)\ *n* : a worker that sews inseams (as on trouser legs or shoes)
**in-season** *adj* **1** *of a female mammal* : being in heat **2** : SEASONAL ⟨*in-season* accommodations⟩ ⟨*in-season* fruits⟩
¹**in·sect** \'in,sekt\ *n* -S [L *insectum*, fr. neut. of *insectus*, past part. of *insecare* to cut into, fr. *in-* ²in- + *secare* to cut; trans. of Gk *entomon* — more at SAW, ENTOMOLOGY] **1 a** : any of numerous small invertebrate animals that are more or less obviously segmented and that include members of the class Insecta and others (as spiders, mites, ticks, centipedes, sowbugs) having superficial resemblance to members of Insecta — not used technically **b** [NL *Insecta*] : a member of the class Insecta (as an ant, bee, fly) **2** *now chiefly substand* : any of various small animals (as an earthworm, coral polyp, turtle) **3** : a small, trivial, or contemptible person

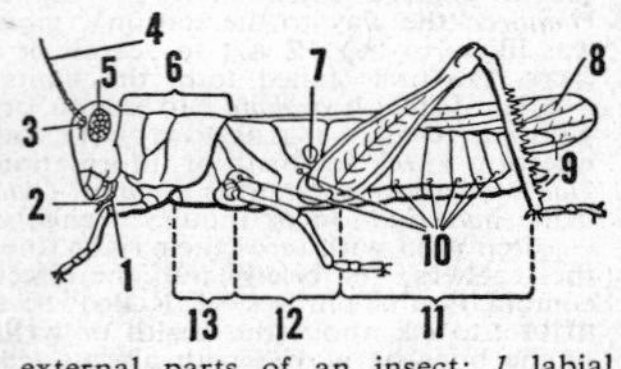


external parts of an insect: *1* labial palpus, *2* maxillary palpus, *3* simple eye, *4* antenna, *5* compound eye, *6* prothorax, *7* tympanum, *8* wing, *9* ovipositor, *10* spiracles, *11* abdomen, *12* metathorax, *13* mesothorax

²**insect** \"\ *adj* **1** : of, relating to, or being insects ⟨~ bites⟩ ⟨~ pests⟩ **2** : used on, for, or against insects ⟨~ pins⟩ ⟨~ powder⟩ ⟨an ~ cabinet⟩ **3** : using or depending on insects ⟨~ feeders⟩ ⟨~ fertilization⟩
**in·sec·ta** \ən'sektə\ *n pl*, *cap* [NL, fr. L, pl. of *insectum* insect] **1** *in former classifications* : a large group of segmented animals including (1) many worms and the arthropods, (2) all the arthropods, (3) the true insects, the myriapods, and the arachnids, or (4) the myriapods and the insects **2** : a class of Arthropoda comprising segmented animals that as adults have a well-defined head bearing a single pair of antennae, three pairs of mouthparts, and usu. a pair of compound eyes, a 3-segmented thorax each segment of which bears a pair of legs ventrally with the second and third often bearing also a pair of dorsolateral wings, and an abdomen usu. of 7 to 10 visible segments without true jointed legs but often with the last segments modified or fitted with specialized extensions (as claspers, stings, ovipositors), that breathe air usu. through a ramifying system of tracheae which open externally through spiracles or gills, that exhibit a variety of life cycles often involving complex metamorphosis, and that include the greater part of all living and extinct animals — see PROTURA; compare COLLEMBOLA
¹**in·sec·tan** \(ˈ)in¦sektən, ən's-\ *adj* [NL *Insecta* + E *-an*] : of or relating to the class Insecta
²**insectan** \"\ *adj* [¹*insect* + *-an*] : of or relating to insects
**in·sec·tary** \'in,sektərē, ən's-, 'in,sek,terē\ *or* **in·sec·tar·i·um** \,=,='ta(a)rēəm\ *n*, *pl* **insectaries** \-ēz\ *or* **insectar·ia** \-ēə\ [NL *insectarium*, fr. L *insecta* + *-arium* -ary] : a place for the keeping or rearing of living insects
**insect bed** *n* : a geologic stratum rich in insect remains
**in·sect·ed** \(ˈ)in¦sektəd, ən's-\ *adj* [L *insectus* (past part. of *insecare* to cut into) + E *-ed*] : cut into : SEGMENTED ⟨the ~ body of a sea anemone⟩
**insect flower** *n* : PYRETHRUM 2a — usu. used in pl.
**insecti-** *comb form* [L *insectum*] : insect ⟨*insecti*ferous⟩ ⟨*insecti*fuge⟩
**in·sec·ti·ci·dal** \ən¦sektə¦sīd°l\ *adj* **1** [*insecti-* + *-cidal*] : destroying or controlling insects **2** [*insecticide* + *-al*] : of or relating to an insecticide — **in·sec·ti·ci·dal·ly** \-°lē\ *adv*
¹**in·sec·ti·cide** \ən'sektə,sīd\ *n* -S [*insecti-* + *-cide* (killing)] : the killing of insects ⟨a carefully controlled mass ~ was going on —*Newsweek*⟩
²**insecticide** \"\ *n* -S [ISV *insecti-* + *-cide* (killer)] : an agent that destroys insects; *broadly* : an agent hostile or repellent to insects — compare LARVICIDE
**in·sec·tic·o·lous** \¦in,sek¦tikələs\ *adj* [*insecti-* + *-colous*] : dwelling on the bodies of insects ⟨~ mites⟩
**in·sec·ti·fuge** \ən'sektə,fyüj\ *n* -S [*insecti-* + *-fuge*] : an agent that drives away insects usu. without destroying them : an insect repellent
¹**in·sec·tile** \(ˈ)in¦sekt°l, ən's-, -,tīl, -(,)til\ *adj* [L *insectum* + E *-ile*] : like or being an insect : consisting of insects ⟨an ~ mixture for feeding songbirds⟩
²**insectile** \"\ *adj* [¹*in-* + L *sectilis* divided, cut, sectile — more at SECTILE] : not sectile : incapable of being divided
**in·sec·tion** \ən'sekshən\ *n* [LL *insection-*, *insectio* incision, fr. L *insectus* (past part. of *insecare* to cut into) + *-ion-*, *-io* -ion — more at INSECT] : a notched or segmented part ⟨~*s* of a leaf margin⟩
**in·sec·ti·val** \¦in,sek¦tīvəl\ *adj* [¹*insect* + *-ive* + *-al*] : typical of an insect
**in·sec·tiv·o·ra** \,in,sek'tivərə\ *n pl*, *cap* [NL, fr. *insecti-* + *-vora*] : an order of mammals comprising the moles, shrews, hedgehogs, and certain related forms that are mostly small, insectivorous, terrestrial or fossorial, and nocturnal — see LIPOTYPHLA, MENOTYPHLA
**in·sec·tiv·o·rae** \-,rē\ *also* **in·sec·tiv·o·ra** \-,rə\ [NL, fr. *insecti-* + *-vorae* (fr. L, fem. pl. of *-vorus* -vorous) *or* *-vora*] *syn of* MICROCHIROPTERA
**in·sec·ti·vore** \ən'sektə,vō(ə)r\ *n* -S **1** [NL *Insectivora*] : a mammal of the order Insectivora **2** [F, fr. *insectivore* insectivorous, fr. *insecti-* + *-vore* (fr. L *-vorus* -vorous)] : an insectivorous plant or animal : a carnivore that feeds on insects
**in·sec·tiv·o·rous** \¦in,sek¦tiv(ə)rəs\ *adj* [L *insectum* insect + E *-ivorous* (as in *carnivorous*)] : feeding on insects : depending on insects as food
**insectivorous plant** *n* : a plant that captures and digests insects either passively (as the common pitcher plant or the sundew) or by the movement of certain organs (as the Venus's-flytrap) — compare DROSERACEAE, LENTIBULARIACEAE, SARRACENIACEAE
**in·sec·tol·o·gy** \,in,sek'täləjē\ *n* -ES [F *insectologie*, fr. *insecte* insect (fr. L *insectum*) + *-o-* + *-logie* -logy — more at INSECT] : ENTOMOLOGY

**insect orchis** *n* : a twayblade of the genus *Listera*
**insect powder** *n* : a powder for the extermination of insects; *esp* : PYRETHRUM 2a
**in·sec·tu·ous** \(,)in¦sekch(əw)əs, ən's-\ *adj* [¹*insect* + *-uous* (as in *contemptuous*)] : involving or full of insects : BUGGY
**insect wax** *n* : a waxlike substance secreted by an insect; *esp* : CHINESE WAX
**in·secure** \¦in+\ *adj* [ML *insecurus*, fr. L *in-* ¹in- + *securus* secure] : lacking security: **a** : not confident or sure : UNCERTAIN ⟨feeling somewhat ~ of his reception⟩ **b** : not effectually guarded, protected, or sustained : exposed to danger : UNSAFE ⟨an ~ investment⟩ ⟨property was very ~ during the riots⟩ **c** : not tightly fastened : not firmly fixed in position : SHAKY ⟨the hinge is ~⟩ **d** : not highly stable or well-adjusted : lacking likelihood of permanence or success : UNSTABLE, UNSURE ⟨a marriage ~ from the beginning⟩ ⟨his fortune was increasingly ~⟩ — **in·se·cure·ly** *adv* — **in·se·cure·ness** *n*
**in·security** \¦in+\ *n* [perh. fr. ML *insecuritas* danger, hazard, fr. L *in-* ¹in- + *securus* secure + *-itas* -ity] : the quality or state of being insecure: as **a** : lack of assurance : APPREHENSIVENESS ⟨a feeling of ~⟩ **b** : lack of safety : HAZARD, RISK ⟨the ~ of his capital⟩ **c** : an insecure condition or circumstance ⟨the minor *insecurities* of life⟩ ⟨noticed the ~ of the lock⟩
**inseeing** \'=¦==\ *adj* [²*in-* + *seeing*, pres. part. of *see*] **1** : having insight **2** : tending to look inward : subjective or egocentric in orientation
**in·sel·berg** \'in(t)səl,bərg, 'inzəl-, 'inzəl,berg\ *n*, *pl* **inselbergs** \-gz\ *or* **inselber·ge** \-gə\ [G, fr. *insel* island + *berg* mountain] : an isolated mountain partly buried by the debris derived from and overlapping its slopes
**in·sem·i·nate** \ən'semə,nāt, *usu* -ād·+V\ *vt* -ED/-ING/-S [L *inseminatus*, past part. of *inseminare*, fr. *in-* ²in- + *seminare* to beget, plant, fr. *semin-*, *semen* seed — more at SEMEN] **1** : to sow or sow in ⟨~ the minds of the young with practical ideals⟩ **2** : to introduce semen into (the female genital tract) by coitus or by other means **syn** see IMPLANT
**in·sem·i·na·tion** \(,)in,semə'nāshən, ən-\ *n* -S : the act or process of inseminating — compare ARTIFICIAL INSEMINATION
**in·sem·i·na·tor** \='==,nād·ə(r), -ātə-\ *n* -S : one that practices the technique of artificial insemination esp. of cattle
**in·sensate** \(ˈ)in¦sen,sā|t, ən's-, -n(t)sə|, *usu* |d·+V\ *adj* [LL *insensatus*, fr. L *in-* ¹in- + LL *sensatus* gifted with sense, intelligent — more at SENSATE] **1** : having no capacity to perceive : INSENTIENT, INANIMATE ⟨the ~ stones⟩ **2** : lacking or marked by lack of sense or understanding ⟨dull ~ rustics⟩ ⟨~ ignorance⟩ : not based on plan or reason : FOOLISH, FATUOUS ⟨this ~ project⟩ **3 a** : lacking awareness, sensibility, or sensitivity : having no conception of or feeling for ⟨~ to beauty⟩ ⟨~ to his privileges and responsibilities **b** : lacking humane feeling : UNFEELING; *broadly* : CRUEL, HARSH, BRUTAL ⟨~ destruction⟩ ⟨~ hatred⟩ — **in·sen·sate·ly** *adv* — **in·sen·sate·ness** *n* -ES
**in·sense** \ən'sen(t)s\ *vt* [ME *ensensen*, fr. MF *ensenser*, fr. OF, fr. *en-* ²in- + *sens* sense, fr. L *sensus* — more at SENSE] *dial Brit* : to give (a person) a sense of the importance or significance of something : impress or imbue firmly with a fact or idea : INSTRUCT, INFORM
**in·sensibility** \(ˌ)in, ən+\ *n* [LL *insensibilitas*, fr. L *insensibilis* insensible + *-itas* -ity] : the quality or state of being insensible: as **a** : an unconscious or comatose state **b** : lack of physical feeling or sensitivity : an unresponsive or unreactive condition : INSENSITIVITY ⟨marked ~ to cold⟩ ⟨increasing ~ to stimuli⟩ **c** : lack of mental or emotional feeling or response : APATHY ⟨her complete ~ to the honor done her⟩
¹**in·sensible** \(ˈ)in, ən+\ *adj* [ME, fr. MF & L; MF, fr. L *insensibilis*, fr. *in-* ¹in- + *sensibilis* sensible] **1** : incapable or bereft of feeling or sensation: as **a** : not endowed with consciousness : INANIMATE, INSENTIENT ⟨~ earth⟩ **b** : deprived of consciousness : UNCONSCIOUS ⟨to fall ~⟩ **c** : lacking sensory perception : failing to react to stimuli either wholly or to some degree ⟨markedly ~ to pain⟩; *also* : deprived of such perception or ability to react ⟨hands ~ from cold⟩ **2** : incapable of being perceived by the senses or perceptible only with difficulty : IMPERCEPTIBLE; *broadly* : MINUTE, SLIGHT, GRADUAL ⟨~ motion⟩ ⟨~ gradations⟩ **3** *archaic* : lacking sense or intelligence : STUPID, SENSELESS, UNREASONING **4** : devoid or insusceptible of emotion or passion : void of feeling : APATHETIC, INDIFFERENT ⟨~ to fear⟩; *also* : UNAWARE ⟨~ of their danger⟩ **5** : not intelligible : MEANINGLESS — used chiefly in law **6** : devoid of sensibility : lacking delicacy or refinement — **in·sensibleness** \"+\ *n* — **in·sensibly** \"+\ *adv*
²**insensible** \"\ *n* -S : one that is insensible
**in·sensitive** \(ˈ)in, ən+\ *adj* [¹*in-* + *sensitive*] : not sensitive: as **a** *obs* : INSENTIENT, INANIMATE **b** : lacking feeling : INSENSIBLE **c** : not physically or chemically sensitive **d** : not morally or mentally sensitive : UNIMPRESSIONABLE — **in·sensitively** \"+\ *adv* — **in·sensitiveness** \"+\ *or* **in·sensitivity** \(ˌ)in, ən+\ *n*
**in·sentience** \(ˈ)in, ən+\ *n* [fr. *insentient*, after E *sentient*: *sentience*] : the quality or state of being insentient
**in·sentient** \"+\ *adj* [¹*in-* + *sentient*] : not sentient : not having perception or feeling : lacking consciousness or animation
**in·separability** \(ˌ)in, ən+\ *n* : the quality or state of being inseparable
¹**in·separable** \(ˈ)in, ən+\ *adj* [ME, fr. L *inseparabilis*, fr. *in-* ¹in- + *separabilis* separable] **1** : not separable : incapable of being separated or disjoined **2** : invariably attached to a word, stem, or root ⟨*un-* is an ~ prefix⟩ — **in·separableness** \"+\ *n* — **in·separably** \"+\ *adv*
²**inseparable** \"\ *n* -S : one that is inseparable from another — usu. used in pl.
**in·separate** \(ˈ)in, ən+\ *adj* [LL *inseparatus*, fr. L *in-* ¹in- + *separatus* separate] : not separate : UNITED; *usu* : INSEPARABLE — **in·separately** \"+\ *adv*
**in·sequent** \(ˈ)in, ən+\ *adj* [¹*in-* + *sequent*] *of the course of a stream* : apparently uncontrolled by the associated rock structure
¹**in·sert** \ən'sər|t, -sə|, -səi|, *usu* |d·+V\ *vb* -ED/-ING/-S [L *insertus*, past part. of *inserere*, fr. *in-* ²in- + *serere* to join, bind together — more at SERIES] *vt* **1 a** : to set (something) in : put or thrust in : INTRODUCE ⟨~*ing* the scions in hardy stocks⟩ ⟨~ a key noiselessly in a lock⟩ **b** : to put or introduce into the body of : INTERPOLATE ⟨~*ed* a few words of description⟩ **c** : to set in and make fast (as a piece of fabric) ⟨~ a patch in a pair of torn trousers⟩ ⟨~ a decorative medallion in a tooled leather cover⟩; *esp* : to insert by sewing between two cut edges ⟨~*ing* bands of lace on the front of the blouse⟩ **2** : to attach or fix in a particular position in the course of natural growth — used only in past part. ⟨the meristem is ~*ed* between more or less differentiated tissue regions —Katherine Esau⟩ ~ *vi*, *of a muscle* : to be in attachment to the part to be moved ⟨retraction is accomplished by two fairly thick bands of retractor muscles which ~ on the lophophore and originate in the body wall —Mary Rogick⟩
²**in·sert** \'in,s-\ *n* -S : something that is inserted or is for insertion : INSERTION, INSET: as **a** : written or printed material inserted (as a map or plate between the leaves of a book, a circular within the folds of a newspaper, an instruction sheet in a carton of merchandise) **b** : a removable portion of a die or mold **c** : a part of a casting placed in the mold and becoming integral with the metal cast around it **d** : a piece of cloth set into a garment for decoration, ease, and additional fullness
**in·sert·able** *or* **in·sert·ible** \ən'sərd·əbəl\ *adj* : capable of being inserted
**inserted** \(ˈ)=¦==\ *adj* [fr. past part. of ¹*insert*] : set in : fitted in: as **a** : having the basal part set into another structure ⟨an insect with ~ mouthparts⟩ **b** : attached by natural growth (as a muscle or tendon or the parts of a flower) **c** : not in one piece with the main body and therefore replaceable ⟨an *inserted*-tooth saw⟩ ⟨an ~ valve seat⟩
**in·sert·er** \ən'sərd·ə(r)\ *n* -S : one that inserts
**in·ser·tion** \ən'sərshən, -səsh-, -səish-\ *n* -S [LL *insertion-*, *insertio*, fr. L *insertus* (past part. of *inserere* to insert) + *-ion-*, *-io* -ion] **1** : the act or process of inserting ⟨the

~ of new ball bearings⟩ **2 :** something that is inserted **:** INSERT: as **a :** the part of a muscle by which it is attached to the part to be moved — distinguished from *origin* **b :** narrow banding (as of lace or embroidery) with finished edges for insertion as ornament between two pieces of fabric **c :** a single appearance of an advertisement (as in a newspaper) **3 :** the mode or place of attachment of an organ or part ⟨the ~ of a muscle⟩ ⟨deep ~ of the petals of a flower⟩ — **in·ser·tion·al** \-shən³l,-shnəl\ *adj*

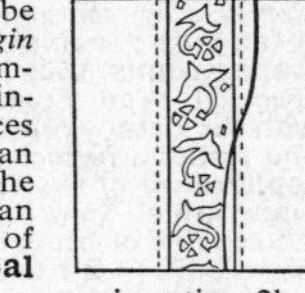
insertion 2b

**in·ser·tive** \ən'sərd·iv\ *adj* [L *insertivus*, fr. *insertus* (past part.) + *-ivus* -ive] **1** *obs* **:** marked by insertion **:** INSERTED **2 :** tending to insert
**in-service** \(')in¦=,ən'=\ *adj* **:** going on or continuing while in service ⟨*in-service* training⟩ ⟨*in-service* care of delicate fabrics⟩
**in·serviceable** \(')in, ən+\ *adj* [¹*in-* + *serviceable*] **:** UNSERVICEABLE
**in·ser·vi·ent** \ən'sərvēənt\ *adj* [L *inservient-, inserviens*, pres. part. of *inservire* to serve, fr. *in-* ²in- + *servire* to serve — more at SERVE] *archaic* **:** serving or subservient to (as an end or purpose) **:** CONDUCIVE
**insession** *n* -s [LL *insession-, insessio*, lit., act of sitting in, act of sitting down, fr. L *insessus* (past part. of *insidēre* to sit in, sit on, fr. *in-* ²in- + *sedēre* to sit) + *-ion-, -io* -ion — more at SIT] *obs* **:** the act of sitting in a bath; *also* **:** SITZ BATH
**in·ses·so·res** \,in,se'sōr(,)ēz\ *n pl, cap* [NL, fr. LL, pl. of *insessor* waylayer (lit., one that sits on), fr. L *insessus* (past part.) + *-or*] *in former classifications* **:** an order of birds that have the feet adapted for perching including the Passeres and many others
**in·ses·so·ri·al** \¦in,se¦sōrēəl\ *adj* **1** [L *insessus* (past part.) + E *-orial*, as in *raptorial*] **:** perching or adapted for perching ⟨~ feet⟩ **2** [NL *Insessores* + E *-ial*] **:** of or relating to the order Insessores
**¹inset** \'=,=\ *n* [⁴*in* + *set* (n.)] **1 a :** a place where something (as water) flows in **:** CHANNEL **b :** a setting in or inflowing (as of a tide) **2 :** something that is inset: as **a :** INSERT a; *esp* **:** one or more separate leaves inserted in a book usu. before binding **b :** a small but not necessarily small-scale graphic representation (as a map or illustration) set within the compass of a larger one **c :** a piece of cloth set into a garment (as for decoration) ⟨a satin skirt with ~s of ruffled chiffon⟩ **d :** a part or section of a utensil that fits into an outer part ⟨the ~ of a double boiler⟩ **e** [intended as trans. of G *einsprengling*] **:** PHENOCRYST
**²inset** \", ən'=\ *vt* **inset** *or* **insetted; inset** *or* **insetted; insetting; insets** [²*in-* + *set* (v.)] **1 :** to set in **:** place in as an insert ⟨~ an embroidered panel⟩ **2 :** to provide with an insert ⟨~ a belt with rhinestones⟩
**in·set·ter** \"+ə(r)\ *n* **:** one that puts in insets (as in a book)
**in·severable** \(')in, ən+\ *adj* [¹*in-* + *severable*] **:** incapable of being severed **:** INDIVISIBLE **:** impossible to separate — **in·sev·er·ably** \-blē\ *adv*
**in·sheathe** *also* **in·sheath** \ən+\ *var of* ENSHEATHE
**inshining** \(')in,=, ən'=\ *n* -s [⁴*in* + *shining*, gerund of *shine*] **:** ILLUMINATION ⟨when the soul feels the divine ~ —H.W. Beecher⟩
**¹inship** *vt* [²*in-* + *ship*] *obs* **:** EMBARK
**²inship** \(')in¦=, ən'=\ *adv* [fr. the phrase *in ship*] **:** on shipboard
**inshipment** \'in,==\ *n* [⁴*in* + *shipment*] **:** IMPORT — usu. used in pl. ⟨~s dropped 4 percent . . . but 8 percent more chicks hatched locally —J.M.Gwin⟩
**inshoot** \'in,=\ *n* [⁴*in* + *shoot*] **:** a pitched baseball that breaks toward a right-handed batter
**¹inshore** *vt* [²*in-* + *shore* (n.)] *obs* **:** to put on or bring to shore
**²inshore** \(')in¦=, ən'=\ *adj* [fr. the phrase *in shore*] **:** situated or carried on near shore **:** moving toward shore ⟨~ fishing⟩ ⟨an ~ wind⟩
**³inshore** \"\ *adv* [fr. the phrase *in shore*] **:** to or toward shore **:** near shore ⟨drifted ~ during the night⟩
**inshore current** *n* **:** an ocean current that flows in or to landward of the zone of breaking waves
**in·shrine** \ən+\ *archaic var of* ENSHRINE
**¹inside** \(')in¦=, ən'=\ *n* [⁴*in* + *side*] **1 :** an inner side or surface: as **a :** the right side of a sword in fencing **b :** the part of a footpath or sidewalk furthest from an adjoining roadway **c :** the concave aspect of a curve **d :** the side of home plate nearer the batter in baseball **2 :** an interior or internal portion or content **:** the part within: as **a :** inward nature, mind, thoughts, or feeling **b :** the inner parts of the body; *usu* **:** VISCERA, ENTRAILS — usu. used in pl. **c :** an inside passenger or seat (as in a stagecoach) **3 :** the middle or principal part of a division of time ⟨the ~ of a week⟩ **4 insides** *pl* **:** the 18 first-quality quires between the outside quires of a ream of writing or drawing paper; *broadly* **:** reams of which all quires or sheets are of first quality — compare OUTSIDE **5 a :** a situation in which information not generally available may be obtained **:** a position of trust and confidence ⟨he was on the ~ in all those deals⟩ ⟨only someone on the ~ could have told⟩ **b** *slang* **:** information not generally available **:** confidential information ⟨has the ~ on what happened at the convention⟩ **6** *or* **inside forward a :** INSIDE LEFT **b :** INSIDE RIGHT
**²inside** \"\ *adj* **1 a :** of, relating to, or being on the inside ⟨an ~ wall⟩ ⟨~ views⟩ **b :** included or enclosed in something ⟨the ~ furnishings⟩ **c :** used inside ⟨~ clothing⟩ **d :** measured from within usu. so as to include the cavity but not the substance ⟨~ diameter⟩ **2 :** employed or working indoors ⟨kept both an ~ man and a gardener⟩ **3 a :** relating or known to a select group **:** coming from an assuredly informed source ⟨~ information⟩ **b :** placed in an organization as an undercover representative of an actually or potentially antagonistic interest ⟨party ~ men in the unions⟩ **4** *of a union* **:** representing the employees of a single employer **syn** see INNER
**³inside** \"\ *prep* **1 a :** within the boundaries of **:** in the interior of ⟨waited ~ the church⟩ ⟨pain originating ~ the muscle⟩ **b :** on the inner side of ⟨place the dot ~ the curve⟩ **2 :** before the end of ⟨answered ~ an hour⟩
**⁴inside** \"\ *adv* **:** on or in the inside **:** INTERNALLY, WITHIN ⟨a house that was spotlessly clean both ~ and outside⟩ ⟨stayed ~ during the storm⟩
**inside and out** *adv* **:** INSIDE OUT
**inside attack** *n* **:** a division of a lacrosse team consisting of the inside home, the outside home, and the first attack — compare INSIDE DEFENSE
**inside ball** *n* **:** baseball play characterized by skillful use of strategy and fine points of technique
**inside caliper** *n* **:** a caliper for measuring dimensions of a cavity (as the inner diameter of an engine cylinder)
**inside clinch** *n* **:** a clinch knot in which the seized end of the line is inside the noose — compare OUTSIDE CLINCH
**inside defense** *n* **:** a division of a lacrosse team consisting of point, cover point, and the first defense — compare INSIDE ATTACK
**inside finish** *n* **:** the final work in a building necessary for its completion (as the adding of doors, paneled jambs, baseboards) — compare OUTSIDE FINISH
**inside form** *n* **:** INNER FORM
**inside half** *n* **:** SCRUM HALF
**inside home** *n* **:** a lacrosse player whose position is on the right side of the opponent's goal — called also *in home*
**inside job** *n* **:** an irregular or criminal act perpetrated by or with the connivance of a person occupying a position of trust in respect to the victim of the act ⟨the payroll robbery was an *inside job*⟩; *also* **:** such an act perpetrated by the apparent victim
**inside left** *n* **:** a forward on a soccer team whose position is between the center forward and the outside left
**inside loop** *n* **:** ²LOOP 2 f
**inside lot** *n* **:** INTERIOR LOT
**insident** *adj* [L *insident-, insidens*, pres. part. of *insidēre* to sit in, sit on — more at INSESSION] *obs* **:** residing in **:** INHERENT
**inside of** *prep* **:** WITHIN **:** in the compass or on the inner side of ⟨*inside of* the city walls⟩ **:** in no more than ⟨back *inside of* an hour⟩
**inside out** *adv* **1 :** in such a manner that the inner surface becomes the outer ⟨peeled her gloves off *inside out*⟩ **2 :** THOROUGHLY ⟨knows his material *inside out*⟩
**inside-out flower** *n* **:** any of several western No. American herbs constituting the genus *Epimedium* of the family Berberidaceae and distinguished by sharply reflexed sepals
**inside quire** *n* **:** a quire of paper lying between the outside quires
**in·sid·er** \(')in'sīdə(r), ən-\ *n* -s [¹*inside* + *-er*] **:** a person recognized or accepted as a member of some group, category, or organization: as **a :** a person having access to confidential information because of his position **b :** an officer or a director of a company or a beneficial owner of 10 percent or more of an equity security registered on an exchange ⟨laws regulating the manipulation of a company's securities by ~s⟩
**inside right** *n* **:** a forward on a soccer team whose position is between the center forward and the outside right
**inside straight** *n* **:** four cards of a poker hand (as 9,8,6,5) that will make a straight if a card of one particular rank is added
**inside stuff** *n, slang* **:** confidential information
**inside track** *n* **1 :** the inner side of a curved racecourse **2 :** a position of advantage in competition ⟨the candidate who had the *inside track*⟩
**inside turn** *n* **:** a normal aircraft turn in which the top surfaces of the aircraft incline toward the inside of the curve
**insidiate** *vb* -ED/-ING/-S [L *insidiatus*, past part. of *insidiari*, fr. *insidiae* ambush, fr. *insidēre* to sit in — more at INSESSION] *vt, obs* **:** to plot or scheme against **:** lie in wait for **~** *vi, obs* **:** to lie in ambush **:** PLOT, SCHEME — **insidiation** *n* -s *obs* — **insidiator** *n* -s *obs*
**in·sid·i·ous** \ən'sidēəs *sometimes* -ijəs\ *adj* [L *insidiosus* insidious, cunning, deceitful, fr. *insidiae* ambush + *-osus* -ous] **1 a :** watching for an opportunity to ensnare ⟨an ~ tempter⟩ **:** lying in wait **:** intended to entrap or trick ⟨an ~ plot⟩ **b :** enticing and deleterious ⟨these ~ drugs⟩ **2 a :** acting by imperceptible degrees **:** having a gradual, cumulative, and usu. hidden effect **:** SUBTLE ⟨~ charm⟩ ⟨the ~ pressures of modern life⟩ ⟨an ~ drink⟩ **b** *of a disease* **:** developing so gradually as to be well established before becoming apparent **syn** see SLY
**in·sid·i·ous·ly** *adv* **:** in an insidious manner **:** GRADUALLY, SLYLY, SECRETIVELY
**in·sid·i·ous·ness** *n* -ES **:** the quality or state of being insidious
**¹insight** \'in,=\ *n* [ME *insight, insiht*, fr. *in* + *sight, siht* sight — more at SIGHT] **1 :** the power or act of seeing into a situation or into oneself **:** DISCERNMENT, PENETRATION, UNDERSTANDING **2 :** the act or fact of apprehending the inner nature of things or of seeing intuitively **:** clear and immediate understanding ⟨an extraordinary ~ into the complexity of women's emotions —*Current Biog.*⟩ **3** *obs* **:** a physical view **:** INSPECTION, LOOK **4 a :** recognition that one is ill esp. in mind (as in many neuroses but usu. not in typical insanities) **b :** comprehension or awareness of the nature of such illness or of the unconscious forces contributing to the emotional conflict involved **5 :** immediate and clear learning that takes place without recourse to overt trial-and-error behavior
**²insight** \"\ *n* -s [ME *insicht*] *archaic Scot* **:** PERSONAL PROPERTY; *esp* **:** household goods
**in·sight·ed** \'=,sīd·əd\ *adj* [¹*insight* + *-ed*] **:** endowed with insight
**in·sight·ful** \'=,sītfəl\ *adj* [¹*insight* + *-ful*] **:** exhibiting or characterized by insight ⟨the chapter . . . is ~ and suggestive of new perspectives —R.C.Angell⟩ — **in·sight·ful·ly** \-fəlē\ *adv*
**in·sig·nia** \ən'signēə\ *also* **insig·ne** \-(,)nē\ *n, pl* **insignia** *or*

Insignia of the United States Army: *1* General Staff; *2* Adjutant General's Corps; *3* Inspector General; *4* Judge Advocate General's Corps; *5* Quartermaster Corps; *6* Finance Corps; *7* Corps of Engineers; *8* Ordnance Corps; *9* Signal Corps; *10* National Guard Bureau; *11* Military Intelligence Reserve; *12* Infantry; *13* Armor; *14* Artillery; *15* Chemical Corps; *16* Transportation Corps; *17* Dental Corps; *18* Veterinary Corps; *19* Army Security Reserve; *20* Army Nurse Corps; *21* Medical Corps; *22* United States Military Academy; *23* Chaplain, Christian faith; *24* Chaplain, Jewish faith; *25* Medical Service Corps; *26* Aide to a Major General; *27* Warrant Officer; *28* Military Police Corps; *29* Civilian Affairs and Military Government

**insignias** [*insignia* fr. L, distinctive marks, badges, signs, pl. of *insigne* distinctive mark, badge, sign, fr. neut. of *insignis* marked, distinguished, fr. *in-* ²in- + *signum* mark, sign — more at SIGN] **1 :** a distinguishing mark of authority, office, or honor **:** BADGE, EMBLEM ⟨the *insignia* of royalty⟩ ⟨a collector of *insignias*⟩ **2 :** a typical and characteristic mark or sign by which something is distinguished ⟨the gay *insigne* of the new fighter squadron⟩ ⟨sports letters were originally *insignia* granted for especial competence in a competitive sport⟩
**in·significance** \¦in+\ *n* [fr. *insignificant*, after E *significant*: *significance*] **:** the quality or state of being insignificant **:** UNIMPORTANCE ⟨the ~ of the sum involved⟩
**in·significancy** \"+\ *n* [¹*in-* + *significancy*] **1 :** INSIGNIFICANCE **2 :** an insignificant thing or person
**¹in·significant** \"+\ *adj* [¹*in-* + *significant*] **:** not significant: as **a :** lacking meaning or import **:** MEANINGLESS ⟨forget this ~ quarrel⟩ **b** *obs* **:** INEFFECTIVE, FUTILE **c :** having no importance **:** UNIMPORTANT ⟨our losses were ~⟩ **d :** lacking weight or position (as from character, social standing, influence) **:** CONTEMPTIBLE ⟨this ~ hanger-on⟩ **e :** of little size or importance **:** SMALL ⟨an ~ town⟩ ⟨hard to believe that this ~ insect could be so deadly⟩ — **in·significantly** \"+\ *adv*
**²insignificant** \"\ *n* **:** something that is insignificant
**insignificative** *adj* [¹*in-* + *significative*] *obs* **:** not significative
**in·sig·nis pine** \ən'signəs-\ *n* [part trans. of NL *Pinus insignis*] *Austral & New Zeal* **:** MONTEREY PINE
**in·simplicity** \¦in+\ *n* [¹*in-* + *simplicity*] **:** lack of simplicity; *also* **:** a thing lacking in simplicity
**in·sincere** \"+\ *adj* [L *insincerus*, fr. *in-* ¹in- + *sincerus* sincere] **:** lacking sincerity or genuineness: as **a** *of a person* **:** not being or expressing what one appears to be or express **:** HYPOCRITICAL ⟨a charming but thoroughly ~ woman whose words could never be taken at face value⟩ **b :** not based on reality, fact, or an honest appraisal ⟨an ~ denial⟩ ⟨the ~ and pity-seeking sigh of a spoilt animal —Arnold Bennett⟩ — **in·sincerely** \"+\ *adv*
**in·sincerity** \"+\ *n* [L *insincerus* insincere + E *-ity*] **1 :** the quality or state of being insincere ⟨the patent ~ of his answer⟩ **2 :** something that is insincere ⟨forgiving her evasions and *insincerities*⟩
**in·sin·u·ant** \ən'sinyəwənt\ *adj* [L *insinuant-, insinuans*, pres. part. of *insinuare* to insinuate] **:** INSINUATING, INSINUATIVE
**in·sin·u·ate** \ən'sinyə,wāt, *usu* -ād·+V\ *vb* -ED/-ING/-S [L *insinuatus*, past part. of *insinuare*, fr. *in-* ²in- + *sinuare* to bend, curve, fr. *sinus* curve, fold — more at SINUS] *vt* **1 a :** to introduce (as an idea or point of view) stealthily, slyly, or artfully **:** convey in a subtle, indirect, or covert way **:** instill imperceptibly ⟨cautiously *insinuating* doubts of his guardian's probity into the mind of the boy⟩ ⟨these fears craftily *insinuated* by enemy propaganda⟩ **b :** to impart or communicate with artful indirect wording or oblique reference and without direct or forthright expression **:** HINT, IMPLY ⟨Newman says of a gentleman that . . . he never . . . ~s evil which he dare not say out —Sir A. T. Quiller-Couch⟩ **2** [ML *insinuatus*, past part. of *insinuare*, fr. L] *Roman & civil law* **:** to register or file for registration (as a will or a gift) **3 :** to introduce (as oneself) by stealthy, smooth, or artful means ⟨*insinuating* himself into the confidence of the villagers⟩ ⟨gently the cat *insinuated* himself into the snug corner between the chairs⟩; *broadly* **:** to introduce gradually or without fuss and turmoil ⟨as time went on saner ideas *insinuated* themselves into the minds of the members⟩ **4** *obs* **:** to draw or attract (as the mind) to something or to a course by artful or indirect means **5 :** to push, work, or introduce slowly, carefully, or by a roundabout way ⟨cautiously *insinuating* herself into the crowd⟩ ⟨~ a car through traffic⟩ **~** *vi* **1** *archaic* **:** to enter gently, slowly, or imperceptibly **:** CREEP, WIND, FLOW **2** *archaic* **:** to ingratiate oneself **:** obtain access subtly **syn** see SUGGEST
**insinuating** *adj* **1 :** tending to gradually cause doubt, distrust, or change of outlook ⟨~ remarks⟩ **2 :** winning favor and confidence by imperceptible degrees ⟨these ~ attentions⟩ **:** INGRATIATING **3** *archaic* **:** entering or penetrating slowly or by a roundabout course — **in·sin·u·at·ing·ly** *adv*
**in·sin·u·a·tion** \ən,sinyə'wāshən\ *n* -s [L *insinuation-, insinuatio*, fr. *insinuatus* (past part.) + *-ion-, -io* -ion] **1 :** the act or process of insinuating: as **a :** stealthy or indirect hinting or suggestion **b** [MF & LL; MF, fr. LL *insinuation-, insinuatio*, fr. L] *Roman & civil law* (1) **:** the copying of an act or legal transaction (as a gift) in a public record (2) **:** the first production of a will for probate **c :** the gaining of favor, affection, or influence by gentle or artful means **:** INGRATIATION **d** *archaic* **:** slow or indirect entry or penetration **2 :** something that is insinuated: as **a :** an utterance intended to hint at or imply something subtly, slyly, or indirectly; *esp* **:** one intended to convey something derogatory ⟨his ~s about the governor's income⟩ **b** *obs* **:** an ingratiating act or speech
**in·sin·u·a·tive** \ən'sinyə,wād·|iv, -wə|, |t|, |ēv *also* |əv\ *adj* [L *insinuatus* (past part.) + E *-ive*] **1 :** tending or intended to insinuate **:** INGRATIATING ⟨a timidly ~ look⟩ **2 :** given to, characterized by, or involving insinuation **:** giving hints **:** INSINUATING ⟨an ~ remark⟩ — **in·sin·u·a·tive·ly** \|əvlē, -li\ *adv*
**in·sin·u·a·tor** \-,wād·ə(r), -ātə-\ *n* -s [LL, warner, fr. L *insinuatus* (past part. of *insinuare* to insinuate) + *-or*] **:** one that insinuates
**in·sin·u·a·to·ry** \-,wə,tōrē, -tȯrē, -ri\ *adj* [*insinuate* + *-ory*] **:** INSINUATIVE
**in·sin·u·en·do** \ən,sinyə'wen(,)dō\ *n* -s [blend of *insinuation* and *innuendo*] **:** INSINUATION 2a
**¹in·sip·id** \ən'sipəd\ *adj* [F & LL; F *insipide*, fr. MF, fr. LL *insipidus*, fr. L *in-* ¹in- + LL *sapidus* well-tasted, savory, wise, prudent — more at SAPID] **1 :** lacking taste or savor to such a degree as to be unpleasing or unappetizing to the palate **:** SAVORLESS, TASTELESS ⟨~ overcooked boiled cabbage⟩ **2 :** lacking in qualities that interest, attract, stimulate, or challenge **:** DULL, UNINTERESTING, STALE, COMMONPLACE ⟨which may give occasion to wit and mirth within that circle, but would seem flat and ~ in any other —Earl of Chesterfield⟩ **3 :** cloyingly sentimental or sweet ⟨manages to be appropriately babyish without becoming ~ —Robert Hatch⟩
**syn** VAPID, FLAT, JEJUNE, INANE, BANAL, WISHY-WASHY: INSIPID indicates a lack of sufficient taste or savor to please, attract, interest, or stimulate; it applies to that which leaves one uninterested or bored ⟨you have so much animation, which is exactly what Miss Andrews wants; for I must confess there is something amazingly *insipid* about her —Jane Austen⟩ ⟨all former delights of turf, mess, hunting field, and gambling-table; all previous loves and courtships . . . were quite *insipid* when compared with the lawful matrimonial pleasures which of late he had enjoyed —W.M.Thackeray⟩ VAPID, often interchangeable with INSIPID, indicates a want of savor, tang, or sparkle likely to please, or liveliness, force, or spirit likely to interest ⟨Sulpicius had a genius for making the most interesting things seem utterly *vapid* and dead —Robert Graves⟩ ⟨his prose is *vapid* and feeble in the essay, and stilted and artificial in the oration —V.L.Parrington⟩ ⟨the *vapid* and silly chatter of ordinary sociability among men and women —J.C.Powys⟩ FLAT is less precisely suggestive of deficiency than the preceding but as strongly condemnatory in indicating want of stimulation, animation, or interest ⟨a thing of frigid conceits worn bare by iteration; of servile borrowings; of artificial sentiment, *flat* as the lees and dregs of wine —J.L.Lowes⟩ ⟨though his men are *flat* his women characters are done with real insight and intuitive understanding —*Times Lit. Supp.*⟩ JEJUNE suggests a meager scantness of substance, a dearth of anything satisfying, nourishing, or strengthening ⟨mere annalists . . . whose work is as colorless as it is *jejune* —J.R.Green⟩ ⟨registration in the universities dwindled as the instruction they offered became increasingly *jejune* and lifeless —S.E.Morison⟩ INANE suggests a vacant emptiness, an utter want of purport, significance, or cogency ⟨the passive, suggestible, mentally monocellular human being whose vast *inane* face is to be met with in all the Broadways and Main Streets of the world, the end product of picture magazines, bad education, mass entertainment, and a vulpine competitive society —Clifton Fadiman⟩ ⟨Blanche's life, begun with who knows what bright hopes and what dreams, might just as well have never been lived. It all seemed useless and *inane* —W.S.Maugham⟩ BANAL indicates complete absence of the freshness that stimulates; it may stress the unrelieved commonplace ⟨the average man, doomed to some *banal* and sordid drudgery all his life long —H.L.Mencken⟩ ⟨the representation of life [in moving pictures] is hollow, stupid, *banal*, childish —J.T.Farrell⟩ WISHY-WASHY may imply weakness through dilution or vacillation ⟨talent is a *wishy-washy* thing unless it is solidly founded on sheer hard work —E.G.Coleman⟩
**²insipid** \"\ *n* -s *archaic* **:** one that is insipid
**in·si·pid·i·ty** \,in(t)sə'pidəd·ē, -ətē, -i\ *n* -ES [F *insipidité*, fr. MF, fr. ML *insipiditas*, fr. LL *insipidus* insipid + L *-itas* -ity] **1 :** the quality or state of being insipid **:** VAPIDITY ⟨the ~ of her thoughts⟩ **2 :** something (as a remark or an idea) that is notably insipid ⟨these *insipidities* of expression⟩
**in·sip·id·ly** *adv* **:** in an insipid manner **:** so as to be insipid ⟨~ expressed thoughts⟩
**in·sip·id·ness** *n* -ES **:** INSIPIDITY
**in·sip·i·ence** \ən'sipēən(t)s\ *n* -s [ME, fr. MF, fr. OF, fr. L *insipientia* folly, fr. *insipient-, insipiens* insipient + *-ia* -y] *archaic* **:** the quality or state of being insipient **:** lack of intelligence
**in·sip·i·ent** \-nt\ *adj* [MF or L; MF, fr. L *insipient-, insipiens*, fr. *in-* ¹in- + *sapient-, sapiens* wise, fr. pres. part. of *sapere* to taste, have taste — more at SAGE] *archaic* **:** lacking wisdom **:** STUPID, FOOLISH
**in·sist** \ən'sist\ *vb* -ED/-ING/-S [MF or L; MF *insister*, fr. L *insistere* to stand upon, persist, dwell upon, fr. *in-* ²in- + *sistere* to stand, cause to stand, fr. *stare* to stand — more at STAND, REST — used with *on* or *upon* **2** *archaic* **:** to continue determinedly or

urgently (as in a course of action) : PERSEVERE, PERSIST **3 a** : to take a stand and refuse to give way : hold firmly to something ⟨~*ed* on the accuracy of his account⟩ **b** : to be persistent, urgent, or pressing ⟨~*ed* on going with them⟩ ~ *vt* : to take a firm stand about : persist in a point of view about — used with a clause as object ⟨~*ed* that we come in⟩ ⟨the moderate confederation may ~ that the radicals be ejected from the government⟩ ⟨~ he had done right⟩

**in·sis·tence** *also* **in·sis·tance** \-tən(t)s\ *n* -s [*insist* + -*ence* or -*ance*] **1** : the act or an instance of insisting ⟨his ~ on coming⟩ **2** : the quality or state of being insistent : PERSISTENCE, URGENCY

**in·sis·ten·cy** \-tənsē, -si\ *n* -ES : INSISTENCE

**¹in·sis·tent** \-tənt\ *adj* [L *insistent-, insistens*, pres. part. of *insistere* to insist, stand upon] **1** *archaic* : standing or resting on something **2 a** : insisting or disposed to insist : PERSISTENT, PERSEVERING ⟨~ demands⟩ **b** : compelling attention : obtrusively conspicuous ⟨working in the ~ heat⟩ ⟨~ pounding of waves⟩ ⟨a bold ~ butte⟩ **3** [F *insistant*, pres. part. of *insister* to insist] *of a bird's hind toe* : inserted so far above the base of other toes that only the tip will reach to the ground — opposed to *incumbent* **syn** see PRESSING

**²insistent** \"\ *n* -s : an insistent person

**in·sis·tent·ly** *adv* : in an insistent manner

**in·sist·er** \-tə(r)\ *n* -s : one that insists

**in·sist·ing·ly** *adv* [fr. *insisting* (pres. part. of *insist*) + -*ly*] : with insistence : INSISTENTLY, URGENTLY

**in·sis·tive** \ən'sistiv\ *adj* : tending to insist or urge

**in·si·tion** \in'sishən\ *n* -s [L *insition-, insitio*, fr. *insitus* (past part.) + -*ion-, -io* -ion] **1** *obs* : the act of grafting or a graft **2** : a taking in or adding as if through grafting (as by inoculation)

**in·si·ti·tious** \¦in(t)sə¦tishəs\ *adj* [L *insiticius*, fr. *insitus*, past part. of *inserere* to engraft, fr. *in-* ²in- + *serere* to plant, sow — more at SOW] : constituting an insertion : INTERPOLATED

**in si·tu** \(')in'sī(,)tü, -sē(-, -si(-, -)chü\ *adv* (*or adj*) [L, in position] : in the natural or original position ⟨motion pictures of the heart beating *in situ*⟩ ⟨combines . . . panels with reinforced concrete *in situ* columns —*London Calling*⟩

**in·snare** \ən+\ *archaic var of* ENSNARE

**insoak** \'in,=\ *n* [⁴*in* + *soak* (after *soak in*, v.)] : the taking up of free surface water by unsaturated soil

**in·sobriety** \¦in+\ *n* [¹*in-* + *sobriety*] : lack of sobriety, moderation, or calmness; *esp* : intemperance in drinking

**in·sociability** \(¦)in, ən+\ *n* : the quality or state of being insociable : lack of sociability

**in·sociable** \(')in, ən+\ *adj* [L *insociabilis*, fr. *in-* ¹in- + *sociabilis* sociable] **1** *obs* : incapable of being combined **2** : not sociable : not companionable : UNSOCIABLE, TACITURN — **in·sociably** \"+\ *adv*

**insocial** *adj* [LL *insocialis*, fr. L *in-* ¹in- + *socialis* social] *obs* : UNSOCIABLE — **insocially** *adv*, *obs*

**insofar** \¦=='=\ *adv* : in such measure : to such extent or degree ⟨pledged himself to follow a party line through thick and thin and ~ abandoned his freedom to think —Sidney Hook⟩

**insofar as** *conj* : in such measure as : to such extent or degree as ⟨we will succeed only *insofar as* we are prepared to sacrifice secondary objectives⟩

**insofar that** *conj* : in the measure that : to the extent or degree that ⟨cooperated fully *insofar that* many of their projects were jointly conducted⟩

**insol** *abbr* insoluble

**in·so·late** \'in(t)(,)sō,lāt, -,sə,-\ *vt* -ED/-ING/-S [L *insolatus*, past part. of *insolare*, fr. *in-* ²in- + *sol* sun — more at SOLAR] : to place in the sunlight : expose to the sun's rays (as for curing, drying, ripening)

**in·so·la·tion** \,=(,)='lāshən\ *n* -s [F or L; F, fr. MF, fr. L *insolation-, insolatio*, fr. *insolatus* (past part.) + -*ion-, -io* -ion] **1** : exposure (as of fruits or drugs) to the rays of the sun usu. to induce curing, drying, maturing **2** : SUNSTROKE **3 a** : solar radiation that has been received (as by the earth) **b** : the rate of delivery of all direct solar energy per unit of horizontal surface

**insole** \'=,=\ *n* [⁴*in* + *sole*] **1** : an inside sole of a shoe **2** : a loose thin strip (as of leather or felt) placed inside a shoe for warmth or ease

**in·so·lence** \'in(t)s(ə)lən(t)s\ *n* -s [ME, fr. L *insolentia*, fr. *insolent-, insolens* insolent + -*ia* -y] **1** : the quality or state of being insolent : HAUGHTINESS, IMPUDENCE : gross disrespect ⟨~ is often an expression of insecurity⟩ **2** : an instance of insolent conduct or treatment : INSULT ⟨unwilling to put up with her petty ~*s*⟩

insole 2

**in·so·len·cy** \-lənsē, -si\ *n* -ES **1** : INSOLENCE **2** *obs* : a strange or unusual thing or occurrence

**¹in·so·lent** \-lənt\ *adj* [ME, fr. L *insolent-, insolens*; akin to L *insolescere* to grow haughty and prob. to L *solēre* to be accustomed, *sodalis* comrade — more at ETHICAL] **1 a** : haughty and contemptuous or brutal in behavior or language : OVERBEARING ⟨how ~ of late he is become —Shak.⟩ **b** : lacking usual or proper respect for rank or position : presumptuously disrespectful or familiar toward equals or superiors : provokingly free or pert ⟨~ street-corner loafers⟩ ⟨I will not tolerate an ~ child⟩ **2** : proceeding from or characterized by insolence ⟨heard out his ~ speech⟩ **3 a** *obs* : exceeding due bounds : EXCESSIVE, EXTRAVAGANT **b** : of such scope as to give an effect of contemptuous self-assurance ⟨the modern world, with its quick material successes and its ~ belief in the boundless possibilities of progress —Bertrand Russell⟩ ⟨mastered the violin with ~ ease⟩ **4** *obs* : not customary : NOVEL, STRANGE, UNUSUAL **syn** see PROUD

**²insolent** \"\ *n* -s : one who is insolent

**in·so·lent·ly** *adv* : in an insolent manner : to an insolent degree

**in·so·lent·ness** *n* -ES : the quality or state of being insolent

**in·solidity** \¦in+\ *n* [¹*in-* + *solidity*] : lack of solidity : weak flimsy form or quality

**in so·li·do** \(')in'sälə,dō\ *also* **in so·li·dum** \-,dəm\ *adv* (*or adj*) [L] : for the whole : involving all — used in civil law of a solidary obligation or contract ⟨an *in solido* obligation⟩ ⟨action may be brought against both the insured and the insurer, jointly and *in solido*⟩; compare JOINT AND SEVERAL

**in·solubility** \(¦)in, ən+\ *n* [LL *insolubilitas*, fr. L *insolubilis* insoluble + -*itas* -ity] : the quality or state of being insoluble: as **a** : INDISSOLUBILITY **b** (1) : INEXPLICABILITY (2) : something inexplicable

**in·solubilization** \"+\ *n* : the process of insolubilizing

**in·solubilize** \(')in, ən+\ *vt* [L *insolubilis* + E -*ize*] : to render insoluble

**¹in·soluble** \(')in, ən+\ *adj* [alter. (influenced by L *insolubilis*) of ME *insolible*, fr. L *insolubilis*, fr. *in-* ¹in- + *solvere* to free, dissolve + -*bilis* -able — more at SOLVE] : not soluble: as **a** *archaic* : incapable of being loosened : INDISSOLUBLE **b** : having or admitting of no solution or explanation : UNSOLVABLE ⟨an ~ doubt⟩ **c** *obs*, *of an argument* : UNANSWERABLE, IRREFUTABLE **d** : incapable of being dissolved in a liquid ⟨chalk is ~ in water⟩; *broadly* : soluble only with difficulty or to a slight degree ⟨a very ~ salt, dissolving no more than 1 part in 500,000 of water⟩ — **in·solubleness** \"+\ *n* — **in·solubly** \"+\ *adv*

**²insoluble** \"\ *n* [alter. (influenced by L *insolubilis*, adj.) of ME *insolible*, fr. *insolible*, adj.] **1** : something (as a problem or difficulty) that cannot be solved **2** : an insoluble substance ⟨the ~*s* in a tanning extract⟩

**in·solvability** \¦in, ən+\ *n* : the quality or state of being insolvable

**in·solvable** \(')in, ən+\ *adj* [¹*in-* + *solvable*] : INSOLUBLE; *esp* : incapable of being solved ⟨an apparently ~ problem⟩ — **in·solv·ably** \-blē,-bli\ *adv*

**in·sol·vence** \(')in¦sälvən(t)s, ən's-\ *n* -s *archaic* : INSOLVENCY

**in·sol·ven·cy** \-vənsē, -si\ *n*, *often attrib* [prob. fr. ML *insolventia*, fr. L *in-* ¹in- + *solvent-*, *solvens* (pres. part. of *solvere* to pay, free, dissolve) + -*ia* -y] **1** : the fact or state of being insolvent : inability to pay debts **2** : insufficiency (as of an estate) to discharge all enforceable debts

**insolvency law** *or* **insolvent law** *or* **insolvency statute** *or* **insolvent statute** *n* : a state statute that affords to an insolvent debtor relief from and sometimes full discharge of debts upon his surrender for the benefit of his creditors of all his property not exempt by law and that is suspended when it conflicts with the Federal Bankruptcy Act or covers a field occupied thereby or affects persons or property within the purview of that act

**¹in·sol·vent** \-vənt\ *adj* [¹*in-* + L *solvent-, solvens* (pres. part.)] **1 a** : unable or having ceased to pay debts as they fall due in the usual course of business; *specif* : having liabilities in excess of a reasonable market value of assets held — compare BANKRUPT **b** : insufficient to pay all debts charged against it ⟨an ~ estate⟩ **c** : IMPOVERISHED, DEFICIENT ⟨these morally ~ teachers⟩ ⟨~ beliefs⟩ **2** : relating to or for the relief of insolvents ⟨~ regulations⟩

**²insolvent** \"\ *n* : an insolvent debtor

**in·som·nia** \ən'sämnēə\ *n* -s [L, fr. *insomnis* sleepless (fr. *in-* ¹in- + *somnus* sleep) + -*ia* — more at SOMNOLENT] : prolonged inability to obtain adequate sleep : abnormal wakefulness : SLEEPLESSNESS

**¹in·som·ni·ac** \-ē,ak\ *n* -s [L *insomnia* + E -*ac* (as in *maniac*)] : a person suffering from insomnia

**²insomniac** \"\ *adj* **1** : affected with insomnia ⟨an ~ boy⟩ **2 a** : characteristic of or occurring during a period of sleeplessness ⟨~ distress⟩ ⟨these tumbling ~ ideas⟩ **b** : associated with or tending to cause sleeplessness ⟨humid ~ nights⟩ ⟨the ~ flapping of the canvas —S.N.Behrman⟩

**in·som·ni·ous** \ən'sämnēəs\ *adj* [L *insomniosus*, fr. *insomnia* + -*osus* -ous] : affected with insomnia : SLEEPLESS

**in·somnolence** *or* **in·somnolency** \(')in, ən+\ *n* [¹*in-* + *somnolence* or *somnolency*] : SLEEPLESSNESS, INSOMNIA

**insomuch** \¦=='=\ *adv* [ME *in so muche*, *in so moche* — more at MUCH] : so much : to such a degree : so — usu. used with *that* or *as* ⟨they made no mistakes at all. *Insomuch* that . . . it is impossible to imagine a more successful outcome —Bernard De Voto⟩

**insomuch as** *conj* : INASMUCH AS ⟨*insomuch as* news reports have irretrievably blackened our motives⟩

**in·sonorous** \(¦)in, ən+\ *adj* [¹*in-* + *sonorous*] : lacking resonance

**in·sooth** \ən'=\ *adv* [ME *in soth*, *in soothe* — more at SOOTH (n.)] *archaic* : in truth or reality : TRULY, ACCURATELY, FACTUALLY

**in·sorb** \ən'sȯ(ə)rb\ *vt* -ED/-ING/-S [²*in-* + L *sorbēre* to suck up — more at ABSORB] : to take in : ABSORB

**in·sordid** \(')in, ən+\ *adj* [¹*in-* + *sordid*] : free from sordidness : GENEROUS

**in·sou·ciance** \ən'süsēən(t)s, -üshən-, *F* aⁿsüsyäⁿs\ *n* -s [F, fr. *in-* ¹in- + *soucier* to trouble, disturb (fr. L *sollicitare* to disturb, agitate, move) + F -*ance* — more at SOLICIT] : freedom from concern or care : absence of studied attention : an attitude of indifference or unconcern esp. to the impression created (as by one's work, conduct, or comportment) on others ⟨moved on with a sort of elegant ~⟩ ⟨the utter ~ of this financial policy⟩ ⟨the light ~ of these lyrics⟩

**in·sou·ciant** \-sēənt,-shənt, *F* -syäⁿ\ *adj* [F, fr. *in-* ¹in- + *souciant*, pres. part. of *soucier*] : exhibiting or characterized by insouciance ⟨an ~ manner⟩ ⟨a gay ~ person⟩ — **in·sou·ciant·ly** \-sēəntlē, -shən-, -li\ *adv*

**insoul** *var of* ENSOUL

**insp** *abbr* inspector

**in·span** \(')inz¦pan, ənz'p-, -n¦sp-\ *vb* [Afrik, fr. MD *inspannen*, fr. *in* in (adv.) + *spannen* to stretch, span, hitch up — more at SPAN] *vt*, *chiefly Africa* : to yoke or harness (draft animals) to a vehicle : hitch draft animals to (a vehicle) ~ *vi*, *chiefly Africa* : to inspan animals or a vehicle ⟨*inspanned* as soon as we had eaten⟩

**inspeak** *vt* **inspoke** *or archaic* **inspake**; **inspoken**; **inspeaking**; **inspeaks** [²*in-* + *speak*; prob. trans. of G *einsprechen*] : to instill or infuse by or as if by speaking

**¹inspect** *n* [L *inspectus*, fr .*inspectus*, past part.] *obs* : INSPECTION

**²in·spect** \ənz'pekt, ən'sp-\ *vb* -ED/-ING/-S [partly fr. L *inspectus*, past part. of *inspicere*, fr. *in-* ²in- + -*spicere* (fr. *specere* to look), & partly fr. L *inspectare*, fr. *inspectus* — more at SPY] *vt* **1** : to view closely and critically (as in order to ascertain quality or state, detect errors, or otherwise appraise) : examine with care : SCRUTINIZE ⟨let us ~ your motives⟩ ⟨~*ed* the herd for ticks⟩ **2** : to view and examine officially (as troops or arms) ~ *vi*, *archaic* : to look carefully : make an examination (as into a situation) : SEARCH **syn** see SCRUTINIZE

**in·spect·able** \-təbəl\ *adj* : capable of being inspected or publicly observed

**in·spect·ing·ly** *adv* : so as to inspect : with an effect of inspecting

**in·spec·tion** \-kshən\ *n* -s [ME *inspeccioun*, fr. MF *inspection*, fr. L *inspection-, inspectio*, fr. *inspectus* (past part.) + -*ion-, -io* -ion] **1** : the act or process of inspecting : a strict or close examination: as **a** (1) : the physical examination of the injured part of a person suing for damages for personal injury (2) : the examination of articles of commerce to determine their fitness for transportation or sale **b** : official examination to determine and report on the condition of military or naval personnel and matériel **c** : visual observation of the body in the course of a medical examination — compare PALPATION **d** : an investigation of an applicant for insurance **e** : an examination or a survey of a community, of premises, or of an installation by an authorized person (as to determine compliance with regulations or susceptibility to fire or other hazards) **2** : INSIGHT, PERCEPTION — obs. except in the philosophy of A. N. Whitehead

**in·spec·tion·al** \-shən°l,-shnəl\ *adj* **1** : of or relating to inspection : by means of or involving inspection ⟨~ services⟩ **2** : being or designed to be comprehensible immediately and without study or analysis ⟨an ~ comparison of two languages⟩

**inspection arms** *n* **1** : a position in the manual of the rifle, carbine, and pistol in which the weapon is held with the chamber open for inspection **2** : the command to take this position

**inspection car** *n* : a small motorized vehicle with flanged wheels for inspecting railroad track and roadway

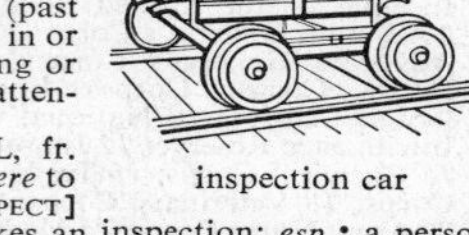

inspection car

**in·spec·tive** \-ktiv\ *adj* [LL *inspectivus*, fr. L *inspectus* (past part.) + -*ivus* -ive] : engaged in or given to inspection : watching or examining closely : visually attentive ⟨an ~ gaze⟩

**in·spec·tor** \-tə(r)\ *n* -s [L, fr. *inspectus* (past part. of *inspicere* to inspect) + -*or* — more at INSPECT] **1** : one that inspects or makes an inspection; *esp* : a person employed to inspect something (as the work of others, goods imported, the state and hazards of buildings) — often used in combination ⟨customs ~⟩ ⟨fire ~⟩; see MINE INSPECTOR **2** : one that oversees or supervises: as **a** : a police officer in charge of a number of precincts and ranking below a superintendent or deputy superintendent **b** : a person appointed to oversee the conduct of an election (as with respect to the provisions of law and propriety)

**in·spec·tor·ate** \-tərət, *usu* -əd·+V\ *n* -s **1** : the office, position, work, or district of an inspector **2** : a body of inspectors

**inspector general** *n*, *pl* **inspectors general** [trans. of F *inspecteur général*] : a person that heads an inspectorate : the supervisor of a body of inspectors or a department or system of inspection (as of an army) ⟨the *inspector general* of agriculture⟩; *also* : an officer of a military corps of inspectors that investigates and reports on organizational matters (as discipline, morale, supply, accounts)

**in·spec·to·ri·al** \¦inz,pek¦tōrēəl, ən-, -n,sp-\ *or* **in·spec·tor·al** \ənz'pekt(ə)rəl, ən'sp-\ *adj* [*inspector* + -*ial* or -*al*] : of, relating to, or involving inspection, an inspector, or an inspector's duties

**in·spec·tor·ship** \ənz'pektə(r),ship, ən'sp-\ *n* : the status or position of an inspector ⟨obtained his ~ at 35⟩

**in·spec·to·scope** \ənz'pektə,skōp, ən'sp-\ *n* [fr. *Inspectoscope*, a trademark] : an x-ray device with fluoroscope designed to detect contraband articles (as on the person or in parcels or baggage)

**in·spec·tress** \-ktrəs\ *n* -ES [*inspector* + -*ess*] : a female inspector; *esp* : a woman who inspects the work of hotel chambermaids and advises the housekeeper of the need for renovation of rooms and replacement of furniture

**in·spec·trix** \-ktriks\ *n* -ES [LL, fem. of L *inspector*] : INSPECTRESS

**inspersion** *n* -s [MF, fr. LL *inspersion-, inspersio*, fr. L *inspersus* (past part. of *inspergere* to sprinkle, fr. *in-* ²in- + -*spergere*, fr. *spargere* to scatter) + -*ion-, -io* -ion — more at SPARK] *obs* : SPRINKLING

**in·spex·i·mus** \ənz'peksəməs, ən'sp-\ *n* -ES [L, we have inspected] : an English charter or letters patent beginning with the Latin word *inspeximus* in which the grantor confirms and recites a former charter

**insphere** *var of* ENSPHERE

**in·spir·able** \ənz'pīrəbəl, ən'sp-\ *adj* [*inspire* + -*able*] **1** : capable of being inspired ⟨while still ~ with a sense of responsibility⟩ **2** : fit for inspiration ⟨barely ~ air⟩

**in·spi·rate** \'inzpə,rāt *sometimes* -(,)pi,- *or* -,pē,- *or chiefly Brit* -,pī,-; 'in(t)(,)sp-\ *vt* -ED/-ING/-S [L *inspiratus*, past part. of *inspirare* to inspire, breathe into] **1** *archaic* : INSPIRE **2** *phonet* : to articulate during inhalation

**in·spi·ra·tion** \,=(,)='rāshən\ *n* -s [ME *inspiracioun*, fr. MF or LL; MF *inspiration*, fr. OF, fr. LL *inspiration-, inspiratio*, fr. L *inspiratus* (past part. of *inspirare* to breathe into, inspire) + -*ion-, -io* -ion] **1** : a divine influence or action upon the lives of certain persons that is believed to qualify them to receive and communicate sacred revelation and is interpreted within Christianity as the direct action of the Holy Spirit **2** [MF or LL; MF, fr. LL *inspiration-, inspiratio*] : the act of breathing in; *specif* : the drawing of air into the lungs — opposed to *expiration* **3 a** : the act or power of moving the intellect or emotions : capacity to inspire ⟨the ~ of this lovely scene⟩ **b** : the act of suggesting or influencing opinions or information esp. on a public matter ⟨the ~ of this rumor was traced to a source near the governor⟩ **4 a** : the quality or state of being inspired ⟨an artist whose ~ came from many sources⟩ ⟨found his ~ weakening⟩ **b** : something that is inspired ⟨had a new ~ as he waited⟩ ⟨a scheme that was a pure ~⟩ **5** : someone or something that inspires : an inspiring agent or influence

**in·spi·ra·tion·al** \¦=='rāshən°l, -shnəl\ *adj* **1** : produced by or moved by inspiration ⟨an ~ speaker⟩ **2** : of or relating to inspiration ⟨the ~ element in Scripture⟩ **3** : communicating inspiration ⟨~ talks⟩ — **in·spi·ra·tion·al·ly** \-°l|ē, -əl|, |i\ *adv*

**in·spi·ra·tion·ist** \,=(,)='rāsh(ə)nəst\ *n* -s : one who holds a theory of or belief in inspiration esp. of Scripture

**in·spira·tive** \ənz'pīrəd·iv, ən'sp-; 'inzpə,rād·iv, 'in(t)sp-\ *adj* [L *inspiratus* (past part.) + E -*ive*] : tending to inspire : INSPIRING

**in·spi·ra·tor** \'inzpə,rād·ə(r), 'in(t)sp-\ *n* -s [LL, fr. L *inspiratus* (past part. of *inspirare* to inspire) + -*or*] **1** : INSPIRER **2** : one that inhales or draws in something: as **a** : INJECTOR **b** : RESPIRATOR

**in·spi·ra·to·ry** \ənz'pīrə,tōrē, ən'sp-, -tōr-, -ri\ *adj* [L *inspiratus* (past part.) + E -*ory*] : relating to, aiding, used for, or associated with inspiration ⟨~ muscles⟩ ⟨the ~ whoop of whooping cough⟩

**in·spire** \ənz'pī(ə)r, ən'sp-, -īə\ *vb* -ED/-ING/-S [ME *inspiren*, *enspiren*, fr. MF & L; MF *inspirer*, *enspirer*, fr. OF, fr. L *inspirare*, fr. *in-* ²in- + *spirare* to breathe — more at SPIRIT] *vt* **1 a** *archaic* : to breathe or blow into or upon **b** *archaic* : to infuse (as life) by breathing ⟨*inspired* into him an active soul —Wisd Sol 15:11⟩ **c** *obs* : to breathe or blow (as air or vapor) into or upon something **2** : to draw in by breathing : breathe in : INHALE ⟨*inspiring* the crisp fall air⟩ ⟨the baby will ~ the mucus down into its lungs —*Fire Manual* (*Mass.*)⟩ ⟨be accomplished by increasing the oxygen percentage in the *inspired* air —H.G.Armstrong⟩ — distinguished from *expire* **3 a** : to influence, move, or guide (as to speech or action) through divine or supernatural agency or power ⟨the gods were believed to ~ the oracles⟩ ⟨spoke like a prophet *inspired* from above⟩ **b** : to have an animating, enlivening, or exalting effect upon esp. in a degree or with a result suggestive of the workings of some extraordinary power or influence ⟨had been *inspired* by his mother⟩ ⟨our ability to ~ the plodder —Ellie Tucker⟩ ⟨Milton and Shakespeare ~ the active life of England . . . through exceptional individuals —W.B.Yeats⟩ ⟨books that have *inspired* countless generations⟩ — often used with *with*; *specif* : to stimulate to creative activity in an art **c** : ENCOURAGE, IMPEL, MOTIVATE — usu. used with *to* ⟨*inspired* them to greater efforts⟩ ⟨a success which *inspired* him to broaden his activities⟩ **d** : AFFECT — usu. used with *with* ⟨experiences that *inspired* him with a yearning for education⟩ ⟨poverty that ~*s* the beholder with pity and disgust⟩ **4 a** : to communicate or impart (as an utterance) to an agent through divine or supernatural power ⟨spoke in words *inspired* by God⟩ **b** : to infuse or introduce into the mind or communicate to the spirit ⟨a steadfastness that *inspired* confidence in his followers⟩ ⟨conduct that ~*s* nothing but disgust⟩ : AROUSE, PROVOKE **5 a** : to bring about : OCCASION, PRODUCE ⟨events that *inspired* a new fashion⟩ ⟨studies that *inspired* several inventions⟩ ⟨hoping that improvement in business would ~ a tax cut⟩ ⟨the attacks *inspired* the passing of stringent food and drug regulations —E.S.Turner⟩ **b** : INCITE, FOMENT ⟨communist-*inspired* riots⟩ **6** : to cause to be said or written by influence and without acknowledgment of actual source or authorship ⟨a rumor that had been *inspired* by interested parties⟩ ~ *vi* **1** : to impart inspiration **2** *obs* : BREATHE, BLOW **3** : to draw in breath : inhale air into the lungs ⟨*inspired* deeply from a small bottle he had taken from his pocket —E.C.Bentley⟩

**inspired** *adj* [ME *enspired*, fr. past part. of *enspiren* to inspire] **1 a** : moved by or as if by a divine or supernatural influence : affected by divine inspiration ⟨~ prophets⟩ **b** : communicated by divine or supernatural inspiration : having divine authority ⟨the ~ books of the Bible⟩ **2** : breathed in : INHALED **3 a** : suggested by someone in power or in a position to know ⟨~ views⟩ **b** : having received or publishing authoritative views or information ⟨an ~ newspaper⟩ **4** : outstanding or brilliant in a way or to a degree suggestive of divine or supernatural inspiration ⟨an ~ mechanic⟩ ⟨an ~ performance of a concerto⟩ ⟨an ~ answer to an awkward question⟩ — **in·spired·ly** \-īrədlē, -ī(ə)rd-\ *adv*

**in·spir·er** \-īrə(r)\ *n* -s [alter. (influenced by -*er*) of ME *inspirour*, fr. *inspiren* to inspire + -*our* -or] : one that inspires

**inspiring** *adj* : that inspires or tends to inspire ⟨~ thoughts⟩ ⟨the music was ~⟩ — **in·spir·ing·ly** *adv*

**in·spirit** \ənz'p-, ən'sp-\ *also* **en·spirit** \", en-\ *vt* -ED/-ING/-S [²*in-* or ¹*en-* + *spirit* (n.)] **1** : to infuse spirit into : fill with courage, determination, hope, vigor, or exaltation : ANIMATE, HEARTEN ⟨unconquerable jests have ~*ed* men's hearts in long periods of disaster —Agnes Repplier⟩ **2** : to cause to be possessed by a spirit **syn** see ENCOURAGE

**in·spir·it·er** \"ə(r)\ *n* -s : one that inspirits

**inspiriting** *adj* : tending or able to inspirit ⟨an ~ letter⟩ — **in·spir·it·ing·ly** *adv*

**in·spi·rom·e·ter** \,inzpə'rämad·ə(r), ,inz,pī-', ,in(t)(,)sp-\ *n* [*inspire* + -*o-* + -*meter*] : an apparatus for measuring air inspired in breathing

**¹in·spis·sate** \(')inz¦pisāt, ənz'p-, -i,sāt, 'inzpə,sāt, -n(t)(¦)sp-\ *or* **in·spis·sat·ed** \-ād·əd\ *adj* [*inspissate* fr. LL *inspissatus* (past part.); *inspissated* fr. past part. of ²*inspissate*] : thickened in consistency; *broadly* : made thick, heavy, or intense ⟨shed a flood of *inspissated* darkness on a cloud of confusing uncertainties —G.B.Barbour⟩ ⟨*inspissated* class-consciousness —Vincent Sheean⟩

**²in·spis·sate** \ənz'pi,sāt, 'inzpə,-, -n(t)(')sp-\ *vb* -ED/-ING/-S [LL *inspissatus*, past part. of *inspissare*, fr. L *in-* ²in- + *spissare* to thicken, fr. *spissus* thick; akin to Gk *aspis* shield — more at ASPID-] *vt* : to bring to a heavier consistency : CONDENSE ⟨*inspissating* the serum in the Petri dishes⟩; *broadly* : to make thick, heavy, or intense ⟨parties of school children and factory girls *inspissating* the gloom of the museum atmosphere —Clive Bell⟩ ~ *vi* : to reach or assume a heavier consistency ⟨sap *inspissating* over a fire⟩ — **in·spis·sa·tor** \-ād·ə(r)\ *n* -s

**in·spis·sa·tion** \,inzpə'sāshən, -(,)pi-, ,in(t)(,)sp-\ *n* -s [F or ML; F, fr. MF, fr. ML *inspissation-, inspissatio*, fr. LL *inspissatus* (past part.) + L -*ion-, -io* -ion] : the act or process of inspissating or the state of being inspissated

**in spite of** *prep* [ME] : without being blocked or prevented by the opposing force of : regardless of the adverse effect of : DESPITE, NOTWITHSTANDING ⟨went *in spite of* the rain⟩ ⟨a handsome man *in spite of* his baldness⟩ ⟨plunged ahead *in spite of* all efforts to stop him⟩

**inspoke** *past of* INSPEAK

**inspoken** *past part of* INSPEAK

**inst** *abbr* 1 installment 2 instant; instantaneous 3 institute; institution 4 instruction; instructor 5 instrument; instrumental

**in·stability** \ˌinztəˈ⸗⸗⸗, ˌin(t)stə-\ *n* [ME *instabilitee*, fr. MF or L; MF *instabilité*, fr. L *instabilitas*, fr. *instabilis* + *-itas* -ity] **:** the quality or state of being unstable: as **a :** lack of physical firmness **:** INSECURITY ⟨the ~ of a building⟩ **b :** lack of determination or uniformity ⟨economic ~⟩ **:** INCONSTANCY ⟨~ of temper⟩ ⟨increasing ~ of cherished institutions⟩; *also* **:** tendency to react violently or explosively ⟨emotional ~⟩ ⟨the extreme ~ of certain chemicals⟩ **c :** an unstable state of the atmosphere that results when the vertical distribution of temperature or moisture is such that an air particle when set in motion will tend to move at increasing speed either upward or downward from its previous position

**in·stable** \(ˈ)inzˈtābəl, -nˈst-\ *adj* [MF or L; MF, fr. L *instabilis*, fr. *in-* ¹in- + *stabilis* firm, stable — more at STABLE] **:** UNSTABLE

**in·stall** *also* **in·stal** \ənˈztȯl, ənˈst-\ *vt* **installed; installed; installing; installs** *also* **instals** [MF *installer*, *instaler*, fr. ML *installare*, fr. L *in-* ²in- + ML *stallum*, *stallus* stall, fr. OHG *stal* place, stall — more at STALL] **1 a :** to place in possession of an office or dignity by seating in a stall or official seat **b :** to place in an office, rank, or order **:** INDUCT ⟨~*ed* the new college president⟩ **2 :** to introduce and establish (oneself or another) in an indicated place, condition, or status ⟨~*ing* himself in the big chair before the fire⟩ ⟨~*ed* his sister as secretary⟩ **3 :** to set up for use or service ⟨the electrician ~*ed* the new fixtures⟩ ⟨had gas heating ~*ed*⟩

**in·stal·lant** \-lənt\ *n* -s [ML *installant-*, *installans*, pres. part of *installare* to install] **:** one that formally installs another to office

**in·stal·la·tion** \ˌinztəˈlāshən, ˌin(t)stə-\ *n* -s [F or ML; F, fr. MF, fr. ML *installation-*, *installatio*, fr. *installatus* (past part. of *installare*) + L *-ion-*, *-io* -ion] **1 :** an act of installing or the state of being installed: as **a :** the giving possession of an office, rank, or order with the usual rites or ceremonies **b :** ESTABLISHMENT **c :** the setting up or placing in position for service or use **2 a :** something that is installed for use ⟨admired the new plumbing ~⟩ **b installations** *pl* **:** APPOINTMENTS, FURNISHINGS, EQUIPMENT ⟨the ~*s* were of excellent quality and in very good taste⟩ **3 :** land and improvements installed thereon devoted to military purposes ⟨forts, training camps, and other army ~*s*⟩

**in·stall·er** \ənˈztȯlə(r), ənˈst-\ *n* -s **:** one that installs ⟨repairmen and ~*s* of new equipment⟩

**installing officer** *n* **:** a person that supervises or conducts a formal installing of an officer of an organization

**¹in·stall·ment** *or* **in·stal·ment** \-lmənt\ *n* -s [*install* or *instal* + *-ment*] **1 :** an act of installing or the state of being installed **2** *obs* **:** the seat or place in which one is installed

**²installment** *also* **instalment** \"\ *n* -s [alter. of earlier *estallment*, *estalment* arrangement for payment by installments, prob. fr. MF *estaler* to stop, place, fix (fr. OF, fr. *estal* stop, place, position, fr. OHG *stal* place, stall) + E *-ment* — more at STALL] **1 a :** one of the portions into which a sum of money or a debt is divided for payment at set and usu. regular intervals ⟨the balance may be paid in three equal quarterly ~*s*⟩ **b :** a payment that is part of a sum owed ⟨surprised to get even an ~ on the money he had loaned⟩ **2 a :** one of several parts (as of a publication) presented at intervals **:** FASCICLE **b :** one portion of a story published serially (as in a magazine)

**³installment** *also* **instalment** \"\ *adj* **:** of, relating to, based on, or involving periodic payments of a fixed sum or of a predetermined percentage of a total ⟨~ buying⟩ ⟨~ credit⟩ ⟨~ loan⟩ ⟨an ~ account⟩

**installment mortgage** *n* **:** a mortgage in which the sum loaned is to be repaid in installments over a period of time

**installment plan** *n* **:** a plan that involves payment by installments

**installment sales insurance** *n* **:** insurance that covers the seller's interest in merchandise which is sold on installment terms

**installment selling** *n* **:** the selling of consumer goods on credit under conditional sales contracts that provide for regular periodic payments after an initial down payment

**¹in·stance** \ˈinztən(t)s, ˈin(t)stə-, ˈinsən-\ *n* -s [ME *instaunce*, fr. MF *instance* act of urging, motive, instant, fr. L *instantia* presence, vehemence in speech, urgency, fr. *instant-*, *instans* (pres. part.) + *-ia* -y — more at INSTANT] **1 a** *archaic* **:** urgent or earnest solicitation **:** urgency or exercise of pressure in either petition or action **b :** INSTIGATION, SUGGESTION, REQUEST ⟨work undertaken at the ~ of the householder⟩ **c** *obs* **:** something that urges **:** an impelling cause or motive **2** [ML *instantia*, trans. of Gk *enstasis*] **a** *archaic* **:** a case or example brought forward in disproof or rebuttal of a generalization **:** EXCEPTION **b :** something that is available or is offered as an illustrative case **:** something cited in proof or as an example ⟨an ~ of true heroism⟩ ⟨carefully documenting each ~ of the use of this diphthong⟩ **c** *obs* **:** TOKEN, SIGN, SYMPTOM **d** *obs* **:** DETAIL, CIRCUMSTANCE **3** [F or LL; F, fr. LL *instantia*, fr. L] **a :** the institution and prosecution of a lawsuit **:** a legal proceeding or process **:** SUIT **b** (1) **:** a demand set forth in a civil law proceeding (2) **:** a specific case referred to as an example (3) **:** a case in an ecclesiastical court that is brought at the request of a party and not upon official request **4 a :** a step, stage, or situation viewed as part of a process or series of events **:** an occasion or period defined by certain events ⟨a well-known writer who prefers, in this ~, to remain anonymous —*Times Lit. Supp.*⟩ ⟨appointments will be made for a three-year period in the first ~⟩ **b :** SUBSTITUTION INSTANCE

**syn** CASE, ILLUSTRATION, EXAMPLE, SAMPLE, SPECIMEN: INSTANCE and CASE are less specific in meaning and suggestion than the others. The former may be used in reference to any particular person, thing, or situation which may be given to illustrate or explain ⟨the *instance* may be rejected, but the principle abides —B.N.Cardozo⟩ ⟨wanted to work out the problem on a definite *instance* —A.L.Guérard⟩ CASE is now very general in meaning and poor in connotative power; it is used to designate a situation or occurrence showing characteristics to be grouped together and viewed as a configuration or pattern ⟨the *case* of payments made under the head of profits to entrepreneurs, financiers, speculators, and middlemen in various markets —J.A.Hobson⟩ ⟨usually isolated *cases* of deaf and dumb, feebleminded, or otherwise unfortunate children —R.W.Murray⟩ ILLUSTRATION is likely to suggest an instance adduced for the sake of clarifying or demonstrating ⟨the resolution of Washington and his men at Valley Forge is an *illustration* of bravery⟩ EXAMPLE suggests a single item or incident taken as typical or representative ⟨perhaps the best of many American *examples* of the creative artist and thinker . . . in a country and an era dominantly materialistic —H.S.Canby⟩ SAMPLE may indicate a part or a unit of a whole taken more or less at random but still presumed to be typical or representative in showing a general nature, character, or quality ⟨so many happy youths . . . so many divers *samples* from the growth of life's sweet season —William Wordsworth⟩ ⟨the barest *sample* of the riches which the gleaner may gather —B.N.Cardozo⟩ SPECIMEN is close to SAMPLE in its meaning but may suggest scientific or otherwise close analysis ⟨made it my business to examine some *specimens* of the writing —Charles Dickens⟩ SPECIMEN may indicate either the typical or representative example or the merely existent instance ⟨there were a few boomtowns in the Middle West, but the finest *specimens* began to be seen only with the discoveries of gold and silver in the Far West —A.F.Harlow⟩ — **for instance** \fəˈ(r)in- *sometimes* ˈfrin-\ *adv* **:** as an example

**²instance** \"\ *vb* -ED/-ING/-S *vt* **1** *obs* **:** URGE, IMPORTUNE **2 :** to illustrate or demonstrate by an instance ⟨his meaning is well *instanced* in the passage quoted⟩ **3 :** to mention as a case or example **:** CITE ⟨we might ~ the increase in delinquency⟩ ~ *vi* **:** to mention an instance **syn** see MENTION

**instance court** *n* **:** a branch of a court of admiralty that has jurisdiction over all maritime contracts and torts except prize cases

**in·stan·cy** \-ənsē, -si\ *n* -ES [L *instantia*] **1 :** URGENCY, INSISTENCE ⟨continued to press his claim with some ~⟩ ⟨the vivid ~ of an involuntary cry —C.E.Montague⟩ **2 :** nearness of approach **:** IMMINENCE ⟨the ~ of peril —*Yale Rev.*⟩ **3 :** immediateness of occurrence or action **:** INSTANTANEOUSNESS ⟨the ~ of their response⟩ ⟨the *instancies* of aviation and television —Mary Madeleva⟩

**¹in·stant** \ˈinztənt, ˈin(t)stə-\ *n* -s [ME, prob. fr. MF, fr. *instant*, adj.] **1 a :** an infinitesimal space of time **:** a point of time ⟨came not an ~ too soon⟩; *esp* **:** a point without temporal duration separating two states each with temporal duration ⟨at the ~ of death⟩ **b :** a point of time present or regarded as present in respect to a particular context **:** MOMENT ⟨the ~ we met⟩ ⟨come here this ~⟩ ⟨the ~ she opened her eyes⟩ **2 :** the present or current month

**²instant** \"\ *adj* [ME, fr. MF or L; MF, fr. L *instant-*, *instans*, fr. pres. part. of *instare* to stand upon, press upon, urge, fr. *in-* ²in- + *stare* to stand — more at STAND] **1 :** INSISTENT, IMPORTUNATE, PRESSING, URGENT ⟨~ in argument⟩ **2 a :** PRESENT, CURRENT ⟨the ~ case being tried⟩ **b :** of or occurring in the present month — abbr. *inst.* ⟨received your letter of the 10th *inst.*⟩; compare PROXIMO, ULTIMO **3 :** closely pressing in respect to time ⟨running an ~ risk of suffocating⟩ **4 :** IMMEDIATE, DIRECT ⟨the ~ dependence of form upon soul —R.W.Emerson⟩ **5 a :** premixed or precooked for easy final preparation ⟨~ cake mix⟩ ⟨~ mashed potatoes⟩ **b :** immediately soluble in water ⟨~ coffee⟩ **syn** see PRESSING

**³instant** \"\ *adv* **:** at once **:** INSTANTLY

**in·stan·ta·ne·i·ty** \ˌinzˌtantᵊnˈēəd-ē, ənz-, -antəˈnē-, ˌinztəntəˈnē-, -n(ˌ)st-\ *n* -ES [*instantaneous* + *-ity*] **:** the quality or state of being instantaneous

**in·stan·ta·neous** \ˌinztənˈtānēəs, ˌin(t)stə-, -ānyəs\ *adj* [ML *instantaneus*, fr. L *instant-*, *instans* (pres. part.) + *-aneus* (as in *subterraneus* subterranean)] **1 :** done, occurring, or acting without any perceptible duration of time ⟨~ death⟩ ⟨~ heaters⟩ **2 a :** done without any delay being introduced purposely ⟨~ action⟩ **b** *of a sound recording* **:** capable of being used as soon as recorded **3 :** occurring or present at a particular instant ⟨~ value⟩ ⟨~ velocity⟩ ⟨~ voltage⟩ — **in·stan·ta·ne·ous·ly** *adv* — **in·stan·ta·ne·ous·ness** *n* -ES

**instantaneous exposure** *n* **:** exposure of photographic materials for a short time by an automatic device — compare TIME EXPOSURE

**in·stan·ter** \ənzˈtantə(r), ənˈsta-\ *adv* [ML, fr. L, earnestly, vehemently, fr. *instant-*, *instans* instant] **:** at once **:** IMMEDIATELY, INSTANTLY

**in·stan·tial** \(ˈ)inzˈtanchəl, ənzˈt-, -nˈsta-\ *adj* [L *instantia* presence, urgency + E *-al* — more at INSTANCE] **:** of, relating to, constituting, or providing an instance ⟨empirical laws for which there is ~ evidence —Arthur Pap⟩

**in·stan·ti·ate** \⸗ˈ⸗chēˌāt\ *vt* -ED/-ING/-S [L *instantia* presence, urgency + E *-ate*] **:** to represent (an abstraction or universal) by a concrete instance — **in·stan·ti·a·tion** \(ˌ)⸗ˌ⸗⸗ˈāshən\ *n* -s

**¹in·stant·ly** *adv* [ME, fr. *instant* (adj.) + *-ly*] **1 :** with urgency or importunity **:** PRESSINGLY **2** *obs* **:** in this or in the most recent moment **:** just now **3 :** without the least delay **:** at once **:** IMMEDIATELY

**²in·stant·ly** \"\ *conj* **:** as soon as **:** IMMEDIATELY, DIRECTLY ⟨recognized her ~ I saw her⟩

**in·stant·ness** *n* -ES **:** the quality or state of being instant

**¹in·star** \ənzˈt-, ənˈst-\ *also* **en·star** \ən-,en-\ *vt* [²in- or ¹en- + *star* (n.)] **1** *archaic* **:** to place as a star **:** turn into a star **2 :** to adorn or stud with or as if with stars ⟨a coronet *instarred* with precious stones⟩

**²in·star** \ˈinˌtär, -nˌst-, -tə(r\ *n* -s [NL, fr. L, figure, form, perh. alter. of *instare* to approach, to be evenly balanced, stand upon — more at INSTANT] **:** a stage in the life of an insect or other arthropod between two successive molts ⟨some insects may have seven or more ~*s*⟩; *also* **:** an individual in a specified instar ⟨collected several third-*instar* larvae⟩

**in·state** \ənzˈtāt, -nˈstāt, *usu* -ād+V\ *also* **en·state** \ən-,en-\ *vt* [²in- or ¹en- + *state* (n.)] **1 :** to set, place, or establish esp. in a rank, office, or status **:** INSTALL ⟨hoped to ~ his sister in her estate⟩ **2** *obs* **a :** INVEST, ENDOW **b :** BESTOW, CONFER

**in·state·ment** \-mənt\ *n* -s **:** INSTALLATION

**in sta·tu nas·cen·di** \ənˈstā(ˌ)tünəˈsendē, -ˈstaˌ ˌ(ˌ)chü-, -ˌdī; -ˈstä(ˌ)tünäˈskendē\ [L, in the state of being born] **:** in the nascent state ⟨produce the aldehyde *in statu nascendi* —C.D.Hurd⟩ **:** in the course of being formed or developed ⟨if . . . isolation can promote the formation of full species, such species must *in statu nascendi* pass through a phase of less than specific distinction —Fridthjof Økland⟩

**in statu quo** \-ˈkwō\ [L] **:** in the state in which something is or was **:** in the former or same state

**in·stau·ra·tion** \ˌinz,tȯˈrāshən, ˌin,st-\ *n* -s [L *instauration-*, *instauratio*, fr. *instauratus* (past part. of *instaurare* to renew, restore) + *-ion-*, *-io* -ion — more at STORE] **1 :** restoration after decay, lapse, or dilapidation **2** *obs* **:** an act of instituting or establishing something

**in·stau·ra·tor** \ˈ⸗⸗ˌrād-ə(r)\ *n* -s [LL, fr. L *instauratus* (past part.) + *-or*] **:** one that engages in instauration

**in·stead** \ənˈsted, ənˈst-, *more often before "of" than in other positions* ÷ -tid\ *adv* [fr. the phrase **instead of**] **1 :** in the place **:** in lieu **:** as a substitute or equivalent ⟨he came ~⟩ **2 :** as an alternative to something expressed or implied **:** in the place of something **:** RATHER ⟨longing ~ for a quiet country life⟩

**instead of** *prep* [ME *in sted of*] **:** as a substitute for or alternative to ⟨had peanut butter *instead of* jelly⟩ ⟨sent his helper *instead of* coming himself⟩

**in·steep** \ənzˈtēp, ənˈst-\ *vt* [²in- + *steep*] **:** STEEP, SOAK **:** IMBRUE

**in·stel·la·tion** \ˌinz,teˈlāshən, ˌin,ste-\ *n* -s [²in- + L *stella* star + E *-ation* — more at STAR] **1 :** a setting among the stars **2 :** a turning into a star

**in·step** \ˈinz,tep, ˈin,step\ *n* [perh. fr. ⁴in + *step*] **1 :** the arched middle portion of the human foot next in front of the ankle joint; *esp* **:** the upper surface of this part **2 :** the part of the hind leg of the horse and related animals between the hock and the pastern joint **3 :** the part of a shoe or stocking over the instep **4 :** something (as the slope of a hill) that is felt to resemble the human instep

**in·sti·gate** \ˈinztəˌgāt, ˈin(t)stə-, *usu* -ād+V\ *vt* -ED/-ING/-S [L *instigatus*, past part. of *instigare* — more at STICK] **:** to goad or urge forward **:** set on **:** PROVOKE, INCITE ⟨his past experience *instigated* him to boldness⟩ ⟨*instigating* a plot to overthrow the government⟩ **syn** see INCITE

**in·sti·gat·ing·ly** *adv* **:** in an instigating manner

**in·sti·ga·tion** \ˌ⸗⸗ˈgāshən\ *n* -s [ME *instigacioun*, fr. MF or L; MF *instigation*, fr. L *instigation-*, *instigatio*, fr. *instigatus* (past part.) + *-ion-*, *-io* -ion] **1 :** an act of instigating or the state of being instigated **:** INCITEMENT ⟨they agreed at our ~ to confer⟩ ⟨the ~ of the new program⟩ **2 :** something that instigates **:** INCENTIVE ⟨his friends' approval was a real ~ to succeed⟩

**in·sti·ga·tive** \ˈ⸗⸗ˌgād-iv\ *adj* [L *instigatus* (past part.) + E *-ive*] **:** tending to instigate

**in·sti·ga·tor** \-ˌgād-ə(r), -ātə-\ *n* -s [L, fr. *instigatus* (past part.) + *-or*] **:** one that instigates

**in·still** *also* **in·stil** \ənzˈtil, ənˈstil\ *vt* **instilled; instilled; instilling; instills** *also* **instils** [MF & L; MF *instiller*, fr. L *instillare*, fr. *in-* ²in- + *stillare* to drip, trickle — more at DISTILL] **1 :** to introduce a drop at a time **:** cause to enter drop by drop ⟨~ a few drops of warm olive oil⟩ **2 :** to impart or introduce gradually **:** cause to be taken in little by little ⟨~*ing* a reverence for honest dealings⟩ ⟨~*ed* the teachings of his own faith⟩ **syn** see IMPLANT

**in·stil·la·tion** \ˌinztəˈlāshən, ˌin(t)stə-\ *n* -s [MF & L; MF, fr. L *instillation-*, *instillatio*, fr. *instillatus* (past part.) + *-ion-*, *-io* -ion] **1 :** an act of instilling **:** introduction by instilling ⟨repeated ~ of penicillin⟩ **2 :** something that is instilled or designed for instillation ⟨an oily ~⟩ ⟨silver ~ for use in the eyes of the newborn⟩

**in·still·er** \ənzˈtilə(r), ənˈsti-\ *n* -s **:** one that instills

**in·still·ment** *also* **in·stil·ment** \-lmənt\ *n* -s **:** INSTILLATION 1

**¹in·stinct** \ˈinz,tiŋ(k)t, -ˌtēŋ-, ˈin(ˌ)st-\ *n* -s [ME, fr. L *instinctus*, fr. *instinctus* (past part.)] **1** *obs* **:** INSTIGATION, IMPULSE **2 :** a natural or inherent aptitude, tendency, impulse, or capacity ⟨an ~ for the right word⟩ ⟨his ~ toward success⟩ ⟨the religious ~*s* of primitive peoples⟩ **3 a :** complex and specific response on the part of an organism to environmental stimuli that is largely hereditary and unalterable though the pattern of behavior through which it is expressed may be modified by learning, that does not involve reason, and that has as its goal the removal of a somatic tension or excitation **b :** behavior that is mediated by reactions (as reflex arcs) below the conscious level — usu. not used technically

**²in·stinct** \(ˈ)inzˈtiŋ(k)t, ənzˈt-, -nˈsti-\ *adj* [L *instinctus*, past part. of *instinguere* to instigate, incite; akin to L *instigare* to instigate, incite — more at STICK] **1** *obs* **:** implanted by nature **:** INNATE **2** *obs* **:** impelled by an inner or animating or exciting agency **3 :** profoundly imbued **:** FILLED, CHARGED — usu. used postpositively and with *with* ⟨a spirit ~ with human kindness⟩ ⟨~ with patriotism⟩

**³instinct** *vt* -ED/-ING/-S [L *instinctus* (past part.)] **1** *obs* **:** INSTIGATE, IMPEL **2** *obs* **:** to implant as an animating power

**in·stinc·tion** \ənˈtiŋ(k)shən, ənˈst-\ *n* -s [obs. E, instigation, inspiration, fr. MF, fr. LL *instinction-*, *instinctio*, fr. L *instinctus* (past part.) + *-ion-*, *-io* -ion] **1** *obs* **:** INSTINCT **2 :** instinctive behavior

**in·stinc·tive** \(ˈ)inzˈtiŋ(k)tiv, ənˈst-, -)tēv *also* -)təv\ *adj* [¹*instinct* + *-ive*] **:** of, relating to, or constituting instinct **:** derived from or prompted by instinct **:** determined by natural impulse or propensity **:** UNLEARNED, UNREASONED ⟨an ~ dread of mice⟩ ⟨~ behavior⟩ **syn** see SPONTANEOUS

**in·stinc·tive·ly** \-təvlē, -li\ *adv* **:** in an instinctive manner **:** as a matter of instinct ⟨reached ~ for some support⟩ ⟨~ proud of their traditions⟩

**¹in·stinc·tiv·ist** \⸗ˈ⸗təvəst, -tēv-\ *n* -s [*instinctive* + *-ist*] **:** one that views society as a manifestation of various instinctive drives; *broadly* **:** one that views human behavior and social adaptation as the resultant of the interplay of various instinctive drives (as for survival) with environmental factors (as group relations)

**²in·stinc·tiv·ist** \(ˈ)⸗ˈ⸗⸗⸗\ *or* **in·stinc·ti·vistic** \(ˌ)⸗ˌ⸗⸗ˈvistik, -tēk\ *adj* **:** based on the predominance of instinct **:** of or relating to instinctivists ⟨~ theories⟩

**in·stinc·tu·al** \(ˈ)⸗ˈ⸗ch(əw)əl\ *adj* [¹*instinct* + *-ual* (as in *actual*)] **:** of, relating to, or based on instincts ⟨~ behavior⟩ ⟨the ~ society of social insects⟩ — **in·stinc·tu·al·ly** \-əlē, -li\ *adv*

**in·sti·tor** \ˈinztəˌtȯ(ə)r, ˈin(t)stə-\ *n* -s [L, fr. *instit-* (perf. stem of *insistere* to occupy a place in, stand upon, persist) + *-or* — more at INSIST] **:** a person (as the manager of a commercial or manufacturing business, a broker, factor, or commission agent) to whom the transaction of some business is committed as agent to such a degree as to bind the principal — used chiefly in Roman and civil law — **in·sti·to·ri·al** \⸗⸗ˈtōrēəl\ *adj*

**¹in·sti·tute** \ˈinztəˌtüt, ˈin(t)stə-, -əˌtyüt, *in rapid speech* ˈinzˌt(y)üt *or* ˈin(t)st(y)-; *usu* -üd+V\ *vt* -ED/-ING/-S [ME *instituten*, fr. L *institutus*, past part. of *instituere*, fr. *in-* ²in- + *-stituere* (fr. *statuere* to stand up, set, place) — more at STATUTE] **1 :** to establish in a particular position or office: as **a :** to invest with spiritual charge of a benefice **:** put (as a pastor) in charge of the care of souls **b :** to appoint as heir under Roman or civil law **2 a :** to originate and get established **:** set up **:** cause to come into existence **:** ORGANIZE ⟨the man that *instituted* these reforms in lexicography⟩ **b :** to set on foot **:** INAUGURATE, INITIATE ⟨*instituting* an investigation of the charges⟩ **3 a** *obs* **:** to ordain or enjoin to be or to be done **b** *archaic* **:** to ground or establish in principles or rudiments **:** INSTRUCT, EDUCATE **syn** see FOUND

**²institute** \"\ *n* -s [L *institutum*, fr. neut. of *institutus* (past part.)] **1** *obs* **:** DESIGN, PLAN, PURPOSE **2** *obs* **:** an act of instituting **3** [MF & L; MF *institut*, fr. L *institutum*] **:** something that is instituted: as **a** (1) **:** an elementary principle **:** a precept or rule recognized as authoritative (2) **institutes** *pl* **:** a collection of such principles and precepts; *esp* **:** a comprehensive summary of legal principles and decisions — compare DIGEST **b** (1) **:** an organization for the promotion of some estimable or learned cause or the welfare of some group ⟨an ~ for the blind⟩ ⟨an ~ for psychical research⟩ (2) **:** an association of persons or organizations that collectively constitute a technical or professional authority in a field of work or study ⟨Horological *Institute* of America⟩ ⟨an ~ of architects⟩ (3) *chiefly Brit* **:** a school or academy esp. for part-time education of workers ⟨teaching in the village ~⟩ (4) **:** an institution for advanced education esp. in science or technology ⟨spent two years at the textile ~⟩ (5) **:** a brief course of instruction or seminars (as for teachers or poultrymen) on business or professional problems **c :** a building or group of buildings occupied by an institute **4** [L *institutus* (past part.)] **a** *Scots law* **:** the person to whom an estate is first given by destination or testament — compare SUBSTITUTE **b** *civil law* **:** an heir appointed by will under a duty to transfer the property to a person designated in the will

**in·sti·tut·er** \-üd-ə(r)\ *n* -s **:** INSTITUTOR

**in·sti·tu·tion** \ˌinztəˈtüshən, ˌin(t)stə-, -təˈtyü-, *in rapid speech* inzˈt(y)ü- *or* in(t)sˈt(y)ü-, *chiefly in substand speech* in(t)səˈ-\ *n* -s [ME *institucioun*, fr. MF & L; MF *institution*, fr. OF, fr. L *institution-*, *institutio* arrangement, custom, instruction, element of instruction, appointment of an heir, fr. *institutus* (past part.) + *-ion-*, *-io* -ion] **1 :** an act or the process of instituting: as **a** [ME *institucioun*, fr. ML *institution-*, *institutio*, fr. L] **:** the investing of a clergyman with the spiritual part of a benefice by which the care of souls is committed to his charge followed in the Church of England by induction **b** (1) **:** the appointment of an heir (2) **:** the appointment of an institute (sense 4a) **c :** ESTABLISHMENT, FOUNDATION, ENACTMENT ⟨the ~ of this custom dates back to the 15th century⟩ **d** *obs* **:** reduction to order or form **:** REGULATION, ORDERING **e** *obs* **:** INSTRUCTION, EDUCATION **f :** the establishment of a sacrament; *usu* **:** the designation, authorization, or ordination by Christ of various signs or ceremonies as sacraments ⟨the words of ~ form part of the eucharistic rite⟩ **2 :** something that serves to instruct (as a textbook or a system of rules or principles) — now usu. restricted to law; compare INSTITUTE 3a **3 :** something that is instituted: as **a** (1) **:** a significant and persistent element (as a practice, a relationship, an organization) in the life of a culture that centers on a fundamental human need, activity, or value, occupies an enduring and cardinal position within a society, and is usu. maintained and stabilized through social regulatory agencies ⟨~ of marriage⟩ ⟨the family is a fundamental social ~⟩ (2) **:** a custom that is usu. widely sanctioned or tolerated and that in some degree contributes to group welfare ⟨the old New England ~ of bundling⟩ ⟨the coffee break has become an ~ in many places⟩ (3) **:** something or someone well established in some customary relationship **:** FIXTURE ⟨the old man was an ~ along the waterfront⟩ ⟨father's Sunday breakfast in bed was a family ~⟩ **b :** an established society or corporation **:** an establishment or foundation esp. of a public character ⟨a literary ~⟩ ⟨the Smithsonian *Institution*⟩ ⟨~*s* of higher learning⟩ **c :** a building or the buildings occupied or used by such organization

**in·sti·tu·tion·al** \ˌ⸗⸗ˈt(y)üshənᵊl, (ˈ)⸗ˈt(y)ü-, -shnəl\ *adj* **1 :** of, relating to, involving, or constituting an institution ⟨an ~ investor⟩ ⟨~ elements of a political system⟩ ⟨~ care of the blind⟩: as **a :** of or relating to the institution of a sacrament **b** *of advertising* **:** designed to create goodwill and prestige for a company and its products rather than to produce immediate sales of specific products **2 :** provided with or characterized by institutions **:** having or sponsoring institutions esp. of a charitable or educational nature ⟨~ society⟩ — **in·sti·tu·tion·al·ly** \-ᵊlē, -əl|, |i\ *adv*

**institutional economics** *n pl but sing or pl in constr* **:** a school of economics that emphasizes the importance of nonmarket factors (as social institutions) in influencing economic behavior, economic analysis being subordinated to consideration of sociological factors, history, and institutional development

**in·sti·tu·tion·al·ism** \ˌ⸗⸗ˈt(y)üshənᵊlˌizəm, ⸗ˈt(y)ü-, -shnə-li-\ *n* -s **1 :** adherence to, upholding of, or acceptance of established institutions (as of society or religion) **:** belief in or dependence on that which is sanctified and given authority as an institution ⟨exhibiting an excessive conventionalism and ~ in religion⟩ **2 a :** a policy or theory favoring extended use of public institutions (as for defectives and criminals);

*also* : such use of public institutions ⟨with declining family solidarity ~ became increasingly important in the care of the sick, the unwanted, the aged⟩ **b** : the characteristics (as regimentation, standardization, and impersonality) that are associated with institutional life ⟨there was no ~ about this happy home⟩ **3 a** : the doctrines and teachings of institutional economics **b** : a theory that regards the establishment and maintenance of institutions (as for education, charity, and social activities) as an essential function of a church

**in·sti·tu·tion·al·ist** \-ᵊləst, -ələ-\ *n* -s **1** : a writer on or of institutes esp. of the law **2** : an adherent to, teacher of, or believer in any form of institutionalism : a defender of traditional institutions

**in·sti·tu·tion·al·iza·tion** \-ᵊlə'zāshən, -ᵊl,ī'z-, -ələ'z-, -ə,lī'z-\ *n* -s **1** : the quality or state of being or becoming institutionalized ⟨a pleasant custom always has a tendency toward ~⟩ **2** : the action or a result of institutionalizing ⟨the ~ of the insane⟩

**in·sti·tu·tion·al·ize** \-ᵊl,īz, -ə,līz\ *vt* -ED/-ING/-S *see -ize in Explan Notes* [*institutional* + *-ize*] **1** : to give the character of an institution to : make into or treat like an institution ⟨modern society tends to ~ its burdens⟩; *esp* : to incorporate into a system of organized and often highly formalized belief, practice, or acceptance ⟨the Japanese *institutionalized* suicide⟩ ⟨*institutionalized* graft⟩ **2** : to place in or commit to the care of a specialized institution (as for the insane, alcoholics, epileptics, delinquent youth, or the aged) **3** : to accustom (a person) so firmly to the care and supervised routine of an institution as to make incapable of managing a life outside

**in·sti·tu·tion·ary** \ˌ==ˈt(y)üshə,nerē, (ˈ)=ˈt(y)ü-, -shnərē, -ri\ *adj* : of or relating to institution in office ⟨an ~ banquet⟩

**in·sti·tu·tion·ize** \ˌ=='t(y)üshə,nīz, ='t(y)-\ [*institution* + *-ize*] *vt* -ED/-ING/-S : INSTITUTIONALIZE 1

**institutions** *pl of* INSTITUTION

**in·sti·tu·tive** \'==,t(y)üd·iv, '=,t(y)-\ *adj* [L *institutus* (past part. of *instituere* to institute) + E *-ive* — more at INSTITUTE] **1** : tending to institute : concerned with or leading to the institution of something ⟨~ factors⟩ ⟨an ~ meeting⟩ **2** *obs* : characterized or formed by institution : CONVENTIONAL

**in·sti·tu·tor** \-üd·ə(r), -ütə-\ *n* -s [L, fr. *institutus* (past part.) + *-or*] : one that institutes: as **a** : FOUNDER, ORDAINER, ESTABLISHER ⟨the ~ of this pleasant custom⟩ **b** *archaic* : TEACHER, INSTRUCTOR **c** : a Protestant Episcopal bishop or a priest delegated by him who institutes a rector or assistant minister into a parish or church

**in·sti·tu·tress** \ˌ==ˈt(y)ü·trəs, (ˈ)=ˈt(y)-\ *also* **in·sti·tu·trix** \-ü·triks\ *n, pl* **institutress·es** \-ü·trəsəz\ *also* **institutrix·es** \-ü·triksəz\ *or* **institutri·ces** \ˌ=='t(y)ü·trə,sēz, ='t(y)-; ,==(,)t(y)ü·'trī(,)sēz\ [*institutress* fr. *instituter* + *-ess*; *institutrix* fr. *institutor*, after such pairs as E *director*: *directrix*] : a female institutor

**instl** *abbr* installation

**instmt** *abbr* instrument

**instn** *abbr* **1** institution **2** instruction

**in store** *adv (or adj)* : at or from the point where stored with subsequent storage and shipping costs to be paid by the buyer ⟨goods sold *in store*⟩ ⟨payment to be made *in store*⟩ — compare EX STORE, FREE ON BOARD

**instore** *vt* [ME *instoren*, fr. ML *instaurare*, fr. L, to renew, restore — more at INSTAURATION] *obs* : FURNISH, PROVIDE

**instr** *abbr* **1** instruction; instructor **2** instrument; instrumental

**¹instreaming** \'inz,t-, 'in,st-\ *adj* [²*in* + *streaming*, pres. part. of *stream* (after *stream in*, v.)] : streaming in : entering like flowing water

**²instreaming** \"\ *n* [⁴*in* + *streaming*, gerund of *stream* (after *stream in*, v.)] : the action of entering like a stream of water : a flowing in ⟨the . . . ~ of beauty and truth —Cecil Sprigge⟩

**in·strength·en** \ənz't-,ən'st-\ *vt* [²*in-* + *strengthen*] : to give an inner strength to : strengthen in body or spirit

**instrn** *abbr* instruction

**instroke** \'inz,t-,'in,st-\ *n* [⁴*in* + *stroke*] : an inward stroke; *specif* : a stroke in which the piston in a steam or other engine is moving away from the crankshaft — opposed to *outstroke*

**¹instruct** *adj* [ME *instructe*, fr. L *instructus* (past part.)] **1** *obs* : INSTRUCTED **2** *obs* : PROVIDED, EQUIPPED

**²in·struct** \ənz'trəkt, ən'st-\ *vb* -ED/-ING/-S [ME *instructen*, fr. L *instructus*, past part. of *instruere*, fr. *in-* ²in- + *struere* to build, establish — more at STRUCTURE] *vt* **1** : to give special knowledge or information to: as **a** : to train in some special field : give skill or knowledge in some art or field of specialization : educate in respect to a particular subject or area of knowledge ⟨had a tutor to ~ him in English⟩ **b** : to provide with information about something : APPRISE ⟨~*ed* us that the toilets were downstairs⟩ ⟨the senses ~ us of most material dangers⟩ **c** : to impart knowledge systematically to ⟨~*ed* three generations of children in the village school⟩ **2 a** : to furnish with directions based on informed or technical awareness of a problem ⟨the judge ~*ed* the jury⟩ **b** : to give an order or command to esp. authoritatively, formally, and with attention to clearness : DIRECT ⟨~*s* the eleven companions to await on the hill the outcome of the fight —R.M.Lumiansky⟩ **3 a** *archaic* : to put in order : PREPARE **b** : to actuate and establish the controls of (an automatic electronic machine) **4** *Scots law* : to prove or establish on the basis of evidence : PROVE, CONFIRM ~ *vi* : to serve as an instructor ⟨~*ed* in the public schools for many years⟩ **syn** see COMMAND, TEACH

**instructed** *adj* **1** : EDUCATED, CULTURED ⟨the ~ person is usually tolerant⟩ ⟨planned by an ~ taste⟩ **2 a** : furnished with and restricted in action by specific instructions ⟨sent ~ delegates to the convention⟩ **b** : ordered by informed authority : DIRECTED ⟨an ~ verdict⟩ — **in·struct·ed·ly** *adv* — **in·struct·ed·ness** *n* -ES

**in·struct·ible** \-ktəbəl\ *adj* [L *instructus* (past part.) + E *-ible*] : capable of being instructed or taught ⟨~ children⟩ ⟨a very ~ subject⟩

**in·struc·tion** \-kshən\ *n* -s [ME *instruccioun*, fr. MF&LL; MF *instruction*, fr. LL *instruction-*, *instructio*, fr. L, act of constructing, act of arranging, fr. *instructus* (past part. of *instruere* to instruct) + *-ion-*, *-io* -ion — more at INSTRUCT] **1** : something that instructs or is imparted in order to instruct: as **a** : LESSON, PRECEPT ⟨children should profit from the ~*s* of their elders⟩ **b** *obs* : INFORMATION, NEWS, REPORT **c** (1) : something given by way of direction or order — usu. used in pl. ⟨gave the maid ~*s* to wait for the grocer⟩ (2) : information in the form of an outline of procedures : DIRECTIONS — usu. used in pl. ⟨the ~*s* for assembling the model⟩ **2** : the action, practice, or profession of one that instructs : TEACHING ⟨new theories of ~⟩ ⟨engaged in ~ rather than active service⟩ **3** : the quality or state of being instructed ⟨where ~ is more widely diffused —Havelock Ellis⟩

**in·struc·tion·al** \-shənᵊl,-shnəl\ *adj* **1** : relating to, serving for, or promoting instruction : EDUCATIONAL ⟨~ methods⟩ ⟨used for ~ purposes⟩ ⟨the director of ~ services⟩ **2** : containing or conveying instruction or information ⟨an ~ film⟩

**instruction card** *n* : JOB SHEET

**in·struc·tive** \-ktiv, -tēv *also* -təv\ *adj* [prob. fr. MF *instructif*, fr. L *instructus* (past part.) + MF *-if* -ive] : conveying knowledge : serving to instruct or inform ⟨experience furnishes very ~ lessons⟩ ⟨such experiences are ~⟩ — **in·struc·tive·ly** \-təvlē, -li\ *adv* — **in·struc·tive·ness** \-tivnəs, -tēv- *also* -təv-\ *n* -ES

**in·struc·tor** \-ktə(r)\ *n* -s [ME *instructour*, fr. MF or ML; MF *instructeur*, fr. ML *instructor*, fr. L, arranger, preparer, fr. *instructus* (past part. of *instruere* to arrange, prepare, instruct) + *-or*] : one that instructs : TEACHER ⟨our older brother was our ~ in woodcraft⟩ ⟨an ~ in the local high school⟩; *specif* : a teacher in a college or university of a rank below any of the various grades of professor ⟨most colleges recognize the following ascending order of ranks: ~, assistant professor, associate professor, professor⟩

**in·struc·to·ri·al** \ˌ=ˌ=ˈtōrēəl\ *adj* : of or relating to an instructor ⟨miserable ~ salaries⟩ ⟨~ carelessness⟩

**in·struc·tor·ship** \ənz'trəktə(r),ship, ən'st-\ *n* : the position or status of an instructor ⟨obtained an ~ at the university⟩

**in·struc·tress** \-ktrəs\ *n* -ES [*instructor* + *-ess*] : a female instructor

**¹in·stru·ment** \'inztrəmənt, 'in(t)strə-\ *n* -s [ME, fr. L *instrumentum*, fr. *instruere* to construct, equip, arrange, instruct + *-mentum* -ment] **1 a** : a means whereby something is achieved, performed, or furthered ⟨the modern university is the ~ for preserving, enlarging, and disseminating our ever-increasing body of knowledge —Harlan Hatcher⟩ **b** : a person or group made use of by another as a means or aid : DUPE, TOOL ⟨suspecting . . . that I only wished to make an ~ of him —W.H.Hudson †1922⟩ **2** : UTENSIL, IMPLEMENT ⟨surgical ~*s*⟩ ⟨~*s* of torture⟩ **3** : an implement used to produce music esp. as distinguished from the human voice — see PERCUSSION INSTRUMENT, STRINGED INSTRUMENT, WIND INSTRUMENT **4** *obs* : an organ of the body **5 a** : a legal document (as a deed, will, bond, lease, agreement, mortgage, note, power of attorney, ticket on carrier, bill of lading, insurance policy, warrant, writ) evidencing legal rights or duties esp. of one party to another **b** : something capable of being presented as evidence to a court for inspection **c** : an act recorded in writing by a notary : a notarial act **6 a** : a measuring device for determining the present value of a quantity under observation; *broadly* : a device (as for controlling, recording, regulating, computing) that functions on data obtained by such a measuring device **b** : an electrical or mechanical device used in navigating an airplane; *specif* : such a device used as the sole means of navigating when there is limited or no visibility **syn** see IMPLEMENT, MEAN — **on instruments** : by means of airplane instruments ⟨flying *on instruments*⟩

**²in·stru·ment** \-,ment, -,mənt — *see* ²-MENT\ *vt* -ED/-ING/-S **1** : to address a legal instrument (as a petition) to **2** : to prepare or score for one or more musical instruments ⟨~ a sonata for orchestra⟩ : ORCHESTRATE **3** : to equip (as a process, machine, or vehicle) with instruments ⟨the whole factory is well ~*ed* —*Farm Chemicals*⟩ ⟨an ~*ed* satellite⟩

**¹in·stru·men·tal** \ˌ==ˈmentᵊl\ *adj* [ME, fr. ML *instrumentalis*, fr. L *instrumentum* + *-alis* -al] **1** : serving as a means or intermediary determining or leading to a particular result : being an instrument that functions in the promotion of some end or purpose ⟨this novel was ~ in bringing on open conflict⟩ ⟨an ~ act leading to a reward⟩ **2** : relating to, composed for, or performed on a musical instrument ⟨~ music⟩ ⟨~ ensemble⟩ — compare VOCAL **3** : of, relating to, or done with an instrument ⟨~ design⟩ ⟨~ navigation⟩ **4 a** : of, relating to, or being a case in grammar expressing means or agency ⟨English shows a surviving trace of the ~ case in *the* of "the more the merrier"⟩ **b** : being a suffixal element that denotes means or agency **5** : based on or in accordance with instrumentalism — **in·stru·men·tal·ly** \-ᵊlē,-ᵊli\ *adv*

**²instrumental** \"\ *n* -s **1** *obs* : INSTRUMENT, MEANS **2** : the instrumental case or a word in that case **3** : a composition played on or for playing on a musical instrument — compare VOCAL

**instrumental goods** *n pl* : PRODUCER GOODS

**in·stru·men·tal·ism** \ˌ=='mentᵊl,izəm\ *n* -s [¹*instrumental* + *-ism*] : a conception that the significant factor of a thing is its value as an instrument; *specif* : the doctrine that ideas are instruments of action and that their usefulness determines their truth

**¹in·stru·men·tal·ist** \-ᵊləst\ *n* -s [¹*instrumental* + *-ist*] **1 a** : a player of a musical instrument **b** : a composer of instrumental music **2** : a proponent of instrumentalism

**²in·stru·men·tal·ist** \ˌ=ˌ===\ *adj* : advocating instrumentalism : INSTRUMENTAL

**in·stru·men·tal·i·ty** \ˌ==,mən'taləd·ē, -,men- -, -lətē, -i\ *n* -ES **1** : the quality or state of being instrumental : a condition of serving as an intermediary ⟨the agreement was reached through the ~ of the governor⟩ **2 a** : something by which an end is achieved : MEANS ⟨precious metals purified through the ~ of heat⟩ ⟨*instrumentalities* of production⟩ ⟨mechanical *instrumentalities*⟩ **b** : something that serves as an intermediary or agent through which one or more functions of a controlling force are carried out : a part, organ, or subsidiary branch esp. of a governing body ⟨the judicial *instrumentalities* of the federal government⟩ ⟨a Chilean government ~ devoted to developing the country's natural resources —*Ethyl News*⟩ **syn** see MEAN

**in·stru·men·tal·ize** \ˌ=='mentᵊl,īz\ *vt* -ED/-ING/-S : to render instrumental : DIRECT, ORGANIZE, ADAPT

**instrumental theory** *n* : INSTRUMENTALISM

**in·stru·men·tar·ium** \,inztrəmən-'ta(a)rēəm, ,inst-, -,men --\ *n, pl* **instrumentar·ia** \-ēə\ [NL, prob. fr. ML, case for storing papers, cartulary, fr. L *instrumentum* instrument + *-arium*] : the equipment needed for a particular surgical, medical, or dental procedure; *also* : the professional instruments of a surgeon, physician, or dentist

**in·stru·men·ta·ry** \ˌ=='mentərē, -n·trē\ *adj* : of or relating to a legal instrument ⟨an ~ witness⟩

**in·stru·men·tate** \'inztrəmən,tāt, 'in(t)strə-\ *vt* -ED/-ING/-S [¹*instrument* + *-ate* (after *orchestrate*)] : INSTRUMENT 2

**in·stru·men·ta·tion** \ˌ==='tāshən, -,men- -\ *n* -s [¹*instrument* + *-ation*] **1** : a use of or operation with instruments: as **a** : the use of one or more instruments in treating a patient (as in the passing of a cystoscope) **b** : the application of instruments esp. for observation, measurement, or control (as in a manufacturing process or the operation of a machine or vehicle) **2** : MEANS, AGENCY, INSTRUMENTALITY **3 a** [F, fr. *instrument* (fr. MF, fr. L *instrumentum* instrument) + *-ation*] : the arrangement or composition of music for instruments esp. for a band or orchestra — compare ORCHESTRATION **b** : the act or manner of playing musical instruments **c** : the arrangement and distribution of instruments (as in a band or orchestra) **4 a** : a branch of science concerned with the development, manufacture, and utilization of instruments **b** : instruments or the group of instruments employed for a particular purpose (as the control of a machine or recording the data about the function of a vehicle)

**in·stru·men·ta·tor** \'==mən,tād·ə(r)\ *n* -s [*instrumentate* + *-or*] : one that arranges a musical score for performance by a specific group of instruments

**instrument board** *or* **instrument panel** *n* : a panel on which instruments are mounted; *esp* : DASHBOARD 2

instrument board

**instrumented** *past of* INSTRUMENT

**instrument flight** *n* : an airplane flight made on instruments : blind flight

**instrument flying** *n* : navigation solely according to information given by instruments within an airplane usu. including radio or radar devices : blind flying — contrasted with *contact flying*

**instrumenting** *pres part of* INSTRUMENT

**instrument landing** *n* : a landing made with no external visibility and solely by means of instruments within an airplane and by ground radio directive devices : blind landing

**instrument landing system** *n* : a system for airplane landings in which the pilot is guided by radio beams — abbr. *ILS*; compare GROUND-CONTROLLED APPROACH

**in·stru·ment·man** \'===,man\ *n, pl* **instrumentmen** : a surveyor who operates a transit, level, or similar instrument

**instrument rating** *n* : a license or rating given to an airplane pilot authorized to do instrument flying

**instruments** *pl of* INSTRUMENT, *pres 3d sing of* INSTRUMENT

**instrument weather** *n* : weather in which the ground is so invisible from the air that instrument flying is required

**instyle** *vt* [²*in-* + *style*] *obs* : CALL, DENOMINATE

**in·suavity** \(ˈ)in, ən+\ *n* [L *insuavitas*, fr. *insuavis* unpleasant (fr. *in-* ¹in- + *suavis* pleasant) + *-itas* -ity — more at SWEET] : lack of suavity : BRUSQUENESS

**in·subjection** \ˌin+\ *n* [¹*in-* + *subjection*] : lack of subjection : a state of disobedience or opposition to authority (as of government)

**in·submergible** *or* **in·submersible** \"+\ *adj* [*insubmergible* fr. ¹*in-* + *submerge* + *-ible*; *insubmersible* prob. fr. F, fr. *in-* ¹in- + L *submersus* (past part. of *submergere* to submerge) + F *-ible*] : incapable of sinking

**in·submissive** \"+\ *adj* [¹*in-* + *submissive*] : unwilling to submit

**¹in·subordinate** \"+\ *adj* [¹*in-* + *subordinate*] : not subordinate: as **a** : unwilling to submit to authority : DISOBEDIENT, MUTINOUS ⟨~ boys⟩ **b** : not holding a lower or inferior position ⟨the bankers of Antwerp placed no limit on their enterprise: economic activity was not subordinate; it had become, from the medieval point of view, ~ —Stringfellow Barr⟩

**syn** REBELLIOUS, MUTINOUS, SEDITIOUS, FACTIOUS, CONTUMACIOUS: INSUBORDINATE applies to disobedience of orders, infraction of rules, or a generally disaffected attitude toward authority, often in military or other organization similarly constituted ⟨*insubordinate* deckhands confined to the brig⟩ ⟨*insubordinate* native troops feeling that they were being discriminated against⟩ REBELLIOUS may suggest forceful resistance to or insurgence against authority in addition to insubordination and temperamental opposition ⟨*rebellious* mountaineers proposing to set up their own independent republic⟩ ⟨temperamentally *rebellious*, instinctively disliking externally imposed authority —Francis Biddle⟩ MUTINOUS suggests either opposing authority by destroying discipline and order or the forceful overthrow of authority ⟨for more than a year Cortes stayed in the new land, a desolate sandy waste, while the *mutinous* soldiers cursed him —*Amer. Guide Series: Calif.*⟩ ⟨the guards might be overpowered, the palace forced, the king a prisoner in the hands of his *mutinous* subjects —T.B.Macaulay⟩ SEDITIOUS suggests treasonable activities, esp. those designed to weaken or overthrow a government or foster separatist tendencies ⟨*seditious* factionalism went on a rampage and began to wreck our foreign policy —Max Ascoli⟩ ⟨revolutions that were not made in Boston, by Boston gentlemen, were quite certain to be wicked and *seditious* —V.L.Parrington⟩ FACTIOUS suggests an addiction to factions with contentious perversity and irreconcilability threatening central constituted authority ⟨Florence . . . wearing out her soul by *factious* struggles —Margaret Oliphant⟩ ⟨the opposition will be vigilant but not *factious*. We shall not oppose merely for the sake of opposition —Clement Attlee⟩ CONTUMACIOUS indicates persistent, willful, or overt defiance of authority and disobedience, sometimes contemptuous, of authority ⟨a fine was appointed for every failure to obey the bishop's summons; he was empowered to excommunicate *contumacious* persons —F.M.Stenton⟩ ⟨magistrates and populace were incensed at a refusal of customary marks of courtesy and respect for the laws, which in their eyes was purely *contumacious* —W.R.Inge⟩

**²insubordinate** \"\ *n* : an insubordinate person

**in·subordinately** \ˌin+\ *adv* : in an insubordinate manner : with insubordination

**in·subordination** \"+\ *n* [prob. fr. F, fr. *in-* ¹in- + *subordination*] : the quality or state of being insubordinate : defiance of authority : MUTINY

**in·substantial** \"+\ *adj* [prob. fr. F *insubstantiel*, fr. LL *insubstantialis*, fr. *in-* ¹in- + *substantialis* substantial] : not substantial: as **a** : lacking substance or reality : IMAGINARY, APPARITIONAL ⟨an ~ mirage floating near the horizon⟩ **b** : lacking firmness or solidity of structure : FLIMSY, FRAIL ⟨delicate ~ wrists and ankles⟩ — **in·substantiality** \"+\ *n*

**in·subvertible** \"+\ *adj* [LL *insubvertibilis*, fr. *in-* ¹in- + L *subvertere* to overturn, overthrow + *-ibilis* -ible — more at SUBVERT] : incapable of being overthrown or altered in course or orientation ⟨the ~ physical laws⟩

**in·success** \"+\ *n* [¹*in-* + *success*] : lack of success : FAILURE

**insucken** \'=,==\ *adj* [¹*in* + *sucken*] *Scot* : situated in or astricted to a sucken

**in·sufferable** \(ˈ)in, ən+\ *adj* [¹*in-* + *sufferable*] : incapable of being endured ⟨an ~ injury⟩ : intolerable esp. by reason of pompous assurance or assumed superiority ⟨~ self-importance⟩ ⟨a thoroughly ~ child⟩ — **in·sufferableness** \"+\ *n* — **in·sufferably** \"+\ *adv*

**in·suf·fi·cience** \ˌinsəˈfishən(t)s\ *n* -s [ME, fr. MF or LL; MF, fr. LL *insufficientia*] : INSUFFICIENCY

**in·suf·fi·cien·cy** \-shensē, -si\ *n* [LL *insufficientia*, fr. *insufficient-*, *insufficiens* insufficient + *-ia* -y] **1** : the quality or state of being insufficient : lack of sufficiency: as **a** : lack of mental or moral fitness : INABILITY, INCOMPETENCY ⟨the ~ of a man for an office⟩ **b** : lack of adequate supply of something (as force, quality, quantity) : INADEQUACY ⟨~ of provisions⟩ **c** : lack of physical power or capacity : IMPOTENCE; *specif* : inability of an organ or body part to function normally ⟨cardiac ~⟩ ⟨renal ~⟩ **2** : something insufficient ⟨sadly aware of his own neglects and *insufficiencies*⟩

**in·suf·fi·cient** \-shənt\ *adj* [ME, fr. MF, fr. LL *insufficient-*, *insufficiens*, fr. *in-* ¹in- + L *sufficient-*, *sufficiens* sufficient — more at SUFFICIENT] : not sufficient: as **a** : lacking in strength, power, ability, capacity, or skill : INCOMPETENT, UNFIT ⟨a person ~ to discharge the duties of an office⟩ **b** *obs* : not sufficiently furnished or supplied : deficient or lacking in something **c** : inadequate to some implied or designated need, use, or purpose ⟨provisions ~ in quantity⟩ — **in·suf·fi·cient·ly** *adv*

**in·suf·flate** \'in(t)sə,flāt, ən'sə-\ *vt* -ED/-ING/-S [LL *insufflatus*, past part. of *insufflare*, fr. L *in-* ²in- + *sufflare* to blow, sufflate — more at SUFFLATE] **1** : to blow or breathe upon or into : subject to insufflation ⟨~ a room with insecticide⟩ **2** : to blow or breathe (something) onto a surface or into a void : practice insufflation of ⟨*insufflated* the metallic powder onto the hot surface⟩ ⟨*insufflated* the drug into the depths of the wound⟩

**in·suf·fla·tion** \,in(t)sə'flāshən\ *n* -s [MF, fr. LL *insufflation-*, *insufflatio*, fr. *insufflatus* (past part.) + L *-ion-*, *-io* -ion] : an act or the action of breathing or blowing on, into, or in: as **a** : the breathing upon a person or thing in the ritual of various liturgical churches to symbolize (as at baptism) the inspiration of a new spiritual life and the expulsion of evil spirits **b** : the act of blowing (as a gas, powder, or vapor) into a cavity of the body ⟨~ of gas into a fallopian tube to determine its patency⟩

**in·suf·fla·tor** \'in(t)sə,flād·ə(r), ən'sə-\ *n* -s [*insufflate* + *-or*] : a device for insufflating: as **a** : an injector for forcing air into a furnace **b** : a device used in medical insufflation (as of a drug) **c** : a device for blowing the powder used in developing latent fingerprints (as in criminal investigation)

**in·su·la** \'in(t)s(y)ələ, 'inshə-\ *n, pl* **in·su·lae** \-,lē, 'in(t)sə,lī\ **1** [L, lit., island — more at ISLE] : an ancient Roman building or a group of buildings standing together forming a block or square and usu. constituting an apartment building **2** [NL, fr. L] : ISLAND OF REIL

**in·su·lant** \'in(t)sələnt *sometimes* 'in(t)syəl- *or* 'inshəl-\ *n* -s [¹*insulate* + *-ant*] : INSULATION

**¹in·su·lar** \-lə(r)\ *adj* [LL *insularis*, fr. L *insula* island + *-aris* -ar — more at ISLE] **1 a** : of or relating to an island : being or having the characteristics of an island : dwelling or situated on or forming an island **b** *usu cap* (1) : of or relating to Great Britain or to the British isles as distinct from the continent of Europe — compare CONTINENTAL (2) : of, relating to, or characteristic of the Insular hand **2 a** : INSULATED, ISOLATED, DETACHED ⟨an ~ building⟩ **b** *of a plant or animal* : having a restricted or isolated natural range or habitat **3 a** : of or relating to the people of an island **b** : resulting from isolation or characteristic of isolated people **c** : NARROW, CIRCUMSCRIBED, ILLIBERAL, PREJUDICED **4** [NL *insula* + E *-ar*] : of or relating to an island of cells or tissue (as the islets of Langerhans or islands of Reil)

**²insular** \"\ *n* -s : ISLANDER

**insular celtic** *n, usu cap I&C* : the Celtic languages excluding Gaulish

**insular hand** *or* **insular script** *n, usu cap I* : a script characterized by thick initial strokes and heavy shading developed from half uncial under the influence of uncial by Irish scribes about the 5th and 6th centuries A.D. and used in England until the Norman conquest and in Ireland with modifications to the present day

**in·su·lar·ism** \-lə,rizəm\ *n* -s : the quality or state of being insular and esp. of exhibiting narrowness and rigidity of outlook or mind

**in·su·lar·i·ty** \ˌ=='larəd·ē, -ətē, -i *also* -'ler-\ *n* -ES **1** : the quality or state of being an island or consisting of islands ⟨the ~ of Great Britain⟩ **2 a** : condition of dwelling on an island or in isolation **b** : narrowness or illiberality of opinion or custom

**in·su·lar·ize** \'==,lə,rīz\ *vt* -ED/-ING/-S [¹*insular* + *-ize*] : to form into or represent as an island

**in·su·lar·ly** *adv* **1** : in an insular manner : NARROWLY, RIGIDLY ⟨an ~ prejudiced mind⟩ **2** : throughout an island ⟨~ distributed Philippine plants⟩

**1in·su·lary** \'==,lerē\ *n* -ES [prob. modif. (influenced by E *-ary*) of F *insulaire*, fr. *insulaire*, adj., insular, fr. LL *insularis*] *archaic* : ISLANDER

**2insulary** \"\ *adj* [prob. modif. (influenced by E *-ary*) of LL *insularis*] *archaic* : INSULAR

**1in·su·late** \'in(t)sə,lāt *sometimes* 'in(t)syə- *or* 'inshə-; *usu* -ād.+V\ *vt* -ED/-ING/-S [L *insula* island + E *-ate* — more at ISLE] **1** *archaic* : to form an island of : isolate by surrounding water **2 a** : to separate or shield (a conductor) from conducting bodies by means of nonconductors so as to prevent transfer of electricity, heat, or sound **b** : to place in a detached situation or in a state of isolation : set apart : SEGREGATE, ISOLATE ⟨hysterical symptoms quite commonly serve to ~ the patient —Norman Cameron⟩ ⟨*insulating* man from the natural world⟩ **c** : to remove (as specie or a commodity) from the open market : STERILIZE ⟨a program designed to ~ the government-held surpluses by using them for special purposes⟩; *also* : to stabilize (a market) by such removal

**2in·su·late** \-,lət, -,lāt\ *adj* [L *insula* island + E *-ate*] : set apart : ISOLATED

**insulating** *adj* : serving to insulate : functioning as insulation ⟨~ material⟩ ⟨an ~ calm⟩

**insulating board** *or* **insulation board** *n* : a board with insulating properties; *esp* : a structural or finish material that consists of sheets of lightly compressed vegetable pulp variously finished and is used esp. for its thermal insulating effect resulting from great numbers of minute included air spaces

**insulating oil** *n* : any of various oily liquids (as a hydrocarbon oil) used as insulators and cooling mediums in transformers, switches, or other electrical equipment

**insulating varnish** *n* : varnish used to insulate electrical apparatus (as certain coils or glass fittings)

**in·su·la·tion** \,==ˈlāshən\ *n* -S **1 a** : an act or action of insulating ⟨work on the ~ of the house⟩ **b** : the quality or state of being insulated ⟨his complete ~ in regard to current events⟩ : ISOLATION ⟨~ as a factor in evolution⟩ **2** : something that insulates; *usu* : material that retards the passage of heat, electricity, or sound : nonconducting material that is used in insulating

**insulation resistance** *n* : the alternating-current resistance between two electrical conductors or two systems of conductors separated by an insulating material

**in·su·la·tive** \'==,lād·iv, -āt|, |ēv *also* |əv\ *adj* : relating to or constituting insulation ⟨~ value⟩ ⟨an ~ effect⟩

**in·su·la·tor** \-,lād·ə(r), -ātə-\ *n* -S **1** : one that insulates; *esp* : a worker that applies electrical or thermal insulation **2 a** : a material or body that is a poor conductor of electricity, heat, or sound **b** : a body of electrically nonconducting material for keeping charged conductors from contact with each other or from grounding and often also for supporting them

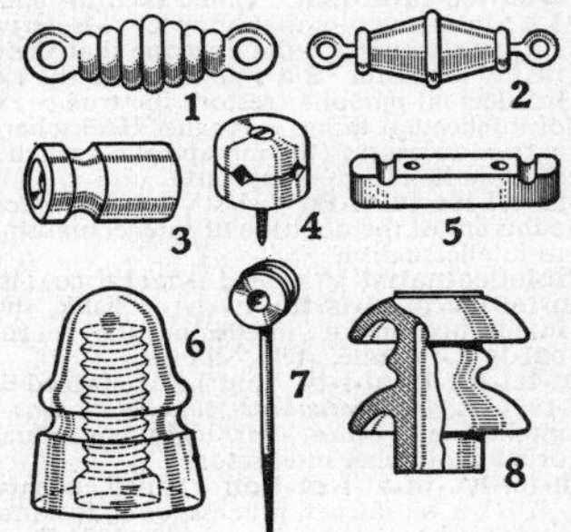

insulators 2b: *1, 2* used with antennas; *3* knob, *4* split-knob, *5* cleat, *6, 8* petticoat, *7* standoff

**in·su·lin** \'in(t)sələn *sometimes* 'in(t)slən *or* 'in(t)syəl- *or* 'inshə-\ *n* -S [NL *insula* + E *-in*] : a protein pancreatic hormone secreted by the islets of Langerhans that is essential esp. for the metabolism of carbohydrates, that is obtained commercially in crystalline form usu. from beef or pork pancreas, and that is used in the treatment and control of diabetes mellitus

**in·su·lin·ase** \-lə,nās, -āz\ *n* -S [*insulin* + *-ase*] : an enzyme found esp. in liver that inactivates insulin

**in·su·lin·ize** \-,nīz\ *vt* -ED/-ING/-S : to treat with insulin

**insulin shock** *n* : hypoglycemia associated with the presence of excessive insulin in the system and characterized by progressive development of coma

**insulin shock therapy** *n* : the treatment of mental disorder (as schizophrenia) by insulin in doses sufficient to produce deep coma — compare INSULIN SHOCK

**in·sulse** \ən'səl(t)s\ *adj* [L *insulsus*, lit., unsalted, fr. *in-* ¹in- + *-sulsus* (fr. *salsus*, past part. of *salere* to salt, fr. *sal* salt) — more at SALT] *archaic* : TASTELESS, FLAT, STUPID — **in·sul·si·ty** \-)səd·ē\ *n* -ES

**1in·sult** \ən'səlt\ *vb* -ED/-ING/-S [MF or L; MF *insulter*, fr. L *insultare*, lit., to spring upon, leap, fr. *in-* ²in- + *-sultare* (fr. *saltare* to leap) — more at SALTANT] *vi* **1** *archaic* : to behave with pride or insolence : display arrogance or contempt : exult or boast usu. insolently or contemptuously : TRIUMPH, VAUNT **2** *obs* : to make an attack or assault **~** *vt* **1 a** : to treat with insolence, indignity, or contempt by word or action : affront wantonly ⟨his impertinences ~*ed* his sister's guests⟩ **b** : to make little of : affect offensively or depreciatively ⟨~*ed* the traditions of the sea by ordering "right" and "left" to be substituted . . . for "starboard" and "port" —Bruce Bliven b.1889⟩ ⟨editorial slovenliness that ~*s* the reader's mind⟩ **2** *obs* : to make an attack on : ASSAULT, ASSAIL; *esp* : to make a sudden military attack on without the usual preliminaries or formalities **syn** see OFFEND

**2in·sult** \'in,səlt\ *n* -S [MF or LL; MF *insult*, *insulte*, fr. LL *insultus*, prob. fr. L *in-* ²in- + *-sultus* (fr. *saltus* leap) (prob. influenced by L *insultare* to insult, spring upon); akin to L *salire* to leap — more at SALLY] **1** *archaic* : an act of attacking : ONSET, ATTACK **2** : a gross indignity offered to another either by word or act : an act or speech of insolence or contempt ⟨his words were a studied ~⟩ ⟨such an offer was an ~ to our intelligence⟩ **3** : damage or an instance of injury to the body or one of its parts ⟨repeated acute vascular ~*s*⟩ ⟨any ~ to the constitution of a patient suffering from active tuberculosis —*Jour. Amer. Med. Assoc.*⟩; *also* : an agent that produces such an insult ⟨a thermal ~⟩ ⟨damage resulting from malnutrition ~*s*⟩ **syn** see AFFRONT

**in·sult·abil·i·ty** \(,)in,səltə'biləd·ē, ən-, -lətē, -i\ *n* -ES : capacity for being or readiness to be insulted

**in·sult·able** \ən'səltəbəl\ *adj* : capable of being insulted; *esp* : easily insulted : OVERSENSITIVE

**in·sul·ta·tion** \,in,səl'tāshən\ *n* -S [MF, fr. L *insultation-*, *insultatio*, fr. *insultatus* (past part. of *insultare* to insult) + *-ion-*, *-io* -ion] **1** *archaic* : an act of insulting : contemptuous or insolent treatment : scornful exultation **2** *obs* : ATTACK, ONSET

**insulted** *adj* [fr. past part. of ¹*insult*] *chiefly dial* : affected with irritation or distaste : OFFENDED, ANNOYED

**in·sult·er** \ən'səltə(r)\ *n* -S : one that insults

**insulting** *adj* : containing, characterized by, or constituting insult ⟨~ language⟩ ⟨the ~ agent in a pathologic process⟩ — **in·sult·ing·ly** *adv* — **in·sult·ing·ness** *n* -ES

**insultproof** \'=,=+,=\ *adj* : not susceptible to insult

**in sunder** *adv (or adj)* [ME, fr. OE *onsundran*, *onsundrum* — more at ASUNDER] *archaic* : ASUNDER ⟨breaketh the bow and cutteth the spear *in sunder* —Ps 46:9 (AV)⟩

**in·superability** \(')in, ən+\ *n* : the quality or state of being insuperable

**in·superable** \(')in, ən+\ *adj* [ME, fr. MF & L; MF, fr. L *insuperabilis*, fr. *in-* ¹in- + *superabilis* superable — more at SUPERABLE] : incapable of being surmounted: as **a** : incapable of being vanquished : INVINCIBLE ⟨these ~ heroes who dared the northern seas⟩ **b** : impossible to overcome ⟨~ difficulties⟩ **c** : incapable of being passed over : IMPASSABLE ⟨an ~ barrier⟩ **d** : UNSURPASSABLE — **in·su·per·a·ble·ness** \-nəs\ *n* — **in·su·per·a·bly** \-blē, -bli\ *adv*

**in·supportability** \;in+\ *n* : INSUPPORTABLENESS

**in·supportable** \"+\ *adj* [MF or LL; MF, fr. LL *insupportabilis*, fr. L *in-* ¹in- + *supportare* to carry, convey + *-abilis* -able — more at SUPPORT] : impossible to support: as **a** : incapable of being borne : UNENDURABLE ⟨~ burdens⟩ ⟨an ~ pain⟩ **b** : incapable of being sustained : UNJUSTIFIABLE ⟨~ charges⟩ **c** *obs* : IRRESISTIBLE — **in·supportably** \"+\ *adv*

**in·supportableness** \"+\ *n* -ES : the quality or state of being insupportable

**in·supposable** \"+\ *adj* [¹*in-* + *supposable*] : impossible to suppose : UNBELIEVABLE

**in·suppressible** \"+\ *adj* [¹*in-* + *suppress* + *-ible*] : impossible to suppress — **in·suppressibly** \"+\ *adv*

**in·suppressive** \"+\ *adj* [¹*in-* + *suppress* + *-ive*] : INSUPPRESSIBLE

**in·sur·abil·i·ty** \ən,shu̇rə'biləd·ē, -lətē, -i\ *n* -ES : the quality or state of being insurable

**in·sur·able** \ən'shu̇rəbəl\ *adj* [*insure* + *-able*] : capable of being or proper to be insured against loss, damage, death ⟨~ property⟩ : affording a sufficient ground for insurance

**insurable interest** *n* : an interest (as based on a blood tie or likelihood of financial injury) that is judged to give an insurance applicant a legal right to enforce the insurance contract against the objection that it is a wagering contract contrary to public policy

**insurable value** *n* : the value of property stated in an insurance contract indicating the limit of indemnity that will be paid at the time of loss

**in·sur·ance** \ən'shu̇r(ə)n(t)s, *chiefly in southern U.S.* 'in,=(=)\ *n* -S *often attrib* [*insure* + *-ance*] **1 a** : the action or process of insuring or the state of being insured usu. against loss or damage by a contingent event (as death, fire, accident, or sickness) **b** : means of insuring against loss or risks ⟨provide ~ against floods⟩ **2 a** : the business of insuring persons or property; *specif* : a device for the elimination or reduction of an economic risk common to all members of a large group and employing a system of equitable contributions out of which losses are paid **b** : coverage by contract whereby for a stipulated consideration one party undertakes to indemnify or guarantee another against loss by a specified contingency or peril **c** : the principles and practices of the business of insuring — see ACCIDENT INSURANCE, AUTOMOBILE INSURANCE, BUSINESS INTERRUPTION INSURANCE, CASUALTY INSURANCE, DISABILITY INSURANCE, FIRE INSURANCE, GROUP INSURANCE, HEALTH INSURANCE, LIABILITY INSURANCE, LIFE INSURANCE, MARINE INSURANCE, SOCIAL INSURANCE, UNEMPLOYMENT INSURANCE, WORKMEN'S COMPENSATION INSURANCE; compare ANNUITY, CORPORATE SURETYSHIP, INSURABLE INTEREST, LOSS, MUTUAL, POLICY, PREMIUM, RATE, REINSURANCE, REPRESENTATION, RESERVE, RISK TONTINE, WARRANTY **3 a** : the premium paid for insuring something **b** : the sum for which something is insured

**insurance adjuster** *n* : a person employed by insurer or insured to determine the loss under an insurance policy

**insurance agent** *n* : an agent of an insurer authorized to negotiate contracts of insurance

**insurance broker** *n* : a broker who usu. acts as the agent of the insured in making contracts of insurance but sometimes as the agent of the insurer for some purposes (as payment of the premium) and of the insured for all other purposes

**insurance certificate** *n* **1** : a certificate issued by an insurer to a shipper as evidence that a shipment of merchandise is covered under a marine policy **2** : CERTIFICATE 5

**insurance reserve** *n* : the part of the reserve of an insurance company to be absorbed from the initial reserve in any year in payment of losses — compare INVESTMENT RESERVE

**insurance trust** *n* : an agreement providing for the receipt and distribution of life insurance proceeds by a trustee

**in·sur·ant** \ən'shu̇r(ə)nt\ *n* -S [*insure* + *-ant*] : a person who takes out a policy of insurance; *also* : one on whose life a policy of life insurance is taken out

**in·sure** \ən'shu̇(ə)r, -u̇ə\ *vb* -ED/-ING/-S [ME *insuren*, prob. alter. (influenced by *in-* ²in-) of *assuren* to assure — more at ASSURE] *vt* **1** *obs* : to declare to with confidence : ASSURE : promise solemnly **2** : to assure against a loss by a contingent event on certain stipulated conditions or at a given rate or premium : give, take, or procure an insurance on or for : enter into or carry a contract of insurance on — used of either the person who pays the insurance premiums or the society, corporation, or underwriter that undertakes the risk as subject and of the thing to which the risk attaches (as life or property) or the sum secured as object **3** : ENSURE 3 **~** *vi* : to contract to give insurance : UNDERWRITE; *also* : to procure or effect insurance **syn** see ENSURE

**insured** *n* -S [fr. *insured*, past part. of *insure*] : a person whose life, physical well-being, or property is the subject of insurance : the owner of a policy of insurance : POLICYHOLDER

**insured plan** *n* : a pension or retirement plan under which contributions are used to purchase life insurance or annuities as a means of funding the benefits promised

**in·sur·er** \ən'shu̇rə(r)\ *n* -S [*insure* + *-er*] **1** : one that makes certain or secure : one that guarantees ⟨these ~*s* of peace⟩ **2** : one that contracts to indemnify another by way of insurance : an insurance company or underwriter **3** *archaic* : INSURED

**1in·surge** \ən+\ *vb* [L *insurgere*, fr. *in-* ¹in- + *surgere* to rise — more at SURGE] *vi* : to become insurgent : behave insurgently **~** *vt* : to make insurgent

**2insurge** \'in+,-\ *n* [⁴*in* + *surge*] : a surging in

**in·sur·gence** \ən'sərjən(t)s, -səj-,-səij-\ *n* -S [prob. fr. F, fr. *insurgent*, n. (fr. E) + *-ence*] : an act or the action of being insurgent : UPRISING, INSURRECTION ⟨the recurrent ~ of the lower house⟩

**in·sur·gen·cy** \-jənsē, -si\ *n* -ES [¹*insurgent* + *-ency*] **1** : the quality or state of being insurgent; *specif* : a condition of revolt against a recognized government that does not reach the proportions of an organized revolutionary government and is not recognized as belligerency **2** : INSURGENCE

**1in·sur·gent** \-nt\ *n* -S [L *insurgent-*, *insurgens*, pres. part. of *insurgere* to rise up, insurge] **1** : a person who rises in revolt against civil authority or an established government : REBEL; *esp* : a rebel not recognized as a belligerent — compare RIOT, TREASON **2** : one that acts contrary to the policies and decisions of his political party

**2in·sur·gent** \"\ *adj* **1** : rising in opposition to civil or political authority or against an established government : INSUBORDINATE, REBELLIOUS **2** : surging in ⟨the quick ~ sea⟩ — **in·sur·gent·ly** *adv*

**in·sur·ges·cence** \,in(t)(,)sər'jesⁿn(t)s\ *n* -S [¹*insurge* + *-escence*] : tendency to make insurrection

**insuring clause** *n* : a clause in an insurance policy that sets out the risk assumed by the insurer or defines the scope of the coverage afforded

**in·surmountable** \;in+\ *adj* [¹*in-* + *surmountable*] : incapable of being surmounted, passed over, or overcome : INSUPERABLE ⟨~ disadvantages⟩ — **in·surmountableness** \"+\ *n* -ES — **in·surmountably** \"+\ *adv*

**in·sur·rect** \,in(t)sə'rekt\ *vi* [back-formation fr. *insurrection*] : to make or engage in insurrection

**in·sur·rec·tion** \,in(t)sə'rekshən\ *n* -S [ME *insurreccioun*, fr. MF *insurrection*, fr. LL *insurrection-*, *insurrectio*, fr. L *insurrectus* (past part. of *insurgere* to rise against, insurge) + *-ion-*, *-io* -ion — more at INSURGE] **1** : an act or instance of revolting against civil or political authority or against an established government **2** : an act or instance of rising up physically **syn** see REBELLION

**in·sur·rec·tion·al·ly** \-ᵊl|ē, -əl|, |i\ *adv* : in respect to insurrection : from an insurrectionary point of view

**in·sur·rec·tion·ary** \-shə,nerē, -ri\ *also* **in·sur·rec·tion·al** \;==ˈrekshənᵊl, -shnəl\ *adj* [*insurrection* + *-ary* or *-al*] : of, relating to, or constituting insurrection : given to or tending to induce insurrection : REBELLIOUS ⟨~ activity⟩ ⟨~ movements⟩

**2insurrectionary** \"\ *n* -ES : a participant in insurrection : INSURGENT

**in·sur·rec·tion·ist** \,==ˈreksh(ə)nəst\ *n* -S : a favorer of or participant in insurrection : INSURGENT

**in·sur·rec·tion·ize** \-shə,nīz\ *vt* -ED/-ING/-S : to cause (as a people) to be insurgent : make insurrection in (a country)

**in·sur·rec·to** \,in(t)sə'rek(,)tō\ *n* -S [Sp, fr. L *insurrectus* (past part.)] : INSURRECTIONARY, INSURGENT, REBEL

**in·susceptibility** \;in+\ *n* : the quality or state of being insusceptible : lack of susceptibility

**in·susceptible** \"+\ *adj* [¹*in-* + *susceptible*] : not susceptible : incapable of being moved, affected, or impressed ⟨~ of pity⟩ ⟨~ to disease⟩ ⟨~ animals⟩ — **in·susceptibly** \"+\ *adv*

**inswarming** \'=,==\ *adj* [²*in* + *swarming*, pres. part. of *swarm* (after *swarm in*, v.)] : entering in or like a swarm

**insweeping** \'=,==\ *adj* [²*in* + *sweeping*, pres. part. of *sweep* (after *sweep in*, v.)] : moving sweepingly in

**inswinger** \'=,=+\ *n* [²*in* + *swing* (v.) + *-er*] : a bowled cricket ball that swerves in the air from off to leg — compare OUTSWINGER

**int** *abbr* **1** intelligence **2** intercept **3** interest **4** interim **5** interior **6** interjection **7** interleaved **8** intermediate **9** internal **10** international **11** interpreter **12** interval **13** interview **14** intransitive

**in·tabulation** \ən·+\ *n* [²*in-* + *tabulation*] : TABLATURE 1a

**in·tact** \ən·'takt\ *adj* [ME *intacte*, fr. L *intactus*, fr. *in-* ¹in- + *tactus*, past part. of *tangere* to touch — more at TANGENT] **1** : untouched esp. by anything that harms or diminishes : left complete or entire : UNINJURED ⟨obtain your uncle's estate ~ —Kenneth Roberts⟩ ⟨houses largely ~ after some 3500 years —Jacquetta & Christopher Hawkes⟩ ⟨the memory of that night remained ~ —Elinor Wylie⟩ **2** *of a living body or its parts* : physically and functionally complete : having no relevant component removed or destroyed: **a** : physically virginal **b** : sexually competent : UNCASTRATED — used chiefly of a domestic animal — **in·tact·ness** \-k(t)nəs\ *n* -ES

**in·ta·gliat·ed** \ən·'tal|,yād·əd, -täl|, |glē,ā-\ *adj* [It *intagliato* (past part. of *intagliare*) + E *-ed*] : engraved in or as if in intaglio

**1in·ta·glio** \ən·'tal|(,)yō, -täl|, |glē,ō\ *n* -S *often attrib* [It, fr. *intagliare* to engrave, carve, cut, fr. ML *intaleare*, fr. L *in-* ²in- + LL *taliare* to cut — more at TAILOR] **1 a** : an engraving or incised figure in stone or other hard material; *specif* : a figure or design depressed below the surface of the material with the normal elevations of the design hollowed out so that an impression from the design yields an image in relief **b** : the art or process of executing intaglios **c** : a process or method of printing from a face in which the ink-carrying part is sunk that produces raised printing (as in die stamping) or plane printing (as in gravure) — compare LETTERPRESS, PLANOGRAPHY, STENCIL **2** : something carved in intaglio or stamped so as to resemble an intaglio carving; *esp* : a carved gem with the figures or designs carved into a generally flat surface — compare CAMEO **3** : a countersunk die for producing a figure in relief

**2intaglio** \"\ *vt* -ED/-ING/-S : to cut or represent in intaglio

**intaglio ri·le·va·to** \-,rēlə'vä(,)tō\ *or* **intaglio ri·lie·vo** \-rē'lē(,)vō, -rēl'yā(-, -ye(-\ *n* [It, fr. *intaglio* + *rilevato* raised or *rilievo* relief] : SUNK RELIEF

**intagliotype** *n* [¹*intaglio* + *type*] : a process for producing from a design drawn on a coated metal plate an intaglio plate for printing; *also* : a print from such a plate

**intake** \'=,=\ *n*, *often attrib* [⁴*in* + *take* (after *take in*, v.)] **1** *dial chiefly Brit* : a portion of land taken in or enclosed from a moor, common, or road : ENCLOSURE : hillside pasture or land reclaimed (as from the sea) **2 a** : an opening through which air, water, steam, or other fluid enters an enclosure ⟨the fuel-mixture ~ of an engine cylinder⟩ ⟨the ~ of an aqueduct⟩ — see JET ENGINE illustration **b** : a main passageway for air in a coal mine **3 a** : the act, process, or an instance of taking in ⟨~ . . . of various life-sustaining material —H.A.Overstreet⟩ ⟨stop the ~ of new clerks —Christopher Strachey⟩ ⟨an ~ of breath⟩ ⟨after the first quick ~ of surprise —Ethel Wilson⟩ ⟨the rate of ~ is an important index —W.F. Mackey⟩; *specif* : initial procedures (as interviews) conducted by a social worker, juvenile-court officer, or clinician in considering a client for treatment or service ⟨the role of the ~ worker⟩ ⟨an ~ official⟩ **b** (1) : the amount taken in ⟨an adequate ~ of food⟩ ⟨strictly limited my ~ during the day —*Sydney (Australia) Bull.*⟩ (2) : energy taken in : INPUT (3) : the persons taken into a group or organization ⟨half the total ~ were the sons of plebeians —J.W.Saunders⟩ (4) *chiefly Brit* : a person taken into a military service : RECRUIT ⟨just arrived with a new ~ —Derek Stanford⟩ **4** *Scot* **a** : SWINDLE **b** : SWINDLER

**intake stroke** *n* : the stroke in the cycle of an internal-combustion engine during which the fuel mixture is drawn in before compression

**int al** *abbr* [L *inter alia*] among other things; [L *inter alios*] among other persons

**in·tangibility** \(;)in·, ən·+\ *n* **1** : the quality or state of being intangible ⟨there is a certain ~ about this problem⟩ **2** : something that is intangible : an intangible element ⟨fond of the pretty *intangibilities* of romance —Hugh Miller b. 1891⟩

**1in·tangible** \(')in·, ən·+\ *adj* [F or ML; F, fr. MF, fr. ML *intangibilis*, fr. L *in-* ¹in- + LL *tangibilis* tangible — more at TANGIBLE] **1** : incapable of being touched or perceived by touch : not tangible : IMPALPABLE, IMPERCEPTIBLE ⟨that more subtle and ~ thing, the soul —John Buchan⟩ ⟨the ~ constituent of energy —James Jeans⟩ **2** : incapable of being defined or determined with certainty or precision : VAGUE, ELUSIVE ⟨with an ~ feeling of impending disaster —Guy Fowler⟩ ⟨this menace from the North was ~ and evasive —John Buchan⟩ — **in·tangibleness** \"+\ *n* — **in·tangibly** \"+\ *adv*

**2intangible** \"\ *n* : something intangible; *specif* : an asset (as goodwill or a patent right) that is not corporeal

**intangible assets** *n pl* : INTANGIBLES

**intangible property** *n* : property having no physical substance apparent to the senses : incorporeal property (as choses in action) often evidenced by documents (as stocks, bonds, notes, judgments, franchises) having no intrinsic value or by rights of action, easements, goodwill, trade secrets

**in·tar·sia** \ən·'tärsēə\ *n* -S [G, prob. modif. (influenced by It *tarsia*) of It *intarsio*, fr. *intarsiare* to inlay, fr. *in-* ²in- + *tarsiare* to inlay, fr. *tarsia* intarsia, fr. Ar *tarṣī*'] **1** : a mosaic usu. of small pieces of wood which are inserted and glued into hollows of a wooden support that was popular in 15th century Italy for decoration featuring esp. scrolls, arabesques, architectural scenes, and flowers **2** : the art or process of making such work — **in·tar·si·ate** \-ē,āt, -ēət\ *adj*

**in·tar·si·a·tu·ra** \ən·,tärsēə'tu̇rə\ *n*, *pl* **intarsiatu·re** \-(,)rā\ [It, fr. *intarsiato* (past part. of *intarsiare*) + *-ura* -ure (fr. L)] : INTARSIA

**in·tar·sio** \-sē,ō\ *n*, *pl* **intar·si** \-(,)sē\ [It] : INTARSIA

**in·tar·sist** \-,səst\ *n* -S [*intarsia* + *-ist*] : a person who works in intarsia

**intcl** *abbr* intercoastal

**in·te·ger** \'intəjə(r), -tēj-\ *n* -S [L, adj., untouched, entire — more at ENTIRE] **1** : any of the natural numbers (as 1, 2, 3, 4, 5), the negatives of these numbers, or 0 **2** : a complete entity ⟨governmental policy is an ~ —Dean Acheson⟩ ⟨they become a whole, an ~, of people who have the same aspirations and hopes —William Faulkner⟩ **syn** see NUMBER

**in·te·gra·bil·i·ty** \,intəgrə'biləd·ē, -lətē, -i\ *n* -ES : the fact or character of being integrable

**in·te·gra·ble** \'intəgrəbəl\ *adj* [³*integrate* + *-able*] : capable of being integrated ⟨a differential equation that is ~⟩ ⟨an ~ function⟩

**1in·te·gral** \'intəgrəl, 'integ- *also* in·'tegrəl *or* ÷'in·trəgəl *or* ÷'in·trēgəl\ *adj* [ME, fr. ML *integralis*, fr. L *integr-*, *integer* untouched, entire + *-alis* -al] **1 a** : of, relating to, or serving to form a whole : essential to completeness : organically joined or linked : CONSTITUENT, INHERENT ⟨science has become an ~ part of his cultural environment —C.I.Glicksberg⟩ ⟨an ~ part of the empire⟩ ⟨in great dramas character is always . . . somehow ~ with plot —T.S.Eliot⟩ ⟨political and economic power are ~ one to the other —*Commonweal*⟩ **b** (1) : of, being, or relating to a mathematical integer (2) : relating to or concerned with mathematical integrals or integration **c** : formed as a unit with another part (as the main part or tool or mechanism ⟨the pin is ~ with the pump body —H.F.Blanchard & Ralph Ritchen⟩ ⟨heat transfer through tubes with ~ spiral fins —*Transactions of Amer. Society of Mech. Engineers*⟩ ⟨the steam chest may be an ~ part of the turbine casing or may be bolted to it —B.G.A.Skrotzki & W.A.Vopat⟩ **2** : composed of constituent parts making a whole : COMPOSITE, INTEGRATED ⟨a hospital, a medical school, and a laboratory of science all in one ~ group —V.G.Heiser⟩ **3** : having nothing omitted or taken away : lacking nothing that belongs to it : COMPLETE,

ENTIRE, PERFECT ⟨if vocations are declining, it is because ~ Catholic living is declining —J.H.Wilson⟩ — **in·te·gral·ly** \-əlē,-əli\ *adv*

**²integral** *n* -s **1 :** an entire thing **:** TOTALITY, WHOLE **2** *obs* **:** an integral part **:** CONSTITUENT, COMPONENT **3 :** the result of a mathematical integration either of a function or of an equation

**integral calculus** *n* [prob. part trans. of NL *calculus integralis*] **:** a branch of mathematics that deals chiefly with the methods of finding indefinite integrals of functions and the evaluation of definite integrals, calculation (as of lengths of curves, areas, volumes, moments of inertia) by definite integration, mean values of functions, and the solution of certain simple types of differential equations

**integral cover** *n* **:** SELF-COVER

**integral equation** *n* **:** an equation in which the dependent variable is included at least once under a definite integral sign

**integral humanism** *n* **:** a Christian humanism based on Thomistic principles and advocated esp. by Jacques Maritain

**in·te·gral·i·ty** \ˌintəˈgraləd·ē\ *n* -ES **:** integral quality or state

**integral rational function** *n* **:** POLYNOMIAL

**integral tripack** *n* **:** a photographic film or plate consisting of three superposed emulsions each sensitive to a different primary color and coated on a single support — called also *monopack;* compare BIPACK

**in·te·grand** \ˈintəˌgrand, ˌ==ˈ=\ *n* -s [L *integrandus,* gerundive of *integrare* to integrate] **:** a mathematical expression to be integrated **:** the function under the integral sign

**¹in·te·grant** \ˈintəgrənt, -tēg-\ *adj* [F or L; F *intégrant,* fr. MF, fr. L *integrant-, integrans,* pres. part. of *integrare* to integrate] **:** INTEGRAL ⟨all these are ~ parts of the republic —Edmund Burke⟩

**²integrant** \"\ *n* -s **:** an integral part **:** COMPONENT **syn** see ELEMENT

**in·te·graph** \-ˌgraf, -râf\ *n* [ISV, blend of *integrate* and *-graph*] **:** an instrument that draws mechanically the graph of an antiderivative of a given mathematical function

**¹in·te·grate** \-ˌgrət, -ˌgrāt\ *adj* [ME *integrat,* fr. L *integratus* (past part.)] **:** INTEGRATED ⟨we may consider logic . . . as an ~ whole —William Hamilton †1856⟩

**²integrate** \"\ *n* -s **:** something that is integrated **:** a complete, organically unified, or perfect entity usu. resulting from a combination of elements **:** WHOLE ⟨an ~ of images which portray the person at his future best —C.K.Kluckhohn & H.A. Murray⟩ ⟨the cell, the molecule are not aggregates but ~*s* —H.J.Muller⟩

**³in·te·grate** \ˈintəˌgrāt, *usu* -ād·+V\ *vb* -ED/-ING/-S [L *integratus,* past part. of *integrare,* fr. *integr-, integer* untouched, entire — more at ENTIRE] *vt* **1** *obs* **:** to make complete **:** CONSTITUTE ⟨the particular doctrines which ~ Christianity —William Chillingworth⟩ **2 :** to form into a more complete, harmonious, or coordinated entity often by the addition or arrangement of parts or elements ⟨that conquest rounded and *integrated* the glorious empire —Thomas De Quincey⟩ ⟨if man is to ~ himself, he must discover his springs of action —P.W.Bridgman⟩ **3 :** to combine to form a more complete, harmonious, or coordinated entity: **a :** to unite (as a part or element) with something else ⟨a system of free enterprise carefully *integrated* with teamwork —J.C.Penney⟩ ⟨he who ~*s* this knowledge with the pattern of culture —David Daiches⟩ **b :** to combine together (as units or elements) ⟨~ the seventeen . . . reports into a few policy statements —E.C.Banfield⟩ ⟨this course . . . is designed to assist him to ~ all of his college experiences —A.C.Eurich⟩ ⟨a customs union that . . . would ~ the economies of the two countries —*Current Biog.*⟩ **c** (1) **:** to incorporate (as an individual or group) into a larger unit or group ⟨~ the West German divisions into the Atlantic defense system —*New Statesman & Nation*⟩ ⟨the South of that era was never *integrated* into the nation —H.W.Odum⟩ ⟨~ hundreds of thousands of Puerto Rican . . . workers into the organized labor movement —*N.Y. Times*⟩ (2) **:** to end the segregation of and bring into common and equal membership in society or an organization ⟨attempt to ~ Negroes into the church in a cautious gradual manner —*Jour. of Social Issues*⟩ ⟨moves . . . to ~ Indian children in the public school systems —*Indian Affairs*⟩ **4 :** DESEGREGATE ⟨a well-staffed state agency managed . . . to ~ forty formerly segregated school districts —Douglass Cater⟩ **5 :** to indicate the whole of **:** give the sum or total of **6 :** to find the integral of (as a function or equation) ~ *vi* **:** to become integrated ⟨some of the white parishioners . . . were willing to go along with the decision to ~ —*Jour. of Social Issues*⟩ ⟨the show begins to ~ again —Alfred Bester⟩ **syn** see UNIFY

**integrated** *adj* **1 :** characterized by integration: **a :** composed of separate parts united together to form a more complete, harmonious, or coordinated entity ⟨her tightly plotted, admirably ~ novel —John Barkham⟩ ⟨an ~ series of twenty-six dams —*Lamp*⟩ **b :** combining elements usu. taught in separate academic courses or departments ⟨to establish the behavior sciences on an ~ footing —J.W.Bennett⟩ ⟨~ courses⟩ **c :** having in common and equal membership individuals or groups differing in some group characteristic (as race) ⟨Negro units were broken up and reassigned in ~ groups —*New Republic*⟩ ⟨an ~ school⟩ **d :** characterized by psychological integration ⟨an ~ personality⟩ **e :** characterized by close cooperation or partial unity of constituent units ⟨a more closely ~ economic and political system —D.D.Eisenhower⟩ ⟨an ~ Europe⟩ ⟨an ~ military staff⟩ **f** (1) **:** operating economically as a single coordinated physically interconnected unit or system usu. confined to a specific region ⟨an ~ public utility system⟩ (2) **:** characterized by possession of sources of supply and continuous control of production and often distribution from raw materials to diversified finished products ⟨an ~ company . . . occupies a favored position as compared with a competitor which is at the mercy of the market —*Financial World*⟩ **g** *of the bar* **:** characterized by the compulsory membership of all lawyers practicing in a specific area (as a state) ⟨the states having an ~ bar have codes of professional ethics enforceable upon all members —*Jour. of the Amer. Judicature Society*⟩ **h :** characterized by social solidarity, coherency of form and function, and moral or psychological unity among members ⟨its culture is . . . more stable and better ~ —A.L.Kroeber⟩ **2 :** incorporated into a group or organization on the basis of common and equal membership despite differing characteristics (as race) ⟨most Indians are ~ with the other residents —W.R.Moore⟩ ⟨Negroes . . . have long been ~ in the police department —Gladwin Hill⟩

**integrated logging** *n* **:** a system of logging planned to remove in one cutting all usable timber and to separate the primary products and distribute them to industries where they will bring the highest returns

**integrating factor** *n* **:** a factor that renders immediately integrable a differential equation multiplied by it

**integrating sphere** *n* **:** a spherical shell used to determine total luminous flux by means of photometric measurement of a spot of light through an aperture in the shell whose white interior produces thorough diffusion of light from a source placed at its center

**integrating wattmeter** *n* **:** WATT-HOUR METER

**in·te·gra·tion** \ˌintəˈgrāshən\ *n* -s [L *integration-, integratio* act of renewing, act of restoring, fr. *integratus* (past part. of *integrare* to renew, integrate) + *-ion-, -io* -ion — more at INTEGRATE] **1 :** the act, process, or an instance of integrating **:** the condition of being formed into a whole by the addition or combination of parts or elements **2 a :** a combination and coordination of separate and diverse elements or units into a more complete or harmonious whole ⟨the automobile is an ~ of a multitude of machine parts —C.C.Furnas⟩ ⟨large-scale ~ of efforts —Oscar Handlin⟩ **b :** a unification and mutual adjustment of diverse groups or elements into a relatively coordinated and harmonious society or culture with a consistent body of normative standards ⟨most urban communities possess some degree of ~ around primary group norms —Kimball Young⟩ ⟨the total ~ of any given culture about its technology —David Bidney⟩ **c :** the organization of teaching matter to interrelate or unify subjects usu. taught in separate academic courses or departments ⟨through ~ it is possible to teach science, health, and safety as part of the regular program —E.J.Goebel⟩ **d :** an arrangement usu. on a hierarchical basis of functions or units of an organization to promote coordination and responsibility ⟨the need for administrative ~ at the county level —C.F.Snider⟩ ⟨an ~ of units previously scattered . . . in departments or otherwise —F.A.Ogg & P.O.Ray⟩ **e :** an incorporation into society or an organization (as a public school) on the basis of common and equal membership of individuals differing in some group characteristic (as race) ⟨ordered ~ of all white and Negro troops in the armed forces —*New Republic*⟩ ⟨the native Polynesian group that strongly objects to ~ with Europeans —*N.Y. Times*⟩ ⟨a positive ~ of the African into the South African community —Margaret Ballinger⟩ **f** (1) **:** the coordination and correlation of the total processes of perception, interpretation, and reaction ensuring a normal effective life ⟨failure of association and failure of ~ take place among neurotic individuals —R.M.Dorcus & G.W. Shaffer⟩ (2) **:** a harmonious coordination of the behavior and personality of an individual with his environment ⟨she attempts to enter the world of her fellow teenagers, and after many mistakes she achieves such ~ —Eleanor Scott⟩ **g :** the establishment of close cooperation among or some degree of unification of distinct entities (as countries or groups of countries) esp. in a specific area (as trade or defense) ⟨West European ~ is the first condition for the survival of every country concerned —William Petersen⟩ ⟨the . . . proposal for the economic ~ of Europe into one single market —*Current Biog.*⟩ **h :** the unified control of a number of successive or similar economic esp. industrial processes formerly carried on independently ⟨~ may result in important cost reductions⟩ **3 :** the operation of finding a function of which the integrand is the derivative of a function or of solving a differential equation **4 :** the sum of the processes by which the developing parts of an organism are formed into a functional and structural whole ⟨at the molecular level of ~ many studies are needed —*Science*⟩

**integration by parts :** a method of integration by means of the reduction formula $\int udv = uv - \int vdu$

**in·te·gra·tion·ist** \-sh(ə)nəst\ *n* -s **:** a person that believes in, advocates, or practices integration ⟨opposition to the ~*s* came from many groups in the small southern town⟩

**in·te·gra·tive** \ˈ==ˌgrād·|iv, -āt|, |ēv *also* |əv\ *adj* [³*integrate* + *-ive*] **1 :** tending to integrate ⟨the ~ action of the nervous system —J.R.Newman⟩ **2 :** favoring or implementing integration ⟨the widespread ~ trend of modern science —Weston La Barre⟩ ⟨anthropology's ~ tools —Abraham Edel⟩

**in·te·gra·tor** \-ād·ə(r), -ātə-\ *n* -s [LL, renewer, restorer, fr. L *integratus* (past part.) + *-or*] **:** one that integrates ⟨religion has been the supreme ~ of intellectual and emotional experience —H.N.Fairchild⟩; *specif* **:** a device (as a planimeter or pedometer) that totalizes by mechanical, electromechanical, electronic, or other physical means a multiplicity of variable quantities in a manner comparable to that in which mathematical solutions are arrived at by means of differential equations or integral calculus

**integri-** *comb form* [L, fr. *integr-, integer* — more at ENTIRE] **:** whole **:** entire ⟨*integri*folious⟩ ⟨*integri*palliate⟩

**in·teg·ri·ty** \ənˈtegrəd·ē, -rətē, -i\ *n* -ES [ME *integrite,* fr. MF & L; MF *integrité,* fr. L *integritat-, integritas,* fr. *integr-, integer* untouched, entire + *-itat-, -itas* -ity] **1 a :** an unimpaired or unmarred condition **:** entire correspondence with an original condition **:** SOUNDNESS ⟨personality function depends greatly upon the ~ of brain function —*Diagnostic & Statistical Manual*⟩ ⟨maintenance of the ship's watertight ~ —*Manual of Seamanship*⟩ ⟨designed to assure structural ~ of the aircraft —*Index to Current Tech. Publications*⟩ ⟨the ~ of the national currency is not dependent on its convertibility —*Current Biog.*⟩ **b :** an uncompromising adherence to a code of moral, artistic, or other values **:** utter sincerity, honesty, and candor **:** avoidance of deception, expediency, artificiality, or shallowness of any kind ⟨an example of great physical vigor, business ~, and thrift —*Current Biog.*⟩ ⟨a writer of ~ has a duty toward his opinions —C.L.Carmer⟩ ⟨a serious reflection on the intellectual ~ of the accusers —C.R.Davenport⟩ ⟨his ~ told him that this would be at variance with the dramatic truth of his opera —Robert Lawrence⟩ ⟨the ~, the clean drive, and the unforced power that distinguishes the good primitive novel —Frederic Morton⟩ **2 :** the quality or state of being complete or undivided **:** material, spiritual, or aesthetic wholeness **:** organic unity **:** ENTIRENESS, COMPLETENESS ⟨the emphasis is always on the ~ and the uniqueness of the finished poem —David Daiches⟩ ⟨has a feeling for the ~ of each separate person —Malcolm Cowley⟩ ⟨seen in its ~ . . . it is a crumbling tower of waste —Charles Dickens⟩ ⟨guarantee the ~ of the British Empire forever —Upton Sinclair⟩ ⟨aesthetic experience is experience in its ~ —John Dewey⟩

**in·teg·u·ment** \ənˈtegyəmənt\ *n* -s [L *integumentum,* fr. *integere* to cover (fr. *in-* ²in- + *tegere* to cover) + *-mentum* -ment — more at THATCH] **1 :** something that covers or encloses **:** COVERING, ENVELOPE ⟨still encased in a dry brittle ~ that had once been leather —A.B.Chandler⟩ ⟨almost any ~ of a book before the age of cloth, is attractive —R.W.Chapman⟩ **2 :** an external coating or investment: as **a :** one of the usu. two envelopes that enclose the nucellus of an ovule, that are often fused, and that sometimes with other parts form the seed coat **b :** an enveloping layer, membrane, or structure (as the skin of a fish or the exoskeleton of an insect)

**in·teg·u·men·tal** \ˌ=ˌ==ˈment[ə]l\ *or* **in·teg·u·men·ta·ry** \-ntərē, -n·trē\ *adj* **:** of or relating to the integument; *esp* **:** CUTANEOUS

**in·tel·lect** \ˈint[ə]lˌekt\ *n* -s [ME, fr. MF or L; MF, fr. L *intellectus,* fr. *intellectus,* past part. of *intellegere, intelligere* to perceive, understand — more at INTELLIGENT] **1 a :** the power or faculty of knowing as distinguished from the power to feel and to will **b** *Aristotelianism* (1) **:** passive reason (2) **:** active reason **c** *Scholasticism* **:** the faculty of penetrating appearances and getting at the substance through abstraction from and elimination of the individual **d** *Thomism* (1) **:** the receptive faculty of cognition that makes apprehensible the phantasms or intelligible forms — called also *passive intellect, possible intellect, potential intellect* (2) **:** the aspect of the soul that is immortal and constitutes the active power of thought operating upon the phantasms or intelligible forms — called also *active intellect, agent intellect* **e :** UNDERSTANDING, REASON **2 a :** a person given to reflective thought or reasoning **:** a person of notable intellect **:** BRAIN ⟨the outstanding ~ of the whole convention —*Hispanic Amer. Hist. Rev.*⟩ **b :** the totality of intellectual persons ⟨the ~ of the country recognized his superiority⟩ **3 intellects** *pl, now chiefly dial* **:** WITS, FACULTIES ⟨she wishes I had more ~*s* —Eden Phillpotts⟩ **syn** see MIND

**in·tel·lec·tion** \ˌint[ə]lˈekshən\ *n* -s [ME *intelleccioun* intellect, understanding, fr. L *intellection-, intellectio* synecdoche, lit., understanding, fr. *intellectus* (past part.) + *-ion-, -io* -ion] **1 :** exercise of the intellect **:** REASONING, COGNITION, APPREHENSION ⟨one of the most sublime acts of ~ of all time —*New Yorker*⟩ **2 :** a specific act of the intellect **:** NOTION, THOUGHT, IDEA ⟨many ~*s* —Alan Devoe⟩

**in·tel·lec·tive** \ˌ==ˈ=tiv\ *adj* [MF or LL; MF *intellectif,* fr. LL *intellectivus,* fr. L *intellectus* (past part.) + *-ivus* -ive] **1 :** relating to, based on, or possessed by the intellect **:** INTELLECTUAL ⟨those more ~ artificial features which find their expression in refined syntax and style —M.A.Pei⟩ **2 :** having intellectual power **:** INTELLIGENT, RATIONAL, COGNITIVE ⟨awareness of a spiritual ~ soul —Beatrice H. Zedler⟩ — **in·tel·lec·tive·ly** \-tə̇vlē\ *adv*

**¹in·tel·lec·tu·al** \ˌint[ə]lˈekch(əw)əl, -ksh-\ *adj* [ME, fr. MF & L; MF *intellectuel,* fr. L *intellectualis,* fr. *intellectus* intellect + *-alis* -al] **1 a :** of, belonging to, or relating to the intellect or its use **:** REFLECTIVE, REASONING ⟨satire is an ~ weapon —Herbert Read⟩ ⟨~ powers⟩ ⟨enabling them to function on the ~ plane —Bruce Bliven b.1889⟩ ⟨began his ~ career as a mathematician —F.S.C.Northrop⟩ — contrasted with *animal* **b :** having its source in or being preeminently guided by the intellect as distinguished from emotion or experience **:** RATIONAL ⟨has a tremendous ~ sympathy for oppressed people —Green Peyton⟩ ⟨think of such playwrights as coldly ~ —E.R.Bentley⟩ ⟨in no sense an ~ or metaphysical painter —Herbert Read⟩ ⟨the most subtle and ~ edifice ever made by man —Weston La Barre⟩ ⟨disseminated the severe and ~ Florentine style —*Nat'l Gallery of Art*⟩ **c :** calling the intellect into play **:** requiring use of the intellect ⟨as abstruse and ~ as a chess problem⟩ ⟨there should be a distinction . . . between manual or copying work and ~ work —K.C.Wheare⟩ **2** *obs* **:** apprehensible by the intellect alone **:** IMMATERIAL, SPIRITUAL, IDEAL **3 a** *archaic* **:** endowed with the power to know and reason **:** INTELLIGENT **b** (1) **:** devoted to matters of the mind and esp. to the arts and letters **:** given to study, reflection, and speculation esp. concerning large or abstract issues ⟨sort of the ~ type, but most of the gang are real people —W.H. Whyte⟩ ⟨maintain a person can be ~ and not be intelligent —Jean Stafford⟩ (2) **:** engaged in activity requiring preeminently the use of the intellect **:** engaged in mental as distinguished from manual labor; *esp* **:** engaged in creative literary, artistic, or scientific labor ⟨~ workers should be able to deduct from their income tax the amounts which they must spend for books, documents, research work, and materials in general —*Report: (Canadian) Royal Commission on Nat'l Development*⟩ (3) **:** reflecting, indicating, or suggesting devotion to matters of the mind **:** intellectual or associated with a studious reflective temper or large mental endowment ⟨had a high ~ forehead —Edmund Wilson⟩ **syn** see MENTAL

**²intellectual** \"\ *n* -s **1** *obs* **:** INTELLECT, UNDERSTANDING **2 intellectuals** *pl, archaic* **:** intellectual powers or faculties **3 a :** a person of superior intelligence **:** a brainy person ⟨an uneducated ~ who had directed his great powers to accumulation and exploitation —S.H.Adams⟩ ⟨an ~ is a person endowed with unusual mental capacity —*Saturday Rev.*⟩ **b** (1) **:** a person devoted to matters of the mind and esp. to the arts and letters **:** one given to study, reflection, and speculation esp. concerning large, profound, or abstract issues ⟨afraid to be an ~ — if you wanted to go to art galleries, you were immediately suspect —P.E.Deutschman⟩ ⟨a friendly manner, a quiet voice, and the face of an ~ —William Ridsdale⟩ (2) **:** a person claiming to belong to an intellectual elite or caste, given to empty theorizing or cerebration, and often inept in the solution of practical problems **:** EGGHEAD ⟨don't go for the ~ who knows nothing but $2 words —J.P.Whitcomb⟩ ⟨that dreary and narrow creature an ~ —*Manchester Guardian Weekly*⟩ ⟨~ is an ugly word . . . it implies consummate snobbery —Russell Kirk⟩ **c :** a person engaged in activity requiring preeminently the use of the intellect **:** one engaged in mental as distinguished from manual labor ⟨~*s* . . . are functioning groups of society, like any of the professionals, such as lawyers, doctors, engineers, professors —F.G.Wilson⟩

**intellectual history** *n* **:** a branch of history that deals with the rise and evolution of ideas **:** history of ideas

**in·tel·lec·tu·al·ism** \ˌint[ə]lˈekch(əw)əˌlizəm, -ksh-\ *n* -s **1 a :** the viewpoint that knowledge is derived from pure reason **:** RATIONALISM **b :** the doctrine that the ultimate principle of reality is reason **2 a :** devotion to the exercise of intellect or intellectual pursuits ⟨restore the true ~; that is to say, a love of intellectual things —August Heckscher⟩ **b :** such devotion carried to excess ⟨the unnatural ~ which society inflicts upon the middle class —Ian Watt⟩

**¹in·tel·lec·tu·al·ist** \-ləst\ *n* -s [¹*intellectual* + *-ist*] **1 :** an adherent of the doctrine of intellectualism **2 :** a person given to intellectualism

**²intellectualist** \"\ *adj* **:** INTELLECTUALISTIC

**in·tel·lec·tu·al·is·tic** \ˌ==ˌ=(=)=ˈlistik, -tēk\ *adj* **:** relating to intellectualism or intellectualists — **in·tel·lec·tu·al·is·ti·cal·ly** \-tə̇k(ə)lē, -tēk-, -li\ *adv*

**in·tel·lec·tu·al·i·ty** \ˌint[ə]lˌekchəˈwaləd·ē, -ksh-, -lətē, -i\ *n* -ES [LL *intellectualitat-, intellectualitas,* fr. L *intellectualis* intellectual + *-itat-, -itas* -ity] **:** intellectual power **:** the quality or state of being intellectual

**in·tel·lec·tu·al·i·za·tion** \ˌint[ə]lˌekchə(wə)lə̇ˈzāshən, -ksh-, -ˌlīˈz-\ *n* -s **:** the act, process, or an instance of intellectualizing ⟨opposed to any ~ of art —Herbert Read⟩

**in·tel·lec·tu·al·ize** \ˌ==ˈ=(=)əˌlīz\ *vb* -ED/-ING/-S *see -ize in Explan Notes* [¹*intellectual* + *-ize*] *vt* **1 :** to give intellectual or rational form or content to **:** treat or analyze intellectually ⟨tendency to ~ . . . problems —*Current Biog.*⟩ ⟨~*s* traditional forms like the sonnet and madrigal —Douglas Bush⟩ **2 :** to avoid (conscious recognition of the emotional basis of an act or feeling) by substituting a superficially plausible explanation ⟨conflicts that are *intellectualized* —L.E.Hinsie⟩ ~ *vi* **:** to engage in intellectual discussion **:** REASON, PHILOSOPHIZE ⟨sat . . . and simply *intellectualized* —Johnny George⟩

**in·tel·lec·tu·al·ly** \ˌint[ə]lˈekch(əw)əlē, -ksh-, -kshlē, -li\ *adv* **:** in an intellectual manner

**in·tel·lec·tu·al·ness** \ˌint[ə]lˈekch(əw)əlnə̇s, -ksh-\ *n* -ES **:** the quality or state of being intellectual

**intellectual virtue** *n, Aristotelianism* **:** a virtue (as wisdom) concerned with the apprehension of rational principles

**¹in·tel·li·gence** \ənˈteləjən(t)s\ *n* -s *often attrib* [ME, fr. MF, fr. OF, fr. L *intelligentia,* fr. *intelligent-, intelligens* (pres. part.) + *-ia* -y — more at INTELLIGENT] **1 a** (1) **:** the faculty of understanding **:** capacity to know or apprehend **:** INTELLECT, REASON ⟨~, which emerged during the revolutionary cycles of matter as the highest form yet achieved —Hermann Reith⟩ ⟨conceived of history as the expression of a divine ~⟩ (2) *Christian Science* **:** the basic eternal quality of divine Mind **b :** the available ability as measured by intelligence tests or by other social criteria to use one's existing knowledge to meet new situations and to solve new problems, to learn, to foresee problems, to use symbols or relationships, to create new relationships, to think abstractly **:** ability to perceive one's environment, to deal with it symbolically, to deal with it effectively, to adjust to it, to work toward a goal **:** the degree of one's alertness, awareness, or acuity **:** ability to use with awareness the mechanism of reasoning whether conceived as a unified intellectual factor or as the aggregate of many intellectual factors or abilities, as intuitive or as analytic, as organismic, biological, physiological, psychological, or social in origin and nature **c :** mental acuteness **:** SAGACITY, SHREWDNESS ⟨did all he was asked to do with ~ and great good humor⟩ **2 a :** an intelligent being; *esp* **:** an incorporeal spirit **:** ANGEL ⟨hierarchies of angelic ~*s* —S.F.Mason⟩ **b :** a person of some intellectual capacity ⟨all those ~*s* we have agreed to call great —*Times Lit. Supp.*⟩ ⟨the greatest all-round ~ writing in England —P.S.O'Hegarty⟩ **3 a :** the act of understanding **:** COMPREHENSION, KNOWLEDGE ⟨faith is necessary to the ~ of the Christian mysteries —*Encyc. Americana*⟩ **b** (1) **:** information communicated **:** NEWS, NOTICE, ADVICE ⟨more weight is laid upon ~ than on editorials —Horace Greeley⟩ ⟨the joyful ~ that there is hope —Georgina Grahame⟩ ⟨from the engine-room voice tube came ~ of more importance —M.S.Boylan⟩ (2) **:** interchange of information **:** COMMUNICATION ⟨accused of maintaining ~ with the enemy⟩ (3) *obs* **:** a piece of information — usu. used in pl. (4) *archaic* **:** common understanding or mutual relations **:** ACQUAINTANCE, INTERCOURSE (5) **:** evaluated information concerning an enemy or possible enemy or a possible theater of operations and the conclusions drawn therefrom; *also* **:** the section, agency, or persons engaged in obtaining such information **:** SECRET SERVICE ⟨investigated me and told me I was qualified for Navy ~ —T.F.Murphy⟩ ⟨an ~ bureau⟩ ⟨available to American and allied ~ organizations —L.W.Doob⟩ **syn** see MIND

**²intelligence** *vt* -ED/-ING/-S *obs* **:** to bring tidings of (something) or to (someone)

**in·tel·li·genced** \-jən(t)st\ *adj* [¹*intelligence* + *-ed*] **1 :** having mental power **:** INTELLIGENT **2 :** having information **:** INFORMED

**intelligence office** *n* **:** an agency where servants (as domestic help) may be hired ⟨you would know the best real estate and *intelligence offices* —Emily Post⟩

**intelligence officer** *n* **:** a staff officer who gathers, evaluates, interprets, and disseminates intelligence and attempts to thwart enemy attempts to gather such information

**intelligence quotient** *n* **:** a number held to express the relative intelligence of a person determined by dividing his mental age by his chronological age with chronological years above 14 or sometimes 16 disregarded and then multiplying by 100 to eliminate decimals —abbr. *IQ, I.Q.*

**in·tel·li·genc·er** \-jənsə(r), -ˌjen(t)s-, ˌ=ˌ==ˈjen-\ *n* -s [¹*intelligence* + *-er*] **:** one that conveys intelligence or news: as **a :** a secret agent **:** SPY **b :** a bringer of news **:** REPORTER ⟨made this wearied ~ sit up and listen —Virgil Thomson⟩ **c :** newspaper — usu. used as the names of newspapers

**intelligence test** *n* **:** any of various tests consisting of standardized questions and tasks designed to determine the mental age of the person examined or his relative capacity to absorb information and solve problems **:** a test designed to measure capacity to learn apart from actual achievement — compare ACHIEVEMENT TEST, APTITUDE TEST

**in·tel·li·gen·cy** \-jənsē, -si\ *n* -ES [L *intelligentia* — more at INTELLIGENCE] *archaic* **:** INTELLIGENCE

**¹in·tel·li·gent** \-nt\ *adj* [L *intelligent-, intelligens*, pres. part. of *intelligere, intellegere* to perceive, understand, fr. *inter-* + *legere* to choose, select, gather — more at LEGEND] **1 a :** possessing intelligence or intellect **:** having the power of reflection or reason ⟨assumes the existence of other worlds peopled by ~ beings⟩ **b :** guided or directed by intelligence or intellect **:** RATIONAL ⟨in the other kind of behavior, often called ~, the animal is able to benefit from its past experience —*New Biology*⟩ **2 a :** having or indicating a high or satisfactory degree of intelligence and mental capacity or powers of perception, consideration, and correct decision **:** not stupid or foolish ⟨Puritanism presupposed an ~ clergy capable of interpreting Scripture —*Amer. Guide Series: Mass.*⟩ ⟨though she could not read, both her face and conversation were ~ —Willa Cather⟩ **b :** well adapted to its purpose **:** being the product of intelligence of a high order **:** revealing or reflecting good judgment or sound and comprehensive thought **:** WISE, SKILLFUL ⟨an ~ decision⟩ ⟨~ propaganda⟩ ⟨an ~ essay⟩ **3 a :** marked by quick active perception and understanding ⟨an ~ person, looking out of his eyes and hearkening in his ears —R.L.Stevenson⟩ **b** *archaic* **:** showing or having some special knowledge, skill, or aptitude

**syn** KNOWING, BRILLIANT, SMART, BRIGHT, QUICK-WITTED, CLEVER, ALERT: INTELLIGENT, limited in connotational range, indicates mental capacity and power, often to a high degree, enabling one to perceive, learn, consider, and judge ⟨what should a mature and *intelligent* nation do in such a crisis? . . . we ought to keep our heads . . . be alert to really serious dangers —Elmer Davis⟩ ⟨it is fairly easy for any *intelligent* mother to know when the baby is hungry —Morris Fishbein⟩ KNOWING may indicate ability to know or possession of special knowledge; it often applies to intimations of special information or sophistication ⟨the *knowing* collectors of records —*Saturday Rev.*⟩ ⟨the two young officers exchanged *knowing* glances —W.M.Thackeray⟩ BRILLIANT indicates uncommon, quick, shining mental keenness, capacity, achievement against difficulty ⟨a shrewd sensible man, only not *brilliant* —George Meredith⟩ ⟨first revealed with bitter and *brilliant* incisiveness the cynical desperation of early postwar adolescents —*Amer. Guide Series: Minn.*⟩ SMART suggests quickness in perceiving, in cannily calculating, or in successful resourcefulness ⟨he was top of the class, and the master said he was the *smartest* lad in the school —D.H.Lawrence⟩ ⟨for hundreds of years the *smartest* businessmen in the world have been coming in to the City of London —D.W.Brogan⟩ SMART may indicate facetious pertness ⟨*smart* retorts are also cherished, especially by the young —L.J.Davidson⟩ BRIGHT indicates a lively alert quickness in learning and understanding ⟨the teachers all knew he was *bright* as brass . . . he took every last one of the prizes —Ellen Glasgow⟩ ⟨foreordained that any *bright* person ought to have seen it coming —*Harper's*⟩ QUICK-WITTED indicates quickness in arising to an occasion, in perceiving and coping with problems or dangers ⟨a *quick-witted* debater hard to entangle or confuse⟩ ⟨making their way through enemy territory under the *quick-witted* leadership of the captain⟩ CLEVER may suggest quick, apt facility at improvising, finding expedients, contriving to cope with problems ⟨*clever* boys and girls like to test their minds on difficulties —Bertrand Russell⟩ ⟨he was a *clever* lawyer . . . and had the jury eating out of his hand —Dorothy Sayers⟩ ALERT indicates a wide-awake care about and concern with any emergent development that might have been unnoticed ⟨*alert* and wary, making off at the first alarm —James Stevenson-Hamilton⟩ ⟨*alert* to this need, Congress authorized five military highways —*Amer. Guide Series: Mich.*⟩ **syn** see in addition MENTAL

**²intelligent** \"\ *n* -S **1** *obs* **:** a person who conveys information **:** SPY **2 :** an intelligent being

**in·tel·li·gen·tial** \ən‚teləˈjenchəl\ *adj* **:** of, like, relating to, or having intelligence **:** exercising or implying understanding ⟨the existential and the ~ elements —Heinrich Zimmer⟩

**in·tel·li·gent·ly** *adv* **:** in an intelligent manner ⟨delivered an ~ reasoned summation⟩

**in·tel·li·gen·tsia** *also* **in·tel·li·gen·tzia** \(ˌ)in‚teləˈjentsēə, ən‚tel- *also* -ˈjench(ē)ə *or* -ˈgentsēə\ *n* -S [Russ *intelligentsiya*, fr. L *intelligentia* intelligence — more at INTELLIGENCE] **1 a :** a class of well-educated articulate persons constituting a distinct, recognized, and self-conscious social stratum within a nation and claiming or assuming for itself the guiding role of an intellectual, social, or political vanguard ⟨the basic function of the Encyclopedists and of all later ~*s* . . . includes both the iconoclastic and the pedagogic, the destructive and the constructive element —Arthur Koestler⟩ ⟨an inferior helot people without any national consciousness, without any ~ —O.D.Tolischus⟩ ⟨it has a restless, unstable, rebellious, and brilliant ~ —R.H.Markham⟩ **b :** a class of persons devoted to matters of the mind and esp. to the arts and letters **:** a class of persons given to study, reflection, and speculation esp. concerning large, profound, or abstract issues ⟨a café where the local ~ gathered⟩ ⟨a trifling comedy scorned by the ~⟩ **2 :** a class of persons engaged in activity requiring preeminently the use of the intellect **:** a class of persons engaged in mental as distinguished from manual labor ⟨best opinion in this country accords to professional men and women the status of ~ —M.L.Cooke⟩

**in·tel·li·gi·bil·i·ty** \(ˌ)=ˌ==jəˈbilədē, -lətē, -i\ *n* -ES **1 :** the quality or state of being intelligible **:** CLARITY, UNDERSTANDABILITY ⟨the immediate ~ of the prose —Richard Eberhart⟩ **2 :** something that is intelligible

**¹in·tel·li·gi·ble** \ənˈteləjəbəl\ *adj* [ME, fr. L *intelligibilis*, fr. *intelligere* to perceive, understand + *-ibilis* -able — more at INTELLIGENT] **1** *obs* **:** INTELLIGENT **2 :** capable of being understood or comprehended ⟨an ~ description⟩ ⟨~ pronunciation⟩ **3 a :** apprehensible by the intellect only **:** purely conceptual ⟨the classical conception, according to which thinking is the inspection of ~ objects —Norman Malcolm⟩ **b :** relating to something that is beyond perception **:** SUPERSENSIBLE, SUPRASENSUOUS ⟨made the ~ world . . . the starting point of their speculations —Frank Thilly⟩ — **in·tel·li·gi·ble·ness** \-nəs\ *n* -ES — **in·tel·li·gi·bly** \-blē, -bli\ *adv*

**²intelligible** \"\ *n* -S **:** an object of the intellect ⟨the intellect's natural capacity for the intuition of ~*s* —L.J.Thro⟩

**intelligible species** *n*, *Thomism* **:** an object as apprehended through an act of intellectual cognition — contrasted with *sensible species*

**in·tem·er·ate** \ənˈteməˌrāt, -rət\ *adj* [L *intemeratus*, fr. *in-* ¹in- + *temeratus*, past part. of *temerare* to violate, defile, fr. *temere* rashly, by chance — more at TEMERITY] **:** INVIOLATE, PURE, UNDEFILED

**in·tem·per·ance** \(ˈ)in, ən+\ *n* [ME *intemperaunce*, fr. L *intemperantia*, fr. *intemperant-, intemperans* intemperate (fr. *in-* ¹in- + *temperant-, temperans* temperate, fr. pres. part. of *temperare* to temper, regulate) + *-ia* -y — more at TEMPER] **1 :** inclemency or severity esp. of weather **2 a :** excess or lack of moderation in an action ⟨much ~ of statement in the current condemnation of our education —F.N.Robinson⟩ and esp. in satisfying an appetite or passion; *specif* **:** habitual or excessive drinking of intoxicants **b :** an intemperate act ⟨these daily ~*s* were disquieting, because men can't talk themselves into permanent rages —*New World*⟩

**intemperancy** *n* -ES [L *intemperantia*] *obs* **:** INTEMPERANCE

**in·tem·per·ate** \(ˈ)in, ən+\ *adj* [ME *intemperat*, fr. L *intemperatus*, fr. *in-* ¹in- + *temperatus* temperate — more at TEMPERATE] **:** not temperate: as **a :** immoderate in satisfying an appetite or passion; *specif* **:** given to excessive use of intoxicating liquors ⟨an ~ drinker⟩ **b :** lacking temperance or moderation **:** EXCESSIVE, INORDINATE, IMMODERATE, VIOLENT ⟨~ language⟩ ⟨~ zeal⟩ ⟨~ attacks⟩ **c :** not mild **:** EXTREME, INCLEMENT, SEVERE ⟨~ weather⟩ ⟨an ~ zone⟩ — **in·tem·per·ate·ly** *adv* — **in·tem·per·ate·ness** *n*

**in·tem·per·a·ture** \ən+\ *n* [¹*in-* + *temperature*] *n*, *archaic* **:** distempered state **:** INTEMPERANCE ⟨this season, the ~ of which may last till the middle of May —Tobias Smollett⟩

**in·tem·pes·tive** \ˌin(ˌ)temˈpestiv\ *adj* [L *intempestivus*, fr. *in-* ¹in- + *tempestivus* tempestive] **:** UNTIMELY, INOPPORTUNE

**in tempo** *adv* (*or adj*) [It] **:** in time **:** a tempo — used as a direction in music

**in·tem·po·ral** \(ˈ)inˈtemp(ə)rəl, ənˈt-\ *adj* [¹*in-* + *temporal*] **:** transcending temporal relations **:** TIMELESS ⟨a cruelly abstract and ~ truth —Claude Vigée⟩ — **in·tem·po·ral·ly** \-rəlē\ *adv*

**in·tend** \ənˈtend\ *vb* -ED/-ING/-S [alter. (influenced by L *in-* ²in-) of ME *entenden*, fr. OF *entendre*, fr. LL *intendere*, fr. L, to intend, attend, stretch out, extend, fr. *in-* ²in- + *tendere* to stretch, stretch out — more at TEND] *vt* **1 a** *archaic* **:** to understand or construe in a certain manner **:** APPREHEND, INTERPRET **b** (1) **:** SIGNIFY, MEAN ⟨what was ~*ed* by that remark⟩ ⟨by teleology is ~*ed* the purposefulness of nature⟩ (2) **:** to have in mind **:** have reference to **:** refer to ⟨this tavern I think must have been the one ~*ed* . . . in his novel —*Notes & Queries*⟩ **2 a** [ME *intenden, entenden*, fr. MF *entendre*, fr. L *intendere*] (1) **:** to have in mind as a design or purpose **:** PLAN ⟨~*s* to do all in his power⟩ ⟨~ not to retrace the march of occupation in detail —Russell Lord⟩ (2) **:** to have in mind as an object to be gained or achieved ⟨~*s* that general opulence to which it gives occasion —Adam Smith⟩ ⟨~*ed* the advantage of a great number of people —H.E. Scudder⟩ ⟨~*s* only his own advancement⟩ **b :** to design for or destine to a specified purpose or future ⟨the engravings are not ~*ed* for sale —Mary Zimmer⟩ ⟨~*ed* him to be the next president⟩ **3** *archaic* **:** to proceed on (one's course or way) **4** [ME *intenden, entenden*, fr. L *intendere*] *archaic* **a :** to direct the mind on **:** attend to **:** take care of ⟨~*s* his brother's will —George Chapman⟩ **b :** to direct (the eyes) toward something **5** *obs* **:** ASSERT, MAINTAIN **:** PRETEND **6** *archaic* **:** to stretch out or forth **:** make tense **:** EXTEND, STRETCH ~ *vi* **1** [ME *entenden*, fr. MF *entendre*] **:** to have an aim or end in mind ⟨none of our first plans . . . could be carried out as we ~*ed* —R.L.Stevenson⟩ **2** *archaic* **a** [ME *intenden, entenden*, fr. L *intendere*] **:** to direct one's course or way **:** PROCEED **b :** to start or set out **:** intend to go or set out

**syn** INTEND, MEAN, DESIGN, PROPOSE, and PURPOSE can mean to have in mind as an end, aim, or function. INTEND implies that the mind is directed to some definite accomplishment or end, often with determination ⟨*intended* 24 books, sketched 14, but left only four —Gilbert Highet⟩ ⟨did not *intend* annexation of Italian land —Hilaire Belloc⟩ or that, in the mind, one conceives a thing as in a particular occupation or function, serving a given purpose, or carrying a particular meaning ⟨the volume was *intended* for reading in the public schools —Agnes Repplier⟩ ⟨was *intended* for the church —L.O. Howard⟩ ⟨the five- and six-year courses are *intended* for pupils likely to proceed to the university —H.C.Dent⟩ ⟨the meaning of the phrase was not what the writers *intended*⟩ MEAN can come close to the sense of INTEND though it carries a weaker implication of determination, often indicating little more than volition or decision ⟨*mean* to pay back a debt⟩ ⟨put something to a use for which it was not *meant*⟩ ⟨*mean* to go to the movies tonight⟩ DESIGN usu. stresses forethought in arriving at an intention, often implying contriving or scheming ⟨*designs* a companion volume in which she will carry further her discussion —Marjorie Nicolson⟩ ⟨plans we had *designed* to put into effect immediately⟩ ⟨putting a machine to uses for which it was not *designed*⟩ ⟨have no protection against *designing* and dishonest people⟩ PROPOSE implies a clear setting forth, in the mind or before others, of one's intention, connoting clear definition or open avowal ⟨*proposed* to live as if the golden age had come again —Van Wyck Brooks⟩ ⟨*proposes* to give a summary of titles at the end of the work —H.O.Taylor⟩ ⟨*proposed* to carry out the preposterous plan —*Lamp*⟩ ⟨the plan turned out better than he had *proposed* at the committee meeting⟩ PURPOSE differs little from PROPOSE except in implying a stronger determination or clearer intent ⟨*purpose* staying there about a month —Mary W. Shelley⟩ ⟨*purpose* to arrange a typical program in this chapter —W.F.Brown b.1903⟩ ⟨*purpose* to write a history of England —T.B.Macaulay⟩

**in·tend·ance** \ənˈtendən(t)s\ *n* -S [F, fr. MF, fr. *intendant* + *-ance*] **1 :** the care, control, or management of an office, department, or other public business **:** SUPERINTENDENCE **2 :** an administrative department esp. of an army; *specif* **:** an army supply service in some countries (as France)

**in·tend·an·cy** *also* **in·tend·en·cy** \-dənsē, -si\ *n* -ES [*intendancy* prob. fr. F *intendance* + E *-y*; *intendency* prob. fr. MF *intendance* + E *-ency*] **1 :** the office, function, or employment of an intendant; *also* **:** a body of intendants **2** *usu intendency* [Sp *intendencia*, fr. *intendente*] **:** a district under an intendant

**in·tend·ant** \ənˈtendənt\ *n* -S [F, fr. MF, fr. L *intendent-, intendens*, pres. part. of *intendere* to intend, attend — more at INTEND] **:** a person who has the charge, direction, or management of some public business: as **a :** an administrator of a French province under the centralized system introduced by Richelieu **b :** an administrative officer next to the governor in Canada under French rule **c :** an official in charge of the colonial treasury sometimes having the governorship of the province in various Spanish and Portuguese colonies **d :** a chief administrative official (as governor of a district or mayor of a city) esp. in some Spanish-American countries

**¹intended** *adj* [fr. past part. of *intend*] **1 a :** PROPOSED ⟨the first volume of an ~ series⟩; *specif* **:** BETROTHED, AFFIANCED ⟨his ~ bride⟩ **b :** INTENTIONAL ⟨an ~ insult⟩ **2** *obs* **:** EXTENDED, STRAINED — **in·tend·ed·ly** *adv* — **in·tend·ed·ness** *n* -ES

**²intended** *n* -S **:** an affianced person **:** BETROTHED ⟨went to the residence of his ~ —D.D.Martin⟩

**in·tend·ence** \ənˈtendən(t)s\ *n* -S [*intend* + *-ence*] **:** ATTENDANCE, ATTENTION

**in·ten·den·cia** \ˌin(ˌ)tenˈden(t)sēə\ *n* -S [Sp, fr. *intendente*] **:** the house, office, or administrative area of an intendant in a country of Spanish or Portuguese speech

**in·ten·den·te** \-ˈdentē\ *n* -S [Sp, fr. F *intendant*] **:** an intendant in a country of Spanish or Portuguese speech

**in·tend·er** \ənˈtendə(r)\ *n* -S **:** a person who intends

**intendiment** *n* -S [ML *intendimentum* meaning, interpretation, hidden purpose, fr. L *intendere* to intend, attend + *-mentum* -ment — more at INTEND] *obs* **:** INTENTION; *also* **:** ATTENTION

**intending** *adj* **:** PROSPECTIVE, ASPIRING ⟨the ~ solicitor has a long and expensive training —T.G.Lund⟩ ⟨~ students⟩

**in·tend·ment** \ənˈten(d)mənt\ *n* -S [alter. (influenced by E *intend*) of ME *entendement*, fr. MF, fr. OF, fr. *entendre* to intend + *-ment* — more at INTEND] **1 :** INTENTION, DESIGN, PURPOSE ⟨voted for it . . . because its ~*s* were good —A.J. Beveridge⟩ **2 a :** MEANING, SIGNIFICANCE ⟨acquired further ~ as later men discerned a broader symbolism in them —H.O. Taylor⟩ **b :** the true meaning, understanding, or intention of a law or other legal instrument — compare COMMON INTENDMENT

**intends** *pres 3d sing of* INTEND

**in·ten·er·ate** \ənˈtenəˌrāt\ *vt* -ED/-ING/-S [²*in-* + L *tener* soft, tender + E *-ate* — more at TENDER] **:** to make tender or sensitive **:** SOFTEN ⟨contrives to ~ the granite —R.W.Emerson⟩ — **in·ten·er·a·tion** \ən‚tenəˈrāshən\ *n* -S

**intens** *abbr* intensive

**in·ten·sate** \ənˈtenˌsāt\ *vt* -ED/-ING/-S [*intense* + *-ate*] **:** INTENSIFY

**in·tense** \ənˈten(t)s\ *adj*, *sometimes* -ER/-EST [ME, fr. MF, fr. L *intensus* stretched, tight, intense, fr. *intensus*, past part. of *intendere* to stretch out, intend] **1 a :** existing in a strained or extreme degree **:** revealed in the height of its distinctive character ⟨an ~ light⟩ ⟨an expression of ~ anxiety —T.B. Costain⟩ ⟨~ cold⟩ **b** *of color* **:** very deep ⟨dyed an ~ blue⟩ **c :** having or showing its characteristic trait in extreme degree ⟨an ~ sun shone down⟩ ⟨the moon, ~ and white as the snow —Eudora Welty⟩ ⟨~ bright frosty stars —John Masefield⟩ **d :** extremely marked or pronounced **:** INTENSIVE ⟨rock alteration is ~, leaving few minerals or rocks in their original condition —*Univ. of Ariz. Record*⟩ ⟨a neurodermatitis with ~ itching and burning of the skin —H.G.Armstrong⟩ **e :** very large **:** CONSIDERABLE ⟨giving off ~ amounts of radiation —Arthur Charlesby⟩ **2 :** strained or straining in or as if in an extreme effort **:** done or performed with great zeal, energy, or eagerness **:** highly concentrated ⟨~ study⟩ ⟨a pursuit of learning *intenser* perhaps than any before or since —Ellery Sedgwick⟩ ⟨listened with ~ attention⟩ **3 a** *obs* **:** INTENT, BENT, RESOLVED — used with *upon* or *about* **b** (1) **:** feeling deeply esp. by nature or temperament **:** exhibiting or reflecting strong feeling or earnestness of purpose ⟨my only love, you are so ~ —Edna S. V. Millay⟩ ⟨so ~ in his moral convictions —G.G.Coulton⟩ ⟨~ in everything he does —*Current Biog.*⟩ ⟨an ~ expression on his face⟩ (2) **:** charged with artistic emotion or intellectual excitement **:** possessing the quality of artistic tension ⟨his style is ~, eloquent, personal to himself —H.O.Taylor⟩ ⟨painted his most mature and ~ work —*Americas*⟩ (3) **:** deeply felt ⟨a man of ~ convictions⟩ — **in·tense·ly** *adv* — **in·tense·ness** *n*

**in·ten·si·fi·ca·tion** \ən‚ten(t)səfəˈkāshən\ *n* -S **:** the act, process, or an instance of intensifying ⟨an ~ of a process that has already been long at work —Barbara Ward⟩

**in·ten·si·fi·er** \ənˈten(t)səˌfī(ə)r\ *n* -S **:** one that intensifies: as **a :** a device (as a two-part cylinder with rigidly connected pistons of different diameters) for stepping up fluid pressure **b :** a photographic intensifying reagent **c :** a gene that enhances the normal effect of another nonallelic gene when both are present **d :** INTENSIVE ⟨words . . . which have been used emotively as ~*s* —William Empson⟩

**in·ten·si·fy** \-ˌfī\ *vb* -ED/-ING/-S [*intense* + *-ify*] *vt* **1 :** to make intense or more intensive **:** STRENGTHEN, INCREASE, DEEPEN ⟨are ~*ing* our sales effort —*Wall Street Jour.*⟩ ⟨~ farming on a wide scale —*Farmer's Weekly (So. Africa)*⟩ **2 a :** to increase the density and contrast of (an image on a photographic film or plate) by treating with any of various reagents that act either by producing an additional deposit or by rendering the original deposit more opaque **b :** to make more acute **:** SHARPEN ⟨~ still more the resultant problems of health and nutrition —R.W.Steel⟩ ~ *vi* **:** to become intense or more intense: as **a :** to grow stronger **:** INCREASE, DEEPEN ⟨within her own narrowed sphere her sympathies seemed to ~ —*McGill News*⟩ **b :** to grow sharper or more acute ⟨the drought has *intensified* and spread —K.S.Davis⟩ ⟨rivalry among the three departments . . . is ~*ing* —*Newsweek*⟩

**syn** AGGRAVATE, HEIGHTEN, ENHANCE: INTENSIFY indicates a deepening or strengthening until very noticeable or unusually deep or strong ⟨in the lustrous air all colors were *intensified* —Mary Webb⟩ ⟨the depression of the early thirties *intensified* his dissatisfaction with the capitalist system —Granville Hicks⟩ AGGRAVATE, often used in connection with the unpleasant or evil, applies to an increase in seriousness and demand for attention ⟨the external symptoms of decline have served to *aggravate* long existing internal tensions —J.G. Colton⟩ ⟨the din of its two small rooms *aggravated* by the peripheral racket that came from the kitchen —Jean Stafford⟩ HEIGHTEN may suggest a lifting above the ordinary or accustomed ⟨a painter discards many trivial points of exactness, in order to *heighten* the truthfulness of a few fundamentals —C.E.Montague⟩ ⟨a dramatic incident may *heighten* the popular indignation that leads toward war —Dexter Perkins⟩ ENHANCE suggests a lifting or strengthening above normal, esp. in attractiveness, desirability, or value ⟨the charm of this wild land is *enhanced* by the presence of deer and the famous forest ponies —S.P.B.Mais⟩ ⟨a blue serge suit freshly pressed which *enhanced* the impression he gave of neatness and cleanliness —Henry Miller⟩ ⟨the political prestige of the C.I.O. was *enhanced* by the election —*Collier's Yr. Bk.*⟩

**intensifying screen** *n* **:** a fluorescent screen placed usu. on each side of an X-ray photographic film so as to augment the direct effect of the X rays between two such screens

**in·ten·sion** \ənˈtenchən\ *n* -S [L *intension-, intensio*, fr. *intensus* (past part. of *intendere* to stretch forth) + *-ion-, -io* -ion — more at INTEND] **1** *archaic* **:** an act of straining, stretching, or bending **:** TENSION **2 a :** degree or marked degree (as of a quality) **:** INTENSITY **b :** increase of power or energy **:** INTENSIFICATION **c :** strong or energetic exercise (as of the mind) **:** INTENTNESS, DETERMINATION **3 :** CONNOTATION 3 ⟨the ~ of "*triangle*" implies or includes that of "plane figure"⟩ — contrasted with *extension*

**in·ten·sion·al** \-chənᵊl, -chnəl\ *adj* **:** of, relating to, or marked by intension; *specif* **:** CONNOTATIVE ⟨literature works by ~ means . . . by the manipulation of the informative and affective connotations of words —S.I.Hayakawa⟩ — **in·ten·sion·al·ly** \-ᵊlē, -əlē, -i\ *adv*

**in·ten·si·tom·e·ter** \ən‚ten(t)səˈtämədə(r)\ *n* [*intensito-* (fr. *intensity*) + *-meter*] **:** an instrument for measuring the intensity of X rays

**in·ten·si·ty** \ənˈten(t)sədē, -ətē, -i\ *n* -ES [*intense* + *-ity*] **1 :** the quality or state of being intense: as **a :** extreme or very high degree **:** extreme strength, force, or energy ⟨the ~ of the sun's rays⟩ ⟨the ~ and accuracy of this fire —S.L.A.Marshall⟩ ⟨strikingly signalizes the ~ of the hope —Bernard De Voto⟩ ⟨rains of unparalleled ~ —W.E.Swinton⟩ **b :** extreme depth of feeling **:** passionate quality **:** extreme sensibility ⟨her ~, which would leave no emotion on a normal plane —D.H. Lawrence⟩ ⟨the most striking feature . . . is the ~ of his nature —R.A.Hall b.1911⟩ ⟨instinctively kept to ~, knowing that without passion no art can live —Louise Bogan⟩ **c :** the quality of aesthetic or intellectual emotion or excitement **:** compactness of artistic statement or expression **:** artistic tension ⟨lacks the ~ and the profundity that the greatest poetry has —R.A.Hall b.1911⟩ ⟨with ~ the poem may survive anything — even archaic language —J.P.Bishop⟩ ⟨compressed into poetic ~ . . . instead of sprawling forth sloppy, formless, and diffuse —Peter Viereck⟩ ⟨a painting of dramatic ~⟩ ⟨impress their poetry with density and ~, cutting out irrelevancies and long-windedness —Mary M. Colum⟩ **d :** depth of conviction ⟨his voice was hoarse with the ~ of his belief —Irwin Shaw⟩ **e :** strenuousness of effort or application **:** ENERGY ⟨the campaign was waged with great ~ by both parties⟩ **2 :** the degree or amount of a quality or condition: as **a :** the relative loudness or softness of a tone or a tonal effect **b :** the energy with which air is propelled through the vocal tract in articulating **:** LOUDNESS **c :** a specified measure of the effect of certain physical agencies expressed as the magnitude of force or energy per unit (as of surface, charge, or mass) — see ELECTRIC INTENSITY, GRAVITATIONAL INTENSITY, LUMINOUS INTENSITY, MAGNETIC INTENSITY, RADIANT INTENSITY, SOUND INTENSITY; compare LUMINOUS-FLUX DENSITY, RADIANT-FLUX DENSITY **d :** SATURATION 4a **e :** a measure of the magnitude of an earthquake **f :** intensive quality **:** INTENSIVENESS ⟨carried on agriculture with varying degrees of ~ —A.C.Parker⟩ **g :** the vividness or strength of a sensation ⟨his shame reached a high degree of ~⟩ **h :** cultural vigor esp. of a primitive people as expressed in quantity of cultural content and complexity and interrelations of cultural patterns ⟨a contrast in the . . . ~ of cultural systems —E.H. Spicer⟩ **3 :** an instance of intense quality, condition, or experience ⟨the *intensities*, the moments of feeling and depths of experience that constitute the fundamental part of living —Leon Edel⟩

**intensity modulation** *n* **:** modulation in which the brightness of the light displayed on a cathode-ray tube varies with the intensity of the signal

**intensity of light :** LUMINOUS-FLUX DENSITY

**intensity of magnetization :** MAGNETIZATION

**intensity of radiation :** RADIANT-FLUX DENSITY

**¹in·ten·sive** \(ˈ)inˈten(t)siv, ənˈt-, -sēv *also* -səv\ *adj* [prob. fr. MF *intensif*, fr. ML *intensivus*, fr. L *intensus* intense, stretched + *-ivus* -ive — more at INTENSE] **1** *obs* **:** INTENSE, VEHEMENT **2 :** of, relating to, or marked by intensity or intensification: as **a :** highly concentrated **:** ZEALOUS, EAGER, EXHAUSTIVE ⟨~ study⟩ ⟨~ effort⟩ **b :** INTENSIFYING; *esp* **:** tending to give force or emphasis ⟨an ~ adverb, as *dreadfully* in "it was *dreadfully* cold"⟩ **c** (1) **:** constituting or relating to a method of cultivation of land designed to increase the productivity of a given area by the expenditure of more capital and labor upon it — opposed to *extensive* (2) **:** constituting or relating to the method of conducting an industry so as to increase its returns by perfecting its methods and appliances rather than by enlarging its scale **d :** relating to intension **e :** involving the use of large doses or substances having great therapeutic activity **f :** presenting a large and concentrated amount of material to be studied intensely ⟨~ course⟩ ⟨~ training⟩ ⟨~ program⟩ — **in·ten·sive·ly** \-sə̇vlē, -li\ *adv* — **in·ten·sive·ness** \-sivnəs, -sēv- *also* -səv-\ *n* -ES

**[2]intensive** \"\ *n* -s : an intensive linguistic element (as a word, particle, or prefix)

**intensive pronoun** *n* **1 :** a pronoun that emphasizes a preceding noun or another pronoun (as *itself* in "borrowing is itself a bad habit") **2 :** a personal pronoun compounded with *-self* and used in apposition with a noun or pronoun or as pronominal adjunct (as *itself* in "the cat looked innocence itself" or *himself* in "he made it himself")

**intensive proposition** *n* **:** a proposition stating a relation of intension between concepts or one whose meaning is to be understood in intension

**[1]in·tent** \ən·ˈtent\ *n* -s [alter. (influenced by L *in-* [2]in-) of ME *entent, entente;* ME *entent*, fr. OF, fr. LL *intentus* aim, purpose, intent, fr. L, act of stretching out, fr. *intentus*, past part. of *intendere* to stretch out, intend; ME *entente*, fr. OF, fr. L *intentus* (past part.) — more at INTEND] **1 a** (1) **:** the act, fact, or an instance of intending **:** PURPOSE, DESIGN ⟨suspect him of hostile ~ —S.M.Crothers⟩ ⟨came with ~ to kill⟩ (2) **:** the design or purpose to commit any wrongful or criminal act that is the natural and probable consequence of other voluntary acts or conduct (3) **:** the state of mind or mental attitude with which an act is done **:** VOLITION **b :** an end or object proposed **:** AIM ⟨used his leisure time to good ~⟩ **2 a :** MEANING, PURPORT, IMPORT, SIGNIFICANCE ⟨paraphrase in speech the ~ of the communication —Edward Sapir⟩; *specif* **:** INTENDMENT 2b **b :** the connotation of a term **syn** see INTENTION — **to all intents and purposes** *also* **to all intents** *or* **to all intent and purpose :** in all applications or senses **:** PRACTICALLY, REALLY, VIRTUALLY ⟨the process is *to all intents and purposes* identical with that practiced today —A.C.Morrison⟩

**[2]intent** \"\ *adj* [L *intentus*, fr. past part. of *intendere* to stretch forth] **1 :** directed with strained or eager attention **:** CONCENTRATED, EARNEST, INTENSE ⟨a gaze so ~ that the girl flushed a little —P.B.Kyne⟩ ⟨his face was ~ as he examined each picture —Lyle Saxon⟩ **2 a** (1) **:** having the mind or attention closely or fixedly directed on something **:** PREOCCUPIED, ENGROSSED ⟨the two men, ~ on their figures, did not notice —Sherwood Anderson⟩ ⟨still too ~ upon his own thoughts —W.M.Thackeray⟩ ⟨so ~ on this fantastic . . . narrative that she had hardly stirred —Walter de la Mare⟩ (2) **:** reflecting or evidencing strained or concentrated attention or preoccupation ⟨her forehead was painfully anxious and ~ as she gave this evidence —Charles Dickens⟩ **b :** having the mind or will concentrated on some end or purpose **:** DETERMINED, RESOLVED, BENT ⟨a selfish interest ~ upon privilege for itself —H.J.Laski⟩ ⟨~ upon making his way in the corporation —Lee Rogow⟩ ⟨~ that we should have a week of climbing —E.A.Weeks⟩

**in·ten·tion** \ən·ˈtenchən\ *n* -s [ME *entencioun, intencioun*, fr. MF & L; MF *entention, intention*, fr. OF, fr. L *intention-, intentio*, lit., act of stretching out, fr. *intentus* (past part.) + *-ion-, -io* -ion] **1 a** (1) **:** an act of intending **:** RESOLVE ⟨announced its ~ to divide its Indian Empire into two dominions —*Current Biog.*⟩ ⟨certainly had no ~ of doing so —Rose Macaulay⟩ (2) **intentions** *pl* **:** purpose with respect to marriage ⟨inquired concerning the young man's ~*s* toward his daughter⟩ (3) **:** a written or printed statement of intention ⟨filed his ~ to run for mayor⟩ **b** (1) **:** the will to administer a sacrament in the form and spirit prescribed by the Roman Catholic Church (2) **:** the will to apply the benefits of a mass or prayers to a particular person or purpose; *also* **:** the person or purpose contemplated **c** (1) *Roman law* **:** the part of a formula in which the plaintiff's claims and the defendant's defenses are stated (2) *old English law* **:** a declaration in a real action **2 :** an intended object **:** AIM, END ⟨complete and final victory was his ~⟩ ⟨his ~ (the intended significance of the poem) . . . and what he actually contrives as a poet to do, conflict —F.R.Leavis⟩ **3 :** the import or meaning of something **:** something that is conveyed or intended to be conveyed to the understanding **:** SIGNIFICANCE ⟨shook his head with a double ~ —James Joyce⟩ **4 a** *archaic* (1) **:** strenuous mental application **:** close attention (2) **:** the act or an instance of straining or tensing (as the eye) **b :** a concept or notion; *esp* **:** a concept considered as the product of attention directed to an object of knowledge — see FIRST INTENTION, SECOND INTENTION **5 :** a process or manner of healing of incised wounds — see FIRST INTENTION, SECOND INTENTION

**syn** INTENT, PURPOSE, DESIGN, AIM, END, OBJECT, OBJECTIVE, GOAL: INTENTION simply indicates what one proposes to do or accomplish ⟨the main *intention* of the poem has been to make dramatically visible the conflict —Allen Tate⟩ ⟨it was Buchanan's *intention* that his administration should be chiefly characterized by a vigorous foreign policy —C.R.Fish⟩ INTENT may imply more deliberate and clear formulation ⟨to tell a lie, also, with *intent* to deceive was a serious offense —Havelock Ellis⟩ ⟨the clear *intent* of the Taft-Hartley law's provision on secondary boycotts —*Wall Street Jour.*⟩ PURPOSE can apply to what one proposes with resolution and determination ⟨the missionary was here for a *purpose*, and he pressed his point —Willa Cather⟩ ⟨writing her excellent period stories for girls, Elizabeth Howard has a well-defined *purpose* in view —*Current Biog.*⟩ DESIGN may suggest careful ordering, calculating, or scheming ⟨that sense of inherent *design* that characterizes the English or the Russian novel —J.A.Michener⟩ ⟨the TVA is substituting order and *design* for haphazard, unplanned, and unintegrated development —*Amer. Guide Series: Tenn.*⟩ ⟨to keep this strategic peninsula out of the hands of any power which might harbor aggressive *designs* —C.A. Fisher⟩ AIM may imply clear and definite singleness of purpose or intention ⟨the theoretical understanding of the world, which is the *aim* of philosophy —Bertrand Russell⟩ ⟨the next *aim* of the company was to secure the St. Louis and Missouri river trade —Grace L. Nute⟩ END stresses intended effect and may subordinate or contrast with notions of means ⟨the final *end* of government is not to exert restraint but to do good —Rufus Choate⟩ ⟨He knows us and our true *end* is to know Him —J.A.Pike⟩ OBJECT is closely synonymous with END but may be used for more individually determined desires or intentions to accomplish ⟨my *object* all sublime I shall achieve in time — to let the punishment fit the crime —W.S.Gilbert⟩ ⟨the *object* of this society is to elevate the architectural profession as such —*Amer. Institute of Architects*⟩ OBJECTIVE may be used in relation to that which is quite concrete and tangible and immediately attainable ⟨getting the child to want to write is the new-style teacher's first *objective* —John Haverstick⟩ ⟨to fight wars of limited *objective* and to make moderate and reasonable peace settlements —W.H.Chamberlin⟩ GOAL may indicate that which is attained by struggle and endurance of hardship ⟨the achievement of understanding, which is man's highest *goal* —Ida C. Merriam⟩ ⟨could not help thinking that this was my *goal*, that I had been brought to this spot with a purpose, that in this wild and solitary retreat some tremendous adventure was about to befall me —W.H.Hudson †1922⟩

**in·ten·tion·al** \-chənᵊl, -chnəl\ *adj* [ML *intentionalis*, fr. L *intention-, intentio* intention, attention + *-alis* -al] **1 :** relating to intention or design **:** having an intention ⟨deeply ~ in its message —Fanny Butcher⟩ **2 :** done by intention or design **:** INTENDED, DESIGNED ⟨~ damage⟩ **3 a :** of, relating to, or based on intention (sense 4b) or a particular conception of intention ⟨a simple categorical statement (for example, "Parsifal sought the Holy Grail") is ~ if it uses a substantival expression (in this instance, "the Holy Grail") without implying either that there is or there isn't anything to which the expression truly applies —R.M.Chisholm⟩ **b :** referring or pointing beyond itself ⟨the ~ structure of consciousness —Hannah Arendt⟩ **syn** see VOLUNTARY

**intentional fallacy** *n* **:** the fallacy that the value or meaning of a work of art (as a poem) may be judged or defined in terms of the artist's intention

**in·ten·tion·al·ism** \-ᵊlˌizəm, -əˌli-\ *n* -s [ISV *intentional* + *-ism*] **:** ACT PSYCHOLOGY

**in·ten·tion·al·i·ty** \ən·ˌtenchəˈnaləd·ē\ *n* -ES [ML *intentionalitat-, intentionalitas*, fr. *intentionalis* intentional + L *-itat-, -itas* -ity] **:** the quality or state of being intentional; *specif* **:** the characteristic of being conscious of intending an object ⟨three forms of ~ or objective reference, idea, judgment, and desire —Vivian J. McGill⟩

**in·ten·tion·al·ly** \ənˈtenchənᵊlē, -chnəlē, -i\ *adv* **:** in an intentional manner **:** with intention **:** PURPOSELY ⟨~ vague and misleading language⟩

**intentional object** *n* **:** something whether actually existing or not that the mind thinks about **:** a referent of consciousness — compare PHENOMENOLOGY

**intentional pass** *n* **:** the act or an instance of deliberately walking a batter in baseball

**intentional species** *n* **:** mental images or forms produced by sensation and cognition — compare SPECIES

**in·ten·tioned** \ən·¦tenchənd\ *adj* **:** having intentions of a specified kind ⟨seriously ~ radio work —Leslie Rees⟩ — often used in combination ⟨justify a well-*intentioned* lie —Lucius Garvin⟩

**in·ten·tion·less** \ən·ˈtenchənləs\ *adj* **:** being without intention

**intentions** *pl of* INTENTION

**intention tremor** *n* **:** a slow tremor of the extremities that increases on attempted voluntary movement and is observed in certain diseases (as multiple sclerosis) of the nervous system

**in·ten·tive** \ənˈtentiv\ *adj* [alter. (influenced by L *in-* [2]in-) of ME *ententif*, fr. OF, fr. LL *intentivus* intensive, fr. L *intentus* (past part. of *intendere* to intend, attend) + *-ivus* -ive — more at INTEND] **:** ATTENTIVE, INTENT — **in·ten·tive·ly** \-əvlē\ *adv* — **in·ten·tive·ness** \-ivnəs\ *n* -ES

**in·tent·ly** *adv* **:** in an intent manner

**in·tent·ness** *n* -ES **:** the quality or state of being intent

**intents** *pl of* INTENT

**in·ter** *R* ən·ˈtər, + *vowel* -tər·; *-R* -tə̄, + *suffixal vowel* -tər· *also* -tə̄r, + *vowel in a following word* -tər· *or* -tə̄ *also* -tə̄r\ *vt* **interred; interred; interring; inters** [alter. (influenced by L *in-* [2]in-) of ME *enteren*, fr. MF *enterrer*, fr. OF, fr. (assumed) VL *interrare*, fr. *in-* [2]in- + L *terra* earth — more at TERRACE] **1 :** to deposit (a dead body) in the earth or in a grave or tomb **:** BURY, INHUME ⟨the good is oft *interred* with their bones —Shak.⟩ **2** *obs* **:** to enclose the dead body of **3** *obs* **:** to put in the ground **:** cover with earth

**inter-** *prefix* [ME *inter-, entre-, enter-;* ME *inter-*, fr. MF & L; MF, fr. L, fr. *inter;* ME *entre-*, fr. OF, fr. L *inter-;* ME *enter-*, fr. MF & L; MF *entre-*, fr. OF, fr. L *inter-*; akin to OHG *untar* between, among, ON *ithrar*, pl., intestines, OIr *etar, eter* between, among, Gk *enteron* intestine, Skt *antar* between, within, in, and OE *in* — more at IN] **1 :** between, among, in the midst ⟨*inter*mediate⟩ ⟨*inter*polar⟩ ⟨*inter*space⟩ **2 :** mutual, reciprocal ⟨*inter*marry⟩ ⟨*inter*mesh⟩ ⟨*inter*relation⟩ ⟨*inter*twine⟩ **3 :** between or among the parts of ⟨*inter*costal⟩ ⟨*inter*dental⟩ **4 :** carried on between ⟨*inter*collegiate⟩ ⟨*inter*communication⟩ ⟨*inter*national⟩ **5 :** occurring between **:** intervening ⟨*inter*glacial⟩ ⟨*inter*tidal⟩ **6 :** shared by or derived from two or more ⟨*inter*departmental⟩ ⟨*inter*faith⟩ **7 :** between the limits of **:** within ⟨*inter*tropical⟩

**inter** *abbr* **1** intermediate **2** interrogative

**in·ter·academic** \¦intə(r)+\ *adj* [*inter-* + *academic*] **:** among or between or common to schools, colleges, or universities ⟨~ exchanges⟩ ⟨~ courtesies⟩

**in·ter·acinous** \"+\ *also* **in·ter·acinar** \"+\ *adj* [*interacinous* fr. *inter-* + *acinous; interacinar* fr. *interacinous* + *-ar*] **:** situated between or among the acini of a gland

**[1]in·ter·act** \ˈintəˌ(r)akt\ *n* [*inter-* + *act;* intended as trans. of F *entr'acte*] **:** ENTR'ACTE ⟨a mask proper was closely associated with an early Tudor play as an afterpiece rather than as an ~ —E.K.Chambers⟩

**[2]in·ter·act** \¦==¦=\ *vi* [*inter-* + *act*] **:** to act upon each other **:** have reciprocal effect or influence ⟨required many generations of ~*ing* human beings to make such discoveries and inventions —P.A.Sorokin⟩

**in·ter·ac·tant** \-ktənt\ *n* -s [[2]*interact* + *-ant*] **:** one that interacts; *specif* **:** one of two or more substances taking part in a chemical reaction **:** REACTANT

**in·ter·ac·tion** \¦intə¦(r)akshən\ *n* **1 :** mutual or reciprocal action or influence ⟨~ of the heart and lungs⟩ ⟨~ of an individual with his social environment⟩ ⟨~ admits causal action between physical events, between mental events, and also between mental and physical events —Vivian J. McGill⟩ **2 :** a measure of how much the effect of one statistical variable upon another is determined by the values of one or more other variables

**in·ter·ac·tion·al** \-shənᵊl, -shnəl\ *adj* **:** of or relating to interaction or to a theory of interaction ⟨~ ecology⟩ — **interactionally** *adv*

**in·ter·ac·tion·ism** \-shəˌnizəm\ *n* -s **1 :** a theory that mind and body are distinct and interact causally upon one another — compare DOUBLE-ASPECT THEORY, PSYCHOPHYSICAL PARALLELISM **2 :** a theory that derives social processes (conflict, competition, cooperation) from human interaction

**in·ter·ac·tion·ist** \-ˌnəst\ *n* **:** a proponent of interactionism

**in·ter·active** \¦intə(r)+\ *adj* [*inter-* + *active*] **1 :** mutually or reciprocally active **2 :** INTERACTIONAL

**in·ter·activity** \"+\ *n* **:** the fact or process of interacting

**in·ter·adaptation** \"+\ *n* [*inter-* + *adaptation*] **:** mutual adaptation

**[1]in·ter·agency** \"+\ *n* [*inter-* + *agency*] **:** the action or function of an intermediary

**[2]interagency** \"\ *adj* [*inter-* + *agency* (n.)] **:** involving two or more public or government agencies ⟨~ dispute⟩ ⟨~ committee⟩

**in·ter·agent** \"+\ *n* [*inter-* + *agent*] **:** an intermediate agent **:** INTERMEDIARY

**in·ter alia** \¦intə¦(r)ālēə, -lyə\ *adv* [L] **:** among other things ⟨the commission recommended, *inter alia*, that:⟩ ⟨rate of progress will depend upon, *inter alia*, the number of . . . engineers available —L.L.Goodman⟩

**inter ali·os** \-lēˌōs\ *adv* [L] **:** among other persons

**in·ter·allied** \¦intə(r)+\ *also* **in·ter·ally** \"+\ *adj* [*inter-* + *allied* (adj.) or *ally* (n.)] **:** involving or relating to all or a number of allies ⟨British policy on both German reparations and *Interallied* debts —*Atlantic*⟩ ⟨~ agreement⟩

**in·ter·ambulacral** \"+\ *adj* [*inter-* + *ambulacral*] **:** situated between ambulacra

**in·ter·ambulacrum** \"+\ *n* [NL, fr. *inter-* + *ambulacrum*] **:** one of the areas between two ambulacra in an echinoderm

**in·ter–american** \"+\ *adj, usu cap A* **:** involving or concerning some or all of the nations of No. and So. America ⟨~ affairs⟩ ⟨~ treaties⟩

**in·ter·am·ni·an** \¦intə¦(r)amnēən\ *adj* [LL *interamnus* interamnian (fr. L *inter-* + *amnis* river) + E *-ian*] **:** situated between or enclosed by rivers

**in·ter·animate** \¦intə(r)+\ *vt* [*inter-* + *animate*] **:** to animate mutually ⟨love with one another so ~*s* two souls —John Donne⟩

**in·ter·animation** \"+\ *n* **:** mutual animation

**in·ter·articular** \"+\ *adj* [*inter-* + *articular*] **:** situated between articulating surfaces ⟨~ cartilage⟩

**in·ter·association** \"+\ *n* [*inter-* + *association*] **:** mutual association **:** INTERRELATION ⟨~ of sense perceptions⟩

**in·ter·astral** \"+\ *adj* [*inter-* + *astral*] **:** situated or occurring between or among stars

**in·ter·atomic** \"+\ *adj* [*inter-* + *atomic*] **:** situated or acting between atoms ⟨~ forces⟩

**in·ter·atrial** \"+\ *adj* [*inter-* + *atrial*] **:** situated between the atria of the heart ⟨~ septum⟩

**in·ter·aural** \"+\ *adj* [*inter-* + *aural*] **:** situated between or connecting the ears ⟨~ plane⟩

**in·ter·availability** \"+\ *n* [*inter-* + *availability*] *Brit* **:** availability mutually extended throughout a specified system or grouping

**in·ter·axial** \"+\ *also* **in·ter·axal** \"+\ *adj* [NL *interaxis* + *-ial* or *-al*] **:** lying between the axes ⟨~ space in an architectural plan⟩

**in·ter·axillary** \"+\ *adj* [*inter-* + *axillary*] **:** situated within or between the axils of leaves

**in·ter·axis** \"+\ *n* [NL, fr. L *inter-* + *axis*] **:** the space between two axes (as of a building plan)

**in·ter·balance** \"+\ *vt* [*inter-* + *balance*] **:** to balance mutually or reciprocally **:** achieve mutual balance among ⟨intricate *interbalancing* of lead, glass, and stone —M.W.Baldwin⟩

**in·ter·banded** \"+\ *adj* [*inter-* + *banded*] **:** deposited in alternating layers of different materials ⟨~ quartz and galena⟩

**in·ter·bank** \"+\ *adj* [*inter-* + *bank* (n.)] **:** involving two or more banks ⟨~ deposits⟩ ⟨~ relations⟩

**[1]in·ter·bed** \"+\ *vb* [*inter-* + *bed*] **:** INTERSTRATIFY

**[2]in·ter·bed** \ˈintə(r)ˌbed\ *n* **:** a typically thin layer of one kind of sedimentary material between layers of another kind

**in·ter·behavior** \"+\ *n* [*inter-* + *behavior*] **:** interaction between two or more individuals **:** social behavior — **in·ter·behavioral** *adj*

**in·ter·bel·la** \¦intə(r)¦belə\ *or* **interbel·lum** \-ləm\ *adj* [NL, fr. L *inter* between, among + *bella* (pl. of *bellum* war) or *bellum* — more at INTER-, BELLICOSE] **:** extending or occurring between wars ⟨~ period⟩ ⟨*interbellum* generation of writers⟩

**in·ter·blend** \¦intə(r)+\ *vb* [*inter-* + *blend*] **:** to blend together **:** INTERMINGLE, COMMINGLE

**in·ter·bonding** \"+\ *n* [*inter-* + *bonding*, gerund of *bond*] **:** a bonding together ⟨~ of concrete and rock⟩

**in·ter·borough** \"+\ *adj* [*inter-* + *borough*] **:** relating to, situated in, or operating between two or more boroughs ⟨~ subway system⟩

**in·ter·bourse** \"+\ *adj* [*inter-* + *bourse* (n.)] **:** issued simultaneously in different countries ⟨~ securities⟩

**in·ter·brain** \ˈintə(r)+ˌ-\ *n* [*inter-* + *brain*] **:** DIENCEPHALON

**in·ter·branch** \¦intə(r)+\ *adj* [*inter-* + *branch* (n.)] **:** occurring between branches ⟨~ rivalry in the armed forces⟩

**in·ter·breed** \"+\ *vb* [*inter-* + *breed*] *vi* **:** to breed together: as **a :** CROSSBREED **b :** to breed within a closed population **:** INBREED ~ *vt* **:** to cause (individuals or groups) to breed together

**in·ter·ca·lary** \ən·ˈtərkəˌlerē, -tə̄k-, -təik-, -ri, ¦intə(r)¦kal(ə)r-\ *adj* [L *intercalarius*, fr. *intercalare* to intercalate + *-arius* -ary; influenced also by L *intercalaris* intercalary, fr. *intercalare* + *-aris* -ar] **1 a** *of a day or month* **:** inserted in a calendar by intercalation **:** INTERCALATED **b** *of a year* **:** containing an intercalary period **2 :** inserted or introduced between the usual or original elements or components **:** INTERPOLATED ⟨~ matter in a text⟩ ⟨~ tissue in a plant⟩ ⟨~ line in a poem⟩

**intercalary meristem** *n* **:** a meristem developing between regions of mature or permanent tissue (as at the base of the grass leaf) — compare APICAL MERISTEM, LATERAL MERISTEM

**in·ter·ca·late** \ən·ˈtərkəˌlāt, -tə̄k-, -təik-, *usu* -ād·+V\ *vt* -ED/-ING/-S [L *intercalatus*, past part. of *intercalare*, fr. *inter-* + *calare* to call, summon — more at LOW] **1 :** to insert (as a day or month) in a calendar by intercalation **2 :** to insert between or among existing elements **:** INTERPOLATE ⟨~ a vowel into a cluster of consonants⟩ ⟨stories *intercalated* into a narrative⟩ **3 :** to insert (as a sheet of lava) between layers or beds of other rock **:** INTERSTRATIFY — usu. used in the past part.

**in·ter·ca·la·tion** \=ˌ==ˈlāshən\ *n* -s [MF or L; MF, fr. L *intercalation-, intercalatio*, fr. *intercalatus* (past part.) + *-ion-, -io* -ion] **1 a :** the insertion of one or more days at regular intervals in a calendar in order to bring it into accord with the solar year **b :** a period so inserted **2 a :** the insertion or introduction of something among other existing or original things **b :** something that is so inserted ⟨the poet was reluctant to vary the metrical arrangement of the poem to accommodate an ~ —A.K.Moore⟩ **3 :** the introduction or existence of a bed or layer between other layers or of a particular fossil horizon between fossil zones of different character; *also* **:** an intercalated bed or lenticular deposit ⟨a few lenses of volcanic ash are present as ~*s*⟩

**in·tercameral** \¦intə(r)+\ *adj* **:** occurring between two chambers of a legislature ⟨~ deadlock⟩

**in·ter·capillary** \"+\ *adj* [*inter-* + *capillary*] **:** situated between capillaries

**[1]in·ter·cardinal** \"+\ *n* [*inter-* + *cardinal*] **:** an intercardinal point of the compass ⟨~*s* are four points from the cardinals and eight points from one another —H.A.Calahan⟩

**[2]intercardinal** \"\ *adj* **:** lying midway between the cardinal points ⟨~ points of the compass⟩

**in·ter·carotid body** \"+...-\ *n* [*inter-* + *carotid*] **:** CAROTID BODY

**in·ter·carpal** \"+\ *adj* [*inter-* + *carpal*] **:** situated between carpal bones

**in·ter·cartilaginous ossification** \"+...-\ *n* [*inter-* + *cartilaginous*] **:** ENDOCHONDRAL OSSIFICATION

**in·ter·caste** \"+\ *adj* [*inter-* + *caste* (n.)] **:** existing between or involving two or more castes ⟨~ education⟩ ⟨~ mobility⟩

**in·ter·catenated** \"+\ *adj* [*inter-* + *catenated*, past part. of *catenate*] **:** chained or linked together ⟨~ ideas⟩

**in·ter·cavernous** \"+\ *adj* [*inter-* + *cavernous*] **:** situated between and connecting the cavernous sinuses behind and in front of the pituitary body ⟨~ sinus⟩

**in·ter·cede** \ˌintə(r)ˈsēd\ *vi* [L *intercedere*, fr. *inter-* + *cedere* to move, go — more at CEDE] **1** *obs* **a :** to get in the way **:** INTERVENE **b :** to come or lie esp. in time or space **2 :** to act between parties with a view to reconciling differences **:** to beg or plead in behalf of another **:** MEDIATE ⟨the Western powers would not ~ in behalf of the people —N.S.Timasheff⟩ ⟨she it was who *interceded* for the old woman with her uncle —Hilaire Belloc⟩

**in·ter·ced·er** \-də(r)\ *n* **:** one that intercedes

**in·ter·cellular** \¦intə(r)+\ *adj* [*inter-* + *cellular*] **:** lying between cells ⟨~ space in plant tissue⟩ ⟨~ canals in lumber⟩

**intercellular substance** *n* **:** MIDDLE LAMELLA

**in·ter·cen·sal** \"+¦sen(t)səl\ *adj* [*inter-* + *census* + *-al*] **:** occurring between censuses ⟨~ study⟩ ⟨~ figures⟩

**in·ter·central** \"+\ *adj* [*inter-* + *central*] **1 :** lying or extending between centers ⟨~ nerve fibers⟩ **2** [NL *intercentrum* + E *-al*] **:** of or relating to an intercentrum

**in·ter·centrum** \"+\ *n* [NL, fr. *inter-* + *centrum*] **1 :** an element of the vertebral column alternating with the true centra of the vertebrae in several different classes of vertebrates **2 :** HYPOCENTRUM **3 :** one of the ossified intervertebral disks characteristic of certain mammals

**[1]in·ter·cept** \ˌintə(r)ˈsept\ *vt* -ED/-ING/-S [L *interceptus*, past part. of *intercipere*, fr. *inter-* + *-cipere* (fr. *capere* to take, seize) — more at HEAVE] **1 :** to take, seize, or stop by the way or before arrival at the destined place **:** stop or interrupt the progress or course of ⟨~ a letter⟩ ⟨telegram will ~ him at Paris⟩ ⟨~ a forward pass⟩ ⟨~ an attacking bomber⟩ **2** *obs* **:** to stop or prevent from doing something **:** HINDER ⟨who ~*s* me in my expedition —Shak.⟩ **3** *obs* **:** to interrupt communication or connection with ⟨while storms vindictive ~ the shore —Alexander Pope⟩ **4 :** to include (part of a curve, surface, or solid) between two points, curves, or surfaces ⟨the part of a circumference ~*ed* between two radii⟩

**[2]in·ter·cept** \ˈ==ˌ=\ *n* -s **1 :** a part intercepted; *specif* **:** the part of a coordinate axis included between the origin and the point where a graph crosses the axis **2 :** an interception of a ball passed or thrown by an opponent (as in lacrosse) **3 :** a picked-up code or message (as one sent by radio)

**in·ter·cept·er** \ˌ==ˈseptə(r)\ *n* -s **:** INTERCEPTOR

**in·ter·cep·tion** \-pshən\ *n* -s [MF or L; MF, fr. L *interception-, interceptio*, fr. *interceptus* (past part.) + *-ion-, -io* -ion] **1 :** the act of intercepting or state of being intercepted ⟨~ of vital information to and from enemy agents —*All Hands*⟩ ⟨rushing skyward like a fighter going up on an ~ —Terrence Horsley⟩ **2 :** an intercepted segment **:** INTERCEPT

**in·ter·cep·tive** \¦==¦septiv\ *adj* [[1]*intercept* + *-ive*] **:** tending to intercept

**in·ter·cep·tor** \ˌ==ˈ=tə(r)\ *n* -s [L, fr. *interceptus* (past part.) + *-or*] **:** one that intercepts: as **a :** a device for preventing the entrance of solid matter, grease, or other material into a drain subject to clogging **b :** a light high-speed fast-climbing fighter plane designed for defense against raiding bombers

**in·ter·cerebral** \¦intə(r)+\ *adj* [*inter-* + *cerebral*] **:** situated between the cerebral hemispheres

**in·ter·ces·sion** \ˌintə(r)ˈseshən\ *n* -s [MF or L; MF, fr. L *intercession-, intercessio* intervention, act of becoming surety, interposition of a veto, fr. *intercessus* (past part. of *intercedere* to intervene, become surety) + *-ion-, -io* -ion — more at INTERCEDE] **1 a :** the act of interceding **:** interposition between parties at variance with a view to reconciliation **:** MEDIATION **b :** prayer, petition, or entreaty in favor of another **2** *Roman & civil law* **:** assumption of liability for the debt of another either by substitution or by the addition of a new debtor or surety — compare ADPROMISSION, CUMULATIVE INTERCESSION, EXPROMISSION, FIDEJUSSION

**in·ter·ces·sion·al** \¦==¦seshənᵊl, -shnəl\ *adj* **:** relating to or characterized by intercession or entreaty

**in·ter·ces·sive** \¦intə(r)¦sesiv\ *adj* [L *intercessus* (past part.) + E *-ive*] **:** INTERCESSORY

**in·ter·ces·sor** \ˈ==ˌsesə(r)\ *n* -s [ME *intercessour*, fr. MF & L; MF *intercesseur*, fr. L *intercessor*, fr. *intercessus* (past part.) + *-or*] **1 :** one who intercedes **:** MEDIATOR **2 :** a bishop who

during a vacancy of the see administers the bishopric till a successor is installed
**in·ter·ces·so·ri·al** \ˌintə(r)səˈsōrēəl, -sȯr-\ *adj* **:** of or belonging to an intercessor
**in·ter·ces·so·ry** \ˌintə(r)ˈses(ə)rē, -ri\ *adj* [ML *intercessorius*, fr. L *intercessus* (past part. of *intercedere* to intercede) + *-orius* -ory — more at INTERCEDE] **:** relating to or marked by intercession ⟨~ prayer⟩
**interchain** *vt* [*inter-* + *chain*] *obs* **:** to link together
[1]**in·ter·change** \ˌintə(r)ˈchānj\ *vb* [alter. (influenced by L *inter-*) of ME *entrechaungen*, fr. MF *entrechangier*, fr. OF, fr. *entre-* inter- + *changier* to change — more at CHANGE] *vt* **1 :** to put each of (two things) in the place of the other ⟨~ two tires⟩ **2 :** to give and take mutually ⟨~ blows⟩ ⟨~ ideas⟩ ⟨~ goods⟩ **3** *archaic* **:** to cause to follow alternately **:** ALTERNATE, VARY ~ *vi* **:** to change places mutually **:** take part in an exchange ⟨vowels on each side of the triangle tend to ~ in accordance with certain specific rules —William Chomsky⟩
[2]**in·ter·change** \ˈ==ˌ=\ *n* [alter. (influenced by L *inter-*) of earlier *enterchange*, *enterchaunge*, fr. MF *entrechange*, fr. *entrechangier*, v.] **1 :** an act of changing each for the other or one for another **:** EXCHANGE ⟨~ of currency between nations⟩ ⟨~ of clothing⟩ ⟨~ of segments between chromosomes⟩ **2 :** an act of mutually giving and receiving ⟨~ of gifts⟩ ⟨~ of notes⟩ **3** *archaic* **:** alternate succession **:** ALTERNATION ⟨sweet ~ of hill and valley —John Milton⟩ **4 a :** a process of moving cars among railroads to provide uninterrupted movement by rail without unloading and reloading **b :** an act of transferring passengers or freight from one carrier to another **5 :** a junction of two or more highways by a system of separate levels that permit traffic to pass from one to another without the crossing at grade of traffic streams — compare CLOVERLEAF, GRADE SEPARATION

interchange 5

**in·ter·change·abil·i·ty** \ˌintə(r)ˌchānjəˈbilədē, -əte, -i\ *n* **:** the quality or state of being interchangeable ⟨standardization and ~ of parts has taken place in a series of small steps —A.D.H.Kaplan⟩ ⟨~ of mass and energy, which has become an essential principle in physics —Bertrand Russell⟩
**in·ter·change·able** \ˌ==ˈchānjəbəl\ *adj* [alter. (influenced by L *inter-*) of ME *entrechaungeable*, *enterchaungable*, fr. MF *entrechangeable*, *entrechangable*, fr. OF, fr. *entrechangier* (v.) + *-able*] **1 :** capable of being interchanged **2** *obs* **:** MUTUAL, RECIPROCAL **3 :** following each other in alternate succession **:** ALTERNATING **4** *obs* **:** CHANGEABLE, VARIABLE **5 :** permitting mutual substitution without loss of function or suitability ⟨same instrument, known in English by the ~ terms virginal and spinet —A.E.Wier⟩ ⟨each car is like every other . . . and parts are so completely standardized that they are ~ —A.M. Sievers⟩ ⟨standard kit consists of . . . four ~ cutting blades —*Steel*⟩ **6 :** capable of being exchanged or bartered ⟨~ bond⟩ — **in·ter·change·able·ness** *n* — **in·ter·change·ably** \-blē, -li\ *adv*
**interchangeable manufacturing** *n* **:** the making of the parts of machines with such tolerances that any of the parts will properly function in any of the machines
**interchangement** *n* [alter. (influenced by L *inter-*) of earlier *enterchangement*, fr. F *entrechangement*, fr. MF, fr. OF, fr. *entrechangier* to interchange + *-ment* — more at INTERCHANGE] *obs* **:** reciprocal exchange ⟨contract . . . strengthened by ~ of your rings —Shak.⟩
**interchange point** *n* **:** a location at which freight in transit is transferred from one carrier to another
**in·ter·chang·er** \ˌ==ˈchānjə(r)\ *n* **:** one that interchanges; *esp* **:** HEAT EXCHANGER
**interchange track** *n* **:** a track for transfer of freight cars moving in interchange
**in·ter·chapter** \ˈintə(r)+ˌ-\ *n* [*inter-* + *chapter*] **:** an intervening or inserted chapter
**in·ter·chromomere** \ˌintə(r)+\ *n* [*inter-* + [2]*chromomere*] **:** a nongenic area of a chromonema thought to alternate with the genic chromomeres
**in·ter·church** \ˈ"+\ *adj* [*inter-* + *church* (n.)] **:** common to or shared by many or all churches **:** emphasizing cooperation and joint action between religious denominations **:** INTERDENOMINATIONAL ⟨~ movement⟩ ⟨~ aid⟩
**intercision** *n* -s [L *intercision-*, *intercisio*, fr. *intercisus* (past part. of *intercidere* to cut apart, fr. *inter-* + *-cidere* — fr. *caedere* to cut, strike, beat) + *-ion-*, *-io* -ion — more at CONCISE] **1** *obs* **:** a cutting off, through, or asunder **:** INTERRUPTION, INTERSECTION **2** *obs* **:** a falling off **:** FAILING
**in·ter·citizenship** \ˌintə(r)+\ *n* [*inter-* + *citizenship*] **:** citizenship or the right to civic privileges in different bodies politic at the same time ⟨~ in different states of the U.S.⟩
**in·ter·city** \ˈ"+\ *adj* [*inter-* + *city* (n.)] **:** extending or operating between cities ⟨~ bus⟩ ⟨~ broadcasting network⟩
**in·ter·civic** \ˈ"+\ *adj* [*inter-* + *civic*] **:** existing or taking place between or among fellow citizens
**in·ter·class** \ˈ"+\ *adj* [*inter-* + *class* (n.)] **:** relating to or involving more than one class ⟨~ religious movement⟩ ⟨~ marriage⟩
**in·ter·clavicle** \ˈ"+\ *n* [*inter-* + *clavicle*] **:** a ventral median membrane bone in front of the sternum and between the clavicles in certain vertebrates (as the monotremes and most reptiles)
**in·ter·clavicular** \ˈ"+\ *adj* [*inter-* + *clavicular*] **1 :** situated between the clavicles **2** [fr. *interclavicle*, after E *clavicle*: *clavicular*] **:** of or relating to the interclavicle
**in·ter·club** \ˈ"+\ *adj* [*inter-* + *club* (n.)] **:** involving or relating to more than one club ⟨~ yacht race⟩
**interclude** *vt* -ED/-ING/-S [L *intercludere*, fr. *inter-* + *-cludere* (fr. *claudere* to close) — more at CLOSE] *obs* **:** to shut off, out, or up **:** INTERCEPT, CONFINE
**in·ter·coastal** \ˈ"+\ *adj* [*inter-* + *coastal*] **:** extending or operating between sea coasts ⟨~ steamers running between Atlantic and Pacific ports⟩ ⟨~ railroad traffic⟩
**in·ter·coccygeal** \ˈ"+\ *adj* [*inter-* + *coccygeal*] **:** lying between the segments of the coccyx
**in·ter·college** \ˈ"+\ *adj* [*inter-* + *college* (n.)] **:** INTERCOLLEGIATE
**in·ter·collegiate** \ˈ"+\ *adj* [*inter-* + *collegiate*] **:** characterized by participation or cooperation of two or more colleges or universities **:** belonging to related colleges ⟨~ athletic competition⟩ — compare EXTRAMURAL
**in·ter·col·line** \ˌintə(r)ˈkälən, -äˌlīn\ *adj* [*inter-* + L *collis* hill + E *-ine* — more at HILL] **:** situated between hills
**in·ter·colonial** \ˌintə(r)+\ *adj* [*inter-* + *colonial*] **:** existing between or among colonies **:** relating to the intercourse or mutual relations of colonies ⟨~ trade⟩ — **in·ter·colonially** \ˈ"+\ *adv*
**in·ter·column** \ˈ"+\ *n* [L *intercolumnium*, fr. *inter-* + *columna* column — more at COLUMN] **:** the space between two columns
**in·ter·columnar** \ˈ"+\ *also* **in·ter·columnal** \ˈ"+\ *adj* [*inter-* + L *columna* column + E *-ar* or *-al*] **:** existing between pillars ⟨~ space⟩

**in·ter·co·lum·ni·a·tion** \ˌintə(r)kəˌləmnēˈāshən\ *also* **in·ter·col·um·na·tion** \ˌintə(r)ˌkäləmˈnāsh-\ *n* [L *intercolumnium* intercolumn + E *-ation*] **1 a :** the clear space between the columns of a series **b :** the distance between the centers of a series of columns measured at the bottom of the shaft **2 :** the system of spacing the columns of a colonnade measured in terms of the base diameter of the shafts — see ARAEOSTYLE, ARAEOSYSTYLE, DIASTYLE, EUSTYLE, PYCNOSTYLE, SYSTYLE

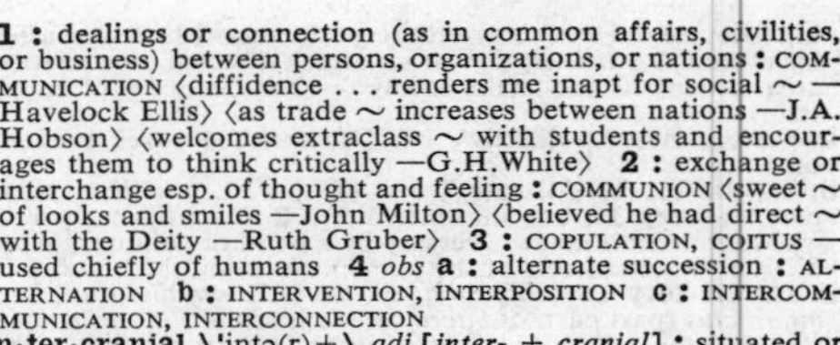

intercolumniation 2 *a* pycnostyle, *b* systyle, *c* eustyle, *d* diastyle, *e* araeostyle

**in·ter·com** \ˈintə(r)ˌkäm\ *n* -s [by shortening] **:** INTERCOMMUNICATION SYSTEM
**in·ter·com·mon** \ˌintə(r)ˈkämən\ *vi* -ED/-ING/-S [ME *intercomounen*, *entercomenen*, fr. AF *entrecomuner*, fr. OF *entre-* inter- + *comuner* to put in common, share — more at COMMUNE] **1** *obs* **:** to have dealings or association **2** *obs* **:** to share with others **:** participate mutually **3 :** to enjoy a right of pasture together
**in·ter·com·mon·age** \-nij\ *n* **:** the practice or right of intercommoning
**in·ter·communal** \ˌintə(r)+\ *adj* [*inter-* + *communal*] **:** existing between communities
**in·ter·com·mune** \ˌintə(r)kəˈmyün\ *vb* [alter. (influenced by L *inter-*) of ME *entrecomunen*, *entrecommunen*, fr. AF *entrecomuner*, *entrecommuner*] *vi* **:** to have mutual communion or intercourse by conversation ~ *vt*, *obs* **:** to deprive of intercourse with other men **:** OUTLAW
**in·ter·communicability** \ˌintə(r)+\ *n* **:** the quality of being mutually communicable ⟨~ of human and bovine disease⟩
**in·ter·communicable** \ˈ"+\ *adj* [fr. *intercommunicate*, after E *communicate*: *communicable*] **:** capable of being mutually communicated
**in·ter·communicate** \ˈ"+\ *vi* [prob. fr. *inter-* + *communicate*] **1 :** to communicate mutually **:** give and receive information **:** hold conversation **2 :** to afford passage from one to another ⟨*intercommunicating* rooms⟩
**in·ter·communication** \ˈ"+\ *n* [prob. fr. *inter-* + *communication*] **:** mutual communication ⟨~ telephone⟩ ⟨unhampered ~ among the scientists of the world⟩
**intercommunication system** *n* **:** a two-way communication system with microphone and loudspeaker at each station for communicating within a limited area (as between offices in the same building or between operating stations on an airplane)
**in·ter·communicator** \ˈ"+\ *n* **:** an instrument for intercommunication
**in·ter·communion** \ˈ"+\ *n* [*inter-* + *communion*] **:** open communion between churches or denominations based on official recognition of other bodies and ratified usu. by an agreement between cooperating parties
[1]**in·ter·community** \ˈ"+\ *n* [*inter-* + *community*] **:** the quality of being common to two or more **:** participation in common ⟨~ of measurements is achieved by the metric system⟩
[2]**intercommunity** \ˈ"\ *adj* [*inter-* + *community* (n.)] **:** existing between two or more communities ⟨~ rivalry⟩
**in·ter·company** \ˈ"+\ *adj* [*inter-* + *company* (n.)] **:** existing between two or more companies ⟨~ agreements⟩
**in·ter·comparable** \ˈ"+\ *adj* [*inter-* + *comparable*] **:** capable of being compared
**in·ter·compare** \ˈ"+\ *vt* [*inter-* + *compare*] **:** to compare (as members of a specified group or their qualities) with one another ⟨to return to the open clusters . . . we can . . . ~ their total luminosities . . . compare them also with the open clusters in our own system — Harlow Shapley⟩
**in·ter·comparison** \ˈ"+\ *n* [*inter-* + *comparison*] **:** reciprocal or mutual comparison
**in·ter·condenser** \ˈ"+\ *n* [*inter-* + *condenser*] **:** one of the intermediate stages in a multistage steam-engine condenser
**in·ter·confessional** \ˈ"+\ *adj* [*inter-* + *confessional*] **:** involving, supported by, or common to groups (as Anglicans and Eastern Orthodox) having different confessions of faith
**in·ter·con·nect** \ˌintə(r)kəˈnekt\ *vt* [*inter-* + *connect*] **:** to connect mutually or with one another ⟨~*ed* generating stations⟩
**in·ter·con·nect·ed·ness** \-tədnəs\ *n* **:** the quality or state of being interconnected **:** INTERRELATEDNESS ⟨the ~ of the interests of all nations has become so great —H.J.Morgenthau⟩
**in·ter·connection** \ˌintə(r)+\ *n* [*inter-* + *connection*] **:** connection between two or more **:** mutual connection ⟨~ of members of an electric power system⟩ ⟨basis of rational belief lies in the ~ of judgments each independently formed —J.H.Muirhead⟩
**in·ter·consonantal** \ˈ"+\ *or* **in·ter·consonantic** \ˈ"+\ *adj* [*inter-* + *consonantal*, *consonantic*] **:** immediately preceded and immediately followed by a consonant
**in·ter·continental** \ˈ"+\ *adj* [*inter-* + *continental*] **1 :** existing or extending between or among continents ⟨~ flight⟩ **:** subsisting or carried on between continents ⟨~ war⟩ **2 :** capable of traveling between continents ⟨~ missile⟩ ⟨~ bomber⟩
**in·ter·conversion** \ˈ"+\ *n* [*inter-* + *conversion*] **:** conversion into one another **:** mutual conversion ⟨~ of chemical compounds⟩
**in·ter·convert** \ˈ"+\ *vt* [*inter-* + *convert*] **:** to change each into the other **:** INTERCHANGE ⟨ordinary and extraordinary rays were ~*ed* when the crystals were placed at right angles —S.F.Mason⟩
**in·ter·convertibility** \ˈ"+\ *n* **:** the quality of being interconvertible ⟨~ of currencies⟩
**in·ter·convertible** \ˈ"+\ *adj* [*inter-* + *convertible*] **:** convertible the one into the other **:** INTERCHANGEABLE ⟨matter and energy are ~⟩ — **in·ter·con·vert·ibly** \-blē, -li\ *adv*
**in·ter·cool** \ˌintə(r)ˈkül\ *vt* [back-formation fr. *intercooler*] **:** to cool (a fluid) in an intercooler
**in·ter·cool·er** \-lə(r)\ *n* [*inter-* + *cooler*] **:** a device for cooling a fluid (as air) between successive heat-generating processes (as in a multistage air compressor)
**in·ter·corporate** \ˌintə(r)+\ *adj* [*inter-* + *corporate*] **:** existing between, involving, or belonging to two or more corporations ⟨~ council⟩ ⟨~ control of stock⟩
**in·ter·correlate** \ˈ"+\ *vt* [*inter-* + *correlate*] **:** to correlate (members of a group) with each other
**in·ter·correlation** \ˈ"+\ *n* [*inter-* + *correlation*] **:** correlation between members of a group; *esp* **:** one of the correlations existing among independent statistical variables excluding the dependent variable criterion
**in·ter·cosmic** \ˈ"+\ *adj* [*inter-* + *cosmic*] **:** situated between or among the planets or stars ⟨~ dust⟩ — **in·ter·cosmically** \ˈ"+\ *adv*
[1]**in·ter·cos·tal** \ˈ"+ˈkästᵊl\ *adj* [NL *intercostalis*, fr. L *inter-* + *costa* rib + *-alis* -al — more at COAST] **1 a :** situated between the ribs **b :** of, relating to, or produced by the intercostal muscles **2 :** situated between the veins or nerves of a leaf **3 :** lying or fitted between the continuous members of a ship's frame ⟨~ plate⟩ ⟨~ keelson⟩ ⟨~ angle iron⟩ — see SHIP illustration — **in·ter·cos·tal·ly** \-ᵊlē, -ᵊli\ *adv*
[2]**intercostal** \ˈ"\ *n* **:** an intercostal part or structure
**intercostal artery** *n* **:** any of the arteries supplying or lying in the intercostal spaces and being mostly branches of the aorta
**intercostal muscle** *n* **:** any of the short muscles that extend between the ribs filling in most of the intervals between them and serving to move the ribs in respiration
**intercostal nerve** *n* **:** one of the anterior divisions of the thoracic nerves that lie in the intercostal spaces
**intercostal vein** *n* **:** one of the veins of the intercostal spaces
**in·ter·cos·to·brachial nerve** \ˌintə(r)ˌkästō+ . . . -\ *n* [*intercostal* + *-o-* + *brachial*] **:** the lateral cutaneous branch of the second intercostal nerve that crosses the axilla and supplies the skin of the inner and back part of the upper half of the arm
**in·ter·country** \ˌintə(r)+\ *adj* [*inter-* + *country* (n.)] **:** INTERNATIONAL
**in·ter·course** \ˈintər,kō(ə)rs, -kȯ(ə)rs, -təˌkōəs, -təˌkȯ(ə)s\ *n* [ME *intercurse*, prob. modif. (influenced by L *inter-*) of MF *entrecours*, fr. OF, fr. ML *intercursus*, fr. L, intervention, act of running between, fr. *intercursus*, past part. of *intercurrere* to run between, fr. *inter-* + *currere* to run — more at CURRENT] **1 :** dealings or connection (as in common affairs, civilities, or business) between persons, organizations, or nations **:** COMMUNICATION ⟨diffidence . . . renders me inapt for social ~ —Havelock Ellis⟩ ⟨as trade ~ increases between nations —J.A. Hobson⟩ ⟨welcomes extraclass ~ with students and encourages them to think critically —G.H.White⟩ **2 :** exchange or interchange esp. of thought and feeling **:** COMMUNION ⟨sweet ~ of looks and smiles —John Milton⟩ ⟨believed he had direct ~ with the Deity —Ruth Gruber⟩ **3 :** COPULATION, COITUS — used chiefly of humans **4** *obs* **a :** alternate succession **:** ALTERNATION **b :** INTERVENTION, INTERPOSITION **c :** INTERCOMMUNICATION, INTERCONNECTION
**in·ter·cranial** \ˌintə(r)+\ *adj* [*inter-* + *cranial*] **:** situated or occurring within the cranium
**in·ter·create** \ˈ"+\ *vt* [*inter-* + *create*] **:** to create jointly with another
**in·ter·creedal** \ˈ"+\ *adj* [*inter-* + *creedal*] **:** INTERDENOMINATIONAL
**in·ter·cres·cence** \ˌintə(r)ˈkresən(t)s\ *n* -s [*inter-* + *-crescence* (as in *excrescence*)] **:** a growing together of tissues
[1]**in·ter·crop** \ˌintə(r)+\ *vb* [*inter-* + *crop*] *vt* **1 :** to grow a crop in between (another) ⟨*intercropped* their tree fruit . . . with market garden crops —*Biol. Abstracts*⟩ **2 :** to use (ground) for a catch crop ~ *vi* **:** to grow two or more crops simultaneously (as in alternate rows) in the same ground
[2]**in·ter·crop** \ˈintə(r)+ˌ-\ *n* **:** CATCH CROP ⟨sweet clover ~⟩
[1]**in·ter·cross** \ˌintə(r)+\ *vb* [*inter-* + *cross*] *vi* **1 :** to cross each other ⟨various shapes and colors . . . ~*ing* without confusion —Earl of Shaftesbury †1713⟩ **2 :** CROSS 5 ~ *vt* **1 :** to place across each other ⟨framed of iron bars ~*ed*, which formed . . . an immense cage —S.T.Coleridge⟩ **2 :** CROSS 9
[2]**in·ter·cross** \ˈintə(r)+ˌ-\ *n* **:** an instance or a product of crossbreeding
**in·ter·crystalline** \ˌintə(r)+\ *adj* [*inter-* + *crystalline*] **:** occurring between crystals ⟨~ crack in a metal⟩ — compare TRANSCRYSTALLINE
**in·ter·crystallization** \ˈ"+\ *n* [*inter-* + *crystallization*] **:** the process of intercrystallizing
**in·ter·crystallize** \ˈ"+\ *vi* [*inter-* + *crystallize*] **:** to crystallize together at the same time with resulting mutual inclusion so that each component retains through the mass its own crystallographic identity including crystallographic and optical orientation; *sometimes* **:** to form a solid solution — used of two or more associated minerals
**in·ter·cultural** \ˈ"+\ *adj* [*inter-* + *cultural*] **1 :** cultivated between the rows of some other crop **2 :** occurring during the growing period ⟨~ tillage⟩ ⟨~ hoeing⟩ **3 :** existing between or relating to two or more cultures ⟨~ contact⟩ ⟨~ tension⟩ ⟨~ education⟩
**in·ter·culture** \ˈintə(r)+ˌ-\ *n* [*inter-* + *culture*] **:** INTERCROPPING
**in·ter·current** \ˌintə(r)+\ *adj* [L *intercurrent-*, *intercurrens*, pres. part. of *intercurrere* to run between — more at INTERCOURSE] **1 :** running between or among **2 a** *obs* **:** coming in between or among **:** lying between **b :** INTERVENING **3 :** occurring in the midst of a process **:** INTERRUPTING ⟨~ sense impressions during a dream⟩ **4 :** occurring in and modifying the course of another disease ⟨~ infection⟩ — **in·ter·cur·rent·ly** *adv*
[1]**in·ter·cut** \ˈ"+\ *vb* [*inter-* + *cut*] *vt* **1 :** to insert a contrasting camera shot into (a take) by cutting ⟨*intercutting* panoramic long shots with closeups of action and expression —*Time*⟩ **2 :** to insert (a contrasting camera shot) into a take by cutting ⟨rapidly ~ news shots and animated maps —*New Republic*⟩ ~ *vi* **:** to alternate contrasting camera shots of the same scene or of different scenes by cutting ⟨*intercutting* for dramatic suspense —Budd Schulberg⟩
[2]**in·ter·cut** \ˈintə(r)+ˌ-\ *n* **:** an intercut camera shot or film sequence ⟨cartoon sequences to be used as ~*s* when the camera fades out on the principals —T.M.Pryor⟩
**in·ter·denominational** \ˌintə(r)+\ *adj* [*inter-* + *denominational*] **:** occurring between or among or common to different denominations ⟨~ cooperation between Methodists and Presbyterians⟩
**in·ter·denominationalism** \ˈ"+\ *n* **:** the principle of fostering intercommunion and cooperative activities among different religious denominations
**in·ter·dental** \ˈ"+\ *adj* [*inter-* + *dental*] **1 :** situated or placed between the teeth **2 :** formed with the tip of the tongue protruded between the upper and lower front teeth ⟨~ consonants⟩ — **in·ter·dentally** \ˈ"+\ *adv*
**in·ter·den·tal·i·ty** \ˌintə(r)(ˌ)denˈtalədē\ *n* [ISV *interdental* + *-ity*] **:** interdental articulation: **a :** substitution of the interdental sounds \th\ and \t͟h\ for \s\ and \z\ respectively **:** LISP **b :** interdental articulation of other alveolars or dentals (as \t\, \d\, \n\, \l\)
**in·ter·dentil** \ˌintə(r)+\ *n* [*inter-* + *dentil*] **:** the space between two dentils
**in·ter·departmental** \ˈ"+\ *adj* [*inter-* + *departmental*] **:** existing, exchanged, or carried on between departments; *esp* **:** characterized by participation or cooperation of two or more departments of an educational institution ⟨~ major⟩ — **in·ter·departmentally** \ˈ"+\ *adv*
**in·ter·depend** \ˈ"+\ *vi* [*inter-* + *depend*] **:** to depend upon one another
**in·ter·dependence** \ˈ"+\ *n* [*inter-* + *dependence*] **:** mutual dependence ⟨~ of members of a family⟩ ⟨~ of statistical variables⟩
**in·ter·dependency** \ˈ"+\ *n* [*inter-* + *dependency*] **:** INTERDEPENDENCE
**in·ter·dependent** \ˈ"+\ *adj* [*inter-* + *dependent*] **:** mutually dependent — **in·ter·de·pend·ent·ly** *adv*
**in·ter·determination** \ˈ"+\ *n* [*inter-* + *determination*] **:** cause and effect operating among several factors **:** multiple causation
**in·ter·determined** \ˈ"+\ *adj* [*inter-* + *determined*, past part. of *determine*] **:** mutually determined
**in·ter·dialect** \ˈ"+\ *or* **in·ter·dialectal** \ˈ"+\ *adj* [*interdialect* fr. *inter-* + *dialect* (n.); *interdialectal* fr. *inter-* + *dialectal*] **:** existing or occurring between dialects ⟨~ loans⟩ ⟨~ influences⟩
[1]**in·ter·dict** \ˈintə(r)ˌdikt *sometimes* -dīt *or* + V -dīd-\ *n* -s [alter. (influenced by L *interdictum*) of ME *entredit*, fr. OF, fr. L *interdictum* prohibition, interdict of a praetor, fr. neut. of *interdictus*, past part. of *interdicere* to interpose, forbid, interdict, fr. *inter* between, among + *dicere* to say — more at INTER-, DICTION] **1 :** an ecclesiastical censure of the Roman Catholic Church barring a person or the people of a region from the sacraments, religious services, and Christian burial **2 :** a prohibitory decree **:** PROHIBITION **3 a** *Roman civil law* (1) **:** an administrative order of the praetor for prevention of encroachments on or wrongs concerning sacred or public property or breaches of the peace (2) **:** an order issued as a remedy in certain cases (as of disputed possession) forbidding certain things to be done **b :** an order in systems founded on Roman civil law corresponding to the injunction of the English law **c** *civil & Scots law* **:** one incompetent to manage his affairs by reason of mental weakness, facility, or insanity **:** one under curatorship as an incompetent **:** an interdicted person **:** one under voluntary or judicial interdiction
[2]**in·ter·dict** \ˌ==ˈ=\ *vt* -ED/-ING/-S [alter. (influenced by L *interdictum*, n., and *interdictus*, past part.) of ME *entrediten*, prob. fr. OF *entredit*, past part. of *entredire*, fr. L *interdicere*] **1 :** to lay under or prohibit by an interdict ⟨~*ed* under heavy penalties the use of the Book of Common Prayer —T.B. Macaulay⟩ **2 :** PROHIBIT, DEBAR ⟨~ trade with a foreign nation⟩ **3 :** to destroy, cut, or damage by ground or aerial firepower (enemy lines of reinforcement, supply, or communication) in order to stop or hamper enemy movement and to destroy or limit enemy effectiveness **syn** see FORBID
[3]**in·ter·dict** \ˌ==ˈ=\ *adj* [ME *interdicte*, fr. L *interdictus*, past part.] *archaic* **:** INTERDICTED
**in·ter·dic·tion** \ˌintə(r)ˈdikshən\ *n* [ME (Scot. dial.) *interdiccioun*, fr. L *interdiction-*, *interdictio*, fr. *interdictus* (past part.) + *-ion-*, *-io* -ion] **1 :** the act of interdicting or state of being interdicted **:** INTERDICT, TABOO ⟨in primitive society . . . the same ~ is very frequently laid on the names of common objects —J.G.Frazer⟩ ⟨so little did he comprehend the rigid ~*s* of Montreal society —Walter O'Meara⟩ **2** *civil & Scots law* **:** a voluntary or judicial restraint placed upon a person suffer-

ing from mental weakness with respect to acts which may affect his estate **3 :** artillery fire or air attack directed on a route or area to deny its use to the enemy ⟨~ bombing⟩ ⟨~ of an airstrip⟩

**in·ter·dic·tive** \¦==¦diktiv\ *adj* [²*interdict* + *-ive*] **:** INTERDICTORY

**in·ter·dic·tor** \,==ˈdiktə(r)\ *n* -s [LL, fr. L *interdictus* (past part.) + *-or*] **1 :** one that interdicts **2** *Scots law* **:** a person whose consent is made necessary by a bond of voluntary interdiction to certain acts of the person executing the bond

**in·ter·dic·to·ry** \,==ˈdikt(ə)rē, -ri\ *adj* [LL *interdictorius*, fr. L *interdictus* (past part. of *interdicere* to interdict) + *-orius* -ory] **:** having the power or effect of interdicting **:** relating or belonging to interdiction **:** PROHIBITORY ⟨~ decree⟩ ⟨coastal road was still under heavy ~ fire —R.E.Lawless⟩

**in·ter·dic·tum** \,==ˈdiktəm\ *n, pl* **interdic·ta** \-tə\ [L] **:** INTERDICT, INJUNCTION

**in·ter·dig·i·tate** \,intə(r)ˈdijə,tāt\ *vb* -ED/-ING/-S [*inter-* + L *digitus* finger + *-ate* — more at TOE] *vi* **:** to interlock like the fingers of folded hands **:** INTERFINGER ⟨forests ~ with the grasslands⟩ **~** *vt* **:** INTERSTRATIFY ⟨fluvial and marine sediments form an *interdigitated* succession —Daniel Wirtz & Henning Illies⟩

**in·ter·dig·i·ta·tion** \,==,==ˈtāshən\ *n* **:** the act of interlocking or the condition of being interlocked or interpenetrated ⟨produce, by ~, alternate strips of warm and cold water —*Encyc. Britannica*⟩

**in·ter·dine** \¦intə(r)+\ *vi* [*inter-* + *dine*] **:** to join in a common meal ⟨subdivided into subcastes which do not intermarry or ~ —D.G.Mandelbaum⟩

**in·ter·disciplinary** \"+\ *adj* [*inter-* + *disciplinary*] **:** characterized by participation or cooperation of two or more disciplines or fields of study ⟨an ~ conference⟩ **:** drawing on or contributing to two or more disciplines ⟨~ approach to anthropology⟩

**in·ter·district** \"+\ *adj* [*inter-* + *district* (n.)] **:** existing between districts ⟨~ athletic contests⟩

**in·ter·dome** \ˈintə(r)+,-\ *n* [*inter-* + *dome*] **:** an open space between the inner and outer shells of a dome or cupola

**in·ter·dotting** \"+,-\ *n* -s [*inter-* + *dotting*, gerund of *dot*] **:** dots applied to an area (as of an engraving) for producing a light shading

**in·ter·epimeral** \¦intə(r)+\ *adj* [*inter-* + *epimeral*] **:** situated between adjacent epimera

**¹interess** *n* -ES [ME *interesse*] *obs* **:** RIGHT, CONCERN, INTEREST

**²interess** *vt* -ED/-ING/-ES **1** *obs* **:** INTEREST; *esp* **:** to admit to a right or privilege **2** [MF *interesser*, fr. L *interesse* to be between, differ, concern] *obs* **:** to affect injuriously **:** INJURE

**in·ter·es·se** \,intəˈresē\ *n* -s [ML] **1 :** a legal interest in property **2 :** interest upon money

**in·ter·es·see** \,intərəˈsē\ *n* -s [²*interess* + *-ee*] **:** a party in interest

**interesse ter·mi·ni** \-ˈtərmə,nī\ *n* [ML, lit., interest of term or end] **:** the right of entry legally conferred by the demise of a leasehold estate before entry is made

**¹in·ter·est** \ˈin·trəst *also* ˈintərəst *or* ˈintə,rest *or* ˈintərst *sometimes* ˈin·,trest\ *n* -s [ME, prob. alter. of earlier *interesse*, fr. AF & ML; AF *interesse*, fr. ML, legal interest, compensation, interest on money, fr. L, to concern, be of importance, fr. *inter-* + *esse* to be; influenced by MF *interest* damage, loss, compensation for damage, fr. OF, damage, loss, fr. L, it concerns, is of importance, 3d pers. sing. pres. indic. of *interesse* — more at IS] **1 a :** right, title, or legal share in something ⟨what exactly is your ~ in this affair⟩ **:** participation in advantage, profit, and responsibility ⟨half ~ in a hardware business⟩ ⟨offered to buy out his ~ in the company⟩ **:** STAKE, CLAIM **b :** something in which one has a share of ownership or control **:** BUSINESS ⟨has ~*s* all over the world⟩ **c** *obs* **:** a share in producing a total effect or result **2 a :** the state of being concerned or affected esp. with respect to advantage or well-being **:** GOOD, BENEFIT, PROFIT ⟨engaged a lawyer to look after his ~*s*⟩ ⟨acting always in his own ~⟩ ⟨each faction made concessions in the common ~⟩ ⟨speed laws passed in the ~ of safety⟩; *specif* **:** SELF-INTEREST ⟨sacrifice of personal ~ by men who believed in the job they were doing —T.W.Arnold⟩ ⟨distinguish fact from fiction . . . ~ from impartiality —Elmer Davis⟩ **b :** something that is the object of desire ⟨natural ~ in seeing his children well educated⟩ **3 a :** the price paid for borrowing money generally expressed as a percentage of the amount borrowed paid in one year ⟨~ on a loan⟩ ⟨~ on a bond⟩ — see COMPOUND INTEREST, SIMPLE INTEREST **b :** the money so paid ⟨~ on certain indebtedness is deductible from taxable income⟩ **c :** the share received by capital from the product of industry as distinguished from rent and profit and wages — see PURE INTEREST **4 :** an excess over and above an exact equivalent ⟨returned the insults with ~⟩ **5 :** the power of influencing ⟨~ with the boss⟩ **6 a :** the persons effectively controlling an enterprise or dominating a field of activity ⟨landed ~⟩ ⟨iron ~⟩ ⟨banking ~⟩ ⟨Protestant ~⟩ **b interests** *pl* **:** the dominating group of owners in a field of business, industry, or finance considered locally, regionally, nationally, or internationally; *sometimes* **:** BIG BUSINESS **7 a :** a feeling that accompanies or causes special attention to some object **:** CURIOSITY, CONCERN ⟨took a lively ~ in the divorce proceedings in court⟩ ⟨lifelong ~ in sports⟩ ⟨~ in arctic exploration⟩ ⟨~ in child welfare⟩ **b :** readiness to attend to and be stirred by a certain class of objects ⟨testing the aptitudes, ~*s*, emotions of the patient⟩ **c :** something that causes or arouses curiosity or concern ⟨campaign of great intrinsic ~ to military students⟩ ⟨question of great philosophic ~⟩ **8 a** *obs* **:** INJURY **b** *obs* **:** compensation for injury **:** DAMAGES

**²interest** \"\ *vt* -ED/-ING/-S **1 :** to cause to share or participate ⟨this holding company through which the public is ~*ed* in the Emperor mine —*Sydney (Australia) Bull.*⟩ **2 :** to involve the interest or welfare of **:** AFFECT, CONCERN — used with *in* ⟨~*ed* herself exuberantly in the progress of the political campaign —Robert Grant †1940⟩ ⟨thanked those who had ~*ed* themselves in his behalf⟩ **3 :** to cause or induce to have a share or interest **:** persuade to participate or engage ⟨city authorities began to ~ themselves in the parking problem⟩ ⟨~ a banker in a loan⟩ ⟨can I ~ you in a game of bridge⟩ **4 :** to engage or attract the attention of **:** arouse interest in ⟨would find some picture that ~*ed* him, in an old magazine —Floyd Dell⟩ ⟨offer a market that ought to ~ any businessman —Andrew Boyd⟩

**interested** *adj* [fr. past part. of ²*interest*] **1 :** having the attention engaged **:** having curiosity or sympathy aroused ⟨~ listeners⟩ ⟨a nice widowed doctor up there who is ~ in her —Hamilton Basso⟩ **2 :** having a share or concern in some affair or project **:** liable to be affected or prejudiced **:** CONCERNED, INVOLVED ⟨in addition to the lender and borrower, the state considers itself an ~ party to these operations —*U.S.Investor*⟩; *esp* **:** having self-interest **:** not disinterested ⟨generosity proceeding from ~ motives⟩ ⟨~ witness⟩ — **in·ter·est·ed·ly** *adv* — **in·ter·est·ed·ness** *n* -ES

**in·ter·esterification** \¦intə(r)+\ *n* [*inter-* + *esterification*] **:** TRANSESTERIFICATION

**interest group** *n* **:** a group of persons having a common identifying interest that often provides a basis for action

**interesting** *adj* [fr. pres. part. of ²*interest*] **1** *obs* **:** of concern **:** IMPORTANT **2 :** engaging the attention **:** capable of arousing interest, curiosity, or emotion ⟨~ news⟩ ⟨~ personality⟩

**syn** ENGROSSING, ABSORBING, INTRIGUING: INTERESTING may imply a power to provoke attentive interest to an unspecified degree through some such quality as curiosity, sympathy, desire to understand, enthusiasm, or vicarious identification ⟨seemed to me to be increasingly *interesting;* she was acquiring new subtleties, complexities, and comprehensions —Rose Macaulay⟩ ⟨the effect of the moonlight on Netta's face was *interesting*. It was even complicated. It emphasized a certain haggardness, a certain battered, woebegone pitifulness in her —J.C.Powys⟩ ENGROSSING may suggest power to divert attention from other matters and to hold it by challenge, stimulation, provocation ⟨an *engrossing* account of his research problems⟩ ⟨an *engrossing* mystery drama⟩ ⟨the fight with the hooked trout is only one phase of the sport, albeit a very *engrossing* one —Alexander MacDonald⟩ ABSORBING may imply power to hold interest and attention utterly, the person concerned being oblivious to all else ⟨but Maugham's skill as a storyteller is so impelling that one must follow through this *absorbing* tale to its end —R.A.Cordell⟩ ⟨when a woman takes up some *absorbing* pursuit, and finds it and its associations more interesting than her husband's company and conversation and friends —G.B.Shaw⟩ INTRIGUING usu. applies to what attracts attention, esp. by arousing curiosity, puzzling one, archly fascinating, or challenging ingenuity ⟨these *intriguing* beginnings stimulated a great research effort —A.G.N.Flew⟩ ⟨her eyes had a definite slant from some Oriental ancestor, and, with her flaxen hair, gave her face an *intriguing* prettiness —Winifred Bambrick⟩

**— in an interesting condition** *of a woman* **:** PREGNANT

**in·ter·est·ing·ly** *adv* **:** in an interesting manner ⟨when he ceases to be just ~ neurotic and . . . gets locked up —*Time*⟩

**in·ter·est·ing·ness** *n* -ES **:** the quality or state of being interesting ⟨others who felt the essential ~ of his writings —*Times Lit. Supp.*⟩

**interest lottery** *n* **:** a lottery that issues bonds for borrowed money at less than the normal rate of interest and gives chances for prizes as the consideration for the low interest

**interest policy** *n* **:** an insurance policy which requires insurable interest in the property covered only at the time of loss and not at the inception of the policy

**interests** *pl of* INTEREST, *pres 3d sing of* INTEREST

**in·ter·estuarine** \¦intə(r)+\ *adj* [*inter-* + *estuarine*] **:** lying between two estuaries

**¹in·ter·face** \ˈintə(r)+,-\ *n* [*inter-* + *face*] **1 :** a plane or other surface forming a common boundary of two bodies or spaces ⟨passage of ~*s* of the diametrically opposed air masses —*Yr. Bk. of General Medicine*⟩ ⟨the ~ between two separate types of oil flowing along a pipeline —*Canadian Banker*⟩ ⟨heat transfer at an air-earth ~ —J.E.Vehrencamp⟩ **2 :** the boundary between two phases in a heterogeneous physical-chemical system ⟨the boundary between . . . two phases is designated as an ~, although the term *surface* is often used with a general meaning which includes all types of interfaces —W.D.Harkins⟩ — compare SURFACE 1

**²in·ter·face** \¦intə(r)+\ *vt* [*inter-* + *face*] **:** to make (a garment) with an interfacing

**in·ter·facial** \"+\ *adj* [*inter-* + *face* + *-ial*] **1 :** included between two plane surfaces or faces ⟨an ~ angle⟩ **2** [*interface* + *-ial*] **:** relating to or situated at an interface ⟨~ layer⟩ ⟨~ strength of felt⟩

**interfacial tension** *n* **:** surface tension at the interface between two liquids

**in·ter·facing** \ˈintə(r)+,-\ *n* [*inter-* + *facing*] **:** a firm cloth shaped and sewn between the facing and outside of a garment for stiffening and shape retention and used esp. in revers, collars, cuffs

**in·ter·factional** \¦intə(r)+\ *adj* [*inter-* + *factional*] **:** existing between factions ⟨~ disputes⟩

**in·ter·faith** \"+\ *adj* [*inter-* + *faith* (n.)] **:** occurring between or among people or organizations of different religious faiths or creeds ⟨~ marriage⟩ ⟨~ conference⟩

**in·ter·family** \"+\ *adj* [*inter-* + *family* (n.)] **:** occurring or existing between families ⟨~ marriage⟩ ⟨~ grafting of plants⟩

**in·ter·fascicular** \"+\ *adj* [*inter-* + *fascicular*] **:** situated between fascicles ⟨~ tissue⟩

**interfascicular cambium** *n* **:** cambium located between vascular bundles — compare FASCICULAR CAMBIUM

**in·ter·felted** \"+\ *adj* [*inter-* + *felted*] **:** pressed closely together ⟨~ fibers⟩ ⟨~ layers of rock⟩

**in·ter·fenestral** \"+\ *adj* [*inter-* + *fenestral*] **:** situated between windows ⟨~ panel⟩

**in·ter·fenestration** \,intə(r)+\ *n* [*inter-* + L *fenestratus* (past part. of *fenestrare* to provide with openings or windows) + E *-ion* — more at FENESTRATED] **1 :** width of pier between two windows **2 :** arrangement of windows with relation to the distance between them from axis to axis or from opening to opening

**in·ter·fe·rant** \,intə(r)ˈfirənt, -fēr-\ *n* -s [*interfere* + *-ant*] **:** the holder of or an applicant for a patent that conflicts with a patent granted earlier

**in·ter·fere** *R* ¦intə(r)¦fi(ə)r, *-R* -tə¦fiə *or* +V -i(ə)r\ *vi* -ED/-ING/-s [alter. (influenced by L *inter-*) of MF (*s'*)*entreferir* to strike each other, fr. OF, fr. *entre-* inter- + *ferir* to strike, fr. L *ferire* — more at BORE (pierce)] **1 :** to strike one foot against the opposite foot or ankle in walking or running — used esp. of horses **2 :** to come in collision **:** to be in opposition **:** to run at cross-purposes **:** CLASH ⟨*interfering* claims⟩ — used with *with* ⟨carbon dioxide ~*s* with the liberation of oxygen to the tissues —H.G.Armstrong⟩ **3 :** to enter into or take a part in the concerns of others **:** INTERMEDDLE, INTERPOSE, INTERVENE **4** *obs* **:** to run into another or each other **:** INTERSECT **5 :** to act reciprocally so as to augment, diminish, or otherwise affect one another — used of waves **6 :** to claim substantially the same invention and thus question the priority of invention between the claimants — distinguished from *infringe* **7** *of a football player* **a :** to run ahead of the ballcarrier and provide allowed blocking protection for him **b :** to hinder illegally an attempt of a player to receive a pass or make a fair catch of a punt **syn** see MEDDLE

**in·ter·fer·ence** \,==ˈfirən(t)s, -fēr-\ *n* -s [*interfere* + *-ence*] **1 :** the act or process of interfering **:** a brushing or kicking of feet or ankles in walking or running **2 :** the act of meddling in or hampering an activity or process ⟨~ in the affairs of another nation⟩ **:** OBSTRUCTION, INHIBITION ⟨cause of our present economic troubles is laid to political ~ with the beneficent workings of private competitive effort for gain —John Dewey⟩ **3 :** the mutual effect on meeting of two wave trains of the same type so that such wave trains of light produce lines, bands, or fringes either alternately light and dark or variously colored and such wave trains of sound produce silence, increased intensity, or beats — compare FRINGE 2e, INTERFERENCE COLORS, INTERFERENCE FIGURE, INTERFERENCE PATTERN, INTERFERENCE SPECTRUM **4 a :** incorrect meshing of gear teeth resulting in contact along other than the proper lines of action **b :** contact so close as to produce deformation and stress **5 :** an instance of interfering with a patent; *also* **:** the proceeding for determining the question of priority involved **6 a :** the act of illegally hampering an opponent (as in football) **b :** the act of protecting a ballcarrier or a passer by blocking would-be tacklers; *also* **:** a player providing this protection **7 :** the inhibiting of coincident crossing over of genes at loci immediately adjacent to a chiasma **8 a :** confusion of received radio signals due to strays or undesired signals **b :** something that produces such confusion **9 :** the disturbing effect exerted by the learning of an act on the performance of a previously learned act with which it is inconsistent **10 :** prevention of typical growth and development of a virus in a suitable host by the presence of another virus in the same host individual — see INTERFERENCE PHENOMENON

**interference colors** *n pl* **:** colors produced by the strengthening or the weakening of certain wavelengths of a composite beam of light in consequence of interference

**interference figure** *n* **:** a figure observed with a conoscope when a section of a doubly refracting crystal is in the path traversed by convergent plane-polarized light (as when a centered black cross is superimposed over a black spot at the center of a series of concentric colored rings)

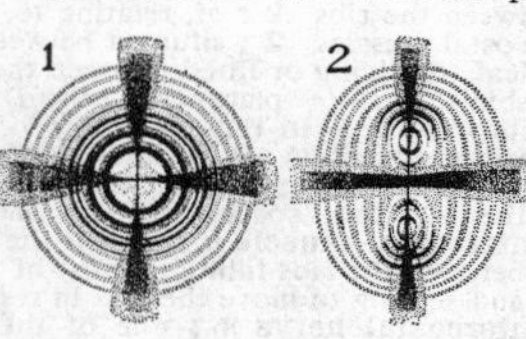

interference figures: *1* produced by a uniaxial crystal; *2* produced by a biaxial crystal when polarizer and analyzer are set at right angles to each other

**interference fringe** *n* **:** FRINGE 2e

**interference pattern** *n* **:** an arrangement of fringes or bands (as Newton's rings) due to interference — compare OPTICAL FLAT

**interference phenomenon** *n* **:** preoccupation of the route of invasion of a pathogenic virus (as by competition for available nutrients) by another virus postulated as the basis of interference — called also *cell-blockade phenomenon*

**interference spectrum** *n* **:** a spectrum (as in a transparent film) in which the dispersion is due to interference of light

**in·ter·fe·ren·tial** \¦intə(r)fə¦renchəl\ *adj* [fr. *interference*, after such pairs as E *difference: differential*] **:** of, relating to, or depending on interference (as of light)

**in·ter·fer·er** *R* ,intə(r)ˈfirər, *-R* -təˈfirə(r\ *n* -s **:** one that interferes

**interfering** *adj* **:** OBSTRUCTING, MEDDLING ⟨~ old woman⟩ — **in·ter·fer·ing·ly** *adv* — **in·ter·fer·ing·ness** *n* -ES

**in·ter·fer·o·gram** \,==ˈfirə,gram\ *n* [*interferometer* + *-gram*] **:** a record made by an interferograph

**in·ter·fer·o·graph** \-raf, -rȧf\ *n* [ISV *interferometer* + *-graph*] **:** an apparatus for making photographic records of optical interference phenomena (as patterns of interference fringes)

**in·ter·fer·om·e·ter** \,==fəˈrämәd·ə(r)\ *n* [ISV *interfero-* (fr. *interfere*) + *-meter*] **:** an instrument for precise determinations of wavelength, spectral fine structure, indices of refraction, and very small linear displacements through the separation of light by means of a system of mirrors and glass plates into two parts that travel unequal optical paths and when reunited consequently interfere with each other — see ACOUSTIC INTERFEROMETER — **in·ter·fer·o·met·ric** \,==¦firə¦me·trik\ *adj* — **in·ter·fer·o·met·ri·cal·ly** \-rək(ə)lē\ *adv* — **in·ter·fer·om·e·try** \,==fəˈrämə·trē\ *n* -ES

**in·ter·fertile** \¦intə(r)+\ *adj* [*inter-* + *fertile*] **:** capable of interbreeding — **in·ter·fertility** \,intə(r)+\ *n*

**in·ter·fibrillar** \"+\ *adj* [*inter-* + *fibrillar*] **:** situated between fibrils

**in·ter·filamentary** \¦intə(r)+\ *adj* [*inter-* + *filamentary*] **:** existing between filaments

**in·ter·file** \"+\ *vt* [*inter-* + *file*] **:** to file among ⟨~ cards in a catalog⟩

**in·ter·finger** \¦intə(r)+\ *vi* [*inter-* + *finger*] *of rocks* **:** to intergrade through a series of interlocking or overlapping wedge-shaped layers **:** INTERPENETRATE, INTERDIGITATE

**in·ter·firm** \¦intə(r)+\ *adj* [*inter-* + *firm* (n.)] **:** INTERCOMPANY

**¹in·ter·flow** \"+\ *vi* [*inter-* + *flow*] **1 :** to flow between **2 :** to pass into one another **:** INTERMINGLE

**²in·ter·flow** \ˈintə(r)+,-\ *n* **:** a flowing into one another **:** INTERMINGLING

**in·ter·flu·ence** \¦intə(r)¦flüən(t)s, ən·ˈtərfləwən(t)s\ *n* -s [fr. *interfluent*, after such pairs as E *confluent: confluence*] **:** INTERFLOW

**in·ter·flu·ent** \-nt\ *adj* [L *interfluent-*, *interfluens*, pres. part. of *interfluere* to flow between, fr. *inter-* + *fluere* to flow — more at FLUID] **:** flowing between or among **:** passing into one another as if by a natural flow **:** INTERMINGLING

**in·ter·flu·mi·nal** \¦intə(r)¦flümənᵊl\ *adj* [*inter-* + L *flumin-*, *flumen* river + E *-al* — more at FLUME] **:** INTERFLUVIAL

**in·ter·flu·ous** \ən·ˈtərfləwəs\ *adj* [L *interfluus*, fr. *interfluere* to flow between] **:** INTERFLUENT

**in·ter·fluve** \ˈintə(r),flüv\ *n* -s [*inter-* + L *fluvius* river, stream, fr. *fluere* to flow] **:** the area between adjacent streams flowing in the same direction

**in·ter·fluvial** \¦intə(r)+\ *adj* [*inter-* + *fluvial*] **:** lying between streams

**¹in·ter·fold** \"+\ *vt* [*inter-* + *fold*] **:** to fold (paper sheets) together **:** INTERLOCK ⟨~*ing* machine⟩

**²interfold** \"\ *adj* **:** arranged in interlocking folded sheets ⟨~ paper towels⟩

**in·ter·foliar** \"+\ *or* **in·ter·foliaceous** \"+\ *adj* [*inter-* + L *folium* leaf + E *-ar* or *-aceous* — more at BLADE] **:** borne between the leaves; *esp* **:** borne between opposite or verticillate leaves ⟨~ stipules in Rubiaceae⟩

**in·ter·fo·li·ate** \,intə(r)ˈfōlē,āt\ *vt* [*inter-* + L *folium* + E *-ate*] **:** INTERLEAVE

**in·ter·fraternity** \¦intə(r)+\ *adj* [*inter-* + *fraternity* (n.)] **:** existing or occurring between fraternities ⟨~ dance⟩ ⟨~ council⟩

**in·ter·fret** \ˈintə(r)+,-\ *n* [*inter-* + *fret* (network)] **:** the interaction between two wind currents of different velocities or directions producing a wave motion of the air often of great amplitude and frequently creating special cloud effects (as mackerel sky or billow clouds)

**in·ter·frontal** \¦intə(r)+\ *adj* [F, fr. *inter-* + *frontal*] **:** lying between the frontal bones

**in·ter·fruitful** \"+\ *adj* [*inter-* + *fruitful*] **:** capable of reciprocal cross-pollination ⟨~ strawberry⟩ — **in·ter·fruit·ful·ness** *n*

**in·ter·fuel** \"+\ *adj* [*inter-* + *fuel* (n.)] **:** existing between fuels ⟨~ competition⟩

**in·ter·fuse** \,intə(r)ˈfyüz\ *vb* [L *interfusus*, past part. of *interfundere* to pour between, fr. *inter-* + *fundere* to pour — more at FOUND] *vt* **1 :** to combine (one thing and another) as if by scattering or mixing **:** combine intimately as if by fusing or blending **:** INTERMINGLE ⟨curricular designs that would seek to ~ the social sciences and humanities rather than subordinate one to another —Theodore Brameld⟩ **2 :** to pass (one thing or element) into or through others by pouring or spreading **:** INFUSE, DIFFUSE ⟨clustered round the texts, *interfused* with the texts, are all the values discovered in them or added to them by students, critics —Malcolm Cowley⟩ **3 :** to enter widely or deeply into **:** blend with **:** PERVADE, PERMEATE ⟨wit that *interfused* all his writings⟩ **~** *vi* **:** BLEND, FUSE ⟨these patterns, which overlap and ~ —R.B.Heilman⟩

**in·ter·fu·sion** \-üzhən\ *n* [LL *interfusion-*, *interfusio* act of flowing between, fr. L *interfusus* (past part.) + *-ion-*, *-io* -ion] **:** the action or result of interfusing ⟨~ of religion and virtue is not in fact so close as to secure their habitual coexistence —James Martineau⟩ ⟨a national culture is the ~ of many elements⟩ ⟨~ of one color into another⟩

**in·ter·galactic** \¦intə(r)+\ *adj* [*inter-* + *galactic*] **:** situated or taking place in the vast spaces between galaxies ⟨~ gas⟩

**intergatory** *n* -ES [by contr.] *obs* **:** INTERROGATORY

**in·ter·generic** \¦intə(r)+\ *adj* [*inter-* + *generic*] **:** existing or occurring between genera ⟨~ hybridization⟩

**in·ter·genic** \"+\ *adj* [*inter-* + *genic*] **:** occurring between genes ⟨~ change⟩ ⟨~ interaction⟩

**in·ter·ge·no·mal** \"+¦jē¦nōməl\ *adj* [*inter-* + *genome* + *-al*] **:** occurring between genomes ⟨~ pairing⟩

**¹in·ter·glacial** \"+\ *adj* [ISV *inter-* + *glacial;* orig. formed in G] **:** occurring or formed between glacial epochs ⟨~ climate⟩

**²interglacial** \"\ *n* -s **:** an age or time of comparatively warm or dry climate between times of glaciation

**in·ter·globular** \"+\ *adj* [*inter-* + *globular*] **:** situated in the peripheral part of the dentine of teeth ⟨the ramifications of the tubules end in ~ spaces⟩

**in·ter·glyph** \ˈintə(r)+,-\ *n* [*inter-* + *glyph*] **:** the space between glyphs

**in·ter·governmental** \¦intə(r)+\ *adj* [*inter-* + *governmental*] **:** between or involving participation by two or more governments or levels of government ⟨~ discussions of commodity stabilization arrangements —Henry Brodie⟩ ⟨an ~ committee⟩

**in·ter·gradation** \"+\ *n* [*inter-* + *gradation*] **1 :** transition through a series of grades, forms, or kinds that vary (as in evolution) only by consecutive and related differences ⟨may merely represent parallel evolution rather than ~ —Charlotte Avers⟩ **2 :** an intermediate or transitional form **:** a member of a continuously varying series — **in·ter·gradational** \"+\ *adj*

**¹in·ter·grade** \"+\ *vi* [*inter-* + *grade*] **:** to merge gradually one with another through a continuous series of intermediate forms, kinds, or types

**²in·ter·grade** \ˈintə(r)+,-\ *n* **:** an intermediate or transitional form

**in·ter·graft** \¦intə(r)+\ *vi* [*inter-* + *graft*] **:** to be reciprocally capable of being grafted **:** to become united by grafting ⟨most plums ~ freely⟩

**in·ter·granular** \"+\ *adj* [*inter-* + *granular*] **:** lying or occurring between grains or granules ⟨~ spaces in metamorphic rocks⟩ ⟨~ corrosion of a metal⟩

**in·ter·grave** \"+\ *vt* [*inter-* + *grave*] **:** to grave or carve between **:** engrave in alternate parts

**in·ter·grind** \"+\ *vt* [*inter-* + *grind*] **:** to grind together with **:** blend in grinding ⟨resin *interground* with cement⟩

**in·ter·group** \"+\ *adj* [*inter-* + *group* (n.)] **:** existing or occurring between two or more social groups

**in·ter·grow** \"+\ *vi* [*inter-* + *grow*] **:** to grow among each other **:** grow intermixed **:** exhibit intergrowth

**in·ter·grown** \"+\ *adj* : characterized by intergrowth ⟨~ knot in timber⟩

**in·ter·growth** \'intə(r)+,-\ *n* [*inter-* + *growth*] **1** : a growing between, among, or together; *also* : the product of such growth **2** : growth by intussusception

**¹in·ter·hemal** \¦intə(r)+\ *adj* [*inter-* + *hemal*] : lying between the hemal arches or hemal spines

**²interhemal** \"\ *n* -s : one of the slender elongated bones extending into the flesh of fishes between the hemal spines

**in·ter·hemispheric** \"+\ *adj* [in sense 1, fr. *inter-* + *hemisphere* + *-ic;* in sense 2, fr. *inter-* + *hemispheric*] **1** : lying between the cerebral hemispheres **2** : extending or occurring between hemispheres ⟨~ air flights⟩ ⟨~ warfare⟩

**in·ter·house** \"+\ *adj* [*inter-* + *house* (n.)] : taking place between dormitories, sorority houses, or fraternity houses ⟨an ~ track meet⟩

**in·ter·human** \"+\ *adj* [*inter-* + *human*] : existing or occurring between human beings ⟨~ relations⟩ ⟨~ contagion⟩

**¹in·ter·im** \'intərəm *also* -tə,rim *sometimes* -n·trəm\ *n* -s [L, adv., meanwhile, fr. *inter* between — more at INTER-] **1** : a time intervening : MEANTIME, INTERVAL ⟨~ between phases of the battle⟩ ⟨~ between arrival and departure⟩ **2** : a provisional decision or arrangement; *specif* : a compromise attempting to settle controversies between Catholics and Protestants ⟨Ratisbon *Interim*⟩ **syn** see BREAK

**²interim** \"\ *adv* [L] : in the meantime : MEANWHILE ⟨had tasted ~ of the life of the sporting gentleman —Adrian Bell⟩

**³interim** \"\ *adj* : belonging to an interim : done, made, or occurring for an interim or meantime : TEMPORARY, PROVISIONAL ⟨~ committee⟩ ⟨~ government⟩ ⟨~ lease⟩

**interim certificate** *n* : a temporary or preliminary certificate (as of securities)

**interim dividend** *n* : a preliminary distribution of profits by way of a dividend before determining the full dividend to be paid for the year; *also* : a dividend declared and paid between regular dividend dates

**interim ethics** *n* : an interpretation of the ethical teachings of Jesus as principles enunciated for governing the conduct of the disciples during the anticipated brief span of time before the coming of the second advent and the passing of the terrestrial world

**in·ter·im·is·tic** \¦intərə¦mistik\ *adj* [¹*interim* + *-istic*] : of or relating to an interim : falling in or designed for an interim : PROVISIONAL

**in·ter·imperial** \¦intə(r)+\ *adj* [*inter-* + *imperial*] : carried on between or concerning empires or parts of an empire ⟨~ trade⟩

**in·ter·industrial** \"+\ *or* **in·ter·industry** \"+\ *adj* [*inter-* + *industrial* or *industry* (n.)] : existing or occurring between industries ⟨~ transactions⟩ ⟨~ commodity flow⟩ or throughout the parts of an industry ⟨~ wage structure⟩

**in·ter·influence** \"+\ *vt* [*inter-* + *influence*] : to influence reciprocally ⟨dialectic *interinfluencing* —Edward Sapir⟩

**in·ter·insular** \"+\ *adj* [*inter-* + *insular*] : existing or occurring between islands ⟨~ currents⟩

**in·ter·insurance** \"+\ *n* [*inter-* + *insurance*] : RECIPROCAL INSURANCE

**in·ter·insurer** \"+\ *n* [*inter-* + *insurer*] : an underwriter of reciprocal insurance

**in·ter·ionic** \"+\ *adj* [*inter-* + *ionic*] : situated or acting between ions ⟨~ distance⟩ ⟨~ force⟩

**¹in·te·ri·or** \(')in¦tirēə(r), ən·'t-, -tēr-\ *adj* [MF & L; MF, fr. L, compar. of (assumed) OL *interus* inward, on the inside; akin to L *inter* between, among — more at INTER-] **1** : being within the limiting surface or boundary ⟨~ communication⟩ : INSIDE, INNER — opposed to *exterior* **2** : remote from the surface, border, or shore : situated toward the center of a mass, area, or structure ⟨~ recesses of the castle⟩ : INLAND ⟨~ lake⟩ ⟨~ markets⟩ **3** : belonging to the inner constitution or operation of something or to its private or concealed nature ⟨~ meaning of a poem⟩ **4** : belonging to mental or spiritual life ⟨~ monologue⟩ : not bodily or worldly **syn** see INNER

**²interior** \"\ *n* -s **1** : something that is within : the internal or inner part of a thing : INSIDE ⟨~ of a house⟩ **2** : the inland part (as of a country, state, kingdom) ⟨deep into the ~ of Australia⟩ **3** : the inner or spiritual nature : inner character **4** : the internal affairs of a state or nation ⟨Department of the *Interior*⟩ **5** : a scene or view of the interior of a building ⟨learned to draw ~*s*⟩ **6** : an indoor setting or scene in a play or motion picture

**interior angle** *n* : an angle formed between two sides within any rectilinear figure (as a polygon) or between either of two parallel lines and the segment of an intersecting line that lies between them

interior angles: a g h, b g h, g h d, g h c

**interior ballistics** *n pl but usu sing in constr* : a branch of ballistics that deals with the combustion of powder in a gun, the pressure developed, and the motion of the projectile along the bore of the gun — compare EXTERIOR BALLISTICS

**interior basin** *n* : a depression from which no stream flows outward to the sea

**interior decorating** *n* : INTERIOR DESIGN

**interior decoration** *n* **1** : INTERIOR DESIGN **2** : the materials and furnishings of the interior of a building

**interior decorator** *n* **1** : INTERIOR DESIGNER **2 a** : one who supplies house furnishings **b** : one who paints or wallpapers building interiors : DECORATOR

**interior design** *n* : the art or practice of selecting and organizing the surface coverings, draperies, furniture, and furnishings of an architectural interior

**interior designer** *n* : one who specializes in interior design

**interior drainage** *n* : drainage toward the center of an interior basin rather than to the sea

**interior guard** *n* : a guard maintained within a military installation (as for keeping order, protecting property, guarding prisoners)

**in·te·ri·or·i·ty** \ən,tirē'ȯrəd·ē, -tēr-, -'är-, -ətē, -i\ *n* -ES [prob. fr. F or ML; F *intériorité,* fr. ML *interioritat-, interioritas,* fr. L *interior* + *-itat-, -itas* -ity] : the quality or state of being interior, internalized, or personal — contrasted with *exteriority*

**in·te·ri·or·iza·tion** \ən,tirēərə'zāshən, -tēr-, -rī'-\ *n* -s : the act or process of interiorizing ⟨~ of social values⟩ ⟨~ of the ideals of womanhood —Margaret Cormack⟩

**in·te·ri·or·ize** \=ˈ==rē,rīz\ *vt* -ED/-ING/-S *see -ize in Explan Notes* [¹*interior* + *-ize*] : to make interior; *esp* : to make a part of one's own inner being or mental structure ⟨explanation may lie in women's having *interiorized* cultural notions of feminine inferiority —Helen M. Hacker⟩

**interior lines** *n pl* : lines of operation of an armed force that is operating from a center against converging forces — compare EXTERIOR LINES

**interior live oak** *n* : an evergreen oak (*Quercus wizlizenii*) of western No. America much resembling the coast live oak but occurring chiefly in the foothills of mountain ranges somewhat removed from the coast and forming an important part of the chaparral

**interior lot** *n* : a lot bounded by a street on only one side — called also *inside lot*

**in·te·ri·or·ly** *adv* : on or toward the inside : INWARDLY ⟨laughing ~⟩ ⟨grooved ~⟩

**interior monologue** *n* : a usu. extended representation in monologue of a fictional character's sequence of thought and feeling ⟨constant shuttling between *interior monologue* and direct narrative —Dan Wickenden⟩

**in·te·ri·or·ness** *n* -ES : the quality or state of being interior

**interior plain** *n* : a plain remote from the borders of a continent — contrasted with *coastal plain*

**interior planet** *n* : INFERIOR PLANET

**interior slope** *n* : the slope connecting the interior crest with the banquette tread in a fortification

**interior spring** *n, Brit* : an innerspring mattress

**in·ter·island** \¦intə(r)+\ *adj* [*inter-* + *island* (n.)] : existing or operating between islands ⟨~ transport⟩

**interj** *abbr* interjection

**in·ter·ja·cen·cy** \¦intə(r)'jāsᵊnsē\ *n* -ES : the state of being interjacent : INTERVENTION

**in·ter·ja·cent** \¦=ˈjāsᵊnt\ *adj* [L *interjacent-, interjacens,* pres. part. of *interjacēre* to lie between, fr. *inter-* + *jacēre* to lie — more at GIST] : lying or being between or among others : INTERVENING, INTERPOLATED ⟨~ remarks⟩

**in·ter·jac·u·late** \,intə(r)'jakyə,lāt\ *vt* -ED/-ING/-S [*inter-* + *-jaculate* (as in *ejaculate*)] : to ejaculate parenthetically

**in·ter·jac·u·la·to·ry** \¦==¦jakyələ,tōrē, -tȯr-, -rē\ *adj* [*inter-* + *-jaculatory* (as in *ejaculatory*)] : thrown in : interspersed parenthetically ⟨~ comment⟩

**in·ter·ject** \,intə(r)'jekt\ *vb* -ED/-ING/-S [L *interjectus,* past part. of *interjacere, interjicere,* fr. *inter-* + *jacere* to throw — more at JET] *vt* : to throw in between or among other things : INTERPOSE, INTERPOLATE ⟨~ a statement⟩ ⟨~ a remark⟩ ~ *vi* **1** : to throw oneself between or among others : come between : INTERPOSE **2** *obs* **a** : to cross one another **b** : INTERVENE

**in·ter·jec·tion** \,==ˈjekshən\ *n* -s [ME *interieccioun,* fr. MF & L; MF *interjection,* fr. L *interjection-, interjectio,* fr. *interjectus* (past part.) + *-ion-, -io* -ion] **1** : the act of interjecting: as **a** : the act of uttering exclamations : EXCLAMATION, EJACULATION **b** : the act of putting in between : INTERPOSITION ⟨~ of new issues into a debate⟩ ⟨~ of a third party into a quarrel⟩ **2** : something that is interjected or that interrupts : an interposed remark or exclamation ⟨editorial ~*s*⟩ ⟨topical ~*s*⟩ **3 a** : an ejaculatory word (as *Heavens! Wonderful!*) or form of speech (as *Alas! eh? ha ha!*) usu. lacking grammatical connection **b** : a cry or inarticulate utterance (as *ouch! phooey! ugh!*) expressing an emotion

**in·ter·jec·tion·al** \¦==¦jekshənᵊl, -shnəl\ *adj* **1** : thrown in between other words : PARENTHETICAL ⟨~ remark⟩ **2** : relating to or of the nature of an interjection : consisting of natural and spontaneous exclamations : EJACULATORY ⟨~ grunts⟩ — **in·ter·jec·tion·al·ly** \-ᵊlē, -əlē, -i\ *adv*

**in·ter·jec·tion·al·ize** \,==ˈjekshənᵊl,īz, -shnə,līz\ *vt* -ED/-ING/-S : to make or turn into an interjection

**in·ter·jec·tion·ary** \¦==¦jekshə,nerē\ *adj* : INTERJECTORY, INTERJECTIONAL

**interjection point** *n* : EXCLAMATION POINT

**in·ter·jec·tor** \,==ˈjektə(r)\ *n* -s : one that interjects

**in·ter·jec·to·ri·ly** \¦==¦jektərəlē\ *adv* : in an interjectory manner

**in·ter·jec·to·ry** \¦==¦jekt(ə)rē, -ri\ *adj* [*interject* + *-ory*] : characterized by interjection : thrust in between

**in·ter·jec·tur·al** \¦==¦jekchərəl, -ksh(ə)rəl\ *adj* [L *interjectura* insertion (fr. *interjectus* — past part. — + *-ura* -ure) + E *-al*] : INTERJECTIONAL

**in·ter·join** \¦intə(r)¦join\ *vt* [*inter-* + *join*] : to join mutually : INTERCONNECT

**in·ter·junc·tion** \,intə(r)'jəŋkshən\ *n* [L *interjunctus* (past part. of *interjungere* to join together, fr. *inter-* + *jungere* to join, yoke) + E *-ion* — more at YOKE] : a joining of two or more things ⟨~ of roads⟩

**in·ter·ki·ne·sis** \,intə(r)kə'nēsəs, -,kī'-\ *n* [NL, fr. *inter-* + *-kinesis*] : the period between any two mitoses of a nucleus (as between the first and second meiotic divisions)

**in·ter·ki·net·ic** \¦==¦ned·ik\ *adj* [fr. NL *interkinesis,* after NL *kinesis:* E *kinetic*] : belonging or relating to interkinesis ⟨~ period⟩

**in·ter·knit** \¦intə(r)+\ *vb* [*inter-* + *knit*] : to knit together : INTERTWINE, INTERRELATE

**in·ter·knot** \"+\ *vt* [*inter-* + *knot*] : to knot together

**¹in·ter·lace** \¦intə(r)¦lās\ *vb* [alter. (influenced by L *inter-*) of ME *entrelacen,* fr. MF *entrelacer,* fr. OF *entrelacier,* fr. *entre* inter- + *lacier* to lace — more at LACE] *vt* **1** : to unite by or as if by lacing together : INTERWEAVE ⟨*interlaced* boughs⟩ ⟨*interlaced* fibers⟩ **2** : to vary or diversify by alternation, interpolation, or intermixture : ALTERNATE, INTERSPERSE, MIX ⟨narrative *interlaced* with anecdotes⟩ ~ *vi* : to cross one another as if woven together : INTERTWINE, INTERLOCK ⟨*interlacing* letters⟩ ⟨*interlacing* circles⟩

**²in·ter·lace** \"=,=\ *n* **a** : a form of surface decoration consisting of a number of straps or ribbons so interwoven as to produce a symmetrical design : INTERLACEMENT **b** : INTERLACED SCANNING

**interlaced** *adj* [fr. past part. of ¹*interlace*] : INTERLINKED, INTERWOVEN, INTERLOCKED

**interlaced scanning** *n* : television scanning in which each frame is scanned in two successive fields each consisting of all the odd or all the even horizontal lines

**in·ter·lace·ment** \,==ˈlāsmənt\ *n* -s [alter. (influenced by L *inter-*) of earlier *enterlacement,* fr. F *entrelacement,* fr. MF, fr. OF, fr. *entrelacier* (v.) + *-ment*] : the process or result of interlacing : a pattern of interlacing elements

**in·ter·lac·er** \¦==¦lāsə(r)\ *n* **1** : one that laces shoes during manufacture **2** : one who makes basketry designs in shoe uppers by cutting slits and weaving in leather strips

**in·ter·lac·ery** \-s(ə)rē\ *n* [¹*interlace* + *-ery*] : interlaced bands, lines, or fibers : INTERLACEMENT

**interlacing** *n* [fr. gerund of ¹*interlace*] : INTERLACED SCANNING

**interlacing arches** *n pl* [fr. pres. part. of ¹*interlace*] : usu. circular arches so constructed that their archivolts intersect and seem to be interlaced

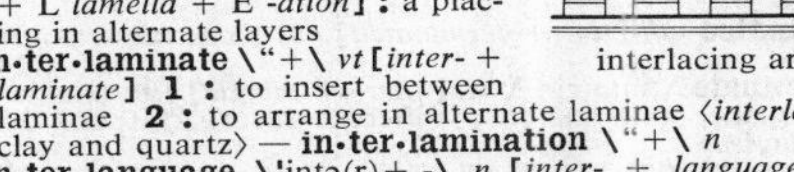

interlacing arches

**in·ter·lacustrine** \¦intə(r)+\ *adj* [*inter-* + *lacustrine*] : situated between lakes

**in·ter·lamellar** \"+\ *adj* [*inter-* + *lamellar*] : situated between lamellae

**in·ter·lamellation** \"+\ *n* [*inter-* + L *lamella* + E *-ation*] : a placing in alternate layers

**in·ter·laminate** \"+\ *vt* [*inter-* + *laminate*] **1** : to insert between laminae **2** : to arrange in alternate laminae ⟨*interlaminated* clay and quartz⟩ — **in·ter·lamination** \"+\ *n*

**in·ter·language** \'intə(r)+,-\ *n* [*inter-* + *language*] : language or a language for international communication

**in·ter·lap** \¦intə(r)+\ *vi* [*inter-* + *lap*] : to lap over one another : OVERLAP ⟨flew with our wings *interlapping* —*Newsweek*⟩

**in·ter·lard** \,intə(r)'lärd, -lȧd\ *vt* [alter. (influenced by L *inter-*) of earlier *enterlard,* fr. MF *enterlarder,* fr. OF, fr. *entre* inter- + *larder* to lard — more at LARD] **1** *obs* : to alternate with layers or strips of fat : insert lard or bacon in : LARD **2** : to insert between : MIX, MINGLE; *esp* : to introduce something that is foreign or irrelevant into ⟨~ a conversation with oaths⟩ ⟨~ a text with photographs⟩ ⟨English ~*ed* with Spanish terms⟩

**¹in·ter·lay** \'intə(r)+,-\ *vt* [*inter-* + *lay*] : to provide (as a mounted printing plate) with an interlay

**²interlay** \"\ *n* : something (as a sheet of tissue) placed between a printing plate and its base to make the plate or certain areas a suitable height for proper impression — compare OVERLAY, UNDERLAY

**¹in·ter·layer** \,intə(r)+\ *vt* [*inter-* + *layer* (n.)] : INTERSTRATIFY, INTERBED

**²in·ter·layer** \'==+,-\ *n* : a layer placed between other layers ⟨plastic ~ in safety glass⟩; *specif* : INTERBED

**¹in·ter·leaf** \,intə(r)+\ *vt* [*inter-* + *leaf* (n.)] : INTERLEAVE

**²in·ter·leaf** \'==+,-\ *n* **1** : a usu. blank leaf inserted or fastened between two leaves of a book (as for written notes or for protecting a color plate) **2** : SLIP SHEET

**in·ter·league** \¦intə(r)+\ *adj* [*inter-* + *league* (n.)] : existing or occurring between leagues ⟨~ trading of players⟩

**in·ter·leave** \,intə(r)'lēv\ *vt* -ED/-ING/-S [*inter-* + *-leave* (back-formation fr. *leaved,* taken as a past participle)] **1 a** : to equip (as a manifold business form) with an interleaf **b** : SLIP-SHEET **2** : INTERLAMINATE, INTERSTRATIFY

**in·ter·lending** \¦intə(r)+\ *adj, Brit* : of or relating to interlibrary loan

**in·ter·lens** \"+\ *adj* [*inter-* + *lens* (n.)] *of a photographic shutter* : situated between lens elements

**in·ter·library** \"+\ *adj* [*inter-* + *library* (n.)] : taking place between libraries ⟨~ loan⟩

**in·ter·light** \"+\ *vt* [*inter-* + *light*] : to light intermittently ⟨misery is *interlit* with flashes of pure joyousness —Edmond Taylor⟩

**¹in·ter·line** \"+\ *vb* [alter. (influenced by L *inter-*) of ME *enterlinen,* fr. ML *interlineare,* fr. L *inter-* + *linea* line — more at LINE] *vt* **1** : to write or insert between lines already written or printed ⟨*interlined* additions to a manuscript⟩ : write or print something between the lines of ⟨~ a page⟩ ⟨~ a book⟩ **2** : to add an interline to (ruled paper) ~ *vi* : to make insertions between written or printed lines

**²interline** \'intə(r),līn\ *n* : a light often broken line ruled between horizontal lines

**³in·ter·line** \¦==+\ *vt* [ME *interlinen,* fr. *inter-* + *linen* to line — more at LINE] : to provide (as a garment) with an interlining

**⁴in·ter·line** \"+\ *adj* [*inter-* + *line* (n.)] : relating to, involving, or carried by two or more transportation lines ⟨~ traffic⟩ ⟨~ freight⟩ ⟨~ haul⟩ ⟨~ costs⟩

**¹in·ter·lin·e·al** \"+¦linēəl\ *adj* [*interlinear* + *-al*] : INTERLINEAR — **in·ter·lin·e·al·ly** \-əlē\ *adv*

**¹in·ter·lin·e·ar** \"+\ *adj* [ME *interliniare,* fr. ML *interlinearis,* fr. L *inter-* + *linearis* linear — more at LINEAR] **1** : situated between lines **2** : inserted between lines already written or printed ⟨~ gloss⟩ ⟨~ corrections⟩ ⟨~ translation⟩ **3 a** : containing insertions between lines ⟨~ manuscript⟩ **b** : written or printed in different languages or texts in alternate lines ⟨~ bible⟩ — **in·ter·lin·e·ar·ly** *adv*

**²interlinear** \"\ *n* -s : a book having interlinear matter; *esp* : a school text of a work in a foreign language with interlinear translation

**¹in·ter·lin·e·ary** \"+¦linē,erē\ *adj* [prob. alter. (influenced by E *-ary*) of ML *interlinearis*] : INTERLINEAR

**²interlineary** \"\ *n* -ES : INTERLINEAR ⟨infinite helps of *interlinearies,* breviaries, synopses —John Milton⟩

**in·ter·lin·e·ate** \,intə(r)'linē,āt\ *vb* -ED/-ING/-S [ML *interlineatus,* past part. of *interlineare* to interline — more at INTERLINE] : INTERLINE

**in·ter·lin·e·a·tion** \,==,==ˈāshən\ *n* [ML *interlineatus* (past part.) + E *-ion*] **1** : the act of interlining **2** : something interlined ⟨~*s* in a later hand⟩ ⟨editorial ~*s*⟩ ⟨a printed form with typewritten ~*s* —*N.Y.Times*⟩

**in·ter·lin·er** \¦==¦līnə(r)\ *n* **1** : one that interlines **2** : INTERLINING ⟨~*s* for arctic and military clothing⟩

**in·ter·lin·gua** \,intə(r)'liŋgwə\ *n* -s [It, fr. *inter-* + *lingua* language, tongue, fr. L — more at TONGUE] **1** : INTERLANGUAGE **2** *usu cap* : an artificial interlanguage that is based on the linguistic elements common to English and the chief Romance languages and is promoted by the International Auxiliary Language Association

**in·ter·lingual** \¦intə(r)+\ *adj* [*inter-* + *lingual*] : of, relating to, or existing between two or more languages ⟨~ alphabet⟩ ⟨~ dictionary⟩ ⟨~ idiom⟩

**in·ter·linguistic** \"+\ *adj* [*inter-* + *linguistic*] **1** : INTERLINGUAL ⟨~ influences⟩ **2** : of or relating to an interlanguage

**in·ter·linguistics** \"+\ *n pl but sing in constr* [ISV *inter-* + *linguistics*] : the study of interlingual similarities and relationships esp. for the purpose of devising an interlanguage

**¹in·ter·lin·ing** \"+¦līniŋ\ *n* [ME, fr. gerund of *interlinen, enterlinen* to interline — more at INTERLINE] : INTERLINEATION

**²in·ter·lining** \"+\ *n* [*inter-* + *lining*] **1** : an inner lining (as of a coat or jacket) consisting of a warm or firm fabric shaped and sewn between the ordinary lining and the outside fabric **2** : any fabric used for making interlinings

**¹in·ter·link** \"+\ *vt* [*inter-* + *link*] : to link together

**²interlink** \"\ *n* : an intermediate or connecting link

**in·ter·linkage** \"+\ *n* **1** : the act of interlinking or state of being interlinked **2** : a system of links ⟨molecular ~⟩

**in·ter·lobate** \"+\ *adj* [*inter-* + *lobate*] : lying between lobes ⟨~ moraines of a retreating glacier⟩

**in·ter·lobular** \"+\ *adj* [*inter-* + *lobular*] : lying between or connecting lobules ⟨~ connective tissue⟩

**in·ter·local** \"+\ *or* **in·ter·locality** \"+\ *adj* [*inter-* + *local* (adj.) or *locality* (n.)] : existing between localities ⟨~ tax differences⟩ — **in·ter·locally** \"+\ *adv*

**in·ter·located** \"+\ *adj* [*inter-* + *located,* past part. of *locate*] : placed between others : INTERPOSED

**¹in·ter·lock** \"+\ *vb* [*inter-* + *lock*] *vi* : to engage or interrelate with one another : lock into one another : interlace firmly ⟨~*ing* fingers⟩ ⟨bolt ~*s* with its striker⟩ ⟨~*ing* stitches⟩ ~ *vt* **1** : to lock together : unite closely ⟨walls . . . contrived to ~ stone with stone without using an ounce of mortar —John McNulty⟩ **2** : to connect in such a way that the motion of any part is constrained by another part; *esp* : to arrange the connections of (as railroad switches or signals) to ensure successive movement in proper sequence

**²in·ter·lock** \'intə(r)+,-\ *n* **1** : the fact or state of being interlocked ⟨~ of corporate directorates⟩ **2** : an arrangement whereby the operation of one part or mechanism automatically brings about or prevents the operation of another ⟨~ on an elevator door⟩ **3** : a mechanism for or the act of synchronizing a motion-picture camera and sound-recording devices

**³in·ter·lock** \¦==+\ *adj* : knitted with interlocking stitches by the use of two alternating sets of needles ⟨~ hosiery⟩

**interlocked grain** *also* **interlocking grain** *n* : a wood grain in which the fibers incline in one direction in a number of annual rings and in a reverse direction in succeeding rings

**in·ter·lock·er** \"+¦läkə(r)\ *n* : one that interlocks

**interlocking director** *n* [fr. pres. part. of ¹*interlock*] : one who serves as a director of two or more corporations at one time

**interlocking directorate** *n* : a directorate linked with that of another corporation by interlocking directors so that the businesses managed by them are to some degree under one control

**in·ter·loculus** \,intə(r)+\ *n* [NL, fr. *inter-* + *loculus*] : a space or part between two loculi

**in·ter·lo·cu·tion** \,intə(r)lō'kyüshən, -lə'-\ *n* [L *interlocution-, interlocutio,* fr. *interlocutus* (past part. of *interloqui* to speak between, fr. *inter-* + *loqui* to speak) + *-ion-, -io* -ion] **1** : interchange of speech : CONVERSATION **2** : an interruptive utterance : INTERRUPTION, INTERPOLATION, PARENTHESIS **3 a** *obs* : responsive reading or recital **b** *obs* : a speech in reply : RESPONSE **c** : mode of intercommunication **4 a** [LL *interlocution-, interlocutio,* fr. L] : the making of an interlocutory legal order or decree; *also* : the order or decree **b** *Roman law* : a constitution of the emperor in the form of an informal expression of the imperial wish

**in·ter·loc·u·tor** \,intə(r)'läkyəd·ə(r), |tə(r)\ *n* -s [L *interlocutus* (past part.) + E *-or*] **1** : one who takes part in dialogue or conversation **2** : a man in the middle of the line in a minstrel show who questions the end men and acts as leader **3** [ML *interlocutorium,* fr. neut. of *interlocutorius,* adj.] *Scots law* : a judgment or order of a court whether interlocutory or finally determining the issues

**¹in·ter·loc·u·to·ry** \¦==¦läkyə,tōrē, -tȯr-, -rē\ *adj* [*interlocution* + *-ory*] **1** : consisting of or having the nature of dialogue : CONVERSATIONAL ⟨~ observations⟩ **2** : of or belonging to an interruptive speech or question : spoken as an interlocution **3** [ME (Scot. dial.), fr. ML *interlocutorius,* fr. LL *interlocutus* (past part. of *interloqui* to pronounce an interlocutory sentence, fr. L, to speak between) + L *-orius* -ory] *law* : not final or definitive : made or done during the progress of an action : INTERMEDIATE, PROVISIONAL ⟨~ decree in a divorce suit⟩ ⟨~ motion⟩

**²in·ter·loc·u·to·ry** *n* -ES *obs* : an interlocutory decree

**in·ter·loc·u·tress** *or* **in·ter·loc·u·trice** \,==ˈläkyə·trəs\ *or* **in·ter·loc·u·trix** \-,triks\ *n, pl* **interlocutresses** \-rəsəz\ *or* **interlocutrices** \,==,==ˈtrī(,)sēz\ [*interlocutress* fr. *interlocutor* + *-ess; interlocutrice* fr. F, fem. of *interlocuteur* interlocutor; *interlocutrix* fr. *interlocutor* + *-trix*] : a female interlocutor

**in·ter·lope** \¦intə(r)¦lōp\ *vb* -ED/-ING/-S [prob. back-formation fr. *interloper*] *vi* **1** : to encroach on the rights (as in trade) of others : trade without a proper license **2** : INTRUDE, INTERMEDDLE, INTERFERE ~ *vt, obs* : INTERPOLATE

**in·ter·lop·er** \'==,lōpə(r), ,==ˈ==\ *n* -s [alter. (influenced by L *inter-*) of earlier *enterloper,* prob. fr. *enter* inter- + *-loper* (as in *landloper*)] **1** : one that interlopes : an unlawful intruder on a property or sphere of action **2** : one that interferes or thrusts himself in wrongfully or officiously

**in·ter·lot** \,intə(r)+\ *vt* [*inter-* + *lot*] : to pool (as star lots of wool) into large lots for auction

**in·ter·lu·ca·tion** \,intə(r)lü'kāshən *also* -)lyü'-\ *n* -s [L *interlucation-, interlucatio* act of pruning, act of thinning, fr. *interlucatus* (past part. of *interlucare* to thin, top, fr. *inter-* + *-lucare* — fr. *luc-, lux* light) + *-ion-, -io* -ion — more at LIGHT] : the cutting of trees from a stand so that the remaining trees will grow rapidly

**in·ter·lu·cent** \¦intə(r)¦lüsənt *also* -)l¦yü-\ *adj* [L *interlucent-, interlucens,* pres. part. of *interlucēre* to shine, fr. *inter-* + *lucēre* to shine — more at LIGHT] **:** shining or glowing between or in the midst of other things

[1]**in·ter·lude** \ˈintə(r),lüd *also* -)l,yüd\ *n* -s [alter. (influenced by L *inter-*) of ME *enterlude,* fr. ML *interludium,* fr. L *inter-* + *ludus* play — more at LUDICROUS] **1 a :** an entertainment of a light or farcical character introduced between the acts of an old mystery or morality play or forming a feature of a festival or fete **b :** one of the farces or comedies derived from these entertainments **2 :** a performance or entertainment between the acts of a play **3 a :** an irrelevant change or happening in a course of events **:** EPISODE ⟨romantic ~⟩ **b :** an intervening or interruptive space of time or such a feature or event **:** INTERVAL ⟨forests with ~s of open meadow⟩ ⟨brief ~ of sanity⟩ ⟨~s of wit and humor in a tragic story⟩ **4 :** a musical composition inserted between the parts of a musical or dramatic entertainment or religious service; *specif* **:** a short organ piece played between verses of a hymn or psalm

[2]**interlude** \"\ *vi* -ED/-ING/-S **1 :** to perform an interlude **2 :** to occur as an interlude

**in·ter·lu·di·al** \¦==¦lüdēəl *also* -)l,yü-\ *adj* **:** of, relating to, or resembling an interlude ⟨~ passage between fugues⟩

**in·ter·lu·nar** \¦intə(r)¦lünə(r) *also* -)l¦yü-\ *also* **in·ter·lu·na·ry** \-nərē\ *adj* [*interlunar* prob. fr. MF *interlunaire,* fr. L *interlunium* interlunation (fr. *inter-* + *luna* moon) + MF *-aire* (fr. L *-aris* -ar); *interlunary* prob. modif. (influenced by E *lunary*) of MF *interlunaire* — more at LUNAR] **:** relating to the interval between old and new moon when the moon is invisible ⟨silent as the moon . . . hid in her vacant ~ cave —John Milton⟩

**in·ter·lunation** \,intə(r)+\ *n* [prob. fr. *inter-* + *lunation*] **1 :** the interlunar period **2 :** a period of darkness or blankness

**in·ter·lying** \¦intə(r)+\ *adj* [*inter-* + *lying,* pres. part. of *lie*] **:** lying in between ⟨~ beds of gravel⟩

**in·ter·mandibular** \¦intə(r)+\ *adj* [*inter-* + *mandibular*] **1 :** situated between the mandibles **2 :** INTERRAMAL

**in·ter·marine** \"+\ *adj* [*inter-* + *marine*] **:** carried on between seas or ships on the sea ⟨~ communication⟩

**in·ter·marriage** \"+\ *n* [*inter-* + *marriage*] **1 :** marriage between members of different racial, social, or religious groups ⟨~ between Negroes and whites⟩ ⟨~ of invaders and the conquered⟩ ⟨Protestant-Catholic ~⟩ **2 a :** INMARRIAGE, ENDOGAMY **b :** INBREEDING

**in·ter·marry** \"+\ *vi* [*inter-* + *marry*] **1 a :** to marry each other — used of a couple or of one of the contracting parties ⟨statute legitimatizing children whose parents *intermarried* after their birth —Morris Ploscowe⟩ **b :** to marry within a group ⟨the deaf are likely to ~ —H.J.Baker⟩ **2 :** to become connected by marriage between their members **:** give and take mutually in marriage — used of families, castes, social or religious or ethnic groups or of their members ⟨if a peeress by marriage should afterwards ~ with a commoner —T.E.May⟩

**in·ter·maxilla** \"+\ *n* [NL, fr. *inter-* + *maxilla*] **:** PREMAXILLA

**in·ter·maxillar** \"+\ *adj* [*inter-* + *maxillar*] **:** INTERMAXILLARY

[1]**in·ter·maxillary** \"+\ *adj* [*inter-* + *maxillary*] **1 :** lying between maxillae; *esp* **:** joining the two maxillary bones ⟨~ suture⟩ **2 :** of or relating to the premaxillae

[2]**intermaxillary** \"\ *n* **:** PREMAXILLA

**intermean** *n* [*inter-* + *mean*] *obs* **:** something intermediate **:** INTERLUDE

**in·ter·meddle** \¦intə(r)+\ *vb* [ME *entermedlen,* fr. MF *entremedler, entremeller, entremesler,* fr. OF, fr. *entre-* inter- + *medler, meller, mesler* to mix — more at MEDDLE] *vt* **1** *obs* **:** INTERMINGLE **2** *obs* **:** INTERPOSE ~ *vi* **:** to meddle with the affairs of others **:** meddle officiously **:** INTERFERE ⟨must know and ~ with mysteries —Mary Webb⟩ ⟨any *intermeddling* with slavery in the federal district —S.E.Morison & H.S.Commager⟩ **syn** see MEDDLE

**in·ter·meddler** \"+\ *n* **1 :** one who intermeddles ⟨out-of-state ~s⟩ **2 a** *obs* **:** INTERMEDIARY **b** *obs* **:** INTERLOPER

**in·ter·mede** \ˈintə(r),mēd\ *n* -s [F *intermède,* fr. It *intermedio,* fr. LL *intermedium* — more at INTERMEDIUM] **1** *archaic* **:** INTERMEDIUM **2** *or* **in·ter·mède** \aⁿtermed\ **:** INTERMEZZO 1

[1]**intermedia** *pl of* INTERMEDIUM

[2]**in·ter·me·dia** \,intə(r)ˈmēdēə\ *n, pl* **intermedi·ae** \-dē,ē\ [NL, fr. L, fem. of *intermedius* intermediate — more at INTERMEDIATE] **:** either member of the middle pair of tail feathers of a bird

**in·ter·me·di·a·cy** \,intə(r)ˈmēdēəsē, -si, *chiefly Brit* -mējəs- *or* -mēdyəs-\ *n* [fr. [2]*intermediate,* after E *immediate: immediacy*] **:** INTERMEDIATENESS

**in·ter·me·di·al** \¦intə(r)¦mēdēəl\ *n* [L *intermedius* + E *-al*] **:** INTERMEDIATE

[1]**in·ter·me·di·ary** \¦intə(r)¦mēdē,erē, -ri, *chiefly Brit* -mējər- *or* -mēdyər-\ *adj* [prob. fr. F *intermédiaire,* fr. L *intermedius* + F *-aire* -ary] **1 :** lying, coming, or done between **:** INTERMEDIATE ⟨~ distribution of perishable products⟩ ⟨importing and other ~ trades⟩ **2 :** acting or capable of acting between others as a mediator ⟨~ agent⟩

[2]**intermediary** \"\ *n* -ES [prob. fr. F *intermédiaire,* fr. *intermédiaire,* adj.] **1 :** one that is intermediate: **a :** MEDIATOR, INTERAGENT, GO-BETWEEN ⟨~ between the people and God⟩ **b :** something that serves as a medium or means **:** mediating agency **2 :** an intermediate form, stage, or product

**intermediary host** *n* **:** INTERMEDIATE HOST

[1]**in·ter·me·di·ate** \,intə(r)ˈmēdē,āt, *usu* -ād.+V\ *vi* [ML *intermediatus,* past part. of *intermediare,* fr. L *inter-* + LL *mediare* to mediate — more at MEDIATE] **1 :** to come between **:** INTERVENE, INTERPOSE **2 :** to act as intermediate agent **:** MEDIATE

[2]**in·ter·me·di·ate** \¦intə(r)¦mēdēət, *chiefly Brit* -mējə- *or* -mēdyə-; *usu* -əd.+V\ *adj* [ML *intermediatus,* fr. L *intermedius* intermediate (fr. *inter-* + *medius* mid, middle) + *-atus* -ate — more at MID] **1 :** lying or being in the middle place or degree **:** between extremes or limits **:** coming or done in between **:** INTERVENING ⟨~ hue⟩ ⟨~ credit⟩ ⟨~ stage of growth⟩ ⟨~ stops on a journey⟩ ⟨~ sizes⟩ **2 a :** of or relating to the period between primary and secondary education usu. comprising the fourth, fifth, and sixth grades **b :** of or relating to the stage between the introductory and advanced stages of a course of study or training ⟨~ French⟩ ⟨~ piano pupil⟩ **c :** taken during the first year after matriculation at a British university other than Oxford or Cambridge ⟨~ examination⟩ ⟨an ~ course⟩ — compare PREVIOUS EXAMINATION, RESPONSION 2b

[3]**intermediate** \"\ *n* -s **1 :** something intermediate **:** a term, member, class, or quality between others of a series **2 :** one that acts between others **:** MEDIATOR, INTERMEDIARY **3 :** an intermediate biological type or form **4 :** a chemical compound formed as an intermediate step between the starting material and the final product (as a dye intermediate) **5 a :** a wool-carding machine that comes between the breaker and the finisher **b :** a machine in cotton manufacture placed between the slubbing billy and the roving frame **6 a :** IDLER WHEEL **b :** the second speed in a vehicle having three forward speeds

[4]**intermediate** \"\ *prep* **:** in the time intervening between — used in law ⟨waste committed ~ the sale and the period when the right to redeem expired —T.M.Cooley⟩

**intermediate carrier** *n* **:** a transportation line participating in a through movement which neither originates nor terminates the passengers or freight

**intermediate disk** *n* **:** KRAUSE'S MEMBRANE

**intermediate frequency** *n* **:** a relatively low frequency to which a signal is converted before demodulation in heterodyne reception — abbr. *i.f.*

**intermediate girl scout** *n* **:** a member of the Girl Scouts in the age group ranging approximately from 10 through 13 years old

**intermediate goods** *n pl* **:** PRODUCER GOODS

**intermediate host** *n* **1 :** a host which is normally used by a parasite in the course of its life cycle and in which it may multiply asexually but not sexually — compare DEFINITIVE HOST **2 :** RESERVOIR 6a; *sometimes* **:** VECTOR 2

**in·ter·me·di·ate·ly** *adv* **1 :** in an intermediate position **:** between things or times **2 :** to an intermediate degree ⟨~ hot⟩ **3 :** not immediately **:** INDIRECTLY

**in·ter·me·di·ate·ness** *n* -ES **:** the quality or state of being intermediate

**intermediate school** *n* **1 :** JUNIOR HIGH SCHOOL **2 :** a school comprising the fourth, fifth, and sixth grades **3 :** a part of the British school system serving children from 12 to 14 years of age — compare JUNIOR SCHOOL, SENIOR SCHOOL

**intermediate stock** *n* **:** a stock grafted between the basal stock and the scion (as in a double-worked apple tree)

**intermediate tissue** *n* **:** CONJUNCTIVE TISSUE

**intermediate wheatgrass** *n* **:** an Asiatic grass (*Agropyron intermedium*) introduced into the rangelands of western U.S. for pasture and fodder use

**intermediate wheel** *n* **:** an idler wheel in the driving train or the dial train of a timepiece

**in·ter·me·di·a·tion** \,intə(r),mēdēˈāshən\ *n* [ML *intermediatus* (past part.) + E *-ion*] **:** the act of coming between **:** INTERVENTION, MEDIATION

**in·ter·me·di·a·tor** \-ˈmēdē,ād.ə(r), -ātə-\ *n* [ML *intermediatus* (past part.) + E *-or*] **:** MEDIATOR

**in·ter·mediatory** \,intə(r)+\ *adj* **:** MEDIATORY

**in·ter·me·din** \,intə(r)ˈmēdᵊn\ *n* -s [ISV *intermed-* (fr. NL *pars intermedia*) + *-in*] **:** a hormone secreted by the pars intermedia or the anterior lobe of the pituitary body that induces expansion of chromatophores in various vertebrates

**intermedio-** *comb form* [L *intermedius*] **:** intermediate and ⟨*intermedio*lateral⟩

**in·ter·me·di·um** \,intə(r)ˈmēdēəm\ *n, pl* **interme·dia** \-dēə\ *or* **intermediums** [LL, fr. L, neut. of *intermedius* intermediate — more at INTERMEDIATE] **1** *obs* **:** an intermediate space or time **:** INTERVAL **2 :** a musical or dance interlude **3 :** an intervening agent **:** INTERMEDIARY, MEDIUM **4 :** a bone or cartilage situated between the radiale and ulnare in the carpus and between the tibiale and fibulare in the tarsus in many vertebrates

**in·ter·me·di·us** \¦==¦mēdēəs\ *adj* [NL, fr. L, intermediate] **:** tending to be moderately virulent — used esp. of strains of diphtheria bacilli — compare GRAVIS, MITIS

**in·ter·mell** \¦==¦mel\ *vb* [ME *entremellen, entermellen,* fr. MF *entremeller* — more at INTERMEDDLE] *archaic* **:** INTERMEDDLE, INTERMINGLE

**in·ter·member** \,intə(r)+\ *vb* -ED/-ING/-S [*inter-* + *member* (n.)] **:** to fit into a uniform or harmonious group ⟨storage cupboard which ~s with the vertical cabinets —Estelle B. Hunter⟩ ⟨filing sections ~*ed* in a stack⟩

**in·ter·membral** \"+\ *adj* [*inter-* + *membral*] **:** existing between members — **in·ter·membrally** \"+\ *adv*

**intermembral index** *n, anthrop* **:** the ratio of the length of the whole arm to the length of the whole leg multiplied by 100

**in·ter·membranous** \"+\ *adj* [*inter-* + *membranous*] **:** situated or occurring between membranes

**intermembranous ossification** *n* **:** ossification that takes place in connective tissue without prior development of cartilage — compare ENDOCHONDRAL OSSIFICATION

**in·ter·meningeal** \"+\ *adj* [*inter-* + *meningeal*] **:** situated or occurring between the meninges ⟨~ hemorrhage⟩

**in·ter·menstrual** \"+\ *adj* [*inter-* + *menstrual*] **:** occurring between the menses ⟨~ pain⟩

**in·ter·ment** \ənˈtərmənt, -tə̄m-\ *n* -s [ME *enterment,* fr. MF *enterrement,* fr. OF, fr. *enterrer* to inter + *-ment* — more at INTER] **1 :** the act or ceremony of depositing a dead body in a grave or tomb **:** BURIAL, SEPULTURE, INHUMATION ⟨change from ~ to cremation⟩ **2 :** the act of removing from sight or consideration ⟨decision . . . will result in the ~ of the women's program —Helen Fuller⟩

**in·ter·mesenteric** \¦intə(r)+\ *adj* [*inter-* + *mesenteric*] **:** situated between mesenteries

**in·ter·mesh** \"+\ *vi* [*inter-* + *mesh*] **:** to mesh with one another ⟨~*ing* twin rotors⟩

**in·ter·metallic** \"+\ *adj* [*inter-* + *metallic*] **:** composed of two or more metals or of a metal and a nonmetal in an alloy

**intermetallic compound** *n* **:** an alloy having a characteristic crystal structure and usu. a definite composition not necessarily conforming with the normal rules of valence — often distinguished from *solid solution*

**in·ter·mewed** \"+\ *adj* [*inter-* + *mewed,* past part. of *mew* (to molt); prob. trans. of MF *entremué*] *of a hawk* **:** having molted once in confinement

**in·ter·mez·zo** \,intə(r)ˈmet(,)sō *sometimes* -ed(,)zō\ *n, pl* **intermez·zi** \-sē, -zē\ *or* **intermezzos** [It, fr. LL *intermedium* — more at INTERMEDIUM] **1 :** a short light sometimes burlesque musical or dramatic piece presented between the acts of serious drama or opera **2 a :** a humorous musical play in the 16th and 17th centuries the acts of which alternated with those of the principal work **b :** a movement coming between the major sections of a symphony or other extended work **c :** a short independent instrumental composition **3 :** DIVERSION, EPISODE, AFFAIR, INTERLUDE ⟨pretty lady who created a domestic ~ —*Newsweek*⟩

**in·ter·micellar** \¦intə(r)+\ *adj* [*inter-* + *micellar*] **:** situated between micelles ⟨~ cavities⟩

**in·ter·migration** \"+\ *n* [*inter-* + *migration*] **:** mutual migration **:** migration in both directions ⟨~ of fauna of neighboring continents⟩

**in·ter·mi·na·bil·i·ty** \ən,tərmənəˈbiləd.ē\ *n* -ES **:** ENDLESSNESS

**in·ter·mi·na·ble** \ənˈtərmənəbəl, -tə̄m-, -təim- *also* -mn-\ *adj* [ME, fr. LL *interminabilis,* fr. L *in-* [1]in- + *terminare* to terminate + *-abilis* -able — more at TERMINATE] **:** having no termination **:** wearisomely protracted **:** BOUNDLESS, ENDLESS ⟨~ sermons⟩ ⟨~ debates⟩ ⟨~ forest⟩ — **in·ter·mi·na·ble·ness** *n* -ES — **in·ter·mi·na·bly** \-blē, -li\ *adv*

**in·ter·mi·nate** \-mə,nāt, -nət\ *adj* [L *interminatus,* fr. *in-* [1]in- + *terminatus,* past part. of *terminare*] *archaic* **:** having no end or limit

**interminated** *adj* [[1]*in-* + *terminated*] *obs* **:** LIMITLESS, BOUNDLESS

**in·ter·mingle** \¦intə(r)+\ *vb* [*inter-* + *mingle*] **:** to mingle or mix together ⟨*intermingling* different races⟩ ⟨fat and lean *intermingled*⟩

**in·ter·ministerial** \"+\ *adj* [*inter-* + *ministerial*] **:** existing between ministries ⟨~ commission⟩

**in·ter·mis·sion** \,intə(r)ˈmishən\ *n* -s [L *intermission-, intermissio,* fr. *intermissus* (past part. of *intermittere* to cease, intermit) + *-ion-, -io* -ion] **1 :** the act of intermitting or state of being intermitted **:** INTERRUPTION, BREAK ⟨~ between acts of a play⟩ **2 :** cessation for a time **:** an intervening period of time **:** INTERVAL ⟨work without ~⟩ **3 :** the space of time between two paroxysms of a disease — distinguished from *remission*

**in·ter·mis·sive** \¦==¦misiv\ *adj* [L *intermissus* + E *-ive*] **:** INTERMITTENT

**in·ter·mit** \,intə(r)ˈmit, *usu* -id.+V\ *vb* **intermitted; intermitted; intermitting; intermits** [L *intermittere,* fr. *inter-* + *mittere* to send — more at SMITE] *vt* **1 :** to cause to cease for a time or at intervals **:** DISCONTINUE, INTERRUPT, SUSPEND ⟨pray to the gods to ~ the plague —Shak.⟩ ⟨never *intermitted* the custom of dressing for dinner⟩ **2 :** to cause (as a spark) to come and go at intervals ~ *vi* **:** to cease at intervals **:** to be intermittent ⟨a fever that *intermitted* with great regularity⟩ **syn** see DEFER

**in·ter·mit·tence** \,==ˈmitᵊn(t)s\ *n* -s **1 :** the quality or state of being intermittent **:** periodic cessation or interruption **:** INTERMITTENCY ⟨~ of the pulse⟩ **2 :** periodic recurrence **:** FITFULNESS ⟨violent ~s of physical passion —Aldous Huxley⟩

**in·ter·mit·ten·cy** \-sē, -si\ *n* -ES **:** intermittent character or condition **:** INTERMITTENCE ⟨~ of employment and uncertainty of wages⟩

**intermittency effect** *n* **:** the photographic effect in which intermittent exposures fail to give the same density as a continuous exposure of the same total energy

**in·ter·mit·tent** \¦==¦mitᵊnt\ *adj* [L *intermittent-, intermittens,* pres. part. of *intermittere* to intermit — more at INTERMIT] **:** coming and going at intervals **:** not continuous **:** ALTERNATING, RECURRENT, PERIODIC ⟨~ fever⟩ ⟨~ rain⟩ ⟨~ publication⟩ ⟨~ stream⟩ ⟨~ spark⟩ — **in·ter·mit·tent·ly** *adv*

**intermittent claudication** *n* **:** cramping pain and weakness in the legs esp. the calves on walking that disappears after rest and is usu. associated with inadequate blood supply to the muscles (as in thromboangiitis obliterans, vascular spasm, or arteriosclerosis)

**intermittent current** *n* **:** an electric current that flows and ceases to flow at regular or irregular intervals but is not reversed

**intermittent light** *n* **:** a signal or beacon light having equal periods of shining and eclipse — compare FLASHLIGHT, OCCULTING LIGHT

**intermittent movement** *n* **:** the motion produced by a mechanical device that advances a motion-picture film one or more frames at a time with stationary intervening periods; *also* **:** any such mechanical device

**intermittent pulse** *n* **:** a pulse that occas. skips a cardiac beat

**intermittent sterilization** *n* **:** sterilization by heating to boiling several times at intervals of about 24 hours in order that any resistant spores may germinate and be destroyed

**in·ter·mit·ter** *or* **in·ter·mit·tor** \,intə(r)ˈmid.ə(r)\ *n* -s **:** one that intermits; *esp* **:** a device for producing intermittent movement

**in·ter·mix** \¦intə(r)+\ *vb* [back-formation fr. earlier *intermixt* intermingled, fr. L *intermixtus,* past part. of *intermiscēre* to intermix, fr. *inter-* + *miscēre* to mix — more at MIX] **:** to mix together **:** INTERMINGLE ⟨coal seams ~*ed* with iron ore⟩

**in·ter·mixable** \"+\ *adj* **:** capable of being mixed or blended together ⟨~ paint colors⟩

**in·ter·mixedly** \"+\ *adv* **:** in a mixed manner

**in·ter·mixture** \"+\ *n* [L *intermixtus* + E *-ure* (as in *mixture*)] **1 a :** the act of mixing together or the state of being mixed together **b :** a mass formed by mixture **:** a mass of ingredients mixed ⟨~ of letters and figures in a cryptogram⟩ **2 :** an additional ingredient **:** ADMIXTURE **3 :** MISCEGENATION

**in·ter·modulation** \"+\ *n* [ISV *inter-* + *modulation*] **:** the production in an electrical device of currents having frequencies equal to the sums and differences of frequencies supplied to the device or of their harmonics; *also* **:** distortion (as of amplified sound) caused by intermodulation

**in·ter·molecular** \"+\ *adj* [*inter-* + *molecular*] **:** existing or acting between molecules ⟨~ forces⟩ ⟨~ condensation⟩ — **in·ter·mo·lec·u·lar·ly** *adv*

**in·ter·mon·tane** \¦intə(r)¦män,tān\ *or* **in·ter·mont** \-¦mänt\ *adj* [*intermontane* fr. *inter-* + L *montanus* of a mountain; *intermont* fr. *inter-* + L *mont-, mons* mountain — more at MOUNTAIN] **:** situated between mountains ⟨~ basin⟩

**in·ter·morainic** \¦intə(r)+\ *adj* [*inter-* + *morainic*] **:** situated between moraines ⟨~ depression⟩

**in·ter·mountain** \"+\ *adj* [*inter-* + *mountain*] **:** INTERMONTANE

**in·ter·mundane** \"+\ *adj* [*inter-* + *mundane*] **:** existing between worlds ⟨~ space⟩

**in·ter·mun·di·al** \"+¦məndēəl\ *or* **in·ter·mun·di·an** \-ēən\ *adj* [L *intermundia* + E *-al* or *-an*] **:** INTERMUNDANE

**in·ter·mun·di·um** \,==ˈməndēəm\ *n, pl* **intermun·dia** \-ēə\ [NL, back-formation fr. L *intermundia,* pl., spaces between worlds, fr. *inter-* + *-mundia* (fr. *mundus* world) — more at MUNDANE] **:** space between worlds

**in·ter·mural** \¦intə(r)+\ *adj* [L *intermuralis,* fr. *inter-* + *muralis* of a wall — more at MURAL] **:** lying between walls — **in·ter·murally** \"+\ *adv*

**in·ter·muscular** \"+\ *adj* [*inter-* + *muscular*] **:** lying between and separating muscles ⟨~ fat⟩

**in·ter·mutual** \"+\ *adj* [*inter-* + *mutual*] **:** MUTUAL — **in·ter·mutually** *adv* \"+\

[1]**in·tern** *or* **in·terne** \(ˈ)in¦tərn, ənˈt-, -tə̄n,-təin\ *adj* [MF *interne,* fr. L *internus* — more at INTERNAL] *archaic* **:** INTERNAL

[2]**intern** \"\ *vt* -ED/-ING/-S [F *interner,* fr. *interne,* adj.] **1 a :** to confine within prescribed limits esp. during a war ⟨the plane was landed safely and the crew was ~*ed* —T.W.Lawson⟩ **b :** to impound esp. during a war ⟨duty of a neutral to ~ belligerent ships and planes⟩ **2 :** to confine to or as if to a hospital ⟨meddling fools who propose to ~ the dear lady —Norman Douglas⟩

[3]**in·tern** \ˈin,t-\ *n* -s **:** a person interned **:** INTERNEE

[4]**intern** \"\ *or* **interne** \"\ *n* -s *often attrib* [F *interne,* fr. *interne,* adj.] **1 a :** an advanced student or recent graduate in a professional field (as teaching) who is getting practical experience under the supervision of an experienced worker **b :** one who after completion of an undergraduate medical curriculum serves in residence at a hospital — compare INTERNIST, RESIDENT **2 :** one trained in a profession allied to medicine (as nursing or dentistry) who undergoes a period of practical clinical experience prior to practicing his profession

[5]**intern** \"\ *vi* -ED/-ING/-S **:** to act as an intern

[1]**in·ter·nal** \(ˈ)in¦tərnᵊl, ənˈt-, -tə̄n-, -təin-\ *adj* [L *internus* internal (fr. *inter* between) + E *-al* — more at INTER-] **1 a :** existing or situated within the limits or surface of something **:** INWARD, INTERIOR ⟨~ structure⟩ ⟨~ parts of the body⟩ ⟨~ regions of the earth⟩ ⟨~ mechanism of a toy⟩ ⟨~ funds of a business⟩ — opposed to *external* **b :** situated near the inside of the body ⟨~ layer of abdominal muscle⟩ **:** situated on the side toward the median plane of the body ⟨the ~ surface of the lung⟩ **2 :** capable of being applied through the stomach by being swallowed ⟨~ remedy⟩ ⟨~ stimulant⟩ **3 :** relating to the inner being or consciousness **:** belonging to or existing within the mind **:** SUBJECTIVE ⟨~ monologue⟩ **:** PRIVATE ⟨~ opinion⟩ ⟨~ resentment⟩ ⟨~ sensations⟩ **4 :** originating in or dependent on the thing itself **:** belonging to the mutual relations of the parts of a thing **:** INTRINSIC, INHERENT ⟨~ evidence of forgery in a document⟩ ⟨test a theory for ~ consistency⟩ **5 a :** present or performed within an organism ⟨~ senses⟩ ⟨~ speech⟩ **b :** arising within a sense organ ⟨~ stimulus⟩ **6 :** of or relating to the domestic affairs or administrative functions of a country or state ⟨~ commerce⟩ ⟨~ discord⟩ ⟨~ improvement⟩ ⟨~ debt⟩ **syn** see INNER

[2]**internal** \"\ *n* -s **1 internals** *pl* **:** the internal organs of the body **:** INNARDS **2 a :** an inner or essential quality or property **b** *obs* **:** spiritual nature **:** SOUL

**internal angle** *n* **:** INTERIOR ANGLE

**internal audit** *n* **1 :** a usu. continuous examination and verification of books of account conducted by employees of a business — contrasted with *independent audit* **2 :** a review of systems of internal check and internal control of a business

**internal auditory meatus** *also* **internal acoustic meatus** *n* **:** a short canal in the petrous portion of the temporal bone through which pass the facial, auditory, and glossopalatine nerves

**internal ballistics** *n pl but usu sing in constr* **:** INTERIOR BALLISTICS

**internal black spot** *n* **:** a breakdown of garden beets due to boron deficiency and characterized by small dark necrotic masses of tissue in the root

**internal brown spot** *or* **internal brown fleck** *n* **:** a nonparasitic disease of the potato that is of unknown cause and is characterized by brown corky spots scattered throughout the interior of the tuber and sometimes by ring-shaped corky surface lesions — called also *corky ring spot*

**internal capsule** *n* **:** CAPSULE 1b (1)

**internal carotid artery** *n* **:** the inner branch of the carotid artery supplying the brain, eyes, and other internal structures of the head

**internal check** *n* **:** an accounting procedure whereby routine entries for transactions are handled by more than one employee in such a manner that the work of one employee is automatically checked against the work of another for detection of errors and irregularities

**internal-combustion engine** *n* **:** a heat engine in which the combustion that generates the heat takes place inside the engine proper instead of in a furnace — compare DIESEL ENGINE, GAS ENGINE, GASOLINE ENGINE, GAS TURBINE, JET ENGINE, ROCKET ENGINE, EXTERNAL-COMBUSTION ENGINE

**internal control** *n* **:** a system or plan of accounting and financial organization within a business comprising all the methods and measures necessary for safeguarding its assets, checking the accuracy of its accounting data or otherwise substantiating its financial statements, and policing previously adopted rules, procedures, and policies as to compliance and effectiveness

**internal conversion** *n* **:** transformation of nuclear gamma-ray energy into electron-emission energy within the atom itself

**internal cork** *n* **1 :** a virus disease of sweet potatoes characterized principally by the small brown to black corky spots which develop within the roots becoming prominent after harvest and storage **2 :** CORK 5

**internal degree** *n* **:** a degree granted by a university to a student who has completed the prescribed course in that university — compare EXTERNAL DEGREE

**internal energy** *n* **:** the total amount of kinetic and potential energy possessed by the molecules of a body and their ultimate parts owing to their relative positions and their motions inside the body and excluding the energy due to the passage of waves through the body and to vibrations of the body

**internal environment** *n* : the fluid medium in which the cells of the body exist

**internal friction** *n* : frictional interaction between adjacent portions in the interior of a substance due to viscous deformation or flow and resulting in the generation of heat

**internal gear** *n* : a gear having teeth on the inside of its circular rim

**in·ter·nal·i·ty** \ˌin(ˌ)tərˈnaləd·ē\ *n* -ES : the quality or state of being internal : INTERIORITY

**in·ter·nal·iza·tion** \ən-ˌtərnᵊlə'zāshən\ *n* -s : the act of internalizing ⟨man's conscience is an ~ of parental . . . authority —Asher Moore⟩

**in·ter·nal·ize** \ən-'tərnᵊlˌīz\ *vt* -ED/-ING/-s *see -ize in Explan Notes* [¹*internal* + *-ize*] : to make internal : give subjective character to : INTERIORIZE; *specif* : to incorporate (as values, patterns of culture, motives, restraints) within the self as conscious or subconscious guiding principles through learning and socialization — compare INTROJECT

internal gear

**internal law** *n* : the law of a state regulating its domestic affairs as opposed to that regulating its foreign affairs

**in·ter·nal·ly** \(ˈ)in·ˈtərnᵊlē, ən-ˈt-, -tᵊn-, -təin-, -li\ *adv* **1** : within the termini, enveloping surface, or boundary of a thing : within the body : beneath the surface : INWARDLY **2** : MENTALLY : SPIRITUALLY **3** : in or in respect to the inner constitution or affairs of something ⟨a doctrine ~ inconsistent⟩

**internally fired boiler** *n* : a boiler whose furnace is wholly or partly surrounded by water — compare EXTERNALLY FIRED BOILER

**internal mammary artery** *n* : a branch of the subclavian artery of each side that runs down along the anterior wall of the thorax and rests against the costal cartilages

**internal mammary vein** *n* : a vein accompanying the internal mammary artery of each side

**internal medicine** *n* : a branch of medicine that deals with the diagnosis and treatment of nonsurgical diseases

**internal navigation** *n* : navigation on inland waterways

**in·ter·nal·ness** *n* -ES : INTERNALITY

**internal oblique** *n* : a sheet of diagonally arranged abdominal muscle lying between the external oblique and transverse layers on either side of the trunk

**internal phase** *n* : DISPERSED PHASE

**internal phloem** *n* : primary phloem internal to the primary xylem and either in contact with it or in discrete strands

**internal porch** *n* : VESTIBULE, LOBBY, NARTHEX 2

**internal pressure** *n* : pressure inside a portion of matter due to attraction between molecules

**internal relation** *n* : a relation that is involved in or essential to the nature of the thing related ⟨logical equivalence of propositions is an *internal relation* —Arthur Pap⟩ — contrasted with *external relation*

**internal respiration** *n* : the exchange of gases (as oxygen and carbon dioxide) between the cells of the body and the blood by way of the fluid bathing the cells — distinguished from *external respiration*

**internal revenue tax** *n* : EXCISE 1b, 1c, 1d

**internal rhyme** *n* : rhyme between a word within a line and another either at the end of the same line or within another line

**internal secretion** *n* : HORMONE

**internal student** *n* : a student studying in the same university from which he expects to receive a degree — compare EXTERNAL STUDENT

**internal thread** *n* : a screw thread on an inner or concave surface (as of a nut that fits on a bolt)

¹**in·ter·nasal** \ˌintə(r)+\ *adj* [*inter-* + *nasal*] : situated between the nostrils ⟨~ septum⟩ ⟨~ scale⟩

²**internasal** \"\ *n* : an internasal part; *esp* : any of certain scales lying just behind the nostril in snakes

¹**in·tern·ation** \ˌin,tər'nāshən\ *n* -s [F, fr. *interner* to intern + *-ation* — more at INTERN] : the act of interning or the state of being interned : INTERNMENT

²**in·ter·nation** \ˌintə(r)+\ *n* [*inter-* + *nation*] : a population composed of or representing several nationalities

³**internation** \"\ *adj* [*inter-* + *nation*] : existing or occurring between nations ⟨~ rivalry⟩

¹**in·ter·na·tion·al** \R ¦intər¦nashənᵊl, -shnəl, -naash-, -naish-, -R ¦intə¦na- *sometimes* ¦intᵊn¦a-\ *adj* [*inter-* + *national*] **1** : existing between or among nations or their citizens : relating to the intercourse of nations : participated in by two or more nations : common to or affecting two or more nations ⟨~ trade⟩ ⟨~ labor union⟩ ⟨~ trade association⟩ **2** : belonging or relating to an organization or association having members in two or more countries ⟨~ congress⟩ ⟨~ movement⟩ **3 a** *of a unit of measurement* : fixed by the mutual agreement of authorized representatives of different countries **b** *of an electrical unit* : accepted by the International Conference in London in 1908 and used as a legal unit prior to 1950 ⟨~ coulomb⟩ **4** : of or relating to the International Code

²**international** \"\ *n* **1** : a person having relations with or obligations to more than one nation (as through citizenship in one and permanent residence in another) **2** : a participant in an international contest **3** : INTERNATIONAL STOCK **4 a** : a party, organization, or association that transcends national limits; *specif* : an international socialist organization **b** : a craft or industrial union with local affiliates in several countries **5** : a class of racing sailboats that are 33 feet long, sloop-rigged, and of one design; *also* : a boat in this class

**international auxiliary language** *n* : INTERLANGUAGE

**international candle** *n* : CANDLE 4a

**international carat** *n* : CARAT 1b

**international code** *n, usu cap I&C* : a marine code adopted by all the leading nations for holding communication at sea by means of 26 flags each standing for a different letter of the Roman alphabet and an additional triangular code flag or answering pennant which are hoisted in various combinations each of which represents according to the code a different word, phrase, or sentence

**international copyright** *n* : copyright secured by treaty between nations

**international crime** *n* : a crime (as piracy, illicit trade in narcotics, slave trading) in violation of international law

**international date line** *n* : DATE LINE

**in·ter·na·tio·nale** \ˌ≈≈shə'nal, -näl, -nâl\ *n* -s [F, fr. fem. of *international*, adj., fr. E] : INTERNATIONAL 4a ⟨a Communist ~⟩

**in·ter·na·tion·al·ism** *pronunc at* ¹INTERNATIONAL + ˌizəm\ *n* **1 a** : international character, principles, interests, or outlook **b** : international organization, influence, or common participation ⟨friction between governments is . . . reduced by administrative ~ —C.J.Friedrich⟩ **c** : COSMOPOLITANISM ⟨~ in art⟩ **2** : the doctrine or belief that world peace may be attained by the friendly association of all nations on a basis of equality and without sacrifice of national character for the securing of international justice and for cooperation in all matters of worldwide interest ⟨the alternatives of outright nationalism and outright ~ —*Fortune*⟩ — compare ISOLATIONISM **3** : the doctrine or belief of an international political association or party ⟨the ~ of the socialists found any barriers of race or nationality repugnant —Oscar Handlin⟩

¹**in·ter·na·tion·al·ist** \"+ˌəst\ *n* [¹*international* + *-ist*] **1** : an advocate of internationalism **2** : a specialist in international law **3** : a member of a team selected from the country at large to play against the team of another country ⟨tennis ~⟩

²**internationalist** \"\ *or* **in·ter·na·tion·al·is·tic** \¦≈≈¦(≈)≈¦istik, -tēk\ *adj* : advocating or influenced by internationalism ⟨~ thought⟩

**in·ter·na·tion·al·i·ty** \ˌ≈≈,≈shə'naləd·ē, -lətē, -i\ *n* : the quality or state of being international ⟨~ of the use of scientific language —Otto Neurath⟩

**in·ter·na·tion·al·iza·tion** \ˌ≈≈¦(≈)≈ə'zāshən, -ˌī'z-\ *n* : an act or process of internationalizing ⟨~ of a waterway⟩

**in·ter·na·tion·al·ize** \ˌ≈≈'≈≈ˌīz\ *vt* [¹*international* + *-ize*] : to make international in relations, effect, or scope ⟨~ a war⟩ ⟨~ a market⟩; *esp* : to place under international control or protection

**international language** *n* : INTERLANGUAGE

**international law** *n* : a body of rules that control or affect the rights of states in their relations with each other and of individuals in their relations to foreign states and with each other when public international factors are involved, that are based in the practice of Great Britain and the U. S. on the customs and usages of civilized nations, treaties, the acts of the executive in international matters, statutes, and judicial decisions esp. including those of international tribunals and in the practice of European continental countries also on the opinions of text writers, and that are generally accepted as binding and enforceable by the participant nations — called also *law of nations*

**international legislation** *n* : the law found in the treaties and international agreements among nations binding the parties thereto but not necessarily being a part of the body of international law binding all nations

**in·ter·na·tion·al·ly** \¦≈≈¦nashᵊnᵊlē, -shnəlē, -naash-, -naish-, -ᵊli, -əli\ *adv* : in an international manner ⟨~ agreed⟩ : from an international point of view ⟨~ famous⟩ : between different nations or their citizens

**international map** *n* : a map of the world at a scale of one to one million having a uniform set of symbols and conventional signs and printed in modified polyconic projection on sheets each covering an area of 4 degrees latitude by 6 degrees longitude except above the 60th parallel where the longitude covered is 12 degrees on each sheet

**international match point** *n* : a scoring unit used in contract bridge tournaments played in Europe and based on but not directly proportional to the winning margin of a board

**international orange** *n* : a vivid reddish orange that is redder and much darker than golden poppy and redder, stronger, and much darker than chrome orange

**international phonetic alphabet** *n, usu cap I, P, & A* : IPA

**international pitch** *n* **1** : DIAPASON NORMAL **2** : the tuning standard adopted in 1939 of 440 vibrations per second for A above middle C

**international private law** *n* : CONFLICT OF LAWS

**international relations** *n pl but sing in constr* : a branch of political science concerned with relations between political units of national rank and dealing primarily with foreign policies, the organization and function of governmental agencies concerned with foreign policy, and the factors (as geography and economics) underlying foreign policies

**international salute** *n* : a salute of 21 guns to a national flag

**international scientific vocabulary** *n, usu cap I&S&V* : a part of the vocabulary of the sciences and other specialized studies that consists of words or other linguistic forms current in two or more languages and differing from New Latin in being adapted to the structure of the individual languages in which they appear — abbr. *ISV*

**international stock** *n* : a stock marketable at financial centers outside as well as within the country of issue

**international style** *n* **1** : a school of painting showing delicate linearity and decorative treatment of surface popular in Europe during the 14th and early 15th centuries **2** : functional architectural design employing the latest of building techniques and avoiding traditional or regional influences

**international temperature scale** *n* : a practical temperature scale defining all temperatures above −183° C by specified formulas relating temperatures at one atmosphere pressure to the indications of instruments calibrated at six reproducible fixed points: the boiling point of oxygen (−182.97° C), the ice point (0° C), the steam point (100° C), the boiling point of sulfur (444.6° C), the freezing point of silver (960.8° C), the freezing point of gold (1063° C)

**international unit** *n* : a quantity of a biological (as a vitamin, hormone, antibiotic, antitoxin) or its equivalent based on bioassay that produces a particular biological effect agreed upon internationally

**interne** *var of* INTERN

**in·ter·necine** \¦intər¦ne¦ˌsēn, -nē¦, ¦ˌsīn, ¦sᵊn, ¦sən; ¦intərnə¦sēn; ən-'tərnəˌsēn, -nəsən, -nəˌsīn\ *adj* [L *internecinus*, fr. *internecare* to destroy, kill (fr. *inter-* + *necare* to kill, fr. *nec-*, *nex* violent death) + *-inus* -ine — more at NOXIOUS] **1 a** : marked by great slaughter : DEADLY ⟨the alternatives only of ~ war or absolute surrender —W.E.Gladstone⟩ **b** : involving or accompanied by mutual slaughter : mutually destructive ⟨zealots who stabbed each other in ~ massacre —F.W.Farrar⟩ **2** : of, relating to, or involving conflict within a group; *broadly* : INTERNAL ⟨absorbed in incurable, rancorous ~ feuds —Barbara Ward⟩ ⟨a bitter ~ struggle among artists —Roger Fry⟩

**in·ter·ne·cion** \¦≈≈'neshən, -nēsh-\ *n* -s [L *internecion-*, *internecio*, fr. *internecare* + *-ion-*, *-io* -ion] : mutual destruction : MASSACRE

**in·ter·necive** \¦≈≈¦nesiv, -nēs-; ən-'tərnəs-\ *adj* [L *internecivus*, fr. *internecare* + *-ivus* -ive] : INTERNECINE

**interned** *past of* INTERN

**in·tern·ee** \ˌin·ˌtər¦nē, -tə̄-, -təi-; ən·'≈ˌ≈\ *n* -s [²*intern* + *-ee*] : a person interned

¹**in·ter·neural** \ˌintə(r)+\ *adj* [*inter-* + *neural*] : situated between neural arches or neural spines

²**interneural** \"\ *n* -s : one of the spiny bones that extend into the flesh of certain fishes between the neural spines and articulate with the rays of the dorsal fins

**in·ter·neuron** \"+\ *also* **in·ter·neurone** \"+\ *n* [*inter-* + *neuron, neurone*] : an internuncial neuron — **in·ter·neuronal** \"+\ *adj*

**interning** *pres part of* INTERN

**in·ter·nist** \ən-'tərnəst, -tᵊn-\ *n* -s [*intern-* (fr. *internal medicine*) + *-ist*] : a specialist in internal medicine : a specialist in the diagnosis and medical treatment of internal diseases

**in·tern·ment** \ən-'tərnmənt, -tᵊn-, -təin-\ *n* -s [F *internement*, fr. *interner* to intern + *-ment* — more at INTERN] : the act of interning or the state of being interned ⟨~ of enemy aliens⟩

**in·ter·nodal** \¦intə(r)+\ *adj* [*inter-* + *nodal*] : lying between nodes ⟨~ stem gall⟩ ⟨~ loop of a vibrating string⟩

**in·ter·node** \'intə(r),nōd\ *n* [L *internodium*, fr. *inter-* + *nodus* knot, joint + *-ium* (n. suffix) — more at NET] : an interval or part between two nodes : SEGMENT

**interns** *pres 3d sing of* INTERN, *pl of* INTERN

**in·tern·ship** *also* **in·terne·ship** \'in·ˌtərn,ship, -tᵊn-, -təin-\ *n* [⁴*intern*, *interne* + *-ship*] **1** : the state or position of being an intern **2 a** : a period of service as an intern **b** : the phase of medical training covered during such service **c** : a training period in actual service as an employee in a technical or business establishment **3** : a grant enabling a student or recent graduate to serve as an intern

**in·ter·nuclear** \¦intə(r)+\ *adj* [*inter-* + *nuclear*] : situated or extending between nuclei ⟨~ distances in molecules⟩

**in·ter·nunce** \'intə(r),nən(t)s\ *n* -s [L *internuntius*, *internuncius* — more at INTERNUNCIO] *archaic* : INTERNUNCIO

¹**in·ter·nun·cial** \¦intə(r)¦nən(t)sēəl, -nün-, ¦sh(ē)əl, ¦ch-\ *adj* [*internuncio* + *-al*] **1** : of or relating to an internuncio : serving as a conveyer of messages **2** : serving to link sensory and motor neurons — **in·ter·nun·cial·ly** \-əlē\ *adv*

²**internuncial** \"\ *or* **internuncial neuron** *n* -s : a nerve fiber intercalated in the path of a reflex arc in the central nervous system and tending to modify the arc and coordinate it with other bodily activities

**in·ter·nun·ci·ary** \¦(t)sēˌerē, ¦shē-, ¦chē-; ¦sharē, ¦chə-\ *adj* [*internuncio* + *-ary*] : INTERNUNCIAL 1

**in·ter·nun·cio** \ˌintə(r)'nən(t)sēˌō, -nün¦, ¦shēˌō, ¦chēˌō\ *n* -s [It *internunzio*, fr. L *internuntius*, *internuncius*, fr. *inter-* + *nuntius*, *nuncius* messenger] **1** : a messenger between two parties : GO-BETWEEN **2** : a diplomatic papal representative of lower rank than a nuncio **3** : a minister formerly representing a government (as the Austrian government) at Constantinople

**in·ter·nun·ci·us** \-ēəs\ *n, pl* **internun·cii** \-ēˌī, -ēˌē\ [L] : INTERNUNCIO

**in·ter·nuptial** \¦intə(r)+\ *adj* [*inter-* + *nuptial*] **1** : relating to intermarriage **2** : intervening between married states

**in·ter·objective distance** \¦intə(r)+ . . . -\ *n* [*inter-* + *objective*] : the distance between the pupils of the two eyes

**in·ter·oceanic** \"+\ *adj* [*inter-* + *oceanic*] : existing or extending between oceans ⟨~ communication⟩

**in·ter·o·cep·tive** \¦intərō¦septiv\ *adj* [*inter-* (as in *interior*) + *-o-* + *-ceptive* (as in *receptive*)] : of, relating to, or functioning as an interoceptor — compare EXTEROCEPTIVE, PROPRIOCEPTIVE

**in·ter·o·cep·tor** \-ptə(r)\ *n* -s [*inter-* (as in *interior*) + *-o-* + *-ceptor* (as in *receptor*)] : a receptor (as in the wall of the alimentary tract) responsive to stimuli originating within the body and esp. in the viscera — compare EXTEROCEPTOR

**in·ter·ocular** \¦intə(r)+\ *adj* [*inter-* + *ocular*] : situated between the eyes

**in·ter·o·fec·tive** \¦intərō¦fektiv\ *adj* [*inter-* (as in *interior*) + *-o-* + *-fective* (as in *effective*)] : of, relating to, dependent on, or constituting the autonomic nervous system — distinguished from *exterofective*

**in·ter·office** \¦intə(r)+\ *adj* [*inter-* + *office*] : existing between the offices of an organization ⟨~ memo⟩

**in·ter·operation** \"+\ *n* [*inter-* + *operation*] : reciprocal operation ⟨~ of factors⟩

**in·ter·oper·cle** \ˌintərō'pərkəl\ *n* [NL *interoperculum*] : the membrane bone between the preopercle and the branchiostegals of a fish

¹**in·ter·oper·cu·lar** \¦≈≈≈¦pərkyələ(r)\ *adj* [NL *interoperculum* + E *-ar*] : of or relating to an interoperculum

²**interopercular** \"\ *n* -s : INTEROPERCLE

**in·ter·oper·cu·lum** \ˌ≈≈≈'≈≈ləm\ *n* [NL, fr. *inter-* + *operculum*] : INTEROPERCLE

**in·ter·optic** \¦intə(r)+\ *adj* [*inter-* + *optic*] : lying between the optic lobes

**in·ter·orbital** \"+\ *adj* [*inter-* + *orbital*] : situated or extending between the orbits of the eyes ⟨~ septum⟩ ⟨~ distance⟩

**interorbital breadth** *n* : the distance between the dacrya

**in·ter·osculant** \"+\ *adj* [*inter-* + *osculant*] *math* : osculating with each other : INTERSECTING ⟨~ curves⟩

**in·ter·osculate** \"+\ *vi* [*inter-* + *osculate*] : to osculate with each other : INTERMIX ⟨*interosculating* blood vessels⟩ — **in·ter·osculation** \"+\ *n*

**in·ter·osseous** \"+\ *adj* [*inter-* + *osseous*] : situated between bones; *esp* : lying between the bones of the leg or forearm ⟨~ membrane⟩ ⟨~ artery of the hand⟩ ⟨~ nerve⟩

**in·ter·os·se·us** \ˌintə'(r)¦äsēəs\ *n, pl* **interos·sei** \-ēˌī\ [NL, fr. *inter-* + L *osseus*, adj., osseous — more at OSSEOUS] : any of various small muscles arising from the metacarpals and metatarsals and inserted into the bases of the first phalanges

**in·ter·ownership** \¦intə(r)+\ *n* [*inter-* + *ownership*] : interlocking ownership

**in·ter·page** \"+\ *vt* [*inter-* + *page*] : to insert or put between pages ⟨*interpaged* translation⟩

**in·ter·parental** \"+\ *adj* [*inter-* + *parental*] : existing between parents ⟨~ tension⟩

¹**in·ter·parietal** \"+\ *adj* [*inter-* + *parietal*] : lying between parietal elements; *esp* : lying between the parietal bones

²**interparietal** \"\ *n* : an interparietal element (as a bone or scale)

**interparietal bone** *n* : a median triangular bone lying at the junction of the parietal and occipital bones and rarely present in man but conspicuous in various lower mammals — see INCA BONE

**in·ter·pa·ri·e·ta·le** \ˌintə(r)pəˌrīə'tālē\ *n* -s [NL, fr. *inter-* + LL *parietale*, neut. of *parietalis* parietal — more at PARIETAL] : an interparietal bone or cartilage

**in·ter·parliamentary** \¦intə(r)+\ *adj* [*inter-* + *parliamentary*] : existing among or involving several national legislatures ⟨~ congress⟩

**in·ter·paroxysmal** \"+\ *adj* [*inter-* + *paroxysmal*] : occurring between paroxysms

**in·ter·party** \"+\ *adj* [*inter-* + *party*] : existing between parties ⟨~ cooperation⟩

**in·ter·peduncular** \"+\ *adj* [*inter-* + *peduncular*] : lying between the peduncles of the brain

**interpeduncular ganglion** *n* : a mass of nerve cells lying between the cerebral peduncles in the median plane just dorsal to the pons

**in·ter·pel** \ˌintə(r)'pel\ *vt* **interpelled; interpelled; interpelling; interpels** [MF *interpeller*, fr. L *interpellare* — more at INTERPELLATE] **1** *obs* : INTERRUPT **2** *Scots law* : PREVENT, PRECLUDE, INTERCEPT

¹**in·ter·pel·lant** \¦≈≈¦pelənt\ *adj* [L *interpellant-*, *interpellans*, pres. part. of *interpellare*] : INTERRUPTING

²**interpellant** \"\ *n* -s : INTERPELLATOR

**in·ter·pel·late** \¦≈≈'pe,lāt, *usu* -ād.+V; ən-'tərpə,-, -tə̄p-, -təip-, *usu* -ād.+V\ *vt* -ED/-ING/-s [L *interpellatus*, past part. of *interpellare*, fr. *inter-* + *-pellare* (fr. *pellere* to drive, beat, push) — more at FELT] **1** *obs* : INTERRUPT **2** : to question formally about a governmental policy or decision

**in·ter·pel·la·tion** \ˌ≈≈pə'lāshən; ≈,≈≈'lāshən\ *n* -s [L *interpellation-*, *interpellatio*, fr. *interpellatus* + *-ion-*, *-io* -ion] **1** *obs* : an act of interposing : INTERCESSION **2** : INTERRUPTION **3** : the act of formally bringing into question (as in a European legislature) a ministerial policy or action ⟨~ . . . is the particular method by which the deputies exercise their power of controlling and dismissing cabinets —Ernest Barker⟩ **4** *Scots law* : INTERCEPTION, PREVENTION

**in·ter·pel·la·tor** \ˌ≈≈'pelād·ə(r); ≈'≈≈,lād·ə(r)\ *n* -s [L, fr. *interpellatus* + *-or*] : one that interpellates

**in·ter·pendent** \¦intə(r)+\ *adj* [*inter-* + *pendent*] **1** *archaic* : hanging between : HESITANT **2** *archaic* : INTERDEPENDENT

**in·ter·penetrable** \"+\ *adj* [*inter-* + *penetrable*] : capable of being mutually penetrated ⟨portrays good and evil as ~ and relative —K.O.Myrick⟩

**in·ter·penetrant** \"+\ *adj* [*inter-* + *penetrant*] : mutually penetrating ⟨~ crystals⟩

**in·ter·penetrate** \"+\ *vb* [*inter-* + *penetrate*] *vt* : to penetrate between, within, or throughout : penetrate thoroughly : PERMEATE ⟨Westerners who *interpenetrated* the East in the nineteenth century —Elmer Davis⟩ ~ *vi* : to penetrate mutually ⟨the territories of the two peoples ~ a good deal —C.D. Forde⟩ **syn** see PERMEATE

**in·ter·penetration** \"+\ *n* [*inter-* + *penetration*] **1** : thorough penetration : PERMEATION **2** : mutual penetration; *esp* : the effect in painting of two or more forms crossing and including shapes in common — compare TRANSPARENCY

**in·ter·penetrative** \"+\ *adj* [*inter-* + *penetrative*] : tending to penetrate mutually ⟨for him realism and mysticism are ~ —B.R.Redman⟩ — **in·ter·penetratively** \"+\ *adv*

**in·ter·personal** \"+\ *adj* [*inter-* + *personal*] **1** : existing between persons ⟨~ situation in which speech occurs —Z.S. Harris⟩ **2** : relating to or involving personal and social relations out of which develop systems of shared expectations, patterns of emotional relatedness, and modes of social adjustment ⟨disrupted ~ relationships —M.J.Pescor⟩ — **in·ter·personally** \"+\ *adv*

**in·ter·petaloid** \"+\ *adj* [*inter-* + *petaloid*] : lying between ambulacral areas ⟨~ spaces on a sea urchin⟩

**in·ter·phalangeal** \"+\ *adj* [*inter-* + *phalangeal*] : existing between phalanges ⟨~ flexion⟩

**in·ter·phase** \'intə(r)+,-\ *n* [*inter-* + *phase*] : INTERKINESIS — **in·ter·phasic** \¦intə(r)+\ *adj*

**in·ter·phone** \'intə(r),fōn\ *n* [fr. *Interphone*, a trademark] : a telephone system (as in an airplane, tank, ship, or office building) for intercommunication between points within a small area

**in·ter·piece** \-,pēs\ *n* [*inter-* + *piece*] : INTERLUDE

**in·ter·pilaster** \ˌintə(r)+\ *n* [*inter-* + *pilaster*] : the space between two pilasters

**interplace** *vt* [*inter-* + *place*] **1** *obs* : to place between or among : INSERT **2** *obs* : to place alternately

**in·ter·plait** \¦intə(r)+\ *vt* [*inter-* + *plait*] : to plait together

**in·ter·plane** \"+\ *adj* [in sense 1, fr. *inter-* + *plane* (section of an airplane); in sense 2, fr. *inter-* + *plane* (airplane)] **1** : situated or extending between the upper and lower wing of an airplane ⟨~ strut⟩ **2** : existing between airplanes ⟨~ communication⟩

**in·ter·planetary** \"+\ *adj* [*inter-* + *planetary*] : existing, carried on, or operating between planets ⟨the density of hydrogen in ~ and interstellar space —*Science*⟩

¹**in·ter·plant** \"+\ *vt* [*inter-* + *plant* (v.)] : to plant (a crop) between plants of another kind : set out (young trees) among existing growth

²**in·ter·plant** \'≈≈+,-\ *n* : a crop planted between plants of another crop

³**in·ter·plant** \¦≈≈+\ *adj* [*inter-* + *plant* (n.)] : existing between manufacturing plants ⟨~ transfer of material⟩

**1in·ter·play** \ˈintə(r)+,-\ *n* [*inter-* + *play*] **:** mutual action or influence **:** reciprocal or contrasting action or effect **:** INTERACTION ⟨bureaucratic controls are imposed upon . . . an ~ of private interests —Irving Howe⟩ ⟨~ of character and circumstance —Hallam Tennyson⟩

**2in·ter·play** \ˌ==+\ *vi* **:** to exert interplay ⟨there enter into imaginative creation three factors which reciprocally ~ —J.L. Lowes⟩

**in·ter·plea** \ˈintə(r)+,-\ *n* [*inter-* + *plea*] **:** the plea of a defendant disclaiming any interest in the subject matter of a controversy and calling for an interpleader proceeding between the true claimants

**in·ter·plead** \ˌintə(r)ˈplēd\ *vb* [AF *enterpleder*, fr. *enter-* inter- + *pleder* to plead, fr. OF *plaidier* — more at PLEAD] *vi* **:** to go to trial with each other in order to determine a right on which the action of a third party depends ~ *vt* **:** to bring (two or more claimants) into court in order to compel the litigation of the ownership of a claim ⟨insurance company, not knowing where the payment should go between the three, ~*ed* the claimants —W.H.Atwell⟩

**1in·ter·plead·er** \-də(r)\ *n* [AF *enterpleder*, fr. *enterpleder*, v.] **:** a proceeding devised to enable a person of whom the same debt, duty, or thing is claimed adversely by two or more parties to compel them to litigate the right or title between themselves and thereby to relieve himself from the suits which they might otherwise bring against him

**2interpleader** \"\ *n* [*interplead* + *-er*] **:** one that interpleads

**in·ter·plical** \ˌintə(r)+\ *adj* [*inter-* + *plical*] **:** lying between folds

**1in·ter·pluvial** \"+\ *adj* [*inter-* + *pluvial*] **:** comparatively dry and occurring between times of greater precipitation ⟨~ age⟩

**2interpluvial** \"\ *n* -s **:** an interpluvial age or time

**in·ter·point** \ˈintə(r)+,-\ *n* [*inter-* + *point*] **:** the printing of braille on both sides of the paper in such a way that the points of one side fall between points of the other side

**in·ter·polar** \ˌintə(r)+\ *adj* [*inter-* + *polar*] **:** situated or extending between poles ⟨~ field of a magnet⟩ ⟨~ wire⟩

**in·ter·po·late** \ənˈtərpə,lāt, -tōp-, -təip-, *usu* -ād.+V\ *vb* -ED/-ING/-S [L *interpolatus*, past part. of *interpolare* to give a new appearance to, alter, interpolate, fr. *inter-* + *-polare* (fr. *polire* to polish, furbish) — more at POLISH] *vt* **1 a :** to alter or corrupt (as a text) by inserting new or foreign matter; *esp* **:** to change by inserting matter that is new or foreign to the purpose of the author ⟨was both *interpolated* and misunderstood —*Modern Language Notes*⟩ **b :** to insert (words) into a text ⟨*interpolated* editorial comment⟩ **:** put in (a remark) in a conversation **2 :** to insert between other things or parts **:** INTERCALATE ⟨letter which I here ~ as a good example of his style —Osbert Sitwell⟩ ⟨~ a layer of insulating material between ceiling and floor⟩ **3 :** to estimate values of (a function) between two known values ~ *vi* **:** to make insertions — compare EXTRAPOLATE

**in·ter·po·lat·er** \-ād.ə(r), -ātə-\ *n* -s **:** one that interpolates

**in·ter·po·la·tion** \ˌ=,==ˈlāshən\ *n* -s [L *interpolation-, interpolatio*, fr. *interpolatus* + *-ion-, -io* -ion] **1 :** an act of interpolating or state of being interpolated **:** introduction or insertion of something spurious or foreign **2 :** something that is introduced or inserted **:** INSERTION **3 :** the process of calculating approximate values by interpolating between values already known

**in·ter·po·la·tor** \ˌ=ˈ==,lād.ə(r), -ātə-\ *n* -s [L, fr. *interpolatus* + *-or*] **1 :** INTERPOLATER **2 :** a mechanically rotated clockwork instrument with two cams worked in conjunction with a relay to secure the correct telegraphic retransmission of any given number of consecutively repeated dots or dashes

**in·ter·pole** \ˈintə(r)+,-\ *n* [*inter-* + *pole*] **:** a supplementary pole placed between the regular poles of a direct-current dynamo or motor in order to regulate commutation — called also *commutating pole*

**in·ter·political** \ˌintə(r)+\ *adj* [*inter-* + *political*] **:** INTERCITY — used of the Greek city-states

**in·ter·polymer** \"+\ *n* [*inter-* + *polymer*] **:** COPOLYMER

**in·ter·polymerization** \"+\ *n* **:** COPOLYMERIZATION

**in·ter·polymerize** \"+\ *vt* [*interpolymer* + *-ize*] **:** COPOLYMERIZE

**in·ter·pone** \ˌintə(r)ˈpōn\ *vt* -ED/-ING/-S [L *interponere* — more at INTERPOSE] *archaic* **:** INTERPOSE

**in·ter·por·tal** \ˌ==+ˈpōrd.ᵊl, -pȯr-\ *adj* [*inter-* + *port* + *-al*] **:** existing between ports of the same country ⟨~ trade⟩

**in·ter·pos·al** \ˌintə(r)ˈpōzəl\ *n* -s [*interpose* + *-al*] **:** the act of interposing **:** INTERPOSITION, INTERVENTION

**in·ter·pose** \-ōz\ *vb* [MF *interposer*, modif. (influenced by *poser* to put, place) of L *interponere* (perfect stem *interpos-*), fr. *inter-* + *ponere* to put, place — more at POSE, POSITION] *vt* **1 a :** to place between or in an intermediate position **:** cause to intervene ⟨dense . . . forests ~ an almost impassable barrier —Samuel Van Valkenburg & Ellsworth Huntington⟩ ⟨tending to ~ objects of worship between God and man —W.R.Inge⟩ **b :** to put (oneself) between **:** thrust in **:** INTRUDE ⟨what watchful cares do ~ themselves betwixt your eyes and night? —Shak.⟩ **2 :** to put forth by way of interference or intervention ⟨prevent a decision's being reached by *interposing* a veto⟩ **3 :** to introduce or throw in between the parts of a conversation or argument ⟨interrupted by questions from the class, and listened to whatever we might so ~ —C.I.Lewis⟩ ⟨~ objections⟩ **4 :** to move (a chessman) so as to shield a checked king or a piece that is directly attacked ~ *vi* **1 :** to be or come between ⟨cut through an *interposing* thicket⟩ **2 :** to step in between parties at variance **:** INTERVENE, MEDIATE ⟨listened . . . to their dispute, and at length *interposed* once more on the old man's side —W.H.Hudson †1922⟩ **3 :** to make an interruption or digression ⟨here Adam *interposed* —John Milton⟩

**in·ter·pos·er** \-zə(r)\ *n* **:** one that interposes

**in·ter·pos·ing·ly** *adv* **:** so as to interpose

**in·ter·po·si·tion** \ˌintə(r)pəˈzishən\ *n* [ME *interposicioun*, fr. MF *interposition*, fr. L *interposition-, interpositio*, fr. *interpositus* (past part. of *interponere*) + *-ion-, -io* -ion] **1 :** the act of interposing or the state of being interposed **:** a being, placing, or coming between **:** MEDIATION, INTERVENTION ⟨~ of the state between the federal government and the citizen of the states⟩ **2 :** something that is interposed

**interposition growth** *n* **:** INTRUSIVE GROWTH

**interposure** *n* -s *obs* **:** INTERPOSITION

**interpr** *abbr* interpreter

**in·ter·pret** \ənˈtərprət, ÷-pət, -tōp-, -təip-, *usu* -əd.+V\ *vb* -ED/-ING/-S [ME *interpreten*, fr. MF & L; MF *interpreter*, fr. L *interpretari*, fr. *interpret-, interpres* broker, negotiator, expounder, interpreter, fr. *inter-* + *-pret-, -pres* (prob. akin to L *pretium* value, price) — more at PRICE] *vt* **1 :** to explain or tell the meaning of **:** translate into intelligible or familiar language or terms **:** EXPOUND, ELUCIDATE, TRANSLATE ⟨Emmanuel, which being ~*ed* is, God with us —Mt. 1:23 (AV)⟩ ⟨~ dreams⟩ ⟨can only ~ his conduct as caused by fear⟩ **2 :** to understand and appreciate in the light of individual belief, judgment, interest, or circumstance **:** CONSTRUE ⟨~ a law⟩ ⟨~ a contract⟩ ⟨the gift was naturally ~*ed* as a bribe⟩ ⟨~ the signs of a coming storm⟩ **3 :** to apprehend and represent by means of art **:** show by illustrative representation **:** bring (a score or script) to active realization by performance ⟨an actor ~*s* a role⟩ ⟨~ a song⟩ ~ *vi* **:** to act as an interpreter **:** TRANSLATE

**in·ter·pret·abil·i·ty** \ˌ=,=p(r)əd.əˈbiləd.ē, -)ətə-, -latē, -i\ *n* -ES **:** the quality or state of being interpretable ⟨~ of signs⟩

**in·ter·pret·able** \ˌ=ˈ=p(r)əd.əbəl, -)ətəb-\ *adj* [LL *interpretabilis*, fr. L *interpretari* + *-abilis* -able] **:** capable of being interpreted or explained ⟨~ as a confession of guilt —P.A. Rollins⟩ — **in·ter·pret·able·ness** *n* -ES — **in·ter·pret·ably** \-blē, -bli\ *adv*

**interpretament** *n* -s [LL *interpretamentum*, fr. L *interpretari* + *-mentum* -ment] *obs* **:** INTERPRETATION

**in·ter·pre·tant** \ˌ=ˈ=p(r)əd.ənt, -)ətə-\ *n* -s [L *interpretant-, interpretans*, pres. part. of *interpretari*] **1 a :** the disposition or readiness of an interpreter to respond to a sign **b :** a sign or set of signs that interprets another sign **c :** the response or reaction to a sign **2 :** INTERPRETER

**in·ter·pre·tate** \-)ə,tāt\ *vi* -ED/-ING/-S [L *interpretatus*, past part. of *interpretari* to interpret — more at INTERPRET] *archaic* **:** INTERPRET

**in·ter·pre·ta·tion** \ən,tərprəˈtāshən, ÷-pə-, -tōp-, -təip-\ *n* -s [ME *interpretacioun*, fr. MF & L; MF *interpretation*, fr. L *interpretation-, interpretatio*, fr. *interpretatus* + *-ion-, -io* -ion] **1 :** the act or the result of interpreting: as **a :** explanation of what is not immediately plain or explicit ⟨~ of a dream⟩ or unmistakable ⟨~ of a law⟩ ⟨~ of a biblical passage⟩ ⟨~ of an aerial photograph⟩ ⟨~ of symptoms of disease⟩ **b :** translation from one language into another — used of oral translation by interpreters **c :** explanation of actions, events, or statements by pointing out or suggesting inner relationships or motives or by relating particulars to general principles ⟨Marxist ~ of history⟩ ⟨allegorical ~ of a novel⟩ ⟨poetic ~*s* of natural phenomena⟩ **2 :** representation in performance, delivery, or criticism of the thought and mood in a work of art or its producer esp. as penetrated by the personality of the interpreter ⟨~ is a transcendental effort . . . in which the player seeks not to reproduce but to re-create the music the composer wrote —C.M.Smith⟩ ⟨famous for her original ~*s* of several dramatic roles⟩ **3 :** a particular adaptation or application of a method or style or set of principles ⟨the stone house . . . shows a naïve and unusual ~ of classical elements —*Amer. Guide Series: Pa.*⟩ ⟨an amusing ~ of the shirt vogue in black cotton —Virginia Pope⟩ **4 :** activity directed toward the enlightenment of the public concerning the significance of the work of a public service or agency; *sometimes* **:** PUBLICITY, PUBLIC RELATIONS ⟨program of ~ developed by a natural-history museum⟩ — **in·ter·pre·ta·tion·al** \ˌ=ˌ=ˈtāshənᵊl, -shnəl\ *adj*

**interpretation clause** *n* **:** a clause inserted in a statute or contract declaring the interpretation that is to be put upon certain words

**in·ter·pre·ta·tive** \ənˈtərp(r)ə,tād.iv, -tōp-,-təip-, |t|, |ēv *also* |əv *sometimes* -)ətə|\ *adj* [*interpret* + *-ative*] **1 :** designed or fitted to interpret **:** EXPLANATORY ⟨~ magazine article⟩ **2 :** according to interpretation ⟨~ distortions in a translation⟩ ⟨~ elasticity of a statute⟩ — **in·ter·pre·ta·tive·ly** \|əvlē, -li\ *adv*

**interpretative bigamy** *n* **:** BIGAMY 2b

**interpretative dance** *or* **interpretive dance** *n* **:** a dance depicting a story or a definite emotion rather than following an abstract pattern

**in·ter·pret·er** \ənˈtərprəd.ə(r), ÷ -pə-, -tōp-, -təip-, -ətə-\ *n* -s [alter. (influenced by *-er*) of ME *interpretour*, fr. *interpreten* to interpret + *-our* -or — more at INTERPRET] **1 :** one that interprets, explains, or expounds ⟨early decipherers and ~*s* of hieroglyphic —W.T.Albright⟩ **2 :** one that translates; *esp* **:** a person who translates orally for parties conversing in different tongues **3 :** a machine that prints on punched cards the symbols recorded in them by perforations

**in·ter·pret·er·ship** \-,ship\ *n* **:** the position of interpreter

**in·ter·pre·tive** \ənˈtərp(r)əd.iv, (-tōp-,-təip-, -)ət|\ *adj* **:** INTERPRETATIVE — **in·ter·pre·tive·ly** \|əvlē, -li\ *adv*

**in·ter·pre·tress** \ənˈtərp(r)ə.trəs\ *also* **in·ter·pret·ess** \-)əd.əs\ *n* -ES **:** a female interpreter

**interprets** *pres 3d sing of* INTERPRET

**in·ter·provincial** \ˌintə(r)+\ *adj* [*inter-* + *provincial*] **:** existing between provinces ⟨~ compact⟩

**in·ter·proximal** \"+\ *also* **in·ter·proximate** \"+\ *adj* [*inter-* + *proximal* or *proximate*] **:** situated between adjacent parts or surfaces; *esp* **:** situated between adjoining teeth ⟨~ space⟩

**in·ter·pulmonary** \"+\ *adj* [*inter-* + *pulmonary*] **:** situated between the lungs

**in·ter·punct** \ˈintə(r),pəŋkt\ *n* -s [L *interpunctus*, past part.] **:** INTERPOINT

**in·ter·punc·tion** \ˌ==ˈpəŋkshən\ *n* -s [L *interpunction-, interpunctio*, fr. *interpunctus* (past part. of *interpungere* to punctuate, interpoint, fr. *inter-* + *pungere* to prick) + *-ion-, -io* -ion — more at PUNGENT] *n* -s **:** PUNCTUATION; *also* **:** PUNCTUATION MARK

**in·ter·punctuate** \ˌintə(r)+\ *vt* [*inter-* + *punctuate*] **:** PUNCTUATE — **in·ter·punctuation** \"+\ *n*

**in·ter·pupillary** \"+\ *adj* [*inter-* + *pupillary*] **:** extending between the pupils of the eyes; *also* **:** extending between the centers of a pair of spectacle lenses ⟨~ distance⟩

**in·ter·quartile range** \"+ . . . -\ *n* [*inter-* + *quartile*] **:** the range of values of the variable in a statistical distribution that lies between the upper and lower quartiles

**in·ter·racial** \"+\ *or* **in·ter·race** \"+\ *adj* [*inter-* + *racial* or *race*] **1 :** existing between or involving two or more races or members of different races ⟨~ understanding⟩ ⟨an ~ conference⟩ **2 :** of, relating to, or designed for two or more races or members of different races ⟨~ housing⟩

**in·ter·radial** \"+\ *adj* [*inter-* + *radial*] **:** of or relating to an interradius — **in·ter·radially** \"+\ *adv*

**in·ter·ra·di·um** \ˌintə(r)ˈrādēəm\ *n, pl* **interra·dia** \-ēə\ [NL, fr. *inter-* + *-radium* (fr. *radius*)] **1 :** one of the areas between radii **2 :** INTERAMBULACRUM

**in·ter·radius** \ˌintə(r)+\ *n, pl* **interradii** [NL, fr. *inter-* + *radius*] **:** a radius in a coelenterate halfway between two perradii

**in·ter·ramal** \"+\ *adj* [*inter-* + *ramal*] **:** situated between rami esp. of the lower jaw

**in·ter·ramification** \"+\ *n* [*inter-* + *ramification*] **:** the union of branches to form a network

**in·ter·react** \"+\ *vi* [*inter-* + *react*] **:** to react reciprocally — **in·ter·reaction** \"+\ *n*

**interred** *past of* INTER

**in·ter·reef** \"+\ *adj* [*inter-* + *reef* (n.)] **:** situated between reefs ⟨~ sedimentation⟩

**in·ter·reflection** \"+\ *n* [*inter-* + *reflection*] **:** reciprocal reflection ⟨~ of light between surfaces of a lens⟩

**in·ter·regional** \"+\ *adj* [*inter-* + *regional*] **:** existing between regions ⟨~ zone⟩

**in·ter·reg·nal** \"+ˈregnᵊl\ *adj* **:** of or relating to an interregnum

**in·ter·reg·num** \-nəm\ *n, pl* **interregnums** \-mz\ *or* **in·terreg·na** \-nə\ [L, fr. *inter-* + *regnum* dominion — more at REIGN] **1** *obs* **:** reign or tenure of power during a temporary vacancy of a throne or suspension of the ordinary government **2 a :** the time during which a throne is vacant between the death, abdication, or expulsion of a sovereign and the accession of his successor **b :** a period between two regimes of the same form or of different forms of government **3 :** a period during which the normal functions of government or control are suspended **4 a :** a period of freedom from customary authority **b :** a lapse, break, or pause in a continuous series

**1in·ter·reign** \ˈintə(r),rān\ *n* [MF *interregne*, fr. L *interregnum*] **:** INTERREGNUM

**2in·ter·reign** \ˌintə(r)+\ *vi* [*inter-* + *reign* (v.)] **:** to reign between other reigns

**in·ter·relate** \"+\ *vb* [*inter-* + *relate*] *vt* **:** to bring into mutual relation ⟨has not yet learned to ~ his characters —*Saturday Rev.*⟩ ~ *vi* **:** to have mutual relationship ⟨the linguistic system ~*s* with the other systems of the culture —H.L. Smith b.1913⟩

**in·ter·related** \"+\ *adj* [*inter-* + *related*] **:** having a mutual or reciprocal relation or parallelism **:** CORRELATIVE — **in·ter·re·lat·ed·ly** *adv* — **in·ter·re·lat·ed·ness** *n*

**in·ter·relation** \"+\ *n* [*inter-* + *relation*] **:** mutual relation **:** INTERRELATEDNESS

**in·ter·relationship** \"+\ *n* **:** mutual relationship **:** CORRESPONDENCE ⟨~*s* of animal structure and function⟩

**in·ter·religious** \"+\ *adj* [*inter-* + *religious*] **:** existing between religions ⟨~ goodwill⟩

**1in·ter·renal** \"+\ *adj* [*inter-* + *renal*] **:** lying between the kidneys

**2interrenal** \"\ *n* -s **:** INTERRENAL BODY

**interrenal body** *or* **interrenal gland** *n* **:** a small body of discrete adrenal cortical tissue lying between the kidneys of certain fishes

**in·ter·rer** \ənˈtər·ə(r) *also* -tərə(r)\ *n* -s **:** one that inters

**in·ter·rex** \ˈintə(r),reks\ *n, pl* **interre·ges** \ˌ==ˈrē(,)jēz\ [L, fr. *inter-* + *rex* king — more at ROYAL] **:** one who exercises supreme or kingly power during an interregnum **:** a provisional ruler

**interring** *pres part of* INTER

**in·ter·ro·ga·ble** \ənˈterəgəbəl, (ˈ)in¦t-\ *adj* [*interrogate* + *-able*] **:** capable of being interrogated

**in·ter·ro·gant** \ənˈterəgənt\ *n* -s [L *interrogant-, interrogans*, pres. part. of *interrogare*] **:** INTERROGATOR

**in·ter·ro·gate** \-rə,gāt, *usu* -ād.+V\ *vb* -ED/-ING/-S [L *interrogatus*, past part. of *interrogare*, fr. *inter-* + *rogare* to ask, request — more at RIGHT] *vt* **1 :** to question typically with formality, command, and thoroughness for full information and circumstantial detail ⟨~ a witness⟩ **2** *obs* **:** to ask questions about **3 :** to examine in detail **:** research into the causes, reasons, nature of ⟨modern potters ~ in their laboratories the glazes used in ancient China —C.E.Montague⟩ ~ *vi* **:** to ask questions of someone **:** conduct an examination ⟨frank I will respond as you ~ —Robert Browning⟩ **syn** see ASK

**in·ter·ro·gat·ing·ly** *adv* **:** QUESTIONINGLY

**in·ter·ro·ga·tion** \ən,terəˈgāshən\ *n* -s [ME *interrogacioun*, fr. MF *interrogation*, fr. L *interrogation-, interrogatio*, fr. *interrogatus* + *-ion-, -io* -ion] **1 a :** the act of interrogating **b :** a question put **:** INQUIRY **2 a :** a question regarded as a type of sentence or unit of discourse **b :** a questioning with the force of an emphatic affirmation or denial **3 :** QUESTION MARK — **in·ter·ro·ga·tion·al** \ˌ=¦==ˈgāshənᵊl, -shnəl\ *adj*

**interrogation point** *or* **interrogation mark** *n* **:** QUESTION MARK

**1in·ter·rog·a·tive** \ˌintəˈrägəd.iv, -ətiv\ *adj* [LL *interrogativus*, fr. L *interrogatus* + *-ivus* -ive] **1 :** having the form or the force of a question ⟨~ sentence⟩ **:** used in a question ⟨~ pronoun⟩ **:** requiring or seeming to require an answer from the hearer or reader ⟨~ inflection in his voice⟩ **2 :** QUESTIONING, INQUISITIVE ⟨had an ~ nose⟩ — **in·ter·rog·a·tive·ly** \-əvlē, -li\ *adv*

**2interrogative** \"\ *n* -s **1 :** an interrogative utterance **:** QUESTION **2 :** a word (as *who, what, which*) or a particle (as Latin *-ne*) used in asking questions

**in·ter·ro·ga·tor** \ənˈterə,gā|d.ə(r), |tə- *sometimes* ˌintəˈrägə\ *n* -s [LL, fr. L *interrogatus* (past part. of *interrogare* to interrogate) + *-or* — more at INTERROGATE] **1 :** one that interrogates **:** QUESTIONER; *specif* **:** one who interrogates prisoners of war ⟨born a German and . . . served as ~ in the American Army —Virginia Peterson⟩ **2 :** a radio transmitter and receiver combined for sending out a signal that triggers a transponder and for receiving and displaying the reply

**1in·ter·rog·a·to·ry** \ˌintəˈrägə,tōrē, -tȯr-, -ri\ *n* -ES [ML *interrogatorium*, fr. neut. of LL *interrogatorius*] **1 :** a formal question or inquiry; *esp* **:** a question put in writing and required by law to be answered under direction of a court **2 :** a question sign or signal denoting interrogation

**2interrogatory** \ˌ¦==¦==,==\ *adj* [LL *interrogatorius*, fr. L *interrogatus* + *-orius* -ory] **:** containing, expressing, or implying a question **:** INTERROGATIVE ⟨ends most of her remarks with an ~ upward inflection —Dan Wickenden⟩

**interrogatory action** *n, Roman law* **:** an action in which preliminary issues are tried before litiscontestation

**in·ter·ro·gee** \ən,terəˈgē\ *n* -s [*interrogate* + *-ee*] **:** someone interrogated

**in ter·ro·rem** \ˌin,teˈrō,rem\ *adv (or adj)* [L, for terror] **:** by way of threat or intimidation ⟨if, after becoming aware of the other party's offense, the injured party could hold it *in terrorem* over his head —Edward Jenks⟩

**in·ter·rupt** \ˌintəˈrəpt\ *vb* -ED/-ING/-S [ME *interrupten*, fr. L *interruptus*, past part. of *interrumpere*, fr. *inter-* + *rumpere* to break — more at REAVE] *vt* **1 :** to stop by breaking in **:** halt, hinder, or interfere with the continuation of (some activity) **:** prevent (one) from proceeding by intrusive or interpolated comment or action ⟨the . . . recovery was ~*ed* by the depression of 1883–85 —F.A.Bradford⟩ ⟨~ a speaker with frequent questions⟩ **2 :** to break or stop the uniformity, continuity, sequence, or course of **:** introduce a difference in ⟨an affair of copious eating and still more copious drinking, ~*ed* by bouts of homemade fun —Aldous Huxley⟩ ⟨the plain narrows and is ~*ed* by broad spurs from the Pennines —L.D.Stamp⟩ **3** *obs* **:** OBSTRUCT, THWART, PREVENT ~ *vi* **:** to break in upon some action or discourse **:** INTERPOLATE; *esp* **:** to break in with questions or remarks while another is speaking ⟨a bad habit of ~*ing*⟩ **syn** see ARREST

**interrupted** *adj* **1 :** broken in upon **:** DISCONTINUOUS ⟨an ~ stripe⟩ ⟨~ suture⟩ **2 :** not uniform **:** broken in arrangement or symmetry ⟨~ inflorescence⟩ **3 :** consisting of or containing a stop in articulation ⟨\k\ is an ~ consonant⟩ ⟨\dzh\ is an ~ phoneme⟩ **4** *of a map projection* **:** not having continuous outlines **:** split (as along meridians) so as to give better shape and scale for each continent or ocean — **in·ter·rupt·ed·ly** *adv* — **in·ter·rupt·ed·ness** *n* -ES

**interrupted cadence** *n* **:** DECEPTIVE CADENCE

**interrupted continuous waves** *n pl* **:** radio waves that are continuous except for periodic interruptions at a materially lower frequency

**interrupted current** *n* **:** a pulsating electric current produced by opening and closing a continuous-current circuit in a regular manner

**interrupted fern** *n* **:** an American fern (*Osmunda claytoniana*) with tall erect pinnate fronds and a few pairs of sporogenous pinnae borne at or near the center of the fertile fronds

**interrupted key** *n, cryptology* **:** an aperiodic keying sequence formed by interrupting a short key at various points and resuming from its beginning each time

**interrupted perforation** *n* **:** perforation on postage stamps for vending machines or dispensers in which there are unperforated spaces between groups of holes

**interrupted screw** *n* **:** a screw from which sectors have been removed by longitudinal cuts through the threads so that it can be thrust into a reciprocally machined mating part and locked by only a fraction of a turn

**in·ter·rupt·er** *also* **in·ter·rup·tor** \ˌintəˈrəptə(r)\ *n* -s **:** one that interrupts: as **a :** a device for periodically and automatically interrupting an electric current **b** *cryptology* **:** a message element or insertion signaling a change of key

**in·ter·rupt·ible** \ˌ==ˈrəptəbəl\ *adj* **:** capable of being interrupted ⟨~ utility service at reduced rates⟩

**in·ter·rup·tion** \ˌ==ˈrəpshən\ *n* -s [ME *interrupcioun*, fr. L *interruption-, interruptio*, fr. *interruptus* + *-ion-, -io* -ion] **1 :** an act of interrupting or state of being interrupted **2 :** a breach or break caused by the abrupt intervention of something foreign **3 :** obstruction caused by breaking in upon a course, current, progress, or motion **:** STOP **4 :** temporary cessation **:** INTERMISSION, SUSPENSION **5** *Scots law* **:** an act or proceeding that defeats an adverse title or claim based on prescription by stopping the running of the period of time required for the perfection of the title or claim and starting it running anew **syn** see BREAK

**in·ter·rup·tive** \ˌ==ˈrəptiv, -tēv *also* -təv\ *also* **in·ter·rup·to·ry** \-tərē\ *adj* [*interrupt* + *-ive* or *-ory*] **:** tending to interrupt — **in·ter·rup·tive·ly** \-təvlē\ *adv*

**inters** *pres 3d sing of* INTER

**1in·ter·scapular** \ˌintə(r)+\ *adj* [*inter-* + *scapular*] **:** situated between the shoulder blades **:** of or relating to the region between the shoulders ⟨~ feathers⟩

**2interscapular** \"\ *n* **:** an interscapular feather

**in·ter·scene** \ˈintə(r)+,-\ *n* [*inter-* + *scene*] **:** a scene (as in a motion picture) inserted between portions of the main narrative ⟨the passing of time has been done very adroitly by the use of cartoon ~*s* —W.H.Rudkin⟩

**in·ter·scholastic** \ˌintə(r)+\ *adj* [*inter-* + *scholastic*] **:** characterized by participation or cooperation of two or more secondary schools ⟨has withdrawn from ~ athletics⟩ — compare EXTRAMURAL

**in·ter·school** \"+\ *adj* [*inter-* + *school*] **:** existing between schools ⟨won first prize in the ~ debating competition⟩ — opposed to *intraschool*

**in·ter se** \ˈintə(r)ˈsē\ *adv (or adj)* [L] **:** among or between themselves ⟨all species will breed *inter se* —*Farmer's Weekly (So. Africa)*⟩ ⟨relations of the several parts of the empire *inter se* are not subject to international law —*Manchester Guardian Weekly*⟩

**in·ter·seamed** \ˌintə(r)¦sēmd\ *adj* [by folk etymology fr. MF *entresemer* to intersperse (fr. *entre-* inter- + *semer* to sow, fr. L *seminare*) + E *-ed* — more at DISSEMINATE] *archaic* **:** INTERSPERSED, SOWN ⟨borders of lilies ~ with roses —Robert Greene⟩

**1in·ter·sect** \ˌintə(r)ˈsekt\ *vb* -ED/-ING/-S [L *intersectus*, past part. of *intersecare*, fr. *inter-* + *secare* to cut — more at SAW] *vt* **1 :** to pierce or divide by passing through or across (a line or area) **:** CROSS ⟨any two diameters of a circle ~ each other⟩ ⟨canals ~ the city in every direction —*Encyc. Americana*⟩ **2 :** to determine the position of by triangulation ⟨opportunity was taken to ~ some twenty odd peaks —*Geog. Jour.*⟩

**3 :** to write (as a shorthand stroke) so as to cut across another or be cut across by another **~** *vi* **1 :** to meet and cross at a point ⟨~*ing* roads⟩ **2 :** to cut into one another so as to share an area in common **:** OVERLAP ⟨where positive law and morals ~ —Herbert Agar⟩

**²intersect** \ˈ==,=\ *n* -S **:** a point or curve of intersection

**in·ter·sec·tant** \ˌ==ˈsektənt\ *adj* **:** INTERSECTING

**intersecting arcade** *n* **:** a Romanesque arcade having interlacing arches

**in·ter·sec·tion** \ˌ==ˈsekshən, *in sense 3* " *or* ˈ==,==\ *n* -S [L *intersection-, intersectio,* fr. *intersectus* + *-ion-, -io* -ion] **1 :** an act, state, or place of intersecting ⟨understand the ~ of visible with invisible worlds —Stephen Spender⟩ **2 :** the sum total of points of a line, surface, or volume that it has in common with another line, surface, or volume ⟨the ~ of a plane with a spherical surface in a circle⟩ **3 :** a place where two or more highways join or cross; *specif* **:** an area of potential collision between vehicles traveling on different roadways that cross

**¹in·ter·sec·tion·al** \ˌ==ˈsekshənᵊl, -shnəl\ *adj* [*intersection* + *-al*] **:** of or relating to an intersection

**²in·ter·sec·tion·al** \"\ *adj* [*inter-* + *sectional*] **:** existing between sections ⟨~ football game⟩

**in·ter·segmental** \ˌintə(r)+\ *adj* [*inter-* + *segmental*] **:** lying between segments; *specif* **:** lying between the primordial segments of the embryo ⟨~ artery⟩

**in·ter·septal** \"+\ *adj* [*inter-* + *septal*] **:** situated between septa ⟨~ space⟩

**intersert** *vt* -ED/-ING/-S [L *intersertus,* past part. of *interserere,* fr. *inter-* + *serere* to join, bind together — more at SERIES] *obs* **:** INTERPOLATE, INSERT — **in·ter·ser·tion** *n* -S *obs*

**in·ter·sertal** \ˌintərˈsərd·ᵊl\ *adj* [G, fr. L *intersertus* + G *-al* (fr. L *-alis* -al)] *of an igneous rock* **:** of an ophitic texture in which the interstitial material is glass or a constituent other than augite

**in·ter·service** \ˌintə(r)+\ *adj* [*inter-* + *service*] **:** occurring between or relating to two or more of the armed services ⟨~ rivalry⟩

**in·ter·sesamoid** \"+\ *adj* [*inter-* + *sesamoid*] **:** situated between sesamoid bones ⟨~ ligament of a horse's fetlock⟩

**in·ter·session** \ˈintə(r)+,-\ *n* [*inter-* + *session*] **:** a period between two academic sessions or terms sometimes utilized (as in an adult education program) for brief concentrated courses — **in·ter·sessional** \ˌ==+\ *adj*

**in·ter·set** \ˌintə(r)+\ *adj* [*inter-* + *set* (past part.)] **1 :** set between or among other things **2 :** set about ⟨hills ~ with white villas⟩

**in·ter·sex** \ˈintə(r)+,-\ *n* [ISV *inter-* + *sex*] **:** an intersexual individual **:** an intergrade between the sexes

**in·ter·sexual** \ˌintə(r)+\ *adj* [ISV *inter-* + *sexual*] **1 :** existing between sexes ⟨~ hostility⟩ **2 :** intermediate in sexual characters between a typical male and a typical female — **in·ter·sexually** \"+\ *adv*

**in·ter·sexuality** \"+\ *or* **in·ter·sexualism** \"+\ *n* [ISV *inter-* + *sexuality* or *sexualism*] **:** the quality or state of being intersexual

**in·ter·shoot** \"+\ *vb* [*inter-* + *shoot*] *vi* **:** to shoot or flash at intervals ⟨hues . . . ~*ing* and to sight lost and recovered —William Wordsworth⟩ **~** *vt* **:** to intermingle with **:** color in streaks ⟨flames ~*ing* the dense smoke⟩

**in·ter·social** \"+\ *adj* [*inter-* + *social*] **:** relating to the mutual intercourse or relations of persons in society

**in·ter·societal** \"+\ *adj* [*inter-* + *societal*] **:** existing or occurring between societies ⟨~ comparisons of culture⟩ ⟨~ diffusion⟩

**intersole** *obs var of* ENTRESOL

**in·ter·sow** \"+\ *vt* [*inter-* + *sow*] **1 :** to sow, scatter, or sprinkle among other things **:** INTERSPERSE **2 :** to intersperse (a planting) with seed of another crop

**¹in·ter·space** \ˈintə(r)+,-\ *n* [*inter-* + *space* (n.); trans. of LL *interspatium*] **1 :** intervening space or time **:** INTERVAL: as **a :** a space between printed letters **b :** an air space in a building **c :** the space between two related body parts whether void or filled by another kind of structure ⟨an ~ between dorsal fins⟩ ⟨the skin of the ~ between the 5th and 6th ribs⟩ **2 :** interplanetary or interstellar space

**²in·ter·space** \ˌ==+\ *vt* [*inter-* + *space* (v.)] **:** to put an interval between (two things) **:** separate (as the members of a series) by spaces ⟨a line of *interspaced* hyphens⟩ ⟨periods of work *interspaced* by drinking sprees⟩

**in·ter·spatial** \"+\ *adj* [LL *interspatium* (fr. L *inter-* + *spatium* space) + E *-al* — more at SPACE] **:** of or relating to an interspace — **in·ter·spatially** \"+\ *adv*

**in·ter·specific** \"+\ *or* **in·ter·species** \"+\ *adj* [*inter-* + *specific* or *species*] **:** existing between species ⟨~ hybrid⟩

**in·ter·sper·sal** \ˌ==ˈspərsəl\ *n* -S [*intersperse* + *-al*] **:** INTERSPERSION

**in·ter·sperse** \ˌintərˈspərs, -təˈspə̄s, -pəis\ *vt* -ED/-ING/-S [L *interspersus* interspersed, fr. *inter-* + *sparsus,* past part. of *spargere* to strew, scatter — more at SPARK] **1 :** to scatter or set here and there among things **:** insert at intervals ⟨~ pictures in a book⟩ **2 :** to diversify or adorn with things set or scattered at intervals **:** place something at intervals in or among ⟨~ a book with pictures⟩

**in·ter·spers·ed·ly** \-sədlē\ *adv* **:** in an interspersed or scattered manner

**in·ter·sper·sion** \ˌintərˈspər\zhən, təˈspə̄\, -pəi\ *Brit usu & US sometimes* \shən\ *n* -S **:** the act or fact of interspersing or state of being interspersed: as **a :** the intermingling of kinds of organisms (as species) within an ecological community **b :** the state or degree of intermingling of one kind of organism with others ⟨certain forbs show a high level of ~ in grasslands⟩

**in·ter·sphere** \ˌintə(r)+\ *vi* [*inter-* + *sphere*] **:** to fall or come within the spheres or influences of one another

**in·ter·spicular** \"+\ *adj* [*inter-* + *spicular*] **:** situated between spicules

**in·ter·spinal** \"+\ *or* **in·ter·spinous** \"+\ *adj* [*inter-* + *spinal* or *spinous*] **:** lying between spines; *esp* **:** lying between the spines of adjacent vertebrae ⟨~ ligament⟩

**in·ter·spi·na·lis** \ˌintə(r)ˌspīˈnaləs, -nāl-, -näl-\ *n, pl* **inter·spina·les** \-a(ˌ)lēz, -ā(ˌ)lēz, -ä,lās\ [NL, fr. *inter-* + LL *spinalis* spinal — more at SPINAL] **:** any of various short muscles connecting the spinous processes of contiguous vertebrae

**in·ter·sporal** \ˌintə(r)+\ *adj* [*inter-* + *sporal*] **:** situated between spores

**in·ter·sprinkle** \"+\ *vt* [*inter-* + *sprinkle*] **:** INTERSPERSE

**in·ter·sta·di·al** \ˌintə(r)ˈstādēəl\ *n* -S [ISV *inter-* + NL *stadium* + ISV *-al*] **:** a substage within a glacial stage marking a temporary retreat of the ice

**in·ter·stage** \ˌintə(r)+\ *adj* [*inter-* + *stage*] **:** placed between the stages ⟨~ steam turbine⟩ ⟨~ radio amplifier⟩

**in·ter·state** \"+\ *also* **in·ter·statal** \"+\ *adj* [*inter-* + *state* or *statal*] **:** relating to the mutual relations of states **:** existing between or including different states — used esp. of the states of the U.S. and of the states of Australia ⟨~ commerce⟩ ⟨~ highway⟩

**interstate extradition** *or* **interstate rendition** *n* **:** extradition from one of the states of the U.S. or one of its territories according to procedure authorized by the U.S. Constitution and by acts of Congress

**in·ter·stellar** \"+\ *adj* [*inter-* + *stellar*] **:** located among the stars of the Milky Way or of other galaxies or passing from one star to another ⟨~ space⟩

**interstellar line** *n* **:** one of the dark spectral lines of a star or other distant celestial body that is caused by the absorption of atoms and molecules in the intervening interstellar gas and that does not partake of the Doppler shift of the spectral lines produced in the star itself

**in·ter·sterile** \"+\ *adj* [*inter-* + *sterile*] **:** characterized by sterility in which pollen of either variety will not fertilize the other **:** mutually incapable of fertilizing ⟨~ subspecies of a plant⟩

**in·ter·sterility** \"+\ *n* [*inter-* + *sterility*] **:** mutual infertility between related groups or individuals

**in·ter·sternite** \"+\ *n* [*inter-* + *sternite*] **:** an intersegmental plate on the undersurface of the insect abdomen

**in·ter·stice** \ən·ˈtərstəs, -təs-,-təis-\ *n, pl* **interstic·es** \÷ -stə,sēz, -stəsəz\ [F, fr. LL *interstitium,* fr. L *interstitus* (past part. of *intersistere* to stand still or stop in the middle of something, fr. *inter-* + *sistere* to place, stand) + *-ium* (n. suffix) — more at SOLSTICE] **1 :** a space that intervenes between one thing and another **:** a space between things (as the parts of a body) closely set **:** CRACK, CREVICE, INTERVAL ⟨~s of a wall⟩ ⟨the ~s of network⟩ **2 a :** an interval of time **b :** the intervals that the canon law requires between the reception of the various degrees of orders in the Roman Catholic Church

**in·ter·sticed** \-stəst\ *adj* **:** provided with interstices **:** having interstices between **:** situated at intervals ⟨~ fence palings⟩

**in·ter·stimulate** \ˌintə(r)+\ *vt* [*inter-* + *stimulate*] **:** to stimulate reciprocally — **in·ter·stimulation** \"+\ *n*

**¹in·ter·sti·tial** *also* **in·ter·sti·cial** \ˌintə(r)ˈstishəl\ *adj* [*interstitial* fr. LL *interstitium* + E *-al; intersticial* alter. (influenced by *interstice*) of *interstitial*] **1 :** relating to or situated in the interstices **2 :** situated within but not restricted to or characteristic of a particular organ or tissue — used chiefly of isolated cells of uncertain origin and function and of the fibrous tissues that bind together cells and tissues **3 :** affecting the interstitial tissues of an organ or part ⟨~ hepatitis⟩ **4 :** relating to, characteristic of, or being a solid structure in which usu. smaller atoms or ions of one or more nonmetals occupy holes between larger metal atoms or ions in a crystal lattice ⟨~ carbides . . . in which the small carbon atoms occupy ~ positions in the crystal lattices of the metals—Therald Moeller⟩ — **in·ter·sti·tial·ly** \-shəlē, -li\ *adv*

**²interstitial** \"\ *n* -S **:** a plant growing in the interstices of an association

**interstitial area** *n* **:** a transitional urban area (as between an industrial and residential district) that may be characterized by a degree of cultural isolation and consequent incidence of crime and delinquency

**interstitial-cell-stimulating hormone** *n* **:** LUTEINIZING HORMONE

**in·ter·sti·tium** \ˌ==ˈstishēəm\ *n, pl* **intersti·tia** \-ēə\ [LL — more at INTERSTICE] **1** *obs* **:** INTERSTICE **2** [NL, fr. LL] **:** interstitial tissue

**in·ter·stock** \ˈintə(r)+,-\ *n* **:** INTERMEDIATE STOCK

**in·ter·stratification** \ˌintə(r)+\ *n* [*inter-* + *stratification*] **:** the state of being interstratified

**in·ter·stratify** \"+\ *vb* [*inter-* + *stratify*] *vt* **:** to insert between other strata **:** arrange in alternate strata ⟨lava flow *interstratified* with sedimentary rock⟩ **~** *vi* **:** to settle in layers between other layers

**in·ter·stream** \"+\ *adj* [*inter-* + *stream*] **:** situated between streams ⟨~ divide⟩

**in·ter·strial** \"+\ *adj* [*inter-* + L *stria* + E *-al*] **:** situated between striae

**in·ter·subjective** \"+\ *adj* [*inter-* + *subjective*] **1 :** connecting or interrelating two consciousnesses or subjectivities ⟨~ communication⟩ **2 :** existing between, accessible to, or capable of being established for two or more subjects **:** OBJECTIVE ⟨~ reality of the physical world⟩ — **in·ter·subjectively** \"+\ *adv* — **in·ter·subjectivity** \"+\ *n*

**in·ter·tangle** \"+\ *vt* [*inter-* + *tangle*] **:** ENTANGLE, INTERTWINE — **in·ter·tanglement** \"+\ *n* -S

**in·ter·tentacular** \"+\ *adj* [*inter-* + *tentacular*] **:** situated between tentacles

**in·ter·tergal** \"+\ *adj* [*inter-* + *tergal*] **:** situated between tergites

**in·ter·tergite** \"+\ *n* [*inter-* + *tergite*] **:** one of the small plates intercalated between the tergites of some insects

**in·ter·terminal switching** \"+...-\ *n, pl* **interterminal switchings** [*inter-* + *terminal*] **:** the moving of cars from a point on one railroad line to a point on another when both points are within the switching limits of the same station or industrial switching district — compare INTRATERMINAL SWITCHING

**in·ter·territorial** \"+\ *adj* [*inter-* + *territorial*] **:** existing or carried on between territories

**in·ter·tessellation** \"+\ *n* [*inter-* + *tessellation*] **:** intricate or complex interrelation comparable to a mosaic design

**in·ter·testamental** \"+\ *adj* [*inter-* + *testamental*] **:** of, relating to, or being the period of approximately two centuries between the composition of the last canonical book of the Old Testament and the writing of the books of the New Testament

**in·ter·texture** \"+\ *n* [*inter-* + *texture*] **1 :** the act of interweaving or state of being interwoven **2 :** something that is interwoven

**in·ter·threaded** \"+\ *adj* [*inter-* + *threaded,* past part. of *thread*] **:** intercrossed by or as if by interwoven threads

**in·ter·tidal** \"+\ *adj* [*inter-* + *tidal*] **:** of, relating to, or being the part of the littoral zone that is above low-tide mark ⟨~ faunal elements⟩

**¹in·ter·tie** \"+\ *vt* [*inter-* + *tie*] **:** to connect or fasten mutually ⟨~ power systems⟩

**²in·ter·tie** \ˈintə(r)+,-\ *n* **1 :** a horizontal tie other than the sill and plate or other principal ties that secures uprights to one another in a framed work **2 :** the act of intertying

**in·ter·till** \ˌintə(r)+\ *vt* [*inter-* + *till*] **1 :** to cultivate between the rows of (a crop) **2 :** INTERCROP

**in·ter·tillage** \"+\ *n* [*inter-* + *tillage*] **:** cultivation between rows of a crop

**in·ter·tissued** \"+\ *adj* [*inter-* + *tissue* + *-ed;* trans. of MF *entretissu*] **:** INTERWOVEN

**in·ter·tone** \ˈintə(r)+,-\ *n* [*inter-* + *tone*] **:** a tone of intermediate pitch heard when two other tones of slightly different pitches are sounded simultaneously

**in·ter·tongue** \"+\ *vi* [*inter-* + *tongue*] **:** INTERLOCK ⟨beds of dark limestone . . . ~ with the white limestone —C.O.Dunbar⟩

**in·ter·tonic** \"+\ *adj* [*inter-* + *tonic*] **:** occurring between stressed syllables (as *-con-* in *uncontested*)

**in·ter·trabecular** \"+\ *adj* [*inter-* + *trabecular*] **:** situated between trabeculae

**in·ter·trade** \"+\ *n* [*inter-* + *trade*] **:** reciprocal trade

**in·ter·traffic** \"+\ *n* [*inter-* + *traffic*] **:** mutual traffic or exchange ⟨legitimate ~ between Russia and the border countries —*Newsweek*⟩ ⟨literary ~ between England and Spain has been sporadic and haphazard —*Times Lit. Supp.*⟩

**in·ter·tra·gi·an** \ˌintə(r)ˈtrājēən\ *adj* [*inter-* + NL *tragus* + E *-ian*] **:** situated between the tragus and antitragus ⟨~ canal⟩

**in·ter·transversalis** \ˌintə(r)+\ *n* [NL, fr. *inter-* + *transversalis*] **:** any of a series of small muscles connecting the transverse processes of contiguous vertebrae and most highly developed in the neck

**in·ter·trappean** \"+\ *adj* [*inter-* + ⁵*trap* + *-ean*] **:** lying between successive basaltic lava flows

**in·ter·tribal** \"+\ *adj* [*inter-* + *tribal*] **:** existing or occurring between tribes ⟨~ warfare⟩ **:** common to or shared by several tribes ⟨~ problems⟩

**in·ter·trig·i·nous** \ˌintə(r)ˈtrijənəs\ *adj* [L *intertriginosus,* fr. *intertrigin-, intertrigo* + *-osus* -ous] **:** exhibiting or affected with intertrigo

**in·ter·triglyph** \ˌintə(r)+\ *n* [*inter-* + *triglyph*] **:** METOPE

**in·ter·tri·go** \ˌintə(r)ˈtrī(ˌ)gō\ *n* -S [L, fr. *inter-* + *-trigo* (fr. *terere* to rub) — more at THROW] **:** inflammation produced by chafing of adjacent areas of skin

**in·ter·trochanteric** \ˌintə(r)+\ *adj* [*inter-* + *trochanteric*] **:** being or lying between trochanters

**in·ter·tropical** \"+\ *also* **in·ter·tropic** \"+\ *adj* [*inter-* + *tropical, tropic*] **:** situated between or within the tropics **:** relating to regions within the tropics **:** TROPICAL

**intertropical front** *n* **:** a zone of convergence of trade winds and equatorial winds often marked by heavy rains in tropical regions — compare DOLDRUM 3

**in·ter·tropics** \"+\ *n pl* **:** the zones between the tropics of Cancer and Capricorn or any region in them

**in·ter·trude** \ˌintə(r)·ˈtrüd\ *vt* -ED/-ING/-S [LL *intertrudere,* fr. L *inter-* + *trudere* to thrust, push — more at THREAT] **:** to bring in intrusively **:** INTERPOLATE

**in·ter·tubercular** \ˌintə(r)+\ *adj* [*inter-* + *tubercular*] **:** situated between tubercles

**in·ter·tubular** \"+\ *adj* [*inter-* + *tubular*] **:** lying between tubules

**in·ter·twine** \ˌintə(r)·ˈtwīn\ *vb* [*inter-* + *twine*] *vt* **:** to unite by twining one with another **:** ENTANGLE, INTERLACE, INTERTWIST ⟨the sex impulse is closely *intertwined* with the life impulse —Susanne K. Langer⟩ **~** *vi* **:** to twine about one another **:** become mutually entangled or involved ⟨theological concepts are inevitably *intertwining* —Robert Root⟩ — **in·ter·twine·ment** \-nmənt\ *n* -S

**in·ter·twin·ing·ly** *adv* **:** in an intertwining manner

**¹in·ter·twist** \ˌintə(r)+\ *vb* [*inter-* + *twist*] *vt* **:** to twist together one with another **:** INTERTWINE ⟨~*ed* roots⟩ ⟨so ~*ed* are our emotions —Roger Fry⟩ **~** *vi* **:** to twist about one another ⟨~*ing* tendrils⟩

**²in·ter·twist** \ˈ==+,-\ *n* **:** an act or fact of intertwisting **:** the state of being intertwisted **:** TANGLE ⟨peering through an ~ of vines and shrubs⟩

**in·ter·university** \ˌintə(r)+\ *adj* [*inter-* + *university*] **:** existing or carried on between universities ⟨~ research⟩

**in·ter·urban** \"+\ *adj* [*inter-* + *urban*] **:** going between or connecting cities or towns ⟨~ electric railways⟩ ⟨~ buses⟩

**in·ter·val** \ˈintə(r)vəl\ *n* -S [ME *intervalle,* fr. MF, fr. L *intervallum* space between ramparts, interval, fr. *inter-* + *vallum* rampart — more at WALL] **1 a :** a space of time between the recurrences of similar conditions or states **:** PAUSE ⟨~ between coughing spells⟩ ⟨~s of sanity⟩ ⟨~ of thousands of years between glaciations⟩ **b** *Brit* **:** INTERMISSION **c :** the time between two events or points of time ⟨firing at ~s of ten minutes⟩ ⟨~ between a lightning flash and the following thunder⟩ **d :** a portion of the total time cycle of a traffic signal during which the signal indications do not change **2 a :** a space between things **:** empty space between objects ⟨posts set up at regular ~s along the road⟩ ⟨buildings placed at wide ~s⟩ **b** (1) **:** the space between elements in military formation in the direction of width — contrasted with *distance* (2) **:** the distance between the foremasts of the guides of adjacent units in a compound naval formation **c :** the relative difference in pitch between two simultaneous or successive notes or tones **3 :** something that breaks or interrupts a uniform series or surface **:** an intervening part ⟨grazing land with brief ~s of forest⟩ ⟨the road follows a winding course except for a few straight ~s⟩ **4** *chiefly NewEng* **:** BOTTOM 6 **5 a :** the totality of numbers belonging to a given set of real numbers **b :** the totality of such numbers between and either including or excluding one or both of two end numbers of the set **c :** the totality of such numbers greater or less than and either including or excluding one of the numbers of the set **d :** a set of points on a line segment that represents one of these totalities **6 :** a gap between different qualities or states that may be ideally filled with intervening grades ⟨~ between savagery and culture⟩ ⟨~ between landlord and tenant, master and servant, was less —T.B.Macaulay⟩ **syn** see BREAK

**in·ter·vale** \-ˌvāl, -vəl\ *n* [fr. obs. E *intervale* interval, fr. ME *intervalle;* influenced in meaning by *vale*] *chiefly NewEng* **:** BOTTOM 6 ⟨~ land⟩

**in·ter·valed** \ˈintə(r)vəld\ *adj* [*interval* + *-ed*] **:** having intervals **:** interrupted at intervals **:** placed at intervals ⟨march is being made with platoons ~ at two yards —Peter Bowman⟩

**in·ter·val·lic** \ˌintə(r)ˈvalik\ *adj* [*interval* + *-ic*] **:** of or relating to an interval ⟨~ relationships of the notes of a melody⟩

**in·ter·val·om·e·ter** \ˌintə(r)vəˈläməd·ə(r)\ *n* [*interval* + *-o-* + *-meter*] **:** a device that operates a control at regular intervals; *specif* **:** an electrical device that regulates the interval between exposures made with an aerial camera

**interval timer** *n* **:** TIMER 1a

**in·ter·varietal** \ˌintə(r)+\ *adj* [*inter-* + *varietal*] **:** obtaining between varieties ⟨~ sterility⟩ ⟨~ differences in basal metabolism⟩

**in·ter·varsity** \"+\ *adj* [*inter-* + *varsity*] *Brit* **:** INTERUNIVERSITY ⟨~ sports⟩

**in·ter·vascular** \"+\ *adj* [*inter-* + *vascular*] **1 :** lying between or surrounded by blood vessels **2 :** situated within a seed vessel or vascular structure

**in·ter·vein** \"+\ *vt* [*inter-* + *vein*] **:** to interlace with or as if with veins

**in·ter·veinal** \"+\ *adj* [*inter-* + *veinal*] **:** situated or occurring between veins

**in·ter·vene** \ˌintə(r)ˈvēn\ *vb* -ED/-ING/-S [L *intervenire,* lit., to come between, fr. *inter-* + *venire* to come — more at COME] *vi* **1 :** to enter or appear as an irrelevant or extraneous feature or circumstance ⟨business seldom follows any projected course exactly, because unforeseeable developments . . . ~ —*Fortune*⟩ **2 :** to occur, fall, or come between points of time or events ⟨an instant *intervened* between the flash and the report⟩ ⟨*intervening* years⟩ **3 :** to come in or between by way of hindrance or modification **:** INTERPOSE ⟨~ to settle a quarrel⟩ ⟨death *intervened* soon after⟩ **4 :** to occur or lie between two things ⟨Paris, where the same city lay on both sides of an *intervening* river —*Amer. Guide Series: N. Y. City*⟩ **5 a :** to become a party to an action or other legal proceeding begun by others for the protection of an alleged interest **b :** to interfere usu. by force or threat of force in another nation's domestic affairs in order to protect the lives or property of the nationals of the interfering nation or to further some other purpose deemed vital to its welfare **~** *vt, obs* **:** to come between **:** interfere with

**in·ter·ven·er** *also* **in·ter·ve·nor** \-nə(r)\ *n* -S **:** one that intervenes

**in·ter·ve·nience** \ˌ==ˈvēnyən(t)s\ *n* -S **:** the act or fact of intervening **:** INTERVENTION

**¹in·ter·ve·nient** \ˌ==ˈvēnyənt\ *adj* [L *intervenient-, interveniens,* pres. part. of *intervenire*] **1 :** being or coming in incidentally or extraneously ⟨~ circumstances⟩ **2 :** situated or occurring between different points or events **:** INTERVENING ⟨deep ~ ravines —C.E.Craddock⟩ **3 :** INTERMEDIARY

**²intervenient** \"\ *n* -S **:** one that intervenes

**in·ter·ven·tion** \ˌ==ˈvenchən\ *n* -S [LL *intervention-, interventio,* fr. L *interventus* (past part. of *intervenire* to intervene) + *-ion-, -io* -ion] **1 :** the act or fact of intervening **:** INTERPOSITION ⟨~ of divine providence⟩ ⟨surgical ~⟩ **2 :** interference that may affect the interests of others: as **a** *civil law* **:** the act of a person who pays commercial paper for honor — called also *payment by intervention* **b :** the act by which a third person in order to protect his own interest interposes and becomes a party to a legal proceeding pending between other parties **c :** the interference of a country in the affairs of another country for the purpose of compelling it to do or forbear doing certain acts or of maintaining or altering the actual condition of its domestic affairs irrespective of its will — compare MEDIATION — **in·ter·ven·tion·al** \ˌ==ˈvenchənᵊl, -chnəl\ *adj*

**in·ter·ven·tion·ism** \-chəˌnizəm\ *n* -S **:** the theory or practice of intervening **:** interference (as by a government) in economic affairs at home or in political affairs of another country — compare ISOLATIONISM, LAISSEZ-FAIRE

**in·ter·ven·tion·ist** \-ˌnəst\ *n* -S **:** one that intervenes or favors intervention

**in·ter·ven·tor** \-ˈventə(r)\ *n* -S [L, fr. *interventus* (past part. of *intervenire* to intervene) + *-or* — more at INTERVENE] **1 :** a person designated by a church to reconcile parties and unite them in the choice of officers **2 :** a temporary administrator (as of a province in Central America or So. America) in time of disturbance

**¹in·ter·ventral** \ˌintə(r)+\ *adj* [*inter-* + *ventral*] **:** of or relating to the posterior pair of primitive ventral structural elements of a typical vertebra

**²interventral** \"\ *n* **:** an interventral cartilage or ossification

**in·ter·ventricular foramen** \"+ . . .-\ *n* [*inter-* + *ventricular*] **:** FORAMEN OF MONRO

**interversion** *n* -S [LL *interversion-, interversio,* fr. L *interversus* (past part. of *intervertere*) + *-ion-, -io* -ion] *obs* **:** MISAPPROPRIATION, EMBEZZLEMENT

**intervert** *vt* -ED/-ING/-S [L *intervertere,* lit., to turn aside, fr. *inter-* + *vertere* to turn — more at WORTH] **1** *obs* **:** to turn to a course or use other than the proper one **:** MISUSE; *esp* **:** EMBEZZLE **2** *obs* **:** CHANGE, INVERT

**in·ter·vertebral** \ˌintə(r)+\ *adj* [*inter-* + *vertebral*] **:** situated between vertebrae — **in·ter·vertebrally** \"+\ *adv*

**intervertebral disk** *n* **:** one of the tough elastic disks that are interposed between the centra of adjoining vertebrae and that consist of an outer fibrous ring enclosing an inner pulpy nucleus

**in·ter·vesicular** \"+\ *adj* [*inter-* + *vesicular*] **:** lying between vesicles

**¹in·ter·view** \ˈintə(r),vyü\ *n* [alter. (influenced by *inter-*) of earlier *enterview,* fr. MF *entrevue,* fr. fem. of *entrevu,* past part. of (*s'*)*entrevoir* to see one another, meet, fr. *entre-* inter- + *voir* to see — more at VIEW] **1 a :** a mutual sight or view **b :** a meeting face to face **:** a private conversation; *usu* **:** a formal meeting for consultation : CONFERENCE ⟨candidates for the position were called in for ~s⟩ **c** : a transient or secret meeting (as of lovers) ⟨the stolen ~s of those spring mornings —William Black⟩ **2 a** : a meeting in which a writer or reporter or radio or television commentator obtains information from someone for publication or broadcast **b** : the statement so obtained **c** : a news story reporting or reproducing such a conversation **3** : a scheduled meeting between a teacher and a student for purposes of instruction or counseling

**²interview** \"\ *vt* : to have an interview with : question or converse with esp. in order to obtain information or ascertain personal qualities ⟨~*ing* job applicants⟩ ⟨~ housewives about their color preferences⟩ ⟨~*ing* witnesses in a criminal investigation⟩ ⟨~*ed* the highest government officials and even strangers on buses —J.M.Mead⟩ ~ *vi* : to carry on an interview ⟨technique of ~*ing*⟩

**in·ter·view·ee** \¦==,vyüˌē\ *n* -s [*²interview* + *-ee*] : one that is interviewed ⟨~s voted 22 percent for giving food to western Europe —*Newsweek*⟩

**in·ter·view·er** \'==,vyüə(r)\ *n* : one that interviews: *specif* : a clerk who does preliminary interviewing of applicants for employment and arranges interviews with the employing officials

**in·ter·villous** \¦intə(r)+\ *adj* [*inter-* + *villous*] : situated between villi

**in·ter·visibility** \"+\ *n* : the quality or state of being mutually visible

**in·ter·visible** \"+\ *adj* [*inter-* + *visible*] : mutually visible ⟨~ surveying stations⟩

**in·ter·visit** \"+\ *vi* [alter. (influenced by *inter-*) of F *entrevisiter*, fr. MF, fr. *entre-* + *visiter* to visit — more at VISIT] : to exchange visits

**in·ter·visitation** \"+\ *n* [*inter-* + *visitation*] : exchange of visits : mutual visiting ⟨classroom ~s of schoolteachers⟩

**in·ter·vital** \"+\ *adj* [*inter-* + *vital*] : occurring between two lives

**in·ter vi·vos** \¦intə(r)¦vēˌvōs, -¦vīˌv-\ *adv* (*or adj*) [L] : between living persons : from one living person to another ⟨transaction *inter vivos*⟩ ⟨*inter vivos* trust⟩ — compare DONATIO MORTIS CAUSA

**in·ter·vo·cal·ic** \¦intə(r)(ˌ)vō¦kalik, -lēk\ *also* **in·ter·vocal** \¦==¦vōkəl\ *adj* [*inter-* + *vocalic* or *vocal*] : immediately preceded and immediately followed by a vowel ⟨~ consonant⟩ — **in·ter·vo·cal·i·cal·ly** \¦==(ˌ)==¦lək(ə)lē, -lēk-, -li\ *adv*

**in·ter·vo·lu·tion** \ˌintə(r)vəˈlüshən\ *n* [fr. *intervolve*, after such pairs as E *revolve*: *revolution*] : the state or fact of being intervolved or coiled up

**in·ter·volve** \¦intə(r)¦välv, -¦vȯlv\ *vb* -ED/-ING/-S [*inter-* + *-volve* (as in *involve*)] *vt* : to involve or roll up one within another ⟨mazes intricate, eccentric, *intervolved* —John Milton⟩ ~ *vi* : to twist or coil within one another

**in·ter·war** \¦intə(r)+\ *adj* [*inter-* + *war* (n.)] : lying between wars ⟨~ years⟩

**¹in·ter·weave** \"+\ *vb* [*inter-* + *weave*] *vt* **1** : to weave together ⟨*interweaving* a wool warp with a silk weft⟩ **2** : to intermingle or blend together ⟨*interweaving* his own insights . . . with letters and memoirs —Phoebe Adams⟩ ~ *vi* : INTERTWINE, INTERMINGLE

**²in·ter·weave** \'intə(r)+,-\ *n* : the act or result of interweaving ⟨~ of caste and religion . . . is so close that each merges into and is part of the other —Andrew Mellon⟩

**in·ter·wed** \¦intə(r)+\ *vi* [*inter-* + *wed*] : INTERMARRY

**in·ter·wind** \"+\ *vb* [*inter-* + *wind*] : INTERTWINE, INTERVOLVE

**in·ter·word** \"+\ *adj* [*inter-* + *word* (n.)] : occurring between words ⟨~ juncture⟩

**in·ter·work** \"+\ *vb* [*inter-* + *work*] *vt* : to work into something else : INTERWEAVE ~ *vi* : to work with or act upon each other : INTERACT

**in·ter·world** \'intə(r)+,-\ *n* [*inter-* + *world*] : a world existing between other worlds ⟨~s of the imagination⟩

**in·ter·wo·ven** \¦intə(r)¦wōvən\ *adj* [fr. past part. of *interweave*] : woven together in texture or construction

**in·ter·wo·ven·ness** \-n(n)əs\ *n* -ES : the quality or state of being interwoven : close or inseparable connection

**in·ter·wreathe** \¦intə(r)+\ *vb* [*inter-* + *wreathe*] : INTERTWINE

**in·ter·wrought** \"+\ *adj* [*inter-* + *wrought*] : worked into or through one another : complexly associated

**in·ter·xylary** \"+\ *adj* [*inter-* + *xylem* + *-ary*] : existing among xylem elements

**in·ter·zonal** \"+\ *or* **in·ter·zone** \"+\ *adj* [*inter-* + *zonal* or *zone*] : occurring or carried on between zones ⟨~ travel⟩ ⟨~ competition⟩

**in·ter·zooecial** \"+\ *adj* [*inter-* + *zooecial*] : existing between or among zooecia

**in·tes·ta·ble** \(ˈ)in¦testəbəl, ənˈt-\ *adj* [LL *intestabilis*, fr. L, execrable, accursed, fr. *in-* ¹in- + *testari* to be a witness, make a will + *-abilis* -able] **1** : not competent to make a will ⟨an ~ minor⟩ ⟨insane and ~⟩ **2** *obs* : incompetent to be a witness

**in·tes·ta·cy** \ənˈtestəsē, -si\ *n* [*¹intestate* + *-cy*] : the quality or state of being or dying intestate

**¹in·tes·tate** \ənˈteˌstā|t, -stə|, *usu* |d+V\ *adj* [ME, fr. L *intestatus*, fr. *in-* ¹in- + *testatus*, past part. of *testari* to be a witness, make a will, fr. *testis* witness — more at TESTAMENT] **1** : having made no valid will ⟨die ~⟩ **2** : not bequeathed or devised : not disposed of by will ⟨an ~ estate⟩ ⟨the administration of ~ property⟩

**²intestate** \"\ *n* -s : one who dies intestate

**in·tes·ti·nal** \ənˈtestᵊnᵊl, *in rapid speech* -s(ᵊ)nəl; *sometimes chiefly Brit* ¦in,te¦stīn-\ *adj* [prob. fr. MF, fr. *intestin* + *-al*] **1 a** : of or relating to the intestine ⟨the ~ tube⟩ ⟨~ ferments⟩ : affecting the intestine ⟨~ catarrh⟩ : taking place in the intestine ⟨~ digestion⟩ **b** : living within the intestine ⟨the ~ flora⟩ ⟨an ~ worm⟩ **2** : suggesting an intestine: as **a** : being internal or subterranean ⟨the rumbling ~ routes of the subways —Molly L. Bar-David⟩ **b** : intricately circuitous or involute ⟨tangled carvings in gluttonous ~ designs —Peggy Bacon⟩ **syn** see INNER

**intestinal calculus** *or* **intestinal concretion** *n* : DUST BALL

**intestinal canal** *n* : INTESTINE

**intestinal flu** *n* : any of various acute usu. transitory gastrointestinal conditions marked by nausea, vomiting, diarrhea, and griping pains

**intestinal fortitude** *n* : COURAGE, STAMINA, GUTS ⟨the qualities we have discussed — common sense, *intestinal fortitude*, leadership . . . are not the only ones desirable in a second lieutenant —*Infantry Jour.*⟩ ⟨only a man of powerful will and *intestinal fortitude* could have done these things —*Newsweek*⟩

**in·tes·ti·nal·ly** \-ᵊlē, -əl|, |i\ *adv* : in or upon the intestines

**¹in·tes·tine** \ənˈtestən, *chiefly dial* -ˌstīn\ *adj* [MF or L; MF *intestin*, fr. L *intestinus*, fr. *intus* within — more at ENT-] **1 a** : of or relating to the internal affairs of a state or country — usu. used of something evil or troublesome ⟨an ~ disorder⟩ ⟨an ~ calamity⟩ ⟨~ war⟩ **b** : of or relating to the internal parts of the body **2** : INWARD ⟨an ~ necessity⟩ **3** *obs* : INTERNAL **syn** see INNER

**²intestine** \"\ *n* -s [MF *intestin*, fr. L *intestinum*, fr. neut. of *intestinus*] **1** : the tubular portion of the alimentary canal that in the vertebrate lies posterior to the stomach from which it is separated by the pyloric valve and consists typically of a slender but long anterior part made up of duodenum, jejunum, and ileum which function in digestion and assimilation of nutrients and a broader shorter posterior part made up usu. of cecum, colon, and rectum which serve chiefly to extract moisture from the by-products of digestion and evaporate them into feces — often used in pl. ⟨the shot pierced his ~s in several places⟩ — see LARGE INTESTINE, SMALL INTESTINE **2** : the entire alimentary canal esp. when more or less straight and tubular (as in many invertebrates)

**in·tes·ti·ni·form** \-stənəˌfȯrm\ *adj* [*²intestine* + *-iform*] : like an intestine in form

**in·tes·ti·no·intestinal** \ən¦testə(ˌ)nō+\ *adj* [*²intestine* + *-o-* + *intestinal*] : originating in and acting on the intestine ⟨an ~ reflex⟩

**in·tes·ti·no·vesical** \"+\ *adj* [*²intestine* + *-o-* + *vesical*] : of or relating to the intestine and bladder

**in·tex·ine** \'inˌtekˌs|ēn, |ᵊn\ *or* **in·tex·tine** \-kˌst|\ *n* -s [*intexine* fr. G, fr. *int-* (fr. L *intus* within) + *exine*; *intextine* alter. (influenced by *extine*) of *intexine*] : the inner membrane of the exine when this exists in two layers

**intg** *abbr* interrogate; interrogator

**inthrall** *or* **inthral** *vt* **inthralled; inthralled; inthralling; inthralls** *or* **inthrals** [by alter. (influenced by *²in-*)] : ENTHRALL

**inthralment** *n* -s *archaic* : ENTHRALLMENT

**inthronization** *n* -s [MF or ML; MF *intronisation*, fr. ML *inthronization-*, *inthronizatio*, fr. LL *inthronizatus* (past part. of *inthronizare* to enthrone, modif. — influenced by L *in-* ²in- — of Gk *enthronizein*) + L *-ion-*, *-io* -ion — more at ENTHRONIZE] : ENTHRONEMENT, ENTHRONIZATION

**¹inthrow** \'==,=\ *n* [*⁴in* + *throw* (after *throw in*, v.)] : the act or process of throwing soil toward the crop by the cultivating gangs of a row-crop cultivator; *also* : the amount of soil thrown

**²inthrow** \"\ *vt* : RIDGE *vt* 2b

**intice** *archaic var of* ENTICE

**in·ti·chi·u·ma** \ˌintēchēˈümə\ *n, pl* **intichiuma** *usu cap* [native name in central Australia] : an Australian magical ceremony having as its object the increase of a clan's totemic species

**in·til** *or* **in·till** \ənˈtil\ *prep* [ME, fr. *²in* + *til*, *till* to — more at TILL] *chiefly Scot* : IN, INTO

**in·ti·ma** \ˈintəmə\ *n, pl* **in·ti·mae** \-ˌmē, -ˌmī\ *or* **intimas** [NL, fr. L, fem. of *intimus* innermost] **1** : the innermost coat of an organ (as a blood vessel or lymphatic) consisting (as in larger blood vessels) of an endothelial lining backed by a layer of connective tissue and one of elastic tissue **2** : the innermost coat of a trachea of an insect — **in·ti·mal** \-məl\ *adj*

**in·ti·ma·cy** \ˈintəməsē, -si\ *n* -ES [*²intimate* + *-cy*] **1** : the state of being intimate: as **a** : close association or connection ⟨the furnishings suggested at least some ~ with the outside world —C.L.Jones⟩ ⟨in the city you are more free from unwelcome ~ —M.R.Cohen⟩ **b** : close personal relationship esp. marked by affection or love (as in close friendship) ⟨a long ~ with the governor of the state⟩ ⟨long continued ~ with the fields and meadows about him —*Encyc. Americana*⟩ ⟨a common danger had made of these two enemies friends . . . and now that the danger had passed their ~ was done —Jack McLaren⟩ **c** : a relationship marked by depth of knowledge or broadness of information ⟨his ~ with the history of the middle ages⟩ **d** : complete intermixture, compounding, or interweaving ⟨would call for some effort to disentangle a relationship of things marked by such ~⟩ **2** : the quality or state of being careful and searching in notation of details ⟨an ~ of observation which few scientists can equal —H.S.Canby⟩ **3 a** : a sexual liberty taken ⟨resented the pawing *intimacies* of the man who was driving the car —Erle Stanley Gardner⟩; *specif* : sexual intercourse ⟨denied charges of having an affair with a married woman . . . though she said ~ between them had taken place about 25 times —*New York Enquirer*⟩ or an instance of it ⟨indications that she had recently experienced an ~ —R.O.Lawson & S.D.Greene⟩ **b** : an objectionable liberty taken with the person ⟨became embarrassingly familiar with the *intimacies* of fame —Green Peyton⟩ **4** : the quality of affecting one in a usu. pleasant intimate personal way ⟨music marked by an ~ of expression⟩ **5** : the state of seeming to be in a close friendly personal relationship — used of inanimate things ⟨the almost cloistered ~ of much of the route —*Amer. Guide Series: Vt.*⟩ **6** : the capacity for establishing oneself quickly in an intimate personal relationship ⟨only one other man possessing this curious ~ with wild things —Edison Marshall⟩

**in·ti·ma·do** \ˌintəˈmä(ˌ)dō\ *n* -s [prob. alter. (influenced by Sp *-ado*, as in *renegado*) of *³intimate*] *archaic* : an intimate friend : INTIMATE

**¹in·ti·mate** \ˈintəˌmāt, *usu* -ād+V\ *vt* -ED/-ING/-S [LL *intimatus*, past part. of *intimare* to make known, fr. L *intimus* innermost, superl. of (assumed) OL *interus* inward, on the inside — more at INTERIOR] **1** : to give notice of : ANNOUNCE, NOTIFY **2** : to impart or communicate with delicate or indirect wording or covert slight gesture without forthright blunt expression ⟨said that he . . . might not be able to say all that he thought, thus *intimating* to his hearers that they might infer that he meant more —O.W.Holmes †1935⟩ **syn** see SUGGEST

**²in·ti·mate** \-mət, *usu* -əd+V\ *adj* [LL *intimatus*, past part. of *intimare* to make known; E *intimate* influenced in meaning by L *intimus* innermost] **1 a** : of or relating to an inner character or essential nature : INNERMOST : characteristic of the genuine core of something ⟨it is in the purposes he entertains . . . that an individual most completely . . . realizes his ~ selfhood —John Dewey⟩ **b** : belonging to or characterizing the inmost true self : indicative of one's deepest nature ⟨his ~ reflections⟩ **2** : marked by a very close physical, mental, or social association, connection, or contact: as **a** : showing complete intermixture, compounding, fusion : thoroughly or closely interconnected, interrelated, interwoven ⟨the ~ relations . . . between economics, politics, and legal principles —V.L.Parrington⟩ ⟨an ~ mixture of rock particles⟩ ⟨an ~ affiliation of house and garden —*Amer. Guide Series: N.Y.*⟩ **b** : showing depth of detailed knowledge and understanding and broadness of information from or as if from long association, near contact, or thorough study and observation ⟨this girl, so ~ with nature —W.H.Hudson †1922⟩ ⟨an ~ knowledge of admiralty law —H.W.H.Knott⟩ **c** : marked by or as if by knowledge of esp. personal details which only an eyewitness or very close confidant might have ⟨of St. Francis and St. Bernard their ~ biographers assure us that . . . they . . . never allowed themselves actual laughter —G.G.Coulton⟩ **d** : marked by or as if by a warmly personal attitude esp. developing through long or close association, by friendliness, unreserved communication, mutual appreciation and interest ⟨pretend that they are in smart society and on ~ terms with people they slander —Oscar Wilde⟩ : manifesting warm personal interest ⟨his voice low, ~, full of meaning —Aurelia Levi⟩ : arousing a warm personal response ⟨a lyrical and ~ painting⟩ **e** : showing or fostering close personal interests and relations rather than those colder and more distant, formal, or routine : suggesting or furthering easy unreserved personal expression, feeling, or relationships through smallness, exclusiveness, limitation, or privacy ⟨an ~ sense of being a member of some mystic brotherhood —W.S.Maugham⟩ ⟨the ~ politics of the eighteenth century were an involved web of human passions —J.H.Plumb⟩ ⟨two plush rooms, one formal, the other cozy and ~ —T.H.Fielding⟩ ⟨an ~ theater that served coffee between its films⟩ ⟨an ~ cocktail lounge⟩; *also* : designed or composed chiefly for presentation to a small group ⟨~ opera⟩ ⟨~ music⟩ **f** : marked by or appropriate to very close personal relationships : marked by or befitting a relationship of love, warm or ardent liking, deep friendship, or mutual cherishing ⟨always ~ relations between a mother and her young child —Edward Westermarck⟩ ⟨their hand grasp was very ~ and mutually comprehending —Arnold Bennett⟩ **g** : of, relating to, or befitting deeply personal (as emotional, familial, or sexual) matters or matters usu. kept private or discreet ⟨to his intensely aristocratic nature this discussion of his ~ family affairs . . . was most abhorrent —A. Conan Doyle⟩ ⟨clean-minded youth horrifies its elders by facing the ~ facts of life —G.A.Bartlett⟩ **h** : engaged in or marked by sexual relations : SEXUAL, MARITAL ⟨ladies were supposed to be without sexual desire . . . in their ~ relations with their husbands they consented graciously —W.E.Woodward⟩ **i** : worn next to the skin ⟨~ underwear⟩ : worn in the home ⟨an ~ negligee⟩ **j** : designed or prepared (as by waterproofing) for immediate contact with something to be wrapped ⟨the efficiency of ~ wraps and carton overwraps in preventing corrosion —*Corrosion & Material Protection*⟩ ⟨aluminum foil laminated to paper finds use as an ~ wrapper for a variety of products —N.A.Cooke⟩ **syn** see FAMILIAR

**³intimate** \"\ *n* -s : one who associates or has associated intimately (as with a person or place) ⟨writes as one who . . . has been an ~ of the Parisian scene —R.J.Goldwater⟩ : an intimate friend or confidant ⟨counted a banker among his ~s⟩ **syn** see FRIEND

**in·ti·mate·ly** \-mətlē, -li\ *adv* : in an intimate manner ⟨the physical and the economic background of poverty are most ~ related —P.E.James⟩ ⟨a city she knows ~ —*Americas*⟩ ⟨every one of which he could have named ~ had he put his memory to it —Kay Boyle⟩ ⟨the author leads his audience easily and ~ —S.W.Reed⟩

**in·ti·mate·ness** \-mətnəs\ *n* -ES : INTIMACY

**in·ti·mat·er** \-ˌmād·ə(r), -ātə-\ *n* -s [*¹intimate* + *-er*] : one that intimates

**in·ti·ma·tion** \ˌintəˈmāshən\ *n* -s [ME *intimacion*, fr. MF *intimation*, fr. LL *intimation-*, *intimatio*, fr. *intimatus* (past part. of *intimare*) + L *-ion-*, *-io* -ion] **1** : the act of intimating or the state of being intimated: as **a** : ANNOUNCEMENT, NOTIFICATION **b** : an indirect usu. hinted suggestion or notice ⟨~s of immortality —William Wordsworth⟩ ⟨gave only ~ of the fact he was guilty of rudeness⟩ **2** : something intimated ⟨never learned what his ~ was⟩

**in·time** \aⁿˈtēm\ *adj* [F, fr. L *intimus* innermost] : INTIMATE

**in·tim·i·date** \ənˈtiməˌdāt, *usu* -ād+V\ *vt* -ED/-ING/-S [ML *intimidatus*, past part. of *intimidare*, fr. L *in-* ²in- + *timidus* timid] : to make timid or fearful : inspire or affect with fear : FRIGHTEN ⟨despite his imposing presence and all the grandeur surrounding him, I was not *intimidated* —Polly Adler⟩; *esp* : to compel to action or inaction (as by threats) ⟨charged with *intimidating* public officials to get the government to buy machine guns he was selling —*Time*⟩

**syn** INTIMIDATE, COW, BULLDOZE, BULLY, BROWBEAT agree in meaning to frighten or coerce by frightening means into submission or obedience. INTIMIDATE suggests a display or application (as of force or learning) so as to cause fear or a sense of inferiority and a consequent submission ⟨most of these officials have been badly *intimidated* by the specter of a summons to appear before a Congressional committee —*New Republic*⟩ ⟨many authors and publishers are not merely *intimidated* by the thought of footnotes; they are positively terrified —G.W. Sherburn⟩ COW implies a reduction to a state where the spirit is broken or all courage lost ⟨*cowed* into cooperation through fear of the gangsters —Michael Blundell⟩ ⟨*cowed* the gang with his detective's star —J.T.Farrell⟩ ⟨a ship's company *cowed* to groveling point —John Masefield⟩ BULLDOZE, in its earliest sense signifying to intimidate or coerce by violence, now often can mean to force into line by an application of great force, not necessarily implying though often involving intimidation ⟨a *bulldozed* people, shaking with the ague of the terrorized —W.L.Sullivan⟩ ⟨the sheer strength of his reputation and the force of his will *bulldozing* them into making loans —F.L. Allen⟩ ⟨the highly reputable gentlemen who were *bulldozed* into taking this responsibility have resigned —Robert Moses⟩ BULLY implies intimidation or attempts to intimidate by swaggering overbearing behavior or by the use of unfair force ⟨a mild, long-suffering woman will permit her husband to *bully* her for years, whereas another woman will react violently to the first beating —Jacob Fried⟩ ⟨inevitable that the older boys should become mischievous louts; they *bullied* and tormented and corrupted the younger boys —H.G.Wells⟩ BROWBEAT implies a cowing by scornful contemptuous treatment, esp. intellectual or moral oppression ⟨were *browbeaten* into the hardest and most menial tasks —F.V.W.Mason⟩ ⟨no wish to *browbeat* the reader into accepting my theory of myself or of anything else —George Santayana⟩ ⟨*browbeat* students by a great display of learning⟩

**in·tim·i·da·tion** \ənˌtiməˈdāshən\ *n* -s [F, fr. MF, fr. *intimider* (fr. ML *intimidare* to intimidate) + *-ation*] : the act of intimidating or the state of being intimidated ⟨the voters were kept from the polls by ~⟩ ⟨cringed to see the woman's ~ before her husband's cruelty⟩

**in·tim·i·da·tor** \ənˈtiməˌdād·ə(r), -ātə-\ *n* -s : one that intimidates

**in·tim·i·da·to·ry** \-ˌdəˌtōrē, *chiefly Brit* ¦==¦dātəri *or* -ā·tri\ *adj* [*intimidate* + *-ory*] : tending to intimidate ⟨an ~ array of obstacles —F.S.Mitchell⟩ : designed to intimidate ⟨the similarity, in some species, between ~ and courtship displays —E.A. Armstrong⟩

**in·ti·mism** \ˈintəˌmizəm\ *n* -s [*intimist* + *-ism*] : a principle or practice among painters (as in early 20th century France) of selecting as subject matter familiar or intimate scenes or occasions from their own everyday life — compare GENRE

**¹in·ti·mist** \-məst\ *n* -s *often cap* [F *intimiste*, fr. *intime* intimate + *-iste* -ist] : an intimist painter

**²intimist** \"\ *adj, often cap* **1** : of, relating to, or practicing intimism **2** *of fiction* : dealing chiefly with intimate and private esp. psychological experiences ⟨the peculiarly modern feeling of individual helplessness that the war brought into . . . people's consciousness, and it made sense that emotion as the ~ novel does not as a rule —Anthony West⟩

**in·tim·i·ty** \ənˈtimədˌē\ *n* -ES [F *intimité*, fr. *intime* intimate + *-ité* -ity] *archaic* : intimate privacy

**in·tinc·tion** \ənˈtiŋ(k)shən\ *n* -s [LL *intinction-*, *intinctio* immersion, fr. L *intinctus* (past part. of *intingere* to dip in, fr. *in* ²in- + *tingere* to dip, moisten) + *-ion-*, *-io* -ion — more at TINGE] : the administration of the sacrament of Communion by dipping the bread in the wine and giving both together to the communicant

**in·tine** \ˈinˌtēn, -tīn\ *n* -s [prob. fr. G, fr. L *intus* within, in — more at ENT-] : the inner of the two layers forming the wall of a spore (as a pollen grain) — called also *endosporium*; compare EXINE, PERINIUM

**intire** *archaic var of* ENTIRE

**in·ti·sy** \ˈintəsē\ *n* -ES [NL (specific epithet of *Euphorbia intisy*)] : a spurge (*Euphorbia intisy*) from which rubber-yielding latex is obtained in limited quantities

**intitle** *archaic var of* ENTITLE

**intitulate** *vt* -ED/-ING/-S [LL *intitulatus*, past part. of *intitulare*, fr. L *in-* ²in- + *titulus* title] *obs* : ENTITLE

**in·tit·u·la·tion** \ənˌtichəˈlāshən\ *n* -s [MF or ML; MF, fr. ML *intitulation-*, *intitulatio* name, title, fr. LL *intitulatus* (past part. of *intitulare*) + L *-ion-*, *-io* -ion] *archaic* : the act of giving a title to; *also* : the title itself

**in·tit·ule** \ənˈti(ˌ)chül, -ˌchəl\ *vt* -ED/-ING/-S [MF *intituler*, fr. LL *intitulare*] *Brit* : to give a title or designation to — now used chiefly of a legislative act

**intl** *abbr* international

**intmd** *abbr* intermediate

**intmt** *abbr* intermittent

**intn** *abbr* intention

**in·to** \ˈintə, -ntü, -n(ˌ)tü, +V *often* -ntəw\ *prep* [ME, fr. OE *intō*, fr. *²in* + *tō* to] **1 a** — used as a function word primarily denoting motion so directed as to terminate, if continued, when the position denoted by *in* has been reached and usu. after a verb that carries the idea of motion or a word implying or suggesting motion or passage to indicate a place or thing entered or penetrated or enterable or penetrable by or as if by a movement from the outside to an interior part ⟨came ~ the house⟩ ⟨the river ran ~ the sea⟩ ⟨traveled ~ the next state⟩ ⟨a route ~ the wilderness⟩ ⟨imports ~ this country⟩ ⟨the mountains merge ~ the plain⟩ ⟨brought ~ membership in the club⟩ ⟨off we go ~ the wide blue yonder⟩ but sometimes in constructions in which the idea of motion is carried by the very use of *into* in preference to *in* ⟨among the first ~ the field —*N. Y. Herald Tribune*⟩ ⟨they were ~ their clothes and on deck — H.A.Chippendale⟩ ⟨the child was ~ the cookie jar as soon as no one was looking⟩ ⟨stores them away ~ an inner pocket — A.J.Coutts⟩ ⟨baptized ~ the Catholic Church⟩ **b** : in toward ⟨sailed the boat ~ the pier⟩ ⟨the batter leaned ~ the pitch⟩ ⟨it stood close ~ a fine cottonwood grove —Willa Cather⟩ ⟨keeping well ~ the foot or lower slopes of the scarpside — S.G.Joseph⟩ **2** *chiefly Scot* : IN 1a(1) ⟨living ~ his new house⟩ **3 a** — used as a function word indicating a state or condition assumed, brought into being (as by force), or allowed to come about ⟨enter ~ bliss⟩ ⟨drive someone ~ despair⟩ ⟨fall ~ decay⟩ ⟨land brought ~ cultivation⟩ ⟨collapses ~ hysterics and quits —H.F. & Katharine Pringle⟩ **b** — used as a function word that usu. follows words carrying an idea of alteration or suggesting or implying alteration and that indicates a form or condition assumed often with loss of original or essential identity and emergence as something else ⟨came ~ being⟩ ⟨develop ~ a butterfly⟩ ⟨compounds resolved ~ simple substances⟩ ⟨translate a book ~ French⟩ ⟨divide a hospital ~ several wards⟩ ⟨fold a paper ~ four⟩ ⟨the barn was remodeled ~ a garage⟩ ⟨the land was plowed ~ broad ridges and hollows —L.D.Stamp⟩ ⟨the book went ~ edition after edition⟩ ⟨divide the theme ~ a beginning, a middle, and an ending⟩ **4** — used as a function word to indicate something accepted or acquired (as for possession) ⟨talked himself ~ a good job⟩ ⟨came ~ an inheritance⟩ **5 a** (1) *obs* : TO, TOWARD (2) : toward and as far as (something considered central) ⟨go ~

town⟩ ⟨go ~ market⟩ **b :** in the direction of ⟨looking ~ the sun⟩ ⟨looked ~ his plate and said nothing⟩ ⟨turned ~ the wind⟩ **c :** up to : as far as ⟨since then — right ~ today — you and I have enjoyed . . . the economic idea of roaring production —Sylvia F. Porter⟩ **d :** AGAINST 2a ⟨run ~ a wall⟩ ⟨fell ~ a fence⟩ ⟨the mixture is run ~ an endless moving wire screen —*Amer. Guide Series: La.*⟩ **6 a** — used as a function word to indicate the dividend in mathematical division ⟨dividing 3 ~ 6 gives 2⟩ **b** *archaic* **:** BY : together with — used with *multiply* **7** — used as a function word to indicate a set of circumstances, a function, action, or occupation entered upon or taken on ⟨get ~ trouble⟩ ⟨go ~ business⟩ ⟨force ~ compliance⟩ ⟨might be tortured ~ divulging military information —G.A. Craig⟩ **8 a** — used as a function word indicating something in which a literal or figurative insertion or introduction is made or in which there is inclusion ⟨pushed the hose ~ the pipe⟩ ⟨read a new meaning ~ a sentence⟩ ⟨water enters ~ the composition of the human body⟩ ⟨marry ~ an influential family⟩ ⟨introduced a bill ~ the legislature⟩ ⟨play a song ~ a microphone⟩ ⟨soon got ~ the act⟩ **b** — used as a function word to indicate something penetrated by the sight or insight or by an intellectual process (as investigation, reflection, or analysis) ⟨peer ~ the distance⟩ ⟨look ~ the future⟩ ⟨search ~ his motives⟩ ⟨inquire ~ his activities⟩ ⟨insights ~ religion and poetry⟩ ⟨seek to look . . . ~ the hopes and fears of men and women —F.D.Roosevelt⟩ **c :** so as to impress, dent, or force inward ⟨pressed the marble ~ the palm of his hand⟩ ⟨force the grease ~ the bearings⟩ **d** — used as a function word to indicate something slowed or stopped in its course or impeded by interruption ⟨~ the path of a train⟩ ⟨stepped ~ a punch on the jaw⟩ ⟨butt ~ their conversation⟩ **e :** so as to permeate or fill ⟨gases expanding ~ a vacuum —S.F.Mason⟩ **f :** in direct connection or contact with ⟨I am ~ a heavy fish . . . have already taken a twelve-inch bass on the same plug —Paul Brooks⟩ **9** — used as a function word indicating a period of time or an extent of space of which a portion is used or occupied ⟨sang far ~ the night⟩ ⟨went some distance ~ the next month before paying the bill⟩ ⟨stretched ~ the distance⟩ **10** — used as a function word to indicate something contributed to, paid, received in exchange, or dealt with by handling in some way ⟨all the sugar we had went ~ the cake⟩ ⟨his pay check went ~ the rent⟩ ⟨their spare cash went ~ some new furniture⟩ ⟨all their brain power went ~ solving the problem⟩ **11 :** so as to include ⟨the company then expanded ~ bakery machines and specialized sewing machines —*Time*⟩

**in·to·cos·trin** \ˌintəˈkästrən\ *n* -s [fr. *Intocostrin*, a trademark] **:** an extract of purified curare

**in·toed** \ˈin-ˌtōd\ *adj* [²*in* + *toed*] **:** having the toes turned inward

**in·tolerability** \(ˌ)in, ən+\ *n* **:** the quality or state of being intolerable

**¹in·tolerable** \(ˈ)in-, ən-+\ *adj* [ME, fr. L *intolerabilis*, fr. *in-* ¹in- + *tolerabilis* tolerable] **1 :** not tolerable **:** not capable of being borne or endured **:** UNBEARABLE ⟨~pain⟩ ⟨~ anguish⟩ ⟨an ~ burden⟩ ⟨an almost ~ beauty —Bernard DeVoto⟩ **2** *archaic* **:** not to be withstood **:** IRRESISTIBLE **3 :** EXTREME, EXCESSIVE ⟨sometimes gives way to an ~ degree of sentimentality over some of his women —C.H.Sykes⟩ ⟨scarcely to have made an impression upon the ~ multitude of volumes which everyone is supposed to have read —Arnold Bennett⟩ ⟨an ~ amount of airless inner space —Lewis Mumford⟩ — **in·tolerableness** \"+\ *n* — **in·tolerably** \"+\ *adv*

**²intolerable** \"\ *adv* **:** INTOLERABLY

**in·tolerance** \"+\ *n* [F *intolérance*, fr. L *intolerantia*, fr. *intolerant-, intolerans* intolerant + *-ia* -y] **1 :** the quality or state of being intolerant: as **a :** the lack of an ability to endure ⟨an ~ of strong light⟩; *specif* **:** exceptional sensitivity to a drug, food, or other substance ⟨~ to quinine⟩ **b :** ILLIBERALITY, BIGOTRY **2 :** an instance of intolerance

**in·tolerancy** \"+\ *n* [L *intolerantia*] *archaic* **:** INTOLERANCE

**¹in·tolerant** \"+\ *adj* [F or L; F *intolérant*, fr. L *intolerant-, intolerans*, fr. *in-* ¹in- + *tolerant-, tolerans* tolerant] **1 :** unable to endure ⟨a plant ~ of direct sunlight⟩ ⟨a constitution ~ of excesses⟩ **2 a :** unwilling to endure ⟨~ of all strangers⟩ **b :** unwilling to tolerate a difference of opinion or feeling esp. in religious matters **:** refusing to allow others the free enjoyment of their opinions or worship **:** BIGOTED **c :** unwilling to grant equal social, political, or professional rights; *specif* **:** unwilling to tolerate social equality with one of another racial group — **in·tol·er·ant·ly** *adv*

**²intolerant** \"\ *n* -s **:** an intolerant person

**in·tolerating** \(ˈ)in-, ən-+\ *adj* [¹*in-* + *tolerating*, pres. part. of *tolerate*] *archaic* **:** INTOLERANT

**in·toleration** \(ˌ)in-, ən-+\ *n* [¹*in-* + *toleration*] **:** INTOLERANCE

**intomb** *archaic var of* ENTOMB

**in·ton·able** \ən-ˈtōnəbəl\ *adj* **:** that can be intoned

**in·to·na·co** \ən-ˈtänəˌkō, -tōn-\ *n* -s [It, fr. *intonacare* to coat with plaster, fr. (assumed) VL *intunicare*, fr. L *in-* ²in- + *tunica* tunic, coating] **:** the finishing coat of fine plaster in fresco painting — compare ARRICCIO

**in·to·nate** \ˈintəˌnāt, -tō-, *usu* -ād·+V\ *vt* -ED/-ING/-S [ML *intonatus*, past part. of *intonare*] **1 :** INTONE **2 :** to sound esp. with a particular intonation **:** UTTER

**in·to·na·tion** \ˌ≈≈ˈnāshən\ *n* -s [ML *intonation-, intonatio*, fr. *intonatus* (past part. of *intonare*) + L *-ion-, -io* -ion] **1 :** the act of intoning: **a (1) :** the act of singing the opening phrase of a plainsong, psalm, or canticle **(2) :** the act of musically reciting usu. in monotone any part of a liturgy **b (1) :** the act of sounding musical tones (as of a scale) **(2) :** the singing and playing of music according to the aural perception of the prevailing standard of accuracy in pitch **c :** the act of reciting in a singing voice usu. in a monotone **2 :** something intoned; *specif* **:** the opening tones of a Gregorian chant preceding the reciting note usu. sung by the priest alone **3 a :** the manner of singing, playing, or uttering tones ⟨spoke with a foreign ~⟩ ⟨played the piece with a romantic ~⟩ **b :** pitch phenomena in speech; *esp* **:** such a phenomenon insofar as it makes a syntactical or emotional distinction (as between a declarative and interrogative statement) — **in·to·na·tion·al** \ˌ≈≈ˈnāshənᵊl, -shnəl\ *adj*

**intonation pattern** *n* **:** a unit of speech melody in a language or dialect that contributes to the total meaning of an utterance ⟨one's *intonation pattern* in the utterance of *dead* may reveal one's emotional reaction to an announcement of death⟩ ⟨one *intonation pattern* makes *leave* a command, another makes it a question⟩

**in·tone** \ən-ˈtōn\ *vb* -ED/-ING/-S [alter. (influenced by ML *intonare*) of earlier *entone*, fr. ME *entonen*, fr. MF *entoner*, fr. ML *intonare*, fr. L *in-* ²in- + *tonus* tone] *vt* **1 a :** to utter in musical or prolonged tones **:** recite in singing tones or in a monotone ⟨~ the service⟩ ⟨~ the hours of the night⟩ ⟨*intoning* the marriage ceremony with the regular orthodox allowance for nasal recitative —T.L.Peacock⟩ **b :** to sing (as a song) or play (as a sonata) with special attention to the continuity of sound **2 :** to sing usu. as a solo or semichorus (the opening phrase of a plainsong, psalm, or canticle) ~ *vi* **:** to utter something in singing tones or in monotone (as in chanting) — **in·ton·er** \-ōnə(r)\ *n*

**in·to·neme** \ən-ˈtōˌnēm\ *n* -s [*intone* + *-eme*] **:** INTONATION PATTERN

**in·tone·ment** \-ōnmənt\ *n* -s **:** the act of intoning or the state of being intoned ⟨the ~ of the service⟩

**intoothed** \ˈ≈ˌ≈\ *adj* [²*in* + *toothed*] **:** having the teeth turned inward

**in·tor·sion** *or* **in·tor·tion** \ən-ˈtȯrshən\ *n* -s [LL *intortion-, intortio* action of curling, fr. L *intortus* (past part. of *intorquēre* to twist, fr. *in-* ²in- + *torquēre* to twist) + *-ion-, -io* -ion — more at TORTURE] **:** a winding, bending, or twisting around (as of the stem of a plant); *specif* **:** inward rotation (as of a body part) about an axis or a fixed point — compare EXTORSION

**in·tort·ed** \-rd·əd\ *adj* [L *intortus* (past part. of *intorquēre*) + E *-ed*] **:** twisted inward or in and out **:** TWINED, WREATHED, TANGLED

**in to·to** \in-ˈtōd·(ˌ)ō, -tō(ˌ)tō\ *adv* [L, on the whole] **:** TOTALLY, ENTIRELY, ALTOGETHER ⟨promised to publish the book *in toto*⟩ ⟨accepted the plan *in toto*⟩

**intower** *vt* [²*in-* + *tower* (n.)] *obs* **:** to imprison in a tower (as the Tower of London)

**intown** \ˈ≈ˌ≈, ≈ˈ≈\ *adj* [¹*in* + *town*] **:** being in the built-up part of a town ⟨an ~ section of the city⟩

**¹in·tox·i·cant** \ən-ˈtäksəkənt, -sēk-\ *n* [ML *intoxicant-, intoxicans*, pres. part. of *intoxicare*] **:** something that intoxicates **:** an intoxicating agent; *esp* **:** an alcoholic drink ⟨felt he should abstain from the use of ~s⟩

**²intoxicant** \"\ *adj* [ML *intoxicant-, intoxicans*, pres. part. of *intoxicare*] **:** INTOXICATING ⟨the drink was warm and ~⟩ ⟨the air comes up from the heights, fine and ~ —Sacheverell Sitwell⟩ — **in·tox·i·cant·ly** *adv*

**¹in·tox·i·cate** \-kə̇t, -ˌkā| *usu* |d·+V\ *adj* [ME *intoxicat*, fr. ML *intoxicatus*, past part. of *intoxicare*] **1** *obs* **:** POISONED **2** *archaic* **:** excited or exhilarated beyond self-control by alcoholic drinks or to the point of enthusiasm or frenzy (as by pleasure) or stupefied by a narcotic

**²in·tox·i·cate** \-ˌkāt, *usu* -ād·+V\ *vt* -ED/-ING/-S [ML *intoxicatus*, past part. of *intoxicare*, fr. L *in-* ²in- + *toxicum* poison — more at TOXIC] **1 :** POISON **2 a :** to excite or stupefy by alcoholic drinks or a narcotic esp. to the point where physical and mental control is markedly diminished **:** make drunk **:** INEBRIATE **b :** to excite to the point of enthusiasm, frenzy, or madness **:** elate strongly and often excessively ⟨found the idea *intoxicating* and ennobling⟩ ⟨*intoxicated* with dreams of fortune —Van Wyck Brooks⟩ ⟨*intoxicated* by success⟩

**intoxicated** *adj* **1 :** being under the marked influence of an intoxicant **:** DRUNK, INEBRIATED **2 :** emotionally excited, elated, or exhilarated (as by great joy or extreme pleasure) **syn** see DRUNK

**in·tox·i·cat·ed·ly** \≈ˈ≈≈ˌ≈≈≈, ≈ˌ≈≈ˈ≈≈≈\ *adv* **:** in an intoxicated manner ⟨found herself ~ striving for that careless, exhilarating blitheness —Harriet LaBarre⟩

**intoxicating** *adj* **:** producing or fitted to produce intoxication ⟨an ~ beverage⟩ ⟨~ flattery⟩ ⟨~ beauty⟩ — **in·tox·i·cat·ing·ly** \≈ˈ≈≈ˌ≈≈≈, ≈ˌ≈≈ˈ≈≈\ *adv*

**in·tox·i·ca·tion** \≈ˌ≈≈ˈkāshən\ *n* -s [ML *intoxication-, intoxicatio* poisoning, fr. ML *intoxicatus* + L *-ion-, -io* -ion] **1 :** poisoning or the abnormal state induced by a chemical agent (as a drug, serum, or toxin) ⟨barbiturate ~ may occur as an intractable dermatitis⟩ ⟨lead ~ is a hazard of some occupations⟩ **2 a :** the quality or state of being drunk **:** INEBRIATION **b :** a strong excitement of mind or feelings (as from joy or pleasure) **:** an elation that rises to enthusiasm, frenzy, or madness **3 :** the act of intoxicating

**in·tox·i·ca·tive** \≈ˈ≈≈ˌkād·iv\ *adj, archaic* **:** of, relating to, or tending to cause intoxication

**In·tox·im·e·ter** \ˌin-ˌtäkˈsimәd·ә(r)\ *trademark* — used for a device used to measure the degree of an individual's intoxication by means of chemical tests of the breath

**intpr** *abbr* interpreter

**intr** *abbr* **1** intransitive **2** introduced; introducing; introduction; introductory

**in·tra-** *in pronunciations below*, ¦≈≈ = ¦in·trə *or* ··(ˌ)trä *or* ··(ˌ)trȧ\ *prefix* [LL, fr. L *intra* within, fr. (assumed) OL *interus* inward, on the inside — more at INTERIOR] **1 a :** within — esp. in adjectives formed from adjectives ⟨*intra*glacial⟩ ⟨*intra*vaginal⟩ ⟨*intra*cellular⟩ ⟨*intra*-European⟩ ⟨*intra*cosmical⟩ **b :** during — esp. in adjectives formed from adjectives ⟨*intra*natal⟩ ⟨*intra*febrile⟩ ⟨*intra*pyretic⟩ ⟨*intra*vital⟩ **c :** between layers of — esp. in adjectives formed from adjectives ⟨*intra*cutaneous⟩ **d :** underneath — esp. in adjectives formed from adjectives ⟨*intra*dural⟩ **2 :** INTRO- ⟨an *intra*muscular injection⟩ ⟨*intra*venation⟩ ⟨*intra*cerebral⟩ **3 :** internal ⟨*intra*selection⟩

**in·tra–abdominal** \¦≈≈+\ *adj* [*intra-* + *abdominal*] **:** being within the abdomen ⟨*intra-abdominal* pressure⟩ or going into the abdomen ⟨an *intra-abdominal* injection⟩ — **in·tra–abdominally** \"+\ *adv*

**in·tra–atomic** \"+\ *adj* [*intra-* + *atomic*] **:** existing within an atom ⟨the project which led to man's first practical utilization of *intra-atomic* energy —Julian Huxley⟩

**in·tra·bi·on·tic** \"+(ˈ)bīˈäntik\ *adj* [prob. irreg. fr. *intra-* + Gk *biount-, biōn* living + E *-ic* — more at -BIONT] **:** existing or occurring within an individual

**in·tra·cartilaginous** \¦≈≈+\ *adj* [*intra-* + *cartilaginous*] *of bone development* **:** taking place within the substance of cartilage **:** ENDOCHONDRAL — compare INTRAMEMBRANOUS

**in·tra·cav·i·tar·i·ly** \"+¦kavəˈterəlē\ *adv* **:** in an intracavitary manner

**in·tra·cav·i·tary** \-ˌterē\ *adj* [*intra-* + *cavity* + *-ary*] **:** being within or from within a body cavity ⟨~ irradiation of cervical cancer⟩

**in·tra·cellular** \¦≈≈+\ *adj* [ISV *intra-* + *cellular*] **:** being or occurring within a body cell or within the body cells **:** ENDOCELLULAR — **in·tra·cellularly** *adv*

**in·tra·cerebral** \"+\ *adj* [ISV *intra-* + *cerebral*] **:** going into the cerebrum ⟨~ inoculation⟩ — **in·tra·cerebrally** \"+\ *adv*

**in·tra·cervical** \"+\ *adj* [ISV *intra-* + *cervical*] **:** situated within the cervix of the uterus

**in·tra·chordal** \"+\ *adj* [*intra-* + *chordal*] **:** being or occurring within a chord (as the notochord)

**in·tra·cisternal** \"+\ *also* **in·tra·cistern** \"+\ *adj* [*intra-* + *cisternal or cistern*] **:** going into or being or occurring within a cisterna — **in·tra·cis·ter·nal·ly** \"+(ˈ)siˈstərnᵊlē *or* +sə¦-\ *adv*

**in·tra·city** \¦≈≈+\ *adj* [*intra-* + *city*] **:** being, occurring, or operating within a particular city ⟨~ buses⟩

**in·tra·coastal** \"+\ *adj* [*intra-* + *coastal*] **:** being within and close to the coast or belonging to the inland waters near the coast ⟨an ~ waterway⟩

**in·tra·company** \"+\ *adj* [*intra-* + *company*] **:** being or occurring within a company ⟨for the sake of ~ relations —*Current Biog.*⟩

**in·tra·continental** \"+\ *adj* [*intra-* + *continental*] **:** being within a particular continent

**in·tra·cortical** \"+\ *adj* [*intra-* + *cortical*] **:** being or situated within the cortex

**in·tra·cranial** \"+\ *adj* [*intra-* + *cranial*] **:** being or occurring within the cranium ⟨~ pressure⟩ — **in·tra·cra·ni·al·ly** \"+¦krānēəlē\ *adv*

**intracranial cast** *n* **:** a cast of the brain cavity in a skull

**in·tra·crystalline** \¦≈≈+\ *adj* [*intra-* + *crystalline*] **:** being or occurring within a crystal ⟨an ~ field⟩

**in·tractability** \(ˌ)in, ən+\ *n* **:** the quality or state of being intractable

**¹in·tractable** \(ˈ)in, ən+\ *adj* [L *intractabilis*, fr. *in-* ¹in- + *tractabilis* tractable] **1 :** not easily governed, managed, or directed **:** not disposed to be taught, disciplined, or tamed **:** OBSTINATE, REFRACTORY ⟨an ~ temper⟩ ⟨an ~ child⟩ **:** unwilling to submit ⟨~ to force⟩ **2 :** not easily manipulated or wrought ⟨an ~ metal⟩ **3 :** not easily relieved or cured ⟨an ~ pain⟩ ⟨an ~ malady⟩ **:** not responsive (as to a medicine) ⟨~ to remedies⟩ **syn** see UNRULY

**²intractable** \"\ *n* -s **:** one that is intractable ⟨most of the group was docile but it did contain ~s⟩

**in·tractableness** \(ˈ)in, ən+\ *n* **:** the quality or state of being intractable **:** STUBBORNNESS, REFRACTORINESS

**in·tractably** \"+\ *adv* **:** in an intractable way

**in·tra·cutaneous** *pronunc at* INTRA- +\ *adj* [ISV *intra-* + *cutaneous*] **:** INTRADERMAL — **in·tra·cutaneously** \"+\ *adv*

**intracutaneous test** *n* **:** a test for immunity or hypersensitivity to a particular antigen made by injecting a minute amount of diluted antigen into the skin — compare PATCH TEST, SCRATCH TEST

**in·tra·cytoplasmic** \¦≈≈+\ *adj* [ISV *intra-* + *cytoplasmic*] **:** lying or occurring in cytoplasm (as of a cell) ⟨~ multiplication of sporozoans⟩

**in·tra·da** \ən-ˈträdə\ *n* -s [modif. of It *intrata, entrata* entrance, introduction, fr. fem. of *intrato, entrato*, past part. of *intrare, entrare* to enter, fr. L *intrare* — more at ENTER] **:** a musical introduction or prelude esp. in 16th and 17th century music **:** ENTRÉE

**in·tra·departmental** *pronunc at* INTRA- +\ *adj* [*intra-* + *departmental*] **:** being or occurring within a department ⟨~ rivalry⟩

**in·tra·dermal** \"+\ *also* **in·tra·dermic** \"+\ *adj* [*intradermal* fr. *intra-* + *dermal*; *intradermic* ISV *intra-* + *dermic*] **:** being within the skin ⟨an ~ nevus⟩ **:** being between the layers of the skin ⟨an ~ injection⟩ — **in·tra·der·mal·ly** \"+¦dərməlē\ *also* **in·tra·der·mi·cal·ly** \-mək(ə)lē\ *adv*

**in·tra·disciplinary** \¦≈≈+\ *adj* [*intra-* + *disciplinary*] **:** being or occurring within the scope of a scholarly or academic discipline or between the people active in such a discipline

**in·tra·district** \"+\ *adj* [*intra-* + *district*] **:** being or occurring within a district ⟨interdistrict and ~ services —D.H.Nucker⟩

**intrado** *n* -s [modif. of Sp *entrada* entry, income, fr. fem. of *entrado*, past part. of *entrar* to enter, fr. L *intrare* — more at ENTER] *obs* **:** INCOME

**in·tra·dos** \ˈin·trəˌdäs, -ˌdōs, -ˌdō; in·ˈträ|ˌdäs, -rä|, |ˌdəs\ *n, pl* **intrados** \-ˌdōz\ *or* **intradoses** \-äsəz, -ōsəz, -əsəz\ [F, fr. L *intra* within + F *dos* back — more at INTRA-, DOSSIER] **1 :** the interior curve of an arch; *esp* **:** the inner curved face of the whole body of voussoirs **2 :** the inner surface of a vault — compare EXTRADOS

*1* intrados 1

**in·tra·ductal** *pronunc at* INTRA- +\ *adj* [*intra-* + *duct* + *-al*] **:** being or occurring within a duct ⟨~ pressure⟩

**in·tra·dural** \"+\ *adj* [ISV *intra-* + *dural*] **:** being or occurring within the dura mater

**in·tra–european** \"+\ *adj, usu cap E* [*intra-* + *european*] **:** being or occurring within the boundaries of Europe or between the countries of Europe ⟨*intra-European* political movements⟩

**in·tra·fascicular** \"+\ *adj* [*intra-* + *fascicular*] **:** being or occurring within a vascular bundle

**in·tra·formational** \"+\ *adj* [*intra-* + *formational*] **:** being or occurring within a geologic formation **:** originating more or less contemporaneously with the enclosing geologic material — see BRECCIOLA

**in·tra·genic** \"+\ *adj* [*intra-* + *genic*] **:** being or occurring within a gene ⟨~ changes⟩

**in·tra·glacial** \"+\ *adj* [*intra-* + *glacial*] **:** being or occurring within a glacier or a glacial stage

**in·tra·granular** \"+\ *adj* [*intra-* + *granular*] **:** being or occurring within a grain ⟨~ microstructures —*Jour. of Geol.*⟩

**in·tra·group** \"+\ *also* **in·tra·group·al** \"+¦grüpəl\ *adj* [*intragroup* fr. *intra-* + *group*; *intragroupal* fr. *intra-* + *group* + *-al*] **:** being or occurring within a single group ⟨increased ~ hostility —J.B.Carroll⟩

**in·tra·hepatic** \"+\ *adj* [ISV *intra-* + *hepatic*] **:** being within or originating in the liver — compare EXTRAHEPATIC

**intrail** *archaic var of* ENTRAIL

**in·tra·imperial** *pronunc at* INTRA- +\ *adj* [*intra-* + *imperial*] **:** being, occurring, or carried on within an empire

**in·tra·individual** \"+\ *adj* [*intra-* + *individual*] **:** being or occurring within the individual

**in·tra–industry** *or* **in·tra·industrial** \"+\ *adj* [*intra-* + *industry* or *industrial*] **:** being or occurring within an industry or between the independent enterprises of an industry

**in·tra·island** \"+\ *adj* [*intra-* + *island*] **:** being within or limited to the confines of an island ⟨~ distances are not great —J.H.S.Billmyer⟩ ⟨~ telephone and courier service —John Hersey⟩

**in·trait** \ˈinˌträ, ˈan-, -\ *n* [F, fr. *in-* ²in- + *-trait* (as in *extrait* extract, fr. MF, fr. past part. of *extraire* to extract, fr. L *extrahere*) — more at EXTRACT] **:** one of a class of extracts prepared from plants in which the enzymes are killed before drying

**in·tra·lamellar** *pronunc at* INTRA- +\ *adj* [*intra-* + *lamellar*] **:** situated within a lamella — used esp. of the trama in agarics

**in·tra·luminal** \"+\ *adj* [*intra-* + *luminal*] **:** being within or arising from within the lumen ⟨~ inflammation of the esophagus⟩

**in·tra·marginal** \"+\ *adj* [*intra-* + *marginal*] **:** being, occurring, or operating within a margin

**in·tra·matrical** \"+\ *adj* [*intra-* + *matrical*] **:** being or occurring within a matrix — **in·tra·matrically** \"+\ *adv*

**in·tra·medullary** \"+\ *adj* [ISV *intra-* + *medullary*] **:** being or lying within a medulla ⟨an ~ tumor of the spinal cord⟩; *esp* **:** involving use of the marrow space of a bone for support ⟨~ pinning of a fracture of the thigh⟩

**in·tra·membranous** \"+\ *adj* [*intra-* + *membranous*] *of bone development* **:** taking place through the ossification of a membrane — compare INTRACARTILAGINOUS

**in·tra·mental** \"+\ *adj* [*intra-* + *mental*] **:** INTRAPSYCHIC

**in·tra·mercurial** *also* **in·tra·mercurian** \"+\ *adj* [*intramercurial* ISV *intra-* + *mercurial*; *intramercurian* fr. *intra-* + *mercurian*] **:** being within the orbit of the planet Mercury

**in·tra·micellar** \"+\ *adj* [*intra-* + *micellar*] **:** being or taking place within a micelle ⟨~ swelling of cellulose by water⟩ — **in·tra·mi·cel·lar·ly** *adv*

**in·tra·molecular** \¦≈≈+\ *adj* [ISV *intra-* + *molecular*] **:** situated or occurring within the molecule ⟨~ rearrangement⟩ **:** formed by reaction between different parts of the same molecule — **in·tra·mo·lec·u·lar·ly** *adv*

**intramolecular respiration** *n* **:** the production of carbon dioxide and of organic acids by aerobic organisms or tissues while deprived of atmospheric oxygen

**intramolecular salt** *n* **:** INNER SALT

**in·tra·montane** \¦≈≈+\ *adj* [ISV *intra-* + *montane*] **:** being within a mountainous region

**in·tra·morainic** \"+\ *adj* [*intra-* + *morainic*] **:** being or occurring within the lobate curve of a moraine

**in·tra·mundane** \"+\ *adj* [*intra-* + *mundane*] **:** being or occurring within the material world — opposed to *extramundane*

**in·tra·mural** \"+\ *adj* [*intra-* + *mural*] **1 :** being, occurring, or undertaken within the limits usu. of a state, community, organization, or institution (as an academic institution) ⟨the most extensive ~ investigation undertaken in the history of our government —W.H.Hale⟩ ⟨an ~ squabble within the corporation⟩ ⟨the ~ conflicts of four generations of a prolific family —Harrison Smith⟩ ⟨the college's ~ sports program⟩ ⟨~ competition between the departments of the state university⟩ — opposed to *extramural* **2 :** being or occurring within the substance of the walls of an organ ⟨~ infarction⟩ ⟨~ circulation⟩ — **in·tra·murally** \"+\ *adv*

**in·tra·muscular** \"+\ *adj* [ISV *intra-* + *muscular*] **:** being within a muscle ⟨~ fat⟩ **:** going into a muscle ⟨~ injection⟩ — **in·tra·muscularly** \"+\ *adv*

**in·tra·nasal** \"+\ *adj* [*intra-* + *nasal*] **:** lying within or going into the nasal structures — **in·tra·nasally** \"+\ *adv*

**in·tra·natal** \"+\ *adj* [*intra-* + *natal*] **:** occurring chiefly with reference to the child during the act of birth ⟨~ accident⟩ — compare INTRAPARTUM, NEONATAL

**in·tra·national** \"+\ *adj* [*intra-* + *national*] **:** being or occurring within a nation ⟨~ movements of the population⟩

**intrance** *archaic var of* ²ENTRANCE

**in·tra·ne·ous** \(ˈ)in-¦trānēəs, ən-ˈt-\ *adj* [LL *intraneus*, fr. L *intra* within — more at INTRA-] **:** being or growing within an area **:** INTERNAL — opposed to *extraneous*

**in·tra·neural** *pronunc at* INTRA- +\ *adj* [*intra-* + *neural*] **:** being or occurring within or going into a nerve or nervous tissue — **in·tra·neurally** \"+\ *adv*

**in·tranquil** \(ˈ)in-, ən-+\ *adj* [¹*in-* + *tranquil*] **:** not tranquil **:** DISTURBED, RESTLESS ⟨an ~ sleep⟩ — **in·tranquillity** \"+\ *n*

**in trans** *abbr* in transit

**intrans** *abbr* intransitive

**in·transferable** \ˌin-, (ˈ)in-, ən+\ *adj* [¹*in-* + *transferable*] **:** incapable of being transferred

**in·transgressible** \ˌin+\ *adj* [¹*in-* + *transgress* + *-ible*] **:** that cannot or may not be transgressed

**in·tran·si·geance** \ən-ˈtran(t)səjən(t)s, -raan- *also* -ra(a)nzəj- *sometimes* ˌin·tra(a)nˈsij(ē)ən(t)s *or* -ˈzi-\ *also* **in·tran·si·gean·cy** \-nsē, -nsi\ *n, pl* **intransigeanc·es** *also* **intransigeancies** [*intransigeance* fr. F, fr. *intransigeant*, after F *-ant: -ance*; *intransigeancy* fr. ²*intransigeant* + *-cy*] **:** INTRANSIGENCE ⟨assume attitudes of bohemian ~ toward society —Philip Rahv⟩

**¹in·tran·si·geant** \-nt\ *n* -s [F (trans. of Sp *intransigente*), fr. *in-* ¹in- + *transigeant*, pres. part. of *transiger* to compromise, fr. L *transigere* to transact] **:** ¹INTRANSIGENT

**²intransigeant** \"\ *adj* [F (trans. of Sp *intransigente*), fr. *in-* ¹in- + *transigeant*, pres. part. of *transiger*] **:** ²INTRANSIGENT — **in·tran·si·geant·ly** *adv*

**in·tran·si·gence** \ən'tran(t)səjən(t)s, -raan- *also* -ra(a)nzəj-\ *also* **in·tran·si·gen·cy** \-nsē,-nsi\ *n, pl* **intransigenc·es** *also* **intransigencies** [*intransigence* fr. ²*intransigent*, after such pairs as E *abstinent: abstinence; intransigency* fr. ²*intransigent* + *-cy*] **:** the quality or state of being intransigent ⟨his absolute ~ on any question —*Current History*⟩ ⟨~ in the face of harsh realities —R.J.Slavin⟩ ⟨the desire not . . . to prejudice the integration and defense of the West by ~ on issues —*Current History*⟩ ⟨who, by their ~, do most to block the peace —*New Republic*⟩

¹**in·tran·si·gent** \-jənt\ *n* -s [Sp *intransigente*, fr. *in-* ¹in- + *transigente*, pres. part. of *transigir* to compromise, fr. L *transigere* to transact — more at TRANSACT] **:** one that is intransigent

²**intransigent** \"\ *adj* [Sp *intransigente*, fr. *in-* ¹in- + *transigente*, pres. part. of *transigir*] **1 a :** refusing to compromise or budge from an often extreme position taken or held **:** preserving an immovable independence of position or attitude **:** UNCOMPROMISING ⟨an ~ imperialist who opposed with great force . . . every liberal tendency —R.P.Casey⟩ ⟨felt the man was ~ because of his youth and would modify his views as he grew older⟩ **b** *of two or more* **:** IRRECONCILABLE ⟨the ~ parties to the dispute⟩ **2 :** befitting one that is uncompromising ⟨its previous ~ attitude toward modern art —*Americana Annual*⟩ — **in·tran·si·gent·ly** *adv*

**in·tran·si·gent·ism** \-nt,izəm, -n‧,ti-\ *n* -s **:** the quality or state of being intransigent or the policy of an intransigent ⟨the militant ~ of the antislavery forces —A.C.Cole⟩

**in–transit** \'‧‧,‧‧, ‧‧'‧‧\ *adj* [fr. the phrase *in transit*] **:** being in transit ⟨worried about *in-transit* passengers to Europe during the storm⟩ **:** of or relating to something in transit ⟨*in-transit* freight rates⟩

**in·transitable** \(')in‧, ən‧+\ *adj* [¹*in-* + *transitable*] **:** not capable of being crossed or passed over ⟨an ~ gorge⟩

¹**in·transitive** \(')in‧, ən‧+\ *adj* [LL *intransitivus*, fr. L *in-* ¹in- + LL *transitivus* transitive] **:** not transitive: as **a** *archaic* **:** not transmitted to another **:** not passing beyond particular limits **b** (1) **:** not passing over directly to an object ⟨an ~ action⟩ (2) **:** expressing an action or state as limited to the agent or subject or as ending in itself **:** not taking a direct object — used of a verb form ⟨the verbs in "the bird flies" and "he runs" are ~⟩; compare ¹ABSOLUTE 4d (3) **:** being a construction containing an intransitive verb form **c :** characterizing a logical relationship between the three statements *x, y,* and *z* that occurs when *x* is related to *y* as *y* but not *x* is related to *z* — **in·transitively** \"+\ *adv* — **in·transitiveness** \"+\ *n*

²**intransitive** \"\ *n* **:** an intransitive verb form or construction

**in·transitivity** \(')in‧, ən‧+\ *n* **:** the quality or state of being intransitive **:** INTRANSITIVENESS

**in·tran·si·tiv·ize** \(')‧'‧(‧)‧,īz\ *vt* -ED/-ING/-S **:** to make intransitive — **in·tran·si·tiv·iz·er** \-zə(r)\ *n* -S

**in tran·si·tu** \(')in'tran(t)sə,tü, -ranzə-\ *adv* [L] **:** during passage from one place to another

**in·translatable** \(')in‧+\ *adj* [¹*in-* + *translate* + *-able*] **:** not translatable

**in·transmissibility** \"+\ *n* **:** the quality or state of being intransmissible

**in·transmissible** \"+\ *adj* [¹*in-* + *transmissible*] **:** not transmissible

**in·transmutable** \"+\ *adj* [¹*in-* + *transmutable*] **:** not transmutable

**in·trant** \'intrənt\ *n* -s [L *intrant-, intrans*, pres. part. of *intrare* to enter — more at ENTER] *archaic* **:** ENTRANT; *esp* **:** one entering an educational institution or a holy or fraternal order

**in·tra·nuclear** *pronunc at* INTRA- +\ *adj* [ISV *intra-* + *nuclear*] **:** being or occurring within or going into a nucleus

**in·tra·ocular** \"+\ *adj* [ISV *intra-* + *ocular*] **:** being or occurring within or going into the eyeball

**in·tra·oral** \"+\ *adj* [*intra-* + *oral*] **:** being or occurring within the mouth

**in·tra·organismal** \"+\ *adj* [*intra-* + *organismal*] **:** situated or originating inside an organism ⟨~ conflicts⟩ ⟨interpretation of ~ processes and relationships — L.A.White⟩

**in·tra·organizational** \"+\ *adj* [*intra-* + *organizational*] **:** being or occurring within an organization

**in·tra·parietal** \"+\ *adj* [*intra-* + *parietal*] **1 :** INTRAMURAL 2 **2 :** located within the parietal lobe of the cerebrum

**in·tra·par·tum** \"+'pärdəm\ *adj* [NL *intra partum*, lit., during birth, fr. L *intra* during, within + *partum*, accus. of *partus* birth — more at INTRA-, ANTEPARTUM] **:** occurring chiefly with reference to a mother during the act of birth — compare INTRANATAL

**in·tra·party** \'‧‧‧+\ *adj* [*intra-* + *party*] **:** being or occurring within the membership or scope of a usu. political party ⟨~ feuding⟩ ⟨~ organization⟩

**in·tra·pelvic** \"+\ *adj* [*intra-* + *pelvic*] **:** situated within the pelvis

**in·tra·pericardiac** \"+\ *adj* [*intra-* + *pericardiac*] **:** situated within or going into the pericardium ⟨~ injections⟩

**in·tra·peritoneal** \"+\ *adj* [ISV *intra-* + *peritoneal*] **:** being within or going into the peritoneal cavity; *also* **:** going through the peritoneum — **in·tra·peritoneally** \"+\ *adv*

**in·tra·petiolar** \"+\ *adj* [ISV *intra-* + *petiolar*] **1 :** enclosed by the expanded base of the petiole ⟨~ leaf buds in the plane tree⟩ **2 :** situated between the petiole and the stem ⟨~ stipules in plants of the family Rubiaceae⟩

**in·tra·pial** \"+\ *adj* [*intra-* + *pial*] **:** being or occurring within the pia mater

**in·tra·plant** \"+\ *adj* [*intra-* + *plant*] **:** being or occurring within an industrial plant ⟨~ working conditions and policies —*Americana Annual*⟩ ⟨~ disputes⟩

**in·tra·psychic** *or* **in·tra·psychical** \"+\ *adj* [*intra-* + *psychic* or *psychical*] **:** being or occurring within the psyche, the mind, or the personality ⟨~ conflicts⟩ ⟨~ processes⟩ — **in·tra·psychically** \"+\ *adv*

**in·tra·pulmonic** \"+\ *adj* [*intra-* + *pulmonic*] **:** occurring within the lungs ⟨~ pressure⟩

**in·tra·school** \"+\ *adj* [*intra-* + *school*] **:** existing within a school ⟨an ~ athletic program⟩ — opposed to *interschool*

**in·tra·selection** \"+\ *n* [ISV *intra-* + *selection*] **:** hypothetical competition between structural elements of a tissue or organ resulting in survival of those best suited to a particular function or situation

**in·tra·service** \"+\ *adj* [*intra-* + *service*] **:** being or occurring within the armed services ⟨~ rivalry⟩ or within a branch of the armed services ⟨~ advancement⟩

**in·tra·shop** \"+\ *adj* [*intra-* + *shop*] **:** being within or confined to a single shop ⟨~ agencies for collective bargaining⟩

**in·tra·species** \"+\ *adj* [*intra-* + *species*] **:** INTRASPECIFIC

**in·tra·specific** \"+\ *adj* [*intra-* + *specific*] **:** being or occurring within a species or involving the members of one species

**in·tra·spinal** \"+\ *adj* [*intra-* + *spinal*] **:** being within or going into a spine; *esp* **:** going into the spinal canal — **in·tra·spinally** \"+\ *adv*

**in·tra·state** \"+\ *adj* [*intra-* + *state*] **:** existing within a state ⟨interstate and ~ commerce⟩

**in·tra·stelar** \"+\ *adj* [*intra-* + *stelar*] **:** being or occurring within a stele

**in·tra·stratal** \"+\ *adj* [*intra-* + *stratal*] **:** being or occurring within strata ⟨~ solution⟩

**in·tra·telluric** \"+\ *adj* [*intra-* + *telluric*; trans. of G *intratellurisch*] **1 :** situated, formed, or occurring deep within the earth — used esp. of a mineral of an igneous rock **2 :** of, relating to, or constituting the period or stage of crystallization of igneous rocks prior to eruption

**intraterminal switching** *n, pl* **intraterminal switchings :** the moving of cars from one place to another on the same railroad line and within the switching limits of one station or industrial switching district — compare INTERTERMINAL SWITCHING

**in·tra·thecal** \"+\ *adj* [*intra-* + *thecal*] **1 a :** being within a sheath **b :** being or going under the membranes covering the brain or spinal cord ⟨an ~ injection⟩ **2 :** being within the theca esp. of a coral — **in·tra·thecally** \"+\ *adv*

**in·tra·thoracic** \"+\ *adj* [ISV *intra-* + *thoracic*] **:** being or occurring within the thorax ⟨~ extension of the disease —Cecil Wakeley⟩ ⟨~ pressure⟩

**in·tratom·ic** \¦in·trə¦tämik\ *adj* [irreg. fr. *intra-* + *atomic*] **:** INTRA-ATOMIC

**in·tra·tracheal** *pronunc at* INTRA- +\ *adj* [ISV *intra-* + *tracheal*] **:** being or occurring within or going into the trachea

**in·tra·tropical** \"+\ *adj* [*intra-* + *tropical*] **:** INTERTROPICAL

**in·tra·uterine** \"+\ *adj* [ISV *intra-* + *uterine*] **:** being or occurring within the uterus; *esp* **:** occurring during the part of development that takes place in the uterus

**in·tra·vaginal** \"+\ *adj* [ISV *intra-* + *vaginal*] **1 :** situated within a sheath — used esp. of branches in grasses **2 :** being or occurring within or going into the vagina

**in·trav·a·sation** \(,)in‧,travə'sāshən\ *n* -s [prob. fr. *intra-* + *-vasation* (as in *extravasation*)] **:** the entrance of foreign matter into a vessel of the body

**in·tra·venous** *pronunc at* INTRA- +\ *adj* [ISV *intra-* + *venous*] **:** being within or going into or by way of the veins ⟨~ feeding⟩ ⟨an ~ inflammation⟩; *also* **:** used in intravenous procedures ⟨an ~ needle⟩ ⟨an ~ solution⟩ — **in·tra·venously** \"+\ *adv*

**in·tra vi·res** \¦in·trə¦vī(,)rēz\ *adv* [NL] *law* **:** within the powers — opposed to *ultra vires*

**in·tra·vital** *pronunc at* INTRA- +\ *adj* [ISV *intra-* + *vital*] **:** INTRAVITAM

**in·tra vi·tam** \¦in·trə'vī,tam, -trä'wē,täm\ *adv* [NL, during life, fr. L *intra* during, within + *vitam*, accus. of *vita* life — more at INTRA-, VITAL] **:** during life **:** while the subject is alive ⟨the symptoms of fatty liver are . . . not sufficient in most cases to make an accurate diagnosis *intra vitam* —O.V.Brumley⟩

**in·tra·vi·tam** \¦‧‧¦‧‧‧\ *adj* [fr. *intra vitam*, adv.] **1 :** performed upon or occurring in a subject that is alive ⟨an ~ diagnosis⟩ ⟨~ blood clotting⟩ **2** *of a stain* **:** having the property of tinting living cells without killing them

**in·tra·vitelline** *pronunc at* INTRA- +\ *adj* [*intra-* + *vitelline*] **:** being or occurring within the yolk of an egg

**in·tra·vitreous** \"+\ *adj* [*intra-* + *vitreous*] **:** being or occurring within the vitreous humor

**in·tra·xylary** \"+\ *adj* [*intra-* + *xylem* + *-ary*] **:** situated within the xylem

**in–tray** \'‧,‧\ *n* [⁴*in* + *tray*] **:** a shallow wood or metal basket usu. placed on a desk and used for holding incoming material (as letters) or material still to be dealt with — distinguished from *out-tray*

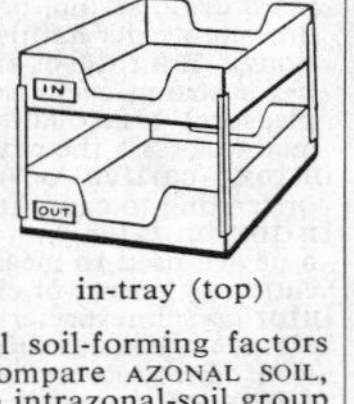

in-tray (top)

**in·tra·zonal** *pronunc at* INTRA- +\ *adj* [*intra-* + *zonal*] **:** of or belonging to intrazonal soil or an intrazonal soil

**intrazonal soil** *n* **1 :** a major soil group classified as a category of the highest rank and including soils with more or less well-developed soil characteristics determined by relatively local factors (as the nature of the parent material) that prevail over the normal soil-forming factors of climate and living organisms — compare AZONAL SOIL, ZONAL SOIL **2 :** a soil belonging to the intrazonal-soil group

**intreat** *archaic var of* ENTREAT

**intrench** *var of* ENTRENCH

**in·trep·id** \(')in·¦trepəd, ən·'t-\ *adj* [L *intrepidus*, fr. *in-* ¹in- + *trepidus* alarmed — more at TREPIDATION] **:** characterized by resolute fearlessness in meeting dangers or hardships and enduring them with fortitude ⟨an ~ explorer⟩ ⟨an ~ attitude⟩ **syn** see BRAVE

**in·tre·pid·i·ty** \,in·trə'pidəd·ē, -tre'-, -idətē, -i\ *n* **:** the quality or state of being intrepid **:** resolute bravery **:** VALOR ⟨a girl of immense ~ and she struggled on gallantly —J.C.Powys⟩

**in·trep·id·ly** *adv* **:** in an intrepid manner

**in·trep·id·ness** *n* -ES **:** INTREPIDITY

**in·tri·ca·cy** \'in·trəkəsē, -trēk-, -si *sometimes* ən·'trik- *or* 'in·,trik-\ *n* -ES [¹*intricate* + *-cy*] **1 :** the quality or state of being intricate **:** complexity or involution in structure or arrangement (as of parts) ⟨these improvements . . . greatly increase the ~ of the mechanisms —Bryan Morgan⟩ ⟨the ~ of his philosophic notions⟩ **2 :** something intricate; *esp* **:** an intricate part, aspect, or relationship ⟨who know and admire the *intricacies* of bullfighting —Murray Sinclair⟩ ⟨with all its *intricacies* of fibers, muscles, and veins —Mary W. Shelley⟩ ⟨involved in the *intricacies* of his own success at law school —Mary Deasy⟩

¹**in·tri·cate** \-kət, *usu* -kəd·+V\ *adj* [ME (Sc), fr. L *intricatus*, past part. of *intricare* to entangle] **1 :** having many interwinding, intermeshing, or nicely or complexly interrelating parts, phases, patterns, or elements and being consequently perplexing and hard to grasp in detail, follow through, or execute ⟨a mazy dance in imitation of the ~ windings of the labyrinth —J.G.Frazer⟩ ⟨the wheels, cogs, levers, all the ~ parts of the hay-loading machine —Sherwood Anderson⟩ ⟨~ interlaced diamonds —*Amer. Guide Series: Md.*⟩ **2 :** showing an involvement or complexity of various detailed considerations or notions and hence requiring precise analysis **:** difficult to cope with, resolve, analyze, solve ⟨the ~ task of reorganizing the economic system on an equitable basis —J.A.Hobson⟩ ⟨our system of civil courts was very ~, and no explanation could be given of it without a long historical preamble —F.W.Maitland⟩ **syn** see COMPLEX

²**in·tri·cate** \'in·trə,kāt, -trē,-, *usu* -ād·+V\ *vt* -ED/-ING/-S [L *intricatus*, past part. of *intricare* to entangle, fr. *in-* ²in- + *tricae* trifles, impediments, perplexities; perh. akin to L *torquēre* to twist — more at TORTURE] **1 a** *obs* **:** ENTANGLE, ENSNARE **b :** INTERRELATE, INTERLOCK, INTERMESH ⟨so consistently *intricated* that one rests on another and so is involved with what was earlier —Marianne Moore⟩ ⟨a career . . . *intricated* with an epoch —Lucien Price⟩ ⟨pseudopodia, reticulated and *intricated* —*Biol. Abstracts*⟩ **2** *archaic* **:** to make intricate **:** COMPLICATE

**in·tri·cate·ly** *pronunc at* ¹INTRICATE +lē *or* li\ *adv* **:** in an intricate manner ⟨an ~ designed floral pattern⟩ ⟨an ~ abstruse philosophical doctrine⟩

**in·tri·cate·ness** \"+nəs\ *n* -ES **:** INTRICACY

**in·tri·ca·tion** \,in·trə'kāshən, -trē'-\ *n* -s [ME *intricacion*, fr. ML *intrication-, intricatio*, fr. L *intricatus* + *-ion-, -io* -ion] **1** *obs* **:** COMPLICATION, COMPLEXITY **2 :** INTERRELATION, INTERMESHING

**in·tri·gant** *or* **in·tri·guant** \¦in·trē¦gänt, ¦an·'t-\ *n* -s [F *intrigant*, fr. *intrigant*, adj., that intrigues, fr. It *intrigante*, pres. part. of *intrigare* to intrigue] **:** one that intrigues **:** INTRIGUER ⟨talked almost in whispers, like ~*s* —E.P.O'Donnell⟩

**in·tri·gante** *or* **in·tri·guante** \"\ *n* -s [F *intrigante*, fem. of *intrigant*] **:** a female intriguer ⟨the most fascinating woman they had ever known, but also . . . an ~ of dark and winding ways —Gertrude Atherton⟩

¹**in·trigue** \ən·'trēg *sometimes* 'in·,t-\ *vb* -ED/-ING/-S [F *intriguer* to puzzle, intrigue, fr. It *intrigare* to intrigue, fr. L *intricare* to entangle] *vt* **1** *archaic* **:** CHEAT, TRICK **2 :** to get, make, or accomplish by intrigue ⟨~ some bill through the senate —Thornton Wilder⟩ ⟨*intrigued* their way through ballrooms and bedrooms —*Time*⟩ ⟨*intrigued* themselves into office —F.M.Ford⟩ **3** *obs* **:** ENTANGLE, COMPLICATE **4 a :** to arouse the interest, desire, or curiosity of (as by beguiling or baffling) **:** BEGUILE ⟨a tale that ~*s* the reader⟩ ⟨an *intriguing* smile⟩ ⟨became *intrigued* with sketching children —*Newsweek*⟩ **b :** to engage by intriguing in this way ⟨has become something distinctive enough to ~ our interest —Charlton Laird⟩ ⟨have *intrigued* my attention and tightly gripped my fancy —Paul Ives⟩ ~ *vi* **:** to carry on an intrigue: as **a :** PLOT, SCHEME ⟨*intrigued* and conspired against him to the end —Hilaire Belloc⟩ **b :** to engage in a clandestine or illicit affair or intimacy

²**in·trigue** \'in·,trēg, ən·'t-\ *n* -s [F, crafty scheme, plot, love affair, fr. It *intrigo* crafty scheme, fr. *intrigare* to intrigue] **1** *obs* **:** INTRICACY, COMPLEXITY **2 a :** a covert and involved scheme to accomplish one's end by devious maneuvering and crafty stratagem ⟨the party politicians . . . reverted to their familiar ~*s* and maneuvers —H.G.Wells⟩ ⟨the ~*s* and conspiracies of the middle ages —Edmond Taylor⟩ **b :** a tendency toward or the practice of engaging in such schemes ⟨jealousy and ~ and backbiting, producing a poisonous atmosphere of underground competition —Bertrand Russell⟩ ⟨ambitious, unscrupulous, and cruel, a master of ~ —Victor Seroff⟩ **3 :** the plot of a literary or dramatic work esp. marked by an intricacy of design or action or a complex interrelation of events ⟨the play rightly shows greater concern for comic ~ than for human probability —*Time*⟩ **4 :** a clandestine affair or intimacy esp. involving a married woman ⟨that hard-to-be-governed passion of youth hurried me frequently into ~*s* with low women —Benjamin Franklin⟩ **syn** see PLOT

**in·trigu·er** \-gə(r)\ *n* -s **:** one that intrigues

**intriguing** \‧'‧‧ *sometimes* '‧,‧‧\ *adj* **:** engaging the interest to a marked degree ⟨rather an ~ poem —William Strachey⟩ **:** FASCINATING ⟨a subject of ~ intricacy⟩ **:** BEGUILING ⟨a small and ~ young woman⟩ **syn** see INTERESTING

**in·trigu·ing·ly** *adv* **:** in an intriguing manner

¹**in·trin·sic** \(')in·¦trinz|ik, ən·'t-, -rin(t)s|, |ēk\ *adj* [MF *intrinsèque* inner, internal, fr. LL *intrinsecus*, fr. L, adv. inwardly, inwards, fr. (assumed) L *intrim* (fr. — assumed — OL *interus* inward, on the inside) + L *-secus* (fr. *sequi* to follow) — more at INTERIOR, SUE] **1** *obs* **:** PRIVATE, SECRET **2 a :** belonging to the inmost constitution or essential nature of a thing **:** essential or inherent and not merely apparent, relative, or accidental ⟨form was treated as something ~, as the very essence of the thing in virtue of the metaphysical structure of the universe —John Dewey⟩ ⟨recommend this book for its ~ interest —Daniel George⟩ ⟨~ merit⟩ ⟨a wide gap between ~ feelings and the social expressions of them —H.J.Muller⟩ — opposed to *extrinsic* **b :** originating or due to causes or factors within a body, organ, or part ⟨~ asthma⟩ **c :** being good in itself or irreducible **:** being desirable or desired for its own sake and without regard to anything else ⟨when anyone says that values are merely matters of opinion or subjective liking, he is speaking only of ~ values —L.W.Beck⟩ **d :** REAL, ACTUAL ⟨a fine big bird, he is . . . but there is no ~ beauty about him —Richard Jefferies⟩ **3 :** originating and included wholly within an organ or part — used esp. of certain muscles; opposed to *extrinsic* — **in·trin·si·cal·ly** \|ək(ə)lē, |ēk-, -li\ *adv* — **in·trin·si·cal·ness** \|əkəlnəs, |ēk-\ *n* -ES

²**intrinsic** *n* -s *obs* **:** an intrinsic quality

**in·trin·si·cal** \|əkəl, |ēk-\ *adj* [alter. (influenced by ¹*intrinsic*) of earlier *intrinsecal*, fr. LL *intrinsecus* + E *-al*] *archaic* **:** INTRINSIC

**intrinsic factor** *n* **:** a substance produced by normal stomach and intestinal mucosa that facilitates absorption of vitamin $B_{12}$ from the gastrointestinal tract and thereby assists in the development and maturation of red blood cells — compare EXTRINSIC FACTOR

**intrinsic fraud** *n* **:** fraud (as by the use of forged documents, false claims, perjured testimony) that misleads a court or jury relying upon it in determining issues and induces the court or jury to find for the party perpetrating the fraud — compare EXTRINSIC FRAUD

**in·tro** \'in·(,)trō\ *n* -s [short for *introduction*] **:** a musical introduction in jazz and popular music

**intro-** *prefix* [ME, fr. MF, fr. L, fr. *intro*, adv., inwardly, to the inside, fr. (assumed) OL *interus* inward, on the inside — more at INTERIOR] **1 :** in **:** into ⟨*intro*jection⟩ **2 :** inward **:** within ⟨*intro*active⟩ ⟨*intro*flex⟩ ⟨*intro*reception⟩ — opposed to *extro-*

**in·tro·cep·tive** \¦in·trə¦septiv, -rō¦-\ *adj* [*intro-* + *-ceptive* (as in *receptive*)] **:** capable of receiving within itself

**introd** *abbr* introduction

**in·tro·duce** \¦in·trə¦d(y)üs, -rō¦d-, *in rapid speech* ¦in(t)ə(r)'d-\ *vt* -ED/-ING/-S [ME *introducen* to initiate, instruct, fr. L *introducere* to introduce, fr. *intro-* + *ducere* to lead — more at TOW] **1 a :** to lead, bring, conduct, or usher in esp. for the first time ⟨~ a person into a drawing room⟩ ⟨~ European birds into America⟩ **b :** to cause to take part or be involved by introducing ⟨the fruits of *introducing* party men into municipal affairs —*Sydney (Australia) Bull.*⟩ **2 a :** to bring into play (as in action or thought) ⟨~ abuses into court practices⟩ **:** bring forward in the course of an action or sequence ⟨~ irrelevancies into the discussion⟩ **:** add or contribute (as a new element or feature) ⟨~ new business into a play⟩ ⟨*introduced* amendments to the draft extension bill —*Current Biog.*⟩ ⟨*introduced* a new and mutually beneficial element into crop and livestock husbandry —N.C.Wright⟩ **b :** to bring into practice or use **:** INSTITUTE ⟨~ a new fashion in hats⟩ ⟨the first officer to ~ gunpowder into the French Army —Edmond Taylor⟩ ⟨*introduced* club cars on certain important business expresses —O.S.Nock⟩ ⟨slow to ~ new processes, slow to adopt new inventions —Leo Wolman⟩ **3** *obs* **:** to cause to exist **:** bring into being **4 :** to lead to or make known by a formal act, announcement, or recommendation: as **a :** to cause to be acquainted **:** cause to know each other personally ⟨~ two strangers⟩ **:** make (one person) known to another ⟨~ the boy to her father⟩ **b :** to present formally at court or into society ⟨a party to ~ his daughter to London society⟩ **c :** to present or announce formally or officially or by an official reading ⟨~ a bill to Congress⟩ **d :** to make preliminary explanatory or laudatory remarks about (as a performer or act in a show) ⟨a master of ceremonies . . . to ~ acts on the bill —*Current Biog.*⟩ **e** (1) **:** to bring (as an actor, singer, or literary character) before the public for the first time (as in a play, a concert, or a novel) ⟨a Hollywood extravaganza *introducing* a young Broadway star⟩ ⟨several excellent mysteries *introducing* a French detective —A.C.Ward⟩ (2) **:** to bring (a commercial product) to the attention of the public (as by an advertising campaign) **5 :** to lead into or preface ⟨*introduces* his study with a detailed description and careful evaluation of the publisher materials used in his report —W.H.Voskuil⟩ **:** START, BEGIN ⟨~ a subject by a long preface⟩ **6 a :** to put or insert into ⟨~ a catheter into a vein⟩ ⟨some 1800 eggs were *introduced* into a tiny drop of sea water —W.C.Allee⟩ **b :** to put (an atom or group of atoms) into a molecule **7 :** to bring to a knowledge of **:** bring into intellectual acquaintanceship with (as by contact, instruction, representation) ⟨~ readers to the poet's works⟩ — **in·tro·duc·er** \-sə(r)\ *n* -S

**in·tro·duce·ment** \,‧‧'‧mənt\ *n* -s *archaic* **:** INTRODUCTION

**in·tro·duc·ible** \¦‧‧¦d(y)üsəbəl\ *adj* **:** capable of being introduced **:** fit to be introduced

**introduct** *vt* -ED/-ING/-S [L *introductus*, past part. of *introducere* to introduce] *obs* **:** INTRODUCE

**in·tro·duc·tion** \,in·trə'dəkshən, -rō'd-, *in rapid speech* ,in(t)ə(r)'d-\ *n* -s [ME *introduccion* act of introducing, fr. MF *introduction*, fr. L *introduction-, introductio*, fr. *introductus* (past part. of *introducere* to introduce) + *-ion-, -io* -ion] **1 :** something that introduces: as **a** *obs* (1) **:** a preliminary step **:** PREPARATION (2) **:** initial instruction **:** a first lesson **:** instruction in rudiments **b** (1) **:** a distinguishable part (as of a book or treatise) that provides explanation, information, or comment preparatory or preliminary to the main portion or subject — compare PREFACE, PROEM (2) **:** a formal or elaborate preliminary treatise esp. introductory to other treatises or to a course or field of study ⟨an ~ to metaphysics⟩ ⟨an ~ to European drama⟩ (3) **:** a course or a subject matter preparatory to a particular study; *specif, cap* **:** a branch of the study of the Bible that applies the contributions of literary and historical criticism to textual problems (as of date, authorship, place of origin, structure, sources, and purpose) of the books of Scripture **c :** a form esp. polite and conventional used in the introduction of one person to another **d :** a series of chords or a short movement or passage preparing the listener for the main body of a musical composition **e :** an initial anticipatory, explanatory, or promotional statement or set of remarks (as in introducing a speaker, an entertainment, or a commercial product) **2 :** the act or process of introducing or the state of being introduced: as **a :** a leading, bringing, conducting, or ushering in or the state of being led, brought, conducted, or ushered in esp. for the first time ⟨responsible for the ~ of aliens into the country⟩ ⟨anticipated his ~ into the dining room⟩ **b :** a causing to take part or be involved ⟨the ~ of crooked politicians into city government⟩ **c :** INSTITUTION ⟨the ~ of new manufacturing processes⟩ ⟨the ~ of a newspaper to cover local events⟩ ⟨the ~ of new rules governing behavior⟩ **d :** a making known or acquainted or a being made known or acquainted ⟨the ~ of the two men to each other⟩ **e :** a formal presentation ⟨the ~ of a young girl to society⟩ ⟨the ~ of a bill into Congress⟩ **f :** a preliminary, preparatory, or initial explaining, talking up, or advertising ⟨an ~ to the subject matter in a preface to a book⟩ ⟨the ~ of an act by a master of ceremonies⟩ ⟨the ~ of a new product on a TV commercial⟩ **g :** a putting in **:** INSERTION ⟨the ~ of new matter into the recipe⟩ ⟨the ~ of a catheter into a vein⟩ ⟨the ~ into the stomach and esophagus of material which is opaque in appearance under the X ray —Morris Fishbein⟩ **h :** a bringing into play or adding or contributing in the course of an action or sequence or the state of being brought, added, or contributed in this way ⟨the ~ of a spirit of bitterness into the discussion⟩ ⟨the ~ of rude remarks into his report⟩ **3 :** something introduced ⟨resented all new ~s into his old methods of doing things⟩; *specif* **:** an exotic plant (as a new variety of horticultural derivation) or an animal brought into a region where it is not native

**in·tro·duc·tive** \¦═¦dəktiv, -tēv *also* -təv\ *adj* [fr. *introduction*, after such pairs as E *induction: inductive*] **:** INTRODUCTORY

**in·tro·duc·tor** \-tə(r)\ *n* -S [LL, fr. L *introductus* (past part. of *introducere* to introduce) + *-or*] *archaic* **:** INTRODUCER

**in·tro·duc·to·ri·ly** \-kt(ə)rəlē, -li\ *adv* **:** in an introductory manner

**in·tro·duc·to·ri·ness** \,═'═t(ə)rēnəs, -rin-\ *n* -ES **:** the quality or state of being introductory

**in·tro·duc·to·ry** \¦═¦═t(ə)rē, -ri\ *adj* [LL *introductorius*, fr. L *introductus* (past part. of *introducere* to introduce) + *-orius* -ory] **:** being or belonging to an introduction or serving to introduce **:** PRELIMINARY, PREFATORY ⟨an ~ section of a book⟩ ⟨an ~ course in mathematics⟩ ⟨remarks ~ to a main speaker⟩

**in·tro·flex** \¦in·trə¦fleks, -rō¦-\ *vb* -ED/-ING/-ES [*intro-* + *flex*] **:** to flex inward

**in·tro·flex·ion** *also* **in·tro·flec·tion** \¦══¦flekshən\ *n* [fr. *introflex*, after E *flex: flection*] **:** inward flexion **:** an act or instance of introflexing

**in·tro·fy** \'══,fī\ *vt* -ED/-ING/-ES [modif. (influenced by E *-fy*) of L *introferre* to carry in, fr. *intro-* + *ferre* to carry — more at BEAR] **:** to increase the impregnating power of (as sulfur for wood pulp)

**in·tro·gres·sion** \,══'greshən\ *n* -S [*intro-* + *-gression* (as in *digression*)] **:** the entry or introduction of a gene from one gene complex into another (as in introgressive hybridization)

**in·tro·gres·sive** \¦══¦gresiv\ *adj* [fr. *introgression*, after such pairs as E *digression: digressive*] **:** of, belonging to, or marked by introgression

**introgressive hybridization** *n* **:** the spread of genes of one species into the gene complex of another as a result of hybridization between numerically dissimilar populations in which extensive backcrossing prevents formation of a single stable population

**in·troit** \'in,trōət, 'in,trȯit, ən'trōət, ən'trȯit *sometimes* 'in·trəwət\ *n* -S [MF *introite*, fr. ML *introitus*, fr. L, entrance, fr. *introitus*, past part. of *introire* to go into, enter, fr. *intro-* + *ire* to go — more at ISSUE] **1** *often cap* **:** the first part of the proper of the mass in the Roman rite consisting orig. of the processional psalm but now usu. consisting of an antiphon and verse from one of the psalms followed by the Gloria Patri **2 :** a psalm, anthem, or hymn sung or played at the beginning of the communion service esp. in Anglican churches **3 :** a choral response sung at the beginning of a worship service

**in·troi·tal** \(')in·'trōəd-ᵊl, ən·'t-, -rȯid- -\ *adj* [*introitus* + *-al*] **:** of or relating to an introitus

**in·troi·tus** \ən·'trōəd-əs, -rȯid- -\ *n, pl* **introitus** [NL, fr. L, entrance] **:** the orifice of a body cavity; *esp* **:** the vaginal opening

**in·tro·ject** \¦in·trə¦jekt, -rō¦-\ *vb* -ED/-ING/-S [back-formation fr. *introjection*] *vt* **1 :** to incorporate or assimilate into oneself subconsciously or unconsciously (attitudes or ideas of others esp. parental figures, or in infantile fancy actual parts or all of another's body) — opposed to *project;* compare INTERNALIZE **2 :** to turn toward oneself (the love felt for another) or against oneself (the hostility felt toward another) ~ *vi* **:** to enter into a situation and play the role either in actuality or in fantasy that the situation suggests or demands

**in·tro·jec·tion** \¦══¦jekshən\ *n* -S [*intro-* + *-jection* (as in *projection*)] **1 :** a throwing in; *esp* **:** a throwing of oneself into some pursuit or action **2** [ISV *intro-* + *-jection* (as in *projection*); orig. formed as G *introjektion*] **:** a theory that sense perceptions are mental counterparts of the objects perceived **3** [ISV *intro-* + *-jection* (as in *projection*); orig. formed as G *introjektion*] **:** the act or process of introjecting attitudes, ideas, or body parts — opposed to *projection*

**in·tro·jec·tive** \¦══¦jektiv\ *adj* **:** of, belonging to, marked by, or given to introjection

**in·tro·mis·si·ble** \¦══¦misəbəl\ *adj* [fr. *intromission*, after such pairs as E *admission: admissible*] **:** capable of intromission

**in·tro·mis·sion** \,══'mishən\ *n* -S [ML *intromission-, intromissio*, fr. *intromissus* (past part. of ML — with reflexive pronoun object — *intromittere*) + L *-ion-, -io* -ion — more at SMITE] **1** *Scots law* **:** an intermeddling with the affairs or effects of another — see LEGAL INTROMISSION, VICIOUS INTROMISSION **2** [F, fr. MF, fr. L *intromissus* (past part. of *intromittere* to send in, let in) + MF *-ion*] **a :** the act of sending, letting, or putting in or the state of being sent, let, or put in **:** INSERTION, ADMISSION; *specif* **:** the introduction of the penis into or its maintenance within the vagina during coitus **b :** the time during which intromission is sustained during coitus

**in·tro·mis·sive** \¦══¦misiv\ *adj* [fr. *intromission*, after such pairs as E *permission: permissive*] **:** of or belonging to intromission

**in·tro·mit** \¦══¦mit\ *vb* **intromitted; intromitted; intromitting; intromits** [ME *intromitten*, fr. ML (with reflexive pronoun object) *intromittere* to concern (oneself), meddle, fr. L *intromittere* to send in, let in, fr. *intro-* + *mittere* to send — more at SMITE] *vi, Scots law* **:** to interfere or intermeddle esp. with the effects or goods of another — compare INTROMISSION 1 ~ *vt* [L *intromittere* to send in, let in] **:** to send or put in **:** INSERT, INTRODUCE; *also* **:** to allow to pass **:** ADMIT — **in·tro·mit·ter** \-mid·ə(r)\ *n* -S

**in·tro·mit·tent** \-mitᵊnt\ *adj* [L *intromittent-, intromittens*, pres. part. of *intromittere* to send in, let in] **:** adapted for or functioning in intromission — used of the copulatory organ of an animal

**in·tro·punitive** \¦in·trō+\ *adj* [*intro-* + *punitive*] **:** tending to blame or to inflict punishment on the self — opposed to *extrapunitive*

**in·trorse** \'in,trȯrs, ən·'trȯ(ə)rs\ *adj* [prob. fr. (assumed) NL *introrsus*, fr. L *introrsus*, adv., inward, contr. of *introversus*, fr. *intro-* + *versus* toward, fr. *versus*, past part. of *vertere* to turn — more at WORTH] **:** facing inward or toward the axis of growth ⟨an ~ anther⟩ **:** having its line of dehiscence toward the gynoecium — compare EXTRORSE — **in·trorse·ly** *adv*

**intros** *pl of* INTRO

**in·tro·spect** \¦in·trə¦spekt, -rō¦-\ *vb* -ED/-ING/-S [L *introspectus*, past part. of *introspicere* to look into, fr. *intro-* + *-spicere* (fr. *specere* to look) — more at SPY] *vt* **:** to look within (as one's own mind or psyche) **:** examine (as oneself) with introspection ~ *vi* **:** to engage in or practice introspection — **in·tro·spec·tor** \-ktə(r)\ *n* -S

**in·tro·spect·able** *or* **in·tro·spect·ible** \-ktəbəl\ *adj* **:** capable of being observed by introspection

**in·tro·spec·tion** \-kshən\ *n* -S [L *introspectus* + E *-ion*] **:** the examination of one's own thought and feeling **:** a looking into oneself **:** SELF-EXAMINATION; *also* **:** such examination including one's sensory and perceptual experience esp. undertaken under controlled conditions of experiment — opposed to *extrospection* — **in·tro·spec·tion·al** \-shənᵊl,-shnəl\ *adj*

**in·tro·spec·tion·ism** \-shə,nizəm\ *n* -S **:** a doctrine that psychology must be based essentially on data derived from introspection — compare BEHAVIORISM

**1in·tro·spec·tion·ist** \-sh(ə)nəst\ *n* -S **1 :** one esp. given to introspection **2 :** an adherent of introspectionism

**2introspectionist** \"\ *or* **in·tro·spec·tion·is·tic** \¦═══¦shə¦nistik\ *adj* **:** of or relating to introspectionism ⟨a special ~ technique was devised —Ethel Albert⟩

**in·tro·spec·tive** \¦══¦spektiv,-tēv *also* -təv\ *adj* [*introspect* + *-ive*] **:** of or belonging to introspection **:** employing, marked by, or tending to introspection — opposed to *extrospective* — **in·tro·spec·tive·ly** \-təvlē, -li\ *adv* — **in·tro·spec·tive·ness** \-tivnəs, -tēv- *also* -təv-\ *n* -ES

**in·tro·susception** \,in·trə, ,in·(,)trō+\ *n* [*intro-* + *susception*] **:** INTUSSUSCEPTION

**in·trou·va·ble** \aⁿ·trüvàbl(ᵊ), -b(lə)\ *adj* [F, fr. *in-* 1in- + *trouvable* capable of being found, fr. MF, fr. *trouver* to find (prob. fr. — assumed — VL *tropare* to compose) + *-able* — more at TROUBADOUR] **:** impossible to find ⟨pamphlets, all now almost ~ —*Times Lit. Supp.*⟩ — **in·trou·va·bly** \ən·'trüvəblē\ *adv*

**in·tro·ver·si·ble** \¦in·trə¦vərsəbəl, -rō¦-\ *adj* [*introversion* + *-ible*] **:** capable of being introverted

**in·tro·ver·sion** \¦in·trə¦vər|zhən, -·trō¦-, -və|, -vəi| *also* |sh-\ *n* -S [*intro-* + *-version* (as in *diversion*)] **1 :** the act of introverting or the state of being introverted ⟨economic ~ —Peter Schmid⟩ ⟨an ~ and not an expansion —D.S.Savage⟩ **2 a :** the act of directing one's attention toward or getting gratification from one's own thoughts and feelings and other intrapsychic experience ⟨neurotic ~ — too much preoccupation with oneself —*Irish Digest*⟩ — opposed to *extroversion* **b :** the state of being wholly or predominantly concerned with and interested in one's own intrapsychic experience **c :** a habitual tendency toward such introversion

**in·tro·ver·sive** \|siv *also* |ziv\ *adj* [*introversion* + *-ive*] **:** characterized by or given to introversion: **a :** turned in upon itself **:** drawn in or invaginated **b :** tending to turn one's attention to one's own experience **:** notably marked by psychological introversion — opposed to *extroversive;* contrasted with *extratensive* — **in·tro·ver·sive·ly** \|səvlē, |zə-\ *adv*

**1in·tro·vert** \'══,vər|t, -və|, -vəi|, ,══'═, *usu* |d·+V\ *vt* -ED/-ING/-S [*intro-* + *-vert* (as in *divert*)] **1 a :** to turn inward or in upon itself: as (1) **:** to bend inward (2) **:** to turn (as the thoughts) introversively **b :** to direct upon oneself ⟨served the purpose of ~*ing* aggressive intentions —Ernst Simmel⟩ **2 :** to draw in or invaginate (one tubular part or organ) within another **3 :** to produce introversion in **:** make an introvert of **:** cause to be introvert

**2in·tro·vert** \'══,═\ *n* -S **1 :** something that is or can be introverted (as the eyestalks of certain snails or the retractile proboscis of a sipunculid worm) **2 :** one whose personality is characterized by introversion — opposed to *extrovert*

**3introvert** \"\ *adj* [2*introvert*] **:** of or belonging to psychological introversion **:** characterized by or tending to introversion ⟨~ tendencies⟩ ⟨~ behavior⟩

**introverted** *adj* [fr. past part. of 1*introvert*] **1 :** INTROVERSIVE: **a :** turned in upon itself ⟨the ~ Old Kingdom did not carry on extensive intercourse with foreign lands —J.W.Curtis⟩ **b :** marked by introversion ⟨the ~ young man given to odd moods and uncommunicativeness⟩ — opposed to *extroverted* **2** *of a quatrain* **:** having an enclosed rhyme

**in·tro·vert·ish** \¦══¦ish\ *adj* [2*introvert* + *-ish*] **:** somewhat introverted

**in·tro·ver·tive** \¦══¦iv\ *adj* [1*introvert* + *-ive*] **:** INTROVERSIVE

**in·trude** \ən·'trüd\ *vb* -ED/-ING/-S [L *intrudere* to force in, fr. *in-* 2in- + *trudere* to thrust, push — more at THREAT] *vi* **1 :** to thrust oneself in **:** come or go in without invitation, permission, or welcome **:** enter by intrusion **:** ENCROACH, TRESPASS ⟨where none might ~ upon his grief —P.B.Kyne⟩ ⟨manifest no wish to ~ on academic prerogatives —*Saturday Rev.*⟩ ⟨abashed at *intruding* on all these busy people —Jule Mannix⟩ **2** *geol* **:** to enter as if by force ~ *vt* **1 :** to thrust or force in, into, on, or upon esp. without permission, welcome, or fitness ⟨~ political theory into his play⟩ ⟨~ these confidences on you —G.B.Shaw⟩ ⟨didn't want to ~ himself upon her uninvited⟩ ⟨improper to ~ the dog into the houses of other people they were calling on —Joseph Conrad⟩ ⟨the right to ~ its judgment upon questions of policy or morals —O.W.Holmes †1935⟩ **2 :** to settle (a minister) in a parish against the will of the people ⟨ecclesiastical adventurers from the Continent were *intruded* by hundreds into lucrative benefices —T.B.Macaulay⟩ **3** *geol* **:** to cause to enter as if by force

**in·trud·er** \-də(r)\ *n* -S **:** one that intrudes ⟨the swarming ~*s* upon the peace of that hill looked like sheep —Kenneth Roberts⟩; *specif* **:** a military aircraft assigned to penetrate alone into enemy territory usu. at night

**in·trud·ing·ly** *adv* [*intruding* (pres. part. of *intrude*) + *-ly*] **:** in the manner of one that intrudes

**in·tru·sion** \ən·'trüzhən\ *n* -S [ME *intrusioun* invasion, usurpation, fr. MF *intrusion* act of intruding, fr. ML *intrusion-, intrusio*, fr. L *intrusus* (past part. of *intrudere* to intrude) + *-ion-, -io* -ion] **:** the act of intruding or the state of being intruded: as **a** (1) **:** the entry of a stranger after a particular estate of freehold is determined before the person who holds it in remainder or reversion has taken possession (2) **:** the act of wrongfully entering upon, seizing, or taking possession of the property of another (as in trespassing upon crown lands or in the usurpation of an office) **b :** a trespassing or encroachment **:** an undesirable or unwelcome bringing in or entering ⟨the fire replenished, and the house shut against ~ —Mary Austin⟩ ⟨that other shattering of illusion which comes by way of the ~ of fact —J.L.Lowes⟩ ⟨resented the man's ~ upon his privacy⟩ **c :** a settlement of a minister in a parish against the wishes of the parishioners **d** (1) **:** the forcible entry of molten rock or magma into or between other rock formations; *also* **:** the body of igneous rock resulting from solidification of the intruded magma (2) **:** the plastic injection of masses of salt into overlying rocks; *also* **:** the intruded salt

**1in·tru·sive** \(')in·¦trüs|iv, ən·'t,-üz|, |ēv *also* |əv\ *adj* [*intrusion* + *-ive*] **1 a :** characterized by intrusion or encroachment ⟨an ~ remark⟩ ⟨far too sensitive to be ~ —Mollie Panter-Downes⟩ ⟨an ~ culture⟩ **b :** showing a tendency to intrusion **:** given to habitual intrusion **:** thrusting one's way into a place, group, or activity where one is not welcome or invited ⟨a loud and ~ individual⟩ **2 a :** thrusting or projecting inward ⟨an ~ arm of the sea⟩ **b :** thrust or forced in: as (1) *of a rock* **:** having been forced while in a plastic or liquid state into cavities or cracks or between layers of other rock — contrasted with *extrusive;* compare 1BOSS 2, 1DIKE 3c, SILL (2) **:** PLUTONIC **3** *of an organism* **:** having a range that extends into an area in which it or the group it represents would not be expected to be found **4** *of an archaeological object* **:** lying in a stratum that is not the place of original deposit **5** *of a sound or letter* **:** having nothing that corresponds to it in orthography or etymon ⟨~ \t\ in \'mints\ for *mince*⟩ ⟨~ *d* in *thunder*⟩ ⟨~ \r\ in the pronunciation \,indēə'riŋk\ for *India ink*⟩ **syn** see IMPERTINENT

**2intrusive** \"\ *n* -S **:** something that is intrusive; *specif* **:** intrusive rock or an intrusive rock

**intrusive growth** *n* **:** differential growth of the wall of a cell resulting in projection of newly formed parts between adjacent cells or into intercellular spaces — compare GLIDING GROWTH, SYMPLASTIC GROWTH

**in·tru·sive·ly** \|əvlē, -li\ *adv* **:** in an intrusive manner

**in·tru·sive·ness** \|ivnəs, |ēv- *also* |əv-\ *n* -ES **:** the quality or state of being intrusive ⟨have lost much of my taste for the special ~ of modern journalism, and it is no longer my opinion that it is necessary for the public to know the whole truth about anybody who has had the misfortune to acquire a little celebrity —Wolcott Gibbs⟩

**intrust** *var of* ENTRUST

**in·tu·bate** \'in·t(y)ü,bāt, ən·'t-\ *vt* -ED/-ING/-S [2*in-* + *tube* + *-ate*] **:** to treat by intubation **:** perform intubation on

**in·tu·ba·tion** \,═,═'bāshən\ *n* -S [2*in-* + *tube* + *-ation*] **:** the introduction of a tube into a hollow organ (as the trachea or intestine) to keep the latter open or to restore its patency if obstructed

**in·tue** \ən·'t(y)ü\ *vt* [L *intueri*] *archaic* **:** INTUIT

**in·tu·ent** \(')in·¦t(y)üənt, in·'t(y)ü-, 'intəwənt, 'in·tyəw-\ *adj* [L *intuent-, intuens*, pres. part. of *intueri*] *archaic* **:** knowing by intuition

**in·tu·it** \(')in·¦t(y)üət, ən·'t(y)ü-, 'intəwət, 'in·tyəw-\ *vb* -ED/-ING/-S [L *intuitus*, past part. of *intueri*] *vt* **:** to know or apprehend directly or by intuition ⟨only through the sensuous can the ideal be ~*ed* —Murray Krieger⟩ ⟨an imaginative artist ~*ing* the motives of men long dead —Howard M. Jones⟩ ~ *vi* **:** to have knowledge directly or by intuition

**in·tu·it·able** \ən·'t(y)üəd·əbəl\ *adj* **:** knowable through intuition

**in·tu·i·tion** \,in·(,)t(y)ü'ishən, ,intə'wi-, ,in·tyə'wi-\ *n* -S [ME *intuycion*, fr. LL *intuition-, intuitio*, fr. L *intuitus* (past part. of *intueri* to look at, contemplate, fr. *in-* 2in + *tueri* to look at) + *-ion-, -io* -ion — more at TUITION] **1 a** *obs* **:** the act of looking upon, regarding, examining, or inspecting **b** *archaic* **:** the act of contemplating or considering **:** CONTEMPLATION, CONSIDERATION **c** *obs* **:** a view, regard, or consideration of something as an ulterior goal or acquisition **2 a :** the act or process of coming to direct knowledge or certainty without reasoning or inferring **:** immediate cognizance or conviction without rational thought **:** revelation by insight or innate knowledge **:** immediate apprehension or cognition **b :** knowledge, perception, or conviction gained by intuition ⟨trusting . . . to what are called ~*s* rather than reasoned conclusions —A.C.Benson⟩ **c :** the power or faculty of attaining to direct knowledge or cognition without rational thought and inference **d** *in Bergsonism* **:** a form of knowing that is akin to instinct or a divining empathy and that gives direct insight into reality as it is in itself and absolutely **e :** quick and ready insight ⟨with one of her quick leaps of ~ she had entered into the other's soul —Edith Wharton⟩ **syn** see REASON

**in·tu·i·tion·al** \¦═(,)═¦(w)ishənᵊl, -shnəl\ *adj* **1 :** of, belonging to, derived from, characterized by, or perceived by intuition **:** INTUITIVE **2 :** of or belonging to intuitionism ⟨an ~ theory⟩ — **in·tu·i·tion·al·ly** \-ᵊlē, -əl|, |li\ *adv*

**in·tu·i·tion·al·ism** \,═(,)═'(w)ishənᵊl,izəm, -shnə,li-\ *n* -S **:** INTUITIONISM

**1in·tu·i·tion·al·ist** \-shənᵊləst, -shnəl-\ *n* -S **:** 1INTUITIONIST

**2in·tu·i·tion·al·ist** \¦═(,)═¦═-\ *or* **in·tu·i·tion·al·is·tic** \¦══-¦(w)ishənᵊl¦istik, -shnə¦li-\ *adj* **:** 2INTUITIONIST

**in·tu·i·tion·ism** \,═(,)═'(w)ishə,nizəm\ *n* -S **1 a :** a doctrine that there are self-evident truths intuitively known which form the basis of human knowledge **b :** a doctrine that objects of perception are intuitively known to be real ⟨radical empiricism, naive realism, and ~ . . . are expressions of an intense longing for reality —Frank Thilly⟩ **2 a :** a doctrine holding that the rightness or wrongness of particular actions or of kinds of actions is immediately intuitable through a special faculty (as the conscience) or that fundamental principles about what is right and wrong can be intuited **b :** a system of ethics that bases its ultimate conceptions on intuitions; *specif* **:** one according to which moral values (as the good) are intuitively apprehended and indefinable or irreducible **3 :** a thesis that mathematics is based upon special intuitions and requires rejection of the law of excluded middle — contrasted with *formalism* and *logicism*

**1in·tu·i·tion·ist** \-sh(ə)nəst\ *n* -S **:** an adherent of intuitionism

**2in·tu·i·tion·ist** \¦═(,)═¦═-\ *or* **in·tu·i·tion·is·tic** \-¦(w)ishə¦nistik\ *adj* **1 :** of, belonging to, or based on intuitionism **2 :** advocated by intuitionists

**intuition line** *n, usu cap I* **:** LINE OF INTUITION

**in·tu·i·tive** \ən·'t(y)üəd-iv, -üət|\ *adj* [ML *intuitivus*, fr. L *intuitus* (past part. of *intueri* to look at, contemplate) + *-ivus* -ive] **1 :** knowing or perceiving by intuition **:** capable of knowing by direct insight or cognition ⟨the ~ faculty⟩ ⟨an ~ power⟩ **2 a :** acquired, known, arrived at, or perceived by intuition ⟨an ~ awareness of another's feelings⟩ ⟨an ~ understanding of the parallelogram of forces —S.F. Mason⟩ ⟨an ~ conviction⟩ **:** known immediately or without the use of inference **:** directly apprehended ⟨~ knowledge⟩ ⟨~ truths⟩ — contrasted with *discursive;* compare INNATE **b :** knowable by intuition **c :** made by intuition or private judgment ⟨the ~ estimates of individuals —H.J.Morgenthau⟩ **3 :** possessing or using intuition or gifted with marked insight ⟨an ~ poet⟩ ⟨an ~ mind⟩ ⟨he was not a systematic critic, but was purely ~ —F.A.Swinnerton⟩ **4 :** 2INTUITIONIST — **in·tu·i·tive·ly** \|əvlē, -li\ *adv* — **in·tu·i·tive·ness** \|ivnəs\ *n* -ES

**intuitive reason** *n* **:** the faculty of apprehending a priori truths or principles — contrasted with *discursive reason;* compare PURE REASON

**in·tu·i·tiv·ism** \|i,vizəm\ *n* -S **:** INTUITIONISM 2

**1in·tu·i·tiv·ist** \-,vəst\ *n* -S **:** 1INTUITIONIST

**2intuitivist** \"\ *adj* **:** 2INTUITIONIST

**in·tu·mesce** \,in·(,)t(y)ü¦mes\ *vi* -ED/-ING/-S [L *intumescere* to swell, rise, fr. *in-* 2in- + *tumescere* to swell, incho. of *tumēre* to swell — more at THUMB] **:** to enlarge, expand, swell, or bubble up (as from being heated)

**in·tu·mes·cence** \,══'mes°n(t)s\ *n* -S [F, fr. L *intumescere* + F *-ence*] **1 a :** an enlarging, swelling, or bubbling up (as under the action of heat) **b :** the state of being swollen **:** marked enlargement **:** INFLATION **2 :** something swollen or enlarged (as a tumor); *specif* **:** an enlargement resembling a knob or pustule and consisting of a group of abnormally enlarged cells appearing on leaves or other plant parts as a result of physiological disturbances

**in·tu·mes·cent** \¦═(,)═¦mesᵊnt\ *adj* [L *intumescent-, intumescens*, pres. part. of *intumescere*] **1 :** marked by intumescence **:** swelling, enlarging, or bubbling up **2** *of paint* **:** swelling and charring when exposed to flame and forming an insulating fire-retardant barrier between the flame and the coated material

**in-turn** \'═,═\ *n* [2*in* + *turn*, after *turn in* v.] **:** a moving curling stone that is rotating clockwise — compare OUT-TURN

**inturned** \'═¦═\ *adj* [2*in* + *turned*, past part. of *turn*] **:** turned inward ⟨ladies' hose with an ~ knitted welt —W.E.Shinn⟩ **:** INTROVERTED ⟨were somewhat dour and ~ —Oliver La Farge⟩

**in·tus·sus·cept** \¦intəsə¦sept\ *vb* -ED/-ING/-S [prob. fr. (assumed) NL *intussusceptus*, past part. of (assumed) NL *intussuscipere*, fr. L *intus* within + *suscipere* to take up — more at ENT-, SUSCEPTIBLE] *vt* **:** to cause to turn inward esp. upon itself or to be received in some other thing or part; *esp* **:** to cause (an intestine) to undergo intussusception ⟨the bowel became ~*ed*⟩ ~ *vi* **:** to undergo intussusception ⟨some 3 ft. of the ileum had ~*ed* through the ileocecal valve into the cecum —*Veterinary Record*⟩

**in·tus·sus·cep·tion** \,═══'sepshən\ *n* -S [prob. fr. NL *intussusception-, intussusceptio*, prob. fr. (assumed) NL *intussusceptus* + L *-ion-, -io* -ion] **1 :** the reception of one part within another **:** INVAGINATION; *esp* **:** the passing of one portion of the intestine into an adjacent portion producing intestinal obstruction **2 :** the deposition of new particles of formative material among those already embodied in a tissue or structure (as in the growth of living organisms) — usu. distinguished from *accretion* and *apposition*

**in·tus·sus·cep·tive** \¦═══¦septiv\ *adj* **:** of, belonging to, or characterized by intussusception

**in·tus·sus·cep·tum** \,═══'septəm\ *n, pl* **intussuscep·ta** \-tə\ [NL, prob. neut. sing. of (assumed) NL *intussusceptus*] **:** the portion of the intestine that passes into another portion in intussusception

**in·tus·sus·cip·i·ens** \-sə'sipē,enz, -ēənz\ *n, pl* **intussus·cipien·tes** \-,sipē'en·(,)tēz\ [NL, prob. fr. pres. part. of (assumed) NL *intussuscipere*] **:** the portion of the intestine that receives the intussusceptum in intussusception

**intwine** *var of* ENTWINE

**intwist** *var of* ENTWIST

**inuendo** *var of* INNUENDO

**inug·suk** \'ēnəg,sük\ *adj, usu cap* **:** of or relating to a stage of Eskimo culture in west Greenland (A.D. 1200–1400) resulting from contact between Thule Eskimo and medieval Norse cultures

**in·u·la** \'inyələ\ *n* [NL, fr. L, elecampane, modif. of Gk *helenion* — more at HELENIUM] **1** -S **:** the dried roots and rhizomes of elecampane used as an aromatic stimulant and esp. formerly as a remedy in pulmonary diseases **2** *cap* **:** a genus of Old World perennial herbaceous or rarely shrubby plants (family Compositae) having large yellow radiate heads with anthers caudate at base — see ELECAMPANE **3** -S **:** any plant or root of the genus *Inula*

**in·u·lase** \'inyə,lās, -āz\ *also* **in·u·lin·ase** \-yələ,nās, -āz\ *n* -S [*inulase* ISV *inul-* (fr. *inulin*) + *-ase; inulinase* ISV *inulin* + *-ase*] **:** an enzyme obtained esp. from molds (as *Aspergillus niger*) and capable of converting inulin into levulose but without action on starch

**in·u·lin** \'inyələn\ *n* -S [prob. fr. G *inulin*, fr. NL *Inula* genus of plants (family Compositae) + G *-in*] **:** a tasteless white nondigestible polysaccharide that occurs usu. in place of starch in many composite and other plants esp. in the tubers or roots of Jerusalem artichoke, dahlia, or chicory, that on hydrolysis yields levulose, and that is used as a source of levulose and as a diagnostic agent in a test for kidney function

**in·um·brate** \'inəm,brāt, ə'nə-\ *vt* -ED/-ING/-S [L *inumbratus*, past part. of *inumbrare*, fr. *in-* 2in- + *umbrare* to shade, fr. *umbra* shadow — more at UMBRAGE] **:** to put in shadow **:** SHADE

**in·unct** \ə'nəŋ(k)t\ *vt* -ED/-ING/-S [L *inunctus*, past part. of *inunguere* — more at ANOINT] **:** ANOINT 1

**in·unc·tion** \ə'nəŋ(k)shən\ *n* -S [ME, fr. L *inunction-, inunctio*, fr. *inunctus* (past part. of *inunguere*) + *-ion-, -io* -ion] **1 :** an act of applying an oil or ointment : ANOINTING; *specif* : the rubbing of an ointment into the skin for therapeutic purposes **2** : OINTMENT, UNGUENT, INUNCTUM

**in·unc·tum** \-ŋ(k)təm\ *n* -S [NL, fr. L, neut. of *inunctus*, past part. of *inunguere*] : an ointment for rapid absorption usu. containing lanolin as a base

**inund** *vt* -ED/-ING/-S [L *inundare*] *obs* : INUNDATE

**in·un·da·ble** \ə'nəndəbəl, 'i(,)nənd-\ *adj* [*inundate* + *-able*] : exposed to inundation

**in·un·dant** \-dənt\ *adj* [L *inundant-, inundans*, pres. part. of *inundare*] : FLOODING, INUNDATING

**in·un·date** \'inən,dāt *sometimes* 'i,nə- *or* ə'nə-; *usu* -ād + V\ *vt* -ED/-ING/-S [L *inundatus*, past part. of *inundare*, fr. *in-* ²in- + *undare* to rise in waves, fr. *unda* wave — more at WATER] **1 a** : to flood with water : SUBMERGE ⟨rising rivers ~ low-lying farms⟩ ⟨a tidal wave ~*s* the island⟩ **b** : to flood as if with water ⟨red blood *inundated* her face, previously so pale —Thomas Hardy⟩ ⟨I have never felt . . . more *inundated* with frustration —John Mason Brown⟩ **2** : to overwhelm by great numbers or a superfluity of something : SWAMP ⟨was *inundated* by calls, telegrams, and letters —Marya Mannes⟩ ⟨*inundated* the nation with carloads of literature —Estes Kefauver⟩

**in·un·da·tion** \,i(,)nən'dāshən\ *n* -S [ME *inundacion*, fr. L *inundation-, inundatio*, fr. *inundatus* (past part. of *inundare*) + *-ion-, -io* -ion] **1** : a rising and spreading of water over land not usu. submerged : FLOOD ⟨the threat of ~ by the sea —Lewis Mumford⟩ ⟨his tears were not drops but a little ~ down his cheeks —Glenway Wescott⟩ ⟨fossil shells give evidence of prehistoric ~*s*⟩ **2** : DELUGE, SWARM ⟨an ~ of telegrams⟩ ⟨an ~ of tourists⟩

**in·un·da·tor** *pronunc at* INUNDATE +ə(r)\ *n* -S : one that inundates

**in·un·da·to·ry** \ə'nəndə,tōrē, -tȯr-, -ri\ *adj* [*inundate* + *-ory*] : tending to inundate

**inu·pik** \ə'nüpik\ *n* -S *cap* : an Eskimo-Aleut language of southwestern Alaska

**in·urbane** \(')in, ən+\ *adj* [L *inurbanus*, fr. *in-* ¹in- + *urbanus* of the city, refined — more at URBAN] : lacking in refinement or courtesy — **in·urbanity** \'in+\ *n*

**in·ure** \ə'n(y)u̇(ə)r, -ùə\ *or* **en·ure** \ə'-, e'-\ *vb* -ED/-ING/-S [*inure* alter. (influenced by ²*in-*) of *enure*, fr. ME *enuren*, fr. ¹*en-* + *ure*, n., use, custom — more at URE] *vt* : ACCUSTOM : discipline to accept something : HABITUATE ⟨*inured* to the smell of the stable⟩ ⟨a public . . . that is *inured* to certain ways of seeing and thinking —John Dewey⟩ ⟨being stationed at an arctic base ~*s* a man to cold⟩ ~ *vi* : to come into operation : become operative ⟨we are dealing with a relation . . . that might virtually ~ by usage only —W.E.Gladstone⟩ : ACCRUE ⟨the profits ~ to the benefit of hospitals for crippled children —D.A. Reed⟩; *specif* : to become legally effective ⟨when there is such an identity of interest between the taxpayers that a refund to one will ~ to the benefit of the other . . . the unsatisfied liability may be recovered —W.T.Plumb⟩ **syn** see HARDEN

**in·ured** \-u̇(ə)rd, -ùəd\ *adj* [fr. past part. of *inure*] : adapted to existing conditions : accustomed to adverse elements : DISCIPLINED, HARDY ⟨our successors . . . may be graver, more ~ and equable men —V.S.Pritchett⟩ ⟨a peasant . . . lean-faced, dark, wind-*inured* —Robert Lynd⟩ — **in·ured·ness** \-u̇rdnəs, -ùəd-, -u̇rəd-\ *n* -ES

**in·ure·ment** \-u̇(ə)rmənt, -ùəm-\ *n* -S : the quality or state of being inured

**in·urn** \ən+\ *vt* -ED/-ING/-S [²*in-* + *urn*, n.] : to enclose in or as if in an urn : ENTOMB ⟨the body was cremated and the ashes ~*ed*⟩ ⟨where . . . storied cenotaphs ~ sweet human hopes —R.W.Emerson⟩ — **in·urn·ment** \-mənt\ *n* -S

**inusitate** *adj* [L *inusitatus*, fr. *in-* ¹in- + *usitatus* usual, customary, fr. past part. of *usitor* to use often, fr. *usus*, past part. of *uti* to use — more at USE] *obs* : UNFAMILIAR

**in·us·tion** \ə'nəschən\ *n* -S [LL *inustion-, inustio* branding, fr. L *inustus* (past part. of *inurere* to brand, burn in, fr. *in-* ²in- + *urere* to burn) + *-ion-, -io* -ion — more at EMBER] *archaic* : CAUTERIZATION

**in ute·ro** \ə'n(y)üdə,rō\ *adv* [L] : in the uterus : before birth ⟨the infection is apparently acquired *in utero* from a mother with a latent disease —*Yr. Bk. of Pediatrics*⟩

**in·utile** \(')in, ən+\ *adj* [ME, fr. MF, fr. L *inutilis*, fr. *in-* ¹in- + *utilis* useful — more at UTILE] : of no practical value : USELESS, UNUSABLE ⟨being myth it is ~ —Donald Davidson⟩ ⟨the large proportion of ~ tree volume due to decay —*Ecology*⟩ — **in·utility** \'in+\ *n*

**in utro·que ju·re** \,inyü·,trōkwē'jùrē, ,inü·,trō(,)kwā'yü·\ *adv* [NL, lit., in both laws] : in or under both canon and civil law

**in·utterable** \(')in, ən+\ *adj* [¹*in-* + *utterable*] *archaic* : UNUTTERABLE

**inv** *abbr* **1** [L *invenit*] he designed; he devised; he invented **2** invented; invention; inventor **3** inventory **4** investment **5** invitation **6** invoice

**in va·cuo** \ən'vakyə,wō\ *adv* [NL] **1** : in a vacuum ⟨this residue may be fractionally distilled *in vacuo* —T.P.Hilditch⟩ **2** : without reference to pertinent facts or materials ⟨the theoretical technique has been evolved *in vacuo* —D.L. Bolinger⟩

**in·vad·able** \ən'vādəbəl\ *adj* : capable of being invaded

**in·vade** \ən'vād\ *vb* -ED/-ING/-S [ME *invaden*, fr. L *invadere*, fr. *in-* ²in- + *vadere* to go — more at WADE] *vt* **1 a** : to enter in a hostile manner : overrun with a view to conquest or plunder ⟨soldiers ~ enemy territory⟩ **b** *obs* : to make a personal attack upon : ASSAULT ⟨what madness could provoke a mortal man to ~ a sleeping god —John Dryden⟩ **2** : to encroach, intrude, or trespass upon : INFRINGE ⟨you can obtain legal counsel to determine if any of your rights have been *invaded* —R.O.Case⟩ ⟨when government ~*s* the traditional area of business —A.L.Nickerson⟩ ⟨during his absence his house was *invaded* and plundered —E.D.Dickinson⟩ ⟨resented these queries as *invading* the family privacy —John Dollard⟩ **3** : to penetrate in the manner of an invader: **a** (1) : to grow over or spread into : PERMEATE ⟨the growing city has *invaded* the surrounding countryside —P.E.James⟩ ⟨the imagery of movement . . . *invaded* secular as well as religious literature —R.W.Southern⟩ ⟨doubts ~ his mind⟩ ⟨an odor of onions ~*s* the room⟩ (2) : to affect injuriously and progressively ⟨gangrene ~*s* healthy tissue⟩ ⟨cholera ~*s* the city⟩ (3) : to push into : enter intrusively ⟨the bow-roofed . . . South Ferry Terminal, its upper deck *invaded* by the el structure —*Amer. Guide Series: N.Y.City*⟩; *specif* : to enter in a molten state ⟨compression . . . forces the granitic part of the crust downward to form a solid root and upward to ~ the thick sediments of the mountain-forming belt as molten rock —W.H.Bucher⟩ **b** : to enter or take possession of : PENETRATE, ENGULF ⟨at midmorning, the sun finally ~*s* the very bottom of the gorge —Lester Womack⟩ ⟨two thousand skiers . . . ~ this alpine region —R.S.Monahan⟩ ⟨layfolk . . . *invaded* ecclesiastical offices and revenues —G.G.Coulton⟩; *specif* : to penetrate steadily by taking up residence in (an area occupied by a population of a different class or ethnic composition) **c** : to raid or take by storm ⟨possums ~ the corn patch⟩ ⟨a young and ambitious small-town girl . . . came to New York to ~ the public-relations field —*Publishers' Weekly*⟩ ~ *vi* : to make an invasion **syn** see TRESPASS

**in·vad·er** \-də(r)\ *n* -S : one that invades

**invading** *adj* : of, relating to, or being an invader ⟨~ army⟩ ⟨~ tourists⟩ ⟨~ culture⟩ ⟨~ virus⟩

**in·vag·i·nate** \ən'vajə,nāt, *usu* -ād+V\ *vb* -ED/-ING/-S [ML *invaginatus*, past part. of *invaginare*, fr. L *in-* ²in- + *vagina* sheath — more at VAGINA] *vt* **1** : ENCLOSE, SHEATHE ⟨external . . . sex organs of the male, contrasted to the *invaginated* organs of the female —*Yr. Bk. of Neurology, Psychiatry & Neurosurgery*⟩ **2** : to fold in so that an outer becomes an inner surface : INTUSSUSCEPT ⟨~ the sac into the lumen —E.A. Graham⟩ ~ *vi* : to become sheathed or infolded ⟨the sphere of cells then *invaginated* to give a cuplike double-walled gastrula —S.F.Mason⟩

**in·vag·i·na·tion** \(,)in,vajə'nāshən, ən,v-\ *n* -S **1** : an act or process of invaginating: as **a** : the formation of a gastrula by an infolding of part of the wall of the blastula **b** : intestinal intussusception **2** : an invaginated part

**¹in·val·id** \(')in'valəd, ən'v-\ *adj* [L *invalidus* not strong, infirm, weak, inadequate, fr. *in-* ¹in- + *validus* strong — more at VALID] **1 a** : being without foundation in fact or truth : INDEFENSIBLE, UNJUSTIFIED ⟨this argument . . . is ~ on two counts —*Monsanto Mag.*⟩ ⟨now that rockets can escape gravity it is ~ to say that what goes up must come down⟩ **b** : lacking in effectiveness : INADEQUATE, WEAK ⟨acceptance of the new method was a tacit admission that the old technique was ~ and inferior⟩ **2** [ML *invalidus*, fr. L] : being without legal force or effect ⟨declared the wills technically ~ because of some legal flaw —Robert Graves⟩

**²invalid** \"\ *vt* -ED/-ING/-S *archaic* : INVALIDATE

**³in·va·lid** \'invələd, *Brit* ¦invə¦lēd\ *adj* [L & F; F *invalide*, fr. L *invalidus*] **1 a** : suffering from disease or disability : SICKLY, DISABLED ⟨hired a nurse to care for his ~ mother⟩ **b** : of, relating, or suited to one that is sick ⟨~ chair⟩ ⟨the whole family lived on ~ fare, on custards and broths and arrowroot pudding —Jean Stafford⟩ **2** : being in poor condition : WEAKENED, UNSOUND ⟨reminding me that, if my chimney was allowed to stand in that ~ condition, my policy of insurance would be void —Herman Melville⟩

**⁴in·va·lid** \'invələd; *Brit* 'invə,lēd *also* ,invə'lēd\ *n* -S : one that is sickly or disabled ⟨arranged a bed table for the ~ —Eden Phillpotts⟩ ⟨an exaggeration to assume that France is a chronic economic ~ —Paul Johnson⟩; *specif*, *archaic* : a member of the armed forces who has become unfit for active duty by illness or injury ⟨his garrison at present consists of a few hundreds of ~*s* —Tobias Smollett⟩

**⁵in·va·lid** \'invələd, *esp before a syllable-increasing suffix* -,lid; *Brit* ¦invə¦lēd\ *vb* -ED/-ING/-S *vt* **1** : to make sickly or disabled ⟨because of a bone ailment, has been ~*ed* since childhood —*Sat. Eve. Post*⟩ **2** : to classify as sick or disabled and remove from active duty ⟨of the 185 firemen . . . sixty were ~*ed* home because of smoke poisoning, burns, or exhaustion —Joseph Millard⟩; *specif* : to release from military service because of illness or injury ⟨~*ed* out of the Norfolk Yeomanry with rheumatic fever —*Saturday Rev.*⟩ ⟨received three bullets through the body, and was due to be ~*ed* home —Joyce Cary⟩ ~ *vi*, *archaic* **1** : to become an invalid ⟨cannot conceal from myself that I am ~*ing* —R.W.Sibthorp⟩ **2** : to become released from active duty because of disability ⟨the conscripts . . . ~ at an inexplicable rate —*Spectator*⟩

**in·val·i·date** \ən'valə,dāt, *usu* -ād+V\ *vt* [¹*invalid* + *-ate*] : to weaken or make valueless : DISCREDIT ⟨how far the facts confirm or ~ this proud claim —Aldous Huxley⟩ ⟨deviation from a rule which does not affect any important rights of the alien should not ~ a deportation hearing —*Harvard Law Rev.*⟩ **syn** see NULLIFY

**in·val·i·da·tion** \(,)in,valə'dāshən, ən,v-\ *n* : the act or process of invalidating or the state of being invalidated

**in·va·lid·ish** \'invələdish, -,lid-, *Brit* ¦invə¦lēd-\ *adj* : resembling or characteristic of an invalid

**in·va·lid·ism** \'invələ,dizəm, *Brit* ¦invə¦lē,d-\ *n* -S : the quality or state of being an invalid : a usu. chronic condition of disability

**in·va·lid·i·ty** \¦invə'lidəd·ē, ¦invə¦-, -idətē, -i\ *n* [MF or ML; MF *invalidité*, fr. ML *invaliditat-, invaliditas*, fr. *invalidus* void, without legal force + L *-itat-, -itas* -ity] **1** : lack of sound foundation or binding legal force **2** [³*invalid* + *-ity*] **a** : incapacity to work because of prolonged illness or disability ⟨insurance for sickness and ~ and for the provision of medical service for the working class —R.V.Sires⟩ **b** : INVALIDISM

**in·val·id·ly** \(')in¦valədlē, ən'v-, -li\ *adv* : in an invalid manner : ILLEGALLY

**in·val·id·ness** *n* : the quality or state of being invalid

**in·valuable** \ən+\ *adj* [¹*in-* + *value*, v. + *-able*] **1** : of an excellence or worth beyond measure : of incalculable value : PRICELESS ⟨fellow townsmen gave him a standing ovation for his ~ services to the community⟩ ⟨a flair for languages is ~ to the career diplomat⟩ ⟨his firsthand knowledge of the area was ~ to the search party⟩ **2** *archaic* : of no value : WORTHLESS ⟨flattered myself I might not be altogether ~ to your ladyship —George Colman †1836⟩ **syn** see COSTLY

**in·valuableness** \"+\ *n* : the quality or state of being invaluable

**in·valuably** \"+\ *adv* : to an invaluable degree : IMMEASURABLY

**in·valued** \"+\ *adj* [¹*in-* + *valued* (past part. of *value*, v.)] *archaic* : INVALUABLE ⟨no vulgar price the ~ treasure brought —John Hoole⟩

**in·var** \'in,vär\ *n* -S [fr. *Invar*, a trademark] : an iron-nickel alloy containing about 36 percent nickel and having a coefficient of linear expansion of approximately 0.000001 inch per inch per degree centigrade at ordinary temperatures

**in·variability** \(')in, ən+\ *n* : the quality or state of being invariable

**¹in·variable** \(')in, ən+\ *adj* [prob. fr. F, fr. MF, fr. *in-* ¹in- + *variable*] : CONSISTENT, UNIFORM : showing no deviation : UNCHANGING, UNFAILING ⟨where many words . . . are relatively ~ in meaning from one sentence to another —I.A. Richards⟩ ⟨after dinner . . . retired to the library, according to his ~ habit —Valentine Williams⟩ ⟨was respected for his ~ courtesy and undoubted integrity —H.W.H.Knott⟩ — **in·variableness** \"+\ *n*

**²invariable** \"\ *n* : one that remains constant

**in·variably** \(')in, ən+\ *adv* : without exception or change : ALWAYS, CONSISTENTLY ⟨those most loved . . . are ~ those who have the capacity for believing in others —W.J.Reilly⟩ ⟨the scene . . . was ~ the room in which I lay —Charles Lamb⟩ ⟨a desire to conduct my life ~ —Arnold Bennett⟩

**in·variance** \"+\ *n* [¹*invariant* + *-ance*] : invariability under prescribed or implied conditions

**¹in·variant** \"+\ *n* [¹*in-* + *variant*] : a constant factor : one that does not change; *specif* : a mathematical expression or magnitude that remains unchanged under prescribed or implied conditions

**²invariant** \"\ *adj* [¹*in-* + *variant*] **1** : CONSTANT, UNCHANGING, UNVARYING, UNIVERSAL ⟨16 subjects were presented, on 4 successive days, with 300 ~ stimuli —*Biol. Abstracts*⟩ ⟨basic human emotions . . . are ~ —H.B.Parkes⟩; *specif* : unaffected by the group of mathematical operations under consideration **2** : having no degree of freedom — used of a physical-chemical system; compare PHASE RULE

**invaried** *adj* [¹*in-* + *varied*] *obs* : UNVARIED

**in·va·sion** \ən'vāzhən\ *n* -S [ME (Sc) *invasioune*, fr. MF *invasion*, fr. LL *invasion-, invasio*, fr. L *invasus* (past part. of *invadere* to invade) + *-ion-, -io* -ion — more at INVADE] **1 a** : a hostile entrance or armed attack on the property or territory of another for conquest or plunder ⟨the ~ of So. Korea resulted in the first police action by United Nations forces⟩ **b** *obs* : an attack on a person : ASSAULT **2** : an inroad of any kind: as **a** : an entry into or establishment in an area not previously occupied ⟨~ of agricultural Lowland Britain by . . . industries from the Highland Margin —L.D. Stamp⟩ ⟨an ~ of catbrier⟩ ⟨~ of sediments by granite —W.H. Bucher⟩ **b** : the introduction or spread of something hurtful or pernicious ⟨~ of locusts⟩; *specif* : the period during which a pathogen multiplies in and is distributed through the body of a host prior to the development of clinically evident disease ⟨vaccine helps to defeat a virus ~ by promoting the production of antibodies in the bloodstream⟩ **c** : a penetration or occupation by an outside force or agency ⟨tourists . . . making their annual ~ of France —James Pope-Hennessy⟩ ⟨insidious ~*s* of experience into the heart —Mark Schorer⟩ ⟨knew I would not disapprove of this ~ of my place by my young cousin —R.H.Davis⟩; *specif* : the penetration and gradual occupation of an area by a population group of different socioeconomic status or racial or cultural origin than its original inhabitants — compare SUCCESSION **d** : VISIT, TOUR ⟨guest ~*s* by famed choreographers —*Time*⟩ ⟨the enterprising candidate made a two-day ~ of nearby tank towns⟩ **3** : ENCROACHMENT, INTRUSION; *specif* : an encroachment upon a right protected by law affording grounds for an action for damages or some other remedy

**in·va·sion·ary** \-zhə,nerē, -ri\ *adj* : INVASIVE

**invasion currency** *or* **invasion money** *n* : paper money issued for use by military forces in an invasion

**in·va·sive** \ən'vāsiv, -āziv\ *adj* [ME (Sc), fr. MF *invasif*, fr. ML *invasivus*, fr. L *invasus* (past part. of *invadere*) + *-ivus* -ive] **1** *obs* : of, relating to, or characterized by military aggression ⟨shall we . . . make compromise, insinuation, parley, and base truce to arms ~ —Shak.⟩ **2** : tending to spread ⟨for years we have been trying to get rid of ~ bulbs —E.H.M.Cox⟩; *specif* : tending to invade healthy tissue ⟨~ cancer cells⟩ — compare PREINVASIVE **3** *archaic* : tending to encroach on or infringe ⟨~ of tribal rights —H.J.S.Maine⟩

**in·va·sive·ness** *n* -ES : the quality or state of being invasive; *specif* : the tendency of a pathogenic organism to penetrate into and grow within the host away from the original site of inoculation ⟨~ is a major factor in virulence⟩

**in·vecked** \(')in¦vekt, ən'v-\ *adj* [modif. (influenced by E ¹-*ed*) of L *invectus*, past part. of *invehere* to carry in, bring in] : INVECTED

**in·vec·ta et il·la·ta** \ən'vektə,ed·ə'lād·ə\ *n pl* [LL, lit., things brought in and things carried in] *Roman & civil & Scots law* : goods of a tenant brought upon the leased premises or goods of others brought there by their consent and for other than temporary use

**in·vect·ed** \(')in¦vektəd, ən'v-\ *adj* [L *invectus* (past part. of *invehere* to carry in, bring in) + E ¹-*ed*] *heraldry* : edged by convex semicircles or arcs : SCALLOPED — compare ENGRAILED

**in·vec·tion** \-kshən\ *n* -S [L *invection-, invectio*, fr. *invectus* (past part. of *invehere* to carry in, bring in) + *-ion-, -io* -ion] : an introduction of something from an outside source ⟨an ~ of . . . battle smoke floated among islands of rose-tinted altocumulus —K.M.Dodson⟩

**¹in·vec·tive** \ən'vektiv, -tēv *also* -təv\ *adj* [ME *invectiff*, fr. MF *invectif*, fr. LL *invectivus*, fr. L *invectus* (past part. of *invehere*) + *-ivus* -ive] : of, relating to, or characterized by insult or abuse : DENUNCIATORY ⟨a sharp corrective message, suitably ~ —Edith G. Blanchard⟩

**²invective** \"\ *n* -S **1** : an abusive expression or diatribe : a vehement verbal attack ⟨replied with ~*s* fierce and scurrilous —J.A.Froude⟩ ⟨thundering ~ against sin —Ernest Beaglehole⟩ **2** : critical or insulting language : violent abuse : VITUPERATION ⟨as his anger mounted, ridicule and ~ poured from his mouth searing and burning all that they touched —D.L.Cohn⟩ **syn** see ABUSE

**in·vec·tive·ly** \-təvlē, -li\ *adv*, *obs* : in an invective manner ⟨thus most ~ he pierceth through the body of our country, swearing —Shak.⟩

**in·veigh** \ən'vā\ *vb* -ED/-ING/-S [L *invehi* to sail into, attack, inveigh, pass. infin. of *invehere* to carry in, bring in, fr. *in-* ²in- + *vehere* to carry — more at WAY] *vi* : to protest bitterly or violently : complain vehemently : RAIL — used with *against* ⟨~ against injustice⟩ ⟨~*s* against the arbitrary character of all such unscientific procedures —G.M.Messing⟩ ~ *vt* : [L *invehere*] *obs* : INVEIGLE

**in·veigh·er** \-āə(r)\ *n* -S : one that inveighs

**in·vei·gle** \ən'vāgəl *also* ən'vēg- *or* ən'veg-\ *vt* **inveigled; inveigled; inveigling** \-g(ə)liŋ\ **inveigles** [modif. (influenced by E ²*in-*) of MF *aveugler* to blind, hoodwink, fr. OF *avogler*, fr. *avogle*, *avugle* blind, fr. ML *ab oculis*, fr. L *ab* from + *oculis*, abl. pl. of *oculus* eye — more at OF, EYE] **1** *obs* : DELUDE, MISLEAD, HOODWINK, BEGUILE ⟨your rhetorical flourishes . . . contributed in an high degree to ~ the jury, and bring that noble lord to the scaffold —Robert Atkyns⟩ **2** : to snare by ingenuity or flattery : ENTICE, CAJOLE ⟨used the most subtle means to ~ the author into the office —Edward Bok⟩ ⟨with patience and diplomacy, she can eventually ~ him into marrying her —Nellie Maher⟩ **3** : to acquire by ingenuity or flattery ⟨over gin and water we *inveigled* from him a pack of well-worn cards —Ernest Beaglehole⟩ **syn** see LURE

**in·vei·gle·ment** \-gəlmənt\ *n* -S : an act, process, or means of inveigling : ENTICEMENT, LURE

**in·vei·gler** \-g(ə)lə(r)\ *n* -S : one that inveigles

**inveil** *var of* ENVEIL

**in·vent** \ən'vent\ *vt* -ED/-ING/-S [ME *inventen*, fr. L *inventus*, past part. of *invenire*, fr. *in-* ²in- + *venire* to come — more at COME] **1** : to search out or come upon : FIND, DISCOVER ⟨must ~ beds for them —Frederick Way⟩ ⟨this polymer was ~*ed* in England and is an outgrowth of earlier research —Leonard Maner & Harry Wechsler⟩ **2** : to think up or imagine : concoct mentally : FABRICATE ⟨his fund of knowledge seemed inexhaustible, for what he didn't know he ~*ed* —Alvin Redman⟩ ⟨preparing in his mind the harshest response he could ~ —W.F.Davis⟩ **3** : to create or produce for the first time : be the author of : DEVISE, ORIGINATE ⟨he ~*ed* and secured a patent . . . for a rock-boring machine —B.A.Soule⟩ ⟨if the Semitic letters were not derived from Egypt they must have been ~*ed* by the Phoenicians —Edward Clodd⟩ ⟨~*ed* an ingenious kind of ball game —Margaret Bean⟩ ⟨has ~*ed* plenty of good tunes of his own —Sigmund Spaeth⟩ **4** *obs* : FOUND, ESTABLISH, INSTITUTE, INITIATE ⟨festival days in old time were ~*ed* for recreation —John Northbrooke⟩ **syn** see CONTRIVE

**in·vent·able** *or* **in·vent·ible** \-təbəl\ *adj* : capable of being invented

**inventary** *n* -ES [LL *inventarium* — more at INVENTORY] *obs* : INVENTORY

**in·ven·tion** \ən'venchən\ *n* -S [ME *invencioun*, fr. MF *invention*, fr. L *invention-, inventio*, fr. *inventus* (past part. of *invenire* to find) + *-ion-, -io* -ion] **1** : an act of finding or of finding out : DISCOVERY ⟨~ of the principle of leverage⟩ **2 a** : the power to conceive new ideas and relationships : productive imagination : INVENTIVENESS ⟨old crates and boxes are often more stimulating to a child's ~ than expensive toys⟩ **b** : a faculty for creative selection of theme and imaginative treatment of design or content ⟨the variety and excellence of the classical legacy demonstrate the abundant ~ of the ancient Greeks⟩ ⟨as a teller of tales he had rich ~ and adroit construction —Brander Matthews⟩ **c** : a product of creative imagination or fertile wit ⟨the ~*s*, the devices which serve a novelist best grow . . . out of his necessity —Caroline Gordon⟩ ⟨a cascade of melodic ~ —Harold Sinclair⟩ ⟨those pillars, that stair and varnished roof . . . were among the worst ~*s* of the Gothic revival —W.B.Yeats⟩ **d** : a musical composition or piece imitative in style, usu. short, and usu. written for the piano or other keyboard instrument **3 a** : an act of mental creation or organization : application of knowledge : CONCEPTION, FORMULATION ⟨~ of agreements or compromises —Weston La Barre⟩ ⟨no continuing agency to interpret the party platform after its slapdash ~ every four years —R.L. Strout⟩ ⟨tried a long play of her own ~ —Leslie Rees⟩ **b** : a product of thought or mental synthesis : IDEA, CONCEPT ⟨the idea that the royal family should be a symbol of respectability was an ~ of Queen Victoria —Fritz Stern⟩ ⟨characterized the Supreme Court as the great political ~ of the framers of the Constitution —Felix Frankfurter⟩ ⟨new social ~*s* are made by those who suffer from the current conditions —Ralph Linton⟩; *specif* : a fictitious idea or statement ⟨race theories are . . . a modern ~ to explain such group conflicts —M.R.Cohen⟩ ⟨the whole purpose of the . . . argument being to invalidate the generally accepted romance and prove it an ~ —E.V.Lucas⟩ **4 a** : the creation of something not previously in existence : purposeful experimentation leading to the development of a new device or process : ORIGINATION ⟨necessity is the mother of ~⟩ ⟨machinery of their own ~ —*Amer. Guide Series: Md.*⟩ **b** : an original device or process ⟨writing was a greater ~ than the steam engine —A.N.Whitehead⟩; *specif*, *U.S. patent law* : a device or process that is not only novel and useful but that reflects creative genius, makes a distinct contribution to and advances science, is recognized by masters of science as such an advance and reveals more than the skill of expert artisans or mechanics in discovering new and useful gadgets or processes of wide commercial application

**inventious** *adj* [fr. *invention*, after such pairs as E *contention: contentious*] : INVENTIVE

**in·ven·tive** \ən'ventiv, -tēv *also* -təv\ *adj* [ME *inventif*, fr. MF, fr. *invention*, after such pairs as MF *action: actif* active] **1** : having the capacity for or being a prolific producer of inventions : CREATIVE, INGENIOUS ⟨an ~ writer⟩ ⟨an ~ composer⟩ ⟨the preposition . . . is a tremendously ~ word —R.M. Weaver⟩ **2** : of, relating to, or characterized by invention ⟨the war gives rise to incidents . . . beyond the ~ power of the human imagination —Maya Deren⟩ ⟨exquisite gold work and ~ ceramics —Angélica Mendoza⟩ ⟨a mechanic of an ~ turn of mind —J.Q.Dealey⟩ — **in·ven·tive·ly** \-təvlē, -li\ *adv*

**in·ven·tive·ness** \-tivnəs, -tēv- *also* -təv-\ *n* -ES : the quality or state of being inventive : INGENUITY, CREATIVITY

**in·ven·tor** *also* **in·vent·er** \ən'ventə(r)\ *n* -S [*inventor* fr. L, fr. *inventus* (past part. of *invenire*) + *-or*; *inventer* alter. (influenced by E ²-*er*) of *inventor*] **1** *obs* : one that finds or finds out : DISCOVERER ⟨first ~ of the nervous system —John Freind⟩ **2 :** one that conceives by creative imagination ⟨~ of a new ballet⟩ ⟨one must be an ~ to read well —S.P.Sherman⟩ ⟨the next step is to discover what makes a man an ~ rather than a passive culture carrier —Ralph Linton⟩ **3 :** one that creates a new device or process : ORIGINATOR ⟨Eli Whitney was the ~ of the cotton gin⟩

**in·ven·to·ri·able** \ˈinvən·ˌtōrēəbəl, -tȯr-, ˌ==ˈ====\ *adj* **1 :** capable of being inventoried **2 :** includable in an inventory or in its valuation

**in·ven·to·ri·al** \ˌ==ˈ=rēəl\ *adj* **:** of or relating to an inventory — **in·ven·to·ri·al·ly** \-rēəlē\ *adv*

**inventorize** *vt* -ED/-ING/-S [MF *inventoriser*, fr. *inventoire* inventory (fr. ML *inventorium*) + *-iser* -ize] *archaic* **:** INVENTORY

**¹in·ven·to·ry** \ˈinvən·ˌtōrē, -tȯr-, -ri\ *n* -ES *often attrib* [alter. (influenced by ML *inventorium*) of ME *invitory*, modif. of ML *inventorium*, alter. (influenced by L *-orium* -ory) of LL *inventarium*, fr. L *inventus* (past part. of *invenire* to find) + *-arium* -ary] **1 :** an itemized list of current assets: as **a :** a written list or catalog usu. made by a fiduciary under oath of the tangible or intangible property of an individual, organization, or estate describing the items or classes of property so as to be identifiable and usu. placing a valuation thereon **b** (1) **:** a list or schedule of raw materials, supplies, work in process, and finished goods on hand as of a given date (2) **:** a list of merchandise held for sale (3) **:** the aggregate value assigned to an inventory **c :** a survey of natural resources; *specif* **:** an estimate or enumeration of the wildlife (as game animals) of a region **d :** a questionnaire designed to provide an index of individual interests or personality traits **2 :** a detailed study or recapitulation : SURVEY, SUMMARY ⟨offered a brief ~ of the chief inventions of the middle ages —Benjamin Farrington⟩ ⟨the replies . . . provide a nearly complete ~ of the ideas which are afloat among the young people —W.J.Cahnman⟩ ⟨Whitman's verses . . . are often more *inventories* than imaginative projections of America —H.S.Canby⟩ **3 a :** the quantity of goods or materials on hand : STOCK, SUPPLY ⟨adequate *inventories* of washing machines to meet local demand⟩ ⟨it took quite an ~ of heavy tools . . . to do all this —George Woodbury⟩ **b :** a surplus of goods or materials accumulated against future needs : RESERVE ⟨there has piled up a 2000 million dollar ~ of foodstuffs —John Boyd Orr⟩ ⟨industry would purchase for a year in advance what would amount to an ~ of labor —Leland Hazard⟩ **4 :** the act or process of taking an inventory ⟨the annual ~ takes two weeks⟩ ⟨depends on a careful and continuing ~ of the entire staff —J.B.Conant⟩ **5 :** a comprehensive list of personality traits, personal preferences, attitudes, interests, or abilities used to measure subjective judgments and to evaluate individual characteristics and skills

**²inventory** \"\ *vb* -ED/-ING/-ES *vt* **1 a :** to make an itemized report or record of : take stock of : CATALOG ⟨~ home troops⟩ ⟨~ waterfowl⟩ ⟨walked in uninvited and *inventoried* the room with one long glance —John Selby⟩; *specif* **:** to count and list the assets of together with their valuation ⟨~ an estate⟩ **b :** to include in a business inventory **2 :** to make a study or recapitulation of : SURVEY, SUMMARIZE ⟨a book of criticism that . . . completely *inventoried* the mind of the age —Rebecca West⟩ ~ *vi* **:** to have a value by inventory ⟨his estate *inventories* at close to half a million⟩

**inventory control** *n* **:** coordination and supervision of the supply, storage, distribution, and recording of materials to maintain quantities adequate for current needs without excessive oversupply or loss

**in·ven·tress** \ənˈven·trəs\ *n* -ES [*inventor* + *-ess*] **:** a female inventor

**in·ven·trix** \-en·triks\ *n* -ES [L, fem. of *inventor* — more at -TRIX] **:** INVENTRESS

**in·veracity** \ˌin+\ *n* [¹*in-* + *veracity*] **1 :** lack of truth : FALSENESS ⟨forced to recognize its inadequacy, its palpable ~ —G.J.Becker⟩ **2 :** an intentional falsehood : LIE ⟨the bogus anecdotes of his conversation were not, I am convinced, plain *inveracities*, but things which he had imagined —Christopher Hollis⟩

**¹in·ver·ness** \ˌinvə(r)ˈnes\ *adj* [fr. *Inverness*, burgh and county in Scotland] **1 :** of or from the burgh of Inverness, Scotland **:** of the kind or style prevalent in Inverness **2 :** INVERNESS-SHIRE

**²inverness** \"\ *n* -ES **:** a loose belted coat having an often detachable shoulder cape with a close-fitting round collar

**inverness-shire** \ˌinvə(r)ˈnes(h),shi(ə)r, -iə, -ˌshə(r)\ *or* **inverness** \ˌinvə(r)ˈnes\ *adj, usu cap I* [fr. *Inverness-shire* or *Inverness*, county in Scotland] **:** of or from the county of Inverness, Scotland **:** of the kind or style prevalent in Inverness

inverness

**¹in·verse** \(ˈ)inˈvərs, ənˈv-, -və̄s, -vəis\ *vt* -ED/-ING/-S [L *inversus*, past part. of *invertere*] **:** INVERT, REVERSE

**²in·verse** \ˈ=,=, =ˈ=\ *adj* [L *inversus*, past part. of *invertere* to invert — more at INVERT] **1** *archaic* **:** being upside down : INVERTED ⟨a tower builded on a lake, mocked by its ~ shadow —Thomas Hood †1845⟩ **2 :** opposite in nature or relationship : CONTRARY, REVERSED ⟨as high as 70 percent . . . were engaged in repair and conversion work, a condition ~ to prewar operation —*Collier's Yr. Bk.*⟩ ⟨attendance of the students . . . is in ~ ratio to the work in the cornfields —Joaquin Noval⟩ **3 a :** opposite in nature and effect — used of two mathematical operations which when both are performed in succession upon any quantity reproduce that quantity ⟨division is the ~ operation of multiplication⟩ **b** *of a mathematical function* **:** expressing the same relationship as another function but from the opposite viewpoint

**³inverse** \"\ *n* -S **1 :** something of a contrary nature or quality : OPPOSITE, REVERSE ⟨had no luck with his experiment so he tried the ~ of this process and got a positive result⟩; *specif* **:** the opposite color from that of the first card dealt in the winning row in the game of rouge et noir — compare COULEUR 2 **2 :** the result of an inversion; *specif* **:** a proposition which is inferred immediately from another and in which the subject term is the negative of the subject of the given proposition and the predicate term is unchanged ⟨the ~ of "no purposeful effort is entirely wasted" is "some not-purposeful effort is entirely wasted"⟩ — compare CONTRAPOSITION **3 :** an inverse function, operation, or point

**inverse cosecant** *n* **:** ARC COSECANT

**inverse cosine** *n* **:** ARC COSINE

**inverse cotangent** *n* **:** ARC COTANGENT

**inverse feedback** *n* **:** NEGATIVE FEEDBACK

**inverse function** *n* **:** either of two mathematical functions such that each is the inverse of the other

**in·verse·ly** \(ˈ)=ˈ==\ *adv* **:** in an inverse order or manner **:** by inversion

**inversely proportional** *adj* **:** having their product constant — used of two variable quantities one of which varies directly as the reciprocal of the other

**inverse point** *n* **:** either of two points on a diametral line of a fixed circle or sphere the product of whose distances from the center equals the square of the radius

**inverse proportion** *n* **:** the relation between two inversely proportional quantities

**inverse ratio** *n* **:** the ratio of the reciprocals of two quantities

**inverse secant** *n* **:** ARC SECANT

**inverse sine** *n* **:** ARC SINE

**inverse spelling** *n* **:** REVERSE SPELLING

**inverse-square** \ˌ=,=ˈ=\ *adj* [fr. the phrase *inverse square*] **:** according with or relating to the inverse-square law

**inverse-square law** *n* **:** a statement in physics: the manner in which a physical quantity (as illumination) varies with the distance from the source is inversely as the square of the distance

**inverse tangent** *n* **:** ARC TANGENT

**inverse taper** *n, of an airfoil* **:** increase in the chord with distance outboard from the root

**inverse-time** \ˌ=,=ˈ=\ *adj* [fr. the phrase *inverse time*] **:** done with a purposely delayed action that decreases as the operating force increases — used esp. of electrical relays

**inverse trigonometric function** *n* **:** the inverse of any of the six trigonometric functions

**inverse voltage** *n* **:** the voltage moving through a rectifier during the reverse half of the alternating-current cycle

**in·ver·sion** \ənˈvərzhən, -və̄, -vəi| *also* |shən\ *n* -S [L *inversion-, inversio*, fr. *inversus* (past part. of *invertere* to invert) + *-ion-, -io* -ion — more at INVERT] **1 :** an act or result of turning inside out or upside down : FLEXURE, DOUBLING: as **a :** a folding back of rock strata upon themselves by which their sequence seems reversed **b :** a dislocation of a bodily organ in which it is turned partially or wholly inside out ⟨~ of the uterus⟩ **c :** a condition of being turned inward ⟨~ of the foot⟩ **d :** RETROFLEXION 3 **2 :** a reversal of position, order, or relationship: as **a :** the reverse of an established pattern ⟨the structure of an insect . . . is an almost complete ~ of what prevails in a vertebrate animal —A.D.Imms⟩ ⟨so strange an ~ of the paternal and filial relations as this proposition of his son to pay him a hundred pounds —George Eliot⟩ **b** (1) **:** INVERTED ORDER (2) **:** ANASTROPHE **c :** a change of cadence by the introduction in a metrical series of a foot in which arsis and thesis have positions symmetrically opposed to the positions they have in the normal esp. adjacent feet of the series **:** shift of cadence from rising to falling or from falling to rising — compare SUBSTITUTION **d** (1) *of an interval* **:** a raising of the lower or dropping of the upper tone by an octave (2) *of a triad or seventh chord* **:** a transposition of the root to some voice other than the bass (3) *of a melody* **:** a repetition of a phrase or subject (as of a fugue) with each ascending interval inverted into a corresponding descending interval and vice versa (4) *in double counterpoint* **:** a transposition of an upper and a lower voice part (5) **:** a transferring of a pedal point from the bass to an upper part **e** *logic* **:** the operation of immediate inference which gives an inverse proposition — see ³INVERSE 2 **f** (1) **:** a breaking off of a chromosome section and its subsequent reattachment in reversed position (2) **:** such a chromosome section **3 a :** a change in the order of the terms of a mathematical proportion effected by inverting each ratio **b :** the operation of inverting or forming the inverse either of a magnitude or of an operation **c :** a change from the order in which elements or parcels of objects are arranged naturally or normally **4 :** HOMOSEXUALITY **5 a :** a conversion of a substance showing dextrorotation into one showing levorotation or vice versa ⟨the ~ of sucrose involves hydrolysis of a dextrorotatory material to an equimolar mixture of D-glucose and D-fructose that is levorotatory⟩ **b :** a substitution of one of the groups attached to the asymmetric atom of an optically active organic molecule so that an original clockwise arrangement of atoms or groups becomes counterclockwise **c :** a change of a crystalline substance from one polymorphic form into another **6 :** a conversion of direct current into alternating current **7 :** a reversal of normal atmospheric temperature gradient **:** increase of temperature of the air with increasing altitude

**in·ver·sion·ist** \-zh(ə)nə̇st, -sh-\ *n* -S **:** one who habitually writes upside down and backward

**inversion point** *n* **1 :** TRANSITION POINT **2 :** a point (as on a temperature scale) at which a physical quantity reaches a maximum or minimum or at which it changes algebraic sign

**inversion spectrum** *n* **:** a microwave absorption spectrum (as of ammonia vapor) attributed in quantum mechanics to quantized changes in molecular structure from one arrangement to another that is the mirror image of the first

**in·ver·sive** \(ˈ)inˈvərsiv, ənˈv-, -rziv\ *adj* [*inversion* + *-ive*] **:** marked by inversion ⟨~ error⟩ ⟨~ personality⟩

**¹in·vert** \ənˈvər|t, -və̄, -vəi, *usu* |d+V\ *vb* -ED/-ING/-S [L *invertere*, fr. *in-* ²in- + *vertere* to turn — more at WORTH] *vt* **1 a :** to turn inside out or upside down ⟨the magician ~s the bag to show it is empty⟩ ⟨the gardener ~s a bell jar over his rose cutting⟩; *specif* **:** to print (a part of a stamp or an overprint) upside down **b :** to turn inward ⟨when a foot is ~*ed* its forepart tends to approach the midline of the body —*Jour. Amer. Med. Assoc.*⟩ **2 :** to reverse in position, order, or relationship ⟨both poems ~ the original affective situation, turning despair into success —Malcolm Brown⟩ ⟨in singing the second half of "Ten Little Indians" you ~ the numbers⟩ ⟨the generality concerning molecular weight may not be ~*ed*, for it is not true that salts with light molecules are invariably salty tasting —F.A.Geldard⟩; *specif* **:** to subject (a melody) to inversion **3 a :** to subject (as sucrose) to inversion **b :** to change (a crystalline compound) from one polymorphous form to another ~ *vi* **:** to undergo inversion ⟨sucrose ~s⟩ ⟨the quartz starts to ~ to cristobalite —F.H.Norton⟩

**²in·vert** \ˈin,v-\ *n* -S **:** one that is characterized by inversion: as **a :** INVERTED ARCH **b :** the lowest point in the internal cross section of an artificial channel **c :** a stamp having an overprint or some portion of its design inverted **d :** HOMOSEXUAL

**³invert** \"\ *adj* **:** subjected to chemical inversion : INVERTED 3 ⟨~ sugar⟩

**invert** *abbr* invertebrate

**in·vert·ase** \ənˈvərd·ˌās, ˈin,v-, -āz\ *n* -S [ISV ¹*invert* + *-ase*; prob. orig. formed in F] **:** an enzyme found in many microorganisms and plants and in animal intestines that is capable of effecting the inversion of sucrose and that is usu. prepared from yeast as a white powder — called also *sucrase*

**in·ver·te·bra·cy** \ənˈvərd·əbrəsē\ *n* -ES [²*invertebrate* + *-cy*] **:** SPINELESSNESS

**in·vertebral** \(ˈ)in, ən+\ *adj* [¹*in-* + *vertebral*] **:** INVERTEBRATE

**in·vertebrata** \(ˌ)in, ən+\ *n pl, cap* [NL, fr. neut. pl. of *invertebratus* invertebrate] *in some esp former classifications* **:** a primary division of the animal kingdom including all except the Vertebrata

**¹in·vertebrate** \(ˈ)in, ən+\ *n* [NL *Invertebrata*] **1 :** an animal having no backbone or internal skeleton ⟨in the lower ~s such as coelenterates —W.H.Dowdeswell⟩ **2 :** one that is weak or indecisive ⟨its new dangers are the innocuous and the ~ —Sacheverell Sitwell⟩

**²invertebrate** \"\ *adj* [NL *invertebratus*, fr. L *in-* ¹in- + NL *vertebratus* vertebrate] **1 :** lacking a spinal column ⟨~ jellyfish⟩ **2 :** lacking in structure or vitality : DISORGANIZED, WEAK ⟨his book is completely ~, breaking sharply in the middle into two books —S.E.Hyman⟩ ⟨moves far beyond the often ~ lyricism . . . into a rhetoric that has intellectual iron —Mark Schorer⟩

**inverted** *adj* **1 a :** turned upside down or inside out ⟨~ rock strata⟩ ⟨~ lumen of the intestine⟩ ⟨the blood rushed to his head as he zoomed across the field in ~ flight⟩ **b :** inverted in relation to the rest of a stamp — used of parts of a stamp or stamp design ⟨~ center⟩ **c** *heraldry* **:** having the tip pointing down — used of a wing ⟨an eagle, wings expanded and ~⟩ **d :** RETROFLEX **2 :** reversed in position, order, or relationship **:** contrary to an established pattern ⟨~ spellings⟩ ⟨~ seasons of the southern hemisphere⟩ ⟨much ~ snobbery in the idealization of the English working class —Roy Lewis & Angus Maude⟩; *specif* **:** based on or characterized by musical inversion ⟨~ melody⟩ **3 :** transformed by inversion **4 :** HOMOSEXUAL — **in·vert·ed·ly** *adv*

**inverted arch** *n* **:** an arch with the crown downward that is much used in foundations, sewers, and tunnels and is often made of solid concrete

**inverted comma** *n* **1 a :** a type comma reversed so as to produce an upside-down comma at the top of the printed line **b :** the comma so printed that is commonly used singly or in pairs to mark the beginning of a quotation **2** *chiefly Brit* **:** QUOTATION MARK

**inverted engine** *n* **:** an engine whose crankshaft is above the cylinders

**inverted interval** *n* **:** a simple musical interval having its lower tone raised or its upper tone lowered an octave

**inverted mordent** *n* **:** PRALLTRILLER

**inverted order** *n* **:** an arrangement of the elements of a sentence (as subject, predicate) that is the reverse of the usual order and is designed to achieve variety or emphasis (as in "among them were the following" "again she called") or to indicate a question (as in "what does he say") — compare ANASTROPHE

**inverted passive** *n* **:** a passive construction in which the subject of the passive verb corresponds to the indirect object of the verb in an active construction (as in "he was awarded a medal by the club")

**inverted perspective** *n* **:** REVERSE PERSPECTIVE

**inverted pleat** *n* **:** a pleat formed by bringing two folded edges toward or to a center point on the outside of the material to form a box pleat on the inside

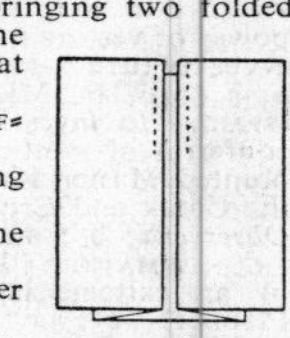

inverted pleat

**inverted-pyramid indention** *n* **:** HALF-DIAMOND INDENTION

**inverted siphon** *n* **:** a pipe for conducting water beneath a depressed place

**inverted talon** *n* **:** an ogee molding with the convex part at the top

**inverted triad** *n* **:** a triad with a tone other than the root in the bass

**in·ver·tend** \ˌin(ˌ)vərˈtend\ *n* -S [L *invertendus*, gerundive of *invertere* to invert — more at INVERT] **:** a proposition upon which the operation of inversion is performed

**in·vert·er** \ənˈvərd·ə(r), -və̄, -vəi|, |tə(r)\ *n* -S **1 :** one that inverts **2 :** a device for converting direct current into alternating current by mechanical or electronic means

**in·vert·ible** \|d·əbəl|, |təbəl\ *adj* **1 :** capable of being inverted or subjected to inversion **2 :** admitting of musical inversion

**in·vert·in** \ənˈvərtᵊn\ *n* -S [ISV ¹*invert* + *-in*] **:** INVERTASE

**inverting** *pres part of* INVERT

**inverting telescope** *n* **:** a telescope in which the image is seen or photographed upside down usu. because it has no optical erecting system

**in·ver·tor** \ənˈvərd·ə(r), -və̄, -vəi, |tə(r)\ *n* -S [NL (influenced in meaning by L *in* and L *vertere* to turn), irreg. fr. L *invertere* to invert + *-or* — more at ¹IN, WORTH] **:** a muscle that turns a part (as the foot) inward

**inverts** *pres 3d sing of* INVERT

**invert soap** *n* **:** CATIONIC DETERGENT

**invert sugar** *n* **:** a mixture of D-glucose and D-fructose that is sweeter than sucrose, that occurs naturally in fruits and honey, that is usu. made commercially from a solution of cane sugar by hydrolysis (as with acid), and that is used chiefly as a difficultly crystallizable syrup in foods and in medicine

**¹in·vest** \ənˈvest\ *vt* -ED/-ING/-S [ML *investire*, fr. L, to clothe, cover, surround, fr. *in-* ²in- + *vestire* to clothe, fr. *vestis* garment — more at WEAR] **1 a :** to array in the symbols of office or honor **:** install in an office or honor with customary ceremonies ⟨was ~*ed* by Queen Elizabeth . . . in a private ceremony —*Springfield (Mass.) Union*⟩ ⟨was ~*ed* with the George Medal, Britain's highest award for civilian heroism —*Charlottetown (Canada) Guardian*⟩ **b :** to furnish with or make a formal grant (as of power or authority) to **:** establish officially ⟨by the Constitution of the United States, the president is ~*ed* with certain important political powers —John Marshall⟩ **c :** to put in possession or control of someone : VEST ⟨provincial life in Tsarist Russia . . . ~*ed* absolute authority in the head of the family —*London Calling*⟩ **2** [L *investire*] **:** to envelop or cover completely : SURROUND, COAT ⟨things are ~*ed* with mystery in the degree that their origins and causes are unknown —Edward Clodd⟩ ⟨could ~ a common murder case with the atmosphere of an Aeschylean drama —Van Wyck Brooks⟩; *specif* **:** to place (a pattern) in refractory material in the process of investment casting ⟨bell-form bowl, ~*ed* with a rich turquoise blue glaze —*Parke-Bernet Galleries Catalog*⟩ — see CIRE PERDUE **3** [L *investire*] **a :** CLOTHE, ADORN ⟨brought a light raincoat with which he now ~*ed* his ample person —John Buchan⟩ ⟨went to the pains of ~*ing* the production richly, for sets and costumes are fabulous —Louise Mace⟩ **b** *obs* **:** to put on : DON ⟨cannot find one this girdle to ~ —Edmund Spenser⟩ **4** [MF *investir*, fr. OIt *investire*, fr. L, to surround] **:** to surround with troops or ships so as to prevent escape or entry **:** lay siege to ⟨Charleston was never besieged, nor was any serious effort made . . . to ~ it on the land side —O.L.Spaulding⟩ **5 :** to endow with some quality or characteristic : INFUSE, ENRICH ⟨talent for ~*ing* the commonplace with significance —Gerald Bullett⟩ ⟨the realist . . . ~s contemporary events with values that are eventually established as history —Bernard Smith⟩ ⟨the tone of his . . . voice which he tried to ~ with candor and modesty —Bernard De Voto⟩ ⟨swept off his hat with a gesture that ~*ed* it with plumes —Edna Ferber⟩

**²invest** \"\ *vb* -ED/-ING/-S [It *investire*, fr. L, to clothe, cover, surround] *vt* **1 a :** to commit (money) for a long period in order to earn a financial return ⟨~*ed* his savings in stocks, bonds, and real estate⟩ **b :** to place (money) with a view to minimizing risk rather than speculating for large gains at greater hazard **2 :** to make use of with particular thought of future benefits or advantages ⟨~*ed* his savings in a year of study —Norman Foerster⟩ ⟨I am avaricious of time and uneasy if I don't ~ it well —O.W.Holmes †1935⟩ ~ *vi* **:** to commit funds for future gain or purchase something of intrinsic value **:** make an investment ⟨anyone who wants to know more before ~*ing* can write the editor —*Monsanto Mag.*⟩ — often used with *in* ⟨decided to ~ in a first edition as a birthday gift for her husband⟩ ⟨the burghers . . . would not ~ in factories —William Petersen⟩

**in·vest·able** *also* **in·vest·ible** \-təbəl\ *adj* [²*invest* + *-able*, *-ible*] **:** available for investment ⟨~ surplus⟩

**investient** *adj* [L *investient-, investiens*, pres. part. of *investire*] *obs* **:** SURROUNDING, ENVELOPING

**in·ves·ti·ga·ble** \ənˈvestəgəbəl, -tēg-\ *adj* [LL *investigabilis*, fr. L *investigare* to investigate + *-abilis* -able] *archaic* **:** INVESTIGATABLE

**in·ves·ti·gat·able** \ənˈvestəˌgād·əbəl, =ˌ==ˈ===\ *adj* **:** capable of being investigated

**in·ves·ti·gate** \ənˈvestəˌgāt, *usu* -ād·+V\ *vb* -ED/-ING/-S [L *investigatus*, past part. of *investigare*, fr. *in-* ²in- + *vestigare* to track, trace; akin to L *vestigium* trace, footprint] *vt* **:** to observe or study closely **:** inquire into systematically : EXAMINE, SCRUTINIZE ⟨the whole brilliance of this novel lies in the fullness with which it ~s a past —Mark Schorer⟩ ⟨a commission to ~ costs of industrial production —Broadus Mitchell⟩ ⟨synthetic resins *investigated* for possible use in printing inks —H.J.Wolfe⟩ ⟨*investigating* every square cubit of terrain which she might have covered —L.C.Douglas⟩; *specif* **:** to subject to an official probe ⟨~ a crime⟩ ⟨~ marine casualties⟩ ⟨the F.B.I. ~s every applicant for federal employment⟩ ~ *vi* **:** to make a systematic examination : STUDY; *specif* **:** to conduct an official inquiry ⟨the power of Congress to ~ is an implied power in the Constitution —*New Republic*⟩

**investigating** *adj* **:** INVESTIGATIVE 2 — **in·ves·ti·gat·ing·ly** \=ˈ==,==, =,==ˈ===\ *adv*

**in·ves·ti·ga·tion** \ən,vestəˈgāshən\ *n* -S [ME *investigacioun*, fr. MF *investigation*, fr. L *investigation-, investigatio*, fr. *investigatus* (past part. of *investigare*) + *-ion-, -io* -ion] **1 :** the action or process of investigating **:** detailed examination : STUDY, RESEARCH ⟨success of the . . . blend in knitwear has led to active ~ of blends with other fibers —*Amer. Fabrics*⟩ ⟨a strong movement to make American universities centers of scholarly work and scientific ~ —J.B.Conant⟩ **2 :** a searching inquiry : EXAMINATION, SURVEY ⟨his doctoral thesis was a penetrating ~ of the causes of race conflict⟩ ⟨carried on energetic ~s of the medicinal flora of Mexico —*Amer. Guide Series: Mich.*⟩; *specif* **:** an official probe ⟨the first Congressional ~ of loyalty in government —Will Herberg⟩

**syn** see INQUIRY

**in·ves·ti·ga·tion·al** \=ˌ==ˈgāshənᵊl, -shnəl\ *adj* **:** INVESTIGATIVE 2

**in·ves·ti·ga·tive** \=ˈ==,gād·|iv, -āt|, |ēv *also* |əv\ *adj* **1 :** characterized by or having a tendency toward investigation ⟨~ scientist⟩ **2 :** of or relating to investigation ⟨~ power⟩ ⟨~ technique⟩

**in·ves·ti·ga·tor** \-,gād·ə(r), -ātə-\ *n* -S [L, fr. *investigatus* (past part. of *investigare*) + *-or*] **:** one that investigates: as **a :** one that conducts systematic inquiries or experiments : STUDENT, RESEARCHER **b :** an insurance claim adjuster or an underwriter **c :** one who is employed to examine the quality of goods or services of a business, its type of personnel, or the condition of its property — called also *spotter* **d :** one who inquires into the history of an applicant for employment to determine his integrity and loyalty **e :** DETECTIVE

**in·ves·ti·ga·to·ry** \-gə,tōrē, -tȯrē, -ri *chiefly Brit* ≈ˈ≈≈-ˈgātəri *or* -ā·tri\ *adj* [*investigate* + *-ory*] : INVESTIGATIVE

**in·ves·ti·tive** \ənˈvestəd·iv\ *adj* [ML *investitus* (past part. of *investire* to invest) + E *-ive*] : of, relating to, or having the power of vesting a right

**in·ves·ti·ture** \-tə,chu̇(ə)r, -,chu̇ə, -,chə(r), -tə,tu̇-, -tə-,tyu̇-\ *n* -s [ME, fr. ML *investitura*, fr. *investitus* (past part. of *investire* to invest) + L *-ura* -ure] **1 a** : the ceremonial conferral of symbols of office or honor ⟨the six newly appointed Master Knights . . . immediately after their ~ with the Cloak and Cross of Malta —*Springfield (Mass.) Catholic Observer*⟩ **b** : an act of ratifying or establishing in office : CONFIRMATION ⟨the ~ of Parliament yesterday was marked by an extreme lack of enthusiasm and applause —Janet Flanner⟩ **c** : LIVERY OF SEIZIN **2** : an act of infusing or enriching **3 a** : an act of clothing or decorating ⟨to dress the sovereign in a linsey-woolsey garb would . . . be a very unsuitable ~ —R.C.Singleton⟩ **b** : something that covers or adorns ⟨the heavy red damask ~ of the four-poster⟩ ⟨regrettable that the drama does not live up to its rich ~ —*Newsweek*⟩ **4** *archaic* : ²INVESTMENT 2 **5** : BLOCKADE, SIEGE ⟨the enemy fleet riding to the ~ of Japan —*This World*⟩

**¹in·vest·ment** \ənˈves(t)mənt\ *n* -s [¹*invest* + *-ment*] **1 a** *archaic* : VESTMENT **b** : an outer layer of any kind : COATING, ENVELOPE: as (1) : an outward habiliment : GUISE ⟨one man asserts his right to grow a beard . . . as the ~ of his motley —*Times Lit. Supp.*⟩ (2) : an external covering of a cell, part, or organism (3) : a layer of heat-resistant material in which a dental appliance (as a bridge or inlay) is cast or in which it is embedded before soldering (4) : refractory material that forms the mold in investment casting **2** : INVESTITURE 1 ⟨~ with the ring has been an integral part of each coronation —*Literary Digest*⟩ **3** : BLOCKADE, SIEGE ⟨his proposals for an attack on Montreal . . . and a complete ~ of Quebec by land and sea —J.B.Brebner⟩

**²investment** \"\ *n* -s *often attrib* [²*invest* + *-ment*] **1 a** : an expenditure of money for income or profit or to purchase something of intrinsic value : capital outlay ⟨~ in common stocks⟩ ⟨~ in a diamond brooch⟩ **b** : the sum invested or the property purchased ⟨has a large ~ in a copper mine⟩ ⟨a fine painting is an ~⟩ **2** : the commitment of funds with a view to minimizing risk and safeguarding capital while earning a return — contrasted with *speculation* **3** : the commitment of something other than money to a long-term interest or project ⟨the job calls for the ~ of a great deal of hard thinking and planning —D.F.Cavers⟩

**investment bank** *n* [²*investment*] : an institution that specializes in buying and selling large blocks of securities (as new issues) and in raising funds for capital expansion — **investment banking** *n*

**investment banker** *n* **1** : a person employed by an investment bank or engaged in investment banking **2** : INVESTMENT BANK

**investment casting** *n* [¹*investment*] : casting by the cire-perdue process

**investment company** *or* **investment trust** *n* [²*investment*] : a company that holds securities of other corporations for investment benefits only — compare HOLDING COMPANY

**investment counselor** *or* **investment adviser** *n* [²*investment*] : an individual or firm that analyzes and makes recommendations on a client's securities for a fee but does not have physical custody of these securities ⟨*investment counselors* or advisers must register under the Investment Advisers Act of 1940 —J.O.Kamm⟩

**investment reserve** *n* [²*investment*] : the terminal reserve of an insurance company in any year — compare INSURANCE RESERVE

**in·ves·tor** \ənˈvestə(r)\ *n* -s [¹*invest* & ²*invest* + *-or*] : one that invests; *specif* : one that seeks to commit funds for long-term profit with a minimum of risk — contrasted with *speculator*

**invests** *pres 3d sing of* INVEST

**in·ves·ture** \ənˈves(h)chə(r)\ *n* -s [¹*invest* + *-ure*] *archaic* : INVESTITURE 1

**in·vet·er·a·cy** \ənˈved·ərəsē, -vetər-,-ve·tr-, -si\ *n* -ES [*inveterate* + *-cy*] *archaic* **1** : prejudiced animosity : HOSTILITY **2** : the quality or state of being obstinate : TENACITY

**¹in·vet·er·ate** \-rət, *usu* -rəd·+V\ *adj* [L *inveteratus*, past part. of *inveterare* to make old, to age, fr. *in-* ²in- + *veter-*, *vetus* old — more at WETHER] **1** *archaic* : obstinately prejudiced or antagonistic : BIASED, HOSTILE ⟨felt ~ against him —Charles Dickens⟩ **2 a** : CONTINUOUS, RECURRENT, CHRONIC ⟨~ bursitis⟩ **b** : deep-rooted or widely accepted : INGRAINED, ESTABLISHED ⟨~ tendency to naturalize foreign words —George Woodcock⟩ ⟨supported by precedent so ~ that the chance of abandonment is small —B.N.Cardozo⟩ ⟨~ and skillful biographer —Marvin Lowenthal⟩ **c** : stubbornly inflexible : ADAMANT, OBSTINATE ⟨~ prejudice⟩ ⟨his ~ demand for the imposition of a severe discipline —C.I.Glicksberg⟩ **d** : long-lasting : PERSISTENT ⟨the ~ smell of ether in a hospital⟩ **3** *obs* : of an advanced age : ANCIENT ⟨rotten wood . . . taken out of an ~ willow tree —John Evelyn⟩ **4** : fixed by long habit or usage : CONFIRMED, HABITUAL ⟨~ sightseers —Astrid Peters⟩ ⟨an ~ love of alcohol —C.B.Nordhoff & J.N.Hall⟩ ⟨the punishment for ~ idleness was a whipping on the bare back —W.E.Woodward⟩

**syn** CHRONIC, CONFIRMED, DEEP-ROOTED, DEEP-SEATED: INVETERATE suggests resolute persistence in an idea or attitude making change or moderation impossible or most unlikely ⟨Frenchmen do not crave a master . . . the average Frenchman is probably the world's most *inveterate* individualist —*Christian Century*⟩ ⟨*inveterate* habits of animistic thinking —Lewis Mumford⟩ ⟨the *inveterate* hostility of "creative" writers to criticism —P.E.More⟩ CHRONIC implies long continuation or frequent recurrence of a usu. detrimental condition or trait but lacks the suggestion of determination that may accompany INVETERATE ⟨his *chronic* state of mental restlessness —George Eliot⟩ ⟨envy and rebellion and class resentments are *chronic* moral diseases with us —G.B.Shaw⟩ ⟨the total lack of adequate means of transportation rendered the problem of a grain market a *chronic* difficulty to the frontier farmers —V.L.Parrington⟩ CONFIRMED suggests a pattern that has become fixed by habit or usage ⟨I am a *confirmed* wanderer —Isaac D'Israeli⟩ ⟨a *confirmed* bachelor⟩ ⟨his intense egoism rendered him impatient of all reproof or instruction and . . . he soon became a victim of *confirmed* mannerisms —*Nation*⟩ DEEP-ROOTED and DEEP-SEATED in general refer to qualities so deeply engrained that they have become part of the core of personal character, or to conditions of deep significance and lasting endurance ⟨Lincoln had a *deep-rooted* aversion to slavery⟩ ⟨the *deep-rooted* causes of Indian discontent —*Current History*⟩ ⟨the conviction of Thomas Aquinas, that between true science and true religion there can be no contradiction, is exceedingly *deep-seated* —J.H.Randall⟩ ⟨*deep-seated* sources of cultural antipathy between Asia and the U.S. —M.W.Straight⟩

**²in·vet·er·ate** \-ved·ə,rāt\ *vt* -ED/-ING/-S [L *inveteratus*, past part. of *inveterare*] *archaic* : to establish firmly : root deeply : CONFIRM

**in·vet·er·ate·ly** \ved·ərətlē, -vetər-,-ve·tr-, -li\ *adv* : in an inveterate manner : PERSISTENTLY

**in·vet·er·ate·ness** \-ətnəs\ *n* -ES : the quality or state of being inveterate : PERSISTENCE

**in·viability** \(ˌ)in, ən+\ *n* : inability to live — used esp. of a genetic constitution that precludes survival ⟨~ of intergeneric hybrids —E.R.Sears⟩

**in·viable** \(ˈ)in, ən+\ *adj* [ISV ¹*in-* + *viable*] : incapable of surviving

**in·vid·i·ous** \ənˈvidēəs\ *adj* [L *invidiosus*, fr. *invidia* envy + *-osus* -ose — more at ENVY] **1** : detrimental to reputation : DEFAMATORY ⟨the ~ implication of the phrase is . . . against those who pursue self-interest through politics —Felix Frankfurter⟩ **2** : likely to cause discontent or animosity or envy ⟨the four confidential advisers of the crown soon found that their position was embarrassing and ~ —T.B. Macaulay⟩ **3** : full of envious resentment : JEALOUS ⟨his professional abilities as an officer . . . had to stand ~ scrutiny —J.G.Cozzens⟩ **4 a** : of an unpleasant or objectionable nature : HATEFUL, OBNOXIOUS ⟨~ remarks that were sometimes neither kind nor true —John Hurkan⟩ **b** : causing harm or resentment : INJURIOUS ⟨would be ~ to select for special mention a more or less haphazard list of names —*Survey Graphic*⟩ ⟨far from our purpose to institute any ~ comparisons between these two gifted women —Eugene Field⟩ **syn** see HATEFUL

**in·vid·i·ous·ly** *adv* : in an invidious manner : ODIOUSLY

**in·vid·i·ous·ness** *n* -ES : the quality or state of being invidious : ODIOUSNESS

**in·vigilancy** \(ˈ)in, ən+\ *n* -ES [¹*in-* + *vigilancy*] *archaic* : lack of vigilance

**in·vig·i·late** \ənˈvijə,lāt\ *vb* -ED/-ING/-S [L *invigilatus*, past part. of *invigilare*, fr. *in-* ²in- + *vigilare* to watch — more at VIGILANT] *vi* : to keep watch ⟨that invisible power that ~s over all things —Henry More⟩; *specif*, *Brit* : to proctor an examination ~ *vt* : to make watchful

**in·vig·i·la·tion** \(ˌ)in,vijəˈlāshən, ən,v-\ *n* -s : an act of surveillance; *specif* : the proctoring of an examination

**in·vig·i·la·tor** \ənˈvijə,lād·ə(r)\ *n* -s *Brit* : PROCTOR 2b

**in·vig·or** *or* **in·vig·our** \ənˈvigə(r)\ *vt* [alter. (influenced by E ²*in-*) of earlier *envigor*, fr. ¹*en-* + *vigor*, n.] *archaic* : INVIGORATE

**in·vig·o·rate** \ənˈvigə,rāt, *usu* -ād·+V\ *vt* -ED/-ING/-S [prob. fr. ²*in-* + obs. E *vigorate* to invigorate, fr. L *vigoratus*, past part. of *vigorare*, fr. *vigor* — more at VIGOR] : to give life and energy to : ANIMATE ⟨a lotion to ~ the skin⟩ ⟨that puzzling out of new possibilities which ~s the imagination —H.A.Overstreet⟩ ⟨an industrial center *invigorated* by defense contracts —R.M.Hodesh⟩ **syn** see STRENGTHEN

**invigorating** *adj* : having an enlivening effect : BRACING, STIMULATING ⟨~ climate⟩ ⟨thought that he would try these ~ berries since he was inclined to fall asleep during his prayers —Charles Cooper⟩ ⟨his writings are tonic and . . . ~ to those who stand in need of inspiration —R.L.Cook⟩ — **in·vig·o·rat·ing·ly** \ˈ≈≈,≈≈≈, ≈,≈≈ˈ≈≈≈\ *adv*

**in·vig·o·ra·tion** \≈,≈≈ˈrāshən\ *n* -s **1** : the act or process of invigorating ⟨demands for . . . ~ of the Articles were made even before they became effective —Allan Nevins⟩ **2** : the quality or state of being invigorated ⟨the ~ that derives from . . . the cultural atmosphere of a great city —A.A.Houghton⟩

**in·vig·o·ra·tor** \≈ˈ≈≈,rād·ə(r), -ātə-\ *n* -s : one that invigorates

**in·vi·nate** \ənˈvī,nāt, ˈin,v-\ *vt* -ED/-ING/-S [prob. fr. (assumed) NL *invinatus*, past part. of (assumed) NL *invinare*, fr. L *in-* ²in- + *vinum* wine — more at WINE] : to make present by invination

**in·vi·na·tion** \,in,vīˈnāshən\ *n* -s [F, prob. fr. (assumed) NL *invination-*, *invinatio*, fr. (assumed) NL *invinatus* + L *-ion-*, *-io* -ion] : the inclusion of the blood of Christ in the eucharistic wine without change in either substance — compare IMPANATION

**in·vin·ci·bil·i·ty** \(ˌ)in,vin(t)səˈbiləd·ē, ən,v-, -lətē, -i\ *n* -ES : the quality or state of being invincible

**¹in·vin·ci·ble** \(ˈ)inˈvin(t)səbəl, ənˈv-\ *adj* [ME, fr. MF, fr. LL *invincibilis*, fr. L *in-* ¹in- + *vincibilis* conquerable — more at VINCIBLE] **1 a** : incapable of being vanquished or subjugated : impervious to attack or conquest : UNBEATABLE ⟨~ army⟩ ⟨has been ~ in eight-oared Olympic rowing —*Collier's Yr. Bk.*⟩ **b** : impossible to overcome or subdue : ABSOLUTE, UNSWERVING ⟨the ~ obscurity of his origins —Joseph Conrad⟩ ⟨a resolute, yet not ~, skepticism —A.G.N.Flew⟩ ⟨~ respect for authority⟩ ⟨man's ~ conviction that a sublime soul cannot be imprisoned —W.L.Sullivan⟩ **2** : beyond an individual's control and so not involving moral responsibility : UNAVOIDABLE — used esp. of lack of knowledge about theological concepts ⟨~ ignorance⟩ — **in·vin·ci·ble·ness** \-nəs\ *n* -ES — **in·vin·ci·bly** \-blē, -bli\ *adv*

**²invincible** \"\ *n* -s : one that is invincible

**in·violability** \(ˌ)in, ən+\ *n* : the quality or state of being inviolable

**in·violable** \(ˈ)in, ən+\ *adj* [MF or L; MF, fr. L *inviolabilis*, fr. *in-* ¹in- + *violabilis* violable] **1** *obs* : incapable of being broken or destroyed : INDESTRUCTIBLE **2 a** : secure from violation or infringement : INCORRUPTIBLE, SACROSANCT ⟨thinking of conscience as an ~ source of moral certitude —Lucius Garvin⟩ ⟨bound by mores more strict, more rigorous, more ~ than most religious denominations would dare to require —Jessie Bernard⟩ **b** : secure from assault or trespass : UNTOUCHABLE, UNASSAILABLE ⟨the person of the king is ~⟩ ⟨~ frontier⟩ ⟨~ green lawns⟩ — **in·vi·o·la·ble·ness** \-nəs\ *n* — **in·vi·o·la·bly** \-blē, -bli\ *adv*

**in·vi·o·la·cy** \ənˈvīələsē, -si\ *n* -ES [*inviolate* + *-cy*] : the quality or state of being inviolate

**in·violate** \(ˈ)inˈvīələ̇t, ənˈv- *also* -,lāt; *usu* |d.+V\ *also* **inviolated** \-,lād·əd, -ātəd\ *adj* [ME *inviolat*, fr. L *inviolatus*, fr. *in-* ¹in- + *violatus*, past part. of *violare* to violate — more at VIOLATE] **1 a** : free from change or blemish : PURE, UNBROKEN ⟨desired the Italian culture to be ~ and predominant —John Buchan⟩ ⟨cease searching for the perfect shell, the whole ~ form —Anne M. Lindbergh⟩ ⟨while I continue to keep this oath ~ —*Hippocratic Oath*⟩ **b** : free from assault or trespass : UNTOUCHED, INTACT ⟨as he had fallen on the plain, ~ he lay —R.C.Trench⟩ ⟨the . . . first white settlers agreed to keep this ground ~ —*Amer. Guide Series: Conn.*⟩ **2** : INVIOLABLE 2 ⟨they . . . regarded their hunting zones as their own ~ property —L.S.B.Leakey⟩ ⟨the confidences of this Club are ~ —R.H.Davis⟩ — **in·vi·o·late·ly** *adv* — **in·vi·o·late·ness** *n* -ES

**invious** *adj* [L *invius*, fr. *in-* ¹in- + *via* road — more at VIA] *obs* : lacking roads : TRACKLESS

**inviron** *obs var of* ENVIRON

**in·vir·tu·ate** \ənˈvərchə,wāt\ *vt* -ED/-ING/-S [²*in-* + *virtue* + *-ate*] *archaic* : to endow with virtue

**in·vis·cate** \ənˈvi,skāt, ˈin,v-\ *vt* -ED/-ING/-S [LL *inviscatus*, past part. of *inviscare* to snare as with birdlime, fr. L *in-* ²in- + *viscare* to smear with birdlime, fr. *viscum* mistletoe, birdlime — more at VISCID] : to encase in a sticky substance : make viscid — **in·vis·ca·tion** \,in,viˈskāshən\ *n* -s

**in·viscid** \(ˈ)in, ən+\ *adj* [¹*in-* + *viscid*] **1** : not having viscosity ⟨~ fluid⟩ **2** : relating to the flow of an inviscid body ⟨~ theory⟩

**in·visibility** \(ˌ)in, ən+\ *n* [LL *invisibilitat-*, *invisibilitas*, fr. L *invisibilis* invisible + *-itat-*, *-itas* -ity] **1** : the quality or state of being invisible **2** : something that is invisible

**¹in·visible** \(ˈ)in, ən+\ *adj* [ME, fr. MF, fr. L *invisibilis*, fr. *in-* ¹in- + *visibilis* visible] **1 a** : incapable of being seen through lack of physical substance : not perceptible by vision : INTANGIBLE, UNSEEN ⟨another thriller about an ~ man⟩ ⟨an angel and a high-frequency wave are equally ~ to the mass of mankind —Lewis Mumford⟩; *specif* : not appearing in published financial statements ⟨~ assets and liabilities⟩ **b** : of or relating to service or capital transactions not reflected in statistics of foreign trade ⟨the nation's greatest ~ export, tourism —T.H.Fielding⟩ ⟨a bit of unconscious humor is the listing of movies among ~ imports —George Soule⟩ ⟨Ireland's trade deficit was met by ~ items, including immigrant remittances —Alzada Comstock⟩ **2** : inaccessible to view : out of sight : HIDDEN ⟨~ hinge⟩ ⟨in stormy weather the seaman's compass takes the place of ~ stars⟩ ⟨the world's largest and finest private or public assemblage of French art . . . is now ~ in the attic of the Hermitage —Janet Flanner⟩ **3** : of such small size or unobtrusive quality as to be hardly noticeable : IMPERCEPTIBLE, INCONSPICUOUS ⟨~ hair net⟩ ⟨~ plaid⟩ ⟨the translation is almost ~ —Stuart Preston⟩ — **in·visible·ness** \"+\ *n* — **in·visibly** \"+\ *adv*

**²invisible** \"\ *n* : one that is invisible ⟨the ~s that lurk in haunted houses⟩ ⟨the present deficit gap . . . must be closed either by greater merchandise exports or larger earnings on ~s —J.B.Cohen⟩

**invisible church** *n* : CHURCH INVISIBLE

**invisible government** *n* : a government controlled by a person (as a boss) or an agency (as a pressure group) holding no official position and usu. held to be unknown to the public ⟨the interlocking control thus created was an *invisible government* —F.L.Paxson⟩

**invisible green** *n* **1** : a very dark green to yellowish green **2** : a dark bluish green that is greener and duller than average teal green and bluer and slightly less strong than duck green

**invisible ink** *n* : SECRET INK

**in·vi·tant** \ˈinvətənt, ənˈvītᵊnt\ *n* -s [*invite* + *-ant*] *archaic* : INVITER

**¹in·vi·ta·tion** \,invəˈtāshən\ *n* -s [MF or L; MF, fr. L *invitation-*, *invitatio*, fr. *invitatus* (past part. of *invitare* to invite) + *-ion-*, *-io* -ion] **1 a** : the act of inviting : the requesting of a person's company or participation ⟨I took the ~ to dinner as a dismissal from tea —O.S.J.Gogarty⟩ ⟨joined the expedition at the ~ of the government⟩ **b** (1) : a written or verbal request to be present or participate ⟨address wedding ~s⟩ ⟨accept an ~ to membership⟩ (2) : a written or verbal request to do or undertake ⟨an ~ to sing at a benefit concert⟩ ⟨an ~ to assume leadership of a project⟩ (3) *often cap* : a brief exhortation immediately preceding the confession in the communion service of the Anglican and other Protestant churches **c** : SUGGESTION, PROPOSAL ⟨the ~s of a master are scarcely to be distinguished from commands —Edward Gibbon⟩ ⟨he refused my ~ to consider the history of Christian intolerance —H.J.Laski⟩ **2 a** : ATTRACTION, STIMULUS, LURE, INCENTIVE ⟨they were forced to move, even though the Sahara desert was no ~ —Emil Lengyel⟩ ⟨good scholarship . . . presents us with evidence which is an ~ to the critical faculty of the reader —T.S.Eliot⟩ **b** : a precipitating factor : INDUCEMENT, CHALLENGE, PROVOCATION ⟨a hatchet painted red was thrown down in a friendly village as an ~ to join in a war —Clark Wissler⟩ ⟨the laws . . . were an ~ to smuggling —Roger Burlingame⟩ ⟨her sultry look was clearly an ~⟩

**²invitation** \ˈ≈≈ˈ≈≈\ *also* **in·vi·ta·tion·al** \ˈ≈≈ˈtāshənᵊl, -shnəl\ *adj* : prepared or entered in response to a request or challenge ⟨~ article⟩ ⟨~ exhibit⟩; *specif* : limited to invited participants ⟨~ tournament⟩

**¹in·vi·ta·to·ry** \ənˈvīd·ə,tōrē\ *adj* [ME, fr. LL *invitatorius*, fr. L *invitatus* (past part. of *invitare*) + *-orius* -ory] : containing an invitation ⟨a brief ~ note⟩ ⟨~ psalm⟩

**²invitatory** \"\ *n* -ES [ME, fr. ML *invitatorium*, fr. LL, neut. of *invitatorius*, adj.] : any of various liturgical forms of invitation used in church services ⟨common *invitatories* are the Venite and Psalm 95⟩

**¹in·vite** \ənˈvīt, *usu* -īd·+V\ *vb* -ED/-ING/-S [MF or L; MF *inviter*, fr. L *invitare*, prob. fr. *in-* ²in- + *-vitare* (prob. akin to Gk *hiesthai* to hasten, long for) — more at GAIN] *vt* **1 a** : to offer an incentive or inducement to : ENTICE, TEMPT ⟨the book ~s interest⟩ ⟨writes about the people and places that ~ his pen —*Atlantic*⟩ ⟨rock-strewn streams ~ the fisherman —*Amer. Guide Series: N.J.*⟩ ⟨virgin spaces of America *invited* colonization —Douglas Bush⟩ ⟨I loaf and ~ my soul —Walt Whitman⟩ **b** : to provide opportunity or occasion for : increase the likelihood of : open the way to ⟨to shrink from responsibility is to ~ social and economic insecurity —H.G. Armstrong⟩ ⟨so long as there is starvation and joblessness in the midst of abundance we are *inviting* the deluge —Ruth Benedict⟩ ⟨lurid emotionalism and tear-jerking nostalgia . . . *inviting* sighs and hisses —Leslie Rees⟩ ⟨wandered slowly along . . . in that wholly relaxed state which always seems to ~ small adventures —William Beebe⟩ **2 a** : to request the presence or participation of : solicit the company of : ASK ⟨~ guests to dinner⟩ ⟨~ educators to a conference⟩ ⟨~ a team to a tournament⟩ ⟨open the door and ~ him in⟩; *esp* : to send a formal invitation to ⟨an affair open only to those who had been *invited*⟩ **b** : to request formally ⟨~ him to be chief executive⟩ ⟨*invited* her to give a talk on flower arrangement⟩ ⟨it is not as yet very clear which . . . are *invited* to consider becoming signatories —I.A.Richards⟩ **c** : to urge politely or indicate a receptiveness to : ENCOURAGE, WELCOME ⟨leaned forward . . . and *invited* me to continue in English —Barbara Henderson⟩ ⟨*inviting* him to put his own motives under examination —Lionel Trilling⟩ ⟨~ bids on a contract⟩ ⟨~s oral suggestions from his three clerks —J.P.Frank⟩ ⟨his manner did not ~ approach —H.E.Starr⟩ ~ *vi* : to issue an invitation ⟨he did not ~: he commanded —Max Beerbohm⟩ ⟨the spacious campus . . . ~s to the enjoyment of the out-of-doors —*Catalog of Hollins Coll.*⟩

**²in·vite** \ˈin,v-\ *n* -s *now chiefly dial* : INVITATION 1 ⟨you sound like you didn't get no ~ to the dance —Richard Bissell⟩

**invited** *adj* [fr. past part. of ¹*invite*] : present or done by invitation ⟨~ guests⟩ ⟨read an ~ paper at the meeting⟩

**in·vi·tee** \,in,vīˈtē, ən,vīˈtē\ *n* -s [*invite* + *-ee*] : an invited person : GUEST; *specif* : a person (as a customer) present in a place by the express or implied invitation of the occupier in control of that place under circumstances such as impose a duty on the occupier to use reasonable care to protect the safety of such person — compare LICENSEE, TRESPASSER

**in·vite·ment** \ənˈvītmənt\ *n* -s **1** *obs* : INVITATION 1 ⟨would not stand upon ~, but came of himself —George Chapman⟩ **2** *archaic* : INVITATION 2 ⟨unable to resist the delicious ~ to repose —Charles Lamb⟩

**in·vit·er** *or* **in·vi·tor** \ənˈvīd·ə(r), -ītə-\ *n* -s : one that invites

**¹inviting** *n* -s [fr. gerund of ¹*invite*] *obs* : INVITATION ⟨he hath sent me an earnest ~ —Shak.⟩

**²inviting** *adj* [fr. pres. part. of ¹*invite*] **1** : giving an invitation ⟨the ~ ship would haul the Stars and Stripes to the peak —H.A.Chippendale⟩ **2** : of an agreeable nature : pleasing to the senses : ATTRACTIVE, TEMPTING ⟨~ climate⟩ ⟨~ prospect⟩ ⟨~ eye⟩ ⟨beautiful binding, ~ type, fine paper —*N.Y. Times Book Rev.*⟩ — **in·vit·ing·ly** *adv* — **in·vit·ing·ness** *n* -ES

**in·vi·tress** \ənˈvī·trəs\ *n* -ES [*inviter* + *-ess*] *archaic* : a female inviter

**in vi·tro** \(ˈ)inˈvē·(,)trō\ *adv* (*or adj*) [NL, lit., in glass] : outside the living body : in a test tube or other artificial environment ⟨*in vitro* cultivation of tissues⟩ — compare IN VIVO

**in vi·vo** \(ˈ)inˈvē(,)vō\ *adv* (*or adj*) [NL, lit., in that which is alive] : in the living body of a plant or animal ⟨*in vivo* synthesis of vitamin D⟩ ⟨microorganisms are not ordinarily destroyed *in vivo* by bacteriostatic drugs —*Jour. Amer. Med. Assoc.*⟩ — compare IN VITRO

**in·vo·ca·ble** \ənˈvōkəbəl, ˈinvək-\ *adj* [irreg. (influenced by L *invocare* to invoke) fr. *invoke* + *-able*] : capable of being invoked

**in·vo·cant** \-kənt\ *n* -s [L *invocant-*, *invocans*, pres. part. of *invocare* to invoke] : one that invokes

**in·vo·cate** \ˈinvə,kāt\ *vb* -ED/-ING/-S [L *invocatus*, past part. of *invocare*] *vt*, *archaic* : INVOKE ⟨still will I ~ his name —John Wesley⟩ ~ *vi* : to make a supplication : PRAY ⟨after that hour to daybreak 'tis held an ungodly thing to ~ —Thomas Herbert⟩

**in·vo·ca·tion** \,invəˈkāshən, -vōˈ-\ *n* -s [ME *invocacioun*, fr. MF *invocation*, fr. L *invocation-*, *invocatio*, fr. *invocatus* (past part. of *invocare* to invoke) + *-ion-*, *-io* -ion] **1 a** : the action or an act of petitioning for help or support : SUPPLICATION, APPEAL ⟨~ to the Muses⟩; *specif*, *often cap* : a prayer of entreaty that is usu. a call for the divine presence and is offered at the beginning of a meeting or service of worship **b** : a summoning up or calling upon for authority or justification ⟨~ of economic reasons . . . to justify postponement of wage increases —Frank Gorrell⟩ ⟨~ of a celebrated piece of advice attributed to Talleyrand —*Times Lit. Supp.*⟩ **2 a** : an act of conjuring ⟨~ of an ancestral spirit⟩ **b** : a formula for conjuring : INCANTATION ⟨~s . . . to bring harm to mother or child —Francis Hackett⟩ **3 a** : a judicial call for papers or evidence from another case — used chiefly in admiralty prize procedure **b** : an act of legal or moral implementation : ENFORCEMENT ⟨~ of treaty provisions⟩ — **in·vo·ca·tion·al** \ˈ≈≈ˈ≈shənᵊl, -shnəl\ *adj*

**in·voca·tive** \ənˈväkəd·iv; ˈinvə,kād·iv, -vō,-\ *adj* [LL *invocativus*, fr. L *invocatus* (past part. of *invocare* to invoke) + *-ivus* -ive] : INVOCATORY

**in·vo·ca·tor** \ˈinvə,kād·ə(r), -vō,-\ *n* -s [LL *invocator*, fr. L *invocatus* (past part. of *invocare* to invoke) + *-or*] : one that invokes

**in·voc·a·to·ry** \ənˈväkə,tōrē\ *adj* [fr. *invocation*, after such pairs as E *revocation: revocatory*] : of, relating to, or characterized by invocation ⟨~ prayer⟩

**¹in·voice** \ˈin,vȯis\ *n* -s *often attrib* [modif. of MF *envois*, pl. of *envoi* action of sending, message — more at ENVOY] **1 a** : an itemized statement furnished to a purchaser by a seller and usu. specifying the price of goods or services and the terms of sale : BILL ⟨prices shown on this ~ are net⟩ **b** : a consignment of merchandise ⟨received a large ~ of broomstraw⟩ **c** : a printed form used for detailing charges : BILLHEAD ⟨a picture of the factory appears on the ~⟩ **2** : BILL OF LADING

**²invoice** \"\ *vb* -ED/-ING/-S *vt* **1 a** : to submit a statement of charges for : BILL ⟨~ desk accessories to the stationery buyer⟩ **b** : to send a consignment of (merchandise) : SHIP ⟨where are the sewing machines *invoiced* me by this steamer —R.H.Davis⟩ **2** : INVENTORY ~ *vi* **1** : to make or render an invoice ⟨please ~ and advise where to pay —*advt*⟩ **2** : to be worth on inventory ⟨his little office would not have *invoiced* more than fifteen hundred dollars —W.A.White⟩

**in·voke** \ənˈvōk\ *vt* -ED/-ING/-S [ME *invoken*, fr. MF *invoquer*, fr. L *invocare*, fr. *in-* ²in- + *vocare* to call, fr. *voc-, vox* voice — more at VOICE] **1 a** : to petition for help or support : call upon for assistance ⟨the gods had to be *invoked* to bring rain —T.E.Sanford⟩ ⟨she would ~ the Travelers' Aid Society, and they would assist her in getting a . . . place to live —Donn Byrne⟩ **b** : to appeal to as furnishing authority or motive : propound as a logical basis ⟨racist doctrines are *invoked* for political ends —Ruth Benedict⟩ ⟨~ the balance-of-payments difficulties to justify . . . import prohibitions —*Economist*⟩ ⟨four theories . . . *invoked* by geographers to explain the origin of the areas —S.A.Cain⟩ ⟨imaginary lesions . . . *invoked* to account for conditions which had a merely psychogenic origin —R.S.Ellery⟩ **2 a** : to call forth by incantation : CONJURE 2 ⟨spokesmen for the two tribes *invoked* the spirits of departed . . . chiefs to tell them they were now as one —*Time*⟩ ⟨~ a plague on all their houses —W.L.Sperry⟩ **b** : to use (a respected name) to imply endorsement by the owner ⟨more misquotations probably have been attributed to Jefferson than to any other American, because many politicians who ~ his name have read him not at all —L.B. Wright⟩ **3 a** : to make an earnest request for : SOLICIT ⟨~ the board's help in getting his old job back —Dixon Wecter⟩ ⟨the student of genetics ~*s* the aid of the physicist and biochemist —J.M.Fogg⟩ **b** : ENTREAT, IMPLORE ⟨~ mercy⟩ ⟨*invoked* their forgiveness⟩ **4 a** : to call for (as papers or other evidence) judicially — used chiefly in admiralty prize procedure **b** : to put into legal effect or call for the observance of : ENFORCE, IMPLEMENT ⟨~ the penalties of the law —Albert Mowbray⟩ ⟨military sanctions may be *invoked* only after economic sanctions have failed —Norman Hill⟩ ⟨*invoked* the veto six times in the dispute —C.D.Fuller⟩ ⟨~ a promise⟩ ⟨unhesitatingly *invoked* the health department's broad powers —Leonard Engel⟩ ⟨because it possesses that right . . . can usually discipline the majority without *invoking* its prerogative —*Foreign Affairs*⟩ **5 a** : to introduce or put into operation : INSTIGATE, EMPLOY ⟨controls alien to . . . peacetime custom will have to be *invoked* —Stacy May⟩ ⟨~ bold visions at a time of unrest —Norman Cousins⟩ ⟨discipline should not be *invoked* . . . without first consulting the union —Earl Brown⟩ ⟨alliteration's artful aid is *invoked* on every page —*Irish Digest*⟩ **b** : to bring about : CAUSE, EXCITE ⟨operations . . . ~ new problems of administration, maintenance and supply —H.H.Arnold & I.C.Eaker⟩ ⟨stabilizing the regime and *invoking* social and patriotic fervor —E.P. Snow⟩

**in·vok·er** \-kə(r)\ *n* -S : one that invokes

**in·volatile** \(ˈ)in, ən+\ *adj* [¹*in-* + *volatile*] : not vaporizing or capable of being vaporized — **in·volatility** \(ˌ)in, ən+\ *n*

**in·vol·u·cel** \ənˈvälyəˌsel\ *n* -S [NL *involucellum*, dim. of *involucrum*] : a secondary involucre (as in each secondary umbel of a compound umbel) — **in·vol·u·cel·late** \(ˌ)in¦välyə¦selət, ən¦v-\ *or* **in·vol·u·cel·lat·ed** \(ˌ)=ˌ==ˈseˌlād·əd\ *adj*

**in·vo·lu·cral** \¦invə¦lükrəl *also* -vəl¦yü-\ *adj* [prob. fr. (assumed) NL *involucralis*, fr. NL *involucrum* involucre + L *-alis* -al] : of, relating to, or resembling an involucre

**in·vo·lu·crate** \-krət\ *adj* [prob. fr. (assumed) NL *involucratus*, fr. NL *involucrum* involucre + L *-atus* -ate] : having an involucre

**in·vo·lu·cre** \ˈinvəˌlükə(r) *also* -vəlˌyü-\ *n* -S [F, fr. NL *involucrum* involucre] : one or more whorls of bracts situated below and close to a flower, flower cluster, or fruit (in a seed plant) : as **a** : a rosette of bracts surrounding a composite flower head (as a daisy) and often resembling a true calyx — see CUPULE 1a **b** : a whorl of bracts subtending the inflorescence in many members of the Umbelliferae

**in·vo·lu·cred** \-kə(r)d\ *adj* [*involucre* + *-ed*] : INVOLUCRATE

**in·vo·lu·cri·form** \¦==¦krəˌfȯrm\ *adj* [prob. fr. (assumed) NL *involucriformis*, fr. NL *involucrum* involucre + L *-iformis* -iform] : having the form or appearance of an involucre

**in·vo·lu·crum** \ˌ==ˈ=krəm\ *n, pl* **involu·cra** \-krə\ [L, fr. *involvere* to wrap, envelop] **1** : a surrounding envelope or sheath ⟨each group has its ~ of space from which it drives any encroaching group —C.S.Coon⟩ **2** [NL, fr. L] : INVOLUCRE **3** [NL, fr. L] : a formation of new bone about a sequestrum (as in osteomyelitis)

**in·voluntarily** \(ˌ)in, ən+\ *adv* : in an involuntary manner

**in·voluntariness** \"+\ *n* -ES : the quality or state of being involuntary

**in·voluntary** \(ˈ)in, ən+\ *adj* [LL *involuntarius*, fr. L ¹*in-* + *voluntarius* voluntary] **1 a** : springing from accident or impulse rather than conscious exercise of the will : UNINTENTIONAL, SPONTANEOUS ⟨an ~ inheritance from her rich and backward husband —Nigel Dennis⟩ ⟨concentration became at first effortless, then ~, then necessitous —Charles Morgan⟩ **b** : dictated by authority or circumstance : COMPULSORY ⟨~ servitude⟩ ⟨~ unemployment⟩ **c** *of bankruptcy* : declared upon petition of creditors **2** : not subject to control of the will : independent of volition : REFLEX ⟨~ contraction⟩ ⟨~ weeping⟩

**involuntary deposit** *n, law* : an accidental or unintentional transference of property to the possession of another without the assent, negligence, or even knowledge of the owner (as of a boat carried onto land by a storm)

**involuntary manslaughter** *n* : manslaughter resulting from the failure to perform a legal duty expressly required to safeguard human life, or from the commission of an unlawful act not constituting a felony, or from the commission of a lawful act in a negligent or improper manner — compare HOMICIDE, MURDER, VOLUNTARY MANSLAUGHTER

**involuntary muscle** *n* : muscle governing reflex functions and not under direct voluntary control : SMOOTH MUSCLE

**involuntary trust** *n* : CONSTRUCTIVE TRUST

¹**in·vo·lute** \ˈinvəˌlüt *also* -vəlˌyüt; ˌ==ˈ=\ *adj* [L *involutus* involved, intricate, fr. past part. of *involvere* to wrap, envelop] **1 a (1)** : curled spirally **(2)** : having the whorls closely coiled ⟨~ shell⟩ **b (1)** : curled or curved inward **(2)** : having the edges rolled over the upper surface toward the midrib ⟨an ~ leaf⟩ — compare CONVOLUTE, REVOLUTE **2** : INVOLUTED 3 ⟨the possible moves . . . not only manifold, but ~ —E.A.Poe⟩ **3** : of or relating to an involute ⟨~ curve⟩ ⟨~ gear cutter⟩ — **in·vo·lute·ly** *adv*

²**involute** \"=\ *n* -S : a curve traced by any point of a perfectly flexible inextensible thread kept taut as it is wound upon or unwound from another curve — compare EVOLUTE

³**involute** \ˌ==ˈ=\ *vi* -ED/-ING/-S **1** : to curl inward : become involute ⟨the leaf margin ~*s*⟩ **2 a** : to return to a former condition ⟨after pregnancy the uterus ~*s*⟩ **b** : to clear up : DISAPPEAR ⟨the disease ~*s* without desquamation —*Annals of N.Y. Academy of Sciences*⟩

involute *a,p,p,p,p,* traced by any point, *p*, of the thread, *t*, unwinding from curve, *c*

**involuted** \ˈ==ˌ==, ˌ==ˈ==\ *adj* [L *involutus* involved, intricate + E *-ed*] **1** : INVOLUTE 1b ⟨~ soil zone⟩ **2** : that has returned to a normal size or condition ⟨~ uterus⟩ **3** : of an involved or complicated nature : ABSTRUSE, INTRICATE ⟨much ~ wordage . . . obscures the fact that the tax law is an issue —Robert Wallace⟩ ⟨a remarkable man, ~, brilliant, and horribly afraid —Charles Neider⟩ — **in·vo·lut·ed·ly** *adv* — **in·vo·lut·ed·ness** *n* -ES

**involute tooth** *n* : a gear tooth that conforms in contact profile to an involute curve, that engages mating teeth with rolling rather than sliding friction, and that transmits motion with speed practically independent of slight changes in center distance

**in·vo·lu·tion** \ˌinvəˈlüshən *also* -vəlˈyü-\ *n* -S [ML *involution-, involutio* envelopment, fr. L, something enveloped, fr. *involutus* (past part. of *involvere* to wrap, envelop) + *-ion-, -io* -ion] **1 a** : the act or an instance of infolding or entangling : INVOLVEMENT ⟨her subsequent Red ~ was probably from idealistic reaction . . . rather than from Marxist conviction —Wilbur Burton⟩ ⟨some ~*s* of the plot I had quite forgotten —Arnold Bennett⟩; *specif* : an involved grammatical construction usu. characterized by the insertion of clauses between the subject and predicate **b** : the quality or state of being involved : ENVELOPMENT, INTRICACY ⟨whatever the degree of ~ . . . tale within tale —*Modern Language Notes*⟩ ⟨his mind . . . is simple; his syntax lacks ~ —Austin Warren⟩ **2** : the act or process of raising a quantity or symbol to any assigned power or affecting it with an assigned exponent — opposed to *evolution* **3 a** : an inward curvature or penetration ⟨~ of a soil deposit⟩ **b** : the formation of a gastrula by ingrowth of cells formed at the dorsal lip **4** : a shrinking or return to a former size ⟨~ of the uterus after pregnancy⟩ **5** : the regressive alterations of a body or its parts that are characteristic of the aging process; *specif* : presenile decline marked by a decrease of bodily vigor and in women by the menopause **6** : a relation of a higher type of reality to a lower type (as mind to matter) upon which it depends

¹**in·vo·lu·tion·al** \¦invə¦lüshənᵊl, -shnəl *also* -vəl¦yü-\ *adj* [*involution* + *-al*] : of or relating to an involutional or to involutional melancholia ⟨~ depression⟩ ⟨~ period⟩

²**involutional** \"\ *n* -S : one that suffers from involutional melancholia

**involutional melancholia** *or* **involutional psychosis** *n* : an agitated depression occurring at the time of the menopause or climacteric and usu. characterized by somatic and nihilistic delusions

**involution form** *n* : an irregular or atypical bacterium formed under unfavorable conditions (as in old cultures) and variously considered as a degenerating cell or as a specialized reproductive body

**in·volve** \ənˈv¦älv, ¦ȯlv *also* ¦ä(ü)v *or* ¦ȯv\ *vt* -ED/-ING/-S [ME *involven*, fr. L *involvere* to wrap, envelop, fr. *in-* ²in- + *volvere* to roll — more at VOLUBLE] **1** *archaic* : to enfold or envelop so as to encumber ⟨the number of difficulties in which this question is *involved* —Benjamin Jowett⟩ **2 a** : to draw in as a participant : ENGAGE, EMPLOY ⟨size of operations and . . . numbers of workmen *involved* —G.M.Trevelyan⟩ ⟨an organization . . . heavily *involved* in the nation's defense program —R.J.Cordiner⟩ ⟨kings were constantly *involved* in Continental affairs —G.G.Coulton⟩ ⟨he got *involved* in a lawsuit⟩ **b** : to oblige to become associated (as in an unpleasant situation) : EMBROIL, ENTANGLE, IMPLICATE ⟨led the English . . . to ~ India in the war —D.W.Brogan⟩ ⟨the controversies . . . moved on in all their ugliness to ~ others —John Mason Brown⟩ **c** : to occupy (oneself) absorbingly; *esp* : to commit (oneself) emotionally — usu. used with *in* or *with* ⟨we simply don't see enough of her characters . . . to feel personally *involved* in what they say or feel or do —Dan Wickenden⟩ ⟨she . . . never had the slightest intention of *involving* herself with him —Aurelia Levi⟩ **3 a** *archaic* : to enclose in a covering : WRAP ⟨the embryo is still farther *involved*, in two membranes —Oliver Goldsmith⟩ **b** : to surround as if with a wrapping : ENVELOP, SHROUD ⟨rights and privileges at the root . . . are discovered to be *involved* in doubt —B.N.Cardozo⟩ ⟨*involved* in a howling dancing crowd —Arthur Morrison⟩ **4 a** *archaic* : to wind, coil, or wreathe about : ENTWINE ⟨around me they *involved* a giddy dance —P.B.Shelley⟩ **b** : to relate closely : CONNECT, LINK ⟨the problem is closely *involved* with the management of pastures —Allan Fraser⟩ **5 a** : to have within or as part of itself : CONTAIN, INCLUDE ⟨tragic opera . . . must ~ convincing treatment of an elemental conflict —*Opera News*⟩ ⟨two late-arriving costumes . . . ~ magnificent brocaded coats covering deceptively casual sheaths —Lois Long⟩ ⟨a community program *involving* recreational, cultural, and economic . . . features —*Amer. Guide Series: N.C.*⟩ ⟨this course ~*s* a discussion of the trial rules of evidence —*Loyola Univ. Bulletin*⟩ **b** : to require as a necessary accompaniment : ENTAIL, IMPLY ⟨building their own roads . . . *involved* the construction of over 200 bridges —Joseph Millard⟩ ⟨diseases . . . which ~ long hospitalization —Cecile Starr⟩ ⟨changing those attitudes *involved* a job of mass education —Stanley Frank⟩ ⟨a mission which ~*s* much danger —T.B. Costain⟩ ⟨fusion ~*s* disparate materials . . . arranged so as to work together —*College English*⟩ ⟨insensitiveness ~*s* a meagerness of imagination in human relations —Albert Dasnoy⟩ **c** : to have an effect on : concern directly : AFFECT ⟨biological processes . . . like breathing and digesting, ~ the whole organism —H.J.Muller⟩ ⟨lacerations that ~ muscles or cause severe hemorrhage —H.G.Armstrong⟩ ⟨the problem . . . ~*s* their future —Harrison Smith⟩ ⟨work stoppages . . . *involved* more than 100 thousand workers —*Collier's Yr. Bk.*⟩ ⟨is never really three-dimensional, hence his conflicts do not ~ the reader —Frances Keene⟩ **6** : FILL ⟨a fire building so *involved* with heat, smoke and flame that immediate access to the interior is not possible —W.Y.Kimball⟩ ⟨drawings . . . *involved* with color become either water colors or pastels —Carlyle Burrows⟩ **7** : to engross or occupy fully : ABSORB ⟨*involved* in these imaginings she knew nothing of time —Thomas Hardy⟩ **syn** see INCLUDE

**involved** *adj* **1** *obs* : COVERT, SECRETIVE, UNDERHAND ⟨plain and direct, not crafty and ~ —Francis Bacon⟩ **2** *obs* : INVOLUTE, TWISTED **3 a** : COMPLICATED, INTRICATE ⟨~ poem⟩ ⟨~ sentence⟩ ⟨the music becomes more ~ —Warwick Braithwaite⟩ ⟨cup with sturdy base and ~ handle —W.E.Cox⟩ **b** : CONFUSED, TANGLED ⟨at his death . . . left his affairs dreadfully ~ —Jane Austen⟩ **4** : AFFECTED, IMPLICATED ⟨far . . . from an ~ understanding of normal human emotions —Robert Bingham⟩ ⟨dealing with . . . the most severely ~ patients —R.J.Thomas⟩ ⟨a heavily ~ fire floor —J.J.McCarthy⟩ **syn** see COMPLEX

**in·volved·ly** \-(l)və(ə)dlē\ *adv* : in an involved manner

**in·volved·ness** \-(l)vədnəs, -(l)v(d)n-\ *n* -ES : INVOLVEMENT

**in·volve·ment** \-(l)vmənt\ *n* -S **1** : the act or an instance of involving ⟨his ~ of others was inexcusable⟩ ⟨~ is uncalled for because there are no moral and spiritual values at stake —M.W.Straight⟩ ⟨there would be no drama in such a story . . . no ~ of the spectator's own inevitable deep divisions —R.P. Warren⟩ ⟨any action . . . which might be interpreted as ~ in the big power conflict —G.S.Bhargava⟩ **2** : the state or fact of being involved ⟨the fluid se[illegible]s' ~ in the world —Muriel Rukeyser⟩ ⟨increasing ~ in [illegible]blic life —Herbert Read⟩ ⟨knowledge of . . . diverse peoples, our ~ with them in practical terms and our commitment to them in terms of brotherhood —J.R.Oppenheimer⟩; *specif* : inclusion in a damaged area ⟨rheumatic fever, with or without heart ~ —*Biol. Abstracts*⟩ ⟨the child's face escaped ~ in the injuries —*Springfield (Mass.) Daily News*⟩ **3** : an involved or entangled condition or situation : COMPLEXITY, CONFUSION ⟨further complaints of obscurity, ~ —John Foster⟩

**in·volv·er** \-(l)və(r)\ *n* -S : one that involves

**invt** *abbr* **1** [L *invenit*] he designed; he devised; he invented **2** inventory

**in·vulnerability** \(ˌ)in, ən+\ *n* : the quality or state of being invulnerable

**in·vulnerable** \(ˈ)in, ən+\ *adj* [L *invulnerabilis*, fr. *in-* ¹in- + *vulnerare* to wound + *-abilis* -able — more at VULNERABLE] **1** : incapable of being wounded, injured, or damaged : immune to physical assault ⟨an armadillo curls up to make himself ~⟩ : IMPREGNABLE ⟨gunners rake the beaches from ~ positions in overhanging cliffs⟩ **2** : immune to or proof against attack : INVINCIBLE, UNASSAILABLE ⟨~ dignity⟩ ⟨though he was now a partner, his position wa[illegible] not ~ —Hamilton Basso⟩ — **in·vulnerably** \"+\ *adv*

**in·vulnerableness** \"+\ *n* : INVULNERABILITY

**inwale** \ˈ=ˌ=\ *n* [⁴*in* + *wale*] : a finishing strip of wood fastened inside the frame of an open boat and extending along the top strake to reinforce the gunwale — compare CLAMP 3

¹**in·wall** \ənˈ+\ *vt* [alter. (influenced by E ²*in-*) of earlier *enwall*, fr. ¹*en-* + *wall*, n.] : to enclose with or as if with a wall

²**in·wall** \ˈin+ˌ-\ *n* [⁴*in* + *wall*] : an inner wall (as of a blast furnace)

¹**in·ward** \ˈinwərd, ˈinwəd\ *adj* [ME *inward*, fr. OE *inweard*, *innerweard*, *innanweard*; OE *inweard* akin to MD *inwaert* inward, OHG *inwert*, all fr. a prehistoric WGmc compound whose first constituent is represented by OE *in*, *inn*, adv., in, and whose second constituent is represented by OE *-weard* -ward; OE *inneweard* fr. *inne* within (akin to OHG & ON *inni* within, Goth *inna*, all fr. a prehistoric Gmc word derived from the word represented by OE *in*, *inn*, adv., in) + *-weard* -ward; OE *innanweard* akin to ON *innanverthr* inward, both fr. a prehistoric NGmc-WGmc compound whose first constituent is represented by OE & ON *innan* within, from within, OHG *innan*, *innana* within, Goth *innana* (all fr. a prehistoric Gmc word derived from the word represented by OE *in*, *inn*, adv., in) and whose second constituent is represented by OE *-weard* -ward — more at IN (adv.), -WARD] **1 a** : situated on the inside : INNER, INTERNAL ⟨~ smile⟩ ⟨the whole body moves in response to some ~ rhythm —Ellen Glasgow⟩ **b** : produced from within : MUFFLED ⟨her words were ~ and indistinct —Ann Radcliffe⟩ **2 a** : of or relating to the mind or spirit : MENTAL, SPIRITUAL ⟨~ peace⟩ ⟨the scholar . . . lives an ~ and unmaterial life —P.E.More⟩ ⟨~ struggle of the heroes to find their own truth —Leslie Rees⟩ **b** : of or relating to religious faith : DEVOUT, PIOUS ⟨monks . . . free the soul from corporeality and make it ~ —José Ortega y Gasset⟩ **3 a** : of or relating to close acquaintance : FAMILIAR, INTIMATE ⟨intimate and ~, not outward from the child —R.L.Shayon⟩ ⟨more ~ with the Tudor-Stuart dramatists than any man . . . before or since —T.S.Eliot⟩ **b** *obs* : CONFIDENTIAL, SECRET ⟨what is ~ between us, let it pass —Shak.⟩ **4** *archaic* : of or relating to the homeland : DOMESTIC ⟨the dangers ~ they foresaw would be from the noblemen removed from the Queen's Council —Robert Norton⟩ **5** : directed toward the interior : INGOING ⟨~ slope of radiator grille —*Car Life*⟩ **syn** see INNER

²**inward** \"\ *or* **inwards** \"\ *adv* [ME *inward*, *inwardes*; ME *inward* fr. OE *inweard*, fr. *inweard*, adj.; ME *inwardes* fr. *inward* + *-es* (adverbially functioning gen. sing. ending of nouns) — more at INWARD (adj.), -'S] **1 a** : toward the inside : toward the center or interior ⟨the sides of the hole seemed to slope ~ until they met —Gwyn Thomas⟩ ⟨ships . . . that tried to run either ~ or outward through the blockade —C.S. Forester⟩; *specif* : HOMEWARD ⟨~ bound⟩ **b** *obs* : on the inside : INTERNALLY ⟨the maple seldom ~ sound —Edmund Spenser⟩ **2** : toward the inner being : into the mind or spirit ⟨his rich emotions began to turn ~ —H.S.Canby⟩

³**inward** \", *in sense 2 usu* ˈinə(r)d\ *n* -S [ME, fr. OE *inneweard*, fr. *inneweard*, adj. — more at INWARD (adj.)] **1** : an inner being or nature : ESSENCE, SPIRIT ⟨make thine ~ like unto thine outward —John Payne⟩ — usu. used in pl. ⟨Jefferson puts the ~*s* of the issue in these terms —Archibald MacLeish⟩ **2** *or* **inwards** : an inside or interior part ⟨their forms fled to the dusky ~ of his mysterious box —Ross Lockridge⟩ ⟨saw him . . . glare down into the mysterious ~*s* of the engine —Wallace Stegner⟩; *specif* : INNARDS ⟨the gastroenterologist manages our nervous ~*s* —Greer Williams⟩ **3** *obs* : an intimate friend : CONFIDANT ⟨I was an ~ of his —Shak.⟩

⁴**in·ward** \ˈinˌwȯrd\ *n* [ML *inwarda*, *inguarda*, prob. fr. (assumed) OE *inweard*, fr. OE *in*, *inn*, adv., in + *weard* ward, action of guarding — more at IN (adv.), WARD (n.)] : bodyguard service rendered to a king by his sokemen when he visits their shire

**inward dive** *n* : a competitive diving category including dives in which the body from a backward standing takeoff position rotates forward around a transverse axis — compare BACK DIVE, FRONT DIVE, REVERSE DIVE, TWIST DIVE

**inward light** *n, usu cap I&L* : INNER LIGHT

**in·ward·ly** *adv* [ME, fr. OE *inweardlice* heartily, fervently, fr. *inweardlic* internal, fr. *inweard*, adj., inward + *-lic* -ly] **1** : in the innermost being : MENTALLY, SPIRITUALLY ⟨women's self-possession is an outward thing; ~ they flutter —Joseph Conrad⟩ ⟨read, mark, and ~ digest —C.L.Becker⟩ **2** *obs* : in a complete or private manner : FULLY, INTIMATELY ⟨acquainting me with the state of affairs, more ~ than I knew before —John Milton⟩ **3 a** : on the inside : INTERNALLY ⟨he had bled ~ —Daniel Defoe⟩ **b** : to oneself : INAUDIBLY, SECRETLY ⟨I'd have thought she'd ~ either cursed or spat —Kenneth Roberts⟩ **4** : toward the center or interior ⟨see ~ and represent the world of the imagination —Herbert Read⟩

**in·ward·ness** *n* -ES [¹*inward* + *-ness*] **1** : close acquaintance : FAMILIARITY, INTIMACY ⟨read his way into a certain ~ with Chaucer's idiom —John Speirs⟩ **2** : fundamental nature or meaning : ESSENCE, SIGNIFICANCE ⟨apprehending the real ~ of a plowman —C.D.Lewis⟩ ⟨could not grasp the ~ of the text —H.J.Laski⟩ ⟨far from . . . certain as to the true ~ of her violent dismissal —Joseph Conrad⟩ **3** : internal quality or substance ⟨became aware of the ~ of my body, of the blood moving in darkness —R.P.Warren⟩ **4 a** : preoccupation with one's own affairs or attitudes : INTROSPECTION, SUBJECTIVITY ⟨the sensitiveness of James's characters, their seeming ~ —Morris Roberts⟩ ⟨voluntary withdrawal . . . was to mean thereafter an ~ of corporate life —W.L.Sperry⟩ **b** : preoccupation with ethical or ideological values : SPIRITUALITY ⟨Socrates' ~, integrity, and inquisitiveness —H.R.Finch⟩

**inwards** *var of* INWARD

**in·weave** \(ˈ)in, ən+\ *or* **en·weave** \ən, (ˈ)en+\ *vt* [²*in-* or ¹*en-* + *weave*, v.] **1 a** : to weave in or together **b** : to decorate by weaving : INSERT, INTERLACE **c** : to mend or patch by reweaving **2** : to incorporate as if by weaving ⟨the vitality of experience which is *inwoven* with their thorniness —J.H. Hanford⟩

¹**inwick** \ˈ=ˌ=\ *n* [⁴*in* + *wick*, n. (port in curling)] : a shot in curling in which a player's stone is made to carom off the inner edge of an intervening stone so as to knock away from the tee the stone nearest it — compare OUTWICK

²**inwick** \"\ *vi* : to make an inwick

**inwind** *var of* ENWIND

**inwit** \ˈ=ˌ=\ *n* [ME, fr. *in*, prep. & adv. + *wit*, n.] : inward knowledge : CONSCIENCE, UNDERSTANDING ⟨acting from ~ —Ezra Pound⟩ ⟨spills his yarns with humor and delight or with an ~ of sadness —I.L.Salomon⟩

**inwith** \ˈ=ˌ=\ *adj (or adv)* [ME, fr. *in*, prep. & adv. + *with*, prep.] *Scot* : INSIDE, BEN

**inworn** \ˈ=ˌ=\ *adj* [²*in* + *worn*, past part. of *wear* (after *wear in*, v.)] : INGRAINED

**in·wound** \(ˈ)in, ən+\ *adj* [²*in* + *wound*, past part. of *wind* (after *wind in*, v.)] : INTERTWINED

**in·woven** \(ˈ)in, ən+\ *or* **en·woven** \ən, (ˈ)en+\ *adj* [fr. past part. of *inweave*] **1 a** : INTERWOVEN **b** : ENTWINED **2** : closely associated ⟨~ with the heath in his boyhood —Thomas Hardy⟩

**inwrap** *var of* ENWRAP

**inwreathe** *var of* ENWREATHE

**in·wrought** \(ˈ)in, ən+\ *or* **en·wrought** \ən, (ˈ)en+\ *adj* [*inwrought* fr. ²*in* + *wrought*, past part. of *work* (after *work in*, v.); *enwrought* alter. (influenced by ¹*en-*) of *inwrought*] **1 a** : having a decorative element worked or woven in : ORNAMENTED ⟨bonnet . . . ~ with figures —John Milton⟩ **b** *archaic* : WORKED, EMBROIDERED ⟨by beauty's hand ~ —Erasmus Darwin⟩ **2** : worked in as a constituent : INTERWOVEN ⟨~ with the tale are some of the great secrets of philosophy —Marianne Moore⟩

**in·ya·la** \ənˈyälə\ *n, pl* **inyala** [Zulu *inxala*] : NYALA 1

**in·yo·ite** \ˈin(ˌ)yōˌīt\ *n* -S [*Inyo* county, California, its locality + E *-ite*] : a mineral $Ca_2B_6O_{11}.13H_2O$ consisting of a hydrous calcium borate occurring in colorless monoclinic crystals (hardness 2, sp. gr. 2)

¹**io** *n* -S [L, interj., fr. Gk *iō*] *obs* : a shout of joy or triumph ⟨rocks, valleys, hills, with splitting ~*s* ring —John Dryden & Nathaniel Lee⟩ — often used interjectionally

²**io** \ˈē(ˌ)ō\ *n* -S [Hawaiian] : a large hawk (*Buteo solitarius*) that is the only indigenous raptorial bird of Hawaii

**IO** *abbr* **1** information officer **2** in order **3** inspecting order **4** intelligence officer

**Io** *symbol* ionium

**ioa** *var of* IWA

**iod** *var of* YODH

**iod-** *or* **iodo-** *comb form* [F *iode* iodine] **1** : iodine ⟨*iod*hydrate⟩ ⟨*iodo*form⟩ **2 a** *now usu* **iodo-** : containing iodine in place of hydrogen — in names of organic compounds ⟨*iodo*acetophenone⟩ **b** *now usu* **iodo-** : containing iodine regarded as replacing hydroxyl or oxygen or as coordinated to a central atom — in names of inorganic acids and salts ⟨*iodo*argentate⟩ ⟨*iodo*bismuthate⟩ **c** : containing iodine as iodide sometimes replacing another element or group — in names of minerals and salts occurring as minerals ⟨*iodo*sulfate⟩

**iod·amoeba** \(ˌ)īˈōd, -ˈäd+\ *n, cap* [NL, fr. *iod-* + *amoeba*] : a genus of amoebas commensal in the intestine of man and other mammals and distinguished by uninucleate cysts containing a large glycogen vacuole that stains characteristically with iodine

**¹io·date** \ˈīə,dāt\ *n* -s [F, fr. *iode* iodine + *-ate*] : a salt of iodic acid

**²iodate** \"\ *vt* -ED/-ING/-S [*iod-* + *-ate*, v. suffix] : to impregnate or treat with iodine — **io·da·tion** \ˌīəˈdāshən\ *n* -s

**iodhydrin** *var of* IODOHYDRIN

**iod·ic** \(ˈ)īˈädik\ *adj* [F *iodique*, fr. *iode* iodine + *-ique* -ic] : of, relating to, or containing iodine — used esp. of compounds in which this element is pentavalent

**iodic acid** *n* : a crystalline oxidizing solid $HIO_3$ formed by oxidation of iodine (as with fuming nitric acid)

**iodic anhydride** *n* : IODINE PENTOXIDE

**io·dide** \ˈīə,dīd, -ˌdəd\ *n* -s [ISV *iod-* + *-ide*] : a binary compound of iodine usu. with a more electropositive element or radical : a salt or ester of hydriodic acid ⟨potassium ~⟩ ⟨ethyl ~⟩

**iodimetry** *var of* IODOMETRY

**io·di·nate** \ˈīədə,nāt\ *vt* -ED/-ING/-S [*iodine* + *-ate*, v. suffix] : to treat or cause to combine with iodine or a compound of iodine : introduce iodine into (as an organic compound)

**iodinated casein** *n* : an iodine-containing preparation that is made from casein, resembles the thyroid hormone in physiological activity, and is used in animal feeds (as to increase milk production of cows)

**io·di·na·tion** \ˌīədəˈnāshən\ *n* -s : the process of iodinating

**io·dine** *also* **io·din** \ˈīə,dīn *also* -ˌdən *or* -dᵊn *or* -ˌdēn\ *n* -s [F *iode* iodine (fr. Gk *ioeidēs* purple, violet colored, fr. *ion* violet + *-oeidēs* -oid) + E ²*-ine* or *-in* — more at VIOLET] : a nonmetallic univalent and polyvalent element belonging to the halogens that is obtained usu. as heavy shining blackish gray crystals subliming to a violet-colored irritating vapor, that occurs naturally only in combination in small quantities esp. in seawater, rocks, soils, and underground brines and in marine plants and animals, that is essential for the normal functioning of the thyroid gland of all vertebrates, that is usu. extracted from the ashes of seaweeds, from Chile saltpeter, or from oil-well brines, and that is used chiefly in medicine (as in antisepsis and in the treatment of cretinism and goiter), photography, and analysis — symbol *I*; see ELEMENT table

**iodine bush** *n* : a shrub (*Allenrolfia occidentalis*) of the family Chenopodiaceae with fleshy jointed stems, leaves resembling scales, and flowers in crowded spikes that grows in moist saline soils in the southwestern U.S. and is used for winter grazing — called also *burroweed, California greasewood, pickleweed*

**iodine number** *or* **iodine value** *n* : a measure of the unsaturation of a substance (as an oil or fat) expressed as the number of grams of iodine or equivalent halogen absorbed by 100 grams of the substance ⟨the *iodine numbers* of linseed oil, olive oil, and coconut oil are approximately 175–201, 77–91, and 8–9.5 respectively⟩

**iodine 131** *n* : a heavy radioactive isotope of iodine having the mass number 131 and a half-life of 8 days that is produced in the fission of uranium or by bombardment of tellurium with neutrons and that is used esp. in the form of sodium radioiodide in the diagnosis of thyroid disease and the treatment of goiter — symbol $I^{131}$ or $^{131}I$; called also *radioiodine*

**iodine pentoxide** *n* : a white crystalline solid $I_2O_5$ formed by the oxidation of iodine or the dehydration of iodic acid and used to oxidize carbon monoxide quantitatively to carbon dioxide — called also *iodic anhydride*

**iodine weed** *n* : INKWEED 1

**io·din·oph·i·lous** \ˌīədəˈnäfələs\ *also* **io·din·o·phil** \ˌīəˈdinə,fil\ *or* **io·din·o·phile** \-,fīl\ *or* **io·din·o·phil·ic** \ˌīəˌdinəˈfilik\ *adj* [*iodinophilous* fr. *iodine* + *-o-* + *-philous*; *iodinophil, iodinophile* fr. *iodine* + *-o-* + *-phile, -phil*; *iodinophilic* prob. fr. *iodinophil* + *-ic*] : taking up or coloring readily with iodine — used esp. of various starchy cell inclusions

**io·dism** \ˈīə,dizəm\ *n* -s [*iod-* + *-ism*; prob. intended as trans. of G *jodkrankheit*] : an abnormal local and systemic condition resulting from overdosage with, prolonged use of, or sensitivity to iodine or iodine compounds

**io·di·za·tion** \ˌīədəˈzāshən, -ˌdīˈz-\ *n* -s : the process of iodizing

**io·dize** \ˈīə,dīz\ *vt* -ED/-ING/-S [*iod-* + *-ize*] : to treat with iodine or an iodide ⟨recommended *iodized* salt as a preventive of thyroid trouble⟩

**iodized oil** *n* : a viscous oily liquid that has an odor like garlic, is made by treating a fatty vegetable oil (as poppy-seed oil) with iodine or hydriodic acid, and is used as a contrast medium in X-ray photography

**io·do** \īˈō(,)dō, ˈīə,dō\ *adj* [*iod-*] : containing iodine — used esp. of organic compounds; compare IOD- 2

**iodo-** — see IOD-

**iodo·acetate** \īˌōdō, īˌädō+\ *n* [ISV *iod-* + *acetate*] : a salt or ester of iodoacetic acid

**iodo·acetic acid** \"+ . . . -\ *n* [*iodoacetic* ISV *iod-* + *acetic*] : a crystalline acid $CH_2ICOOH$ made by reaction of chloroacetic acid and a metallic iodide and used in biochemical research esp. because of its inhibiting effect on many enzymes (as in glycolysis in muscle extracts)

**iodo·behenate** \īˌōdə, īˌädə+\ *n* [*iod-* + *behenate*] : a salt of iodobehenic acid

**iodo·behenic acid** \"+. . -\ *n* [*iodobehenic* ISV *iod-* + *behenic* (in *behenic acid*)] : a solid mono-iodo derivative $C_{21}H_{42}ICOOH$ of behenic acid made by reaction of erucic acid and hydriodic acid

**iodo·benzene** \īˌōdə, īˌädə+\ *n* [ISV *iod-* + *benzene*] : a colorless liquid $C_6H_5I$ made usu. from benzene by reaction with iodine and nitric acid — called also *phenyl iodide*

**iodo·bromide** \"+\ *n* : BROMOIODIDE

**iodo·bromite** \"+\ *n* -s [obs. G *iodobromit* (now *jodobromit*), fr. obs. G *iod-* (now *jod-*) + G *bromit* bromyrite, fr. *brom-* + *-it* -ite] : a mineral Ag(Br,Cl,I) consisting of chloride, iodide, and bromide of silver that is isomorphous with cerargyrite and bromyrite

**iodo·casein** \"+\ *n* : IODINATED CASEIN

**iodo·chloride** \"+\ *n* : CHLOROIODIDE

**iodo·ethane** \īˌōdō, īˌädō+\ *n* : ETHYL IODIDE

**iodo·form** \īˈōdə,fórm, īˈäd-\ *n* -s [ISV *iod-* + *-form* (as in *chloroform*)] : a yellow crystalline volatile compound $CHI_3$ that has a penetrating persistent odor, is made usu. by electrolysis of an alkaline solution of a metallic iodide in alcohol or acetone, and is sometimes used as an antiseptic dressing; tri-iodo-methane

**iodo·gor·go·ic acid** \īˌōdəˌgórˈgōik, īˌäd-\ *n* [*iodogorgoic* fr. *iod-* + *gorgo-* (fr. *gorgonin*) + *-ic*] : DIIODOTYROSINE

**iodo·hy·drin** \ī,ōdəˈhīdrən, ī,äd-\ *also* **iod·hy·drin** \ī,ōdˈh-, ī,äd-\ *n* -s [ISV *iod-* + *-hydrin*] : any of a class of iodine compounds analogous to the chlorohydrins

**iodo·mer·cu·rate** \īˌōdəˌmərkyərət, īˌäd-, -ˌrāt\ *also* **iodo·mer·cu·ri·ate** \-(,)mərˈkyu̇rēət, -ē,āt\ *n* -s [ISV *iod-* + *mercur-* or *mercuri-* + *-ate*] : any of a series of complex salts containing iodine and mercury in the anion

**iodo·metric** \"+\ *adj* [ISV *iodometry* + *-ic*] : of, relating to, or by means of iodometry — **iodo·metrically** \"+\ *adv*

**io·dom·e·try** \ˌīəˈdämə·trē\ *also* **io·dim·e·try** \-dim-\ *n* -ES [*iodometry* ISV *iod-* + *-metry*; *iodimetry* alter. (influenced by E *-i-*) of *iodometry*] **1** : the volumetric determination of iodine usu. by titration with a standard solution of sodium thiosulfate using starch as indicator **2** : a method of quantitative analysis involving the use of a standard solution of iodine or the liberation of iodine from an iodide

**io·do·ni·um** \ˌīəˈdōnēəm\ *n* -s [ISV *iod-* + *-onium*; orig. formed as G *iodonium*] : the univalent cation $H_2I^+$ derived from hydrogen iodide and known only in disubstituted form

**¹iodo·phile** \īˈōdə,fīl, īˈäd-\ *or* **iodo·phil·ic** \-ˌ≈≈ˈfilik\ *adj* [*iodophile* ISV *iod-* + *-phile*; *iodophilic* fr. *iodophile* + *-ic*] : staining in a characteristic manner with iodine — used esp. of starch-containing cells staining blue with iodine

**²iodophile** \"\ *n* -s : an iodophile cell or individual

**iodo·phthalein** \ī,ōdə, ī,ädə+\ *n* : a symmetrical tetraiodo derivative of phenolphthalein or its soluble blue-violet crystalline disodium salt $C_{19}H_8I_4O(ONa)COONa$ used to render the gall bladder opaque to X rays and to treat typhoid carriers

**iodo·protein** \"+\ *n* : an iodine-containing protein (as iodinated casein) — compare THYROPROTEIN

**io·dop·sin** \ˌīəˈdäpsən\ *n* -s [*iod-* (fr. Gk *ioeidēs* violet-colored + *ops-* (fr. Gk *opsis* sight) + *-in* — more at IODINE, -OPSIS] : a photosensitive violet pigment in the retinal cones of most animals that is similar to rhodopsin but more labile, that is formed from vitamin $A_1$, and that is important in daylight vision

**iodo·pyr·a·cet** \ī,ōdōˈpirə,set, ī,äd-\ *n* -s [d*iiodo-pyr*idone-N-*acet*ic acid] : a salt $C_8H_{19}I_2N_2O_3$ administered intravenously in aqueous solution as a contrast medium for radiography esp. of the urinary tract; the diethanolamine salt of 3,5-diiodo-4-pyridone-*N*-acetic acid — called also *diodone*

**iodoso-** *comb form* [ISV *iodos-* (fr. *iodous*) + *-o-*] : containing the univalent radical —IO consisting of one atom each of iodine and oxygen, esp. replacing hydrogen ⟨*iodoso*benzoic acid $C_6H_4(IO)COOH$⟩

**io·do·so·benzene** \ˌīəˈdō(,)sō+\ *n* [ISV *iodoso-* + *benzene*] : an amorphous solid compound $C_6H_5IO$ that explodes when heated and is formed by treating iodobenzene with chlorine and then with a caustic alkali

**iodous** \īˈōdəs, īˈäd-, ˈīəd-\ *adj* [ISV *iod-* + *-ous*] : relating to or containing iodine and esp. iodine with a valence of three ⟨~ acid $HIO_2$⟩

**iodoxy-** *comb form* [ISV *iod-* + *oxy-*] : containing the univalent radical —$IO_2$ of iodic acid, esp. replacing hydrogen ⟨*iodoxy*benzoic acid $C_6H_4(IO_2)COOH$⟩

**io·doxy·benzene** \ˌīəˈdäksē+\ *n* [*iodoxy-* + *benzene*] : a crystalline compound $C_6H_5IO_2$ that explodes when heated and is obtained by oxidation of iodosobenzene

**iod·y·rite** \īˈädə,rīt\ *n* -s [*iod-* + argyr- + *-ite*] : a yellowish or greenish hexagonal mineral AgI consisting of native silver iodide usu. occurring in thin plates

**io·lite** \ˈīə,līt\ *n* -s [G *iolith*, fr. *io-* (fr. Gk *ion* violet) + *-lith* -lite, -lith — more at VIOLET] : CORDIERITE

**IOM** *abbr* interoffice minute

**io moth** \ˈī(,)ō-\ *n* [NL *io* (specific epithet of *Automeris io*), fr. L *Io*, mythical priestess of Argos who was loved by Zeus, fr. Gk *Iō*] : a large yellowish American moth (*Automeris io*) having a large ocellate spot on each hind wing and a larva covered with fascicles of spines that sting like nettles

**ion** \ˈīən *also* ˈī,än\ *n* -s [Gk, neut. of *iōn*, pres. part. of *ienai* to go — more at ISSUE] **1** : an atom or group of atoms when combined in a radical or molecule that carries a positive or negative electric charge as a result of having lost or gained one or more electrons and that may exist in solution usu. in combination with molecules of the solvent or out of solution, that may be formed during electrolysis and migrate to the electrode of opposite charge, or that may be formed in a gas and be capable of carrying an electric current through the gas — see ANION, CATION; compare HYDROGEN ION **2** : a free electron or other charged subatomic particle

**-ion** *n suffix* -s [ME *-ioun, -ion, -iun*, fr. OF *-ion, -iun*, fr. L *-ion-, -io*] **1 a** : act or process ⟨acidulat*ion*⟩ ⟨rebell*ion*⟩ **b** : result of an act or process ⟨construct*ion*⟩ **2 a** : state or condition subject*ion*⟩ **b** : thing acted upon or conditioned ⟨ambit*ion*⟩

**ion chamber** *n* : IONIZATION CHAMBER

**ion engine** *n* : a jet engine deriving thrust from a stream of ionized particles

**ion exchange** *n* : a reversible interchange that takes place between ions of like charge and usu. between ions present on an insoluble solid and ions present in a solution surrounding the solid and that may occur naturally or be applied for various purposes — see ANION EXCHANGE, CATION EXCHANGE

**ion exchanger** *n* **1** : a solid agent (as a zeolite or a synthetic resin) used in ion exchange — compare ANION EXCHANGER, CATION EXCHANGER **2** : an apparatus or piece of equipment for effecting ion exchange

**ion-exchange resin** *n* : an insoluble material of high molecular weight that contains either acidic groups for exchanging cations or basic groups for exchanging anions and that may be used in medicine (as for reducing the sodium content of the body or the acidity of the stomach) and in ion exclusion as well as in the usual ion-exchange processes

**ion exclusion** *n* : a process of separating materials in solution by means of an ion-exchange resin that excludes highly ionized particles and takes up slightly ionized particles or particles not ionized

**¹io·ni·an** \īˈōnēən\ *n* -s *usu cap* [L *ionius*, adj. + E *-an*, n. suffix] **1** : a native or inhabitant of Ionia; *esp* : one of the Greek people descended from an early group of Hellenic invaders of Greece **2** : a member of a school of philosophers of ancient Greece consisting chiefly of the Milesians but including also the philosophers Heraclitus and Xenophanes

**²ionian** \(ˈ)≈ˈ≈≈≈\ *adj, usu cap* [L *ionius* Ionian (fr. *Ionia*, ancient district including the south central part of the west coast of Asia Minor and several nearby Aegean islands such as Chios and Samos, fr. Gk *Iōnia*, fr. *Iōn*, n., Ionian + *-ia*) + E *-an*, adj. suffix] **1 a** : of, relating to, or characteristic of Ionia **b** : of, relating to, or characteristic of the people of Ionia **2** : of or relating to the Ionian group of Greek philosophers ⟨resumed the *Ionian* tradition of scientific research —Benjamin Farrington⟩

**ionian mode** *n, usu cap I* **1** : the Greek hypophrygian mode **2** : an authentic ecclesiastical mode consisting of a pentachord and an upper conjunct tetrachord represented on the white keys of the piano by an ascending diatonic scale from C to C — called also *Ionic mode*; see MODE illustration

**¹ion·ic** \(ˈ)īˈänik, -nēk\ *adj* [L & MF; MF *ionique*, fr. L *ionicus*, fr. Gk *iōnikos*, fr. *Iōnia* Ionia + *-ikos* -ic] **1** *usu cap* : IONIAN **2** *usu cap* : belonging to or resembling the Ionic order of architecture that is lighter and more graceful than Doric and is characterized esp. by the spiral volutes of its capital — see CAPITAL illustration **3** : of, relating to, or consisting of ionics

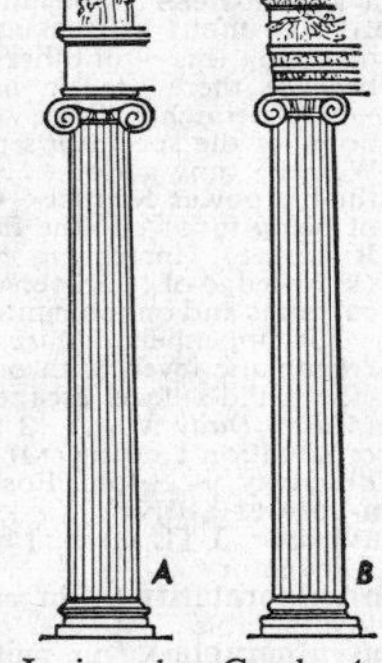


Ionic order: Greek, *A*; Roman, *B*

**²ionic** \"\ *n* -s **1** *cap* : a dialect of ancient Greek used in Ionia that was the vehicle of an important body of literature **2** [LL *ionicus*, fr. L *ionicus*, adj.] **a** : a foot of verse that consists either of (1) two long and two short syllables or (2) two short and two long syllables — called also respectively (1) *major ionic* and (2) *minor ionic* **b** : a verse or meter consisting of ionics

**³ionic** \"\ *adj* [ISV *ion* + *-ic*] **1** : of, relating to, existing in the form of, or characterized by ions ⟨~ charge⟩ ⟨~ hydrogen⟩ ⟨~ crystals⟩ **2** : operated by, utilizing, or taking place by means of ions ⟨~ loudspeaker⟩ ⟨~ conduction⟩

**ionic alphabet** *n, usu cap I* [¹*ionic*] : a variety of the eastern form of the ancient Greek alphabet having 24 letters in its developed form and officially accepted late in the 5th cent. B.C. at Athens from which its use in time extended throughout the Greek-speaking world

**ionic bond** *n* [³*ionic*] : ELECTROVALENT BOND

**ionic displacement** *n* [¹*ionic*] : the occurrence in iambic meter of a pyrrhic foot followed or sometimes preceded by a spondaic foot that together create an ionic cadence (as in the third and fourth feet in Shakespeare's line "when to the sessions of sweet silent thought" ŏo|ŏó|oo|óó|oó)

**ion·i·cism** \īˈänə,sizəm\ *n* -s *usu cap* [¹*ionic* + *-ism*] **1** : an Ionic feature; *esp* : a characteristic feature of the Ionic dialect — called also *Ionism* **2** : the quality or state of being Ionic

**ion·i·cize** \-,sīz\ *vt* -ED/-ING/-S *often cap* [¹*ionic* + *-ize*] : to make Ionic

**ionic mode** *n, usu cap I* : IONIAN MODE

**ionic valence** *n* [³*ionic*] : ELECTROVALENCE

**io·nism** \ˈīə,nizəm\ *n* -s *usu cap* [prob. fr. L *Iones* Ionians (fr. Gk *Iōnes*, pl. of *Iōn* Ionian) + E *-ism*] : IONICISM

**io·ni·um** \īˈōnēəm\ *n* -s [*ion* + *-ium*; so called fr. its ionizing action] : a naturally occurring radioactive isotope of thorium having mass 230 — symbol $Th^{230}$ or *Io*; see URANIUM SERIES

**ion·iza·tion** \ˌīənəˈzāshən, -ˌnīˈz-\ *n* -s [ISV ²*ionize* + *-ation*] : the process of ionizing or the state of being ionized — compare DISSOCIATION

**ionization chamber** *n* : a partially evacuated tube provided with electrodes so that its conductivity due to the ionization of the residual gas reveals the presence of ionizing radiation (as X rays or beta rays)

**ionization constant** *n* : a constant that depends upon the equilibrium between the ions and the molecules that are not ionized in a solution or liquid — symbol *K*; called also *dissociation constant*

**ionization current** *n* : an electric current produced in an ionized gas subjected to an electric field

**ionization gauge** *n* : a low-pressure vacuum gauge in which the pressure is indicated by the ionization current between two specified electrodes at a prescribed voltage

**ionization potential** *n* : the potential difference corresponding to the energy in electron volts that is just sufficient to ionize a gas molecule

**¹io·nize** \ˈīə,nīz\ *vt* -ED/-ING/-S *often cap* [Gk *iōnizein* to speak Ionic, fr. *Iōn*, n., Ionian + *-izein* -ize] : IONICIZE

**²ion·ize** \"\ *vb* -ED/-ING/-S [ISV *ion* + *-ize*] *vt* : to convert wholly or partly into ions ⟨a charged particle . . . ~*s* the air molecules with which it collides —G.W.Gray b. 1886⟩ ⟨*ionized* calcium⟩ ~ *vi* : to become converted wholly or partly into ions ⟨a salt ~*s* in water⟩

**ion·o·gen** \īˈänəjən, -,jen\ *n* -s [ISV *ion* + *-o-* + *-gen*] **1** : a compound capable of forming ions : ELECTROLYTE 2 **2** : an atom or group capable of being ionized

**ion·o·gen·ic** \ī,änəˈjenik\ *adj* [*ion* + *-o-* + *-genic*] : capable of ionizing

**ion·og·ra·phy** \ˌīəˈnägrəfē\ *n* -ES [*ion* + *-o-* + *-graphy*] : electrochromatography involving the migration of ions (as on wet filter paper)

**Io·none** \ˈīə,nōn\ *trademark* — used for either of two oily liquid isomeric ketones $C_{13}H_{20}O$ that have a strong violet odor, are found esp. in the essential oil of an Australian shrub (*Boronia megastigma*) but are usu. obtained from citral, and are used esp. in perfumes

**ion·o·pho·re·sis** \ī,änəfəˈrēsəs\ *n, pl* **ionophore·ses** \-ē,sēz\ [NL, fr. *ion* (fr. E) + *-o-* + *-phoresis*] : ELECTROPHORESIS; *esp* : the movement of relatively small ions — **ion·o·pho·ret·ic** \ī,änəfəˈred·ik\ *adj*

**ion·o·sphere** \īˈänə+,-\ *n* [*ion* + *-o-* + *-sphere*] : the part of the earth's atmosphere beginning at an altitude of about 25 miles and extending outward 250 miles or more, containing free electrically charged particles by means of which radio waves are transmitted to great distances around the earth, and consisting of several regions within which occur one or more layers that vary in height and ionization with time of day, season, and the solar cycle, the gases in this part of the earth's atmosphere being ionized by ultraviolet rays from the sun and to a lesser extent by charged particles from the sun — see D REGION, E REGION, F REGION — **ion·o·spher·ic** \ī,änəˈsfirik, -fer-\ *adj*

**io·not·ro·py** \ˌīəˈnä·trəpē\ *n* -ES [*ion* + *-o-* + *-tropy*] : TAUTOMERISM

**ion·oxalis** \ˌīən+\ *n, cap* [NL, fr. Gk *ion* violet + NL *Oxalis*] : a genus of chiefly tropical American herbs (family Oxalidaceae)

**ions** *pl of* ION

**-ions** *pl of* -ION

**ionto-** *comb form* [NL, fr. Gk *iont-*, *iōn*, pres. part. of *ienai* to go — more at ISSUE] : ion ⟨*ionto*quantimeter⟩ ⟨*ionto*therapy⟩

**ion·to·pho·re·sis** \ī,äntəfəˈrēsəs\ *n, pl* **iontophore·ses** \-ē,sēz\ [NL, fr. *ionto-* + *-phoresis*] **1** : ELECTROPHORESIS **2** : the introduction of drugs through intact skin by the transfer of ions effected by means of the application of a direct electric current—**ion·to·pho·ret·ic** \ī,äntəfəˈred·ik\ *adj*

**ion trap** *n* : a device that prevents the formation of a discolored spot on a television screen by diverting the negative ions from the cathode that would cause it

**io·ra** \īˈōrə, ēˈō-\ *n* -s [origin unknown] : any of several small bright-colored Asiatic songbirds that are related to the bulbuls and that constitute a genus (*Aegithina*)

**ios** *pl of* IO

**io·ta** \īˈōd·ə, -ōtə, *in sense 1 sometimes* ēˈō-\ *n* -s [L *iota, jota*, fr. Gk *iōta* — more at JOT] **1** : the ninth and smallest letter of the Greek alphabet — symbol I or ι; see ALPHABET table **2** : an infinitesimal amount : a very small degree : JOT ⟨of statesmanship he had not an ~ —S.H.Adams⟩ ⟨he had used a lance . . . nicely, to extract the last ~ of pain —F.V.W.Mason⟩

**iota adscript** *n* : the unpronounced iota of a Greek improper diphthong when written on the line after the long vowel — used in standard printing practice only when the long vowel is a capital

**io·ta·cism** \-,sizəm\ *n* -s [LL *iotacismus*, fr. Gk *iōtakismos*, fr. *iōta* iota] : excessive use of the letter iota or I or a too frequent repetition of its sound; *specif* : the use in modern Greek of the sound of iota (Eng. *ē* in *bē*) in speaking words written with other vowels or diphthongs (as *ē, y, ei, oi*) — compare ITACISM

**iota subscript** *n* : the unpronounced iota of a Greek improper diphthong when written small beneath the preceding long vowel [as ᾳ (*āi*), ῃ (*ēi*), ῳ (*ōi*)]

**I O U** \ˌī(,)ōˈyü\ *n* -s [fr. the pronunciation of *I owe you*] : a paper that has on it the letters IOU and a signature as an acknowledgment of debt, that names a sum of money, and that is sometimes used as the equivalent of a promissory note

**-ious** *adj suffix* [ME, partly fr. OF *-ious, -ios, -ieus, -ieux*, fr. L *-iosus*, fr. *-i-* (penultimate vowel in nouns such as *religio* religion, *malitia* malice, *species* species, appearance, *spatium* space) + *-osus* -ose, and partly fr. L *-ius* (final portion of the nom. sing. masc. form of adjectives such as *meritorius* that brings in money)] : -OUS ⟨edacious⟩

**¹io·wa** *also* **io·way** \ˈīəwə, -,wā\ *n, pl* **iowa** *or* **iowas** *usu cap* [Dakota *Ayuhwa*, lit., sleepy ones] **1 a** : a Siouan people of Iowa, Minnesota, and Missouri **b** : a member of such people **2** : a dialect of the Chiwere language

**²io·wa** \ˈīəwə, ÷ˈīə,wā, *by outsiders sometimes* īˈōə\ *adj, usu cap* [*Iowa*, state in the north central U. S., fr. ¹*iowa*] : of or from the state of Iowa ⟨an *Iowa* cornfield⟩ : of the kind or style prevalent in Iowa : IOWAN

**iowa crab** *or* **iowa crab apple** *n, usu cap I* [²*iowa*] : a wild crab apple (*Malus ioensis*) of the western U. S. with fragrant pink flowers — called also *western crab apple*

**¹io·wan** \ˈīəwən\ *adj, usu cap* [*Iowa*, state in the north central U. S. + E *-an*, adj. suffix] **1** : of, relating to, or characteristic of the state of Iowa **2** : of, relating to, or characteristic of the people of Iowa

**²iowan** \"\ *n* -s *cap* [*Iowa*, state in the north central U. S. + E *-an*, n. suffix] **1** : a native or resident of Iowa **2 a** : a substage of the Wisconsin glacial stage **b** : the drift of such substage

**IP** *abbr* **1** ice point **2** India paper **3** initial point **4** innings pitched **5** installment paid **6** intermediate pressure

**ipa** \ˈēpə\ *n* -s *usu cap* [AmerSp, of AmerInd origin] **1** : a people of the Vilela group **2** : a member of the Ipa people

**IPA** \ˌī(,)pēˈā\ *n* -s [International Phonetic Alphabet] : an alphabet designed to represent each human speech sound with a unique symbol

**IPA** *abbr* **1** including particular average **2** intermediate power amplifier

**IPC** *n* -s [isopropyl N-phenylcarbamate] : a crystalline herbicide $C_6H_5NHCOOCH(CH_3)_2$ that is poisonous to grasses but not to broad-leaved plants; isopropyl carbanilate

**IPD** *abbr* individual package delivery

**ip·e·cac** \ˈipə,kak, ˈipē-\ *or* **ipe·cacu·nha** \,≈≈,kakyəˈwan(y)ə, ē,pākəˈkwanyə\ *n* -s [*ipecac* short for *ipecacuanha*, fr. Pg, fr. Tupi *ipekaaguéne*] **1** : a tropical So. American creeping plant (*Cephaelis ipecacuanha*) with drooping flowers **2 a** : the dried rhizome and roots of ipecac formerly used as a medicine and now valued as the source of emetine — called also *Brazilian ipecac* **b** : the dried roots of any of several plants used like ipecac roots — see BASTARD IPECAC, WHITE IPECAC

**ipecac spurge** *n* **:** a spurge (*Euphorbia ipecacuanhae*) of the eastern U. S. with a root that is emetic and purgative — called also *American white ipecac*

**ip·e·cac·u·a·nhic** \ˌipəˌkakyəˈwan(y)ik, ¦ipē,-\ *adj* **:** of or relating to ipecac

**ipf** *abbr* imperfect

**iph·i·ge·nia** \ˌifəjəˈnīə\ *n, cap* [NL, fr. L *Iphigenia*, daughter of Agamemnon, fr. Gk *Iphigeneia*] **:** a genus of tropical bivalve mollusks related to *Donax*

**IPI** *abbr* [L *in partibus infidelium*] in the regions of unbelievers

**¹ip·id** \ˈipəd\ *adj* [NL *Ipidae*] **:** of or relating to the Scolytidae

**²ipid** \"\ *n* -s [NL *Ipidae*] **:** a member of the Scolytidae

**ip·i·dae** \ˈipəˌdē\ [NL, fr. *Ip-, Ips*, type genus + *-idae*] *syn of* SCOLYTIDAE

**ipil** \ˈēpəl\ *or* **ifil** \ˈēfəl\ *n* -s [Sp *ipil*, fr. Tag] **1 :** a Philippine and Pacific island tree (*Intsia bijuga*) yielding a valuable brown dye and having a very hard and durable dark wood **2 :** the wood of the ipil

**ipil·ipil** \ˌēpəˈlēpəl\ *n* -s [Tag *ipil ipil*] **:** a tropical leguminous shrub (*Leucaena glauca*) used esp. in the Philippines as a means of controlling various undesirable grasses in pastures and rangelands

**ipin** \(ˈ)ē¦pin, -pēn\ *adj, usu cap* [fr. *Ipin*, city in south central China] **:** of or from the city of Ipin, China **:** of the kind or style prevalent in Ipin

**ip·i·ti** \ˈipəd·ē\ *n* -s [Xhosa & Zulu *i puti*] **:** BLUE DUIKER

**ip·i·u·tak** \ˌipēˈyüˌtak\ *adj, usu cap* [*Ipiutak*, locality near Point Hope, northwest Alaska, where remains of the culture were discovered] **:** of or relating to an Eskimo culture in western Alaska of about A.D.100–600 characterized by ivory carvings, finely chipped stone implements resembling Siberian artifacts, and villages of semiunderground earth lodges

**IPM** *abbr, often not cap* inches per minute

**ip·o·moea** \ˌipəˈmēə\ *n* [NL, fr. Gk *ip-, ips* worm + NL *-omoea* (fr. Gk *homoios* like); fr. the twining habit of the plants — more at HOME-] **1** *cap* **:** a genus of herbaceous vines (family Convolvulaceae) having showy campanulate or funnelform flowers with capitate stigmas — see MORNING GLORY, SWEET POTATO **2** *also* **ip·o·mea** \"\ -s **:** a plant or flower of the genus *Ipomoea* **3** *usu* **ipomea** -s **:** the dried root of a scammony (*Ipomoea orizabensis*)

**IPP** *abbr* India paper proofs

**ip·pi·ap·pa** \ˌipēˈapə\ *n* -s [by alter.] **:** JIPIJAPA

**IPR** *abbr, often not cap* inches per revolution

**ips** \ˈips\ [NL *Ip-, Ips*, fr. Gk *ip-, ips* woodworm] *syn of* SCOLYTUS

**IPS** *abbr* **1** *often not cap* inches per second **2** iron pipe size

**ip·se dix·it** \ˌipsēˈdiksət\ *n, pl* **ipse dixits** [L, lit., he himself said it, trans. of Gk (Dor) *autos epha*; fr. the use of this expression by the Pythagoreans in reference to statements made by Pythagoras himself] **:** an assertion made on authority but not proved **:** DICTUM ⟨has had a good many followers ready to accept his *ipse dixit* —D.W.Hering⟩

**ip·se·dix·it·ism** \-səd·ˌizəm\ *n* -s **:** dogmatic assertion or assertiveness ⟨denounces all appeals to a moral faculty as sheer ~ —James Martineau⟩

**ip·se·ity** \ipˈsēəd·ē\ *n* -ES *sometimes cap* [L *ipse* self, himself + E *-ity*] **:** individual identity **:** SELFHOOD ⟨those heavenly moments . . . when a sense of the divine ~ invades me—L.P. Smith⟩

**ip·si·lateral** *also* **ip·se·lateral** \ˌipsē, -sə+ *or* **ip·so·lateral** \-(ˌ)sō+\ *adj* [ISV *ipsi-, ipse-, ipso-* (fr. L *ipse*) + *lateral*] **:** situated or appearing on or affecting the same side of the body — compare CONTRALATERAL — **ip·si·laterally** \"+\ *adv*

**ip·so fac·to** \ˌip(ˌ)sōˈfak(ˌ)tō\ *adv* [NL] **:** by the fact or act itself **:** as the result of the mere act or fact **:** by the very nature of the case ⟨does one, *ipso facto*, become a censor when he warns against such censorship —H.C.Gardiner⟩ ⟨training in speech . . . is *ipso facto* training in personality —A.T.Weaver⟩

**ipso ju·re** \-ˈjürē, -ˈyü-\ *adv* [L] **:** by the law itself **:** by operation of law

**ips·wich** \ˈip(ˌ)swich, -ˌswēch\ *adj, usu cap* [fr. *Ipswich*, county borough of East Suffolk, England] **:** of or from the county borough of Ipswich, England **:** of the kind or style prevalent in Ipswich

**ipswich sparrow** *n, usu cap I* [fr. *Ipswich*, town in northeastern Massachusetts where it was observed] **:** a sparrow (*Passerculus princeps*) similar to the Savannah sparrow but larger and paler that breeds on Sable island off the coast of Nova Scotia and migrates south along the Atlantic coast to Georgia

**IPT** *abbr* indexed, paged, and titled

**ipu·ri·ná** \ˌēpərēˈnä\ *n, pl* **ipuriná** *or* **ipurinás** *usu cap* **1 a :** an Arawakan people of northwestern Brazil **b :** a member of such people **2 :** the language of the Ipuriná people

**ipv** *abbr* **1** imperative **2** improve

**IPW** *abbr* interrogation prisoner of war

**IQ** \(ˈ)ī¦kyü\ *abbr or n* -s intelligence quotient

**IQ** *abbr, often not cap* [L *idem quod*] the same as

**IQED** *abbr* [L *id quod erat demonstrandum*] that which was to be proved

**iqui·to** \ēˈkēd·(ˌ)ō\ *n, pl* **iquito** *or* **iquitos** *usu cap* [AmerSp] **1 :** a Zaparo people of the upper Amazon **2 :** a member of the Iquito people

**ir-** — see IN-

**IR** *abbr* **1** infrared **2** inland revenue; internal revenue **3** intelligence ratio **4** interim report **5** interrogator-responder **6** insoluble residue

**Ir** *symbol* iridium

**ira·cund** \ˈīrəˌkənd\ *adj* [L *iracundus*, fr. *ira* anger — more at IRE] *archaic* **:** easily provoked to anger **:** IRASCIBLE

**ira·cun·di·ty** \ˌīrəˈkəndəd·ē\ *n* -ES *archaic* **:** the quality or state of being iracund **:** ANGER

**ira·de** \ēˈrädē\ *n* -s [Turk, lit., will, wish, fr. Ar *irādah*] **:** a decree of a Muhammadan ruler

**i rail** *n, cap I* **:** an I-shaped rail

**iran** \(ˈ)ī¦ran, -raa(ə)n *sometimes* (ˈ)ī¦- *or* (ˈ)ē¦-; (ˈ)ī¦rän, (ˈ)ē¦-, -ˈrän\ *adj, usu cap* [fr. *Iran*, country in southwestern Asia] **:** of or from Iran **:** of the kind or style prevalent in Iran

**:** IRANIAN, PERSIAN

**¹ira·ni** \=ˈ=ē, -i\ *n* -s *cap* [Per *īrānī*, fr. *īrān* Iran] **:** IRANIAN 1

**²irani** \"\ *adj, usu cap* **:** IRANIAN, PERSIAN

**¹ira·ni·an** \iˈrānēən, *sometimes* -ran- *or* -raan- *or* -rän- *or* (ˈ)ī¦rā- *or* (ˈ)ī¦ra(a)-\ *adj, usu cap* [*Iran* + E *-ian*] **:** of or relating to Iran or the Iranians or their speech

**²iranian** \"\ *n* -s *cap* **1 :** a native or inhabitant of Iran — see PERSIAN 1 **2 :** a branch of the Indo-European family of languages that includes Avestan, Old Persian, Median, Scythian, Middle Iranian, and Persian — see INDO-EUROPEAN LANGUAGES table

**iran·ic** \iˈranik, (ˈ)ī¦r-\ *adj, usu cap* [*Iran* + E *-ic*] **:** IRANIAN

**irano-** *comb form, usu cap* [*Iran*] **:** Iranian and ⟨*Irano*-British⟩

**¹irano-afghan** \iˈra(ˌ)nō, -rä-, -rā-, ī¦ra-, ē¦rä-, ē¦rā-+\ *adj, usu cap I&A* [*Irano-* + *Afghan*] **:** of, relating to, or characteristic of the people that constitute the chief element in the population of the upland territory extending from western Iran to northern India

**²irano-afghan** \"\ *n, cap I&A* **:** one of the Irano-Afghan people

**iraq** *also* **irak** \(ˈ)i¦räk, -rak,-rāk\ *adj, usu cap* [fr. *Iraq* (*Irak*), country in southwestern Asia] **:** of or from Iraq (*Iraq* oil fields) **:** of the kind or style prevalent in Iraq

**¹iraqi** *also* **iraki** \=ˈ=ē, -i\ *n* -s *cap* [Ar *ˈirāqīy*, fr. *ˈIrāq* Iraq] **1 :** a native or resident of Iraq **2 :** the dialect of Modern Arabic spoken in Iraq

**²iraqi** *also* **iraki** \"\ *adj, usu cap* **1 a :** of, relating to, or characteristic of Iraq **b :** of, relating to, or characteristic of the Iraqis **2 :** of, relating to, or characteristic of the Iraqi language

**iraq·i·an** *also* **irak·i·an** \-ēən\ *n or adj, usu cap* [*Iraq* (*Irak*) + E *-ian*] **:** IRAQI

**iras·ci·bil·i·ty** \ə̇ˌrasəˈbiləd·ē, (ˌ)ī¦ras-, -raas-, -ləté, -i\ *n* -ES [F *irascibilité*, fr. MF, fr. *irascible* + *-ité* -ity] **:** the quality or state of being irascible **:** proneness to anger **:** IRASCIBLENESS

**iras·ci·ble** \ə̇ˈrasəbəl, (ˈ)ī¦r-, -raas-\ *adj* [MF, fr. LL *irascibilis*, fr. L *irasci* to be angry (fr. *ira* anger) + *-ibilis* -ible — more at IRE] **1 :** marked by hot temper and resentful anger **:** having or showing a disposition to be easily incensed ⟨his proud, ~ individualism that went out of its way to pick a quarrel —V. L.Parrington⟩ ⟨became so ~ that within six months he lost his wife and half of his office staff —Herman Wouk⟩ **2 a :** moved by desire for that which is attained only with difficulty or danger **b :** stirred by combative emotions (as anger, pride, courage, fear) — opposed to *concupiscible*

**syn** CHOLERIC, SPLENETIC, CROSS, TESTY, CRANKY, TOUCHY, TECHY, TETCHY: IRASCIBLE stresses a tendency to fiery anger ⟨the *irascible* but kindhearted deity who indulges in copious curses to ease his feelings —M.R.Cohen⟩ CHOLERIC may convey suggestions of impatience and unreasonableness, in addition to indicating hot temper ⟨that fiery formula which has sprung from the lips of so many *choleric* old gentlemen . . . "I shall write to *The Times*" —Max Beerbohm⟩ SPLENETIC may suggest a strong inclination to quick anger coupled with moroseness, sullenness, malice, vindictiveness, or crusty peevishness ⟨a very queer character, by turns *splenetic* and benevolent —*Times Lit. Supp.*⟩ ⟨that *splenetic* temper, which seems to grudge brightness to the flames of hell —W.S.Landor⟩ CROSS is likely to indicate a snappish grumpy irritability ⟨I am determined I will not be *cross;* it is not a little matter that puts me out of temper —Jane Austen⟩ TESTY may indicate quick anger inspiring sharp acid comment and inspired by relatively trivial irritations ⟨he raged . . . he was ever more autocratic, more *testy* —Sinclair Lewis⟩ ⟨the *testy* major was in fume to find no hunter standing waiting —John Masefield⟩ CRANKY may indicate an irritable temper blended with fretfulness or capriciousness ⟨how *cranky* you are . . . don't be so absurd as . . . to act like a child —Anthony Trollope⟩ ⟨she's going to have a kid, and of course women . . . get *cranky* when they're that way —Sinclair Lewis⟩ TOUCHY, TETCHY, and TECHY, the first now being the most common, indicate an over sensitiveness making for irritability, defensiveness, likelihood of taking offense or being hurt ⟨*techy* and impatient of contradiction, sore with wounded pride —W.H.Hazlitt⟩ ⟨a man who had grown too *touchy* to make judicious decisions —*Time*⟩

**iras·ci·ble·ness** *n* -ES **:** the quality or state of being irascible

**iras·ci·bly** \-blē,-bli\ *adv* **:** in an irascible manner

**irate** \(ˈ)ī¦rāt, *usu* -ād·+V\ *adj, sometimes* -ER/-EST [L *iratus*, fr. *ira* anger + *-atus* -ate — more at IRE] **1 :** roused to or given to ire **:** feeling and showing a high degree of anger **:** WRATHFUL, INCENSED ⟨a neighborhood ~ over continued acts of vandalism⟩ ⟨never had enough money to meet his bills, and he was not used to dodging ~ grocers —Sinclair Lewis⟩ ⟨~ against the practice of usury —E.L.Surtz⟩ **2 :** arising from anger ⟨~ words⟩ ⟨an ~ glare⟩ ⟨started to splutter an ~ objection —W.H.Wright⟩ **syn** see ANGRY

**irate·ly** *adv* **:** in an irate manner **:** ANGRILY

**irate·ness** *n* -ES **:** the quality or state of being irate

**ira·va** \iˈrävə\ *n, pl* **irava** *or* **iravas** *cap* [native name in India] **1 :** an untouchable Hindu caste of the Malabar coast region of southwest India **2 :** a member of the Irava caste

**ira·ya** \iˈrāyə, -rīə\ *n, pl* **iraya** *or* **irayas** *usu cap* [Sp, fr. Iraya, person, human being] **1 a :** a predominantly pagan people inhabiting the mountainous interior of northern Mindoro in the Philippines **b :** a member of such people **2 :** the Austronesian language of the Iraya people

**ir·bis** \(ˌ)ərˈbēs, irˈ-\ *n, pl* **irbis** *or* **irbises** [Russ, fr. Mongol *irbis* & Kalmuck *irwş*] **:** SNOW LEOPARD

**IRBM** *abbr or n* -s **:** an intermediate range ballistic missile

**IRC** *abbr* irregular route carrier

**ir drop** \(ˈ)ī¦är-\ *n, usu cap I&R* [*I*, symbol for effective current in amperes + *R*, symbol for resistance in ohms] **:** the voltage drop due to energy losses in a resistor

**¹ire** \ˈī(ə)r, ˈīə\ *n* -s [ME, fr. OF, fr. L *ira;* akin to OE *ofost* haste, zeal, OS *obast* haste, zeal, ON *eisa* to race forward, Gk *hieros* powerful, supernatural, holy, sacred, *inein, inan* to empty out, defecate, *oistros* gadfly, frenzy, Skt *iṣṇāti, iṣyati* he sets in motion, swings; basic meaning: moving rapidly] **:** ANGER, WRATH ⟨provocation enough to arouse the ~ of a saint⟩ **syn** see ANGER

**²ire** \"\ *vt* -ED/-ING/-S **:** to provoke to anger **:** arouse ire in ⟨reads a piece in his local newspaper that ~s him —Sidney Atkinson⟩ **:** ANGER, IRRITATE

**³ire** \"\ *n* -s [by shortening] *dial* **:** IRON

**ire·ful** \ˈī(ə)rfəl, ˈīəf-\ *adj* [ME, fr. *ire* + *-ful*] **1 :** full of ire **:** marked by ire **:** ANGRY, WRATHFUL ⟨an ~ mood⟩ **2 :** given to ire **:** easily angered **:** IRASCIBLE, CHOLERIC ⟨an ill-tempered ~ old man⟩ — **ire·ful·ly** \-fəlē, -li\ *adv* — **ire·ful·ness** *n* -ES

**ire·land** \ˈī(ə)rlənd, ˈīəl-\ *adj, usu cap* [fr. *Ireland*, one of the British Isles] **1 :** of or from the island of Ireland **:** of the kind or style prevalent in the island of Ireland **2 :** of or from the republic of Ireland **:** of the kind or style prevalent in the republic of Ireland

**ire·land·er** \-ləndə(r), -ˌlan-,-ˌlaan-\ *n* -s *cap* [*Ireland* + E *-er*] **:** a native of Ireland

**ireland king of arms** *cap I & usu cap K&A* **:** a king of arms for heraldic supervision in Ireland appointed by the king of England and holding an office of which there is record from the reign of Richard II until that of Edward IV — compare ULSTER KING OF ARMS

**ire·less** \ˈī(ə)rləs, ˈīəl-\ *adj* **:** being without ire — **ire·less·ly** *adv* — **ire·less·ness** *n* -ES

**ire·na** \īˈrēnə\ *n, cap* [NL, fr. Gk *eirēnē* peace] **:** a genus of birds (family Aegithinidae) consisting of the fairy bluebirds of India

**irene** \ˈīˌrēn, =ˈ=\ *n* -s [ISV *irone* + *-ene*] **:** a liquid hydrocarbon $(CH_3)_4C_{10}H_8$ derived from naphthalene and obtained by reduction and cyclization of irone with hydriodic acid and phosphorus

**irenic** *or* **ei·renic** \(ˈ)ī¦renik, -rēn-\ *also* **ireni·cal** \-nəkəl\ *adj* [Gk *eirēnikos*, fr. *eirēnē* peace (prob. of non-IE origin) + *-ikos* -ic, -ical] **:** conducive to or operating toward peace, moderation, harmony, and conciliation and away from contention and partisanship esp. among disputants ⟨~ measures⟩ ⟨~ without being namby-pamby —*Chicago Theol. Seminary Register*⟩ ⟨the viewpoint is ~ and the author seeks to show the best features of each religion and church in turn —N.K. Burger⟩ **syn** see PACIFIC

**ireni·cal·ly** \-nək(ə)lē\ *adv* **:** in an irenic manner **:** in a way calculated to conciliate or to promote peace

**ireni·cism** \=ˈ=nəˌsizəm\ *n* -s **:** a social temper or condition or a state of public opinion making for peace

**irenicon** *var of* EIRENICON

**irenics** \īˈreniks, -rēn-\ *n pl but usu sing in constr, also* **irenic** \-nik\ **:** irenic theology as distinguished from polemic theology **:** theology concerned with securing Christian unity

**ire·si·ne** \ˌirəˈsī(ˌ)nē\ *n* [NL, modif. of Gk *eiresiōnē* branch of olive or laurel wound round with wool and hung with fruits; fr. the woolly calyx] **1** *cap* **:** a genus of tropical American opposite-leaved herbs (family Amaranthaceae) having small spicate or paniculate scarious flowers and often colored foliage — see ACHYRANTHES 2 **2 -s :** any plant of the genus *Iresine*

**ir·gun·ist** \irˈgünəst\ *n* -s *usu cap* [NHeb *Irgun* (*Ṣ bai Leumi*), lit., national military organization (fr. *irgun* organization + *ṣbai* military + *leumi* national) + E *-ist*] **:** a member of a militant rightist underground group of Zionists

**iri·ar·tea** \ˌirēˈärd·ēə\ *n, cap* [NL, after Bernardo de Iriarte †1814 Span. diplomat and amateur botanist] **:** a small genus of tall pinnate-leaved chiefly Brazilian palms with smooth trunk and crown of leaves supported by long slender prop roots — see STILT PALM

**iri·cism** \ˈīrəˌsizəm\ *n* -s *usu cap* [¹*Irish* + *-cism* (as in *Scotticism*)] **:** IRISHISM

**iri·cize** \-ˌsīz\ *vb* -ED/-ING/-S *sometimes cap* [¹*Irish* + *-cize* (as in *scotticize*)] **:** IRISHIZE

**irid** \ˈīrəd\ *n* -s [NL *Irid-, Iris*] **:** a plant of the family Iridaceae

**irid-** *or* **irido-** *comb form* [L *irid-, iris* — more at IRIS] **1 :** rainbow ⟨*iridal*⟩ ⟨*iridescent*⟩ **2** [NL *irid-, iris*] **:** iris of the eye ⟨*iridectomy*⟩ ⟨*iridoparalysis*⟩ **:** iris and ⟨*iridocyclitis*⟩ **3** [*iridescent*] **:** iridescent ⟨*iridize*⟩ ⟨*iridocyte*⟩ **4** [NL *Irid-, Iris*] **:** the genus Iris ⟨*iridin*⟩ **5** [NL *iridium*] **:** iridium **:** iridium and ⟨*iridosmine*⟩

**iri·da·ce·ae** \ˌirəˈdāsēˌē, ˌīr-\ *n pl, cap* [NL, fr. *Irid-, Iris*, type genus + *-aceae*] **:** a family of perennial herbs (order Liliales) with usu. only basal ensiform leaves and flowers in racemes or panicles that are subtended individually or in clusters by two spathose bracts and have the perianth petaloid and the ovary inferior

**iri·da·ceous** \¦=ˈ=¦dāshəs\ *adj* [NL *Iridaceae* + E *-ous*] **1 :** of or relating to the family Iridaceae or esp. the genus *Iris* **2 :** resembling an iris ⟨silvery blue ~ flowers⟩

**iri·dal** \ˈirədᵊl, ˈīr-\ *adj* [*irid-* + *-al*] **1 :** of or relating to the rainbow **:** IRIDIAN **2 :** of or relating to the iris of the eye **:** IRIDIC

**iri·dec·to·mize** \ˌirəˈdektəˌmīz, ˌīr-\ *vt* -ED/-ING/-S **:** to subject to iridectomy

**iri·dec·to·my** \-ˌmē\ *n* -ES [*irid-* + *-ectomy*] **:** the surgical removal of part of the iris of the eye

**irides** *pl of* IRIS

**ir·i·desce** \ˌirə¦des\ *vi* -ED/-ING/-S [back-formation fr. ¹*iridescent*] **:** to be iridescent

**ir·i·des·cence** \ˌirəˈdesᵊn(t)s\ *n* -s [*irid-* + *-escence*] **1 :** a play of structural colors producing rainbow effects that is exhibited in various bodies as a result of interference in a thin film (as of a soap bubble or mother-of-pearl) or of diffraction of light reflected from a closely ribbed or corrugated surface (as of the plumage of certain birds) and is readily distinguished from the inherent colors of substances by its variation with the angle of incidence of the illumination **2 :** a display or effect suggestive of the play of colors on an iridescent surface in gleaming or glistening or in subtly shifting and changing shades and hues ⟨paled before the ~ of the best of his earlier plays —*Americana Annual*⟩ ⟨a certain ~ of glamor and superiority —Margaret Landon⟩ ⟨no apple tang, no citrous clarity, but the ~ of the papaya, the opaline evanescence of the guava —Waldo Frank⟩ **:** GLITTER, SHEEN, LUSTER, OPALESCENCE

**¹ir·i·des·cent** \¦irə¦desᵊnt\ *adj* [*irid-* + *-escent*] **1 :** having iridescence **:** showing colors like those of the rainbow esp. in shifting patterns of hues and shades that vary with a change of light or point of view ⟨a beetle with an ~ back⟩ ⟨as softly ~ as the rays from a jewel —Ellen Glasgow⟩ ⟨smart, lean glass towers with ~ washrooms —Brooks Atkinson⟩ ⟨crunchy, ~, lovely snow —Elaine W. Neal⟩ **:** NACREOUS, OPALESCENT **2 a :** having a gleaming or glittering quality suggestive of the phenomenon of iridescence **:** BRILLIANT, FLASHING ⟨two wickedly witty and ~ novels —*Time*⟩ ⟨a man for whom the map of the present was always ~ with the glories of the past —H.C.Wolfe⟩ ⟨his ~ performance as an art, music, and drama critic —John Mason Brown⟩ **b :** having the constantly shifting fluid character of an iridescence ⟨the life of ~ revery —Edmund Wilson⟩ ⟨that ~ play of meanings —Susanne K. Langer⟩ **3** *of a fabric* **:** CHANGEABLE 4 ⟨curtains of an ~ material, purple in one light, golden brown in another —Howard Moss⟩ ⟨a filmy ~ green carpet —*Amer. Guide Series: Tenn.*⟩

**²iridescent** \"\ *n* -s **:** an iridescent fabric, trimming, or accessory ⟨the green-blue ~s are featured in rayon organdy for a party dress —*Women's Wear Daily*⟩

**ir·i·des·cent·ly** *adv* **:** in an iridescent manner

**irid·i·al** \īˈridēəl, əˈr-\ *adj* [*irid-* + *-ial*] **:** of or relating to an iris esp. of the eye **:** IRIDIC

**irid·i·an** \-ēən\ *adj* [*irid-* + *-ian*] **1 :** of or relating to the iris of the eye **:** IRIDIC **2 a :** resembling a rainbow **b :** having the colors of the rainbow **3 :** containing iridium

**irid·ic** \(ˈ)ī¦ridik, əˈr-\ *adj* [*irid-* + *-ic*] **1 :** of, relating to, or derived from iridium — used esp. of a compound in which iridium is tetravalent **2 :** of or relating to the iris of the eye ⟨~ grains and a flood of intraocular fluid —*Time*⟩

**iri·din** \ˈirədᵊn, ˈīr-, -dən\ *n* -s [ISV *irid-* + *-in*] **1 :** a crystalline glucoside $C_{24}H_{26}O_{13}$ occurring esp. in orrisroot **2 :** an oleoresin prepared from the common blue flag for use as a purgative and liver stimulant

**irid·io-platinum** \ī¦ridē(ˌ)ō, ə̇¦r-+\ *n* [*iridio-* (fr. NL *iridium*) + *platinum*] **:** a hard alloy of iridium and platinum

**irid·i·um** \īˈridēəm, əˈr-\ *n* -s *often attrib* [NL, fr. *irid-* + *-ium;* fr. the colorful appearance of some of its solutions] **:** a silver-white hard brittle very heavy chiefly trivalent and tetravalent metallic element of the platinum group that occurs usu. as a native alloy with platinum or with osmium in iridosmine, is resistant to chemical attack at ordinary temperatures, and is used esp. in hardening platinum for alloys suitable for surgical instruments, electrical and other scientific apparatus, jewelry, and the points of gold pens — symbol *Ir;* see ELEMENT table

**iri·di·za·tion** \ˌirədəˈzāshən, ˌīr-, -ˌdīˈz-\ *n* -s **1 :** the action or process of making iridescent **:** IRISATION **2 :** the action or process of exhibiting iridescence **3 :** a semblance of a halo around a light observed by persons affected with glaucoma

**iri·dize** \ˈirəˌdīz, ˈīr-\ *vt* -ED/-ING/-S [*irid-* + *-ize*] **:** to make iridescent

**irido-** — see IRID-

**iri·do·choroiditis** \¦irə(ˌ)dō, ¦īr-+\ *n* [NL, fr. *irid-* + *choroiditis*] **:** inflammation of the iris and the choroid

**iri·do·cyclitis** \"+\ *n* [NL, fr. *irid-* + *cyclitis*] **:** inflammation of the iris and the ciliary body

**irid·o·cyte** \īˈridəˌsīt, əˈr-\ *n* -s [*irid-* + *-cyte*] **:** a cell that occurs esp. in the skin of fishes and reptiles and appears iridescent greenish from included guanine — compare GUANOPHORE

**iri·do·do·ne·sis** \ˌirə(ˌ)dōdəˈnēsəs, ˌīr-\ *n, pl* **iridodone·ses** \-ēˌsēz\ [NL, fr. *irid-* + Gk *donein* to shake + NL *-sis*] **:** tremulousness of the iris **:** HIPPUS

**iri·do·myr·mex** \-ˈmərˌmeks\ *n, cap* [NL, fr. *irid-* + GK *myrmēx* ant — more at PISMIRE] **:** a genus containing the Argentine ant

**irid·o·phore** \īˈridəˌfō(ə)r, əˈr-\ *n* -s [*irid-* + *-phore*] **:** an iridescent chromatophore — compare IRIDOCYTE

**iri·dos·mine** \ˌirəˈdäzˌmēn, ˌīr-, -ˌmən\ *n* -s [G *iridosmin*, fr. *irid-* + NL *osmium* + G *-in* -ine] **:** a mineral consisting of a native iridium osmium alloy usu. containing some rhodium and platinum and found in tin-white or steel-gray grains isomorphous with iridium

**iri·dos·mi·um** \-ˌmēəm\ *n* -s [NL, fr. *irid-* + *osmium*] **:** IRIDOSMINE

**irids** *pl of* IRID

**iring** *pres part of* IRE

**i ring** *n, cap I* **:** a band or hoop secured around the circumference of a metal drum as a reinforcement

**¹iris** \ˈīrəs\ *n, pl* **iris·es** \-rəsəz\ *or* **iri·des** \ˈirəˌdēz, ˈīr-\ [ME, fr. L, fr. Gk (basic meaning: rainbow) — more at WIRE] **1 :** a prismatic crystal; *esp* **:** a quartz that is iridescent because of internal cracks **2 a :** RAINBOW **b :** a play of colors resembling a rainbow **:** a circle or arch of rainbow hues **3** [NL, fr. Gk] **a :** the opaque muscular contractile diaphragm that is suspended in the aqueous humor in front of the lens of the eye, is perforated by the pupil and is continuous peripherally with the ciliary body, has a deeply pigmented posterior surface which excludes the entrance of light except through the pupil and a variously colored anterior surface in different individuals which determines the color of the eyes — see EYE illustration **b** (1) **:** IRIS DIAPHRAGM; *esp* **:** one used on a motion-picture camera in fading pictures in or out (2) **:** a masking device having a circular opening of which the diameter can be varied

**²iris** \"\ *n* [NL, fr. L, iris, any of various plants of the family Iridaceae] **1** *cap* **:** the type genus of the family Iridaceae comprising perennial herbaceous plants that develop from rhizomes or bulbs, have linear or sword-shaped mostly basal leaves, erect stalks on which the flowers are borne, and short-lived usu. brightly colored flowers with the three inner perianth segments erect and the three outer spreading or drooping, and include many widely cultivated ornamentals **2** *pl* **irises** *or* **iris** *also* **irides :** any plant or flower of the genus *Iris* — see BEARDED IRIS, BEARDLESS IRIS; DUTCH IRIS, ENGLISH IRIS, GERMAN IRIS, JAPANESE IRIS, SPANISH IRIS **3** *or* **iris blue :** a pale blue to pale purple — called also *endive blue*

**³iris** \"\ *vt* -ED/-ING/-S **1 :** to make iridescent **:** give the form or appearance of a rainbow to ⟨spray ~*ed* above the falls⟩ **2 :** to operate the iris of a motion-picture camera so as to fade (a picture) — used with *in* or *out*

**iris·at·ed** \ˈīrəˌsād·əd\ *adj* **:** IRISED, IRIDESCENT ⟨~ crystal beads⟩

**iris·ation** \ˌīrəˈsāshən\ *n* -s **1 :** the act or process of making iridescent ⟨the ~ of a culture plate by developing bacteria⟩ **2 :** IRIDESCENCE ⟨~s in a cloud are evidence that it is composed of water droplets —D.W.Perrie⟩ ⟨in the area of the sun beautiful ~s may occur⟩

**iris borer** *n* **:** a large brown-headed pinkish grub that is the larva of a noctuid moth (*Macronoctua onusta*) and that is destructive to the rhizomes and crowns of various irises

**iris diaphragm** *n* **:** an adjustable diaphragm of thin opaque plates that can be turned by a ring so as to change the diameter of a central opening usu. to regulate the aperture of a lens (as in a camera or microscope)

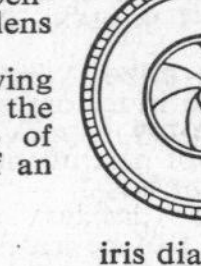
iris diaphragm

**irised** \ˈīrəst\ *adj* [¹*iris* + *-ed*] **1 :** having or characterized by colors like those of the rainbow **:** IRIDESCENT ⟨the ~ sweep of northern lights⟩ **2 :** having an iris of an indicated kind ⟨pale-*irised* eyes⟩

**irises** *pl of* IRIS, *pres 3d sing of* IRIS

**iris family** *n* **:** IRIDACEAE

**iris green** *n* **:** MALACHITE GREEN 3

**¹irish** \ˈīrish, -rēsh\ *adj, usu cap* [ME, fr. (assumed) OE *Īrisc*, fr. OE *Īras* Irishmen (of Celt origin; akin to OIr *Ēriu* Ireland) + *-isc* -ish] **1 :** of, relating to, or characteristic of Ireland or its inhabitants **:** produced in or native or peculiar to Ireland **2 a :** being or belonging to the Celtic speech of Ireland **:** IRISH-GAELIC **b** *obs* **:** SCOTTISH-GAELIC

**²irish** \"\ *n* -ES *see sense 1a* **1** *cap* **a** *pl in constr* **:** natives or inhabitants of Ireland or their immediate descendants esp. when of Celtic speech or culture — compare CELT, GAEL **b** *obs* **:** IRISHMAN, IRISHWOMAN **2** *cap* **:** the Irish language: **a :** the Irish branch of Goidelic **:** the Goidelic speech of the Celts in Ireland **:** IRISH GAELIC — see MIDDLE IRISH, OLD IRISH; INDO-EUROPEAN LANGUAGES table **b** *obs* **:** SCOTTISH GAELIC **c :** English as spoken by the Irish with more or less dialect change and brogue **3** *usu cap, obs* **:** an old game resembling backgammon **4** *usu cap* **a :** IRISH LINEN **b :** IRISH WHISKEY **5** *usu cap* **:** TEMPER, ANGER ⟨don't get your *Irish* up over a little thing like that⟩ **6** *usu cap* **:** a tap-dance step consisting of a shuffle, hop, and step

**irish alphabet** *n, usu cap I* **:** a modified form of the Latin alphabet used by the ancient Britons and still employed in writing and printing Irish — compare INSULAR HAND

**irish blight** *n, usu cap I* **:** LATE BLIGHT

**irish broom** *n, usu cap I* **1 :** a low Iberian shrub (*Cytisus patens*) **2 :** SCOTCH BROOM

**irish bull** *n, usu cap I* [⁵*bull*] **:** an expression containing apparent congruity but actual incongruity of ideas ⟨"it was hereditary in his family to have no children" is a well-known *Irish bull*⟩

**irish chippendale** *n, usu cap I&C* **:** ornate carved furniture made prob. in Ireland about the middle of the 18th century and based on Chippendale designs

**irish christian brother** *n, usu cap I&C&B* **:** BROTHER OF THE CHRISTIAN SCHOOLS

**irish coffee** *n, usu cap I* **:** a mixed drink consisting of hot sugared coffee liberally laced with Irish whiskey and topped with whipped cream

**irish confetti** *n, usu cap I* [so called fr. the tradition that Irishmen often throw bricks in a fight] **:** a rock, brick, or fragment of rock or brick

**irish crochet** *n, usu cap I* **:** a heavy lace of Irish origin that is hand-crocheted or machine-made with rose or leaf designs on a square mesh ground and is used esp. for insertion, edging, and trimming

**irish diamond** *n, usu cap I* **:** CRYSTAL 2

**irish dividend** *n, usu cap I* **:** an assessment on stock

**irish elk** *or* **irish deer** *n, usu cap I* **:** a large extinct Pleistocene deer (*Megaloceros hibernicus*) remains of which are found esp. under the peat of Ireland and England

**irish·er** \ˈīrishə(r), -rēsh-\ *n* -S *cap* **:** IRISHMAN

**irish furze** *n, usu cap I* **:** a columnar compact sparse-flowering shrub (*Ulex europaeus strictus*)

**irish gaelic** *n, cap I&G* **:** the Goidelic speech of the Celts of Ireland esp. as used since the end of the medieval period — compare MIDDLE IRISH, OLD IRISH; see INDO-EUROPEAN LANGUAGES table

**irish-gaelic** \ˌ≈≈ˈ≈≈\ *adj, usu cap I&G* **:** of, relating to, or characteristic of the Goidelic speech of the Celts of Ireland

**irish grazier** *n, usu cap I, sometimes cap G* **:** TAMWORTH

**irish green** *n, often cap I* **:** a deep green

**irish harp** *n, usu cap I* **:** CLARSACH

**irish heath** *n, usu cap I* **:** a low evergreen European shrub (*Daboecia cantabrica*) of the family Ericaceae that has slender leaves dark green above and whitish below and small nodding bell-shaped white or sometimes rosy or purplish flowers borne in erect terminal racemes — called also *St.-Dabeoc's-heath*

**irish·ism** \ˈīri,shizəm, -rē-\ *n* -S *usu cap* **1 :** a word, phrase, or mode of expression distinctive of the Irish **2 :** IRISH BULL

**irish ivy** *n, usu cap 1st I* **:** a European ivy (*Hedera helix hibernica*) that is a variety of English ivy distinguished by larger leaves and fruit

**irish·ize** \ˈīri,shīz, -rē-\ *vt* -ED/-ING/-S *often cap* **:** to make Irish in quality or traits ⟨~ the music⟩

**irish juniper** *n, usu cap I* **:** a narrow columnar ornamental juniper (*Juniperus communis hibernica*) that is a horticultural variety of the common juniper

**irish linen** *n, usu cap I* **:** a fine lightweight linen fabric made in Ireland and used esp. for clothing

**irish lord** *n, usu cap I* **:** any of several sculpins (genus *Hemilepidotus*) of the Bering sea region that are locally important as food fishes

**irish·ly** *adv, often cap* **:** in the style or way of the Irish

**irish mail** *n, usu cap I* **:** a 3-wheeled or 4-wheeled toy vehicle activated by a hand lever somewhat on the principle of a manually operated railway handcar

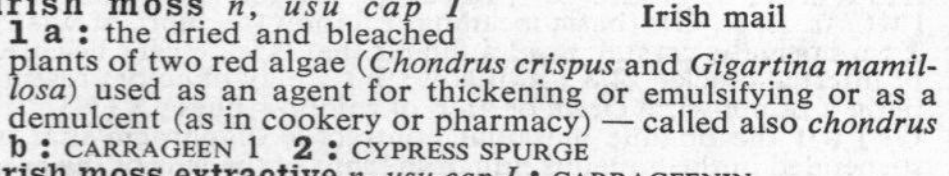
Irish mail

**irish·man** \ˈ≈≈mən\ *n, pl* **irishmen** *cap* [ME, fr. *Irish* + *man*] **1 :** a native or inhabitant of Ireland **:** HIBERNIAN **2 :** one that is of Irish descent **3 :** TUMATAKURU

**irish mile** *n, usu cap I* **:** an old Irish unit of distance equal to 1.273 statute miles

**irish moss** *n, usu cap I* **1 a :** the dried and bleached plants of two red algae (*Chondrus crispus* and *Gigartina mamillosa*) used as an agent for thickening or emulsifying or as a demulcent (as in cookery or pharmacy) — called also *chondrus* **b :** CARRAGEEN 1 **2 :** CYPRESS SPURGE

**irish moss extractive** *n, usu cap I* **:** CARRAGEENIN

**irish·ness** *n* -ES *usu cap* **:** the quality or state of being Irish

**irish pennant** *or* **irish pendant** *n, usu cap I* **:** a loose untidy object about a ship or naval installation; *esp* **:** the end of a line left hanging loose or out of place

**irish poplin** *n, usu cap I* **:** a fabric with silk warp and worsted filling made orig. in Ireland

**irish potato** *n, usu cap I* **:** POTATO 2 a (2)

**irish·ry** \ˈīrishrē, -rēsh-, -ri\ *n* -ES *usu cap* [ME *Irisherie, Irishrie*, fr. *Irish* + *-erie* -ery or *-rie* -ry] **1 :** IRISH 1a **2 a :** Irish quality or character ⟨~ of temperament⟩ **b :** an Irish peculiarity or trait ⟨a deliberate ~⟩

**irish setter** *n* **1** *usu cap I&S* **:** a breed of bird dogs that are in general comparable to English setters but have a chestnut-brown or mahogany-red coat **2** *usu cap I, often cap S* **:** a dog of the Irish Setter breed

**irish snipe** *n, usu cap I* **:** an avocet (*Recurvirostra americana*) of No. America

**irish stew** *n, usu cap I* **:** a stew having as its principal ingredients meat, potatoes, and onions in a thick gravy

**irish strawberry** *n, usu cap I, Austral* **:** STRAWBERRY TREE

**irish system** *n, usu cap I* **:** a system of prison management developed for Ireland by Sir Walter Crofton and noted for its mark system and commutation of sentences, classification of prisoners, military discipline, trade and academic training, preparation for free self-control, and release under police supervision

**irish terrier** *n* **1** *usu cap I&T* **:** a breed of active medium-sized terriers that originated in Ireland and is characterized by a dense close wiry coat of red, golden red, or reddish wheaten **2** *usu cap I & sometimes cap T* **:** a dog of the Irish Terrier breed

**irish water spaniel** *n* **1** *usu cap I&W&S* **:** a breed of large retrievers developed in Ireland by interbreeding various sporting dogs and the poodle and characterized by a heavy coat of liver-colored curls, a topknot of long curls, and a nearly hairless rattail **2** *usu cap I & sometimes cap W&S* **:** a dog of the Irish Water Spaniel breed

**irish whiskey** *n, usu cap I* **:** whiskey made in Ireland chiefly of barley

**irish wolfhound** *n, usu cap I & sometimes cap W* **:** a very large tall hound that in general resembles the deerhound but is much larger and stronger, weighs upward from 90 pounds, and has a shoulder height from 31 inches in the male and 28 inches in the female

**irishwoman** \ˈ≈≈,≈≈\ *n, pl* **irishwomen** *cap* **:** a woman born in Ireland or of Irish descent

**irishy** \ˈīrishē, -rēsh-, -shi\ *adj, often cap* **:** suggesting or characteristic of the Irish ⟨~ blue eyes⟩

**irish yew** *n, usu cap I* **:** a hardy columnar yew (*Taxus baccata stricta*) that has erect branches and dark green foliage and is a horticultural variety of the common Old World yew

**iri·sin** \ˈīrəsən\ *n* -S [ISV *iris* + *-in*; orig. formed in G] **:** a polysaccharide $(C_6H_{10}O_5)_x$ occurring esp. in the rhizomes of some irises and like inulin yielding levulose on hydrolysis

**irising** *pres part of* IRIS

**iris mauve** *n* **:** a grayish yellowish pink that is yellower and slightly less strong than cloud pink

**irisroot** \ˈ≈≈,≈\ *n* **:** ORRISROOT

**iris whitefly** *n* **:** a whitefly (*Aleyrodes spiraeoides*) that is sometimes a pest on late potatoes in the northwestern U.S.

**iri·tis** \ī'rīd·əs\ *n* -ES [NL, irreg. fr. *iris* + *-itis*] **:** inflammation of the iris of the eye

**¹irk** \ˈərk, ˈək, ˈəik\ *adj* [ME] *now dial* **:** weary and disgusted

**²irk** \"\ *vb* -ED/-ING/-S [ME *irken*] *vi, now chiefly Scot* **:** to become tired or wearied esp. to the point of being bored or disgusted or unwilling to do or submit to something ~ *vt* **1** *obs* **:** to be tired of or disgusted with **2 :** to irritate or disgust (as a person) usu. by reason of tiresome or wearying qualities ⟨restrictions that ~*ed* buyers⟩ ⟨it ~*s* me to see such waste⟩ **syn** see ANNOY

**³irk** \"\ *n* -S **1 :** IRKSOMENESS, TEDIUM ⟨the ~ of a narrow existence⟩ **2 :** a cause or source of annoyance or disgust ⟨the main ~ is the wage level⟩

**irk·some** \-səm\ *adj* [ME *irksom*, fr. *irken* to irk + *-som* -some] **1** *obs* **:** WEARY, VEXED, DISGUSTED **2 :** tending to irk ⟨an ~ task⟩ **:** IRRITATING, TEDIOUS ⟨such ~ caution⟩ — **irk·some·ly** *adv* — **irk·some·ness** *n* -ES

**ir·kutsk** \(ˈ)ir¦kütsk, ¦ər¦-\ *adj, usu cap* [fr. *Irkutsk*, U.S.S.R.] **:** of or from the city of Irkutsk, U.S.S.R. **:** of the kind or style prevalent in Irkutsk

**irne** *archaic var of* IRON

**IRO** *abbr* inland revenue officer; internal revenue officer

**iro·ha** \ˌi(ˌ)rō¦hä, ≈ˈ≈(ˌ)≈\ *also* **iro·fa** \-fä\ *n* -S [Jap, fr. *i* + *ro* + *ha* or *fa*, its first three syllables] **:** the Japanese kana in its popular order in distinction from the scientific arrangement which is based on that of Sanskrit

**iro·ko** \əˈrō(ˌ)kō\ *n* -S [Yoruba *ìrókò*] **1 :** a very large timber tree (*Chlorophora excelsa*) of tropical western Africa with strong durable streaky lustrous light brown to dark brown wood that is extremely resistant to termite attack and often used as a substitute for teak **2 :** the wood of an iroko tree

**¹iron** \ˈī(ə)rn, ˈīən *sometimes chiefly for the sake of the meter in a line of poetry* ˈīrən\ *n* -S [ME *iren, iron*, fr. OE *īren, īsen, īsern*; akin to OHG *īsan, īsarn* iron, ON *īsarn, jārn*, Goth *eisarn*; all fr. a prehistoric Gmc word prob. of Venetic or Illyrian origin like OIr *īarn* iron, W *haearn*; akin to Venetic *Isaras*, a river; akin to L *ira* anger — more at IRE] **1 a :** a heavy malleable ductile magnetic chiefly bivalent and trivalent metallic element that is silver-white when pure but readily rusts in moist air and is chemically active in other respects (as toward dilute acids), that occurs native in meteorites and combined in most igneous rocks, that is usu. extracted from its ores by smelting with coke and limestone in a blast furnace, that is the most used of metals (as in construction, armaments, tools), and that plays a vital role in biological processes (as in transport of oxygen in the animal body) — symbol *Fe*; see CAST IRON, INGOT IRON, IRON ORE, PIG IRON, STEEL, WROUGHT IRON; ELEMENT table; compare FERRITE **b :** iron in some particular physical or chemical state: as (1) **:** iron chemically combined ⟨~ in the blood⟩ ⟨a tonic of ~ and wine⟩ (2) **:** iron that cannot be hardened by quenching (as wrought iron, pig iron) — distinguished from *steel* ⟨the ~ and steel industry⟩ **2 :** something (as an instrument, appliance, or tool) made of or commonly, customarily, or orig. made of iron: as **a** (1) **:** an iron weapon; *esp* **:** SWORD (2) **:** armed might **:** WEAPONRY (3) *slang* **:** a portable firearm **:** PISTOL **b** (1) **:** something (as chains, handcuffs, shackles) used to bind, confine, or restrain — usu. used in pl. ⟨kept the prisoner in ~*s*⟩ (2) *archaic* **:** BONDS, CAPTIVITY **c :** a branding or cauterizing iron **d irons** *pl, archaic* **:** dies used in striking coins **e :** HARPOON **f :** a heatable device usu. with a flat metal base of some weight that is used to smooth, finish, or press (as cloth) **:** FLATIRON **g :** STIRRUP **h :** SOLDERING IRON **i :** an iron weight with a handle sometimes used in curling instead of the customary stone **j :** the cutter in a tool (as a plane) **k :** one of a series of golf clubs numbered 1 through 9 that have heads of iron or occas. other metal laid back at a progressively greater angle so as to give progressively greater height and less distance to the flight of the ball **3 :** resemblance to iron in some quality (as strength, inflexibility, hardness, durability) ⟨the ~ of that spirit⟩; *also* **:** a quality of exhibiting such resemblance ⟨muscles of ~⟩ **4 :** a unit of measurement equal to one forty-eighth of an inch used in measuring thickness of a shoe sole ⟨a six-*iron* sole⟩ **5 :** MINERAL BROWN **6 :** the iron industry or its production esp. as a market factor ⟨~ has remained steady⟩ — **in irons** *or* **into irons 1** *of a sailing vessel while tacking* **:** having the head to the wind and unable to fill away on either tack **:** incapable of coming about or filling away **2 :** in chains or fetters **:** in confinement — **iron in the fire 1 :** a matter requiring close oversight or attention **:** ENTERPRISE ⟨was a businessman and had other *irons in the fire* —J.D.Beresford⟩ **2 :** a prospective course of action **:** a project not yet realized ⟨got several *irons in the fire* and I'm hoping to land something before very long —W.S.Maugham⟩

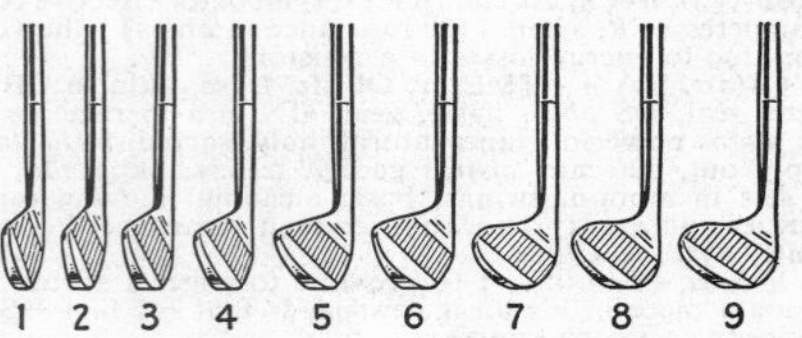
1 2 3 4 5 6 7 8 9
irons 2k: *1* driving iron, *2* midiron, *3* mid-mashie, *4* mashie iron, *5* mashie, *6* mashie niblick, *7* pitcher, *8* pitching niblick, *9* niblick

**²iron** \"\ *adj* [ME *iren*, fr. OE *īren, īsen, īsern* (akin to OHG *īsarnīn*, adj., iron, Goth *eisarneins*), fr. *īren, īsen, īsern*, n.] **1 :** of, relating to, or derived from iron **:** made of or containing iron ⟨an ~ bar⟩; *broadly* **:** made of or consisting of steel or other modified iron **2 :** resembling iron in appearance or color ⟨a grim ~ sky⟩ **3 :** resembling iron in some quality (as hardness, strength, impenetrability, endurance, insensibility): as **a :** having great physical hardness or strength **b :** RUDE, HARD, SEVERE **c :** strong and healthy **:** ROBUST ⟨an ~ constitution⟩ ⟨~ digestions⟩ **d :** INFLEXIBLE, UNRELENTING ⟨~ determination⟩ **e :** holding or binding fast **:** not to be broken ⟨the ~ ties of kinship⟩ **f :** metallic in tone **:** HARSH ⟨an ~ voice⟩ **4** *of a golf shot* **:** played with an iron

**³iron** \"\ *vb* -ED/-ING/-S [ME *irenen*, fr. *iren*, n.] *vt* **1 :** to furnish, arm, or cover with iron ⟨~*ed* the new wheel⟩ **2 a :** to shackle with irons **:** FETTER, HANDCUFF **b :** to attach or make fast with fittings of iron ⟨~ the toolbox to the truck⟩ **3 a :** to smooth with or as if with an instrument of iron; *esp* **:** to press (as cloth) with a heated flatiron **b :** to remove by ironing — usu. used with an adverb of direction ⟨gently ~*ing* away the wrinkles⟩ **4 :** to take (as a fish) with a gaff or harpoon **5 :** to thin the walls of (a deep-drawn metal article) by reducing the clearance between punch and die ~ *vi* **:** to iron clothes ⟨~*ed* all morning⟩

**iron age** *n, usu cap I&A* **:** the period of human culture characterized by the smelting of iron and its almost universal use in industry beginning about 1000 B.C. in southern Europe and somewhat earlier in western Asia and Egypt — compare BRONZE AGE, STONE AGE; see HALLSTATT, LA TÈNE

**iron alum** *n* **1 :** an alum containing iron as the trivalent constituent; *esp* **:** ammonium ferric alum $NH_4Fe(SO_4)_2.12H_2O$ **2** [¹*alum* (aluminum sulfate)] **:** HALOTRICHITE

**ironback** \ˈ≈(ə),≈\ *n* **:** a plate of iron for the back of a fireplace

**iron bacteria** *n* **:** any of various bacteria of the order Chlamydobacteriales that act upon iron compounds and produce deposits of ocher and bog ore

**ironbark** \ˈ≈(ə),≈\ *n* **1** *or* **ironbark tree :** any of several Australian eucalypts (as *Eucalyptus sideroxylon, E. paniculata, E. siderophloia, E. resinifera*) having hard gray bark and useful timber and in some cases yielding eucalyptus gum **2 :** the extremely heavy hard strong durable wood of an ironbark which is commonly available in large sizes and is extensively used in heavy construction

**ironbark acacia** *n* **:** an Australian timber tree (*Acacia excelsa*) with very hard dark-grained wood

**ironbark box** *n* [¹*box*] **:** any of several Australian eucalypts; *esp* **:** a widely distributed stringybark (*Eucalyptus obliqua*)

**iron black** *n* **:** a powder consisting of precipitated antimony which is used in coating various objects to give them the appearance of polished iron or steel

**iron blue** *n* **1 :** STEEL GRAY **2 :** any of various strongly colored pigments that range in masstone from reddish blue to jet black and possess good hiding power, that are now usu. made by bringing together solutions of ferrous sulfate, ammonium sulfate, and sodium ferrocyanide and oxidizing the white precipitate formed, that consist of complex compounds regarded as both ferrocyanides and ferricyanides containing positive ions (as ammonium and sodium ions), and that are used chiefly in blueprints, inks, laundry blues, paints and enamels, crayons, and linoleum: as **a :** PRUSSIAN BLUE **b :** TURNBULL'S BLUE

**ironbound** \ˈ≈(ə)¦≈\ *adj* [ME *irenbounden*, fr. *iren* iron + *bounden* bound — more at IRON, BOUND] **:** bound with or as if with iron: as **a :** HARSH, RUGGED ⟨an ~ coast⟩ **b :** bound with irons **:** SHACKLED ⟨an ~ prisoner⟩ **c :** RIGID, UNYIELDING, RIGOROUS ⟨~ traditions⟩ ⟨an ~ climate⟩

**iron brown** *n* **:** MINERAL BROWN

**iron buff** *n* **:** a fast dye composed of hydrated ferric oxide formed on the fiber by the action of an alkali on an iron salt

**iron carbide** *n* **:** a binary compound of iron with carbon; *esp* **:** CEMENTITE

**iron carbonate** *n* **:** a carbonate of iron; *esp* **:** FERROUS CARBONATE

**iron carbonyl** *n* **:** a compound formed by reaction of metallic iron with carbon monoxide; *esp* **:** the flammable unstable poisonous liquid pentacarbonyl $Fe(CO)_5$ used chiefly in making iron powder and pure iron for use as a catalyst

**iron cement** *n* **:** a mixture of small cast-iron borings or turnings usu. with ammonium chloride used moist as a cement to make rust joints

**iron chink** *n* [⁷*chink*; fr. its performance of tasks formerly done by Chinese] **:** a machine for rapidly cleaning and dressing fish (as salmon) at a cannery

**iron chloride** *n* **:** a chloride of iron: as **a :** FERRIC CHLORIDE **b :** FERROUS CHLORIDE

**¹ironclad** \ˈ≈(ə)¦≈\ *adj* [¹*iron* + *clad*] **1 :** sheathed in, protected by, or having an exterior of iron — used esp. of naval vessels **2 a :** RIGOROUS, SEVERE, EXACTING ⟨an ~ oath⟩ ⟨~ controls⟩ **b :** INFLEXIBLE, RIGID ⟨an ~ rule⟩ ⟨~ caste distinctions⟩ **c :** vigorously determined **:** fixed and unshakable ⟨an ~ patriot⟩ ⟨an ~ defense⟩ **3** *of a plant* **:** highly resistant to unfavorable environmental factors (as cold) ⟨only the most ~ roses thrive so far north⟩ ⟨developed several ~ apricots for the North Central states⟩

**²ironclad** \ˈ≈(ə),≈\ *n* -S **1 :** an armored naval vessel **2 :** one (as a knight in armor or a person of precise and rigid morality) that is felt to resemble an armored vessel

**iron curtain** *n, often cap I&C* [trans. of G *eiserner vorhang* iron fireproof theatrical curtain] **1 :** a political, military, and ideological barrier that cuts off and isolates an area (as of Soviet-controlled territory) preventing free communication and contact with differently oriented areas **2 a :** an intangible barrier against communication of information or ideas; *esp* **:** one that is set up for concealment and bars any opportunity for penetration **b :** a bar to the crossing of a mental or cultural borderline

**iron-deficiency anemia** *n* **1 :** hypochromic anemia in which deficiency of hemoglobin in the individual red blood cells is the characteristic abnormality — see CHLOROSIS **2 :** HYPOCHROMIC ANEMIA

**irone** \ˈī,rōn, ≈ˈ≈\ *n* -S [ISV *iris* + *-one*; orig. formed as G *iron*] **:** any of several oily liquid isomeric ketones $C_{14}H_{22}O$ or a mixture of some of them that have a strong odor of violet and orrisroot, that occur in orris oil, and that are used in perfumes

**ironed** *past of* IRON

**iron·er** \ˈī(ə)rnə(r), ˈīən-\ *n* -S **:** one that irons: as **a :** a person who presses or shapes something (as clothes, hats, gloves) with a hand or automatic iron or on a heated form **b :** a machine for ironing fabrics **:** MANGLE

**ironfisted** \ˈ≈(ə)¦≈≈\ *adj* **1 :** STINGY, MEAN, MISERLY **2 :** harsh and ruthless ⟨~ methods⟩

**iron-free** \ˈ≈(ə)¦≈\ *adj* **:** containing no iron

**iron front** *n* **:** a cast-iron facade for a building

**iron glance** *n* [part trans., part modif. of G *eisenglanz*, fr. *eisen* iron + *glanz* brightness] **:** HEMATITE

**iron grass** *n* **:** VERNAL SEDGE

**iron gray** *n* **:** a nearly neutral very slightly greenish dark gray — called also *bat*

**iron hand** *n* **:** stern or rigorous control

**ironhanded** \ˈ≈(ə)¦≈≈\ *adj* **:** having or acting or governing with a strong or heavy hand **:** INFLEXIBLE, RIGOROUS — **iron·hand·ed·ly** *adv* — **iron·hand·ed·ness** *n* -ES

**ironhard** \ˈ≈(ə)¦≈\ *adj* **:** having the hardness of iron **:** very hard or severe ⟨an ~ frost⟩ ⟨an ~ beak⟩

**iron hat** *n* [ME *iren hat*, fr. *iren* iron + *hat* — more at IRON, HAT] **1 a :** a headpiece of iron or steel used as armor during the middle ages **b** *slang* **:** DERBY 2a **c :** a metal or plastic safety hat **2 :** GOSSAN

**ironhead** \ˈ≈(ə),≈\ *n* **1 a :** WOOD IBIS 1 **b :** AMERICAN GOLDENEYE **2 :** a stupid person

**ironheaded** \ˈ≈(ə)¦≈≈\ *adj* **1 :** furnished or tipped with a head, top, or point of iron **2 :** very hardheaded

**ironheads** \ˈ≈(ə),≈\ *n pl but sing or pl in constr, also* **ironhead** *dial chiefly Eng* **:** KNAPWEED

**ironhearted** \ˈ≈(ə)¦≈≈\ *adj* **:** HARDHEARTED, UNFEELING, CRUEL ⟨an ~ master⟩

**iron horse** *n* **:** a locomotive engine

**iron hydroxide** *n* **:** a hydroxide of iron: as **a :** FERRIC HYDROXIDE **b :** FERROUS HYDROXIDE

**iron·ic** \(ˈ)ī¦ränik, -nēk *sometimes* əˈr-\ *or* **iron·i·cal** \-nəkəl, -nēk-\ *adj* [LL *ironicus*, fr. Gk *eirōnikos* dissembling, fr. *eirōneia* dissimulation + *-ikos* -ic, -ical — more at IRONY] **1 :** of or relating to irony **:** containing, expressing, or constituting irony ⟨an ~ remark⟩ ⟨it was ~ that he should enter then⟩ **2 :** addicted to the use of irony **:** given to irony ⟨a very ~ man⟩ **3** *obs* **:** DISSEMBLING, PRETENDED **syn** see SARCASTIC

**iron·i·cal·ly** \-nək(ə)lē, -nēk-, -li\ *adv* **:** in an ironical manner **:** with or so as to constitute irony ⟨~ enough the well-planned scheme failed completely⟩ ⟨answered ~⟩

**iron·i·cal·ness** \-kəlnəs\ *n* -ES **:** the quality or state of being ironical

**ironing** *n* -S **1 :** the action or process of smoothing or pressing with or as if with a hot flatiron **2 :** clothes and linens ironed or to be ironed ⟨found the dampened ~ waiting in a basket⟩ ⟨folded and put away the ~⟩

**ironing board** *also* **ironing table** *n* **:** a flat padded cloth-covered surface on which clothes are ironed that was orig. of wood but is now often of ventilated metal, has one end tapered so that gar-

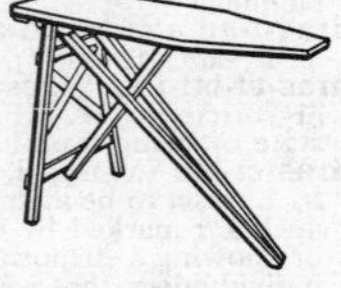
ironing board

ments may be fitted over it, and is usu. equipped with an adjustable support by which it may be held rigid at a convenient working height

**iron·ish** \'ī(ə)rnish, 'īən-, -nēsh\ *adj* **:** resembling or resembling that of iron ⟨an ~ taste⟩

**iro·nist** \'īrənəst\ *n* -s [*irony* + *-ist*] **:** one given to irony **:** a user of irony esp. in the development of a literary work or theme

**iro·nize** \-ˌnīz\ *vb* -ED/-ING/-S [*ironic* + *-ize*] *vt* **:** to make ironic **:** give an appearance or effect of irony to ⟨*ironizing* her account of the meeting⟩ ~ *vi* **:** to use irony **:** speak or behave ironically ⟨why ~ over such trivia⟩

**iron–jawed** \'=(=)¦=\ *adj* **1 :** having a jaw like or of iron ⟨*iron-jawed* pincers⟩ ⟨an *iron-jawed* boxer⟩ **2 :** rigorously determined ⟨an *iron-jawed* disposition⟩

**iron law** *n* **:** a law or controlling principle that is incontrovertible and inexorable ⟨*iron laws* of historical necessity⟩

**iron law of wages** [intended as trans. of G *ehernes lohngesetz*, lit., brazen law of wages] **:** a statement in economics: wages naturally tend to fall to the minimum level necessary for subsistence — called also *brazen law of wages*

**iron·less** \'ī(ə)rnləs, 'īən-\ *adj* **:** having no iron ⟨an ~ culture⟩ **:** free from iron ⟨~ diets⟩

**ironlike** \'=(=)ˌ=\ *adj* **:** resembling iron **:** exhibiting strength or hardness like that of iron ⟨~ determination⟩

**iron liquor** *n* **:** a black liquid consisting of a solution of crude ferrous acetate $Fe(C_2H_3O_2)_2$ usu. obtained by treating scrap iron with pyroligneous acid and used chiefly as a mordant in dyeing — called also *black liquor*

**iron loss** *n* **:** the loss of available energy by hysteresis and eddy currents in an electromagnetic apparatus (as a transformer) — compare COPPER LOSS

**iron lung** *n* **:** a device for artificial respiration in which rhythmic alternations in the air pressure in a chamber surrounding a patient's chest force air into and out of the lungs esp. when the nerves governing the chest muscles fail to function because of poliomyelitis

**iron man** *in senses 1 & 2* '=(=)ˌman *or* -ˌmaa(ə)n *or* -ˌmən, *in senses 3,4, & 5* '=(=)'man *or* -'maa(ə)n\ *n* **1 :** a maker or manufacturer of iron ⟨*iron men* are uncertain about carloadings⟩; *esp* **:** a worker engaged in the manufacture or processing of iron **2 a :** a railroad worker who handles the rails in tracklaying **b :** a cement worker who weighs out ground iron ore and adds it to slurry or dry-ground rock as it goes into the kiln **c :** a worker who makes iron facsimiles of paper shoe-part models for use in cutting cardboard patterns **3 :** a man of unusual physical endurance ⟨took pride in his mastery of the pitching art, in the reputation he bore as the *iron man* —*Collier's*⟩ **4** *slang* **:** DOLLAR; *esp* **:** a silver dollar **5** *slang* **:** a machine or device that does something formerly performed by hand **:** ROBOT

**ironmaster** \'=(=)ˌ==\ *n* **:** one that conducts or manages the founding or manufacture of iron esp. on a large scale

**iron mike** *n, slang* **:** an automatic pilot on a ship or airplane

**iron minium** *n* **:** BERLIN BROWN

**iron mold** *n* [[1]*iron* + *mold*, alter. of *mole* (spot)] **:** a spot (as on cloth) due to staining by rusty iron or by ink

**iron–mold** \'=(=)¦=\ *vt* **:** to stain with iron mold

**ironmonger** \'=(=)ˌ==\ *n* [ME *irenmonger*, fr. *iren* iron + *monger* — more at IRON, MONGER] *Brit* **:** a dealer in iron and hardware

**ironmongery** \'=(=)ˌ=(=)=\ *n* -ES **1** *Brit* **:** HARDWARE **2** *Brit* **:** a hardware store or business **3 :** the craft or technical art of a worker in metals **:** SMITHING ⟨a whole new craft of delicate, precise ~ that had to be developed —A.L.Kroeber⟩

**iron–monticellite** \¦=(=)ˌ==ˈ=ˌ=\ *n* **:** a silicate $CaFeSiO_4$ of iron and calcium that is isomorphous with monticellite

**iron mountain** *n* **:** a mountain that contains large or economically important amounts of iron ore

**iron·ness** \'ī(ə)rnnəs, 'īənn-\ *n* -ES **:** the quality or state of being iron ⟨an ~ of constitution⟩ ⟨such ~ of will⟩

**iron oak** *n* **1 :** any of several American oaks (as the blackjack or the common post oak) having notably hard tough durable wood **2 :** a European Turkey oak

**iron ore** *n* **:** a native compound of iron (as hematite, limonite, magnetite, siderite, goethite, and the bog and clay iron ores) from which the metal may be profitably extracted

**iron–ore cement** *n* **:** a German cement in which iron ore is substituted for the clay or shale used in making portland cement

**iron out** *vt* **1 a :** to make smooth or straight ⟨*ironed out* the curves in the highway⟩ ⟨*ironing* the crumpled paper *out*⟩ **b :** to make uniform ⟨*ironing out* irregularities in the wage scale⟩ **2 :** to make tolerable or harmonious by suppression or modification of extremes (as discordant views or aspirations, technical difficulties, or divergent theories) ⟨conferences will *iron out* any conflicts of interest⟩

**iron oxide** *n* **:** any of several natural or synthetic oxides or hydrated oxides of iron: as **a :** anhydrous or hydrated ferric oxide varying in color from red, brown, or black to orange or yellow depending in part on the degree of hydration and the purity and used esp. as a pigment — compare OCHER, SIENNA **b :** FERROSOFERRIC OXIDE **c :** FERROUS OXIDE **d :** GOETHITE

**iron–oxide red** *n* **:** a strong brown to reddish brown — called also *agate, Spanish red, tarragona*

**iron pan** *n* **:** a hard soil layer that is cemented with iron oxides and that usu. consists of sand or sand and gravel

**iron pentacarbonyl** *n* **:** the iron carbonyl $Fe(CO)_5$

**iron pot** *n* **:** SCOTER

**iron putty** *n* **:** an acid-resistant putty prepared from ferric oxide and boiled linseed oil

**iron pyrites** *or* **iron pyrite** *n* **:** PYRITE 2

**iron range** *n* **:** any of several highly productive iron-ore districts of the U.S. and Canada in the general vicinity of Lake Superior ⟨the Mesabi *iron range*⟩

**iron ration** *n* **:** an emergency ration

**iron red** *n* **1 :** a natural or synthetic red pigment (as Indian red or Venetian red) consisting wholly or in part of iron oxide — compare ROUGE 2a **2 :** any of the colors oxide red; *esp* **:** INDIAN RED — compare IRON-OXIDE RED

**irons** *pl of* IRON, *pres 3d sing of* IRON

**iron safe clause** *n* **:** a clause in a fire insurance policy covering merchandise that requires inventory records to be kept in a fireproof safe

**iron sand** *n* **:** sand rich in iron ore (as that of certain New Zealand coastal areas)

**iron scale** *n* **:** SCALE 4a(1)

**iron scrap** *n* **1 :** waste pieces or disused articles of wrought iron suitable for reworking **2 :** cast iron or castings suitable only for remelting

**ironshod** \'=(=)¦=\ *adj* **:** shod, cased, or tipped with iron or steel ⟨~ hooves⟩ ⟨an ~ wheel⟩ ⟨~ barge poles⟩

**ironshot** \'=(=)ˌ=\ *adj, of a mineral* **:** streaked or speckled with iron or an iron ore

**ironside** \'=(=)ˌ=\ *n* **1 :** a man of great strength or bravery **2 a ironsides** *pl, usu cap* **:** any of various bodies of hardy veteran troops **b :** a member of Cromwell's Ironsides cavalry during the English Civil War or of a similar force; *broadly* **:** a hardy veteran puritan soldier **3 ironsides** *pl but sing or pl in constr* **:** an ironclad ship

**iron sight** *n* **:** a metallic sight for a gun as distinguished from a sight depending on an optical or computing system — compare TELESCOPE SIGHT

**iron skull** *n, slang* **:** a railway boilermaker

**ironsmith** \'=(=)ˌ=\ *n* [ME *iren smyth*, fr. *iren* iron + *smyth*, smith — more at IRON, SMITH] **1 :** IRONWORKER, BLACKSMITH **2 :** any of several East Indian barbets (as *Megalaima oorti faber*) having notes that resemble the sounds made by a blacksmith

**iron spinel** *n* **:** HERCYNITE

**iron stand** *n* **:** a raised and usu. ventilated metal stand on which a hot flatiron may be rested when not in use

**ironstone** \'=(=)ˌ=\ *n* **1 :** a hard sedimentary rock rich in iron; *esp* **:** a siderite in a coal region **2 :** IRONSTONE CHINA

**ironstone china** *n* **:** a hard white stoneware pottery developed in England during the 18th century as a cheaper substitute for bone china and orig. highly decorated but used most extensively as plain white inexpensive tableware throughout much of the 19th century

**iron sulfate** *n* **:** a sulfate of iron: as **a :** FERRIC SULFATE **b :** FERROUS SULFATE

**iron sulfide** *n* **:** any of several compounds of iron and sulfur: as **a :** FERROUS SULFIDE **b :** the disulfide $FeS_2$ occurring in nature as pyrite and marcasite

**iron tree** *n* **:** a tree of the genus *Metrosideros* (esp. *M. vera*) with notably hard wood

**iron–vane meter** *n* **:** MOVING-IRON METER

**ironware** \'=(=)ˌ=\ *n* [ME *irenware*, fr. *iren* iron + *ware* — more at IRON, WARE] **:** articles made of iron; *esp* **:** iron household utensils (as cooking vessels or cutlery)

**ironweed** \'=(=)ˌ=\ *n* **:** any of several chiefly weedy plants: as **a :** KNAPWEED **b :** BLUEWEED 1 **c :** BLUE VERVAIN **d** *chiefly Brit* **:** RAGWEED 2 **e :** any of several American plants of the genus *Vernonia*

**ironwood** \'=(=)ˌ=\ *n* **1 :** any of numerous trees and shrubs (as various ebonies, hornbeams, or acacias) with exceptionally tough or hard wood — compare BASTARD IRONWOOD, BLACK IRONWOOD, WHITE IRONWOOD **2 :** the wood of an ironwood

**ironwood wattle** *n* **:** IRONBARK ACACIA

**ironwork** \'=(=)ˌ=\ *n* [ME *irenwerk*, fr. *iren* iron + *werk* work — more at IRON, WORK] **1 a :** work in iron **:** beat, smithed, or dressed iron ⟨did all the ~⟩ ⟨a balcony of lacy ~⟩ **b :** the part of something (as a building, a ship, or a wheel) that is made of iron ⟨the ~ of the carriage was forged locally⟩ **c :** iron articles ⟨dealt in ~⟩ **2 ironworks** *pl but sing or pl in constr* **:** a mill or building where iron or steel is smelted or heavy iron or steel products are made

**ironworker** \'=(=)ˌ==\ *n* **:** a worker in iron: as **a :** a person employed at an ironworks **b :** a shopworker who fabricates structural steel parts **c :** one who builds with structural steel or iron

**ironworking** \'=(=)ˌ==\ *n* **:** the process of fashioning things from iron

**ironwort** \'=(=)ˌ=\ *n* [so called fr. the belief that such mints cure sword wounds] **1 :** any of several shrubby or subshrubby mints that constitute the genus *Sideritis*, often have yellow flowers and whitish woolly stem or leaves, and are chiefly native to the eastern Mediterranean region **2 :** HEMP NETTLE

[1]**irony** \'ī(ə)rnē, 'īənē, -ni\ *adj* [ME *yrony*, fr. *yron*, *iren* iron + *-y* — more at IRON] **1 :** made or consisting of iron **:** containing or abounding in iron ⟨~ sands⟩ ⟨~ chains⟩ **2 :** resembling iron in some quality (as taste or hardness) ⟨an ~ flavor⟩

[2]**iro·ny** \'īrənē, -ni *sometimes* 'īərn-\ *n* -ES [L *ironia*, fr. Gk *eirōneia*, fr. *eirōn* dissembler (perh. fr. *eirein* to say) + *-eia* -y — more at WORD] **1 a :** feigned ignorance designed to confound or provoke an antagonist **:** DISSIMULATION — compare SOCRATIC IRONY **b :** DRAMATIC IRONY **2 a :** humor, ridicule, or light sarcasm that adopts a mode of speech the intended implication of which is the opposite of the literal sense of the words (as when expressions of praise are used where blame is meant) **b :** this mode of expression as a literary style or form ⟨a gift for ~⟩ **c :** an ironic utterance or expression **3 :** a state of affairs or events that is the reverse of what was or was to be expected **:** a result opposite to and as if in mockery of the appropriate result ⟨the ~ of fate⟩ **syn** see WIT

**iron yellow** *n* **1 :** any of several permanent synthetic yellow to orange pigments (as Mars yellow) consisting wholly or in part of hydrated iron oxide **2 :** MARS YELLOW 2

[1]**Ir·o·quoi·an** \ˌirəˈkwȯi(y)ən, -wāyən\ *adj, usu cap* [[2]*Iroquois* + *-an*] **1 :** of, relating to, or characteristic of the language family Iroquoian or one of its members **2 :** of, relating to, or characteristic of the Iroquois

[2]**iroquoian** \"\ *n* -s *cap* **1 :** a language family of eastern No. America including Cayuga, Cherokee, Conestoga, Erie, Huron, Mohawk, Onondaga, Oneida, Seneca, Tuscarora **2 :** a member of any of the peoples constituting the Iroquois

[1]**Ir·o·quois** \'irəˌkwȯi, -wä *sometimes* -wȯiz\ *adj, usu cap* [Fr, adj. & n., fr. Algonquin *Irinakhoiw*, lit., real adders] **1 :** of, relating to, or characteristic of the Iroquois **2 :** of, relating to, or characteristic of the language of the Iroquois

[2]**iroquois** \"\ *n, pl* **iroquois** \-ȯi(z), -ä(z)\ *usu cap* [F] **1 a :** an Indian people comprising a confederacy of five peoples that consisted orig. of the Cayuga, Mohawk, Oneida, Onondaga, and Seneca of central New York and later included the Tuscarora and fragments of various other peoples **b :** a member of any of such peoples **2 :** any of the languages of the Iroquois

**ir·pex** \'ərˌpeks\ *n, cap* [NL, fr. L *irpex*, *hirpex* harrow — more at HEARSE] **:** a genus of tooth fungi (family Hydnaceae) that have shelving or resupinate sporophores and include some forms associated with decay of woody plant tissue

**irr** *abbr* **1** irredeemable **2** irregular

**ir·radiance** \ə+\ *n* **1** *obs* **:** emission of rays (as of light) **2 :** something (as intellectual or spiritual illumination) that is emitted like rays of light ⟨informed . . . with so splendid a spiritual ~ —J.P.Bishop⟩ **3 :** radiant flux density on a given surface usu. expressed in watts per square centimeter or square meter

**ir·radiancy** \"+\ *n* **1 :** the quality or state of being irradiant **2 :** IRRADIANCE 3

**ir·radiant** \"+\ *adj* [L *irradiant-*, *irradians*, pres. part. of *irradiare*] **:** emitting rays of light **:** serving to or able to illuminate or brighten

[1]**ir·radiate** \"+\ *adj* [L *irradiatus*, past part.] **:** made bright with or as if with light **:** ILLUMINATED ⟨a countenance ~ with love⟩

[2]**ir·radiate** \"+\ *vb* -ED \-ING\-S [L *irradiatus*, past part. of *irradiare*, fr. *in-* [2]in- + *radiare* to radiate — more at RADIATE] *vt* **1 a :** to throw rays of light upon **:** shine upon **:** ILLUMINATE, BRIGHTEN ⟨moonlight *irradiating* the placid water⟩ **b :** to enlighten intellectually or spiritually **:** make clear or brilliant ⟨wisdom *irradiated* his counsel⟩ **c :** to affect or treat by radiant heat or other radiant energy; *specif* **:** to treat by exposure to radiation (as of ultraviolet light or radium) **2 :** to send forth like rays of light **:** RADIATE, SHED, DIFFUSE ⟨*irradiating* strength and comfort⟩ ~ *vi* **1** *archaic* **:** to emit rays **:** SHINE **2** *archaic* **:** to issue in rays

**irradiated** *adj* **1** *of an heraldic figure or device* **:** represented as surrounded with rays of light **2 :** treated, prepared, or altered by exposure to a specific radiation ⟨~ milk⟩ ⟨~ tissues⟩

**ir·ra·di·at·ing·ly** \¦=ˈ==ˌ===, =ˌ==ˈ===\ *adv* **:** so as to irradiate

**ir·radiation** \(ˌ)i, ə+\ *n* -s [MF, fr. LL *irradiation-*, *irradiatio*, fr. L *irradiatus* + *-ion-*, *-io* -ion] **1 a** *archaic* **:** a giving off of rays of light **b :** the emission of radiant energy (as heat) **c :** an emanation, diffusion, or radiation of something from a common center or point of origin or a result of such activity: as (1) **:** the radiation of a physiologically active agent from a point of origin within the body; *esp* **:** the spread of a nervous impulse beyond the usual conduction path (2) *obs* **:** emission of a supposed influence or immaterial fluid from the eyes (3) **:** apparent enlargement of a light or bright object or surface when displayed against a dark background; *esp* **:** the spreading of light by the grains of a photographic emulsion causing the developed image to be larger and more diffuse at the edges than the optical image — called also *diffusion* **2 a** *archaic* **:** a ray of light **b :** mental or spiritual illumination **3 a :** exposure to rays (as ultraviolet light, X rays, or alpha rays) **b :** application of X rays, radium rays, or other radiation (as for therapeutic purposes) **4 :** IRRADIANCE 3

**irradiation sickness** *n* **:** RADIATION SICKNESS

**ir·radiative** \ə+\ *adj* **:** tending to irradiate

**ir·radiator** \ə+\ *n* -s **:** one that irradiates; *esp* **:** an apparatus for applying irradiations (as X rays)

**ir·rad·i·ca·ble** \(')iˈradəkəbəl, əˈra-, (')i¦ra-, (')iə¦ra-\ *adj* [ML *irradicabilis*, fr. L *in-* [2]in- + *radicare* to take root + *-abilis* -able — more at RADICATE] **:** impossible to eradicate **:** DEEP-ROOTED — **ir·rad·i·ca·bly** \-blē\ *adv*

**ir·rad·i·cate** \əˈradəˌkāt\ *vt* -ED/-ING/-S [[2]*in-* + *radicate*] **:** to root deeply

**irrationable** *adj* [L *irrationabilis*, fr. *in-* [1]in- + *rationabilis* rationable — more at RATIONABLE] **1** *obs* **:** lacking the power of reason **2** *archaic* **:** UNREASONABLE, UNSUITABLE

[1]**ir·rational** \(')i, ə, (')ir, (')iə+\ *adj* [ME *irrationall*, fr. L *irrationalis*, fr. *in-* [1]in- + *rationalis* rational — more at RATIONAL] **:** not rational: as **a** (1) **:** not endowed with reason **:** lacking powers of reasoning or understanding ⟨the lower animals are commonly described as ~⟩ (2) **:** lacking usual or normal mental clarity or coherence ⟨was ~ for several days after the accident⟩ **b :** not governed by or according to reason ⟨~ . . . is a neutral term meaning either what is outside the scope of reason or what has not yet been tested by reason —*Times Lit. Supp.*⟩ **c** *Greek & Latin prosody* (1) *of a syllable* **:** having a quantity other than that required by the meter (2) *of a foot* **:** containing such a syllable (3) *of a meter* **:** containing such feet **d** *of a number* **:** real but not expressible as the quotient of two integers ⟨$\pi$ and $\sqrt{3}$ are ~ numbers⟩

[2]**irrational** \"+\ *n* -s **1 :** an irrational being **:** a being not acting according to reason **2 :** an irrational quantity or number **:** SURD

**ir·rationalism** \"+\ *n* **1 :** a viewpoint or system of belief emphasizing the use of intuition, instinct, feeling, or faith rather than a reliance upon reason or holding that the universe is governed by irrational, volitional, or mysterious forces instead of by reason **2 :** the quality or state of being irrational

[1]**ir·rationalist** \"+\ *adj* **:** of, relating to, or advocating irrationalism

[2]**irrationalist** \"\ *n* **:** a proponent of irrationalism

**ir·rationalistic** \(¦)i, ə, (¦)ir, (¦)iə+\ *adj* **:** not based on reason **:** ILLOGICAL; *sometimes* **:** IRRATIONALIST

**ir·rationality** \"+\ *n* [ML or NL *irrationalitas*, fr. L *irrationalis* irrational + *-itas* -ity — more at IRRATIONAL] **1 :** the quality or state of being irrational: as **a :** lack of being endowed with reason **b :** lack of accordance with reason **:** UNREASONABLENESS, FOOLISHNESS **2 :** something that is irrational **:** ABSURDITY **3 :** inequality of dispersion of different colors in refraction spectra (as between crown and flint glass)

**ir·rationalize** \i, ə, ir, iə+\ *vt* **:** to make irrational

**ir·rationally** \(')i, ə, (')ir, (')iə+\ *adv* **:** so as to be or appear irrational **:** without or beyond the bounds of reason ⟨~ jealous⟩

**ir·rationalness** \"+\ *n* **:** the quality or state of being irrational

**ir·real** \"+\ *adj* [[1]*in-* + *real*] **:** not real

**ir·reality** \¦i, ¦ir, ¦iə+\ *n* [[1]*in-* + *reality*] **:** UNREALITY

**ir·realizable** \(¦)i, ə, (¦)ir, (¦)iə+\ *adj* [[1]*in-* + *realizable*] **:** UNREALIZABLE, UNATTAINABLE

**ir·rebuttable** \¦i, ¦ir, ¦iə+\ *adj* [[1]*in-* + *rebut* + *-able*] **:** impossible to rebut **:** not subject to rebuttal ⟨an ~ argument⟩

**irrebuttable presumption** *n* **:** a presumption that the law does not allow to be rebutted **:** a conclusive presumption

**ir·receptive** \"+\ *adj* [[1]*in-* + *receptive*] **:** UNRECEPTIVE

**ir·reciprocal** \"+\ *adj* [[1]*in-* + *reciprocal*] **:** not reciprocal **:** UNILATERAL ⟨~ permeability⟩

**ir·reclaimable** \"+\ *adj* [[1]*in-* + *reclaim* + *-able*] **:** incapable of being reclaimed ⟨~ swamps⟩; *esp* **:** bad beyond any possibility of redemption ⟨vicious ~ boys⟩ — **ir·reclaimably** \"+\ *adv*

**ir·reclaimed** \"+\ *adj* [[1]*in-* + *reclaimed*] **:** UNRECLAIMED; *esp* **:** not brought under cultivation ⟨~ wasteland⟩

**ir·recognition** \(¦)i, ə, ¦ir, ¦iə+\ *n* [[1]*in* + *recognition*] **:** failure to recognize **:** absence of recognition

**ir·recognizable** \(¦)i, ə, (¦)ir, (¦)iə+\ *adj* [[1]*in-* + *recognizable*] **:** UNRECOGNIZABLE — **ir·recognizably** \"+\ *adv*

**ir·recollection** \(¦)i, ə, ¦ir, ¦iə+\ *n* [[1]*in-* + *recollection*] *archaic* **:** failure to recollect **:** FORGETFULNESS

**irrecompensable** *adj* [MF, fr. *in-* [1]in- + *recompensable* — more at RECOMPENSABLE] *obs* **:** impossible to requite — **irrecompensably** *adv, obs*

**ir·reconcilability** \(¦)i, ə, ¦ir, ¦iə+\ *n* **:** the quality or state of being irreconcilable **:** IRRECONCILABLENESS

[1]**ir·reconcilable** \(¦)i, ə, (¦)ir, (¦)iə+\ *adj* [[1]*in-* + *reconcile* + *-able*] **1 :** impossible to bring into friendly accord or understanding **:** hostile beyond the possibility of reconciliation ⟨~ enemies⟩ ⟨~ factions⟩ **2 :** impossible to make consistent or harmonious ⟨these ~ accounts⟩

[2]**irreconcilable** \"\ *n* -s **:** one that is irreconcilable; *esp* **:** a member of a group (as a political party) that vigorously opposes compromise or other collaborative techniques

**ir·reconcilableness** \"+\ *n* **:** the quality or state of being irreconcilable

**ir·reconcilably** \"+\ *adv* **:** so as to be irreconcilable **:** beyond the possibility of reaching agreement ⟨~ opposed⟩

**irreconcile** *vt* [[1]*in-* + *reconcile*] *obs* **:** to put at variance **:** ESTRANGE

**ir·reconciliable** \(¦)i, ə, (¦)ir, (¦)iə+\ *adj* [MF, fr. LL *irreconciliabilis*, fr. L *in-* [1]in- + *reconciliare* to reconcile + *-abilis* -able — more at RECONCILE] *archaic* **:** IRRECONCILABLE — **ir·reconciliably** \"+\ *adv, obs*

**ir·reconciliation** \(¦)i, ə, ¦ir, ¦iə+\ *n* [[1]*in-* + *reconciliation*] **:** lack of reconciliation

**ir·recoverable** \¦i, ¦ir, ¦iə+\ *adj* [[1]*in-* + *recoverable*] **1 :** not capable of being recovered, regained, remedied, or rectified **:** IRREPARABLE ⟨an ~ debt⟩ ⟨suffered an ~ injury⟩ **2** *obs* **:** IRREVOCABLE **3** *archaic* **:** incapable of being restored to health or life — **ir·recoverableness** \"+\ *n*

**ir·recoverably** \"+\ *adv* **1 :** so as to be irrecoverable **:** beyond any possibility of being recovered, regained, remedied, or rectified ⟨~ lost⟩ ⟨~ ill⟩ ⟨disposed of the evidence finally and ~⟩ **2 :** IRREVOCABLY ⟨determination to commit themselves ~ —J.A.Froude⟩

**irrecuperable** *adj* [ME, fr. LL *irrecuperabilis*, fr. L *in-* [1]in- + *recuperare* to take back, recover + *-abilis* -able — more at RECOVER] *obs* **:** IRRECOVERABLE — **irrecuperably** *adv, obs*

**ir·re·cu·sa·ble** \¦irē¦kyüzəbəl\ *adj* [LL *irrecusabilis*, fr. L *in-* [1]in- + LL *recusabilis* capable of being rejected, fr. L *recusare* to reject, refuse + *-abilis* -able — more at RECUSANT] **:** not subject to exception or rejection ⟨an ~ proposition⟩ — **ir·re·cu·sa·bly** \-blē\ *adv*

**ir·redeemable** \¦i, ¦ir, ¦iə+\ *adj* [[1]*in-* + *redeem* + *-able*] **1 :** not redeemable: as **a** (1) *of mortgaged goods* **:** not recoverable on payment of what is due (2) **:** not terminable by payment of the principal — used of a debt or annuity (3) *of a bond with stated maturity* **:** not callable before maturity **b** *of paper money* **:** not convertible into specie at the pleasure of the holder **:** INCONVERTIBLE **2 a :** admitting of no change or release **:** ABSOLUTE, HOPELESS ⟨~ gloom⟩ **b :** insusceptible of redemption or reform **:** utterly and hopelessly bad **:** IRRECLAIMABLE ⟨~ sinners⟩ — **ir·redeemably** \"+\ *adv*

**ir·re·den·ta** *or* **ir·ri·den·ta** \ˌirəˈdentə\ *n* -s [It *irredenta* (in *Italia irredenta*, lit., unredeemed Italy — used to refer to Italian-speaking areas not incorporated in Italy), fem. of *irredento* unredeemed, fr. *in-* [1]in- (fr. L) + *redento* redeemed, fr. L *redemptus*, past part. of *redimere* to redeem — more at REDEEM] **:** a region related historically or ethnically to one state but politically subject to another ⟨a frontier ~⟩ ⟨treaty inequities that created needless ~*s*⟩

**ir·re·den·tism** \-nˌtizəm\ *n* -s [It. *irredentismo*, the policy of the Italian Irredentists, fr. (*Italia*) *irredenta* + *-ismo* -ism] **:** the principles, policy, or practice of a party or of persons that seek to incorporate within their national boundary territory of which their nation has been deprived or of which the population is ethnically closely related to that of their nation

[1]**ir·re·den·tist** \-ntəst\ *n* -s [It *irredentista* one advocating the incorporation of Italia irredenta into Italy, fr. (*Italia*) *irredenta* + *-ista* -ist] **:** an advocate of irredentism

[2]**irredentist** \¦==¦==\ *adj* **1 :** of, relating to, or involving irredentists or irredentism ⟨an ~ movement⟩ ⟨~ sentiments⟩ **2 :** living in an irredenta ⟨~ populations⟩ **:** concerning the people of an irredenta ⟨~ problems⟩

**ir·reducibility** \¦i, ¦ir, ¦iə+\ *n* **:** the quality or state of being irreducible ⟨the ~ of psychological phenomena⟩

**ir·reducible** \"+\ *adj* [[1]*in-* + *reducible*] **1 :** impossible to bring into a desired state, form, or condition ⟨an ~ hernia⟩ **2 a :** impossible to simplify or make easier or clearer ⟨an ~ formula⟩ ⟨an ~ racial or cultural idiosyncrasy —Abram Kardiner⟩ **b :** impossible to make less or smaller ⟨an ~ minimum⟩ — **ir·reducibly** \"+\ *adv*

**irreducible equation** *n* **:** a mathematical equation equivalent to one formed by equating an irreducible function to zero

**irreducible function** *n* **:** an integral rational function of a polynomial that cannot be resolved into integral rational factors of lower degree with coefficients in the same number field

**ir·re·duc·ti·ble** \¦i(r)rə¦dəktəbəl, ¦iərə-\ *adj* [[1]*in-* + *reduct* + *-ible*] **:** IRREDUCIBLE

**ir·referable** \(¦)i, ə, (¦)ir, (¦)iə+\ *adj* [[1]*in-* + *referable*] **:** not referable

**ir·reflection** *also* **ir·reflexion** \¦i, ¦ir, ¦iə+\ *n* [F *irréflexion*, fr. *in-* ¹in- + *réflexion* — more at REFLECTION] **:** lack of mental consideration (as of a project or course of action)

**ir·reflective** \"+\ *adj* [¹*in-* + *reflective*] **:** not based on reflection **:** UNTHINKING, HEEDLESS ⟨an ~ delight⟩ — **ir·reflectively** \"+\ *adv* — **ir·reflectiveness** \"+\ *n*

**ir·reflexive** \"+\ *adj* [¹*in-* + *reflexive*] **1 :** not reflexive **2** *of a logical or mathematical relation* **:** never relating a term to itself — **ir·reflexivity** \(ˈ)i, ə, ¦ir, ¦iə\ *n*

**ir·reformable** \¦i, ¦ir, ¦iə+\ *adj* [¹*in-* + *reformable*] **1 :** incapable of being reformed **:** INCORRIGIBLE ⟨an ~ rascal⟩ **2 :** not subject to revision or alteration **:** final or perfect beyond the possibility of improvement ⟨~ dogma⟩ ⟨an ~ judgment⟩

**ir·ref·ra·ga·bil·i·ty** \(ˌ)i(r),refrəgəˈbiləd·ē, əˌ-, (ˌ)iəˌ-\ *n* **:** the quality or state of being irrefragable

**ir·ref·ra·ga·ble** \(ˈ)i(r)ˈrefrəgəbəl, əˈ-, (ˈ)iəˈ-\ *adj* [LL *irrefragabilis*, fr. L *in-* ¹in- + *refragari* to resist, oppose (fr. *re-* + *-fragari* — as in *suffragari* to vote for, support) + *-abilis* -able — more at SUFFRAGE] **1 :** impossible to gainsay, deny, or refute ⟨~ arguments⟩ ⟨~ data⟩ ⟨these ~ authorities⟩ **2 :** impossible to break or alter **:** INVIOLABLE, INDESTRUCTIBLE ⟨~ rules⟩ ⟨an ~ cement⟩ — **ir·ref·ra·ga·bly** \-blē\ *adv*

**ir·refrangible** \¦i, ¦ir, ¦iə+\ *adj* [¹*in-* + *refrangible*] **1 :** IRREFRAGABLE 2 **2 :** not capable of being refracted — used of visible light and other radiations

**ir·refusable** \"+\ *adj* [¹*in-* + *refusable*] **:** impossible to refuse

**ir·refutability** \(ˌ)i, ə, (ˌ)ir, (ˌ)iə+\ *n* **:** the quality or state of being irrefutable

**ir·refutable** \"+\ *adj* [LL *irrefutabilis*, fr. L *in-* ¹in- + LL *refutabilis* refutable — more at REFUTABLE] **:** impossible to refute **:** INCONTROVERTIBLE ⟨an ~ argument⟩ — **ir·refutably** \"+\ *adv*

**ir·regardless** \¦i, ¦ir, ¦iə+\ *adv* [prob. blend of *irrespective* and *regardless*] *nonstand* **:** REGARDLESS

**ir·regenerate** \"+\ *adj* [¹*in-* + *regenerate*] *archaic* **:** UNREGENERATE

¹**ir·regular** \(ˈ)i, ə, (ˈ)ir, (ˈ)iə+\ *adj* [ME *irreguler*, fr. MF, fr. LL *irregularis*, fr. L *in-* ¹in- + LL *regularis* regular — more at REGULAR] **1** *of a person* **a** *Roman Catholicism* **:** prevented by an impediment or bar from receiving or exercising clerical orders or offices **b :** behaving without regard to established laws, customs, or moral principles ⟨a wild ~ man in his youth⟩ **c :** not belonging to or not having satisfied the requirements of some particular group or organized body ⟨an ~ physician⟩ **2 a :** failing to accord with what is usual, proper, accepted, or right ⟨~ conduct⟩ **:** contrary to rule or custom ⟨some of his documents were ~⟩ ⟨although it was ~ we accepted the excuse⟩ **b** *of a word or inflection* **:** not conforming to the normal or usual manner of inflection ⟨*sell*, *cast*, *feed* are ~ verbs⟩; *specif* **:** STRONG 16a **c (1) :** improper or inadequate because of failure to conform to a prescribed course **(2)** **:** *of a marriage under Eng or Scots law* **:** celebrated without either proclamation of the banns or publication of intention to marry **:** CLANDESTINE **d :** not belonging to the regular army organization but raised for a special purpose ⟨~ troops are often used as independent commands to harass the enemy⟩ **3 a :** lacking perfect symmetry of form **:** not straight, smooth, even, regular ⟨a rough ~ terrain⟩ ⟨a long ~ coastline⟩ ⟨~ teeth⟩ **b** *of a flower or its parts* **:** lacking uniformity ⟨an ~ corolla⟩; *specif* **:** ZYGOMORPHIC **4 a :** lacking continuity or regularity of occurrence, activity, or function ⟨~ payments⟩ ⟨~ intervals⟩ ⟨an ~ worker⟩ **b** *of a physiological function* **:** failing to occur at regular or normal intervals ⟨~ menstruation⟩ ⟨have your bowels been ~⟩ **c** *of an individual* **:** failing to defecate at such intervals ⟨was constipated and very ~⟩ **d** *of a market* **:** characterized by individual price movements in both directions without establishment of an overall trend ⟨cotton futures were ~⟩

²**irregular** \"\ *n* **:** one that is irregular: as **a :** a soldier (as a guerrilla or partisan) who is not a member of a regular military force — usu. used in pl. **b irregulars** *pl* **:** merchandise that has imperfections or that falls below the manufacturer's usual standard or specifications and is usu. sold unbranded and at a concession in price — compare ²SECOND 4

³**irregular** \"\ *adj* [NL *Irregularia*] **:** EXOCYCLIC

**irregular carrier** *n* **:** a common carrier that operates without regular schedule or over routes not specified in the certificate or permit

**irregular deposit** *n* **:** a deposit of money (as for safekeeping) made with the understanding that an equivalent amount but not necessarily the identical money is to be returned to the depositor

**ir·regularia** \(ˌ)i, ə, ¦ir, ¦iə+\ [NL, fr. LL, neut. pl. of *irregularis*] *syn of* EXOCYCLOIDA

**ir·regularity** \"+\ *n* [ME *irregularite*, fr. OF *irregularité*, fr. ML *irregularitat-*, *irregularitas*, fr. LL *irregularis* irregular + L *-itat-*, *-itas* -ity — more at IRREGULAR] **1 :** the quality or state of being irregular **2 :** something that is irregular; *esp* **:** lack of proper and honest conduct (as in respect to a position of trust) — usu. used in pl. ⟨alleged *irregularities* in the city government⟩ ⟨*irregularities* in his accounts⟩

**ir·regularly** \(ˈ)i, ə, (ˈ)ir, (ˈ)iə+\ *adv* **:** in an irregular manner **:** at irregular intervals **:** so as to be irregular ⟨came to school very ~⟩

**irregular ode** *n* **:** an ode characterized by irregularity of verse and stanzaic structure and by lack of correspondence between parts — called also *pseudo-Pindaric ode*

**irregular peloria** *n* **:** peloria in which symmetry is attained by increase in number of some part — compare REGULAR PELORIA

**irregular variable** *n* **:** a variable star whose light fluctuations are nonperiodic

¹**irregulate** *adj* [ML *irregulatus*, fr. L *in-* ¹in- + LL *regulatus*, past part. of *regulare* to regulate — more at REGULATE] *obs* **:** not regulated

²**irregulate** *vt*, *obs* **:** to make irregular **:** DISORDER

**ir·regulated** \(ˈ)i, ə, (ˈ)ir, (ˈ)iə+\ *adj* [¹*in-* + *regulated*] **:** not regulated or controlled ⟨~ moods⟩

**ir·relate** *or* **ir·related** \¦i, ¦ir, ¦iə+\ *adj* [*irrelate* fr. ¹*in-* + L *relatus*, suppletive past part. of *referre* to relate; *irrelated* fr. ¹*in-* + *related* — more at RELATE] **:** not related

**ir·relation** \"+\ *n* [¹*in-* + *relation*] **:** UNRELATEDNESS

**ir·relative** \(ˈ)i, ə, (ˈ)ir, (ˈ)iə+\ *adj* [¹*in-* + *relative*] **:** not relative: as **a :** not related or connected **:** lacking mutual relationship ⟨remote and ~ regions —Douglas Carruthers⟩ **b :** not pertinent or relevant ⟨making ~ statements⟩ — **ir·relatively** \"+\ *adv*

**ir·relevance** *or* **ir·relevancy** \"+\ *n*, *pl* **irrelevances** *or* **irrelevancies 1 :** the quality or state of being irrelevant ⟨the ~ of these remarks⟩ **2 :** something irrelevant ⟨a plot full of *irrelevancies* and digressions⟩

**ir·relevant** \"+\ *adj* [¹*in-* + *relevant*] **:** not relevant **:** not applicable or pertinent **:** FOREIGN, EXTRANEOUS ⟨~ allegations⟩ ⟨~ to the matter in hand⟩

**ir·relevantly** \"+\ *adv* **:** in an irrelevant manner **:** so as to be irrelevant ⟨spoke idly and ~⟩

**ir·relievable** \¦i, ¦ir, ¦iə+\ *adj* [¹*in-* + *relieve* + *-able*] **:** impossible to relieve ⟨~ suffering⟩

**ir·religion** \"+\ *n* [MF or L; MF, fr. L *irreligion-*, *irreligio*, fr. *in-* ¹in- + *religion-*, *religio* religion — more at RELIGION] **1 :** the quality or state of being irreligious **:** lack of religion **:** IMPIETY **2** *obs* **:** a false religion **:** a perverted form of religion

**ir·religionist** \"+\ *n* **:** a supporter or practicer of irreligion

**ir·religiosity** \"+\ *n* [LL *irreligiositas*, fr. L *irreligiosus* + *-itas* -ity] **:** the quality or state of being irreligious

**ir·religious** \"+\ *adj* [L *irreligiosus*, fr. *in-* ¹in- + *religiosus* religious — more at RELIGIOUS] **1 :** lacking recognized religious emotions, doctrines, or practices **:** UNGODLY **2 :** of or constituting irreligion **:** PROFANE ⟨~ speech⟩ **3** *obs* **:** relating to, believing in, or practicing a false religion — **ir·religiously** \"+\ *adv*

**ir·re·me·able** \(ˈ)iˌrēmēəbəl, əˈr-, (ˈ)irˈr-, (ˈ)iəˈr-\ *adj* [L *irremeabilis*, fr. *in-* ¹in- + *remeare* to go back (fr. *re-* + *meare* to go) + *-abilis* -able — more at PERMEATE] **1 :** offering no possibility of return ⟨an ~ path⟩ **2 :** unable to return to a former place or state **:** IRREVERSIBLE ⟨an ~ stream⟩ ⟨~ tissue degeneration⟩ — **ir·re·me·ably** \-blē\ *adv*

**ir·remediable** \¦i, ¦ir, ¦iə+\ *adj* [L *irremediabilis*, fr. *in-* ¹in- + *remediabilis* remediable — more at REMEDIABLE] **:** impossible to remedy, correct, redress, alter, cure ⟨an ~ error⟩ ⟨~ defects of character⟩ — **ir·remediableness** \"+\ *n* — **ir·remediably** \"+\ *adv*

**irremediless** *adj* [¹*in-* + *remediless*] *obs* **:** REMEDILESS

**ir·remissible** \¦i, ¦ir, ¦iə+\ *adj* [MF, fr. LL *irremissibilis*, fr. L *in-* ¹in- + LL *remissibilis* remissible — more at REMISSIBLE] **:** not remissible: as **a :** impossible to overlook or forgive **:** UNPARDONABLE ⟨~ crimes⟩ **b :** impossible to refrain from or escape **:** OBLIGATORY ⟨~ duties⟩ ⟨an ~ responsibility⟩ — **ir·remissibly** \"+\ *adv*

**ir·remissive** \"+\ *adj* [¹*in-* + *remissive*] **:** not remissive

**ir·removability** \"+\ *n* **:** the quality or state of being irremovable

**ir·removable** \"+\ *adj* [¹*in-* + *removable*] **:** not removable: as **a :** impossible to remove or take away **:** not displaceable **b (1) :** impossible to remove or dismiss from office or position ⟨an ~ officer⟩ **(2) :** appointed for or granted for life tenure — used of an incumbent of a benefice who cannot be transferred or dismissed except for a grave crime and by canonical process or to a benefice so held **c :** IMMOVABLE, INFLEXIBLE — **irremovably** *adv*

**ir·repair** \"+\ *n* [¹*in-* + *repair*] **:** DISREPAIR

**irrepairable** *adj* [¹*in-* + *repairable*] **:** not capable of being repaired

**ir·reparable** \(ˌ)i, ə, (ˌ)ir, (ˌ)iə+\ *adj* [ME *irreperable*, fr. MF *irreparable*, fr. L *irreparabilis*, fr. *in-* ¹in- + *reparabilis* reparable — more at REPARABLE] **:** not reparable **:** impossible to make good, undo, repair, or remedy **:** IRRETRIEVABLE ⟨an ~ loss⟩ ⟨~ harm⟩ ⟨~ tissue changes⟩

**ir·reparableness** \"+\ *n* -ES **:** the quality or state of being irreparable

**ir·reparably** \"+\ *adv* **:** in an irreparable manner or to an irreparable degree

**ir·re·pa·tri·a·ble** \¦i(r)rēˈpā·trēəbəl ¦iərē-, -rēˌ-\ *n* -S [¹*in-* + *repatriate* + *-able*] **:** a person who cannot be repatriated usu. for political reasons

**ir·repealability** \¦i, ¦ir, ¦iə+\ *n* **:** the quality or state of being irrepealable

**ir·repealable** \"+\ *adj* [¹*in-* + *repealable*] **:** not capable of being repealed **:** impossible to revoke ⟨~ provisions of the statute⟩

**ir·repentance** \"+\ *n* [¹*in-* + *repentance*] **:** IMPENITENCE

**ir·replaceable** \"+\ *adj* [¹*in-* + *replaceable*] **:** not replaceable — **ir·replaceableness** \"+\ *n* -ES — **ir·replaceably** \"+\ *adv*

**ir·repleviable** \"+\ *adj* [¹*in-* + *replevin* + *-able*] **:** not subject to replevin

**ir·replevisable** \"+\ *adj* [¹*in-* + *replevisable*] **:** IRREPLEVIABLE

**ir·reprehensible** \(ˌ)i, ə, ¦ir, ¦iə+\ *adj* [ME, fr. LL *irreprehensibilis*, fr. L *in-* ¹in- + *reprehensus* (past part. of *reprehendere* to reprehend) + *-ibilis* -ible — more at REPREHEND] **:** not reprehensible **:** free from blame or reproach ⟨conduct in all respects ~⟩

**ir·representable** \"+\ *adj* [¹*in-* + *representable*] **:** not representable

**ir·repressibility** \¦i, ¦ir, ¦iə+\ *n* -ES **:** the quality or state of being irrepressible ⟨his constant ~⟩

¹**ir·repressible** \"+\ *adj* [¹*in-* + *repress* + *-able*] **:** impossible to repress, restrain, or control ⟨~ joy⟩ ⟨~ conflict⟩ ⟨an ~ chatterbox⟩

²**irrepressible** \"\ *n* -S **:** an irrepressible person

**ir·repressibleness** \"+\ *n* -ES **:** IRREPRESSIBILITY

**ir·repressibly** \"+\ *adv* **:** in an irrepressible manner **:** so as to be irrepressible ⟨~ gay⟩

**ir·repressive** \"+\ *adj* [¹*in-* + *repressive*] **:** IRREPRESSIBLE

**ir·reproachability** \"+\ *n* **:** the quality or state of being irreproachable

**ir·reproachable** \"+\ *adj* [¹*in-* + *reproachable*] **:** not subject to or deserving of reproach **:** BLAMELESS, FAULTLESS, IMPECCABLE ⟨~ manners⟩ ⟨an ~ character⟩

**ir·reproachableness** \"+\ *n* -ES **:** IRREPROACHABILITY

**ir·reproachably** \"+\ *adv* **:** so as to be beyond reproach **:** in an irreproachable manner

**ir·reproducible** \(ˌ)i, ə, ¦ir, ¦iə+\ *adj* [¹*in-* + *reproducible*] **:** not reproducible **:** impossible to duplicate

**ir·reprovable** \¦i, ¦ir, ¦iə+\ *adj* [¹*in-* + *reprovable*] **1 :** IRREPROACHABLE **2** *obs* **:** INDISPUTABLE

**ir·rep·tion** \əˈrepshən\ *n* -S [LL *irreption-*, *irreptio*, fr. L *irreptus* (past part. of *irrepere* to creep in, fr. *in-* ²in- + *repere* to creep) + *-ion-*, *-io* -ion — more at REPTILE] **:** an act or instance of entering by stealth or inadvertence ⟨the ~ of pseudo-classical plurals in technical language⟩

**ir·rep·ti·tious** \ˌi,repˈtishəs\ *adj* [L *irreptus* + E *-itious*] **:** marked by or resulting from irreption ⟨an ~ error in transliterating⟩ ⟨~ words in a text⟩

**ir·resistance** \¦i, ¦ir, ¦iə+\ *n* [¹*in-* + *resistance*] **:** lack of resistance **:** SUBMISSIVENESS

**ir·resistibility** \"+\ *n* **:** the quality or state of being irresistible

¹**ir·resistible** *or* **ir·resistable** \"+\ *adj* [¹*in-* + *resist* + *-ible*, *-able*] **:** impossible to successfully resist **:** superior to opposition ⟨an ~ attraction⟩

²**irresistible** \"\ *n* -S **:** an irresistible person or thing

**ir·resistibleness** \"+\ *n* **:** IRRESISTIBILITY

**ir·resistibly** \"+\ *adv* **:** to an irresistible extent or degree **:** so as to be irresistible

**ir·resistless** \"+\ *adj* [blend of *irrestible* and *resistless*] *archaic* **:** IRRESISTIBLE

**ir·resoluble** \(ˌ)i, (ˌ)ir, (ˌ)iə, ə+\ *adj* [L *irresolubilis*, fr. *in-* ¹in- + *resolvere* to resolve + *-bilis* -ble — more at RESOLVE] **1** *archaic* **:** incapable of being dissolved or resolved into parts **:** INSOLUBLE **2** *archaic* **:** incapable of being relieved or dispelled **3 :** incapable of being solved **:** impossible to make open, clear, or simple ⟨the question is ~ on the evidence at hand⟩

**ir·resolute** \(ˈ)i, ə, (ˈ)ir, (ˈ)iə+\ *adj* [¹*in-* + *resolute*] **1** *obs* **:** not resolved or solved **:** UNEXPLAINED **2 a :** uncertain how to act or proceed ⟨stood ~ waiting for some inspiration⟩ **b :** lacking strength of purpose or decisiveness of character **:** weak and vacillating ⟨a kindly man but very ~⟩

**ir·resolutely** \"+\ *adv* **:** in an irresolute manner **:** so as to be or appear irresolute

**ir·resoluteness** \"+\ *n* **:** the quality or state of being irresolute

**ir·resolution** \(ˌ)i, ə, ¦ir, ¦iə+\ *n* [prob. fr. MF, fr. *in-* ¹in- + *resolution* — more at RESOLUTION] **1** *obs* **:** the quality or state of not having formed a decided opinion **:** DOUBT, UNCERTAINTY **2 :** lack of resolution **:** a fluctuation of mind (as in doubt or between hope and fear) **:** INDECISION, VACILLATION

**ir·resolvable** \¦i, ¦ir, ¦iə+\ *adj* [¹*in-* + *resolvable*] **:** incapable of being resolved; *esp* **:** impossible to separate into component parts

**ir·resolved** \"+\ *adj* [¹*in-* + *resolved*] **:** not resolved **:** lacking in certainty, assurance, or decision ⟨a troubled and ~ heart⟩ — **ir·resolvedly** \"+\ *adv*

**ir·respective** \"+\ *adj* [¹*in-* + *respective*] **1** *obs* **:** lacking in respect **:** DISRESPECTFUL **2** *archaic* **:** functioning without or having no regard for persons, conditions, circumstances, or consequences ⟨oversteps in his ~ zeal every decency and every right —S.T.Coleridge⟩

**irrespectively** \"+\ *adv*, *obs* **:** in an irrespective manner

**irrespective of** *also* **irrespectively of** *prep* **:** without respect or regard to **:** independent or regardless of ⟨values his friends *irrespective of* what he may hope to gain from them⟩ ⟨this payment is made *irrespective of* any settlement the court may order⟩

**ir·respirable** \"+; (ˌ)i, ə, (ˌ)ir, (ˌ)iə+\ *adj* [F, fr. LL *irrespirabilis*, fr. L *in-* ¹in + *respirare* to breathe, respire + *-abilis* -able — more at RESPIRE] **:** unfit for breathing ⟨an ~ vapor⟩

**ir·responsibility** \¦i, ¦ir, ¦iə+\ *n* **:** the quality or state of being irresponsible

¹**ir·responsible** \"+\ *adj* [¹*in-* + *responsible*] **:** not responsible: as **a :** not required to answer to some higher authority **:** not liable to be called into question **:** subject to no oversight or control ⟨shall the planning be done by some ~ dictatorship or by democratic representatives whose acts are subject to discussion and criticism —M.R.Cohen⟩ ⟨the state is ~ and exempt from all ordinary controls⟩ **b :** not based on sound reasoned considerations ⟨~ optimism⟩ ⟨~ dreams⟩; *esp* **:** uttered without regard to truth, propriety, or fairness ⟨~ gossip⟩ ⟨these ~ charges⟩ **c (1) :** lacking a proper or adequate sense of responsibility ⟨~ jacks-in-office⟩ **(2) :** mentally inadequate to bear responsibility in an acceptable or normal manner ⟨the mother . . . was finally declared ~ and of too low intelligence to care for her large brood of children —Eda & Lawrence LeShan⟩ **d :** unprepared or unwilling to meet financial responsibilities ⟨financially ~ drivers⟩

²**irresponsible** \"\ *n* **:** one who is irresponsible

**ir·responsibleness** \"+\ *n* **:** IRRESPONSIBILITY

**ir·responsibly** \"+\ *adv* **:** so as to be or appear irresponsible **:** in an irresponsible degree

**ir·responsive** \"+\ *adj* [¹*in-* + *responsive*] **:** not responsive: as **a :** not able, ready, or inclined to respond ⟨the patient was ~ to treatment⟩ ⟨~ to control⟩ **b :** IRRESPONSIBLE a — **ir·responsiveness** \"+\ *n*

**ir·restrainable** \"+\ *adj* [¹*in-* + *restrain* + *-able*] **:** UNRESTRAINABLE — **ir·restrainably** \"+\ *adv*

**ir·resultive** \"+\ *adj* [¹*in-* + *result* + *-ive*] **:** lacking result **:** ABORTIVE

**ir·resuscitable** \"+\ *adj* [¹*in-* + *resuscitable*] **:** impossible to restore to life or activity — **ir·resuscitably** \"+\ *adv*

**ir·retention** \"+\ *n* [¹*in-* + *retention*] **:** failure of retention

**ir·retentive** \"+\ *adj* [¹*in-* + *retentive*] **:** lacking ability to retain something ⟨a casual ~ mind⟩ — **ir·retentiveness** \"+\ *n*

**ir·reticence** \(ˈ)i, ə, (ˈ)ir, (ˈ)iə+\ *n* [¹*in-* + *reticence*] **:** something lacking in reticence ⟨the ~*s* that are inseparable from military life⟩

**ir·retraceable** \¦i, ¦ir, ¦iə+\ *adj* [¹*in-* + *retrace* + *-able*] **:** impossible to retrace

**ir·retractile** \"+\ *adj* [¹*in-* + *retractile*] **:** not retractile

**ir·retrievability** \"+\ *n* **:** the quality or state of being irretrievable

**ir·retrievable** \"+\ *adj* [¹*in-* + *retrieve* + *-able*] **:** not retrievable **:** impossible to recoup, repair, or overcome ⟨an ~ loss⟩ ⟨~ errors in judgment⟩ ⟨~ ruin⟩

**ir·retrievableness** \"+\ *n* -ES **:** IRRETRIEVABILITY

**ir·retrievably** \"+\ *adv* **:** so as to be irretrievable **:** to an irretrievable degree or in an irretrievable manner ⟨manuscript ~ lost⟩

**ir·rev·e·lant** *or* **ir·rev·a·lent** \(ˈ)i(r)ˈrevələnt, əˈr-, (ˈ)iəˈr-\ *adj* [by alter.] *substand* **:** IRRELEVANT

**ir·reverence** \(ˈ)i, ə, (ˈ)ir, (ˈ)iə+\ *n* -S [ME, fr. L *irreverentia*, fr. *irreverent-*, *irreverens* + *-ia* -y] **1 a :** the quality or state of being irreverent **:** failure to offer due respect to that which is generally reverenced **b :** an irreverent act or utterance ⟨these pert ~*s*⟩ **2 :** condition of being without reverence **:** dishonored or neglected state **:** DISREGARD ⟨treating their elders with complete ~⟩

**ir·reverency** \"+\ *n* -ES **:** IRREVERENCE 1

**ir·reverend** \"+\ *adj* [¹*in-* + *reverend*] **1 :** not reverend **:** not worthy of reverence **2** *archaic* **:** IRREVERENT — **ir·reverendly** \"+\ *adv*

**ir·reverent** \"+\ *adj* [L *irreverent-*, *irreverens*, fr. *in-* ¹in- + *reverent-*, *reverens* reverent — more at REVERENT] **:** not reverent: as **a :** failing in proper reverence to something entitled to veneration or respect ⟨~ scholars mocking sacred things⟩ **b :** characterized by a lightly pert or exuberant quality or manner ⟨a certain ~ gaiety and ease of manner⟩ — **ir·reverently** \"+\ *adv*

**ir·reverential** \(ˌ)i, ə, ¦ir, ¦iə+\ *adj* [¹*in-* + *reverential*] **:** lacking in due respect or reverence **:** IRREVERENT — **ir·reverentially** \"+\ *adv*

**ir·reverentialism** \"+\ *n* -S **:** the quality or state of being irreverent

**ir·reversibility** \¦i, ¦ir, ¦iə+\ *n* **:** the quality or state of being irreversible

**ir·reversible** \"+\ *adj* [¹*in-* + *reverse* + *-ible*] **:** incapable of being reversed: as **a :** impossible to recall, repeal, or annul ⟨an ~ decree⟩ **b :** impossible to turn about, back, or upside down ⟨an ~ cover⟩ ⟨~ cushions⟩ **c :** impossible to make run or take place backward ⟨an ~ engine⟩ ⟨~ chemical syntheses⟩ **d** *of a colloid* **:** incapable of undergoing transformation from sol to gel or vice versa **e :** unsymmetrical with respect to constituent elements or terms ⟨an ~ relation⟩ **f** *of a pathological process* **:** of such severity that recovery is impossible ⟨~ shock⟩ ⟨~ anoxic damage to the brain⟩ — **ir·reversibly** \"+\ *adv*

**ir·revocability** \(ˌ)i, ə, ¦ir, ¦iə+\ *n* **:** the quality or state of being irrevocable

**ir·revocable** \(ˌ)i, ə, (ˌ)ir, (ˌ)iə+\ *adj* [ME, fr. L *irrevocabilis*, fr. *in-* ¹in- + *revocabilis* revocable — more at REVOCABLE] **:** incapable of being recalled or revoked **:** past recall **:** UNALTERABLE ⟨an ~ promise⟩ ⟨firm and ~ is my doom —Shak.⟩

**ir·revocableness** \"+\ *n* **:** IRREVOCABILITY

**ir·revocably** \"+\ *adv* **:** so as to be irrevocable **:** beyond any possibility of change ⟨~ determined⟩

**ir·revoluble** \"+\ *adj* [¹*in-* + *revoluble*] *archaic* **:** having no finite period of revolution

**irridenta** *var of* IRREDENTA

**ir·ri·ga·ble** \ˈirəgəbəl, -rēg-\ *also* **ir·ri·gat·able** \ˈirəˌgād·əbəl, -ātə-, ˌ==ˈ==\ *adj* [*irrigate* + *-able*] **:** possible to irrigate **:** susceptible of or suitable for irrigation ⟨~ land⟩ — **ir·ri·ga·bly** \ˈirəgəblē, -rēg-, -bli\ *adv*

**ir·ri·gate** \ˈirə,gāt, *usu* -ād·+V\ *vb* -ED/-ING/-S [L *irrigatus*, past part. of *irrigare*, fr. *in-* ²in- + *rigare* to water — more at RAIN] *vt* **1 :** WET, MOISTEN ⟨secretions that ~ mucous surfaces⟩; as **a :** to supply (as land or crops) with water by artificial means (as by diverting streams, digging canals, flooding, or spraying) **b :** to apply a continuous stream of liquid to (a part of the body) for a therapeutic purpose **2 :** to refresh or make fertile as if by watering ~ *vi* **1 :** to practice irrigation (as of land) **2** *slang* **:** to drink intoxicating liquor **:** IMBIBE

**ir·ri·ga·tion** \ˌirəˈgāshən\ *n* -S *often attrib* [L *irrigation-*, *irrigatio*, fr. *irrigatus* + *-ion-*, *-io* -ion] **1 :** the action or process of irrigating: as **a :** the artificial watering of land (as by canals, ditches, pipes, or flooding) to supply moisture for plant growth ⟨~ ditches⟩ ⟨growing crops by ~⟩; *also* **:** a single watering by such means ⟨the berries will need another ~ if it doesn't rain soon⟩ **b :** application of a continuous stream of liquid to a part of the body for a therapeutic purpose ⟨wound ~⟩ **2 :** a refreshing or making fertile as if by watering

**ir·ri·ga·tion·al** \ˌirəˈgāshən³l, -shnəl\ *adj* **:** of or relating to irrigation

**irrigation efficiency** *n* **:** the ratio between irrigation water actually utilized by growing crops and water diverted from a source (as a stream) in order to supply such irrigation water

**ir·ri·ga·tion·ist** \ˌirəˈgāsh(ə)nəst\ *n* -S **:** a user or advocate of irrigation esp. in farming

**ir·ri·ga·tive** \ˈirəˌgād·iv\ *adj* **:** IRRIGATIONAL

**ir·ri·ga·tor** \-ād·ə(r), -ātə-\ *n* -S **:** one that irrigates: as **a :** an agriculturist who employs irrigation in the growing of crops **b :** a device, apparatus, or system used to irrigate something (as a wound or a crop) **c :** a worker who supervises agricultural irrigation or irrigating equipment

**ir·rig·u·ous** \əˈrigyəwəs\ *adj* [L *irriguus*, fr. *irrigare* to irrigate — more at IRRIGATE] **1** *archaic* **:** IRRIGATED, MOISTENED; *esp* **:** well-watered **2 :** serving to irrigate or water ⟨slow ~ streams⟩

**ir·ri·sion** \əˈrizhən\ *n* -S [L *irrision-*, *irrisio*, fr. *irrisus* (past part. of *irridēre* to laugh at, fr. *in-* ²in- + *ridēre* to laugh) + *-ion-*, *-io* -ion — more at RIDICULOUS] **:** a laughing at a person or thing **:** DERISION

¹**ir·ri·sor** \əˈrīzər\ [NL, fr. L, mocker, scoffer, fr. *irrisus* + *-or*] *syn of* PHOENICULUS

²**irrisor** \"\ *n* -S **:** a bird of the genus *Phoeniculus* **:** WOOD HOOPOE

**ir·ri·sor·i·dae** \ˌirəˈsōrəˌdē, -ˈzō-\ [NL, fr. *Irrisor*, type genus + *-idae*] *syn of* PHOENICULIDAE

**ir·riso·ry** \-īsərē, -īzə-,-izə-\ *adj* [LL *irrisorius*, fr. L *irrisus* (past part. of *irridēre* to laugh at) + *-orius* -ory — more at IRRISION] **:** given to derision **:** DERISIVE

**ir·ri·ta·bil·i·ty** \ˌirəd·əˈbiləd·ē, -rətə-, -lətē, -i\ *n* -ES [L *irritabilitas*, fr. *irritabilis* + *-itas* -ity] **:** the quality or state of being irritable: as **a :** quick excitability to annoyance, impatience, or anger **:** PETULANCE, FRETFULNESS ⟨~ of temper⟩ ⟨showing increasing ~ as he waited⟩ **b :** abnormal excitability of an organ or part of the body (as the stomach or bladder) **:** heightened responsiveness **c :** the property of protoplasm and of living organisms that permits them to react to environmental changes (as by specific orientation, change of shape, or production or cessation of movement)

**ir·ri·ta·ble** \ˈirəd·əbəl, -rətə-\ *adj, sometimes* -ER/-EST [L *irritabilis*, fr. *irritare* to irritate + *-abilis* -able — more at IRRITATE] **:** capable of being irritated: as **a :** likely to become impatient, angry, or disturbed **:** easily exasperated ⟨an ~ disposition⟩ ⟨such ~ neurotic people⟩; *broadly* **:** easily excitable **b :** excessively or unduly sensitive to irritants or stimuli **:** exhibiting abnormal irritability ⟨an ~ colon⟩ **c** *of protoplasm or a living organism* **:** responsive to stimuli

**syn** FRACTIOUS, PEEVISH, SNAPPISH, WASPISH, PETULANT, PETTISH, HUFFY, HUFFISH, FRETFUL, QUERULOUS: IRRITABLE implies ready, impatient excitability whereby one is angered and exasperated easily ⟨a hot day and the clerk in the store was *irritable* . . . had not slept much the night before and he had a headache —Lyle Saxon⟩ FRACTIOUS may suggest a wilful or truculent unruliness or perverse crossness ⟨those who are spoilt and *fractious*, who must have everything their own way —F.A.Swinnerton⟩ ⟨a wary, querulous, grumbling, vain, testy, self-righteous, honorable man, a defiant and *fractious* servant and a high-handed and mistrustful master —Arthur Schlesinger b.1917⟩ PEEVISH may suggest childish irritability about petty matters ⟨*peevish* because he called her and she did not come, and he threw his bowl of tea on the ground like a willful child —Pearl Buck⟩ ⟨*peevish*, and wrathful, often insolent, and quarrelsome —Charles Kingsley⟩ SNAPPISH may apply to an irritability manifesting itself in sharp, tart, sarcastic objections and rejoinders ⟨a little *snappish* at reflecting how many miles he had to post —Samuel Butler †1902⟩ WASPISH may connote testy, resentful, stinging irascibility ⟨a little *waspish* woman who would have been ahead of me snapped out at a man who seemed to be with her —C.S.Lewis⟩ PETULANT may suggest sulky and capricious dissatisfaction and complaint as though resolved to be displeased ⟨in his youth the spoiled child of Boston, in middle life he was *petulant* and irritable, inclined to sulk when his will was crossed —V.L. Parrington⟩ PETTISH may apply to childish, sulky ill humor of or as if of one slighted ⟨she heard Amy's voice in *pettish* exclamation: "Oh, get out, you!" —Arnold Bennett⟩ HUFFY or HUFFISH may suggest a tending to take undue offense or to have one's arrogant pride hurt and to parade one's blustering irritation ⟨rather *huffy*, and somewhat on the high-and-mighty order with him —Harriet B. Stowe⟩ FRETFUL suggests ill-humored continuing irritability and complaining or whining peevishness ⟨his voice was peevish, almost whining, and there were certain overtones in it which recalled the *fretful* complaining voice —W.H.Wright⟩ QUERULOUS stresses the idea of discontented whining complaining, often childishly futile, resentful, and arising from determined inclination to be displeased ⟨the man himself grew old and *querulous* and hysterical with failure and repeated disappointment and chronic poverty —Aldous Huxley⟩

**irritable heart** *n* **:** CARDIAC NEUROSIS

**ir·ri·ta·ble·ness** *n* -ES **:** IRRITABILITY

**ir·ri·ta·bly** \-blē, -bli\ *adv* **:** in an irritable manner **:** with irritability

**ir·ri·ta·ment** \ˈirəd·əmənt, əˈrid·-\ *n* -S [F, fr. LL *irritamentum*, fr. *irritare* to irritate, provoke + *-mentum* -ment] *archaic* **:** INCITEMENT, IRRITANT

**¹ir·ri·tan·cy** \ˈirəd·ənsē, -ətən-, -si *also* -ətᵊn-\ *n* -ES [¹*irritant* + *-cy*] *Roman, civil, & Scots law* **:** a making or the quality or state of being made null and void **:** INVALIDATION; *also* **:** IRRITANT CLAUSE

**²irritancy** \"\ *n* -ES [²*irritant* + *-cy*] **:** the quality or state of being irritating

**¹ir·ri·tant** \-ənt,-ᵊnt\ *adj* [MF, fr. LL *irritant-, irritans*, pres. part. of *irritare* to invalidate, fr. L *irritus* invalid, fr. *in-* ¹in- + *-ritus* (fr. *ratus* valid, fr. past part. of *reri* to reckon, calculate) — more at REASON] **:** making null and void — compare IRRITANT CLAUSE

**²irritant** \"\ *adj* [F, fr. MF, fr. L *irritant-, irritans*, pres. part. of *irritare* to irritate, provoke — more at IRRITATE] **:** IRRITATING; *specif* **:** tending to produce irritation or inflammation

**³irritant** \"\ *n* -S **:** something that irritates or excites; *specif* **:** an agent by which irritation is produced ⟨a chemical ~⟩

**irritant clause** *n* [¹*irritant*] *Scots law* **:** a clause in an instrument providing that if certain specified events shall take place the instrument shall be void

**¹ir·ri·tate** \ˈirəˌtāt, *usu* -ād·+V\ *vb* -ED/-ING/-S [L *irritatus*, past part. of *irritare*, fr. *in-* ²in- + *-ritare* (perh. akin to L *oriri* to rise) — more at RISE] *vt* **1** *obs* **:** to increase the action of **:** heighten excitement in **:** AGGRAVATE **2 :** to excite impatience, anger, or displeasure in **:** PROVOKE, EXASPERATE, ANNOY ⟨*irritated* by the child's insolence⟩ **3 :** to cause (an organ or tissue) to be irritable **:** produce irritation in ⟨harsh soaps may ~ the skin⟩ ⟨avoid *irritating* the sensitive laryngeal reflexes —*Anesthesia Digest*⟩ **4 :** to produce excitation in (as a nerve) **:** STIMULATE **:** cause (as a muscle) to contract ~ *vi* **:** to cause or induce displeasure or irritation ⟨it's the petty things of life that ~ most⟩ ⟨a soothing lotion for burns that is guaranteed not to ~⟩

**syn** EXASPERATE, NETTLE, ROIL, RILE, PEEVE, AGGRAVATE, PROVOKE: IRRITATE means to arouse angry annoyance or great displeasure evoking feelings ranging from impatience to rage ⟨it *irritated* him that she peered so into everything that was his, searching him out —D.H.Lawrence⟩ ⟨a Mexican carpenter will *irritate* newcomers beyond endurance by taking a three-hour siesta —Green Peyton⟩ EXASPERATE suggests galling vexation or angry annoyance ⟨her unexplained departure had *exasperated* him —Edith Wharton⟩ NETTLE usu. indicates a stinging pique, sometimes a rankling irritation ⟨a touch of light scorn in her tone *nettled* me —W.J.Locke⟩ ROIL and its variant RILE suggest inducing an angry or resentful state of agitated disturbance ⟨her manner of ignoring him. That *roiled* him inexpressibly —C.S.Forester⟩ ⟨with raucous taunting and ribald remarks to *rile* up the proprietor —W.A.White⟩ PEEVE applies to arousing fretful irritation, sometimes petty or querulous ⟨when she ventured to criticize it, even mildly, he was *peeved* —Louis Auchincloss⟩ AGGRAVATE may apply to repeated action or condition that intensifies anger or irritation ⟨he did not sweat and pray over each card as she must, but he did keep an eye out for reneging and demanded a cut now and then just to *aggravate* her —J.F.Powers⟩ PROVOKE may suggest irritation or anger that excites to action ⟨don't think I am trying to *provoke* you or to make fun of what you revere —Ann Bridge⟩ ⟨a Tory resident who *provoked* local animosities and was charged with high treason —*Amer. Guide Series: Conn.*⟩

**²irritate** \"\ *vt* [LL *irritatus*, past part. of *irritare* to invalidate — more at IRRITANT] **:** to make null and void **:** DEFEAT

**irritated** *adj* [fr. past part. of ¹*irritate*] **:** subjected to irritation: as **a :** roused to anger **:** ANNOYED ⟨that tired ~ father⟩ **b :** roughened, reddened, or inflamed by some irritating agent ⟨an ~ skin⟩ ⟨hiding her ~ eyes behind dark glasses⟩ — **ir·ri·tat·ed·ly** \ˈ==,===, ,=ˈ===\ *adv*

**irritating** *adj* **:** causing displeasure or annoyance **:** PROVOKING — **ir·ri·tat·ing·ly** \ˈ==,===, ,=ˈ===\ *adv*

**ir·ri·ta·tion** \ˌirəˈtāshən\ *n* -S [MF, fr. L *irritation-, irritatio*, fr. *irritatus* (past part. of *irritare* to irritate, provoke) + *-ion-, -io* -ion — more at IRRITATE] **1 :** an act of irritating or a state of being irritated: as **a :** excitement to activity **:** STIMULATION **b :** excitement of impatience, anger, or passion **:** ANNOYANCE **c :** IRRITABILITY b **2 :** EXCITATION 3; *esp* **:** the act of exciting a muscle to contraction by artificial stimulation

**ir·ri·ta·tive** \ˈirəˌtād·|iv, -ət|, |ēv *also* |əv\ *adj* [¹*irritate* + *-ive*] **1 :** serving to excite **:** IRRITATING ⟨an ~ agent⟩ **2 :** accompanied with or produced by increased action or irritation ⟨an ~ cough⟩

**ir·ri·ta·tor** \-ād·ə(r), -ātə-\ *n* -S **:** one that irritates

**ir·ri·to·motility** \ˌirətō+\ *n* [*irritation* + *-o-* + *motility*] **:** response of plant tissues to external stimuli by means of movements or curvatures

**irrogate** *vt* -ED/-ING/-S [L *irrogatus*, past part. of *irrogare* to propose against, impose, fr. *in-* ²in- + *rogare* to ask, request — more at RIGHT] *obs Scot* **:** to impose (a penalty) legally — **irrogation** *n* -S *obs*

**¹irrorate** *vt* -ED/-ING/-S [L *irroratus*, past part. of *irrorare*, fr. *in-* ²in- + *rorare* to moisten, shed moisture, fr. *ror-, ros* dew — more at RORIC] *obs* **:** BEDEW, MOISTEN — **irroration** *n* -S *obs*

**²ir·ro·rate** \ˈirəˌrāt, ǝˈrōrǝt\ *also* **ir·ro·rat·ed** \ˈirəˌrād·əd\ *adj* [*irrorate* fr. L *irroratus*, past part.; *irrorated* fr. L *irroratus* + E *-ed*] **:** covered with little spots **:** SPECKLED ⟨a tawny butterfly with black-*irrorate* wings⟩

**ir·rotational** \ˌi, |ir, |iə+\ *adj* [¹*in-* + *rotational*] **:** not involving rotation **:** free from vortices ⟨~ flow⟩ ⟨an ~ electrostatic field⟩ — **ir·rotationally** \"+\ *adv*

**ir·rubrical** \(ˈ)i, ə, (ˈ)ir, (ˈ)iə+\ *adj* [¹*in-* + *rubrical*] **:** not rubrical

**ir·ru·ma·tion** \ˌirüˈmāshən\ *n* -S [L *irrumation-, irrumatio*, fr. *irrumatus* (past part. of *irrumare* to give suck, extend the penis for fellatio, fr. *in-* ²in- + *-rumare*, fr. *ruma, rumis* breast, teat) + *-ion-, -io* -ion] **:** FELLATIO

**ir·rupt** \əˈrəpt\ *vb* -ED/-ING/-S [L *irruptus*, past part. of *irrumpere*, lit., to break in, fr. ¹*in-* in + *rumpere* to break — more at RUPTURE] *vi* **1 a :** to enter forceably or suddenly **:** appear without warning **:** INTRUDE ⟨the sea had once ~*ed* into the cavern⟩ ⟨the merchants constituted a very tight caste, rarely ~*ing* into social groups either above or below —G.W. Johnson⟩ **b** *of an animal population* **:** to undergo a sudden upsurge in numbers esp. when natural ecological balances and checks are disturbed **2 :** ERUPT 1c ⟨the crowd ~*ed* in a fervor of patriotism —*Time*⟩ ~ *vt* **:** INTRUDE 3 — opposed to *erupt*

**ir·rup·ti·ble** \(ˈ)i(r)ˈrəptəbəl, əˈr-, (ˈ)iə|r-\ *adj* **:** UNBREAKABLE

**ir·rup·tion** \əˈrəpshən\ *n* -S [L *irruption-, irruptio*, fr. *irruptus* + *-ion-, -io* -ion] **:** an act or instance of irrupting: as **a :** a sudden violent or forceable entry **:** a rushing or bursting in ⟨the current ~ of bad manners into everyday life⟩ ⟨an ~ of water through a break in the dike⟩ **b :** a sudden and violent invasion ⟨the ~*s* of the Goths into Italy⟩ **c :** ERUPTION 1 **d :** a sudden sharp increase in the relative numbers of a natural population usu. associated with favorable alteration of the environment

**ir·rup·tive** \-ptiv\ *adj* **:** irrupting or tending to irrupt ⟨~ forces⟩: as **a :** rushing or bursting in or upon **:** entering forceably or violently ⟨the ~ roar of new engines —J.G. Cozzens⟩ **b** *of an igneous rock* **:** INTRUSIVE **c :** marked by irruption ⟨the ~ stage of rabbit increase⟩ **:** undergoing irruption ⟨the ~ deer herds of the state⟩ — compare CYCLIC — **ir·rup·tive·ly** \-tәvlē\ *adv*

**IRU** *abbr* **1** international radium unit **2** international rat unit

**irul** \ˈēˌrül\ *n* -S [Tamil *iruḷ*] **:** ACLE 1,2

**iru·la** \ˈirələ\ *n, pl* **irulas** *or* **irula** *usu cap* **:** a primitive Veddoid people inhabiting the Deccan plateau of India and being one of the pre-Dravidian peoples of India

**irus·ka** \əˈrüskə\ *n* -S [Pawnee, lit., the fire is in me] **:** a dance of a fire-handling sacred male society of the Pawnee Indians that is the precursor of the grass dance

**ir·ving·ite** \ˈərviŋˌīt\ *n* -S *usu cap* [Edward *Irving* †1834 Scot. clergyman + E *-ite*] **:** a member of the Catholic Apostolic Church — often taken to be offensive

**¹is** [ME (3d pers. sing. pres. indic. and — northern dial. — 1st & 2d pers. sing. pres. indic. and — northern dial. — 1st & 2d & 3d pers. pl. pres. indic. of *been* — suppletive infinitive — to be), fr. OE (3d pers. sing. pres. indic. of *bēon* — suppletive infinitive — to be); akin to OHG *ist* (3d pers. sing. pres. indic. of *sīn* to be), ON *es, er* (3d pers. sing. pres. indic. of *vesa, vera* — suppletive infinitive — to be), Goth *ist* (3d pers. sing. pres. indic. of *wisan* — suppletive infinitive — to be), L *est* (3d pers. sing. pres. indic. of *esse* to be), Gk *esti* (3d pers. sing. pres. indic. of *einai* to be), Skt *asti* is, he is, Hitt *eszi*] *pres 3d sing of* BE, *dial pres 1st & 2d sing of* BE, *substand pres pl of* BE

**²is** \ˈiz\ *n* -ES **:** that which is; *specif* **:** that which is factual, empirical, actually the case, or spatiotemporal — contrasted with *ought*

**is-** *or* **iso-** *comb form* [LL, fr. Gk, fr. *isos* equal] **1 :** equal **:** homogeneous **:** uniform ⟨*is*energic⟩ ⟨*is*acoustic⟩ ⟨*iso*cephaly⟩ ⟨*iso*type⟩ **2** *usu* **iso- a :** isomer of a (specified) compound ⟨*iso*cyanuric acid $C_3(NH)_3O_3$⟩ ⟨*iso*vanillin $CH_3OC_6H_4(OH)CHO$⟩ **b** (1) **:** of, relating to, or having a branched chain of carbon atoms ⟨*iso*hydrocarbons⟩ ⟨*iso*synthesis⟩ — compare NORMAL 10e (2) **:** having a straight chain of carbon atoms to which one branching methyl group is attached in the position next to one end ⟨*iso*hexyl $(CH_3)_2CHCH_2CH_2CH_2$—⟩ **3** *usu* **iso- :** for or from different individuals of the same species ⟨*iso*antigen⟩ ⟨*iso*antibody⟩

**is** *abbr* island; isle

**IS** *abbr* **1** interservice **2** interstate

**i's** *or* **is** *pl of* I

**is·a·be·li·ta** \ˌizəbəˈlēd·ə\ *or* **is·a·bel·ite** \-ˈbeˌlīt\ *n* -S [AmerSp *isabelita*, fr. Sp *Isabelita* (feminine nickname), dim. of *Isabel* (feminine name)] **:** any of various fishes belonging to a genus *Angelichthys* of the family Chaetodontidae; *esp* **:** an angelfish (*A. ciliaris*) colored orange red, sky blue, and golden that is common in the West Indies

**is·a·bel·la** \ˌizəˈbelə\ *also* **is·a·bel** \ˈizəˌbel\ *n* -S *often cap* [MF *isabelle*, fr. *Isabelle* (feminine name)] **:** a moderate yellowish brown to light olive brown that is lighter and stronger than clay drab or medal bronze

**isabella grape** \ˌ==ˈ==-\ *also* **isabella** *n* -S *usu cap I* [prob. after *Isabella* Gibbs, 19th cent. Am. woman who introduced it into Brooklyn from North Carolina] **:** FOX GRAPE c

**isabella moth** *n, usu cap I* [NL *isabella* (specific epithet of *Isia isabella*), perh. fr. E *isabella*] **:** a common stout-bodied snuff-colored American arctiid moth (*Isia isabella*) having the hind wings often tinged with orange or red

**is·a·bel·line** \ˌizəˈbelən, -ˌlīn, -ˌlēn\ *adj* [*isabella* + *-ine*] **:** of the color Isabella

**isabelline bear** *n* **:** RED BEAR

**is·abnormal** \ˈīs *also* ˈīz+\ *or* **iso·abnormal** \ˌī(ˌ)sō *also* -)zō+\ *n* [*is-* + *abnormal*, adj.] **:** an imaginary line or a line on a chart that connects or marks places on the surface of the earth having equal differences in a given time from the normal temperature of these places or that indicates differences between the calculated and actual temperatures of the different parallels of latitude

**is·acoustic** \"+\ *adj* [*is-* + *acoustic*] **:** of or relating to equal intensity of sound

**is·adelphous** \"+\ *adj* [prob. fr. (assumed) NL *isadelphus*, fr. NL *is-* + *-adelphus* -adelphous] **:** having the separate bundles of stamens in a diadelphous flower equal in number

**is·a·go·ge** \ˈīsəˌgōjē, ˌ==ˈ==\ *n* -S [L, fr. Gk *eisagōgē*, fr. *eisagein* to introduce, fr. *eis* into + *agein* to lead; akin to Gk *en* in — more at IN, AGENT] **:** a scholarly introduction to a branch of study or research — **isa·gog·ic** \ˌ==ˈgäjik\ *or* **isa·gog·i·cal** \-jəkəl\ *adj*

**isa·gog·ics** \ˌ==ˈgäjiks\ *n pl but usu sing in constr, also* **isa·gog·ic** \-ik\ [*isagoge* + *-ics*] **:** introductory studies; *esp* **:** a branch of theology that is preliminary to actual exegesis and deals with the literary and external history of the Bible

**is·a·ian** \īˈzāən, *chiefly Brit* -zīən\ *or* **isa·ian·ic** \ˌī=(ˌ)=ˈanik\ *adj, usu cap* [*isaian* fr. Isaiah, 8th cent. B.C. major Hebrew prophet + E *-an*, adj. suffix; *isaianic* fr. *Isaiah* + E *-an*, adj. suffix + *-ic*] **:** of, relating to, or having the characteristics of Isaiah or the book of Isaiah ⟨the *Isaianic* character of this prophesy —Robert Gordis⟩ ⟨the somber and threatening, the almost *Isaian*, utterance —Edmund Wilson⟩

**is·allobar** \(ˈ)īs *also* (ˈ)īz+\ *n* [ISV *is-* + *all-* + *-bar* (as in *isobar*)] **:** an imaginary line or a line on a chart connecting the places of equal change of atmospheric pressure within a specified time — **is·al·lo·bar·ic** \(ˌ)īˌsaləˈbärik, (ˌ)īˌza-, -bar-\ *adj*

**is·al·lo·therm** \īˈsaləˌthərm *also* īˈza-\ *n* [ISV *is-* + *all-* + *-therm*] **:** an imaginary line or a line on a chart connecting the places of equal change of temperature within a specified time

**is·an·drous** \(ˈ)īˈsandrəs *also* (ˈ)īˈza-\ *adj* [*is-* + *-androus*] **:** having the stamens similar and equal in number to the petals

**is·an·e·mone** \īˈsanəˌmōn, ˌīsəˈnemə(ˌ)nē *also* īˈza- *or* ˌīzə-\ *n* [ISV *is-* + *-anemone* (irreg. fr. Gk *anemos* wind) — more at ANIMATE] **:** an isogram of wind speed

**is·anom·al** \ˌīsəˈnäməl *also* ˌīzə-\ *n* -S [ISV *is-* + *-anomal* (fr. LL *anomalus* dissimilar) — more at ANOMALOUS] **:** an imaginary line or a line on a chart connecting places that have the same anomalies esp. of temperature or pressure

**is·anomalous** \ˈīs *also* ˈīz+\ *adj* [*isanomal* + *-ous*] **:** relating to an isabnormal or an isanomal

**isa·no oil** \əˈsä(ˌ)nō-\ *n* [*isano* prob. native name (of the tree *Ongokea klaineana*) in the Congo region of West Africa] **:** an unsaturated fatty oil that is obtained from the kernel of the nuts of a West African tree (*Ongokea klaineana*) of the family Oleoceae, that polymerizes readily, and that is used in coatings

**is·an·thous** \(ˈ)īˈsan(t)thəs *also* -ˈza-\ *adj* [NL *isanthus*, fr. *is-* + *-anthus* -anthous] **:** having the flowers regular

**is·apostolic** \(ˈ)īs *also* (ˈ)īz+\ *adj* [LGk *isapostolos* isapostolic (fr. Gk *is-* + *apostolos* apostle) + E *-ic* — more at APOSTLE] **:** equal to or contemporaneous with the apostles — used esp. of bishops consecrated by the apostles

**isard** *var of* IZARD

**isar·ia** \īˈsa(a)rēə\ *n, cap* [NL, fr. *is-* + *-aria*] **:** a form genus of imperfect fungi (family Stilbellaceae) that are parasitic on insects and have the conidia borne terminally on slender hyphae that cover the coremiums

**isa·rithm** \ˈīsəˌriṯhəm, -th- *also* ˈīzə-\ *n* -S [ISV *is-* + *-arithm* (fr. Gk *arithmos* number); orig. formed as G *isarithmus* — more at ARITHMO-] **:** a line drawn on a map or chart to connect points having equal numerical values (as of temperature, elevation, or density of population)

**isa·tin** \ˈīsətən, -əd·ən\ *n* -S [ISV *isat-* (fr. NL *Isatis*) + *-in*] **:** an orange red crystalline compound $C_8H_5NO_2$ obtained by oxidation of indigo or oxindole or by various syntheses and used as an intermediate for indigoid dyes

**isa·tin·ic acid** \ˌīsəˈtinik-\ *or* **isat·ic acid** \(ˈ)īˈsad·ik-\ *n* [*isatinic* ISV *isatin* + *-ic*; *isatic* ISV *isatin* + *-ic*] **:** a white solid amino acid $NH_2C_6H_4COCOOH$ obtained by hydrolysis of isatin

**-isation** — see -IZATION

**isa·tis** \ˈīsəd·əs\ *n, cap* [NL, fr. L, woad, fr. Gk — more at WOAD] **:** a large genus of herbs (family Cruciferae) having entire leaves, small yellow flowers, and compressed oblong or orbicular pods — see WOAD

**isat·o·gen** \īˈsad·əjən, -ˌjen\ *n* -S [ISV *isatin* + *-o-* + *-gen*] **:** a parent compound $C_8H_5NO_2$ isomeric with isatin and known in the form of various colored derivatives that are made by treating an *ortho*-nitro-phenyl-acetylene with sulfuric acid

**isa·to·ic anhydride** \ˌīsəˈtōik-\ *n* [*isatoic* ISV *isatin* + *-o-* + *-ic*] **:** a high-melting dicarboxylic acid anhydride $C_8H_5NO_3$ made by oxidation of isatin or by reaction of anthranilic acid with phosgene

**¹isau·ri·an** \īˈsȯrēən\ *n* -S *cap* [*Isauria*, ancient district in south central Asia Minor + E *-an*, n. suffix] **:** a native or inhabitant of Isauria

**²isaurian** \(ˈ)=ˈ===\ *adj, usu cap* [*Isauria* + E *-an*, adj. suffix] **1 :** of, relating to, or characteristic of Isauria **2 :** of, relating to, or characteristic of the people of Isauria

**is·auxesis** \ˈīs *also* ˈīz+\ *n* [NL, fr. *is-* + *auxesis*] **:** ISOGONY — **is·auxetic** \"+\ *adj*

**isa·wa** \əˈsäwə\ *or* **isa·wi·ya** \ˌēsəˈwē(y)ə\ *or* **ais·sa·wa** \īˈsäwə\ *n pl, usu cap* [Ar *ʿīsawīyah*, an order of dervishes] **:** members of a Muslim religious brotherhood founded in Morocco about 1500

**is·ba** *also* **iz·ba** \əzˈbä\ *n* -S [Russ *izba*, fr. Old Russian *istŭba* bathing room, prob. of Gmc origin; akin to OHG *stuba* heated room — more at STOVE] **:** a Russian log hut

**ISC** *abbr* interstate commerce

**is·car·i·ot·ic** \(ˌ)iˌskarēˈäd·ik, əˌsk-\ *or* **is·car·i·ot·i·cal** \-d·əkəl\ *adj* [Judas *Iscariot*, apostle that betrayed Jesus + E *-ic* or *-ical*] **:** of, relating to, or having the characteristics of Judas Iscariot; *specif* **:** TREACHEROUS

**is·che·mia** *also* **is·chae·mia** \əˈskēmēə\ *n* -S [NL *ischaemia*, fr. *ischaemus* styptic, stopping blood (fr. Gk *ischaimos*, fr. *ischein* to check, restrain + *haima* blood) + *-ia*; akin to Gk *echein* to have, hold — more at SCHEME, HEM-] **:** localized tissue anemia due to obstruction of the inflow of arterial blood (as by the narrowing of arteries by spasm or disease) ⟨cerebral ~⟩ ⟨renal ~⟩ ⟨myocardial ~⟩ — **is·che·mic** *also* **is·chae·mic** \(ˈ)iˈskēmik, əˈs-\ *adj*

**ischemic contracture** *n* **:** shortening and degeneration of a muscle resulting from deficient blood supply

**ischi-** *or* **ischio-** *comb form* [L *ischi-*, fr. Gk, fr. *ischion* hip joint] **1 :** ischium ⟨*ischi*algia⟩ ⟨*ischio*podite⟩ **2 :** ischial and ⟨*ischio*caudal⟩ **3 :** resembling a hip joint ⟨*ischio*cerite⟩

**is·chi·ad·ic** \ˌiskēˈadik\ *adj* [L *ischiadicus* of pain in the hip, fr. Gk *ischiadikos*, fr. *ischiad-, ischias* sciatica (fr. *ischion* hip joint) + *-ikos* -ic] **:** ISCHIAL

**is·chi·al** \ˈiskēəl\ *adj* [prob. fr. (assumed) NL *ischialis*, fr. L *ischi-* + *-alis* -al] **:** of, relating to, or situated near the ischium

**is·chi·at·ic** \ˌiskēˈad·ik, -atik\ *adj* [LL *ischiaticus* of pain in the hip, alter. (influenced by adjectives ending in *-aticus* such as LL *dramaticus* dramatic) of L *ischiadicus*] **:** ISCHIAL

**is·chio·capsular** \ˌiskē(ˌ)ō+\ *adj* [*ischi-* + *capsular*] **:** of, relating to, or being an accessory ligament of the hip joint passing from the ischium below the acetabulum to blend with the capsular ligament

**is·chio·cav·er·no·sus** \ˌiskē(ˌ)ōˌkavə(r)ˈnōsəs\ *n* -ES [NL, fr. *ischi-* + *-cavernosus* belonging to the corpus cavernosum, fr. L *cavernosus* cavernous] **:** a muscle covering the crus of the penis or clitoris

**is·chi·oc·er·ite** \ˌiskēˈäsəˌrīt\ *n* [*ischi-* + Gk *keras* horn, antenna + E *-ite* — more at HORN] **:** a joint of the antenna of a crustacean

**is·chi·op·o·dite** \-ˈäpəˌdīt\ *n* [ISV *ischi-* + *-podite*] **:** the third joint from the base of certain limbs of crustaceans (as the thoracic legs of decapods)

**is·chio·rectal** \ˌiskē(ˌ)ō+\ *adj* **:** of, relating to, or adjacent to both ischium and rectum

**is·chi·um** \ˈiskēəm\ *n, pl* **is·chia** \-kēə\ [L, hip joint, fr. Gk *ischion*; perh. akin to Skt *sakthi* thigh] **1 :** the dorsal and posterior of the three principal bones composing either half of the pelvis consisting in man of a thick portion, a large rough eminence on which the body rests when sitting, and a forwardly directed ramus which joins that of the pubis **2 :** ISCHIOPODITE

**is·chy·o·dus** \əˈskīədəs\ *n, cap* [NL, fr. *ischy-* (fr. Gk *ischys* strength) + *-odus*; akin to Gk *echein* to have, hold — more at SCHEME] **:** a genus of Jurassic and Cretaceous chimaeroid fishes of Europe and New Zealand

**is·chy·ro·my·i·dae** \ˌiskərōˈmīəˌdē\ *n pl, cap* [NL, fr. *Ischyromys*, type genus (fr. Gk *ischyros* strong + *mys* mouse) + *-idae*; akin to Gk *echein* to have, hold — more at MOUSE] **:** a family of primitive extinct sciuromorph rodents widely distributed in the northern hemisphere from the Lower Eocene to the Upper Oligocene, distantly related to the mountain beaver, and distinguished by low-crowned generalized cheek teeth

**ise** *or* **i'se** \(ˌ)īz\ *usu cap* [contr. of E dial. *I is* I am, fr. E *I* + E dial. *is* — more at IS] *dial* **:** I am

**-ise** \ˌīz\ *vb suffix* **:** -IZE — see -IZE in Explan Notes

**is·en·trope** \ˈīsᵊnˌtrōp, ˈīzᵊn-\ *also* **is·en·trop·ic** \ˌ==-ˈträpik\ *n* -S [*isentrope* ISV prob. back-formation fr. *isentropic*, adj.; *isentropic*, n. fr. *isentropic*, adj.] **:** an isentropic line or surface (as on a meteorological chart or engineering diagram)

**is·en·trop·ic** \ˌ==-ˈträpik, ˌīˌsen-, ˌīˌzen-\ *adj* [ISV *is-* + *entropy* + *-ic*] **:** having or indicating constant entropy ⟨the ~ chart, a map of the air unaffected by surface heating and cooling, aids in identifying the air from one map to the next —T.M.Longstreth⟩ **:** taking place without change of entropy ⟨if steam could be expanded in a turbine with no friction or other losses, expansion would be ~ —A.G.Christie⟩ — **is·en·trop·i·cal·ly** \-pək(ə)lē\ *adv*

**is·ep·ipte·sis** \ˌīˌsepə(p)ˈtēsəs, ˌīˌze-\ *n, pl* **isepipte·ses** \-ēˌsēz\ [NL, fr. *is-* + *epi-* + Gk *ptēsis* flight, fr. *petesthai* to fly — more at FEATHER] **:** a line on a map or chart connecting localities reached at one date by different individuals of a species of migratory bird

**ises** *pl of* IS

**is·ethi·o·nate** \ˌīˌseˈthīəˌnāt, ˌīˌze-\ *n* [ISV *isethion-* (fr. *isethionic*) + *-ate*] **:** a salt or ester of isethionic acid

**is·ethionic acid** \(ˈ)īs, (ˈ)īz+ . . . -\ *n* [*isethionic* ISV *is-* + *ethionic*] **:** a crystalline sulfonic acid $HOC_2H_4SO_3H$ obtained by action of sulfur trioxide on alcohol or ether and used in making surface-active agents

**is·fa·han** \ˈisfəˌhän, -han, ˌ==ˈ=\ *adj, usu cap* [fr. *Isfahan*, city in west central Iran] **:** of or from the city of Isfahan, Iran **:** of the kind or style prevalent in Isfahan

**ISG** *abbr, often not cap* imperial standard gallon

**ish** \ˈish\ *n* -ES [ME (Sc) *ische*, fr. ME *ischen, isshen* to come out, go out, fr. MF *issir* — more at ISSUE] **1** *Scots law* **:** right of exit **:** ISSUE, EXIT ⟨~ and entry⟩ **2** *Scots law* **:** time of expiry (as of a lease) **:** EXPIRY, TERMINATION

**-ish** \ish, ēsh\ *adj suffix* [ME, fr. OE *-isc;* akin to OHG *-isc, -isk* -ish, ON *-skr,* Goth *-isks* -ish, Gk *-iskos,* dim. n. suffix] **1 :** of or belonging to — chiefly in adjectives indicating nationality or ethnic group ⟨Finn*ish*⟩ ⟨Gaul*ish*⟩ ⟨Turk*ish*⟩ **2 a :** characteristic or typical of ⟨boy*ish*⟩ ⟨London*ish*⟩ **:** having the undesirable qualities of ⟨amateur*ish*⟩ ⟨mul*ish*⟩ **b** (1) **:** having a touch or trace of ⟨summer*ish*⟩ **:** somewhat ⟨purpl*ish*⟩ ⟨lat*ish*⟩ (2) **:** having the approximate age of ⟨forty*ish*⟩ (3) **:** being or occurring at the approximate time of — esp. in words formed from numerals indicating an hour of the day or night ⟨five*ish*⟩ ⟨eight*ish*⟩

**ish·er·wood system** \'ishə(r),wu̇d-\ *n, usu cap I* [after Benjamin F. *Isherwood* †1915 Am. naval engineer] **:** a technique of ship construction employing large transverse frames widely spaced and light longitudinal members closely spaced — called also *longitudinal framing*

**ishi·ha·ra test** \,ishē'härə-\ *n, usu cap I* [after Shinobu *Ishihara* b1879 Jap. ophthalmologist who devised it] **:** a widely used test for the detection of color blindness

**ishi·ka·wa·ite** \,ishē'käwə,īt\ *n* -s [*Ishikawa* district, north central Honshu, Japan, its locality + E *-ite*] **:** a rare mineral (U, Fe, Y, etc.)(Nb, Ta)$O_4$ consisting of an oxide of uranium, iron, niobium, tantalum, yttrium, and the rare-earth metals

**ish·kash·mi** \ish'käsh(,)mē\ *n, pl* **ishkashmi** *or* **ishkashmis** *usu cap* **1 :** an Iranian people of the highlands of the southwestern Pamir mountains **2 :** a member of the Ishkashmi people

**ish·kyl·dite** *or* **ish·kil·dite** \'ishkəl,dīt\ *n* -s [Russ *ishkil'dit,* fr. *Ishkyldino,* Middle Volga district, U.S.S.R., its locality + Russ *-it* -ite] **:** a mineral $Mg_{15}Si_{11}O_{27}(OH)_{20}$ consisting of a basic silicate of magnesium

**ish·ma·el** \'ishmēəl, -(,)mā-\ *n* -s *usu cap* [after *Ishmael* (AV), *Ismael* (DV), son of Abraham by his concubine Hagar; fr. the statement made concerning him in Gen 16:12 (AV) that "his hand will be against every man, and every man's hand against him"] **:** one at odds with or as if with society **:** OUTCAST, OUTLAW, OUTSIDER ⟨I am an *Ishmael* by instinct —Samuel Butler †1902⟩ ⟨the murder novel, . . . long the *Ishmael* of fiction, shows every sign of rejoining the main fold of literature —Anthony Boucher⟩

**ish·ma·el·ite** \-ēə,līt, -āə-\ *n* -s *usu cap* **1 :** a descendant of Ishmael **2 :** ISHMAEL ⟨individual animals which as *Ishmaelites* lived a solitary life and ranged alone —P.A.Rollins⟩

**ish·ma·el·it·ish** \ˌ=(,)==,līd·ish, ˌ=(,)===\ *adj, usu cap* **:** of, relating to, or having the characteristics of an Ishmaelite ⟨the wretched, fearful, *Ishmaelitish* condition of every man against his fellowmen —Hastings Lyon⟩

**isi·ac** \'isē,ak, 'izē-,'isē-\ *or* **isi·a·cal** \ə'sīəkəl, (')ī'sī-\ *adj, usu cap* [*isiac* fr. L *isiacus,* fr. Gk *isiakos,* fr. *Isis,* orig. Egyptian goddess of motherhood and the family whose cult spread throughout the Mediterranean world in Hellenistic times; *isiacal* fr. L *isiacus* + E *-al*] **:** of or relating to Isis or the cult of Isis

**isi·dae** \'īsə,dē, 'izə-\ *n pl, cap* [NL, fr. *Isis,* type genus (fr. Gk, orig. Egyptian goddess of motherhood and the family) + *-idae*] **:** a family of gorgonians having an axis composed of alternating horny and calcareous joints

**isid·i·if·er·ous** \ī,sidē'if(ə)rəs\ *or* **isid·i·of·er·ous** \-ē'äf-\ *adj* [*isidiiferous* fr. *isidium* + *-i-* + *-ferous; isidioferous* fr. *isidium* + *-o-* + *-ferous*] **:** bearing isidia

**isid·i·oid** \ī'sidē,ȯid\ *adj* [*isidium* + *-oid*] **:** of, relating to, or resembling an isidium

**isid·i·ose** \-ē,ōs\ *adj* [*isidium* + *-ose*] **:** of or relating to isidia

**isid·i·um** \ī'sidēəm\ *n, pl* **isid·ia** \-ēə\ [NL, fr. *Isidium,* supposed genus of lichens, irreg. fr. *Isis* genus of gorgonians + Gk *eidos* form; fr. the resemblance of lichens that have isidia to gorgonians — more at IDOL] **:** an outgrowth from the surface of the thallus in certain lichens that resembles a soredium

**is·i·do·ri·an** *or* **is·i·do·re·an** \ˌizə'dōrēən\ *adj, usu cap* [*Isidore* of Seville †A.D.636 Span. prelate and scholar + E *-an,* adj. suffix] **:** of, relating to, or characteristic of Isidore of Seville

**isi·nai** *also* **isi·nay** \ˌēsə'nī\ *n, pl* **isinai** *or* **isinais** *usu cap* **1 a :** a Christianized people of Nueva Vizcaya, Luzon, Philippines **b :** a member of such people **2 :** the Austronesian language of the Isinai people

**isin·glass** \'īzᵊn,glas, 'īziŋ,g-, -zēŋ-, -laa(ə)s, -lais, -lȧs\ *n* -ES [prob. by folk etymology (influence of E *glass*) fr. obs. D *huizenblas,* fr. MD *huusblase,* fr. *huus* sturgeon + *blase* bladder; akin to OHG *hūso* beluga and to OHG *blāsan* to blow — more at HUSO, BLAST] **1 :** a semitransparent whitish substance consisting of a very pure form of gelatin orig. prepared from the air bladders of sturgeons from the rivers of western Russia but now largely made from those of sturgeons of other areas or of various other fishes and used chiefly as a clarifying agent and in making jellies and glue — called also *fish gelatin, fish glue* **2 :** mica esp. when in thin transparent sheets **3 :** a colloidal extractive substance (as agar) from various algae

**is·lam** \i'släm, -iz'läm, -lam, -laa(ə)m, -lȧm, 'ˌ=,= also 'izləm *or* 'isləm\ *n* -s *cap* [Ar *islām* submission (to the will of God), fr. *aslama* to surrender] **1 :** the religious faith of Muslims who profess belief in Allah as the sole deity and in Muhammad as the prophet of Allah ⟨*Islam* . . . is the religion of judgment —J.E.Turner⟩ ⟨*Islam* was a fellowship —J.C.Archer⟩ **2 a :** the cultural system or civilization erected in history upon the foundations of Islamic religious faith ⟨for nine centuries the Turks were the principal champions of *Islam* —Emil Lengyel⟩ ⟨the grafting of the spirit of modern nationalism upon the ancient trunk of *Islam* —H.L.Hoskins⟩ **b :** the national political units of the modern world that share the Muslim religion ⟨*Islam* is the principal problem of three hundred million people who might be . . . our friends —Mortimer Graves⟩

**is·lam·ic** \(')iz'slämik, (')iz'l-, -lam-,-lȧm-, -mēk\ *adj, usu cap* [F *islamique,* fr. *islam* (fr. Ar *islām*) + *-ique* -ic] **:** of, relating to, or characteristic of Islam ⟨*Islamic* traditions⟩ ⟨an *Islamic* republic⟩

**is·lam·ics** \=ˈ=miks, -mēks\ *n pl but sing in constr, usu cap* **:** the academic study of Islam

**is·lam·ism** \=ˈ=,mizəm, 'izlə,mi-, 'islə,-\ *n* -s *usu cap* **:** the faith, doctrine, or cause of Islam

**is·lam·ist** \-,məst\ *n* -s *usu cap* **1 :** an orthodox Muslim **2 :** a student or scholar of Islamics

**is·lam·ite** \-,mīt, *usu* -īd·+V\ *n* -s *usu cap* [F, fr. *islam* + *-ite*] **:** MUSLIM

**is·lam·it·ic** \ˌizlə'mid·ik, ˌisl-, -it|, |ēk\ *adj, usu cap* **:** of, relating to, or characteristic of Islamism **:** MUSLIM

**is·lam·iza·tion** \,izləmə'zāshən, ,islə-, -,mī'z-, i,slämə'-, i,slamə'-, i,slȧmə'-\ *n* -s *usu cap* **:** the act or process of islamizing or being islamized

**is·lam·ize** \'izlə,mīz, 'islə-, i'slä,m-, i'sla,-, i'slȧ,-\ *vt* -ED/-ING/-s *often cap* **1 :** to make Islamic in quality, traits, or way of thinking or acting; *esp* **:** to convert to Islamism ⟨*Islamizing* the religion of these semibarbarous hordes —P.K. Hitti⟩ **2 :** to bring under the control of Islam

**¹is·land** \'īlənd\ *n* -s *often attrib* [alter. (influenced by E ¹isle) of earlier *iland,* fr. ME, fr. OE *īgland;* akin to OFris *eiland* island, ON *eyland;* all fr. a prehistoric NGmc-WGmc compound whose first constituent is represented by OE *īg, īeg* island and whose second constituent is represented by OE *land;* OE *īg, īeg* island akin to OE *ēa* river, OHG *ouwa* land by water, meadow, *aha* river, ON *ey* island, *ā* river, Goth *ahwa* river, L *aqua* water — more at LAND] **1 a :** a tract of land surrounded by water and smaller than a continent **b** *dial* **:** a tract of land cut off on two or more sides by water **:** PENINSULA **2 :** something resembling an island by its isolated, surrounded, or sequestered position: as **a** (1) **:** an elevated piece of land surrounded by swamp or alluvial land ⟨thousands were marooned on ~s of high ground —*Time*⟩ (2) **:** a piece of woodland surrounded by flat open country **b :** ISLET 2 c — compare ISLAND OF REIL **c** (1) **:** a small isolated space between lines in a fingerprint (2) **:** a lanceolate interruption in a line on the palm held to be a sign in palmistry ⟨when the line has an ~ in the center . . . it foretells some trouble —Alice D. Jennings⟩ **d** (1) **:** a showcase, counter, or platform standing apart and approachable on all sides ⟨only fast turnover items can be placed on ~s —*Printers' Ink*⟩ ⟨double built-in cooking top in an ~ arrangement —*Amer. Builder Catalog Directory*⟩ (2) *or* **island platform :** a platform at a railway station that has tracks on each side of it **e** (1) **:** SAFETY ISLAND (2) **:** SAFETY ZONE **f :** a superstructure on the deck of an aircraft (as the forecastle, bridge, or poop) on the deck of an aircraft carrier or other ship **3 :** a group or area isolated from its environment by specific characteristics or conditions: as **a :** an isolated ethnological group ⟨the Hungarian colony . . . is a picturesque racial ~ —*Amer. Guide Series: Mich.*⟩ ⟨there are many cultural ~s in the United States —David Riesman⟩ **b :** SPEECH ISLAND

**²island** \"\ *vt* -ED/-ING/-s **1 :** to make into or as if into an island ⟨a clear brown stream . . . ~*ing* a purple and white rock with an amber pool —John Ruskin⟩ **2 :** to dot with or as if with islands ⟨a fair expanse of level pasture ~*ed* with groves —William Wordsworth⟩ ⟨groups of people ~*ed* upon the dark grass —F.D.Ommanney⟩ **3 :** to place on or as if on an island **:** ISOLATE ⟨the great mystery in whose midst we are ~*ed* —Arthur Symons⟩

**island arc** *n* **:** an arcuate chain of islands

**island carib** *n, usu cap I&C* **1 :** an Indian of the Lesser Antilles **2 :** the Arawakan language of the Island Caribs and their modern descendants in British Honduras, Guatemala, and Honduras

**island chain** *n* **:** a line of islands

**island continent** *n* **:** an island as large or nearly as large as a continent ⟨the *island continent* of Greenland⟩

**is·land·er** \'īləndə(r)\ *n* -s **:** a native or inhabitant of an island

**island-hop** \'==,=\ *vi* **:** to go from island to island ⟨our *island-hopping,* creek-exploring houseboat life —A.W.Baum⟩; *esp* **:** to seize island after island in a military offensive ⟨instead of *island-hopping,* he suggested that we should employ . . . massive strokes —Joseph Driscoll⟩

**is·land·ish** \'īlәndish\ *adj* **:** of, relating to, or having the characteristics of an island

**is·land·less** \-n(d)ləs\ *adj* **:** having no islands **:** lacking islands ⟨a stretch of ~ ocean fully 500 miles across —F.C.Lincoln⟩

**is·land·man** \-n(d)mən\ *n, pl* **islandmen** *now chiefly Irish* **:** ISLANDER ⟨comparing them with the *islandmen* who walked up and down as cool and fresh-looking as the sea gulls —J.M. Synge⟩

**island of langerhans** *usu cap L* [after Paul *Langerhans* †1888 — more at ISLET OF LANGERHANS] **:** ISLET OF LANGERHANS

**island of reil** \-'rī(ə)l\ *usu cap R* [after Johann C. *Reil* †1813 Ger. physician born in Holland] **:** the central lobe of the cerebral hemisphere that is situated deeply between the lips of the lateral fissure

**island of resistance :** a strongpoint in a defensive position that is organized for perimeter military defense and normally is capable of mutual support with other similar positions

**is·land·ol·o·gy** \,īlən'däləjē\ *n* -ES **:** a study of islands

**island universe** *n* **:** a galaxy other than the Milky Way system but not necessarily smaller or less important

**is·lay** \(')iz'lī\ *n* -s [AmerSp] **:** a California wild plum (*Prunus ilicifolia*)

**¹isle** \'īl, *esp before pause or consonant* 'īəl\ *n* -s [ME *isle, ile,* fr. OF, fr. L *insula,* perh. fr. *in* + *-sula* (akin to L *salum* sea, *sal* salt) — more at IN, SALT] **:** ISLAND; *esp* **:** a small island ⟨Australian seas are rich in ~s —C.L.Barrett⟩ ⟨this 54-acre ~ is an exclusive residential district —*Amer. Guide Series: Minn.*⟩

**²isle** \"\ *vt* -ED/-ING/-s **1 :** to make an isle of **2 :** to place on or as if on an isle ⟨the faun is *isled* within the spotted wood —Randall Jarrell⟩

**isle·less** \'ī(ə)lləs\ *adj* **:** having no islands

**isle·man** \'ī(ə)lmən\ *n, pl* **islemen :** ISLANDER

**isle of wight disease** \-'wīt-\ *usu cap I&W* [*Isle of Wight,* island in the English channel constituting a county of England] **:** a serious European disease of adult honeybees caused by a minute mite (*Acarapis woodi*)

**isles·man** \'ī(ə)lzmən\ *n, pl* **islesmen** [*isles* (pl. of ¹isle) + *man*] **:** a native or inhabitant of a group of islands (as the Hebrides or Shetland isles)

**is·let** \'īlət, *usu* -əd·+V\ *n* -s [MF *islette,* fr. *isle* + *-ette*] **1 :** a small island **:** ISLE **2 :** something resembling a small island esp. in its isolation or elevation: **a :** ISLAND 2a **b** *chiefly Brit* **:** ISLAND 2c **c :** a small isolated mass of one type of tissue within a different type; *specif* **:** ISLET OF LANGERHANS

**is·le·ta** \iz'lād·ə\ *n, pl* **isleta** *or* **isletas** *usu cap* [*Isleta,* Indian village and pueblo in central New Mexico occupied by the Isleta people, fr. Sp *isleta* islet, dim. of *isla* island, fr. L *insula*] **1 a :** a Tanoan people of New Mexico **b :** a member of such people **2 :** the language of the Isleta people — compare TIWA

**is·let·ed** \'īləd·əd\ *adj* **:** set like an islet or furnished with islets

**islet of lang·er·hans** \-'läŋə(r),hän(t)s, -hänz\ *usu cap L* [after Paul *Langerhans* †1888 Ger. physician] **:** any of the groups of small slightly granular endocrine cells that form anastomosing trabeculae among the tubules and alveoli of the pancreas and secrete the hormone insulin

**is·lot** \'īlət\ *n* -s [F *îlot,* fr. MF *islot,* dim. of *isle*] *archaic* **:** ISLET

**ism** \'izəm\ *n* -s [*-ism*] **:** a distinctive doctrine, cause, system, or theory — often used disparagingly ⟨against any ~ that isn't Americanism —J.F.O'Neill⟩ ⟨futurism and cubism and all the other ~s —J.L.Lowes⟩

**-ism** \,izəm\ *n suffix* -s [ME *-isme,* fr. MF & L; MF *-isme,* partly fr. L *-isma* (fr. Gk), & partly fr. L *-ismus,* fr. Gk *-ismos*] **1 a :** act, practice, or process — esp. in nouns corresponding to verbs in *-ize* ⟨critic*ism*⟩ ⟨hypnot*ism*⟩ ⟨plagiar*ism*⟩ **b :** manner of action or behavior characteristic of a (specified) person or thing ⟨animal*ism*⟩ ⟨Micawber*ism*⟩ **2 a :** state, condition, or property ⟨barbarian*ism*⟩ ⟨polymorph*ism*⟩ **b :** abnormal state or condition resulting from excess of a (specified) thing ⟨alcohol*ism*⟩ ⟨morphin*ism*⟩ **c :** abnormal state or condition characterized by resemblance to a (specified) person or thing ⟨mongol*ism*⟩ **3 a :** doctrine, theory, or cult ⟨Buddh*ism*⟩ ⟨Calvin*ism*⟩ ⟨Platon*ism*⟩ ⟨salvation*ism*⟩ ⟨vegetarian*ism*⟩ **b :** adherence to a system or a class of principles ⟨neutral*ism*⟩ ⟨real*ism*⟩ ⟨social*ism*⟩ ⟨stoic*ism*⟩ **4 :** characteristic or peculiar feature or trait ⟨colloquial*ism*⟩ ⟨latin*ism*⟩ ⟨poetic*ism*⟩

**is·ma·el·ism** \'izmēə,lizəm, -z(,)mā,-\ *n* -s *usu cap* [*Ismael* (DV), *Ishmael* (AV), son of Abraham by his concubine Hagar + E *-ism;* so called fr. a belief that the Arabs are descendants of Ishmael] **:** ISLAMISM

**is·ma·ili** *or* **is·ma'·i·li** \,izmä'ē(,)lē, ,ism-, -mə'ē-\ *also* **is·ma·ili·an** \-lēən\ *n* -s *usu cap* [*Ismaili, Isma'ili* fr. Ar *Isma'īlīy,* fr. *Isma'īl* †A.D.760 son of the sixth imam Jafar al-Sadiq and in the opinion of the Ismailis his true successor; *Ismailian* fr. Ar *Isma'īlīy* + E *-an*] **:** one of a Shi'a sect composed of those who recognize the Aga Khan as imam

**is·ma·ilism** \-'ē,lizəm\ *n* -s *usu cap* [*Isma'īl* †A.D.760 + E *-ism*] **:** the Ismaili movement or its doctrines

**is·ma·ilite** \-'ē,līt\ *n* -s *usu cap* [*Isma'īl* †A.D.760 + E *-ite*] **:** ISMAILI

**is·ma·ilit·ic** \ˌizmēə'lid·ik\ *adj, usu cap* **:** of or relating to the Ismailis

**is·me·ne** \iz'mē(,)nē\ *n* [NL, fr. L *Ismene,* daughter of Oedipus, fr. Gk *Ismēnē*] **1** *cap, in some classifications* **:** a genus of So. American bulbous perennial herbs that have incurved filaments projecting beyond the margin of the floral cup and are usu. included in the genus *Hemerocallis* **2** -s **:** PERUVIAN DAFFODIL

**is·nad** \i'snäd, iz'n-\ *n* -s [Ar *isnād*] **:** the chain of authorities attesting to the historical authenticity of a particular hadith

**is·neg** \'iz,neg, ˌ='=\ *n, pl* **isneg** *or* **isnegs** *usu cap* [Apayao] **:** APAYAO

**is·ness** \'iznəs\ *n* -ES [¹*is* + *-ness*] **1 :** the fact that a thing is ⟨at the very outset there is no ~ to life —*Yale Rev.*⟩ **b :** the quality or state of elemental or factual existence **2 :** the state of things as they are ⟨the economics of the soldier who accepts a rough equation between ~ and oughtness —H.J.Laski⟩ — contrasted with *oughtness*

**is·n't** \'izᵊn(t), *in rapid speech* 'id|\ [by contr.] **:** is not

**iso** \'ī(,)sō\ *adj* [*is-*] **:** ISOMERIC; *esp* **:** having a branched chain ⟨~ acids with branching methyl groups⟩ — compare IS- 2

**iso-** *in pronunciations below,* ˌ=(,)= = ˌī(,)sō *also* ˌī(,)zō, ˌ== = ˌīsō, ˌīsə *also* ˌīzō, ˌīzə\ — see IS-

**iso·abnormal** *var of* ISABNORMAL

**iso·agglutination** \"+\ *n* [ISV *is-* + *agglutination*] **:** agglutination of an agglutinogen of one individual by the serum of another of the same species — **iso·agglutinative** \"+\ *adj*

**iso·agglutinin** \"+\ *n* [ISV *is-* + *agglutinin*] **:** an agglutinin specific for the cells of another individual of the same species

**iso·agglutinogen** \"+\ *n* [*isoagglutinin* + *-o-* + *-gen*] **:** a substance capable of provoking formation of or reacting with an isoagglutinin

**iso·allele** \"+\ *n* **:** a member of a pair of alleles each of which produces such a like result as to be indistinguishable by ordinary means

**iso·alloxazine** \"+\ *n* **:** a yellow solid $C_{10}H_6N_4O_2$ that differs from alloxazine only in the position of one hydrogen atom attached to nitrogen and that is the parent compound of riboflavin and other flavins

**iso·amyl** \"+\ *n* [ISV *is-* + *amyl*] **1 :** ISOPENTYL **2 :** AMYL 2a

**isoamyl acetate** *n* **:** the acetic ester $CH_3COOC_5H_{11}$ of amyl alcohol from fusel oil — called also *amyl acetate, banana oil, pear oil;* not used systematically

**isoamyl alcohol** *n* **1 :** ISOPENTYL ALCOHOL **2 :** AMYL ALCOHOL 2a

**iso·amylene** \ˌ=(,)= *at* ISO-+\ *n* [ISV *is-* + *amylene*] **:** a branched-chain amylene; *esp* **:** AMYLENE a

**isoamyl nitrite** *n* **:** AMYL NITRITE

**isoamyl salicylate** *n* **:** AMYL SALICYLATE

**iso·antibody** \ˌ=(,)= *at* ISO- +\ *n* **:** an antibody against an antigen sometimes present in members of a species that is produced by a member of the species lacking that antigen when exposed to it ⟨production of an anti-Rh ~ by an Rh-negative person⟩ — compare RH FACTOR

**iso·antigen** \"+\ *n* [ISV *is-* + *antigen*] **:** an antigen capable of inducing the production of an isoantibody; *specif* **:** any of several closely similar antigens only one of which may occur in an individual and each of which is capable of inducing the formation of antibodies to any other antigen of its group — **iso·antigenic** \"+\ *adj*

**iso·bar** \'== *at* ISO- + ,bär\ *n* [ISV *is-* + *-bar* (fr. Gk *baros* weight) — more at GRIEVE] **1 :** an imaginary line or a line on a map or chart connecting or marking places on the surface of the earth where the height of the barometer reduced to sea level is the same either at a given time or for a certain period **2 a** *also* **iso·bare** \-,ba(a)(ə)r\ **:** one of two or more atoms having practically the same atomic weights but different atomic numbers and hence different chemical properties ⟨carbon 14 and ordinary nitrogen 14 are ~s⟩ **b :** one of two or more nuclides having the same mass numbers but different atomic numbers — **iso·bar·ism** \-,bä,rizəm, -,ba(a)r,-\ *n* -s

**iso·barbaloin** \ˌ=(,)= *at* ISO- +\ *n* **:** a crystalline compound $C_{20}H_{18}O_9$ isomeric with barbaloin and isolated with it from aloin

**iso·bar·ic** \ˌ== *at* ISO- + ˌbarik\ *adj* [ISV *isobar* + *-ic*] **1 :** showing equal pressure: as **a :** showing points in the atmosphere having equal barometric pressure ⟨~ lines⟩ **b :** taking place without change of pressure ⟨~ expansion⟩ ⟨~ process⟩ **2 :** of, relating to, or having the relationship of an isobar

**iso·barometric** \ˌ=(,)=+\ *adj* [ISV *is-* + *barometric*] **:** ISOBARIC

**iso·base** \'==,bās\ *n* [ISV *is-* + *base*] **:** an imaginary line or a line on a map or chart passing through all points that have been elevated to the same extent since some specified time (as the Glacial epoch)

**¹iso·bath** \-,bath\ *n* [ISV *is-* + *-bath* (fr. Gk *bathos* depth); akin to Gk *bathys* deep — more at BATHY-] **1 :** an imaginary line or a line on a map or chart that connects all points having the same depth below a water surface (as of an ocean, sea, or lake) **2 :** a line similar to an isobath indicating depth below the earth's surface of an aquifer or other geological horizon

**²isobath** \"\ *or* **iso·bath·ic** \ˌ==ˈbathik\ *adj* [*isobath* ISV *is-* + *-bath* (fr. Gk *bathos* depth); *isobathic* fr. ¹*isobath* + *-ic*] **:** having constant depth

**iso·bathy·therm** \,=='bathə,thərm\ *n* [*is-* + *bathy-* + *-therm*] **:** a line connecting points on the earth's surface where a certain temperature is found at the same depth — **iso·bathy·ther·mal** \ˌ==ˌ==ˈthərməl\ — **iso·bathy·ther·mic** \-mik\ *adj*

**iso·bilateral** \ˌ=(,)= *at* ISO- +\ *adj* **:** bilateral with the corresponding opposite parts alike

**iso·borneol** \ˌ==+\ *n* [ISV *is-* + *borneol*] **:** a volatile crystalline alcohol $C_{10}H_{17}OH$ stereoisomeric with borneol, synthetically obtainable from alpha-pinene or camphene, and yielding camphor on oxidation

**iso·bornyl** \"+\ *n* [ISV *is-* + *bornyl*] **:** the univalent radical $C_{10}H_{17}$ derived from isoborneol

**iso·bront** \'==,bränt\ *also* **iso·bron·ton** \-äntən, ,=='==, ,=='brän,tän\ *n* [*isobront* ISV *is-* + *-bront* (fr. Gk *brontē* thunder); *isobronton* fr. *is-* + *-bronton* (fr. Gk *brontē* thunder) — more at BRONT-] **:** a line on a chart marking the simultaneous development of a thunderstorm at different points on the earth's surface

**iso·bryales** \ˌ==+\ *n pl, cap* [NL, fr. *is-* + *Bryales*] **:** a large widely distributed order of Musci comprising mosses that have branched creeping gametophores on which the leaves are so twisted as to appear to be in two rows and usu. pleurocarpous sporophytes with erect capsule and double peristome

**iso·butane** \"+\ *n* [ISV *is-* + *butane*] **:** a gaseous branched-chain hydrocarbon $(CH_3)_3CH$ usu. accompanying normal butane and used chiefly as an alkylating agent and as a fuel gas; 2-methyl-propane

**iso·butene** \"+\ *n* [*is-* + *butene*] **:** ISOBUTYLENE — not used systematically

**iso·butyl** \"+\ *n* [ISV *is-* + *butyl*] **:** the primary alkyl radical $(CH_3)_2CHCH_2-$ derived from isobutane

**isobutyl alcohol** *n* **:** the branched-chain primary butyl alcohol $(CH_3)_2CH_2CH_2OH$ synthetically made usu. from carbon monoxide and hydrogen; 2-methyl-1-propanol

**iso·bu·tyl·carbinol** \ˌ==ˌ==+\ *n* [*isobutyl* + *carbinol*] **:** ISOPENTYL ALCOHOL

**iso·butylene** \ˌ== *at* ISO- +\ *n* [ISV *is-* + *butylene*] **:** the branched-chain gaseous butylene $(CH_3)_2C{=}CH_2$ obtainable from isobutane by dehydrogenation and used chiefly in making butyl rubber and gasoline components and in alkylating aromatic hydrocarbons — called also *2-methylpropene*

**isobutyr-** *or* **isobutyro-** *comb form* [ISV, fr. *isobutyric* (in *isobutyric acid*)] **:** ISOBUTYRIC **:** related to isobutyric acid ⟨*isobutyr*amide⟩ ⟨*isobutyro*nitrile⟩

**iso·butyrate** \ˌ== *at* ISO- + *n* -s [*isobutyr-* + *-ate*] **:** a salt or ester of isobutyric acid

**iso·butyric acid** \"+ . . . -\ *n* [*isobutyric* ISV *is-* + *butyric*] **:** a colorless liquid acid $(CH_3)_2CHCOOH$ made by the oxidation of isobutyl alcohol and used chiefly in making esters for use as flavoring materials

**iso·butyryl** \"+\ *n* [ISV *isobutyr-* + *-yl*] **:** the radical $(CH_3)_2CHCO-$ of isobutyric acid

**iso·caloric** \"+\ *adj* **:** having similar caloric value ⟨~ diets⟩ — **iso·calorically** \"+\ *adv*

**iso·candle diagram** \'==+, . . . -\ *n* [*isocandle* fr. *is-* + *candle*] **:** a system of isocandle lines for various candlepowers of a source of light

**isocandle line** *n* **:** a line showing in suitable coordinates all directions in space in which a given source of light has a specified candlepower

**iso·car·pic** \ˌ=='kärpik\ *also* **iso·car·pous** \-pəs\ *adj* [*isocarpic* fr. *is-* + *-carpic* (fr. ¹*carp-* + *-ic*); *isocarpous* fr. *is-* + *-carpous*] **:** having carpels equaling the perianth divisions in number — compare ANISOCARPIC

**iso·cellular** \ˌ==+\ *adj* **:** consisting of similar cells

**iso·center** \'==+,-\ *n* [*is-* + *center*] **:** the point on an aerial photograph intersected by the bisector of the angle between the plumb line and the perpendicular to the photograph

**iso·ce·phal·ic** \ˌ=(,)=sə'falik\ *also* **iso·ceph·a·lous** \ˌ=='sefələs\ *adj* [*is-* + *-cephalic* or *-cephalous*] **:** having the heads of the figures in a composition brought to the same level — used esp. of a bas-relief — **iso·ceph·a·ly** \ˌ=='sefəlē\ *n* -ES

**iso·ce·rau·nic** \ˌ=(,)=sə'rȯnik\ *or* **iso·ke·rau·nic** \-kə'-\ *adj* [*isoceraunic* fr. *is-* + *ceraun-* + *-ic; isokeraunic* fr. *is-* + *keraun-* (fr. Gk *keraunos* thunderbolt) + *-ic* — more at CERAUN-] **:** showing or having equal frequency or severity or simultaneous occurrence of thunderstorms ⟨~ maps⟩

**iso·cer·cal** \¦=‚=¦sərkəl\ *adj* [*is-* + *-cercal*] **1 :** having symmetrical upper and lower lobes and a gradually tapering vertebral column — used of the tail fin of a fish **2 :** having or relating to an isocercal tail fin — **iso·cer·cy** \'=‚=‚sərsē, -rkē\ *n* -ES

**iso·cheim** \'== *at* ISO- +‚kīm\ *n* -S [prob. modif. (influenced by Gk *cheimōn* winter) of F *isochimène*, fr. *is-* + *-chimène* (fr. Gk *cheimainein* to be stormy, be winter); akin to Gk *cheimōn* winter — more at HIBERNATE] **:** a line joining points on the earth's surface having the same mean winter temperature — compare ISOTHERE

**iso·chela** \¦==+\ *n* [NL, fr. *is-* + *chela*] **:** a chelate spicule having both ends alike

**iso·chor** \'==‚kō(ə)r\ *also* **iso·chore** \-‚kō(ə)r\ *n* -S [ISV *is-* + *-chor* (fr. Gk *chōros* place, clear space) — more at CHOR-] **:** a line representing the variation of pressure with temperature when the volume of the substance operated on is constant — **iso·chor·ic** \¦==¦kȯrik, -¦kōr-\ *adj*

**iso·chro·mat** \¦==krō¦mat, ‚==krō‚m-\ *n* -S [*is-* + *-chromat* (fr. Gk *chrōmat-*, *chrōma* color) — more at CHROMATIC] **:** a graph showing intensity as a function of voltage for a given wavelength of the output from an X-ray source

**iso·chromatic** \¦==+\ *adj* [ISV *is-* + *chromatic*] **1 a :** of or corresponding to constant color ⟨the ~ variation of refractive index with density for a given wavelength⟩ **b :** connecting points of the same color **c :** coincident with a line of equal stress in a photoelastic stress pattern **2 :** ORTHOCHROMATIC **3** *of cells or tissues* **:** having the same color; *specif* **:** staining similarly with like dyes

**iso·chromosome** \¦==+\ *n* **:** a chromosome with identical arms believed to be derived from a telocentric chromosome by fusion of two daughter chromosomes

**isoch·ro·nal** \(')ī¦säkrən^əl\ *adj* [Gk *isochronos* isochronous + E *-al*] **1 :** uniform in time **:** having equal duration **:** recurring at regular intervals **:** ISOCHRONOUS **2** [*isochrone* + *-al*] **:** ISOCHRONIC

**iso·chrone** \'== *at* ISO- +‚krōn\ *n* -S [ISV *is-* + *-chrone* (fr. Gk *chronos* time)] **:** a line on a map or chart connecting points at which an event occurs simultaneously or which represent the same time or time difference (as a line showing the distances that may be reached from a central point in a city in the same length of time)

**iso·chron·ic** \¦==¦kränik, -rōn-\ *adj* [*isochrone* + *-ic*] **1 :** having isochrones ⟨~ map⟩ **2** [ISV *isochron-* (fr. Gk *isochronos* isochronous) + *-ic*] **:** exhibiting isochronism ⟨a muscle and its nerve must be ~ —Alexis Carrel⟩

**isochro·nism** \ī'säkrə‚nizəm; ‚īsə'krō‚n- *also* ‚īzə'krō‚n-\ *n* -S [F *isochronisme*, fr. Gk *isochronos* isochronous + F *-isme* -ism] **1 a :** the condition or property of having a uniform period of vibration — used of a pendulum or a watch balance **b :** uniformity of rate of operation — used of a timepiece **2 a :** equal duration of units or measures in prosody **b :** emphasis on stable rhythmic units in poetry **3** [*is-* + *chron-* + *-ism*] **:** the condition of having identical chronaxies — used of excitable structures (as motor neurones and muscle fibers)

**isoch·ro·nous** \(')ī¦säkrənəs\ *adj* [Gk *isochronos* isochronous (fr. *is-* + *chronos* time) + E *-ous*] **:** equal in duration, interval, or metrical length **:** ISOCHRONAL ⟨the oscillations of a spiral hairspring were ~ —S.F.Mason⟩ ⟨free oscillations of an elastic system were ~ —Adrien Jaquerod⟩ — **isoch·ro·nous·ly** *adv*

**isochronous governor** *n* **:** a governor that maintains the same speed in the mechanism controlled regardless of the load

**iso·citric acid** \¦== *at* ISO- + . . . -\ *n* **:** a crystalline acid HOOCCH(OH)CH(COOH)$CH_2$COOH isomeric with citric acid that is found esp. in the leaves of various air plants of the genus *Kalanchoe* and in blackberry juice and is recognized as an intermediate stage in the metabolism of fats and carbohydrates; 2-hydroxy-1,2,3-propane-tricarboxylic acid

**iso·cla·site** \‚īsō'klā‚sīt, ī'säklə-, -‚zīt\ *n* [G *isoklas* isoclasite (fr. *is-* + *-klas* -clase) + E *-ite*] **:** a mineral $Ca_2(PO_4)(OH)$.$2H_2O$ consisting of a basic hydrous calcium phosphate occurring in small white crystals or columnar forms

[1]**iso·cli·nal** \¦== *at* ISO- + ¦klīn^əl\ *adj* [ISV *is-* + *-clinal*] **:** relating to, having, or indicating equality of inclination or dip: as **a** *also* **isoclinic :** being or relating to an isocline **b :** being or relating to an isoclinic line — **iso·cli·nal·ly** \-^əlē\ *adv*

[2]**isoclinal** \"\ *n* -S **:** ISOCLINIC LINE

**isoclinal fold** *n* **:** an isocline or a fold so closely compressed that it approximates an isocline

**iso·cline** \'==‚klīn\ *n* -S [*is-* + *-cline*] **:** an anticline or syncline so closely folded that the rock beds of the two sides have the same dip

**iso·clin·ic line** \¦==¦klinik-\ *also* **isoclinic** *n* [*isoclinic* ISV *is-* + *-clinic*] **:** a line on a map or chart joining points on the earth's surface at which a dip needle has the same inclination to the plumb line — compare ACLINIC LINE

**iso·colon** \¦==+\ *n* [Gk *isokōlon*, fr. neut. of *isokōlos* of equal members, fr. *is-* + *kōlon* limb, member — more at CALK] **1 a :** period consisting of cola of equal length **2 :** the use of equal cola in immediate succession

**iso·con·tae** *syn of* ISOKONTAE

**iso·cortex** \¦== *at* ISO- + \ *n* [NL, fr. *is-* + L *cortex* bark — more at CORTEX] **:** NEOPALLIUM

**iso·corydine** \"+\ *n* **:** a crystalline alkaloid $C_{20}H_{23}NO_4$ isomeric with corydine and occurring with it

**iso·cra·cy** \ī'säkrəsē\ *n* -ES [Gk *isokratia*, fr. *isokratēs* having equal power or equal rights (fr. *is-* + *kratos* strength, power) + *-ia* -y — more at HARD] **:** equality of power or rule; *esp* **:** a system of government in which all have equal political power

**iso·cryme** \'== *at* ISO + ‚krīm *or* -‚krim\ *n* -S [ISV *is-* + Gk *krymos* frost, icy cold — more at CRUST] **:** an imaginary line or a line on a map or chart connecting points having the same mean temperature for a specified coldest time of the year

**isocyan-** *or* **isocyano-** *comb form* [ISV, fr. *isocyanic* (in *isocyanic acid*)] **:** containing the univalent group —NC isomeric with cyanogen and present in isocyanides ⟨*isocyano*benzene $C_6H_5NC$⟩

**iso·cyanate** \¦== *at* ISO- + \ *n* -S [ISV *isocyan-* + *-ate*] **:** a compound containing the univalent radical —NCO consisting of an isocyano group united with oxygen **:** a salt or ester of isocyanic acid ⟨phenyl ~ $C_6H_5NCO$⟩

**iso·cyanic acid** \¦== + . . . -\ *n* [ISV *is-* + *cyanic acid*] **:** cyanic acid regarded as having the formula HNCO and usu. prepared (as by the reaction of phosgene with the salt of a primary amine) in the form of esters of which some are used in making polyurethans and other resins, plastics, foams, and adhesives

**iso·cyanide** \"+\ *n* [*is-* + *cyanide*] **:** any of a class of compounds that are isomeric with the normal cyanides, that have the structure RNC, and that are in general colorless volatile poisonous liquids of strong offensive odor ⟨phenyl ~ $C_6H_5$-NC⟩ — called also *carbylamine*

**iso·cyanine** \"+\ *n* [ISV *is-* + *cyanine*] **:** any of several simple cyanine dyes in whose structure the carbon atom joining the two quinoline or other heterocyclic rings is attached at different positions in the two rings

**iso·cyano** \"+\ *adj* [*isocyan-*] **:** relating to or containing the group —NC isomeric with cyanogen — used esp. of organic compounds

**iso·cyclic** \"+\ *adj* [ISV *is-* + *cyclic*] **:** relating to, characterized by, or being a ring composed of atoms of only one element; *esp* **:** CARBOCYCLIC — distinguished from *heterocyclic*

**iso·diametric** \"+\ *adj* [ISV *is-* + *diametric*] **1 a :** having equal diameters **b :** having dimensions that are equal in all directions ⟨~ parenchyma cells⟩ **2 :** having lateral axes that are equal ⟨~ crystals⟩

**iso·di·a·phere** \¦==¦dīə‚fi(ə)r\ *n* -S [*is-* + *-diaphere* (fr. Gk *diapherein* to differ, carry across, fr. *dia-* + *pherein* to carry) — more at BEAR] **:** a nuclear species that has the same isotopic number as one or more other nuclear species

**iso·dimorphism** \¦== *at* ISO- + \ *n* [ISV *is-* + *dimorphism*] **:** isomorphism between the two forms of two dimorphous substances (as iron sulfide and cobalt arsenide) in such a way that each form of one is isomorphous with a form of the other — **iso·dimorphous** \"+\ *adj*

**iso·dom·ic** \¦==¦dämik\ *or* **isod·o·mous** \(')ī¦sädəməs\ *adj* [*isodomon* + *-ic* or *-ous*] **:** of or relating to isodomon

**isod·o·mon** \ī'sädə‚män, -‚mən\ *or* **isod·o·mum** \-‚məm\ *n* -S [L & Gk; L *isodomum*, fr. Gk *isodomon*, neut. of *isodomos* of equal courses, fr. *is-* + *domos* course of masonry, house — more at TIMBER] **:** masonry having blocks of equal length and thickness laid in courses so that each vertical joint of a course comes over the middle of a block just below

**iso·dont** \'== *at* ISO- +‚dänt\ *also* **iso·don·tous** \¦==¦däntəs\ *adj* [*isodont* ISV *is-* + *-odont*; *isodontous* prob. fr. F *isodonte* isodont + E *-ous*] **1 :** having the teeth all alike **2** *of a snake* **:** having the maxillary teeth of equal length

**iso·dose** \'==‚dōs\ *adj* [ISV *is-* + *dose*, n.] **:** of or relating to points or zones in a medium that receive equal doses of radiation ⟨an ~ chart⟩ ⟨the ~ rate lines are in units of roentgens per hour —G.M.Dunning⟩

**iso·drin** \'==‚drən\ *n* -S [*is-* + *-drin* (fr. *aldrin*)] **:** a crystalline insecticide $C_{12}H_8Cl_6$ that is a stereoisomer of aldrin and resembles aldrin in properties

**iso·durene** \¦==+\ *n* **:** a liquid aromatic hydrocarbon $C_6H_2(CH_3)_4$ isomeric with durene; 1,2,3,5-tetramethyl-benzene

**iso·dynamic** \¦=(‚)=+\ *adj* [ISV *is-* + *dynamic*] **:** of or relating to equality or uniformity of force

**isodynamic line** *n* **:** an imaginary line or a line on a map connecting points on the earth's surface at which the horizontal magnetic intensity is the same — called also *isogam*

**iso·electric** \"+\ *adj* [ISV *is-* + *electric*] **:** having or representing zero difference of electric potential

**isoelectric point** *n* **:** the point or narrow range on a pH scale at which the concentration of the anionic part of an ampholyte equals that of the cationic part **:** the pH at which the ampholyte will not migrate in an electrical field ⟨the *isoelectric points* of most proteins range from pH values of 4 to 7⟩

**iso·electronic** \"+\ *adj* [ISV *is-* + *electronic*] **1 :** having the same number of electrons ⟨the fluoride ion, the neon atom, and the sodium ion are ~⟩ — used of atoms or their ions **2 :** having the same number of valency electrons ⟨the carbon dioxide molecule and the cyanate ion are ~⟩ — used of molecules or radicals or ions composed of two or more atoms — **iso·electronically** \"+\ *adv*

**iso·eta·les** \‚=(‚)=ə'tā(‚)lēz\ *n pl, cap* [NL, fr. *Isoetes* + *-ales*] **:** an order of plants that is assigned to the class Lycopodineae or occas. to the class Filicineae, is known to have existed since the Cenozoic, and comprises *Isoetes* and possibly various extinct genera

**iso·etes** \ī'sōə‚tēz\ *n* [NL, fr. L, houseleek, fr. Gk, fr. neut. of *isoetēs* equal in years, fr. *is-* + *etos* year — more at WETHER] **1** *cap* **:** a large widely distributed genus (coextensive with the family Isoetaceae) of fern allies comprising the aquatic or marsh-growing quillworts that have a short buried lobed stem from which arises a tuft of quill-shaped leaves bearing sporangia in their axils — see ISOETALES **2** *pl* **isoetes :** any plant of the genus *Isoetes* **:** QUILLWORT 1

**iso·eugenol** \¦=(‚)= *at* ISO- + \ *n* [ISV *is-* + *eugenol*, prob. orig. formed in G] **:** an aromatic liquid phenol $CH_3CH$=C-$HC_6H_3(OCH_3)$OH found esp. in ilang-ilang oil and nutmeg oil, obtained also from eugenol by isomerization with alkali, and used chiefly in perfumes and in the synthesis of vanillin; 4-propenyl-guaiacol

**iso·flavone** \"+\ *n* [*is-* + *flavone*] **:** a colorless cyrstalline ketone $C_{15}H_{10}O_2$ that occurs as hydroxy derivatives in many plants often in the form of glycosides (as genistin, prunitrin)

**iso·flu·ro·phate** \‚=='flürə‚fāt\ *n* -S [by shortening] **:** DIISOPROPYL FLUOROPHOSPHATE

**iso·gam** \'==‚gam\ *n* -S [ISV *is-* + *-gam* (fr. *gamma*)] **:** ISODYNAMIC LINE

**iso·gamete** \¦==+\ *n* [ISV *is-* + *gamete*] **:** a gamete showing no differentiation in form or size or behavior from another gamete with which it is capable of uniting to form a zygote — compare HETEROGAMETE — **iso·gametic** \"+\ *adj*

**isog·amous** \(')ī¦sägəməs\ *also* **iso·gam·ic** \¦== *at* ISO- + ¦gamik\ *adj* [*isogamous* prob. fr. (assumed) NL *isogamus*, fr. NL *is-* + *-gamus* -gamous; *isogamic* prob. fr. *is-* + *-gamic*] **1** *of sexual reproduction* **:** characterized by fusion of like individuals or gametes — compare ANISOGAMOUS, HETEROGAMOUS, OOGAMOUS **2 :** having isogamous reproduction ⟨the ~ aquatic forms⟩

**isog·a·my** \ī'sägəmē\ *n* -ES [ISV *is-* + *-gamy*] **:** isogamous reproduction

**iso·gen** \'== *at* ISO- + jən, ‚jen\ *n* -S [back-formation fr. *isogenous*] **:** an isogenous structure

**iso·ge·ne·ic** \‚==jə'nēik\ *adj* [by alter. (influenced by *isogeneity*)] **:** ISOGENIC

**iso·ge·ne·ity** \‚==jə'nēəd·ē\ *n* -ES [*is-* + *-geneity* (irreg. — prob. influenced by *heterogeneity* — fr. *gene*)] **:** the quality or state of being isogenic

**iso·gen·er·a·tae** \‚=(‚)=‚jenə'rā‚tē, -rä-, -'\ *n pl, cap* [NL, fr. *is-* + L *generatae* (fem. pl. of *generatus*, past part. of *generare* to beget) — more at GENERATE] **:** a class of brown algae including those that have two alternating generations similar in vegetative structure and size — compare HETEROGENERATAE

**iso·genesis** \¦==+\ *n* [NL, fr. *is-* + L *genesis*] **:** similarity of origin or development

**iso·genic** \¦==¦jenik\ *adj* **:** having the same genic constitution: **a :** HOMOZYGOUS **b :** having all or certain specified genes the same — used of separate individuals

**isog·e·nism** \ī'säjə‚nizəm\ *n* -S [*is-* + *gene* + *-ism*] **:** ISOGENEITY

**iso·genotypic** \¦== *at* ISO- + \ *adj* [*is-* + *genotypic*] **:** based on a single genotype — used of two or more generic names

**isog·e·nous** \(')ī¦säjənəs\ *adj* [*is-* + *-genous*] **:** having the same origin

**iso·geotherm** \¦== *at* ISO- + \ *n* -S [ISV *is-* + *ge-* + *-therm*] **:** an imaginary line or curved surface beneath the earth's surface through points having the same mean temperature — called also *geoisotherm* — **iso·geothermal** \"+\ *adj* — **iso·geothermic** \"+\ *adj*

**iso·gloss** \'==‚gläs, -lȯs\ *n* -ES [ISV *is-* + *-gloss* (fr. Gk *glōssa* language, tongue) — more at GLOSS] **1 :** a boundary line between places or regions that differ in a particular linguistic feature ⟨the ~ separating Low German *maken* "to make" from High German *machen*⟩ ⟨dialect boundaries can be established only by means of ~*es* —Hans Kurath⟩ **2 :** a line on a map representing an isogloss — **iso·gloss·al** \¦==¦=əl\ *adj*

[1]**iso·gon·ic** \¦==+¦gänik\ *also* **isog·o·nal** \(')ī¦sägən^əl\ *adj* [ISV *is-* + *-gon* (fr. Gk *gōnia* angle) + *-ic* or *-al* — more at *-GON*] **:** of, relating to, or having equal angles

[2]**isogonic** \"\ *or* **isogonal** \"\ *n* -S **:** ISOGONIC LINE

[3]**isogonic** \"\ *adj* [*is-* + *gon-* + *-ic*] **:** of, relating to, or marked by isogonism or isogony

**isogonic line** *n* [[1]*isogonic*] **:** an imaginary line or a line on a map joining points on the earth's surface at which magnetic declination is the same — compare ACLINIC LINE, AGONIC LINE

**isog·o·nism** \ī'sägə‚nizəm\ *n* -S [*is-* + *gon-* + *-ism*] **:** the quality or state of having similar medusae or gonophores — used of hydroids of different genera

**isog·o·ny** \-‚nē\ *n* -ES [*is-* + *-gony*] **:** equivalent relative growth of parts in such a way that relative size differences remain constant — compare HETEROGONY

**iso·graft** \'== *at* ISO- +‚-\ *n* -S [*is-* + *graft*] **:** HOMOGRAFT

**iso·gram** \'==‚gram\ *n* -S [*is-* + *-gram*] **:** a line on a map or chart along which there is a constant value (as of temperature, pressure, or rainfall)

**iso·graph** \-‚graf, -räf\ *n* -S [*is-* + *-graph*] **1 :** an instrument consisting of two short straightedges connected by a large circular joint marked with angular degrees that combines the functions of a protractor and a set square **2 :** an electronic calculator for finding both real and imaginary roots of algebraic equations

**iso·griv** \-‚griv\ *n* -S [*is-* + *-griv* (fr. *grivation*)] **:** a line on a map or chart connecting points of equal grivation

**isog·y·nous** \(')ī¦säjənəs\ *adj* [ISV *is-* + *-gynous*] **:** ISOCARPIC

**iso·gyre** \¦== *at* ISO- + ‚-\ *n* [ISV *is-* + *gyre*] **:** the dark shadow in an interference figure representing the locus of all points that correspond to directions of transmission through the crystal plate in which the state of polarization of the incident rays is unchanged by passage through the plate

**iso·haline** \‚=='hā‚lēn, -'ha‚-, -‚līn\ *or* **iso·hal·sine** \-'hal‚sēn, -‚sīn\ *n* -S [*isohaline* ISV *is-* + *-haline* (fr. Gk *halinos* of salt, fr. *hal-*, *hals* salt + *-inos* -ine); *isohalsine* fr. *is-* + *-halsine* (irreg. fr. Gk *hal-*, *hals* salt) — more at SALT] **:** a line or surface drawn on a map or chart to indicate connecting points of equal salinity in the ocean

**iso·hel** \'==‚hel\ *n* -S [*is-* + *-hel* (fr. Gk *hēlios* sun) — more at SOLAR] **:** a line drawn on a map or chart connecting places of equal duration of sunshine

**iso·hemagglutination** \¦==+\ *n* [*is-* + *hemagglutination*] **:** isoagglutination of red blood cells

**iso·hemagglutinin** \"+\ *n* [*is-* + *hemagglutinin*] **:** a hemagglutinin causing isoagglutination

**iso·hemagglutinogen** \"+\ *n* -S [*isohemagglutinin* + *-o-* + *-gen*] **:** an antigen inducing the production of or reacting with specific isohemagglutinins

**iso·hemolysin** \"+\ *n* [ISV *is-* + *hemolysin*] **:** a hemolysin that causes isohemolysis

**iso·hemolysis** \"+\ *n* [NL, fr. *is-* + *hemolysis*] **:** the lysis of the red blood cells of one individual of a species by specific antibodies in the serum of another (as in human erythroblastosis fetalis)

**iso·hydric** \"+\ *adj* [ISV *is-* + *hydr-* + *-ic*] **:** relating to or being solutions of electrolytes having equal concentration of a common ion (as a hydrogen ion) not affecting one another's conductivity on being mixed

**iso·hyet** \¦==+¦hīət\ *also* **iso·hyetal** \¦==+\ *n* -S [*isohyet* ISV *is-* + *-hyet* (fr. Gk *hyetos* rain); *isohyetal* fr. *isohyetal*, adj. — more at HYET-] **:** an isohyetal line on a map or chart

**iso·hyetal** \¦==+\ *adj* [prob. fr. *isohyet* + *-al*] **:** relating to or indicating equal rainfall ⟨~ lines⟩

**iso·immunization** \¦==+\ *n* [ISV *is-* + *immunization*] **:** production by an individual of antibodies against constituents of the tissues of others of his own species (as when transfused with blood from one belonging to a different blood group)

**iso·ionic point** \¦==+...-\ *n* [*isoionic* ISV *is-* + *ionic*] **:** the hydrogen-ion concentration expressed usu. as the pH value at which the ionization of an amphoteric substance as an acid equals the ionization as a base and becomes identical with the isoelectric point in the absence of foreign inorganic ions

**isokeraunic** *var of* ISOCERAUNIC

**iso·kon·tae** \‚=='kän‚tē\ *n pl, cap* [NL, fr. *is-* + *-kontae* (fr. Gk *kontos* punting pole, fr. *kentein* to prick, goad); fr. the equal length of the flagella — more at CENTER] *in some classifications* **:** a class of green algae comprising forms without motile stages or with flagella of equal length and including most of those now usu. placed in Chlorophyceae — compare HETEROKONTAE

**iso·la·bil·i·ty** \‚īsələ'biləd·ē *also* ‚isə- *sometimes* ‚īzə-\ *n* -ES **:** the quality or state of being isolable

**iso·la·ble** \'==ləbəl\ *also* **iso·lat·able** \'==‚lād·əbəl, -ātə-, ‚=='===\ *adj* [*isolable* fr. [1]*isolate* + *-able*; *isolatable* fr. [1]*isolate* + *-able*] **:** capable of being isolated

**iso·lant** \'==‚lənt\ *n* -S [[1]*isolate* + *-ant*] **:** [3]ISOLATE 4, 5

[1]**iso·late** \'īsə‚lāt *also* 'isə- *sometimes* 'īzə-; *usu* -ād.+V\ *vb* -ED/-ING/-S [back-formation fr. *isolated*] *vt* **1 a** (1) **:** to set apart from others **:** cause to be detached from others and alone **:** place alone **:** make solitary ⟨a tiny village that had been *isolated* from civilization⟩ (2) **:** to cause to be stranded **:** cut off ⟨*isolated* what was left of the fleeing army⟩ **b :** to keep apart or away from others so as to minimize or wholly reduce any effect on others; *specif* **:** to separate (one with a contagious disease) from others not similarly infected ⟨kept very close track of all carriers and *isolated* them whenever they gave positive results —V.G.Heiser⟩ — compare QUARANTINE **c :** to single out **:** PINPOINT ⟨*isolating* the most important sense of a word⟩ **2 :** to separate (as a chemical compound) from all other substances **:** obtain pure or in a free state **3 :** INSULATE 2a ~ *vi* **:** to cause something to be isolated

[2]**iso·late** \-‚lāt, -‚lət, -lə\, *usu* \d·+V\ *adj* [prob. fr. [1]*isolate*, after such pairs as *appropriate*, v.: *appropriate*, adj.] **:** ISOLATED

[3]**isolate** \"\ *n* -S **1 :** an isolated factor, function, or process ⟨the smallest human ~ is a culture —J.K.Feibleman⟩ ⟨no one historical epoch and no one cultural ~ can present the permanent features of society —Georgiana Melvin⟩ **2 :** something singled out for observation **:** ABSTRACT 3 ⟨~*s* which could be described . . . as if they completely represented the physical world from which they had been extracted —Lewis Mumford⟩ **3 :** a chemical compound (as geraniol) separated from an essential oil for use in perfumes **4 a :** a spore, single organism, or viable part of an organism that has been isolated (as from diseased tissue, contaminated water, or the air); *often* **:** a pure culture produced from such an isolate **b :** an individual or strain isolated from a natural population (as for the study of a pathogenic fungus or bacterium) **5 :** a relatively homogeneous population separated from related populations by geographic or biologic or social factors or by the intervention of man — compare BIOTYPE, CLONE, ISOLATION 2 **6 :** an individual living in isolation from particular phases of an environment; *esp* **:** an individual socially withdrawn or removed from society through rejection of or incapacity for interpersonal relationships

**isolated** *adj* [F *isolé* isolated (fr. It *isolato*, fr. *isola* island — fr. L *insula* — + *-ato* -ate) + E *-ate* + *-ed* — more at ISLE] **1 a :** placed alone or apart **:** being alone **:** SOLITARY ⟨could not remain the ~ figure he had been —Sherwood Anderson⟩ **b :** caused to be alone or apart **:** cut off **:** STRANDED ⟨if attacked the ~ pawn can be defended —*New Complete Hoyle*⟩ **2 a :** occurring alone or once **:** UNIQUE ⟨some ~ incident not likely to recur —Dorothy Barclay⟩ **b :** SPORADIC ⟨the reader who has an ~ rather than overall interest —R.S.Browne⟩ ⟨~ instances of ill behavior —Eugene Burr⟩ **3 :** not bonded (as by cement) to an adjacent structure ⟨~ buildings⟩ ⟨an ~ pier⟩ **4 :** separated by more than one single bond in a system of at least two double bonds in a molecule **:** not conjugated ⟨~ double bonds⟩ — **iso·lat·ed·ly** \'==‚==, ‚=='===\ *adv*

**isolating** *adj* [fr. pres. part. of [1]*isolate*] **:** of, relating to, or being a language in which each word typically expresses a distinct idea and in which variations in parts of speech and syntactical relations are determined almost exclusively by the order in which words are joined and by the use of particles so that a sentence typically consists of a string of formally independent words ⟨an ~ language⟩ ⟨the ~ form of speech of the Sino-Tibetan languages⟩ — distinguished from *agglutinative* and *inflectional*; compare ANALYTIC 4

**isolating mechanism** *n* **:** something (as a geographical, ecological, physiological, anatomical, or psychological barrier) that limits interbreeding between groups and is thereby a major factor in the differentiation of biologic units (as races or species)

**iso·la·tion** \‚=='lāshən\ *n* -S [F, fr. *isoler* to isolate (fr. *isolé* isolated) + *-ation*] **1 :** the action of isolating or condition of being isolated **2 :** a segregation of a group of organisms from related forms in such a manner as to prevent crossing

**isolation booth** *n* **:** a small soundproof booth used (as in a television studio) as a small studio within a larger studio

**iso·la·tion·ism** \-shə‚nizəm\ *n* -S **1 a :** a policy directed toward the isolation of a nation from other nations by a deliberate abstention from alliances and other international political and economic relations ⟨American foreign policy was set on a course of ~ —Dorothy B. Goebel⟩ ⟨a peculiarly hopeless kind of new Asian ~ —H.R.Isaacs⟩ **b :** a disposition or tendency to isolate deliberately an individual or group (as a political party) or a field of endeavor (as education or intellectual activity) from outside and esp. foreign relations or influences ⟨uncontrolled ~ would estrange the party from . . . the leaders of friendly cooperative non-Communist parties —H.A.Steiner⟩ ⟨ivory-tower cultural ~ —Leslie Rees⟩ **2 :** an attitude or conviction favoring adherence to a policy of deliberate isolation ⟨~ can never again dominate America —G.W.Chapman⟩ ⟨the hard core of ~ in the United States has been ethnic and emotional —Samuel Lubell⟩ — compare INTERNATIONALISM, INTERVENTIONISM

[1]**iso·la·tion·ist** \‚=='lāsh(ə)nəst\ *n* -S **:** one that advocates or believes in isolationism ⟨criticism . . . not from ~*s* but from internationalists —*Atlantic*⟩ ⟨anthropological ~*s*⟩

[2]**isolationist** \¦==(=)=¦\ *adj* **:** of, characterized by, or favoring isolationism ⟨the orthodox believe that much money can be saved, especially of what now goes to foreign aid, by a more ~ foreign policy —Walter Lippmann⟩ ⟨the country was in an overwhelmingly ~ mood —F.L.Allen⟩ ⟨culturally as well as politically ~ —Christian Gauss⟩

**iso·la·tive** \'==‚lād·iv, -ātil, |ēv *also* |əv\ *adj* **1** *of a sound change* **:** occurring in isolation **:** not dependent on phonetic environment ⟨OE \stāān\ *stān* became by ~ change Modern English \stōn*stone*⟩ — compare COMBINATIVE **2 :** ISOLATING

**iso·la·tor** \-ād·ə(r), -ātə-\ *n* -s **:** one that isolates; *specif* **:** a device that absorbs or prevents the transmission of noise or vibration (as of machinery)

**iso·lecithal** \¦ī(,)sō *at* ISO-+\ *adj* [ISV *is-* + *lecithal*] **:** HOMOLECITHAL

**iso·lette** \,īsə¦let *also* ¦is-\ *n* -s [fr. *Isolette*, a trademark] **:** an incubator for premature infants that is designed to provide controlled temperature, humidity, and oxygen supply and to permit feeding and care under aseptic conditions with a minimum of handling

**iso·leucine** \¦ī(,)sō *at* ISO-+\ *n* [ISV *is-* + *leucine*] **:** a crystalline amino acid $C_2H_5CH(CH_3)CH(NH_2)COOH$ that is isomeric with leucine, that occurs in its dextrorotatory L-form in most dietary proteins but is usu. obtained from the waste from the recovery of sugar from beet molasses, and that like leucine is essential in the nutrition of animals and man; α-amino-β-methyl-valeric acid

**iso·line** \ˈīsə+,līn\ *n* [*is-* + *line*] **:** ISOGRAM

**isol·o·gous** \(ˈ)ī¦säləgəs\ *adj* [ISV *is-* + *-logous* (as in *homologous*)] **:** relating to or being any of two or more closely related chemical compounds in a series whose successive members possess a regular difference in composition other than a difference of one carbon and two hydrogen atoms — sometimes distinguished from *homologous*

**iso·logue** *or* **iso·log** \ˈīsə *at* ISO-+,lȯg *also* ,läg\ *n* -s [ISV, fr. *isologous*, after such pairs as E *analogous: analogue*] **:** a compound, such as isologous with one or more other compounds

**¹iso·lo·ma** \,īsə'lōmə\ [NL, fr. *is-* + Gk *lōma* fringe; akin to Gk *eilein* to wind, roll — more at VOLUBLE] *syn of* KOHLERIA

**²isoloma** \"\ *n* -s [NL *Isoloma*] **:** a plant of the genus *Kohleria*

**iso·lux** \ˈīsə *at* ISO-+,ləks\ *n* -ES [*is-* + L *lux* light — more at LIGHT] **:** ISOPHOTE

**¹iso·magnetic** \¦ī(,)sō *at* ISO-+\ *adj* [ISV *is-* + *magnetic*] **:** of, relating to, or marked by points of equal magnetic intensity or points of equal value of a component of such intensity ⟨an ~ chart⟩

**²isomagnetic** \"\ *n* **:** a line on a map or chart of the earth's surface connecting points of equal magnetic intensity or points of equal value of a component of such intensity

**iso·maltose** \¦īsō+\ *n* [ISV *is-* + *maltose*] **:** a syrupy disaccharide $C_{12}H_{22}O_{11}$ isomeric with maltose, present in hydrol (sense 3), and obtainable also from dextran by acid hydrolysis, from glucose by reaction with acids, and from gentiobiose octaacetate by rearrangement

**iso·mer** \ˈīsə *at* ISO-+,mə(r)\ *n* -s [ISV, back-formation fr. *isomeric*; prob. orig. formed in G] **1 :** a compound, radical, or ion isomeric with one or more others **2 :** a nuclide isomeric with one or more others ⟨a metastable ~⟩ — called also *nuclear isomer*

**isom·er·ase** \īˈsäməˌrās, -āz\ *n* -s [ISV *isomer* + *-ase*] **:** any of various enzymes that catalyze isomerization (as of glucose phosphate to fructose phosphate) — compare MUTASE 2

**iso·mere** \ˈīsə *at* ISO-+,mi(ə)r\ *n* -s [*is-* + *-mere*] **:** a corresponding part or segment

**iso·mer·ic** \¦īsə¦merik\ *adj* [ISV *isomer-* (fr. Gk *isomerēs* equally divided, fr. *is-* + *meros* part, share) + *-ic* — more at MERIT] **:** of, relating to, or exhibiting isomerism ⟨butane and isobutane are ~ compounds⟩ ⟨the thiocyanate and isothiocyanate radicals are ~⟩ — **iso·mer·i·cal·ly** \-rək(ə)lē\ *adv*

**isom·er·ide** \īˈsäməˌrīd\ *n* -s [*isomeric* + *-ide*] **:** ISOMER 1

**isom·er·ism** \-,rizəm\ *n* -s [ISV *isomeric* + *-ism*] **1 :** the phenomenon exhibited by two or more chemical compounds, radicals, or ions of containing the same numbers of atoms of the same elements in the molecule, radical, or ion and hence having the same molecular formula but differing in the structural arrangement of the atoms and consequently in one or more properties ⟨the ~ of the butyl alcohols⟩ — compare GEOMETRIC ISOMERISM, OPTICAL ISOMERISM, POSITION ISOMERISM, STEREOISOMERISM, TAUTOMERISM **2 :** the phenomenon exhibited by two or more nuclides of having the same mass numbers and the same atomic numbers but of differing in energy state and rate of radioactive decay — called also *nuclear isomerism* **3** [prob. fr. *isomerous* + *-ism*] **:** the condition of having or being made up of corresponding parts or segments; *esp* **:** the condition (as of a plant having the members of each floral whorl equal in number) of having two or more comparable parts made up of identical numbers of similar segments

**isom·er·i·za·tion** \ī,säməˌrəˈzāshən, -,rīˈz-\ *n* -s [ISV *isomer* + *-ization*] **:** the process of isomerizing (as of the straight-chain hydrocarbon butane to the branched-chain hydrocarbon isobutane of higher octane number for gasoline)

**isom·er·ize** \īˈsäməˌrīz\ *vb* -ED/-ING/-S [ISV *isomer* + *-ize*] *vi* **:** to become changed into an isomeric form ~ *vt* **:** to cause to change into an isomeric form

**isom·er·ous** \(ˈ)ī¦säm(ə)rəs\ *adj* [ISV *is-* + *-merous*] **:** exhibiting isomerism — opposed to *heteromerous*

**isom·ery** \īˈsämərē\ *n* -ES [ISV *isomeric* + *-y*] **:** ISOMERISM 1

**¹iso·metric** \¦īsə *at* ISO-+\ *also* **iso·metrical** \"+\ *adj* [*is-* + *metr-* (fr. Gk *metron* measure) + *-ic* or *-ical* — more at MEASURE] **:** of, relating to, or characterized by equality of measure: as **a :** of, relating to, or having the form of an isometric drawing **b :** EQUIGRANULAR **c :** taking place at constant volume ⟨an ~ change of temperature and pressure⟩ **d** *of muscular contraction* **:** taking place against resistance, without significant shortening of muscle fibers, and with marked increase in muscle tone — compare ISOTONIC **e** *of a stanza or strophe* **:** having lines of equal measure — **iso·metrically** \"+\ *adv*

**²isometric** \"\ *n* -s **:** ISOMETRIC LINE

**isometric drawing** *n* **:** the representation of an object on a single plane (as a sheet of paper) with the object placed as in isometric projection but disregarding the foreshortening of the edges parallel to the three principal axes of the typical rectangular solid, lines parallel to these axes appearing in their true lengths and producing an appearance of distortion

**isometric line** *n* **1 :** a line (as a contour line) drawn on a map and indicating a true constant value throughout its extent **2 :** a line representing changes of pressure or temperature under conditions of constant volume

**isometric projection** *n* **:** an axonometric projection in which the three spatial axes of the object are represented as equally inclined to the drawing surface and equal distances along the axes are drawn equal

**isometric system** *n* **:** a crystal system characterized by three equal axes at right angles (as in the cube and regular octahedron) — see CRYSTAL SYSTEM illustration

cube as seen in isometric projection

**iso·me·tro·pia** \,ī(,)sō *at* ISO-+məˈtrōpēə\ *n* -s [NL, fr. Gk *isometros* of equal measure (fr. *is-* + *metron*) + NL *-opia*] **:** equality in refraction in the two eyes

**iso·morph** \ˈīsə,mȯrf\ *n* -s [ISV *is-* + *-morph*] **:** something identical with or similar to something else in form or shape or structure: as **a :** one of two or more substances related by isomorphism **b :** an individual or group exhibiting isomorphism **c :** a ciphertext pattern recurring with different constituent letters ⟨FXEXRF and PZMZTP are ~*s*⟩

**iso·mor·phic** \¦īsə¦mȯrfik\ *adj* [ISV *is-* + *-morphic*] **:** being of identical or similar form or shape or structure **:** exhibiting isomorphism; *esp* **:** having sporophytic and gametophytic generations alike in shape and size ⟨some algae and fungi are ~⟩ — compare HETEROMORPHIC

**iso·mor·phism** \¦īsə¦fizəm\ *n* -s [ISV *is-* + *-morphism*; prob. orig. formed as G *isomorphismus*] **1 :** the quality or state of being isomorphic: as **a :** similarity in organisms of different ancestry resulting from convergence **b** (1) **:** similarity of crystalline form and structure between substances of similar compositions (as between sulfates of barium $BaSO_4$ and of strontium $SrSO_4$) — sometimes used only of substances that are so closely similar that they can form a more or less continuous series of solid solutions; compare HETEROMORPHISM 2 (2) **:** HOMEOMORPHISM 1 **2 :** a hypothetical identity of psychological manifestation and brain process

**iso·mor·phous** \-fəs\ *adj* [ISV *is-* + *-morphous*] **:** ISOMORPHIC; *esp* **:** isostructural and capable of forming solid solutions together ⟨the ~ components forsterite and fayalite of olivine⟩ ⟨strontium sulfate is ~ with barium sulfate⟩ — used of minerals and other crystalline substances

**iso·mor·phy** \ˈīsə,fē\ *n* -ES [ISV *is-* + *-morphy*] **:** HOMOPLASY

**iso·myaria** \¦īsō+\ *n pl, cap* [NL, fr. *is-* + *-myaria*] *in some classifications* **:** a division of Lamellibranchia comprising bivalve mollusks having two adductor muscles of nearly equal size — compare HETEROMYARIA, MONOMYARIA — **iso·my·ar·i·an** \¦ī(,)sō¦mīˈarēən\ *adj*

**iso·neph** \ˈīsə,nef\ *n* -s [ISV *is-* + *-neph* (fr. Gk *nephos* cloud) — more at NEBULA] **:** a line on a map connecting points that have the same average percentage of cloudiness

**iso·ni·a·zid** \,īsəˈnīəzəd\ *n* -s [*isonicotinic acid hydrazide*] **:** a crystalline compound $C_5H_4NCONHNH_2$ used orally or intramuscularly in the treatment of tuberculosis often in conjunction with streptomycin or dihydrostreptomycin and para-aminosalicylic acid; isonicotinic acid hydrazide

**iso·nicotinic acid** \¦īsō+…-\ *n* [*isonicotinic* ISV *is-* + *nicotinic*] **:** a crystalline acid $C_5H_4NCOOH$ made usu. by oxidation of the corresponding picoline or ethyl-pyridine and used chiefly in making isoniazid; 4-pyridine-carboxylic acid

**iso·nic·o·ti·no·yl·hydrazine** \,īsō,nikə,tēnəwəl+\ *or* **iso·nicotinyl·hydrazine** \,īsō,nikə,tēnᵊl+\ *n* [*isonicotinoylhydrazine* fr. *isonicotin-* (fr. *isonicotinic acid*) + *-o-* + *-yl* + *hydrazine*; *isonicotinylhydrazine* fr. *isonicotin-* (fr. *isonicotinic acid*) + *-yl* + *hydrazine*] **:** ISONIAZID

**iso·nip·e·caine** \,īsəˈnipə,kān\ *n* -s [prob. fr. *isonipe-* (fr. *isonipecotic acid* isomer of nipecotic acid, fr. *is-* + *nipecotic acid*) + *-caine*] **:** meperidine or its hydrochloride

**iso·nitrile** \¦īsō+\ *n* [ISV *is-* + *nitrile*] **:** ISOCYANIDE

**iso·ni·tro** \¦īsə¦nī-(,)trō\ *adj* [*isonitro-*] **:** containing the acid bivalent group $=NO(OH)$

**isonitro-** *comb form* [*is-* + *nitr-*] **:** containing the acid bivalent group $=NO(OH)$ related to the nitro group ⟨*isonitro*ethane $CH_3CH{=}NO(OH)$⟩ — compare ACI-

**iso·ni·tro·so** \¦īsə,nī-¦trō(,)sō *also* ¦īzə-\ *adj* [*isonitroso-*] **:** containing the bivalent hydroxy-imino group $=NOH$

**isonitroso-** *comb form* [ISV *is-* + *nitroso-*] **:** containing the bivalent hydroxy-imino group $=NOH$ related to the nitroso group and characteristic of oximes ⟨*isonitroso*acetone $CH_3COCH{=}NOH$⟩

**ison·o·my** \īˈsänəmē\ *n* -ES [Gk *isonomia*, fr. *isonomos* characterized by equality before the law (fr. *is-* + *nomos* right, law) + *-ia* -y — more at NIMBLE] **:** equality before the law

**iso·nuclear** \¦īsō *at* ISO-+\ *adj* [*is-* + *nuclear*] **:** relating to or attached to the same nucleus or ring in the molecule of a chemical compound ⟨an ~ bromo-nitro-naphthalene⟩

**iso·octane** \¦īsō+\ *n* [ISV *is-* + *octane*] **:** an octane of branched-chain structure or a mixture of such octanes: as **a :** the flammable liquid hydrocarbon $(CH_3)_2CH(CH_2)_4CH_3$ in whose molecule there is branching only at one end of the chain; 2-methyl-heptane **b :** a flammable liquid hydrocarbon $(CH_3)_2CHCH_2C(CH_3)_3$ made usu. by hydrogenation of diisobutylene and used esp. as a standard in rating motor fuels by their octane number; 2,2,4-trimethyl-pentane — not used technically **c :** HYDROCODIMER — used chiefly commercially

**iso·oc·tyl alcohol** \¦īsō+…-\ *n* [*isooctyl* fr. *is-* + *octyl*] **:** an octyl alcohol of branched-chain structure or a mixture of such alcohols; *esp* **:** a mixture of isomeric primary alcohols $C_7H_{15}CH_2OH$ obtained by reaction of heptylenes with carbon monoxide and hydrogen and used esp. in synthesis (as of plasticizers) — not used scientifically

**iso·pach** \ˈīsə,pak\ *n* -s [*is-* + *-pach* (fr. Gk *pachys* thick) — more at PACHY-] **:** an isogram that connects points of equal thickness of a particular geological stratum formation or group of formations

**iso·pach·ous** \¦īsə¦pakəs, (ˈ)ī¦säpək-\ *adj* **:** of, relating to, or having an isopach ⟨~ contours⟩ ⟨an ~ map⟩

**iso·pag** \ˈīsə *at* ISO-+,pag\ *n* -s [*is-* + *-pag* (fr. Gk *pagos* frost; akin to Gk *pēgnynai* to fasten) — more at PACT] **:** an equiglacial line on a map or chart that connects the points where ice is present for approximately the same number of days in winter

**iso·paraffin** \¦īsō¦+\ *n* [*is-* + *paraffin*] **:** a paraffin hydrocarbon of branched-chain structure — **iso·paraffinic** \"+\ *adj*

**iso·pec·tic** \,īsəˈpektik\ *n* -s [*is-* + *pect-* (fr. Gk *pēktos* fixed, frozen, fr. *pēgnynai* to fasten) + *-ic*] **:** an equiglacial line on a map or chart connecting points where ice begins to form at the beginning of winter

**iso·pelletierine** \¦īsō+\ *n* [ISV *is-* + *pelletierine*] **:** a liquid alkaloid $C_8H_{15}NO$ from the root bark of pomegranate; 2-acetonyl-piperidine

**iso·pentane** \"+\ *n* [*is-* + *pentane*] **:** a volatile flammable liquid hydrocarbon $(CH_3)_2CHC_2H_5$ found in petroleum and used in gasoline and as a solvent

**iso·pentyl** \"+\ *n* [*is-* + *pentyl*] **:** the pentyl radical $(CH_3)_2CHCH_2CH_2-$ derived from isopentane; 3-methyl-butyl — called also *isoamyl*

**isopentyl alcohol** *n* **:** a primary pentyl alcohol $(CH_3)_2CHCH_2CH_2OH$ that has a disagreeable odor and pungent taste and is obtained from fusel oil; 3-methyl-1-butanol — called also *isoamyl alcohol, isobutylcarbinol*

**iso·perimetric** *also* **iso·perimetrical** \"+\ *adj* [Gk *isoperimetros* isoperimetric (fr. *is-* + *perimetros* perimeter) + E *-ic* or *-ical* — more at PERIMETER] **1 :** of, relating to, or having equal perimeters — used esp. of geometrical figures **2 :** having a constant scale — used of a line on a map

**iso·phen·al** \¦īsə¦fēnᵊl\ *adj* [*isophene* + *-al*] **:** of, relating to, or having an isophene

**iso·phene** \ˈīsə,fēn\ *also* **iso·phane** \-,fān\ *n* -s [*isophene* fr. *is-* + *-phene* (fr. Gk *phainein* to show); *isophane* ISV *is-* + *-phane* (fr. Gk *phainein* to show) — more at FANCY] **1 :** a line on a map or chart connecting places within a region at which a particular biological phenomenon (as the flowering of a given plant) occurs at one time **2 :** PHENOCONTOUR

**iso·phe·nous** \¦īsə¦fēnəs\ *adj* [*isophene* + *-ous*] **:** having the same phenotype

**iso·phone** \ˈīsə,fōn\ *n* [ISV *is-* + *-phone*] **1 :** a phonetic isogloss (sense 1) **2 :** a phonetic feature shared by some but not all of the speakers of a dialect, language, or group of related languages

**iso·pho·ria** \,īsəˈfōrēə\ *n* -s [NL, fr. *is-* + *-phoria*] **:** the quality or state of having the visual axes of the two eyes in the same horizontal plane

**iso·phorone** \¦īsō+\ *n* [ISV *is-* + *phorone*] **:** a high-boiling liquid ketone $C_9H_{14}O$ made by condensation of acetone and used as a solvent; 3,5,5-trimethyl-2-cyclohexen-one

**iso·phote** \ˈīsə,fōt\ *also* **iso·phot** \-,fät\ *n* -s [ISV *is-* + *-phote, -phot* (fr. Gk *phōt-, phōs* light) — more at FANCY] **:** a line or surface on a chart forming the locus of points of equal illumination or light intensity from a given source

**iso·pho·tic line** \¦īsə¦fōd·ik-\ *n* [*isophotic* fr. *isophote* + *-ic*] **:** ISOPHOTE

**iso·phthal·ic acid** \¦īsō *at* ISO-+¦thalik-\ *n* [*isophthalic* ISV *is-* + *phthalic*] **:** a crystalline diacid $C_6H_4(COOH)_2$ isomeric with phthalic acid made usu. by oxidation of *meta*-xylene and used in making synthetic resins and esters for use as plasticizers; *meta*-benzene-dicarboxylic acid

**iso·phyl·lia** \,īsəˈfilēə\ *n, cap* [NL, fr. *is-* + *phyll-* + *-ia*] **:** a genus of madrepores comprising the rose corals

**iso·phyl·lous** \¦īsə¦filəs\ *adj* [ISV *is-* + *-phyllous*] **:** having foliage leaves of like form on the same plant or stem — compare ANISOPHYLLOUS

**iso·phyl·ly** \ˈīsə,filē\ *n* -ES [*isophyllous* + *-y*, n. suffix] **:** the quality or state of being isophyllous

**iso·pi·es·tic** \¦ī(,)sō,pīˈestik\ *adj* [*is-* + *piest-* (fr. Gk *piestos* compressible, fr. *piezein* to press) + *-ic* — more at PIEZO-] **:** of, relating to, or marked by equal pressure **:** ISOBARIC

**iso·plastic graft** \¦īsō+…-\ *n* [*isoplastic* fr. *is-* + *plastic*] **:** HOMOGRAFT

**iso·pleth** \ˈīsə,pleth\ *n* -s [ISV *is-* + *-pleth* (fr. Gk *plēthos* quantity, multitude); akin to Gk *plēthein* to be full — more at FULL] **1 :** an isogram on a graph showing the occurrence or frequency of a phenomenon as a function of two variables — often used of meteorological elements **2 :** a line on a map connecting points at which a given variable has a specified constant value ⟨~*s* such as isothermal lines or topographic contour lines⟩

**iso·pleu·ra** \,īsəˈplürə\ [NL, fr. *is-* + *-pleura*] *syn of* AMPHINEURA

**iso·ploid** \ˈīsə,plȯid\ *adj* [*is-* + *-ploid*] **:** having an even number of genomes in somatic cells

**iso·pluvial** \¦īsō+\ *adj* [*is-* + *pluvial*] **:** of, relating to, or marked by equal rainfall ⟨an ~ line⟩

**iso·pod** \ˈīsə,päd\ *n* -s [NL *Isopoda*] **:** one of the Isopoda

**isop·o·da** \īˈsäpədə\ *n pl, cap* [NL, fr. *is-* + *-poda*] **:** a large order of small sessile-eyed malacostracan crustaceans (superorder Peracarida) that lack a carapace, have a body usu. depressed with seven free thoracic segments each bearing a pair of similar legs, and that occur in marine, freshwater, or terrestrial habitats or as parasites on invertebrates and fish — compare TANAIDACEA — **isop·o·dan** \(ˈ)ī¦sä pədᵊn, -əd°n\ *adj or n* — **isop·o·dous** \-dəs\ *adj*

**iso·pod·i·form** \¦īsə¦pädə,fȯrm *also* ¦īzə-\ *adj* [NL *isopodiformis*, fr. *Isopoda* + L *-iformis* -iform] **:** resembling an isopod in form

**iso·po·go·nous** \¦īsō *at* ISO- + pə¦gōnəs, ¦pāgən-\ *adj* [NL *isopogonus*, fr. *is-* + *-pogonus* (fr. Gk *pōgōn* beard) — more at -POGON] **:** having feathers whose two webs are equal

**iso·polity** \,īsō+\ *n* -ES [Gk *isopoliteia*, fr. *isopolitēs* having equal or reciprocal political rights (fr. *is-* + *politēs* citizen) + *-ia* -y — more at POLICE] **:** equality or reciprocity of rights or privileges (as of citizenship) ⟨an agreement between two countries establishing ~ for their citizens⟩

**isopoly-** *comb form* [ISV *is-* + *poly-*] **:** containing several groups or ions of the same acid-forming element **:** POLY- 2b — in names of complex inorganic acids and their salts ⟨*isopoly*-molybdates⟩ — compare HETEROPOLY-

**iso·poly acid** \¦īsə¦pälē-\ *n* [*isopoly* ISV *isopoly-*] **:** any of a large group of complex oxygen-containing acids derived from a single inorganic acid by elimination of water from two or more molecules — distinguished from *heteropoly acid*

**iso·por** \ˈīsə,pō(ə)r\ *n* -s [*is-* + *-por* (fr. Gk *poros* passage, path) — more at FARE] **:** an imaginary line or a line on a map of the earth's surface connecting points of equal annual change in one of the magnetic elements

**iso·por·ic** \¦īsə¦pȯrik\ *adj* **:** of, relating to, or indicating an isopor

**iso·pren·a·line** \,īsəˈprenᵊlən, -ᵊl,ēn\ *n* -s [prob. fr. *isopropyl* + *adrenaline*] **:** ISOPROTERENOL

**iso·prene** \ˈīsə,prēn\ *n* -s [prob. fr. *is-* + *pr-* (fr. *propyl*) + *-ene*] **:** a flammable liquid diolefin hydrocarbon $CH_2{=}C(CH_3)CH{=}CH_2$ obtained usu. by heating rubber or turpentine (sense 2) or in cracking petroleum and used chiefly in making synthetic rubber; 2-methyl-1,3-butadiene — see POLYISOPRENE, TERPENE

**¹iso·pre·noid** \¦īsə¦prē,nȯid\ *adj* [*isoprene* + *-oid*] **:** relating to, containing, or being the branched-chain grouping $(C)_2$-C–C–C of five carbon atoms that is characteristic of isoprene and that recurs in the molecules of many natural compounds (as rubber, terpenes, vitamin A, vitamin E, phytol)

**²isoprenoid** \"\ *n* -s **:** an isoprenoid compound

**iso·pro·pa·nol** \,īsəˈprōpə,nōl, -nōl\ *n* -s [*is-* + *propane* + *-ol*] **:** ISOPROPYL ALCOHOL — not used systematically

**iso·pro·pe·nyl** \-ōpənᵊl, -,nil\ *n* [ISV *is-* + *propenyl*] **:** the univalent radical $CH_2{=}C(CH_3)-$ isomeric with propenyl ⟨*isopropenyl*-isopropylidene isomerism . . . is typical of many terpenoids —W.S.Ropp⟩

**iso·pro·pox·ide** \,īsə,prōˈpäk,sīd, -səd\ *n* -s [prob. fr. *is-* + *propox-* (fr. *propoxyl*) + *-ide*] **:** a binary compound of the radical $(CH_3)_2CHO-$ isomeric with propoxyl; *esp* **:** a base formed from isopropyl alcohol by replacement of the hydroxyl hydrogen with a metal ⟨aluminum ~ $[(CH_3)_2CHO]_3Al$⟩

**iso·propyl** \¦īsō+\ *n* [ISV *is-* + *propyl*] **:** the alkyl radical $(CH_3)_2CH-$ isomeric with normal propyl

**isopropyl alcohol** *n* **:** a volatile flammable liquid secondary alcohol $(CH_3)_2CHOH$ made usu. by hydration of propylene by means of sulfuric acid and used as a solvent and rubbing alcohol and as a source of acetone by dehydrogenation; 2-propanol

**iso·pro·pyl·arterenol** \¦īsə¦prōpəl+\ *n* [*isopropyl* + *arterenol*] **:** ISOPROTERENOL

**iso·pro·pyl·ate** \,īsəˈprōpə,lāt\ *n* -s [*isopropyl* + *-ate*] **:** ISOPROPOXIDE

**isopropyl ether** *n* **:** a colorless volatile flammable water-insoluble liquid $[(CH_3)_2CH]_2O$ made from propylene or isopropyl alcohol and used as a solvent

**iso·propylidene** \¦ī(,)sō+\ *n* [ISV *is-* + *propylidene*] **:** the bivalent radical $(CH_3)_2C<$ isomeric with propylidene — compare ISOPROPENYL

**iso·pro·te·re·nol** \,īsə,prōd·əˈrē,nōl, -nōl\ *n* -s [short for *isopropylarterenol*] **:** a crystalline compound $C_{11}H_{17}NO_3$ that is the isopropyl homologue of racemic epinephrine and that is used in the treatment of asthma — called also *isopropylarterenol*

**isop·tera** \īˈsäptərə\ *n pl, cap* [NL, fr. *is-* + *-ptera*] **:** an order of social insects consisting of the termites — **isop·te·rous** \(ˈ)ī¦säptərəs\ *adj*

**iso·pulegol** \¦īsō *at* ISO- +\ *n* [ISV *is-* + *pulegol*] **:** a liquid terpenoid alcohol $C_{10}H_{17}OH$ that has an odor like that of menthol and that is used as an intermediate in the synthesis of menthol from citronellol

**¹iso·pyc·nic** \¦īsə¦piknik\ *also* **iso·pyc·nal** \-nəl\ *adj* [*is-* + *pycn-* + *-ic* or *-al*] **:** of, relating to, or marked by equal density

**²isopycnic** \"\ *or* **isopycnal** \"\ *n* -s **:** a line or surface on a map connecting points of equal density (as of water, air)

**iso·quercitrin** \¦īsō+\ *n* [*is-* + *quercitrin*] **:** a pale-yellow crystalline glucoside $C_{21}H_{20}O_{12}$ occurring esp. in cotton flowers and maize and yielding quercetin and glucose on hydrolysis

**iso·quinoline** \"+\ *n* [ISV *is-* + *quinoline*] **:** a low-melting crystalline or liquid nitrogenous base $C_9H_7N$ that is associated with its isomer quinoline in coal tar and that is the parent structure in many alkaloids (as narcotine, papaverine)

**iso·rhythm** \ˈīsō+,-\ *n* [*is-* + *rhythm*] **:** a single fixed rhythmic pattern typically long and complex that is reiterated throughout the whole of a sung voice part which is usu. the tenor ⟨~ in late medieval motets⟩ — **iso·rhythmic** \¦īsō¦+\ *adj*

**iso·safrole** \¦īsō+\ *n* [ISV *is-* + *safrole*] **:** a liquid acetal $(CH_2O_2)C_6H_3CH{=}CHCH_3$ that has an odor like that of anise, that is obtained from the essential oils of ilang-ilang and the fruit of Japanese star anise and synthetically from safrole and hot alkali, and that is used chiefly in making piperonal

**isos·ce·les** \(ˈ)ī¦säsə,lēz\ *adj* [LL, fr. Gk *isoskelēs*, fr. *is-* + *skelos* leg — more at CYLINDER] *of a triangle* **:** having two equal sides — see TRIANGLE illustration

**isosceles trapezoid** *n* **:** a trapezoid with its two nonparallel sides equal

**iso·sebacic acid** \¦īsō *at* ISO- + . . . -\ *n* [*isosebacic* fr. *is-* + *sebacic*] **:** a solid mixture of sebacic acid and two isomeric dicarboxylic acids $C_8H_{16}(COOH)_2$ obtainable by reaction of butadiene with sodium, carbon dioxide, and finally hydrogen and useful esp. for making plasticizers and alkyd resins

**¹iso·seismal** \"+\ *adj* [*is-* + *seismal*] **:** of, relating to, or marked by equal intensity of earthquake shock ⟨an ~ line⟩

**²isoseismal** \"\ *n* -s **:** an isoseismal line on a map or chart of the earth's surface connecting points of equal intensity of earthquake shock

**iso·seismic** \"+\ *adj* [*is-* + *seismic*] **:** ISOSEISMAL

**iso·osmotic** \¦īs *also* ¦īz+\ *adj* [ISV *is-* + *osmotic*] **:** of, relating to, or exhibiting equal osmotic pressure ⟨~ solutions⟩

**iso·spon·dyl** \ˈīsō *at* ISO -+¦spänd°l\ *n* -s [NL *Isospondyli*] **:** a fish of the order Isospondyli

**iso·spon·dy·li** \,īsəˈspändə,lī\ *n pl, cap* [NL, fr. *is-* + *spondyli*] **:** a large order of teleost fishes that is the most primitive group of teleosts and that includes about 50 living families (as of the herrings and salmons) whose fishes have soft-rayed fins, an air bladder connected with the alimentary canal by a duct, abdominal pelvic fins, the anterior vertebrae unmodified and similar to the others, and usu. a mesocoracoid or precoracoid arch — **iso·spon·dy·lous** \¦īsə¦spändələs\ *adj*

**isos·po·ra** \īˈsäspərə\ *n, cap* [NL, fr. *is-* + *-spora*] **:** a genus of Coccidia closely related to *Eimeria* and including the only species (*I. hominis*) of coccidium known to be parasitic in man

**iso·spore** \ˈīsō *at* ISO-+,-\ *n* [ISV *is-* + *spore*] **1 :** one of the spores produced by a homosporous organism **2 :** a sexual spore exhibiting no sexual dimorphism

**iso·spor·ic** \¦īsə¦spȯrik\ *adj* [*isospore* + *-ic*] **:** ISOSPOROUS

**iso·spor·ous** \¦īsə¦spōrəs, (ˈ)ī¦säspərəs\ *adj* [*is-* + *-sporous*] **:** of, relating to, or having isospores

**iso·spo·ry** \ˈ==ˌ at ISO- + ˌspōrē; īˈsäspərē\ *n* -ES [ISV *is-* + *-spory*] **:** the quality or state of being isosporous

**isos·ta·sist** \īˈsästəsəst\ *n* -S **:** a specialist in the study of isostasy

**isos·ta·sy** *also* **isos·ta·cy** \-təsē\ *n* -ES [*isostasy* ISV *is-* + *-stasy* (fr. Gk *-stasia*); *isostacy* alter. (influenced by E *-cy*) of *isostasy* — more at -STASIA] **1 :** the quality or state of being isostatic **2 :** general equilibrium in the earth's crust maintained by a yielding flow of rock material beneath the surface under gravitative stress and by the approximate equality in mass of each unit column of the earth from the surface to a depth of about 70 miles — compare ISOSTATIC COMPENSATION

**iso·static** \ˈ== *at* ISO- + \ *adj* [ISV *is-* + *static;* orig. formed as F *isostatique*] **1 a :** subjected to equal pressure from every side **b :** being in hydrostatic equilibrium **2 :** relating to or characterized by isostasy

**isostatic compensation** *n* **:** the deficiency of mass in the earth's crust below sea level that exactly balances the mass above sea level

**iso·stemo·nous** \ˌ==ˈstēmənəs, -stem-\ *adj* [ISV *is-* + *-stemonous*] **:** having stamens equal in number to the perianth divisions

**iso·stemo·ny** \ˌ==ˈstēmənē, -stem-\ *n* -ES [ISV *isostemonous* + *-y*] **:** the quality or state of being isostemonous

**iso·stere** \ˈ==ˌsti(ə)r\ *also* **iso·ster** \-ˌste(ə)r\ *n* -S [*is-* + *-stere, -ster* (fr. Gk *stereos* solid) — more at STARE] **1 :** a line on a map or chart connecting points of equal atmospheric density **2** [prob. back-formation fr. *isosteric*] **:** one of two or more substances related by isosterism

**iso·ster·ic** \ˌ==ˈsterik\ *adj* [*is-* + *ster-* (fr. Gk *stereos* solid) + *-ic*] **1 :** of, relating to, or exhibiting isosterism **2 :** of, relating to, or marked by equal atmospheric density

**isos·ter·ism** \īˈsästəˌrizəm; ˈ== *at* ISO- + ˌstiˌrizəm *or* ˌsteˌr-\ *n* -S [*is-* + *ster-* (fr. Gk *stereos* solid) + *-ism*] **:** the phenomenon of similarity of structure and of resulting similarity of some properties exhibited by two or more molecules or groups or ions containing different atoms though not necessarily the same number of atoms but having the same number of total or valence electrons in the same arrangement (as in carbon monoxide and gaseous nitrogen or in the cyanide and acetylide ions)

**iso·structural** \ˈ== *at* ISO- + \ *adj* **:** relating to or having a similar crystal structure in that the atoms correspond in position and function although there may not be close chemical relationship **:** ISOTYPIC 2 — used of minerals and other crystalline substances ⟨calcite and sodium nitrate are ~⟩; compare ISOMORPHOUS

**iso·tac** \ˈ==ˌtak\ *n* -S [*is-* + *-tac* (fr. Gk *takēnai* to melt, be dissolved, pass. aor. infin. of *tēkein* to melt, dissolve) — more at THAW] **:** an equiglacial line on a map or chart connecting points where ice melts at the same time in spring

**iso·tach** \-ˌtak\ *n* -S [ISV *is-* + *-tach* (fr. Gk *tachys* quick) — more at TACHY-] **:** a line on a map or chart connecting points of equal wind speed

**iso·tac·tic** \ˌ==ˈtaktik\ *adj* [ISV *is-* + *-tactic*] **:** of, relating to, or having a stereochemical regularity of structure in the repeating units of a polymer — compare SYNDYOTACTIC

**isote** *var of* IZOTE

**iso·ther·al** \ˈ== *at* ISO- + ˈthirəl\ *adj* [F *isothère* isothere + E *-al*] **:** of, relating to, or marked by the same mean summer temperature ⟨an ~ line⟩

**iso·there** \ˈ==ˌthi(ə)r\ *n* -S [F *isothère*, fr. *is-* + *-thère* (fr. Gk *theros* summer); akin to Gk *thermos* hot] **:** a line on a map or chart of the earth's surface connecting points having the same mean summer temperature

**iso·therm** \-ˌthərm\ *n* -S [F *isotherme*, adj., isothermal, fr. *is-* + *-therme* (fr. Gk *thermē* heat, fr. *thermos* hot) — more at WARM] **1 :** a line on a map or chart of the earth's surface connecting points having the same temperature at a given time or the same mean temperature for a given period **2 :** a line on a chart representing changes of volume or pressure under conditions of constant temperature

**¹iso·ther·mal** \ˌ==ˈthərməl\ *adj* [F *isotherme*, adj. + E *-al*] **1 :** of, relating to, or marked by equality of temperature **2 :** of, relating to, or marked by changes of volume or pressure under conditions of constant temperature

**²isothermal** \"\ *n* -S **:** ISOTHERM 1

**isothermal curve** *n* **:** ISOTHERM 2

**isothermal line** *n* **:** ISOTHERM 1

**isothermal region** *n* **:** STRATOSPHERE

**iso·ther·mic** \-mik\ *adj* [ISV *isotherm* + *-ic*] **:** ISOTHERMAL — **iso·ther·mi·cal·ly** \-mək(ə)lē\ *adv*

**iso·ther·mo·bath** \ˌ==ˈthərməˌbath\ *n* -S [*isotherm* + *-o-* + *-bath* (fr. Gk *bathos* depth); akin to Gk *bathys* deep — more at BATHY-] **:** a line on a diagram of a vertical section of the ocean connecting points of equal temperature

**isothiocyan-** *or* **isothiocyano-** *comb form* [ISV *is-* + *thiocyan-*] **:** containing the univalent radical —NCS isomeric with the thiocyano radical and present in isothiocyanates ⟨*isothiocyano*amines⟩

**iso·thio·cyanate** \ˌ==ˌthīō+\ *n* -S [ISV *isothiocyan-* + *-ate*] **:** a compound containing the univalent radical —NCS consisting of an isocyano group united with sulfur **:** a salt or ester of isothiocyanic acid — compare MUSTARD OIL 2

**isothiocyanato-** *comb form* [*isothiocyanate* + *-o-*] **:** ISOTHIOCYAN- — esp. in names of coordination complexes

**iso·thiocyanic acid** \ˌ==ˌthīō+ . . .-\ *n* [*isothiocyanic* ISV *is-* + *thiocyanic*] **:** thiocyanic acid regarded as having the formula HNCS and usu. prepared in the form of esters

**iso·tone** \ˈ==ˌtōn\ *n* -S [*is-* + *-tone* (prob. fr. Gk *tonos* tension, stretching) — more at TONE] **:** one of two or more nuclides having the same number of neutrons

**iso·ton·ic** \ˌ==ˈtänik\ *adj* [ISV *is-* + *tonic*] **1 :** of, relating to, or exhibiting equal tension; *specif, of muscular contraction* **:** taking place in the absence of significant resistance with marked shortening of muscle fibers and without great increase in muscle tone — compare ISOMETRIC **2 :** having the same or equal osmotic pressure **:** ISOSMOTIC — used of solutions ⟨an ~ salt solution in which blood cells are counted⟩; compare HYPERTONIC, HYPOTONIC — **iso·ton·i·cal·ly** \-nək(ə)lē\ *adv*

**iso·tonicity** \ˌ== *at* ISO- + \ *n* [*isotonic* + *-ity*] **:** the quality or state of being isotonic

**iso·to·nize** \ˈ==ˌtōˌnīz\ *vt* -ED/-ING/-S [*isotonic* + *-ize*] **:** to make isotonic

**iso·tope** \ˈ==ˌtōp\ *n* -S [*is-* + *-tope* (fr. Gk *topos* place) — more at TOPIC] **1 a :** one of two or more species of atoms of the same chemical element that have the same atomic number and occupy the same position in the periodic table and that are nearly identical in chemical behavior but differ in atomic mass or mass number and so behave differently in the mass spectrograph, in radioactive transformations, and in physical properties (as diffusibility in the gaseous state) and may be detected and separated by means of these differences ⟨deuterium and tritium are ~*s* of hydrogen⟩; *esp* **:** one such species of atom or a mixture of such species of atoms prepared for use as a tracer or in medicine — usu. indicated for a specific element by the mass number following the name of the element or written superior to the symbol of the element (as carbon 14, $C^{14}$, or $^{14}C$); compare RADIOISOTOPE **b :** the nucleus of such a species of atom **2 :** NUCLIDE

**isotope effect** *n* **:** the variation of certain characteristics (as density and spectrum) of an element in accordance with the mass of the isotopes involved

**iso·topic** \ˌ==ˈtäpik, -ˈtōp-\ *adj* [ISV *isotope* + *-ic*] **:** of, relating to, or having the relationship of an isotope — **iso·topi·cal·ly** \-pək(ə)lē\ *adv*

**isotopic number** *n* **:** the number of neutrons minus the number of protons in an atomic nucleus

**iso·to·py** \ˈ==ˌtōpē, īˈsädəpē\ *n* -ES [ISV *isotope* + *-y*, n. suffix] **:** the quality or state of being isotopic

**isot·ria** \īˈsä·trēə\ *n, cap* [NL, fr. *is-* + Gk *tria* three, neut. of *treis* three — more at THREE] **:** a small genus of terrestrial orchids of eastern No. America that are sometimes included in *Pogonia* and that have a nearly terminal whorl of leaves and a usu. solitary greenish yellow flower with long linear sepal — see WHORLED POGONIA

**iso·tron** \ˈ== *at* ISO- + -ˌträn\ *n* -S [prob. fr. *isotope* + *-tron*] **:** an electromagnetic apparatus for separating isotopes introduced as ions from an extended source which group according to their masses under the combined effect of a strong direct field and weak fields that vary at radio frequency

**iso·tropic** \ˌ==ˈträpik, -rōp-\ *adj* [ISV *is-* + *-tropic;* orig. formed as F *isotropique*] **1 :** exhibiting properties (as velocity of light transmission, conductivity of heat or electricity, compressibility) with the same values when measured along axes in all directions ⟨an ~ crystal⟩ — compare ANISOTROPIC 1 **2 :** exhibiting equal tendencies to growth in all directions **:** lacking predetermined axes ⟨~ eggs⟩

**isot·ro·pism** \īˈsä·trəˌpizəm\ *n* -S [*isotropic* + *-ism*] **:** ISOTROPY

**isot·ro·pous** \(ˈ)=ˈ==pəs\ *adj* [*isotropic* + *-ous*] **:** ISOTROPIC

**isot·ro·py** \=ˈ==pē\ *n* -ES [ISV *isotropic* + *-y*, n. suffix] **:** the quality or state of being isotropic

**iso·type** \ˈ== *at* ISO- + ˌtīp\ *n* [ISV *is-* + *type*] **1 a :** an animal or plant or group common to two or more countries or life regions **b** (1) **:** PARATYPE 1 — usu. used in plant taxonomy (2) **:** a type that is or is considered for technical purposes to be the duplicate of a holotype **2 a :** a conventionalized pictographic symbol (as a drawing or outline or silhouette of a human figure or of a building or of a product) designed to represent (as by repetition or fractionalizing of each symbol or as by scaling each symbol to significantly the same size or to contrasted sizes) a fixed number or quantity of or other unitary fact about the thing symbolized ⟨each ~ of a soldier in that diagram represents an entire army division⟩ or designed to convey other information ⟨public telephones often have a large ~ of a bell over the booths as a directional guide to the booths⟩ and typically used in graphic statistical representations (as diagrams, charts) **b :** a graphic statistical representation (as a chart) that utilizes such isotypes

**iso·typ·ic** \ˌ==ˈtipik\ *or* **iso·typ·i·cal** \-pəkəl\ *adj* [*isotype* + *-ic* or *-ical*] **1** *usu isotypical* **:** of or relating to an isotype **2 :** relating to or having a chemical formula analogous to and a crystal structure like that of another specified compound **:** ISOSTRUCTURAL — used of minerals and other crystalline substances ⟨some phosphates and silicates are ~⟩

**iso·urea** \ˌ=(ˌ)=+\ *n* [NL, fr. *is-* + *urea*] **:** PSEUDOUREA

**iso·valerate** \ˌ=(ˌ)=+\ *n* -S [ISV *isovaleric* (in *isovaleric acid*) + *-ate*] **:** a salt or ester of isovaleric acid

**iso·valerianic acid** \"+ . . .-\ *n* [*isovalerianic* ISV *is-* + *valerianic*] **:** ISOVALERIC ACID

**iso·valeric acid** \"+ . . .-\ *n* [*isovaleric* ISV *is-* + *valeric*] **:** a liquid acid $(CH_3)_2CHCH_2COOH$ that has a disagreeable odor, that occurs esp. in valerian root in the free state and in some essential oils and marine-animal oils in the form of esters, that is made by oxidation of isopentyl alcohol, and that is used chiefly in making esters for use in flavoring materials; β-methyl-butyric acid

**iso·valeryl** \"+\ *n* -S [ISV *isovaler-* (in *isovaleric acid*) + *-yl*] **:** the radical $(CH_3)_2CHCH_2CO—$ of isovaleric acid

**is·oxazole** \(ˈ)īs *also* (ˈ)īz+\ *n* [ISV *is-* + *oxazole*] **1 :** a liquid heterocyclic compound $C_3H_3NO$ that is isomeric with oxazole, has a penetrating odor like that of pyridine, and is made by the action of hydroxylamine on propiolaldehyde **2 :** a derivative of isoxazole

**iso·zooid** \ˌ== *at* ISO- + \ *n* [*is-* + *zooid*] **:** a zooid resembling its parent — opposed to *allozooid*

**is·pa·ghul** \ˈispəˌgül, -ˌgəl\ *n* -S [Per *ispaghōl, aspaghōl*, lit., horse's ear, fr. *asp* horse (fr. MPer) + *ghōl* ear; fr. the shape of the leaf; akin to Skt *aśva* horse — more at EQUINE] **:** an Old World plantain (*Plantago ovata*) with mucilaginous seeds that are used in preparing a beverage

**is·pa·han** \ˈispəˌhän, -han, ˌ==ˈ=\ *n* -S *often cap* [*Ispahan, Isfahan*, city in west central Iran] **:** a handmade Persian rug that is typically deep red or blue or green with floral or animal patterns in antique design and that is usu. long and narrow

**i spy** \ˈī-\ *n, cap I* [prob. alter. (influenced by E *I*, pron.) of *hy spy*] **:** HIDE-AND-SEEK

**¹is·ra·el** \ˈizˌrēəl *also* ˈis| *or* |(ˌ)rāəl *or* |ˌrīl *or* ÷|ˌrōl *sometimes* |(ˌ)rāˌel *or* |(ˌ)räˌel *or* |ˌrīˌel *or* |(ˌ)rāˌel\ *n* -S *cap* [ME, fr. OE, fr. LL, fr. Gk *Israēl*, fr. Heb *Yisrā'ēl*, lit., let God contend, fr. *sārāh* to fight + *ēl* God] **1 a** (1) **:** the ancient Hebrew people descended from the patriarch Jacob (2) **:** the group of 10 Hebrew tribes anciently inhabiting the northern part of Palestine and constituting a kingdom independent of Judah **b :** the Jewish people of past and present **2 :** a body of individuals (as members of the Jewish or Christian faiths) regarded by itself or others as the actual or spiritual chosen people of God **:** ELECT

**²israel** \"\ *adj, usu cap* [*Israel*, independent Jewish state in Palestine, fr. Heb *Yisrā'ēl*] **:** ISRAELI

**¹is·rae·li** \izˈrālē, *sometimes* is| *or* ˌ=ˌreˌā- *or* ˌ=|ˌrəˌā-\ *adj, usu cap* [NHeb *yiśrě'ēlī*, fr. Heb, Israelite, Israelitic, fr. *Yisrā'ēl*] **:** of or from the republic of Israel **:** of the kind or style prevalent in Israel

**²israeli** \"\ *n, pl* **israelis** *also* **israeli** *cap* **:** a native or inhabitant of the republic of Israel

**israeli hebrew** *n, cap I&H* **:** the Hebrew language in colloquial use in present-day Israel

**¹is·ra·el·ite** *pronunc at* ¹ISRAEL +ˌīt; *usu* -īd·+V\ *n* -S *cap* [ME, fr. LL *Israelita, Israelites*, fr. Gk *Israēlitēs*, fr. *Israēl* Israel + *-itēs* -ite] **1 a** (1) **:** a member of the ancient Hebrew people descended from the patriarch Jacob (2) **:** a member of one of the 10 Hebrew tribes anciently inhabiting the northern part of Palestine — compare SAMARITAN **b :** a member of the Jewish people of past or present **:** JEW **2 :** a member of a body of individuals regarded by itself or others as the actual or spiritual chosen people of God

**²israelite** \"\ *also* **is·ra·el·it·ic** \ˌ=(ˌ)=(=)ˈid·ik\ *or* **is·ra·el·it·ish** \-ˌīd·|ish, -ˌīt|, |ēsh\ *adj, usu cap* [*²israelite* fr. *¹israelite; israelitic* fr. LL *israeliticus*, fr. *Israelita, Israelites* + L *-icus* -ic; *israelitish* fr. ¹*israelite* + *-ish*] **:** of or relating to Israel ⟨*Israelite* conquests in Canaan⟩ ⟨*Israelite* prophets⟩

**iss** *abbr* issue

**is·sa** \ˈēˌsä, iˈ-\ *n, pl* **issas** \-ˌsä(z)\ *or* **issa** *usu cap* **1 :** a Hamitic people of the French territory of the Afars and the Issas **2 :** a member of the Issa people

**is·sa·char·ite** \ˈisəˌkäˌrīt\ *n* -S *usu cap* [*Issachar*, ninth son of Jacob and ancestor of the tribe (fr. LL, fr. Heb *Yissākhār*) + E *-ite*] **:** a member of the Hebrew tribe of Issachar

**is·sei** \(ˈ)ēˈsā\ *n, pl* **issei** *also* **isseis** *often cap* [Jap, lit., first generation, fr. *is* first + *sei* generation] **:** a Japanese immigrant to America and esp. to the U. S. — compare NISEI

**is·su·able** \ˈish(y)əwəbəl, ˈi(ˌ)shüəb-, *chiefly Brit* ˈisyəwəb- *or* ˈi(ˌ)syüəb-\ *adj* **1 :** that is of such a kind as to admit issue being taken or joined ⟨an ~ matter⟩ ⟨~ terms⟩ **2 :** that is authorized for issuing ⟨~ goods⟩ ⟨~ currency⟩ **3 :** that may accrue ⟨~ profits⟩ — **is·su·ably** \-blē,-bli\ *adv*

**issuable plea** *n* **:** a plea on the merits on which an adverse party may take issue and go to trial

**is·su·ance** \-əwən(t)s, -üən-\ *n* -S **1 :** ISSUE 9a, 9b **2 :** ISSUE 2a

**is·su·ant** \-nt\ *adj* **1** *archaic* **:** coming forth from a specified place or source ⟨~ from the eternal throne, came like a cloud of light, the bright response —P.J.Bailey⟩ **2** *heraldry* **a :** depicted or shown as coming forth ⟨a panther with flames ~ from the mouth⟩ **b :** depicted or shown as rising upward (as from the top or bottom line of an ordinary or from another bearing or from the base of an escutcheon) ⟨two sprigs ~⟩ **c** *of an animal figure* **:** rising upward and having only the upper part visible ⟨a lion rampant ~ from a fess⟩

**¹is·sue** \ˈi(ˌ)shü, ˈish(ˌ)yü, ˈi(ˌ)shü, ˈish(ˌ)yü, *before a vowel often* -ˌsh(y)əw; *chiefly in the southern U. S.* -ˌsh(y)ə *before a consonant or pause or before a vowel in a following word; chiefly Brit* ˈi(ˌ)syü *or* ˈi(ˌ)syü *or* ˈisyəw\ *n* -S [ME, fr. MF, way out, exit, proceeds, fr. OF *eissue, issue*, fr. fem. of *eissu, issu*, past part. of *eissir, issir* to come out, go out, fr. L *exire* to go out, fr. *ex-* ¹ex- + *ire* to go; akin to Goth *iddja* he went, Gk *ienai* to go, Skt *eti* he goes, and prob. to OE *ēode* he went] **1 issues** *pl* **:** proceeds from a source of revenue (as an estate) ⟨rents, profits, and ~*s*⟩ **2 a** (1) **:** the action of going out or coming out or flowing out from something **:** OUTGOING, EGRESS, OUTFLOW ⟨the ~ of water from a broken pipe⟩ ⟨a constant entrance and ~ of visitors⟩ ⟨the river's place of ~⟩ (2) **:** the action of coming forth from or as if from something in which one is immersed **:** EMERGENCE ⟨the ~ of a people from barbarism into a civilized way of life⟩ **b :** the power to go out or come out or flow out from something ⟨potentialities that remain repressed for lack of ~⟩ **3 a :** a means of going out from something **:** EXIT, OUTLET, VENT ⟨a dark labyrinth that had no ~⟩ **b :** a place where something goes out from something **:** place of egress ⟨at the northern ~ of the plaza a beautiful boulevard begins⟩; *specif* **:** the point at which a body of water flows out into another usu. larger body of water ⟨a river whose source and ~ were unknown⟩ **4 :** OFFSPRING, PROGENY ⟨died without ~⟩; *specif* **:** one or more persons descended from a common ancestor **5 a :** final outcome **:** RESULT, CONSEQUENCE ⟨no chance at all of a happy ~ —C.P. Snow⟩ **b** *obs* **:** a final conclusion or decision about something arrived at after consideration **c** *archaic* **:** TERMINATION, END ⟨to hope that his enterprise would have a prosperous ~ —T. B.Macaulay⟩ **6 a :** a point in question of law or fact; *specif* **:** a single material point of law or fact depending in a suit that is affirmed by one side and denied by the other and that is presented for determination at the conclusion of the pleadings **b** (1) **:** a matter that is in dispute between two or more parties or that is to be disputed by the parties **:** a point of debate or controversy ⟨the ~ over which of them was to be leader⟩ ⟨seemed to want to make an ~ of almost everything⟩ (2) **:** a matter not yet finally settled and on the settlement of which something else depends **:** a pregnant unsettled matter **:** vital question ⟨burning ~*s* of the day⟩ ⟨an ~ that could make or wreck careers —T.H.White b. 1915⟩ ⟨to judge of each ~ . . . in the light of fact —Rose Macaulay⟩ **:** PROBLEM ⟨in every genuine metaphysical debate some practical ~, however conjectural and remote, is involved —William James⟩ **:** a controverted subject or topic ⟨the ~ of desegregation⟩ **c :** something entailing alternatives between which to choose or decide **:** something involving judgments or decisions ⟨a situation seen in terms of the ~ it presents —Archibald MacLeish⟩ **d :** the point at which an unsettled matter is ready for a decision **:** the point at which a question is ripe for decision ⟨quickly brought the matter to an ~⟩ **e :** a means of settling a point of debate or controversy; *specif* **:** a test or trial by means of which a question can be settled — used with *put* ⟨the theory was challenged and finally put to the ~⟩ **7 a :** a discharge (as of blood) from the body that is caused by disease or other physical disorder or that is produced artificially ⟨had long suffered from an ~ of blood⟩ **b :** an incision made to produce such a discharge **8 a :** something proceeding or coming forth from a usu. specified source ⟨an ~ of smoke from a chimney⟩; *esp* **:** something proceeding from a usu. specified source by or as if by flowing out or emanating or emerging from it ⟨hallucinations and other ~*s* of a disordered imagination⟩ **b** *obs* **:** something done by a specified agent **:** DEED **9 a** (1) **:** the act of officially putting forth or getting out or printing (as new currency or postage stamps) or making available or distributing (as supplies or material) or giving out or granting (as licenses) or proclaiming or promulgating (as a written order or directive) ⟨eagerly awaiting the next ~ of commemorative stamps⟩ ⟨~ of supplies by the quartermaster⟩ (2) **:** the act of bringing out (as a new book or a revised edition of a book or a new number of a magazine or a fresh printing of a newspaper) for distribution to or sale or circulation among the public **:** PUBLICATION ⟨~ of the enlarged edition is awaited with interest⟩ ⟨the many details involved in each day's ~ of a newspaper⟩ (3) **:** the act of offering securities for sale to investors ⟨a new ~ of government bonds⟩ (4) *chiefly Brit* **:** CIRCULATION 8a, 8c **b :** the condition or fact of being produced or made available by such action ⟨the book's ~ at such a time took everyone by surprise⟩ **c :** the thing (as a bank note or a security or an item of supplies or an individual's license or a copy of a book, magazine, newspaper) or the whole quantity of things (as all the postage stamps put forth with a certain design or the whole extent of supplies given out on a certain date or all the copies of a periodical printed for a specific day or month) produced or made available at one time or on a certain date by such action and usu. distinguished (as in date, design, content, nature) from those produced or made available at some other time ⟨waiting for the next ~ of the magazine⟩ ⟨bought specimens of each new ~ of stamps⟩ **d** *chiefly Brit* **:** CIRCULATION 8b **10 :** the first delivery of a negotiable instrument complete in form (as a bill or note) to a person who takes it as a holder **syn** see EFFECT — **at issue** *adv* **1 :** in a state of controversy **:** at variance **:** at a point where opposing viewpoints are held **:** in disagreement ⟨for years they remained *at issue* with each other⟩ **2** *also* **in issue :** in the process of being critically discussed or questioned **:** under discussion or in question or in dispute ⟨proceeded to inform them of the point *at issue*⟩

**²issue** \"\ *vb* -ED/-ING/-S [ME *issuen*, fr. MF *issu*, past part. of *issir* to come out, go out — more at ¹ISSUE] *vi* **1 a :** to go out or come out or flow out ⟨they *issued* out into the street⟩ ⟨a great sigh of relief *issued* from the ancient lungs —T.B.Costain⟩ ⟨the narrow coastal plain into which the Congo ~*s* —Tom Marvel⟩ **b :** to come forth from or as if from something in which one is immersed **:** EMERGE ⟨the external acts which . . . from these precepts —R.W.Southern⟩ **c :** to come to an issue of law or fact in pleading **2 :** ACCRUE ⟨profits *issuing* out of sale of the stock⟩ **3 :** to come forth by way of descent from a specified parent or ancestor **:** become descended **:** be an offspring of a specified parent or ancestor ⟨children that shall ~ from thee — Isa 39:7 (DV)⟩ **4 a :** to proceed or come forth from a usu. specified source ⟨from the dining room *issued* the sound of two voices —Louis Bromfield⟩ ⟨his enmity *issued* from the old man's fear of a possible young rival —C.S.Forester⟩; *esp* **:** to proceed or come forth from a usu. specified source by or as if by flowing out or emanating or emerging from it ⟨blood *issued* from the cut and trickled down his forehead⟩ **b** (1) **:** to be or have a consequence or final outcome **:** RESULT ⟨social unrest *issuing* in several serious conflicts —C.B.Roden⟩ ⟨any unhappiness that we experience ~*s* generally from our circumstances —W.F.Hambly⟩ (2) **:** to be of such a kind or to have such a nature as to have or tend toward a specified end or consequence or outcome **:** turn out to have a certain result **:** end up by being something specified ⟨such a theory of ethics ~*s* in three crucial problems —Iredell Jenkins⟩ ⟨*issuing* in necessary and immutable results —J.H.Newman⟩ **:** EVENTUATE ⟨this change in policy *issued* in a permanent institution — W.R.Inge⟩ **5 a :** to appear or become available through being officially put forth or distributed or granted or proclaimed or promulgated **:** appear through issuance ⟨were astonished at the flood of currency *issuing* each year⟩ **b :** to appear or become available through being brought out for distribution to or sale or circulation among the public **:** appear through publication ⟨no new editions are expected to ~ from that press⟩ **c :** to go forth by authority ⟨there must be an affidavit made showing reasonable grounds before the warrant can ~ —Paul Wilson⟩ ~ *vt* **1 :** to cause to come forth **:** give vent to **:** DISCHARGE, EMIT ⟨a volcano *issuing* smoke and fire⟩ **2** *obs* **:** to bring forth (offspring) **3 a :** to cause to appear or become available by officially putting forth or distributing or granting or proclaiming or promulgating **:** cause to appear through issuance ⟨the government *issued* a new airmail stamp⟩ ⟨*issued* a decree⟩ ⟨*issued* a formal letter to his adherents⟩ ⟨*issued* rifles and rations⟩ **b :** to cause to appear or become available by bringing out for distribution to or sale or circulation among the public **:** PUBLISH ⟨*issued* the book shortly after the author's death⟩ **4 a** *obs* **:** TERMINATE, SETTLE **b** *archaic* **:** to cause to have a specified consequence or final outcome or result **:** cause to end up in something specified **syn** see SPRING

**is·sue·less** \-ülės, -ül-,-əl-\ *adj* [ME *issules*, fr. *issu, issue* issue + *-les, -lees* -less — more at ¹ISSUE] **:** being without issue: **a :** having no offspring ⟨died ~⟩ **b :** producing no result ⟨an ~ effort⟩ **c :** not maintaining or marked by any stand that would arouse debate or controversy ⟨an ~ piece of writing⟩

**issue of fact :** FACT IN ISSUE

**issue of law :** a question involving primarily the application of principles of law as distinguished from an issue involving primarily the determination of facts in a case **:** a question of law rather than of fact — compare FACT IN ISSUE

**issue pea** *n* **:** a small globular object (as a dried garden pea or a wooden bead) formerly placed in an abscess or ulcer so as to induce or increase a suppurative discharge

**is·su·er** \-əwə(r), -üə(r), -üə(r)\ *n* -S **:** one that issues something (as securities, currency, books)

**ist** \ˈist\ *n, pl* **ists** \ˈis(t)s\ *n* -S [¹*-ist*] **:** one that professes or adheres to or specializes in an ism — usu. used disparagingly

**¹-ist** \əst *sometimes* ˌist\ *n suffix, pl* **-ists** \-s(t)s\ [ME *-iste*, fr. OF & L; OF *-iste*, fr. L *-ista*, fr. Gk *-istēs*, fr. *-is-* (fr. verb stems in *-izein -ize*) + *-tēs* (suffix forming agent nouns)] **1 a :** one that does : one that performs a (specified) action ⟨cycl*ist*⟩ ⟨balloon*ist*⟩ ⟨duell*ist*⟩ : one that makes or produces ⟨novel*ist*⟩ ⟨syllog*ist*⟩ **b :** one that plays a (specified) musical instrument ⟨organ*ist*⟩ ⟨violin*ist*⟩ **c :** one that operates a (specified) mechanical instrument or contrivance ⟨telegraph*ist*⟩ **2 a :** one that practices or studies or specializes in a (specified) art or science or particular field of knowledge or particular skill ⟨geolog*ist*⟩ ⟨mytholog*ist*⟩ ⟨algebra*ist*⟩ ⟨ventriloqu*ist*⟩ **b** (1) **:** one that is usu. professionally occupied with or interested in ⟨fashion*ist*⟩ ⟨color*ist*⟩ (2) **:** one that toys with or dabbles in ⟨controvert*ist*⟩ ⟨speculat*ist*⟩ **3 :** one that professes or adheres to or advocates a (specified) doctrine or theory or system or policy or code of behavior or procedure ⟨de*ist*⟩ ⟨social*ist*⟩ ⟨roya*list*⟩ ⟨hedon*ist*⟩ ⟨pur*ist*⟩ or that supports the doctrine or theory or system or policy or code of behavior or procedure of a (specified) individual ⟨Calvin*ist*⟩ ⟨Darwin*ist*⟩ ⟨Hitler*ist*⟩ — esp. in nouns corresponding to nouns in *-ism* **4 :** one that is marked by ⟨pessim*ist*⟩ ⟨fatal*ist*⟩ — esp. in nouns corresponding to nouns in *-ism*

**²-ist** \"\ *adj suffix* **:** of, relating to, or characteristic of (something indicated) ⟨dilettant*ist*⟩

**is't** \(ˈ)ist\ [by contr.] *archaic* **:** is it

**is·tan·bul** \ˌistə̇n|bül, -ˌstä|, -ˌstal, -ˌstaal, -ˌstäl, |n|b-, -bül *also* ˌē(ˌ)s-\ *adj, usu cap* [fr. *İstanbul*, city on the European side of the Bosporus in Turkey] **:** of or from the city of Istanbul, Turkey **:** of the kind or style prevalent in Istanbul

**¹isth·mi·an** \ˈismēən\ *n* -s [L *isthmius*, adj., isthmian (fr. Gk *isthmios*, fr. *isthmos* isthmus) + E *-an*, n. suffix] **1 :** a native or inhabitant of an isthmus **2** *usu cap* **:** a native or inhabitant of the Isthmus of Panama

**²isthmian** \"\ *adj* [L *isthmius*, adj., isthmian + E *-an*, adj. suffix] **:** of, relating to, or situated in or near an isthmus ⟨an ~ route⟩ ⟨an ~ people⟩: as **a** *often cap* **:** of or relating to the Isthmus of Corinth in Greece or the games anciently held there ⟨the *Isthmian* festival⟩ **b** *often cap* **:** of or relating to the Isthmus of Panama connecting the No. American and So. American continents ⟨the *Isthmian* canal⟩

**isth·mi·ate** \-mēˌāt\ *adj* [NL *isthmiatus*, fr. *isthmi-* (fr. *isthmus*) + L *-atus* -ate] **:** having an isthmus (sense 2)

**isth·mic** \-mik\ *adj* [L *isthmicus*, fr. Gk *isthmikos*, fr. *isthmos* isthmus + *-ikos* -ic] **1 :** ISTHMIAN **2** *also* **isth·mal** \-məl\ [*isthmus* + *-ic* or *-al*] **:** of, relating to, or taking place in a bodily isthmus ⟨~ ectopic pregnancy⟩

**isth·moid** \-ˌmȯid\ *adj* [prob. fr. (assumed) NL *isthmoides*, fr. NL *isthm-* (fr. *isthmus*) + L *-oides* -oid] **:** resembling an isthmus

**isth·mus** \ˈisməs, *chiefly Brit sometimes* ˈistm-\ *n* -ES [L, fr. Gk *isthmos*; perh. akin to ON *eith* isthmus, Gk *ithma* step, motion, *ienai* to go — more at ISSUE] **1 :** a narrow strip of land running through a body of water and having the water lying at each side and connecting two larger land areas (as two continents or a peninsula and the mainland) **2 :** a contracted part or passage connecting two larger structures or cavities: as **a :** a sharp constriction separating midbrain from hindbrain **b :** the lower portion of the uterine corpus **c :** the fleshy area on the throat of a fish between the gills **d :** a narrow intermediate portion of the pharynx of many nematodes **e :** the constricted connection between the main parts of a desmid

**isthmus of the fauces :** FAUCES 1

**-is·tic** \ˈistik, -tēk\ *also* **-is·ti·cal** \-tə̇kəl, -tēk-\ *adj suffix* [-istic fr. MF & L & Gk; MF *-istique*, fr. L *-isticus*, fr. Gk *-istikos*, fr. *-istēs* -ist + *-ikos* -ic; *-istical* fr. MF *-istique* & L *-isticus* & Gk *-istikos* + E *-al*] **:** of, relating to, or characteristic of ⟨panoist*ic*⟩ — often in adjectives corresponding to nouns in *-ism* or nouns in *-ist* ⟨altru*istic*⟩

**is·ti·o·phor·i·dae** \ˌistēōˈfȯrəˌdē\ *n pl, cap* [NL, fr. *Istiophorus*, type genus + *-idae*] **:** a family of large vigorous marine scombroid fishes comprising important food and sport fishes (as sailfishes, spearfishes, and marlins)

**is·ti·oph·o·rus** \ˌistēˈäfərəs\ *n, cap* [NL, irreg. fr. Gk *histion* sail + NL *-phorus*; akin to Gk *histanai* to cause to stand — more at STAND] **:** a small but widely distributed genus of fishes comprising the sailfishes (sense 1) and being type of the family Istiophoridae

**is·tle** *also* **ix·tle** \ˈis(t)lē\ *n* -s [AmerSp *ixtle*, fr. Nahuatl *ichtli*] **:** a fiber obtained from any of various tropical American plants: as **a :** a fiber obtained from the leaves of an epiphytic bromeliad (*Bromelia sylvestris*) **b :** a fiber obtained from any of several Mexican plants of the genus *Agave* (esp. *A. ixtli*) and used esp. for cordage and basketry

**¹is·tri·an** \ˈistrēən\ *adj, usu cap* [*Istria* + E *-an*, adj. suffix] **1 :** of, relating to, or characteristic of Istria, a peninsula on the northeast coast of the Adriatic sea **2 :** of, relating to, or characteristic of the people of Istria

**²istrian** \"\ *n* -s *cap* [*Istria* + E *-an*, n. suffix] **:** a native or inhabitant of Istria

**ists** *pl of* IST

**-ists** *pl of* -IST

**isu·rus** \īˈsu̇rəs\ *n, cap* [NL, fr. *is-* + *-urus*] **:** a genus of large voracious sharks that is sometimes made the type of a separate family but usu. included in Lamnidae — see MACKEREL SHARK

**ISV** *abbr* International Scientific Vocabulary

**ISWG** *abbr* imperial standard wire gauge

**¹it** \(ˈ)i|t, ə|, *usu* |d·+V\ *pron* [ME *it, hit*, fr. OE *hit* — more at HE] **1 a :** that one — used as neuter pronoun of the third person singular that is the subject or direct object or indirect object of a verb or the object of a preposition and usu. used in reference to (1) a lifeless thing ⟨took a quick look at the house and noticed ~ was very old⟩ ⟨saw the corpse and walked over to ~⟩ ⟨~ is now no more —E.H.Collis⟩ or (2) a plant ⟨there is a rosebush near the fence and ~ is now blooming⟩ or (3) an insect ⟨felt a fly land on her neck and squirmed as ~ crawled down⟩ or an animal whose sex is unknown or disregarded ⟨saw the horse break away and watched ~ gallop into the canyon⟩ or (4) an infant or child whose sex is unknown or disregarded ⟨if a child were severely beaten every time ~ sneezed —Bertrand Russell⟩ ⟨heard the baby crying and brought ~ some milk⟩ or (5) a group or classification of individuals or things ⟨the football team is in top form and ~ is sure of victory⟩ ⟨buy a bag of apricots . . . plums and grapes for fifteen cents, wash . . . and eat ~ on our way —Claudia Cassidy⟩ or (6) an abstract noun ⟨beauty is everywhere and ~ is a source of joy⟩ or (7) a word viewed as a word ⟨*machine* is a common word and ~ can be applied to a variety of things⟩ or (8) a phrase or clause ⟨"Go ahead," she said, but he didn't hear ~⟩; sometimes used pleonastically together with a noun as subject of a verb esp. in ballad poetry ⟨our love ~ was stronger by far —E.A.Poe⟩ and in substandard speech ⟨the horse ~ ran away⟩; often used with a present participle like the adjective *its* with a gerund in a way that makes distinction between the two constructions impossible except by arbitrary analysis ⟨wet it before applying to the seal, to prevent ~ sticking —H.S. Kingsford⟩ ⟨there was a doubt about ~ being available — Valentine Heywood⟩; see ITS; compare HE, SHE, THEY **b** (1) **:** that male or female one whose identity is unknown or uncertain — used esp. in indirect or direct questions in reference to one that is usu. not directly indicated (as by pointing) or otherwise clearly specified (as by a qualifying clause or phrase) ⟨don't know who ~ is⟩ ⟨the knocking at the door continued and she finally said "who is ~?"⟩ ⟨someone appeared dimly in the fog and ~ looks like my brother⟩ (2) **:** that male or female one whose identity is known — sometimes used in the speech of children or usu. disparagingly in the speech of others as a subject or object in reference to any person ⟨just look at my daddy and the big car ~ has⟩ ⟨what a little haughty prude ~ is —W.M.Thackeray⟩ ⟨just listen to ~ talk⟩ **c :** YOU — used in speaking to or as if to a baby ⟨did ~ hurt its little knees and chin⟩ — compare HE 4 **d :** ITSELF — used as indirect or direct object of a verb or as object of a preposition ⟨the plane plunged to earth carrying all its occupants with ~⟩ **2 a** — used as an expletive subject of an impersonal verb that expresses a simple condition or an action without direct or implied reference to an agent in statements or questions about (1) the weather ⟨~ is raining⟩ ⟨~ is getting cold⟩ ⟨is ~ a pretty day —Agnes S. Turnbull⟩ or (2) the time ⟨~'s eleven o'clock⟩ ⟨~ is late⟩ or divisions or points of time (as seasons, holidays, generalized parts of day or night) ⟨~'s only a few months until spring —C.W.Morton⟩ ⟨~ will soon be Christmas⟩ ⟨~ is getting on toward evening⟩ ⟨~ will dawn early tomorrow⟩ or (3) physical or mental conditions ⟨~ hurts when I look at a bright light⟩ ⟨~ makes him sad if he thinks about her too much⟩ or (4) an extent of distance or space ⟨~ is five miles to the next town⟩ **b** — used as an expletive subject in other statements or questions having an undefined subject ⟨if ~ hadn't been for you, I don't know what I would have done⟩ ⟨they have what ~ takes⟩ **3 a** (1) — used as an anticipatory subject of a verb whose logical subject is another word or a phrase or a clause ⟨~ is me⟩ ⟨~ is he who is responsible⟩ ⟨~ is the mayor they like⟩ ⟨~ is well you found out in time⟩ ⟨~ is necessary to repeat the whole thing⟩ ⟨~ is said the danger is great⟩ ⟨~ is a wonderful vacation spot, that town⟩ ⟨~ happened that they were away⟩; often used as subject of a periphrasis to shift emphasis from a logical subject to some other part of a statement ⟨~ was in this city that the treaty was signed⟩ (2) — used as an anticipatory object of a verb whose logical object is another word or a phrase or a clause ⟨I take ~ that there was some kind of rift —Hamilton Basso⟩ ⟨he made ~ clear, that answer of his⟩ ⟨found ~ necessary to continue⟩ ⟨made ~ evident that we needed help⟩ **b** *now chiefly dial* — used with the verb *be* where *there* is now used ⟨are so proud, so censorious, that ~ is no living with them —Paul Bayne⟩ ⟨~ was an English lady bright, and she would marry a Scottish knight —Sir Walter Scott⟩ ⟨~'s nobody here but me⟩ **c** — used with many transitive verbs as a direct object with little or no meaning and an almost entirely expletive or reinforcing function ⟨really living ~ up⟩ ⟨decided to rough ~ on his vacation⟩ or with many intransitive verbs as an apparent direct object with the same function ⟨footed ~ back to camp⟩ ⟨the satellites were free to go ~ alone —*Newsweek*⟩ or with some words used as nonce verbs as an apparent direct object with the same function ⟨decided that we would . . . hotel ~ —J.K. Jerome⟩ ⟨a man who likes to chef ~ now and then —Gerald Movius⟩ **4 a** (1) **:** a matter discussed or considered or about to be discussed or considered ⟨remembered she had told him about ~⟩ ⟨~ being agreed then —Walter Goodman⟩ (2) **:** a situation referred to either directly or by implication or about to be referred to either directly or by implication ⟨thought ~ was splendid⟩ ⟨doubted ~ would happen⟩ ⟨~ added up to a strangeness for which nothing in the previous frontier culture was a preparation —Bernard DeVoto⟩ (3) **:** a statement or idea or similar object of attention referred to either directly or by implication or about to be referred to either directly or by implication ⟨if you remember these points ~ will help you⟩ **b :** something read (as a passage in a book, words on a sign) ⟨~ tells in the book about the American Revolution⟩ ⟨~ says in the papers he expects to win the election⟩ ⟨a mile back ~ said to take a right turn⟩ or something looked at (as a traffic signal, a directional arrow) ⟨come on, ~ says to go⟩ **5 :** the general state of affairs or circumstances **:** general situation ⟨~ hasn't gone so well today⟩ ⟨came to that remote place to fish, get away from ~ all —Robert Murphy⟩ ⟨remember me, when ~ is well with you —Gen 40:14 (RSV)⟩ **6 a** (1) **:** something that has been done ⟨do ~ some more⟩ or is being done ⟨quit ~⟩ ⟨cut ~ out⟩ or is to be done ⟨go to ~⟩ ⟨he'll do ~ the right way⟩ ⟨decided to make a long weekend of ~ —Rebecca West⟩ (2) **:** some unpleasant or dreaded eventuality ⟨in for ~ now⟩; *specif* **:** punishment or chastisement or retribution ⟨going to catch ~⟩ ⟨put up with his sneers as long as possible and then let him have ~⟩ **b** (1) **:** all that one can desire or experience ⟨claims he's had ~ and that life is now pretty much a bore⟩ (2) **:** all that one can endure or suffer ⟨had a terrible day and swore he'd really had ~⟩ (3) **:** all that one is going to be allowed to have or do ⟨he's had ~ — I'm not going to put up with that nonsense any longer⟩ **c :** all that is required **:** the total extent of something needed or wanted ⟨when you've finished that job, that's ~ and you can go home⟩ ⟨everyone passes by, shakes hands and that's ~ —D.E.Weinland⟩ **d :** an expenditure of effort in attempting to attain an objective **:** STRUGGLE, CONTEST ⟨stick to ~ and you'll win out⟩ **7 :** a way out of a difficulty **:** answer to a problem **:** SOLUTION ⟨I have ~! This is what we'll do⟩ **8 a :** what is important or essential or tenaciously held to or sought after **:** what counts **:** what matters ⟨haven't got a chance and you should realize ~ is all over now⟩; *specif* **:** LIFE ⟨had stopped breathing and I could see ~ was all over⟩ **b** (1) **:** a crucial moment when much is at stake **:** a crisis on whose outcome much or everything depends ⟨an offensive was about to be launched and headquarters felt that this was ~⟩ (2) **:** a point at which the end of life or the end of everything that matters is imminent ⟨this is ~. From now on no power on earth can save the doomed city — F.V.Drake⟩ **9 a :** a quality or group of qualities requisite or desirable for or evidenced in a particular situation ⟨the legislators had ~ on most of the other delegates in convention maneuvering —Bill Hatch⟩ **b :** something that is expected or desired **:** something suitable or satisfactory ⟨that's ~, you're doing fine⟩ **c** (1) **:** something that perfectly or nearly perfectly meets the requirements of a situation **:** the very thing needed or required **:** just the thing wanted ⟨here's a suggestion for a Christmas gift that is really ~⟩ (2) **:** something that is without equal **:** something peerless ⟨stop acting as though you were ~⟩ ⟨she just seems to think she's ~⟩ (3) **:** something beyond which one cannot go **:** the ultimate **:** PINNACLE, ACME ⟨when it comes to graciousness, she's really ~⟩ **10 :** SEXUAL INTERCOURSE ⟨if I wanted to let you touch me I would . . . can't you see I don't want ~ —Morley Callaghan⟩

**²it** \"\ *adj* [ME *hit*, fr. *hit* (pron.)] *now chiefly dial* **:** ITS

**³it** \ˈit, *usu* ˈid·+V\ *n* -s [¹*it*] **1 :** the player in a game who performs a key active or passive function (as trying to catch others in a game of tag or to answer questions in a guessing game) essential to the nature of the game **2 :** physical allure esp. when accompanied by personal magnetism and charm **:** SEX APPEAL

**-it** \ə̇t, ə̇d\ *vb suffix* [ME, alter. of *-ed*] *Scot var of* -ED

**it** *abbr* item

**IT** *abbr* **1** immediate transportation **2** immunity test **3** income tax **4** internal thread **5** international tolerance **6** *often not cap* [L *in transitu*] in transit

**ita** \ˈēd·ə\ *n, pl* **ita** *or* **itas** *usu cap* [Tag] **:** AETA

**ita·bi·rite** \ˌēd·əˈbiˌrīt\ *n* -s [*Itabira* (now, Presidente Vargas), town in Minas Gerais state, Brazil) + E *-ite*] **:** a quartzite containing micaceous hematite

**ita·cism** \ˈēd·əˌsizəm\ *n* -s [modif. of Gk *ēta* eta + *-cism* (as in *iotacism*) — more at ETA] **1 :** pronunciation of Greek eta as \ē\ **2 :** IOTACISM

**ita·cist** \-ˌsə̇st\ *n* -s **:** one that practices or favors itacism — **ita·cis·tic** \¦≈≈¦sistik\ *adj*

**it·a·col·u·mite** \ˌid·əˈkäl(y)əˌmīt\ *n* -s [*Itacolumi*, mountain in Minas Gerais state, Brazil + E *-ite*] **:** a schistose micaceous quartzite that is flexible when split into thin slabs

**it·a·con·ate** \ˌid·əˈkäˌnāt\ *n* -s [*itaconic* (acid) + *-ate*] **:** a salt or ester of itaconic acid

**it·a·con·ic acid** \¦≈≈¦≈nik-\ *n* [ISV, anagram of *aconitic*] **:** a crystalline dicarboxylic acid $HOOCC(=CH_2)CH_2COOH$ obtained by decomposing aconitic acid or usu. by fermentation of sugars with molds of the genus *Aspergillus* and used as a monomer for both vinyl-type polymers and polyesters; methylene-succinic acid

**ital-** *or* **italo-** *comb form, usu cap* [*Ital-* fr. L *Italus*; *Italo-* fr. It or L; It, fr. *italo*, fr. L *Italus*] **1 :** Italian ⟨*Ital*american⟩ **2 :** Italian and ⟨*Italo*-Austrian⟩

**ital** *abbr* italic

**¹ital·ian** \əˈtalyən, *chiefly dial or substand or disparaging* (ˈ)īˈt-\ *n* -s *cap* [ME, fr. L *Italia* Italy (fr. Gk *Italia*) + ME *-an*] **1 a :** a native or inhabitant of Italy **b :** one that is of Italian descent **2 :** the language of the Italians developed from the Vulgar Latin of ancient times

**²italian** \"\ *adj, usu cap* **1 a :** of, relating to, or characteristic of Italy **b :** of, relating to, or characteristic of Italians **2 :** of, relating to, or characteristic of the Italian language

**¹ital·ian·ate** \-ˌnāt\ *vt* -ED/-ING/-S [prob. fr. It *italianato*, adj.] **:** ITALIANIZE

**²ital·ian·ate** \-nə̇t, -ˌnāt\ *adj, usu cap* [It *italianato*, fr. *italiano* Italian (fr. *Italia* Italy — fr. L — + *-ano* — fr. L *-anus* -an) + *-ato* (fr. L *-atus* -ate)] **1 :** ITALIANIZED ⟨an *Italianate* Englishman⟩ **2 :** having an Italian quality **:** marked by Italian characteristics or influence ⟨*Italianate* architecture⟩

**italian bee** *n, usu cap I* **:** a honeybee predominantly yellowish in color that resembles the Carniolan bee in habits

**italian blue** *n, often cap I* **:** a vivid greenish blue

**italian chestnut** *n, usu cap I* **:** SPANISH CHESTNUT

**italian clover** *n, usu cap I* **:** CRIMSON CLOVER

**italian corn salad** *n, usu cap I* **:** a southern European succulent plant (*Valerianella eriocarpa*) used as a salad vegetable

**italian cypress** *n, usu cap I* **:** a Eurasian tree (*Cupressus sempervirens*) with thin gray bark and erect or ascending branches and dark green leaves resembling scales — called also *Mediterranean cypress*

**italian earth** *n, often cap I* **1 :** RAW SIENNA **2 :** BURNT SIENNA

**italian fennel** *n, usu cap I* **:** CAROSELLA

**italian green** *n* **1** *often cap I* **:** TERRE VERTE 2 **2** *usu cap I&G* **:** a sulfur dye — see DYE table I (under *Sulfur Green 11*)

**italian greyhound** *n, usu cap I* **:** a toy dog of a breed developed by selective breeding from the standard-sized greyhound

**italian hand** *n, usu cap I* **1 :** a book hand characterized by roundness and a fine sloping line developed about the 12th century A.D. in Italy from the Roman cursive and revived by calligraphers in the early 15th century and used as the model for the first Italian printers and for modern English handwriting — compare ITALIC **2 :** craftiness or subtlety in the conduct of political, business, or personal affairs — usu. used in the phrase *fine Italian hand*

**italian honeysuckle** *n, usu cap I* **:** ITALIAN WOODBINE

**ital·ian·ism** \-yəˌnizəm\ *n* -s *usu cap* [prob. fr. MF *italianisme*, fr. OIt *italiano* Italian + MF *-isme* -ism — more at ITALIANATE] **1 a :** a quality or group of qualities distinctive of Italy or the Italian people **b :** a linguistic feature (as a pronunciation or a word or a phrase or an idiom) borrowed from or suggestive of the Italian language **2 a :** specialized interest in or emulation of Italian qualities or achievements **b :** attachment to or furtherance of Italian policies or ideals

**ital·ian·ist** \-nə̇st\ *n* -s *usu cap* **1 :** a specialist in the study of Italy or the Italian people or the Italian language **2 :** one that is attached to or seeks to further Italian policies or ideals

**ital·ian·i·ty** \ə̇ˌtalēˈanəd·ē, -lˈya-\ *n* -ES *usu cap* **:** the quality or state of being Italian (as in character or allegiance)

**ital·ian·iza·tion** \ə̇ˌtalyənə̇ˈzāshən, -ˌnīˈz-\ *n* -s *usu cap* **1 :** the action or process of italianizing or of becoming italianized **2 :** something (as a name or word) that has been italianized

**ital·ian·ize** \ə̇ˈtalyəˌnīz\ *vb* -ED/-ING/-s *often cap, see -ize in Explan Notes* [prob. fr. F *italianiser*, fr. MF, fr. OIt *italiano* Italian + MF *-iser* -ize — more at ITALIANATE] *vi* **:** to act in a fashion regarded as distinctive of Italians; *specif* **:** to follow (as in style or technique) recognized Italian painters ⟨the *italianizing* masters of Antwerp⟩ **~** *vt* **1 :** to make Italian (as in behavior, appearance, culture, style) ⟨foreigners gradually *italianized* by residence in Italy⟩ **:** cause to have Italian characteristics ⟨*italianizing* a style of architecture⟩ **2 :** to change or modify (as a word or expression foreign to Italian) so as to make conform (as in spelling or pronunciation) to characteristics of the Italian language ⟨an *italianized* family name⟩

**ital·ian·iz·er** \-zə(r)\ *n* -s *often cap* **:** one that italianizes

**italian kale** *n, usu cap I* **:** SEVEN-TOP TURNIP

**italian lake** *n, often cap I* **:** YELLOW OCHER 2

**ital·ian·ly** *adv, usu cap* **:** in an Italian manner

**italian millet** *n, usu cap I* **:** FOXTAIL MILLET

**italian ocher** *n, often cap I* **:** RAW SIENNA 2

**italian paste** *n, usu cap I* **:** ALIMENTARY PASTE

**italian pear scale** *n, usu cap I* **:** a reddish to purple hard scale (*Epidiaspis piricola*) that is sometimes destructive to various fruit and nut trees in California

**italian pink** *n, often cap I* **:** DUTCH PINK 2

**italian pool** *n, usu cap I* **:** pin pool played with four balls

**italian poplar** *n, usu cap I* **:** LOMBARDY POPLAR

**italian roast** *n, usu cap I* **:** coffee of an extremely dark roast

**italian ryegrass** *also* **italian rye** *n, usu cap I* **:** a European grass (*Lolium multiflorum*) much used for hay and in the U.S. also for turf and green-manuring

**italians** *pl of* ITALIAN

**italian sixth** *n, usu cap I* **:** an augmented sixth chord consisting of a musical tone with a major third and an augmented sixth above the lowest tone (as A-flat, C, F-sharp)

**italian sonnet** *n, usu cap I* **:** PETRARCHAN SONNET

**italian stone pine** *n, usu cap I* **:** STONE PINE 2

**italian thistle** *n, usu cap I* **:** a hoary thistle (*Carduus pycnocephalus*) native to the Mediterranean region but established as a weed in the southwestern U.S.

**italian turnip** *or* **italian turnip broccoli** *n, usu cap I* **:** an annual or biennial (*Brassica ruvo*) prob. of European origin but grown elsewhere for its tops and tender flower shoots which are used as greens — called also *broccoli rab*

**italian vegetable marrow** *n, usu cap I* **:** COCOZELLE

**italian vermouth** *n, usu cap I* **:** sweet vermouth

**italian walnut** *n, usu cap I* **:** ENGLISH WALNUT

**italian woodbine** *n, usu cap I* **:** a Eurasian honeysuckle (*Lonicera caprifolium*) sometimes escaped in America and having the upper leaves connate and the flowers usu. in sessile whorls in the axils

**¹ital·ic** \ə̇ˈtalik, -lēk *also* (ˈ)īˈt-\ *adj* [L *Italicus* Italian, of Italy, fr. Gk *Italikos*, fr. *Italia* Italy + *-ikos* -ic] **1** *usu cap* **a** [NL *Italica*, fr. L, fem. of *Italicus*] **:** COMPOSITE **b** *of handwriting* **:** characterized by a sloping angle suggestive of italics ⟨written in a medieval *Italic* script⟩ — compare GOTHIC 3 **c** (1) **:** of, relating to, or characteristic of ancient Italy (2) **:** of, relating to, or characteristic of the peoples of ancient Italy ⟨vanished *Italic* cultures⟩ **d** (1) **:** of, relating to, or characteristic of a branch of the Indo-European language family that includes Latin and other languages (as Oscan, Umbrian) spoken by the peoples of ancient Italy and that also includes the Romance languages (as Italian, French, Spanish) descended from Latin (2) **:** of, relating to, or characteristic of the ancient languages of the Italic branch of the Indo-European language family as contrasted with the modern Romance languages (3) **:** of, relating to, or characteristic of Osco-Umbrian **2** *sometimes cap* **:** of, relating to, produced in, or characteristic of a style of distinctively printed letters or numbers or other characters that slant upward to the right (as in "*these words are italic*") and that are sometimes distinguished from other faces (as some obliques) having about the same degree of slant by the form of the letter *a* and that are typically used to give emphasis to a word or group of words or to refer to words as words or to indicate words or phrases foreign to the language of a context or to refer to titles of long works ⟨beautifully printed ~ letters⟩ ⟨paragraphs beginning with ~ capitals⟩

**²italic** \"\ *n* -s **1** *sometimes cap* **a :** an italic character **:** italic type ⟨an ~ is used at the beginning of each subdivision⟩ ⟨introduced ~s as a device for achieving emphasis⟩ ⟨printed in ~⟩ ⟨a font of ~s⟩ **b :** a written letter or number or other character (as in a handwritten or typed manuscript) that is underscored for emphasis or for some other purpose achieved in print by the use of italic type or that is so underscored (as in a handwritten or typed manuscript sent to a printer) to indicate that the matter underscored is to be set in italic type ⟨each ~ is clearly underlined⟩ ⟨writes a delighted "*yes!*" with ~s and a mark of exclamation —R.G.F.Robinson⟩ ⟨after the underscored sentence in the manuscript the author writes "~s mine"⟩ **c** *usu* **italics** *pl but sometimes sing in constr* **:** exaggerated intonation or some similar oral speech device by which one or more words is heavily and usu. affectedly emphasized or otherwise given sharp prominence ⟨was yapping, her silly voice fraught with ~s —Margaret Long⟩ ⟨a woman who has an irritating way of speaking in ~s —W.J. Locke⟩ **2** *cap* **a :** a branch of the Indo-European language family that includes Latin and other languages (as Oscan, Umbrian) spoken by the peoples of ancient Italy and that also includes the Romance languages (as Italian, French, Spanish) descended from Latin — see INDO-EUROPEAN LANGUAGES table **b :** the group of ancient languages of this branch as contrasted with the modern Romance languages **c :** OSCO-UMBRIAN

**ital·i·cism** \-ləˌsizəm\ *n* -s *usu cap* [¹*italic* + *-ism*] **:** ITALIANISM 1b

**ital·i·ci·za·tion** \ə̇ˌtaləsə̇ˈzāshən, -ˌsīˈ *also* ī,-\ *n* [*italicize* + *-ation*] **:** the use of italics or a single underscore in printing or writing

**ital·i·cize** \-ˌsīz\ *vb* -ED/-ING/-S *see -ize in Explan Notes* [¹*italic* + *-ize*] *vt* **1 a :** to print in italics ⟨the printer *italicized* the whole passage⟩ **b :** to underscore with a single line for emphasis or for some other purpose achieved in print by the use of italic type or so as to indicate that the matter underscored is to be set in italic type ⟨annoyingly *italicizes* sentence after sentence in her notes⟩ **2 :** ACCENTUATE, EMPHASIZE, STRESS: as **a :** to give sharp prominence to (spoken words) usu. affectedly by the use of some oral speech device esp. exaggerated intonation ⟨she was *italicizing* every other word with that deadly, glittering brightness that a woman puts on —George Orwell⟩ ⟨*italicized* words and even phrases surged about in her conversation —Ngaio Marsh⟩ **b :** to bring out strongly or cause to be highlighted **:** play up ⟨decorative features that ~ the building's perfect symmetry⟩ ⟨his scorn for the orthodox language and logic of the law is *italicized* by such wry remarks —Fred Rodell⟩ ⟨serves especially to ~ the principle —N.F.Adkins⟩ ⟨dramatically *italicizes* the movie's theme —*Newsweek*⟩ **c :** to outline sharply **:** bring into sharp relief ⟨the little carmine smudge of her *italicized* lips —Bruce Marshall⟩ ~ *vi* **:** to use italics ⟨has a habit of *italicizing*⟩

[1]**ital·i·ote** \ə'talē,ōt, -ēət\ *also* **ital·i·ot** \-ēət, -ē,ät\ *n* -s *usu cap* [Gk *Italiōtēs*, fr. *Italia* Italy + *-ōtēs* -ote] **:** a Greek inhabitant of ancient Italy

[2]**italiote** \"\ *adj, usu cap* **:** of or relating to the Italiotes

**italo-** — see ITAL-

[1]**italo·phile** \ə'talə,fīl, 'id-ᵊlō,f-\ *also* **italo·phil** \-,fil\ *adj, usu cap* [*Ital-* + *-phile* or *-phil*] **:** friendly to or favoring what is Italian ⟨~ policies⟩

[2]**italophile** \"\ *n* -s *usu cap* **:** one that is friendly to or favors what is Italian

**it·a·ly** \'id-ᵊlē, 'itᵊl-, -li, *in rapid speech* 'itl-\ *adj, usu cap* [fr. *Italy*, country in southern Europe] **:** of or from Italy **:** of the kind or style prevalent in Italy

**ita palm** *or* **eta palm** \'ēd-ə-\ *n* [of Arawakan origin; akin to Arawak (Guiana) *ité* ita palm, Baniva *itéui*] **:** MIRITI PALM

**itas** *pl of* ITA

**ita·uba** \,ēd-ə'übə, ,id-\ *n* -s [Pg *itaúba*, fr. Tupi *itauba*] **1 :** a large South American tree (*Mezilaurus itauba*) of the family Lauraceae that yields a durable russet-brown wood much used in marine and general construction **2 :** the wood of the itauba

[1]**itch** \'ich\ *n* -ES [ME *icche, yicche*, fr. OE *gicce*, fr. *giccan*, v.] **1 a :** a localized or generalized uneasy sensation (as of a crawling, prickling, stinging) in the upper surface of the skin usu. considered to result from mild stimulation of pain receptors and producing a feeling of irritation in the affected area and eliciting an urge to relieve the affected area by scratching **:** ITCHING, PRURITUS ⟨had an ~ and scratched it⟩ **b :** a skin disorder (as a mange) accompanied by such a sensation; *esp* **:** a contagious eruption in man and animals that is marked by this sensation experienced to an intense degree and by surface lesions and that is caused by invasion of the skin by an itch mite (*Sarcoptes scabiei*) that forms minute galleries in the skin and keeps up a constant irritation — usu. used with *the* ⟨has the ~⟩; compare MANGE **2 a (1) :** a restless usu. constant often compulsive desire for or hankering after something **:** restless longing **:** uneasy craving ⟨a compelling ~ for money and success —Lee Rogow⟩ ⟨the ~ to travel⟩ ⟨the same restless ~ to be always doing something else —Bertrand Russell⟩ ⟨was uninfected by the ~ of publicity —V.L.Parrington⟩ **(2) :** a restless craving for sensual esp. sexual gratification **:** LUST, PRURIENCE ⟨the ~ of the senses —Bruce Marshall⟩ ⟨with meaty good looks and the gross ~ they often portend —*Time*⟩ ⟨had aroused in him only the vague adolescent ~ of desire which almost any personable woman could satisfy —Aldous Huxley⟩ **b :** a restless usu. constant inclination toward something **:** restless propensity **:** uneasy predisposition or overreadiness ⟨the ~ to justify all conduct on logical grounds —H.J.Muller⟩ ⟨an ~ for activity —Raymond Holden⟩ **3 :** a condition of restless ferment **:** seething agitation **:** STEW ⟨the ~ of aggressive nationalism —Karl Robson⟩ ⟨was in an ~ to be off —Bruce Marshall⟩ ⟨lived in a constant ~ of irritation —Hesketh Pearson⟩

[2]**itch** \"\ *vb* -ED/-ING/-S [ME *ichen, icchen, yicchen*, fr. OE *giccan*; akin to OHG *jucchen* to itch, MD *joken*] *vi* **1 a :** to have a localized or generalized uneasy sensation (as of a crawling, prickling, stinging) in the upper surface of the skin **:** have an itch ⟨seemed to ~ all over⟩ ⟨her arm ~*ed*⟩ **b :** to produce such a sensation ⟨heavy winter underwear that ~*ed*⟩ **2 a :** to have a restless usu. constant often compulsive desire for or hankering after something **:** long restlessly for something **:** crave something uneasily ⟨and ~ to get their hands on a juicy morsel —D.L.Cohn⟩ ⟨way ~*ing* to take immediate action —W.F.Hambly⟩ ⟨~*ed* to see the world⟩ **b :** to have a restless usu. constant inclination toward something **:** have a restless propensity for or uneasy predisposition to something **:** be impatiently eager **:** be overready ⟨killers who ~*ed* to kill again —Hal Burton⟩ **3 :** to be in a restless ferment **:** SEETHE, STEW ⟨~ with one curiosity —Milton Bracker⟩ ⟨~*es* with lechery —J.I.Cope⟩ ~ *vt* **1 :** to cause to have a localized or generalized uneasy sensation (as of a crawling, prickling, stinging) in the upper surface of the skin **:** cause to have an itch ⟨felt it ~ his leg —Joan Williams⟩ ⟨wool socks that ~*ed* his feet⟩ **2 :** IRK, VEX, IRRITATE ⟨that always has been amused . . . where the others were ~*ed* —Sinclair Lewis⟩

[3]**itch** \"\ *var of* ECHE

**itch·i·ly** \'ichəlē, -li\ *adv* **:** in an itchy manner **:** NERVOUSLY, RESTLESSLY ⟨holding it ~, as if it were a snake —*Time*⟩

**itch·i·ness** \-chēnəs, -chin-\ *n* -ES **:** the quality or state of being itchy

[1]**itching** *adj* [fr. pres. part. of [2]*itch*] **:** that itches: **a :** having, producing, or marked by an uneasy sensation in the skin ⟨bothered with an ~ back⟩ ⟨an ~ skin eruption⟩ **b (1) :** having or marked by a restless desire or craving or longing for something ⟨always glad to cater to her ~ public⟩ **(2) :** restlessly or insatiably seeking after what is novel and different ⟨the time is coming when people will not endure sound teaching, but having ~ ears they will accumulate for themselves teachers to suit their own likings —2 Tim 4:3 (RSV)⟩ **(3) :** restlessly or insatiably seeking after acquisitions esp. money **:** AVARICIOUS ⟨had ~ fingers always ready for a bribe⟩ ⟨an ~ palm⟩ **c :** having or marked by a restless inclination toward or predisposition to something **:** impatiently eager ⟨~ anxiety —G.M.Trevelyan⟩ ⟨an ~ impulse —B.A.Williams⟩; *specif* **:** restlessly disposed to travel about and not to remain long in any one place ⟨born . . . with an ~ foot, he started drifting down through the cattle ranges —W.C.Tuttle⟩ ⟨having had ~ feet in his journalistic days, he had at least six different home towns —Volta Torrey⟩ **d :** being in a restless ferment **:** SEETHING, STEWING ⟨~ adolescents⟩

[2]**itching** *n* -s [ME *icchinge, yicching*, fr. gerund of *icchen, yicchen* to itch — more at ITCH] **:** ITCH 1a, 2

**itch mite** *n* **1 :** any of several minute parasitic mites that burrow into the skin of man and animals and cause itch; *esp* **:** a mite of any of several varieties of a species (*Sarcoptes scabiei*) that causes the itch, is about 1/60 of an inch long, and has a round-ovate body and three-jointed legs and mandibles resembling minute needles **2** *Austral* **:** CHIGGER

**itchweed** \'ˌ=ˌ=\ *n* **:** a white hellebore (*Veratrum album*) of Europe

**itchwood** \'ˌ=ˌ=\ *also* **itchwood tree** *n* **:** a tree (*Semecarpus vitiensis*) of the Pacific islands with an irritant milky juice

**itchy** \'ichē, -chi\ *adj, usu* -ER/-EST **1 :** ITCHING: as **a :** having, affected by, or resembling an itch or the itch ⟨dirty ~ vagabonds⟩ ⟨an ~ disease⟩ **b :** that causes or tends to cause itching ⟨an ~ sweater⟩ ⟨the thermometer leaped in a day from wind-bitten chill to ~ warmth —Sinclair Lewis⟩ **c (1) :** filled with restless desire or longing or craving for something ⟨fresh out of high school and ~ for excitement —*Time*⟩ **(2) :** restlessly craving sensual esp. sexual gratification **:** LUSTING, PRURIENT ⟨~ young profligates⟩ **d :** restlessly or compulsively driven toward action **:** impatiently eager ⟨an ~ reformer —W.L.Sullivan⟩ ⟨when some local rifleman shows evidence of an ~ trigger finger —Horace Sutton⟩ **2 :** nervously restless **:** JUMPY, RESTIVE ⟨gets ~ if you're not around⟩

[1]**-ite** \,īt, *usu* ,īd-+V\ *n suffix* -s [ME, fr. OF & L; OF, fr. L *-ita, -ites*, fr. Gk *-itēs* (n. & adj. suffix)] **1 a :** native **:** inhabitant **:** resident ⟨Gotham*ite*⟩ ⟨Brooklyn*ite*⟩ ⟨New Hampshir*ite*⟩ **:** occupant **:** dweller ⟨flat*ite*⟩ ⟨trailer*ite*⟩ **b :** descendant **:** offspring ⟨Adam*ite*⟩ **c (1) :** adherent **:** follower **:** supporter ⟨Jacob*ite*⟩ **:** advocate ⟨Darwin*ite*⟩ **:** devotee ⟨Browning*ite*⟩ **(2) :** member of a (specified) group or organization or movement ⟨Pusey*ite*⟩ **2 a (1) :** substance produced through some (specified) process ⟨anabol*ite*⟩ ⟨catabol*ite*⟩ **(2) :** commercially manufactured product ⟨ebon*ite*⟩ ⟨lydd*ite*⟩ ⟨vulcan*ite*⟩ **b :** -ITOL — esp. in commercial names ⟨dulc*ite*⟩ **3** [NL *-ites*, fr. L] **:** fossil ⟨coral*lite*⟩ ⟨filic*ite*⟩ **4 :** mineral ⟨erythr*ite*⟩ **:** rock ⟨chromit*ite*⟩ **5** [F, fr. L *-ita, -ites*] **:** segment or constituent part of a body or of a bodily part ⟨som*ite*⟩ ⟨dendr*ite*⟩

[2]**-ite** \"\ *n suffix* -s [F, alter. of *-ate* (fr. NL *-atum*) — more at -ATE] **:** salt or ester of an acid with a name ending in *-ous* ⟨nitr*ite*⟩ ⟨sulf*ite*⟩

**itea** \'id-ēə, 'id-\ *n* [NL, fr. Gk, willow — more at WITHY] **1** *cap* **:** a genus of shrubs (family Saxifragaceae) having racemes of small white flowers with linear petals and a 2-valved capsular fruit — see VIRGINIA WILLOW **2** -s **:** any plant of the genus *Itea*

[1]**item** \'īd-əm, 'ītəm, 'ī,tem\ *adv* [ME, fr. L, fr. *ita* thus, prob. after L *id* it, that: *idem* the same — more at ITERATE] **1 :** and in addition **:** LIKEWISE, ALSO — used to introduce and call special attention to a new fact or particular or statement ⟨a length of chain, ~ a hook —Philip Guedalla⟩ **2 a** — used to introduce and call special attention to an initial statement and to each of the new statements that follow that are viewed as forming a related series with the initial statement **b** — used to introduce and call special attention to a single statement that is not viewed as one of a related series **c** — used **(1)** to introduce and signalize an initial particular or detail and each of the new particulars or details that follow that are viewed as forming a related group with the initial particular or detail or **(2)** to introduce and signalize each individual thing (as an article of household goods, an article of apparel, an object in an art collection, a book in a library) belonging to an aggregate of individual things that are being listed one after the other in an enumeration (as in an inventory or similar list)

[2]**item** \'īd-əm, 'ītəm\ *n* -s [MF, fr. *item* (adv.), fr. L] **1 a** *obs* **:** an admonition or warning **b** *now dial* **:** HINT, INTIMATION, INKLING **2 a (1) :** an individual particular or detail singled out from a group of related particulars or details ⟨support him down to the ~ —*Time*⟩; *esp* **:** a small or tiny detail ⟨a courteous writer will stop short of rubbing into our minds the last ~ of all that he means —C.E.Montague⟩ **(2) :** a detail of information **:** piece of information ⟨gave names and addresses and other relevant ~*s*⟩ **(3) :** an individualizing or distinguishing mark or part or quality or characteristic ⟨an ~ of his customary appearance —Bernard DeVoto⟩ **:** FEATURE ⟨carefully studied each ~ in the landscape⟩ ⟨more than one ~ in the decorative features of the room was highly original⟩ **:** TRAIT ⟨he was pleased by every unlikeness to things American, by every ~ he could hail as characteristic —H.G.Wells⟩ ⟨inherited ~*s* from both ancestral lines, whether hair color or intelligence —Ruth Benedict⟩ **b (1) :** an individual thing (as an article of household goods, an article of apparel, an object in an art collection, a book in a library) singled out from an aggregate of individual things (as those being enumerated in a bill or inventory or similar list) ⟨was charged for three ~*s*⟩ ⟨glanced at each ~ in the list⟩ **:** individual object **:** ARTICLE ⟨cherished ~*s* of Americana —Jerome Weidman⟩ **(2) :** something singled out from a specified or implied category of things of the same kind ⟨bread, meat, and other food ~*s*⟩ ⟨an important ~ of international trade⟩ ⟨various ~*s* of clothing⟩ ⟨thousands of ~*s* of mail⟩ **(3) :** a thing of a particular class or kind as contrasted with a related thing of another class or kind ⟨the real ~ in the series —H.J.Laski⟩ **(4) :** something produced by manufacturing or manual labor or in some other way **:** a piece of goods **:** PRODUCT, COMMODITY ⟨a fast-selling ~⟩ ⟨marketing a variety of ~*s*⟩ ⟨where only a very few ~*s* are sold in bulk —A.S.Igleheart⟩ **(5) :** a check or draft or other financial instrument **c :** SHOW **c (1) :** a film or stage presentation or similar production **:** SHOW ⟨a bright new ~ on Broadway⟩ ⟨had seen this ~ brilliantly danced —Winthrop Sargeant⟩ **(2) :** one of the parts of such a production ⟨the main ~ of the show was to be a program of native dances —Ursula G. Bower⟩ **d** *Brit* **:** a selection of instrumental or sung music **:** musical selection **:** piece of music ⟨before even the first ~ is played listeners are relaxed and receptive —Clifford Lawson-Reece⟩ **3 a :** an object of attention or concern or interest to a specified degree ⟨an ~ of great importance⟩ or in a specified field ⟨an essential ~ for every home⟩ or to a specified individual ⟨excellent pictures add to the value of this book as a shipman's ~ —George Horne b. 1902⟩ ⟨an ~ of historical interest to the collector —Edith Diehl⟩ — compare COLLECTOR'S ITEM **b :** one of usu. two or more points of discussion or consideration **:** TOPIC, SUBJECT, MATTER ⟨there was one more ~ he wanted to speak about⟩ ⟨the index of the book listed all ~*s* covered⟩ ⟨added another ~ to the agenda⟩ **4 a (1) :** something that forms a contributory or component part or section of something specified ⟨mentioned a separate ~ of income⟩ ⟨obliteration of religion as an ~ of state policy —Hartzell Spence⟩ **(2) :** one of the elements or circumstances or influences that contributes to producing an indicated result **:** FACTOR ⟨a major ~ of school expense⟩ **(3) :** a subdivision of a cultural trait **:** a particular cultural factor or small group of such factors **b :** something usu. written down that forms part of a larger whole: as **(1) :** one of a series of separate listings (as each of the separate details given in a statement of charges for goods ordered or as each of the separate credits or debits detailed in a book of account) **:** ENTRY **(2) :** a brief line (as a remark, observation, comment) or a paragraph or two having a largely self-contained theme or subject and forming a contributory part of a more extensive piece of writing (as a newspaper column, diary, journal) **(3) :** a brief news bulletin or news report **:** a brief piece of news ⟨one ~ of news reached him after another, each more harassing than the one before —C.S.Forester⟩ **(4) :** a piece of writing (as an article, story, poem) usu. relatively short in length that forms a contributory part of a longer work (as an anthology, reference book, periodical) ⟨contributed a couple of ~*s* to the magazine⟩ **(5) :** a subordinate provision **:** CLAUSE ⟨may also veto ~*s* of proposed legislation and accept the parts of which they approve —A.N.Christensen⟩ **c (1) :** a unit of measurement (as a question, statement) in a test or scale (as of mental aptitude) **(2) :** a unit of correlated information (as the data indicated on a business punched card) about an individual person or thing **5 a :** something unspecified **:** an indeterminate thing ⟨her shopping bag was loaded with miscellaneous ~*s* she had bought⟩ **b :** something routine in a group of routine things **:** a run-of-the-mill thing ⟨just one more ~ in a busy day⟩ ⟨is an event, not a mere ~ in the year's publishing list —D.W.Brogan⟩

**syn** ITEM, DETAIL, and PARTICULAR can signify one of the things, either separate and distinct or considered so, that constitute a whole. ITEM applies chiefly to each thing in a list of things or in a group of things that lend themselves to listing ⟨an *item* in a laundry list⟩ ⟨each *item* of income⟩ ⟨an *item* in an inventory⟩ ⟨the first *item* confronting the mason in the building of footings and foundations for a new building is the excavation —J.R.Dalzell⟩ DETAIL in this connection applies to each separate thing which enters into the building, form, or construction of something as a house, a painting, narrative, or operation ⟨*details* of the building's architecture⟩ ⟨the *details* of modern life which pass daily under our eyes —Matthew Arnold⟩ ⟨the *details* of my employment —Mary W. Shelley⟩ ⟨a painter's fine execution of *details*⟩ PARTICULAR in this connection implies a relationship with any whole and stresses that relationship more than ITEM or DETAIL, emphasizing the smallness, singleness, and concreteness of each item or detail in the whole ⟨we know nothing of their language, and only . . . minor *particulars* of their social customs and religion —R.W. Murray⟩ ⟨the real question is what is the world . . . and that can be revealed only by the study of all nature's *particulars* —William James⟩ ⟨things are necessary or probable in kinds or species not simply as *particulars* —John Dewey⟩

[3]**item** \"\ *vt* -ED/-ING/-S **1** *archaic* **:** to figure up **:** COMPUTE, RECKON **2** *archaic* **:** to set down the particular details of **:** make a note or memorandum of

[4]**item** \"\ *usu cap* — a communications code word for the letter *i*

**iteming** *n* -s [prob. fr. E dial. *iteming* (taken as pres. part.) trifling, fidgeting, fr. [2]*item* + *-ing*] *dial Eng* **:** lack of earnestness **:** FRIVOLITY

**item·iza·tion** \,īd-əmə'zāshən, ,ītə-, -,mī'z-\ *n* -s **:** the action of itemizing

**item·ize** \'ˌ=ˌ,mīz\ *vt* -ED/-ING/-S *see -ize in Explan Notes* [[2]*item* + *-ize*] **1 a (1) :** to set down item by item **:** analyze or arrange or present item by item ⟨*itemizing* the cost⟩ ⟨*itemized* all expenses⟩ **(2) :** to specify the separate items of **:** list each item of ⟨*itemized* their contributions to charity⟩ **b :** to make due note of as an item **:** list as an item ⟨must ~ each piece of property —R.B.Gehman⟩ **2 :** to note or state the separate particulars or details of item by item ⟨*itemized* in a glowing eulogy his contribution to science⟩ — **item·iz·er** \-zə(r)\ *n* -s

**itemized** *adj* **:** arranged or presented with each item listed and detailed ⟨asked for an ~ bill⟩ ⟨an ~ account⟩ **syn** see CIRCUMSTANTIAL

**item veto** *n* **:** power of an executive (as a governor) to veto separate items of a bill (as an appropriation bill) without vetoing the entire bill

**iter** \'ī,te(ə)r, 'ī,-\ *n* -s *see sense 2* [L, journey, way, passage, right of way, fr. *ire* to go — more at ISSUE] **1** [ML, fr. L] **:** EYRE **2** *pl* **iti·nera** \ə'tinərə, ī'-\ *or* **iters a :** an ancient Roman road **b** *Roman law* **:** the right to pass over another's land on foot or by horseback — compare ACTUS **3 :** an anatomical passage; *specif* **:** AQUEDUCT OF SYLVIUS

**it·er·ance** \'id-ərən(t)s, 'itər-\ *n* -s [*iterate* + *-ance* (prob. after *utterance*)] **:** REPETITION, REITERATION, REPETITIOUSNESS, RECURRENCE

**it·er·an·cy** \-nsē, -nsi\ *n* -ES **:** the quality of being iterant **:** REPETITION, REITERATION, REPETITIOUSNESS, RECURRENCE

**it·er·ant** \-nt\ *adj* [L *iterant-, iterans*, pres. part. of *iterare*] **:** marked by repetition or reiteration or by repetitiousness or recurrence ⟨~ echoes⟩

**it·er·ate** \-ə,rāt, *usu* -ād-+V\ *vt* -ED/-ING/-S [L *iteratus*, past part. of *iterare* to iterate, fr. *iterum* again, anew; akin to L *is* he, that, *ita* thus, Skt *itara* the other, *iti* thus] **:** REITERATE ⟨*iterated* his complaint⟩ **syn** see REPEAT

**iterated integral** *n* **:** an integral of a function of several variables that is evaluated by finding the definite integral with respect to one variable and then the definite integral of the result with respect to the second and so continuing until the desired accuracy is achieved

**it·er·a·tion** \,=ˌ='rāshən\ *n* -s [ME *iteracioun*, fr. L *iteration-, iteratio*, fr. *iteratus* (past part.) + *-ion-, -io* -ion] **:** the action of repeating or reiterating **:** REPETITION, REITERATION ⟨constant ~ of the theme of a world out of joint —R.C.Carpenter⟩

[1]**it·er·a·tive** \'ˌ=ˌ,rā|d-|iv, ,rə|, |t|, |ēv *also* |əv\ *adj* [MF *iteratif*, fr. LL *iterativus* frequentative, fr. L *iteratus* (past part.) + *-ivus* -ive] **1 :** marked by or involving repetition or reiteration or repetitiousness or recurrence ⟨~ methods⟩ ⟨~ poetic imagery⟩ **2 :** serving or tending to repeat; *specif, of a verb form or aspect* **:** expressing repetition of an action — compare FREQUENTATIVE, REDUPLICATIVE — **it·er·a·tive·ly** \|əvlē, -li\ *adv* — **it·er·a·tive·ness** \|ivnəs, |ēv- *also* |əv-\ *n* -ES

[2]**iterative** \"\ *n* -s **:** a word expressing repetition of an action

[1]**-i·tes** \'īd-(,)ēz, 'ī(,)tēz\ *n suffix, pl* **-ites** [NL — more at [1]-ITE] **:** organism or fossil like (a specified group) or from (an indicated place) — chiefly in generic names usu. of fossils ⟨*Agavites*⟩ ⟨*Malayites*⟩

[2]**-ites** *pl of* -ITIS

**ith·a·gine** \'ithə,jīn\ *n* -s [NL *Ithaginis*] **:** BLOOD PHEASANT

**ithag·i·nis** \ə'thajənəs\ *n, cap* [NL, irreg. fr. Gk *ithagenēs* legitimate, aboriginal] **:** a genus consisting of the blood pheasants

[1]**ith·er** \'ithə(r)\ *dial Brit var of* OTHER

[2]**ither** \"\ *dial Brit var of* EITHER

**ithu·ri·el's spear** \ə'th(y)ürēəlz-\ *n, usu cap I* [so called fr. the phrase *Ithuriel with his spear* in *Paradise Lost* (4:810) by John Milton †1674, Eng. poet] **:** GRASSNUT 2

[1]**ithy·phal·lic** \,ithə'falik\ *n* -s [LL *ithyphallicus*, adj.] **1 :** a piece of verse having an ithyphallic meter **2 :** an obscene piece of verse

[2]**ithyphallic** \'ˌ=ˌ=ˌ=\ *adj* [LL *ithyphallicus*, fr. Gk *ithyphallikos*, fr. *ithyphallos* phallus + *-ikos* -ic] **1 a :** having a meter typically used in hymns sung at ancient festivals honoring the Greek and Roman god of revelry Bacchus ⟨written in ~ verse⟩; *specif* **:** having the meter of a trochaic dimeter brachycatalectic (–◡–◡––) **b (1) :** of or relating to festivals anciently celebrated in honor of Bacchus ⟨~ processions⟩ **(2) :** of or relating to the phallus carried in processions held during these festivals **2 a :** having an erect or tumid penis — usu. used of figures in an art representation (as a statue or drawing) ⟨the curious and enigmatical semidisguised human figures are ~ —G.Baldwin Brown⟩ ⟨sketches of ~ bulls⟩ **b (1) :** LUSTFUL **(2) :** OBSCENE

**ithy·phal·lus** \,=ˌ='faləs\ [NL, fr. Gk *ithyphallos* phallus, erect penis, fr. *ithys* straight + *phallos* penis — more at ATHROGENIC, BLOW (move)] *syn of* PHALLUS

**-it·ic** \|id-|ik, |it|, |ēk\ *adj suffix* [F *-itique*, fr. MF, fr. L *-iticus*, fr. Gk *-itikos*, fr. *-itis* (n. & adj. suffix) + *-ikos* -ic] **:** of, resembling, or marked by — in adjectives formed from nouns usu. ending in *-ite* ⟨dendr*itic*⟩ and *-itis* ⟨bronch*itic*⟩ and sometimes from other nouns ⟨dactyl*itic*⟩

**-itides** *pl of* -ITIS

**itie** \'īd-ē, 'ī,tī\ *n* -s *usu cap* [by alter. and shortening] **:** ITALIAN — usu. used disparagingly

**-ities** *pl of* -ITY

**itinera** *pl of* ITER

**itin·er·a·cy** \ī'tin(ə)rəsē, -si *also* ə't-\ *n* -ES [[2]*itinerate* + *-cy*] **:** ITINERANCY

**itin·er·an·cy** \-rənsē, -si\ *n* -ES **1 a (1) :** the action of itinerating ⟨preached to many people in the course of his ~⟩ **(2) :** the condition of being itinerant ⟨the ~ of a medieval minstrel⟩ **b :** a system (as in the Methodist Church) of rotating ministers who itinerate ⟨features of the episcopacy and the ~ —F.S. Mead⟩ **2 a :** official work or duty that involves traveling about from place to place (as in covering a preaching circuit) ⟨returned to the ~ —J.W.Johnston⟩ **b :** a group of persons (as preachers, judges) having such work or duty ⟨a member of the ~⟩

[1]**itin·er·ant** \-rənt\ *adj* [LL *itinerant-, itinerans*, pres. part. of *itinerari* to journey, fr. L *itiner-, iter* journey — more at ITER] **1 :** that travels about from place to place ⟨an ~ agricultural worker⟩ ⟨an ~ theatrical troupe⟩; *esp* **:** that travels about in covering a circuit ⟨an ~ preacher⟩ **2 :** marked by itinerancy ⟨lived an ~ life⟩ ⟨the ~ ministry⟩ **:** given or done or held in the course of traveling about from place to place ⟨~ discourses⟩ ⟨~ sketching⟩ ⟨~ tent meetings⟩ — **itin·er·ant·ly** *adv*

[2]**itinerant** \"\ *n* -s **:** one that travels about from place to place; *esp* **:** one that travels about in covering a circuit

**itin·er·ar·i·um** \(,)ī,tinə'ra(a)rēəm, ə,t-\ *or* **itinerary** *n, pl* **itineraria** *or* **itinerariums** *or* **itineraries** [ML *itinerarium* (also, account of a journey, itinerary), fr. LL] **:** a prayer given in the Roman Catholic breviary that is used for a person who is about to travel

[1]**itin·er·ary** \ī'tinə,rerē, -,reri *also* ə't- *or* -nərē *or* -nəri\ *n* -ES [ME *itinerarie*, fr. LL *itinerarium*, neut. of *itinerarius* of a journey, itinerary] **1 a (1) :** a course of travel **:** route of a journey or tour or trip ⟨an ~ that took them through Canada⟩ **(2) :** an official or royal tour or circuit or visitation **:** PROGRESS ⟨when Queen Elizabeth I made one of her periodical *itineraries* of Kent —Richard Church⟩ **b :** a plan or outline of a prospective route to be followed in the course of traveling or touring **:** sketch of the prospective course of a journey or trip ⟨discussed their ~ before leaving⟩ **2 a :** a travel account **:** record of a journey or tour or trip **:** travel diary ⟨wrote the ~ in the course of the expedition⟩ **b :** a guidebook with information designed for travelers or tourists **:** ROADBOOK ⟨a helpful ~⟩ **3** *archaic* **:** ITINERANT

[2]**itinerary** \"\ *adj* [LL *itinerarius*, fr. L *itiner-, iter* journey + *-arius* -ary] **1 :** of or relating to traveling or journeying or touring; *specif* **:** of or relating to routes or roads followed in traveling or journeying or touring ⟨the ~ system developed by the ancient Romans⟩ **2** *archaic* **:** ITINERANT

[1]**itin·er·ate** \ī'tinə,rāt *also* ə't-; *usu* -ād-+V\ *vb* -ED/-ING/-S [LL *itineratus*, past part. of *itinerari* to journey — more at ITINERANT] *vi* **:** to travel about from place to place; *esp* **:** to travel about in covering a circuit ⟨*itinerating* missionaries⟩ ⟨*itinerating* judges⟩ ~ *vt, archaic* **:** to travel through **:** TRAVERSE ⟨~ the country —G.F.Townsend⟩ — **itin·er·a·tion** \(,)ī,tinə'rāshən *also* ə,t-\ *n* -s

[2]**itin·er·ate** \-,rət, -,rāt\ *adj* [LL *itineratus* (past part.)] **:** ITINERANT ⟨~ newspapermen —Turner Catledge⟩

**-i·tious** \ˈishəs\ *adj suffix* [L *-icius, -itius,* adjective suffix added to the base of a noun or past participle] **:** of, relating to, or having the characteristics or properties of (something specified) ⟨excrement*itious*⟩ ⟨cement*itious*⟩

**-i·tis** \ˈīd·əs, |təs *sometimes* ˈē\ *n suffix, pl* **-i·tis·es** \ˈīd·əsəz, |təs- *also* **-i·ti·des** \ˈid·ə,dēz, ˈitə-\ *sometimes* **-i·tes** \ˈīd·-(,)ēz, |(,)tēz *sometimes* ˈē\ [NL, fr. L & Gk; L, fr. Gk, n. & adj. suffix] **1 :** disease usu. inflammatory of a (specified) part or organ **:** inflammation of ⟨laryng*itis*⟩ ⟨bronch*itis*⟩ **2** *pl usu* **-itises a** (1) **:** malady arising ⟨appendic*itis*⟩ ⟨neur*itis*⟩ **2 :** affliction with (something specified) ⟨too-much-money*itis*⟩ ⟨vacation-from (something specified) ⟨too-much-money*itis*⟩ (2) **:** affliction with (something specified) **:** forced endurance or suffering of ⟨television*itis*⟩ — chiefly in nonce formations **b** (1) **:** tendency esp. when excessive to or toward (something specified) **:** marked proneness to ⟨accident*itis*⟩ (2) **:** marked fondness for or obsession with (something specified) **:** weakness for **:** infatuation with ⟨adjectiv*itis*⟩ ⟨jazz*itis*⟩ (3) **:** excessive concern for or promotion or advocacy of or reliance on (something specified) ⟨education*itis*⟩ — chiefly in nonce formations **c :** quality or state of being marked to an often excessive degree by certain typical characteristics of (something specified) ⟨big-business*itis*⟩ — chiefly in nonce formations

**it·mo** \ˈit(,)mō\ *or* **ik·mo** \ˈik(-\ *n* -s [Tag] **:** BETEL

**it·neg** \ˈit,neg\ *n, pl* **itneg** *or* **itnegs** *usu cap* [Tinggian] **:** TINGGIAN

**-i·tol** \ə,tȯl, -tōl\ *n suffix* -s [ISV *-it-* (fr. [1]*-ite*) + *-ol*] **:** polyhydroxy alcohol usu. related to a sugar ⟨mann*itol*⟩ ⟨inos*itol*⟩

**ito·na·ma** \,ēd·əˈnämə\ *n, pl* **itonama** *or* **itonamas** *usu cap* [AmerSp, of AmerInd origin] **1 a :** a people of northeastern Bolivia **b :** a member of such people **2 :** the language of the Itonama people

**it·o·nid·idae** \,id·əˈnid·ə,dē\ [NL, fr. *Itonida,* genus of gall midges (prob. fr. L, title of the goddess Minerva, irreg. fr. Gk *Itōnid-, Itōnis,* title of the goddess Athena) + *-idae*] *syn of* CECIDOMYIIDAE

[1]**its** \(ˌ)its, əts\ *adj* [[1]*it* + *-s* (possessive case ending)] **1 :** of or belonging to it or itself as possessor **:** inherent in it **:** associated or connected with it ⟨going to ~ kennel⟩ ⟨~ weird howl⟩ ⟨did it bump ~ little head⟩ **2 :** of or relating to it or itself as author, doer, giver, or agent **:** effected by it **:** experienced by it as subject **:** that it is capable of ⟨a little child proudly showing the teacher ~ first drawings⟩ ⟨~ remarkable speed⟩ ⟨~ spasmodic reactions⟩ ⟨did ~ very best⟩ **3 :** of or relating to it or itself as object of an action **:** experienced by it as object ⟨this proposal and ~ final enactment into law⟩ ⟨intending ~ betterment⟩ **4 :** that it has to do with or is supposed to possess or to have knowledge of or a share or some special interest in ⟨a dog that knows ~ master⟩ **5 :** that is esp. significant for it or **:** that brings it good fortune or prominence — used with *day* or sometimes with other words indicating a division of time ⟨the football team was having ~ day⟩

[2]**its** \ˈits\ *pron, sing or pl in constr* **:** its one or its ones — used occas. without a following noun as a pronoun equivalent in meaning to the adjective *its* ⟨women take to a thing, any thing, and go deep enough, and they're ~ —A.S.M.Hutchinson⟩ — compare [3]HIS

[3]**its** \(ˌ)its, əts\ [by alter.] *substand* **:** [1]IT'S

[4]**its** *pl of* IT

[1]**it's** \(ˌ)its, əts\ [by contr.] **1 :** it is ⟨*it's* good⟩ **2 :** it has ⟨*it's* been a long time⟩

[2]**it's** \"\ *adj* [by alter.] *now substand* **:** ITS

**it·sel** \ətˈsel\ *dial var of* ITSELF

[1]**it·self** \ət+\ *pron* [ME, fr. OE *hit self,* fr. *hit* it + *self* — more at HE] **1 :** that identical one — compare [1]IT 1a; used (1) reflexively as object of a preposition or direct or indirect object of a verb ⟨the dog will have to look out for ~ while its master is gone⟩ ⟨hurt ~ crossing the street⟩ ⟨watched the cat giving ~ a bath⟩; (2) for emphasis in apposition with *it, which, that, this,* or a noun ⟨it is attractive ~⟩ ⟨which ~ is reason enough⟩ ⟨a bookbinding that ~ is valuable⟩ ⟨this ~ was sufficient excuse⟩ ⟨the letter ~ was missing⟩; (3) for emphasis instead of nonreflexive *it* as object of a preposition or direct or indirect object of a verb ⟨its agility is a source of amusement to its master and is a protection for ~⟩; (4) for emphasis instead of *it* or instead of *it itself* as subject of a verb ⟨never used for any purpose other than what ~ was designed for⟩ or as predicate nominative ⟨an animal is generally concerned for just one thing and that is ~⟩ or in comparisons after *than* or *as* ⟨a dog being chased by an animal smaller than ~⟩; (5) in absolute constructions ⟨~ a splendid specimen of classic art, it is sure to be exhibited throughout the world⟩ **2 :** its normal, healthy, or sane condition ⟨the dog seemed quite ill at first but soon came to ~⟩ **:** its normal, healthy, or sane self ⟨fed the little creature milk and it was soon ~⟩ **3 :** YOURSELF — used in speaking to or as if to a baby ⟨did it hurt ~⟩ — compare [1]IT 1c

[2]**itself** \"\ *adv* **1** *Irish* **:** in very fact **:** INDEED — used as an intensive usu. at the end of a clause ⟨where is he ~ —J.M. Synge⟩ **2** *Irish* **:** ACTUALLY, EVEN — used as an intensive usu. at the end of a clause ⟨though you were to have no hand on your poor mother ~ —Gerald O'Donovan⟩

**it·ty-bit·ty** \ˌid·ēˈbid·ē\ *or* **it·sy-bit·sy** \ˌitsēˈbitsē\ *adj* [prob. fr. baby talk for *little bit*] **:** extremely small **:** TINY ⟨an *itty-bitty* piece of cake⟩ — not in formal use

**it·u·re·an** \,ichəˈrēən\ *n* -s *usu cap* [L *Ituraeus* Iturean (fr. Gk *Ityraios,* adj., of Iturea, country in ancient Palestine) + E *-an*] **:** a native or inhabitant of Iturea, an Arab kingdom in ancient Palestine south of Damascus

**itu·ri·te fiber** \,ēd·əˈrēd·ē-\ *n* [origin unknown] **:** the fiber of a So. American herb (*Ischnosiphon obliquus*) of the family Marantaceae

**-i·ty** \əd·ē, ətē, -i; *when* s, *less often when* r, *precedes, the first vowel is sometimes lost, as in* kəˈpastē *for* "capacity"\ *n suffix* -ES [ME *-ite,* fr. OF or L; OF *-ité,* fr. L *-itat-, -itas,* fr. *-i-* (thematic or, rarely, connective vowel) + *-tat-, -tas* -ty] **:** quality **:** state **:** degree ⟨asinin*ity*⟩ ⟨theatrical*ity*⟩

**it·za** \ətˈsä\ *n, pl* **itza** *or* **itzas** *usu cap* [Sp *itzá,* of AmerInd origin] **1 a :** a division of the Yucatec people of Petén, Guatemala **b :** a member of such division **2 :** a dialect of Yucatec

**IU** *abbr* **1** immunizing unit **2** international unit

**iu·li·dae** \(ī)ˈyülə,dē\ [NL, fr. *Iulus,* type genus + *-idae*] *syn of* JULIDAE

**iu·lus** \-ləs\ [NL, alter. of *Julus*] *syn of* JULUS

**-ium** *n suffix* **1** -s [NL, perh. after such words as L *medium*] **a** (1) **:** chemical element ⟨sod*ium*⟩ ⟨uran*ium*⟩ (2) **:** chemical radical ⟨ammon*ium*⟩ **b :** an ion having a positive charge — in names of complex cations (as those derived from an organic base) ⟨imidazol*ium* [$C_3H_4N_2H$]$^+$⟩ ⟨pyridin*ium*⟩ ⟨nitrosyl*ium* $NO^+$⟩ — compare -ONIUM **2** *pl* **-iums** *also* **-ia** [NL, fr. L, fr. Gk *-ion* (n. suffix, often of diminutive force)] **:** small one **:** mass — esp. in biological terms ⟨onch*ium*⟩ ⟨pollin*ium*⟩

**ius** *var of* JUS

**IV** *abbr* **1** *often not cap* increased value **2** *often not cap* initial velocity **3** intravenous **4** *often not cap* [L *in verbo; in voce*] under the word **5** *often not cap* invoice value **6** iodine value

**iva** \ˈīvə, ˈēvə\ *n* [NL, fr. *iva* (specific epithet of *Ajuga iva*), prob. fr. F *ive* ground pine, fr. MF, fr. OF *yve,* fr. *if* yew, of Celt origin; fr. its similarity in smell; akin to OHG *īwa* yew — more at YEW] **1** *cap* **:** a small genus of American herbs or shrubs (family Ambrosiaceae) with mostly opposite leaves and small greenish flowers and with the staminate and pistillate both in the same head **2** -s **:** any plant of the genus *Iva* — see MARSH ELDER 2

**ivan** \ˈīvən *also* ēˈvän\ *n* -s *usu cap* [Russ *Ivan,* proper name, John, fr. ORuss *Ioannŭ,* fr. Gk *Iōannēs* — more at JOHN] **:** RUSSIAN; *esp* **:** a Russian soldier

**iva·no·vo** \ēˈvänə,vō, -,vəv\ *adj, usu cap* [fr. *Ivanovo,* city in U.S.S.R.] **:** of or from the city of Ivanovo, U.S.S.R. **:** of the kind or style prevalent in Ivanovo

**iva·tan** \ˌēvəˈtän\ *n, pl* **ivatan** *or* **ivatans** *usu cap* [native name in the Batan Islands] **1 a :** a people inhabiting the Batan islands of the Philippines **b :** a member of such people **2 :** an Austronesian language of the Ivatan people

[1]**-ive** \iv, ēv *also* əv\ *adj suffix* [ME *-if, -ive,* fr. MF & L; MF *-if,* fr. L *-ivus;* akin to (assumed) Gk *-eiwos* (whence Gk *-eios* -ive)] **:** that performs or tends toward or serves to accomplish an (indicated) action esp. regularly or lastingly ⟨amus*ive*⟩ ⟨co-ordinat*ive*⟩

[2]**-ive** \"\ *n suffix* -s [ME *-if, -ive,* fr. MF & L; MF *-if,* fr. L *-ivus,* fr. *-ivus,* adj. suffix] **:** something that performs or tends toward or serves to accomplish an (indicated) action esp. regularly or lastingly ⟨sedat*ive*⟩ ⟨correct*ive*⟩

**ivied** \ˈīvēd, -vid\ *adj* [[1]*ivy* + *-ed*] **:** covered with ivy ⟨~ walls⟩ ⟨~ ruins⟩

**ivies** *pl of* IVY

**ivin** \ˈīvən, ˈiv-\ *n* -s [alter. of earlier *iven,* fr. ME, fr. OE *īfegn, īfig* — more at IVY] *dial Eng* **:** IVY

**ivo·ried** \ˈīv(ə)rēd, -rid\ *adj* **1** *archaic* **:** made of or covered with ivory **2** *archaic* **:** resembling ivory (as in color, smoothness)

**ivo·rine** \ˈīvə,rēn, ˌ==ˈ=\ *n* -s *often attrib* [fr. *Ivorine,* a trademark] **:** a substance resembling ivory in color and texture

[1]**ivo·ry** \ˈīv(ə)rē, -ri\ *n* -ES *see senses 3, 4* [ME *ivor, ivorie,* fr. OF *ivore, ivoire, ivurie,* fr. L *eboreus,* adj., of ivory, fr. *ebor-, ebur* ivory, of Hamitic origin; akin to Egypt *ʾbw* elephant, ivory] **1 a** (1) **:** the hard creamy-white opaque fine-grained elastic modified dentine that composes the tusks of an elephant (2) **:** the dentine of the tusks of large mammals (as narwhals, walruses) other than elephants (3) **:** the dentine of any tooth **b :** a tusk of an elephant or other large mammal **2 a :** creamy whiteness **b** *or* **ivory yellow** *or* **ivory white** (1) **:** a variable color averaging a pale yellow that is darker, slightly redder, and very slightly less strong than cream, paler and slightly redder than straw, and paler and slightly greener than leghorn (2) *of textiles* **:** a yellowish white that is stronger and slightly redder than milk white and redder and slightly less strong than average shell tint **3** *pl* **ivories** *or* **ivory** *slang* **:** TOOTH ⟨fell down and broke one of his *ivories*⟩ ⟨snarled and showed his ~⟩ **4** *pl* **ivories** *or* **ivory :** something made of ivory or of a substance resembling or suggestive of ivory: as **a** *slang* **:** DIE 1a ⟨rattling the ~⟩ ⟨picked up one of the *ivories*⟩ **b :** a carving in ivory ⟨the museum has a remarkable collection of *ivories*⟩ **c** *slang* **:** a pool or billiard ball ⟨watched them shoot the *ivories* around⟩ **d** *slang* **:** one of the keys of a piano keyboard or of the keyboard of a similar instrument (as an accordion) ⟨tickling the *ivories*⟩

[2]**ivory** \"\ *adj* [ME *iver,* fr. *iver, ivor,* n.] **1 a :** made of ivory **:** consisting of ivory ⟨an ~ figurine⟩ ⟨a tiny ~ box⟩ **b :** resembling or suggestive of ivory **:** having a finish suggestive of the surface of ivory ⟨a fine-grained wood with a highly polished ~ surface⟩ ⟨~ porcelain⟩; *esp* **:** having a creamy whiteness and smoothness suggestive of ivory ⟨admired her ~ arms and shoulders⟩ **c :** of the color ivory **2 :** IVORY-TOWERED ⟨little men in ~ offices, who . . . fear to carry out their instructions in a liberal and imaginative way —Edward Sackville-West⟩

[3]**ivory** \"\ *dial var of* IVY

**ivory–billed woodpecker** \ˌ=(=)=ˌ=-\ *or* **ivorybill** \ˈ=(=)=,=\ *n* **:** a nearly extinct large woodpecker (*Campephilus principalis*) having plumage that is glossy black with white along the neck and wings, a large ivory-white bill, and in the male a large scarlet crest

**ivory black** *n* **:** a fine black pigment prepared by calcining ivory scrap **2 :** a bone black usu. of high quality

**ivory board** *n* **:** a highly finished paperboard coated on both sides

**ivory brown** *n* **1 :** a brown pigment made by partially carbonizing ivory **2 :** BONE BROWN 2

**ivory coast** *adj, usu cap I&C* [fr. *Ivory Coast Republic*] **:** of or relating to the Ivory Coast Republic **:** of the kind or style prevalent in the Ivory Coast Republic

**ivory coast·er** \-ˈkōstə(r)\ *n* -s *cap I&C* [*Ivory Coast,* country in West Africa + E *-er*] **:** a native or inhabitant of the Ivory Coast

**ivory coral** *n* **:** any of several hard and branching madrepores (family Oculinidae) with widely spaced polyps and firm skeleton

**ivory–dome** \ˈ=(=)=,=\ *n* **:** BONEHEAD

**ivory gull** *n* **:** a gull (*Pagophila eburnea*) that is circumpolar in distribution and migrates as far south as New Brunswick and England

**ivory–leaves** *also* **ivory–leaf** \ˈ=(=)=,=\ *n, pl* **ivory–leaves :** WINTERGREEN 2a

**ivory nut** *n* **1 :** the nutlike seed of a So. American palm (*Phytelephas macrocarpa*) containing a very hard endosperm — see VEGETABLE IVORY **2 :** APPLENUT

**ivory palm** *or* **ivory–nut palm** *also* **ivory plant** *n* **:** a palm yielding ivory nuts

**ivory plum** *n* **1 a :** CREEPING SNOWBERRY **b :** the fruit of creeping snowberry **2 :** WINTERGREEN 2a

**ivory shell** *n* **:** any of several tropical whelks (family Buccinidae) with ivory-white shells spotted and mottled with orange or brown or red

**ivory tint** *n* **:** a yellowish gray that is greener and duller than sand and greener and paler than natural

**ivory tower** *n* [trans. of F *tour d'ivoire;* orig. used by C. A. Sainte-Beuve †1869 Fr. poet & critic with reference to Alfred de Vigny †1863 Fr. poet & novelist] **1 a :** a nonrealistic often escapist or visionary attitude marked by usu. studied aloofness from and lack of concern with practical matters or urgent problems **:** a dreamy impractical attitude divorced from reality and often marked by limited vision or narrow-mindedness ⟨her safe *ivory tower* of aloofness from life —Dorothy C. Fisher⟩ **b :** an often complacently blind preoccupation with what is wholly or nearly wholly speculative or theoretical or abstract or esoteric ⟨the *ivory tower* of speculation —J.L.Liebman⟩ **c :** a state of mental withdrawal from and nonparticipation in practical matters and surrounding activity **:** a retreat from concern with or interest in reality and the world outside the self ⟨living in an *ivory tower*⟩ **2 :** something (as a secluded place or environment or a psychological withdrawal into oneself) that affords a means of retreating from reality and practical issues ⟨viewing college as an *ivory tower*⟩ ⟨she entered the *ivory tower* of her deafness and closed the door —Aldous Huxley⟩ ⟨still seek to preserve an *ivory tower* of intellectual sterility —David Worcester⟩

**ivory–tower** \ˌ=(=)=ˈ=\ *adj* **1 :** marked by failure or refusal to face or cope with reality and practical matters **:** NONREALISTIC, IMPRACTICAL, DREAMY, ESCAPIST ⟨her thinking is *ivory-tower* —J.F.Dinneen⟩ ⟨were this the only result, the work would indeed have been *ivory-tower* —A.A.Twichell⟩ ⟨the *ivory-tower* point of view of certain academicians and librarians —John Farrar⟩ ⟨*ivory-tower* seclusion of the scholar —Sergius Yakobson⟩ **2 :** preoccupied with what is wholly or nearly wholly speculative or theoretical or abstract or esoteric ⟨*ivory-tower* writers and artists⟩

**ivory–towered** \ˌ=(=)=ˈ=\ *adj* **1 :** divorced from reality and practical matters **:** living in or surrounded by an ivory tower **:** nurturing an ivory-tower outlook or approach **:** cultivating an ivory-tower method of living or acting ⟨*ivory-towered* esthetic antagonists —Bennett Cerf⟩ ⟨an *ivory-towered* recluse⟩ **2 :** far removed from the outside world and everyday activity **:** REMOTE, SOLITARY, ISOLATED ⟨any college town, however inland and *ivory-towered* —Nell G. Ahern⟩ **:** SHELTERED ⟨an *ivory-towered* home —*Newsweek*⟩

**ivory–tower·ish** \ˌ=(=)=ˈtaù(ə)rish\ *adj* **:** rather unrealistic or impractical **:** inclined toward aloofness and preoccupation with what is abstract or esoteric ⟨a young man, naive, scholarly, somewhat *ivory-towerish* —Clifton Fadiman⟩ ⟨fall between the one extreme of being too superficial and the other of becoming esoteric and therefore *ivory-towerish* —R.J.Leach⟩ — **ivory–tower·ish·ness** *n* -ES

**ivory–tower·ism** \ˌ=(=)=ˈtaù(ə),rizəm\ *n* **:** cultivation of or attachment to an ivory-tower attitude or way of living or acting ⟨an *ivory-towerism* that many young Americans reared in a practical tradition view with mistrust —*Newsweek*⟩ ⟨defend contemporary American criticism from preoccupation with aesthetics and *ivory-towerism* —*Amer. Literature*⟩

**ivory–tower·ist** \-ˌrəst\ *or* **ivory–tower·ite** \-,rīt\ *n* -s **:** one marked by ivory-towerism ⟨ignore the insipidities of the *ivory-towerites* and try to build a new literature —William Small⟩

**ivory tree** *n* **:** any of several trees of the family Apocynaceae; *esp* **:** an East Indian tree (*Holarrhena antidysenterica*) with hard white wood and a bark formerly much used as a remedy for diarrhea and dysentery

**ivorywood** \ˈ=(=)=,=\ *n* **:** an Australian timber tree (*Siphonodon australis*) of the family Celastraceae — called also *native guava*

**ivory yellow** *or* **ivory white** *n* **:** IVORY 2b

**ivray** *also* **ivraie** \ēvˈrā\ *n* -s [MF *ivraie*] **:** BEARDED DARNEL

**iv·ver** \ˈivə(r)\ *dial var of* EVER

[1]**ivy** \ˈīvē, -vi\ *n* -ES [ME, fr. OE *īfig;* akin to OHG *ebahewi, ebah* ivy, and perh. to L *ibex* (lit., climber), Gk *iphyon,* a plant] **1 a :** a widely cultivated ornamental climbing or prostrate or sometimes shrubby vine (*Hedera helix*) native to Europe and Asia that has evergreen leaves and small yellowish flowers and black berries and that clings to upright surfaces (as of walls, rocks, trees) by means of numerous aerial roots having tiny adhering disks — called also *English ivy* **b** (1) **:** MOUNTAIN LAUREL (2) **:** POISON IVY **2 :** a variable color averaging a dark grayish green that is yellower and duller than Persian green and yellower and paler than hemlock green

ivy

[2]**ivy** \"\ *adj* **1 :** ACADEMIC 2, 5 ⟨the situation has grown so acute that it is no longer confined to the ~ towers but creeps out into open public discussion —*Music Educators Jour.*⟩ **2 :** IVY LEAGUE ⟨~ college boys⟩

**ivy–arum** \ˈ==ˈ==\ *n* **:** any of various woody vines constituting the genus *Scindapsus* and often cultivated as ornamentals for their glossy often slotted and variegated foliage; *esp* **:** a much-branched tall climber (*S. aureus*) native to the Solomon islands that has large leathery cordate leaves spotted and lined with golden yellow and that climbs by aerial rootlets arising from the nodes — called also *Ceylon creeper*

**ivybells** \ˈ==,=\ *n, pl* **ivybells :** a slender creeping European bellflower (*Wahlbergia hederacea*) of the family Campanulaceae that has petioled suborbicular to cordate and sometimes obscurely lobed leaves and small pale blue often nodding flowers and that is widely distributed in damp acid peaty areas throughout western Europe

**ivyberry** \ˈ=,==\ — *see* BERRY\ *n* **:** WINTERGREEN 2a

**ivy bindweed** *n* **:** BLACK BINDWEED 1

**ivy family** *n* **:** ARALIACEAE

**ivy geranium** *also* **ivy–leaved geranium** \ˈ==ˈ=-\ *n* **:** a commonly cultivated trailing So. African plant (*Pelargonium peltatum*) with peltate to nearly orbicular leaves and usu. rosy carmine flowers

**ivy gourd** *n* **1 :** a tropical Asiatic vine (*Coccinia cordifolia*) of the family Cucurbitaceae with triangular leaves and large white flowers and scarlet fruit **2 :** the fruit of the ivy gourd

**ivy green** *n* **:** a variable color averaging a grayish olive green that is yellower and slightly darker and stronger than bronze green and yellower and stronger than privet

**ivy league** *adj, usu cap I&L* **1 a :** belonging to or characteristic of or derived from one or more of a group of long-established eastern U.S. colleges widely regarded as high in scholastic and social prestige ⟨the manager was young, *Ivy League,* and hoping for an early vice-presidency —Jay Wilson⟩ ⟨leaders with *Ivy League* backgrounds —E.J.Kahn⟩ **b :** belonging to an athletic association made up of teams representing these colleges ⟨a couple of *Ivy League* teams⟩ ⟨likely to become an *Ivy League* champion⟩ **2 :** belonging to or characteristic of the students of Ivy League colleges ⟨the *Ivy League* look⟩ ⟨an *Ivy League* suit⟩

**ivy leaguer** *n, usu cap I&L* **:** a student at or graduate of an Ivy League college

**ivy–leaved speedwell** \ˈ==ˈ=-\ *also* **ivy speedwell** *n* **:** a speedwell (*Veronica hederaefolia*) having reniform leaves with two or three small lobes on each side of the base

**ivy–leaved toadflax** *n* **:** KENILWORTH IVY

**ivy owl** *n* **:** BARN OWL

**ivy scale** *n* **:** OLEANDER SCALE

**ivy–tod** \ˈ==,=\ *n* **:** a growth or clump of ivy

**ivy tree** *n* **1 :** a small often shrubby New Zealand evergreen tree (*Nothopanax arboreum*) of the family Araliaceae having glossy palmate leaves with 3 to 7 leaflets and large doubly compound umbels of small greenish brown flowers; *broadly* **:** any of several other New Zealand trees or shrubs of the genus *Nothopanax* **2** *dial* **:** MOUNTAIN LAUREL

**ivy vine** *n* **1 :** a woody vine (*Ampelopsis cordata*) of the central U.S. **2 :** VIRGINIA CREEPER

**ivyweed** \ˈ==,=\ *n* **:** KENILWORTH IVY

**ivywood** \ˈ==,=\ *n, dial* **:** MOUNTAIN LAUREL

**IW** *abbr* **1** inside width **2** isotopic weight

**iwa** *or* **ioa** \ˈēwə\ *n* -s [Hawaiian] **:** FRIGATE BIRD

**iwan** \ˈē,wän\ *n* -s [origin unknown] **:** a large hall or audience chamber often open on one side and found in Parthian architecture

**iwis** \ēˈwis, ÷īˈw-\ *adv* [ME, fr. OE *gewis* certain; akin to OHG *giwisso* certainly, ON *viss* certain, Goth *unwiss* uncertain, unsure, Gk *aistos* unknown, and the prehistoric root of OE *witan* to know — more at Y-, WIT] *archaic* **:** CERTAINLY, INDEED, TRULY

**ix·ia** \ˈiksēə\ *n* [NL, fr. Gk *ixos* mistletoe, birdlime + NL *-ia;* akin to L *viscum* mistletoe, birdlime] **1** *cap* **:** a genus of southern African bulbous plants (family Iridaceae) having linear sword-shaped leaves and very showy spikes of mostly pink or purple flowers **2** -s **:** any plant of the genus *Ixia* — called also *corn lily*

**ix·i·a·ce·ae** \,iksēˈāsē,ē\ [NL, fr. *Ixia,* type genus + *-aceae*] *syn of* IRIDACEAE

**ixil** \ēˈshē(ə)l\ *n, pl* **ixil** \"\ *or* **ixils** \-lz\ *or* **ixi·les** \-shē(,)-lās\ *usu cap* **1 a :** an Indian people of central Guatemala **b :** a member of such people **2 :** a Mayan language of the Ixil people

**ix·o·des** \ikˈsō(,)dēz\ *n, cap* [NL, fr. Gk *ixōdēs* like birdlime, sticky, fr. *ixos* birdlime + *-ōdēs* -ode] **:** a widespread genus (the type of the family Ixodidae) of ticks that suck the blood of man and of many domesticated and wild mammals, transmit diseases of cattle and sheep, and sometimes cause paralysis or other severe reactions

**ix·odic** \-ˈsädik, -ˈsōd-\ *adj* [NL *Ixodes* + E *-ic*] **:** IXODID

[1]**ix·odid** \-dəd\ *adj* [NL *Ixodidae*] **:** of, relating to, or caused by ticks of the genus *Ixodes*

[2]**ixodid** \"\ *n* -s **:** a tick of the genus *Ixodes*

**ix·od·i·dae** \-ˈsädə,dē\ *n, pl, cap* [NL, fr. *Ixodes* + *-idae*] **:** a family of ticks distinguished by the presence of a dorsal chitinous shield — see IXODES

**ix·o·doid** \ˈiksə,dȯid\ *adj* [NL *Ixodoidea*] **:** of, like, or relating to the Ixodoidea

**ix·o·doi·dea** \ˌ==ˈdȯidēə\ *n pl, cap* [NL, fr. *Ixodes,* type genus + *-oidea*] **:** a superfamily of Acarina comprising the ticks — compare ARGASIDAE, IXODIDAE

**ix·o·ra** \ˈiksərə\ *n* [NL, irreg. fr. *Ishvara,* Hindu divinity, fr. Skt *īśvara* ruler, lord] **1** *cap* **:** a large genus of tropical shrubs or small trees (family Rubiaceae) that have leathery evergreen leaves and terminal corymbs of showy salver-shaped flowers and are often cultivated as ornamentals in the warm greenhouse **2** -s **:** any plant of the genus *Ixora*

**ixtle** *var of* ISTLE

**iyar** *or* **iy·yar** \ˈē,yär, -,yər\ *n* -s *usu cap* [Heb] **:** the 8th month of the civil year or the 2d month of the ecclesiastical year in the Jewish calendar — see MONTH table

**iynx** \ˈīiŋks, ˈyiŋ-\ *n* -ES [L, fr. Gk] **:** WRYNECK 1

**iyo** \ˈē(,)yō\ *n* [origin unknown] **1 :** African piassava **2 :** a Philippine woody vine (*Tetrastigma harmandii*) of the family Vitaceae having sour but edible fruit

**izar** \əˈzär\ *n* -s [Hindi *izār,* fr. Ar, veil, covering] **:** a voluminous outer garment of Muslim women that covers the whole body

**izard** *also* **isard** \ēˈzär(d)\ *n, pl* **izard** \"\ *or* **izards** \-r(z), -rdz\ [F, fr. MF, fr. MF dial. (Gascony) *isart*] **:** a chamois found in the Pyrenees

**-ization** *also* **-isation** \əˈzāshən *also* ˌīˈz-\ *n suffix* -s [*-ize* or *-ise* + *-ation*] **:** action or process ⟨desulfur*ization*⟩ ⟨euchromat*ization*⟩ ⟨con*ization*⟩ **:** state or result ⟨dimer*ization*⟩ ⟨immiser*ization*⟩

**izba** *var of* ISBA

**-ize** \ˌīz *sometimes, as in* "baptize", ˈīz\ *vb suffix* -ED/-ING/-S *see -ize in Explan Notes* [ME *-isen,* fr. OF *-iser,* fr. LL *-izare,* fr. Gk *-izein*] **1 a** (1) **:** to cause to be or become or conform to or be like or resemble (something specified) ⟨system*ize*⟩ ⟨american*ize*⟩ ⟨liquid*ize*⟩ **:** cause to be formed into ⟨union*ize*⟩

⟨diphthong*ize*⟩ (2) **:** to subject to action by or treatment of (something specified) ⟨critic*ize*⟩ **:** subject to a (specified) action ⟨plagiar*ize*⟩ (3) **:** to cause to have or appear to have some (specified) quality ⟨rational*ize*⟩ **:** act upon in such a way as to produce a (specified) result in ⟨brutal*ize*⟩ ⟨commercial*ize*⟩ (4) **:** to impregnate or treat or combine with (something specified) ⟨albumin*ize*⟩ ⟨hydrogen*ize*⟩ (5) **:** to adapt to (something specified) **:** modify by means of ⟨avian*ize*⟩ **b :** to make (a specified thing) of **:** treat like ⟨idol*ize*⟩ ⟨lion*ize*⟩ **c :** to treat in the manner of or according to the method or process of (a specified individual) ⟨bowdler*ize*⟩ ⟨mesmer*ize*⟩ **2 a :** to become or become like (something specified) ⟨crystall*ize*⟩ **b :** to be productive in or of (something specified) ⟨theor*ize*⟩ **:** engage in or carry on a (specified) activity ⟨botan*ize*⟩ ⟨philosoph*ize*⟩ ⟨attitudin*ize*⟩ ⟨concert*ize*⟩ **c :** to follow after someone or something (specified) **:** adopt or spread the manner of activity or the outlook or teaching of someone ⟨calvin*ize*⟩

**izhevsk** \'ē,zhe|fsk, |vzk, |vsk, ≈'≈; 'ēzhə̇|\ *adj, usu cap* [fr. *Izhevsk,* city in U.S.S.R.] **:** of or from the city of Izhevsk, U.S.S.R. **:** of the kind or style prevalent in Izhevsk

**iz·mir** \(')iz¦mi(ə)r\ *adj, usu cap* [fr. *İzmir* (formerly Smyrna), Turkey] **:** of or from the city of Izmir, Turkey **:** of the kind or style prevalent in Izmir

**izod test** \'ī,zäd-, 'īzəd-\ *n, usu cap I* [after E. G. *Izod,* 20th cent. Eng. mechanical engineer] **:** a test of a metal's or plastic's resistance to impact that is made by determining the amount of energy in foot-pounds needed by a swinging hammer to fracture a notched test piece of the material held in a vertical position and supported at its lower end

**izo·te** *also* **iso·te** \ə̇'zōd·ē\ *n* -s [MexSp, fr. Nahuatl *iczotl*] **1 :** any of several Mexican plants of the genus *Yucca; esp* **:** SPANISH BAYONET **2 :** the coarse hard fiber of an izote resembling istle

**iz·zard** \'izə(r)d\ *n* -s [alter. of earlier *ezod, ezed,* prob. fr. MF *et zède* and Z — more at ZED] *now chiefly dial* **:** the letter z

**iz·zat** \'izət\ *n* -s [Hindi *'izzat,* fr. Ar *'izzah* glory] **1 :** personal dignity or respect **:** HONOR ⟨is against my ∼ —Rudyard Kipling⟩ **2 :** power to command admiration **:** PRESTIGE ⟨afraid of losing ∼⟩

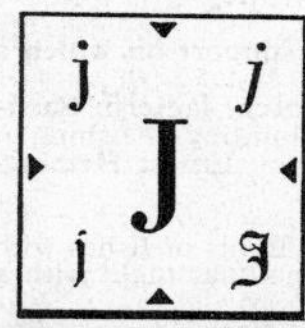

**[1]j** \'jā\ *n, pl* **j's** *or* **js** \'jāz\ *often cap, often attrib* **1 a :** the 10th letter of the English alphabet **b :** an instance of this letter printed, written, or otherwise represented **c :** a speech counterpart of orthographic *j* (as *j* in *jump, ajar,* German *ja,* Spanish *jefe*) **2 a :** a printer's type, a stamp, or some other instrument for reproducing the letter *j* **b :** ONE — see NUMBER table **c :** a unit vector parallel to the y-axis **3 :** someone or something arbitrarily or conveniently designated *j* esp. as the 10th in order or class **4 :** something having the shape of the letter J

**[2]j** *abbr, often cap* **1** jack **2** January **3** join **4** joule **5** journal; journalism **6** [L *judex*] judge **7** July **8** June **9** junior **10** [L *jus*] law **11** justice **12** juvenile

**[3]j** *symbol, cap* **1** Yahwistic or Judean — used in biblical criticism to designate Yahwistic material esp. from an ancient epic constituting the earliest and a main source of the Hexateuch ⟨the *J* passages in the creation story⟩ ⟨the *J* text⟩ — compare D, E, P **2** *ital* mechanical equivalent of heat **3** *ital* radiant intensity

**JA** *abbr* **1** joint account **2** joint agent **3** judge advocate

**jaag·siek·te** *also* **jaag·ziek·te** *or* **jag·siek·te** *or* **jag·ziek·te** \'yäg,sēktə, -,zēk-\ *n* -s [Afrik *jagsiekte,* fr. *jag* hunt + *siekte* sickness] **:** an apparently infectious disease of sheep that is characterized by proliferation of the pulmonary alveolar epithelium and occlusion of the alveoli and terminal bronchioles and that is usu. held to be caused by an unidentified filterable virus

**ja·al goat** \'jāəl, 'yäəl\ *n* [Heb *yā'ēl* wild goat] **:** an ibex (*Capra nubiana*) of the mountains of Ethiopia, Upper Egypt, and Arabia with long slender horns

**[1]jab** \'jab, 'jaa(ə)b\ *vb* **jabbed; jabbed; jabbing; jabs** [alter. of *job* (to strike)] *vt* **1 a :** to pierce with or as if with something sharp **:** STAB ⟨got *jabbed* in the lower part of his chest, seriously if not fatally —*Westminster Gazette*⟩ **b :** to poke quickly or abruptly **:** THRUST ⟨*jabbing* the poker among the gray ashes —Rebecca Caudill⟩ **2 :** to give a short straight blow to (as a boxing opponent) with the fist ∼ *vi* **1 :** to make quick or abrupt thrusts with something sharp ⟨*jabbed* around with my spear, knocking off the stalks of dead mulleins —John Moore⟩ ⟨took up his list of dates and *jabbed* at it with a pencil —Dorothy Sayers⟩ **2 :** to strike a person with a short straight blow ⟨hooking when he should have *jabbed,* . . . his head sometimes a craning target —*Time*⟩

**[2]jab** \"\ *n* -s **:** an act of jabbing **:** a quick or abrupt thrust, stab, or punch; *specif* **:** a short straight punch in boxing delivered with the leading hand

**já·ba·lí** \,häbə'lē\ *or* **ja·va·li** \-ävə-\ *n* -ES [AmerSp *jabalí,* fr. Sp, wild boar, fr. Ar *jabalīy,* short for *khinzīr jabalīy,* fr. *khinzīr* pig + *jabal* mountain] **:** PECCARY

**ja·ba·li·na** \,häbə'lēnə\ *or* **jave·li·na** \-ävə-\ *n* -s **:** PECCARY

**jabalpur** *usu cap, var of* JUBBULPORE

**jab·a·rite** \'jabə,rīt\ *n* -s *usu cap* [Ar *jabarīy* (fr. *jabr* power, force) + E *-ite*] **:** a member of an early school of Muslim determinists who denied that man has freedom of choice and affirmed an absolute predestination fashioned by Allah

**[1]jab·ber** \'jabə(r)\ *vb* **jabbered; jabbered; jabbering** \-b(ə)riŋ\ **jabbers** [ME *jaberen,* of imit. origin] *vi* **:** to talk rapidly, indistinctly, or unintelligibly **:** utter gibberish or nonsense **:** CHATTER ⟨∼*ing* in incomprehensible tongues —F.L. Allen⟩ ⟨kept ∼*ing* away —Edita Morris⟩ ∼ *vt* **:** to speak rapidly or indistinctly ⟨∼ half a dozen languages —F.L. Lucas⟩

**[2]jabber** \"\ *n* -s **:** an act of jabbering **:** rapid, incoherent, or trivial talk with indistinct utterance **:** GIBBERISH, CHATTER ⟨must we fall into the ∼ and babel of discord —Sir Winston Churchill⟩

**jab·ber·er** \-b(ə)rə(r)\ *n* -s **:** one that jabbers ⟨sweep the ∼*s* out of the way of civilization —G.B.Shaw⟩

**jabbering** *adj* **:** tending to or given to jabber **:** BABBLING ⟨a ∼ fool⟩ ⟨was the father of three ∼ daughters⟩ — **jab·ber·ing·ly** *adv*

**jabbernowl** \'jäbə(r),nōl, 'jab-\ *var of* JOBBERNOWL

**jab·ber·wocky** \'jabə(r),wäkē, -ki\ *also* **jab·ber·wock** \-äk\ *n, pl* **jabberwockies** *also* **jabberwocks** *often attrib* [*jabberwocky* fr. *Jabberwocky,* a nonsense poem in *Through the Looking Glass* by Lewis Carroll (Charles L. Dodgson) †1898 Eng. author and mathematician; *jabberwock* fr. *Jabberwock,* the fabulous monster in the poem *Jabberwocky*] **:** meaningless speech, writing, or patter **:** GIBBERISH ⟨bringing the house down with . . . his ∼ patter and his energetic clowning —*Life*⟩ ⟨began to babble in ∼ —Leo Rosten⟩ ⟨carries on his heated conversations . . . in a sort of *jabberwock* —Arthur Knight⟩

**jabbing** *adj* [fr. pres. part. of [1]*jab*] **:** THRUSTING, STABBING ⟨a neat, crisp, ∼ bitterness —*Horizon*⟩

**[1]jab·ble** \'jabəl\ *vb* -ED/-ING/-S [imit.] *vt, Brit* **:** AGITATE, SPLASH ⟨*jabbled* coffee on his saucer —Michael McLaverty⟩ ∼ *vi, Brit* **:** to break in small waves **:** RIPPLE

**[2]jabble** \"\ *n* -s **1** *Brit* **:** an agitation on the surface of water **:** SPLASHING, DASHING, RIPPLING **:** CHOPPINESS **2** *Brit* **:** a mental or emotional agitation or turmoil

**jabim** *usu cap, var of* YABIM

**jab·i·ru** \¦jabə¦rü\ *n* -s [Pg *jabiru, jabirú,* fr. Tupi & Guarani *jaburú, jabirú*] **1 :** a large stork (*Jabiru mycteria*) of tropical America **2 a :** WOOD IBIS 1 **b :** the saddle-billed stork of Africa or a related stork of the genus *Xenorhynchus* of the East Indies and Australia

**jab·o·ran·di** \,jabə'randē\ *n* -s [Pg *jaborandi, jaborandí,* fr. Tupi *yaborandí*] **1 a :** the dried leaves of a So. American rutaceous shrub (*Pilocarpus jaborandi*) that are a source of pilocarpine — called also *Pernambuco jaborandi* **b :** the dried leaves of a closely related shrub (*P. microphyllus*) that are similarly used — called also *Maranham jaborandi* **2 :** the root of a Brazilian plant (*Piper jaborandi*) that is a source of pilocarpine

**ja·bot** \zha'bō, ja'-, '≈(,)≈\ *n* -s [F, crop, jabot, fr. MF, prob. fr. a dial. word akin to OF *gave* throat, crop] **1 :** a single or tiered fall of lace, cloth, or both attached to the front of a neckband, worn esp. by men in the 18th century, and still worn by some English counsels **2 a :** a ruffle or pleated frill of cloth, lace, or both attached down the center front of a shirt, blouse, or dress bodice **b :** a similar fall of material in drapery

jabot 2a

**ja·bot·i·ca·ba** \jə,bäd·ə'käbə\ *n* -s [Pg *jaboticaba, jabuticaba,* fr. Tupi] **1 :** a large shrub or small tree (*Myrciaria cauliflora*) of the family Myrtaceae native to Brazil and the West Indies but introduced into the southern U.S. having flowers and fruit borne all along the trunk and main branches and purplish fruit that resembles grapes in appearance and flavor but has tough thick skin and is borne singly or in small clusters **2 :** the fruit of the jaboticaba

**jabs** *pres 3d sing of* JAB, *pl of* JAB

**ja·ca** \'jäkə\ *n* -s [Pg — more at JACKFRUIT] **:** JACKFRUIT

**ja·cal** \hə'käl\ *n, pl* **jaca·les** \-ä(,)lās\ *also* **jacals** [MexSp, fr. Nahuatl *xacalli,* fr. *xamitl* adobe + *calli* house] **1 :** a crude house or hut in Mexico and southwestern U.S. with a thatched roof and walls made of upright poles or sticks covered and chinked with mud or clay **2 :** the method of construction used in building a jacal

**ja·cal·tec** \,häkəl'täk\ *or* **ja·cal·te·ca** \-kə\ *n, pl* **jacaltec** *or* **jacaltecs** *or* **jacalteca** *or* **jacaltecas** *usu cap* [Sp *jacalteca,* of AmerInd origin] **1 a :** an Indian people of western Guatemala **b :** a member of such people **2 :** a Mayan language of the Jacaltec people

**jac·a·mar** \'jakə,mär\ *n* -s [F, fr. Tupi *jacamá-ciri*] **:** any of many picarian birds of the family Galbulidae inhabiting tropical forests from Mexico to Argentina, being usu. brilliant metallic green or bronze above and rufescent below with a white throat, having a long sharp bill, and feeding on insects which they catch on the wing

**jac·a·mar·al·cy·on** \,jakə,mä'ralsēən\ *n, cap* [NL, fr. F *jacamar* + Gk *alkyōn, halkyōn* kingfisher] **:** a genus of jacamars having only three toes and including a single Brazilian form (*J. tridactyla*)

**jac·a·me·ro·pine** \¦jakə¦mirə¦pīn, -,pə̇n\ *adj* [NL *Jacamerops* + E *-ine*] **:** of or relating to the genus *Jacamerops*

**jac·a·me·rops** \,≈≈'mē,räps\ *n, cap* [NL, irreg. fr. F *jacamar* + NL *-ops*] **:** a genus of birds comprising the largest of the jacamars which are about 10 inches long

**[1]jac·a·na** \'jakənə\ *n* [modif. of Pg *jaçanã,* fr. Tupi & Guarani] **1** -s **:** any of several wading birds that chiefly frequent coastal freshwater marshes and ponds in warm regions, that have long slender legs and very long toes by means of which they run about over floating vegetation, a pointed bill with a frontal shield between the eyes, and usu. a sharp spur at the bend of the wing, and that constitute the nearly tropicopolitan family Jacanidae **2** *cap* [NL, fr. Pg *jaçanã*] **:** the type genus of Jacanidae comprising the New World jacanas

**[2]ja·ca·na** \'häkənə\ *n* -s [AmerSp *jácana, ácana, jacana, acana,* prob. fr. Taino] **:** a West Indian timber tree (*Pouteria multiflora*) the hard dark wood of which is valued for furniture

**ja·can·i·dae** \jə'kanə,dē\ *n pl, cap* [NL *Jacana,* type genus + *-idae*] **:** a small but widely distributed family of birds (suborder Charadrii) that are related to the plovers and sandpipers and comprise the jacanas

**[1]jac·a·ran·da** \¦jakərən¦dä, ,jakə'randə\ *n* -s [Pg *jacarandá,* fr. Tupi *yacarandá*] **1 :** any of several Brazilian timber trees (as Brazilian rosewood) with heavy dark wood that resembles rosewood **2 :** the wood of a jacaranda

**[2]jac·a·ran·da** \,jakə'randə\ *n* [NL & Pg; NL (the genus), fr. Pg (a tree of this genus)] **1** *cap* **:** a genus of pinnate-leaved tropical American trees (family Bignoniaceae) with showy blue flowers in panicles **2** -s **:** a tree of the genus *Jacaranda*

**jac·a·re** \'jakə,rā, ,≈≈'≈\ *n* -s [Pg, fr. Tupi *jacaré, yacaré*] **:** CAIMAN

**ja·ca·te** \hə'kä,tā\ *n* -s [MexSp] **:** a stout shrub (*Hymenoclea monogyra*) of the family Compositae of the southwestern U.S. and adjacent Mexico, having alternate leaves and heads of greenish flowers and forming dense thickets in sandy arroyos

**jacent** *adj, obs* [L *jacent-, jacens,* pres. part. of *jacēre* to lie — more at ADJACENT] **:** RECUMBENT, PRONE

**j acid** *n, usu cap J* **:** a crystalline sulfonic acid $NH_2C_{10}H_5(OH)SO_3H$ made by alkaline fusion of a disulfonic acid of beta-naphthylamine and used as an intermediate esp. for direct azo dyes; 6-amino-1-naphthol-3-sulfonic acid

**[1]ja·cinth** \'jāsə̇n(t)th, 'jas-\ *n* -s [ME *iacinct, iacynth,* fr. OF *jacincte, jacinte, jacinthe,* fr. L *hyacinthus,* a precious stone, a flowering plant — more at HYACINTH] **:** HYACINTH; *sometimes* **:** a gem more nearly pure orange in color than a hyacinth

**[2]jacinth** \"\ *adj* **1 :** being like a jacinth **2 a** *obs* **:** HYACINTHINE **b :** being of the color jacinthe **c :** TAWNY

**ja·cinthe** \"\ *n* -s [F *jacinthe,* lit., hyacinth] **:** a moderate orange that is yellower and stronger than honeydew and yellower and slightly lighter than Persian orange

**jac·i·ta·ra palm** \¦jasə¦tärə-\ *also* **jacitara** *n* -s [Pg *jacitara,* fr. Tupi] **:** a Brazilian palm of the genus *Desmoncus* the distal pinnae of whose leaves are represented by retrorse hooks that enable the stem to climb — see TIPITI

**[1]jack** \'jak\ *n* -s *often attrib* [ME *jacke,* fr. *Jacke,* nickname for *Johan* (John)] **1 a** (1) *cap, obs* **:** a man of the common people; *also* **:** an impertinent or rude fellow ⟨familiar both with peers and *Jacks* —*Brit. Mag.*⟩ (2) *sometimes cap* **:** a human being **:** MAN — used as an intensive in such phrases as *every man jack* ⟨virtually every man ∼ —*Time*⟩ or *every jack one* ⟨dead, dead every ∼ one of them —W.S.Maugham⟩ (3) *cap, slang* **:** PAL, BUDDY, GUY — usu. used in address ⟨what they get you for, *Jack* —Thurston Scott⟩ ⟨I love it all, *Jack* —Chandler Brossard⟩ **b** (1) *often cap* **:** SAILOR — called also *jack-tar* (2) *sometimes cap* **:** LABORER, SERVANT, ATTENDANT (3) **:** LUMBERJACK (4) *Austral* **:** POLICEMAN **c** (1) **:** a playing card carrying the figure of a servant or soldier and ranking usu. below the queen — called also *knave* (2) [by shortening] **:** JACKPOT 1a(4) (3) **:** a player's bet in a lottery that he can name all five numbers that will be drawn **2 a :** a figure usu. of a man that strikes the time on a bell esp. in a turret clock **b** (1) **:** any of various portable hand-operated machines for lifting heavy weights or otherwise exerting great force by utilizing the principle of the lever, screw, toggle joint, or hydraulic press (2) **:** a clamp commonly of the screw type for holding work firmly in a desired position (as in a machine) (3) **:** a usu. triangular wooden brace fastened to the floor by means of a foot iron and a stage screw and hinged to the back of a wall or other scenic unit in a stage set in order to prop it up from behind **c :** a contrivance for turning a spit **d :** an intermediate upright piece of wood at the inner end of each key in any of several keyboard instruments (as a harpsichord or piano) com-

jack 2e(3)

municating its action to the string by means of a quill, a metal tangent, or a hammer **e** (1) **:** a small white target ball at which bowls are rolled in lawn bowling (2) [prob. short for *jackstone*] **:** a small round stone **:** PEBBLE; *esp* **:** one used in the game of jacks (3) **:** a small six-pointed usu. metal object used in the game of jacks (4) **jacks** *pl but sing in constr* **:** a game played with a set of small objects (as stones, bones, or metal pieces, and often a ball) in which the players toss, catch, and move these objects in a variety of figures requiring coordination of hand and eye (5) [by shortening] **:** JACKKNIFE 2 **f :** a bat to close a masonry course **g** (1) *dial Eng* **:** one fourth of a pint; *also* **:** HALF-PINT (2) [by shortening] **:** APPLEJACK ⟨a side of beef and a gallon of ~ to wash it down —G.A.Chamberlain⟩; *also* **:** BRANDY ⟨the stuff tasted like raisin ~ —Gore Vidal⟩ ⟨an extra supply of prune ~ —*Amer. Guide Series: Pa.*⟩ **h** (1) **:** a lever for depressing the sinkers which push the loops down on the needles in a knitting machine (2) **:** a lever that raises a harness esp. on dobby looms (3) **:** CREEL 3 (4) **:** a machine like a fly frame to handle fine cotton roving **i :** a small flag showing nationality flown by a ship usu. on a jack staff at the bowsprit cap or at the bow but elsewhere in making certain signals **j** (1) **:** a bar of iron athwartships at a topgallant masthead to support a royal mast and spread the royal shrouds (2) **:** LAZY JACK 2 **k :** a pan or frame for the fuel of a torch used in hunting or fishing at night; *also* **:** the torch itself **:** JACKLIGHT **l** (1) **:** a receptacle with one or more connections to electric circuits arranged for convenient plugging in of connections to other circuits (2) **:** a female metallic terminal or junction piece by means of which instruments may be quickly inserted in a line or telephone circuits quickly joined at the central office or exchange **m :** SPHALERITE **n** *slang* **:** MONEY ⟨hadn't that much ~ —Nevil Shute⟩ **3 :** something smaller than the usual or typical of its kind — used in combination ⟨~ rafter⟩ ⟨*jack*shaft⟩ **4 a :** any of several fishes: as (1) **:** PIKE, PICKEREL; *esp* **:** a young or small pike (2) **:** WALLEYED PIKE (3) **:** a fish of the family Carangidae; *esp* **:** a crevalle (*Caranx hippos*) (4) **:** a young male fish ⟨a ~ salmon⟩ **b :** the male of various animals esp. of the domestic ass or donkey **c :** any of several birds: as (1) [by shortening] **:** JACKDAW (2) [by shortening] **:** JACKSNIPE **d :** BONE SPAVIN **e** [by shortening] **:** JACKRABBIT **syn** see FLAG

[2]**jack** \"\ *vb* -ED/-ING/-S *vi* **1 :** to hunt or fish at night with a jacklight; *specif* **:** to hunt game esp. deer illegally at night by shining a spotlight that dazzles and holds immobile **2** *slang chiefly Brit* **:** to give up suddenly or readily — used with *up* **~** *vt* **1 :** to hunt or fish at night with a jacklight **:** kill with the aid of a jacklight ⟨a buck that had been ~*ed* on his own land —*N.Y. Herald Tribune*⟩ **2 a :** to move or lift by or as if by means of a jack — usu. used with *up* ⟨~ up an automobile⟩ ⟨~*ed* up my shorts —Harold Robbins⟩ **b :** RAISE, INCREASE ⟨decided to ~ their fees —*Wall Street Jour.*⟩ — usu. used with *up* ⟨stepped in to ~ up . . . the prices he got —F.L. Allen⟩ **c :** to raise the level or quality of **:** BOLSTER — usu. used with *up* ⟨~*ing* up discipline —R.M.Neal⟩ ⟨has ideas about ~*ing* up audiences —*New Yorker*⟩ ⟨this whole business of ~*ing* up the soul —P.G.Wodehouse⟩ **d :** to take to task **:** call to account **:** reprimand or scold sharply — used with *up* ⟨~*ed* up two or three men of the company —R.P.Reeder⟩ **3 :** to pass (boards) up to a piler on top of a lumber pile

[3]**jack** \"\ *n* -S [ME *jakke*, fr. MF *jaque, jaques* — more at JACKET] **1 :** a coarse cheap body garment worn for defense during the medieval period; *esp* **:** one made of leather and sometimes lined with metal **2 :** a vessel for holding liquor made orig. of waxed leather and coated on the outside with tar or pitch **:** JUG, TANKARD

[4]**jack** *var of* JACKFRUIT

[5]**jack** *var of* JACK CHEESE

**jack-a-dan·dy** \ˌjakəˈdandē\ *n, pl* **jack-a-dandies** [[1]*jack* + *a* (of) + *dandy*] **:** a little dandy **:** a little foppish impertinent fellow

[1]**jack·al** \ˈjakəl *also* -ˌkȯl\ *n* -S *often attrib* [Turk *çakal*, fr. Per *shagāl, shaghāl*, fr. Skt *sṛgāla, śṛgāla*] **1 a :** any of several wild dogs of the Old World, smaller, usu. more yellowish, and less daring than wolves, sometimes hunting in packs at night but more usu. singly or in pairs, and feeding on carrion and small animals (as poultry); *esp* **:** a common wild dog (*Canis aureus*) of southeastern Europe, southern Asia, and northern Africa **b :** the fur or pelt of this animal **2 a :** a person who tends to the routine needs of or performs menial tasks for another **:** DRUDGE **b :** an individual who for mercenary or self-seeking ends serves or collaborates with another esp. in the commission of base or sordid acts ⟨blackmailed by one of his ~*s* —Edmund Wilson⟩ ⟨denounced these ~ tactics —Stringfellow Barr⟩

[2]**jac·kal** \hәˈkäl\ *n* -S [by alter.] **:** JACAL

**jack-a'-lantern** *var of* JACK-O'-LANTERN

**jackal buzzard** *n* **:** a southern African hawk (*Buteo rufofuscus*)

**jack·a·legs** \ˈjakəˌlegz\ *n pl but sing in constr* [alter. of *jockteleg*] *chiefly Scot* **:** a large clasp knife

**jack-a-lent** \ˈjakəˌlent\ *n, pl* **jack-a-lents** *usu cap J&L* [[1]*jack* + *a* (of) + *Lent*] **1 :** a small stuffed puppet set up to be pelted as a sport in Lent **2 :** a simple or insignificant fellow **:** PUPPET

**jack·a·napes** \ˈjakəˌnāps\ *n* -ES [ME *Jack Napis, Jac Napes*, nickname for William de la Pole †1450 4th earl and 1st duke of Suffolk] **1 :** MONKEY, APE **2 a :** an impertinent or conceited fellow **:** COXCOMB ⟨beribboned ~ —Frank Yerby⟩ **b :** a pert or mischievous child

**jack arch** *n* [[1]*jack* (something smaller)] **:** a flat arch (as a lintel with a keystone)

**jack-a-roo** \ˌjakəˈrü\ *var of* JACKEROO

**jack·ass** \ˈjaˌkas, -kaa(ə)s, -kais *also* -kȧs *in New Eng & Brit esp (in Brit at least) in sense 2*\ *n* [[1]*jack* + *ass*] **1 a :** a male ass; *also* **:** DONKEY **b** *Austral* **:** KOOKABURRA **2 :** a stupid person **:** FOOL, DOLT ⟨a conceited ~⟩ **3 :** HAWSE BAG

**jackass bark** *n* **1 :** a 3-masted ship square-rigged on the foremast, setting square topsails and topgallant sails over a fore-and-aft mainsail, and fore-and-aft rigged on the mizzen **2 :** a 4-masted ship square-rigged on the foremast and mainmast and gaff-rigged on the mizzen and jiggermast **3 :** a sailing ship with three or more masts and a combination of gaffsails and square sails in addition to complete square rig on its foremast

**jackass bat** *n* **:** a large spotted bat (*Euderma maculata*) occurring in the southwestern U. S. and having enormous ears joined across the forehead by a low band

**jackass brig** *n* **:** a brig-rigged ship not setting a square mainsail and having a fore-topmast and fore-topgallant mast made of one spar

**jackass clover** *n* **1 :** CALIFORNIA BUR CLOVER **2 :** a rank-scented annual herb (*Wislizenia refracta*) of the family Capparidaceae that has trifoliolate leaves and long-stalked yellow flowers and is found in the western U. S.

**jackass deer** *n* **1 :** KOB **2 :** MULE DEER

**jack·ass·ery** \-sərē\ *n* -ES **:** a piece of stupidity or folly **:** DOLTISHNESS ⟨the most preposterous ~ we ever heard of —Hubert Kay⟩

**jackass fish** *n* **:** a morwong (*Dactylopagrus macropterus*) of Australia, Tasmania, and New Zealand

**jackass hare** *or* **jackass rabbit** *n* **:** JACK RABBIT

**jackass kingfisher** *n* **:** KOOKABURRA

**jack·ass·ness** *n* -ES **:** the quality or state of being a jackass

**jackass penguin** *n* **:** a penguin (*Spheniscus demersus*) of western So. America and southern Africa whose note suggests the braying of an ass

**jackass rig** *n* **:** a rig differing in some particular from the type of rig to which it mainly belongs

**jack bean** *n* **1 :** a bushy semierect annual tropical American plant of the genus *Canavalia*; *esp* **:** a plant (*C. ensiformis*) having long pods with white seeds and grown esp. for forage — compare SWORD BEAN **2 :** the seed of the jack bean

**jackbird** \ˈ=ˌ=\ *n* **1 :** a passerine bird (*Callaeas cinerea*) of South Island, New Zealand, resembling the starling **2 :** SADDLEBACK 2d

**jack block** *n* **:** a block fixed aloft for raising and lowering the topgallant and royal yards of a ship

**jackboot** \ˈ=ˌ=\ *n* **1 :** a heavy military boot esp. of glossy black leather extending well above the knee and having a wide flaring top and worn esp. during the 17th and 18th centuries **2 :** a boot similar in shape to the military jackboot worn esp. by fishermen

**jack box** *n* **:** a connection box containing one or more jacks into which a piece of electric equipment (as a telephone or loudspeaker) may be plugged

jackboot 1

**jackboy** \ˈ=ˌ=\ *n, archaic* **:** a boy (as a stableboy) who does menial work

**jack-by-the-hedge** \ˈ===ˌ=\ *n, usu cap J, dial Eng* **:** GARLIC MUSTARD

**jack chain** *n* **1 :** a light wire chain whose links are set at right angles to each other resembling a figure eight or having the end of each loop bent round to meet the end of the other loop **2 :** an endless toothed chain for moving logs usu. from the millpond into the sawmill

**jack cheese** *also* **jack** *n*, -S *often cap J* **:** a semisoft whole-milk cheese with high moisture content

**jack crevalle** *n* **:** a crevalle (*Caranx hippos*)

**jack crow** *n* **:** a rare West African bird (*Picathartes gymnocephalus*) resembling a crow and having bluish gray back and wings, white underparts, and a bright yellow and black naked head

**jack curlew** *n* **1 :** WHIMBREL **2 :** HUDSONIAN CURLEW

**jackdaw** \ˈ=ˌ=\ *n* [[1]*jack* + *daw*] **1 :** a common bird (*Corvus monedula*) of Europe and parts of Asia that is closely related to but smaller than the common crow, is glossy black above and dark gray below with silvery gray markings on head and neck, is a clever mimic capable of learning to imitate the human voice, is gregarious in habits usu. nesting in and about buildings, and is readily tamed **2 :** GRACKLE 2; *esp* **:** BOAT-TAILED GRACKLE

**jacked** *past of* JACK

**jack·een** \jaˈkēn\ *n* -S [[1]*jack* + *-een* (fr. IrGael *-īn*, dim. suffix)] *Irish* **:** an obnoxious self-assertive dude ⟨a jaunty little ~ with a rich brogue —R.B.D.French⟩

**jack·er** \ˈjakə(r)\ *n* -S **:** one that jacks: as **a :** a person who hunts or fishes at night with a jacklight **b :** a worker who smooths and toughens leather by rolling it under pressure in a rolling jack **c** (1) **:** a sawmill pondman who guides logs into the jack chain that moves them to the log deck of the mill — called also *jackerman, slipman* (2) **:** JACK CHAIN

[1]**jack·e·roo** \ˌjakəˈrü\ *n* -S [alter. of *jackaroo*, fr. [1]*jack* + *-aroo* (as in *kangaroo*)] *Austral* **:** a green hand working as an apprentice on a sheep ranch

[2]**jack·e·roo** \"\ *vi* **jackerooed; jackerooed; jackerooing; jackeroos** *Austral* **:** to work as a jackeroo

[1]**jack·et** \ˈjakət, *usu* -əd·+V\ *n* -S *often attrib* [ME *jaket*, fr. MF *jaquet*, dim. of *jaque, jaques* short jacket, pourpoint, jack, fr. *jacques, jacque* peasant, fr. the name *Jacques* James, Jacob] **1 a** (1) **:** a garment like a coat for the upper body usu. having a front opening, collar, lapels, sleeves, and pockets, made in varying lengths from waist to hip, and worn separately or as part of a suit ⟨cardigan ~⟩ ⟨an embroidered pajama ~⟩ (2) *Midland* **:** a man's vest **b :** something worn or fastened around the body but not for use as clothing: as (1) **:** CORK JACKET (2) **:** STRAITJACKET (3) **:** a casing for the upper part of the body usu. made of plaster and serving a supportive, corrective, or restraining purpose **2 a** (1) **:** the natural covering of an animal (as the skin of a snake or fish) (2) **:** the fur or wool of a mammal sometimes together with the skin ⟨a flock with a fine even ~ of wool⟩ (3) **:** a young seal **b :** the skin of a potato — used chiefly of cooked potatoes in the phrase *in their jackets* **3 :** an outer covering or casing: as **a :** a thermally nonconducting cover or lagging (as for a tank, pipe, or engine cylinder); *also* **:** a covering that encloses an intermediate space through which a temperature-controlling fluid may be circulated (as in water-cooling a gasoline-engine cylinder) **b** (1) **:** a cylindrical hollow forging in a built-up gun that is concentric with and shrunk usu. directly upon the tube, extends from the breech usu. to a little forward of the trunnions, and usu. contains the seat for the breechblock or breech plug (2) **:** the tough cold-worked metal casing which forms the outer shell of a built-up bullet and into which lead is swaged to form the complete projectile **c** (1) **:** a cloth covering for a machine roller usu. woven or felted in tubular form (2) **:** a felt cover for a couch roll in a papermaking machine **d :** an easily removable form that supports a foundry mold on all four sides during pouring **e** (1) **:** a wrapper or open envelope for a document (as a letter, dispatch, or the case-history file or personal record of a prisoner, serviceman, or agency client) on which are put directions for its disposition and notations as to its contents, dates of being sent and received, or other details (2) **:** an envelope for enclosing registered mail during delivery from one post office to another **f** (1) **:** a detachable protective wrapper for a book typically consisting of a rectangular sheet of paper elaborately printed with descriptive or promotional material, cut flush at head and foot, and folded around the binding with ends tucked between cover board and free endpaper — called also *book jacket, book wrapper, dust cover, dust jacket, dust wrapper, wrapper* (2) **:** the cover of a paperbound book esp. when folded and tucked under at the fore edge (3) **:** the outside leaves for a booklet, pamphlet, or catalog which is to be stitched or wired through the saddle (4) **:** a paper or paperboard envelope for a phonograph record

[2]**jacket** \"\ *vt* -ED/-ING/-S **:** to put a jacket on **:** enclose in or with a jacket ⟨reports which had been ~*ed* —C.R.Cooper⟩

**jacket crown** *n* **:** an artificial crown that is placed over the remains of a natural tooth

**jacketed** *adj* **1 :** wearing or having a jacket ⟨~ boys on the road⟩ **2 :** enclosed in or by a jacket ⟨~ bullets⟩

**jacketing** *n* -S **1 a :** fabric used for jackets **b :** JACKET 3a, 3b **2 :** BEATING ⟨gave him an awful ~⟩

**jack·field ware** \ˈjakˌfēld-\ *n, usu cap J* [fr. *Jackfield*, England] **:** pottery made at Jackfield, Shropshire, England, in the 18th century and distinguished esp. by its thick brilliant black glaze applied over a common red clay

**jackfish** \ˈ=ˌ=\ *n* [[1]*jack* + *fish*] **:** JACK 4a (1)

**jack fishing** *n* **1 :** fishing for jacks (as pike) **2 :** fishing with a jacklight

**jack-fool** \ˈ=ˈ=\ *n, usu cap J* [ME *Jakke fool*] **:** TOMFOOL

**jack frost** *n, cap J&F* **:** frost or frosty weather personified

**jack·fruit** \ˈjakˌfrüt\ *or* **jack** *or* **jak** \ˈjak\ *or* **jak·fruit** \ˈjakˌ-\ *n* -S [*jackfruit, jakfruit* fr. Pg *jaca* jackfruit (fr. Malayalam *cakka*) + E *fruit; jack, jak* fr. Pg *jaca*] **1 :** a large East Indian tree (*Artocarpus heterophyllus*) that is distinguished from the closely related breadfruit by its entire leaves, yields a fine-grained yellow wood, and is widely cultivated in the tropics for its immense fruits which contain an edible but insipid pulp and nutritious seeds that are commonly roasted **2 :** the fruit of the jackfruit **3 :** DURIAN

**jackhammer** \ˈ=ˌ==\ *n* **1 :** a rock drill of the hammer type usu. held in the hands of the operator **2 :** AIR HAMMER

**jack hor·ner pie** \ˈjakˈhȯrnə(r)-\ *n, usu cap J&H* [after (*Little*) *Jack Horner*, a nursery-rhyme character depicted as pulling a plum out of a pie] **:** an ornamental pie-shaped container from which favors or toys are extracted often by pulling a ribbon at a party

**jack-hunting** \ˈ=ˌ==\ *n* **:** hunting with a jacklight

**jackies** *pl of* JACKY

**jack-in-a-bottle** \ˈ===ˌ==\ *n, pl* **jacks-in-a-bottle :** LONG-TAILED TIT

**jack-in-a-box** \ˈ===ˌ=\ *n, pl* **jacks-in-a-box 1 :** a tropical East Indian tree (*Hernandia sonora*) which bears a drupe that rattles in the inflated calyx when dry **2** *Brit* **:** CUCKOOPINT

**jacking** *n* -S **1 :** a process in spinning for giving extra twist or draft or both to the roving often done on a mule **2 :** the practice or act of hunting or fishing with a jacklight ⟨an effort to stop deer ~ —L.S.Marceau⟩

**jack-in-office** \ˈ===ˌ==\ *n, pl* **jacks-in-office** *sometimes cap J* **:** an insolent fellow in authority ⟨some little *jack-in-office* of a clerk —O.S.J.Gogarty⟩

**jack-in-the-box** \ˈ===ˌ=\ *n, pl* **jack-in-the-boxes** *also* **jacks-in-the-box** *sometimes cap J* **1** *obs* **:** SHARPER, CHEAT **2 :** a child's toy consisting of a box out of which a figure springs when the lid is raised **3 :** any of several mechanical contrivances: as **a :** DIFFERENTIAL GEAR **b :** a large wooden screw turning in a nut attached to the cross-piece of a rude press **c :** a lifting jack **:** JACKSCREW **d :** a burglar's tool for opening doors or safes by means of a small but powerful screw **e :** a jim-crow reversing tool **f :** SUN-AND-PLANET MOTION

jack-in-the-box 2

**jack-in-the-green** \ˈ===ˌ=\ *n, pl* **jack-in-the-greens** *or* **jacks-in-the-green** *usu cap J&G* **1 :** a man or boy enclosed in a conical framework covered with leaves and boughs to take a prominent part in the May Day games of English chimney sweeps **2 :** an English primrose having sepals resembling leaves

**jack-in-the-pulpit** \ˈ===ˈ=(ˌ)=\ *n, pl* **jack-in-the-pulpits** *or* **jacks-in-the-pulpit 1 :** any of several plants of the genus *Arisaema*; *esp* **:** an American spring-flowering woodland herb (*A. atrorubens*) with sheathing leaves, an upright club-shaped spadix with open overarching green and purple spathe, and fruit consisting of a mass of bright scarlet berries — see GREEN DRAGON 2 **2 :** TURK'S-CAP LILY b **3 :** LOVE-IN-A-MIST 1 **4 :** a figwort (*Scrophularia californica*) of western No. America with dull red flowers **5 :** PRAIRIE WAKE-ROBIN

**jack jumper** *n* **:** a sled that consists of one thick runner curved much like a barrel stave to which is attached an upright with a seat having grips on either side of its undersurface and that is used on a slope; *also* **:** a person who rides a jack jumper

**jack ketch** \ˈjakˈkech\ *n, usu cap J&K* [after *Jack* (John) *Ketch* †1686 Eng. executioner] *Brit* **:** a public executioner; *specif* **:** HANGMAN

[1]**jackknife** \ˈ=ˌ=\ *n* [prob. fr. [1]*jack* + *knife*] **1 :** a large strong clasp knife for the pocket **2 :** a dive executed headfirst either forward or backward in which the diver beginning usu. at the highest point of the dive bends from the waist and touches or clasps his ankles while holding his knees unflexed before straightening out to enter the water

jackknife 1

[2]**jackknife** \"\ *vt* **1 :** to cut with a jackknife **2 :** to double up like a jackknife ⟨willing to ~ himself to get in and out —*Springfield (Mass.) Republican*⟩ **3 :** to cause to jackknife ⟨the tractor and trailer were *jackknifed* by the diesel —*Springfield (Mass.) Union*⟩ **~** *vi* **1 :** to double up like a jackknife ⟨~ on the sofa beside the Christmas tree —D.C.Peattie⟩ **2 :** to turn or rise and form an angle of 90 degrees or less with each other — used esp. of a pair of vehicles one of which is attached to and follows the other (as a tractor and its trailer or two railroad cars)

[3]**jackknife** \"\ *adj* **:** resembling a jackknife esp. in its manner of opening and closing ⟨a ~ drawbridge⟩ ⟨a ~ door⟩

**jackknife clam** *n* **:** RAZOR CLAM

**jack ladder** *n* **1 :** a ship's ladder with wooden rungs and side ropes **2 a :** an inclined plane up which logs are moved from pond to sawmill typically consisting of a V-shaped trough within which an endless chain carries the logs upward **b :** JACK CHAIN

**jack lagging** *n* **:** rough temporary lagging used in arch centering and brought to the true curve of the intrados to take the weight of the voussoirs

[1]**jack·leg** \ˈjaˌkleg\ *adj* [[1]*jack* + *-leg* (as in *blackleg* "sharper")] **1 a :** characterized by lack of skill or training **:** AMATEUR ⟨simplifies the labors of the ~ editor —D.L.Cohn⟩ ⟨a fair ~ carpenter —Stanley Walker⟩ **b :** characterized by unscrupulousness, dishonesty, or lack of professional standards ⟨two ~ lawyers and a cigar-eating judge —F.B.Gipson⟩ **2 :** designed for use as a temporary expedient **:** MAKESHIFT ⟨rigged up a ~ system of landing lights —W.L.White⟩

[2]**jackleg** \"\ *n* **:** one who is jackleg

[3]**jackleg** \"\ *n* [*jackhammer* + *leg*] **:** a support on which a jackhammer is mounted while drilling

[1]**jacklight** \ˈ=ˌ=\ *n* [[1]*jack* + *light*] **:** a torch, lantern, flashlight, or other artificial light used esp. in hunting or fishing at night ⟨spearing fish in the bay with a ~ —Ernest Hemingway⟩

[2]**jacklight** \"\ *vb* **:** JACK

**jack·light·er** \"+ə(r)\ *n* **:** a person who hunts or fishes with a jacklight; *esp* **:** one who hunts deer illegally at night with a jacklight

**jack line** *n* [[1]*jack* (something smaller)] **1 :** a small rope or line **2 :** a rod or steel cable connecting a central pumping engine with each of two or more oil wells which it powers

**jack mackerel** *n* **:** either of two fishes of the genus *Trachurus:* **a :** a California market fish (*T. symmetricus*) that is iridescent green or bluish above and silvery below **b :** a closely related Australian fish (*T. novaezelandiae*)

**jack·man** \ˈjakmən\ *n, pl* **jackmen 1 :** a textile worker who puts copper printing shells into machines that print cloth **2 :** SCREWMAN **3 :** a repairer of shoes

**jack mormon** *n, sometimes cap J & usu cap M* **1 :** a non-Mormon living in a Mormon community and sympathetic to or on friendly terms with his neighbors **2 :** a Mormon inactive in the church or not adhering strictly to Mormon tenets **:** a backsliding or nominal Mormon ⟨always paid his tithes — only he had to have his coffee so some called him a *jack Mormon* —*Amer. Guide Series: Ariz.*⟩ ⟨a *jack Mormon*, which means that . . . he no longer pays tithes or holds with the tenet of total abstinence —A.J.Liebling⟩

**jacko** *var of* JOCKO

**jack oak** *n* **1 :** BLACKJACK 5 **2 :** an extremely variable oak (*Quercus ellipsoidalis*) of east central No. America having leaves with sharply pointed lobes and ashy gray turbinate to goblet-shaped acorn cups with persistent dull pubescence

**jack-of-all-trades** \ˌ=ˈ=ˈ=\ *n, pl* **jacks-of-all-trades** *sometimes cap J* **:** a person who can do passable work at various trades **:** a handy or versatile individual ⟨was expected to be a *jack-of-all-trades* —Patricia M. Johnson⟩ ⟨every man would be something of a *jack-of-all-trades* —A.L.Kroeber⟩

**jack off** *vi* **:** MASTURBATE — usu. considered vulgar

**jack-o'-lantern** *or* **jack-a-lantern** *also* **jack-o'-lanthorn** \ˈjakəˌ\ *or* **jack-with-a-lantern** \ˈ===ˌ==\ *n* **1 a** *obs* **:** a man carrying a lantern **:** a night watchman **b :** IGNIS FATUUS **c :** SAINT ELMO'S FIRE **d :** a lantern made of a pumpkin or other vegetable so prepared as to show in illumination features of a human face **2 :** a large luminescent mushroom (*Clitocybe illudens*)

jack-o'-lantern 1d

**jack-over-the-ground** \ˈ=ˈ==ˌ=\ *n, pl* **jacks-over-the-ground :** GROUND IVY 1

**jack pike** *n* **:** JACK 4a (1)

**jack pine** *n* **1 :** a slender No. American pine (*Pinus banksiana*) having two stout twisted leaves in each fascicle, one-sided curved cones with spiny-tipped scales, and wood that is used esp. for boxwood and pulpwood **2 :** BRISTLECONE PINE **3 :** LODGEPOLE PINE **4 :** LIMBER PINE

**jack-pine sawfly** *n* **:** an American sawfly (*Neodiprion pratti banksianae* or *N. banksianae*) having a larva that is a serious defoliator of pine (as jack pine)

**jack plane** *n* **:** a medium-sized general-purpose bench plane usu. somewhat over a foot in length — see PLANE illustration

**jack post** *n* **:** either of the posts supporting the crankshaft of a deep-well-boring apparatus

**jackpot** \ˈ=ˌ=\ *n, often attrib* [[1]*jack* (playing card) + *pot*] **1 a** (1) **:** a hand of draw poker in which every player antes in order to increase the gain to the winner and in which no player may open without a pair of jacks or better (2) **:** a game of draw poker in which a pair of jacks or better is required to open — compare ROODLE (3) **jackpots** *pl but sing or pl in constr* **:** draw poker in which every pot is a jackpot (4) **:** an unusually large pot (as in the game of poker) formed by accumulation of stakes from previous play in which no decision was reached **b** (1) **:** a combination on a slot machine which wins for a player a top prize or all the coins in the machine; *also* **:** the sum so won (2) **:** a large fund of money or other impressive reward formed by the accumulation of unwon prizes (as in a quiz contest) ⟨lost TV's biggest ~ so far —*Newsweek*⟩ ⟨the ~ question⟩ (3) **:** an impressive often unexpected success or reward ⟨lecturing all over the country with an occasional ~ in a friendly town —H.S.Canby⟩ **2 a :** a pool or fund contributed by a number of persons ⟨a ~ which sent the family on their way rejoicing —*Emporia (Kan.) Gazette*⟩ **b :** mail for distant separations for which a postal clerk does not immediately have room in his case and which he masses together in one box or sack for later distribution when space is available **3** *chiefly West* **:** a tight spot **:** JAM, SCRAPE ⟨apt to get himself and his friends into a ~ —Ross Santee⟩

**jack–pudding** \ˈ=ˈ=\ *n, sometimes cap J* **:** BUFFOON, CLOWN, MERRY-ANDREW

[1]**jackrabbit** \ˈ=,==\ *n* [[1]*jack* (jackass) + *rabbit;* fr. its long ears] **:** any of several large hares (genus *Lepus*) of western No. America having very long ears and long hind legs and living in open country sometimes in such large numbers as to do much injury to forage and crops

[2]**jackrabbit** \"\ *vi* -ED/-ING/-S **:** to make a sudden lurch or jump or a fast start ⟨a car ~*ing* down the street —Paul Jones⟩

**jack rafter** *n* [[1]*jack* (something smaller)] **:** a short rafter: **a :** one of the shorter rafters used in a hip or valley roof **b :** a secondary roof timber (as a common rafter resting on purlins); *also* **:** one of the pieces simulating extended rafters under the eaves in some styles of building

**jackrod** \ˈ=,=\ *n* **:** JACKSTAY

**jack·roll** \ˈja,krōl\ *vt* [back-formation fr. *jackroller*] **:** ROLL 7

**jack·roll·er** \-lə(r)\ *n* [[1]*jack* + *roller*] **:** one who robs a drunken or sleeping person

**jack rope** *n* **:** a rope fastening the foot of a fore-and-aft sail to a boom

**jack rose** *n* [fr. *jack rose,* a variety of red rose, alter. of *jacqueminot rose* — more at JACQUEMINOT] **1 :** a vivid red that is bluer and deeper than apple red or scarlet and bluer and stronger than carmine **2** *usu cap J&R* **:** a cocktail consisting of lemon juice, apple brandy, and grenadine shaken in ice and strained before serving

**jacks** *pl of* JACK, *pres 3d sing of* JACK

**jack saddle** *n* **:** the saddle of a harness

**jack salmon** *n* **1 :** WALLEYED PIKE **2** *western No. America* **:** GRILSE; *also* **:** SILVER SALMON

**jackscrew** \ˈ=,=\ *n* **:** a screw-operated jack for lifting or for exerting pressure

**jackshaft** \ˈ=,=\ *n* [[1]*jack* (something smaller) + *shaft*] **:** COUNTERSHAFT; *specif* **:** the intermediate driving shaft in an automobile

jackscrew

**jack·shay** *also* **jack·shea** \ˈjak,shā\ *n* -S [origin unknown] *Austral* **:** a bushman's quart pot used esp. for boiling water

**jacks–in–the–box** *pl of* JACK-IN-THE-BOX

**jacks–in–the–green** *pl of* JACK-IN-THE-GREEN

**jacks–in–the–pulpit** *pl of* JACK-IN-THE-PULPIT

**jacksmelt** \ˈ=,=\ *n* [[1]*jack* + *smelt*] **:** a large silversides (*Atherinopsis californiensis*) of the Pacific coast of No. America that sometimes attains a length of 18 inches and is the chief commercial smelt of the California markets

**jacksnipe** \ˈ=,=\ *n, pl* **jacksnipe** *or* **jacksnipes** [[1]*jack* + *snipe*] **1 :** a true snipe (*Limnocryptes minima*) of Europe and other parts of the Old World that is smaller and more highly colored than the common snipe **2 a :** PECTORAL SANDPIPER **b :** WILSON'S SNIPE **c :** any of several other snipes

**jacks–of–all–trades** *pl of* JACK-OF-ALL-TRADES

**jack·son** \ˈjaksən\ *adj, usu cap* [fr. *Jackson,* Miss.] **:** of or from Jackson, the capital of Mississippi ⟨*Jackson* merchants⟩ **:** of the kind or style prevalent in Jackson

**jackson cent** *n, usu cap J* [after Andrew *Jackson* †1845 7th U. S. president] **:** HARD-TIMES TOKEN

**jackson day** *n, usu cap J&D* [after Andrew *Jackson*] **:** the anniversary on January 8 of the successful defense of New Orleans by General Jackson in 1815 which is a legal holiday in Louisiana and generally observed by Democrats throughout the U. S.

**jackson haines** \-ˈhānz\ *n, usu cap J&H* [after *Jackson Haines* †1875, Amer. figure skater] **:** a figure-skating spin executed on the flat of one skate in which the body gradually assumes a low sitting position with the free leg held in front with knee bent and then gradually straightens to an erect position — called also *sit spin*

**jack·so·nia** \jakˈsōnēə\ *n, cap* [NL, fr. George *Jackson* 19th cent Brit. botanist + NL *-ia*] **:** a large genus of yellow-flowered Australian shrubs (family Leguminosae) with very variable leaves some of which are like needles and others merely phyllodia

[1]**jack·so·ni·an** \(ˈ)jak¦sōnēən\ *adj, usu cap* [Andrew *Jackson* 7th president of the U. S. (1829–37) + E *-ian*] **:** of or relating to Andrew Jackson, his views or policies, or his era ⟨stunned by the sheer restlessness of *Jacksonian* America —G.W.Pierson⟩; *esp* **:** relating to a body of political ideas commonly associated with Andrew Jackson and vigorously championing the right and ability of the common man to participate in politics and administration and opposing the aristocratic principle of government ⟨*Jacksonian* democracy⟩

[2]**jacksonian** \"\ *n -s usu cap* **:** a follower of Andrew Jackson **:** an adherent of Jackson's principles or policies

[3]**jacksonian** \"\ *adj, often cap* [*Jacksonian* (*epilepsy*)] **:** of or resembling Jacksonian epilepsy

**jacksonian epilepsy** *n, usu cap J* [John H. *Jackson* †1911 Eng. neurologist + E *-ian*] **:** symptomatic epilepsy produced by injury to the brain (as by trauma or toxic agents) and manifesting symptoms that vary with the part of the brain injured

**jack·son·ism** \ˈjaksə,nizəm\ *n* -S, *usu cap* [Andrew *Jackson* + E *-ism*] **:** Jacksonian political principles and policies ⟨the sophisticated public, which had had too much of *Jacksonism,* was bored by stories of woodsmen and sailors —Van Wyck Brooks⟩

**jack·son·ite** \-sə,nīt\ *n* -S *usu cap* [Andrew *Jackson* + E *-ite*] **:** JACKSONIAN

**jack·son·ville** \ˈjaksən,vil, *esp S* -,vəl\ *adj, usu cap* [fr. *Jacksonville,* Fla.] **:** of or from the city of Jacksonville, Fla. ⟨a *Jacksonville* garden⟩ **:** of the kind or style prevalent in Jacksonville

**jackson vine** *n, usu cap J* [fr. the name *Jackson*] **:** MATRIMONY VINE

**jackson white** *n, cap J & usu cap W* [prob. after Capt. *Jackson,* Am. slave trader in colonial times] **:** one of a group of people of mixed Negro, Indian, and white ancestry in the Ramapo mountains of New York and New Jersey

**jacks–over–the–ground** *pl of* JACK-OVER-THE-GROUND

**jack spavin** *n* **:** BONE SPAVIN

**jack spool** *n* **:** a large wooden spool on which is wound woolen sliver from a carding machine or woolen yarn for dyeing or warping

**jack staff** *n* [[1]*jack* (flag)] **:** a staff which is fixed on the bowsprit cap or in the bows of a ship and upon which the jack is hoisted

**jackstay** \ˈ=,=\ *n* **1 a :** an iron rod, wooden bar, or wire rope stretching along a yard of a ship to which the sails are fastened **b :** a support of wood, iron, or rope running up and down a mast on which the parrel of a yard travels **c :** a reefing rope stretching along the reef band of a square sail from hole to hole **d :** a fixed bar or rope for hanging esp. clothes bags or for securing awning stops (as around a barbette) **2 a :** a longitudinal rigging provided to maintain the correct distance between the heads of various riggings on an airship

**jackstock** \ˈ=,=\ *n* [[1]*jack* (ass) + *stock*] **:** male asses

**jack·stone** \ˈjak,stōn\ *n* [alter. of earlier *chackstone,* alter. of *checkstone,* sing. of *checkstones*] **1 :** JACK 2e (4) — usu. used in pl. **2 :** JACK 2e (3)

**jackstraw** \ˈ=,=\ *n* [[1]*jack* + *straw*] **1** *obs* **:** a man without property, worth, or influence **2 a :** one of the pieces used in the game jackstraws **b jackstraws** *pl but sing in constr* **:** a game in which a set of straws or strips (as of bone or wood) are let fall in a heap and each player in turn tries to remove them one at a time with a small instrument and without disturbing the rest of the pile **3** *dial Eng* **:** any of several small European birds using bedstraw in their nests: as **a :** WHITETHROAT **b :** GARDEN WARBLER **c :** BLACKCAP

**jack stringer** *n* [[1]*jack* (something smaller)] **:** a bridge stringer placed outside the main stringers

**jack–tar** \ˈ=ˈ=\ *n, often cap J* **:** JACK 1b(1)

**jack timber** *n* [[1]*jack* (something smaller)] **:** a timber (as a rafter, rib, or studding) that from being intercepted is shorter than the others with which it is used

**jack tree** *n* [[4]*jack*] **:** JACKFRUIT 1

**jack truss** *n* [[1]*jack* (something smaller)] **:** a minor truss in a hip roof used where the roof has not its full section

**jack wax** *n* **:** a chewy confection made by pouring boiling maple syrup over snow

**jack weight** *n, archaic* **:** a weight attached to an endless chain and forming part of a roasting jack

**jack–with–a–lantern** *var of* JACK-O'-LANTERN

**jackwood** \ˈ=,=\ *n* [[4]*jack* + *wood*] **:** the wood of the jackfruit tree

**jacky** \ˈjakī\ *n* -ES [[1]*jack* (quarter pint) + *-y*] *Brit* **:** GIN ⟨snuff . . . and excellent ~ —W.S.Gilbert⟩

**jack yard** *n* [[1]*jack* (something smaller)] **:** a spar to extend a fore-and-aft topsail beyond the gaff

**jacky winter** \ˈjakē-\ *n* [fr. *Jacky,* dim. of *Jack*] **:** a small brown flycatcher (*Microeca fascinans*) of Australia

**ja·cob** \ˈjākəb *sometimes* -əp\ *n* -S *cap* [LL, fr. Gk *Iakōb,* fr. Heb *Ya'ăqōbh,* after *Ya'ăqōbh* (Jacob) in the Bible (Gen. 25:20 ff.), the eponymous ancestor of the Israelites] **:** the ancient Hebrew nation **:** ISRAEL ⟨yet you did not call upon me, O *Jacob;* but you have been weary of me, O Israel —Isa 43:22 (RSV)⟩

[1]**ja·co·be·an** \¦jakə¦bēən *also* ¦jāk- *sometimes* jəˈkōb-\ *adj, usu cap* [NL *jacobaeus* Jacobean (fr. *Jacobus* —James I —†1625 king of England) + E *-an*] **:** of or relating to James I of England, his reign, or his times: as **a :** relating to or representing an early 17th century style of architecture that continued the Elizabethan style with freer use of the classical orders **b :** relating to or exemplifying an early 17th century style in furniture influenced by Renaissance models but somewhat simpler and lighter **c :** of, relating to, or typical of writers or literature of the early 17th century ⟨*Jacobean* drama⟩

[2]**jacobean** \"\ *n* -S *usu cap* **:** a Jacobean statesman or writer

[3]**jacobean** \"\ *adj, usu cap* [NL *jacobaeus* Jacobean (fr. LL *Jacobus* St. James — in the Bible, Gal 1:19, Jas 1:1, et al. —, fr. Gk *Iakōbos,* fr. Heb *Ya'ăqōbh* Jacob) + E *-an*] **:** of or relating to the New Testament Epistle of James or to its author

**jacobean lily** *n, often cap J* [[3]*Jacobean*] **:** a Mexican bulbous herb (*Sprekelia formosissima*) of the family Amaryllidaceae cultivated for its handsome bright red solitary flower — called also *Aztec lily*

**ja·co·bi·an** \jəˈkōbēən, yə-\ *also* **jacobian determinant** *n* -S *usu cap J* [K. G. J. *Jacobi* †1851 Ger. mathematician + E *-an*] **:** a determinant in which the elements of the first column are the partial derivatives of the first of a set of *n* functions with respect to each of *n* independent variables, those of the second column the partial derivatives of the second function with respect to each independent variable, and so on

**jaco·bin** \ˈjakəbən *sometimes* ˈjāk- *or* jəˈkōb-\ *n* -S *usu cap* [ME, fr. MF, fr. ML *Jacobinus,* fr. LL *Jacobus* St. James, + L *-inus* -ine; fr. the location of the first Dominican convent in the street of St. James (Rue St.-Jacques) in Paris] **1 :** DOMINICAN **2** [F, fr. *Jacobin* Dominican; fr. the group's having been founded in the Dominican convent in Paris in 1789] **a :** a member of an extremist political group advocating equalitarian democracy and famous for its terrorist policies during the French Revolution of 1789 **b :** a political extremist or radical; *esp* **:** one that advocates the attainment of equalitarian democracy usu. by revolutionary or violent methods ⟨the children of the Boston Federalists grew up under the impression that Democrats, or *Jacobins,* as they were called, were repulsive creatures —C.G.Bowers⟩ **3 a :** a breed of fancy pigeons whose neck feathers are reversed and so form a fluffy hood **b** [F, fr. *Jacobin,* Dominican; fr. the resemblance of the head and neck of such birds to the hood of a Dominican] **:** a tropical American hummingbird of the genus *Florisuga* (esp. *F. mellivora*)

**jaco·bin·ia** \,jakəˈbinēə, ,jāk-\ *n* [NL, fr. *Jacobina,* Brazil + NL *-ia*] **1** *cap* **:** a genus of tropical American herbs and shrubs (family Acanthaceae) having tubular red or orange bilabiate flowers with two stamens **2** -S **:** any plant of the genus *Jacobinia*

**jaco·bin·ic** \¦jakə¦binik, -nēk *sometimes* ¦jāk-\ *or* **jaco·bin·i·cal** \-nəkəl, -nēk-\ *adj, usu cap* **:** of or relating to the Jacobins or Jacobinism — **jaco·bin·i·cal·ly** \-nək(ə)lē, -nēk-, -li\ *adv, usu cap*

**jaco·bin·ism** \ˈ==,bə,nizəm\ *n* -S *usu cap* [F *jacobinisme,* fr. *jacobin* + *-isme* -ism] **:** the principles and practice of the Jacobins: **a :** the egalitarianism and terrorism of the Jacobins of the French Revolution of 1789 **b :** any violent or revolutionary political extremism ⟨*Jacobinism* . . . means in practice government by a rabble —G.H.Sabine⟩

**jaco·bin·ize** \-,nīz\ *vt* -ED/-ING/-S *often cap* **:** to make Jacobinic **:** convert to Jacobinism

[1]**jaco·bite** \ˈjakə,bīt *also* ˈjāk-; *usu* -īd.+V\ *n* -S *usu cap* **1** [ME, fr. ML *Jacobita,* fr. *Jacobus* Baradaeus (Jacob Baradai) †578 Syrian monk, founder of the Jacobite Church + L *-ita* -ite] **:** a member of a Syrian monophysite church **2** [ML *Jacobita,* fr. LL *Jacobus* St. James + L *-ita* -ite — more at JACOBIN] **:** DOMINICAN **3** [*Jacobus* (James II) †1701 king of England + E *-ite*] **:** a partisan of James II of England or the Stuarts after the revolution of 1688

[2]**jacobite** \"\ *adj, usu cap* **:** of or relating to the Jacobites

**jaco·bit·i·cal** \¦==¦bid·əkəl, -it|, |ēk-\ *also* **jaco·bit·ish** \ˈ==,bīd·|ish, -īt|, |ēsh\ *adj, usu cap* [[1]*Jacobite* + *-ical* or *-ish*] **:** of or relating to the Stuart pretenders to the English crown or their adherents

**jaco·bit·ism** \ˈ==,bīd·,izəm\ *n* -S *usu cap* [[1]*Jacobite* + *-ism*] **:** the cause and activities of the English Jacobites

**ja·cobs·ite** \ˈjākəb,zīt *sometimes* -kəp,sīt\ *n* -S [F *jakobsite,* fr. *Jakobsberg,* Sweden, its locality + F *-ite*] **:** a black magnetic isometric mineral $MnFe_2O_4$ consisting of an oxide of manganese and iron and constituting a member of the magnetite series

**jacob's ladder** *n, usu cap J* [after *Jacob* (Israel), the eponymous ancestor of the twelve tribes of Israel in the Bible, who in a dream saw a ladder extending from earth to heaven (Gen 28:12), fr. LL, fr. Gk *Iakōb,* fr. Heb *Ya'ăqōbh*] **1 a :** a pinnate-leaved European perennial herb (*Polemonium caeruleum*) with bright blue or white flowers —called also *charity, Greek valerian* **b :** any of several related American herbs (as *P. vanbruntiae*) **2 :** CARRION FLOWER 1 **3 :** a marine ladder of rope or chain with wooden or iron rungs **4 :** an elevator consisting typically of an endless chain and buckets used in lifting coal and other materials

jacob's ladder 3

**ja·cob·son's cartilage** \ˈjākəbs|ənz-, -kəps|\ *or* **jacobson's turbinal** *n, usu cap J* [after Ludvig L. *Jacobson* †1843 Danish surgeon and anatomist] **:** a narrow process of cartilage between the vomer and the cartilage of the nasal septum

**jacobson's nerve** *n, usu cap J* [after L.L.*Jacobson*] **:** TYMPANIC NERVE 1

**jacobson's organ** *n, usu cap J* [after L.L.*Jacobson*] **:** a slender horizontal canal in the nasal mucosa that ends in a blind pouch, has an olfactory function, and is rudimentary in adult man but highly developed in most reptiles

**jacob's–rod** \ˈ==¦=\ *n, pl* **jacob's–rods** *usu cap J* [after *Jacob* in the Bible, who is mentioned as peeling rods of poplar (Gen 30:37)] **:** an asphodel of the genus *Asphodeline*

**jacob's staff** *n, usu cap J* [after *Jacob* St. James, symbolized in religious art by a pilgrim's staff — more at JACOBIN] **1** *obs* **:** a pilgrim's staff **2 a** *obs* **:** CROSS-STAFF **2 b** *also* **jacob staff :** a short square rod with a cursor used for measuring heights and distances **c** *also* **jacob staff :** a straight rod or staff pointed and shod with iron at the bottom for insertion in the ground, having a socket joint at the top, and used instead of a tripod for supporting a compass **3** *obs* **:** a staff with a sword or dagger concealed in it

**jacob's–staff** \ˈ==¦=\ *n, pl* **jacob's–staffs** *usu cap J* [*Jacob's staff* (pilgrim's staff)] **1 :** GREAT MULLEIN **2 :** a plant of the genus *Fouquieria*

**ja·co·bus** \jəˈkōbəs\ *n* -ES *usu cap J* [after *Jacobus* (King James I) †1625 king of England, during whose reign unites were coined] **:** UNITE

**jac·o·net** \ˈjakə,net, -,nōt, ,==ˈnet\ *n* -S [modif. of Urdu *jagannāthī,* fr. *Jagannāth* (Puri), India, where such cloth was first made] **:** a lightweight cotton cloth resembling lawn that is used with or without a semiglaze for clothing and is given a waterproof finish for use in bandages

**ja·co·pev·er** \,yäkəˈpevə(r)\ *n* -S [Afrik *jakopewer,* prob. irreg. fr. *Jacob Evertsen,* 17th cent. Du. sea captain with bulging eyes and red face] **:** any of several large-eyed reddish food fishes of southern Africa; *esp* **:** a common scorpaenid fish (*Sebastichthys capensis*)

**ja·cot tool** \zhaˈkō, ja-, ˈ=(,)=\ *n, usu cap J* [prob. intended as trans. of F *tour Jacot,* lit., Jacot lathe, prob. fr. the name *Jacot*] **:** a small hand lathe in which watch pivots are burnished or polished

**jac·quard** \ˈja,kärd, jəˈk-, -kȧd\ *n* -S *often cap* [after Joseph M. *Jacquard* †1834 French inventor] **1 a :** a loom apparatus or head for weaving figured fabrics that has a mechanism controlled by a chain of variously perforated cards which cause the warp threads to be lifted in the proper sequence for producing figures **b** *or* **jacquard loom :** a loom having a jacquard **2 :** a fabric of jacquard weave or jacquard-knitted pattern

**jacquard board** *n, often cap J* **:** a tough and very stiff jute board or pressboard used for making jacquard cards

**jacquard knitting** *n, often cap J* **:** machine knitting with a jacquard attachment that makes patterns by the use of colored yarns

**jacquard weave** *n, often cap J* **:** an intricate variegated weave made on a jacquard loom and used for brocade, tapestry, and damask

**jacque·mi·not** \ˈjakmə,nō\ *n* -S [*Jacqueminot* or *General Jacqueminot,* a variety of red rose, after Viscount Jean François *Jacqueminot* †1865 French general] **:** RASPBERRY RED

**jacque·rie** \zhäˈkrē\ *n* -S *often cap* [F, fr. *jacquerie,* the 1358 peasant revolt in France, fr. MF, fr. *jacques, jacque* peasant + *-erie* -ery — more at JACKET] **1 :** a peasants' revolt **2 :** the peasant class ⟨stormed and sacked by a famished *Jacquerie* —*Times Lit. Supp.*⟩

**jac·tance** \ˈjaktən(t)s\ *or* **jac·tan·cy** \-nsē\ *n, pl* **jactances** *or* **jactancies** [MF & L; MF *jactance,* fr. L *jactantia,* fr. *jactant-, jactans* (pres. part. of *jactare* to throw, shake, speak out, boast) + *-ia* -y — more at JET] **:** vainglorious boasting ⟨~, vanity, peculation to the ruin of 20 years' labor —Ezra Pound⟩

**jac·ta·tion** \jakˈtāshən\ *n* -S [L *jactation-, jactatio,* fr. *jactatus* (past part. of *jactare*) + *-ion, -io* -ion] **1 :** boastful declaration or display ⟨one of his familiar ~*s* of imperfection —George Saintsbury⟩ **2** [prob. fr. F, fr. L] **:** a throwing or tossing of the body; *specif* **:** JACTITATION

**jac·ti·tate** \ˈjaktə,tāt\ *vi* -ED/-ING/-S [LL *jactitatus,* past part. of *jactitare,* freq. of L *jactare*] **:** to toss or jerk the body about

**jac·ti·ta·tion** \,==ˈtāshən\ *n* -S [LL *jactitation-, jactitatio,* fr. *jactitatus* + *-ion,* -io -ion] **1 a** *archaic* **:** boastful public assertion or ostentation **b :** false boasting or claim or other false assertion made or repeated to the prejudice of another person: as (1) *or* **jactitation of marriage :** false and actionable pretension that one is married to someone (2) **:** SLANDER OF TITLE **2 :** a tossing to and fro or jerking and twitching of the body or its parts **:** excessive restlessness esp. in certain psychiatric disorders

**ja·cu** \jəˈkü\ *n* -S [Pg *jacu, jacú,* fr. Tupi *jacú*] **:** a So. American guan (esp. *Penelope obscura jacquaçu*)

**jacua** *var of* JAGUA

**jac·u·late** \ˈjakyə,lāt\ *vt* -ED/-ING/-S [L *jaculatus,* past part. of *jaculari* — more at EJACULATE] **:** to throw or hurl forward (as a dart)

**jac·u·la·tion** \,==ˈlāshən\ *n* -S [L *jaculation-, jaculatio,* fr. *jaculatus* + *-ion-, -io* -ion] **:** the act of pitching, throwing, or hurling ⟨hills hurled to and fro with ~ dire —John Milton⟩

**ja·cun·da** \,jäkünˈdä\ *n, pl* **jacunda** *or* **jacundas** *usu cap* [Pg *jacundá,* of AmerInd origin] **1 a :** a Tupian Indian people of northern Brazil **b :** a member of such people **2 :** the language of the Jacunda people

**jac·u·tin·ga** \,jakyəˈtiŋgə\ *n* -S [Pg, fr. Tupi, lit., white jacu] **1 :** a So. American guan (*Pipile jacutinga*) **2** [Pg, fr. *Jacutinga,* village in the state of Rio de Janeiro, Brazil, its locality] **:** a hematitic iron ore that occurs in Brazil and is characterized by thin bedding or lamination

[1]**jade** \ˈjād\ *n* -S [ME] **1 :** a broken-down, vicious, or worthless horse **:** PLUG ⟨struck his armed heels against the panting sides of his poor ~ —Shak.⟩ **2 a :** a low or shrewish woman **:** WENCH, TERMAGANT ⟨the painted ~ into which inevitably she degenerated —Maurice Valency⟩ **b :** a flirtatious girl **:** MINX ⟨a laughing ~ of not ungentle mold —J.G.Saxe⟩

[2]**jade** \"\ *vt* -ED/-ING/-S **1 a :** to make a jade of (a horse) **:** wear out by overwork or abuse ⟨when a horse approaches the goal, he does not, unless he is *jaded,* slacken his pace —William Cowper⟩ **b :** to tire by severe or tedious tasks **:** FATIGUE, FAG ⟨constant repetition of often trivial material ~*s* one's palate —Thomas Heinitz⟩ **2** *obs* **:** to make ridiculous or expose to scorn ⟨do not now fool myself, to let imagination ~ me —Shak.⟩ **~** *vi* **:** to become weary **:** lose heart **:** FLAG ⟨when I feel my Muse beginning to ~, I retire to the solitary fireside of my study — Robert Burns⟩ **syn** see TIRE

[3]**jade** \"\ *n* -S [F, fr. obs. Sp (*piedra de la*) *ijada,* lit., loin stone; Sp *ijada* loin, fr. L *ilia,* pl. of *ilium, ileum* groin, viscera; fr. the belief that jade cures renal colic — more at ILEUM] **1 :** a tough compact gemstone that is commonly green but sometimes whitish and takes a high polish: **a :** jade derived from jadeite — called also *imperial jade, true jade* **b :** jade derived from nephrite **2 :** JADE GREEN

**jaded** *adj* [fr. past part. of [2]*jade*] **1 :** fatigued by overwork or abuse **:** WORN OUT, EXHAUSTED ⟨come in plenty ~, looking as thin and gaunt as a gutted snowbird —F.B.Gipson⟩ **2 :** dulled by surfeit or excess **:** SATIATED ⟨might pall on ~ appetites —*Americana Annual*⟩ ⟨all the gilded corruption of a ~ and perverted group of men and women —Pamela Taylor⟩ — **jad·ed·ly** *adv* — **jad·ed·ness** *n* -ES

**jade gray** *n* **:** a variable color averaging a grayish green that is bluer and duller than average bayberry, bluer, lighter, and stronger than slate green, and yellower and slightly darker than average blue spruce (sense 2a)

**jade green** *n* **1 :** a variable color averaging a light bluish green that is greener and deeper than robin's-egg blue (sense 2), Eton blue, or turquoise (sense 2b) **2** *of textiles* **:** a variable color averaging a moderate yellowish green that is yellower, lighter, and stronger than tarragon, yellower, lighter, and slightly less strong than malachite green, and yellower and stronger than verdigris

**jade·ite** \ˈjā,dīt\ *n* -S [F, fr. *jade* + *-ite*] **1 :** a monoclinic mineral $NaAlSi_2O_6$ found chiefly in Burma that consists of a sodium aluminum silicate and when cut constitutes a valuable variety of jade **2 :** a light green that is bluer and deeper than average mint green and bluer and paler than serpentine

**jade plant** *n* **:** any of various plants of the genus *Crassula* (as *C. argentea* and *C. arborescens*)

**jadesheen** \ˈ=,=\ *n* **:** AMERICAN GREEN

**jadestone** \ˈ=,=\ *n* **:** [3]JADE 1

**jad·ish** \ˈjādish\ *adj* [[1]*jade* + *-ish*] **:** having the qualities or characteristics of a jade — **jad·ish·ly** *adv* — **jad·ish·ness** *n* -ES

**jady** \ˈjādē\ *adj, usu* -ER/-EST [[1]*jade* + *-y*] **:** JADISH

**jae·ger** *also* **ja·ger** \ˈyāgə(r)\ *n* -S [G *jäger,* lit., hunter, fr. OHG *jagāri,* fr. *jagōn* to hunt + *-āri* -er — more at YACHT] **1** *or* **jä·ger** \"\ **:** a German or Austrian rifleman: **a :** one belonging to a military unit composed chiefly of huntsmen using their own weapons **b :** one belonging to a mobile light-infantry unit **2** *or* **jäger a :** HUNTER, HUNTSMAN **b :** an attendant on a person of rank or wealth dressed in hunter's costume **3 :** any of several large and spirited rapacious birds of the family Stercorariidae (as *Stercorarius parasiticus*) that inhabit the northern seas, are usu. blackish brown above and lighter below or chiefly sooty brown or blackish with the bill hooked and cered, are strong flyers, and harass weaker birds until they drop or disgorge their prey — called also *marlinespike;* compare PARASITIC JAEGER, POMARINE JAEGER

**1jag** \ˈjag, -aa(ə)-, -ai-\ *n* -S [ME *jagge*] **1 a :** one of a series of dangling tabs along the edge of a garment used esp. for ornamentation of medieval apparel **:** DAG **b :** a slashed section or slit of a garment revealing an underlying piece of another color used esp. in Renaissance apparel **2** *now dial* **:** SHRED, RAG, TATTER **3** *now dial Eng* **:** a projecting hair or bristle or a hairy or bristly outgrowth (as the awn of oats) **4 :** a sharp projecting part or protuberance **:** TOOTH, BARB **5** *chiefly Scot* **:** PRICK, STAB, JAB **6 :** a piece of metal screwed on the ramrod of a rifle to hold a rag or tow and used for cleaning the barrel **7 :** JAG BOLT

**2jag** \ˈ"\ *vb* **jagged** \-gd\ **jagged** \ˈ"; *see* JAGGED *adj*\ **jagging; jags** [ME *jaggen,* fr. *jagge,* n.] *vt* **1** *now dial* **:** STAB, JAB **2 a :** to slash or pink (a garment) with jags **b :** to cut teeth or other indentations into **c :** to make (an edge) ragged by cutting or notching **:** cut unevenly ⟨his hand shook and *jagged* the leaf⟩ ~ *vi* **1 :** PRICK, THRUST ⟨blackest jealousy *jagging* at their hearts —Llewelyn Powys⟩ **2 :** to move in jerks ⟨a blunt tool not only ~*s* and takes longer to cut but . . . will not cut cleanly —Albert Toft⟩ **:** JOG

**3jag** \ˈ"\ *n* -S [origin unknown] **1 a :** a small or part load ⟨a ~ of hay⟩ **b :** a trip for fetching a jag ⟨on the last ~ before dark⟩ **c** *chiefly dial* **:** PORTION, QUANTITY ⟨give the bay mare a ~ of oats⟩ ⟨people bought ~*s* of things they didn't need⟩ **2 a :** a state or feeling of exhilaration or intoxication esp. when induced by liquor **:** an inebriating load (as of liquor) ⟨had a good ~ on when he left the bar⟩ **:** THRILL ⟨takes the stuff because it gives him a ~⟩ **b :** a period of unrestrained indulgence (as in liquor or an emotion) **:** BENDER, SPREE ⟨went on a weekend ~ to forget his troubles⟩ ⟨addicts on marijuana ~*s*⟩ ⟨enjoying a sentimental ~⟩ **:** SPELL ⟨bringing them to tears . . . and ending in a crying ~ himself —Dixon Wecter⟩ **3** *chiefly Scot* **:** a leather bag or pouch

**4jag** \ˈ"\ *vt, dial* **:** to convey (a load of something) from one place to another **:** CARRY

**JAG** *abbr* judge advocate general

**ja·ga·tai** \ˌjagəˈtī\ *n* -S *usu cap* [fr. *Jagatai,* region in central Asia approximately equivalent to Turkistan, fr. *Jagatai* †1242 Mongol ruler who governed it] **1 :** any of various Eastern Turkic languages: as **a :** UIGHUR 2a **b :** UZBEK 2 **2 :** the Eastern Turkic languages collectively

**jag bolt** *n* [1*jag*] **:** an anchor bolt with a barbed flaring shank which resists retraction when leaded into stone or set in concrete — called also *hacked bolt, rag bolt*

**jageer** *var of* JAGIR

**ja·gel·lo** \yäˈgeˌ(ˌ)lō\ *or* **ja·giel·lo** \yägˈye-\ *n* -S *usu cap* [after Ladislas II (or V) *Jagello* (Pol *Jagiełło*) †1434 grand duke of Lithuania and king of Poland] **:** a member of a dynasty ruling in Lithuania, Poland, Hungary, and Bohemia during the 14th, 15th, and 16th centuries

**ja·gel·lo·ni·an** \ˌyägəˈlōnēən\ *or* **ja·giel·lo·ni·an** \-gyə¦-\ *or* **ja·gel·lon** \ˌyägə¦lōn\ *or* **ja·giel·lon** \-gyə¦-\ *adj, usu cap* **:** of or relating to the Jagellos

**1jager** *or* **jäger** *var of* JAEGER

**2ja·ger** *or* **jae·ger** \ˈyägə(r)\ *n* -S [fr. *Jagersfontein,* town in southwestern Orange Free State, Union of So. Africa, where such diamonds are mined] **:** a high-quality diamond of bluish white grade

**jaggar** *var of* JUGGER

**1jag·ged** \ˈjagəd, -aag-,-aig-\ *adj, often* -ER/-EST [ME, fr. *jagge* jag + *-ed*] **1 :** having a sharply uneven edge or surface **:** marked by jags ⟨the ~ skyline of the city⟩ ⟨a ~ coastline with deep coves and rocky points⟩ ⟨a ~ bolt of lightning⟩ ⟨blasted out great ~ chunks of stone⟩ **2 :** having a harsh or rough quality **:** RAGGED ⟨her voice was ~ with excitement —Sinclair Lewis⟩ **:** RUGGED ⟨some of his ideas, once so ~ and uncompromising, have been smoothed by time —Herbert Kupferberg⟩ **3 :** marked by sharply broken or violently varying movement **:** abruptly irregular ⟨harsh, stubborn harmonies, his ~ rhythms —*Time*⟩

**2jagged** \-gd\ *adj* [3*jag* + *-ed*] *slang* **:** DRUNK

**jag·ged chickweed** \-gəd-\ *n* **:** a European herb (*Holosteum umbellatum*) naturalized in eastern No. America and having several white flowers in a long-stalked umbel

**jag·ged·ly** \-gədlē, -li\ *adv* **:** in a jagged manner

**jag·ged·ness** \-gədnəs\ *n* -ES **:** the quality or state of being jagged

**1jag·ger** \-gə(r)\ *n* -S [2*jag* + *-er*] **1 :** one that jags; *specif* **:** JAGGING WHEEL **2** *chiefly dial* **:** something sharp or prickly: as **a :** BRAMBLE, THORN **b :** a frayed bit of wire on a worn cable

**2jagger** \ˈ"\ *n* -S [3*jag* + *-er*] *dial Brit* **:** one that carries a jag: as **a :** an itinerant peddler **b :** PACKHORSE

**3jagger** \ˈ"\ *n* -S [D *jager,* lit., hunter, fr. MD, fr. *jagen* to hunt + *-er* — more at YACHT] *archaic* **:** a boat accompanying a fishing fleet to supply and empty the boats

**jag·gery** *also* **jag·ghery** *or* **jag·ga·ry** \-gərē\ *n* -ES [Hindi *jāgrī;* perh. akin to Skt *śarkarā* gravel, grit, sugar — more at SUGAR] **:** an unrefined brown sugar made esp. from palm sap (as in India)

**jaggery palm** *n* **:** an East Indian palm (*Caryota urens*) having stout-petioled pinnate leaves with wedge-shaped divisions and being a chief source of jaggery — called also *toddy palm*

**jagging** *pres part of* JAG

**jagging wheel** *n* [fr. pres. part. of 2*jag*] **:** a wheel with a zigzag or jagged edge for cutting cakes or pastry into ornamental figures

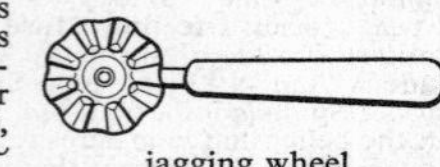
jagging wheel

**jag·gy** \-gē\ *adj* **jaggier; jaggiest** [1*jag* + *-y*] **1 :** having or abounding in jags **:** JAGGED, NOTCHED, UNEVEN, ROUGH ⟨~ teeth⟩ **2** *chiefly Scot* **:** PRICKLY

**ja·gir** *also* **ja·ghir** *or* **ja·ghire** *or* **ja·geer** *or* **ja·gheer** \jəˈgi(ə)r\ *n* -S [Per *jāgīr,* fr. *jā* place + *-gīr* keeping, holding (fr. *giriftan* to seize, hold)] **:** a grant of the public revenues of a district in northern India or Pakistan to a person with power to collect and enjoy them and to administer the government in the district; *also* **:** the district so assigned, the revenue from it, or the tenure by which it is held — compare ENAM

**ja·gir·dar** *also* **ja·ghir·dar** *or* **ja·ghire·dar** *or* **ja·geer·dar** *or* **ja·gheer·dar** \-ˌdär\ *n* -S [Per *jāgīrdār,* fr. *jāgīr* + *-dār* holder — more at BHUMIDAR] **:** the holder of a jagir

**ja·gla** \ˈjäglə\ *n* -S [of Indic origin; akin to Skt *chāgala* goat] **:** SEROW

**jag·less** \ˈjagləs, -aag-,-aig-\ *adj* [3*jag* + *-less*] **:** having or producing no jag ⟨a stimulating but ~ beverage⟩

**jags** *pl of* JAG, *pres 3d sing of* JAG

**jagsiekte** *or* **jagziekte** *var of* JAAGSIEKTE

**jag spike** *n* [1*jag*] **:** BOLT

**1ja·gua** \ˈhägwə\ *also* **ja·cua** \-äkwə\ *n* -S [Sp *jagua,* fr. Taino *ṡawa*] **:** GENIPAP

**2ja·gua** \ˈ", ˈyä-\ *n* -S [modif. of Sp *yagua* — more at YAGUA] **:** INAJA

**jag·uar** \ˈjag¦ˌwär, ˈjaig¦, ¦ˌwå(r *also* -gyə¦ *sometimes* ¦ˌwə(r) *or* ÷ -gə¦\ *n, pl* **jaguars** *also* **jaguar** [Sp & Pg; Sp *yaguar, jaguar* & Pg *jaguar* fr. Tupi *jaguara* & Guarani *yaguara*] **:** a large powerful cat (*Felis onca*) ranging from Texas to Paraguay but extremely rare in the northern part of its range, having a larger head, heavier body, and shorter thicker legs than the leopard or the cougar, and being of brownish yellow or buff color marked with black spots each of which is surrounded by a somewhat broken ring of smaller ones

jaguar

**jag·ua·run·di** \ˌjagwəˈrəndē, ˌjaig-, -gyəw-\ *also* **jag·ua·ron·di** \-rän-\ *n* -S [Amer Sp & Pg, fr. Guarani *yaguarundi* & Tupi *jaguarundi*] **:** a slender long-tailed short-legged grayish wildcat (*Felis jaguarondi*) widely distributed from Mexico to Patagonia — see EYRA

**ja·güey** \häˈgwā\ *n* -S [Amer Sp, fr. Taino] **:** any of several trees of the genus *Ficus; esp* **:** BANYAN

**jah** \ˈy|ä, ˈj|, |å\ *cap, var of* YAH

**ja·hi·li·ya** \ˌjähəˈlē(y)ə\ *n, cap* [Ar *jāhilīyah*] **:** the pre-Islamic period in Arabia

**jahrzeit** *often cap, var of* YAHRZEIT

**jahve** *or* **jahveh** *cap, var of* YAHWEH

**jahvism** *or* **jahwism** *cap, var of* YAHWISM

**jahvist** *or* **jahwist** *usu cap, var of* YAHWIST

**jahwe** *or* **jahweh** *cap, var of* YAHWEH

**jai alai** \ˈhī,lī *also* ¦hīə¦lī\ *n, pl* **jai alais** [Sp, fr. Basque, fr. *jai* festival + *alai* merry] **:** a game of Basque origin resembling handball and played (as in Spain and Latin America) on a large walled court by usu. two or four players who use a long curved wicker basket strapped to the right wrist to catch and hurl the ball against the front wall to make it rebound in such a way that the opponent cannot return it before it has bounced more than once — see CESTA, FRONTON, PELOTA

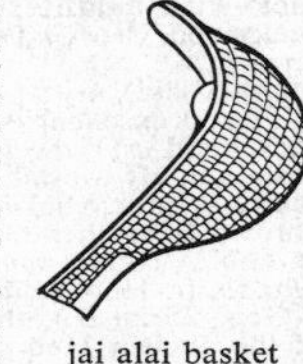
jai alai basket

**1jail** \ˈjāl, *esp before pause or consonant* -āəl\ *n* -S [ME *jaiole, jaile,* fr. OF *jaiole,* fr. (assumed) VL *caveola,* dim. of L *cavea* cavity, cage — more at CAGE] **1 :** PRISON **2 :** a building for the confinement of persons held in lawful custody (as for minor offenses or some future judicial proceeding) **:** LOCKUP **3 :** confinement in a jail ⟨kept in ~ until he posted bond⟩ ⟨sentenced to ~ for 30 days⟩

**2jail** \ˈ"\ *vt* -ED/-ING/-S **:** to confine in or as if in a jail **:** lock up **:** IMPRISON

**jailbait** \ˈ=,=\ *n* **1 :** a temptation to commit an offense for which one can be jailed **2** *slang* **:** a girl under the age of consent with whom unlawful sexual intercourse constitutes statutory rape ⟨knocked up some little ~ —Maritta Wolff⟩

**jailbird** \ˈ=,=\ *n* **:** a person who is or has been confined in jail; *specif* **:** one jailed long or often

**jailbreak** \ˈ=,=\ *n* **:** a forcible escape from jail

**jail delivery** *n* **1 :** the clearing of a jail by bringing the prisoners to trial or by having the legality of their commitments reviewed **2 :** the freeing esp. by force of prisoners in a jail

**jail·er** *or* **jail·or** \ˈjālə(r)\ *n* -S [ME *jailer,* fr. OF *jaiolier,* fr. *jaiole* + *-ier* -er] **1 :** a keeper of a jail or prison **:** GUARD **2 :** one that restricts another's liberty as if by imprisonment

**jail fever** *n* **:** TYPHUS 1a

**jailhouse** \ˈ=,=\ *n* **:** JAIL

**jail liberties** *or* **jail limits** *n pl* **:** a space or district around a jail which is legally considered as part of the prison and within which a prisoner (as a debtor) is allowed to go at large under a bond of security

**1jain** \ˈjīn, ˈjān\ *also* **jai·na** \-nə\ *or* **jain·ist** \-nəst\ *n* -S *usu cap* [*jain* fr. Hindi, fr. Skt *jaina,* fr. *jina* saint, victorious, fr. *jayati* he conquers; *jaina* fr. Skt; *jainist* fr. Hindi *jain* + E *-ist;* akin to Gk *bia* force] **:** an adherent of Jainism

**2jain** \ˈ"\ *or* **jaina** \ˈ"\ *also* **jainist** \ˈ"\ *adj, usu cap* **:** of or relating to the Jains or Jainism

**jain·ism** \-ˌnizəm\ *n* -S *usu cap* **:** a religion of India historically traceable to the jina Vardhamana Mahavira of the 6th century B.C. having scriptures, temples, a cultus, and a monastic class and being characterized by the belief that while gods control the realm of time and matter no being higher than an absolutely perfect human soul is necessary for the creation or moral regulation of the universe, and by the personal ideal of the kevalin worked toward through usu. numerous lives in the pursuit of right knowledge, right faith, and right conduct including ahimsa and in veneration of the jinas often involving images — compare DIGAMBARA, SVETAMBARA

**jai·pur** \ˈjī,pu̇(ə)r, =ˈ=\ *adj, usu cap* [fr. *Jaipur,* India] **:** of or from the city of Jaipur, India **:** of the kind or style prevalent in Jaipur

**jai·puri** \ˈjīpə(ˌ)rē, jīˈpu̇rē\ *n, usu cap* [Hindi *jaipurī* fr. Jaipur, fr. Jaipur, city in India] **:** a dialect of Rajasthani

**jaj·man** \ˈjəjˈmän\ *n, pl* **jaj·mans** \-nz\ *or* **jaj·ma·ni** \-nē\ [Hindi *jajmān,* fr. Skt *yajamāna,* pres. part. of *yajati* he sacrifices; akin to Av *yasna* sacrifice] **:** one of a fixed circle of persons in a Hindu caste system whom a member of an occupational group (as a barber) serves as an exclusive and hereditary right

**jajoba** *var of* JOJOBA

**jak** *or* **jakfruit** *var of* JACKFRUIT

**jakarta** *usu cap, var of* DJAKARTA

**1jake** \ˈjāk\ *n* -S [fr. *Jake,* nickname for *Jacob*] **:** an uncouth country fellow **:** HICK; *broadly* **:** FELLOW — often used disparagingly

**2jake** \ˈ"\ *adj* [origin unknown] *slang* **:** ALL RIGHT, FINE ⟨it was pretty hot . . . otherwise everything was ~ —Philip Hamburger⟩

**3jake** \ˈ"\ *also* **ja·key** \ˈjākē\ *n, pl* **jakes** *also* **jakeys** [by shortening & alter. fr. *Jamaica (ginger)*] *slang* **:** an alcoholic extract of Jamaica ginger used as a beverage during the prohibition era

**jake leg** *n* [3*jake*] **:** a paralysis caused by drinking jake or some other strong liquor

**jakes** \ˈjāks\ *n pl but usu sing in constr* [perh. fr. the F name *Jacques*] **1** *chiefly dial* **:** PRIVY 2 ⟨the fir trees . . . planted to shelter the garden ~ —Llewelyn Powys⟩ **2** *dial Brit* **:** a dirty mess **:** EXCREMENT

**ja·khals·bes·sie** *also* **jak·kals·bes·sie** *or* **ja·kaals-bes·sie** \ˌjaˌkȯlzˈbesē, -ˌkəl-\ *n* -S [Afrik *jakkalsbessie,* fr. *jakkals* jackal + *bessie* berry] **:** an African ebony (*Diospyros mespiliformis*) with evergreen leaves

**jako** \ˈja(ˌ)kō\ *n* -S [origin unknown] **:** AFRICAN GRAY

**jak tree** *n* **:** JACKFRUIT 1

**ja·kun** \jəˈkün\ *n, pl* **jakun** *or* **jakuns** *usu cap* **1 a :** an aboriginal people of the southern part of the Malay peninsula **b :** a member of such people **2 :** the Mon-Khmer language of the Jakun people

**jal·ap** \ˈjaləp, ˈjäl-\ *n* -S [F & Sp; F *jalop,* fr. Sp *jalapa,* fr. *Jalapa,* town in Mexico] **1** *also* **ja·la·pa** \jəˈläpə, hə'-\ **a :** the dried purgative tuberous root of a Mexican plant (*Exogonium purga*) or the powdered drug prepared from it that contains the resinous glycosides convolvulin and jalapin and is the official jalap — compare JICAMA **b :** the root or derived drug of related plants constituting an inferior source of the jalap resins **2 :** any of various plants yielding jalap

**ja·la·pe·ño** \ˌhäləˈpān(ˌ)yō\ *n* -S [MexSp] **:** a Mexican pepper

**jala·pin** \ˈjaləpən, ˈjäl-; jəˈläp-\ *n* -S [*jalap* + *-in*] **:** a cathartic glucosidic constituent of true jalap resin and scammony resin

**ja·lee work** \ˈjä(ˌ)lē-\ *n* [Hindi *jālī* network, latticework, fr. Skt *jāla* net] **:** carving esp. in marble in the form of a pierced screen **:** LATTICEWORK

**ja·leo** \həˈlā(ˌ)ō\ *n* -S [Sp, fr. *jalear* to cheer a dancer or singer, fr. *hala,* interj. used to cheer or urge on] **:** a lively Spanish solo dance accompanied by castanets

**ja·lopy** *also* **jal·lopy** *or* **ja·lop·py** \jəˈläpē, -pi\ *n* -ES [origin unknown] **1** *also* **ja·lop** \-p\ **:** a dilapidated automobile ⟨roaring around in a battered old ~⟩ **2 :** an outdated often mechanically inferior model (as of an airplane)

**ja·louse** \jəˈlüz\ *vt* -ED/-ING/-S [F *jalouser* to envy, be jealous of, fr. OF, fr. *jalos, jalous, jelous* jealous — more at JEALOUS] **1** *chiefly Scot* **:** SUSPECT, SURMISE ⟨*jaloused* frae your last discourse that ye were perplexed —John Buchan⟩ **2 :** to be jealous of or begrudge jealously ⟨*jaloused* him and planned to do him a harm —Sir Richard Burton⟩

**jal·ou·sie** \ˈjaləsē, -si *sometimes* ¦==¦sē\ *n* -S [F, lit., jealousy, fr. OF *jalousie, jelousie* — more at JEALOUSY] **1 :** a blind or shutter having horizontal slats that are adjustable or fixed at an angle to admit light and air while excluding sun and rain and to permit looking out from behind them without being visible to the outside **2** *or* **jalousie window :** a window made of adjustable glass louvers that control ventilation

**jal·ou·sied** \ˈ"d\ *adj* **:** equipped with jalousies ⟨a ~ porch⟩ **:** having horizontal slats ⟨~ shutters⟩

**jal·pa·ite** \ˈjalpəˌīt\ *n* -S [G *jalpait,* fr. *Jalpa,* Zacatecas, Mexico, its locality + G *-it* -ite] **:** a mineral consisting of cupriferous argentite

**1jam** *also* **jamb** \ˈjam, -aa(ə)-\ *vb* **jammed** *also* **jambed; jammed** *also* **jambed; jamming** *also* **jambing; jams** *also* **jambs** [perh. of imit. origin] *vt* **1 a :** to press into a close or tight position **:** wedge in ⟨~*s* the piano between the sides of the doorway⟩ **:** fix tightly ⟨~ his hat on his head⟩ ⟨~ his teeth together to stop their chattering⟩ **:** SQUEEZE ⟨~ 50 people into a bus designed for 30⟩ **b (1) :** to cause (as some movable part of a machine) to become wedged or fixed so as to be unworkable ⟨a misstroke will ~ the typewriter keys⟩ **(2) :** to make (as a machine) unworkable by such jamming ⟨crashed when a loose nut *jammed* the controls⟩ **c :** to impede or block passage of or along **:** OBSTRUCT ⟨could not get through because traffic was completely *jammed* by the crowd⟩ ⟨the communications channels were *jammed* up with priority messages —Ira Wolfert⟩ **d :** to fill or cause to fill closely or to excess **:** PACK ⟨fans ~ the stadium⟩ ⟨newspaper columns were *jammed* with election propaganda⟩ ⟨~*s* authentic details into his stories⟩ **2 :** to push or apply forcibly **:** force violently ⟨*jammed* himself through the porthole⟩ ⟨*jammed* his spurs into the horse's flanks⟩ ⟨~ the bill through a reluctant legislature by party discipline⟩ ⟨*jamming* political opinions down students' throats —Kenneth Roberts⟩; *specif* **:** to apply (the brakes) suddenly with full force — usu. used with *on* ⟨would ~ the brakes on and throw the passengers forward⟩ **3 :** CRUSH, BRUISE ⟨got his right hand severely *jammed* in the door⟩ **4 :** to bring (a boat) close to the wind so that the upper sails are shaking or laid aback ⟨~ the boat into the wind to avoid collision⟩ **5 a :** to cause interference in (radio or radar signals) **:** make unintelligible (as a radio program or broadcast) by intentionally sending out signals or messages in an interfering manner **b :** to make (as a radio or radar apparatus) ineffective by jamming radio or radar signals or by causing reflection of radar waves from a special device ~ *vi* **1 a :** to become blocked, wedged, or fixed **:** stick fast ⟨an odd cartridge may ~ in the gun⟩ ⟨the line *jammed* and the boat hung useless⟩ **b :** to become unworkable through the jamming of a movable part ⟨the overheated machine *jammed*⟩ **2 :** to force one's way esp. into a restricted space **:** mass together tightly **:** CROWD ⟨continued to ~ into the already crowded hall⟩ ⟨the children *jammed* forward to claim their treats⟩ **3 :** to improvise on a musical instrument with a group **:** take part in a jam session ⟨gathered after hours with their instruments and *jammed* all night⟩ **syn** see PRESS

**2jam** \ˈ"\ *n* -S **1 :** something made closely packed, immovable, or unusable by jamming **:** an instance of jamming ⟨lost the pistol match due to a ~ during the rapid fire⟩; *specif* **:** a crowded mass of people or things causing impedance or blockage ⟨a log ~ in the river⟩ ⟨a flood caused by an ice ~⟩ ⟨delayed an hour by a traffic ~⟩ **2 a :** the quality or state of being jammed **:** STOPPAGE, CONGESTION ⟨the ~ of the legislature caused by the piling up of new bills in the final days⟩ **b :** the pressure or congestion of a crowd of people or things **:** CRUSH ⟨escape from the clangor and ~ of the city streets⟩ **3 :** an involved and embarrassing state of affairs **:** DIFFICULTY, MESS, FIX **:** a tight spot ⟨made him late for his date and got him in a ~ with his girl friend⟩ ⟨can get out of its ~ by finding new foreign markets for its products⟩ **4 :** JAM SESSION **syn** see PREDICAMENT

**3jam** \ˈ"\ *adv* **:** COMPLETELY, CLEAR ⟨filled the jar ~ full⟩ ⟨threw the ball ~ across the field⟩

**4jam** \ˈ"\ *n* -S [prob. fr. 1*jam*] **1 :** a product made by boiling fruit and sugar to a thick consistency without preserving the shape of the fruit ⟨spread raspberry ~ on a slice of bread⟩ **2** *chiefly Brit* **:** something agreeable or easy ⟨this job isn't all ~; it has its headaches⟩ ⟨the test was ~ for him and he finished first⟩ **3** [so called fr. its scent that resembles that of raspberry jam] **:** a shrubby acacia (*Acacia acuminata*) with elongated slender phyllodes and cylindrical axillary spikes of yellow flowers that is an important browse plant in much of Western Australia

**5jam** \ˈ"\ *vt* **jammed; jammed; jamming; jams 1 :** to spread with jam ⟨munching *jammed* bread⟩ **2 :** to make into jam ⟨fresh, preserved, or *jammed* fruit⟩

**6jam** \ˈjäm\ *n* -S [Hindi *jām*] **:** the ruler in some northwest Indian states in the region of Cutch, Kathiawar, and the lower Indus

**ja·ma** *also* **ja·mah** \ˈjämə\ *n* -S [Hindi *jāma,* lit., garment, fr. Per] **:** a long-sleeved cotton coat of at least knee length worn by men in northern India and Pakistan

**jamadar** *var of* JEMADAR

**1ja·mai·ca** \jəˈmākə\ *adj, usu cap* [fr. *Jamaica,* island in the West Indies] **:** of or from the island of Jamaica **:** of the kind or style prevalent in Jamaica **:** JAMAICAN

**2jamaica** \ˈ"\ *n* -S *usu cap* [by shortening] **:** JAMAICA RUM

**jamaica apple** *n, usu cap J* **1 :** CHERIMOYA **2 :** CUSTARD APPLE

**jamaica banana** *n, usu cap J* **:** the large yellow commercial banana of the Caribbean region

**jamaica bayberry** *n, usu cap J* **:** BAYBERRY 1a

**jamaica bloodwood** *n, usu cap J* **:** FALSE LOGWOOD

**jamaica buckthorn** *n, usu cap J* **:** CHEROKEE ROSE

**jamaica bullace plum** *n, usu cap J* **:** GENIP 2

**jamaica cherry** *n, usu cap J* **1 :** a West Indian fig (*Ficus laevigata*) having globose edible fruits the size of a cherry **2 :** CALABUR TREE

**jamaica cucumber** *n, usu cap J* **:** GHERKIN

**jamaica dogwood** *n, usu cap J* **:** a West Indian tree (*Piscidia erythrina*) the narcotic root of which is used as a fish poison in Jamaica

**jamaica ginger** *n, usu cap J* **1 :** a high grade of ginger grown in Jamaica **2 a :** an alcoholic extract of ginger used as a flavoring essence **b :** the powdered root of ginger used as an infusion in medicine (as in colic or diarrhea)

**jamaica honeysuckle** *n, usu cap J* **:** a West Indian passionflower (*Passiflora laurifolia*) having fragrant flowers, somewhat astringent leaves, and yellow edible fruit — called also *bell apple, sweet cup, water lemon*

**jamaica ironwood** *n, usu cap J* **:** a small tropical American tree (*Erythroxylon areolatum*) with yellowish white flowers, red drupes, and hard wood

**jamaica mignonette** *n, usu cap J, West Indies* **:** HENNA

**1ja·mai·can** \jəˈmākən\ *adj, usu cap J* [*Jamaica,* island in the West Indies + E *-an*] **:** of or relating to Jamaica

**2jamaican** \ˈ"\ *n* -S *cap* **:** a native or inhabitant of Jamaica

**jamaica pepper** *n, usu cap J* **:** ALLSPICE

**jamaica plum** *n, usu cap J* **:** a hog plum (*Spondias mombin*) of the West Indies

**jamaica quassia** *n, usu cap J* **1 :** BITTERWOOD 1a **2 :** quassia obtained from bitterwood

**jamaica rum** *n, usu cap J* **:** a heavy-bodied rum made in Jamaica by slow fermentation using dunder and usu. having a pungent bouquet — see GERMAN RUM

**jamaica sarsaparilla** *n, usu cap J* **1** [so called fr. its once being shipped from Jamaica] **:** SARSAPARILLA 1 **2 :** an inferior sarsaparilla grown in Jamaica

**jamaica seal** *n, usu cap J* **:** WEST INDIA SEAL

**jamaica senna tree** *n, usu cap J* **:** a tropical Old World herb (*Cassia obovata*) commonly naturalized in tropical America and having glaucous foliage and bright yellow flowers

**jamaica sorrel** *n, usu cap J* **:** ROSELLE

**jamaica thistle** *n, usu cap J* **:** PRICKLY POPPY

**jamaica vervain** *n, usu cap J* **:** a cosmopolitan tropical weed (*Stachytarpheta anoides jamaicensis*) with oblong leaves and bright blue flowers in slender spikes

**jamaica walnut** *n, usu cap J* **:** a small Jamaican tree (*Picrodendron baccatum*) with hard heavy strong dark olive to nearly black very bitter waxy wood and a fruit that is a drupe with thin bitter flesh, woody endocarp, and a rugose seed

**ja·man** \ˈjämən\ *n* -S [Hindi *jāman, jāmun,* fr. Skt *jambula,* fr. *jambu*] **:** JAVA PLUM

**1jamb** \ˈjam, -aa(ə)-\ *n* -S [ME *jambe,* fr. MF, lit., leg, fr. LL *gamba, camba* hock (of a horse), leg — more at GAMBOL] **1 :** an upright piece or surface forming the side of an opening (as a doorway, window, fireplace) **2 :** a projecting columnar part (as of a masonry wall) or mass (as of ore) **3 :** LEG, SHANK — used chiefly in heraldry **4** *also* **jambe** \ˈ"\ **:** JAMBEAU

**2jamb** *var of* JAM

**jam·ba** \ˈjämbə\ *n* -s [prob. native name in India] : ACLE 1

**jam·ba·laya** \ˌjəmbəˈlīə, -līyə\ *n* -s [LaF, fr. Prov *jambalaia, jabalaia, jambaraia* stew of rice and fowl] **1** : rice cooked with ham, sausage, chicken, shrimp, or oysters and usu. tomato and seasoned with herbs **2** : a mixture of diverse elements : POTPOURRI

**jamb brick** *n* : a brick with the corner of one end and side rounded for use on the vertical side of an opening in a brick wall

**jam·beau** \ˈjam(ˌ)bō, ═ˈ═\ *n, pl* **jam·beaux** \-ō(z)\ [ME, fr. (assumed) AF, fr. OF *jambe* leg — more at JAMB] : a piece of medieval plate armor for the leg below the knee : GREAVE — see ARMOR illustration

**jam·bee** \ˈjamˌbē, ═ˈ═\ *n* -s [fr. *Jambi* (Djambi), district and town, Sumatra, Indonesia] *archaic* : a walking stick made from East Indian rattans (genus *Calamus*) and popular in the reign of Queen Anne

**jam·ber** \ˈjambə(r)\ *n* -s [ME, fr. MF *jambiere*, fr. OF, fr. *jambe* leg] : JAMBEAU

**jam·bo** \ˈjam(ˌ)bō\ *or* **jam·bou** *also* **jam·bu** \-)bü\ *n* -s [Hindi *jambū, jambu*, fr. Skt] : ROSE APPLE 1

**jam·bok** \(ˈ)zhamˈbäk\ *var of* SJAMBOK

**jam·bo·lan** \ˌjambəˈlan\ *or* **jambolan plum** *also* **jam·bo·la·na** \ˌ══ˈlänə\ *n* [Pg *jambolão*, fr. Hindi *jambūl*] : JAVA PLUM

**jam·bone** \ˈjamˌbōn\ *n* [origin unknown] : a lone euchre hand that is played with the bidder's cards exposed on the table

**jam·bool** *or* **jam·bul** \ˌjəmˈbül\ *n* -s [Hindi *jambūl*, fr. Skt *jambūla*, fr. *jambū, jambu*] **1** : JAVA PLUM **2** : a drug obtained from the bark and seeds of Java plum and formerly believed to be of value in treating diabetes

**jamborandi** *var of* JABORANDI

**jam·bo·ree** \ˌjambəˈrē, ˌjaam-\ *n* -s [origin unknown] **1** : a euchre hand containing the five highest trumps **2** : a noisy or unrestrained carousal or frolic : SPREE ⟨got on a ~ last Tuesday and . . . drank repeatedly at every saloon, insulted every person they encountered, brandished pistols and discharged them —D.D.Martin⟩ **3 a** : a large festive gathering (as of a political party or a league of sports teams) often involving a program of variety entertainment or exhibition performances **b** : a national or international camping assembly of boy scouts — compare CAMPOREE **4** : a long mixed program of entertainment ⟨the summer program also includes Sunday matinees of concerts and fountain play . . . plus four special night ~s featuring fireworks —Janet Flanner⟩

**jam·bos** \ˈjamˌbäs, -bōs\ *n* [NL, fr. E *jambo*] **1** *cap, in some classifications* : a genus of woody plants (family Myrtaceae) with opposite leathery leaves and panicles or corymbs of showy flowers that includes the Java plum, Malay apple, and rose apple which are usu. placed in the genus *Eugenia* **2** *also* **jam·bo·sa** \jamˈbōsə\ *pl* **jambos** *also* **jambosas** [*jambosa* fr. NL *Jambosa*, syn. of *Jambos*] : ROSE APPLE 1

**jamb peg** *n* : a device used in faceting gems comprising a piece of wood containing a series of holes in which a dop stick can be fixed at varying angles

**jambs** *pl of* JAMB, *pres 3d sing of* JAMB

**jamb shaft** *n* : a free or engaged column decorating the jamb of a door opening or window opening (as in medieval architecture) — see ESCONSON

**jambstone** \ˈ═,═\ *n* : a stone set vertically at the edge of a window or door opening so that one of its faces forms a jamb or part of a jamb

**jamb stove** *n* : a stove used in the U. S. in the middle of the 18th century made of five cast-iron plates forming a box and built into a fireplace wall so that the front opens into the fireplace to receive live coals and the back warms an adjoining room

diagram of jamb stove: *1* fireplace room, *2* stove room, *3* end plate, *4* side plate, *5* stove leg, *6* stove hole, *7* flue for stove, *8* chimney of fireplace, *9* lintel beam

**jam cleat** *n* [²*jam*] : a cleat with a hinged top for belaying with a single turn of rope and without hitches

**james** *n* -ES [after *James* I †1625 king of England] *slang* : ¹SOVEREIGN 2

**james·ian** *also* **james·ean** \ˈjāmzēən\ *adj, usu cap* **1** [William *James* †1910 Am. philosopher and psychologist + E *-ian* or *-ean*] : of, relating to, or resembling William James or his philosophical or psychological teachings (as pragmatism, radical empiricism) **2** [Henry *James* †1916 Am. writer + E *-ian* or *-ean*] : of, relating to, or resembling Henry James or his writings ⟨a *Jamesian* revival⟩ ⟨has written a *Jamesian* novel of psychological tension⟩

**james–lange theory** \ˈjāmzˈläŋə-\ *n, usu cap J&L* [after William *James* and Carl Georg *Lange* †1900 Dan. physician and psychologist] : a theory in psychology: the affective component of emotion follows rather than precedes the attendant physiological changes

**jame·son·ite** \ˈjām(p)səˌnīt, -məs-\ *n* -s [Robert *Jameson* †1854 Scot. mineralogist + E *-ite*] : a gray orthorhombic mineral $Pb_4FeSb_6S_{14}$ consisting of a lead antimony iron sulfide, having a metallic luster, and occurring in fibrous masses

**james's powder** *or* **james' powder** \ˈjāmz(əz)-\ *n, usu cap J* [after Robert *James* †1776 Eng. physician] : ANTIMONIAL POWDER

**james·town lily** \ˈjāmzˌtaun\ *n, often cap J* [fr. *Jamestown*, Va.] : JIMSONWEED

**jamestown weed** *often cap J, var of* JIMSONWEED

**jammed** *past of* JAM

**jam·mer** \ˈjamə(r), -aam-\ *n* -s [¹*jam* + *-er*] : one that jams: as **a** (1) : a vehicular hoist used to load logs by animal or tractor power (2) : one that operates such a jammer **b** : a usu. modulated transmitter that emits a signal that is intended to interfere with or make unintelligible radio or radar signals

**jamming** *pres part of* JAM

**jam·my** \ˈjamē, -aam-, -mi\ *adj* -ER/-EST [⁴*jam* + *-y*] **1** : sticky with jam ⟨fended off the child's ~ hands⟩ **2** *Brit* : DELIGHTFUL, EASY ⟨a way of singing that's just ~⟩

**jam nut** *n* [²*jam*] : LOCKNUT 1

**ja·moke** \jəˈmōk\ *n* -s [alter. of earlier *jamocha*, blend of *java* and *mocha*] *slang* : COFFEE 1a

**jam–pack** \ˈ═,═\ *vt* [¹*jam* + *pack*] : to fill to overflowing : fill by crowding in as much as possible : pack tightly : CRAM ⟨vacationists *jam-packed* the trains⟩ ⟨*jam-packs* his columns with useful information⟩

**jam·pan** \ˈjamˌpan\ *n* -s [Beng *jhāpān*] : a sedan with two poles used in the hill country of India

**jam riveter** *n* [²*jam*] : a pneumatic riveting hammer designed for use in a restricted space

**jam·ro·sade** \ˌjamrōˈzād\ *n* -s [*jambo* + *rose* + *-ade*] : the fruit of the rose apple

**jams** *pres 3d sing of* JAM, *pl of* JAM

**jam session** *n* [²*jam*] : an impromptu performance by a group of jazz musicians typically for the players' own enjoyment and characterized by group improvisation

**jam·shed·pur** \ˈjämˌshedˌpu̇(ə)r\ *adj, usu cap* [fr. *Jamshedpur*, India] : of or from the city of Jamshedpur, India : of the kind or style prevalent in Jamshedpur

**¹jam–up** \ˈ═,═\ *adj* [prob. fr. *jam up*, v.] : very good : FIRST-RATE : BANG-UP ⟨after one course in psychology you turn out to be a whiz-bang, *jam-up* mind reader —J.S.Redding⟩

**²jam–up** \ˈ"\ *n* -s [fr. *jam up*, v.] : ²JAM 1

**jam weld** *n* [²*jam*] : BUTT WELD

**jamwood** \ˈ═,═\ *n* [⁴*jam* + *wood*] : the raspberry-scented wood of the jam used by the aboriginal inhabitants of Australia for spears

**JAN** *abbr* joint army-navy

**ja·nam·bre** \həˈnämˌ(ˌ)brā\ *n, pl* **janambre** *or* **janambres** *usu cap* [Sp, of AmerInd origin] **1 a** : an Indian people of northeastern Mexico **b** : a member of such people **2** : the language of the Janambre people, perhaps Coahuiltecan

**jan·a·pa** \ˈjanəpə\ *also* **jan·a·pan** \-pən\ *n* -s [Tamil *caṇappu, caṇappai*] : SUNN 2

**jan·ders** \ˈjandə(r)z, ˈjȯn-,ˈjän-,ˈjaan-,ˈjȧn-\ *dial var of* JAUNDICE

**J and WO** *abbr* jettison and washing overboard

**¹jane** \ˈjān\ *n* -s *usu cap* [ME, prob. modif. of MF *Genes* Genoa, Italy] : a small Genoese coin circulating in England during the 14th and 15th centuries

**²jane** \ˈ"\ *n* -s [fr. the name *Jane*] *slang* : GIRL, WOMAN

**jane doe** \-ˈdō\ *n, usu cap J&D* [*Jane* + *Doe* (as in *John Doe*)] : a female party to legal proceedings whose true name is unknown — called also *Mary Major*; compare JOHN DOE

**jane·ite** *also* **jan·ite** \ˈjāˌnīt\ *n* -s [*Jane* Austen †1817 Eng. novelist + E *-ite*] : an enthusiastic admirer of Jane Austen's writings

**janes** \ˈjānz\ *dial var of* JEANS

**jan·ga·da** \janˈgädə, -aŋ-\ *n* -s [Pg, fr. Tamil *caṅkaṭam* or Malayalam *caṅṅāṭam*, fr. Skt *saṁghāta* joining of timber, union] : a raft made of logs of light wood with a sail, seat, steering oar, and dagger boards and used by fishermen along the northeast coast of Brazil : CATAMARAN

jangada

**jangada fiber** *n* : the bast fiber from the tibourbou

**jan·ga·dei·ro** \ˌjaŋgəˈdā(ˌ)rō\ *n* -s [Pg, fr. *jangada* + *-eiro* -er (fr. L *-arius*)] : a Brazilian fisherman who sails a jangada

**¹jan·gle** \ˈjaŋgəl, ˈjaiŋ-\ *vb* **jangled**; **jangled**; **jangling** \-g(ə)liŋ\ **jangles** [ME *janglen*, fr. OF *jangler*, of Gmc origin; akin to MD *jangelen* to grumble, whine, haggle, *janken* to yelp, whine, squeal, G dial. *jangeln* to talk in a whining manner] *vi* **1** *archaic* : to talk idly : BABBLE, CHATTER ⟨some . . . have turned aside unto vain *jangling* —1 Tim 1:6 (AV)⟩ **2** : to quarrel in words : ALTERCATE, WRANGLE ⟨must ~ till at last we fought —A.E.Housman⟩ **3** : to sound harshly or discordantly ⟨the alarm clock *jangled* loudly⟩ ~ *vt* **1** : to utter or sound discordantly or in a babbling or chattering way ⟨the telephone *jangled* a summons⟩ **2 a** : to cause to sound harshly or inharmoniously ⟨~ a bunch of keys⟩ **b** : to excite to tense and discordant irritation ⟨the whimsy that had sometimes *jangled* the nerves of American newsmen —John Lardner⟩

**²jangle** \ˈ"\ *n* -s [ME, fr. MF, fr. OF, fr. *jangler*] **1** : idle talk : CHATTER, BABBLE ⟨his eternal ~ about being the average father of an average American family —Louis Auchincloss⟩ **2** : noisy altercation : CONTENTION, WRANGLING ⟨she hated . . . a shrill squabble of shrews, a degrading ~ between servant and mistress —Jean Stafford⟩ **3** : discordant sound : a confused ringing ⟨music that seemed to be a chaotic ~⟩ ⟨the ~ of sleigh bells⟩ : DISCORD ⟨a haven of calm amid the ~ of modern civilization⟩

**jan·gler** \-g(ə)lə(r)\ *n* -s [ME, fr. *janglen* + *-er*] : one that jangles

**jan·gly** \-g(ə)lē, -li\ *adj, sometimes* -ER/-EST [¹*jangle* + *-y*] : marked by jangling ⟨~ costume jewelry⟩ : having a jangling quality ⟨the ~ music of the dance hall piano⟩

**jani·ceps** \ˈjanəˌseps ˈjān-\ *n* -ES [NL, fr. L *Janus*, a two-faced Roman god + *-ceps* headed, fr. *caput* head — more at JANUARY, HEAD] : a double fetal monster joined at thorax and skull and having two equal faces looking in opposite directions

**jani·form** \-ˌfȯrm\ *adj* [*Janus* + E *-iform*] : having a face on each of two sides ⟨a coin bearing a ~ head⟩

**jan·is·sary** *or* **jan·i·zary** \ˈjanəˌserē, -ˌze-, -ri\ *n* -ES [It *giannizzero*, fr. Turk *yeniçeri*, fr. *yeni* new, inexperienced + *çeri* soldier, military force] **1** *often cap* **a** : a soldier of an elite corps of Turkish troops orig. organized in the 14th century as the sultan's guard, drawn chiefly from subject Christian boys seized in tribute, and continuing as the largest and strongest unit of the army until abolished after revolting in 1826 **b** : a Turkish soldier **2** : a member of a group of loyal or subservient troops, officials, or supporters ⟨a politician with the help of a large following of *janissaries* ready to carry out his personal will⟩ **3** : a West Indian wrasse (*Clepticus parrae*) that is mostly reddish brown with the caudal region green

**janissary music** *n, often cap J* **1 a** : music of military bands formed on the Turkish model and featuring shrill fifes and loud oboes and drums, cymbals, triangles, and Turkish crescents **b** : orchestral or other music imitating this music or its qualities — called also *Turkish music* **2** : BATTERY 12

**¹jan·i·tor** \ˈjanəd·ə(r), -nətə-\ *n* -s [L, fr. *janua* door, fr. *janus* arch, gate; perh. akin to Skt *yāna* road, *yāti* he goes, Lith *joti* to ride, L *ire* to go — more at ISSUE] **1** : DOORKEEPER **2** : one that keeps the premises of an apartment, office, or other building clean and free of refuse, tends the heating system, and makes minor repairs

**²janitor** \ˈ"\ *vi* **janitored**; **janitored**; **janitoring** \-əriŋ, ˈjanəˌtriŋ\ **janitors** : to work as a janitor

**jan·i·to·ri·al** \ˌjanəˈtōrēəl, -tȯr-\ *adj* : of or belonging to a janitor : CUSTODIAL ⟨~ duties⟩ ⟨the ~ staff⟩

**jan·i·tress** \ˈjanəˌtrəs\ *n* -ES [*janitor* + *-ess*] : a female janitor : CHARWOMAN

**jan·i·trix** \-nə-,(ˌ)triks\ *n* -ES [L, fem. of *janitor*] : JANITRESS

**jan·ker** \ˈjaŋkər\ *n* -s [origin unknown] *Scot* : a long pole on two wheels used esp. for hauling logs

**jan·kers** \ˈjaŋkə(r)z\ *n pl but sing in constr* [origin unknown] *Brit* : confinement, fatigue duty, or drill imposed as punishment on a member of the armed forces

**jan·ko keyboard** \ˈyäŋ(ˌ)kō-\ *n, usu cap J* [after Paul von *Jankó* †1919 Hungarian pianist] : a pianoforte keyboard invented in 1882 consisting of six rows of keys with three digitals to each note, those of each row being at whole-step intervals

**jan·mash·ta·mi** \ˌjənˈmäshtəˌmē\ *n* -s *usu cap* [Skt *janmāṣṭamī*, fr. *janma* birth (fr. *janati* he begets) + *aṣṭama* eighth, fr. *aṣṭā* eight — more at KIN, EIGHT] : a Hindu festival celebrating the birthday of the deified hero Krishna

**jann** *n* -s [Ar *jānn*] : JINN

**jan·ney coupler** \ˈjanē-\ *n, usu cap J* [after Eli H. *Janney* †1912 Am. inventor] : a device for coupling railroad cars and locomotives invented in the early 1880s and employed in principle in the standard automatic coupler of today

**¹jan·nock** \ˈjanək\ *n* -s [ME *ianock*] *dial Brit* : BANNOCK

**²jannock** \ˈ"\ *adj* [origin unknown] *dial Brit* : straightforward and fair : UPRIGHT, DECENT ⟨to give a lover a chance of a final scene before leaving him . . . was ~ —F.M.Ford⟩

**jan·sen·ism** \ˈjan(t)səˌnizəm\ *n* -s *usu cap* [F *jansénisme*, fr. Cornelis *Jansen* (Cornelius Jansenius) †1638 Dutch theologian + F *-isme* -ism] **1** : a theological doctrine condemned by the Roman Catholic Church as heretical that flourished esp. in France in the 17th and 18th centuries maintaining among its principal tenets that freedom of the will (as in accepting or resisting grace) is nonexistent and that the redemption of mankind through the death of Jesus Christ was limited to only a part of mankind and that those not so redeemed are by the positive will of God inescapably condemned to hell **2** : a negative rigoristic moral attitude (as toward sex) associated with adherents of Jansenism : PURITANISM

**¹jan·sen·ist** \-ˌnəst\ *n* -s *usu cap* [F *janséniste*, fr. C. *Jansen* + F *-iste* -ist] **1** : an adherent of Jansenism **2** : a member of the Church of Utrecht in Holland originating by schism from the Roman Catholic Church in 1723 and forming part of the Old Catholic Church since 1889

**²jansenist** \ˈ"\ *also* **jan·sen·is·tic** \ˌ══ˈnistik\ *adj, usu cap* : of, relating to, or characteristic of the Jansenists or Jansenism

**jan·thi·na** \ˈjan(t)thənə\ *n* [NL, fr. L *ianthina*, fem. of *ianthinus* violet-blue, fr. Gk *ianthinos*, fr. *ion* violet + *anthos* flower — more at VIOLET, ANTHOLOGY] **1** *cap* : the type genus of Janthinidae comprising pelagic snails of warm seas that have a thin spiral purple shell, a large head, and protrusible gills **2** -s : any snail of the genus *Janthina*

**jan·thin·i·dae** \janˈthinəˌdē\ *n pl, cap* [NL, fr. *Janthina*, type genus + *-idae*] : a family of marine snails (suborder Taenioglossa) comprising the violet snails and floating at the surface by means of a raft of air bubbles enclosed in hardened mucus secreted by the foot — see JANTHINA

**janty** *also* **jantee** *archaic var of* JAUNTY

**jan·u·ary** \ˈjanyəˌwerē, -ri *also* ÷ˈjen-, *dial* -nə,w-\ *n, pl*

**januaries** *or* **januarys** *usu cap* [ME *Januarie*, fr. L *Januarius*, first month of the ancient Roman year, fr. *Janus*, two-faced god or numen of gates and doors and therefore of beginnings (fr. *janus* arch, gate) + *-arius* -ary — more at JANITOR] : the first month of the Gregorian calendar — abbr. *Jan.*; see MONTH table

**janus–faced** \ˈjānəˌsfāst\ *or* **janus** *adj, usu cap J* [after *Janus*, the god or numen] **1** : looking in opposite directions ⟨a *Janus-faced* look at the past and future of our national economy⟩ **2** : having two contrasting aspects ⟨a *Janus-faced* alternation of melodic variations in major and minor throughout the movement⟩ **3** : TWO-FACED, DECEITFUL

**janus green** *or* **janus green B** *n, usu cap J* : a basic monoazo azine dye made from safranine and dimethylaniline and used chiefly as a biological stain

**ja·nus·like** \ˈjānəˌslīk\ *adj, usu cap* : looking or acting in opposite or contrasting ways ⟨the *Januslike* quality of Soviet foreign policy created confusion . . . among western statesmen —F.C.Barghoorn⟩

**jan·war** \ˈjanwər\ *usu cap, Scot var of* JANUARY

**jap** \ˈjap\ *n* -s *usu cap, often attrib* [by shortening] : JAPANESE — often used disparagingly

**¹ja·pan** \jəˈpan, -paa(ə)n *also* (ˈ)jaˌp-\ *adj* [fr. *Japan*, country consisting of an island chain in the western Pacific off the eastern coast of Asia] **1** *usu cap* : of or from Japan : of the kind or style prevalent in Japan : JAPANESE **2 a** : of, resembling, or characteristic of Japanese lacquered work **b** : coated or treated with japan

**²japan** \ˈ"\ *n* -s [fr. *Japan*, whence it orig. came] **1 a** : a varnish yielding a hard brilliant coating on such surfaces as metal or wood **b** *or* **japan drier** : a varnish that contains a large percentage of resins and driers and that is used as a grinding liquid for paste colors or as a liquid drier for paints **c** *or* **japan black** : a quick-drying black varnish consisting usu. of asphaltum, linseed oil, and thinner that is used for coating metal and that is usu. hardened by baking **2 a** : work varnished and figured in the Japanese manner ⟨the likeness of His Majesty . . . was housed in a circular container of its own, of black ~ —John Godley⟩ **b** : Japanese china or silk

**³japan** \ˈ"\ *vt* **japanned**; **japanned**; **japanning**; **japans** **1** : to cover with a coat of japan or with some other hard brilliant varnish in the manner of the Japanese : LACQUER **2** : to give a high gloss to with varnish supplemented by heating; *specif* : to give a glossy black to (as leather)

**japan allspice** *n, usu cap J* : a Japanese shrub (*Chimonanthus praecox*) cultivated for its fragrant yellow flowers that blossom before the leaves appear — called also *Japanese allspice*

**japan ashberry** *n, usu cap J* : an Asiatic evergreen shrub (*Mahonia japonica*) with handsome foliage and yellow flowers

**japan bittersweet** *n, usu cap J* : JAPANESE BITTERSWEET

**japan blue** *n, often cap J* : a dark blue that is redder and duller than Peking blue, redder and deeper than Flemish blue, and stronger and slightly redder than Majolica blue (sense 1)

**japan camphor** *n, usu cap J* : dextrorotatory camphor

**japan cedar** *n, usu cap J* : JAPANESE CEDAR

**japan clover** *n, usu cap J* : an annual lespedeza (*Lespedeza striata*) sometimes used as a forage, soil-improving, and pasture crop esp. in the southeastern U.S. — called also *Japanese clover, Jap clover*

**¹jap·a·nese** \ˌjapəˈnēz, -ēs, *in rapid speech attributively sometimes* ˈjap,n-\ *adj, usu cap* [*Japan* + *-ese*] **1 a** : of, relating to, or characteristic of Japan **b** : of, relating to, or characteristic of the Japanese **2** : of, relating to, or characteristic of the Japanese language

**²japanese** \ˈ"\ *n, cap* **1** *pl* **japanese** : a native or inhabitant of Japan or one of his descendants **2** -s : the language of the Japanese

**japanese acid clay** *or* **japanese acid earth** *n, usu cap J* : fuller's earth occurring in Japan — called also *Kambara earth*

**japanese allspice** *n, usu cap J* : JAPAN ALLSPICE

**japanese andromeda** *n, usu cap J* : a broad-leaved evergreen Asiatic shrub (*Pieris japonica*) with glossy leaves and drooping clusters of whitish flowers that is used as an ornamental — called also *andromeda*

**japanese anemone** *n, usu cap J* : an Asiatic garden plant (*Anemone nupehensis*) having compound leaves and large showy flowers — called also *Japanese windflower*

**japanese angelica tree** *n, usu cap J* : a shrub or small tree (*Aralia elata*) having a much-compounded inflorescence with a short main axis and spreading secondary axes

**japanese ape** *n, usu cap J* : a small brownish ape (*Macaca speciosa*) of Japan that has a naked face and red ischial callosities

**japanese apricot** *n, usu cap J* : a Japanese ornamental tree (*Prunus mume*) with fragrant white flowers and yellow inedible fruits somewhat smaller than those of the common apricot

**japanese arborvitae** *n, usu cap J* : a Japanese evergreen tree (*Thuja standishii*) with reddish brown bark, spreading or somewhat upright branches bearing thick compressed branchlets, and leaves that are bright green above with white triangular markings below and that are of two types, those of the main axes terminating in sharp rigid points and those of the lateral branches ending obtusely

**japanese artichoke** *n, usu cap J* : CHINESE ARTICHOKE

**japanese ash** *n, usu cap J* **1** : an Asiatic tree (*Fraxinus mandschurica*) having light yellowish wood with a grain resembling that of oak **2** : the wood of Japanese ash used esp. for veneer and joinery — called also *tamo*

**japanese aspen** *n, usu cap J* : a medium-sized Japanese tree (*Populus sieboldii*) with tomentose twigs and thick leaves

**japanese azalea** *n, usu cap J* : any of several ornamental azaleas from Japan and China (esp. *Rhododendron japonica*) — compare KURUME AZALEA

**japanese banana** *n, usu cap J* : an Asiatic banana (*Musa basjoo*) that is cultivated as a foliage plant in Japan

**japanese barberry** *n, usu cap J* : a compact ornamental Japanese shrub (*Berberis thunbergii*) that has simple spines, entire oblong or spatulate leaves, yellowish flowers either solitary or in small umbels, and bright red persistent berries and that is widespread in cultivation esp. for hedges — compare COMMON BARBERRY

**japanese barnyard millet** *n, usu cap J* : JAPANESE MILLET

**japanese bear** *n, usu cap J* : a small black bear (*Ursus japonicus*) of northern Japan that has a small white breast marking

**japanese beauty–berry** *n, usu cap J* : a Japanese shrub (*Callicarpa japonica*) with long pointed leaves, cymes of pink flowers, and ornamental violet fruit

**japanese beech** *n, usu cap J* : a beech that is native to Japan and is distinguished from the European beech esp. by its soft light yellowish brown wood

**japanese beetle** *n, usu cap J* : a small metallic green and brown scarabaeid beetle (*Popillia japonica*) introduced into America from Japan that as a grub feeds on the roots of grasses and decaying vegetation and as an adult eats foliage and fruits and is a serious pest — see MILKY DISEASE

**japanese b encephalitis** *n, usu cap J&B* : an encephalitis that occurs epidemically in Japan esp. in summer and is caused by an insect-transmitted virus

**japanese bitterling** *n, usu cap J* : any of several small east Asian cyprinid fishes (genus *Acheilognathus*) characterized by development in the female of a very long ovipositor during the breeding season

**japanese bittersweet** *n, usu cap J* : an ornamental Asiatic woody vine (*Celastrus articulata*) that has showy orange-yellow fruit with a persistent scarlet aril — called also *Japan bittersweet*

**japanese black pine** *n, usu cap J* : a large Japanese ornamental tree (*Pinus thunbergii*) having orange-yellow branchlets, leaves three inches or more in length and in bundles of two, and the scales of the cone armed with prickles — called also *black pine*

**japanese blue** *or* **japanese green** *n, often cap J* : a grayish green that is bluer and deeper than slate green and yellower and duller than average blue spruce (sense 2a)

**japanese cane** *n, usu cap J* : a sugarcane that usu. has slender stalks and is widely grown for forage

**japanese cedar** *n, usu cap J* : a large evergreen tree (*Cryptomeria japonica*) grown esp. in Japan and China for its valuable soft wood — called also *Japan cedar*

**japanese cherry** *n, usu cap J* : JAPANESE FLOWERING CHERRY

**japanese chestnut** *n, usu cap J* **1** : a Japanese nut tree (*Castanea crenata*) **2** : the fruit of the Japanese chestnut that is larger than the American chestnut but not so sweet

**japanese climbing fern** *n, usu cap J* : a slender twining fern (*Lygodium japonicum*) with finely divided fronds

**japanese clock** *n, usu cap J* : a Japanese timepiece indicating six sunrise and six sunset divisions of time whose length varies with the change of seasons

**japanese clover** *n, usu cap J* : JAPAN CLOVER

**japanese cornel** *also* **japanese cornel dogwood** *n, usu cap J* : a Japanese dogwood (*Cornus officinalis*) that has scaly bark and is used as an ornamental

[1]**japanese crab** *n, usu cap J* [[1]*crab*] : GIANT CRAB 1

[2]**japanese crab** *or* **japanese crab apple** *n, usu cap J* [[4]*crab*] : SHOWY CRAB APPLE

**japanese cypress** *n, usu cap J* : any of several Japanese evergreens of the genus *Chamaecyparis; esp* : SUN TREE

**japanese deer** *n, usu cap J* : a small deer (*Cervus nippon* syn. *C. sika*) of Japan having slightly forked round antlers and a coat that is spotted with white in summer and plain grayish brown in winter — called also *sika*

**japanese flood fever** *n, usu cap J* : TSUTSUGAMUSHI DISEASE

**japanese flowering cherry** *n, usu cap J* : any of certain ornamental hybrid cherries developed in Japan chiefly from two species (*Prunus serrulata* and *P. sieboldii*) that bear a profusion of white or pink usu. double and often fragrant flowers followed by small inedible fruit, that have long been admired and revered by the Japanese, and that are now widespread in cultivation in regions of moderate climate — called also *Japanese cherry*

**japanese fold** *n, usu cap J* : FRENCH FOLD

**japanese fowl** *n, usu cap J* : one of a Japanese breed of fancy fowls resembling game fowls but having long hackles and tail feathers

**japanese gelatin** *n, usu cap J* : AGAR 1a

**japanese ginger** *n, usu cap J* : a commercial ginger root prepared from a Japanese ginger (*Zingiber mioga*) and usu. marketed unscraped and coated with lime

**japanese gut** *n, usu cap J* : material for fishing leaders made from raw silk fibers bonded with gelatin

**japanese hawthorn** *n, usu cap J* : an evergreen shrub (*Raphiolepis umbellata*) of China and Japan with glossy dark green leaves and showy white fragrant flowers

**japanese hazel** *n, usu cap J* : a Japanese shrub (*Corylus sieboldiana*) with edible nuts in a long tubular involucre

**japanese hemlock** *n, usu cap J* : a Japanese hemlock (*Tsuga diversifolia*) with pubescent branchlets and glossy dark green foliage

**japanese herring** *n, usu cap J* : a round herring (*Etrumeus micropus*)

**japanese holly** *n, usu cap J* : a Japanese shrub (*Ilex crenata*) with evergreen, crenate, but not prickly leaves

**japanese honeysuckle** *n, usu cap J* : an Asiatic twining or trailing honeysuckle (*Lonicera japonica*) that has half-evergreen leaves and fragrant white flowers changing to yellow and that although planted orig. for ornamental purposes has become a troublesome weed in some areas — see HALL'S HONEYSUCKLE

**japanese hop** *n, usu cap J* : an ornamental climbing vine (*Humulus japonicus*) commonly cultivated for its variegated foliage

**japanese horse chestnut** *n, usu cap J* : a Japanese tree (*Aesculus turbinata*) sometimes cultivated for its showy, yellowish white, red-spotted flowers

**japanese horseradish** *n, usu cap J* : WASABI

**japanese iris** *n, usu cap J* : any of various beardless garden irises that are developed chiefly from two species (*Iris laevigata* and *I. kaempferi*) of eastern Asia and that have ensiform leaves and very large handsome white, blue, reddish purple, or violet flowers with spreading falls and standards

**japanese isinglass** *n, usu cap J* : AGAR 1a

**japanese ivy** *n, usu cap J* : BOSTON IVY

**japanese kerria** *n, usu cap J* : JAPANESE ROSE 1

**japanese knot** *n, usu cap J* : [3]KNOT c

**japanese knotweed** *n, usu cap J* : a stout perennial Japanese herb (*Polygonum cuspidatum*) having cordate leaves and panicles of greenish white flowers

**japanese lacquer** *n, usu cap J* : LACQUER 1b

**japanese lacquer tree** *n, usu cap J* : JAPANESE VARNISH TREE

**japanese lantern** *n, usu cap J* : CHINESE LANTERN

**japanese lantern plant** *n, usu cap J* : CHINESE LANTERN PLANT

**japanese larch** *n, usu cap J* : a Japanese ornamental tree (*Larix leptolepis*) having leaves with two white bands beneath and each cone scale reflexed at its apex

**japanese laurel** *n, usu cap J* **1** : an Asiatic dioecious evergreen shrub (*Aucuba japonica*) that has ovate to obtusely acuminate dark green shining leaves often blotched with yellow and that is used as an ornamental — called also *Japan laurel* **2** : JAPANESE RUBBER PLANT

**japanese lawn grass** *n, usu cap J* : KOREAN LAWN GRASS

**japanese leaf** *n, usu cap J* : CHINESE EVERGREEN

**japanese lilac** *n, usu cap J* **1** : a Chinese lilac (*Syringa villosa*) with profuse rose-lilac or whitish late-blooming flowers **2** : JAPANESE TREE LILAC

**japanese linden** *n, usu cap J* : a Japanese tree (*Tilia japonica*) used as an ornamental

**japanese mackerel** *n, usu cap J* : a widely distributed mackerel (*Pneumatophorus japonicus*) of the western Pacific — called also *opelu*

**japanese maple** *n, usu cap J* : a shrub or small tree (*Acer palmatum*) of Japan and Korea that has purple flowers and in most varieties deeply parted green leaves and that is used as an ornamental — called also *full-moon maple*

**japanese medlar** *n, usu cap J* : LOQUAT

**japanese millet** *n, usu cap J* : a coarse annual grass with thick appressed purplish inflorescence and awnless spikelets that is considered to be a variety of barnyard grass or a distinct species (*Echinochloa frumentacea*), is cultivated esp. in Japan and southeastern Asia for its edible seeds which resemble millet and for forage, and is an important wildlife food in parts of the U.S. — called also *billion-dollar grass, Japanese barnyard millet, sanwa millet*

**japanese mink** *n, usu cap J* **1** : an Asiatic weasel (*Mustela sibirica*) **2** *or* **jap mink** : the pale yellowish brown fur of the Japanese mink that is commonly dyed to resemble mink

**japanese mint** *or* **japanese peppermint** *n, usu cap J* : a Japanese mint (*Mentha arvensis piperascens*) that is a variety of the common mint of Europe

**japanese mint oil** *or* **japanese peppermint oil** *n, usu cap J* : an essential oil obtained from corn mint and used chiefly as a source of menthol

**japanese morning glory** *n, usu cap J* : any of certain cultivated morning glories that are derived from an Old World tropical species (*Ipomoea nil*) and are distinguished by a wide color range and by the occurrence of crested, frilled, or double flowers

**japanese moss** *n, usu cap J* : BABY'S TEARS

**japanese mustard** *n, usu cap J* : INDIAN MUSTARD

**japanese nightingale** *n, usu cap J* : an Asiatic hill tit (*Leiothrix lutea*) that is chiefly olivaceous brown with a yellow breast and red bill and feet and that is often kept as a cage bird — called also *Japanese robin*

**japanese nutmeg** *n, usu cap J* : a Japanese tree (*Torreya nucifera*) with edible seeds

**japanese oak** *n, usu cap J* : any of several oaks that are native to, grown in, or shipped as timber from Japan: as **a** : an evergreen oak (*Lithocarpus glabra*) closely related to and resembling the tanbark oak of the American Pacific coast **b** : any of several oaks of the genus *Quercus* (esp. *Q. grosseserrata*) with moderately light, fine-grained, even-textured wood

**japanese oyster** *n, usu cap J* : a large oyster (*Ostrea gigas*) that is native to the coast of Japan and that has been introduced along the Pacific coast of No. America where it is maintained by repeated planting of spat from the natural habitat

**japanese pagoda tree** *n, usu cap J* : an ornamental Chinese and Japanese tree (*Sophora japonica*) with compound dark green leaves and profuse panicles of yellowish white flowers — called also *Chinese scholartree*

**japanese paper** *n, usu cap J* : a long-fibered paper made orig. in Japan and often used for printing engravings — called also *Japan paper*

**japanese parasol fir** *n, usu cap J* : UMBRELLA PINE 1

**japanese pear** *n, usu cap J* : SAND PEAR 2a

**japanese persimmon** *n, usu cap J* **1** : an Asiatic persimmon (*Diospyros kaki*) that is prob. native to China but has been developed into numerous horticultural forms esp. in Japan **2** : the fruit of the Japanese persimmon which is usu. larger than native American persimmons

**japanese pheasant** *n, usu cap J* : a pheasant (*Phasianus colchicus versicolor*)

**japanese pine** *n, usu cap J* : any of several eastern Asiatic ornamental pines (esp. *Pinus thunbergii* and *P. densiflora*)

**japanese pink** *n, usu cap J* : a China pink (*Dianthus chinensis heddewigii*) distinguished by dentate or jagged-edged petals

**japanese pittosporum** *n, usu cap J* : TOBIRA

**japanese plum** *n, usu cap J* **1** : any of numerous large showy usu. yellow to light red cultivated plums that are sometimes inferior to European plums in flavor **2** : any of numerous plum trees derived from a Chinese tree (*Prunus salicina*) that are somewhat less hardy than most European and American plum trees and produce Japanese plums **3** : LOQUAT

**japanese print** *n, usu cap J* : a color print executed from wood blocks in water-based inks and developed to a high degree of artistry by the Japanese esp. in the late 18th and early 19th centuries

**japanese privet** *n, usu cap J* : either of two Asiatic evergreen privets: **a** : an erect shrub or small tree (*Ligustrum lucidum*) of China, Korea, and Japan with glabrous dark green usu. acuminate leaves and flowers in long erect panicles **b** : a somewhat smaller shrub (*L. japonicum*) of Korea and Japan with usu. more obtuse darker green leaves and flowers in looser more lax panicles

**japanese quince** *n, usu cap J* **1** : LOQUAT **2** : a hardy Chinese shrub (*Chaenomeles lagenaria*) that is distinguished from the common quinces by its scarlet flowers and large stipules and is grown mostly for ornament — called also *Japonica*; compare DWARF JAPANESE QUINCE

**japanese radish** *n, usu cap J* : DAIKON

**japanese raisin tree** *n, usu cap J* : a deciduous shrub or small tree (*Hovenia dulcis*) of eastern Asia having a spicy odor, ovate leaves, and reddish edible fruit stalks — called also *honey tree*

**japanese red** *n, often cap J* : INDIAN RED 2a

**japanese red pine** *n, usu cap J* : a Japanese ornamental pine (*Pinus densiflora*) that has orange-red bark, yellowish young branches, and minutely serrulate leaves in fascicles of two with the leaf sheaths ending in two long points

**japanese river fever** *n, usu cap J* : TSUTSUGAMUSHI DISEASE

**japanese robin** *n, usu cap J* **1** : JAPANESE NIGHTINGALE **2** : a small Japanese bird (*Erithacus akahige*) related to the nightingale

**japanese rose** *n, usu cap J* **1** : a slender Chinese shrub (*Kerria japonica*) cultivated for its bright yellow often globular flowers — called also *Japan globeflower* **2** : MULTIFLORA ROSE

**japanese rubber plant** *n, usu cap J* : a succulent shrub (*Crassula argentea*) having very thick shiny green leaves and white or rosy red flowers in close panicles — called also *Japanese laurel*

**jap·a·nes·ery** \ˌjapəˈnēzərē, -ēsərē\ *n* -ES *sometimes cap* [[1]*Japanese* + *-ery*] : a Japanese ornament : BAUBLE — usu. used in pl. ⟨a shelf full of *japaneseries*⟩

**japaneses** *pl of* JAPANESE

**japanese sago palm** *n, usu cap J* : SAGO PALM 2a

**japanese sand pear** *n, usu cap J* : SAND PEAR 2a

**japanese snail** *n, usu cap J* : an ovoviviparous freshwater snail (*Viviparus malleatus*) that is native to Japan and is often kept in aquariums where it is a valuable scavenger

**japanese snowball** *n, usu cap J* **1 a** : a handsome cultivated shrub (*Viburnum plicatum*) with large globose clusters of sterile flowers very similar to those of the guelder rose **b** : the flower cluster of the Japanese snowball **2** *also* **japanese snowbell** : a deciduous shrub or small tree (*Styrax japonica*) having flowers in short glabrous racemes

**japanese snowflower** *n, usu cap J* : a Japanese shrub (*Deutzia gracilis*) with slender arching branches covered in spring with a profusion of white flowers

**japanese spaniel** *n, usu cap J* **1** : a toy dog originating in Japan that is bred chiefly as a pet, that differs from the pekingese in its proportions of body and legs, and that is characterized by a silky coat and black and white or red and white coloring **2** : a breed of dogs comprising the Japanese spaniels

**japanese spider crab** *n, usu cap J* : GIANT CRAB 1

**japanese spruce** *n, usu cap J* **1** : a Japanese fir (*Abies mariesii*) with densely rusty pubescent twigs **2** : YEDDO SPRUCE

**japanese spurge** *n, usu cap J* : a low Japanese herb or subshrub (*Pachysandra terminalis*) that has white flowers in terminal spikes and is often used as a ground cover — compare ALLEGHENY SPURGE

**japanese star anise** *n, usu cap J* : a Japanese evergreen tree (*Illicium anisatum*) with poisonous fruit

**japanese storax** *n, usu cap J* : JAPANESE SNOWBALL 2

**japanese table pine** *n, usu cap J* : an umbrella-shaped evergreen shrub (*Pinus densiflora umbraculifera*) grown as an ornamental — called also *Japanese umbrella pine*

**japanese tissue** *n, usu cap J* : a thin strong lightweight paper orig. handmade in Japan from long native fibers and used for mending tears in book pages and for cleaning lenses

**japanese tree lilac** *n, usu cap J* : an arborescent lilac (*Syringa amurensis japonica*) of Japan having showy yellowish white flowers — called also *Japanese lilac, Japan tree lilac*

**japanese tung oil** *or* **japanese wood oil** *n, usu cap J* : a drying oil obtained from a Japanese tung tree (*Aleurites cordata*)

**japanese umbrella pine** *n, usu cap J* **1** : UMBRELLA PINE 1 **2** : JAPANESE TABLE PINE

**japanese varnish tree** *n, usu cap J* **1** *or* **japanese sumac** : a Japanese sumac (*Rhus verniciflua*) that resembles the poison sumac and is a source of the natural Japan varnish or Japan lacquer — called also *Japanese lacquer tree* **2** : CHINESE PARASOL TREE

**japanese walnut** *n, usu cap J* : a valuable Japanese nut tree (*Juglans cordiformis ailanthifolia*) that bears a heart-shaped nut and is used as a walnut stock because of its hardiness — called also *heartnut, Japan walnut*

**japanese wax** *n, usu cap J* : JAPAN WAX

**japanese wax tree** *n, usu cap J* : a Japanese sumac (*Rhus succedanea*)

**japanese white pine** *n, usu cap J* : an evergreen tree (*Pinus parviflora*) used esp. in dwarf form as an ornamental in Japanese gardens

**japanese windflower** *n, usu cap J* : JAPANESE ANEMONE

**japanese wistaria** *n, usu cap J* : a Japanese deciduous shrub (*Wisteria floribunda*) that is widely cultivated for ornament and has twining branches and velvety pubescent pods

**japanese witch hazel** *n, usu cap J* : a Japanese shrub or small tree (*Hamamelis japonica*) that resembles the American witch hazel but bears reddish yellow flowers in midwinter and that is used as an ornamental

**japanese wolf** *n, usu cap J* : an Asiatic wolf (*Canis hodophylax*)

**japanese yellow** *n, often cap J* : CHINESE ORANGE 2

**japanese yew** *n, usu cap J* : a shrubby hardy evergreen (*Taxus cuspidata*) of China and Japan that has lustrous dark green foliage and is cultivated in many horticultural forms

**jap·a·nesque** \ˌjapəˈnesk, jəˌpa¦-, ˈja,pa¦-\ *adj, often cap* [*Japan* + *-esque*] : JAPANESY ⟨intensely white and intensely *Japanesque* egrets —William Beebe⟩

**jap·a·nesy** \ˌjapəˈnēzē, -nēsē\ *adj, usu cap J* [[1]*Japanese* + *-y*] : having or suggesting a Japanese manner or style : resembling what is Japanese ⟨some of the houses had columned verandas and *Japanesy* curved gables —Joseph Wechsberg⟩

**japan fox** *n, usu cap J* : the pelt of the raccoon dog processed to simulate fox

**japan globeflower** *n, usu cap J* : JAPANESE ROSE 1

**ja·pan·ism** \jəˈpa,nizəm, -paa,- *also* jaˈp-\ *n* -S *usu cap* [*Japan* + *-ism*] **1** : a trait or characteristic distinctive of the Japanese or of their civilization or art ⟨modern trend in fine art toward skeletal frameworks . . . can be traced back to the *Japanism* of the 70s —Edgar Kaufmann⟩ **2** : Japanese nationalism ⟨a rising tide of *Japanism* which was soon to overwhelm foreign missionaries —Hugh Byas⟩

**jap·a·ni·za·tion** \ˌjapənəˈzāshən, -ˌnīˈz-\ *n* -S *often cap* : the act or process of japanizing

**jap·a·nize** \ˈ==,nīz\ *vt* -ED/-ING/-S *often cap* [*Japan* + *-ize*] **1** : to make Japanese: **a** : to cause to acquire traits or characteristics that are or are believed to be distinctively Japanese **b** : to bring into close conformity with Japanese national customs and institutions : change in behavior and attitude to suit the Japanese way of life **2** : to bring (an area) under the political, cultural, or commercial influence of Japan

**japan lacquer** *n, usu cap J* : JAPAN 1a

**japan laurel** *n, usu cap J* : JAPANESE LAUREL

**japan leather** *n, usu cap J* : JAPANNED LEATHER

**japan lily** *n, usu cap J* : any of several Japanese lilies (as *Lilium auratum, L. japonicum, L. speciosum*)

**japan medlar** *or* **japan plum** *n, usu cap J* **1** : LOQUAT **2** : JAPANESE PERSIMMON

**japanned** *past of* JAPAN

**japanned leather** *n* [fr. past part. of [3]*japan*] : leather having a smooth shiny usu. black surface obtained by coating with japan — compare PATENT LEATHER

**japanned peacock** *or* **japanned peafowl** *n* [fr. past part. of [3]*japan*; fr. the lustrous quality of the feathers] : a peafowl which is usu. considered a variety of the Indian peacock and in which the wings of the male are largely deep blue

**ja·pan·ner** \jəˈpanə(r), -paan- *also* jaˈp-\ *n* -S [*Japan* + *-er*] **1** *usu cap, obs* **a** : JAPANESE 1 **b** : a Japanese ship **2** [[3]*japan* + *-er*] : a worker who applies coatings of enamel or varnish in making japanned leather or other japanned articles

**japanners' brown** *n* : an iron oxide that contains chiefly ferric oxide and is used as a drier for oils esp. in the patent-leather and oilcloth industries

**ja·pan·nery** \jəˈpanərē *also* jaˈp-\ *n* -ES [[3]*japan* + *-ery*] : a room or other place where leather is japanned

**japanning** *n* -S [fr. gerund of [3]*japan*] : the process of varnishing with japan; *also* : the material used

**japano-** *comb form, usu cap* [*Japan* (the country)] : Japanese ⟨*Japano*logist⟩ ⟨*Japano*phile⟩

**ja·pan·o·phile** \jəˈpanə,fīl *also* jaˈp-\ *n* -S *usu cap* [*Japano-* + *-phile*] : one who esp. admires and likes Japan or Japanese ways

**japan paper** *n, usu cap J* : JAPANESE PAPER

**japan quince** *n, usu cap J* : JAPANESE QUINCE

**japan rose** *n, usu cap J* **1 a** : any of several Japanese roses (as *Rosa multiflora* and *R. rugosa*) **b** : CAMELLIA 2 **2** : a moderate yellowish pink to orange

**japans** *pl of* JAPAN, *pres 3d sing of* JAPAN

**japan tea** *n, usu cap J* : unfermented Japanese tea of a light color

**japan tree lilac** *n, usu cap J* : JAPANESE TREE LILAC

**japan varnish** *n, usu cap J* : the natural varnish obtained from the Japanese varnish tree

**japan walnut** *n, usu cap J* : JAPANESE WALNUT

**japan wax** *or* **japan tallow** *n, usu cap J* : a yellowish fat obtained from the berries of sumac (as *Rhus verniciflua*) and used chiefly in polishes and textile finishes

**jap clover** *n, usu cap J* : JAPAN CLOVER

[1]**jape** \ˈjāp\ *vb* -ED/-ING/-S [ME *japen*, perh. fr. MF *japper* to bark at, nag, of imit. origin] *vi* **1** : to say or do something jokingly or mockingly : play tricks : JEER ⟨wondering why you ~ at him⟩ **2** *now chiefly dial* : to have sexual intercourse ~ *vt* : to make mocking fun of : GIBE, TAUNT ⟨*japed* the actors from the balcony⟩

[2]**jape** \"\ *n* -S [ME *jape*, fr. *japen*] : something designed to arouse amusement or laughter: as **a** : an amusing literary or dramatic production ⟨a merry little ~ that was cribbed from a 1940 movie —*Time*⟩ **b** : JOKE, GIBE ⟨volumes of quips, jests, ~*s*, boners, sallies, and bright sayings —Lee Rogow⟩ **c** : a trick played in jest : PRACTICAL JOKE ⟨~*s* and feats of ingenious devilry —Thomas Wood †1950⟩ **syn** see JOKE

**jap·er** \-pə(r)\ *n* -S [ME, fr. *japen* + *-er*] : one that japes; *esp* : a professional jester

**jap·ery** \-p(ə)rē\ *n* -ES [ME *japerie*, fr. *japen* + *-erie* -ery] **1** : jesting talk : JOKES ⟨the patterned wheezes and stylized ~ that have stood them in such good stead during nearly two decades of burlesque —Gladwin Hill⟩ **2** : JOKE, JEST ⟨the sort of man who goes in for flippant *japeries* —*Springfield (Mass.) Union*⟩

[1]**ja·phet·ic** \jəˈfed·ik, (ˈ)ja¦f-\ *adj, usu cap* [*Japheth* (Japetus), one of the sons of Noah in the Bible (Gen 5:32 ff.) + E *-ic*] **1** : relating to or derived from Japheth who was a son of Noah — used vaguely as an ethnological epithet for the Caucasians of Europe and some adjacent parts of Asia **2** : of, relating to, or constituting a group of early non-Indo-European languages in Europe and western Asia assumed by some to form one family with the Caucasian languages and including Basque, Etruscan, Minoan, and sometimes Sumerian and Elamite — compare ASIANIC

[2]**japhetic** \"\ *n* -S *cap* **1** : the Japhetic languages **2** : a Japhetic language

**jap mink** *n, usu cap J* : JAPANESE MINK 2

**japonian** *n* -S *usu cap* [*Japon* (obs. var. of *Japan*) + E *-ian*] *obs* : JAPANESE

**ja·pon·ic** \jəˈpänik, jaˈp-\ *adj, usu cap* [*Japon* + E *-ic*] : JAPANESE

**ja·pon·i·ca** \-nəkə\ *n* -S [NL, fr. fem. of *Japonicus* Japanese, fr. *Japonia* Japan + L *-icus* -ic] **1** : CAMELLIA 2 **2** : JAPANESE QUINCE 2 **3** : CRAPE MYRTLE

**jap·o·nism** \ˈjapə,nizəm\ *n* -S *usu cap* [F *japonisme*, fr. *Japon* Japan + F *-isme* -ism] : JAPANISM

**japs** *pl of* JAP

[1]**ja·pyg·id** \jəˈpijəd\ *adj* [NL *Japygidae*] : of or relating to the family Japygidae

[2]**japygid** \"\ *n* -S : an insect of the family Japygidae

**ja·pyg·i·dae** \-jə,dē\ *n pl, cap* [NL, fr. *Japyg-, Japyx*, type genus + *-idae*] : a family of soil-inhabiting insects (order Entotrophi) with the anal appendages forcepslike rather than filamentous

**ja·pyx** \ˈjāpiks\ *n, cap* [NL, prob. after *Japyx*, mythical founder of Japygia, ancient kingdom in southeastern Italy] : the type genus of the family Japygidae

**ja·qui·ma** \ˈhakəmə\ *n* -S [Sp *jáquima* — more at HACKAMORE] *Southwest* : the headstall of a halter

[1]**jar** \ˈjär, ˈjȧ(r\ *vb* **jarred**; **jarred**; **jarring**; **jars** [prob. of imit. origin] *vi* **1 a** : to make a harsh or discordant sound : GRATE ⟨winced as the iron gate *jarred* against the sidewalk⟩ : RATTLE ⟨an explosion that made the windows ~⟩ **b** : to be out of harmony or in conflict : CLASH — usu. used with *with* ⟨the slapstick tone ~*s* with the underlying seriousness —Leo Marx⟩; *specif* : BICKER ⟨two of the men had been *jarring* at each other . . . — some old feud —Agnes M. Cleaveland⟩ **c** : to have a harshly disagreeable or disconcerting effect ⟨an unexpected pettiness that ~*s*⟩ — often used with *on* or *upon* ⟨resounding harmonies that ~ on unaccustomed ears⟩ ⟨savage expressions that ~ upon the sensitivity of some readers⟩ **2** : to shake or vibrate severely (as from a blow) ⟨bolt had *jarred* loose⟩ ⟨the platform ~*s* as a train rumbles by⟩ ~ *vt* **1** : to cause to jar : affect disagreeably ⟨the din ~*s* her nerves⟩ : shake up ⟨the boat ride will ~ the patient less⟩ : UNSETTLE ⟨the violent opposition *jarred* his resolve⟩ ⟨soldiering had *jarred* men loose from birthplace and habit as nothing else could have done —Dixon Wecter⟩ **2** : to drill (a well) by repeated percussion **3** : to collect or remove (insects) from a plant by jarring or shaking

[2]**jar** \"\ *n* -S **1 a** : a harsh grating sound ⟨the loose floorboard that was lifted with a slight groaning ~ —Arthur Morrison⟩ **b** : a state or manifestation of discord or conflict : CLASH, DISSENSION ⟨except for a ~ in the case of Hyderabad, this revolution has taken place . . . smoothly and peacefully —*White Paper on Indian States*⟩; *esp* : a petty quarrel ⟨heard the loud harsh words of a family ~⟩ **2 a** : a rough shaking (as from a sharp impact) ⟨lenses should be protected from ~*s* and jolts —*Kodak Reference Handbook*⟩ **b** : an unsettling blow (as to the mind or feelings) ⟨gave his nerves the ~ needed to break the habit⟩ ⟨gave a ~ to his composure⟩ **c** : a break or conflict in rhythm, flow, movement, or transition typically rough, abrupt, crude, or disconcerting : an unpleasant discontinuity or incongruity ⟨works persistently, swiftly, without ~ —Sinclair Lewis⟩ **3** : a connecting link between a

well-drill cable and the drilling tool so constructed that when the tool sticks the next upward pull causes a sharp jerk tending to dislodge the tool **syn** see IMPACT

³**jar** \"\ *n* -s [MF *jarre*, fr. OProv *jarra*, fr. Ar *jarrah* earthen water vessel] **1 :** a rigid container having a wide mouth and often no neck and made typically of earthenware or glass ⟨a ~ that had held jam⟩ ⟨a tobacco ~⟩ ⟨an ornamental cold-cream ~⟩ — compare BOTTLE **2 :** JARFUL ⟨buy pickles by the ~⟩ ⟨enough plums to make a dozen ~s of jelly⟩

jar 1

⁴**jar** \"\ *vt* **jarred; jarred; jarring; jars :** to put in a jar; *specif* **:** to preserve (as fruit) by canning in glass jars

⁵**jar** \"\ *n* -s [alter. of earlier *char* — more at CHARE] *archaic* **:** TURN — used esp. in the phrase *on the jar* ⟨the door was on the ~ and, gently opening it, I entered —Henry Brooke⟩

**ja·ra·be** \hə'rä(,)bā\ *n* -s [AmerSp, fr. Sp, syrup, fr. Ar *sharāb* — more at SYRUP] **:** any of several provincial Mexican couple dances (as the hat dance) that have the zapateado as their basic step

**ja·ra·gua** \¦zharə¦gwä\ *or* **jaragua grass** *n* -s [Pg *jaraguá*, fr. Tupi] **:** a tall forage grass (*Hyparrhenia rufa*) native to Brazil but now used elsewhere for hay and forage

¹**ja·ra·na** \hə'ränə\ *n* -s [AmerSp] **1 :** a large Central American manbarklak (*Eschweilera jarana*) with hard heavy durable wood used chiefly for heavy construction **2 :** the salmon pink to reddish brown variegated wood of the jarana

²**jarana** \"\ *n* -s [AmerSp, fr. Sp, fun, merrymaking, trick, deceit, alter. of *harana*, *arana* trick, deceit] **1 :** a couple dance of Yucatan that is performed with waltz and zapateado steps **2 :** a stringed instrument of Mexico resembling a ukulele

**ja·ra·ra·ca** \,zharə'räkə\ *n* -s [Pg, fr. Tupi *jararaca* & Guarani *yararaca*] **:** any of various So. American pit vipers

**ja·ra·ra·cus·su** *or* **ja·ra·ra·cu·çu** \,zharə,räkə'sü\ *n* -s [Pg *jararacuçu*, *jararacuçú*, fr. Tupi *jararaca wassu* & Guarani *yararaca wassu*, lit., big jararaca] **:** a venomous pit viper (*Bothrops jararacussu*) of Brazil that is related to the fer-de-lance

**jar·a·wa** \'jarə,wä\ *n, pl* **jarawa** *or* **jarawas** *usu cap* **1 :** an Andamanese people of So. Andaman Island **2 :** a member of the Jarawa people

**jarbird** \'⸗,⸗\ *n* [²*jar* + *bird*; fr. the noise it makes with its beak on dead branches] **:** a nuthatch (*Sitta caesia*)

**jar·bot** \'järbət\ *n* -s [origin unknown] **:** dilatation of the esophagus in the horse

**jar·di·niere** *or* **jar·di·nière** \¦järdᵊn¦i(ə)r, \|äd-, -dᵊn¦(y)e(ə)r, -iə,-eə *also* ¦zh|\ *n* -s [F *jardinière*, lit., female gardener, fem. of *jardinier* gardener, fr. OF, fr. *jardin* garden (fr. *jart* garden, of Gmc origin; akin to OHG *gart* enclosure) + *-ier* -er — more at YARD] **1 a :** an ornamental stand for plants or flowers **b :** a large round usu. decorative ceramic flowerpot **2 :** a garnish for meat consisting of several vegetables cubed and cooked separately or together

jardiniere 1b

**jar·ed·ite** \'ja(a)rə,dīt\ *n* -s *cap* [*Jared*, the eponymous ancestor of the Jaredites according to the *Book of Mormon* (Ether 1:31 ff) + E *-ite*] **:** one of a group of people that according to Mormon belief settled America after the general dispersal accompanying the confusion of tongues at Babel — compare NEPHITE

**jarfly** \'⸗,⸗\ *n* [²*jar* + *fly*; fr. the harsh whirring noise it produces] **:** CICADA

**jar·ful** \'⸗,fůl\ *n, pl* **jar·fuls** *also* **jars·ful** \'jär,fůlz, 'jä,fůlz, -ärz,fůl, -äz,fůl\ [³*jar* + *-ful*] **:** the quantity held by a jar ⟨mixed several ~s of juice in the bowl⟩

¹**jar·gon** \'järgən, 'jäg- *also* -,gän\ *n* -s [ME *jargoun*, fr. MF *jargon*, prob. of imit. origin] **1 :** chatter or twitter esp. of a bird or animal **2 a :** confused unintelligible language **:** GIBBERISH; *specif* **:** JARGON APHASIA **b :** a strange, outlandish, or barbarous language or dialect ⟨foreign languages were considered rude ~s⟩ **c :** a hybrid language or dialect arising from a mixture of languages that is typically much simplified in vocabulary and grammar (as pidgin English) and is used for communication between peoples of different speech; *specif, usu cap* **:** CHINOOK JARGON — compare LINGUA FRANCA **3 a :** the technical terminology or characteristic idiom of specialists or workers in a particular activity or area of knowledge; *often* **:** a pretentious or unnecessarily obscure and esoteric terminology **b :** a special vocabulary or idiom fashionable in a particular group or clique **4 :** language vague in meaning and full of circumlocutions and long high-sounding words **syn** see DIALECT

²**jargon** \"\ *vi* -ED/-ING/-S [ME *jargounen*, fr. *jargoun*, n.] **1 :** TWITTER, WARBLE ⟨the birds would begin their early-morning ~*ing* —Elizabeth M. Roberts⟩ **2 :** JARGONIZE

**jargon aphasia** *n* **:** the fluent use of words that bear no relation to the meaning intended

**jargon code** *n* **:** a full set of code names for use in otherwise plain language communication in order to conceal persons, things, or actions being discussed ⟨in a *jargon code* of Louis XIII, the pope is referred to as "the rose", Rome as "the garden"⟩

**jar·gon·ist** \'⸗gənəst\ *or* **jar·gon·eer** \¦⸗⸗¦ni(ə)r, -iə\ *n* -s **:** one that is addicted to jargon

**jar·gon·is·tic** \¦⸗⸗¦nistik, -tēk\ *adj* **:** characterized by the use of jargon **:** phrased in jargon

**jar·gon·ize** \'⸗⸗,nīz\ *vb* -ED/-ING/-S *vi* **:** to speak or write jargon ~ *vt* **1 :** to express in jargon **2 :** to make into jargon or into a jargon ⟨developed a *jargonized* form of Dutch in communication with native Africans —Leonard Bloomfield⟩

**jar·goon** \(')jär¦gün, (')jä¦g-\ *or* **jar·gon** \'jär,gän\ *n* -s [F *jargon* — more at ZIRCON] **:** a colorless or pale yellow or smoky zircon

**jarhead** \'⸗,⸗\ *n* [³*jar* + *head*] *chiefly Midland* **:** MULE; *esp* **:** an army mule

**ja·ri·na** \zhə'rēnə\ *n* -s [Pg] **:** IVORY NUT 1

**ja·risch–herx·hei·mer reaction** \'yärish'herks,hīmər-\ *n, usu cap J&H* [after Adolf *Jarisch* †1902 Austrian dermatologist & Karl *Herxheimer* †1944 Ger. dermatologist] **:** HERXHEIMER REACTION

**jark** \'järk\ *n* -s [origin unknown] *archaic* **:** the seal of a counterfeit document

**jark·man** \-mən\ *n, pl* **jarkmen** *archaic* **:** a vagabond counterfeiter of documents (as licenses, passes, certificates)

**jarl** \R 'yär(ə)l, -R 'yäl\ *n* -s [ON — more at EARL] **:** a Scandinavian noble ranking immediately below the king — used also of the chiefs of Orkney and Shetland; compare EARL

¹**jar·less** \'järləs, 'jäl-\ *adj* [²*jar* + *-less*] **:** free from jar ⟨a smooth ~ ride⟩

²**jarless** \"\ *adj* [³*jar* + *-less*] **:** not having or requiring jars ⟨the ~ methods of preserving⟩

**jarl·ite** \'yär,līt\ *n* -s [C. F. *Jarl*, 20th cent. Danish official in the cryolite industry + E *-ite*] **:** a mineral $NaSr_3Al_3F_{16}$ consisting of an alumino-fluoride of sodium and strontium

**jar mill** *n* [²*jar*] **:** a small ball mill for pulverizing plastic materials (as paint)

**jar·mo·ite** \'jär(,)mō,īt\ *n* -s *usu cap* [*Jarmo*, site of a prehistoric town in northeastern Iraq + E *-ite*] **:** a member of a prehistoric people inhabiting the foothills of southern Kurdistan

**ja·rool** \jə'rül\ *n* -s [Hindi *jarūl*] **:** QUEEN'S CRAPE MYRTLE

**ja·ro·site** \jə'rō,sīt, 'jarə,s-\ *n* -s [G *jarosit*, fr. Barranco *Jaroso*, Almería, Spain + G *-it* -ite] **:** an ocher-yellow or brown mineral $KFe_3(SO_4)_2(OH)_6$ consisting of basic sulfate of potassium and iron and occurring in minute rhombohedral crystals or in masses — compare AMMONIOJAROSITE, ARGENTOJAROSITE, NATROJAROSITE, PLUMBOJAROSITE

**jaro·vi·zation** \,yärəvə'zāshən, ,yar-, -,vī'z-\ *n* -s **:** VERNALIZATION

**jaro·vize** *or* **iaro·vize** *or* **yaro·vize** \'⸗⸗,vīz\ *vt* -ED/-ING/-S [Russ *yarovoe* spring grain (fr. *yara* spring) + E *-ize*; akin to Gk *hōra* season — more at HOUR] **:** VERNALIZE

**jar–owl** \'⸗,⸗\ *n* [²*jar*; fr. the harsh noise it makes] **:** a European goatsucker

**jar·rah** \'jarə\ *n* -s [native name in Australia] **1 :** an Australian eucalypt (*Eucalyptus marginata*) with rough bark and ovate leaves **2 :** a red gum (*Eucalyptus rostrata*) **3 :** the wood of jarrah

**jarred** *past of* JAR

**jarring** *pres part of* JAR

**jar·ring·ly** *adv* **:** in a jarring manner ⟨a piano ~ out of tune⟩

**jar·ring·ness** *n* -ES **:** the quality or state of being jarring

**jars** *pres 3d sing of* JAR, *pl of* JAR

**jar·vey** *also* **jar·vie** \'järvē\ *n, pl* **jarveys** *also* **jarvies** [fr. *Jarvey*, nickname for *Jarvis*] **1** *chiefly Irish* **:** the driver of a hackney coach or of a jaunting car **2 :** HACKNEY COACH

**ja·sey** \'jāzē\ *n* -s [prob. alter. of *jersey*] *Brit* **:** a wig made usu. of worsted

**jasi·o·ne** \,ja|sē'ō(,)nē, ,jā|, |zē-\ *n* [NL, fr. Gk *iasiōnē* bindweed] *cap* **:** a genus of European herbs (family Campanulaceae) having alternate leaves and blue flowers in a solitary involucrate head — see SHEEP'S-BIT

**jasm** \'jazəm\ *n* -s [origin unknown] **:** zest for accomplishment **:** DRIVE, ENERGY ⟨you must have ~ if you want to amount to anything in this world —*Linotype News*⟩

**jas·mi·na·ce·ae** \,jazmə'nāsē,ē, -asm-\ [NL, fr. *Jasminum*, type genus + *-aceae*] *syn of* OLEACEAE

**jas·mine** \'jazmən *sometimes* 'jas- *or* 'jaas-\ *or* **jes·sa·mine** \'jes(ə)mən\ *also* **jas·min** *like* JASMINE\ *n* -s [F *jasmin*, fr. Ar *yāsamīn* (colloq. *yāsmīn*), fr. Per] **1 a** (1) **:** any of numerous usu. limber and often climbing shrubs of temperate and warm regions that constitute the genus *Jasminum* and usu. have extremely fragrant flowers (2) *usu jessamine* **:** a tall-climbing semi-evergreen Asiatic shrub (*J. officinale*) with slender shoots and fragrant white flowers from which a perfume is extracted **b :** any of numerous other plants having sweet-scented flowers — usu. used with preceding qualifier ⟨cape ~⟩ ⟨red ~⟩ **c** *usu jessamine* **:** YELLOW JESSAMINE 2 **d :** MATRIMONY VINE **2 a :** a perfume having an odor like that of jasmine **b :** a constituent of such a perfume consisting of jasmine oil or a formulated preparation with a similar odor **3 :** a light yellow that is greener, lighter, and stronger than average maize, redder, stronger, and slightly lighter than popcorn, and redder and slightly deeper than chrome lemon — compare BUTTER YELLOW

jasmine

**jasmine family** *n* **:** OLEACEAE

**jasmine mango** *or* **jasmine tree** *n* **:** FRANGIPANI

**jasmine oil** *n* **:** a fragrant essential oil obtained from flowers of a jasmine (as *Jasminum officinale* or *J. grandiflorum*) and used in perfumery

**jasmine orange** *n* **:** ORANGE JESSAMINE

**jasmine tea** *n* **:** tea scented by being packed with or fired with jasmine flowers — compare SCENTED TEA

**jasminewood** \'⸗⸗,⸗\ *n* **1 :** the fragrant wood of a tree (*Ochna mauritiana*) of Mauritius **2 :** the tree that yields jasminewood

**jasmine yellow** *n* **:** BUTTER YELLOW — compare JASMINE 3

**jas·mi·num** \'jazmənəm, -asm-\ *n, cap* [NL, fr. F *jasmin* jasmine — more at JASMINE] **:** a large genus of tropical chiefly East Indian woody vines or shrubs of the family Oleaceae having mostly pinnate leaves and flowers shaped like salvers

**jas·mone** \'jaz,mōn, -as,m-\ *n* -s [ISV *jasmine* + *-one*] **:** a liquid ketone $C_{11}H_{16}O$ that is derived from cyclopentene, has an odor like that of jasmine, is found esp. in jasmine oil, and is used in perfumery

**jasp** \'jasp\ *n* -s [ME *jaspe* — more at JASPER] *archaic* **:** JASPER

**jas·pa·chate** \'jaspə,kāt\ *or* **jasp·agate** \'jas,pagət\ *n* -s [F & L; F *jaspagate*, fr. L *iaspachates*, fr. Gk *iaspachatēs*, fr. *iaspis* jasper + *achatēs* agate] **:** AGATE JASPER

**jas·pé** \(')zha¦spā, (')ja-\ *adj* [F, fr. past part. of *jasper* to mottle, fr. *jaspe* jasper] **:** resembling jasper in blending of colors **:** clouded in streaks of contrasting colors; *specif* **:** variegated in weaving by the use of warp yarns of differing shades together with single-color filling yarns

¹**jas·per** \'jaspə(r), -aas-, -ais- *sometimes* -ȧs-\ *n* -s [ME *jaspre*, *jaspe*, fr. MF *jaspre*, *jaspe*, fr. L *jaspis*, fr. Gk *iaspis*, of Sem origin; akin to Ar *yashb* jasper, Heb *yāshpheh*] **1 :** an opaque cryptocrystalline quartz of any of several colors (as red, brown, green, yellow) ⟨the wall was built of ~, while the city was pure gold, clear as glass —Rev 21:18 (RSV)⟩; *esp* **:** green chalcedony ⟨one block, pure green as a pistachio nut, there's plenty ~ somewhere in the world —Robert Browning⟩ **2 :** a hard fine-grained ceramic ware containing a high percentage of barium salts and ordinarily stained (as blue or green) with metallic oxides and decorated with sprigged ornamentation **3 :** a blackish green that is bluer than cannon — compare JASPER GREEN

²**jasper** \"\ *adj* **1 :** relating to or composed of jasper **2 :** PEPPER-AND-SALT

³**jasper** \"\ *n* -s [fr. the name *Jasper*] **:** FELLOW, GUY ⟨aim to stay sober . . . till I work that ~ over —Ross Santee⟩

**jasper bar** *n* [¹*jasper*] **:** ¹BAR 8

**jas·pered** \-pə(r)d\ *adj, archaic* **:** of mottled or variegated color **:** SPECKLED

**jasper green** *n* **:** a moderate green that is yellower and paler than sea green (sense 1a), bluer and paler than myrtle (sense 3a), and bluer, lighter, and stronger than average laurel green (sense 1) — compare JASPER

**jas·per·ize** \-pə,rīz\ *vt* -ED/-ING/-S **:** to convert into or make to resemble jasper

¹**jas·per·oid** \-,rȯid\ *adj* [¹*jasper* + *-oid*] **:** resembling jasper

²**jasperoid** \"\ *n* -s **:** ¹JASPER 1

**jasper opal** *n* **:** a yellow opal resembling jasper

**jasper pink** *n* **:** a strong yellowish pink that is redder and darker than salmon pink, redder and deeper than melon, and redder than peach red

**jasper red** *n* **:** a moderate red that is yellower and paler than cerise, claret (sense 3a), average strawberry (sense 2a), or Turkey red and lighter and stronger than pepper red — called also *old coral*

**jasper slip** *or* **jasper stone** *n* **:** a slip or stone of reddish quartz that is used in polishing watch parts

**jas·per·ware** \'⸗⸗,⸗\ *n* **:** JASPER 2

**jas·pery** \-p(ə)rē, -ri\ *adj* **:** of, resembling, or containing jasper

**jas·pid·e·an** \(')ja¦spidēən\ *or* **jas·pid·e·ous** \-ēəs\ *adj* [L *jaspid-*, *jaspis* jasper + E *-ean*, *-eous* — more at JASPER] **:** JASPERY

**jas·pi·lite** *also* **jas·pi·lyte** \'jaspə,līt\ *n* -s [¹*jasper* + *-i-* + *-lite* or *-lyte*] **:** a compact siliceous rock rich in hematite and resembling jasper

**jas·pis** \'jaspəs\ *n* -ES [ME, fr. L — more at JASPER] **:** JASPER 1

**jas·po·nyx** \'jaspə(,)niks, -,späniks\ *n* -ES [L *iasponyx*, fr. Gk, fr. *iaspis* jasper + *onyx* — more at ONYX] **:** an onyx part or all of whose layers consist of jasper

**jasp·opal** \'ja,spōpəl\ *n* [by contr.] **:** JASPER OPAL

**jasps** *pl of* JASP

**jass** \'yäs\ *n* -ES [G dial. (Switzerland)] **1 a :** a two-handed game played with a 36-card or 32-card pack in which points are scored by melding certain combinations and by taking scoring cards in tricks **b :** KLABERJASS **2** *or* **jasz** \"\ **:** the jack of trumps as top card in jass or klaberjass

**jas·sach·ni** \jə'säknē\ *n, pl* **jassachni** *or* **jassachnis** *usu cap* **1 :** a Buryat people of southern Transbaikalia in Siberia **2 :** a member of the Jassachni people

¹**jas·sid** \'jasəd\ *adj* [NL *Jassidae*] **:** of or relating to the Jassidae

²**jassid** \"\ *n* -s **:** a leafhopper of the family Jassidae; *broadly* **:** LEAFHOPPER

**jas·si·dae** \'jasə,dē\ *n pl, cap* [NL, fr. *Jassus*, type genus (fr. L *Iassus*, *Iasus*, ancient town in southwestern Asia Minor, fr. Gk *Iassos*, *Iasos*) + *-idae*] **:** a family of leafhoppers: **a** *in some classifications* **:** a family coextensive with Cicadellidae **b :** a large cosmopolitan family of small usu. slender leafhoppers that have the ocelli near the margin of the vertex and that include many economically significant pests of cultivated plants some of which (as the beet leafhopper) transmit plant diseases — compare TETTIGELLIDAE

**ja·ssy** \'yäsē\ *adj, usu cap* [fr. *Jassy* (*Iaşi*), Romania] **:** IASI

**ja·sus** \'jāsəs\ *n, cap* [NL, fr. L *Iassus*, *Iasus* ancient town] **:** a genus of spiny lobsters including the Cape crawfish

**jat** \'jät\ *n* -s *usu cap* [Hindi *jāṭ*] **1 :** an Indo-Aryan people of the Punjab and Uttar Pradesh **2 :** a member of the Jat people

**ja·ta·co** \hə'tä(,)kō\ *n* -s [AmerSp] **:** an amaranth (*Amaranthus caudatus*) sometimes used as a food plant in tropical America

**ja·ta·ka** \'jädəkə\ *n* -s *usu cap* [Skt *jātaka*, fr. *jāta* born, fr. *janati* he begets — more at KIN] **:** any of some 550 birth stories or narratives of former incarnations of Gautama Buddha collected in Buddhist sacred writings

**jat·eo·rhi·za** \,jad·ēō'rīzə\ [NL, fr. Gk *iatēr*, *iatēs* physician + NL *-o-* + *-rhiza*] *syn of* JATRORRHIZA

**ja·tha** \jə'tä\ *n* -s [Panjabi *jathā*] **:** an armed band or organized company esp. of Sikhs

**jat·ki** \'jätkē\ *n* -s *cap* **:** a dialect of Lahnda

**jat·ni** \'jätnē\ *n* -s *usu cap* [Hindi *jāṭnī*, fr. *jāṭ*] **:** a female Jat

**JATO** \'jād·(,)ō, -ā(,)tō\ *abbr, often not cap* jet-assisted takeoff

**ja·to·be** \,'zhad·ə¦bā\ *n* -s [Pg *jatobá*, fr. Tupi] **:** COURBARIL

**jato unit** *n* **:** a unit for assisting the takeoff of an airplane consisting of one or more rocket engines that are usu. discarded after the fuel has been consumed

**jat·ro·gua** \'ja·trəfə\ *n, cap* [NL, fr. Gk *iatros* physician + *trophē* food, fr. *trephein* to nourish — more at ATROPHY] **:** a widely distributed mainly tropical American genus of herbs, shrubs, and trees (family Euphorbiaceae) usu. having lobed leaves and inconspicuous cymose flowers — see PHYSIC NUT

**ja·troph·ic** \jə'träfik\ *adj* [NL *Jatropha* + E *-ic*] **:** of or relating to physic nuts

**jat·ror·rhi·za** \,ja·trə'rīzə\ *n, cap* [NL, fr. *jatro-* (var. of *iatr-*) + *-rhiza*] **:** a genus of woody vines (family Menispermaceae) of eastern Africa and Mauritius having lobed leaves and long loose racemes of flowers — see CALUMBA

**jat·ror·rhi·zine** \,ja·trə'rī,zēn, -īzᵊn\ *or* **jat·eo·rhi·zine** \,jad·ēō'r-\ *n* -s [ISV *jatrorrhiz-*, *jateorhiz-* (fr. NL *Jatrorrhiza* or *Jateorhiza*, genus name of *Jatrorrhiza palmata* or *Jateorhiza palmata*) + *-ine*] **:** an alkaloid $C_{20}H_{21}NO_5$ that occurs in calumba and is related in structure to berberine

**jaud** \'jȯd, 'jäd\ *Scot var of* JADE

**jau·die** \-di\ *n* -s [alter. of ME *chaudoun*, *chaudern* — more at CHAWDRON] **1** *chiefly Scot* **:** edible entrails; *esp* **:** a pig's stomach **2** *chiefly Scot* **:** a pudding made of jaudie

**jaug** \'jȯg, 'jäg\ *Scot var of* JAG

**jauk** \'jȯk, 'jäk\ *vi* -ED/-ING/-S [ME (Sc dial.) *jaken*] *Scot* **:** DALLY, DAWDLE

**jau·ling·ite** \'yaůliŋ,īt\ *n* -s [G *jaulingit*, fr. the *Jauling*, Austria + G *-it*] **:** a fossil resin high in oxygen content

**jaun** \'jän, -ȯ-, -ȧ-\ *n* -s [Beng *jān*, fr. Skt *yāna* going, vehicle — more at HINAYANA] **:** a small Calcutta palanquin

¹**jaunce** \'jȯn(t)s, -ä-,-ȧ-\ *vi* -ED/-ING/-S [origin unknown] *archaic* **:** PRANCE ⟨spurgalled and tired by *jauncing* Bolingbroke —Shak.⟩

²**jaunce** \"\ *n* -s *now dial Eng* **:** a tiring jaunt or journey

**jaun·der** \'jȯndər, 'jän-\ *vi* -ED/-ING/-S [origin unknown] *Scot* **:** PRATTLE, GABBLE

**jaun·ders** \'jȯndə(r)z, 'jän-,'jan-,'jaan-,'jän-\ *dial var of* JAUNDICE

¹**jaun·dice** \'jȯndəs, 'jän-,'jän- *chiefly dial* 'jan- *or* 'jaan- *or* -də(r)z\ *n* -s [ME *jaunis*, *jaundis*, fr. MF *jaunisse*, fr. *jaune* yellow (fr. L *galbinus* yellowish green, fr. *galbus* yellow) + *-isse* -ice] **1 :** yellowish pigmentation of the skin, tissues, and certain body fluids caused by the deposition of bile pigments that follows interference with normal production and discharge of bile (as in certain liver diseases) or excessive breakdown of red blood cells (as after internal hemorrhage or in various hemolytic states) **2 :** a disease or abnormal condition that is characterized by jaundice: as **a :** INFECTIOUS HEPATITIS 1 **b :** LEPTOSPIROSIS **c :** TOXEMIC JAUNDICE **3 :** a state or attitude characterized by satiety, distaste, or hostility ⟨looked at me with some ~ in her eye —Kenneth Roberts⟩ **4 :** GRASSERIE

²**jaundice** \"\ *vt* -ED/-ING/-S **:** to affect with envy, hostility, or distaste **:** PREJUDICE ⟨my own experience, as a minor poet, may have *jaundiced* my outlook —T.S.Eliot⟩

**jaundice berry** *n* [so called fr. its use as a remedy for jaundice] **:** the fruit of a barberry (*Berberis vulgaris*)

**jaundiced** *adj* **1 a :** yellowed by or as if by jaundice ⟨all looks yellow to the ~ eye —Alexander Pope⟩ **b :** YELLOW ⟨barred windows with ~ borders —John Ruskin⟩ **2 :** exhibiting or affected by envy, distaste, or hostility ⟨long ago looked with a ~ eye on the growth of regimentation —Irwin Edman⟩

**jaundice root** *n* **:** GOLDENSEAL

**jaune bril·lant** *also* **jaune bril·liant** \¦zhōnbrē¦(y)äⁿ\ *n, pl* **jaunes brillants** \-äⁿ(z)\ [F *jaune brillant*, lit., brilliant yellow] **:** any of several yellow pigments used esp. as artists' colors: as **a :** NAPLES YELLOW 1a **b :** cadmium sulfide either alone or in a mixture (as cadmium yellow)

¹**jaunt** \'jȯnt, -ä-,-ȧ-, *chiefly dial* -a- *or* -aa-\ *vi* -ED/-ING/-S [origin unknown] **1** *archaic* **:** to trudge or trip tediously about ⟨catch my death with ~*ing* up and down —Shak.⟩ **2 :** to make a usu. short journey (as an excursion) for pleasure ⟨~ through orchards and gardens —*Newsweek*⟩

²**jaunt** \"\ *n* -s **1** *archaic* **:** a difficult or tiring trip or journey ⟨a very long and troublesome ~ —George Washington⟩ **2 :** an excursion undertaken for pleasure ⟨a ~ to the shore or the hills —F.L.Allen⟩

**jaun·ti·ly** \'jȯntᵊlē, 'jän-,'jän-, -tə̇l|, |i, *chiefly dial & archaic* 'jan- *or* 'jaan-\ *adv* **:** in a light or carefree manner **:** AIRILY ⟨~ concluded that life was an affliction —Harry Levin⟩

**jaun·ti·ness** \-tēnəs, -tin-\ *n* -ES **:** the quality or state of being jaunty **:** SPRIGHTLINESS, UNCONCERN ⟨the synthetic optimism, the false ~ —Bruce Bliven b. 1889⟩

**jaunting car** *also* **jaunty car** *n, Irish* **:** a light horse-drawn two-wheeled open vehicle with seats placed lengthwise either face-to-face or back to back — called also *outside car*, *sidecar*

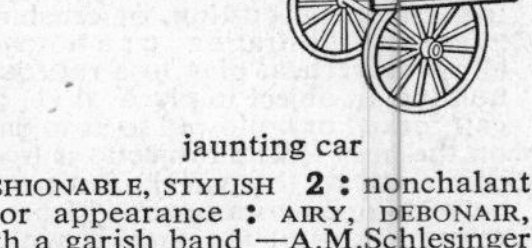
jaunting car

**jaunt·ing·ly** *adv* **:** JAUNTILY

¹**jaun·ty** \-tē,-ti\ *adj* -ER/-EST [alter. of earlier *jentee*, fr. F *gentil* — more at GENTLE] **1** *archaic* **a :** GENTEEL **b :** FASHIONABLE, STYLISH **2 :** nonchalant or sprightly in manner or appearance **:** AIRY, DEBONAIR, PERKY ⟨a ~ straw hat with a garish band —A.M.Schlesinger b. 1917⟩ ⟨a shrewdly ~ optimist —H.E.Clurman⟩ ⟨such writing jars with its ~ banality —C.C.Abbott⟩

²**jaun·ty** \'jȯnti, 'jän-\ *n* -ES [perh. modif. of F *gendarme* — more at GENDARME] *Brit* **:** the master-at-arms aboard a naval vessel

¹**jaup** \'jȯp, 'jäp\ *vb* -ED/-ING/-S [prob. of imit. origin] *chiefly Scot* **:** SPLASH, SPATTER

²**jaup** \"\ *n* -s *chiefly Scot* **:** a splash or spatter esp. of dirty water

¹**java** \'jävə, 'javə, 'jȧvə\ *adj, usu cap* [fr. *Java*, island in Indonesia] **:** of or from the island of Java **:** of the kind or style prevalent in Java **:** JAVANESE

²**java** \", *in sense 1 usu* 'java\ *n* -s **1** -s *often cap* **:** COFFEE ⟨the boys came down and found me crying into my ~ —John Dos Passos⟩ **2** *usu cap* **a :** a breed of large general-purpose domestic fowls developed in America from oriental stock **b** -s **:** a bird of this breed

**java almond** *n, usu cap J* **1 :** a large East Indian tree (*Canarium commune*) that has large unequally pinnate leaves and white flowers in clustered terminal panicles followed by ovoid drupaceous fruits and that is a source of elemi **2 :** the rich oily seed of the Java almond that is used as food and as a source of cooking and illuminating oils but having an integument that causes diarrhea

**java bean** *n, usu cap J* **:** a strain or race of the sieva bean grown in southeastern Asia but dangerous as a feed because of the presence of a cyanogenetic glucoside in the seeds

**java black rot** *or* **java dry rot** *n, usu cap J* **:** a storage disease of the sweet potato caused by a fungus (*Diplodia tubericola*) that makes the inside of a root black and brittle

**java citronella oil** *n, usu cap J* **:** CITRONELLA OIL b

**java cotton** *n, usu cap J* **:** KAPOK

**java grass** *n, usu cap J* **:** a grass (*Polytrias praemorsa*) found in the West Indies and cultivated in Panama and in some parts of the U. S. as a lawn grass
**java jute** *n, usu cap 1st J* **:** KENAF
**javali** *var of* JABALÍ
**java man** *n, usu cap J* **:** either of two prehistoric men of primitive form (*Pithecanthropus erectus* and *P. robustus*) known chiefly from more or less fragmentary skulls found in Trinil, Java — called also *Trinil man*
**¹javan** \ˈjävən, ˈjav-,ˈjäv-\ *adj, usu cap* [*Java*, island in Indonesia + E *-an*] **:** JAVANESE
**²javan** \"\ *n* -s *cap* **:** a native or inhabitant of Java
**¹java·nese** \ˌjavəˈnēz, ˌjäv-, ˌjäv-, -ēs\ *adj, usu cap* [*Java* + *-nese* (as in *Japanese*)] **1 a :** of, relating to, or characteristic of Java **b :** of, relating to, or characteristic of the Javanese **2 :** of, relating to, or characteristic of the Javanese language
**²javanese** \"\ *n, pl* **javanese** *usu cap* **1 a :** an Indonesian people inhabiting mainly the island of Java **b :** a member of such people **2 :** an Austronesian language of the Javanese people — compare MADURESE, SUNDANESE
**javanese skunk** *n, usu cap J* **:** TELEDU
**javan ox** *n, usu cap J* **:** a domesticated banteng of Java
**javan peacock** *or* **javan peafowl** *n, usu cap J* **:** a peafowl (*Pavo muticus*) of southeastern Asia in which the plumage is predominantly metallic green with ocellations and markings of blue and coppery yellow — compare INDIAN PEACOCK
**javan rhinoceros** *n, usu cap J* **:** a small one-horned rhinoceros (*Rhinoceros sondaicus*) of Java, Sumatra, and the Indian region west to Calcutta
**javan squirrel** *n, usu cap J* **:** JELERANG
**javan·thro·pus** \jəˈvan(t)thrəpəs; ˌjäˌvanˈthrōpəs, ˌja-, ˌjä-\ *n, cap* [NL, fr. *Java* + *-anthropus*] *in some classifications* **:** a genus of Hominidae comprising the Solo man
**java pepper** *n, usu cap J* **:** a climbing or somewhat arborescent East Indian pepper (*Piper cubeba*) that is sometimes cultivated for its fruits which are the source of cubeb
**java plum** *n, usu cap J* **:** a large tree (*Eugenia jambolana*) that is found chiefly in the East Indies and Australia and has strongly astringent seeds and bark used as a drug in India
**java skull** *n, usu cap J* **:** the skull of Java man
**java sparrow** *n, usu cap J* **:** a weaverbird (*Padda oryzivora*) that is native to Java, has glaucous gray and black upper parts, pinkish underparts, white cheeks, and large pink bill, resembles a finch, and is a common cage bird
**java tea** *n, usu cap J* **1 a :** the dried leaves of an East Indian mint (*Orthosiphon stamineus*) from which a powerful diuretic is obtained **b :** the mint that bears such leaves **2 :** any of several black teas grown in Java or resembling those grown there
**java teak** *n, usu cap J* **:** TEAK 1
**ja·vé** \ˈyä(ˌ)vā, ˈyä-, -ve\ *cap, var of* YAHWEH
**jav·el** \ˈjavəl\ *n* -s [ME *javel, javell*] *archaic* **:** a vagabond or worthless fellow
**ja·vel green** \(ˈ)zhaˈ|vel, zhəˈ|\ *n, often cap J* [*javel (water)*] **:** a moderate greenish yellow that is greener and duller than citron yellow and greener and deeper than linden green — called also *eau de Javel green*
**¹jav·e·lin** \ˈjav(ə)lən\ *n* -s [MF *javeline*, alter. of *javelot*, of Celt origin; akin to W *gaflach* spear, OIr *gabul* forked stick, fork — more at GAFFLE] **1 a :** a light spear cast usu. by hand as a weapon of war or in hunting wild boar and other big game **b** *archaic* **:** a long-shafted combat weapon (as a pike) tipped with metal and used for thrusting **2** *or* **javelin man :** a man armed with a javelin; *esp* **:** a javelin-bearing member of the escort of an English judge **3 a :** a slender shaft of wood not less than 260 centimeters long, tipped with iron or steel, and intended to be thrown for distance as an athletic feat or exercise **b** *or* **javelin throw :** an athletic field event in which a javelin is thrown for distance **4** *or* **javelin formation :** a formation of military airplanes (as bombers) in which the elements fly one behind the other in line though not always at the same altitude
**²javelin** \"\ *vt* -ED/-ING/-S **1 :** to pierce with or as if with a javelin ⟨lightning ~*s* the hills⟩ **2 :** to throw or hurl like a javelin ⟨pieces of tin and board stuck in the mud where they had been ~*ed* by the heavy explosions —H.D.Skidmore⟩
**javelina** *var of* JABALINA
**javelin bat** *n* **:** a large carnivorous spearnose bat (*Phyllostomus hastatus*) of tropical America distinguished by a triangular prolongation of the nose leaf
**jav·e·lin·eer** \ˌjav(ə)ləˈni(ə)r, -iə\ *n* -s **:** a soldier armed with a javelin
**ja·velle water** *or* **ja·vel water** \(ˈ)zhaˈ|vel, zhəˈ|\ *n, usu cap J* [*Javel*, former town now included in Paris, France; trans. of F *eau de Javel, eau de Javelle*] **:** either of two aqueous solutions of hypochlorite used as a disinfectant or a bleaching agent and in photography: **a :** a solution of potassium hypochlorite now little used **b :** a solution of sodium hypochlorite
**ja·vell·iza·tion** \ˌzhaˌveləˈzāshən\ *n* -s [*Javelle (water)* + *-ization*] **:** chlorination of water with Javelle water
**jav·er** \ˈjavə(r)\ *dial var of* JABBER
**¹jaw** \ˈjȯ\ *n* -s [ME *jow, jowe, jaw, jawe*, prob. fr. MF *joe, joue* cheek] **1 a :** either of two complex cartilaginous or bony structures in most vertebrates that border the mouth, support the soft parts enclosing it, and usu. bear teeth on their oral margin comprising (1) an upper more or less firmly fused with the skull and (2) a lower hinged, movable, and articulated by a pair of condyles with the temporal bone of either side — called also respectively (1) *upper jaw, maxilla*, (2) *lower jaw, mandible* **b :** the bones, muscles, nerves, and other parts constituting the walls of the mouth and serving to open and close it — usu. used in pl. **c :** any of various organs of invertebrates that perform the function (as the biting or masticating of food) of the vertebrate jaws — compare CHELICERA, MANDIBLE 2, MASTAX **2 :** something resembling the jaw of an animal in form or action: as **a :** one of the sides of a narrow opening (as of a gorge) **b :** either of two or more opposing parts (as of a vise, measuring machine, pair of pliers, stone crusher) movable so as to open and close for holding, grasping, clamping, cutting, or crushing something between them — see VISE illustration **c :** a notched or forked part (as a guide allowing vertical play to a railroad-car axle box) adapted for holding an object in place **d** (1) **:** the inner end of a boom or gaff forked or hollowed so as to partly encircle and move freely on the mast (2) **:** projections from a yard at the slings often connected by the parrel **3 a :** a space lying between or as if between open jaws ⟨escaped from out of the ~*s* of the whale⟩ ⟨close the ~ of the shackle with a bolt⟩ **b :** a position or situation in which one is threatened (as with death) ⟨rode into the ~*s* of danger⟩ **4** *slang* **a :** TALK ⟨no time for ~⟩; *esp* **:** impudent or offensive talk **:** SCOLDING ⟨hold your ~ and be off⟩ ⟨don't have to take any of his ~⟩ **b :** a friendly talk **:** CHAT ⟨looked up his friend and had a good long ~⟩ **5 :** the pitch of a helix formed by a strand of a rope ⟨soft-laid, tarred hemp, 3-stranded with rather long ~ —C.W.T.Layton⟩
**²jaw** \"\ *vb* -ED/-ING/-S *vt* **1 :** to exercise the jaws upon ⟨~*ed* her bubble gum⟩ **2** *slang* **:** to scold at ⟨~*ed* him all evening about the accident⟩ **3** *slang* **:** to talk at tiresomely ⟨~ the customer till his resistance is broken down⟩ ~ *vi* **1 :** to speak abusively or indignantly and at length ⟨left when she began ~*ing* at him⟩ ⟨quit ~*ing* about it⟩ **2 :** to talk at length **:** CHAT, GAB ⟨~*ed* together all day about old times⟩ **syn** see SCOLD
**³jaw** \"\ *n* -s [origin unknown] *chiefly Scot* **:** WAVE, SPLASH
**⁴jaw** \"\ *vt* -ED/-ING/-S *chiefly Scot* **:** to throw (liquid) in quantity
**ja·wab** \jəˈwäb, -wȯb\ *n* -s [Hindi *jawāb*, fr. Ar] **:** a building (as the false mosque of the Taj Mahal) erected to correspond to or balance another
**jaw·ba·tion** \jȯˈbāshən\ *n* -s [alter. (influenced by ¹*jaw*) of *jobation*] *dial Eng* **:** a long tiresome reproof **:** JAWING
**jaw bit** *n, chiefly Brit* **:** a bar across the jaws of a pedestal underneath an axle box of a railway car
**jawbone** \ˈ≈,≈\ *n* **1 :** JAW 1a; *esp* **:** MANDIBLE **2** *slang* **:** CREDIT, TRUST ⟨got his winter's supplies on ~⟩ ⟨prohibit further ~ at post exchanges —*Newsweek*⟩
**jawbreaker** \ˈ≈,≈≈\ *n* **1 :** a word difficult to pronounce **2 :** a round hard candy made from sugar syrup **3 :** JAW CRUSHER
**jawbreaking** \ˈ≈,≈≈\ *adj* **:** difficult to pronounce ⟨a foreign city with a ~ name⟩ — **jaw·break·ing·ly** *adv*
**jaw clutch** *n* **1 :** DOG CLUTCH **2** *also* **jaw coupling :** CLAW CLUTCH
**jaw crusher** *n* **:** a machine for crushing rock or ore between two heavy steel jaws
**jawed** \ˈjȯd\ *adj* [¹*jaw* + *-ed*] **:** having a specified kind of jaw — usu. used in combination ⟨lean-*jawed*⟩ ⟨lantern-*jawed*⟩
**jawfish** \ˈ≈,≈\ *n* **:** a fish of the percoid family Opisthognathidae comprising tropical marine fishes with a single dorsal fin, a single lateral line, and very large mouth
**jawfoot** \ˈ≈,≈\ *n* **:** MAXILLIPED
**jawhole** \ˈ≈,≈\ *n* [⁴*jaw* + *hole*] *Scot* **:** SEWER, CESSPOOL
**jawing** *pres part of* JAW
**jaw·less** \ˈjȯləs\ *adj* **:** having no jaw
**jawless fish** *n* **:** any of the primitive vertebrates comprising the superclass Agnatha
**jawlike** \ˈ≈,≈\ *adj* **:** resembling a jaw or pair of jaws in appearance, function, or action
**jawline** \ˈ≈,≈\ *n* **:** the outline of the lower jaw as a facial feature
**jaw rope** *n* **:** a rope holding the jaws of a gaff to the mast **:** PARREL
**jaws** *pl of* JAW, *pres 3d sing of* JAW
**jaw sealer** *n* **:** a machine for sealing flexible package materials by applying pressure with heated bars movable by jaw action
**jawsmith** \ˈ≈,≈\ *n* **:** a professional talker **:** DEMAGOGUE
**¹jay** \ˈjā\ *n* -s [ME, fr. MF *jai*, fr. LL *gaius*, prob. fr. the name *Gaius*] **1 a :** a predominantly fawn-colored Old World bird (*Garrulus glandarius*) with a black-and-white crest and wings marked with black, white, and blue **b :** any of numerous typically brightly colored and frequently largely blue birds that with the common Old World jay constitute a subfamily of the family Corvidae, are distinguished from the related crows by smaller size, more arboreal habits, and frequently by possession of an elongated tail and a definite crest, have roving habits, pugnacious ways, and harsh voices, and are often destructive to the eggs and young of other birds — see BLUE JAY, CANADA JAY **2 a :** an impertinent chatterer **b :** a gaudily or flashily dressed person **:** WANTON, DANDY **c :** a person lacking experience (as in city ways) or polish **:** an unsophisticated, countrified, or gullible person **:** GREENHORN, RUBE **3** *or* **jay blue :** a moderate blue that is greener and duller than average copen, redder and slightly duller than azurite blue, redder and duller than Dresden blue, and redder and paler than bluebird
**²jay** \"\ *adj* -ER/-EST **:** unsophisticated or countrified in character **:** BACKWARD, UNSKILLED, RUSTIC ⟨~*er* than a real hick⟩
**³jay** \ˈjā\ *n* -s **:** the letter *j*
**jaybird** \ˈ≈,≈\ *n, chiefly Midland* **:** JAY 1, 2 ⟨naked as a ~⟩
**jaycee** \ˈ≈ˈ≈\ *n* -s *usu cap* [³*jay* + *cee* (letter); fr. the initials of *junior chamber*] **:** a member of a junior chamber of commerce
**jaygee** \ˈ≈ˈ≈\ *n* -s [³*jay* + *gee* (the letter); fr. the initials of *junior grade*] **:** LIEUTENANT JUNIOR GRADE
**¹jayhawk** \ˈ≈,≈\ *n* [¹*jay* + *hawk*] **1 :** JAYHAWKER **2 :** a fictitious bird with a large beak used as an emblem in Kansas
**²jayhawk** \"\ *vt* -ED/-ING/-S **:** to make a predatory attack on **:** RAID
**jay·hawk·er** \"ə(r)\ *n* **1 a** *often cap* **:** a member of one of the bands of antislavery guerrillas of the Kansas border in raids on Missouri before and during the Civil War **b :** a member of one of the bands of outlaws engaged in raiding in the West following the Civil War **2** *usu cap* **:** KANSAN — used as a nickname
**jaypie** \ˈ≈,≈\ *or* **jaypiet** \ˈ≈,≈≈\ *n* [¹*jay* + *pie, piet*] **1 :** a European jay **2** *dial Eng* **:** MISTLE THRUSH
**jay teal** *n, dial Eng* **:** a European teal (*Nettion crecca*)
**jayvee** \ˈ≈ˈ≈\ *n* -s [³*jay* + *vee* (the letter); fr. the initials of *junior varsity*] **1 :** JUNIOR VARSITY **2 :** a member of a junior varsity team — usu. used in pl.
**jaywalk** \ˈ≈,≈\ *vi* [¹*jay* + *walk*] **:** to cross a street carelessly or at an unusual or inappropriate place or in a dangerous or illegal direction so as to be endangered by the traffic — **jay·walker** \ˈ≈,≈≈\ *n*
**jaz·er·ant** \ˈjazərənt\ *also* **jaz·er·an** \-n\ *n* -s [ME *jesseraunt*, fr. MF *jaseran, jazerenc*, fr. Ar. *jazā'irī* Algerian, fr. *al-Jazā'ir* Algiers] **1 :** a coat of armor made of small overlapping metal plates usu. mounted on linen or other lining **2 :** armor of the jazerant type
**jaz·y·ges** \ˈjazəˌjēz, -ˌgēz\ *n, pl* **jazyges** *usu cap* [L *Jazyges, Iazyges*, fr. Gk *Iazyges*] **1 :** a Sarmatian people orig. occupying the shores of the Black sea **2 :** a member of the Jazyges people
**¹jazz** \ˈjaz, -aa(ə)-\ *vb* -ED/-ING/-ES [origin unknown] *vt* **1 :** to copulate with — usu. considered vulgar **2 a :** to increase the appeal or excitement of **:** ENLIVEN, POPULARIZE ⟨the newsman who ~*es* a story to sell himself to editor and public —C.K. Streit⟩ — usu. used with *up* ⟨drank bootleg gin to ~ me up —J.D.Hart⟩ **b :** to increase the speed of **:** ACCELERATE ⟨~ the motor⟩ **3 :** to play (music) in the manner of jazz **:** make jazz of ⟨pep up old tunes by ~*ing* them⟩ ~ *vi* **1 :** COPULATE — usu. considered vulgar **2 :** to go seeking pleasure **:** GAD — used with *around* **3 a :** to dance or perform jazz ⟨~*ing* to the music of the band⟩ ⟨a saxophonist who ~*es* at a nightclub⟩ **b :** to dance around in a jazzy manner ⟨chairs and tables . . . ~*ing* crazily to and fro across the cabin —Shevawn Lynam⟩
**²jazz** \"\ *n* -ES **1 :** COPULATION — usu. considered vulgar **2 a :** American music developed from religious and secular songs (as spirituals, shout songs), blues, ragtime, and other popular music (as brass-band marches) and characterized by improvisation, syncopated rhythms, contrapuntal ensemble playing, special melodic features (as flatted notes, blue notes) peculiar to the individual interpretation of the player, and the introduction of vocal techniques (as portamento) into instrumental performance — see BOP, DIXIELAND; compare SWING **b :** popular dance music influenced by jazz and played (as in the late 1920s) in a loud rhythmic manner **c :** a dance to jazz music with incisive rhythms and often acrobatic and grotesque steps — compare JITTERBUG 1 **3 :** excessively earnest and enthusiastic talk or preoccupation **:** stuffy foolishness ⟨BUNKUM ⟨spouted all the scientific ~ at him —Pete Martin⟩
**³jazz** \"\ *adj* [²*jazz*] **1 :** of, relating to, or having the characteristics of jazz ⟨~ music⟩ ⟨~ fans⟩ **2 :** MOTTLED ⟨the room will be done in ~ colors —Upton Sinclair⟩
**jazz ballet** *n* **:** a ballet or dance performance in jazz style
**jazzbow** \ˈ≈,≈\ *n* **:** a ready-made bow tie
**jazz·i·ly** \-zəlē, -li\ *adv* **:** in a jazzy manner
**jazz·i·ness** \-zēnəs, -zin-\ *n* -ES **:** the quality or state of being jazzy
**jazz·ist** \-zəst\ *n* -s **:** a lover of jazz
**jazz·man** \-zmən, -zˌman\ *n, pl* **jazzmen :** a performer of jazz
**jazzy** \-zē, -zi\ *adj* -ER/-EST **1 :** having the character of jazz ⟨loud fast ~ music⟩ **2 :** of an unrestrained, animated, or flashy character ⟨a ~ good-time city⟩ ⟨tuned out the highbrow program for something more ~⟩ ⟨a ~ Hawaiian shirt⟩
**JB** *abbr* **1** joint board **2** joint bond **3** junction box
**j–bar lift** \ˈ≈,≈ ~\ *or* **j–bar** \ˈ≈,≈\ *n, cap J* **:** a ski tow consisting of an overhead moving cable carrying a series of suspended bars of J shape on the base of which skiers may half sit and half lean while being pulled uphill
**j boat** *n, usu cap J* **1 :** a large yacht of the 76-foot rating class **2 :** a small sailboat raced by children
**j bolt** *n, cap J* **:** a bolt the shape of the letter J with threads usu. only on the longer leg
**j–box** \ˈ≈,≈\ *n, cap J* **:** a container having the form of an upright J through which a textile is passed in a wet finishing process (as bleaching)
**jc** *abbr* junction
**JC** *abbr* **1** [L *jurisconsultus*] jurisconsult **2** justice clerk **3** junior court
**JCB** *abbr or n* -s [L *juris canonici baccalaureus*] **:** a bachelor of canon law
**JCD** *abbr or n* -s [L *juris canonici doctor*] **:** a doctor of canon law
**JCL** *abbr or n* -s [L *juris canonici licentiatus*] **:** a licentiate in canon law
**JC of C** *abbr* junior chamber of commerce
**JCR** *abbr* junior common room
**JCS** *abbr* joint chiefs of staff
**jct** *or* **jctn** *abbr* junction
**jd** *abbr* joined
**JD** *abbr or n* -s **1** [L *juris doctor*] **:** a doctor of law **2** [L *jurum doctor*] **:** a doctor of laws
**JD** *abbr* **1** Julian day **2** junior deacon **3** junior dean **4** justice department **5** juvenile delinquent
**JEA** *abbr* joint export agent
**jeal·ous** \ˈjeləs\ *adj* [ME *jelous*, fr. OF *jalos, jalous, jelous*, fr. (assumed) VL *zelosus*, fr. LL *zelus* zeal + L *-osus* -ous — more at ZEAL] **1 a :** intolerant of rivalry or unfaithfulness ⟨shall worship no other god, for the Lord . . . is a ~ God —Exod 34:14 (RSV)⟩ ⟨~ of the slightest interference in household management —Havelock Ellis⟩ **b :** disposed to suspect rivalry or unfaithfulness (as in love) **:** apprehensive of the loss of another's devotion ⟨so ~ she wouldn't let him dance with anyone else⟩ **c :** hostile toward a rival or one believed to enjoy an advantage (as a possession or attainment) **:** ENVIOUS, RESENTFUL ⟨~ because her coat isn't as nice as yours⟩ **2 :** zealous in guarding (as a possession) **:** VIGILANT ⟨this ~ love of privacy and independence —J.W.Beach⟩ **:** SOLICITOUS ⟨students . . . were like sons to him, he was ~ for their welfare —Ellwood Hendrick⟩ **3 :** distrustfully watchful **:** apprehensive of harm or fraud **:** SUSPICIOUS ⟨the ~ caution of New England —Van Wyck Brooks⟩ **syn** see ENVIOUS
**jea·louse** \jəˈlüz\ *vt* -ED/-ING/-S [modif. (influenced by *jealous*) of F *jalouser* to envy, be jealous of — more at JALOUSE] *archaic* **:** SUSPECT, MISTRUST
**jeal·ous·ly** \ˈjeləslē, -sli\ *adv* [ME *jelously*, fr. *jelous* jealous + *-ly*] **:** in a jealous manner ⟨a ~ guarded right⟩ ⟨his absorption in a career she ~ hated —Oscar Handlin⟩
**jeal·ous·ness** *n* -ES [ME *jelousnes*, fr. *jelous* + *-nes* -ness] **:** JEALOUSY
**jeal·ou·sy** \ˈjeləsē, -si\ *n* -ES [ME *jelousie*, fr. OF *jalosie, jalousie, jelousie*, fr. *jalos, jalous, jelous* jealous + *-ie* -y — more at JEALOUS] **1 a :** a jealous disposition or state of mind **:** a jealous nature, attitude, or feeling ⟨blinded by ~ to the skill of his fellow workers⟩ ⟨felt a natural ~ toward the winner⟩ **:** hostile rivalry ⟨intense local *jealousies* among existing villages —R.A.Billington⟩ **b** *now dial Brit* **:** SUSPICION, MISTRUST **2 :** zealous vigilance ⟨cherish their official political freedom with fierce ~ —Paul Blanshard⟩ **3** [trans. of F *jalousie*] **:** JALOUSIE
**jean** \ˈjēn *chiefly Brit* ˈjān\ *n* -s [short for *jean fustian*, fr. ME *Jene, Gene* Genoa, Italy (fr. MF *Genes*) + *fustian*] **1** *also* **jeans** *pl but sing in constr* **:** a durable twilled cotton cloth usu. in solid colors or stripes used esp. for sportswear and work clothes — compare DENIM, ⁹DRILL **2 jeans** *pl* **a :** pants usu. made of jean or denim and worn for work or sports — compare BLUE JEANS **b :** TROUSERS ⟨had to dig into his ~*s* to pay for the rest of the albums —*Down Beat*⟩
jeans 2a
**jean·pau·lia** \jēnˈpȯlēə\ *n* [NL, prob. fr. *Jean Paul* Richter †1825 Ger. author + NL *-ia*] *syn of* BAIERA
**jebel** *var of* DJEBEL
**jeb·u·site** \ˈjebyəˌsīt *sometimes* -ˌzīt *or* ˈjēbə-ˌsīt\ *n* -s *usu cap* [*Jebus*, ancient city in Palestine (fr. Heb *Yĕbūs*) + E *-ite*] **:** a member of a Canaanite people living in and around the ancient city of Jebus on the site of Jerusalem
**jec·o·rin** \ˈjekərən\ *n* -s [ISV *jecor-* (fr. L *jecor-, jecur* liver) + *-in*] **:** a complex lipoidal substance $C_{105}H_{186}N_5O_{46}P_3S$ somewhat resembling lecithin, orig. isolated from liver tissue, and occurring in small quantities in blood and in various tissues
**jec·o·rize** \ˈjekəˌrīz\ *vt* -ED/-ING/-S [L *jecor-, jecur* liver + E *-ize* — more at HEPATIC] **:** to impart to (fats or oils) some of the properties of cod-liver oil (as by irradiation with ultraviolet light)
**jed·burgh cast** \ˈjedˌbərə-, -ˌb(ə)rə-\ *also* **jed·dart cast** \ˈjedə(r)t-\ *n, usu cap J* [fr. *Jedburgh* or *Jeddart*, town in Roxburgh, Scotland, where in the 17th century a band of marauders was summarily executed] *Scot* **:** a court trial after punishment has been inflicted
**jedburgh justice** *also* **jeddart justice** *n, usu cap 1st J* **1** *Scot* **:** justice that punishes first and tries afterwards **:** LYNCH LAW **2** *Scot* **:** wholesale punishment or acquittal
**jed·ding ax** \ˈjediŋ-\ *n* [*jedding* alter. of *jadding*, pres. part. of *jad* to make a long deep hole in a rock, fr. *jad*, such a hole, of unknown origin] **:** a stonecutter's ax with a flat face and a pointed peen
**jee** *var of* GEE
**jeel** \ˈjē(ə)l\ *n* -s [ME (Sc dial.) *giell*, fr. MF *gel, giel* frost, jelly, fr. L *gelus, gelu* frost — more at COLD] *Scot* **:** JELLY
**¹jeep** \ˈjēp\ *n* -s [prob. alter. (influenced by Eugene the *Jeep*, a small fanciful wonder-working animal in the comic strip *Thimble Theatre* by Elzie C. Segar †1938 Am. cartoonist) of *gee pee*, fr. *gee* + *pee* (the letter); fr. the initials *g. p.* of *general purpose*] **1 a** (1) **:** a diminutive multipurpose motor vehicle of 80-inch wheelbase and ¼-ton capacity equipped with four-wheel drive and used by the U. S. Army in World War II — called also *peep* (2) **:** a modified U. S. Army vehicle of this kind having greater horsepower, more comfortable springs, longer wheelbase, increased fuel capacity, and a higher hood **b :** a 1½-ton command car used in the armored divisions of the U. S. Army during World War II **2** *or* **jeep carrier :** ESCORT CARRIER

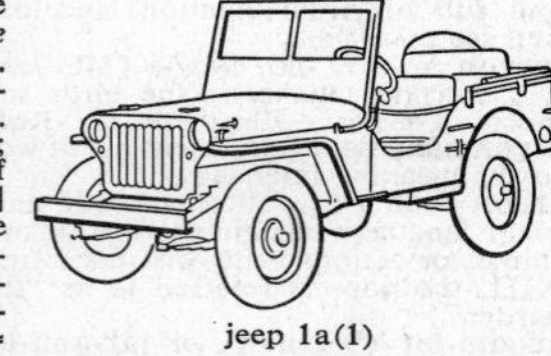
jeep 1a(1)

**²jeep** \"\ *vb* -ED/-ING/-S *vi* **:** to travel in a jeep ~ *vt* **:** to convey in a jeep
**Jeep** \"\ *trademark* — used for a civilian automotive vehicle
**jeep·able** \-pəbəl\ *adj* [¹*jeep* + *-able*] **:** so rough or narrow as to be impassable to motor vehicles except jeeps ⟨a ~ road⟩
**jee·pers** \ˈjēpə(r)z\ *also* **jeepers cree·pers** \ˌ≈≈ˈkrēpə(r)z\ *interj* [*jeepers* euphemism for *Jesus*; *jeepers creepers* euphemism for *Jesus Christ*] — used as a mild oath
**jeep·ney** \ˈjēpnē\ *n* -s [fr. *jeep* + *jitney*] **:** a Philippine jitney bus converted from a jeep
**¹jeer** \ˈji(ə)r, -iə\ *vb* -ED/-ING/-S [origin unknown] *vi* **:** to speak or cry out with derision or mockery **:** show contempt or scorn in often loud or coarse ridicule or sarcasm ⟨the fellows would ~ at him for knowing a girl —Hugh MacLennan⟩ ⟨~*ed* when he struck out⟩ ~ *vt* **:** DERIDE, MOCK, RIDICULE ⟨~*ed* the umpire's decision⟩ ⟨~*ed* his opponent when he tried to speak⟩ **syn** see SCOFF
**²jeer** \"\ *n* -s **1 :** a jeering remark or sound **:** TAUNT ⟨the tough kid's ~: "If they're good they're probably phony" —*Time*⟩ **2 :** the quality or state of jeering ⟨knew he was angry, though his voice showed nothing but a gentle ~ —Richard Llewellyn⟩
**jeer·er** \ˈjirə(r)\ *n* -s **:** one that jeers
**jeer·ing·ly** *adv* **:** in a jeering manner
**jeers** \ˈji(ə)rz, -iəz\ *n pl* [ME *jeres*] **:** a combination of tackles for hoisting or lowering the lower yards
**jeez** *also* **geez** \ˈjēz\ *interj* [euphemism for *Jesus*] — used as a mild oath
**je·fe** \ˈhā(ˌ)fā\ *n* -s [Sp, fr. F *chef* — more at CHIEF] *Southwest* **:** CHIEF, LEADER ⟨labor ~*s* willing to forgive, forget —*Santa Fe New Mexican*⟩
**jef·fer·is·ite** \ˈjef(ə)rəˌsīt\ *n* -s [William W. *Jefferis* †1906 Am. banker + E *-ite*] **:** a mineral consisting of a vermiculite containing iron, aluminum, and magnesium
**jef·fer·son city** \ˈjefə(r)sən-\ *adj, usu cap J&C* [fr. *Jefferson City*, Missouri] **:** of or from Jefferson City, the capital of Missouri ⟨*Jefferson City* schools⟩ **:** of the kind or style prevalent in Jefferson City
**jefferson da·vis's birthday** \-ˈdāvəs(əz)-\ *n, usu cap J&D&B* [after *Jefferson Davis* †1889 president of the Confederate States of America] **:** June 3 observed as a holiday in most of the southern states
**jefferson day** *n, usu cap J&D* [after Thomas *Jefferson* †1826 Am. president] **:** April 13 observed as a holiday in Alabama, Missouri, and Oklahoma in honor of the birthday of Thomas Jefferson

**jef·fer·so·nia** \ˌjefə(r)ˈsōnēə, -nyə\ *n, cap* [NL, fr. Thomas *Jefferson* + NL *-ia*] **:** a genus of North American and Asiatic herbs (family Berberidaceae) with basal palmately lobed leaves, solitary white flowers, and capsular fruit — see TWINLEAF

**¹jef·fer·so·nian** \ˌ;;ˈsōnēən, -nyən\ *adj, usu cap* [Thomas *Jefferson* + E *-ian*] **:** of, associated with, or favoring Thomas Jefferson or Jeffersonianism ⟨the *Jeffersonian* states' rights school —R.G.McCloskey⟩ ⟨the underlying assumptions of *Jeffersonian* democracy —Gerald Stourzh⟩

**²jeffersonian** \"\ *n* -s *usu cap* **:** a follower of Thomas Jefferson **:** an adherent of Jeffersonianism ⟨continuity between the Federalists and the *Jeffersonians* — *Times Lit. Supp.*⟩ ⟨modern *Jeffersonians* . . . believe in government intervention in economic life —Reinhold Niebuhr⟩

**jef·fer·so·nian·ism** \ˌ;;ˈsōnēəˌnizəm, -ōnyəˌn-\ *n* -s *usu cap* **:** the political principles and ideas held by Thomas Jefferson or later associated with his name and centering around a belief in states' rights, a strict construction of the federal Constitution, confidence in the political ability of the common man, and an agrarian as opposed to an industrial or commercial economy

**jef·fer·son·ite** \ˈjefə(r)səˌnīt\ *n* -s [Thomas *Jefferson* + E *-ite*] **:** a mineral Ca(Mn,Zn,Fe)$Si_2O_6$ consisting of a dark green or greenish black pyroxene

**jef·frey pine** \ˈjefrē-\ *also* **jef·frey's pine** \-ēz-\ *n, usu cap J* [after John *Jeffrey*, 19th cent. Scot. gardener and botanical explorer] **:** a tall symmetrical pine (*Pinus jeffreyi*) of western No. America that has long blue-green needles in groups of three and elongated cones borne on spreading or somewhat pendulous branches and that is sometimes classified as a variety of the ponderosa pine from which it differs chiefly in lighter color of bark and needles

**jeffrey pine beetle** *n, usu cap J* **:** a bark beetle (*Dendroctonus ponderosae*) destructive to Jeffrey pine in California

**jehad** *sometimes cap, var of* JIHAD

**je·ho·vah** \jiˈhōvə\ *n* -s *cap* [NL, intended as a transliteration of Heb *Yahweh*, the vowel points of Heb *'ădhōnāy* my lord being erroneously substituted for those of *Yahweh;* fr. the fact that in some Heb manuscripts the vowel points of *'ădhōnāy* (used as a euphemism for *Yahweh*) were written under the consonants *yhwh* of *Yahweh* to indicate that *'ădhōnāy* was to be substituted in oral reading for *Yahweh*] **:** ²GOD — a Christian transliteration of the tetragrammaton long assumed by many Christians to be the authentic reproduction of the Hebrew sacred name for God but now recognized to be a late hybrid form never used by the Jews; compare YAHWEH

**jehovah god** *n, cap J&G* **:** a supreme deity recognized and the only deity worshiped by Jehovah's Witnesses

**jehovah's witnesses** *n pl, cap J & usu cap W* **:** members of a group that witness by distributing literature and by personal evangelism to beliefs in the theocratic rule of God, the sinfulness of organized religions and governments, and an imminent millennium

**je·ho·vism** \jəˈhōˌvizəm\ *n* -s *cap* **:** YAHWISM

**¹je·ho·vist** \-ˌvəst\ *n* -s *usu cap* [*Jehovah* + *-ist*] **:** YAHWIST 1

**²jehovist** \"\ *adj, usu cap* **:** YAHWISTIC 1

**je·ho·vis·tic** \jəˌhōˈvistik, ˌjēˌhōˈv-\ *adj, usu cap* **1 :** of or relating to the religion of Jehovah **2 :** YAHWISTIC

**je·hu** \ˈjē(ˌ)h(y)ü, ˈjē(ˌ)yü, ˈjā(-\ *n* -s *sometimes cap* [fr. *Jehu* †*ab* 816 B.C. king of Israel who was noted for his furious attacks in a chariot (2 Kings 9:20)] **:** a driver esp. of a cab or coach; *specif* **:** one who drives fast or recklessly ⟨a tattered ~ . . . who took the dune road to Dhaid as though the devil himself were after him —Ralph Hammond-Innes⟩

**jeis·tic·cor** \ˈjēstiˌkō(ə)r\ *Scot var of* JUSTAUCORPS

**jejun-** *or* **jejuno-** *comb form* [*jejunum*] **1 :** jejunum ⟨*jejun*ectomy⟩ **2 :** jejunal and ⟨*jejuno*duodenal⟩

**je·ju·nal** \jəˈjünᵊl, (ˈ)jēˌjü-\ *adj* [*jejun-* + *-al*] **:** of or relating to the jejunum

**je·june** \jəˈjün, (ˈ)jēˌjün\ *adj* [L *jejunus*] **1** *obs* **:** lacking food **:** HUNGRY **2 :** inadequate to nourish the body or relieve hunger **:** wanting nutritive value ⟨the ~ diets of the very poor⟩ **3 a :** devoid of interest or significance **:** DULL, FLAT, INANE, VAPID ⟨the lectures . . . seemed ~ and platitudinous —John Buchan⟩ ⟨literary history without evaluative criteria becomes ~ and sterile —C.I.Glicksberg⟩ **b :** giving evidence of lack of experience or information ⟨a singularly brief, all too ~, note on the historical events that occasioned the document —*Times Lit. Supp.*⟩ ⟨not appointed because they are qualified in investment or economics, but their comments on such matters need not be ~ —*Economist*⟩ **c :** IMMATURE, JUVENILE, PUERILE ⟨the ~ behavior of an adolescent boy⟩ ⟨~ remarks on world affairs by one who possessed no relevant knowledge⟩
**syn** see INSIPID

**je·june·ly** *adv* **:** in a jejune manner

**je·june·ness** \-ünnəs\ *n* -ES **:** the quality or state of being jejune

**je·ju·ni·ty** \jəˈjünəd·ē, jēˈjü-\ *n* -ES [L *jejunitas*, fr. *jejunus* jejune + *-itas* -ity] **:** the quality or state of being jejune

**je·ju·nos·to·my** \jəˌjüˈnästəmē, (ˌ)jēˌjü-\ *n* -ES [ISV *jejun-* + *-stomy*] **1 :** the surgical formation of an opening through the abdominal wall into the jejunum **2 :** the opening made by jejunostomy

**je·ju·num** \jəˈjünəm, jēˈ-\ *n, pl* **jeju·na** \-nə\ [L (trans. of Gk *nēstis*, fr. *nēstis* fasting), fr. neut. of *jejunus;* fr. the belief that it is empty after death] **:** the first two fifths of the small intestine beyond the duodenum usu. merging almost imperceptibly with the ileum though somewhat larger, thicker-walled, and more vascular and having more numerous circular folds and fewer Peyer's patches

**jekyll-and-hyde** \ˈjekələn(d)ˈhīd *also* ˈjēk- *or* ˈjāk-\ *adj, usu cap J&H* [after Dr. *Jekyll* and Mr. *Hyde*, the two sides of the split personality of the chief character in *The Strange Case of Dr. Jekyll and Mr. Hyde* (1886) by Robert Louis Stevenson †1894 Scot. writer] **:** of, relating to, or resembling a person who leads a double life or who has two apparently distinct characters one of which is good and the other evil ⟨the hooded bandit was a *Jekyll-and-Hyde* character —M.D. Portman⟩

**jelatong** *var of* JELUTONG

**jel·er·ang** \ˈjeləˌraŋ\ *n* -s [origin unknown] **:** a giant squirrel (*Ratufa bicolor*) of Java and southern Asia

**jel·ick** \ˈyelik\ *n* -s [Turk *yelek*] **:** the bodice or vest of a Turkish woman's dress

**¹jell** \ˈjel\ *vb* -ED/-ING/-S [back-formation fr. *jelly*] *vi* **1 :** to reach the consistency of jelly **:** CONGEAL, SET ⟨the grapes ~*ed* readily⟩ **2 :** to achieve distinctness **:** take shape **:** CRYSTALLIZE, SOLIDIFY ⟨romantic interludes that somehow fail to ~ —Hoffman Birney⟩ ⟨both thought and expression require time to ~ —A.T.Weaver⟩ ⟨long after the public's opinion has ~*ed* —J.W.Irwin⟩ ~ *vt* **:** to give distinctness to **:** cause to take form ⟨it was this discovery which did most to ~ his thought after it had been fluid during two decades —Hunter Mead⟩

**²jell** \"\ *n* -s **:** JELLY

**jel·la·ba** *or* **djel·la·ba** \jəˈläbə\ *also* **je·lab** \-b\ *n* -s [Ar *jallabah* & *jallāb*, alter. of *jallābīyah*] **:** a full loose garment (as of wool or cotton) with a hood and with sleeves and skirt of varying length orig. worn chiefly in Morocco

**jellied gasoline** *n* **:** NAPALM

**jel·li·fi·ca·tion** \ˌjeləfəˈkāshən\ *n* -s **:** the act or process of jellifying or the state of being jellified

**jel·li·fy** \ˈ;;ˌfī\ *vb* -ED/-ING/-ES [*jelly* + *-fy*] *vt* **1 :** to make gelatinous **:** JELLY ⟨the red buttery mud is . . . *jellified* —Negley Farson⟩ **2 :** to reduce to slackness or weakness ⟨I turned, all *jellified* at her voice —Eugene Walter⟩ ~ *vi* **:** to become jelly or like jelly ⟨the lazy ear and the ~*ing* mind —*New Republic*⟩

**Jell-O** \ˈje(ˌ)lō\ *trademark* — used for a gelatin dessert often given the flavor and color of any of various fruits

**jelloped** *var of* JOLLOPED

**¹jel·ly** \ˈjelē, -li\ *n* -ES [ME *gelly, gellie*, fr. MF *gelee* frost, jelly, fr. fem. of *gelé* (past part. of *geler* to freeze, congeal), fr. L *gelatus*, past part. of *gelare* to freeze, congeal — more at COLD] **1 :** a semitransparent easily melted food preparation having a soft somewhat elastic consistency due to the presence of gelatin, pectin, or a similar substance: as **a :** ³ASPIC **b :** a dessert made usu. by adding gelatin to fruit juices **c :** a fruit product made by boiling sugar and the juice of fruit containing pectin **2 :** a substance resembling jelly esp. in consistency: as **a :** a transparent elastic gel **b :** a semisolid medicated or cosmetic preparation often having a gum base and usu. intended for local application ⟨ephedrine ~⟩ **c :** a jellylike preparation used in electrocardiography to obtain better conduction of electricity ⟨electrode ~⟩ **3 :** a gelatinous blue-green alga of the genus *Nostoc* found on damp ground esp. after a rain **4 :** JELLYFISH **5 :** a gelatin screen used to color or diffuse light (as of a theater spotlight) **6 :** a moral or emotional state felt to resemble jelly; *esp* **:** a state of fear or irresolution ⟨reduced to quivering ~ at the decisive moment⟩ **7 :** a shapeless structureless mass **:** PULP

**²jelly** \"\ *vb* -ED/-ING/-ES *vi* **1 :** to become jelly **:** come to the consistency of jelly **:** SET — compare ²GEL **2 :** to make jelly ⟨will be ~*ing* for days —Elizabeth Janeway⟩ ~ *vt* **:** to bring to the consistency of jelly — compare GELATINIZE

**³jelly** \"\ *adj* [alter. of *jolly*] *Scot* **:** POMPOUS, PROUD

**jelly bag** *n* **:** a bag typically of cheesecloth or flannel through which the juices for jelly are strained

**jelly bean** *n* **1 :** a sugar-coated candy bean with a gum or jelly center **2 :** a weak, spineless, or effeminate person ⟨this 50-year-old *jelly bean* —Shelby Foote⟩

**jellybread** \ˈ;;ˌ;\ *n, North* **:** a piece of bread and jelly

**jelly doughnut** *n* **:** a raised doughnut with jelly filling

**jelly end rot** *n* **:** a fungous disease of the potato that is caused by fungi of the genera *Fusarium* and *Rhizoctonia* and that produces a soft rot of the stem end of the tubers

**jellyfish** \ˈ;;ˌ;\ *n* **1 a :** any of various usu. marine and free-swimming coelenterates that constitute the sexually reproducing form of hydrozoans and scyphozoans which exhibit alternation of a sexual and an asexual generation and that have a nearly transparent saucer-shaped body with a mouth on the underside which extends by radially situated gastrovascular canals to the margin of the body, extensile marginal tentacles studded with stinging cells, and various sense organs distributed along the margin of the body — called also *sea nettle* **b :** SIPHONOPHORE **c :** CTENOPHORE — not used technically **2 :** a person lacking backbone or firmness ⟨if I should yield to threats . . . I should be a ~ by this time —Elinore M. Herrick⟩

**jelly fungus** *n* **:** any of various fungi whose appearance or consistency suggests jelly; *specif* **:** any fungus of the order Tremellales

**jellyleaf** \ˈ;;ˌ;\ *n* **:** QUEENSLAND HEMP

**jelly lichen** *n* **:** a lichen with a gelatinous thallus; *esp* **:** any of numerous lichens having an algal component belonging to the genus *Nostoc*

**jellylike** \ˈ;;ˌ;\ *adj* **:** resembling jelly in appearance or consistency **:** GELATINOUS

**jelly of whar·ton** \-ˈhwȯrtᵊn *also* -ˈwȯ-\ *n, usu cap W* [after Thomas *Wharton* †1673 Eng. anatomist] **:** WHARTON'S JELLY

**jelly plant** *n* **1 :** an Australian edible seaweed (*Eucheuma speciosum*) used in making jelly **2 :** KEI APPLE

**jelly powder** *n* **:** commercial gelatin mixed with sugar, flavoring, and color for use in making jellied desserts

**jelly roll** *n* **:** a thin sheet of sponge cake spread with jelly and rolled up while hot

**jelly strength** *n* **:** the strength of a gel or jelly (as gelatin or glue) expressed often as the weight in grams required to force a plunger into a test sample under specified conditions — called also *gel strength*

**jel·u·tong** *also* **jel·a·tong** *or* **jel·o·tong** \ˈjeləˌtȯŋ, -täŋ, ˌ;;ˈ;\ *n* -s [Malay *jĕlutong*] **1 :** any of several trees constituting a genus (*Dyera*) of the family Apocynaceae **2 :** a glutinous milky juice that is obtained from various jelutongs (esp. *Dyera costulata*), resembles chicle, and is used chiefly in waterproofing, in rubber compounds, and in chewing gum

**jem·a·dar** \ˈjeməˌdär\ *or* **jam·a·dar** \ˈjəm-\ *n* -s [Hindi *jama'dar, jam'dar* (influenced in meaning by Per *jamā'at* body of troops), fr. Ar *jam'* collections, assemblage + Per *dār* having] **1 :** an officer in the army of India having a rank corresponding to that of lieutenant in the English army **2 :** any of several police or other officials of the government of India

**je·mez** \ˈhāməs\ *n, pl* **jemez** *usu cap* [Sp *jemez, jemes*, of AmerInd origin] **1 :** a group of Tanoan Amerindian peoples of New Mexico **2 :** a member of a Jemez people

**jem·lah goat** \ˈjemlə-\ *n, usu cap J* [*jemlah* prob. native name in the Himalayas] **:** TAHR

**¹jem·my** \ˈjemi\ *adj* [alter. (influenced by the nickname *Jemmy*) of *jimp* + *-y*] *now dial Eng* **:** SPRUCE, NEAT, SNAPPY

**²jemmy** \"\ *n* -ES [fr. *Jemmy*, nickname for *James*] **1** *Brit* **:** JIMMY 1 ⟨*jemmies* in action, stealthy footsteps creeping upstairs and down —Rose Macaulay⟩ **2** *Brit* **:** a sheep's head used for food **3** *dial Eng* **:** GREATCOAT

**jen** \ˈrən\ *n* -s [Chin (Pek) *jen*²] **:** the cardinal Confucian virtue of benevolence to one's fellowmen

**je·na glass** \ˈyānə-\ *n, usu cap J* [fr. *Jena*, Germany] **:** glass of fine quality esp. suited for chemical and optical ware and other scientific and industrial applications

**je ne sais quoi** \zhənəˌsāˈkwä\ *n* **:** something that cannot be adequately described or expressed

**jen·ne·ri·an** \(ˈ)jeˈnirēən\ *adj, usu cap* [Edward *Jenner* †1823 Eng. physician + E *-ian*] **:** of or relating to Edward Jenner **:** by the method of Jenner ⟨*Jennerian* vaccination⟩

**jen·net** \ˈjenət\ *n* -s [ME *genett, jennett*, fr. MF *genet*, fr. Catal *ginet, genet* Zenete (member of a Berber people), mounted soldier, a kind of horse, fr. colloq. Ar *zinētī* (Ar *zanātīy*) of the Zenetes, fr. *Zanātah* the Zenete people] **1** *also* **gen·et** \"\ **:** a small Spanish horse **2** [influenced in meaning by ¹*jenny*] **a :** a female donkey **b :** HINNY

**jen·nie harp** \ˈjenē-, -ni-\ *n* [*jennie* alter. of ¹*jenny*] **:** the female harp seal

**jen·ny** \ˈjenē, -ni\ *n* -ES [fr. *Jenny*, nickname fr. the name Jane] **1 a :** a female bird or animal — often used in combination ⟨*jenny* wren⟩ **b :** a female donkey **2 :** SPINNING JENNY **3 :** a traveling crane; *esp* **:** a locomotive crane **4 :** JINNY **5** *or* **jen·nie** \"\ **:** a losing hazard in English billiards made at an acute angle to a long side of the table — see LONG JENNY, SHORT JENNY **6** *or* **jennie** -s *usu cap* [so called fr. its having the designation *JN*] **:** a training airplane used in World War I **7 :** a machine for cleaning grease or paint from surfaces by means of a jet of steam

**jenny ass** *n* **:** JENNET 2a

**jenny cutthroat** *n, dial Eng* **:** a whitethroat (*Sylvia communis*)

**jenny howlet** *n, dial Eng* **:** OWL

**jenny lind bed** \ˈ;;ˈlin(d)-\ *n, usu cap J&L* [after *Jenny* (Johanna Maria) *Lind* †1887 Swed. operatic soprano who successfully toured the U.S. (1850–52)] **:** an American spool bed

**jenny wood** *n, usu cap J* **:** FREIJO

**jenny wren** *n* **1 :** WREN **2 :** HERB ROBERT

**jen·o·ar** \ˈjenəˌwär\ *n* -s [native name in the East Indies] **:** any of several snappers of the Indian ocean; *esp* **:** a snapper (*Lutjanus sebae*) that is a popular food and game fish

**jens** *pl of* JEN

**jeo·fail** \ˈjeˌfā(ə)l\ *n* -s [AF *jeo fail, jo faill* I am at fault, I mistake] *archaic* **:** a mistake or oversight in legal pleading or other proceeding or the acknowledgment of such an error

**jeop·ard** \ˈjepə(r)d\ *vt* -ED/-ING/-S [ME *juparten, jeoparten, jeoparden*, back-formation fr. *jupartie, jeopartie, jeopardie* jeopardy] **:** JEOPARDIZE

**jeop·ar·dize** \-ˌdīz\ *vt* -ED/-ING/-S [*jeopardy* + *-ize*] **:** to expose to danger (as of imminent loss, defeat, or serious harm) **:** IMPERIL ⟨~ his life⟩ ⟨laws *jeopardizing* freedom of speech⟩ ⟨reforms too long delayed or denied have *jeopardized* peace, undermined democracy and swept away civil and religious liberty —F.D.Roosevelt⟩ **syn** see VENTURE

**jeop·ar·dous** \-dəs\ *adj* [ME *jupartous, jeopartous*, fr. *jupartie, jeopartie* + *-ous*] **:** marked by risk or danger **:** PERILOUS, HAZARDOUS ⟨takes such ~ episodes philosophically . . . as occupational liabilities —*Natural History*⟩

**¹jeop·ar·dy** \-ˌdē, -ˌdi\ *n* -ES [ME *jupartie, jeopartie, jeopardie*, fr. AF *juparti, jeu parti*, fr. OF, alternative, poem treating amorous problems in dialogue form, fr. *ju, jeu* game, play (fr. L *jocus* joke, jest, game) + *parti*, past part. of *partir* to divide — more at JOKE, PART] **1** *obs* **:** PROBLEM, DILEMMA; *also, obs* **:** TRICK **2 :** exposure to or imminence of death, loss, or injury **:** DANGER, HAZARD ⟨place a fortune in ~ by gambling⟩ **3 :** the danger that an accused person is subjected to when duly put upon trial for a criminal offense **syn** see DANGER

**²jeopardy** \"\ *vt* -ED/-ING/-ES **:** JEOPARDIZE, IMPERIL

**jeopardy assessment** *n* **:** a special assessment under the U.S. income-tax laws levied to collect an alleged deficiency when the taxing officer believes that delay may jeopardize the collection of the claim

**je·quir·i·ty** \jəˈkwirəd·ē\ *or* **jequirity bean** *n* -ES [Pg *jequiriti, jequiriti*, perh. of Indic origin; akin to Hindi *ratti* ratti — more at RUTTEE] **1 :** the scarlet and black seed of Indian licorice used in India and other tropical regions for beads in rosaries and necklaces and as a standard weight **2 :** INDIAN LICORICE

**je·qui·ti·ba** \jəˌkēd·əˈbä, zhəˌ;ˈ-\ *n* -s [Pg *jequitibá*, fr. Tupi] **1 :** a So. American tree (*Cariniana legalis*) that yields a valuable hardwood similar to Colombian mahogany **2 :** the wood of the jequitiba — called also *Brazilian mahogany*

**jer·boa** \jərˈbōə, jer-\ *n* -s [Ar *yarbū'*] **1 :** any of several social nocturnal jumping rodents (family Dipodidae) inhabiting arid parts of the Old World, having long hind legs, long tail, and often large leaflike ears, and being mostly yellowish brown with white underparts and black-tipped tail **2 :** any of various jumping rodents (as a kangaroo rat or a pouched mouse)

jerboa

**jerboa kangaroo** *n* **:** any of several brush-tailed rat kangaroos (genus *Bettongia*)

**jerboa mouse** *n* **:** any of various leaping rodents usu. with elongated hind legs (as the sciuromorph pocket mice and kangaroo rats or the myomorph broad-toothed rat)

**jerboa pouched mouse** *n* **:** any of several small slender leaping marsupials (genus *Antechinomys*) of the central desert of Australia

**jerboa rat** *n* **:** any of several relatively large Australian rats (family Muridae) with hind legs adapted to leaping (as members of the genus *Conilurus*)

**jer·e·me·jev·ite** *also* **er·e·me·yev·ite** \ˌ(y)erəˈmā(y)əˌvīt, ˌfīt\ *n* -s [F *jérémeiéwite*, fr. Pavel V. Eremeev (*Jeremeiew*) †1899 Russ. mineralogist + F *-ite* -ite] **:** a mineral $AlBO_3$ consisting of aluminum borate in colorless or yellowish hexagonal crystals (hardness 6.5, sp. gr. 3.28)

**jer·e·mi·ad** \ˌjerəˈmīəd, -īˌad\ *n* -s [F *jérémiade*, fr. *Jérémie* Jeremiah (fr. LL *Jeremias*) + *-ade* -ad] **:** a lamenting and denunciatory complaint **:** a doleful story **:** a dolorous tirade ⟨a ~ against a civilization that values knowledge above wisdom —Lawrence Durrell⟩

**jer·e·mi·ah** \-īə\ *n* -s *usu cap* [after *Jeremiah* †*ab*585 B.C. Heb prophet known for his pessimism, fr. LL *Jeremias, Hieremias*, fr. Gk *Hieremias*, fr. Heb *Yirmĕyāh*] **:** a person who complains about the evil, decay, and disaster that he sees about him and who foresees and predicts a calamitous future ⟨*Jeremiahs* lamenting the decline of public morals⟩

**jer·e·mi·an·ic** \ˌjerəˌmīˈanik\ *also* **jer·e·mi·an** \-ˈmīən\ *adj, usu cap* [*Jeremianic* fr. *Jeremiah* + E *-an* + *-ic; Jeremian* fr. *Jeremiah* + E *-an*] **:** of, relating to, or suggestive of the prophet Jeremiah or the biblical material of Jeremiah ⟨a *Jeremianic* discourse⟩ ⟨a *Jeremianic* tone⟩

**je·rez** \hāˈrās, -rāth\ *adj, usu cap* [fr. *Jerez*, Spain] **:** of or from the city of Jerez, Spain **:** of the kind or style prevalent in Jerez

**jerfalcon** *var of* GYRFALCON

**jerican** *var of* JERRICAN

**¹jerk** \ˈjərk, -ək, -əik\ *vb* -ED/-ING/-S [prob. alter. of *yerk*] *vt* **1** *obs* **:** to strike with or as if with a whip **2 :** to give a quick and suddenly arrested thrust, push, pull, or twist to ⟨~ a rope⟩ ⟨~ a coat off⟩ ⟨~ out a pistol⟩ **3 :** to throw with a quick motion suddenly arrested ⟨~ money on a table⟩; *specif* **:** to bowl (a cricket ball) illegally (as by bending the arm) **4 :** to utter in an abrupt, snappy, or sharply broken manner ⟨~ out words⟩ **5 :** to prepare and dispense (sodas) ~ *vi* **1 :** to make a sudden spasmodic motion or series of such motions **:** move with a start or starts ⟨fish ~*ing* and tumbling on the deck of a boat⟩ **2 :** to move in short abrupt motions ⟨a cripple ~*ing* along a street⟩ **:** move along with frequent jolts ⟨a train ~*ing* past a station⟩ **3 :** to throw an object with a jerk; *specif* **:** to jerk the ball in bowling in the game of cricket **4** *obs* **:** SNEER

**syn** SNAP, TWITCH, YANK: JERK indicates sudden, sharp, quick, graceless, forceful movement begun or ended abruptly ⟨thought the train would never start, but at last the whistle blew and the carriages *jerked* forward —G.G.Carter⟩ ⟨*jerked* her head back as if she'd been struck in the face —Dorothy Baker⟩ SNAP may apply to a quite quick action abruptly terminated, as biting or trying to bite sharply or seizing, clutching, snatching, locking, or breaking suddenly ⟨the hounds were fine beasts . . . lank and swift as they bent over the food to *snap* it into their jaws and swallow it quickly —Elizabeth M. Roberts⟩ ⟨the syndicate *snapping* up land as soon as it is for sale⟩ ⟨*snapped* at her because Theophilus did not eat enough —Margaret Deland⟩ TWITCH may indicate quick, sometimes spasmodic, and often light action combining tugging and jerking ⟨shrunken body continued to jerk and quiver, fingers *twitching* at his gray beard —Gerald Beaumont⟩ ⟨one Pan ready to *twitch* the nymph's last garment off —Robert Browning⟩ ⟨put out his hand to *twitch* off a twig as he passed —Willa Cather⟩ YANK indicates quick and heavy tugging and pulling ⟨watches her two-year-old stand passive while another child *yanks* his toy out of his hand —Margaret Mead⟩ ⟨she *yanked* the corset strings viciously —D.B.Chidsey⟩ ⟨by means of long blocks and tackle they set to *yanking* out logs —S.E.White⟩

**²jerk** \"\ *n* -s *often attrib* **1** *obs* **:** a stroke esp. of a whip **:** LASH **2 :** a single quick motion usu. of short duration and length (as a suddenly arrested pull, thrust, push, or jolt) ⟨get up with a ~⟩ **3 a :** jolting, bouncing, or thrusting motions ⟨a rustic dance full of ~ and rhythm⟩ **b :** tendency to produce spasmodic motions ⟨a car with little ~ and noise⟩ **4 a :** an involuntary spasmodic muscular movement due to reflex action; *esp* **:** one induced by an external stimulus — see KNEE JERK **b jerks** *pl* (1) **:** CHOREA (2) **:** involuntary twitchings due to nervous excitement (as in the dancing mania and sometimes in religious revivals) **5** [prob. fr. *jerk* "masturbator", fr. *jerk (off)*] **:** a stupid, foolish, naïve, or unconventional person ⟨these ~s . . . who didn't know anything outside their rank and serial number —J.G.Cozzens⟩ ⟨soapbox orators who . . . vary from philosophers to out-and-out ~s —Richard Joseph⟩ **6 :** the pushing of a weight from shoulder height to a position overhead **:** the second phase of the clean and jerk in weight lifting

**³jerk** \"\ *vt* -ED/-ING/-S [back-formation fr. ³*jerky*] **:** to cut into long slices or strips and dry in the sun ⟨~ beef⟩ — see CHARQUI

**jerked** *past of* JERK

**jerk·er** \-kə(r)\ *n* -s **:** one that jerks

**jerk·i·ly** \-kəlē, -li\ *adv* **:** in a jerky manner ⟨bowed ~, first to the orchestra, then to the audience —*Time*⟩

**¹jer·kin** \-kən\ *n* -s [origin unknown] **1 :** a close-fitting hip-length jacket made without sleeves or with extended shoulders, being usu. collarless and belted, and cut like the 16th century doublet over which it was orig. worn **2 :** any of various adaptations of the 16th century jerkin often worn now by both men and women

**²jerkin** \"\ *n* -s [prob. fr. *gerfalcon* + *-kin*] **:** a male gyrfalcon

**jerk·i·ness** \-kēnəs, -kin-\ *n* -ES **:** the quality or state of being jerky

**jerking** *pres part of* JERK

**jerk·ing·ly** *adv* **:** JERKILY

**jerkinhead** \ˈ;;ˌ;\ *n* [prob. alter. (influenced by ¹*jerkin*) of *kirkinhead*] **:** a hipped part of a roof which is hipped only for a part of its height leaving a truncated gable

**jerk line** *n* **:** a single rein used orig. in the western U.S. that was fastened to the brake handle and ran through the driver's hand to the bit of the lead animal

jerkinhead

**jerk off** *vb* **:** MASTURBATE — usu. considered vulgar

**jerk pump** *n* **:** a fuel-injection pump in an oil engine which

supplies impulsively an accurately metered charge to the nozzle at the time of the opening of the inlet valve
**jerks** pres 3d sing of JERK, pl of JERK
**jerkwater** \ˈ=,=\ or **jerk** adj [¹jerk + water; fr. the fact that rural trains took on water that was carried in buckets from the source of supply] **1 :** insignificant and remote ⟨a ~ town⟩ ⟨a ~ college⟩ **2 :** contemptibly petty, narrow, or trivial : PIDDLING ⟨a ~ carnival act⟩ ⟨a ~ politician⟩
¹**jerky** \ˈjərkē, ˈjə̄k-, ˈjəik-, -ki\ adj -ER/-EST [²jerk + -y] **1 a :** moving along with or accompanied by fits and starts : JOLTING ⟨a ~ vehicle⟩ **b :** characterized by abrupt or awkward transitions ⟨a ~ prose style⟩ **2 a :** INANE, FOOLISH ⟨~ adolescents hanging around drugstores⟩ **b :** contemptibly weak or ineffectual ⟨the ~ policies of an ignorant governor⟩
²**jerky** \"\ n -ES : a horse-drawn wagon usu. without springs that is used for carrying passengers
³**jer·ky** \"\ n -ES [modif. of Sp *charqui* — more at CHARQUI] : meat (as beef) that has been jerked
**jer·mo·nal** \ˌjərməˈnäl\ n -S [prob. fr. Hindi *jar* cold + *munāl* pheasant] : HIMALAYAN SNOW COCK
**jer·o·bo·am** \ˌjerəˈbōəm\ n -S *sometimes cap* [after *Jeroboam* I †ab912 B.C. king of the northern kingdom of Israel referred to as the "mighty man of valor" (1 Kings 11:28—AV)] **1 :** an oversize wine bottle holding about four quarts ⟨a ~ of champagne⟩ **2** *Brit* : CHAMBER POT
**je·ro·mi·an** \jəˈrōmēən\ adj, *usu cap* [St. *Jerome* (Eusebius *Hieronymus*) †420 church father + E *-ian*] : of or relating to St. Jerome or his works
**jer·ri·can** or **jerry can** *also* **jeri·can** \ˈjerē,kan\ n [²jerry + can] : a 5-gallon fluid container
¹**jer·ry** \ˈjerē, -ri\ n -ES [fr. *Jerry*, nickname for the names *Jeremy & Jeremiah*] **1** *archaic* : the noise that according to custom was made (as by hammering, beating, or rattling) to celebrate the end of someone's term of apprenticeship in the printing trade **2** [by shortening & alter. fr. *jeroboam*] *Brit* : CHAMBER POT
²**jerry** \"\ n -ES *usu cap* [alter. (influenced by ¹jerry and the name *Jerry*) of *German*] *chiefly Brit* : GERMAN
³**jerry** \"\ adj -ER/-EST [back-formation fr. *jerry-built*] : POOR, SLIPSHOD, MAKESHIFT ⟨~ workmanship⟩
**jerry-build** \ˈ=,=,=\ vb [back-formation fr. *jerry-built*] vt **1 :** to build (as a house) flimsily of materials of poor quality **2 :** to put together, contrive, or devise with insufficient care or planning ⟨attempt to *jerry-build* a military pact —Denis Healey⟩ ⟨*jerry-builds* the English language as if it were the English countryside —Cyril Connolly⟩ **~** vi : to put up a jerry-built structure : do building cheaply and with inferior materials
**jerry-builder** \ˈ==,==\ n : one that jerry-builds; *esp* : a builder who erects cheap buildings of poor materials and unsubstantial construction esp. on speculation for quick sale
**jerry-built** \ˈ==,=\ adj [*jerry* prob. fr. *Jerry*, nickname for *Jeremy & Jeremiah*] **1 :** built cheaply and unsubstantially of poor or insufficient materials ⟨*jerry-built* wharves⟩ ⟨buying sagging old houses or *jerry-built* new ones —Vera Connolly⟩ ⟨mean-looking little houses, very *jerry-built* —John Morris⟩ ⟨600 acres of *jerry-built* shacks —Emory Ross⟩ ⟨the thin walls of the *jerry-built* house —Virginia Woolf⟩ **2 :** carelessly or hastily put together : constructed without due thought or care : unsound in planning or execution : FLIMSY; *often* : constructed or devised at haphazard ⟨*jerry-built* tax legislation —*N.Y. Times*⟩ ⟨the political empire of Rome became more and more *jerry-built* —Weston La Barre⟩ ⟨the movie is a particularly unsatisfying, *jerry-built* affair —Manny Farber⟩
**jerry-come-tumble** \ˌ==(,)=ˈ==\ *also* **jerry-go-nimble** \ˌ==(,)=ˈ==\ n -S *usu cap J* **1** *dial Eng* : TUMBLER **2** *dial Eng* : CIRCUS
**jerry man** n : a wasteman in a mine
**jerrymander** var of GERRYMANDER
¹**jer·sey** \ˈjərzē, ˈjə̄z-, ˈjəiz-, -zi, *dial* ˈjärz- or ˈjäz-\ adj, *usu cap* [fr. *Jersey*, one of the Channel islands] : of or from the island of Jersey : of the kind or style prevalent in Jersey
²**jersey** \"\ n, *often attrib* **1** *also* **jersey cloth** -S **a :** a plain weft-knitted fabric in tubular form made of wool, cotton, nylon, rayon, or silk and used for underwear, dresses, sportswear **b :** TRICOT 1 **2** -S : any of various close-fitting usu. circular-knitted garments: as **a :** a man's sleeveless cotton undershirt **b :** a pullover with short or long sleeves worn esp. by children, athletes, or sailors **3 a** *usu cap* : a breed of rather small short-horned dairy cattle originating on the island of Jersey in the English channel and now widely distributed, being in color predominantly yellowish brown or fawn although sometimes ranging from silvery gray or pale buff to black with occasional white marking, and being noted for the high fat content of their milk **b** -S *often cap* : an animal of the Jersey breed
³**jersey** \"\ adj, *usu cap* [fr. (*New*) *Jersey*, fr. *Jersey*, the Channel island] : NEW JERSEY
¹**jer·sey·an** \-zēən, -ziən\ n -S *usu cap* [(*New*) *Jersey* + E *-an*] : a native or resident of the state of New Jersey
²**jerseyan** \"\ adj, *usu cap* : of, relating to, or characteristic of New Jersey or New Jerseyites
**jersey city** adj, *usu cap J&C* [fr. *Jersey City*, New Jersey] : of or from Jersey City, N.J. ⟨a *Jersey City* physician⟩ : of the kind or style prevalent in Jersey City
**jersey cream** n, *often cap J* [²*Jersey* (cattle)] : POLAR BEAR 2
**jersey elm** n, *usu cap J* [¹*Jersey*] : an elm that is a variety (*Ulmus campestris wheatleyi*) of the English elm with erect branches and broader leaves — called also *Guernsey elm*
**jersey giant** n [³*Jersey*] **1** *usu cap J&G* : a breed of very large domestic fowls developed in New Jersey by interbreeding large Asiatic fowls with Langshans and being orig. solid black but now having a white variety **2** *usu cap J & often cap G* : a bird of the Jersey Giant breed
**jer·sey·ite** \-zē,īt, -zi,īt\ n -S *usu cap* [(*New*) *Jersey* + E *-ite*] : a native or resident of the state of New Jersey
**jersey justice** n, *usu cap 1st J* [³*Jersey*; fr. the supposedly more efficient legal system in New Jersey] : speedy and effective justice (as in criminal cases)
**jersey lightning** n, *usu cap J* [³*Jersey*] *slang* : APPLEJACK
**jersey·man** \ˈ==mən\ n, pl **jerseymen** *usu cap* [*Jersey*, the island + *man*] **1 :** a native or resident of the island of Jersey **2 :** NEW JERSEYITE
**jersey pine** n, *usu cap J* [³*Jersey*] : a common open or straggling pine (*Pinus virginiana*) of the eastern U.S. having leaves only an inch or two long
**jersey tea** n, *usu cap J* [³*Jersey*] **1 :** NEW JERSEY TEA **2 :** WINTERGREEN 2a
**jert** \ˈjərt\ *chiefly Scot var of* JERK
**je·ru·sa·lem** \jəˈrüs(ə)ləm *also* -üz| *or* |ə,lem\ adj, *usu cap* [fr. *Jerusalem*, Palestine, fr. LL *Jerusalem*, *Hierusalem*, fr. Gk *Ierousalēm*, *Hierousalēm*, fr. Heb *Yĕrūshālaim*] : of or from Jerusalem, a city of Palestine now divided between the Republic of Israel of which it is the capital and the Hashimite Kingdom of Jordan : of the kind or style prevalent in Jerusalem
**jerusalem artichoke** n, *usu cap J* [*Jerusalem* by folk etymology fr. It *girasole* — more at GIRASOL] **1 :** a perennial American sunflower (*Helianthus tuberosus*) widely cultivated and often occurring as an escape **2 :** the tuber of Jerusalem artichoke used as a vegetable, as a feed for livestock, and as a source of levulose
**jerusalem cherry** n, *usu cap J* : either of two plants of the genus *Solanum* (*S. pseudo-capsicum* or *S. capsicastrum*) cultivated as ornamental house plants for their bright orange to red berries
**jerusalem corn** n, *usu cap J* : DURRA
**jerusalem cricket** n, *usu cap J* : a burrowing nocturnal insect (*Stenopelmatus fuscus*) of the southwestern U.S. related to the katydids and having a large head and transverse black abdominal stripes — called also *sand cricket*
**jerusalem cross** n, *cap J* **1 :** a cross potent with a small Greek cross in each of the four spaces between the arms **2** [so called fr. the resemblance of the arrangement of the leaves to the shape of the Jerusalem cross] : MALTESE CROSS 2

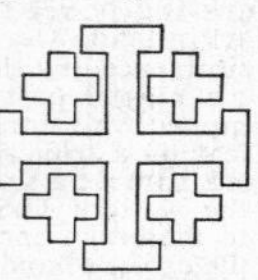
Jerusalem cross

**jerusalem haddock** n, *usu cap J, West* : OPAH
**jerusalem oak** n, *usu cap J* **1 :** an aromatic oak-leaved goosefoot (*Chenopodium botrys*) **2 :** MEXICAN TEA
**jerusalem pea** n, *usu cap J* : an East Indian perennial bean (*Phaseolus trinervius*) that is closely related to and sometimes considered a variety of the urd bean
**jerusalem pine** n, *usu cap J* : ALEPPO PINE
**jerusalem sage** n, *usu cap J* : any of several plants of the genus *Phlomis* (as *P. fruticosa* or *P. tuberosa*) often cultivated and having dense axillary whorls of purple flowers
**jerusalem star** n, *usu cap J* **1 :** SALSIFY **2 :** SNOW-IN-SUMMER **3 :** a Eurasian evergreen subshrub (*Hypericum calycinum*) with large showy yellow flowers
**jerusalem sunday** n, *usu cap J&S* : MID-LENT SUNDAY
**jerusalem tea** n, *usu cap J* : MEXICAN TEA
**jerusalem thorn** n, *usu cap J* **1 :** CHRIST'S-THORN **2 :** a large shrub or shrubby tree (*Parkinsonia aculeata*) that is native to tropical America but naturalized in the southern and southwestern U.S., that has pinnate leaves with small deciduous leaflets, sharp spines, and showy racemose yellow flowers, and that is used for hedging and as emergency food for livestock esp. in dry regions — called also *horsebean* **3 :** CATECHU 2
**jer·vine** \ˈjər,vēn, -vən\ n -S [NL *jervina*, fr. Sp *yervina*, perh. fr. *yervo* vetch, chick-pea (fr. L *ervum*) + *-ina* -ine] : a crystalline alkaloid $C_{26}H_{39}NO_3$ related in structure to the steroids and found in the rhizomes and roots of white hellebore, American hellebore, and other species of the genus *Veratrum*
**jes** \ˈjes\ n -ES [prob. native name in West Africa] : OTTER SHREW
¹**jess** *or* **jesse** \ˈjes\ n, pl **jesses** [ME *ges*, *gesse*, fr. MF *gies*, *giez*, fr. pl. of *giet*, *get*, *jet* throw — more at JET] : either of two short straps of leather or other material secured on the legs of a hawk used in falconry and usu. provided with a ring for attaching a swiveled leash
²**jess** \"\ vt -ED/-ING/-ES : to attach jesses to (a hawk)
**jessamine** var of JASMINE
**jes·sa·my** \ˈjesəmē, -mi\ n -ES [modif. of *jessamine*] **1** *dial Eng* : JASMINE **2** [so called fr. the use of perfume] : DANDY, FOP

jesses: *1* ring for leash, *2* swivel, *3* ring for jesses, *4* jesses

**jes·sant-de-lis** *also* **jes·sant-de-lys** \ˌjesᵊn(t)dəˈlē\ adj [*jessant* (prob. alter. of *jacent*) + *fleur-de-lis*] : having the upper points of a fleur-de-lis arising from the mouth of a heraldic leopard's face
**jes·se** *also* **jes·sie** *or* **jes·sy** \ˈjesē, -si\ n, pl **jesses** *also* **jessies** [prob. after *Jesse*, father of David in the Bible; fr. "And there shall come forth a rod out of the stem of Jesse" (Isa 11:1—AV)] *chiefly dial* : a severe scolding or beating ⟨just as soon as I go home I'll give you ~ —Alice Cary⟩
**jessed** \ˈjest\ adj [¹*jess* + *-ed*] : having on jesses
**jes·se tree** \ˈjesē-, -si-\ *or* **jesse** n -S *usu cap J* [after *Jesse*, father of David in the Bible] : a genealogical tree in which the lineage of Christ is represented in sculpture and decorative art — called also *tree of Jesse*
**jesse window** n, *usu cap J* [after *Jesse* in the Bible] : a decorative window in which a Jesse tree is a principal subject of the design
**jes·sur** \ˈjesə(r)\ n -S [perh. fr. Beng] : RUSSELL'S VIPER
¹**jest** \ˈjest\ n -S [ME *geste*, fr. OF *geste*, *jeste*, fr. L *gesta* deeds, fr. neut. pl. of *gestus*, past part. of *gerere* to bear, wage, cherish, accomplish — more at CAST] **1 a** *obs* : ACT, DEED, EXPLOIT **b :** an act intended to provoke laughter : PRANK ⟨began as a ~ and ended as a tragedy⟩ ⟨signs marking the city limits . . . pranksters carry off and plant in remote spots as a ~ —*Amer. Guide Series: Calif.*⟩ **c :** a ludicrous circumstance or incident ⟨a proper ~, and never heard before, that Suffolk should demand a whole fifteenth for costs and charges —Shak.⟩ **2 a :** a jeering remark : GIBE, TAUNT ⟨many a foul ribald ~ at the expense of the prisoner —J.L.Motley⟩ **b :** a witty remark : clever quip : MOT ⟨the kind of wry ~ that had sent the ancient gods into peals of ironic laughter —T.B. Costain⟩ **3 a :** a frivolous mood or manner — usu. used with *in* ⟨done in ~ and not supposed to be taken seriously⟩ ⟨many a true word is spoken in ~⟩ **b :** GAIETY, MERRIMENT ⟨I knew him, Horatio: a fellow of infinite ~, of excellent fancy —Shak.⟩ **4 :** the butt of a joke : LAUGHINGSTOCK ⟨to be the standing ~ of all one's acquaintance —R.B.Sheridan⟩ **syn** see FUN, JOKE
²**jest** \"\ vb -ED/-ING/-S [ME *gesten* to tell a tale, recite a romance, fr. *geste*, n.] vi **1 :** to utter taunts : jeer and mock : GIBE ⟨mock not nor ~ at anything of importance —George Washington⟩ ⟨~s at scars that never felt a wound —Shak.⟩ **2 :** to speak or act without seriousness or in a frivolous manner ⟨you surely ~, interrupted I; I am a foreigner, and you would abuse my ignorance —Oliver Goldsmith⟩ **3 :** to make a witty remark : say something amusing : QUIP, JOKE ⟨~*ed* with her in a low voice —Anne D. Sedgwick⟩ **4** *obs* : to make merry ⟨as gentle and as jocund as to ~ go I to fight —Shak.⟩ **~** vt : to jeer and mock at : make fun of : RIDICULE, BANTER ⟨~*ed* his friend over his fondness for horses⟩
**jestbook** \ˈ=,=\ n : a book containing jests and jokes — called also *jokebook*
**jest·ee** \(ˈ)jeˈstē\ n -S : a person subjected to jesting
**jest·er** \ˈjestə(r)\ n -S [alter. of ME *gestour*, fr. *gesten* + *-our* -or] **1** *archaic* : a professional teller of gests ⟨harper's strain and ~'s tale went round in vain —Sir Walter Scott⟩ **2 :** FOOL 2a ⟨a court ~⟩ ⟨the world never has believed its ~s even when they knew more than its kings —James Street⟩ **3 :** one given to uttering jests or playing the clown ⟨has played to perfection the role of the world's . . . ~ —*Time*⟩
**jest·ing·ly** adv : in a jesting manner
¹**jesu·it** \ˈjezh(ə)wət *also* -ez| *or* |wət; *usu* -əd· + V\ n -S *usu cap* [NL *Jesuita*, fr. LL *Jesus* + L *-ita* -ite] **1 :** a member of a religious society for men founded by St. Ignatius Loyola in 1534 **2 :** one given to intrigue or equivocation : a crafty person : CASUIST ⟨one fourth of all power is in these ignorant masses, and they are in the hands of the political *Jesuits* of the South —*No. Amer. Rev.*⟩
²**jesuit** \"\ adj, *usu cap* : of or relating to the Jesuits or Jesuitism
**jesuit berry** n, *usu cap J* : PARTRIDGEBERRY 1
**jesu·it·ed** \-(,)wid·əd, -wəd-\ adj, *usu cap*, *archaic* : JESUITIC
**jesu·it·ic** \ˌ==ˈwid·|ik, -ˈ|wit|, |ēk\ *or* **jesu·it·i·cal** \|əkəl, |ēk-\ adj **1** *usu cap* : of or relating to the Jesuits, Jesuitism, or jesuitry **2** *often cap* : having qualities thought to resemble those of a Jesuit — usu. used disparagingly ⟨the low cunning and *Jesuitical* trick with which she deludes her husband —S.T. Coleridge⟩ — **jesu·it·i·cal·ly** \|ək(ə)lē, |ēk-, -li\ adv, *often cap*
**jesu·it·ism** \ˈ==,wəd·,izəm, -wə,ti-\ n -S **1** *usu cap* : the system, doctrine, or practices of Jesuits **2** *often cap* : JESUITRY
**jesu·it·ize** \-əd·,īz, -ə,tīz\ vb -ED/-ING/-S *often cap*, vi : to act or teach in the actual or ascribed manner of a Jesuit **~** vt : to indoctrinate with actual or ascribed Jesuit principles — usu. used disparagingly
**jesu·it·ry** \-ətrē, -ri\ n -ES *often cap* : principles or practices ascribed to the Jesuits (as the practice of mental reservation, casuistry, and equivocation) — usu. used disparagingly
**jesuits' bark** *also* **jesuit bark** n, *usu cap J* [so called fr. the fact that it was brought into Europe from the Jesuit missions in So. America] : CINCHONA 3
**jesuits' drops** n pl, *usu cap J* : FRIAR'S BALSAM
**jesuits' nut** n, *usu cap J* : WATER CHESTNUT 1
**jesuits' tea** *also* **jesuit tea** n, *usu cap J* **1 :** MATÉ **2 :** MEXICAN TEA
**jesuit style** n, *usu cap J* : a baroque style of architecture in ecclesiastical buildings of the 16th and 17th centuries
**jesuits' water nut** n, *usu cap J* : WATER CHESTNUT 1
**je·sus bug** \ˈjēzəs- *also* -zəz-\ n, *usu cap J* [after *Jesus* Christ; fr. the allusion to his walking on water (Mt 14:25)] : WATER STRIDER 1
¹**jet** \ˈjet, *usu* -ed· + V\ n -S [ME *get*, *jet*, fr. MF *jaiet*, *geet*, *gest*, fr. L *gagates*, fr. Gk *gagatēs*, fr. *Gagas*, river and ancient town in the district of Lycia in southern Asia Minor] **1 :** a very compact velvet-black mineral of the nature of coal that is often used for jewelry **2 :** JET BLACK
²**jet** \"\ adj [ME *get*, fr. *get*, *jet*, n.] **1 :** made of jet **2 :** of the color jet
³**jet** \"\ vi **jetted**; **jetted**; **jetting**; **jets** [ME *jetten*, perh. fr. MF *jeter* to throw, but influenced in meaning by L *jactare* to throw, boast] **1** *obs* : to walk with a haughty or pompous air : STRUT, SWAGGER ⟨how he ~s under his advanced plumes —Shak.⟩ ⟨when the stage of the world was hung with black they *jetted* up and down like proud tragedians —Thomas Dekker⟩ **2 a** *archaic* : to walk along slowly : STROLL **b** *obs* : to walk in a sprightly manner : CAPER, TRIP **3 :** to move about very quickly : DART ⟨hoped to see . . . the wingless squirrel ~ from tree to tree —James Montgomery⟩
⁴**jet** \"\ n -S *archaic* : an artificial way of walking : HITCH, SWAGGER ⟨the genteel trip and the agreeable ~ as they are now practiced at the court of France —Eustace Budgell⟩
⁵**jet** \"\ vb **jetted**; **jetted**; **jetting**; **jets** [MF *jeter*, lit., to throw, fr. L *jactare* to throw, shake, speak out, boast, fr. *jactus*, past part. of *jacere* to throw; akin to Gk *hienai* to send, Toch A *ya-* to make, do, Hitt *ijami* I make, I do] vi **1 a** *obs* : INTRUDE, ENCROACH ⟨insulting tyranny begins to ~ upon the innocent and aweless throne —Shak.⟩ **b :** to project or jut prominently ⟨the rock *jetted* out over the deep canyon⟩ **2 :** to spout forth : emit a jet : GUSH, SPURT ⟨molten material from the bowels of earth ~s up between sedimented water-laid rocks —Russell Lord⟩ ⟨flame and smoke *jetted* from the sides of the five warships —Kenneth Roberts⟩ **~** vt **1 :** to make projections on (as a building) : cause to project ⟨the second stories of the houses were *jetted*, shadowing the street from the sun⟩ **2** *now dial Eng* : to throw (as a ball) with a jerk **3 :** to emit in a stream : blow out : SPOUT ⟨while I waited . . . the other gun *jetted* smoke —Kenneth Roberts⟩ ⟨*jetted* a powerful stream of water at the burning building⟩ **4 a :** to place (as a pile or caisson) in the ground by means of a jet of water acting at the lower end **b** (1) : to bore (as a well) by means of a high-pressure jet of air or water (2) : to flush out the drillings from (a well) by means of a jet of water **5 :** to apply an insecticide to (an animal) in small jets under pressure
⁶**jet** \"\ n -S [MF, fr. *jeter*] **1 a** (1) : a forceful rush of liquid, gas, or vapor through a narrow or restricted opening in spurts or in a continuous flow ⟨trained the powerful ~ of water on the fire⟩ ⟨saw a practical use for these burning ~s of gas escaping from the earth's fissures —Gardiner Symonds⟩ (2) : a usu. high-speed stream of fluid that is discharged from a nozzle or orifice in a body and that produces reaction forces tending to propel the body in the direction opposite to that of the discharge — see JET PROPULSION **b :** a nozzle for a jet of gas, water, or other fluid ⟨a garden fountain with more than 200 ~s —F.J.Taylor⟩ **c :** something issuing in or as if in a jet ⟨sometimes the whole story is a ~ of irony —H.M.Reynolds⟩ ⟨talk poured from her in a brilliant ~ —*Time*⟩ **2** *dial Eng* : a large ladle **3 :** a projection at the bottom of a piece of foundry type as it comes from the mold that is planed off in finishing — called also *tail*, *tang* **4 a :** JET AIRPLANE **b :** JET ENGINE
⁷**jet** \"\ vi **jetted**; **jetted**; **jetting**; **jets** : to travel by jet airplane ⟨*jetted* to London to see the show —*Newsweek*⟩
⁸**jet** \"\ n -S [prob. alter. of *gist*] : the main point : GIST ⟨but . . . I don't see the ~ of your scheme —R.B.Sheridan⟩
**jet airplane** *also* **jet plane** n : an airplane powered by a jet engine that utilizes the surrounding air in the combustion of fuel or by a rocket-type jet engine that carries its fuel and all the oxygen needed for combustion
**jetbead** \ˈ=,=\ n : a shrub (*Rhodotypos scandens*) that has black shining fruit and is used as an ornamental
**jet black** n : a very dark black
**jet coal** n : CANNEL COAL
**je·té** \zhəˈtā\ n -S [F, fr. past part. of *jeter* to throw, hurl — more at JET] : a sharp leap in ballet with an outward thrust of the working leg — see GRAND JETÉ, TOUR JETÉ
**jeté en tour·nant** \-,äⁿ,tu̇rˈnäⁿ\ n [F, lit., jeté while turning] : TOUR JETÉ
**jet engine** *also* **jet motor** n : an engine that produces motion as a result of the rearward discharge of a jet of fluid; *specif* : an airplane engine having one or more exhaust nozzles for discharging rearward a continuous jet or intermittent jets usu. of heated air and exhaust gases to produce forward propulsion — see ROCKET 4

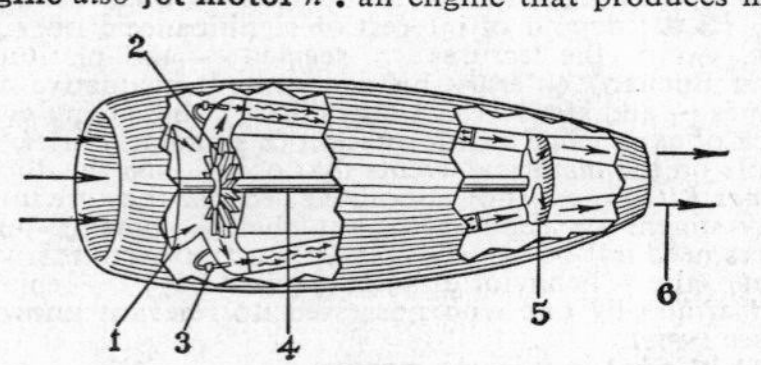

jet engine (simplified cutaway): *1* air intake, *2* impeller or compressor, *3* fuel injection, *4* drive shaft, *5* turbine, *6* exhaust

**jeth** \ˈjet\ n -S *usu cap* [Hindi *Jēṭh*, fr. Skt *Jyaiṣṭha*] : a month of the Hindu year — see MONTH table
**Jet Liner** \ˈ=ˈ=\ *trademark* — used for a jet-propelled airliner
**jet·ness** n -ES [²*jet* + *-ness*] : the quality or state of being the color jet black
**jeton** \ˈjetᵊn, zhəˈtōⁿ *or* **jet·ton** \ˈjetᵊn\ n, pl **jetons** *or* **jettons** \-tᵊnz, -tōⁿ(z)\ [F *jeton*, fr. MF, fr. *jeter* to throw, cast up (accounts), calculate — more at JET] : ¹COUNTER 1a
**jet-pile** \ˈ=,=\ n : a pile placed in position by means of a jet of water under high pressure acting at the toe of the pile to form a space for settling of the pile
**jetport** \ˈ=,=\ n : an airport designed esp. for jet planes
**jet power** n : power derived from jet engines
**jet-propelled** \ˈ==ˈ=\ adj **1 :** propelled by one or more jet engines ⟨*jet-propelled* bomb⟩ ⟨*jet-propelled* airplane⟩ **2 :** suggestive of the speed and force of a jet airplane : HIGH-POWERED ⟨a good and successful novelist producing his works at *jet-propelled* speed —Antonia White⟩ ⟨she possesses enthusiasm and restless energy, her songs are *jet-propelled* —*Punch*⟩
**jet propulsion** n : propulsion of a body by means of a jet of fluid (as in the motion given to an inflated toy balloon when the compressed air is allowed to escape through the neck or the motion given to a rocket by the rearward discharge of a high-speed stream of hot gases produced by the rocket fuel); *specif* : propulsion of an airplane by one or more jet engines
**jet pump** n : a pump in which a small jet of steam, air, water, or other fluid in rapid motion lifts or otherwise moves by its impulse a large quantity of the fluid with which it mingles
**jets** pl of JET, pres 3d sing of JET
**jet·sam** \ˈjetsəm\ n -S [alter. of ¹*jettison*] **1** *archaic* : JETTISON **2 :** the part of a ship, its equipment, or cargo that is cast overboard by the master to lighten the load in time of distress and that sinks or is grounded — distinguished esp. in law from *flotsam* and *lagan* **3 :** FLOTSAM 2
**jet·son** \ˈjetsən\ *or* **jet·som** \-səm\ *archaic var of* JETTISON
**jet stream** n : a long narrow meandering current of high-speed winds near the tropopause blowing from a generally westerly direction and often exceeding a speed of 250 miles per hour
**jet·tage** \ˈjed·ij\ n -S [¹*jetty* + *-age*] : dues levied on a ship for the use of a jetty or pier
**jet·teau** \(,)jeˈtō\ n -S [modif. of F *jet d'eau*] : a jet of water
¹**jet·ted** \ˈjed·əd\ adj [¹*jet* + *-ed*] : having ornaments of jet
²**jetted** \"\ adj [fr. past part. of ⁵*jet*] *Brit* : PIPED, BOUND — used esp. of pockets
¹**jet·ter** \ˈjed·ə(r)\ n -S [³*jet* + *-er*] : one that digs jet
²**jetter** \"\ n -S [⁵*jet* + *-er*] : one (as a geyser) that sends out a jet
**jet thrust** n : THRUST 3c(2)
**jetting** pres part of JET
¹**jet·ti·son** \ˈjed·əsən, ˈjet|, |-əzən\ n -S [ME *jetteson*, fr. AF *getteson*, fr. OF *getaison*, *getaisson* action of throwing, fr. L *jactation-*, *jactatio* — more at JACTATION] **1** *marine insurance* : a voluntary sacrifice of cargo of a ship necessitated by immediately impending danger threatening the general interest —

compare GENERAL AVERAGE **2 :** a casting overboard or away (as of an object, a person, an idea) **:** ABANDONMENT ⟨illustrates more forcibly than any election that has yet taken place the ~ of convictions, of honor, of patriotism —*Saturday Rev.*⟩

**²jettison** \"\ *vt* -ED/-ING/-S **1** *maritime law* **:** to make flotsam and jetsam of ⟨deck loads were so heavy that many carriers had to ~ cargo when they got into a stiff blow —D.H.Clark⟩ **2 :** to cast off as an encumbrance **:** get rid of **:** throw away **:** ABANDON, DISCARD ⟨if a diver does not know how to control his equipment or to ~ it in an emergency . . . he courts disaster —Byron Porterfield⟩ ⟨the obsolete has been calmly ~*ed;* the translation into the contemporary is complete —J.L.Lowes⟩ ⟨an army too soft to ~ its weaklings is on the way out —*Infantry Jour.*⟩ **3 :** to drop (as auxiliary equipment, bombs, cargo, or fuel) from an airplane in flight (as for lightening the load or providing greater safety) ⟨external long-range fuel tanks which are ~*ed* in combat —Peter Masefield⟩

**jet·ti·son·able** \-nəbəl\ *adj* **:** designed for being jettisoned or capable of being easily jettisoned from an airplane ⟨~ fuel tanks⟩

**jet·to** \'je,tō\ *n* -S [It *getto,* fr. *gettare* to throw, fr. L *jactare* — more at JET] **:** JETTEAU

**jetton** *var of* JETON

**jet·tru** \'je·(,)trü\ *n* -S *usu cap* **:** a union of seven Turkish peoples of central Asia formed at the end of the 17th or beginning of the 18th century under one khan

**¹jet·ty** \'jed·ē, -etl, |i\ *n* -ES [ME *getee, jettee,* fr. MF *jetee* action of throwing or thrusting, jetty, fr. fem. of *jeté,* past part. of *jeter* to throw — more at JET] **1 a :** a structure (as a pier or mole of wood or stone) extended into a sea, lake, or river to influence the current or tide or to protect a harbor; *also* **:** a protecting frame of a pier **b :** a landing wharf or pier often of framed woodwork **2 :** a part of a building that projects beyond the rest ⟨one of the most common features of New England colonial architecture was the overhanging second story or ~ as it was called —H.S.Morrison⟩ **3 :** a protecting outwork **:** BASTION, BULWARK **4** *dial Eng* **:** a narrow passage or raised footpath **syn** see WHARF

**²jetty** \"\ *vi* -ED/-ING/-ES **1 :** PROJECT, JUT — used esp. of a part of a building **2 :** to extend like a jetty for a distance into a body of water ⟨the great Municipal Pier which *jetties* out nearly a mile into the lake —*Time*⟩

**³jetty** \"\ *adj* [¹*jet* + -*y*] **:** having the color jet black ⟨the sky was of a ~ black, and the stars were brilliantly visible —E.A. Poe⟩ ⟨a wine-red lined cowl which she wore demurely over her ~ hair —Herman Wouk⟩

**jetware** \'=,=\ *n* **:** pottery usu. of red clay covered with a jet-black glaze

**jeu** \'zhə, |ər(·), |ə, *F* |œ\ *n, pl* **jeux** \|ə(z), |ərz, |ər(·), |ə(z), |œ\ [F, fr. L *jocus* joke, jest, game — more at JOKE] **:** GAME

**jeu d'es·prit** \,=də'sprē\ *n, pl* **jeux d'esprit** [F, lit., play of the mind] **:** a play or piece of writing displaying cleverness or wit ⟨senseless to ignore as a mistaken *jeu d'esprit* the labor that went into those parodies —Hugh Kenner⟩

**jeune fille** \,zhə(r)n'fē, -ən-, *or as F*\ *n, pl* **jeunes filles** \"\ [F] **:** a young girl

**jeune pre·mier** \-prəm'yā\ *n, pl* **jeunes premiers** \-ā(z)\ [F] **:** the juvenile lead in a play ⟨bowed low . . . as if he were indeed some real *jeune premier* —H.E.Bates⟩

**jeu·nesse do·rée** \,zhə(r)'nesdə'rā, zhə;-, -(,)dȯ'-, -dō'-, *or as F*\ *n* [F, gilded youth] **:** young people of wealth and fashion ⟨one might have taken him for the type of the *jeunesse dorée* of Virginia surrounded with tutors, servants, horses, and dogs —Van Wyck Brooks⟩ ⟨artists are beginning to contest the occupation of that territory with the *jeunesse dorée* —Stuart Preston⟩

**¹jew** \'jü\ *n* -S [ME *Gyu, Jewe, Jew,* fr. OF *gyu, jeu, jué, juef,* fr. L *Judaeus,* adj. & n., fr. Gk *Ioudaios,* fr. Heb *Yĕhūdhī,* fr. *Yĕhūdhāh* Judah, Jewish kingdom in southern Palestine, after *Yĕhūdhāh* Judah, 4th son of Jacob and ancestor of the Judahites] **1** *usu cap* **a :** JUDAHITE **b :** ISRAELITE 1 **2** *cap* **:** a member of the nation existing in Palestine from the 6th century B.C. to the 1st century A.D. within which the elements of Judaism largely developed **3** *cap* **:** a person belonging to the worldwide group constituting a continuation through descent or conversion of the ancient Jewish people and characterized by a sense of community; *esp* **:** one whose religion is Judaism — see ASHKENAZI, SEPHARDI **4** *usu cap* **:** a person believed to drive a hard bargain

**²jew** \"\ *adj, usu cap* **:** JEWISH — usu. taken to be offensive

**³jew** \"\ *vt* -ED/-ING/-S *sometimes cap* **:** to cheat by sharp business practice — usu. taken to be offensive

**jewbird** \'=,=\ *n* [¹*jew* + *bird;* fr. its conspicuous beak] **:** ANI

**jewbush** \'=,=\ *n* [¹*jew* + *bush;* prob. fr. the shape of the involucres] **:** either of two tropical American low shrubs of the genus *Pedilanthus* (*P. tithymaloides* and *P. padifolius*) possessing powerful emetic and drastic properties

**jew crow** *n* [prob. so called fr. its prominent curved beak] *dial Eng* **:** CHOUGH

**jew down** *vt, sometimes cap J* **:** to induce (a seller) by haggling to lower his price **:** get (a price or a sum) reduced by haggling — usu. taken to be offensive

**¹jew·el** \'jüəl, 'jü| also |l, *chiefly Brit* |(,)il\ *n* -S *often attrib* [ME *juel, jowel, jewel,* fr. OF *juel, joel, joiel,* dim. of *ju, jo, jeu* game, play — more at JEOPARDY] **1** *archaic* **:** an article with intrinsic value usu. used for adornment ⟨here, wear this ~ for me; 'tis my picture —Shak.⟩ **2 a :** a precious stone; *esp* **:** a stone cut and polished for use as an ornament ⟨they shall fetch thee ~s from the deep —Shak.⟩ **b** (1) **:** one that is highly esteemed or prized ⟨had our prince, ~ of children, seen this hour —Shak.⟩ (2) **:** something that resembles a jewel ⟨this lake — a ~ nestling amid mountains —H.J.Laski⟩ ⟨presenting the ~ of truth in a pleasing setting —R.A.Hall b.1911⟩ **3 a :** an ornament of precious metal usu. gold or silver, often set with stones or finished with enamel work and now usu. worn as an accessory of dress or as the badge of an order **b :** an article of costume jewelry **4 a :** a bearing for a pivot in a watch or a delicate instrument (as a compass) made of a crystal or a precious stone (as a ruby or sapphire) or of glass **b :** a lining of brass or other soft metal for a bearing (as on a railroad car) **5 :** an ornamental boss of colored glass

**²jewel** \"\ *vt* **jeweled** *or* **jewelled; jeweled** *or* **jewelled; jeweling** *or* **jewelling; jewels 1 a :** to adorn with jewels ⟨you are as well ~*ed* as any of them —Ben Jonson⟩ ⟨the kings go by with ~*ed* crowns —John Masefield⟩ **b :** to equip with jewels ⟨company sells more ~*ed* watches than any other in the U.S. —*Time*⟩ ⟨building precision ~*ed* engines by mass-production methods —*Newsweek*⟩ **c :** to trim with jeweling ⟨lacy white wool . . . heavily ~*ed* with iridescent sequins —*Women's Wear Daily*⟩ **2 :** to give beauty or perfection to as if by adorning with jewels ⟨the still swamp water was dark . . . but in open patches it was ~*ed* with reflected stars —Myrtle R. White⟩ ⟨~*ing* all this outer zone of the marsh are the little birds —D.C.Peattie⟩ ⟨a dazzling blaze of ~*ed* words and flashing images —*Times Lit. Supp.*⟩

**jewel beetle** *n* **:** any of various usu. brightly colored beetles of the family Buprestidae

**jewel block** *n* **:** a block at the extremity of a yard through which the halyard of a studding sail is rove

**jewel box** *or* **jewel case** *n* **1 :** a small chest designed to hold jewelry **2 :** something small and exquisite ⟨his house . . . a *jewel box,* quite the most desirable upon the seaside drive —D.C.Peattie⟩

**jewel cloth** *n* **:** a usu. gauzy fabric with sparkling metallic bits sprinkled over its surface that is used chiefly for stage costumes and window displays

jewel box 1

**jew·el·er** *or* **jew·el·ler** \-lə(r)\ *n* -S [ME *jueler, joweler,* fr. *juel, jowel* jewel + -*er* — more at JEWEL] **1 a :** an artist who designs and makes jewelry — compare GOLDSMITH **b :** one who repairs jewelry **2 :** one who deals in precious and costume jewelry, precious stones, watches, and usu. silverware, china, and giftwares **3 :** one who specializes in the construction and repair of highly sensitive scientific instruments

**jewelers' block insurance** *n* **:** all-risk insurance covering jewelers' stocks including property of others in the custody of the insured

**jewelers' putty** *n* **:** PUTTY POWDER

**jewelers' rouge** *n* **:** rouge that is of fine quality and fine particle size

**jewel fish** *n* **:** a small scarlet and olive African cichlid fish (*Hemichromis bimaculatus*) irregularly speckled with emerald green or sapphire that is sometimes kept in a tropical aquarium

**jeweling** *or* **jewelling** *n* -S **1 :** the act or art of working in or of applying jewels **2 :** the ornamentation of pottery with bosses of glass or glaze **3 :** an arrangement of real or imitation jewels used as a trimming on a dress

**jew·el·lery** \-lri\ *chiefly Brit var of* JEWELRY

**jew·el·ry** \-lrē,-lri\ *n* -ES [ME *juelrie, jowelrie,* fr. *juel, jowel* jewel + -*rie* -ry] **1 :** ornamental pieces (as rings, necklaces, bracelets) made of materials that may or may not be precious (gold, silver, glass, plastic) often set with genuine or imitation gems and worn for personal adornment — see COSTUME JEWELRY **2 :** something like jewelry (as in beautifying or adorning) ⟨I wished to see the snow and ice, the divine ~ of winter —John Muir †1914⟩

**jewels** *pl of* JEWEL, *pres 3d sing of* JEWEL

**jewelweed** \'=(=),=\ *n* **:** a plant of the genus *Impatiens* **:** BALSAM 4: as **a :** a somewhat glaucous annual herb (*I. capensis*) of No. America that occurs from Newfoundland to Alaska and south to Florida chiefly on wet rather acid soil and has extremely variable but typically crimson-spotted orange open flowers and sometimes minute cleistogamous flowers — called also *celandine* **b :** a glaucous annual herb (*I. pallida*) that occurs on wet and usu. calcareous soil in much of eastern and central No. America and has canary yellow to creamy white flowers sometimes spotted with brownish red — called also *snapweed, touch-me-not*

**jewelweed family** *n* **:** BALSAMINACEAE

**jew·ely** *or* **jew·el·ly** *pronunc at* JEWEL + ē *or* i\ *adj* **1 :** having or wearing jewels **2 :** resembling a jewel **:** having the brilliance and sparkle of a jewel ⟨the ~ star of life had descended too far —Thomas De Quincy⟩

**jew·ess** \'jüəs\ *n* -ES *usu cap* [ME *Jewesse,* fr. *Gyu, Jewe, Jew* Jew + -*esse* -ess — more at JEW] **:** a female Jew

**jewfish** \'=,=\ *n* **1 :** any of various large groupers usu. dusky green or blackish, thickheaded, and rough-scaled, with a voracious but sluggish disposition: as **a :** GIANT BASS **b :** SPOTTED JEWFISH **c :** BLACK JEWFISH **2 :** any of various other large percoid fishes: as **a :** a western Australian lutjanid (*Glaucosoma hebraicum*) **b :** MULLOWAY

**jewing** *pres part of* JEW

**¹jew·ish** \'jüish, -üēsh\ *adj, usu cap* **:** of, relating to, or characteristic of a Jew — **jew·ish·ly** *adv, usu cap*

**²jewish** \"\ *n* -ES *cap* **:** YIDDISH

**jewish calendar** *n, usu cap J* **:** a lunisolar calendar in use among Jewish peoples which is reckoned from the year 3761 B.C., which received its present form from Hillel II about A.D.360, and in which 19 years constitute a metonic cycle — see MONTH table, YEAR table

**jew·ish·ness** *n* -ES *usu cap* **:** the quality or state of being Jewish

**jewish science** *n, cap J&S* **:** a healing cult adapted from Christian Science to persons with a Jewish background

**jew·ism** \'jü,izəm\ *n* -S *usu cap* **1 :** JUDAISM **2 :** something characteristic of Jews

**jew lizard** *n, usu cap J* **:** an Australian agamid lizard (*Amphibolurus barbatus*)

**jew monkey** *n, usu cap J* [prob. so called fr. its beard] **:** any of several sakis and macaques

**jew nail** *n* **:** CORRUGATED FASTENER

**jew plum** *n, usu cap J* **:** OTAHEITE APPLE

**jew·ry** \'jürē, 'jürē, -ri\ *n* -ES *usu cap* [ME *Gywerie, Jewerie, Jewrie,* fr. OF *juierie, juiverie,* fr. *gyu, jeu, jué, juif* Jew + -*erie* -ery — more at JEW] **1 :** a quarter or district of a city or town inhabited by Jews **:** GHETTO **2** *archaic* **:** the land of Judea ⟨let me have a child . . . to whom Herod of *Jewry* may do homage —Shak.⟩ **3 a :** the part of the population of a country that adheres to Judaism ⟨the titular head of Scotch *Jewry* was both a classical scholar and a Hebraist —Maurice Samuel⟩ **b :** the world Jewish community ⟨the recognition of Israel as the focus of Jewish civilization, the cultural center of the world *Jewry* —*Reconstructionist*⟩

**jews** *pl of* JEW, *pres 3d sing of* JEW

**jew's-ear** \'=,=\ *n, pl* **jew's-ears** *usu cap J* [intended as trans. of NL *auricula Judae,* lit., ear of Judas, after *Judas* Iscariot, apostle that betrayed Jesus; fr. its resemblance to a human ear and its frequent growth on elder trees, on one of which Judas reputedly hanged himself] **:** a widely distributed edible fungus (*Auricularia auricula-judae*) growing on decaying wood

**jew's harp** \'jüz *also* ÷ 'jüs+,-\ *or* **jews' harp** *n, usu cap J* [perh. so called fr. their being purveyed by Jewish peddlers] **1 :** a small lyre-shaped instrument placed between the teeth and played by twanging an elastic metal tongue whose tone is modified by changing the size and shape of the mouth cavity **2** *also* **jews-harp-plant** \'=,=,=\ **:** NODDING TRILLIUM **3 :** the ring of an anchor

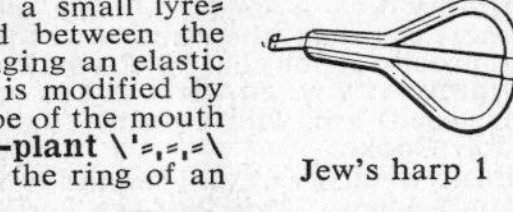

Jew's harp 1

**jews' houses** *n pl, usu cap J* **:** the remains of ancient tin-smelting furnaces and miners' houses in Cornwall and Devon

**jew's mallow** *n, usu cap J* **1 :** a stout herb (*Corchorus olitorius*) cultivated in Syria and Egypt as a potherb and in India for its jute fiber **2 :** JUTE 1

**jew's-stone** \'=,=\ *n, pl* **jew's-stones** *usu cap J* [trans. of ML *lapis Judaicus*] **1 :** a large fossil clavate spine of a sea urchin **2 :** MARCASITE 2

**jews'-thorn** \'=,=\ *n, usu cap J* [so called fr. the belief that it was used to crown Christ] **:** CHRIST'S-THORN

**jew's trump** *n, usu cap J* **:** JEW'S HARP 1

**jew-tongo** \'=;täŋ(,)gō\ *n, usu cap J&T* [prob. fr. Jew-Tongo, fr. *jew* (fr. E *Jew*) + -*tongo* (as in *ningre-tongo*); perh. fr. the existence among its original speakers of former slaves who had been owned by Portuguese Jews] **:** an English-based creole language of Surinam

**jewy** \'jüē, -üi\ *adj* -ER/-EST *usu cap* **:** JEWISH — usu. used disparagingly

**je·zail** \jə'zī(ə)l, -zā(-\ *n* -S [Per *jazā'il*] **:** a long heavy Afghan rifle

**jez·e·bel** \'jezə,bel *also* -,bəl\ *n* -S *often cap* [fr. *Jezebel,* 9th cent. B.C. Phoenician princess and wife of Ahab, king of Israel, known for her wicked conduct (1 Kings 16:31 ff)] **:** an impudent, shameless, or abandoned woman ⟨painted, screaming ~s hauled away by the raiding constables —Albert Parry⟩ — **jez·e·bel·ish** \-ish,-ēsh\ *adj, often cap*

**jez·ek·ite** \'jez(h)ə,kīt\ *n* -S [F *ježekite,* fr. Bohuslav *Ježek* 20th cent. Czech mineralogist + F -*ite*] **:** a mineral $Na_4CaAl_2(PO_4)_2(OH)_2F_2O(?)$ consisting of a basic aluminum calcium sodium fluophosphate occurring in colorless to white monoclinic crystals (hardness 4.5, sp. gr. 2.9)

**JG** *abbr or n* -S *often not cap* **:** junior grade **:** LIEUTENANT JUNIOR GRADE

**jhang·ar** \'jəŋə(r)\ *adj, usu cap* [*Jhang,* district in the Punjab where artifacts were found + E -*ar*] **:** of or relating to a culture in the Indus valley of about 2000 B.C. characterized by a crude handmade gray or black pottery having incised geometric ornamentation

**jhan·si** \'jän(t)sē\ *adj, usu cap* [fr. *Jhansi,* India] **:** of or from the city of Jhansi, India **:** of the kind or style prevalent in Jhansi

**jha·ral** \'järəl\ *n* -S [Nepali *jhāral*] **:** TAHR

**jheel** *or* **jhil** \'jē(ə)l\ *n* -S [Hindi *jhīl*] *India* **:** a pool, marsh, or lake esp. remaining from inundation

**JHS** *var of* IHS

**jhu·kar** \'jükər, -,kär\ *adj, usu cap* [fr. *Jhukar,* Sind, Pakistan, where artifacts were found] **:** of or relating to a culture of the Indus valley about 2500 B.C. and later, known from settlements built upon those of Harappa, and characterized by buildings inferior to Harappa and round crudely decorated seals or seal amulets of pottery

**JHVH** *or* **JHWH** *var of* YHWH

**¹jib** \'jib\ *n* -S [origin unknown] **1 :** a triangular sail set upon a stay or its own luff and extending from the head of the foremast or foretopmast to the bowsprit or the jibboom — see SAIL illustration **2** *dial Eng* **:** the lower lip or jaw

**²jib** \"\ *vb* **jibbed; jibbed; jibbing; jibs** *vt* **:** to cause to swing (as a sail or yard) from one side of a sailing vessel to another (as in tacking) ~ *vi* **1 :** to shift across or swing round from one side of a vessel to the other — used of a ship's sail, yard, or boom **2 :** to shift or swing in a way resembling jibbing ⟨the value of dollars, francs, and pounds sterling *jibbed* this way and that —*Time*⟩

**³jib** \"\ *n* -S [prob. by shortening & alter. fr. *gibbet*] **:** the projecting arm of a crane; *also* **:** a derrick boom

**⁴jib** \"\ *also* **gib** \"\ *vi* **jibbed** *also* **gibbed; jibbed** *also* **gibbed; jibbing** *also* **gibbing; jibs** *also* **gibs** [prob. fr. ²*jib*] **1 :** to move restively backward or sidewise **:** refuse to go; *also* **:** to stop short or back out **:** SHY — used of an animal in harness **2 a :** to show hesitation or a tendency to refuse to proceed further or act in a particular way **:** BALK ⟨he *jibbed* on singing because the women were there —Joseph Furphy⟩ ⟨never *jibbed* at the stiffest climb —Roy Saunders⟩ **b :** to show objection **:** balk in opposition ⟨it was only the middle classes at which he *jibbed* for he was genuinely devoted to his servants —Eric Keown⟩ ⟨*jibbed* at all grief which could not be brushed aside —Elizabeth Taylor⟩ **syn** see DEMUR

**⁵jib** \"\ *n* -S **:** JIBBER

**¹jibaro** *usu cap, var of* JIVARO

**²ji·ba·ro** *or* **gi·ba·ro** \'hēbə,rō\ *n* -S [AmerSp *jíbaro, gíbaro,* prob. fr. *jíbaro* Jivaro] **:** a Puerto Rican small farmer, rural worker, or laborer esp. of mountainous regions

**jib·ba** *or* **djib·bah** *also* **jib·bah** \'jibə\ *n* -S [Egyptian Ar *jibbah,* var. of Ar *jubbah*] **:** a long loose cloth coat usu. with long sleeves worn esp. by Muslims

**¹jibber** *var of* GIBBER

**²jib·ber** \'jibə(r)\ *n* -S [⁴*jib* + -*er*] **:** one that jibs; *esp* **:** a balky horse

**jib·bings** \'jibənz, -biŋz\ *n pl* [fr. gerund of Sc *jib* to milk a cow dry (of unknown origin) + -*s*] *Scot* **:** strippings from a cow

**jib·boom** \(')ji(b)'büm\ *n* [¹*jib* + *boom*] **:** a spar which serves as an extension of the bowsprit and is sometimes itself extended by a flying jibboom — see SHIP illustration

**jib crane** *n* [³*jib*] **:** a crane having a jib

**jib door** \'jib-\ *n* [*jib* of unknown origin] **:** a door made flush with a wall without dressings or moldings and often disguised by continuing the finishings or decorations of the wall across its surface

**¹jibe** *or* **gybe** \'jīb\ *vb* -ED/-ING/-S [perh. modif. (influenced by ¹*jib*) of D *gijben, gijpen*] *vi* **1** *of a fore-and-aft sail or its boom* **:** to shift suddenly and with force from one side to the other when a ship is steered off the wind until the sail fills on the opposite side **2 :** to change the course of a vessel so that the sail jibes — compare TACK 1a ~ *vt* **:** to cause to jibe

**²jibe** *or* **gybe** \"\ *n* -S **:** the swing of a sail or its boom in jibing or the turn of a sailboat so that its sail jibes

**³jibe** \"\ *var of* GIBE

**⁴jibe** *also* **gibe** \"\ *vi* -ED/-ING/-S [origin unknown] **:** to be in accord ⟨his account of the accident ~s pretty well with other accounts⟩ ⟨their inferior status did not ~ with democratic ideals —E.N.Palmer⟩ **syn** see AGREE

**jibe-o** \'jī(,)bō, jī'bō\ *interj* [¹*jibe* + -*o*] — used by the man at the tiller or wheel of a sailboat in warning that the boat is about to jibe

**jib guy** *n* [¹*jib*] **:** one of two or more lateral stays running to the head of the jibboom — see SHIP illustration

**jibhead** \'=,=\ *n* [¹*jib* + *head*] **:** a small iron bar for stretching the head of a jib when the point of the sail has been cut off

**jib-headed** \'=;==\ *adj* [¹*jib*] *of a sail* **:** running up to a point at the head like a jib **:** TRIANGULAR — compare GAFF-HEADED

**jib-header** \'=;==\ *n* **:** a jib-headed topsail

**ji·bi** \'jē(,)bē\ *n* -S [origin unknown] **:** a small chiefly yellowish green extinct bird (*Hemignathus obscurus ellisianus*) of Oahu

**jib iron** *n* [¹*jib*] **:** JIB TRAVELER

**jiblet** *var of* GIBLET

**jib netting** *n* [¹*jib*] **:** a triangular safety netting rigged under a jibboom — see SHIP illustration

**ji·boa** \jə'bōə\ *also* **ji·bo·ya** \-ō(y)ə\ *n* -S [Pg *jibóia,* fr. Tupi] **:** any of several large So. American boas

**ji-o-jib** \'jibə, jib\ *n* -S [¹*jib* + *o* (of) + *jib*] **:** a small jib set outside of the flying jib

**jibs** *pl of* JIB, *pres 3d sing of* JIB

**jib sheet** *n* [¹*jib*] **:** either of two ropes which lead from the clew of a jib to port and starboard respectively and by which the sail is trimmed

**jibstay** \'=,=\ *n* [¹*jib* + *stay*] **:** a stay on which a jib is set

**jib topsail** *n* [¹*jib*] **:** a small jib occas. used and set above and outside of all the other jibs

**jib traveler** *n* [¹*jib*] **:** an iron ring to which the tack of the jib on some cutters is made fast and which travels on the bowsprit

**JIC** *abbr* **1** joint industrial council **2** joint intelligence committee

**ji·ca·ma** \'hēkəmə\ *n* -S [MexSp *jícama,* fr. Nahuatl *xicama, xicamatl*] **1 :** a tall-climbing Mexican vine (*Exogonium bracteatum*) with showy flowers and a sweet watery root that is sometimes eaten raw or cooked — compare JALAP **2 :** YAM BEAN **3 :** a small dahlia (*Dahlia coccinea*) with yellow, orange, or scarlet flowers that is sometimes cultivated and is an ancestor of some improved horticultural dahlias

**ji·ca·que** *or* **xi·ca·que** \hē'kä(,)kā\ *n, pl* **jicaque** *or* **jicaques** *or* **xicaque** *or* **xicaques** *usu cap* [Sp, fr. Nahuatl *xicaque,* lit., ancient person] **1 a :** an Indian people of northern Honduras **b :** a member of such people **2 :** the language of the Jicaque people

**ji·ca·que·an** \-,kēən\ *n* -S *usu cap* **:** a language family of the Hokan stock in Honduras comprising only the Jicaque language

**ji·ca·ra** \'hēkərə\ *n* -S [MexSp *jícara,* fr. Nahuatl *xicalli*] **1 :** CALABASH 2a **2 :** a cup or bowl made from the fruit of a calabash tree

**ji·ca·ri·lla** \,hēkə'rē(y)ə\ *n, pl* **jicarilla** *or* **jicarillas** *usu cap* [Sp, fr. MexSp, little basket, dim. of *jícara;* fr. the proficiency of the women in basketmaking] **1 a :** an Apache people of the western group ranging through southeastern Colorado, northern New Mexico, and adjacent sections of Kansas, Oklahoma, and Texas **b :** a member of such people **2 :** the language of the Jicarilla people

**jiff** \'jif\ *n* -S [by shortening] *slang* **:** JIFFY

**jif·fle** \'jifəl\ *vi* [origin unknown] *dial Eng* **:** to move restlessly **:** FIDGET

**jif·fy** \'jifē, -fi\ *n* -ES [origin unknown] **:** MOMENT, INSTANT — used chiefly in the phrase *in a jiffy*

**¹jig** \'jig\ *n* -S [prob. fr. MF *giguer* to dance, jig, gambol about, frolic, fr. *gigue* fiddle, of Gmc origin; akin to OHG *gīga* fiddle; akin to ON *geiga* to turn aside — more at GIG] **1 a :** any of several lively springy dances in triple rhythm, popular in 16th and 17th century England and Scotland and still commonly danced in Ireland in a way characterized by intricate and dexterous motions of the feet **b :** music to which a jig may be danced **c :** GIGUE 3 **d :** a rapid usu. jerky up-and-down or to-and-fro motion ⟨the ~ of popcorn in a popper⟩ **2** *obs* **a :** a lively usu. jesting or mocking song **b :** a lively or comic act used at the end of a play or as an interlude **3 :** TRICK, STRATAGEM, GAME — now used chiefly in the phrase *the jig is up* **4 a :** any of several fishing devices (as a spoon hook) that are jerked up and down or drawn through the water — compare SQUID **b :** a device used to maintain mechanically the correct positional relationship between a piece of work and the tool working on it or between parts of work during their assembly **c :** a device in which crushed ore is concentrated or coal is cleaned in water by a rapid reciprocating vertical motion imparted to the substance either by mechanical means or by a pulsating water column **d :** a machine for dyeing piece goods by passing them at full width through the dye liquor by means of rollers **5** *also* **jigg** \"\ **:** NEGRO — often taken to be offensive — **in jig time** *adv* **:** with expeditiousness **:** RAPIDLY ⟨the tire was whipped off and changed in *jig time* —Dillon Ripley⟩

**²jig** \"\ *vb* **jigged; jigged; jigging; jigs** [prob. fr. MF *giguer*] *vt* **1 :** to dance in the rapid and lively manner of a jig ⟨~ a morris⟩ **2 a :** to give a rapid jerky up-and-down or to-and-fro motion to ⟨*jigged* his feet —Michael McLaverty⟩ ⟨a handful of coins that he rattled by *jigging* his thumb along the table —Saul Bellow⟩ **:** cause to jig ⟨grabbed a girl and started to ~ her around the yard —C.T.Jackson⟩ **b :** to separate (as ore from gangue or coal from slate) by a rapid up-and-down motion usu. in water **3 :** to catch (a fish) with a jig or by jerking a hook into the body **4 :** to drill (as a well) with a spring pole **5 :** to machine, form, or set in place by means of a jig-controlled tool operation ~ *vi* **1 a :** to dance a jig **:** execute a lively dance or dance step **b :** to move with a jigging motion or with rapid usu. jerky motions up and down or to and fro ⟨*jigged* furiously up and down to limber his leg muscles —A.J.Liebling⟩ **2 :** to fish with a jig ⟨several men in canoes *jigging* for cod —N.C.McDonald⟩ **3 :** to work with the aid of a jig

**³jig** \"\ — a communications code word for the letter *j*

**jig·a·boo** \ˈjigə,bü\ *n* -s [¹*jig* + *-aboo* (as in *bugaboo*)] **:** NEGRO — often taken to be offensive

**jig-a-jig** *or* **jig-a-jog** *var of* JIG-JOG

**jig·a·ma·ree** \ˈjigəmə,rē, ,==ˈ=\ *n* -s [¹*jig* + *-amaree*, of unknown origin] *slang* **:** something (as a device or contrivance) felt to be too fanciful, difficult, or small in value to designate accurately

**jig-back** \ˈ=,=\ *adj* [fr. the phrase *jig back*] **:** having two carriers that alternately ascend and descend — used of an aerial tramway

**jig borer** *n* [¹*jig*] **:** a precision machine tool resembling a vertical milling machine, equipped with sensitive adjustments for the table and the position of the cutting tool, and used esp. for locating and drilling or boring holes in jigs

**¹jig·ger** \ˈjigə(r)\ *n* -s [¹ and ²*jig* + *-er*] **1 :** one that jigs **:** one that operates a jig: as **a :** one that concentrates ore by jigging — called also *jigman* **b :** one that shakes down the grain into sacks during bagging **c :** the operator of a dyeing jig — called also *jigman, vatman* **2 :** a light tackle usu. consisting of a double and single block and fall **:** WATCH TACKLE **3 :** ¹JIG 4a **4 a :** a small boat rigged like a yawl **b** *or* **jiggermast** \ˈ=,=\ (1) **:** a small mast stepped in the stern (as in a yawl or ketch) (2) **:** the aftermost mast of a four-masted ship **c :** a sail set on a jiggermast **5 a :** a mechanical contrivance esp. operating with a jerky reciprocating motion: as (1) **:** a machine carrying a revolving mold in which the clay for ceramics is shaped by a profile (2) **:** a machine for slicking or pebbling leather (3) **:** a tool for polishing the upper leather or the edge of a boot sole **b :** something (as a contrivance, device, or gewgaw) too complex, tricky, or trivial to designate accurately **:** GADGET **6 :** a measure used in mixing drinks and holding usu. one and one half ounces **7 :** JIG 4d **8 :** a cooper's drawknife **9 :** a golf iron with a narrow fairly well lofted face used esp. for approach shots **10 :** a part of a commercial fish trap that impounds the fish **11 :** ¹BRIDGE 3e

jigger 6

**²jigger** \"\ *vb* **jiggered; jiggered; jiggering** \-g(ə)riŋ\ **jiggers** [freq. of ²*jig*] *vi, of a fish* **:** to give repeated tugs on a line ~ *vt* **1 :** to jerk up and down **:** give a series of tugs on **2 :** to alter or rearrange sometimes by manipulating ⟨~*ed* the records to cover up his theft⟩ **3** [¹*jigger*] **:** to shape with a jigger in ceramics

**³jigger** \"\ *n* -s [of African origin; akin to Wolof *jiga* insect, Yoruba *ji'ga³* jigger] **:** CHIGGER

**jig·gered** \ˈjigə(r)d\ *adj* [origin unknown] **:** DAMNED — used in mild oaths usu. in the phrase *I'll be jiggered*

**jigger flea** *n* [³*jigger*] **:** CHIGOE

**jiggering** *n* -s [fr. gerund of ²*jigger*] **:** the process of forming ceramic ware by means of a jigger

**jigger·man** \ˈjigə(r)mən, -,man\ *n, pl* **jiggermen 1 :** one who forms pottery on a jigger **2 :** one who resurfaces and sharpens large grindstones on a stone-dressing lathe

**jigger pump** *n* [¹*jigger*] **:** a pump to force beer into vats

**jig·gers** \ˈjigə(r)z\ *interj* [origin unknown] — used as a warning esp. that police are coming

**jigger saw** *n* [by alter.] **:** JIG SAW

**jigger up** *vt, slang* **:** to throw into confusion ⟨won't have the camp arrangements *jiggered up* any more than they are —C.S. Forester⟩ **:** foul up ⟨the machinery was all *jiggered up*⟩

**jiggery-pokery** \ˈjigərē¦pōkərē\ *n* -ES [alter. of *joukery-pawkery*] **1** *chiefly Brit* **:** HUMBUG, NONSENSE **2 :** underhanded dealings, conniving, or manipulations **:** MONKEY BUSINESS, SKULDUGGERY

**jig·get** \ˈjigət\ *vi* **jiggeted** *or* **jiggetted; jiggeted** *or* **jiggetted; jiggeting** *or* **jiggetting; jiggets** [²*jig* + *-et* (as in *fidget*)] **:** to move in a jigging or jerky way **:** JIG

**jig·gety** \-gəd·ē\ *adj, sometimes* -ER/-EST **:** JERKY, UNSTEADY

**jigging** *pres part of* JIG

**jig·gish** \ˈjigish, -gēsh\ *adj* **:** resembling or suitable for a jig or lively movement

**¹jig·gle** \ˈjigəl\ *vb* **jiggled; jiggled; jiggling** \-g(ə)liŋ\ **jiggles** [freq. of ²*jig*] *vi* **:** to move with quick little continuous jerks or oscillating motions back and forth or up and down ⟨*jiggling* like a doll on a coiled spring —Raymond Chandler⟩ ~ *vt* **:** to cause to jiggle ⟨*jiggled* the cup to mix the milk and the coffee —Wirt Williams⟩

**²jiggle** \"\ *n* -s **1 :** the motion of one that jiggles **2 :** a brief contrived fluctuation in the price of a stock more limited than a pool operation

**jig·gly** \ˈjig(ə)lē, -li\ *adj, often* -ER/-EST **:** tending to jiggle **:** UNSTEADY, JIGGLING ⟨the short leg of a ~ table —*New Yorker*⟩ **:** marked by a jiggling motion ⟨a ~ ride in a bus⟩

**jig grinder** *n* [²*jig*] **:** a precision grinding machine with fine adjustments for work requiring great accuracy (as in the fabrication of jigs and dies)

**jiggumbob** *n* -s [²*jig* + *-umbob* (of unknown origin)] *obs* **:** a contrivance or trifle felt to be too fanciful, difficult, or trivial to designate accurately

**jig·gy** \ˈjigē, -gi\ *adj, often* -ER/-EST **:** suggesting or having the effect of a jig

**¹jig-jog** \ˈjig,jäg\ *also* **jig-jig** \-,jig\ *or* **jig-a-jog** \ˈjigə,jäg\ *or* **jig-a-jig** \ˈ==,=\ *vi* [¹*jig* + *jog*] **:** to move with jigs or jogs **:** bounce jerkily up and down in proceeding **:** jolt repeatedly up and down

**²jig-jog** *also* **jig-jig** *or* **jig-a-jog** *or* **jig-a-jig** \"\ *n* **:** the movement of something that jig-jogs

**³jig-jog** *also* **jig-jig** *or* **jig-a-jog** *or* **jig-a-jig** \"\ *adv* **:** in the manner of one that jig-jogs ⟨trotted *jig-jog* down the road⟩

**jig-joggy** \ˈjig,jägē\ *adj* **:** jolting or bouncing jerkily up and down **:** JOGGING

**jig·man** \ˈjigmən\ *n, pl* **jigmen** [¹*jig* + *man*] **:** JIGGER 1a, 1c

**jigs** *pl of* JIG, *pres 3d sing of* JIG

**¹jigsaw** \ˈ=,=\ *n* [¹*jig* + *saw*] **1 a :** a machine saw with a narrow vertically reciprocating blade for cutting curved and irregular lines or ornamental patterns in openwork **b :** SCROLL SAW **2 :** JIGSAW PUZZLE ⟨broken up like a ~ loose in its box —Wright Morris⟩ ⟨as the pieces of the ~ are fitted together —*Economist*⟩

jigsaw 1a

**²jigsaw** \"\ *vt* **1 :** to cut or form by or as if by a jigsaw ⟨coat and skirt ~*ed* out of her deceased father's Sunday suit —Francis & Katharine Drake⟩ **2 :** to arrange or place in an intricate or interlocking way in the manner of the parts of a jigsaw puzzle ⟨giant industrial plants ~*ed* together —Cameron Hawley⟩ ⟨the place was full of planes, ~*ed* into every foot of space —Frank Harvey⟩

**³jigsaw** \"\ *adj* **1 :** made up of pieces cut by a jigsaw **2 a :** consisting of intricate scrollwork ⟨~ detail around the eaves and windows⟩ ⟨gables decorated with ~ frills —*Amer. Guide Series: Tenn.*⟩ **b :** marked by the use of intricate scrollwork as decoration ⟨ornamental architecture of the ~ period —W.A. White⟩ **c** (1) **:** suggesting intricate scrollwork ⟨its spectacular ~ pattern of islands and inland waterways —W.R.Moore⟩ ⟨driving through its ~ streets —Kamala Markandaya⟩ ⟨transactions . . . of ~ complexity —*Lamp*⟩ (2) **:** suggesting a jigsaw puzzle or its separate pieces ⟨the witness may get history across at last in ~ bits —Mitchell Dawson⟩

**jigsaw puzzle** *n* **:** a puzzle made by sawing or cutting a picture into small pieces to be fitted together — called also *picture puzzle*

**ji·gua** \ˈhēgwə\ *n* -s [AmerSp, fr. Carib] **:** any of several tropical American trees of the genera *Ocotea* and *Nectandra*

**jigue** *var of* JIQUI

**ji·had** *also* **je·had** \jəˈhäd, -had\ *n* -s *sometimes cap* [Ar *jihād*] **:** a holy war waged on behalf of Islam as a religious duty; *broadly* **:** a bitter strife or crusade undertaken in the spirit of a holy war

**ji·kun·gu** \jəˈküŋ(,)gü\ *n* -s [Shambala *zikungu, nkungu*, pl. of *lukungu*] **:** a tropical African plant (*Telfairia pedata*) of the family Cucurbitaceae cultivated for its edible seeds which also yield an oil

**¹jill** *often cap, var of* GILL

**²jill** \ˈjil\ *n* -s [¹*jill*] **:** a female ferret

**jill·et** \ˈjilət\ *n* -s [¹*jill* + *-et*] *now Scot* **:** a vexatiously flirtatious girl **:** WENCH

**¹jil·lion** \ˈjilyən\ *n* -s [*j-* + *-illion* (as in *million, billion*)] **:** an indeterminately large number ⟨any number of spots from one to a ~ —Alfred Bester⟩

**²jillion** \"\ *adj* **:** very great many ⟨climbing those stairs a ~ times a day —Jean Stafford⟩

**¹jilt** \ˈjilt\ *n* -s [alter. of *jillet*] **1** *obs* **:** an unchaste woman **:** WHORE **2 a :** a woman who capriciously casts off one previously accepted as a lover **b :** a man who is capricious and irresponsible in love relations ⟨a young ~ who switched from one woman to another every few months⟩

**²jilt** \"\ *vt* -ED/-ING/-S **1 a :** to cast off or reject (as a lover) capriciously or unfeelingly **b :** to sever close relations with **2** *obs* **:** DECEIVE, CHEAT

**jilt·ee** \(ˈ)jil¦tē\ *n* -s **:** one who has been jilted

**jilt·er** \ˈjiltə(r)\ *n* -s **:** one that jilts

**jim·ber-jawed** \ˈjimbə(r)¦=\ *adj* [prob. alter. of *gimbal* + *jawed*] **:** having a projecting lower jaw

**jimcrack** *var of* GIMCRACK

**¹jim crow** \ˈjimˈkrō\ *n, often cap J&C* [after *Jim Crow*, a stereotype Negro in a song-and-dance act presented by Thomas D. Rice †1860 Am. entertainer that was based on an anonymous song of the early 19th cent. called *Jim Crow*] **1 :** NEGRO — usu. taken to be offensive **2 :** discrimination (as in educational opportunity, social rights, or transportation facilities) against a racial or ethnic group other than white and esp. against the Negro in the southern U.S. by either legal enforcement or traditional sanctions and usu. by restrictive measures designed to prevent intermingling (as of Negroes with whites) on equal terms in public places ⟨the Supreme Court decision outlawing *Jim Crow* in dining cars on interstate trains —*Time*⟩ **3 a :** a machine for bending or straightening rails **b :** a planing machine with a reversing tool that can plane both ways

**²jim crow** \ˈ=¦=\ *adj, often cap J&C* **1 :** upholding jim crow ⟨gradual relinquishment of *Jim Crow* laws —Raymond Moley⟩ **:** practicing jim crow ⟨a *jim crow* school⟩ ⟨a *jim crow* town⟩ **:** marked by jim crow ⟨this *Jim Crow* environment —H.M.Gloster⟩ **2 :** set aside for the use of a racial or ethnic group (as the Negro in the southern U.S.) that is being discriminated against ⟨a *jim crow* railroad car⟩

**³jim crow** \"\ *vt, often cap J&C* **:** to subject to jim crow ⟨the exploited and *jim crowed* life of the Negro —Sidney Finkelstein⟩ ⟨many . . . states *jim crow* the Indians —Oliver La Farge⟩

**jim crow·ism** \ˈ=ˈ=,izəm\ *n, often cap J&C* **:** racial segregation

**¹jim-dandy** \ˈjimˈ=\ *n* [*Jim* (nickname for *James*) + *dandy*] **:** something fine or wonderful of its kind ⟨the bicycle he got as a gift was a *jim-dandy*⟩

**²jim-dandy** \ˈ=¦=\ *adj* **:** fine or wonderful of its kind ⟨had a *jim-dandy* voice⟩ ⟨a *jim-dandy* invention⟩

**jim dash** \ˈ=,=\ *n* [prob. fr. the name *Jim*] **:** a short printed dash usu. used to separate the decks of a newspaper headline, individual items under one newspaper heading, or separate stories dealing with one event if they follow each other in the same column

**jim fish** \ˈ=¦=\ *n, usu cap J&F* [*Jim* (nickname for *James*) + *fish*] *SoAfr* **:** NEGRO — usu. taken to be offensive

**jim hill mustard** \ˈ=¦hil-\ *n, usu cap J&H* [after *Jim* (James J.) *Hill* †1916 Am. railroad promoter; fr. the growth of the weed along railroad lines J. Hill promoted] **:** TUMBLE MUSTARD

**jim·i·ny** *or* **jim·mi·ny** \ˈjimənē, ˈjēm-, -ni\ *interj* [alter. of *gemini*] — used as a mild oath often in the phrases *by jiminy, jiminy crickets, jiminy Christmas*

**jim·jams** \ˈjim,jamz, -,jaa(ə)mz\ *n pl* [perh. alter. of *delirium tremens*] *slang* **:** DELIRIUM TREMENS; *also* **:** a markedly nervous, overwrought, or depressed condition esp. arising from excess or fear ⟨drink so much coffee I get the ~ —*New Yorker*⟩ ⟨attack the January ~ with love and laughter —*Mademoiselle*⟩

**jimmer** *var of* GIMMER

**jim·mies** \ˈjimēz, -miz\ *n pl* [alter. of *jimjams*] **1** *slang* **a :** DELIRIUM TREMENS — used with *the* **b :** extreme nervousness or depression **2 :** a fern poisoning of sheep, cattle, and goats marked by seizures of severe trembling often followed by acute respiratory paralysis and death

**¹jim·my** \ˈjimē, -mi\ *var of* JEMMY

**²jimmy** \"\ *n* -ES [fr. *Jimmy*, nickname for *James*] **1 :** a short crowbar ⟨the window was pried open with a ~⟩ **2 :** a railroad car for coal **3 :** SPOT 7

**³jimmy** \"\ *vt* -ED/-ING/-ES **:** to pry or force open (something fastened) esp. with a jimmy ⟨did he ~ a window or door —T.G.Cooke⟩

**jimmyweed** \ˈ==,=\ *n* [*jimmies* + *weed*] **:** RAYLESS GOLDENROD

**¹jimp** \ˈjimp\ *adj* -ER/-EST [origin unknown] **1** *dial Brit* **a :** slender and trim **b :** neat and spruce **2** *dial Brit* **:** SCANTY, SKIMPY — **jimp·ly** \-lē\ *adv*

**²jimp** \"\ *vt* -ED/-ING/-S *dial Brit* **:** to cut short **:** SKIMP

**³jimp** \"\ *adv, dial Brit* **:** BARELY, SCARCELY

**jim·son·weed** \ˈjim(p)sən,=\ *or* **james·town weed** \ˈjāmz,taůn-\ *or* **jimson** *or* **jimp·son·weed** *also* **jimpson** *n* -s *often cap J* [fr. *Jamestown*, Va.] **:** an intensely poisonous tall coarse annual weed (*Datura stramonium*) of tropical and perhaps Asiatic origin now naturalized in many parts of the world and having rank-smelling foliage and large white or violet trumpet-shaped flowers that are succeeded by globose prickly fruits — called also *apple of Peru*

jimsonweed

**jim·swing·er** \ˈjim,swiŋə(r)\ *n* [origin unknown] *South & Midland* **:** a long-tailed coat

**ji·na** \ˈjinə\ *n* -s *usu cap* [Skt, saint, victorious — more at JAIN] **:** one who according to Jainism has conquered temporal and material existence through self-discipline and attained a transcendent and eternal state of bliss; *esp* **:** one venerated as a tirthankara

**jin·dy·wor·o·bak** \,jindēˈwórə,bak\ *n* -s [prob. fr. native name in Australia] **:** one of a group of strongly nationalistic Australians seeking to promote native ideas and traditions esp. in literature

**ji·ne·te** \hēˈnād·ē\ *n* -s [MexSp, fr. Sp, Zenete, mounted soldier, horseman, one skilled at horsemanship, fr. colloq. Ar *zinētī* of the Zenetes — more at JENNET] **:** one who trains young horses to the bridle and saddle

**jing** \ˈjiŋ\ *interj* [short for ¹*jingo*] — a mild oath usu. used in the phrase *by jing*

**jing·bang** \ˈjiŋ,baŋ\ *n* -s [origin unknown] *slang* **:** COMPANY, CROWD — used in the phrase *the whole jingbang*

**¹jin·gle** \ˈjiŋgəl\ *vb* **jingled; jingled; jingling** \-g(ə)liŋ\ **jingles** [ME *ginglen*, of imit. origin] *vi* **1 :** to make a usu. light sharp continued clinking or varied and mingled tinkling usu. metallic sound ⟨sleigh bells ~⟩ ⟨coins in his pocket *jingled* as he walked⟩ ⟨innumerable pottery bracelets *jingled* up and down upon her arms —Scott Fitzgerald⟩ **2 :** to sound in a way chiefly characterized by continued catchy repetition (as of rhyme, phrase, cadence) — used esp. of verse ~ *vt* **:** to cause to jingle ⟨*jingled* the coins in his pocket as he talked⟩ ⟨loved to ~ his spurs —Owen Wister⟩ — **jin·gler** \-g(ə)lə(r)\ *n* -s

**²jingle** \"\ *n* -s **1 :** a metallic jingling sound ⟨the ~ of the small bells⟩ **:** a rhythmical cadence ⟨the ~ of the verse as he read it⟩ **2 a :** something that jingles or is designed to jingle ⟨a toy tambourine set about with little ~*s*⟩ **b** (1) **:** a short verse marked esp. by catchy repetition (as of rhyme, alliterative sounds, cadences) ⟨not so much a poet as a writer of ~*s*⟩ (2) **:** a short catchy song usu. using such a verse ⟨composing ~*s* for TV advertising⟩ (3) **:** an incomplete verse used in a contest in which the entrants supply the missing lines **3 :** a two-wheeled covered vehicle used in parts of Ireland and Australia as a public conveyance **4 :** JINGLE SHELL

**jingle bell** *n* **1 :** a bell mounted on a spring and used to signal the engine room for all speed available **2 a :** CASCABEL **b :** SLEIGH BELL **3 :** a signal bell used on a shop door to announce the entrance of customers

**jinglebob** \ˈ==,=\ *n* [¹*jingle* + *bob*] **:** a cattle marking consisting of an ear slashed so that the halves dangle beside the head; *also* **:** a steer with such a marking

**jin·gled** \ˈjiŋgəld\ *adj, slang* **:** mildly drunk

**¹jin·gle-jan·gle** \ˈjiŋgəl¦jaŋgəl\ *n* -s [redupl. of ²*jingle*] **:** a jingling and jangling sound ⟨the unpleasant ~ of metallic objects in the back of the car truck⟩

**²jinglejangle** \"\ *vi* **:** to make a jinglejangle ⟨~ like goat bells on the Alps —Rose Macaulay⟩

**jingle shell** *n* **:** a mollusk of the genus *Anomia* or sometimes of the family Anomiidae having thin flat translucent shell valves that produce noise when dried and shaken together

**jingle stick** *n* **:** a usu. toy percussion instrument formed of a stick on which are mounted small metal disks

**jin·glet** \ˈjiŋglət\ *n* -s [²*jingle* + *-et*] **:** the ball clapper of a sleigh bell

**¹jingling** *n* [ME *gingling*, fr. gerund of *ginglen* to jingle — more at JINGLE] **1 :** the act or process of producing a jingle **2 :** JINGLE 1

**²jingling** *adj* [fr. pres. part. of ¹*jingle*] **:** making the sound of something that jingles

**jingling johnny** *n, usu cap 2d J* **:** PAVILLON CHINOIS

**jin·gling·ly** *adv* **:** in a jingling manner

**jingling match** *n* **:** an old English game in which blindfolded players try to catch one not blindfolded player who keeps jingling a bell

**jin·gly** \ˈjiŋ(g)(ə)lē, -li\ *adj, sometimes* -ER/-EST [²*jingle* + *-y*] **:** having a jingling quality **:** sounding like a jingle ⟨a ~ sound from a vibrating metallic part⟩ ⟨a ~ verse⟩

**¹jin·go** \ˈjiŋ(,)gō\ *interj* [prob. euphemism for *Jesus*] — used formerly as an exclamation by conjurers when producing something by sleight of hand; now used as a mild oath usu. in the phrase *by jingo*

**²jingo** \"\ *n* -ES [fr. *Jingo* supporter of the British belligerent attitude toward Russia in 1878, fr. ¹*jingo*; fr. the fact that the phrase *by jingo* appeared in the refrain of a chauvinistic song sung by the Jingoes] **:** one characterized by jingoism **:** a clamorous and belligerent chauvinist ⟨~*es* clamored for war —Ethel Drus⟩

**³jingo** \"\ *adj* **:** of or relating to a jingo **:** marked by jingoism ⟨a ~ nationalism⟩

**jin·go·ish** \-ish\ *adj* [²*jingo* + *-ish*] **:** tending to jingoism ⟨a ~ statesman⟩ **:** marked by jingoism ⟨the ~ remarks of the nationalists⟩

**jin·go·ism** \-,izəm\ *n* -s [²*jingo* + *-ism*] **:** clamorous chauvinism or arrogant nationalism esp. marked by a belligerent foreign policy ⟨warfare generates ~ —Barbara Ward⟩ ⟨belligerent ~ and narrow isolationism —J.F.Kennedy⟩

**¹jin·go·ist** \-,əst\ *n* -s [²*jingo* + *-ist*] **:** JINGO ⟨the magniloquent parrot cries of the ~ —*Spectator*⟩

**²jingoist** \"\ *or* **jin·go·is·tic** \¦=(,)=¦istik\ *adj* **:** JINGO ⟨a ~ slogan advocating war⟩ ⟨*jingoistic* national pride —*New Republic*⟩ — **jin·go·is·ti·cal·ly** \-tək(ə)lē\ *adv*

**jingo ring** *n* [¹*jingo*] *Scot* **:** a singing game in which children join hands and dance around one in the center

**jinjili** *var of* GINGELLY

**¹jink** \ˈjiŋk\ *n* -s [origin unknown] **1 jinks** \ˈjiŋ(k)s\ *pl* **:** PRANKS, FROLICS ⟨operettas in which the ~*s* of a prewar military aristocracy were reclothed in the fashions of 1932 —Christopher Isherwood⟩ ⟨the ~*s* of a gang of youthful pranksters⟩ **2 :** the act or movement of one that jinks **:** a dodging away **:** SLIP

**²jink** \"\ *vb* -ED/-ING/-S *vi* **1 a :** to move quickly with sudden turns or changes of direction (as in dancing or dodging) ⟨is constantly flying at fast speed, and is forever ~*ing* all over the sky, twisting, turning, weaving, trying to avoid the flak from below —J.S.Childers⟩ **b :** to run away esp. by agile movements ⟨the bear had ~*ed* sideways and vanished into a cave —Christine Weston⟩ ⟨these little white grouse ~ out over the snowy sidings —Richard Perry⟩ **2** *chiefly Scot* **:** to play tricks and frolic **3 :** to play for five tricks in spoil five after winning three at the risk of losing if unsuccessful the tricks already taken — used with *it* ~ *vt* **1** *chiefly Scot* **:** to escape by dodging or ducking **2** *chiefly Scot* **:** to defeat by cheating or trickery

**³jink** \"\ *n* -s [by *alter.*] *dial Eng* **:** ³CHINK

**⁴jink** \"\ *vb* -ED/-ING/-S *dial Eng* **:** ⁴CHINK ⟨a shunt engine groaned, and ~*ed* the buffers of the freight trucks —Robert Westerby⟩

**jin·ker** \ˈjiŋkə(r)\ *n* -s [alter. of *janker*] **1** *Austral* **:** a contrivance like a cart having either two or four wheels and used esp. for log and timber carrying **2** *Austral* **:** a two-wheeled racing sulky

**jin·ket** \ˈjiŋkət\ *Scot var of* JUNKET

**jinks** \ˈjiŋ(k)s\ *n pl but sing in constr* [origin unknown] **:** CHECKERBERRY

**jinn** \ˈjin\ *also* **jin·ni** *or* **jin·nee** \jəˈnē, ˈjinē\ *or* **djin** *or* **djinn** \ˈjin\ *or* **djin·ni** *n, pl* **jinns** *or* **jinn** [Ar *jinnīy* demon, spirit] **1 :** one of a class of beneficent or malevolent spirits in Islam that inhabit the earth, that are capable of assuming various forms, and that exercise supernatural power **2 :** a supernatural spirit ⟨some ~ of the air made visible for a moment —Osbert Sitwell⟩ ⟨scoffing at the idea of casting out a ~ —Alan Villiers⟩; *esp* **:** one that takes on human form and serves the one who summons him ⟨magically summoning his private ~ —Hamilton Basso⟩

**jin·nah cap** \ˈjinə-\ *n, usu cap J* [after Mohammed Ali *Jinnah* †1948 Pakistani statesman] **:** a hat shaped like a fez but made of real or imitation karakul and worn by Pakistani Muslims

**jin·ny** \ˈjinē, -ni\ *n* -ES [alter. of *jenny*] **:** a block carriage on a crane that sustains pulley blocks hung from an eyebar or crosscar — called also *jenny*

**jin·rik·i·sha** *also* **jin·rik·sha** \(jən)ˈrik(,)shó *also* -kə,shó\ *n* -s [Jap, fr. *jin* man + *riki* strength, power + *sha* carriage] **:** a small light two-wheeled usu. passenger vehicle drawn by one man and orig. used in Japan

jinrikisha

**¹jinx** \ˈjiŋ(k)s\ *n* -ES [prob. alter of *jynx*; fr. the wryneck's being used in witchcraft] **:** something that unaccountably foredooms one or is felt to foredoom to failure or misfortune **:** something that is felt to bring bad luck; *esp* **:** an evil spell or intangible force ⟨felt he had finally broken the ~ that kept him from achieving fame⟩

**²jinx** \"\ *vt* -ED/-ING/-ES **1 :** to foredoom unaccountably to failure or misfortune **:** bring bad luck upon ⟨the general belief was that his ghost had ~*ed* the ship —James Dugan⟩ ⟨his race and his color have seemed to ~ his personal life —R.G.Hubler⟩ **2 :** to put a stop or end to **:** make worthless or pointless ⟨~*ed* my story —F.J.Taylor⟩

**ji·pi·ja·pa** \,hēpēˈhäpə\ *also* **jippi-jappa** \,hip-\ *n* -s [Sp *jipijapa*, fr. *Jipijapa*, Ecuador] **1 :** a Central and So. American plant (*Carludovica palmata*) resembling a palm — called also *toquilla* **2 :** a hat made from fiber from the young leaves of jipijapa

**ji·qui** \hēˈkē\ *or* **ji·que** \-kā\ *n* -s [AmerSp *jiquí*] **1 :** SABICU **2 :** a Cuban timber tree (*Malpighia obovata*) with hard wood very resistant to moisture

**ji·ra·ja·ra** \,hirəˈhärə\ *n, pl* **jirajara** *or* **jirajaras** *usu cap* [Sp, of AmerInd origin] **1 a :** a group of peoples of northwestern Venezuela **b :** a member of any of such peoples **2 :** the language of the Jirajara peoples constituting a language family

**jird** \ˈji(ə)rd\ *n* -s [Berber *agherda, gherda*] **:** any of several No. African gerbils constituting a genus (*Meriones*) of the Cricetidae

**jir·ga** *or* **jir·gah** \ˈjərgə, ˈji(ə)r-\ *n* -s [Pashto, prob. of Mongol origin like Per *jarga* circle of men or beasts] **:** a council of Afghan tribal leaders

**jir·kin·et** \ˌjərkə̇ˈnet\ *n* -s [alter. of *jerkin* + *-et*] *Scot* : a jacket or blouse worn by women

**jirt** \ˈjərt\ *Scot var of* JERK

**jism** *or* **gism** \ˈjizəm\ *n* -s [origin unknown] : SEMEN — usu. considered vulgar

**jit·ney** \ˈjitnē, -ni\ *n* -s [origin unknown] **1** *slang* : NICKEL 2a **2** [so called fr. the original 5 cent fare] **a** : BUS 1; *esp* : a small bus designed to carry paying passengers over a regular route according to a flexible schedule **b** : a small electric truck designed for transporting or towing around a train station, air or bus terminal, or a dock

[1]**jit·ter** \ˈjid·ə(r), -itə-\ *vb* -ED/-ING/-S [origin unknown] *vi* **1** : to be nervous or act in a nervous way ⟨~*ed* around backstage on the opening night —*Newsweek*⟩; *esp* : to experience the jitters ⟨bears his awful responsibility without ~*ing* —*Time*⟩ **2** : to jog or jig continuously : make continuous fast repetitive movements ⟨the wash . . . still ~*ed*, stiff and yellowish on the wire line —Raymond Chandler⟩; *also* : to progress in short fast repetitive movements ~ *vt* : to cause to jitter; *also* : cause to move in jittering movements

[2]**jitter** \"\ *n* -s **1** : the state of mind or the movement of one that jitters **2 jitters** *pl but sing or pl in constr* : extreme nervousness : a sense of panic — often used with *the* ⟨experienced a bad case of the ~*s* before playing the solo⟩ **3** : irregular random variation in a signal usu. evidenced by variation in the position of a spot on a radar or television screen

[1]**jitterbug** \ˈ≈≈,≈\ *n* [[1]*jitter* + [1]*bug*] **1** : a dance in which couples two-step, balance, and twirl in standardized patterns or with vigorous acrobatics originating in Harlem in the 1920s and persisting in many variants through the periods of lindy, swing, boogie-woogie, and bop — compare JAZZ 2c **2 a** : one who dances the jitterbug **b** : a devotee of jazz music; *esp* : one who sways and gestures in time to jazz music

[2]**jitterbug** \"\ *vi* : to dance the jitterbug

**jit·ter·i·ness** \-ərēnə̇s, -rin-\ *n* -ES : the quality or state of being jittery

**jit·tery** \-rē,-ri\ *adj* **1** : suffering from the jitters ⟨our ~ guards began to question everyone at rifle points —F.E. Fox⟩ ⟨he is tense, ~ — a mass of jangled nerves — his fingers tremble as he lights one cigarette after another —S.N.Behrman⟩ **2** : marked by jittering movements : tending to jitter ⟨warblers . . . are small and ~, and stay hidden in the leaves —J.W. Krutch⟩

**jiujitsu** *or* **jiujutsu** *var of* JUJITSU

**ji·va** \ˈjēvə\ *n* -s *sometimes cap* [Skt *jīva*, fr. *jīva* living, alive — more at QUICK] **1** *Hinduism* **a** : the vital energy of life **b** : the individual soul **2** *Jainism* **a** : the individual life monad or separate individual self **b** : the aggregate of all life monads or separate selves : LIFE

**ji·van·muk·ta** \ˌjēvənˈmu̇ktə\ *n* -s [Skt *jīvanmukta*, fr. *jīvan-* (fr. *jīvati* he lives) + *mukta* emancipated, set free, fr. *muñcati* he frees, releases; akin to Skt *jīva* living — more at MUCUS] *Hinduism* : one who has attained jivanmukti

**ji·van·muk·ti** \-(ˌ)tē\ *n* -s [Skt *jīvanmukti*, fr. *jīvan-* + *mukti* release, liberation, fr. *muñcati*] *Hinduism* : spiritual release or salvation achieved while still alive — compare MOKSHA

**ji·va·ran** \ˈhēvərən\ *adj, usu cap* [*Jivaro* + *-an*] : JIVAROAN

**ji·va·ro** \ˈhēvə,rō\ *or* **ji·ba·ro** \-ēbə-\ *n, pl* **jivaro** *or* **jivaros** *or* **jibaro** *or* **jibaros** *usu cap* [Sp *jíbaro*, of AmerInd origin] **1 a** : a group of peoples of northwestern Peru and southern Ecuador **b** : a member of any of such peoples **2** : the language of the Jivaro peoples constituting a language family — **ji·va·ro·an** \ˌ≈≈ˈrōən\ *adj, usu cap*

[1]**jive** \ˈjīv\ *n* -s [origin unknown] **1 a** *slang* : glib, deceptive, or foolish talk **b** : the jargon of narcotics addicts or of jazz music and nightclub life **c** : a special jargon of difficult or slang terms ⟨a sort of academic ~ interlarded with lengthy and undigested quotations —Dwight MacDonald⟩ **2** : hot jazz or the jitterbugging sometimes performed to it

[2]**jive** \"\ *vb* -ED/-ING/-S *vi* **1** *slang* : to talk jive : fool around : KID **2 a** : to dance to hot jazz; *esp* : JITTERBUG **b** : to play hot jazz ~ *vt* **1** *slang* : TEASE, KID **2** : to play (music) hot ⟨small bands *jiving* in cellar clubs⟩

**jiz·ya** *also* **jiz·yah** \ˈjizyə\ *n* -s [Ar *jizyah*] : a capitation tax formerly levied on non-Muslims by the Islamic state

**JJ** *abbr* **1** judges **2** justices

**jl** *abbr* journal

**JMA** *abbr* junior military aviator

**JMJ** *abbr* Jesus, Mary, Joseph

**JMT** *abbr* job methods training

**jn** *abbr* **1** join **2** junction

**jna·na** \jəˈnänə\ *n* -s [Skt *jñāna*, fr. *jānāti* he knows — more at KNOW] *Hinduism* : KNOWLEDGE

**jnana–marga** \jə,nänəˈmärgə\ *n* -s [Skt *jñānamārga*, fr. *jñāna* + *mārga* road, way] : the Hindu approach to salvation by the way of knowledge developed in the Upanishads and the philosophic systems (as Sankhya, Vedanta, Yoga) and involving mental and ascetic self-discipline often in the companionship of a guru — compare KARMA-MARGA

**jnana–yoga** \-ˈyōgə\ *n* [Skt *jñānayoga*, fr. *jñāna* + *yoga* — more at YOGA] *Hinduism* : spiritual discipline attained by philosophical knowledge

**jna·ni** \jəˈnä(ˌ)nē\ *n* -s [Skt *jñānī, fr. jñāna*] : a devotee of jnana-marga

**jnc** *abbr* junction

**JND** *abbr* just noticeable difference

**jnl** *abbr* journal

**jnlst** *abbr* journalist

**jnr** *abbr* junior

**jnt** *abbr* joint

[1]**jo** \ˈjō\ *n* -ES [Sc *jo* joy, alter. of *joy*] *chiefly Scot* : SWEETHEART, DEAR — often used in addressing a person ⟨John Anderson, my ~ John —Robert Burns⟩

[2]**jo** *var of* JOE

**JO** *abbr* **1** joint organization **2** junior officer

**jo·a·chim·ite** \ˈjōə,ki,mīt\ *n* -s *usu cap* [*Joachim* of Floris †*ab* 1202 Ital. mystic + E *-ite*] : a follower of Joachim of Floris who divided all time into the three ages of the Father, Son, and Holy Spirit of which the second age lasted from A.D. 1 to 1260 and whose doctrine of a spiritual elite destined to convert the world in the third age influenced the Fraticelli

**jo·a·chism** \ˈjōə,kizəm\ *n* -s *usu cap* [*Joachim* of Floris + E *-ism*] : adherence to the doctrines of the Joachimites

**joan** \ˈjō(ə)n, jōˈan\ *n* -s *usu cap* [fr. the name *Joan*] : a country girl

**joannes** *var of* JOHANNES

**joan silverpin** \-ˈ≈≈,≈\ *n, usu cap J* [prob. fr. E dial. *Joan's silver pin* article of beauty in a sordid setting; fr. the fact that this showy flower is often found among weeds] : any of several poppies; *esp* : OPIUM POPPY

**joa·quin·ite** \wäˈkē,nīt, wōˈ-\ *n* -s [fr. *Joaquin* ridge, San Benito co., Calif. + E *-ite*] : a mineral consisting of a sodium iron titanium silicate and occurring in honey-yellow orthorhombic crystals

**jo·ar** \jəˈwär\ *var of* JOWAR

[1]**job** \ˈjäb\ *n* -s [perh. fr. obs. E, lump, fr. ME *jobbe*, perh. alter. of *gobbe* — more at GOB] **1 a** : a piece of work ⟨did odd ~*s* for the neighborhood housewives⟩ ⟨gave up the marriage as a bad ~ —the before her, that of phrasing and rephrasing a fugue —Osbert Sitwell⟩ ⟨the bridge was a bigger and longer ~ than the firm expected⟩ : PERFORMANCE, ACHIEVEMENT ⟨the new biography is a superb ~⟩ ⟨too lazy to turn out an honest ~⟩; *specif* : a small miscellaneous piece of work undertaken on order at a stated rate ⟨have two offset ~*s* to print up today⟩ ⟨the car needed a brake ~⟩ **b** : a quality, product, or result of work ⟨do a better ~ next time⟩ ⟨a more uniform dye ~ is obtained in skeins —H.R.Mauersberger⟩ **c** : an example of a usu. specified type : ITEM ⟨at the truck stop were three tractor-trailer ~*s*⟩ ⟨the blonde ~ sitting at the bar⟩ **2** : something done for private advantage : DEAL; *esp* : a collusive piece of business ⟨his appointment as judge was a flagrant ~⟩ ⟨suspected the whole incident was a put-up ~⟩ **3** *chiefly Brit* : a state or turn of affairs : a piece of luck : THING — used with *bad* or *good* ⟨it was a good ~ you didn't hit the old man —E.L.Thomas⟩ **4** : a criminal enterprise; *specif* : ROBBERY ⟨the gang that pulled the bank ~⟩ **5 a** : a regular remunerative employment : POSITION, SITUATION ⟨got a part-time ~ as a waiter in a café⟩ ⟨holds a key ~ in the government⟩ **b** : a specific duty, role, or function : work customarily performed ⟨the stokers' ~ was to feed coal into the furnaces⟩ ⟨the white blood cells . . . have the ~ of fighting infection —Morris Fishbein⟩ ⟨when more light is needed a stronger bulb will do the ~⟩; *specif* : an activity or group of related activities contributing to a larger process ⟨divide the manufacturing process into a number of carefully defined ~*s* assigned to individual workers⟩ **6** : an undertaking requiring unusual exertion : EFFORT ⟨the radio whined so loud that it was a ~ to talk through it —Rose Macaulay⟩ **7** : the object or material on which work is being done ⟨held the ~ with tongs while he hammered it⟩ **8** : the actual process of doing a piece of work : the activity of a job ⟨learned plumbing on the ~ itself⟩ ⟨get on with the ~ of planning the trip⟩ ⟨stuck to the ~ till the tire was off⟩ **9** : the area used in carrying on a job (as of construction) ⟨lumber stored in piles on the ~⟩ **10 jobs** *pl* : defective or slow-selling goods (as publishers' remainders) sold at reduced prices **11** *slang* : a thoroughly damaging piece of work : a job of destruction or disablement — usu. used in the phrase *do a job on* ⟨the collision really did a ~ on their car⟩ ⟨did a ~ on his rival in the third game, letting him score only one point⟩ **syn** see TASK — **on the job** : attending to one's work ⟨a mechanical servant that is right *on the job* day and night⟩

[2]**job** \"\ *vb* **jobbed; jobbed; jobbing; jobs** *vi* **1 a** : to do odd or occasional pieces of work for hire : work by the piece ⟨supported himself by *jobbing* in local orchestras⟩ **b** : to do job work **2 a** : to direct or carry on public business so as to secure private advantage or graft **b** : to seek or give a political favor in return for secret influence or graft ⟨a bit of *jobbing* . . . got a grand jury presentment to make a road which served nobody's interest but his own —Samuel Lover⟩ **3** : to carry on the business of a middleman : trade in wholesale lots ⟨his company ~*s* and doesn't sell to the homeowner⟩ ~ *vt* **1** : to buy and sell (as stock) or let (as a property) for profit : SPECULATE **2** : to hire or let by the job or for a period of service ⟨~ a carriage for the time he would be in the city⟩ **3** : to make a job of (a matter of public trust or duty) : get, deal with, or effect by jobbery **4** : to do or cause to be done by separate portions or lots : SUBLET ⟨~ the city paving to the lowest bidders⟩ **5** : to do a job on : SWINDLE, TRICK ⟨claimed he had been *jobbed* out of the championship⟩ : dispose of (as by political intrigue) ⟨assured his election by *jobbing* his political rival⟩

[3]**job** \"\ *adj* **1** *Brit* : that is for hire by the job or for a given service or period ⟨~ carriage at 2 guineas a day⟩ ⟨a ~ gardener⟩ **2 a** : used in or suitable for job work ⟨~ type⟩ **b** : engaged in job work ⟨~ printer⟩ ⟨~ shop⟩ **c** : done as job work ⟨~ printing⟩ **3** : of or relating to a job or to employment ⟨guarantee of ~ security⟩ ⟨gloom in the ~ market⟩

[4]**job** \"\ *vb* **jobbed; jobbed; jobbing; jobs** [ME *jobben*] *vi, chiefly dial* : JAB ~ *vt* **1** *chiefly dial* : JAB **2** *chiefly Austral* : to strike or hit esp. with a heavy blow

[5]**job** \"\ *n* -s : a one-handed stroke used in field hockey by a tackler to push the ball away from an opponent's stick

**job analysis** *n* : determination of the precise characteristics of a job or position through detailed observation and critical examination of the sequential activities, facilities required, conditions of work, and the qualifications needed in a worker usu. as a preparatory step toward a job description

**job analyst** *n* : a specialist in job analysis

**jo·ba·tion** \jōˈbāshən\ *n* -s [*jobe* + *-ation*] *chiefly Brit* : a long tedious reproof : SCOLDING, LECTURE

**job·ber** \ˈjäbə(r)\ *n* -s [[2]*job* + *-er*] : one that jobs: as **a** (1) *chiefly Brit* : one that buys livestock from farmers and sells to consumers or other dealers ⟨if the ~ comes you can sell the pig —J.M.Synge⟩ (2) : STOCKJOBBER (3) : WHOLESALER; *specif* : a wholesaler in some trades who operates on a small scale or who sells only to retailers and institutions rather than to other wholesale organizations **b** (1) : one that works by the job or on job work (2) : one that contracts with lumbermen to do one or more parts of a logging operation (3) : JOB PRESS

**job·ber·nowl** \ˈjäbə(r),nōl\ *n* -s [prob. alter. of obs. *jobard* blockhead (fr. ME, fr. MF, fr. *Job*, Old Testament patriarch + MF *-ard*) + *nowl*, alter. of *noll*] *Brit* : NUMSKULL, NINCOMPOOP

**jobber's drill** *n* : a straight-shank drill somewhat shorter than the taper-shank drill of the same diameter

**jobber's reamer** *n* : a reamer that may be used either in a machine or when provided with a suitable holder as a hand tool

**job·bery** \ˈjäb(ə)rē, -ri\ *n* -ES [[2]*job* + *-ery*] : the act or practice of jobbing : official corruption : political intrigue or graft ⟨all the public posts were filled by ~ —Szyman Askenazy⟩

**jobbing** *pres part of* JOB

[1]**job·ble** \ˈjäbəl\ *var of* JABBLE

[2]**jobble** *n* -s [[1]*job* + *-le*] *dial Eng* : a small quantity or load

**job card** *n* : a card in a cost-accounting system on which the detailed costs of an order are accumulated : COST SHEET

**job case** *n* : any of a class of typecases carrying with some exceptions both capital and lower-case letters — see CALIFORNIA JOB CASE

**job classification** *n* : the grouping of jobs into classes usu. on the basis of type of work or level of pay

**job control** *n* : union influence over the employment practices of an establishment exercised through contract clauses regulating hiring, promotion, transfer, layoff, and discharge and directed toward union security

**job description** *n* : an orderly record of the essential activities involved in the performance of a task that is abstracted from a job analysis and used in classifying and evaluating jobs and in the selection and placement of employees

**jobe** \ˈjōb\ *vt* -ED/-ING/-S [after *Job*, Old Testament patriarch; fr. the scolding tone of his friends' speeches] *archaic* : SCOLD, REPROVE, LECTURE

**job evaluation** *or* **job rating** *n* : systematic qualitative appraisal of each job or position in an establishment either through the assignment of points for job characteristics or through comparison of job factors (as mental effort, experience, and responsibility required) for the purpose of determining the relative position of the job in the job hierarchy and for fixing wage rates

**jobholder** \ˈ≈,≈≈\ *n* : one that has a regular job; *specif* : a government employee

**job·less** \ˈjäblə̇s\ *adj* **1** : having no employment **2** : of or benefiting those who are jobless ⟨~ insurance⟩ — **job·less·ness** *n* -ES

**jo block** \ˈjō-\ *n, usu cap J* [by contr.] : JOHANSSON BLOCK

**job lot** *n* **1 a** : a miscellaneous collection of goods for sale as a lot usu. to a retailer at a reduced price **b** : a miscellaneous sometimes inferior group ⟨get a *job lot* of deans, dowagers, cabinet ministers, and ambassadors to meet them —W.J.Locke⟩ **2** : a smaller than normal unit of commodities, goods, or production **3** : an odd quantity of paper offered for sale at a discount because discontinued or otherwise nonstandard — **in job lots** *adv* : in an extensive and often indiscriminate manner : WHOLESALE ⟨organizations in elaborate regalia and . . . degrees marketed *in job lots* —C.W.Ferguson⟩

**job·mas·ter** \ˈjäb,mastə(r)\ *n* [[1]*job* + *master*] *Brit* : the keeper of a livery stable

**jo·bo** \ˈhō(ˌ)bō\ *n* -s [Sp, fr. Taino *hobo*] **1** *West Indies & Mexico* : HOG PLUM 1 **2** *West Indies & Mexico* : GUMBO-LIMBO 1

**job of work** *chiefly Brit* : JOB 1a ⟨an absence which generally occurred when there was a *job of work* to be done —R.H. Sampson⟩

**job order** *n* : the written authority given a worker or shop to perform certain work

**job press** *n* : PLATEN PRESS; *also* : a relatively small press — called also *jobber*

**job rotation** *n* : the assigning of an employee to a variety of tasks in turn to provide diversified experience during training or to counteract boredom

**jobs** *pl of* JOB, *pres 3d sing of* JOB

**job's comforter** \ˈjōbz-\ *n, usu cap J* [after *Job*, Old Testament patriarch; fr. the scolding tone of his friends' speeches] **1** : one that increases (as by tactless or malicious remarks) a person's distress while supposedly comforting him **2** : FURUNCLE

**job sheet** *n* **1** : a page of instruction to aid a worker in performing a task — called also *instruction card* **2** : JOB CARD

**jobsite** \ˈ≈,≈\ *n* [[1]*job* + *site*] : JOB 9

**job specification** *n* : a specialized job description designed by emphasizing mental and physical qualifications and special skills required in an operative to facilitate selection and placement of employees

**job's tears** *n pl, usu cap J* [after *Job*, Old Testament patriarch who wept because of his many afflictions (Job 16:16 ff)] **1** : hard pearly white seeds often sold as beads or strung in necklaces **2** *sing in constr* : an Asiatic grass (*Coix lacryma-jobi*) now widely cultivated in the tropics that produces Job's tears in ornamental and edible varieties — called also *tear grass*

**job ticket** *n* **1** : an auxiliary printed form that may accompany a job order to a workshop to be used variously for recording worker's time, identifying material, giving brief instructions as to procedure, routing, tools, and destination **2** : JOB ORDER

**job work** *n* : commercial printing of orders (as for letterheads, circulars, cards, booklets) — compare BOOKWORK

**joc** *abbr* **1** jocose **2** jocular

**JOC** *abbr* joint operations center

**joch** \ˈyȯk\ *n* -s [G, lit., yoke, fr. OHG *joh* — more at YOKE] : COL 1

**jo·cism** \ˈjō,sizəm\ *n* -s *usu cap* [F *jocisme*, fr. Jeunesse Ouvière Chrétienne (lit., Christian Working Youth), a Catholic youth organization + *-isme* -ism] : a Roman Catholic movement among young workers directed toward christianizing the ranks of labor and founded in Belgium during the period 1912–1924 by Canon Joseph Cardijn

[1]**jo·cist** \ˈjōsə̇st\ *n* -s *usu cap* [F *jociste*, fr. Jeunesse Ouvière Chrétienne + *-iste* -ist] : a member of the Jocist movement

[2]**jocist** \"\ *adj, usu cap* : of or relating to Jocism

[1]**jock** \ˈjäk\ *n* -s *often cap* [fr. *Jock*, Sc & Ir nickname for *John*] **1** *Scot & Irish* : a country boy : LAD **2** : a soldier in a Scottish regiment

[2]**jock** \"\ *n* -s [short for [1]*jockey*] **1** : JOCKEY 2a ⟨any one of two dozen top ~*s* will get home with the best horse in a race —Eddie Arcaro⟩ **2** : DISC JOCKEY

[3]**jock** \"\ *var of* JOCKSTRAP

**jock·er** \ˈjäkə(r)\ *n* -s [E slang *jock* penis + *-er* — more at JOCKSTRAP] *slang* : a male homosexual

[1]**jock·ey** \ˈjäkē, -ki\ *n, pl* **jockeys** [fr. *Jockey*, chiefly Sc nickname for *John*] **1** *Brit* : LADDIE, CHAPPIE, FELLOW ⟨a mischievous ~⟩ ⟨a tough old ~ of a colonel⟩ **2 a** : one who rides or drives a horse; *esp* : a professional rider in a horse race **b** *archaic* : one who handles or deals in horses : HORSE TRADER **c** : a person who operates or manipulates an often specified vehicle or other object : DRIVER, OPERATOR ⟨a truck ~⟩ ⟨an elevator ~⟩ ⟨a typewriter ~⟩; *specif* : one who parks cars or trucks in a storage garage — compare DISC JOCKEY **3** : a sometimes padded leather flap on a saddle that covers the point of attachment of the stirrup leather or serves as ornament — see STOCK SADDLE illustration **4** : HARVARD CRIMSON 1

[2]**jockey** \"\ *vb* **jockeyed; jockeyed; jockeying; jockeys** *vt* **1** : to deal shrewdly or fraudulently with : get the better of by craft : OUTWIT, TRICK, GULL ⟨dozens of unprincipled hucksters at the resort who ~ the unwary for fair⟩ ⟨the newly established method of party horse trading ~*ed* them out of many deputies —Janet Flanner⟩ **2 a** : to ride (a horse) as a jockey ⟨the winning horse was ~*ed* by his son⟩ **b** : to be the driver, pilot, or operator (a vehicle or other mechanism) ⟨~s a taxi for a living⟩ **3 a** : to maneuver or manipulate (as a person) by adroit or devious means ⟨proposals for public works were ~*ed* through Parliament by a combination of members —E.H. Collis⟩ ⟨trying to ~ you into some sort of trap —Erle Stanley Gardner⟩ **b** : to change the position of esp. by a series of movements : MANIPULATE ⟨~*ed* the camera back and forth till he got just the right angle⟩ : MANEUVER ⟨~ the furniture around the living room⟩; *specif* : to bring by jockeying ⟨~ a car into a parking space⟩ ⟨flew close to ~ the other plane out of formation⟩ ~ *vi* **1** : to act as a jockey ⟨~*ed* in races till he was too heavy for the horse⟩ **2** : to maneuver for advantage ⟨~ for position as the horses race the first lap⟩ ⟨watch the racing fleets . . . ~ for the favoring wind —E.A.Weeks⟩ ⟨behind the scenes ~*ing* . . . to determine the Democratic party's candidate for lieutenant governor —*N.Y.Times*⟩

**jockey boot** *n* : TOP BOOT

**jockey cap** *n* : a lightweight cap with a long visor worn esp. by jockeys

jockey cap

**jockey club** *n* : an association of persons interested in horse racing usu. regulating races in a certain district

**jockey coat** *n, chiefly Scot* : GREATCOAT; *esp* : one of broadcloth with wide sleeves

**jockey pulley** *or* **jockey wheel** *n* : IDLER PULLEY

**jock·ey·ship** \ˈ≈≈,ship\ *n* : the art or practice of jockeying

**jockey stick** *n* : a stick fastened to the hame of the near horse and the bit of the off horse for use in driving with a single rein to prevent crowding

**jockey weight** *n* : a weight that rides on the beam of scales or the lever of a testing machine to provide fine adjustment

**jock itch** *or* **jockey itch** *n* [[3]*jock* or *jockey (strap)*] : ringworm of the crotch : TINEA CRURIS

**jocko** \ˈjä(ˌ)kō\ *or* **jacko** \ˈja(-\ *n* -s [F *jocko*, of African origin; akin to Efik *id³iok¹* chimpanzee] **1** : CHIMPANZEE **2** : MONKEY

**jocks** *pl of* JOCK

**jock·strap** \ˈjäk,strap\ *also* **jock** *or* **jockey strap** *n* -s [*jockstrap* fr. E slang *jock* penis (short for earlier *jockam, jockum*, of unknown origin) + *strap*; *jock* short for *jockstrap*; *jockey strap* alter. of *jockstrap*] : a supporter for the genitals worn by men participating in sports or strenuous activities : an athletic supporter

**jock·te·leg** \ˈjäktə,leg\ *n* -s [origin unknown] *Scot* : a large clasp knife

**jo·co** \ˈjō(ˌ)kō\ *adj* [by shortening] *Scot* : JOCOSE

**jo·cose** \(ˈ)jōˈkōs\ *adj* [L *jocosus*, fr. *jocus* jest, joke + *-osus* -ose — more at JOKE] **1** : given to jokes and jesting : abounding in jokes ⟨felt the preacher was too ~ for his serious position⟩ **2** : having the character of or containing a joke : sportively humorous ⟨made ~ remarks about things the others didn't consider funny at all⟩ **syn** see WITTY

**jo·cose·ly** *adv* : in a jocose manner : JOKINGLY

**jo·cose·ness** *n* -ES : JOCOSITY

**jo·cos·i·ty** \jōˈkäsəd·ē, -ətē, -i\ *n* -ES [L *jocosus* + E *-ity*] **1** : the quality or state of being jocose ⟨talking with loud ~ —Bruce Marshall⟩ **2** : a jocose act or saying ⟨a book of . . . sly and devastating *jocosities* —*Amer. Mercury*⟩

**jo·co·te** \hōˈkō(ˌ)tā\ *n* -s [AmerSp, fr. Nahuatl *xocotl*] : MOMBIN

**jocote de mi·co** \-dāˈmē(ˌ)kō\ *n* [AmerSp, lit., monkey jocote] : BARBAS

**jo·cu** \hōˈkü\ *n* -s [AmerSp (Cuba) *jocú*] : DOG SNAPPER

**joc·u·lar** \ˈjäkyələ(r)\ *adj* [L *jocularis*, fr. *joculus* little jest, little joke, dim. of *jocus* jest, joke + *-aris* -ar — more at JOKE] **1** : given or disposed to jesting : acting in jest : overtly jocose ⟨grew ~ and began to tease the others about their fears⟩ **2** : said or done in joke : of, containing, or of the character of a joke : PLAYFUL, MERRY ⟨set the table laughing with his ~ remarks⟩ ⟨the more solemn dances were organized by the chiefs . . . the more ~ ones, however, took place without authority —Irving Rouse⟩ **syn** see WITTY

**joc·u·lar·i·ty** \ˌjäkyəˈlarəd·ē, -ətē, -i *also* -ler-\ *n* -ES [LL *jocularitas*, fr. L *jocularis* + *-itas* -ity] **1** : the quality or state of being jocular ⟨a singular display of ~, in which irrelevancy and sheer bad taste are especially conspicuous —N.F.Adkins⟩ **2** : an instance of being jocular : JEST ⟨interspersed . . . were axioms and proverbs and *jocularities* —*New Yorker*⟩

**joc·u·lar·ly** *adv* : in a jocular manner ⟨a subject they had generally avoided or else tried to deal with ~ —Richard Blaker⟩

**joc·u·lar·ness** *n* -ES : JOCULARITY

**joc·u·la·tor** \ˈjäkyə,lād·ə(r)\ *n, pl* **joc·u·la·to·res** \ˌjäkyələˈtōr(ˌ)ēz\ *or* **joculators** [ML, fr. L, jester, joker — more at JUGGLER] : a wandering entertainer of medieval Europe who for hire practiced the arts of minstrelsy, narration, dancing, juggling, and mime

**jo·cum** \hōˈküm\ *also* **jo·cu·ma** \-mə\ *n* -s [AmerSp *jocuma*, prob. fr. Taino] : MASTIC BULLY

**joc·und** \ˈjäkənd *sometimes* ˈjōk-\ *adj* [ME *jocound, jocund,* fr. LL *jocundus*, alter. (influenced by L *jocus* joke) of L *jucundus*, fr. *juvare* to help] **:** feeling, exhibiting, or characteristic of mirth or good cheer **:** CHEERFUL, GAY, LIVELY ⟨singing, dancing, and ~ feasting⟩ ⟨a small and ~ blaze upon the hearth —Elinor Wylie⟩ **syn** see MERRY

**jo·cun·di·ty** \jō'kəndəd·ē, -ətē, -i\ *n* -ES [LL *jocunditas*, fr. *jocundus* + L *-itas* -ity] **1 :** JOCUNDNESS **2 :** a jocund action or speech **:** PLEASANTRY

**joc·und·ly** *adv* [ME, fr. *jocund* + *-ly*] **:** in a jocund manner

**joc·und·ness** *n* -ES [ME *jocundnes*, fr. *jocund* + *-nes* -ness] **:** the quality or state of being jocund

**jod** *var of* YODH

**jo-dart·er** *or* **joe dart·er** \'jō'därd·ər\ *n* **:** JIM-DANDY

**jodel** *var of* YODEL

¹**jodh·pur** \'jädpə(r), 'jōd-, -,pu̇(ə)r, -u̇ə\ *adj, usu cap* [fr. *Jodhpur*, Rajputana, India] **:** of or from the city of Jodhpur, India **:** of the kind or style prevalent in Jodhpur

²**jodh·pur** \'jädpə(r) *also* ÷ -dfə-\ *n* -s **1** *also* **jodhpur breeches :** pants for horseback riding cut full through the hips, close-fitting from knee to ankle, and usu. having a strap under the foot — usu. used in pl. **2** *or* **jodhpur boot** *also* **jodhpur shoe :** a short riding boot; *esp* **:** an ankle-high boot fastened with a strap that is buckled at the side — compare CHUKKA

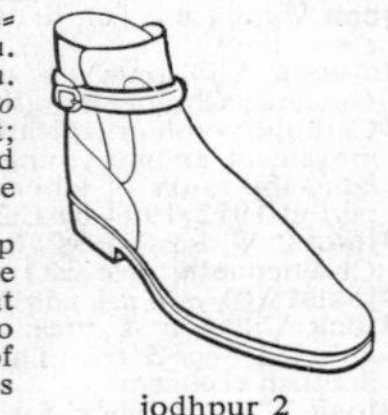
jodhpur 2

**jo·do** \'jō(,)dō\ *n* -s *usu cap* [Jap *jōdo*] **1 :** PURE LAND **2 :** a Japanese Buddhist sect founded 1175 that promises rebirth in the Pure Land to all those who invoke the name of Amida Buddha and live a righteous life

¹**joe** \'jō\ *var of* ¹JO

²**joe** *or* **jo** \"\ *n, pl* **joes** [short for *johannes*] **:** a gold dobra worth 12,800 reis

³**joe** *also* **jo** \"\ *n* -s [prob. alter. of *java*] *slang* **:** COFFEE

⁴**joe** \"\ *n* -s *often cap* [fr. *Joe*, nickname for *Joseph*] **1** — used informally to address a man whose name the speaker does not know **2** *slang* **:** GUY, FELLOW ⟨he's a good ~⟩ ⟨just an average ~⟩ ⟨a couple of ~s here who don't play a too crippled game of bridge —Al Hine⟩

**joe blow** *n, usu cap J&B* [*Joe* + *blow* (prob. arbitrarily chosen to rhyme with *Joe*)] *slang* **:** an ordinary man; *specif* **:** one who is self-important

**joebush** \'=,=\ *n* [*joe* (origin unknown) + *bush*] **:** JOEWOOD

**joe college** *n, usu cap J&C* [*Joe* + *college*] **:** a college boy; *esp* **:** one devoted to amusement

**joe doakes** \-'dōks\ *n, pl* **joe doakes** *usu cap J&D* [*Joe* + the name *Doakes*] **1 :** an average man **2 :** SO-AND-SO

**joe mil·ler** \-'milə(r)\ *n, usu cap J&M* [fr. *Joe Miller's Jest-book* (1739), a collection of jokes by John Mottley †1750 Eng. writer, after *Joe Miller* †1738 Eng. comedian] **1 :** a book of jokes **2 :** JOKE; *esp* **:** a stale joke

**joe-pye weed** \'jō'pī-\ *n, often cap J&P* [origin unknown] **:** BONESET 1; *esp* **:** either of two tall perennial American herbs (*Eupatorium maculatum* and *E. purpureum*) with stems usu. purplish or blotched with purple, whorled leaves, and terminal clusters of heads of typically purple tubular flowers — see MARSH MILKWEED

**joe rocker** *n* [origin unknown] **:** GREEN CRAB

**joes** *pl of* JO

**joewood** \'=,=\ *n* [*joe* (origin unknown) + *wood*] **:** a West Indian shrub or small tree (*Jacquinia keyensis*) of the family Theophrastaceae with leathery saponaceous leaves and an extremely hard wood — called also *barbasco*

¹**jo·ey** \'jōē, -ōi,ōi\ *n* -s [native name in Australia] **1** *Austral* **a :** a baby kangaroo ⟨shot a doe with a ~⟩ **b :** a baby animal **c :** a young child **2** *Austral* **:** ODD-JOBMAN

²**joey** \"\ *n* -s *usu cap* [fr. *Joey*, nickname for *Joseph*] **1** [after *Joseph* Hume †1855 Eng. politician who urged the issue of fourpenny pieces] *Brit* **a :** a fourpenny piece **b :** a threepenny piece **2** [after *Joseph* Grimaldi †1837 Eng. pantomimist and clown] **:** a circus clown

¹**jog** \'jäg *also* 'jȯg\ *vb* **jogged; jogged; jogging; jogs** [prob. alter. of *shog*] *vt* **1 :** to push or shake by prodding (as with the elbow or hand) **:** JOSTLE, NUDGE; *esp* **:** to push or touch in order to give notice, to excite attention, or to warn ⟨*jogged* the reins and the horses started up⟩ ⟨~ you with my elbow when it's time to go⟩ **2 :** to rouse to alertness or action ⟨tied a string on his finger to ~ his memory⟩ **:** REMIND ⟨~ their customers two or three times a year —Paul Friggens⟩ **3 a :** to cause to jog **:** drive (as a horse) at a jog ⟨an exercise boy . . . ~s the colt around the track —F.A.Wrensch⟩ **b :** to cause (a machine) to operate for an instant ⟨a button permits *jogging* the . . . motor to facilitate positioning tools —*Sweet's Catalog Service*⟩ **4 :** to align the edges of (piled sheets of paper) usu. by winding and knocking on or with a flat surface ~ *vi* **1 :** to move up and down or about with a short often heavy motion ⟨walked away quickly, his white-painted holster *jogging* against his hip —Thomas Williams⟩ **2 :** to run or ride at a slow jogging trot ⟨a substitute *jogged* out to the referee⟩ **3 :** to go at a slow, leisurely, or monotonous pace **:** TRUDGE, PLOD, POKE ⟨a team of oxen *jogged* along . . . drawing a vehicle —O.E.Rölvaag⟩ ⟨prefer to ~ along . . . in stagecoaches instead of whizzing past in a cloud of dust and cinders —Margaret Deland⟩ ⟨under easy sail the fleet *jogged* along before a moderate trade —S.E.Morison⟩ ⟨from then on her life *jogged* peacefully along —C.M.L.Beuf⟩ **4 :** to go one's way **:** JOURNEY ⟨figured I would just ~ back . . . and let you get away —Owen Wister⟩

²**jog** \"\ *n* -s **1 :** SHAKE, PUSH, JOLT ⟨gave the dispenser a ~ in hopes of jarring the coin loose⟩; *specif* **:** one intended to give notice or awaken attention ⟨gave his sleeping buddy a ~ as the officer approached⟩ ⟨seeing the book there gave his memory a ~⟩ **2 a :** a jogging movement, gait, or trip ⟨getting . . . under weigh for a ~ down to the breakwater and beyond to have a look at the weather —Llewellyn Howland⟩ **b :** a slow pace with marked beats — used of a horse

³**jog** \"\ *n* -s [prob. alter. of ¹*jag*] **1 :** ¹JAG 4 **2 a :** a short part (as of a line, road, or wall) interrupting the direction of the rest ⟨a window in the ~ facing south⟩ **:** an often right-angled projection, notch, or step ⟨a ~ in the wall enclosing pipes⟩ **b :** the space in the angle of a jog ⟨built shelves in the ~ between chimney and wall⟩ **c :** a brief abrupt change in direction ⟨where the highway makes a ~ around the courthouse square⟩ **3 :** a narrow theatrical flat used in an interior setting (as to form an offset in a wall)

⁴**jog** \"\ *vi* **jogged; jogged; jogging; jogs :** to form or make a jog ⟨the road ~s to the right over the hill⟩

**jog cart** *n* [¹*jog*] **:** a training sulky that is narrower and has longer shafts than a racing sulky

**jog·ger** \-gə(r)\ *n* -s [¹*jog* + *-er*] **:** one that jogs ⟨a memory ~⟩; *specif* **:** LAYBOY

¹**jog·gle** \'jägəl\ *vb* **joggled; joggled; joggling** \-g(ə)liŋ\ **joggles** [freq. of ¹*jog*] *vt* **:** to shake slightly **:** push suddenly but slightly so as to cause to shake or totter **:** JOSTLE, JOG ⟨skate up to the muskrat house and ~ it —Pete Barrett⟩ ⟨don't want anything . . . that might even ~ your precious status quo —Louis Auchincloss⟩ ~ *vi* **:** to have or go with a shaking or jerking motion **:** shake slightly to and fro or up and down ⟨the faint sounds of rifles *joggling* on backs —Robert De Vries⟩ ⟨when empty, they *joggled* . . . violently on their iron-shod wheels —Christopher Rand⟩

²**joggle** \"\ *n* -s **:** a joggling motion

³**joggle** \"\ *n* -s [³*jog* + *-le* (dim. suffix)] **1 a :** a notch or tooth in the joining surface of a piece of building material to prevent slipping **b :** a slight step-shaped offset formed into a flat piece of metal (as for providing a flange) **2 :** a dowel for joining two adjacent blocks of masonry **3 :** a joint that is formed by joggles

⁴**joggle** \"\ *vt* **joggled; joggled; joggling; joggles 1 :** to join by means of a joggle so as to prevent sliding apart **2 :** to offset (sheet metal) at a corner or edge for improved fit

**joggle beam** *n* [³*joggle*] **:** a built-up beam or flitch beam secured by joggling

**joggle piece** *n* [³*joggle*] **:** a vertical member in a truss supporting one end of a brace or strut by a shoulder or joggle

**joggle plating** *n* [³*joggle*] **:** plating construction for steel ships in which one edge or both edges of a plate are joggled over the edge of an adjoining one

**joggle post** *n* [³*joggle*] **1 :** JOGGLE PIECE **2 :** a post made of timbers joggled together

**jog·gler** \-g(ə)lə(r)\ *n* -s [⁴*joggle* + *-er*] **:** an operator of a machine for joggling

**jogglework** \'=,=\ *n* [³*joggle* + *work*] **:** work (as in masonry) done in joggled courses

**joggling board** *n* [fr. pres. part. of ¹*joggle*] **:** a board suspended between end supports on which one may joggle for play or exercise **:** SPRINGBOARD

joggling board

**jogi** *var of* YOGI

**jogjakarta** *or* **jokyakarta** *usu cap, var of* DJOKJAKARTA

**jogs** *pl of* JOG, *pres 3d sing of* JOG

**jog trot** *n* [²*jog* + *trot*] **1 :** a slow regular jolting gait **2 :** a routine habit or method persistently adhered to **:** a slow easygoing way or course of action ⟨the sober *jog trot* of domestic bliss —John Galsworthy⟩

**jog-trot** \'=,=\ *adj* [*jog trot*] **:** having the character of a jog trot **:** HUMDRUM ⟨the contrast between their violence and our own *jog-trot* existences —Walter de la Mare⟩

**jogtrot** \"\ *vi* **jogtrotted; jogtrotted; jogtrotting; jogtrots** [*jog trot*] **:** to go at a jog trot ⟨~ all the way home⟩

**jo·han·nes** *also* **jo·an·nes** \jō'(h)anəs\ *n, pl* **johannes** *also* **joannes** [after *Johannes* or *Joannes* John (or João) V †1750 king of Portugal who first issued such coins and whose name appeared on them] **:** an old Portuguese gold coin first issued in the 18th century and equivalent to 6400 reis — called also *half joe*; compare DOBRA

**jo·han·nes·burg** \jō'hanəs,bərg, jə'-, -hän-, -nəz,-, -bə̄g,-bəig *sometimes* yō'-\ *adj, usu cap* [fr. *Johannesburg*, Union of So. Africa] **:** of or from the city of Johannesburg, Union of So. Africa **:** of the kind or style prevalent in Johannesburg

**jo·han·nes·burg·er** \-gə(r)\ *n* -s *cap* [Afrik, fr. *Johannesburg* + Afrik *-er*] **:** a native or inhabitant of Johannesburg, Union of So. Africa

**jo·han·nine** \(')jō¦hanən, jō'hə,nīn\ *adj, usu cap* [*Johannes* (John), one of the twelve apostles of Christ + E *-ine*] **:** of, relating to, or having the characteristics of the Apostle John or the New Testament books whose authorship is ascribed to him

**jo·han·nite** \jō'ha,nīt\ *n* -s [G *johannit*, fr. Archduke *Johann* (John) of Austria †1859 Austrian general, founder of a museum in Graz, Austria + G *-it* -ite] **:** a mineral $Cu(UO_2)_2(SO_4)(OH)_2.6H_2O$ consisting of a green hydrous basic uranyl copper sulfate that occurs in massive form

**jo·hann·sen·ite** \jō'han(t)sə,nīt\ *n* -s [Albert *Johannsen* †1950 Am. geologist + E *-ite*] **:** a mineral $CaMnSi_2O_6$ consisting of a silicate of calcium and manganese belonging to the pyroxene group

**jo·hans·son block** \(')jō¦han(t)sən-\ *n, usu cap J* [after C. E. *Johansson*, 20th cent. Swed. engineer] **:** one of a set of gauge blocks ground to an accuracy of one hundred-thousandth of an inch or better — called also *Jo block*

**john** \'jän\ *n* -s [fr. the name *John*, fr. ME *Johan, Jon, John*, fr. LL *Joannes, Johannes*, fr. Gk *Iōannēs*, fr. Heb *Yōḥānān*] **1 a** *often cap* **:** FELLOW, GUY, CHAP ⟨these Wall Street ~s can be trimmed —Carl Van Vechten⟩ **b** *usu cap* **:** a Chinese man ⟨the melancholy *Johns* with glazed caps and black pigtails —J.H.Beadle⟩ **c** *usu cap, now chiefly Austral* **:** COP, POLICEMAN ⟨a wild-eyed boy rushed in . . . and volunteered to direct the *Johns* to the body —*Sydney (Australia) Bull.*⟩ **2 :** TOILET ⟨have three bathrooms and only two ~s —Mary Manning⟩

**john a. grindle** *n, usu cap J&A&G* [fr. the name *John* + the initial *A.* (prob. fr. *a* "of") + *grindle*] **:** BOWFIN

**john-a-nokes** *or* **john-a-noakes** \,jänə'nōks\ *n, usu cap J&N* [alter. of earlier *John at Noke*, fr. the name *John* + *at Noke*, prob. fr. ME *atten ok* at the oak tree] *archaic* **:** a party to legal proceedings whose true name is unknown ⟨as willing to plead for *John-a-Nokes* as for the first noble of the land —Sir Walter Scott⟩ — compare JOHN-A-STILES

**john-apple** \'=,==\ *n, usu cap J* [fr. the name *John* + *apple*] *archaic* **:** APPLEJOHN

**john-a-stiles** *or* **john-a-styles** \,jänə'stī(ə)lz\ *n, usu cap J&S* [alter. of earlier *John at Stile*, fr. the name *John* + *at Stile*, prob. fr. ME *atte stile* at the stile] *archaic* **:** the second party to legal proceedings when the true names of both parties are unknown — compare JOHN-A-NOKES

**john barleycorn** *n, usu cap J&B* [fr. the name *John* + *barleycorn*] **:** alcoholic liquor personified

**johnboat** \'=,=\ *n* [fr. the name *John* + *boat*] **:** a narrow flat-

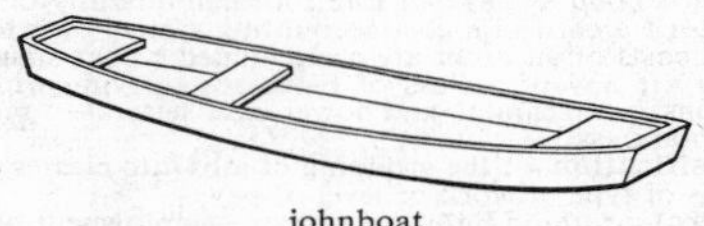
johnboat

bottomed square-ended boat usu. propelled by a pole or paddle and much used on inland rivers and streams ⟨boys on rafts and in ~s —E.W.Smith⟩

**john brown** *n, usu cap J&B* [fr. the name *John Brown*; prob. trans. of Afrik *Jan Bruin*] **:** a small plump deep-bodied sparid fish (*Gymnocrotaphus curvidens*) of southern Africa that is yellowish to bronzy brown and prized as a sport and food fish

**john bull** *n, usu cap J&B* [after *John Bull*, a character supposed to typify the English nation in *The History of John Bull*, a satire by John Arbuthnot †1735 Scot. physician and writer] **1 :** the English nation personified **:** the English people ⟨*John Bull* had been weakened by the war —F.A.Magruder⟩ **2 :** a typical or average Englishman ⟨a pipe-smoking *John Bull* astride a bicycle⟩ ⟨he was *John Bull* in a Benedictine robe —Shane Leslie⟩ — **john bull·ish** \-'bu̇lish\ *adj, usu cap J&B* — **john bull·ish·ness** *n, usu cap J&B* — **john bull·ism** \-'bu̇,lizəm\ *n, usu cap J&B*

**john chinaman** *n, usu cap J&C* [fr. the name *John* + *Chinaman*] **1 :** the Chinese nation personified **:** the Chinese people — usu. taken to be offensive **2 :** a Chinese immigrant; *esp* **:** one living in the U.S. or in Australia — usu. taken to be offensive

**john citizen** *n, usu cap J&C* [fr. the name *John* + *citizen*] **:** a typical or average citizen **:** JOHN DOE

**john crow** *n, usu cap J&C* [fr. the name *John* + *crow*] *British West Indies* **:** TURKEY BUZZARD

**john doe** *n, usu cap J&D* [fr. the name *John Doe*] **1 :** a party to legal proceedings whose true name is unknown; *esp* **:** the first such party when two or more are unknown — compare JOHN STILES, RICHARD MILES, RICHARD ROE **2 :** an anonymous, undistinguished, or average man ⟨brilliant educators and plain *John Does* —K.D.Wells⟩ ⟨the authors of those remarks are now so many *John Does* —Norman Cousins⟩

**john dory** *n, pl* **john dorys** *usu cap J&D* [fr. the name *John* + *dory* (fish)] **:** a marine fish of the family Zeidae: as **a :** a common European food fish (*Zeus faber*) that is yellow to olive in color and has an oval compressed body, long dorsal spines, and a dark spot on each side **b :** a closely related and possibly identical fish that is sometimes considered a separate species (*Z. capensis*) and is widely distributed in southern seas, being taken often in some quantity off southern Africa, Australia, and New Zealand

**john down** *n, usu cap J&D* [fr. the name *John* + *down* (feathers)] *Newfoundland* **:** FULMAR 1

**jo·hne's bacillus** \'yōnəz-\ *n, usu cap J* [after Heinrich A. *Johne* †1910 Ger. bacteriologist] **:** a bacillus (*Mycobacterium paratuberculosis*) that causes Johne's disease

**johne's disease** *n, usu cap J* [after Heinrich A. *Johne*] **:** a chronic often fatal enteritis of cattle and less commonly of sheep, goats, and horses that is caused by Johne's bacillus and is characterized by persistent diarrhea and gradual emaciation — called also *paratuberculosis*

**john-go-to-bed-at-noon** \'=,=,=,=,'=\ *n, usu cap J* [fr. the name *John*] **:** any of several plants whose flowers close about noon; *esp* **:** GOATSBEARD 1

**john han·cock** \-'han,käk\ *n, usu cap J&H* [after *John Hancock* †1793 Am. statesman; fr. the size and prominence of his signature on the U.S. Declaration of Independence] **:** an autograph signature ⟨put your *John Hancock* on that line —Sinclair Lewis⟩

**john henry** *n, usu cap J&H* [fr. the name *John Henry*] **:** an autograph signature ⟨would give anything to scratch his *John Henry* off that . . . sheet of paper —Richard Hallet⟩

**joh·nin** \'yōnən\ *n* -s [*john-* (fr. *Johne's bacillus*) + *-in*] **:** a sterile solution of the growth products of Johne's bacillus made in the same manner as tuberculin and used to identify Johne's disease by skin tests, conjunctival reactions, or intravenous injection

**john law** *n, usu cap J&L* [fr. the name *John* + *law*] **:** a law officer **:** POLICEMAN

**john ma·rig·gle** \-mə'rigəl\ *n, usu cap J&M* [fr. the name *John* + *marigle*, of unknown origin] **:** TENPOUNDER 1

**john·ny** *also* **john·nie** \'jänē, -ni\ *n, pl* **johnnies** [fr. *Johnny*, nickname for *John*] **1** *often cap* **a :** JOHN 1a ⟨one of these gilded *johnnies* who used to sell cars on commission —Dorothy Sayers⟩ **b** *now chiefly Austral* **:** JOHN 1c **2 :** JOHN 2 ⟨wash basins, sinks, and, of course, the ~ —S.S.Rabl⟩ **3 :** a short gown with no collar and with an opening in the back for wear by hospital bed patients ⟨the one string at the back of the neck of the ~ was undone —R.M.Keith⟩

**johnnycake** \'=,=,=\ *also* **jon·ny cake** \'jänē,-\ *n* [prob. fr. the name *Johnny* + *cake*] **1 a :** a bread made of white or yellow cornmeal mixed with salt and water or milk and either baked thin in a pan or dropped by spoonfuls onto a hot greased griddle **b :** a bread made of cornmeal, water or milk, and leavening with or without shortening and eggs **2** *Austral* **:** a bread either baked as small cakes in hot ashes or fried

**johnny collar** \'==,==\ *n, often cap J* **:** a small round or pointed dress collar that has a front split and that fits close to the neck

**johnny-come-lately** *also* **johnnie-come-lately** \'==,='==\ *n, pl* **johnny-come-latelies** *or* **johnnies-come-lately** *usu cap J* [fr. the name *Johnny*] **:** a late or recent arrival **:** NEWCOMER ⟨*Johnny-come-latelies* bringing up the rear —*N.Y. Times*⟩ ⟨the *Johnny-come-latelies* climbed the bandwagon —*Chicago Daily News*⟩

**johnny cra·paud** *or* **johnny cra·peau** \-kra'pō, -'=(,)=\ *n, usu cap J&C* [fr. the name *Johnny* + F *crapaud* toad; fr. the reputation of the French for eating frogs — more at CRAPAUD] **1 :** the French people **2 :** FRENCHMAN

**johnny darter** *n, usu cap J* [fr. the name *Johnny* + *darter*] **:** a small darter (*Boleosoma nigrum*) found in streams of the central U.S.

**johnny house** *n* [*johnny* + *house*] *chiefly Midland* **:** an outdoor toilet

**johnny jump** *n, usu cap 1st J* [fr. the name *Johnny* + *jump*, v.; fr. the rapid growth] **:** SHOOTING STAR

**johnny-jump-up** \'==='=\ *n* -s *usu cap 1st J* [fr. the name *Johnny* + *jump up*, v.; fr. the rapid growth] **1 :** WILD PANSY; *broadly* **:** any of various chiefly small-flowered cultivated pansies **2 :** any of various American violets (as a bird's-foot violet)

**johnny-on-the-spot** \'==,=='=\ *n, usu cap J* [fr. the name *Johnny* + the phrase *on the spot*] **:** one who is on hand and ready esp. to perform a service or respond to an emergency ⟨luckily he was *Johnny-on-the-spot* . . . and was given his highly important post —John Dean⟩

**johnny raw** *n, usu cap J&R* [fr. the name *Johnny* + *raw*] **:** a raw recruit **:** GREENHORN

**johnny reb** *n, usu cap J&R* [fr. the name *Johnny* + *reb*] **:** a Confederate soldier in the Civil War

**johnny rook** *n, usu cap J* [fr. the name *Johnny* + *rook*] **:** a hawk (*Phalcoboenus australis*) of the Falkland islands that is related to the caracaras

**johnny smokers** *n pl but sing or pl in constr, usu cap J* [fr. the name *Johnny* + *smokers*; fr. the appearance of the feathery styles of the fruit] **:** PRAIRIE SMOKE 1

**johnny verde** \¦=¦vərd\ *n, usu cap J* [fr. the name *Johnny* + Sp *verde* green, fr. L *viridis* — more at VERDANT] **:** SAND BASS 1a

**john q. public** *also* **john q.** *or* **john q. citizen** *n, usu cap J&Q&P&C* [fr. the name *John* + the initial *Q.* + *public* or *citizen*] **1 :** a member of the public or the community **:** PERSON, CITIZEN ⟨just another *John Q. Citizen* on the road —*Springfield (Mass.) Union*⟩ **2 :** the public or the community personified ⟨Mr. and Mrs. *John Q. Public* suffered no great deprivations —*Domestic Commerce*⟩

**johns** *pl of* JOHN

**john·son bar** \'jän(t)sən-\ *n, usu cap J* [fr. the name *Johnson*] **:** the reverse gear lever of a railroad steam locomotive

**john·son·ese** \,jän(t)sə¦nēz, -ēs\ *n* -s *usu cap* [Samuel *Johnson* †1784 Eng. lexicographer and writer + E *-ese*] **:** a literary style characterized by balanced phraseology and excessively Latinic diction ⟨fell into the pompous rhythm of the later eighteenth century . . . into *Johnsonese* —Hastings Lyon⟩

**johnson grass** *n, usu cap J* [after William *Johnston* †1859 Am. farmer] **:** a tall perennial sorghum (*Sorghum halepense*) that spreads by scaly creeping rhizomes, has been widely introduced as a hay and forage grass, and has become naturalized in many warm regions (as the southern U.S.) where it is a serious pest on cultivated land

¹**john·so·ni·an** \(')jän¦sōnēən\ *adj, usu cap* [Samuel *Johnson* + E *-ian*] **1 :** of, relating to, or characteristic of Samuel Johnson ⟨a thoroughly *Johnsonian* conception of decorum —Donald Davie⟩ **2 :** of, relating to, or resembling the literary style of Samuel Johnson: as **a :** marked by purity, elevation, and grace ⟨the high style is the style that one thinks of as *Johnsonian* —Lillian De La Torre⟩ **b :** marked by balanced phraseology and excessively Latinic diction ⟨in prolix and *Johnsonian* style —Dinah M. Mulock⟩

²**johnsonian** \"\ *n* -s *usu cap* **:** a student, follower, or imitator of Samuel Johnson or his writings

**john·so·ni·ana** \jän,sōnē'anə, -'ānə, -'änə *also* -'änə\ *n pl, usu cap* [Samuel *Johnson* + E *-i-* + *-ana*] **:** collected items by, about, or relating to Samuel Johnson

**johnson noise** *n, usu cap J* [after John B. *Johnson* b1887 Am. physicist] **:** THERMAL NOISE

**john stiles** \-'stī(ə)lz\ *n, usu cap J&S* [alter. of *john-a-stiles*] **:** a party to legal proceedings whose true name is unknown; *esp* **:** the third such party when three are unknown — compare JOHN DOE, RICHARD MILES, RICHARD ROE

**john·ston's organ** \'jän(t)stənz-\ *n, usu cap J* [after Christopher *Johnston* †1891 Am. physician] **:** a sense organ in the second antennal segment of insects that responds to movements of the antennal flagellum and serves as a flight-speed indicator

**john·strup·ite** \'jän,strə,pīt\ *n* -s [G *johnstrupit*, fr. Frederik *Johnstrup* †1894 Danish mineralogist + G *-it* -ite] **:** a mineral approximately $(Ca,Na)_3(Ce,Ti,Zr)Si_2O_8F$ consisting of a complex silicate of cerium and other metals in prismatic crystals (sp. gr. 3.29)

**john's-wort** \'=,=\ *n, pl* **john's-worts** *usu cap J* [after St. *John*, one of the twelve apostles of Christ; fr. its having been gathered on the eve of the Feast of St. John (June 24)] **:** SAINT-JOHN'S-WORT

**john to·whit** \-tü'(h)wit\ *n, usu cap J* [fr. the name *John* + *towhit*, of imit. origin] **:** a West Indian vireo (*Vireo altiloquus*)

**john trot** *n, usu cap J&T* [fr. the name *John Trot*] **:** a dull man **:** BUMPKIN, BOOR

**joie de vi·vre** \,zhwädə'vēvr(ᵊ), -vēv(rə)\ *n* [F, lit., joy of living] **:** keen or buoyant enjoyment of life ⟨youthfully innocent *joie de vivre* —John Beaufort⟩

¹**join** \'jȯin *dial* 'jīn\ *vb* -ED/-ING/-S [ME *joinen*, fr. OF *join-, joign-*, stem of *joindre*, fr. L *jungere* — more at YOKE] *vt* **1 a :** to put or bring together and fasten, connect, or relate so as to form a single unit, a whole, or a continuity **:** COMBINE, LINK ⟨~ two blocks of wood with glue⟩ ⟨two moral forces, separate and yet ~*ed*⟩ ⟨~ forces in an effort to stamp out vice⟩ ⟨a bridge ~*ing* the two halves of the city⟩ **b :** to connect (as points) by a line (as a straight line) **c :** ADJOIN ⟨his studio there ~*ed* that of the famous sculptor —J.T.Marshall⟩ **2 :** to put or bring into close contact, association, or relationship **:** ATTACH, UNITE, COUPLE ⟨was later ~*ed* to another battalion⟩ ⟨the agitation of his mind, ~*ed* to the pain of his wound, kept him awake —Francis Parkman⟩ ⟨~*ed* in marriage by a local minister⟩ **3 :** to enter into or engage in (battle) **4 a** (1) **:** to

come into the company of : come into local contact or association with ⟨~s his wife and three children around the breakfast table —Stuart Chase⟩ ⟨~*ed* us for lunch⟩ (2) : to come to ⟨at the next town we ~ another route⟩ **b** : to connect or associate oneself with: (1) : to participate in : enter into ⟨~*ed* the defense of Paris as commander of naval antiaircraft batteries —*Current Biog.*⟩ (2) : to ally oneself with ⟨~ the government in condemning foreign aggression⟩ (3) : BOARD ⟨~a vehicle⟩; *esp* : to go aboard (a ship) usu. as a member of the personnel ⟨~*ed* the destroyer as executive officer⟩ (4) : to become a member or associate of ⟨~ a church⟩ ⟨~ a faculty⟩ ⟨ran away from school to ~ a traveling tent show —*Current Biog.*⟩ ~ *vi* **1 a** : to come together so as to be connected or united ⟨English nouns ~ easily to form compounds⟩ **b** : ADJOIN ⟨at this point the two estates ~⟩ **2** : to come into close association or relationship: as **a** : to form or enter into an alliance or league ⟨business interests ~*ed* to maintain the consolidated system —*Amer. Guide Series: Minn.*⟩ — often used with *up* ⟨the three clubs ~*ed* up to improve the town's playground facilities⟩ **b** : to become a member of a group or organization ⟨an ambulance service was organized and I ~*ed* in as a stretcher bearer —Nevil Shute⟩ ⟨he is now a Mason but he did not ~ until last year⟩ ⟨two weeks after he ~*ed* up he was sent into the fighting area and saw immediate action⟩ **c** : to enter into or take part in a collective activity ⟨~ in singing the national anthem⟩ ⟨when there was group dancing . . . they all ~*ed* in together —Cabell Phillips⟩

**syn** CONJOIN, LINK, CONNECT, RELATE, ASSOCIATE, COMBINE, UNITE all signify a bringing or coming together into a more or less close union. RELATE and ASSOCIATE suggest the loosest and most unspecific of unions; LINK, JOIN, CONJOIN, and CONNECT suggest a closer contact to the point of a physical or moral attachment; COMBINE and UNITE suggest a union to the point of some loss of identity or a complete loss of identity of the separate elements. Of the pair RELATE and ASSOCIATE, ASSOCIATE emphasizes the mere fact of the bringing, coming, or being together of two or more persons or things although it suggests by customary implication some kind of unspecified often intangible but compatible or companionable interaction ⟨*associate* with shady characters⟩ ⟨*associate* the sense of hunger and the search for food⟩ ⟨was *associated* with the hospital from 1889 until 1919 —*Amer. Guide Series: Md.*⟩ ⟨the smooth ultralegato style now often *associated* with English music of the period —E.T.Canby⟩ RELATE can signify a bringing or coming together in any number of ways so that the two or more things have some generally only implied physical, moral, or logical bearing on each other ⟨the wing of a bird and the arm of a man are historically *related*⟩ ⟨an interrogation point which *relates* the title closely to the text —G.W.Johnson⟩ ⟨not the least merit of the book is that it *relates* the history of science to other thought currents —F.L.Baumer⟩ ⟨their ability to *relate* what they observe to what they know or have previously observed —Gertrude H. Hildreth⟩ Although they are used to signify a more specific union, LINK, CONNECT, JOIN, and CONJOIN in their nonphysical application may suggest a bringing or coming together as general and unspecified as that implied by RELATE or ASSOCIATE but tend more, esp. in physical application, to signify a junction of some kind, often an inseparable junction as by a chain or by bonding. CONNECT is the most general of these four and suggests a loose attachment, esp. one that preserves the identity of the elements and the evidence of the connection ⟨*connect* the two ends of the pipe⟩ ⟨*connect* the two houses by a path⟩ ⟨the criminal activity has been *connected* with the names of several prominent men⟩ ⟨a number of articles *connected* with her life —*Amer. Guide Series: R.I.*⟩ LINK suggests a slightly closer coupling esp. in the physical application of the word in which is implied inseparability but of still clearly identifiably separate elements ⟨the bridge *linking* the islands of North Hero and Grand Isle —*Amer. Guide Series: Vt.*⟩ ⟨none of the subjects that *linked* us together could be talked about in a bar —Nevil Shute⟩ ⟨eight Anarchists were condemned to death or life imprisonment in a trial that *linked* them to this Haymarket Riot —J.D.Hart⟩ JOIN usu. suggests strongly the idea of physical or moral contact or junction or the making of a continuity of two or more things ⟨apply glue to the edges to be *joined*⟩ ⟨*join* the ends of the wires with solder⟩ ⟨a common purpose *joined* their efforts⟩ CONJOIN usu. emphasizes both the togetherness of a joining and the separateness of the things joined ⟨three *conjoined* quadrangular beakers with a common cover —*Parke-Bernet Galleries Catalog*⟩ ⟨a scientific realism, based on mechanism, is *conjoined* with an unwavering belief in the world of men . . . as being composed of self-determining organisms —A.N.Whitehead⟩ COMBINE and UNITE usu. emphasize the first a mingling and the second a union or integration in which individual identity is lost in a common aim or in the formation of a new product from the mingling or integration. COMBINE stresses a merging by intermixture ⟨*combine* ingredients in making a cake⟩ ⟨*combines* Georgian Colonial and Classical Revival designs —*Amer. Guide Series: Pa.*⟩ ⟨beauty and melody and graceful motion . . . were *combined* in her —W.H.Hudson †1922⟩ UNITE strongly emphasizes the singleness resulting from the junction of persons or elements ⟨*unite* the separated army divisions⟩ ⟨certain chemical elements *unite* to form gases⟩ ⟨*unite* two people in a common purpose⟩ ⟨*unite* a couple in marriage⟩ ⟨a cooperative community in which manual and intellectual labor might be *united* —Allan MacDonald⟩

— **join hands 1** : to clasp or shake hands in token of agreement or affection **2 a** : to make contact : come together ⟨*joined hands* with forces coming from the east⟩ **b** : to join together in an alliance or corporate enterprise or to a common end ⟨the clergy *joined hands* with the laity in maintaining the inherited verse forms —Kemp Malone⟩ — **join out** *or* **join out the odds** *slang* : to engage in the business of procuring : turn pimp — **join the issue** *or* **join issue 1** : to submit a legal issue jointly for decision **2 a** : to accept, fix on, or clearly define a particular issue as the basis of a controversy or other struggle ⟨*the issue* was clearly *joined* —K.S.Latourette⟩ ⟨the Senator did not endorse unfair play, injustice, and indecency, and thus *join the issue* —W.L.Miller⟩ ⟨the minority report was read and *the issue joined* —Walter Goodman⟩ **b** : to take an opposed or contrary position on some question : take issue ⟨it is with his conclusions that we today would *join issue* —K.H. Hartley⟩

**²join** \"\ *n* -s **1** : something that joins : a place or line where joining occurs : JOINT ⟨ensure accurately matching ~s —W.P. Matthew⟩ ⟨the ~s between the veins and the arteries, the capillaries —S.F.Mason⟩ ⟨the ~ of lid and box⟩ **2** : a splice in magnetic recording tape

**join·able** \-nəbəl\ *adj* : capable of being joined

**join·der** \ˈjȯində(r)\ *n* -s [F *joindre* to join — more at JOIN] **1** : act of joining : a putting together : CONJUNCTION ⟨simultaneous production and ~ of these two pieces at the Argentine Embassy —*Blue Bk. on Argentina*⟩ **2 a** : a joining of parties as plaintiffs or defendants in a suit **b** : acceptance of an issue tendered **c** : a joining of causes of action or defense or of parties in an indictment **d** : a joining of two or more parties in a common transaction

**joined** *past of* JOIN

**¹join·er** \ˈjȯinə(r) *dial* ˈjīn-\ *n* -s [ME *joinour, joiner,* fr. AF *joignour*, fr. OF *joign-, join-* (stem of *joindre* to join) + AF *-our* -or — more at JOIN] **1** : one that joins: as **a** : a person whose occupation is to construct articles by joining pieces of wood : one who does the woodwork (as doors or stairs) necessary for the finishing of buildings — compare CARPENTER **b** : a worker who stitches together the parts of garments **c** : a worker who prepares sheets of glass for grinding and polishing by arranging them on a plaster-covered table **d** : a worker who inserts sections of stained glass into leads preparatory to their placement in windows **e** : a worker who by hand or by machine shapes the edge of the shank sole of shoes at the joint between the shank and heel — called also *jointer* **f** : a worker who fits and joins the parts of interior furnishings of boats and installs the completed units **g** : a worker who puts rubber articles (as baby pants) through a roller-cutter that joins and trims the edges **2** : JOINTER a(1) **3** : a typically gregarious or civic-minded person who joins many organizations : a person temperamentally given to joining many organizations ⟨the young businessman is not markedly a civic ~ —W.H.Whyte⟩ ⟨when it comes to clubs and organizations, she is not a ~ —*Current Biog.*⟩

**²joiner** \"\ *vi* -ED/-ING/-S : to work as a joiner

**joiner work** *n* : JOINERY

**join·ery** \ˈjȯinərē, -ri\ *n* -ES [¹*joiner* + *-y*] **1** : the art or trade of a joiner **2** : work done by a joiner; *also* : things made by a joiner

**joining** *n* -s [fr. gerund of ¹*join*] **1 a** : the act or an instance of joining one thing to another ⟨an easy ~ is always possible —L.A.Leslie⟩ **b** : the condition or fact of being joined together : JUNCTURE ⟨apt to name each separate confluence with its own name, since their later ~s are unknown to him —A.A. Hill⟩ **2 a** : the place or manner of being joined together : JOIN, JOINT ⟨the ~ is hardly visible⟩ **b** : something that joins two things together **3** : the practice of joining many organizations ⟨used to be the fashion to decry all forms of American ~ —W.S.Lynch⟩

**joins** *pres 3d sing of* JOIN, *pl of* JOIN

**¹joint** \ˈjȯint *dial* ˈjīnt\ *n* -s [ME *joint, jointe,* partly fr. OF *jointe* joint of the body, fr. fem. of *joint*, past part. of *joindre* to join; partly fr. MF *joint* joint (place where two parts meet), fr. past part. of *joindre* — more at JOIN] **1 a** (1) : the point of contact between elements of an animal skeleton (as femur and hipbone) whether movable or rigidly fixed together with the parts (as membranes, tendons, ligaments) that surround and support it ⟨the capsule of the shoulder ~⟩ ⟨the antennal ~s of a cockroach⟩ (2) : such a structure regarded as a particular type of mechanism ⟨the ball-and-socket ~ of the hip⟩ (3) : NODE 4a ⟨the ~s of a stem of grass⟩ **b** : a part or space included between two articulations, knots, or nodes ⟨the first ~ of the arm⟩ ⟨a ~ of cane⟩ **c** : a large piece of meat for roasting **2 a** : a place where two things or parts are joined or united : a union of two or more smooth or even surfaces admitting of a close fitting or junction whether movable or immovable : JUNCTION ⟨a ~ between two pieces of timber⟩ ⟨a ~ in a pipe⟩ **b** : a space between the adjacent surfaces of two bodies (as bricks) joined and held together by means of cement, mortar, or other material ⟨a thin ~⟩ **c** : a fracture or crack in rock not accompanied by dislocation being generally one of many arranged in a systematic pattern, occurring in all firm coherent rocks, and dividing them into blocks **d** : the flexing portion of a cover along either backbone edge of a book; *also* : the groove where the cover hinges — called also *hinge* **e** : the junction of two or more members of a framed structure **f** : a union formed by two abutting rails in a track including the bars, bolts, and other elements necessary to hold the abutting rails together **g** : an area at which two ends, surfaces, or edges are attached (as by adhesive, tape, nails, or staples) **3 a** (1) : a shabby or disreputable place of entertainment or other public house ⟨make a tour of the tough ~s —W.S.Maugham⟩ ⟨I wouldn't go there; that place is a ~⟩ (2) : a place (as a nightclub, restaurant, or hotel) open to the public ⟨I'll have you know this is a respectable ~ —William Grampp⟩ ⟨it depended on the social tone of the ~ —Scott Fitzgerald⟩ (3) : PLACE, ESTABLISHMENT, DWELLING ⟨there now are buffaloes all over the ~ —R.M.Yoder⟩ ⟨this is certainly an intellectual ~ —Sinclair Lewis⟩ ⟨come on over to my ~⟩ **b** *slang* : a concession stand at a circus or fair **c** *slang* (1) : a marijuana cigarette (2) : a hypodermic needle; *also* : the needle, dropper, and connection used in taking drugs hypodermically — **out of joint 1 a** *of a bone* : having the head slipped from its socket **b** : being out of adjustment or harmony : being at odds : UNSUITABLE, INCONSISTENT ⟨production costs are now entirely *out of joint* with retail prices —Jack Morpurgo⟩ ⟨impractical, romantic, and wholly *out of joint* with their times —W.P.Webb⟩ **2 a** : being in an unsatisfactory or disordered state : UNPROPITIOUS ⟨the times are *out of joint*⟩ **b** : being out of humor : DISGRUNTLED, DISSATISFIED ⟨find themselves a little *out of joint* with the party arrangements —Sir Winston Churchill⟩ ⟨the Ministry are much *out of joint* —Thomas Gray⟩ ⟨must have been many noses put *out of joint* —Alvin Johnson⟩

joints used in masonry: *1* struck; *2* weathered; *3* flush; *4* raked, *5* tooled, concave; *6* tooled, "V"

**²joint** \"\ *adj* [ME, fr. MF, fr. past part. of *joindre* — more at JOIN] **1** : JOINED, UNITED, COMBINED ⟨subjected to the ~ influences of culture and climate⟩ **2** : common to two or more: as **a** (1) : involving the united activity of two or more : done or produced by two or more working together ⟨issued a ~ report⟩ ⟨achieved through our ~ efforts⟩ (2) : constituting an activity, operation, or organization in which elements of more than one armed service participate ⟨the *Joint* Chiefs of Staff⟩ (3) : constituting an action or expression in which two or more governments unite as distinguished from an identic action or expression ⟨a ~ intervention⟩ ⟨a ~ note⟩ **b** (1) : shared by or affecting two or more : held or obligating or obligated in common ⟨~ property⟩ ⟨a ~ fine⟩ (2) : united in right, status, interest, power, privilege, duty, or obligation (3) : of or relating to the right of survivorship in property held in joint tenancy or by the entirety as distinguished from that held as tenants in common — compare CORREAL, JOINT AND SEVERAL, SEVERAL, SOLIDARITY **3** : united, joined, or sharing with another (as in a right, obligation, status, or activity) : not solitary in interest or action : holding in common with an associate : acting together ⟨~ heir⟩ ⟨~ creditor⟩ **4** : of or relating to a joint family

**³joint** \"\ *vb* -ED/-ING/-S [¹*joint*] *vt* **1 a** *obs* : JOIN, UNITE, COMBINE ⟨~*ing* their force —Shak.⟩ **b** : to unite by a joint : fit together ⟨~ boards⟩ ⟨her elbows and shoulders are ~*ed* wrong —*Irish Digest*⟩ **c** : to provide with a joint : ARTICULATE **d** : to prepare (as a board) for joining by planing the edge to be joined **e** : to file down (saw teeth) to a correct height **2** : to separate the joints of : divide at the joint : cut up into joints ⟨lamb should present little difficulty if thoroughly ~*ed* beforehand —Noreen Routledge⟩ ~ *vi* **1** : to fit as if by joints : coalesce as joints do ⟨the stones ~ neatly⟩ **2** : to form joints as a stage in growth (as of winter wheat and other small grains)

**joint account** *n* : a bank or brokerage account owned jointly by two or more persons either of whom may withdraw funds or effect transactions on his signature alone

**joint adventure** *n* : a partnership or cooperative agreement between two or more persons restricted to a single specific undertaking — called also *joint undertaking;* compare SYNDICATE

**joint and several** *adj* : constituting or relating to rights which two or more persons entitled thereto may assert either together or separately or to duties and liabilities of two or more persons for which they may be held liable either together or separately (as a note where all makers or any one of them can be held for the full amount) — compare CORREAL, IN SOLIDO, JOINT 2b(3), SEVERAL, SOLIDARITY

**joint and survivor annuity** *n* : JOINT LIFE AND SURVIVOR ANNUITY

**joint annuity** *n* : JOINT LIFE ANNUITY

**joint assertion** *n* : CONJUNCTION 7a

**joint author** *n* : a person who collaborates with one or more persons in the production of a literary work ⟨*joint authors* of a widely used text⟩

**joint bar** *n* : a steel member embodying beam strength and stiffness by its structural shape and material and commonly used in pairs to splice rail ends together

**joint-bedded** \ˈ=¦==\ *adj, of a quarried stone* : bedded in the wall so that its natural bed is set in a joint — compare FACE-BEDDED

**joint chair** *n* [¹*joint*] *Brit* : a chair supporting the ends of abutting rails

**joint committee** *n* : a committee appointed by both houses of a legislature usu. for the purpose of considering joint action or resolving differences between the houses — compare CONFERENCE 3b

**joint contributory** *adj* : CONTRIBUTORY

**joint convention** *n* : a meeting together of both branches of the U.S. Congress or of a state legislature

**joint denial** *n* : the complex proposition asserting that neither of two propositions is true ⟨the *joint denial* "not *p* and not *q*" is true only if *p* and *q* are false⟩ — compare ALTERNATIVE DENIAL

**jointed** *adj* [ME, fr. *joint, jointe* joint + *-ed*] : having joints : ARTICULATED ⟨a ~ doll⟩ — often used in combination ⟨loose-jointed⟩ ⟨well-jointed⟩

**jointed cactus** *n* : a cactus of the genus *Opuntia*

**jointed charlock** *n* : a Eurasian weed (*Raphanus raphanistrum*) closely related to the common radish and having seed pods that are prominently constricted

**jointed fern** *n* : HORSETAIL 2

**joint·ed·ly** *adv* : in a jointed manner

**joint·ed·ness** *n* -ES : the quality or state of being jointed

**joint enterprise** *n* **1** : JOINT ADVENTURE **2 a** : an undertaking of two or more persons for a common object under circumstances giving each an equal right to control a vehicle or instrumentality and making all chargeable with the negligence of anyone exercising actual control and causing harm to another in actions between the third person and the parties to the enterprise **b** : an undertaking of two or more persons for mutual benefit or pleasure

**joint·er** \ˈjȯintə(r)\ *n* -s : one that joints: as **a** (1) : a hand or power planer for smoothing a sawed surface for jointing or mortising (2) : a tool used for filing the points of saw teeth to a uniform height **b** (1) : a bent piece of iron inserted to strengthen joints (2) : a tool for pointing joints (3) : a tool for cutting grooves to indicate joints in freshly laid surfaces of cement **c** : a triangular-shaped edged attachment to a plow beam for covering trash and organic matter in plowing **d** (1) : a worker who joints (as wires, pipes, or scissors blades) (2) : a worker who operates an abrasive saw or wheel for cutting structural stone true for fit in construction (3) : JOINER 1e

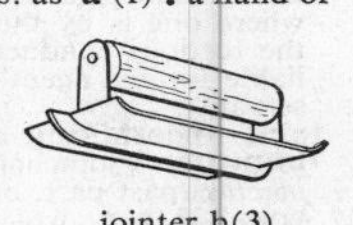
jointer b(3)

**jointer gauge** *n* : an attachment clamped to one side of a bench plane and made adjustable to secure any desired angle between the edge of a board being planed and its face

**jointer plane** *n* : a woodworker's plane about 2 feet long used for smoothing long surfaces (as the edges of boards in preparation for joining them)

**joint evil** *or* **joint ill** *n* : NAVEL ILL

**joint facility** *n* : railway property that two or more carriers jointly own, maintain, or operate by formal agreement

**joint family** *or* **joint household** *n* : a consanguineal family unit that includes two or more generations of kindred related through either the paternal or maternal line who maintain a common residence and are subject to common social, economic, and religious regulations

**joint fir** *n* [¹*joint;* fr. the leafless jointed stems] : any of various plants of the family Gnetaceae and esp. of the genera *Gnetum* and *Ephedra* with small scalelike leaves resembling those of some evergreens

**joint-fir family** *n* : GNETACEAE

**joint gap** *n* [¹*joint*] : the distance in 64ths of an inch between the ends of contiguous rails measured at a point about ⅝ inch below the top of the rail

**joint grass** *n* [¹*joint*] **1** : a coarse creeping grass (*Paspalum distichum*) that roots at the joints and is used as fodder and as a soil binder **2** : HORSETAIL **3** : YELLOW BEDSTRAW

**jointing** *n* -s [fr. gerund of ³*joint*] **1** : the act or process or an instance of making a joint; *also* : the joint thus produced **2** : the process of filling and finishing the joints in masonry with a special caulking material **3** : a condition or structure in rock characterized by the presence of joints

**jointing rule** *n* : a long straight rule used by bricklayers for securing straight joints and faces

**joint·less** \ˈjȯintləs *dial* ˈjīnt-\ *adj* : constituting one piece : having no seam or joint

**joint life and survivor annuity** *n* : an annuity payable as long as any of two or more designated persons shall live

**joint life annuity** *n* : an annuity payable only until the death of the first of two or more designated persons

**joint life insurance** *n* : a policy providing for payment of the proceeds upon the first occurrence of death among the persons insured

**joint·ly** *adv* [ME, fr. *joint* + *-ly*] **1** : in a joint manner: as **a** : TOGETHER, UNITEDLY ⟨activities carried on ~ with other societies —*Mech. Engineering*⟩ ⟨written ~ with other scientists —*Current Biog.*⟩ ⟨owned ~ by several companies⟩; *specif* : so as to be or become liable to a joint obligation **b** : in joint tenancy or in tenancy by the entirety, or with the right of survivorship **2** : in proportion to the product

**joint mouse** *n* [¹*joint;* fr. the fact that its movement suggests that of a mouse] : a loose fragment (as of cartilage) within a synovial space

**joint·ness** *n* -ES : the quality or state of being common to two or more persons

**joint obligation** *n* : an obligation binding each of the obligors to the performance of the entire obligation

**joint oil** *n* [¹*joint*] : SYNOVIA

**joint plant** *n* [¹*joint*] : a wandering Jew (*Tradescantia fluminensis*) with green or green and white striped leaves

**joint product** *n* **1** : a product of joint effort ⟨view this report as truly a *joint product* —C.E.Osgood & T.A.Sebeok⟩ **2** : one of two or more products of substantial importance derived from the same raw material (as gas and coke from coal) — distinguished from *by-product*

**joint rate** *n* : a rate from a point on one transport carrier to a point on another line made by agreement and published in a concurrent tariff

**joint resolution** *n* : a resolution passed by both branches of a legislative body; *esp* : one passed by both houses of the U.S. Congress and having the force of law when signed by the president or passed by a two-thirds majority of both houses over the president's veto ⟨a *joint resolution,* requiring mere congressional majorities, has been resorted to when the treaty-making process . . . broke down —F.A.Ogg & P.O.Ray⟩ — compare BILL 3, CONCURRENT RESOLUTION

**joint·ress** \ˈjȯin·trəs\ *n* -ES [obs. E *jointer* man who holds a jointure (fr. *jointure* + *-er*) + *-ess*] : a woman who has a legal jointure

**joint ring** *n* [¹*joint*] *obs* : GEMEL 2

**joint runner** *n* [¹*joint*] : a piece of asbestos rope with clamps placed around a pipe or tile joint to serve as a dam for the retention of poured molten metal later to be caulked in

**joint rust** *n* [¹*joint*] : a disease of grasses caused by the cattail fungus and characterized by the development of fungal stromata esp. about the joints of an affected plant — compare CHOKE 5

**joints** *pl of* JOINT, *pres 3d sing of* JOINT

**joint session** *or* **joint meeting** *n* : a session of the two houses of a legislature meeting together and acting as one body

**joint shingle** *n* [¹*joint*] : a short wooden shingle formerly applied by nailing edge to edge instead of overlapping

**joint snake** *n* [¹*joint;* fr. the deep lateral fold on the body] : GLASS SNAKE

**joint splice** *n* [¹*joint*] : a reinforce at a joint intended to hold the parts in their true relation

**joint stock** *n* : stock or capital held in company : capital held as a common stock or fund

**joint-stock bank** *n* **1** : a bank organized as a joint-stock association **2** : an English or Australian bank whose capital is subscribed by private persons under statutory law as distinguished from a government bank

**joint-stock company** *n* **1** : a company or association consisting of a number of individuals organized to conduct a business for gain with a joint stock, the shares owned by any member being transferable without the consent of the rest **2** *also* **joint-stock association** : a form of partnership differing from the ordinary form of partnership by the transferability of shares (as in a corporation), by the fact that the death of a stockholder does not dissolve the company, and by the fact that the managing of the company is limited to persons specially authorized — compare CORPORATION, LIMITED LIABILITY

**joint stock land bank** *n, usu cap J&S&L&B* : any of several corporations organized to make mortgage loans direct to farmers and to issue bonds similar to farm loan bonds

**joint stool** *n* [¹*joint*] **:** a stool formed of parts held together by pegged mortise-and-tenon joints **:** a stool made by a joiner

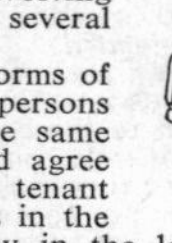
joint stool

**joint tariff** *n* **:** a schedule of rates agreed upon by two or more carriers involving charges between points on their several lines

**joint tenancy** *n* **:** one of several forms of tenure in which two or more persons hold in concurrent ownership the same estate in realty or personalty and agree that upon the death of one joint tenant the full title to the estate remains in the surviving joint tenants and finally in the last survivor — compare TENANCY BY THE ENTIRETY, TENANCY IN COMMON

**joint tenant** *n* **:** one who holds an estate by or in joint tenancy

**joint tortfeasor** *n* **1 :** one of two or more persons acting in concert in the commission of a tort **2 a :** one of two or more persons who may be joined as defendants in the same single cause of action to recover damage for a tort **b :** one of two or more persons jointly and severally fully responsible for all the damage to a third person caused by their concurring though independent tortious acts **c :** one of two tortfeasors where one is by the policy of the law vicariously liable for the tortious conduct of the other (as where the principal is liable for his agent's conduct or the master for that of his servant)

**joint undertaking** *or* **joint venture** *n* **:** JOINT ADVENTURE

¹**join·ture** \ˈjȯinchə(r)\ *n* -s [ME, fr. MF, fr. L *junctura*, fr. *junctus* (past part. of *jungere* to join) + *-ura* -ure — more at YOKE] **1 a :** an act of joining **:** the state of being joined **:** UNION ⟨the ∼ of two odd names in marriage —E.C.Smith⟩ ⟨the battle seemed on its way to ∼ —*Time*⟩ **b :** JOINT, JUNCTURE **2 a** *obs* (1) **:** the joint tenancy of an estate (2) **:** the estate so held **b** (1) **:** an estate settled on a wife to be taken by her in lieu of dower (2) **:** a settlement upon the wife of a freehold estate (as in lands or tenements) for her lifetime at least to take effect upon the decease of the husband and to act as a bar to dower — called also *legal jointure;* compare EQUITABLE DOWER

²**jointure** \"\ *vt* -ED/-ING/-S **:** to settle a jointure upon

**join·tur·ess** \-chərə̇s\ *n* -ES [alter. (influenced by ¹*jointure*) of *jointress*] **:** JOINTRESS

**joint vein** *n* [¹*joint*] **:** a small geological vein occupying a joint

**joint vetch** *n* [¹*joint;* fr. the jointed pod] **:** a plant of the genus *Aeschynomene*

**joint water** *n* [¹*joint;* trans. of G *gelenkwasser*] **:** SYNOVIA

**jointweed** \ˈ=,=\ *n* [¹*joint* + *weed*] **:** a plant of the genus *Polygonella; esp* **:** an American herb (*P. articulata*) with jointed almost leafless stems and spikelike racemes of small white flowers

**joint wire** *n* [¹*joint*] **:** hollow wire that is used for joints (as in a watchcase)

**jointwood** \ˈ=,=\ *n* [¹*joint* + *wood*] **:** an East Indian tree (*Cassia nodosa*) with dense showy racemes of pink or red flowers

**joint wood berry** *n* **:** CRANBERRY BUSH 2

**jointworm** \ˈ=,=\ *n* [¹*joint* + *worm*] **1 :** the larva of any of several small chalcid flies of the family Eurytomidae and genus *Harmolita* which attack the stems of grain and cause swellings like galls usu. at or just above the first joint **2** [so called fr. its jointed appearance] **:** BAMBOO WORM

¹**joist** \ˈjȯist *dial* ˈjīst\ *n* -s [ME *giste, geste,* fr. MF *giste,* fr. (assumed) VL *jacitum,* fr. L *jacēre* to lie + *-itum* (neut. of *-itus,* past participial ending) — more at GIST] **1 a :** any of the small rectangular-sectioned timbers or rolled iron or steel beams ranged parallel from wall to wall in a structure or resting on beams or girders to support the planking, pavement, tiling, or flagging of a floor or the laths or furring strips of a ceiling — see BINDING JOIST, BRIDGING JOIST, CEILING JOIST, TRIMMING JOIST **b :** a similar timber supporting the floor of a bridge or other structure **2 :** a stud or scantling about 3 by 4 inches in section

²**joist** \"\ *vt* -ED/-ING/-S **:** to furnish with joists

**joisting** *n* -s [¹*joist* + *-ing*] **:** joists esp. when in position supporting a floor

**jo·jo·ba** \hōˈhōbə, həˈ-\ *or* **ja·jo·ba** \həˈ-\ *n* [MexSp *jojoba*] **:** a shrub or small tree (*Simmondsia californica*) of the family Buxaceae of southwestern No. America with edible seeds that contain a valuable oil

**jo-jotte** \jōˈjät\ *n* -s [fr. *Jo-Jotte,* a trademark] **:** a card game based on belotte or klaberjass with some features (as doubling and slam bonuses) of bridge

¹**joke** \ˈjōk\ *n* -s [L *jocus* jest, joke, game; akin to OS *gehan* to say, speak, OHG *gehan, jehan* to say, speak, MW *ieith* language, Toch A & B *yask-* to demand, beg, Skt *yācati* he implores; basic meaning: speaking] **1 a :** something said or done to amuse or provoke laughter **:** something funny or humorous ⟨a tune which can be played backward — a ∼ —Edward Sackville-West⟩ ⟨the use of primarily visual ∼*s* —*Current Biog.*⟩; *esp* **:** a brief usu. oral narrative designed to provoke laughter and typically having a climactic humorous twist or denouement ⟨had a great fund of off-color ∼*s*⟩ **b** (1) **:** the spirit of humor or raillery in which something is said or done ⟨knew they were meant in ∼ —James Jones⟩ (2) **:** the humorous or ridiculous element in something ⟨the ∼ of it was that the matter was so entirely his own choice —S.E.White⟩ (3) **:** LAUGHTER, RAILLERY, KIDDING — often used in the phrase *take a joke* ⟨the most valuable thing she taught me was to take a ∼ —Polly Adler⟩ **c :** PRACTICAL JOKE ⟨mustn't play ∼*s* on poor old ladies⟩ **d :** a person or thing that is the object of laughter or ridicule **:** LAUGHINGSTOCK ⟨why, he's the ∼ of the whole town⟩ ⟨was still . . . a national ∼ —Van Wyck Brooks⟩ **2 a :** something lacking substance, genuineness, or quality **:** something not to be taken seriously **:** a trivial or trifling matter ⟨palaces and haunts . . . in which the state religion is a ∼ —Ray Alan⟩ ⟨consider his skiing a ∼ —Harold Callender⟩ — often used in negative construction ⟨it is no ∼ . . . to encounter week after week a player of settled reputation —Bernard Darwin⟩ **b :** something presenting no difficulty **:** something accomplished with ridiculous ease ⟨that exam was a ∼⟩

**syn** JOKE, JEST, JAPE, QUIP, WITTICISM, WISECRACK, CRACK, GAG can mean, in common, a remark, story, or action intended to evoke laughter. JOKE, when applied to a story or remark, suggests something designed to promote good humor, esp. an anecdote with a humorous twist at the end; when applied to an action, it often signifies a practical joke, usu. suggesting a fooling or deceiving of someone at his expense, generally though not necessarily good humored in intent ⟨everyone knows the old *joke,* that "black horses eat more than white horses", a puzzling condition which is finally cleared up by the statement that "there are more black horses" —W.J.Reilly⟩ ⟨issues had become a hopeless muddle and national politics a biennial *joke* —Dixon Wecter⟩ ⟨a child hiding mother's pocketbook as a *joke*⟩ ⟨the whole tale turns out to be a monstrous *joke,* a deception of matchless cruelty —B.R.Redman⟩ JEST, now literary or affected, in an older sense still connotes raillery or sarcasm but generally today suggests humor that is light and sportive, as banter ⟨continually . . . making a *jest* of his ignorance —J.D.Beresford⟩ ⟨won fame by *jests* at the foibles of his time, but . . . his pen was more playful than caustic —S.T.Williams & J.A.Pollard⟩ JAPE, usu. of literary occurrence, orig. signified an amusing anecdote but today is identical with JEST or JOKE ⟨the merry *japes* of fundamentally irresponsible young men —Edmund Fuller⟩ ⟨the *japes* about sex still strike me as being prurient rather than funny —John McCarten⟩ QUIP suggests a quick, neatly turned, witty remark ⟨full of wise saws and homely illustrations, the epigram, the *quip,* the jest —B.N.Cardozo⟩ ⟨many *quips* at the expense of individuals and their villages —Margaret Mead⟩ ⟨enlivened their reviews with *quips* —W.H. Dunham⟩ WITTICISM is a bookish and WISECRACK or CRACK the more general term for a clever or witty, esp. a biting or sarcastic, remark, generally a retort ⟨all the charming *witticisms* of English lecturers —Eric Sevareid⟩ ⟨a vicious *witticism* at the expense of a political opponent⟩ ⟨merely strolls by, makes a goofy *wisecrack* or screwball suggestion —Hugh Humphrey⟩ ⟨though the gravity of the situation forbade their utterance, I was thinking of at least three priceless *cracks* I could make —P.G.Wodehouse⟩ GAG, orig. in this connection and still signifying an interpolated joke or laugh-provoking piece of business, more generally today applies to any remark, story, or piece of business considered funny, esp. one written into a theatrical, movie, radio, or television script, and sometimes has extended its meaning to signify any trick whether funny or not but usu. one considered foolish ⟨*gags* grown venerable in the service of the music halls —*Times Lit. Supp.*⟩ ⟨the *gag* was not meant to be entirely funny —*Newsweek*⟩ ⟨gave a party the other night and pulled a really constructive *gag* . . . had every guest in the place vaccinated against smallpox —*Hollywood Reporter*⟩ ⟨a frivolous person, given to *gags* and foolishness⟩

²**joke** \"\ *vb* -ED/-ING/-S [L *jocari,* fr. *jocus*] *vi* **:** to make jokes **:** say or do something as a joke **:** JEST ⟨*joked* about the possibility of . . . lead poisoning due to bullets —Morris Fishbein⟩ ∼ *vt* **1 :** to make jokes upon **:** poke fun at **:** KID, BANTER ⟨beginning to ∼ him a bit about a nice young lady —Ethel Wilson⟩ **2 :** to obtain by joking ⟨∼ a beggar's penny out of you —Robert Lynd⟩

**jokebook** \ˈ=,=\ *n* **:** JESTBOOK

**joke·less** \ˈjōklə̇s\ *adj* **:** lacking jokes

**joke·let** \-lə̇t\ *n* -s **:** a little joke

**jok·er** \ˈjōkə(r)\ *n* -s **1 a :** a person given to joking **:** JESTER, HUMORIST, WAG ⟨a ∼ with an original turn of mind —*New Yorker*⟩ ⟨one of the town ∼*s* put her reluctance to marry down to a hereditary distaste for contracts —Frank O'Connor⟩ **b :** GUY, BLOKE, FELLOW ⟨in walks a ∼ very skinny and tall —Garson Kanin⟩ ⟨what a soft bloody job some ∼*s* have —David Ballantyne⟩; *sometimes* **:** an insignificant, obnoxious, or incompetent person **:** SLOB ⟨a shame to let a ∼ like this win —Harold Robbins⟩ ⟨know just what to do with that ∼ —Maxwell Griffith⟩ **2 a :** a small object (as a ball or pea) used in playing thimblerig — called also *little joker* **b** (1) **:** a playing card usu. marked on its face with a picture of a jester and often added to a pack of playing cards as a wild card (as in poker or canasta) or as the highest-ranking card (as in five hundred) (2) **:** a card designated as wild — see BIG JOKER **c** (1) **:** a clause that is ambiguous or apparently immaterial inserted in a legislative bill to make it inoperative or uncertain in some respect without arousing opposition at the time of its passage (2) **:** an unsuspected, misleading, or misunderstood clause, phrase, or word in an agreement, contract, statement, or other document that in effect nullifies or greatly alters its apparent terms or purport (3) **:** something (as an expedient or stratagem) held in reserve to gain one's end or escape from a difficult situation ⟨retained one ∼: they could appeal from a Greek legal decision to Roman law —Jaques-Yves Cousteau⟩ (4) **:** a fact, factor, or condition unsuspected or not apparent at first that thwarts or nullifies an apparent advantage ⟨depreciation: the ∼ in mechanization —Herrele DeGraff & Ladd Haystead⟩ ⟨the ∼ . . . is that we have a pretty persistent and devastating way of getting in the way of ourselves —H.A.Overstreet⟩

**joker trap** *n* **:** SKEE TRAP

**jokes** *pl of* JOKE, *pres 3d sing of* JOKE

**jokesmith** \ˈ=,=\ *n* **:** a joke writer

**joke·ster** \ˈjōkstə(r)\ *n* -s **:** JOKER

**jokey** *or* **joky** \ˈjōkē\ *adj, often* **jokier;** *often* **jokiest :** given to joking **:** WAGGISH ⟨a ∼ old bird —Sinclair Lewis⟩

**jok·ing·ly** *adv* **:** in a joking manner

**joking relationship** *n* **:** an institutionalized relationship of pronounced familiarity between specified relatives widely found among primitive peoples and involving the exchange of frequently sexually colored banter, jocular insults, and the playing of tricks upon one another — compare AVOIDANCE 5

**jö·kul** \ˈyō,ku̇l\ *also* **jö·kul** \ˈyœ̄,-\ *n* -s [Icel *jökull* icicle, glacier, fr. ON — more at ICICLE] **:** an Icelandic mountain covered with ice and snow **:** an Icelandic snow mountain

**jokyakarta** *usu cap, var of* DJOKJAKARTA

**joll** \ˈjäl\ *vi* -ED/-ING/-S [origin unknown] *dial Eng* **:** to move or walk clumsily **:** LURCH

**jolley** *also* **jollie** *var of* JOLLY

**jol·li·er** \ˈjälēə(r)\ *n* -s **1 :** a person who jollies, flatters, or banters **2 :** a worker who uses a jolly to make pottery hollow ware **3 :** a worker who operates a rotary pounding machine for flattening the lower edge of the shoe upper where it folds over the insole and smoothing the bottom for attachment of the outsole

**jol·li·fi·ca·tion** \,jäləfəˈkāshən\ *n* -s [¹*jolly* + *-fication*] **:** FESTIVITY, MERRYMAKING ⟨a pageant and general ∼ will begin at noon —*N.Y. Times*⟩

**jol·li·fy** \ˈjälə,fī\ *vi* -ED/-ING/-ES [¹*jolly* + *-fy*] **:** to make merry **:** CAROUSE

**jol·li·ly** \-lə̇lē, -lī\ *adv* [ME *jolifly, jolily,* fr. *jolif, joly* + *-ly*] **:** in a jolly manner **:** CHEERFULLY ⟨passing ∼ along the street —Laurence Sterne⟩

**jol·li·ness** \-lēnə̇s, -lin-\ *n* -ES [ME *jolifnesse, jolynesse,* fr. *jolif, joly* + *-nesse* -ness] **:** the quality or state of being jolly ⟨could not wholly eradicate that inherent English ∼ —Roy Lewis & Angus Maude⟩

**jol·li·ty** \ˈjäləd·ē, -ətē, -i\ *n* -ES [ME *jolifte, jolite,* fr. OF *jolivete, jolifte, jolite,* fr. *jolif, joli* + *-té* -ty] **1 :** the quality or state of being jolly **:** GAIETY, MERRIMENT, CHEER ⟨put on a show of bluff ∼ —Irwin Shaw⟩ **2** *Brit* **:** a festive gathering, meeting, or entertainment ⟨the occasion was a ∼ of the Bursley Burial Club —Arnold Bennett⟩ **3** *obs* **:** SPLENDOR, MAGNIFICENCE

**jol·loped** \ˈjäləpt\ *or* **jel·loped** \ˈjel-\ *adj* [obs. E *jollop, jellop* dewlap (prob. fr. *joll,* var. of *jowl* + *lap*) + *-ed*] *heraldry* **:** WATTLED

¹**jol·ly** \ˈjälē, -li\ *adj* -ER/-EST [ME *jolif, joli,* fr. OF *jolif, joli, jol-* (prob. of Scand origin; akin to ON *jōl* Yule, feast) + *-if* -ive — more at YULE] **1 a** (1) **:** full of high spirits **:** GAY, JOYOUS ⟨think no more, lad; laugh, be ∼ —A.E. Housman⟩ ⟨seems pretty comfortable and ∼ —Rachel Henning⟩ (2) **:** given to conviviality **:** FESTIVE, JOVIAL ⟨a ∼ and carefree companion —R.W.Pickford⟩ ⟨∼ sportsmen . . . reserved time enough to frolic —*Amer. Guide Series: Mass.*⟩ **b :** attended or marked by mirth or gaiety **:** expressing, suggesting, inspiring, or reflecting a mood of gaiety **:** CHEERFUL, BRIGHT ⟨impressed by his ∼ air of success —Arnold Bennett⟩ ⟨the last movement is a ∼ rondo —Virgil Thomson⟩ ⟨entirely in the right of it to lead a ∼ life —George Eliot⟩ ⟨had a ∼ time⟩ ⟨thickets of hawthorn and holly with ∼ little streams —S.P.B.Mais⟩ ⟨the countryside has a ∼ quality —Rebecca West⟩ **2** *now dial Eng* **a :** gay and attractive in manner and appearance **b :** appearing healthy or in good condition **:** SLEEK, PLUMP, LARGE **3 :** extremely pleasant or agreeable **:** DELIGHTFUL, SPLENDID, BULLY ⟨∼ little open carriages —O.S.Nock⟩ ⟨what a ∼ new world it is —T.R. Ybarra⟩ ⟨studying the . . . ∼ curve of her cheek —Vera Caspary⟩ ⟨why, that's real ∼⟩ **syn** see MERRY

²**jolly** \"\ *adv* **:** VERY, REMARKABLY ⟨did a lot of things that were ∼ foolish —R.H.Newman⟩ ⟨hoped it would be a ∼ good lesson to them —Dorothy Sayers⟩ — often used as an intensive ⟨they would kindly do as they were ∼ well told —John Stockbridge⟩

³**jolly** \"\ *vb* -ED/-ING/-ES *vi* **:** to engage in good-natured banter or raillery **:** CHAFF, KID ⟨*jollied* and joked with sailors in the street —Dixon Wecter⟩ ∼ *vt* **1 :** to put or seek to put in good humor esp. to gain some end **:** COAX, WHEEDLE, INDULGE ⟨∼*ing* the illiterate populace along towards the new age —Roland Mathias⟩ ⟨*jollied* my mother by joining her on the sofa —Peter De Vries⟩ ⟨do be good . . . and ∼ him along —Robertson Davies⟩ ⟨try to pay for their entertainment by ∼*ing* us along —S.E.White⟩ **2 :** to form or shape with a jolly

⁴**jolly** \"\ *n* -ES **1** *Brit* **:** MARINE **2** *chiefly Brit* **:** a sociable good time **:** JOLLIFICATION **3** *or* **jol·ley** *also* **jol·lie** \"\ -s **:** a potter's machine like a jigger used for flatware (as plates or saucers) and hollow ware

**jol·ly balance** \ˈjälē-, ˈyälē-\ *n, usu cap J* [After Philipp von *Jolly* †1884 Ger. physicist] **:** a very delicate spring balance used esp. for the determination of densities by the method of weighing in air and in water

**jol·ly boat** \ˈjälē-\ *or* **jolly** *n* -ES [origin unknown] **:** a boat of medium size belonging to a ship and used for general rough or small work

**jolly rog·er** \-ˈräjə(r)\ *n, usu cap J&R* [¹*jolly* + *Roger* (the name)] **:** a flag in any of various color combinations bearing one or more emblems of mortality (as a skeleton, a skull and crossbones, or an hourglass) and raised on a pirate ship of the 17th and 18th centuries as a signal that quarter would be given if no resistance were offered but now often believed to have been used by pirates as their ensign; *specif* **:** a black flag bearing a white skull and crossbones — compare BLACK FLAG

Jolly Roger

**jolof** *usu cap, var of* WOLOF

¹**jolt** \ˈjōlt\ *vb* -ED/-ING/-S [prob. blend of *joll* (obs. var. of ⁴*jowl*) and obs. *jot* to bump, prob. of imit. origin] *vt* **1 :** to cause to move with a sudden and jerky motion by a push or series of pushes **:** JOUNCE ⟨the lumbering coach ∼*ed* its passengers over the miserable road⟩ ⟨∼*ed* about by the car's swift turns⟩ **2 a :** to give a sharp knock to so as to dislodge or move ⟨∼ it crosswise and lengthwise with a rawhide hammer —H.F.Blanchard & Ralph Ritchen⟩ **b :** to jar in boxing with a quick or hard blow **3 a :** to administer a psychological shock to **:** disturb the composure of ⟨crudely ∼*ed* out of that mood —Virginia Woolf⟩ ⟨trying to ∼ the world into looking at the future —*New Yorker*⟩ **b :** to shake or interfere with roughly, abruptly, and disconcertingly **:** upset the even tenor or stability of ⟨determination to pursue his own course was ∼*ed* badly —F.L. Paxson⟩ ⟨her parents' plans, however, were rudely ∼*ed* —Clyde Gilmour⟩ ∼ *vi* **1 a** *of a vehicle* **:** to move with a jolt or a series of jolts ⟨the train ∼*ed* to a stop —Nathaniel Benchley⟩ ⟨the wagon ∼*ed* up the slope —Ellen Glasgow⟩ **b :** to ride or move on foot with a succession of jolts ⟨on into South Carolina they ∼*ed* —Dixon Wecter⟩ ⟨my body ∼*s* and jars, for I have not got into the trick of drifting slackly down a hillside —Wynford Vaughn-Thomas⟩ ⟨climbed into the tonga and ∼*ed* away —John Masters⟩ **2** *slang* **:** to take jolts of narcotics; *esp* **:** to take jolts of heroin ⟨was she still ∼*ing* —Wenzell Brown⟩

²**jolt** \"\ *n* -s **1 a :** an abrupt sharp jerky blow or movement knocking or shaking violently and tending to unsettle or dislodge **:** JOUNCE ⟨well packed for protection against ∼*s* in shipment⟩ ⟨received the full ∼ from each explosion —L.D. de La Penne & Virgilio Spigai⟩ **b :** a jarring blow in boxing **c** (1) **:** a sudden feeling of shock, surprise, or disappointment caused by some novel or unexpected event or development **:** a psychological blow or shock ⟨that a few men have such far-reaching power gave the people quite a ∼ —Paul Wooton⟩ ⟨will give an exciting and much-needed ∼ to the complacency of those laymen —J.F.Wharton⟩ ⟨this kind of discussion gives a healthy ∼ —David Daiches⟩ ⟨the affair dealt quite a ∼ to his pride⟩; *also* **:** an event or development causing such a feeling ⟨his mother's death was quite a ∼ to the boy⟩ (2) **:** a damaging but nonphysical blow **:** SETBACK, REVERSE ⟨the . . . argument for evolution had received a severe ∼ —R.W.Murray⟩ ⟨had a severe financial ∼⟩ **2** *slang* **:** a term in jail **3 a :** a small potent or bracing portion of something **:** SHOT ⟨a reassuring ∼ of fresh air —*Atlantic*⟩ ⟨poured a ∼ of brandy —Dorothy Baker⟩ ⟨a new perfume that contains a ∼ of gardenia —*New Yorker*⟩ **b** *slang* **:** a unit of a narcotic (as heroin) for hypodermic injection ⟨a ∼ can be had for a nod and a price —J.B.Clayton⟩ **syn** see IMPACT

**jolt·er** \ˈjōltə(r)\ *n* -s **:** one that jolts

**jolter-head** \ˈ==,=\ *also* **jolt-head** \ˈ=,=\ *n* [*jolter-head* alter. of *jolt-head; jolt-head* prob. fr. ²*jolt* + *head*] **1** *archaic* **:** a large or heavy head **2** *now dial chiefly Eng* **:** DUNCE, BOOBY, BLOCKHEAD

**jolter-headed** \¦==¦==\ *also* **jolt-headed** \ˈ=¦==\ *adj* **1** *archaic* **:** having a large or heavy head **2** *now dial chiefly Eng* **:** STUPID, DULL

**jolthead porgy** \ˈ=,=-\ *also* **jolthead** *n* **:** a large yellow blue-marked porgy (*Calamus bajonado*) of the tropical western Atlantic

**jolt·i·ness** \ˈjōltēnə̇s\ *n* -ES **:** the quality or state of being jolty

**jolting** *adj* **:** tending to jolt **:** attended by or producing jolts ⟨a ∼ ride⟩ ⟨a ∼ experience⟩ — **jolt·ing·ly** *adv*

**jolt·less** \ˈjōltlə̇s\ *adj* **:** free from jolts

**jolt-wagon** \ˈ=,==\ *n, Midland* **:** a farm wagon

**jolty** \ˈjōltē\ *adj* -ER/-EST **:** causing jolts **:** tending to jolt ⟨a ∼ wagon⟩

¹**jo·nah** \ˈjōnə\ *n* -s *usu cap J* [after *Jonah,* Old Testament prophet who by disobeying God's command caused a storm to endanger the ship he was traveling in (Jon 1:4 ff), fr. Heb *Yōnāh*] **:** one believed to bring bad luck or misfortune ⟨perhaps I was the *Jonah* — at least I was the thirteenth man —Arthur Langford⟩ ⟨her left foot was her *Jonah;* nothing had ever happened to her right foot —John Hersey⟩

²**jonah** \"\ *vt* -ED/-ING/-S *often cap J* **:** to bring bad luck to **:** JINX ⟨ordered the boy on shore again, accusing him of wanting to ∼ the whole trip —*Youth's Companion*⟩

**jonah crab** *n, usu cap J* **:** a large reddish crab (*Cancer borealis*) of the eastern coast of No. America that is sometimes found along rocky shores but is more common in deep water

**jon·a·than** \ˈjänəthən\ *n* -s *usu cap* [fr. the name *Jonathan;* prob. fr. the frequent use of Old Testament given names among the English colonists in America] **:** AMERICAN; *esp* **:** NEW ENGLANDER ⟨*Jonathans* are antislavery, but not against foreigners —*Chicago Democrat*⟩ — compare BROTHER JONATHAN

**jonathan freckle** *n, usu cap J* [fr. *Jonathan,* a variety of apple to which the disease is especially destructive, after *Jonathan* Hasbrouck †1846 Am. jurist] **:** a nonparasitic storage disease of apples that produces small circular skin-deep discolorations

**jonathan spot** *n, usu cap J* [fr. *Jonathan,* a variety of apple to which this disease is especially destructive] **:** a nonparasitic disease of apples that produces circular depressed necrotic areas around the lenticels — called also *spot rot*

**jones reductor** \ˈjōnz-\ *n, usu cap J* [after Clemens *Jones,* 19th cent. Am. metallurgist] **:** a reductor that consists essentially of a long upright tube filled with granular zinc through which a solution to be reduced (as a ferric salt) is poured

**jong** \ˈyäŋ\ *n* -s [Afrik, fr. MD *jonge,* fr. *jonc* young; akin to OHG *jung* young — more at YOUNG] *southern Africa* **:** a young man

**jon·glery** \ˈjäŋglərē\ *n* -ES [F *jonglerie,* fr. MF, alter. of OF *joglerie* — more at JUGGLERY] **:** entertainment provided by a jongleur

**jon·gleur** \(ˈ)zhōⁿ¦glœr(·), ˈjäŋglər\ *n* -s [F, fr. MF, alter. of OF *jogleour* — more at JUGGLER] **1 :** an accompanist for a troubadour in the 12th and 13th centuries **2 :** an itinerant medieval minstrel reciting and singing for hire

**jonnock** *var of* JANNOCK

**jonny cake** *var of* JOHNNYCAKE

**jon·quil** \ˈjän,kwə̇l, ˈjäŋk- *sometimes* ˈjə̇\ *n* -s [NL & F; NL *junquilia,* fr. F or Sp; F *jonquille,* fr. Sp *junquillo,* dim. of *junco* rush, reed (fr. the appearance of the leaves), fr. L *juncus;* akin to ON *einir* juniper, Sw *en,* L *juniperus* juniper, MIr *ain* reed] **1 a :** a perennial bulbous herb (*Narcissus jonquilla*) native to southern Europe and northern Africa that has long slender leaves resembling those of a rush and is widely cultivated for its yellow or white fragrant clustered flowers which are smaller than those of typical daffodils and have the corona much shortened — compare NARCISSUS 2 **b :** a narcissus or daffodil with a yellow corona — used chiefly in the florist trade **2 a :** DAFFODIL 2 **b :** a light to moderate yellow that is redder and less strong than amber yellow or apricot yellow and redder and stronger than buff (sense 4a)

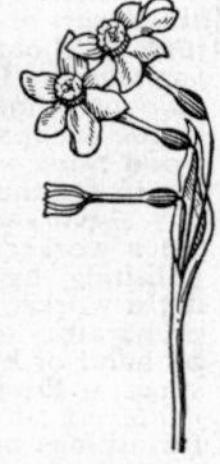
jonquil

**jon·so·nian** \(ˈ)jän¦sōnēən\ *adj, usu cap* [Ben *Jonson* †1637 Eng. dramatist + E *-ian*] **:** of, relating to, or characteristic of Ben Jonson or his works

**jon·ty** \ˈjäntē, ˈjän-, -ti\ *Brit var of* ²JAUNTY

¹**jook** *var of* JOUK

²**jook** \'jük\ *n* -s [Gullah *juke, joog* disorderly — more at JUKE JOINT] *South* : JUKE JOINT ⟨a ~ from which she was trying to extricate her husband —Marjorie K. Rawlings⟩

**jookerie** or **jookery** *var of* JOUKERY

**jook organ** *n, South* : JUKEBOX

¹**jor·dan** \'jȯrdᵊn, 'jȯ(ə)d-\ *n* -s [ME (also, a vessel used by physicians and alchemists), prob. fr. the river *Jordan* in Palestine; perh. fr. medieval pilgrims' bringing water from the Jordan back to England] *dial Brit* : CHAMBER POT

²**jordan** \"*, southern US often* 'jərd- *or* 'jəd- *or* 'jəid-\ *adj, usu cap* [fr. *Jordan*, country in southwestern Asia] : of or from the Hashemite Kingdom of Jordan : of the kind or style prevalent in Jordan : JORDANIAN

³**jordan** \" *also* **jordan engine** *or* **jordan refiner** *n* -s *sometimes cap J* [after Joseph *Jordan*, 19th cent. Am. inventor] : a machine for refining paper pulp that consists of a stationary hollow cone having projecting knives on its interior surface and fitting over a rapidly rotating adjustable cone having similar knives on its outside surface

⁴**jordan** \"\ *vt* **jordaned** *also* **jordanned; jordaned** *also* **jordanned; jordaning** *also* **jordanning** \-dᵊniŋ\ **jordans** : to refine in a jordan

**jordan almond** *n, usu cap J* [by folk etymology fr. ME *jardin almande*, fr. MF *jardin* garden + ME *almande* almond — more at JARDINIÈRE, ALMOND] **1** : an almond imported from Malaga and used extensively in confectionery **2** : an almond coated with sugar of various colors

**jordan chest** *n, often cap J* [after Joseph *Jordan*, 19th cent. Am. inventor] : a stock chest that holds paper stock ready to be jordaned

**jor·dan curve** \(')zhȯ(ə)r¦däⁿ-\ *n, usu cap J* [after Camille *Jordan* †1922 Fr. mathematician] : a closed plane curve (as a circle or an ellipse) that does not intersect itself

¹**jor·da·ni·an** \(')jȯ(r)¦dānēən, -nyən *sometimes* -dan-\ *adj, usu cap* [*Jordan*, country in southwestern Asia + E *-ian*] **1** : of, relating to, or characteristic of Jordan **2** : of, relating to, or characteristic of the people of Jordan

²**jordanian** \"\ *n* -s *cap* : a native or inhabitant of Jordan

**jor·dan·ite** \'jȯ(r)dᵊn,īt\ *n* -s [G *jordanit*, fr. Dr. *Jordan*, 19th cent. Ger. scientist + G *-it* -ite] : a mineral $Pb_{14}As_7S_{24}$(?) consisting of a lead-gray monoclinic lead arsenic sulfide (sp. gr. 6.39)

**jor·danon** \'jȯ(r)dᵊn,än\ *n* -s [NL, fr. David S. *Jordan* †1931 Am. naturalist + Gk *-on* (neuter n. & adj. suffix)] : MICROSPECIES

**jordan's law** *n, usu cap J* [after David S. *Jordan*] : a generalization in evolutionary biology: closely related organisms tend to occupy adjacent rather than identical or distant ranges

**jo·ree** \jə'rē\ *also* **joree-bird** *n* -s [imit.] *chiefly Midland* : CHEWINK

**jo·rist** \'jōrəst\ *n* -s [Jan David *Joris* (*Joriszoon*) †1536 Dutch Anabaptist leader + E *-ist*] *usu cap* : DAVIDIST 2

**jor·na·da** \hȯ(r)'nädə\ *n* -s [Sp, fr. OSp, fr. OProv *jornada*, fr. *jorn* day, fr. LL *diurnum* — more at JOURNEY] *Southwest* : an arduous usu. one-day journey across a stretch of desert ⟨almost perished for lack of water on this grim ~ —R.G.Cleland⟩

**jo·ro·ba·do** \¦hȯrə¦baü\ *n* -s [AmerSp, fr. Sp, humpbacked, fr. *joroba* humpback (fr. OSp *hadruba*, fr. Ar dial. — Spain — *haduba, hudūba*, fr. Ar *hadaba*) + *-ado* -ate (fr. L *-atus*)] : either of two moonfishes (*Vomer setipinnis* and *Selene vomer*)

**jo·ro·po** \hə'rō(,)pō\ *n* -s [AmerSp] : the national ballroom dance of Venezuela marked by lilting stamping steps in three-quarter time

**jor·ram** \'yürəm, 'yȯr-\ *n* -s [ScGael *iorram*] *Scot* : a Gaelic boat song

**jo·rum** \'jōrəm, 'jȯr-\ *n* -s [perh. after *Joram* in the Bible who "brought with him vessels of silver . . . gold, and . . . brass" (2 Sam 8:10 — AV)] **1 a** : a large drinking vessel (as a jug or bowl) ⟨the host smiled . . . and shortly afterwards returned with a steaming ~ —Charles Dickens⟩ **b** : the contents of such a vessel ⟨drinking a ~ of hot whiskey and water —J.E.Agate⟩ **2** : a large quantity ⟨a ~ of ink —Margery Sharp⟩

**jo·sef** *or* **jo·seph** \'jōzəf\ *or* **jo·sup** \-zəp\ *n* -s [Afrik *josef*, prob. after *Josef* (Joseph), Old Testament patriarch; fr. the brilliant colors of the fish, reminiscent of Joseph's coat of many colors (Gen 37:3 — AV)] : an elephant fish (*Callorynchus capensis*) of southern Africa

**jo·se·ite** \zhə'zā,īt\ *n* -s [G *joseit*, fr. São *José* do Paraiso, Minas Gerais, Brazil + G *-it* -ite] : a mineral $Bi_3Te(Se,S)$ consisting of a telluride of bismuth that also contains sulfur and selenium

**jo·seph** \'jōzəf *also* -ōsəf\ *n* -s [prob. after *Joseph*, Old Testament patriarch; fr. his coat of many colors (Gen 37:3 — AV)] : a long cloak; *esp* : an 18th century woman's riding coat buttoning down the front

**joseph-and-mary** \¦==+==\ *n, usu cap J&M* [after *Joseph* and *Mary*, parents of Jesus; fr. the red and blue flowers that suggested representations of the Holy Family in which Joseph was pictured in red and Mary in blue] *dial Eng* : LUNGWORT 2a

**jo·se·phine** \'jōzə,fēn *also* -ōsə-\ *n* -s *often cap* [fr. the name *Josephine*] : BLUSH 4a

**josephine's-lily** *also* **josephine lily** \¦==,=¦==\ *n, pl* **josephine's-lilies** *also* **josephine lilies** *usu cap J* [after *Joséphine* de Beauharnais †1814 empress of France] : a southern African bulbous herb (*Brunsvigia josephinae*) of the family Amaryllidaceae with bright red flowers

**jo·se·phin·ite** \'jōzə¦fē,nīt *also* -ōsə-\ *n* -s [*Josephine* co., Oregon + E *-ite*] : a natural alloy of iron and nickel occurring in stream gravel — compare AWARUITE

**jo·seph·ite** \'jōzə,fīt *also* -ōsə-\ *n* -s *usu cap* **1** [*Joseph* of Volokolamsk, 16th cent. leader in the Russian Orthodox Church + E *-ite*] : a member of a monastic party rising to prominence in the Russian Orthodox Church in the 16th century, adhering to strict forms of ritualism and asceticism, and believing in a close union between church and state — called also *Possessor* **2** [*Joseph* Smith †1914 Mormon leader + E *-ite*] : a member of the Reorganized Church of Jesus Christ of Latter-day Saints

**joseph's coat** *n, usu cap J* [after *Joseph*, Old Testament patriarch; fr. his coat of many colors (Gen 37:3—AV)] **1** : a coat of many colors ⟨a country as dappled and patchy as *Joseph's coat* —T.H.Fielding⟩ **2** : any of certain plants with variegated foliage: as **a** : a tampala with red and green variegated leaves grown as an ornamental **b** : COLEUS 2

¹**josh** \'jäsh *also* 'jȯsh\ *vb* -ED/-ING/-ES [origin unknown] *vt* : to make fun of : tease good-naturedly : joke with ⟨whenever they ~*ed* her, she could laugh at herself as much as they could laugh at her —Edward Kimbrough⟩ ⟨climbed into our bus and ~*ed* the women schoolteachers —G.P.Musselman⟩ ~ *vi* : to banter lightly : JOKE ⟨~*ed* with the cameramen and was evidently in fine spirits —*N.Y. Times*⟩

²**josh** \"\ *n* -ES : light and good-humored joking : JEST, JOKE ⟨thoroughly enjoyed all the chatter and ~⟩

**josh·er** \-shə(r)\ *n* -s : one that joshes ⟨a great little ~ . . . when it comes to kidding —Sinclair Lewis⟩

**josh·ua tree** \'jäsh(ə)wə-, ÷|sh,wə- *also* 'jȯ|\ *also* **joshua** *n* -s *usu cap J* [prob. after *Joshua*, Old Testament patriarch; fr. the grotesquely extended branches, reminiscent of the outstretched arm of Joshua as he pointed with his spear toward the city of Ai (Josh 8:18—AV)] : a branched arborescent yucca (*Yucca brevifolia*) of the southwestern U. S. that has short leaves and clustered greenish white flowers and often grows to a height of 25 feet

**jo·si·an·ic** \¦jō,sī¦anik, -ōzē-\ *adj, usu cap* [*Josiah* †ab608 B.C. king of Judah noted for his reforming spirit + connective *-n-* + E *-ic*] : of or relating to Josiah

**jo·sie** \'jōzē, -ōsē\ *n* -s [*joseph* + *-ie*] : a fitted outer waist formerly worn by women

**jos·kin** \'jäskən\ *n* -s [perh. fr. the name *Joseph* + *-kin* (as in *bumpkin*)] : BUMPKIN

¹**joss** \'jäs, 'jȯs\ *n* -ES [pidgin English, fr. Pg *deus* god, fr. L — more at DEITY] : a Chinese idol or cult image

²**joss** \'jäs\ *n* -ES [origin unknown] *dial Eng* : FOREMAN

³**joss** \"\ *vi* -ED/-ING/-ES [prob. short for *jostle*] *dial Eng* : JOSTLE, CROWD

**jos·ser** \-sə(r)\ *n* -s [origin unknown] *Brit* : FELLOW, CHAP ⟨an absurd old ~ whom her mother made a fool of —G.B.Shaw⟩

**joss flower** *n* [¹*joss*] : CHINESE SACRED LILY

**joss house** *n* [¹*joss*] : a Chinese temple or house of idol worship

**joss paper** *n* [¹*joss*] : gold and silver paper cut to resemble money and burned in front of a joss

**joss stick** *n* [¹*joss*] : a slender stick of incense burned in front of a joss

¹**jos·tle** \'jäsəl *also* 'jȯs-\ *also* **jus·tle** \'jəs-\ *vb* **jostled** *also* **justled; jostled** *also* **justled; jostling** *also* **justling** \-s(ə)liŋ\ **jostles** *also* **justles** [*jostle* alter. of *justle; justle* freq. of ¹*joust, just*] *vi* **1 a** (1) : to come in contact or into collision : push and shove ⟨all drift and ~ and barge against one another —J.C.Powys⟩ ⟨wanted to get back to the bright lights . . . to ~ with the crowds —Harold Griffin⟩ (2) : to crowd or push or shove another horse in racing ⟨the stewards may disqualify the winner for crossing or *jostling* —Dennis Craig⟩ **b** : to make one's way by pushing and shoving or crowding ⟨men in pearl-buttoned waistcoats and flared trousers *jostling* round the street market —Osbert Lancaster⟩ **c** : to exist in close proximity : rub elbows ⟨study of the great groups that have *jostled* and migrated around America —Priscilla Robertson⟩ ⟨survivals of barbaric codes of law *jostled* with varying mixtures of Roman law, local custom, and violence —R.W. Southern⟩ **2 a** *obs* : to run atilt in a tournament : JOUST **b** : to vie or struggle in gaining an objective : CONTEND ⟨tribes began to ~ with one another for room —Daniel Defoe⟩ ⟨a novel good enough to ~ with the others in the great stream —Douglas Stewart⟩ ~ *vt* **1 a** (1) : to come in contact or into collision with : push and shove against ⟨*jostled* each other in the dance or at the board —W.M. Thackeray⟩ (2) : to push or shove against (another horse) in racing **b** : to drive or force by or as if by pushing : ELBOW ⟨shrugged his shoulders and *jostled* his way out of the hall —John Buchan⟩ **c** : to stir up : AGITATE, DISTURB ⟨a mind *jostled* once more into uncertainty —Owen Wister⟩ **d** *obs* : to bring into or as if into contact or collision ⟨the churches . . . clash and ~ supremacies with the civil magistrate —John Milton⟩ **e** : to exist in close proximity with : rub elbows with ⟨Europe, where a number of languages ~ each other —D.G. Mandelbaum⟩ ⟨fishing vessels lying close-packed at the moorings, *jostling* each other —Nevil Shute⟩ **2** : to vie or struggle with in attaining an objective : contend with ⟨both men were *jostling* each other for nomination⟩

²**jostle** \"\ *also* **justle** \"\ *n* -s **1** : an encounter that jostles ⟨might glide through . . . life among them without a ~ —Thomas Jefferson⟩ **2 a** : the state of being crowded and jostled together ⟨away from the hustle and the ~ that ought to have been congenial to me —Max Beerbohm⟩ **b** : the act of pushing or shoving in horse racing : INTERFERENCE ⟨the ~ was wholly caused by the fault of some other horse or jockey —Dan Parker⟩

**jos·tle·ment** \-lmənt\ *n* -s : disturbance by pushing and shoving ⟨bursting in his full-blown way along the pavement, to the ~ of all weaker people —Charles Dickens⟩

**jos·tler** \-s(ə)lə(r)\ *n* -s : one that jostles

**josup** *var of* JOSEF

¹**jot** \'jät, *usu* -äd·+V\ *n* -s [L *jota* iota, jot, fr. Gk *iōta*, of Sem origin; akin to Heb *yōdh* yodh] **1** : an instance of iota esp. as the smallest letter of the Greek alphabet — used in translation of the Bible or in allusion to such translation ⟨till heaven and earth pass, one ~ or one tittle shall in no wise pass from the law, till all be fulfilled —Mt 5:18 (AV)⟩ **2** : the least bit : smallest amount : IOTA ⟨he who adds a ~ to such knowledge creates new mind —G.B.Shaw⟩

²**jot** \"\ *vt* **jotted; jotted; jotting; jots** : to write briefly or hurriedly : set down in or as if in the form of a note ⟨wake up six times during the night and ~ another name on the pad —G.S.Perry⟩ — usu. used with *down* ⟨*jotted* down a summary of all their private interviews —Peter Quennell⟩

**jo·ta** \'hōd·ə, -ō(,)tä\ *n* -s [Sp, prob. fr. OSp *sota* dance, fr. *sotar* to dance, fr. L *saltare* — more at SALTANT] **1** : a Spanish folk dance in ¾ time performed by a man and a woman to intricate castanet and heel rhythms **2** : the music of the jota

**jot·ni·an** \'jätnēən\ *adj, usu cap* [ON *jötn-, jötunn* giant + E *-ian*; akin to OE *eoten* giant, MLG *eteninne* giantess, and perh. to OE *etan* to eat — more at EAT] : of, relating to, or constituting a division of the Precambrian — see GEOLOGIC TIME table

**jot·ter** \'jäd·ə(r)\ *n* -s **1** : one that jots down memoranda ⟨a quick ~ of notes —Jack Alexander⟩ **2** : a memorandum book

**jot·ting** *n* -s : a brief note : MEMORANDUM ⟨made rapid ~*s* on chance bits of paper —Walter Pach⟩

**jougs** \'jügz\ *n pl but sing in constr, also* **joug** \'jüg\ [alter. of earlier *jogis, jougis*, perh. modif. of MF *joug* yoke, fr. L *jugum* — more at YOKE] : an iron collar fastened to a wall or post and used in Scotland as a pillory

**jouissance** *n* -s [MF, fr. *jouiss-* (stem of *jouir* to enjoy, fr. L *gaudēre* to rejoice) + *-ance* — more at JOY] *obs* : USE, ENJOYMENT; *also* : JOLLITY

¹**jouk** \'jük\ *vb* -ED/-ING/-S [origin unknown] *vi* **1** *dial* **a** : DUCK, DODGE **b** : to evade work **2** *dial* : FAWN, CRINGE **3** *dial* : CHEAT, DECEIVE ~ *vt* **1** *dial* **a** : DUCK, DODGE **b** : to get out of (work) by evasion **2** *dial* : CHEAT, DECEIVE

²**jouk** \"\ *n* -s *chiefly Scot* : SWOOP, SWERVE, JERK

**jouk·ery** \'jükərē\ *n* -ES *chiefly Scot* : SWINDLING, TRICKERY

**joukerypawkery** \¦===¦==\ *n* -ES [*joukery* + *pawkery*] *Scot* : JIGGERY-POKERY

**joule** \'jül, 'jaü(ə)l *sometimes* 'jōl; *the first seems to have been the physicist's own pronunc*\ *n* -s [after James P. *Joule* †1889 Eng. physicist] **1** : the absolute mks unit of work or energy equal to $10^7$ ergs or approximately 0.7375 foot-pounds or 0.2390 gram calorie and taken as standard in U. S. **2** : a unit of work or energy that is equal to about 1.00017 absolute joules and that was formerly taken as a standard in U. S. — called also *international joule*

**joule effect** *n, usu cap J* [after J. P. *Joule*] : production of heat by mechanical work, an electric current, or change in length due to magnetization — compare MAGNETOSTRICTION

**joule heat** *also* **joulean heat** \'jül|ēən-, 'jaül| *sometimes* 'jōl|\ *n, usu cap J* [after J. P. *Joule*] : heat resulting from an electric current through a resistance

**joule's cycle** *n, usu cap J* [after J. P. *Joule*] : BRAYTON CYCLE

**joule's equivalent** *n, usu cap J* [after J. P. *Joule*] : MECHANICAL EQUIVALENT OF HEAT

**joule's law** *n, usu cap J* [after J. P. *Joule*] : either of two statements in physics: (1) the rate at which heat is produced by a steady current in any part of an electric circuit is jointly proportional to the resistance and the square of the current (2) the internal energy of an ideal gas depends only upon its temperature irrespective of volume and pressure — compare JOULE-THOMSON EFFECT

**joule-thom·son effect** \'=-'täm(p)sən-\ *n, usu cap J&T* [after J. P. *Joule* and Sir William *Thomson* (Lord Kelvin) †1907 Brit. physicist] : the change in temperature of a gas on expansion through a porous plug from a high pressure to a lower one under adiabatic conditions, the observation of this change proving among other things that Joule's second law is only approximately true

¹**jounce** \'jaün(t)s\ *vb* -ED/-ING/-S [ME *jouncen*] *vi* **1** : to fall, drop, or bounce so as to shake **2** : to move or proceed in jounces ⟨the truck *jounced* off across the concrete and the weeds —Josephine Johnson⟩ ⟨*jounced* over a rut —William Attwood⟩ ~ *vt* : to cause to jounce

²**jounce** \"\ *n* -s : a shaking fall or bump : JOLT

**jouncy** \-sē\ *adj, usu* -ER/-EST : marked by a jouncing motion or effect ⟨innumerable ~ elevator rides —*New Yorker*⟩

**jour** *abbr* **1** journal; journalism; journalist **2** journey **3** journeyman

¹**jour·nal** \'jərnᵊl, 'jōn-, 'jəin-\ *n* -s [ME, fr. MF, fr. *journal*, adj., daily, fr. L *diurnalis*, fr. *diurnus* of the day, daily (fr. *dies* day + *-urnus*, as in *nocturnus* nocturnal) + *-alis* -al — more at DEITY, NOCTURNAL] **1 a** : a usu. daily record of a journey **b** : a record of current transactions usu. kept daily or regularly: as (1) : DAYBOOK 2 (2) : a book of original entry in double-entry bookkeeping either for recording transactions of a particular class (as sales or cash transactions) or for recording transactions not cared for in specialized books **c** : an account of usu. day-to-day events written down regularly or as they occur or presented as if written down in this way **d** : a record of experiences, ideas, or reflections kept regularly for private use **e** : a record of transactions kept by a deliberative body or an assembly; *specif* : the record of daily proceedings of a legislative body kept by the clerk **f** : LOGBOOK, LOG **2** [F, fr. *journal* (record)] **a** : a daily newspaper **b** : a periodical publication esp. dealing with matters of current interest ⟨the editor of a weekly news ~⟩ — often used of official or semiofficial publications of special groups ⟨the *Journal of the American Medical Association*⟩ **3** : the part of a rotating shaft, axle, roll, or spindle that turns in a bearing

²**journal** *adj* [MF — more at ¹JOURNAL] *obs* : DIURNAL

³**journal** *like* ¹JOURNAL\ *vt* -ED/-ING/-S [¹*journal*] **1** : to support on, provide with, or make into a journal : support on a bearing ⟨~ a pulley on a shaft⟩ **2** : to connect by means of a journal ⟨a connecting rod ~*ed* to one end of a walking beam⟩

**jour·nal·ary** \-ᵊl,erē\ *adj* **1** *obs* : DAILY, DIURNAL **2** : of or belonging to a journal : recorded in or as if in a journal ⟨the ~ form of the novel —A.D.Henderson⟩

**journal bearing** *n* : BEARING 4c

**journal box** *n* : a metal housing to support and protect a journal bearing (as on a railroad-car wheel axle)

**jour·nal·ese** \¦jərnᵊl¦ēz, ¦jōn-, ¦jəin-, -ēs\ *n* -s [¹*journal* + *-ese*] **1** : a style of writing held to be characteristic of newspapers **2** : writing marked by simple, informal, and usu. loose sentence structure, the frequent use of clichés, sensationalism in the presentation of material, and superficiality of thought and reasoning

**jour·nal·ism** \'==,izəm\ *n* -s [F *journalisme*, fr. *journal* (n.) + *-isme* -ism] **1 a** : the collection and editing of material of current interest for presentation through the media of newspapers, magazines, newsreels, radio, or television **b** : the editorial or business management of a newspaper, magazine, or other agency engaged in the collection and dissemination of news **c** : an academic study concerned with the collection and editing of news or the editorial or business management of a news medium **2** : journalistic writing: **a** : writing designed for publication in a newspaper or popular magazine **b** : writing characterized by a direct presentation of facts or description of events without an attempt at interpretation **c** : writing designed to appeal to current popular taste or current public interest **3** : newspapers and magazines **4** : the presentation of events or ideas (as in a painting or play) in a manner regarded as similar to that of journalism

**jour·nal·ist** \-ᵊst\ *n* -s [¹*journal* + *-ist*] **1 a** : one engaged in journalism; *esp* : one employed to write or edit the subject matter of a news medium **b** : a writer who aims or is felt to aim chiefly at a mass audience or strives for immediate popular appeal in his writings **c** : an enlisted man (as in the U.S. Navy) who performs public information duties **2** : one who keeps a journal

**jour·nal·is·tic** \¦==¦istik, -tēk\ *adj* : of, relating to, or having the characteristics of journalism or journalists ⟨the brilliant and amusing example of ~ acumen —*N.Y. Times*⟩ ⟨these ~ illustrations . . . had great aesthetic vitality —Lewis Mumford⟩ ⟨resorted to the ~ device of gingering up the actual records —*New Yorker*⟩; *esp* : marked by literary qualities appropriate to newspapers and popular magazines — **journal·is·ti·cal·ly** \-tək(ə)lē, -tēk-, -li\ *adv*

**jour·nal·ize** \'==,īz\ *vb* -ED/-ING/-S *see -ize in Explan Notes* [¹*journal* + *-ize*] *vt* : to enter or record in a journal ~ *vi* **1** : to keep a journal in accounting **2** : to keep a personal journal : write down daily or regularly reflections, observations, or ideas — **jour·nal·iz·er** \-zə(r)\ *n* -s

**journal voucher** *n* : a paper in accounting that authorizes an entry in a journal or a paper that constitutes an authorized entry for direct posting

¹**jour·ney** \'jərnē, 'jōn-, 'jəin-, -ni\ *n* -s [ME *jurne, jorne, journey*, fr. OF *jornee, journee* day, fr. *jor, jour* day, fr. LL *diurnum*, fr. neut. of L *diurnus* of the day, daily — more at JOURNAL] **1 a** : travel or passage from one place to another : TRIP ⟨a three-day ~⟩ **b** *now chiefly dial* : a day's travel; *also* : the distance traveled during a day **c** *archaic* : a stage of a journey : a portion of a trip undertaken at one time **d** : something suggesting travel or passage from one place to another: as (1) : the course of one's life from birth to death (2) *obs* : the daily course of the sun across the sky (3) : an often extended experience that provides new information or knowledge beyond that which one might normally acquire ⟨a ~ into higher mathematics⟩ ⟨a ~ into the customs of another country⟩ ⟨an inviting and pleasant mental ~ for the reader —Frank Mortimer⟩ ⟨his ~ into faith —Florence Bullock⟩ **2 a** *chiefly dial* : a day's labor or a fixed amount of work as an equivalent **b** : a weight of metal (as 15 pounds troy of gold or 60 pounds troy of silver) that was the supply for one day's minting of coins by hand in the British mint and that made up into coin constitutes the unit out of which one coin is set aside for the trial of the pyx **c** : a cycle of work done in glass manufacturing in converting a quantity of material into glass or glass products **3** *obs* **a** : FIGHT, BATTLE **b** : a military expedition : SIEGE, CAMPAIGN

²**journey** \"\ *vb* **journeyed; journeyed; journeying; journeys** [ME *jorneyen, journeyen*, fr. MF *journoier*, fr. *journee*] *vi* : to go on a journey ⟨spent the summer ~*ing*⟩ : go from home to a distant place ⟨packed his belongings and ~*ed* to another country⟩ : TRAVEL ⟨~ from place to place in search of treasure⟩ ⟨most of us ~ to work by bus, tram, train —Agnes M. Miall⟩ ~ *vt* **1** : to travel over or through : TRAVERSE ⟨~*ed* many a land —Sir Walter Scott⟩ **2** : to separate (coins in the British mint) into journeys

**journey-bated** *adj, obs* : worn out with journeying

**journeycake** \'==,=\ *n* [prob. by folk etymology fr. *johnnycake*] : JOHNNYCAKE

**jour·ney·man** \'==mən\ *n, pl* **journeymen** *often attrib* [ME, fr. *jurne, journey* + *man*] **1 a** : a worker who has learned a handicraft or trade and is qualified to work at it usu. for another by the day — distinguished from *apprentice* and *master* **b** : an experienced usu. competent or reliable workman in any field usu. as distinguished from one that is brilliant or colorful ⟨a good, reliable ~ of the theatre —*Theatre Arts*⟩ ⟨a good ~ trumpeter —*New Yorker*⟩ ⟨~ work, competent but without much distinction —J.G.Villa⟩ ⟨~*'s* work too slick and trite to prove itself —K.P.Kempton⟩ ⟨*journeymen* rather than first-rate artists —H.E.Clurman⟩ **2** *archaic* : one hired to work for another : HIRELING **3** : the first rank earned by members of a Camp Fire Girls Horizon Club — compare ARTISAN

**journeys accounts** *n pl* : the number of days required for travel to a court formerly considered in English law as the fewest within which a new writ could be obtained after the abatement of a previous one

**journey weight** *n* : a journey of coins in the British mint

**journeywoman** \'==,=\ *n, pl* **journeywomen** : a female journeyman

**journeywork** \'==,=\ *n* **1 a** : work done by a journeyman esp. by the day **b** : work done for hire **2** : necessary routine and often servile work : HACKWORK

¹**joust** \'jaüst *sometimes* 'jəst *or* 'jüst\ *or* **just** \'jəst\ *n* -s [ME, fr. OF *joste, juste, jouste*, fr. *joster, juster, jouster*] **1 a** : a combat on horseback between two knights with lances esp. in the lists or an enclosed field; *specif* : an often combat of this kind as part of a tournament or display mock combat — **tilt b jousts** *or* **justs** *pl* : TOURNAMENT **2** : an action resembling that of a man or of men jousting esp. in being personal combat or competition ⟨young people in their ~*s* with ideas —William Van Til⟩ ⟨the producer's Academy Award-winning ~ against anti-Semitism —*Newsweek*⟩ ⟨the ancient ritual of the ~ from boats, striving to knock each other into the water —Paul Engle⟩

²**joust** \"\ *or* **just** \"\ *vi* -ED/-ING/-S [ME *jousten, justen*, fr. OF *joster, juster, jouster* to gather, unite, joust, fr. (assumed) VL *juxtare*, fr. L *juxta* near, nearby; akin to L *jungere* to join — more at YOKE] **1** : to fight on horseback as a knight or man-at-arms **2 a** : to engage in combat with lances on horseback : engage in a joust : TILT ⟨two knights ~*ing* in the lists⟩ **b** : to participate in an action resembling a joust : engage in personal combat or competition ⟨cars no longer ~*ing* and jostling at the crossings —R.M.Coates⟩ ⟨passenger-~*ing* and jostling at the mighty business car manufacturers⟩ ~ like surly giants over the mighty business of making and selling millions of motorcars —A.W.Baum⟩ — **joust·er** *or* **just·er** \-tə(r)\ *n* -s

**jousting** *also* **justing** *n* -s [ME, fr. the gerund of ME *justen, jousten*] : the action or sport of one that jousts : JOUST, TILT

**jousting helmet** *or* **jousting helm** *n* : TILTING HELMET

**jou·vence blue** \(')zhü¦vä(ⁿ)ⁿs-\ *n* [*jouvence* fr. F, youth (in *fontaine de jouvence* fountain of youth), fr. MF, alter. of *jouvente*, fr. L *juventa*, fr. *juvenis* young — more at YOUNG] **:** a moderate bluish green to greenish blue that is deeper than gendarme or cyan blue and duller than parrot blue

**jouy print** \zhə'wē-, 'zhwē-\ *n*, *usu cap J* [*Jouy*-en-Josas, France, its original place of manufacture] **:** TOILE DE JOUY

**jo·va** \'hōvə\ *n*, *pl* **jova** *or* **jovas** *usu cap* [Sp, of AmerInd origin] **1 :** an important division of the Piman peoples of northeastern Sonora **2 :** a member of the Jova people

**jove** \'jōv\ *interj*, *usu cap* [fr. *Jove* (Jupiter), ancient Roman god of the sky, fr. L *Jov-*, *Juppiter* — more at DEITY] — used typically to express surprise or agreement esp. in the phrase *by Jove*

**jove's-beard** \'=,=\ *n*, *pl* **jove's-beards** *usu cap J* **:** JUPITER'S-BEARD

**jove's-flower** \'=,=\ *n*, *pl* **jove's-flowers** *usu cap J* **:** CLOVE PINK

**jove's-fruit** \'=,=\ *n*, *pl* **jove's-fruits** *usu cap J* **1 :** a spicebush (*Benzoin melissaefolium*) of the southern U.S. **2 :** PERSIMMON

**jo·vial** \'jōvēəl, -vyəl\ *adj* [MF & LL; MF, fr. LL *jovialis* of the god Jupiter, fr. *Jov-*, *Juppiter* Jupiter, ancient Roman god of the sky + L *-alis* -al — more at DEITY] **1 a** *obs* **:** JOVIAN **b :** having the nature, disposition, or aspect that according to astrology is determined by Jupiter as natal or ruling planet **2 :** characterized by or showing marked good humor esp. as exhibited in mirth, hilarity, or conviviality **:** JOYFUL, JOLLY ⟨a ~ portly gentleman⟩ ⟨a ~ grin⟩ **syn** see MERRY

**jovialist** *n* -s **1** *obs* **:** one born under the planet Jupiter **2** *obs* **:** one having a jovial disposition

**jo·vial·i·ty** \,jōvē'aləd·ē, jōv'ya-, -lətē, -i\ *n* -ES **:** the quality or state of being jovial ⟨greeted him with customary ~ —S.E.White⟩ ⟨liked the ~ of the gathering⟩

**jo·vial·ize** \'jōvēə,līz, -vyə-\ *vb* -ED/-ING/-S *vt*, *archaic* **:** to make jovial ~ *vi*, *obs* **:** to act in a jovial way

**jo·vial·ly** \-əlē,-əli\ *adv* **:** in a jovial manner

**jo·vial·ness** *n* -ES **:** JOVIALITY

**jo·vi·an** \'jōvēən\ *adj*, *usu cap* [L *Jovius* of Jupiter (fr. *Jov-*, *Juppiter*) + E *-an*] **1 :** of, relating to, or befitting the chief ancient Roman god Jupiter ⟨*Jovian* thunderbolts⟩ ⟨*Jovian* wrath⟩ ⟨the committee's *Jovian* attitude toward justifying its decisions —Paul Moor⟩ ⟨resolved the trouble by *Jovian* fiat —Agnes de Mille⟩ ⟨a *Jovian* detachment from the pressure of events —H.R.Tolley⟩ **2** [L *Jov-*, *Juppiter*, the planet Jupiter (fr. *Jov-*, *Juppiter*, the god Jupiter) + E *-ian*] **:** relating to the planet Jupiter ⟨the *Jovian* satellites⟩

**jo·vi·cen·tric** \,jōvə'sen·trik\ *also* **jo·vi·cen·tri·cal** \-rəkəl\ *adj*, *usu cap* [L *Jov-*, *Juppiter*, the planet Jupiter + E *-i-* + *-centric* or *centrical*] **:** centered upon or revolving around the planet Jupiter **:** appearing as viewed from the center of Jupiter — **jo·vi·cen·tri·cal·ly** \-rək(ə)lē\ *adv*

**¹jow** \'jaů, 'jō\ *vb* -ED/-ING/-S [alter. of ⁴*jowl*] *vt* **1** *dial Brit* **:** to give a blow to **:** STRIKE **2** *dial Brit* **:** to cause (a bell) to ring or toll ~ *vi*, *dial Brit*, *of a bell* **:** TOLL, RING

**²jow** \"\ *n* -s *chiefly Scot* **:** STROKE, KNOCK, TOLL ⟨and every ~ the dead bell gave cried woe to Barbara Allen —*Barbara Allen*⟩

**jo·war** \jə'wär\ *n* -s [Hindi *joār*, *jawār*; akin to Skt *yava* barley] *India* **:** DURRA

**¹jow·er** \'jaů(ə)r\ *vi* -ED/-ING/-S [perh. of imit. origin] *chiefly dial* **:** QUARREL, WRANGLE

**²jower** \"\ *n* -s *dial* **:** QUARREL, SPAT

**¹jowl** \'jaůl *also* 'jōl *sometimes* 'jȯl\ *n* -s [alter. (prob. influenced by ¹*jaw*) of ME *chavel*, *chauel*, *chawl*, fr. OE *ceafl*; akin to MHG *kivel*, *kiver* jaw, OS *kaflos*, pl., jaws, ON *kjaptr* jaw, OIr *gop* beak, mouth, Av *zafar-*, *zafan-* mouth] **1 a :** JAW; *esp* **:** MANDIBLE **b :** one of the lateral halves of the mandible **2 a :** CHEEK 1 **b :** the boneless cheek meat of a hog ⟨a dinner of boiled ~ and black-eyed peas⟩ — see PORK illustration

**²jowl** \"\ *n* -s [alter. (prob. influenced by ¹*jaw*) of ME *cholle*, prob. fr. OE *ceole* throat — more at GLUTTON] **1 a :** the pendulous part of a double chin **b :** the flesh hanging under the jaw of a fat pig **c :** the dewlap of cattle **d :** the wattle of a fowl **e :** a marked fullness and looseness of the flesh about the lower cheek and jaw usu. associated with aging — usu. used in pl. **2 :** the space and the soft tissues filling it between the branches of the lower jaw of a horse

**³jowl** \"\ *n* -s [ME *choll*, *cholle*, *jol*, *jolle*] **1** *obs* **:** HEAD 1 **2 :** a cut or dish of fish consisting of the head and usu. adjacent parts

**⁴jowl** \'jaů(ə)l, 'jōl\ *vb* -ED/-ING/-S [ME *chollen*, *jollen*, perh. fr. *choll*, *cholle*, *jol*, *jolle* head] *dial* **:** ¹JOW

**⁵jowl** \"\ *n* -s *dial* **:** ²JOW

**jowled** \'jaů(ə)ld *also* 'jōld *sometimes* 'jȯld\ *adj* [²*jowl* + *-ed*] **:** JOWLY ⟨his big, ~ countenance —W.A.White⟩

**jowl·er** \-lər\ *n* -s [¹*jowl*, ²*jowl* + *-er*] *chiefly Scot* **:** a dog having extremely large jaws or jowls

**jowly** \'jaůlē, -li *also* 'jōl- *sometimes* 'jȯl-\ *adj*, *often* -ER/-EST [²*jowl* + *-y*] **:** having marked jowls **:** full and usu. saggy of flesh about the lower cheeks and jaw area ⟨a silver-haired elderly man with a disillusioned ~ face, wrinkled as a leaky balloon —John Dos Passos⟩

**jows·er** \'jaůzə(r) *sometimes* -aůsə-\ *dial Eng var of* ¹DOWSER

**jow·ter** \'jaůtə(r)\ *n* -s [origin unknown] *dial Eng* **:** a peddler or hawker esp. of fish

**¹joy** \'jȯi\ *n* -s [ME *joye*, *joy*, fr. OF *joie*, *joye*, fr. L *gaudia*, pl. of *gaudium* joy, fr. *gaudēre* to rejoice; akin to Gk *gēthein* to rejoice, *gauros* proud, MIr *guāire* noble, Toch B *kāw-* to desire, Lith *džiaugiuos* I rejoice] **1 a :** the emotion excited by the acquisition or expectation of good **:** pleasurable feelings or emotions caused by well-being, success, or good fortune or by the prospect of possessing what one loves or desires **:** GLADNESS, DELIGHT **b :** an experience of such emotion **:** ENJOYMENT ⟨the ~ of books —Van Wyck Brooks⟩ **c :** the sign or exhibition of joy **:** GAIETY, JUBILATION, MERRIMENT ⟨after the victory there was great ~ in the town⟩ **d** — used interjectionally as an exclamation of delight esp. in the phrase *oh joy* **2 :** a state of happiness or felicity **:** BLISS **3 a :** a source or cause of joy ⟨motherhood is a ~ rather than a job —Kathleen H. Seib⟩ ⟨found many ~*s* in . . . rustic life —Ella E. Clark⟩ ⟨this book . . . is a ~ and an instruction —J.A.Michener⟩ ⟨a ~ to look at⟩ **b :** a small endearing or loved child **4** *of a planet* **:** astrological position in a house of agreeable quality or condition **:** an accidental dignity **syn** see PLEASURE

**²joy** \"\ *vb* -ED/-ING/-S [ME *joyen*, fr. OF *joir*, *jouir*, fr. L *gaudēre* to rejoice] *vi* **:** to experience or show pleasure or great delight **:** REJOICE, EXULT ⟨a happily married couple ~*ing* in a common ambition —Louise Mace⟩ ⟨could ~ in the purity of tone —W.M.Clark⟩ ~ *vt* **1** *obs* **:** to make joyful or happy **:** DELIGHT, GLADDEN **2** *archaic* **:** ENJOY **3** *obs* **a :** to greet with joy or welcome with honor **b :** CONGRATULATE **4** *obs* **:** to rejoice at

**joy·ance** \'jȯiən(t)s\ *also* **joy·an·cy** \-nsē\ *n*, *pl* **joyances** *also* **joyancies** [*joy* + *-ance*, *-ancy*] **1 :** the action of enjoying oneself **:** FESTIVITY, JUBILATION **2 a :** JOY, PLEASURE, DELIGHT **b** *archaic* **:** ENJOYMENT

**¹joyc·ean** \'jȯisēən\ *adj*, *usu cap* [James *Joyce* †1941 Ir. writer + E *-an*] **:** of, relating to, or befitting the writer Joyce or his writings ⟨*Joycean* passages⟩ ⟨*Joycean* stream of consciousness⟩ ⟨*Joycean* bitterness —Ann F. Wolfe⟩

**²joycean** \"\ *n* -s *usu cap* **1 :** a specialist in the life and writings of James Joyce **2 a :** an imitator of the style or methods of writing of James Joyce **b :** one that is prone to defend Joyce against criticism or that favors Joyce's style or methods

**joy·ful** \'jȯifəl\ *adj*, *sometimes* **joyfuller**; *sometimes* **joyfullest** [ME, fr. *joye*, *joy* + *-ful*] **:** marked by joy: **a :** experiencing pleasure or delight **:** HAPPY, JUBILANT ⟨a mother who is ~ on the return of her lost son⟩ **b :** bringing or causing joy ⟨~ news⟩ **:** inspiring joy ⟨a ~ occasion⟩ **c :** showing joy ⟨a ~ countenance⟩ **syn** see GLAD

**joy·ful·ly** \-f(ə)lē, -li\ *adv* [ME *joyfully*, fr. *joyful* + *-ly*] **:** in a joyful manner ⟨~ singing Christmas carols⟩

**joy·ful·ness** \-fəlnəs\ *n* -ES [ME *joyfulnesse*, fr. *joyful* + *-nesse* -ness] **:** JOY

**joy girl** *n*, *slang* **:** PROSTITUTE

**joyhouse** \'=,=\ *n*, *slang* **:** BROTHEL

**joy-juice** \'=,=\ *n*, *slang* **:** an alcoholic liquor

**joy·less** \'jȯiləs\ *adj* [ME *joyles*, fr. *joy* + *-les* -less] **:** not experiencing joy ⟨a ~ man⟩ **:** not inspiring or causing joy ⟨a ~ occasion⟩ **:** UNENJOYABLE ⟨a ~ trip⟩ ⟨a ~ season⟩ — **joy·less·ly** *adv* — **joy·less·ness** *n* -ES

**joy·ous** \'jȯiəs\ *adj* [ME, fr. MF *joyeus*, fr. OF *joios*, fr. *joie*, *joye* joy + *-os* -ous — more at JOY] **:** JOYFUL **syn** see GLAD

**joy·ous·ly** *adv* **:** JOYFULLY, HAPPILY, MERRILY

**joy·ous·ness** *n* -ES **:** JOYFULNESS, MERRIMENT, JUBILATION

**joy·pop** \'=,päp\ *vi*, *slang* **:** to use drugs only occasionally **:** use drugs as a joypopper

**joy·pop·per** \-äpə(r)\ *n*, *slang* **:** an occasional user of drugs **:** a drug user who is not yet totally addicted

**¹joyride** \'=,=\ *n* [¹*joy* + *ride*] **1 :** a ride (as in car or plane) purely for pleasure **2 a :** a joyride taken esp. in a stolen car without regard for safety or consequences to oneself or others ⟨having stolen an automobile for a ~ —E.D.Radin⟩ **b :** any course of conduct or action marked by a seeking of pleasure with a reckless disregard of cost or consequences ⟨went on a ~, spending his inheritance heedlessly and improvidently⟩

**²joyride** \"\ *vi* **:** to go on a joyride ⟨after luncheon . . . I could ~ in a plane —C.L.Baldridge⟩ ⟨*joyriding* around in his car all evening⟩ — **joyrider** \'=,==\ *n*

**joys** *pl of* JOY, *pres 3d sing of* JOY

**joy·some** \'jȯisəm\ *adj* **:** JOYFUL — **joy·some·ly** *adv*

**joy stick** *n* [perh. fr. E slang *joy stick* penis; fr. its position between the knees of the aviator] **:** CONTROL STICK

**JP** *abbr* **1** Japan paper **2** jet-propelled; jet propulsion

**JP** *abbr or n* -s *often not cap* justice of the peace

**JPP** *abbr* Japan paper proofs

**jr** *abbr* **1** journal **2** *often cap J* junior **3** juror

**JS** *abbr* joint support

**j's** *or* **js** *pl of* J

**JSC** *abbr* joint-stock company

**JSD** *abbr or n* -s **:** a doctor of juristic science

**j-stick** \'=,=\ *n* **:** J-BAR LIFT

**j-stroke** \'=,=\ *n*, *cap J* **:** a canoeing stroke in which the path of the paddle resembles the letter J used by a lone paddler to keep a straight course while paddling on one side of the canoe only

**jt** *abbr* joint

**JTC** *abbr* junior training corps

**jtly** *abbr* jointly

**jua·ma·ve** \(h)wə'mävē\ *also* **juamave istle** *n* -s [perh. irreg. fr. *Jaumave*, town in eastern Mexico] **:** a high-grade istle derived from a Mexican agave (*Agave funkiana*) and characterized by long pale flexible fibers

**jua·ne·ño** \(h)wə'nān(,)yō\ *n*, *pl* **juaneño** *or* **juaneños** *usu cap* [AmerSp, fr. *San Juan Capistrano*, Spanish mission in what is now southwestern California] **1 :** an extinct Shoshonean people of southwestern California speaking a dialect of Luiseño **2 :** a member of the Juaneño people

**ju·ang** \'jü,äŋ\ *n*, *pl* **juang** *or* **juangs** *usu cap* **1 a :** a Kol people of Orissa, India **b :** a member of such people **2 :** the Munda language of the Juang people

**ju·ar** \jə'wär\ *var of* JOWAR

**juárez** *or* **juarez** *adj*, *usu cap* **:** CIUDAD JUÁREZ

**ju·ba** \'jübə\ *n* -s [origin unknown] **1 :** a Haitian dance of African origin having drum and stick accompaniment and performed as a work dance or as a dance for the dead **2 :** a dance of plantation Negroes in the South accompanied by complexly rhythmic hand clapping and slapping of the knees and thighs ⟨the sudden silence after the singing and ~ —R.P. Warren⟩

**juba's-brush** *or* **juba's-bush** \'jübəz;=\ *n*, *pl* **juba's-brushes** *or* **juba's-bushes** *usu cap J* [perh. fr. *Juba's*, genitive case of a name *Juba*] **:** an annual weed (*Iresine paniculata*) of the central U.S. and tropical America

**ju·bate** \'jü,bāt\ *adj* [NL *jubatus*, fr. L, having a mane, fr. *juba* mane + *-atus* -ate; akin to L *jubēre* to command — more at JUSSIVE] **:** fringed with long pendent hairs like a mane

**jub·bah** *or* **jub·ba** \'jübə, 'jəbə\ *n* -s [Ar *jubbah*] **:** a long outer garment resembling an open coat, having long sleeves, and formerly worn in Muslim countries esp. by public officials and professional people ⟨arrayed in white cloth robes, a black ~, and a gold sash —John Buchan⟩

**jub·bul·pore** \'jəbəl,pō(ə)r\ *or* **ja·bal·pur** \'jəbəl,pů(ə)r\ *adj*, *usu cap* [fr. *Jubbulpore*, *Jabalpur*, city in Jubbulpore district, Madhya Pradesh, India] **:** of or from the city of Jubbulpore, India **:** of the kind or style prevalent in Jubbulpore

**jubbulpore hemp** *n*, *usu cap J* [fr. *Jubbulpore* district, Madhya Pradesh, India, where it is grown] **:** SUNN

**ju·be** \'yü(,)bā\ *n* -s [F *jubé*, fr. MF, fr. ML *Jube*, *Domine*, *benedicere* Deign, O Lord, to bless; prob. fr. the fact that in the medieval church the deacon stood at the rood screen or on the rood loft when pronouncing this benediction before the reading of the Gospel] **1 :** ROOD SCREEN **2 :** the gallery above a rood screen

**ju·ber·ous** \'jüb(ə)rəs, -bə(r)s\ *adj* [alter. of *dubious*] *South and Midland* **:** doubtful and hesitating **:** DUBIOUS

**ju·bi·lance** \'jübələn(t)s\ *n* -s [*jubilant* + *-ance*] **:** the quality or state of being jubilant **:** EXULTATION

**ju·bi·lant** \-nt\ *adj* [L *jubilant-*, *jubilans*, pres. part. of *jubilare* to jubilate] **1 :** making noises and demonstrations of joy or triumph ⟨shots fired by ~ cowboys in celebration of frontier legal victories —*Amer. Guide Series: Texas*⟩ **2 :** manifesting or expressing exultation or gladness ⟨~ strings and ceremonious percussion —Irving Kolodin⟩ ⟨the walls . . . were covered with ~ childish drawings —Oliver La Farge⟩ — **ju·bi·lant·ly** *adv*

**ju·bi·lar·i·an** \,==lar·(a)rēən\ *n* -s [ML *jubilarius* jubilarian (fr. LL *jubilaeus* jubilee + L *-arius* -ary) + E *-an*, n. suffix] **:** one that celebrates a jubilee commemorating personal service in a state of life or profession; *esp* **:** a religious observing a jubilee

**¹ju·bi·late** \'==,lāt\ *vi* -ED/-ING/-S [L *jubilatus*, past part. of *jubilare*; akin to MHG *jū*, *jūch* (exclamation of joy), *jōlen* to yodel, Gk *iygē* shout, howling, Lith *yvas* owl] **:** to utter sounds or make demonstrations of joy and exultation ⟨the war was not officially ended but . . . a war-weary nation *jubilated* —Dixon Wecter⟩

**²ju·bi·la·te** \,yübə'lä(,)tā, ,jü-\ *n* -s [L, 2d pers. pl. imper. of *jubilare*; fr. the occurrence of this word at the beginning of Ps 99 in the Vulgate (Ps 100 AV and RSV)] **1 :** a song or outburst of joy and gladness ⟨Heaven's grand courts with ~*s* rang —*Tinsley's Mag.*⟩ **2** [L, 2d pers. pl. imper. of *jubilare*; fr. the occurrence of this word at the beginning of Ps 65 in the Vulgate (Ps 66 AV and RSV), used as the introit for the third Sunday after Easter] *usu cap* **:** the third Sunday after Easter

**ju·bi·la·tio** \,yübə'lätsē,ō\ *n* -s [L, jubilation] **:** JUBILUS

**ju·bi·la·tion** \,jübə'lāshən\ *n* -s [ME *jubilacioun*, fr. L *jubilation-*, *jubilatio*, fr. *jubilatus* (past part. of *jubilare* to jubilate) + *-ion-*, *-io* -ion] **1 :** the action of jubilating ⟨we must not rejoice or give way to ~ —Sir Winston Churchill⟩ **b :** the state of being jubilant ⟨he expelled his pent-up ~ in a long whistle —F.G.Slaughter⟩ **2 :** an expression of joy or exultation ⟨the ~*s* of the garrison were short-lived —C.R.Low⟩

**ju·bi·le·an** \jübə'lēən\ *adj* [¹*jubilee* + *-an*] **:** of or relating to a jubilee

**¹ju·bi·lee** \'jübə,lē\ ,==ˈ=\ *n* -s [ME, fr. MF & LL; MF *jubilé*, fr. LL *jubilaeus*, modif. (influenced by L *jubilare* to jubilate) of LGk *iōbēlaios*, fr. Heb *yōbhēl* ram's horn, trumpet, jubilee] **1** *also* **ju·bi·le** \"\ *often cap* **:** a year of emancipation and restoration provided by ancient Hebrew law for celebration every fifty years and held to be characterized by emancipation of Hebrew slaves, restoration of alienated lands to their former owners, and omission of all cultivation of the land — used esp. in the phrase *year of jubilee* ⟨the year of ~ . . . appears to have been calculated but not observed —T.W. Manson⟩ ⟨you shall hallow the fiftieth year . . . it shall be a ~ for you —Lev 25:10 (RSV)⟩ ⟨in this year of ~ ye shall return every man unto his possession —Lev 25:13 (AV)⟩ — compare SABBATICAL YEAR **2 a** (1) **:** a fiftieth anniversary or the completion of fifty years in an office, position, or condition ⟨the Australian florin commemorating the ~ of the constitution of the commonwealth —Lionel Thompson⟩ ⟨the ~ . . . of King George the Third in 1810 —E.J.Shears⟩ (2) **:** a special anniversary or the completion of a significant length of service involving a period other than fifty years — usu. used with qualifying adjective ⟨the seventieth ~ of the reign of the Emperor Francis Joseph —Hans Meyerhoff⟩ ⟨the approach of his thirty-year ~ may have supplied a . . . motive for retirement —W.F.Edgerton⟩ — compare DIAMOND JUBILEE, SILVER JUBILEE **b :** a celebration or commemoration of such an anniversary or of the completion of such a period of service ⟨the sesquicentennial vacation ~ scheduled for this year —*Stamps*⟩ **3 a :** a period of time (as a year) proclaimed by the Roman Catholic pope every 25 years or during a time of rejoicing (as an anniversary) as a time of special solemnity during which a special indulgence may be gained ⟨the first ~ was proclaimed in the year 1300 —Percy Winner⟩ **b** *or* **jubilee indulgence :** a special plenary indulgence granted during a year of jubilee to Roman Catholics who perform certain specified works of repentance and piety usu. including a pilgrimage to Rome ⟨the precise conditions for gaining each ~ are determined by the Roman pontiff —Herbert Thurston⟩ **4** [influenced in meaning by *jubilation*] **:** a state of joy or rejoicing **:** JUBILATION ⟨they . . . only thought of their triumph and abandoned themselves to ~ —W.H.Prescott⟩ **5** [influenced in meaning by *jubilation*] **:** the sound of jubilation **:** joyous shouting ⟨all along the crowded way was ~ and loud huzza —Sir Walter Scott⟩ **6 a** *obs* **:** a period of remission or restitution and sometimes license ⟨moved . . . a general ~ shall be for the debts —*House of Lords Debates*⟩ **b** [influenced in meaning by *jubilation*] **:** a season or occasion of celebration or rejoicing ⟨during the wild ~ of the Restoration —T.B.Macaulay⟩ ⟨we had a big ~ . . . to celebrate our victory —A.F.Harlow⟩ **7** *obs*, *often cap* **:** a period of fifty years ⟨I have lived among you almost a *Jubilee* —Ephraim Pagitt⟩ **8 :** a Negro folk song characterized by references to a future happy time or a time of deliverance from trials and tribulations ⟨the weary field hollers of the slaves were mingled with another elements of the ~*s* —*N. Y. Times Book Rev.*⟩ — compare HOLLER 3

**²jubilee** \"\ *adj* **:** FLAMBÉ 2 ⟨cherries ~⟩

**ju·bi·lize** \'==,līz\ *vi* -ED/-ING/-S [prob. fr. ¹*jubilee* + *-ize*] *archaic* **:** ¹JUBILATE

**ju·bi·lus** \-ləs\ *n*, *pl* **jubi·li** \-,lī\ [ML, fr. LL, cry of joy, fr. L *jubilum*, fr. *jubilare* to jubilate] **:** the melisma on the last *a* of *alleluia* from which the sequence of the mass developed — called also *jubilatio*

**ju·bus** \'jübəs\ *var of* JUBEROUS

**juca** *var of* YUCA

**juck** \'jək\ *vi* -ED/-ING/-S [imit.] **:** to make the natural noise of a partridge settling down for the night

**juco** *abbr* junior college

**jud** *abbr* **1** judge; judgment **2** judicial; judiciary

**judaean** *var of* JUDEAN

**judaeo-** — see JUDEO-

**¹ju·dah·ite** \'jüdə,īt\ *n* -s *usu cap* [*Judah*, 4th son of Jacob (Gen 29:35), the eponymous ancestor of the Judahites (Josh 15) + E *-ite*] **1 :** a member of the Hebrew tribe of Judah **2 :** a member of the Kingdom of Judah composed of the tribes of Judah and Benjamin

**²judahite** \"\ *adj*, *usu cap* **:** of or relating to the tribe or the Kingdom of Judah ⟨a place in *Judahite* territory —N.H. Snaith⟩ ⟨edited to suit a *Judahite* audience —L.A.Weigle⟩

**ju·da·ic** \(')jü'dāik, -āek\ *adj*, *usu cap* [L *judaicus*, fr. Gk *ioudaikos*, fr. *Ioudaios* Jew + *-ikos* -ic — more at JEW] **:** of, relating to, or characteristic of Jews or Judaism ⟨the . . . idea of particularism in *Judaic* thinking —F.S.Nichols⟩

**ju·da·i·ca** \jü'dāəkə\ *n pl*, *usu cap* [L, neut. pl. of *judaicus* Judaic] **:** things Jewish; *esp* **:** literary or historical materials relating to Jews or Judaism ⟨a new publication devoted to *Judaica* —W.S.La Sor⟩ ⟨a large collection of *Judaica*⟩

**ju·da·i·cal** \(')jü'dāəkəl\ *adj*, *usu cap* [ME *judeicall*, fr. L *judaicus* + ME *-al*] **:** JUDAIC — **ju·da·i·cal·ly** \-k(ə)lē, -li\ *adv*

**ju·da·ism** \'jüdə,izəm, -dē,i- *sometimes* -(,)dā,i- *or* -,dizəm\ *n* [LL *judaismus*, fr. Gk *ioudaismos*, fr. *Ioudaios* Jew + *-ismos* -ism] **1** *cap* **:** the religion of the Jews characterized by belief in one God and in the mission of Jews to teach the Fatherhood of God as revealed in the Hebrew Scriptures — see CONSERVATIVE JUDAISM, ORTHODOX JUDAISM, RECONSTRUCTIONISM, REFORM JUDAISM **2** *usu cap* **:** the quality or state of being a Jew **:** conformity to Jewish rites, ceremonies, and practices **:** adherence to the religion or culture of the Jews ⟨declared their *Judaism* openly —Cecil Roth⟩ **3** *usu cap* **:** the total complex of cultural, social, and religious beliefs and practices of the Jews **4** *usu cap* **:** the whole body of Jews **:** the Jewish community ⟨losses sustained by *Judaism* . . . by the oppression of Jews in Russia and Rumania —Herbert Loewe⟩

**ju·da·ist** \'jüdə·əst, -dēə-, -(,)dāə-\ *n* -s *usu cap* [*judaism* + *-ist*] **:** one that believes in or practices Judaism — **ju·da·is·tic** \;==;istik, -tēk\ *adj* — **ju·da·is·ti·cal·ly** \-tək(ə)lē, -tēk-, -li\ *adv*

**ju·da·iza·tion** \,jüdə·ə'zāshən, ,jüdē,-(,)dā, ,jü(,)dā, ,jü,dā, |,ī'z-\ *n* -s *usu cap* **:** the act or process of judaizing or being judaized

**ju·da·ize** \'jüdə,īz, -dē,-, -(,)dā,-\ *vb* -ED/-ING/-S *often cap* [LL *judaizare*, fr. Gk *ioudaizein*, fr. *Ioudaios* Jew + *-izein* -ize] *vi* **:** to adopt the customs, beliefs, or character of a Jew **:** become Jewish ⟨they . . . prevailed on the Galatians to *Judaize* so far as to observe the rites of Moses in various instances —Joseph Milner⟩ ~ *vt* **1 :** to imbue with or deeply affect by the doctrines or practices of Judaism ⟨attempts to ~ the Christian Sunday into a sabbath⟩ **2 :** to make Jewish **:** convert to Judaism ⟨descendants of Slav tribes *Judaized* long after the Dispersal —Evelyn Waugh⟩

**ju·da·iz·er** \-,zə(r)\ *n* -s *usu cap* **1 :** a Jewish Christian of the apostolic age who attempted to enforce conformity by all Christians to the precepts and practices of Judaism ⟨the *Judaizers* . . . thought that Gentiles, in order to be Christians, should be circumcised —J.W.Hunkin⟩ **2 :** a member of an heretical group arising in the Russian Orthodox Church in the 15th century and favoring an increased emphasis upon the doctrines and rituals of Judaism ⟨the *Judaizers* conducted a campaign of subversive activity within the church —Serge Bolshakoff⟩

**¹ju·das** \'jüdəs\ *n* -ES *often attrib* [after *Judas* Iscariot, apostle that betrayed Jesus] **1** *usu cap* **:** TRAITOR; *esp* **:** one that betrays under the pretense of friendship ⟨some *Judas* . . . gave the story to the one-party press —G.W. Johnson⟩ **2** *or* **judas window** *also* **judas-hole** *sometimes cap J* **:** a peephole usu. constituted by an aperture resembling a window with a sliding panel and used chiefly for inspection (as in the door of a house or a prison cell) ⟨the guard sprang to reconnoiter through a ~ —*N.Y.Sun*⟩ ⟨peering through the broken ~ in the door of the cell —John Hersey⟩ ⟨after a considerable time a ~ was opened —W.S.Maugham⟩ ⟨the *judas window* of the cell door slammed down —Dickey Chapelle⟩

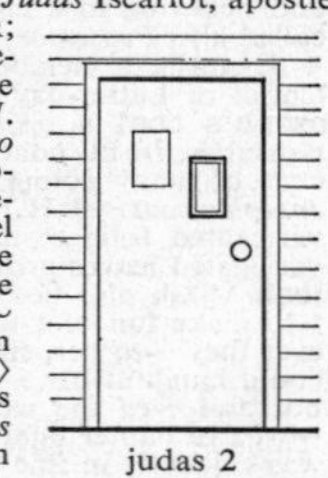

judas 2

**²judas** \"\ *adj*, *usu cap* **:** of, relating to, or being an animal used as a decoy or to lead other animals to slaughter ⟨a *Judas* duck⟩ ⟨as sheep are led by a *Judas* goat —James Reach⟩

**judas-colored** \'==;==\ *adj*, *usu cap J* [so called fr. a belief that Judas Iscariot was red haired] **:** RED, REDDISH — usu. used of hair ⟨there's treachery in that *Judas-colored* beard —John Dryden⟩

**judas-ear** \'==,=\ *n*, *pl* **judas-ears** *usu cap J* [trans. of NL *auricula Judae* — more at JEW'S-EAR] **:** JEW'S-EAR

**judas priest** *interj*, *often cap J&P* [euphemism for *Jesus Christ*] — used as a mild oath

**judas thorn** *n*, *usu cap J* **:** a Judas tree (*Cercis siliquastrum*)

**judas tree** *n*, *usu cap J* [so called fr. a belief that Judas Iscariot hanged himself on a tree of this kind] **:** an often shrubby Eurasian tree (*Cercis siliquastrum*) that has glabrous shoots and rounded deeply cordate leaves and is widely cultivated in mild regions for its abundant purplish rose flowers which appear in early spring; *broadly* **:** a tree or shrub of the genus *Cercis*

**jud·cock** \'jəd,=\ *n* -s [perh. irreg. fr. *ged* + *cock*] **:** JACKSNIPE

**¹jud·der** \'jədə(r)\ *vi* -ED/-ING/-S [prob. alter. (prob. influenced by *jar*) of *shudder*] **:** to vibrate with intensity **:** jar strongly ⟨the motors which clattered protestingly to life, backfiring and ~*ing* —J.L.Rhys⟩

**²judder** \"\ *n* -s **:** the action or sound of juddering ⟨they . . . found some comfort in the ~ of the engines —Audrey Barker⟩

**¹ju·de·an** *also* **ju·dae·an** \(')jü'dēən\ *adj*, *usu cap* [*Judea*, *Judaea*, southern division of Palestine under Persian, Greek, and Roman rule + E *-an*, adj. suffix] : of, relating to, or characteristic of ancient Judea ⟨*Judean* mountains⟩ ⟨the background of *Judaean* history —J.W.Jack⟩

[2]**judean** *also* **judaean** \"\ *n* -s *usu cap* [*Judea, Judaea* + E *-an*, n. suffix] : an inhabitant of ancient Judea ⟨the Israelites and *Judeans* . . . disclosed no interest in theoretical questions universal in scope —R.H.Pfeiffer⟩

**judeo-** *also* **judaeo-** *comb form, usu cap* [L *judaeus* Jewish, Jew — more at JEW] **1** : of or relating to the Jews or Judaism ⟨*Judeo*phobia⟩ **2** : Jewish and ⟨*Judeo*-Christian⟩ ⟨*Judeo*-Persian⟩

**judeo-german** \jü¦dā(,)ō, ¦jüdē(,)ō, jü¦dē(,)ō+\ *n, cap J&G* : YIDDISH

**judeo-spanish** \jü¦dā(,)ō, ¦jüdē(,)ō, jü¦dē(,)ō+\ *n, cap J&S* : the Romance language of Sephardic Jews in the Balkans, Greece, and Asia Minor

**ju·dex** \'jü,deks\ *n, pl* **judi·ces** \-‚də,sēz\ [L *judic-, judex*] **1** : a private person appointed in Roman law to hear and determine a case and corresponding most nearly to a modern referee or arbitrator appointed by the court **2** : JUDGE

**judex or·di·na·ri·us** \-,ȯ(r)dᵊn'a(a)rēəs\ *n, pl* **judices ordina·rii** \-rē,ī\ [ML, lit., regular judge] : a judicial magistrate having jurisdiction in his own right as a judge as distinguished from a judex appointed for a particular case

**judex pe·da·ne·us** \-pə'dānēəs\ *n, pl* **judices peda·nei** \-ē,ī\ [LL, lit., petty judex] : a judex appointed to hear petty causes

[1]**judge** \'jəj, *dial* 'jej\ *vb* -ED/-ING/-S [ME *juggen*, fr. OF *jugier*, fr. L *judicare*, fr. *judic-, judex* judex, judge] *vt* **1** : to form an authoritative opinion about : decide on the merits of ⟨a wall must be *judged* by the way it is built —Paul Potts⟩ ⟨humanity *judged* these authors . . . and found them worthy of enduring fame —Van Wyck Brooks⟩ **2** : to hear and determine (as a litigated question) or decide in the case of (as a person) in or as if in a court of justice : sit in judgment upon : TRY ⟨the power of the court to ~ cases in interstate commerce⟩ ⟨*judged* and condemned to death for killing his mother —John Milton⟩ ⟨He shall come to ~ the quick and the dead —*Bk. of Com. Prayer*⟩ **3** *obs* : CONDEMN 3a ⟨some whose offenses are pilfering . . . they ~ to be whipped —Francis Bacon⟩ **4** : to consider or pronounce to be usu. after inquiry and deliberation ⟨recommend . . . such measures as he shall ~ necessary and expedient —*U.S.Constitution*⟩ ⟨youngsters *judged* delinquent —Dorothy Barclay⟩ **5** : to exercise paramount civil and military authority over : GOVERN, RULE — used of a Hebrew tribal leader in biblical times ⟨and he *judged* Israel in the days of the Philistines twenty years —Judg 15: 20 (RSV)⟩ **6** : to form an estimate or appraisal of ⟨he could ~ pace to a nicety —*Irish Digest*⟩ ⟨we ~ the distance from remembered comparisons —Weston La Barre⟩ **7** : to hold as an opinion : THINK ⟨I ~ she was right —B.A.Williams⟩ ~ *vi* **1** : to form an opinion: as **a** : to estimate esp. on the basis of a comparison of facts or ideas ⟨as near as I could ~, we were not twenty yards from the rocks —Frederick Marryat⟩ **b** : to form a conclusion from evidence ⟨when the mind assents to a proposition it ~*s* —J.S. Mill⟩ **c** : to form a critical evaluation — often used with *of* ⟨it is hard to ~ of the general style of the painting from such small portions —O. Elfrida Saunders⟩ **2** : to hear and determine (as in causes on trial) : decide as a judge : pronounce judgment ⟨may the Lord ~ between you and me —Gen 16:5 (RSV)⟩ **syn** see INFER

[2]**judge** \"\ *n* -s [ME *juge*, fr. MF, fr. L *judic-, judex* judex, judge, fr. *ju-* (fr. *jus* right, law) + *-dic-, -dex* (fr. *dicere* to determine, say) — more at JUST, DICTION] : one that judges: **a** (1) : a public official invested with authority to hear and determine litigated questions; *esp* : the presiding magistrate in a court of justice usu. so named in his commission ⟨the ~ declares the law, the jury finds the facts —Edward Jenks⟩ ⟨European ~*s* are members of a hierarchically organized bureaucracy —C.J.Friedrich⟩ (2) : a person who performs one or more functions of such an official (as a justice of the peace or referee) or of any judicial officer — sometimes used as an honorific or courtesy title without much significance ⟨American law early . . . dignified every magistrate by calling him ~ —H.S.Commager⟩ **b** *cap* : GOD, CHRIST ⟨the coming of the Lord is at hand . . . behold, the *Judge* is standing at the doors —Jas 5: 8-9 (RSV)⟩ **c** *often cap* : a tribal hero exercising paramount civil and military authority over the Hebrews in the biblical period of more than 400 years following the death of Joshua ⟨the Lord raised up ~*s*, who saved them out of the power of those who plundered them —Judg 2:16 (RSV)⟩ **d** : one appointed to decide in a contest or competition (as a trial of skill or speed between two or more parties) : UMPIRE ⟨the *Judge* . . . must occupy the judges' box at the time the horses pass the winning post —Dan Parker⟩ ⟨on election day the ~ helps decide disputes at the polls⟩ **e** : one that decides or determines any question, point at issue, or controversy : one that gives an authoritative opinion ⟨each house shall be the ~ of the . . . qualifications of its own members —*U.S.Constitution*⟩ ⟨the board shall be the ~ of what constitutes unprofessional conduct —G.B.Cummings⟩ ⟨the best ~ of what his book was about —Ellen Glasgow⟩ **f** : one that has sufficient knowledge or experience to decide on the merits of or to form an authoritative opinion about something (as a question or a work of art) : CONNOISSEUR, CRITIC ⟨was an extraordinary ~ of character —C.F.Smith⟩ ⟨a good ~ of poetry —John Dryden⟩

**judge advocate** *n, pl* **judge advocates** : a legal officer charged with the administration of military justice (as by acting as legal adviser or as prosecutor at a court-martial) and usu. serving on the staff of a military commander ⟨*judge advocates* shall perform their duties under the direction of the Judge Advocate General —*U.S.Code*⟩

**judge advocate general** *n, pl* **judge advocate generals** *or* **judge advocates general** : the senior legal officer and chief legal adviser in an entire military establishment (as the U.S. Department of Defense or the British army) ⟨the *Judge Advocate General* has ordered the case forwarded to the court for review —J.F.Spindler⟩

**judge delegate** *n, pl* **judges delegate** : a judge having delegated authority ⟨an extraordinary and rarely constituted court of *judges delegate* —*Nation*⟩ — compare JUDGE ORDINARY

**judge lynch** *n, usu cap J&L* : the lynch law personified ⟨*Judge Lynch* is not the sovereign spirit of America —*Nation*⟩

**judge-made** \'=¦=\ *adj* : created by judges or judicial decision — used esp. of law applied or established by the judicial interpretation of statutes so as to extend or restrict their scope

**judge ordinary** *n, pl* **judges ordinary** [trans. of ML *judex ordinarius*] **1** : a judge having jurisdiction in his own right ⟨English prelates who were sitting . . . not as *judges ordinary* but as mere delegates of the pope —Frederick Pollock & F.W. Maitland⟩ — compare JUDGE DELEGATE **2** : a judge having ecclesiastical or probate jurisdiction

**judge·ship** \'jəj,ship\ *n* : the jurisdiction or office of a judge ⟨the ~ for the western district of Pennsylvania provided for by the act —*U.S.Code*⟩ ⟨appointed him to a ~ in the circuit court of the United States —W.C.Ford⟩

**judg·ess** \'jəjəs\ *n* -ES : a female judge

**judg·mat·i·cal** \(')jəj¦mad·əkəl\ *also* **judg·mat·ic** \-d·ik\ *adj* [prob. irreg. (influenced by such words as *dogmatical, dogmatic*) fr. *judgment* + *-ical* or *-ic*] : JUDICIOUS ⟨his ~ introduction to this brief selection . . . of shorter poems —Leonard Bacon⟩ ⟨he . . . is nicely *judgmatic* for a man still in his twenties —E.A.Weeks⟩

**judg·mat·i·cal·ly** \-d·ək(ə)lē\ *adv* : in the manner of a judge : GRAVELY ⟨they need to be interpreted ~ —E.L.Bernays⟩

**judg·ment** *or* **judge·ment** \'jəjmənt\ *n* -s [ME *juggement*, fr. OF *jugement*, fr. *jugier* to judge + *-ment* — more at JUDGE] **1 a** : a formal utterance or pronouncing of an authoritative opinion after judging **b** : an opinion so pronounced; *esp* : an adverse opinion : CENSURE, CRITICISM **2 a** (1) : a formal decision or determination given in a cause by a court of law or other tribunal : COURT ORDER, SENTENCE — compare DECREE 3b(1), SUMMARY JUDGMENT (2) *Brit* : a record or statement of the reasons for a specific judicial decision — compare OPINION **b** (1) : an obligation (as a debt) created by decree of a court ⟨collection of . . . automobile ~*s* from uninsured motorists —*Harvard Law Rev.*⟩ — compare ESTOPPEL, QUASI CONTRACT (2) : an official certificate evidencing such a decision or decree **c** *archaic* : a definitive or authoritative decision usu. pronounced formally as if in a court of justice **3 a** *obs* : the action of trying a person or a cause in or as if in a court of justice : TRIAL **b** *usu cap* (1) : the final judging of mankind by God in which reward or punishment is meted out to each individual according to his deserts — usu. used with *the* ⟨the expected letting loose of . . . anger at the *Judgment* —C.A.Scott⟩ ⟨the dead . . . biding *Judgment*, in its fold have slept —Walter de la Mare⟩ (2) : JUDGMENT DAY 1a **4 a** : a divine sentence or decision; *specif* : a calamity held to be sent by God as a punishment for wrong committed or as a symbol of divine displeasure **b** : a divine decree : a law divinely given ⟨hear, O Israel, the statutes and ~*s* which I speak in your ears this day —Deut 5:1 (AV)⟩ **5** *obs* : JUSTICE, RIGHTEOUSNESS ⟨for I the Lord love ~, I hate robbery —Isa 61:8 (AV)⟩ **6 a** : the action of judging : the mental or intellectual process of forming an opinion or evaluation by discerning and comparing ⟨the author has sought to exercise some rigor of *judgement* —Ernest Barker⟩ **b** : an opinion or estimate so formed ⟨an economist should form an independent ~ on currency questions —Bertrand Russell⟩ **c** *obs* : a religious belief or opinion of a sectarian nature : PERSUASION ⟨those of the Presbyterian ~ —Oliver Cromwell⟩ **7 a** : the capacity for judging : the power or ability to decide on the basis of evidence ⟨~ is the highest of the human faculties —E.L.Godkin⟩ ⟨some of the sharpest men in argument are notoriously unsound in ~ —O.W.Holmes †1894⟩ ⟨a steadying and composing effect upon their ~ —Matthew Arnold⟩ **b** (1) : the exercise of the capacity to judge ⟨in cases where poor ~ was displayed —Harold Koontz & Cyril O'Donnell⟩ ⟨sound professional ~ —*Jour. of Accountancy*⟩ (2) : the wise or just exercise of this capacity : DISCERNMENT, DISCRETION — used without qualifier ⟨he was not a man of ~ and he allowed personal feeling to influence his action —Hilaire Belloc⟩ ⟨displays . . . tact, clarity, and ~ —*Saturday Rev.*⟩ **8** *obs* : one possessing good judgment : [2]JUDGE f ⟨he's one o' th' soundest ~*s* in Troy . . . and a proper man —Shak.⟩ **9** *logic* **a** : the action of mentally establishing a relation between two or more terms; *esp* : the affirmation or denial of a predicate with respect to a subject — compare APPREHENSION **b** : a formal expression embodying such a logical conclusion; *esp* : a proposition viewed as a statement of something believed or asserted **10** *philos* : the capacity, power, or faculty of judging: as **a** *Scholasticism* : the capacity to arrive at a decision about the value of things **b** *Kantianism* (1) : the power of relating particular to general terms or concepts — see DETERMINATIVE JUDGMENT, REFLECTIVE JUDGMENT (2) : a capacity mediating between reason and the understanding; *broadly* : the critical faculty — **judgment not withstanding the verdict** *or* **judgment non ob·stan·te ve·re·dic·to** \-,nänəb'stantē,verə'dik(,)tō, -,nōn-\ : a legal judgment entered for one party because law and justice require it notwithstanding a verdict of the jury in favor of an opposing party **syn** see SENSE

**judg·men·tal** \(')jəj¦mentᵊl\ *adj* : of, relating to, or involving judgment ⟨emphasizing the ~ aspect of morality —Sing-nan Fen⟩ ⟨the right to correct ~ errors —H.F.Taggart⟩

**judgment book** *n* **1** : a book in which the clerk of a court of record enters judgments **2** *usu cap J&B* : the record of all human acts to be opened at the Last Judgment ⟨the leaves of the *Judgment Book* unfold —Bayard Taylor⟩

**judgment by default** : a judgment entered as a result of the failure of a party to appear or to file a pleading or to perform some other act of an interlocutory nature required by law within the time allowed

**judgment cap** *n* : BLACK CAP

**judgment creditor** *n* : a creditor having a legal right to enforce execution of a judgment for a sum of money ⟨a suit in equity by two *judgment creditors* of an insolvent . . . corporation —*Corporation Jour.*⟩ — compare JUDGMENT DEBTOR

**judgment day** *n* **1 a** *usu cap J&D* : the day of the Last Judgment : DOOMSDAY 1 ⟨belief in . . . the *Judgment Day* at the end of the world —E.R.Pike⟩ **b** : a day of final judgment ⟨driven Congress . . . for the sake of a completed record before the *judgment day* of election —F.L.Paxon⟩ **2** : the day fixed by statute, rule, or custom of a court on which judgments are pronounced or entered upon the court records

**judgment debt** *n* : a legal obligation to pay a debt or damages evidenced by a judgment entered in a court of record and enforceable by execution or other judicial process — compare QUASI CONTRACT

**judgment debtor** *n* : one whose obligation to pay a judgment debt remains unsatisfied ⟨order the appearance of a *judgment debtor* for supplementary examination as to financial ability —F.H.Myers⟩ — compare JUDGMENT CREDITOR

**judgment lien** *n* : a statutory lien usu. upon the real estate of a judgment debtor that becomes effective upon entry of a judgment by a court of record or upon filing notice of the judgment with the appropriate public official

**judgment note** *n* : a promissory note of a kind illegal in some states of the U.S. upon which the holder is enabled to enter judgment and take out execution ex parte in case of default in payment

**judgment-proof** \¦==¦=\ *adj* : of or being one (as a judgment debtor) from whom nothing can be recovered because he has no property or has fraudulently concealed or removed his property from the jurisdiction of the judgment ⟨an insolvent, *judgment-proof* tort-feasor —R.E.Keeton⟩

**judgment rate** *n* : an insurance rate based on the judgment of the rater instead of on a prescribed schedule

**judgment roll** *n* **1** : a parchment roll or a book containing a record of the proceedings and judgment of a case in a court of law ⟨the cost of transcribing the *judgment roll* —*Ward v. Cruse*⟩ **2** : a roll of papers constituted by a collection of the original records of a judicial proceeding

**judgment seat** *n, often cap J* : the seat of judgment where all are to be tried in the presence of God at the time of the Last Judgment ⟨we must all appear before the *judgment seat* of Christ —2 Cor 5:10 (RSV)⟩

**judgment summons** *n* : a summons issued in an English county court requiring a judgment debtor to appear and show cause why he should not be imprisoned

**judgt** *abbr* judgment

**ju·di·ca·ble** \'jüdəkəbəl\ *adj* [LL *judicabilis*, fr. L *judicare* to judge + *-abilis* -able — more at JUDGE] : capable of being or liable to be judged ⟨a ~ dispute⟩

**ju·di·ca·tive** \-,kād·iv\ *adj* [ML *judicativus*, fr. L *judicatus* (past part. of *judicare* to judge) + *-ivus* -ive] : having the power to judge : JUDICIAL ⟨all the ~ authority of the House of Lords —David Hume †1776⟩

**ju·di·ca·tor** \-ād·ə(r)\ *n* -s [LL, fr. L *judicatus* (past part. of *judicare*) + *-or*] : one that judges or acts as a judge ⟨the authority of its ~*s* called in question —William Robertson †1686⟩

**ju·di·ca·to·ry** \-‚kə,tōrē\ *n* -ES [ML *judicatorium* court of law, fr. L *judicatus* (past part. of *judicare*) + *-orium* -ory] **1** : JUDICIARY 1a ⟨evidence in the Saxon *Judicatory* sometimes consisted in the . . . testimony of the fact itself —Nathaniel Bacon⟩ **2** : JUDICATURE 2 ⟨the treaties of the U.S. had been . . . put in execution by state *judicatories* —Alexander Hamilton⟩ **3** : one of the four governing bodies of the Presbyterian Church ⟨the General Assembly is the highest ~ of this Church —*Constitution of the United Presbyterian Church in the U.S.A.*⟩ — compare GENERAL ASSEMBLY, PRESBYTERY, SESSION, SYNOD

**ju·di·ca·ture** \-kə,chu̇(ə)r, -kəchər, -,kāchər\ *n* -s [MF, fr. ML *judicatura*, fr. L *judicatus* (past part. of *judicare*) + *-ura* -ure] **1** : the action of judging : the administration of justice (as by courts of law) ⟨~ is nothing else but an interpretation of the laws —Thomas Hobbes⟩ ⟨the Supreme Court of *Judicature* in England⟩ **2** : a court of justice : a legal tribunal ⟨the Court of the Lord Lyon in Scotland is one of the ~*s* of that country —F.J.Grant⟩ **3** : JUDICIARY 1 ⟨the Lyon Court is a . . . part of the ~ of Scotland —L.G.Pine⟩

**judices** *pl of* JUDEX

**ju·di·cial** \(')jü¦dishəl\ *adj* [ME, fr. L *judicialis*, fr. *judicium* judgment (fr. *judic-, judex* judex, judge) + *-alis* -al — more at JUDGE] **1** : of, relating to, or concerned with a judgment, the function of judging, the administration of justice, or the judiciary ⟨the ~ powers of Congress —W.S.Sayre⟩ ⟨the new ~ code⟩ ⟨a ~ circuit⟩ — compare ADMINISTRATIVE, EXECUTIVE, LEGISLATIVE **2** : of or relating to judgment concerning the supposed influence of the heavenly bodies on things human ⟨prosecuted . . . for lecturing in ~ astrology —*Times Lit. Supp.*⟩ **3** : ordered or enforced by a court or other legal tribunal ⟨it could not be the end of the law, whether moral or ~, to license a sin —John Milton⟩ ⟨a ~ sale⟩ — compare CONVENTIONAL **4** *obs* : JUDICIOUS ⟨showed himself so ~ and industrious as gave great satisfaction —John Smith †1631⟩ **5** : of, characterized by, or expressing judgment : CRITICAL 1 c ⟨gave a cold, ~ look at his lapel —Claud Cockburn⟩ ⟨a biography . . . appreciative and yet ~ in purpose —Tyler Dennett⟩ **6** : arising from a judgment of God : coming as a divine punishment ⟨a ~ pestilence⟩ **7** : belonging or appropriate to a judge or the judiciary ⟨with stern ~ frame of mind —W.S.Gilbert⟩ ⟨weight of his ~ wig —Frank Yerby⟩

[2]**judicial** *n* -s [ME, fr. *judicial*, adj.] *obs* : a law or ordinance that is subject to enforcement by the courts — compare MORAL LAW

**judicial act** *n* : an act involving the exercise of judicial power; *esp* : one that determines controversies or questions of right or obligation

**judicial administration** *n* **1** : the dispensing of justice according to law esp. through the functioning of a system of courts ⟨the people . . . see the processes of *judicial administration* at close range in thousands of local courts —E.F.Johnson⟩ **2** : the management of the internal affairs of a system of courts ⟨effective *judicial administration* requires the establishment of businesslike methods —F.M.Vinson⟩

**judicial astrology** *n* : a branch of astrology that professes to foretell the fate and acts of nations and individuals — called also *mundane astrology*

**judicial bond** *n* : COURT BOND ⟨a *judicial bond* given where the law does not require any is not binding —*Hartford Accident & Indemnity Co. v. Abdalla*⟩

**judicial combat** *n* : TRIAL BY BATTLE

**judicial committee of the privy council** *usu cap J&P & both Cs* : a committee of the British Privy Council composed of leading jurists usu. from Great Britain and occasionally from Commonwealth countries that acts as the highest court of appeal from British colonies and from some of the nations of the Commonwealth ⟨appeal to the *Judicial Committee of the Privy Council* still lies from Ceylonese courts —Maurice Duverger⟩

**judicial conference** *n* : a conference composed of judges and sometimes other public officials and leaders of the bar and meeting to study problems and suggest reforms and improvements in the administration of the judicial system in a specific area ⟨each circuit has a *Judicial Conference* of the Circuit —F.M.Vinson⟩

**judicial council** *n* : a governmental agency usu. composed of judges and lawyers and established to study and make recommendations to the legislature on alterations in the laws and in the administration of the courts ⟨*judicial councils* . . . devise ways of simplifying judicial procedure —A.F.MacDonald⟩

**judicial discretion** *n* : the choice among possible decisions exercised by a judge according to the principles of justice and equity in the absence of a specific rule of law governing the case

**judicial factor** *n* : an administrator of an estate appointed under Scots law by the Court of Session — compare RECEIVER

**ju·di·ci·al·i·ty** \(,)jü,dishē'aləd·ē\ *n* -ES : the quality or state of being judicial ⟨characterized by Olympian ~⟩

**judicial legislation** *n* : laws held to be created by the pronouncements of a judge who departs from a strict interpretation of a law according to the manifest intention of the legislature — compare JUDGE-MADE

**ju·di·cial·ly** \(')jü¦dish(ə)lē, -li\ *adv* : in a judicial manner

**judicial murder** *n* : death caused by a court sentence held to be legal but unjust ⟨a revolution . . . with no massacres or *judicial murders* of people on the losing side —H.B.Parkes⟩

**judicial notice** *n* : the recognition by a court for the purposes of a case of the existence or truth of certain facts as being self-evident or common knowledge ⟨no evidence is necessary as to any matters of which the court takes *judicial notice* —H.J. Stephen⟩

**judicial oath** *n* : an oath required in the course of judicial proceedings esp. in a court — compare PERJURY

**judicial process** *n* : the series of steps in the course of the administration of justice through the established system of courts ⟨no valid basis within the *judicial process* for pursuing review of my rulings in the case —L.W.Youngdahl⟩

**judicial review** *n* **1** : REVIEW 5 ⟨deportation orders shall not become final until the completion of *judicial review* —*Harvard Law Rev.*⟩ **2** : a constitutional doctrine that gives to a court system and esp. to a supreme court the power to annul legislative or executive acts which the judges declare are contrary to the provisions of the constitution ⟨*judicial review* has . . . been termed America's distinctive contribution to the science of politics —F.A.Ogg & P.O.Ray⟩

**judicial separation** *n* : a separation of husband and wife sanctioned by an order of a court : a divorce a mensa et thoro — called also *legal separation*

**judicial sequestration** *n* : a mandate of a Louisiana court directing a sheriff to take possession of property in a dispute to await the order of the court as to who is entitled to possession

**judicial township** *n* : a political division of a county in some western states of the U.S. — compare CIVIL DISTRICT, ELECTION DISTRICT 2

**judicial veto** *n* : the power possessed by a court system and esp. a supreme court to annul legislative and executive acts by declaring them unconstitutional ⟨the explicit assumption . . . that the *judicial veto* is basically undemocratic —*Amer. Polit. Sci. Rev.*⟩

**judicial writ** *n* : a writ issued by a court under its own seal for judicial purposes — compare ORIGINAL WRIT

[1]**ju·di·ciary** \jü'dishē,erē, -ri *also* -shər-\ *adj* [L *judiciarius*, fr. *judicium* judgment + *-arius* -ary — more at JUDICIAL] : of, concerned with, or relating to the judiciary : JUDICIAL ⟨the general principle of English ~ law —Edward Jenks⟩ ⟨the appointment of more women to higher ~ positions —*Current Biog.*⟩ ⟨the ~ committee⟩

[2]**judiciary** \"\ *n* -ES **1 a** : a system of courts of law in an area (as a nation or state) ⟨the judges are career members of the Italian ~ —Charles Fairman⟩ ⟨the federal ~ is responsible for the trial of cases involving federal laws —W.S.Sayre⟩ **b** : the persons (as the body of judges) constituting this system as an active agency ⟨in England . . . the ~ are recruited primarily from the ranks of practicing barristers —T.G.Lund⟩ **2** : a branch of government in which judicial power is vested ⟨organization of the government into legislative, *judiciary* and executive —Thomas Jefferson⟩ ⟨the senate committee on the ~⟩ — compare EXECUTIVE 1, LEGISLATIVE

**ju·di·cious** \(')jü¦dishəs\ *adj* [MF *judicieux*, fr. L *judicium* judgment + MF *-eux* -ous] **1** : having or exercising sound judgment ⟨a careful and ~ man —C.H.Lincoln⟩ ⟨this critic is admirably ~ —Milton Rugoff⟩ **2** : directed or governed by sound usu. dispassionate judgment : characterized by discretion ⟨a ~ series of investments —Samuel Butler †1902⟩ ⟨the healthiest trees . . . have had the most ~ pruning —A.S. Igleheart⟩ ⟨compounded by a ~ mixture of ingredients —Malcolm Cowley⟩ **syn** see WISE

**ju·di·cious·ly** *adv* : in a judicious manner : with good judgment : WISELY ⟨the quality of hay can be . . . improved by ~ fertilizing the fields —*Farmer's Weekly* (*So. Africa*)⟩ ⟨an occasional word ~ designed to draw out reactions from others —A.T.Weaver⟩

**ju·di·cious·ness** *n* -ES : the quality or state of being judicious : sound judgment : SAGACITY ⟨~ is . . . apparent in the excellent job of selection —David Riesman⟩

**ju·di·ci·um** \yü'dikēəm\ *n, pl* **judi·cii** \-kē,ē\ [L] : JUDGMENT

**ju·do** \'jü(,)dō\ *n* -s [Jap *jūdō*, fr. *jū* weakness, gentleness (fr. Chin — Pek — *jou*[2] soft, gentle) + *dō* road, art, fr. Chin (Pek) *tao*[4] road, way] : a modern refined form of jujitsu utilizing special applications of principles of movement, balance, and leverage

**ju·do·ka** \'jüdō,kä, ,=='=\ *n, pl* **judoka** [Jap *jūdōka*, fr. *jūdō*] : one who participates in judo

**ju·do·pho·bia** \,jüdə'fōbēə\ *n, usu cap* [prob. fr. *judo-* (alter. of *judeo-*) + *-phobia*] : ANTI-SEMITISM

**ju·dy** \'jüdē\ *n* -ES *usu cap* [fr. *Judy*, nickname for the name *Judith*] : GIRL ⟨as hep as the average *Judy* about such matters —John & Ward Hawkins⟩

**juey** \'hwā\ *n* -s [AmerSp] *Puerto Rico* : GREAT LAND CRAB

**¹jug** \ˈjəg\ *n* -s [imit.] **:** a sound or note made by a bird (as the nightingale) ⟨the pretty birds do sing, cuckoo, *jug-jug* —Thomas Nash⟩

**²jug** \ˈ"\ *vi* **jugged; jugged; jugging; jugs :** to make the natural sound of a nightingale

**³jug** \ˈ"\ *n* -s [perh. fr. *Jug*, nickname for the name *Joan*] **1 a** *chiefly Brit* **:** a small pitcher usu. used as part of a table service ⟨holding the cream ~ poised above a cup —Frances Towers⟩ **b :** a large deep container usu. of earthenware or glass that has a narrow mouth, is fitted with a handle, and is used to hold liquids — compare BOTTLE **c :** the contents of a jug **2 :** JAIL, PRISON ⟨told them politely to discontinue their operations and get out of town or get thrown in the ~ —Frank Frederick⟩ **3** *slang* **:** BANK

jug 1b

**⁴jug** \ˈ"\ *vb* **jugged; jugged; jugging; jugs** *vt* **1 :** to stew in an earthenware vessel ⟨can ~ a rabbit well enough —Robert Browning⟩ **2 :** to commit to jail **:** IMPRISON ⟨is rudely pinched for stealing . . . and is *jugged* in an English jail —Edmund Gilligan⟩ ~ *vi* **:** to fish usu. for catfish by means of a hook and line attached to a floating jug

**⁵jug** \ˈ"\ *n* -s [fr. *Jug*, nickname for the name *Joan*] *obs* **:** WOMAN ⟨whoops, *Jug*, I love thee —Shak.⟩

**⁶jug** \ˈ"\ *vi* **jugged; jugged; jugging; jugs** [perh. fr. ²*jug*] *of quail or partridge* **:** to nestle or collect in a covey

**juga** *pl of* JUGUM

**¹ju·gal** \ˈjügəl\ *adj* [L *jugalis*, lit., of a yoke, fr. *jugum* yoke + *-alis* -al — more at YOKE] **:** MALAR

**²jugal** \ˈ"\ *n* -s **:** a bone lying below the orbit in lower vertebrates and forming part of the cheekbone in some higher forms

**jugal lobe** *n* [*jugal* fr. *jugum* + *-al*] **:** the modified jugum of a primitive lepidopterous insect

**jugal point** *also* **ju·ga·le** \jüˈga(,)lē, -gä(-, -gā(-\ *n* -s [*jugal point* fr. ¹*jugal* + *point*; *jugale* fr. NL, fr. L, neut. of *jugalis* jugal] **:** the point at which lines following the margin of the frontal and temporal processes of the zygomatic bone are joined

**ju·ga·tae** \jüˈgād·(,)ē, -ˈgäd·(,)ē\ *n pl*, *cap* [NL, fr. fem. pl. of *jugatus* jugate] *in some classifications* **:** a division of Lepidoptera that is equivalent to Homoneura and consists of moths having the front wings provided with a jugum

**ju·gate** \ˈjü,gāt, -gət\ *also* **ju·gat·ed** \-gād·əd\ *adj* [*jugate* prob. fr. (assumed) NL *jugatus*, fr. NL *jugum* + L *-atus* -ate; *jugated* fr. *jugate* + *-ed* — more at JUGUM] **1 a :** PAIRED **b :** having a jugum **2** [*jugate* fr. L *jugatus*, past part. of *jugare* to join, connect, fr. *jugum* yoke; *jugated* fr. L *jugatus* + E *-ed*] **:** CONJOINED, OVERLAPPING ⟨~ busts on a coin⟩

**ju·ga·tion** \jüˈgāshən\ *n* -s **:** the quality or state of being jugate

**jug–eared** \ˈ=,=\ *adj* **:** having protuberant ears

**juge d'in·struc·tion** \zhüezhdaⁿstrüeksyōⁿ\ *n, pl* **juges d'instruction** \ˈ"\ [F, lit., judge of preliminary investigation] *French law* **:** a magistrate for criminal cases to whom complaints are made and who interrogates parties and witnesses, conducts investigations, and formulates charges

**ju·gend·stil** \ˈyügənt,shtēl\ *n* -s *usu cap J* [G, lit., style of *Jugend*, fr. *Jugend*, illustrated periodical founded in Munich in 1896 + G *stil* style, fr. MHG, style, stylus, fr. L *stilus* — more at STYLE] **:** a late 19th century and early 20th century German decorative style parallel to art nouveau

**ju·ger** \ˈjüg(ə(r), ˈyüg|, ˈjüj|\ *n, pl* **jugers** \|ə(r)z\ *or* **ju·ge·ra** \ˈyügərə\ [L *jugerum*; akin to MHG *jiuch* morgen, Gk *zeugos* team, yoke (of oxen), L *jugum* yoke] **:** an ancient Roman unit of land area equal to 28,800 square Roman feet or 0.622 acre

**jug·ful** \ˈjəg,fu̇l\ *n, pl* **jugfuls** *or* **jugs·ful** \-g,fu̇lz, -gz,fu̇l\ **1 :** the quantity held by a jug **2 :** GREAT DEAL — used in the phrase *not by a jugful* ⟨haven't seen anything yet — not by a ~⟩

**jugged** *past of* JUG

**jug·ger** *or* **jag·gar** \ˈjəgə(r)\ *n* -s [Hindi *jhagar*] **:** LUGGAR

**¹jug·ger·naut** \ˈjəgə(r),nȯt, -nät, *usu* |d·+V\ *n* -s [Hindi *Jagannāth* lord of the world (i.e. Vishnu, one of the principal Hindu gods), fr. Skt *Jagannātha*, fr. *jagat* world (fr. *jagat* adj., moving, living) + *nātha* lord; fr. a former belief that devotees of Vishnu sometimes allowed themselves to be crushed beneath the wheels of the car on which his image was being drawn in procession; akin to Skt *jigāti* he goes, *gamati* — more at COME] **:** a massive inexorable force or object that advances irresistibly and crushes whatever is in its path ⟨war has always been represented as a ~ —H.L.Matthews⟩ ⟨the tank . . . a formidable ~, is the modern scientific equivalent of the armored knight —G.R.Harrison⟩

**²juggernaut** \ˈ"\ *vt* -ED/-ING/-S **:** to crush under a juggernaut

**jugging** *pres part of* JUG

**jug·gins** \ˈjəgənz\ *n* -ES [prob. fr. the name *Juggins*] **:** one easily victimized **:** SIMPLETON ⟨was a clumsy ~ and let the ladder get out of control —Edith C. Rivett⟩

**¹jug·gle** \ˈjəgəl\ *vb* **juggled; juggled; juggling** \-g(ə)liŋ\ **juggles** [ME *jogelen*, fr. MF *jogler* to joke, sing, fr. L *joculari* to joke, fr. *joculus* little joke, fr. *jocus* joke + *-ulus* — more at JOKE] *vi* **1 :** to perform the tricks of a juggler **:** engage in feats of manual dexterity ⟨the conjurer ~s with two oranges —R.L.Stevenson⟩ **2 :** to practice deceit **:** CHEAT, TRICK ⟨never ~s or plays tricks with her understanding —Charles Lamb⟩ **3 a :** to engage in manipulation esp. for the purpose of achieving a desired end ⟨the facts were unchangeable — it was useless to ~ with them —O.E.Rölvaag⟩ **b :** to make necessary adjustments **:** JIGGLE ⟨pilot bent to the instrument panel and ~*ed* quickly with his massed controls —Nevil Shute⟩ **4 :** to advance a ball by means of a juggle (as in girls' basketball) ~ *vt* **1 a** (1) **:** to practice deceit or trickery on **:** BEGUILE ⟨is't possible the spells of France should ~ men into such strange mysteries —Shak.⟩ (2) **:** to gain by deceit or trickery — usu. used with *out of* ⟨was simply ~*ing* money out of the pockets of the poor —S.E.Morison & H.S.Commager⟩ **b :** to engage in manipulation with esp. for the purpose of achieving a desired end ⟨~*ed* railroads as though they were letters in a Scrabble game —Bennett Cerf⟩ ⟨could ~ mathematical formulas in such a way as to make the ordinary man dizzy —A.W.Long⟩ **2 a :** to toss in or as if in the manner of a juggler ⟨~s nine balls at the same time⟩ ⟨a huge fire would already be ~*ing* its golden coronets in the fireplace —Osbert Sitwell⟩ **b :** to hold or balance insecurely or precariously ⟨tried to catch the ball but only *juggled* it⟩ **c :** to twist and turn **:** jiggle with ⟨~s the steering wheel to straighten the car⟩ **3 :** to advance (as a basketball) by means of a juggle

**²juggle** \ˈ"\ *n* -s **1 :** an act or instance of juggling: **a :** a trick of magic **b :** a show of manual dexterity **c :** an act of manipulation esp. for the purpose of achieving a desired end **:** DECEPTION, TRICKERY ⟨quieted by a ~ the apprehension about the size of the public debt —T.B.Macaulay⟩ ⟨a result of their royal father's unscrupulous ~ with the coinage —G.M.Trevelyan⟩ **2 :** the act of advancing a ball by tossing or tapping it into the air and catching it again usu. after taking several steps to gain ground (as in speedball or girls' basketball)

**³juggle** \ˈ"\ *n* -s [perh. alter. of ³*joggle*] **:** a block of timber cut to a specified length

**⁴juggle** \ˈ"\ *dial Eng var of* JOGGLE

**jug·gler** \ˈjəg(ə)lə(r)\ *n* -s [ME *jogelour, joglere*, fr. OE *geogelere*, fr. OF *joglere* joker (accus. *jogleour*), fr. L *joculator*, fr. *joculatus* (past part. of *joculari* to joke) + *-or*] **1 a :** one that performs tricks or acts of magic ⟨one of England's best generals with more tricks up his sleeve than a roving ~ —F.V.W.Mason⟩ **b :** one that is practiced in acts of manual dexterity; *esp* **:** one skilled in keeping several objects in motion in the air at the same time by alternately tossing and catching them **2 :** one that manipulates or deceives esp. for the purpose of achieving a desired end ⟨suave and unscrupulous ~ of words —H.J.Muller⟩

**jug·glery** \-glərē, -ri\ *n* -ES [ME *jogelrye*, fr. OF *joglerie*, fr. *jogler* to joke, sing, + *-erie* -ery] **1 :** the art or practice of a juggler ⟨dances, acts of ~, prayers, and songs are climaxed by the weird fire dance —*Nat'l Geographic*⟩ **2 :** manipulation or trickery often designed to achieve a desired end ⟨the bill merely looks like a rather disingenuous piece of ~ —*Economist*⟩ ⟨the ~ with which . . . he proved whatever he had a mind to —W.S.Maugham⟩

**jug-handled** \ˈ=,==\ *adj* [³*jug*] **:** not properly or fairly proportioned **:** ONE-SIDED ⟨trade between Canada and the U. S. is distinctly *jug-handled* —*Boston Herald*⟩

**jughead** \ˈ=,=\ *n* **1** *chiefly West & Midland* **a :** MULE **b :** a wild or stubborn horse **2** *chiefly West & Midland* **:** a stupid person **:** LUNKHEAD

**ju·glan·da·ce·ae** \,jü,glanˈdāsē,ē, -,glən-\ *n pl*, *cap* [NL, fr. *Jugland-*, *Juglans*, type genus + *-aceae*] **:** a family of trees (order Juglandales) that include the walnuts and hickories and are characterized by odd-pinnate leaves, apetalous staminate flowers in catkins, pistillate flowers with a perianth and solitary or few in a cluster, and a drupe with a fibrous or woody epicarp and a nutlike seed — **ju·glan·da·ceous** \ˌ=(,)=ˈdāshəs\ *adj*

**ju·glan·da·les** \,=(,)=ˈdā(,)lēz\ *n pl*, *cap* [NL, fr. *Jugland-*, *Juglans* + *-ales*] **:** an order or other group of Dicotyledoneae coextensive with the family Juglandaceae

**ju·glans** \ˈjü,glanz\ *n*, *cap* [NL *Jugland-*, *Juglans*, fr. L *juglandis*, *juglans* walnut, fr. *ju-* (fr. *Juppiter*, god of the sky) + *gland-*, *glans* acorn — more at DEITY, GLAND] **:** a genus (the type of the family Juglandaceae) of walnut trees characterized by the separation of the pith of the branchlets into thin plates and by the indehiscent husk and furrowed shell of the fruit — see BLACK WALNUT, BUTTERNUT, ENGLISH WALNUT

**ju·glar** \(ˈ)zhüˈglär\ *n* -s *usu cap* [after Joseph C. *Juglar* †1905 Fr. economist] **:** a business cycle of approximately nine years

**ju·glone** \ˈjü,glōn\ *n* -s [ISV *jugl-* (fr. NL *Juglans*) + *-one*; orig. formed as G *juglon*] **:** a reddish yellow crystalline compound $C_{10}H_5O_2(OH)$ that is obtained esp. from green shucks of walnuts and is the chief active principle of the brown hair dye from walnuts; 5-hydroxy-1,4-naphthoquinone

**jugoslavia** *usu cap, var of* YUGOSLAVIA

**jug plant** *n* **:** a perennial evergreen herb (*Asarum arifolium*) having solitary basal flowers shaped like an urn

**jugs** *pl of* JUG, *pres 3d sing of* JUG

**¹jugu·lar** \ˈjəgyələ(r)\ *sometimes* ˈjüg-, *chiefly in substand speech* ˈjəg(ə)l-\ *adj* [LL *jugularis*, fr. L *jugulum* collarbone, neck, throat; akin to L *jungere* to join — more at YOKE] **1 a :** of or relating to the throat or neck **b :** of or relating to the jugular vein ⟨~ pulsations⟩ **2 a** *of a fish* **:** having the ventral fins located on the throat anterior to the pectorals **b** *of a fin* **:** located on the throat **c :** of or relating to the fishes that have jugular fins

**²jugular** \ˈ"\ *n* -s **1 :** JUGULAR VEIN **2 :** a jugular fish

**jugu·la·res** \,jəgyəˈla(a)(,)rēz, ,jüg-\ *n pl*, *cap* [NL, fr. L, pl. of *jugularis* jugular] *in some esp former classifications* **:** an order or other group comprising teleost fishes with the ventral fins well forward on the throat that are now generally included in the order Percomorphi

**jugular foramen** *n* **:** a large irregular opening from the posterior cranial fossa that is bounded anteriorly by the petrous part of the temporal bone and posteriorly by the jugular notch of the occipital and that transmits the inferior petrosal sinus, the glossopharyngeal, vagus, and accessory nerves, and the internal jugular vein

**jugular fossa** *n* **:** a depression on the basilar surface of the petrous portion of the temporal bone

**jugular ganglion** *n* **:** SUPERIOR GANGLION

**jugular process** *n* **:** a lateral process of the occipital bone near each condyle articulating with the temporal bone

**jugular vein** *n* **:** any of several veins of each side of the neck: as **a :** a vein in man that collects the blood from the interior of the cranium, the superficial part of the face, and the neck, runs down the neck on the outside of the internal and common carotid arteries, and unites with the subclavian forms the innominate vein — called also *internal jugular vein* **b :** a smaller and more superficial vein in man that collects most of the blood from the exterior of the cranium and deep parts of the face and opens into the subclavian vein — called also *external jugular vein* **c :** a vein in man that commences near the hyoid bone and joins the terminal part of the external jugular or the subclavian — called also *anterior jugular vein*

**jugu·late** \ˈjəgyə,lāt, ˈjüg-\ *vt* -ED/-ING/-S [L *jugulatus*, past part. of *jugulare*, fr. *jugulum* collarbone, neck, throat] **:** to kill esp. by cutting the throat

**jugu·lum** \-ləm, ˈyügyəl-\ *n, pl* **jugu·la** \-lə\ [NL, fr. L, collarbone, neck, throat] **1 :** the lower throat or the part of the neck just above the breast of a bird **2 :** the jugum of an insect

**ju·gum** \ˈjügəm, ˈyü-\ *n, pl* **ju·ga** \-gə\ *or* **jugums** [NL, fr. L, yoke — more at YOKE] **1 a :** one of the ridges commonly found on fruits of plants of the family Ammiaceae **b :** a pair of the opposite leaflets of a pinnate leaf **2 :** the most posterior and basal region of an insect's wing that is modified in the primitive Lepidoptera as a backwardly directed basal lobe on the inner margin of the fore wings and that serves to couple the fore and hind wings during flight **3 :** a more or less complicated crossbar linking the two arms of the brachidium of certain brachiopods

**ju·gur·thine** \jüˈgərthən, -,thīn\ *adj*, *usu cap* [L *jugurthinus*, fr. *Jugurtha* †104 B.C. king of Numidia defeated and captured by the Romans + L *-inus* -ine] **:** of or relating to Jugurtha or his reign ⟨the *Jugurthine* War⟩

**¹juice** \ˈjüs\ *n* -s [ME *juis, jus*, fr. OF *jus* broth, gravy, juice, fr. L; akin to ON *ostr* cheese, Skt *yūṣa* soup, broth] **1 :** the extractable fluid contents of plant cells or plant structures ⟨tomato ~⟩ ⟨lime ~⟩ **2 a :** the extractable fluid contents of animal cells and flesh ⟨press all the ~ from the meat⟩ **b :** the natural fluids of an animal body (as blood, lymph, and secretions) **c :** the liquid or moisture contained in or coming from something ⟨mineral ~s in the earth —John Woodward †1728⟩ **3 a :** the inherent quality of a thing **:** inner warmth and vitality **:** ESSENCE ⟨merely as literary productions, they are bursting with authentic human ~s —G.W.Johnson⟩ **b :** robust life **:** strength and vigor **:** VITALITY ⟨in the old days there were the pioneers . . . full of ~ and jests —Sinclair Lewis⟩ ⟨dismiss any writing with the ~ of life in it as mere journalism —J.D.Adams⟩ **4 :** a fluid or medium (as electricity, gasoline, oil) that supplies power ⟨ship's scout-bombing groups had traveled just enough farther . . . to leave them short of ~ to get home —Fletcher Pratt⟩

**²juice** \ˈ"\ *vt* -ED/-ING/-S **1 a :** to extract the juice of ⟨*juiced* and canned the tomatoes⟩ **b** *dial* **:** MILK **2 :** to add juice to **:** supply with juice ⟨*juiced* the apple pies⟩

**juiced rehearsal** *n* **:** a dress rehearsal of a television program in which the mechanical equipment is used as if for the final production

**juice·less** \ˈjüsləs\ *adj* **1 :** lacking moisture **:** DRY **2 :** lacking interest or stimulation **:** LIFELESS ⟨dull and ~ as only book knowledge can be when it is unrelated to . . . life —John Mason Brown⟩

**juice pear** *also* **juicy pear** *n* **:** JUNEBERRY

**juic·er** \ˈjüsə(r)\ *n* -s **1 :** an electrician who arranges the lighting for a stage set (as for a theater or television) **2 :** an appliance with which juice is extracted from fruit or vegetables

**juice up** *vt* **:** to give life, energy, or spirit to **:** ANIMATE ⟨the show is *juiced up* by its stars —Wendell Brogen⟩ ⟨*juice up* an otherwise dull evening⟩

**juic·i·ly** \ˈjüsəlē, -li\ *adv* **:** in a juicy manner ⟨"how about a nice thick steak," she said ~ —Thomas Wolfe⟩

**juic·i·ness** \-sēnəs, -sin-\ *n* -ES **:** the quality or state of being juicy

**juicy** \ˈjüsē, -si\ *adj* -ER/-EST [ME *jousy*, fr. *jous, juis, jus* juice + *-y*] **1 :** abounding with juice **:** SUCCULENT ⟨ate red beef and ~ pork —F.V.W.Mason⟩ **2 :** having a high profit potential **:** financially rewarding **:** FAT **3 a** ⟨found the rewards of business *juicier* than the rewards of politics —Josephine Pinckney⟩ ⟨route over the old Spanish Main is a ~ strip for commercial flying —*Harper's*⟩ **3 a :** RAINY, MOIST, DAMP **b :** wet and sloppy underfoot ⟨sun was shining palely upon . . . roads ~ with black mud —Arnold Bennett⟩ **4 a :** rich in interest **:** COLORFUL, DISTINCTIVE ⟨~ human tradition that produced the masculine brown harmonies of the English pub —Lewis Mumford⟩ **b :** RACY, PIQUANT ⟨the story had all the elements of a ~ scandal —W.A.White⟩ **c :** lusty and full-blown **:** full of vitality ⟨as ripe and ~ a canteen manageress . . . as ever wore frilly crepe de chine —John Metcalf⟩ **d :** VIGOROUS ⟨had the distinct impression . . . that this particular kick had been a ~ one —E.F.Benson⟩

**ju·ji·tsu** *or* **ju·jut·su** *or* **jiu·jit·su** *or* **jiu·jut·su** \jüˈjit(,)sü *sometimes* -ˈjət- *or* -ˈjüt-\ *n* -s [Jap *jūjutsu*, fr. *jū* weakness, gentleness (fr. Chin—Pek—*jou²* soft, gentle) + *jutsu* art, fr. Chin (Pek) *shu⁴*] **:** the Japanese art of self-defense without weapons that depends for its efficiency largely upon the principle of making use of an opponent's strength and weight to disable or injure him — see JUDO

**ju·ju** \ˈjü(,)jü\ *n* -s [of West African origin; akin to Hausa *djudju* fetish, evil spirit] **1 :** a fetish, charm, or amulet of West African tribes ⟨the ~ consisted of a bunch of chicken feathers well soaked in chicken blood and held together by strips of snakeskin —*Time*⟩ **2 :** the magic attributed to or associated with the use of a juju ⟨no one ever would have thought that the old man . . . was in any way connected with ~ —H.L.Ballowe⟩

**ju·jube** \ˈjü,jüb\ *n* -s [ME, fr. ML *jujuba*, alter. of L *zizyphum*, fr. Gk *zizyphon*] **1 a :** an edible drupaceous fruit of a tree of the genus *Ziziphus* **:** CHINESE DATE **b** *also* **jujube tree :** a tree that produces jujubes; *broadly* **:** a tree of the genus *Ziziphus* **2 :** a fruit-flavored gumdrop or lozenge

**juke** \ˈjük, ˈju̇k\ *vi* -ED/-ING/-S [prob. alter. of ¹*jouk*] *chiefly South* **:** to mess around

**juke·box** \ˈjük,bäks, *chiefly southern US* ˈju̇k,- *or* ˈjüt,-\ *or* **juke** *n, pl* **jukeboxes** *or* **jukes** [Gullah *juke, joog* disorderly, wicked] **:** a cabinet containing an automatic player and numerous phonograph records that are played by inserting a coin in a slot and usu. pushing a button to choose a record

**juke joint** *n* [Gullah *juke, joog* disorderly, wicked (in *juke house* brothel), of West African origin; akin to Wolof *dzug* to lead a disorderly life, Bambara *dzugu* wicked] **:** an establishment having a jukebox; *esp* **:** a small inexpensive establishment for eating, drinking, or dancing to the music of a jukebox

**jukes** \ˈjüks\ *n, pl* **jukes** \ˈ"\ *also* **jukeses** \-ksəz\ *usu cap* [*Jukes*, fictitious name of a family that was the subject of a study of hereditary tendencies to crime, immorality, disease, and poverty by Richard L. Dugdale †1883 Am. sociologist] **:** a stupid person ⟨before the Revolution, more than fifty thousand of England's *Jukes* . . . poured into the colonies —Charles Hamilton⟩ — compare KALLIKAK

**ju·lep** \ˈjüləp\ *n* -s [ME, fr. MF, fr. Ar *julāb*, fr. Per *gulāb* rose water, julep, fr. *gul* rose + *āb* water — more at ABKAR] **1 :** a drink consisting usu. of sweet syrup, flavoring, and water designed to soothe or stimulate ⟨a very soft well-flavored pleasant saccharine ~ —W.S.Coleman⟩ **2 a :** a tall drink made from gin, rum, or other alcoholic liquor and sometimes flavored with citrus juice ⟨gin ~⟩ ⟨orange ~⟩ **b :** a tall drink consisting of bourbon, sugar, and mint served in a frosted tumbler filled with finely crushed ice — called also *mint julep*

**ju·lian** \ˈjülyən\ *adj*, *usu cap* [L *julianus*, fr. Gaius *Julius* Caesar †44 B.C. Roman general and statesman + L *-anus* -an] **:** of, relating to, or characteristic of Julius Caesar

**julian calendar** *n*, *usu cap J* **:** a calendar introduced in Rome in 46 B.C. establishing the twelve-month year of 365 days with each fourth year having 366 days, the months each having 31 or 30 days except for February which has 28 or in leap years 29 days — compare GREGORIAN CALENDAR

**julian day calendar** *n*, *usu cap J* **:** a system used esp. by astronomers of numbering days consecutively from the arbitrarily selected point of the year 4713 B.C. instead of by cycles of days

**julian day number** *n*, *usu cap J* **:** the number of a day in the Julian day calendar (as 2,436,934 for Jan. 1, 1960)

**ju·lian·ist** \ˈjülyənəst\ *n* -s *usu cap* [*Julian*, 6th cent. bishop of Halicarnassus + E *-ist*] **:** a follower of Julian the Monophysite — compare APHTHARTODOCETAE

**julian period** *n*, *usu cap J* [*julian*, adj.] **:** a chronological period of 7980 Julian years that combines the solar and lunar cycles and the Roman indiction cycle and is reckoned from the year 4713 B.C. when the first years of these cycles coincided

**julian year** *n*, *usu cap J* **:** the year of exactly 365 days, 6 hours adopted in the Julian calendar

**¹ju·lid** \ˈjüləd\ *adj* [NL *Julidae*] **:** of or relating to the Julidae

**²julid** \ˈ"\ *n* -s [NL *Julidae*] **:** a millipede of the family Julidae

**ju·li·dae** \ˈjülə,dē\ *n pl*, *cap* [NL, fr. *Julus*, type genus + *-idae*] **:** a family of millipedes (class Diplopoda) having a cylindrical body composed of more than 30 rings and many eyes usu. crowded together in a cluster

**ju·lien·ite** \ˈjülyə,nīt\ *n* -s [Flem *juliëniet*, fr. Henry *Julien* †1920 Belg. geologist + Flem *-iet* -ite] **:** a mineral $Na_2Co(SCN)_4.8H_2O$ consisting of a hydrous thiocyanate of sodium and cobalt that occurs in small blue needlelike crystals

**¹ju·lienne** \,jüleˈen, (ˈ)jülˈyen, ˈzhü-, (ˈ)zhü-\ *n* -s [F, prob. fr. the name *Julienne*] **:** a clear soup containing julienne vegetables

**²julienne** \ˈ"\ *adj* **:** cut in long thin strips — used esp. of vegetables and fruit ⟨~ potatoes⟩ ⟨~ peaches⟩ ⟨garnished with ~ carrots⟩

**ju·liet** \ˈjülyət, ˈjüle͵et\ *also* ˈjüleə| *or* (ˈ)jülˈyet; *usu* |d·+V\ *n* -s [*Juliet*, heroine of Shakespeare's tragedy *Romeo and Juliet* (1594–95)] **:** a woman's slipper with a high front and back and low-cut sides — compare ROMEO

**juliet cap** *n*, *usu cap J* **:** a woman's skullcap that is often made of elaborately decorated mesh and used esp. for semiformal and bridal wear

Juliet cap

**ju·li·ett** \ˈjüle͵et\ *usu cap* [prob. irreg. fr. *Juliet*] — a communications code word for the letter *j*

**ju·lio** *or* **giu·lio** \ˈjül(,)yō\ *n* -s [It *giulio*, after Pope *Julius* II †1513 (It *Giulio* II)] **:** an Italian silver coin

**ju·lius cae·sar cipher** \ˈjülyə(s)ˈsēzə(r)-\ *n*, *usu cap J & 1st C* [after Gaius *Julius Caesar* †44 B.C. Roman general and statesman] **:** a substitution cipher replacing each plaintext letter by one that stands later in the alphabet

**jul·lun·dur** \ˈjələndə(r)\ *adj*, *usu cap* [fr. *Jullundur*, city in northwestern India] **:** of or from the city of Jullundur, India **:** of the kind or style prevalent in Jullundur

**ju·lus** \ˈjüləs\ *n*, *cap* [NL, fr. Gk *ioulos* catkin, down, wood louse; perh. akin to L *volvere* to roll — more at VOLUBLE] **:** a widely distributed genus of millipedes that is the type of the family Julidae

**ju·ly** \(ˈ)jüˈlī, jəˈlī, jüˈ-\ *n* -s *usu cap* [ME *julie*, fr. OE *julius*, fr. L, after Gaius *Julius* Caesar †44 B.C. Roman general and statesman who was born in this month] **:** the seventh month of the Gregorian year — see MONTH table

**july hound** *n*, *usu cap J* **:** a small chiefly white hound of U. S. origin

**ju·ma·da** \jəˈmädə\ *n* -s *usu cap* [Ar *jumādā*] **:** one of the two months Jumada I and Jumada II of the Muhammadan year — see MONTH table

**ju·ma·no** \,zhüməˈnō\ *n, pl* **jumano** *or* **jumanos** *usu cap* **1 :** a Uto-Aztecan people of northwestern Chihuahua, Mexico, and prob. a subdivision of the Suma **2 :** a member of the Jumano people

**ju·mart** \ˈjü,mart\ *n* -s [F, fr. Prov *gimerro, jamerro, chimarro*, fr. OProv *jumerra*, fr. L *chimaera* chimera] **:** a mythical offspring of a bull and a mare or an ass or of a horse or ass and a cow

**¹jum·ble** \ˈjəmbəl\ *vb* **jumbled; jumbled; jumbling** \-b(ə)liŋ\ **jumbles** [perh. of imit. origin] *vi* **1 :** to move in a confused or disordered mass **:** move in pell-mell fashion ⟨the soldiers *jumbled* through the door —Robert McLaughlin⟩ **2 a** *archaic* **:** to make discordant sounds **b :** to mingle in a confused or disordered manner **:** form a jumble ⟨entrances and exits tended to ~ —*Time*⟩ **3** *archaic* **:** to travel with jolts ~ *vt* **1 :** to mix in a confused mass **:** put or throw together without order — often used with *up* ⟨~s the stories up, giving no indication of when they were written —Edmund Wilson⟩ ⟨*jumbled* up the members of the chorus . . . to suit his pictorial effect —Edward Sackville-West⟩ **2** *archaic* **:** to stir, agitate, or jolt about **:** shake up ⟨a beast . . . whose trot would ~ me —William Cowper⟩

**²jumble** \ˈ"\ *n* -s **1 :** an assemblage of things mingled together without order, coherence, sequence, or plan **:** a confused, amorphous, or disordered mass **:** MEDLEY ⟨picturesque ~s of steep roofs, balconies, gables, dormers, and many chimneys —T.E.Tallmadge⟩ ⟨a ~ of fishing craft —Martin

Chisholm⟩ ⟨a thick ~ of technical terms and apparatus —Shirley A. Briggs⟩ ⟨our plans fell into a ~ —Carleton Beals⟩ ⟨an architectural ~⟩ **2** *archaic* : an instance of jolting or of being jolted : SHOCK, JOLT **3** *Brit* : articles for a rummage sale ⟨most of the stuff was very inferior ~ —Nigel Balchin⟩; *also* : RUMMAGE SALE ⟨they had a pair at the ~ —H.E.Bates⟩ **syn** see CONFUSION

**³jumble** *or* **jum·bal** \"\ *n* -s [*jumble* alter. (prob. influenced by ¹*jumble*) of earlier *jumbal*, prob. alter. of obs. *gimbal* finger ring — more at GIMBAL] : a small thin sugared cake usu. shaped like a ring

**jumbled** *adj* : lacking order, coherence, sequence, or plan : constituting a jumble ⟨a vast ~ waste —Henry Miller⟩ ⟨put his feet on the ~ desk —David Wagoner⟩ ⟨a ~ neighborhood of tenement houses, cheap stores —*New Yorker*⟩ ⟨my ~ memories fall harmoniously into patterns —David Daiches⟩

**jum·ble·ment** \-lmənt\ *n* -s : the act or an instance of jumbling : the fact of being jumbled

**jumble sale** *n, Brit* : RUMMAGE SALE

**jum·bling·ly** *adv* : in a jumbling manner

**jum·bly** \-blē\ *adj* : JUMBLED, CONFUSED

**¹jum·bo** \ˈjəm(ˌ)bō\ *n* -s [fr. *Jumbo*, an elephant exhibited by P.T.Barnum] **1** : a very large or huge specimen of its kind ⟨their size varies from the circumference of a small orange to ~s larger than a basketball —Charlotte D. Widrig⟩ **2 a** : a traveling carriage for mounting drills or saws or for transporting excavated material (as in tunnel driving) **b** (1) : a main-lead logging block (2) : a tongueless double sled used esp. for hauling logs short distances **c** (1) : a forestaysail esp. on an American schooner (2) : a triangular sail set point downward on the foreyard of a square-rigged ship or a topsail schooner in place of the regular foresail **d** : a record of car movements as posted on oversize sheets of paper maintained in a loose-leaf binder

**²jumbo** \"\ *adj* : being a very large specimen of its kind : HUGE ⟨a symphony does not need a ~ orchestra for its performance —Ross Parmenter⟩ ⟨flashed their ~ diamonds —Dawn Powell⟩

**jum·bo·ism** \-mbōˌizəm\ *n* -s : admiration for or worship of bigness ⟨too many Americans today are afflicted with ~ —*Springfield (Mass.) Union*⟩

**jumbo roll** *n* **1** : the full-width roll of trimmed paper as it comes from the paper machine **2** : a large roll of paper that is over 10 (or sometimes 12) inches in diameter and is to be used in converting operations

**jum·buck** \ˈjəmˌbək\ *n* [native name in Australia] *Austral* : SHEEP

**jum·by** *or* **jum·bie** \ˈjəmbē\ *n, pl* **jumbies** [modif. of Kongo *zumbi* fetish, spirit] *dial* : an evil spirit, ghost, or minor demon esp. in Negro belief and folklore

**jumby bean** *or* **jumby tree** *n* **1 a** : a West Indian necklace tree (*Ormosia monosperma*) **b** *West Indies* : the common lead tree (*Leucaena glauca*) **2** *or* **jumby bead** : the seed of a jumby bean

**ju·melle** \(ˈ)jüˈmel\ *adj* [F, fem. of *jumeau*, fr. MF, fr. OF *jumel*, fr. L *gemellus*, adj. & n., twin, dim. of *geminus* — more at GEMINATE] : TWIN, PAIRED — used of objects made or formed in pairs ⟨a ~ window opened upon the little balcony —John Bennett⟩

**ju·ment** \ˈjümənt\ *n* -s [ME, fr. L *jumentum*; akin to L *jungere* to join — more at YOKE] *archaic* : BEAST; *esp* : BEAST OF BURDEN

**jum·ma** \ˈjəmə\ *n* -s [Hindi *jama* collection, amount, fr. Ar *jamaʿ* total, aggregate] *India* : ASSESSMENT

**jum·na·pa·ri** \ˌjəmnəˈpärē\ *n, usu cap* [Hindi] : an Indian breed of milch goats

**¹jump** \ˈjəmp\ *vb* -ED/-ING/-S [prob. akin to Sw *gumpa* to jump, LG *gumpen*] *vi* **1 a** (1) : to move or throw itself into or through the air ⟨a pretty stream ~*ing* and twisting down to sea⟩ : REAR ⟨the light ~*ed* up —Guy McCrone⟩ (2) : to rise and fall agitatedly or abruptly ⟨the formerly placid waters were . . . ~*ing* —Francis Birtles⟩ ⟨the snow ~*ed* in tiny cloud puffs —Victor Canning⟩ **b** (1) : to spring free from the ground or some other environing medium by the muscular action of the feet and legs or in some animals the tail : project oneself through the air : SPRING, LEAP, HOP ⟨a trout will ~ several feet —John Burroughs⟩ ⟨~*ed* on a moving bus⟩ ⟨~*ed* out of bed⟩ ⟨~*ed* down from the tree⟩; *also* : to rise to one's feet with a bound or other energetic movement ⟨~*ed* up and vigorously protested the chairman's action⟩ (2) : to make a sudden spasmodic movement as a result of surprise or other nervous shock : START ⟨~*ed* at his unexpected entry⟩ (3) *in board games* : to move over a position occupied by an opponent's man to a vacant one beyond and capture the man (as in checkers) or to so move merely to facilitate progress to one's goal (as in Chinese checkers) (4) : to pass over a regular or proper stopping point : SKIP ⟨this typewriter ~s and needs repairing⟩ (5) *of a published item* : to continue from one column or page to another (6) : to undergo a vertical or lateral displacement owing to improper alignment of the film on a projector mechanism ⟨images ~ on the screen⟩ (7) : to drop from an airborne airplane with a parachute (8) : to commence or launch upon a drive, march, expedition, or other enterprise : start out : BEGIN — used with *off* ⟨the campaign ~*ed* off to a good start⟩ ⟨~*ed* off for the distant mining country⟩; *specif* : to start forward in a military attack ⟨at 11:01 a.m. the assault companies ~*ed* off —P.W.Thompson⟩ ⟨the attack ~*ed* off in good weather —*Military Engineer*⟩ (9) : to move, obey, or act with energy or alacrity : HUSTLE ⟨when he spoke he expected people to ~ —T.O.Thoman⟩ ⟨said he wanted them to ~ to it —Earle Birney⟩ ⟨the first thing the new bureaucrat learns is this: when the phone rings — ~ —*Newsweek*⟩ **2** : COINCIDE, AGREE, ACCORD — usu. used with *with* ⟨it ~s with my humor —Shak.⟩ ⟨that choice ~s with the spirit of the age —J.C.Powys⟩ **3 a** (1) : to pass or move haphazardly or aimlessly from one thing or state to another : shift abruptly ⟨the author ~s from region to region —*Geog. Jour.*⟩ ⟨~*ing* from job to job —Albert Deutsch⟩ (2) : to change or abandon employment esp. in violation of contract ⟨~*ed* to the Mexican League . . . and drew a five-year ban —*Springfield (Mass.) Daily News*⟩ ⟨~*ed* without notice —Fred Bradna & Hartzell Spence⟩ (3) : to rise or climb abruptly from one rank, status, or condition to another often with omission of intermediate stages ⟨~*ed* rapidly from captain through all the grades to colonel —H.H.Arnold & I.C. Eaker⟩ ⟨~*ed* from the Stone Age to the Iron Age without any intervening copper or bronze culture period —R.W.Murray⟩ (4) : to increase suddenly and sharply ⟨recruiting began to ~ that very evening —W.G.Shepherd⟩ ⟨population is ~*ing* —W.A.Bridges⟩ (5) : to make a jump bid in bridge **b** (1) : to make a judgment precipitately or without careful study of one's premises : make a mental leap ⟨inclined to ~ from some general observation to the first possible solution —W.J. Reilly⟩ ⟨before you ~ to that happy but unwarranted assumption —S.L.Payne⟩ ⟨no impressionist who ~s hastily to conclusions —C.I.Glicksberg⟩ (2) : to accept eagerly : take quick or immediate advantage — usu. used with *at* ⟨~*ed* at the job⟩ ⟨~*ed* at the chance⟩ (3) : to join, enter, or intervene with eagerness or alacrity — usu. used with *in* or *into* ⟨as unhealthy as if . . . the military ~*ed* in, in the recognition that a literate and educated population was important for the quality of future draftees —R.L.Meier & Eugene Rabinowitch⟩ ⟨~*ed* into this . . . business on twenty-four hour notice —F.D.Roosevelt⟩ and in such phrases as *jump aboard* ⟨finally ~*ed* aboard bolshevism —A.M.Rosenthal⟩ and *jump on the bandwagon* ⟨exhibiting a desire to ~ on the bandwagon —M. F.A.Montagu⟩ **4 a** : to attack suddenly or without warning : POUNCE — often used with *on* or *upon* ⟨~*ed* upon them without reason —*Pasadena (Calif.) Independent*⟩ **b** : to give a tongue-lashing : level severe criticism or censure ⟨~*ed* all over me for it⟩ — often used with *on* or *upon* ⟨people who ~ on modern poetry as obscure —*Time*⟩ or in the phrase *jump down one's throat* ⟨whenever I opened my mouth he ~s down my throat —W.S.Gilbert⟩ **5 a** : SWING ⟨the jazz they do blow is interesting and ~s —*Metronome Yearbook*⟩ ⟨whole thing ~s splendidly —*Jazz Jour.*⟩ **b** : to be very lively : bustle with gaiety or activity ⟨the joint was really ~*ing* with kids —Maritta Wolff⟩ ⟨the town was ~*ing* —*Springfield (Mass.) Daily News*⟩ ⟨the place is beginning to ~ already —Chandler Brossard⟩ ⟨Saturday night ~*ed* —Langston Hughes⟩ ~ *vt* **1 a** (1) : to pass over or across (a space or object) by or as if by a spring or leap : CLEAR ⟨~ a brook⟩ ⟨~ a hurdle⟩ ⟨took eight years before field trials ~*ed* the Atlantic —W.F.Brown b. 1903⟩ ⟨often ~ the border again the same day —*N.Y. Times*⟩ (2) *obs* : to expose to danger : RISK, HAZARD ⟨~ a body with dangerous physic —Shak.⟩ **b** *in board games* : to move over (a man) by jumping **c** (1) : to skip over or pass by : BYPASS ⟨the transmission of certain characteristics may ~ one or more . . . generations —Henry Wynmalen⟩ ⟨~ electrical connections⟩ (2) : to continue (as a newspaper story or article) from one column or page to another (3) : ANTICIPATE ⟨~ the green light⟩ ⟨~ the gun⟩ **d** (1) : to escape or run away from ⟨couldn't ~ his color —Thurston Scott⟩ (2) : to abandon or leave esp. hastily or furtively ⟨~ town without paying their bills —Hamilton Basso⟩ ⟨~*ed* their reservation and were on the warpath —P.A.Rollins⟩ (3) : to leave (employment) esp. in violation of contract or other obligation : breach (a labor contract) by leaving or taking other employment ⟨draft-age men ~*ing* essential war jobs —*Newsweek*⟩ ⟨wanted to ~ the show —Fred Bradna & Hartzell Spence⟩ ⟨~*ed* ship and settled in the United States —David Dodge⟩ ⟨~*ed* their indentures and bobbed up as journeymen in distant cities —*Newsweek*⟩ ⟨~ contract when tempted by more money —Harriot B. Barbour⟩ (4) : to turn off from (one's normal or appointed track or course) ⟨streams that ~*ed* their beds in the flood —*Springfield (Mass.) Union*⟩ ⟨a train ~*ed* the track⟩ (5) : to get aboard typically by jumping ⟨~*ed* a freight and rode it to town⟩ ⟨~ a crowded bus —W.J.Finn⟩ **2 a** (1) : to attack suddenly or unexpectedly : pounce upon ⟨thought he was snooping around and ~*ed* him —Lillian Hellman⟩ ⟨intended to ~ him, sitting or no —Shelby Foote⟩ ⟨suddenly ~*ed* by an enemy patrol party —Ed Cunningham⟩; *specif* : to attack (a target) suddenly with military aircraft (2) : to scold or criticize severely : assail verbally : bawl out ⟨that she would never do . . . unless she were ~*ed* into it —F. M.Ford⟩ — often used with *out* ⟨~*ed* the little foreman out —Ross Santee⟩ ⟨went down to ~ the inspector out —F.B. Gipson⟩ **b** : to seize or take possession of in violation of another's rights : occupy illegally ⟨~ another man's claim⟩ ⟨~*ing* an assignment for the first time in his life —Michael Foster⟩ **c** : to have coitus with — usu. considered vulgar **3 a** (1) : to cause to jump ⟨the wind can ~ those flames one mile or five —Stirling Silliphant⟩ ⟨it ~s me out of bed —J.W. Noble⟩ ⟨had to ~ her from the stiles —Jane Austen⟩ (2) : to cause (game) to break cover : START, FLUSH ⟨~*ed* a mule deer —D.C. Peattie⟩ (3) : to come upon suddenly ⟨~*ed* the trail and took cover —H.L.Davis⟩ **b** (1) : to elevate in rank esp. by skipping intermediate ranks ⟨one of many junior officers ~*ed* several ranks to fill the void —*Newsweek*⟩ ⟨~*ed* him from instructor to full professor in two years —*Time*⟩ (2) : to raise (a bridge partner's bid) by more than one rank (3) : to increase esp. swiftly or sharply ⟨~*ed* admission prices from fifty cents to a dollar —F.B.Gipson⟩ **4** : to bore with a jumper (as in quarrying)

**syn** JUMP, LEAP, SPRING, BOUND, VAULT, and SALTATE mean, in common, to project oneself upward or through space by or as if by quick muscle action. JUMP, the most general, implies a muscular propelling, or any action resembling a muscular propelling, of the body upward or to a spot other than the one one is in, whether upward, on a level, or below one, or over some obstacle ⟨*jump* with fright⟩ ⟨*jump* three feet across a brook⟩ ⟨*jump* up onto a platform⟩ ⟨*jump* down from the truck⟩ ⟨*jump* over a wall⟩ LEAP, often interchangeable with JUMP, generally suggests a much greater muscular propulsion or a more spectacular result ⟨*leap* a high fence⟩ ⟨*leap* down from a platform⟩ ⟨go *leaping* across a field⟩ SPRING adds to JUMP or LEAP the idea of elasticity, lightness, or grace, stressing more the movement than the going to or over ⟨*spring* up into the air⟩ ⟨*spring* out of a cage⟩ ⟨a deer *springing* across the open field⟩ BOUND, like SPRING, emphasizes the movement but suggests vigor or strength and, often, a consequent forceful speed achieved by fast successive leaps forward ⟨a herd of antelope *bounding* gracefully across the plain⟩ ⟨the speaker, a large vigorous man, came *bounding* down the aisle and up onto the stage⟩ VAULT suggests a leap upward or over something with the aid of the hands laid on an object or with similar assistance ⟨rose to his feet . . . grabbed the sturdy milking stool by one leg, *vaulted* the fence, and plunged into the woods —C.G.D.Roberts⟩ ⟨an acrobat . . . was *vaulting* over chair backs —Margaret Deland⟩ SALTATE implies a jumping or leaping from place to place as in certain ballet movements

— **jump bail** : to abscond while at liberty under bail bonds — **jump over the broomstick** *or* **jump the broom** *dial* : to get married ⟨we ought to *jump the broom* —J.H.Stuart⟩ — **jump rope** : to jump over a rope held by its two ends by the jumper or by two other persons and swung around the jumper from head to foot, or back and forth under the feet — **jump the queue** *Brit* **1** : to go ahead of a waiting line (as at a theater window) ⟨attempt to *jump the queue* is to court disaster —*London Calling*⟩ **2** : to seek to obtain something in advance of one's turn : obtain preferential treatment ⟨*jumping the* allied *queue* and seeking a special arrangement —*Economist*⟩ — **jump the traces 1** *of a horse* : to jump over the traces **2** : to cast off restraint : display a rebellious or nonconformist spirit ⟨might *jump the traces* and precipitate a new round of fighting —Lindesay Parrott⟩ ⟨*jumped the traces* more than once —Maurice Ries⟩

**²jump** *adv, obs* : EXACTLY, PAT

**³jump** \ˈjəmp\ *n* -s **1 a** (1) : an act of jumping : LEAP, SPRING, BOUND ⟨cleared the fence with a running ~⟩ (2) : any of several sports competitions featuring a leap, spring, or bound — see BROAD JUMP, HIGH JUMP (3) : a space cleared or traversed by a leap (4) : an obstacle to be jumped over (as on the course of a steeplechase) simulating natural obstructions met in fox hunting and of varied construction, dimensions, and number **b** (1) : a sudden spasmodic movement (as from surprise or other nervous shock) : START, TWITCH ⟨gave a ~ as she entered the room⟩ (2) : **jumps** *pl* : FIDGETS, WILLIES, NERVOUSNESS ⟨this place fairly gives me the ~s —G.K. Chesterton⟩ ⟨just got the ~s, I guess —Gore Vidal⟩ **c** *in board games* : a move made by jumping **d** : a descent by parachute from an airplane **e** : an act of coitus — usu considered vulgar **2** *obs* **a** : a critical point or crisis **b** : VENTURE, HAZARD **3 a** (1) : a movement made by the tube of a gun before a fired projectile leaves the muzzle (2) : a vertical deviation of the path of the trajectory from the line of elevation **b** : an abrupt interruption of level in a piece of brickwork or masonry **c** (1) : ⁴BORE (2) : BREAKER 3a **d** (1) : a sharp or sudden increase ⟨the ~ in the size of the entering freshman class —J. K.Folger⟩ (2) : JUMP BID (3) : a sudden change : a qualitative or quantitative leap : an abrupt transition ⟨social progress proceeds by ~s⟩ ⟨the ~ from the liquid to the gaseous state⟩ (4) : the continuation of a published item (as a newspaper story or article) from one column or page to another; *also* : the portion of a published item comprising such a continuation — compare BREAKOVER **e** (1) : a quick or short journey esp. by air : HOP ⟨reluctant to start a new round of . . . plane ~s —*Newsweek*⟩ ⟨a convenient one-night ~ from either St. Louis or Memphis —*Amer. Guide Series: Ark.*⟩ (2) : one in a series of moves from one place to another ⟨usually going farther west at each ~ —Dixon Wecter⟩ ⟨kept one ~ ahead of the sheriff⟩ **4** : an advantage esp. in time : START — usu. used in the phrase *get the jump* ⟨might get the ~ on the United States in the development of nuclear power —*N.Y. Times*⟩ ⟨desirous of getting the ~ on the competition —Elmer Davis⟩

**syn** JUMP, LEAP, SPRING, BOUND, and VAULT signify a single movement achieved by the corresponding action signified by the verb. SALTATION may indicate a sequence or group of such actions **syn** see in addition ¹JUMP

— **on the jump** *adv (or adj)* : on the go : very busy ⟨kept so much *on the jump* by the motel trade —W.L.Gresham⟩

**⁴jump** \"\ *adj* [prob. fr. ²*jump*] **1** *obs* : EXACT, FITTING, PRECISE **2** : constituting a jump bid in bridge ⟨~ response⟩ **3** : SWING ⟨a ~ band⟩

**⁵jump** \ˈjəmp, ˈjəmp\ *n* -s [prob. alter. of *jupe*] **1** *dial Brit* : a loose jacket for men **2** *dial Brit* : an underbodice worn — usu. instead of stays by women — usu. used in pl.

**jump·able** \ˈjəmpəbəl\ *adj* : capable of being jumped

**jump ball** *n* : a method of putting a basketball into play by tossing it in the air between two opponents who jump up and tap it; *also* : a ball put into play in this manner

**jump bid** *n* : a bridge bid of more tricks than are necessary in the denomination specified to overcall the preceding bid — called also *jump*

**jump boot** *n* : a boot worn by paratroopers

**jump dam** *n* : a dam designed to prevent the migration of fishes into unsuitable spawning waters

**jumped** *past of* JUMP

**jumped–up** \ˈ=ˌ=\ *adj* : newly or recently sprung up or arisen ⟨this unconcern for pedigree leads people to suppose that the English lords are a *jumped-up* lot —Nancy Mitford⟩ ⟨the hatred of *jumped-up* genius —Hesketh Pearson⟩

**¹jump·er** \ˈjəmpə(r)\ *n* -s [¹*jump* + *-er*] **1** : a person who jumps: as **a** *usu cap* : one of a revivalistic sect whose members jump, skip, hop up and down, clap their hands, shout, or otherwise demonstrate an intense spiritual excitation in their meetings — called also *Holy Jumper* **b** : a person who jumps another's claim **c** : a miner who drills with a jumper **d** : a person who quits his employment esp. in violation of contract or other obligation ⟨the special Army camp for drafted job ~s —*Newsweek*⟩ **e** : a delivery-route driver's helper **f** : an experienced employee who can help or substitute for one or more of the workers engaged in an industrial process — called also *handyman, utility man* **g** : a person who competes in a jumping event (as the broad jump or a ski jump) **2 a** : a drill or boring tool consisting of a bar which is jumped up and down in the borehole **b** : any of several sleds (as used by boys in coasting or for hauling merchandise over bare ground) **c** : JUMPER SLED **d** : a plowshare specially fitted for rough soil (as by having an upturned colter to cut roots); *also* : a plow having a moldboard so attached that it jumps out of the ground when it hits a stump **e** : SWAGE 2b **f** : stones used for leveling courses esp. in random-coursed ashlar **g** (1) : a short wire used to close a break or cut out part of a circuit (2) : the removable member of a train-line or truck-trailer coupling consisting usu. of two coupling plugs and a connecting cable **h** : HOSE BRIDGE **3** : any of several jumping animals: as **a** : a saddle horse trained to jump obstacles **b** : SMALLMOUTH BLACK BASS

**²jumper** \"\ *n* -s *often attrib* [prob. fr. ⁵*jump* + *-er*] **1 a** : a loose blouse, jacket, or smock worn esp. by workmen on the job **b** : a sleeveless dress or a skirt with a bib for women and girls worn usu. with a blouse or sweater **2 a** : a child's one-piece coverall for play or sleeping — usu. used in pl. **b** : a sailor's blouse having long sleeves and a broad square collar tapering to a V neck in front **c** *chiefly Brit* : a sweater for women or girls

jumper 1b

**jumper sled** *n* : a log sled having a high crosspiece on which one end of a log is supported while being dragged

**jumper stay** *n* : a stay or tackle set up esp. in heavy weather to prevent a yard or boom from jumping

**jump fire** *n* : a forest fire started some distance ahead of the main front of a larger fire by burning material carried ahead by wind

**jump head** *n* : a headline or heading identifying a jump (sense 3d[4])

**jump–hop** \ˈ=ˌ=\ *n* : a spring from both feet followed by a hop on one foot

**jumpier** *comparative of* JUMPY

**jumpiest** *superlative of* JUMPY

**jump·i·ness** \ˈjəmpēnəs, -pin-\ *n* -ES : the quality or state of being jumpy : NERVOUSNESS ⟨was better able to master his ~ —C.S.Forester⟩

**jumping** *adj* [fr. pres. part. of ¹*jump*] **1 a** : given to or characterized by making jumps ⟨a ~ animal⟩ **b** : used in making jumps ⟨a ~ pole⟩ **c** : featuring jumps ⟨a ~ race⟩ **2** : SWING ⟨a ~ band⟩

**jumping bean** *or* **jumping seed** *n* : a seed of any of several Mexican shrubs of the genera *Sebastiania* and *Sapium* of the family Euphorbiaceae that tumbles about because of movements of the contained larva of a small moth (*Carpocapsa saltitans*)

**jumping cactus** *also* **jumping cholla** *n* : CHOLLA

**jumping deer** *n* : MULE DEER

**jumping hare** *n* [trans. of Afrik *springhaas*, fr. D *springen* to jump + *haas* hare] : a sciuromorph rodent (*Pedetes cafer*) of southern and eastern Africa that resembles a kangaroo in form, that is about two feet long, and that is tawny brown in color and of nocturnal and social habits — called also *springhaas*

**jumping jack** *n* : a toy figure of a man jointed and made to jump or dance by means of strings or a sliding stick

**jump·ing·ly** *adv* : in a jumping manner

**jumping mouse** *n* : any of several small hibernating No. American myomorph rodents (family Zapodidae) with long hind legs and tail and no cheek pouches

**jumping mullet** *n* : a very active Australian gray mullet (*Mugil argenteus*) reputed to leap into boats

**jumping net** *or* **jumping sheet** *n, chiefly Brit* : LIFE NET

**jumping–off place** \ˌ==ˈ=ˌ=\ *n* **1 a** : a place regarded as marking the farthest limit of civilization : a remote or isolated place **b** : the end or edge of the world ⟨seemed suddenly to be at the end of the world, the *jumping-off place* —*Nat'l Geographic*⟩ **2** : a place from which some enterprise is launched : a point of departure ⟨a *jumping-off place* for the conquest of the rest of Europe —P.E.Mosely⟩ ⟨a *jumping-off place* for reflection —Maurice Valency⟩

**jumping orchid** *n* [so called fr. its habit of suddenly ejecting its pollen masses] : an orchid of the genus *Catasetum*

**jumping pit** *n* : the landing area for the high and broad jump and the pole vault events consisting of a pit filled with sawdust or soft loam to cushion the impact

**jumping plant louse** *n* [*jumping* + *plant louse*] : any of numerous plant lice constituting the family Psyllidae

**jumping rabbit** *n* : FIVE-TOED JERBOA

**jumping rat** *n* : any of numerous jumping rodents (as the jerboa, jumping mouse, and kangaroo rat)

**jumping shrew** *n* : ELEPHANT SHREW

**jumping spider** *n* : a spider of the family Salticidae

**jumping viper** *n* : a small rough-skinned stout-bodied pit viper (*Bothrops nummifer*) of Central America and Mexico that slides its body forward when striking thereby considerably increasing its attacking range

**jump joint** *n* [¹*jump*] **1** : BUTT JOINT **2** : a flush joint (as of plank or masonry)

**jump line** *n* : a directional line of print (as "continued on page 7, column 2") at the end of the first part of a divided story or article in a newspaper or periodical or a line (as "continued from page 1") at the continuation

**jumpmaster** \ˈ=ˌ==\ *n* : a person in charge of the jumping (as of parachute troops)

**jump–off** \ˈ=ˌ=\ *n* -s **1** : an act of jumping off : a place from which to jump off : the start of a race or an attack ⟨the *jump-off* was at twelve —Dan Levin⟩ **2** : an additional round of competition to determine the winner when two or more horses are tied after completion of the first round of jumping

**jump page** *n* : a page on which the continuation of a newspaper article appears

**jump pass** *n* : a pass executed by a player who jumps into the air and releases the ball before landing (as in football and basketball)

**jump ring** *n* : a circle of wire with ends meeting and not welded used as a connecting link in jewelry

**jump rope** *also* **jumping rope** *n* : a rope used in jumping rope — called also *skipping rope*

**jumps** *pres 3d sing of* JUMP, *pl of* JUMP

**jump saw** *n* : a crosscut circular saw in a sawmill that can be raised or lowered and is used for crosscutting timbers, boards, or slabs

**jump scrape** *n* : an implement resembling a plow that is used to complete ridges or levees for the check system of irrigation

**jump seat** *n* **1** : a movable carriage seat **2** : a folding seat between front and rear seats of a closed passenger automobile

**jumpseed** \'=,=\ *n* : VIRGINIA KNOTWEED
**jump shot** *n* **1** : a shot in billiards in which the cue ball is made to jump over an object ball **2** *also* **jump stroke** : a croquet shot made with a downward stroke of the mallet so that the ball jumps over an obstacle **3** : a shot made by a basketball player who jumps into the air and releases the ball with one or both hands at the peak of his jump
**jump spark** *n* : a spark produced by the jumping of electricity across a gap
**jump suit** *n* : a uniform worn by paratroopers for jumping
**jump turn** *n* **1** : a turn in the air executed by a skier who crouches, places the inner pole or both poles near the tip of the lower ski, pulls the knees up, jumps around the pole or poles, and lands in a crouch with the skis edged inward **2** : a turn in the air executed by a dancer who takes off with and lands on both feet
**jump weld** *n* : a butt weld in which one member is welded at right angles to a relatively larger part
**jumpy** \'jəmpē, -pi\ *adj* -ER -EST **1** : jumping or inducing to jump ⟨a ~ carriage⟩ : characterized by jumps or sudden variations ⟨the story . . . gets rather jerky and ~ —A.F.W. Plumptre⟩ **2** : NERVOUS, IRRITABLE, JITTERY ⟨if you didn't drink so much, you wouldn't be so ~ —Barnaby Conrad⟩ ⟨~ nerves⟩ : nervously apprehensive ⟨apprehension that bribes will be uncovered . . . makes senators as ~ as they are —R.H.Rovere⟩
**jun** *abbr* junior
**junc** *abbr* junction
**jun·ca·ceae** \,jəŋ'kāsē,ē\ *n pl, cap* [NL, fr. *Juncus*, type genus + *-aceae*] : a large widely distributed family of typically tufted herbs (order Liliales) resembling grasses and having a chaffy 6-parted perianth and a capsular fruit — **jun·ca·ceous** \;=;kāshəs\ *adj*
**jun·cag·i·na·ce·ae** \,jəŋ,kajə'nāsē,ē\ *n pl, cap* [NL, fr. *Juncagin-, Juncago*, type genus (fr. *Juncus*) + *-aceae*] : a family of marsh or bog herbs (order Naiadales) having leaves resembling rushes and small perfect flowers with 3 to 6 stamens and 3 to 6 carpels which separate at maturity
**jun·co** \'jəŋ(,)kō\ *n* [NL, fr. Sp, a bird, rush — more at JONQUIL] **1 a** *cap* : a genus of small American finches found from the arctic circle to Costa Rica usu. having a pink bill, ashy gray head and back, conspicuous white lateral tail feathers and often reddish brown on the back and sides **b** *pl* **juncos** *or* **juncoes** : any bird of this genus — see CAROLINA JUNCO, SLATE-COLORED JUNCO **2** *pl* **juncos** *or* **juncoes** [AmerSp, fr. Sp, rush] : ALLTHORN
**jun·coi·des** \,jəŋ'kȯi(,)dēz\ [NL, fr. *Juncus*, genus of marsh plants + L *-oides* -oid] *syn of* LUZULA
**¹junc·tion** \'jəŋ(k)shən\ *n* -S [L *junction-, junctio*, fr. *junctus* (past part. of *jungere* to join) + *-ion-, -io* -ion — more at YOKE] **1** : the act or an instance of joining or meeting : the state of being joined ⟨a ~ of two armies⟩ ⟨operates a ~ between the French spirit and German ideas and . . . culture —MatthewArnold⟩ **2 a** : a place or point of union or meeting ⟨at the ~ of two . . . fences —Thomas Hardy⟩ **b** *or* **junction point** : a place or point at which carrier lines meet or interchange traffic **c** : an intersection of roads or highways esp. where one of the highways terminates **3** : something that joins: as **a** : JUNCTION BOX **b** : a logical connective **c** : a grammatical unit formed by qualified and qualifying terms (as "the red barn") — compare NEXUS, RANK
**²junction** \"\ *vb* -ED/-ING/-S : to join at a junction
**junc·tion·al** \-shən³l, -shnəl\ *adj* : relating to junction
**junctional nevus** *n* : a nevus that develops at the junction of the dermis and epidermis and is potentially cancerous
**junction box** *n* : a box (as of metal) for enclosing the junction of electric wires and cables
**junc·tur·al** \'jəŋ(k)chərəl, -)sh(ə)rəl\ *adj* : of or relating to grammatical juncture
**junc·ture** \'jəŋ(k)chə(r), -(k)shə(r)\ *n* -S [ME, fr. L *junctura*, fr. *junctus* (past part. of *jungere* to join) + *-ura* -ure — more at YOKE] **1** : an instance of joining : UNION, JUNCTION ⟨at the ~ of four fields —*Think*⟩ ⟨the ~ of the American Third and Seventh armies —E.K.Lindley & Edward Weintal⟩ ⟨emphasizes the ~ of poetry and music —Gilbert Highet⟩ **2 a** : JOINT, ARTICULATION, CONNECTION, SEAM **b** : the manner of transition between two consecutive speech sounds or between a speech sound and a pause **3** : a point of time; *esp* : one made critical or important by a concurrence of circumstances ⟨at certain ~s in the dancing, the scalps were raised high in the air —G.H.Fathauer⟩ ⟨at this ~ in history⟩
**syn** PASS, EXIGENCY, EMERGENCY, CONTINGENCY, PINCH, STRAIT (OR STRAITS), CRISIS: these nouns all denote a critical or crucial time or state of affairs, as in the life of a person, an institution, or a country's history. JUNCTURE emphasizes the usu. significant concurrence or convergence of events ⟨we may now be at a vital *juncture* where the ideals of liberalism can best be achieved through separate institutions and not the omnicompetent state —P.W.Kurtz⟩ ⟨occasions when there may be genuine uncertainty as to who should become prime minister. At such a *juncture* it is highly desirable to have someone charged with the duty of inviting a suitable person to form a government —R.M.Dawson⟩ PASS is stronger than JUNCTURE in implying an evil or distressing concurrence or convergence of events or the condition induced by such a concurrence, or, sometimes, a dilemma brought about by it ⟨they did in a desperate *pass* the best they knew —J.J.Mallon⟩ ⟨the frightful *pass* to which destiny had brought her —Arnold Bennett⟩ EXIGENCY emphasizes the pressures brought to bear or the urgency of the demands created by a special situation, esp. a juncture or pass ⟨the *exigencies* of war⟩ ⟨such travel *exigencies* as having to scout around for a room when you're tired and want to hole up for the night —Richard Joseph⟩ ⟨social contacts for a presidential couple are pretty well restricted by official *exigencies* —S.H.Adams⟩ EMERGENCY, implying more of a crucial nature but less necessary difficulty than EXIGENCY, is a sudden, unforeseen juncture or pass calling for immediate action to avoid disaster ⟨a national *emergency*⟩ ⟨aid in helping to meet the *emergency* of a large number of unemployed youths —*Amer. Guide Series: Minn.*⟩ ⟨a great social *emergency*, teen-age delinquency —D.W.Maurer & V.H. Vogel⟩ CONTINGENCY is an event or concurrence of events that is fortuitous, only remotely possible, or uncertain of occurrence ⟨sense and ingenuity may be relied upon to cope with special *contingencies* —R.F.Heizer⟩ ⟨the bank had accumulated a surplus . . . which it held against future *contingencies* and risks —*Collier's Yr. Bk.*⟩ PINCH implies pressure or the need for action but without quite the same intensity as EMERGENCY or EXIGENCY ⟨could always in a *pinch* pawn my microscope for three pounds —W.S.Maugham⟩ ⟨ready in a *pinch* to ride roughshod over opposition —William Power⟩ STRAIT, now commonly STRAITS, applies to a troublesome situation from which escape is difficult because of hampering or binding circumstances ⟨a moment of financial *strait* —F.L. Paxson⟩ ⟨her father died and the family was left in dire financial *straits* —*Current Biog.*⟩ ⟨the army's truly desperate *straits* —F.V.W.Mason⟩ CRISIS applies to a juncture or pass whose outcome will make a decisive difference, esp. serving as a turning point as in a life, history, or the course of a disease ⟨her adolescence had passed without the trace of a religious *crisis* —Aldous Huxley⟩
**jun·cus** \'jəŋkəs\ *n* [NL, fr. L, rush — more at JONQUIL] **1** *cap* : a genus (the type of the family Juncaceae) of chiefly marsh plants of temperate regions that are perennial tufted glabrous herbs with mostly terete or channeled leaves **2** -ES : any plant of the genus *Juncus* — see RUSH
**¹jundy** *or* **jun·die** \'jəndi\ *n, pl* **jundies** [origin unknown] *Scot* : JOSTLE, JOG
**²jundy** *or* **jundie** \"\ *vb* **jundied; jundied; jundying; jundies** *Scot* : JOSTLE, JOG
**¹june** \'jün\ *n* -S *usu cap, often attrib* [ME *Junius, Juyn, June;* ME *Junius*, fr. OE & L; OE, fr. L, prob. fr. *Junius*, name of a Roman gens; ME *Juyn, June*, fr. MF & L; MF *juin*, fr. OF, fr. L *Junius*; prob. akin to L *Juno*, ancient Italian goddess] : the 6th month of the Gregorian calendar — see MONTH table
**²june** \"\ *vb* -ED/-ING/-S [origin unknown] *dial* : to drive briskly
**ju·neau** \'jü(,)nō\ *adj, usu cap* [fr. *Juneau*, Alaska] : of or from Juneau, the capital of Alaska : of the kind or style prevalent in Juneau

**june beetle** *or* **june bug** *n, often cap J* : any of numerous rather large leaf-eating scarabaeoid beetles that fly chiefly in late spring and have as larvae white grubs that live in soil and feed chiefly on the roots of grasses and other plants: as **a** : any of various large brown beetles (genus *Phyllophaga*) of eastern No. America **b** : GREEN JUNE BEETLE **c** : any of several European beetles (genus *Phyllopertha*) that are similar in appearance and habits to members of *Phyllophaga* **d** : any of several white-striped beetles (genus *Polyphylla*) of western No. America
**june·berry** \'jün — *see* BERRY\ *n, usu cap* **1** : any of various No. American trees and shrubs that constitute the genus *Amelanchier* and are sometimes cultivated for their showy white flowers or edible usu. purple or red fruits **2** : the fruit of a Juneberry
**junebud** \'=,=\ *n, usu cap* : REDBUD
**june drop** *n, usu cap J* : the falling of young fruit due to improper or incomplete fertilization, disease, or environmental factors at a maximum about June
**junefish** \'=,=\ *n* : SPOTTED JEWFISH
**juneflower** \'=,=\ *n, usu cap* : CANADA VIOLET
**june grass** *n, usu cap J* **1** : KENTUCKY BLUEGRASS **2** : a tufted grass (*Koeleria cristata*) abundant on prairies having narrow leaves and densely flowered terminal panicles like spikes — called also *crested hair grass, prairie June grass*
**june pink** *n, usu cap J* : SWAMP AZALEA
**june·teenth** \,jün·'tēn(t)th\ *n* -S *usu cap* [¹*june* + nine*teenth*] : June 19 observed as a general holiday by Negroes in Texas in celebration of the anniversary of the emancipation of slaves in the state
**june week** *n, usu cap J&W* : graduation week at West Point, Annapolis, and the U.S. Air Force Academy
**june yellows** *n pl but sing in constr, usu cap J* : a nonparasitic disease of strawberries due to a hereditary factor in some varieties and characterized esp. by yellow and green mottling and streaking of the leaves
**jung** \'jůŋ\ *n, pl* **jung** *or* **jungs** *usu cap* **1** : an ancient Tatar people of northwest China related to the Hsiung-nu, the Hu, and the Ti **2** : a member of the Jung people
**jun·ger·man·nia** \,jəŋgə(r)'manēə\ *n, cap* [NL, fr. Ludwig *Jungermann* †1653 Ger. botanist + NL *-ia*] : a formerly recognized genus of liverworts whose members are now included among various genera of the family Jungermanniaceae
**jun·ger·man·ni·a·ce·ae** \,==,=,manē'āsē,ē\ *n pl, cap* [NL, fr. *Jungermannia*, type genus + *-aceae*] : a family of liverworts comprising the acrogynous leafy members of the order Jungermanniales or in some esp. former classifications being coextensive with the order — see ACROGYNAE, ANACROGYNAE — **jun·ger·man·ni·a·ceous** \;==;=;=;āshəs\ *adj*
**jun·ger·man·ni·a·les** \,==,=,manē'ā(,)lēz\ *n pl, cap* [NL, fr. *Jungermannia*, genus of liverworts + *-ales*] : a large and widely distributed order of predominantly tropical liverworts that grow from a definite apical cell, that are characterized by marked diversity of form but with simple primitive tissue organization, and that include the leafy liverworts together with certain lower forms with terrestrial habits and a simple branching thallus or a leafless thalloid shoot — compare ACROGYNAE, ANACROGYNAE; see JUNGERMANNIACEAE
**¹jung·i·an** \'yůŋēən\ *n* -S *usu cap* [Carl G. *Jung* †1961 Swiss psychologist and psychiatrist + E *-ian*] : an adherent of the psychological doctrines of C. G. Jung
**²jungian** \"\ *adj, usu cap* **1** : of or relating to C. G. Jung whose psychological doctrines stress the opposition of introversion and extroversion and the concept of mythology and cultural and racial inheritance in the psychology of individuals **2** : of, relating to, or having the characteristics of the psychological doctrines of Jung
**¹jun·gle** \'jəŋgəl\ *n* -S *often attrib* [Hindi *jaṅgal*, fr. Skt *jāṅgala*] **1** *India* **a** : uncultivated ground **b** : land overgrown (as with brushwood) **2 a** : an impenetrable thicket or tangled mass of tropical vegetation some parts of which can be lived in by native people or wild animals **b** : a tract overgrown with thickets or masses of vegetation **3** : a hobo camp ⟨stays here all the time and runs this ~ —Burl Ives⟩ **4 a** (1) : a confused or chaotic mass or assemblage of objects : TANGLE, JUMBLE ⟨a ~ of gigantic tanks and curiously shaped pipes —*Amer. Guide Series: Ark.*⟩ ⟨an old-fashioned used-car junkyard ~ —N.F.Busch⟩ (2) : something that baffles, perplexes, or frustrates by its tangled, complex, or deviously intricate character : MAZE ⟨a perfect ~ of minute regulations —John Buchan⟩ ⟨~s of official indifference and red tape —*Time*⟩ ⟨a bureaucratic ~ of double-talk and evasions —P.B.Williamson⟩ ⟨difficult . . . to find one's way through the medieval ~ —G.G.Coulton⟩ **b** : a place or scene of ruthless struggle for survival ⟨turned international economy into a ~ —W.L.Clayton⟩ ⟨the ~ philosophy of big-business capitalism —T.E.N.Driberg⟩ ⟨a tale of teen-age gang violence in the concrete ~ —Arthur Gelb⟩
**²jungle** \"\ *vi* -ED/-ING/-S **1** : to inhabit a jungle ⟨tiny beasts that have *jungled* in that pale forest —John Galsworthy⟩ **2** : to camp in a hobo jungle ⟨*jungled* up with four others beside a creek —Nelson Algren⟩
**jungle ballot** *n* : BLANKET BALLOT
**jungle bear** *n* : SLOTH BEAR
**jungle cat** *n* : a small grayish to tawny Asiatic wildcat (*Felis chaus*) with slightly crested back, somewhat tufted ears, and obscure blotching and striping
**jungle cock** *n* : a male jungle fowl
**jun·gled** \-ld\ *adj* [¹*jungle* + *-ed*] : overgrown with jungle
**jungle fowl** *n* **1** : any of several Asiatic wild birds of the genus *Gallus; esp* : a bird (*G. gallus*) of southeastern Asia from which domestic fowls are believed to have descended **2 a** : an Australian megapode (*Megapodius reinwardtii tumulus*) **b** : any Australian species of the genus *Megapodius*
**jungle green** *n* : a very dark green
**jungle gym** *n* [fr. *Junglegym*, a trademark] : a three-dimensional structure of vertical and horizontal bars upon which children can climb and play

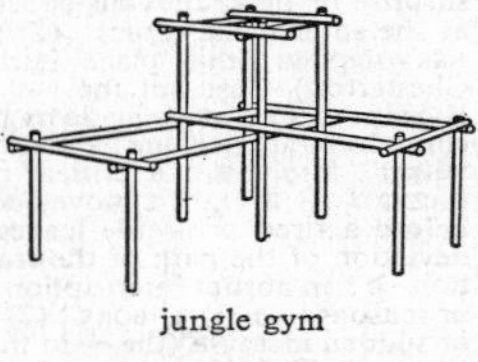
jungle gym

**jungle hen** *n* : a female jungle fowl
**jungle juice** *n* : a homemade or improvised alcoholic beverage; *esp* : one concocted by military personnel ⟨apt to be brewing on the ship fifteen different batches of *jungle juice* —T. O.Heggen⟩
**jungle mouse** *n* : any of several long-snouted often spiny-furred mice of southeastern Asia constituting the genus *Leggada*
**jungle rice** *n* : SHAMA MILLET
**jungle yellow fever** *n* : yellow fever endemic in or near forest or jungle areas in Africa and So. America and transmitted by mosquitoes other than members of the genus *Aedes* and esp. by those of the genus *Haemagogus*
**¹jun·gli** \'jəŋglē\ *n* -S [¹*jungle* + *-i* (as in *Hindi*)] : an inhabitant of an Indian jungle
**²jungli** *or* **jun·gly** \"\ *adj* **1** : inhabiting an Indian jungle : being or belonging to or characteristic of an inhabitant of such a jungle ⟨the ~ dialect was the only language we heard —S.T.Moyer⟩ **2** *India* : UNCOUTH, UNREFINED ⟨a rude, ~ individual —Alan Moorehead⟩
**jun·gly** \'jəŋg(ə)lē\ *adj* : of, relating to, or like a jungle ⟨an overgrown ~ garden⟩ ⟨a ~ world of high-pressure pluggers —*Time*⟩
**juning** *pres part of* JUNE
**¹jun·ior** \'jünyə(r)\ *n* -S [L, n. & adj.] **1 a** (1) : a person who is younger than another ⟨my ~s were already asleep —Jimmy O'Dea⟩ ⟨told his ~ that theological research was not compatible with longevity —H.J.Laski⟩ (2) *sometimes cap* [LL, fr. L] : a male child : SON ⟨in summer months ~ wears a coat of tan and nothing more —*N.Y. Herald Tribune*⟩ ⟨just as good for mother and the girls as for ~ —S.L.A.Marshall⟩ ⟨~ is improving in his understanding of numbers —Paul Woodring⟩ **b** (1) : a young person; *esp* : JUNIOR MISS ⟨coats and even skirts for teens and ~s —*Springfield (Mass.) Union*⟩ (2) : a clothing size for dresses, coats, and suits usu. for women and girls with slight figures that have youthful designs and little fullness in the bodice **c** : an immature or young animal — used esp. of small and pet stock **2** [ML, fr. L] **a** : a person holding a position of lesser standing in a hierarchy of ranks ⟨executives told their ~s that the day of the order taker was over—F.L.Allen⟩ ⟨the newest ~ on the staff—Albert Christen⟩ ⟨an officer one grade his ~ —Wirt Williams⟩ **b** (1) : a student in his next-to-the-last year before graduating from an educational institution (2) : a student in his third year or having third-year standing at a senior college (3) : a student in his first year at a junior college (4) : a student in his third year at a secondary school (5) : a pupil in a junior school (6) : a member of a church school or Sunday school age-level division that generally includes children of the ages 9 to 11 **3** : a barrister who has not taken silk **4** : a player (as the dealer in piquet) who receives cards later in the deal
**²junior** \"\ *adj* [L, compar. of *juvenis* young — more at YOUNG] **1 a** : less advanced in age than another : YOUNGER — used chiefly and often cap. to distinguish a son with the same given name as his father; opposed to *senior;* abbr. *Jr* or *jr* **b** (1) : of or relating to youth : YOUTHFUL, YOUNG ⟨some relatively ~ skins are as dry as bone —*Mademoiselle*⟩ (2) : designed for young people esp. of the adolescent age group ⟨a worthwhile ~ novel —Louise S. Bechtel⟩ **c** : of more recent date ⟨only six years ~ to Boston —H.L.Mencken⟩; *specif* : of more recent date and therefore inferior or subordinate as to right of preference ⟨a ~ lien⟩ **d** : ranking below another in point of time of service ⟨the ~ senator from Illinois⟩; *specif* : having less seniority than another ⟨resented having a ~ man get to be an engineer before him⟩ **2 a** [ML, fr. L] : lower in standing or in rank esp. in a hierarchy of ranks ⟨a ~ partner⟩ ⟨made a ~ member —G.A.Wagner⟩ ⟨shifted himself, as ~ officer, to the general's left —J.G.Cozzens⟩ ⟨the task of teaching such courses is customarily assigned to ~ members of the staff —*Times Lit. Supp.*⟩ **b** : associated with another in a secondary or auxiliary role ⟨the ~ author of a methodological study⟩ **c** : duplicating or suggesting on a smaller or diminished scale something typically large or powerful ⟨the ~ hurricane that swept in —Mollie Panter-Downes⟩ ⟨the new store will be a . . . ~ department store —*Retailing Daily*⟩ **3 a** : composed of juniors ⟨the ~ class⟩ : of or relating to juniors, a junior class, or a junior school **b** : of or relating to a church school or Sunday school age-level division of juniors ⟨the ~ curriculum lessons⟩
**jun·ior·ate** *n* -S **1** : a course of high school or college study for the priesthood, brotherhood, or sisterhood; *specif* : one preparatory to the course in philosophy **2** : a seminary for juniorate training
**junior captain** *n* : a lieutenant in a fire department
**junior church** *n* : a program of worship, study, or project work for children carried on in churches during part or all of the adult worship service
**junior college** *n* **1** : an educational institution of post-high-school rank that offers two years of studies corresponding to the first two years of a senior college and prepares for transfer to such a college **2** : an institution complete in itself that serves the adults of its community by offering technical and vocational studies as well as courses in liberal education — compare COMMUNITY COLLEGE
**junior common room** *n* : a common room at a British college reserved for the use of undergraduates
**junior high school** *also* **junior high** *n* : a school organized to facilitate the transition from the elementary school to the high school usu. including the 7th and 8th grades of the elementary school and the 1st year of the high school — contrasted with *senior high school*
**ju·nior·i·ty** \jün'yȯrəd-ē, -yär-, -ətē, -i\ *n* -ES : the quality, state, or relation of being junior ⟨terms indicating relative rank of seniority or ~ —J.F.Embree & W.L.Thomas⟩
**junior leaguer** *n, often cap J&L* : a member of a league of young women organized for intelligent participation in civic affairs esp. through direct volunteer service to civic and social organizations and agencies for community betterment
**junior levirate** *n* : a form of the levirate in which a younger brother (as the next eldest one) marries the widow of the deceased husband
**junior library** *n, Brit* : a children's library
**junior matriculation** *n* : a certificate awarded to students who have successfully completed the ordinary course at a Canadian high school — compare SENIOR MATRICULATION
**junior miss** *n* **1** : an adolescent girl ⟨dresses in sizes for misses and *junior misses* —*N.Y. Times*⟩ **2** : JUNIOR 1b(2)
**junior mortgage** *n* : a second, third, or later mortgage
**junior optime** *n* : a man in the optime class at Cambridge University ranking one step below the senior optime and two steps below the wranglers
**junior republic** *n, usu cap J&R* : a self-governing industrial community for neglected or delinquent children
**junior right** *n* : the law of descent to the youngest son or in the absence of any issue to the youngest brother formerly existing by Anglo-Saxon custom in parts of England : BOROUGH-ENGLISH — compare PRIMOGENITURE, ULTIMOGENITURE
**junior school** *n* : a part of the British school system serving children from 7 to 11 years of age — compare INTERMEDIATE SCHOOL, SENIOR SCHOOL
**junior seminary** *n* : PREPARATORY SEMINARY
**junior soldier** *n* : a boy or girl between the ages of 7 and 13 who has met the requirements for enrollment as a junior member of the Salvation Army
**junior varsity** *n* : the members of a varsity squad lacking the experience or class qualification for the first team
**junior yearling** *n* : an animal of an age between 12 and 18 months on a date of the year specified by rules for livestock exhibits of the season
**ju·ni·per** \'jünəpə(r)\ *n* -S [ME *junipere, junipur*, fr. L *juniperus* — more at JONQUIL] **1 a** [NL *Juniperus*] : an evergreen shrub or tree of the genus *Juniperus; esp* : one having a prostrate or shrubby habit — see TREE illustration **b** : any of several coniferous trees resembling the juniper: as (1) : a white cedar (*Chamaecyparis thyoides*) (2) : LARCH **c** : RETEM **d** : BOX HUCKLEBERRY **2** : a dark grayish green that is bluer, lighter, and stronger than average ivy, lighter than Persian green, and yellower and lighter than hemlock green
**juniper bay** *n* [*juniper* + ⁹*bay*] : a swamp in which white cedar (*Chamaecyparis thyoides*) predominates and which often contains sweet bay
**juniper berry** *n* **1** : the fruit of a plant of the genus *Juniperus* (as the blue berrylike pungent-tasting cone of the common juniper) **2** : BOX HUCKLEBERRY
**ju·ni·per·ic acid** \,jünə¦perik-\ *n* [ISV *juniper-* (fr. NL *Juniperus*, genus that produces it) + *-ic*] : a crystalline hydroxy acid $HOCH_2(CH_2)_{14}COOH$ found in the waxy exudation from several conifers (as *Juniperus sabina*)
**juniper oil** *or* **juniper-berry oil** *n* : an acrid essential oil obtained from the dried ripe fruit of common juniper and used chiefly in gin flavors and liqueurs and esp. formerly in medicine as a diuretic and stimulant
**juniper scale** *n* : a tiny dull whitish round scale (*Diaspis carueli*) that feeds on junipers and related trees esp. in ornamental plantings
**juniper-tar oil** *or* **juniper tar** *n* : CADE OIL
**juniper tree** *n* **1** : a tree of the genus *Juniperus* **2** : TAMARACK 1a(1)
**ju·nip·er·us** \jü'nipərəs\ *n, cap* [NL, fr. L, juniper] : a large genus of evergreen shrubs or trees (family Cupressaceae) that have small appressed scale leaves or esp. on juvenile growth acerose leaves, minute solitary terminal flowers, and small cones resembling berries and that include some cultivated as ornamentals and some valued for their timber — see PENCIL CEDAR
**juniper webworm** *n* : the larva of either of two destructive European tortricid moths (*Phalonia rutilana* and *Dichomeris marginella*) introduced into No. America that devours the foliage of several junipers
**¹junk** \'jəŋk\ *n* -S *often attrib* [ME *jonke*] **1 a** *obs* : a piece of worn or poor rope or cable **b** : pieces of old cable or old cordage used for making such articles as gaskets, mats, swabs, or oakum **c** *chiefly Brit* : a thick piece or chunk of something : HUNK ⟨a ~ of cold salt mutton —E.O.Schlunke⟩ **d** : hard salted beef supplied to ships **e** : a part of the head of a sperm

whale between the case and the white horse containing oil and spermaceti **2 a** (1) **:** old iron, glass, paper, cordage, or other waste that may be treated so as to be used again in some form ⟨one third of the cars . . . are close to ~ in value —*Nation's Business*⟩ ⟨sold the old wreck for ~⟩ (2) **:** secondhand, worn, or discarded articles of any kind having little or no commercial value ⟨furnished the room with ~ obtained from relatives⟩ **b :** a product regarded as shoddy, cheap, or specious **:** something without intrinsic value **:** TRASH; *specif* **:** JUNK JEWELRY ⟨real jewelry, not ~ from Paris —Rose Thurburn⟩ ⟨newest ~ trinkets . . . made for her in Paris —Lois Long⟩ **c :** something devoid of meaning or significance **:** something that is intellectually worthless **:** BUNK, HOKUM, NONSENSE ⟨read no more ~ —Nathaniel Benchley⟩ ⟨will have nothing to do with protocol, formalities, and all that ~⟩ **3 :** FISH 5e **4** *slang* **:** NARCOTICS; *esp* **:** HEROIN

**²junk** \ˈ"\ *vt* -ED/-ING/-S **:** to abandon or get rid of as no longer of value or use **:** SCRAP ⟨a dislike to ~ partially depreciated equipment —Harold Koontz & Cyril O'Donnell⟩ ⟨became the first big maker of electric appliances to ~ fair-trade pricing —*Newsweek*⟩ **syn** see DISCARD

**³junk** \ˈ"\ *n* -S [Pg *junco*, fr. Jav *joŋ*] **:** any of various characteristic boats of Chinese and neighboring waters having as common features bluff lines, very high poop and overhanging stem, little or no keel, usu. high pole masts carrying lug sails with battens running entirely across, and a rudder usu. dropping below the keel

junk

**junk bottle** *n* [¹*junk*] **:** a stout bottle of thick dark-colored glass

**¹jun·ker** \ˈyu̇ŋkə(r)\ *n* -S *usu cap, often attrib* [G, fr. OHG *junchērro*, fr. *junc* young + *hērro* lord, master — more at YOUNG, YOUNKER] **1 :** a young German noble **2 :** a member of the Prussian landed aristocracy characterized by extreme militarism, nationalism, and antidemocratic views ⟨the *Junkers*, the hard, ambitious governing class —*Auckland (New Zealand) Weekly News*⟩ ⟨*Junker* influence . . . in the German army —Hajo Halborn⟩

**²junk·er** \ˈjəŋkə(r)\ *n* -S [¹*junk* + -*er*] **1** *slang* **:** a narcotics addict **2 :** an automobile of such age and condition as to be ready for scrapping ⟨wanted an old ~ —Gregor Felsen⟩

**jun·ker·dom** \ˈyu̇ŋkə(r)dəm\ *n* -S *usu cap* [¹*junker* + -*dom*] **:** the body of Junkers **:** Junker society ⟨lost in the anonymity of Prussian *Junkerdom* —V.L.Albjerg⟩

**jun·ker·ism** \-kə,rizəm\ *n* -S *usu cap* [¹*junker* + -*ism*] **:** the Junker system of government **:** Junker principles or policies ⟨*Junkerism* has greatly declined in influence —*N.Y. Times*⟩

**¹jun·ket** \ˈjuŋkət, ˈjəŋ-\ *n* -S [ME *jonket, junket*, fr. (assumed) ONF *jonquette* rush basket, dim. of OF *jonchee, jonchie*, fr. *jonc* rush, fr. L *juncus* — more at JONQUIL] *dial Brit* **:** BASKET; *esp* **:** one for carrying or catching fish

**²jun·ket** \ˈjəŋkət, *usu* -əd·+V\ *n* -S [ME *ioncate*, prob. fr. OIt *giuncata* cream cheese, fr. (assumed) VL *juncata*, fr. L *juncus* rush] **1 a :** a cream cheese or a dish of curds and cream **b :** a dessert of sweetened, flavored milk that is set in a smooth jelly by rennet **c** *obs* **:** a sweet dish, confection, or other delicacy **2 a :** a festive social affair **:** FEAST, BANQUET, PARTY ⟨the farm kitchen frequently was the setting for a country dance or ~ —Marilyn Fenno⟩ **b** (1) **:** a pleasure trip, cruise, or outing ⟨the ~s . . . attract hundreds of vacationers —Charles Rawlings⟩ ⟨a high-speed ~ to a tropical port —William McFee⟩ ⟨our first ~ by Italy's railroad system —Claudia Cassidy⟩ (2) **:** a pleasure trip or tour made by an official at public expense ostensibly for purposes of inspection, investigation, or other public business ⟨unnecessary ~s by state employees are taking big hunks out of the pockets of . . . taxpayers —*Springfield (Mass.) Union*⟩ ⟨this journey clearly is more than a ~ —W.H.Lawrence⟩ (3) **:** a tour or journey of any kind ⟨the best description of a lecturing ~ ever written —E.A.Weeks⟩ ⟨an agricultural ~ through nine European countries —*Newsweek*⟩ ⟨back from a business ~ through the eastern United States —E.T.Sager⟩

**³junket** \ˈ"\ *vb* -ED/-ING/-S *vi* **1 :** to make an entertainment **:** FEAST, BANQUET **2 :** to go on a junket **:** TOUR ⟨~*ed* like contemporary tourists —*N.Y. Herald Tribune*⟩ ~ *vt* **:** ENTERTAIN, FEAST ⟨these cowled academicians ~*ed* and entertained princes —Norman Douglas⟩

**jun·ke·teer** \ˌjəŋkəˈti(ə)r, -iə\ *also* **jun·ket·er** \ˈjəŋkəd·ə(r)\ *n* -S [³*junket* + -*eer* or -*er*] **:** a person who junkets; *esp* **:** an official who makes a pleasure trip at public expense ostensibly for purposes of inspection or other official business ⟨true ~*s* . . . are a small, potent minority who reflect on every study mission —H.A.Williams⟩

**junketing** *n* -S **1 :** the act or an instance of junketing ⟨it will be political ~ —L.C.Wilson⟩ **2** *chiefly Brit* **:** FESTIVITY, FEASTING, CELEBRATION ⟨the feasting and ~ went on for days —Harold Albert⟩ ⟨there are to be big ~*s* —*Scots Mag.*⟩

**junk·ie** \ˈjəŋkē, -ki\ *n* -S [¹*junk* + -*ie*] **1 :** JUNKMAN **2** *or* **junky** -ES \ˈ"\ *slang* **:** a narcotics peddler or addict

**junk jewelry** *n* [¹*junk*] **:** inexpensive costume jewelry

**junk mail** *n* [¹*junk*] **:** third-class mail (as circulars, leaflets, and other advertising matter) bearing no direct address or not bearing the recipient's name and typically addressed to "occupant", "householder", or "boxholder"

**¹junk·man** \ˈjəŋkmən\ *n, pl* **junkmen** [³*junk* + *man*] **:** a member of the crew of a junk

**²junk·man** \ˈjəŋk,man\ *n, pl* **junkmen** [¹*junk* + *man*] **:** a person who deals in resalable junk

**junk ring** *n* [¹*junk*; fr. its orig. use in confining the hemp packing round the piston of a steam engine] **:** a wide ring around the piston of an internal-combustion engine forming the base for piston rings

**junks** *pl of* JUNK, *pres 3d sing of* JUNK

**junky** \ˈjəŋkē, -ki\ *adj* -ER/-EST [¹*junk* + -*y* (adj. suffix)] **:** having the character of junk **:** constituting junk ⟨a ~ copy of a painting —John Howard⟩

**junkyard** \ˈ=,=\ *n* [¹*junk* + *yard*] **:** a yard used to keep usu. resalable junk

**ju·no·esque** \ˌjünōˈesk\ *adj, usu cap* [*Juno*, ancient Italian goddess, wife of Jupiter (fr. L) + E -*esque*] **1 :** marked by stately or voluptuous beauty and generous proportions ⟨beautiful in a fine *Junoesque* fashion —Louis Bromfield⟩ ⟨her neck and head are *Junoesque* —P.B.Kyne⟩ **2 :** PLUMP, BUXOM ⟨for the *Junoesque* figure —*Good Housekeeping*⟩ ⟨a *Junoesque* size 40 —*Women's Wear Daily*⟩

**¹ju·no·nia** \jüˈnōnēə\ [NL, fr. LL *Junonia (ales)* peacock (lit., Juno's bird), fr. L *Junonia*, fem. of *Junonius* of Juno, fr. *Junon-, Juno*] *syn of* PRECIS

**²junonia** \ˈ"\ *n* -S [NL, fr. *junonia* (specific epithet of *Scaphella junonia*)] **:** a rare volute mollusk (*Scaphella junonia*) that is creamy white with brown or orange markings, that is much sought by shell collectors, and that is known to occur only in deep water off the coasts of Florida

**ju·no's bird** \ˈjü(,)nōz-\ *n, cap J* [trans. of L *Junonis volucris* or LL *Junonia ales*] **:** PEACOCK

**junr** *abbr* junior

**junt** \ˈjənt\ *n* -S [prob. alter. (influenced by *chunk*) of *joint*] *chiefly Scot* **:** large amount **:** CHUNK

**jun·ta** \ˈhu̇ntə *also* ˈhün- *or* ˈjən- *sometimes* ˈhu̇n·(,)tä *or* ˈhün(,)tä *or* ˈhəntə *or* ˈjüntə\ *n* -S [Sp, fr. fem. of *junto* together, joined, fr. L *junctus*, past part. of *jungere* to join — more at YOKE] **1 :** a council or committee for political or governmental purposes ⟨government by ~ is a characteristic feature —L.K. Caldwell⟩ ⟨abetted by the propaganda of exile ~*s* —G.W. Johnson⟩; *esp* **:** a closely knit group of persons composing or dominating a government esp. after a revolutionary seizure of power ⟨a military ~ with the trappings of a constitutional monarchy —E.K.Lindley⟩ ⟨called to account by a revolutionary ~ —Barbara Henderson⟩ ⟨some of the ruling ~*s* in the Arab countries —David Ben-Gurion⟩ **2 :** a closely knit group of persons combined for some common purpose **:** JUNTO ⟨a literary ~⟩

**jun·to** \ˈjənt·(,)ō, -n·(,)tō\ *n* -S [prob. alter. of *junta*] **:** a closely knit group of persons combined for some common purpose and usu. meeting secretly or privately **:** CABAL, FACTION

**ju·pa·ti** *or* **ju·pa·ty** \ˈjüpəd·ē\ *or* **jupati palm** *n* -S [Pg *jupati*, fr. Tupi *jupati, jubati*] **:** a Brazilian palm (*Raphia taedigera*) attaining an overall height of 70 feet of which not more than 6 or 8 feet represents stem, the remainder consisting of extremely large leathery pinnatisect leaves that are arranged in a terminal crown and rise from long strong stems which are used locally for various structural purposes

**jupe** \ˈjüp\ *n* -S [ME *juype*, fr. OF *jupe*, fr. Ar *jubbah*] **1** *chiefly Scot* **:** a man's coat, jacket, or tunic **2** [F] *chiefly Scot* **a :** a man's shirt **b :** a woman's bodice **c :** STAYS — usu. used in pl. **3 :** a woman's skirt

**ju·pi·te·ri·an** \ˌjüpəˈtirēən\ *n* -S *usu cap* [(*Mount of*) *Jupiter* + E -*ian*] **:** a person that has a well-developed Mount of Jupiter and a long and large finger of Jupiter and that is usu. held by palmists to be characterized by ambition, leadership, and a religious nature ⟨with all his vanity the *Jupiterian* is warm-hearted —W.G.Benham †1944⟩

**ju·pi·ter's-beard** \ˈjüpəd·ə(r)z-\ *n, pl* **jupiter's-beards** *cap* [after *Jupiter*, ancient Roman god of the sky, fr. L *Juppiter*; trans. of L *barba Jovis* — more at DEITY] **1 :** HOUSELEEK **2 :** a silvery hairy European shrub (*Anthyllis barba-jovis*) with evergreen foliage and pale yellow flowers **3 :** a fungus (*Hydnum barba-jovis*) **4 :** RED VALERIAN

**ju·pon** \jüˈpän, ˈ=,=\ *n* -S [ME *iopoun, iupone, iopon*, fr. MF *jupon*, fr. OF *jupe*] **:** a tight-fitting garment like a shirt often padded and quilted and worn under medieval armor; *also* **:** a late medieval jacket similar to the surcoat

**jur** \ˈjər\ *vb* -ED/-ING/-S [imit.] *dial chiefly Eng* **:** PUSH, JAR, BUTT

**¹ju·ra** \ˈyu̇rə\ *n pl* [L, pl. of *jur-, jus* law, right] **:** RIGHTS

**²ju·ra** \ˈju̇rə\ *n, cap* [prob. fr. G, after *Jura*, mountain range between France and Switzerland, fr. L] **:** the Jurassic geological period or the rocks belonging to it

**ju·ral** \ˈju̇rəl\ *adj* [L *jur-, jus* law, right + E -*al*] **:** of or relating to law **:** JURISTIC; *also* **:** of or relating to rights or obligations — **ju·ral·ly** \-əlē, -li\ *adv*

**ju·ra·ment** \ˈju̇rəmənt\ *n* -S [L *juramentum*, fr. *jurare* to swear + -*mentum* -ment] *archaic* **:** OATH

**ju·ra·men·ta·do** \ˌhu̇rəmənˈtä(,)dō, ˌjü-\ *n* -S [Sp, bound by oath] **:** a Muslim Moro who has taken an oath to die while engaged in killing Christians — compare AMOK

**ju·ra·men·tum** \ˌju̇rəˈmentəm, ˌyu̇-\ *n, pl* **juramenta** \-tə\ [LL] *Roman, civil, & canon law* **:** OATH

**ju·rane** \ˈju̇ˌrān\ *adj, usu cap* [ML *Juranus*, fr. *Jura* mountains + L -*anus* -ane] **1 :** of or relating to the Jura mountains **2 :** of or relating to the medieval duchy of Burgundy

**ju·ra·ra** \zhəˈrärə, ˌzhu̇rəˈrä\ *n* -S [Pg *jurará*, fr. Tupi *jurára, yurará*] **:** ARRAU

**ju·ras·sic** \jəˈrasik, jüˈ-, -sēk\ *adj, usu cap* [F *jurassique*, fr. *Jura*, mountain range between France and Switzerland (fr. L) + -*ique* -ic] **:** constituting or relating to the period of the Mesozoic era preceding the Comanchean and succeeding the Triassic and the corresponding system of rocks — see GEOLOGIC TIME table

**²jurassic** \ˈ"\ *n* -S *usu cap* **:** the Jurassic period or system of rocks

**ju·rat** \ˈju̇,rat\ *n* -S [ME *jurate*, fr. ML *juratus*, fr. L, past part. of *jurare* to swear — more at JURY] **1 :** any of several public officials: as **a :** a municipal officer similar to an alderman in some English towns (as the Cinque Ports) **b :** a magistrate chosen for life in the Channel islands **2 :** a person who has taken an oath; *specif* **:** one in late medieval England sworn to assist the administration of justice (as by giving information about crimes committed in his neighborhood) **3** [short for L *juratum (est)* it has been sworn] **:** a certificate added to an affidavit stating when, before whom, and in British practice where it was made

**ju·ra·ta** \jəˈrād·ə\ *n* -S [ML] **1** *Old Eng law* **:** a jury of 12 men existing at common law and not by statute — compare ASSIZE **2 :** JURAT 3

**ju·ra·tion** \jəˈrāshən\ *n* -S [LL *juration-, juratio*, fr. L *juratus* (past part.) + -*ion*, -*io* -ion] **:** a taking or an administration of an oath

**ju·ra·to·ry** \ˈju̇rə,tōrē\ *adj* [LL *juratorius*, fr. L *juratus* (past part.) + -*orius* -ory] **:** relating to or comprising or expressed in an oath ⟨~ obligation⟩

**juratory caution** *n* [prob. trans. of F *caution juratoire*, trans. of LL *cautio juratoria*] **1** *Scots law* **:** a security consisting of a sworn inventory and pledge of the goods of the affiant **2** *admiralty law* **:** a suit in forma pauperis

**jura–trias** \ˈ=ˈ=ˈ=\ *n* -ES *usu cap J&T* [²*jura* + *trias*] **:** the Jurassic and Triassic together

**jura–triassic** \ˈ=ˈ=ˈ=\ *adj, usu cap J&T* **:** of or relating to the Jura-Trias

**jure** \ˈjü(ə)r\ *vt* -ED/-ING/-S [back-formation fr. *juror*] **:** to make a juror of

**ju·rel** \hüˈrel\ *n* -S [Sp, fr. Sp. dial. *shurel* or Catal *sorell* fr. LL *saurus* horse mackerel, fr. Gk *sauros* horse mackerel, lizard — more at SAURIA] **:** any of several carangid food fishes of warm seas: as **a :** BLUE RUNNER **b :** a crevalle (*Caranx hippos*)

**ju·re ux·o·ris** \ˌjü(ˌ)rē,ekˈsōrəs\ *adv* [L] **:** in or by the right of a wife (as in a conveyance by a husband at common law of his wife's estate)

**ju·rid·ic** \jəˈridik, (ˈ)jüˈr-, -dēk\ *adj* [L *juridicus*, fr. *jur-, jus* right, law + -*dicus* (fr. *dicere* to say)] **:** JURIDICAL

**ju·rid·i·cal** \-dəkəl, -dēk-\ *adj* [L *juridicus* + E -*al*] **1 :** of or relating to the administration of justice or the office of a judge **:** acting or used in the administration of justice **2 :** of or relating to law in general or jurisprudence **:** LEGAL — **ju·rid·i·cal·ly** \-dək(ə)lē, -dēk-, -li\ *adv*

**juridical days** *n pl* [trans. of L *dies juridici*] **:** days on which courts are open

**juridical person** *n* **:** JURISTIC PERSON

**juried** *adj* **:** selected for exhibition by an art jury ⟨a ~ show of fine quality —*Craft Horizons*⟩

**juries** *pl of* JURY, *pres 3d sing of* JURY

**ju·rin's law** \ˈjürənz-\ *n, cap J* [after James *Jurin* †1750 Eng. physician] **:** a law of physics: the height of a capillary column of a liquid at a particular temperature is inversely proportional to the diameter of the tube

**ju·ris·con·sult** \ˌju̇rəˈskän,səlt ,ju̇rəskənˈs-\ *n* -S [L *jurisconsultus*, fr. *juris* (gen. of *jus* law, right) + *consultus*, past part. of *consulere* to consult] **:** a man learned in law, esp. international and public law

**ju·ris·dic·tion** \ˌju̇rəsˈdikshən, -əz', -əˈsti-\ *n* -S [ME *jurisdiccioun, jurediccioun*, fr. OF & L; OF *juridiction, juredicion*, fr. L *jurisdiction-, jurisdictio*, fr. *juris* (gen. of *jus* right, law) + *diction-, dictio* act of saying, delivery in public speaking — more at JUST, DICTION] **1 :** the legal power, right, or authority to hear and determine a cause considered either in general or with reference to a particular matter **:** legal power to interpret and administer the law in the premises **2 :** authority of a sovereign power to govern or legislate **:** power or right to exercise authority ⟨territory subject to the ~ of the U.S. —G.W. Johnson⟩ **3 :** the limits or territory within which any particular power may be exercised **:** sphere of authority ⟨head of one of the world's smallest Masonic ~*s* —*Associated Press*⟩ **:** CONTROL ⟨an American theatrical trade union having ~ over dancers and singers —Anatole Chujoy⟩; *specif* **:** an assignment of organizing rights by a national labor federation to a constituent union **syn** see POWER

**ju·ris·dic·tion·al** \ˌ=ˈ=ˈdikshənᵊl, -ˈsti-, -shnəl\ *adj* **:** of or relating to jurisdiction **:** involving a question of jurisdiction; *specif* **:** involving the right of one of two or more unions to organize and represent the employees of a plant, trade, or industry, the right to exclusive control over certain work, or the territorial limits of such jurisdiction ⟨a ~ dispute⟩ ⟨a ~ strike⟩ — **ju·ris·dic·tion·al·ly** \-ᵊlē, -əlē, -i\ *adv*

**ju·ris·dic·tive** \-ktiv\ *adj* [*jurisdiction* + -*ive*] **:** of, relating to, or having jurisdiction

**ju·ris·prude** \ˈju̇rə,sprüd\ *n* -S [back-formation (influenced by *prude*) fr. *jurisprudence*] **:** a person who makes ostentatious show of learning in jurisprudence and the philosophy of law or who regards legal doctrine with undue solemnity or veneration ⟨disclaims being a ~ —*New Republic*⟩

**ju·ris·pru·dence** \ˌju̇rəˈsprüdᵊn(t)s, ˌjür- *also* ˈ=ˈ=,=\ *n* -S [F & L; F, fr. MF, fr. LL *jurisprudentia*, fr. L *prudentia juris*] **1** *archaic* **:** knowledge of or skill in law **2 a :** a system or body of law **:** a department of law ⟨an exponent of sociological ~⟩ ⟨Roman ~⟩ — compare ANALYTICAL JURISPRUDENCE, FORENSIC MEDICINE **b :** the science or philosophy of law ⟨devoted himself to the study of ~⟩ **c** (1) **:** the course of court decisions as distinguished from legislation and doctrine ⟨a tendency that has become apparent in the ~ of the American courts —Bernard Schwartz⟩ (2) **:** the collected decisions of a court **:** REPORTS

**ju·ris·pru·dent** \ˈ=ˈ=ˈsprüdᵊnt\ *n* -S [LL *jurisprudent-, jurisprudens*, fr. L *juris* (gen. of *jus* right, law) + *prudent-, prudens* foreseeing, skilled, prudent — more at PRUDENT] **:** a person skilled in jurisprudence **:** JURIST

**ju·ris·pru·den·tial** \ˌju̇rə(,)sprüˈdenchəl\ *adj* [LL *jurisprudentia* + E -*al*] **:** of or relating to jurisprudence — **ju·ris·pru·den·tial·ly** \-əlē\ *adv*

**ju·rist** \ˈju̇rəst, ˈjür-\ *n* -S [MF *juriste*, fr. ML *jurista*, fr. L *jur-, jus* law, right + -*ista* -ist — more at JUST] **1 a :** a person who practices law **:** LAWYER **b :** JUDGE ⟨replaced a ~ then under fire —R.G.Spivack⟩ **2 :** a person skilled in the philosophy or science of the law **:** a scholar in the law ⟨19th century philosophical ~*s* —Roscoe Pound⟩

**ju·ris·tic** \jəˈristik, (ˈ)jüˈr-, -tēk\ *adj* **:** of or relating to a jurist or jurisprudence **:** relating to, created by, or recognized in law ⟨~ theory⟩ ⟨a ~ being⟩ — **ju·ris·ti·cal·ly** \-tək(ə)lē, -tēk-, -li\ *adv*

**juristic act** *n* **:** an act of a private individual directed to the origin, termination, or alteration of a right

**juristic person** *n* **:** a body of persons, a corporation, a partnership, or other legal entity that is recognized by law as the subject of rights and duties — called also *artificial person, conventional person, fictitious person*

**ju·ror** \ˈju̇rə(r), ˈjü- *also* -,rō(ə)r *or* -ō(ə)\ *n* -S [ME *jurour, jurrour*, fr. AF *jurour*, fr. OF *jurer* to swear + -*our* -or — more at JURY] **1 a :** one of a number of men sworn to deliver a verdict as a body **:** a member of a jury **b :** a person designated and summoned to serve on a jury **2 :** a person who takes oath esp. of allegiance **3 :** a member of a jury for awarding prizes or determining relative merit at a contest or exhibition

**jurr** *var of* JUR

**juruk** *usu cap, var of* YURUK

**ju·ru·pa·ite** \həˈrüpə,īt\ *n* -S [*Jurupa* mts., Riverside co., Calif. + E -*ite*] **:** a hydrous calcium magnesium silicate $(Ca,Mg)_2(Si_2O_5)(OH)_2$

**¹ju·ry** \ˈju̇rē, ˈjür-, -ri\ *n* -ES [ME *jure, jurie*, fr. AF *juree*, fr. OF *jurer* to swear, fr. L *jurare, jurari*, fr. *jur-, jus* law, right — more at JUST] **1 :** a body of men sworn to give a verdict upon some matter submitted to them; *esp* **:** a body of men selected according to law, impaneled and sworn to inquire into and try any matter of fact, and to give their verdict according to the evidence legally produced — compare GRAND JURY, PETIT JURY, TRIAL JURY **2 :** the body of dicasts of ancient Athens **3 a :** a committee for determining relative merit or awarding prizes at an exhibition or competition ⟨two *juries* for its third annual national exhibition —*Americana Annual*⟩ **b :** the director and four judges responsible for officiating at a fencing bout

**²jury** \ˈ"\ *vt* -ED/-ING/-ES **:** to select entries for (an art exhibit) ⟨inviting one man to ~ . . . its quadrennial exhibitions of contemporary American art —Aline B. Saarinen⟩ **:** judge the relative merits of (entries in an art exhibit) ⟨~*ing* the submissions at the invitation of the foundations —G.A.Wagner⟩

**³jury** \ˈ"\ *adj* [origin unknown] **:** improvised for temporary use esp. in an emergency **:** MAKESHIFT ⟨a ~ mast⟩ ⟨a ~ anchor⟩ ⟨a ~ rig⟩ ⟨~ repairs completed, they started again —Will Irwin⟩

**jury box** *n* **:** the place usu. enclosed by paneling where the jury sits at the trial of a court case

**jury chancellor** *n, Scots law* **:** the foreman of a jury

**jury commission** *n* **:** a body of public officers entrusted with the task of ascertaining the names and addresses of persons qualified by law to act as jurors and sometimes of actually selecting by lot a panel of such jurors

**ju·ry·less** \ˈ=ˈ=ləs\ *adj* **:** being without a jury

**jury list** *n* **:** a list of persons qualified to be drawn for jury service, summoned to court to serve as jurors, or sworn to act as jurors in a particular case

**ju·ry·man** \ˈ==mən\ *n, pl* **jurymen** **1 :** a person summoned to a sitting of a court to act as a juror if chosen **2 :** JUROR

**jury of the vicinage :** a jury formerly drawn from the neighborhood and now drawn from the political subdivision in which the court is held

**jury–packing** \ˈ=ˈ=,==\ *n* **:** the practice or an instance of illegally or corruptly influencing a jury by making available for jury service persons known to be biased or partial in a particular case to be tried

**jury–rigged** \ˈ=ˈ=\ *adj* [³*jury*] **:** rigged for temporary service

**jury room** *n* [¹*jury*] **:** the place where a jury in arriving at a verdict deliberates in private

**jury strut** *n* [³*jury*] **:** an auxiliary strut used as a support for a primary strut

**jury wheel** *n* [¹*jury*] **:** a revolving device or circular box from which the names of persons to serve as jurymen may be drawn by chance

**jurywoman** \ˈ==,==\ *n, pl* **jurywomen :** a female member of a jury

**¹jus** \ˈjəs\ *or* **ius** \ˈyüs\ *n, pl* **ju·ra** \ˈju̇rə\ *or* **iu·ra** \ˈyu̇-\ [L — more at JUST] **1 :** LAW **2 :** a legal principle, right, or power

**²jus** \ˈzhüs, ˈjüs, F ˈzhᵫ\ *n, pl* **jus** [F — more at JUICE] **:** JUICE, GRAVY — compare AU JUS

**jus** *abbr* justice

**jus ab·u·ten·di** \-,abyəˈtendē, -,dī\ *n* [L, right of abusing] *Roman & civil law* **:** a right to make full use of property even to wasting or destroying it **:** absolute and unlimited ownership with the power of free alienation — compare JUS UTENDI

**jus ac·cre·scen·di** \-,akrəˈsendē, -,dī\ *n* [L, lit., right of increasing] *Roman & civil law* **:** a right of accrual (as the right of survivorship)

**jus ad rem** \-(ˈ)aˈdrem\ *n* [ML, right to a thing] *civil & canon law* **:** a right to acquire particular property arising out of another's legal duty **:** a jus in personam as distinguished from a jus in rem based on full ownership or possession of particular property **:** an inchoate as distinguished from a perfected right

**jus ae·di·li·um** \-ēˈdilēəm\ *or* **jus ae·di·li·ci·um** \-,ēdəˈlis(h)ēəm\ *n* [L, law of the aediles or law of an aedile] *Roman law* **:** the law of the curule aediles set forth in their edicts usu. relating to police and market regulations

**jus al·ba·na·gii** \-,albəˈnājē,ī\ *n* [ML, right of alien confiscation] **:** DROIT D'AUBAINE

**jus an·ga·ri·ae** \-(,)anˈga(a)rē,ē\ *n* [LL, lit., right of angaria] **:** ANGARY

**jus ca·non·i·cum** \-kəˈnänəkəm\ *n* [ML] **:** CANON LAW

**jus ci·vi·le** \-səˈvī(,)lē\ *n* [L] **:** CIVIL LAW

**jus com·mer·cii** \-kəˈmərshē,ī\ *n* [L, right of commerce] *Roman & civil law* **:** a right to make contracts, acquire, hold, and transfer property, and have business dealings

**jus com·mu·ne** \-kəˈmyü(,)nē\ *n* [L] **1 :** the common law of England **2 :** the common or public law or right as opposed to the jus singulare established for special cases

**jus co·nu·bii** *or* **jus con·nu·bii** \-kəˈn(y)übē,ī\ *n* [L, lit., right of marriage, right of intermarriage] **1 :** CONNUBIUM 2 **2 :** the body of rules and conventions of a people or community governing intermarriage

**jus de·li·be·ran·di** \-də,libəˈrandē, -n,dī\ *n* [L, right of deliberating] *Roman & civil law* **:** a right granted to an heir to take a certain time to decide whether to accept the inheritance or not

**jus dis·po·nen·di** \-,dispəˈnendē, -,dī\ *n* [L, right of disposing] **:** a right of disposal as of property **:** power of alienation

**jus ec·cle·si·as·ti·cum** \-ə,klēzēˈastəkəm, -e,k-\ *n* [LL] **:** ECCLESIASTICAL LAW

**jus edi·cen·di** \-,edəˈsendē, -n,dī\ *n* [L, right of decreeing] *Roman law* **:** a right belonging to the curule aediles, praetors, and quaestors and presidents in the provinces of making edicts

**jus fru·en·di** \-früˈendē, -,dī\ *n* [L, right of enjoying] *Roman & civil law* **:** a right of enjoyment of another's property without destroying its substance

**jus gen·ti·um** \-ˈjenchēəm\ *n* [L, law of aliens, law of nations] **1 :** a body of legal rules for the government of aliens subject to Rome and of the intercourse of Roman citizens with aliens **2 :** INTERNATIONAL LAW

**jus ho·no·ra·ri·um** \-,änəˈra(a)rēəm\ *n* [L, magisterial law] *Roman law* **:** the law established by the edicts of the magistrates consisting chiefly of the praetorian law and the law of the curule aediles

**ju·si** *or* **hu·si** \'hüsē\ *n* -s [PhilSp, fr. Tag *husi*] **:** a fine sheer Philippine fabric for dresses or shirts that is made in plain weave from silk and vegetable fibers

**jus in per·so·nam** \'j'ə,sinpə(r)'sō,nam\ *n* [L, right against a person] **:** a right of legal action against or to enforce a legal duty of a particular person or group of persons — compare JUS IN REM

**jus in re** \-'rē\ *n* [ML, lit., right in a thing] **:** JUS IN REM

**jus in rem** \-'rem\ *n* [L, right against a thing] **:** a right enforceable against anyone in the world interfering with that right founded on some specific relationship, status, or particular property accorded legal protection from interference by anyone (as the right to be free from slander or to enjoy one's property)

**jus in·ter gen·tes** \-,intə(r)'jen·,tēz\ *n* [L, law among nations] **:** JUS GENTIUM

**jus la·tii** \-'lāshē,ī\ *n*, *cap L* [L, lit., right of Latium, ancient country of Italy] **:** the right of a person (as a Latin not a citizen of Rome) who has certain rights of or to Roman citizenship

**jus na·tu·rae** \-nə'tü(,)rē, -nə·'tyü-\ *n* [L, lit., law of nature] **:** NATURAL LAW

**jus na·tu·ra·le** \-,nachə'ra(,)lē, -rā(-, -rä(-\ *n* [L] **:** NATURAL LAW

**jus per·so·na·rum** \-,pərsə'na(a)rəm\ *n* [L, law of persons] **:** the law of persons occupying special relations to one another (as parent and child, husband and wife, guardian and ward) or of persons with limited rights (as aliens, minors, slaves, incompetent or insane persons)

**jus post·li·mi·ni·i** \-,pōstlə'minē,ī\ *n* [L, right of return to one's threshold] *Roman law* **:** POSTLIMINIUM

**jus pri·mae noc·tis** \-,prī(,)mē'näktəs\ *n* [L, right of first night] **1 :** DROIT DU SEIGNEUR **2 :** a right granted by the law or custom of a primitive people to some person other than the bridegroom of deflowering the bride

**jus pro·pri·e·ta·tis** \-p(r)ə,prīə'tād·əs\ *n* [ML, lit., right of ownership] **:** a right based on ownership of property irrespective of actual possession

**jus pub·li·cum** \-'pəbləkəm\ *n* [L] **:** public law including in Roman law the criminal and sacred law

**jus re·lic·tae** \-rə'lik(,)tē\ *n* [ML, right of a widow] *Scots law* **:** a widow's right to a share in the free movable estate of her deceased husband to the extent of one third if there are children and otherwise one half

**jus re·lic·ti** \-,tī\ *n* [ML, right of a widower] *Scots law* **:** a widower's right to share in the free movable estate of his deceased wife since 1881 to the extent of one third if there are children and otherwise one half

**juss** *abbr* jussive

**jus san·gui·nis** \-'saŋgwənəs\ *n* [L, right of blood] **:** a rule that the citizenship of the child is determined by the citizenship of its parents

**jus·si·aea** \,jəsē'ēə\ *n*, *cap* [NL, irreg. fr. Bernard de *Jussieu* †1777 Fr. botanist] **:** a genus of chiefly tropical aquatic or semiaquatic herbs (family Onagraceae) that are closely related to the evening primroses and have a many-seeded capsule and usu. entire alternate leaves — see PRIMROSE WILLOW

**jus·si·ae·an** \¦==¦ēən\ *or* **jus·si·eu·an** \-¦yüən\ *also* **jus·si·e·an** \-¦ēən\ *adj*, *usu cap* [fr. or irreg. fr. Bernard de *Jussieu* †1777 or Antoine Laurent de *Jussieu* †1836 Fr. botanists + E *-an*] **:** of or relating to the French botanists Bernard de Jussieu or Antoine Laurent de Jussieu ⟨*Jussiaean* classification⟩

**jus sin·gu·la·re** \-,siŋgyə'la(a)rē\ *n* [L, individual law, particular law] *Roman & civil law* **:** a law or right established for special cases as opposed to the jus commune

[1]**jus·sive** \'jəsiv, -sēv *also* səv\ *adj* [L *jussus* (past part. of *jubēre* to order) + E *-ive;* akin to W *udd* lord, Gk *hysminē* fight, battle, Skt ud*yōdhati* it boils up, rages, *yudhyati* he fights] **:** expressing or having the effect of a command

[2]**jussive** \"\ *n* -s **:** a word, form, case, or mood expressing command

**jus so·li** \'jəs'sō,lī\ *n* [L, right of the soil] **:** a rule of the common law that determines the allegiance or citizenship of a child by the place of its birth — compare ALLEGIANCE

[1]**just** *var of* JOUST

[2]**just** \'jəst\ *adj often* -ER/-EST [ME *just*, *juste*, fr. MF & L; MF *juste*, fr. OF, fr. L *justus*, fr. *jus* right, law, justice, fr. OL *jous;* akin to OIr *huisse*, *uisse* right, just, Skt *yos* welfare, and perh. to L *jungere* to bind, join; basic meaning: tie, obligation — more at YOKE] **1 a** (1) **:** having a basis in fact **:** REASONABLE, WELL-FOUNDED, JUSTIFIED ⟨felt a ~ fear of the consequences of his actions⟩ (2) **:** conforming to fact or reason **:** not false **:** RIGHT, TRUE, ACCURATE ⟨had a very ~ notion of the boy's abilities⟩ ⟨one element in a ~ discrimination —John Dewey⟩ (3) *archaic* **:** agreeing closely or exactly with a pattern, model, or other original **:** FAITHFUL **b** *obs* **:** adapted to some end or purpose **:** APPROPRIATE, SUITABLE **c** (1) *obs* **:** regular or exact in operation **:** CONSTANT, UNIFORM (2) *obs* **:** being exactly the specified measure, dimension, quantity, or other result of calculation **:** not approximate but exact (3) **:** conforming to some standard of correctness **:** CORRECT, PROPER, FITTING ⟨tended to distort some of the concerto's ~ proportions —Winthrop Sargeant⟩ ⟨react in ~ measure against this naturalism —Irving Babbitt⟩ ⟨combines wit and sentiment in ~ proportions —Douglas Watt⟩ (4) *obs* **:** EQUAL, EVEN (5) **:** giving or sounding musical tones at the mathematically exact intervals of their vibration ratios ⟨~ intonation⟩ ⟨~ scale⟩ — compare TEMPERED **d** *archaic* **:** lacking nothing needed for completeness **:** COMPLETE, FULL **2 a :** righteous before God **b** (1) **:** acting or being in conformity with what is morally right or good **:** RIGHTEOUS, EQUITABLE ⟨a reward directed his way by a ~ providence —W.H.Whyte⟩ ⟨a ~ war⟩ ⟨that is justice, even if it is not ~ —Alan Paton⟩ ⟨his decisions quick and instinctively ~ —Norman Mailer⟩ (2) **:** MERITED, DESERVED ⟨won him that ~ affection and popularity —F.J.Mather⟩ ⟨received his ~ punishment⟩ **c :** conforming to or consonant with what is legal or lawful **:** legally right ⟨a ~ title⟩ ⟨~ compensation⟩ ⟨a ~ proceeding⟩ **syn** see FAIR, UPRIGHT

[3]**just** \(¦)jəs(t), (¦)jis(t), (¦)jes(t), *in rapid speech sometimes* (,)dis(t)\ *adv* [ME, fr. *just*, adj.] **1 a :** EXACTLY, PRECISELY ⟨some indication of ~ how nervous she was —C.B.Flood⟩ ⟨~ the words we often have to look up in a dictionary —G.A. Miller⟩ ⟨capturing . . . ~ the expression of terror which had baffled him —Laurence Binyon⟩ ⟨must always have his meals served ~ so⟩ ⟨has ~ the thing you need⟩ ⟨that's ~ the point in dispute⟩ ⟨you must take me ~ as I am⟩ ⟨an apartment project . . . that cost ~ $20 million —*Wall Street Jour.*⟩ **b** (1) **:** precisely at the time referred to or implied ⟨was ~ ten when he came in⟩ ⟨not here ~ now⟩ (2) **:** but a very short time ago **:** very recently ⟨has ~ been published⟩ ⟨was ~ here⟩ — often used in the phrase *just now* ⟨saw him ~ now⟩ **c** *Brit* **:** on the point of being — often used with *on* ⟨it was now ~ on eight o'clock —Paul Jennings⟩ **2** *obs* **:** in a precise or accurate manner **:** CORRECTLY, ACCURATELY **3 a :** by a very small margin **:** BARELY ⟨had only ~ time to get back —F.W.Crafts⟩ ⟨could ~ see the very high weathercock of the church —Arnold Bennett⟩ ⟨~ short of the record —*Current Biog.*⟩ ⟨it was ~ over fifty years ago —Alan Devoe⟩ ⟨should be adjusted to ~ clear the dial —W.E.Shinn⟩ ⟨has an entrance ~ within the . . . county line —*Amer. Guide Series: N.Y. City*⟩ **b :** in immediate proximity **:** IMMEDIATELY, DIRECTLY ⟨lies ~ west of here⟩ ⟨~ across from the campus⟩ ⟨~ down the hall —J.K.Blake⟩ **4 a :** ONLY, MERELY, SIMPLY ⟨~ a note to let you know⟩ ⟨turn it into ~ another automobile —R.C.Ruark⟩ ⟨to them it's ~ a business —*Irish Digest*⟩ ⟨asked for a copy and got it — ~ like that —M.S.Mayer⟩ ⟨there was ~ lots of scenery —J.F.Dobie⟩ ⟨seems incredibly large for ~ the aristocracy —H.P.Becker⟩ ⟨I'm ~ your interpreter —Ernest Hemingway⟩ ⟨I don't think about it; I ~ go —J.J.Godwin⟩ **b** (1) **:** QUITE, VERY, ABSOLUTELY, REALLY — used as an intensive ⟨that's ~ ducky⟩ ⟨~ had a wonderful time⟩ (2) *chiefly dial* **:** INDEED, TRULY ⟨I tried a master; but he confused me, ~ —Willa Cather⟩ ⟨couldn't he play the violin, ~ —*Wesfarmers News*⟩ — **just about** *adv* **:** ALMOST, APPROXIMATELY ⟨passes *just about* through the middle of the region —P.E.James⟩ ⟨is the work done? *just about*⟩ ⟨shown to *just about* every audience you can name —Cecile Starr⟩ — **just in case** *adv* **:** by way of precaution against a possible or anticipated eventuality ⟨surrounded the area *just in case* —*Springfield* (*Mass.*) *Union*⟩

**just** *abbr* justice

**just·au·corps** \¦zhüstə¦kō(ə)r\ *or* **jus·ti·coat** \'jəstə,kōt\ *n*, *pl* **justaucorps** \-r(z)\ *or* **justicoats** \-ts\ [*justaucorps* fr. F, fr. *juste au corps* close to the body; *justicoat*, alter. (influenced by E *coat*) of *justaucorps*] **:** a fitted coat or jacket; *specif* **:** a man's knee-length coat with flaring and stiffened skirts worn in the late 17th and early 18th centuries

justaucorps

**juste-mi·lieu** \¦zhüstmēl¦yə, -yər(·), -yə̄\ *n*, *pl* **juste-milieux** \-yə(z), -yər(·), -yərz, -yə̄(z)\ [F] **:** the just or golden mean; *esp* **:** a governmental policy characterized by moderation and compromise

**jus·tice** \'jəstəs\ *n* -s *often attrib* [ME *justice*, *justise*, fr. OE & OF; OE *justise*, fr. OF *justice*, *justise*, fr. L *justitia*, fr. *justus* just + *-itia* -ice] **1 a :** the maintenance or administration of what is just **:** impartial adjustment of conflicting claims **:** the assignment of merited rewards or punishments **:** just treatment ⟨meting out evenhanded ~⟩ ⟨the natural aspiration for ~ in the human heart —W.A.White⟩ ⟨a splendid example of divine ~ —M.W.Fishwick⟩ ⟨social ~⟩ **b** [ME *justice*, *justise*, fr. AF & ML; AF *justice*, fr. ML *justitia*, fr. L] **:** a person duly commissioned to hold courts or to try and decide controversies and administer justice: as (1) **:** a judge of the Supreme Court of Judicature in England, or formerly of the Court of King's Bench, Common Pleas, or Exchequer (2) **:** a judge of a common-law court or a superior court of record (3) **:** a justice of the peace **:** an inferior magistrate ⟨a police ~⟩ ⟨traffic court ~⟩ **c** (1) **:** administration of law **:** the establishment or determination of rights according to the rules of law or equity (2) **:** infliction of punishment ⟨promises the indulgence of the jury to the husband who has himself executed ~ —H.M.Parshley⟩ **2 a** (1) **:** the quality or characteristic of being just, impartial, or fair **:** FAIRNESS, INTEGRITY, HONESTY ⟨possessed a keen sense of honor and ~⟩ ⟨pointed out, with equal ~, that . . . there are good businesses and bad —D.W.Brogan⟩ ⟨"it was nobody's fault . . .," she added, with scrupulous ~ —Ellen Glasgow⟩ ⟨the same standards used in steel must in ~ be applied to other industries —Mary K. Hammond⟩ (2) **:** the principle or ideal of just dealing or right action ⟨the courts are not helped as they . . . ought to be in the adaptation of law to ~ —B.N.Cardozo⟩ (3) **:** conformity to such principle or ideal **:** RIGHTEOUSNESS ⟨defends the ~ of his cause⟩ **b** (1) *in Platonism* **:** the condition of harmony existing in a state between its members when each citizen occupies a place in accordance with his merit **:** the highest of the four cardinal virtues (2) *in Aristotelianism* **:** the practice of virtue toward others — see COMMUTATIVE JUSTICE, DISTRIBUTIVE JUSTICE, RETRIBUTIVE JUSTICE (3) **:** that virtue which gives to each his due **c** (1) **:** the quality of conforming to positive law (2) **:** the quality of conforming to positive law and also to divine or natural law **3 :** conformity to truth, fact, or reason **:** CORRECTNESS, RIGHTFULNESS ⟨complained with ~ that English waxes and wanes like the moon —*English Language Arts*⟩ ⟨admitted that there was much ~ in these observations —T.L.Peacock⟩ — **bring to justice :** to cause to be brought before a proper tribunal for trial — **do justice 1** *obs* **:** to pledge in drinking **2 a :** to do what is just **:** administer justice **:** act justly ⟨longed to *do justice* in the world —*Time*⟩ **b :** to treat fairly or according to merit ⟨to *do* the man *justice*, his writing is brilliant⟩ **c** (1) **:** to treat or handle adequately or properly ⟨not *doing* full *justice* to his material —Carl Van Doren⟩ ⟨a full schedule may not permit him to *do justice* to his studies —Bates Boyle⟩ ⟨open for experienced salesmen who can *do justice* to America's outstanding line of small leather goods —*Luggage & Leather Goods*⟩ (2) **:** to consume in a manner showing due appreciation ⟨*do* the food *justice*⟩ ⟨after he likewise had *done* the liquor *justice* —Winston Churchill⟩ **3 :** to acquit in a way that is worthy of one's powers ⟨in the concerto he clearly did not *do* himself *justice*⟩

**justice clerk** *n*, *pl* **justice clerks** [ME] **:** the vice-president of the High Court of Justiciary and the presiding officer of the Outer House of the Court of Session in Scotland — called also *lord justice clerk*

**justice court** *or* **justice's court** *n* **:** an inferior court not of record having limited criminal or civil jurisdiction, presided over by a justice of the peace, and existing in some states from which appeal usu. may be claimed

**justice general** *n*, *pl* **justices general** [ME] **:** the former presiding officer of the High Court of Justiciary in Scotland whose duties are now entrusted to the lord president of the Court of Session — called also *lord justice general*

**justice in eyre** *n* [ME, trans. of AF *justice en eire*] **:** an itinerant judge riding the circuit to hold court in the different counties

**justice of the peace** [ME] **:** a subordinate magistrate for the conservation of the peace in a specified district with sometimes other incidental administrative and financial powers specified in his commission and with the principal duties of administering summary justice in minor cases, of committing for trial in a superior court on cause shown, and in Great Britain of granting licenses and acting if a county justice as judge at quarter sessions

**jus·tic·er** \-sə(r)\ *n* -s [ME *justiser*, fr. MF *justicier*, fr. OF, fr. *justice*] *archaic* **:** one who maintains or administers justice **:** JUDGE

**jus·tice·ship** \-s,ship\ *n* **:** the office or dignity of a judge

**justice's warrant** *n* **:** a warrant issued by an inferior magistrate (such as a justice of the peace, alderman, or federal commissioner) as distinguished from a bench warrant issued by a court of record

**justiceweed** \'==,=\ *n* **:** a slender white-flowered herb (*Eupatorium leucolepis*) of the eastern U. S.

**jus·ti·cia** \,jə'stishēə\ *n*, *cap* [NL, fr. James *Justice*, 18th cent. Scot. horticulturist + NL *-ia*] **:** a genus of perennial herbs or shrubs (family Acanthaceae) growing in water or wet places and having entire leaves and small flowers in long-peduncled axillary spikes or heads — see WATER WILLOW

**jus·ti·cia·bil·i·ty** \,jə,stish(ē)ə'bilad·ē\ *n* -ES **:** the quality of being justiciable

**jus·ti·cia·ble** \¦jə¦stish(ē)əbəl\ *adj* [F, fr. MF] **:** capable of being decided by legal principles or by a court of justice **:** liable to trial in a court of justice ⟨a ~ case⟩

**jus·ti·ci·ar** \,jə'stishēə(r)\ *n* -s [ME, fr. (influenced by ME *-ar*) ML *justiciarius*, *justitiarius*, fr. L *justitia* justice + *-arius* -ary — more at JUSTICE] **1 :** a high royal judicial officer in medieval England; *esp* **:** a justice of one of the superior courts **2** [ML *justiciarius*, *justitiarius*] **:** the chief political and judicial officer of the Norman and later kings of England until the 13th century — called also *capital justiciar* **3 :** either of two chief judges under early Scotch kings and with jurisdiction north and south respectively of Forth

**jus·ti·ci·ar·ship** \-(r),ship\ *n* **:** the office or dignity of a justiciar

**jus·ti·ci·ary** \,jə'stishē,erē, -ri\ *n* -ES [ME *justiciarie*, fr. ML *justiciaria*, *justitiaria*, fr. L *justitia* justice + *-aria* -ary] **1 :** the jurisdiction of a justiciar or of the High Court of Justiciary which consists of original and appellate jurisdiction in serious criminal cases and appellate jurisdiction from sheriff's decisions in civil matters in the small-debts court **2** [ML *justiciarius*, *justitiarius*] **:** JUSTICIAR

**jus·ti·ci·es** \,jə'stishē,ēz\ *n*, *pl* **justicies** [ML, lit., you may bring to trial, 2d pers. sing. pres. subj. of *justiciare*, *justitiare* to bring to trial, fr. L *justitia* justice] *Eng law* **:** a writ addressed to a sheriff ordering him to do justice in a case (as trespass, vi et armis, or personal action involving not more than 40 shillings) he otherwise could not try

**justicoat** *var of* JUSTAUCORPS

**jus·ti·fi·abil·i·ty** \,jəstə,fīə'bilad·ē, -ətē, -i\ *n* -ES **:** the quality of being justifiable

**jus·ti·fi·able** \'jəstə,fīəbəl, ,=='===\ *adj* [*justify* + *-able*] **:** capable of being justified **:** EXCUSABLE, DEFENSIBLE ⟨~ family pride —*Current Biog.*⟩

**justifiable homicide** *n* **:** a homicide (as by accident, by misadventure, in self-defense, in performing a legal duty like quelling a mob or carrying out a death sentence, in preventing a felony involving great bodily harm, or in defense of one's home or members of one's family) justified or excused by law for which no criminal punishment is imposed

**jus·ti·fi·able·ness** *n* -ES **:** the quality or state of being justifiable

**jus·ti·fi·ably** \-blē, -li\ *adv* **:** in a justifiable manner **:** DEFENSIBLY, EXCUSABLY ⟨~ classified as secret —D.W.Mitchell⟩ ⟨~ expects early action —H.S.Truman⟩

**jus·ti·fi·can·dum** \,jəstəfə'kandəm\ *n*, *pl* **justifican·da** \-də\ [LL, neut. of *justificandus*, gerundive of *justificare* to justify — more at JUSTIFY] **:** something that is to be justified — compare JUSTIFICANS

**jus·ti·fi·cans** \,jəstəfə'kanz\ *n*, *pl* **justifican·tia** \-nchēə\ [LL, pres. part. of *justificare*] **:** something (as a principle) that serves to justify

**jus·ti·fi·ca·tion** \,jəstəfə'kāshən\ *n* -s [ME *justificacioun*, fr. LL *justification-*, *justificatio*, fr. *justificatus* (past part. of *justificare* to justify) + *-ion-*, *io* -ion] **1 a :** the act, process, or state of being justified by God **b :** the terms under which one is so justified **2 a** (1) **:** the act or an instance of justifying **:** VINDICATION, DEFENSE ⟨the ~ of barbarous means by holy ends —H.J.Muller⟩ (2) **:** the condition of being justified ⟨doubted the historical ~ of the Confiteor . . . in any Lutheran liturgy —S.G.Hefelbower⟩ (3) **:** something that justifies ⟨finds in it the ~ . . . of his own work —A.P.d'Entrèves⟩ ⟨its only logical ~ would have been swift military success —Hugh Gaitskell⟩ **b** (1) **:** the showing in court of a sufficient lawful reason why a party charged or accused did or failed to do that for which he is called to answer (2) **:** something that constitutes such a reason (3) **:** the justifying of sureties (as on a bail bond) **c :** the act or an instance of verifying or proving ⟨the purpose of ~ is to produce conviction in the hearer —John Ladd⟩ **3 :** the process or result of justifying (as a line of type)

**jus·ti·fi·ca·tive** \'jəstəfə,kād·iv, ,jə'stifə,kād·iv, ¦jəstə¦fikəd·iv\ *adj* [prob. fr. F *justificatif*, fr. MF, fr. LL *justificatus* (past part.) + MF *-if* -ive] **:** serving to justify **:** JUSTIFICATORY

**jus·tif·i·ca·to·ry** \,jə'stifəkə,tōrē, ¦jəstə¦fikə,-, 'jəstəfəkə,-, -tȯr-, -ri, *esp Brit* ¦jəstifi¦kātəri *or* -ā·tri\ *adj* [LL *justificatus* (past part.) + E *-ory*] **:** tending or serving to justify **:** VINDICATORY

**jus·ti·fi·er** \'jəstə,fī(ə)r, -īə\ *n* -s **:** one that justifies: as **a :** a person who vindicates or absolves **b :** a graver for trimming the walls in enamel work

**jus·ti·fy** \'jəstə,fī\ *vb* -ED/-ING/-S [ME *justifien*, fr. MF or LL; MF *justifier*, fr. OF, fr. LL *justificare*, fr. L *justus* just + *-ficare* -fy — more at JUST] *vt* **1 a** (1) **:** to prove or show to be just, desirable, warranted, or useful **:** VINDICATE ⟨science *justifies* itself when it contributes to the desire to know —*Scientific American Reader*⟩ ⟨*justified* to herself his every fault —Ruth Park⟩ ⟨most cats must ~ themselves by catching mice —Charlton Laird⟩ ⟨~ the ways of God to man —John Milton⟩ ⟨undertaking to ~ a single scale of rates for the entire country —*Collier's Yr. Bk.*⟩ ⟨the welcome he received *justified* his visit —A.R.Forde⟩ (2) *obs* **:** to confirm, maintain, or acknowledge as true, lawful, or legitimate **b :** to prove or show to be valid, sound, or conforming to fact or reason **:** furnish grounds or evidence for **:** CONFIRM, SUPPORT, VERIFY ⟨their immediate jubilant reaction has been abundantly *justified* by the sales —Peter Forster⟩ ⟨attempts to ~ his definition of cartography —*Geographical Journal*⟩ ⟨insinuation of personal interest as a determining factor seems to me not *justified* by the facts shown —O.W.Holmes †1935⟩ ⟨*justified* my fondest hopes —D.G.Gerahty⟩ **c** (1) **:** to show to have had a sufficient legal reason (as that the libel charged is true or that the trespass charged was by license of the possessor) for (an act made the subject of a charge or accusation) (2) **:** to qualify (oneself) as a surety by taking oath to the ownership of sufficient property **2 a** *archaic* **:** to execute justice upon **:** administer justice to **b** *archaic* **:** to pronounce free from guilt or blame **:** ABSOLVE ⟨I think — or at least hope — you would have *justified* me —George Meredith⟩ **c :** to judge, regard, or treat as righteous, worthy of salvation, or as freed from the future penalty of sin ⟨God *justifies* with his forgiveness and grace the man who comes to him —Will Herberg⟩ **3 a :** to make level and square the body of (a typefounder's strike) **b :** to set to fit the measure or space closely (as a line of type, matrices, photocomposition, typewriting) or so that all full lines are of equal length and flush right and left (as typewritten matter) **c :** to cause to align evenly at the bottom (as letters of different size) **d :** to adjust to fit and lock up securely (set letterpress matter) ~ *vi* **1 a :** to show a sufficient lawful reason (as that the plaintiff consented to an act alleged to be a trespass) for an act done or not done **b :** to qualify as bail or surety by taking oath to the ownership of sufficient property ⟨the surety *justified* on the bail bond⟩ **2 :** to accept and receive as just or righteous those who respond in wholehearted faith to God as revealed by Jesus Christ ⟨believing with all their being that God *justified* through faith —John Dillenberger & Claude Welch⟩ **3** *printing* **a :** to be capable of or susceptible of justification **b :** to become justified **syn** see EXPLAIN, MAINTAIN

**justifying space** *or* **justification space** *n* **:** a space that is set by striking the spacebar of a keyboard typesetting machine and that has no predetermined width

**justing** *var of* JOUSTING

**jus·tin·i·a·ni·an** *or* **jus·tin·i·a·ne·an** \,jə¦stinē¦ānēən\ *adj*, *usu cap* [*Justinianian* fr. *Justinian* I †565 Byzantine emperor (fr. LL *Justinianus*) + E *-ian; Justinianean* fr. LL *Justinianeus* of Justinian (fr. *Justinianus* Justinian) + E *-an*] **:** of or relating to the Byzantine emperor Justinian under whom much of the Western Empire was reconquered and the laws codified in the Justinian Code ⟨the *Justinianean* ordinances on the subject of divorce were revived —B.J.Kidd⟩

**justle** *var of* JOSTLE

**just·ly** *adv* [ME, fr. *just* (adj.) + *-ly*] **:** in a just manner: as **a** *chiefly dial* **:** EXACTLY, PRECISELY, QUITE ⟨do not ~ know what your taste in reasons may be —Thomas Gray⟩ **b :** in conformity with law or justice **:** FAIRLY ⟨treated all his employees ~⟩ **c :** in conformity with fact or reason **:** CORRECTLY, PROPERLY ⟨~ ranked among the most wonderful efforts of the human hand —H.T.Buckle⟩ ⟨helps them to reason more ~ —M.R.Cohen⟩ **d :** in a manner appropriate to or required by the case **:** RIGHTLY, FITTINGLY, ACCURATELY ⟨essential that it be well developed and ~ proportioned to the other body measurements —H.G.Armstrong⟩ ⟨expresses quivering nervous strain more ~ than any player we have —*Current Biog.*⟩

**just·ness** \'jəs(t)nəs\ *n* -ES [ME *justnesse*, fr. *just* (adj.) + *-nesse* -ness] **:** the quality or state of being just: as **a :** RIGHTEOUSNESS, UPRIGHTNESS ⟨address as Jehovah a composite idea of authority, fatherhood, ~ —Joseph Macleod⟩ **b :** conformity with truth or reason **:** VALIDITY, FAIRNESS, SOUNDNESS ⟨the ~ and propriety of their sentiments —William Cowper⟩ **c :** conformity with some standard of aesthetic correctness or propriety **:** RIGHTNESS, ACCURACY, PRECISION, NICETY ⟨set forth with a ~ and care that proclaimed him a master orchestral artisan —Winthrop Sargeant⟩ ⟨estimating the ~ of the imitation —Irving Babbitt⟩ ⟨impressive in the absolute ~ of its design —R.M.Coates⟩ ⟨which he renders with a memorable ~ and beauty —Edward Sackville-West⟩

**just-noticeable difference** *n* **:** the minimum difference perceptible in any part of a series of sensory qualities ordinarily determined by reference to the corresponding stimulus conditions **:** the smallest perceptible change in a stimulus situation

**just price** *n* [trans. of ML *justum pretium*] **1 :** a price conforming to the doctrine developed in antiquity and elaborated in the medieval period that price should in general correspond to the cost of production **2 :** a price approved by common estimate, determined by a legal maximum, or conforming to some other standard of rightness or equity

**justs** *pl of* JUST

**just the same** *adv* **:** even so **:** NEVERTHELESS ⟨*just the same* I would trust him implicitly⟩

**jus uten·di** \¦jəsyü'tendē, -,dī\ *n* [L, right of using] **:** a personal right or servitude of one gratuitously for the needs of himself and his family and without profit to make use of another's property without consuming it or destroying its substance or capacity for future profit

[1]**jut** \'jət, *usu* -əd•+V\ *vb* **jutted; jutted; jutting; juts** [perh. back-formation fr. [1]*jutty*] *vi* **:** to shoot out or forward **:** PROTRUDE ⟨a cigar *jutting* from his teeth —J.A.Michener⟩ ⟨narrow bony shoulders *jutting* from his undershirt —James Jones⟩ ⟨cliffs *jutting* straight up —Peggy Durdin⟩ ⟨hurdles that ~ into the river —Murray Schumach⟩ **~** *vt* **:** to cause to jut ⟨*jutting* out his jaw humorously —Phelim Brady⟩ **syn** see BULGE

[2]**jut** \"\ *n* -s **:** something that projects or juts **:** PROJECTION ⟨passed behind a ~ of the shore —B.A.Williams⟩

[1]**jute** \'jüt, *usu* -üd•+V\ *n* -s *cap* [ME *Jute*, fr. ML *Jutae*, *Juti*, pl., Jutes, of Gmc origin; akin to OE *Eotas*, *Eotenas*, *Iotas* Jutes, ON *Jōtar*] **:** a member of one of the Low German peoples of Jutland of whom some settled in Kent in the 5th century — **jut•ish** \-üd•ish\ *adj*, *usu cap*

[2]**jute** \"\ *n* -s *often attrib* [Hindi & Bengali *jūṭ*, prob. fr. Skt *jūṭa* matted hair] **1 :** the glossy fiber of either of two East Indian plants (*Corchorus olitorius* and *C. capsularis*) used chiefly for sacking, burlap, and the cheaper varieties of twine **2 :** either of the two plants producing this fiber; *also* **:** any other plant of the genus *Corchorus*

**jute board** *n* **:** a strong plyboard containing no jute fiber but made typically from sulfate and wastepaper pulps and used esp. for shipping containers

**jute butts** *n pl* **:** fiber from the thick woody butt of the jute stalk used for bagging, twine, paper stock

**jute paper** *n* **:** a strong paper made largely from jute fiber — compare JUTE BOARD

**jutia** *var of* HUTIA

**jut–jawed** \'=¦=\ *adj* **:** having a jutting jaw ⟨his head was big, *jut-jawed* —Will Henry⟩

[1]**jut•lan•dic** \¦jət¦landik\ *adj*, *usu cap* [*Jutland*, Denmark + E *-ic*] **1 a :** of, relating to, or characteristic of Jutland **b :** of, relating to, or characteristic of the people of Jutland **2 :** of, relating to, or characteristic of the Jutlandic dialect

[2]**jutlandic** \"\ *n* -s *cap* **:** the Danish dialect of Jutland in western Denmark

**jutting** *adj* **:** PROJECTING, PROTRUDING ⟨the powerful ~ jaw —A.L.Kroeber⟩ — **jut•ting•ly** *adv*

[1]**jut•ty** \'jəd•ē\ *vb* -ED/-ING/-ES [ME *jutteyen*] *archaic* **:** to project beyond **:** JUT

[2]**jutty** \"\ *n* -ES [ME *jutte*, *jutty*, perh. alter. of *jette* jetty] **1** *archaic* **:** PIER, JETTY **2 :** a projecting part of a building ⟨an ugly assortment of *jutties*, ornaments, and blind windows —Joseph Wechsberg⟩

**juv** *abbr* **1** [L *juvenis*] young **2** juvenile

[1]**ju•ve•nal** \'jüvən$^{ə}$l\ *n* -s [L *juvenalis*, adj.] *archaic* **:** YOUTH ⟨forever . . . ~*s* in limb and spirit —*Observer*⟩

[2]**juvenal** \"\ *adj* [L *juvenalis*, fr. *juvenis* young person + *-alis* -al] **:** of, relating to, or being a juvenile ⟨~ bobwhite quail —*Wildlife Rev.*⟩

[3]**juvenal** \"\ *n* -s *usu cap* [after *Juvenal* † *ab* A.D. 140 Roman lawyer and satirist (fr. L D. Junius *Juvenalis*)] **:** a writer resembling or suggestive of the Roman poet Juvenal in his use of biting satire and pungent realism — **ju•ve•na•li•an** \¦jüvə¦nālēən\ *adj*, *usu cap*

**juvenal plumage** *n* [[2]*juvenal*] **:** the plumage of a bird immediately succeeding the natal down

**ju•ve•nes•cence** \,jüvə'nes$^{ə}$n(t)s\ *n* -s [[2]*juvenal* + *-escence*] **:** the state of being youthful or of growing young ⟨if she gave any evidence of ~, he had managed to overlook it —Josephine Pinckney⟩

[1]**ju•ve•nile** \'jüvə,nīl, -,n$^{ə}$l *sometimes* -(,)nil\ *adj* [F or L; F *juvénile*, fr. L *juvenilis*, fr. *juvenis* young person (fr. *juvenis* young) + *-ilis* -ile — more at YOUNG] **1 a :** of, relating to, or being a juvenile **:** physiologically immature or undeveloped **:** YOUNG ⟨the baby snake varies in color and markings from the ~ —*Farmer's Weekly* (*So. Africa*)⟩ ⟨his appearance was ~ —Elinor Wylie⟩ ⟨a ~ period that is essentially asexual —W.C.Allee⟩ ⟨gave her a most ~ and engaging look —Edna Ferber⟩ ⟨ten ~ years of my life —F.N.Souza⟩ **b :** being or remaining in a youthful stage of development; *specif* **:** being a plant in which the leaves are assumed to be similar to ancestral adult forms **c :** MAGMATIC ⟨~ waters⟩ **2 a :** of, relating to, characteristic of, or suitable for children or young people ⟨a ~ book⟩ ⟨a ~ phase of love not yet warmed into passion —C.W.Cunnington⟩ ⟨a ~ membership of 82,111 —C.W.Ferguson⟩ **b :** being or relating to an actor who plays a youthful part ⟨played the ~ lead in a new hit⟩ **3 :** reflecting psychological or intellectual immaturity **:** unworthy of an adult **:** CHILDISH ⟨the ~ customs of fraternities —Harold Taylor⟩ ⟨regarded their desperate rebellion as ~ melodrama —Paul Blanshard⟩ ⟨~ behavior⟩ **syn** see YOUTHFUL

[2]**juvenile** \"\ *n* -s **1 a :** a young person **:** CHILD, YOUTH ⟨observed some of the evil effects of factory labor upon ~*s* —Paul Woodring⟩ ⟨leader of a gang of ~*s* who stole a car recently —*Springfield* (*Mass.*) *Daily News*⟩ **b :** a book for children or young people ⟨a general trade book as well as a ~ —*Publishers' Weekly*⟩ **2 a :** a young individual fundamentally like an adult of its kind except in size and reproductive activity **b :** a bird in juvenal plumage **c :** a 2-year old racehorse **3 :** an actor who plays youthful parts; *sometimes* **:** an actress who plays such parts

**juvenile court** *n* **:** a court having special jurisdiction over delinquent and dependent children usu. up to the age of 18 and emphasizing in practice clinical and casework techniques with goals of delinquency prevention and rehabilitation of the child rather than punishment

**juvenile delinquency** *n* **1 :** a status in a juvenile characterized by antisocial behavior (as truancy, waywardness, incorrigibility) that is beyond parental control and therefore subject to legal action **2 :** a violation of the law of the U.S. that is committed by a juvenile and that is not punishable by death or life imprisonment

**juvenile delinquent** *n* **:** a person adjudged to be a delinquent under an age fixed by law (as 16 or 18 years or 21 years in a few states)

**juvenile insurance** *n* **:** insurance upon the life of a child usu. issued to a parent who signs the application and pays the early premiums

**juvenile officer** *n* **:** a police officer charged with the detection, prosecution, and care of juvenile delinquents — compare PROBATION OFFICER

**ju•ve•ni•lia** \,jüvə'nilēə\ *n pl but sometimes sing in constr* [L, neut. pl. of *juvenilis* juvenile] **1 :** artistic or literary compositions produced in the author's youth and typically marked by immaturity of style, treatment, or thought **:** youthful writing or other artistic work ⟨essentially ~ and are only interesting as such —*Times Lit. Supp.*⟩ ⟨a curious piece of ~ —Milton Crane⟩ ⟨is still ~ — magnificent ~ —Graham Greene⟩ **2 a :** artistic or literary compositions suited to or designed for the young ⟨the crown jewels of ~ —*Saturday Rev.*⟩ **b :** a book, film, or other composition of such character ⟨endow this ~ with what little verisimilitude it has —*Newsweek*⟩

**ju•ve•nil•i•ty** \,jüvə'niləd•ē, -ətē, -i\ *n* -ES [L *juvenilitat-*, *juvenilitas*, fr. *juvenilis* juvenile + *-itat-*, *-itas* -ity] **1 :** youthful condition or manner **2 a :** immaturity of thought or conduct **:** CHILDISHNESS ⟨reveals the fatal ~ . . . beneath the sophisticated surface —D.S.Savage⟩ ⟨the ~ of grown-up people —B.I.Bell⟩ **b :** an instance of such immaturity — usu. used in pl. ⟨pettiness, *juvenilities* —John Adams⟩

**ju•via** \'hüvēə, 'zhü-\ *n* -s [Sp & Pg, of Arawakan origin; akin to Baniva *iuíya*, *yuvíya* juvia, Baré *yuhíya*] **:** BRAZIL NUT

**juxta-** *comb form* [L *juxta*, adv. & prep., near, nearby — more at JOUST] **:** situated near ⟨*juxta*-articular⟩ ⟨*juxta*medullary⟩

**jux•ta•pose** \'jəkstə,pōz *sometimes* ,=='=\ *vt* [prob. fr. E *juxtaposition*, after such pairs as *interposition: interpose*] **:** to place side by side **:** place in juxtaposition ⟨the huts were never closely *juxtaposed* —V.G.Childe⟩ ⟨words perpetually *juxtaposed* in new and sudden combinations —T.S.Eliot⟩ ⟨pain has been . . . *juxtaposed* to pleasure as a form of emotion —F.A.Geldard⟩

**juxtaposed** *adj* **:** placed side by side **:** being in juxtaposition **syn** see ADJACENT

**jux•ta•pos•it** \,=='päzət\ *vt* -ED/-ING/-S [L *juxta* near + *positus*, past part. of *ponere* to place — more at POSITION] **:** JUXTAPOSE

**jux•ta•po•si•tion** \,jəkstəpə'zishən\ *n* -s [L *juxta* near + E *position*] **:** the act or an instance of placing two or more objects in a close spatial or ideal relationship ⟨the proper ~ of rocks, trees —D.C.Buchanan⟩ ⟨the ~ of abstract with concrete, of the homely with the far-fetched —C.D.Lewis⟩; *also* **:** the condition of being so placed ⟨forested mountains and the sea were in ~ —A.L.Kroeber⟩ ⟨the resulting ~ of popular epic and village song —G.F.Jones⟩ — **jux•ta•po•si•tion•al** \¦===¦zishən$^{ə}$l, -shnəl\ *adj*

**JV** *abbr* **1** Japanese vellum **2** junior varsity

**JVP** *abbr* Japanese vellum proofs

**JW** *abbr* junior warden

**jwlr** *abbr* jeweler

**jyn•gine** \'jin,jīn, -njən\ *adj* [NL *Jyng-*, *Jynx* + E *-ine*] **:** of or relating to the genus *Jynx*

**jynx** \'jiŋ(k)s\ *n* [L *iynx*, fr. Gk] **1** -ES **:** WRYNECK **2** *cap* [NL, fr. L *iynx*] **:** a genus of woodpeckers consisting of the wrynecks

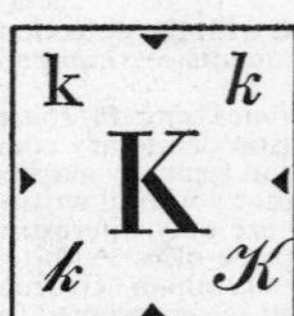

**¹k** \'kā\ *n, pl* **k's** *or* **ks** \'kāz\ *often cap, often attrib* **1 a :** the 11th letter of the English alphabet **b :** an instance of this letter printed, written, or otherwise represented **c :** a speech counterpart of orthographic *k* (as *k* in *kill, skill, like, joked,* or German *kühn*) **2 :** a printer's type, a stamp, or some other instrument for reproducing the letter *k* **3 :** someone or something arbitrarily or conveniently designated *k* esp. as the 10th or when j is used for the 10th the 11th in order or class **4 :** something having the shape of the letter K **5 :** a unit vector parallel to the z-axis

**²k** *abbr, often cap* **1** [L *kalendae*] calends **2** karat **3** [*kathode*] cathode **4** keel **5** keg **6** Kelvin **7** key **8** kilo- **9** kilogram **10** king **11** kip **12** kitchen **13** knight **14** knit **15** knot **16** kopeck **17** koruna **18** kran **19** krona **20** krone **21** kroon **22** kurus

**³k** *symbol* **1** *cap* [NL *kalium*] potassium **2** *often cap* constant **3** [G *konstant*] Boltzman's constant **4** thermal conductivity **5 a** key — used as a cryptographic subscript ⟨$B_p$ ($D_K$) = $E_e$ means that D was used as the key letter when B was enciphered into E⟩; see VIGENÈRE CIPHER **b** *cap* a cryptographic numerical keying element or the numerical value of a key letter when the normal alphabet is numbered from 0 to 25 ⟨P + C = K is the Beaufort keying method⟩ **6** *cap* **:** dissociation constant **7** *cap* **:** ionization constant

**¹ka** *var of* KAY

**²ka** \'kō, 'kä\ *chiefly Scot var of* CALL

**³ka** \'kä\ *n* -s [Egypt] **:** the personality double believed in ancient Egypt to be born with an individual and after death to reside in the statue of the deceased in the tomb dependent upon the preservation and nourishment of the body

**⁴ka** *usu cap, var of* KHA

**ka** *abbr* [*kathode*] cathode

**KA** *abbr* king of arms

**kaa·ba** *or* **ka'·ba** *also* **ka'·bah** *or* **caa·ba** \'käbə, 'kȧbə\ *adj, usu cap* [Ar *ka'bah,* lit., square building, fr. *ka'b* cube] **:** of or relating to the Islamic shrine in Mecca that incorporates a sacred black stone and is the goal of Islamic pilgrimage and the point toward which all Muslims turn in praying — see QIBLA

**kaa·ma** \'kämə\ *n* -s [Hottentot (Nama dial.) ʘxamap, *Kamāb*] **:** HARTEBEEST

**kaa·wi yam** \'käwē\ *n* [origin unknown] **:** a yam (*Dioscorea aculeata*) of southern Asia and Polynesia with prickly stems and sweet tubers

**kab** *var of* CAB

**ka·babish** \kə'babish, -'bäb-\ *n, pl* **kababish** *or* **kababishes** *usu cap* **1 :** a nomadic Arab people in the Anglo-Egyptian Sudan **2 :** a member of the Kababish people

**ka·ba·ka** \kə'bäkə\ *n* -s [native name in Uganda] **:** the native king of Buganda in Uganda ⟨the Colonial Office a year ago exiled the *Kabaka* . . . of Buganda —*N.Y. Times*⟩

**kabala** *or* **kabbala** *often cap, var of* CABALA

**kabalassou** *var of* CABALASSOU

**kabalist** *var of* CABALIST

**ka·ba·ra·go·ya** \kə,bärə'gōyə\ *n* -s [origin unknown] **:** a large water monitor (*Varanus salvator*) of southeastern Asia, the Malay archipelago, and the Philippines that sometimes reaches a length of seven feet

**ka·bar·din** \¦kabər¦dēn, ¦käbər-, ¦kä,bär-\ *also* **ka·bard** \kə'bärd\ *n* -s *cap* **1 :** a member of a Circassian people of the Caucasus mountains who comprise over half the population of the Kabardino-Balkarian Autonomous Soviet Socialist Republic and whose religion is Islam **2** *or* **ka·bar·di·an** \kə'bärdēən\ **:** the Caucasic language of the Kabardins — **ka·bar·din·i·an** \¦kabər¦dinēən\ *adj, usu cap*

**kabassou** *var of* CABASSOU

**kab·ba·lah** \kə'bälə\ *n* -s [Heb *qabbālāh,* lit., received, fr. *qābēl* to receive] **:** a written certificate issued by a rabbi to a prospective shohet who has passed an examination testing his knowledge of and expertness in shehitah

**kabbalist** *var of* CABALIST

**ka·bel·jou** *also* **ka·bel·jau** *or* **ka·bel·jauw** \'käbəl,yaů, 'kab-\ *n* -s [Afrik *kabeljou,* fr. D *kabeljauw* cod] **:** a large South African sciaenid food fish (*Johnius hololepidotus*) having a liver extremely rich in vitamin A that is closely related to and sometimes held identical with the European maigre

**kabinda** *usu cap, var of* CABINDA

**ka·bir·pan·thi** \kə,bir'pən·,tē\ *n* -s *usu cap* [Hindi *kabīrpanthī* fr. *Kabīr* †1518 Hindu mystic poet + *panthī* follower] **:** a member of a reform sect of India originating in the 15th century with doctrines based on the teachings of Kabir

**ka·bi·stan** \¦käbə¦stän, ¦kabə¦stan\ *n* -s *usu cap* [*Kabistan, Kabristan,* locality in southeastern Dagestan, U.S.S.R.] **:** ¹KUBA

**ka·bob** *also* **ka·bab** *or* **ke·bab** *or* **ke·bob** *or* **ca·bob** \'kä,bäb, kə'bäb; *when "shish" precedes,* kə,bäb\ *n* -s [Per, Hindi, Ar, & Turk; Per & Hindi *kabāb,* fr. Ar, fr. Turk *kebap*] **:** cubes of meat (as lamb) marinated and cooked with onions, tomatoes, or other vegetables esp. on a skewer — usu. used in pl.

**kaboodle** *var of* CABOODLE

**ka·bui** \kə'büē\ *n, pl* **kabui** *or* **kabuis** *cap* **1 :** a Naga people of the Naga hills on the Burma-Assam frontier west and northwest of Manipur valley **2 :** a member of the Kabui people

**kab·u·kal·li** \,kabə'kalē\ *n* -s [native name in British Guiana] **:** CUPIUBA

**ka·bu·ki** \kə¦bükē, -'bükē, *Jap approximately* 'käbü(,)kē\ *n, usu cap* [Jap, lit., art of singing and dancing] **:** traditional Japanese popular drama with singing and dancing performed in a highly stylized manner

**ka·bul** \'käbəl, -,bül, -,bůl; kə'bül, ka'-, -'bůl\ *adj, usu cap* [fr. *Kabul,* city in eastern Afghanistan, capital of Afghanistan] **:** of or from Kabul, the capital of Afghanistan **:** of the kind or style prevalent in Kabul

**¹ka·bu·li** \'käbə(,)lē; kə'bülē, -'bůlē\ *adj, usu cap* [Per *kābulī,* fr. *Kābul* Kabul] **:** of or belonging to Kabul, Afghanistan

**²kabuli** \"\ *n* -s *cap* **:** a native or resident of Kabul

**ka·bu·ri** \kə'bürē\ *n* -s [origin unknown] **:** a land crab (*Ucides cordatus*) common in mangrove swamps from the West Indies to southern Brazil

**ka·byl** *also* **ka·byle** \kə'bī(ə)l, -bē(ə)l\ *n* -s *usu cap* [Ar *qabā'il,* pl. of *qabīlah* tribe] **1 :** a Berber belonging to a Muslim agricultural people of the mountainous coastal area east of Algiers including blond and brunet types and now speaking chiefly Arabic **2 :** the Berber language of the Kabyles

**kacha** *or* **kachcha** *var of* KUTCHA

**ka·cha na·ga** \¦kächə¦nägə\ *n, pl* **kacha nagas** *usu cap K&N* **1 :** a group of three allied Naga peoples including the Kabui, the Lyeng, and the Zemi and inhabiting the Naga hills near Manipur **2 :** a member of a Kacha Naga people

**kachari** *usu cap, var of* CACHARI

**kache** *usu cap, var of* KHA

**kach·e·mak bay** \¦kachə,mak¦bā\ *adj, usu cap K&B* [*Kachemak Bay,* locality south of Anchorage, south central Alaska, where remains of the culture were discovered] **:** of or relating to a Pacific Eskimo and Aleutian culture of about A.D. 100–1700 characterized by sealing and by the development of southwest Alaskan types of artifacts and the introduction of foreign traits

**¹ka·chin** \kə'chin\ *n, pl* **kachin** *or* **kachins** *usu cap* **1 :** CHINGPAW **2 :** the Tibeto-Burman language of the Chingpaw people

**²kach·in** \'kachən\ *n* -s [perh. alter. of *catechin*] **:** pyrocatechol used as a photographic developer

**ka·chi·na** *or* **ka·tci·na** *also* **ka·tchi·na** *or* **ca·chi·na** \kə'chēnə\ *n* -s [Hopi *qačina* supernatural] **1 :** one of the deified ancestral spirits believed among the Hopi and other Pueblo Indians to visit the pueblos at intervals (as to bring rain) **2 :** one of the elaborately masked impersonators of the kachinas that dance at agricultural ceremonies **3** *or* **kachina doll :** a doll representing a kachina made from cottonwood root and given to Hopi children by the kachina dancers

**k acid** *n, cap K* **:** a crystalline sulfonic acid $NH_2C_{10}H_4$-(OH)$(SO_3H)_2$ isomeric with H acid that is used as a dye intermediate; 8-amino-1-naphthol-3,5-disulfonic acid

**kackle** *var of* KECKLE

**ka·da·ga** \kə'dägə\ *n, pl* **kadaga** *or* **kadagas** *usu cap* **:** COORG

**ka·dai** \kä,dī\ *n* -s *usu cap* **:** a language family of southern China and northern Vietnam held to be related to Thai

**ka·dam·ba** \kə'dambə\ *n* -s [Skt, of Dravidian origin; akin to Tamil-Malayalam *kaṭampu*] **1 :** an East Indian shade tree (*Anthocephalus cadamba*) of the family Rubiaceae having hard yellowish wood and globose clusters of flowers **2 :** the wood of the kadamba

**kadarite** *usu cap, var of* QADARITE

**ka·da·ya gum** \kə'dīə-\ *n* [*kadaya* modif. of Hindi *karāyal* resin] **:** STERCULIA GUM

**kad·dish** \'kädish\ *n, pl* **kad·di·shim** \kä'dishəm, -(,)-shēm\ *often cap* [Aram *qaddīsh* holy] **1 :** an ancient Jewish prayer in Aramaic recited in several forms by the cantor in the daily ritual of the synagogue and adopted for use on various occasions; *specif* **:** a mourner's prayer recited daily at public services during the first 11 months after the death of a parent or other close relative and on subsequent anniversaries of the death **2 :** the person (as traditionally a son) who recites the mourner's kaddish for the deceased

**kadet** *var of* ²CADET

**kadi** *also* **kadhi** *var of* QADI

**kadiak bear** *usu cap K, var of* KODIAK BEAR

**ka·dir** *also* **kha·dar** *or* **kha·dir** \'kädə(r)\ *n, pl* **kadir** *or* **kadirs** *usu cap* **:** a primitive jungle-dwelling people somewhat negroid in appearance who are remnants of the pre-Dravidian peoples of India and inhabit the Deccan plateau

**ka·do·ha·da·cho** \kə,dōhədə'chō\ *n, pl* **kadohadacho** *or* **kadohadachos** *usu cap* [Caddo *Kädohädächo,* lit., real chiefs] **1 :** a Caddoan confederacy of northeastern Texas and southwestern Arkansas including the Cahinnio, Kadohadacho proper, and Upper Natchitoches **2 :** a member of any one of the peoples of the Kadohadacho confederacy

**kad·su·ra** \'kädsərə, 'käts-\ *n* -s [modif. of Jap *katsura*] **:** KATSURA TREE

**ka·du** \'kä(,)dü\ *n, pl* **kadu** *or* **kadus** *usu cap* **1 a :** a people inhabiting chiefly the Katha district of Upper Burma east of Manipur, Assam **b :** a member of such people **2 :** the Tibeto-Burman language of the Kadu people

**ka·dy** *or* **ka·ty** *also* **ca·dy** \'kād¦ē, -ät¦, ¦i\ *or* **cad·dy** \'kad|\ *n* -ES [perh. alter. of *caddie;* fr. its being worn by boys] **:** a man's hat (as a straw hat or derby)

**kae** \'kā\ *n* -s [ME (northern dial.) *ka;* akin to MD *ca* jackdaw, OHG *kāa, kā* — more at CHOUGH] *chiefly Scot* **:** JACKDAW

**kae·ding petrel** \'kādiŋ-\ *or* **kaeding's petrel** *n, usu cap K* [after Henry B. *Kaeding* †1913 Am. mining engineer] **:** a petrel (*Oceanodroma leucorhoa kaedingi*) of the coast and islands of Lower California that is closely related to the Leach's petrel but smaller and with a less forked tail

**kaemp·fer·ol** \'kempfə,rōl, -rōl\ *also* **kamp·fer·ol** \'kam-\ *n* -s [Engelbert *Kämpfer* †1716 Ger. physician + ISV *-ol*] **:** a yellow crystalline flavonol coloring matter $C_{15}H_{10}O_6$ found in the free form or in glycosidic combination in many plants

**kaf** *var of* KAPH

**ka·fa** *or* **kaf·fa** \'käfə, 'kafə\ *n, pl* **kafa** *or* **kaffa** *usu cap* **1 :** a native or inhabitant of the Kafa region in southwestern Ethiopia **2 :** the Cushitic language of the Kafa

**kaf·er·i·ta** \,kafə'rēd·ə\ *n* -s [blend of *kaffir* and *feterita*] **:** a hybrid between kafir and feterita

**kaf·fa** \'käfə, 'kafə\ *n* -s *often cap* [*Kaffa, Kafa,* region and former province in southwestern Ethiopia] **:** a grayish reddish brown that is yellower and lighter than liver and redder and stronger than average taupe brown

**kaf·fee·klatsch** \'käfā,kläch, -fē,-, -lach\ *n* -ES *often cap* [G, fr. *Kaffee* coffee + *Klatsch* gossip] **:** COFFEE KLATCH

**kaf·fir** *or* **kaf·ir** \'kafə(r)\ *n* [Ar *kāfir* infidel] **1** *also* **caf·fer** *or* **caf·fre** \"\ *pl* **kaffir** *or* **kaffirs** *or* **kafir** *or* **kafirs a** *usu cap* **:** a member of a group of southern African Bantu-speaking peoples of Ngoni stock **b** *sometimes cap* **:** a South African of negroid ancestry — usu. used disparagingly **2** *also* **caffer** *or* **caffre** -s *sometimes cap* **:** one who is not a Muslim — usu. used disparagingly **3** -s *usu cap* **:** XHOSA — often used disparagingly **4** -s *usu cap* **:** a South African stock (as a land or mining share) traded on the London stock exchange — usu. used in pl. **5** *usu* **kafir** *or* **kafir corn** -s *sometimes cap K* **:** any of various grain sorghums that have stout short-jointed somewhat juicy stalks and erect heads

**kaffir bean** *n, usu cap K, Africa* **:** COWPEA

**kaffir beer** *n, usu cap K* **:** a beer prepared by the native population of southern Africa from grain

**kaffir boom** \-,bōm, -,büm\ *n, often cap K* [part trans. of Afrik *kafferboom,* fr. *Kaffer* Kaffir + *boom* tree, fr. D, fr. MD; akin to OE *bēam* tree — more at BEAM] *Africa* **:** CORAL TREE; *esp* **:** a coral tree (*Erythrina caffra*) with scarlet flowers and light soft wood sometimes used for fence posts or shingles

**kaffir bread** *n, usu cap K* **1 :** the farinaceous pith of the fruit of a plant of the genus *Encephalartos* (esp. *E. caffer*) used as food in southern Africa **2 :** a plant that bears Kaffir bread

**kaffir cat** *also* **caffer cat** *or* **caffre cat** *n, usu cap K or 1st C* **:** a widely distributed wildcat (*Felis ocreata,* syn. *F. caffra*) of Africa and Asia Minor that has a tawny striped coat and is regarded as one of the chief ancestors of domesticated cats

**kaffir crane** *n, usu cap K* **:** a slaty gray crane (*Balearica regulorum*) of southern Africa that has a crown of velvety black plumes

**kaffir lily** *n, usu cap K* **1 :** CRIMSON FLAG **2 :** a plant of the genus *Clivia; esp* **:** a plant (*C. miniata*) of southern Africa cultivated for its showy flowers

**kaffir orange** *n, usu cap K* **1 :** an East African tree (*Strychnos spinosa*) having rough bark, grayish green foliage, and dark green round aromatic fruit with hard rind and soft pulp **2 :** the fruit of the Kaffir orange

**kaffir piano** *n, usu cap K* **:** a marimba of southern Africa

**kaffir plum** *or* **kaffir date** *n, usu cap K* **1 :** an African tree (*Harpephyllum caffrum*) of the family Anacardiaceae **2 :** the edible fruit of Kaffir plum

**kaf·fi·yeh** *also* **kef·fi·yeh** \kə'fē(y)ə\ *n* -s [Ar *kūfīyah, kaffīyah* — more at CAFFA] **:** an Arab headdress consisting of a square of cloth folded to form a triangle and bound on the head with an agal

**kaf·frar·i·an** *also* **caf·frar·i·an** \ka'fra(a)rēən, kə'-\ *adj, usu cap* [*Kaffraria,* region of Cape Province, Union of South Africa + E *-an*] **:** of, relating to, or being the biogeographic province or subregion that includes the Union of South Africa and adjacent areas

**kaf·ir** \'kafə(r)\ *n, pl* **kafir** *or* **kafirs** *usu cap* [Ar *kāfir* infidel] **1 :** a people of the Hindu Kush in northeastern Afghanistan **2 :** a member of the Kafir people

**kafi·ri** \'kafərē, kə'firē\ *n* -s *usu cap* **:** the Dard language of the Kafir people

**kaftan** *var of* CAFTAN

**ka·fu·an** \kə'füən\ *adj, usu cap* [*Kafu* River, Uganda + E *-an*] **:** of, relating to, or being a Lower Pleistocene culture of Uganda typified by crudely chipped pebble tools

**kagaba** *usu cap, var of* CÁGABA

**ka·go** \'kä(,)gō\ *n* -s [Jap] **:** an open palanquin used in Japan

**ka·go·shi·ma** \¦kägə¦shēmə\ *adj, usu cap* [fr. *Kagoshima,* city on the south coast of Kyushu, Japan] **:** of or from the city of Kagoshima, Japan **:** of the kind or style prevalent in Kagoshima

**ka·gu** \'kä(,)gü\ *n* -s [native name in New Caledonia] **:** a crested flightless gruiform bird (*Rhynochetos jubatus*) confined to New Caledonia that is slaty gray with orange-red bill and feet and concealed bars of black, white, and rufous on the wings

**ka·gu·ra** \'kägə(,)rä\ *n* -s [Jap] **:** a stately dance of the Shinto religion that now forms a part of Japanese village festivals

**ka·ha** \'kä(,)hä, ='=\ *or* **ka·hau** \-,haů, ='=\ *n* -s [native name in Borneo; fr. its cry] **:** PROBOSCIS MONKEY

**ka·hal** \'kä,häl\ *n* -s [Heb *qāhal* community, gathering] **:** the local governing body of a former European Jewish community administering religious, legal, and communal affairs

**ka·ha·la** \kə'hälə\ *n* -s [Hawaiian] **:** an amberfish (*Seriola dumerili*) of Hawaiian waters

**ka·har** \kə'här\ *n* -s [Hindi *kahār*] **:** one of a Hindu caste whose caste occupation is that of a carrier

**ka·ha·wai** \'kähə,wī\ *n* -s [Maori] **:** AUSTRALIAN SALMON

**ka·hi·ka·tea** \'kīkə,tēə, 'kak-\ *n* -s [Maori] **:** a New Zealand evergreen tree (*Podocarpus dacrydioides*) valued for its light soft easily worked wood, its resin, and the sweet edible aril surrounding its seed — called also *white pine*

**ka·hi·li** \kə'hēlē\ *n* -s [Hawaiian] **:** a long pole decorated at one end with a cluster of feather plumes and used as a ceremonial emblem in Hawaii

**kahili ginger** *n, Hawaii* **:** a butterfly lily (*Hedychium gardnerianum*) that is native to northern India and is cultivated for its long spikes of lemon yellow flowers with bright red stamens

**kahn test** \'kän-\ *or* **kahn reaction** *or* **kahn** *n* -s *usu cap K* [after Reuben L. *Kahn* *b*1887 Am. bacteriologist] **:** a serum-precipitation reaction for the diagnosis of syphilis

**ka·hu** \'kä(,)hü\ *n* -s [Maori] **:** a common harrier (*Circus approximans*) represented by several distinct races in Australasia and the East Indies

**ka·hu·na** \kə'hünə\ *n* -s [Hawaiian] **1** *Hawaii* **:** a native master of a craft or vocation **2** *Hawaii* **:** a native medicine man **:** a master of Hawaiian religious lore and ceremonial

**kahuna ana·ana** \ə'nä,ə,nä\ *n, pl* **kahuna anaana** [Hawaiian, fr. *kahuna* + *'anā'anā* black magic] *Hawaii* **:** SORCERER; *esp* **:** one who prays his victims to death

**kahuna la·pa·au** \-lə'pä,aů\ *n, pl* **kahuna lapaau** [Hawaiian, fr. *kahuna* + *lapa'au* medicinal] *Hawaii* **:** a medical practitioner esp. skilled in herbal medicine

**kai** \'kī\ *n, pl* **kai** *or* **kais** *usu cap* **1 a :** a people on the Huon gulf, Territory of New Guinea **b :** a member of such people **2 :** the Melanesian language of the Kai people **3 :** KATE

**kaibal** *usu cap, var of* KOIBAL

**kai·bar·tha** *or* **kai·bart·ta** \kī'bərd·ə, -'bär-\ *n* -s *usu cap* [Beng *kaibartta,* fr. Skt *kaivarta* fisherman] **:** a member of a low caste of Mongoloid origin that is numerous in Assam and Bengal

**kaid** \'kīd, 'kä,ēd\ *n* -s [Ar *qā'id* leader, commander in chief, fr. *qād* to command] **:** a tribal chief or governor of a district or group of villages in northern Africa

**kai·feng** \'kī¦fəŋ\ *adj, usu cap* [fr. *Kaifeng,* city in east central China] **:** of or from the city of Kaifeng, China **:** of the kind or style prevalent in Kaifeng

**¹kai–kai** \'kī,kī\ *n, pl* **kai–kai** [Marquesan; akin to Hawaiian & Samoan *'ai* food, Maori & Tongan *kai*] **1** *or* **kai** *Austral* **:** FOOD **2** *Austral* **:** FEASTING

**²kai–kai** \"\ *or* **kai** *vt* -ED/-ING/-s *Austral* **:** EAT

**kai·ka·ra** \kī'kärə\ *n* -s [modif. of Ar *karākīy,* pl. of *kurkīy* demoiselle] **:** DEMOISELLE 2a

**kai·ka·wa·ka** \'kīkə,wäkə\ *n* -s [Maori] **:** either of two New Zealand evergreen trees of the genus *Libocedrus:* **a :** KAWAKA **b :** MOUNTAIN PINE 3b

**kail** *var of* KALE

**kails** \'kāəlz\ *n pl* [ME *kayles;* akin to MD *kegel* cone, ninepin, OHG *kegil* stake, peg, ON *kaggi* keg — more at KEG] **1** *dial Brit* **:** a set of bone or wooden pins used in playing ninepins **2** *usu sing in constr, dial Brit* **:** a game played with kails

**¹kail·yard** \'kā(ə)l,=\ *n* [Sc, fr. *kale, kail* + E *yard* — more at KALE] *Scot* **:** KITCHEN GARDEN

**²kailyard** \"\ *adj, often cap, of a school of writers* **:** characterized by sentimental description of Scottish life and considerable use of Scots dialect ⟨such various aspects of Scottish life as whiskey, deerstalking, salmon fishing, the *Kailyard* school of writers —Janet Adams Smith⟩

**kail·yard·er** \-də(r)\ *n* -s *often cap* **:** a writer of the kailyard school

**kaim** \'kām\ *chiefly Scot var of* COMB

**kai·ma·kam** *also* **qai·ma·qam** *or* **qaim·ma·qam** \¦kīmə¦käm\ *n* -s [Turk *kaymakam,* fr. Ar *qā'im maqām* deputy, fr. *qā'im* standing + *maqām* place] **:** a lieutenant or deputy in the service of the Ottoman Empire

**kai·mi clover** \'kīmē-\ *n* [origin unknown] **:** a West Indian tick trefoil (*Desmodium canum*) used as a pasture plant esp. in the humid tropics

**¹kain** *var of* ²CAIN

**²kain** \'kīn\ *n* -s [Malay] **:** SARONG

**kai·nah** \'kīnə\ *n, pl* **kainah** *or* **kainahs** *usu cap* [Blackfoot *ah-kai-nah,* lit., many chiefs] **:** BLOOD 9

**kainga** \'kīŋə\ *n* -s [Maori] **:** a Maori village usu. located on low ground — compare PA

**kaingang** *cap, var of* CAINGANG

**¹ka·ing·in** *also* **ca·ing·in** *or* **ca·iñg·in** \kä'ēŋən\ *n* -s [Tag *kaingin*] *Philippines* **:** SWIDDEN ⟨some lonely farmer hewing out a ~ in the jungle —Wallace Stegner⟩

**²kaingin** \"\ *adj, Philippines* **:** employing a technique of clearing land by slashing and burning underbrush and trees and plowing the ashes under for fertilizer ⟨well-known ~ system which has been enormously destructive of valuable timber —A.L.Kroeber⟩

**kai·nite** \'kī,nīt, 'kā,-\ *also* **kai·nit** \kī'nēt\ *n* -s [G *kainit,* fr. Gk *kainos* new, recent + G *-it* -ite — more at RECENT] **:** a natural salt $KMg(SO_4)Cl.3H_2O$ consisting of a hydrous sulfate and chloride of magnesium and potassium that occurs impure in irregular granular masses, whose color as determined by purity is white, gray, pink, violet, or black, and that is used as a fertilizer and as a source of potassium and magnesium compounds

**kai·nos·ite** \'kīnə,sīt, 'kān-\ *n* -s [Sw *kainosit,* fr. Gk *kainos* + Sw *-it* -ite] **:** a mineral $Ca_2(Ce,Y)_2(SiO_4)_3CO_3.H_2O$ consisting of hydrous silicate and carbonate of calcium, cerium, and yttrium

**kainozoic** *var of* CENOZOIC

**kai·ros** \(')kī¦räs\ *n, pl* **kai·roi** \-rȯi\ [Gk, fitness, opportunity, time; perh. akin to Gk *keirein* to cut — more at SHEAR] **:** a time when conditions are right for the accomplishment of a crucial action **:** the opportune and decisive moment

**kais** *pl of* KAI

**kai·ser** \'kīzə(r)\ *n* -s [ME *keiser,* fr. ON *keisari;* akin to OE *cāsere* emperor, OHG *keisur,* Goth *kaisar;* all fr. a prehistoric Gmc word borrowed fr. L *Caesar,* cognomen of Gaius Julius Caesar †44 B.C. Roman general and statesman] **:** EMPEROR: as **a :** the head of an ancient or medieval empire (as the Roman Empire or the Holy Roman Empire) **b** [G, fr. OHG *keisur*] **:** the sovereign of Austria from 1804 to 1918 ⟨all the countries over which the Hapsburg ~s claimed personal lordship —*Century Mag.*⟩ **c** [G, fr. OHG *keisur*] **:** the ruler of Germany from 1871 to 1918 ⟨the appointment of the chancellor of the German Empire by the ~⟩

**kaiser brown** *n, often cap K* **:** GINGER 5

**kai·ser·dom** \-dəm\ *n* -s [prob. trans. of G *kaisertum*] **1 :** the office or authority of a kaiser ⟨opposition to ~ among many American groups⟩ **2 :** the territory ruled by a kaiser ⟨the most efficient economists of ~ —*N.Y. Times Mag.*⟩

**kai·se·rin** \'kīzərən\ *n* -s [G, fem. of *kaiser*] **:** the wife of a kaiser

**kai·ser·ism** \-,rizəm\ *n* -s *often cap* **:** a political system and practices existing under or symbolized by the rule of the German kaiser ⟨that *Kaiserism* must be repudiated in favor of some new and more liberal political system —F.A.Ogg & Harold Zink⟩ ⟨the . . . absolute political dogmas with which *Kaiserism* is associated —*New Republic*⟩

**kai·ser·ship** \-zə(r),ship\ *n* -s **:** the office of kaiser

**kai·ta·ka** \kī'täkə\ *n* -s [Maori] **:** a mat of fine flax worn as a cloak by the Maoris

**kai·thi** \'kīd·ē\ *n* -s *usu cap* [Hindi *kaithī, kāyathī* used by the Kayasths, fr. *kāyath* Kayasth, fr. Skt *kāyastha*] **:** an alphabet of Nagari type that is used in writing Bihari and eastern Hindi

**kai·val·ya** \kī'vəlyə\ *n* -s [Skt, fr. *kevala* exclusively one's own, alone, whole — more at CELIBATE] **:** the final state of Jain and Vedantic salvation characterized as absolute release of one's jiva from all entanglements with ajiva **:** self-directed liberation

**kajak** *var of* KAYAK

**ka·jar** \kə'jär, 'kä,j-\ *n, pl* **kajar** *or* **kajars** *usu cap* [Per *Qājār,* of Turk origin] **1 :** a people of northern Iran holding political supremacy through the dynasty ruling Persia from 1794 to 1925 **2 :** a member of the Kajar people

**ka·ja·wah** \kə'jäwə\ *also* **ke·dja·ve** \-ävə\ *n* -s [Hindi *kajāwa,* fr. Per] **:** a pannier used in pairs on camels and mules esp. in India

**ka·ka** \'käkə\ *n* -s [Maori] **:** an olive brown New Zealand parrot (*Nestor meridionalis*) that is marked with gray on the

crown and red on the face, neck, abdomen, rump, and underwing coverts and that talks and mimics well in captivity
**kaka beak** *or* **kaka bill** *n* : an evergreen glory pea (*Clianthus puniceus*) that is a climbing shrub sometimes exceeding 12 feet in height, has brilliant red flowers growing in pendulous axillary racemes and distinguished by the very long pointed keel, and is native to New Zealand but now rare except in cultivation
**ka·kap je·ram** \ˌkäˌkäpjəˈräm\ *n* [Malay *kakap jĕram*] : a fishing boat of the Malayan east coast
**ka·ka·po** \ˈkäkəˌpō\ *n* -s [Maori] : a New Zealand parrot (*Strigops habroptilus*) with soft green and brown barred plumage that has well-developed wings but little power of flight, lives in holes or burrows in the ground, and has nocturnal habits — called also *owl parrot*
**ka·kar** *or* **ka·kur** \ˈkäkə(r)\ *n* -s [Hindi *kakar*] : MUNTJAC 1
**kak·a·ral·li** *also* **kak·a·rali** *or* **kak·e·ral·li** \ˌkakəˈralē\ *n* -s [native name in British Guiana] **1** *in British Guiana* : SAPUCAIA **2** *in British Guiana* : MANBARKLAK
**ka·ka·ri·ki** \ˈkäkəˌrēkē\ *or* **ka·ka·wa·ri·ki** \ˈkäkəwəˌ-\ *n* -s [Maori] **1** : either of two green parakeets of New Zealand: **a** : one (*Cyanorhamphus novae-zelandiae*) having a red crown **b** : one (*Cyanorhamphus auriceps*) having a yellow crown **2** : a small green New Zealand lizard of the genus *Lygosoma*
**kak·a·toe** \ˌkakəˈtō(ˌ)ē\ *n, cap* [NL, perh. modif. of D *kaketoe* cockatoo — more at COCKATOO] : a genus of moderately large to very large parrots that are widely distributed in the Australasian area, are usu. predominantly white, and include numerous widely known cockatoos (as the pink cockatoo and the sulphur-crested cockatoo)
**ka·ka·wa·hie** \ˌkäkəwəˈhēˌā\ *n* -s [Hawaiian] : a bright scarlet flower-pecker (*Loxops maculata flammea*) of Molokai Island
**ka·ke·mo·no** \ˌkäkəˈmō(ˌ)nō, ˌkak-, -mōnə\ *n* -s [Jap] : a picture or writing on silk or paper that is suitable for hanging and that usu. has a roller at its lower edge — compare MAKIMONO
**¹ka·ki** \ˈkä(ˌ)kē\ *n* -s [Jap] : JAPANESE PERSIMMON
**²ka·ki** \ˈkäˈkē\ *n* -s [Maori] : a blackish stilt of New Zealand that is usu. considered a color phase of the white-headed stilt but is sometimes assigned to a separate species (*Himantopus novae-zelandiae*)
**kak·i·dro·sis** \ˌkakəˈdrōsəs\ *n, pl* **kakidro·ses** \-ōˌsēz\ [NL, fr. *kak-*, *cac-* cac- + *-idrosis*] : secretion of sweat of a disagreeable odor
**ka·ki·emon** \ˌkäkēˈ(y)āˌmän\ *n* -s *usu cap* [after Sakaida *Kakiemon fl* 1650 Jap. potter] **1** : a Japanese porcelain made in Arita and much copied in Europe **2** : porcelain decoration in the manner of Kakiemon painted usu. in iron red, blue green, light blue, violet, or grayish yellow
**kak·is·toc·ra·cy** \ˌkakəˈstäkrəsē\ *n* -ES [Gk *kakistos* (superl. of *kakos* bad) + E *-cracy* — more at CACK] : government by the worst men
**kak·kak** \ˈkaˌkak\ *n* -s [Chamorro] : a small bittern (*Ixobrychus sinensis*) of Guam
**kako-** — see CAC-
**kak·o·gen·ic** \ˌkakəˈjenik\ *adj* [*cac-* + *-genic*] : DYSGENIC
**ka·kor·tok·ite** \kəˈkō(r)dəˌkīt\ *n* -s [*Kakortok* (Greenland Eskimo name for Julianehaab), Greenland + E *-ite*] : a rock of variable composition occurring in Greenland in black, white, and red sheets — see AGPAITE
**ka·ku** \ˈkä(ˌ)kü\ *n* -s [Hawaiian] *Hawaii* : GREAT BARRACUDA
**kal** *abbr* [L *kalendae*] calends
**ka·la azar** \ˌkäləˌəˈzär\ *n* [Hindi *kālā-āzār* black disease, fr. Hindi *kālā* black + Per *āzār* disease] : a severe infectious disease chiefly of eastern and southern Asia that is marked by fever, progressive anemia, leukopenia, and enlargement of the spleen and liver and is caused by a flagellate (*Leishmania donovani*) which is transmitted by the bite of sand flies (genus *Phlebotomus*) and which proliferates in reticuloendothelial cells — called also *visceral leishmaniasis*
**ka·lam** \kəˈläm\ *n* -s [Ar *kalām* word, speech] : Muslim scholastic theology — compare MUTAKALLIMUN, SHARI'A
**Kal·a·mein** \ˈkaləˌmīn\ *trademark* — used for sheet metal used esp. on wooden doors to prevent the passage of fire
**ka·la·mian** \ˌkäləmˈyän\ *n, pl* **kalamian** *or* **kalamians** *usu cap* [native name in northern Sulu Sea] **1** : a Christianized people inhabiting the Calamian islands of the Philippines **2** : a member of the Kalamian people
**kalan·choe** \ˌkalənˈkōē, kəˈlaŋkə(ˌ)wē\ *n* [NL] **1** *cap* : a genus of chiefly African and Australian tropical herbs or shrubs (family Crassulaceae) having a four-parted calyx and including numerous forms cultivated as ornamentals **2** -s : any plant of the genus *Kalanchoe*
**ka·lan·tas** *or* **ca·lan·tas** \ˌkälənˈtäs\ *n* -ES [Tag *kalantas*] : PHILIPPINE CEDAR
**kal·a·poo·ia** *or* **kal·a·pu·ya** *also* **cal·a·poo·ya** *or* **cal·a·pu·ya** \ˌkaləˈpüyə\ *n, pl* **kalapooia** *or* **kalapooias** *or* **kalapuya** *or* **kalapuyas** *usu cap* **1 a** : an Indian people of the Willamette basin, Oregon **b** : a member of such people **2 a** : a language family of Oregon including Kalapooia and Yoncalla **b** : a language of the Kalapooia family formerly spoken in the Willamette basin, Oregon
**kal·a·poo·ian** *or* **kal·a·pu·yan** \ˌ≈≈ˈ≈yən\ *adj, usu cap* : of or relating to the Kalapooia or their language
**ka·la·sie** \ˌkäləˈsē\ *n* -s [Dayak (Ngadju dial.) *kalasi*] : a long-tailed monkey of Borneo (*Pygathrix rubicunda*) that has a tuft of long hair on the head
**kale** *or* **kail** \ˈkāl, *esp before pause or consonant* -āəl\ *n* -s [Sc, fr. ME (northern dial.) *cal, cale*, fr. OE *cāl* — more at COLE] **1 a** : COLE 1 **b** : a very hardy cabbage (*Brassica oleracea acephala*) that has curled often finely cut leaves which do not form a dense head and that is considered by some to be the original form of the cultivated cabbage **c** *Scot* : a plant of the family Cruciferae **2** *Scot* : BROTH, SOUP; *esp* : soup made with kale **3** *chiefly Scot* **a** : FOOD **b** : MEAL **4** *slang* : MONEY ⟨a ritzy neighborhood where everybody had the ∼ —J.T.Farrell⟩
**kaleege** *or* **kaleej** *var of* KALIJ
**¹ka·lei·do·scope** \kəˈlīdəˌskōp *sometimes* -lēd-\ *n* [Gk *kalos* beautiful + *eidos* form + E *-scope* — more at CALLI-, IDOL] **1** : an instrument that contains loose fragments of colored glass confined between two flat plates and two plane mirrors placed at an angle of 60° so that changes of position exhibit its contents in an endless variety of symmetrical varicolored forms **2** : something resembling a kaleidoscope: as **a** : a variegated changing pattern or scene ⟨the lake a ∼ of changing colors —Robert Gibbings⟩ **b** : a succession of changing phases or actions ⟨reduce all experience to a shifting ∼ of meaningless incidents —John Dewey⟩ ⟨her day ... became a ∼ of things embarked upon and left for other things —Adrian Bell⟩
**²kaleidoscope** \"\ *vb* -ED/-ING/-S *vi* : to appear as if in a kaleidoscope ⟨pictures of the lights and the planes spinning and crashing ... *kaleidoscoped* through his mind —Howard Hunt⟩ ∼ *vt* : to view as if in a kaleidoscope ⟨poking ... fun at our banalities and shortsightednesses as he ∼s them with the long view of man's cultural achievement —Henry Hewes⟩
**ka·lei·do·scop·ic** \≈ˌ≈≈ˈskäpik, -pēk\ *also* **ka·lei·do·scop·i·cal** \-pəkəl, -pēk-\ *adj* **1** : of, relating to, or formed by a kaleidoscope ⟨gazed raptly at the ∼ patterns within the instrument⟩ **2** : having changing tints or variegated color ⟨∼ color of the clouds at sunset⟩ **3 a** : constantly changing : rapidly shifting ⟨air was fretted with a ∼ network of swifts ... with swallows, martins, and if late enough, nighthawks —William Beebe⟩ ⟨a year of ∼ change, of breathtaking developments crowding so rapidly one upon the other —Allan Taylor⟩ **b** : having infinite variety : possessing many facets ⟨such a being of ∼ versatility ... we call contemptuously a jack-of-all-trades —Havelock Ellis⟩ ⟨shocking inhumanity of the slave trade has been compressed within the pages of this ∼ novel with romance and sea adventure —*N.Y. Herald Tribune*⟩ — **ka·lei·do·scop·i·cal·ly** \-pək(ə)lē, -pēk-, -li\ *adv*
**ka·le·ma** \kəˈlāmə\ *n* -s [Pg] : a violent surf that occurs on the coast of the Guinea region, West Africa
**kalendar** *var of* CALENDAR — used esp. of ecclesiastical calendars ⟨the Episcopal ∼⟩
**kalends** *var of* CALENDS

**kale runt** *or* **kale stock** *n* : the stem of kale
**kaleyard** \≈ˌ≈\ *chiefly Scot var of* KAILYARD
**kal·gan** \(ˈ)kalˌgan, (ˈ)kälˌgän\ *adj, usu cap* [fr. *Kalgan*, city in northern China] : of or from the city of Kalgan, China : of the kind or style prevalent in Kalgan
**kalian** *var of* CALEAN
**ka·li·bo·rite** \ˌkaləˈbōrˌīt\ *n* -s [G *kaliborit*, fr. *kali-* (fr. NL *kalium*) + *bor-* + *-it* -ite] : a mineral $KMg_2B_{11}O_{19}.9H_2O$ consisting of a hydrous borate of potassium and magnesium
**ka·lic·i·nite** \kəˈlisənˌīt\ *n* -s [G *kalicinit*, fr. F *kalicine* kalicinite (irreg. fr. NL *kalium* + F *-ine*) + G *-it* -ite] : a mineral $KHCO_3$ consisting of an acid carbonate or bicarbonate of potassium
**ka·lig·e·nous** \kəˈlijənəs, (ˈ)kaˌl-\ *adj* [ISV *kali* alkali (fr. NL) + *-genous*] : forming alkalies — used of the alkali metals
**kalij** *or* **kaleege** *also* **kaleej** *or* **kal·lege** \ˈkalij, ˈkäl-, ˈkal-, -(ˌ)lēj\ *n, pl* **kalij·es** *or* **kaleeg·es** *also* **kaleej·es** *or* **kalleg·es** [Nepali & Pahari *kālij*] : any of several related crested Indian pheasants (genus *Lophura* or *Gennaeus*) that are related to the Chinese silver pheasant
**ka·li·na** \kəˈlēnə\ *n, pl* **kalina** *or* **kalinas** *usu cap* [Carib *calina* Caribs, strong men — more at CANNIBAL] : GALIBI
**ka·lin·ga** *also* **ka·ling·ga** \kəˈliŋgə\ *n, pl* **kalinga** *or* **kalingas** *usu cap* [native name in northern Luzon] **1 a** : any of several peoples inhabiting northern Luzon, Philippines **b** : a member of such people **2** : the Austronesian language of the Kalinga people
**ka·li·nin** \kəˈlēnən, kəlˈyēnyən\ *adj, usu cap* [fr. *Kalinin*, city in the west central part of European Russia, U.S.S.R.] : of or from the city of Kalinin, U.S.S.R. : of the kind or style prevalent in Kalinin
**ka·li·nin·grad** \-ˌgrad\ *adj, usu cap* [fr. *Kaliningrad*, city in the western part of European Russia, U.S.S.R.] : of or from the city of Kaliningrad, U.S.S.R. : of the kind or style prevalent in Kaliningrad
**kali·nite** \ˈkaləˌnīt, ˈkäl-\ *n* -s [*kali-* (fr. NL *kalium*) + connective *-n-* + *-ite*] : a mineral $KAl(SO_4)_2.11H_2O$ consisting of a fibrous and birefringent hydrous sulfate of potassium and aluminum that is distinct from alum in crystallization and water content
**kali·oph·i·lite** \ˌkalēˈäfəˌlīt, ˌkäl-\ *n* -s [G *kaliophilit*, fr. *kalio-* (fr. NL *kalium*) + *-phil* -phile + *-it* -ite] : a colorless mineral $KAlSiO_4$ of volcanic origin consisting of potassium aluminum silicate that occurs in acicular crystals or fine threads (hardness 6, sp. gr. 2.5–2.6)
**kal·i·spel** \ˌkaləˈspel\ *n, pl* **kalispel** *or* **kalispels** *usu cap* [Kalispel, lit., camas] **1 a** : a Salishan people of northern Idaho and northwestern Montana **b** : a member of such people **2** : a language of the Kalispel and Spokan peoples — called also *Pend d'Oreille*
**ka·li·um** \ˈkālēəm\ *n* -s [NL, fr. NL *kali* alkali, potassium (fr. Ar *qily* saltwort) + *-ium*] : POTASSIUM — symbol *K*
**ka·li yu·ga** \ˌkəlēˈyügə\ *n, usu cap K&Y* [Skt *kaliyuga*, fr. *kali* ace on a die + *yuga* yoke, age of the world; fr. the fact that the ace is the unluckiest throw in dice games — more at YOKE] : the depraved fourth and final age of a Hindu world cycle : dark age
**kalka** *usu cap, var of* KHALKHA
**kal·kow·skite** \kalˈkōfˌskīt\ *n* -s [G *kalkowskyn* (irreg. fr. E. L. *Kalkowsky* †1938 Ger. mineralogist + G *-in* -ine) + E *-ite*] : a mineral $Fe_2Ti_3O_9$(?) consisting of an oxide of iron and titanium and usu. containing small amounts of rare-earth elements, niobium, and tantalum
**kalk·vis** \ˈkälkˌfis\ *n* -ES [Afrik, fr. *kalk* lime (fr. D, fr. MD *calc*) + *vis* fish, fr. D, fr. MD *visch*; akin to OHG *kalk* lime and to OHG *fisc* fish — more at CHALK, FISH] : a cutlass fish (*Lepidopus caudatus*) of southern Africa
**kal·li·kak** \ˈkaləˌkak\ *n* -s *usu cap* [*Kallikak*, fictitious name of a family having one branch consisting mainly of intelligent and successful persons and another branch containing a large proportion of mentally deficient and immoral persons that was studied by H. H. Goddard †1957 Am. psychologist, fr. Gk *kalli-* calli- + *kak-* cac-] : a stupid person ⟨rubber masks by means of which an ordinary citizen can transform himself into demon, witch ... *Kallikak*, bumpkin —Bernard Wolfe⟩ — compare JUKES
**kal·li·ma** \ˈkaləmə\ *n, cap* [NL, prob. irreg. fr. Gk *kallimos* beautiful, fr. *kallos* beauty — more at CALLI-] : a genus of highly mimetic nymphalid butterflies of southern Asia and the Pacific islands that are often brilliantly colored above but when at rest with wings folded resemble dead leaves in color and markings
**kal·li·type** \ˈkaləˌtīp\ *n* [ISV *kalli-* (fr. Gk *kalli-* calli-) + *type*] : a contact printing-out photographic process that uses paper sensitized with a ferric salt and silver nitrate and a developer containing borax and Rochelle salt
**kal·mia** \ˈkalmēə\ *n* [NL, fr. Peter *Kalm* †1779 Swed. botanist + NL *-ia*] **1** *cap* : a genus of No. American evergreen shrubs (family Ericaceae) with oblong to linear leaves and showy flowers that are borne in clusters in the axils of leaves or bracts and have a saucer-shaped basally 10-saccate corolla with an anther resting in each sac — see MOUNTAIN LAUREL, SHEEP LAUREL **2** -s : any plant of the genus *Kalmia*
**kal·muck** *or* **kal·muk** \ˈkalˌmək, ≈ˈ≈\ *or* **kal·myk** \ˈkal(ˌ)mik, ≈ˈ≈\ *also* **cal·muck** \ˈkalˌmək, ≈ˈ≈\ *n* -s *usu cap* [Russ *Kalmyk*, fr. Kazan Tatar] **1** : a member of a Buddhist Mongol people orig. of Dzungaria — called also *Eleut* **2** : the Mongolian language of the Kalmucks
**ka·lo** \ˈkä(ˌ)lō\ *n* -s [Hawaiian] : TARO
**ka·lon** \kəˈlän, (ˈ)kaˌl-\ *n* -s [Gk, fr. neut. of *kalos* good, beautiful — more at CALLI-] : the ideal of physical and moral beauty esp. as conceived by the philosophers of classical Greece
**ka·long** \ˈkaˌlȯŋ, ˈkäˌl-, kəˈl-, -läŋ\ *n* -s [Jav] : a large fruit bat of the Malay archipelago
**ka·lop·a·nax** \kəˈläpəˌnaks\ *n* -ES [NL, fr. *kalo-* (fr. Gk *kalos* beautiful) + Gk *panax* panacea, fr. *panakēs* all-healing — more at PANACEA] : a showy Japanese tree (*Kalopanax ricinifolium*) of the family Araliaceae that has foliage like that of the castor-oil plant
**kal·o·ter·mes** \ˌkaləˈtər(ˌ)mēz\ *n, cap* [NL, fr. *kalo-* (fr. Gk *kalos*) + *Termes*] : the type genus of Kalotermitidae comprising many termites that are destructive pests of living trees or of dry timber — see CRYPTOTERMES
**¹kal·o·ter·mi·tid** *also* **cal·o·ter·mi·tid** \ˌ≈≈ˈ≈məd·əd\ *adj* [NL *Kalotermitidae*] : of or relating to the Kalotermitidae
**²kalotermitid** *also* **calotermitid** \"\ *n* -s [NL *Kalotermitidae*] : a termite of the family Kalotermitidae
**kal·o·ter·mit·i·dae** \ˌ≈≈(ˌ)tərˈmid·əˌdē\ *n pl, cap* [NL, fr. *Kalotermit-*, *Kalotermes*, type genus + *-idae*] : a family of primitive termites occurring in most warm regions and including many serious destroyers of wood and growing trees — compare CRYPTOTERMES; see DRY-WOOD TERMITE
**ka·lox·y·lon** \kəˈläksəˌlän, -lən\ *n, cap* [NL, fr. *kalo-* (fr. Gk *kalos*) + *-xylon*] : a form genus of fossil plants based only on roots
**kal·pa** \ˈkəlpə\ *n* -s [Skt] : a duration of time in Hinduism covering a complete cosmic cycle from the origination to the destruction of a world system — compare YUGA
**kalpak** *var of* CALPAC
**kal·pis** \ˈkalpəs\ *n* -ES [Gk; akin to OIr *cilornn* jar] : a hydria having a rounded shoulder and a small back handle
**kal·si·lite** \ˈkalsəˌlīt *also* -lts-\ *n* -s [prob. fr. *kalium* + *aluminum* + *silicon* + *-ite*] : a rare mineral $KAlSiO_4$ consisting of aluminosilicate of potassium
**kalsomine** *var of* CALCIMINE
**ka·lua** \käˈlüə\ *adj* [Hawaiian *kālua*, fr. *kālua* to bake in a ground oven] *Hawaii* : baked in an earth oven ⟨∼ pig⟩
**ka·lum·pang** \ˌkäləmˈpäŋ\ *n* -s [Tag *kalumpáng*] *Philippines* : a large tropical Old World tree (*Sterculia foetida*) having foul-smelling blossoms that are followed by red pods enclosing oil-rich and protein-rich seeds sometimes used as food and yielding light soft wood that is sometimes used for carving
**ka·lum·pit** *also* **ca·lum·pit** \-ˈpēt\ *n* -s [Tag *kalumpit*] : a common Philippine tree (*Terminalia edulis*) that yields a soft wood and dark red fleshy fruits used for preserves
**ka·lun·ti** \kəˈlüntē\ *n* -s [Taw-Sug] : a lauan (*Shorea kalunti*) with yellow wood
**kal·war** \(ˌ)kəlˈwō(ə)r\ *n* -s *usu cap* [Hindi *kalvār*, lit., liquor seller, fr. Skt *kalyapāla*, fr. *kalya* liquor + *pāla* guard, keeper] : a member of a Hindu caste engaging in trade
**kalymma** *var of* CALYMMA
**kam** *dial var of* ²CAM
**ka·ma** \ˈkämə\ *n* -s [Skt *kāma* love, wish, desire — more at CHARITY] **1** : enjoyment of the world of the senses constituting one of the ends of man in Hinduism : PLEASURE **2** *in Buddhism & Theosophy* : the human principle of desire — compare KAMARUPA
**ka·ma·ai·na** \ˌkäməˈīnə\ *n* -s [Hawaiian, fr. *kama* person + *'āina* land] : a long-time resident of Hawaii
**ka·ma·chi·le** \ˌkäməˈchilē\ *or* **ka·man·chi·le** \ˌkämənˈ-\ *var of* CAMACHILE
**kam·a·cite** \ˈkaməˌsīt\ *n* -s [obs. G *kamacit* (now *kamazit*), fr. Gk *kamak-*, *kamax* vine pole, shaft + G *-it* -ite; akin to MHG *hamel* pole, Skt *śamyā* stick, staff] : a mineral consisting of a nickel-iron alloy forming with taenite the mass of most meteoric iron
**ka·ma·hi** \kəˈmähē\ *n* -s [Maori] : a New Zealand tree (*Weinmannia racemosa*) of the family Cunoniaceae that yields timber and firewood — called also *towai*
**ka·ma·la** *also* **ka·me·la** *or* **ka·mi·la** \ˈkəmələ\ *n* -s [Skt *kamala*, prob. of Dravidian origin; akin to Kanarese *kōmale*, *kōval*] **1** : an East Indian tree (*Mallotus philippinensis*) **2** : a reddish cathartic powder from the capsules of the kamala tree that contains rottlerin and is used as an orange dye for silk and wool and as a vermifuge chiefly in veterinary practice
**ka·ma·ni** \kəˈmänē\ *n* -s [Hawaiian] **1** : MALABAR ALMOND **2** : MASTWOOD
**kamansi** *var of* CAMANSI
**ka·mao** \kəˈmäˌō, -ˈmaů\ *n* -s [Hawaiian *kama'o*] : a bird (*Phaeornis obscura myadestina*) of the family Turdidae found on Kauai Island, Hawaii
**ka·mar** \kəˈmär\ *n, pl* **kamar** *or* **kamars** *usu cap* **1** : a people of central India now engaged in the practice of plow agriculture **2** : a member of the Kamar people
**ka·ma·res** *or* **ka·ma·rais** \kəˈmäˌres, -ˌrəs\ *n, pl* **kamares** *or* **kamarais** *usu cap* [fr. *Kamares*, cave on the south slope of Mount Ida, Crete, where it was discovered] : a gaily colored Minoan pottery reaching its peak of excellence about 2000 B.C.
**ka·mar·e·zite** \kəˈmarəˌzīt\ *n* -s [G *kamarezit*, fr. *Kamareza*, *Kamariza*, near Laurium, Greece + G *-it* -ite] : a mineral $Cu_3(SO_4)(OH)_4.6H_2O$(?) consisting of a hydrous basic copper sulfate
**ka·ma·rin·ska·ia** \kəˈmärənzkəyə, -mar-, -nsk-\ *n* -s [Russ] : a Russian folk dance that is characterized by acrobatic knee bends, leaps, and leg extensions
**ka·ma·ru·pa** \ˌkäməˈrüpə\ *n* -s [Skt *kāmarūpa*, fr. *kāma* desire + *rūpa* form] *Theosophy* : the form assumed by the kama after a person's death — compare ASTRAL BODY — **ka·ma·ru·pic** \ˌ≈≈ˈ≈pik\ *adj*
**¹kamas** *or* **kamass** *var of* CAMAS
**²kamas** *pl of* KAMA
**ka·ma·sin** \ˌkäməˈsēn, ˌkam-, -sin\ *also* **ka·mass** \ˈkäməs, ˈkam-\ *or* **ka·mas·sian** \kəˈmashən, -asēən\ *or* **ka·mas·sin** *like* KAMASIN\ *n, pl* **kamasin** *or* **kamasins** *usu cap* [*Kamasin*, *Kamass*, *Kamassin* fr. Russ *Kamasintsy* (pl.), fr. Kamasin *Kangmāžə*; *Kamassian* prob. fr. *Kamass* + *-ian*] **1 a** : a Samoyed people on the upper Yenisei river, Siberia, who are ethnically largely extinct or absorbed into the Russian culture by intermarriage **b** : a member of such people **2** : the Uralic language of the Kamasin people
**ka·mas·si** \kəˈmäsē\ *n* -s [Afrik *kamassie*, prob. modif. of Xhosa *kamamasane*] **1** : a tree (*Gonioma kamassi*) of the family Apocynaceae of southern Africa **2** : the hard yellow wood of the kamassi
**kam·ba** \ˈkämbə\ *n, pl* **kamba** *or* **kambas** *usu cap* **1 a** : a Bantu people of central Kenya **b** : a member of such people **2** : a Bantu language of the Kamba people
**kam·bal** \ˈkəmbəl\ *n* -s [Hindi, fr. Skt *kambala*] : a coarse woolen blanket or shawl worn in India
**kam·ba·la** \kəmˈbälə\ *n* -s [Burmese] **1 a** : an East Indian tree (*Sonneratia apetala*) with strong reddish wood **b** : the wood of the kambala **2** : IROKO
**kam·ba·ra earth** \kəmˈbärə-\ *n, usu cap K* [fr. *Kambara*, town in Japan] : JAPANESE ACID CLAY
**kam·boh** \ˈkəm(ˌ)bō, ˈkäm-\ *n* -s [Per] : a member of a low caste in the Punjab engaged chiefly in agriculture
**kam·cha·dal** *also* **kam·cha·dale** \ˌkämchəˈdäl\ *or* **kamchadele** \-del, -dē(ə)l\ *n, pl* **kamchadal** *or* **kamchadals** *usu cap* [Russ *Kamchadal* Kamchatkan] **1 a** : a Paleo-Asiatic people of southern Kamchatka who are chiefly hunters and fishers **b** : a member of such people **2** : a Luorawetlan language of the Kamchadal people
**¹kam·chat·kan** \(ˈ)kamˈchatkən\ *adj, usu cap* [*Kamchatka*, peninsula in the northeastern U.S.S.R. + E *-an*, adj. suffix] : of or relating to the Kamchatka peninsula
**²kamchatkan** \"\ *n* -s *usu cap* [*Kamchatka* + E *-an*, n. suffix] : KAMCHADAL
**kamchatkan sea eagle** *n, usu cap K* : an eagle (*Haliaeetus pelagicus*) that has white shoulders, rump, and tail when adult, feeds largely on fish, and is found on the coasts of the western North Pacific — called also *Steller's sea eagle*
**¹kame** \ˈkām\ *n now dial var of* COMB
**²kame** \"\ *n* -s [Sc, kame, comb, fr. ME (northern dial.) *camb* comb, fr. OE *camb* — more at COMB] : a short ridge, hill, or mound of stratified drift deposited by glacial meltwater — compare ESKER
**ka·meel** \kəˈmē(ə)l, -mā(-\ *n* -s [Afrik, fr. D, camel, fr. MD *cameel*, fr. L *camelus* — more at CAMEL] *Africa* : GIRAFFE
**ka·meel·doorn** \-ˌdōrn\ *also* **ka·meel·do·ring bush** \-ˌdōriŋ-\ *or* **ka·meel·thorn** \-ˌthōrn\ *n, pl* **kameeldoorns** *also* **kameelthorns** [*kameeldoorn* fr. obs. Afrik *kameeldoorn* (now *kameeldoring*), fr. Afrik *kameel* + obs. Afrik *doorn* thorn, fr. D, fr. MD *dorn*; *kameeldoring bush* fr. Afrik *kameeldoring* + E *bush*; *kameelthorn* part trans. of Afrik *kameeldoring*; akin to OE *thorn* — more at THORN] *Africa* : any of several acacia trees; *esp* : a tall tree (*Acacia giraffae*) on which the giraffe often browses
**ka·me·ha·me·ha day** \kəˌmāəˈmā(ˌ)hä-\ *n, usu cap K&D* [after *Kamehameha* I †1819 king of Hawaii] : June 11 observed as a holiday in Hawaii in celebration of the anniversary of the birth of Kamehameha I
**kamela** *or* **kamila** *var of* KAMALA
**ka·me·lau·ki·on** \ˌkäməˈlaůkˌyȯn, -aůkēˌȯn\ *n* -s [MGk *kamēlaukion*, alter. (prob. influenced by Gk *kamēlos* camel) of LGk *kamelaukion*] : a tall brimless hat worn by priests and monks in some Oriental rites
**ka·me·rad** \ˌkäməˈräːt\ *interj* [G, lit., comrade, fr. MF *camarade* companion — more at COMRADE] — used by German soldiers in World War I as a cry of surrender

kamelaukions

**kame terrace** *n* [²*kame*] : a terrace of stratified sand and gravel deposited by streams between a glacier and an adjacent valley wall
**ka·mi** \ˈkäˈmi\ *n, pl* **kami** [Jap, god] : a sacred power or force; *esp* : one of the Shinto deities including mythological beings, spirits of distinguished men, and forces of nature
**ka·mia** \ˈkämēə\ *n, pl* **kamia** *or* **kamias** *usu cap* [Kamia *Kamiyai*, *Kamiyahi*] **1 a** : an Indian people of southeastern California and northwestern Mexico **b** : a member of such people **2** : a Yuman language of the Kamia people
**ka·mi·as** \kəmˈyäs\ *n* -s [Tag *kamyás*] *Philippines* : BILIMBI
**ka·mik** \ˈkämik\ *n* -s [Esk] : an Eskimo sealskin boot
**¹ka·mi·ka·ze** \ˌkäməˈkäzē\ *n* -s [Jap, lit., divine wind, fr. *kami* god + *kaze* wind] **1** *often cap* : a member of a Japanese air attack corps assigned to make a suicidal crash on a target (as a ship) **2** : an airplane containing explosives to be flown in a suicide crash on a target
**²kamikaze** \ˌ≈≈ˈ≈\ *adj, sometimes cap* **1** : of, relating to, or resembling that of a kamikaze ⟨extending the ∼ way of fighting to whole nations —Norbert Wiener⟩ **2** : SUICIDAL ⟨the city's ∼ taxi drivers⟩
**kam·lei·ka** \kamˈlīkə\ *also* **kam·e·lai·ka** \ˌkaməˈl-\ *n* -s [Esk *kamleika*] : a waterproof pullover shirt made of dried animal intestines and worn in the Aleutians

**kam·loops trout** \'kam,lüps-\ also **kamloops** n, usu cap K [fr. *Kamloops*, city in Brit. Columbia] : a large black-spotted rainbow trout native chiefly to Lake Pend Oreille, Idaho, and widely introduced in western streams and lakes

**käm·mer·er·ite** \'kemərə,rīt\ n -s [Sw *kämmererit*, fr. A. A. *Kämmerer* 19th cent. scientist in St. Petersburg (Leningrad) + Sw *-it* -ite] : a reddish penninite

**kampferol** var of KAEMPFEROL

**kam·pi·lan** or **cam·pi·lan** \käm'pē,län\ n -s [Tag *kampilan*] : a long straight-edged sheathed cutlass broadening toward the point that is used by the Moro peoples of Mindanao and Sulu

**kam·pong** or **cam·pong** \'käm,pȯŋ, -päŋ, ='=\ n -s [Malay *kampong*] : a native hamlet or village in a Malay-speaking country

**kamp·to·zoa** \,kam(p)tə'zōə\ [NL, fr. *kampto-* (fr. Gk *kamptos* flexible) + NL *-zoa* — more at CAMPTO-] syn of ENTOPROCTA

**ka·muk** \kə'mük\ n, pl **kamuk** or **kamuks** usu cap : a mountain people of northeast Thailand who practice primitive shifting agriculture and are related to the Kha of Vietnam

**ka·mu·ning** or **ca·mu·ning** \¦kämü¦nēŋ\ n -s [Tag *kamuning*] **1** : a tropical Asiatic tree (*Murraya exotica*) **2** : the wood of the kamuning noted for its hardness

**ka·na** \'känə\ n, pl **kana** or **kanas** often attrib [Jap] **1 a** : a Japanese system of syllabic writing dating from the 8th or 9th century A.D. and having characters that can be used exclusively for writing the language but are normally used only for foreign words, for grammatical inflections and function words not represented by kanji, or at the side of kanji to indicate pronunciation **b** : either of the two different but equivalent sets of characters that are used in the kana system and that each have 48 characters increased by the use of two diacritics to 73 — see HIRAGANA, KATAKANA **2** : a single character belonging to the kana system of writing

**kana-a** \¦känə¦ä\ adj, usu cap [origin unknown] : of or relating to a hard thin white to slate gray pottery of the Developmental Pueblo period that is either plain or decorated with black lines

**kanaf** also **kanaff** var of KENAF

**ka·nai·ma** \kə'nīmə\ n -s [native name in British Guiana] : an evil spirit or a person possessed by an evil spirit believed by Indians of British Guiana and northwestern Brazil to be an avenger

**ka·naka** \kə'nakə, -nakə; *in Hawaiian, sing & pl are both "kanaka" but sing is* ='== *& pl is* '=== \ n -s often cap [Hawaiian, person, human being] : POLYNESIAN, MICRONESIAN, MELANESIAN : SOUTH SEA ISLANDER

**kana-majiri** \¦=='mäjərē\ n -s [Jap, fr. *kana* + *majiri* mixture] : the standard form of Japanese writing consisting of kanji supplemented by hiragana characters to indicate inflectional endings and function words and to show pronunciation esp. when that would otherwise be doubtful

**ka·nam man** \kə'nam-\ n, usu cap K [fr. *Kanam*, locality on Lake Victoria, Kenya, where the type was discovered] : an extinct East African man known from a fragmentary fossil jaw and associated teeth found in early Pleistocene lake beds

**kan·a·rese** also **can·a·rese** \¦kanə¦rēz, -ēs\ n, pl **kanarese** also **canarese** usu cap [*Kanara*, district in southwest India + E *-ese*] **1 a** : a Kanada-speaking people of Mysore, south India **b** : a member of such people **2** : KANNADA **3** : the script normally used to write Kannada

**ka·na·ri** also **ca·na·ri** \kə'närē\ n -s [Malay *kĕnari*] : JAVA ALMOND

**ka·nau·ri** \kə'naurē\ or **ka·na·wa·ri** \-näwərē\ n -s usu cap : a Tibeto-Burman language of Himachal Pradesh, India

**ka·na·za·wa** \kə'näzəwə\ adj, usu cap [fr. *Kanazawa*, city in western Honshu, Japan] : of or from the city of Kanazawa, Japan : of the kind or style prevalent in Kanazawa

**kan·chil** \'känchəl\ n -s [Malay] : any of several small chevrotains of southeastern Asia formerly regarded as constituting several species but now usu. held to be varieties of one (*Tragulus kanchil*)

**kan·de·lia** \kan'dēlēə, -lyə\ n, cap [NL, fr. Malayalam *kandel* tree of the genus *Kandelia* + NL *-ia*] : a genus of East Indian trees (family Rhizophoraceae) that are related to and resemble the common mangroves but have laciniate petals and 5-parted or 6-parted calyx

**kandh** usu cap, var of KHOND

**¹kan·dy·an** \'kandēən\ adj, usu cap [*Kandy*, town in central Ceylon, + E *-an*, adj. suffix] **1** : of, relating to, or characteristic of Kandy, Ceylon **2** : of, relating to, or characteristic of the people of Kandy

**²kandyan** \"\ n -s usu cap [*Kandy* + E *-an*, n. suffix] : a native or resident of Kandy, Ceylon

**ka·neel·hart** \kə'nā(ə)l,härt\ n -s [prob. fr. D, fr. *kaneel* cinnamon (fr. MD *caneel*, *canele*, fr. MF *cannelle*, fr. ML *canella*) + D *hart* heart, fr. MD *herte*, *harte*; akin to OE *heorte* heart — more at CANELLA, HEART] **1** : a tropical tree (*Licania cayenensis*) of Central and So. America **2** : the very strong wood of kaneelhart

**ka·nesh·ite** \'käni,shīt\ n -s usu cap [*Kanesh*, *Kanish*, ancient city of eastern Asia Minor + E *-ite*] **1** : an inhabitant of ancient Kanesh in eastern Asia Minor **2** or **ka·nish·ite** \"\ : the principal dialect of Hittite — called also *Kanesian*

**ka·ne·sian** \kə'nēzhən\ or **ka·ni·sian** \-nizh-\ adj, usu cap [irreg. fr. *Kanesh*, *Kanish* + E *-ian*] : of, relating to, or characteristic of the Kaneshites

**kang** or **k'ang** \'käŋ\ n -s [Chin (Pek) *k'ang⁴*] : a brick platform built across one side or end of a room in a house in northern China or Manchuria, warmed by a fire beneath, and used for sleeping

**kan·ga·ny** or **kan·ga·ni** \kəŋ'gänē\ n, pl **kanganies** or **kanganis** [Tamil *kankāṇi*, lit., one who sees with the eyes, fr. *kaṇ* eye + *kāṇ* to see] : an overseer of labor in Ceylon, India, and Malaya

**¹kan·ga·roo** \¦kaŋgə¦rü, ¦kaiŋ-\ n -s [prob. native name in Queensland, Australia] **1 a** : any of various herbivorous leaping marsupial mammals (family Macropodidae) of Australia, New Guinea, and adjacent islands that have a small head, large ears, long powerful hind legs with the two larger hind toes armed with heavy nails, a long thick tail used as a support and in balancing, and rather small forelegs not used in progression — see MARSUPIALIA, WALLABY **b** (1) : the pelt or fur of the kangaroo (2) : leather made from the skin of the kangaroo resembling glazed kid in appearance **2** *Austral* : wild young cattle — usu. used in the pl. **3** *Brit* : AUSTRALIAN **4** : KANGAROO CLOSURE ⟨the ~ saves parliamentary time —Derek Walker-Smith⟩

kangaroo

**²kangaroo** \"\ adj : of or relating to a kangaroo court ⟨these ~ qualities of justice that even of the courtroom . . . can make a jungle —Herbert Feinstein⟩

**kangaroo acacia** or **kangaroo thorn** n : a thorny Australian acacia (*Acacia armata*) often used for hedges

**kangaroo apple** n **1** : an edible yellow egg-shaped fruit of Australia and New Zealand that has a mealy subacid pulp **2** : a shrubby or herbaceous perennial plant (*Solanum aviculare*) that is sometimes cultivated in warm regions for its racemes of purple flowers and for the kangaroo apples that it bears

**kangaroo bear** n : KOALA

**kangaroo beetle** n : any of certain brilliantly colored Old World beetles with thick hind legs constituting the genus *Sagra* that is included in Chrysomelidae or made the type of a separate family

**kangaroo closure** n : the restriction of debate to those amendments judged by the presiding officer of a legislative body to be most appropriate ⟨the New Zealand House has not had to adopt . . . the *kangaroo closure* —Walter Nash⟩ — compare GUILLOTINE

**kangaroo court** n **1** : a mock court in which the principles of law and justice are disregarded or perverted: **a** : one held by vagabonds or by prisoners in a jail or prison camp ⟨*kangaroo courts* . . . are vicious organizations controlled by the most perverted and brutal prisoners —J.V.B.Bennett⟩ ⟨non-Communist prisoners sentenced to death by Red *kangaroo courts* —*Army-Navy-Air Force Jour.*⟩ **b** : one involving comic procedures and ludicrous penalties designed for the amusement of the participants and spectators ⟨*kangaroo courts* — to which anyone not in Western garb can be hauled and fined —Helen Gould⟩ **2** : a court or a similar body (as a legislative investigating committee) characterized by irresponsible, unauthorized, or irregular status or procedures ⟨in Czechoslovakia . . . *kangaroo courts* have been handing down stiff sentences for "labor sabotage" —C.L.Sulzberger⟩ ⟨two committee jobs which put him . . . in the position of conducting his own *kangaroo court* —*Atlantic*⟩

**kangaroo dog** n : an Australian breed of rough-haired dogs that resemble greyhounds and that are used for hunting kangaroos

**kangaroo feathers** n pl, *Austral* : NONSENSE

**kangaroo grass** n : any of several grasses of the genus *Themeda*: as **a** : a common perennial forage grass (*Themeda australis*) that is usu. held to occur from Australia across southern Asia and into eastern Africa and that is very closely related to and perhaps a variety of the African rooigras **b** : ULLA GRASS

**kangaroo hare** n : HARE WALLABY

**kangaroo jerboa** n : RAT KANGAROO

**kangaroo mouse** n : any of various small leaping rodents (as dwarf pocket rat, jumping mouse, or pocket mouse)

**kangaroo paw** n : an Australian sedgelike spring-flowering herb (*Anigozanthos manglesii*) of the family Amaryllidaceae having the clustered flowers covered with greenish wool except at their red bases — called also *kangaroo's-foot*

**kangaroo rat** n **1** : RAT KANGAROO **2** : any of numerous pouched nocturnal burrowing rodents (genus *Dipodomys*) of arid parts of the western U.S.

**kangaroo's-foot** \,==',=\ or **kangaroo-foot plant** \,=='=,=-\ n, pl **kangaroo's-foots** : KANGAROO PAW

**kangaroo vine** or **kangaroo grape** n : an Australian woody vine (*Cissus antarctica*) sometimes used as a houseplant

**kan·ga·yam** \¦kaŋgə¦yäm\ n [*Kangayam*, cattle-breeding center in Madras state, southern India] **1** usu cap : an Indian breed of brown or gray cattle used chiefly for draft **2** -s often cap : an animal of the Kangayam breed

**k'ang hsi** \'käŋ'shē\ adj, usu cap K&H [after *K'ang-hsi* †1722 Chin. emperor, second of the Ch'ing dynasty] : of, relating to, or having the characteristics of Chinese ceramic art or Chinese porcelain wares of the latter half of the 17th century or the first quarter of the 18th century

**kang·li** \'käŋ'lē\ also **kang·la** \-lä\ n -s usu cap : one of the major divisions of the Great Horde

**kan·gri** \'kəŋ(,)grē\ n -s [Hindi *kaṅgrī*] : a small portable earthenware-lined wicker basket used as a warming stove in Kashmir

**kangs** pl of KANG

**k'angs** pl of K'ANG

**kan·ho·bal** \¦känō¦bäl\ n -s usu cap **1 a** : an Indian people of western Guatemala **b** : a member of such people **2** : a Mayan language of the Kanhobal people

**ka·nin** \'känən\ n -s [Tag, fr. *kain* to eat] *Philippines* : boiled rice

**kanishite** usu cap, var of KANESHITE

**kanisian** usu cap, var of KANESIAN

**kan·je·ra man** \'känjərə-\ n, usu cap K [fr. *Kanjera*, locality in Kenya where the type was discovered] : an extinct East African man known from parts of four thick-walled dolichocephalic skulls found in association with artifacts of Abbevillian type and regarded as a primitive form of *Homo sapiens* possibly belonging to the Middle Pleistocene

**kan·ji** \'kän(,)jē\ n, pl **kanji** or **kanjis** [Jap] **1** : a Japanese system of writing based on the Chinese one and composed principally of characters borrowed or adapted from Chinese — see KANA, KANA-MAJIRI **2** : a single character belonging to the kanji system of writing

**kan·ka·nai** \¦käŋkə¦nī\ n, pl **kankanai** or **kankanais** usu cap [native name in northern Luzon] **1 a** : a people inhabiting the southern part of Mountain Province of northern Luzon, Philippines — compare IGOROT **b** : a member of such people **2** : an Austronesian language of the Kankanai people

**kan·krej** \'kän,krej\ n -ES [origin unknown] : GUZERAT

**kan·na·da** \'känədə, 'kan-\ n -s usu cap [Kanarese *kannaḍa*] : the major Dravidian language of Mysore, south India

**ka·no** \'kä(,)nō\ adj, usu cap [fr. *Kano*, city in northern Nigeria] : of or from the city of Kano, Nigeria : of the kind or style prevalent in Kano

**kanon** var of CANON

**ka·no·ne** \kə'nōnə\ n, pl **kano·nen** \-ōnən\ [G, lit., cannon, fr. It *cannone* — more at CANNON] : an expert skier

**ka·noon** \kä'nün\ n -s [Turk *kānun* — more at CANUN] : ZITHER

**kanpur** usu cap, var of CAWNPORE

**kans** \'kän(t)s\ also **kans grass** n, pl **kans** [Hindi *kās*, fr. Skt *kāśa*] : a common Indian grass (*Saccharum spontaneum*) found also in the West Indies that is used for thatching and for forage and in some areas is a troublesome weed — called also *glagah*

**kan·sa** \'kanzə, -n(t)sə\ or **kan·sas** *like* KANSAS\ n, pl **kansa** or **kansas** usu cap [native name in the Kansas river valley] **1 a** : a Siouan people of the Kansas river valley, Kansas **b** : a member of such people **2** : a dialect of Dhegiha

**¹kan·san** \'kanzən, 'kaan- *sometimes* -n(t)sən *or* 'kain(t)s-\ n -s cap [*Kansas*, state in the central U.S. + E *-an*, n. suffix] : a native or resident of Kansas

**²kansan** \"\ adj, usu cap [*Kansas* + E *-an*, adj. suffix] **1 a** : of, relating to, or characteristic of the state of Kansas **b** : of, relating to, or characteristic of the people of Kansas **2** : of or relating to the second glacial stage during the glacial epoch in No. America

**kan·sas** \-nzəs *also* -nzəz *sometimes* -n(t)səs *or* -zis *or* -ziz *or* -sis\ adj, usu cap [fr. *Kansas*, state in the central U.S., fr. *Kansa*, *Kansas* (Siouan people)] : of or from the state of Kansas ⟨*Kansas* wheatfields⟩ : of the kind or style prevalent in Kansas : KANSAN

**kansas cit·i·an** also **kansas city·an** \¦=zə(s)¦sid·ēən, -itē- *also* -zəz¦si- *sometimes* -sə(s)¦si-\ n, cap K&C : a native or resident of Kansas City

**kansas city** \¦==¦sid·|ē, -it|, |i, *in rapid speech* (')kanz¦si- *or* (')kaan-\ adj, usu cap K&C **1** [fr. *Kansas City*, city in western Missouri] : of or from Kansas City, Mo. : of the kind or style prevalent in Kansas City **2** [fr. *Kansas City*, city in northeastern Kansas] : of or from Kansas City, Kans. : of the kind or style prevalent in Kansas City

**kansas gay-feather** n, usu cap K : a perennial herb (*Liatris pycnostachya*) having spikes of purplish flowers — called also *prairie button snakeroot*

**kansas horse plague** n, usu cap K : contagious equine encephalomyelitis

**kansas thistle** n, usu cap K : BUFFALO BUR

**kan·tar** or **can·tar** or **qan·tar** \kan·'tär, kən-·\ n -s [Ar *qinṭār*, fr. LGk *kentēnarion* weight of 100 pounds, fr. LL *centenarium*, *centenarius* — more at CENTENARY] : any of various units of weight used in Mediterranean countries (as an Egyptian unit equal to about 99 pounds and a Turkish unit equal to about 124½ pounds)

**kan·te·le** also **kan·te·la** \'känt°lə, 'kan-\ n -s [Finn *kantele*] : a traditional Finnish harp orig. having 5 strings but now having as many as 20 to 30 strings

**kan·ten** \'kan,ten\ n -s [Jap, lit., cold weather, fr. *kan* midwinter + *ten* sky] : AGAR 1a

**kantharos** var of CANTHAROS

**¹kant·ian** \'kantēən, 'kän- *also* -nchən\ adj, usu cap [Immanuel *Kant* †1804 Ger. philosopher + E *-ian*] **1** : of or relating to the German philosopher Immanuel Kant **2** : of or relating to Kantianism

**²kantian** \"\ n -s usu cap : a follower of Kant or adherent to Kantianism

**kant·ian·ism** \-,nizəm\ n -s usu cap : the philosophy of Immanuel Kant that endeavors to synthesize the tradition of continental rationalism and British empiricism by holding that phenomenal knowledge is the joint product of percepts given to us through sensations organized under the forms of intuition of space and time and of concepts or categories of the understanding but that reason involves itself in fallacies if it tries to apply to the noumenal the principles of the understanding applicable only to the phenomenal so that the speculative ideas of God, the world, and the self although having heuristic import represent regulative knowledge as distinguished from the constitutive knowledge about the phenomenal at the same time that the ideas of God, freedom, and immortality represent necessary presuppositions for morality — compare CATEGORICAL IMPERATIVE, NOUMENON, PHENOMENON

**kan·ti·ara** \,kantē'a(a)rə\ n -s [origin unknown] : a spinose plant (*Carthamus oxycantha*) resembling the safflower that grows in troublesome clumps in Indian grasslands but can be made edible for livestock by beating off the spines

**kantikoy** var of CANTICO

**kant·ism** \'kant-,izəm, 'kän-\ n -s usu cap : KANTIANISM

**kant·ist** \-ntəst\ n -s usu cap : KANTIAN

**kantuta** var of CANTUTA

**ka·nuck** also **ka·nuk** \kə'nək\ cap, var of CANUCK

**ka·nu·ka** \'känəkə\ n -s [Maori] : a shrubby New Zealand tree (*Leptospermum ericoides*) with strong resistant wood that is used for making fences — compare MANUKA

**kanun** var of CANUN

**ka·nu·ri** \kə'nürē\ n, pl **kanuri** or **kanuris** usu cap **1 a** : a Negro people of the Muslim kingdom of Bornu west of Lake Chad whose history of dominance in that area goes back more than 500 years — compare TIBBU **b** : a member of such people **2** : the language of the Kanuri people

**kan·war** \(')kan¦wär\ n, pl **kanwar** or **kanwars** usu cap **1** : an indigenous people of central India esp. in the Bilaspur district many of whom are large landholders **2** : a member of the Kanwar people

**kan·ya butter** \'kanyə-\ n [*kanya* perh. modif. of Hausa *ka³'da³nya¹* shea tree] : SHEA BUTTER

**kanya tree** n [*kanya* perh. modif. of Hausa *ka³'da³nya¹*] : SHEA TREE

**kanyaw** var of CANAO

**kan·zu** \'kan(,)zü\ n -s [Swahili] : a long white robe worn by African men (as the Swahili)

**kao-chü-li** \¦kaùchə¦lē\ n, pl **kao-chü-li** usu cap : a people of probable Tungusic affinities inhabiting the Yalu river region of Korea and Manchuria from the 1st to the 7th centuries A.D.

**kaoh·siung** \¦kaùshē¦ùŋ, ¦gaù-\ adj, usu cap [fr. *Kaohsiung*, city in Formosa, China] : of or from the city of Kaohsiung, Formosa, China : of the kind or style prevalent in Kaohsiung

**kao·liang** \¦kaùlē¦äŋ\ also **koa·liang** \¦kōl-\ or **kow·liang** \¦kaùl-, ¦kōl-\ n -s [Chin (Pek) *kao¹* *liang²*, lit., tall grain, fr. *kao¹* high, tall + *liang²* grain] **1** : any of various grain sorghums that have slender dry pithy stalks, open erect panicles, and small white or brown seeds and are grown chiefly in China and Manchuria for their grain which is used for food and stalks which are used for fodder, thatching, and fuel **2** : a spirituous liquor made in China from the juice of kaoliang stalks

**ka·olin** also **ka·oline** \'kāələn, kā'ōl-\ n -s [F *kaolin*, fr. *Kao-ling*, hill in Kiangsi province, southeast China, where it was originally obtained] : a fine usu. white clay resulting from extreme weathering of aluminous minerals (as feldspar) that contains kaolinite as its principal constituent, that remains white on firing, and that is used chiefly in ceramics and refractories, as an adsorbent, as a filler or extender (as in paper or rubber or pigments), and in medicine — see CHINA CLAY; compare FIRECLAY

**ka·olin·ic** \¦kāə¦linik\ adj [ISV *kaolin* + *-ic*] : of, relating to, or resembling kaolin

**ka·olin·ite** \'kāələ,nīt, kā'ōl-\ n -s [*kaolin* + *-ite*] : a mineral $Al_2Si_2O_5(OH)_4$ consisting of a hydrous silicate of aluminum that is polymorphous with dickite and nacrite and constitutes the principal mineral in kaolin

**ka·olin·it·ic** \¦kāələ¦nid·ik, kā,ōl-\ adj : of, relating to, containing, or resembling kaolinite

**ka·olin·iza·tion** \,kāələnə'zāshən, ,kāə,lin-, kā,ōlən-, -,nī'z-\ n -s [ISV *kaolinize* + *-ation*] : the development of kaolin by metasomatism

**ka·olin·ize** \'kāələ,nīz, kā'ōl-\ vt -ED/-ING/-S [ISV *kaolin* + *-ize*] : to convert (as feldspar) into kaolin

**kaori** var of KAURI

**ka·pa** \'käpə\ n -s [Hawaiian] *Hawaii* : TAPA

**ka·pai** \kə'pī\ adj [Maori] *New Zeal* : GOOD

**ka·pel·le** also **ca·pel·le** \kə'pelə\ n, pl **kapel·len** also **capel·len** \-lən\ often cap [G *kapelle*, fr. It *cappella* choir, chapel, fr. ML, chapel — more at CHAPEL] **1** : the choir or orchestra of a royal or papal chapel **2** : a musical organization; *esp* : ORCHESTRA

**ka·pell·meis·ter** also **ca·pell·meis·ter** \kə'pel,mīstər\ n, pl **kapellmeister** often cap [G *kapellmeister*, fr. *kapelle* + *meister* master, fr. OHG *meistar*, fr. L *magister* — more at MASTER] : the musical director of a kapelle

**kapellmeister music** n, often cap K : music of uninspired correctness — usu. used disparagingly

**kaph** also **caph** or **kaf** \'käf, 'kōf\ n -s [Heb *kaph*, lit., palm of the hand] **1** : the 11th letter of the Hebrew alphabet — symbol כ or ך; see ALPHABET table **2** : a letter of the Phoenician or another Semitic alphabet corresponding to Hebrew kaph

**ka·pok** also **ca·poc** \'kā,päk\ n -s [Malay *kapok*] : a mass of silky fibers that clothe the seeds of the ceiba tree and are used commercially as a filling for mattresses, cushions, life preservers, and sleeping bags and as insulation — called also *ceiba*, *Java cotton*, *silk cotton*

**kapok oil** n : a light-yellow semidrying oil obtained from the seeds of the kapok tree and used in foods and in soapmaking

**kapok tree** n : SILK-COTTON TREE

**ka·po·te** \kə'pōd·ə\ n -s [Yiddish, fr. F *capote* — more at CAPOTE] : a man's long coat of medieval origin worn esp. by Jews of eastern Europe — compare CAPOTE

**¹kap·pa** \'kapə\ n -s [Gk, of Sem origin; akin to Heb *kaph*] : the 10th letter of the Greek alphabet — symbol K or κ; see ALPHABET table

**²kappa** \"\ n -s [NL, fr. Gk *kappa*] : a cytoplasmic factor in certain paramecia that mediates production of paramecin and thereby makes the medium in which such animals are grown toxic to members of strains not possessing the factor

**kap·pa·rah** \,käpä'rä, kä'pȯrə\ n, pl **kap·pa·roth** or **kap·pa·rot** \,käpä'rōt(h), kä'pȯrəs\ [Heb, lit., atonement] **1** : a symbolic ceremony practiced by some Orthodox Jews on the eve of Yom Kippur in which typically a cock, hen, or coin is swung around the head and offered in atonement or as ransom for one's sins **2** : SACRIFICE; *specif* : something used as a symbolic sacrifice in the kapparah ceremony

**kap·pie** \'kapē, 'käpē\ n -s [Afrik, fr. D *kapje* small cap, dim. of *kap* cap, fr. MD *cappe*, fr. LL *cappa* head covering — more at CAP] *Africa* : SUNBONNET ⟨her hair . . . covered by a big black linen ~ which came down over her shoulders —Stuart Cloete⟩

**ka·pu** \'kä(,)pü\ n -s [Hawaiian] *Hawaii* : TABOO

**ka·pu·ka** \'käpəkə\ n -s [Maori] : a rather small New Zealand broadleaf evergreen tree (*Griselinia littoralis*) sometimes cultivated in warm regions as an ornamental

**ka·pur** \kə'pù(ə)r\ or **ka·por** \-pō(ə)r\ n -s [Hindi *kapūr*, fr. Skt *karpūra* camphor — more at CAMPHOR] : a tree (*Dryobalanops aromatica*) that produces Borneo camphor

**ka·put** also **ka·putt** \kä'put, kə'-, -püt\ adj [G, fr. F *capot* not having made a trick at piquet — more at CAPOT] **1** : utterly defeated or destroyed : FINISHED, DONE FOR, RUINED ⟨after weeks of bombardment the city was ~⟩ **2** : made useless or unable to function ⟨the TV production masterminds were caught with their cables and cameras ~ —R.L.Shayon⟩ **3** : hopelessly outmoded or set aside ⟨the notion that reading is ~ each time a mammoth entertainment medium catches hold —Harvey Breit⟩ ⟨all those curls that used to take hours to do are ~ —Ethel Merman⟩

**ka·ra·bagh** \¦karə¦bä\ n -s usu cap [fr. *Karabagh*, region in Azerbaidzhan, U.S.S.R.] : a small Caucasian rug showing considerable Persian influence in pattern and usu. having magenta, turquoise, and pale green as the prevailing colors

**karabiner** var of CARABINER

**ka·ra·chai** also **ka·ra·tchai** \¦karə¦chī\ or **ka·ra·cha·yevt**

\ˌ≈≈ˈchäyəft\ *n, pl* **karachai** *or* **karachais** *usu cap* [*karachai, karatchai* fr. *Karachai*, region on the northern slope of the western Caucasus mountains, U.S.S.R.; *karachayevt* fr. Russ *Karachayevtsi* (pl.) Karachai people, fr. *Karachai*] **1 :** a Turkic-speaking people of the Caucasus **2 :** a member of the Karachai people

**ka·ra·chi** \kəˈrächē *also* -rachē\ *adj, usu cap* [fr. *Karachi*, Pakistan] **:** of or from the city of Karachi, Pakistan **:** of the kind or style prevalent in Karachi

**ka·ra·dagh** \ˈkärəˌdäg\ *n* -s *usu cap* [fr. *Karadagh*, mountain range in Azerbaidzhan province, northwestern Iran] **:** a Persian rug having a bold design and rich coloring

**ka·ra·gan·da** \ˌkarəganˈdä\ *adj, usu cap* [fr. *Karaganda*, city in the central U.S.S.R.] **:** of or from the city of Karaganda, U.S.S.R. **:** of the kind or style prevalent in Karaganda

**kara·ism** \ˈka(a)rəˌizəm\ *or* **kara·it·ism** \-rəˌīd·ˌizəm\ *n* -s *usu cap* [*karaism* fr. *kara-* (fr. LHeb *qĕrāīm* Karaites, fr. Heb *qārā* to read) + *-ism*; *karaitism* fr. *karaite* + *-ism*] **:** a Jewish doctrine originating in Baghdad in the 8th century that rejects rabbinism and talmudism and bases its tenets on interpretation of the Scriptures

**karait** *var of* KRAIT

**kara·ite** \-rəˌīt\ *n* -s *usu cap* [*kara-* (fr. L Heb *qĕrāīm* Karaites) + *-ite*] **1 :** an adherent of Karaism **2 :** a Turkic dialect spoken by Karaite people from Crimea

**karajá** *or* **karaya** *usu cap, var of* CARAJÁ

**ka·ra·ka** \ˈkärəkə\ *n* -s [Maori] **:** a New Zealand tree (*Corynocarpus laevigata*) having orange-colored fruit with edible pulp and poisonous seeds that when cooked and dried are also edible and form an important article of native diet

**kara·kal·pak** *or* **qara·qal·paq** \ˌkarəkəlˈpak, -rəkälˈ-\ *n, pl* **karakalpak** *or* **karakalpaks** *or* **qaraqalpaq** *or* **qaraqalpaqs** *usu cap* [Kirghiz, lit., black cap, fr. *kara* black + *kalpak* cap] **1 a :** a Turkic people living near Lake Aral, Central Asia **b :** a member of such people **2 :** the Turkic language of the Karakalpak people

**kara kir·ghiz** \ˌkarə(ˌ)kərˈgēz, -arə,kirˈ-\ *n, usu cap both Ks* [Kirghiz *Karakyrghyz*, lit., black Kirghiz, fr. *kara* black + *Kyrghyz* Kirghiz] **1 :** a Kirghiz people closely resembling the Mongols and dwelling chiefly in the Tien Shan highlands and the Great Pamir — called also *Black Kirghiz, Burut* **2 :** a member of the Kara Kirghiz people

**kar·a·kul** *also* **car·a·cul** \ˈkarəkəl *also* ˈker-\ *n* [fr. *Karakul*, village in Uzbekistan, U.S.S.R., where the breed originated] **1 a** *usu cap* **:** a breed of hardy slender fat-tailed sheep from Bukhara with coarse wiry brown fur **b** -s *often cap* **:** a sheep of this breed **2** -s **:** the tightly curled glossy black coat of the newborn lamb of the Karakul breed valued as fur — compare ASTRAKHAN, BROADTAIL, PERSIAN LAMB

**kar·a·kurt** \ˈkarəˌku̇(ə)rt\ *n* -s [Turki, fr. *kara* black + *kurt* wolf] **:** a venomous spider (*Latrodectus tredecimguttatus*) of eastern Europe and Siberia — called also *black wolf*

**ka·ra·mo·jong** \ˌkarəˈmōˌjäŋ\ *or* **ka·ra·mo·jo** \-(ˌ)jō\ *n, pl* **karamojong** *or* **karamojongs** *or* **karamojo** *or* **karamojos** *usu cap* **1 a :** a pastoral people of northeast Uganda **b :** a member of such people **2 :** a Nilotic language of the Karamojong people

**kar·a·mu** \ˈkarəˌmü\ *n* -s [Maori] **:** a New Zealand shrub or tree of the genus *Coprosma*

**ka·ran·da** \kəˈrəndə, -ˌdä\ *var of* CARAUNDA

**ka·ran·ka·wa** \kəˈraŋkəˌwȯ\ *n, pl* **karankawa** *or* **karankawas** *usu cap* **1 a :** an Indian people of the Gulf coast in Texas **b :** a member of such people **2 :** a language of the Karankawa people **3 :** a language family perhaps related to Coahuiltecan and Tonkawan that comprises the Karankawa language

**kar·at** *or* **car·at** \ˈkarət *also* ˈker-\ *n* -s [prob. fr. MF *carat*, fr. ML *carratus* unit of weight for precious stones — more at CARAT] **:** a unit of fineness for gold equal to 1/24 part of pure gold in an alloy ⟨16-*karat* gold contains 16/24 pure gold⟩ ⟨24-*karat* gold is pure⟩ — abbr. *k* or *kt*

**kar·a·tas** \ˈkarəˌtas\ *n* [NL, fr. Tupi *carautá, caragoatá* karatas] **1** *cap* **:** a genus of tropical American plants (family Bromeliaceae) with the flowers in dense terminal heads **2** -ES **:** any plant of the genus *Karatas* (esp. *K. plumieri*) **3** -ES **:** SILK GRASS 3b

**ka·ra·te** \kəˈrätē\ *n* -s [Jap, lit., empty hand] **:** a Japanese art of self-defense in which kicks and openhanded blows are delivered esp. to vulnerable parts of the body

**karatto** *var of* KERATTO

**karaya** *usu cap, var of* CARAJÁ

**ka·rava gum** *also* **karaya** \kəˈrīə-\ *n* -s [*karaya* modif. of Hindi *karāyal* resin] **:** STERCULIA GUM; *esp* **:** a gum derived from an Indian tree (*Sterculia urens*)

**¹kar·bi** \ˈkärbē\ *n* -s [native name in Queensland, Australia] **:** a small stingless wild bee (*Trigona carbonaria*) of Australia that makes a spiral mass of honeycomb

**²karbi** \"\ *n, pl* **karbi** [Gujarati *kaḍbī*] *India* **:** dried stalks of Indian corn

**ka·rel** \kəˈrel, ˈkarəl\ *n* -s *cap* [back-formation fr. *karelian*] **:** KARELIAN 2

**ka·re·la** \ˈkərələ\ *n* -s [Hindi *karelā*, fr. Skt *kāravella, kāravellaka*] *India* **:** a large balsam apple (*Momordica charantia*) with an elongated warty yellowish to coppery fruit

**¹ka·re·lian** *also* **ca·re·lian** \kəˈrēlēən, -lyən\ *adj, usu cap* [*Karelia*, region in northwestern U.S.S.R. + E *-an*, adj. suffix] **1 :** of, relating to, or characteristic of Karelia, a region of the northwestern U.S.S.R. and the adjoining borders of eastern Finland **2 :** of, relating to, or characteristic of the people of Karelia **3 :** of, relating to, or characteristic of the language of the Karelians

**²karelian** *also* **carelian** \"\ *n* -s *cap* [*Karelia* + E *-an*, n. suffix] **1 :** a native or inhabitant of Karelia **2 :** the Finno-Ugric language of the Karelian people that is closely related to Finnish and sometimes treated as a dialect of it

**ka·ren** \kəˈren\ *n, pl* **karen** *or* **karens** *usu cap* **1 a :** a group of peoples of eastern and southern Burma **b :** a member of any of such peoples **2 a :** a group of languages spoken by the Karen peoples that is held to be related to the Tibeto-Burman, Thai, or Mon-Khmer language groups **b :** a language of this group

**ka·ren·ni** \kəˈrenē\ *n, pl* **karenni** *or* **karennis** *usu cap* **1 :** one of several Karen peoples of eastern Burma the women of which elongate their necks by heavy coils of brass that thrust the head away from the body **2 :** a member of a Karenni people

**ka·rez** \käˈrez, ˈ≈ˌ≈\ *n, pl* **karez** [Per *kārez*] **1 :** an underground irrigation tunnel bored horizontally into rock slopes in Baluchistan **2 :** a system of irrigation by underground tunnels

**kari** *var of* KARRI

**kar·i·era** \ˌkarēˈerə\ *n, pl* **kariera** *or* **karieras** *usu cap* **1 :** a people of Western Australia **2 :** a member of the Kariera people

**kar·in·gho·ta** \ˌkarənˈgōd·ə\ *n* -s [origin unknown] **:** NIEPA 1

**kariri** *usu cap, var of* CARIRI

**kar·i·te** *or* **kar·i·ti** \ˈkarəd·ē\ *n* -s [F *karité*, of Niger-Congo origin; akin to Wolof *karité* karite] **:** SHEA TREE

**karite butter** *or* **karite oil** *n* **:** SHEA BUTTER

**karl fisch·er reagent** \ˈkärlˈfishər-\ *n, usu cap K&F* [after *Karl Fischer*, 20th cent. Ger. chemist] **:** a colored solution of pyridine, sulfur dioxide, iodine, and anhydrous methanol that reacts quantitatively with water to form a colorless solution and is used to determine the amount of water in numerous substances

**karls·bad salt** \ˈkärlzˌbad-, -l(t)sˌbät-\ *n, usu cap K* [trans. of G *karlsbader salz*, fr. *Karlsbad* (*Karlovy Vary*), town in western Czechoslovakia renowned for its sulfur springs] **1 :** a mixture of mineral salts including esp. potassium sulfate and sodium sulfate that is obtained from the water of certain springs **2 :** an artificial mixture of potassium sulfate, sodium sulfate, sodium chloride, and sodium bicarbonate

**karls·ru·he** \ˈkärlzˌrüə, -l(t)sˌr-\ *adj, usu cap* [fr. *Karlsruhe*, city in southwest Germany] **:** of or from the city of Karlsruhe, Germany **:** of the kind or style prevalent in Karlsruhe

**kar·ma** \ˈkärmə, ˈkər-\ *n* -s *often cap* [Skt *karman* (nom. *karma*) karma, work, office, fr. *karoti* he does, makes; akin to OIr *cruth* form, Lith *kurti* to build, Skt *kāra* doing, *kr̥noti* he does, makes] **1 :** the force generated by a person's actions that is held in Hinduism and Buddhism to be the motive power for the round of rebirths and deaths endured by him until he has achieved spiritual liberation and freed himself from the effects of such force ⟨release from the ~ of recurrent existences —John Baillie⟩ — compare NIRVANA, SAMSARA **2 :** the sum total of the ethical consequences of a person's good or bad actions comprising thoughts, words, and deeds that is held in Hinduism and Buddhism to determine his specific destiny in his next existence ⟨as our desires shape themselves, so we act and build up our coming fate, our ~ —P.E.More⟩ **3 :** a subtle form of matter held in Jainism to develop in the soul and vitiate its purity, to lengthen the course of individual transmigration, and to postpone the possibility of final salvation ⟨the soul's chief problem . . . of managing to throw off or expel ~ matter from itself —J.B.Noss⟩ — **kar·mic** \-mik\ *adj, often cap*

**kar·ma·dha·ra·ya** \ˌkərməˈdärēə, -ärəyə\ *n* -s [Skt *karmadhāraya*, fr. *karma-* (fr. *karman*) + *dhāraya* that holds, that maintains; perh. fr. the fact that such words maintain the same function throughout, inasmuch as the syntactic function of the entire compound is the same as the syntactic function of its final constituent would be if used alone; akin to Skt *dhārayati* he holds, carries, keeps — more at FIRM] **:** a class of compound words typically having a noun as second constituent and a descriptive adjective as first constituent (as *bluegrass, blackberry*), a noun as second constituent and an attributive noun as first constituent (as *houseboat*), or an adjective as second constituent and an adverb as first constituent (as *everlasting, widespread*) and having meanings that follow the formula "*A B* that is *A*" for nouns or "*B* in the manner expressed by *A*" for adjectives, where *A* stands for the first constituent and *B* for the second; *also* **:** a compound word belonging to this class

**karma-marga** \-ˈmärgə\ *n* -s [Skt, fr. *karma-* (fr. *karman*) + *mārga* path, fr. *mr̥ga* deer, gazelle] **:** the strict observation of caste regulations and ritual duties regarded in Hinduism as one path to a happier life in an individual's next incarnation **:** salvation by works — compare BHAKTI-MARGA, JNANA-MARGA

**karmatian** *or* **karmathian** *usu cap, var of* QARMATIAN

**karma-yoga** \ˈ≈≈ˌ≈≈\ *n* [Skt *karmayoga*, fr. *karma-* (fr. *karman*) + *yoga*] **:** yoga through disinterested service or the selfless performance of duties

**kar·mouth** *or* **kar·mout** \(ˈ)kärˈmüt\ *n* -s [Ar *qarmūṭ*] **:** any of several African siluroid fishes (genera *Clarias* and *Heterobranchus*) that have an accessory breathing organ enabling them to live for a time out of water

**karn** \ˈkärn\ *var of* CAIRN

**ka·ro** \ˈkä(ˌ)rō\ *n* -s [Maori] **:** either of two New Zealand plants of the genus *Pittosporum*: **a :** a shrub or small tree (*P. crassifolium*) with fastigiate branches **b :** an epiphyte (*P. cornifolium*) with whorled leaves

**ka·rok** \kəˈräk\ *n, pl* **karok** *or* **karoks** *usu cap* [Karok *karuk* upstream] **1 a :** an Indian people of the Klamath river valley, California **b :** a member of such people **2 :** the Quoratean language of the Karok people **3 :** QUORATEAN

**karolin** *var of* CAROLIN

**ka·ross** \kəˈräs\ *n* -ES [Afrik *karos*, perh. alter. of D *kuras* cuirass, fr. MF *curasse, cuirasse* — more at CUIRASS] **:** a simple garment or rug of animal skins usu. used by native tribesmen of southern Africa

**kar·pas** \ˈkärˌpäs\ *n* -ES [Heb *karpās*, fr. Aram *karpas*] **:** a piece of parsley, celery, or lettuce placed on the Passover seder plate as a symbol of spring or hope and dipped in salt water in remembrance of the hyssop and blood of the Passover in Egypt

**kar·ree** \kəˈrē, -rā\ *also* **karree boom** \-ˌbüm, -ˌbōm\ *or* **kar·roo·boom** \-ˈrüˌb-\ *n* -s [*karree* fr. Afrik, prob. fr. Hottentot *karib*; *karree boom, karrooboom* fr. Afrik *karreeboom*, fr. *karree* + *boom* tree, fr. D, fr. MD; akin to OE *bēam* tree — more at BEAM] **:** a plant of the genus *Rhus* (esp. *R. viminalis*) of southern Africa

**kar·ren** \ˈkärən\ *n* -s [G] **:** a ribbed and fluted rock surface resulting at least in part from differential solution

**kar·ri** *or* **kari** \ˈkarē\ *n* -s [native name in Western Australia] **1 :** a large gum tree (*Eucalyptus diversicolor*) of Western Australia **2 :** the hard durable red wood of karri that constitutes one of the principal commercial timbers of Australia

**karri-tree** \ˈkarē,\ *n* [origin unknown] **:** PRINCESS-TREE

**kar·roo** *or* **ka·roo** \kəˈrü\ *n* -s [Afrik *karo*, perh. fr. Hottentot *garo* desert] **:** a dry tableland of southern Africa that often rises in terraces to a considerable elevation

**karroo bush** *also* **karroo shrub** *n* **1 :** a thorny acacia (*Acacia horrida*) that yields cape gum **2 :** a plant of the genus *Tetragonia* (esp. *T. arbuscula*)

**karroo caterpillar** *n* **:** the larva of a pyralidid moth (*Loxostege frustralis*) that seriously damages fodder in sheep-farming regions of southern Africa

**kar·ru·sel** \ˌkarəˈsel, ˈ≈≈ˌ≈ *also* ˈker- *or* -zel\ *n* -s [prob. alter. of *carrousel*] **:** a revolving escapement that is designed to reduce position errors in a watch and is mounted in a carriage similar to that of a tourbillion but differs from it in slower speed of rotation and in having the fourth wheel contained inside the carriage

**kar·shu·ni** *also* **car·shu·ni** \kärˈshünē\ *or* **gar·shu·ni** \gär-\ *n* -s *usu cap* [Ar *karshūnīy*, prob. fr. Syr *gershūn* alien, foreign + Ar *-īy* belonging to] **:** Arabic written in Syriac characters esp. as used in the Maronite ritual

**karst** \ˈkärst\ *n* -s [G] **:** a limestone region marked by sinks and interspersed with abrupt ridges, irregular protuberant rocks, caverns, and underground streams — **karst·ic** \-tik\ *adj*

**kar·tik** \ˈkard·ik\ *n* -s *usu cap* [Hindi *kārtik*, fr. Skt *kārttika*, fr. *kr̥ttikā* Pleiades; perh. akin to Skt *kr̥ṇatti* he spins — more at HURDLE] **:** a month of the Hindu year — see MONTH table

**kart·ve·lian** \(ˈ)kärtˈvēlēən, -lyən\ *also* **karth·li** \ˈkärtlē\ *or* **kart·vel** \ˈkärtˌvel\ *n* -s *usu cap* **1 :** a member of a group of related peoples of the Caucasus **2 :** the South Caucasic language family including Georgian, Mingrelian, Svanetian, and Laz

**ka·ru·na** \ˈkəru̇ˌnä\ *n* -s [Skt *karuṇā* compassion; perh. akin to OE *hrēowan* to grieve, repent — more at RUE] **:** compassion that is a fundamental quality in the bodhisattva ideal of Mahayana Buddhism

**kar·win·skia** \kärˈwinzkēə, -n(t)sk-\ *n, cap* [NL, fr. Wilhelm *Karwinsky* von Karwin †1855 Ger. traveler + NL *-ia*] **:** a genus of shrubs or small trees (family Rhamnaceae) that are chiefly native to Mexico and the southwestern U.S. and have flowers with small hooded short-clawed petals and fleshy drupes

**kary-** *or* **karyo-** *also* **cary-** *or* **caryo-** *comb form* [NL, fr. Gk *kary-, karyo-* walnut, nut, kernel, fr. *karyon* — more at CAREEN] **1 :** nucleus of a cell ⟨*kary*enchyma⟩ ⟨*karyo*kinesis⟩ — in cytological terms **2 :** nut **:** kernel ⟨*caryo*psis⟩

**kary·en·chy·ma** \ˌkarēˈeŋkəmə, -enk-\ *n* -s [NL, fr. *kary-* + *-enchyma*] **:** KARYOLYMPH

**kar·yo·chy·le·ma** \ˌkarē(ˌ)ōˌkīˈlēmə\ *n* -s [NL, fr. *kary-* + *-chylema* (as in *enchylema*)] **:** KARYOLYMPH

**kar·yo·clasic** \ˌ≈≈ˈklāsik, -las-\ *or* **kar·yo·clas·tic** \-lastik\ *adj* [*karyoclasic* ISV *karyoclas-* (fr. NL *karyoclasis*) + *-ic*; *karyoclastic* fr. *kary-* + *-clastic*] **:** of or relating to karyoclasis

**kar·y·oc·la·sis** *or* **kar·y·ok·la·sis** \ˌkarēˈäkləsəs\ *n, pl* **karyocla·ses** *or* **karyokla·ses** \-əˌsēz\ [NL *karyoclasis*, fr. *kary-* + *-clasis*] **1 :** disintegration of the cell nucleus **2 :** interruption of mitosis (as in colchicine poisoning)

**kar·yo·gam·ic** \ˌkarēōˈgamik\ *adj* **:** of or relating to karyogamy

**kar·y·og·a·my** \ˌkarēˈägəmē\ *n* -ES [ISV *kary-* + *-gamy*] **:** the fusion of cell nuclei (as in fertilization) — compare PLASMOGAMY

**kar·yo·kinesis** \ˌkarē(ˌ)ō+\ *n* [NL, fr. *kary-* + *-kinesis*] **1 :** the nuclear phenomena characteristic of mitosis **2 :** the whole process of mitosis — compare CYTOKINESIS — **kar·yo·kinetic** \"+\ *adj*

**karyokinetic figure** *n* [*karyokinetic* ISV *kary-* + *kinetic*] *biol* **:** ACHROMATIC FIGURE

**kar·y·o·log·ic** \ˌkarēəˈläjik\ *or* **kar·y·o·log·i·cal** \-jəkəl\ *adj* **:** of or relating to karyology — **kar·y·o·log·i·cal·ly** \-jək(ə)lē\ *adv*

**kar·y·ol·o·gy** \ˌkarēˈäləjē\ *n* -ES [ISV *kary-* + *-logy*] **:** a branch of cytology that deals with the minute anatomy of cell nuclei and esp. the nature and structure of chromosomes

**kar·yo·lymph** \ˈkarēō+ˌ-\ *n* [ISV *kary-* + *lymph*; prob. orig. formed as G *karyolymphe*] **:** the clear homogeneous ground substance of a cell nucleus — called also *enchylema, nuclear sap*; opposed to *karyotin*

**kar·y·ol·y·sis** \ˌkarēˈäləsəs\ *n* [NL, fr. *kary-* + *-lysis*] **:** dissolution of the cell nucleus with loss of its affinity for basic stains sometimes occurring normally but usu. in necrosis — **kar·yo·lyt·ic** \ˌkarēəˈlid·ik\ *adj*

**kar·y·ol·y·sus** \-ləsəs\ *n, cap* [NL, fr. *kary-* + *-lysus* (fr. Gk *lyein* to loose, dissolve) — more at LOSE] **:** a genus of haemogregarines parasitic in reptiles

**kar·yo·mere** \ˈ≈≈≈ˌmi(ə)r\ *n* -s [ISV *kary* + *-mere*] **1 a :** ²CHROMOMERE **b :** a sperm head **2 :** a swollen vesicular chromosome (as in certain embryonic tissues) — called also *chromosomal vesicle*

**kar·y·om·er·ite** \ˌkarēˈäməˌrīt\ *n* -s [ISV *kary-* + *-mere* + *-ite*; prob. orig. formed as G *karyomerit*] **:** KARYOMERE 2

**kar·yo·microsome** \ˌkarē(ˌ)ō+\ *n* **:** a nuclear microsome

**kar·yo·mi·to·ic** \ˌkarēōˌmīˈtōik\ *or* **kar·yo·mi·tot·ic** \ˌkarēō+\ *adj* [*karyomitoic* fr. *karyomitosis* + *-ic*; *karyomitotic* fr. *kary-* + *mitotic*] **:** of or relating to karyomitosis

**kar·yo·mitome** \ˌkarēō+\ *n* [ISV *kary-* + *mitome*] **:** the nuclear reticulum of a cell

**kar·yo·mitosis** \"+\ *n* [NL, fr. *kary-* + *mitosis*] **:** mitotic division of the nucleus of a cell

**kar·y·on** \ˈkarēˌän\ *n* -s [NL, fr. Gk *karyon* nut — more at CAREEN] **:** the nucleus of a cell — **kar·y·on·tic** \ˌkarēˈäntik\ *adj*

**kar·yo·plasm** \ˈkarēə+ˌ-\ *also* **kar·yo·plas·ma** \ˌ≈≈≈+\ *n* -s [ISV *kary-* + *-plasm, -plasma*; orig. formed as G *karyoplasma*] **:** NUCLEOPLASM 1 — **kar·y·o·plasmic** \ˌ≈≈(ˌ)≈+\ *or* **kar·y·o·plasmatic** \"+\ *adj*

**kar·yo·pyc·nosis** \ˌkarē(ˌ)ō+\ *n* [NL, fr. *kary-* + *pycnosis*] **:** KARYOCLASIS 1 — **kar·yo·pycnotic** \"+\ *adj*

**kar·y·or·rhec·tic** \ˌkarēəˈrektik\ *adj* [*kary-* + Gk *rhēktikos* apt to burst, fr. *rhēktos* that can be broken (fr. *rhēgnynai* to break) + *-ikos* -ic] **:** of or relating to karyorrhexis

**kar·y·or·rhex·is** \ˌkarēəˈreksəs\ *n, pl* **karyorrhex·es** \-kˌsēz\ [NL, fr. *kary-* + *-rrhexis*] **:** KARYOCLASIS 1

**kar·y·os·chi·sis** \ˌkarēˈäskəsəs\ *n, pl* **karyoschi·ses** \-əˌsēz\ [NL, fr. *kary-* + *-schisis*] **:** KARYOCLASIS 1

**kar·yo·some** \ˈkarēəˌsōm\ *n* -s [ISV *kary-* + *-some*; orig. formed as G *karyosom*] **1 :** CHROMOCENTER **2 :** ENDOSOME; *esp* **:** an endosome consisting of a nucleolar mass of heterochromatin as distinguished from one that is a plasmosome

**kar·yo·systematic** \ˌkarē(ˌ)ō+\ *adj* **:** of or relating to karyosystematics

**kar·yo·systematics** \"+\ *n pl but sing in constr* **:** a branch of systematics that seeks to determine natural relationships by the study of karyotypes

**kar·yo·the·ca** \ˌkarēō+\ *n* -s [NL, fr. *kary-* + *-theca*] **:** a nuclear membrane

**kar·y·o·tin** \ˈkarēətən, -ˌtin\ *n* -s [ISV *kary-* + *-tin* (fr. *chromatin*); orig. formed as G *caryotin* (now *karyotin*)] **:** the reticular usu. stainable material of the cell nucleus — opposed to *karyolymph*

**kar·yo·type** \-ˌtīp\ *n* [ISV *kary-* + *type*; prob. orig. formed as F *caryotype*] **1 :** the sum of the specific characteristics of a cell nucleus including chromosome number, form, size, and points of spindle-fiber attachment **2 :** a diagrammatic representation of a physical karyotype — **kar·yo·typ·ic** \ˌkarēōˈtipik\ *or* **kar·yo·typ·i·cal** \-pəkəl\ *adj*

**¹kas** *pl of* KA

**²kas** \ˈkäs\ *n, pl* **kas** [D, fr. MD *casse, cas* chest, box, fr. ONF *casse* — more at CASE] **:** a Dutch cupboard or wardrobe common in the late 17th and the 18th centuries in the New Netherlands colony in America, often paneled, sometimes painted with floral designs, and equipped with two doors, heavy cornices, and usu. a drawer at the bottom

**kasbah** *or* **kasba** *usu cap, var of* CASBAH

**kas·cam·i·ol** \kaˈskamēˌōl\ *n* -s [origin unknown] **:** a purple gallinule (*Porphyrula martinicas*) of the West Indies

**ka·sha** \ˈkäshə\ *n* -s [Russ; akin to Pol *kasza* kasha, Lith *košti* to strain] **1 :** a mush made from coarse cracked buckwheat, barley, millet, or wheat **2 :** kasha grain before cooking

**Kasha** \ˈkashə\ *trademark* — used for a soft napped twilled fabric of fine wool and hair having a slight crosswise streaked effect

**ka·shan** \kəˈshän\ *n* -s *usu cap* [fr. *Kashan*, city in central Iran] **1 :** a Persian rug of fine quality, soft color, and fluid floral designs **2 :** a heavy glazed pottery produced in eastern Mediterranean lands during the 16th, 17th, and 18th centuries

**¹kasher** *var of* KOSHER

**²ka·sher** \käˈshe(ə)r, -eə\ *or* **ko·sher** \ˈkōshə(r)\ *vt* -ED/-ING/-S [*kasher* fr. Heb *kāshēr* to make kosher; *kosher* fr. Yiddish, n., kosher, fr. Heb *kāshēr* kosher, fit, proper] **:** to make (meat or utensils) kosher for use according to Jewish law

**kash·gai** *also* **khash·gai** \ˈkashˌgī\ *n* -s *usu cap* **1 :** a Turkic often nomadic people of southern Iran **2 :** a member of the Kashgai people

**ka·shi** \ˈkäshē\ *n* -s [Ar *qāshīy* belonging to Kashan, fr. *Qāshān* Kashan, city in central Iran] **:** a Persian enameled tile made esp. in the 16th and 17th centuries

**ka·shim** \ˈkashəm\ *n* -s [Esk] **:** an Eskimo house of assembly

**kash·mir** \ˈkazhˌmi(ə)r, -aizh-, -iə; -ash-, -aa-,-ai-\ *var of* CASHMERE

**kashmir goat** *n, usu cap K* [fr. *Kashmir*, region in the northern part of the Indian subcontinent] **:** an Indian goat raised chiefly for its undercoat of fine soft wool that constitutes the cashmere wool of commerce

**kash·miri** *or* **cash·miri** \≈ˈmirē\ *n, pl* **kashmiris** *or* **kashmiri** *usu cap* **1 :** a native or inhabitant of Kashmir **2 :** the Dard language of the Kashmiri people

**¹kash·mir·ian** \(ˈ)≈ˈmirēən\ *adj, usu cap* **1 :** of, relating to, or characteristic of Kashmir **2 :** of, relating to, or characteristic of the people of Kashmir

**²kashmirian** \"\ *n* -s *cap* **:** KASHMIRI

**ka·shou·bish** \kəˈshübish\ *n* -ES *cap* **:** the Kashubian language

**kash·ruth** *or* **kash·rut** \käˈshrüt(h), ˈ≈ˌ≈\ *also* **kash·rus** \ˈkäshrəs, -rüs\ *n* -s [*kashruth, kashrut* fr. Heb *kashrūth, kashrūt*, lit., fitness, fr. *kāshēr* kosher, fit, proper; *kashrus* fr. Yiddish, fr. Heb *kashrūth*] **1 :** the state of being kosher according to Jewish religious law ⟨rabbinical approval of the ~ of the new scroll of the Torah⟩ **2 :** the Jewish dietary laws ⟨meals for Orthodox Jews who observe ~⟩ — compare HECHSHER

**kashua** *var of* CACHUA

**ka·shube** *or* **ka·shub** \kəˈshüb\ *n* -s *cap* **1 :** a member of a Slavonic Pomeranian people who live just west of the mouth of the Vistula river **2 :** KASHUBIAN

**ka·shu·bi·an** \kəˈshübēən\ *or* **kasubian** *or* **kas·su·bi·an** *also* **cas·su·bi·an** *or* **ca·su·bi·an** \kəˈsü-\ *n* -s *cap* [*Kashube* + E *-ian*, n. suffix] **1 :** KASHUBE 1 **2 :** a West Slavic language closely related to Polish and spoken in the region of Danzig

**kasida** *var of* QASIDA

**kas·ka** \ˈkaskə\ *n, pl* **kaska** *or* **kaskas** *usu cap* **1 a :** an Athapaskan people of the Liard river valley of the Yukon and British Columbia **b :** a member of such people **2 :** the language of the Kaska people — called also *Nahane*; see MONTAGNARD

**kaso·lite** \ˈkasəˌlīt, kəˈsōˌl-\ *n* -s [*Kasolo*, Katanga, Belgian Congo, its locality + E *-ite*] **:** a mineral $Pb(UO_2)SiO_4H_2O$ consisting of a hydrous uranium lead silicate that occurs in yellow-ocher monoclinic crystals

**kas·sel** *also* **cas·sel** \ˈkasəl, ˈkäs-\ *adj, usu cap* [fr. *Kassel*, city in central Germany] **:** of or from the city of Kassel, Germany **:** of the kind or style prevalent in Kassel

**kas·site** *or* **cas·site** \ˈkaˌsīt\ *n* -s *usu cap* **1 :** a member of a people inhabiting parts of the Iranian plateau south of the Caspian sea and ruling Babylon between 1600 and 1200 B.C. **2 :** the Elamite language of the Kassite people

**kas·tu·ra** \kəˈstu̇rə\ *n* -s [Hindi *kastūrī*, fr. Skt *kastūrikā*, fr. Gk *kastorion* castor, fr. neut. of *kastoreios, kastorios* of a beaver, fr. *kastor-, kastōr* beaver — more at CASTOR] **:** MUSK DEER

**kaswa** *var of* CACHUA

**kat** *or* **khat** *or* **qat** *or* **q'at** *or* **quat** *or* **cat** \ˈkät\ *n* -s [Ar *qāt*] **:** a shrub (*Catha edulis*) cultivated by the Arabs for its leaves that act as a stimulant narcotic when chewed or used as a tea — called also *African tea, Arabian tea*

**ka·ta** \ˈkä(ˌ)tä\ *n* -s [Jap] **:** form practice in judo **:** a set of exercises in judo — compare RANDORI

**kata-** *or* **kat-** *prefix* [Gk — more at CATA-] **:** CATA-

**katabanian** *usu cap, var of* QATABANIAN

**ka·tab·a·sis** *or* **ca·tab·a·sis** \kəˈtabəsəs\ *n, pl* **kataba·ses** *or* **cataba·ses** \-bə,sēz\ [Gk *katabasis* descent, fr. *katabainein* to go down, fr. *kata-* cata- + *bainein* to go — more at COME] **1 :** a going or marching down or back **:** RETREAT; *esp* **:** a military retreat ⟨the Russian anabasis and ~ of Napoleon —Thomas DeQuincey⟩ ⟨the tragic and precipitate ~ of the UN troops —H.L.Ickes⟩ **2 :** a troparion sung after the two sides of the choir descend to the middle of the church at the end of each ode of the canon at matins in the Eastern Orthodox Church

**kat·a·bat·ic** \ˌkad·əˌbad·ik\ *adj* [LGk *katabatikos* of descent, fr. Gk *katabatos* descending (fr. *katabainein* to descend) + *-ikos* -ic] **:** of or relating to the downward motion of air (as in air drainage induced by surface cooling)

**kat·a·bel·la** \ˌkatəˈbelə\ *n* -s [origin unknown] *dial Brit* **:** HEN HARRIER

**katabolism** *var of* CATABOLISM

**kata·chro·ma·sis** *or* **cata·chro·ma·sis** \ˌkad·əˈkrōməsəs\ *n, pl* **katachroma·ses** *or* **catachroma·ses** \-mə,sēz\ [NL, fr. *kata-* or *cata-* + *chrom-* + connective *-a-* + *-sis*] **:** the mitotic nuclear transformations leading to formation of daughter nuclei from the chromosome groups separated in anaphase — compare ANACHROMASIS

**katagenesis** *var of* CATAGENESIS

**ka·ta·ka·na** \ˌkäd·əˈkänə\ *n* -s [Jap, fr. *kata* side + *kana*] **:** a set of symbols for writing Japanese kana having characters that are in general squarer and more angular than those of the hiragana

**kata·mor·phism** *or* **cata·mor·phism** \ˌkad·əˈmȯr,fizəm\ *n* -s [*kata-* or *cata-* + *-morphism*] **:** the breaking down of rock by chemical or mechanical processes — compare ANAMORPHISM, METAMORPHISM

**kata·mor·pho·sis** \ˌkad·əˈmȯrfəsəs *sometimes* -ˌmȯrˈfōs-\ *n* [NL, fr. *kata-* + *morphosis*] **:** evolutionary change based on or involving hypomorphosis

**ka·ta·na** \kəˈtänə\ *n* -s [Jap] **:** a single-edged sword that is the longer of a pair worn by the Japanese samurai

**ka·tang** \kəˈtäŋ\ *n, pl* **katang** *or* **katangs** *usu cap* **1 :** a Moi people of northern Vietnam **2 :** a member of the Katang people

**katastate** *var of* CATASTATE

**kata·thermometer** *or* **cata·thermometer** \ˈkad·ə+\ *n* [*kata-* or *cata-* + *thermometer*] **:** a large-bulbed alcohol thermometer used to measure the cooling effect of particular atmospheric conditions or to measure moderate air velocities by means of the cooling effect

**katatonic** *var of* CATATONIC

**ka·ta·ya·ma** \ˌkäd·əˈyämə\ *n, cap* [NL, prob. fr. *Katayama*, town in western Honshu, Japan] **:** a genus of Oriental freshwater snails (family Bulimidae) including important intermediate hosts of a human schistosome (*Schistosoma japonicum*) — see ONCOMELANIA

**katcina** *or* **katchina** *var of* KACHINA

**¹kate** \ˈkāt, *usu* -ād·+V\ *n* -s [fr. *Kate*, nickname for the name *Catherine*] **1** *dial Eng* **:** HAWFINCH **2 :** PILEATED WOODPECKER

**²kâ·te** \ˈkätə\ *n, pl* **kâte** *or* **kâtes** *usu cap* **1 a :** a people of the Huon peninsula of the Territory of New Guinea **b :** a member of such people **2 :** the Papuan language of the Kâte people

**kate green·a·way** \ˌkātˈgrēnə,wā\ *adj, usu cap K&G* [after *Kate* (Catherine) *Greenaway* †1901 Eng. painter and illustrator of children's books] *of clothing* **:** having a long full skirt, short waist and sleeves, round neck, and usu. a sash and ruffled edges ⟨in her green *Kate Greenaway* pelisse, with the long band of soft beaver running from neck to hem —Victoria Lincoln⟩

**ka·tel** \ˈkäd·ᵊl\ *n* -s [Afrik, fr. Pg *catel, catre* cot, fr. Tamil-Malayalam *kaṭṭil* bedstead, bier — more at COT] **:** a wooden hammock used in Africa as a bed in a wagon

**ka·ter's pendulum** \ˈkād·ə(r)z-\ *n, usu cap K* [after Henry *Kater* †1835 Eng. scientist] **:** a compound pendulum with adjustable knife edges placed respectively at the center of suspension and near the center of oscillation and used to determine acceleration of gravity by means of the period of oscillation

**ka·thak** \kəˈtäk\ *n* -s [Beng, professional storyteller, fr. Skt *kathaka*, fr. *kathayati* he tells, narrates, fr. *kathā* talk, story, fr. *kathā* how; akin to Skt *ka* who? — more at WHO] **:** an intricate dance of northern India that includes passages of narrative pantomime — compare BHARATA NATYA, KATHAKALI, MANIPURI

**ka·tha·ka·li** \ˌkäd·əˈkälē\ *n* -s [Malayalam *kathakaḷi* drama, fr. *katha* story (fr. Skt *kathā* talk, fr. *kathā* how) + *kaḷi* play; Skt *kathā* how akin to Skt *ka* who? — more at WHO] **:** a spectacular lyric dance drama of southern India based on Hindu literature and performed with acrobatic energy and highly stylized pantomime — compare BHARATA NATYA, KATHAK, MANIPURI

**kat·hal** \ˈkət,həl\ *n* -s [Hindi *kaṭ-hal*, fr. Skt *kaṇṭakaphala*, fr. *kaṇṭaka* thorn + *phala* fruit] **:** JACKFRUIT 1

**ka·tha·re·vu·sa** *or* **ka·tha·re·vou·sa** \ˌkäthəˈrevə(ˌ)sä\ *n* -s *cap* [NGk *kathareuousa*, fr. Gk, fem. of *kathareuōn*, pres. part. of *kathareuein* to be pure, fr. *katharos* pure] **:** modern Greek conforming to classic Greek usage and tending to reject non-Greek vocabulary — compare DEMOTIC 3

**kath·a·robe** \ˈkathə,rōb\ *n* -s [ISV *katharo-* (fr. Gk *katharos* pure) + *-be* (as in *microbe*)] **:** a katharobic organism

**kath·a·robic** \ˌ≈≈ˈrōbik, -ˈräb-\ *adj* [*katharobe* + *-ic*] **:** living in or being a highly oxygenated medium free from organic matter — compare MESOSAPROBIC, SAPROBIC

**kath·a·rom·e·ter** \ˌ≈≈ˈrämad·ə(r)\ *n* [Gk *katharos* pure + E *-meter*] **:** an apparatus for determining the composition of a gas mixture by measuring thermal conductivity

**katharsis** *var of* CATHARSIS

**kathen·o·theism** \(ˈ)kat¦henōthē,izəm, kaˈthe-; (¦)kat¦henō·¦th-, kaˈthenō¦th-\ *n* [*katheno-* (fr. Gk *kath' hena* one at a time, fr. *kata* down, according to, by + *hena*, acc. sing. masc. of *heis* one) + *theism* — more at CATA-, SAME] **:** the worship of one god at a time as supreme without denying the existence of other gods and including the tendency to make different gods supreme one after the other — compare HENOTHEISM

**kathen·o·the·ist** \-ˌəst\ *n* [*kathenotheism* + *-ist*] **:** one whose worship exemplifies kathenotheism

**ka·thi·a·wa·ri** \ˌkäd·ēəˈwärē\ *n, usu cap* [prob. fr. Hindi or Gujarati *kāṭhiāwāḍī* of Kāthiāwār (Kathiawar), peninsula on the western coast of India] **1 :** a breed of small hardy horses of India of partially Arab ancestry **2** *-s often cap* **:** a horse of the Kathiawari breed

**ka·this·ma** *also* **ca·this·ma** \kəˈthizmə\ *n, pl* **kathisma·ta** \kāˈthēzmətə\ [MGk *kathisma*, fr. Gk, sinking, settling down, fr. *kathizein* to seat, sit down, fr. *kata-* cata- + *hizein* to seat; akin to Gk *hezesthai* to sit — more at SIT] **:** one of the 20 sections into which the Psalter is divided for liturgical use in the Eastern Orthodox Church

**kathodic** *var of* CATHODIC

**katholikos** *var of* CATHOLICOS

**¹kati** *var of* CATTY

**²ka·ti** \ˈkäd·ē\ *n, pl* **kati** *or* **katis** *usu cap* **1 :** a Kafir people of easternmost Kafiristan in the Hindu Kush mountains of Afghanistan **2 :** a member of the Kati people

**ka·tik** \ˈkäd·ik\ *n* -s *cap* [Hindi *kātik*, fr. Skt *kārttika* — more at KARTIK] **:** KARTIK

**katin** *usu cap, var of* KHATIN

**kati·po** \ˈkäd·ə,pō, ˈkad-\ *n* -s [Maori] **:** a small venomous spider (*Latrodectus hasselti* or *L. scelio*) of eastern Asia, Australia, and New Zealand related to the American black widow and commonly black with a red stripe on the abdomen — see REDBACK SPIDER

**kat·man·du** \¦kat,manˌdü, -ˌmən- *also* ¦kät,män- *or* ¦kätmən-\ *adj, usu cap* [fr. *Katmandu*, Nepal] **:** of or from Katmandu, the capital of Nepal **:** of the kind or style prevalent in Katmandu

**ka·to** \ˈkäd·(ˌ)ō\ *n, pl* **kato** *or* **katos** *usu cap* [Pomo, lake] **1 a :** an Athapaskan people of northwestern California **b :** a member of such people **2 :** a language of the Kato and Wailaki peoples

**ka·tong lu·ang** \ˈkä,tōŋləˈwäŋ\ *or* **ka·ton luang** \-tōnl-\ *n, pl* **katong luang** *or* **katon luang** *usu cap K&L* [Siamese, lit., savages of the yellow leaf] **1 :** a migratory pygmy people of mountainous regions of Thailand **2 :** a member of the Katong Luang people

**ka·ton·kel** \kəˈtäŋkəl\ *n* -s [Afrik] **1** *Africa* **:** BARRACUDA 2 **2** *Africa* **:** ATLANTIC BONITO

**katoptrite** *var of* CATOPTRITE

**ka·to·wi·ce** \ˌkäd·əˈvētsə\ *adj, usu cap* [fr. *Katowice*, city in southern Poland] **:** of or from the city of Katowice, Poland **:** of the kind or style prevalent in Katowice

**kats** *pl of* KAT

**ka·tsu** \ˈkät(ˌ)sü\ *n* -s [Jap] **:** resuscitation of an unconscious judoka

**katsup** *var of* CATSUP

**kat·su·ra tree** \ˈkätsərə-\ *also* **katsura** *n* -s [Jap *katsura*] **:** a deciduous tree (*Cercidiphyllum japonicum*) of the order Ranales that has short spurs on its branches, broadly ovate leaves with crenate-serrate margins, and fruit which is a pod enclosing many winged seeds and that is sometimes cultivated as an ornamental esp. for its dark blue-green foliage which turns bright yellow or red in autumn

**kat·su·won·i·dae** \ˌkatsəˈwänə,dē\ *n pl, cap* [NL, fr. *Katsuwonus*, type genus (fr. Jap *katsuo* victorfish) + *-idae*] *in some classifications* **:** a family of scombroid fishes comprising the oceanic bonitos and closely related forms and including a type genus (*Katsuwonus*) that is commonly placed in the family Scombridae

**ka·tu·ka** \ˈkəd·əkə\ *n* -s [perh. fr. Skt *kaṭuka* sharp, bitter, fierce, fr. *kaṭu*, prob. of Dravidian origin; akin to Tamil *kaṭu* to be pungent, ache, Malayalam *kaṭu* pungent, extreme] **:** RUSSELL'S VIPER

**ka·tun** \ˈkä,tün\ *n* -s [Maya, fr. *ka* 20 + *tun* year of 360 days] **:** a period of 20 tuns in the Maya calendar — compare BAKTUN, PICTUN

**katy** *var of* KADY

**ka·ty·did** *also* **ca·ty·did** \ˈkād·|ē,did, -ˌāt|, |i,- *sometimes* ,≈≈ˈ≈\ *n* -s [imit.] **1 :** LONG-HORNED GRASSHOPPER; *esp* **:** any of several large green American long-horned grasshoppers that have greatly elongated antennae, a long ovipositor, long hind legs, and stridulating organs on the fore wings of the males with which a loud shrill sound is produced **2 :** a pair of wheels usu. from 7 to 12 feet in diameter used with a heavy axle to transport logs in lumbering

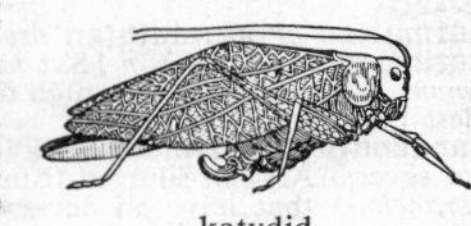
katydid

**katz·en·jam·mer** \ˈkatsən,jamə(r)\ *n* -s [G, fr. *katzen* (pl. of *katze* cat, fr. OHG *kazza*) + *jammer* distress, misery, fr. OHG *jāmar*, fr. *jāmar*, adj., sad; akin to OE *geōmor* sad, OS *jāmar* — more at CAT] **1 :** the nausea, headache, and debility that often follow dissipation or drunkenness **:** HANGOVER ⟨asking you what you prescribe for a slight case of ~ —Malcolm Lowry⟩ **2 :** distress, depression, or confusion resembling that caused by a hangover ⟨forgetting the spiritual ~s from which men of culture periodically suffer in new . . . countries —*New Republic*⟩ **3 :** a discordant clamor ⟨during all this ~, divers . . . have been reconnoitering around the craft to learn the identity of its owner —S.J.Perelman⟩

**kauch** \ˈkäk\ *var of* KIAUGH

**kau·mog·ra·pher** \kȯˈmägrəfə(r)\ *n* -s [Gk *kauma* burning heat (fr. *kaiein* to burn) + E *-o-* + *-grapher* — more at CAUSTIC] **:** a worker who transfers designs, trademarks, or other printed material to cloth articles with a hot iron

**kau·nas** \ˈkaůnəs\ *adj, usu cap* [fr. *Kaunas*, Lithuania] **:** of or from the city of Kaunas, Lithuania **:** of the kind or style prevalent in Kaunas

**kau·ri** *also* **kau·rie** *or* **kau·ry** *or* **kaw·rie** *or* **kaw·ry** *or* **cow·rie** *or* **kao·ri** \ˈkaůrē\ *n, pl* **kauris** *also* **kauries** [Maori *kawri*] **1** *or* **kauri pine :** a tree of the genus *Agathis*; *esp* **:** a tall timber tree (*A. australis*) of New Zealand having fine white straight-grained wood **2 :** the wood of the kauri tree **3** *or* **kauri resin** *or* **kauri gum** *or* **kauri copal :** a light-colored to brown copal from the kauri tree found usu. as a fossil in the ground but also collected by tapping living trees and used chiefly in making varnishes and linoleum

**kauri-butanol value** *n* **:** a measure of the solvent power of a petroleum thinner for paints and varnishes that is determined as the number of milliliters of the thinner just causing turbidity in a standard solution of a hard kauri in normal butyl alcohol

**ka·va** *or* **ca·va** \ˈkävə\ *also* **ka·va·ka·va** \ˌ≈≈ˈ≈≈\ *n* -s [Tongan & Marquesan *kava*, lit., bitter] **1 a :** an Australasian shrubby pepper (*Piper methysticum*) from whose crushed root an intoxicating beverage is made **b :** the beverage made from kava **2 :** the dried rhizome and roots of the kava shrub formerly used as a diuretic and genitourinary antiseptic

**ka·vass** \kəˈväs\ *n* -ES [Turk *kavas*, fr. Ar *qawwās* bowman] **1 :** an armed constable or courier in Turkey **2 :** a consular guard in the countries of the eastern Mediterranean

**ka·vi·ka** \kəˈvēkə\ *n* -s [origin unknown] **:** MALAY APPLE

**kavil** *var of* CAVEL

**ka·vi·ron·do** \ˌkävəˈrän(ˌ)dō\ *n, pl* **kavirondo** *or* **kavirondos** *usu cap* **:** BANTU KAVIRONDO

**kav·va·nah** *or* **kaw·wa·nah** \¦kävə¦nä\ *n, pl* **kav·va·noth** *or* **kav·va·not** *or* **kaw·wa·noth** *or* **kaw·wa·not** \-¦nōt(h), -ōs\ [Heb *kawwānāh*, fr. *kawwēn* to devote, intend] *Jewish relig* **:** intention to carry out a divine command or precept **:** devotion or fervor in prayer ⟨the women prayed with complete ~⟩

**kav·ya** \ˈkävyə\ *n* -s [Skt *kāvya*, fr. *kāvya*, adj., poetical] **:** poetic composition in Sanskrit and other Indic languages characterized by decorative elaboration

**¹kaw** \ˈkȯ\ *n* -s *usu cap* **:** KANSA

**²kaw** \"\ *n, pl* **kaw** *or* **kaws** *usu cap* **:** AKHA

**ka·wa** \kəˈwä\ *n* -s *usu cap* **:** WA

**ka·wa·gu·chi** \kəˈwägə(ˌ)chē\ *adj, usu cap* [fr. *Kawaguchi*, city in southeastern Honshu, Japan] **:** of or from the city of Kawaguchi, Japan **:** of the kind or style prevalent in Kawaguchi

**ka·wai·isu** \kəˈwīə(ˌ)sü\ *n, pl* **kawaiisu** *or* **kawaiisus** *usu cap* **1 :** a Shoshonean people of the Tehachapi mountains of southern California **2 :** a member of the Kawaiisu people

**ka·wa·ka** \kəˈwäkə\ *n* -s [Maori] **:** a New Zealand timber tree (*Libocedrus plumosa*)

**¹ka·wa·ka·wa** \¦käwə¦käwə\ *or* **kawa** *n* -s [Maori] **1 :** KAVA 1 **2 :** a shrub or small tree (*Piper excelsum*) chiefly of New Zealand that has cordate to ovate aromatic leaves and is held to be sacred by the Maoris

**²kawakawa** \"\ *n, pl* **kawakawa** [Hawaiian] *Hawaii* **:** LITTLE TUNA

**kaw·chot·ti·ne** *also* **kaw·chod·in·ne** \kȯˈchädənē\ *n, pl* **kawchottine** *or* **kawchottines** *usu cap* **:** HARE 3

**ka·wi** \ˈkäwē\ *or* **ka·vi** \-ävē\ *n* -s *usu cap* [Jav *kawi* poem, poetical, fr. Skt *kavi* wise, learned, poet or Skt *kāvya* poetical (fr. *kavi*); prob. akin to Gk *akouein* to hear — more at HEAR] **:** the ancient Austronesian language of Java

**¹kay** \ˈkā\ *adj* [ME, left] *dial Eng* **:** LEFT, SINISTER

**²kay** *var of* KEY

**³kay** *also* **ka** \ˈkā\ *n* -s **1 :** the letter *k* **2 :** something having the shape of the letter K

**kaya** \ˈkīə, ˈkäyə\ *n* -s [Jap] **:** a Japanese tree (*Torreya nucifera*) with light red bark and yellow lustrous close-grained wood

**¹kay·ak** *also* **ky·ak** *or* **cay·ak** *or* **ka·jak** \ˈkī,ak *also* -ī,yak\ *n* -s [Esk (Greenland dial.) *qajaq*] **1 :** a fully decked-in Eskimo skin canoe propelled by a double-bladed paddle — compare UMIAK **2 :** a canvas-covered portable canoe that resembles a kayak and is paddled or sailed widely in the U. S. — compare FALTBOAT

kayak 1

**²kayak** \"\ *vi* -ED/-ING/-s **:** to paddle or sail a kayak ⟨I was out ~ing for seal —D.B.Putnam⟩ — **kay·ak·er** \-akə(r)\ *n* -s

**kay·an** \ˈkīən\ *n, pl* **kayan** *or* **kayans** *usu cap* [native name in northern Borneo] **1 :** a Dayak people of north central Borneo sometimes regarded with the Kenya as a subdivision of the Bahau **2 :** a member of the Kayan people

**kayapo** *usu cap, var of* CAYAPO

**ka·yasth** \ˈkäyəst\ *or* **ka·yas·tha** \-stə\ *n* -s *usu cap* [Skt *kāyastha*, prob. fr. *kāya* body, group + *-stha* standing, being in; akin to Skt *cinoti* he gathers, heaps up and to Skt *tiṣṭhati* he stands — more at POET, STAND] **:** a member of a high Hindu caste esp. numerous in Bengal and Uttar Pradesh whose caste occupation is that of clerks, writers, and accountants

**kay·en·ta** \kīˈ(y)entə\ *adj, usu cap* [fr. *Kayenta*, village in northeastern Arizona, where remains of the culture were found] **:** of or belonging to the northern Arizona branch of the Anasazi culture that provides a record from the period of the earth-lodge villages to the Great Pueblo centers

**kayles** *var of* KAILS

**¹kayo** \(ˈ)kā¦ō\ *n* -s [pronunciation of *KO*, abbr. or n.] **:** KNOCKOUT

**²kayo** \"\ *vt* **kayoed; kayoed; kayoing; kayoes** *or* **kayos :** to knock out

**kayuvava** *or* **kayubaba** *usu cap, var of* CAYUVAVA

**ka·zak** \kəˈzak, -zäk\ *n* -s *usu cap* [Kazak, lit., free person, adventurer, vagabond] **1** *or* **ka·zakh** \"\ **a :** a Turko-Tatar Muslim people of central Asia **b :** a member of the Kazak people **2** *or* **kazakh** *or* **qa·zaq** \"\ **:** TURKI **3 :** a bright-colored all-wool Caucasian rug woven by nomads often in sawtooth patterns or highly stylized plant or animal designs **4 :** OXBLOOD

**ka·zan** \kəˈzan, -zän\ *adj, usu cap* [fr. *Kazan*, city in the eastern part of European Russia, U.S.S.R.] **:** of or from the city of Kazan, U.S.S.R. **:** of the kind or style prevalent in Kazan

**kazan tatar** *n, usu cap K&T* **1 :** a member of a group of Tatars living in the Tatar Republic, U.S.S.R. **2 :** the Turkic language of the Kazan people

**kazarian** *usu cap, var of* KHAZAR

**kazi** *var of* QADI

**ka·zoo** \kəˈzü\ *also* **ga·zoo** \gə-\ *n* -s [imit.] **:** a device into which a person sings or hums and which consists usu. of an open-ended tube with a membrane-covered side hole ⟨the ~ is that noisemaking toy that comes nowadays in Christmas stockings —Harlan Cleveland⟩ — called also *eunuch flute, mirliton, Tommy talker, zarah*

**KB** *abbr* **1** King's Bench **2** kitchen and bathroom **3** kite balloon **4** knight bachelor

**KBP** *abbr* kite balloon pilot

**kc** *abbr* **1** kilocycle **2** kilocycles per second

**KC** *abbr* **1** kennel club **2** king's counsel **3** knight commander

**KČ** *abbr* [Czech *koruna československý*] koruna

**kcal** *abbr* kilocalorie; kilogram calorie

**k-capture** \ˈ≈,≈≈\ *also* **k-electron capture** \¦≈≈¦≈(ˌ)≈-\ *n, usu cap K* **:** the capture by an atomic nucleus of an electron from an inner energy level or orbit of the extranuclear electrons

**kd** *abbr* killed

**KD** *abbr* **1** kiln-dried **2** knocked down

**KDCL** *abbr* knocked down, in carloads

**KDF** *abbr* knocked down flat

**KDLCL** *abbr* knocked down, in less than carloads

**kdm** *abbr* kingdom

**KE** *abbr* kinetic energy

**ke-** — see KER-

**kea** \ˈkeə, ˈkēə\ *n* -s [Maori] **:** a large parrot (*Nestor notabilis*) of South Island, New Zealand, that is predominantly green with a very long heavy bill and that is normally insectivorous but sometimes attacks sheep, slashing the back to reach the kidney fat on which it feeds

**kea·corn** \ˈkā,kȯrn\ *n* -s [origin unknown] **1** *dial* **:** WINDPIPE **2** *dial* **:** GULLET

**keat** *var of* KEET

**keats·ian** \ˈkētsēən\ *adj, usu cap* [John *Keats* †1821 Eng. poet + E *-ian*] **:** of, relating to, or characteristic of the poet Keats or his poetry ⟨the manner of Keats is imitated to excess . . . and there is a similar profusion of *Keatsian* classical allusions —W.H.Gardner⟩

**keawe** *var of* KIAWE

**kebab** *or* **kebob** *var of* KABOB

**keb·bie** \ˈkebi\ *n* -s [prob. alter. of earlier *kibble*, fr. ME *kyble*] *chiefly Scot* **:** a rough hook-headed walking stick

**keb·buck** *also* **keb·bock** \ˈkebək\ *n* -s [ME (Sc dial.) *cabok*, fr. ScGael *ceapag* (also, piece of sod, barrow wheel)] *dial Brit* **:** a whole cheese

**keb·yar** \ˈkeb,yär\ *n* -s [Balinese] **:** a Balinese solo dance performed with the upper part of the body from a sitting position with crossed ankles

**kechua** *usu cap, var of* QUECHUA

**kech·u·ma·ran** \ˌkechəmə¦rän\ *n* -s *usu cap* [*Kechua* + *Aymaran*] **:** a language stock comprising Aymara and Quechua

**¹keck** \ˈkek\ *vi* -ED/-ING/-s [imit.] **:** to make the sounds of retching

**²keck** \"\ *n* -s [back-formation fr. ¹*kex*] *Brit* **:** WILD CHERVIL 1

**¹keck·le** \ˈkekəl\ *dial var of* CACKLE

**²keckle** \"\ *also* **kack·le** \ˈkak-\ *vt* -ED/-ING/-s [origin unknown] **:** to wind with rope to prevent chafing

**keck·ling** \ˈkek(ə)liŋ\ *n* -s **:** old rope wound around a cable to prevent chafing

**keck·sy** \ˈkeksi\ *n* -ES [¹*kex* + *-y*] *chiefly dial Eng* **:** KEX

**ked** \ˈked\ *n* -s [origin unknown] **:** SHEEP KED

**ked·dah** \ˈkedə, kəˈdä\ *n* -s [Hindi *kheḍā*] *in India* **:** an enclosure constructed to trap wild elephants

**¹kedge** \ˈkej\ *adj* [ME *kygge*] *chiefly Scot* **:** BRISK, LIVELY

**²kedge** \"\ *vt* -ED/-ING/-s [ME *caggen*] **:** to move (a ship) from one position to another by means of a line attached to a kedge dropped at the distance and in the direction desired

**³kedge** \"\ *or* **kedge anchor** \"-\ *also* **kedg·er** \ˈkejə(r)\ *n* -s **:** a small anchor that is used in kedging or other light work

**ked·ger·ee** *or* **keg·er·ee** \ˈkejə,rē, ,≈≈ˈ≈\ *n* -s [Hindi *khicṛī*, fr. Skt *khiccā*] **1** *in India* **:** a mixture of rice, beans, lentils, and seasonings sometimes with smoked fish **2 :** cooked flaked fish, rice, hard-boiled eggs, and seasoning heated in cream

**kedgy** \ˈkejē, -ji\ *chiefly Scot var of* CADGY 1

**kedjavé** *var of* KAJAWAH

**ked·lock** \ˈked,läk, -ˌlək\ *n* -s [ME *ketelok*, fr. OE *cedelc*] **1 :** CHARLOCK **2 :** WHITE MUSTARD

**ke·du·shah** \kəˈdůshə\ *n, pl* **kedu·shoth** *or* **kedu·shot** \-,shōt(h), -ōs\ *usu cap* [Heb *qědhushshāh* holiness] **:** a recital of a prayer in the Jewish ritual introduced into the third benediction of the Amidah and sometimes including the responses

**keech** \ˈkēch\ *n* -ES [origin unknown] *dial Eng* **:** a fatty lump

**¹keek** \ˈkēk\ *vi* -ED/-ING/-s [ME *kiken, keken*, prob. fr. MD *kīken* to look; akin to MLG *kīken* to look] *chiefly Scot* **:** PEEP, LOOK ⟨opened the low door and ~*ed* into the room —Alasdair Carmichael⟩

**²keek** \"\ *n* -s *chiefly Scot* **:** PEEP, LOOK ⟨take another ~ at the redcoats —R.L.Stevenson⟩

**keekwilee-house** \ˈkēkwə(ˌ)lē-\ *n* [Chinook jargon *keekwilee* below, fr. Chinook *gigwalix*] **:** an earth lodge partially below the surface of the ground used by the Indians of the northwest coast of No. America — compare BARRABORA

**¹keel** \ˈkēl, *esp before pause or consonant* -ēəl\ *vb* -ED/-ING/-s [ME *kelen*, fr. OE *cēlan*, fr. *cōl* cool — more at COOL] *vt* **1** *now dial* **:** COOL; *specif* **:** to keep by stirring or skimming from boiling over ⟨while greasy Joan doth ~ the pot —*Shak.*⟩ **2** *obs* **:** to make less ardent or violent in feeling ~ *vi* **1** *now dial* **:** ⁴COOL **2** *now dial* **:** to become less ardent or violent in feeling

**²keel** \"\ *n* -s [ME *kele*, fr. MD *kiel*; akin to OE *cēol* ship, OS & OHG *kiol*, ON *kjōll* ship, Gk *gaulos* milk pail, kind of ship, OE *cot* small house — more at COT] **1 a (1) :** a flat-bottomed ship; *esp* **:** a barge used on the Tyne to carry coal from Newcastle **(2) :** a barge load of coal **b :** a British unit of weight for coal based on the amount one keel can hold now equal to 21.2 long tons **2 :** a long ship of the early Norsemen

**³keel** \"\ *n* -s [ME *kele, keole*, fr. ON *kil-, kjölr*; akin to MD & MLG *kiel, keel* keel, OE *ceole* throat, beak of a ship — more at GLUTTON] **1 a (1) :** a longitudinal timber or series of timbers scarfed together extending from stem to stern along the center of the bottom of a boat, often projecting below the bottom, and constituting the boat's principal timber to which the ribs are attached on each side — compare CENTERBOARD, FALSE KEEL; see SHIP illustration **(2) :** a bar keel or plate keel on a metal ship **(3) :** KEELSON **(4) :** BILGE KEEL **b (1) :** BOAT, SHIP **(2) :** a boat or ship having a keel as opposed to one having a centerboard or a flat bottom ⟨the shipyard laid down ten new ~s in a year⟩ **c :** the assembly of members at the bottom of the hull of a semirigid or rigid airship that provides special strength to resist hogging and sagging and serves to distribute the effect of concentrated loads along the hull **2 :** a projection suggesting a keel **:** RIDGE: as **a :** a biological process forming a ridge **:** CARINA **b :** a keel molding or the ridge of one

**[4]keel** \"\ *vb* -ED/-ING/-S *vt* **1 :** to cause to turn or tip to the side away from a vertical plane or over esp. so that the bottom shows **:** OVERTURN, CAPSIZE — usu. used with *over* or *up* ⟨sailing vessels lying ~*ed* over at low tide in the harbors —Richard Joseph⟩ **2 :** to cause to collapse or faint — usu. used with *over* ⟨the continued heat ~*ed* over quite a few of the summer visitors⟩ ~ *vi* **1 :** to turn or tip away from a vertical plane or over esp. so that the bottom shows ⟨sailing craft ~ to the lee rail in a spanking breeze —*Amer. Guide Series: Conn.*⟩ **:** OVERTURN, CAPSIZE — usu. used with *over* or *up* ⟨the yacht swung across wind and ~*ed* over⟩ ⟨brakes squealing and slipping on the rails and engines ~*ing* over into drifts —Helen Rich⟩ **2 :** to fall in or as if in a faint **:** SWOON — usu. used with *over* ⟨so tired he ~*ed* over onto the bed⟩ ⟨just one drink, and ~*ed* right over —George Spanner⟩

**[5]keel** \"\ *or* **keel disease** *n* -s [[4]*keel*] **:** acute septicemic salmonellosis or paratyphoid of ducklings marked by sudden collapse and death of apparently healthy birds

**[6]keel** \"\ *n* -s [ME (Sc dial.) *keyle*, prob. fr. ScGael *cīl*] **1** *now chiefly dial* **:** a red ocher used for marking something (as lumber or sheep) **:** RUDDLE; *also* **:** a mark made with this material (as at the end of a warp of yarn to show whether the weaver has used the full length) **2 :** a colored marking chalk or crayon used by engineers and surveyors

**[7]keel** \"\ *vt* -ED/-ING/-S *Scot* **:** to mark with keel

**keel·age** \'kēlij\ *n* -s [[3]*keel* + *-age*] **:** a toll for a ship entering and anchoring or mooring in a port esp. in Great Britain

**keelback** \'ˌˌ\ *also* **keelback snake** *n* [[3]*keel* + *back*] **:** a small aquatic Indian snake (*Natrix piscator*) with strongly keeled dorsal scales

**keelbill** *or* **keelbird** \'ˌˌ\ *n* [[3]*keel* + *bill* or *bird*] **:** ANI

**keelblock** \'ˌˌ\ *n* [[3]*keel* + *block*] **:** a block of hard wood used to support the keel of a ship when under construction or when docked

**keelboat** \'ˌˌ\ *n* [[3]*keel* + *boat*] **1 :** a shallow covered riverboat with a keel that is usu. rowed, poled, or towed and used for freight **2 :** a yacht or other sailboat having a keel as distinguished from one having a centerboard

**keel·boat·man** \"mən\ *n, pl* **keelboatmen :** a member of the crew of a keelboat

**keel–bully** \'ˌˌˌ\ *n* [[2]*keel* + *bully*] *Brit* **:** one of the crew of a keel

**keeled** \'kē(ə)ld\ *adj* [[3]*keel* + *-ed*] **:** having a carina ⟨~ breastbone⟩ ⟨~ flower⟩

**keeled snake** *n* **:** a snake with strongly keeled scales; *esp* **:** a venomous Australian elapid (*Tropidechis carinatus*)

**[1]keel·er** \'kēlə(r)\ *n* -s [ME *kelare*, a tub used for cooling liquids, fr. *kelen* to cool + *-are* -er — more at KEEL] *now chiefly dial* **:** a broad shallow tub (as for a liquid or washing something)

**[2]keeler** \"\ *n* -s [[2]*keel* + *-er*] *dial Eng* **:** KEELMAN

**[3]keeler** \"\ *n* -s [[3]*keel* + *-er*] **:** a boat having a keel; *esp* **:** KEELBOAT

**kee·ler polygraph** \"-\ *n, usu cap K* [after Leonarde *Keeler* †1949 Amer. criminologist, its inventor] **:** an instrument for making a graphic record of the changes in blood pressure and pulse and respiration rate of someone being questioned under or as if under suspicion of guilt — called also *lie detector*

**keel·haul** \'kē(ə)l,hȯl\ *also* **keel·hale** \-hāl, *esp before pause or consonant* -āəl\ *vt* [D *kielhalen*, fr. *kiel* keel (fr. MD) + *halen* to fetch, draw, pull, fr. MD — more at KEEL, HAUL] **1 :** to haul (a person) under the keel of a ship either athwartships or from bow to stern by ropes in punishment (as on a naval vessel) or torture (as by pirates) **2 :** to rebuke with great severity

**kee·lie** \'kēlē, -li\ *n* -s [imit.] **1 :** KESTREL **2** *dial Brit* **:** a street urchin **:** LOAFER

**[1]keeling** *pres part of* KEEL

**[2]kee·ling** \'kēliŋ\ *n* -s [ME *keling*, perh. of Scand origin; akin to Icel *keila* cusk, ON, arm of the sea; akin to OHG *kīl* wedge — more at CHINE] *chiefly Scot* **:** CODFISH; *esp* **:** a large codfish

**kee·li·vine** \'kēli,vīn\ *n* -s [origin unknown] *Scot* **:** PENCIL; *esp* **:** one of black lead

**keel·less** \'kē(ə)lləs\ *adj* [[3]*keel* + *-less*] **:** having no keel ⟨a ~ boat⟩

**keel line** *n* [[3]*keel* + *line*] **:** the bottom or lowest line of a boat esp. along the keel

**keel·man** \'kē(ə)lmən\ *n, pl* **keelmen** [[2]*keel* + *man*] **:** a member of the crew of a keel

**keel molding** *n* [[3]*keel*] **:** a brace molding with a central projecting fillet resembling a keel

**keels** *pres 3d sing of* KEEL, *pl of* KEEL

**keel–shaped scraper** \'ˌˌ-\ *n* **:** a prehistoric flint scraper consisting of a small core chipped at both ends and sides and resembling the bottom of a boat in shape

keel molding

**keel·son** *also* **kel·son** \'kelsən, 'kē(ə)l-*also* -lts-\ *n* -s [prob. of Scand origin; akin to Dan & Norw *kjølsvin*, Sw *kölsvin*, Norw dial. *kjølsvill*, prob. fr. *kjøl*, *köl* keel (fr. ON *kǫlr*) + *svin* pig, fr. ON *svīn* — more at KEEL, SWINE] **:** a longitudinal structure in the framing of a ship to contribute stiffness, prevent local deformations, and distribute over a considerable length the effect of concentrated loads: **a :** a structure of timbers in a wooden ship parallel with and above the keel and fastened to it by long bolts passing through the floor timbers **b :** a deep continuous structure of plates and bars in a metal ship usu. in the form of a strong I beam secured at its ends to the stem and the sternpost and connected at its upper and lower edges to the reverse frames and keel plates respectively — called also *middle-line keelson, vertical keel*; see BILGE KEELSON, SIDE KEELSON; SHIP illustration

**kee·lung** \'kē¦lüŋ\ *adj, usu cap* [fr. *Keelung*, Formosa] **:** of or from the city of Keelung, Formosa, China **:** of the kind or style prevalent in Keelung

**kee·mun** \'kā¦mün, 'kē¦mən\ *n* -s *usu cap* [fr. *Keemun* (Ch'imen) district in Anhwei province, China] **:** CONGOU

**[1]keen** \'kēn\ *adj* -ER/-EST [ME *kene* wise, bold, brave, sharp, fr. OE *cēne* wise, bold, brave; akin to OHG *kuoni* bold, strong, MD *coene* bold, brave, ON *kœnn* wise, skillful, clever, OE *cnāwan* to know — more at KNOW] **1 a :** having a fine edge or point **:** SHARP ⟨a ~ blade⟩ ⟨a ~ sword⟩ **b :** affecting one as if by cutting **:** causing great distress to the mind or sensibilities ⟨~ sarcasm⟩ ⟨a ~ sense of guilt⟩ **c** (1) **:** affecting the senses or creating physical discomfort as if by cutting **:** PENETRATING, PIERCING ⟨a ~ wind⟩ ⟨~, cold winters —Edith Hamilton⟩ **:** STINGING ⟨a ~ slap⟩ **:** SHRILL ⟨a high ~ sound⟩ (2) **:** sharp or pungent to the sense ⟨a ~ scent⟩ **2 a :** characterized by intense interest, feeling, or desire **:** showing a quick and ardent responsiveness **:** EAGER, ENTHUSIASTIC ⟨a ~ swimmer⟩ ⟨fiery and dominant natures, eager to conquer, ~ to impress —A.C.Benson⟩ ⟨~ to go on a picnic⟩ ⟨both of them were ~ on skiing⟩ ⟨very ~ about the girl⟩; *also* **:** giving evidence of such qualities ⟨the features lean and ~ from restless intellectual energy —J.A.Froude⟩ **b** *of emotion or feeling* **:** INTENSE, GREAT ⟨a ~ desire to be in the forefront of activity⟩ ⟨the ~ delight in the chase —F.W.Maitland⟩ ⟨a ~ personal interest in the boy⟩ ⟨the ~ dread of the gods —M.R.Cohen⟩ **3 a :** acute or quick and penetrating (as in mental power) ⟨a ~ mind⟩ ⟨~ in their bargain —H.E.Scudder⟩ **:** intellectually sharp or incisive ⟨a ~ wit⟩ ⟨~ questions⟩ **:** ASTUTE ⟨~ businessmen —Gilbert Highet⟩; *also* **:** giving evidence of astuteness or the play of alert or carefully calculating minds ⟨~ competition⟩ ⟨debate was not as ~ as it might have been —Winston Churchill⟩ **b :** extremely sensitive in perception or in perceiving distinctions ⟨a ~ eyesight⟩ ⟨a ~ sense of smell⟩ **c :** marked by fine and extremely precise distinctions ⟨~ refinements of logic⟩ **4** *of ice in curling* **:** hard and clear **5** *Brit, of a price* **:** favorable to the purchaser **:** LOW ⟨outfits for all ranks and services at very ~ prices —*Nautical Mag.*⟩ **6** *slang* **:** WONDERFUL, DESIRABLE — a generalized expression of approval **syn** see EAGER, SHARP

**[2]keen** \"\ *adv* [ME *kene*, fr. *kene*, adj.] **:** KEENLY ⟨businessmen ~ set on practical affairs —J.W.Beach⟩

**[3]keen** \"\ *vt* -ED/-ING/-S [[1]*keen*] **:** to put a sharp edge on **:** SHARPEN ⟨the cutting edge of the knife is first ~*ed* up —J.V.A.Long⟩ ⟨~ the razor —Christopher Morley⟩

**[4]keen** \"\ *vb* -ED/-ING/-S [IrGael *caoinim* (I) lament, fr. OIr *coīnim*] *vi* **1 a :** to wail or bewail with a keen ⟨~*ed* like a squaw bereft —Minnie H. Moody⟩ **b :** to make a sound suggesting a keen ⟨the soft ~*ing* of the screech owls —A.W. Derleth⟩ ⟨the night was rent by ~*ing* sirens —*Time*⟩ ⟨the ~*ing* in the aerials rose to a witches' chorus —T.H.Raddall⟩ ⟨violins ~*ed* in the shadows —Albert Hubbell⟩ **2 :** to lament, mourn, or complain loudly ~ *vt* **:** to utter by keening ⟨~*ed* our sorrow —*Punch*⟩

**[5]keen** \"\ *n* -s [IrGael *caoine*] **1 a :** a lamentation or dirge for the dead uttered in a loud wailing voice **b :** a rhythmic recounting of the life and character of a dead person or an exhortation to vengeance for his death — compare CORONACH **2 :** a lamentation or cry of grief

**keen·er** \-nə(r)\ *n* -s [[4]*keen* + *-er*] **:** one that keens; *esp* **:** a professional usu. female mourner at a wake or funeral

**keene's cement** \'kēnz-\ *n, usu cap K* [after Richard W. *Keene*, 19th cent. Eng. inventor] **:** a hard-finish gypsum plaster to which alum has been added and which is used chiefly as a gauging plaster in lime mortar for walls (as of hospitals, stores, railroad stations) where an unusually tough and durable plaster is required

**[1]keening** *adj* [fr. pres. part. of [4]*keen*] **:** having the quality of or suggesting a keen ⟨the . . . cicada and his ~ cry —K.F. Weaver⟩ ⟨a long ~ scream like a rabbit caught in a gin trap —Hartley Howard⟩

**[2]keening** *n* -s [fr. gerund of [4]*keen*] **1 :** the act of keening ⟨mourning . . . is celebrated by self-laceration, the destruction of property, and daily ~ —William Lipkind⟩ ⟨~ was not confined to the period of death —Alfred Métraux⟩ ⟨the ~ of bagpipes —Lyn Harrington⟩ **2 :** [5]KEEN ⟨never had heard a ~ —Mary Deasy⟩

**keen·ly** *adv* [ME *kenely* boldly, bravely, sharply, fr. *kene* wise, bold, brave, sharp + *-ly* — more at KEEN] **:** in a keen manner ⟨stared at him ~ —Nevil Shute⟩ ⟨~ aware of the evils of the society —H.R.G.Greaves⟩ ⟨cleverly construed and ~ written —*Time*⟩

**keen·ness** \'kēnnəs\ *n* -ES [[1]*keen* + *-ness*] **:** the quality or state of being keen ⟨exhibited a ~ of judgment unusual in one his age⟩ ⟨the ~ of his desire to succeed⟩

**keen–scented** \'ˌˌˌ\ *adj* **:** having a keen sense of smell ⟨a *keen-scented* hound⟩

**[1]keep** \'kēp\ *vb* **kept** \'kept\ **kept; keeping; keeps** [ME *kepen* to observe, heed, seek, seize, keep, fr. OE *cēpan* to observe, heed, seek, seize; akin to OE *capian* to look, OS *kapōn*, OHG *chapfēn* to look, ON *kōpa* to stare, and perh. to Russ *zabota* care, worry] *vt* **1 a :** to observe or fulfill (something prescribed or obligatory) **:** adhere to or not swerve from or violate (as a faith) **:** practice or perform as a duty **:** not neglect **:** be faithful to (as a promise): as (1) **:** to notice with due, approved, or customary actions and feelings **:** act fittingly in relation to by refraining from anything inappropriate or unsuitable ⟨~*ing* a Sabbath day by ceasing from all work —H.G.Cowan⟩ (2) **:** to conform to in habits or conduct (as by regular attendance to or the performance of appropriate duties) or adjust one's schedule of activities to include ⟨~ chapel⟩ ⟨~ early hours⟩ (3) **:** to act (as in playing an instrument, singing, marching) in accord with (as a preestablished time, tempo, or rhythm) ⟨asked the musicians to ~ time with the metronome⟩ ⟨could not ~ the tricky rhythm of the Latin-American dance⟩ **b :** to reside at a British university long enough to complete the requirements of (a term); *esp* **:** to eat a sufficient number of dinners in hall at the Inns of Court to make (a term) count for the purpose of being called to the bar **2 :** PRESERVE, MAINTAIN: as **a :** to watch over and defend esp. from danger, harm, or loss ⟨prayed God to ~ and help his family⟩ ⟨anxious to ~ his son from illness and accident⟩ ⟨his sanguine nature *kept* him from worry⟩ **b** (1) **:** to have the care of **:** be responsible for **:** TEND ⟨the shepherd boy *kept* sheep on the moors at night⟩ ⟨*kept* a garden for his parents⟩ ⟨was paid to ~ the furnace⟩ (2) **:** to support by providing with a home, food, clothing, or other requisites of existence ⟨the foster parents *kept* the child for a year until his real parents could be found⟩ (3) **:** to maintain in a good, fitting, or orderly condition ⟨objected to ~*ing* the house⟩ ⟨a meticulously *kept* orchard⟩ (4) **:** to maintain habitually by undertaking the expense of ⟨what sort of table do they ~ —Jane Austen⟩ **c :** to continue to maintain **:** not cease from or intermit ⟨~ silence⟩ ⟨~ guard over the child⟩ **d** (1) **:** to cause to remain in a given place, situation, or condition **:** maintain unchanged **:** hold or preserve in a particular state ⟨~ valuables under lock and key⟩ ⟨*kept* all perishable food cold⟩ ⟨~ a person waiting⟩ — often used with a following prepositional phrase or adverb indicating place or direction ⟨*kept* the boys away from the house⟩ ⟨*kept* the top of the box down with weights⟩ ⟨*kept* the dog in the house⟩ ⟨*kept* the children in⟩ ⟨*kept* the cat out⟩ ⟨~ the birds off the antenna⟩ (2) **:** to preserve (food) in an unspoiled condition ⟨~ meat by packing it in ice⟩ ⟨~ potatoes in storage in a cool cellar⟩ **e** (1) **:** to have or retain in one's service or in an established position or relationship ⟨~ a maid and a butler⟩ ⟨~*s* two assistants⟩ — often used with *on* ⟨*kept* the cook on until she could find a new employer⟩ (2) **:** to possess (as a domestic animal) usu. for certain services or advantages ⟨~*s* a horse⟩ ⟨~*s* several head of cattle⟩ (3) **:** to maintain in exchange for sexual favors ⟨never married but *kept* a mistress for several years⟩ ⟨found the woman was ~*ing* a man several years her junior⟩ (4) **:** to control totally the policy, principles, and ideas of (as a newspaper) by one's money or economic power ⟨a *kept* press⟩ **f** (1) **:** to maintain a record in (as of daily occurrences or transactions) ⟨~ a journal⟩ ⟨~ books for a business firm⟩ (2) **:** to enter (as an account or record) in a book **g :** to have customarily in stock for sale ⟨bought the best sherry the store *kept*⟩ **3 a :** to restrain from departure or removal **:** not let go of **:** HOLD, DETAIN ⟨~ him as a prisoner for a week⟩ ⟨*kept* the children after school for disobedience⟩ ⟨nothing to ~ me in the hot city⟩ **b :** to hold back **:** RESTRAIN, PREVENT ⟨tried to ~ him from going out at night⟩ ⟨nothing *kept* him from going through with it⟩ **c :** SAVE, RESERVE, STORE ⟨asked the grocer to ~ a good cut of beef for her each week⟩ ⟨*kept* the hardest questions until the end of the examination⟩ **d :** to refrain from communicating, revealing, or betraying **:** not divulge ⟨~ a secret⟩ ⟨~ his counsel⟩ **4 a :** to retain or continue to have in one's possession or power esp. by conscious or purposive policy ⟨were able to conquer the island but were unable to ~ it⟩ ⟨found the money and figured he could ~ it⟩ ⟨the court decided the couple could ~ the child⟩ **b :** WITHHOLD ⟨*kept* most of his inheritance from him⟩ ⟨*kept* the sad news from the parents⟩ **c :** to have in control **:** not lose ⟨~ one's temper⟩ **5 :** to keep to ⟨ill and ~*s* her room —Jane Austen⟩ ⟨with a cold that has left her weak, so that she has *kept* the house for over a fortnight —O.W.Holmes †1935⟩ **6 a :** to continue in (as a course) **:** not deviate from ⟨~ the path rather than strike off through the woods⟩ ⟨~ the center of the road⟩ **b :** to stay or remain on or in in usu. against opposition ⟨~ your seat⟩ ⟨~ the saddle despite the bucking of the horse⟩ ⟨~ the field under fire⟩ ⟨*kept* his ground even though attacked again and again⟩ **7 a :** CONDUCT, MANAGE ⟨~ a meeting⟩ **:** carry on ⟨~ a business⟩ ⟨the chairman was not there to ~ the yearly assembly⟩ ⟨*kept* a small tearoom⟩ **b** *archaic* **:** to keep up **c :** to make out or manage in respect to the welfare of (oneself) ⟨how have you been ~*ing* yourself⟩ **8 :** to associate with (company) ⟨concerned about the company she was ~*ing*⟩ **9** *dial Eng* **:** to frighten or scare away (birds) ~ *vi* **1** *now Brit* **:** LIVE, LODGE ⟨could not find where the man *kept* in town⟩ **2 a :** to maintain a course, direction, or progress **:** persevere in going ⟨~ along the main route for 10 miles⟩ ⟨*kept* to the south all day⟩ **b :** to continue usu. without interruption a particular action ⟨the fire *kept* burning all night⟩ ⟨~ smiling⟩ — often used with *on* ⟨*kept* on talking until he was told to stop⟩ **c :** to persist resolutely or stubbornly in a practice or a course of action often in spite of opposition or warning **:** continue firmly or obstinately ⟨~*s* asking us to go swimming⟩ — often used with *on* ⟨*kept* on drinking after the doctor told him to stop⟩ **3 a :** to stay or remain (as in a particular place or condition) ⟨~ in the house if it rains⟩ ⟨the wind *kept* to the east⟩ ⟨~ in a happy frame of mind⟩ ⟨~ out of the way⟩ ⟨~ in touch with friends⟩ ⟨*kept* warm with blankets and hot soup⟩ ⟨*kept* clean by washing daily⟩ **b :** to be in regard to health ⟨how are you ~*ing*⟩ **c :** to keep up ⟨was unable to ~ with the older boys on the hike⟩ ⟨it follows the herring schools and sometimes ~*s* with them for days —F.G.Kay⟩ **4 :** ABSTAIN, REFRAIN ⟨couldn't ~ from talking⟩ **5 a :** to remain in good condition **:** not go bad or deteriorate ⟨the food will ~ for a long time under refrigeration⟩ ⟨knowledge does not ~ any better than fish —A.N.Whitehead⟩ **b :** to remain undivulged ⟨knew the secret would ~ if he told nobody⟩ **c :** to call for no immediate action ⟨the matter will ~ until morning when we can see a lawyer⟩ **6 :** to be or remain in session ⟨school ~*s* five days a week⟩ **7 :** to keep wicket

**syn** KEEP, KEEP (*back*), KEEP (*out*), RETAIN, DETAIN, WITHHOLD, RESERVE, HOLD, and HOLD (*back*) can mean, in common, not to relinquish one's possession, custody, or control. KEEP is the most general term, carrying the common meaning ⟨*keep* one's car for another year⟩ ⟨*keep* one's balance⟩ ⟨*keep* one's right to vote⟩ KEEP (*back*) is interchangeable with any of the remaining terms ⟨*keep back* a part of an employee's pay⟩ ⟨*keep back* a person who wants to rush out into a storm⟩ ⟨*keep back* some tickets for a friend⟩ KEEP (*out*) applies to the keeping of some portion of a whole ⟨*keep out* a part of a week's pay for emergencies⟩ RETAIN implies continued keeping esp. against a threatened taking or loss ⟨*retain* one's possessions even in war⟩ ⟨*retain* one's sanity⟩ ⟨*retain* control of a company⟩ DETAIN implies a delay in letting go from one's control ⟨*detain* a man suspected of a crime⟩ ⟨*detain* a ship in quarantine⟩ WITHHOLD implies a delay in letting go or a refusal to give or let go ⟨*withhold* information⟩ ⟨*withhold* payments on a house⟩ ⟨*withhold* one's help⟩ RESERVE implies either a keeping in store or withholding from present use esp. for some future or special need or purpose ⟨*reserve* a certain percentage for emergencies⟩ ⟨*reserve* a space in a house for a playroom⟩ ⟨*reserve* seats at an opera⟩ HOLD and HOLD (*back*) are often used in place of WITHHOLD or KEEP (*back*) and sometimes in place of DETAIN or RESERVE when restraint in letting go is implied ⟨*hold* a portion of a week's pay as a fine⟩ ⟨*hold* a person suspected of a crime⟩ ⟨*hold back* some tickets that are on sale as a favor to a friend⟩ ⟨*hold* one's condemnation until a later date⟩ ⟨*hold back* one's judgment until all the evidence has been considered⟩

**syn** OBSERVE, CELEBRATE, SOLEMNIZE, COMMEMORATE: KEEP, along with others in this set, can mean the noticing or honoring of a day or occasion fittingly or duly. KEEP is rather mild in its implications and may suggest merely a customary or wonted notice without anything untoward or inappropriate; it implies opposition to *break* ⟨his build was all compact, for force, well-knit . . . he *kept* no Lent to make him meager —John Masefield⟩ OBSERVE may indicate a heightened solemnity, attention to correct details, and a proper attitude ⟨knowing that the usual ritual would have to be *observed* —T. B.Costain⟩ ⟨New Hampshire *observes* one holiday not possessed by any other state —*Amer. Guide Series: N.H.*⟩ In today's English and esp. in nonreligious contexts CELEBRATE is likely to suggest notice of an occasion by festivity or indulgence ⟨*celebrate* New Year's Eve⟩ ⟨*celebrating* a friend's good fortune⟩ ⟨many parties *celebrating* a football victory⟩ SOLEMNIZE is likely to carry a contrasting suggestion, that of grave dignity or splendid ceremony ⟨mysterious rites were *solemnized*, and . . . of those terrific idols some received such dismal service —William Wordsworth⟩ ⟨this blessed day ever . . . shall be kept festival: to *solemnize* this day the glorious sun stays in his course —Shak.⟩ COMMEMORATE stresses the idea of remembrance and suggests observance or ceremony, or a symbol or monument designed to ensure against forgetfulness and oblivion ⟨the first time it had ever been rung to *commemorate* the death of a monarch —*New Yorker*⟩ ⟨their six children all died in early youth, and the Bradleys determined to *commemorate* them by founding an educational institution —Marie A. Kasten⟩

— **keep an eye on :** to watch carefully although not continuously ⟨*keep an eye on* the pot so it doesn't boil over⟩ ⟨*keep an eye on* the children while I'm away⟩ — **keep at :** to persevere or persist in doing or concerning oneself with — **keep bach** *slang* **:** to live as a bachelor; *esp* **:** to keep house in the absence of one's wife — **keep cases 1 :** to be in charge of the casebox **2 :** to keep a watch on **:** keep tabs on — **keep company :** to go together as frequent companions or in courtship ⟨after marriage they could look back with pleasure on the time they were *keeping company*⟩ — **keep** (one) **company :** to stay or travel with (one) to provide companionship — **keep cut** *obs* **:** to keep one's distance **:** act warily — **keep face :** to retain one's poise or equanimity esp. under circumstances that would tend to destroy it — **keep faith :** to observe and live up to one's moral commitments (to something) **:** show steady loyalty — often used with *with* ⟨*keep faith* with one's religion⟩ ⟨*keep faith* with one's children⟩ — **keep hands off :** to refrain from interfering ⟨requested that the government *keep hands off* in the internal affairs of other countries⟩ — **keep house 1 :** to occupy or maintain a separate house or establishment as opposed to living with parents or relatives or boarding out ⟨is married and *keeping house*⟩ **2** *Brit* **:** to remain secluded at home to evade creditors — **keep mind** *Scot* **:** to keep in mind **:** REMEMBER — **keep one's end up** *or* **keep up one's end 1 :** to do one's fair share in an enterprise involving two and often more people or participants ⟨could *keep his end up* in a conversation on almost any subject⟩ **2 :** to preserve one's wicket by defensive play — used of a batsman in cricket — **keep one's feet :** to stay upright **:** keep one's balance — **keep one's hand in :** to keep in practice ⟨tried to *keep his hand in* at tennis by playing a little at least once a week⟩ — **keep pace :** to keep up ⟨had no trouble *keeping pace* with the faster runners⟩ ⟨did not wish to *keep pace* with the neighbors in social life⟩ — **keep standing :** to hold intact (as set type) — **keep step :** to keep in step ⟨*keep step* with the other marchers⟩ ⟨*keep step* with the times and turn it to your sales advantage —*Women's Wear Daily*⟩ — **keep the field :** to continue a campaign — **keep the peace :** to avoid or prevent a breach of the peace or any crime likely to result in such a breach — **keep to 1 a :** to confine oneself to **:** remain in **:** not leave ⟨*kept to* the house during his convalescence⟩ ⟨*kept to* the main roads in his travels⟩ **b :** to limit oneself to (as a particular kind of diet) **2 :** to abide by ⟨*keep to* the rules of the game⟩ **:** conform to ⟨*keep to* the hour decided on —Agnes M. Miall⟩ **:** not deviate from ⟨*keep to* the point⟩ — **keep to oneself 1 :** to keep secret ⟨knew what the facts were but *kept* them *to himself*⟩ ⟨*kept* their knowledge . . . *to themselves* and made no attempt to spread it —Sean MacCormac⟩ **2 :** to remain solitary or apart from other people **:** avoid social relations ⟨a shy girl who *kept* pretty much *to herself*⟩ — **keep wicket :** to play as wicketkeeper in cricket

**[2]keep** \"\ *n* -s [ME *kep*, *keep*, fr. *kepen* to keep — more at KEEP] **1** *archaic* **:** HEED, NOTICE — usu. used in the phrases *give keep, take keep* **2 :** the act of keeping or the state of being kept: as **a** *archaic* **:** CUSTODY, GUARD, CHARGE **b :** MAINTENANCE **3 :** one that keeps or protects: as **a :** STRONGHOLD, FORTRESS, CASTLE; *specif* **:** the strongest and securest part of a medieval castle often used as a place of residence esp. during a siege **b :** KEEPER ⟨has been made the ~ of an anticritical defensive system —F.R.Leavis⟩ **c :** PRISON, JAIL **d :** a cap or other mechanical device for retaining anything in place; *specif* **:** a light iron casting resting on the hanger at the bottom of a locomotive axle box to keep the lubricating pad in position **4 a :** the means or provisions by which one is kept ⟨the horse was hardly worth its ~⟩ **b** *Brit* **:** pasture for grazing or the grass in such pasture **c :** a conditioning tonic or regimen for game cocks **5 keeps** *pl but sing in constr* **:** a game of marbles played for keeps **6 :** a football play in which the quarterback fakes a pass but keeps the ball and runs with it **syn** see LIVING — **for keeps** *adv* **1 a :** with the provision that one keep what he has won ⟨the two men were playing the game *for keeps*⟩ **b :** with deadly seriousness ⟨with the firm intention of winning or overcoming if at all possible ⟨found out that his rival was not fooling but competing with him *for keeps*⟩ **2 :** with the intention of remaining in a particular state or relationship for good **:** PERMANENTLY ⟨after his experience in foreign countries he came home *for keeps*⟩

3 : with finality : with the result of ending the matter ⟨stole their crown jewels . . . and *for keeps* —Ethel M. Thornbury⟩ ⟨plugged *for keeps* in a gun duel with a desperado —John McCarten⟩

**keep·able** \-pəbəl\ *adj* : capable of being kept for some time without deterioration ⟨some foods are ~ under refrigeration⟩

**keep away** *vi* : to sail less close to the wind ~ *vt* : to cause (a sailing ship) to keep away

**keep back** *vt* **1** : RESTRAIN ⟨had a hard time *keeping* her *back*⟩ ⟨*kept* the man *back* from committing the crime⟩ : hold back : RETARD ⟨*kept* the completion of the plan *back* by a year⟩ **2 a** : to refrain from giving : WITHHOLD ⟨*kept* a portion of his pay *back*⟩ **b** : to refrain from divulging ⟨*kept* the information *back* until he was paid for it⟩ **c** : RESERVE, SAVE ⟨*kept* rare items *back* for customers who would pay the best prices⟩ ~ *vi* : to refrain from approaching or advancing near (as to something dangerous) ⟨asked the children to *keep back* while the fireworks were exploding⟩ **syn** see KEEP

**keep down** *vt* **1 a** : to hold in subjection : SUPPRESS ⟨had trouble *keeping* the insurgents *down*⟩ **b** : to keep in control ⟨*kept* the horse *down* with the curb⟩ **c** : LIMIT, RESTRICT ⟨tried to *keep* expenses *down*⟩ **d** : to prevent from growing, advancing, or succeeding ⟨can't *keep* a good man *down*⟩ **2** : to prevent from regurgitating or vomiting ⟨felt sick but succeeded in *keeping* his dinner *down*⟩ **3** : to set or leave set in lowercase in printing

[1]**keep·er** \-pə(r)\ *n* -s [ME *keper*, fr. *kepen* to keep + *-er* — more at KEEP] **1** : one that keeps something (as by watching over, guarding, maintaining, supporting, restraining): as **a** : GUARDIAN, PROTECTOR ⟨am I my brother's ~ —Gen 4:9 (RSV)⟩ **b** : one that conforms to or abides by (as a custom, rite, or law) ⟨a ~ of the Lord's commandments⟩ : one that fulfills (as a promise or pledge) **c** : one that has charge of (as a prison, prisoners, inmates of an institution, the grounds or buildings of an estate, animals in a zoo); *specif* : GAMEKEEPER **d** : one that owns, maintains, or carries on (as a boarding house, castle, store) **e** : GUARD **f** *obs* : one that keeps a mistress **g** : one whose vocation or avocation is the care of (as bees) **h** : WICKETKEEPER **i** : CURATOR ⟨a ~ of manuscripts in a library⟩ **j** : one whose job is to keep something in good or satisfactory condition ⟨a boat ~⟩ ⟨a greenhouse ~⟩ **k** : an armature that preserves the intensity of magnetization of a permanent magnet **2** : a device that keeps something in position: as **a** : LATCH **b** : the strike of a lock **c** : GUARD RING **d** : LOCKNUT **e** : a loop of string tied in the eye of a bowstring to keep it in place when the bow is unbraced **f** : the keep in a locomotive axle box **g** : a leather loop on a rifle sling for holding the sling tight on the arm when firing with the sling **3** : a fruit or vegetable that keeps well **4** : a fish large enough to be legally caught

[2]**keeper** \"\ *vt* -ED/-ING/-S *Brit* : to maintain (a game preserve) under the care of a keeper ⟨marsh . . . strictly ~*ed* and alive with fowl —*Country Life*⟩

**keep·er·ing** \-p(ə)riŋ\ *n* -s *Brit* : the occupation or work of a keeper (as a gamekeeper)

**keeper of the broad seal** *obs* : KEEPER OF THE GREAT SEAL

**keeper of the great seal** *or* **keeper of the seal** : a high officer of state in England and Scotland who has custody of the great seal : LORD CHANCELLOR

**keeper of the privy purse** : PRIVY PURSE 2

**keeper of the privy seal** [ME *keper of the prive seale*] **1** : LORD PRIVY SEAL **2** : an officer in Scotland and Cornwall analogous to the English lord privy seal

**keep·er·ship** \'kēpə(r),ship\ *n* : the office or position of keeper

**keep in** *vt* **1 a** : to keep from expressing : hold back ⟨*kept* his feelings *in* until he nearly burst⟩ ⟨was unable to *keep* the secret *in*⟩ **b** : to detain in the school after regular school hours as a punishment ⟨*kept* the children *in* for disobedience⟩ **2** *archaic* : to keep (a fire) burning ~ *vi* **1** *of a fire* : to keep burning **2** : to stay on good or favorable terms ⟨anxious to *keep in* with the boss⟩

[1]**keeping** *n* -s [ME *keping*, fr. gerund of *kepen* to keep — more at KEEP] **1** : the act of one that keeps: as **a** : CUSTODY, GUARD, MAINTENANCE ⟨left the small child in the woman's ~⟩ ⟨the ~ of the lighthouse⟩ **b** : the observance of a rule, obligation, or rite **c** : a reserving or preserving for future use **d** *obs* : the maintaining of a mistress **2 a** : the means by which something is kept : KEEP, SUPPORT, PROVISION, FEED ⟨provided good ~ for the cattle⟩ **b** : the state of being kept or the condition in which something is kept ⟨the house is in good ~⟩ **3** : CONFORMITY, CONGRUITY, HARMONY, CONSISTENCY — usu. used in the phrases *in keeping* or *out of keeping* ⟨behavior in ~ with the solemnity of the occasion⟩ ⟨simplicity and restraint is in admirable ~ with the earnest purpose of the pioneers —*Amer. Guide Series: Minn.*⟩ ⟨a doctrine so out of ~ with the facts of Japanese life —Kazuo Kawai⟩

[2]**keeping** *adj* [ME *keping*, fr. pres. part. of *kepen* to keep] : of or relating to something that remains unspoiled over a period of time ⟨apples with good ~ quality⟩

**keeping room** *n*, *dial* : a family living room

**keep off** *vt* **1** : to keep away : keep back ⟨had a hard time *keeping* the children *off* when he brought out the pony⟩ **2** : to ward off : AVERT ⟨a charm to *keep off* disease and misfortune⟩ ~ *vi* : to keep back ⟨asked the spectators to *keep off* because the animal was unpredictable⟩

**keep out** *vt* : to keep back : WITHHOLD ⟨*kept* a portion of a man's paycheck *out*⟩; *also* : RESERVE, SAVE ⟨*keep* some of the best cuts of meat *out* for a good customer⟩ **syn** see KEEP

**keeps** *pres 3d sing of* KEEP, *pl of* KEEP

**keep·sake** \'kēp,sāk\ *n* [[1]*keep* + *-sake* (as in *namesake*)] **1** : something kept or given to be kept as a memento (as of a friend or a happy occasion) **2** : GIFTBOOK 2 **3** : a giftbook made up for a particular group or occasion and serving as a specimen of fine printing

**keep under** *vt* : to hold in subjection ⟨*kept* the conquered people *under* for 50 years⟩

**keep up** *vt* **1** : to go on with : persevere in : continue usu. with persistence ⟨*kept* the talk *up* until midnight⟩ ⟨*kept* his criminal activity *up* until he was caught⟩ ⟨*kept up* their correspondence⟩ : MAINTAIN, SUSTAIN ⟨*kept up* a front for Mama, who was not to be worried —Andrea Parke⟩ ⟨*kept* their standards *up*⟩ **2** : to prevent from diminishing or deteriorating : keep in good condition ⟨worked every day to *keep* the garden *up*⟩ ⟨*kept* his credit *up* by paying his bills regularly⟩ **3** *archaic* : to keep confined or penned up ~ *vi* **1** : to stay even (as in acts of strength, endurance, or speed) ⟨although he was small he could *keep up* with the larger boys in sports⟩ : stay along (as in thoughts or studies) ⟨able to *keep up* with his class in school⟩ **2** : to keep adequately informed — used with *on* or *with* ⟨*kept up* with the affairs of the office⟩ ⟨*keep up* on international relations⟩ **3** : to continue without interruption : maintain a particular course, condition, or series of actions ⟨the rain *kept up* all night⟩ **4** : to match one's neighbors or contemporaries in accomplishment or in the acquisition of material goods : be in fashion — usu. used with *with* ⟨*keeping up* with the professors —*Yale Rev.*⟩ ⟨farm folk seem to place less emphasis than city folk upon competitive consumption, or spending to *keep up* with the Joneses —Day Monroe⟩

**keesh** *var of* KISH

**kees·hond** \'kās,händ, -hȯn-, -nt\ *n* [D, prob. fr. *Kees* (nickname for *Cornelis* Cornelius) + *hond* dog, fr. MD; akin to OHG *hunt* dog — more at HOUND] **1** *usu cap* : a breed of small heavy-coated dogs like the pomeranians but larger, of uncertain origin, and long used in Holland on barges esp. as watchdogs and ratters **2** *pl* **kees·hon·den** \-ndən\ *often cap* : an animal of the Keeshond breed

**keest** \'kēst\ *n* -s [D, kernel, pit, marrow, fr. MD *keest*, *keeste*] *Scot* : inner vital substance : MARROW ⟨cold to the ~⟩

**keester** *var of* KEISTER

**keet** *or* **keat** \'kēt\ *n* -s [imit.] : GUINEA FOWL; *esp* : a young guinea fowl

**keeve** *or* **kieve** \'kēv\ *n* -s [ME *kive*, *keve*, fr. OE *cȳf*, prob. borrowed in prehistoric times fr. (assumed) VL *cupia*, fr. L *cupa* tub, vat — more at HIVE] **1** : a tub or vat esp. for liquids (as a bleaching kier or dolly tub) **2** *Brit* : a rock basin hollowed out by water

**kee·wa·tin** \(')kē¦wātᵊn\ *adj*, *usu cap* [fr. *Keewatin* district, Northwest Territories, Canada] : of or relating to a division of the Archeozoic — see GEOLOGIC TIME table

**kef** \'kef, 'kāf\ *or* **kif** \'kif\ *n* -s [colloq. Ar *kēf* (*kayf*) enjoyment, pleasure] **1** : a state of dreamy tranquillity : LANGUOR **2** : a smoking material (as Indian hemp) that produces kef ⟨basks there . . . smoking . . . his ~ —Hendrik de Leeuw⟩

**kef·fel** \'kefəl\ *n* -s [W *ceffyl* horse, fr. L *caballus* horse, nag — more at CAVALCADE] *dial Brit* : a usu. old or worthless horse : NAG

**keffiyeh** *var of* KAFFIYEH

**ke·fir** *also* **ke·phir** \ke'fi(ə)r, kə'f-, 'kefər\ *n* -s [Russ *kefir*, fr. a native name in the Caucasus] : a slightly effervescent acidulous beverage of low alcoholic content made chiefly in southern Russia of cow's milk that is fermented by means of kefir grains

**kefir grain** *n* : a small mass resembling a tiny cauliflower, occurring in kefir, containing casein and other milk solids together with the yeasts and lactobacilli that cause the characteristic kefir fermentation, and serving as a starter to induce this fermentation when introduced into fresh milk

**keg** \'keg, -ā-, ÷ -a-, ÷ -ai-\ *n* -s [alter. of earlier *cag*, fr. ME *kag*, of Scand origin; akin to ON *kaggi*, *-kaggr* keg, cask, Sw & Dan *kagge*; prob. akin to OHG *kegil* stake, peg, MD *kegge* wedge, Sw dial. *kage* tree stump, and perh. to Lith *žãgaras* dry twig; basic meaning: branch, stake] **1** : a small cask or barrel having a capacity of 30 gallons or less **2** : the contents of a keg

**kegeree** *var of* KEDGEREE

**keg·ler** *also* **kegel·er** *or* **kegel·ler** \'keg(ə)lə(r), 'kāg-\ *n* -s [G *kegler*, fr. *kegeln* to bowl (fr. *kegel* bowling pin, cone, fr. OHG *kegil* stake, peg) + *-er* — more at KEG] : [1]BOWLER

**keg·ling** *also* **kegel·ing** *or* **kegel·ling** \-g(ə)liŋ\ *n* -s [G *kegeln* to bowl + E *-ing*] : BOWLING

**keg·meg** \'keg,meg\ *var of* CAGMAG

**ke·gon** \'kā,gän, -gȯn\ *adj*, *usu cap* [Jap, fr. *ke* lotus + *gon* glory] : of, relating to, or being a sect of Japanese Buddhism originating in the 8th century and teaching the unreality of phenomenal antitheses and the ultimate unity of all reality in and through the Buddha

**ke·hil·lah** *or* **ke·hil·la** \kə'hilə\ *n*, *pl* **kehil·loth** *or* **kehil·lot** \-,lōt(h), -ōs\ [Heb *qĕhillāh* assembly, community] : the Jewish community of a city organized for the administration of charities and communal work

**ke·hoe·ite** \'kē(,)(h)ō,īt\ *n* -s [Henry *Kehoe*, 19th cent. Am. mineralogist + E *-ite*] : a mineral $Al_8(Zn,Ca)_3(PO_4)_6(OH)_{12}$-$21H_2O$(?) consisting of a massive basic hydrous calcium aluminum zinc phosphate (sp. gr. 2.3)

**kei apple** \'kā-, 'kī-, 'kəi-\ *n*, *usu cap K* [fr. Great *Kei* river, Cape Province, Union of South Africa] **1** : the edible fruit of a southern African shrub (*Dovyalis caffra*) of the family Flacourtiaceae that is shaped like a small apple and is used for pickles and preserves **2** : the shrub that bears the Kei apple

**keik** \kēk\ *var of* KEEK

**kei·ki** \'kākē\ *n* -s [Hawaiian] **1** *Hawaii* : CHILD **2** *Hawaii* : an immature plant

**keist** \'kāst\ *Scot var of* CAST

**keis·ter** \'kēstə(r), 'kīs-\ *or* **kees·ter** \'kēs-\ *n* -s [origin unknown] **1** : SATCHEL, SUITCASE; *specif* : one carried by an itinerant peddler **2** *slang* : BUTTOCKS

**keit·loa** \'kītləwə, 'kāt-, ⸗'lōə\ *n* -s [Sechuana *kgetlwa*, *khetlwa*] : a black rhinoceros that has a posterior horn which equals or exceeds the anterior in length and that has been considered to constitute a distinct species

**kek·chi** *or* **quek·chi** \'kek(,)chē\ *n*, *pl* **kekchi** *or* **kekchis** *or* **quekchi** *or* **quekchis** *usu cap* **1 a** : an Indian people of north central Guatemala **b** : a member of such people **2** : the Mayan language of the Kekchi people

**ke·ku·lé formula** \'kākə,lā-\ *n*, *usu cap K* [after Friedrich August *Kekule* von Stradonitz †1896 Ger. chemist] : a structural formula for an organic compound that depicts each valence bond as a short line; *esp* : the hexagonal ring formula for benzene — see BENZENE RING illustration

**ke·ku·ne oil** *or* **ke·ku·na oil** \kə'künə-\ *n* [prob. native name in Ceylon] : CANDLENUT OIL

**ke·la·bit** \kə'läbət\ *n*, *pl* **kelabit** *or* **kelabits** *usu cap* [native name in Sarawak] **1** : a Dayak people of northern Sarawak **2** : a member of the Kelabit people

**kelb–el–bahr** \¦kel,bel¦bär\ *n* -s [Ar *kalb al-baḥr*, lit., the dog of the sea (river, Nile)] : any of several large formidable characin fishes of the Nile and rivers and lakes of tropical Africa that constitute the genus *Hydrocyon*, reach a length of about three feet, have strong teeth, and in form resemble a salmon

**keld** \'keld\ *n* -s [prob. of Scand origin; akin to ON *kelda* spring, marshy place, prob. fr. *kaldr* cold — more at COLD] **1** *dial Eng* : SPRING, FOUNTAIN **2** *dial Eng* : the still part of a body of water

**kel·e·be** \'kelə(,)bē\ *n* -s [Gk *kelebē*, prob. of non-IE origin] : an ovoid krater having handles that drop almost vertically to the shoulder from horizontal extensions on the rim

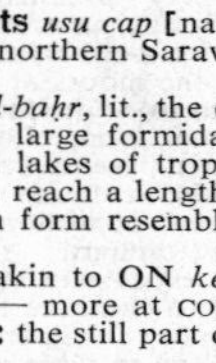

kelebe

**k electron** *n*, *usu cap K* : an electron in the K-shell

**k–electron capture** *usu cap K*, *var of* K-CAPTURE

**ke·lep** \kə'lep\ *n* -s [Kekchi *kelép*] : a Central American stinging ant (*Ectatomma tuberculatum*) that lives in small colonies in the ground esp. near clearings

**kell** \'kel\ *n* -s [ME (northern dial.) *kelle*, alter. of *calle* — more at CAUL] *dial Brit* : CAUL; *specif* : a net cap worn by women

**kelleg** *or* **kellock** *var of* KILLICK

**kellin** *var of* KHELLIN

**kel·li·on** \ke'lē,än, -ē,ȯn\ *n*, *pl* **kel·lia** \-ēə, -ē(,)ä\ [LGk, lit., little cell, fr. L *cella* cell + Gk *-ion* (dim. suffix) — more at CELL] : a small religious house of the Eastern Church occupied by not more than three monks and three lay brothers

**kel·logg oak** \'ke,lȯg-, -,läg-, -,ləg-\ *or* **kellogg's oak** *n*, *usu cap K* [after Albert *Kellogg* †1887 Am. botanist] : CALIFORNIA BLACK OAK

**kel·lup·weed** \'keləp,⸗\ *n* [*kellup* (alter. of *kelp*) + *weed*] : OXEYE 1d

[1]**kel·ly** \'kelē, -li\ *n* -ES [prob. by folk etymology (influence of the name *Kelly*) fr. *callow*] : the topsoil removed in order to secure clay for brickmaking

[2]**kelly** \"\ *vt* -ED/-ING/-ES : to cover (as a molding floor for bricks) with kelly

[3]**kelly** \"\ *or* **kel·lie** \"\ *var of* KILLIE

[4]**kelly** *n*, *pl* **kellies** *or* **kellys** [prob. fr. the name *Kelly*] : a man's stiff hat (as a derby or a flat-topped straw hat) ⟨only the dudes wore straw *kellies* —*New Yorker*⟩

[5]**kelly** \"\ *or* **kelly green** *n*, *often cap K* [fr. the common Irish name *Kelly*; fr. green's being a traditional Irish color] : a variable color averaging a strong yellowish green that is greener and duller than cyprus green and greener, stronger, and slightly lighter than emerald (sense 2b) ⟨comes in red, ~, white, or black —*Women's Wear Daily*⟩

[6]**kelly** \"\ *n* -s [prob. alter. of E dial. *kelp*, of unknown origin] *Austral* : CROW ⟨gave the ~*s* a rare blessing and left them to their feast —*Sydney* (*Australia*) *Bull.*⟩

[7]**kelly** \"\ *also* **kelly joint** *n* -s [prob. fr. the name *Kelly*] : GRIEF STEM

**kelly pool** *n*, *usu cap K* : a pool game in which each player draws a number and while playing on the object balls in numerical order aims to pocket the ball having his number on it and thereby win the game but if his ball is pocketed by another player he loses his chance of winning and continues to play with the aim of pocketing the balls of other players

**kelm·scott** \'ke(l)mzkət, 'keüm-, -m(p)sk-; -mz,kät, -m(p),sk-\ *adj*, *usu cap* [fr. the *Kelmscott* Press, publishing firm in Hammersmith, England, fr. *Kelmscott*, England, home of William Morris †1896 Eng. poet and artist, its founder] : produced by the Kelmscott Press ⟨*Kelmscott* books⟩ ⟨the *Kelmscott* Chaucer⟩

**ke·loid** *also* **che·loid** \'kē,lȯid\ *n* -s [F *kiloïde*, *chéloïde*, fr. Gk *chēlē* claw + F *-oïde* -oid] : a thick scar resulting from excessive growth of fibrous tissue and occurring esp. after burns or radiation injury — **ke·loi·dal** \(')kē¦lȯidᵊl\ *adj*

**kelp** \'kelp, 'keüp\ *n* -s [ME *culp*] **1 a** : any of various large brown seaweeds of the orders Laminariales and Fucales — see GIANT KELP **b** : a mass or growth of large seaweeds; *esp* : a mass of those burned for the ashes **2** *also* **kelp ash** : the ashes of seaweed used formerly as a source of alkali and now as a source of iodine

**kelp bass** *n* : a dusky sea bass (*Paralabrax clathratus*) that is blotched with darker brown or gray above and silvery or yellowish below, is common in kelp beds along the California coast, and is an esteemed sport fish

**kelp crab** *n* : any of several spider crabs common among algae and eelgrass along the Pacific coast of No. America: as **a** : the common kelp crab (*Pugettia producta* syn. *Epialtus productus*) **b** : GRACEFUL KELP CRAB **c** : SHEEP CRAB

**kelp·er** \-pə(r)\ *n* -s : one that gathers or prepares kelp

**kelpfish** \'⸗,⸗\ *n* : any of various fishes inhabiting kelp beds: as **a** : a large variably colored blenny (*Heterostichus rostratus*) found among kelp or eelgrass along the California coast or another member of the family Clinidae **b** : any of several brilliantly colored percoid fishes of the family Odacidae found along the coasts of Australia and New Zealand — called also *rock whiting*

**kelp fly** \'⸗,⸗\ *n* : any of various rather large flattened two-winged flies that constitute the family Coelopidae and have larvae that feed on kelp

**kelp goose** *n* : a goose (*Chloephaga hybrida*) of littoral habits found in the Falkland islands and adjacent So. America

**kelp greenling** *n* : GREENLING 1a(2)

**kelp gull** *n* : a black-backed gull (*Larus dominicanus*) of the southern hemisphere

**kelp hen** *n* : a weka of South Island of New Zealand that feeds on marine animals and prob. represents a dark phase of a species (*Gallirallus australis*) though sometimes considered a separate species (*G. brachypterus*)

[1]**kel·pie** *also* **kel·py** \'kelpē, 'keüp-\ *n*, *pl* **kelpies** [prob. of Celt origin; akin to ScGael *cailpeach*, *calpach*, *colpach* heifer, steer, colt, *colpa* cow, horse] : a water spirit usu. equine in form that is held esp. in Scottish folklore to delight in or bring about the drowning of travelers

[2]**kelpie** \"\ *n* -s [after *Kelpie*, an early specimen] : an Australian sheep dog of a breed developed in the 19th century in New South Wales by crossing the dingo with various British sheep dogs

**kelp pigeon** *n* : a sheathbill (*Chionis alba*) having a pinkish or yellowish black-tipped bill and occurring from the Falkland islands south to parts of Antarctica

**kelp plover** *n* : DOWITCHER

**kelp raft** *n* : a mass of floating kelp

**kelpwort** \'⸗,⸗\ *n* : GLASSWORT 2

**kelpy** \'kelpē, 'keüp-\ *adj*, *sometimes* -ER/-EST [*kelp* + *-y*] : abounding in or characterized by kelp

**kel·sey locust** \'kelsē- *also* -ltsē-\ *n*, *usu cap K* [after Harlan P. *Kelsey* b1872 Am. horticulturist] : an American shrub (*Robinia kelseyi*) having rose or purple flowers, glabrous branches, and glandular hispid pods

**kelson** *var of* KEELSON

[1]**kelt** \'kelt\ *n* -s [ME (northern dial.), prob. fr. ScGael *cealt*] : a salmon or sea trout that is weak and emaciated after spawning

[2]**kelt** \"\ *n* -s [ScGael *cealt*] *dial Brit* : homespun frieze cloth usu. of black wool with a mixture of white

[3]**kelt** \"\ *cap*, *var of* CELT

[1]**kelter** *var of* KILTER

[2]**kel·ter** \'keltər\ *vi* -ED/-ING/-S [origin unknown] *chiefly Scot* : to move restlessly : UNDULATE

[3]**kel·ter** \'kəltə(r)\ *n* -s [origin unknown] **1** *dial Eng* : property of any kind; *esp* : MONEY **2** : RUBBISH, TRASH

**keltic** *usu cap*, *var of* CELTIC

**kel·ty** \'kelti\ *n* -ES [origin unknown] *Scot* : an additional glass of liquor forced upon a reluctant drinker

**kel·vin** \'kelvən\ *adj*, *usu cap* [after William Thomson, Lord *Kelvin* †1907 Brit. physicist] : relating to, conforming to, or having a thermometric scale on which the unit of measurement equals the centigrade degree and according to which absolute zero is 0°, the equivalent of −273.16°C, and water freezes at 273.16° and boils at 373.16°

**kelvin balance** *n*, *usu cap K* [after Lord *Kelvin*] : a device for comparing the force produced by an electric current flowing through fixed and movable coils and the force of gravity

**kelvin's law** *n*, *usu cap K* [after Lord *Kelvin*] : a statement in electrical economics: the most economical cross-section area for an electric conductor is that for which the cost of energy lost in a given period equals the interest for the same period of the capital involved

**ke·mal·ism** \kə'mä,lizəm\ *n* -s *usu cap* [*Kemal* Atatürk (Mustafa Kemal) †1938 Turkish general and statesman + E *-ism*] : the political, economic, and social principles advocated by Kemal Atatürk and designed to create a modern republican secular Turkish state out of a portion of the Ottoman empire

[1]**ke·mal·ist** \-,ləst\ *n* -s *usu cap* [*Kemal* Atatürk + E *-ist*] : a follower of Kemal Atatürk : an adherent of Kemalism ⟨the economic policies of the *Kemalists*⟩

[2]**kemalist** \"\ *adj*, *usu cap* : of, relating to, or having the characteristics of Kemalism or Kemalists ⟨the modern *Kemalist* pattern of revolution —*Atlantic*⟩ ⟨the Ottoman empire collapsed and *Kemalist* Turkey was born — Necmeddin Sadak⟩

**ke·man·cha** \kə'mänchə\ *n* -s [Ar *kamanjah*, fr. Per] : an Arabian violin that has usu. a single string and a gourd resonator and is held vertically when played

[1]**kemb** \'kem\ *vt* **kembed** \-md\ *or* **kempt** \-m(p)t\ **kembed** *or* **kempt**; **kembing**; **kembs** [ME *kemben*, fr. OE *cemban*; akin to OS *kembian* to comb, OHG *kemben*, *chempen*, ON *kemba*; denominatives fr. the root of E [1]*comb*] *dial* : COMB

[2]**kemb** \"\ *n* -s *dial* : COMB

**ke·me·ro·vo** \'kemə,rō(,)vō\ *adj*, *usu cap* [fr. *Kemerovo*, U.S.S.R.] : of or from the city of Kemerovo, U.S.S.R. : of the kind or style prevalent in Kemerovo

**ke·mi·ri nut** \kə'mirē-\ *also* **kemiri** *n* -s [Jav *kĕmiri*] : CANDLENUT 1

[1]**kemp** \'kemp\ *n* -s [ME *kempe*, fr. OE *cempa*; akin to OS *kempio* warrior, OHG *kempho*, ON *kappi*; all fr. a prehistoric WGmc-NGmc word derived fr. a word meaning "combat", "battle"; akin to OE *camp*, *comp* combat, battle, OHG *kamph* combat, battle, ON *kapp* contest, zeal; all borrowed fr. L *campus* plain, field, battlefield — more at CAMP] **1 a** *dial Brit* : a strong and worthy warrior or athlete : CHAMPION **b** *dial Eng* : an impetuous rogue **2** *dial Brit* : a competition or contest esp. among reapers in a harvest field

[2]**kemp** \"\ *vi* -ED/-ING/-S [ME *kempen*, prob. fr. *kempe*, n.] *chiefly Scot* : to contend or compete for championship esp. in a reaping contest

[3]**kemp** \"\ *n* -s [ME *kempe* coarse hair, of Scand origin; akin to ON *kampr* mustache; akin to OE *cenep* mustache, OFris *kenep* mustache, MD *canef*been cheekbone, and perh. to ON *knefill* pole, stake — more at KNAVE] : a coarse dead fiber esp. of wool or mohair that is usu. short, wavy, and white, has little affinity for dye, and is used in mixed wools (as in carpets or for novelty effects)

**kem·pas** \'kempəs\ *n* -ES [Malay *kĕmpas*] **1** : a leguminous Malayan tree (*Koompassia malaccensis*) with very hard heavy strong wood **2** : the wood of the kempas

**kemp·ite** \'kem,pīt\ *n* -s [James F. *Kemp* †1926 Am. geologist + E *-ite*] : a mineral $Mn_2(OH)_3Cl$ consisting of a basic manganese oxychloride occurring in small emerald green orthorhombic crystals

**kem·ple** \'kempəl\ *n* -s [alter. of earlier *kimple*, of Scand origin; akin to ON *-kimbull* bundle, Icel *kimbill* small bundle, small haystack, Norw dial. *kimbel* bundle of grass] : a Scotch unit of measure for straw varying around 400 pounds

**kemp's loggerhead** *or* **kemp's turtle** \'kemps-\ *n*, *usu cap K* [fr. the name *Kemp*] : RIDLEY

**kempt** \'kem(p)t\ *adj* [ME, fr. past part. of *kemben* to comb — more at KEMB] : neatly kept : TRIM ⟨lips . . . unsmiling above the faintly grizzled and elegantly ~ imperial —Jean Stafford⟩

**kempy** \'kempē\ *adj*, *sometimes* -ER/-EST [[3]*kemp* + *-y*] : containing or resembling kemp ⟨a lean hairy animal . . . whose ~ wool brings only the lowest market prices —C.A.Amsden⟩

[1]**ken** \'ken\ *vb* **kenned** *also* **kend** \-nd\ *or* **kent** \-nt\ **kenned** *also* **kend** *or* **kent**; **kenning**; **kens** [ME *kennen*; partly fr. OE *cennan* to make known, declare, acknowledge; partly fr. ON *kenna* to perceive, know; both akin to OHG *kennen* to make known, Goth *kannjan*; causatives fr. the root of OE *cunnan* to know — more at CAN] *vt* **1** *archaic* : to have

sight of : SEE ⟨as far as I could ~ thy chalky cliffs, . . . I stood upon the hatches in the storm —Shak.⟩ **2** *now dial* : to recognize by or as if by sight : DISCERN ⟨*kenned* in the beautiful lady the child of his friend —S.T.Coleridge⟩ **3** *now chiefly Scot* **a** : to have acquaintance with ⟨have *kend* every wench in the Halidome of St. Mary's —Sir Walter Scott⟩ **b** : to have knowledge of ⟨it was getting dark, and they didn't ~ the ground like us —John Buchan⟩ **c** : to have awareness or understanding of ⟨do ye ~ what ye're saying, man? —William Black⟩ **4** *Scots law* : to admit to ownership of heritable property ~ *vi* **1** *now chiefly Scot* : to have knowledge : KNOW ⟨it was his father then ye *kent* of —Sir Walter Scott⟩ **2** *obs* : to have the power of sight ⟨spaces distant from them as far as a man may ~ —Marchamont Needham⟩

**²ken** \"\ *n* -s **1** *obs* : the distance that bounds the range of ordinary vision esp. at sea ⟨are safely come within a ~ of Dover —John Lyly⟩ **2 a** : the range of vision ⟨then felt I like some watcher of the skies when a new planet swims into his ~ —John Keats⟩ **b** : the sight or view esp. of a place or person ⟨'tis double death to drown in ~ of shore —Shak.⟩ **c** : the power or exercise of vision ⟨searched with fixed ~ to know what place it was wherein I stood —H.F.Cary⟩ **3** : the range of recognition, comprehension, perception, understanding, or knowledge ⟨abstract words that are beyond the ~ of young children —Lois M. Rettie⟩ ⟨all knowledge and experience come within the historian's ~ —W.G.Carleton⟩ **syn** see RANGE

**³ken** \"\ *n* -s [prob. short for *kennel*] : HOUSE; *esp* : a rowdy resort for thieves and beggars ⟨has fishwives and boozing ~*s* enough to supply all of America —Kenneth Roberts⟩

**⁴ken** \"\ *n* -s [Jap, lit., fist] : a Japanese game of forfeits

**ken-** *or* **keno-** *comb form* [Gk, fr. *kenos*; akin to Arm *sin* empty, vain] : empty ⟨*kenotron*⟩

**ke·naf** *also* **ka·naf** *or* **ka·naff** \kə'naf\ *n* -s [Per] **1** : a valuable fiber plant (*Hibiscus cannabinus*) of the East Indies now widespread in cultivation **2** : the fiber of kenaf used for cordage and canvas manufacture — called also *ambari, bastard jute, Bombay hemp, deccan hemp, Java jute*

**kench** \'kench\ *n* -ES [origin unknown] : a bin or enclosure in which fish or skins are salted

**ken·dal green** \'kendᵊl-\ *also* **kendal** *n* -s *usu cap K* [ME, fr. *Kendal*, borough of Westmorland, England] : a green woolen cloth resembling homespun or tweed

**kendal sneck bent** *n, usu cap K* [prob. fr. *Kendal*, England] : a fishhook of wide squarish and curved pattern — see FISHHOOK illustration

**ken·dle** \'ken(d)ᵊl\ *dial var of* KINDLE

**kend·na** \'ken(d)nə\ [*kend* (past of ¹*ken*) + *na*] *chiefly Scot* : did not know

**ken·do** \'ken(,)dō\ *n* -s [Jap *kendō*] : a Japanese sport of fencing with staves

**ken·dyr** *or* **ken·dir** \(')ken¦di(ə)r\ *n* -s [Russ & Turk; Russ *kendyr'*, fr. Turk *kendir*] **1** : a strong bast fiber that resembles Indian hemp and is used in Asia as cordage and as a substitute for cotton and hemp **2** : an Old World dogbane (*Apocynum venetum*) cultivated chiefly in Asiatic Russia for the kendyr that it produces

**ken·il·worth ivy** \'kenᵊl,wərth-\ *n, usu cap K* [fr. *Kenilworth* Castle, Warwickshire, Eng.] : a delicate trailing Old World plant (*Cymbalaria muralis*) of the family Scrophulariaceae with palmately lobed and veined leaves and small pale violet flowers with a yellow palate

**ke·nite** \'kē,nīt\ *n* -s *usu cap* : a member of an ancient people of southern Palestine related to the Amalekites

**ken·na** \'ken(n)ə\ [¹*ken* + *na*] *chiefly Scot* : do not know

**kenned** \'kend\ *adj* [ME *kend*, fr. past part. of *kennen* to know — more at KEN] *chiefly Scot* : WELL-KNOWN, FAMILIAR ⟨wearying terribly for the sight of a ~ face —John Buchan⟩

**ken·ne·dya** \kə'nēdēə, 'kenə,dēə\ *n, cap* [NL, after Lewis *Kennedy* †1818, Eng. nurseryman] : a genus of Australian woody vines (family Leguminosae) bearing showy red or purplish flowers whose corolla has a long keel

**¹ken·nel** \'kenᵊl\ *n* -s [ME *kenel*, fr. (assumed) ONF *kenil*, fr. (assumed) VL *canile* (whence OF *chenil* kennel, F dial. *cani*), fr. L *canis* dog — more at HOUND] **1 a** (1) : a house for a dog or pack of hounds (2) : an establishment for the breeding or boarding of dogs — usu. used in pl. **b** : a house or other dwelling place regarded as unfit for human residence **2 a** : a pack of dogs or other animals **b** : a group of persons ⟨literary agent who has a ~ of eccentric clients —Martin Levin⟩ **3** : a bed or den of an animal (as a fox or otter) **4** : GABLE 2b

kennel 1a(1)

**²kennel** \"\ *vb* **kenneled** *or* **kennelled; kenneled** *or* **kennelled; kenneling** *or* **kennelling; kennels** *vi* **1** : to take shelter or lie in a kennel ⟨the fox ~*s* on the hillside⟩ **2** : to lodge in a dwelling place regarded as unfit for human residence ⟨the dull sodden faces of the man and woman who ~*ed* there —E.P.Roe⟩ ~ *vt* **1 a** : to put or keep in a kennel ⟨~ your hound for he has been well whipped —J.H.Wheelwright⟩ ⟨the apple trees under which the dogs were ~*ed* —Eve Langley⟩ **b** : to provide with a dwelling place regarded as unfit for human residence ⟨that quarter of the town where they are ~*ed* is . . . inhabited by strangers —Richard Steele⟩ **2** : to provide or seek lodging or shelter for esp. in a secluded place ⟨writers and painters . . . ~*ing* themselves in the depths of the country —*Times Lit. Supp.*⟩ **3** : to keep within bounds or under control : CONFINE, RESTRAIN ⟨indulge our enthusiasms while keeping our angers and envies ~*ed* —Brand Blanshard⟩ ⟨constantly striving to keep his quickly roused temper ~*ed*⟩

**³kennel** \"\ *n* -s [alter. of ²*cannel*] : a gutter in a street ⟨streets were ill-paved and . . . sloped down on both sides to the ~*s* —G.M.Trevelyan⟩

**kennel club** *n* : an association of dog fanciers concerned esp. with advancing the interests of one or more breeds of dogs usu. by establishing standards, providing competitions, or recording pedigrees

**ken·nel·ly-heav·i·side layer** \'kenᵊlē'hevē,sīd-\ *n, usu cap K&H* [after Arthur W. *Kennelly* †1939 Am. electrical engineer and Oliver *Heaviside* †1925 Eng. physicist, its discoverers] : IONOSPHERE

**kennelmaid** \'==,=\ *n* : a woman who takes care of kennels

**ken·nel·man** \'kenᵊlmən\ *n, pl* **kennelmen** : one who takes care of kennels

**ken·ner·ly's salmon** \'kenərl|ēz-, -*R* -nəl| *or* -nᵊl|\ *n, usu cap K* [fr. the name *Kennerly*] : KOKANEE

**ken·ni·cott's willow warbler** \'kenəkəts-, -ə,käts-\ *n, usu cap K* [fr. the name *Kennicott*] : a warbler (*Acanthopneuste borealis kennicotti*) that breeds in Alaska

**¹ken·ning** \'keniŋ\ *n* -s [ME, fr. gerund of *kennen* to ken — more at KEN] **1** *obs* : range of sight : VIEW **2** *chiefly Scot* **a** : COGNITION, RECOGNITION **b** : a perceptible but small amount : LITTLE ⟨his father was . . . a ~ on the wrong side of the law —R.L.Stevenson⟩

**²kenning** \"\ *n* -s [ON, fr. *kenna* to perceive, know, name, name with a kenning + *-ing* — more at KEN] : a metaphorical compound word or phrase used esp. in Old English and Old Norse poetry ⟨Germanic verse . . . laid main stress upon the trope known as ~; the ocean is the "whale's bath," the "foaming fields", the "sea-street" —F.B.Gummere⟩

**kenningwort** \'==,=\ *n* [¹*kenning* + *wort*] : CELANDINE 1

**ken·ny method** *or* **ken·ny treatment** \'kenē-\ *n, usu cap K* [after Elizabeth *Kenny* †1952 Australian nurse, its developer] : a method of treating poliomyelitis consisting of application of hot fomentations to relax spasmodic contraction of affected muscles, reeducation through guided passive movement of the separate muscles with reestablishment of the patient's awareness of them, and guided active coordination

**ke·no** \'kē(,)nō\ *n* -s [modif. of F *quine* set of five winning numbers in a lottery, fr. OF *quines*, pl., throw at dice where each die shows 5, fr. L *quini* five each, fr. *quinque* five — more at FIVE] : a game resembling lotto in which numbers printed on pellets taken from a keno goose are announced to the players who cover the same numbers on cards and in which five numbers covered in the same horizontal row win for the player — see BINGO

**keno-** — see KEN-

**keno goose** *n* : a flexible sack with a narrow neck that releases one numbered pellet at a time for use in playing keno — called also *goose*

**ke·no·sis** \kə'nōsəs, kē'-\ *n* -ES [LGk *kenōsis*, fr. Gk, evacuation, action of emptying, fr. *kenoun* to purge, empty (fr. *kenos* empty) + *-sis* — more at KEN-] **1** : the act of Christ in emptying himself of the form of God, taking the form of a servant, and humbling himself to the extent of suffering death **2** : the act of voluntarily giving up personal rights and ambitions and accepting suffering as a follower of Christ

**ke·not·ic** \-nät·ik, -ät|, |ēk\ *adj* [Gk *kenōtikos* purgative, emptying, fr. (assumed) Gk *kenōtos* (verbal of Gk *kenoun*) + Gk *-ikos* -ic] : of, affirming, or marked by kenosis ⟨~ theories of the Incarnation that stem from Philippians 2:7⟩ ⟨a ~ Christology⟩ ⟨the ~ character of Russian Christianity⟩

**ke·not·i·cism** \|ə,sizəm\ *n* -s : the doctrine of or belief in the kenosis of Christ

**ke·not·i·cist** \-,səst\ *n* -s : an advocate or adherent of kenoticism

**ken·o·tron** \'kenə,trän\ *n* -s [*ken-* + *-tron*] : a high-vacuum diode used as a rectifier in appliances (as X-ray equipment and electrostatic precipitators) where high voltage and low current are required

**kens** *pres 3d sing of* KEN, *pl of* KEN

**ken·sing·ton** \'kenziŋtən, -n(t)siŋ-\ *n* -s [fr. the name *Kensington*] *dial* : a covered-dish supper

**ken·speck·le** \'kenz,pekəl, -n,sp-\ *or* **ken·speck** \-pek\ *adj* [prob. of Scand origin; akin to Norw *kjennspak* quick at recognizing, fr. *kjenne* to know, recognize (fr. ON *kenna*) + *spak* wise, gentle, tractable, fr. ON *spakr* — more at KEN] *chiefly Scot* : having a distinctive appearance : CONSPICUOUS

**¹kent** *past of* KEN

**²kent** \'kent\ *adj, usu cap* [fr. *Kent* county, England] : of or from the county of Kent, England : of the kind or style prevalent in Kent : KENTISH

**³kent** \"\ *n* -s [alter. of *quant*] *chiefly Scot* : STAFF, POLE: as **a** : a shepherd's staff **b** : a punting pole with a flange near the end

**⁴kent** \"\ *vb* -ED/-ING/-S *vi, chiefly Scot* : to push or propel a boat with a kent ~ *vt, chiefly Scot* : to push or propel with a kent

**kent bugle** *n, usu cap K* [prob. after Edward Augustus †1820 1st duke of *Kent*, Eng. soldier] : KEY BUGLE

**ken·tia** \'kentēə\ *n* [NL, fr. William *Kent* †*ab* 1828 Dutch gardener and traveler in the Orient + NL *-ia*] **1** *cap* : a genus of pinnate-leaved palms that are natives of Australia and the East Indies and have spadices with angled branchlets and flowers with six stamens **2** -s : any of several palms formerly assigned to the genus *Kentia*: as **a** : either of two feather palms (*Howea forsteriana* and *H. belmoriana*) from Lord Howe Island that are extensively cultivated for their ornamental foliage **b** : UMBRELLA PALM 1

**kent·i·cism** \'kentə,sizəm\ *n* -s *usu cap* [*Kent* county + *-icism* (as in *Anglicism*)] : a word or phrase peculiar to the Kentish dialect

**kent·ish** \'kentish\ *adj, usu cap* [ME, fr. OE *Centisc*, fr. *Cent* Kent + OE *-isc* -ish] **1** : of, relating to, or characteristic of the county of Kent, England **2** : of, relating to, or characteristic of the people of Kent

**kentish glory** *n, usu cap K* : an orange-brown moth (*Endromis versicolor*) with black-and-white markings that is common in parts of England and whose larva feeds on birch

**kent·ish·man** \-shmən\ *n, pl* **kentishmen** *cap* : a native or inhabitant of Kent

**kentish nightingale** *n, usu cap K, dial Eng* : BLACKCAP 2a

**kentish plover** *n, usu cap K* : a widely distributed ring plover (*Charadrius alexandrinus*) that sometimes breeds on the east coast of England

**ken·tle** \'kentᵊl\ *n* -s [by alter.] : QUINTAL

**kent·ledge** \'kent,lej\ *n* -s [origin unknown] : pig iron or scrap metal used as ballast

**ken·tro·gon** \'ken·trə,gän\ *n* -s [Gk *kentron* sharp point, center of a circle + E *-gon* — more at CENTER] : a larva of a parasitic barnacle (order Rhizocephala)

**ken·tro·lite** \'ken·trə,līt\ *n* -s [G *kentrolith*, fr. Gk *kentron* sharp point + G *-lith* -lite] : a dark reddish brown mineral $Pb_2Mn_2Si_2O_9$ consisting of a lead manganese silicate

**¹ken·tuck** \kən·'tək, (')ken·¦t-, (')kān·¦t-\ *adj, usu cap* [fr. *Kentucky*, the state] *dial* : KENTUCKIAN

**²kentuck** \"\ *n* -s *cap, dial* : KENTUCKIAN

**¹ken·tuck·i·an** \kən·'təkēən, -təkiən *sometimes* ken··\ *adj, usu cap* [*Kentucky* + E *-an*] **1** : of, relating to, or characteristic of Kentucky **2** : of, relating to, or characteristic of the people of Kentucky

**²kentuckian** \"\ *n* -s *cap* : a native or resident of Kentucky

**ken·tucky** \-təkē, -ki\ *adj, usu cap* [*Kentucky*, state in the U. S., prob. of Iroquoian origin; akin to Iroquois *kenta* level, prairie] : of or from the state of Kentucky : of the kind or style prevalent in Kentucky : KENTUCKIAN

**kentucky bass** *or* **kentucky black bass** *n, usu cap K* : SPOTTED BLACK BASS

**kentucky bluegrass** *also* **kentucky blue** *n, usu cap K* : a valuable pasture and meadow grass (*Poa pratensis*) that has tall stalks and slender bright green leaves, is one of the chief constituents in mixtures of seed for lawns, and is found in both Europe and America where it reaches its finest development in the central U.S. — called also *bluegrass, June grass, meadow grass, smooth meadow grass*

**kentucky cardinal** *n, usu cap K* : ²CARDINAL 5

**kentucky coffee tree** *n, usu cap K* : a tall No. American tree (*Gymnocladus dioica*) of the family Leguminosae with bipinnate leaves and large woody brown pods whose seeds have been used as a substitute for coffee — called also *bonduc*

**kentucky flat** *n, usu cap K* : ARK 2b

**kentucky green** *n, often cap K* : a dark yellowish green that is yellower and less strong than holly green (sense 1), lighter and stronger than deep chrome green, yellower and darker than golf green, and yellower, lighter, and stronger than average hunter green

**kentucky jean** *n, usu cap K* **1** : a homemade jean woven with a cotton warp and a wool weft **2** : a garment of Kentucky jean

**kentucky rifle** *n, usu cap K* : a long-barreled flintlock of relatively small caliber developed in the early 18th century in Pennsylvania and extensively used on the American frontier

**kentucky warbler** *n, usu cap K* : a warbler (*Oporornis formosus*) of the eastern U.S. that is olive green above and yellow below and has the head marked with black

**kentucky windage** *n, usu cap K* [*Kentucky* (*rifle*)] : a windage correction made by aiming a firearm to the right or left of the target rather than by adjustment of the sights

**¹ken·ya** \'kenyə *also* 'kēn-\ *adj, usu cap* [fr. *Kenya*, country in eastern Africa] : of or from Kenya : of the kind or style prevalent in Kenya : KENYAN

**²ken·ya** *or* **ken·yah** \'kenyə\ *n, pl* **kenya** *or* **kenyas** *or* **kenyah** *or* **kenyahs** *usu cap* [native name in northern Borneo] **1** : a Dayak people of north central Borneo sometimes held with the Kayan to constitute a subdivision of the Bahau **2** : a member of the Kenya people

**¹ken·yan** \'kenyən *also* 'kēn-\ *adj, usu cap* [*Kenya* + E *-an*] **1** : of, relating to, or characteristic of Kenya **2** : of, relating to, or characteristic of the people of Kenya

**²kenyan** \"\ *n* -s *cap* : a native or inhabitant of Kenya

**¹kep** \'kep\ *vt* **kepped** \-pt\ **kep·pen** \-pən\ *or* **kip·pen** \'kipən\ **kepping; keps** [ME *keppen*, alter. of *kepen* to observe, heed, seek, seize, keep — more at KEEP] **1** *dial Brit* : to intercept and hinder ⟨~ him on his way home⟩ **2** *dial Brit* : to make a catch of : serve as a catch for

**²kep** \"\ *n* -s *dial Brit* : CATCH, HAUL

**keph·a·lin** \'kefəlin\ *var of* CEPHALIN

**kephir** *var of* KEFIR

**kepi** \'kāpē, 'kepē\ *n* -s [F *képi*, fr. G dial. (Switzerland) *käppi*, dim. of *kappe* cap, fr. OHG *kappa* cloak, cape, fr. LL *cappa* head covering, cloak — more at CAP] : a military cap having a close-fitting band, a round flat top sloping toward the front, and a visor ⟨the forage cap was the American version of the French ~ —W.F.Harris⟩

**kep·le·ri·an** \(')ke¦plirēən\ *adj, usu cap* [Johannes *Kepler* †1630 Ger. astronomer + E *-ian*] **1** : of or relating to the astronomer Kepler **2** : being in accord with Kepler's laws

**keplerian telescope** *n, usu cap K* : a refracting telescope usu. used in astronomical observations including a positive objective lens and a positive eyepiece and giving an inverted image and a relatively wide field of view

**kep·ler's law** \'keplə(r)z-\ *n, usu cap K* [after Johannes *Kepler*] **1** : a statement in astronomy: the orbit of each planet is an ellipse that has the sun at one focus **2** : a statement in astronomy: the radius vector from the sun to each planet generates equal orbital areas in equal times **3** : a statement in astronomy: the ratio of the square of the revolution period to the cube of the orbital major axis is the same for all the planets

**kept** *past of* KEEP

**ker-** *also* **ke-** *prefix* [imit.] — used in onomatopoeic or echoic forms imitating the noise of a falling object ⟨*kerplop*⟩

**ke·ra·lan** \'kerələn\ *n* -s *cap* [*Kerala* state, India + E *-an*] : a native or inhabitant of Kerala state, southern India

**ke·ra·na** *or* **ker·ra·na** \kə'rānə\ *n* -s [modif. of Per *karranāi*, fr. *nāi* reed, reed pipe] : a long Persian trumpet

**ker·a·sin** \'kerəsən\ *n* -s [ISV *keras-* (prob. fr. Gk *keras* horn) + *-in* — more at HORN] : a cerebroside $C_{48}H_{93}NO_8$ that occurs esp. in Gaucher's disease and that yields lignoceric acid on hydrolysis

**kerat-** *or* **kerato-** — see CERAT-

**ker·a·ter·pe·ton** \,kerə'tərpə,tän\ *n, cap* [NL, fr. *kerat-* + Gk *herpeton* creeping thing, snake] : a genus of broad-headed extinct amphibians similar to salamanders found in the Carboniferous of Ohio and Ireland

**ker·a·tin** \'kerəd·ən, -ətən\ *also* **ceratin** \'se-\ *n* -s [ISV *kerat-, cerat-* + *-in*] : any of various sulfur-containing fibrous proteins that form the chemical basis of epidermal tissues (as horn, hair, wool, nails, feathers), that are insoluble in most solvents and unlike collagen and other proteins are typically not digested by enzymes of the gastrointestinal tract, and that produce elastic properties of fibers — compare PSEUDOKERATIN

**ker·a·tin·i·za·tion** \,kerəd·ənə'zāshən\ *n* -s [ISV *keratinize* + *-ation*] : conversion into keratin or keratinous tissue

**ker·a·tin·ize** \'kerəd·ə,nīz\ *vb* -ED/-ING/-S [ISV *keratin* + *-ize*] *vt* : to make keratinous ⟨tissues *keratinized* by friction⟩ ~ *vi* : to become keratinous or converted into keratin ⟨a *keratinizing* scar⟩

**ke·rat·i·no·phil·ic** \kə¦rat³nō¦filik\ *adj* [*keratin* + *-o-* + *-philic*] : showing strong affinity for hair, skin, feathers, horns, and other keratinized material — used chiefly of fungi capable of growing on such materials

**ke·rat·i·nous** \kə'rat³nəs\ *adj* [Gk *keratinos*, fr. *kerat-*, *keras* horn — more at HORN] : HORNY

**ker·a·ti·tis** \,kerə'tīd·əs\ *n* -ES [NL, fr. *kerat-* + *-itis*] : inflammation of the cornea of the eye characterized by burning or smarting, blurring of vision, and sensitiveness to light and caused by infectious or noninfectious agents — compare KERATOCONJUNCTIVITIS

**ker·a·to·conjunctivitis** \¦kerəd·ō+\ *or* **cer·a·to·conjunctivitis** \¦serəd·ō+\ *n* [NL, fr. *kerat-*, or *cerat-* + *conjunctivitis*] : combined inflammation of the cornea and conjunctiva: **a** : a virus disease of man often epidemic and marked by pain, redness, and swelling with tenderness of adjacent lymph nodes and profuse watery discharge from the eyes — called also *pinkeye* **b** : a highly contagious rickettsial disease of cattle marked by inflammation of the conjunctiva and cornea and infective discharge from eyes and nose

**ker·a·to·der·ma** \,kerəd·ō'dərmə\ *n* [NL, fr. *kerat-* + *-derma*] : a horny condition of the skin

**ker·a·to·gen·ic** \¦===¦jenik\ *adj* [*kerat-* + *-genic*] : capable of inducing proliferation of epidermal tissues

**ker·a·tog·e·nous** \¦kerə¦täjənəs\ *adj* [*kerat-* + *-genous*] : producing horn or horny tissue

**ker·a·toid** \'kerə,tȯid\ *adj* [ISV *kerat-* + *-oid*] : HORNY

**ker·a·toi·dea** \,kerə'tȯidēə\ [NL, fr. *kerat-* + *-oidea*] *syn of* KERATOSA

**Ker·a·tol** \'kerə,tȯl, -tōl\ *trademark* — used for a pyroxylin-coated waterproof material used esp. in bookbinding

**ker·a·tol·y·sis** \,kerə'täləsəs\ *n* [NL, fr. ISV *keratin* + NL *-o-* + *-lysis*] **1** : the process of breaking down or dissolving keratin **2** [NL, fr. *kerat-* + *-lysis*] : a skin disease marked by peeling of the horny layer of the epidermis

**¹ker·a·to·lyt·ic** \¦kerəd·ō¦lid·ik\ *adj* [ISV *kerat-* + *-lytic*] : relating to or causing keratolysis

**²keratolytic** \"\ *n* -s : a keratolytic agent (as salicylic acid)

**ker·a·to·ma·la·cia** \,kerəd·ōmə'lās(h)ēə\ *n* -s [NL, fr. *kerat-* + *-malacia*] : a softening and ulceration of the cornea of the eye resulting from severe systemic deficiency of vitamin A — compare XEROPHTHALMIA

**ker·a·to·phyre** \'kerəd·ō,fī(ə)r\ *n* -s [ISV *kerat-* + *-phyre*; orig. formed as G *keratophyr*] **1** : any of various rocks resembling hornfels **2** : a compact porphyritic rock with anorthoclase as its prevailing feldspar and with or without quartz

**ker·a·to·plas·ty** \-,plastē\ *n* -ES [ISV *kerat-* + *-plasty*] : plastic surgery on the cornea; *esp* : corneal grafting

**ker·a·tosa** \,kerə'tōsə, -ōzə\ *n pl, cap* [NL, fr. *kerat-* + L *-osa* (neut. pl. of *-osus* -ous)] : an order of Demospongiae comprising the horny sponges with a spongin skeleton and without spicules and including the commercially important family Spongiidae

**ker·a·tose** \'kerə,tōs\ *or* **cer·a·tose** \'se-\ *adj* [NL *Keratosa*] : of or relating to the Keratosa

**ker·a·to·sis** \,kerə'tōsəs\ *n, pl* **kerato·ses** \-ō,sēz\ [NL, fr. *kerat-* + *-osis*] **1** : a disease of the skin marked by overgrowth of horny tissue **2** : an area of the skin affected by keratosis

**ker·a·tot·ic** \¦==¦täd·ik\ *adj* [fr. NL *keratosis*, after such pairs as NL *hypnosis*: E *hypnotic*] : of or relating to keratosis : affected by keratosis

**ke·rat·to** \kə'rad·(,)ō\ *also* **ka·rat·to** \kə'rad·(,)ō\ *n* -s [prob. native name in the West Indies] **1** : any of several West Indian agaves (esp. *Agave keratto*) **2** : the fiber from keratto

**ke·rau·lo·phon** \kə'rȯlə,fän\ *also* **ke·rau·lo·phone** \-fōn\ *n* -s [*keraulophon* fr. G, fr. E *keraulophone*; *keraulophone* fr. Gk *keras* horn + *aulos* reed instrument like an oboe + E *-phone* — more at HORN, ALVEOLUS] : a labial pipe-organ stop of 8-foot pitch having metal pipes

**kerauno-** *comb form* [Gk — more at CERAUN-] : thunder

**ke·rau·no·graph** \kə'rȯnə,graf, -rȧf\ *n* [ISV *kerauno-* + *-graph*] **1** : a figure impressed by lightning upon a body or material **2** : CERAUNOGRAPH — **ke·rau·no·graph·ic** \=¦==¦grafik\ *adj* — **ker·au·nog·ra·phy** \,kerə'nägrəfē\ *n* -ES

**kerb** \'kərb\ *n* -s [by alter.] *Brit* : CURB 5 g, 6

**ker·bau** \'kər,bau̇\ *n* -s [Malay] *in Malaysia* : WATER BUFFALO; *esp* : a usu. black wide-horned variety of Siamese origin used chiefly in rice cultivation

**¹kerch** \'kərch\ *n* -ES [ME *kerche*, short for *kerchef*] : KERCHIEF 1a

**²kerch** \'kerch\ *adj, usu cap* [fr. *Kerch*, Crimea, U.S.S.R.] : of or from the city of Kerch, U.S.S.R. : of the kind or style prevalent in Kerch

**ker·cher** \'kəchə(r)\ *n* -s [ME *kevercher*, *kercher*, modif. of MF *cuevrechief*, *cuerchief*] *dial Eng* : HANDKERCHIEF

**¹ker·chief** \'kərchə̇f, 'kəch-, 'kəich-, -,chē|\ *n, pl* **kerchiefs** *also* **ker·chieves** \|fs, |vz; *see pl at* HANDKERCHIEF\ [ME *courchef*, *kerchef*, *coverchief*, fr. OF *cuevrechef*, *couvrechef*, *cuerchief*, fr. *covrir* to cover + *chief*, *chef* head — more at COVER, CHIEF] **1 a** : a square of cloth worn usu. folded by women as a head covering **b** : a similar cloth worn about the neck or shoulders **2** : HANDKERCHIEF 1

kerchief 1a

**²kerchief** \"\ *vt* -ED/-ING/-S : to put a kerchief over ⟨~*ed* her hair before going out into the rain⟩

**ker·chief·like** \-f,līk\ *adj* : resembling a kerchief

**¹ker·choo** \kə'chü\ *n* -s [imit.] : the characteristic sound of a person sneezing

**²kerchoo** *vi* -ED/-ING/-S : to make a kerchoo

**ke·re** *or* **qe·re** \kə'rē\ *also* **qre** \'krē\ *n* -s [Heb *qĕrī* imper. of *qārā'* to read] : a reading that in the traditional

Jewish mode of reading the Hebrew Bible is substituted for one actually standing in the consonantal text with the consonants of the word or phrase to be read being usu. given in the margin and the vowel points if the text is vocalized being inserted in the text — called also *keri;* compare KETHIB

**ke·rek** \kəˈrek\ *n, pl* **kerek** *or* **kereks** *usu cap* **1 a :** a people constituting a small branch of the Kamchadal-Koryak ethnic group **b :** a member of such people **2 :** the language of the Kerek containing elements of Eskimo

**kere per·pe·tu·um** \-pə(r)ˈpechəwəm\ *n* [NL, lit., perpetual kere] **:** a kere which is always substituted for a particular word in the Hebrew Bible and whose consonants are not written in the margin but are supplied by the reader from memory

**ke·res** \ˈkā,rās\ *n, pl* **keres** *usu cap* **1 a :** a Pueblo people of New Mexico including the Acoma, Cochiti, Laguna, San Felipe, Santa Ana, Santo Domingo, and Sia **b :** a member of the Keres people **2 :** the language of the Keres people constituting the Keresan family

**ker·e·san** \ˈkerəsən\ *n, pl* **keresan** *usu cap* **:** a language family consisting of Keres only and having no close relationship to any other language group

**ke·re·wa** \kəˈrāwə\ *n, pl* **kerewa** *or* **kerewas** *usu cap* **1 a :** a Papuan people on the Gulf of Papua **b :** a member of such people **2 :** the language of the Kerewa people

**¹kerf** \ˈkərf, ˈkə̄f\ *n* -s [ME *kirf, kerf* (also, action of cutting), fr. OE *cyrf* action of cutting, something cut off; akin to MHG *kerbe, kerp* notch, OE *ceorfan* to carve — more at CARVE] **1 a :** a slit or notch made in cutting usu. by a saw or cutting torch **b :** the width of cut that a saw or cutting torch makes in wood or other material **2 :** GROOVE 2a(4) **3 :** a deep narrow cut in a face of coal (as to facilitate mining or to remove clay or dirt seams)

**²kerf** \"\ *vt* -ED/-ING/-S **:** to make a kerf in esp. by sawing; *specif* **:** to cut (as a beam) transversely along the underside in order to permit bending

**kerf graft** *n* **:** a graft similar to a cleft graft except that the cut in the stock is made with a saw

**ker·flop** \kə(r)ˈfläp\ *adv* [*ker-* + *flop*] **:** with or as if with a flop

**ker·gue·len cabbage** \ˈkərgələn-, ¦kərgə¦len-\ *n, usu cap K* [fr. *Kerguelen* island in the southern Indian ocean] **:** an herb (*Pringlea antiscorbutica*) of the family Cruciferae of the island of Kerguelen that is unique in its family in being wind-pollinated

**ke·ri** *or* **qe·ri** \kəˈrē\ *also* **k'ri** *or* **kri** *or* **q'ri** *or* **qri** \ˈkrē\ *n* -s [Heb *qĕri* — more at KERE] **:** KERE

**ke·ri·ah** \kəˈrēə\ *n, pl* **keri·oth** *or* **keri·ot** \-ē,ōt(h), -ōs\ [Heb *qĕrīʿāh*] **:** the traditional act or ceremony among Jews of rending one's garment at the funeral of a near relative as a symbol of mourning

**ke·ri·on** \ˈkirē,än\ *n* -s [NL, fr. Gk *kērion* honeycomb — more at CERION] **:** inflammatory ringworm of the hair follicles of the beard and scalp usu. accompanied by secondary bacterial infection and marked by spongy swelling and the exudation of sticky pus from the hair follicles

**keri perpetuum** *n* [NL, lit., perpetual keri] **:** KERE PERPETUUM

**ker·lock** \ˈkəələk\ *dial Eng var of* CHARLOCK

**kerman** *usu cap, var of* KIRMAN

**ker·man·ji** \kə(r)ˈmänjē\ *n* -s *cap* [Kurdish] **1 :** the western dialect of the Kurdish language spoken in the region of eastern Turkey **2 :** the Kurdish language

**¹ker·man·shah** \¦kərmən¦shä, kərˈmän,-\ *adj, usu cap* [fr. *Kermanshah,* Iran] **:** of or from the city of Kermanshah, Iran **:** of the kind or style prevalent in Kermanshah

**²kermanshah** *usu cap, var of* KIRMANSHAH

**³kermanshah** \"\ *n* -s *often cap* **:** COCONUT 4

**ker·mes** \ˈkər(,)mēz, -,məs; kərˈmes; *in sense 1b* ˈkər(,)mēz\ *n* [F *kermès,* fr. Ar *qirmiz* — more at CRIMSON] **1 a** *pl* **kermes :** the dried bodies of the females of various scales (genus *Kermes*) that are found on the kermes oak of the Mediterranean region, are round and about the size of a pea, and constitute the oldest dyestuff known producing a red color resembling but much inferior to that of cochineal **b** *cap* [NL, fr. F *kermès* or E *kermes*] **:** a genus (the type of the family Kermesidae) of scales comprising those that form kermes and various related No. American and Australian scales **2** *pl* **kermes :** KERMES MINERAL **3** *or* **kermes scarlet** *pl* **kermes :** a somewhat variable color averaging scarlet

**ker·mes·ite** \ˈkərmē,zīt, -mə,sīt; kərˈme,sīt\ *n* -s [F *kermésite,* fr. *kermès* + *-ite*] **:** a mineral $Sb_2S_2O$ consisting of antimony oxysulfide occurring usu. as tufts of cherry-red capillary crystals and resulting from the alteration of stibnite

**kermes mineral** *also* **kermes** *n* **:** a soft brown-red powder consisting essentially of antimony trisulfide and antimony trioxide and used formerly as an alterative, diaphoretic, and emetic

**kermes oak** *also* **kermes** *n* **:** a dwarf often shrubby evergreen oak (*Quercus coccinea*) of the Mediterranean region that is the host of the kermes insect and has a bark rich in tannin

**ker·mis** \ˈkərməs, ˈke(ə)rm-\ *or* **ker·mess** \", kərˈmes\ *or* **kir·mess** \kərˈmes\ *n* -ES [D *kermis,* fr. MD *kercmisse, kermisse,* fr. *kerke, kerc* church + *misse* mass, church festival] **1 :** a local outdoor festival of the Low Countries orig. held annually on the feast day of the local patron saint **2 :** an entertainment and fair usu. given for the purpose of raising money

**¹kern** \ˈkərn, ˈkə̄n\ *vb* -ED/-ING/-S [ME *curnen, kernen,* fr. (assumed) OE *cyrnen,* fr. OE *corn* — more at CORN] *vi, dial Eng* **:** to form kernels ⟨good weather for the grain to ~⟩ ~ *vt, dial Eng* **:** to form or set (as a crop of fruit) ⟨trees that had ~*ed* their best crop in years⟩

**²kern** \"\ *n* -s *dial Eng* **:** KERNEL, GRAIN ⟨~ of corn⟩ ⟨~*s* of sand⟩

**³kern** \"\ *also* **kerne** \", ˈke(ə)rn, ˈkeən\ *n* -s [ME *kerne,* fr. MIr *cethern* band of soldiers, fr. *cath* battle, fr. OIr; akin to Gaulish *catu-* battle, W *cad,* OE *heatho-,* OHG *hadu-,* ON *hōth-* battle, Skt *śatru* enemy] **1 :** a foot soldier; *esp* **:** a light-armed soldier of medieval Ireland or Scotland ⟨those rough rugheaded ~*s* —Shak.⟩ — compare GALLOWGLASS **2 :** a rude or boorish countryman esp. from Scotland or Ireland

**⁴kern** \ˈkərn, ˈkə̄n\ *chiefly dial var of* KIRN

**⁵kern** \", ˈkəin\ *n* -s [modif. of F *carne* corner, projecting angle, fr. F dial. (Picardy & Normandy), fr. L *cardin-, cardo* hinge — more at CARDINAL] **1 :** a part of the face of a typecast letter that projects beyond the body (as the upper or lower extremity of *f* or the tail of *Q*) **2 :** a corresponding part of a printed letter

**⁶kern** \"\ *vb* -ED/-ING/-S *vt* **1 :** to form with a kern (as a letter) **2 :** to smooth (type) about the kern ~ *vi* **:** to become kerned — used of a letter or some part of a letter

**⁷kern** \"\ *n* -s [G, core, kernel, nucleus, fr. OHG *kerno;* akin to ON *kjarni* kernel, core, OE *corn*] **:** NUCLEUS 2*l*

**¹ker·nel** \ˈkərnᵊl, ˈkə̄n-,ˈkəin-\ *n* -s [ME *curnel, kirnel, kernel,* fr. OE *cyrnel,* dim. of *corn* grain, seed — more at CORN] **1** *chiefly dial* **:** a fruit seed ⟨beaten . . . for picking a ~ out of a pomegranate —Shak.⟩ **2 :** the inner portion of a seed within the integuments — usu. used of edible seeds and of the contents of the endocarp in nuts, drupes, and similar fruits ⟨peach ~*s*⟩ ⟨as brown in hue as hazelnuts, and sweeter than ~*s* —Shak.⟩ **3 :** a whole grain or seed of a cereal ⟨~ of corn⟩ ⟨wheat and barley ~*s*⟩ **4** *chiefly dial* **a :** a hard swelling under the surface of the skin **b :** a small gland or body resembling a gland **5 :** a central or essential part: as **a :** the gist of a concept or idea ⟨a ~ of recognizable truth . . . which commands respect —*Wall Street Jour.*⟩ ⟨the ~ of this argument is made out to be a mere matter of logic —O.P.Wood⟩ ⟨recent tendency to regard myth, ritual, and magic as the ~ instead of the husk of religion —W.R.Inge⟩ **b :** the core of a structure or organization ⟨its position as a world power and the ~ of a great empire —Vera M. Dean⟩ **6 :** ¹CORE 1*t*

**²kernel** \"\ *vb* **kerneled** *or* **kernelled; kerneled** *or* **kernelled; kerneling** *or* **kernelling; kernels** [ME *kyrnellen,* fr. *curnel, kirnel, kernel,* n.] *vi* **:** to form or produce kernels **:** ripen into kernels ~ *vt* **:** to envelop or enclose as a kernel ⟨great artist ~*ed* in the . . . man of the world —Osbert Sitwell⟩

**³kernel** \"\ *vt* **kerneled** *or* **kernelled; kerneled** *or* **kernelled; kerneling** *or* **kernelling; kernels** [ME *kernelen,* fr. MF *querneler, kerneler,* var. of *creneler* — more at CRENEL] **:** CRENELLATE

**ker·neled** *or* **ker·nelled** \-ᵊld\ *adj* [¹*kernel* + *-ed*] **:** having a kernel ⟨farms in this section produce a red ~ corn —*Amer. Guide Series: Pa.*⟩

**ker·nel·late** \ˈkərnᵊl,āt\ *vt* -ED/-ING/-S [ML *kernellatus,* past part. of *kernellare,* fr. ME *kernelen*] **:** CRENELLATE

**ker·nel·ly** \ˈkərnᵊlē\ *adj* [¹*kernel* + *-y*] **1 :** having kernels or many kernels **2 :** resembling kernels

**kernel smut** *n* **:** COVERED SMUT

**kernel spot** *n* **:** a disease of the pecan kernel caused by a fungus (*Coniothyrium caryogenum*) and characterized by irregularly roundish dull brown spots

**ker·nic·ter·us** \kə(r)ˈniktərəs\ *n* -ES [NL, fr. G *kern* core, kernel, nucleus + NL *icterus* — more at KERN] **:** a condition marked by the deposit of bile pigments in the nuclei of the brain and spinal cord and by degeneration of nerve cells that occurs usu. in infants as a part of the syndrome of erythroblastosis fetalis

**ker·nig sign** \ˈkərnig-\ *or* **kernig's sign** *n, usu cap K* [after Vladimir *Kernig* †1917 Russ. physician] **:** an indication usu. present in meningitis that consists of pain and resistance on attempting to extend the leg at the knee with the thigh flexed at the hip

**kerning** *pres part of* KERN

**kern·ite** \ˈkər,nīt\ *n* -s [fr. *Kern* co., Calif. + E *-ite*] **:** a mineral $Na_2B_4O_7.4H_2O$ that consists of a hydrous sodium borate occurring in colorless to white crystals and cleavage masses and that is an important source of borax — called also *rasorite*

**ker·nos** \ˈkər,näs\ *n, pl* **ker·noi** \-nȯi\ [Gk] **:** an ancient Greek vessel consisting of several small cups joined on a pottery ring or attached to the rim of a vase

kernos in cross section

**kern river indian** \ˈkərn-\ *n, usu cap K&R&I* [fr. the *Kern river,* in California] **:** an Indian of the Tübatulabal or a related people living on the Kern river in California

**kern river trout** *n, usu cap K&R* [fr. the *Kern river* in California] **:** a variety of rainbow trout occurring only in the Kern river in California

**kerns** *pres 3d sing of* KERN, *pl of* KERN

**ker·o·gen** \ˈkerəjən, -,jen\ *n* -s [Gk *kēros* wax + E *-gen* — more at CEREUS] **:** bituminous material occurring esp. in oil shale and yielding oil when heated — **ke·rog·e·nous** \kəˈräjənəs\ *adj*

**ker·o·sine** *or* **ker·o·sene** \ˈkerə,sēn, ˈkar-, ,==ˈ=\ *n* -s [*kerosine* alter. of *kerosene; kerosene* fr. Gk *kēros* wax + E *-ene* (as in *camphene*); fr. the use of paraffin in its manufacture — more at CEREUS] **:** a flammable hydrocarbon oil that is less volatile than gasoline, that is usu. obtained by distillation of petroleum, and that is used for burning in lamps and heaters or furnaces, as a fuel or fuel component for jet engines, and as a solvent or thinner (as in insecticide emulsions or paints) — see LAMP illustration

**ker·plunk** \kə(r)ˈpləŋk\ *adv* [imit.] **:** with a loud dull sound **:** with a thud ⟨a coconut which fell ~ at his feet⟩

**kerrana** *var of* KERANA

**kerr cell** \ˈkär-, ˈkər-\ *n, usu cap K* [after John *Kerr* †1907 Scot. physicist] **:** a cell that contains electrodes immersed in nitrobenzene or other liquid, that exhibits double refraction in a high degree and with short time lag, and that is used in devices where the intensity of light is to be changed rapidly in accordance with the voltage applied to the electrodes (as in the recording of sound tracks for motion pictures) — compare KERR EFFECT 1

**kerr effect** *n, usu cap K* [after John *Kerr*] **1 :** the production of double refraction in various dielectrics when placed in a strong electric field **2 :** the rotation of the plane of polarization when plane-polarized light is reflected from the end of a magnet

**¹ker·ria** \ˈkerēə\ *n* [NL, fr. William *Kerr* †1814 Eng. gardener + NL *-ia*] **1** *cap* **:** a genus of Chinese shrubs (family Rosaceae) with solitary yellow often double flowers **2** -s **:** any shrub of the genus *Kerria*

**²kerria** \"\ *n, cap* [NL, fr. Robert *Kerr* †1813 Eng. scientific writer + NL *-ia*] **:** a genus of aquatic New World oligochaete worms

**ker·rie** \ˈkerē\ *n* -s **:** KNOBKERRIE

**ker·ril** \ˈkerəl\ *n* -s [native name in India] **:** a sea snake (*Kerilia jerdoni*) of the Asiatic coast from the Persian gulf to Japan

**¹kerry** \ˈkerē, -ri\ *adj, usu cap* [fr. County *Kerry,* Ireland] **:** of or from County Kerry, Ireland **:** of the kind or style prevalent in County Kerry

**²kerry** \"\ *n, usu cap* **1 :** an Irish breed of small hardy long-lived black cattle noted for their milk **2** -ES *often cap* **:** an animal of the Kerry breed

**kerry blue terrier** *n* **1** *usu cap K & B & T* **:** an Irish breed of medium-sized terriers of uncertain ancestry that has a long head, a deep chest, and a silky coat of blue of any shade, stands about 18 inches high, and weighs from 30 to 38 pounds **2** *usu cap K* **:** a dog of the Kerry blue terrier breed

**kerry hill** *n, usu cap K&H* [fr. *Kerry Hill* in Kerry, town in Wales] **:** a breed of hardy English mutton-type sheep

**kers** \ˈkərs, ˈkärs\ *dial var of* CRESS

**ker·sen·neh** \kə(r)ˈsenə\ *also* **ker·san·né** \-sanä\ *n* -s [Ar *kirsannah*] **:** ERS

**¹ker·sey** \ˈkərzē, ˈkə̄z-, -zi\ *n, pl* **kerseys** *also* **kersies** [ME, fr. *Kersey,* village in Suffolk, Eng.] **1 a :** a coarse ribbed woolen cloth for hose and work clothes woven first in medieval England **b :** a heavy wool or wool and cotton fabric made in plain or twill weave with a smooth surface and used esp. for uniforms and coats **2 :** a garment of kersey

**²kersey** \"\ *adj* **1 :** made of kersey **2** *obs* **:** HOMESPUN

**ker·sey·mere** \ˈ==,mi(ə)r, -iə\ *n* -s [alter. (influenced by ¹*kersey*) of *cassimere*] **:** a fine woolen fabric with a close nap made in fancy twill weaves

**ker·u·ing** \ˈkerəwiŋ\ *n* -s [Malay *kĕruing*] **:** APITONG

**ke·ryg·ma** \kəˈrigmə, kēˈ-\ *also* **ke·rug·ma** \-rəg-\ *n, pl* **kerygma·ta** *also* **kerugma·ta** \-mədə\ [Gk *kērygma,* fr. *kēryssein* to proclaim, preach] **1 :** the preaching or proclamation of the Christian gospel esp. in the form found in the primitive Christian church **2 :** the original Christian gospel preached by the apostles

**ker·yg·mat·ic** \¦kerig¦mad·ik\ *adj* [Gk *kērygmat-, kērygma* + E *-ic*] **:** of, relating to, or based upon the kerygma

**ker·yl** \ˈkerəl\ *n* -s [*kerosine* + *-yl*] **:** a mixture of alkyl radicals that is derived from kerosine specially purified for making sulfonated anionic detergents and that consists chiefly of one or more radicals ranging in size from decyl to tetradecyl or hexadecyl ⟨condensation of ~ chloride with benzene yields keryl-benzene⟩

**ke·rys·tic** \kəˈristik, kēˈ-\ *adj* [fr. (assumed) Gk *kērystos* (verbal of Gk *kēryssein* to preach) + E *-ic*] **:** HOMILETIC

**ke·sar** \ˈkāzə(r)\ *archaic var of* KAISER

**kest** \ˈkest\ *dial Brit var of* CAST

**kes·trel** \ˈkestrəl\ *n* -s [ME *castrel,* fr. MF *cresserele, crecerelle, quercelle,* fr. *crecelle, cresselle* rattle, fr. (assumed) VL *crepicella,* alter. (influenced by L *crepare* to crack, rattle) of L *crepitacillum,* fr. *crepitare* to rattle, crackle — more at CREPITATE] **:** a common small European falcon (*Falco tinnunculus*) that is noted for its habit of hovering in the air against a wind, is about a foot long, and is bluish gray above in the male and reddish brown in the female; *broadly* **:** any of various related small Old World falcons — compare SPARROW HAWK

**¹ket** \ˈket\ *n, pl* **ket** [ME, flesh, meat, of Scand origin; akin to ON *kjöt* flesh, meat, OSw *köt, kiot, kiöt;* perh. akin to Skt *guda* bowel, rectum — more at COT] **1** *dial Brit* **a :** CARRION **b :** FILTH, RUBBISH **2** *dial Brit* **:** a good-for-nothing person

**²ket** \"\ *n, pl* **ket** [prob. alter. of ³*cot*] *Scot* **:** a fleece of wool

**³ket** \"\ *n, pl* **ket** *or* **kets** *cap* **1 a :** a people of the middle Yenisei region of Siberia that constitutes the only western Paleo-Asiatic group **b :** a member of such people **2 :** the Yeniseian language of the Ket people

**ket-** *or* **keto-** *comb form* [ISV, fr. *ketone*] **1** *usu* **keto- a :** containing the ketone group ⟨*keto*hexose⟩ — in names of classes of compounds; compare ALD- 1 **b :** containing a ketone group regarded as formed by replacement of two hydrogen atoms in a methylene group by oxygen — in names of specific organic compounds ⟨*keto*propionic acid⟩; compare OXO- **c** *usu ital* **:** containing an unmodified ketone group — in names of open-chain ketonic forms of specific sugars ⟨*keto*-D-fructose⟩ — compare ALDEHYDO- 1 **2 :** related to a ketone ⟨*ket*oxime⟩ — compare ALD- 2

**ke·ta** \ˈkēd·ə\ *n* -s [Russ] **:** DOG SALMON 1

**ke·tal** \ˈkē,tal\ *n* -s [*ket-* + *-al*] **:** an acetal derived from a ketone

**ket·a·pang** \ˈked·ə,paŋ\ *n* -s [Malay *kĕtapang*] **:** a low-grade variety of gutta

**ke·ta·zine** \ˈkēd·ə,zēn, -zᵊn\ *n* [ISV *ket-* + *azine*] **:** an azine $R_2C{=}NN{=}CR_2$ formed from a ketone

**ketch** \ˈkech\ *n* -ES [alter. of earlier *catch,* fr. ME *cache,* prob. fr. *cacchen* to chase, catch — more at CATCH] **:** a fore-and-aft-rigged boat similar to a yawl but having a larger mizzen and having the mizzenmast stepped farther forward typically of the rudderhead or of the after end of the waterline

ketch

**ketchup** *var of* CATSUP

**ket·e·lee·ria** \,ked·ᵊlˈirēə\ *n, cap* [NL, fr. J.B.*Keteleer,* 19th cent. Belgian gardener + NL *-ia*] **:** a genus of Asiatic conifers (family Pinaceae) that resemble firs and have persistent cone scales and keeled upper leaf surfaces

**ket·em·bil·la** \,ked·əmˈbilə\ *or* **kit·am·bil·la** \,kid-·\ *n* -s [Singhalese *kätämbilla*] **1 :** a hairy purple acid tropical fruit that is used esp. for preserves and is closely related to the kei apple **2 :** a small shrubby tree (*Dovyalis hebecarpa*) of the family Flacourtiaceae that is native to Ceylon and is cultivated in various tropical areas for the ketembillas it bears

**ke·tene** \ˈkē,tēn\ *n* -s [ISV *ket-* + *-ene;* orig. formed as G *keten*] **:** a colorless poisonous gaseous compound $CH_2{=}C{=}O$ of penetrating odor that is made by pyrolysis of acetic acid or acetone and used as an acetylating agent (as in making acetic anhydride from acetic acid or acetic esters from alcohols); *also* **:** any of various derivatives of this compound — see DIKETENE

**ke·thib** *or* **ke·thibh** *also* **ke·thiv** *or* **ke·tib** *or* **k'thib** *or* **kthib** *or* **k'thibh** *or* **kthibh** \kəˈt(h)ēv\ *n* -s [Heb *kĕthībh,* fr. Aram, written] **:** a reading in the consonantal text of the Hebrew Bible for which in traditional Jewish practice there is substituted a different reading whose consonants are usu. given in the margin — compare KERE

**kethubah** *var of* KETUBAH

**ke·ti·mine** \ˈkēd·ə,mēn, -,mən\ *n* [ISV *ket-* + *imine*] **:** a Schiff base of the general formula $R_2C{=}NH$ or $R_2C{=}NR'$ formed by condensation of a ketone with ammonia or a primary amine

**ke·to** \ˈkēd·(,)ō, -ē(,)tō\ *adj* [*ket-*] **:** of or relating to a ketone **:** being or containing the ketone group — compare OXO

**keto-** — see KET-

**keto acid** *n* **:** a compound that is both a ketone and an acid ⟨acetoacetic acid is a beta *keto acid*⟩

**ke·to·bem·i·done** \,kēd·ōˈbemə,dōn\ *n* -s [*ket-* + *car*bethoxy + methyl + *-id* + *-one*] **:** a narcotic ketone $C_{15}H_{21}NO_2$ related chemically to meperidine

**ke·to-enol tautomerism** \ˈkēd·ō+ . . . -\ *n* [*ket-* + *enol*] **:** tautomerism in which the keto and enol forms of a compound (as ethyl acetoacetate) are in equilibrium

**ke·to·gen·e·sis** \¦kēd·ō+\ *n* [NL, fr. *ket-* + L *genesis*] **:** the production of ketone bodies (as in diabetes and other conditions of impaired metabolism)

**ke·to·genic** \¦kēd·əˈjenik\ *adj* [ISV *ket-* + *-genic*] **:** producing ketone bodies

**ketogenic diet** *n* **:** a diet that supplies a large amount of fat and minimal amounts of carbohydrate and protein and that is used esp. in epilepsy to produce a ketosis and alter the degree of bodily alkalinity

**ke·to·glutaric acid** \¦kēd·ō+(,)=¦== . . . -\ *n* [ISV *ket-* + *glutaric*] **:** either of two crystalline keto derivatives of glutaric acid; *esp* **:** the alpha keto isomer $HOOCCH_2CH_2COCOOH$ formed in various metabolic processes (as the Krebs cycle and transaminations involving glutamic acid)

**ke·to·heptose** \"+\ *n* [*ket-* + *heptose*] **:** a heptose of a ketonic nature — see HEPTULOSE

**ke·to·hexose** \"+\ *n* [ISV *ket-* + *hexose*] **:** a hexose (as fructose or sorbose) of a ketonic nature — see HEXULOSE

**ke·tol** \ˈkē,tōl, -tōl\ *n* -s [ISV *ket-* + *-ol*] **:** a compound (as an acyloin) that is both a ketone and an alcohol **:** HYDROXY KETONE

**ke·tol·y·sis** \kēˈtäləsəs\ *n* [NL, fr. *ket-* + *-lysis*] **:** the decomposition of ketones

**ke·to·lyt·ic** \¦kēd·əˈlid·ik\ *adj* [ISV *ket-* + *-lytic*] **:** of, relating to, or characterized by ketolysis

**ke·tone** \ˈkē,tōn\ *n* -s [G *keton,* alter. of *azeton* acetone — more at ACETONE] **:** any of a class of organic compounds (as acetone) that are characterized by a carbonyl group attached to two carbon atoms usu. contained in hydrocarbon radicals (as in the general formula RCOR) or in a single bivalent radical and that are similar to aldehydes but are less reactive

**ketone body** *n* **:** any of the three compounds acetoacetic acid, acetone, and beta-hydroxybutyric acid recognized as products of fatty-acid catabolism and found in the blood and urine in abnormal amounts in diabetes mellitus and other conditions of impaired metabolism — called also *acetone body*

**ketone group** *n* **:** the characteristic group of ketones consisting of carbonyl attached to two carbon atoms

**ke·to·ne·mia** *or* **ke·to·nae·mia** \,kēd·əˈnēmēə\ *n* -s [NL, fr. ISV *ketone* + NL *-emia, -aemia*] **1 :** a condition marked by an abnormal increase of ketone bodies in the circulating blood **2 :** KETOSIS 2 — **ke·to·ne·mic** \¦==¦nēmik\ *adj*

**ke·ton·ic** \kēˈtänik\ *adj* [ISV *ketone* + *-ic*] **:** relating to, containing, or derived from a ketone

**ke·ton·imine** \¦kē,tōn+\ *n* [ISV *ketone* + *imine*] **:** KETIMINE — used esp. of dyes

**ke·to·nize** \ˈkē,tō,nīz\ *vb* -ED/-ING/-S [*ketone* + *-ize*] *vt* **:** to convert into a ketone ~ *vi* **:** to become converted into a ketone

**ke·to·nu·ria** \,kēd·əˈn(y)u̇rēə\ *n* -s [NL, fr. ISV *ketone* + NL *-uria*] **:** the presence in man and domestic animals of excess ketone bodies in the urine (as in diabetes mellitus, starvation acidosis, or other conditions involving reduced or disturbed carbohydrate metabolism)

**ke·tose** \ˈkē,tōs\ *n* -s [ISV *ket-* + *-ose*] **:** a sugar (as fructose or sorbose) containing one ketone group per molecule — contrasted with *aldose;* see MONOSACCHARIDE

**ke·to·side** \ˈkēd·ə,sīd\ *n* -s [*ket-* + *glycoside*] **:** a glycoside that on hydrolysis yields a ketose

**ke·to·sis** \kēˈtōsəs\ *n, pl* **keto·ses** \-ō,sēz\ [NL, fr. *ket-* + *-osis*] **1 :** an abnormal increase of ketone bodies in the body in conditions of reduced or disturbed carbohydrate metabolism (as in uncontrolled diabetes mellitus) **2 :** a nutritional disease of cattle and sometimes sheep, goats, or swine that is marked by reduction of blood sugar and the presence of ketone bodies in the blood, tissues, milk, and urine, that is associated with digestive and nervous disturbances, that usu. results from long-continued feeding of coarse rations low in available sugar or from liver inefficiency associated with vitamin A deficiency, and that is esp. likely to occur in heavy milkers shortly after parturition — compare MILK FEVER 2a

**ke·to·steroid** \¦kēd·ō+\ *n* [ISV *ket-* + *steroid*] **:** a steroid (as androsterone, cortisone, or estrone) containing a ketone group ⟨excretion of 17-*ketosteroids* in the urine⟩

**ke·tot·ic** \kēˈtäd·ik\ *adj* [fr. NL *ketosis,* after such pairs as NL *hypnosis:* E *hypnotic*] **:** of or relating to ketosis **:** affected with ketosis

**ke·tox·ime** \kēˈtäk,sēm\ *n* [ISV *ket-* + *oxime*] **:** an oxime of a ketone

**ket·tle** \ˈke\|d·ᵊl, \|tᵊl, ÷ ˈki\|; *some who have* ¦ki\| *in "teakettle" and/or "kettle of fish" have* ¦ke\| *in other contexts*\ *n* -s [ME *ketel,* fr. ON *ketill;* akin to OE *cietel* kettle, OHG *kezzil,* Goth *katilē* (gen. pl.); all fr. a prehistoric Gmc word borrowed fr. L *catillus* small bowl, dish, dim. of *catinus* bowl, pot; perh. akin to Gk *kotylē* cup, small vessel] **1 a** (1) : a metallic vessel in which liquids or semifluid masses are boiled; *esp* : TEAKETTLE (2) : a cooking utensil with a bail handle **b** : a quantity cooked in a kettle at one time ⟨could eat a whole ~ of stew⟩ **2 a** *obs* : KETTLEDRUM 1 ⟨let the ~ to the trumpet speak —Shak.⟩ **b** : the metallic bowl of a kettledrum across which the parchment head is stretched **3 a** : POTHOLE **b** : a steep-sided hollow without surface drainage esp. in a deposit of glacial drift and often containing a lake or swamp **4** *North* : a shallow metal pail ⟨dinner ~⟩

**kettle base** *adj* : ²BOMBÉ

**kettle-bottomed** \ˈ==ˌ==\ *adj, of a ship* : having a flat hull

**kettledrum** \ˈ==ˌ=\ *n* **1** : a percussion instrument that consists of a hollow brass or copper hemisphere with a parchment head the tension of which can be changed by hand screws or foot pedal to vary the pitch, that is played with a pair of sticks with large padded heads, and that is used in pairs, threes, or fours of different sizes in both orchestra and concert band — see TIMPANI **2** *obs* : KETTLEDRUMMER **3** : an informal party at which light refreshments are usu. served

kettledrum 1

**ket·tle·drum·mer** \"ə(r)\ *n* : one that plays the kettledrums

**kettle front** *adj* : ²BOMBÉ

**ket·tle·man** \ˈ==mən\ *n, pl* **kettlemen** : an industrial worker who melts, cooks, or dyes substances in a heated container: as **a** : a brewery worker who makes the wort that is the basis for beer **b** : one who refines impure lead to secure a commercial grade **c** : one who cooks the ingredients of paints, varnishes, or oils **d** : BURNER MAN

**kettle of fish** *see* KETTLE\ **1** : a bad state of affairs : MESS, PREDICAMENT ⟨here's a pretty how-de-do, here's a pretty *kettle of fish* —W.S.Gilbert⟩ **2** : a thing to be considered or reckoned with : MATTER, AFFAIR ⟨books and discs . . . were two very different *kettles of fish* —Roland Gelatt⟩ ⟨a far different *kettle of fish* from the fictionalized life stories of Hollywood —Lee Rogow⟩

**ket·tler** \ˈke|d·ᵊlə(r), |t(ᵊ)lə-, ÷ˈki|\ *n* -s : a textile worker who prepares gums for use in mixing printing colors

**ket·tle stitch** \ˈked·ᵊl-, -etᵊl-\ *n* [part trans. of G *kettelstich*, fr. *kettel* small chain (dim. of *kette* chain, fr. OHG *ketīna*, fr. L *catena*) + *stich* stitch — more at CHAIN] *bookbinding* : a knot formed in the sewing thread at the ends of the sections to hold them together — called also *catch stitch*

**ke·tu·bah** *or* **ke·thu·bah** \ˌke,t(h)üˈvä, kəˈsüvə\ *n, pl* **ketuboth** *or* **ketu·bot** \-,t(h)üˈvōt(h), -ˈsü,v-, -ōs\ *or* **ketubahs** *or* **kethuboth** *or* **kethubot** *or* **kethubahs** [Heb *kĕthūbhāh* document] : a formal Jewish marriage contract that provides for a money settlement payable to the wife in the event of divorce or at the husband's death

**ke·tu·pa** \kəˈtüpə\ *n* [NL, prob. fr. Malay *kĕtupok* fish owl] **1** *cap* : a genus of large chiefly tropical owls that is closely related to *Bubo* and contains various fish owls **2** -s : FISH OWL

**ke·tyl** \ˈkēd·ᵊl\ *n* -s [*ket-* + *-yl*] : any of a class of unstable compounds made by treating ketones with a metal (as sodium)

**keuper** \ˈkȯipə(r)\ *adj, usu cap* [G] : of or relating to the upper division of the German Trias — see GEOLOGIC TIME table

**keur·boom** \ˈkər,büm\ *also* **keur** \ˈkər\ *n* -s [Afrik *keurboom*, fr. *keur* choice + *boom* tree] : a pinnate-leaved shrub (*Virgilia capensis*) of southern Africa having purple flowers and being of the family Leguminosae

**KEV** *abbr, often not cap* kilo electron volt

**ke·va·lin** \ˈkāvələn\ *n* -s [Skt, fr. *kevala* alone, pure, absolute — more at CELIBATE] *Jainism* : one who is set free from matter : a liberated soul

**keva·zin·go** \ˌkevəˈziŋ(ˌ)gō, ˌkāv-\ *also* **ke·wa·sin·go** \ˌkäwəˈsi-, -əˈzi-\ *or* **ke·wa·sin·ga** \-ŋgə\ *n* -s [native name in western Africa] **1** : any of various African bubingas of the genus *Copaifera* **2** : the wood of a kevazingo used esp. for decorative veneers

**¹kev·el** \ˈkevəl\ *or* **cav·el** \ˈkav-\ *n* -s [ME *kevile* pin, hasp, peg, fr. ONF *keville*, fr. L *clavicula* small key — more at CLAVICLE] : a strong timber, bollard, or cleat (as a cross timber in a bollard or a timber bolted across two stanchions)

**²kev·el** \ˈkevəl\ *n* -s [of Scand origin; akin to ON *kefli* stick of wood, *kafli* cut-off piece, Norw *kavle, kjevle* piece of wood, roller; akin to OFris *kavelia* to cast lots, MD *kavele* piece of wood for casting lots, Lith *žabas* branch, bunch of twigs] : CUDGEL, STAFF

**³kevel** \"\ *n* -s [ME *kevell*] : a hammer for roughly shaping or breaking stone

**ke·wee·naw·an** \ˈkēwē¦nȯən\ *adj, usu cap* [*Keweenaw* Point, Mich. + E *-an*] : of or relating to a division of the Proterozoic see GEOLOGIC TIME table

**kew·pie** \ˈkyüpē, -pi\ *n* -s [alter. of *cupid*] : a fairy conceived of as a good-natured chubby winged baby with a topknot of hair

**Kewpie** \"\ *trademark* — used for a small chubby doll with a topknot of hair

**kew weed** \ˈkyü-\ *n* [prob. fr. *Kew* Gardens (Royal Botanic Gardens), London, Eng.] : FRENCHWEED 2

**¹kex** \ˈkeks\ *n* -ES [ME] *dial chiefly Eng* : the dry stalk of various hollow-stemmed plants (as cow parsnip)

**²kex** \"\ *adj, dial Eng* : resembling kex : dry and hollow

**³kex** \"\ *n* -ES [Maya] : a Maya therapeutic rite in which an ailing person pledges an offering of food to the force or agency of his illness in return for his health

**¹key** \ˈkē\ *n* -s *often attrib* [ME *key, kay, keye*, fr. OE *cǣg, cǣge, cǣga*; akin to OFris *kēi, kāi* key, MLG *keie, keige* spear, and perh. to OHG *kīl* wedge — more at CHINE] **1 a** : an instrument usu. of metal so designed that it may be inserted in a lock in order to operate the bolt or catch **b** : a tool with a shaft that fits into printers' quoins and is rotated to tighten or loosen them **c** : a small metal piece with a slot in one end used to roll up a strip of metal (as on a can of sardines) or to roll up the body of a collapsible metal tube (as a tube of toothpaste) **2** : something that affords or prevents entrance, possession, or control **3 a** : something that serves to reveal or solve a problem, difficulty, or mystery ⟨the ~ to a riddle⟩ **b** : a simplified version that accompanies something as a clue to its explanation (as an outline map, a word-for-word translation, a book containing solutions to problems); *specif* : a list of words or phrases giving the value of symbols (as a pronunciation alphabet) **c** : an arrangement of the salient characters of a group of plants or animals or of species or genera for the purpose of determining the names and taxonomic relationships of unidentified members of a group **d** : the matter used to key an advertisement **e** : a map legend **4 keys** *pl* : spiritual authority in a Christian religion ⟨power of the ~s⟩; *specif* : the power or jurisdiction of the presidency in the Mormon Church **5** : a tool or device used to transfer, wind, or otherwise move usu. in order to secure or tighten: as **a** (1) : COTTER PIN (2) : COTTER **b** : a keystone in an arch **c** : a wedge used to make a dovetail joint **d** : a wedge between two feathers to break a stone **e** : the last board laid in a floor **f** : a tapered block driven into a recess in a scarf joint between two timbers so as to draw them more firmly together **g** : a small wooden wedge that is forced into the dovetail joint at a corner of a stretcher frame of a painting in order to tighten the canvas **h** : a wedge used to split a tenon in a mortise or the upper end of a tool handle (as a hammer or ax) for the purpose of tightening **i** : any of the metal U-shaped devices used to secure the bands or cords in position in a bookbinder's sewing press **j** : a strip of wood inserted in a timber across the grain to prevent casting **k** : a small usu. metal parallel-sided piece that is flat or tapered on top and that is used for securing a part (as a pulley, crank, or hub) **6 a** : one of the levers (as a digital or pedal) of a keyboard musical instrument that actuates the mechanism and produces the tones **b** : a lever by which a vent is opened or closed in the side of a woodwind instrument (as a clarinet or bassoon) or a valve or piston is controlled in a brass instrument (as a French horn or trumpet) **c** : a depressible digital that serves as one unit of a keyboard and that works usu. by lever action to set in motion a character (as in a typewriter) or an escapement (as in some typesetting machines) **7** : SAMARA **8 a** : a leading, prominent, or critical individual or principle ⟨a ~ actor⟩ ⟨the ~ features of a new car⟩ **b** : a component of a liquid mixture that is being separated by fractional distillation ⟨the least volatile of these components is the heavy ~ and the most volatile is the light ~ —E.G.Scheibel⟩ **9** [trans. of ML *clavis*] **a** *obs* : the lowest note or keynote of a scale **b** (1) : a system of seven tones based on their relationship to a keynote or tonic; *specif* : the tonality of a scale (2) : the total harmonic and melodic relations of such a system **10 a** : characteristic style, tone, or intensity of thought, feeling, or action **b** : the tone or pitch of a voice ⟨speaking in a plaintive ~⟩ **c** : the pervading tone and intensity of color (as in a painting) **d** : the predominant tone of a photograph with respect to its lightness or darkness — compare HIGH-KEY, LOW-KEY **11** : a decoration or charm resembling a key **12 a** (1) : plastering forced between laths to hold the rest in place (2) : the hold that plaster has on a wall (3) : the roughness of a wall that causes plaster to adhere to it **b** : a hollow in a brick or tile to hold mortar **c** : the rough surface on the wrong side of a veneer to hold the glue **13 a** : a metallic lever for rapidly and easily opening and closing the circuit of telegraphic-station equipment **b** : a small switch for opening or closing an electric circuit **14** : a projecting portion used to prevent movement at a construction joint (as of a floor, wall, pavement, footing, dam) into the adjacent section **15** *or* **keymove** \ˈ=ˌ=\ : the first move in the solution of a chess problem or combination **16 a** : the control of a cryptographic process (as a code book, grille, cipher alphabet, or set of alphabets) **b** : the enciphering or deciphering instructions for a cryptogram: as (1) : the settings of a ciphering machine (2) : the column sequence of a transposition (3) : KEYING SEQUENCE (4) : KEY WORD (5) : KEY LETTER (6) : an element in a keying sequence — see PERIODIC KEY, PERIOD KEY, RUNNING KEY, SPECIFIC KEY, VIGENÈRE CIPHER **17** : KEYHOLE 4

keys 1a

**²key** \"\ *vb* -ED/-ING/-S [ME *keyen*, fr. *key, kay, keye*, n.] *vt* **1** : to lock with or as if with a key : FASTEN: as **a** : to secure by a key (as a hammerhead to a handle, a pulley on a shaft, plaster to lathing) **b** : to finish off (an arch) by inserting a keystone **c** : to expand and tighten (as a canvas stretcher on a painting) with keys **2 a** : to fix or determine the musical key of **b** : to regulate the musical pitch of ⟨~ the strings⟩ **c** : to control (a process) in cryptography ⟨in ~*ed* columnar transposition the column sequence is controlled by a key word⟩ — compare KEYING SEQUENCE **3** : to apply color to (as a painting) in a particular key **4** : HARMONIZE, ATTUNE ⟨remarks ~*ed* to a situation⟩ **5** : to transmit by means of a telegraph key **6** : to identify (a biological specimen) by means of a key **7** : to insert in (an advertisement) some direction or other matter intended to identify answers : apply a symbol to (an advertisement) by means of which identification is effected **8** : to produce or cause nervous tension in — used with *up* ⟨~*ed* up over an impending operation⟩ ~ *vi* : to use a key: as **a** : to permit of identification by means of a key — often used with *out* ⟨the specimen ~*s* out to a genus of common starfish⟩ **b** : to operate a telegraph key

**³key** \"\ *archaic var of* QUAY

**⁴key** \"\ *also* **kay** *like* ¹CAY\ *n* -s [modif. (influenced by ³*key*) of Sp *cayo*, fr. Lucayo *cayo*] : a low island or reef; *specif* : one of the coral islets off the southern coast of Florida

**key·age** \ˈkēij\ *archaic var of* QUAYAGE

**keyaki** *var of* KIAKI

**ke·yau·wee** \kəˈyaù(ˌ)wē\ *n, pl* **keyauwee** *or* **keyauwees** *usu cap* **1** : an extinct people of northern No. Carolina presumed to have been Siouan **2** : a member of the Keyauwee people

**keybank** \ˈ=ˌ=\ *n* : a rectangular set of keys comprising one of the removable setting-key units of a monotype keyboard

**key bargain** *n* : the terms of a collective agreement that set a precedent for other companies or industries

**key bed** *n, geol* : a distinctive stratum or group of strata that serves to facilitate correlation in field mapping or subsurface studies : the horizon or bed on which elevations are taken or to which elevations are referred in making a structure contour map — called also *key horizon*

**key bit** *n* : the projection on a key for operating a tumbler lock

**key block** *n, chiefly Brit* : KEY PLATE

**¹keyboard** \ˈ=ˌ=\ *n, often attrib* [¹*key* + *board*] **1 a** : a bank of keys on which the performer on a musical instrument (as a piano) plays and which consists of a double row of seven white and five raised black keys to the octave **b** : one of several such banks constituting a set : MANUAL **c** : a set of manuals **2** : an assemblage of systematically arranged keys by which a machine (as a typewriter) is operated **3** : a board on which keys for locks (as of hotel rooms) are hung

part of the keyboard of a piano

**²keyboard** \"\ *vb* -ED/-ING/-S *vi* : to operate a keyboard typesetting machine ~ *vt* : to set by means of a keyboard typesetting machine — **keyboarder** *n*

**keyboard paper** *n* : a continuous roll of paper for use as a ribbon for a Monotype machine

**key bolt** *n* : a bolt secured at one end by a key or cotter

**key brick** *n* : a brick made so that each narrow side is inclined at the same angle toward the end of the brick

**key bugle** *n* : a bugle having six keys and a chromatic range of about two octaves

**key button** *n* : a lettered or numbered cover attachable to a key of a typewriter or typesetting machine

**key chord** *n, music* : a tonic triad

**key-cold** \ˈ=¦=\ *adj, now dial Brit* : cold as a metal key : devoid of the warmth of life: as **a** : cold in death **b** : apathetic and indifferent

**key deer** *n, usu cap K* [⁴*key*] : a nearly extinct race of very small white-tailed deer native to the Florida keys

**key desk** *n* : CONSOLE 3a

**key drawing** \ˈ=ˌ==\ *n* : an outline drawing that indicates position of printed matter or that serves as a guide for color separation

**keyed** \ˈkēd\ *adj* [partly fr. ¹*key* + *-ed*; partly fr. past part. of ²*key*] **1** : furnished with keys ⟨a ~ instrument⟩ **2** : reinforced by a key or keystone ⟨a ~ arch⟩ **3** : set to a key (as a tune) **4** : ADJUSTED, ATTUNED, FITTED ⟨~ to the present situation⟩ ⟨every thought ~ to the reaction of the strangers —Agnes S. Turnbull⟩

**keyed bugle** *n* : KEY BUGLE

**keyed horn** *n* : BASS HORN

**key·er** \ˈkēə(r)\ *n* -s : a device (as a mechanical key or vacuum tube) that turns an electronic circuit on or off

**key form** *n* : the form that is run first of a set of forms used to print work in two or more colors

**key fossil** *n* : INDEX FOSSIL

**key fruit** *n* [so called fr. its growing in bunches suggesting a hanging bunch of keys] : SAMARA

**key harp** *n* : a keyboard musical instrument having tuning forks as vibrators

**¹keyhole** \ˈ=ˌ=\ *n* [¹*key* + *hole*] **1** : a hole or aperture (as in a door or lock) for receiving a key **2 a** : a hole or groove in beams intended to be joined together to receive the key that fastens them **b** : a slot for a key or cotter **3** : a hole made by a bullet that has keyholed **4** : the free-throw area in basketball

**²keyhole** \"\ *vi* [¹*keyhole*; fr. the shape of the hole made by the bullet] *of a bullet* : to strike a target when (as from tumbling or ricocheting) the long axis of the bullet is not in the same line as the line of flight

**³keyhole** \"\ *adj* [¹*keyhole*] **1** : revealingly intimate : INSIDE ⟨a ~ report⟩ ⟨a ~ view of private lives⟩ ⟨intimate, almost ~ narrative portrait —*New Yorker*⟩ **2** : intent on revealing intimate details ⟨a ~ reporter⟩

**keyhole limpet** *n* [so called fr. the perforation at the apex of its shell] : a limpet of the genus *Fissurella*

**keyhole neckline** *n* : a neckline in the shape of a keyhole

**keyhole saw** *n* : a saw used for cutting short-radius curves that is similar to a compass saw but usu. has a narrower blade and finer teeth — see PISTOL GRIP illustration

keyhole neckline

**keyhole urchin** *n* : a flat sea urchin of the order Exocycloida with long narrow apertures occurring near the margin of the test

**key horizon** *n* : KEY BED

**key industry** *n* : an industry (as the production of machine tools or chemicals) whose output is essential to the successful operation of many other industries

**¹key·ing** \ˈkēiŋ -ē·ēŋ\ *n* -s [¹*key* + *-ing* (n. suffix)] : the process of turning an electronic circuit off or on either manually or automatically ⟨such ~ represents the simplest possible form of modulation, and is applicable to all kinds of oscillators —W.A.Edson⟩

**²keying** \"\ *adj* : possessing the ability to turn an electronic circuit off or on ⟨a ~ device⟩

**keying by** *n* [fr. the gerund of *key by*, v.] : the action of clearing an automatic stop in an emergency and permitting a train to pass a signal set at danger

**keying sequence** *n* [fr. pres. part. of ²*key*] : a sequence of numbers or letters that enciphers or deciphers a polyalphabetic substitution cipher letter by letter

**key job** *n* **1** : a critical or vital job **2** : a job that can be evaluated accurately and then used as representative of other similar jobs

**key·less** \ˈkēləs\ *adj* [¹*key* + *-less*] : lacking or not requiring a key

**keyless watch** *n, Brit* : STEM-WINDER

**key letter** \ˈ=ˌ==\ *n* : a letter (as a letter of a repeated key word) functioning as an element in a cryptographic keying sequence

**key light** *n* : the main light illuminating a subject in photography

**key line** *n* : a line (as at the foot of a printed page) listing and explaining symbols used

**keylock** \ˈ=ˌ=\ *n* **1** : a lock opened by a key **2** : a wrestling hold in which a contestant uses both arms to lock an opponent's arm in a bent position

**key·man** \ˈkē¦man, -maa(ə)n\ *n, pl* **keymen** : a person doing work of vital importance (as in a business organization) ⟨within ministry and cabinet alike, the prime minister is the ~ —F.A.Ogg & Harold Zink⟩

**keyman insurance** *n* : insurance upon the life of a valuable employee naming the employing firm as beneficiary — compare BUSINESS LIFE INSURANCE

**key money** *n* **1** *Brit* : a payment required of a tenant esp. of an apartment on taking possession of the key **2** : a bribe paid by a prospective tenant in order to obtain housing ⟨the *key money* for an average studio in Paris is in the neighborhood of one thousand dollars —Paul Bowles⟩

**keymove** *var of* KEY

**¹keynes·i·an** \ˈkānzēən\ *adj, usu cap* [John M. *Keynes* †1946 Eng. economist + E *-ian*] : of or relating to Keynesianism

**²keynesian** \"\ *n* -s *usu cap* : an adherent or advocate of Keynesianism

**keynes·i·an·ism** \-ēə,nizəm\ *n* -s *usu cap* : the economic theories and programs ascribed to John Maynard Keynes and his followers; *specif* : the advocacy of monetary and fiscal programs by government to increase employment

**¹keynote** \ˈ=ˌ=, *in sense 1 sometimes* ˈ=ˈ=\ *n* [¹*key* + *note*] **1** : the first and harmonically fundamental tone of a scale : TONIC **2** : the fundamental or leading fact or idea : the prevailing tone ⟨this simple statement may be taken as the . . . ~ of the whole system —C.H.Driver⟩ ⟨sadness is the ~ of this little collection —*Books Abroad*⟩

**²keynote** \ˈ=ˌ=\ *vt* **1** : to set a keynote in ⟨the mood of compassion that ~*s* most of her writing —Ann F. Wolfe⟩ ⟨~ the overall color scheme . . . with a romantic mural —*N.Y. Herald Tribune*⟩ **2 a** : to deliver the keynote address at ⟨~ a Midwest farm political rally —*Wall Street Jour.*⟩ **b** : to declare in or as if in a keynote address ⟨"we want peace . . .," the secretary *keynoted* —*Newsweek*⟩

**keynote address** *or* **keynote speech** *n* : an address (as at a political convention) intended to present the issues of primary interest to the assembly but often concentrated upon arousing unity and enthusiasm ⟨the *keynote address* . . . is a highly emotional performance —D.D.McKean⟩ ⟨highlighting the convention's opening day is tonight's *keynote speech* —*TV Guide*⟩

**key·not·er** \ˈkē,nōd·ə(r), -ōtə-\ *n* : one that sets the keynote; *esp* : one that delivers a keynote speech ⟨to serve as temporary chairman and ~ of the Republican national convention —*Current Biog.*⟩

**keynote speaker** *n* : KEYNOTER

**key of art** : ALEMBROTH

**key of life** : ANKH

**key pad** *n* : a pad on a key of a wind instrument (as a flute or clarinet) making the hole leakproof

**key pattern** *n* : a Greek fret first found in the Geometric period and used throughout the classical era

**key pipe** *n* : a tubular opening in a lock for the shank of the key

**key plate** *n* **1** : the part of a stove top in which the lids are placed **2** : a protective usu. metal plate surrounding a keyhole **3** : a plate that prints the central design on a bicolor postage stamp — compare DUTY PLATE **4** : one of a set of color-printing plates that contains greater detail than the others and that is often the black plate

**key plug** *n* : the part of a lock into which the key is inserted

**key punch** *n* : a machine actuated by a keyboard and used to cut holes or notches in punched cards

**keypunch** \ˈ=ˌ=\ *vt* [*key punch*] : to cut holes or notches in (a punched card) with a key punch

**keys** *pl of* KEY, *pres 3d sing of* KEY

**key seat** *n* : a bed or groove in a mechanical part to receive a key

**keyseat** \ˈ=ˌ=\ *vt* [*key seat*] : to supply (as a mechanical part) with a key seat ⟨a ~*ed* shaft⟩

**key·seat·er** \ˈkē,sēd·ə(r)\ *n* **1** : a machine for keyseating machine parts **2** : one that operates a keyseating machine

**key-sequence** \ˈ=ˌ==\ *n* : KEYING SEQUENCE

**key signature** *n* : one or more sharps or flats placed immediately after the clef to designate the musical scale to be understood on the staff that in turn establishes the tonality

**keyslot** \ˈ=ˌ=\ *n* : a keyway esp. in a shaft

**keysmith** \ˈ=ˌ=\ *n* **1** : a person who makes or repairs keys **2** : an operator of a key-duplicating machine

**key station** *n* : a broadcasting station at which a network program originates

**¹keystone** \ˈ=ˌ=\ *n* [¹*key* + *stone*] **1** : the wedge-shaped piece at the crown of an arch; *esp* : such a piece inserted last and locking the other pieces in place **2** : something analogous to the keystone of an arch in position or function : a part or force on which associated things depend for support ⟨the ~ of his faith⟩ ⟨~ of a system of defense⟩: as **a** : crushed stone of small size used in bituminous bound roads to fill the voids of the large aggregate — compare COVER STONE **b** : a bondstone in masonry **c** *or* **keystone sack** : second base in baseball

keystone 1

**²keystone** \"\ *vt* : to support by means of a keystone

**keystone effect** *n* : a type of distortion in a television picture whereby a square pattern appears larger at the top than at the bottom

**key·ston·er** \ˈkē,stōnə(r)\ *n, usu cap* [*Keystone State*, nickname for Pennsylvania (fr. its central position among the original 13 states) + *-er*] : PENNSYLVANIAN 1 — used as a nickname

**Key·tain·er** \ˈkē,tānə(r)\ *trademark* — used for a small usu. leather case for carrying keys (as in the pocket)

**key·trumpet** *n* : a trumpet with side holes covered with keys that control its pitch

**key turner** *n, obs* : TURNKEY
**key–type** \ˈ=,=\ *n* : a single design used on the stamps of different colonies of a country
**key valve** *n* : a valve designed to be operated by a removable key to prevent unauthorized operation
**keyway** \ˈ=,=\ *n* **1** : a groove or channel for a key (as in a shaft or the hub of a pulley) : KEY SEAT **2** : the aperture for the key in a lock having a flat metal key **3** : a groove or channel for a key in a construction joint (as in a floor or wall) or underneath a retaining wall or dam
**key word** *n* : a word that is a key: **a** : a word exemplifying the meaning or value of a letter or symbol (as *then* in the statement "*th-* as in *then*") **b** : a word used as a cipher key: as (1) : a word that governs a transposition procedure (2) : a word from which a mixed alphabet is derived (3) : a word repeated to form a keying sequence
**kg** *abbr* **1** keg **2** kilogram **3** king
**KGC** *abbr* **1** knight grand commander **2** knight grand cross
**kgm** *abbr* **1** kilogram **2** kilogram-meter
**KGPS** *abbr, usu not cap* kilograms per second
**k–gun** \ˈ=,=\ *n, usu cap K* [¹*k*] : a naval depth-charge projector
**kha** *or* **ka** \ˈkä\ *also* **ka·che** \ˈkä(,)chā\ *n, pl* **kha** *or* **khas** *or* **ka** *or* **kas** *usu cap* **1 a** : a people of Nepal of mixed Mongoloid and Indo-Aryan blood **b** : a member of such people **2 a** : an agrarian aboriginal people of Laos **b** : a member of such people
**kha·ba·rovsk** \kəˈbärəfsk, -rəvzk\ *adj, usu cap* [fr. *Khabarovsk*, U.S.S.R.] : of or from the city of Khabarovsk, U.S.S.R. : of the kind or style prevalent in Khabarovsk
**khadar** *or* **khadir** *var of* KADIR
**khad·dar** \ˈkädə(r)\ *also* **kha·di** \ˈkädē\ *n* -s [Hindi *khādar*, *khādī*] : homespun cotton cloth worn by adherents of the movement for autonomy in India instead of the mill-made foreign product — compare SWADESHI, SWARAJ
**kha·gan** \käˈ(g)än\ *also* **kha·kan** \-ˈ(k)än\ *n* -s [Turk *kağan*] : KHAN
**khair** \ˈkī(ə)r\ *n* -s [Hindi, fr. Skt *khadira*] : CATECHU 2
¹**khaki** *also* **khakee** \ˈka\|kē, ˈkä\|, ˈkȧ\|, \|ki, *Canadian often* ˈkär\|\ *n* -s [Hindi *khākī* dusty, dust-colored, fr. *khāk* dust, fr. Per] **1 a** : a khaki-colored cloth; *esp* : a durable cotton or woolen cloth used for military uniforms **b** : a garment of khaki-colored cloth; *esp* : a military uniform — usu. used in pl. ⟨covered with mud to the eyes, in old ~*s* —F.M.Ford⟩ **2** : a light yellowish brown that is yellower and duller than walnut brown, yellower and less strong than cinnamon, and duller and slightly yellower than manila or fallow
²**khaki** *also* **khakee** \"\ *adj* : of the color khaki — used esp. of cloth
**khaki bush** *also* **khaki·bos** \-,bäs, -,bȯs\ *n* [*khakibos* fr. Afrik, fr. *khaki* + *bos* bush] *chiefly Africa* : AFRICAN MARIGOLD
**khaki camp·bell** \-ˈkam(b)əl, -aambəl\ *n* [after Mrs. Adale *Campbell*, 19th cent. Brit. duck breeder] **1** *usu cap K&C* : an English breed of small brownish upright ducks noted for their extensive production of large white eggs **2** -s *often cap K&C* : a bird of the Khaki Campbell breed
**khaki election** *n* : an election held during or shortly after a war in the expectation that the party in power will benefit from war enthusiasm
**khaki weed** *n, chiefly Austral* : CHAFF-FLOWER
**khak·sar** \(ˈ)käkˈsär\ *n* -s *usu cap* [Hindi *khāksār*, fr. Per *khāksār* humble, prob. fr. *khāk* dust + *-sār* like] : a member of a militant Muslim nationalist movement of India
**kha·lal** \kəˈläl\ *adj* [Ar *khalāl*] : of, relating to, or constituting the second of four recognized stages in the ripening of a date in which it reaches its full size and changes from green to red or yellow or a combination of the two colors — compare KIMRI, RUTAB, TAMAR
**kha·lat** *or* **khi·lat** \kəˈlat\ *n* -s [Hindi *khal'at*, *khil'at*, fr. Ar *khil'ah*] : a robe presented by a person of rank and worn as a mark of distinction in India
**kha·lif** \kəˈlēf\ *or* **kha·li·fa** \kəˈlēfə\ *var of* CALIPH
**khal·kha** *also* **khal·ka** *or* **kal·ka** \ˈkalkə\ *n* -s *usu cap* **1** : a member of a Mongol people inhabiting all but the western part of Outer Mongolia **2** : the language of the Khalkha people used as the official language of the Mongolian People's Republic
**khal·sa** \ˈkäl(t)sə\ *n* -s [Hindi *khāliṣa*, *khālsa* pure, genuine, fr. Per, fr. Ar *khāliṣah*] **1** : the exchequer of an Indian state **2** *usu cap* : a militant theocracy arising in the late 17th century and continuing today as one of the significant divisions of the Sikhs — compare NANAKPANTHI
**kham·bu** \ˈkäm(,)bü\ *also* **kham·ba** \-,bə\ *n, pl* **khambu** *or* **khambus** *also* **khamba** *or* **khambas** *usu cap* **1** : a Tibetan Mongoloid people of the southern slopes of the Himalayas **2** : a member of the Khambu people
**kha·mir** \kəˈmi(ə)r\ *n* -s *usu cap* : a dialect of the Cushitic language Agau
**kham·sin** *also* **kham·seen** *or* **cham·sin** \kamˈsēn\ *n* -s [Ar (*rīḥ al-*) *khamsīn* the wind of the fifty (days between Easter and Pentecost)] : a hot southerly Egyptian wind coming from the Sahara usu. in the spring and often carrying fine particles of sand ⟨the ~ . . . has been known to take paint off cars and force fine sand into camera shutters —G.E.Edgerton⟩ — compare SIROCCO
**kham·ti** \ˈkäm(p)tē\ *n, pl* **khamti** *or* **khamtis** *usu cap* **1 a** : a Tai people of northeastern Assam and Burma related to the Thais **b** : a member of such people **2** : a Thai language of the Khamti people
¹**khan** \ˈkän, -a-, -aa(ə)-, -ȧ-\ *also* **cham** \ˈkam, -aa(ə)-\ *n* -s [ME *caan*, fr. MF, of Turkic origin; akin to Jagatai *khān*, Turk *han* prince, khan] **1** : a medieval sovereign of China and ruler over the Turkish, Tatar, and Mongol tribes ⟨at the critical moment . . . the great ~ died —Sir Winston Churchill⟩ **2** : a local chieftain or man of rank esp. in Afghanistan, Iran, and some areas of central Asia — used sometimes as a title of respect
²**khan** \"\ *n* -s [Ar *khān*, fr. Per] : a caravansary or rest house in some Asian countries ⟨huge ~*s* . . . still receive shipments of goods that wind into Aleppo by camel train —*N.Y.Times*⟩
**khan·ate** \-,nāt, -,nət, *usu* \|d·+V\ *n* -s *sometimes cap* [¹*khan* + *-ate*] : the dominion or jurisdiction of a khan ⟨the capital of a semi-independent ~ —E.D.Laborde⟩
**khan·jar** \ˈkan,jär\ *or* **han·djar** \ˈha-\ *n* -s [Ar *khanjar*] : a short curved dagger of Muslim countries ⟨the broad silver-sheathed ~*s* — the mark of authority in the northern deserts —Ralph Hammond-Innes⟩
**khan·kah** \ˈkäŋkə\ *n* -s [Hindi *khānaqāh*, fr. Per *khāna* house + *gāh* place] : a dervish monastery
**khan·sa·mah** *or* **khan·sa·ma** \ˈkänsə,mä, känˈsämə\ *n* -s [Hindi *khānsāmān*, fr. Per, fr. *khān* lord + *sāmān* stores] : a male servant in India: **a** : HOUSE STEWARD **b** : BUTLER **c** : COOK
**khan·ty** \ˈkäntē\ *n* -ES *usu cap* : OSTYAK
**kha·num** *or* **ha·num** \ˈhänəm, ˈkä-, =ˈnəm, =ˈnüm\ *n* -s [Per & Turk; Per *khānum*, fr. Turk *hanım*, fem. of *han* prince, sovereign, khan] : a woman of rank or position esp. in Turkey and Iran
**kha·pra beetle** \ˈkä\|prə, ˈka\|\ *n* [Hindi *khaprā*, lit., destroyer, fr. Skt *kṣapayati* he destroys; akin to Skt *kṣiṇoti* he destroys — more at PHTHISIS] : a dermestid beetle (*Trogoderma granarium*) native to the Indian subcontinent and now a serious pest of stored grain in most parts of the world
**kha·ria** \ˈkärēə\ *n* -s *usu cap* **1** : a member of a people of western Bengal **2** : the Munda language of the Kharia people
**kha·rif** \kəˈrēf\ *adj* [Hindi *kharīf*, fr. Ar *kharīf* gathered, autumn, autumnal crop, fr. *kharafa* to gather] : of, relating to, or constituting India's autumn and lesser crop that consists chiefly of pearl millet, durra, and maize and that is sown in June just before the monsoon rains and is harvested from August on — compare RABI
**kha·ri·jite** \ˈkärə,jīt\ *n* -s *usu cap* [Ar *khārijī* one that departs, dissenter + E *-ite*] : a member of a Muslim secessionist sect establishing a radically democratic and puritanical reform community in the 7th century
**khar·kov** \ˈkär,kȯ\|f, -rkə\|, \|v\ *adj, usu cap* [fr. *Kharkov*, U.S.S.R.] : of or from the city of Kharkov, U.S.S.R. : of the kind or style prevalent in Kharkov
¹**kha·rosh·thi** \kəˈrōshtē\ *n* -s *usu cap* [Skt *kharoṣṭī*] : a cursive script of Aramaic origin used in northwestern India, Afghanistan, and Turkistan from about 300 B.C. to at least the middle of the 5th century A.D.
²**kharoshthi** \"\ *adj, usu cap* : of, relating to, or written in the script Kharoshthi
**khar·toum** \(ˈ)kärˈtüm\ *adj, usu cap* [fr. *Khartoum*, Sudan] : of or from Khartoum, capital of the Sudan : of the kind or style prevailing in Khartoum
**khar·toum·er** *also* **khar·tum·er** \=ˈ=ə(r)\ *n* -s *cap* [*Khartoum*, Sudan + E *-er*] : a native or inhabitant of Khartoum; *specif* : one of an organized Arab slaving company of the 19th century
**khar·war** \(,)kərˈwär\ *n, pl* **kharwar** *or* **kharwars** *usu cap* [Santali *kharwār*] **1** : a Bengal people speaking a Munda language **2** : a member of the Kharwar people
**khashgai** *usu cap, var of* KASHGAI
**kha·si** \ˈkäsē\ *or* **kha·sia** \-ēə\ *n* -s *usu cap* **1** : a member of any of several Mongoloid peoples of the Khasi and Jaintia hills of Assam **2** : the Mon-Khmer language of the Khasi people
**khas–kura** \ˈkäsˈku̇rə\ *n* -s *usu cap* : an Indic dialect of Nepal
**khat** *var of* KAT
**kha·tin** *or* **ka·tin** \kəˈtin\ *n, pl* **khatin** *or* **khatins** *or* **katin** *or* **katins** *usu cap* : ⁴TIN
**kha·tri** \ˈkə·trē\ *n* -s [Hindi *khatrī*, *khattrī*, fr. Skt *kṣatriya* — more at KSHATRIYA] : a member of a Hindu caste employed in trade who claim Kshatriya origin
**khatti** *usu cap, var of* HATTI
**kha·tun** \(ˈ)käˈtün\ *n* -s [Hindi *khātūn*, fr. Per *khānum*] : a woman of rank or position in Muslim countries
**kha·wa·rij** \kəˈwärij\ *n pl, usu cap* [Ar *khawārij*, pl. of *khārijī* one that departs, dissenter] : KHARIJITES
**khaya** \ˈkīə, ˈkāə\ *n* [NL, fr. Wolof *khaye* khaya tree] **1** *cap* : a genus of African timber trees (family Meliaceae) with wood closely resembling mahogany **2** -s : any tree of the genus *Khaya*
**kha·zar** *also* **kho·zar** *or* **cha·zar** \kəˈzär\ *or* **ka·za·ri·an** \-rēən\ *n, pl* **khazar** *or* **khazars** *usu cap* **1** : a Tatar people existing as a nation in the Caucasus and southeastern Russia from about the end of the 2d century A.D. to the end of the 11th century **2** : a member of the Khazar people
**khe·dive** \kəˈdēv, keˈ-\ *n* -s [F *khédive*, fr. Turk *hidiv*, fr. Per *khidīw* prince] : the ruler of Egypt from 1867 to 1914 governing as a semi-independent viceroy of the sultan of Turkey
**khe·di·vi·al** \-vēəl\ *also* **khe·div·al** \-vəl\ *adj, often cap* : of or relating to a khedive ⟨a bribe to some ~ minister —A.J. Liebling⟩ ⟨a *Khedival* decree —Salma Bishlawy⟩
**khe·di·vi·ate** \-vēət, -vē,āt\ *also* **khe·div·ate** \-vət, -,vāt\ *n* -s *often cap* : the government or dominion of a khedive
**khel·la** \ˈkelə\ *n* -s [Ar *akhillah*] : a bishop's-weed (*Ammi visnaga*)
**khel·lin** *also* **kel·lin** \ˈkelən\ *n* -s [*khella* + *-in*] : a crystalline compound $C_{14}H_{12}O_5$ obtained from the fruit of khella and used as an antispasmodic in asthma and a coronary vasodilator in angina pectoris
**kher·wa·ri** \kə(r)ˈwärē\ *n* -s *usu cap* : any of a group of closely related Munda languages including Ho, Mundari, and Santali
**khe·sa·ri** \kəˈsärē\ *or* **khesari gram** *n* -s [Hindi *khesārī*, *khisārī*, *kisārī*] *India* : GRASS PEA
**kheth** *var of* HETH
**khid·mat·gar** *or* **khid·mut·gar** \ˈkidmət,gär\ *or* **khit·mat·gar** *or* **khit·mut·gar** \ˈkitm-\ *n* -s [Hindi *khidmatgār*, fr. Ar *khidmah* service + Per *-gār* (suffix denoting possession or agency)] *India* : a male waiter
**khi·la·fat** \ˈkilə,fat, kəˈläfət\ *n* -s [Turk *hilâfet*, fr. Ar *khilāfah* caliphate] : the chief spiritual authority of Islam as exercised by the Turkish sultans
**khilat** *var of* KHALAT
**khirghiz** *usu cap, var of* KIRGHIZ
**khi·tan** *or* **ki·tan** \ˈkēˈtän\ *also* **chi–dan** *or* **chi–tan** \ˈchēˈdän\ *n, pl* **khitan** *or* **khitans** *or* **kitan** *or* **kitans** *usu cap* **1 a** : a conquering Tatar people maintaining hegemony of northern China in the Liao dynasty from the 10th to the 12th centuries **2** : a member of the Khitan people
**khlyst** \ˈklist\ *n, pl* **khlys·ty** \kliˈstē\ *or* **khlysts** *usu cap* [Russ, lit., whip, prob. of imit. origin] : a member of a secret Russian Christian sect that originated in the 17th century or earlier, taught that God becomes incarnate in many Christs through their suffering, and followed ascetic and ecstatic practices
**khmer** *or* **kmer** \kəˈme(ə)r\ *n, pl* **khmer** *or* **khmers** *or* **kmer** *or* **kmers** *usu cap* **1 a** : an aboriginal people of Cambodia noted for their architectural achievements ⟨the mighty *Khmer* empire . . . ruled most of Indo-China and bequeathed the matchless jungle temple of Angkor Wat to posterity —*Time*⟩ **b** : a member of such people **2** : a Mon-Khmer language of the Khmer people that is the official language of Cambodia — **khmeri·an** \-merēən, -mir-\ *adj, usu cap*
**khmu** \kəˈmü\ *n, pl* **khmu** *or* **khmus** *usu cap* **1** : the most numerous group of the Kha people of northern Laos **2** : a member of the Khmu people
**khoa** \kəˈwä\ *n* -s [Hindi *khoā*] : a semidehydrated whole-milk product of India
**khoi·san** \ˈkȯi,sän\ *n* -s *usu cap* **1** : a group of African peoples speaking Khoisan languages **2** : a subfamily of African languages comprising Hottentot and the several languages known as Bushman and related to Sandawe and Hatsa with which it forms the Macro-Khoisan family
**kho·ja** *or* **kho·jah** \ˈkōjə\ *n* -s [Turk & Per; Turk *hoca*, fr. Per *khwāja*] **1** *also* **ho·dja** \ˈhō-\ **a** : a member of any of various classes (as wealthy merchants) in Muslim lands — used as a title of respect **b** : a Muhammadan teacher **2** *cap* [Hindi *khoja*, fr. Per *khwāja*] *India* : a member of an Ismaili sect surviving as a subsect of the ancient Assassins
**kho·ka·ni** \kōˈkänē\ *n, pl* **khokani** *or* **khokanis** *usu cap* **1** : a Durani people of Afghanistan **2** : a member of the Khokani people
**khond** *or* **kandh** \ˈkänd\ *n, pl* **khond** *or* **khonds** *or* **kandh** *or* **kandhs** *usu cap* **1** : any of several Dravidian peoples of Orissa, India **2** : a member of a Khond people
**khon·di** \-dē\ *n* -s *usu cap* : KUI
**khor** \ˈkō(ə)r\ *n* -s [Ar *khawr*] : WATERCOURSE, RAVINE
**kho·ras·san** \ˌkōrəˈsan\ *also* **khu·ra·san** \ˌku̇r-\ *n, pl* **khorassan** *or* **khorassans** *usu cap* [fr. *Khorassan* or *Khurasan*, province of Iran] : a Persian rug or carpet often of Herat or animal pattern and vivid coloring
**kho·shot** \ˈkō,shät\ *n, pl* **khoshot** *or* **khoshots** *usu cap* **1** : a Kalmuck people converted to Lamaism in the early 17th century **2** : a member of the Khoshot people
**kho·ta·na** \kōˈtänə\ *n, pl* **khotana** *or* **khotanas** *usu cap* : KOYUKON
**kho·ta·nese** *n, pl* **kho·ta·nese** \ˌkōtᵊnˈēz, -ēs\ *usu cap* [*Khotan*, region in Turkistan, central Asia + E *-ese*] : an Iranian language of central Asia found in documents from the eighth century to the tenth century
**kho·war** \ˈkō,wär\ *n* -s *usu cap* : a Dard language of Chitral, northwest Pakistan
**khozar** *usu cap, var of* KHAZAR
**khud** \ˈkəd\ *n* -s [Hindi *khaḍ*] *India* : RAVINE, PRECIPICE
**khun·nong** \kəˈnȯŋ, -näŋ\ *n, pl* **khunnong** *or* **khunnongs** *usu cap* **1** : a Tibeto-Burman people occupying the upper tributary region of the Irrawaddy river and dwelling in communal houses **2** : a member of the Khunnong people
**khus·khus** \ˈkəskəs\ *or* **khuskhus grass** *also* **khus** \ˈkəs\ *or* **kus·kus** *or* **cus·cus** \ˈkəskəs\ *n* -ES [Per & Hindi *khaskhas*] : an aromatic grass (*Andropogon zizamoides*) whose esp. fragrant roots yield an oil used in perfumery and are also made into mats in tropical India — called also *vetiver*
**khut·bah** *or* **khut·ba** \ˈku̇tbə\ *n* -s [Ar *khuṭbah*] : a pulpit address of prescribed form that is read in mosques on Fridays at noon prayer and contains an acknowledgment of the sovereignty of the reigning prince
¹**khwa·raz·mi·an** \kwəˈrazmēən, kwäˈ-\ *adj, usu cap* [*Khwarazm*, province of ancient Persia + E *-ian*] **1** : of or relating to Khwarazm **2** : of or relating to the Khwarazmian people
²**khwarazmian** \"\ *or* **khwa·rez·mi·an** \-rez-\ *or* **khwa·riz·mi·an** \-riz-\ *n* -s *usu cap* **1** : an Uzbek people **2** : a member of the Khwarazmian people
**kHz** *abbr* kilohertz
**ki** *var of* TI
**ki** *abbr* **1** kilocycle **2** king **3** kitchen
**KIA** *abbr* killed in action
**ki·aat** \kēˈät\ *n* -s [Afrik, prob. fr. native name in southern Africa] : a tree (*Pterocarpus angolensis*) of southern Africa having heavy strong durable wood that is used for furniture, joinery, and flooring
**ki·a·boo·ca** *or* **ki·a·boo·ka** *or* **ky·a·boo·ka** *also* **kya–bouka** \ˌkīəˈbükə\ *n* -s [origin unknown] : AMBOYNA 1
**ki·aki** *or* **ke·ya·ki** \kēˈ(y)äkē\ *n* -s [Jap *kiaki*] : a Japanese timber tree (*Zelkova serrata*) with fine hard wood
**kia·mu·sze** \jēˈämə,sə(r), -sə̄\ *adj, usu cap* [fr. *Kiamusze*, Manchuria] : of or from the city of Kiamusze, Manchuria : of the kind or style prevalent in Kiamusze
**ki·ang** *also* **ky·ang** *or* **ki·yang** \kēˈ(y)äŋ\ *n, pl* **kiangs** *also* **kiang** [Tibetan *kyaṅ* (written *rkyaṅ*)] : an Asiatic wild ass (*Equus hemionus*) typically having reddish back and sides, white underparts, muzzle, and legs, and a dusky stripe along the spine and occurring in many local races most of which have at various times been considered separate species
**kia ora** \ˌkēəˈōrə\ *interj* [Maori *kia ora*, lit., be well] — used as a salutation or toast in Australia and New Zealand
**kiaugh** \ˈkyäk\ *n* -s [prob. fr. ScGael *cabhag* hurry, troubles] *Scot* : TROUBLE, ANXIETY, STIR
**ki·a·we** *or* **ke·a·we** \kēˈäwā\ *n* -s [Hawaiian *kiawe*] : any of several mesquites introduced into and to some extent naturalized in Hawaii
**kib·be** *also* **kib·beh** \ˈkibə\ *n* -s [Ar *kubbah*] : ground lamb and wheat baked as a cake
¹**kib·ble** \ˈkibəl\ *n* -s [G *kübel* tub, bucket, fr. OHG *-chubilī*, modif. of (assumed) VL *cupia* — more at KEEVE] *Brit* : a hoisting bucket used in mining
²**kibble** \"\ *vt* **kibbled**; **kibbled**; **kibbling** \-b(ə)liŋ\ **kibbles** [origin unknown] : to grind coarsely ⟨*kibbled* dog biscuit⟩ ⟨*kibbled* grain⟩
³**kibble** \"\ *n* -s : coarsely ground meal or grain
**kib·butz** \kiˈbu̇ts, -üts\ *n, pl* **kib·but·zim** \(,)ki,bu̇tˈsēm, -büt-\ [NHeb *qibbūṣ*, fr. Heb, gathering] : a collective farm or settlement in Israel cooperatively owned and managed by the members and organized on a communal basis ⟨the ~ is one of four main types of agricultural settlement —John Hersey⟩ ⟨in each ~ the . . . living arrangements are centralized with a common dining hall and children's quarters —Joan Comay⟩
**kib·butz·nik** \kiˈbu̇tsnik, -büt-\ *n* -s [Yiddish *kibutsnik*, fr. *kibuts* kibbutz (fr. NHeb *qibbuṣ*) + *-nik* (n. suffix denoting a person engaged in or connected with — something specified —, fr. Pol & Russ)] : a member of a kibbutz
¹**kibe** \ˈkīb\ *n* -s [ME *kybe*] : a chap or crack in the flesh caused by cold : an ulcerated chilblain esp. on the heel ⟨the clouted shoe of the peasant galls the ~ of the courtier —Sir Walter Scott⟩
²**kibe** \"\ *vt* -ED/-ING/-s : to affect with kibes ⟨make me as angry as a *kibed* heel —T.B.Costain⟩
**ki·bei** \(ˈ)kēˈbā\ *n, pl* **kibei** *also* **kibeis** *often cap* [Jap] : a son or daughter of issei parents who is born in America and esp. in the U.S. and educated largely in Japan — distinguished from *nisei*; compare SANSEI
**ki·bit·ka** \kəˈbitkə\ *n* -s [Russ, of Turkic origin; akin to Kazan Tatar *kibit* booth, stall, tent, Uighur *käbit*] **1** : a Kirghiz circular tent of latticework and felt **2** : a Russian covered vehicle on wheels or runners
**kibitz** \ˈkibəts *also* kəˈbits\ *vb* -ED/-ING/-ES [Yiddish *kibitsen*, fr. G *kiebitzen*, fr. *kiebitz* pewit, busybody, fr. MHG *gībitz* pewit, of imit. origin] *vi* : to act as a kibitzer ⟨observation which amounts, if not to democratic control, at least to democratic ~*ing* —Elmer Davis⟩ ⟨an awful thing to ~ on a man and his wife, and hear what they really talk about —J.M.Cain⟩ ~ *vt* : to observe as a kibitzer: **a** : to be a kibitzer at ⟨~*ing* a Pullman card game —Bob Broeg⟩ **b** : to watch the performance of as a kibitzer ⟨~*ed* him at poker —Theodore Sturgeon⟩
**kibitz·er** \-sə(r)\ *n* -s [Yiddish *kibitser*, fr. *kibitsen* + *-er*] : an outsider or nonparticipant who looks on and may offer unwanted advice or comment esp. at a card game ⟨contract bridge has achieved a following both of ~*s* and players probably never surpassed in the history of any nonathletic game —*N.Y. World-Telegram*⟩ ⟨nothing can be more of a trial at the scene of an illness or an accident than a ~ —Robert Rice⟩
**kibla** *or* **kiblah** *var of* QIBLA
¹**ki·bosh** *also* **ky·bosh** \ˈkī,bäsh, kəˈbäsh\ *n* -ES [origin unknown] : something that serves as a check or stop — used chiefly in the phrase *to put the kibosh on* ⟨the directive puts the ~ on one of the few potentially valuable efforts that the United States has been making in the field of psychological warfare —R.H.Rovere⟩ ⟨might even be able to put the ~ on the plan before it was put into operation⟩
²**kibosh** \"\ *vt* -ED/-ING/-ES : BLOCK, FRUSTRATE ⟨a limited . . . budget ~*ed* the architects' first proposal —*Architectural Forum*⟩
**ki·chai** \ˈkē,chī\ *n, pl* **kichai** *or* **kichais** *usu cap* **1** : a Caddo people of north-central Texas **2** : a member of the Kichai people
**kich·el** \ˈkikəl\ *n, pl* **kich·lach** \-klək\ *or* **kichel** [Yiddish *kikhel* small cake, dim. of *kukhen* cake, fr. OHG *kuocho* — more at CAKE] : a semisweet baked product made of eggs, flour, and sugar usu. rolled and cut in diamond shape and baked until puffed
**kichua** *usu cap, var of* QUECHUA
¹**kick** \ˈkik\ *vb* -ED/-ING/-s [ME *kiken*] *vi* **1 a** (1) : to thrust out the foot or feet with force : strike out with the foot or feet (as in defense or bad temper or in effecting a swimming stroke); *esp* : to give impetus to something with a usu. fast blow with the foot (2) : THRUST, DRIVE ⟨the bomber's engines ~ with a 350,000-pound thrust⟩ **b** : to have a habit of kicking ⟨the horse ~*s* when men approach him with a saddle⟩ ⟨the boy ~*s* when he gets into fights⟩ **c** : to execute a kick in dancing **d** : to try to score or gain ground in a game of football by kicking the ball **e** : to engage in small annoying or harassing tactics ⟨~*ing* at neighboring countries to distract their own people from internal problems⟩ **2 a** : to show opposition : REBEL ⟨tends to ~ against authority⟩ **b** : to express discontent : COMPLAIN ⟨had studied very little and so had no reason to ~ about low grades⟩ **3** *slang* : DIE — compare KICK IN, KICK OFF **4** *of a firearm* : to recoil when fired — often used with *back* **5 a** *of a cricket pitch* : to cause a bowled ball to rebound erratically **b** *of a bowled ball in cricket* : to rebound erratically — often used with *up* **6** : to function with vitality and energy ⟨still alive and ~*ing* at 75 years⟩ ⟨continue to flourish and . . . wax fat and ~ —*Dock Leaves*⟩ **7 a** : to move or go erratically or jerkily as if being kicked ⟨an engine that ~*ed* a good deal when it was started in cold weather⟩ ⟨the jumping jack ~*ed* about on the floor until it ran down⟩ **b** : to move from one to another of or stay or rest in various successive places as circumstance or whim dictates ⟨an old chair that ~*ed* around the house for years⟩ ⟨during winters ~*ed* about Florida and other warm areas⟩ ~ *vt* **1 a** : to strike, thrust, or hit with the foot usu. with force **b** : to strike usu. suddenly with force as if kicking **c** : to impel or drive as if by kicking; *specif* : to cause (a railroad car) to be carried by momentum to a particular track position by uncoupling while still moving **d** : to cause (a racehorse or racing car) to show a sudden burst of speed ⟨~*ed* his car into the lead —*Newsweek*⟩ **2** : to score (a goal or point) by kicking the ball in a game of football **3** *chiefly dial* : to refuse (a person) after an invitation or an offer of marriage : JILT ⟨took to drink after being ~*ed* in favor of a rival⟩ **4** *slang* : to heap reproaches upon (oneself) ⟨~*ed* himself every time he thought of the lost opportunity⟩ **5** : RAISE 17a **6** *slang* : to free oneself of or break (a drug habit) **syn** see OBJECT — **kick against the pricks** : to feel or show usu. pointless opposition to or resentment of an often necessary authority one is subject to — **kick downstairs** : to kick out : EJECT — **kick one's heels** : to while or pass the time aimlessly or futilely — **kick over the traces** : to cast off restraint : become insubordinate : throw off authority or control — **kick the beam 1** : to be extremely lightly weighted **2** : to become or be of extremely small value ⟨the prices of building plots *kicked the beam* —Marguerite Steen⟩ — **kick the bucket** *slang* : DIE — **kick up one's heels 1** : to show sudden extreme delight or energy inspired by such delight **b** : to have a lively time ⟨had no time to take a holiday and *kick up my heels* when I came back from the war —Rebecca West⟩ **2** *slang* : DIE
²**kick** \"\ *n* -s **1 a** : an act of kicking : a blow or sudden force-

ful thrust with the foot and esp. the toe ⟨felt the ~ so strongly that a pain shot up his leg⟩; *specif* : a sudden propelling (as of a ball) with a blow of the foot esp. in football — see DROP-KICK, FREE KICK, PLACE-KICK **b** : a forceful thrust or sudden drive ⟨the engine drove the car ahead in a series of ~*s*⟩ **c** : a vigorous elevation of a leg (as in dancing) ⟨a high ~ and then a pirouette⟩ **d** : the power to kick : degree of force in kicking **e** : a rhythmic often forceful motion of the legs used alone or in conjunction with arm movements to propel a swimmer through the water **f** : a burst of speed or the ability to exhibit a burst of speed in racing esp. as unleashed in the last part of a race **2** *slang Brit* : SIXPENCE **3** *archaic slang* : the latest fashion or style **4 a** : a sudden forceful jolt, jerk, jog, or thrust suggesting a kick ⟨felt the sudden ~ of the drill in his hand as the power was turned on⟩ ⟨a noticeable upward ~ in the barograph trace —G.H.T.Kimble⟩; *specif* : the recoil of a gun **b** : an electrical impulse or the deflection on a meter that records it **c** : a single automatic operation of a business machine **5** *slang* : DISMISSAL, DISCHARGE; *specif* : a dishonorable discharge from the armed forces ⟨the maximum penalty is . . . a year and a ~ —F.B.Wiener⟩ — compare ³BOOT 8b **6** *slang* : POCKET, POCKETBOOK ⟨without a dime in his ~ for a cup of coffee⟩ **7** *chiefly Brit* : KICKER 1b ⟨not a powerful ~, he is very accurate —Len Smith⟩ **8** : an indentation at the bottom of a molded glass bottle to lessen its holding capacity **9** *chiefly Brit* : a projection on a stock board or brick mold for forming a frog in the brick; *also* : the frog so formed **10 a** : a feeling of opposition or objection ⟨had a ~ against the new schedule⟩ **b** : an expression of opposition or objection ⟨heard all sorts of ~*s* against the administration⟩ **c** : the grounds for objection ⟨trying to find out what the ~ was⟩ **11 a** : a quick and forcible effect suggestive of a kick: as (1) : the effect or force of an explosive when exploded ⟨the high-test gasoline had quite a ~⟩ (2) : a marked physical effect (as of stimulation by alcohol) ⟨got a quick ~ out of drinking⟩; *also* : ability to produce such an effect ⟨a drink with no ~ in it⟩ **b** (1) : a feeling of pleasure or of marked enjoyment : THRILL ⟨get a ~ out of that music⟩ (2) : a source of such pleasure ⟨the play had a dramatic ~ that made it very successful⟩ **c kicks** *pl, slang* : PLEASURE, THRILLS, FUN ⟨playing for ~*s*, not money⟩ **d** *slang* : way of getting one's pleasure or livelihood : manner or style of behaving or performing ⟨the band is on a Dixieland ~⟩ ⟨went on a mystery-reading ~ —*Time*⟩ **12** : a sudden and striking surprise, revelation, or turn of events : TWIST ⟨the novel ended with an ironical ~⟩ **13** *slang* : RAISE ⟨a demand for a salary ~ —Pete Martin⟩ — **kick in the pants** : a humbling setback — **kick in the teeth** : a sudden usu. violent often contemptuous setback ⟨the pleased delegation . . . got a delayed *kick in the teeth* —*Time*⟩

**kick·able** \-kəbəl\ *adj* : capable of being kicked : fit or deserving to be kicked

**kick·a·poo** \ˈkikə,pü\ *n, pl* **kickapoo** *or* **kickapoos** *usu cap* [Kickapoo *kiwĕgapawa*, lit., he stands about] **1 a** : an Indian people orig. of Wisconsin but now living in Oklahoma and Chihuahua, Mexico **b** : a member of such people **2** : a dialect of Fox

**kick around** *vt* **1 a** : to treat in an inconsiderate or high-handed fashion ⟨business was so good he felt he could *kick* the customers *around* a little⟩ ⟨*kicks* his children *around* a good deal⟩ ⟨men and women who are so frequently *kicked around*, abused, misunderstood, and unappreciated —William Benton⟩ **b** *slang* : to treat in a casual, unsystematic, or experimental way ⟨*kicked* the music *around* for a while, trying it out⟩ **2** *slang* : to consider, examine, or discuss (as an idea) from all angles usu. by random suggestion or discussion ⟨*kicked* the notion *around* for an hour or so to see if it might be feasible⟩ ~ *vi* : to work in a hit-or-miss fashion or wherever work offers itself ⟨*kicked around* in stock companies —R.F.Shepard⟩

**kick back** *vi* **1** : to recoil upon one usu. in an unexpected way ⟨his accusations *kicked back* and he found himself in jail⟩ **2** : to pay a kickback ⟨forced to *kick back* out of every paycheck⟩ ~ *vt* **1** : to restore (something stolen) to the owner **2** : to give back (money) as a kickback ⟨asked to *kick* a dollar *back* each week⟩

**kickback** \ˈ=,=\ *n* -S [*kick back*] **1** : the action or the effect of kicking back: as **a** (1) : the starting backward of an internal-combustion engine while being cranked (2) : the backward thrust of a piece of work being fed into a machine (as a circular saw) — called also *backkick* **b** : a strong esp. unfavorable reaction ⟨was unable to take the medicine because of a marked ~⟩ — called also *backkick* **2** : REFUND: as **a** : a percentage payment exacted as a condition for granting assistance by one in a position to open up or control a source of income or gain ⟨appointees paid a ~ to the ward boss out of each paycheck⟩ **b** : a usu. secret rebate of part of a purchase price by the seller to the buyer or to the one who directed or influenced the purchaser to buy from such seller **c** : a rebate given to a seller (as an automobile dealer) by a finance company that purchases the buyer's promissory note or installment paper **3** : high voltage produced (as in a radio transmitting set) by the sudden interruption of current in a low-voltage circuit — called also *backkick* **4** : KICKBOARD 1

**kickball** \ˈ=,=\ *n* : a children's game that resembles baseball and is played with an inflated ball which is kicked instead of batted

**kickboard** \ˈ=,=\ *n* **1** : one of two high boards on either side of the pit end of a bowling alley that separate adjacent alleys and keep flying pins in the right alley **2** : a buoyant rectangular board grasped with the hands by a swimmer while developing kicking techniques — called also *flutterboard*

**kickdown** \ˈ=,=\ *n* -S [fr. *kick down*, v.] : a change to lower gear in an automotive vehicle; *also* : the manually operated or automatic device for making such a change

**kicked** *past of* KICK

**kick·er** \ˈkikə(r)\ *n* -S **1** : one that kicks: as **a** : an animal having the habit of kicking **b** : a member of a football team who makes or is designated to make dropkicks, place-kicks, or punts **c** : a person who protests, complains, or grumbles esp. habitually **d** : a sawmill device for throwing logs from the conveyor trough onto the log deck **e** : a mechanical part that gives a sharp push to some object (as for feeding or ejecting work from a machine) **f** : a device for opening a stove door or other object by pressure applied with the foot **g** : a ball (as in cricket and tennis) that rebounds erratically or high **h** : WILD-OAT KICKER **i** : a small internal-combustion engine in a boat; *also* : a boat driven by such an engine **j** : an aircrewman who releases or propels out of a cargo airplane bundles to be parachuted to a drop zone on the ground **2** : TEDDER **3** : a protective covering for the toes and instep of a goalkeeper in field hockey usu. made of canvas or soft leather with a padding of felt or sponge rubber **4** : an unmatched card retained with a pair or three of a kind when drawing cards in draw poker **5** : a machine for softening skins in tanning **6** : a line of newspaper type set above a headline usu. in a different typeface and intended to provoke interest in, editorialize about, or provide orientation for the matter in the copy it heads **7** : KICK 12

**kickier** *comparative of* KICKY

**kickiest** *superlative of* KICKY

**kick in** *vt, slang* : CONTRIBUTE ⟨asked to *kick* a dollar *in* for a present for the boss⟩ ~ *vi* **1** *slang* : DIE ⟨*kicked in* at the ripe old age of 90⟩ **2** *slang* : to make a contribution ⟨an unknown contributor *kicked in* with $1000⟩

**kick-in** \ˈ=,=\ *n* -S [fr. *kick in*, v.] : a free kick in soccer used to put the ball in play after it has gone out of bounds over a sideline

**kicking** *pres part of* KICK

**kicking-colt** \ˈ==,=\ *n* : JEWELWEED a

**kicking-horses** \ˈ==,==\ *n pl but usu sing in constr* : JEWELWEED a

**kick·ish** \ˈkikish\ *adj, now dial Eng* : IRRITABLE, CANTANKEROUS

**kick off** *vi* **1** : to start or restart the play in football by a place-kick from a point close to or at the center of the field **2** : to begin proceedings or undertake the initial move or action ⟨the entertainers *kicked off* with a fast song and dance⟩ **3** *slang* : DIE ⟨worth a cool million when he *kicked off*⟩ ~ *vt* : to start or signalize the beginning of (a concerted effort) ⟨*kick* the drive for funds *off* with a nationwide broadcast⟩

**kickoff** \ˈ=,=\ *n* -S [*kick off*] **1** : the act of kicking off: as **a** : a kick that puts the ball into play in a football or soccer game **b** : COMMENCEMENT ⟨makes no bones about it being the ~ for his big bid for the Democratic Presidential nod —*Newsweek*⟩ ⟨is also hoping to round up some of its oldest living customers for this ~ party —Bennett Cerf⟩ **2** : a device (as a power-operated lever) for casting work off a machine table out of a cavity in a die

**kick out** *vi* **1** : to kick the ball deliberately over a touchline (as when stalling for time) in a soccer game **2** : to take a free kick after a touchback or safety in a game of football ~ *vt* : to turn out, dismiss, or eject usu. forcefully or summarily ⟨tried to keep the lad in his employ but finally had to *kick* him *out*⟩ ⟨when he entered the house he was *kicked out* immediately⟩ ⟨suggested *kicking* all enemy aliens *out*⟩

**kickout** \ˈ=,=\ *n* -S [*kick out*] : the act of kicking out or of kicking something out

**kick over** *vi* : to begin to fire — used of an internal-combustion engine ⟨after a moment of cranking the motor *kicked over*⟩ ~ *vt* : to cause (an internal-combustion engine) to turn over and usu. begin to fire ⟨could not *kick* the motor *over*⟩

**kickpipe** \ˈ=,=\ *n* : a short section of pipe to protect an electric cable from mechanical damage where it emerges from a floor or deck

**kickplate** \ˈ=,=\ *n* : a protective plate (as of metal or plastic) applied to the bottom of a door or cabinet or to the riser of a step to prevent marring of the finish by shoe marks

**kick pleat** *n* : a short inverted pleat used to give breadth (as at the bottom of a skirt for ease in walking or at the bottom of a slipcover for ease in fitting the band around corners)

**kicks** *pres 3d sing of* KICK, *pl of* KICK

**kick·shaw** \ˈkik,shȯ\ *n* -S [by folk etymology fr. F *quelque chose* something, anything] **1** *or* **kickshaws** *pl but usu sing in constr* **a** : a fancy dish in cookery : TIDBIT, DELICACY **b** : something elegant but trifling : TRIFLE, TOY **2** *archaic* : a fantastic person

**kick·sies** \ˈkiksiz\ *n pl* [*kicks* trousers (fr. pl. of ²*kick*) + -*ie* + -*s*] *slang Brit* : TROUSERS, PANTS

**kick-sled** \ˈ=,=\ *n* : a sled popular in Scandinavia that consists usu. of a low seat on runners and that is propelled usu. by one holding the back of the seat, standing on a runner with one foot, and pushing with the other

**kicksorter** \ˈ=,==\ *n* : a device that sorts and records electrical pulses of given intensities (as pulses from an ionization chamber)

**kickstand** \ˈ=,=\ *n* : a device for holding up a bicycle or motorcycle when not in use consisting of a metal bar or rod that is attached by a swivel device to the frame and may be kicked to a vertical position as a prop

**kick starter** *or* **kick start** *n* : a motor starter (as on a motorcycle) that is activated by a thrust of the foot usu. assisted by the body weight

**kick through** *vi* **1** *slang* : to kick in **2** *slang* : to make a confession ⟨*kick through* and tell me what it is —Erle Stanley Gardner⟩

**kick turn** *n* : a standing half turn in skiing made by raising one ski so that it is nearly vertical to the ground, turning the ski outward and downward so that it is brought down pointed backward, and bringing the other ski around parallel to it

**kick up** *vt* **1** : to cause to rise or be propelled upward forcefully ⟨the tires *kicked* little stones *up*⟩ ⟨clouds of dust *kicked up* by passing cars⟩ **2 a** : RAISE ⟨signal the auctioneer quietly and *kick* the bid *up* another thousand —Grant Cannon⟩ **b** : to stir up : PROVOKE ⟨*kicked* a row *up* over nothing⟩ ⟨*kick up* a fuss⟩ ~ *vi* **1** : to give evidence of disorder ⟨felt his stomach start to *kick up*⟩ **2** : to become insubordinate : act in a protesting or unexpectedly independent way ⟨when the New Woman began *kicking up* on the American scene in the middle of the 19th century —Lois Long⟩

**kickup** \ˈ=,=\ *n* -S [*kick up*] **1** : a noisy quarrel : DISTURBANCE, ROW **2 a** : KICK 1c **b** : a method in speedball of converting a ground ball to an aerial ball by means of the foot **3** : KICK 8 **4** : an upward bend made in the frame of a motor vehicle to clear the rear axle

**kick wheel** *n* : a potter's wheel worked by a foot pedal or by kicking a heavy disk at the foot of the vertical shaft

**kickx·ia** \ˈkiksēə\ *n, cap* [NL, fr. Jean *Kickx* †1831 and his son Jean *Kickx* †1864 Belgian botanists + NL -*ia*] : a small genus of Old World creeping pubescent herbs (family Scrophulariaceae) having pinnately veined oval leaves and flowers with a prominent palate — see CANCERWORT

**kicky** \ˈkikē\ *adj* -ER/-EST **1** *chiefly dial* : SASSY, CONTRARY **2** : likely to kick

¹**kid** \ˈkid\ *n* -S [ME *kide*, of Scand origin; akin to ON *kith* kid, OSw *kidh*; akin to OHG *kizzī* kid; prob., like MIr *cit* sheep, Alb *qith* young male goat, fr. a cry to goats and sheep to return to the fold] **1 a** (1) : a young goat usu. under one year old (2) : a young individual of various related animals (as many antelopes and some deer) **b** : a young individual of various other animals ⟨a sea-otter ~⟩ **2 a** : the flesh, fur, or skin of a kid **b** : something made of kid: as (1) : KIDSKIN (2) : KID LEATHER (3) : KID GLOVE **3** : CHILD, YOUNGSTER ⟨took the ~*s* to the playground⟩ ⟨a ~ of eighteen —Dan Cushman⟩ ⟨grade-school ~*s*⟩ **4** *slang* : a young person marked by proficiency or expertness ⟨quite some ~ when it comes to staying in the public eye⟩

²**kid** \"\ *vi* **kidded**; **kidded**; **kidding**; **kids** [ME *kidden*, fr. *kide*, n.] : to bring forth young — used of a goat or an antelope

³**kid** \"\ *adj* [¹*kid*] **1** : of, relating to, or made of kid **2** : YOUNGER — used in the phrases *kid brother* and *kid sister*

⁴**kid** \"\ *vb* **kidded**; **kidded**; **kidding**; **kids** [prob. fr. ¹*kid*] *vt* **1** : DECEIVE, FOOL **2** : to make fun of usu. good-humoredly and often by innocent deception ⟨used to ~ him then about his intellectual face —G.W.Brace⟩ ⟨a medicine-show barker *kidding* the crowd⟩ ⟨any nation that could ~ its own foibles was . . . new and pleasant —*Time*⟩ ⟨*kidded* him into thinking the police were inquiring about him⟩ ~ *vi* **1** : to make fun of someone or something **2 a** : JOKE **b** : to indulge in good-humored fooling or horseplay — often used with *around* — **kid·der** \-də(r)\ *n* -S

⁵**kid** \"\ *n* -S [ME *kidde*, *kid*] *dial Eng* : a bundle of heath and twigs : FAGOT

⁶**kid** \"\ *vt* **kidded**; **kidded**; **kidding**; **kids** : to bind (fagots) in bundles

⁷**kid** \"\ *vi* **kidded**; **kidded**; **kidding**; **kids** [prob. alter. of earlier *cod*, fr. ¹*cod*] *dial Eng* : to form pods — used of a legume

⁸**kid** \"\ *n* -S [prob. alter. of ¹*cod*] *dial Eng* : the seed pod of a legume

⁹**kid** \"\ *n* -S [prob. alter. of ¹*kit*] : a small wooden tub; *esp* : a sailor's mess tub

**kidcote** \ˈ=,=\ *n* [prob. fr. ¹*kid* (young goat) + *cote* (shed for animals); fr. the use of any available shed in small towns to house lawbreakers] *archaic* : JAIL

**kid·der·min·ster** \ˈkidə(r),minztə(r), -n(t)st-\ *or* **kidderminster carpet** *n* -S *usu cap* [fr. *Kidderminster*, borough in Worcester county, England] : ingrain carpet — called also *Scotch carpet*

**kid·di·er** \ˈkidēə(r)\ *also* **kid·der** \-də(r)\ *n* -S [origin unknown] *dial Eng* : a huckster esp. of agricultural produce

**kid·ding·ly** *adv* : in the manner of one that is kidding

**kid·dish** \ˈkidish, -dēsh\ *adj* : CHILDISH ⟨beginning to come along as well with her ~ admirers —W.C.Williams⟩ — **kid·dish·ly** *adv* — **kid·dish·ness** *n* -ES

¹**kid·dle** \ˈkidᵊl\ *n* -S [ME *kydle*, fr. ONF *quidel*, fr. MLG *kiedel*] : a barrier that extends across a river and that is designed to deflect the water and river fish through an opening across which a fishnet may be stretched

²**kiddle** \"\ *dial Eng var of* CUDDLE

**kid·do** \ˈki(,)dō\ *n, pl* **kiddos** *or* **kiddoes** [¹*kid* + -*o*] — used as a familiar form of address ⟨don't worry about me, ~ —Max Arnold⟩ ⟨this means war, and ~, you're right in the middle —H.L.Spinner⟩

**kid·dush** \ˈki(,)dùsh, -dəsh; kəˈdüsh\ *n* -ES [Heb *qiddūsh* sanctification] : a Jewish ceremony that proclaims the holiness of the incoming Sabbath or festival and that consists of a benediction pronounced customarily before the evening meal over a cup of wine or two loaves of white Sabbath bread ⟨hurried home in time for ~ on Friday evening⟩

**kiddush ha·shem** \-həˈshām\ *n* [Heb *qiddūsh hashshēm* sanctification of the name (of God)] : a religious or moral act according to Jewish religion that causes others to reverence God : religious martyrdom — compare HILLUL HASHEM

**kid·du·shin** \kəˈdüshən, ==ˈshēn\ *n* -S [Aram *qiddūshīn*, pl. of Heb *qiddūsh*] : a betrothal ceremony preceding the Jewish marriage ceremony

**kid·dy** *or* **kid·die** \ˈkidē, -di\ *n, pl* **kiddies** [¹*kid* + -*y*, -*ie*] : a small child

**kid finish** *n* : a bookbinding finish of paper or boards resembling the surface of undressed kid leather

**kid glove** *n* : a dress glove made of kidskin or of some leather that resembles kidskin — **with kid gloves** *adv* : with special consideration : in a tactful manner ⟨never threatened to abuse or discriminate against him, instead treated him *with kid gloves* —*Time*⟩

**kid-glove** \ˈ=ˈ=\ *adj* [*kid glove*] **1** *or* **kid-gloved** \ˈ=ˈ=\ **a** : marked by a calculated fastidiousness and delicacy esp. in the avoidance of the rough or the uncouth in talk or action **b** : marked by extreme considerateness, care, and gentleness (as in handling) ⟨would no longer expect *kid-glove* treatment for their monarchist activities —*New Internat'l Yr. Bk.*⟩ ⟨I never thought I'd have a situation that called for such *kid-gloved* treatment —Francis Towle⟩ **2** *of a citrus fruit* : having an easily removable skin

**kid-glove orange** *n* : MANDARIN 4b(1)

**kid leather** *n* **1** : soft pliable leather made from either goatskin or kidskin and used for shoes, gloves, garments, and handbags **2** : a chrome tanned grain glove leather made from goatskin or lambskin

**kid·let** \ˈkidlə̇t\ *n* -S [¹*kid* + -*let*] *slang* : KIDDY

¹**kid·nap** \ˈkid,nap\ *vt* **kidnaped** *or* **kidnapped**; **kidnaped** *or* **kidnaped**; **kidnapping** *or* **kidnaping**; **kidnaps** [prob. back-formation fr. *kidnapper*] **1** *obs* : to carry off to enforced labor esp. in the British colonies in America **2 a** : to carry (an unwilling person) away by unlawful force or fraud or to seize and detain for the purpose of so carrying away — compare ABDUCTION 2 **b** : to seize and carry or take away often wrongly ⟨*kidnapped* the children for the afternoon⟩ ⟨quite a business *kidnapping* pet dogs and watching the "Lost" columns for reward notices —T.W.Duncan⟩ ⟨*kidnapping* a sizable coastwise steamer —*Nat'l Geographic*⟩

²**kidnap** \"\ *adj* : of, relating to, or being a kidnapping ⟨a ~ plot⟩ ⟨the ~ car⟩

**kid·nap·per** *or* **kid·nap·er** \-pə(r)\ *n* -S [¹*kid* (child) + obs. *napper* thief, fr. *nap* (to seize) + -*er*] : one that kidnaps; *esp* : one that abducts a child for ransom

**kidnapping** *or* **kidnaping** *n* -S [fr. gerund of ¹*kidnap*] : the act or an instance of stealing, abducting, or carrying away a person by force or fraud often with a demand for ransom

**kid·ney** \ˈkidnē, -ni\ *n* -S *often attrib* [ME *kidenei*, *kidney*, fr. *kiden-*, *kidn-* (origin unknown) + *ei*, *ey* egg, fr. OE *ǣg* — more at EGG] **1 a** : one of a pair of vertebrate organs situated in the body cavity near the spinal column that serve to excrete urea, uric acid, and other waste products of metabolism, that in man are bean-shaped organs about 4½ inches long lying behind the peritoneum of the posterior part of the abdomen and embedded in a mass of fatty tissue, and that consist chiefly of nephrons by which urine is secreted, collected, and finally discharged into the pelvis of the kidney whence it is conveyed by the ureter to the bladder to be periodically discharged — compare MESONEPHROS, METANEPHROS, PRONEPHROS **b** : any of various more or less complex excretory organs of invertebrate animals — see GREEN GLAND; compare NEPHRIDIUM **2** : sort or kind esp. as regards persuasion, disposition, or temperament ⟨a nice helpful guy, of a different ~ entirely from the ubiquitous Secret Police functionaries —Paula Lecler⟩ **3** : a kidney-shaped aggregate of ore **syn** see TYPE

**kidney bean** *n* **1** : the seed of any cultivated bean derived from the common species (*Phaseolus vulgaris*); *esp* : any of certain rather large dark red kidney-shaped beans **2** : a plant producing kidney beans

**kidney chop** *n* : a loin chop (as of lamb or veal) containing a kidney whole or in part — see VEAL illustration

**kidney corpuscle** *n* : MALPIGHIAN CORPUSCLE

**kidney cotton** *n* [so called fr. the shape of the mass in which the seeds are found] **1** : a shrub or small tree (*Gossypium brasiliense*) yielding a long-staple cotton **2** : the fiber obtained from kidney cotton

**kidney desk** *n* : a desk that is kidney-shaped in top and horizontal section

**kidney ore** *n* [so called fr. its occurrence in kidney-shaped masses] : a mineral consisting of a variety of hematite

**kidneyroot** \ˈ==,=\ *n* [so called fr. the belief that such plants cure kidney diseases] **1** : JOE-PYE WEED **2** : COYOTE BRUSH

**kidney-shaped** \ˈ==,=\ *adj* : shaped like a kidney : RENIFORM

**kidney stone** *n* **1** : a kidney-shaped pebble **2** : RENAL CALCULUS

kidney desk

**kidney table** *n* : a usu. small side table with a kidney-shaped top

**kidney vetch** *n* : a perennial Eurasian herb (*Anthyllis vulneraria*) having heads of red or yellow flowers and formerly used as a remedy for renal disorders

**kidney worm** *n* : any of several nematode worms parasitic in the kidneys: as **a** : GIANT KIDNEY WORM **b** : a common and destructive black-and-white worm (*Stephanurus dentatus*) that is related to the gapeworm but attains a length of two inches and is parasitic in the kidneys, lungs, and other viscera of the hog in warm regions — called also *lardworm*

**kidneywort** \ˈ==,=\ *n* [so called fr. the use of such plants to cure kidney diseases] **1** : NAVELWORT 1 **2** : STAR SAXIFRAGE **3** : COYOTE BRUSH

**kids** *pl of* KID, *pres 3d sing of* KID

**kidskin** \ˈ=,=\ *n* [¹*kid* + *skin*] **1** : the skin of a young goat **2** : KID LEATHER

**kid stuff** *n* **1** : something befitting or appropriate only to children ⟨realized that all that saluting and about-facing was *kid stuff* —T.W.Duncan⟩ **2** : something extremely simple or easy ⟨convinced him that running for the town council would be *kid stuff*⟩

**kie·kie** \ˈkēə,kēə, ˈkē,kē, ˈkī,kī\ *n* -S [Maori] : a New Zealand climbing shrub (*Freycinetia banksii*) with edible berries

**kiel** \ˈkēl, *esp before pause or consonant* -ēəl\ *adj, usu cap* [fr. *Kiel*, Germany] : of or from the city of Kiel, Germany : of the kind or style prevalent in Kiel

**kiel·ba·sa** \kilˈbäsə, k(y)el-, kēl-\ *n, pl* **kielbasas** \-səz\ *also* **kielba·sy** \-sē\ [Pol *kiełbasa* sausage; akin to Russ *kolbasa* sausage, Czech & Slovenian *klobasa*] : an uncooked smoked sausage

**kier** \ˈki(ə)r\ *n* -S [prob. of Scand origin; akin to ON *ker* tub, vessel, Norw dial. *kjer*; akin to OHG *char* vessel, bowl, Goth *kas* vessel] : a large metal vat in which fibers, yarns, and fabrics are boiled off, bleached, or dyed

**kier-boil** \ˈ=,=\ *vt* : to scour (as cotton) by boiling in a kier usu. with an alkaline solution

**kier·ing** \ˈkiriŋ\ *n* -S : the process of treating in a kier

¹**kier·ke·gaard·ian** \ˌkirkəˌgärdēən, ˌkyerkəˌgȯrēən\ *adj, usu cap* [Sören Aabye *Kierkegaard* †1855 Danish philosopher + E -*ian*] : of or relating to the Danish philosopher Kierkegaard or his existentialist philosophy ⟨discourage the growth of a *Kierkegaardian* cult —James Collins⟩ — compare CHRISTIAN EXISTENTIALISM

²**kierkegaardian** \"\ *n* -S *usu cap* : a follower of Kierkegaard : an adherent of Kierkegaardian philosophy

**kier·man** \ˈkirmən\ *n, pl* **kiermen** : one who works at a kier

**kie·sel·guhr** *or* **kie·sel·gur** \ˈkēzəl,gü(ə)r, -ùə\ *n* -S [G *kieselgur*, fr. *kiesel* pebble, flint + *guhr*, *gur* guhr] : loose or porous diatomite — compare TRIPOLI

**kie·ser·ite** \ˈkēzə,rīt\ *n* -S [G *kieserit*, fr. Dietrich G. *Kieser* †1862 Ger. physician + G -*it* -ite] : a mineral $MgSO_4 \cdot H_2O$ that consists of hydrous magnesium sulfate and is white when pure

**ki·ev** \ˈkē,(y)e\|f, -ēyə\|, \|v\ *adj, usu cap* [fr. *Kiev*, U.S.S.R.] : of or from the city of Kiev, U.S.S.R. : of the kind or style prevalent in Kiev

[1]**ki·ev·an** \'kē,(y)efən, -evən\ *adj, usu cap* [*Kiev*, U.S.S.R. + E *-an*] **:** of or relating to Kiev, U.S.S.R.; *esp* **:** of the 11th and 12th centuries of Kiev's supremacy ⟨*Kievan* Russia⟩
[2]**kievan** \"\ *n* -s *cap* **:** a native or inhabitant of Kiev, U.S.S.R.
**kieve** *var of* KEEVE
**kif** *var of* KEF
**Ki·ja·fa** \kē'(y)afə, -)äfə\ *trademark* — used for a wine made from the juice and flavored with the pits of a small black Danish cherry
**ki·kar** \'kēkə(r), 'kik-\ *n* -s [Hindi *kīkar*] **:** GUM ARABIC TREE
**kike** \'kīk\ *n* -s [prob. alter. of *kiki*, redupl. of *-ki*, common ending of names of Jews who lived in Slavic countries] **:** JEW — usu. taken to be offensive
**ki·ke·pa** \kē'kāpə\ *n* -s [Hawaiian] **:** a tapa or sarong worn by Hawaiian women with the top under one arm and over the shoulder of the opposite arm
**ki·kon·go** \kē'käŋ(,)gō\ *n, usu cap* **:** KONGO
**ki·ku** \'kē(,)kü\ *n* -s [Jap] **:** CHRYSANTHEMUM 1
**kiku·mon** \'kikə,män, 'kēk-\ *n* -s [Jap, fr. *kiku* + *mon* badge, crest] **:** CHRYSANTHEMUM 3
**ki·ku·yu** \kə'kü(,)yü, kē'-\ *n, pl* **kikuyu** *or* **kikuyus** *usu cap* **1 a :** a Bantu-speaking agricultural negroid people of Kenya **b :** a member of such people **2 :** a Bantu language of the Kikuyu people
**kikuyu grass** *n, often cap K* **:** a southern African forage grass (*Pennisetum clandestinum*) introduced into Australia and So. America
**kil** *abbr* **1** kilderkin **2** kilogram **3** kilometer
**kild** *abbr* kilderkin
**kil·dare** \(')kil¦da(a)|(ə)r, -de|, |ə\ *adj, usu cap* [fr. County *Kildare*, Ireland] **:** of or from County Kildare, Ireland **:** of the kind or style prevalent in County Kildare
**kildare green** *n, often cap K* **:** a moderate yellow green that is greener, lighter, and stronger than average moss green, yellower and lighter than average pea green, and yellower and paler than apple green (sense 1)
**kil·dee** \'kildē\ *dial var of* KILLDEER
**kildeer** *var of* KILLDEER
**kil·der·kin** \'kildə(r)kən\ *n* -s [ME *kinderkin, kilderkin*, fr. MD *kindekijn, kinnekijn*, fr. ML *quintale* quintal + MD *-kijn* (dim. suffix) — more at QUINTAL, -KIN] **1 :** a cask about half the size of a common barrel and sometimes smaller **2 :** an English unit of capacity equal to ½ barrel or 18 imperial gallons
**kiley** *var of* KYLIE
**kil·hig** \'kil,hig\ *or* **kil·lig** \'kilig\ *n* -s [origin unknown] **:** a short thick pole used in logging to direct the fall of a tree
**ki·lim** \kē'lēm\ *n* -s [Turk, fr. Per *kilīm*] **:** a pileless tapestry-woven carpet, mat, or spread made in Turkey, Kurdistan, the Caucasus, Iran, and western Turkestan
**ki·li·wa** \kə'lēwə\ *or* **ki·li·wi** \-wē\ *n, pl* **kiliwa** *or* **kiliwas** *or* **kiliwi** *or* **kiliwis** *usu cap* **1 a :** an Indian people of northern Lower California, Mexico **b :** a member of such people **2 :** a Yuman language of the Kiliwa people
**kil·ken·ny** \(')kil¦kenē, -ni\ *adj, usu cap* [fr. County *Kilkenny*, Ireland] **:** of or from County Kilkenny, Ireland **:** of the kind or style prevalent in County Kilkenny
[1]**kill** \'kil\ *vb* **killed** \-ld\ *or chiefly dial* **kilt** \-lt\ **killed** *or chiefly dial* **kilt**; **killing**; **kills** [ME *cullen, killen* to strike, beat, kill; perh. akin to OE *cwellan* to kill — more at QUELL] *vt* **1 a :** to deprive of life **:** put to death **:** cause the death of ⟨~*ed* by enemy fire⟩ ⟨this poison ~*s* rats⟩ ⟨the accident ~*ed* six people⟩; *also* **:** to terminate suddenly the life processes of (as in preparing tissue for fixing and microscopic examination) **b :** to destroy as if by killing ⟨~*s* whatever core of human decency he ever had in him —Aldous Huxley⟩ ⟨an industry ~*ed* by competition⟩ ⟨an unfavorable report would . . . ~ any chance of getting a license —*Wall Street Jour.*⟩ **c :** to slaughter (as a hog) for food **:** convert a food animal into (as pork) by slaughtering **d** (1) **:** to shatter (a clay target) by hitting in skeet shooting (2) *of a ship* **:** SINK ⟨~*ed* ships and . . . wounded ships staggering away from battle —Ira Wolfert⟩ **e :** to subvert completely the plans and hopes of **:** outwit with the result of putting in a hopeless position ⟨the calamitous failure of his plan ~*ed* him more than if he had lost all his money⟩ **2 a :** to put an end to esp. abruptly **:** cause to cease **:** stop esp. with finality ⟨knew he could not ~ the evil in the world⟩ ⟨~ the enterprise by denying it the money necessary to proceed⟩ ⟨the censors ~*ed* the play after its first week⟩ ⟨~*ed* the engine and got out of the car⟩ ⟨a snack to ~ her hunger⟩ ⟨the fire-*killing* power of the chemical⟩ **b :** to get rid of **:** ELIMINATE ⟨~ foam in pulp in paper mills⟩ **c :** DEFEAT, VETO ⟨the bill was ~*ed* on the first vote⟩ ⟨asked for a transfer but his petition was ~*ed*⟩ **d** (1) **:** to take out or omit or mark for omission (something published as in a newspaper or presented as on a stage) **:** mark for deletion (something designed for publication or presentation) ⟨~*ed* a good part of the article for political reasons⟩ ⟨~*ed* the story as it was written for the late edition⟩ ⟨~*ed* the second act and substituted a new one after the second week⟩; *also* **:** to order (as set type) to be destroyed or distributed (2) **:** to stop the use of (as a stage prop or broadcast microphone) or the functioning of (as a stage light) **3 a :** to destroy the vital or active or essential quality of ⟨~ a disease with antibiotics⟩ ⟨~*ed* the pain with drugs⟩ ⟨the heat ~*ed* the yeast⟩ ⟨believed that to explain a joke is to ~ it⟩ **b :** NEUTRALIZE ⟨threw an alkali in the solution to ~ the acid⟩ **c :** to deprive of the power to germinate ⟨~ the seed⟩ **d :** to do damage or injury to (as flour) by overheating **e :** SPOIL, RUIN ⟨the addition of the wrong color totally ~*ed* the portrait⟩ **f** (1) **:** to injure or hurt severely **:** cause extreme pain to ⟨my feet are ~*ing* me⟩ (2) *chiefly Irish* **:** to knock unconscious ⟨got ~*ed* in a fight and didn't come to until morning⟩ **g :** to tire or exhaust esp. almost to the point of collapse ⟨the heat and the heavy work ~*ed* him and he had to lie down for a while⟩ ⟨no use ~*ing* ourselves getting to the train —J.P. Marquand⟩ **h :** to lessen or impede markedly ⟨the frantic maneuver ~*ed* her speed —Joseph Millard⟩ **i :** to impress a cancellation mark upon (a stamp) ⟨the stamp was ~*ed* with a blue grid —E.R.Guilford⟩ **4 a :** to make a markedly favorable impression on **:** affect strongly ⟨on her first stage appearance she ~*ed* the audience⟩ **b** *slang* **:** to impress as hilariously funny or ridiculous ⟨his jokes ~*ed* me⟩ **5 :** to occupy oneself in some convenient way merely to pass (time or a unit of time) **:** fill in (time or a unit of time) ⟨ways in which to ~ an hour until train time⟩ ⟨~ an entire afternoon over a pot of tea —Lin Yutang⟩; *also* **:** to provide or serve as a convenient occupation or distraction to help pass (time or a unit of time) ⟨reading ~*ed* a good deal of time during the trip⟩ **6 a :** to treat in such a manner as to destroy undesirable properties and so make suitable for further treatment or for a specific purpose ⟨~ soap stock by boiling with alkali⟩ ⟨~ fur by means of chemicals in preparation for dyeing⟩ **b :** to cause (molten steel) to become quiet and free from bubbling by adding a strong deoxidizing agent (as aluminum) that combines with oxygen and minimizes reaction between oxygen and carbon during solidification **c :** KNOT 5 **d :** DE-ENERGIZE ⟨~ a live electrical circuit⟩ **e :** to reduce the strength of (plaster of paris) by mixing with an excess of water **7 :** to break or burn (an object in a mortuary rite of a nonliterate culture) for the purpose of separating from the material substance the spirit which may then accompany and serve the spirit of a recently deceased person **8 :** to play (a return shot) so hard in a racket game that one's opponent cannot make return — compare SMASH **9 a :** to consume (as an alcoholic beverage) totally ⟨~*ed* his drink and held out the glass —W.L.Gresham⟩ **b :** to consume the total contents of (as a bottle of liquor) ⟨~*ed* two bottles of wine over dinner⟩ ~ *vi* **1 a :** to perform the act of killing something **:** commit murder or slaughter **b :** to make an irresistible impression ⟨dressed to ~⟩ **c :** to produce exhaustion or fatigue ⟨a ~*ing* occupation⟩ **2 :** to undergo killing or slaughter — usu. used of a food animal
**syn** KILL, SLAY, MURDER, ASSASSINATE, DISPATCH, EXECUTE all mean, in common, to put to death. KILL merely states the fact ⟨*kill* a rabbit⟩ ⟨a man *killed* by a twenty-foot fall⟩ ⟨the drought *killed* most of the vegetation⟩ ⟨*kill* a proposal⟩ SLAY in being a more literary word implies a force and wantonness and a generally more dramatic action ⟨the law which forbade the sinful *slaying* of a cat —Agnes Repplier⟩ ⟨his heavy tales of how Dion O'Banion was *slain* in his flower shop —Herman Kogan⟩ ⟨in 1258 the terrible conqueror Hulagu swept over Baghdad and *slew* the Caliph with 80,000 of the faithful —*Times Lit. Supp.*⟩ MURDER implies motive and usu. premeditation in a criminal human act ⟨*murder* a wealthy man for his money⟩ ⟨the fear which drove Rome to *murder* Carthage and Corinth and her own character as well —Herbert Agar⟩ ⟨that theory is *murdered* by the brutal fact that there are many among the older generation who will not believe —G.W. Johnson⟩ ASSASSINATE implies the killing of a person by stealth or treachery, esp. of a person in governmental or political power ⟨*assassinate* a monarch⟩ DISPATCH in this connection stresses speed and directness in murdering or otherwise putting to death and is usu. used intentionally to avoid the violent or odious connotations of the other terms ⟨eight to twelve otters were *dispatched* before the main herd dispersed —*Nature Mag.*⟩ ⟨one of his first tasks was to *dispatch* a sick and dying horse with a sledgehammer —*Times Lit. Supp.*⟩ ⟨then reached up, caught Wright by the coat, drew him down on to him, and at one stab *dispatched* him —*Amer. Guide Series: La.*⟩ EXECUTE is the term used for putting to death one condemned to death by a legal or quasi-legal process ⟨*execute* a man convicted of murder⟩ ⟨the mob summarily *executed* the horse thief⟩
[2]**kill** \"\ *n* -s **1 a :** KILLING 1 ⟨an animal moving in for the ~⟩ ⟨indicted a man for a ~ in the downtown section of the city⟩ **b :** an act of hunting with the intent of killing for food ⟨an animal on a ~⟩ **c** (1) **:** the death or killing (as of weeds) by weed killers, insecticides, or other lethal preparations (2) **:** the ability to kill **:** a killing force (as of a weed killer) ⟨the residual ~ of DDT⟩ **2 :** something killed: as **a :** an animal or bird shot in a hunt; *collectively* **:** the animals or birds shot in a hunt, during a season, or in a particular period of time ⟨the annual ~ of cock pheasants is estimated at 750,000 —*Amer. Guide Series: Mich.*⟩ **b :** an enemy airplane shot down or otherwise destroyed by military action while in flight ⟨a group captain's determination to get maximum ~*s* at his fighter station —*Sydney (Australia) Bull.*⟩; *also* **:** an enemy submarine or ship destroyed **c :** something to be destroyed (as by gunfire) ⟨guide missiles to the ~ —J.J. Haggerty⟩ **d :** copy that has been omitted or marked for omission from a publication (as a newspaper) **e :** a return shot in a racket game that has been driven so hard that one's opponent cannot handle it **3 :** an order or instruction to kill (as set type matter or a news story) **4 :** KILLING 3 **5 :** an animal used as bait in big-game hunting — **on the kill 1** *of an animal* **:** having the intention of killing (as for food) **2 :** intending to stop at almost nothing to achieve one's end ⟨politicians *on the kill* in an election year⟩
[3]**kill** \"\ *n* -s *often cap* [D *kil*, fr. MD *kille*; akin to East Fris. *kille* watercourse, ON *kill* small bay, arm of the sea, and perh. to OHG *kil* wedge — more at CHINE] **:** CHANNEL, CREEK, RIVER, STREAM — used chiefly in place names in Delaware and the state of New York (as Catskill mountains)
**kill·able** \'kiləbəl\ *adj* **:** capable of being killed esp. legally **:** fit to kill
[1]**kil·lar·ney** \kə'lärnē, -lȧn-, -ni\ *adj, usu cap* [fr. *Killarney* mountains, Ontario, Canada] **:** of, relating to, or constituting mountain-making movements near the end of the Proterozoic era — see GEOLOGIC TIME table
[2]**killarney** \"\ *or* **killarney green** *n* -s *often cap K* [fr. *Killarney*, district in County Kerry, Ireland] **:** a moderate yellowish green to green that is stronger than Gretna green
**kil·las** \'kiləs\ *n* -ES [Corn *kyllas*] *Cornwall* **:** argillaceous slate
**kill back** *vt* **:** to kill (a tree or shrub) at the top ⟨low temperature *killed* the tree *back*⟩ ⟨the tops of all the garden shrubs were *killed back* by the storm⟩
**kill-courtesy** *n, obs* **:** BOOR
**kill-cow** \'⸗,⸗\ *n* **1** *now dial* **:** a man of real or fancied importance **:** PERSONAGE **2** *now dial* **:** a serious or consequential matter
**kill·crop** \'kil,kräp\ *n* [LG *kilkrop*] **:** a voracious infant **:** a fairy changeling
**kill·dee** \'kildē\ *dial var of* KILLDEER
**kill·deer** *or* **kil·deer** \'kil,di(ə)r, -iə\ *n, pl* **killdeers** *or* **killdeer** *or* **kildeers** *or* **kildeer** [imit.] **:** a plover (*Charadrius vociferus* syn. *Oxyechus vociferus*) found throughout temperate No. America and in southern areas in migration to So. America, being about 10 inches long, grayish brown above, ferruginous in the rump, and white below and with two black bands on the breast and neck, and having a much-repeated cry that is plaintive and penetrating
**kill-devil** \'⸗,⸗⸗\ *n* **1** *dial* **:** West Indian rum **2 :** liquor that is cheap or poor in quality
**killed** *past of* KILL
**kil·le·fer** *also* **kil·li·fer** \'kiləfə(r)\ *n* -s [fr. the name *Killefer*] **:** a tractor-drawn agricultural machine that is used for deep tillage and loosening of the subsoil and consists essentially of one or more wheel-mounted pointed horizontal knives or chisels
**kill·er** \'kilə(r)\ *n* -s *often attrib* [[1]*kill* + *-er*] **1 :** one that kills: **a :** MURDERER; *esp* **:** a homicidal criminal or maniac **b :** SLAUGHTERER; *also* **:** one who buys animals for slaughter ⟨~*s* took a big share of the choice of low prime yearlings —*Chicago Daily Drovers Jour.*⟩ **c :** an effective bait in fishing **d :** something that has a forceful and usu. violent impact ⟨a backhand stroke that was a ~⟩ ⟨his punch was a ~⟩ **e** *slang* **:** one who gives an admirable or irresistible personal or sartorial impression ⟨she was no ~ on looks —Garson Kanin⟩ **2 :** an animal to be killed for food or other use **3** *or* **killer whale :** a fierce carnivorous gregarious whale (*Orcinus orca* syn. *Orca orca*) 20 to 30 feet long that is black with yellowish white areas on sides and underparts, has a high dorsal fin, powerful tail, and sharp strong teeth, and preys on large fishes, seals, and even in groups on the larger whales **4 :** a postal canceling stamp; *also* **:** a cancellation mark on a postage stamp

killer 4

**killer bar** *n* **:** a bar or line on a postmarking stamp or in the postmark it produces
**killer boat** *also* **killer ship** *n* **:** one of the small fast boats accompanying a factory ship in whaling and responsible for the pursuit and capture of a whale
**killer-diller** \¦kilə(r)¦dilə(r)\ *n* -s [redupl. of *killer*] *slang* **:** something highly and usu. factitiously sensational of its kind ⟨plot hocus-pocus and *killer-diller* battles between good and evil —Jean Garrigue⟩ ⟨*killer-diller* love scenes —C.J.Rolo⟩
**killer plant** *n* **:** an East African plant (*Adenia sinensis*) of the family Passifloraceae that contains a highly poisonous alkaloid — called also *modecca flower*
**kil·lick** \'kilik\ *also* **kel·leg** \'keləg\ *or* **kel·lock** \'kelək\ *or* **kil·lock** \'kilək\ *n* -s [origin unknown] **1 :** ANCHOR; *esp* **:** a small anchor **2 :** a jury anchor formed by a stone usu. bound within sticks of wood
**killickinnic** *or* **killikinick** *or* **killickinnick** *var of* KINNIKINNICK
**kil·lie** *also* **kil·ly** \'kilē\ *or* **kel·ly** *or* **kel·lie** \'kelē\ *n, pl* **killies** *or* **kellies** [[3]*kill* + *-ie, -y*] **:** KILLIFISH
**kil·li·fish** \'kilē,fish, -li,-\ *n* [*killie* + *fish*] **1 :** any of numerous small oviparous fishes of the family Cyprinodontidae which are usu. striped or barred with black, which are much used as bait and in mosquito control, and some of which live equally well in fresh and brackish water or even in the sea — see GUDGEON, MAYFISH, MUMMICHOG **2 :** TOPMINNOW 1
**killig** *var of* KILHIG
[1]**kill·ing** \'kiliŋ, -lēŋ\ *n* -s [ME, fr. gerund of *killen* to strike, kill — more at KILL] **1 :** the act of one that kills; *esp* **:** MURDER, HOMICIDE **2 :** KILL 2a **3 :** a sudden notable success esp. in stock speculation or business ⟨a ~ he made in railway securities —Robert Shaplen⟩
[2]**killing** \"\ *adj* [fr. pres. part. of [1]*kill*] **1 :** having the effect of killing: as **a :** producing death **:** FATAL, DEADLY ⟨a ~ disease⟩ ⟨a ~ drink⟩ **b :** having a marked deleterious or painful effect or impact extremely difficult to endure **:** ⟨the strain of concentration was ~, so he gave up⟩; *also* **:** calling for great strength, stamina, or endurance ⟨a ~ pace⟩ **c :** having an irresistible and notable effect ⟨a ~ humor⟩ ⟨a ~ dress⟩ **2 :** arousing the desire to kill ⟨as ~ a hatred between them as though they were two jungle beasts —Jean Stafford⟩
**killing bottle** *n* **:** a bottle containing a poisonous vapor (as cyanide) for killing insects to be preserved as specimens
**killing frost** *n* **:** a frost low enough in temperature to kill most exposed garden vegetation and fruit buds
**kill·ing·ly** *adv* **:** in a killing manner
**kil·lin·ite** \'kilə,nīt\ *n* -s [*Killiney*, bay and village, County Dublin, Ireland + E *-ite*] **:** a mineral consisting of a variety of pinite
**killjoy** \'⸗,⸗\ *n* [[1]*kill* + *joy*] **:** one that inspires gloom or counteracts joy or high spirits **:** one that tends to pessimism or a depressing solemnness esp. among people that are happy or optimistic **:** one that dispirits ⟨professional ~*s* whose chief fear it is that people . . . might get some fun out of life —T.P.Whitney⟩
**kill-kid** \'⸗,⸗\ *n* [[1]*kill* + *kid* (young goat); fr. the poisonous foliage] **:** SHEEP LAUREL
**kill off** *vt* **1 :** to destroy in large numbers or totally ⟨the flood of hunters *killed* the buffalo *off* rapidly until only a few were left⟩ ⟨the flowers were *killed off* by the first frost⟩ ⟨the lack of enthusiasm *killed* the project *off* quickly⟩ **2 :** to get rid of **:** ELIMINATE ⟨the low prices they asked *killed* their competition *off*⟩
**kil·lo·gie** \kə'lōgi\ *n* -s [perh. irreg. fr. Sc *kill* kiln, fr. ME, alter. of *kilne* — more at KILN] *chiefly Scot* **:** the sheltered space before a kiln fire
**kill out** *vt* **:** to complete the curing of (tobacco) by exposing to high temperature to dry out the stem and stop further chemical change
**kills** *pres 3d sing of* KILL, *pl of* KILL
**kill-time** \'⸗,⸗\ *n* **:** an occupation that serves to kill time
**kill-wart** \'⸗,⸗\ *or* **killwort** \'⸗,⸗\ *n* [*kill-wart* fr. [1]*kill* + *wart*; fr. its use to remove warts; *killwort* by folk etymology fr. *kill-wart*] **:** CELANDINE 1
**killy fish** *n* **:** KILLIFISH
**kil·ly hawk** \'kilē-\ *n* [*killy* of imit. origin] **:** SPARROW HAWK 2
**kil·mar·nock willow** \(')kil¦märnək-\ *n, usu cap K* [fr. *Kilmarnock*, burgh in Ayr county, Scotland] **:** a small Old World willow that is a variety (*Salix caprea pendula*) of the great sallow with crooked pendulous branches
[1]**kiln** \'kil(n)\ *n* -s *often attrib* [ME *kilne*, fr. OE *cyln, cylen*, fr. L *culina* kitchen, fr. *coquere* to cook — more at COOK] **:** an oven, furnace, or heated enclosure used for processing a substance by burning, firing, or drying: as **a :** LIMEKILN **b :** BRICKKILN **c :** an oven with a heat-resistant lining used to fire ceramics **d :** a room or shed through which warm air is circulated for the removal of moisture (as from grain, lumber, or tobacco) — compare KILN EVAPORATOR
[2]**kiln** \"\ *vt* -ED/-ING/-s **:** to burn, fire, or dry in a kiln
**kiln-dried** \'⸗¦⸗\ *adj* **:** dried or cured in a kiln ⟨*kiln-dried* lumber⟩
**kiln-dry** \'⸗¦⸗\ *vt* **:** to dry (wood) in a kiln **:** season artificially
**kiln evaporator** *n* **:** a room with a slatted floor through which heat is circulated for drying fruit
**kilneye** \'⸗,⸗\ *or* **kilnhole** \'⸗,⸗\ *n* **:** the mouth of a kiln; *specif* **:** an opening in a limekiln for removal of the lime
**kiln·man** \'⸗mən\ *n, pl* **kilnmen :** one who loads or fires a kiln or controls the drying or baking done therein
**kiln-run** \'⸗,⸗\ *adj* **:** as taken from the kiln **:** not sorted as to quality ⟨*kiln-run* brick⟩
**kiln scum** *n* **:** WHITEWASH 3
[1]**ki·lo** \'kē(,)lō, 'ki(-\ *n* -s **1 a** [by shortening] **:** KILOGRAM **b :** KILOWARE **2** [by shortening] **:** KILOMETER
[2]**kilo** \"\ *usu cap* — a communications code word for the letter *k*
**kilo-** *comb form* [F, modif. of Gk *chilioi* — more at MILE] **:** thousand — chiefly in names of units in the metric system ⟨*kilo*ampere⟩ ⟨*kilo*gauss⟩ ⟨*kilo*joule⟩
**kilo·calorie** \'kilō+,-\ *n* [ISV *kilo-* + *calorie*] **:** CALORIE b(1)
**kilo·cy·cle** \'kilə,sīkəl\ *n* [ISV *kilo-* + *cycle*] **:** one thousand cycles; *esp* **:** one thousand cycles per second — used as a unit of radio frequency ⟨broadcasting on a frequency of 1250 ~*s*⟩; abbr. *kc*
**kilo·gram** *or* **kilo·gramme** \-,gram, -raa(ə)m\ *n* [F *kilogramme*, fr. *kilo-* + *gramme* gram — more at GRAM] **1 :** the basic metric unit of mass and weight equal to the mass of a platinum-iridium cylinder kept at the International Bureau of Weights and Measures near Paris and nearly equal to 1000 cubic centimeters of water at the temperature of its maximum density — see METRIC SYSTEM table; abbr. *kg* **2 :** a unit of force equal to the weight of a kilogram under standard gravity
**kilogram calorie** *n* **:** CALORIE b(1)
**kilogram-meter** \'⸗⸗,⸗'⸗⸗\ *n* **:** the mks gravitational unit of work and energy equal to the work done by a kilogram force acting through a distance of one meter in the direction of the force **:** about 7.235 foot-pounds
**kilo·hertz** \'kilə +,-\ *n* [ISV *kilo-* + *hertz*] **:** a unit of frequency equal to one thousand hertz — abbr. *kHz*
**kilo·liter** \'kilə+,-\ *n* [F *kilolitre*, fr. *kilo-* + *litre* liter — more at LITER] **:** a metric unit of capacity equal to 1000 liters — see METRIC SYSTEM table; abbr. *kl*
**kilome·ter** \÷kə'läməd·ə(r), |tə- *also* 'kilə,mē|\ *n* [F *kilomètre*, fr. *kilo-* + *mètre* meter — more at METER] **:** a metric unit of length equal to 1000 meters — see METRIC SYSTEM table; abbr. *km*
**kilo·parsec** \'kilə+\ *n* **:** one thousand parsecs
**kilo·ton** \'kilə,tən\ *n* [*kilo-* + *ton*] **1 :** one thousand tons **2 :** an explosive force equivalent to that of one thousand tons of TNT — used esp. in reference to an atom or hydrogen bomb — abbr. *kt*
**kil·o·var** \-,vär\ *n* -s [*kilo*volt + *a*mpere + *r*eactive] **:** the part of a kilovolt-ampere contributed by reactance
**kilo·volt** \'kilə,vōlt\ *n* [ISV *kilo-* + *volt*] **:** a unit of electromotive force equal to one thousand volts — abbr. *kv*
**kilo·volt·age** \-tij\ *n* **:** potential difference expressed in kilovolts
**kilovolt-ampere** \'⸗⸗,⸗'⸗,⸗\ *n* **:** a unit of apparent power in an electric circuit equal to 1000 volt-amperes
**kilo·ware** \'kilə+,-\ *n* [*kilo* + *ware*] **1 :** packaged mixtures of unsorted postage stamps accumulated esp. by European post offices largely from parcel tags and sold by the kilogram **2 :** a package of unsorted stamps usu. sealed by the government to indicate that the mixture is as orig. assembled by the post office
**kilo·watt** \'kilə,wät, *usu* -äd·+V\ *n* [ISV *kilo-* + *watt*] **:** a unit of power equal to 1000 watts or about 1.34 horsepower — abbr. *kw*
**kilowatt-hour** \'⸗⸗,⸗'⸗\ *n* **:** a unit of work or energy equal to that expended in one hour at a steady rate of one kilowatt or to $3.6 \times 10^6$ joules
**kilp** \'kilp\ *dial Eng var of* KELP
**kil·roy** \'kil,rȯi\ *n* -s *usu cap* [after *Kilroy*, mythical soldier of World War II whose name was inscribed in unlikely places all over the world by Amer. soldiers] **:** an inveterate traveler ⟨like the roamers *Kilroy* and Ulysses —Peter Viereck⟩; *esp* **:** a transient soldier ⟨of all the *Kilroys* of history who have passed through here . . . it was Napoleon who best summed up the strategic importance of Malta —J.P.O'Donnell⟩
[1]**kilt** \'kilt\ *vb* -ED/-ING/-s [ME *kilten*, of Scand origin; akin to Dan *kilte (op)* to gather up (as a skirt), Sw dial. *kilta (sej)* to gather up one's skirts, ON *kjalta* fold made by a gathered skirt, OSw *kilta* lap, and perh. to Goth *kilthei* womb — more at CHILD] *vt* **1** *now chiefly dial* **:** to gather up or tuck in (as a skirt) for protection or freedom of action **2** *archaic* **:** to truss up **:** HANG ⟨brought the country to order by ~*ing* thieves and banditti with strings —Sir Walter Scott⟩ **3 :** to equip with a kilt ⟨insists that nominees prove Scottish relationship or extraction, or they don't get ~*ed* —*Sat. Eve. Post*⟩ ~ *vi* **:** to move nimbly
[2]**kilt** \"\ *n* -s **1 :** a pleated wraparound skirt usu. of tartan reaching from the waist to the knees worn by men and boys in Scotland and esp. by Scottish regiments in the British armies **2 :** something that resembles a Scottish kilt; *esp* **:** a short plaid skirt for women or girls
[3]**kilt** *chiefly dial past of* KILL
[1]**kilt·ed** \'kiltəd\ *adj* [fr. past part. of [1]*kilt*] **1 :** gathered in or tucked up ⟨clam diggers with ~ skirts⟩ **2 :** gathered in vertical pleats **:** KNIFE-PLEATED ⟨yoke of ~ nylon⟩
[2]**kilted** \"\ *adj* [[2]*kilt* + *-ed*] **:** wearing a kilt ⟨a tall ~ Highlander⟩ ⟨~ regiment⟩

**kil·ter** \'kiltə(r)\ *also* **kel·ter** \'kel-\ *n* -S [origin unknown] **1 a :** good working condition **:** ORDER, ADJUSTMENT — usu. used in the phrase *out of kilter* ⟨the car wouldn't go because the engine was out of ~⟩ ⟨his nerves are out of ~ —James Hilton⟩ **b :** BALANCE, ALIGNMENT ⟨unexpected expenses threw the budget out of ~⟩ ⟨a truck rammed the house and pushed it out of ~⟩ **2 :** 4SKEET

**kilt·ie** \'kiltē, -ti\ *n* -S [2*kilt* + *-ie*] **1** *or* **kilty** \"\ -ES *often cap* **:** one who wears a kilt; *specif* **:** a member of a Highland regiment **2 a :** a shoe with a long slashed tongue that folds over the instep to cover the lacing **b :** SHAWL TONGUE

kiltie 2a

**kim·ber·ley** \'kimbə(r)lē\ *n* -S *often cap* [fr. *Kimberley*, town in northern Cape Province, Union of So. Africa] **:** a commercial grade of white diamond ranking below Wesselton

**kimberley horse disease** *n, usu cap K* [fr. *Kimberley*, district of Western Australia] **:** WALKABOUT DISEASE

**kim·ber·lin** \'kimbələn\ *n* -S [prob. alter. of ME *kymeling*, *comling* — more at COMELING] *dial Eng* **:** NEWCOMER, STRANGER

**kim·ber·lite** \'kimbə(r),līt\ *n* -S [*Kimberley*, Union of So. Africa + E *-ite*] **:** an agglomerate biotite-peridotite that occurs in pipes in southern Africa and less extensively in Kentucky and that is weathered yellow at the surface, is blue farther down, and often contains diamonds — called also *blue earth, blue ground, blue stuff*

**kim·bun·du** \kim'bün(,)dü\ *n, usu cap* **:** a Bantu language of northern Angola — called also *Mbundu*

**kim·chi** *also* **kim·ch'i** *or* **kim·chee** \'kimchē\ *n* -S [Korean] **:** a vegetable pickle seasoned with garlic, red pepper, and ginger that is the national dish of Korea

**kim·mer** \'kimər\ *var of* CUMMER

**kim·me·ri·an** \kə'mirēən, -mēr-\ *usu cap, var of* CIMMERIAN

**kim·nel** \'kimn(ə)l\ *n* -S [ME *kymelyn, kymnelle*, prob. fr. OE *cumb*, a liquid measure — more at COOMB] *now dial Eng* **:** a large wooden tub for brewing, kneading, and salting meat

**ki·mo·no** \kə'mōnə *sometimes* -ō(,)nō\ *or* **ki·mo·na** \-ōnə\ *n* -S [Jap *kimono* clothes] **1 :** a loose wraparound robe with wide sleeves and a broad sash traditionally worn by Japanese men and women ⟨a neat waiting maid in striped ~ —*Outlook*⟩ **2 :** a loose dressing gown copied from the Japanese robe and worn chiefly by women and babies — **ki·mo·noed** \-nəd,-nōd\ *or* **ki·mo·naed** \-nəd\ *adj*

kimono 2

**kimono sleeve** *n* **:** a sleeve cut in one piece with the bodice

**kim·ri** \'kimrē\ *adj* [Ar] **:** of, relating to, or constituting the first of four recognized stages in the ripening of a date in which it makes its most rapid growth and remains green — compare KHALAL, RUTAB, TAMAR

**kim·squit** \'kimzkwət, -im(p)skw-\ *n, pl* **kimsquit** *or* **kimsquits** *usu cap* **1 :** a Bellacoola people of Dean Inlet on the Kimsquit river, British Columbia **2 :** a member of the Kimsquit people

1**kin** \'kin\ *n, pl* **kin** *see sense 1a* [ME, fr. OE *cyn;* akin to OHG *kind* child, *chunni* family, race, ON *kyn*, Goth *kuni* family, race, L *genus* kind, race, *gignere* to beget, Gk *genea* birth, race, family, *genos* race, kin, kind, *gignesthai* to be born, Skt *janati* he begets, *jana* person] **1 a** *pl* **kins :** a group of persons of common ancestry **:** CLAN, STOCK ⟨chiefs of the ~*s* —P.A.Sorokin⟩ **b** *archaic* **:** LINEAGE, EXTRACTION, BIRTH ⟨some one perhaps of gentle ~ —Edmund Spenser⟩ **2 a :** one's immediate family **:** RELATIVES, KINDRED ⟨an outcast among . . . the ~ of his father —Ruth Benedict⟩ **b :** a blood relation **:** KINSMAN ⟨he wasn't any ~ to you —Jean Stafford⟩ — compare CONSANGUINITY **3** *obs* **:** the quality or state of being related **:** KINSHIP ⟨without a crime, except his ~ to me —John Dryden⟩ **4 a :** a related group **:** similar kind **:** ILK ⟨the positivists and their ~ —W.V.Quine⟩ **b :** one having community of interest or close affinity with another ⟨abstraction and generalization have always been recognized as close ~ —John Dewey⟩ — **of kin :** closely related **:** AKIN ⟨he was *of kin* to the . . . prizefighter —*Times Lit. Supp.*⟩

2**kin** \"\ *adj* **:** of the same nature or family **:** having affinity **:** KINDRED, RELATED ⟨Germany . . . is the ~ land of these people of Pennsylvania —G.P.Musselman⟩

3**kin** \'kīn\ *chiefly Scot var of* KIND

4**kin** \'kin\ *n* -S [ME *kyne, kynne*, alter. of *chin, chine* crack, fissure, chasm — more at CHINE] *dial Eng* **:** CRACK, CREVICE; *specif* **:** a chap in the skin

5**kin** \'kin\ *n, pl* **kin** [Jap] **:** CATTY

6**kin** \"\ *n* -S [Chin (Pek) *ch'in²*] **:** an ancient Chinese musical instrument resembling a zither and having from 5 to 25 silk strings — compare KOTO

7**kin** \'jin\ *n* -S *usu cap* [Chin (Pek) *Chin¹*] **1 :** a Tatar people founding an 11th century dynasty in China and being ancestral to the Manchus **2 :** a member of the Kin people

**kin-** *or* **kine-** *or* **kino-** *or* **cin-** *or* **cino-** *comb form* [Gk *kinēma* motion — more at CINEMATOGRAPH] **:** motion **:** action ⟨*kin*esthesia⟩ ⟨*kino*plasm⟩ ⟨*kine*plasty⟩

**-kin** \kən\ *also* **-kins** \-nz\ *n suffix, pl* **-kins** [*-kin* fr. ME, fr. MD *-kin, -ken, -kijn;* akin to OS *-kīn*, dim. suffix, OHG *-chīn; -kins* fr. ME, suffix used to form surnames (as *Jenkins*), fr. *-kin* + *-s*, patronymic suffix (as in *Roberts*)] **:** little ⟨cat*kin*⟩ ⟨baby*kins*⟩

**kinaesthesia** *or* **kinaesthesis** *var of* KINESTHESIA

**ki·nah** *also* **qi·nah** \kē'nä\ *n, pl* **ki·noth** *or* **ki·not** *also* **qi·noth** *or* **qi·not** \-nōt(h)\ [Heb *qīnāh* dirge, lamentation] **1 :** a Hebrew elegy chanted traditionally on the Ninth of Ab **2 :** a dirge or lament esp. as sung by Jewish professional mourning women

**kinah meter** *n* **:** a Hebrew poetic meter typically having the line divided into two stichs with three stresses in the first stich and two stresses in the second

**ki·nase** \'kī,nās, 'ki,-\ *n* -S [ISV *kin*etic + *-ase;* orig. formed in G] **1 :** a substance (as enterokinase) that converts a zymogen into an enzyme — compare COENZYME **2 :** any of various enzymes (as hexokinases) that promote phosphorylation processes ⟨adenylic ~ or myosine catalyzes the transfer of phosphate groups among the adenosine phosphates⟩ — compare PHOSPHORYLASE

**kin·car·dine·shire** \kən'kärd(ə)n,shi(ə)r, kiŋ'-, -,shər\ *or* **kincardine** *adj, usu cap* [fr. *Kincardineshire* or *Kincardine* county, Scotland] **:** of or from the county of Kincardine, Scotland **:** of the kind or style prevalent in Kincardine

**kinch** \'kinch\ *n* -ES [alter. of 3*kink*] *chiefly Scot* **:** a noose or loop in a rope

**kin·chin** \'kinchən\ *n* -S [G *kindchen*, dim. of *kind* child, fr. OHG — more at KIN] *slang* **:** CHILD ⟨~*s* . . . sent on errands by their mothers —Charles Dickens⟩

**kin·cob** *also* **kin·kob** *or* **kin·khab** \'kin,käb, -iŋ,-\ *n* -S [Hindi *kimkhāb, kamkhwāb*, fr. Per] **:** an Indian brocade usu. of gold or silver or both

1**kind** \'kīnd\ *n* -S [ME *kind, kinde*, fr. OE *cynd, gecynd;* akin to OE *cyn* kin — more at KIN] **1 a** *archaic* **:** a universal order or inherent tendency in nature ⟨God holds us by laws of ~ —Nathaniel Fairfax⟩ ⟨lovers wanting sight shall follow ~ —Thomas Watson †1592⟩; *specif* **:** natural disposition **b :** a natural grouping without taxonomic connotations **:** SPECIES ⟨people . . . cut off by the desert or the frozen north from communication with their ~ —Ellen Glasgow⟩ ⟨the ways that mud turtles had found best for their ~ —J.W.Krutch⟩ ⟨search for the real essences of natural ~*s* —Stuart Hampshire⟩ **c** *archaic* **:** FAMILY, LINEAGE ⟨of a gentle ~ and noble stock —Shak.⟩ **d** *archaic* **:** a related grouping **:** SECT ⟨poets ever were a careless ~ —William Collins †1759⟩ **2 a** *archaic* **:** STYLE, ASPECT, MANNER, WISE ⟨mirthful . . . but in a stately ~ —Alfred Tennyson⟩ ⟨in no ~ desirous that his majesty should be under any obligation —Thomas Hale⟩ **b** *South & Midland* **:** WAY — used with superlative ⟨he's heartburning the worst ~ over that little gal —*Amer. Guide Series: Tenn.*⟩ ⟨he's goin' to coax his father the hardest ~ —W.D.Howells⟩ **3 a** *obs* **:** SEX ⟨ask . . . what inquest made her dissemble her disguised ~ —Edmund Spenser⟩ **b** *archaic* **:** innate character **:** INSTINCT ⟨though fickle she prove, a woman has't by ~ —Robert Burns⟩ **c :** fundamental nature or quality **:** ESSENCE ⟨problems of social science differ from problems of individual behavior in degree . . . not in ~ —Edward Sapir⟩ **4 a :** a group united by common traits or interests **:** CATEGORY, CLASS ⟨examples of ~*s* of steel are: crucible, Bessemer, basic open-hearth —S.E.Rusinoff⟩ ⟨colonial houses . . . perfect of their ~ —R.W.Hatch⟩ ⟨there are ~*s* of madness which are really forms of inspiration —R.M.Weaver⟩ ⟨the ~ is satire —*Times Lit. Supp.*⟩ ⟨turned to Washington . . . to find companionship among his own ~ —Allen Johnson⟩ ⟨the people I have in mind are the ~ who assume most of the responsibility for unpaid . . . civic duties —J.W.Hoffman⟩ — sometimes used as a zero plural with a preceding *these* or *those* and a following *of* ⟨these ~ of sensational statements —Sir Winston Churchill⟩ **b** (1) **:** a specific variety **:** TYPE, BRAND ⟨one ~ of uniform for all . . . troops —L.H. Smith⟩ ⟨the ~ of analysis followed —W.D.Preston⟩ ⟨what ~ of car do you drive⟩ — often used in the phrase *kind of a* ⟨some ~ of a house is the first requirement of civilized man —L.F.Salzman⟩ ⟨what ~ of an organization —H.E.Gaston⟩ ⟨consider the ~ of a community in which they have faith —Eric Goldman⟩ ⟨that ~ of a girl —Hamilton Basso⟩ (2) **:** a recognized or desirable variety ⟨novel which won all ~*s* of praise —*Saturday Rev.*⟩ ⟨can be more ~*s* of a fool in a short time —W.C.Tuttle⟩ ⟨didn't figure that was any ~ of a life —H.S.Chippendale⟩ **c :** a doubtful or barely admissible member of a specified category — used with *of* and the indefinite article ⟨gave a ~ of snort —John Dos Passos⟩ ⟨the whole universe . . . turned a ~ of gray —H.A.Chippendale⟩ ⟨it's ~ of a vacation —W.H.Whyte⟩ ⟨~ of a blend of humor and pathos⟩ **d :** the same rank — used of playing cards ⟨four of a ~⟩ **5** *Christian relig* **:** either of the elements bread or wine used in the Eucharist ⟨Communion is given in one ~ only in Germany —C.B.Moss⟩ **6 a :** goods or commodities as distinguished from money ⟨economic measures providing aid in ~ rather than in cash —Frank Lorimer⟩ **b :** the equivalent of what has been offered or received ⟨reply in ~⟩ ⟨it hadn't seemed such a terrible thing to hurt him until she was paid back in ~ —William Heuman⟩ **7 :** AMOUNT — used in the phrase *that kind of money* ⟨he's got to be good to pull down that ~ of money —Richard Llewellyn⟩ **syn** see TYPE

2**kind** \"\ *adj* -ER/-EST [ME *kinde, kind*, fr. OE *gecynde*, fr. *cynd, gecynd*, n.] **1** *obs* **:** consistent with nature **:** NATURAL, FITTING ⟨is but ~ for a cock's head to breed a comb —Stephen Gosson⟩ **2** *now dial* **:** of a good variety or in thriving condition — used of crops ⟨graft . . . ~ fruits upon thorns —John Hales⟩ ⟨the cultivation having been perfect, the barley crop will be ~ —S.C.Scrivener⟩ **3** *now chiefly dial* **a :** of an affectionate nature **:** FOND, INTIMATE ⟨reserve your ~ looks and language for private hours —Jonathan Swift⟩ **b :** GRATEFUL ⟨should declare himself . . . ~ for all those benefits —*Homilies*⟩ **4 a :** of a sympathetic nature **:** FRIENDLY, OBLIGING ⟨was always ~ to the boy —A. Conan Doyle⟩ ⟨everyone is so friendly and ~ —A.J.McConnell⟩ **b :** of a forbearing nature **:** governed by consideration and compassion **:** GENTLE, LENIENT ⟨naturally you are ~ to pets —*Boy Scout Handbook*⟩ ⟨generally was ~ in his judgment of me —O.W.Holmes †1935⟩ **c :** arising from or characterized by sympathy or forbearance ⟨a ~ act⟩ **5** *now chiefly dial* **a :** of a pleasant nature **:** AGREEABLE ⟨the soft green . . . countryside is so ~ to your eyes —Richard Joseph⟩ **b :** soft and yielding to the touch ⟨the wool was . . . ~ to handle —*Westralian Farmers Co-op. Gazette*⟩

**syn** KIND, KINDLY, BENIGN, and BENIGNANT can mean, in common, having or manifesting a nature that is gentle, considerate, and inclined to benevolent or beneficent actions. KIND and KINDLY, often interchangeable, both suggest gentleness, humaneness, and a sympathetic interest in the welfare of others, KIND applying more often to the disposition to sympathy and helpfulness, KINDLY stressing more the expression of a sympathetic, helpful nature, mood, or impulse ⟨a *kind* person with a *kindly* interest in the problems of others⟩ ⟨a person *kind* to animals⟩ ⟨the *kindly* attentions of an elderly stranger⟩ ⟨the critics were by no means *kind* to the play —J.K.Newnham⟩ ⟨felt *kindly* and protective and superior —Christopher Isherwood⟩ BENIGN and BENIGNANT stress mildness and mercifulness and apply more often to the acts, utterances, or policies, gracious or patronizing, of a superior rather than an equal ⟨a *benign* master⟩ ⟨the *benign* rule of a benevolent despot⟩ ⟨the transformation of a *benign* personality into a belligerent one —Lewis Mumford⟩ ⟨looked up into his *benignant* face, as if she had come thither for his pardon and paternal affection —Nathaniel Hawthorne⟩ ⟨heaven was divinely merciful, infinitely *benignant*. It spared him, pardoned his weakness —Virginia Woolf⟩

3**kind** \"\ *adv, now dial* **:** KINDLY ⟨how ~ he puts it —Charles Dickens⟩

4**kind** *vt* -ED/-ING/-S [prob. fr. 1*kind*] *obs* **:** BEGET

**kind** *abbr* kindergarten

**kin·dal** \'kind(ə)l\ *n* -S [native name in India] **1 :** an Indian tree (*Terminalia paniculata*) with hard gray or grayish-brown wood that resembles black walnut **2 :** the wood of the kindal tree

**kinder** *comparative of* KIND

**kin·der·be·weijs** *also* **kin·der·be·wys** \,kində(r)bə'vīs\ *n* -ES [D *kinderbewijs*, fr. *kinder* (pl. of *kind* child) + *bewijs* proof] *Roman Dutch law* **:** a deed by a surviving spouse certifying and securing the amounts due to minor children out of the estate of a deceased

1**kin·der·gar·ten** *R* 'kində(r),gär|t(ə)n, |d(ə)n, –*R* -də,gȧ|\ *n* -S [G, fr. *kinder* (pl. of *kind* child) + *garten* garden] **1 :** a school or division of a school below the first grade usu. serving pupils of the 4 to 6 age group and fostering their natural growth and social development through constructive play with blocks, clay, crayons and by group games, songs, and exercise **2 :** the room or building in which a kindergarten is housed

2**kindergarten** \"\ *adj* **1 :** of or relating to a kindergarten ⟨teaching at the ~ level⟩ **2 :** of or relating to an elementary level or initial phase ⟨a ~ lecture on the meaning of nationhood —Robert Trumbull⟩ ⟨have as yet only reached the ~ stage in learning how to manage our complex economic problems —A.H.Hansen⟩

**kin·der·gart·ner** *also* **kin·der·gar·ten·er** \|t(ə)nə(r), |d(ə)n-\ *n* -S [G *kindergärtner*, fr. *kindergarten* + *-er*] **1 :** a child attending kindergarten or of kindergarten age ⟨~*s* and first graders⟩ ⟨pajamas and robes for toddlers and ~*s* —*Parents Mag.*⟩ **2 :** a teacher at the kindergarten level ⟨~, experienced, summer camp —*N.Y.Times*⟩

**kin·der·hook** \'kində(r),hu̇k\ *or* **kin·der·hook·ian** \¦==-¦hu̇kēən\ *adj, usu cap* [fr. *Kinderhook*, Pike county, Ill.] **:** of or relating to the lowest formational division of the Mississippian series in the Mississippi valley or the epoch of its deposition — see GEOLOGIC TIME table

**kindest** *superlative of* KIND

**kindhearted** \'=¦==\ *adj* **:** having a sympathetic nature **:** HUMANE, COMPASSIONATE ⟨a ~ landlord — ever anxious to ameliorate the condition of the poor —Anthony Trollope⟩ — **kind·heart·ed·ly** *adv*

**kind·heart·ed·ness** *n* -ES **:** the quality or state of being kindhearted

1**kin·dle** \'kind(ə)l, *rapid* -n(ə)l\ *vb* **kindled; kindled; kindling** \-(ə)liŋ\ **kindles** [ME *kindlen*, fr. ON *kynda* to kindle + ME *-len* -le; akin to MHG *künten, künden* to kindle, OHG *cuntesal* fire] *vt* **1 :** to start (a fire) burning **:** LIGHT, IGNITE ⟨~ a fire with a match⟩ **2 a :** to awaken or intensify to awareness ⟨armies cannot be raised . . . unless the rage of the people is first *kindled* by lies and name-calling —Kenneth Roberts⟩ ⟨these two delightful . . . handbooks should ~ a child's imagination —Muna Lee⟩ **b :** to stir up **:** AROUSE, INSPIRE ⟨his enthusiasm ~*s* his comrades⟩ ⟨hopes that . . . *kindled* close to half of France —Janet Flanner⟩ **c :** to bring into being **:** INSTITUTE ⟨the Good Neighbor policy . . . which was *kindled* by Sumner Welles —A.C.Wilgus⟩ **3 :** to cause to glow **:** ILLUMINATE ⟨animation *kindling* his pale face —A.J.Cronin⟩ ⟨*kindling* with color the pale lichens —Thomas Vance⟩ ~ *vi* **1 a :** to start a fire ⟨some fire to ~ with —Stith Thompson⟩ **b :** to begin to burn **:** catch fire ⟨dry leaves ~ at the touch of flame⟩ **2 a :** to flare up **:** gather intensity ⟨their mutual resentment again *kindled* —Edward Gibbon⟩ **b :** to grow warm or animated **:** become stirred emotionally ⟨no boy will fail to ~ to the struggles of his California youth —Ethna Sheehan⟩ **3 :** to sparkle or become illuminated as if with fire **:** GLOW ⟨light *kindled* in the liquor —Frances G. Patton⟩ ⟨could see her eyes widen, ~ and flinch —John Fountain⟩

2**kindle** \"\ *n* -S [ME, prob. fr. *kinde, kind*, n., kind + *-le* — more at KIND] *now dial* **:** the young of an animal **:** LITTER ⟨a ~ of kittens⟩ — **in kindle :** PREGNANT — used chiefly of a rabbit

3**kindle** \"\ *vb* **kindled; kindled; kindling; kindles** [ME *kindlen*, prob. fr. *kindle*, n.] *vt* **:** to give birth to **:** BEAR ⟨one of our does *kindled* a single rabbit —*Amer. Small Stock Farmer*⟩ ~ *vi* **:** to bring forth young ⟨bred one of the Angora does to ~ about the time I would be making the move —*Standard Rabbit Jour.*⟩ — now used chiefly of a rabbit

**kindle-coal** *or* **kindle-fire** *n* [1*kindle*] *obs* **:** one that stirs up strife ⟨Satan is the great *kindle-coal* —William Gurnall⟩

**kin·dler** \'kind(ə)lə(r), *rapid* -n(ə)l-\ *n* -S [ME, fr. *kindlen* + *-er*] **1 :** one that kindles **2 :** KINDLING 2

**kind·less** \'kīndləs, *rapid* -nl-\ *adj* [1*kind* + *-less*] **1** *obs* **:** INHUMAN ⟨remorseless, treacherous, lecherous, ~ villain —Shak.⟩ **2 :** DISAGREEABLE, UNSYMPATHETIC, UNCONGENIAL ⟨no thought less kindly — toward even thee that are ~ —A.C. Swinburne⟩ ⟨the unreturned of ~ land and sea —Walter de la Mare⟩ — **kind·less·ly** *adv*

**kind·li·ness** \'kīndlēnəs, -lin-, *rapid* -nl-\ *n* -ES [ME *kindlinesse*, fr. *kindly* + *-nesse* -ness] **1 :** the quality or state of being kindly **:** FRIENDLINESS, BENEVOLENCE **2 :** the quality or state of being agreeable or manageable **:** PLEASANTNESS, TRACTABILITY ⟨~ of climate⟩ ⟨~ of feel . . . makes esparto papers preeminent for their printing qualities —F.H.Norris⟩ ⟨steel of the future will be very different in ~ of working —William Metcalf⟩

1**kin·dling** \'kindliŋ, -lēŋ, *rapid* -nl-\ *n* -S [ME, fr. gerund of *kindlen* to kindle (ignite) — more at 1KINDLE] **1 a :** an act or instance of igniting ⟨the ~ of a bonfire⟩ **b :** an act or instance of exciting or causing to glow ⟨a ~ of enthusiasm⟩ ⟨looking at the sunset, watching the ~ of the clouds —Susan Ertz⟩ **2 :** easily combustible material of a convenient size for starting a fire ⟨crumpled paper makes good ~ for the stove⟩ ⟨a famous old covered bridge that was carried away and crushed to ~ . . . in the spring flood —*Amer. Guide Series: Conn.*⟩

2**kindling** \"\ *n* -S [ME, fr. gerund of *kindlen* (to give birth) — more at 3KINDLE] **:** an act of giving birth — used chiefly of a rabbit

**kindling temperature** *or* **kindling point** *n* **:** IGNITION TEMPERATURE

**kindling wood** *n* **:** wood of a size or kind to kindle readily — called also *fat pine, lightwood, pine, pitch pine, rich-pine*

1**kind·ly** \'kīndlē, -li, *rapid* -nl-\ *adj* -ER/-EST [ME, fr. OE *cyndelīc, gecyndelīc*, fr. *cynd, gecynd* kind + *-līc* -ly — more at KIND] **1 a** *obs* **:** consistent with nature **:** NATURAL, APPROPRIATE ⟨the earth shall sooner leave her ~ skill to bring forth fruit —Edmund Spenser⟩ **b** *archaic* **:** related by birth or blood **:** HEREDITARY, LEGITIMATE ⟨their ~ possessions which . . . their predecessors and they had kept —John Spalding⟩ ⟨he must be a genuine or ~ son —W.E.Hearn⟩ **2 :** of an agreeable or beneficial nature **:** PLEASANT, FAVORABLE ⟨~ climate⟩ ⟨the soil is ~ to my feet —K.M.Dodson⟩ ⟨a ~ half century —Sinclair Lewis⟩ ⟨two of these periods . . . were most ~ toward his profession of architect —*Times Lit. Supp.*⟩ **3 :** KIND 2 **4 a :** of a sympathetic or generous nature **:** FRIENDLY, BENEVOLENT ⟨was greatly pleased and for that day . . . more ~ with her —Pearl Buck⟩ ⟨benefited greatly from their charity and ~ interest in him —Raymond Holden⟩ ⟨homespun, ~, shrewd men whose strength resided in their neighborliness —Norman Cousins⟩ **b :** expressive of a sympathetic nature ⟨~ look⟩ ⟨~ eye⟩ **5 :** SEA-KINDLY **syn** see KIND

2**kindly** \"\ *adv, sometimes* -ER/-EST [ME, fr. OE *cyndelīce, gecyndelīce*, fr. *cyndelīc, gecyndelīc*, adj.] **1 a :** in the normal way **:** NATURALLY ⟨old wounds which had healed ~ —*Amer. Mercury*⟩ **b :** in a natural way **:** READILY, SPONTANEOUSLY ⟨nearing the three furlongs he . . . was galloping ~ —*Sydney (Australia) Sunday Telegraph*⟩ — often used with *take to* ⟨a wild, fleet-footed people, who did not take ~ to restraint —R.A.Billington⟩ ⟨unadorned styles which some audiences take to more ~ than to . . . polished grace —Robert Bendiner⟩ **2 a :** in a kind manner **:** SYMPATHETICALLY, GENEROUSLY ⟨treats his horse ~ and never uses spurs⟩ ⟨the foundation is not looking ~ upon requests for grants⟩ **b :** in an appreciative manner **:** as a gesture of good will ⟨takes criticism ~⟩ ⟨would take it ~ if you would put in a good word for the boy⟩ **c :** in a gracious or considerate manner **:** COURTEOUSLY, OBLIGINGLY ⟨the party which I was ~ invited to join —Anthony Trollope⟩ ⟨the encipherer had ~ divided the words of his message off with commas —Fletcher Pratt⟩ ⟨~ fill out the attached questionnaire⟩ **3** *chiefly South* **:** in a way **:** RATHER ⟨going up the hollow was ~ like going up a big green tunnel —J.H.Stuart⟩

**kindly tenant** *n, Scots law, obs* **:** a tenant favored with a low or easy rent because his landlord wanted to favor him or believed him a descendant of an original possessor of the land

**kind·ness** \'kīnnəs *also* -ndnəs\ *n* -ES [ME *kindenesse*, fr. *kinde, kind* + *-nesse* -ness] **1 :** an act or instance of being kind **:** FAVOR ⟨a well-established lawyer did a great ~ in taking into his office this young man —Ruth P. Randall⟩ **2 a :** the quality or state of being kind **:** SYMPATHY, CLEMENCY ⟨man's supreme manifestation of the spirit is ~ —Albert Schweitzer⟩ ⟨cooler air . . . enwrapped him in its ~ —Joseph Whitehill⟩ **b** *archaic* **:** a feeling of fondness **:** AFFECTION, LOVE ⟨a lady for whom he had once entertained a sneaking ~ —Washington Irving⟩

**kind of** \¦kīndə(v), -dē,-di,-dər\ *adv* **:** to a moderate degree or extent **:** RATHER, PARTLY ⟨I *kind of* like you all the same —Robert Westerby⟩ ⟨the wind *kind of* slowed up after while —Vance Randolph⟩

1**kin·dred** \'kindrəd\ *n, pl* **kindred** *see sense 1a* [ME *kinrede, kindrede*, fr. 1*kin* + *-rede* (fr. OE *rǣden* condition, rule, estimation, fr. *rǣdan* to advise, rule, guess, read) — more at READ] **1 a** *pl* **kindreds :** a natural grouping **:** PEOPLE, POPULATION ⟨every ~, every tribe on this terrestrial ball —Edward Perronet⟩ ⟨among the winter-scourged ~*s* —C.G.D.Roberts⟩ **b** (1) **:** a group of related individuals **:** FAMILY, CLAN ⟨the ~ has an organic quality; what happens to the individual member is felt by the whole group —A.D.Rees⟩ (2) **:** RELATIVES ⟨if his ~ still remain to him —Alexis de Tocqueville⟩ **c :** a genealogical group **:** LINEAGE ⟨study the incidence of cancer among members of a ~⟩ **2** *archaic* **a :** relationship by blood or marriage **:** KINSHIP ⟨a secret match . . . raised him to ~ with the throne —J.R.Green⟩ **b :** possession of similar qualities **:** AFFINITY ⟨thy ~ with the great of old — Alfred Tennyson⟩

2**kindred** \"\ *adj* **1 a :** of an allied nature **:** SIMILAR ⟨pamphlets of a ~ sort —G.C.Sellery⟩ ⟨an auditorium for concerts, lectures, and ~ events⟩ **b :** having common qualities or stemming from the same source **:** CONGENIAL, RELATED ⟨~ spirit⟩ ⟨~ arts of music, painting and letters —Elinor Wylie⟩ ⟨~ Germanic languages⟩ ⟨sound waves . . . penetrate to the listener's inner ear and there set up ~ vibrations —Charlton Laird⟩ **2** *archaic* **a :** of the same ancestry **:** COGNATE ⟨countries . . . already occupied by their ~ tribes —Edward Gibbon⟩ **b :** of, relating to, or done by a kinsman ⟨what ~ crime . . . am I decreed to expiate —Tobias Smollett⟩

**kin·dred·less** \-ədləs\ *adj* **:** not having kindred

**kin·dred·ness** *n* -ES **:** the quality or state of being related **:** KINSHIP

**kin·dred·ship** \-əd,ship\ *n* **:** KINSHIP

**kinds** *pl of* KIND, *pres 3d sing of* KIND

1**kine** \'kīn\ *archaic pl of* COW

2**kine** \'kinē\ *var of* CINE

3**kine** \"\ *n* -S [by shortening] **:** KINESCOPE

**kine-** — see KIN-

**kin·e·ma** \'kinəmə\ *var of* CINEMA

**kinema red** *n* **:** GOYA

1**kin·e·mat·ic** \¦kinə¦mad·|ik, ¦kīn-, -at|, |ēk\ *also* **kin·e·mat·i·cal** \|əkəl, |ēk-\ *adj* [back-formation fr. *kinematics*] **1 :** of or relating to kinematics or the motions of bodies **2 :** of or relating to mechanical elements having relative motion — compare PAIR 2a(8) — **kin·e·mat·i·cal·ly** \|ək(ə)lē, |ēk-, -li\ *adv*

2**kinematic** \"\ *var of* CINEMATIC

**kin·e·mat·ics** \|iks, |ēks\ *also* **cin·e·mat·ics** \'sin-\ *n pl but sing in constr* [modif. (influenced by Gk *kinēmat-, kinēma* motion) of F *cinématique*, fr. Gk *kinēmat-, kinēma* + F *-ique* -ics — more at CINEMATOGRAPH] **:** a branch of dynamics that deals with aspects of motion (as acceleration and velocity) apart from considerations of mass and force

**kinematic viscosity** *n* **:** COEFFICIENT OF KINEMATIC VISCOSITY
**kin·e·mat·o·graph** \ˌkinəˈmadəˌgraf, ˌkīn-, -atə-, -ˌräf\ *var of* CINEMATOGRAPH
**kin·e·ma·tog·ra·phy** \ˌkinəməˈtägrəfē, ˌkīn-, -fi\ *var of* CINEMATOGRAPHY
**kin·e·plas·ty** \ˈkinəˌplastē, ˈkīn-\ *var of* CINEPLASTY
**kinepox** \ˈ=,=\ *n* [¹*kine* + *pox*] **:** COWPOX
**kin·e·sal·gia** \ˌkinəˈsalj(ē)ə, ˌkīn-\ *n* -S [NL, fr. *kinesis* + *-algia*] **:** pain occurring in conjunction with muscle action
**¹kin·e·scope** \ˈkinəˌskōp\ *n* [fr. *Kinescope*, a trademark] **1 :** a cathode-ray tube having at one end a screen of luminescent material on which are produced visible images (as television pictures or oscillograph curves) **2 :** a motion picture made from a kinescope image
**²kinescope** \ʺ\ *vt* **kinescoped; kinescoped; kinescoping; kinescopes :** to make a kinescope of (a television program)
**kinesi-** *or* **kinesio-** *comb form* [Gk *kinēsi-*, fr. *kinēsis* motion — more at KINESIS] **:** movement **:** motion ⟨*kinesimeter*⟩ ⟨*kinesiology*⟩
**-ki·ne·sia** \kəˈnēzh(ē)ə, ˌkī-\ *or* **-ci·ne·sia** \sə-, ˌsī-\ *n comb form* -S [NL, fr. Gk *-kinēsia*, fr. *kinēsis*] **:** movement **:** motion ⟨hyper*kinesia*⟩ ⟨para*kinesia*⟩
**ki·ne·si·at·rics** \kəˌnēsēˈa·triks, kī,-, -ēzē-\ *n pl but sing in constr* [ISV *kinesi-* + *-iatrics*] **:** KINESITHERAPY
**ki·ne·sic** \kəˈnēsik (ˈ)kī;n-, -ēz|\ *adj* [Gk *kinēsis* + E *-ic*] **:** of or relating to kinesics ⟨~ investigation⟩ — **ki·ne·si·cal·ly** \|ək(ə)lē\ *adv*
**ki·ne·sics** \kəˈnēsiks, kī-, -ēzi-\ *n pl but sing in constr* [Gk *kinēsis* + E *-ics*] **:** a systematic study of nonlinguistic body motion (as blushes, shrugs, waves) in its relation to communication ⟨man did not become truly human until he developed spoken language but one might guess that for millennia ~ was the . . . mode of communication —Stuart Chase⟩
**kin·e·sim·e·ter** \ˌkinəˈsimədə(r), ˌkīn-\ *also* **ki·ne·si·om·e·ter** \kəˌnēsēˈäm-, kī,-, -ēzē-\ *n* [*kinesi-* + *-meter*] **:** an instrument for measuring bodily movements
**ki·ne·si·o·log·ic** \kəˌnēsēəˈläjik, kīˌn-, -ēzē-\ *or* **ki·ne·si·o·log·i·cal** \-jəkəl\ *adj* **:** of, relating to, or involving the methods of kinesiology
**ki·ne·si·ol·o·gy** \=ˌnēsēˈäləjē, -ēzē-\ *n* -ES [*kinesi-* + *-logy*] **1 :** study of the principles of mechanics and anatomy in relation to human movement ⟨~ of corrective exercise⟩ ⟨~ of the ethnic dance⟩ **2 :** KINESITHERAPY
**ki·ne·sis** \kəˈnēsəs, kī-\ *or* **ci·ne·sis** \sə-, sī-\ *n, pl* **kineses** *or* **cineses** \-ē,sēz\ [NL, fr. Gk *kinēsis* motion, fr. *kinein* to move + *-sis*; akin to L *ciēre* to move — more at CITE] **1 :** physical movement including quantitative, qualitative, and positional change **2 :** movement that is induced by stimulation (as by light) and is not specifically orienting — compare TAXIS
**-ki·ne·sis** \kəˈnēsəs, -kī-\ *n comb form, pl* **-kineses** [NL, fr. Gk *kinēsis*] **1 :** activation ⟨chemo*kinesis*⟩ ⟨photo*kinesis*⟩ **2 :** division ⟨karyo*kinesis*⟩
**ki·ne·si·therapy** \kəˈnēsē, kīˌnēsē+\ *n* [ISV *kinesi-* + *therapy*] **:** the therapeutic and corrective application of passive and active movements (as by massage) and of exercise
**kin·es·the·sia** \ˌkinəsˈthēzh(ē)ə *sometimes* ˌkīn-\ *or* **kin·es·the·sis** \-thēsəs\ *also* **kin·aes·the·sia** *or* **kin·aes·the·sis** \ˌkinəs- *sometimes* ˌkīn-\ *n, pl* **kinesthesias** *or* **kinestheses** [NL, fr. *kin-* + *esthesia or esthesis*] **1 :** a sense mediated by end organs that lie in the muscles, tendons, and joints and are stimulated by bodily movements and tensions **:** MUSCLE SENSE **2 :** the sensory experience derived from the muscle sense
**kin·es·thet·ic** *also* **kin·aes·thet·ic** \ˌ=ˌ=ˈthed-ik, -et|, |ēk\ *adj* [fr. NL *kinesthesia*, after such pairs as NL *anesthesia*: E *anesthetic*] **:** of or relating to bodily reaction or motor memory ⟨get ~ pleasure from watching skaters waltz⟩ ⟨seldom had a ~ image of the first weight at the moment of lifting . . . the second —R.S.Woodworth⟩ — **kin·es·thet·i·cal·ly** *also* **kin·aes·thet·i·cal·ly** \|ək(ə)lē, |ēk-, -li\ *adv*
**kinet-** *or* **kineto-** *also* **cinet-** *or* **cineto-** *comb form* [Gk *kinētos* moving — more at KINETIC] **:** movement **:** motion ⟨*kinetogenic*⟩
**ki·net·ic** \kəˈned-|ik, (ˈ)kī;n-, -et|, |ēk\ *adj* [Gk *kinētikos* of motion, fr. *kinētos* moving (fr. *kinein* to move) + *-ikos* -ic — more at KINESIS] **1 :** relating to kinetics or to the motion of material bodies and the forces and energy associated therewith **2 a :** of or relating to motion **:** ACTIVE, LIVELY ⟨modern dance has been called ~ pantomime⟩ ⟨a ~ world with mobility . . . as its keynote —F.D.Graham⟩ **b :** supplying motive force **:** ENERGIZING, DYNAMIC ⟨jumped to attention . . . upon the ~ arrival of the master —S.N.Behrman⟩ ⟨a ~ artist . . . inflames the passions of readers —*Saturday Rev.*⟩ ⟨a ~, creative force —*N.Y.Times*⟩ ⟨the complex civilization of which Rome was the ~ center —H.O.Taylor⟩ **3 :** of or relating to kinesis ⟨~ occupational therapy⟩ ⟨response to light may be ~ —V.B. Wigglesworth⟩ **4 :** KINESTHETIC ⟨in the concert hall . . . listening to actual musical sound enriched by the ~ force of human participation —Goddard Lieberson⟩
**ki·net·i·cal·ly** \|ək(ə)lē\ *adv* **:** in a kinetic manner
**kinetic energy** *n* **:** energy (sense 5) that is associated with motion
**kinetic friction** *n* **:** SLIDING FRICTION
**kinetic potential** *n* **:** the difference between the kinetic energy and the potential energy of a dynamic system expressed as a function of the position coordinates and their time derivatives — called also *Lagrangian function*
**ki·netics** \kəˈned-|iks, kīˈ-, -et|, |ēks\ *n pl but sing or pl in constr* **1 :** a branch of dynamics that deals with the effects of forces upon the motions of material bodies **2 a :** a branch of physical science that deals with the rate of change in a physical or chemical system; *specif* **:** REACTION KINETICS **b :** the rate of change or reaction in such a system **c :** the mechanism by which a physical or chemical change is effected ⟨the ~ of the acid-catalyzed reaction between organic acids and alcohols —C.E.Leyes⟩
**kinetic theory** *n* **:** a theory in physics: the minute particles of a substance are in vigorous motion on the assumptions that (1) the particles of a gas move in straight lines with high average velocity, continually encounter one another and thus change their individual velocities and directions, and cause pressure by their impact against the walls of a container and that (2) the temperature of a substance increases with an increase in either the average kinetic energy of the particles or the average potential energy of separation (as in fusion) of the particles or in both when heat is added — called also respectively (1) *kinetic theory of gases*, (2) *kinetic theory of heat*
**ki·ne·to·chore** \kəˈned-|ə,kō(ə)r, kī-, -ne|, |t|, |ō,-, -kȯ(ə)r\ *n* -S [*kinet-* + Gk *chōros* place — more at CHOR-] **:** CENTROMERE
**ki·ne·to·gen·e·sis** \=,=ˈjenəsəs\ *n* [NL, fr. *kinet-* + L *genesis*] **:** evolution of animal structures presumed to be due to animal movements — **ki·ne·to·ge·net·ic** \=ˌ=jəˈned-ik\ *adj* — **ki·ne·to·ge·net·i·cal·ly** \-d-ək(ə)lē\ *adv*
**ki·ne·to·graph** \=ˈ=,graf, -ˌräf\ *n* [*kinet-* + *-graph*] **:** an apparatus for taking a series of photographs of moving objects for examination with the kinetoscope — **ki·ne·to·graph·ic** \=ˌ=ˈgrafik\ *adj*
**ki·ne·to·ne·ma** \=,=ˈnēmə\ *n, pl* **kinetonema·ta** \-məd-ə\ [NL, fr. *kinet-* + *-nema*] **:** a modified portion of chromonema associated with the centromere
**ki·ne·to·nucleus** \=ˈ=+\ *n* [NL, fr. *kinet-* + *nucleus*] **:** a kinetoplast formerly thought to be a secondary nucleus exclusively concerned with motor activities — compare TROPHONUCLEUS
**ki·ne·to·phone** \=ˈ=,fōn\ *n* [*kinet-* + *-phone*] **:** a machine combining a kinetoscope and a phonograph synchronized so as to produce the illusion of motion in a scene with accompanying sounds
**ki·ne·to·phonograph** \=ˈ=+\ *n* [*kinet-* + *phonograph*] **:** KINETOPHONE
**ki·ne·to·plast** \=ˈ=,plast\ *also* **ci·ne·to·plast** \sə-, sī-\ *n* -S [ISV *kinet-* + *-plast*] **:** a complex cell structure made up of basal granules, associated fibrils, and related bodies found in association with the base of certain flagella and undulating membranes and regarded as actively concerned with the motility of these structures
**Ki·ne·to·scope** \kəˈ==,skōp, kī-\ *trademark* — used for a device for viewing through a magnifying lens a sequence of pictures of a changing scene on an endless band of film moved continuously over a light source and a rapidly rotating shutter that creates an illusion of motion
**kin·e·to·sis** \ˌkinəˈtōsəs, ˌkī-\ *n, pl* **kineto·ses** \-ō,sēz\ [NL, fr. *kinet-* + *-osis*] **:** MOTION SICKNESS
**kin·folk** \ˈkin,fōk\ *also* **kins·folk** \-nz,-\ *n pl* [*kinfolk* alter. of *kinsfolk*; *kinsfolk* fr. ME *kynsefolke*, fr. *kynse*, *kinnes* (gen. of ¹*kin*) + *folke*, *folk* folk] **:** RELATIVES
**¹king** \ˈkiŋ\ *n* -S *except sense 13a, often attrib* [ME, fr. OE *kyning, cyning*; akin to OS & OHG *kuning*, *kunig* king, ON *konungr*; all fr. a prehistoric WGmc-NGmc compound whose first constituent is represented by E ¹*kin*, and whose second constituent is represented by E *-ing* (n. suffix)] **1 a :** a male monarch who reigns over a major territorial unit **:** the ruler of a kingdom ⟨~s were makers of the laws —James I⟩ ⟨distinguish between the ~ and the crown —C.H.McIlwain⟩ ⟨in . . . Britain the sovereign is not the *King* but the King-in-Parliament —W.H.Wickwar⟩ **b :** the paramount or an esp. important chief (as the head of an Indian or African tribe) ⟨occupied by Shingess, ~ of the Delawares —A.S.Withers⟩ **2** *cap* **:** GOD, CHRIST 1 ⟨to worship the *King*, the Lord of hosts —Zech 14:16 (RSV)⟩ ⟨that the *King* of glory may come in —Ps 24:7 (RSV)⟩ **3 :** one that holds a supreme or preeminent position in a particular sphere or class; *esp* **:** a chief among competitors ⟨the cattle ~s rode up from the south —Alan Moorehead⟩ ⟨even if no longer ~, cotton remains the chief cash crop —Howell Walker⟩ ⟨this ~ of books —*Brit. Bk. Centre*⟩ ⟨their ~s of steel and oil and chemicals —*Nation*⟩ **4** *obs* **:** QUEEN BEE **5 :** the principal piece in a set of chessmen that may move ordinarily one square in any direction and has the power of capture but is obliged never to enter or remain in exposure to capture **6 :** a playing card marked with a stylized figure of a king and usu. the initial letter K **7 :** one that occupies a position like that of or plays the part of a male monarch — often used in real or mock titles ⟨*King* of Arms of the Order of the Garter —A.L.Wagner⟩ ⟨a decorated float carrying the *King* of Misrule —*Springfield (Mass.) Daily News*⟩ ⟨in all the school games he was the ~ —Robert Graves⟩ ⟨~ of the club's annual hobby show —*Springfield (Mass.) Union*⟩ ⟨public opinion is ~ —L.W.Doob⟩ **8 :** any of a class of fuller's teasels **9 :** a checker that as a result of reaching an opponent's king row has been crowned and given the power of moving backward as well as forward **10 :** the second officer in a Royal Arch chapter of Masons **11 :** a sexually mature male termite **12 :** KING SALMON ⟨fisherman who come . . . to catch the ~s —R.L.Haig-Brown⟩ **13 a** *usu cap* **:** an American breed of large vigorous utility pigeons developed to produce large numbers of squabs that weigh about one pound at four weeks of age **b** *often cap* **:** any pigeon of the King breed ⟨not bred so extensively as the white *King* —Rudolph Seiden⟩ **14 :** a king-size cigarette
**²king** \ʺ\ *vb* -ED/-ING/-S [ME *kingen*, fr. *king*, n.] *vi* **:** to act the king **:** RULE — usu. used with *it* ⟨in our . . . country science ~s it over the realm of intellectual discourse —Clifton Fadiman⟩ ~ *vt* **1 :** to cause to be a king ⟨then am I ~*ed* again —Shak.⟩ **2** *archaic* **:** GOVERN ⟨England . . . is so idly ~*ed* —Shak.⟩
**³king** \ʺ\ *usu cap* — a communications code word for the letter *k*
**king al·fred's candle** \-ˈalfrədz-\ *n, usu cap K&A* [after *Alfred* the Great †901 king of the West Saxons in England; fr. the belief that he developed such a device] **:** an early time-telling device consisting of a candle marked off in time bands to show the passage of time by the amount the candle burns down
**king at arms** *often cap K&A* **:** KING OF ARMS — not in official use
**king auk** *n* **1 :** GREAT AUK **2 :** DOVEKIE 2
**king ball** *n* **:** a red or black ball that is placed on a white spot in front of the holes on a bagatelle board and that must be struck by one of the other balls before a score can be made
**kingbird** \ˈ=,=\ *n, often cap* **:** any of various American tyrant flycatchers — see ARKANSAS KINGBIRD, CASSIN'S KINGBIRD, EASTERN KINGBIRD, GRAY KINGBIRD
**king blossom** *n* **:** the large central flower in a cluster of apple flowers on the fruiting spur
**kingbolt** \ˈ=,=\ *n* **1 :** a vertical bolt by which the forward axle and wheels of a vehicle or the trucks of a railroad car are connected with the other parts **2 :** an iron tie rod used in place of a king post in the construction of a roof
**king carp** *n* **:** MIRROR CARP
**king charles's head** \-ˈchärlz(əz)-\ *n, usu cap K&C* [after *Charles* I †1649 king of England, who was beheaded; fr. the habit of Mr. Dick, character in *David Copperfield*, novel by Charles Dickens †1870 Eng. novelist, of introducing the subject of King Charles's head into all discussions] **:** OBSESSION 3 ⟨that *King Charles's head* of modern America, the menace of Communism —*Times Lit. Supp.*⟩
**king charles spaniel** \-lz-\ *n, usu cap K&C* [after *Charles* II †1685 king of England, who was fond of such dogs] **:** a dog of a black and tan variety of the English toy spaniel
**king closer** *n* **:** a closer bigger than half a brick; *specif* **:** a brick with one corner cut away making the header at that end half the width of the brick — compare QUEEN CLOSER
**king cobra** *n* **:** a large and very venomous elapid snake (*Naja hannah*) found from India to southern China and the Philippines and attaining a length of 12 feet or more — called also *hamadryad*
**king conch** *n* **:** a large conch (*Strombus gigas*) with a pink outer shell often used in cameo cutting; *also* **:** any of certain other large conchs or helmet shells — compare QUEEN CONCH
**king crab** *n* **1 :** any of several closely related large marine arthropods of eastern No. America and eastern Asia constituting the only surviving members of the order Xiphosura and class Merostomata and having a broad crescentic cephalothorax with a pair of large compound eyes and two simple eyes on the upper surface and six pairs of legs arising from the lower surface about the centrally placed mouth, a small abdomen articulated to the cephalothorax with its segments fused into a single piece, swimming appendages to which the flat leaflike gills are attached, and a long stiff movably articulated caudal spine; *esp* **:** an arthropod (*Limulus polyphemus* syn. *Xiphosurus polyphemus*) found on sandy and muddy bottoms on the coasts of No. America from Maine to Mexico and the West Indies that attains a length of nearly two feet — called also *horseshoe crab* **2 a :** a large European spider crab (*Maia squinado*) **b :** a large scarlet anomuran crab (*Lopholithodes mandtii*) of shallow water from California to Alaska **c :** the largest of the edible crabs (*Paralithodes camtschaticus*) often measuring five feet from claw tip to claw tip, weighing up to 15 pounds, and widely distributed in the No. Pacific
**kingcraft** \ˈ=,=\ *n* **1 :** the art of governing as a king; *esp* **:** the use of clever tactics or cunning in exercising the functions of kingship ⟨a sort of correspondence course in ~ —Dorothy M. Stuart⟩ **2 :** the craft or profession of a king ⟨to abolish ~, priestcraft, caste, monopoly —Walt Whitman⟩
**king crow** *n* **:** BLACK DRONGO
**kingcup** \ˈ=,=\ *also* **kingcob** \ˈ=,=\ *n* **1 :** any of various common buttercups (as *Ranunculus bulbosus*, *R. acris*, or *R. repens*) **2 :** a marsh marigold (*Caltha palustris*)
**king devil** *n* **:** any of various European hawkweeds (esp. *Hieracium praealtum*) that have been introduced into and are locally troublesome weeds in the northeastern U.S.
**king·dom** \ˈkiŋdəm\ *n* -S [ME, fr. OE *cyningdōm*, fr. *cyning* king + *-dōm* -dom — more at KING] **1** *obs* **:** KINGSHIP **2 a :** a major territorial unit subject to a monarchical form of government usu. headed by a king or queen **:** the realm of a king ⟨inclusion of additional provinces in the Italian ~⟩ ⟨when plantations were like small ~s —William Beebe⟩ ⟨this through the ~s of Europe⟩ — compare EMPIRE 1a, PRINCIPALITY **3 :** a politically organized community (as a nation or state) having a monarchical form of government usu. headed by a king ⟨the new Christian ~s found themselves at war with the Barbary —C.S.Forester⟩ ⟨decreed Spain a ~ (without a king) —S.G.Rich⟩ **4** *often cap* **a :** the eternal kingship or sovereignty of God ⟨Jesus, to whom the authority of the ~ is delegated, heals sickness —R.H.Strachan⟩ **b :** the spiritual realm over which God reigns as king **:** HEAVEN ⟨all I now have is what my Father is keeping . . . for us in His ~ —*Voice of Prophecy News*⟩ **c :** the fulfillment on earth of God's will esp. in complete perfection ⟨the time is fulfilled, and the ~ of God is at hand —Mk 1:14 (RSV)⟩ **d :** the invisible society of human beings in which God is held to be obeyed ⟨members of the ~ were to strive to be examples of the life which God deemed ideal for men —K.S.Latourette⟩ **5 :** a realm or region in which something is dominant ⟨the rise of a ~ of wheat in the Old Northwest —W.O.Lynch⟩ ⟨in the untroubled ~ of reason —Bertrand Russell⟩ ⟨a cattle ~⟩ **6 :** one of the three primary divisions into which natural objects are commonly classified — see ANIMAL KINGDOM, MINERAL KINGDOM, PLANT KINGDOM **7 :** an area or sphere in which one exercises authority like a king ⟨his gambling ~ —Dean Jennings⟩ ⟨busy . . . increasing the size and ornamentations of our personal ~s —*Saturday Rev.*⟩ **8 :** a hostel for men or for women that provides living quarters at low cost to members of a religious movement among Negroes in the U.S. known as Father Divine's Peace Mission Movement ⟨with Father Divine . . . at a meeting in one of his ~s —M.L.Bach⟩
**kingdom come** *n* [fr. the phrase *Thy kingdom come* in the *Lord's Prayer*] **:** the next world **:** HEAVEN ⟨the guns that would blow everyone to *kingdom come* —Meridel Le Sueur⟩
**king·domed** \ˈkiŋdəmd\ *adj* **1 :** ROYAL ⟨~ Achilles in commotion rages —Shak.⟩ **2 :** consisting of more than one kingdom — often used in combination ⟨a multi*kingdomed* confederation⟩
**kingdom hall** *n, usu cap K&H* **:** a local Jehovah's Witnesses meeting place where religious services are held
**kingdomtide** \ˈ==,=\ *n, often cap* **:** a season of the church year preceding Advent and observed by some Christians as a time for emphasizing the message of the kingdom of God
**king eagle** *n* **:** IMPERIAL EAGLE
**kinged** *past of* KING
**king eider** *or* **king duck** *n* **:** a circumpolar eider duck (*Somateria spectabilis*) having very large lateral gibbous processes at the base of the bill
**king-emperor** \ˈ=ˈ=(=)=\ *n* **:** a king who is also ruler of an empire; *specif* **:** the British monarch in his onetime capacity as emperor of India ⟨the darling of the Saxon *king-emperors* —F.H.Cramer⟩ ⟨the . . . *king-emperor* of one fourth of the world —*Literary Digest*⟩
**king fern** *n* **:** ROYAL FERN
**kingfish** \ˈ=,=\ *n* **1 a :** any of several marine croakers of the family Sciaenidae: as (1) **:** a whiting (*Menticirrhus saxatilis*) of the No. American Atlantic coast (2) **:** a small silvery California food fish (*Genyonemus lineatus*) — called also *chenfish* (3) **:** MULLOWAY **b :** any of various scombroid fishes; *esp* **:** CERO **c :** any of various marine percoid fishes esp. of the family Carangidae (as an amberfish) **2 :** an undisputed master in an area or group **:** COCK OF THE WALK ⟨the ~ in the gem trade in the whole Persian gulf —*Amarillo (Texas) Sunday News-Globe*⟩ ⟨the ~ of San Antonio's underworld —*Survey Graphic*⟩
**king·fish·er** \ˈkiŋ,fishə(r)\ *n* **:** any of numerous nonpasserine birds constituting the family Alcedinidae that are usu. crested and bright-colored with a rather short tail, long stout sharp bill, and weak syndactyl feet — see ALCEDO, BELTED KINGFISHER, DACELO, KOOKABURRA
**kingfisher daisy** *n* **:** a densely hairy annual herb (*Felicia bergeriana*) of the family Compositae found in southern Africa that is used as an ornamental and has bright blue ray flowers and a yellow disk
**king hair** *n* **:** GUARD HAIR
**king har·ry** \-ˈhari\ *n, usu cap K&H* [after one of the *King Henrys* of England; so called fr. its conspicuous crown] *dial Eng* **:** GOLDFINCH
**kinghead** \ˈ=,=\ *n* **:** GREAT RAGWEED
**king·hood** \ˈkiŋ,hu̇d\ *n* [ME, fr. *king* + *-hood*] **:** KINGSHIP
**kinghunter** \ˈ=,==\ *n* **:** KOOKABURRA
**king-in-council** \ˈ==ˈ==\ *n, pl* **kings-in-council** *often cap K &C* **:** the British monarch acting with the advice and consent of the privy council usu. as a formal means of giving legal effect to cabinet decisions ⟨executive decisions are reached by the *king-in-council*⟩
**kinging** *pres part of* KING
**king-in-parliament** \ˈ==ˈ===\ *n, pl* **kings-in-parliament** *often cap K&P* **:** the collective legal entity composed of the British monarch and the two houses of parliament acting together that constitutes the supreme legislative authority of the United Kingdom ⟨the lawmaking function is vested in the *King-in-Parliament* —F.A.Ogg & Harold Zink⟩
**king-killer** \ˈ=,==\ *n* **:** REGICIDE
**king·klip** \ˈkiŋ,klip\ *n* -S [short for *kingklipfish*, fr. *king* + *klipfish*; trans. of Afrik *koningklipvis*] **:** a mottled cusk eel of southern Africa (*Genypterus capensis*) that attains a length of five feet and is highly esteemed as food ⟨~ liver is of a delicacy and flavor unsurpassed by even chicken liver —J.L.B.Smith⟩
**king·less** \ˈkiŋləs\ *adj* [ME *kingles*, fr. *king* + *-les* -less] **:** lacking a king ⟨a ~ people —Lord Byron⟩
**king·let** \-lət\ *n* -S **1 :** a weak or petty king; *esp* **:** one that rules over a small territory ⟨four eastern ~s receiving investiture at the hands of the emperor —*Century Mag.*⟩ **2 :** any of several very small birds of the genus *Regulus* that resemble the warblers but have some of the habits of titmice — see GOLDCREST, GOLDEN-CRESTED KINGLET, GOLDEN-CROWNED KINGLET, RUBY-CROWNED KINGLET
**king·li·ness** \ˈkiŋlēnəs\ *n* -ES **:** the quality or state of being kingly
**king·ling** \-liŋ\ *n* -S [¹*king* + *-ling*] **:** a little or petty king ⟨Germany has had more kings, ~s, and knights —*American*⟩
**king lory** *n* **:** KING PARROT
**¹king·ly** \ˈkiŋlē, -li\ *adj* -ER/-EST [ME *kingly*, fr. *king* + *-ly*] **1 :** having the status of king or royal rank ⟨before the murder of her ~ guest —William Stephenson⟩ **2 :** of, suitable for, or usu. associated with a king ⟨symbolizing ~ power and justice —*N.Y.Herald Tribune*⟩ ⟨veneration of the ~ office —Charles Beadle⟩ ⟨venison was considered a ~ food —G.B.Saul⟩ ⟨a mere soldier, with few ~ qualities —J.R.Green⟩ **3 :** having the character, qualities, or attributes of or usu. associated with a king ⟨a ~, i.e. self-ruling people —K.R.Popper⟩ **4 :** characterized by having a king as ruler or as head of the state **:** MONARCHICAL ⟨the ~ form of government —Connop Thirlwall⟩
**²kingly** \ʺ\ *adv, often* -ER/-EST **:** in a kingly manner ⟨and heard him ~ speak —Alfred Tennyson⟩
**king mackerel** *n* **:** a cero (*Scomberomorus cavalla*) esp. noted as a sport fish
**kingmaker** \ˈ=,==\ *n* **:** one that uses his power and influence to cause another to become a king; *esp* **:** one that exerts great influence over the selection of candidates for political office ⟨that great ~ Warwick —Samuel Daniel⟩ ⟨the chief financiers of some campaigns have been persons of great wealth, with no . . . ax to grind save the desire to be ~s —V.O.Key⟩
**king monkey** *n* **:** a guereza (*Colobus polykomus*) of Sierra Leone having a white forehead suggesting a crown
**king mullet** *n* **:** YELLOW GOATFISH
**king nut** *or* **king nut hickory** *n* **:** BIG SHELLBARK
**king of arms** *often cap K&A* [ME *king of armes*] **:** an officer of arms of the highest rank **:** a principal herald — called also *king at arms*
**king of beasts** [ME *king of bestes*] **:** LION
**king of birds :** EAGLE
**king of heralds :** a principal herald in medieval Europe
**king of kings** [ME *king of kinges*] **:** a monarch having other monarchs under him: as **a :** an earthly sovereign ⟨this forthright declaration by the *king of kings* . . . forms a fitting conclusion to the long story of Justinian's wars —P.N.Ure⟩ **b** *cap 1st K, often 2d K* **:** GOD, CHRIST 1 ⟨the blessed and only Sovereign, the *King of kings* and Lord of lords —1 Tim 6:15 (RSV)⟩ ⟨the deity is treated as the *King of Kings* —D.S. Sarma⟩
**king of the anteaters :** a So. American antbird (*Grallaria varia* syn. *G. rex*)
**king-of-the-herrings** \ˈ===ˈ=\ *n* **:** OARFISH
**king of the mackerels :** either of two large pelagic fishes of the family Molidae: **a :** a fish (*Ranzania truncata*) of the Atlantic ocean **b :** a fish (*Ranzania makua*) of the Pacific ocean
**king of the mullets 1 :** a European bass (*Labrax lupus*) **2 :** CARDINAL FISH
**king-of-the-salmon** \ˈ===ˈ=\ *n* **:** a dealfish (*Trachypterus rex-salmonorum*) of the northern Pacific ocean

**king of the vultures :** KING VULTURE
**king orange** *n* **1 :** a citrus tree that produces a moderate sized fruit with a rich savory pulp enclosed in a thick deep orange-yellow to orange tuberculated rind and that may be a variety of the mandarin or a hybrid possibly between this and the sweet orange **2 :** the fruit of the king orange
**king ortolan** *n* **1 :** KING RAIL **2 :** FLORIDA GALLINULE
**king parrot** *n* **:** any of various Australian birds (genus *Alisterus*) of the family Psittacidae; *esp* **:** an Australian parrot (*A. scapulatus*) about 16 inches long that is chiefly bright scarlet on the head and underparts and green above
**king penguin** *n* **:** a large penguin (*Aptenodytes patagonica*) of the Falklands and Kerguelen

king penguin

**kingpin** \ˈ=,=\ *n* **1 :** any of several bowling pins: as **a :** HEADPIN **b :** the number 5 pin **2 :** one that holds a chief or most prominent place in a group or undertaking ⟨~ of the great steel industry —F.L.Allen⟩ ⟨sought by the government . . . as the ~ of dope peddlers —*Associated Press*⟩ ⟨recognized ~ in the tailor-made car field —*Ethyl News*⟩ **3 a :** KINGBOLT 1 **b :** KNUCKLE PIN **4 :** one that holds together a complex system or arrangement ⟨the . . . chancellor is fully aware of the fact that he is the ~ of the constitutional setup —C.J.Friedrich & H.J. Spiro⟩
**king plank** *n* **:** the center plank of a wooden deck
**king post** *n* **1 :** a vertical member connecting the apex of a triangular truss (as of a roof) with the base — called also *crown post;* see ROOF illustration **2 :** a short strong tubular mast that supports the cargo boom of a shipboard derrick — called also *derrick post, samson post*
**king-post truss** *n* **:** a truss having a vertical central strut

*1* king post

**king quail** *n, Austral* **:** PAINTED QUAIL b
**king rail** *n* **:** a rather large long-billed No. American rail (*Rallus elegans*) having plumage streaked above with black and tawny olive and a rufous or cinnamon-red breast when in full plumage
**king rod** *n* **:** KINGBOLT 2
**king row** *n* **1 :** a row of four playing squares on the edge of a checkerboard nearest each player **2 :** the men on a king row at the start of a game of checkers ⟨to keep a *king row* intact⟩
**king rummy** *n* **:** a card game of the contract rummy group
**kings** *pl of* KING, *pres 3d sing of* KING
**king salmon** *n* **:** a large usu. red-fleshed salmon (*Oncorhynchus tshawytscha*) of the northern Pacific ocean that attains an average weight of about 20 pounds but is reported to sometimes exceed 100 pounds and is of great commercial importance — called also *black salmon, Chinook salmon, quinnat salmon*
**king's beadsman** *n* **:** BEADSMAN 2b
**king's bench** *n, usu cap K&B* [ME *kyngesbenche*] **:** COURT OF KING'S BENCH
**king's birthday** *n, usu cap K&B* **:** the legal holiday on which the British monarch's birthday is publicly celebrated in the United Kingdom and many other parts of the Commonwealth and Empire
**king's blue** *n* **1 :** a light to moderate blue that is greener and less strong than bluet **2 :** SMALT 2 **3 :** COBALT BLUE 1a
**king's books** *n pl* **:** the crown taxation list of ecclesiastical benefices and preferments in England
**king's champion** *n, usu cap K&C* **:** one who formerly at the coronation of the sovereign of England declared his readiness to defend the sovereign's title to the crown against any challenger
**king's color** *n, often cap K&C* **1 :** a union jack carried on the right of the regimental color by most British regiments **2 a :** a white ensign bearing the royal cipher used on ceremonial occasions by the Royal Navy
**king's counsel** *n, usu cap K&C* **1 :** a group of barristers of preeminence selected upon nomination of the lord chancellor to serve as counsel to the British crown and as such entitled to certain honorary privileges (as the wearing of a silk gown) **2 :** a member of this group of barristers ⟨the first woman attorney to win the high legal distinction of being a *King's Counsel* —P.J.Noel-Baker⟩
**king's english** *n, usu cap K&E* **1 :** standard, pure, or correct English speech or usage ⟨can think as speedily in classic Greek as . . . in the *King's English* —*Saturday Rev.*⟩ **2 :** English speech used by educated persons in southern England ⟨separating the *King's English* from the American language —M.A. Pei⟩
**king's evidence** *n, usu cap K* **:** one who gives evidence for the crown in British criminal proceedings ⟨willingness to turn *King's evidence*⟩ — compare STATE'S EVIDENCE
**king's evil** *n, often cap K&E* [ME *kinges evil;* fr. the belief that it could be healed by the touch of a king] **:** SCROFULA
**king's-fern** \ˈ=,=\ *n, pl* **king's-ferns :** ROYAL FERN
**king's friends** *n pl, often cap K&F* **:** members of the British parliament supporting the attempts of George III to increase the personal power of the monarch ⟨the *King's Friends* . . . were in the main recruited from the ranks of the Tories —Sidney Low & F.S.Pulling⟩
**king's-fruit** \ˈ=,=\ *n, pl* **king's-fruits :** MANGOSTEEN
**king's grith** *n* **:** KING'S PEACE 1
**king·ship** \ˈkiŋ,ship\ *n* **1 :** the office of king ⟨the traditional attributes of ~ —D.W.S.Lidderdale⟩ ⟨~ . . . has always been a symbol of national unity —Ernest Barker⟩ **2 :** the quality or state of being a king **:** MAJESTY ⟨the king is thus divested of his ~ and . . . becomes merely a corpse —J.G.Frazer⟩ **3 :** government by a king **:** a monarchical form of government headed by a king ⟨the medieval theory of ~ —G.H.Sabine⟩ ⟨whose contribution to the cause of ~ was less . . . enduring —Hector Bolitho⟩
**king-size** \ˈ=,=\ *or* **king-sized** \ˈ=ˈ=\ *adj* **1 :** longer than the regular or standard size — used of a cigarette ⟨about the length of a *king-sized* cigarette —*Scientific Monthly*⟩ **2 :** much larger in size than is usual for a particular class of things **:** OVERSIZE ⟨regular or *king-size* portions —*N.Y.Times*⟩ ⟨a *king-size* cocktail⟩ ⟨*king-size* bed six by seven feet⟩ **3 :** exceeding others of the kind in some conspicuous quality **:** EXTRAORDINARY ⟨a *king-size* hobby —Barbara Lenox⟩ ⟨a *king-size* movie⟩ ⟨a *king-size* lightning storm⟩
**king's man** *n* **1 :** an adherent of the king; *esp* **:** a supporter of the British cause during the American Revolution ⟨neither *king's man* nor rebel —*Sat. Eve. Post*⟩ **2 :** a customhouse officer
**king's mark** *n, usu cap K* **:** an official mark consisting of a leopard's or lion's head crowned that is used as part of a hallmark
**king snake** *n* **:** any of numerous brightly marked colubrid snakes (genus *Lampropeltis*) of the southern and central U.S. that are voracious consumers of rodents — called also *milk snake*
**king snapper** *n* [so called fr. the markings on the young which suggest the mark the British Board of Ordance places upon government stores] **:** GOVERNMENT BREAM
**king sora** *n* **:** FLORIDA GALLINULE
**king's paprika** *n* [trans. of G *königspaprika*] **:** Hungarian paprika that is made from whole peppers including seeds and stalks
**king's peace** *n, sometimes cap K&P* [ME *kynges pees*] **1 :** the special protection secured by the monarch in Anglo-Saxon and medieval England to particular persons (as members of the royal household) or places (as the king's highway) and occas. to specific periods of time (as coronation days) ⟨the *king's peace* was to abide in his assembly and . . . extend to the members in coming to it and returning from it —T.E.May⟩ **2 :** the general peace for the protection of persons and property secured in medieval times to large areas and later to the entire royal domain by the law administered by authority of the British monarch ⟨the *king's peace* had . . . grown from an occasional privilege into a common right —Frederick Pollock⟩
**king spoke** *n* **:** the spoke of the steering wheel of a ship that is upright when the rudder is fore and aft and is usu. distinguished by a Turk's head
**king's proctor** *n, usu cap K&P* **:** an officer of the judiciary in England who may intervene in actions for divorce chiefly to prevent collusive proceedings
**king's purple** *n* **:** ROYAL PURPLE 2
**king's ransom** *n* **:** a very large sum of money ⟨a rare book sometimes sells for a *king's ransom* —R.D.Altick⟩
**king's regulations** *n pl, usu cap K&R* **:** regulations for the British armed forces issued by the crown
**king's remembrancer** *n, usu cap K&R* **:** an officer of the British judiciary who is responsible for the collection of debts due to the monarch
**king's scholar** *n, usu cap K&S* **:** a student in an English school or college who is supported by a foundation created by or under the auspices of a king ⟨a *King's Scholar* at Cambridge⟩
**king's scout** *n, usu cap K&S* **:** a boy scout who has achieved the highest rating in British scouting by earning ten proficiency badges including four from a required list
**king's shilling** *n* **:** a shilling whose acceptance by a recruit from a recruiting officer constituted until 1879 a binding enlistment in the British army ⟨he's taken the *king's shilling*⟩
**king's silver** *n, usu cap K* **:** POST-FINE
**king's spear** *n, Brit* **:** JACOB'S-ROD
**kings·ton** \ˈkiŋztən, -ŋ(k)st-\ *adj, usu cap* [fr. *Kingston, Jamaica*] **:** of or from Kingston, the capital of Jamaica **:** of the kind or style prevalent in Kingston
**kingston valve** *n, usu cap K* [prob. fr. the F. C. *Kingston* Co., Los Angeles, Calif.] **:** a conical valve opening outward from a ship and closed by the underwater pressure of the sea that is used esp. on a ballast tank of a submarine
**king's x** *interj, usu cap K&X* [prob. short for *king's excuse*] — used as a cry in children's games to claim exemption from being tagged or caught or to call for a time out ⟨how they make haste to cry with fingers crossed *King's X* — no fairs to use it any more —Robert Frost⟩
**king's yellow** *n* **1 :** arsenic trisulfide used as a pigment **2 :** ORPIMENT 2
**king tody** *n* **:** ROYAL FLYCATCHER
**king truss** *n* **:** a truss framed with a king post
**king turtle** *n* **:** a large No. American soft-shelled turtle (*Amyda spinifera*)
**king vulture** *n* **:** a large vulture (*Sarcoramphus papa*) ranging from Mexico to Paraguay that is creamy white in color with wings, rump, and tail black and the carunculate head and the neck colored scarlet, yellow, orange, and blue
**king·wa·na** \kiŋˈwänə\ *n, pl* **kingwana** *or* **kingwanas** *usu cap* **:** a dialect of Swahili widely used in the eastern Congo as a trade language
**king whiting** *n* **:** a whiting (*Menticirrhus americanus*) of the east coast of No. America from Maryland to Texas
**king wil·liam pine** \-ˈwilyəm-\ *n, usu cap K&W* [after *William* IV †1837 king of England] **:** a Tasmanian tree (*Athrotaxis selaginoides*) of the family Taxodiaceae with sharp-pointed leaves that curve inward and overlap loosely
**kingwood** \ˈ=,=\ *n* **1 :** the wood of any of various trees esp. of the genus *Dalbergia; specif* **:** a handsome Brazilian wood from a tree (*D. cearensis*) of Ceará **2 :** a tree that yields kingwood **3 :** GONCALO ALVES 2
**¹kink** \ˈkiŋk\ *vi* -ED/-ING/-S [ME *kinken* — more at CHINK] *dial* **:** to be seized with a kink **:** gasp convulsively (as in laughing or coughing)
**²kink** \ˈ"\ *n* -s *dial* **:** a fit or paroxysm of coughing or laughter ⟨the sister was in ~s of laughter —Donagh MacDonagh⟩
**³kink** \ˈ"\ *n* -s [D; akin to MLG *kinke* kink — more at CONGER] **1 a :** a short and often tight twist or curl caused by a doubling or winding of something (as a rope or hair) upon itself ⟨looped hose should be changed . . . to reverse folds and prevent ~s —G.E. Stecher⟩ **b :** a bend in something (as a line) otherwise straight **:** INDENTATION, PROJECTION ⟨a dozen curly streets with ~s in them —Thomas Wood †1950⟩ ⟨a ~ in a line on a graph⟩ **c :** a buckling of a railroad track due to longitudinal movement of the rails by creeping or expanding **2 a :** a twist or turn in a person's nature or disposition **:** a mental or physical peculiarity **:** ECCENTRICITY, QUIRK ⟨the ~ in his psychology which made him such a menace to society —P.G.Wodehouse⟩ ⟨a suspicious contempt for the intellectual life . . . is a ~ in the American character —J.J.Wright⟩ **b :** an odd notion **:** WHIM ⟨got a ~ in her head that diamonds she must have —Julian Hawthorne⟩ **3 :** a clever and often unusual idea or method of doing something ⟨every ~ . . . time-saver, or quality-improvement suggestion entered in the contest —*Textile Industries*⟩ ⟨cost-cutting shop ~s —*U.S. Daily*⟩ **4 :** a cramp or stiffness in some part of the body **:** CRICK ⟨taking the ~s out of his legs —Sinclair Lewis⟩ **5 a :** an imperfection (as in design or construction) that is likely to cause difficulties in the operation of something ⟨to spot the ~ . . . that get into an airplane as a result of faulty design —G.W.Gray b. 1886⟩ ⟨number of ~s . . . to be ironed out of the system —Cecile Starr⟩ **b :** a particular type of imperfection in a crystal that is important in the theoretical study of plastic deformation

kinks 1a

**⁴kink** \ˈ"\ *vb* -ED/-ING/-S *vi* **:** to wind into or form a kink **:** become tightly twisted at one or more points ⟨vinyl hose . . . will not ~ —*Monsanto Mag.*⟩ ~ *vt* **:** to cause to form a kink **:** make a kink in ⟨the sinkers are projected forward to ~ the yarn around the needles —*Full-Fashioned Knitting Machine Primer*⟩
**kin·kaid·er** \kinˈkādə(r)\ *n* -s *usu cap* [Moses P. *Kinkaid* †1922 Am. congressman + E *-er*] **:** a settler on free land in Nebraska under terms of the Kinkaid Act in 1904 which allowed each bona fide settler 640 acres upon payment of a filing fee of 14 dollars ⟨the place *Kinkaiders* make their home and prairie chickens freely roam —Carl Sandburg⟩
**kin·ka·jou** \ˈkiŋkə,jü\ *n* -s [F, of Algonquian origin; akin to Ojibwa *qwingwâage* wolverine — more at QUICKHATCH] **:** a nocturnal arboreal carnivorous mammal (*Potos caudivolvulus* syn. *Cercoleptes caudivolvulus*) of the family Procyonidae inhabiting Mexico and Central and So. America that is about three feet long with a slender body, long prehensile tail, large lustrous eyes, and soft woolly yellowish brown fur
**kinkcough** \ˈ=,=\ *n* [¹*kink* + *cough*] **:** WHOOPING COUGH
**kink·er** \ˈkiŋkə(r)\ *n* -s [prob. fr. ⁴*kink* + *-er*] **:** an acrobat or other performer in a circus
**kinkhab** *var of* KINCOB
**kink·host** \ˈkiŋk,hōst\ *n* [ME (northern dial.), fr. *kinken* to gasp + *host* cough — more at CHINK, HOAST] *archaic Scot* **:** WHOOPING COUGH
**kin·kle** \ˈkiŋkəl\ *n* -s [³*kink* + *-le*] **:** a little kink ⟨to shake the ~s out o' back an' legs —J.R.Lowell⟩
**kin·kled** \-ld\ *adj* **:** having kinkles **:** KINKY ⟨~ hair⟩
**kinkob** *var of* KINCOB
**kinks** *pl of* KINK, *pres 3d sing of* KINK
**kinky** \ˈkiŋkē, -ki\ *adj* -ER/-EST **1 :** having or full of kinks **:** closely twisted or curled ⟨the Negro in Africa has short tight ~ hair —Weston La Barre⟩ **2 :** LIVELY, SPIRITED ⟨fresh and ~ horses —Will James⟩ **3 :** CROOKED 2 ⟨professional calligraphic swindler and ~ penman —*Graphic Arts Monthly*⟩
**kin·less** \ˈkinləs\ *adj* **:** having no relatives ⟨left for friendless and ~ souls —E.B.Tylor⟩
**kin·nery** \ˈkin(ə)rē\ *n* [¹*kin* + *-ery*] *South & Midland* **:** KINFOLK, RELATIVES
**kin·ni·kin·nick** *also* **kin·ni·ki·nic** *or* **kin·ni·ki·nick** *or* **kin·ni·kin·nic** *or* **kin·ni·kin·nik** \ˌkinəkəˈnik\ *or* **kil·lic·kin·nic** *or* **kil·li·ki·nick** *or* **kil·lic·kin·nick** \ˌkilək-\ *n* -s [of Algonquian origin; akin to Natick *kinukkinuk* mixture, Ojibwa *kinikinige* he mixes by hand] **1 :** a mixture of the dried leaves and bark of certain plants (as sumac leaves and the inner bark of a dogwood, esp. the silky cornel) and sometimes tobacco smoked by the Indians and pioneers in the Ohio valley and the region of the Great Lakes **2 :** a plant used in kinnikinnick: as **a :** BEARBERRY **b :** SILKY CORNEL **c :** RED OSIER **d :** either of two sumacs (*Rhus virens* and *R. microphylla*) chiefly of the southwestern U.S. and Mexico
**kin·nle** \ˈkinᵊl\ *Scot var of* ²KINDLE
**kin·nor** \kēˈnō(ə)r\ *n* -s [Heb *kinnōr*] **:** an ancient Jewish lyre
**¹ki·no** \ˈkē(,)nō\ *also* **kino gum** *n* -s [of African origin; akin to Mandingo *keno, kano* African kino] **1 :** any of several dark red to black tannin-containing dried juices or extracts obtained from various tropical trees: as **a :** the dried juice obtained usu. from the trunk of an East Indian tree (*Pterocarpus marsupium*) as brown or black fragments and used as an astringent in diarrhea — called also *East India kino, Malabar kino* **b :** BUTEA GUM **c :** EUCALYPTUS GUM **2 :** a tree that produces kino (esp. *Pterocarpus marsupium*)
**²kino** \ˈ"\ *n* -s [G, short for *kinematograph*, fr. F *cinématographe* — more at CINEMATOGRAPH] **:** a motion-picture theater in Europe ⟨fond of going to the ~ —Truman Capote⟩
**kino-** — see KIN-
**kin·o·mere** \ˈkinə,mi(ə)r, ˈkīn-, -nō,-\ *n* -s [*kin-* + *-mere*] **:** CENTROMERE
**kin·o·plasm** \-,plazəm\ *also* **kin·o·plas·ma** \ˌ==ˈplazmə\ *n* [ISV *kin-* + *-plasm, -plasma;* orig. formed as G *kinoplasma*] **:** an active protoplasmic component held to form filaments and mobile structures (as cilia or spindle fibers) — opposed to *trophoplasm*
**kin·o·rhynch** \ˈ===,riŋk\ *n* -s [NL *Kinorhyncha*] **:** a worm of the class Kinorhyncha
**kin·o·rhyn·cha** \ˌ===ˈriŋkə\ *n pl, cap* [NL, fr. *kin-* + *-rhyncha* (fr. Gk *rhynchos* snout, proboscis)] **:** a class of Aschelminthes comprising minute marine worms of uncertain systematic position having certain resemblances to arthropods and annelids but prob. more closely related to the nematodes — see ECHINODERES
**kin·o·ster·ni·dae** \ˌ==ˈstə(r)nə,dē\ *n pl, cap* [NL, fr. *Kinosternon*, type genus + *-idae*] **:** a small family of No. American freshwater turtles comprising the mud turtles
**kin·o·ster·non** \-)nən\ *n, cap* [NL, fr. *kin-* + Gk *sternon* breast — more at STERNUM] **:** a genus (the type of the family Kinosternidae) of No. American freshwater turtles distinguished by fully hinged plastral lobes capable of completely closing the shell
**kinot** *or* **kinoth** *pl of* KINAH
**kin·ross-shire** \kinˈrȯs(h),shi(ə)r, -,shər\ *or* **kin·ross** \kinˈrȯs\ *adj, usu cap K* [fr. *Kinross-shire* or *Kinross* county, Scotland] **:** of or from the county of Kinross, Scotland **:** of the kind or style prevalent in Kinross
**kins** *pl of* KIN
**-kins** — see -KIN
**kinsfolk** *var of* KINFOLK
**kin·sha·sa** \kinˈshäsə\ *adj, usu cap* [fr. *Kinshasa* (formerly *Léopoldville*), capital of Congo] **:** of or from Kinshasa **:** of the kind or style prevalent in Kinshasa
**kin·ship** \ˈkin,ship\ *n* [¹*kin* + *-ship*] **:** the quality or state of being kin: as **a :** personal relationship by blood and sometimes by marriage ⟨her ~ with no less than twelve sovereigns —A.P. Stanley⟩ **b :** relationship by descent from a common ancestor or membership in a common group (as a clan) ⟨the Negroes . . . were already conscious of ~ with other men similarly marked throughout the world —Oscar Handlin⟩ ⟨the instinctive British feelings of ~ and common freedom —Barbara Ward⟩ ⟨a ~ of man with other animals —Weston La Barre⟩ **c :** the socially recognized relationship between people in a culture who are or are held to be biologically related or who are given the status of relatives by ritual **d :** a likeness in character or qualities **:** possession of common features ⟨its mineral waters . . . carry startling ~ to seawater —Helen A. Levin⟩ ⟨in . . . his character studies critics have found a ~ with the early Flemish masters —*Amer. Guide Series: Mich.*⟩ **e :** a community of interest; *esp* **:** a sense of oneness ⟨acquiescence when negation seems to question our ~ with the crowd —B.N.Cardozo⟩ ⟨a sense of professional ~ —Douglas Bush⟩ **f :** a close connection between things that resembles a blood relationship ⟨anthropology's ~ with the humanities⟩
**kinship system** *n* **:** the system of social relationships connecting people in a culture who are or are held to be related and defining and regulating their reciprocal obligations ⟨*kinship systems* vary in different forms of social organization —Thomas Gladwin⟩
**kins·man** \ˈkinzmən\ *n, pl* **kinsmen** [ME *kinnesman*, fr. *kinnes* (gen. of ¹*kin*) + *man*] **:** a man of the same race or family **:** one related by blood or sometimes by marriage **:** RELATION, RELATIVE ⟨Polynesians, distant *kinsmen* of the New Zealand Maori —Ernest Beaglehole⟩ ⟨a very great . . . American whom I am proud to call my ~ —A.E.Stevenson †1965⟩
**kins·man·ship** \-ən,ship\ *n* **:** KINSHIP
**kins·people** \ˈkinz+,-\ *n, pl* **kinspeople :** RELATIVES ⟨reach their sick ~ in Germany —B.J.Hendrick⟩
**kins·woman** \ˈ"+,-\ *n, pl* **kinswomen** [ME *kinneswoman*, fr. *kinnes* (gen. of ¹*kin*) + *woman*] **:** a female relative ⟨the murdered prince had married a ~ of the earl —E.A.Freeman⟩
**kin·tra** \ˈkin·trə\ *Scot var of* COUNTRY
**kin·try** \-ri\ *Scot var of* COUNTRY
**ki·nu·ra** \kəˈnürə\ *n* -s [prob. irreg. fr. Gk *kinyra*, a kind of lyre, fr. Heb *kinnōr*] **:** a small-scaled reed-organ pipe of thin nasal tone that is used in theater pipe organs for comic effects
**ki·o·ea** \ˌkēōˈāə\ *n* -s [Hawaiian] **:** BRISTLE-THIGHED CURLEW
**ki·o·ko** \kēˈō(,)kō\ *n, pl* **kioko** *or* **kiokos** *usu cap* **:** CHOKWE 1
**ki·o·re** \kēˈōrē\ *n* -s [Maori] **:** the native rat (*Rattus exulan*) of New Zealand now wholly or nearly replaced by the introduced Norwegian and black rats
**ki·osk** *also* **ki·osque** \ˈkē,äsk *sometimes* ==ˈ= *or* ˈkī,äsk\ *n* -s [Turk *köşk*, fr. Per *kūshk* portico, palace] **1 :** an open summerhouse or pavilion often having a roof supported by pillars and usu. built in gardens and parks ⟨~s on the heights above the Bosporus —*Manchester Guardian Weekly*⟩ **2** [F *kiosque*, fr. Turk *köşk*] **:** a structure resembling or felt to resemble a kiosk: as **a :** an outdoor newsstand ⟨the bountiful supply of newspapers displayed on every ~ —I.F.Fraser⟩ **b :** a structure housing the entrance to a subway **c** *chiefly Brit* **:** a stand or booth at which merchandise is sold or information is provided ⟨bought tea and buns at the station ~ —Lionel Shapiro⟩ ⟨the ticket ~ closed —T.W.Duncan⟩ ⟨a little information ~ —*Irish Digest*⟩ **d :** TELEPHONE BOOTH ⟨the red telephone ~s . . . at the side of the road —Richard Joseph⟩ **e :** a structure used as a receptacle or as housing for machinery ⟨transformer ~s for the distribution of electricity —*World*⟩

kiosk 1

**ki·o·wa** \ˈkīə,wä, -,wā, -əwə\ *n, pl* **kiowa** *or* **kiowas** *usu cap* [Kiowa *Gâ-i-gwŭ, Kâ-i-gwŭ*, lit., principal people] **1 a :** a Tanoan people in adjoining parts of Oklahoma, Kansas, Colorado, New Mexico, and Texas **b :** a member of such people **2 :** the language of the Kiowa people
**kiowa apache** *n, usu cap K&A* **1 a :** an Athapascan people associated with the Kiowa **b :** a member of such people **2 :** the language of the Kiowa Apache people
**¹kip** \ˈkip\ *n* -s [obs. D, bundle of hides, bundle of flax, fr. MD; akin to MLG *kip* bundle of hides, bunch of fish, ON *kippi* bundle, sheaf] **1 :** a set or bundle of undressed hides of young or small animals (as calves, lambs, colts) **2 :** one of the undressed hides in a kip; *specif* **:** a skin coming from a bovine animal in size between a calf and a matured animal and weighing from 16 to 25 pounds in green salted condition
**²kip** \ˈ"\ *n* -s [origin unknown] *dial Eng* **:** the common tern
**³kip** \ˈ"\ *n* -s [perh. fr. Dan *kippe* cheap tavern] **1 :** BED ⟨ready for the ~ after this screwball day —K.M.Dodson⟩ ⟨was in ~ —Richard Llewellyn⟩ **2 :** SLEEP ⟨get some ~ —Paul Scott⟩
**⁴kip** \ˈ"\ *vi* **kipped; kipped; kipping; kips :** to lie in bed **:** SLEEP ⟨a ragged blanket to ~ in by nights —Richard Dehan⟩ — sometimes used with *down* ⟨you can ~ down . . . and get a bit of sleep —Edith Sitwell⟩
**⁵kip** \ˈ"\ *n* -s [G *kippe* edge, seesaw, arm of a balance, kip, fr. LG, point, edge, fr. L *cippus* stake, post — more at CEPE] **1 a :** a gymnastic feat that is executed when hanging by the hands from a piece of apparatus and consists of moving from

a position in which the legs are above the head to one with the head above the feet by flexing the hips and swinging the legs forward and upward above the head, then arching the back and thrusting with the chest and forcibly kicking the legs downward to raise the body — called also *upstart* **b :** a similar movement executed from a cross seat on the parallel bars by dropping backward with straight arms into position **2 :** a synchronized swimming stunt in which from a back layout position both knees are drawn to the chest and the trunk is submerged backward to a head down vertical position followed by extension of the legs and complete submersion of the body

**⁶kip** \"\ *vi* **kipped; kipped; kipping; kips :** to perform a kip in gymnastics or swimming

**⁷kip** \"\ *n* -s [*kilo* + *pound*] **:** a unit of weight equal to 1000 pounds used to express deadweight load

**⁸kip** \"\ *n* -s [origin unknown] **:** a small piece of wood from which the pennies are tossed in the Australian game of two-up

**⁹kip** \"\ *n* -s [Siamese] **:** the basic monetary unit of Laos from 1955 divided into 100 at — see MONEY table

**kip·chak** \kip'chäk\ *n* -s *usu cap* [Russ, fr. Jagatai] **1 a :** one of the ancient Turkic peoples of the Golden Horde related to the Uighurs and Kirghiz **b :** a member of the Kipchak people **2 :** the Turkic language of the Kipchak people

**kipe** \'kīp\ *n* -s [ME, fr. OE *cȳpa, cȳpe*; akin to MLG *kīpe* basket, Norw dial. *kaup* wooden vessel, OE *cot* (hut) — more at COT] *dial Eng* **:** a large basket used usu. for a measure

**kip·fel** \'kipfəl\ *n* -s [G, dim. of *kipf* wagon post, kipfel, fr. OHG *kipfa, chipf* wagon post, fr. L *cippus* post — more at CEPE] **:** a crescent-shaped cookie or roll

**kip·ling·ese** \,kipliŋ'ēz, -ēs\ *n* -s *usu cap* [Rudyard *Kipling* †1936 Eng. poet and novelist + E *-ese*] **:** the literary style of Rudyard Kipling ⟨write a chanty in *Kiplingese* —*Dial*⟩

**kip·ling·esque** \¦==¦esk\ *adj, usu cap* [Rudyard *Kipling* + E *-esque*] **1 :** of, resembling, or having the characteristics of the literary style of Rudyard Kipling ⟨the poems . . . were direct, *Kiplingesque* —Gertrude Stein⟩ **2 :** characterized by an attitude of superiority over and a responsibility for nonwhite peoples often associated with the writings of Rudyard Kipling ⟨a *Kiplingesque* condescension toward China —F.J.Brown & J.S.Roucek⟩

**kip·page** \'kipij\ *n* -s [modif. of F *équipage* (as in *être en piteux équipage* to be in a sorry plight) — more at EQUIPAGE] *Scot* **:** an excited or irritated state **:** COMMOTION, CONFUSION ⟨dinna pit yoursell into a ~ —Sir Walter Scott⟩

**kip·peen** \ki'pēn\ *n* -s [IrGael *cipīn*] *chiefly Irish* **:** a short thin stick **:** SWITCH

**kippen** *past part of* KEP

**¹kip·per** \'kipə(r)\ *n* -s [ME *kypre*, fr. OE *cypera*, prob. fr. *coper* copper; fr. the color — more at COPPER] **1 :** a male salmon or sea trout during or after the spawning season **2 :** a kippered herring or salmon

**²kipper** \"\ *vt* -ED/-ING/-S **:** to cure by splitting, cleaning, salting, and smoking

**³kipper** \"\ *adj* [origin unknown] *dial* **:** CHIPPER

**⁴kipper** \"\ *n* -s [native name in Australia] **:** a young Australian aborigine who has passed through the initiatory rite

**kip·per·er** \-pərə(r)\ *n* -s **:** one that kippers fish

**kipp generator** \'kip-\ *n, usu cap K* [after Petrus Jacobus *Kipp* †1864 Du. druggist and chemist] **:** a glass laboratory apparatus for generating a gas (as hydrogen sulfide by the action of an acid on ferrous sulfide)

Kipp generator

**kipping** *pres part of* KIP

**kips** *pl of* KIP, *pres 3d sing of* KIP

**kip·si·gis** \kip'sēgəs\ *or* **kip·si·kis** \-ēkəs\ *n, pl* **kipsigis** *or* **kipsikis** *usu cap* **1 a :** a predominantly pastoral people of west-central Kenya **b :** a member of such people **2 :** NANDI

**kipskin** \'=,=\ *n* [¹*kip* + *skin*] **:** ¹KIP 2

**ki·pu·ka** \kē'pükə\ *n* -s [Hawaiian] **:** an area of older land ranging in size from a few square feet to several square miles surrounded by later lava flows ⟨~*s* result from either topographic irregularities or the viscosity of the lava —H.T.Stearns & G.A.Macdonald⟩

**kip-up** *n* -s [fr. *kip up*, v.] **:** a kip executed from a supine position on the mat in tumbling

**ki·ran·ti** \kē'räntē\ *n* -s *usu cap* **:** a group of Tibeto-Burman dialects centering in eastern Nepal

**kir·by** \'kərbē\ *or* **kirby hook** *n* -s [fr. the name *Kirby*] **:** a fishhook of evenly curved pattern — see FISHHOOK illustration

**kirch·hoff's law** \'kirḵ,hōfs-\ *n, usu cap K* [after Gustav R. *Kirchhoff* †1887 Ger. physicist] **1 :** a statement in physics: in an electric network the algebraic sum of the currents in all the branches that meet at any point is zero **2 :** a statement in physics: if any closed circuit is chosen from the branches of an electric network, the algebraic sum of the products formed by multiplying the resistance of each branch by the current in that branch is equal to the algebraic sum of the electromotive forces in the several branches forming the circuit **3 :** a statement in physics: the ratio of the emissive power to the absorptivity is the same for all bodies at the same temperature and equals the emissive power of a black body at that temperature

**kir·ghiz** *or* **kir·ghese** *or* **kir·ghis** *or* **kir·giz** *or* **khir·ghiz** \kir'gēz, kiə'-\ *n, pl* **kirghiz** *or* **kirghizes** *or* **kirghese** *or* **kirgheses** *or* **kirghis** *or* **kirghises** *or* **kirgiz** *or* **kirgizes** *or* **khirghiz** *or* **khirghizes** *usu cap* [Kirghiz *Kyrghyz*] **1 a :** a widespread people of Turkic speech and Mongolian race prob. with some Caucasian intermixture inhabiting chiefly the Central Asian steppes and related to the steppe-dwelling Kazak — see KARA-KIRGHIZ **b :** a member of the Kirghiz people **2 :** the Turkic language of the Kirghiz

**ki·ri** \'kērē\ *n* -s [Jap] **1 :** a paulownia (*Paulownia tomentosa*) **2 :** the light soft straight-grained pale brown wood of the kiri that is easily worked and very resistant to shrinking and swelling and that is used in Japan esp. as a base for lacquer work and in lining fine cabinetry

**ki·ril·li·tsa** \kə'rilətsə\ *n* -s *usu cap* [Russ, fr. *Kirill* (Cyril) — more at CYRILLIC] **:** CYRILLIC ALPHABET

**kiri·mon** \'kirə,män, 'kērə,m-\ *n* -s [Jap, fr. *kiri* + *mon* badge, crest] **:** one of the two imperial badges of Japan consisting of three leaves of the paulownia surmounted by three budding stems — compare CHRYSANTHEMUM 3

kirimon

**ki·rin** \'kē'rin\ *adj, usu cap* [fr. *Kirin*, Manchuria] **:** of or from the city of Kirin, Manchuria **:** of the kind or style prevalent in Kirin

**ki·ri·ri** \¦kēre¦rē\ *usu cap, var of* CARIRI

**ki·ri·wi·na** \,kērē'vēnə\ *n, pl* **kiriwina** *or* **kiriwinas** *usu cap* **:** an Austronesian language of the Trobriand islands

**¹kirk** *also* **kurk** \'ki(ə)rk, 'kərk, 'kiək, 'kək\ *n* -s *often attrib* [ME (northern dial.) *kirke, kirk*, fr. ON *kirkja*, fr. OE *cirice* — more at CHURCH] **1** *chiefly Scot* **:** CHURCH ⟨bells in the city ~*s* —*Christian Century*⟩ ⟨coming to the ~ this morning —Guy McCrone⟩ **2** *usu cap* **:** the Church of Scotland as distinguished from the Church of England or the Episcopal Church in Scotland — usu. used with *the* ⟨the essential autonomy of the *Kirk* —J.Y.Evans⟩

**²kirk** \"\ *vt* **kirked** \-kt\ *or* **kirk·it** \-kət\ **kirked** *or* **kirkit; kirking; kirks** [ME (Sc dial.) *kirken*, fr. *kirke, kirk*, n.] **1** *chiefly Scot* **:** CHURCH **2** *Scot* **:** to take (a bride or couple) to church for the first time after the wedding ceremony ⟨I'm to be married the morn and *kirkit* on Sunday —Sir Walter Scott⟩

**kirk·cud·bright·shire** \,kər'kübri,shi(ə)r, -,shər\ *or* **kirk·cud·bright** \,=¦=bri\ *adj, usu cap* [fr. *Kirkcudbrightshire* or *Kirkcudbright* county, Scotland] **:** of or from the county of Kirkcudbright, Scotland **:** of the kind or style prevalent in Kirkcudbright

**kirk·er** \'kərkər\ *n* -s *usu cap* [¹*kirk* + *-er*] **:** a member or adherent of the Church of Scotland — see AULD KIRKER, FREE KIRKER

**kirk·in·head** \'kərkən,hed\ *n* [perh. irreg. fr. ¹*kirk* + *head*] **:** JERKINHEAD

**kirk keeper** *n, Scot* **:** one that attends a kirk regularly

**kirk·man** \'kirkmən, 'kər-\ *n, pl* **kirkmen** [ME (northern dial.), fr. *kirk* + *man*] **1** *chiefly Scot* **:** CHURCHMAN **2 :** a member or adherent of the Church of Scotland

**kirk·shot** \'kərk,shät\ *n* [alter. of OE *ciricsceat* — more at CHURCHSCOT] **:** CHURCHSCOT

**kirk·town** \'kərk, taun\ *also* **kirk·ton** \-,tən\ *n* [ME (Sc dial.) *kirktoun*, fr. *kirke, kirk* + *toun* town — more at TOWN] **1 :** the hamlet in the immediate neighborhood of the parish church in country parishes of Scotland **2 :** GLEBE 2a

**kirk·yard** \'kirk,yärd, 'kərk-\ *n* [ME (northern dial.) *kirkyard*, fr. *kirk* + *yard*] *chiefly Scot* **:** CHURCHYARD

**kir·man** \kir'män\ *or* **ker·man** \kər-, ker-\ *n* -s *usu cap* [fr. *Kirman* or *Kerman* province, Iran] **:** a Persian carpet or rug characterized by elaborate fluid designs and soft colors ⟨a *Kirman* is the only Persian carpet that looks feminine —Rumer Godden⟩

**kir·man·shah** \¦kirmən¦shä, kər'män,shä\ *or* **ker·man·shah** \¦kermən¦-, kər'män,-\ *n* -s *usu cap* **:** KIRMAN

**kirmess** *var of* KERMIS

**¹kirn** \'kirn, 'kərn\ *n* -s [ME (northern dial.) *kirne*, fr. ON *kirna*; akin to ON *kjarni* churn — more at CHURN] *chiefly Scot* **:** CHURN

**²kirn** \"\ *vb* -ED/-ING/-S *chiefly Scot* **:** CHURN

**³kirn** \"\ *n* -s [perh. of Scand origin; akin to ON *korn* grain — more at CORN] **1** *chiefly Scot* **:** HARVEST HOME **2** ⟨the good old custom of the ~ —J.G.Lockhart⟩ **2** *chiefly Scot* **:** the last handful or sheaf reaped at the harvest — called also *mell*

**kirn baby** *or* **kirn doll** *or* **kirn maiden** *n* [³*kirn*] **:** HARVEST DOLL

**ki·rom·bo** \kə'räm(,)bō\ *also* **ki·roum·ba** \-raumbə\ *n* -s [Malagasy *kiròmbo*] **:** a crested conspicuously colored coraciiform bird (*Leptosomus discolor*) of Madagascar related to the rollers

**ki·rov** \'kērəf\ *adj, usu cap* [fr. *Kirov*, U.S.S.R.] **:** of or from the city of Kirov, U.S.S.R. **:** of the kind or style prevalent in Kirov

**ki·rov·ite** \'kērə,vīt\ *n* -s [Russ *kirovit*, fr. Sergei M. *Kirov* †1934 Russ. revolutionary leader + Russ *-it* -ite] **:** a mineral $Fe,MgSO_4 7H_2O$ consisting of a hydrous sulfate of iron and magnesium isomorphous with melanterite and pisanite

**ki·ro·vo·grad** \kə'rōvə,grad\ *adj, usu cap* [fr. *Kirovograd*, U.S.S.R.] **:** of or from the city of Kirovograd, U.S.S.R. **:** of the kind or style prevalent in Kirovograd

**kir·pan** \kir'pän, kər-\ *n* -s [Panjabi & Hindi *kirpān*, fr. Skt *kṛpāṇa* sword — more at HARVEST] **:** the sacred dagger of the Sikhs ⟨the right of every Sikh . . . to wear a ~ —J.C.Archer⟩

**kirsch** \'kirsh, -iəsh\ *also* **kirsch·was·ser** \-sh,väsə(r)\ *n, pl* **kirsches** *also* **kirschwassers** [*kirsch* fr. G, short for *kirschwasser; kirschwasser* fr. G, fr. *kirsche* cherry + *wasser* water] **:** a dry colorless brandy made in the Black Forest region of Germany, in Alsace, France, and in Switzerland that is distilled from the fermented juice of the black morello cherry and has a bitter almond flavor derived from the ground cherry pits placed in the juice prior to distillation

**kirsch·ner value** \'kirshnər-\ *n, usu cap K* [fr. the name *Kirschner*] **:** a value similar to a Reichert value that indicates the content in a fat of the water-soluble fatty acids (as butyric acid) having soluble silver salts

**kir·se·baer** \'kirsə,ba(a)(ə)r\ *n* -s [Dan *kirsebær*, short for *kirsebærbrændevin*, fr. *kirsebær* cherry + *brændevin* brandy] **:** a Danish cherry liqueur

**kir·sen** \'kərsᵊn\ *now dial var of* ²CHRISTEN

**kirt·land's owl** \'kərtlən(d)z-\ *n, usu cap K* [after Jared P. *Kirtland* †1877 Am. naturalist] **:** SAW-WHET OWL

**kirtland's warbler** *n, usu cap K* [after Jared P. *Kirtland*] **:** a rare warbler (*Dendroica kirtlandii*) of northeastern No. America that breeds in Michigan and winters in the Bahamas and that is gray above and yellow beneath with long pointed wings and notched tail

**¹kir·tle** \'kər|dᵊl, 'kə|, 'kəi|, |tᵊl\ *n* -s [ME *kirtel*, fr. OE *cyrtel*, fr. (assumed) OE *curt* short; akin to OS *kurt*, OHG *kurz*; all fr. a prehistoric WGmc word borrowed fr. L *curtus* shortened — more at SHEAR] **1 :** a garment resembling a tunic or coat usu. reaching to the knees and worn by men often as the principal body garment until the 16th century **2 :** a long gown or dress worn during the middle ages by women usu. beneath a cloak and also in modern times as part of coronation robes ⟨wearing her . . . ~ of blue —H.W.Longfellow⟩

**²kirtle** \"\ *vt* -ED/-ING/-S **:** to cover or enwrap (as in a kirtle) ⟨the wild Albanian *kirtled* to his knee —Lord Byron⟩

**kirve** \'kərv\ *vi* -ED/-ING/-S [prob. alter. of *carve*] **:** to undercut coal in a mine

**ki·saeng** *also* **ki·sang** \'kē,saŋ\ *n, pl* **kisaengs** *or* **kisaeng** [Korean *kisaeng*] **:** a Korean professional singing and dancing girl

**ki·san** \kē'sän\ *n* -s [Hindi *kisān*, fr. Skt *kṛṣāṇa* one who plows, fr. *karṣati* he plows] **:** a small farmer or agricultural worker in India **:** PEASANT

**¹kish** \'kish\ *n* -ES [IrGael *cis*, fr. MIr *cess*] **:** a large square wicker basket used in Ireland for carrying peat

**²kish** \"\ *also* **keesh** \'kēsh\ *n* -ES [prob. modif. of G *kies* gravel, pyrites, fr. MHG *kis*; akin to OHG *kisil* pebble — more at CHISEL] **:** graphite that separates on slow cooling of molten cast iron or pig iron rich in carbon

**kish·en** *or* **kish·on** \'kishən\ *n, pl* **kishen** *or* **kishon** [Manx *kishan*] **:** a Manx unit of capacity equal to 1.03 U. S. pecks or 1 British peck

**kish·i·nev** \'kishə,nef\ *adj, usu cap* [fr. *Kishinev*, U.S.S.R.] **:** of or from the city of Kishinev, U.S.S.R. **:** of the kind or style prevalent in Kishinev

**kish·ke** \'kishkə\ *n* -s [Yiddish, gut, sausage, of Slav origin; akin to Pol *kiszka* gut, sausage, Ukrainian *kyška*, Russ *kishka* gut; akin to Gk *kysthos* vulva — more at HOARD] **:** beef or fowl casing stuffed with a savory filling (as of matzoth flour, chicken fat, and onion) and roasted **:** stuffed derma

**ki·si** \'kēsē\ *n* -s [Hopi] **:** a bower of interwoven branches used for keeping snakes before a Hopi snake dance

**kis·ka·dee** \'kiskə(,)dē\ *n* -s [imit.] **:** DERBY FLYCATCHER

**kis kilim** \'kēs-\ *n, often cap both Ks* [fr. *Kis Kilim*, a kind of carpet, fr. Turk *kızkilim*, fr. *kız* girl + *kilim*] **:** RUSSIAN CALF

**kis·lev** *or* **chis·lev** \'kisləf\ *n* -s *usu cap* [Heb *Kislēw*] **:** the 3d month of the civil year or the 9th month of the ecclesiastical year in the Jewish calendar — see MONTH table

**kis·met** \'kiz,met, -,mət\ *also* **kis·mat** \-,mət\ *n* -s *often cap* [Turk *kısmet*, fr. Ar *qismah* portion, lot] **:** FATE 1, 2a

**¹kiss** \'kis\ *vb* **kissed** *also archaic* **kist** \'kist\ **kissed** *also archaic* **kist; kissing; kisses** [ME *kissen*, fr. OE *cyssan*; akin to OHG *kussen* to kiss, ON *kyssa*, Goth *kukjan*; denominatives fr. the root of OE *coss* kiss, OHG *kus, kuss*, ON *koss*; prob. akin (with phonological conservation due to the imit. nature of the word) to Gk *kynein* to kiss, Hitt *kuwassanzi* they kiss, Skt *cuṃati* he sucks] *vt* **1 a :** to touch or press with the lips (as in affection, greeting, reverence) **:** salute or caress with the lips ⟨~*ed* his wife on the mouth and the baby on the cheek⟩ ⟨~ the foot of the image⟩ **b :** to kiss with a smack ⟨~*ed* her loudly⟩ ⟨~ the children good-night⟩ **2 :** to put or effect by kissing ⟨~ away her tears⟩ **3 a :** to touch gently as if fondly or caressingly ⟨a soft wind that ~*es* the flowers⟩ **b :** to touch or hit lightly; *specif* **:** to contact (another billiard ball) lightly ~ *vi* **1 :** to make or give salutation with the lips **:** to salute or caress one another with the lips ⟨~ and be friends⟩ **2 :** to come in contact, touch, or collide gently **:** REBOUND ⟨the cue ball ~*es* from the red ball⟩ **3** *of duodenal ulcers* **:** to be directly opposite or lie against one another — **kiss good-bye 1 :** to take one's leave of **:** LEAVE ⟨*kissing* the old dump *good-bye* tonight —J.T.Farrell⟩ **2 :** to resign oneself to the loss of **:** part with ⟨whenever you have a ship ashore you can *kiss* a million bucks *good-bye* —J.W. Noble⟩ — **kiss hands :** to touch the hand of a sovereign or superior with the lips as a ceremonial sign of homage or submission (as on meeting or parting) ⟨was sent for by the king and *kissed hands* as prime minister⟩ — **kiss my foot** — used to express contempt (as in denying a request) — **kiss one's hand :** to kiss one's own hand with a motion toward another person in sign of affection — **kiss the book :** to touch with the lips the Bible, New Testament, or Gospels in taking an oath — **kiss the ground :** to prostrate oneself as a sign of homage — **kiss the rod :** to accept punishment or correction submissively

**²kiss** \"\ *n* -ES [ME, alter. (influenced by *kissen*, v.) of *cos*, fr. OE *coss* — more at ¹KISS] **1 :** the act of kissing **:** a salute or caress with the lips **:** SMACK **2 a :** a gentle touch or contact **b :** the light contact or interference of one billiard ball with another — called also *kiss-off* **3 a :** a meringue sometimes with shredded coconut or other material added **b :** a bite-size piece of candy often wrapped in paper or foil ⟨chocolate ~⟩

**kiss·abil·i·ty** \,kisə'biləd·ē\ *n* **:** the quality or state of being kissable

**kiss·able** \'kisəbəl\ *adj* **:** so attractive as to invite kissing ⟨a ~ mouth⟩ — **kiss·able·ness** *n* -ES — **kiss·ably** \-blē\ *adv*

**kis·sar** \'kisə(r)\ *n* -s [colloq. Ar *qīsār* (Ar *qīthār*)] **:** a five-stringed lyre of northern Africa and Ethiopia

**kiss-curl** \'=,=\ *n* **:** a loose curl falling across the forehead or along the cheek

**kiss·er** \'kisə(r)\ *n* -s **1 :** one that kisses **2** *slang* **:** MOUTH ⟨a poke in the ~⟩ **3** *slang* **:** FACE ⟨threw the money in his ~⟩

**kis·si** \'kisē\ *n, pl* **kissi** *or* **kissis** *usu cap* **1 a :** an agricultural people of French Guinea, Liberia, and Sierra Leone **b :** a member of such people **2 :** a West-Atlantic language of the Kissi people

**kiss impression** *n* **:** impression (as of paper against an inked printing surface) that is extremely light

**kissing bug** *n* **:** CONENOSE

**kissing cousin** *or* **kissing kin** *n* **:** a cousin or other collateral relative whom one knows just well enough to kiss more or less formally upon occasional meeting ⟨distantly related but not *kissing cousins*⟩

**kissing dance** *n* **:** a social couple dance culminating in a kiss

**kissing gate** *n, dial Eng* **:** a gate swinging in a V-shaped enclosure that allows only one person to pass at a time

**kiss·ing·ly** *adv* **:** in a lightly touching manner

**kiss-in-the-ring** \'===,=\ *n* **:** drop the handkerchief in which the pursuing player may kiss the player he catches

**kiss-me** \'=,=\ *n* -s **:** any of various plants: as **a :** WILD PANSY **b :** LONDON PRIDE 1 **c :** HERB ROBERT

**kiss-me-at-the-gate** \'====¦=\ *n* **:** a fragrant Chinese honeysuckle (*Lonicera fragrantissima*) grown in the southern U.S. for ornament

**kiss-me-over-the-garden-gate** \'==,===¦==¦=\ *n* **:** any of various plants: as **a :** PRINCE'S-FEATHER 2 **b :** ACHIMENES 2

**kiss-me-quick** \'==,=\ *n* -s **:** a small bonnet worn off the face esp. in the latter half of the 19th century

**kiss of death** [so called fr. the betraying kiss with which Judas pointed out Jesus in the garden of Gethsemane (Mark 14: 44–45)] **:** an act or association ultimately causing ruin ⟨track bucks baseball but this need not be the automatic *kiss of death* —Tommy O'Brien⟩ ⟨for an American to offer . . . friendship meant the *kiss of death* — for the Russian —Gouverneur Paulding⟩

**kiss off** *vt* **:** DISMISS ⟨*kisses* the other performers *off* as mere amateurs⟩

**kiss-off** \'=,=\ *n* -s [*kiss off*] **1 :** KISS 2b **2 a :** an event marking the end (as of a relationship) **b :** an act of dismissal

**kiss of peace :** a religious ceremonial kiss symbolizing fraternal unity and originating in the early church

**kiss spot** *n* **:** a spot appearing on vegetable-tanned leather caused by contact with another hide in tanning

**¹kist** *archaic past of* KISS

**²kist** \'kist\ *n* -s [ME *kiste*, fr. ON *kista* — more at CHEST] *chiefly dial* **:** any of various chests: as **a :** a clothes or linen trunk **b :** COFFIN

**³kist** \"\ *var of* CIST

**⁴kist** \"\ *n* -s [Ar *qist*] *India* **:** an installment (as of land revenue) or the time for paying it

**kist·vaen** \'kist,vīn\ *n* -s [modif. of W *cistfaen*, fr. *cist* chest + *faen*, mutated form of *maen* stone] **:** ¹CIST 1

**kis·wa** *or* **kis·wah** \'ki,swä\ *n* -s [Ar *kiswah*] **:** a black cloth covering the Kaaba

**¹kit** \'kit, *usu* -id·+V\ *n* -s [ME *kitt, kyt*, prob. fr. MD *kitte*, *kit* jug, vessel] **1 a** *dial Brit* **:** a wooden tub or small barrel (as for butter, milk, water, fish) **b :** a round shipping container of wood or metal usu. having tapered sides, a solid bottom on the larger end, and a closure at or in the smaller end and holding about five gallons **2 a** (1) **:** a collection of equipment and often supplies typically carried in a box or bag **:** an outfit of necessary implements, effects, or materials ⟨a plumber's ~⟩ ⟨a first-aid ~⟩ (2) **:** a container (as a bag, box, or folder) for such a collection ⟨essential medical supplies in a clear plastic ~⟩ ⟨a big green ~ bulging with leaflets⟩ **b** *chiefly Brit* **:** an outfit of clothing and accouterments **:** UNIFORM, REGALIA ⟨troops in full battle ~ —Hal Lehrman⟩ ⟨the first game is won by players wearing their own ~ —Denzil Batchelor⟩ **:** DRESS, WEAR ⟨dressed in riding ~, a sleeveless brown silk shirt, breeches, and high boots —Eve Langley⟩ **c** *chiefly Brit* **:** EQUIPMENT, GEAR ⟨run over to my billet and get some overnight ~ —Lionel Shapiro⟩ **d :** a commercially packaged set of parts (as of a scale model, boat, or automobile accessory) usu. ready to assemble and often accompanied by finishing materials and tools **e :** a collection of printed material giving information or instruction on one subject and assembled (as in a folder) for distribution ⟨a free ~ which includes just about everything a prospective visitor should know about the state —*Springfield (Mass.) Republican*⟩ ⟨sent instruction ~*s* to every high school so youngsters can learn how to make out income-tax returns —*Newsweek*⟩ **3** *or* **kit and biling** *or* **kit and boodle** *or* **kit and caboodle :** a group of persons or things **:** LOT — used with *whole* ⟨sent the whole *kit and caboodle* of them home⟩ **4** *dial Eng* **:** BASKET; *esp* **:** one used for fish **5 :** a group of pigeons trained to fly together

**²kit** \"\ *vt* **kitted; kitted; kitting; kits** *chiefly Brit* **:** EQUIP, OUTFIT — often used with *up* ⟨enlisted in the Navy and went . . . to be *kitted up* —A.P.Herbert⟩

**³kit** \"\ *n* -s [origin unknown] **:** a small violin formerly used by dancing masters

**⁴kit** *also* **kitt** \"\ *n* -s [short for *kitten*] **1 :** KITTEN 1 **2 a :** a young immature or much undersized individual of one of the smaller fur-bearing animals ⟨fox ~⟩ **b :** the skin or pelt of such an animal

**⁵kit** \"\ *vi* **kitted; kitted; kitting; kits :** to give birth to kits

**ki·tab** \kē'täb\ *n* -s [Ar *kitāb* book] *Islam* **:** a book esp. of sacred scripture and usu. of the scripture of the Jews, Christians, Zoroastrians, or Muslims

**ki·ta·bi** \-bē\ *n* -s [Ar *kitābī*, fr. *kitāb*] *Islam* **:** one who believes in a book of sacred scripture and with whom a Muslim may marry in what is deemed a lawful marriage

**kit·a·mat** *or* **kit·i·mat** \,kid·ə'mat\ *n, pl* **kitamat** *or* **kitamats** *or* **kitimat** *or* **kitimats** *usu cap* **1 :** a Wakashan people of Douglas Channel, British Columbia **2 :** a member of the Kitamat people

**kitambilla** *var of* KETEMBILLA

**kitan** *usu cap, var of* KHITAN

**ki·ta·ne·muk** \kə'tanə,mək\ *n, pl* **kitanemuk** *or* **kitanemuks** *usu cap* **1 :** a Shoshonean people living between the Tehachapi mountains and the Mojave desert, Calif. **2 :** a member of the Kitanemuk people

**ki·tar** *or* **kit·tar** \kə'tär\ *n* -s [Ar *qītār, qīthār* — more at GUITAR] **:** an Arabian guitar

**kit bag** *n* **1 :** KNAPSACK **2 :** a rectangular usu. leather traveling bag with sides that come together and fasten at the top or open to the full width of the bag and with two straps that wrap around the bag to secure it

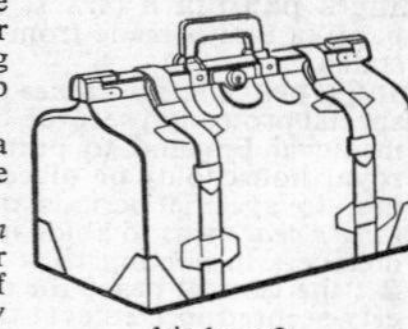
kit bag 2

**kit boat** *n* **:** precut parts of a boat that can be assembled by the purchaser into a complete boat

**kit-cat** *or* **kit-kat** \'kit,kat\ *n* [after *Kit* (*Christopher*) *Cat* or *Catling*, 18th cent. Eng. keeper of the tavern where the club originally met] **1** *usu cap K&C or both Ks* **:** a member of an early 18th century London club of Whig politicians and men of letters **2** [prob. so called fr. the portraits hung in a dining room of the Kit-cat club whose low ceiling made the smaller size necessary] **:** a portrait of less than half length but including the hands ⟨some thirty major portraits hanging on the walls, besides *kit-cats,* heads, sketches . . . and all the lesser oddities of a collection many years in the making —Clemence Dane⟩

**¹kitch·en** \ˈkichən\ *n* -s [ME *kichene, kichen,* fr. OE *cycene;* akin to OHG *chuhhina* kitchen, MLG *kökene,* MD *cokene, cökene;* all fr. a prehistoric WGmc word borrowed fr. LL *coquina,* fr. L, fem. of *coquinus* of cooking, fr. *coquere* to cook + *-inus* -ine — more at COOK] **1 a :** a room or some other space (as a wall area or separate building) with facilities for cooking **:** a place for preparing meals ⟨living room, dining room, and the ~⟩ ⟨a soup ~ where the starving villagers were fed⟩ ⟨a mobile ~ for soldiers in the field⟩ **b :** the personnel that prepares, cooks, and serves food ⟨send orders to the ~⟩ ⟨the ~ sent up a meal⟩ **c :** a combination of kitchen fixtures including cabinets and often stove, refrigerator, and sink marketed as a unit and installed as built-in equipment **2** *now chiefly Scot* **:** food from the kitchen; *specif* **:** food eaten as a side dish with other food **3 a :** any of a series of compartments in which sublimed arsenic fumes from a furnace for treating arsenical ore and baghouse dust are condensed **b :** the laboratory of a reverberatory furnace

**²kitchen** \ˈ"\ *adj* **1 :** of, relating to, or of a kind suitable for use in a kitchen ⟨mop the ~ floor⟩ ⟨~ clock⟩ ⟨a ~ stove⟩ **2 :** that works in a kitchen ⟨a ~ maid⟩ **3 :** used as a kitchen ⟨soldiers bringing supplies to the ~ tent⟩ **4 a :** constituting or having the characteristics of a pidgin language that is used largely for communication between servants and their employers when the two groups are not native speakers of the same language **b :** constituting or having the characteristics of a language as spoken by uneducated speakers ⟨want official acceptance of their language — a sort of ~ Dutch —Serge Fliegers⟩

**³kitchen** \ˈ"\ *vt* -ED/-ING/-s **1** *obs* **:** to furnish food to **:** entertain with kitchen fare **2** *chiefly Scot* **a :** to make palatable **:** SEASON **b :** to serve (food) as kitchen

**Kitchen Bouquet** *trademark* — used for bouquet garni

**kitchen cabinet** *n* **1 :** a cupboard with drawers and shelves designed to hold within easy reach utensils and materials used in preparing food **2 :** an unofficial and informal group of advisers to the head of a government who are held to have more influence with him than his official cabinet ⟨certain of our Presidents have turned to *kitchen Cabinets* to aid them —*Fortune*⟩

**kitchen dresser** *n, Brit* **:** KITCHEN CABINET 1

**kitch·en·er** \-ch(ə)nə(r)\ *n* -s [¹*kitchen* + *-er*] **1 :** the person in charge of a monastery kitchen **2** *Brit* **:** a cooking range

**kitch·en·ette** *also* **kitch·en·et** \ˌkichəˈnet, *usu* -ed·+V\ *n* -s [¹*kitchen* + *-ette*] **:** a very small compactly arranged room or an alcove containing cooking facilities

**kitchen garden** *n* **:** a household garden in which vegetables and often fruits and herbs are cultivated ⟨a flower garden on one side and a *kitchen garden* at the back⟩

**kitchen kaffir** *n, usu cap both Ks* [²*kitchen*] **:** a pidgin language based on Xhosa, Afrikaans, and English and sometimes used in communication between Europeans and Africans in So. Africa

**kitchen match** *n* **:** a wooden splint match that can be lighted by any friction surface

**kitchen midden** *n* [trans. of Dan *kökkenmödding*] **:** a refuse heap; *specif* **:** a mound (as a Neolithic shell heap) marking the site of a primitive human habitation ⟨army engineers, excavating for a mess hall . . . dig unexpectedly into the refuse heap of a prehistoric *kitchen midden* —Corey Ford⟩

**kitchen police** *n* **1 :** enlisted men detailed to assist the cooks in an army mess **2 :** the work of kitchen police — abbr. *K.P.*

**kitchen rose** *n* **:** CINNAMON ROSE

**kitchen stuff** *n* **1 :** food for cooking **:** kitchen requisites (as vegetables) **2 :** kitchen refuse or waste; *esp* **:** fat collected from pots and pans

**kitchenware** \ˈ==,=\ *n* **:** hardware (as cutlery and cooking utensils) for kitchen use

**kitch·ie** \ˈkichi\ *Scot var of* KITCHEN

**kitch·in** \ˈkichən\ *n* -s *usu cap* [after Joseph A. *Kitchin* *b*1910 Amer. political scientist] **:** a business cycle formed by a recession of about three and a half years during a prosperity phase ⟨the *Kitchins* can be best observed, for all countries, on the chart of rates of changes —J.A.Schumpeter⟩

**¹kite** \ˈkīt, *usu* -īd·+V\ *n* -s [ME, fr. OE *cȳta;* akin to MHG *küze* owl, ON *kȳta* to quarrel, Gk *goan* to lament, Lith *gausti* to sound, drone — more at COMELY] **1 :** any of various usu. rather small hawks of the family Accipitridae that have long narrow wings, a deeply forked tail, a weak bill, and feet adapted for taking such prey as insects and small reptiles, that feed also on offal, and that are noted for graceful sustained flight; *specif* **:** a common comparatively large European scavenger (*Milvus milvus*) with chiefly reddish brown plumage — compare BLACK KITE, BLACK-SHOULDERED KITE, SWALLOW-TAILED KITE, WHITE-TAILED KITE **2 :** a person that preys on others **3 :** a contrivance consisting of a surface of a light material stretched over a light often diamond-shaped framework, often provided with a balancing tail, and intended to be flown in the air at the end of a long string — see BOX KITE **4 a :** ACCOMMODATION BILL **b :** a check drawn against uncollected funds in a bank account **c :** a check that has been fraudulently raised before cashing **5 kites** *pl* **:** the lightest and usu. the loftiest sails (as skysails, spinnakers) ordinarily carried only in a light breeze — called also *flying kites* **6 :** something suggested or tried in order to see how people react **:** a tentative proposal or venture **:** TRIAL BALLOON, FEELER ⟨published what has all the appearance of being a ~ for his whole project —Peter Ure⟩ **7 a :** a drag to be towed under water at any depth up to about 40 fathoms that on striking bottom is upset and rises to the surface — called also *sentry* **b :** a device (as a heavy wooden platform) attached to a submerged line towed by a mine sweeper or between two vessels to make the line tow at a predetermined depth for clearing mined areas **8 a :** a heavier-than-air aircraft which is without propelling means other than the towline pull and whose support is derived from the force of the wind moving past its surfaces **b** *slang Brit* **:** AIRPLANE **9 :** a step cut for a gem having a diamond shape and eight quadrilateral facets **10 :** a letter smuggled past prison censorship

kite 3

**²kite** \ˈ"\ *vb* -ED/-ING/-s *vi* **1 :** to get money or credit by a kite; *specif* **:** to create a false bank balance by manipulating deposit accounts **2 :** to go in a rapid, carefree, or flighty manner: **a :** run or move very fast ⟨that dog went *kiting* down the street traveling all of 20 knots —Kenneth Roberts⟩ **b :** GALLIVANT ⟨would ~ off to the movies just about dish-washing time⟩ ⟨used to ~ around with the other kids in the evening⟩ **c :** rise rapidly **:** SOAR ⟨tin prices *kited* in world markets . . . to another record high —*Wall Street Jour.*⟩ **d :** leave suddenly **:** DECAMP ⟨walked out on me . . . took the boys and *kited* —Vance Bourjaily⟩ **3 :** to fly a hawk-shaped paper kite over the haunts of game birds (as grouse) to frighten them into lying close ~ *vt* **1 :** to cause to soar; *specif* **:** to inflate (as a price) in amount ⟨war-risk insurance has *kited* shipping costs skyward —*Time*⟩ **2 :** to use (a kite) to get money or credit ⟨had *kited* the worthless draft on innocent victims —M.M.Hunt⟩; *specif* **:** to raise the amount of (a check) by fraud before cashing it ⟨a $27.50 check could be *kited* to $327.50 —*Newsweek*⟩

**kite balloon** *n* **:** an elongated captive balloon with lobes that keep it headed into the wind for increased lift — abbr. *KB*

**kite eagle** *n* **:** a nearly black East Indian eagle (*Ictinaëtus malayensis*) having a short crest and a very large claw on the inner toe

**kite falcon** *n* **:** CUCKOO FALCON

**kiteflying** \ˈ=,==\ *n* **:** the issuing of political news in such form that it may later be disavowed

**kit·er** \ˈkīd·ə(r)\ *n* -s **:** one that kites

**kite-shaped** \ˈ=,=\ *adj, of a shield* **:** having a bowed top, long straight sides, and a pointed bottom

**kite track** *n* **:** a racetrack with only one turn and with the stretches converging to a point

kite track

**kit fox** *n* [⁴*kit*] **1 a :** a small fox (*Vulpes velox*) of the plains of western No. America **b :** a related species (*V. macrotis*) of the southwestern U.S. **2 :** the fur or pelt of the kit fox

**kith** \ˈkith\ *n* -s [ME *kiththe, kith,* fr. OE *cȳththu, cȳthth,* fr. *cūth* known — more at UNCOUTH] **1 :** familiar friends, neighbors, fellow countrymen, or acquaintances **2 :** KINDRED **3 :** a culturally homogeneous social group tending to be endogamous

**kith and kin** *n pl* [ME] **1 :** friends and kindred **2 :** KINDRED, RELATIONS

**kith·a·ra** \ˈkithərə, kiˈthärə\ *var of* CITHARA

**kithe** *or* **kythe** \ˈkīth\ *vb* -ED/-ING/-s [ME *kithen, kythen,* fr. OE *cȳthan,* fr. *cūth* known — more at UNCOUTH] *vt, chiefly Scot* **:** to make known **:** MANIFEST, DECLARE ~ *vi, chiefly Scot* **:** to become known or manifest **:** APPEAR

**kitimat** *usu cap, var of* KITAMAT

**kit-kat** *var of* KIT-CAT

**kit·ke·hah·ki** \ˈkitkə,häkē\ *n, pl* **kitkehahki** *or* **kitkehahkis** *usu cap* **1 :** a people of the Pawnee confederacy **2 :** a member of the Kitkehahki people

**kit·ksan** \ˌkitkəˈsan\ *n, pl* **kitksan** *or* **kitksans** *usu cap* [Tsimshian, lit., people of the Skeena river] **1 a :** a division of the Tsimshian people in the upper Skeena river valley, British Columbia **b :** a member of such people **2 :** a dialect of Tsimshian

**kit·ling** \ˈkitlən\ *n* -s [ME, fr. ON *ketlingr,* fr. *katt-, kötte* cat + *-lingr* -ling — more at CAT] *dial Brit* **:** KITTEN

**kit·man** \ˈkitmən, -ˌman\ *n, pl* **kitmen** [¹*kit* + *man*] **:** an automobile-factory stock clerk who assembles matched hardware for each car

**kitmutgar** *var of* KHIDMATGAR

**ki·tol** \ˈkē,tȯl, -tōl\ *n* -s [irreg. fr. Gk *kētos* sea monster, whale + E *-ol*] **:** a crystalline alcohol $C_{40}H_{58}(OH)_2$ obtainable esp. from whale-liver oil and capable of yielding vitamin A (as by heating)

**kitool** *var of* KITTUL

**kits** *pl of* KIT, *pres 3d sing of* KIT

**kitsch** \ˈkich\ *n* -ES [G, fr. *kitschen* to slap (a work of art) together, fr. G dial., to scrape up mud from the street] **:** artistic or literary material held to be of low quality, often produced to appeal to popular taste, and marked esp. by sentimentalism, sensationalism, and slickness ⟨the traditional gap . . . between ~ and literature —William Phillips b.1907⟩

**kitt** *var of* KIT

**kittar** *var of* KITAR

**kitted** *past of* KIT

**kit·tel** \ˈkid·ᵊl\ *n, pl* **kittel** [Yiddish *kitel,* fr. MHG *kitel, kietel* cotton or hempen outer garment, prob. fr. Ar *quṭn* cotton] **:** a white cotton or linen robe worn by Orthodox Jews on Rosh Hashana and Yom Kippur and at the Passover Seder and also used as a burial shroud

**¹kit·ten** \ˈkitᵊn\ *n* -s [ME *kitoun,* modif. (influenced by *kitling*) of (assumed) ONF *caton* (whence F dial. — Normandy — *caton*), dim. of ONF *cat,* fr. LL *cattus* — more at CAT] **1 a** (1) **:** a young cat (2) **:** a cat less than nine months old — used esp. in relation to competitive showing **b :** an immature individual of various other small mammals ⟨hamster ~⟩ ⟨rabbit ~⟩ **2 :** ⁴KIT 2b **3** *chiefly dial* **:** one of the rolls of dust that collect under furniture — usu. used in pl.

**²kitten** \ˈ"\ *vb* -ED/-ING/-s [ME *kytnen* fr. *kitoun,* n.] *vi* **:** to give birth to kittens **:** LITTER ~ *vt* **:** to give birth to ⟨that's what I've been called since I was ~*ed* —*Irish Statesman*⟩

**kittenball** \ˈ==,=\ *n* **:** SOFTBALL

**kitten-breeches** \ˈ==,==\ *n pl but sing or pl in constr* [so called fr. the shape of the blossoms] **:** DUTCHMAN'S-BREECHES

**kit·ten·ish** \ˈkit(ᵊ)nish, -nēsh\ *adj* **1 :** resembling or like that of a kitten **2 :** marked by coy or affected playfulness ⟨she was fat and over forty, but still ~ —*Farmer's Weekly* (So. Africa)⟩ — **kit·ten·ish·ly** *adv* — **kit·ten·ish·ness** *n* -ES

**kit·ten·less** \ˈkitᵊnləs\ *adj* **:** having no kitten ⟨a ~ cat⟩

**kit·ter·een** \ˌkid·əˈrēn\ *n* -s [origin unknown] **:** a two-wheeled one-horse carriage with a movable top

**kitting** *pres part of* KIT

**kit·ti·wake** \ˈkid·ē,wāk\ *n* -s [imit.] **:** any of various gulls of the genus *Rissa* having the hind toe short or rudimentary; *esp* **:** ATLANTIC KITTIWAKE

**¹kit·tle** \ˈkid·ᵊl, ˈkitᵊl\ *vt* -ED/-ING/-s [ME (northern dial.) *kytyllen,* prob. fr. ON *kitla* — more at TICKLE] **1** *chiefly Scot* **:** TICKLE **2** *chiefly Scot* **:** ENLIVEN, TITILLATE **3** *chiefly Scot* **:** to flatter and please **4** *chiefly Scot* **:** to keep guessing **:** PERPLEX

**²kittle** \ˈ"\ *adj* -ER/-EST **1** *chiefly Scot* **a :** easily excited **:** TOUCHY, SKITTISH, FIDGETY **b :** QUICK, APT ⟨she's ~ of her hands —George Meriton⟩ **c :** VARIABLE, CAPRICIOUS ⟨Fortune will play ~ tricks —John Barr⟩ **d :** nicely balanced **:** DELICATE **2** *chiefly Scot* **:** hard or risky to deal with or do **:** TICKLISH ⟨to paint an angel's ~ work —Robert Burns⟩ ⟨it's a ~ thing to keep the likes o' him waitin' —S.R.Crockett⟩

**³kittle** \ˈ"\ *vi* -ED/-ING/-s [prob. of Scand origin; akin to Norw dial. *kjetla* to kitten, fr. *kjetling* kitten, fr. ON *ketlingr* — more at KITLING] **1** *chiefly Scot* **:** KITTEN **2** *chiefly Scot* **:** GENERATE, ARISE

**kittle cattle** *n, pl* **kittle cattle** *usu pl in constr* [²*kittle*] *chiefly dial* **:** a group of people that are difficult to manage and inclined to be capricious ⟨*kittle cattle* who do rather unpredictable things —*Country Life*⟩

**kit·tling** \ˈkitlən\ *var of* KITLING

**kit·tlish** \ˈkitlish\ *also* **kit·tly** \-li\ *adj* [¹*kittle* + *-ish* or *-y*] *chiefly Scot* **:** TICKLISH, KITTLE

**kitt·litz's murrelet** \ˈkitləts(əz)-\ *n, usu cap K* [after Baron Friedrich von *Kittlitz* †1874 Ger. officer, ornithologist, and traveler] **:** a murrelet (*Brachyramphus brevirostre*) having buff spots and ranging from Japan and Kamchatka to Alaska

**kit·tly-benders** \ˈkitlē+,-\ *n pl* [*kittly* (perh. fr. ¹*kittle* + *-y*) + *benders,* pl. of *bender*] **:** thin bending ice; *also* **:** the act of running over such ice

**kit·tul** *also* **kit·tool** *or* **ki·tul** \kəˈtül\ *n* -s [Sinhalese *kitul, hitul,* fr. Skt *hintāla*] **1 a :** a brownish black fiber resembling horsehair yielded by the leafstalks of the Asiatic jaggery palm and used chiefly in making brushes for polishing linens and cottons and for brushing velvets — called also *black fiber* **b :** JAGGERY PALM **2 a :** a fiber derived from the gomuti palm resembling kittul **b :** GOMUTI PALM

**¹kit·ty** \ˈkid·ē, -it|, |i\ *n* -ES [fr. *Kitty,* nickname for *Catherine*] **1** *also* **kittie** \ˈ"\ -s *chiefly Scot* **:** a girl of easy virtue **:** WENCH **2 :** KITTY WREN

**²kitty** \ˈ"\ *n* -ES [⁴*kit* + *-y*] **:** CAT 1a; *esp* **:** KITTEN

**³kitty** \ˈ"\ *n* -ES [¹*kit* + *-y*] **1 :** a small bowl or other receptacle **2 a** (1) **:** a fund in a poker game accumulated by taking one or two chips from each large pot and used (as to pay expenses or buy refreshments) for the players (2) **:** a pool that belongs to all players in a game but that participates in the scoring or settlement of certain hands as though it were a player opposed to the bidder **b :** a sum of money or collection of goods usu. accumulated by occasional small contributions and often administered by or for the contributors **:** POOL, FUND ⟨enough in the ~ to make the trip —E.K.Gann⟩ ⟨a campaign ~ raised by oil and utility companies —*Time*⟩ ⟨the ground crew's ~ of cigarettes —Saul Levitt⟩ **c :** the widow in skat, pinochle, and other games — called also *blind* **3 :** JACK 2e(1)

**⁴kitty** \ˈ"\ *n* -ES [prob. alter. of *kidcote*] *dial chiefly Eng* **:** JAIL

**⁵kitty** \ˈ"\ *n* -ES [by shortening & alter.] **:** KITTIWAKE

**kitty-corner** *or* **kitty-cornered** *var of* CATERCORNER

**kitty wren** *n* [fr. the name *Kitty*] **:** a wren (*Troglodytes troglodytes*)

**ki·tu·na·han** \kəˈtünəhən\ *n* -s *usu cap* **:** a language family of western Canada and northwestern U.S. comprising Kutenai

**ki·va** \ˈkēvə\ *n* -s [Hopi] **:** a Pueblo Indian structure used as a ceremonial, council, work, and lounging room for men that is usu. round and is at least partly underground with entrance and lighting usu. from the roof and that includes a fireplace, altar space, and sipapu

**¹kiv·er** \ˈkivə(r)\ *n* -s [ME *kevere,* alter. of *keve, kive* keeve — more at KEEVE] *dial Eng* **:** a shallow vessel or wooden tub

**²kiver** \ˈ"\ *dial var of* COVER

**ki·wai** \kēˈwäē\ *n, pl* **kiwai** *or* **kiwais** *usu cap* **1 a :** a Papuan people inhabiting islands at the mouth of the Fly River, Territory of Papua **b :** a member of such people **2 :** the language of the Kiwai people

**ki·wa·ni·an** \kəˈwänēən\ *n* -s *usu cap* [*Kiwanis* (*club*) + E *-an*] **:** a member of one of the major service clubs

**ki·wi** \ˈkē(,)wē\ *n* -s [Maori, of imit. origin] **1** *also* **kiwi-kiwi** \ˈ=(,)=ˈ=(,)=\ **:** a flightless New Zealand bird of the genus *Apteryx* that is about the size of a domestic chicken, has very rudimentary wings, stout legs, a long straight or slightly curved bill with nostrils near the tip, and hairlike plumage of various shades of gray and brown, nests in burrows, and lays eggs as large as one fourth its weight which are incubated by the male **2** *usu cap* **:** NEW ZEALANDER — used as a nickname

kiwi

**kiyang** *var of* KIANG

**¹ki-yi** \(ˈ)kīˈyī\ *interj* [origin unknown] — used to express exultation

**²ki-yi** \ˈ"\ *vi* **ki-yied; ki-yied; ki-yiing; ki-yis** [imit.] **:** YELP ⟨a . . . dog ran *ki-yiing* past us —Klondy Nelson & Corey Ford⟩

**³ki-yi** \ˈ"\ *n* -s **1 :** a bark or yelp (as of a dog) **2 :** DOG

**⁴ki-yi** \ˈ"\ *n* -s [origin unknown] *in the U.S. Navy* **:** a small brush for scrubbing clothing or canvas

**ki·yi** \ˈkē(,)yē\ *n* -s [origin unknown] **:** a small chub (*Leucichthys kiyi*) abundant in deep water in the Great Lakes

**ki·zil** \kəˈzil\ *n, pl* **kizil** *or* **kizils** *usu cap* **1 :** a Russianized Mongolo-Tatar people around Achinsk, central Siberia **2 :** a member of the Kizil people

**kiz·il·bash** \ˌkizəlˈbäsh\ *n, pl* **kizilbash** *or* **kizilbashes** *usu cap* [Turk *kızılbaş,* fr. *kızıl* red + *baş* head] **1 :** a Persianized Turk of a class devoted to business and professional pursuits in Afghanistan; *also* **:** a member of a community of Turkish or mixed-race colonists in Asia Minor **2 :** a community of Kurdish Turks in eastern Turkey who are Christians and whose women refuse to veil their faces **3 :** a nomadic people in the plains around Ankara, Karahisar, and Tokat professing the Muslim religion but practicing ancient pagan rites

**kj** *abbr* kilojoule

**kjel·dahl** \ˈkel,däl\ *adj, usu cap* [after Johan G. C. T. *Kjeldahl* †1900 Dan. chemist] **:** of, relating to, or being a method for determining the amount of nitrogen (as in an organic substance) by digesting a sample with boiling concentrated sulfuric acid and other reagents or by adding an excess of alkali, distilling, and collecting the ammonia expelled or by determining the ammonia by titration

**kjeldahl flask** *n, usu cap K* [after Johan G. C. T. *Kjeldahl*] **:** a round-bottomed usu. long-necked glass flask for use in digesting the sample in the Kjeldahl method

**kjel·dahl·iza·tion** \ˌkel,däləˈzāshən\ *n* -s *sometimes cap* **:** the process of kjeldahlizing

**kjel·dahl·ize** \ˈkel,dä,līz\ *vt* -ED/-ING/-s *sometimes cap* [*Kjeldahl* (*method*) + *-ize*] **:** to subject to the Kjeldahl method or a modification of this method

Kjeldahl flask

**kl** *abbr* kiloliter

**klab** \ˈkläb\ *n* -s [by shortening] **:** KLABERJASS

**kla·ber·jass** \ˈkläbə(r),yäs\ *n* [G] **:** a two-handed game played with 32 cards in which a player scores by holding a higher sequence than his opponent, by holding both the king and queen of trumps, by taking the last trick, and by taking scoring cards in tricks — called also *clabber, clob, clobber, jass, klab, klob*

**klallam** *usu cap, var of* CLALLAM

**kla·man·tan** *or* **kle·man·tan** \kləˈmän·,tän\ *n, pl* **klamantan** *or* **klamantans** *or* **klemantan** *or* **klemantans** *usu cap* [native name in Borneo; akin to Indonesian *Kalimantan* Borneo] **1 :** any of numerous Dayak peoples living in western, central, and northern Borneo **2 :** a member of any of the Klamantan peoples

**klam·ath** \ˈklaməth\ *n, pl* **klamath** *or* **klamaths** *usu cap* **1 a :** a Lutuamian people of southeastern Oregon and northern California **b :** a member of such people **2 :** a language of the Klamath people

**klamath weed** *n, usu cap K* [fr. *Klamath* river, Oregon and California] **:** a cosmopolitan yellow-flowered perennial St.-John's-wort (*Hypericum perforatum*) common in fields and waste places and useful for wildlife but a noxious weed when established in rangelands

**klan** \ˈklan, -aa(ə)n\ *n* -s *usu cap* [fr. (*Ku Klux*) *Klan,* a secret organization — more at KU KLUX] **1 :** an organization of Ku Kluxers **2 :** a subordinate unit of the Ku Kluxers' organization

**klan·ism** \ˈkla,nizəm, -laa,n-\ *n* -s *usu cap* **:** the beliefs or practices of Ku Kluxers

**klans·man** \ˈklanzmən, -laanz-\ *n, pl* **klansmen** *usu cap* **:** KU KLUXER

**klap·match** *or* **clap·match** \ˈklap,mach\ *n* [by folk etymology fr. D *klapmuts* cap with earflaps, hooded seal, fr. *klap, klep* brim, earflap + *muts* cap] **:** a female seal

**klap·roth·ite** \ˈkläprə,thīt\ *or* **klap·roth·o·lite** \kläˈpröthə,līt\ *n* -s [*klaprothite* fr. G *klaprothit,* fr. Martin H. *Klaproth* †1817 German chemist + G *-it* -ite; *klaprotholite* alter. of *klaprothite*] **:** a steel-gray mineral $Cu_6Bi_4S_9$ consisting of a sulfide of copper and bismuth

**klatch** *or* **klatsch** \ˈklach, -ä-\ *n* -ES [G *klatsch* gossip, action of gossiping, fr. *klatschen* to gossip, of imit. origin] **:** a gathering characterized by informal conversation ⟨you meet him at a literary cocktail ~ —Victor Riesel⟩

**klav·ern** \ˈklavə(r)n\ *n* -s [blend of *klan* and *cavern*] **1 :** a meeting place of Ku Kluxers ⟨sallies forth to the ~ and there dons his resplendent robe —Stetson Kennedy⟩ **2 :** a local unit of the Ku Kluxers' organization

**kla·vier** \kləˈvi(ə)r, klaˈ-, -iə\ *n* -s [G, fr. F *clavier* — more at CLAVIER] **:** CLAVIER 2

**kla·vier·stück** \-,shtik, *G* kläˈvēr,shtœk\ *n* [G, fr. *klavier* piano + *stück* piece] **:** a piano piece

**Klax·on** \ˈklaksən\ *trademark* — used for an electrically operated horn or warning signal

**klea·gle** \ˈklēgəl\ *n* -s *often cap* [*klan* + *eagle*] **:** a high-ranking officer in the hierarchy of the Ku Kluxers' organization

**kle·bels·berg·ite** \ˈklabəlz,bər,gīt\ *n* -s [Hung *klebelsbergit,* fr. Kuno *Klebelsberg* †1932 Hung. statesman + Hung *-it* *-ite*] **:** a mineral consisting of a basic antimony sulfate found in the interstices between crystals in columnar aggregates of stibnite

**kleb·si·el·la** \ˌklebzēˈelə, -epsē-\ *n* [NL, fr. Edwin *Klebs* †1913 Ger. pathologist + NL *-i-* + *-ella*] **1** *cap* **:** a genus of plump nonmotile gram-negative frequently encapsulated bacterial rods (family Enterobacteriaceae) commonly held to comprise a single variable species — see PNEUMOBACILLUS **2** -s **:** an organism of the genus *Klebsiella*

**klebs-löff·ler bacillus** \ˈkläps|ˈleflə(r)-, ˈklebz|\ *n, usu cap K&L* [after Edwin *Klebs* and Friedrich A. J. *Löffler* †1915 Ger. bacteriologist] **:** a bacterium (*Corynebacterium diphtheriae*) that causes human diphtheria

**kleene·boc** \ˈklīn(ə),bäk, -lān-\ *n* -s [Afrik *kleinbok,* fr. *klein* small + *bok* male antelope] **:** ROYAL ANTELOPE

**Klee·nex** \ˈklē,neks\ *trademark* — used for a cleansing tissue

**klein bottle** \ˈklīn-\ *n, usu cap K* [after Felix *Klein* †1925 Ger. mathematician and inventor] **:** a surface that is closed in such a way that it is possible to pass from a point on one side to the corresponding point on the opposite side without passing through the surface and that is formed by passing the nar-

Klein bottle

row end of a tapered tube through the side of the tube and flaring this end out to join the other end

**klein·ite** \ˈklī,nīt\ n -s [G *kleinit*, fr. Karl *Klein* †1907 Ger. mineralogist + G *-it* -ite] : a mineral approximately $Hg_{2-}(NH_4)_6SO_4Cl_6(OH)_3O_3$ consisting of a basic oxide, sulfate, and chloride of mercury and ammonium

**kleist·ian jar** \ˈklīstēən-\ n, usu cap K [Ewald J. von *Kleist* †1748 Ger. scientist and dean of the cathedral of Kamin, Pomerania, one of its discoverers] : LEYDEN JAR

**klemantan** *usu cap, var of* KLAMANTAN

**klen·du·sic** \(ˈ)klen¦d(y)üsik\ *also* **klen·du·sive** \-siv\ *adj* [*klendusity* + *-ic* or *-ive*] : characterized by klendusity

**klen·du·si·ty** \-ˈ==sədē\ n -ES [irreg. fr. Gk *kleidoun* to lock up (fr. *kleid-, kleis* key) + *endysis* entry, act of putting on + E *-ity* — more at CLOSE, ENDYSIS] : the tendency of a plant or variety to escape infection as a result of having some property (as a thick cuticle or hairy surface) that prevents or hinders inoculation : disease-escaping ability

**klepht** *or* **clepht** \ˈkleft\ n -s *often cap* [NGk *klephtēs*, lit., robber, fr. Gk *kleptēs* robber, fr. *kleptein* to steal] : a Greek belonging to one of several independent armed sometimes brigandish communities formed after the Turkish conquest of Greece — **kleph·tic** \-tik\ *adj, usu cap*

**klept-** *or* **klepto-** *comb form* [Gk, fr. *kleptein* to steal; akin to Goth *hlifan* to steal, L *clepere* to steal, OPruss *auklipts* concealed] : stealing : theft ⟨*klept*istic⟩ ⟨*klepto*mania⟩

**klep·to·ma·nia** *or* **clep·to·ma·nia** \,kleptəˈmānēə, -nyə\ n [NL, fr. *klept-* + LL *mania*] : a persistent neurotic impulse to steal esp. without economic motive in which the object stolen is usu. believed to have symbolic significance to the kleptomaniac

[1]**klep·to·ma·ni·ac** *or* **clep·to·ma·ni·ac** \-nē,ak\ n [*klept-* + *maniac*] : a person exhibiting kleptomania

[2]**kleptomaniac** *or* **cleptomaniac** \¦==¦==,=\ *adj* : of, relating to, or having the characteristics of kleptomania or a kleptomaniac

**k-level** \ˈ=,==\ n, *usu cap K* : the energy level of an electron in a K-shell

**klez·mer** \ˈklezmər\ n, *pl* **klez·mo·rim** \klezˈmȯrəm\ *or* **klezmer** [Yiddish, modif. of Heb *kĕlēy zemer* musical instruments] : a Jewish instrumentalist; *specif* : a member of a band of folk musicians in eastern Europe hired to play at Jewish weddings and gatherings

**klick·i·tat** *also* **klik·i·tat** \ˈklikə,tat\ n, *pl* **klickitat** *or* **klickitats** *usu cap* [Chinook, lit., beyond (the Cascade mountains)] **1 a** : a Shahaptian people of southern Washington **b** : a member of such people **2** : a language of the Klickitat people

**klieg eyes** *or* **kleig eyes** \ˈklēg-\ n *pl, sometimes cap K* [*klieg* (*light*) or *kleig* (*light*)] : a condition marked by conjunctivitis and watering of the eyes resulting from excessive exposure to intense light

**klieg light** *or* **kleig light** n, *sometimes cap K* [after John H. *Kliegl* †1959 & his brother Anton T. *Kliegl* †1927 Amer. lighting experts born in Germany] : a carbon arc lamp used in taking motion pictures

**kline reaction** *or* **kline test** \ˈklīn-\ n, *usu cap K* [after Benjamin S. *Kline* b1886 Amer. pathologist] : a rapid precipitation test for the diagnosis of syphilis

**kling** \ˈkliŋ\ n -s *usu cap* [Malay *kĕling*] : a Dravidian prob. of Tamil origin of the seaports of southeastern Asia and Malaysia

**klink** *var of* CLINK

**kli·no·kinesis** \¦klī(,)nō+\ n [NL, fr. Gk *klinein* to lean, slope + NL *-o-* + *kinesis* — more at LEAN] : movement that is induced by stimulation and that involves essentially random alteration of direction

**kli·no·kinetic** \"+\ *adj* [Gk *klinein* + E *-o-* + *kinetic*] : of or relating to klinokinesis

**klinostat** n -s [G, fr. *klino-* clin- + *-stat*] : CLINOSTAT

**kli·no·taxis** \¦klīnə+\ n [NL, fr. Gk *klinein* + NL *-o-* + *-taxis*] : directional orientation involving turning toward a stimulus

**klip·bok** \ˈklip,bäk\ n -s [Afrik, fr. *klip* cliff, rock + *bok* male antelope] : KLIPSPRINGER

**klip·das·sie** \ˈklip,däsē\ *or* **klip·das** \-äs\ n, *pl* **klipdassies** *or* **klipdases** [Afrik, fr. *klip* + *dassie* or *das*] : a hyrax (*Procavia capensis*) of southern Africa

**klip·fish** *or* **clip·fish** \ˈklip,fish\ n [in sense 1, part trans. of Dan *klipfisk*, Norw *klippfisk* & G *klippfisch*; Dan & Norw, prob. fr. G, fr. *klippe* rock near the sea, cliff + *fisch* fish; in sense 2, part trans. of Afrik *klipvis*, fr. *klip* rock, stone (fr. MD *klippe*) + *vis* fish; akin to OE *clif* cliff — more at CLIFF] **1** : a fish (as cod) split open, salted, and dried **2** : a fish of the family Clinidae : KELPFISH

**klip·haas** \ˈklip,häs\ n -ES [Afrik, fr. *klip* + *haas* hare] : ROCK HARE

[1]**klip·pe** \ˈklipə\ n -s [G, fr. Sw *klippa* to cut, shear, clip, fr. ON] : a coin with a square or lozenge-shaped flan (as in 17th century German necessity money)

[2]**klippe** \"\ *or* **klip** \ˈklip\ n, *pl* **klip·pen** \-pən\ *or* **klips** [G *klippe* cliff, crag, rock near the sea, fr. MHG, fr. MLG; akin to OE *clif* cliff — more at CLIFF] : an outlying isolated remnant of an overthrust rock mass owing its isolation to erosion : OUTLIER

**klip·salamander** \ˈklip,==,==\ n [Afrik, fr. *klip* + *salamander*] : a spiny girdle-tailed lizard (*Cordylus cordylus*) that is widely distributed in rocky uplands of southern Africa and that exhibits black and yellowish or reddish color phases; *broadly* : GIRDLETAILED LIZARD

**klip·spring·er** \ˈklip,spriŋə(r)\ n [Afrik, fr. *klip* + *springer* springer, leaper] : a small antelope (*Oreotragus oreotragus*) that is somewhat like the chamois in habits and is found from Cape Colony to Somaliland — called also *klipbok*

**klis·mos** \ˈkliz,mäs, -məs\ n -ES [Gk, fr. *klinein* to lean, recline — more at LEAN] : a chair of Greek design having a concavely curved back rail and curved legs

**klis·ter** \ˈklistə(r)\ n -s [Norw, lit., paste, fr. MLG *klīster*; akin to OE *clǣg* clay — more at CLAY] : a soft wax used on skis esp. for corn snow or crust

**klm** *abbr* kilometer

**klob** \ˈkläb\ n -s [by shortening and alter.] : KLABERJASS

**klock·mann·ite** \ˈkläkmə,nīt\ n -s [G *klockmannit*, fr. Friedrich *Klockmann* †1937 Ger. mineralogist + G *-it* -ite] : a mineral CuSe consisting of a selenide of copper found in tarnished blue-black granular aggregates

**klomp** \ˈklämp\ n, *pl* **klom·pen** \-pən\ [D *klomp* lump, wooden shoe, fr. MD *clompe* clod, block; akin to LG *klump* lump, clump — more at CLUMP] : a wooden shoe worn in the Low Countries

klomp

**klompen dance** n [part trans. of D *klompendans*, fr. *klomp* + *dans* dance] : a Dutch folk dance performed in wooden shoes

**klon·dike** \ˈklän,dīk\ n -s *usu cap* [fr. *Klondike*, region in Yukon territory, Canada, where a gold rush took place (1897=99)] **1** : a source of valuable material or wealth ⟨every new road a *Klondike* to the country through which it passes —Cy Warman⟩ ⟨Yiddish represents a potential *Klondike* of barely tapped resources for Germanic and Slavic specialists —H.H. Paper⟩ **2** : solitaire in which 28 cards are laid out in 7 piles consisting respectively of 1 to 7 cards with the top card of each pile face up and the remaining cards of the pack built in descending sequence of alternate colors as the player goes once through the rest of the pack one card at a time with the object of removing aces from the tableau as they become available and of building on them up to kings — called also *Canfield*

**klon·dik·er** \-kə(r)\ n -s *usu cap* [*Klondike* region + E *-er*] : an inhabitant of the Klondike region of northwestern Canada; *esp* : one who prospects for gold

**klong** \ˈklȯŋ, -äŋ\ n -s [native name in Thailand] : a canal in Thailand used for transportation and drainage ⟨the pond . . . narrowed into a ~ that rimmed the far width of the compound —Kathryn Grondahl⟩

**kloof** \ˈklüf, *Afrik* ˈklu̇əf\ n -s [Afrik, fr. MD *clove* cleft, crevice; akin to OHG *klobo* forked stick, fetter, OS *klobo* shackle for the foot, ON *klofi* cleft, OHG *klioban* to split — more at CLEAVE (split)] *Africa* : a deep glen : GORGE, RAVINE ⟨the narrow ~s of the echoing hills —Stuart Cloete⟩

**klootch·man** \ˈklüchmən\ *also* **klooch** \-ch\ n, *pl* **klootchmen** *also* **klooches** [Chinook Jargon *klootshman*, fr. Nootka *łotssma* woman; wife] : an Indian woman of northwestern No. America

**klop-klop** *var of* CLOP-CLOP

**klös·se** *or* **kloes·se** \ˈklāsə, *among speakers of German descent in US often* ˈklās *or* ˈglās\ n *pl* [G *klösse*, pl. of *kloss* lump, clod, dumpling, fr. MHG *klōz* lump — more at CLOUT] : DUMPLINGS

**kluck·er** \ˈkləkə(r)\ n -s *usu cap* [by shortening & alter.] : KU KLUXER

**klu·kia** \ˈklükēə\ n, *cap* [NL] : a genus of early Mesozoic fossil ferns having large much divided fronds and sporangia arranged in spikes (as in ferns of the genus *Schizaea*)

**klunk** *var of* CLUNK

**klux** \ˈkləks\ *vt* -ED/-ING/-ES *often cap* [by shortening] : KU-KLUX

**klux·er** \ˈkləksə(r)\ n -s *usu cap* [by shortening] : KU KLUXER

**klux·ery** \-sərē\ n -ES *usu cap* [short for *Ku-Kluxery*] : KLANISM

**klux·ism** \-,sizəm\ n -s *usu cap* [short for *Ku-Kluxism*] : KLANISM

**Kly·don·o·graph** \klīˈdänə,graf, -räf\ *trademark* — used for an instrument that makes a photographic record of electric surges in power lines

**klys·tron** \ˈklīsträn\ n -s [fr. *Klystron*, a trademark] : an electron tube in which bunching of electrons is produced by subjecting them to acceleration and deceleration by high potential across a gap and which is used for the generation and amplification of ultrahigh-frequency current (as in radar)

**km** *abbr* **1** kilometer **2** kingdom

**kmer** *usu cap, var of* KHMER

**KMPS** *abbr, often not cap* kilometers per second

**kmw** *abbr* kilomegawatt

**kmwh** *abbr* kilomegawatt-hour

**kn** *abbr* knot

[1]**knack** \ˈnak\ n -s [ME *knak, knakke*] **1 a** : a task or chore requiring adroitness and dexterity **b** : a clever way of doing something **c** : TRICK, SCHEME, STRATAGEM **2 a** : a special ready capacity that is hard to analyze or teach for dexterous adroit performance esp. of the unusual, technical, or difficult ⟨the ~ of writing unforgettable, irresistible melodies —Roland Gelatt⟩ **b** : TRAIT, TENDENCY, INCLINATION; *esp* : one strictly individual and difficult to explain or analyze ⟨these rents in the interior of the earth had a ~ of enlarging themselves —Norman Douglas⟩ **3 a** *archaic* : an ingenious device : a cleverly made contrivance; *broadly* : TOY, TRINKET, KNICKKNACK **b** *obs* : a dainty article of food : DELICACY **c** *obs* : an ingenious literary device : CONCEIT **syn** see GIFT

[2]**knack** \"\ n -s [ME *knak*, of imit. origin like MHG *knacken* to make a cracking noise, OE *cnocian* to knock — more at KNOCK] : a sharp sound (as of the snapping of a finger)

[3]**knack** \"\ *vb* -ED/-ING/-S *vt, dial Brit* : to strike together so as to make a sharp snapping noise ~ *vi, now dial* : to make a sharp abrupt snapping noise : CRACK

**knack·a·way** \ˈnakə,wā, ˈnäk-\ *also* **knock·a·way** \ˈnäk-\ n [by folk etymology fr. MexSp *anacua* — more at ANAQUA] : ANAQUA

**knäck·e·bröd** \(kə)ˈnekə,brə(r)d, -bərd,-brəd,-bred\ n -s [Sw, fr. *knäcka* to break + *bröd* bread] : a very crisp and brittle unleavened rye bread made in large flat circular pieces often with a hole in the center

[1]**knack·er** \ˈnakə(r)\ n -s [[3]*knack* + *-er*] : something (as a castanet) used to make a sharp sound or noise; *esp* : one of two pieces of bone or wood held loosely between the fingers and struck together by moving the hand — usu. used in pl.

[2]**knacker** \"\ n -s [prob. fr. E dial. *knacker, nacker* harnessmaker, saddle maker, prob. of Scand origin; akin to Icel *hnakkur* saddle; akin to ON *hnakki, hnakkr* back of the neck — more at NECK] **1** *also* **knacker·man** \-mən\ *Brit* : one that buys worn-out domestic animals or their carcasses and disposes of the products for other purposes than use as human food (as for animal food or fertilizer) ⟨Jones will sell you to the ~, who will cut your throat and boil you down for the foxhounds —George Orwell⟩ **2** *Brit* : one that buys up old structures (as buildings or ships) for their constituent materials **3** *dial Eng* : an old worn-out domestic animal (as a horse)

**knack·ery** \ˈnakərī\ n -ES [[2]*knacker* + *-y*] *Brit* : the place of business of a knacker : RENDERING PLANT

**knack·wurst** *or* **knock·wurst** \ˈnäk,=\ n -s [G *knackwurst*, fr. *knacken* to make a cracking noise (fr. MHG) + *wurst* sausage — more at KNACK, BRATWURST] : a sausage that is shorter and thicker than a frankfurter and more heavily seasoned

**knacky** \ˈnakē\ *adj* -ER/-EST [[1]*knack* + *-y*] *chiefly dial* : HANDY, INGENIOUS, CLEVER

**knag** \ˈnag\ n -s [ME *knagge, knagg*; akin to MLG *knagge* knot in wood, pin, peg, Sw *knagg* knot in wood, lump, Norw *knagg, knagge* pin, peg, handle, and perh. to OE *cnotta* knot — more at KNOT] **1 a** *obs* : a short projection or spur esp. from a tree trunk or branch **b** *archaic* : a wooden peg for hanging things on **2** *obs* : a prong of an antler

**knagged** *adj* [ME, fr. *knagge, knagg* + *-ed*] *obs* : KNAGGY

**knag·gy** \ˈnagē\ *adj* -ER/-EST : full of or covered with gnarled knotty protuberances : CRAGGY, RUGGED, ROUGH ⟨the old dark ~ skull —Isak Dinesen⟩

**knai·del** \kəˈnādəl, ˈknā-\ n, *pl* **knai·dlach** \-dlək\ [Yiddish *kneydel*, fr. MHG *knödel* — more at KNÖDEL] : DUMPLING 1a

[1]**knap** \ˈnap\ n -s [ME *knap*, fr. OE *cnæpp*; akin to OFris *knapp* button, MLG, knob, heel of a shoe, ON *knappr* button, OE *cnotta* knot — more at KNOT] *chiefly dial* : a top or crest of a hill : SUMMIT; *also* : a small hill or knoll

[2]**knap** *also* **nap** \"\ n -s [ME, of imit. origin] : a sharp or abrupt blow : RAP, KNOCK

[3]**knap** \"\ *vb* **knapped**; **knapped**; **knapping**; **knaps** [ME *knappen*, of imit. origin like MD *cnappen* to make a snapping noise, LG *knappen*] *vt* **1** *dial Brit* : to strike a sharp crisp blow to or with ⟨*knapped* his knuckles against the gatepost⟩ : RAP **2** *also* **nap** : to break with a quick jerk or blow; *esp* : to break up or dress (as flints) **3** *chiefly dial Brit* : to bite sharply or eagerly at : SNAP, CROP ⟨sheep *knapping* the new flush⟩ **4** *dial Brit* : to speak or utter brightly or affectedly : CHATTER ~ *vi* **1** *chiefly dial Brit* : to bite sharply or eagerly **2** *dial Brit* : to chatter smartly : BABBLE

**knap·per** *also* **nap·per** \-pə(r)\ n -s [[3]*knap* + *-er*] : one that knaps; *esp* : one that dresses flints or other stone by knapping

**knap·ping hammer** *also* **nap·ping hammer** \ˈnapiŋ-\ n : a hammer having a medium-weight head with two slightly convex faces used for knapping stone

[1]**knap·sack** \ˈnap,sak\ n [LG *knappsack* or D *knapzak*, fr. LG & D *knappen* to make a snapping noise, bite into, eat + LG *sack* (fr. MLG *sak*) & D *zak* bag, sack, fr. MD *sac* — more at KNAP, SACK] **1** : a bag or case often of canvas supported on the back by a strap over each shoulder and used esp. for carrying supplies while on a march **2** *or* **knapsack tank** : a container equipped with pressurizing and spraying devices, carried on the back, and used to transport materials (as insecticides or fire-extinguishing chemicals) to the point of application

knapsack 1

[2]**knapsack** \"\ *vb* -ED/-ING/-S *vt* : to equip with a knapsack ⟨~*ed* travelers⟩ ~ *vi* : to travel on foot dependent for supplies on the contents of a knapsack

**knapsack sprayer** *or* **knapsack pump** n : a spraying apparatus consisting of a knapsack tank together with pressurizing device, line, and sprayer nozzle, used chiefly in fire control and in spraying fungicides or insecticides

**knapscull** *also* **knapscap** n [ME *knapescall*] *obs Scot* : HELMET

**knap·weed** \ˈnap,=\ n [ME *knopwed*, fr. *knop* + *wed*, *weed* weed — more at KNOP, WEED] : any of various plants of the genus *Centaurea*; *esp* : a weedy perennial (*C. nigra*) that is native to Europe but widely naturalized and that has tough wiry stems and knobby heads of purple flowers

**knarl** *archaic var of* GNARL

**knar·ry** \ˈnärē\ *also* **knarred** \-rd\ *adj* [*knarry* fr. ME, fr. *knarre* + *-y*; *knarred* fr. *knar* + *-ed*] : KNOTTY, GNARLED

**knat** *or* **knatte** *archaic var of* GNAT

**knaur** \ˈnȯ(ə)r\ *or* **knar** \ˈnär\ n -s [ME *knarre* rough stone, knot in wood — more at KNUR] : a knot or burl on wood

**knau·tia** \ˈnau̇dēə\ [NL, fr. Christian *Knaut* †1716 Ger. physician + NL *-ia*] *syn of* SCABIOSA

[1]**knave** \ˈnāv\ n -s [ME (also, boy), fr. OE *cnafa* boy, male servant; akin to OHG *knabo* boy, OHG *knebil* piece of wood used in fastenings, ON *knefill* stick, pole, and prob. to OE *cnotta* knot — more at KNOT] **1** *archaic* **a** : a serving boy **b** : a male servant or menial **c** : a man of humble birth or position **2** : a tricky deceitful fellow : an unscrupulous person : ROGUE, RASCAL **3** : JACK 1 c (1) **syn** see VILLAIN

[2]**knave** \"\ *vb* -ED/-ING/-S *vt* **1** *obs* : to give the name of knave to **2** *obs* : to make a knave of (as oneself) ~ *vi, archaic* : to behave knavishly

**knave bairn** n [ME *knavebarn*, fr. *knave* + *barn* child — more at BAIRN] *chiefly Scot* : a male child

**knav·ery** \ˈnāv(ə)rē, -ri\ n -ES **1 a** : the practices of a knave : petty villainy : knavish action : FRAUD, TRICKERY, RASCALITY **b** : a roguish or mischievous trick : a rascally scheme — usu. used in pl. **2** *obs* : tricks of dress : quaint ornaments : TRINKETRY **3** *obs* : mischievous sportiveness : roguish mischief

**knave·ship** \ˈnāv,ship\ n **1** : the condition of being a knave : the personality of a knave **2** *Scots law* : a small customary due formerly paid in meal to the miller's servant at a thirlage mill in return for grinding a quantity of grain

**knav·ess** \ˈnāvəs\ n -ES : a female knave

**knav·ish** \-vish, -vēsh\ *adj* [ME *knavyssh*, fr. *knave* + *-yssh*, *-ish* -ish] : having the characteristics of or appropriate to a knave: **a** *obs* : MISCHIEVOUS, ROGUISH ⟨a ~ lad, thus to make poor females mad —Shak.⟩ **b** : DISHONEST, FRAUDULENT ⟨~ booksellers put forth volumes of trash —T.B.Macaulay⟩

**knav·ish·ly** *adv* : in a knavish manner

**knav·ish·ness** n -ES : the quality or state of being knavish : KNAVERY

**knaw** \ˈnȯ, ˈnä\ *dial Brit var of* KNOW

**knaw·el** \ˈnȯ(ə)l\ n -s [modif. of G *knäuel, knauel*, lit., ball of yarn, fr. MHG *kniuwel*, alter. of *kliuwel*, dim. of *kliuwe* ball of yarn, fr. OHG *kliuwa* — more at CLEW] : a low spreading Old World annual weed (*Scleranthus annuus*) with inconspicuous greenish flowers that is now widely distributed in No. America; *also* : any of several other weedy plants of this genus

**knead** \ˈnēd\ *vb* -ED/-ING/-S [ME *kneden*, fr. OE *cnedan*; akin to OS *knedan* to knead, OHG *knetan*, ON *knotha* to knead, OSlav *gnesti* to press, OPruss *gnode* trough for kneading bread, OE *cnotta* knot — more at KNOT] *vt* **1 a** : to work and press into a mass with or as if with the hands ⟨~*ing* clay to perfect smoothness⟩ **b** : to mix (as the materials of bread) into a well-blended whole by or as if by repeatedly drawing out and pressing together **c** : to make (as bread) by such a process **2** : to manipulate or work on with or as if with a kneading motion ⟨~*ed* the shoulder muscles to relieve the stiffness⟩ : alter or affect with or as if with repeated small pressures ⟨gradually ~*ing* the idea into shape⟩ **3** : to make kneading movements with ⟨~*ing* her fists into her waist —J.S. Redding⟩ ~ *vi* : to make kneading movements : perform the action of kneading with or as if with the hands ⟨a kitten ~*ing* on the bed⟩ ⟨~*ed* away at the cheeks —Constance Foley⟩

**knead·able** \-dəbəl\ *adj* : suitable for kneading; *esp* : having the proper texture for kneading with the hands ⟨flour that produces an excellent ~ dough⟩

**kneaded eraser** *also* **kneaded rubber** n : a soft pliable eraser of unvulcanized rubber used esp. to remove graphite or charcoal marks from drawing paper

**knead·er** \ˈnēdə(r)\ n -s : one that kneads

**knead·ing·ly** *adv* : in the manner of one that kneads : with a kneading movement ⟨pressed her fingers ~ against the cushion⟩

**kneading table** n : DOUGH TRAY

**knead·man** \ˈnēdmən\ n, *pl* **kneadmen** : a worker that tends a machine which kneads flour paste for macaroni products

**kne·bel·ite** \ˈnābə,līt\ n -s [G *knebelit*, fr. Karl Ludwig von *Knebel* †1834 Ger. translator + G *-it* -ite] : a variously colored mineral $(Fe,Mn)_2SiO_4$ consisting of iron manganese silicate and occurring esp. in Sweden (sp. gr. 4.1)

[1]**knee** \ˈnē\ n -s *often attrib* [ME *kne, knee*, fr. OE *cnēow, cnēo*; akin to OHG *kneo* knee, ON *knē*, Goth *kniu*, L *genu*, Gk *gony*, Skt *jānu*] **1 a** (1) : a joint of the ginglymus type in the middle part of the human leg that is the articulation between the femur, tibia, and patella (2) : the part of the leg that includes this joint ⟨scrubbing the floor on hands and ~*s*⟩ **b** : the corresponding joint in the hind limb of a quadrupedal vertebrate formed by the femur above and the tibia or tibia and fibula below **2 a** : a bending of the knee (as in respect or courtesy) ⟨a man of parts well able to make a good ~⟩ **b** : a blow with the bent knee — usu. used with *the* ⟨got the ~ in the face as he tried to get up⟩ **3** : something felt to resemble the human knee esp. in its angular bent form: as **a** (1) : a crook in a tree branch (2) : a piece of timber naturally or artificially bent for use in supporting structures coming together at an angle (as the framing and deck beams of a ship) (3) : a piece of metal of similar form and corresponding function **b** *archaic* : an angular joint in a grass **c** : a rounded or somewhat conical process arising from the roots of a few swamp-growing trees (as the bald cypress and tupelo gum) and projecting above the surrounding water — compare BUTTRESS ROOT **d** : the part of a cabriole furniture leg that curves outward immediately below the junction of leg and frame **e** : a vertical curve in a stair handrail that is convex on top — compare RAMP **f** : the part of the head block of a sawmill that is attached to the dogs holding a log **g** : the part of a composing stick which is attached and at right angles to the back rim and with which the measure is set **h** : an abrupt change in direction in a curve (as on a graph); *esp* : one approaching a right angle in shape **4** : any of several bodily parts that are structurally or functionally comparable to the human knee: as **a** : the carpal joint of the forelimb of a quadrupedal vertebrate corresponding to the wrist in man — see HORSE illustration **b** (1) : the tarsal joint of a bird corresponding to the ankle of man (2) : the corresponding joint of a quadrupedal mammal — not used technically **c** : the joint between the femur and tibia of an insect **5** : the part of a garment that covers the knee — **on one's knees** : in a state of serious or irremediable defeat or failure ⟨a great nation economically *on its knees*⟩ — **on the knees of the gods** [trans. of Gk *theōn en gounasi*] : beyond human control or knowledge — **over in the knees** : KNEE-SPRUNG — **to one's knees** : into a state of submission or defeat ⟨forced *to his knees* by competition⟩

[2]**knee** \"\ *vb* **kneed**; **kneed**; **kneeing**; **knees** [ME *knewen*, fr. OE *cnēowian*, fr. *cnēow, cnēo* knee] *vi* **1** *obs* : to bend the knee : bow low : KNEEL **2** : to bend like a knee — often used with *over* ⟨heavy-headed grain may lodge or ~ over⟩ ~ *vt* **1** *archaic* : to bend the knee to in supplication or deference **2** : to go over or traverse on the knees ⟨painfully ~*ing* his way up the stairs⟩ **3 a** : to strike or touch with the knee ⟨*kneed* his opponent repeatedly⟩ **b** : to move or cause to move with the knee ⟨*kneed* the door open⟩ **c** : to press the flanks of (a saddle horse) with the knees in alerting or encouraging **4** : to repair or replace the knee of (as a garment) **5** : to cut the knee of so as to disable ⟨~ a steer⟩ **6** : to secure by a knee ⟨transoms must be *kneed* to the horn timber —Edwin Monk⟩

**knee action** n : a front-wheel suspension (as of an automobile) permitting independent vertical movement of each front wheel

**knee baby** n, *dial* : a baby barely able to walk ⟨a *knee baby* and a lap baby⟩

**knee bend** n : an exercise performed by dropping from an upright to a squatting position and resuming an upright position without aid of the hands

**kneeboard** \ˈ=,=\ n : a low wall surrounding a riding ring

**knee bone** n : PATELLA

**knee boot** n **1** : a cover for a knee or for the knees: **a** : a carriage boot for protecting the knees from rain or splatter **b** : a protective boot of padded leather used on the knees of a horse that tends to overreach or strike himself in the knee **2** : a boot reaching to the knee ⟨wading in *knee boots*⟩

**knee brace** n : a bracing member of a structure that is placed diagonally from one to another of two adjoining principal members

**knee breeches** n *pl* : BREECHES

**kneebrush** \ˈ=,=\ n **1** : a tuft or brush of hair on the knees of some antelopes and other animals **2** : POLLEN BRUSH

**knee buckle** *n* **:** a buckle used to fasten knee breeches at or just below the knee

**kneecap** \'ˌ=,=\ *n* **1 :** PATELLA **2 :** a protective cover for the knee

**knee colter** *n* **:** a knee-shaped colter

**knee–crooking** \'=,==\ *adj* **:** OBSEQUIOUS, FAWNING

**kneed** \'nēd\ *adj* [¹*knee* + *-ed*] **1 :** having a knee or knees ⟨a graceful ~ table⟩ — often used in combination ⟨a knobby-*kneed* boy⟩ **2 :** having a bend or angle like that of the bent human knee **:** GENICULATE ⟨steep ~ gables⟩

**knee–deep** \'=;'=\ *adj* [ME *kne-depe*, fr. *kne*, *knee* knee + *depe*, *deep* deep — more at KNEE, DEEP] **1 :** rising to the knees **:** KNEE-HIGH ⟨*knee-deep* snow⟩ **2 a :** sunk to the knees ⟨men *knee-deep* in water⟩ **b :** deeply engaged or occupied **:** OVERWHELMED ⟨*knee-deep* in turmoil⟩ ⟨*knee-deep* in war⟩

**knee drill** *n* **:** a special Salvation Army service at which most of the time is spent on the knees in prayer

**knee drop** *n* **:** a fundamental trampoline stunt in which the performer drops to his knees on the bed and then rebounds to a standing position

**knee–halter** \'=,==\ *vt* **:** to restrain (a horse) by passing a line from the halter or bridle to the knee of a foreleg so as to permit grazing but prevent free or fast movement

**knee–high** \'=;'=\ *adj* **:** rising or reaching upward to the knees ⟨*knee-high* stockings⟩

**knee–high blackberry** *n* **:** SAND BLACKBERRY

**kneehole** \'=,=\ *n* **:** an open space (as under a desk) for the knees

**kneehole desk** *n* **:** a flat-topped desk having a kneehole with flanking tiers of drawers

**kneeing** *pres part of* KNEE

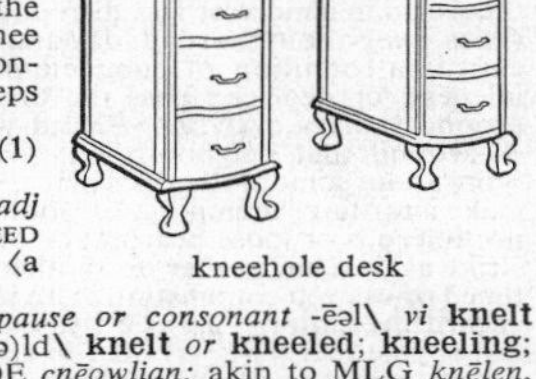
kneehole desk

**knee jerk** *n* **:** an involuntary forward jerk or kick induced by a light blow or sudden strain upon the patellar tendon of the knee that causes a reflex contraction of the quadriceps muscle

**knee joint** *n* **1 :** KNEE 1a(1) **2 :** TOGGLE JOINT

**knee–jointed** \'=;'==\ *adj* **1 :** GENICULATE, KNEED **2 :** having jointed knees ⟨a *knee-jointed* doll⟩

¹**kneel** \'nēl, *esp before pause or consonant* -ēəl\ *vi* **knelt** \'nelt\ *or* **kneeled** \'nē(ə)ld\ **knelt** *or* **kneeled**; **kneeling**; **kneels** [ME *knelen*, fr. OE *cnēowlian;* akin to MLG *knēlen*, MD *cnielen;* denominatives fr. the root of E ¹*knee*] **1 :** to bend the knee **:** fall or rest on the knees ⟨*knelt* to drink from the spring⟩ — sometimes used with *down* ⟨*kneeling* down to pray⟩ **2** *of a rifleman* **a :** to assume a position formerly used in extended-order infantry drill in which the individual while half-faced to the right kneels on the right knee, rests the left forearm across the left thigh, and grasps a rifle in the position of order arms with the right hand above the lower band **b :** to support oneself on the knees while or for the purpose of firing a rifle

²**kneel** \"\ *n* -s **:** an act or instance of kneeling

**kneel·er** \'nēlə(r)\ *n* -s [ME *knelere*, fr. *knelen* to kneel + *-ere* -er] **1 :** one that kneels (as in worship) **2 :** something (as a cushion, stool, board) to kneel on **3 a :** a stone cut to provide a change of direction in masonry **b :** a stone so cut as to support and retain the coping of the slope of a gable

**knee·let** \'nēlət\ *n* -s [¹*knee* + *-let*] **:** a protective covering for the knee

¹**kneeling** *n* -s [ME *kneling*, fr. gerund of *knelen* to kneel — more at KNEEL] **1 :** the act of one that kneels **:** GENUFLECTION **2 :** a place or space for kneeling (as in a church)

²**kneeling** *adj* **:** suitable for use in kneeling ⟨a ~ cushion⟩ **:** designed to be used while kneeling ⟨~ desks⟩

**kneel·ing·ly** *adv* **:** in or from a kneeling position

**knee mortar** *n* **:** a light grenade discharger used by the Japanese during World War II

**knee of head :** an arrangement of timbers outside the stem and below the bowsprit that forms an overhanging bow in a wooden ship

**kneepad** \'=,=\ *n* **:** a protective pad for the knee sometimes attached to a garment

**kneepan** \'=,=\ *n* [ME *knepanne*, fr. *kne* knee + *panne* pan — more at KNEE, PAN] **1 :** PATELLA **2 :** a concavity at the distal end of the femur of an insect

**knee plate** *n* **1 :** a broad steel plate covering the thigh and projecting on each side and used chiefly in body armor for tilting **2 :** a plate for connecting a beam or girder to the frame of a ship

**knee rafter** *n* **:** a diagonal brace between a principal rafter and a tie beam

**knee roll** *n* **:** a padded margin sometimes introduced on the forepart of the skirt of an English saddle to keep a rider's leg from slipping forward

**knee roof** *n* **:** CURB ROOF

**knees** *pl of* KNEE, *pres 3d sing of* KNEE

**knee·sie** \'nēzē\ *n* -s [*knees* (pl. of ¹*knee*) + *-ie*] *slang* **:** an action of flirting or becoming friendly or intimate ⟨played ~s under the table —Lane Foster⟩

**knee–sprung** \'=,=\ *adj, of a horse* **:** having the knees bent when they should normally be straight; *esp* **:** having the knees protruding too far forward — compare BUCK KNEE

**kneestone** \'=,=\ *n* **:** a kneeler for a gable slope

**knee strap** *n* **1 :** a strap to hold a shoe on a cobbler's knee **2 :** an iron strap or facing for a knee timber

**knee–tied** \'=,=\ *adj, of a horse* **:** having a poor conformation in the front legs with the anteroposterior diameter of the leg just below the knee too narrow

**knee timber** *n* **1 :** timber with natural knees or angles in it **2 :** a piece of timber with a knee or angle in it

**knee tool** *n* **:** a knee-shaped tool holder; *usu* **:** a turret-lathe or screw-machine tool holder that supports tools for simultaneous turning and internal-cutting operations

**knee wall** *n* **:** a partition for supporting roof rafters when the span is great or for forming a side wall (as of a second-story room) under a pitched roof

**kneif·fia** \'nīfēə\ *n, cap* [NL, fr. F. G. *Kneiff* †1832 Ger. physician and botanist + NL *-ia*] *in some classifications* **:** a genus of No. American day-blooming herbs (family Onagraceae) having stamens of unequal length and a 4-angled ovary and often included in *Oenothera* — compare SUNDROPS

**kneipp·ism** \'nī,pizəm\ *also* **kneipp's cure** \'nīps-\ *or* **kneipp cure** *n, usu cap K* [*Kneippism* fr. Sebastian *Kneipp* †1897 Ger. priest who developed it + E *-ism; Kneipp's cure* or *Kneipp cure* after S. *Kneipp*, trans. of G *Kneippsche kur* or *Kneipp-kur*] **:** treatment of disease by forms of hydrotherapy (as walking barefoot in morning dew)

¹**knell** \'nel\ *vb* -ED/-ING/-S [ME *knillen, knellen*, fr. OE *cnyllan;* akin to MHG *erknellen* to resound, toll, MHG *knüllen* to strike, beat, ON *knylla*, and prob. to OE *cnotta* knot — more at KNOT] *vt* **1** *obs* **:** to ring (a bell) with slow solemnity **:** TOLL **2 :** to summon by or as if by a knell **3 :** to announce or proclaim by or as if by a knell ⟨the bell buoy ~s your hour —Marguerite J. Adams⟩ ~ *vi* **1 a** *of a bell* **:** RING; *esp* **:** to toll at a death, funeral, or disaster **b :** to sound a knell **2 a :** to give forth a sound like a knell ⟨the owl at its ~*ing* —Dylan Thomas⟩ **b :** to sound a warning or have a sound or import of evil omen

²**knell** \"\ *n* -s [ME *cnul, knel*, fr. OE *cnyll*, fr. *cnyllan*, v.] **1 :** a stroke or sound of a bell (as when tolled at a funeral or at the death of a person) **:** a death signal or passing bell **2 :** a warning of or a sound indicating the passing away of something ⟨this decision sounded the ~ of our hopes⟩

**knelt** *past of* KNEEL

**kne·mi·do·kop·tes** \,nēmədō'käp(,)tēz\ *n, cap* [NL, fr. Gk *knēmid-, knēmis* greave, legging + NL *-o-* + *-koptes* (fr. Gk *koptein* to smite, cut off); akin to Gk *knēmē* shinbone — more at CAPON, HAM] **:** a genus of itch mites attacking birds — see DEPLUMING MITE, SCALY-LEG MITE; compare SCALY LEG — **kne·mi·do·kop·tic** \'====;tik\ *adj*

**knet** *dial past of* KNIT

**knettle** *var of* NETTLE

**knew** *past or dial past part of* KNOW

**knez** \kə'nez\ *n, pl* **knezes** *also* **knezi** [of Slav origin; akin to Serbo-Croatian *knez* prince, Russ *knyaz'*, OSlav *kŭnędzĭ*, of Gmc origin; akin to OHG *kuning* king — more at KING] **:** a Slavic prince or duke

**knib** \'nib\ *n* -s [by alter.] **:** NIB 6a, 6b

**knicht** *archaic var of* KNIGHT

**knick** \'nik\ *n* -s [*knick*point] **:** NICK 6

**knick·er** \-kə(r)\ *n* -s *often attrib* [short for *knickerbocker*] **1 knickers** *pl* **:** KNICKERBOCKERS **2 knickers** *pl* **:** pants for women or girls: as **a :** bloomers with fullness gathered on a band at the knee **b** *chiefly Brit* **:** UNDERPANTS **c :** sport or leisure pants similar in design to knickerbockers

**knick·er·bock·er** \R 'nikə(r),bäkər, —R 'nikə,bäkə(r\ *n* -s *often attrib* [after Diedrich *Knickerbocker*, pretended author of *History of New York* (1809), by Washington Irving †1859 Am. author] **1** *usu cap* **:** a descendant of the old Dutch settlers of New York; *broadly* **:** NEW YORKER **2 a :** loose-fitting knee-length pants gathered at the knee on a band for sports and informal wear by men and boys — usu. used in pl. ⟨~s for golfing⟩ ⟨wearing a ~ suit⟩ **b :** KNICKER 2c **3 :** a wool and cotton clothing fabric resembling tweed and made from nubby yarns with flecks of color

knickerbockers 2a

**knick·er·bock·ered** \-äkə(r)d\ *adj* **:** wearing knickerbockers

**knick·ered** \'nikə(r)d\ *adj* **:** wearing knickers

**knick·knack** \'nik,nak\ *n* [redupl. of *knack*] **1** *obs* **:** a petty trick or artifice **2** *or* **nick·nack** *or* **nic·nac :** a small or trivial article (as of furniture or dress) intended rather for ornament than for use; *esp* **:** a small functionless souvenir

**knick·knack·ato·ry** \-ə,tōrē\ *n* -ES [*knickknack* + *-atory* (as in *conservatory*)] *archaic* **:** a repository or collection of knickknacks

**knick·knack·ery** \-ak(ə)rē\ *n* -ES **:** a knickknack or knickknacks

**knick·knacky** \-akē\ *adj* **1 :** devoted to, characterized by, or concerned with knickknacks ⟨a cluttered ~ room⟩ ⟨such a ~ taste⟩ **2 :** FINICAL, TRIFLING, TRIVIAL

**knickline** \'=,=\ *n* **:** a line formed by the point or angle of a nick in a slope (as of a hill)

**knickpoint** \'nik,=\ *n* [part transl. of G *knickpunkt*, fr. *knicken* to bend + *punkt* point] **:** a place in a stream bed where a nick occurs

¹**knife** \'nīf\ *n, pl* **knives** \-īvz\ [ME *knif*, fr. OE *cnīf*, prob. fr. ON *knīfr;* akin to MLG *knīf* knife, MD *cnijf*, OE *cnotta* knot — more at KNOT] **1 a :** a simple instrument used for cutting consisting of a sharp-edged usu. steel blade provided with a handle **b :** a weapon consisting of or resembling a knife **c :** a culinary utensil consisting of a knife usu. with blade of silver or steel and a handle of metal, ceramic, bone, or pearl ⟨dinner *knives*⟩ ⟨dainty fruit *knives*⟩ **d :** a sharp cutting blade or tool in a machine (as a band saw, a wood-planing machine, or a mowing machine) **e :** any of various instruments used in surgery primarily to sever tissues whether having the form of a conventional knife or scalpel or cutting by other means (as electric or radio-frequency currents); *also* **:** SURGERY — used with *the* ⟨finally decided to submit to the ~⟩ ⟨was under the ~ for several hours⟩ **2 :** MUMBLETY-PEG **3 :** the shape of an envelope flap as produced by the knife on the cutting machine ⟨the size, ~, and watermark of a stamped envelope⟩

²**knife** \"\ *vb* -ED/-ING/-S *vt* **1 :** to use a knife on: as **a :** to stab, slash, or wound with a knife **b :** to prune with a knife **2 a :** to cut or mark with a knife: as (1) **:** to shape or cut out (as shoe uppers) with a knife (2) **:** to trim (as shoe soles) with a knife **b :** to spread (as paint) with a knife **3 :** to try to defeat by underhand means (as a political candidate of one's own party) **:** to work secretly against ⟨one justified in expecting support⟩ **:** UNDERMINE ⟨aiding today those he knows will ~ him tomorrow⟩ **4 a :** to move like a knife in ⟨birds *knifing* the autumn sky⟩ **b :** to impart an action like that of a knife to ⟨*knifed* his hand against his opponent's neck⟩ ~ *vi* **:** to progress or cut a way with or as if with the blade of a knife ⟨the cruiser *knifed* through heavy seas⟩ ⟨a hot sun *knifing* down through the haze⟩ ⟨*knifed* rapidly along the bone⟩

**knife and fork** *n* **1** *Brit* **:** one that eats **:** TRENCHERMAN ⟨a good *knife and fork*⟩ **2 a knives and forks** *pl* (1) **:** paired and solitary cones of the common club moss (*Lycopodium clavatum*) (2) **:** a club moss that bears knives and forks **b :** a key fruit of the sycamore maple — usu. used in pl.

**knife bar** *n* **:** CUTTER BAR

**knife bayonet** *n* **:** a bayonet with considerable breadth of blade and a handle that enables it to be used as a knife, dagger, or entrenching tool

**knifeboard** \'=,=\ *n* **1 :** a board on which knives are cleaned or polished **2** *Brit* **:** a seat on the roof of an old-fashioned omnibus

**knife box** *also* **knife case :** a receptacle for knives and other table cutlery: as **a :** an often ornate wooden container with sloping top used esp. during the 18th century in pairs for the storage of knives and spoons **b :** an open usu. handled tray or rack for the storage of table cutlery

**knife–boy** \'=,=\ *n, Brit* **:** an underservant occupied primarily with the care of knives and general odd jobs about a large household

**knife–edge** \'=,=\ *n* **:** a sharp narrow edge or margin like that of a knife: as **a :** a sharp wedge of steel or other hard material used as a fulcrum or axis of motion for a lever arm or beam in a machine or instrument of precision (as a scale, testing machine, pendulum) to minimize friction **b :** a narrow ridge (as of rock, ice, or sand) **c :** GIRDLE d

**knife–edged** \'=,=\ *adj* **:** having an edge like a knife; *usu* **:** extremely sharp or precise ⟨*knife-edged* pleats⟩ ⟨a *knife-edged* wit⟩

**knife file** *n* **:** a tapered file with a triangular cross section suggesting that of a knife blade

**knife fish** *n* **:** any of several fishes sometimes kept in the tropical aquarium; *esp* **:** a small brownish green fish (*Gymnotus carapo*) from So. America related to the electric eel but lacking electric organs

**knife·ful** \'nīf,fu̇l\ *n, pl* **knives·ful** *or* **knife·fuls** \-īvz,fu̇l, -īf,fu̇lz\ **:** the quantity a knife will hold or convey

**knife grinder** *n* **1 :** one that grinds knives: as **a :** an itinerant tradesman who sharpens knives or other edged tools **b :** a device (as a grindstone or emery wheel) used for grinding or sharpening knives or other edged tools **2 :** a European nightjar (*Caprimulgus europaeus*)

**knife–handle** \'=,==\ *n* **:** RAZOR CLAM

**knife hook** *n, obs* **:** SICKLE 1a

**knife key** *n* **:** a compass key having a knife at one end

**knife lanyard** *n* **:** LANYARD 3a

**knife·less** \'nīfləs\ *adj* **:** lacking a knife

**knifelike** \'=,=\ *adj* **:** resembling or suggesting a knife: **a :** having a sharp edge or ridge ⟨a ~ ridge of land⟩ ⟨a narrow ~ profile⟩ **b :** keen and incisive ⟨icy ~ reasoning⟩ **c :** sharp and penetrating **:** PIERCING ⟨~ pains⟩ ⟨a ~ cold⟩

**knife·man** \'nīfmən\ *n, pl* **knifemen :** a man that uses or works on or works with knives (as a knife fighter or a knife grinder)

**knife money** *n* **:** ancient Chinese bronze money having the shape of knives

**knife pleat** *n* **:** one of a series of narrow sharply pressed pleats all turned in one direction

**knif·er** \'nīfə(r)\ *n* -s **:** one that knifes; *esp* **:** a person who stabs or slashes another with a knife

**knife rest** *n* **1 :** CHEVAL-DE-FRISE **2 :** a support on which a carving knife may be rested on the dining table when not in use

**knif·er·man** \'nīfə(r)mən\ *n, pl* **knifermen :** a slaughterhouse worker who severs hog heads and lets them hang by a thin strip of meat to expose neck glands for government inspection

**knifes** *pres 3d sing of* KNIFE

**knifesmith** \'=,=\ *n* **:** a maker of knives **:** CUTLER

**knife stone** *n* **:** HONE 1; *esp* **:** a fine-grained whetstone for setting and finishing an edge

**knife switch** *n* **:** an electric switch in which contact is made by pushing one or more flat metal blades between the jaws of spring clips

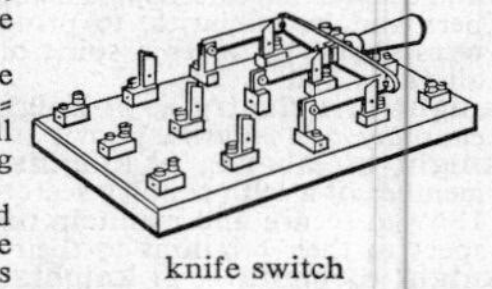
knife switch

**knife tool** *n* **:** a tool suggestive of a knife: as **a :** a knife-shaped graver **b :** a small wheel used in seal engraving for cutting fine lines

**knife urn** *n* **:** an urn-shaped knife box popular in the late 18th and early 19th centuries

**knifeway** \'=,=\ *n* **:** a long tapering usu. hardened straight bar (as a V bar)

**knif·fin system** \'nifən-\ *n, usu cap K* [after Wm. *Kniffin*, 19th cent. Am. horticulturist] **:** a system or method of training grapevines whereby a trunk is carried to the upper of two braced supporting wires along which the annually renewed fruiting canes are tied and from which the bearing branches are allowed to hang down

**knifing** *pres part of* KNIFE

¹**knight** \'nīt, *usu* -īd·+V\ *n* -s [ME, boy, youth, knight, fr. OE *cniht, cneoht* boy, youth, military follower; akin to OS & OHG *kneht* boy, youth, military follower, OE *cnotta* knot — more at KNOT] **1 a** (1) **:** a mounted man-at-arms of the European feudal period serving a king or other superior usu. in return for a tenure of land; *esp* **:** a man ceremonially inducted by a feudal superior into special military rank commonly immediately below that of baron usu. available only after completing regular periods of service as page and squire — compare DUB *vt* 1a (2) **:** a man upon whom a corresponding dignity has been conferred by a sovereign in recognition of personal merit (3) **:** a member of an order of knighthood or of chivalry ⟨a *Knight* of the Garter⟩ (4) **:** a member of a social or fraternal order ⟨*Knights* of Labor⟩; *also* **:** a member of such an order holding a particular degree or rank that is officially so designated ⟨members, acolytes, and ~s of the Inner Tabernacle⟩ **b** (1) **:** a person of ancient history or mythology of a rank equivalent to that of knight — often used to translate Latin *miles* (2) **:** EQUES **c :** KNIGHT OF THE SHIRE **d :** a man who devotes himself to a lady as her attendant or champion **e :** a man associated in his personal or professional character with something specified (as an implement, tool, place, material) — often used in trade or craft nicknames ⟨those petty rascals often called ~s of the bridewell⟩ ⟨a ~ of the quill earning a pittance by his writings⟩ **2 a :** a chess piece that may cross occupied squares and that has an L-shaped move of three squares of which two are in a horizontal or vertical row and one is perpendicular to the row **b :** a face card ranking between the queen and the jack in many European packs of playing cards **3 :** a small bitt with sheaves through which the running rigging of a ship is passed

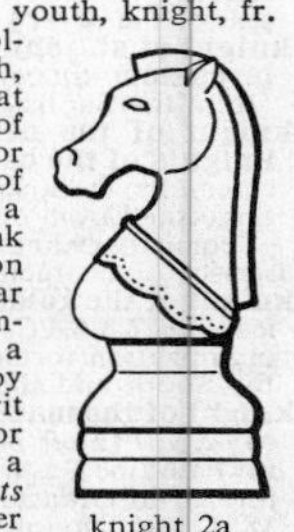
knight 2a

²**knight** \"\ *vt* -ED/-ING/-S [ME *knighten*, fr. *knight*, n.] **:** to make a knight of **:** induct into the state or an order of knighthood **:** DUB

**knight·age** \-d·ij\ *n* -s **1 :** knights or a body of knights ⟨the king and all his ~⟩ **2 :** a register and account of knights ⟨the several ~s and peerages that register men of nobility and note⟩ **3 :** KNIGHTHOOD ⟨hardy service may win a commoner ~⟩

**knight bachelor** *n, pl* **knights bachelors** *also* **knights bachelor :** a knight belonging to the most ancient but the lowest order of English knights and not a member of an order of chivalry — see KNIGHT BANNERET

**knight banneret** *n, pl* **knights bannerets** *also* **knights banneret** [ME] **:** a knight of an ancient English order of knighthood that was commonly conferred as a reward for valor on the field of battle and that entitled the holder to bear a banner rather than the pennon of a knight bachelor

**knight baronet** *n, pl* **knights baronets :** BARONET

**knight commander** *n, pl* **knights commanders :** a member of the second class in an honorary order (as the Order of the Bath) with more than one class of membership ranking below a knight grand cross and above a companion

**knight–companion** \'=='==\ *n, pl* **knights–companions** *also* **knight–companions :** a knight belonging to an order of knighthood having only one class ⟨the Order of the Garter . . . consists of the sovereign and twenty-five *knights-companions* —Valentine Heywood⟩

**knight–errant** \'='==\ *n, pl* **knights–errant** [ME *knight erraunt*] **:** a wandering knight; *esp* **:** one traveling at random in search of adventures in which to exhibit military skill, prowess, and generosity

**knight–errantry** \'='===\ *n, pl* **knight–errantries 1 a :** the character or actions of a knight-errant **:** the practice of wandering in quest of adventures **b :** quixotic conduct **:** a quixotic or romantic adventure or scheme **2 :** KNIGHTS-ERRANT

**knight·ess** \'nīd·əs\ *n* -ES **1** *obs* **:** a woman filling the role of a knight either as a fighter or as a member of an order of chivalric import **:** female knight **2 :** the wife of a knight

**knight·ful·ly** \'nītfəlē\ *adv* **:** in the manner of a knight **:** BRAVELY, CHIVALROUSLY

**knight grand commander** *n, pl* **knights grand commanders :** a member of an honorary order (as the Star of India) that admits other than Christians to membership corresponding in rank to a knight grand cross

**knight grand cross** *n, pl* **knights grand cross :** a member of the highest class in an honorary order (as the Bath) with more than one class of membership — see KNIGHT COMMANDER

**knighthead** \'=,=\ *n* [so called fr. its having been carved to represent knights] **1 :** one of two timbers rising in the bows of a wooden ship just within the stem with one on each side of the bowsprit — called also *bollard timber* **2 :** a triangular bulkhead just abaft the cutwater with a hole through which the bowsprit of a ship passes

**knight·hood** \'nīt,hu̇d\ *n* [ME *knighthod*, fr. *knight* + *-hod* -hood] **1 :** the rank, dignity, condition, profession, or vocation of a knight or of knights as a class ⟨won a ~ for his devotion to civic reform⟩ ⟨~ was at one time both a social obligation and a symbol of maturity⟩ **2 :** the character of a knight **:** qualities befitting a knight or knights as a class **:** KNIGHTLINESS, CHIVALRY **3 a :** knights as a class ⟨the early ~ held a place distinct from the great lords on the one hand and the working peasantry on the other⟩ **b :** a body of knights ⟨the legendary ~ of King Arthur⟩

**knighthood–errant** \'='==\ *n* **:** KNIGHTS-ERRANT

**knight hospitaler** *n, pl* **knights hospitalers** *usu cap K&H* **:** HOSPITALER

**knight·ia** \'nīd·ēə\ *n, cap* [NL, fr. Thomas A. *Knight* †1838 Eng. plant physiologist + NL *-ia*] **:** a small genus of Australasian trees or shrubs (family Proteaceae) with alternate leathery leaves, showy racemose flowers, and follicular fruit — see REWA-REWA

**knightless** *adj, obs* **:** unbecoming a knight **:** UNCHIVALROUS

**knight·li·hood** \'nītlē,hu̇d\ *n* **:** KNIGHTLINESS

**knightlike** \'=,=\ *adj* [ME *knightlik*, fr. *knight* + *-lik* -like] **:** KNIGHTLY 1

**knight·li·ness** \'nītlēnəs\ *n* -ES **:** the quality or state of being knightly; *broadly* **:** chivalrous courtesy or gracious kindness ⟨a natural ~ characterized all his relations with others⟩

**knight·ling** \'nītliŋ\ *n* -s **:** a knight of little worth or importance **:** petty knight

¹**knight·ly** \'nītlē, -li\ *adj* [ME, fr. *knight* + *-ly*] **1 a :** of or relating to a knight **b :** befitting a knight **:** CHIVALROUS **2 :** consisting or made up of knights

²**knightly** \"\ *adv* [ME, fr. *knightly*, adj.] **:** in a manner becoming a knight

**knight marshal** *n, pl* **knights marshals 1 :** a former military officer analogous to the modern quartermaster **2 :** a onetime officer of the British royal household who had judicial cognizance of transgressions committed in the royal household or verge and of contracts to which a member of the king's household was a party

**knight of columbus** *n, pl* **knights of columbus** *usu cap K&C* [after Christopher *Columbus* — more at COLUMBUS] **:** a member of a fraternal and benevolent society of Roman Catholic men founded at New Haven, Conn., in 1882 to promote social and intellectual intercourse among its members, to aid its members and beneficiaries, to protect and promote Catholic interests, and to foster a spirit of fraternity among citizens of all races and creeds

**knight of industry** *n, pl* **knights of industry** [trans. of F *chevalier de l'industrie*] *obs* : SWINDLER

**knight of labor** *n, pl* **knights of labor** *usu cap K&L* : a member of a 19th century secret labor organization formed in 1869 to secure and maintain the rights of workingmen in respect to their relations to their employers

**knight of malta** *n, pl* **knights of malta** *usu cap K&M* [fr. *Malta*, island in the Mediterranean, the seat of the order from 1530–1798] : HOSPITALER

**knight of pyth·i·as** \-'pithēəs\ *n, pl* **knights of pythias** *usu cap K&P* [after *Pythias*, 4th cent. B.C. Pythagorean philosopher whose devotion to his friend Damon is legendary] : a member of a secret fraternal order founded at Washington, D.C., in 1864 for social and charitable purposes

**knight of rhodes** \-'rōdz\ *n, pl* **knights of rhodes** *usu cap K&R* [fr. *Rhodes*, city and island in the Aegean sea, former seat of the order] : HOSPITALER

**knight of st. john of jerusalem** *n, pl* **knights of st. john of jerusalem** *usu cap K&S & both Js* [after *St. John of Jerusalem* (John the Baptist), cousin of Jesus] : HOSPITALER

**knight of the carpet** *also* **knight of the chamber** *n, pl* **knights of the carpet** **1** : a knight who is knighted in formal ceremony (as kneeling in a royal audience chamber) as distinguished from one knighted informally on the field of battle — compare CARPET KNIGHT **2** : a recipient of knighthood for service or distinction other than military

**knight of the golden circle** *n, pl* **knights of the golden circle** *usu cap K&G&C* : a member of a former American secret organization formed about 1855 to promote the interests of the South and the slavery cause

**knight of the maccabees** *n, pl* **knights of the maccabees** *usu cap K&M* [after *Maccabees*, 2d & 1st cent. B.C. Jewish family in Palestine] : a member of a secret beneficiary society formed in Ontario in 1878 and introduced into the U. S. in 1881 and having a ritual based on characteristics of the ancient Maccabean family

**knight of the pestle** *n, pl* **knights of the pestle** : APOTHECARY

**knight of the post** *n, pl* **knights of the post** : a professional false witness of 15th to 17th century England

**knight of the road** *n, pl* **knights of the road** **1** *obs* : HIGHWAYMAN **2** : TRAVELING SALESMAN **3** : TRAMP

**knight of the round table** *n, pl* **knights of the round table** *usu cap K&R&T* : a knight belonging to the legendary order instituted by King Arthur

**knight of the shire** *n, pl* **knights of the shire** [ME] **1** : a knight selected by the freeholders to represent a shire in the House of Commons esp. in medieval times ⟨the *knight of the shire* was the connecting link between the baron and the shopkeeper —T.B.Macaulay⟩ **2** : a parliamentary representative from a shire or county as distinguished from a representative of a city or a borough ⟨the number of *knights of the shire* was increased to 159 —T.E.May⟩

**knight of the sword** *n, pl* **knights of the sword** *usu cap K&S* : a member of a German religious order of knights founded in 1202 by Bishop Albert of Riga in Livonia to convert the heathen Estonians and Livonians and appropriate their lands, confirmed by the pope in 1204, and merged into the Teutonic Order in 1237

**knight of the temple** *n, pl* **knights of the temple** *usu cap K&T* : TEMPLAR 1

**knights** *pl of* KNIGHT, *pres 3d sing of* KNIGHT

**knight service** *also* **knight's service** *n* [ME *knightes service*] **1** : the military service by rendering which a knight held his lands; *also* : the tenure of lands held on condition of performing military service **2** : service such as a knight can or should render; *broadly* : good or valuable service

**knight's fee** *n* [ME *knightes fee*] : the amount of land the holding of which imposed the obligation of knight service, being sometimes a hide or less and sometimes six or more hides

**knight's–spur** \'=,=\ *n, pl* **knight's–spurs** : LARKSPUR 1a

**knight's–star** \'=,=\ *or* **knight's–star lily** *n, pl* **knight's–stars** *or* **knight's–star lilies** : BARBADOS LILY

**knight's tour** *n* : a chess problem in which a knight makes a circuit of the board touching each square once

**knight templar** *n, pl* **knights templars** *or* **knights templar** *also* **knight templars** *usu cap K&T* **1** TEMPLAR 1 **2** : a member of the Knights Templars, an order of Freemasonry conferring three degrees in the York rite — compare CHIVALRIC RITE

**knip·ho·fia** \nip'hōfēə, nī'fō-\ *n* [NL, fr. Johan H. *Kniphof* †1763 Ger. botanist + NL *-ia*] **1** *cap* : a genus of showy African herbs (family Liliaceae) having clumps of long radical leaves and tall scapes of red or yellow drooping flowers with reflexed perianths **2** -s : a plant of the genus *Kniphofia* — called also *tritoma*

**knish** \kə'nish\ *n* -ES [Yiddish, fr. Russ *knish, knysh*, a kind of cake; akin to Ukrainian *knyš*, Pol *knysz*] : a round or square of rich baking-powder dough folded over a savory meat or cheese filling and baked or fried

**knis·te·neaux** \kə,nistə'nō\ *n pl but sing in constr, usu cap* [modif. of F *Christenaux* — more at CREE] : CREE

**¹knit** \'nit, *usu* -id·+V\ *vb* **knit** *or* **knitted** *or dial* **knet** \'net, *usu* -ed·+V\ **knit** *or* **knitted** *or dial* **knet**; **knitting**; **knits** [ME *knitten*, fr. OE *cnyttan*; akin to MLG *knütten* to knit, knot together; denominatives fr. the root of E ¹*knot*] *vt* **1** *now chiefly dial* : to make fast or join with knots : tie together : form into a knot or into knots **2** : to cause to unite in a functional whole as if by knitting or knotting: as **a** : to link firmly or closely (as by interlocking, intertwining, or intertying) ⟨*knitted* her hands until the knuckles blanched⟩ : CONJOIN, CEMENT, CONSOLIDATE ⟨~ the timbers into a sturdy frame⟩ **b** : to cause to grow together ⟨time and rest will ~ the fractured bone⟩ **c** : to bind by immaterial (as social or legal) ties ⟨~ together by common interests⟩ **d** : to draw together : contract into wrinkles ⟨*knitting* his brow in thought⟩ **3 a** : to form (as a fabric or a garment) by the interlacing of a yarn or yarns in a series of connected loops by means of hand or machine needles ⟨*knitting* socks to match the sweater⟩ **b** : to form or bring into being (some immaterial tie) ⟨a new philosophy that *knitted* a new understanding between the classes⟩ ~ *vi* **1** : to make knitted fabrics or objects : do knitting ⟨some women ~, others sew⟩ **2** : to unite into a functional whole as if by being knitted or knotted: as **a** : to become compact : CONSOLIDATE **b** : to grow together ⟨fractures in old bones ~ slowly⟩ **c** : to become drawn together : contract into wrinkles **3** *now dial Brit* **a** (1) *of fruit* : SET (2) *of a plant* : to grow or set fruit **b** *of bees* : SWARM **4** *obs* : EFFERVESCE, FOAM

**²knit** \"\ *n* -s *often attrib* **1 a** : a knitting or style of knitting **b** : knitted material **c** : KNIT STITCH **2** : a contraction or wrinkling up (as of the brow)

**knitback** \'=,=\ *n* [so called fr. its use to heal broken bones] : a coarse branching hairy comfrey (*Symphytum officinale*) sometimes cultivated for its white, yellowish, purple, or rose flowers

**knitch** \'nich, kə'n-\ *n* -ES [ME *knytche, knucche*, fr. OE *gecnycc* bond; akin to MHG *knocke* bundle, MHG *knock* back of the neck, *knoche* bone — more at KNUCKLE] *dial Eng* : BUNDLE, FAGOT

**knit goods** *n pl* **1** : knitted fabrics; *esp* : fabrics made on a knitting machine and used for underwear, hosiery, and other clothing **2** : articles made from such fabrics : knitted garments

**knit stitch** *n* : a basic knitting stitch usu. made with the yarn at the back of the work by inserting the right needle into the front part of a loop on the left needle, catching the yarn from the left side with the point of the right needle, and bringing it through the first loop to form a new loop — compare PURL STITCH

**knit·ted** \'nid·əd, -itəd\ *adj* : made or characterized by knitting ⟨~ garments⟩ — often used in combination ⟨hand-*knitted* woolens⟩

**knit·ter** \'nid·ə(r), -itə-\ *n* -s [ME, fr. *knitten* to knit + *-er* — more at KNIT] **1** : a person that knits by hand or operates a knitting machine **2** : a machine for making knit goods (as hose, jersey, sweaters)

**knit·ting** \'nid·|iŋ, -it|, |ēŋ\ *n* -s [ME, fr. gerund of *knitten* to knit] **1** : the action or method of one that knits by hand or machine; *also* : the action of a machine that knits **2** : work in progress or products made by a person or machine that knits **3** : the occupation of operating a machine that knits **4** *obs* : FASTENING; *esp* : KNOT — **stick to one's knitting** *or* **tend to one's knitting** *also* **mind one's knitting** : to mind one's business : avoid interfering in or involving oneself with the affairs of others

**knitting machine** *n* : a machine for mechanically knitting fabrics (as jersey or tricot) and articles of wear (as sweaters or hosiery) — see CIRCULAR-KNIT, FLAT-KNIT

**knitting needle** *n* **1** : one of two or more slender rods with one or both ends pointed or a flexible rod with both ends pointed used for hand knitting and made usu. of metal, bone, or plastic — see NEEDLE illustration **2** : a spring needle or a latch needle used for machine knitting

**knitting pin** *n* : a single-pointed needle for hand knitting

**knittle** *var of* NETTLE

**knit up** *vt* **1 a** : to tie up : SECURE, UNITE **b** : to make or repair by knitting ⟨*knit up* several pairs of Christmas mittens⟩ ⟨*knit* a torn sleeve *up*⟩ **2** : to bring to an end : CONCLUDE ⟨to *knit* these remarks *up* briefly⟩

**knitwear** \'=,=\ *n* : knitted clothing including hosiery, underwear, and outerwear

**knive** \'nīv\ *vb* -ED/-ING/-S [fr. ¹*knife*, after such pairs as E *wife: wive*] : KNIFE

**knives** *pl of* KNIFE

**knives and forks** *pl of* KNIFE AND FORK

**knivesful** *pl of* KNIFEFUL

**¹knob** *also* **nob** \'näb\ *n* -s [ME *knobbe*; akin to MLG *knubbe*, *knobbe* knot on a tree, knob, Norw *knubb* block, ME *knoppe*, *knopp* bud, knob — more at KNOP] **1 a** (1) : a relatively small usu. rounded mass typically projecting from the surface or extremity of something : a usu. rounded projection or protuberance or protrusion ⟨a heavy club with ~s at one end⟩ ⟨his nose ends in a puggy ~ —N.M.Clark⟩ ⟨a skull having a couple of peculiar ~s⟩ (2) *archaic* : a small rather hard swelling (as a bump, pimple, pustule) on the surface of the skin (3) : a twisted knot or hard excrescence or protuberance esp. of wood : GNARL ⟨~s in the trunk of a tree⟩ (4) : a tiny ball, loop, or tuft (as of thread or hair) formed by twisting or coiling or otherwise tightly drawing together one or more strands; *specif* : KNOP c ⟨little ~s of wool or cotton in different colors —Mary Thomas⟩ (5) : ³BUN 2 ⟨dark hair drawn into a tight little ~ on the neck —Flora Thompson⟩ **b** (1) : a small rounded mass of often carved ornamental work (as a boss at the intersection of the ribs in a vaulting) topping or capping a larger piece of work or serving as a contrastive detail (2) : a small globular usu. ornamental body typically at the top or other extremity of something (as at the top or end of a finial or on the hilt of a sword or at the front and top of a saddlebow) : POMMEL (3) : FINIAL **c** (1) : a usu. rounded projection by which something can be grasped or otherwise manipulated or moved ⟨a metal bar with a ~ at one end⟩; *specif* : a usu. rounded handle (as of a drawer or door) ⟨a door with a heavy ~ of wrought metal⟩ (2) : a usu. rounded projection or a disk or dial typically having a guide mark or series of guide marks around the edge and capable of being turned or pulled or pushed so as to actuate or otherwise operate or control something (as a radio or television set) ⟨he reached to turn on the radio but she pushed his hand from the ~ almost angrily —E.K.Gann⟩ ⟨an expert at knocking ~s off safes —Paul McClung⟩ ⟨turns a control ~ on the instrument panel —T.W.Rodes⟩ **d** : a spool-shaped porcelain insulator for supporting electric wires — see INSULATOR illustration **2 a** (1) : a usu. rounded land prominence (as a knoll, hillock, hill, small mountain) with usu. steep sides; *esp* : an isolated prominent rounded hill (2) **knobs** *pl* : an area marked by a group of such prominences ⟨a rifleman from the east Kentucky ~s —I.S.Cobb⟩ **b** (1) : a usu. tapering upward projection from the summit of a hill or mountain : PEAK ⟨bare crags and ~s —W.M.Davis⟩ (2) : something (as a boulder or group of boulders or a stony area) projecting from the summit or sides of a hill or mountain ⟨erosion wore down the mountains, exposing ~s of harder granite —*Amer. Guide Series: Minn.*⟩ ⟨patches of ragged grass and ~s of boulders —Dixon Wecter⟩ **3** *chiefly Brit* : a small lump of something : a small piece ⟨a scraggly looking salad and a few ~s of cheese —Dawn Powell⟩ ⟨a ~ of coal⟩; *esp* : a small cube ⟨a ~ of sugar⟩ ⟨dropped a ~ of ice into the glass⟩ **4** *archaic* : HEAD ⟨a diminutive head like the ~ of a mannikin —George Santayana⟩ — **with knobs on** *adv* : in an esp. eminent manner : to an esp. notable degree ⟨anglophile though the first three pictures were, the new one is more so *with knobs on* —*Newsweek*⟩ ⟨whatever problem a town can have . . . we have it — *with knobs on* —Sam Pollock⟩

**²knob** *also* **nob** \"\ *vt* **knobbed**; **knobbed**; **knobbing**; **knobs** **1** : to cause to have knobs : form knobs upon ⟨*knobbing* a sheet of metal⟩ **2** : to provide with a knob ⟨wrought-iron gates, *knobbed* on either side with stone balls —Edmund Wilson⟩

**knob and tube wiring** *n* : open electric-wiring work in which the wires are supported on knobs or cleats and encased in tubes where they pass through beams or partitions

**knobbed** \'näb(ə)d\ *adj* [ME, fr. *knobbe* knob + *-ed*] **1** : having a knob or knobs ⟨a ~ stick⟩; *specif* : ending in a knob ⟨a pole ~ at each extremity⟩ **2** : covered with knobs : KNOBBY ⟨a ~ tree trunk⟩

**knobbed crab** *n* : a spiny spider crab (*Mithrax caribbaeus*) of the West Indies and the northern coast of So. America

**knobbed goose** *n* : CHINESE GOOSE 2

**knobbed wrack** *n* : a common brown alga (*Ascophyllum nodosum*) of northern oceans

**knob·ber** \'näbə(r\ *n* -s [¹*knob* + *-er*] *Brit* : a two-year-old male deer

**knob·bi·ly** \'näbəlē\ *adv* : in such a way as to form protuberances ⟨her ~ corseted bulk —Marcia Davenport⟩

**knob·bi·ness** \-bēnəs\ *n* -ES : the quality or state of being knobby

**knob·bish** \-bish\ *adj* : rather knobby ⟨skinny as a rail, and kind of ~ at the joints —Helen Eustis⟩

**knob·ble** \'näbəl\ *n* -s [ME *knoble*, fr. *knob* + *-le* (dim. suffix)] : a little knob or lump

**knob·bled** \-ld\ *adj* : KNOBBLY

**knob·bly** *or* **nob·bly** \'näblē, -li\ *adj, often* -ER/-EST [¹*knob* + *-ly*] : KNOBBY; *esp* : having or covered with very small knobs ⟨a ~ pane of translucent glass⟩

**¹knob·by** \'näbē, -bi\ *adj, usu* **knobbier**; *usu* **knobbiest** [¹*knob* + *-y*] **1 a** : having knobs : having several or many knobs : covered with knobs: as (1) : having protuberances, projections, or protrusions ⟨~ bones⟩ ⟨~ knees⟩ ⟨~ knuckles⟩ : BUMPY ⟨grinned toothlessly and extended a ~ hand —Dorothy Sayers⟩ (2) : having usu. rounded land prominences : HILLY ⟨~ farmland⟩ **b** : shaped like or suggestive of a knob ⟨little ~ noses —Joseph Conrad⟩ **2 a** : involving difficulties : PERPLEXING, INTRICATE, KNOTTY ⟨some of the ~ problems of publishing —Harvey Breit⟩ **b** : resisting compromise or evasion or unequivocal solution : stubbornly unyielding : HARD, OBSTINATE ⟨prefer to turn away from the ~ facts of life —*Time*⟩

**²knobby** \"\ *var of* NOBBY

**knob celery** *n* : CELERIAC

**knob·cone pine** \'=,=-\ *n* : a pine (*Pinus attenuata*) native to the Pacific coast of the U.S. with a prominent knob on each scale of the cone

**knob grass** *n* : HORSE BALM 1

**knob·ker·rie** *also* **knob·ker·ry** \'näb,kerē\ *n, pl* **knobkerries** [modif. (influenced by ¹*knob*) of Afrik *knopkierie*, fr. *knop* knob, bud (fr. MD *cnoppe*) + *kierie* stick, club, fr. Hottentot *kirri* — more at KNOP] : a rather short wooden club with a heavy round knob at one end that may be thrown as a missile or used in close attack and that is used esp. by aborigines of southern Africa

knob-ker-rie

**knob lock** *n* : a door lock with a spring bolt operated by a knob and a dead bolt operated by a key

**knobs** *pl of* KNOB, *pres 3d sing of* KNOB

**knobstick** \'=,=\ *n* **1** : a stick, cane, or club with a rounded knob at its head; *specif* : KNOBKERRIE **2** *Brit* : STRIKEBREAKER, SCAB

**knob·thorn** *also* **knob·thorne** \'näb,thȯ(ə)rn\ *n* -s : an acacia (*Acacia nigrescens*) of southern Africa having a bark often dotted with thorn-tipped knobs

**knobweed** \'=,=\ *n* **1** : KNAPWEED **2** : HORSE BALM 1

**knobwood** \'=,=\ *n* **1** : a tree (*Zanthoxylum capense*) of southern Africa with compound leaves and greenish paniculate flowers **2** : the wood of the knobwood

**¹knock** \'näk\ *vb* -ED/-ING/-S [ME *knoken, knokken*, fr. OE *cnocian, cnucian*; akin to MHG *knochen* to press, ON *knoka* to hit, beat; all of imit. origin] *vi* **1** : to strike upon the surface of something (as a door) with a short sharp fairly heavy blow (as with the knuckles) esp. so as to indicate one's desire to gain admittance (as into a room) or otherwise to attract attention : RAP ⟨~*ed* on the green painted door and it was opened almost at once —Louis Bromfield⟩ ⟨stood there ~*ing* on the gate⟩ ⟨~*ed* on the table before beginning to speak⟩ **2** : to collide fairly heavily or jarringly with something : strike against or bump into something ⟨~*ed* into one person after another in the crowd⟩ ⟨his ~*ing* knees belied the bluster of his talk —W.F.Hambly⟩ **3 a** : to stir about or move along briskly, usu. noisily, and often clumsily or haphazardly : BUSTLE ⟨heard him ~*ing* round in the kitchen —Lucy M. Montgomery⟩ ⟨went ~*ing* rapidly down the road⟩ ⟨go ~*ing* along at a reasonable rate —Dillon Anderson⟩ **b** : to go or move about in an irregular, haphazard, or aimless way : travel about in a careless or indifferent manner and often with no particular objective : WANDER, ROAM, ROVE — usu. used with *about, around* ⟨~*ing* idly up and down the country⟩ ⟨decided to ~ around the world awhile⟩ ⟨~*ed* about the mountains for a couple of weeks⟩ ⟨spent a couple of hours ~*ing* around town⟩ **c** (1) : to lead an irregular life often in straitened difficult circumstances : live like a vagrant — used with *about, around* ⟨content to ~ about the world in a more or less disreputable way —R.W.Southern⟩ ⟨goes ~*ing* about the roads day and night —W.B.Yeats⟩ (2) : to exist in a condition of complete or nearly complete inaction, idleness, or neglect : pass the time inactively or idly : hang around : LOITER, DAWDLE — used with *about, around* ⟨used to ~ around that neighborhood⟩ ⟨would you have my pictures ~*ing* about some art dealer's place —Louis Bromfield⟩ **4 a** : to make a rattling, thumping, or pounding noise (as of loose connecting rods or loose bearings or other parts in a machine that strike against each other or another surface or as of improperly timed or uneven combustion in an internal-combustion engine) ⟨heard the motor ~*ing*⟩ **b** : to undergo detonation (sense 2) ⟨an engine fuel that ~s⟩ **5** : to speak ill of something esp. in a petty way : find fault with or criticize something adversely and often captiously ⟨malcontents who were perpetually ~*ing*⟩ **6** : to end the play in a card game (as gin rummy) and call for a comparison of hands ⟨at this point the player may ~⟩ ~ *vt* **1 a** (1) : to deal a short sharp fairly heavy blow to : strike sharply : deal a jarring blow to : HIT, RAP, BUFFET ⟨~*ed* him on the chin⟩ ⟨~s it about more than any rough road will ever do —Hardiman Scott⟩ (2) : to get rid of by or as if by dealing a stunning blow to : knock out : knock on the head ⟨he can ~ the worry if he takes a Scotch and soda —Ernest Hemingway⟩ ⟨an effective remedy for ~*ing* colds⟩ (3) : to affect in an indicated way by or as if by striking sharply, beating, battering, hammering, or pounding ⟨would ~ any road to pieces —Tom Wintringham⟩ ⟨~*ed* it apart⟩ (4) : to produce or make by so striking or battering ⟨~*ed* a hole in the wall⟩ ⟨a workroom composed of two or three servants' bedrooms ~*ed* into one —C.D.Lewis⟩ **b** (1) : to set forcibly into sudden movement ⟨kept ~*ing* the croquet ball along with her mallet⟩ or send flying ⟨swung hard with his bat and ~*ed* the baseball over the fence⟩ or drive in an indicated direction ⟨~*ed* the book away from his face⟩ or to, into, or onto an indicated thing, place, or position by a short sharp blow, thrust, or stroke or a series of such blows or thrusts ⟨~*ed* a nail up into the ceiling⟩ : give a sudden impetus to by driving with a short sharp blow : impel or propel suddenly and swiftly (2) : to drive out by so striking : force out or expel by or as if by a blow ⟨was ~*ing* the dust out of his clothes —Henry Baerlein⟩ ⟨threatened to ~ his brains out⟩ ⟨will ~ such notions out of your head —T.B.Costain⟩ ⟨can ~ all the interest out of it —H.L.Davis⟩ (3) : to drive forcibly off or down by or as if by so striking : cause to be so removed ⟨~*ed* the head off the statue⟩ ⟨~*ed* a considerable sum off the price⟩ (4) *of a dog* : to drive (game birds) from cover : FLUSH ⟨moved in and ~*ed* the birds —*Amer. Field*⟩ **c** : SHAKE, UPSET, BOTHER, DISTURB ⟨never gives up the idea that he can win, and nothing can ~ him —D.W.Maurer⟩ **d** *chiefly Brit* (1) : to knock out (sense 2a) ⟨struck him under the right eye with her clenched fist and ~*ed* him —Sigerson Clifford⟩ (2) : to make a strong impression on : produce a strong effect in; *esp* : to move to admiration or applause ⟨nothing ~s a country audience like a hornpipe —J.K.Jerome⟩ **2** : to cause to collide fairly heavily or jarringly with something : cause to strike against, run into, or bump into something ⟨~*ed* two oil drums against each other —Vicki Baum⟩ ⟨didn't look where they were going and ~*ed* their heads together⟩ **3** : to speak ill of esp. in a petty way : find fault with or criticize adversely and often captiously ⟨can satirize the manners and morals of our times and even ~ the government —Lee Rogow⟩ ⟨instructions were to keep smiling, ~ nobody —S.H.Adams⟩ **4** : to obtain by or as if by striking or beating ⟨a young man who can ~ some fun out of life —A.J.Cronin⟩ — **knock cold** : to knock out (sense 2a) ⟨ran his head into the wall and was *knocked cold*⟩ — **knock dead** : to move strongly esp. to admiration or applause : knock over ⟨a comedian who really *knocks* them *dead*⟩ — **knock for a goal** : to knock for a loop — **knock for a loop** **1 a** : to overcome utterly : completely vanquish : ROUT ⟨*knocked* his opponent *for a loop*⟩ **b** : to make short work of : get rid of or demolish ⟨*knocked* his faith in human nature *for a loop*⟩ **2** : to make speechless : cause to be at a complete loss : OVERWHELM, BEWILDER, AMAZE, DUMBFOUND ⟨the news *knocked* them *for a loop*⟩ — **knock into a cocked hat** **1 a** : to utterly demolish : RUIN ⟨*knocked* all our plans *into a cocked hat*⟩ ⟨threatened to *knock* the industry *into a cocked hat*⟩ **b** : to prove to be false : utterly disprove ⟨a theory that was finally *knocked into a cocked hat*⟩ **2** : to surpass eminently : excel by far ⟨something that'll *knock* all the other achievements of man *into a cocked hat* —John Galsworthy⟩ — **knock on the head** *or* **knock in the head** **1** : to stun or kill by a blow on the head ⟨had been *knocked on the head* some dark night —R.L.Stevenson⟩ **2** : to check (as a plan, project, procedure) effectively or put an end to : SQUELCH, SQUASH ⟨has *knocked* this rumor *in the head* —*U.S. News & World Report*⟩ — **knock out of the box** : to cause (an opposing pitcher) to retire from a baseball game by hitting pitched balls with marked effectiveness — **knock spots off** *or* **knock the spots off** *also* **knock spots out of** : to surpass eminently : excel by far ⟨she *knocks spots off* anybody I've seen in London —J.B.Priestley⟩ — **knock together** : to make or assemble esp. hurriedly or in a makeshift way ⟨*knocked together* his own desk and bookcase⟩

**²knock** \"\ *n* -s [ME *knokke, knok*, fr. *knokken, knoken*, v.] **1 a** : a short sharp fairly heavy blow : RAP ⟨a loud ~ on the door⟩ **b** (1) : a blow of misfortune or hard treatment ⟨the school of hard ~s had given him a tenacious grasp on reality —Dixon Wecter⟩ ⟨some of the disappointments and hard ~s life has dealt —A.B.Herr⟩ ⟨takes the ~s of the world —M.N. Todd⟩ (2) : something that checks, interrupts, or reverses good conditions or progress : SETBACK, REVERSAL, UPSET ⟨appeared to receive a damaging ~ from the events —Mollie Panter-Downes⟩ **2 a** : a rattling, thumping, or pounding noise (as of loose connecting rods in a machine or as of uneven combustion in an internal-combustion engine) ⟨was worried by the ~ in his car⟩ **b** : DETONATION 2 ⟨a motor fuel that is not subject to ~⟩ **3** : a piece of often petty faultfinding or of adverse and often captious criticism ⟨likes praise but can't stand the ~s⟩ ⟨can take the ~s, not worrying what people say —Stella Molony⟩ **4** : an innings in cricket ⟨won the toss and decided to take first ~⟩

**knock about** *or* **knock around** *vt* **1** : to cause to move irregularly and abruptly from one point to another by or as if by repeated blows : JOLT, JAR ⟨the crowd pushed and shoved and the two boys got *knocked about*⟩ **2** : to treat roughly or subject to difficulties and hardship : mistreat physically or mentally ⟨has been pretty badly *knocked around* during his life⟩ ⟨come into life with large preconceived ideas and are *knocked about* in consequence —Lionel Trilling⟩

**1knockabout** \ˈ⸗⸗ˌ⸗\ *adj* [*knock about*] **1 :** designed or suitable for rough or casual informal use ⟨a ~ clothing⟩ ⟨a ~ travel valise⟩ **2 a :** noisy and rough **:** boisterously violent ⟨was especially fond of ~ games⟩ ⟨~ diversions⟩ **b :** marked by, given to, or skilled at boisterously funny antics and farce and often extravagant burlesque or slapstick ⟨a ~ film comedy⟩ ⟨a ~ vaudeville act⟩ ⟨~ comedians in baggy pants —*Time*⟩ **3 :** marked by or given to irregular, haphazard, or aimless wandering about **:** traveling about carelessly or like a vagrant **:** ROAMING ⟨are afraid the place is full of ~ single men —O.E. Rölvaag⟩

**2knockabout** \ʺ\ *n* -s [partly fr. *1knockabout;* partly fr. *knock about*] **1 a** (1) **:** a performer of knockabout comedy ⟨a couple of vaudeville ~*s*⟩ (2) **:** a performance or instance of knockabout comedy ⟨a grave ceremony that gradually turned into hilarious ~⟩ **b :** boisterous farcical humor of the kind found in knockabout comedy ⟨the rehearsal scene was good ~ —Leslie Rees⟩ **2 a** *Austral* **:** a handyman on a sheep station **b :** one that wanders about or travels in an irregular, haphazard, or aimless way **:** WANDERER, VAGRANT ⟨a man without family, a ~ —D.C.Peattie⟩ **3 :** a sloop with a simplified rig marked by absence of bowsprit and topmast and by having a single headsail on the forestay **4 :** something designed or suitable for rough or casual informal use: as **a :** an article of clothing (as a coat, hat) designed or suitable for such use **b :** an unpretentious vehicle esp. designed or suitable for short trips or other casual informal use ⟨a secondhand car that will serve as a ~⟩ ⟨was now in a one-cylinder ~ which in every way lived up to its name —William Beebe⟩

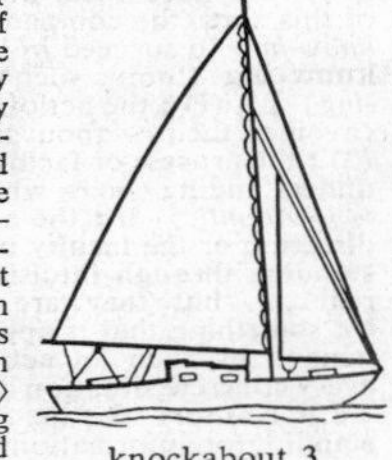
knockabout 3

**knockaway** *var of* KNACKAWAY

**knock back** *vt, chiefly Brit* **:** SWALLOW; *specif* **:** to toss down (an alcoholic beverage) ⟨smelt of the brandy they had just been *knocking back* —Bruce Marshall⟩

**knock-back** \ˈ⸗ˌ⸗\ *n* -s [fr. *knock back,* v.] *Austral* **:** REBUFF, REFUSAL ⟨he's had a *knock-back* from his old man —John Morrison⟩

**knock down** *vt* **1 a** (1) **:** to strike to the ground or lay low with or as if with a short sharp blow **:** FELL, PROSTRATE ⟨hit him on the chin and *knocked* him *down*⟩ (2) **:** to lower in degree **:** tone down **:** put down ⟨needs to have his self-esteem *knocked down*⟩ **:** HUMBLE, HUMILIATE ⟨try not to frustrate him or *knock down* his cap —*Education Digest*⟩ **b :** to hit with or as if with a projectile or other missile and cause to fall **:** shoot down ⟨thinking of ways to *knock* planes *down* from the skies —J.P. Baxter b.1893⟩ **:** bring down by a shot **:** POT ⟨*knocking down* game birds⟩ **c** (1) **:** to dispose of effectively **:** put out of the way **:** get rid of **:** ELIMINATE, QUASH ⟨each objection had been *knocked down* —*Times Lit. Supp.*⟩ (2) *Austral* **:** to spend (money) with abandon ⟨*knock down* their checks there —George Farwell⟩ **d :** to check or abate (flames or heat) at the edges of a blazing area **e :** to cause (a vessel) to heel over or list heavily or beyond recovery ⟨lets the wind blow on both sides of the sail . . . and the boat cannot be *knocked down* —Peter Heaton⟩ **2 :** to dispose of to or as if to a bidder at an auction sale ⟨*knocked* the clock *down* for a trifling sum⟩ **3 :** to take apart (something assembled) typically for convenience of moving, packing, storing, or shipping **:** DISASSEMBLE ⟨*knocked* the table *down* before boxing it⟩ **4 a** *slang* (1) **:** to appropriate dishonestly **:** STEAL ⟨*knocked down* plenty of the cash without getting caught⟩ (2) **:** ROB ⟨*knocked down* a bank⟩ **b :** to receive as income or salary **:** make by earning **:** EARN, DRAW, GET ⟨positions where they were able to *knock down* good money —*Infantry Jour.*⟩ ⟨were *knocking down* close to $150,000 a year —*Newsweek*⟩ **5 :** to hammer out the round and joints of (a book to be rebound) after removal of the cover; *also* **:** to flatten out the frayed ends of (cords or bands) after lacing in **6 :** to make a reduction in (an amount) **:** REDUCE, LOWER ⟨*knocked* the price *down* a dollar or two⟩ **7 :** LOWERCASE ⟨*knocking down* an initial letter that had been printed as a capital⟩ ~ *vi* **1 :** to be adaptable to being knocked down ⟨a portable device that easily *knocks down*⟩ **2** *of wind or a body of water* **:** to become tranquil **:** SUBSIDE ⟨the sea was *knocking down* steadily —R.F.Mirvish⟩

**1knockdown** \ˈ⸗ˌ⸗\ *n* -s [*knock down*] **1 a** (1) **:** the action of knocking down ⟨a general ~ of prices —*Newsweek*⟩ (2) **:** the condition of being knocked down; *specif* **:** the condition of a ship (as a sailboat) that is heeling over, listing heavily, or beyond recovery from the impact of wind or water **b** (1) **:** a temporary or permanent disordered state that is produced in an insect by an insecticide or other control agent and that is marked by cessation of the insect's normal activity and often followed by the insect's death (2) **:** the degree to which an insecticide or other control agent successfully incapacitates or kills insects (3) **:** the percentage of a test group of insects that is successfully incapacitated or killed by an insecticide or other control agent — compare KILL 1c **2 a :** a blow that knocks down ⟨watched for the first ~ in the fight⟩ **b :** an overwhelming or crushing blow (as of misfortune) **:** a severe setback ⟨it was a bad ~ for both of us —Lucien Price⟩ **3 :** something (as a piece of furniture) that can easily be assembled or disassembled **4** *slang* **:** an introduction to a person ⟨give a guy a ~ to your girl friends —Jerome Weidman⟩

**2knockdown** \ʺ\ *adj* [partly fr. *knock down;* partly fr. *1knockdown*] **1 a :** that knocks down or is capable of knocking down ⟨a ~ jab to the jaw⟩ **:** having such force or strength as to strike down **:** PROSTRATING, INCAPACITATING ⟨his schemes have met a ~ blow —Amy Lowell⟩ ⟨the ~ power of an insecticide⟩ **b** (1) **:** that cannot be successfully opposed **:** OVERWHELMING, OVERPOWERING ⟨a bewildering assortment of ~ arguments —J.W.Krutch⟩ ⟨would provide an almost ~ proof —A.G.N.Flew⟩ **:** CRUSHING ⟨a ~ defeat⟩ (2) **:** pushing hindrances or objections relentlessly aside by sheer force or drive **:** BULLDOZING ⟨his ~ style of polemics —W.E.Woodward⟩ **:** bluntly assured **:** CATEGORICAL ⟨he had his ~ answer for anyone who questioned his qualifications —Van Wyck Brooks⟩ **c :** KNOCK-DOWN-AND-DRAG-OUT ⟨can explode any moment into a ~ fight —*Newsweek*⟩ **2 a :** that can easily be put together or taken apart (as for convenience of storing or shipping) **:** made up of parts that are readily assembled or disassembled ⟨a ~ piece of furniture⟩ **b :** KNOCKED-DOWN **3 a :** lowest possible **:** MINIMUM ⟨the auctioneer set the ~ bid at $5.00⟩ **b :** extremely low ⟨can make the trip at ~ cost⟩ **:** REDUCED ⟨bought supplies at ~ prices⟩

**1knock-down-and-drag-out** \ˈ⸗ˌ⸗⸗ˌ⸗ˌ⸗\ *or* **knock-down, drag-out** \ˈ⸗ˌ⸗ˈ⸗ˌ⸗\ *adj* [*knock down* + *and* + *drag out,* v.] **:** marked by extreme violence or bitterness and by the giving of no quarter **:** carried to the last extremity ⟨a *knock-down-and-drag-out* fight⟩ ⟨*knock-down-and-drag-out* political debates⟩ ⟨one of the toughest *knock-down, drag-out* little battles ever fought —*Infantry Jour.*⟩

**2knock-down-and-drag-out** \ʺ\ *n* -s **:** a knock-down-and-drag-out fight or controversy ⟨are both spoiling for a real *knock-down-and-drag-out* on this issue —*New Republic*⟩

**knocked** *past of* KNOCK

**knocked-down** \ˈ⸗ˈ⸗\ *adj* [fr. past part. of *knock down*] **:** not assembled or only partly assembled **:** consisting of parts that can be assembled ⟨prefabricated *knocked-down* buildings⟩ — abbr. *K.D.*

**knock·er** \ˈnäkə(r)\ *n* -s [ME *knokker,* fr. *knokken* to knock + *-er* — more at KNOCK] **1 :** one that knocks: as **a :** a usu. ornamental fixture attached to the outer surface of a door and consisting typically of a metal plate to which a metal ring or bar or hammer is hinged that may be raised and lowered with sharp force against the surface of the plate or door so as to produce a rapping noise designed to indicate one's desire to gain admittance **b** *dial Eng* **:** a spirit or goblin believed to dwell in mines and to show by knocking where ore is **c :** a faultfinder or a person given to adverse often captious criticism ⟨when I see a ~ and a troublemaker I let him know what I think of him —L.B.Salomon⟩ **d** (1) **:** a slaughterhouse worker who stuns cattle with a sledgehammer before they are killed (2) **:** one that knocks ripe fruit (as prunes, olives, nuts) from trees typically with a rubber mallet and a pole (3) **:** CAKE PULLER **2 :** BREAST — often considered vulgar **3 :** TESTIS — often considered vulgar **4** *slang* **:** FELLOW ⟨that fish is a big ~⟩ **:** GUY ⟨hit the dirty ~ right in the jaw⟩ — **up to the knocker** *slang Brit* **1 :** up to par ⟨didn't feel *up to the knocker*⟩ **2 :** up to the fullest or best possible extent or degree ⟨was prepared *up to the knocker*⟩

knocker 1a

**knocker–off** \ˈ⸗⸗ˈ⸗\ *n, pl* **knockers–off** *or* **knocker–offs** [*knock off* + *-er*] **1 :** a worker who knocks temporary hoops from barrels by hand or by machine after heads and permanent hoops have been placed **2 :** a worker who uses a chisel to break apart castings and remove sprues from molded and cast articles

**knocking** *pres part of* KNOCK

**knocking over** *n, pl* **knockings over** *or* **knocking overs** [fr. gerund of *knock over*] **:** the action of a knitting machine device that pushes the newly formed loops off the needles

**knocking shop** *n* [fr. gerund of *knock* "to copulate with", fr. *1knock*] *slang Brit* **:** BROTHEL

**knock–knee** \ˈ⸗ˌ⸗\ *n* **:** a condition in which the legs curve inward at the knees as a result of disease or unphysiologic stresses on the bones ⟨afflicted with *knock-knee*⟩

**knock–kneed** \ˈ⸗ˈ⸗\ *adj* **1 :** having knock-knee ⟨an emaciated *knock-kneed* child⟩ **2 a :** functioning or moving awkwardly or jerkily or laboriously ⟨a *knock-kneed* mind⟩ ⟨*knock-kneed* lines of verse⟩ **:** LIMPING, LAME, INEPT, WEAK ⟨a *knock-kneed* excuse⟩ **b :** devoid of smoothness and grace **:** CLUMSY, GAUCHE ⟨a *knock-kneed* collection of provincial practitioners —*Times Lit. Supp.*⟩ ⟨a *knock-kneed* vase in the foreground —H.L.Mencken⟩

**knock–knees** \ˈ⸗ˌ⸗\ *n pl* **:** knees that approach each other or knock together because of knock-knee ⟨developed *knock-knees* at an early age⟩

**knock·less** \ˈnäkləs\ *adj* **:** having or producing no knock ⟨a ~ motor fuel⟩ **:** devoid of knocks ⟨the easy sheltered ~ unshocked life —*Forum*⟩

**knock–me–down** \ˈ⸗⸗ˌ⸗\ *adj* **:** that overpowers or overwhelms **:** BULLDOZING ⟨*knock-me-down* Johnsonian pragmatism —George Saintsbury⟩ ⟨a *knock-me-down* doctrine —Joseph Conrad⟩

**knockmeter** \ˈ⸗ˌ⸗⸗\ *n* **:** an instrument that measures the intensity of knock (sense 2)

**knock off** *vi* **1 :** to discontinue doing something; *specif* **:** to cease from work or some other occupation ⟨*knocks off* for several days and lolls about in pajamas —E.P.Snow⟩ **2** *slang* **:** DIE ~ *vt* **1 a :** to do esp. in a hurried or routine way **:** take care of **:** get through with **:** attend to **:** DISPATCH ⟨*knocking off* routine duties with very little thought⟩ **b :** to produce esp. roughly or hastily **:** turn out hurriedly ⟨*knocks off* one book after another⟩ **2 a** (1) **:** to discontinue (work or some other occupation) **:** leave off ⟨arranged that they should *knock off* work at five —Nevil Shute⟩ **:** desist from **:** STOP, QUIT (2) **:** to cause to leave off from (work or some other indicated occupation) **:** DISMISS ⟨the foreman *knocked off* the workers for lunch⟩ ⟨told them he was tired of their talking and that he wished they would *knock it off*⟩ **b :** to dispense with **:** pass over **:** SKIP ⟨hoped that the usual inspection would be *knocked off*⟩ **3 :** DEDUCT ⟨*knocked off* 20 cents to make the price more attractive⟩ **4 a :** to take into custody **:** SEIZE, ARREST, NAB ⟨had enough sense not to get *knocked off* by the police —Richard Llewellyn⟩ **b :** RAID ⟨*knocked off* a gambling joint⟩ **5 a :** KILL, MURDER ⟨*knocked off* two men, purely on mercenary grounds —Lewis Baker⟩ **b :** OVERCOME, DESTROY ⟨*knocked off* each center of rebellion⟩ **c :** to get rid of **:** ELIMINATE ⟨*knocked off* every objection⟩ ⟨usually has to *knock off* only one or two opponents —W.S.Carlson⟩ **d :** to dispose of to or as if to a bidder at an auction sale **:** knock down **6 a** *slang* (1) **:** STEAL ⟨*knocked off* a few trinkets in the store⟩ (2) **:** ROB ⟨*knocked off* a couple of banks⟩ **b :** RECEIVE, GET, OBTAIN ⟨*knocks off* a Nobel prize —Ethel Merman⟩ **7 :** to swallow down **:** toss off **:** finish off ⟨ordered a schooner of beer and *knocked* it *off* with unaffected enthusiasm —A.J. Liebling⟩

**knock–off** \ˈ⸗ˌ⸗\ *n, pl* **knock–offs** [*knock off*] **1 :** the action of knocking off; *esp* **:** the automatic coming to a halt of a machine or of a part of a machine through the action of a device actuated when the functioning of the machine becomes faulty **2 :** a cam or other device designed to safeguard a machine or part of a machine from continuing to function when operation becomes faulty **3 :** the time set for leaving off from work or from some other occupation ⟨finished the greater part of the job long before *knock-off*⟩

**knock on** *vt* **:** to knock onward **:** knock forward; *specif* **:** to knock (the ball in rugby) forward in the direction of the opponents' dead-ball line with the hand or arm

**1knock–on** \ˈ⸗ˌ⸗\ *n, pl* **knock–ons** [*knock on*] **:** the action of knocking on

**2knock–on** \ʺ\ *adj* [*knock on*] **:** produced or projected as a result of the collision of an energetic particle (as a neutron or fission fragment) from outside an atom with an elementary particle inside ⟨a *knock-on* shower of particles⟩ ⟨a *knock-on* atom⟩ ⟨a *knock-on* electron⟩

**knock out** *vt* **1 a :** to produce esp. roughly or hastily **:** turn out hurriedly ⟨in that same month he *knocked out* eleven novelettes —*Time*⟩ **b :** to get through with **:** take care of esp. in a hurried or routine way **:** attend to **:** DISPATCH ⟨quickly *knocked out* the few things that had to be looked after⟩ **2 a** (1) **:** to fell (a boxing opponent) by hitting esp. on the chin and making unconscious or otherwise unable to rise or continue within a specified time ⟨*knocked* him *out* in the first round⟩ (2) **:** to make unconscious or to stupefy esp. by hitting on the head ⟨the flowerpot hit him on the head and *knocked* him *out*⟩ **b** (1) **:** to make the further use of impossible without replacement or repair **:** put out of commission **:** make inoperative ⟨telephone communications had been *knocked out*⟩ **:** DEMOLISH, DESTROY ⟨*knocking out* the bridges and an ammunition dump —Lee Rogow⟩ ⟨*knocked out* twelve transport aircraft —*Time*⟩ (2) **:** to put an effective end to **:** get rid of **:** ELIMINATE, CRUSH, SQUASH, SQUELCH ⟨*knocked out* commercial gambling —A.E.Stevenson †1965⟩ **3 a :** to make (as oneself) exhausted **:** tire out **:** wear out ⟨*knocked* themselves *out* with excessive work⟩ **b :** to exert (as oneself) to the breaking point or beyond endurance **:** exert to the utmost **:** drive to the point of exhaustion ⟨*knocking* myself *out* to get top grades —W.H.Whyte⟩ ⟨*knocked* ourselves *out* preparing for the grand opening —Polly Adler⟩ **4 :** to strike (the inverted bowl of a pipe of tobacco) on something or with something so as to cause burning or burned tobacco to fall out ⟨*knocked* his pipe *out* before refilling it⟩ **5 :** to knock out of the box ⟨the pitcher was *knocked out* in the fifth inning⟩

**1knockout** \ˈ⸗ˌ⸗\ *n* -s [*knock out*] **1** *Brit* **:** an auction or sale or similar transaction at which a combination (as of bidders) illegitimately forces out other potential competitors and arranges by prior agreement to have one member of the combination secure at a set price the thing being offered so as later to profitably dispose of the thing (as by reauctioning) **2 a** (1) **:** the act of knocking out or the condition of being knocked out (2) **:** a blow or attack that knocks out ⟨won the fight by a ~⟩ ⟨an attempted early ~ by the enemy —R.W. Stokley⟩ **b** (1) **:** termination of a bout in boxing that occurs when an opponent is knocked out (2) **:** TECHNICAL KNOCKOUT **3 :** something sensationally striking or attractive **:** something altogether out of the ordinary or superlatively excellent ⟨she combines looks with poise and is a ~ at any party⟩ ⟨a hilarious book that is a real ~⟩ ⟨has produced a new film that is a ~⟩ **4 a :** something (as a set of pins in a die) that can be loosened or forced out typically to release or force out something else (as work in a punch or die) **b** (1) **:** a partially punched-out or cutout piece esp. in metal or plastic designed to be forced out when an opening is required; *esp* **:** such a partially punched piece in the side of a junction box (2) **:** the hole produced when such a piece is forced out

**2knockout** \ʺ\ *adj* [partly fr. *knock out;* partly fr. *1knockout*] **1 a :** that knocks out: as (1) **:** that makes unconscious or stupefies ⟨delivered a ~ blow to the head⟩ ⟨mixed a ~ drink⟩ (2) **:** that incapacitates or puts out of commission or demolishes or destroys ⟨planned a ~ offensive against the enemy⟩ ⟨a ~ air attack⟩ (3) **:** that eliminates from competition ⟨only three teams were left in the running after the preliminary ~ matches⟩ **b :** that can be loosened or forced out ⟨removal of hot work from a press by means of ~ pins in the die⟩ or that is equipped with pieces that can be loosened or forced out ⟨metal file cases that are punched with ~ holes⟩ **2 :** sensationally striking or attractive or unusual or excellent ⟨wore a ~ dress⟩ ⟨ideas for a ~ gift⟩

**knockout drops** *n pl* **:** drops of a solution of a drug (as chloral hydrate) put into a drink and designed to make the drinker unconscious or stupefied

**knock over** *vt* **1 a** (1) **:** FELL, PROSTRATE **:** knock down ⟨*knocked* him *over* with one blow⟩ (2) **:** to upset badly **:** greatly disturb **:** OVERWHELM ⟨was *knocked over* by the news⟩ **b :** to get rid of **:** dispose of **:** ELIMINATE ⟨*knocked over* every difficulty⟩ **c :** to get through with **:** finish up with **:** DISPATCH ⟨*knocked over* a book a day —R.L.Taylor⟩ **2 a :** STEAL; *esp* **:** HIJACK ⟨*knocks over* a truckload of merchandise —J.B. Martin⟩ **b :** ROB ⟨*knocking over* a jewelry store —John McCarten⟩ **3 :** to receive as income or salary ⟨*knocks over* a good sum each year⟩ **4 :** to move strongly esp. to admiration or applause ⟨which for really brilliant suddenness of perception *knocks* one *over* completely —H.J.Laski⟩

**knockover** \ˈ⸗ˌ⸗⸗\ *n* -s [*knock over*] **:** the act of knocking over **:** the condition of being knocked over

**knock poker** *n* **:** a card game in which each player holds five cards and attempts to build a good poker hand but draws and discards as in rummy and may end the play by knocking

**knock rummy** *n* **:** rummy played by two to six players in which the winner is the player with the lowest count in unmatched cards and in which a player may end the play by knocking

**knocks** *pres 3d sing of* KNOCK, *pl of* KNOCK

**knock under** *vi, archaic* **:** to admit defeat **:** give in **:** give up **:** YIELD ⟨why should we *knock under* and go with the stream —H.D.Thoreau⟩

**knock up** *vt* **1 a** (1) **:** to arrange or devise esp. hurriedly or with little thought ⟨decided to *knock up* a tennis match⟩ **:** prepare quickly or without much care ⟨*knock up* a meal for us —Irwin Shaw⟩ (2) **:** to strike up casually ⟨*knocked up* an acquaintance with a few people⟩ **b :** to knock together ⟨two small wooden buildings, casually *knocked up* —Josephine Pinckney⟩ **c :** to practice informally with (as a tennis ball, shuttlecock) in warming up before a match (as in tennis, badminton, squash) **2** *Brit* **:** ROUSE, SUMMON; *specif* **:** to cause (as by knocking at the door) to awaken or rise from sleep or rest **3 a :** to make exhausted **:** knock out ⟨hurried too fast and it *knocked* me *up* —G.M.Hopkins⟩ **b** (1) **:** to put out of top condition **:** cause to deteriorate ⟨too much food and idleness had *knocked* them *up*⟩ (2) **:** to bring to an end **:** DESTROY ⟨unfair competition had *knocked up* the once flourishing business⟩ **c :** WOUND, HURT ⟨got pretty badly *knocked up*⟩ ⟨if I'm killed over there — that isn't likely, I'm more of the damned sort that gets *knocked up* —Ellen Glasgow⟩ **4 a :** to run up (as a score) **:** MAKE, ACHIEVE ⟨*knocking up* a good score⟩ **b** *Brit* **:** to receive as income or salary **:** EARN, GET **5** *slang* **:** to make pregnant ⟨no girls get married around here till they're *knocked up* —Ernest Hemingway⟩ **6 :** to make uneasy **:** DISTURB, BOTHER ⟨felt rather *knocked up* by the news⟩ **7 a** *Brit* **:** to knock down (sense 5) **b :** JOG 4 ~ *vi* **1 :** to become totally exhausted or otherwise unfit **:** break down ⟨a few of the beasts had *knocked up* and had to be abandoned —I.L. Idriess⟩ **2 :** to chance upon or meet up with something indicated — used with *against* ⟨*knocked up* against formidable difficulties⟩ ⟨happened to *knock up* against an old friend⟩ **3 :** to practice informally (as by volleying) in warming up before a match (as in tennis, badminton, squash)

**knockup** \ˈ⸗ˌ⸗\ *n* -s [*knock up*] **:** informal practice (as by volleying) in warming up before a match

**knockwurst** *var of* KNACKWURST

**knod·den** \ˈnäd³n, kə'n-\ *adj* [fr. obs. past part. of *knead*] *dial Eng* **:** KNEADED

**knö·del** *or* **knoe·del** \kə'nōedᵊl\ *n, pl* **knödel** *or* **knödels** *or* **knoedel** *or* **knoedels** [G *knödel,* fr. MHG, dim. of *knode* knot, fr. OHG *knodo* — more at KNOT] **:** DUMPLING

**knoe·ve·na·gel reaction** \kə'nə(r)vəˌnägəl-, kə'nōv-\ *or* **knoevenagel condensation** *n, usu cap K* [after Emil *Knoevenagel* †1921 Ger. chemist] **:** an aldol-type condensation catalyzed by amines that takes place between an aldehyde or ketone and a compound containing an active methylene group (as in esters of acetoacetic acid, malonic acid, or cyanoacetic acid)

**1knoll** \ˈnōl\ *n* -s [ME *knol,* fr. OE *cnoll;* akin to MHG *knolle* clod, lump, tuber, ON *knollr* mountaintop, OE *cnotta* knot — more at KNOT] **1 a** *now dial Eng* **:** the top of a hill **b** (1) **:** a usu. small rounded submerged elevation rising from the floor of a body of water; *esp* **:** the upper part or top of such an elevation (2) **:** a usu. rounded submerged projection of a shoal, reef, bank, or bar **2 :** a usu. small rounded land eminence **:** MOUND, HILLOCK

**2knoll** \ʺ\ *n* -s [ME, prob. alter. of *knel* — more at KNELL] *archaic* **:** KNELL

**3knoll** \ʺ\ *vb* -ED/-ING/-S [ME *knollen,* prob. alter. of *knellen* — more at KNELL] *archaic* **:** KNELL

**knolly** \-lē\ *adj* **:** marked by knolls ⟨a ~ section of the country⟩

**knoop hardness** \ˈnüp-\ *n, usu cap K* [after F. *Knoop,* 20th cent. Am. chemist] **:** the relative hardness of a material (as a metal) that is determined by the depth to which the bluntly pointed diamond pyramid of a special instrument will penetrate it

**knop** \ˈnäp\ *n* -s [ME *knoppe, knop,* fr. OE *-cnoppa;* akin to MLG *knuppe, knoppe* bud, MD *cnoppe* knob, bud, OHG *knopf* knot, bud, knob, ON *knyfill* short horn, OIr *gnobh* knot in wood, OE *cnotta* knot — more at KNOT] **:** a usu. ornamental knob: as **a :** a small rounded or angular ornamental enlargement or protuberance that is usu. at the mid or upper part of the stem of a vessel (as a chalice, goblet) or at the same part of the shank or shaft of some other object (as a candlestick, andiron) and that usu. serves as an aid in grasping or holding **b :** KNOB 1b **c :** a tiny ball, loop, or tuft of a fiber (as wool, silk, cotton) that is formed in or on a yarn, thread, or cloth and that is often of a color varying from that of the yarn, thread, or cloth or from that of other balls, loops, or tufts formed in or on the yarn, thread, or cloth

**knop·ite** \ˈnäˌpīt\ *n* -s [G *knopit,* fr. Adolf *Knop* †1893 Ger. mineralogist + G *-it* -ite] **:** perovskite containing cerium

**knopped** \ˈnäpt\ *adj* [ME, fr. *knoppe* + *-ed*] **:** having one or more knops ⟨a glass bowl with a ~ stem⟩ ⟨~ yarn⟩

**knop·per** \ˈnäpə(r)\ *n* -s [G; akin to OHG *knopf* knot, bud, knob] **:** a gall that is formed by a gall wasp on the leaves and immature acorns of various oaks and that is used in tanning and dyeing

**knop·pie spider** \ˈnäpē-\ *n* [Afrik *knoppie,* dim. of *knop* knob, bud — more at KNOBKERRIE] **:** either of two venomous spiders (*Latrodectus geometricus* and *L. indistinctus*) of southern Africa that are closely related to the American black widow

**knop's solution** \ˈnäps-, kəˈnōps-\ *n, usu cap K* [after J. A. L. W. *Knop* †1891 Ger. chemist] **:** a nutrient solution used in growth experiments with higher plants and containing definite proportions of calcium nitrate, potassium nitrate, magnesium sulfate, monobasic potassium phosphate, and potassium chloride dissolved in water

**knop yarn** *n* **:** a ply yarn with knops that is often made by twisting one ply faster than another

**korhaan** *also* **knoorhaan** *var of* KORHAAN

**knor·ria** \ˈnōrēə, ˈnär-\ *n, cap* [NL, fr. Georg W. *Knorr* †1761 Ger. collector of petrified objects + NL *-ia*] **:** a form genus based on fossil stems of Carboniferous age that are intermediate in structure between those typical of the Lepidodendraceae and the Sigillariaceae

**knosp** \ˈnäsp\ *n* -s [G *knospe,* lit., bud; akin to OHG *knopf* knot, bud, knob — more at KNOP] *archaic* **:** KNOP

**knos·si·an** *also* **cnos·si·an** \(kə)ˈnäsēən, *chiefly Brit* -nōs-\ *adj, usu cap* [*Knossos* or *Cnossus,* city in ancient Crete (fr. Gk *Knōssos*) + E *-ian*] **:** of, relating to, or characteristic of the city of Knossos

[1]**knot** \ˈnät, *usu* -äd·+V\ *n* -s [ME *knotte, knot,* fr. OE *cnotta;* akin to OHG *knoto* & *knodo* knot, ON *knūtr* knot, *knūta* top of a bone, knuckle, Lith *gniùsti* to press, *gniùtulas* bale, paper, lump; basic meaning: to press together; something clumped together] **1 a** (1) **:** an intertwining, looping, bending, hitching, folding, gathering together, or tangling of one or more parts of a pliant relatively slender length of something in such a way as to produce a tying together, fastening, binding, or connecting of the length on, to, or with itself, another length, or some other thing ⟨a cord with ~*s* in it⟩ ⟨one rope was attached to another by a loose ~⟩ (2) **:** the interlacement or other disposition or arrangement or formation produced in a length by such manipulation ⟨wondered how to undo the ~⟩ (3) **:** a specific localized point or mass produced in a length by such manipulation; *esp* **:** a lump or knob or some other relatively tight mass produced in a length by such manipulation ⟨made heavy ~*s* in the rope every five feet⟩ (4) **:** a bow or rosette or cockade or epaulet or some other ornamental arrangement of a material (as ribbon) produced by such manipulation ⟨wore a faded red worsted ~, the emblem of his rank, on his left shoulder —F.V.W.Mason⟩ (5) **:** a length of hair rolled or coiled or twisted into a usu. tight mass on the head **:** BUN ⟨with iron-gray hair in a ~ on top of her head —Marcia Davenport⟩ **b :** something perplexingly intricate or involved or difficult **:** a problem or complication that cannot be easily solved ⟨a matter full of legal ~*s*⟩ **c :** something that ties or binds together **:** a bond of union ⟨the two nations renewed the ~ between them —R.W.Van Alstyne⟩; *esp* **:** the bond of marriage ⟨hoped to loose the ~ by divorce⟩ **d :** the central point or heart of something **:** the hard center **:** NUB, CORE, ESSENCE ⟨confront the ~ of meaning—*Western Rev.*⟩ ⟨the very ~ and center of my being —R.L.Stevenson⟩; *esp* **:** the heart of something complicated or problematical ⟨the very ~ of the difficulty —W.E.Gladstone⟩ **2 a** (1) **:** a usu. firm or hard lump or swelling or protuberance in or on a part of an animal body or bone or process ⟨a ~ in a gland⟩ ⟨a pendulous fold of flesh full of ~*s*⟩ ⟨a bone with two or three ~*s*⟩ ⟨a ~ at the end of the animal's horn⟩; *esp* **:** an often contorted lump or swelling or protuberance in a muscle ⟨strained at the oars until the muscles of their arms stood out in ~*s*⟩ (2) **:** a puckering or furrowing or wrinkling of the lower central area of the forehead typically occurring in deep concentration or as an indication of displeasure ⟨went over it slowly with the ~ between his brows —Vincent McHugh⟩ (3) **:** a tight constriction or the sensation of such a constriction ⟨music that dissolved the ~*s* in their minds —Van Wyck Brooks⟩ ⟨his throat caught in a dry ~, his head felt leaden —Marcia Davenport⟩ ⟨moving slowly, as in a dream, his stomach in a ~ —Gregor Felsen⟩ (4) **:** a constricted or contorted mass **:** a tight bundle ⟨I was tired and tense, my nerves were in ~*s* —Polly Adler⟩ **b :** a lump or swelling or protuberance in or on a part of a plant: as (1) **:** the node of a grass (2) **:** a protuberance or an excrescence on a stem or branch or root; *esp* **:** a hard irregular lump formed at the point where a branch grows out of the trunk of a tree ⟨the first American settlers employed . . . pine ~*s*, which were dipped in pitch and burned with a bright but smoky flame —A.L.Powell⟩ (3) *chiefly dial Brit* **:** BUD, BLOOM — used esp. in the phrase *in the knot* ⟨now the hawthorn is coming in the ~⟩ **c :** a relatively small concreted mass that may occur in rocks or in precious stones or in glass or in similar objects or substances and that is typically harder than the surrounding material or that otherwise differs (as in the direction of its grain) from the surrounding material **d :** a cross section of the hard lump on a tree trunk from which a branch grows out and which appears in a board as a rounded usu. cross-grained area that may fall out and leave an irregular hole **e :** a fungous disease of trees marked by the development of abnormal excrescences **3 a :** an ornamental usu. carved or hammered knob, boss, or stud **b :** an ornamental often functional mass (as a corbel or similar member or as the capital of a column) used in architecture and consisting typically of carved or sculptured foliage **4** *now dial Brit* **:** a hill or similar land eminence of moderate height; *esp* **:** a rocky hill of moderate height **5 a :** a small group of persons closely clustered together ⟨~*s* of people talking and arguing on street corners —S.V.Benét⟩ ⟨a chatty little ~ at the back of PTA meetings —Bice Clemow⟩ **b :** CLUMP ⟨a ~ of palm trees⟩ **:** BUNCH ⟨a ~ of drooping dandelions⟩ **6** *now chiefly dial* **:** KNOT GARDEN **7 :** a measured length of yarn, thread, or cord **8 a** (1) **:** one of the lengths marked off on a log line each of which is 47 feet 3 inches in extent and has the same relation to one nautical mile as 28 seconds has to one hour so that the number of such divisions running out from the log reel within a 28-second interval will indicate that the identical number of nautical miles will be covered within one hour by the ship if it maintains the same speed (2) **:** the point marking the dividing line between each such length **b :** one nautical mile per hour — used as a unit of measurement in expressing the rate of speed of seagoing ships and of airplanes and in expressing the relative strength of water currents and the degree of intensity of air currents ⟨a ship that logs 10 ~*s*⟩ ⟨a plane traveling 450 ~*s*⟩ ⟨a 30-*knot* wind⟩; abbr. *kn., kt., k.* **c :** one nautical mile ⟨the ship reached a speed of 12 ~*s* an hour⟩ — not used technically **9 :** an elevated land region formed by the juncture of several mountain regions **10 :** a space curve that is closed

[2]**knot** \"\ *vb* **knotted; knotted; knotting; knots** [ME *knott*] *vt* **1 a** (1) **:** to tie, fasten, bind, or connect with a knot **:** do up or secure with a knot ⟨*knotted* his clothes into a tight bundle⟩ (2) **:** to tie into a knot **:** form into a knot ⟨*knotted* the shoelace and couldn't untie it⟩ **b** (1) **:** to make a knot in or cause to be full of knots ⟨broad soft neckties, which he *knotted* in large loose bows —Laura Krey⟩ ⟨*knotted* the rope every five feet⟩ (2) **:** to make (lace, net, or other fancywork) by twisting and looping thread into knots to form designs **2 a** (1) **:** to unite closely or bind firmly together **:** cause to be closely joined or associated ⟨the ties of blood that were *knotted* into all the relationships of communal life —Oscar Handlin⟩ (2) **:** to group closely together ⟨their horses were *knotted* about an instructor —Hugh MacLennan⟩ (3) **:** to pull together ⟨official and private problems ~ the plot into an intriguing pattern —Fanny Butcher⟩ **b :** to cause to be joined in a confused or tangled way **:** ENTANGLE ⟨ligatures, i.e. combinations in which two or more letters are *knotted* together and lose their original shape —E.H.Minns⟩ ⟨creepers of many kinds . . . *knotting* the undergrowth into impenetrable thickets —C.D. Forde⟩ **3 :** to cause (the forehead or brows) to become knitted ⟨saw him ~ and unknot his eyebrows —Donn Byrne⟩ **4 :** to make (the score of an athletic contest or other competition) even **:** tie up **:** EQUALIZE ⟨slammed in a 30-footer to ~ it again at 3 all —John Drebinger⟩ **5 :** to cover the knots of (wood) with a conditioning preparation (as shellac) before painting ~ *vi* **1 a :** to form knots **:** become knotted ⟨wet cords tend to ~⟩ ⟨took a long drink, the raw alcohol *knotting* and burning in his chest —Irwin Shaw⟩ ⟨the men bent forward, grunting deep in their lungs, their belly muscles *knotting* with the pull of the oars —Frank Yerby⟩ — often used with *up* ⟨the tendons of his legs began to ~ up —Andrew Hamilton⟩ **b :** to form a constricted or contorted mass **:** form lumps ⟨planets . . . were formed by a process of shriveling and *knotting* —Waldemar Kaempffert⟩ **2 :** to become gathered together into a small group **:** cluster together ⟨commandomen, who roamed here and there, *knotting* into groups for the exchange of experiences —John Brophy⟩ **3 :** to make lace, net, or other fancywork by twisting and looping thread into knots to form designs

[3]**knot** \"\ *n* -s **:** any of several sandpipers (genus *Calidris*) that breed in the Arctic and winter in temperate or warm parts of the New and Old World: as **a :** a stocky gregarious Old World bird (*C. canutus*) whose plumage in the breeding season is chestnut and black above and that has a russet head and russet underparts **b :** a similar American bird that forms a subspecies (*C. canutus rufus*) and that is predominantly gray and spotted with black and ruddy brown above and that has a pale brown head and pale brown underparts **c :** a bird (*C. tenuirostris*) that is grayish brown to dark brown above with white underparts and white bars on the wings and tail and that breeds in northeastern Asia and winters southward to Australia — called also *great knot, Japanese knot*

**knot bindweed** *n* **:** BLACK BINDWEED 1

**knot garden** *n* **1 :** an elaborately designed garden esp. of flowers or herbs **2 :** a piece of ground marked by shrubbery or small trees arranged in an intricately formal pattern and typically trimmed into ornamental and often bizarre shapes **:** TOPIARY

**knotgrass** \ˈ=,=\ *n* **1 :** a common cosmopolitan weed (*Polygonum aviculare*) with jointed stems, prominent sheathing stipules, and minute flowers **2 :** any of several grasses (as fiorin oat grass) with geniculate stems; *esp* **:** JOINT GRASS 1

**knothead** \ˈ=,=\ *n* **:** a dull-witted blunderer **:** DUMBBELL, SIMPLETON

**knothole** \ˈ=,=\ *n* **:** a hole in a board or tree trunk where a knot or branch has come out

**knot·less** \ˈnätləs\ *adj* **:** devoid of knots

**knotroot** \ˈ=,=\ *n* **1 :** CHINESE ARTICHOKE **2 :** HORSE BALM 1

**knotroot grass** *n* **:** a No. American grass (*Muhlenbergia mexicana*) used as a soil binder and as hay

**knots** *pl of* KNOT, *pres 3d sing of* KNOT

**knot sawyer** *n* **:** one who saws defective parts from lumber

**knot·ted** \ˈnäd·əd, -ätəd\ *adj* [ME, fr. *knotte, knot* knot + *-ed*] **:** KNOTTY; *esp* **:** twisted or contorted and marked by swollen joints ⟨had been wringing nothing but a scanty living from the soil with their gnarled and ~ hands —C.A. & Mary Beard⟩

**knot·ter** \ˈäd·ə(r), -ätə-\ *n* -s **1 :** one that makes knots: as **a :** a worker who makes nets by hand **b :** a device that knots threads **2 :** one that removes knots: as **a :** a device used in papermaking by which lumps are removed from paper pulp **b :** LIMBER

**knotter bill** *or* **knotter hook** *n* **:** KNOTTING BILL

**knot·ti·ly** \-äd·əlē\ *adv* **:** in a knotty manner ⟨a ~ involved problem⟩

**knot·ti·ness** \-äd·|ēnəs, -ät|, |in-\ *n* -ES **:** the quality or state of being knotty ⟨bewildered by the ~ of the legal points involved⟩

**knotting** *n* -s **1 :** fancywork produced by twisting and looping thread into knots to form designs **2 :** a conditioning preparation (as shellac) used to cover the knots of wood before painting

**knotting bill** *or* **knotting hook** *n* **:** a metal hook with a blunt point on which is formed the knot that secures a quantity of grain gathered up by a grain binder

**knot·ty** \ˈnäd·|ē, -ät|, |i\ *adj, usu* -ER/-EST [ME *knotty*, fr. *knotte*, *knot* knot + *-y* — more at KNOT] **:** marked by or full of knots: as **a :** full of difficulties or complications **:** hard to solve or understand **:** INVOLVED, PUZZLING, INTRICATE ⟨the ~ problems of a complex society —V.L.Parrington⟩ ⟨~ points of international law —Lisle Bell⟩ **b :** tied in or with knots ⟨a ~ rope⟩ **c** (1) **:** twisted or contorted and marked by protuberances **:** GNARLED ⟨ancient ~ trees⟩ **:** BUMPY, KNOBBY ⟨her old ~ hands⟩ (2) **:** having many hard irregular lumps at the points where branches grow out ⟨cut down a ~ tree trunk⟩ (3) **:** showing cross sections of such lumps or having knotholes ⟨~ pieces of lumber⟩ **d :** marked by or indicative of robustness or ruggedness **:** WIRY, TOUGH ⟨a sinewy ~ strength —Jack London⟩ **syn** see COMPLEX

**knotty brake** *n* **:** MALE FERN

**knotty gut** *n* **:** NODULAR DISEASE

**knotty guts** *n pl* **1** *sing or pl in constr* **:** NODULAR DISEASE **2 :** intestines affected with nodular disease

**knotty pine** *n* **1 :** LODGEPOLE PINE **2 :** pine wood marked by an esp. decorative distribution of knots when finished for use unpainted esp. on walls or ceilings

**knotty rhatany** *n* **:** PERUVIAN RHATANY

**knotweed** \ˈ=,=\ *n* **:** any of several plants of the genus *Polygonum; esp* **:** KNOTGRASS 1

**knotweed spurge** *n* **:** SEASIDE SPURGE

[1]**knout** \ˈnau̇t, ˈnüt\ *n* -s [Russ *knut*, of Scand origin; akin to ON *knūtr* knot — more at KNOT] **:** a flogging whip with a lash of leather thongs twisted with wire used for punishing criminals

[2]**knout** \"\ *vt* -ED/-ING/-S **:** to flog with a knout

[1]**know** \ˈnō\ *vb* **knew** \ˈn(y)ü\ *or dial* **knowed** \ˈnōd\ **known** \ˈnōn *sometimes* -ōən\ *also dial* **knowed; knowing; knows** [ME *knowen, knawen,* fr. OE *cnāwan;* akin to OHG *bichnāan* to recognize, ON *knā* I can, L *gnoscere, noscere* to become acquainted with, come to know, Gk *gignōskein* to come to know, perceive, OSlav *znati* to know, Skt *jānāti* he knows] *vt* **1 a** (1) **:** to apprehend immediately with the mind or with the senses **:** perceive directly **:** have direct unambiguous cognition of ⟨taught that one could come to ~ objective truth⟩ (2) **:** to have perception, cognition, or understanding of esp. to an extensive or complete extent ⟨learning to ~ one's mind —Virgil Thomson⟩ ⟨insisted on the importance of ~*ing* oneself⟩ (3) **:** to recognize the quality of **:** see clearly the character of **:** DISCERN ⟨*knew* him for what he was⟩ ⟨~*s* him as honest and reliable⟩ (4) **:** to recognize in a specific capacity ⟨one glance and they ~ him as the one destined to lead them⟩ **b** (1) **:** to apprehend as being the same as something previously apprehended **:** recognize as being an object of perception identical with a previous object of perception **:** recognize as familiar ⟨*knew* her father as soon as she saw him⟩ ⟨said they would ~ that face anywhere⟩ (2) **:** to have acquaintance or familiarity with through experience or acquisition of information or hearsay ⟨*knew* no such restraints —Hugh Seton-Watson⟩ ⟨*knew* the law fairly well⟩ ⟨~*s* foreign languages⟩; *specif* **:** to have personal acquaintance with (a person) ⟨whom he had learned to ~ and love —Allen Johnson⟩ ⟨recognizes many people by sight but doesn't ~ them all⟩ (3) **:** to have experience of ⟨the region has *known* a steadily increasing . . . number of visitors —S.H.Holbrook⟩ ⟨*knew* great delight⟩ ⟨did not ~ happiness with the woman he married —Ruth P. Randall⟩ **c :** to apprehend as being distinct from something previously apprehended **:** recognize as being an object of perception distinct from a previous object of perception **:** recognize as distinct **:** DISTINGUISH ⟨barely able to ~ one thing from another⟩ **2 a :** to have cognizance, consciousness, or awareness of **:** have within the mind as something apprehended, learned, or understood ⟨*knew* they could never have what city folks had —M.W.Straight⟩ ⟨~*s* that this is quite true⟩ ⟨*knew* many would not believe him⟩ ⟨didn't ~ who she was or where she was going⟩ ⟨was *known* to be a friend of hers⟩ **b :** to have a practical understanding of or a distinct skill in through instruction, study, practice, or experience ⟨~*s* how to write vividly —William Clerk⟩ ⟨~*s* the fundamentals perfectly⟩ **3 :** to apprehend with certitude as true, factual, sure, or valid **:** perceive or have within the mind's grasp with clarity and the conviction of certainty **:** have certitude about and clear comprehension of ⟨~ what they want and intend to get it⟩ ⟨*knew* the solution to almost any problem⟩ **4** *archaic* **:** to have sexual intercourse with ~ *vi* **1 a :** to have perception or cognition or understanding of something esp. to an extensive or complete extent ⟨you ~ better⟩ ⟨people who ~ will not waste their time that way⟩ ⟨we want to ~, we will not be content with a fairy tale of love —L.O.Coxe⟩ **b :** to have cognizance, consciousness, or awareness of something **:** be aware of the existence or fact of something ⟨*knew* of her but had not yet met her⟩ ⟨*knew* about what had happened⟩ **2 :** to have information **:** have acquaintance with facts ⟨*knew* differently and therefore refused the offer⟩ **3 :** to have something within the mind's grasp with certitude and clarity ⟨do you ~, or is that only your opinion⟩ — **know one's onions :** to know one's stuff — **know one's stuff :** to be thoroughly proficient or highly skilled in a field of activity or an area of knowledge **:** know the ropes ⟨can rely on her completely because she really *knows her stuff*⟩ — **know the ropes :** to have experience and understanding of the details, methods, and procedures involved in accomplishing or furthering something esp. without unnecessary delay ⟨*knew the ropes* and soon had everything organized smoothly⟩ — **not know from nothing** *slang* **:** to know nothing about something **:** be completely ignorant ⟨*don't know from nothing* —Erskine Caldwell⟩

[2]**know** \"\ *n* -s **:** the fact of knowing **:** KNOWLEDGE ⟨the inside ~ of a journalist —Douglass Cater⟩ — **in the know** *adv* (*or adj*) **:** in possession of confidential or otherwise relatively limited or exclusive knowledge, information, or awareness ⟨the sense of importance which comes from a feeling that one is *in the know* —Stanley Walker⟩ ⟨*in-the-know* intellectuals⟩

**know·abil·i·ty** \ˌnōəˈbiləd·ē\ *n* **:** capability of being known ⟨the question of the ~ of the external world —*Humanist*⟩

**know·able** \ˈnōəbəl\ *adj* **:** capable of being known ⟨the philosophical proposition that the external physical world around us and all its laws are fully ~ —*Atlantic*⟩ — **know·able·ness** *n* -ES

**know-all** *var of* KNOW-IT-ALL

**knowe** *or* **know** \ˈnō, ˈnau̇\ *chiefly Scot var of* KNOLL

**knowed** *past of* KNOW

**know·er** \ˈnōə(r)\ *n* -s [ME, fr. *knowen* to know + *-er* — more at KNOW] **:** one that knows

**know-how** \ˈ=,=\ *n* -s [fr. the phrase *know how*] **:** practical knowledge of how to do or accomplish something with smoothness and efficiency **:** ability to get something done with a minimum of wasted effort **:** accumulated practical skill or expertness ⟨business *know-how*⟩ ⟨needed the *know-how* of a good carpenter⟩ ⟨salesmanship *know-how*⟩ ⟨the *know-how* involved in producing a play⟩ ⟨developed his bowling *know-how*⟩; *esp* **:** technical knowledge, ability, skill, or expertness of this sort ⟨the company needed to use all its ingenuity and *know-how* to succeed in laying the oil lines⟩

[1]**know·ing** \ˈnōiŋ, -ōēŋ\ *n* -s [ME, fr. *knowen* to know + *-ing*] **1 a** (1) **:** the action or fact of knowing or understanding ⟨avoided their ~ about this⟩ ⟨her ~ was a source of comfort⟩ (2) **:** the process or faculty of getting to know or of arriving at understanding ⟨no ~ what may happen⟩ ⟨a power beyond his ~ —*Atlantic*⟩ **b :** the action of knowing by intuition or indirection or the faculty of getting to know or arrive at understanding through intuition or indirection ⟨the ~*s* of art are real . . . but they are not utterly reliable —H.J.Muller⟩ **c :** something that is apprehended or capable of being apprehended by such an action, process, or faculty ⟨underlying every concrete situation he sees the fusion of ~*s* and the known —J.R.Kantor⟩ **2 :** the condition or fact of possessing understanding or information or of being aware of something ⟨in private, in secret ~ —N.L.Rothman⟩

[2]**knowing** \"\ *adj, sometimes* -ER/-EST [ME, fr. pres. part. of *knowen* to know] **1 a :** having or reflecting knowledge, information, or insight **:** marked by understanding and intelligence **:** well-informed and marked by a ready capacity for further learning **:** KNOWLEDGEABLE ⟨a ~ student⟩ ⟨a ~ instructor⟩ **b** (1) **:** having or reflecting the keen awareness and insight and power of discernment typical of the specialist or expert **:** highly perceptive esp. in a specialized or exclusive field ⟨a ~ collector of rare books⟩ ⟨has done an excellent and ~ job in selecting the material for this book —J.C. Smith⟩ (2) **:** having or reflecting distinct skill ⟨~ brushwork on ceiling and doors —Claudia Cassidy⟩ **c** (1) **:** that indicates or is marked by awareness of and careful conformity to what is chic and currently in style **:** SMART ⟨a ~ selection of gloves and accessories⟩ (2) **:** marked by sophistication or snobbishness ⟨a distasteful air of pretentious smartness, of being altogether too ~ —Herbert Read⟩ **2 a** (1) **:** shrewd and keenly alert **:** QUICK-WITTED, ASTUTE ⟨a ~ handling of the business deal⟩ **:** WIDE-AWAKE ⟨any ~ person could have seen what was going on⟩ (2) **:** WORLDLY-WISE ⟨produces ~ chuckles —E.R.Bentley⟩ ⟨perhaps a bit too ~ and sensuous —Robert Lawrence⟩ **b :** that reflects or is designed to indicate possession of confidential, secret, or otherwise exclusive inside knowledge or information ⟨poised her fork and gave her guest a ~ look —Louis Bromfield⟩ ⟨a ~ wink⟩ ⟨maintain a discreet and ~ silence on the subject —Harry Gordon⟩ **:** that indicates an awareness or insight not generally shared ⟨the two young officers exchanged ~ glances —W.M.Thackeray⟩ **3 a :** that knows, is capable of knowing, or is the means of knowing **:** COGNITIVE ⟨in full possession of the ordinary ~ faculties⟩ **b** *archaic* **:** COGNIZANT ⟨~ to and familiar with the whole circumstances —George Catlin⟩ **4 :** that is done with awareness or deliberateness **:** that is intentional ⟨indiscriminate classification of innocent with ~ activity —*Civil Liberties*⟩ **syn** see INTELLIGENT

**know·ing·ly** *adv* [ME, fr. *knowing* + *-ly*] **:** in a knowing manner ⟨smiled ~⟩; *esp* **:** with awareness, deliberateness, or intention ⟨had never ~ hurt him —Max Peacock⟩

**know·ing·ness** *n* -ES **:** the quality or state of being knowing ⟨the brisk ~ of a competent journalist —C.J.Rolo⟩

[1]**know-it-all** \ˈ=,=,=\ *also* **know-all** \ˈ=,=\ *n, pl* **know-it-alls** *also* **know-alls :** one that rashly and annoyingly claims to know or acts as if knowing all about everything or nearly everything **:** one to whom nothing new can apparently be told or who views any advice or suggestion from others as of little or no value or as something that had already been considered and acted on or rejected ⟨loud cocky *know-it-alls*⟩ ⟨a humbling enigma for the *know-alls* —D.B.W.Lewis⟩

[2]**know-it-all** \"\ *also* **know-all** \"\ *adj* [[1]*know-it-all, know-all*] **:** of, relating to, or having the characteristics of a know-it-all ⟨a *know-it-all* attitude⟩ ⟨a *know-all* manner⟩ ⟨should not be so *know-it-all* about what the Almighty was up to —Gretchen Finletter⟩

**knowledgable** *var of* KNOWLEDGEABLE

[1]**knowl·edge** \ˈnälij, -lēj, -ləj, *Brit sometimes* ˈnōl-\ *vt* -ED/-ING/-S [ME *knawlechen, knowlechen,* irreg. fr. *knowen, knawen* to know — more at KNOW] **1** *obs* **:** to recognize as being something indicated **:** admit the status, claims, or authority of **:** ACKNOWLEDGE **2** *obs* **:** to recognize, admit, or confess the fact or truth of

[2]**knowledge** \"\ *n* -s [ME *knawlage, knowlage, knawlege, knowlege,* fr. *knawlechen, knowlechen,* v.] **1** *obs* **a :** ACKNOWLEDGMENT **b :** COGNIZANCE **2 :** the fact or condition of knowing: as **a** (1) **:** the fact or condition of knowing something with a considerable degree of familiarity gained through experience of or contact or association with the individual or thing so known ⟨a thorough ~ of life and its problems⟩ ⟨has a fair ~ of the people of that country⟩ ⟨a remarkable ~ of human nature⟩ (2) **:** acquaintance with or theoretical or practical understanding of some branch of science, art, learning, or other area involving study, research, or practice and the acquisition of skills ⟨~ of advanced mathematics⟩ ⟨has little ~ of the techniques of drawing and painting⟩ ⟨a ~ of foreign languages⟩ **b** (1) **:** the fact or condition of being cognizant, conscious, or aware of something ⟨was elated by ~ of their success⟩ ⟨the ~ that it was really important⟩ ⟨his ~ of what she had had to endure⟩ (2) **:** the particular existent range of one's information or acquaintance with facts **:** the scope of one's awareness **:** extent of one's understanding ⟨said that to the best of his ~ the matter had not yet been attended to⟩ **c :** the fact or condition of apprehending truth, fact, or reality immediately with the mind or senses **:** PERCEPTION, COGNITION ⟨intellective ~⟩ ⟨the nature of ~⟩ **:** COMPREHENSION, UNDERSTANDING ⟨intuitive ~⟩ ⟨proceeding from the lower to the higher degrees of ~⟩ **d :** the fact or condition of possessing within mental grasp through instruction, study, research, or experience one or more truths, facts, principles, or other objects of perception **:** the fact or condition of having information or of being learned or erudite ⟨a man of great ~⟩ ⟨always seeking after more and more ~⟩ **3** *archaic* **:** CARNAL KNOWLEDGE **4 a :** the sum total of what is known **:** the whole body of truth, fact, information, principles, or other objects of cognition acquired by mankind ⟨adding to the vast store of ~⟩ ⟨all branches of ~⟩ **b** *archaic* **:** a branch of learning **:** ART, SCIENCE

**syn** KNOWLEDGE, SCIENCE, LEARNING, ERUDITION, SCHOLARSHIP, INFORMATION, and LORE agree in signifying what is or can be known. KNOWLEDGE applies to any body of known facts or to any body of ideas inferred from such facts or accepted as truths on good grounds ⟨a *knowledge* of languages⟩ ⟨a *knowledge* of the habits of snakes⟩ ⟨a *knowledge* of modern chemistry⟩ ⟨to benefit by the accumulated *knowledge* of centuries⟩ SCIENCE still sometimes interchanges with KNOWLEDGE but commonly applies to a body of systematized knowledge comprising facts carefully gathered and general truths carefully inferred from them, often underlying a practice, usu. connoting exactness, and often denoting knowledge of unquestionable certainty ⟨must bear in mind that geographic discovery also is *science*, and it was a scientific theory that impelled the venture of Columbus —I.M.Price⟩ ⟨the defense of nations had become a *science* and a calling —T.B.Macaulay⟩ ⟨the *science* of administration —A.S.Link⟩ ⟨the art of feeding preceded the *science* of nutrition by many centuries —F.B. Hadley⟩ ⟨the diagnosis of disease is no longer primarily guesswork but rather a *science*⟩ LEARNING applies to knowledge gained by study, often long and careful and sometimes connoting comprehensiveness and profundity ⟨to expose children to as much *learning* as possible⟩ ⟨a full, rich, human book, packed with information lightly dispensed and fortified with *learning* easily worn —Honor Tracy⟩ ⟨a man of great and profound *learning* but little common sense⟩ ERUDITION usu. stresses wide, profound, or recondite learning, sometimes suggesting pedantry ⟨often flabbergast their elders with their *erudition* — a scholarly but lively sense of words, a sound background in history and economics, the ability to translate or even to speak two or three foreign languages —Stanley Walker⟩ ⟨all the encyclopedic *erudition* of the middle ages —J.L.Lowes⟩ ⟨balancing an immense load of *erudition* upon a precarious foundation of fact —*Times Lit. Supp.*⟩ SCHOLARSHIP implies the learning, careful mastery of detail, esp. of a given field, and the critical acumen characteristic of a good scholar ⟨the immense and rapidly expanding *scholarship* not only in psychology but in history, sociology, and anthropology as well, which illuminates the study of the family —Lynn White⟩ ⟨unusually equipped in both scientific and classical *scholarship* in addition to his command of his own field, a brilliant and powerful lecturer —E.S.Bates⟩ ⟨his learning and general *scholarship* were universally recognized, and in his special sphere of law he had no peer in this country —T.D. Bacon⟩ INFORMATION generally applies to knowledge, commonly accepted as true, of a factual kind usu. gathered from others or from books ⟨this book, packed with *information* of the life and movements of big game —*Times Lit. Supp.*⟩ ⟨to seek *information* about a man from friends and credit records⟩ ⟨a book of *information* about early river boats⟩ LORE suggests special, often arcane, knowledge, usu. of a traditional, anecdotal character and of a particular subject ⟨fairy *lore*⟩ ⟨one of the most bizarre occurrences in railroad *lore* —Bennett Cerf⟩ ⟨bird *lore*⟩ ⟨taught the *lore* of medicinal herbs —*Amer. Guide Series: La.*⟩

**knowl·edge·abil·i·ty** *also* **knowl·edg·abil·i·ty** \\ˌ⸗⸗əˈbiləd·ē, -lətē, -i\\ *n* **:** the quality or state of being knowledgeable

**knowl·edge·able** *also* **knowl·edg·able** \\ˈ⸗⸗əbəl\\ *adj* [²*knowledge* + *-able*] **1 a :** marked by or indicating intelligence or knowledge **:** mentally alert and well-informed **:** KNOWING ⟨~ about the technique of painting —Herbert Read⟩ ⟨the keenest and most ~ questions —Norman Cousins⟩ ⟨limousines with ~ chauffeur-guides —*advt*⟩ **b :** marked by a keen sense of discernment **:** marked by notable ability to evaluate and discriminate **:** highly perceptive **:** having awareness and insight ⟨a ~ critic⟩ ⟨sparse but ~ comments —*Newsweek*⟩ **2 a :** marked by an open receptive mind **:** not narrow-minded or otherwise intellectually cramped **:** not provincial in outlook **:** BROAD-MINDED, LIBERAL ⟨addressed himself to a ~ audience that he knew would not be shocked⟩ **b :** responsive and alive to intellectual or cultural stimulation ⟨an eager, ~ group of students⟩ **3 :** marked by deliberateness or awareness **:** INTENTIONAL, CONSCIOUS ⟨an intolerably ~ affectation —Eric Partridge⟩ ⟨not influenced by his ~ prejudices —A.C.Gimson⟩ — **knowl·edge·able·ness** *also* **knowl·edg·able·ness** *n* -ES — **knowl·edge·ably** *also* **knowl·edg·ably** \\-blē, -bli\\ *adv*

**knowl·edged** \\-jd\\ *adj* [²*knowledge* + *-ed*] **:** marked by or equipped with knowledge ⟨trained — at least in his own fashion — and ~ in our ways —S.E.White⟩

**knowl·edge·less** \\-jləs\\ *adj* **:** devoid of knowledge **:** IGNORANT ⟨naked and ~ —Carl Sandburg⟩

**knowledges** *pres 3d sing of* KNOWLEDGE, *pl of* KNOWLEDGE

**knowledging** *pres part of* KNOWLEDGE

¹**known** \\ˈnōn *sometimes* -ōən\\ *adj* [ME *knowen, knawen,* fr. past part. of *knowen, knawen* to know — more at KNOW] **:** that is apprehended or perceived by the mind or senses **:** that has become a part of knowledge ⟨a ~ truth that no one denies⟩ **:** familiar through knowledge or experience ⟨beyond the limits of the ~ world —A.C.Whitehead⟩; *esp* **:** generally recognized ⟨a ~ authority in this matter⟩

²**known** \\"\\ *n* -S **1 :** something known **:** something familiar or recognized; *specif* **:** a substance of known composition — used esp. in chemical analysis ⟨chemical determinations performed on ~s —A.A.Benedetti-Pichler⟩ **2 :** a letter (as in $a^2+2ab$) or some other symbol (as $\pi$) used in a mathematical equation to represent a known number or quantity

¹**know-noth·ing** \\ˈnō,nəthiŋ, -thēŋ\\ *adj* **1 :** extremely ignorant ⟨a *know-nothing* blunderer⟩ **2** *often cap K&N* **:** of, relating to, or characterized by know-nothingism ⟨the *Know-Nothing* party . . . proposed the political proscription of Roman Catholics —W.L.Sperry⟩ ⟨the *know-nothing* anti-intellectualism that parades . . . as anti-Communism —Stringfellow Barr⟩

²**know-nothing** \\"\\ *n, pl* **know-nothings 1 :** one that knows little or nothing **:** IGNORAMUS **2** *usu cap K&N* [so called fr. the fact that some members of the organization replied "I don't know" to any questions that were asked them about it] **:** a member of a 19th century short-lived secret American political organization prominent in the decade before the Civil War and hostile to the political influence of recent immigrants and Roman Catholics **3 :** AGNOSTIC **4 :** an exponent or adherent of 20th century political know-nothingism ⟨counting on the *know-nothings* . . . to exploit the present atmosphere of uncertainty and insecurity —Norman Cousins⟩ ⟨assaults upon intellectuals by political *know-nothings* —Richard Robbins⟩

**know-noth·ing·ism** \\-ŋ,izəm\\ *n* -S **1** *usu cap K&N* **:** the principles and policies of the 19th century Know-Nothings **2 :** the fact or condition of knowing nothing or of desiring to know nothing or the conviction that nothing can be known with certitude esp. in religion or morality ⟨an ethical *know-nothingism* in which there is no longer any certainty . . . as to what is and what is not evil —F.B.Millett⟩ **3** *sometimes cap K&N* **:** a political attitude or philosophy of the mid-twentieth century characterized chiefly by anti-intellectualism and exaggerated patriotism and by fear of foreign and subversive influences ⟨fighting the battle inside the government against the forces of hysteria and *know-nothingism* —Reed Harris⟩

**knows** *pres 3d sing of* KNOW, *pl of* KNOW

**know-what** \\ˈ⸗,⸗\\ *n, pl* **know-whats** [fr. the phrase *know what*] **:** clear recognition of the objective of a selected course of action ⟨the know-why and the *know-what* which businessmen find necessary for all persons in administrative or executive positions —C.E.Henson⟩

**know-why** \\ˈ⸗,⸗\\ *n, pl* **know-whys** [fr. the phrase *know why*] **:** understanding of the reasons underlying something (as a course of action) ⟨our frontier past and our industrialized present both incline us toward a preoccupation with technique, with know-how rather than *know-why* —Dwight Macdonald⟩

**knox·ville** \\ˈnäks,vil *esp S* -vəl\\ *adj, usu cap* [fr. *Knoxville, Tenn.*] **:** of or from the city of Knoxville, Tenn. ⟨a *Knoxville* industry⟩ **:** of the kind or style prevalent in Knoxville

**knox·vil·lite** \\-vi,līt, -və,-\\ *n* -S [*Knoxville,* town in Napa county, Calif. + E *-ite*] **:** MAGNESIOCOPIAPITE

**knt** *abbr* knight

**knub** \\ˈnəb\\ *n* -S [prob. fr. LG *knubbe,* fr. MLG *knubbe, knobbe,* knot on a tree, knob — more at KNOB] **1 a** *dial* **:** KNOB **b :** NUB 4 **2** *or* **knubs** *pl but sing or pl in constr* **:** FRISON

**knubbly** *var of* NUBBLY

**knubby** *var of* NUBBY

¹**knuck·le** \\ˈnəkəl\\ *n* -S [ME *knokel;* akin to MLG *knökel* knuckle, MHG *knöchel, knüchel;* diminutives fr. the root of MLG *knoke* bone, MLG *knoche;* akin to OE *cnycled* bent, ON *knykill* small knot, OE *cnotta* knot — more at KNOT] **1 a** (1) **:** the joint where the ends of two bones meet or articulate (2) **:** the tarsal or carpal joint and the parts including the flesh immediately above or below in a quadruped (as a pig) used for food **:** the knee or hock joint and adjoining parts of a quadruped; *often* **:** the shank of a quadruped used as food (3) **:** the shoulder joint of a whale **b** (1) **:** a rounded prominence formed by bending a joint where two bones meet or articulate; *esp* **:** one of the prominences formed at each of the joints and bases of the fingers of the human hand when the hand is shut or when the fingers are clenched (2) **:** a projection at the carpal or tarsal joints of a quadruped **2 :** something that protrudes like a knuckle, that is shaped like a knuckle, or that is otherwise suggestive of a knuckle: as **a :** a sharply flexed loop of intestines incarcerated in a hernia **b** (1) **:** one of the joining parts of a hinge through which a pin or rivet passes (2) **:** KNUCKLE JOINT (3) **:** the rotating piece used for the coupling device in various forms of automatic car couplings (as the rotating hook of a railroad-car coupler designed to hook up with the coupler of another car) **c** (1) **:** the meeting of two surfaces at a sharp angle (as in a roof or as in the timbers of a ship) (2) **:** the outer part of a sharply angled jetty, a breakwater, or other construction at or along a shore **d :** a small, decorative, carved, or rolled terminal part esp. on a piece of furniture (as at the end of one of the arms of a chair) **e :** a chunk or knob of rock ⟨their bodies calloused by ~s of falling rock —Robert Payne⟩ **f :** a point or support on which something pivots or turns **:** pivotal point ⟨the ship used the end of the pier as a ~ for swinging around⟩ **3 knuckles** *pl but sing or pl in constr* **:** BRASS KNUCKLES — **near the knuckle 1 :** near the permitted, accepted, or tolerable limit of what can be said or done: as **a :** verging on the border line between decency and indecency ⟨jokes that were embarrassingly *near the knuckle*⟩ **b :** verging on what is offensive or injurious to one's sensibilities ⟨accusations too *near the knuckle* for them to ignore⟩ **2 :** near to what is of greatest importance, interest, or concern ⟨the real reasons for doing this are, perhaps, *nearer the knuckle* than they think —John Holloway⟩

²**knuckle** \\"\\ *vb* **knuckled; knuckled; knuckling** \\-k(ə)liŋ\\ **knuckles** *vi* **1 :** to knuckle under ⟨*knuckled* to no pressure groups —*Newsweek*⟩ **2 :** to project or protrude like a knuckle **3 :** to be affected with cocked ankles — usu. used of a horse or of an affected fetlock joint and often with *over* ⟨~s over badly on the off hind leg⟩ ⟨the fetlocks of colts may ~ for some time after birth without permanent harm⟩ ~ *vt* **1 :** to strike ⟨the seaman *knuckled* his forehead and wheeled around —Clark Russell⟩ or press or rub with the knuckles ⟨shook himself and rose, *knuckling* his eyes —Lawrence Durrell⟩ ⟨he *knuckled* his hair and he frowned —Thurston Scott⟩ **2 :** to shoot (a marble) from between the knuckle of the thumb and the bent forefinger **3 :** to form a bend or a knuckle joint in (as steel plates or wire fencing)

**knuckle ball** *n* **:** a baseball pitch made by gripping the ball with the knuckles or fingernails of the index and second and sometimes third fingers pressed against the top of the ball and thrown usu. with little speed or spin so as to give it a typically erratic course

**knuck·le·ball·er** \\ˈnəkəl,bȯlə(r)\\ *n* -S **:** a baseball pitcher that specializes in pitching knuckle balls

**knucklebone** \\ˈ⸗⸗,⸗\\ *n* [ME *knokylle bone,* fr. *knokylle, knokel* knuckle + *bone, bon* bone] **1 a :** one of the bones forming a knuckle of a human finger **b :** a long bone with a knobbed end (as a femur or humerus); *also* **:** the knob of such a bone — now used only of animals **2 a :** the tetrahedral metacarpal or metatarsal bone of a sheep; *esp* **:** such a bone marked on its surfaces and used in ancient times in gaming and divination usu. through being tossed like one of a pair of dice **b knucklebones** *pl but sing in constr* **:** a game played with such marked bones or with small metal objects resembling such bones; *esp* **:** JACKS

**knuck·led** \\ˈnəkəld\\ *adj* **:** having knuckles

**knuckle down** *vi* **1 :** to place the knuckles on the ground preparatory to shooting a marble ⟨*knuckled down* and shot for the center hole⟩ **2 :** to apply oneself with seriousness or concentration **:** apply oneself earnestly ⟨let's have no more nonsense and *knuckle down* to business⟩ **3 :** to knuckle under

**knuck·le-dust** \\ˈnəkəl,dəst\\ *vt* [back-formation fr. *knuckle-duster*] **:** to strike with the fist; *specif* **:** to strike with brass knuckles

**knuck·le-dust·er** \\-tə(r)\\ *n* -S **1 :** BRASS KNUCKLES **2 :** one that specializes in or is given to attacking with the fists; *specif* **:** one that uses brass knuckles

**knucklehead** \\ˈ⸗⸗,⸗\\ *n* **:** a stupid blunderer **:** DUMBBELL — **knuckleheaded** \\ˈ⸗⸗ˈ⸗⸗\\ *adj*

**knuckle joint** *n* **:** a hinge joint in which a projection with an eye on one piece enters a jaw between two corresponding projections with eyes on another piece and is retained by a pin or rivet

knuckle joint

**knuckle-kneed** \\ˈ⸗⸗ˈ⸗\\ *adj* **:** having projecting or bulging knees

**knuckle line** *n* **:** the line of meeting of two surfaces of a ship at an angle

**knuckle man** *or* **knuckle boy** *n* **:** a mine-car clipper who works at the top of a haulage slope attaching and detaching mine cars to and from cables and coupling trains of cars

**knuckle pin** *n* **:** a pin or rivet connecting the two parts of a knuckle joint

**knuckle post** *n* **:** the vertical post of an automobile steering knuckle on which the knuckle is pivoted

**knuckle press** *or* **knuckle-joint press** *n* **:** a punch press using a toggle joint **:** TOGGLE-JOINT PRESS

**knuck·ler** \\ˈnək(ə)lə(r)\\ *n* -S **1 a :** a marble that a player knuckles **b :** KNUCKLE BALL **2 :** a hydraulic-press operator who shapes steel parts for use in shipbuilding

**knuckles** *pl of* KNUCKLE, *pres 3d sing of* KNUCKLE

**knuck·le·some** \\ˈnəkəlsəm\\ *adj* **:** KNUCKLY

**knuckle under** *vi* **:** to admit defeat **:** give in **:** give up **:** YIELD, SUBMIT ⟨if it hadn't been for her pride, she'd have *knuckled under* and gone back home —Jane Woodfin⟩

**knuckling** *n* -S [fr. gerund of ²*knuckle*] **:** COCKED ANKLES

**knuck·ly** \\ˈnək(ə)lē\\ *adj, often* -ER/-EST **:** having bony protuberances; *specif* **:** having prominent knuckles ⟨~ fingers⟩

**knucks** \\ˈnəks\\ *n pl* [alter. of *knuckles,* pl. of ¹*knuckle*] **1** *sing in constr* **:** a game of marbles at the end of which the winner has the option of shooting a marble at the opponent's knuckles held on the ground **2** *sing or pl in constr* **:** BRASS KNUCKLES

**knull·ing** \\ˈnəliŋ\\ *n* -S [by alter.] **:** KNURLING

**knur** \\ˈnər(·)\\ *n* -S [ME *knorre;* akin to ME *knarre* rough stone, knot in wood; akin to MHG & MLG *knorre* burl, knot, OHG *chniurig* knotty, solid, Norw *knart, knort* knot, burl, OE *cnotta* knot — more at KNOT] **1 :** a hard excrescence (as on a tree trunk or stone) **:** GNARL **2** *dial Brit* **:** a usu. wooden ball (as used in the game of knur and spell)

**knur and spell** *n* **:** a game played in northern England that resembles trapball

¹**knurl** \\ˈnərl, *esp before pause or consonant* ˈnər·əl; ˈnəl, ˈnəil\\ *n* -S [prob. blend of *knur* and *gnarl*] **1 a** (1) **:** a small protuberance, excrescence, or knob (2) **:** a small ridge or bead; *esp* **:** one of a series of small ridges or beads used on a usu. metal surface (as of a thumbscrew) as a means of ensuring a firm grip or as a decorative feature **b :** a contorted knot in wood **2 a** *chiefly Scot* **:** a short thickset person; *esp* **:** DWARF **b** *Scot* **:** a tangled mass (as of hair) **:** SNARL **3 :** a tool for knurling

²**knurl** \\"\\ *vt* -ED/-ING/-S **:** to provide (as a thumbscrew) with small ridges or beading (as for ensuring a firm grip) **:** make knurls on **:** MILL

**knurled** *adj* **1 :** GNARLED ⟨the ~ swollen knuckles of his other hand —Norman Mailer⟩ **2 :** provided with knurls ⟨a ~ thumbscrew⟩

**knurling** *n* -S **1 a :** the making of knurls **b :** the ridges on knurled work **:** knurled work **2 a :** a breaking up of a rounded molding as if for a bead and reel but usu. with more elaboration **b :** molding so treated

**knurly** \\-ərlē, -əl-, -əil-, -li\\ *adj, often* -ER/-EST [¹*knurl* + *-y*] **1 :** GNARLY **2 :** DWARFISH

**knurry** *adj* [*knur* + *-y*] *obs* **:** KNURLY

**knut** \\(kə)ˈnət\\ *n* -S [prob. alter. of ¹*nut*] **:** a fop of the late 19th or early 20th century

**knys·na boxwood** \\(kə)ˈniznə-\\ *or* **knysna** *n* -S [fr. *Knysna,* Union of So. Africa] **:** EAST LONDON BOXWOOD

**ko** \\ˈkō, ˈgō\\ *n* -S *usu cap* [Chin (Pek) *ko¹* elder brother] **:** a Chinese porcelain produced in the 12th century and distinguished by its dark clay and fine crackle

¹**KO** \\(ˈ)kāˈō\\ *abbr or n, pl* **KO's** \\-ōz\\ *sometimes not cap* **:** KNOCKOUT

²**KO** \\"\\ *vt* **KO'd** \\-ōd\\ **KO'd; KO'ing; KO's** *sometimes not cap* **:** to knock out

**KO** *abbr* keep off

**koa** \\ˈkōə\\ *n* -S [Hawaiian] **1 :** a Hawaiian timber tree (*Acacia koa*) with light gray bark, crescent-shaped leaves, and white flowers in small round heads **2 :** the fine-grained red wood of the koa now used esp. for furniture

**ko·ae** \\kōˈä,ā\\ *n* -S [Hawaiian] *Hawaii* **:** TROPIC BIRD

**koa finch** *n* **:** any of several Hawaiian birds of the genera *Pseudonestor* and *Psittirostra* (family Drepaniidae) that resemble the finches

**koa ha·o·le** \\-häˈō(,)lā\\ *n* [Hawaiian] **:** LEAD TREE

**ko·ala** *also* **koala bear** *or* **co·ala** \\kōˈälə, kəˈwä-\\ *n* -S [*koala* native name in Australia] **1 :** a sluggish Australian arboreal marsupial (*Phascolarctos cinereus*) that is about two feet long and has large hairy ears, thick ashy gray fur, and sharp claws and that feeds on eucalyptus leaves — called also *kangaroo bear, native bear* **2 :** the pelt of the koala

**ko·a·li** \\kōˈälē, kəˈwä-\\ *n* -S [Hawaiian] **:** any of several tropical morning glories of the genus *Ipomoea* (as *I. tuberculata* or *I. insularis*) used in Hawaii as cordage

**koaliang** *var of* KAOLIANG

**ko·an** \\ˈkō,än\\ *n, pl* **koans** *or* **koan** [Jap *kōan,* lit., public plan, fr. *kō* public + *an* proposal, plan] **:** a paradox used in Zen Buddhism as an instrument of meditation in training monks to despair of an ultimate dependence upon reason and to force them into sudden intuitive enlightenment

**ko·asa·ti** \\,kōəˈsäd·ē\\ *n, pl* **koasati** *or* **koasatis** *usu cap* **1 a :** a Muskogean people of northern Alabama **b :** a member of such people **2 :** the language of the Koasati people

¹**kob** \\ˈkäb, ˈkōb\\ *also* **ko·ba** \\ˈkōbə\\ *n, pl* **kob** *or* **kobs** [of Niger-Congo origin; akin to Wolof *koba* roan antelope, Fulani *kōba*] **:** any of various African antelopes (genus *Adenota*) related to the waterbucks

²**kob** \\ˈkäb\\ *n* -S [by shortening & alter.] **:** KABELJOU

**ko·ban** \\ˈkō,bän\\ *also* **co·bang** *or* **ko·bang** \\-băŋ\\ *n* -S [Jap *koban,* fr. *ko* small + *ban* size, format] **:** an oval Japanese gold coin of widely varying value issued from the 17th century to the 19th century

**ko·be** \\ˈkōbē\\ *adj, usu cap* [fr. *Kobe,* city in western Honshu, Japan] **:** of or from the city of Kobe, Japan **:** of the kind or style prevalent in Kobe

**ko·bell·ite** \\ˈkōbə,līt\\ *n* -S [Sw *kobellit,* fr. Franz von *Kobell* †1882 Ger. mineralogist and poet + Sw *-it* -ite] **:** a mineral $Pb_2(Bi,Sb)_2S_5$ consisting of a blackish gray sulfide of antimony, bismuth, and lead

**ko·bird** *also* **kow·bird** \\ˈkō,⸗\\ *n* [*ko-, kow-* (prob. imit.) + *bird*] **:** YELLOW-BILLED CUCKOO

**ko·bold** \\ˈkō,bōld, -bȯld\\ *n* -S [G — more at COBALT] **1 :** a gnome held esp. in German folklore to inhabit underground places ⟨looked like ~s from some magic mine —Rudyard Kipling⟩ **2 :** a domestic spirit often held in Germanic folklore to be mischievous

**ko·bus** \\ˈkōbəs\\ *n, cap* [NL, fr. E ¹*kob*] **:** a genus of antelopes containing the typical waterbucks

**koch** \\ˈkōch\\ *n, pl* **koches** *usu cap* **:** a member of a hinduized Mongoloid people of Assam

**ko·chi** \\ˈkōchē\\ *adj, usu cap* [fr. *Kochi,* city on south coast of Shikoku, Japan] **:** of or from the city of Kochi, Japan **:** of the kind or style prevalent in Kochi

**ko·chia** \\ˈkōkēə\\ *n* [NL, fr. W. D. J. *Koch* †1849 Ger. botanist + NL *-ia*] **1** *cap* **:** a genus of herbs (family Chenopodiaceae) having a turbinate perianth and broadly winged fruit — see SUMMER CYPRESS **2** -S **:** a plant of the genus *Kochia*

**koch phenomenon** \\ˈkȯk-, ˈkȯḵ-,ˈkōk-,ˈkäk-\\ *n, usu cap K* [after Robert *Koch* †1910 Ger. bacteriologist] **:** the response of a tuberculous animal to reinfection with tubercle bacilli marked by necrotic lesions that develop rapidly and heal quickly and caused by hypersensitivity to products of the tubercle bacilis

**koch's bacillus** *or* **koch bacillus** *n, usu cap K* **:** a bacillus (*Mycobacterium tuberculosis*) that causes human tuberculosis

**koch's postulates** *also* **koch's laws** *n pl, usu cap K* **:** a statement of the steps required to establish a microorganism as the cause of a disease: (1) it must be found in all cases of the disease; (2) it must be isolated from the host and grown in pure culture; (3) it must reproduce the original disease when introduced into a susceptible host; (4) it must be found present in the experimental host so infected

**koch-weeks bacillus** \\-ˈwēks-\\ *n, usu cap K&W* [after Robert *Koch* †1910 and John E. *Weeks* †1949 Am. ophthalmologist, who discovered it independently] **:** a bacterium of the genus *Hemophilus* associated with human conjunctivitis

**KO'd** *past of* KO

**ko·da·gu** \\ˈkōdə,gü\\ *n, pl* **kodagu** *or* **kodagus** *usu cap* **1 a :** an aboriginal people of the mountainous region of Coorg in southern India **b :** a member of such people **2 :** the Dravidian language of the Kodagu people

**ko·dak** \\ˈkō,dak\\ *vb* -ED/-ING/-S [*Kodak*] *vi* **:** to take photographs with a Kodak camera ~ *vt* **:** to take a photograph of with a Kodak camera

**Kodak** \\"\\ *trademark* — used for a small hand camera

**ko·da millet** *also* **koda** \\ˈkōdə\\ *or* **ko·dra** \\-drə\\ *n* -S [*koda, kodra* fr. Panjabi *kodā, kodrā,* fr. Skt *kodrava*] **:** DITCH MILLET

**ko·di·ak bear** \\ˈkōdē,ak\\ *also* **ka·diak bear** \\kədˈyak-, -yäk\\ *or* **kodiak** *n* -S *usu cap K* [fr. *Kodiak* Island, southern Alaska, its habitat] **:** a brown bear (*Ursus middendorffi*) of Alaska that is larger and has shorter thicker claws than the grizzly and feeds largely on salmon

**kod·kod** \\ˈkōd,kōd\\ *n* -S [perh. native name in Chile or Argentina] **:** PAMPAS CAT

**koe·ber·lin·ia** \\,kōbə(r)ˈlinēə\\ *n, cap* [NL, fr. C. L. *Köberlin,* 19th cent. Ger. clergyman and amateur botanist + NL *-ia*] **:** a monotypic genus of nearly leafless thorny shrubs of dry parts of the southwestern U.S. and adjacent Mexico that bear racemes of small white flowers and tend to form dense thickets and that are placed in the family Capparidaceae or sometimes isolated in a separate family

**koech·lin·ite** \\ˈkeklə,nīt\\ *n* -S [Rudolf *Koechlin* †1939 Austrian mineralogist + E *-ite*] **:** a mineral $Bi_2MoO_6$ consisting of a bismuth molybdate

**ko·el** *or* **ko·il** \\ˈkōəl, ˈkȯi(ə)l\\ *n* -S [Hindi *koel, koil,* fr. Skt *kokila* — more at CUCKOO] **:** any of several cuckoos (genus *Eudynamys*) of India, the East Indies, and Australia — called also *long-tailed cuckoo*

**koel·lia** \\ˈkelēə\\ [NL, fr. Johann L. C. *Kölle* †1797 Ger. physician and botanist + NL *-ia*] *syn of* PYCNANTHEMUM

**koel·reu·te·ria** \\,kel,rȯiˈtirēə, -rü'-\\ *n* [NL, fr. Josef G. *Kölreuter* †1806 Ger. botanist + NL *-ia*] **1** *cap* **:** a small genus of Asiatic trees (family Sapindaceae) distinguished by large terminal panicles of flowers and inflated papery capsular fruit — see GOLDENRAIN TREE **2** -S **:** any tree of the genus *Koelreuteria*

**koe·nen·ite** \\ˈkānə,nīt\\ *n* -S [G *koenenit,* fr. Adolf von *Koenen* †1915 Ger. geologist + G *-it* -ite] **:** a mineral $Mg_5Al_2(OH)_{12}Cl_4$ consisting of a basic chloride of aluminum and magnesium

**koenigsberg** *usu cap, var of* KÖNIGSBERG

**koe·pang·er** \\ˈkü,päŋə(r)\\ *n* -S *usu cap* [*Koepang, Kupang,* city at the southwestern end of Timor + E *-er*] **:** a native or inhabitant of the city of Kupang on the Indonesian island of Timor

**ko·e·ri** *or* **ko·i·ri** \\ˈkōərē\\ *n, pl* **koeri** *or* **koeris** *or* **koiri** *or* **koiris** *usu cap* **1 :** an agricultural Aryo-Dravidian people of northeastern Hindustan **2 :** a member of the Koeri people

**koet·tig·ite** *or* **köt·tig·ite** \\ˈked·i,gīt\\ *n* -S [Otto *Köttig,* 19th cent. Ger. chemist + E *-ite*] **:** a mineral $Zn_3(AsO_4)_2.8H_2O$ consisting of a hydrous arsenate of zinc

**koettstorfer value** *usu cap K, var of* KÖTTSTORFER VALUE

**koft·ga·ri** \\ˈkōftgə(,)rē\\ *n* -S [Hindi *koftgarī,* fr. Per *kōftgarī,* fr. *kōftgar* maker of koftgari, fr. *kōft* blow, beating + *-gar* doing; akin to Skt *kāra* doing — more at KARMA] **:** Indian damascene work in which steel is inlaid with gold

**ko·fu** \\ˈkō(,)fü\\ *adj, usu cap* [fr. *Kofu,* city in south central Honshu, Japan] **:** of or from the city of Kofu, Japan **:** of the kind or style prevalent in Kofu

**ko·gas·in** \\kōˈgasən, ˈkō,g-\\ *n* -S [G, fr. *ko-* (fr. *koks* coke, irreg. fr. E *coke*) + *gas* (fr. NL) + *-in* (fr. *benzin* benzine, gasoline)] **:** a liquid mixture of saturated and unsaturated aliphatic hydrocarbons made by reaction of carbon monoxide and hydrogen in the Fischer-Tropsch process

**ko·gia** \\ˈkōjēə\\ *n, cap* [NL] **:** a genus of whales consisting of the pygmy sperm whales

**kogon** *var of* COGON

**ko·he·ko·he** \\ˌkōēˈkōē\\ *n* -S [Maori] **:** a New Zealand tree (*Dysoxylum spectabile*) of the family Neliaceae whose wood is used for furniture and interior finish

**ko-hemp** \\ˈkō,⸗\\ *n* [Chin *ko²* kudzu + E *hemp*] **1 :** KUDZU **2 :** a fiber of the kudzu vine

**kohen** *n, pl* **kohanim** *also* **kohens** *usu cap, var of* COHEN

**koh-i-noor** \\ˈkōə,nu̇(ə)r\\ *n, pl* **koh-i-noors** *often cap* [fr. *Koh-i-noor,* famous diamond that became part of the British crown jewels after the annexation of Punjab by Great Britain in 1849, fr. Per *Kōh-i-nūr,* lit., mountain of light] **:** something that is or is felt to be the best of its kind; *esp* **:** a usu. large and valuable diamond ⟨a young Spaniard with a *Koh-i-noor* of a diamond on his finger and pearls the size of camphor balls in his shirt front —W.J.Locke⟩

**ko·hi·sta·ni** \ˌkō(h)əˈstänē, -tanē\ *n* -s *usu cap* **1 a :** a Himalayan people of northern Pakistan **b :** a member of such people **2 :** a Dard language of the Kohistani people

[1]**kohl** \ˈkōl\ *also* **co·hol** \ˈkōəl\ *or* **ko·hol** \ˈkōəl\ *n* -s [Ar *kuḥl*] **:** a preparation (as of antimony or soot mixed with other ingredients) used esp. in Arabia and Egypt to darken the edges of the eyelids

[2]**kohl** *usu cap, var of* KOL

**koh·le·ria** \kōˈlirēə\ *n, cap* [NL, fr. Michael *Kohler*, 19th cent. Swiss naturalist + NL *-ia*] **:** a genus of rhizomatous often shrubby tropical American herbs (family Gesneriaceae) that are widely cultivated for their soft velvety foliage and showy often scarlet flowers with four or five stamens and partly inferior ovary

**kohl·rabi** \kōlˈrabē, -räbē, ˈ=ˌ==\ *n, pl* **kohlrabies** [G, modif. (influenced by G *kohl* cabbage) of It *cavoli rape*, pl. of *cavolo rapa* kohlrabi, fr. *cavolo* cabbage (fr. L *caulis*) + *rapa* turnip, fr. L — more at HOLE, RAPE] **1 a :** any of a race of cabbages having an edible stem that becomes greatly enlarged, fleshy, and turnip-shaped **b :** any plant of the kohlrabi type **2 :** BROMATIUM

kohlrabi

**kohl·rausch flask** \ˈkōlˌrau̇sh-\ *n, usu cap K* [after Rudolf H. A. *Kohlrausch* †1858 Ger. physicist] **:** a volumetric flask that has an enlarged neck and usu. holds 100 or 200 milliliters

**kohlrausch's law** *n, usu cap K* [after Friedrich W. G. *Kohlrausch* †1910 Ger. physicist] **:** a statement in physical chemistry: the migration of an ion at infinite dilution is dependent on the nature of the solvent and on the potential gradient but not on the other ions present

**kohs blocks** *n pl, usu cap K* [after Samuel C. *Kohs* *b*1890 Am. psychologist] **:** a set of small variously colored blocks that are used to form test patterns in psychodiagnostic examination

**ko·hua** \kōˈhüə\ *n* -s [Maori] **:** a Maori earth oven

**ko·hua·na** \kōˈwänə\ *n, pl* **kohuana** *or* **kohuanas** *usu cap* **1 :** a Yuman people of the Colorado river valley in Arizona, California, and Mexico **2 :** a member of the Kohuana people

**koi** \ˈkȯi\ *n* -s [Jap] **:** CARP 1a

**koi·a·ri** \kȯiˈ(y)ärē\ *n, pl* **koiari** *or* **koiaris** *usu cap* **1 a :** a Papuan people inhabiting Papua **b :** a member of such people **2 :** the language of the Koiari people

**koi·bal** \(ˈ)kȯiˈbäl\ *also* **kai·bal** \(ˈ)kī;-\ *n, pl* **koibal** *or* **koibals** *usu cap* **1 :** a tatarized Samoyed people of the East Siberian region **2 :** a member of the Koibal people

**koil** *var of* KOEL

**koil·onych·ia** \ˌkȯilōˈnikēə\ *n* -s [NL, fr. Gk *koilos* hollow + NL *-onychia* — more at CAVE] **:** abnormal thinness and concavity of fingernails occurring esp. in hypochromic anemias — called also *spoon nail*

**koi·lo·rach·ic** *or* **koi·lor·rhach·ic** \ˌkȯilōˈrakik, -lə;-\ *adj* [*koilo-* (fr. Gk *koilos* hollow) + *rach-, rrhach-* (fr. Gk *rhachis* spine) + *-ic* — more at RACHI-] **:** having the lumbar region of the spinal column concave ventrally

**koi·me·sis** \ˈkēmēsəs\ *n* -ES [MGk *koimēsis*, fr. Gk, sleep, sleep of death, fr. *koiman* to put to sleep — more at CEMETERY] **:** a feast in the Eastern Orthodox Church commemorating the death and the corporeal assumption of the Virgin Mary now celebrated on August 15

**koi·ne** \(ˈ)kȯiˈnā *also* ˈkȯiˌnē\ *n* -s [Gk *koinē*, fr. fem. of *koinos* common — more at CO-] **1** *usu cap* **:** the Greek language commonly spoken and written by the Greek-speaking population of eastern Mediterranean countries in the Hellenistic and Roman periods **2 :** a dialect or language of a region, country, or people that has become the common or standard language of a larger area and of other peoples — compare LINGUA FRANCA

**KO'ing** *pres part of* KO

**koi·non** \kȯiˈnän\ *n* -s [Gk, neut. of *koinos* common] **:** the common element in an apo koinou construction

**koi·no·nia** \ˌkȯinəˈnēə, ˌkēnə-\ *n* -s [Gk *koinōnia* communion, association, partnership, fr. *koinos* common] **1 :** the Christian fellowship or body of believers **2 :** intimate spiritual communion and participative sharing in a common religious commitment and spiritual community ⟨the ~ of the disciples with each other and with their Lord⟩

**koiri** *usu cap, var of* KOERI

**koi·ro·pot·a·mus** \ˌkȯirōˈpädəməs\ *n, cap* [NL, irreg. fr. Gk *choiros* pig + *potamos* river; akin to Gk *piptein* to fall — more at -CHOERUS, FEATHER] **:** a genus of wild hogs comprising the African river hogs

**ko·ji** \ˈkōjē\ *n* -s [Jap *kōji*] **1 :** a yeast or other starter prepared in Japan from rice inoculated with the spores of a mold (*Aspergillus oryzae*) and permitted to develop a mycelium **2 :** an enzyme preparation from koji that is similar to diastase from malt

**ko·jic acid** \ˈkōjik-\ *n* [*kojic* fr. *koji* + *-ic*] **:** a crystalline water-soluble phenolic-type toxic antibiotic $HOC_5H_2O_2CH_2OH$ derived from gamma-pyrone and made by fermentation (as of glucose with molds of the genus *Aspergillus*)

**ko·ka·ko** \kōˈkä(ˌ)kō\ *n* -s [Maori] *New Zeal* **:** WATTLE CROW

**ko·kam** \kōˈkäm\ *n* -s [Malay *kukang, kongkang*] **:** LORIS 1b

**ko·ka·ma** \kōˈkämə\ *n* -s [Tswana *kukama*] **:** GEMSBOK

**ko·kan** \ˈkōkən\ *n* -s [Hindi] **:** an East Indian timber tree (*Duabanga sonneratioides*) of the family Sonneratiaceae

**ko·kan·ee** \kōˈkanē\ *also* **kokanee salmon** *n* -s [prob. fr. *Kokanee* creek, southeastern British Columbia] **:** a small landlocked sockeye salmon that rarely reaches a pound in weight but that is an important forage fish in certain inland waters

**ko·ker·boom** \ˈkōkə(r)ˌbüm, -bōm\ *n* [Afrik, fr. D *koker* quiver, sheath (fr. MD *coker*) + *boom* tree, fr. MD; akin to OE *cocer* quiver and to OE *bēam* tree — more at COCKER, BEAM] **:** QUIVER TREE

**ko·kil** \ˈkōkəl\ *or* **ko·ki·la** \-kələ\ *n* -s [Skt *kokila* — more at CUCKOO] **:** a koel (*Eudynamys scolopacea honorata*) of India

**ko·klas** *or* **ko·klass** \ˈkōkləs\ *n* -ES [native name in Nepal] **:** PUKRAS

[1]**ko·ko** \ˈkō(ˌ)kō\ *n* -s [prob. of Niger-Congo origin; akin to Twi *kɔ̄ˈkɔ̄* koko] **1 :** any of several araceous plants including the taro that are cultivated in tropical western Africa for their starchy edible roots **2** *also* **kok·ko** \ˈkä(ˌ)kō\ [origin unknown] **:** LEBBEK

[2]**koko** \"\ *n* -s [Maori] **:** TUI

[3]**koko** \"\ *n, pl* **koko** *or* **kokos** *usu cap* **1 :** a group of numerous aboriginal peoples of northern Queensland **2 :** a member of any of the Koko peoples

**ko·koon** \kəˈkün\ *n* -s [Tswana *kgokoñ*] **:** BRINDLED GNU

**ko·koo·na** \kəˈkünə\ *n* [NL, fr. Singhalese *kokuṅ* kokoona] **1** *cap* **:** a genus of East Indian trees (family Celastraceae) having flowers with a 3-celled ovary and producing 3-angled fruit **2** -s **:** any tree of the genus *Kokoona*

**ko·ko·pu** \ˈkōkəˌpü\ *n* -s [Maori] **:** any of various New Zealand fishes of the genus *Galaxias* that resemble the trout — compare GALAXIIDAE

**ko·ko·wai** \ˈkōkəˌwī\ *n* -s [Maori] **1 :** red ocher used in New Zealand as a pigment esp. on woodwork **2 :** the earth from which kokowai is obtained

**kokra** \ˈkōkrə, ˈkäk-\ *also* **kokra wood** *n* -s [origin unknown] **1 :** COCOWOOD 1 **2 :** COCUSWOOD

**kok-saghyz** *or* **kok-sagyz** \ˌkōksəˈgēz, ˌkäk-, -giz\ *n* -ES [Russ *kok-sagyz*, fr. Turki *kok-sagïz*, fr. *kok* root + *sagïz* rubber, gum] **:** a perennial dandelion (*Taraxacum kok-saghyz*) native to the Kazakh republic of Russia that has fleshier leaves and more numerous flower heads than the common dandelion of No. America and Europe and is cultivated for its fleshy roots which have a high rubber content — called also *Russian dandelion*

**kok·ta·ite** \ˈkäktəˌīt\ *n* -s [Czech *koktait*, fr. Jaroslav *Kokta*, 20th cent. Czechoslovak mineralogist + Czech *-it* -ite] **:** a mineral $(NH_4)_2Ca(SO_4)_2.H_2O$ consisting of a hydrous sulfate of calcium and ammonium

**ko·ku** \ˈkō(ˌ)kü\ *n, pl* **koku** [Jap] **:** any of three Japanese units of capacity: **a :** a unit for dry measure equal to 5.12 bushels **b :** a unit for liquid measure equal to 47.65 gallons **c :** a unit for vessels equal to 10 cubic feet

**ko·kum butter** \ˈkōkəm-\ *also* **kokum** *or* **co·cum** \ˈkō-\ *n* -s [*kokum, cocum*, fr. Marathi *kokam, kokamb* mangosteen] **:** a semisolid fat or liquid oil obtained from the seeds of a small East Indian tree (*Garcinia indica*) and used in India for food — called also *Goa butter*

**ko·ku·ra** \ˈkōkərə, kōˈku̇rə\ *adj, usu cap* [fr. *Kokura*, city in northern Kyushu, Japan] **:** of or from the city of Kokura, Japan **:** of the kind or style prevalent in Kokura

**kol** *or* **kohl** \ˈkōl\ *n, pl* **kol** *or* **kols** *or* **kohl** *or* **kohls** *usu cap* **1 :** a people of Bengal and Chota Nagpur, India **2 :** a member of such people

**kola** *var of* COLA

**ko·lac·ky** \kəˈläch(k)ē\ *or* **ko·lach** \ˈkōˌläch\ *also* **ko·la·ce** \kəˈlächē\ *or* **ko·latch** \ˈkōˌläch\ *n, pl* **kolacky** *or* **kolaches** [Czech *koláč*; akin to Russ *kolach* kolacky, Bulg *koláč* kolacky, OSlav *kolo* wheel — more at WHEEL] **:** a bun made of rich sweet yeast-leavened dough filled with jam or fruit pulp

**ko·lam** \kōˈläm\ *n, pl* **kolam** *or* **kolams** *usu cap* **1 :** a people of the Gond ethnic group in central India **2 :** a member of the Kolam people

**ko·la·mi** \kəˈlämē\ *n* -s **:** the Dravidian language of the Kolam people

**ko·la nut** *also* **kola** *or* **co·la nut** \ˈkōlə-\ *n* -s [[2]*cola* + *nut*] **:** the bitter caffeine-containing seed of a kola tree that is approximately the size of a chestnut and is chewed as a condiment and stimulant — see [2]COLA 2a

**ko·lar gold fields** \ˈkōˌlär-\ *adj, usu cap K&G&F* [fr. *Kolar Gold Fields*, city in southern India] **:** of or from the city of Kolar Gold Fields, India **:** of the kind or style prevalent in Kolar Gold Fields

**ko·lar·i·an** *also* **co·lar·i·an** \kōˈla(a)rēən\ *n* -s *usu cap* [prob. fr. *Kolar*, town in southern India + E *-ian*] **:** KOL

**kola tree** *or* **cola tree** *n* [[2]*cola* + *tree*] **:** a tree of the genus *Cola* (esp. *C. nitida*) native to tropical Africa but now cultivated in tropical America and Asia — see KOLA NUT

**ko·lat·tam** \kōˈläd·əm\ *n* -s [Tamil *kōl* stick + *āṭṭam* dance] **:** a folk dance of southern India accompanied by the striking together of sticks

**kol·beck·ite** \ˈkōlˌbeˌkīt\ *n* -s [G *kolbeckit*, fr. Friedrich *Kolbeck* †1943 Ger. mineralogist + G *-it* -ite] **:** a mineral consisting of a hydrous silicate and phosphate of beryllium, aluminum, and calcium

**kol·be reaction** \ˈkōlbə-\ *or* **kolbe synthesis** *n, usu cap K* [after A. W. Hermann *Kolbe* †1884 Ger. organic chemist] **1 :** the synthesis of a hydrocarbon (as ethane) by the electrolysis of a salt (as sodium acetate) **2 :** the synthesis of salicylic acid by heating a mixture of sodium phenoxide and carbon dioxide under pressure at 180° to 200°C

**kolbe-schmitt reaction** *or* **kolbe-schmitt synthesis** \-ˈshmit-\ *n, usu cap K & 1st S* [after A. W. Hermann *Kolbe* †1884 and Rudolf *Schmitt* †1898 Ger. chemist] **:** a modified Kolbe reaction for synthesizing salicylic acid and other phenolic acids at temperatures of from 130° to 140°C

**ko·lea** \kōˈlāə\ *n* -s [Hawaiian] *Hawaii* **:** a golden plover (*Pluvialis dominica fulva*) that commonly passes through Hawaii in its migratory flights

**ko·lek** \ˈkōˌlek\ *n* -s [Malay] **:** a Malayan canoe often rigged with a rectangular sail

**ko·lel** \ˈkōˌlāl\ *n, pl* **ko·le·lim** \kōˈlāləm, -ālēm\ *also* **kolels** [NHeb *kōlēl*, fr. Heb *kālal* to comprise, include] **:** also a community or congregation of Jewish settlers in Palestine receiving financial support from the halukkah fund

**kole·ro·ga** \ˌkōləˈrōgə, ˌkäl-\ *n* -s [Kannada *koḷerōga*, fr. *koḷe* rot + Skt *roga* disease] **:** a disease of an areca palm (*Areca catechu*) caused by a fungus (*Phytophthora arecae*)

**kol·ha·pur** \ˈkōləˌpu̇(ə)r\ *adj, usu cap* [fr. *Kolhapur*, city in western India] **:** of or from the city of Kolhapur, India **:** of the kind or style prevalent in Kolhapur

**ko·li** \ˈkōlē\ *n, pl* **koli** *or* **kolis** *usu cap* **1 :** a low-caste people of Bombay, Mysore, Andhra Pradesh, Madhya Pradesh, Rajasthan, and the Punjab, India **2 :** a member of the Koli people

**ko·lin·sky** \kəˈlinzkē, -n(t)skē\ *n* -ES [Russ *kolinskiĭ* of Kola, fr. *Kola*, town and peninsula in northwestern U.S.S.R.] **1** *or* **kolinski** \"\ **a :** any of several Asiatic minks (esp. *Mustela sibirica*) **b :** the fur or pelt of any of these minks — called also *red sable, Tatar sable* **2 :** LEAFMOLD

**kol·khoz** *also* **kol·koz** *or* **kol·khos** \(ˌ)kälˈkȯz, kōl-, ˌkäl-, -ȯs\ *n, pl* **kolkho·zy** \-ȯzē\ *or* **kolkhozes** [Russ *kolkhoz*, short for *kollektivnoe khozyaĭstvo* collective farm, fr. *kollektivnoe* (neut. of *kollektivnyĭ* collective) + *khozyaĭstvo* household, economy, farm] **1 :** a collective farm of the U.S.S.R. **2 :** a system of collectivized agriculture based on the kolkhoz and developed or enforced esp. among satellite countries

**kol·khoz·nik** \-ȯznik\ *n, pl* **kolkhozni·ki** \-nəkē\ *or* **kolkhozniks** [Russ, fr. *kolkhoz* + *-nik* (suffix indicating a person)] **:** a member of a kolkhoz

**kolk·witz·ia** \kōlˈkwitsēə, käl-\ *n* [NL, fr. Richard *Kolkwitz* *b*1873 Ger. biologist + NL *-ia*] **1** *cap* **:** a genus of Chinese shrubs of the family Caprifoliaceae having short-stipuled leaves and tubular flowers succeeded by ovoid bristly achenes **2** -s **:** any plant of the genus *Kolkwitzia*; *esp* **:** BEAUTY BUSH

**kol·ler·gang** \ˈkälə(r)ˌgaŋ\ *n* [G, fr. *kollern* to roll + *gang* motion, course, route, fr. OHG, act of going — more at GANG] **:** EDGE RUNNER 2

**kolm** \ˈkō(l)m\ *n* -s [Sw] **:** a Swedish shale exceptionally high in uranium oxide $U_3O_8$

**kol·mer reaction** \ˈkōlmə(r)-\ *or* **kolmer test** *n* -s *usu cap K* [after John A. *Kolmer* *b*1886 Am. pathologist] **:** a complement fixation test for the diagnosis of syphilis

**kol ni·dre** \kōlˈni(ˌ)drā, kōl-, -ˌdrē, -ˌdrə, ˌ=ˌniˈdrā\ *n, usu cap K&N* [Aram *kol nidhrē* all the vows; fr. the opening phrase of the prayer] **1 :** the recital of an Aramaic prayer in the synagogue on the eve of Yom Kippur asking for annulment of vows to God and forgiveness of transgressions **2 :** a traditional melody to which the words of Kol Nidre are sung or chanted

**ko·lo** \ˈkō(ˌ)lō\ *n* -s [Serbo-Croatian, fr. OSlav, wheel — more at WHEEL] **:** a central European folk dance in which dancers form a circle and progress slowly to right and left while one or more solo dancers perform elaborate steps in the center

**ko·loa ma·pu** \kəˌlōəˈmä(ˌ)pü\ *n* [Hawaiian, fr. *koloa* duck + *mapu* floating] *Hawaii* **:** PINTAIL 1a

**koloa mo·ha** \-ˈmō(ˌ)hä\ *n* [Hawaiian, fr. *koloa* duck + *moha* shining] *Hawaii* **:** SHOVELER 2

**kols** *pl of* KOL

**kol·skite** \ˈkōlzˌkīt, -lˌsk-\ *n* -s [Russ *kolskit*, perh. fr. *Kolskiĭ Poluostrov* Kola Peninsula, northwestern U.S.S.R. + Russ *-it* -ite] **:** a mineral $Mg_5Si_4O_{13}.4H_2O$(?) consisting of a serpentine

**kol·son** *or* **kol·sun** \ˈkōlsən\ *n* -s [native name in India] **:** DHOLE

**ko·lusch·an** \kōˈləshən, -lu̇sh-\ *n* -s *usu cap* [perh. irreg. fr. Aleut *kalukaq* wooden utensil, trough; fr. the trough-shaped labrets worn by Tlingit women] **:** TLINGIT 3

**ko·mat·ik** \kōˈmad·ik\ *n* -s [Esk (Labrador dial.)] **:** an Eskimo sledge with wooden runners and crossbars lashed with rawhide

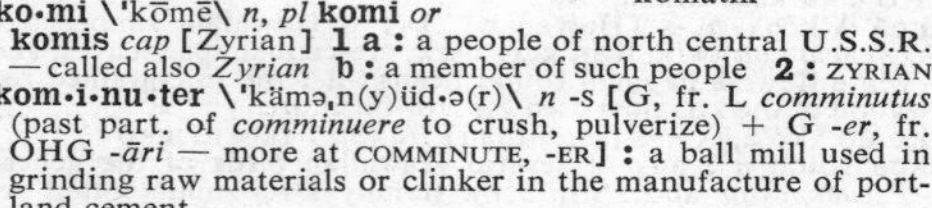

komatik

**kom·bu** \ˈkämˌ(ˌ)bü\ *n* -s [Jap, kombu, kelp, tangle] **:** a food prepared esp. in Japan from various broad-fronded kelps of the family Laminariaceae

**ko·mi** \ˈkōmē\ *n, pl* **komi** *or* **komis** *cap* [Zyrian] **1 a :** a people of north central U.S.S.R. — called also *Zyrian* **b :** a member of such people **2 :** ZYRIAN

**kom·i·nu·ter** \ˈkäməˌn(y)üd·ə(r)\ *n* -s [G, fr. L *comminutus* (past part. of *comminuere* to crush, pulverize) + G *-er*, fr. OHG *-āri* — more at COMMINUTE, -ER] **:** a ball mill used in grinding raw materials or clinker in the manufacture of portland cement

**ko·mi·tad·ji** *or* **co·mi·tad·ji** *also* **ko·mi·ta·ji** \ˌkōməˈtäjē, ˌkäm-\ *n* -s [Turk *komitacı* rebel, member of a secret revolutionary society, fr. *komita* revolutionary committee, secret society] **:** a member of a guerrilla band in Macedonia or the Balkan countries

**kom·man·da·tu·ra** \kəˌmandəˈtu̇rə\ *also* **kom·man·dan·tur** \ˌkämənˌdanˌtu̇(ə)r\ *or* **kom·man·dan·tu·ra** \ˌkämənˌdan-ˈtu̇rə\ *n* -s *usu cap* [*kommandatura, kommandantura* prob. modif. of G *kommandantur* command post, fr. *kommandant* commandant (fr. F *commandant*) + *-ur* -ure; *kommandantur* fr. G, command post] **:** a military government headquarters; *esp* **:** a Russian or interallied headquarters in a European city subsequent to World War II

**kommers** *often cap, var of* COMMERS

**kom·me·tje** *or* **co·mi·tje** \ˈkäməchē\ *n* -s [obs. Afrik (now *kommetjie*), lit., mug, cup, fr. D, dim. of *kom* basin, bowl, fr. MD *com, comme*; akin to MHG *kumpf* bowl — more at COOMB] **:** a small depression common in parts of the African veld

**kom·mos** *or* **com·mos** \kəˈmäs, käˈ-; ˈkäˌmäs, -məs\ *n* -ES [Gk *kommos* kommos, beating of the breast, fr. *koptein* to beat, smite — more at CAPON] **:** a lament in Greek tragedy sung in parts alternating between chief actor and chorus

**ko·mo·do dragon** \kəˈmō(ˌ)dō-\ *or* **komodo lizard** *n, usu cap K* [fr. *Komodo* Island, Indonesia] **:** a dull brown or black monitor lizard (*Varanus komodoensis*) of Komodo and adjacent small islands lying east of Java that attains a length of 10 feet, weighs up to 300 pounds, and feeds largely on eggs but occas. on animals as large as wild pigs or small deer

**ko·mon·dor** \ˈkämənˌdȯ(ə)r\ *n* [Hung] **1** *usu cap* **:** a Hungarian breed of large powerful shaggy-coated white dogs with black nose and dark brown eyes that are used as guard dogs and as herd dogs **2** *pl* **komondors** \-rz\ *also* **komondo·rock** *or* **komondo·rok** \-dȯrək\ *often cap* **:** a dog of the Komondor breed

**kom·so·mol** *or* **com·so·mol** \ˌkäm(p)səˈmȯl\ *also* **con·so·mol** \ˌkän(t)s-\ *n* -s *usu cap* [Russ *komsomol*, short for *Kommunisticheskiĭ Soyuz Molodezhi* Communist Union of Youth, fr. *kommunisticheskiĭ* communist + *soyuz* union + *molodezhi*, gen. of *molodezh'* youth] **:** a member of a Russian Communist youth organization with members between the ages of 16 and 23 years

**ko·na** \ˈkōnə\ *or* **kona storm** *n* -s [Hawaiian *kona*] **:** a storm of southerly or southwesterly winds and heavy rains in Hawaii

**ko·nak** \kōˈnäk\ *n* -s [Turk] **:** a large house in Turkey; *esp* **:** one used as an official residence ⟨we went to visit the big white ~ . . . which I loved so dearly —Selma Ekrem⟩

**konakri** *or* **konakry** *usu cap, var of* CONAKRI

**ko·nar·i·ot** \kəˈna(a)rēˌōt, -ēət\ *or* **ko·nar·i·ote** \-ēˌōt, -ēət\ *n* -s *usu cap* [perh. irreg. fr. *Konya*, city and district in southwest central Turkey] **:** a Turk orig. from the Konya district of Asia Minor now settled in Macedonia

**kond** *or* **kondh** *usu cap, var of* KHOND

**kon·de** \ˈkän(ˌ)dā\ *n, pl* **konde** *or* **kondes** *usu cap* **1 a :** a Bantu people of Nyasaland **b :** a member of such people **2 a :** a Bantu people of Tanganyika **b :** a member of such people **3 :** a Bantu language of either of the Konde peoples

**kon·di·to·rei** \ˈkȯndētōˌrī\ *n* -s *often cap* [G, fr. *konditor* confectioner (blend of earlier *kanditor* confectioner — fr. *kandieren* to candy, fr. F *candir* or It *candire*, both fr. Ar *qandī* candied — and *kondieren* to preserve, fr. L *condire*) + *-ei* -y, fr. MHG *-īe*, fr. OF *-ie* — more at CANDY, CONDITE] **:** a shop selling confectionery or pastry

**kon·dra·ti·eff** \kənˈdrädˌēˌef\ *n* -s *usu cap* [after Nikolai D. *Kondratev* *b*1892 Russ. economist] **:** a business cycle with a periodicity of between 50 and 60 years

**kon·fyt** \kənˈfīt\ *n* -s [Afrik *konfyt*, fr. D *konfijt*, fr. MD *confijt*, fr. MF *confit* — more at COMFIT] *chiefly Africa* **:** PRESERVES

**kon·go** \ˈkän(ˌ)gō\ *n, pl* **kongo** *or* **kongos** *usu cap* **1 a :** a Bantu people of the lower Congo river **b :** a member of such people **2 :** a Bantu language of the Kongo people used as a trade language in the western Congo and adjacent parts of western equatorial Africa and Angola — compare TSHILUBA

**kon·go·ni** *also* **con·go·ni** \käŋˈgōnē\ *n, pl* **kongoni** [Swahili] **:** a hartebeest (*Alcelaphus cokei*) of East Africa

**kongs·berg·ite** \ˈkäŋzˌ(ˌ)bərˌgīt\ *n* -s [F, fr. *Kongsberg*, town in southern Norway + F *-ite*] **:** a mineral consisting of a native silver mercury amalgam

**ko·nia** *or* **ko·ni·eh** \ˈkōnēə\ *n* -s *usu cap* [fr. *Konia, Konya*, district in southwest central Turkey] **:** a Turkish rug woven usu. in soft shades of red, blue, and yellow

**kö·nigs·berg** *or* **ko·nigs·berg** *or* **koe·nigs·berg** \ˈkānigz-ˌbərg, ˈkə(r)n-, ˈkən-, ˈkœniksˌberk\ *adj, usu cap* [fr. *Königsberg* (now *Kaliningrad*), city in the former province of East Prussia, Germany] **:** of or from Königsberg **:** of the kind or style prevalent in Königsberg

**ko·nim·e·ter** \kōˈnimədə(r)\ *also* **co·ni·om·e·ter** \ˌkōnē-ˈämədə(r)\ *n* [*koni-* or *conio-* (fr. Gk *konia* dust) + *-meter* — more at INCINERATE] **:** a device for estimating the dust content of air (as in a mine or a cement mill)

**ko·ninck·ite** \ˈkōniŋˌkīt, -nənˌk-\ *n* -s [F *koninckite*, fr. L. G. de *Koninck* †1887 Belg. geologist + F *-ite*] **:** a mineral $FePO_4.3H_2O$ consisting of hydrous ferric phosphate in yellow aggregates of radiated structure

**ko·nini** \kəˈninē, -ˈnēnē\ *n* -s [Maori] **:** a tree fuchsia (*Fuchsia excorticata*) of New Zealand that often attains a height of 40 feet and that has pendulous showy flowers — called also *native fuchsia*

**ko·nio·cortex** \ˌkōnē(ˌ)ō+\ *n* [*konio-* (fr. Gk *konia* dust) + *cortex*] **:** granular-appearing cerebral cortex esp. characteristic of sensory areas

**ko·ni·ol·o·gy** *also* **co·ni·ol·o·gy** \ˌkōnēˈäləjē\ *n* -ES [*konio-, conio-* (fr. Gk *konia* dust) + *-logy*] **:** a science that deals with atmospheric dust and its effects on plant and animal life

**kon·jak** \ˈkänˌjak\ *n* -s [Jap *konjaku*] **:** a large aroid (*Amorphophallus rivieri*) grown in Japan for its large tuberous corms used for making flour

**konk** *var of* CONK

**kon·ka·ni** \ˈkäŋkə(ˌ)nē, ˈkōŋ-\ *n* -s *usu cap* [Marathi *Koṅkaṇī*, fr. *Koṅkaṇ* Konkan, coast region of western India where it is spoken] **:** an Indic language of the west coast of India sometimes considered a dialect of Marathi

**konk·er tree** \ˈkäŋ|kə(r)-, ˈkōŋ|\ *n* [[1]*conker* + *tree*] **:** HORSE CHESTNUT 1a

**ko·no** \ˈkō(ˌ)nō\ *n, pl* **kono** *or* **konos** *usu cap* **1 a :** a peasant people of Sierra Leone **b :** a member of such people **2 :** a Mande language of the Kono people closely related to Vai

**ko·no·hi·ki** \ˌkōnəˈhēkē\ *n* -s [Hawaiian] **1 :** a headman of a Hawaiian land division who also controls fishing rights in adjacent waters **2 :** a Hawaiian land division with its accompanying fishing rights

**kon·seal** \ˈkänˌsē(ə)l\ *n* [fr. *Konseals*, a trademark] **:** CACHET 3

**-kont** \ˌkänt\ *n comb form* -s [ISV, fr. Gk *kontos* pole, fr. *kentein* to prick — more at CENTER] **:** flagellum of a cell

**kon·ta·kion** *or* **con·ta·kion** \kənˈtäkyōn\ *n, pl* **konta·kia** *or* **conta·kia** \-yə\ [MGk *kontakion*, lit., scroll, prob. dim. of LGk *kontak-, kontax* pole, fr. Gk *kontos*] **:** a short hymn in the Eastern Orthodox Church in praise of a saint

**kon·yak** \ˈkänˌyak\ *n, pl* **konyak** *or* **konyaks** *usu cap* **1 a :** a people of the Assam-Burma frontier area **b :** a member of such people **2 :** the Tibeto-Burman language of the Konyak people

**kon·ze** \ˈkänzə\ *n* -s [Konde *nkonzhe*] **:** an African hartebeest (*Alcelaphus lichtensteini*) of the Zambesi and Nyasa regions

**koo·doo** *or* **ku·du** *also* **kou·dou** \ˈkü(ˌ)dü\ *n* -s [Afrik *koedoe*, prob. fr. Xhosa *iqudu, iquda*] **:** a large African antelope (*Strepsiceros strepsiceros* syn. *kudo*) that has large annulated spirally twisted horns and is grayish brown with vertical white stripes on the sides — compare LESSER KOODOO

**koofah** *var of* GUFA

**kook·a·bur·ra** \ˈku̇kəˌbərə\ *n* -s [native name in Australia] **:** a kingfisher (*Dacelo gigas*) of Australia that is about the size of a crow, has a call resembling loud laughter, and feeds in part on reptiles — called also *kinghunter, laughing jackass*

**koo·le·tah** \ˈküləˌtä\ *n* -s [Esk (Greenland dial.)] **:** an Eskimo coat made of caribou skin

**koo·li·man** \ˈküləˌman, -ˌmən\ *var of* COOLAMON

**koo·lo·kam·ba** \ˌküləˈkambə, -käm-\ *n* -s [native name on the Gabon river, Gabon, equatorial Africa] **:** a dark-faced West African chimpanzee sometimes regarded as a separate species (*Pan koolokamba*)

**koom·bar** \'kümbə(r)\ *n* -s [Tamil *kumir*] : an East Indian timber tree (*Gmelina arborea*) used esp. for building foundations and for boat decks

**koom·kie** \'kümkē\ *or* **koon·kie** \-üŋkē,-üŋkē\ *n* -s [Hindi *kumakī* helper, fr. Per] : a trained usu. female elephant used in India to decoy and train wild male elephants

**koorajong** *var of* KURRAJONG

**koorhaan** *var of* KORHAAN

**koor·ka** \'ku̇rkə\ *n* -s [origin unknown] : a coleus (*Coleus parviflorus*) native to Africa but cultivated widely in India for its edible tubers

**kootch** *var of* COOCH

**koo·tcha** \'küchə\ *or* **koo·tchar** \-chə(r)\ *n* -s [native name in Australia] : a small stingless wild Australian honeybee of the genus *Trigona*

**kootenai** *usu cap, var of* KUTENAI

**kope** \'kōp\ *chiefly Midland var of* ³COOP

**ko·peck** *or* **ko·pek** *or* **co·peck** \'kō,pek\ *n* -s [Russ *kopeĭka*, fr. *kop'e* lance; fr. the fact that the Czar was orig. depicted on the coin with a lance in his hand; akin to Russ *kopat'* to dig, hollow, Gk *koptein* to smite, cut off — more at CAPON] **1** : a Russian unit of monetary value equal to 1/100 of a ruble — see MONEY table **2** : a coin orig. of base silver representing one kopeck

**koph** *var of* QOPH

**ko·pi** \'kōpē\ *n* -s [Moriori] *New Zeal* : KARAKA

**kop·je** *or* **kop·pie** \'käpē\ *n* -s [Afrik *koppie* kopje, cup, fr. D *kopje* small head, cup, dim. of *kop* head, cup, fr. MD *cop, coppe* — more at CUP] : a small hill found esp. on the African veld sometimes reaching 100 feet above the surrounding country and often covered with scrub

**kop·lik's spots** \'käpliks-\ *also* **koplik spots** *n pl, usu cap K* [after Henry *Koplik* †1927 Am. pediatrician] : small bluish white dots surrounded by a reddish zone that appear on the mucous membrane of the cheeks and lips before the appearance of the skin eruption in a case of measles

**kop·pa** \'käpə\ *n* -s [Gk, of Sem origin; akin to Heb *qōph* qoph] : a letter of the early Greek alphabet replaced by kappa in the eastern Greek alphabet except for use as a numeral with the value 90 but retained in the western Greek alphabet and ultimately becoming the Latin letter *Q*

**kop·pel·flö·te** \'käpəl,flādə, -flēdə, *G* 'kȯpəl,flœtə\ *n* -s [G, fr. *koppel* tie, connection (fr. MHG *koppel, kuppel*, fr. OF *cople, couple* pair, bond) + *flöte* flute, fr. MHG *vloite*, fr. OF *flaute, fleute* — more at COUPLE, FLUTE] : an open flute stop in a pipe organ having a neutral tone and serving as a basis upon which to erect tonal pyramids of mutation ranks

**kopp·ite** \'kä,pīt\ *n* -s [G *koppit*, fr. Hermann F. M. *Kopp* †1892 Ger. chemist + G *-it* -ite] : a mineral consisting of a pyrochlore containing cerium, iron, and potassium

**kopt** *cap, var of* COPT

**kor** *also* **cor** *or* **core** \'kȯ(ə)r, 'kō(ə)r\ *n* -s [Heb *kōr*] : an ancient Hebrew and Phoenician unit of measure of capacity identical with the homer but used in later Old Testament times only in liquid measurement

**ko·ra** \'kōrə\ *n* -s [origin unknown] : WATER COCK

**ko·rah·ite** \'kōrə,īt\ *n* -s *usu cap* [*Korah*, great-grandson of Levi (Exod 6:21 (AV)) + E *-ite*] : a descendant of the biblical Levite Korah who founded a line of prominent temple musicians

**ko·rai period** \'kōr,ī-\ *n, usu cap K* [*Korai, Koryu*, dynasty ruling Korea from about A.D. 918 to 1392] : the historical and stylistic period from about A.D. 918 to 1392 in Korea

**korait** *var of* KRAIT

**ko·ra·kan** \'kōrə,kän\ *or* **ku·rak·kan** \'ku̇rə,kän\ *n* -s [Tamil *kurakkan*, fr. Sinhalese *kurakkan* raggee] : RAGGEE

**ko·ran** *or* **qur·'an** *or* **qu·ran** *or* **qo·ran** \kə'ran, (')kō;r-, (')kȯ;r-, (')kü;r-, -rän, -raa(ə)n, -rȧn *sometimes* 'kōrən *or* 'kȯrən\ *n* -s *usu cap* [Ar *qur'ān*, fr. *qara'a* to read, recite] : the book composed of writings accepted by Muslims as revelations made to Muhammad by Allah and as the divinely authorized basis for the religious, social, civil, commercial, military, and legal regulations of the Islamic world

**ko·ra·na** \kə'ränə\ *n, pl* **korana** *or* **koranas** *usu cap* **1 a** : any of a group of racially mixed Hottentot peoples living along the Orange, Vaal, and Modder rivers in southern Africa **b** : a member of any of such peoples **2** : a dialect of Hottentot spoken by the Korana peoples

**ko·ran·ic** *or* **qur·'an·ic** \kə'ranik, kō'-,kȯ'-,kü'-, -rän-,-raan-,-rȧn-\ *adj, usu cap* : of, relating to, or prescribed by the Muslim sacred scriptures contained in the Koran ⟨they come to be able to sip alcoholic drinks without *Koranic* scandal —Hal Lehrman⟩

**ko·ra·ri** \'kōrə,rē\ *n* -s [Maori] : NEW ZEALAND FLAX

**korban** *var of* CORBAN

**kor·dax** *or* **cor·dax** \'kȯ(ə)r,daks\ *n* -ES [L *cordax*, fr. Gk *kordax*; akin to Gk *kradan* to shake, brandish — more at CARDINAL] **1** : a phallic dance by nude horned figures in the Dionysian orgies of ancient Greece **2** : a lewd coarse dance derived from the Dionysian kordax and incorporated into Greek and Latin comedy **3** : any of various lively Renaissance court dances

**kor·do·fan gum** \'kȯrdə,fan-\ *n, usu cap K* [fr. *Kordofan* province, Republic of the Sudan] : a superior gum arabic from the Kordofan district of the Republic of the Sudan

**kor·do·fan·ian** \,kȯrdə'fanēən\ *n, cap* [*Kordofan* province, Republic of the Sudan + E *-ian*] : a small group of languages spoken in the Kordofan district of the Republic of the Sudan apparently constituting a language family

**ko·rea** \kə'rēə, *in rapid speech* 'krēə, *chiefly southern US* (')kō;rēə\ *adj, usu cap* [fr. *Korea*, country in eastern Asia] : of or from Korea : of the kind or style prevalent in Korea : KOREAN

¹**ko·re·an** *also* **co·re·an** \-ēən\ *adj, usu cap* [*Korea* + E *-an*, adj. suffix] **1 a** : of, relating to, or characteristic of Korea **b** : of, relating to, or characteristic of the Koreans **2** : of, relating to, or characteristic of the Korean language

²**korean** *also* **corean** \"\ *n* -s *cap* [*Korea* + E *-an*, n. suffix] **1** : a native or inhabitant of Korea **2** : the language of the Korean people now usu. written in the Hankul alphabet

**korean box** *or* **korean boxwood** *n, usu cap K* : a compact slow-growing notably hardy box (*Buxus microphylla koreana*) with conspicuously winged branches and obovate leaves ¼ to ½ inch long

**korean lawn grass** *n, usu cap K* : an Asiatic grass (*Zoisia japonica*) used in China and Japan and more recently in America as a lawn grass — called also *Japanese lawn grass*

**korean lespedeza** *n, usu cap K* : a much-branched annual lespedeza (*Lespedeza stipulacea*) that is native to Korea but is widely cultivated for hay and forage esp. in regions of hot dry climate

**korean pine** *n, usu cap K* : a pine (*Pinus koraiensis*) of eastern Asia having reddish gray bark and differing from Swiss pine in having longer leaves with the margins toothed to the apex and cones four to six inches long

**koreanspice viburnum** \=;==;=-\ *n, usu cap K* : a much-branched spreading deciduous spring-flowering shrub (*Viburnum carlesii*) having both its young branchlets and its inflorescence tomentose and having clove-scented flowers with a cylindrical corolla tube

**korean velvet grass** *n, usu cap K* : MASCARENE GRASS

**koreish** *usu cap, var of* QURAISH

**ko·resh·an** \kō'reshən\ *adj, usu cap* [Heb *Kōresh* Cyrus (after *Cyrus* R. Teed †1908 Am. physician who founded Koreshanity) + E *-an*, adj. suffix] : of or relating to Koreshanity

**ko·resh·an·i·ty** \,kō,re'shanədē\ *n* -ES *usu cap* [*koreshan* + *-ity*] : the doctrines and beliefs of a communal religious society founded in 1886 by Cyrus R. Teed to reestablish church and state upon a basis of divine fellowship

**kor·haan** \'kō(ə)r,hän\ *or* **knor·haan** *also* **knoor·haan** \'nō-\ *or* **koor·haan** \'kō-\ *n, pl* **korhaan** *or* **korhaans** *or* **knorhaan** *or* **knorhaans** [*korhaan, koorhaan* fr. Afrik *korhaan*, fr. D, black grouse, fr. *korren* to coo (fr. MD *curren*, prob. of imit. origin) + *haan* cock, rooster, fr. MD *hane*; *knorhaan, knoorhaan* fr. Afrik *knorhaan*, fr. D, black grouse, alter. (influenced by *knorren* to grumble, fr. MD *cnorren*, prob. of imit. origin) of *korhaan*; akin to OE *hana* rooster — more at CHANT] **1** : any of several African bustards **2** *usu knoorhaan* [so called fr. the sound they make when taken out of the water] **a** : any of several gurnards of southern Africa **b** : a large grunt (*Pomadasys operculare*) of the Indian ocean that is a food and game fish in southern Africa

**koriak** *usu cap, var of* KORYAK

**ko·ri bustard** \'kōrē-\ *n* [*kori* fr. a native name in southern Africa] : GOM-PAAUW

**ko·ri·ma·ko** \,kōrə'mä(,)kō\ *n* -s [Maori] : a New Zealand bellbird (*Anthornis melanura*)

**ko·rin** \'kōrən\ *n* -s [origin unknown] : a gazelle (*Gazella rufifrons*) of Senegambia, West Africa

**Ko·ri·na** \kə'rēnə\ *trademark* — used for limba wood

**kor·ku** \'kȯ(ə)r(,)kü\ *n, pl* **korku** *or* **korkus** *usu cap* **1 a** : a people inhabiting the forested hills of southern Madhya Pradesh, India **b** : a member of such people **2** : the Munda language of the Korku people

**kor·nel·ite** \'kȯ(r)nᵊl,īt\ *n* -s [Hung *kornelit*, fr. *Kornel* Hlavacsek, 19th cent. person otherwise unidentified + Hung *-it* -ite] : a mineral $Fe_2(SO_4)_3 \cdot 7H_2O$ consisting of a ferric sulfate heptahydrate

**kor·ne·rup·ine** \,kȯ(r)nə'rü,pēn, -,pən\ *n* -s [Dan *kornerupin*, fr. A. N. *Kornerup*, 19th cent. Dan. geologist + Dan *-in* -ine] : a mineral $(Mg,Fe,Al)_{20}(Si,B)_9O_{43}$ consisting of a magnesium aluminum iron borosilicate resembling sillimanite in appearance

**ko·ro** \'kōr(,)ō\ *n* -s [Jap *kōro*, fr. *kō* incense + *ro* hearth, furnace] : a squat broad-mouthed jar with bulging shoulder and usu. of porcelain or jade

**ko·roa** \kə'rōə\ *n, pl* **koroa** *or* **koroas** *usu cap* **1** : a Tunican people of the Yazoo and Mississippi river valleys, Mississippi **2** : a member of the Koroa people

**kor·o·mi·ko** \,kȯrə'mē(,)kō\ *also* **kor·o·mi·ka** \-ēkə\ *n* -s [Maori] **1** : any of several shrubs of the genus *Veronica* (esp. *V. salicifolia* and *V. parviflora*) **2** : a drug obtained from a koromiko plant

**ko·ro·na** \'kȯrə,nō\ *n, pl* **korona** *or* **koronas** [Hung, lit., crown, fr. L *corona* — more at CROWN] **1** : the basic monetary unit of Hungary 1892–1925 **2** : a silver coin representing one korona

**Kor·o·seal** \'kȯrə,sē(ə)l\ *trademark* — used for a thermoplastic composition of polyvinyl chloride that is rubberlike and resistant to oil, sunlight, and flame and is used esp. in insulation, tank linings, gaskets, and coatings for textiles and paper

**kor·ri·gan** \'kȯrə,gän\ *n* -s [Bret, fem. of *korrig* gnome, dim. of *korr* dwarf] : a long-haired nocturnal often malevolent Breton fairy sorceress

**kor·ri·gum** \'kärəgəm\ *n* -s [modif. of Kanuri *kargum*] : a reddish fawn antelope (*Damaliscus korrigum*) of western Africa with black markings

**kors** *pl of* KOR

**kor·sa·koff's psychosis** *or* **korsakoff's syndrome** *also* **kor·sa·kow's psychosis** *or* **kor·sa·kow's syndrome** \'kȯ(r)sə,kȯfs-, -,kävz-\ *n, usu cap K* [after Sergei *Korsakov* †1900 Russ. psychiatrist] : an abnormal mental condition that is usu. a sequel of chronic alcoholism, is often associated with polyneuritis, and is characterized by an irregular memory loss for which the patient attempts to compensate through confabulation

**ko·ru·na** \'kȯrə,nä\ *n, pl* **ko·run** \-,rün\ *or* **ko·ru·ny** \-,rənē\ *also* **korunas** \-,rə,näz\ [Czech, lit., crown, fr. L *corona*] **1** : the basic monetary unit of Czechoslovakia — see MONEY table **2** : a coin representing one koruna

**kor·wa** \'kȯ(ə)rwə\ *n, pl* **korwa** *or* **korwas** *usu cap* **1 a** : a people of the western Chota Nagpur region of southwestern Bihar, India, apparently related to the Mundas **b** : a member of such people **2** : the Munda language of the Korwa people

**kor·yak** *or* **kor·iak** \'kȯ(ə)rē,yak\ *n, pl* **koryak** *or* **koryaks** *or* **koriak** *or* **koriaks** *usu cap* **1 a** : an Americanoid people of northeastern Siberia **b** : a member of such people **2** : the Luorawetlan language of the Koryak people

**KO's** *pl of* KO, *pres 3d sing of* KO

**ko·sam** \'kō,sam\ *n* -s [origin unknown] : a small evergreen shrub (*Brucea amarissima*) of the family Simaroubaceae that is widely distributed in open country in much of southeastern Asia and in northern Australia, is noted for the bitterness of all its parts, and has various uses esp. in local medicine — see KOSAM SEED

**kosam seed** *n* : the very bitter fruit of the kosam sometimes used in the treatment of various diarrheas and dysenteries

**ko·share** \kō'sha(a)(ə)r\ *n, pl* **koshare** *or* **koshares** *often cap* [Keres] **1** : a Pueblo Indian clown society representing ancestral spirits in ceremonies invoking rain and fertility **2** : a member of the koshare

¹**ko·sher** \'kōshə(r)\ *or* **ka·sher** \kä'she(ə)r, -eə\ *adj* [Yiddish *kosher*, fr. Heb *kāshēr* fit, proper] **1** : sanctioned by Jewish law; ritually fit, clean, or prepared for use according to Jewish law ⟨~ meat⟩ ⟨a ~ scroll of the law⟩ **2** : selling, serving, or using food that is ritually fit according to Jewish law ⟨a ~ restaurant⟩ ⟨she keeps a ~ house⟩ **3** : GENUINE, LEGITIMATE, PROPER ⟨a strong minority feeling that Piltdown was not a very ~ specimen —*New Yorker*⟩ ⟨tried to stop me from withdrawing the money, sensing that something was not ~, but I wouldn't listen —Polly Adler⟩ ⟨the rifle report that followed shortly after seemed perfectly ~ at the time; after all, they do fire guns at army bases —Frederic Ramsey⟩

²**kosher** *var of* KASHER

**kosher hide** *n* : the hide of an animal slaughtered in accordance with rabbinical law by crosswise cutting of the throat — called also *cutthroat*

**ko·sin** \'kōsᵊn\ *n* -s [ISV *kos-* (fr. ¹*koso*) + *-in*] : a yellowish brown amorphous anthelmintic powder containing all of the constituents of brayera — called also *brayerin*

**kosmos** *var of* COSMOS

¹**ko·so** \'kō(,)sō\ *or* **kos·so** \'kä(-\ *or* **kous·so** \'kü(-\ *n* -s [prob. fr. Galla *kosso*] : BRAYERA

²**koso** \'kō(,)sō\ *n, pl* **koso** *or* **kosos** *usu cap* **1** : a Shoshonean people of southeastern California **2** : a member of the Koso people

**kos·suth hat** \(')kä;süth-, (')kȯ;süth-, 'kȯ,shu̇t-\ *n* [after Lajos *Kossuth* †1894 Hung. patriot and statesman] : a hat with a flat-topped crown and rolled brim

kossuth hat

**kos·te·letz·kya** \,kästə'letskēə\ *n, cap* [NL, fr. V. F. *Kosteletzky* †1887 Bohemian botanist] : a small genus of herbs of the family Malvaceae that are native chiefly to the southern U.S. and tropical America and that differ from the mallows in having a single ovule in each cell of the ovary

**ko·stro·ma** \'kästrə;mä\ *adj, usu cap* [fr. *Kostroma*, city in north central part of European Russia, U.S.S.R.] : of or from the city of Kostroma, U.S.S.R. : of the kind or style prevalent in Kostroma

**kot** \'kät, 'kȯt\ *n, pl* **kot** *or* **kots** *usu cap* **1 a** : an extinct people once living along the Agul river tributary of the Yenisei river in Siberia **b** : a member of the Kot people **2** : the Yeniseian language of the Kot people

¹**ko·ta** \'kōdə\ *or* **ko·tar** \'kō,tär\ *n, pl* **kota** *or* **kotas** *or* **kotar** *or* **kotars** *usu cap* **1 a** : an artisan and buffalo-herding people of the Nilgiri hills of southwestern India **b** : a member of such people **2** : the Dravidian language of the Kota people

²**kota** \"\ *n, pl* **kota** *or* **kotas** *usu cap* **1** : a Bantu-speaking people of the interior of French Equatorial Africa noted in recent times for the quality of their carving esp. of wooden religious masks **2** : a member of the Kota people

**ko·thor·nos** \'käthər,näs, kō'thȯrnəs\ *n* -ES [Gk] : COTHURNUS 1

**ko·to** \'kōd(,)ō\ *n* -s [Jap] : a long Japanese zither having 13 silk strings — compare ⁶KIN

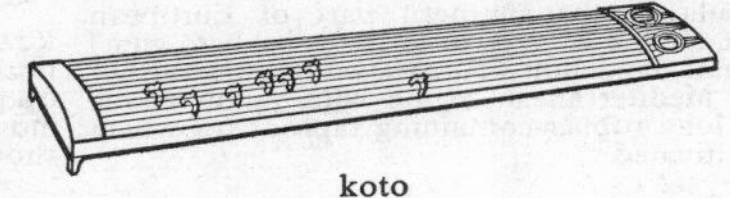
koto

**ko·to·ite** \'kōdə,wīt\ *n* -s [G *kotoit*, fr. Bundjiro *Koto* †1935 Jap. geologist and petrographer + G *-it* -ite] : a mineral $Mg_3(BO_3)_2$ consisting of a borate of magnesium

**ko·to·ko** \kə'tō(,)kō\ *n, pl* **kotoko** *or* **kotokos** *usu cap* **1** : a people of the lower Shari-Logoni basin in the environs of Lake Chad **2** : a member of the Kotoko people

**kotow** *var of* KOWTOW

**ko·tschu·be·ite** \kə'chübē,īt\ *n* -s [F *kotchoubeïte*, fr. P. A. v. *Kochubey*, 19th cent. Russ. count + F *-ite*] : a rose-red mineral consisting of a chrome-bearing clinochlore

**köttigite** *var of* KOETTIGITE

**kötts·torf·er value** *or* **koetts·torf·er value** \'ket,stȯrfər-\ *n, usu cap K* [prob. fr. the name *Köttstorfer, Koettstorfer*] : SAPONIFICATION VALUE

**ko·tu·ku** \'kōdə,kü\ *n* -s [Maori] *NewZeal* : GREAT WHITE HERON 1

**kot·wal** *or* **cot·wal** \'kōt,wäl\ *n* -s [Hindi *kotwāl*, fr. Per] : a chief police officer or town magistrate in India

**kot·wa·lee** \'kōt,wälē\ *n* -s [Hindi *kotwālī*, fr. Per, fr. *kotwāl*] : a police station in India

**kotyliform** *var of* COTYLIFORM

**kou** \'kau̇\ *n* -s [Hawaiian] *Hawaii* : a tree (*Cordia subcordata*) of the Pacific islands whose wood is used for making household utensils

**koudou** *var of* KOODOO

**koulan** *var of* KULAN

**kou·miss** *or* **ku·miss** *or* **ku·mys** *or* **ku·myss** \kü'mis, 'küməs\ *n* -ES [Russ *kumys*, fr. Kazan Tatar & Kirghiz *kumyz*] : a fermented beverage made orig. by the nomadic peoples of central Asia from mare's milk and now also from cow's milk elsewhere — compare LEBEN

**kou·prey** \'kü(,)prā\ *also* **kou·proh** \-rō\ *n* -s [native name in Cambodia] : a blackish brown short-haired forest ox (*Bibos sauveli* or *Novibos sauveli*) of Cambodia that attains a large size, that has a long tail, large dewlap, and spreading recurved horns like those of the yak, and that may be an ancestor of the zebus

**kourbash** *var of* KURBASH

**kou·ros** \'kü,rȯs\ *n, pl* **kou·roi** \-rȯi\ [Gk *koros, kouros* boy — more at CRESCENT] : a sculptured figure of a Greek youth (as an athlete) of which many examples dating from classical antiquity are extant

¹**kouse** *also* **kous** \'kau̇(ə)s\ *n, pl* **kous·es** [by alter.] : COUS

²**kouse** *also* **kous** \'kau̇s\ *n, pl* **kous·es** [origin unknown] : PEARL MILLET

**kouskous** *var of* COUSCOUS

**kousso** *var of* KOSO

**kousso flower** *n* [*kousso* prob. fr. Galla *kosso* brayera] : BRAYERA

**kov·no** \'kȯv(,)nō, -,nə\ *adj, usu cap* [fr. *Kovno* (*Kaunas*), Lithuania] : KAUNAS

**kowbird** *var of* KOBIRD

**ko·whai** \'kō,wī\ *n* -s [Maori] : a shrub or small tree (*Sophora tetraptera*) of Australasia and Chile that yields a hard strong wood

**kowliang** *var of* KAOLIANG

¹**kow·tow** *or* **ko·tow** \(')kau̇;tau̇ *sometimes* kō'tau̇\ *n* -s [Chin (Pek) *k'o¹ t'ou²*, fr. *k'o¹* to strike, bump + *t'ou²* head] : an act of kowtowing

²**kowtow** *or* **kotow** \"\ *vi* -ED/-ING/-S **1** : to kneel and touch the forehead to the ground (as in old Chinese custom) in token of homage, worship, or deep respect ⟨everyone should ~ to the abbot, even the chief, but no one receives the abbot's kowtow —Ju-K'ang T'ien⟩ **2** : to show obsequious deference : FAWN ⟨you'll never find a Swiss ~*ing* or bootlicking —T.H. Fielding⟩ ⟨a brilliant scholar . . . ~*ed* to the regime and became an empty, self-hating shell of a man —*Time*⟩

**ko·yem·shi** \kō'yem(p)shē\ *n, pl* **koyemshi** *or* **koyemshis** *often cap* [Zuñi] **1** : a Zuñi Indian clown society whose members wear the mask of the mudhead and are credited with curing illness by their dancing and clowning **2** : a member of the koyemshi

**ko·yu·kon** \kō'yü,kän\ *n, pl* **koyukon** *or* **koyukons** *usu cap* **1 a** : an Athapaskan people of the Yukon river valley of west central Alaska **b** : a member of such people **2** : the language of the Koyukon people — called also *Khotana, Ten'a*

**ko·zhi·kode** \'kōzhə,kōd\ *adj, usu cap* [fr. *Kozhikode* (*Calicut*), India] : CALICUT

**ko·zo** \'kō(,)zō\ *n* -s [Jap *kōzo*] : PAPER MULBERRY

**KP** *abbr or n* -s kitchen police

**KP** *abbr* **1** king post **2** King's Proctor **3** knotty pine

**kpel·le** \kə'pelə\ *n, pl* **kpelle** *or* **kpelles** *usu cap* **1 a** : a people of central Liberia **b** : a member of the Kpelle people **2** : a Mande language of the Kpelle people

**KPH** *abbr* kilometers per hour

**kr** *abbr* **1** kiloroentgen **2** kran **3** kreuzer **4** krona **5** krone **6** kroon

**Kr** *symbol* krypton

**kra** \'krä\ *n* -s [Malay *kera*] : CRAB-EATING MACAQUE

¹**kraal** \'kräl, -ȧ-\ *n* -s [Afrik, fr. Pg *curral* pen for cattle, enclosure, fr. (assumed) VL *currale* enclosure for vehicles — more at CORRAL] **1 a** : a village of southern African natives (as Hottentots or Kaffirs) **b** : the organized social unit that the kraal represents : the native village community **2 a** : a single hut or group of huts in which natives in southern Africa live **b** : an enclosure for domestic animals in southern Africa **c** : an elephant corral in Ceylon, India, or Thailand **d** [D, fr. Pg *curral*] : an enclosure for keeping turtles, lobsters, or sponges alive in shallow water — called also *manyatta*

²**kraal** \"\ *vt* -ED/-ING/-S : to pen in a kraal

**krae·pe·lin·i·an** \,krepə;linēən *also* -rap-\ *adj, usu cap* [Emil *Kraepelin* †1926, Ger. psychiatrist + E *-ian*] : of or relating to Emil Kraepelin or to his system of psychiatric classification

**kraft** \'kraft, -aa(ə)-, -ai-, -ȧ-\ *n* -s *often attrib* [G, lit., strength, fr. OHG — more at CRAVE] : a strong paper (as most brown wrapping and bag papers) or board made from sulfate pulp ⟨~ paper⟩ ⟨~ process⟩ ⟨~ liner⟩

**krait** *or* **ko·rait** *also* **ka·rait** \'krīt, kə'r-\ *n* -s [Hindi *karait*] : any of several brightly banded unaggressive but extremely venomous nocturnal elapid snakes of the genus *Bungarus* that are native to eastern Asia and adjacent islands and frequent cultivated land and human habitations and feed esp. on other snakes

**kra·ken** \'kräkən\ *n* -s [Norw dial., the kraken, fr. Norw dial. *krake* kraken + Norw *-n* (suffixed definite article)] : a fabulous Scandinavian sea monster perhaps imagined on the basis of chance sightings of giant squids

**krakow** *usu cap, var of* CRACOW

**kra·ko·wi·ak** \krə'kōvē,ak\ *n* -s [Pol, fr. *Krakow, Cracow*, city and department in southern Poland] : a Polish usu. group folk dance that combines elements of the ancient round, the more recent square, and the modern polka ⟨tread out bouncing ~ measures to the accompaniment of flute, fiddle, and accordion —H.M.Robinson⟩

¹**kra·ma** \'krämə\ *n* -s [Gk, mixture, mixed wine, fr. *kerannynai* to mix — more at CRATER] : the mingled and consecrated wine and water into which the consecrated bread is broken at the Eucharist in the Eastern Orthodox Church

²**krama** \"\ *or* **kro·mo** \'krō(,)mō\ *n* -s *usu cap* [Jav *krama*] : the form of Javanese used in speaking to or in the presence of social superiors

**kra·me·ria** \krə'mirēə\ *n* [NL, fr. J. G. H. and W. H. *Kramer*, 18th cent. Ger. botanists + NL *-ia*] **1** *cap* : a genus of shrubs that are usu. placed in the family Leguminosae but have sometimes been included among the Polygalaceae or isolated in a monotypic family, that have flowers with irregular petals and a one-celled ovary which are followed by indehiscent prickly fruits, and that in some cases have astringent roots which are sometimes used in pharmacy and tanning **2** -s : the dried roots of certain plants of the genus *Krameria* — see RHATANY — **kra·me·ri·a·ceous** \=;==;āshəs\ *adj*

**kran** \'krän\ *n* -s [Per *qrān*] **1** : the basic monetary unit of Persia from 1826 to 1932 **2** : a silver coin representing one kran

**krang** *var of* KRENG

**krantz** *also* **krans** \'kran(t)s, -ä-\ *n* -ES [Afrik *krans*, lit., wreath, fr. D, fr. MD *crans* — more at CRANCE] : a sheer cliff or precipice in southern Africa ⟨crawled forward and looked over the edge of the ~ —Stuart Cloete⟩

**krantz·ite** \'kran(t),sīt\ *n* -s [G *krantzit*, fr. A. *Krantz*, 19th cent. Ger. mineralogist + G *-it* -ite] **:** a fossil resin similar to amber

**krap·fen** \'kräpfən\ *n, pl* **krap·fen** [G *krapfen*, fr. OHG *krāpfo* hook, fritter — more at CRAVE] **:** BISMARCK

**kra·pi·na man** \'kräpənə-\ *n, usu cap K* [*Krapina*, locality in northern Croatia, Yugoslavia] **:** an early broad-headed Neanderthal man known from several fragmentary skeletons found associated with Mousterian artifacts in a rock shelter in northern Croatia

**kra·sis** \'kräsəs\ *n, pl* **kra·seis** \-ä(,)sēs\ [Gk, mixing, combination, fr. *kerannynai* to mix — more at CRATER] **:** the act or practice of mingling water with wine in the Eastern Orthodox Eucharist **:** MIXED CHALICE — compare KRAMA

**kras·no·dar** \'kraznə,där, ¦==¦=\ *adj, usu cap* [fr. *Krasnodar*, city in southern part of European Russia, U.S.S.R.] **:** of or from the city of Krasnodar, U.S.S.R. **:** of the kind or style prevalent in Krasnodar

**kras·no·yarsk** \'kraznə,yärsk, ¦==¦=\ *adj, usu cap* [fr. *Krasnoyarsk*, city in west central Siberia, U.S.S.R.] **:** of or from the city of Krasnoyarsk, U.S.S.R. **:** of the kind or style prevalent in Krasnoyarsk

**kra·ter** *or* **cra·ter** \'kräd·ər, krä'tā(ə)r\ *n* -s [Gk *kratēr* mixing bowl, krater — more at CRATER] **:** a vessel of Greek and Roman antiquity resembling an amphora but having a larger body and a wide mouth and used for mixing wine and water — compare KELEBE

kraters

**k ration** *n, usu cap K* **:** a lightweight packaged ration of emergency foods developed for U.S. armed forces in World War II

**kratoch·vil·ite** \krə'tächvə,līt, 'krad·ək,vi,l-\ *n* -s [ISV *kratochvil-* (prob. fr. Josef *Kratochvíl* b1878 Czechoslovak petrographer) + *-ite*] **:** FLUORENE

**krat·o·gen** \'krad·əjən, -,jen\ *n* -s [G, fr. *krato-* (fr. Gk *kratos* mastery, strength) + *-gen* — more at HARD] **:** a region that has remained undisturbed while an adjacent area has been affected by mountain-making movements — compare OROGEN — **krat·o·gen·ic** \¦==¦jenik\ *adj*

**kra·ton** \'krā,tän, -ra,t-\ *n* -s [ISV, perh. alter. of *kratogen*] **:** KRATOGEN

**krau·rite** \'kraů,rīt\ *n* -s [G *kraurit*, fr. Gk *krauros* brittle + G *-it* -ite] **:** DUFRENITE

**krau·ro·sis** \krò'rōsəs\ *n, pl* **krau·ro·ses** \-ō,sēz\ [NL, fr. Gk *krauros* brittle + NL *-osis*] **:** atrophy and shriveling of the skin or mucous membrane esp. of the vulva where it is often a precancerous lesion — **krau·rot·ic** \(')=¦räd·ik\ *adj*

**¹krau·sen** \'kròiz°n\ *vt* -ED/-ING/-S [G *kräusen* to add herbs to brewing beer, fr. *krausen*, *kräusen* to curl back from the edge (said of foam), curl, fr. MHG *krūsen* to curl, fr. *krūs* curly — more at CURL] **:** to add strong newly fermenting wort (to beer) to produce natural carbonation — compare GYLE

**²krausen** \"\ *n* -s **:** fermenting wort

**krau·se's corpuscle** \'kraůzəz-\ *n, usu cap K* [after Wilhelm *Krause* †1910 Ger. anatomist] **:** any of various rounded sensory end organs occurring in mucous membranes (as of the conjunctiva or genitals)

**krause's end-bulb** *n, usu cap K* **:** KRAUSE'S CORPUSCLE

**krause's membrane** *n, usu cap K* **:** one of the isotropic cross bands in a striated muscle fiber that consists of disks of sarcoplasm linking the individual fibrils

**kraus·ite** \'kraů,sīt\ *n* -s [Edward Henry *Kraus* b1875 Am. mineralogist + E *-ite*] **:** a mineral $KFe(SO_4)_2.H_2O$ consisting of a hydrous sulfate of potassium and iron

**kraut** \'kraůt, *usu* -aůd·+V\ *n* -s [G, sauerkraut, cabbage, plant, herb, fr. OHG *krūt* herb, cabbage — more at SAUERKRAUT] **1 a :** SAUERKRAUT **b :** turnips cured in the same way as cabbage kraut **2** *often cap* **:** a German soldier or civilian — usu. used disparagingly ⟨one of the . . . techniques of annoying the ~ today is to whistle at him —*Atlantic*⟩

**kraut grass** \'kraůt,=\ *also* **kraut weed** \-aůt-,=\ *n* [prob. alter. (influenced by *kraut*) of *crowd grass, crowdweed*] **:** CHARLOCK

**krebs cycle** \'krebz-\ *n, usu cap K* [after H. A. *Krebs* b1900 Eng. biochemist] **:** a cyclic sequence of reactions occurring in the living organism (as in muscle tissue) and forming a phase of the metabolic function in which acetic acid or acetyl equivalent is oxidized through a series of intermediate acids to carbon dioxide and water and thus provides energy for storage in the form of energy-rich phosphate bonds (as in adenosine triphosphate) that can make it available for use in other vital processes (as muscular work) — called also *citric acid cycle, tricarboxylic acid cycle*

**kreef** \'krāf\ *n* -s [Afrik, fr. D *kreeft* lobster, crayfish, fr. MD *creeft*; akin to OHG *krebiz* crab — more at CRAB] **:** CAPE CRAWFISH

**kre·feld** \'krā,felt, -ld\ *adj, usu cap* [fr. *Krefeld*, Germany] **:** of or from the city of Krefeld, Germany **:** of the kind or style prevalent in Krefeld

**kreis** \'krīs\ *n, pl* **krei·se** \-īzə\ [G, lit., circle, fr. OHG *kreiz*; akin to MLG *kreit*, circle, *krēt* circle, *krit* enclosed combat area — more at KULTURKREIS] **:** a unit of local government in Germany corresponding to a county

**kreit·to·nite** \'krīt°n,īt, -rāt-\ *n* -s [G *kreittonit*, fr. Gk *kreittōn* stronger (compar. of *kratys* strong) + G *-it* -ite — more at HARD] **:** a black gahnite

**kremers·ite** \'kremər,zīt, 'krām-\ *n* -s [G *kremersit*, after P. *Kremers*, 19th cent. Ger. chemist who described it + G *-it* -ite] **:** a volcanic mineral product $[(NH_4),K]_2FeCl_5.H_2O$ consisting of a hydrous chloride of potassium, ammonium, and iron that occurs in red octahedrons

**¹krem·lin** \'kremlən\ *n* -s [earlier *cremelena, cremelina*, prob. modif. of obs. G *kremelin*, modif. of Russ *kreml'*] **1 :** the citadel or fortress of a Russian city or town ⟨the ensembles of the fortified monasteries and ~s —Arthur Voyce⟩ **2** *usu cap* [fr. the *Kremlin*, citadel of Moscow now serving as the governing center of the U.S.S.R.] **a :** a governing center or executive stronghold usu. regarded as secretive and impenetrable ⟨there are many *Kremlins* outside Russia, whose secrets, too, are guarded —Irwin Edman⟩ ⟨some of the permanent secretaries and undersecretaries live in an invisible *Kremlin* —*Economist*⟩ **b :** the supreme governing oligarchy of Soviet Russia ⟨on both sides of the Iron Curtain the battle between *Kremlin* and Vatican continues —C.L.Sulzberger⟩

**²kremlin** \"\ *adj, usu cap* **:** of or relating to the Kremlin esp. as symbolizing the central government of the U.S.S.R. or its policies ⟨*Kremlin* leaders⟩

**krem·lin·ism** \-,nizəm\ *n* -s *usu cap* **:** the policies and practices characteristic of the Soviet Russian government ⟨*Kremlinism* threatens the security and even the physical existence of mankind by keeping alive the global anarchy —H.D.Lasswell⟩

**krem·nitz white** *or* **crem·nitz white** \'kremnəts-\ *n, usu cap K&C* [fr. *Kremnitz, Kremnica*, east central Czechoslovakia] **:** a white lead suitable esp. for use in inks and as an artist's color — called also *Krems white*

**krems white** *or* **crems white** \'kremz-, -m(p)s-\ *n, usu cap K&C* [fr. *Krems*, city in Austria] **:** KREMNITZ WHITE

**kreng** \'kreŋ\ *or* **krang** *or* **crang** \'kraŋ\ *n* -s [D *kreng*, fr. MD *crenge* carrion, carcass; perh. akin to OE *cringan* to yield, fall in battle, die — more at CRINGE] **:** the carcass of a whale after removal of the blubber and baleen

**kreng·ing hook** \'kreŋiŋ-\ *or* **crang·ing hook** \'kraŋiŋ-\ *n* [*krenging, cranging* fr. *kreng, crang* + *-ing*] **:** a hook for holding the blubber of a whale while cutting it away

**kren·ner·ite** \'krenə,rīt\ *n* -s [G *krennerit*, fr. J. S. *Krenner* †1920 Hung. mineralogist + G *-it* -ite] **:** a mineral $AuTe_2$ consisting of a gold telluride

**kreo-** — see CRE-

**krep·lach** *or* **krep·lech** *or* **crep·lich** \'krepləḵ\ *n, pl* **kreplach** *or* **kreplech** *or* **creplich** [Yiddish *kreplech*, pl. of *krepel*, fr. (assumed) MHG dial. *kreppel* (whence G dial. *kräppel* fritter), dim. of MHG dial. *krape*, *krāpe* fritter; akin to OHG *krāpfo* hook, fritter — more at CRAVE] **:** triangular pockets of noodle dough filled with chopped meat or cheese, boiled, and eaten with soup or as a side dish

**kreu·zer** *also* **kreut·zer** *or* **creut·zer** \'krȯitsə(r)\ *n* -s [G *kreuzer*, fr. MHG *kriuzer* (trans. of ML *denarius cruciatus, cruciger*, fr. the cross marking them), fr. *kriuze* cross, fr. OHG *krūzi*, fr. L *cruc-, crux* — more at RIDGE] **:** a small coin of silver and later of copper used in Austria, Germany, and Hungary from the 13th to the mid-19th centuries

**krex** \'kreks, 'gr-\ *vi* -ED/-ING/-S [prob. fr. PaG *greckse* to grunt, ail, fr. G *krächzen* to croak, fr. *krachen* to crack, crash, roar, fr. OHG *krahhōn* to crack — more at CRACK] *dial* **:** GRUMBLE, COMPLAIN ⟨always something to ~ about⟩

**k'ri** *or* **kri** *var of* KERI

**krib·er·gite** \'kribər,gīt\ *n* -s [Sw *kribergit*, prob. irreg. fr. *Kristineberg* mine, Västerbotten province, northern Sweden, its locality + Sw *-it* -ite] **:** a mineral approximately $Al_{16}(PO_4)_8(SO_4)_3(OH)_{18}.10H_2O$ consisting of a hydrous basic sulfate and phosphate of aluminum

**kri·der's hawk** \'krīdə(r)z-\ *n, usu cap K* [fr. the name *Krider*] **:** a hawk of the central U.S. that is a variety (*Buteo jamaicensis kriderii*) of the red-tailed hawk and has the underparts almost pure white

**krieg·spiel** \'krēgz,pē(ə)l, -ēg,sp-, -ēk,sp-\ *n* [G *kriegsspiel*, fr. *krieg* war + *spiel* game] **1 :** a game in which blocks, pins, and flags representing contending forces and guns are moved about according to rules based on war conditions **2 :** chess in which neither player sees the other's board but is given some information as to the opponent's moves by a referee who keeps track of all moves on a third board

**krie·ker** \'krēkə(r)\ *n* -s [perh. fr. D *krieken* to chirp, peep (of imit. origin) + E *-er*] **:** PECTORAL SANDPIPER

**krig·ia** \'krigēə\ *n* [NL, fr. David *Krig*, 18th cent. Am. plant collector + NL *-ia*] **1** *cap* **:** a genus of small branched yellow-flowered No. American herbs that are related to the chicories but resemble dandelions and have a pappus of both bristles and chaff and short achenes **2** -s **:** any plant of the genus *Krigia* — called also *dwarf dandelion*

**krill** \'kril\ *n* -s [Norw *kril* young fry of fish] **:** planktonic crustaceans and larvae that constitute the principal food of whalebone whales which feed by straining krill-containing water through their plates of baleen

**krim·mer** *also* **crim·mer** \'krimə(r)\ *n* -s [G *krimmer*, fr. *Krim* Crimea, peninsula in the southern part of European Russia, U.S.S.R.] **1 :** a gray fur resembling astrakhan or Persian lamb that is made from the pelts of young lambs of the Crimean peninsula region — compare BROADTAIL, KARAKUL **2 :** a pile fabric resembling krimmer fur

**krim-saghyz** *var of* KRYM-SAGHYZ

**kris** *or* **kriss** *also* **creese** \'krēs *sometimes* 'kris\ *n, pl* **krises** *or* **krisses** [Malay *kĕris*] **:** a Malay or Indonesian dagger often with two scalloped cutting edges and ridged serpentine blade ⟨the ~ of a noble or high-class family is a sacred possession —Virginia A. Oakes⟩

kris

**kris dance** *n* **:** a Balinese trance dance in which the dancer attacks himself with a kris

**krish·na·ism** \'krishnə,izəm\ *n* -s *usu cap* [*Krishna*, eighth avatar of Vishnu, one of the principal Hindu gods + E *-ism*] **:** a widespread form of Hindu worship addressed to Krishna as eighth avatar of Vishnu

**kri·ta yu·ga** \,krid·ə'yügə\ *n, usu cap K&Y* [Skt *kṛtayuga*, fr. *kṛta* best throw at dice (that of the four) + *yuga* yoke, age of the world — more at YOKE] **:** the first and best age of a Hindu world cycle

**kri·voi rog** \,kri,vȯi¦rōg, kri¦vȯi'rȯk\ *adj, usu cap K&R* [fr. *Krivoi Rog*, city in southeast central Ukraine, U.S.S.R.] **:** of or from the city of Krivoi Rog, U.S.S.R. **:** of the kind or style prevalent in Krivoi Rog

**kroehn·kite** *or* **kröhn·kite** \'kreŋ,kīt\ *n* -s [modif. of Sp *krönnkite*, fr. B. *Kröhnke*, 19th cent. Ger. mineralogist + Sp *-ite*] **:** a mineral $Na_2Cu(SO_4)_2.2H_2O$ consisting of an azure-blue hydrous copper sodium sulfate that occurs massive

**krom·draai ape-man** \'kräm,drī-\ *also* **kromdraai man** *n, usu cap K* [*Kromdraai*, town in Transvaal, So. Africa, site of the finds] **:** an australopithecine (*Paranthropus robustus* or *Australopithecus robustus*) known from skull and skeletal fragments from southern Africa and distinguished by an extraordinarily massive jaw — compare SWARTKRANZ APE-MAN

**kro·mes·ki** *or* **kro·mes·ky** *also* **cro·mes·ki** *or* **cro·mes·qui** \krō'meskē\ *n, pl* **kromeskis** *or* **kromeskies** [modif. of Russ *kromochki*, pl. of *kromochka* slice of bread, dim. of *kroma* slice of bread] **:** a croquette wrapped in bacon, dipped in batter, and fried

**krom·nek disease** \'kräm,nek-\ *n* [Afrik *kromnek*, fr. *krom* crooked (fr. D, fr. MD *crom, cromb*) + *nek* neck, fr. D, fr. MD *necke* nape of the neck; akin to OE *crumb* crooked and to OE *hnecca* neck — more at CRUMP, NECK] *in southern Africa* **:** TOMATO STREAK

**kromo** *usu cap, var of* KRAMA

**kro·mo·gram** \'krōmə,gram\ *n* [alter. of *chromogram*] **:** the set of three photographic positives used in a chromoscope — called also *chromogram*

**¹kro·na** \'krōnə\ *n, pl* **kro·nur** \-nə(r)\ [Icel *krōna*, lit., crown, fr. ON *krūna, krōna*, fr. MLG *krūne, krōne*, prob. fr. OF *corone, corune* — more at CROWN] **1 :** the basic monetary unit of Iceland — see MONEY table **2 :** a coin representing one krona

**²kro·na** \", 'krünə\ *n, pl* **kro·nor** \-,nō(ə)r\ [Sw, lit., crown, fr. OSw *krūna, krōna*, fr. MLG *krūne, krōne*] **1 :** the basic monetary unit of Sweden — see MONEY table **2 :** a coin representing one krona

**¹kro·ne** \'krōnə\ *n, pl* **kro·nen** \-nən\ [G, lit., crown, fr. OHG *corōna*, fr. L *corona* — more at CROWN] **1 :** the basic monetary unit of Austria from 1892 to 1925 **2 :** a coin representing one krone

**²krone** \"\ *n, pl* **kro·ner** \-nə(r)\ [Dan, lit., crown, fr. ODan *krūne, krōne*, fr. MLG] **1 a :** the basic monetary unit of Denmark — see MONEY table **b :** a coin representing one Danish krone **2 a :** the basic monetary unit of Norway — see MONEY table **b :** a coin representing one Norwegian krone

**kroo** \'krü\ *or* **kroo·boy** \-,bȯi\ *n, pl* **kroo** *or* **krooboys** *usu cap* [*Kroo* alter. of *Kru*] **:** KRU 1b

**kroon** \'krün\ *n, pl* **kroo·ni** \-nē\ *or* **kroons** [Estonian *kroon*, fr. G *krone*] **1 :** the basic monetary unit of Estonia from 1928 to 1940 **2 :** a coin or note representing one kroon

**kru** \'krü\ *n, pl* **kru** *or* **krus** *usu cap* **1 a :** an indigenous Negro people of Liberia skilled as boatmen **b :** a member of the Kru people — called also *Kruman* **2 :** a Kwa language of the Kru people **3 :** a language group containing Kru, Bassa, and Grebo

**kru·bi** \'krübē\ *n* -s [prob. native name in Sumatra] **:** a tropical East Indian aroid (*Amorphophallus titanum*) having a spathe that resembles the corolla of a morning glory and attains a diameter of several feet

**kru·ken·berg tumor** \'krükən,bərg-\ *n, usu cap K* [after Friedrich E. *Krukenberg* b1871 Ger. pathologist] **:** a metastatic ovarian tumor of mucin-producing epithelial cells usu. derived from a primary gastrointestinal tumor

**kru·man** *or* **kroo·man** \'krümən\ *n, pl* **krumen** *or* **kroomen** *usu cap* **:** KRU 1b

**krumm·holz** \'krům,hōlts\ *n, pl* **krummholz** *usu cap* [G, fr. *krumm* crooked (fr. OHG *krumb, krump*) + *holz* wood, fr. OHG — more at CRUMP, HOLT] **:** stunted forest characteristic of most alpine regions — called also *elfinwood*

**krumm·horn** *also* **krum·horn** \-,hȯrn\ *n* [G *krummhorn* — more at CROMORNE] **1 :** an obsolete reed wind instrument with a curved tube — called also *cromorne* **2 :** CROMORNA

krummhorn with cap removed to show reed

**krym-saghyz** *or* **krim-saghyz** \¦krimsə¦gēz, -giz\ *n* -ES [Russ *krym-sagyz*, fr. *Krym* Crimea, peninsula in the southern part of European Russia, U.S.S.R. + Turki *sagīz* rubber, gum] **:** a small dandelion (*Taraxacum megalorrhizon*) of the Mediterranean region with yellow heads and a long rubber-containing taproot for which it is cultivated

**kryo-** — see CRY-

**kry·o·gen yellow G** \'krīəjən-, -,jen-\ *n, usu cap K&Y* [*kryogen* perh. fr. *cry-* + *-gen*] **:** a sulfur dye — see DYE table I (under *Sulfur Yellow 3*)

**kryokonite** *var of* CRYOCONITE

**kryolite** *var of* CRYOLITE

**krypt-** *or* **krypto-** — see CRYPT-

**kryp·ton** \'krip,tän, -,tən\ *n* -s [Gk, neut. of *kryptos* hidden — more at CRYPT] **:** a colorless inert gaseous element that occurs in air to the extent of about one part per million by volume and in gases from thermal springs and other natural gases, that is obtained by separating from liquid air, and that is used in electric lamps (as small quartz lamps for extremely brilliant illumination) — symbol *Kr*; see ELEMENT table

**k's** *or* **ks** *pl of* K

**KS** *abbr* **1** keep standing **2** king's scholar

**KSF** *abbr, often not cap* kips per square foot

**ksha·tri·ya** *also* **kshat·tri·ya** *or* **ksat·ri·ya** \(kə)'sha·trē(y)ə, (kə)'shə-, 'ksh- *sometimes* 'ch-\ *n* -s *usu cap* [Skt *kṣatriya*, fr. *kṣatra* dominion, fr. *kṣayati* he possesses, rules — more at CHECK] **1 :** a twice-born Hindu of the second ancient varna assigned by classical law to a governing or military occupation **2 :** a twice-born Hindu belonging to one of a large group of modern upper castes traditionally derived from the ancient Kshatriya varna — compare SUDRA, VAISYA

**k-shell** \'=,=\ *n, usu cap K* **:** the innermost shell of electrons surrounding an atomic nucleus and constituting the lowest available energy level for the electrons — compare L-SHELL, M-SHELL

**k star** *n, usu cap K* **:** a star of spectral type K — see SPECTRAL TYPE table

**kt** *abbr* **1** karat **2** kiloton **3** knight **4** knot

**k'thib** *or* **kthib** *or* **k'thibh** *or* **kthibh** *var of* KETHIB

**KTL** *abbr, often not cap* [Gk *kai ta loipa*] et cetera

**k truss** *n, usu cap K* **:** a building truss in which the vertical member and two oblique members in each panel form a K

**kua·la lum·pur** \'kwälə'lům,pů(ə)r, 'kwəl-, -'ləm-\ *adj, usu cap K&L* [fr. *Kuala Lumpur*, Federation of Malaya] **:** of or from Kuala Lumpur, capital of the Federation of Malaya **:** of the kind or style prevalent in Kuala Lumpur

**kuan** \'gwän, 'kw-\ *n* -s *usu cap* [Chin (Pek) *kuan*¹ official] **1 :** a type of Chinese pottery of the Sung period in the 12th century **2 :** imperial porcelain made at Ching-tê-chên

**kuan hua** \'gwän'(h)wä\ *n, usu cap K&H* [Chin (Pek) *kuan*¹ *hua*⁴, fr. *kuan*¹ official + *hua*⁴ speech, language] **:** MANDARIN

**¹ku·ba** \kü'bä\ *n* -s *usu cap* [fr. *Kuba*, town in northeast Azerbaidzhan, U.S.S.R.] **:** an eastern Caucasian carpet of coarse but firm weave resembling the Shirvan in design — called also *Kabistan*

**²ku·ba** \'kübə\ *n, pl* **kuba** *or* **kubas** *usu cap* **1 :** a Bantu-speaking people of the central Congo **2 :** a member of the Kuba people

**ku·ba·chi** \kü'bächē\ *n, pl* **kubachi** *or* **kubachis** *usu cap* **1 :** a Caucasian people of Dagestan **2 :** a member of the Kubachi people

**ku·bong** \'kü,bȯŋ, -bäŋ\ *n, pl* **kubong** [Malay] **:** FLYING LEMUR

**ku·bu** \'kü(,)bü\ *n, pl* **kubu** *or* **kubus** *usu cap* [native name in Sumatra] **1 :** an Indonesian Veddoid people of Sumatra **2 :** a member of the Kubu people

**ku·che·an** \(')kü¦chēən\ *n* -s *usu cap* [*Kuche, Kucha*, town and oasis in west central Sinkiang, China + E *-an*] **:** TOCHARIAN B

**ku·chen** \'kükən, 'küḵ-\ *n, pl* **kuchen** [G, cake, fr. OHG *kuocho, chuohho* — more at CAKE] **:** any of several varieties of coffee cake typically made from sweet yeast dough and variously shaped, flavored, and frosted

**ku·dize** \'k(y)ü,dīz\ *vt* -ED/-ING/-S [*kudos* + *-ize*] **:** grant honors to **:** PRAISE

**ku·dos** \-,däs, -,dōs\ *n, pl* **ku·dos** \-,dōz\ [Gk *kydos*; akin to OSlav *čudo* wonder, Gk *akouein* to hear — more at HEAR] **1 :** fame and renown resulting from an act or achievement **:** PRESTIGE ⟨occupations linked to inferior castes in Africa and India bring no ~ to their practitioners, no matter how skilled the craftsman —E.A.Hoebel⟩ ⟨the curate's undaunted demeanor . . . was generally supposed to have terrified the burglars into flight and much ~ accrued to him thereby —Kenneth Grahame⟩ **2 :** praise given for achievement **:** ACCOLADE 3c ⟨a masterly study of primitive versus industrial society . . . with the ~ going to the pagan man —Betty Kirk⟩ ⟨they will compel new respect and admiration far beyond the ~ civilization finds itself obliged to pay —*Collier's*⟩

**kudu** *var of* KOODOO

**kud·zu** \'küd(,)zü\ *also* **kudzu vine** *n* -s [Jap *kuzu*] **:** a prostrate vine (*Pueraria thunbergiana*) of China and Japan that is used widely for hay and forage and for erosion control and soil improvement and that has tuberous edible roots and stems which yield a fiber — see KO-HEMP

**kue** *also* **ku** \'kyü\ *n* -s **:** the letter *q*

**kufa** *var of* GUFA

**¹ku·fic** *also* **cu·fic** \'k(y)üfik\ *adj, usu cap* [*Al Kufa*, town in south central Iraq + E *-ic*] **1 :** of, relating to, or characteristic of Al Kufa, a city of Mesopotamia or of its inhabitants **2 :** constituting, belonging to, characteristic of, or written in the Arabic script Kufic

**²kufic** *also* **cufic** \"\ *n, usu cap* **1 :** a highly angular form of the Arabic alphabet orig. used at Al Kufa esp. for costly copies of the Koran **2 :** any angular variety of the Arabic alphabet — compare NESKHI

**ku·gel** \'kügəl\ *n* -s [Yiddish, lit., ball, fr. MHG *kugel, kugele* — more at CUDGEL] **:** a suet pudding made of noodles, potatoes, or bread, sometimes with raisins added

**ku·gel·hof** \-,hōf\ *n* -s [modif. of G *gugelhupf, gugelhopf* — more at GUGELHUPF] **:** GUGELHUPF

**ku·hio day** \kü'hēō-, ¦==¦=-\ *n, usu cap K&D* [after Prince Jonah *Kuhio* Kalanianaole †1922 Hawaiian delegate to the U.S. Congress] **:** March 26 that is observed as a holiday in Hawaii to commemorate the birthday of Prince Jonah Kuhio Kalanianaole

**kuh·lia** \'külēə, -lyə\ *n, cap* [NL, fr. Heinrich *Kuhl* †1821 Ger. naturalist + NL *-ia*] **:** the type genus of Kuhliidae — see AHOLEHOLE

**kuh·li·idae** \kü'līə,dē\ *n pl, cap* [NL, fr. *Kuhlia*, type genus + *-idae*] **:** a family of small Indo-Pacific marine and freshwater percoid fishes — see KUHLIA

**kuh·nia** \'k(y)ünēə\ *n, cap* [NL, fr. Adam *Kuhn* †1817 Am. physician and botanist + NL *-ia*] **:** a genus of No. American perennial herbs (family Compositae) with alternate resinous leaves and heads of cream-colored tubular flowers

**kui** \'küē\ *n, pl* **kui** *or* **kuis** *usu cap* **1 a :** a people of southeastern Thailand and adjacent Cambodia who are brachycephalic and of short stature **b :** a people of the Shan states **c :** a Dravidian people of central India **2 :** the Dravidian language of the Kui people of India

**kui·by·shev** \'kwēbə,shef, 'küēb-, -ev\ *adj, usu cap* [fr. *Kuibyshev*, city in the eastern part of European Russia, U.S.S.R.] **:** of or from the city of Kuibyshev, U.S.S.R. **:** of the kind or style prevalent in Kuibyshev

**ku·itsh** \kü'ēch\ *n, pl* **kuitsh** *or* **kuitshes** *usu cap* **1 a :** an Indian people of the Pacific coast in Oregon **b :** a member of such people **2 :** a dialect of Siuslaw

**ku·ja·wi·ak** \kü'yävē,ak\ *n* -s [Pol, fr. *Kujawy*, region in north central Poland] **:** a Polish couple dance resembling a waltz with lilting arm and body movements

**kuke** \'kyük\ *n* -s *usu cap* [by alter.] **:** KIKUYU

**ku·ki** \'kükē\ *n, pl* **kuki** *or* **kukis** *usu cap* **1 a :** any of numerous hill peoples in southern Assam, India **b :** a member of a Kuki people **2 :** a language of a Kuki people

**kuki-chin** \,kükē'chin\ *n* -s *usu cap K&C* **:** a group of Tibeto-Burman languages spoken by the Kuki and Chin peoples

**ku-klux** \'k(y)ü,kləks, *often* ÷ 'klü- *by assimilation to the* kl *of "Klux" & "Klan"*\ *vt* -ED/-ING/-ES *often cap both Ks* [fr. *Ku-Klux, Ku-Klux Klan*, secret organization originating in the southern U.S. after the Civil War and advocating maintenance of white supremacy by violent methods] **:** to maltreat or terrorize in a way thought to be typical of Ku Kluxers ⟨*ku-kluxed* him by shooting him with bird shot —R.H.Collins⟩

**ku klux·er** \-əksə(r)\ *n, pl* **ku kluxers** *usu cap both Ks* **1** *also* **ku klux** *pl* **ku kluxes :** a member of a secret society advocating white supremacy and often using violent methods to intimidate Negroes in the South in the period following the Civil War **2 :** a member of a secret fraternal group achieving prominence in many parts of the U.S. in the second decade of the 20th century and believed to confine its membership to native Protestant whites ⟨wilder than the . . . stories about Catholics which are afloat among our own *Ku Kluxers* —*New Republic*⟩

**ku klux·ism** \-ək,sizəm\ *also* **ku klux·ery** \-əksərē\ *n, usu cap both Ks* **:** the principles and practices of Ku Kluxers ⟨the bitterness of the days of reconstruction and *Ku Kluxism* —*Amer. Missionary*⟩ ⟨the spirit of *Ku Kluxism* . . . among the older American elements —Samuel Lubell⟩

**kuk·ri** *also* **kuk·eri** \'ku̇k(ə)rē\ *n* -s [Hindi *kukrī*] **:** a curved short sword with a broad blade used principally by the Gurkhas of India

kukri

**kuk·su** \'ku̇k(,)sü\ *adj, usu cap* [origin unknown] **:** of or relating to an Indian religious cult or its rites practiced in the southern Sacramento valley of California

**ku·ku** \'kü(,)kü\ *n* -s [Maori] **:** a New Zealand fruit dove (*Hemiphaga novae-seelandiae*) that is locally important as a game bird — called also *kukupa*

**ku·kui** \kü'küē\ *n* -s [Hawaiian] **:** CANDLENUT 2

**kukui oil** *n* **:** CANDLENUT OIL

**ku·ku·ku·ku** \,kükə'kü(,)kü\ *n, pl* **kukukuku** *or* **kukukukus** *usu cap* **1 :** a people inhabiting parts of Morabe and Papua in eastern New Guinea **2 :** a member of the Kukukuku people

**ku·ku·pa** \'kükəpə\ *n* -s [Maori] **:** KUKU

**ku·la** \'külə\ *n, pl* **kula** [of Melanesian origin] **:** a Melanesian interisland system of exchange in which prestige items (as necklaces and arm shells) are ceremoniously exchanged with a concomitant trade in useful goods — compare EXCHANGE 1b

**ku·lah** \(')kü¦lä\ *n* -s *usu cap* [fr. *Kula*, town in western Turkey in Asia] **:** a Turkish rug that is often a prayer rug and that uses the Ghiordes knot

**ku·lak** \(')kü¦lak, -¦läk *also* (')kyü¦lak\ *n, pl* **kulaks** \-ks\ *also* **kula·ki** \=='lakē, =='läkē\ [Russ, lit., fist, of Turkic origin; akin to Turk *kol* arm] **1 :** a prosperous or wealthy peasant farmer in 19th century Russia often associated with gaining profit from renting land, usury, or acting as a middleman in the sale of the products of other farmers **2 :** a farmer characterized by Communists as having excessive wealth usu. by possession of more than a minimal amount of property and ability to hire laborers or sometimes merely by unwillingness to join a collective farm and as a result denounced as an oppressor of less fortunate farmers and subjected to severe penalties (as heavy fines and confiscation of property) ⟨a large proportion of the ~s of the twenties were liquidated —L.K.Soth⟩

**ku·la·man** \'külə,män\ *n, pl* **kulaman** *or* **kulamans** *usu cap* [native name in southern Mindanao] **1 a :** a people inhabiting southern Mindanao, Philippines **b :** a member of such people **2 :** an Austronesian language of the Kulaman people

**ku·lan** *or* **kou·lan** \'kü,län\ *n* -s [Kirghiz *kulan*] **:** the wild ass of the Kirghiz steppe that is prob. a variety of the kiang

**ku·la·na·pan** \kü'lanəpən\ *n* -s *usu cap* **:** a language family of the Hokan stock comprising several languages all known as Pomo

**kula ring** *n* **1 :** KULA **2 :** the circle of Melanesian islands participating in the kula exchange

**kul·li** \'kəlē\ *adj, usu cap* [fr. *Kulli*, locality in southern Baluchistan, Pakistan, site of the finds] **:** of or relating to a prehistoric culture of southern Baluchistan characterized by polychrome vases and small objects modeled in clay (as figurines of women and animals, bird whistles, carts)

**kul·tur** \ku̇l'tu̇(ə)r\ *n* -s *often cap* [G, fr. L *cultura* culture — more at CULTURE] **1 :** CULTURE 5b ⟨the dwindling survivors of New England *Kultur* —H.L.Mencken⟩ ⟨our ~ should have its own characteristics —*Irish Statesman*⟩ **2 :** culture chiefly of late 19th century Germans that is a state of civilization characterized by an emphasis on practical efficiency rather than on humanitarian refinements and subordination of the individual to a highly organized state **3 :** culture that is an ideal state of civilization unique to Germany chiefly to militant German expansionists during the Nazi and late Hohenzollern periods usu. to emphasize an alleged superiority of German material and political development over the cultures of other nations and peoples ⟨the ethnocentric doctrine of Germanic *Kultur* . . . utilized for political purposes to justify cultural and political absolutism —David Bidney⟩ ⟨German textbooks were fine-combed for the propaganda of *Kultur* —*Amer. Mercury*⟩

**kul·tur·kampf** \-,käm(p)f\ *n* -s *usu cap* [G, fr. *kultur* + *kampf* conflict, struggle, fr. OHG *kamph* combat — more at KEMP] **:** conflict between civil government and religious authorities esp. over control of education and church appointments ⟨the *Kulturkampf* . . . frets the life of practically every continental nation —*Christian Century*⟩ ⟨planning a protracted *Kulturkampf* against the Church —*Time*⟩

**kul·tur·kreis** \-,krīs\ *n, pl* **kulturkrei·se** \-īzə\ *usu cap* [G, fr. *kultur* + *kreis* area, circle, fr. OHG *kreiz* circular line, encirclement, district; akin to MLG *kreit*, *krēt* circle, enclosed dueling space, OHG *krizzōn* to scratch in (as letters), *krazzōn* to scratch — more at SCRATCH] **:** a culture complex developing in successive epochs from its center of origin and becoming diffused over large areas of the world ⟨the horse-raising peoples in the primary herding *Kulturkreise* —Lawrence Krader⟩ ⟨the concept of the *Kulturkreise* developed by the Vienna school of ethnology⟩

**ku·ma·mo·to** \,küma¦mō(,)tō\ *adj, usu cap* [fr. *Kumamoto*, city in western Kyushu, Japan] **:** of or from the city of Kumamoto, Japan **:** of the kind or style prevalent in Kumamoto

**kuman** *usu cap, var of* CUMAN

**ku·ma·ra** \'kümərə\ *n* -s [Maori] *New Zealand* **:** SWEET POTATO

**ku·ma·ra·hou** \¦===¦hau̇\ *n* -s [Maori] *New Zealand* **:** any of several native woody plants: as **a :** a branching shrub (*Pomaderris elliptica*) with leaves lustrous above and whitish tomentose below and cymes of fragrant pale yellow flowers **b :** a small sometimes shrubby tree (*Quintinia serrata*) that is more or less covered with whitish scales and has shining leathery serrated leaves and cymes of pale lilac flowers

**ku·ma·so** \kü'mä(,)sō\ *n, pl* **kumaso** *or* **kumasos** *usu cap* **:** an indigenous Caucasoid people of Japan formerly inhabiting Kyushu — compare AINU

**kumbh me·la** \'ku̇mmə,lä\ *n, usu cap K&M* [Hindi *kumbh melā* festival in the sign of the zodiac Aquarius, fr. Skt *kumbha* pot, Aquarius + *melā* assembly — more at HUMP, MILITATE] **:** a Hindu festival occurring once every 12 years in one of four sacred sites where bathing for purification of sin is considered esp. efficacious

**kum·bi** \'ku̇mbē\ *n* -s [origin unknown] *India* **:** the silky fiber of the white silk cotton tree

**kum·buk** \'ku̇m,bu̇k\ *n* -s [origin unknown] **:** ARJUN

**kum·har** \(')ku̇m¦här\ *n* -s *usu cap* [Hindi *kumhār*, fr. Skt *kumbhakāra*, fr. *kumbha* pot + *kāra* maker; akin to Skt *kṛṇoti* he does, makes — more at HUMP, KARMA] **:** a member of a potter caste of India

**kumiss** *or* **kumys** *or* **kumyss** *var of* KOUMISS

**kum·kum** \'ku̇m,ku̇m\ *n* -s [Hindi *kuṅkum*, fr. Skt *kuṅkuma* saffron, perh. of Sem origin; akin to Heb *karkōm* saffron, crocus — more at CROCUS] **1 :** red turmeric powder used for making the distinctive Hindu mark on the forehead **2 :** the mark on the forehead made with kumkum

**küm·mel** \'kiməl\ *n* -s [G, lit., caraway seed, fr. OHG *kumil*, *kumīn* cumin — more at CUMIN] **:** a colorless aromatic liqueur flavored principally with caraway seeds

**kumni** *usu cap, var of* KURMI

**kum·quat** *also* **cum·quat** \'kəm,kwät\ *n* -s [Chin (Cant) *kam kwat*, fr. *kam* gold + *kwat* orange] **1 a :** any of several small yellow to orange citrus fruits with sweet spongy rind and somewhat acid pulp that are used chiefly candied or in preserves **b :** a tree or shrub of the genus *Fortunella* that bears kumquats: as (1) **:** a Chinese tree (*F. margarita*) that is widely cultivated in warm regions and that bears ovoid orange-colored kumquats (2) **:** a tree (*F. japonica*) that is known only in cultivation and that bears spherical golden yellow kumquats **2** *Austral* **:** DESERT LEMON

**ku·myk** *also* **ku·mik** \(')kü¦mik\ *or* **ku·muk** \-¦mək\ *n* -s *usu cap* **1 a :** a Turkish people of the Caucasus **b :** a member of such people **2 :** the Turkic language of the Kumyk people

**ku·nai** \'kü,nī\ *n* -s [native name in eastern New Guinea] *New Guinea* **:** COGON

**ku·na·ma** \kü'nämə\ *n* -s *usu cap* **1 :** a language spoken in northern Ethiopia **2 :** a branch of the Chari-Nile language family containing only the Kunama language

**kunbi** *usu cap, var of* KURMI

**kundt tube** \'ku̇nt-\ *n, usu cap K* [after August *Kundt* †1894 Ger. physicist] **:** an acoustically resonating horizontal glass tube in which the standing-wave nodes are exhibited by the distribution of a fine powder and that is used to measure the velocity of sound in gases

**kung** *usu cap, var of* QUNG

**kun·gu cake** \'ku̇ŋ(,)gü\ *n* [*kungu* fr. Nyanja *nkungu* kungu fly] **:** a food made by the natives about Lake Nyasa consisting of compressed cakes of kungu flies

**kungu fly** *n* **:** any of certain small mayflies (genus *Caenis*) and midges (genus *Corethra*) that breed on Lake Nyasa — see KUNGU CAKE

**kun·kur** *or* **kun·kar** \'kəŋkə(r)\ *also* **con·ker** \'käŋ-\ *n* -s [Hindi *kaṅkar*, fr. Skt *karkara*] **:** a limestone used esp. in India for making lime and building roads

**kunst·lied** \'ku̇nzt,lēt, -n(t)st-\ *n* -s [G, fr. *kunst* art (fr. OHG, skill, knowledge) + *lied* song, fr. OHG *liod*; OHG *kunst* akin to OFris *kunst* knowledge, MD *const*, *cunst*, OS *kunst*, all fr. a prehistoric derivative of the verb represented by OHG *kunnan* to know, be able — more at CAN, LAUD] **:** ART SONG

**kunz·ite** \'ku̇nt,sīt\ *n* -s [George F. *Kunz* †1932 Am. gem expert + E *-ite*] **:** a variety of spodumene that occurs in beautiful pinkish lilac crystals and is used as a gem

**kuo-yü** \'gwō'yüē\ *n* -s *usu cap* [Chin (Pek) *kuo*² *yü*³, lit., national language, fr. *kuo*² nation + *yü*³ language] **:** a form of Mandarin taught in the schools and used as a standard language

**kupf·fer cell** \'ku̇pfə(r)-\ *also* **kupf·fer's cell** *n, usu cap K* [after Karl Wilhelm von *Kupffer* †1903 Ger. anatomist] **:** a fixed histiocyte of the walls of the liver sinusoids that is stellate with large oval nucleus and the cytoplasm commonly packed with fragments resulting from phagocytic action

**kupf·fer·ite** \-fə,rīt\ *n* -s [ISV *kupffer-* (fr. Adolph T. *Kupffer* †1865 Russ. physicist) + *-ite*] **:** a green aluminous variety of amphibole

**ku·phar** \'küfə(r)\ *n* -s [Ar *quffah* basket] **:** GUFA

**ku·ping tael** \¦gü,piŋ-\ *n* [Chin (Pek) *k'u*⁴ *p'ing*² treasury scale for silver (fr. *k'u*⁴ treasury + *p'ing*² level, standard weight) + E *tael*] **:** the tael used for reckoning taxes and dues other than customs

**kup·per** \'kəpə(r)\ *n* -s [perh. fr. Sindhi *kapar*] **:** SAW-SCALED VIPER

**ku·ra clover** \kə'rä-, 'ku̇rə-\ *n, usu cap K* [perh. fr. *Kura*, river in Georgia and Azerbaidzhan, U.S.S.R.] **:** a perennial clover (*Trifolium ambiguum*) native to the Caucasus and Romania and introduced into America — called also *honey clover*, *pellett clover*

**kurakkan** *var of* KORAKAN

**kur·bash** *or* **kour·bash** *or* **cour·bash** *or* **cur·bash** \'ku̇(ə)r-,bash, ='=\ *n* -ES [Turk *kırbaç*] **:** a lash or whip of hide used as an instrument of punishment

**kur·chee bark** *or* **kur·chi bark** \'ku̇rchē-\ *n* [*kurchee*, *kurchi* perh. of Indic origin; akin to Skt *kūrca* beard, bunch, bundle of grass — more at QUILT] **:** a Tellicherry bark from a tree (*Holarrhena antidysenterica*) of the family Apocynaceae that contains conessine and other alkaloids

**kurd** \'ku̇(ə)rd, 'kərd\ *n* -s *usu cap* **1 :** one of a numerous pastoral and agricultural people inhabiting a large mountainous plateau region in adjoining parts of Turkey, Iran, Iraq, and Syria and in the Armenian and Azerbaidzhan sectors of the Soviet Caucasus **2 :** KURDISH

¹**kurd·ish** \-dish\ *adj, usu cap* **1 :** of, relating to, or characteristic of the region inhabited by the Kurds **2 :** of, relating to, or characteristic of the Kurds or their language

²**kurdish** \"\ *n* -ES *usu cap* **:** the Iranian language of the Kurds

**kur·di·stan** \¦ku̇rdə¦stan, ¦kər-; ¦ku̇rdə¦stän\ *n* -s *usu cap* [fr. *Kurdistan*, region inhabited by Kurds in Turkey in Asia, Iraq, and Iran] **:** one of the several varieties of rugs woven by the Kurds whose best examples are noted for fine colors and durability

**ku·re** \'k(y)u̇rē, 'kü(,)rā\ *adj, usu cap* [fr. *Kure*, city in southwest Honshu, Japan] **:** of or from the city of Kure, Japan **:** of the kind or style prevalent in Kure

**kur·gan** \(')kü(ə)r¦gän\ *n* -s [Russ, of Turkic origin; akin to Turk *kurgan* fortress, castle] **:** a burial mound of eastern Europe or Siberia

**ku·rie plot** \'kyu̇rē-\ *n, usu cap K* [after F. N. D. *Kurie b*1907 Am. physicist] **:** a graphic means of comparing theoretical and observed momentum distributions in continuous beta-ray spectra

¹**ku·ril·ian** \k(y)ü'rilēən, -rēl-\ *adj, usu cap* [*Kuril* islands, group of islands south of Kamchatka belonging to the U.S.S.R. + E *-ian*, adj. suffix] **1 :** of, relating to, or characteristic of the Kuril islands **2 :** of, relating to, or characteristic of the people of the Kuril islands

²**kurilian** \"\ *n* -s *cap* [*Kuril* islands + E *-ian*, n. suffix] **:** a native or inhabitant of the Kuril islands

**kurios** *usu cap, var of* KYRIOS

**kurk** *var of* KIRK

**kur·ku** \'ku̇(ə)r(,)kü\ *n, pl* **kurku** *or* **kurkus** *usu cap* **:** KORKU

**kur·mi** \'ku̇rmē\ *also* **kum·ni** \'ku̇mnē\ *or* **kun·bi** \'ku̇mbē, -ünbē\ *n* -s *usu cap* [Hindi *Kurmī*] **:** a member of an important agricultural caste distributed throughout India with the exception of the extreme south

**kur·nai** \'ku̇(ə)r,nī\ *n, pl* **kurnai** *or* **kurnais** *usu cap* **1 a :** a people of the southeastern coast of Australia living in permanent villages **b :** a member of such people **2 :** the language of the Kurnai people

**kur·na·kov·ite** \ku̇r'näkə,vīt\ *n* -s [Russ *kurnakovit*, fr. N. S. *Kurnakov* †1941 Russ. mineralogist + Russ *-it* -ite] **:** a mineral $Mg_2B_6O_{11}.13H_2O$ consisting of hydrous borate of magnesium

**kur·ra·jong** \'kərə,jȯŋ, -jäŋ\ *also* **koo·ra·jong** \'ku̇r-\ *or* **cur·ra·jong** \'kər-\ *n* -s [native name in Australia] **:** any of certain Australian shrubs or trees esp. of the family Sterculiaceae that have strong tough bast fibers used by the aborigines for making cordage, nets, and matting **:** BOTTLE TREE: as **a :** FLAME TREE a(1) **b :** a widely distributed eastern Australian tree (*Brachychiton populneum*) with soft light attractively grained wood sometimes used for interior finish, flowers whitish without and red and yellow within, and foliage that is an important emergency food for cattle — compare GREEN KURRAJONG

**kurrajong leaf roller** *n* **:** the destructive larva of an Australian pyralidid moth (*Sylepta clytalis*) feeding on kurrajong foliage

**kur·rol's salt** \'kərˌəlz-, 'ku̇r|\ *n, usu cap K* [perh. fr. the name *Kurrol*] **:** an insoluble sodium metaphosphate or potassium metaphosphate; *esp* **:** a fibrous crystalline sodium metaphosphate $NaPO_3$ IV formed by seeding a melt at 550° C

**kursk** \'ku̇(ə)rsk\ *adj, usu cap* [fr. *Kursk*, city in central part of European Russia, U.S.S.R.] **:** of or from the city of Kursk, U.S.S.R. **:** of the kind or style prevalent in Kursk

**kur·to·rach·ic** \¦kərd·ə¦rakik\ *adj* [*kurto-* (irreg. fr. Gk *kyrtos* bulging, convex) + *rach-* (fr. Gk *rhachis* spine) + *-ic* — more at CYRT-] **:** having the lumbar region of the spinal column concave dorsally

**kur·to·sis** \,kər'tōsəs\ *n* -ES [Gk *kyrtōsis* convexity, fr. *kyrtos* convex + *-ōsis* -osis] **:** the state or quality of peakedness or flatness of the graphic representation of a statistical distribution

**ku·ru·ba** \kə'rübə\ *n, pl* **kuruba** *or* **kurubas** *usu cap* **:** a member of a pastoral people in Mysore and other parts of southern India

**ku·rukh** \'ku̇rək\ *n, pl* **kurukh** *or* **kurukhs** *usu cap* **1 a :** a primitive people of central India who antedate the Dravidians in India — called also *Oraon* **b :** a member of such people **2 :** the Dravidian language of the Kurukh people

**ku·ru·ma** \'ku̇rəmə\ *n* -s [Jap] **:** JINRIKISHA

**ku·rum·ba** \kə'rümbə\ *n, pl* **kurumba** *or* **kurumbas** *usu cap* **1 :** a member of a jungle people living on the slopes of the Nilgiri hills of southern India who are remnants of the oldest pre-Dravidian population of the Deccan **2 :** a member of a shepherd caste of southern India who are known for a variety of blanket that they weave

**ku·ru·me azalea** \'ku̇rə,mā-\ *n, often cap K* [fr. *Kurume*, city in northern Kyushu, Japan] **:** any of certain garden azaleas of variable hardiness with white, pink, rose, scarlet, or lavender flowers originating in Japan chiefly by selection from or hybridization of a native Japanese azalea (*Rhododendron obtusum*) with hairy shoots and evergreen or deciduous leaves

**ku·rus** \kə'rüsh\ *n, pl* **kurus** [Turk *kuruş*] **:** a Turkish piaster equal to ¹⁄₁₀₀ lira — see MONEY table

**kur·vey** \kə(r)'vā\ *vi* **kurveyed; kurveyed; kurveying; kurveys** [Afrik *karwei*, prob. fr. D *karweien* to do odd jobs, fr. *karwei* job, task, fr. MD *corweye* corvée, fr. MF *corvee* — more at CORVÉE] **:** to carry goods about in an ox wagon in southern Africa

**kur·vey·or** \-āə(r)\ *n* -s [modif. (influenced by E *-or*) of Afrik *karweier*, fr. *karwei* to kurvey + *-er* (fr. D, akin to OE *-ere* -er)] **:** a traveling trader in southern Africa who carries goods about in a large ox wagon

**kus** *pl of* KU

**ku·sa** *also* **ku·sha** \'ku̇(,)s(h)ä\ *n* -s [Hindi *kusā*, fr. Skt *kuśa*] **1 :** a grass (*Eragrostis cynosuroides*) of India used in Hindu ceremonies — called also *darbha* **2 :** KANS

**ku·sai·an** \(')kü¦sīən\ *n* -s *cap* [*Kusaie*, island in the eastern Caroline islands + E *-an*, n. suffix] **:** a Micronesian native or inhabitant of Kusaie in the eastern Caroline islands

**ku·sam** \'kü,sam\ *n* -s [origin unknown] **:** a tree (*Schleichera oleosa*) of the family Sapindaceae that grows in dry forests of southeastern Asia, has pinnate leaves, apetalous flowers, and dry fruits surrounded by pulpy arils and that yields a hard heavy reddish brown timber and from its seeds an oil that is used locally for cooking, illumination, and medicine — see MACASSAR OIL

**ku·san** \'küsᵊn\ *n, pl* **kusan** *or* **kusans** *usu cap* **1 a :** an Indian people of Oregon **b :** a member of such people **2 :** a language family in western Oregon including Coos

**ku·shan** \'kü,shän\ *n, pl* **kushan** *or* **kushans** *usu cap* **:** a Saka people invading India from central Asia, formerly having a ruling house with control extending over northwest India, much of present-day west Pakistan, and the Ganges valley to Benares, and eventually becoming absorbed as Kshatriyas or Sudras

**ku·si·man·se** \,küsə'man(t)sə\ *or* **ku·si·man·sel** \-səl\ *n* -s [prob. native name in Liberia] **:** a small dark brown burrowing carnivorous mammal that is a native of West Africa and related to the mongoose

¹**kuskus** *var of* KHUSKHUS

²**kus·kus** \'kü,skǜs\ *var of* COUSCOUS

**kuss·maul breathing** \'ku̇,smau̇l-\ *or* **kussmaul respiration** *n, usu cap K* [after Adolf *Kussmaul* †1902 Ger. physician] **:** abnormally slow deep respiration characteristic of air hunger and occurring esp. in acidotic states

**kus·ti** \'ku̇(,)stē, ='=\ *n* -s [Per *kustī*, *kushtī*, fr. *kusht* waist, side, fr. MPer *kust*, *kustak*] **:** the sacred cord or girdle worn by Parsis as a mark of their faith — compare SACRED SHIRT

**ku·su** \'kü(,)sü\ *n* -s [origin unknown] **:** any of several African striped mice

**ku·sum** \kə'süm\ *n* -s [Hindi, fr. Skt *kusumbha*] *India* **:** SAFFLOWER

**kutch** *var of* CUTCH

**kutcha** *or* **ka·cha** *or* **kach·cha** \'kəchə\ *adj* [Hindi *kaccā*] **:** being in a crude or raw state **:** MAKESHIFT, UNFINISHED ⟨where they cannot get a pukka railway, they take a ~ one —Lord Elgin⟩

**ku·tchin** \kü'chin\ *n, pl* **kutchin** *or* **kutchins** *usu cap* **1 a :** an Athapaskan people of the Yukon and Mackenzie river valleys, Alaska and northwestern Canada **b :** a member of such people **2 :** a language of the Kutchin people — called also *Loucheux*

**ku·te·nai** *or* **ku·te·nay** *also* **koo·te·nai** \'kütᵊn,ā, -t(,)nā, -tnē\ *n, pl* **kutenai** *or* **kutenais** *or* **kutenay** *or* **kutenays** *usu cap* **1 a :** a people of the Rocky mountains on both sides of the U.S.–Canada boundary **b :** a member of such people **2 :** the Kitunahan language of the Kutenai people

**ku·ti·ra gum** *also* **ku·tee·ra gum** \kə'tirə-\ *n* [Hindi *katīrā*] **:** any of several sterculia gums

**kut·na·ho·rite** \,kətnə'hȯr,īt, ,ku̇t-\ *n* -s [G *kutnahorit*, fr. *Kutná Hora*, western Czechoslovakia, its locality + G *-it* -ite] **:** a mineral $Ca(Mn,Mg,Fe)CO_3$ that consists of a carbonate of calcium, manganese, magnesium, and iron and that is isomorphous with either dolomite or calcite

**kut·tar** \kə'tär\ *n* -s [Hindi *kaṭār*, fr. Skt (prob. Prakrit) *kaṭṭāra*, fr. Skt *kartati* he cuts — more at SHEAR] **:** a short dagger used in India with a handle consisting of two parallel bars joined by a crosspiece that is gripped with the hand

**ku·vasz** \'ku̇,väs, 'kü,-\ *n* [Hung, fr. Turk *kavas* armed constable, guard, doorkeeper, fr. Ar *qawwās* bowman] **1** *usu cap* **:** a long-established Hungarian breed of tall and light-footed but sturdy white dogs **2** *pl* **ku·va·szok** \,vä,sȯk\ *often cap* **:** any dog of the Kuvasz breed used for centuries as guard and hunting dogs

**ku·wait** \kə'wāt\ *adj, usu cap* [fr. *Kuwait*, country on the Persian gulf] **:** of or from the country of Kuwait **:** of the kind or style prevalent in Kuwait

¹**ku·wai·ti** \-wād·ē\ *adj, usu cap* [Ar *kuwaytīy*, fr. *Kuwayt* Kuwait] **1 :** of, relating to, or characteristic of Kuwait, a country on the Persian gulf **2 :** of, relating to, or characteristic of the people of Kuwait

²**kuwaiti** \"\ *n* -s *cap* **:** a native or inhabitant of Kuwait

**ku·yo·non** \'küyō,nän\ *n, pl* **kuyonon** *or* **kuyonons** *usu cap* [Kuyonon, fr. *Kuyo* Cuyo, island in the central Philippines + Kuyonon *-non* people, language] **1 a :** a Christianized people inhabiting Cuyo and eastern Palawan islands and parts of other islands in the northern Sulu sea **b :** a member of such people **2 :** an Austronesian language of the Kuyonon people

kuttar

**kv** *abbr* kilovolt

**kva** *abbr* kilovolt-ampere

**kvah** *abbr* kilovolt-ampere-hour

**kvar** *abbr* kilovar

**kvarh** *abbr* kilovar-hour

**kvass** *also* **kvas** \kə'väs, 'kfäs\ *or* **quass** *or* **quas** \", 'kwäs\ *n* -ES [Russ *kvas*; akin to OSlav *kvasŭ* sour drink — more at CHEESE] **:** a weak homemade beer of Eastern European countries (as Russia) made by pouring warm water over a mixture of cereals and allowing it to ferment

**kvu·tzah** *or* **kvu·tza** \kə,vüt'sä, ='=(,)=\ *n, pl* **kvu·tzoth** *or* **kvu·tzot** \-sōt(h), -sōs\ *also* **kvutzahs** *or* **kvutzas** [NHeb *qĕbhūṣāh* (pl. *qĕbhūṣōth*), fr. Heb, group, gathering] **:** a Jewish communal and cooperative farm or settlement in Israel that is usu. smaller than a kibbutz and established on state-owned land

**kw** *abbr* kilowatt

**kwa** \'kwä\ *n, pl* **kwa** *usu cap* **:** a branch of the Niger-Congo language family that contains the Akan languages and Agni, Ga, Fon, Ewe, Yoruba, Ibo, Edo, and Nupe, and less certainly Kru, Bassa, and Grebo and that is spoken along the coast and a short distance inland from Liberia to Nigeria

**kwa·ki·utl** \¦kwäkē¦(y)üdᵊl, (')kwä¦k(y)ü-\ *n, pl* **kwakiutl** *or* **kwakiutls** *usu cap* **1 a :** a Wakashan people on both shores of Queen Charlotte Sound and on northern Vancouver Island **b :** a member of such people **2 :** the language of the Kwakiutl people

**kwal·hi·o·qua** \,kwäl(h)ē'ōkwə\ *n, pl* **kwalhioqua** *or* **kwalhioquas** *usu cap* **1 :** an Athapaskan people of southwestern Washington **2 :** a member of the Kwalhioqua people

**kwang·ju** \'gwäŋ¦jü, 'kw-\ *adj, usu cap* [fr. *Kwangju*, Korea] **:** of or from the city of Kwangju, Korea **:** of the kind or style prevalent in Kwangju

**kwang·tung ware** \'gwäŋ¦du̇ŋ-, 'kw-, -¦tu̇ŋ-\ *n, usu cap K* [fr. *Kwangtung*, province in southeast China] **:** a Chinese porcelanous stoneware that possibly originated in Sung times varying from almost white to dark brown or red and usu. having a variegated glaze

**kwapa** *usu cap, var of* QUAPAW

**kwa·shi·or·kor** \¦kwäshē¦ȯrkər, -ē,ȯr¦kō(ə)r\ *n* -s [native name in Ghana] **:** severe malnutrition in infants and children that is characterized by failure to grow and develop, changes in the pigmentation of the skin and hair, edema, fatty degeneration of the liver, anemia, and apathy and is caused by a diet excessively high in carbohydrate and extremely low in protein

**kwa·tu·ma** \kwä'tümə\ *n* -s [native name in southern Africa] **:** any of several moray eels (genus *Lycodontis*) of southern Africa

**kwa·zo·ku** \'kwäzō,kü, kwä'zō(,)kü\ *n, pl* **kwazoku** [Jap] **:** the class of nobility of both civil and feudal origin in the Japanese social scale — compare HEIMIN, SHIZOKU

**kweek** \'kwāk\ *n* -s [Afrik, fr. D, couch grass; akin to OE *cwice* couch grass — more at QUITCH] **1** *southern Africa* **:** a grass of the genus *Cynodon* **2** *also* **kweekgrass** \'=,=\ *southern Africa* **:** COUCH GRASS 1a

**kwei·lin** \'gwā;lin, 'kw-\ *adj, usu cap* [fr. *Kweilin,* city in southeast China] **:** of or from the city of Kweilin, China **:** of the kind or style prevalent in Kweilin

**kwei·yang** \'gwā;yäŋ, 'kw-\ *adj, usu cap* [fr. *Kweiyang,* city in southern China] **:** of or from the city of Kweiyang, China **:** of the kind or style prevalent in Kweiyang

**kwe·ni** \'kwānē\ *n, pl* **kweni** *or* **kwenis** *usu cap* **:** GURO

**kwe·ri** *also* **kwiri** \'kwirē\ *n* -s *usu cap* **:** a people of the southern British Cameroons

**kwh** *abbr* kilowatt-hour

**kwo·ma** \'kwōmə\ *n, pl* **kwoma** *or* **kwomas** *usu cap* **1 a :** a Papuan people of the Sepik district, Territory of New Guinea **b :** a member of such people **2 :** the language of the Kwoma

**kyabooka** *also* **kya–bouka** *var of* KIABOOCA

**ky·ack** \'kī,ak *also* -ī,yak\ *n* -s [origin unknown] **:** a packsack to be swung on either side of a packsaddle

**kyah** \kē'(y)ä\ *n* -s [Beng] **:** an Indian partridge (*Francolinus gularis*) having a strong spur

**kyak** *var of* KAYAK

**kyang** *var of* KIANG

**kyanite** *var of* CYANITE

**ky·a·nize** \'kīə,nīz\ *vt* -ED/-ING/-S [fr. John H. *Kyan* †1850 Eng. inventor + E *-ize*] **:** to preserve (wood) by steeping in a solution of corrosive sublimate

**kyat** \kē'(y)ät\ *n* -s [Burmese] **1 :** the basic monetary unit of Burma established in 1952 — see MONEY table **2 :** a coin representing one kyat

**kyathos** *var of* CYATHUS

**kybosh** *var of* KIBOSH

**kye** \'kī\ *n pl* [ME *ky,* fr. OE *cȳ* — more at COW] *now dial* **:** KINE

**kyle** \'kī(ə)l\ *n* -s [ScGael *caol,* fr. *caol* narrow; akin to OIr *cōil, cōel* narrow, Latvian *kaîls* naked, bald] *Scot* **:** CHANNEL, SOUND, STRAIT ⟨at the widening mouth of the ~ —David Innes⟩

**ky·lie** *or* **ki·ley** \'kīlē\ *n, pl* **kylies** *or* **kileys** [native name in Australia] **:** an Australian boomerang having one side flat and the other convex

**ky·lin** \'kē'lin\ *n* -s [modif. of Chin (Pek) *ch'i*$^{2}$ *lin*$^{2}$, fr. *ch'i*$^{2}$ male kylin + *lin*$^{2}$ female kylin] **:** a unicorn of Chinese myth depicted with the tail of an ox and the legs and body of a deer — see FÊNG HUANG

**ky·lix** \'kīliks, 'kil-\ *or* **cy·lix** \'sīl-,'sil-\ *n, pl* **kyl·i·kes** \'kilə,kēz\ *or* **cyl·i·ces** \'sil-\ [Gk *kylix;* akin to Gk *kalyx* calyx — more at CHALICE] **:** a drinking cup that has two looped handles on a shallow bowl set upon a slender center foot

kylix

**ky·loe** \'kī(,)lō\ *n* -s *usu cap* [origin unknown] **:** WEST HIGHLAND

**kym-** *or* **kymo-** — see CYM-

**ky·mat·i·on** \kī'mad·ē,än, kə̇'-\ *var of* CYMATIUM

**kym·ba·lon** \'kimbə,län\ *n* -s [Gk — more at CYMBAL] **:** CYMBAL 1a

**ky·mo·gram** \'kīmə,gram\ *n* [ISV *cym-* + *-gram*] **:** a record made by a kymograph

**ky·mo·graph** \-raf,-ráf\ *or* **cy·mo·graph** \'sī-\ *n* [ISV *cym-* + *-graph*] **1 :** a recording device including an electric motor or clockwork that drives a usu. slowly revolving drum which carries a roll of plain or smoked paper and also having an arrangement for tracing on the paper by means of a stylus a graphic record of motion or pressure (as of the organs of speech, blood pressure, or respiration) often in relation to particular intervals of time **2 :** a device for recording on a moving X-ray film the motion of an organ (as the heart) by means of a series of still images — **ky·mo·graph·ic** \;==;grafik\ *adj*

**ky·mog·ra·phy** \kī'mägrəfē\ *n* -ES [ISV *cym-* + *-graphy*] **:** the making of kymographic records

**kymric** *usu cap, var of* CYMRIC

**kyn·uren·ic acid** \;ki|nyə;renik-, ;kī|\ *n* [*kynurenic* ISV *kyn-* (fr. Gk *kyn-, kyōn* dog) + *-uren-* (irreg. fr. Gk *ouron* urine) + *-ic* — more at HOUND, URINE] **:** a crystalline acid $C_9H_5N(OH)COOH$ occurring in the urine of dogs and other animals as one of the normal products of tryptophan metabolism

**kyn·uren·ine** \,=='re,nēn, -,nə̇n\ *n* -s [ISV *kynuren-* (fr. *kynurenic*) + *-ine*] **:** an amino acid $NH_2C_6H_4COCH_2CH(NH_2)COOH$ occurring in the urine of various animals as one of the normal products of tryptophan metabolism and capable of forming kynurenic acid and other products; 3-anthranoyl-alanine

**ky·oo·dle** \(')kī;(y)üdᵊl\ *vi* **kyoodled; kyoodled; kyoodling** \-d(ᵊ)liŋ\ **kyoodles** [imit.] **:** to make loud useless noises **:** HOLLER, YAP ⟨the dogs waved their tails happily and sought out a rabbit and went *kyoodling* after it —John Steinbeck⟩ ⟨quit listening to all this *kyoodling* from behind the fence —Sinclair Lewis⟩

**kyo·to** \kē'(y)ōd·(,)ō, -ō(,)tō *sometimes* 'kyō-\ *adj, usu cap* [fr. *Kyoto,* city in west central Honshu, Japan] **:** of or from the city of Kyoto, Japan **:** of the kind or style prevalent in Kyoto

**ky·pho·scoliosis** \;kī(,)fō+\ *n, pl* **kyphoscolioses** [NL, fr. *kypho-* (fr. *kyphosis*) + *scoliosis*] **:** backward and lateral curvature of the spine

**ky·pho·scoliotic** \"+\ *adj* [fr. NL *kyphoscoliosis,* after such pairs as NL *hypnosis:* E *hypnotic*] **:** of, relating to, or marked by kyphoscoliosis

**ky·phos·i·dae** \kī'fäsə,dē\ *n pl, cap* [NL, fr. *Kyphosus,* type genus + *-idae*] **:** a family of chiefly tropical percoid shore fishes resembling bass and including a number of important herbivorous food fishes — see KYPHOSUS, RUDDERFISH

**ky·pho·sis** \kī'fōsə̇s\ *n, pl* **kypho·ses** \-ō,sēz\ [NL, fr. Gk *kyphōsis,* fr. *kyphos* humpbacked, bent + *-ōsis* -osis — more at CYPHELLA] **1 :** abnormal backward curvature of the spine — opposed to *lordosis* **2 :** the state of one who is affected with kyphosis — **ky·phot·ic** \(')=;fäd·ik\ *adj*

**ky·pho·sus** \kī'fōsəs\ *n, cap* [NL, fr. Gk *kyphos* + L *-osus* -ose] **:** a genus that includes the Bermuda chub and is the type of the family Kyphosidae

**kyr·i·a·le** \,kirē'ä(,)lā\ *also* **kyr·i·al** \'kirēəl\ *n* -s *usu cap* [NL *kyriale,* fr. *kyrie* + ML *-ale* (as in *missale* missal)] **:** a liturgical book containing the text and plainsong notation of the parts of the ordinary of the mass (as the Kyrie, Sanctus, Agnus Dei) that are sung by the congregation

**ky·rie elei·son** \;kirē,āə'lā(ə),sän, -lāsᵊn,-lāəsən, *in rapid speech* ,kirēə'l-\ *or* **kyrie** \'kirē,ā\ *n, pl* **kyrie eleisons** *or* **kyries** *often cap K&E* [*kyrie eleison* fr. LL, fr. Gk *Kyrie eleēson* Lord, have mercy; *kyrie* fr. NL, fr. LL *kyrie eleison*] **1 :** a petitionary invocation (as in the ordinary of the mass and in the breviary) addressed to the Trinity and beginning with the words "kyrie eleison" **2 :** either of two Anglican liturgical responses beginning with the words "Lord, have mercy upon us": **a :** one accompanying the decalogue **b :** one following the summary of the Law

**kyr·i·elle** \;kirē;el\ *n, pl* **kyrielle** [F, fr. OF *kyriele,* lit., kyrie eleison, fr. LL *kyrie eleison*] **:** a French verse form in short usu. octosyllabic rhyming couplets often paired in quatrains and characterized by a refrain which is sometimes a single word or sometimes the full second line of the couplet or fourth line of the quatrain

**ky·ri·os** \'kirē,äs\ *also* **ku·ri·os** \'kúr-\ *n, pl* **kyri·oi** \-ē,ȯi\ *or* **kyrios·es** \-ē,äsə̇z\ *also* **kuri·oi** *or* **kurios·es** *usu cap* [Gk *kyrios* lord, master, fr. *kyros* power, might — more at CURIOLOGIC] **:** LORD ⟨early Christians confessed Jesus Christ as their ~ instead of the emperor⟩

**kyte** \'kīt\ *n* -s [prob. fr. LG *küt* bowel; akin to MD *cuy* calf of the leg, *cuut* fish roe, MLG *kūt* calf of the leg, fish roe, G dial. (Bavarian) *kütz* part of the entrails, Skt *guda* bowel — more at COT] *chiefly Scot* **:** STOMACH, BELLY ⟨sit down and fill your ~ —R.L.Stevenson⟩

**kythe** *var of* KITHE

**kyu·rin** \kyə'rēn\ *n, pl* **kyurin** *or* **kyurins** *usu cap* **:** a member of a Lezghian people of the Caucasus mountains

**[1]l** \'el\ *n, pl* **l's** *or* **ls** *often cap, often attrib* **1 a :** the 12th letter of the English alphabet **b :** an instance of this letter printed, written, or otherwise represented **c :** a speech counterpart of orthographic *l* (as clear *l* in *lean* or Polish *lipa,* dark *l* in *cool* and Polish *łapa*) **2 :** 50 — see NUMBER table **3 :** a printer's type, a stamp, or some other instrument for reproducing the letter *l* **4 :** someone or something arbitrarily or conveniently designated *l* esp. as the 11th or when j is used for the 10th the 12th in order or class **5 :** something having the shape of the capital letter L: as **a :** [2]ELL 2 **b :** [2]ELL 3 **6 :** ELEVATED RAILROAD ⟨riding on the *L*⟩ ⟨an *L* train⟩

**[2]l** *abbr, often cap* **1** lady **2** lake **3** lambert **4** land **5** landing **6** landplane **7** large **8** lat **9** late **10** Latin **11** latitude **12** launch **13** law **14** leaf **15** league **16** learner **17** leather **18** leave **19** left **20** legitimate **21** lempira **22** length **23** letter **24** leu **25** lev **26** lewisite **27** [L *lex*] law **28** liaison **29** [L *liber*] book **30** Liberal **31** [L *libra*] pound **32** licentiate **33** lift **34** light **35** lightning **36** line **37** liner **38** link **39** liquid **40** lira **41** lit **42** liter **43** [L *loco*] in the place; [L *locus*] place **44** lodge **45** long **46** longitude **47** lord **48** lost **49** low **50** lumen

**[3]l** *symbol, cap* **1** *ital* inductance **2** *ital* kinetic potential

**l-** *in sense 1* ¦lē(,)vō *or* ¦el, *in sense 2* ¦el\ *prefix* [ISV, fr. *lev-*] **1 :** levorotatory — usu. printed in italic ⟨*l*-tartaric acid⟩; compare LEV- **2 :** having a similar configuration at a selected carbon atom in an optically active molecule to the configuration of levorotatory glyceraldehyde — usu. printed as a small capital ⟨L-fructose⟩

**[1]la** \'lä\ *n* -s [ME, fr. ML, fr. L *la*bii lip's, a word sung to this note in a medieval hymn to St. John the Baptist] **1 :** the sixth tone of the diatonic scale in solmization **2 :** the tone A in the fixed-do system

**[2]la** \'lȯ, 'lä\ *interj* [ME (northern dial.), fr. OE *lā*] **1** *now chiefly dial* — used for emphasis ⟨indeed, ~, 'tis a noble child —Shak.⟩ ⟨~! Yes, I've heard tell about that old mortar —*Ford Times*⟩ **2** *now chiefly dial* — used to express surprise ⟨~ . . . how very smirking —Charles Dickens⟩

**[3]la** \'lä\ *adj, usu cap* [F, fem. of *le,* def. art., the, fr. L *ille* that one, that — more at LARIAT] **:** THE — used with the family name of a woman ⟨shrugged elaborately — a crib . . . from *La* Dietrich —Nicholas Monsarrat⟩

**la** *abbr* last

**LA** *abbr* **1** landing account **2** law agent **3** leading aircraftsman **4** legislative assembly **5** letter of authority **6** library association **7** lighter than air **8** lightning arrester **9** local agent **10** local authority **11** low altitude

**La** *symbol* lanthanum

**LAA** *abbr* light antiaircraft

**laad** \'läd\ *Scot var of* LAD

**[1]laa·ger** \'lägə(r)\ *n* -s [obs. Afrik *lager* (now, *laer*), fr. G, camp, couch, lair, fr. OHG *legar* couch, lair — more at LAIR] **1** *Africa* **:** CAMP; *esp* **:** a travelers' encampment protected by a circle of wagons **2 :** a military encampment or defensive position protected by a ring of armored vehicles

**[2]laager** \"\ *vi* -ED/-ING/-S **:** to form or camp in a laager **:** ENCAMP

**laag·te** \'läktə\ *n* -s [Afrik, fr. *laag* low; akin to ON *lāgr* low — more at LOW] *Africa* **:** a usu. relatively wide and level valley in the veld

**laap** *var of* LERP

**laa·ven·ite** \'lävə,nīt\ *also* **lav·en·ite** \'lav-\ *n* -s [Norw *låvenit,* fr. *Låven,* island in the Langesund fiord, Norway + Norw *-it* -ite] **:** a mineral consisting of a complex silicate of zirconium, calcium, manganese, and sometimes other elements occurring in prismatic crystals

**[1]lab** \'lab, -aa(ə)b\ *n* -s [ME *labbe,* fr. *labben* to blab] *archaic* **:** [1]BLAB 1

**[2]lab** \"\ *n* -s [by shortening] **:** LABORATORY

**lab** *abbr* labor

**lab·a·dism** \'labə,dizəm\ *n* -s *usu cap* [F *labadisme,* fr. Jean de *Labadie* †1674 Fr. religious reformer + F *-isme* -ism] **:** the doctrines and practices of Labadists

**[1]lab·a·dist** \-,dəst\ *n* -s *usu cap* [Jean de *Labadie* †1674 + E *-ist*] **:** a member of a communistic sect of radical Pietists of the 17th and 18th centuries emphasizing spiritual rebirth and the inner illumination of the Holy Spirit as religious necessities

**[2]labadist** \"\ *adj, usu cap* **:** of or relating to Labadists or to their doctrines and practices

**la bamba** \lä-\ *n* -s *often cap L&B* [AmerSp, the bamba] **:** BAMBA

**la·ban system** \'lābən-\ *n, usu cap L* [after Rudolf *Laban* †1958 Swiss dancing instructor] **:** a method of recording bodily movement (as in a dance) on a staff by means of direction and other symbols that can be aligned with musical accompaniment — see ICOSAHEDRON

**la·ba·ria** \lə'bärēə\ *also* **la·bar·ri** \-rē\ *or* **la·bar·ria** *or* **la·ba·rea** \-rēə\ *n* -s [AmerSp *labaria*] **:** a So. American venomous snake variously identified as a coral snake or any of several pit vipers

**la·bar·raque's solution** \¦labə¦rak(s)-\ *n, usu cap L* [after Antoine G. *Labarraque* †1850 Fr. chemist and pharmacist] **:** JAVELLE WATER b

**lab·a·rum** \'labərəm\ *n* -s [LL] **1 :** an imperial standard of the later Roman emperors resembling the vexillum; *esp* **:** the standard adopted by Constantine after his conversion to Christianity consisting of a purple silk banner hanging from a crosspiece on a pike and surmounted by a golden crown bearing the chi-rho **2 :** any symbolical standard or banner

**lab·ba** \'labə\ *n* -s [of Arawakan origin; akin to Arawak *labba* paca] **:** PACA

**lab·ber** \'labə(r)\ *vb* -ED/-ING/-S [perh. of imit. origin] *dial Eng* **:** SPLASH, WET

**lab·da·num** \'labdənəm\ *or* **lad·a·num** \-adᵊn-\ *n* -s [ML *lapdanum,* fr. L *ladanum, ledanum,* fr. Gk *ladanon, lēdanon,* fr. *lēdon* rockrose, of Sem origin] **:** a soft blackish brown to greenish oleoresin that is obtained from various rockroses (as *Cistus ladanum, C. creticus*), has a fragrant odor and bitter taste, and is used in perfumes esp. as a fixative

**-labe** \,lāb *sometimes* ,lab *or* ,laa(ə)b\ *n comb form* -s [ME, fr. MF, fr. ML *-labium,* fr. LGk *-labion,* dim. of Gk *-labos* (fr. *lambanein* to take) — more at LEMMA] **:** instrument **:** implement ⟨cosmo*labe*⟩

**lab·e·fac·tion** \,labə'fakshən\ *n* -s [LL *labefaction-, labefactio,* fr. L *labefactus* (past part. of *labefacere* to cause to totter, shake, fr. *labare* to totter + *facere* to make) + *-ion-, -io* -ion] **:** a weakening or impairment esp. of moral principles or civil order **:** DOWNFALL, OVERTHROW

**[1]la·bel** \'lābəl\ *n* -s *often attrib* [ME fr. MF, fr. OF *label* ribbon, fringe, label in heraldry, prob. of Gmc origin; akin to OHG *lappa* flap, lappet — more at LAP] **1** *archaic* **:** a narrow piece (as of cloth) **:** STRIP, RIBBON, LAPPET; *specif* **:** one attached to a document to hold an appended seal **2** *obs* **:** a rider or appendix orig. appended to a document on an attached strip **3 :** a heraldic charge consisting of a narrow bar with usu. three pendants and used esp. as a cadency mark to distinguish an eldest or only son during his father's life — called also *file* **4 :** a representation (as in medieval art) of a band or scroll containing an inscription **5 a :** a slip (as of paper, parchment, cloth, leather, metal) that is inscribed and affixed to something for identification, direction, or description **:** TAG, STICKER ⟨write your name on the ~ and tie it to the basket⟩ ⟨books with gilt-lettered red morocco ~*s*⟩ **b :** written, printed, or graphic matter attached to or accompanying an article or inscribed on its container or wrapper identifying the contents or giving other appropriate information (as the destination of a parcel, the use of a medicine, the title of a book) ⟨read the ~ on the bottle⟩ **c :** a descriptive, classifying, or identifying word or phrase: as (1) **:** EPITHET ⟨the term stream of consciousness . . . is already established as a literary ~ —Robert Humphrey⟩ ⟨acquired the ~ of "playboy" which seemed to stick —Brian Crozier⟩ ⟨hanging the subversive ~ on their own liberal clergy —Ralph Winnett⟩ (2) **:** a word or phrase used with but not as part of a dictionary definition usu. in abbreviated form and distinctive type to provide information (as grammatical function or area or level of usage) about the word defined ⟨the ~ *obsolete* is abbreviated *obs*⟩ (3) **:** a newspaper headline merely identifying the subject matter of an article rather than summarizing action **6 :** a projecting molding by the sides and over the top of an opening; *specif* **:** a dripstone of square form characteristic of late Gothic work in England **7 :** an adhesive stamp: **a :** POSTAGE STAMP **b :** a stamp issued for some purpose (as revenue, notification of postage due) other than postage **8 :** PANEL 3f(3) **9 :** a labeled atom in a molecule **10 a** (1) **:** a brand of commercial recordings issued under a usu. trademarked name ⟨there are now available to record buyers more than 10,000 different ~*s* —Joel Turner⟩ ⟨from the Decca group we have, on the parent ~, Liszt's "Faust" Symphony —Thomas Heinitz⟩ (2) **:** one of the commercial recordings so issued ⟨issue . . . compositions first on classical ~*s* and then as "pops" singles —*Current Biog.*⟩ **b :** a company issuing commercial recordings under one or more brand names ⟨spent practically their entire recording careers with one ~ —J.S.Wilson b. 1913⟩ ⟨most of the recordings made by these jazzmen were for small ~*s* —Bill Simon⟩

**[2]label** \"\ *vt* **labeled** *or* **labelled; labeled** *or* **labelled; labeling** *or* **labelling** \-b(ə)liŋ\ **labels 1 :** to give a label to: **a :** to affix a label to **:** mark with a label ⟨~ a bottle⟩ **b :** to describe or designate with a label ⟨subdivides his discussions . . . by sections ~*ed* with numerals and letters —Robert Halsband⟩ ⟨many girls ~*ed* "bad" turned out to be . . . mentally ill —Marjorie Rittwagen⟩ **2 a :** to distinguish (an element or atom) by using a radioactive isotope or an isotope of unusual mass for tracing through chemical reactions or biological processes ⟨the distribution of ~*ed* phosphorus [radiophosphorus] in a moth larva —E.O.Lawrence⟩ **b :** to distinguish (as a compound or molecule) esp. by introducing a labeled atom ⟨glycine ~*ed* with carbon 14 in the carboxyl group⟩

**label clause** *or* **labels clause** *n* **:** a clause in marine insurance limiting the liability of the assurer when only labels, capsules, or wrappers are damaged to the cost of reconditioning to an amount not exceeding the insured value of the goods

**la·bel·er** *or* **la·bel·ler** \-b(ə)lə(r)\ *n* -s **:** one that labels; *esp* **:** one who labels (as a product) by hand or by machine

**la·bel·late** \lə'be,lāt\ *adj* [NL *labell*um + E *-ate*] **:** having a labellum

**la·bel·loid** \-lȯid\ *adj* [NL *labell*um + E *-oid*] **:** resembling a labellum

**la·bel·lum** \lə'beləm\ *n, pl* **labella** \-lə\ [NL, fr. L, small lip, dim. of *labrum* lip — more at LIP] **1 :** the median membrane of the corolla of an orchid often differing markedly from the other two petals in shape and size, occasionally spurred, and while morphologically inner becoming by torsion of the ovary the outer or lower member **2 a :** a prolongation of the labrum of various beetles and true bugs that covers the basal part of the rostrum **b :** either of a pair of sensitive fleshy lobes in two-winged flies that terminate the proboscis sheath and consist of the expanded end of the elongated labium

**labels** *pl of* LABEL, *pres 3d sing of* LABEL

**label stop** *n* **:** a finishing boss at either end of a label, sill, or sill course

**-labes** *pl of* -LABE

**labia** *pl of* LABIUM

**[1]la·bi·al** \'lābēəl\ *adj* [ML *labialis,* fr. L *labium* lip + *-alis* -al — more at LIP] **1 :** of or relating to the lips or labia ⟨a ~ gland⟩ ⟨a ~ scale⟩ **2 :** giving its tones from impact of an air current on a lip or liplike edge ⟨a ~ instrument like the flute⟩ **3 :** produced with the participation of one or both lips — used of consonants (as \f\, \v\, \p\, \b\) and of rounded vowels (as \ü\) and semivowels (as \w\) — compare BILABIAL, LABIODENTAL

**[2]labial** \"\ *n* -s **1 :** FLUE PIPE **2 :** a labial consonant **3 :** one of the small scales that border the lips of most snakes and many other reptiles

**labial gland** *n* **1 :** one of the small tubular mucous and serous glands lying beneath the mucous membrane of the lips **2 :** one of the glands opening at the base of the labium of insects usu. functioning as salivary glands but in some groups producing silk or some other substance

**la·bi·al·i·ty** \,lābē'aləd·ē\ *n* -ES **:** the quality or state of being labial

**la·bi·al·iza·tion** \,lābēələ'zāshən\ *n* -s [[1]*labial* + *-ization*] **:** the action or result of labializing **:** ROUNDING

**la·bi·al·ize** \'lābēə,līz\ *vt* -ED/-ING/-S [[1]*labial* + *-ize*] **:** to make labial: **a :** ROUND 1c(2) **b :** to replace with a sound that is labial ⟨in Spanish *auto,* from Latin *actus,* a velar stop has been *labialized*⟩

**la·bi·al·ly** \'lābēəlē, -li\ *adv* **:** in a labial manner **:** with or by means of the lips

**labial palp** *n* **:** a palp of a bivalve mollusk

**labial palpus** *n* [part trans. of NL *palpus labialis*] **:** either of the jointed appendages on the front of the mentum of an insect — see INSECT illustration

**labial stop** *n* **:** a pipe-organ stop composed of labial pipes

**labial teeth** *n pl* **:** the incisor and canine teeth

**la·bia ma·jo·ra** \'lābēəmə'jōrə, -jȯrə\ *n pl* [NL, lit., larger lips] **:** the outer fatty folds bounding the vulva

**labia mi·no·ra** \-mə'nōrə, -nȯrə\ *n pl* [NL, lit., smaller lips] **:** the inner highly vascular largely connective-tissue folds bounding the vulva

**la·bi·a·tae** \,lābē'ā,tē\ *n pl* [NL, fr. fem. pl. of *labiatus* labiate] *cap* **:** a family of mostly aromatic herbs, shrubs, or rarely trees (order Polemoniales) distinguished esp. by the four-lobed ovary which becomes four one-seeded nutlets in fruit — see MINT

**[1]la·bi·ate** \'lābēət, -ē,āt, *usu* -d·+V\ *adj* [NL *labiatus,* fr. L *labium* lip + *-atus* -ate — more at LIP] **1 :** having lips **:** LIPPED: **a :** having the limb of a tubular corolla or calyx divided into two unequal parts projecting one over the other like the lips of a mouth (as in the snapdragon, sage, catnip) **b** *anat* **:** having thickened fleshy margins **2 :** belonging to the Labiatae

**[2]la·bi·ate** \'lābē,āt\ *n* -s [NL *Labiatae*] **:** a plant of the Labiatae

**labiate bear** *n* [prob. trans. of NL *Ursus labiatus;* fr. its prominent lips] **:** SLOTH BEAR

**la·bi·at·ed** \'lābē,ād·əd\ *adj* **:** LABIATE

**lab·i·dog·na·tha** \,labə'dägnəthə\ [NL, fr. Gk *labid-, labis* handle, forceps + NL *-gnatha*] *syn of* ARANEAE VERAE

**la·bi·el·la** \,lābē'elə\ *n, pl* **labiel·lae** \-e(,)lē\ [NL, dim. of L *labium* lip] **:** HYPOPHARYNX

**la·bile** \'lābəl, 'lā,bīl *also* -,bēl\ *adj* [ME *labyl,* fr. MF *labile,* fr. LL *labilis* fleeting, transient, apt to slip, fr. L *labi* to slip, fall + *-ilis* -ile — more at SLEEP] **1** *obs* **:** prone to slip, err, or lapse **2** [F, fr. MF] **:** characterized by a ready tendency toward or capability for change **:** CHANGEABLE, UNSTABLE ⟨an emotionally ~ patient⟩ **:** ADAPTABLE ⟨has so ~ a face that some of her scenes . . . rock with emotion —Manny Farber⟩ **3 :** readily or continually undergoing chemical or physical or biological change or breakdown (as in the presence of a specified factor) ⟨heat-*labile* and heat-stable antigens⟩ ⟨the germinative plasma of the eggs is ~, producing under the influence of various conditions of nourishment different results —Auguste Lameere⟩ ⟨~ diabetes⟩ **:** fluctuating widely ⟨~ blood pressure in hypertensives⟩: as **a :** readily undergoing cleavage or molecular rearrangement or other chemical modification ⟨one of the chlorine atoms is readily removed as hydrogen chloride and is termed ~ or hydrolyzable chlorine —H.L.Haller & Ruth L. Busbey⟩ ⟨acid-*labile* phosphate⟩ — compare UNSTABLE **b :** characterized by shifting interchange (as of component material) without alteration in kind ⟨~ equilibrium of a fluid⟩ **c** *psychol* **:** tending to discharge rather than to retain affect **d** *geol* **:** unstable mechanically or chemically ⟨stable and ~ minerals⟩ ⟨a ~ stratum⟩

**la·bil·i·ty** \lə'biləd·ē\ *n* -ES **:** the quality or state of being labile ⟨believe that a fall in population level . . . might enhance evolutionary ~ —N.E.Collias & C.H.Southwick⟩

**la·bi·li·za·tion** \,lābələ'zāshən\ *n* -s **:** the action or process of labilizing

**la·bi·lize** \'lābə,līz\ *vt* -ED/-ING/-S [*labile* + *-ize*] **:** to render labile (as in chemical structure)

**labio-** *comb form* [L *labium* lip — more at LIP] **1 :** the lips ⟨*labio*graph⟩ ⟨*labio*plasty⟩ **2 :** labial and ⟨*labio*nasal⟩ ⟨*labio*velar⟩

**[1]la·bio·dental** \¦lābē(,)ō+\ *adj* [*labio-* + *dental*] **:** produced with the participation of lip and teeth or lips and teeth (as the lower lip and the upper front teeth) ⟨the ~ fricative \f\ and \v\⟩ **:** DENTILABIAL — compare BILABIAL, DENTAL, LABIAL

**[2]labiodental** \"\ *n* **:** a labiodental sound

**[1]la·bio·nasal** \"+\ *adj* [ISV *labio-* + *nasal*] **:** both labial and nasal — used of the sound \m\

**[2]labionasal** \"\ *n* **:** the sound \m\

**[1]la·bio·velar** \"+\ *adj* [ISV *labio-* + *velar*] **:** both labial and velar ⟨the ~ sound \w\⟩

**[2]labiovelar** \"\ *n* **:** a labiovelar sound

**la·bio·ve·lar·iza·tion** \,lābēō,vēlərə'zāshən\ *n* -s **:** the action or result of labiovelarizing

**la·bio·ve·lar·ize** \,===='vēlə,rīz\ *vt* [[1]*labiovelar* + *-ize*] **:** to make labiovelar

**la·bite** \'lā,bīt\ *n* -s [ISV *lab-* (fr. *Laba* river, the Caucasus, U.S.S.R.) + *-ite;* orig. formed as Russ *labit*] **:** a mineral $MgSi_3O_6(OH)_2.H_2O$ consisting of hydrous basic silicate of magnesium

**la·bi·um** \'lābēəm\ *n, pl* **labia** \-ēə\ [NL, fr. L, lip — more at LIP] **1 :** any of the folds at the margin of the vulva — compare LABIA MAJORA, LABIA MINORA **2 a :** the lower lip of a labiate corolla — compare GALEA **b :** the liplike lower margin of the foveola in plants of the genus *Isoetes* **3 a :** the lower lip of an insect that is formed by the second pair of maxillae united in the middle line and variously modified in different insects but consists typically of a submentum, mentum, and ligula and bears two labial palpi **b :** the coalescent pedipalpi of some mites **c :** a liplike part of a neuropodium in a polychaete worm **d :** the metastoma of a crustacean **e :** the columellar part of the aperture of a gastropod shell **f :** the movable sclerite forming the ventral wall of the head of a spider

**lab·lab** \'la,blab\ *n* -s [Ar *lablāb*] **:** any of several vines of the genus *Dolichos* or related genera; *specif* **:** HYACINTH BEAN

**lab–lab** \"\ *n* -s [Tag, lit., quagmire, marsh] *Philippines* **:** a mass of microscopic algae chiefly of the Myxophyceae found on the mud in fishponds and used as food by the fry

**[1]la·bor** \'lābə(r)\ *n* -s *see -or in Explan Notes* [ME *labour, labor,* fr. OF, fr. L *labor* drudgery, hardship, work; prob. akin to L *labi* to slip, slide — more at SLEEP] **1 a :** TOIL, WORK: (1) **:** expenditure of physical or mental effort esp. when fatiguing, difficult, or compulsory ⟨with ~ I excavated a pit —W.H. Hudson †1922⟩ ⟨with enormous ~*s* he made himself into a popular writer —Carl van Doren⟩ ⟨sentenced to six months at hard ~⟩ (2) **:** human activity that produces the goods or provides the services in demand in an economy **:** the services performed by workers for wages as distinguished from those rendered by entrepreneurs for profits ⟨each entrepreneur is eager to buy all the kinds of specific ~ he needs —Ludwig Von Mises⟩ **b** (1) **:** the physical activities involved in parturition consisting essentially of a prolonged series of involuntary contractions of the uterine musculature together with both reflex and voluntary contractions of the abdominal wall ⟨drugs that induce ~⟩ ⟨the record of her previous pregnancies and ~*s*⟩ ⟨went into ~ after a fall⟩ (2) **:** the period of time during which such labor takes place ⟨a 12-hour ~⟩ **c :** heavy pitching and rolling of a ship under way **2 :** an act or process requiring labor **:** TASK ⟨translation is a ~ that must be done afresh for each succeeding age —J.C.Swaim⟩ **3 :** a product of labor ⟨muddy waters had swept inland . . . submerging in one implacable tide the ~ of years —William Beebe⟩ ⟨inspecting his completed ~*s* with a critical eye⟩ **4 a :** an economic group comprising those who do manual labor or work for wages ⟨the native ~ is a floating population —*Geog. Jour.*⟩ **:** workingmen as an economic or political force ⟨~ has the right to assemble, to bargain collectively, and to strike —Curtis Bok⟩ ⟨win the vote of ~ in the coming elections⟩ **b :** workers employed in an establishment or available for employment **:** hired help ⟨the injection of ourselves and all our ~ against bubonic plague —*Think*⟩ **:** MANPOWER ⟨a plentiful supply of cheap ~ from across the border⟩ **c :** the organizations or officials (as unions or union leadership) representing groups of workers **:** organized labor ⟨those in ~ who advocate profit sharing by employees⟩ ⟨a conference between ~ and management⟩ **5** *usu* **labour** *usu cap* **a :** the Labour party of the United Kingdom ⟨when *Labour* is in a position to form a government, the sovereign . . . calls the leader as prime minister —R.T.McKenzie⟩ **b :** the Labour party in another nation of the British Commonwealth (as Australia or New Zealand) ⟨*Labour* won its first signal political triumph in the New South Wales elections —Alexander Brady⟩ **syn** see WORK

**[2]labor** \"\ *vb* **labored; labored; laboring** \-b(ə)riŋ\ **labors** *see -or in Explan Notes* [ME *labouren, laboren,* fr. MF *labourer,* fr. OF *laborer, labourer,* fr. L *laborare* to suffer, toil, work, fr. *labor,* n.] *vi* **1 :** to exert one's powers of body or mind esp. with painful or strenuous effort **:** to perform labor **:** WORK, STRIVE ⟨~*ed* to pull their wagons along the slushy road —F.V.W.Mason⟩ ⟨when a writer ~*s* long over a single passage⟩ ⟨began to ~ on the creation of a treaty system —D.J.Dallin⟩ ⟨~*ed* as a miner⟩ ⟨~*s* for the restoration of normal conditions⟩ **2 :** to move with great effort (as against opposition or under a burden) ⟨the boat ~*ed* upriver —Sherwood Anderson⟩ ⟨the ponderous woman ~*ed* puffingly up one flight of stairs —J.B. Benefield⟩ ⟨I had ~*ed* through the *Prometheus* with a Greek dictionary —H.J.Laski⟩ **3 :** to be in or enter into labor in the bearing of a child or young **4 :** to suffer from some disadvantage or distress — usu. used with *under* ⟨~*ed* under the handicap of arthritis⟩ ⟨~ under a delusion⟩ **5** *of a ship* **:** to pitch or roll heavily ⟨~*ed* heavily in a chopping sea —J.L. Motley⟩ **~** *vt* **1** *dial Brit* **:** TILL, CULTIVATE ⟨the cultivated area . . . is ~*ed* by some 65,000 farmers —J.M.Mogey⟩ **2 :** BURDEN, TIRE, DISTRESS ⟨the details . . . are endless and I won't ~ you with them —Horace Sutton⟩ **:** make laborious ⟨anxiety . . . troubled and ~*ed* her mature work —Sara H. Hay⟩ **3** *archaic* **a :** to spend labor on or produce by labor ⟨anvils ~*ed* by the Cyclops' hands —John Dryden⟩ **b :** to strive to effect or achieve **:** work for ⟨earnestly . . . ~*ed* that reunion —Edmund Burke⟩ **4 :** to treat or work out in often laborious detail **:** develop fully **:** ELABORATE ⟨no need to ~ the obvious —Bernard DeVoto⟩ **5** *obs* **:** to use one's influence or favor with or for **:** URGE ⟨the Devil . . . ~*s* all he can to bring them into the same pit —Robert Burton⟩ **6 :** to cause to labor ⟨poets ~*ing* their wits on tasks like these —Gilbert Highet⟩ **7** *obs* **:** BEAT, POUND, RUB ⟨take the white of an egg and ~ the same —*Book of St. Albans*⟩ ⟨the ass . . . if he be ~*ed* with a cudgel —Richard Carew⟩ **8** *obs* **:** to bring by labor or endeavor to a specified position or state ⟨~*ed* him out of his house —Robert Crowley⟩

**[3]labor** \"\ *adj, see -or in Explan Notes* [[1]*labor*] **1 a :** of or relating to labor ⟨~ costs⟩ ⟨an ample ~ supply⟩ ⟨~ legislation⟩ **b :** of, representing the views or interests of, or dominated by organized labor ⟨~ political activity⟩ ⟨editorials in the ~ press⟩ ⟨a ~ leader⟩ ⟨districts that are traditionally liberal and ~ —*NewRepublic*⟩ **c :** affecting labor and management ⟨a ~ contract⟩ **2** *usu cap* **:** of, relating to, or constituted by a political party that claims to represent the interests of working men and women or that is characterized by a membership in which organized labor groups predominate: as **a :** of, relating to, or constituted by one of several minor political parties usu. having a brief period of activity in the U.S. during the late 19th and 20th centuries — usu. used in combination ⟨the Farmer-*Labor* party of Minnesota⟩ ⟨the American *Labor* party in New York state . . . constituted an important political bloc —H.S.Gilbertson⟩ **b** *usu* **labour** (1) **:** of, relating to, or constituted by a major political party of the United Kingdom in the 20th century associated with socialistic policies (as the nationalization of basic industries) and characterized by an organization in which trade unions are predominant ⟨election of a *Labour* candidate to the London County Council⟩ ⟨a *Labour* majority in the House of Commons⟩ (2) **:** of, relating to, or constituted by a political party in another nation of the British Commonwealth that is usu. similar in membership to the Labour party of the United Kingdom ⟨the power of the *Labour* caucus in Australia⟩ ⟨New Zealand's first *Labour* government⟩

**[4]la·bor** \lə'bō(ə)r, -bȯ(ə)r\ *n* -s [MexSp, fr. Sp, farming, tilling, work, fr. L, work] **:** an old Texas unit of land area equal to about 177 acres

**lab·o·ra·to·ri·al** \¦lab(ə)rə¦tōrēəl, -tȯr-\ *adj* **:** of, utilizing, or resembling a laboratory — **lab·o·ra·to·ri·al·ly** \-ēəlē\ *adv*

**lab·o·ra·to·ri·an** \,=(=)='=rēən\ *n* -s **:** a laboratory worker

**¹lab·o·ra·to·ry** \'labrə,tōrē, -tȯr-, -ri *sometimes* 'labər-, *chiefly in substand speech by r-dissimilation* 'labə,t-, *chiefly Brit* lə'bärə·tri *or* -ärətəri\ *n* -ES [ML *laboratorium*, fr. L *laboratus* (past part. of *laborare* to labor) + *-orium* -ory — more at LABOR] **1 a :** a place devoted to experimental study in any branch of natural science or to the application of scientific principles in testing and analysis or in the preparation usu. on a small scale of drugs, chemicals, explosives, or other products or substances ⟨a chemical ~⟩ ⟨a biological ~⟩ ⟨a rolling crime ~⟩ ⟨the weather research plane, a powerful flying ~ —Walter Hayward⟩ **b :** a place equipped for or an organized activity involving experimentation or observation in a field of study (as child development) or practice in a skill (as reading) ⟨was equipped with a psychology ~⟩ ⟨composition ~ . . . for students requiring special help in English fundamentals —*King College Bull.*⟩ **c :** a period in an academic schedule set aside for laboratory work ⟨a course with two lectures and one ~ a week⟩ **2 a :** something resembling a laboratory in carrying on a process of production or testing ⟨the ~ of the mind⟩ ⟨the ~ of ongoing human experience —L.A.Weigle⟩ **b :** an environment that provides opportunity for systematic observation, experimentation, or practice ⟨a settlement house serving as a sociological ~⟩ ⟨the new nation of Israel, a social ~⟩ **3 :** the hearth of a reverberatory furnace

**²laboratory** \"\ *adj* **1 :** of, working, used, or done in a laboratory ⟨get ~ approval for the new appliance⟩ ⟨a ~ assistant in accounting⟩ ⟨a ~ manual⟩ ⟨perform ~ experiments⟩ **2 :** befitting, suggestive of, or resembling that of a laboratory ⟨insisted on . . . ~ conditions in an election —*N.Y. Times*⟩ ⟨a cheap liquor . . . had a fierce ~ flavor —Norman Lewis⟩ ⟨a kind of ~ method in fiction —Robert Humphrey⟩ **3 :** of or involving observation or experimentation or practice for educational purposes ⟨a ~ period⟩ ⟨a ~ course⟩

**laboratory school** *n* **:** a school operated by a college or university and used esp. for student teaching and the demonstration of classroom practices

**labor bank** *n* **:** a bank owned and operated by a labor union

**labor camp** *n* **1 :** a penal colony (as in the U.S.S.R.) where forced labor is performed **2 :** living facilities (as in the western U.S.) for migratory labor

**labor court** *n* **:** a governmental agency established to adjudicate a management-labor dispute not resolved by the parties involved or any dispute over contract interpretation; *also* **:** a similar agency empowered only to subject disputants to compulsory investigation

**labor day** *n* **1** *usu cap L&D* **:** a day set aside for special recognition of the workingman: as **a :** the first Monday in September, observed in the U.S. and Canada as a legal holiday **b :** May 1 in many countries **2** [trans. of Russ *trudoden*, fr. *trud* labor + *den* day] **:** a Soviet unit of labor crediting a collective-farm worker with more or less than his actual working time according to his skill and productivity

**labored** *adj* [fr. past part. of ²*labor*] **:** produced or performed with labor ⟨breathing of the men . . . seemed immensely loud and ~ —Irwin Shaw⟩ **:** bearing marks of labor and effort **:** elaborately wrought **:** not easy or natural ⟨a ~ signature that would seem to indicate only the most rudimentary kind of schooling —Hamilton Basso⟩ ⟨the cumbersome paraphernalia of expression which make his poetry so ~ and artificial —M.R. Adams⟩ — **la·bored·ly** *adv* — **la·bored·ness** *n* -ES

**la·bor·er** \'lābərə(r)\ *n* -S [ME *laborer*, *labourer*, fr. MF *laboureur*, fr. OF *laboreor*, fr. *laborer* to labor + *-eor* -or — more at LABOR] **1 :** one that labors; *specif* **:** a person who does unskilled physical work for wages sometimes as assistant to a skilled artisan ⟨a bricklayer's ~⟩ **2** *archaic* **:** WORKER 3

**labor exchange** *n* **1 :** an exchange for direct transfer of products according to the amount of labor expended in making them without the intervention of money **2 a :** EMPLOYMENT AGENCY **b** *chiefly Brit* **:** EMPLOYMENT EXCHANGE

**labor force** *n* **1 :** a body of employed workers (as of a corporation or in an industry) at a particular place or period of time **2 :** the total number of employable workers ⟨a national *labor force*⟩; *specif* **:** the number of persons in the U.S. at least 14 years of age who are actually employed or are seeking employment

**labor grade** *n* **:** one of a series of wage groupings of the jobs within a plant or company that are considered of approximately equal worth on the basis of job evaluation

**labor income** *n* **:** the annual income of a farmer after business expenses and an interest charge for capital invested are subtracted ⟨to compare *labor income* with city salaries, the value of house rent and the products used must be added —H.E. Botsford⟩

**laboring** *pres part of* LABOR

**la·bor·ing·ly** *adv* **:** in a laboring manner **:** LABORIOUSLY

**laboring oar** *n* [fr. *laboring*, pres. part. of ²*labor*] **:** a part or task requiring greater effort than others ⟨the officer who pulls the *laboring oar* in the club's activities⟩

**la·bo·ri·ous** \lə'bōrēəs, -bȯr-\ *adj* [ME, fr. MF or L; MF *laborieux*, fr. L *laboriosus*, fr. *labor* + *-iosus* -ious] **1 :** devoted to labor **:** INDUSTRIOUS, HARDWORKING, DILIGENT ⟨as men of research . . . they are magnificently ~ and accurate —Aldous Huxley⟩ **2 :** involving or characterized by hard or toilsome effort or by detailed elaboration **:** LABORED ⟨months of ~ research⟩ ⟨slow and ~ transportation⟩ ⟨~ and futile negotiations⟩ ⟨several ~, overlong, painfully "arty" stories —William Peden⟩ ⟨picturesque scenery painted with ~ literalism —*Amer. Guide Series: Pa.*⟩ **3** *chiefly Brit* **:** doing unskilled labor **:** LABORING ⟨cottages for the ~ and industrious part of the community —G.E.Fussell⟩ — **la·bo·ri·ous·ly** *adv* — **la·bo·ri·ous·ness** *n* -ES

**la·bor·ism** \'lābə,rizəm\ *n* -S **1** *usu cap* **a :** the principles and policies of the Labour party **b :** the Labour party or its members **2 :** a system characterized by policies and attitudes favoring a predominance of labor and its interests in economics and politics ⟨~ and not . . . imperialism is the policy of the latest stage of capitalism —J.A.Schumpeter⟩

**la·bor·is·tic** \¦lābə¦ristik\ *adj* [¹*labor* + *-istic*] **:** characterized by policies or attitudes favorable to labor ⟨this chamber . . . turned out to be so much more Fascist than ~ —H.R.Spencer⟩ ⟨a ~ society⟩

**la·bor·ite** \'==,rīt, *usu* -īd·+V\ *n* -S **1 :** a member of a group favoring the interests of labor ⟨one of those radical ~*s* who shunned association with any but wage earners —*Public*⟩ **2** *usu cap* **a :** a member of a political party that claims to be devoted chiefly to the interests of labor ⟨Illinois *Laborites* . . . demand 44-hour week —*N.Y. Times*⟩ **b** *usu* **labourite :** a member of the British Labour party ⟨Liberal, *Laborite* and Conservative are all maneuvering for position —*So. Atlantic Quarterly*⟩ ⟨the British *Labourites* look forward to an industrial democracy —J.H.Randall⟩

**la·bor·less** \'lābə(r)ləs\ *adj* **:** involving or doing no labor **:** EASY, IDLE

**labor market** *n* **1 :** the institutions and processes through which employment and wages are determined ⟨groups excluded from the *labor market*⟩ **2 :** the factors affecting the supply of and demand for labor ⟨a *labor market* favorable to employers⟩ **3 :** the area within which workers compete for jobs and employers compete for workers ⟨draw workers from a large *labor market*⟩

**labor movement** *n* **1 :** an organized effort on the part of workers to improve their economic and social status by united action through the medium of labor unions **2 :** the activities of labor unions to further the cause of organized labor

**labor of love :** a labor voluntarily undertaken or performed without consideration of any benefit or reward

**labor organization** *n* **:** an organization, agency, or representative committee in which employees participate for the purpose of engaging in collective bargaining with employers

**labor relations** *n pl* **:** relations between management and labor esp. as involved in collective bargaining and maintenance of contract

**labors** *pl of* LABOR, *pres 3d sing of* LABOR

**laborsaving** \'==,==\ *adj* **1 :** adapted to supersede or diminish labor ⟨~ devices⟩ ⟨a ~ plan of work⟩ **2** *printing* **a :** ready cut or cast in multiples of a standard size (as the pica) — used of a rule, slug, or furniture **b :** having mortised ends — used of metal furniture

**labor skate** *n, slang* **:** a member of a labor union

**la·bor·some** \'lābə(r)səm\ *adj* [¹*labor* + *-some*] **:** LABORIOUS 2 — **la·bor·some·ly** *adv*

**labor spy** *n* **:** an agent of an employer hired to report on union activities **:** STOOL PIGEON

**labor theory of value :** a theory of value holding that the quantity of labor in a product regulates its value and utilized by Marx to claim for labor the sole rightful claim to production

**labor union** *n* **:** a labor organization created for the purpose of advancing (as by collective bargaining) its members' interests (as in respect to wages and working conditions) — compare CRAFT UNION; see INDUSTRIAL UNION

**la·bou·chère** \,labü'sher\ *n* -S *usu cap* [prob. after Henry du Pré *Labouchère* †1912 Eng. journalist and political leader] **:** a system of betting on roulette, faro, and other games whereby the bettor takes a column of consecutive numbers consistent with the amount he is willing to risk and bets the sum of the top and bottom numbers, canceling the numbers involved in any bet won and adding to the series the amount of each bet lost

**la·boul·be·nia** \lə,bül'bēnēə, ,la,b-, ,lä,b-\ *n, usu cap* [NL, fr. Jean J. A. *Laboulbène* †1898 Fr. physician and entomologist + NL *-ia*] **:** the type genus of the family Laboulbeniaceae

**la·boul·be·ni·a·ce·ae** \(,)=,=,bēnē'āsē,ē\ *n pl, cap* [NL, fr. *Laboulbenia*, type genus + *-aceae*] **:** a family of minute fungi (order Laboulbeniales) living as parasites upon insects and having a thallus consisting of only a few cells and a spermatial type of sexual reproduction resembling that of the red algae — **la·boul·be·ni·a·ceous** \¦=¦==¦āshəs, ¦=,=¦==-\ *adj*

**la·boul·be·ni·a·les** \=,===¦ā(,)lēz\ *n pl, cap* [NL, fr. *Laboulbenia* + *-ales*] **:** an order of euascomycetous fungi coextensive with the family Laboulbeniaceae

**labour** *Brit var of* LABOR

**la·bour·din** *or* **la·bour·dine** \lə'bu̇(ə)rdᵊn, -r,dēn\ *n* -S *cap* [prob. fr. F, fr. *Labourd*, department of Basses Pyrénées, France] **:** a dialect of Basque spoken largely in the extreme west of the Department of Basses Pyrénées in France

**labouring** *n* -S [fr. *labouring*, *laboring*, gerund of *labour*, *labor*] *Scot* **:** FARM

**la·bour·ist** \'lābərəst\ *n* -S *usu cap* **:** LABORITE 2

**labourite** *usu cap, var of* LABORITE

**¹lab·ra·dor** \'labrə,dȯ(ə)r, -ȯ(ə)\ *adj, usu cap* [fr. *Labrador*, peninsula, Newfoundland and Quebec provinces in Canada] **:** of or from Labrador **:** of the kind or style prevalent in Labrador **:** LABRADOREAN

**²labrador** \"\ *n* -S **1** *or* **labrador blue** *often cap L* **:** a dark grayish to blackish blue **2** *usu cap* **:** LABRADOR RETRIEVER

**labrador duck** *n, usu cap L* **:** an extinct black-and-white sea duck (*Camptorhynchus labradorius*) related to the eiders

**¹lab·ra·dor·e·an** *or* **lab·ra·dor·i·an** \¦=¦=¦dȯrēən\ *adj, usu cap* [*Labrador*, peninsula, Canada + E *-an*] **1 :** of or relating to Labrador **2 :** of or forming the continental ice sheets of the Pleistocene epoch whose centers were located east or southeast of Hudson Bay

**²labradorean** *or* **labradorian** \"\ *n* -S *cap* **:** a native or inhabitant of Labrador

**lab·ra·dor·es·cence** \,=,=,dȯ'resᵊn(t)s\ *n* -S [*labradorite* + *-escence* (as in *fluorescence*)] **:** a play of colors or colored reflections exhibited esp. by labradorite and caused by internal structures that selectively reflect only certain colors

**lab·ra·dor·ite** \'=,=,dȯ,rīt\ *n* -S [*Labrador*, peninsula, Canada, its locality + E *-ite*] **:** a mineral consisting of a plagioclase feldspar in which the ratio of albite to anorthite lies between 5:5 and 3:7 and which commonly shows a beautiful play of gray, blue, green, and other colors and is hence much used for ornamental purposes — **lab·ra·dor·it·ic** \¦=,=,dȯ¦rid·ik\ *adj*

**labrador jay** *n, usu cap L* **:** a Canada jay of northeastern Canada that is usu. considered to be a distinct race

**labrador pine** *n, usu cap L* **:** JACK PINE 1

**labrador retriever** *n, usu cap L* **:** a retriever largely developed in England from stock originating in Newfoundland and characterized by a short dense hard unwaved usu. black coat, notable breadth of head, chest, and rib cage, and superior ability as a retriever of both waterfowl and upland game

**labrador spar** *or* **labrador stone** *n, usu cap L* **:** LABRADORITE

**labrador tea** *n, usu cap L* **:** either of two shrubs of the genus *Ledum*: **a :** a low-growing evergreen (*L. groenlandicum*) of eastern No. America having white or creamy bell-shaped flowers and leaves clothed beneath with rusty hairs and sometimes used for making a tea **b :** a related Rocky mountain shrub (*L. glandulosum*)

**la·bral** \'lābrəl\ *adj* [NL *labrum* + E *-al*] **:** of or relating to a labrum

**la·bret** \'lā,bret\ *n* -S [L *labrum* lip + E *-et*] **:** an ornament (as of wood, shell, or stone) worn by some primitive peoples in a perforation of the lip

**¹labrid** \'labrəd, 'lab-\ *adj* [NL *Labridae*] **:** of or relating to the family Labridae

**²labrid** \"\ *n* -S **:** a fish of the family Labridae

**lab·ri·dae** \'labrə,dē\ *n pl, cap* [NL, fr. *Labrus*, type genus + *-idae*] **:** a large and important family of percoid fishes having the palate toothless, the anterior teeth of the jaws separate and usu. strong, and the lower pharyngeals completely united into one bone with conical or tubercular teeth — see WRASSE

**¹la·broid** \'lā,brȯid, 'la,b-\ *adj* [NL *Labrus* + E *-oid*] **:** related to or resembling fishes of the family Labridae

**²labroid** \"\ *n* -S **:** a labroid fish

**la·brum** \'lābrəm, 'lab-\ *n* -S [NL, fr. L, lip, edge — more at LIP] **1 :** the upper or anterior lip of insects and crustaceans and other arthropods consisting of a single median piece or flap immediately in front of or above the mandibles **2 :** the external margin of a gastropod shell **3 :** the labium of an arachnid

**la·brus** \'lābrəs\ *n, cap* [NL, fr. L *labrus*, *labros*, a fish] **:** the type genus of the family Labridae

**la·brus·ca** \lə'brəskə\ *adj, often cap* [NL, fr. *labrusca* (specific epithet of *Vitis labrusca*) fr. L, wild vine] **:** of, relating to, or derived from an American fox grape (*Vitis labrusca*) that has been important in the development of hardy cultivated grapes ⟨several new ~ hybrids⟩ ⟨a hardy ~ grape⟩

**la·brys** \'lābrəs, 'lab-\ *n* -ES [Gk, prob. of Carian origin] **:** an ancient Cretan sacred double ax

**labs** *pl of* LAB

**la·bur·num** \lə'bərnəm, -bənn-\ *n* [NL, fr. L, laburnum, bean trefoil] **1** *cap* **:** a small genus of Eurasian poisonous shrubs and trees (family Leguminosae) having trifoliolate leaves and pendulous racemes of bright yellow flowers **2** -S **:** any plant of the genus *Laburnum*; *esp* **:** an ornamental tree (*L. anagyroides*) often cultivated for Easter decoration — called also *bean trefoil, golden chain, golden rain* **3** -S [L] **:** any of several similar plants of related genera (as *Cytisus*)

**lab·y·rinth** \'labə,rin(t)th, -,rən-\ *n, pl* **labyrinths** \-n(t)s, -n(t)ths\ [alter. (influenced by L *labyrinthus*) of ME *laborintus*, fr. L *labyrinthus*, fr. Gk *labyrinthos*, prob. of Carian origin; akin to Gk *labrys* double ax] **1 a :** a structure full of intricate passageways that make it difficult to find the way from the interior to the entrance or from the entrance to the center ⟨the ~ constructed by Daedalus for Minos, king of Crete, in which the Minotaur was confined⟩ **b :** a maze in a park or garden formed by paths separated by high thick hedges **2 a :** something often bewilderingly involved or tortuous in structure, arrangement, or character **:** a complex that baffles exploration ⟨a ~ of swamps and shifting channels —P.E.James⟩ ⟨the ~ of a great novel —E.K.Brown⟩ **b :** a situation or state (as of mind) from which it is difficult to extricate oneself ⟨a ~ of despair⟩ ⟨sank into the blissful ~ of a dream —Earle Birney⟩ **c :** INTRICACY, PERPLEXITY — usu. used in pl. ⟨sustain the reader through the analytical ~*s* —Hunter Mead⟩ ⟨guided them through the ~*s* of city life —Paul Blanshard⟩ **3 a :** the internal ear or its bony or membranous part — see BONY LABYRINTH, MEMBRANOUS LABYRINTH **b :** the portions of the cortex of the kidney consisting of tortuous uriniferous tubules **c :** a body structure (as the accessory respiratory organ of a labyrinth fish) made up of a maze of cavities and canals **4 :** an intricate sometimes symbolic pattern; *specif* **:** such a pattern inlaid in the pavement of a medieval church **5 a :** a device consisting of an arrangement (as a succession of grooves and collars, grooves and rings, tortuous passageways) usu. for the purpose of offering resistance to fluid flow (as to prevent leakage, promote condensation, separate component elements according to specific gravities) **b :** an enclosure consisting of an undulatory passage connected to the rear of a loudspeaker and providing improved low-frequency response — called also *acoustical labyrinth*

**lab·y·rin·thal** \¦==¦rin(t)thəl\ *adj* **:** LABYRINTHINE

**labyrinth fish** *n* [NL *Labyrinthici*] **:** a fish of the order Labyrinthici; *esp* **:** any of various fish of this order that are often kept in the tropical aquarium — see CROAKING GOURAMI

**lab·y·rin·thi·an** \-thēən\ *adj* **:** LABYRINTHINE

**lab·y·rin·thic** \-thik, -thēk\ *also* **lab·y·rin·thi·cal** \-thəkəl, -thēk-\ *adj* [*labyrinthic* fr. LL *labyrinthicus*, fr. L *labyrinthus* labyrinth + *-icus* -ic; *labyrinthical* fr. LL *labyrinthicus* + E *-al*] **:** LABYRINTHINE — **lab·y·rin·thi·cal·ly** \-thək(ə)lē\ *adv*

**lab·y·rin·thi·ci** \¦==¦rin(t)thə,sī\ *n pl, cap* [NL, fr. pl. of LL *labyrinthicus* of a labyrinth, labyrinthine] *in former classifications* **:** an order of freshwater and brackish water fishes chiefly of southeastern Asia that are now usu. included among the Percomorphi and that are adapted to meet unfavorable conditions by a labyrinthine outpocketing of the gill chamber permitting them to take oxygen from the air as well as from water — compare ANABAS, LABYRINTH FISH

**lab·y·rin·thine** \¦==¦rin(t)thən, -),thēn, -thīn\ *adj* [*labyrinth* + *-ine*] **1 :** of, like, or like that of a labyrinth **:** marked by extreme intricacy or ramification ⟨a ~ network of tortuous footways —R.T.Hopkins⟩ ⟨a ~ bureaucracy⟩ **:** INVOLVED ⟨sprawling ~ sentences —A.L.Scott⟩ **:** CIRCUITOUS ⟨got his way by ~ maneuvering⟩ **2 :** of, relating to, affecting, or originating in the internal ear ⟨~ deafness⟩ ⟨~ function⟩ **3** [NL *Labyrinthici* + E *-ine*] **:** belonging to or characteristic of the Labyrinthici

**labyrinthine sense** *n* **:** a complex sense concerned with the perception of bodily position and motion, mediated by end organs in the vestibular apparatus and the semicircular canals, and stimulated by alterations in the pull of gravity and by head movements — compare VESTIBULAR SENSE

**labyrinthine tooth** *n* **:** a tooth characteristic of the Labyrinthodontia having the dentin enfolded into complex patterns and ridges

**lab·y·rin·thi·tis** \,labərən'thīd·əs\ *n* -ES [NL, fr. E *labyrinth* + NL *-itis*] **:** inflammation of a labyrinth (as of the internal ear)

**¹lab·y·rin·tho·dont** \¦labə¦rin(t)thə,dänt\ *adj* [NL *Labyrinthodontia*] **1 :** of or relating to the Labyrinthodontia **2 :** having labyrinthine teeth

**²labyrinthodont** \"\ *n* -S **:** an amphibian of the group Labyrinthodontia

**lab·y·rin·tho·don·ta** \,==,==¦däntə\ [NL, fr. Gk *labyrinthos* labyrinth + NL *-odonta*] *syn of* LABYRINTHODONTIA

**lab·y·rin·tho·don·tia** \-änch(ē)ə\ *n pl, cap* [NL, fr. Gk *labyrinthos* labyrinth + NL *-odontia* — more at LABYRINTH] **1 :** a superorder of Amphibia comprising extinct amphibians of the Devonian, Upper Paleozoic, and Triassic that are extremely variable in form and size but typically resemble rather heavy-bodied salamanders or crocodiles, that have the centra of the vertebrae ossified from blocks or arches of cartilage, a completely roofed bony skull, and usu. labyrinthine teeth, that are known chiefly from fragmentary remains, and that are considered to be the earliest true tetrapods and in some respects to bridge the gap between the crossopterygians and the most primitive reptiles **2** *in some classifications* **:** a subdivision of Stegocephalia that comprises forms with labyrinthine teeth and is nearly equivalent to Temnospondyli — **lab·y·rin·tho·don·tid** \,==,==¦däntəd\ *adj or n* — **lab·y·rin·tho·don·toid** \-än,tȯid\ *adj*

**lab·y·rin·thu·la** \,==¦rin(t)thyələ\ *n, cap* [NL, dim. of L *labyrinthus* labyrinth] **:** a genus of rhizopods parasitic in aquatic plants, the individuals forming pseudoplasmodia by anastomosis of filar pseudopodia but encysting independently and sometimes passing through transient flagellate stages — see LABYRINTHULALES

**lab·y·rin·thu·la·les** \,==,==¦lā(,)lēz\ *n pl, cap* [NL, fr. *Labyrinthula* + *-ales*] **:** an obscure order of Myxomycetes comprising *Labyrinthula* and a few related parasites of aquatic plants when these are considered plants rather than protozoans

**¹lac** *also* **lack** \'lak\ *n* -S [Per *lak* & Hindi *lākh*, fr. Skt *lākṣā*] **1 :** a resinous substance secreted by the lac insect and used chiefly in the form of shellac — see SEED LAC, STICK LAC **2 :** any of various plant or animal substances that yield hard coatings resembling lac and shellac

**²lac** *var of* LAKH

**LAC** *abbr* leading aircraftsman

**la·can·don** \,läkän'dōn\ *n, pl* **lacandon** \"\ *or* **lacando·nes** \-ō,nās\ *usu cap* [MexSp, of AmerInd origin] **1 a :** an Indian people of Yucatan and Chiapas, Mexico **b :** a member of such people **2 :** a dialect of Yucatec

**lac·ca** \'lakə\ *n* -S [NL & It; NL, prob. fr. It, fr. ML, fr. Ar *lakk*, fr. Per *lak* — more at LAC] **:** LAC

**lac·case** \'la,kās\ *n* -S [ISV *lacc-* (prob. fr. NL *lacca*) + *-ase*; orig. formed in F] **:** a blue copper-containing oxidase occurring esp. in the sap of lacquer trees and having an ability to produce lacquer from the sap and induce oxidation of certain polyhydroxy phenols (as urushiol)

**lac·cate** \'la,kāt\ *adj* [NL *lacca* + E *-ate*] **:** having a varnished or lacquered appearance ⟨a bracket fungus with shining ~ surface⟩

**lac·ci·fer** \'laksəfə(r)\ *n, cap* [NL, fr. *lacca* + *-i-* + *-fer*] **:** a genus (the type of the family Lacciferidae) that comprises the commercially important lac insects

**lac·col** \'la,kȯl, -kōl\ *n* -S [ISV *lacc-* (fr. NL *lacca*) + *-ol*] **:** a crystalline phenol $C_{17}H_{31}C_6H_3(OH)_2$ occurring in the sap of lacquer trees

**lac·co·lith** \'lakə,lith\ *also* **lac·co·lite** \-līt\ *n* -S [Gk *lakkos* cistern, pit + E *-lith* or *-lite*] **:** a mass of igneous rock intruded between sedimentary beds and producing a domic bulging of the overlying strata — **lac·co·lith·ic** \¦==¦lithik\ *also* **lac·co·lit·ic** \-id·ik\ *adj*

**lac dye** *n* **:** a scarlet dye like cochineal used formerly in dyeing and pigment making and obtained from stick lac by extraction with alkali — see ⁴LAKE 1a(1)

**¹lace** \'lās\ *n* -S [ME *las*, *lace*, fr. OF *laz*, fr. L *laqueus* snare — more at DELIGHT] **1** *obs* **:** SNARE, NET **2 :** a cord or string used for drawing together two edges (as of a garment, a shoe, a machine belt) **3 :** an ornamental braid for trimming men's hats, coats, or uniforms ⟨gold ~⟩ ⟨silver ~⟩ **4 a :** a fine openwork fabric with a ground of mesh or net on which patterns may be worked at the same time as the ground or applied later and which is made of thread by looping, twisting, or knitting either by hand with a needle or bobbin or by machinery — see BOBBIN LACE, NEEDLEPOINT **b :** a similar fabric made by crocheting, tatting, darning, embroidering, weaving, or knitting — see HAIRPIN LACE, LIMERICK LACE **5** *obs* **:** a dash of spirits added (as to coffee)

**²lace** \"\ *vb* -ED/-ING/-S [ME *lacen*, fr. OF *lacier*, fr. L *laqueare* to ensnare, fr. *laqueus*] *vt* **1 :** to draw together the edges of by or as if by means of a lace passed through eyelet holes **:** TIE — often used with *up* ⟨*laced* up their shoes⟩ **2 :** to twine, draw, or pass as a lace **:** THREAD, INTERTWINE, EMBROIDER **3 :** to confine or compress by tightening laces esp. of a corset ⟨the old custom of *lacing* children in whalebone bodices⟩ ⟨*laced* her waist out of vanity⟩ **4 :** to adorn or trim with or as if with lace or decorative braid ⟨cloth *laced* with silver⟩ ⟨the landscape . . . was *laced* with countless creeks —D.C.Peattie⟩ **5 a :** BEAT, LASH, THRASH ⟨~ my quivering palm —Charlotte Brontë⟩ ⟨*laced* the bushes with flails —*Springfield (Mass.) Daily News*⟩ **b :** BEST, DEFEAT ⟨*laced* his opponent in a hard-fought game⟩ ⟨was *laced* in the primaries⟩ **6 a :** to add a dash of an alcoholic liquor to (a food or beverage) ⟨*laced* his coffee with rum —Hugh Cave⟩ ⟨lobster Newburg *laced* with sherry —*Publishers' Weekly*⟩ **b :** to add savor, zest, or spice to **:** LIVEN ⟨the book *laced* with irreverent and therefore readable notes on the involvements of English history —*Saturday Rev.*⟩ **7 :** to throw or drive (a ball) hard and usu. in a straight line ⟨*laced* his ball straight down the middle of the fairway⟩ ⟨*laced* his second homer of the game into the stands⟩ **8** *in bookbinding* **:** to draw the tapes or sewing cords through (the boards of the cover) — usu. used with *in* ~ *vi* **1 :** to compress or confine the waist (as with a corset) **2 :** to admit of lacing or tying ⟨covered with a tarpaulin that *laced* up the middle⟩ **3 :** to make a physical or verbal attack — usu. used with *into* ⟨I had a riding whip with me and . . . I rushed at the fellow and fairly *laced* into him —Robert Graves⟩ ⟨reviewers *laced* into the play —*Time*⟩

**lacebark** \'ˌ=,=\ *or* **lacebark tree** *n* [¹*lace* + *bark*] **1 :** a West Indian tree (*Lagetta lintearia*) **2 :** an Australian Kurrajong (*Sterculia acerifolia*) with interlaced bast fibers **3 :** RIBBON TREE **4 :** RIBBONWOOD 1

**lacebark pine** *n* **:** a Chinese tree (*Pinus bungeana*) that is often shrubby in cultivation and has flaky bark that becomes chalky-white, leaves in clusters of three, and cone scales with a recurved umbo resembling a spine

**lace bryozoan** *or* **lace coral** *n* **:** a member of the family Fenestellidae

**lace bug** *n* **:** any of the small bugs that constitute the large hemipterous family Tingidae, that have bodies and wings covered with a lacy network of raised lines, and that include many that suck plant juices and are serious pests

**lace–curtain** \'ˌ=,==\ *adj* **:** having social or economic standing **:** FASHIONABLE — often used to imply ostentation or pushing parvenu traits; compare SHANTY ⟨stickin' up his nose and actin' like he was highbrow, *lace-curtain* Irish —J.T.Farrell⟩ ⟨full of fine writing and *lace-curtain* English —Malcolm Cowley⟩

**laced** *adj* [fr. past part. of ²*lace*] **1 a :** tied or fastened with a lace **b :** trimmed or decorated with lace **2 a :** streaked with color — used esp. of a flower **b :** edged with a band of color differing from the body color — used esp. of a bird's feather

¹**lac·e·dae·mo·ni·an** *also* **lac·e·de·mo·ni·an** \ˌlasədə-ˈmōnēən, -dēˈ-, -nyən\ *adj, usu cap* [L *lacedaemonius* Lacedaemonian (fr. Gk *lakedaimonios,* fr. *Lakedaimōn* Lacedaemon, Sparta, ancient city of Greece) + E *-an*] **1 :** of or relating to Lacedaemon **:** SPARTAN **2 :** LACONIC

²**lacedaemonian** \"\ *n* -s *usu cap* **:** SPARTAN

**laced mutton** *n* [fr. *laced,* past part. of ²*lace*] *obs* **:** PROSTITUTE

**lace fern** *n* **:** any of several American ferns of the genus *Cheilanthes* with finely dissected bipinnate fronds

**lace flower** *n* **1 :** WILD CARROT **2 :** a Rocky mountain herb (*Tiarella unifoliata*) **3 :** BLUE LACE FLOWER

**lace fly** *n* **:** LACEWING

**lace glass** *n* **:** glass having patterns resembling lace

**lace grass** *n* **:** a slender grass (*Eragrostis capillaris*) of the eastern U.S. with a large panicle on branches that resemble hairs

**laceleaf** \'ˌ=,=\ *n* **:** LATTICE PLANT

**lace·less** \'lāsləs\ *adj* **:** lacking lace

**lacelike** \'ˌ=,=\ *adj* **:** resembling lace **:** LACY ⟨~ branches —Elizabeth A. Martin⟩

**lace lizard** *n* **:** either of two large monitors (*Varanus varius* and *V. giganteus*) of Australia

**lace paper** *n* **:** a strong clean paper suitable for perforation with an openwork design in imitation of lace

**lace pillow** *n* **:** PILLOW 3

**lace plant** *n* **1 :** LATTICE PLANT **2 :** ARTILLERY PLANT

**lacepod** \'ˌ=,=\ *n* **:** FRINGEPOD

**lac·er** \'lāsə(r)\ *n* -s **:** one that laces (as shoes or footballs during manufacture or book covers during binding)

**lac·er·a·bil·i·ty** \ˌlasərəˈbiləd·ē\ *n* **:** the quality or state of being vulnerable to laceration

**lac·er·a·ble** \'lasərəbəl\ *adj* [L *lacerabilis,* fr. L *lacerare* to lacerate + *-abilis* -able] **:** capable of being lacerated

¹**lac·er·ate** \'lasə,rāt, *usu* -ād·+V\ *adj* [L *laceratus,* past part.] **:** LACERATED

²**lacerate** \"\ *vt* -ED/-ING/-S [L *laceratus,* past part. of *lacerare* to tear, prob. fr. *lacer* mangled; akin to Gk *lakis* rent] **1 :** to tear or rend roughly **:** wound jaggedly ⟨my feet *lacerated* and swollen —Herbert Passin⟩ ⟨oil smears trail on the blue water from her *lacerated* flank as a torpedo strikes home —H.W. Baldwin⟩ ⟨*lacerated* by rocks —Claud Cockburn⟩ ⟨enlarge and ~ the heart —Sacheverell Sitwell⟩ **2 :** to cause sharp mental or emotional pain to **:** PIERCE, HARROW, TORMENT ⟨Puritan susceptibilities had been *lacerated* —Arnold Bennett⟩ ⟨delighted in *lacerating* frauds and crackpots —Richard Maney⟩ — **lac·er·a·tive** \-ˌrād·iv, -rəd·-\ *adj*

**lacerated** *adj* **1 a :** torn jaggedly **:** RENT **b :** HARROWED, TORTURED ⟨may well conceal ~ pity —Pier-Maria Pasinetti⟩ **2 :** having the margin or apex deeply and irregularly cut or incised

**lac·er·a·tion** \ˌlasəˈrāshən\ *n* -s [MF, fr. L *laceration-, laceratio,* fr. *laceratus* (past part.) + *-ion-, -io* -ion] **1 :** the act of lacerating **2 :** a breach or wound made by lacerating

**la·cer·ta** \ləˈsərd·ə\ *n, cap* [NL, fr. L, lizard — more at LEG] **:** a genus (the type of the family Lacertidae) of lizards formerly including nearly all known lizards but now restricted to certain typical Old World forms — see GREEN LIZARD, SAND LIZARD

**la·cer·tae** \-d·(ˌ)ē\ *n pl, cap* [NL, fr. pl. of L *lacerta* lizard] **:** a division of Lacertilia comprising the typical lizards as distinguished from the chameleons and geckos

**la·cer·tian** \ləˈsərsh(ē)ən\ *adj or n* [L *lacerta* lizard + E *-ian*] **:** LACERTILIAN

¹**la·cer·tid** \ləˈsərd·əd\ *adj* [NL *Lacertidae*] **:** of or relating to the genus *Lacerta* or family Lacertidae

²**lacertid** \"\ *n* -s **:** a lacertid lizard

**la·cer·ti·dae** \-d·ə,dē\ *n pl, cap* [NL, fr. *Lacerta,* type genus + *-idae*] **:** a large Old World family of terrestrial zoophagous lizards with well-developed limbs, pleurodont dentition, and deeply notched tongue

**la·cer·ti·form** \-ˌfȯrm\ *adj* [prob. fr. F *lacertiforme,* fr. L *lacerta* lizard + F *-iforme* -iform] **:** having the form or structure of a typical lizard

**lac·er·til·ia** \ˌlasə(r)ˈtilēə\ *n pl, cap* [NL *Lacerta* + *-ilia* (as in NL *Reptilia*)] **:** a division of Reptilia (usu. a suborder of Squamata) comprising the true lizards, chameleons, geckos, and various related limbless forms all related closely to the snakes in structure and of origin no earlier apparently than the Jurassic and typically distinguished by a tapering tail, well-developed pentadactyl limbs, a scaly or tuberculated skin, and movable eyelids — compare GILA MONSTER

¹**lac·er·til·i·an** \ˌ==ˈtilēən\ *adj* [NL *Lacertilia* + E *-an*] **:** of or relating to the Lacertilia or to a lizard

²**lacertilian** \"\ *n* -s **:** one of the Lacertilia **:** LIZARD

**la·cer·ti·loid** \ləˈsərd·ə,lȯid\ *adj* [NL *Lacertilia* + E *-oid*] **:** like or relating to the Lacertilia

**lac·er·tine** \'lasə(r),tīn, -ˌtən\ *adj* [L *lacerta* lizard + E *-ine*] **1 :** resembling a lizard **:** LACERTILIAN **2 :** adorned with interlacings suggestive of lizard forms

**la·cer·toid** \ləˈsər,tȯid\ *adj* [L *lacerta* lizard + E *-oid* — more at LEG] **:** resembling a lizard

**la·cer·tus fi·bro·sus** \ləˈsərd·əsfīˈbrōsəs\ *n* [NL, lit., fibrous forearm] **:** an aponeurotic expansion from the medial border of the biceps tendon to the fascia of the ulnar side of the forearm

**lac·ery** \'lās(ə)rē\ *n* -ES **:** a lacy appearance or pattern ⟨~ of impermanent girders —Frank Clune⟩ ⟨the ~ of intertwined trees —Nora Waln⟩

**laces** *pl of* LACE, *pres 3d sing of* LACE

**lace stitch** *n* **:** a loose open stitch used in the lighter parts of a design

**lacewing** \'ˌ=,=\ *also* **lacewing fly** *or* **lacewinged fly** \'ˌ=,=-\ *n* **:** any of various neuropterous insects of *Chrysopa, Hemerobius,* and related genera having delicate lacelike wing venation, long antennae, and brilliant eyes and producing larvae useful in destroying aphids and other small insects — see APHIS LION

**lacewood** \'ˌ=,=\ *n* **1 :** LACEBARK 2 **2 :** SYCAMORE 3b — used esp. of the quartersawed wood **3 :** SILK OAK

**lacework** \'ˌ=,=\ *n* **:** forms consisting of or resembling lace ⟨the sculptured sections of the church facades seem to be covered with delicate ~ —Sirarpie Der Nersessian⟩

**lacey** *var of* LACY

**lach·e·na·lia** \ˌlashəˈnālēə\ *n* [NL, fr. W. de *Lachenal* †1800 Swiss botanist + NL *-ia*] **1** *cap* **:** a genus of bulbous plants (family Liliaceae) of southern Africa with ligulate basal leaves and tubular red and yellow flowers **2** -s **:** any plant of the genus *Lachenalia* — see CAPE COWSLIP, LEOPARD LILY

**lach·es** \'lachəz, 'lāch-,'lash-\ *n, pl* **laches** \"\ [ME *lachesse,* fr. MF *laschesse,* fr. OF *lasche* lax, indolent, fr. *laschier* to loosen, fr. LL *laxicare* to become shaky, fr. L *laxare* to loosen — more at LAXATE] **1 :** slackness or carelessness toward duty or opportunity **:** NEGLIGENCE, REMISSNESS ⟨not to be saved by the most liberal allowance of trisyllabic feet, for libertine accentuation, and for other ~ of the kind —George Saintsbury⟩ **2 a** *in equity* **:** neglect to do a thing at the proper time **:** undue delay in asserting a right or claiming a privilege — compare STATUTE OF LIMITATIONS **b :** culpable negligence

**lach·e·sis** \'lakəsəs\ *n, cap* [NL, fr. Gk, Lachesis, one of the three Fates, disposer of lots, fr. *lachein,* 2d aoristic infinitive of *lanchanein* to obtain by lot] **:** a genus of American pit vipers comprising the bushmaster and related snakes that are sometimes included in the genus *Trimeresurus*

**lach·nan·thes** \lakˈnan(t)(ˌ)thēz\ *n, cap* [NL, fr. Gk *lachnos, lachnē* soft woolly hair + NL *-anthes;* akin to OSlav *vlasŭ* hair; fr. the woolly flowers] **:** a genus of No. American herbs (family Haemodoraceae) having leaves both clustered at the base and scattered on the stem and loosely woolly flowers in a compound cyme — see REDROOT

**lach·no·ster·na** \ˌlaknōˈstərnə\ [NL, fr. Gk *lachnos, lachnē* soft woolly hair + *sternon* breast, chest — more at STERNUM] *syn of* PHYLLOPHAGA

**lachrymable** *adj* [L *lacrimabilis,* fr. *lacrima,* tear + *-abilis* -able — more at TEAR (of the eye)] *obs* **:** LAMENTABLE, TEARFUL

**lach·ry·ma chris·ti** *or* **lac·ri·ma chris·ti** \ˌlakrəməˈkri(ˌ)stē, -ˌstī\ *n, pl* **lachry·mae christi** *or* **lacri·mae christi** \-(ˌ)mē-ˈkri(ˌ)stē, -ˌstī; -ˌmīˈkri(ˌ)stē\ *usu cap L&C* [ML, Christ's tear, fr. L *lacrima Christi*] **:** a still Italian wine produced from grapes grown near Vesuvius that is white, red, or rosé and sweet or dry

**lach·ry·mal** *or* **lac·ri·mal** \'lakrəməl\ *adj* [MF or ML; MF *lacrymal,* fr. ML *lacrimalis,* fr. L *lacrima* tear + *-alis* -al] **1** *usu lacrimal* **:** of, relating to, or situated near the organs that produce tears **2 :** marked by tears **:** LACHRYMOSE ⟨a ~ farewell⟩ **3 :** of or relating to tears ⟨~ effusions⟩

**lachrymation** *var of* LACRIMATION

**lachrymator** *var of* LACRIMATOR

**lachrymatory** *var of* LACRIMATORY

**lach·ry·mist** \'lakrəməst\ *n* -s [L *lacrima, lacruma* tear + E *-ist*] *archaic* **:** one given to weeping

**lach·ry·mose** \'lakrə,mōs\ *adj* [L *lacrimosus,* fr. *lacrima* tear + *-osus* -ose — more at TEAR (of the eye)] **1 :** given to tears or weeping **:** suffused with tears **:** TEARFUL **2 :** fit to bring tears or induce mournfulness **:** DISMAL, MELANCHOLY ⟨their songs were sentimental and ~, full of dying heroes and parted lovers —Bernard DeVoto⟩ — **lach·ry·mose·ly** *adv* — **lach·ry·mos·i·ty** \ˌ==ˈmäsəd·ē\ *n* -ES

**lachs·schin·ken** \'läks(h)ˌshiŋkən\ *n, pl* **lachsschinken** *or* **lachsschinkens** [G, lit., salmon ham, fr. *lachs* salmon + *schinken* ham; prob. fr. its color and appearance] **:** a boned double loin of pork that is rolled, mild-cured, slightly smoked, and pressed into a casing

**l acid** *n, usu cap L* **:** a crystalline acid $HOC_{10}H_6SO_3H$ used as an intermediate for azo dyes; 1-naphthol-5-sulfonic acid

**lacier** *comparative of* LACY

**laciest** *superlative of* LACY

**lac·i·ly** \'lāsəlē\ *adj* **:** in a lacy fashion or manner

**lac·i·ness** \-sēnəs\ *n* -ES **:** the quality or state of being lacy

**lac·ing** \'lāsiŋ, -sēŋ\ *n* -s [ME *lacinge,* gerund of *lacen* to lace — more at LACE] **1 :** the action of one that laces (as by tying, tightening, beating) **2 a :** a fastening lace for clothing ⟨shoe ~⟩ ⟨corset ~⟩ **b :** ornamental braid or trimming for uniforms or clothing **c :** a thong of thin leather or a series of metal clips used to join the ends of a machine-driving belt **3 :** a marginal band of color contrasting with the chief color (as on the ear of a rabbit or on a feather) **4 a :** a dash of alcoholic liquor in a food or beverage ⟨coffee with a ~ of whiskey⟩ **b :** a trace or sprinkling that enlivens or adds spice or savor ⟨sprinkles the whole sound track with a ~ of simpering snorts —Goodman Ace⟩ ⟨the committee was made up of old Bostonians with a ~ of others —Francis Russell⟩ **5 a** *or* **lacing line :** a rope or line laced through eyelets along the edge of a sail or awning to attach it to a boom, gaff, or yard **b :** a knee timber fitted behind a ship's figurehead **6 :** BATTERING, TROUNCING ⟨gave the marble thief a quick but thorough ~ —*Argosy*⟩ ⟨what kind of a ~ will the taxpayers take —B.M.Bowie⟩

**lacing course** *n* **:** a course usu. of brick built into a wall constructed of stone or other irregularly shaped material to bond and level it

**la·cin·ia** \ləˈsinēə\ *n, pl* **lacini·ae** \-ē,ē\ *or* **lacinias** [NL, fr. L, lappet, flap; akin to L *lacer* mangled — more at LACERATE] **1 :** a narrow incised segment in a leaf or other similar structure **2 a :** the inner process of the stipes of an insect's maxilla and esp. of its first maxilla **b :** a slender fleshy process on the head of a fish

**la·cin·i·ate** \ləˈsinē,āt\ *or* **la·cin·i·at·ed** \-ˌād·əd\ *adj* [L *lacinia* lappet, flap + E *-ate* or *-ated* (fr. *-ate* + *-ed*)] **:** bordered with a fringe **:** cut into deep irregular usu. pointed lobes **:** narrowly incised with divisions coarser than fimbriate — used of a plant or animal part

**la·cin·i·a·tion** \ˌ=ˌ==ˈāshən\ *n* -s [NL *lacinia* + E *-ation*] **1 :** LACINIA **2 :** the quality or state of being laciniate

**la·cin·i·ose** \ləˈsinē,ōs\ *adj* [L *laciniosus,* fr. *lacinia* lappet, flap + *-osus* -ose] **:** LACINIATE, FRINGED

**lac insect** *n* **:** a scale (*Laccifer lacca*) of southeast Asia that produces lac; *broadly* **:** any of various related scales

**la·cin·u·la** \ləˈsinyələ\ *n, pl* **lacinu·lae** \-yə,lē\ *or* **lacinulas** [NL, dim. of L *lacinia* lappet, flap] **:** a small lacinia — **la·cin·u·late** \-yə,lāt\ *adj* — **la·cin·u·lose** \-ˌlōs\ *adj*

**la·cis** \'lāsəs\ *n* -ES [F, fr. MF, fr. OF, fr. *lacier* to lace — more at LACE] **:** NETWORK, NET; *specif* **:** a square-meshed lace with darned patterns

¹**lack** \'lak, *chiefly southern US dial* 'lik\ *vb* -ED/-ING/-S [ME *laken,* fr. MD, to be lacking, to blame; akin to MD *lac* lack, fault] *vi* **1 :** to be wanting or missing **:** FAIL ⟨nothing is ~*ing* but the will⟩ ⟨space ~*s* for a linguistic analysis —Eric Partridge⟩ ⟨the sense of distance ~*s;* a ridge nearby can be a far-off mountain range —Paul Bowles⟩ **2 :** to want supply or satisfaction **:** be short ⟨enjoined the tapster to see to it that no one ~*ed* for his thirst —Arnold Bennett⟩ ⟨such language is comparatively ~*ing* in responsibility —R.M.Weaver⟩ ~ *vt* **1 :** to be void or destitute of **:** be without or deficient in ⟨what . . . the church ~*s* is democracy —Leo Pfeffer⟩ ⟨~*ed* the ability to become a great singer —W.J.Reilly⟩ ⟨this statement, like all simple statements, ~*s* detail —Charlton Laird⟩ ⟨her voice may be flexible enough, but ~*s* the requisite strength —Lafcadio Hearn⟩ **2** *obs* **:** to feel the absence of **:** MISS ⟨you're loved, sir. They that least lend it you shall ~ you first —Shak.⟩ **3 :** to stand in need of **:** REQUIRE, WANT — used formerly in the vendor's cry *what do you lack?*

**syn** LACK, WANT, NEED, and REQUIRE can imply the absence of something, esp. essential or to be desired. LACK implies such an absence, esp. due to shortage of supply ⟨blankets were made of sage bark cords when rabbit skins were *lacking* —C.D.Forde⟩ ⟨a delicacy of design that larger houses often *lack* —*Amer. Guide Series: N.H.*⟩ ⟨many languages *lack* grammatical person entirely —Weston La Barre⟩ WANT in this application stresses a deplorable lack or adds to LACK the idea of pressing desire or urgent necessity ⟨an age *wanting* in moral grandeur —Matthew Arnold⟩ ⟨an American truck that *wanted* only a few repairs —Richard Llewellyn⟩ ⟨poverty-stricken and *wanting* even the necessities of existence⟩ NEED is used more commonly than WANT in this context to stress necessity ⟨what the business and industrial world most *need* and seek —R.W.McEwen⟩ ⟨assist an increasing number of American families in finding the things they *need* and want —*Annual Report J. C. Penney Corp.*⟩ ⟨both of these bridges are badly *needed* —*Americana Annual*⟩ ⟨it only *needed* that the letter should be correctly addressed —H.E.Scudder⟩ ⟨*need* food and clothing⟩ REQUIRE, similar to if not stronger than NEED in implying necessity, can also suggest the importunity of urgent desire or craving ⟨he found his studies too easy to *require* serious attention —E.S.Bates⟩ ⟨so ill as to *require* constant attendance⟩ ⟨the continuing deficit *requires* either higher rates or a sales tax —*New Republic*⟩ ⟨the reactor *requires* radically new metals to withstand great heats —Tris Coffin⟩

²**lack** \"\ *n* -s [ME *lac,* fr. MD, lack, fault; akin to MLG *lak* lack, error, ON *lakr* lacking, defective, OFris *lec* damage, ON *leka* to leak — more at LEAK] **1 :** the fact or state of being wanting or deficient **:** inadequate or missing supply or provision **:** DEFICIENCY, FAILURE, WANT ⟨explain the comparative ~ of simian fossils —R.W.Murray⟩ ⟨~ of true insight into human passion —A.T.Quiller-Couch⟩ **2 :** that which is lacking **:** the thing needed ⟨green forage is a ~ of desert regions⟩ **syn** see ABSENCE

³**lack** *var of* LAC

**lack·a·dai·si·cal** \ˌlakəˈdāzəkəl, |ēk- *sometimes* -ās|\ *adj* [by folk etymology fr. *lackaday* + *-ical*] **:** lacking life, spirit, or zest **:** devoid of energy or purpose **:** IDLE, VACUOUS ⟨communism is in deadly earnest, whereas the so-called "free world" is ~ —J.F.Dulles⟩ ⟨a mere ~, spiritless young man-about-town —P.G.Wodehouse⟩ **syn** see LANGUID

**lack·a·dai·si·cal·ly** \-k(ə)lē, -li\ *adv* **:** in a lackadaisical manner

¹**lack·a·dai·sy** \'lakə,dāzē\ *n* -ES [by folk etymology fr. *lackaday*] **:** INDIFFERENCE, LASSITUDE

²**lackadaisy** \"\ *interj, archaic* — used to express sorrow or regret

**lack·a·day** \'lakə,dā\ *interj* [by alter. and shortening fr. *alack the day*] *archaic* — used to express sorrow or regret

**lacker** *var of* LACQUER

¹**lack·ey** *or* **lac·quey** \'lakē, -ki\ *n* -s [MF *laquais,* perh. fr. Catal *lacayo, alacayo*] **1 :** a liveried retainer **:** FLUNKY, FOOTMAN ⟨there was jumping of ~*s,* a slamming of car doors, a glare of headlights —Winifred Bambrick⟩ **2 :** a servile follower **:** HANGER-ON, TOADY ⟨join him in refusing to be ~*s* of an appointive official —M.W.Straight⟩ ⟨continued to caricature him as a ~ of capitalism —*Time*⟩

²**lackey** *or* **lacquey** \"\ *vb* -ED/-ING/-S *vi, obs* **:** to play the lackey **:** dance attendance **:** TOADY ~ *vt* **:** to wait upon **:** serve obsequiously **:** ATTEND ⟨a thousand liveried angels ~ her —John Milton⟩ ⟨stop ~*ing* and valeting the spirit of the age —W.L.Sullivan⟩

**lackey moth** *also* **lackey** *n* -s [so called fr. the resemblance of the caterpillar's coat to a footman's livery] **:** a European moth (*Malacosoma neustria*) with a larva that is a tent caterpillar sometimes injurious to orchard trees and other woody plants

**lacking** *prep* [fr. *lacking,* pres. part. of ¹*lack*] **:** WANTING

¹**lackland** \'ˌ=,=\ *n* [¹*lack* + *land*] **:** a person owning no land

²**lackland** \"\ *adj* **:** owning no land **:** LANDLESS, PROPERTYLESS ⟨~ adventurers are honored above men of honest birth —T.B. Costain⟩

¹**lackluster** \'ˌ=,==\ *adj* [¹*lack* + *luster* (n.)] **:** lacking in sheen, radiance, or vitality **:** DULL, UNINSPIRED ⟨looked into space with ~ eyes —Bram Stoker⟩ ⟨the town has ~ dirt streets and plenty of stray dogs —W.A. Krauss⟩ ⟨eager new recruits too often are beaten down to the hangdog, ~ average —Bennett Cerf⟩

²**lackluster** \"\ *n* **:** absence or want of luster ⟨attempts to justify the ~ of psychoanalytic biography —R.M.Wendlinger⟩

**lackmoid** *var of* LACMOID

**lacks** *pres 3d sing of* LACK, *pl of* LACK

¹**lackwit** \'ˌ=,=\ *n* [¹*lack* + *wit*] **:** a dull or witless person **:** BLOCKHEAD, FOOL ⟨appealed strongly to the throng of ~*s* —H.L.Wilson⟩ ⟨the ~*s* who repeat these snappy sayings scarcely comprehend the distinction —*Springfield (Mass.) Union*⟩

²**lackwit** \"\ *adj* **:** lacking intelligence ⟨saddled with a ~ assistant —*Time*⟩

**lac lake** *n* [¹*lac*] **:** INDIAN LAKE

**lac·moid** *also* **lack·moid** \'lak,mȯid\ *n* -s [*lacmoid,* ISV *lacm-* (fr. *lacmus*) + *-oid;* prob. orig. formed as G *lakmoid; lackmoid,* alter. of *lacmoid*] **:** a violet-blue dye resembling litmus that is made by the action of nitrites on resorcinol and is used as an indicator in titration

**lac·mus** *or* **lak·mus** \'lakməs\ *n* -ES [D *lakmoes,* fr. MD *leecmōs,* fr. *lēken* to drip (akin to OE *leccan* to moisten) + *mōs* green vegetables, mushy foods; akin to OE, OS, OFris *mōs* food, OHG *muos,* OE *mete* food — more at LEAK, MEAT] **:** LITMUS

¹**la·co·ni·an** \ləˈkōnēən\ *adj, usu cap* [L *Laconia,* region of ancient Greece (fr. Gk *Lakōn,* n. & adj., Laconian) + E *-an*] **1 :** of, relating to, or characteristic of Laconia, a region of ancient Greece **2 :** of, relating to, or characteristic of the people of Laconia

²**laconian** \"\ *n* -s *cap* **:** a native or inhabitant of Laconia

**la·con·ic** \ləˈkänik, -nēk\ *adj* [L *Laconicus,* fr. Gk *Lakōnikos,* fr. *Lakōn* Laconian + *-ikos* -ic] **1** *archaic, usu cap* **:** of or relating to Laconia or the Laconians **:** SPARTAN **2 a :** speaking or writing with Spartan brevity **:** CURT, TERSE, UNDEMONSTRATIVE ⟨~, these Indians —Weston La Barre⟩ ⟨an antiseptic romance between Jones and a ~ young widow —Martin Levin⟩ **b :** spoken, written, or expressed briefly or sententiously **:** PITHY ⟨the tone of the commentary ~ and masculine —*Times Lit. Supp.*⟩ ⟨a ~ derby-hatted interlude that stops the show —Henry Hewes⟩ **syn** see CONCISE

²**laconic** \"\ *n* -s **1** *obs* **:** a laconic person **2 a :** curt or concise expression **b laconics** *pl* **:** concise sentences

**laconical** *adj* [L *Laconicus* + E *-al*] *archaic* **:** LACONIC

**la·con·i·cal·ly** \-nək(ə)lē, -nēk-, -li\ *adv* **:** in a laconic manner

**la·con·i·cism** \ləˈkänə,sizəm\ *n* -s [¹*laconic* + *-ism*] **:** LACONISM ⟨one of the most heroic ~*s* of all literature —D.C. Smith⟩

**la·con·i·cum** \ləˈkänəkəm\ *n, pl* **laconi·ca** \-ə̇kə\ [L, fr. neut. of *Laconicus* Laconic] **:** the sweating room of an ancient Roman bath

**lac·o·nism** \'lakə,nizəm\ *n* -s [MF & Gk; MF *laconisme,* fr. Gk *lakōnismos* imitation of Lacedaemonian manners, esp. in terseness of expression, fr. *lakōnizein* to speak laconically, laconize] **1 :** brevity or terseness of expression ⟨the provocative ~ of the newspaper headline, which conceals meaning almost as often as it expresses it —B.R.Redman⟩ **2 :** a laconic expression

**lac·o·nize** \'lakə,nīz\ *vb* -ED/-ING/-S [Gk *lakōnizein,* fr. *Lakōn* Laconian + *-izein* -ize] *vi* **:** to incline to the Spartan course or manner ~ *vt* **:** to subject to Spartan rule

**la co·ru·na** \ˌläkəˈrün(y)ə\ *or* **la co·ru·ña** \-ünyə\ *adj, usu. cap L&C* [fr. *La Coruña,* Spain] **:** of or from the city of La Coruna, Spain **:** of the kind or style prevalent in La Coruna

**lac·o·so·mat·i·dae** \ˌlakōsəˈmad·ə,dē\ [NL, fr. *Lacosomat-, Lacosoma,* genus of moths (fr. Gk *lakkos* pit, tank, pond + *sōmat-, sōma* body) + *-idae*] *syn of* MIMALLONIDAE

¹**lac·quer** *also* **lack·er** \'lakə(r)\ *n* -s [*lacquer,* alter. (prob. influenced by F *laque* lac) of earlier *lacker,* fr. obs. *leckar, laker, lacre* lac, fr. OPg *lacra, lacre, lácar,* variants of *laca,* fr. Ar *lakk* — more at LACCA] **1 a :** a spirit varnish (as shellac) often colored and used esp. for coating brass and other metals to heighten their luster or prevent tarnishing **b :** any of various tough durable natural varnishes; *esp* **:** a varnish obtained by tapping the Japanese varnish tree — called also *Chinese lacquer, Japanese lacquer;* compare BURMESE LACQUER **c :** any of various clear or colored synthetic liquid organic coatings that typically dry to form a film by evaporation of a volatile constituent and are used for many industrial purposes; *esp* **:** a coating in which a cellulose derivative (as cellulose nitrate) serves to form such a film with or without a natural or synthetic resin (as an alkyd) ⟨automotive ~*s* are sprayed on⟩ — compare ENAMEL 3, VARNISH 1a **d :** a highly glazed finish for fabrics usu. applied in patterns on a plain ground **e :** a resinous coating applied to flat sheet metal or formed metal cans and usu. dried by baking **2** *or* **lacquer ware :** a decorative article made of wood coated with Japanese or other Oriental lacquer and often inlaid with ivory or metal; *collectively* **:** such articles or ware **3** *or* **lacquer red :** a variable color averaging a dark reddish orange that is redder, stronger, and slightly lighter than ocher red and redder, stronger, and slightly lighter than burnt sienna **4 a :** a dressing (as an alcoholic solution of a gum or resin) for the hair usu. applied by spraying and intended to keep the hair smooth and in place **b :** NAIL POLISH

²**lacquer** *also* **lacker** \"\ *vt* -ED/-ING/-S **1 :** to coat with lacquer **:** VARNISH **2 :** to give a smooth finish or appearance to **:** to make glossy **:** POLISH ⟨wound up with a virtuosity that ~*ed* over any rough patches that had been laid bare in the White Paper —B.A.Young⟩ ⟨does not . . . ~ the phrase as did some of the accusers —Jerome Mellquist⟩

**lacquer disc** *n* **:** a phonograph record made usu. from a nitrocellulose lacquer

**lacquered** *adj* **:** coated with or as if with lacquer **:** GLOSSY, POLISHED, VARNISHED

**lac·quer·er** \-kərə(r)\ *n* -s **:** one that lacquers

**lacquer film** *n* **:** a lamination of lacquer, rubber cement, and waxed paper used for stencils in a silk-screen process

**lacquering** *n* -s **1 :** the application of lacquer **2 :** a lacquer finish

**lacquer man** *n* **:** one who mixes and tints lacquer paints

**lacquer tree** *or* **lacquer plant** *n* **:** a tree yielding lacquer or

Japan wax; *specif* : JAPANESE VARNISH TREE — compare VARNISH TREE

**lacquerwork** \'⸗⸗,⸗\ *n* : LACQUER 2

**lacquey** *var of* LACKEY

**lacrima christi** *usu cap L&C, var of* LACHRYMA CHRISTI

**lac·ri·mal** *var of* LACHRYMAL

**lacrimal bone** *n* : a small thin bone making up part of the front inner wall of each orbit and giving passage to the lacrimal duct

**lacrimal canal** *n* **1** : LACRIMAL DUCT 1 **2** : the bony passage lodging the nasolacrimal duct

**lacrimal caruncle** *n* : a small reddish follicular elevation at the medial angle of the eye

**lacrimal duct** *n* **1** : a short canal leading from a minute orifice on a small elevation at the medial angle of each eyelid **2** : any of several small ducts leading from the lacrimal gland to the lateral angle of the eye

**lac·ri·ma·le** \,lakrə'mā(,)lē, -mä(-, -mä(-\ *n* -s [NL, fr. neut. sing. of ML *lacrimalis* lachrymal — more at LACHRYMAL] : the point where the posterior edge of the lacrimal bone intersects the fronto-lacrimal suture

**lacrimal gland** *n* : an acinous gland that is about the size and shape of an almond and secretes tears

**lacrimal sac** *n* : a dilatation resembling a pouch that is located within the medial canthus of the eye, receives tears from the two lacrimal ducts (sense 1), and transmits them to the nasolacrimal duct

**lacrimal sinus** *n* : TEARPIT

**la·cri·man·do** \,läkrə'män(,)dō, ¦lak-\ *adj (or adv)* [It, lit., weeping, lamenting, fr. L *lacrimandus,* gerundive of *lacrimare* to weep, shed tears] : DOLOROSO, LAMENTING, PLAINTIVE — used as a direction in music

**lac·ri·ma·tion** *also* **lach·ry·ma·tion** \,lakrə'māshən\ *n* -s [L *lacrimation-, lacrimatio,* fr. *lacrimatus* (past part. of *lacrimare* to weep) + *-ion-, -io* -ion] : the secretion of tears : WEEPING; *specif* : abnormal or excessive secretion of tears due to local or systemic disease

**lac·ri·ma·tor** *or* **lach·ry·ma·tor** \'⸗⸗,mād·ə(r)\ *n* -s [*lacrimation* or *lachrymation* + *-or*] : a tear-producing substance (as chloroacetophenone) : TEAR GAS

[1]**lac·ri·ma·to·ry** *or* **lach·ry·ma·to·ry** \'lakrəmə,tōrē, -tȯr-, -ri\ *n* -ES [prob. fr. NL *lachrymatorium,* fr. neut. of *lachrymatorius,* adj., lacrimatory] : a vase found in ancient Roman tombs and formerly regarded as meant for the tears of mourners but now believed to have been a perfume bottle — called also *tear bottle*

[2]**lacrimatory** *or* **lachrymatory** \"\ *adj* [ML & LL; ML *lachrymatorius,* fr. LL *lacrimatorius,* fr. L *lacrimatus* (past part. of *lacrimare* to shed tears, weep, fr. *lacrima* tear) + *-orius* -ory — more at TEAR (of the eye)] **1** : of, relating to, or prompting tears **2** : meant to contain tears

**lac·ri·mi·form** \'lakrəmə,fȯrm\ *adj* [L *lacrima* tear + E *-iform*] : shaped like a teardrop

**lac·ri·moid** \'lakrə,mȯid\ *adj* [L *lacrima* tear + E *-oid*] : resembling a teardrop

**la·cri·mo·so** \¦läkrə¦mō(,)sō, ¦lak-\ *adj (or adv)* [It, lit., tearful, lachrymose, fr. L *lacrimosus* — more at LACHRYMOSE] : marked by a plaintive style — used as a direction in music

**la·croix·ite** \lə'krwä,zīt\ *n* -s [F, fr. F. A. Alfred *Lacroix* †1948 Fr. mineralogist + F *-ite*] : a mineral approximately $Na(Ca,Mn)AlPO_4(OH)_3$ that consists of a basic phosphate of aluminum, calcium, manganese, and sodium often containing fluorine and that occurs in pale yellowish green crystals (hardness 4.1)

**la·crosse** \lə'krȯs *also* -räs\ *n* -s *often attrib* [CanF *la crosse,* lit., the crosier, the hooked stick] : a game originating among the No. American Indians that is played on a turfed field by 2 teams of 10 players each of whom uses a long-handled racket with which the ball is caught, carried, and thrown with the object being to throw the ball into the opponents' goal — compare CROSSE

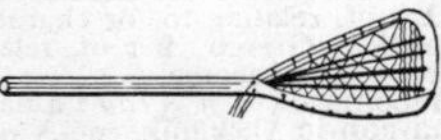
racket used in lacrosse

**lacrosse stick** *n* : CROSSE

**lacs** *pl of* LAC

**lact-** *or* **lacti-** *or* **lacto-** *comb form* [*lact-* fr. F&L; F, fr. L, fr. *lact-, lac; lacti-* fr. F & LL; F, fr. LL, fr. L *lact-, lac; lacto-* fr. *lact-* + *-o-* — more at GALAXY] **1** : milk ⟨*lact*albumin⟩ ⟨*lacto*meter⟩ ⟨*lact*igenic⟩ **2 a** : lactate and ⟨*lacto*phosphate⟩ **b** : lactic acid ⟨*lact*amide⟩ ⟨*lacto*nitrite⟩ **c** : lactose ⟨*lact*itol⟩ ⟨*lacto*bionic acid⟩

**lac·ta·gogue** \'laktə,gäg *sometimes* -gȯg\ *n* -s [*lact-* + *-agogue*] : GALACTAGOGUE

**lact·al·bu·min** \,lak,tal'byümən, -ü,min *sometimes* lak'talbyə-\ *n* -s [ISV *lact-* + *albumin*] : an albumin that is similar to serum albumin and is obtained from the whey of milk; *esp* : a protein fraction from whey including beta⸗lactoglobulin used in foods and in preparing protein hydrolysates

**lac·tam** \'lak,tam, ⸗'⸗\ *n* -s [ISV *lact*one + *am*ide; orig. formed in G] : any of a class of inner amides of amino carboxylic acids formed by the loss of a molecule of water from the amino and carboxyl groups and characterized by the carbonyl⸗imido grouping —CONH— in a ring — compare LACTIM, LACTONE, SULTAM

**lac·ta·ri·us** \lak'ta(a)rēəs, -ter-, -tär-\ *n, cap* [NL, fr. L, milky] : a large genus of white-spored agarics (family Agaricaceae) that exude a white or colored milky juice when cut or broken and that include an edible species (*L. deliciosus*) and some poisonous ones

**lac·ta·ry** \'laktərē\ *adj* [L *lactarius,* fr. *lact-* + *-arius* -ary] *archaic* : of or relating to milk : yielding a white milky juice

**lac·tase** \'lak,tās, -āz\ *n* -s [ISV *lact-* + *-ase*] : an enzyme that hydrolyzes lactose and other beta-galactosides and occurs esp. in the intestines of young mammals and in yeasts

[1]**lac·tate** \-āt, *usu* -ād·+V\ *n* -s [*lact-* + *-ate*] : a salt or ester of lactic acid

[2]**lactate** \"\ *vi* -ED/-ING/-S [L *lactatus,* past part. of *lactare* to suckle, secrete milk, fr. *lact-, lac* milk] : to secrete milk

**lac·ta·tion** \lak'tāshən\ *n* -s [prob. fr. F, fr. LL *lactation-, lactatio* suckling, fr. L *lactatus* (past part.) + *-ion-, -io* -ion] **1** : the secretion and yielding of milk by the mammary gland **2** : one complete period of lactation extending from about the time of parturition to weaning — **lac·ta·tion·al** \(')lak¦tāshənᵊl, -shnəl\ *adj* — **lac·ta·tion·al·ly** \-ᵊlē, -əlē, ¦i\ *adv*

**lactation tetany** *n* : MILK FEVER 1

[1]**lac·te·al** \'laktēəl\ *adj* [L *lacteus* of milk (fr. *lact-, lac* milk) + E *-al* — more at GALAXY] **1** : relating to, consisting of, producing, or resembling milk ⟨~ fluid⟩ ⟨~ organs⟩ **2 a** : conveying or containing a milky fluid (as chyle) ⟨a ~ channel⟩ **b** : of or relating to the lacteals ⟨impaired ~ function⟩

[2]**lacteal** \"\ *n* -s : one of the lymphatic vessels arising from the lymphatic radicles of the villi of the small intestine and conveying chyle from the intestine through the mesenteric glands to the thoracic duct

**lacteal gland** *n* : a lymph gland situated upon a lacteal vessel

**lac·te·nin** \'laktənən\ *n* -s [perh. fr. *lact-* + nitro*gen* + *-in*] : a nitrogenous substance present in milk that inhibits bacterial growth

**lac·te·ous** \'laktēəs\ *adj* [L *lacteus* of milk, milky, fr. *lact-, lac* milk] **1** *archaic* : MILKY, WHITE **2** : LACTEAL

**lactescence** *n* -s [L *lactescere* to turn to milk + E *-ence*] **1** : MILKINESS **2** : a copious flow of milky sap

**lac·tes·cent** \(')lak¦tesᵊnt\ *adj* [L *lactescent-, lactescens,* pres. part. of *lactescere* to turn to milk, inchō. of *lactēre* to be milky, fr. *lact-, lac* milk] **1** : becoming or appearing milky **2 a** : secreting milk **b** : yielding a milky juice — used of a plant

**lacti-** — see LACT-

**lac·tic** \'laktik, -tēk\ *adj* [F *lactique,* fr. *lact-* + *-ique* -ic] **1** : of or relating to milk : obtained from sour milk or whey **2** : involving the production of lactic acid ⟨~ fermentation⟩

**lactic acid** *n* [part trans. of F *acide lactique*] : a hygroscopic usu. syrupy alpha-hydroxy acid $CH_3CH(OH)COOH$ that readily undergoes self-esterification when heated and is known in three optically isomeric forms: (1) the dextrorotatory L⸗form present normally in blood and muscle tissue as a product of the metabolism of glucose and glycogen; (2) the levorotatory D-form obtained by biological fermentation of sucrose; and (3) the racemic DL-form present in sour milk, beer, sauerkraut, pickles, and other food products and made usu. by bacterial fermentation (as of whey, molasses, raw sugar, or starch hydrolysates) but also synthetically, and used chiefly in foods and beverages, in medicine, in tanning and dyeing, and in making esters for use as solvents and plasticizers — called also respectively (1) *dextro-lactic acid or sarcolactic acid,* (2) *levo-lactic acid,* (3) *dl-lactic acid or ordinary lactic acid;* compare HYDRACRYLIC ACID

**lactic acid bacterium** *or* **lactic bacterium** *n* : any of various bacteria chiefly of the genera *Lactobacillus* and *Streptococcus* that produce predominantly lactic fermentation on suitable media and some of which are used in the commercial production of lactic acid and as cheese and butter starters

**lactic casein** *n* : acid casein precipitated from milk by lactic acid

**lactic fermentation** *n* : fermentation in which lactic acid is produced from carbohydrate materials (as lactose in whey) by the action of any of various organisms but esp. the lactic acid bacteria

**lac·tide** \'lak,tīd, -təd\ *n* -s [ISV *lact-* + anhy*dride;* prob. orig. formed in F] **1** : a crystalline dilactone $C_6H_8O_4$ formed from two molecules of lactic acid by self-esterification **2** : a dilactone formed from an alpha-hydroxy acid other than lactic acid

**lac·tif·er·ous** \(')lak¦tif(ə)rəs\ *adj* [F or LL; F *lactifère* lactiferous, fr. LL *lactifer* (fr. *lacti-* — fr. L *lact-, lac* milk — + L *-fer* — adj. comb. form) + E *-ous* — more at GALAXY, -FER] **1** : secreting or conveying milk **2 a** : yielding a milky juice **b** : LATICIFEROUS — **lac·tif·er·ous·ness** *n* -ES

**lac·tif·ic** \-fik\ *also* **lac·tif·i·cal** \-fəkəl\ *adj* [*lactific* fr. F *lactifique,* fr. *lacti-* lact- + *-fique* -fic; *lactifical* fr. F *lactifique* + E *-al*] : producing milk

**lac·ti·fy** \'laktə,fī\ *vt* -ED/-ING/-ES [*lact-* + *-fy*] : to transform by lactic fermentation.

**lac·tim** \'lak,tim, ⸗'⸗\ *n* -s [ISV *lact*one + *im*ide; orig. formed in G] : any of a class of hydroxy imides tautomeric with lactams and characterized by the enolic grouping —C(OH)=N—

**lac·ti·tol** \'laktə,tȯl, -tōl\ *n* -s [*lact-* + *-itol*] : a crystalline alcohol $C_{12}H_{24}O_{11}$ obtained by hydrogenation of lactose

**lac·tiv·o·rous** \(')lak¦tiv(ə)rəs\ *adj* [*lact-* + *-vorous*] : feeding on milk

**lacto-** — see LACT-

**lac·to·bac·il·la·ce·ae** \,laktō,basə'lāsē,ē\ *n pl, cap* [NL, fr. *Lactobacillus,* type genus + *-aceae*] : a large family of rod⸗shaped or spherical gram-negative usu. microaerophilic and nonmotile bacteria that require carbohydrates for growth, fermenting them chiefly to lactic acid, and include the lactic acid bacteria as well as important pathogens — see DIPLOCOCCUS, LACTOBACILLUS, STREPTOCOCCUS

**lac·to·bacillus** \¦lak(,)tō+\ *n* [NL, fr. *lact-* + *Bacillus,* genus of bacteria] **1** *cap* : a genus of gram-positive nonmotile lactic-acid-forming bacteria (family Lactobacillaceae) including various commercially important lactic acid bacteria **2** *pl* **lactobacilli** : any bacterium of the genus *Lactobacillus*

**lactobacillus ca·sei factor** \-'kāsē,ī-\ *n, cap L* [NL *Lactobacillus casei* (lit., *Lactobacillus* of cheese), species of *Lactobacillus* that produces it] : folic acid or a higher conjugated pteroylglutamic acid

**lac·to·bac·te·ri·a·ce·ae** \,laktō(,)bak,tirē'āsē,ē\ [NL, irreg. fr. *Lactobacter,* syn. of *Lactobacillus* (fr. *lact-* + *-bacter*) + *-aceae*] *syn of* LACTOBACILLACEAE

**lac·to·bi·on·ic acid** \¦laktō¦bī¦änik-\ *n* [ISV *lactobi*ose lactose (fr. *lact-* + *biose*) + *-onic*] : a syrupy acid $C_{11}H_{21}O_{10}$-COOH obtained by oxidation of lactose

**lac·to·chrome** \'laktə,krōm\ *n* [*lact-* + *-chrome*] : RIBOFLAVIN

**lac·to·flavin** \¦lak(,)tō+\ *n* [ISV *lact-* + *flavin*] : RIBOFLAVIN

**lac·to·gen** \'laktəjən, -,jen\ *n* -s [*lact-* + *-gen*] : LACTOGENIC HORMONE

**lac·to·genesis** \¦lak(,)tō+\ *n* [NL, fr. *lact-* + *genesis*] : initiation of lactation

**lac·to·gen·ic** \¦laktə¦jenik\ *adj* [*lact-* + *-genic*] : inducing lactation

**lactogenic hormone** *n* : a crystalline protein of the anterior lobe of the pituitary body that induces lactation, maintains the corpora lutea in a functioning state in mammals, and stimulates the crop gland in birds — called also *luteotrophin, prolactin*

**lac·to·globulin** \¦lak(,)tō+\ *n* [ISV *lact-* + *globulin;* prob. orig. formed in Sw] : a crystalline protein fraction that is obtained from the whey of milk and is soluble in half-saturated ammonium sulfate solution but insoluble in pure water — called also *beta-lactoglobulin;* compare LACTALBUMIN

**lac·tom·e·ter** \lak'tämәd·ə(r)\ *n* [*lact-* + *meter*] : a hydrometer for determining the specific gravity of milk

**lac·tone** \'lak,tōn\ *n* -s [ISV *lact-* + *-one*] : any of a class of inner esters of hydroxy carboxylic acids formed typically by the loss of a molecule of water from the hydroxyl and carboxyl groups of the acids, characterized by the carbonyl-oxy grouping —OCO— in a ring, and classed according to the position of the hydroxyl group in the parent acid ⟨gamma-*lactones* from gamma-hydroxy acids contain five-membered rings and delta-*lactones* from delta-hydroxy acids contain 6-membered rings⟩ — compare SULTONE — **lac·ton·ic** \(')lak¦tänik\ *adj*

**lac·to·nitrile** \¦lak(,)tō+\ *n* [ISV *lact-* + *nitrile*] : a liquid $CH_3CH(OH)CN$ made by addition of hydrogen cyanide to acetaldehyde and used in making esters of lactic acid; acetaldehyde cyanohydrin

**lac·to·ni·za·tion** \,laktōnə'zāshən\ *n* -s : the process of lactonizing

**lac·to·nize** \'laktō,nīz\ *vb* -ED/-ING/-S [*lactone* + *-ize*] *vt* : to convert into a lactone ~ *vi* : to become converted into a lactone

**lac·to·phosphate** \¦lak(,)tō+\ *n* [*lact-* + *phosphate*] : a mixture of a lactate and a phosphate ⟨calcium ~⟩

**lac·to·prene** \'laktə,prēn\ *n* -s [*lact-* + iso*prene*] : any of several synthetic rubbers that are polymers or copolymers of an acrylic ester (as ethyl acrylate) and are characterized by good resistance to flexing and ozone, weather, and heat but not to low temperatures

**lac·tose** \'lak,tōs\ *n* -s [ISV *lact-* + *-ose;* prob. orig. formed in F] : a slightly sweet dextrorotatory reducing disaccharide sugar $C_{12}H_{22}O_{11}$ that is present in milk, that is less soluble in water than glucose or sucrose, that on hydrolysis yields glucose and galactose and on fermentation by various organisms yields esp. lactic acid (as in the souring of milk), that is usu. obtained from whey by evaporation as hard crystals of the alpha form containing a molecule of water, and that is used chiefly in foods, medicines, and culture media (as for the manufacture of penicillin); 4-β-galactosyl-glucose

**lac·to·side** \'laktə,sīd\ *n* -s [*lactose* + *-ide*] : a glycoside that yields lactose on hydrolysis

**lac·tos·uria** \,laktō's(h)ürēə, -ōs'yü-\ *n* -s [NL, fr. ISV *lactose* + NL *-uria*] : the presence of lactose in the urine

**lac·to-vegetarian** \¦lak(,)tō+\ *adj* [*lact-* + *vegetarian*] : of or relating to a diet of milk and vegetables and sometimes eggs

**lac·to·yl** \'laktə,wil\ *or* **lac·tyl** \'lak,til\ *n* -s [ISV *lact-* + *-oyl* or *-yl*] : the radical $CH_3CH(OH)CO$— of lactic acid

**lac tree** *n* [¹*lac*] : LACQUER TREE

**lac·tu·ca** \lak'tükə, -k'tyü-\ *n, cap* [NL, fr. L, lettuce — more at LETTUCE] : a genus of widely distributed milky-juiced herbs (family Compositae) having a beaked achene and soft white multiseriate pappus — see LETTUCE, PRICKLY LETTUCE

**lac·tu·ca·ri·um** \,laktə'ka(a)rēəm, -'ker-, -'kär-\ *n* -s [NL, fr. *Lactuca,* genus that produces it + L *-arium*] : the dried milky juice of a prickly lettuce (*Lactuca virosa*) resembling opium in physical properties and formerly used as a sedative

**la·cu·na** \lə'k(y)ünə\ *n, pl* **lacu·nae** \-k(y)ü(,)nē, -kü,nī\ *or* **lacunas** \-k(y)ünəz\ [L, pit, cleft, pool — more at LAGOON] **1** : a blank space : GAP, HOLE : a missing part : DEFECT, FLAW ⟨despite the *lacunae* in substantive information —P.M.Hauser⟩ ⟨with a cultured man there is no gap or ~ between his opinions and his life —J.C.Powys⟩ **2** [NL, fr. L] **a** : one of the follicles in the mucous membrane of the urethra **b** : one of the minute cavities in bone or cartilage occupied by the cells **c (1)** : one of the small pits on the surface of some of the lichens **(2)** : a gap in the protoxylem resulting from breakdown of protoxylem elements during elongation of a root or shoot — called also *carinal canal* **(3)** : a depressed space or pit on the outer surface of a pollen grain **d** : one of the spaces among the tissues of lower animals that serve in place of vessels for the circulation of the body fluids **3** [NL, fr. L] *cap* : a large cosmopolitan genus of chinks that is the type of the family Lacunidae but was often formerly included in Littorinidae **syn** see BREAK

**la·cu·nal** \-k(y)ünᵊl\ *or* **la·cu·nar** \-nə(r)\ *adj* [*lacuna* + *-al* or *-ar*] : LACUNARY

**la·cu·nar** \"\ *n, pl* **lacunars** \-nə(r)z\ *or* **lac·u·nar·ia** \,lakyə'na(a)rēə\ [L, fr. *lacuna* pit] **1** *pl* **lacunars** : a vault or ceiling constructed with recessed panels **2** *pl* **lacunaria** : a recessed panel forming part of a regularly patterned ceiling, vault, or soffit : COFFER

**lacu·nary** \'lakyə,nerē, lə'k(y)ünərē\ *adj* [*lacuna* + *-ary*] : of, relating to, or including lacunae

**lacu·nate** \lə'k(y)ü,nāt, 'lakyə,n-\ *adj* [NL *lacuna* + E *-ate*] : LACUNARY

**la·cune** \lə'k(y)ün\ *n* -s [F or L; F *lacune,* fr. L *lacuna* pit, cleft, pool — more at LAGOON] : LACUNA

**la·cu·ni·dae** \-nə,dē\ *n pl, cap* [NL, fr. *Lacuna,* type genus + *-idae*] : a cosmopolitan family of marine gastropods (suborder Taenioglossa) that comprise the chinks and are characterized by a conical umbilicate shell with a slit leading to the umbilicus

**lac·u·nome** \'lakyə,nōm\ *n* -s [It *lacunoma,* fr. NL *lacuna* + *-oma*] : a system of lacunar spaces sometimes demonstrable in some animal cells and suggested to be comparable to the vacuolar apparatus of the typical plant cell

**la·cu·nule** \lə'k(y)ü,nyül\ *n* -s [*lacuna* + *-ule*] : a small lacuna

**la·cu·nu·lose** \-)ünyə,lōs\ *adj* [*lacunule* + *-ule* + *-ose*] : having minute lacunae

**la·cus·tral** \lə'kəstrəl\ *adj* [*lacustrine* + *-al*] : LACUSTRINE

[1]**la·cus·tri·an** \-rēən\ *adj* [*lacustrine* + *-an*] : LACUSTRINE

[2]**lacustrian** \"\ *n* -s : LAKE DWELLER

**la·cus·trine** \-rən\ *adj* [prob. fr. F or It *lacustre* lacustrine (fr. L *lacus* lake; prob. influenced by L *paluster, palustris* marshy) + E *-ine* — more at LAKE] **1** : of, relating to, or formed in lakes ⟨~ waters⟩ ⟨~ deposits⟩ **2** : growing or living in lakes ⟨a ~ flora⟩ ⟨~ fishes⟩ **3** : of or relating to dwellings built on piles in lakes esp. in prehistoric central Europe, Scotland, and Ireland

**LACW** *abbr* leading aircraftswoman

**lac wax** *n* : SHELLAC WAX

**lacy** *or* **lacey** \'lāsē, -si\ *adj* **lac·i·er; lac·i·est** : resembling, exhibiting, or consisting of lace : LACELIKE ⟨a ~ lady from the past with a passion for the future —*Newsweek*⟩ ⟨ended with ~, upper-register piano notes —Whitney Balliett⟩ ⟨you start out . . . to look at the ~ iron balconies and the old houses —R.M.Hodesh⟩

**lad** \'lad, aa(ə)d\ *n* -s [ME *ladde*] **1 a** *obs* : a male attendant : MANSERVANT **b** *obs* : a man of low station : VARLET, KNAVE **c** *Brit* : a stableboy in a racing stable : GROOM **2 a** : a male person of any age between early boyhood and maturity : BOY, YOUTH, STRIPLING ⟨a young country ~⟩ ⟨a ~ not yet twenty⟩ ⟨all the local ~*s* and lasses⟩ **b** : a male child : SON ⟨~*s,* less often girls, are named after nephews or nieces —J.G.Frazer⟩ **3** : MAN, FELLOW, CHAP — often used familiarly or in affection or admiration ⟨here's luck, ~⟩ ⟨a great ~ with the ladies⟩ ⟨a couple of likely ~*s* for a brawl⟩ **4** : SWEETHEART ⟨have ye seen aught of my bonnie ~⟩

**la·da·khi** *also* **la·da·ki** \lə'däkē\ *n, pl* **ladakhi** *or* **ladakhis** *also* **ladaki** *or* **ladakis** *usu cap* **1** : a native or inhabitant of Ladakh, a region of eastern Kashmir **2** : a Tibetan dialect of Ladakh

**la·dang** \'lä,däŋ\ *n* -s [D, fr. Malay] *Indonesia* : MILPA 1

**ladanum** *var of* LABDANUM

[1]**lad·der** \'ladə(r)\ *n* -s *often attrib* [ME, fr. OE *hlǣdder, hlǣder;* akin to MD *lēder* ladder, OHG *leitara* ladder, ON *hlith* swinging gate, Goth *hleithra* hut, tent, and to OE *hlinian, hleonian* to lean — more at LEAN (incline)] **1 a** : a usu. portable structure for use in climbing up or down that consists commonly of two parallel sidepieces of wood, metal, or rope joined at short intervals by a series of crosspieces that serve as rests for the feet — see AERIAL LADDER, EXTENSION LADDER, STEPLADDER **b** *obs* : the steps leading to a gallows **c** : a set of vertical or inclined steps on a ship : ship's stairway — see ACCOMMODATION LADDER; compare COMPANIONWAY **2** : a means of rising or climbing ⟨the ladder by which one attains to a higher position or status ⟨the only ~ is education in a technical school —Roger Burlingame⟩ ⟨~*s* used by the unscrupulously ambitious —T.H.Eliot⟩ ⟨the societal organizations and the institutions that serve . . . as social ~*s* —*Social Forces*⟩ ⟨the pathetic conviction that learning alone was the ~ to political power —Roy Lewis & Angus Maude⟩ — compare STEPPING-STONE **3** : something that resembles or suggests a ladder in form or use: as **a** *chiefly Brit* : RUN 12a **b** : FISH LADDER **c** : CONVEYER 2a(6) **d** : a series of cross straps attached to the backs of venetian-blind tapes to support the slats **e** : BACKBONE 5, LADDER TRACK **f** : a succession of gunfire salvos fired with uniform differences in range to determine the proper range for achieving hits **g** : a cultivating implement of India resembling a harrow **4** : a series of usu. ascending steps or stages : a scheme of comparative rank or order : SCALE ⟨trying to better his position on the social ~⟩ ⟨ranked objectively in a ~ of economic desirability —*Jour. of Accountancy*⟩ ⟨a toehold on the academic ~ —Lynn White⟩ ⟨has slipped down the power ~ —C.L.Sulzberger⟩ ⟨a world whose standards appear to be at the bottom of the ~ —P.M.Mazur⟩ **5 a** : LADDER COMPANY **b** : LADDER TRUCK

ladder 1a

[2]**ladder** \"\ *vb* **laddered; laddered; laddering** \-d(ə)riŋ\ **ladders** *vt* **1** : to provide with ladders : scale by means of a ladder ⟨~ a building⟩ **2** : to provide with a fish ladder ⟨~ a falls⟩ **3** *chiefly Brit* : to cause or develop a ladder in ⟨~ a stocking⟩ **4** *India* : to work (land) with a ladder : HARROW **5** : to mark transversely as if with rungs of a ladder : BAR, STRIPE ⟨slant rays ~*ed* the lofty shade —D.C.Peattie⟩ ~ *vi* **1** *chiefly Brit* : to develop a ladder : RUN ⟨stockings which ~*ed* the first time they were worn⟩ **2** : to rise like or as if on the successive rungs of a ladder ⟨dusty leaves ~*ing* up a goldenrod stem —W.O.Mitchell⟩ ⟨~*ing* up the bestseller list —*Time*⟩

**ladder-back** \'⸗⸗,⸗\ *adj, of furniture* : having a back consisting of two upright posts connected by horizontal slats : LADDER⸗BACKED ⟨a *ladder-back* chair⟩

**ladder-backed** \¦⸗⸗¦⸗\ *adj* : having a back resembling a ladder; *esp* : having barred markings on the back that are suggestive of the rungs of a ladder ⟨*ladder-backed* woodpeckers⟩

**ladder chain** *n* : a chain resembling a ladder in shape

**ladder company** *n* : a fire department unit comprising the firemen to operate a ladder truck

**laddered** *adj* **1** : provided with a ladder ⟨a ~ loft⟩ **2** : that has developed a ladder ⟨a ~ stocking⟩

**ladder fire** *n* : a method of adjusting artillery or mortar fire by firing in rapid succession three rounds with the same deflection but at different ranges

**laddering** *n* -s : ladders or material for ladders

**ladder jack** *n* : a bracket for supporting a platform or scaffold from a ladder

**lad·der·less** \'lad·ə(r)ləs\ *adj* **1** : having no ladder ⟨a ~ loft⟩ **2** *chiefly Brit* : free from ladders : resistant to laddering ⟨~ stockings⟩

**ladderlike** \'⸗⸗,⸗\ *adj* : resembling a ladder (as in form or appearance or in being graduated or progressive) : SCALAR, SCALARIFORM

**lad·der·man** \'ladə(r)mən, -,man\ *n, pl* **laddermen** : a member of a ladder company

**ladders** *pl of* LADDER, *pres 3d sing of* LADDER

**ladder shell** *n* : a prominently ribbed spiral marine shell of *Epitonium* or related genera : WENTLETRAP

**ladder snake** *n* : a southern European rat snake (*Elaphe scalaris*) with ladderlike markings on back and sides

**ladder tape** *n* **:** a tape support for a venetian blind that consists of two long strips of a woven or plastic fabric joined at intervals by narrow cross strips on which the slats of the blind rest

**ladder tournament** *n* **:** a tournament in which the names of all contestants are drawn and arranged one above the other on a posted list and in which each entrant is entitled to challenge one of the two contestants directly above him and if victorious to assume his opponent's place in the ranking

**ladder track** *n* **:** a main track connecting successive body tracks in a railroad yard **:** BACKBONE 5

**ladder truck** *n* **:** a piece of mobile fire apparatus carrying ladders and usu. other fire-fighting and rescue equipment

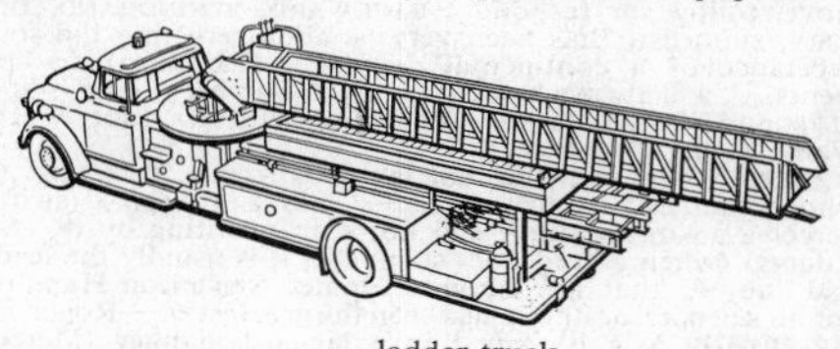

ladder truck

**ladderway** \ˈ≈,≈\ *n* **:** a series of ladders for passage up or down in a mine; *also* **:** a compartment in which ladders are used

**lad·dery** \ˈlad(ə)rē\ *adj* **:** resembling a ladder

**lad·die** \ˈladē, -di\ *n* -s [dim. of *lad*] **:** a young lad

**lad·dish** \ˈladish\ *adj* **:** resembling or belonging to a lad **:** BOYISH, IMMATURE, YOUTHFUL — **lad·dish·ness** *n* -ES

[1]**lade** \ˈlād\ *vb* **laded; lad·ed** \-dəd\ *or in vt sense 1* **lad·en** \-dᵊn\ **lading; lades** [ME *laden*, fr. OE *hladan*, *ladan* to heap, load, draw water; akin to OHG *hladan* to load, ON *hlatha*, Goth *afhlathan* to load, OSlav *klasti* to load, place] *vt* **1 a :** to put a load or burden on or in **:** furnish with freight or cargo **:** LOAD ⟨~ a vessel⟩ ⟨*laded* their asses with the corn —Gen 42:26 (AV)⟩ ⟨the lighter a ship is *laden* the greater will be the effects of an uneven trim —*Manual of Seamanship*⟩ ⟨countless ore-*laden* motor trucks —Tom Marvel⟩ **b :** to put or place as a load or burden esp. for shipment or carriage **:** take aboard **:** PACK, SHIP, STOW ⟨*lading* tea and silks from Canton —F.R.Dulles⟩ ⟨exclude from the protection of their policies cargo *laden* on deck —W.D.Winter⟩ ⟨bring to town their produce, *laden* in wagons —*Amer. Guide Series: Pa.*⟩ **c :** to load heavily: (1) **:** to provide or supply abundantly or to repleteness **:** CHARGE, CRAM, FILL ⟨their breasts were *laden* with decorations and medals —F.J.Mather⟩ ⟨packed with annotations and statistics and *laden* with footnotes —*Times Lit. Supp.*⟩ ⟨let the air with joy be *laden* —W.S.Gilbert⟩ ⟨silt-*laden* soil —R.A.Billington⟩ ⟨the suspense-*laden* room —Cortland Fitzsimmons⟩ (2) **:** to weigh down **:** weigh upon heavily **:** BURDEN, OPPRESS ⟨weak and heavy *laden* —Joseph Scriven⟩ ⟨*laden* with the deep, nostalgic morbidness of youth —Walter O'Meara⟩ ⟨three misery-*laden* men —Albert Deutsch⟩ **2 :** to lift or throw (a liquid) in or out with or as if with a ladle or dipper **:** DIP, DRAW, LADLE ⟨*laded* several dippers of water into a basin⟩ ⟨*laded* metal⟩ ⟨the molten glass is *laded* from the pot to the forming table⟩ ~ *vi* **1 :** to take on cargo **:** LOAD **2 :** to take up or convey a liquid by dipping **syn** see BURDEN

[2]**lade** *now dial var of* LOAD

[3]**lade** \ˈlād\ *n* -s [ME, fr. OE *lād* course, way — more at LODE] **1** *chiefly Scot* **:** MILLRACE **2 a :** the mouth of a river **b :** WATERCOURSE

[1]**lad·en** \ˈlādᵊn\ *vt* **ladened; ladened; ladening** \-d(ᵊ)niŋ\ **ladens** [[1]*lade* + *-en*] **:** LADE ⟨heavily ~*ed* with equipment —Isabel M. Lewis⟩

[2]**laden** *adj* [fr. *laden*, past part. of [1]*lade*] **:** BURDENED, CHARGED, LOADED ⟨leading a ~ mule —Arthur Loveridge⟩ ⟨a ~ silence . . . prevailed —Osbert Sitwell⟩ ⟨a ~ heart⟩

**la·den·burg flask** \ˈlädᵊn,bərg\ *n, usu cap L* [after Albert *Ladenburg* †1911 Ger. chemist] **:** a distilling flask with bulbed neck

**lad·er** \ˈlādə(r)\ *n* -s **:** one that lades

**lad·hood** \ˈlad,hu̇d\ *n* **:** BOYHOOD

[1]**la-di-da** *also* **la-de-da** *or* **la-di-dah** \ˌlädēˈdä\ *vi* -ED/-ING/-S [perh. alter. of *lardy-dardy*, adj.] **:** to speak or act in a la-di-da manner **:** behave in an affectedly refined or elegant manner

[2]**la-di-da** *also* **la-de-da** *or* **la-di-dah** \"\ *or* **lah-di-dah** \"\ *n* -s **1 :** a person who affects gentility or elegance **:** a pretentious imitator of cultivated speech or manners **2 :** behavior characteristic of a la-di-da **:** affected gentility or gentility so exaggerated as to seem affected **:** GENTEELNESS; *esp* **:** an exaggeratedly genteel accent or a mincing prissiness of expression ⟨with your car and your *la-di-da* and Honorable and all the rest of it —Nigel Balchin⟩ ⟨the soldier's blasphemy takes the curse off the aesthete's *la-di-da* —J.W.Beach⟩

[3]**la-di-da** *also* **la-de-da** *or* **la-di-dah** *or* **lah-di-dah** \"\ *adj* **1 :** characteristic of a la-di-da **:** affectedly refined or polished **:** exaggeratedly upper-class in speech and manners **:** GENTEEL ⟨with their gentlemen's voices and *la-di-da* manners —C.S.Forester⟩ ⟨the exotic and inscrutable Chinese . . . is no more true to life than the *la-di-da* Englishman —Owen Lattimore⟩ ⟨complaints against the *la-de-da* pronunciation of some of their hirelings —H.L.Mencken⟩ **2 a :** HIGHFALUTIN, PRETENTIOUS ⟨collecting and drinking wine . . . a dandy hobby, if the vocabulary weren't so *la-di-da* —Clifton Fadiman⟩ **b :** MINCING, SISSIFIED ⟨a *la-di-da* book about men's clothes —G.T.Hellman⟩ **3 :** characteristic of the world of fashion and wealth **:** ELEGANT, HIGH-TONED, STYLISH ⟨the *la-di-da* doings of high society —J.P.O'Donnell⟩ **:** EXTRAVAGANT, LAVISH ⟨*la-de-da* parties and glamour girls —*Time*⟩

**ladies** *pl of* LADY

**ladies aid** *n, usu cap L&A* **:** a local organization of church-women for the purpose of assisting financially the church to which they belong — compare AID 3c

**ladies auxiliary** *n, usu cap L&A* **:** an organization of women that is auxiliary usu. to a men's fraternal or social organization — compare AUXILIARY 9

**ladies chain** *n, often cap L&C* **:** a square-dance figure in which the women give their right hands to each other as they cross over to the opposite men who take their left hands and swing them as they arrive

**ladies' cloth** *var of* LADY'S CLOTH

**ladies' day** *n, often cap L&D* **:** a day on which women receive a special privilege (as attendance as guests at a meeting of a men's club or free admission to a baseball game)

**ladies'-delight** *var of* LADY'S-DELIGHT

**ladies'-eardrop** *var of* LADY'S-EARDROP

**ladies' ladder** *var of* LADY'S LADDER

**ladies' man** *also* **lady's man** *n* **:** a man who shows a marked fondness for the company of women or is very gallant in his attentions to women

**ladies'-pocket** *var of* LADY'S-POCKET

**ladies' room** *n* **:** a women's lavatory esp. in a public or semipublic building or establishment (as a theater or restaurant)

**ladies' slipper** *var of* LADY'S SLIPPER

**la·dies'-streamer** \ˌlādē(z)+ˌ-\ *n* [by folk etymology fr. NL *Lagerstroemia*, genus name] **:** CRAPE MYRTLE

**ladies'-tobacco** *also* **lady's-tobacco** \ˌ≈≈≈ˌ≈≈\ *n* **:** a plant of the genus *Antennaria*

**ladies' tresses** *also* **lady's tresses** *or* **lady's traces** \ˌ≈≈ˌ≈\ *n pl but sing or pl in constr* **:** an orchid of the genus *Spiranthes*

**la·di·fy** *or* **la·dy·fy** \ˈlādə,fī, -dē,-\ *vt* -ED/-ING/-ES **1 :** to make a lady of **:** treat as a lady **:** call by the title *Lady* **2 :** to make ladylike; *esp* **:** to make suitable for a lady ⟨manners that had been carefully *ladified*⟩ ⟨*ladified* copies of a man's best briars —*advt*⟩

**la·dik** \läˈdēk\ *n* -s *usu cap* [fr. *Ladik*, village in Turkey] **:** a rug of fine texture woven in and near Ladik in central Anatolia

**la·din** \ləˈdēn\ *n* -s *cap* [Rhaeto-Romanic, fr. L *Latinum* Latin — more at LATIN (n.)] **1 :** ROMANSH **2 :** one speaking Ladin as a mother tongue

**la·di·na** \ləˈdēnə\ *n* -s *often cap* [AmerSp, fem. of *ladino*] **:** a female ladino

**lading** *n* -s [fr. *lading*, gerund of [1]*lade*] **1 a :** LOADING 1a **b :** an act of bailing, dipping, or ladling **2 :** something that lades **:** a load or something that makes up a load (as the contents of a shipment) **:** CARGO, FREIGHT, BURDEN

[1]**la·di·no** \ləˈdē(,)nō\ *n* -s [Sp, fr. *ladino*, adj., cunning, learned, lit., Latin, fr. L *latinus* Latin — more at LATIN (adj.)] **1** *cap* **:** JUDEO-SPANISH **2** *often cap* [AmerSp, fr. Sp *ladino*, adj.] **a :** a westernized Spanish-speaking Latin American who is not of pure Spanish extraction; *esp* **:** MESTIZO **b :** a Central American of mixed or pure Spanish descent who does not belong to an Indian community **3** [AmerSp, fr. Sp *ladino*, adj.] *Southwest* **:** a cunningly vicious horse or steer **4** *cap* **:** a Judeo-Spanish-speaking Jew of the Balkan or Mediterranean countries; *also* **:** SPAGNUOLO

[2]**la·di·no** \ləˈdī(,)nō, -dē(,)nō, -dīnə\ *or* **ladino clover** *n* -s *often cap L* [prob. fr. It *ladino* of Graubünden, canton of Switzerland] **:** a large nutritious rapidly growing clover that is a horticultural variety of white clover reaching two to four times the size of common white clover and widely planted for hay, ensilage, and grazing and as a cover crop

[1]**lad·kin** \ˈladkən\ *n* -s **:** a little lad

[2]**ladkin** \"\ *n* -s [origin unknown] **:** a glazier's tool for opening cames

[1]**la·dle** \ˈlādᵊl\ *n* -s [ME *ladel*, fr. OE *hlædel*, fr. *hladan* to lade — more at LADE] **1 :** a deep-bowled long-handled spoon used esp. for dipping up and conveying liquids **2 :** an instrument or device resembling a ladle in form or function: as **a :** a vessel with a pouring lip or nozzle for conveying liquid metal from a furnace to another apparatus for further treatment or to a mold for casting **b** (1) **:** a copper scoop attached to a staff and used with muzzle-loading cannon to withdraw the projectile and charge from a loaded piece (2) **:** a ring with handles used for carrying spherical shot **c :** a long-handled box for taking up collections in church

ladle 1

[2]**ladle** \"\ *vt* **ladled; ladled; ladling** \-d(ᵊ)liŋ\ **ladles :** to take up and convey in a ladle **:** dip with or as if with a ladle ⟨*ladled* a bowl of stew for himself —A.B.Mayse⟩ ⟨*ladled* the fish into the weir boat —Mary H. Varse⟩ ⟨information-*ladling* college professors —H.A.Overstreet⟩

**la·dle·ful** \ˈlādᵊl,fu̇l\ *n* -s [ME *ladel-ful*, fr. *ladel* ladle + *-ful*] **:** the quantity held by a ladle

**ladle in** *vt* **:** to put in with or as if with a ladle **:** INSERT ⟨*ladled in* a few such scriptural phrases —Mark Twain⟩

**ladle out** *vt* **:** to dish out **:** FURNISH, GIVE, PROVIDE ⟨*ladle out* two bowls of porridge —Margaret Kennedy⟩ ⟨*ladle it out* slowly⟩ ⟨a more dynamic socialism than the one being officially *ladled out* —Mollie Panter-Downes⟩ ⟨charm is sometimes *ladled out* in too much profusion —C.H.Sykes⟩

**la·dler** \ˈlād(ᵊ)lə(r)\ *n* -s **:** one that ladles

**ladle up** *vt* **:** to serve with or as if with a ladle ⟨lustily singing out for someone to *ladle him up* —Herman Melville⟩

**lad o' pairts** \ˌladəˈpärts, -per-\ *Scot* **:** a clever or talented fellow **:** MAN OF PARTS

**ladp** *abbr* ladyship

**la·drone** *or* **la·dron** *in sense 1* ˈladrən *or* ˈladrən, *in sense 2* ləˈdrōn\ *n, pl* **ladrones** *or* **ladrons** [prob. fr. MF *ladron* thief, robber, fr. L *latron-, latro*] **1** *usu* **ladrone**, *chiefly Scot* **:** BLACKGUARD, ROGUE **2** *usu* **ladron** [Sp *ladrón*, fr. L *latron-, latro*] *Southwest* **:** THIEF, ROBBER

**lads** *pl of* LAD

**lad's-love** \ˈ≈,≈\ *n* **:** BOY'S-LOVE

[1]**la·dy** \ˈlādē, -di\ *n* -ES *often attrib* [ME *lady, lavedi, lafdi*, fr. OE *hlǣfdīge*, fr. *hlāf* bread + *-dīge* (fr. root of a prehistoric verb meaning to knead); akin to OE *dǣge* maid, kneader of bread — more at LOAF, DAIRY] **1** *obs* **:** a mistress of servants **:** a woman who looks after the domestic affairs of a family **:** female head of a household **2 a :** a woman having proprietary rights, rule, or authority **:** a woman to whom obedience or homage is owed as a ruler or feudal superior — usu. used chiefly in the phrase *lady of the manor;* compare LORD 1 **b** (1) **:** a woman receiving the particular homage of a knight (2) **:** a woman who is the object of a lover's devotion **:** LADYLOVE, MISTRESS, SWEETHEART **3 a :** a woman of good family or of a superior social position ⟨inclined to remind you that she was a ~ by birth —W.S.Maugham⟩ ⟨some ~ trifles —Shak.⟩ ⟨and five bastards by a ~ of Seville —Rafael Altamira y Crevea⟩ ⟨a ~ airs⟩ ⟨a ~ housekeeper⟩ ⟨once a ~ could not be a stenographer or a shopgirl —Katharine F. Gerould⟩ — compare GENTLEMAN 1b; used also of a woman in a courteous mode of reference ⟨show this ~ to a seat⟩ ⟨the *ladies'* singles championship⟩ or usu. in the pl. of address ⟨that will be all, *ladies*⟩ ⟨*ladies* and gentlemen⟩ **b :** a woman of refinement and gentle manners **:** a woman whose conduct conforms to a certain standard of propriety or correct behavior **:** well-bred woman ⟨with a *lady's* respect for tranquillity she forbore to discuss these troubles —Frances G. Patton⟩ ⟨no woman with a bosom could be quite a ~ in his eyes —Hugh MacLennan⟩ ⟨a ~ . . . quiet, reserved, gracious, continent . . . gentle, and a woman —W.D.Steele⟩ — compare GENTLEMAN 1c **c :** a woman irrespective of social status or personal qualities **:** FEMALE ⟨a ~ doctor⟩ ⟨a char*lady*⟩ ⟨a two-headed boy and a bearded ~⟩ ⟨~ novelists⟩ ⟨the iceman, the blackberry ~, and the poor blind man with the brooms —Eudora Welty⟩ ⟨noticed the cold eye of the ~ behind the bar —Margery Allingham⟩ ⟨as fit as a ~ sharpshooter —Ethel Merman⟩ **4 :** WIFE ⟨the president and his ~⟩ ⟨his daughter was now a general's ~ —John De Meyer⟩ ⟨fashionable doctors and their *ladies* —Gene Baro⟩ **5** — used as a title prefixed to the names of various supernatural beings and personified abstractions ⟨*Lady* Venus⟩ ⟨*Lady* Luck⟩; compare DAME 1c **6 a :** any of various titled women in Great Britain — used as a courtesy title for the daughter of a duke, marquess, or earl ⟨*Lady* Philippa Stewart, daughter of the fourteenth Duke of Norfolk⟩ and for the wife of a younger son of a duke or marquess ⟨*Lady* Randolph Churchill, wife of a younger son of the Duke of Marlborough⟩ and as a mode of reference for a marchioness, countess, viscountess, or baroness ⟨the Marchioness of Lothian, addressed as *Lady* Lothian⟩ and for the wife of a baronet or knight ⟨Sir William and *Lady* Craigie⟩ **b :** a female member of certain orders of knighthood or chivalry ⟨Her Majesty is *Lady* of the Most Noble Order of the Garter —*Burke's Peerage*⟩ ⟨appointed by Pope Pius as a ~ of the grand cross of the Equestrian Order of the Holy Sepulchre —*Springfield (Mass.) Union*⟩ — compare DAME 1g **7 a** *obs* **:** the queen in a set of chess men **b** *slang* **:** a queen in a deck of playing cards **8** [so called fr. the fancied resemblance to the outline of a seated woman's figure] **:** the triturating apparatus in the stomach of a lobster **9 :** a gunner's mate in charge of the lady's hole on a man-of-war **10 a :** a female animal ⟨one was a ~, her swimmerets . . . covered with black eggs —Robert Hunter⟩ ⟨a ~ goat⟩ ⟨the male trout are handsome, the ~ trout pretty and available —*Ford Times*⟩ **b :** a female harlequin duck — compare LORD-AND-LADY **11 ladies** *pl but sing in constr, chiefly Brit* **:** LADIES' ROOM ⟨slipped into the *ladies* to powder her nose⟩

[2]**lady** \"\ *vb* -ED/-ING/-ES *vt, obs* **:** to make a lady of or to make ladylike ~ *vi* **:** to play the lady — used with *it* ⟨~*ing* it over her former friends⟩

**lady altar** *n, usu cap L* **:** an altar dedicated in honor of the Virgin Mary

**lady am·herst's pheasant** \-ˈam(,)ərs(t)s-\ *n, usu cap L&A* [after Sarah E. *Lady Amherst* †1876 Brit. amateur naturalist] **:** a pheasant (*Chrysolophus amherstiae*) native to western China and Tibet and having a green crown, red crest, and black-barred white cape and a white breast and abdomen

**lady baltimore cake** *n, usu cap L&B* [prob. after *Lady Baltimore*, wife of Lord Baltimore †1632 — more at BALTIMORE] **:** a usu. white butter cake with boiled frosting and a filling of chopped raisins, figs, and nuts — compare LORD BALTIMORE CAKE

**lady beetle** *n* **:** LADYBUG

**ladybird** \ˈ≈,≈\ *n* **1** *also* **ladybird beetle :** LADYBUG **2 :** PINTAIL 1 **3 :** SWEETHEART

**lady bountiful** *n, pl* **lady bountifuls** *or* **ladies bountiful,** *often cap L&B* [after *Lady Bountiful*, character in *The Beaux' Stratagem* (1707), play by George Farquhar †1707 British dramatist born in Ireland] **:** a woman notable for or conspicuous in her benevolences

**lady bracken** *or* **lady brake** *n* [[1]*lady*] **:** a common brake (*Pteridium aquilinum*)

**ladybug** \ˈ≈,≈\ *n* [after Our *Lady*, the Virgin Mary] **:** any of the small more or less hemispherical often brightly colored beetles that constitute the family Coccinellidae, are distributed throughout temperate and tropical regions, and with the exception of a few herbivorous forms feed in both larval and adult stages upon small insects and the eggs of larger ones — see VEDALIA

**lady chair** *n* **1 :** a seat formed by the interlocked hands and wrists of two persons **2 :** an upholstered chair without arms or with very low only slightly projecting arms

**lady chapel** *n, usu cap L & often cap C* [ME (*oure*) *lady chapell*, fr. *oure lady* Our Lady, the Virgin Mary + *chapell* chapel] **:** a chapel dedicated to the Virgin Mary, containing a Lady altar, and located usu. in a cathedral or parish church but sometimes in a separate building

**lady court** *n* **:** a court held by a lady of a manor

**lady crab** *n* **1 :** a brightly spotted swimming crab (*Ovalipes ocellatus*) that is very common on the sandy shores of the Atlantic coast of the U.S. **2 :** a crab (*Portunus puber*) of the English coasts that is closely related and similar to the American lady crab

**lady cracker** *n* **:** a diminutive firecracker

**lady day** *n, usu cap L&D* [ME (*oure*) *lady day*, fr. *oure lady* Our Lady, the Virgin Mary + *day*] **:** a feast of the Virgin Mary; *specif* **:** ANNUNCIATION DAY

**lady fern** *n* **:** a widely distributed fern (*Athyrium filix-femina*) with slender bipinnate fronds showing considerable variation in form; *broadly* **:** any fern of the genus *Athyrium* — usu. used with a qualifying term

**ladyfinger** \ˈ≈,≈≈\ *n* **1 a :** LADY'S-FINGER **b ladyfingers** *pl but sing or pl in constr* **:** a foxglove (*Digitalis purpurea*) **2 :** a small finger-shaped sponge cake **3 :** any of several small-fruited bananas **4 :** a large elongated dessert grape of European origin and superior flavor

**ladyfish** \ˈ≈,≈\ *n* **:** any of several marine fishes: as **a :** a bonefish (*Albula vulpes*) **b :** a crimson and gold wrasse (*Bodianus rufus*) of Florida and the West Indies and south to Brazil — called also *Spanish hogfish* **c :** TENPOUNDER

**lady friend** *n* **1 :** a female friend ⟨no other relatives . . . no *lady friend* with whom you could stay —William Black⟩ ⟨less a secretary than an intimate *lady friend* —H.J.Laski⟩ **2 :** a man's female companion ⟨soldiers, and bankers, and their wives and *lady friends* —*New Yorker*⟩ ⟨spending the day at the beach with his *lady friend*⟩ **3 :** the female partner in an intimate esp. an illicit relationship **:** LOVER, MISTRESS

**ladyfy** *var of* LADIFY

**lady-help** \ˈ≈≈ˈ≈\ *n, Brit* **:** a woman who performs domestic duties at a usu. low wage in consideration of recognition as the social equal of her employer

**la·dy·hood** \ˈlādē,hu̇d\ *n* **1 :** the state of being a lady **:** quality or nature of a lady ⟨the changing status of woman from ~ to the position of political citizen —Amy Loveman⟩ **2 :** LADIES ⟨representative of the ~ of her day⟩

**ladying** *pres part of* LADY

**lady-in-waiting** \ˈ≈≈≈ˈ≈≈\ *n, pl* **ladies-in-waiting :** a lady of a queen's or a princess's household appointed to wait upon or attend her

**la·dy·ish** \ˈlādēish\ *adj* **:** somewhat like a lady; *esp* **:** having or showing undesirable ladylike characteristics — **la·dy·ish·ly** *adv* — **la·dy·ish·ness** *n* -ES

**lady-killer** \ˈ≈≈,≈≈\ *n* **:** a man who captivates women or who has the reputation of being fascinating to women

**lady-killing** \ˈ≈≈,≈≈\ *n* **:** the activities or arts of a lady-killer

**la·dy·kin** \ˈlādēkən\ *n* -s [[1]*lady* + *-kin*] **:** a little lady — sometimes used as an endearment

**la·dy·kind** \-ē,kīnd\ *n* [[1]*lady* + *-kind* (as in *womankind*)] **:** LADIES — compare WOMANKIND

**la·dy·less** \-ēləs\ *adj* **:** lacking ladies **:** not accompanied by a lady

**ladylike** \ˈ≈≈,≈\ *adj* **1 :** resembling a lady in appearance or manners **:** WELL-BRED ⟨editorials urging our girls to be ~ —Virgil Henry⟩ ⟨one establishment may appeal to the conservative ~ type —Lois Long⟩ **2 :** becoming or suitable to a lady **:** marked by conformity to a lady's standards ⟨in a ~ manner she was sick —Sinclair Lewis⟩ ⟨bought her something ~ to put on her back —Eudora Welty⟩ **3 :** foolishly or weakly like a woman: **a :** feeling or showing too much concern about elegance or propriety ⟨~ embarrassment at not being the wife of a real doctor —Lewis Vogler⟩ **b :** lacking in strength, force, or virility **:** WEAK, SOFT, YIELDING ⟨the average puncher was womanly though Heaven knows he was in no wise ~ —P.A.Rollins⟩ **syn** see FEMALE

**la·dy·like·ness** *n* -ES **:** the quality or state of being ladylike ⟨Spanish fans, the acme of ~ —*New Yorker*⟩

**ladylove** \ˈ≈≈,≈\ *n* **:** SWEETHEART, MISTRESS

**lady mass** *n, usu cap L & often cap M* [orig. ME *masse of our Lady*] **:** a mass said in honor of the Virgin Mary

**lady mayoress** *n* **:** a lord mayor's wife

**lady of loretto** *usu cap both Ls* **:** LORETTO NUN

**lady of pleasure :** PROSTITUTE

**lady of the bedchamber :** one of the ladies of noble family holding the official position of personal attendant on a British queen or princess

**lady of the evening :** PROSTITUTE

**lady of the house :** a mistress of a dwelling **:** HOUSEWIFE — used with *the* ⟨is the *lady of the house* at home⟩

**lady-of-the-night** \ˌ≈≈≈ˈ≈\ *n* **:** a West Indian shrub (*Brunfelsia americana*) with fragrant showy yellowish white flowers

**lady palm** *n* **:** an Asiatic fan palm of the genus *Rhapis* with clustered slender reedy stems

**lady paramount** *n, pl* **ladies paramount 1 :** the official in charge of the women's division of an archery tournament **2 :** the chief official of a women's archery tournament

**lady pea** *n* **:** COWPEA

**lady's bedstraw** *n* [fr. earlier *our lady's bedstraw*, after *Our Lady*, the Virgin Mary] **:** YELLOW BEDSTRAW

**lady's bower** *n* **:** a traveler's-joy (*Clematis vitalba*)

**lady's chair** *n* **:** LADY CHAIR 1

**lady's cloth** *or* **ladies' cloth** *n* **:** a closely woven lightweight woolen cloth of fine quality for women's wear

**lady's-comb** \ˈ≈≈ˌ≈\ *n, pl* **lady's-combs** [intended as trans. of L *pecten Veneris*, lit., Venus' comb] **:** a European herb (*Scandix pectenveneris*) with slender pointed fruits

**lady's-delight** *or* **ladies'-delight** \ˌ≈≈≈ˈ≈\ *n, pl* **lady's-delights** *or* **ladies'-delights :** WILD PANSY

**lady's-eardrop** *or* **ladies'-eardrop** \ˌ≈≈ˈ≈,≈\ *n, pl* **lady's-eardrops** *or* **ladies'-eardrops** *but sing or pl in constr* **1 :** any of several plants of the genus *Fuchsia* (esp. *F. coccinea*) **2 :** SPOTTED JEWELWEED **3 :** BLEEDING HEART

**lady's-finger** \ˌ≈≈ˈ≈≈\ *n, pl* **lady's-fingers :** any of various plants with finger-shaped parts: as **a :** any of several legumes (as kidney vetch or bird's-foot trefoil) **b** *dial Eng* **:** CUCKOOPINT **c :** OKRA

**lady's-glove** \ˌ≈≈ˈ≈\ *n, pl* **lady's-gloves 1 :** FOXGLOVE **2** *dial Eng* **a :** FLEAWORT **b :** BIRD'S-FOOT TREFOIL 1a

**lady's gown** *n, Scots law* **:** a present made by a purchaser of real estate to the wife of the grantor on her renouncing her life interest in the property sold

**lady's-grass** \ˌ≈≈ˈ≈\ *n, pl* **lady's-grasses** *Austral* **:** a crab grass (*Digitaria sanguinalis*)

**la·dy·ship** \ˈlādē,ship, -di,-\ *n* [ME *ladishippe, lafdischipe*, fr. *ladi, lafdi* lady + *-shippe, -schipe* -ship] **1 :** the condition of being a lady **:** rank of lady **2** *often cap* **:** the personality of a woman having the rank or title of Lady — used in a mode of reference ⟨her *Ladyship*⟩ or of address ⟨your *Ladyship*⟩

**lady's hole** *n* **:** a place in an old-time man-of-war for keeping gunner's small stores

**lady's-laces** \ˌ≈≈ˈ≈\ *n, pl* **lady's-laces 1 :** REED CANARY GRASS **2 :** RIBBON GRASS

**lady's ladder** *or* **ladies' ladder** *n* **:** shrouds in which the ratlines are placed unusually close together

**lady's-lint** \ˌ≈≈ˈ≈\ *n, pl* **lady's-lints :** GREATER STITCHWORT

**lady's maid** *n* **:** a woman servant who cares for a lady's clothes and assists her in making her toilet

**lady's-maid** \ˈ≈≈ˈ≈\ *vb* [*lady's maid*] **:** to serve or attend as a lady's maid **:** MAID

**lady's man** *var of* LADIES' MAN
**lady's–mantle** \ˈ=ˌ=\ *n, pl* **lady's–mantles** [after *Our Lady*, the Virgin Mary] **:** any of several plants of the genus *Alchemilla; esp* **:** a common European herb (*A. xanthochlora*) having stems and petioles densely covered with spreading hairs
**lady's–nightcap** \ˈ=ˌ=\ *n, pl* **lady's–nightcaps** **1 :** WOOD ANEMONE b **2 :** HEDGE BINDWEED **3 :** a Canterbury bell (*Campanula medium*)
**lady's–paintbrush** \ˈ=ˌ=\ *n, pl* **lady's–paintbrushes** **:** ORANGE HAWKWEED
**lady's–pocket** \ˈ=ˌ=\ *also* **ladies' pocket** *n, pl* **lady's–pockets** *also* **ladies' pockets** **:** SPOTTED JEWELWEED
**lady's–purse** \ˈ=ˌ=\ *n, pl* **lady's–purses** **:** SHEPHERD'S PURSE
**lady's slipper** *or* **lady–slipper** *also* **ladies' slipper** \ˈlādē(z)-ˌ=\ *n* **1 :** any of several No. American temperate-zone orchids esp. of the genus *Cypripedium* having flowers whose shape suggests a slipper **2 :** GARDEN BALSAM **3** *dial Eng* **:** BIRD'S-FOOT TREFOIL 1a **4** *usu pl* **:** GARDEN COLUMBINE
**lady's–smock** \ˈlādē(z)ˌ=\ *also* **lady smock** *n, pl* **lady's–smocks** *also* **lady smocks** **1 :** any of several plants of the genus *Cardamine; esp* **:** CUCKOOFLOWER **2** *dial Eng* **:** HEDGE BINDWEED **3 :** a California toothwort (*Dentaria integrifolia*)
**lady's–sorrel** \ˈ=ˌ=\ *n, pl* **lady's–sorrels** **:** YELLOW WOOD SORREL
**lady's–thimble** \ˈ=ˌ=\ *n, pl* **lady's–thimbles** **1 :** HAREBELL 1 **2 :** FOXGLOVE 1

lady's slipper

**lady's thumb** *n* **:** a common widely distributed erect branched weedy annual herb (*Polygonum persicaria*) with purplish stems, racemes of small pink flowers, and large lanceolate leaves often with a blackish blotch suggesting a thumbprint
**lady's–tobacco** *var of* LADIES'-TOBACCO
**lady's tresses** *or* **lady's traces** *var of* LADIES' TRESSES
**lady's woman** *n* **:** LADY'S MAID
**lady tulip** *n* **:** a Eurasian tulip (*Tulipa clusiana*) with smooth glabrous stems and small flowers that are white tinged with rose — called also *candlestick tulip*
**lady washington geranium** *n, usu cap L&W* [after Martha *Washington* †1802, wife of George Washington †1799 and first lady of the White House] **:** MARTHA WASHINGTON GERANIUM
**lady wrack** *n* **:** BLADDER WRACK
**lae·lap·ti·dae** \lēˈlaptəˌdē\ *n pl, cap* [NL, irreg. fr. *Laelap-, Laelaps*, type genus (fr. L, name of a dog, fr. Gk *lailap-, lailaps* hurricane) + *-idae*] **:** a family of mites living as ectoparasites on animals
**lae·lia** \ˈlēlēə\ *n* [NL, perh. fr. Caius *Laelius fl* 2d cent. B.C. Roman statesman + NL *-ia*] **1** *cap* **:** a genus of Central and So. American orchids having solitary or racemose variously colored flowers with a 3-lobed labellum and pseudobulbs bearing one or two oblong leaves **2** *-s* **:** any plant of the genus *Laelia*
**laelia pink** *n, often cap L* **:** a dark purplish pink to light grayish purplish red
**laemmergeyer** *var of* LAMMERGEIER
**lae·mo·dip·o·da** \ˌlēməˈdipədə\ *n pl, cap* [NL, fr. *laemo-* (fr. Gk *laimos* throat, gullet) + *-dipoda* (fr. Gk *dipod-, dipous* having two feet) — more at GYMNOLAEMATA, DIPODOMYS] *in some classifications* **:** a division of Amphipoda comprising crustaceans (as the whale lice and members of the genus *Caprella*) in which the abdomen is small and rudimentary and the legs are often reduced to five pairs
**laender** *pl of* LAND
**laen·nec's cirrhosis** \(ˈ)lā¦nek(s)-, (ˈ)lē¦, ¦lā,ā¦\ *n, usu cap L* [after René T. H. *Laënnec* †1826 French physician] **:** hepatic cirrhosis in which increased connective tissue spreads out from the portal spaces compressing and distorting the lobules, causing impairment of liver function, and ultimately producing the typical hobnail liver
**lae·o·trop·ic** \¦lēə¦träpik\ *or* **lae·ot·ro·pous** \lēˈä·trəpəs\ *or* **lei·o·trop·ic** \¦līə¦träpik\ *adj* [*laeotropic* or *laeotropous* fr. Gk *laios* left + E *-tropic* or *-tropous*; *leiotropic* irreg. fr. Gk *laios* left + E *-tropic* — more at LEV-] **:** turning to the left **:** SINISTRAL — used esp. of various shells, of spiral cleavage patterns, or of the movement of volvox colonies
**lae·sio enor·mis** \ˈlēshēˌōēˈnȯrməs\ *or* **laesio ultra di·mi·di·um** \-ˈdəˈmidēəm\ *or* **laesio ultra du·plum** \-ˈd(y)üpləm\ *n* [*laesio enormis*, LL, lit., enormous injury; *laesio ultra dimidium*, L, injury over half; *laesio ultra duplum*, L, injury over double] *Roman & civil law* **:** the injury that is suffered by a vendor who has sold something for less than half its value or in some civil-law systems by a purchaser who has bought something at more than double its price and that in most cases gives the right of rescinding the sale
**laet** \ˈlat\ *n* -s [OE *lǣt*; perh. akin to OE *lǣtan* to let] **:** one of a class composed chiefly of freedmen with a status between tribesmen and slaves in ancient Kent
**lae·ta·re sunday** \lāˈtärē-, -ˌ(ˌ)rā-\ *n, usu cap L&S* [L *laetare* rejoice, 2d pers. sing. pres. imper. pass. of *laetare* to make glad, fr. the fact that *laetare* is the opening word of the introit for that day] **:** the fourth Sunday in Lent
**laetation** *n* -s [LL *laetatus* (past part. of *laetare* to fertilize, manure, fr. L, to make glad, fr. *laetus* glad, fertile) + E *-ion* — more at LARD] *obs* **:** MANURE
**lae·tic** \ˈlēd·ik\ *adj* [LL *laeticus* — more at LIEGE] **:** of or relating to a class of non-Roman cultivators of the soil during the later Roman empire who paid tribute for the lands which they occupied
**laev-** *or* **laevo-** — see LEV-
**lae·vi·gra·da** \ˌlēvəˈgrādə\ [NL, neut. pl., fr. *laevi-* (prob. irreg. fr. L *levis* light) + *-grada* (fr. L *gradi* to walk, step)] *syn of* PYCNOGONIDA
**laevo** *var of* LEVO
**la·farge cement** \ləˈfärzh-, -rj-\ *n* [fr. *Lafarge*, a trademark] **:** a nonstaining cement composed of plaster of paris, lime, and marble dust and used in mortar for setting marble and limestone
**la·fay·ette** \ˌläfēˈet, ˌlaf-\ *n* -s [after Marquis de *Lafayette* †1834 French statesman] **1 :** a butterfish (*Poronotus triacanthus*) **2 :** a spot (*Leiostomus xanthurus*)
**la flèche** \ləˈflesh\ *n, usu cap L&F* [fr. *La Flèche*, commune, Sarthe dept., France] **:** a domestic fowl of a French breed that is greenish black with a large V-shaped comb
**la france pink** *n, often cap L&F* [so called fr. *La France*, a variety of rose] **:** a moderate pink that is yellower and darker than arbutus pink and bluer and deeper than hydrangea pink — called also *debutante pink*
**laft** \ˈlaft\ *Scot var of* ¹LOFT
¹**lag** \ˈlag, -aa(ə)g, -aig\ *vb* **lagged; lagged; lagging; lags** [prob of Scand origin; akin to Norw *lagga* to go slowly] *vi* **1 :** to stay or fall behind **:** fail to keep up: **a** (1) **:** to move slowly **:** hang back **:** LINGER, LOITER ⟨as he neared the old home, his steps *lagged* —L.C.Douglas⟩ ⟨*lagged* behind intent on my collecting —David Fairchild⟩ ⟨*lagging* a step or two behind in embarrassment —Harold Sinclair⟩ ⟨at no time in my life have seconds *lagged* so much —T.B.Bruff⟩ ⟨business continued to ~ —*Wall Street Jour.*⟩ (2) **:** DELAY, PROCRASTINATE ⟨this will let applicants ~ a bit in providing this information —*Wall Street Jour.*⟩ **b :** to move, function, or develop with comparative slowness: (1) **:** to be slow or become retarded esp. by comparison with something closely associated or related — usu. used with *behind* ⟨accomplishment *lagging* behind purpose⟩ ⟨rents *lagged* far behind prices —W.P.Webb⟩ ⟨new hospital construction continues to ~ behind the need —D.D. Eisenhower⟩ ⟨through inattention, she *lagged* behind at school —Elizabeth Taylor⟩ (2) **:** to become retarded in attaining maximum value or development ⟨the current ~*s* behind the voltage⟩ ⟨insulin of the modified protamine type has relatively quick action, for it ~*s* two hours only —*Yr. Bk. of Endocrinology*⟩ **c :** to slacken or weaken little by little **:** FLAG ⟨interest in the fascinating drama of French politics never *lagged* —C.G.Bowers⟩ ⟨that concern with French books and reading has never *lagged* —Ruth Gagliardo⟩ **2 a :** to shoot a taw or toss a jack toward a line marked on the ground to determine the order of play in ringer or jacks **b :** to cause a cue ball to rebound from the foot cushion of a billiard table so as to stop as near as possible to the head cushion or sometimes the head string (as for determining order of play) **:** STRING **c :** to throw coins or counters to decide possession by relative closeness to a fixed mark ⟨gambling with Bryan and McKinley buttons, *lagging* at a line —C.L.Baldridge⟩ ~ *vt* **1** *obs* **:** to cause to lag **:** RETARD **2 :** to lag behind ⟨a circuit in which the current ~*s* the voltage —A.E.Fitzgerald⟩ ⟨the one that reaches a particular point in a cycle last is said to ~ the other —N.M.Cooke & John Markus⟩ **3 :** to pitch or shoot (as a coin, counter, marble) at a mark ⟨beer corks *lagged*, in lieu of pennies, along the sidewalk cracks —Nelson Algren⟩ ⟨~ aggies —P.D. Boles⟩ **syn** see DELAY
²**lag** \ˈ"\ *n* -s **1 :** one that lags **:** one that is last ⟨the ~ of all the flock —Alexander Pope⟩ **2 lags** *pl, obs* **:** DREGS, LEES **3** *obs* **:** the lowest class ⟨the common ~ of people —Shak.⟩ **4 a :** the action or the condition of lagging **:** a falling or staying behind ⟨a region marked in the recent past by relative conservatism, inertia, and ~ —Hylan Lewis⟩ ⟨a series of spurts and ~*s* —*Times Lit. Supp.*⟩ ⟨this work must go forward without ~ —D.D.Eisenhower⟩ ⟨a definite ~ had come in business and industry —W.A.White⟩ ⟨a considerable ~ of the blood pressure curve behind the G curve —H.G.Armstrong⟩ **b :** comparative slowness or retardation (as in movement, operation, development) ⟨the social and political ~ that makes the world go on operating in terms of old antagonisms —*Saturday Rev.*⟩ ⟨adjustments for price ~ —*Collier's Yr. Bk.*⟩ ⟨this apparent ~ behind American practice —O.S.Nock⟩ ⟨their intellectual ~ in comparison with the rest of Europe —S.H.Cross⟩ **c :** a falling behind or retardation of one phenomenon with respect to another phenomenon to which it is closely related; *esp* **:** delay of a physical effect behind its cause or of the response of an indicating instrument behind the changed condition it registers ⟨the ~ of sound in some opera houses —Warwick Braithwaite⟩ ⟨the ~ of an alternating current in an inductive circuit behind the impressed voltage⟩ ⟨~ of strain behind stress in an imperfectly elastic material under varying stress⟩ ⟨because they have no ~ and indicate an error as it occurs, the horizon and gyro are a tremendous aid in flying the airplane more easily and precisely —H.L.Redfield⟩ **d** (1) **:** an amount of lag or the time during which lagging continues **:** degree or length of retardation or delay ⟨the ~ between the present and the latest reasonably accurate figures may be four or five years —E.W.Miller⟩ ⟨during this ~ the government should provide help —H.S.Truman⟩ ⟨in Scotland the ~ was a longer one —Ian Finlay⟩ ⟨made up more than two thirds of the ~ behind whites with which they came North —A.L.Kroeber⟩ (2) **:** a space or period of time esp. between related events or phenomena **:** INTERVAL ⟨the ~ between composition and publication is not a uniform one —*Nation*⟩ ⟨in the ~ between basketball season and baseball —Norman Mailer⟩ ⟨in the ~*s* of silence which fell over the shouts —Lawrence Durrell⟩ **5 :** the action of lagging for opening shot (as in ringer or billiards)
³**lag** \ˈ"\ *adj* **1 :** LAST, HINDMOST — used chiefly in the phrase *lag end* ⟨the *lag* end of my life —Shak.⟩ **2** *chiefly dial* **:** coming tardily after or behind **:** BELATED, LATE
⁴**lag** \ˈ"\ *vt* **lagged; lagged; lagging; lags** [origin unknown] **1** *obs* **:** STEAL **2** *slang* **a :** to transport for crime or send to penal servitude; *broadly* **:** to send to jail **:** IMPRISON ⟨the first big-timers to be *lagged* for using the mails —D.W.Maurer⟩ **b** *slang chiefly Brit* **:** ARREST, APPREHEND ⟨don't kindle a fire, unless you want to get *lagged* —Joseph Furphy⟩
⁵**lag** \ˈlag\ *n* -s [⁴*lag*] **1 a** *slang chiefly Brit* **:** a person transported for crime or sent to penal servitude **:** one who is serving or has served a term in prison **:** CONVICT, JAILBIRD ⟨the typical young ~ —*Times Lit. Supp.*⟩ **b** *Austral* **:** EX-CONVICT; *esp* **:** a convict immigrant to Australia ⟨impossible for him not to know that his father was a ~ —Rex Ingamells⟩ **2** *slang chiefly Brit* **:** a term of transportation or penal servitude **:** jail sentence **:** STRETCH
⁶**lag** \ˈlag, -aa(ə)g, -aig\ *n* -s [prob. of Scand origin; akin to ON *lögg* rim of a barrel, Sw *lagg* stave] **1 :** a barrel stave **2 a :** a wooden stave or slat forming part of a covering for a cylindrical object (as a boiler or a carding-machine cylinder) **b :** a strip of any of various materials (as felt or asbestos) used in making a covering or casing esp. for a cylindrical structure **3 :** a bearing strip in an arch or vault centering **4** *textile manuf* **a :** a wooden link in a pattern chain **b :** a large pin in the revolving cylinder of a picker
⁷**lag** \ˈ"\ *vt* **lagged; lagged; lagging; lags** **1 :** to cover or provide with lags or lagging (as for protection against wear or thermal insulation) **2 :** to fasten with lag screws ⟨~ a machine to a bench⟩
**lag-** *or* **lago-** *comb form* [NL, fr. L, fr. Gk *lagō-*, fr. *lagōs*] **:** hare ⟨*lagophthalmos*⟩ ⟨*lagopous*⟩
**lag·an** \ˈlagən\ *also* **lag·end** \-nd\ *or* **lag·on** \-n\ *or* **li·gan** *or* **li·gen** \ˈlīgən\ *or* **lo·gan** \ˈlōg-\ *n* -s [MF *lagan, lagand*, or ML *laganum* debris washed up from the sea, the right to possess such debris, prob. of Gmc origin; akin to ON *lōg* law — more at LAW] **:** goods thrown into the sea with a buoy attached in order that they may be found again — distinguished esp. in law from *flotsam* and *jetsam*
**lag bolt** *n* [⁶*lag*] **:** LAG SCREW
**lag–bolt** \ˈ=ˌ=\ *vt* [*lag bolt*] **:** LAG-SCREW
**lag b'omer** *or* **lag be·omer** *or* **lag ba·omer** \ˈlägˈbōmə(r), -gbəˈō-\ *n, usu cap L&O* [Heb, 33d in omer] **:** a Jewish holiday falling on the 33d day of the omer and commemorating the heroism of Bar Cocheba and Akiba — see OMER 2b
**la·gen** \ˈlägən\ *n* -s [L *lagena* large flask] **:** an obsolete unit of capacity for liquids
**la·ge·na** \ləˈjēnə\ *n* [L, large flask, fr. Gk *lagynos*] **1** *pl* **lagenas** \-nəz\ *or* **lage·nae** \-ē(ˌ)nē\ **:** FLASK, BOTTLE **2** *pl* **lagenae** [NL, fr. L, large flask] **:** the terminal part of the cochlea; *esp* **:** a knob-shaped appendage of the sacculus of a bird or reptile corresponding to the cochlea of a fish or amphibian **3** *cap* [NL, fr. L, large flask] **:** a genus of Foraminifera having a single-chambered often flask-shaped test
**lag·e·na·ri·a** \ˌlajəˈna(a)rēə\ *n, cap* [NL, fr. L *lagena* large flask + NL *-aria*] **:** a genus of herbaceous vines (family Cucurbitaceae) characterized by more or less bottle-shaped fruit and having as its only species the bottle gourd
**lag·e·nid·i·a·ce·ae** \ˌlajəˌnidēˈāsēˌē\ *n pl, cap* [NL, fr. *Lagenidium*, type genus (fr. L *lagena* large flask + NL *-idium*) + *-aceae*] **:** a family of freshwater aquatic fungi (order Lagenidiales) having zoospores that are formed in a vesicle or that complete their development in a vesicle
**lag·e·nid·i·a·les** \-ˈā(ˌ)lēz\ *n pl, cap* [NL, fr. *Lagenidium* + *-ales*] **:** an order of chiefly aquatic fungi (subclass Oomycetes) that are mostly parasitic in algae and water molds and that have a simple or somewhat branched holocarpic thallus
**la·ge·ni·form** \ləˈjēnəˌfȯrm\ *adj* [L *lagena* large flask + E *-iform*] **:** shaped like a flask **:** dilated below and tapering to a slender neck above
**lag·e·noph·o·ra** \ˌlajəˈnäf(ə)rə\ *n, cap* [NL, fr. *lageno-* (fr. Gk *lagēnos, lagynos* large flask) + *-phora*] **:** a small genus of composite herbs of New Zealand and Australia that have small solitary flower heads with white or light blue ray flowers and yellow disk flowers and that differ from members of the genus *Bellis* by possession of terminally beaked achenes
**lag·e·nos·to·ma** \-ˈästəmə\ *n, cap* [NL, fr. *lageno-* (fr. Gk *lagēnos* flask) + *-stoma*] **:** a form genus of Carboniferous seed ferns based on fossil seeds
¹**la·ger** \ˈlägə(r), ˈlȧg-\ *also* **lager beer** *n* -s [*lager*, short for *lager beer*, part trans. of G *lagerbier* beer made for storage, fr. *lager* camp, couch, lair (fr. OHG *legar* couch, bed) + *bier* beer (fr. OHG *bior*) — more at LAIR, BEER] **:** a beer brewed by bottom fermentation and stored in refrigerated cellars for clarification and maturing and usu. dry, light in color, and well carbonated
²**lager** \ˈ"\ *vt* -ED/-ING/-S **:** to store (beer) during a period of aging often accompanied by a secondary fermentation
**lager** *var of* LAAGER
**la·ger·stroe·mia** \ˌlägə(r)ˈstrēmēə, ˌläg-, ˌlag-\ *n, cap* [NL, fr. Magnus *Lagerstroem* †1759 Swedish naturalist and merchant + NL *-ia*] **:** a genus of shrubs (family Lythraceae) of tropical Asia and Africa with usu. showy paniculate flowers and capsular fruits with winged seeds — see CRAPE MYRTLE
**la·get·ta** \ləˈjed·ə\ *n, cap* [NL, fr. AmerSp *lageto* lagetto] **:** a genus of West Indian shrubs or small trees (family Thymelaeaceae) with large alternate leaves and spicate or racemose white flowers
**la·get·to** \ləˈged·(ˌ)ō\ *n* -s [AmerSp *lageto*] *Jamaica* **:** LACEBARK
**lag fault** *n* [¹*lag*] **:** a minor low-angle thrust fault resulting within an overthrust mass from one part of the mass being thrust farther than an adjacent higher or lower part
**lag·gar** \ˈlagə(r)\ *n* -s [Hindi] **:** LUGGAR; *esp* **:** a female luggar
¹**lag·gard** \ˈlagə(r)d, ˈlaag-, ˈlaig-\ *adj* [¹*lag* + *-ard* (n. suffix)] **:** lagging or tending to lag **:** slow or relatively slow to act, move, follow, or respond **:** BACKWARD, BEHINDHAND, DILATORY, SLUGGISH ⟨has been very ~ about erecting the sound substance of a continental defense —R.E.Lapp⟩ ⟨~ payments . . . will always be with us —T.A.Sumberg⟩ ⟨the ~ speed of sound —C.G.Burke⟩ ⟨entering, with ~ foot —Hugh Walpole⟩ **syn** see SLOW
²**laggard** \ˈ"\ *n* -s **:** one that lags **:** LOITERER, LINGERER ⟨~*s* who detain us on our course —*Times Lit. Supp.*⟩ ⟨swift to perceive an opportunity and no ~ in profiting by it —S.H. Adams⟩ ⟨when a herd does stampede, it is usually the leaders and the ~*s* that are caught —James Stevenson-Hamilton⟩ ⟨of all sciences, aesthetic has been the greatest ~ —Roger Fry⟩
¹**lag·gard·ly** \-lē, -li\ *adv* **:** in a laggard manner ⟨Mercury, setting ~ in the west —William Beebe⟩
²**laggardly** \ˈ"\ *adj* **:** being laggard or a laggard ⟨choked on a ~ crumb —Monica Stirling⟩ ⟨the ~ employer . . . should learn to take advantage of government assistance —*Manchester Guardian Weekly*⟩
**lag·gard·ness** *n* -ES **:** the quality or state of being laggard ⟨the long ~ of social legislation —R.E.Montgomery⟩
**lagged** *adj* [fr. past part. of ¹*lag*] **:** affected by lagging **:** showing or reflecting a lag (as in time) **:** DELAYED, RETARDED, TARDY ⟨the influence of disposable income is partially ~ —E.C. Bratt⟩
¹**lag·ger** \ˈlagə(r), -aag-, -aig-\ *n* -s [¹*lag* + *-er*] **:** one that lags or falls behind **:** LAGGARD, LOITERER
²**lagger** *vi* -ED/-ING/-S *obs* **:** LAG, LOITER
³**lag·ger** \ˈlagə(r)\ *n* -s [⁴*lag* + *-er*] *slang chiefly Brit* **:** CONVICT, EX-CONVICT
⁴**lag·ger** \ˈlagə(r), -aag-, -aig-\ *n* -s [⁷*lag* + *-er*] **:** one that covers or provides with lags or lagging
**lag·gin** *or* **lag·gen** \ˈlagən\ *n* -s [prob. of Scand origin; akin to ON *lögg* rim of a barrel] *chiefly Scot* **:** the staves of a hooped vessel (as a barrel or cask) esp. at their bottom — usu. used in pl.
¹**lag·ging** \ˈlagiŋ\ *n* -s [fr. *lagging*, gerund of ⁴*lag*] *slang chiefly Brit* **:** a term or sentence of imprisonment, transportation, or penal servitude
²**lag·ging** \ˈ", -aag-, -aig-\ *n* -s [⁶*lag* + *-ing*] **:** a lag or material used for making lags: as **a :** material applied for thermal insulation esp. around a cylindrical object ⟨during cold weather, the oil tank and the oil lines may be covered with asbestos padding, called ~, to keep the oil warm during flight —B.A.Shields⟩ **b :** poles or planking erected to prevent cave-ins in earthwork (as in a mine or tunnel) **c :** wooden strips for transferring to the centering form the weight of an arch under construction **d :** a detachable protective surface (as on a pulley or a drum)
**lag·ging·ly** *adv* [fr. *lagging*, pres. part. of ¹*lag* + *-ly*] **:** in a lagging manner **:** LOITERINGLY, TARDILY
**lag gravel** *n* [²*lag*] **1 :** residual gravel remaining on a surface after finer materials have been removed by winds **2 :** gravel rolled or dragged along a stream bed at a slower rate than the finer particles of sediment
**la·gid·i·um** \ləˈjidēəm\ *n, cap* [NL, fr. Gk *lagidion*, dim. of *lagōs* hare] **:** a genus of histricomorph rodents (family Chinchillidae) comprising the mountain vizcachas
**laglast** \ˈ=ˌ=\ *n* **:** one that lags or lingers to the last ⟨~ stragglers⟩
**lag line** *n* [¹*lag*] **:** a line toward which players lag (as in marbles)
**-lag·nia** \ˈlagnēə, ˈlaig-\ *n comb form* -s [NL, fr. Gk *lagneia*] **:** lust ⟨copro*lagnia*⟩
**la·gniappe** \ˈlanˌyap, =ˈ=\ *n* -s [AmerF (Louisiana), fr. AmerSp *la ñapa* the lagniappe, fr. Sp *la* (the fem. of *el*, def. art., the) + AmerSp *ñapa, yapa* lagniappe, fr. Quechua *yápa* addition — more at LARIAT] **1 a** *chiefly Louisiana* **:** a small gift given a customer by a merchant at the time of a purchase ⟨a sack of lemon drops for ~ with the groceries⟩ ⟨giving her half a yard extra for ~ —Lyle Saxon⟩ **b :** something given or obtained gratuitously or by way of bonus or good measure ⟨the . . . beautiful widow from whom he first accepts a reward of five thousand dollars, and later her love as a sort of ~ —Neal Cross⟩ **2 :** a gratuity of any kind **:** TIP
**-lag·ny** \¦lagnē, -ni\ *n comb form* -ES [ISV, fr. NL *-lagnia*] **:** -LAGNIA
**lago-** — see LAG-
**la·goa san·ta man** \ləˈgōəˈsantə-\ *n, usu cap L&S* [fr. *Lagoa Santa*, city in Brazil, near where the remains were found] **:** an extinct So. American man with a markedly long, narrow, and high-vaulted cranium known from skeletal remains found in Brazilian caves and orig. regarded as an extremely primitive human type but now usu. held to be a product of inbreeding of the original Mongoloid American stock
**lag·o·chi·las·ca·ris** \ˌlagōkīˈlaskərəs\ *n, cap* [NL, fr. *lag-* + *chil-* + *Ascaris*] **:** a genus of nematode worms believed to be normally parasitic in the intestine of the clouded leopard but in a few instances encountered as a subcutaneous parasite of man in Trinidad and Dutch Guiana
**lag of the tide :** the interval by which the time of high or low water falls behind the mean time in the 2d and 4th quarters of the moon — opposed to *priming of the tide*
**lag·o·morph** \ˈlagəˌmȯrf\ *n* -s [NL *Lagomorpha*] **:** an animal of the order Lagomorpha **:** HARE, RABBIT, PIKA
**lag·o·mor·pha** \ˌ==ˈmȯrfə\ *n pl, cap* [NL, fr. *lag-* + *-morpha*] **:** an order of Eutheria comprising gnawing mammals (as the rabbits, hares, and pikas) that resemble the rodents but have two pairs of upper incisors one behind the other, being formerly regarded as rodents, and then constituting a suborder (Duplicidentata) of Rodentia — **lag·o·mor·phic** \¦==¦mȯrfik\ *adj* — **lag·o·mor·phous** \-fəs\ *adj*
**lag·o·my·i·dae** \ˌlagəˈmīəˌdē\ [NL, fr. *Lagomys* (syn. of *Ochotona*) (fr. *lag-* + *-mys*) + *-idae*] *syn of* OCHOTONIDAE
**lagon** *var of* LAGAN
¹**la·goon** *also* **la·gune** \ləˈgün\ *n* -s *often attrib* [F & It; F *lagune*, fr. It *laguna*, fr. L *lacuna* pit, pool, pond, fr. *lacus* lake — more at LAKE] **1 a :** a shallow sound, channel, pond, or lake near or communicating with the sea ⟨~*s* of Venice⟩ ⟨the ~ of a coral island⟩ — see ATOLL **b :** a shallow freshwater pond or lake usu. near or communicating with a larger lake or a river ⟨long freshwater ~*s* yellow with lagoon flowers —Willa Cather⟩ ⟨riverbed ~*s* —*Amer. Guide Series: Ark.*⟩ **2** [It *lagone*, aug. of *lago*, fr. L *lacus*] **:** a pool esp. in a basin formed by a hot spring **3 :** a shallow artificial pond for the natural oxidation of sewage and ultimate drying of the sludge
²**lagoon** \ˈ"\ *vt* -ED/-ING/-S **:** to subject (sewage) to natural oxidation and drying in a lagoon
**la·goon·al** \-nᵊl\ *adj* **:** of or relating to a lagoon ⟨~ and basinal areas —*Jour. of Geol.*⟩ ⟨a ~ sedimentary origin is indicated —A.M.Bateman⟩
**la·goon·side** \-nˌsīd\ *n* **:** the land bordering on a lagoon
**lag·oph·thal·mos** *or* **lag·oph·thal·mus** \ˌlaˌgäfˈthalməs\ *n* -ES [NL, fr. L & Gk; L *lagophthalmos* person afflicted with lagophthalmos, fr. Gk *lagōphthalmos*, adj., hare-eyed, unable to close the eye, fr. *lagōs* hare + *ophthalmos* eye] **:** pathological incomplete closure of the eyelids **:** inability to close the eyelids fully
**la·go·pous** \ləˈgōpəs\ *adj* [Gk *lagōpous* ptarmigan, a plant (lit., rough-footed like a hare)] **:** having hairy rhizomes suggestive of the foot of a hare
**la·go·pus** \ˈ"\ *n, cap* [NL, fr. L, ptarmigan, a plant, fr. Gk *lagōpous*, fr. *lagōs* hare + *pous* foot] **:** a genus of northern game birds (family Tetraonidae) comprising the ptarmigans and the red grouse
**lag·or·ches·tes** \ˌlaˌgȯ(r)ˈkeˌstēz\ *n, cap* [NL, fr. *lag-* + Gk *orchēstēs* dancer, fr. *orcheisthai* to dance — more at ORCHESTRA] **:** a genus consisting of the hare wallabies

**la·gos** \'lä,gäs\ *adj, usu cap* [fr. *Lagos*, city in Nigeria] **:** of or from Lagos, the capital of Nigeria **:** of the kind or style prevalent in Lagos

**lagos ebony** *n, usu cap L* [fr. *Lagos*, former province of Nigeria] **:** a West African timber tree (*Diospyros dendo*) with hard black heartwood

**lagos rubber** *n, usu cap L* [fr. *Lagos*, former province of Nigeria] **:** high-grade rubber yielded in moderate quantity by a tropical African tree (*Funtumia elastica*) sometimes cultivated prior to the general cultivation of Brazilian rubber trees

**la·gos·to·mus** \lə'gästəməs\ *n, cap* [NL, fr. *lag-* + *-stomus*] **:** a genus of hystricomorph rodents (family Chinchillidae) comprising the plains vizcacha

**lag·o·thrix** \'lagə,thriks\ *n, cap* [NL, fr. *lag-* + *-thrix*] **:** a genus consisting of the woolly monkeys

**la·gran·gi·an function** \lə'granjēən-\ *n, usu cap L* [Joseph L. *Lagrange* †1813 Italian-born geometer and astronomer in France + E *-ian*] **:** KINETIC POTENTIAL

**lag·ri·man·do** \,lägrə¦män(,)dō, ¦lag-\ *adj (or adv)* [It, lit., weeping, lamenting, fr. L *lacrimandus*, gerundive of *lacrimare* to weep, shed tears — more at LACRIMATORY] **:** LACRIMANDO

**lag·ri·mo·so** \-mō(-\ *adj (or adv)* [It, lit., tearful, lachrymose, fr. L *lacrimosus* — more at LACHRYMOSE] **:** LACRIMOSO

**la grippe** \lə'grip, lä'-\ *n* [F, the grippe] **:** GRIPPE

**lags** *pl of* LAG, *pres 3d sing of* LAG

**lag screw** *n* [⁶*lag*; fr. its original use in securing lags to drums or cylinders] **:** a screw having a wrench head and woodscrew threads terminating in a point — called also *lag bolt*

lag screw

**lag–screw** \'=,=\ *vt* [*lag screw*] **:** to fasten or join with a lag screw

**lag·ting** *or* **lag·thing** \'läg,tiŋ\ *n* -s *often cap* [Norw *lagting*, fr. *lag* company, society (fr. ON, layer, due place, *lög*, pl., law) + *ting* parliament, thing (fr. ON *thing*) — more at LAW, THING] **:** a Scandinavian legislative body: **a :** the upper section of the Norwegian parliament **b :** the legislature of the Faeroe islands

**¹la·gu·na** \lə'günə\ *n* -s [Sp, fr. L *lacuna* — more at LAGOON] **:** LAGOON, LAKE, POND ⟨salt lakes and ~s within the tropics almost always have foul bottom waters —W.C.Krumbein & R.M.Garrels⟩

**²laguna** \"\ *n, pl* **laguna** *or* **lagunas** *usu cap* [Sp, pond, lagoon; fr. the lagoon near the site of the tribe's pueblo] **1 a :** a Keres pueblo people of New Mexico **b :** a member of such people **2 :** the language of the Laguna people

**lagune** *var of* LAGOON

**la·gu·ne·ro** \,lägü'nā(,)rō\ *n, pl* **lagunero** *or* **laguneros** *usu cap* [MexSp, fr. Sp *lagunero*, adj., of a lagoon, fr. *laguna* lagoon] **1 :** an extinct Uto-Aztecan people or group of peoples of northern Mexico **2 :** a member of a Lagunero people

**la·gu·rus** \lə'gyürəs\ *n, cap* [NL, fr. *lag-* + *-urus*] **:** a genus of European grasses with the spikelets in woolly heads — see HARE'S-TAIL GRASS

**la·hai·na disease** \lə'hīnə-\ *n, usu cap L* [fr. *Lahaina*, district and city in Maui, Hawaii] **:** a fungal root disease of sugar cane

**la·har** \'lä,här\ *n* -s [Jav] **:** a mudflow containing much volcanic debris

**lah–di–dah** *var of* LA-DI-DA

**lahn·da** \'ländə\ *n* -s *cap* **:** an Indic language of West Punjab

**la·hore** \lə'hō(ə)r, -hȯ(ə)r\ *adj, usu cap* [fr. *Lahore*, city in Pakistan] **:** of or from the city of Lahore, Pakistan **:** of the kind or style prevalent in Lahore

**la·hu** \'lä,hü\ *n, pl* **lahu** *or* **lahus** *usu cap* **1 a :** a widespread group of peoples inhabiting the hilly region between the Salween and Mekong rivers in northern Thailand, Laos, southern Yunnan, and the Shan States of Burma **b :** a member of any of such peoples **2 :** the Tibeto-Burman language of the Lahu people

**la·hu·li** \'lähə,lē\ *n, pl* **lahuli** *or* **lahulis** *cap* **1 :** a native or inhabitant of Lahul, northern Kashmir **2 :** the Tibetan dialect of the Lahuli

**¹lai** \'lā\ *n* -s [F, fr. OF — more at LAY] **1 :** a medieval type of short tale in French literature that is usu. in octosyllabic verse and deals with subjects of Celtic origin often connected with Arthur or the Round Table **2 :** a medieval type of lyric poem revived in the 17th century and composed in unsymmetrical couplets each sung to its own melody

**²lai** \'lī\ *n, pl* **lai** *or* **lais** *usu cap* **1 a :** a Mongoloid people of the Chin Hills in Burma **b :** a member of such people **2 :** the Tibeto-Burman language of the Lai people

**la·ic** \'lāik\ *n* -s [LL *laicus*, adj. & n., fr. LGk *laikos*, fr. Gk, of the people, fr. *laos* people + *-ikos* -ic] **:** a member of the laity **:** LAYMAN ⟨the book has a place . . . not in the cloisters but among the ~s —G.W.Johnson⟩

**la·i·cal** \-ə̇kəl\ *also* **la·ic** \-āik\ *adj* [*laical* fr. LL *laicalis*, fr. *laicus* + L *-alis* -al; *laic* fr. LL *laicus*] **:** of or relating to a layman or the laity ⟨taking off his collar, which till now he has worn in clerical fashion . . . and setting it in *laical* position —Rebecca West⟩ — **la·i·cal·ly** \-ə̇k(ə)lē\ *adv*

**laich** \'läk\ *Scot var of* LOW

**la·i·cism** \'lāə,sizəm\ *n* -s [*laic* + *-ism*] **:** the nonclerical control or administration of a political system or a social function

**la·ic·i·ty** \lā'isəd·ē\ *n* -ES [F *laïcité*, fr. LL *laicus* + F *-ité* -ity] **:** control or influence by the laity

**la·i·ci·za·tion** \,lāəsə'zāshən, -,sī'-\ *n* -s **:** the process or act of laicizing

**la·i·cize** \'lāə,sīz\ *vt* -ED/-ING/-s [*laic* + *-ize*] **:** to make lay **:** put under the direction of or throw open to laymen ⟨resisting efforts of the state to ~ education —*New Republic*⟩

**¹laid** \'lād\ *Scot var of* LOAD

**²laid** \"\ *adj* [fr. past part. of ¹*lay*] **1** *of paper* **:** watermarked with laid lines — compare WOVE **2** *of embroidery* **:** made by couching

**laid fabric** *n* **:** a fabric lacking weft threads and having the warp threads bonded together by rubber latex or other binding material

**laid line** *n* **:** any of the closely spaced parallel lines in laid paper made by laid wires

**laid·ly** \'lādli\ *chiefly Scot var of* LOATHLY

**laid wire** *n* **:** any of the wires on the surface of a dandy roll running parallel with its axis

**laigh** \'läk\ *Scot var of* LOW

**laik** \'läk\ *Scot var of* LACK

**lain** *past part of* LIE

**lainch** \'länch\ *chiefly Scot var of* LAUNCH

**laine** \'lān\ *n* -s [F, fr. L *lana* wool — more at WOOL] **:** woolen cloth **:** WOOL

**¹lair** \'la(a)(ə)r, 'le|, |ə, *Scot* 'lār\ *n* -s [ME *lair, leir*, fr. OE *leger*; akin to OHG *legar* bed, act of lying, cohabitation, ON *legr* grave, cohabitation, Goth *ligrs* bed; derivative fr. the root of E ¹*lie*] **1** *Scot* **:** a burial lot in a graveyard **2 a** *dial Brit* **:** a resting or sleeping place **:** BED ⟨upon a ~ composed of straw with a blanket stretched over it —Sir Walter Scott⟩ **b** *dial Brit* **:** a place where pastured livestock lie or rest **c** *Brit* **:** a pen or shed for cattle on the way to market or kept for slaughtering **3 a :** the bed or living place of a wild animal **:** DEN **b :** something that resembles the den of an animal: as (1) **:** a hidden base of operations ⟨the sinking of a boat by the . . . pirates to cut off approach to their ~ —*Amer. Guide Series: La.*⟩ ⟨believed to be at least one of the other ~s from which the zeppelins sallied forth to the attack —*Times Hist. of the War*⟩ (2) **:** a secret place **:** HIDEAWAY ⟨got up from her ~ among the strawberries and wandered across the meadow —John Buchan⟩ ⟨the children followed the grown-ups into the house, and retiring to their ~ under the sewing machine studied the new personage from safety —Oliver La Farge⟩

**²lair** \"\ *vi* -ED/-ING/-s **:** to make or go to a lair **:** REST ⟨where shall we ~ today for from now we follow new trails —Rudyard Kipling⟩ ⟨carnivores of the late Wisconsin period undoubtedly ~ed . . . intermittently with human occupation —F.C.Hibben⟩

**³lair** \"\ *n* -s [Sc, fr. ME (northern dial.) *lar* learning, fr. OE *lār* lore — more at LORE] *chiefly Scot* **:** LORE; *esp* **:** knowledge acquired through instruction

**⁴lair** \"\ *n* -s [ME, fr. ON *leir* loam, clay; akin to ON *līm* lime — more at LIME] *chiefly Scot* **:** MIRE, MUD

**⁵lair** \"\ *vb* -ED/-ING/-s *vt, chiefly Scot* **:** to cause to sink in the mire ⟨watery flows in which sheep and cattle sometimes ~ themselves —William McIlwraith⟩ ~ *vi, chiefly Scot* **:** WALLOW

**laird** \'la(a)(ə)rd, 'le|, |əd, *Scot* 'lārd\ *n* -s [ME (northern dial.) *lard, laverd* lord — more at LORD] *Scot* **:** a landed proprietor; *esp* **:** the owner of a small estate

**laird·ship** \-,ship\ *n* [*laird* + *-ship*] **:** the estate belonging to a laird

**lairstone** \'=,=\ *n* [¹*lair* + *stone*] *Scot* **:** GRAVESTONE

**lais** *pl of* LAI

**laisse** \'les, 'lās\ *n* -s [F, fr. OF, lit., string, leash — more at LEASH] **:** the irregular strophe of Old French poetry; *esp* **:** a strophe of the chansons de geste

**¹laissez–faire** *also* **laisser–faire** \,le|(,)sā¦fa(a)|(ə)r, ¦la|, -fe|, |ə *also* |(,)zā¦f- *sometimes* |sē¦f- *or* |si¦f- *or* |zē¦f- *or* |zi¦f-\ *adj* [*laissez-faire* fr. F *laissez faire* let (people) do (as they choose) (motto of 18th cent. Fr. economists who protested excessive government regulation of industry); *laisser-faire* fr. F *laisser faire* to let (people) do (as they choose)] **:** of, adhering to, or favoring the doctrine or practice of laissez-faire ⟨in economic philosophy the High Victorians were mainly *laissez-faire* —*Saturday Rev.*⟩ ⟨economic liberalism of the *laissez-faire* type —Frank Thilly⟩ ⟨the social disorganization and *laisser-faire* purposelessness . . . present in the cultural life of these young people —Ernest & Pearl Beaglehole⟩

**²laissez–faire** *also* **laisser–faire** \"\ *n* -s **1 :** a doctrine opposing governmental interference (as by regulation or subsidy) in economic affairs beyond the minimum necessary for the maintenance of peace and property rights ⟨the reaction against free trade and *laissez-faire* —*Atlantic*⟩ ⟨few people . . . hold that *laisser-faire* could solve the economic problems of the British community —*Economist*⟩ ⟨a central position between *laissez-faire* and a planned economy —J.S.Schapiro⟩ — compare FREE ENTERPRISE, MERCANTILISM, PLANNED ECONOMY **2 :** a philosophy or practice characterized by a usu. deliberate abstention from direction or planning **:** a policy of noninterference esp. with individual freedom of choice and action ⟨a poverty that proclaimed *laissez-faire* in ethics —Francis Hackett⟩ ⟨the unhampered elective system which is merely the pedagogical form of . . . *laisser-faire* —P.E.More⟩ ⟨a policy of *laisser-faire* towards the artists—*Times Lit Supp.*⟩ — compare MANAGERIALISM

**laissez–faire·ism** \|(ə),rizəm\ *n* -s **:** the doctrine of laissez-faire ⟨the classic statement of the judicial version of *laissez-faireism* —E.S.Corwin⟩

**laissez–passer** \-,pa¦sā, -,pá¦-, -,pä¦-\ *n* -s [F, fr. *laissez passer* let (someone) pass] **:** PERMIT, PASS ⟨thought a *laissez-passer* rendered him immune to search —John Gunther⟩ ⟨a new *laissez-passer* to the frontiers of the universe —Ritchie Calder⟩ ⟨agreements to enable officials . . . to use the United Nations *laissez-passer* for official travel —*New Internat'l Yr. Bk.*⟩

**lait** \'lāt\ *vb* -ED/-ING/-s [ME *laiten*, fr. ON *leita*, causative fr. the root of ON *līta* to look — more at LITMUS] *vt, dial Eng* **:** to search for ~ *vi, dial Eng* **:** SEARCH

**lai·tance** \'lāt°n(t)s\ *n* -s [F, fr. *lait* milk (fr. L *lact-, lac*) + *-ance* — more at GALAXY] **:** an accumulation of fine particles on the surface of freshly placed concrete occurring when there is an upward movement of water through the concrete due to the presence of too much mixing water, to excessive tamping, or to vibration of the concrete

**¹laith** \'lāth\ *Brit var of* LATHE

**²laith** \'lāth\ *Scot var of* LOATH

**³laith** \'lāth\ *Scot var of* LOATHE

**la·i·ty** \'lāəd·ē, -ətē, -i\ *n* -ES [⁵*lay* + *-ty*] **1 :** the great body of the people of a religious faith as distinguished from its clergy **2 :** the great body of the people as distinguished from those of a particular profession (as medicine or law) or those specially skilled ⟨writers who can interpret this wholeness, both to their colleagues and the ~ —P.B.Sears⟩

**lak·a·toi** \'lakə¦tȯi\ *n* -s [Papuan] **:** a dugout double canoe used by natives of Australasia

**¹lake** \'lāk\ *n* -s *often attrib* [in sense 1, fr. ME *lak*, fr. OE *lacu* stream, pool; akin to OHG *lahha* puddle, MLG & MD *lake* puddle, stagnant pool, ON *lækr* brook, OE *leccan* to moisten; in sense 2, fr. ME *lac, lak, lake*, partly fr. OE *lacu*; partly fr. OF *lac* lake, pond, fr. L *lacus* basin, pond, lake; akin to OE & OS *lagu* sea, water, ON *lögr* sea, water, OIr *loch* lake, pond, Gk *lakkos* pond, cistern, reservoir, OSlav *loky* pool, cistern — more at LEAK] **1** *dial Eng* **:** a small stream or channel **:** BROOK, RIVULET **2 a :** a considerable inland body of standing water, an expanded part of a river, a reservoir formed by a dam, or a lake basin intermittently or formerly covered by water — see LAGOON 1, POND **b :** a pool of other liquid (as lava, oil, or pitch) **c :** something resembling a lake ⟨surrounded by a rosy ~ of azaleas —*Christian Science Monitor*⟩

**²lake** \"\ *n* -s [ME *leyk, laik*, fr. ON *leikr* play; akin to OE *lāc* warlike activity, play, booty, OHG *leih* play, melody, song, Goth *laiks* dance, ON *leika* to play — more at ³LAKE] *dial Eng* **:** AMUSEMENT

**³lake** \"\ *vi* -ED/-ING/-s [ME *leyken, laiken*, fr. ON *leika* to play, deceive, dance; akin to OE *lācan* to leap, spring, fight, MHG *leichen* to hop, make a fool of, Goth *laikan* to hop, jump, OIr *loig* calf, Gk *elelizein* to cause to vibrate, to quiver, Skt *rejate* he trembles] *dial Eng* **:** to amuse oneself **:** PLAY, FROLIC ⟨a toy for the baby to ~ with⟩

**⁴lake** \"\ *n* -s [F *laque* lac, lake, fr. MF, fr. OProv *laca*, fr. Ar *lakk*, fr. Per *lak* — more at LAC] **1 a** (1) **:** a purplish red pigment prepared from lac dye or cochineal by precipitation of the coloring matter with a metallic compound (2) **:** the color of this lake **b :** any of a large group of organic pigments that are usu. bright in color and more or less translucent when in the form of an oil paint, that are composed essentially of a soluble dye rendered insoluble by adsorption on or chemical combination with an inorganic carrier, and that were first prepared from natural dyes (as madder) and later from alizarin but are now usu. prepared from many types of synthetic dyes by precipitation (as with a soluble alkaline earth metal salt or a phosphotungstate or a molybdotungstate or tannin) on a carrier (as hydrated alumina) — called also *color lake*; see DYE table I (under *Organic pigments*); compare MORDANT 1, TONER **2 :** a transparent or semitransparent appearance produced by the use of lakes or resembling that produced by lakes **3 :** CARMINE 2

**⁵lake** \"\ *vb* -ED/-ING/-s *vi, of blood* **:** to alter so that the hemoglobin is dissolved in the plasma ~ *vt* **:** to cause (blood) to lake

**lake ball** *n* **:** a compact rounded mass of organic material sometimes formed in sediment on a lake bottom

**lake basin** *n* **1 :** the depression occupied by a lake **2 :** the area from which drainage reaches a lake

**lake bass** *n* **:** LARGEMOUTH BLACK BASS

**lake bed** *n* **:** LAKE BASIN 1

**lake bordeaux B** *n, usu cap L&B* [⁴*lake*] **:** an organic pigment — see DYE table I (under *Pigment Red 63*)

**lake cress** *n* **:** an aquatic herb (*Armoracia aquatica*) of the mustard family of No. America with submersed or prostrate stems

**lake duck** *n* **1 :** LESSER SCAUP **2 :** MALLARD

**lake dweller** *n* **:** one that lives in a lake dwelling

**lake dwelling** *n* **:** a dwelling built on piles in a lake; *specif* **:** one built in prehistoric times

**lake fly** *n* **1 :** any of numerous midges of the genus *Chironomus* and related genera **2 :** MAYFLY

**lakefront** \'=,=\ *n* **:** land that usu. is developed, has buildings, and fronts on a lake ⟨a row of neat summer cottages on the ~⟩

**lakehead** \'=,=\ *n* **:** the part of a lake most distant from its outlet

**lake herring** *n* **:** a cisco (*Leucichthys artedi*) found from Lake Memphremagog to Lake Superior and northward and important as a commercial food fish; *broadly* **:** CISCO

**lake indian** *n, usu cap L&I* **:** SENIJEXTEE

**lake lamprey** *n* **:** SEA LAMPREY

**lakeland** \'=,land, -lənd\ *n* **:** a region that has many lakes

**lakeland terrier** *n* [fr. *Lakeland* (Lake district), mountainous region in northwestern England where the breed was developed] **1** *usu cap L* **:** an English breed of rather small harsh-coated straight-legged terriers **2** *sometimes cap L* **:** a dog of the Lakeland terrier breed

**lake lawyer** *n* **:** LAWYER 2b

**lake·let** \'lāklə̇t\ *n* -s **:** a little lake ⟨a luxuriant sunken garden surrounding a ~ —Aubrey Drury⟩

**la·ken·vel·der** \'läkən,veldə(r)\ *n* [modif. of G *Lakenfelder*] **1** *usu cap* **:** a German breed of strikingly marked black-and-white domestic fowls somewhat resembling leghorns **2** -s *sometimes cap* **:** a bird of the Lakenvelder breed

**lake perch** *n* **:** YELLOW PERCH

**lake pickerel** *n* **1 :** ⁴PIKE 1a **2 :** CHAIN PICKEREL

**lake pitch** *n* **:** a soft Trinidad asphalt rich in bituminous matter and soluble in petroleum spirit — compare LAND PITCH

**lak·er** \'lākə(r)\ *n* -s [¹*lake* + *-er*] **:** one associated with a lake or lakes: as **a :** a visitor to a lake; *esp* **:** a visitor to the Lake district in England **b** *usu cap* [*Lake (school)*, a group of 19th cent. Eng. poets (fr. *Lake* district, region in northwestern England) + E *-er*] **:** a poet of the Lake School **c :** a fish living in or taken from a lake; *esp* **:** LAKE TROUT **d** (1) **:** a person familiar with sailing on a lake; *esp* **:** a sailor on a Great Lakes ship (2) **:** a boat for lake navigation; *esp* **:** a ship esp. designed as to draft, beam, length, or structure to operate on the Great Lakes and associated canals **e** *North* **:** an expert at driving logs on lakes

**lake red** *n, usu cap L&R* [⁴*lake*] **:** any of several organic pigments — see DYE table I (under *Pigment Red 50* and *53*)

**lakes** *pl of* LAKE, *pres 3d sing of* LAKE

**lake salmon** *n* **1 :** LANDLOCKED SALMON **2 :** LAKE TROUT b

**lake sheepshead** *n* **:** FRESHWATER DRUM

**lakeshore** \'=,=\ *n* **:** the land adjacent to or bordering a lake; *esp* **:** the beach of a lake ⟨on the ~ fishing boats bumped their prows —Rumer Godden⟩

**lake shore disease** *n, north* **:** pine of cattle

**lake shrimp** *n* **:** a common commercial salt-water shrimp (*Penaeus setiferus*)

**lakeside** \'=,=\ *n* **:** LAKESHORE ⟨in this little graveyard by the ~ —Amy Lowell⟩

**lake sturgeon** *n* **:** a sturgeon (*Acipenser fulvescens*) of the Great Lakes and Mississippi river that becomes four to six feet long and is now rare over much of its former range

**lake trout** *n* **:** any of various trout and salmon found in lakes: as **a :** any of several European trouts that are varieties of the brown trout **b :** a large dark No. American char (*Cristivomer namaycush*) that is highly variable in skin and flesh color, sometimes exceeds 50 pounds in weight, and is an important commercial food fish in northern lakes — called also *namaycush, salmon trout, togue*

**lake village** *n* **:** a group of lake dwellings

**lake·ward** \'lākwə(r)d\ *adj* **:** directed toward a lake ⟨wall of high buildings aligned along the ~ side of the city —A.J. Liebling⟩

**lake water cress** *n* **:** LAKE CRESS

**lakeweed** \'=,=\ *n* **:** WATER PEPPER

**lake whitefish** *or* **lake whiting** *n* **:** a large predominantly pale green whitefish (*Coregonus clupeaformis*) that is a superior food and sport fish esp. of the Great Lakes

**¹lakh** *also* **lac** \'läk, 'lak\ *n* -s [Hindi *lākh*, fr. Skt *lakṣa*, lit., mark, sign] **1** *India* **:** one hundred thousand ⟨a population of 20 ~s⟩ ⟨50 ~s of rupees⟩ **2** *India* **:** a great number ⟨we need ~s of schools . . . for our illiteracy is disgraceful —J.A. Michener⟩

**²lakh** \"\ *adj, India* **:** hundred thousand ⟨10 ~ rupees⟩

**³lakh** \"\ *n, pl* **lakh** *or* **lakhs** *usu cap* **1 :** a member of a division of the Lezghians in central Dagestan **2 :** the North Caucasic language of the Lakh people

**la·kher** \'läkə(r)\ *n, pl* **lakher** *or* **lakhers** *usu cap* **:** a member of a head-hunting people of southern Assam and western Burma who are predominantly agricultural

**lakh·mid** \'lakməd\ *n* -s *cap* [*Lakhm*, great-great-grandfather of 'Amr ibn-'Adi, 3d cent. A.D. founder of the dynasty + E *-id*] **:** a northeastern Arabian dynasty strongly allied with Persia at the rise of Islam

**la·kie** \'lākē\ *or* **lakie tide** *n* -s [prob. fr. ¹*lake* + *-ie*] **:** a temporary retrograde movement of the tide observed in the Firth of Forth

**lak·in** \'lākə̇n\ *or* **lak·ing** \-kə̇n,-kiŋ\ *n* -s [of Scand origin; akin to ON *leika* toy, doll, fr. *leika* to play — more at LAKE] *dial Brit* **:** TOY, PLAYTHING

**laking** *pres part of* LAKE

**lak·ish** \'lākish\ *adj, often cap L* [*Lake (school)* + E *-ish* — more at LAKER] **:** of, relating to, or in the style of the Lake School of poetry ⟨did not accuse him of the *Lakish* fault of mysticism —J.R.Derby⟩

**lak·ist** \-kə̇st\ *n* -s *often cap* [*Lake (school)* + E *-ist*] **:** one of the poets of the Lake School or one of their adherents

**lak·miut** \'lak,myüt, -,mē,(y)üt\ *n, pl* **lakmiut** *or* **lakmiuts** *usu cap* **1 :** a Kalapooian people formerly on Lakmiut river, Oregon **2 :** a member of the Lakmiut people

**lakmus** *var of* LACMUS

**la·ko·ta** \lə'kōd·ə\ *n, pl* **lakota** *or* **lakotas** *usu cap* **:** DAKOTA

**laky** \'lākē\ *adj* -ER/-EST [⁴*lake* + *-y*] **:** of, relating to, or resembling lake; *specif, of blood* **:** LAKED

**la·lang** \'lä,läŋ\ *also* **lalang grass** *or* **lal·lang grass** \"+,-\ *n* -s [Malay *lalang*] **1** *Malaya* **:** COGON **2 :** savannah lands of eastern Asia characterized by the presence of cogon

**la·la·pa·loo·za** *or* **lal·la·pa·loo·za** *or* **lol·la·pa·loo·sa** \,läləpə'lüzə\ *n* -s [origin unknown] *slang* **:** something superior or unusual **:** an outstanding example ⟨a filing system for keeping track of things that is . . . a ~ —H.R.Medina⟩

**la·li** \'lälē\ *n* -s [Fijian, Tongan, & Samoan] **:** a large drum made of a hollowed log and used in ceremonies and to summon to church and meetings in Western Polynesia and Fiji

**-la·lia** \'lālēə\ *n comb form* -s [NL, fr. Gk *lalia* chatter, prattle, fr. *lalein* to chat, talk (prob. of imit. origin like G *lallen* to babble, stammer, L *lallare* to sing a lullaby) + *-ia* -y] **:** speech disorder (of a specified type esp. relating to the articulation of speech sounds) ⟨brady*lalia*⟩ ⟨rhino*lalia*⟩ — compare -PHASIA, -PHEMIA, -PHONY 2

**La·lique** *trademark* — used for an elaborate French art glass typically made by a combination of pressing, blowing, frosting, and cutting

**lal·lan** \'lalən\ *or* **lal·land** \-n(d)\ *Scot var of* LOWLAND

**lal·lans** \-nz\ *n, pl* **lallans** *or* **lallanses** *usu cap* **:** LOWLAND SCOTS

**lal·la·tion** \la'lāshən\ *n* -s [L *lallare* to sing a lullaby + E *-tion* — more at -LALIA] **1 :** infantile utterance whether in infants or in older speakers (as by retardation or mimicry) **2 :** a defective articulation of the letter *l*, the substitution of \l\ for another sound, or the substitution of another sound for \l\ — compare LAMBDACISM

**Lal·ly** \'lalē, -li\ *trademark* — used for a concrete-filled cylindrical steel structural column

**lal·ly·gag** *or* **lol·ly·gag** \'lälē,gag, -gaa(ə)g, -gaig\ *vi* **lallygagged** *or* **lollygagged; lallygagged** *or* **lollygagged; lallygagging** *or* **lollygagging; lallygags** *or* **lollygags** [origin unknown] **1** *dial* **:** to fool around **:** LOITER, DAWDLE ⟨*lollygagging* around on some shore station —Maxwell Griffith⟩ **2** *dial* **:** to neck esp. in public **:** SMOOCH **3 :** to chatter incessantly

**la·lo** \'lä(,)lō\ *n* -s [origin unknown] **:** a shoot that arises when the tip is removed from a sugarcane culm

**lalo-** *comb form* [NL, fr. Gk *lalos* talkative, prattling, fr. *lalein* to chat, talk — more at -LALIA] **:** speech **:** the speech organs

**la·lop·a·thy** \la'läpəthē\ *n* -ES [ISV *lalo-* + *-pathy*] **:** a disorder of speech

**lal·o·ple·gia** \,laləˈplēj(ē)ə\ *n* -s [NL, fr. *lalo-* + *-plegia*] **:** paralysis of the muscles involved in speech

**-la·ly** \,lalē, ,lalē, -li\ *n comb form* -ES [NL *-lalia*] **:** -LALIA

**¹lam** \'lam, 'laa(ə)m\ *vb* **lammed; lammed; lamming; lams** [of Scand origin; akin to ON *lemja* to thrash, flog, beat; akin to OE *lemman* to lame, OHG *lemmen*; causative denominatives fr. the root of E ¹*lame*] *vt* **:** to beat soundly **:** THRASH, STRIKE, WHACK ~ *vi* **1 :** STRIKE, THRASH — usu. used with *into* or *out* ⟨*lammed out* wildly at them⟩ **2 :** to flee hastily **:** beat it **:** SCRAM ⟨let's ~ out of here⟩

**²lam** \"\ *n* -s **:** FLIGHT — used in the phrase *on the lam* ⟨to hide a former lover, now on the ~ from Dartmoor —Robert Hatch⟩ ⟨that so-and-so of a promoter had taken it on the ~ —Irene Kuhn⟩

**³lam** \"\ *also* **lamm** \"\ *n* -s [F *lame* lamina, blade, lam — more at LAME] **:** any of the lower levers connected by cords between harnesses and treadles in various looms to enable the weaver to bring down several harnesses with one foot

**lam** *abbr* laminated

**¹la·ma** \ˈlämə, ˈlȧmə\ *n* -s [Tibetan *blama*] **:** a priest or monk of Tibetan Buddhism

**²lama** \"\ *n* [NL, fr. F, llama, fr. Sp *llama* — more at LLAMA] **1** *cap* **:** a genus of mammals (family Camelidae) that includes the llama, alpaca, guanaco, and other living and extinct So. American mountain ruminants with heavy woolly coats **2** -s **:** a dark grayish yellowish brown that is stronger and slightly yellower and lighter than seal, slightly redder and lighter than sepia brown, lighter and stronger than otter brown, and very slightly redder and deeper than bison — called also *elk, goose*

**la·ma·ism** \-məˌizəm\ *n* -s *usu cap* [¹*lama* + *-ism*] **:** a form of Mahayana Buddhism that is found esp. in Tibet and is notable for the variety and elaboration of its ritual practices and the complexity of its hierarchical organization

**la·ma·ist** \-məəst\ *n* -s *usu cap, often attrib* **:** an adherent of Lamaism — **la·ma·is·tic** \ˌ⸗⸗ˈistik\ *adj, usu cap*

**la·man·ite** \ˈlāməˌnīt\ *n* -s *usu cap* [*Laman*, eponymous ancestor of the Lamanites in the *Book of Mormon* (Jacob 3:5) + E *-ite*] *Mormonism* **:** a member of a people descended from Laman, a son of the Jewish prophet Lehi, and identified as the ancestors of the American Indians — compare NEPHITE

**la·man·tin** \ləˈmantᵊn\ *n* -s [F, alter. (resulting from incorrect division) of *la manati* the manatee, fr. *la* the + *manati* manatee, fr. Sp *manatí* — more at MANATEE] **:** MANATEE

**la·marck·ian** \ləˈmärkēən\ *adj, usu cap* [J. B. de Monet *Lamarck* †1829 Fr. botanist and biologist + E *-ian*] **:** of or relating to Lamarckism

**la·marck·ian·ism** \-ēəˌnizəm\ *n* -s *usu cap* **:** LAMARCKISM

**la·marck·ism** \-ärˌkizəm\ *n* -s *usu cap* [J. B. de Monet *Lamarck*, its formulator + E *-ism*] **:** a theory of organic evolution asserting that environmental changes cause structural changes in animals and plants esp. by inducing new or increased use of organs or parts resulting in adaptive modification or greater development and similarly cause disuse and eventual atrophy of other parts and that such changes are transmitted to offspring — compare DARWINISM, EVOLUTION 5 b, NEO-LAMARCKISM

**la·ma·sery** \ˈläməˌserē, ˈlȧm-\ *n* -ES [F *lamaserie*, fr. *lama* + *-serie* (fr. Per *sarāī* palace, large house) — more at CARAVANSARY] **:** a monastery of lamas

**¹lamb** \ˈlam, ˈlaa(ə)m\ *n* -s *often attrib* [ME, fr. OE; akin to OHG, ON, Goth *lamb*, OHG *elaho* elk — more at ELK] **1 a :** a young sheep esp. less than one year old or with no permanent teeth developed **b :** the young of various other animals; *esp* **:** those of some of the smaller antelopes **2** *cap* **a :** LAMB OF GOD **b** *Eastern Church* **:** the Eucharistic Host cut from a holy loaf of the oblation and consecrated **3 a :** a person innocent, gentle, or weak as a lamb ⟨I didn't need to lie, for he took it like a ~ —John Buchan⟩ **b :** DEAR, PET ⟨you're a ~, but it isn't fair —Dorothy Sayers⟩ **c :** a person easily cheated or deceived **:** DUPE; *esp* **:** an inexperienced trader (as in securities) who is readily fleeced ⟨the ~s of every college faculty are subject to the temptation of finance—R.M.Lovett⟩ **4 a :** the flesh of a lamb used as food **b :** LAMBSKIN **5 :** a fierce cruel person **:** RUFFIAN — **in lamb :** PREGNANT — used of a ewe

lamb 4a: *A* wholesale cuts: *1* leg, *2* loin, *3* rack, *4* breast, *5* shank, *6* shoulder; *B* retail cuts: *a* leg; *b* sirloin chops and roast; *c* loin chops and rolled loin roast; *d* patties and chopped roast; *e* rib chops and crown roast; *f* riblets, stew, and stuffed or rolled breast; *g* square-cut shoulder roast, cushion roast, Saratoga chops, rolled shoulder, boneless shoulder chops; *h* neck slices; *i* shanks; *k* blade chops; *m* arm chops

**²lamb** \"\ *vb* -ED/-ING/-S *vi* **:** to bring forth a lamb ~ *vt* **1 :** to bring forth (a lamb) **2 :** to tend (ewes) at lambing time **3 :** to put lambs to graze on (as a field) — often used with *down*

**¹lam·ba** \ˈlambə, ˈläm-\ *n* -s [Malagasy] **:** a large wrap resembling a shawl that is worn by natives of Madagascar and is made of various fabrics in solid colors or patterns

**²lamba** \"\ *n, pl* **lamba** *or* **lambas** *usu cap* **1 a :** a Bantu people of northern Rhodesia **b :** a member of the Lamba people **2 :** a Bantu language of the Lamba people

**lambale** \ˈ⸗,⸗\ *n* -s [¹*lamb* + *ale*] **:** a feast formerly held in England at the time of shearing lambs about Whitsuntide

**lam·baste** *or* **lam·bast** \(ˈ)lamˈbāst, (ˈ)laam-, -baa(ə)st, -baist, -bȧst\ *vt* -ED/-ING/-S [prob. fr. ¹*lam* + *baste* (to beat)] **1 :** to assault violently **:** BEAT, POUND, WHIP ⟨nothing pleased him so much as to get a big logging chain . . . and go at a budmash mate and ~ the evil spirits out of him —*McClure's*⟩ ⟨give a thorough *lambasting* to the Japanese in the First Battle of the Philippines —P.J.Searles⟩ **2 :** to administer a verbal or written thrashing to **:** tear into **:** EXCORIATE ⟨has been much *lambasted* for his ideas —*Ebony*⟩ ⟨approves in principle every major administration policy and ~s certain details —J.H. Crider⟩ ⟨politicians who shout and fear, point with pride, and ~ with abandon —Read Bain⟩

**lamb·da** \ˈlamdə, ˈlaam-\ *n* -s [Gk *labda, lambda*, of Sem origin; akin to Heb *lāmedh* lamedh] **1 :** the 11th letter of the Greek alphabet — symbol Λ or λ; see ALPHABET table **2** [back-formation fr. *lambdoid*] **:** the point of junction of the sagittal and lambdoid sutures of the skull — see CRANIOMETRY illustration **3 :** one thousandth of a cubic centimeter

**lamb·da·cism** \-dəˌsizəm\ *n* -s [LL *labdacismus*, fr. Gk *labdakismos*, fr. *labda, lambda* lambda + connective *-k-* + *-ismos* -ism] **1 :** excessive use of the letter *l* or the sound \l\ (as in alliteration) **2 :** defective articulation of \l\ or substitution of other sounds for it **3 :** substitution of \l\ for another sound (as \r\ when a Chinese says \ˈchelē\ for English *cherry*) — compare LALLATION

**lambda point** *n* **:** the temperature of approximately 2.19°K at which the transition from helium I to helium II takes place — often printed with Greek lambda ⟨λ-*point*⟩

**lamb·doid** \ˈ⸗ˌdȯid\ *or* **lamb·doi·dal** \(ˈ)⸗ˈdȯidᵊl\ *adj* [*lambdoid* fr. F *lambdoïde*, fr. MF, fr. Gk *labdoeidēs, lambdoeidēs*, lit., lambda-shaped, fr. *labda, lambda* + *-oeidēs* -oid; *lambdoidal* fr. F *lambdoïde* + E *-al*] **:** of or relating to a suture that connects the occipital and parietal bones

**lam·ben·cy** \ˈlambənsē, ˈlaam-, -si\ *n* -ES [*lambent* + *-cy*] **:** the quality or state of being lambent **:** something that is lambent

**lam·bent** \-nt\ *adj* [L *lambent-, lambens*, pres. part. of *lambere* to lick — more at LAP] **1 :** playing lightly on or over a surface **:** gliding over **:** WAVERING, FLICKERING ⟨a fire of resinous wood . . . began to crackle and throw ~ shadows about the brass andirons —Hervey Allen⟩ **2 :** softly bright or radiant ⟨her eyes are ~ with love —Francis Yeats-Brown⟩ **3 :** light and brilliant ⟨the play of the author's ~ wit reminds one of the effect of sunshine on rippling water —B.R.Redman⟩ ⟨the coda . . . is brisk and ~ —Vernon Young⟩ **syn** see BRIGHT

**lam·bent·ly** *adv* **:** in a lambent manner

**lamb·er** \ˈlamə(r), ˈlaam-\ *n* -s [²*lamb* + *-er*] **1 :** a person who tends ewes at lambing time **2 :** a ewe that is lambing

**lam·bert** \ˈlambə(r)t, ˈlaam-\ *n* -s [after Johann H. *Lambert* †1777 Ger. physicist] **:** the cgs unit of brightness equal to the brightness of a perfectly diffusing surface that radiates or reflects one lumen per square centimeter

**lambert conformal conic projection** *or* **lambert conformal projection** *n, usu cap L* [after J. H. *Lambert*] **:** a conformal conic map projection with straight-line meridians that meet at a common center beyond the limits of the map and with parallels of which two are standard that are arcs of circles intersecting the meridians at right angles

**lambert pine** *n, usu cap L* [after Aylmer B. *Lambert* †1842 Eng. botanist] **:** SUGAR PINE

**lambert's blue** *n, often cap L* [after J. H. *Lambert*] **:** AZURITE BLUE

**lambert's law** *n, usu cap L* [after J. H. *Lambert*, its formulator] **:** either of two laws in physics: **a :** COSINE LAW **b :** the negative logarithm of the transmittance of a layer of substance is proportional to the thickness of the layer, the constant of proportionality for natural logarithms being the absorption coefficient — called also *Bouguer's law*

**lam·beth conference** \ˈlambəth-, -ˌbeth-\ *n, usu cap L* [fr. *Lambeth* palace, London, residence of the archbishop of Canterbury] **:** a conference of the bishops of the worldwide Anglican communion called usu. about every 10 years by the archbishop of Canterbury to consult but not to legislate for the constituent churches

**lambeth delft** *n, usu cap L&D* [fr. *Lambeth*, metropolitan borough, London] **:** English glazed earthenware of the 17th century — compare FAIENCE

**lambeth walk** *n, usu cap L&W* [fr. *Lambeth Walk* (1937), song by Douglas Furber †1961 Brit. author and Noel Gay †1954 Brit. musician, fr. *Lambeth Walk*, a street in London, England] **:** a jaunty ballroom dance combining a strutting march with figures resembling those of a square dance

**lamb·ie** \ˈlamē, ˈlaam-, -mi\ *n* -s [¹*lamb* + *-ie*] **:** LAMB — used as an endearment

**lambing** *pres part of* LAMB

**lambing paralysis** *n* **:** PREGNANCY DISEASE

**lambing sickness** *n* **:** milk fever in sheep

**lam·bis** \ˈlambəs\ *n, cap* [NL] **:** a genus of conchs (family Strombidae) comprising the scorpion shells of shallow waters of the tropical eastern hemisphere

**lambitive** *adj* [L *lambitus* (past part. of *lambere* to lick) + E *-ive* — more at LAP] *obs* **:** taken by licking with the tongue — used of medicines

**lambkill** \ˈ⸗,⸗\ *n* -s [¹*lamb* + *kill* (v.); fr. their poisonous effect on grazing sheep] **1 :** SHEEP LAUREL **2 :** STAGGERBUSH

**lamb·kin** \-kən\ *n* -s [¹*lamb* + *-kin*] **1 :** a little lamb **2 :** INNOCENT, CHILD — used as an endearment

**lam·blia** \ˈlamblēə\ [NL, fr. Wilhelm Dusan *Lambl* †1895 Austrian physician + NL *-ia*] *syn of* GIARDIA

**lam·bli·a·sis** \lamˈblīəsəs\ *n* [NL *Lamblia* + *-iasis*] **:** GIARDIASIS

**lamblike** \ˈ⸗,⸗\ *adj* **:** resembling a lamb **:** GENTLE, MEEK

**lamb·ling** \ˈlamləŋ\ *n* -s [¹*lamb* + *-ling*] **:** LAMBKIN

**lamb mint** *n* **1 :** SPEARMINT **2 :** PEPPERMINT

**lamb of god** *cap L&G* [ME] **:** a figurative representation of Christ

**lamb plant** *n* [so called fr. its shaggy appearance] **:** SCYTHIAN LAMB

**lam·bre·quin** \ˈlambə(r)kən, -brək-\ *n* -s [F, fr. MF *lampequin, lambequin*, fr. (assumed) MD *lamperkijn*, dim. of *lampers, lamper*, a kind of fine glossy crape, veil made of this material; prob. akin to MD *lamfeter* hood for a hunting bird] **1 :** a scarf usu. with slashed edges used to cover a knight's helmet as protection from sun and rain **2 a :** MANTLING 1 **b :** a short decorative drapery for a shelf edge or for the top of a window casing **:** VALANCE **c :** a scalloped color pattern used esp. at the edge of porcelain tableware

**lambs** *pl of* LAMB, *pres 3d sing of* LAMB

**lamb's-cress** \ˈ⸗,⸗\ *n, pl* **lamb's-cresses :** a bitter cress (*Cardamine hirsuta*)

**lambsdown** \ˈ⸗,⸗\ *n* [*lamb's* (gen. of ¹*lamb*) + *down*] **:** a knitted fabric that is usu. made with a cotton back and a heavily napped woolen face and used esp. for children's clothes and blankets

**lamb's ears** *n pl but usu sing in constr* **:** a perennial hedge nettle (*Stachys olympica*) densely covered with whitish silky wool — called also *woolly hedge nettle*

**lamb's-foot** *n, pl* **lamb's-foots :** a common plantain (*Plantago major*)

**lambskin** \ˈ⸗,⸗\ *n* [ME *lambeskin* fr. *lamb* + *skin*] **1 a :** a lamb's skin or a small fine-grade sheepskin or the leather made from either **b :** such a skin dressed with the wool on and used esp. for winter clothing **2 :** a cotton or wool cloth made to imitate lamb's wool; *esp* **:** a cotton with a satin-weave face and a napped back **3 :** a white leather apron worn as a badge by a Freemason

**lamb's-lettuce** \ˈ⸗ˌ⸗⸗\ *n, pl* **lamb's-lettuces :** CORN SALAD

**lamb's-mint** \ˈ⸗,⸗\ *n, pl* **lamb's-mints :** LAMB MINT

**lamb's-quarters** \ˈ⸗,⸗⸗\ *n pl but sing or pl in constr, also* **lamb's-quarter** \ˈ⸗,⸗⸗\ **1 :** a common weedy goosefoot (*Chenopodium album*) with glaucous foliage that is sometimes used as a potherb and has been introduced from Europe into No. America **2 :** any of several oraches; *esp* **:** GARDEN ORACHE

**lamb's-tongue** \ˈ⸗,⸗\ *n, pl* **lamb's-tongues 1 a :** HOARY PLANTAIN 1 **b :** LAMB'S-QUARTERS 1 **c :** an American dogtooth violet **2 a :** a molding having a tapering tongue-shaped section or half such a section **b :** an ovolo and fillet worked alternately along the edge of a board

**lamb succory** *n* **:** a small European herb (*Arnoseris minima*) of the family Compositae with leaves in a basal rosette and small yellow flower heads — called also *dwarf nipplewort*

**lamb's wool** *n* **1 a :** the soft elastic wool shorn from lambs seven or eight months old **b :** the superior woolen woven from lamb's wool **2 :** a sugared and spiced hot ale beverage containing the pulp of roasted apples

**lamb's-wool sponge** \ˈ⸗,⸗-\ *n* **:** WOOL SPONGE

**lamb tail** *n* **:** a stout perennial weedy herb (*Trichinium exaltatum*) of the family Amaranthaceae that is common in Australia

**lam·dan** \lämˈdän, ˈlämdən\ *also* **lam·den** \ˈlämdən\ *n, pl* **lam·da·nim** \ˌlämˌdäˈnēm; lämˈdänəm, -dȯn-, -(ˌ)nēm\ [*lamdan* fr. Heb *lamdān*, lit., one who has learned, fr. *lāmadh* to learn; *lamden* fr. Yiddish, fr. Heb *lamdān*] **:** a man learned in Jewish law **:** a Talmudic scholar

**¹lame** \ˈlām\ *adj, usu* -ER/-EST [ME, fr. OE *lama*; akin to OS & OHG *lam* lame, crippled, ON *lami* lame, MW *llyveithin* tired, Lith *limti* to break down, and perh. to Gk *nōlemes* untiringly] **1 a :** physically disabled; *also* **:** having a part and esp. a limb so disabled as to impair freedom of movement **b :** halting in movement **:** LIMPING **2 :** lacking needful parts **:** ill composed **:** WEAK, INARTICULATE, HALTING ⟨put up some story to the rector — it must have been a pretty ~ one —Dorothy Sayers⟩ ⟨a broken leg is not so bad as a ~ intellect —Irving Bacheller⟩ ⟨machines, at their best, are ~ counterfeits of living organisms —Lewis Mumford⟩

**²lame** \"\ *vt* -ED/-ING/-S [ME *lamen*, fr. *lame*, adj.] **1 :** to make lame **:** CRIPPLE ⟨was *lamed* for life, and could never ride horseback again —Willa Cather⟩ **2 :** to make impotent or vain **:** DISABLE, FRUSTRATE, HAMSTRING, MAIM, NULLIFY, UNDERCUT ⟨*lamed* the productive and recuperative capacities of Europe generally —G.F.Kennan⟩ ⟨that would ~ your power of bargaining with him —G.B.Shaw⟩ ⟨schools *lamed* by losses of staff —C.E.Montague⟩

**³lame** \"\ *chiefly Scot var of* LOAM

**⁴lame** \"\ *n* -s [MF, fr. L *lamina*] **1 :** a thin plate (as of metal) **:** LAMINA **2 lames** *pl* **:** small overlapping steel plates joined to slide on one another and form a piece of medieval armor

**⁵la·mé** \(ˈ)laˈmā, (ˈ)lä¦-, lə'-\ *n* -s [F, fr. *lamé*, adj., worked with silver or gold thread, fr. *lame* lame, silver or gold thread + *-é* (fr. L *-atus* -ate)] **:** a brocaded clothing fabric sometimes in plain weave made from any of various fibers combined with tinsel filling threads often gold or silver which form the pattern or the ground

**lame-brain** \ˈ⸗,⸗\ *n* **:** a dull-witted or erratic person **:** CRACKPOT, DOLT, NUMSKULL ⟨a reception desk outside the city room on most papers to keep out the *lame-brains* —John McNulty⟩

**la·medh** *or* **la·med** \ˈläˌmed\ *n* -s [Heb *lāmedh*, lit., oxgoad] **1 :** the 12th letter of the Hebrew alphabet — symbol ל; see ALPHABET table **2 :** a letter of the Phoenician or some other Semitic alphabets corresponding to Hebrew lamedh

**lame duck** *n* **1 :** a person unable to meet financial obligations — used esp. of a speculator on an exchange **2 :** an elected officer or group (as a legislature) continuing to hold political office during a usu. brief interim between defeat for reelection and the inauguration of a successor ⟨the president nominated for the Interstate Commerce Commission a *lame duck* —E.W. Carter & C.C.Rohlfing⟩ ⟨the 20th amendment abolished the *lame-duck* sessions of Congress⟩ **3 :** one that falls behind in ability or performance sometimes because of injury or deprivation **:** NE'ER-DO-WELL, STRAGGLER, VICTIM, WEAK SISTER ⟨*lame ducks* and neglected possibilities —George Santayana⟩ ⟨*lame ducks* and half-talents . . . used to be granted solo appearances —*New Republic*⟩ ⟨she always has to have a *lame duck* to look after —Louis Auchincloss⟩

**lam·el** \ˈlaməl\ *n* -s [in sense 1, fr. L *lamella*; in sense 2, fr. NL *lamella*] **1 :** a thin plate **2 :** LAMELLA 2

**lamell-** *or* **lamelli-** *comb form* [NL, fr. *lamella*] **:** lamella ⟨*lamellose*⟩ ⟨*lamelliferous*⟩ ⟨*lamelliform*⟩

**la·mel·la** \ləˈmelə\ *n, pl* **lamel·lae** \-ˌlē, -ˌlī\ *also* **lamellas** [NL, fr. L, small metal plate, dim. of *lamina* thin plate] **1 :** an organ, process, or part resembling a plate: as **a :** one of the thin plates composing the gills of a bivalve mollusk — see BRACHIOPOD illustration **b :** one of the bony concentric layers surrounding the Haversian canals in bone **c :** a gill in fungi of the order Agaricales **2 :** a small medicated disk prepared from gelatin and glycerin for use esp. in the eyes ⟨*lamellae of atropine*⟩

**lamel·lar** \ləˈmelə(r), ˈlaməl-\ *adj* [*lamell-* + *-ar*] **:** composed of or arranged in lamellae **:** LAMELLATE — **lamel·lar·ly** *adv*

**la·mel·la·ri·idae** \ˌlaməˈrīəˌdē\ *n pl, cap* [NL, fr. *Lamellaria*, type genus (fr. *lamell-* + *-aria*) + *-idae*] **:** a family of marine gastropod mollusks (suborder Taenioglossa) having a delicate shell which is often completely enclosed within the mantle

**lamel·late** \ˈlaməˌlāt, ləˈmel-, -ˌlāt\ *adj* [NL *lamellatus*, fr. *lamell-* + L *-atus* -ate] **1 :** composed of or furnished with lamellae **2 :** LAMELLIFORM — **lam·el·late·ly** *adv*

**lamel·lat·ed** \-ˌlādəd\ *adj* [*lamell-* + *-ate* + *-ed*] **:** LAMELLATE

**lam·el·la·tion** \ˌlaməˈlāshən\ *n* -s [*lamell-* + *-ation*] **1 :** formation or division into lamellae **2 :** LAMELLA

**lamelli-** — see LAMELL-

**¹la·mel·li·branch** \ləˈmeləˌbraŋk\ *adj* [NL *Lamellibranchia*] **:** of or relating to the Lamellibranchia

**²lamellibranch** \"\ *n* -s **:** one of the Lamellibranchia **:** a bivalve mollusk

**la·mel·li·bran·chia** \⸗ˌ⸗⸗ˈbraŋkēə\ *n pl, cap* [NL, fr. *lamell-* + *-branchia*] **:** a class of Mollusca including the clams, oysters, and mussels, having the body bilaterally symmetrical, compressed, and more or less completely enclosed within the mantle that secretes a bivalved shell whose right and left parts are connected by a hinge over the animal's back, having no distinct head, usu. two lamelliform gills on each side of the body, and the ventral region differentiated in most of the forms into a muscular plowshare or tongue-shaped foot by means of which the animal burrows or moves about, and having the posterior margins of the mantle lobes drawn out in the burrowing species into tubes through which water passes into and out of the mantle cavity — **la·mel·li·bran·chi·ate** \⸗ˌ⸗⸗ˈbraŋkēət, -ēˌāt\ *adj or n*

**la·mel·li·bran·chi·a·ta** \⸗ˌ⸗⸗ˌbraŋkēˈädə, -ˈād-ə\ [NL, fr. *lamell-* + *-branchiata*] *syn of* LAMELLIBRANCHIA

**¹la·mel·li·corn** \⸗ˈ⸗⸗ˌkȯrn\ *adj* [NL *Lamellicornia*] **1 a** *of an antenna* **:** having the form characteristic of the Lamellicornia **b** *of an insect* **:** having lamellicorn antennae **2 :** of or relating to the Lamellicornia

**²lamellicorn** \"\ *n* -s **:** a lamellicorn beetle

**la·mel·li·cor·nia** \⸗ˌ⸗⸗ˈkȯrnēə\ *n pl* [NL, fr. *lamell-* + L *-cornia*, neut. pl. of *-cornis* -corn] *cap* **:** a superfamily or other group of beetles that are distinguished by 5-jointed tarsi and by having three or more of the terminal segments of the antennae expanded into flattened plates which give the antennae a club-shaped appearance and that include the stag beetles, dung beetles, leaf beetles, and related forms — see SCARABAEOIDEA

**la·mel·li·form** \⸗ˈ⸗⸗ˌfȯrm\ *adj* [*lamell-* + *-form*] **:** having the form of a thin plate

**la·mel·li·rostral** \⸗ˌ⸗⸗+\ *adj* [*lamell-* + *rostral*] **:** having a bill with transverse toothlike ridges inside the edges ⟨ducks and other ~ birds⟩

**la·mel·li·ros·tres** \⸗ˌ⸗⸗ˈrä(ˌ)strēz\ *n pl, cap* [NL, fr. *lamell-* + *-rostres* (fr. L *rostrum* beak) — more at ROSTRUM] *in some classifications* **:** a group of birds including the ducks, geese, swans, mergansers, and usu. the flamingos and having transverse ridges like teeth just inside the edges of the bill — compare ANSERES

**la·mel·loid** \ləˈmeˌlȯid, ˈlaməˌ-\ *adj* [*lamell-* + *-oid*] **:** resembling a lamella

**la·mel·lose** \-ˌlōs\ *adj* [*lamell-* + *-ose*] **:** LAMELLATE — **lam·el·los·i·ty** \ˌlaməˈläsədē\ *n* -ES

**la·mel·lule** \ləˈmel(ˌ)yül\ *n* -s [L *lamellula* small metal plate, dim. of *lamella* small metal plate — more at LAMELLA] **:** a small lamella

**lame·ly** *adv* **:** in a lame manner **:** in the manner of one who is lame

**lamen** *var of* LAMIN

**lame·ness** *n* -ES **:** the quality or state of being lame

**¹la·ment** \ləˈment *sometimes* laˈ-\ *vb* -ED/-ING/-S [MF & L; MF *lamenter*, fr. L *lamentari*, fr. *lamentum*] *vi* **:** to mourn vocally **:** sorrow aloud **:** WAIL, WEEP ⟨the millions ~*ed*; for ages they had sorrowed —Virginia Woolf⟩ ⟨nightingales ~ without ceasing —L.P.Smith⟩ ~ *vt* **1 :** to express sorrow for **:** BEWAIL, MOURN ⟨must regret the imprudence, ~ the result —Jane Austen⟩ ⟨katydids were ~*ing* fall's approach —E.W. Smith⟩ ⟨~*ed* that this particular piano should be so seldom played on —W.F.De Morgan⟩ **2** *archaic* **:** to express sorrow for (oneself) **syn** see DEPLORE

**²lament** \"\ *n* -s [MF or L; MF, fr. L *lamentum*; akin to ON *lō* sandpiper, *lōmr* loon, Goth *lailōun* they reviled, L *latrare* to bark, Gk *lēros* trash, nonsense, delirium, Arm *lam* I weep, Skt *rāyati* he barks] **1 :** a crying out in grief **:** COMPLAINT, SORROWING, WAILING ⟨let reason govern thy ~ —Shak.⟩ ⟨the ~ of the professionals who disapproved —E.O.Hauser⟩ **2 :** a lament crystallized in song or in literary form **:** DIRGE, ELEGY ⟨bagpipes skirled, . . . playing at first a ~ for him —Raymond Daniell⟩ ⟨the dance band . . . was wailing a . . . ~ —Raymond Chandler⟩ ⟨learned a lot of blues songs and ~s —James Jones⟩

**la·men·ta·bi·le** \ˌlämən·ˈtäbəˌlā\ *adv* (*or adj*) [It, fr. L *lamentabilis* lamentable] **:** SADLY, PLAINTIVELY — used as a direction in music

**lam·en·ta·ble** \ˈlaməntəbəl *also* ÷ləˈmen-\ *adj* [ME, fr. MF & L; MF, fr. L *lamentabilis*, fr. *lamentari* to lament + *-abilis* -able] **1 :** to be regretted or lamented **:** DEPLORABLE, PITIABLE ⟨a ~ breakdown in transport organization —Philip Gibbs⟩ ⟨that afternoon, so untouched by premonition, was yet full of ~ fate —Osbert Sitwell⟩ **2 :** expressing grief **:** DOLEFUL, MOURNFUL, SORROWFUL ⟨a faint and ~ cry —Walter de la Mare⟩ ⟨made her ~ complaint —H.O.Taylor⟩ — **lam·en·ta·ble·ness** \-bəlnəs\ *n* -ES — **lam·en·ta·bly** \-blē, -bli\ *adv*

**lam·en·ta·tion** \ˌlamənˈtāshən *sometimes* ˌmen-\ *n* -s [ME *lamentacioun*, fr. MF & L; MF *lamentation*, fr. L *lamentation-, lamentatio*, fr. *lamentatus* (past part. of *lamentari* to lament) + *-ion-, -io* -ion — more at LAMENT] **:** the act of lamenting or bewailing **:** vocal expression of sorrow **:** COMPLAINT ⟨such a scene of frenzy and ~ as Rome had rarely witnessed —John Buchan⟩ ⟨great consternation and ~ among business people when the bank rate goes up —G.B.Shaw⟩

**lamented** *adj* **:** mourned for ⟨the imprint of our wise and ~ friend —A.E.Stevenson b1900⟩ — **la·ment·ed·ly** *adv*

**la·ment·er** \ləˈmentə(r)\ *n* -s **:** one that laments

**la·men·to·so** \ˌlämənˈtō(ˌ)sō, ˌlam-, -)zō\ *adv* (*or adj*) [It, fr. LL *lamentosus* fr. L *lamentum* lament + *-osus* -ous] **:** PLAINTIVELY, SADLY — used as a direction in music

**lamer** *comparative of* LAME

**lames** *pres 3d sing of* LAME, *pl of* LAME

**lamés** *pl of* LAME

**lame sickness** *n* [trans. of Afrik *lamsiekte*] **:** LAMSIEKTE

**lamest** *superlative of* LAME

**la·met** \läˈmet\ *n, pl* **lamet** *or* **lamets** *usu cap* **:** KHA

**lam·e·ter** \ˈlāmətər\ *n* -s [irreg. fr. ¹*lame*] *now Scot* **:** a lame person **:** CRIPPLE

**la·mia** \ˈlāmēə\ *n, pl* **lamias** \-ēəz\ *or* **lami·ae** \-ēˌē\ [ME, fr. L, fr. Gk, devouring monster — more at LEMUR] **:** WITCH, SHE-DEMON, VAMPIRE ⟨a ~ with a British accent —Carlo Baker⟩

**la·mi·a·ce·ae** \ˌlāmēˈāsēˌē\ *n pl*, [NL, fr. *Lamium* + *-aceae* — more at LAMIUM] *syn of* LABIATAE

**la·mi·a·ceous** \⸗ˈāshəs\ *adj* [NL *Lamiaceae* + E *-ous*] **:** LABIATE 2

**la·mi·idae** \ləˈmīəˌdē\ *n pl, cap* [NL, fr. *Lamia*, type genus (fr. Gk *lamia* devouring monster) + *-idae*] **:** a family of beetles closely related to and often included among the Cerambycidae — see OBEREA

**lam·in** \'lamən\ *n* -s [L & NL *lamina*] **1 :** LAMINA **2 :** an astrologer's charm consisting of a thin metal plate

**lamin-** *or* **lamini-** *or* **lamino-** *comb form* [*lamina*] **:** lamina ⟨*laminar*⟩ ⟨*laminiferous*⟩

**lam·i·na** \'lamənə\ *n, pl* **lami·nae** \-,nē, -,nī\ *or* **laminas** [in sense 1, fr. L; in other senses, NL, fr. L] **1 :** a thin plate or scale **:** FLAKE, LAYER **2 a :** the part of the neural arch of a vertebra extending from the pedicle to the median line **b** (1) **:** the blade or expanded part of a foliage leaf — distinguished from *petiole* (2) **:** a foliose expansion (as of the thallus in an alga) **c :** one of the narrow thin parallel plates of soft vascular sensitive tissue that cover the pododerm of the walls of an animal's hoof and fit between corresponding horny laminae on the inside of the wall of the hoof — called also *sensitive lamina* **3 a :** a minor layer of a stratified rock usu. separable and produced by intermittent deposit **b :** a thin layer between cleavage planes in slate or schist **4 :** a plane section of a body having infinitesimal thickness

**lamina cri·bro·sa** \-kri'brōsə\ *n, pl* **laminae cribro·sae** \-,sē, -,sī\ [NL, lit., cribrose lamina] **:** any of several anatomical structures having the form of a perforated plate: as **a :** the cribriform plate of the ethmoid bone **b :** the part of the scleroid coat of the eye penetrated by the fibers of the optic nerve **c :** a perforated plate that closes the internal auditory meatus

**lam·i·na·gram** *or* **lam·i·no·gram** \'lamənə,gram\ *n* [NL *lamina* or E *lamin-* + *-gram*] **:** a roentgenogram of a layer of the body made by means of a laminagraph

**lam·i·na·graph** *or* **lam·i·no·graph** \-raf, -räf\ *n* [NL *lamina* or E *lamin-* + *-graph*] **:** an X-ray machine that makes roentgenography of a body tissue possible at any desired depth — **lam·i·na·graph·ic** *or* **lam·i·no·graph·ic** \;==;grafik\ *adj* — **lam·i·nag·ra·phy** \,=='nagrəfē\ *or* **lam·i·nog·ra·phy** \-'näg-\ *n* -ES

**lam·i·nal** \'lamənᵊl\ *adj* [*lamin-* + *-al*] **1 :** LAMINAR **2 :** produced with the participation of the front upper surface of the tongue (as \sh\, \zh\, \ch\, \j\, \y\)

**lamina pro·pria** \-'prōprēə\ *n, pl* **laminae propri·ae** \-rē,ē, -rē,ī\ [NL, lit., one's own lamina] **:** BASEMENT MEMBRANE

**lam·i·nar** \'lamənə(r)\ *adj* [*lamin-* + *-ar*] **1 :** arranged in, consisting of, or like laminae ⟨cut felt parts exhibit no tendency to separate into layers, despite the ~ formation of the batt from which the material was fabricated —*Story of Felt*⟩ **2 :** of, relating to, or being a streamline flow ⟨the ~ motion of a fluid about a sphere —J.K.Vennard⟩

**laminar flow** *n* **:** streamline flow in a viscous fluid near a solid boundary — contrasted with *turbulent flow*

**lam·i·nar·ia** \,lamə'na(a)rēə\ *n* [NL, fr. *lamin-* + *-aria*] **1** *cap* **:** the type genus of the family Laminariaceae comprising chiefly perennial kelps with an unbranched cylindrical or flattened stipe and a smooth or convoluted blade that is either simple or deeply incised into segments **2** -s **:** any kelp of the genus *Laminaria; broadly* **:** any kelp of the order Laminariales — **lam·i·nar·i·oid** \;==;==,ȯid\ *adj*

**lam·i·nar·i·a·ce·ae** \,==,=='āsē,ē\ *n pl, cap* [NL, fr. *Laminaria*, type genus + *-aceae*] **:** a large family of kelps (order Laminariales) that includes many large kelps chiefly of northern waters and in some classifications is considered coextensive with the order — **lam·i·nar·i·a·ceous** \;==;==;āshəs\ *adj*

**lam·i·nar·i·a·les** \,==,=='ā(,)lēz\ *n pl, cap* [NL, fr. *Laminaria* + *-ales*] **:** an order of marine brown algae that include many economically important kelps, are largely restricted to cold or polar seas, are distinguished by a complex and often very large sporophyte which is usu. differentiated into well-defined holdfast, stipe, and blade, and have microscopic gametophytes

**lam·i·nar·i·an** \;==;na(a)rēən\ *adj* [NL *Laminaria* + E *-an*] **:** of, relating to, or characterized by the presence of kelps of the genus *Laminaria*

**lam·i·nar·in** \,=='na(a)rən\ *n* -s [ISV *laminar-* (fr. NL *Laminaria*) + *-in*] **:** a polysaccharide found in various brown algae that like starch yields only glucose on hydrolysis but differs from starch in molecular structure and properties

**lam·i·narite** \'lamənə,rīt, ,=='na(a),r-\ *n* -s [NL *Laminaria* + E *-ite*] **:** a fossil plant that is supposedly a seaweed related to the kelps of the genus *Laminaria*

**lam·i·nary** \'lamə,nerē\ *adj* [*lamin-* + *-ary*] **:** LAMINAR

**¹lam·i·nate** \-,nāt, *usu* -ād+V\ *vb* -ED/-ING/-S [*lamina* + *-ate* (v. suffix)] *vt* **1 :** to roll or compress (as metal or plastic) into a thin plate **2 :** to separate into laminae **3 a :** to make by uniting superposed layers of one or more materials (as by means of an adhesive or bolts) — compare LAMINATED GLASS, LAMINATED PLASTIC, LAMINATED WOOD **b :** to unite (superposed layers of material) by an adhesive or other means ⟨asphalt is used to ~ sheets of paper —*Science*⟩ ⟨polyethylene film has been *laminated* to paper for waterproof bags —*Chem. & Engineering News*⟩ ~ *vi* **:** to divide into laminae

**²lam·i·nate** \-nə̇t, -,nāt, *usu* |d+V\ *adj* [*lamina* + *-ate* (adj. suffix)] **1 :** consisting of a lamina or laminae **:** LAMINATED **2 :** bearing or covered with laminae

**³laminate** \"\ *n* -s [¹*laminate*] **:** a product made by laminating; *specif* **:** LAMINATED PLASTIC

**lam·i·nat·ed** \-,nād·əd, -ātəd\ *adj* [*lamina* + *-ate* + *-ed*] **1 :** LAMINATE 1 ⟨shale is ~ clay —*Chem. Industries*⟩ ⟨chocolate cake ~ in very fine layers with a light creamy paste between —Edmund Wilson⟩ **2** [fr. past part. of ¹*laminate*] **:** made by laminating **:** composed of layers of firmly united material ⟨glued ~ arches are ideal for many kinds of buildings —*Architectural Record*⟩

**laminated glass** *n* **:** plate consisting of two or more sheets of glass with plastic sheeting bonded between to resist shattering — called also *safety glass, shatterproof glass*

**laminated plastic** *n* **:** a plastic made of superposed layers of paper, wood, or fabric bonded or impregnated with resin and compressed under heat

**laminated spring** *n* **:** LEAF SPRING

**laminated wood** *n* **:** layers of wood glued or otherwise united with the grains parallel to form boards or timbers — compare PLYWOOD

**lam·i·na·tion** \,lamə'nāshən\ *n* -s **1 a :** the process of laminating **b :** the quality or state of being laminated **c :** a laminated structure **d :** LAMINA — compare STRATIFICATION **2 :** a crack parallel to the principal surfaces of sheet metal **3** *or* **la·mi·a·tion** \,lāmē'āshən\ **:** a single stratum of a stratified ecological community

**lam·i·na·tor** \'lamə,nād·ə(r), -ātə-\ *n* -s **:** one that laminates; *esp* **:** one that makes a laminated plastic

**lam·in·board** \'lamən,=\ *n* [*lamin-* + *board*] **:** a veneered wood consisting of a core of parallel sheets cemented together and faced with plies with the grain of the latter usu. at right angles to that of the core

**lam·i·nec·to·my** \,lamə'nektəmē\ *n* -ES [ISV *lamin-* + *-ectomy*] **:** surgical removal of the posterior arch of a vertebra

**laming** *pres part of* LAME

**lamini-** — see LAMIN-

**lam·i·ni·plantar** \,lamənə+\ *adj* [*lamin-* + *plantar*] **:** having a side of the tarsus covered with a single horny plate which meets that of the other side in a ridge behind (as in most singing birds except the larks) — opposed to *scutelliplantar* — **lam·i·ni·plantation** \,===+\ *n* -s

**lam·i·ni·tis** \,lamə'nīd·əs\ *n* -ES [NL, fr. *lamin-* + *-itis*] **:** inflammation of a lamina esp. of a horse's foot that is accompanied by heat, pain, and lameness and is caused by overexertion on hard footing or more often is secondary to some other condition (as digestive disturbances due to overeating) **:** ³FOUNDER 1

**lamino-** — see LAMIN-

**laminogram** *var of* LAMINAGRAM

**laminograph** *var of* LAMINAGRAPH

**lam·i·nose** \'lamə,nōs\ *adj* [*lamin-* + *-ose*] **:** LAMINATE

**lam·i·no·si·op·tes** \,==(,)nō,sī'äp(,)tēz\ *n, cap* [NL, fr. *lamin-* + *-sioptes* (prob. fr. Gk *siōpan* to keep quiet, be still)] **:** a genus of oval sarcoptoid mites that live subcutaneously in poultry and other birds and apparently cause no damage to the host

**lam·i·nous** \'lamənəs\ *adj* [*lamin-* + *-ous*] **:** LAMINATE

**lam·ish** \'lāmish\ *adj* [¹*lame* + *-ish*] **:** somewhat lame

**lamister** *var of* LAMSTER

**lam·i·ter** *var of* LAMETER

**la·mi·um** \'lāmēəm\ *n, cap* [NL, fr. L, dead nettle, fr. (assumed) Gk *lamion*, dim. of *lamia* monster — more at LEMUR] **:** a genus of Old World herbs (family Labiatae) having cordate dentate leaves and showy galeate flowers with basal style and 3-sided nutlets — see DEAD NETTLE, HENBIT

**lamm** *var of* LAM

**¹lam·mas** \'laməs\ *n* -ES [ME *Lammasse, Lammesse*, fr. OE *hlāfmæsse*, fr. *hlāf* bread, loaf + *mæsse* mass; fr. the fact that formerly loaves made from the first ripe grain were consecrated on this day — more at LOAF, MASS] **1** *or* **lammas day** *usu cap L & D* **:** the first day of August **2** *or* **lam·mas·tide** \-mə,stīd\ *usu cap* **:** the time of year around Lammas day

**²lammas** \"\ *vi* [¹*lammas* (influenced in meaning by ¹*lam*)] *dial Eng* **:** to go or depart esp. in a hurry

**lammas lands** *or* **lammas meadows** *n pl, usu cap 1st L* [so called fr. their becoming common on Lammas day] *Eng law* **:** lands or meadows held in severalty during the crop-raising period but subject to rights of common at other times (as for pasturage)

**lammas shoot** *n, often cap L* **:** a young leafy shoot produced usu. in late summer by a woody plant (as an oak) from a bud that would normally open the following spring

**lammed** *past of* LAM

**lam·mer** \'lamər\ *n* -s [ME (northern dial.) *lambre, laumbre*, fr. MF *l'ambre* the amber, fr. *l', le* the + *ambre* amber, ambergris — more at AMBER] *chiefly Scot* **:** AMBER

**lam·mer·gei·er** *or* **lam·mer·gey·er** *also* **lam·mer·geir** *or* **laem·mer·gei·er** \'lamə(r),gī(ə)r, 'lem-\ *n* -s [G *lämmergeier*, fr. *lämmer* (pl. of *lamm* lamb, fr. OHG *lamb*) + *geier* vulture, fr. OHG *gīr* — more at LAMB, GIER-EAGLE] **:** the largest European bird of prey (*Gypaetus barbatus aureus*) indigenous to mountain regions from the Pyrenees to northern China, having a length of about 3½ feet and often a wingspread of nearly 10 feet, and resembling both the eagles and the vultures — called also *bearded vulture*

**lamming** *pres part of* LAM

**lam·na** \'lamnə\ *n, cap* [NL, fr. Gk, a shark, prob. alter. of *lamia* devouring monster (or, a shark) — more at LEMUR] **:** the type genus of the family Lamnidae comprising the porbeagle and a few related forms

**lam·ni·dae** \-nə,dē\ *n pl, cap* [NL, fr. *Lamna*, type genus + *-idae*] **:** a family of large fierce pelagic sharks including the porbeagle and related forms — see MACKEREL SHARK — **lam·noid** \-,nȯid\ *adj or n*

**la·mo·na** \lə'mōnə\ *n* [prob. fr. *Lamona*, Wash.] **1** *usu cap* **:** an American breed of white, short-legged domestic fowls **2** -s *often cap* **:** any bird of the Lamona breed

**¹lamp** \'lamp, -aa(ə)-, -ai-\ *n* -s [ME *lampe, lamp*, fr. OF *lampe*, fr. L *lampas*, fr. Gk, torch, lamp, fr. *lampein* to give light, shine; akin to OIr *lassaim* I flame, OPruss *lopis*, Hitt *lap-* to glow, be hot, ON *leiptr* lightning] **1 a :** a light-giving device: as (1) **:** a device with an oil reservoir and a wick that gives light as it burns (2) **:** a glass bulb enclosing a filament that glows because of its resistance to electric current (3) **:** any of various other devices that produce artificial light ⟨gas ~⟩ ⟨acetylene ~⟩ ⟨fluorescent ~⟩ **b :** a source of natural light (as the sun, the moon, or a star) ⟨the ~s of heaven⟩ **c :** any of various devices for the application of heat: as (1) **:** an apparatus for drying foundry molds during their fabrication (2) **:** a therapeutic heat lamp **2 :** a source of intellectual, moral, or spiritual illumination ⟨thy word is a ~ to my feet and a light to my path —Ps 119:105 (RSV)⟩ ⟨wanted them to be ~s unto themselves —Emma Hawkridge⟩ **3 :** EYE ⟨my wasting ~s —Shak.⟩ ⟨turned her hot ~s on me —R.P.Warren⟩ ⟨imagine walking up to the altar with one ~ in deep mourning —H.C.Witwer⟩ — **of the lamp** *adv (or adj)* **:** of laborious study or excogitation **:** of strain or effort **:** without spontaneity, inspiration, or reality ⟨refined or artificial, smelling a little *of the lamp* —B.N. Cardozo⟩ ⟨"overgrazing" is a theory born *of the lamp* —Russell Lord⟩

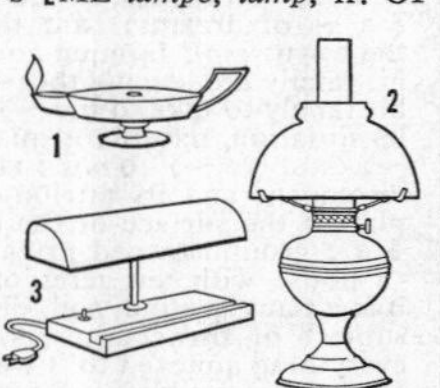

lamps 1a: *1* ancient oil lamp, *2* kerosine lamp, *3* electric desk lamp

**²lamp** \"\ *vb* -ED/-ING/-S *vt* **1** *archaic* **:** to furnish with lamps **2 :** to light or brighten by or as if by lamps ⟨scattered lights ~*ing* the rush and roll of the abyss —Robert Browning⟩ **3** *slang* **:** to look at **:** EYE, SEE ⟨I've ~*ed* two dicks — had their eye on us all day —Elmer Davis⟩ ⟨for the love of Patrick Henry, ~ that! —*Cosmopolitan*⟩ ~ *vi* **:** to shine as or like a lamp ⟨the Spirit-Seven companioning God's throne they ~ before —Robert Browning⟩

**³lamp** \"\ *vi* -ED/-ING/-S [prob. of imit. origin] *chiefly Scot* **:** to walk quickly taking long strides

**lam·pad** \'lam,pad\ *n* -s [L *lampad-, lampas* — more at LAMP] **:** LAMP, CANDLESTICK — used of the seven lamps of fire in Rev 4:5 ⟨till wheeling round the throne the ~s seven (the mystic words of heaven) permissive signal make —S.T.Coleridge⟩

**lam·pa·dite** \'lampə,dīt\ *n* -s [F, fr. Wilhelm A. *Lampadius* †1842 Ger. chemist + F *-ite*] **:** a bog manganese containing copper and often cobalt oxides

**lam·pa·ra** \'lampərə\ *or* **lampara net** *n* -s [prob. fr. Sp *lámpara*, lit., lamp, fr. OSp *lámpada*, fr. L *lampad-, lampas* — more at LAMP] **:** a fishing net that somewhat resembles a purse seine and is used esp. for taking bait fishes

**¹lam·pas** \'lampəs\ *n* -ES [ME *lawmpas*, a kind of glossy crape, fr. MD *lampers* — more at LAMBREQUIN] **:** a brocaded fabric of silk and rayon or cotton having jacquard-woven designs in two or more colors and used chiefly for upholstery

**²lampas** \", -pəz\ *n* -ES [MF, fr. OF] **:** a congestion of the mucous membrane of the hard palate just posterior to the incisor teeth of the horse due to irritation and bruising from harsh coarse feeds

**lam·pat·ia** \lam'pad·ēə\ *n* -s [Nepali *lāmpatiyā*, fr. *lām* long (fr. Skt *lamba* pendent, long, fr. *lambate* it hangs down) + *pāt* leaf, fr. Skt *pattra* wing, feather, leaf; akin to Skt *patati* he flies, falls — more at FEATHER, LIMP] **:** KOKAN

**¹lampblack** \'=,=\ *n* [¹*lamp* + *black*] **1 :** a fine bulky black soot deposited (as from the flame of a smoking oil lamp) in incomplete combustion of carbonaceous materials; *esp* **:** a soot obtained by burning liquid hydrocarbons (as creosote oil or petroleum fuel oils) that is characterized by a duller less intense black than channel black and other carbon blacks, by a blue undertone, and by a content of varying amounts of oily matter in addition to carbon and that is used chiefly as a pigment (as in paints, enamels, printing inks, and concrete) and as a source of carbon for electric brushes — usu. distinguished from *carbon black* **2 :** a nearly neutral slightly bluish black that is darker and slightly greener than Quaker blue

**²lampblack** \"\ *vt* **:** to cover, coat, or smear with lampblack **:** blacken with lampblack ⟨~*ed* platinum —Agnes M. Clerke⟩

**lampbrush chromosome** \'=,=-\ *n* **:** a greatly enlarged pachytene chromosome having apparently filamentous granular loops extending from the chromomeres that is esp. characteristic of certain animal oocytes

**lam·per** \'lampə(r)\ *vi* -ED/-ING/-S [³*lamp* + *-er*] *dial Eng* **:** to walk or go heavily

**lam·per eel** \;lampə;r(ē)l\ *n* [*lamper* alter. of *lamprey*] **1** *or* **lamper** -s **:** LAMPREY **2 :** CONGO SNAKE

**lam·pern** \'lampə(r)n\ *n* -s [ME *lamproun, lampurn*, fr. MF *lamprion, lampreon*, dim. of *lamproie* lamprey — more at LAMPREY] **:** a European river lamprey (*Lampetra fluviatilis*)

**lam·pers** \'lampə(r)z\ *n* -ES [by alter.] **:** ²LAMPAS

**lamp furnace** *n, obs* **:** a furnace heated by a lamp

**lamp holder** *n* **:** an electric lamp socket

**lamphole** \'=,=\ *n* **:** a vertical pipe or shaft between manholes into which a light may be lowered for inspecting a sewer

**lamphouse** \'=,=\ *n* **:** a light housing on an instrument (as a motion-picture projector, photographic enlarger, microscope)

**lamping** *adj* [fr. pres. part. of ²*lamp*] *archaic* **:** SHINING, FLASHING

**lam·pi·on** \'lampēən\ *n* -s [F, fr. It *lampione*, aug. of *lampa* lamp, fr. F *lampe* — more at LAMP] *archaic* **:** a small lamp (as a pot of oil with a wick) formerly used at illuminations

**lamp-iron** \'=,=(=)\ *n* **:** a projecting iron rod from which to hang a lamp

**lamp·ist** \'lampə̇st\ *n* -s [F *lampiste*, fr. *lampe* lamp + *-iste* -ist] **:** a maker or tender of lamps

**lamp·ist·ry** \-trē\ *n* -ES [F *lampisterie*, fr. *lampiste* + *-erie* -ery] **:** the work of a lampist

**lamp·less** \'lampləs\ *adj* **:** lacking lamps **:** DARKENED, UNLIGHTED

**lamp·let** \-plət\ *n* -s **:** a small lamp

**lamplight** \'=,=\ *n* **:** the light of a lamp ⟨the ~ seemed to brighten —Willa Cather⟩

**lamplighter** \'=,==\ *n* **1 :** one that lights a lamp: as **a :** a person who lights streetlights **b :** a spill of paper or wood for lighting lamps **2 :** any of certain fishes of the genus *Pomoxis; esp* **:** WHITE CRAPPIE

**lamplit** \'=,=\ *adj* **:** lighted by a lamp ⟨solitude had come again . . . and the ~ paper —Virginia Woolf⟩

**lamp·man** \'lampmən\ *n, pl* **lampmen :** a workman who takes care of lamps (as in a mine or on a railway)

**lamp oil** *n* **1 :** oil for use in lamps **2** *chiefly Midland* **:** KEROSINE

**lam·pong** \'läm,pȯŋ\ *n, pl* **lampong** *or* **lampongs** *usu cap* [Malay] **1 a :** an Indonesian people inhabiting southern Sumatra **b :** a member of such people **2 :** the Austronesian language of the Lampong people

**¹lam·poon** \(')lam¦pün, (')laam-\ *n* -s [F *lampon*, prob. fr. *lampons!* let us guzzle! (a frequent refrain in 17th cent. French satirical poems), 1st pers. pl. imperative of *lamper* to guzzle, fr. MF, of imit. origin] **1 :** a polemic satire usu. directed against an individual ⟨had written a "scurrilous ~" in Latin verse about him —Douglas Stewart⟩ ⟨corridors hung with colored ~s of English barristers —Louis Auchincloss⟩ — compare PASQUINADE **2 :** a light mocking satire ⟨the old farces and later musical ~s —G.J.Nathan⟩

**²lampoon** \"\ *vt* -ED/-ING/-S **:** to make the subject of a lampoon **:** RIDICULE, SATIRIZE ⟨apart from her singing satires, she also ~s piano styles —Clyde Gilmour⟩ ⟨was viciously ~*ed* by the cartoonists —*Newsweek*⟩ ⟨the aristocracy he had ~*ed* mercilessly for many years rose to his defense —*Current Biog.*⟩

**lam·poon·er** \-nə(r)\ *n* -s **:** a maker of lampoons

**lam·poon·ery** \=='pün(ə)rē, -ri\ *n* -ES **:** the satire of a lampooner

**lam·poon·ist** \-nə̇st\ *n* -s **:** LAMPOONER

**lamppost** \'=,=\ *n* **:** a post supporting a usu. outdoor lamp or lantern (as a streetlight)

**lam·prey** \'lamprē\ *or* **lamprey eel** *n* -s [ME, fr. OF *lampreie, lamproie*, fr. ML *lampreda*, alter. of LL *naupreda, nauprida*, prob. fr. Gaulish] **:** any of various freshwater and salt-water vertebrates that constitute the order Hyperoartia, are widely distributed in temperate and subarctic regions, and resemble eels but have a large circular jawless suctorial mouth with numerous small conical teeth in a cuplike cavity and one to three larger ones on the palate, a single nostril consisting of a blind sac, seven gill pouches opening internally into a canal lying below and communicating with the esophagus just behind the mouth, and small eggs which produce toothless eyeless ammocoetes larvae — see PETROMYZON, SEA LAMPREY

**lam·prid·i·dae** \lam'pridə,dē\ *n pl, cap* [NL, fr. *Lamprid-, Lampris*, type genus (fr. Gk *lampros* bright) + *-idae*] **:** a family of fishes (order Allotriognathi) comprising a single genus and including solely the opah

**lampro-** *comb form* [NL, fr. Gk, fr. *lampros* bright, fr. *lampein* to give light, shine — more at LAMP] **:** bright ⟨*lamprophyre*⟩

**lam·pro·pel·tis** \,lamprə'peltəs\ *n, cap* [NL, fr. *lampro-* + *-peltis* (fr. Gk *peltē* small shield) — more at PELTA] **:** a genus of American colubrid snakes comprising the king snakes

**lam·pro·phyl·lite** \-'fi,līt\ *n* -s [*lampro-* + *phyll-* + *-ite*] **:** a rare mineral $Na_2SrTiSi_2O_8$ consisting of a silicate of titanium, strontium, and sodium

**lam·pro·phyre** \'lamprə,fī(ə)r\ *n* -s [ISV *lampro-* + *-phyre*; orig. formed as G *lamprophyr*] **:** any of a series of dark rocks of basaltic habit that resemble trap, occur usu. in narrow dikes, and sometimes contain glittering plates of biotite — **lam·pro·phyric** \;==;firik, -fīr-\ *adj*

**lamps** *pl of* LAMP, *pres 3d sing of* LAMP

**lampshade** \'=,=\ *n* **:** a shade arranged to soften or direct lamplight

**lamp shell** *n* **:** a brachiopod shell esp. of the genus *Terebratula* or a related genus

**lamp·si·lis** \'lampsələs\ *n, cap* [NL, alter. of *Lasmacampsilis*, prob. fr. *lasma-* (intended as latinization of F *lame* lamina) + Gk *kampsis* action of bending (fr. *kamptein* to bend, fr. *kampē* bend, turning) + L *-ilis* (adj. ending) — more at CAMP] **:** a genus of No. American freshwater mussels including the yellowback and the pocketbook

**lampstand** \'=,=\ *n* **:** a pillar, tripod, or stand for supporting or holding a lamp

**lampwick** \'=,=\ *n* **1 :** a wick or wicking for a lamp **2 :** a European mint (*Phlomis lychnitis*)

**lampworker** \'=,==\ *n* **:** a glassblower who fashions objects (as vials, radio tubes, artistic novelties) by lampworking

**lampworking** \'=,==\ *n* **:** the process of fashioning objects from glass tubing and cane softened to workability over the flame of a small lamp — compare GLASSBLOWING

**¹lam·py·rid** \'lampərə̇d\ *adj* [NL *Lampyridae*] **:** of or relating to the Lampyridae

**²lampyrid** \"\ *n* -s **:** a beetle or firefly of the family Lampyridae

**lam·pyr·i·dae** \lam'pirə,dē\ *n pl, cap* [NL, fr. *Lampyris*, type genus + *-idae*] **:** a family of beetles of medium or small size having usu. an elongate form and rather soft wing covers which do not clasp the sides of the abdomen and including many nocturnal species with luminous organs as well as some species with wingless females — see CANTHARIDAE, GLOWWORM

**lam·py·ris** \'lampərə̇s\ *n, cap* [NL, fr. L, glowworm, fr. Gk, fr. *lampein* to shine — more at LAMP] **:** a genus (the type of the family Lampyridae) including common European fireflies

**lams** *pl of* LAM, *pres 3d sing of* LAM

**lam·siek·te** \'lam,sēktə, 'läm-\ *or* **lam·ziek·te** \-,zē-\ *n* -s [Afrik *lamsiekte*, fr. *lam* lame, (fr. MD) + *siekte* disease, sickness, fr. MD, fr. *siek* ill, sick; akin to OHG *lam* lame and to OHG *sioh* sick, ill — more at LAME, SICK] *Africa* **:** botulism of phosphorus-deficient cattle due to ingestion of bones and carrion containing clostridial toxins

**lam·ster** \'lamztə(r), -m(p)st-\ *or* **lam·is·ter** \-məstə(r)\ *n* -s [²*lam* + *-ster* or *-ister* (as in *barrister*)] **:** FUGITIVE; *esp* **:** one fleeing or hiding from the police ⟨fled to Canada, fought extradition, and has remained a ~ ever since —D.W.Maurer⟩ ⟨most people here are *lamisters* . . . away from home because they didn't have it good enough —A.J.Liebling⟩

**la·mut** \lə'müt\ *n, pl* **lamut** *or* **lamuts** *usu cap* **1 a :** a Tungus maritime people dwelling about the Sea of Okhotsk **b :** a member of such people **2 :** the Tungusic language of the Lamut people

**län** \'len\ *n, pl* **län** *or* **läns** [Sw, fr. OSw *læn* fee, fief, fr. MLG *lēn*; akin to ON *lān* loan — more at LOAN] **:** an administrative district, province, or county from which members of the First Chamber of the Swedish parliament are elected on a proportional basis

**lan-** *or* **lani-** *or* **lano-** *comb form* [L *lan-, lani-*, fr. *lana* — more at WOOL] **:** wool ⟨*lanolin*⟩ ⟨*lanthionine*⟩ ⟨*laniferous*⟩ ⟨*lanosterol*⟩

**LAN** *abbr* local apparent noon

**lan·ac** \'la,nak\ *n* -s [*laminar air navigation and anticollision*] **:** a system of radar navigation that enables an airplane to avoid collisions and to fly at desired altitudes before landing

**la·nai** \lə'nī, -nä,ē\ *n* -s [Hawaiian] **:** a living room open in part to the outdoors **:** an outdoor space used as a living room **:** a lounging terrace **:** PORCH, VERANDA

**la·nao** \lə'nau̇\ *n, pl* **lanao** *or* **lanaos** *usu cap* **:** MARANAO

**la·nar·kia** \lə'närkēə\ *n, cap* [NL, fr. *Lanark* county, Scotland, its locality + NL *-ia*] **:** a genus of fossil ostracoderms from Silurian beds having the body covered with small pointed hollow spines

**lan·ark·ite** \'lanə(r),kīt\ *n* -s [F, fr. *Lanark* county, Scotland + F *-ite*] **:** a mineral $Pb_2OSO_4$ consisting of a basic lead sulfate occurring massive or in monoclinic crystals

**lan·ark·shire** \'lanə(r)k,shi(ə)r, -,shiə, -,shə(r)\ *or* **lanark** *adj, usu cap* [fr. *Lanarkshire* or *Lanark* county, Scotland] **:** of or from the county of Lanark, Scotland **:** of the kind or style prevalent in Lanark

**lan·as** \'lanəs\ *or* **lanas disease** *n* -ES [Jav, soft, melted] **:** BLACK SHANK

**la·nate** \ˈlā,nāt\ *also* **la·nat·ed** \-nād·əd\ *adj* [L *lanatus*, fr. *lana* wool + *-atus* -ate, -ated — more at WOOL] **:** covered with fine hair or hairlike filaments **:** WOOLLY

**la·nat·o·side** \ləˈnad·ə,sīd\ *n* -s [NL *lanata* (specific epithet of *Digitalis lanata*, fr. L, fem. of *lanatus* woolly) + E *-oside*] **:** any of three poisonous crystalline cardiac steroid glycosides occurring in the leaves of a foxglove (*Digitalis lanata*): **a :** the glycoside $C_{49}H_{76}O_{19}$ yielding digitoxin, glucose, and acetic acid on hydrolysis — called also *lanatoside A* **b :** the glycoside $C_{49}H_{76}O_{20}$ yielding gitoxin, glucose, and acetic acid on hydrolysis — called also *lanatoside B* **c :** the bitter glycoside $C_{49}H_{76}O_{20}$ yielding digoxin, glucose, and acetic acid on hydrolysis and used similarly to digitalis — called also *lanatoside C*

**¹lan·ca·shire** \ˈlaŋkə,shi(ə)r, ˈlaiŋ-, -,shiə, -,shə(r)\ *adj, usu cap* [fr. *Lancashire*, England] **:** of or from Lancashire, England **:** of the kind or style prevalent in Lancashire

**²lancashire** \"\ *or* **lancashire cheese** *n* -s *usu cap L* **:** a white moist cheese of loose friable texture from finely cut curds of different ages

**lancashire wrestling** *n, usu cap L* **:** a British style of wrestling whose object is to bring the opponent to the mat from a prescribed standing position

**lan·cas·ter** \ˈlaŋkəstə(r), ˈlaiŋ-; ˈlan,ka(i)s-, ˈlaan,kaas-, ˈlaŋ,ka(a)s-, ˈlaiŋ,kais-\ *adj, usu cap* **1** [fr. *Lancaster* borough, England] **:** of or from the municipal borough of Lancaster, England **:** of the kind or style prevalent in Lancaster **2** [fr. *Lancaster* county, England] **:** LANCASHIRE

**lan·cas·te·ri·an** \ˌ≈,ka(a)ˈstirēən, -,kaiˈ-, -,kəˈ-, -tēr-\ *or* **lan·cas·tri·an** \(ˈ)≈ˈka(a)strēən, -ˈkais-\ *adj, usu cap* [Joseph *Lancaster* †1838 Eng. educationist + E *-ian*] **:** of or relating to a monitorial system of instruction in which advanced pupils in a school teach pupils below them

**¹lancastrian** \"\ *adj, usu cap* [fr. House of *Lancaster*, English royal family, after John of Gaunt, duke of *Lancaster* †1399 + E *-ian*] **:** of or relating to the English royal house of Lancaster

**²lancastrian** \"\ *n* -s *usu cap* **:** a member or supporter of the English royal house of Lancaster that derived from the fourth son of the Plantagenet King Edward III and included Henry IV, Henry V, and Henry VI — compare YORKIST

**³lancastrian** \"\ *adj, usu cap* [*Lancaster* county & *Lancaster* borough, England + E *-ian*] **:** of or relating to Lancashire or Lancaster

**⁴lancastrian** \"\ *n* -s, *cap* **:** a native or inhabitant of Lancashire or Lancaster

**¹lance** \ˈlan(t)s, -aa(ə)-, -ai-, -á-\ *n* -s [ME *launce*, fr. OF *lance*, fr. L *lancea*] **1 :** a weapon of war consisting of a long shaft with a sharp steel head and carried by mounted knights or light cavalry **2 a :** LANCET 2 **b :** a spear with a sharp point and keen cutting edges used by whalers; *also* **:** a similar implement for spearing fish **c :** a small implement used in the Eastern Orthodox Church to cut particles from loaves of altar bread **d :** a pointed blade or tooth in a router or other tool for cutting the grain along or around the path of the tool **3 a :** a medieval military unit comprising a knight and his retinue **b :** a soldier armed with a lance **:** LANCER **4** *obs* **:** a shoot of a tree **5 :** a small iron rod that suspends the core of a foundry mold in casting a shell **6 :** one of the small paper cases filled with combustible composition used esp. for marking the outlines of a fireworks set piece **7 :** OXYGEN LANCE

**²lance** \"\ *vb* -ED/-ING/-S [ME *launcen*, fr. MF *lancier, lancer*, fr. LL *lanceare* to handle a lance, pierce with a lance, fr. L *lancea* lance] *vt* **1 :** to pierce with a lance or similar weapon **2 :** to open with or as if with a lancet **:** to make an incision in or into ⟨~ a boil⟩ ⟨~ a vein⟩ **3 :** LAUNCH, HURL, FLING ⟨signal lamps *lanced* spreading cones —Wirt Williams⟩ ⟨~ himself short and straight, lower the muleta so the bull would follow it, and . . . put the sword in —Ernest Hemingway⟩ ~ *vi* **:** to move forward by or as if by cutting one's way ⟨bombers would buzz overhead and ~ toward shore —Norman Mailer⟩ ⟨tanks *lanced* on into the German bulge —*Time*⟩

**³lance** *var of* LAUNCE

**lance bucket** *n* **:** a socket attached to a saddle for holding the butt of a cavalry lance

**lance corporal** *n* [*lance* (as in *lancepesade*) + *corporal*] **1 :** a private appointed to perform temporarily the duties of a corporal **:** an acting corporal **2 :** a marine enlistee just below the lowest noncommissioned officer and above a private first class

**lanced** \-n(t)st, -nsəd\ *adj* [¹*lance* + *-ed*] **:** shaped and pointed like a lance ⟨~ foliage⟩

**lance·field group** \-n(t)ˌsfēld-\ *also* **lancefield's group** *or* **lancefield grouping** *n, usu cap L* [after Rebecca *Lancefield* *b*1895 Am. bacteriologist] **:** one of the serologically distinguishable groups (as group A, group B) into which streptococci can be divided

**lance·gay** \-n(t)s,gā\ *n* -s [ME *launcegay*, fr. MF *lancegaie*, fr. *lance* + *-gaie* (as in *archegaie, azagaie*, a kind of lance) — more at ASSEGAI] **:** a medieval lance or throwing spear

**lance head** \ˈ≈,≈\ *or* **lance-headed snake** \ˈ≈,≈≈-\ *n* [trans. of F *fer-de-lance*] **:** FER-DE-LANCE

**lance-jack** \ˈ≈,≈\ *n* [*lance* (as in *lancepesade*) + *jack*] *chiefly Brit* **:** LANCE CORPORAL

**lance-knight** \ˈ≈,≈\ *n* [intended as trans. of G *lanzknecht*, by folk etymology (influence of *lanze* lance) fr. *landsknecht* — more at LANSQUENET] **:** LANSQUENET 1

**lance·let** \-n(t)slət\ *n* -s [¹*lance* + *-let*] **1** *obs* **:** LANCET **2 :** any of certain small elongate translucent marine animals that constitute *Branchiostoma* and related genera making up the Cephalochorda and that become from half an inch to four inches long and are found burrowing in the sand in shallow waters on the coasts of warm and warm-temperate seas in many parts of the world — see AMPHIOXUS

**lancelike** \ˈ≈,≈\ *adj* **:** slender and pointed like a lance

**lance-linear** \ˈ≈ˌ≈≈≈\ *adj* **:** narrowly lanceolate

**lance·man** \-n(t)smən\ *n, pl* **lancemen :** a soldier armed with a lance or pike

**lance-oblong** \ˈ≈ˌ≈,≈\ *adj* **:** oblong and lanceolate ⟨*lance-oblong* leaf⟩

**lan·ce·o·lar** \ˈlan(t)sēələ(r)\ lanˈsē-\ *adj* [L *lanceola* (dim. of *lancea* lance) + E *-ar*] **:** LANCEOLATE

**lan·ce·o·late** \-lət, -,lāt\ *also* **lan·ce·o·lat·ed** \-,lād·əd\ *adj* [*lanceolate* fr. LL *lanceolatus*, fr. L *lanceola* + *-atus* -ate; *lanceolated* fr. LL *lanceolatus* + E *-ed*] **:** shaped like a lance head **:** tapering to a point at the apex and sometimes at the base ⟨~ leaf⟩ ⟨~ prism⟩ — **lan·ce·o·late·ly** *adv*

**lancepesade** *n* -s [MF & OIt; MF *lancepessade*, fr. OIt *lancia spezzata* battle-trained or seasoned soldier, select soldier, lit., broken lance, fr. *lancia* lance (fr. L *lancea*) + *spezzata*, fem. of *spezzato*, past part. of *spezzare* to break into pieces, fr. *s-* dis- (fr. L *dis-*) + *pèzza* piece, fr. ML *petia* — more at PIECE] *obs* **:** LANCE CORPORAL

**lancepod** \ˈ≈,≈\ *n* **:** an Australian leguminous plant of the genus *Lonchocarpus*; *esp* **:** BLOODY BARK

**lanc·er** \ˈlan(t)sə(r), -aan-,-ain-,-án-\ *n* -s [MF *lancier*, fr. *lance* + *-ier* -er — more at LANCE] **1 :** one who carries a lance; *specif* **:** a light cavalry soldier armed with a lance ⟨the 16th (Queen's) *Lancers*⟩ **2 lancers** *pl but sing in constr* [F *lancier*, fr. MF] **a :** a set of five quadrilles each in a different meter **b :** the music for the lancers

**lances** *pl of* LANX *or of* LANCE, *pres 3d sing of* LANCE

**lance sergeant** *n* **:** a corporal appointed to perform temporarily the duties of a sergeant **:** acting sergeant

**lance snake** *n* **:** FER-DE-LANCE

**lan·cet** \ˈlan(t)sət, -aan-,-ain-,-án-\ *n* -s [ME *lancette*, fr. MF, dim. of *lance*] **1** *obs* **a :** LANCE **b :** DART, JAVELIN **2 :** a sharp-pointed and commonly two-edged surgical instrument of various forms used to make small incisions (as in a vein or a boil) **3 a** (1) **:** LANCET WINDOW (2) **:** a single light in a traceried window having the shape of a lancet window **b :** LANCET ARCH **4 :** an iron bar for tapping a melting furnace

**lancet arch** *n* **:** an acutely pointed arch — see ARCH illustration

**lancet architecture** *n* **:** the early Gothic in England

**lan·cet·ed** \-səd·əd\ *adj* **:** having a lancet arch or lancet windows

**lancet fish** *n* **1 :** any of several large voracious deep-sea fishes of the genus *Alepisaurus* (as *A. ferox*) having long pointed teeth and a long high dorsal fin **2 :** SURGEONFISH

**lancet fluke** *n* **:** a small liver fluke (*Dicrocoelium dendriticum* or *D. lanceolatum*) widely distributed in sheep and cattle and rarely occurring in man

**lancet window** *n* **:** a high narrow window with an acutely pointed head and without tracery

**lancewood** \ˈ≈,≈\ *n* **1 :** tough elastic wood of various trees that is used esp. for carriage shafts, archery bows, fishing rods, and cabinetwork **2 :** a tropical American tree (*Oxandra lanceolata*) of the family Annonaceae that furnishes most of the lancewood of commerce

lancet window

**lanch** \ˈlanch, -aa(ə)-,-ai-,-á-\ *dial var of* LANCE

**lan·cha** \ˈlanchə\ *or* **lan·chara** \lanˈchärə, -charə\ *n* -s [*lancha* fr. Sp or Pg; Sp, fr. Pg, fr. Malay *lancharan*, fr. *lanchar* effortless speed; *lanchara* fr. Pg, fr. Malay *lancharan*] **:** a light sailing ship largely used for trading in the East Indian archipelago and the Philippines

**lan·chow** \ˈlänˈjō\ *adj, usu cap* [fr. *Lanchow*, China] **:** of or from the city of Lanchow, China **:** of the kind or style prevalent in Lanchow

**lan·ci·form** \ˈlan(t)sə,fȯrm\ *adj* [ISV ¹*lance* + *-iform*] **:** shaped like a lance or lancet ⟨~ window⟩

**lan·ci·nate** \ˈlan(t)sə,nāt\ *vb* -ED/-ING/-S [L *lancinatus*, past part. of *lancinare* to lacerate; akin to *lacer* mangled — more at LACERATE] **:** PIERCE, STAB, LACERATE — **lan·ci·na·tion** \ˌ≈≈ˈnāshən\ *n* -s

**lancing** *pres part of* LANCE

**¹land** \ˈland, -aa(ə)nd\ *; when a consonant follows without pause the d is sometimes lost, as in -nz for "lands" and -n,slīd for "landslide"* \ *n* -s *often attrib* [ME *land, lond*, fr. OE *land, lond*; akin to OHG *lant* land, ON & Goth *land*, OIr *land* open space, area, OPruss *lindan* (acc.) valley, ORuss *lyadina* weed, underbrush] **1 :** the solid part of the surface of the earth in contrast to the water of oceans and seas ⟨sailing out of sight of ~⟩ ⟨a narrow isthmus connecting two great ~ masses⟩ ⟨~ animals⟩ ⟨~ birds⟩ ⟨travel by ~⟩ or to the air ⟨air bombing prepared for the advance of ~ forces⟩ ⟨attacked by ~, sea, and air⟩ **2 a :** a portion (as a country, estate, farm, or tract) of the earth's solid surface considered by itself or as belonging to an individual or a people ⟨out of the ~ of Egypt⟩ ⟨people of faraway ~s⟩ **b :** the people of a country ⟨the ~ rose in rebellion⟩ **c :** REALM, DOMAIN ⟨no longer in the ~ of the living⟩ ⟨a ~ of dreams⟩ **d :** the country as distinguished from the town; *esp* **:** farming country ⟨the independent farmer and his family are leaving the ~ —Eric Sevareid⟩ ⟨the only one of his family to take to the ~⟩ **3 a :** ground or soil in respect to its situation, nature, or quality ⟨wet ~⟩ ⟨good ~⟩ ⟨mountain ~⟩ ⟨stubble ~⟩ **b** *obs* **:** FLOOR, GROUND **c :** the natural environment and its attributes within which production takes place **:** the surface of the earth and all its natural resources **4 a :** ground owned privately or publicly **:** landed property ⟨a house with ten acres of ~⟩ ⟨to divide ~s among heirs⟩ **b** *law* **:** any ground, soil, or earth whatsoever regarded as the subject of ownership (as meadows, pastures, woods) and everything annexed to it whether by nature (as trees, water) or by man (as buildings, fences) extending indefinitely vertically upwards and downwards **c :** an interest or estate in land; *broadly* **:** TENEMENT, HEREDITAMENT — compare REAL ESTATE **d** *Scot* **:** a building having a common entry but several flats or tenements each containing one household **5 a :** ground left unplowed between furrows **b :** any of several portions into which a field is divided for convenience in plowing **c :** the unplowed portion of a field being plowed **d :** a strip of land marked off by furrows; *also* **:** the length of such a strip used as a measure of surface or length **e** *Africa* **:** the portions of a farm suitable for cultivation **:** FIELD, PATCH ⟨mealie ~⟩ **6 :** an area of a surface partly machined (as with holes, indentations, furrows, or grooves) that is left without such machining: as **a :** the level part of a millstone between two furrows **b :** the surface of the bore of a rifle between consecutive grooves **c :** the metal between the flutes of a twist drill **d :** the uncut surface between two adjacent grooves of a phonograph record **7 :** the lap of the strakes in a clinker-built boat or of plates in a steel ship — called also *landing*

**²land** \"\ *vb* -ED/-ING/-S *vt* **1 :** to set or put on shore from a ship or other watercraft after a voyage or water trip **:** DISEMBARK, DEBARK ⟨I'll undertake to ~ them on our coast —Shak.⟩ **2 a :** to set down after conveying ⟨the cab ~*ed* him at the station⟩ **b :** to cause to reach or come to rest in a particular place, position, or condition ⟨his recklessness ~*ed* him in trouble⟩ ⟨unable to ~ a solid punch in the early rounds⟩ ⟨~*ed* the quoit near the stake⟩ **c :** to bring (an airplane) to a landing **3 a :** to catch and bring to shore or into a boat ⟨~ a fish⟩ **b :** to win, gain, capture, or secure usu. as the result of artful effort or competition ⟨~ a job⟩ ⟨salesman ~*ed* the order⟩ ⟨a treaty ~*ed* after long parleys⟩ ⟨~ a racing prize⟩ ⟨~ a husband⟩ **c** *Brit* **:** to put in difficulties **:** EMBARRASS ⟨committee found itself ~*ed* with a witness whose tactics baffled and embarrassed it —*New Statesman & Nation*⟩ ~ *vi* **1 a :** to go ashore from a ship or boat; DISEMBARK **b** *of a ship or boat* **:** to touch at a place on shore **:** come to shore **2 a :** to come to the end of a course or to a stage in a journey **:** come to rest **:** ARRIVE ⟨late that night we ~*ed* at a motel⟩ — often used with *up* ⟨more likely ~ up in the desert —Greville Texidor⟩ **b :** to strike or meet the ground (as after a fall, leap, flight) ⟨~*ed* in a heap at the bottom of the stairs⟩ ⟨the ball must ~ inside the lines of the service court⟩ ⟨fell off the porch and ~*ed* on his head⟩ **c** *of an airplane* **:** to alight on the ground, the water, or other surface — **land on :** to come down on **:** criticize or scold sharply ⟨came in late for dinner and the whole family ~*ed* on him⟩

**³land** \"\ *or* **lands** \-dz\ *interj* [euphemism fr. *Lord, Lord's*] — used to express surprise or wonder ⟨~ sakes, why did you do that⟩ ⟨~ knows where he went⟩

**⁴land** \ˈlänt\ *n, pl* **län·der** *or* **laen·der** \ˈlendə(r)\ [G, land, country, province, fr. OHG *lant* land — more at ¹LAND] **:** a unit of local government in Germany corresponding to a state

**land agent** *n* **1** *Brit* **:** one who manages the lands of an estate **2 a :** an official administering public lands **b :** a broker acting in the claiming or purchase of public or private land (as by settlers)

**land·art** \ˈlandərt\ *Scot var of* LANDWARD

**lan·dau** \ˈlan,dau̇ *also* -dȯ *sometimes* -dō\ *n* -s [fr. *Landau*, Bavaria, Germany, where it was first manufactured] **:** a four-wheeled covered carriage with a top divided into two sections the back section of which can be let down or thrown back while the front section can be removed or left stationary; *also* **:** a closed automobile body with provision for opening or folding the rear quarter

landau

**lan·dau·let** *also* **lan·dau·lette** \ˌlandəˈlet\ *n* -s [*landaulet* fr. *landau* + *-let*; *landaulette* alter. (influenced by *-ette*) of *landaulet*] **1 :** a small landau **:** a coupé with a folding top **2 :** an automobile body with an open driver's seat and an enclosed rear section having one cross seat and a collapsible roof

**land bank** *n* **1 :** a bank issuing its currency upon real property **2 :** a bank (as the Federal Land Bank) that invests in farm mortgages and issues its own bonds to secure funds for the purpose

**land battleship** *or* **land cruiser** *n* **:** ¹TANK 3

**landblink** \ˈ≈,≈\ *n* [¹*land* + *blink* (as in *iceblink*)] **:** a glow that is yellower than iceblink and that is seen in arctic regions over snow-covered land

**land·book** \ˈlan(d),bu̇k\ *or* **land·boc** \-,bāk\ *n* -s [landbook trans. of OE *landbōc*; *landboc* fr. OE *landbōc*, fr. *land* + *bōc* book — more at LAND, BOOK] **:** an early English charter granting land

**land-bred** \ˈ≈ˈ≈\ *adj* **:** not seafaring

**land breeze** *n* **:** a breeze blowing usu. at night toward the sea from the more rapidly cooling land

**land bridge** *n* **:** a strip of land connecting two landmasses (as two continents or a continent and an island)

**land broker** *n, Brit* **:** a real-estate broker

**land caltrop** *n* **:** a common tropical weed (*Tribulus terrestris*) with yellow flowers and spiny fruit

**land certificate** *n* **1 :** a document issued by a government evidencing the official registration of the record of a title to real property **2 :** a preliminary or intermediate document issued by a government evidencing that the grantee named therein will become entitled to a patent or grant of specified land upon fulfilling named conditions

**land court** *n* **:** a court having jurisdiction over registration of title to land and matters incidental thereto

**land crab** *n* **1 :** any of certain crabs chiefly of the family Gecarinidae of the coasts of warm countries that live mostly upon land and breed in the sea and that include many forms (as *Gecarinus ruricola*) that attain considerable size and are eaten by man **2** *Austral* **:** a burrowing crawfish (*Eugaeus fossor*)

**land crake** *n, Brit* **:** CORNCRAKE

**land cress** *n* **1 :** WINTER CRESS **2 :** BITTER CRESS 1 **3** *NewZeal* **:** an annual swine cress (*Coronopus didymus*) having trailing stems and causing taint of milk in cows

**land crocodile** *n* **:** MONITOR 3

**L and D** *abbr* **1** loans and discounts **2** loss and damage

**land dayak** *n, usu cap L&D* [perh. by folk etymology fr. *Landak*, a subdivision of the Land Dayak, in western Borneo] **1 :** a Dayak people inhabiting western Borneo **2 :** a member of the Land Dayak people

**land diameter** *n* [¹*land* (surface of a rifle bore)] **:** the diameter of a rifled firearm measured between diametrically opposite lands — compare CALIBER 1a

**land drake** *n, Brit* **:** CORNCRAKE

**land·drost** \ˈlan(d),drȯst\ *also* **land·trost** \-,tr-\ *n* -s [Afrik *landdros* (formerly spelled *landdrost*), fr. *land* land, country (fr. MD) + *drost* sheriff; akin to OHG *lant* land — more at LAND, DROSTDY] **:** a Boer magistrate in a rural district of South Africa prior to the establishment of British administration ⟨the special court . . . of three ~s with a jury —Manfred Nathan⟩

**lande** \ˈlän͞d\ *n* -s [F — more at LAUND] **1 :** an infertile moor **2 landes** *pl* **:** sandy barrens bordering the sea in southwestern France

**land·ed** \ˈlandəd, -aan-\ *adj* [in sense 1, fr. ME *londed, landed*, fr. *land, lond* land + *-ed*; in sense 2, fr. past part. of ²*land*] **1 :** having an estate in land ⟨~ gentry⟩ ⟨~ interest⟩ **:** consisting in land or real estate or its possession **:** derived from land ⟨~ estate⟩ **2 :** DELIVERED ⟨~ cost of merchandise⟩

**¹land·er** \ˈlandə(r), -aan-\ *n* -s [²*land* + *-er*] **1 :** a worker stationed at one of the levels of a mine shaft to unload rock from the bucket or cage and load drilling and blasting supplies to be lowered to the crew **2 :** a quarry worker who guides and steadies blocks of stone as they are hoisted from the quarry and loaded on trucks or railroad cars

**²länder** *pl of* LAND

**land·ert** \ˈlandərt\ *Scot var of* LANDWARD

**lan·des·ite** \ˈlandə,sīt\ *n* -s [Kenneth K. *Landes* *b*1899 Am. geologist + E *-ite*] **:** a mineral $Fe_6Mn_{20}(PO_4)_{16}.27H_2O(?)$ consisting of a rare hydrous ferromanganese phosphate occurring as a brown alteration crust on reddingite

**landfall** \ˈ≈,≈\ *n* **1 a :** a sighting of land when at sea; *esp* **:** the first sight of land after a voyage ⟨time of ~ is the most interesting period in the voyage for the navigator —Benjamin Dutton⟩ ⟨run your easting down and make your ~ —Alan Villiers⟩ **b :** the first sight of land after a water crossing by airplane **c :** a shore sighted from a ship at sea or an airplane over water ⟨saw the bright island ~s blooming under a sunny sky —David Dodge⟩ **2 :** an approach to or landing on a shore ⟨if the weather be thick, hesitate to attempt a dangerous ~ until the weather clears —G.W.Mixter⟩ **3 :** LANDSLIDE

**landfang** *n* [¹*land* + *fang* (catching)] *obs* **:** firm holding ground for an anchor

**landfast** \ˈ≈,≈\ *adj* **:** fast on the shore ⟨~ ice⟩

**landfill** \ˈ≈,≈\ *n* **:** disposal of trash and garbage by burying it under layers of earth in low ground

**landflood** \ˈ≈,≈\ *n* [ME *londflod*, fr. *lond* land + *flod* flood — more at LAND, FLOOD] **:** an overflowing of land by inland water

**landfolk** \ˈ≈,≈\ *n, archaic* **:** the people of a country

**land force** *n* **:** a military force serving on land as distinguished from naval or air forces

**landform** \ˈ≈,≈\ *n* **:** a feature of the earth's surface due to natural causes ⟨plains, plateaus, and mountain ranges are major ~s⟩ ⟨hills, canyons, sea cliffs, alluvial fans, moraines, eskers, and dunes are among the innumerable minor ~s⟩

**land-gav·el** *or* **land·gaf·ol** \ˈlan(d),gavəl\ *n* -s [ME & OE; ME *londgavel, landgavel*, fr. OE *landgafol, londgafol*, fr. *land, lond* land + *gafol* gavel — more at GAVEL] **:** land rent in early England

**land girl** *n, Brit* **:** a woman farm worker doing work to replace a man absent in military service

**land-grabber** \ˈ≈,≈≈\ *n* **:** one that seizes land illegally, unfairly, or selfishly: as **a :** one who secures public land by misrepresentation or fraud **b** *Ireland* **:** one who takes the holding of an evicted tenant

**land-grant college** \ˈ≈,≈-\ *or* **land-grant university** *n* **:** one of certain institutions for higher education receiving federal aid under the Morrill acts of 1862 and 1890

**land-grant deduction** *n* **:** a deduction in freight and passenger rates formerly received by the federal government on its traffic over a railroad in consideration of land grants

**land-grant road** *n* **:** a railroad that under federal Land Grant acts was aided in construction by grants of land

**land·grave** \ˈlan(d),grāv\ *n* -s [modif. of G *landgraf*, fr. MHG *lantgrave*, fr. *lant* land, country, province (fr. OHG, land) + *grāve* count — more at LAND, BURGRAVE] **1 :** a German count having a certain territorial jurisdiction — compare BURGRAVE **2 :** a county nobleman in the Carolina colony ranking just below the proprietary

**land·grave·ship** \-v,ship\ *n* **:** LANDGRAVIATE

**land·grav·ess** \-vəs\ *n* -ES [*landgrave* + *-ess*] **:** LANDGRAVINE

**land·gra·vi·ate** \lan(d)ˈgrāvē,āt, ˈ≈,≈vē,āt, -ēət\ *n* -s [MF *landgraviat*, fr. ML *landgravius, lantgravius* landgrave (fr. MHG *lantgrāve*) + MF *-at* (fr. L *-atus* -ate)] **:** the office, jurisdiction, or authority of a landgrave

**land·gra·vine** \ˈlan(d)grə,vēn\ *n* -s [modif. of G *landgräfin*, fr. MHG *lantgrævinne*, fr. *lantgrāve* + *-inne* (fem. suffix)] **:** the wife of a landgrave or a woman holding the rank and position of a landgrave

**landholder** \ˈ≈,≈≈\ *n* **:** a holder or owner of land

**landholding** \ˈ≈,≈≈\ *n* **1 :** the state or fact of holding or owning land **2 :** property in land

**land-horse** \ˈ≈,≈\ *n* **:** the horse on a plow's land side

**landing** *n* -s **1 a :** a going or bringing on or to shore or land **b :** an act of alighting or falling on the earth or other surface ⟨airplane ~⟩ ⟨forced ~⟩ **2 a :** a place for landing and taking on passengers and cargo **b :** a place or platform where logs are collected preparatory to further transportation by water or land **3 :** a level part of a staircase at the end of a flight of stairs or connecting one flight with another **4 :** a place usu. the bank where the ore is discharged from a mine **5 :** LAND 7

**landing angle** *n* **:** the angle of attack of the main supporting surfaces of an airplane at the instant of touching the ground in a three-point landing

**landing beam** *n* **:** a radio beam projected from a landing field to indicate to the pilot of an airplane his height above the ground and the proper path for a landing approach

**landing circle** *n* **:** a roughly circular course flown by an airplane just prior to landing esp. on a carrier

**landing craft** *n* **:** any of numerous naval craft specially designed for putting ashore troops and equipment esp. in amphibious beach assault

**landing field** *n* **:** an area of land prepared for the landing and takeoff of airplanes

**landing flap** *n* **:** a flap that is mounted on the undersurface near the trailing edge of an airplane wing and that when lowered increases both the drag and the lift and thus permits landing at lower speed

**landing force** *n* **1 :** LANDING PARTY **2 :** the army or marine component of an amphibious attack force

**landing gear** *n* **1 :** the understructure that absorbs the landing shock and supports the weight of an aircraft when in contact with the land or water **2 :** a retractable support for the forward end of a semitrailer when parked without the tractor unit

**landing light** *n* **:** a floodlight mounted usu. in the wing edge of an airplane for night landings
**landing man** *n* **:** a worker who bunches logs at a landing
**landing mat** *n* **:** a mat of metal mesh or interlocking pierced steel planking used for making quickly assembled all-weather airplane runways
**landing net** *n* **1 :** a dip net used in fishing to take the captured fish from the water **2 :** a rope net dropped from the deck of a transport to enable troops to descend to landing craft

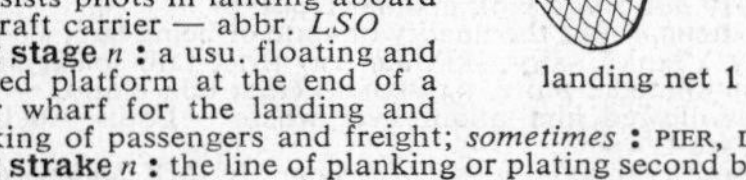
landing net 1

**landing party** *n* **:** a detachment of a ship's company organized for emergency or ceremonial duty ashore
**landing ship** *n* **:** any of numerous ocean-going naval vessels designed for amphibious landings
**landing signal officer** *n* **:** an officer who assists pilots in landing aboard an aircraft carrier — abbr. *LSO*
**landing stage** *n* **:** a usu. floating and anchored platform at the end of a pier or wharf for the landing and embarking of passengers and freight; *sometimes* **:** PIER, DOCK
**landing strake** *n* **:** the line of planking or plating second below the gunwale of a ship
**landing strip** *n* **:** AIRSTRIP
**landing surveyor** *n* **:** a British customs officer who appoints and oversees the landwaiters
**landing T** *or* **landing tee** *n* **:** WIND TEE
**landing waiter** *n* **:** LANDWAITER
**landjumper** \'=,==\ *n* ['*land* + *jumper*] **:** one that unlawfully takes possession of land either owned by or in the possession of another
**landlady** \'=,==\ *n* **1 :** a woman who owns real estate which she rents or leases to others **2 :** a woman who owns or manages an inn, rooming house, or boardinghouse **3** *Scot* **:** the mistress of a private house **:** HOSTESS
**land law** *n* **:** law relating to property in land
**land lead** *n* **:** a passage of water through an ice field
**land league** *n* **1 :** a league used as a land unit equal to three statute miles — compare MARINE LEAGUE **2 :** [1]LEAGUE 2
**land leech** *n* **:** any of various bloodsucking leeches chiefly of moist tropical regions that live on land and are often troublesome to man and other animals; *esp* **:** a leech of the gnathobdellid genus *Haemadipsa*
**länd·ler** \'lentlə(r)\ *n, pl* **ländler** *or* **ländlers** [G, fr. G dial. *Landl* upper Austria, where it originated + G *-er* (fr. OHG *-āri*)] **1 :** an Austrian couple dance of rural origin in triple time that was a precursor of the waltz but slower and performed with stamping somewhat dragging steps **2 :** music for the ländler
**land·less** \'landləs *rapid* -nl-\ *adj* **1 :** having no property or estate in land ⟨~ peasantry⟩ **2 :** containing no land ⟨~ seas⟩ — **land·less·ness** *n* -ES
**landlike** \'=,=\ *adj* **:** resembling land ⟨crimson cloud that ~ slept along the deep —Alfred Tennyson⟩
**landline** \'=,=\ *n* **1 :** a line of transportation or of communication (as by telegraph) on land **2 :** the boundary between land and water or sky ⟨sun came up too: it broke clear of the ~ —Shelby Foote⟩
[1]**land·lock** \'lan(d),läk\ *n* [prob. back-formation fr. *landlocked*] **:** a landlocked state or place
[2]**landlock** \"\ *vt* [back-formation fr. *landlocked*] **:** to cause to be landlocked **:** enclose within land
**land·locked** \'=,=\ *adj* ['*land* + *locked*] **1 :** enclosed or nearly enclosed by land ⟨~ harbor⟩ ⟨~ country⟩ **2 :** confined to fresh water by or as if by some barrier — used of fish that ordinarily seek the sea after spawning
**landlocked salmon** *n* **1 :** a landlocked phase that is sometimes regarded as a distinct variety (*Salmo salar sebago*) or a separate species (*S. sebago*) of the salmon of the Atlantic and is native to lakes of eastern No. America from New Hampshire to New Brunswick — called also *Sebago salmon* **2 :** LAKE TROUT
**landlooker** \'=,==\ *n* **:** CRUISER 4a
**land·loper** *or* **land·loup·er** \'lan(d),lōpə(r), -lōp-, -lüp-\ *n* -S [D *landloper*, fr. MD, fr. *land* + *loper* runner, fr. *lopen* to run + *-er;* akin to OHG *lant* land and to OHG *loufan* to run — more at LAND, LEAP] **1 :** VAGABOND, VAGRANT **2** *obs* **:** LANDLUBBER
**land·lord** \'lan(d),lȯrd, -aan-, -lȯ(ə)d\ *n* [ME, fr. '*land* + *lord*] **1 :** one who lets land to another **:** the owner or holder of land or houses which he leases or rents to another — compare LESSOR ⟨*landlord*-ridden countryside⟩ **2 :** the master of an inn or lodging house ⟨my companion fetched out the jolly ~ —Joseph Addison⟩ **3** *Scot* **:** a host in a private house
**land·lord·ism** \-ȯr,dizəm\ *n* **1 :** the state of being a landlord **:** characteristics of a landlord in action, opinions, or speech **2 :** the relations of landlords to tenants esp. as to leased agricultural lands **:** the system or doctrine of the ownership of the soil being vested in one who leases it to the cultivators ⟨evils of absentee ~⟩
**land·lord·ly** \-ȯrdlē\ *adj* **:** of, relating to, or characteristic of a landlord ⟨~ manner⟩ ⟨~ rights⟩
**land·lord·ry** \-drē\ *n* -ES **:** landlords as a group or class
**land·lord·ship** \-d,ship\ *n* **:** the condition or position of a landlord
**land·lub·ber** \'lan(d),ləbə(r), -aan-\ *n* ['*land* + *lubber*] **1 :** one who passes his life on land **:** LANDSMAN **2 :** one who is unacquainted with the sea or unskilled in seamanship — **land·lub·ber·ish** \-bərish\ *adj* — **land·lub·ber·ly** \-rlē\ *adj*
**land·lub·bing** \-biŋ\ *adj* [*landlubb*er + *-ing*] **:** living as a landlubber **:** LANDLUBBERLY
**land·man** \'lan(d)mən, -,man\ *n, pl* **landmen 1** *obs* **:** one of a particular or specified country **2** *archaic* **:** FARMER, RUSTIC, COUNTRYMAN **3 :** LANDSMAN 2 **4 :** LEASEMAN 1
**landmark** \'=,=\ *n* **1 :** a mark for designating the boundary of land **:** a fixed object (as a monument of any sort, a river, marked tree, stone, ditch) by which the limits of a farm, a town, or other portion of territory may be known and preserved **2 a :** a conspicuous object on land that serves as a guide to navigation at sea **b :** a natural object or man-made structure that marks a course or characterizes a locality ⟨the Armory remains — a solid fortlike ~ of weathered brick —*Amer. Guide Series: Minn.*⟩ ⟨a huge crooked tree was so prominent a ~ for early French voyageurs — *Amer. Guide Series: Mich.*⟩ **c** (1) **:** an anatomical structure used as a point of orientation in locating other structures (as in surgical procedures) (2) *anthrop* **:** a point on the body or skeleton from which measurements are taken **3 :** an event, achievement, characteristic, or modification that marks a turning point or a stage ⟨forty years after its composition the essay stands as a ~ in American criticism —Lionel Trilling⟩ ⟨a ~ in the shift of American values —W.H.Whyte⟩ **4 :** a traditional guiding precept or principle ⟨the new generation is abandoning the old ~*s*⟩
**landmark baptist** \'=,=-\ *or* **landmarker** \'=,==\ *n, usu cap L&B* [so called fr. the stress laid on what this sect regards as the landmarks of Baptist Christianity] **:** a Baptist of the strictly denominational American Baptist Association which originated in Texas and Arkansas in 1905 and took its present name in 1924
**landmass** \'=,=\ *n* **:** a large area of land
**land measure** *n* **:** a unit or series of units of area (as square rod, acre) used esp. in measuring land
**land-mere** *n* -S *obs* **:** BOUNDARY
**land mine** *n* **1 :** a mine that is placed on or just below the surface of the ground and is usu. designed to be exploded by the weight of vehicles or troops passing over it **2 :** AERIAL MINE 2
**land·oc·ra·cy** \lan'däkrəsē\ *n* -ES ['*land* + *-o-* + *-cracy*] **:** a class gaining prominence or power through the possession of land
**land office** *n* **:** a government office in which the entries upon and sales of public land are registered and other business respecting the public lands is transacted
**land-office business** *n* **:** extensive and rapid business **:** rush of sales or transactions ⟨travel agencies had done a *land-office business* —*Time*⟩ ⟨three hotels are doing a *land-office business* —*New Republic*⟩
**land of nod** *usu cap N* [fr. the *Land of Nod* in the Bible (Gen 4:16); influenced in meaning by '*nod;* fr. the nodding in drowsiness] **:** the state of sleep ⟨a friendly fat toad . . . who had lately taken himself off to the *Land of Nod* under the rough bank fringing my lawn —David Gunston⟩
**land of the leal** *usu cap both Ls, Scot* **:** HEAVEN
**lan·dol·phia** \lan'dälfēə, -dȯl-\ *n* [NL, fr. J. F. *Landolphe* †1825 Fr. ship captain + NL *-ia*] **1** *cap* **:** a genus of Old World tropical woody vines (family Apocynaceae) having large yellow or white cymose flowers with narrow lobes succeeded by large berrylike fruits — see CONGO RUBBER **2** -S **:** any plant of the genus *Landolphia*
**landolphia rubber** *n* **:** CONGO RUBBER
**landolt ring** *n, usu cap L* [after Hans *Landolt* †1910 Swiss physical chemist] **:** one of a series of incomplete rings or circles used in studying visual discrimination or acuity
**land otter** *n* **:** any of various otters of *Lutra* and related genera that are primarily terrestrial in contrast to the sea otter
**land·own·er** \'lan,dōnə(r), -aan,-\ *n* **:** an owner of land
**land·own·er·ship** \-(r),ship\ *n* **:** ownership of land ⟨remnants of feudal ~ —J.P.Warbury⟩
**landowning** \'=,==\ *adj* **:** having property in land ⟨~ nobility⟩ **:** relating to landowners ⟨~ interests⟩
**land pike** *n* **1 :** HELLBENDER 1 **2 :** RAZORBACK 2
**land pirate** *n* **1** *obs* **:** a literary pirate **2 :** one who robs on land: as **a :** HIGHWAYMAN **b :** LAND SHARK **3 :** LAND-GRABBER a
**land pitch** *n* **:** a hard Trinidad asphalt — compare LAKE PITCH
**landplane** \'=,=\ *n* ['*land* + *airplane*] **:** an airplane designed to land on and take off from land
**land plaster** *n* **:** gypsum or gypsiferous rock ground fine for use as a fertilizer and for correcting a puddled soil condition caused by the presence of sodium and potassium carbonates
**land-poor** \'=;=\ *adj* **:** pecuniarily embarrassed through owning much unprofitable or encumbered land ⟨a thousand acres and we couldn't afford to buy a cow. Do you know what it means to be *land-poor* —Ellen Glasgow⟩
**land power** *n* **1 :** military strength **2 :** a nation having great military strength — compare SEA POWER
**L and R** *abbr* lake and rail
**land·race** \'lan,drās\ *n* [Dan, fr. *land* land, country + *race*] **1** *usu cap* **:** any of several locally developed breeds or races of swine of northern Europe; *esp* **:** a Danish breed of long-bodied white bacon-type swine — called also *Danish Landrace* **2** *often cap* -S **:** any animal of a Landrace breed
**land rail** *n* **1 :** CORNCRAKE **2 :** an Australasian rail (*Rallus philippensis*)
**landraker** *n, obs* **:** FOOTPAD, HIGHWAYMAN, TRAMP
**landreeve** \'=,=\ *n* **:** a subordinate officer on an extensive estate who acts as the steward's assistant
**land reform** *n* **:** legislative or other measures for effecting a more equitable distribution of agricultural land esp. by dividing large estates into small holdings
**landright** \'=,=\ *n* [OE *landriht* (akin to OHG *lantreht* law of the land, OS *landreht*, OFris *landriucht*), fr. *land, lond* land + *riht* right — more at LAND, RIGHT] **:** right or obligation connected with occupation of or property in land
**lan·dry's paralysis** \'landrēz-\ *n, usu cap L* [after Jean Baptiste *Landry* †1865 Fr. physician] **:** motor paralysis beginning in the legs and rapidly extending to the trunk and arms and finally to the muscles of respiration **:** acute ascending paralysis
[1]**lands** *pl of* LAND, *pres 3d sing of* LAND
[2]**lands** *var of* LAND
[1]**land·scape** \'lanz,kāp, -aan-, -n(d),sk-\ *n, often attrib* [D *landschap*, fr. MD *landscap* region, tract of land (akin to OE *landscipe* region, OHG *lantscaf*, ON *landskapr*), fr. *land* + *-scap* -ship; akin to OHG *lant* land and to OHG *-scap* -ship — more at LAND, -SHIP] **1 a :** a picture representing a view of natural scenery (as fields, hills, forests, water) ⟨~ painting⟩ — compare MARINE 5; SEASCAPE **b :** the art of depicting such scenery **2 a :** the surface of the earth **:** the landforms of a region in the aggregate esp. as produced or modified by geologic forces ⟨most ~*s* are complex rather than simple —Leland Horberg⟩ ⟨glacial ~*s*⟩ ⟨lunar ~⟩ **b :** a portion of land or territory that the eye can comprehend in a single view including all the objects so seen ⟨plans for altering the ~⟩ ⟨~ engineering⟩ **3 a** *obs* **:** VISTA, PROSPECT **b** *obs* **:** a faint sketch **:** ADUMBRATION **4** *obs* **:** EPITOME, COMPENDIUM
[2]**landscape** \"\ *vb* -ED/-ING/-S *vt* **:** to make a landscape of **:** to improve by landscape architecture or gardening ~ *vi* **:** to engage in landscape gardening
**landscape architect** *n* **:** one whose profession is the arrangement of land for human use and enjoyment involving the placement of structures, vehicular and pedestrian circulation, plantings, and relationships with adjacent areas
**landscape architecture** *n* **:** the planning and design of landscape by a landscape architect
**landscape engineer** *n* **:** one who is concerned with the problems of engineering in the field of landscape architecture
**landscape gardener** *n* **:** one who is skilled in the development and decorative planting of gardens and grounds
**landscape management** *n* **:** the care and maintenance of landscape or ornamental plantings
**landscape marble** *n* **:** a close-grained limestone with dark dendritic markings suggesting natural scenery
**landscape mirror** *n* **:** CLAUDE LORRAINE GLASS
**landscape panel** *n* **:** a wooden panel so placed that the grain runs horizontally
**land·scap·er** \-pə(r)\ *n* -S **:** LANDSCAPE GARDENER
**land·scap·ist** \-pəst\ *n* -S **:** a painter of landscapes
**land scrip** *n* **:** a certificate entitling the holder to obtain a certain portion of the public land either by entry or the payment of a portion of the price
**land seal** *n* **:** HARBOR SEAL
**land·seer newfoundland** \'lan(d),si(ə)r-\ *or* **landseer** *n* -S *usu cap L&N* [after Sir Edwin H. *Landseer* †1873 Eng. animal painter] **:** a black-and-white Newfoundland dog
**land's end** *n* **:** the extreme point of a country or region
**land settlement** *n, India* **:** the act of arranging the terms and incidence of the land tax in specific areas
**land·shard** \'lan(d)shə(r)d\ *n* ['*land* + *shard*] *dial Eng* **:** a strip of unplowed land between two pieces of plowed land
**land shark** *n* **1 :** a swindler of sailors on shore **2 :** LAND-GRABBER a
**landship** \'=,=\ *n* **1 :** a large transport wagon **:** COVERED WAGON **2 :** TANK 3
**landside** \'=,=\ *n* **1 :** the side of something near water that is turned toward the land **2** *obs* **:** SHORE **3 :** the side of a furrow next to the land in plowing **4 :** a sidepiece opposite the plow moldboard sometimes forming a V with the share edge (as in a bar share) or consisting of a revolving disk wheel that guides the plow and receives the side pressure when the furrow is turned — see PLOW illustration
**land·skip** \'lanz,kip, -n(d),sk-\ *archaic var of* LANDSCAPE
**lands·knecht** \'läntskə,nekt\ *n* -S [G — more at LANSQUENET] **:** LANSQUENET
**land-slater** \'=,==\ *n* **:** WOOD LOUSE 1
**landsleit** [Yiddish *landslayt* compatriots (suppletive pl. of *landsman*), fr. MHG *lantsliute* alter. of *lantliute* natives, compatriots, fr. *lant* land (fr. OHG) + *liute* people, fr. OHG *liuti*, pl. of *liut* person, people — more at LAND, LIBERAL] *pl of* LANDSMAN
[1]**landslide** \'=,=\ *n* ['*land* + *slide*] **1 :** the rapid downward movement under the influence of gravity of a mass of rock, earth, or artificial fill on a slope; *also* **:** the mass that moves or has moved down **2 :** a great majority of votes for one side; *esp* **:** a one-sided election
[2]**landslide** \"\ *vi* **1 :** to produce a landslide **2 :** to win an election by a heavy majority
**landslip** \'=,=\ *n* **:** LANDSLIDE 1
**lands·mål** *or* **lands·maal** \'län(t),smōl\ *n* -S *often cap* [Norw *landsmål* (formerly spelled *landsmaal*), fr. *land* country, land + *mål* speech] **:** a literary form of Norwegian based on the spoken dialects of Norway that dates from a grammar and dictionary by Ivar Aasen about 1850 and was designed as a national language distinct from that of Denmark — called also *New Norwegian;* compare RIKSMÅL
[1]**lands·man** \'lan(d)zmən\ *n, pl* **landsmen** [*land's* (gen. of '*land*) + *man*] **1 :** a fellow countryman **2 :** one who lives on the land; *esp* **:** one who knows little or nothing of the sea **3 a** *obs* **:** a sailor on his first voyage **b :** a sailor who has had little experience and is rated below an ordinary seaman
[2]**lands·man** \'läntsmən\ *n, pl* **lands·leit** \-t,slīt\ [Yiddish, compatriot, fr. MHG *lantsman*, alter. of *lantman*, fr. OHG, fr. *lant* land + *man* — more at LAND, MAN] **:** a fellow Jew orig. from the same town or section esp. of eastern Europe ⟨friendly advice to a newly arrived ~⟩
**lands·man·shaft** \'läntsmən,shäft\ *n, pl* **landsmanshaf·ten** \-ftən\ [Yiddish, fr. G *landsmannschaft* association of compatriots, fr. *landsmann* compatriot (fr. MHG *lantsman*) + *-schaft* (fr. OHG *scaf-* ship)] **:** a Jewish association of landsleit organized esp. for social and philanthropic purposes
**land snail** *n* **:** a terrestrial gastropod usu. belonging to the pulmonate suborder Stylommatophora
**landspout** \'=,=\ *n* **:** a phenomenon like a waterspout but occurring over land — compare TORNADO, WHIRLWIND
**land station** *n* **:** a radio transmitting station on land for communicating with mobile stations — compare AERONAUTICAL STATION
**land steward** *n* **:** a person who acts for another in management of land
**land·sturm** \'länt,shtu̇rm\ *n* -S [G, orig., call to arms rendered by storm-warning bells, fr. *land* land (fr. OHG *lant*) + *sturm* storm (fr. OHG) — more at LAND, STORM] **1 :** a calling out of the militia **:** a general levy in time of war **2 :** MILITIA, HOME RESERVES
**land-taxer** \'=,==\ *n* **:** an advocate of land taxes
**land-tax parish** *n* **:** a district in Great Britain separately assessed for the land tax
**land tie** *n* **:** a tie rod or chain used to connect a retaining wall, an outside flight of steps, or other structure to an anchor plate embedded in the earth behind it
**land tortoise** *or* **land turtle** *n* **:** any of various tortoises (family Testudinidae) that are usu. slow and clumsy in their movements and habitually live on dry land
**land trash** *n* **:** broken ice near shore
**landtrost** *var of* LANDDROST
**land trust** *n* **:** an unincorporated association for holding real estate by putting the title in one or more trustees for the benefit of the members
**land up** *vt* **:** to fill, surround, cover, or block with earth ⟨a channel that had been partly *landed up*⟩
**land urchin** *n* **:** HEDGEHOG
**land·vogt** \'länt,fōkt\ *n* -S [G, fr. *land* land, province, country (fr. OHG *lant* land) + *vogt* bailiff, fr. OHG *fogat*, fr. ML *vocatus* legal representative — more at LAND, FOUD] **:** the governor of a German royal province or district
**landwaiter** \'=,==\ *n* **:** a customs officer in England who takes account of imports for purposes of taxation and watches over and certifies to the observance of the prescribed form in the shipping of exports
[1]**land·ward** \'landwə(r)d, -aan-\ *also* **land·wards** \-)dz\ *adv* [*landward* fr. ME, fr. *land* + *-ward; landwards* fr. *landward* + *-s*] **:** toward the land — **to landward** *adv* **:** toward land **:** toward or on the landside
[2]**land·ward** \'landərd\ *adj* **1** *Scot* **:** relating to or indicating the country **:** RURAL ⟨a decrease in the ~ population⟩ ⟨*landward*-bred⟩ **2 :** lying or being toward the land **:** being on the side toward the land ⟨on the ~ side Oslo is encircled by hills —Frederick Arnold⟩
**land warrant** *n* **:** a transferable certificate from the land office authorizing a person to assume possession of a specified quantity of public land
**landwash** \'=,=\ *n* **1 :** the line of high tide **2 :** the wash of the sea on the shore
**landway** \'=,=\ *n* **:** a path, road, or route on land ⟨seaways and ~*s* would continue to fulfil vital functions —William Walton⟩ ⟨upwarping of continents creates ~*s* over which terrestrial plants and animals may migrate —F.E.Clements & R.W.Cheney⟩
**land·wehr** \'länt,vār\ *n* -S [G, fr. MHG *lantwer* forces called for defense of the land, fr. OHG *lantweri* defense of the land, fr. *lant* land + *weri* defense — more at LAND, WEIR] **:** the part of the organized national armed forces (as in the former German and Austrian empires, Japan, Switzerland) that has completed the required service with the colors and constitutes the second line of defense
**land wheel** *n* **:** the wheel of a sulky plow which travels on the unplowed land
**land·whin** \'land,hwin, -n,dw-\ *n* -S *dial Eng* **:** RESTHARROW
**land wind** *n* **:** LAND BREEZE
**landwire** \'=,=\ *n* **:** an electric service or communication line strung over the ground
**landworker** \'=,==\ *n* **:** FARMHAND
**landwrack** *or* **landwreck** *n, obs* **:** destruction of something on land **:** RUIN, DEVASTATION
**land yard** *n, dial Eng* **:** a measure of length equal to a rod or a little more
[1]**lane** \'lān\ *n* -S [ME, fr. OE *lane, lanu;* akin to OFris *lāne* lane, MD *lāne* lane, ON *lǫn* row of houses, and perh. to Gk *elan* to drive — more at ELASTIC] **1 a :** a narrow passageway between fences or hedges that is not traveled as a highroad **b :** an alley between buildings **c :** a narrow way among trees, rocks, or other objects ⟨~ between rows of machines in a factory⟩ ⟨traffic ~ of a department store⟩ **2 :** a narrow passageway or track ⟨a ~ between lines of men⟩ **3 a** *or* **lane route :** a route across an ocean between specified degrees of latitude or longitude in which all steamers traveling in the same direction are supposed to keep in order to avoid collisions **b :** a channel of water in a floe or field of ice **c :** a strip of roadway adequate to accommodate a single line of vehicles **d :** AIR LANE **e :** any of several parallel courses marked out on a running track, rowing course, or swimming tank in which a competitor must stay during a race **f :** a bowling alley
[2]**lane** \"\ *vb* -ED/-ING/-S *vi* **:** to form a lane ⟨long sash of bloodred sun *laning* to the ship⟩ **:** separate into lanes ⟨*laning* of flowing liquids⟩ ~ *vt* **:** to make into lanes ⟨the road has been four-*laned*⟩
[3]**lane** \"\ *Scot var of* LONE
**lane·ly** \'lānli\ *Scot var of* LONELY
**lane snapper** \'lān-\ *n* [prob. fr. the name *Lane*] **:** a small snapper (*Lutjanus synagris*) found from Florida to northern Brazil
**lane·some** \'lān(t)səm\ *Scot var of* LONESOME
**la·ne·te** \'lanə;tē\ *n* -S [Tag *laniti*] **:** any of several Philippine trees or their wood: **a :** a valuable timber tree (*Wrightia laniti* of the family Apocynaceae) with soft wood that is used for carving and for musical instruments **b :** a tree (*Allaeanthus luzonicus*) of the family Moraceae having leaves and flowers that are cooked for food
**laneway** \'=,=\ *n* ['*lane* + *way*] *Brit* **:** LANE
[1]**lang** \'laŋ\ *now chiefly dial var of* LONG
[2]**lang** \", -ä-\ *n* -S [native name in India] **:** GRASS PEA
**lang** *abbr* language
**lan·ga·ha** \läŋ'gä(,)hä\ *n* -S [origin unknown] **:** a brownish red opisthoglyphous snake (*Langaha nasuta*) of Madagascar
**lang·ban·ite** \'lōŋbə,nīt\ *n* -S [Sw *långbanit*, fr. *Långban*, Värmland, Sweden, its locality + Sw *-it* -ite] **:** a hexagonal mineral $(Mn,Sb,Ca,Fe,Mg)_9O_8(SiO_4)$(?) occurring in iron-black prismatic crystals consisting of a manganese, iron, and antimony silicate and oxide (hardness 6.5; sp. gr. 4.92)
**lang·bein·ite** \'läŋ,bī,nīt\ *n* -S [G *langbeinit*, fr. A. *Langbein*, 19th cent. Ger. chemist + G *-it* -ite] **:** a mineral $K_2Mg_2(SO_4)_3$ much used in the fertilizer industry consisting of potassium magnesium double sulfate in colorless isometric crystals
**lang·hans' layer** \'läŋ,hänz-, -n(t)s\ *n, usu cap 1st L* [after Theodor *Langhans* †1915 Ger. pathologist] **:** CYTOTROPHOBLAST
**lang·ite** \'laŋ,īt\ *n* -S [Victor von *Lang* †1921 Austrian physicist + E *-ite*] **:** a mineral $Cu_4(SO_4)(OH)_6{\cdot}H_2O$ (?) composed of a basic hydrous sulfate of copper
**lang·lauf** \'läŋ,lau̇f\ *n* -S [G, fr. G *lang* long (fr. OHG) + *lauf* race, run, running, fr. OHG *hlouf* — more at LONG, LEAP] **:** cross-country running or racing on skis — compare DAUERLAUF
**lang·läu·fer** \-,lȯifə(r)\ *n, pl* **langläufer** *or* **langläufers** [G, fr. *lang* + *läufer* runner, racer, fr. MHG *loufære, löufære*,

fr. *loufen* to run (fr. OHG *hlouffan*) + *-ære* -er — more at LEAP] **:** a cross-country skier

**lang lay** \ˈlaŋ-\ *n* [prob. fr. ¹*lang*] **:** a lay of a wire rope in which the wires in each strand are twisted in the same direction as the strands in the rope

**lang·ley** \ˈlaŋlē\ *n* -s [after Samuel P. *Langley* †1906 Am. astronomer] **:** a unit of solar radiation equivalent to one gram calorie per square centimeter of irradiated surface

**lan·go** \ˈlaŋ(,)gō\ *n, pl* **lango** *or* **langos** *usu cap* **1 a :** one of a group of Negro peoples in Uganda speaking dialects of a distinct language **b :** a member of such people **2 :** a Nilotic language of the Lango people

**lan·go·bard** \ˈlaŋgə,bärd\ *n* -s *cap* [L *Langobardi*, pl. — more at LOMBARD] **:** LOMBARD 1

¹**lan·go·bar·dic** \ˌ══ˈbärdik\ *adj, usu cap* [L *Langobardi* + E *-ic*] **:** of or relating to the Lombards

²**langobardic** \"\ *or* **lan·go·bar·di·an** \-dēən\ *n* -s *cap* **:** the West Germanic language of the Lombard people

**langoon** *n* -s [fr. *Langon*, town in southwestern France, its locality] *obs* **:** a French white wine

**lan·goo·ty** \ˌlaŋˈgüd·ē\ *n* -ES [Hindi *lāgoṭī*] **:** a piece of cloth hanging in front from a waistband worn by lower-class people in India

**lan·gos·ta** \laŋˈgȯstə\ *n* -s [AmerSp, fr. Sp, locust, European lobster, fr. (assumed) VL *lacusta*, alter. of L *locusta* — more at LOCUST] **:** a So. or Central American spiny lobster of the genus *Panulirus*

**lan·gouste** \(ˈ)läⁿ¦güst\ *n* -s [F, fr. MF, fr. OProv *langosta*, fr. (assumed) VL *lacusta*] **:** SPINY LOBSTER; *esp* **:** the common European lobster (*Palinurus vulgaris*)

**lan·grage** \ˈlaŋgrij\ *also* **lan·grel** \-rəl\ *n* -s [origin unknown] **:** shot formerly used in naval warfare for tearing sails and rigging and consisting of bolts, nails, and other pieces of iron fastened together or enclosed in a canister

**lang·sat** \ˈläŋ,sät\ *or* **lang·set** \-set\ *n* -s [Malay *langsat*] **:** LANSEH

**langs·dorf·fia** \(ˈ)laŋzˈdȯ(r)fēə\ *n, cap* [NL, fr. G. H. von *Langsdorff* †1852 Ger. physician + NL *-ia*] **:** a genus of parasitic fleshy yellow herbs (family Balanophoraceae) with purplish scales and flowers

**lang·shan** \ˈlaŋ,shan\ *n* [fr. *Langshan*, locality near Shanghai, China] **1** *usu cap* **:** an Asiatic breed of large single-combed domestic usu. black or white fowls resembling the Cochins but with longer neck, tail, and legs **2** -s *often cap* **:** any bird of the Langshan breed

**lang·spiel** *also* **lang·spil** \ˈlaŋz,pē(ə)l, -ŋ(k),sp-\ *n* -s [Norw *langspil*, *langspel*, fr. *lang* long (fr. ON *langr*) + *spil*, *spel* play, fr. MLG *spil*; akin to OHG *spil* play — more at LONG, SPIEL] **:** a harp formerly played in the Shetland islands and Iceland

¹**lang syne** \(ˈ)laŋˈzīn, (ˈ)laiŋ-, -ˈsīn\ *adv* (*or adj*) [ME (Sc) *lang sine*, fr. *lang* long + *sine*, *syne* since — more at LONG, SYNE] *chiefly Scot* **:** at a distant time in the past

²**lang syne** \"\ *n, chiefly Scot* **:** times past **:** old times ⟨old men sat . . . and talked politics, racing, or *lang syne* —Ruth Park⟩

¹**lan·guage** \ˈlaŋgwij, ˈlaiŋ-, -wēj *sometimes* -ŋw-\ *n* -s *often attrib* [ME *langage*, *language*, fr. OF, fr. *langue* tongue, language (fr. L *lingua*) + *-age* — more at TONGUE] **1 :** the words, their pronunciation, and the methods of combining them used and understood by a considerable community and established by long usage ⟨French ~⟩ ⟨Bantu group of ~*s*⟩ ⟨classical Latin is a dead ~⟩ ⟨~ barrier between two countries⟩ **2 a :** audible, articulate, meaningful sound as produced by the action of the vocal organs **b :** a systematic means of communicating ideas or feelings by the use of conventionalized signs, sounds, gestures, or marks having understood meanings ⟨finger ~⟩ ⟨~ of flowers⟩ ⟨~ of painting⟩ ⟨mathematics is a universally understood ~⟩ **c :** an artificially constructed primarily formal system of signs and symbols (as symbolic logic) including rules for the formation of admissible expressions and for their transformation — compare METALANGUAGE, OBJECT LANGUAGE, PHYSICAL LANGUAGE, SENSE-DATUM LANGUAGE, THING-LANGUAGE **d :** the means by which animals communicate or are thought to communicate with each other ⟨~ of the birds⟩ ⟨dog ~⟩ **3 a :** the faculty of verbal expression and the use of words in human intercourse ⟨~ exists only when it is listened to as well as spoken —John Dewey⟩ **:** significant communication **b** *archaic* **:** the faculty of speech; *esp* **:** ability to speak a foreign tongue **4 :** a special manner of use of expression: as **a :** form or manner of verbal expression ⟨elegant ~⟩ **:** characteristic mode of expression of an individual speaker or writer **:** STYLE ⟨figurative ~⟩ **b :** the vocabulary and phraseology belonging to an art or department of knowledge ⟨legal ~⟩ ⟨~ of chemistry⟩ ⟨~ of diplomacy⟩ ⟨a deep-voiced six-footer who talks the farmer's ~ —*Time*⟩ **c :** abusive epithets **:** PROFANITY ⟨shouldn't of blamed the fellers if they'd cut loose with some ~ —Ring Lardner⟩ **5** *obs* **:** TALK; *esp* **:** CENSURE, ABUSE ⟨safely venture to hold ~ —T.B.Macaulay⟩ **6 a** *archaic* **:** a people or nation as distinguished by its speech ⟨all the people, the nations, and the ~, fell down and worshiped the golden image —Dan 3: 7(AV)⟩ **b :** a national division of an international order ⟨~ of Aragon of the Hospitalers⟩

**syn** TONGUE, SPEECH, IDIOM, DIALECT: LANGUAGE is likely to indicate a more general and established and less specific and individual means of communication ⟨English and French are *languages*, that is to say they are systems of habits of speech, exactly like Eskimo or Hottentot or any other *language* —R.A.Hall b. 1911⟩ ⟨the noble *language* of Milton and Burke would have remained a rustic dialect, without a literature, without a fixed grammar, or a fixed orthography —T.B.Macaulay⟩ TONGUE may suggest a more specific and narrowed concept than LANGUAGE ⟨a common language was the ancestor of both of these *tongues* [English and German] —*Publ's Mod. Lang. Assoc. of Amer.*⟩ SPEECH may call attention to the spoken rather than the written communication ⟨they argued, corresponded, delivered speeches, made jokes, and wrote satires in Latin. It was not a dead language but a living *speech* —Gilbert Highet⟩ IDIOM may suggest the more individual, specific, peculiar, and different from the general ⟨the French-English *idiom* of Louisiana as Mr. Cable presents it; the Negro-English idiom of the upper South as Mr. Harris presents it —A.J.Nock⟩ ⟨returning to the *idiom* of the Icelandic saga and to the metric of Langland —C.D.Lewis⟩ DIALECT may refer to a variant of a language, esp. one restricted to a limited area and one not entirely unintelligible to speakers of the language of which it is a phase ⟨the situation with regard to the American Indian languages, with many tribes speaking apparently unrelated languages which are in turn subdivided into *dialects*, is extremely complex —Thomas Pyles⟩ ⟨this language was once a *dialect* developed from a language which may be reconstructed from the historic tongues, and which is conventionally termed Proto-Teutonic —L. H.Gray⟩. In general literary use these terms are often interchangeable ⟨from her early years she must have treasured up those pithy bits of local *speech*, of native *idiom*, which enrich and enliven her pages. The *language* her people speak to each other is a native *tongue* —Willa Cather⟩

²**language** \"\ *vt* -ED/-ING/-S *dial* **:** to express in language

³**language** \"\ *n* -s [by folk etymology fr. *languet*] **:** LANGUET 2a

**language arts** *n pl* **:** the subjects (as reading, spelling, literature, composition, debate, dramatics) taught in elementary and secondary schools that aim at developing the learner's comprehension of written and oral language as well as his use of it for communication and expression

**languaged** \-jd; *stressed* ˈ══\ *adj* [ME *langaged*, fr. *langage* language + ¹*-ed*] **1 :** skilled in language **:** learned in languages **:** having a language **:** using a specified kind of speech — used usu. with a qualifying word ⟨well-*languaged* man⟩ **2 :** expressed in language ⟨beautifully ~ sermons⟩

**lan·guage·less** *pronunc at* ¹LANGUAGE + ləs\ *adj* **:** having no language

**langue** \ˈläⁿg\ *n* -s [F — more at LANGUAGE] **1 :** LANGUAGE 6b **2 :** language that is a system of elements or a set of habits common to a community of speakers — contrasted with *parole*

**langued** \ˈlaŋd\ *adj* [MF *langue* + E *-ed*] *heraldry* **:** having the tongue visible and of a specified tincture ⟨lion armed and ~ gules⟩

**langue de boeuf** \ˌläŋdəˈbə(r)f, -bəf\ *n, pl* **langues de boeuf** \"\ [ME *lange de boef*, fr. MF *langue de bœuf*, lit., ox tongue] **:** a pike with a blade very wide at the head and tapering rapidly to a point used esp. in the 15th century; *also* **:** a short sword or dagger of this shape

**langue d'oc** *or* **langue·doc** \läŋˈdȯk, läⁿgdȯk\ *n* [F, fr. OF, lit., language of *oc*; fr. the use of the word *oc* for "yes" in contrast to the use of the word *oil* for "yes" in northern France] **:** PROVENÇAL

¹**langue·do·cian** \ˌlaŋ(g)(w)əˈdōshən, (ˈ)laŋˈd-\ *adj, usu cap* [*Languedoc*, region in south central France + E *-ian*] **:** of or relating to Languedoc

²**languedocian** \"\ *n* -s *cap* **1 :** a native or inhabitant of Languedoc **2** [F *langue d'oc* + E *-ian*] **:** the Provençal dialect

**langue d'oïl** \läŋˈdȯi(ə)l; läⁿgdȯil, -dōēl, -dȯy\ *n* [F, fr. OF, lit., language of *oïl*; fr. the use of the word *oïl* for "yes" in contrast to the use of the word *oc* for "yes" in Provençal] **:** FRENCH 1

**lan·gues·cent** \(ˈ)laŋˈgwesᵊnt\ *adj* [L *languescent-*, *languescens*, pres. part. of *languescere* to become faint, incho. of *languēre* to be faint — more at SLACK] **:** becoming languid or fatigued

**lan·guet** *also* **lan·guette** \ˈlaŋgwət, (ˈ)laŋˈgwet\ *n* -s [ME *languet*, *languette*, fr. MF *languete*, *languette*, dim. of *langue* tongue — more at LANGUAGE] **:** something resembling the tongue in form or function: as **a :** LATCHET 2 **b :** a part of a sword hilt that overlaps the scabbard **c :** a tongue of land **2 a :** the inner tongue or flat plate opposite the mouth of an organ flue pipe — called also *languid* **b :** the tongue of a harmonium or organ reed **c :** the finger key of a wind instrument **d :** the tongue of a harpsichord jack **3 :** one of the small pointed processes on the median line of the branchial sac of certain ascidians

¹**lan·guid** \ˈlaŋgwəd, ˈlaiŋ-\ *adj* [MF *languide*, fr. L *languidus*, fr. *languēre* to languish, be languid — more at SLACK] **1 :** drooping or flagging from or as if from exhaustion **:** lacking vigor **:** WEAK ⟨arms too ~ with happiness to embrace him —John Galsworthy⟩ **2 :** sluggish in character or disposition **:** DULL, LISTLESS ⟨~ enjoyment of the daydream —Nathaniel Hawthorne⟩ ⟨stretched out a ~ hand —Dorothy Sayers⟩ **3 :** lacking force or vividness **:** SLOW ⟨heard . . . in a moment of exhausted or ~ interest —A.T.Quiller-Couch⟩ ⟨contrast between his huge bulk and his ~, almost effeminate, demeanor —Robert Hichens⟩

**syn** LANGUISHING, LANGUOROUS, LACKADAISICAL, LISTLESS, SPIRITLESS, ENERVATED: LANGUID may indicate an inability or indisposition to exert or concern oneself owing to weakness, malaise, or ennui ⟨she turned and walked from the room with *languid* deliberate steps; her air was curiously apathetic, and she moved as though she were intolerably weary —Elinor Wylie⟩ ⟨struck by something *languid* and inelastic in her attitude, and wondered if the deadly monotony of their lives had laid its weight on her also —Edith Wharton⟩ LANGUISHING may suggest delicate indolence, often accompanying boredom or futilely wistful pensiveness ⟨the pair had completely lost their pallid looks and *languishing* manners; they were as bright-eyed and agile as the hares —Elinor Wylie⟩ LANGUOROUS may suggest the debilitated languidness characteristic of soft, delicate living, effete shrinking from exertion, and indulgence in emotionalism and sentimentality or an atmosphere compatible with such languidness ⟨reclining on the couch reading a novel in *languorous* ease⟩ LACKADAISICAL suggests an indifferent or apathetic and inattentive attitude militating against exertion and for futile, halfhearted performance ⟨had the gift of instilling a corresponding vigor into all his *lackadaisical* black soldiers, who at first sight seemed to be hopelessly addicted to lolling under a bush, and inflexibly determined to do nothing —Kenneth Roberts⟩ LISTLESS suggests combined lack of sustained interest and appearance of languor, esp. as brought about by ennui, boredom, or illness ⟨was struck by her *listless* attitude: she sat there as if she had nothing else to do —Edith Wharton⟩ ⟨struck with the *listless*, slovenly behavior of these men; there was nothing of the national vivacity in their movements; nothing of the quick precision perceptible on the deck of a thoroughly disciplined armed vessel —Herman Melville⟩ SPIRITLESS applies to utter lack of fire, animation, or force ⟨for once she did not greet him with flowery excitement but with a noncommittal "Hello". She seemed *spiritless* —Sinclair Lewis⟩ ⟨dominated the starving, *spiritless* wretches under him with savage enjoyment —F.V.W.Mason⟩ ENERVATED implies a tiring out, exhausting, and sapping, often by luxury or sloth ⟨the *enervated* and sickly habits of the literary class —R.W.Emerson⟩ ⟨*enervated* by licentiousness, ruined by prodigality and enslaved by sycophants —T.B.Macaulay⟩

²**languid** \"\ *n* -s [by alter.] **:** LANGUET 2a

**lan·guid·ly** *adv* **:** in a languid manner

**lan·guid·ness** *n* -ES **:** the quality or state of being languid

¹**lan·guish** \ˈlaŋgwish, ˈlaiŋ-, -wēsh, *esp in pres part* -wəsh\ *vi* -ED/-ING/-ES [ME *languishen*, *languissen*, fr. MF *languiss-*, stem of *languir*, fr. (assumed) VL *languire*, fr. L *languēre*] **1 :** to become languid **:** lose strength or animation **:** be or become dull, feeble, or spiritless **:** lose force or vividness ⟨conversation ~*ed*⟩ **:** FADE ⟨plants ~ in the drought⟩ **2 :** to be or live in a state of lessened or lessening strength or vitality **:** DROOP ⟨~*ing* spirits⟩ **:** pine with longing ⟨~ for years in prison⟩ **:** suffer neglect ⟨contract . . . has ~*ed* in committee ever since —*Newsweek*⟩ **3 :** to assume an expression of weariness or tender grief or emotion appealing for sympathy ⟨~ at him through screwed-up eyes —Edith Wharton⟩

²**languish** \"\ *n* -ES [ME, fr. *languishen*, v.] *archaic* **1 :** the act or state of languishing ⟨one desperate grief cures with another's ~ —Shak.⟩ **2 :** a languishing tender look or expression ⟨the warm, dark ~ of her eyes —J.G.Whittier⟩

**lan·guish·er** \-shə(r)\ *n* -s **:** one that languishes

**lan·guish·ing** *adj* [ME, fr. pres. part. of *languishen* to languish] **1 a :** losing health and strength ⟨could not rouse him from his ~ state⟩ **b :** LINGERING ⟨~ illness⟩ **2 :** expressing longing, desire, or tender sentiment ⟨exchanged ~ glances⟩ **syn** see LANGUID

**lan·guish·ing·ly** *adv* **:** in a languishing manner ⟨drooped her eyelids ~⟩

**lan·guish·ment** \-shmənt\ *n* -s [MF *languissement*, fr. *languiss-* + *-ment*] **1** *archaic* **:** the act or state of languishing **:** ILLNESS, WEAKNESS, SADNESS, LASSITUDE **2** *archaic* **:** tenderness of look or bearing **:** amorous pensiveness

**lan·guor** \ˈlaŋ(g)ə(r), ˈlaiŋ-\ *n* -s [ME *langour*, *langor*, fr. OF, fr. L *languor*, fr. *languēre* to feel faint, languish — more at SLACK] **1** *obs* **:** enfeebling disease **:** SUFFERING **2 :** a state of the body or mind caused by exhaustion or disease and characterized by a languid feeling **:** LASSITUDE ⟨~ of convalescence⟩ **3 :** listless indolence **:** DREAMINESS ⟨certain ~ in the air hinted at an early summer —James Purdy⟩ **4 :** DULLNESS, SLUGGISHNESS **:** lack of vigor **:** STAGNATION ⟨from ~ she passed to the lightest vivacity —Elinor Wylie⟩

**lan·guor·ous** \-ŋ(g)(ə)rəs\ *adj* [MF *langoureux*, fr. *langour* + *-eux* -ous] **1** *obs* **:** GRIEVOUS, SORROWFUL **2 :** producing or tending to produce languor ⟨~ climate⟩ **:** characterized by languor ⟨haunting ~ verse —*Times Lit. Supp.*⟩ **syn** see LANGUID

**lan·guor·ous·ly** *adv* **:** in a languorous manner ⟨sprawling ~ on a sofa⟩

**lan·gur** *also* **lun·goor** \ˌləŋˈgu̇(ə)r\ *n* -s [Hindi *lãgūr*, prob. fr. Skt *lāṅgūlin* having a (long) tail] **:** any of various Asiatic long-tailed monkeys that with the proboscis monkey and the African guerezas constitute a family (Colobidae) and are of slender build, usu. gray or brownish gray in color, and have bushy eyebrows and a chin tuft

**lani-** — see LAN-

**laniard** *var of* LANYARD

**lani·ar·i·us** \ˌlānēˈa(a)rēəs, ˌlan-\ *n, cap* [NL, fr. L, butcher, fr. *laniarius* of a butcher] **:** a genus of African shrikes comprising the boubous

**lani·ary** \ˈ══ˌerē\ *adj* [L *laniarius* of a butcher, fr. *lanius* butcher (prob. of Etruscan origin like L *lanista*) + *-arius* -ary] *of teeth* **:** adapted for tearing **:** CANINE

**lani·ate** \-ē,āt\ *vt* -ED/-ING/-S [L *laniatus*, past part. of *laniare* to rend, prob. fr. *lanius* butcher] **:** to tear in pieces

**la·ni·idae** \ləˈnīə,dē\ *n pl, cap* [NL, fr. *Lanius*, type genus + *-idae*] **:** a family of dentirostral oscine birds consisting of the true shrikes and various related birds

**laning** *pres part of* LANE

**la·nis·ta** \ləˈnistə\ *n, pl* **lanis·tae** \-,stē, -,stī\ [L, of Etruscan origin] **:** a trainer of gladiators in ancient Rome

**la·ni·us** \ˈlānēəs\ *n, cap* [NL, fr. L, butcher] **:** a genus consisting of the typical shrikes

**lank** \ˈlaŋk, -aiŋk\ *adj* -ER/-EST [fr. (assumed) ME *lank*, fr. OE *hlanc*; akin to OHG *hlanca* loin, flank, ON *hlykkr* bend, noose, L *clingere* to girdle, OSlav *klęčati* to kneel; basic meaning: bending] **1 :** slender and thin **:** not well filled out **:** not plump ⟨meager and ~ with fasting grown —Jonathan Swift⟩ ⟨~ cattle⟩ **:** SCANTY, MEAGRE ⟨~ grass⟩ **2** *archaic* **:** LANGUID, DROOPING ⟨reared her ~ head —John Milton⟩ **3** *of hair* **:** hanging straight and limp without spring or curl **syn** see LEAN

**lank·i·ly** \-kəlē, -li\ *adv* **:** in a lanky manner **:** so as to suggest lankiness

**lank·i·ness** \-kēnəs, -kin-\ *n* -ES **:** the quality or state of being lanky

**lank·ish** \-kish,-kēsh\ *adj* **:** somewhat lank

**lank·ly** *adv* **:** in a lank manner **:** LIMPLY

**lank·ness** *n* -ES **:** the quality or state of being lank

**lanky** \ˈlaŋkē, -aiŋ-, -ki\ *adj* -ER/-EST **:** tall, spare, and usu. loose-jointed **:** BONY, RAWBONED ⟨that tall, blond, ~ girl who had followed him about everywhere —Louis Auchincloss⟩ **syn** see LEAN

**lan·ner** \ˈlanə(r)\ *n* -s [ME *laner*, fr. MF *lanier*, short for *faucon lanier*, fr. OF, fr. *faucon* falcon + *lanier* cowardly, fr. *lanier* woolworker, coward, fr. L *lanarius* woolworker, fr. *lana* wool + *-arius* -ary — more at WOOL] **:** a falcon (*Falco biarmicus feldeggii*) of southern Europe or a member of a related variety in southwestern Asia or Africa that resembles the American prairie falcon; *specif* **:** the female of one of these falcons

**lan·ner·et** \ˌlanəˈret\ *n* -s [ME *lanerette*, *lanret*, fr. MF *laneret*, dim. of *lanier* lanner] **:** a male lanner

**lano-** — see LAN-

**lan·o·ceric acid** \ˌlanəˈsi(ə)rik-, -se|\ *n* [ISV *lan-* + *cer-* + *-ic*] **:** a crystalline dihydroxy acid $(HO)_2C_{29}H_{57}COOH$ found as an ester in wool grease

**lan·o·lat·ed** \ˈlanᵊl,ād·əd\ *adj* [*lanolin* + *-ate* + *-ed*] **:** containing lanolin ⟨~ hand cream⟩ ⟨~ soap⟩

**lan·o·lin** \ˈlanᵊlən\ *also* **lan·o·line** \", -ᵊl,ēn\ *n* -s [ISV *lan-* + *-ol* + *-in*, *-ine*; orig. formed as G *lanolin*] **:** wool grease refined for use chiefly in ointments and cosmetics: **a :** a yellowish sticky unctuous mass absorbable by the skin and containing incorporated water — called also *hydrous wool fat* **b :** a similar brownish yellow anhydrous mass — called also *anhydrous lanolin*, *refined wool fat*

**lan·o·lize** \-ᵊl,īz\ *vt* -ED/-ING/-S [*lanolin* + *-ize*] **:** to add lanolin or lanolin derivatives to (as soap)

**la·nose** \ˈlā,nōs\ *adj* [L *lanosus*, fr. *lana* wool + *-osus* -ose — more at WOOL] **:** LANATE, WOOLLY — **la·nos·i·ty** \lāˈnäsəd·ē, lə-\ *n* -ES

**la·nos·ter·ol** \ləˈnästə,rōl, -rōl\ *n* -s [*lan-* + *sterol*] **:** a crystalline tetracyclic alcohol $C_{30}H_{49}OH$ that occurs in wool grease and yeast and may be regarded as a triterpenoid sterol

**lans** *pl of* LAN

**Lans·downe** \ˈlanz,dau̇n\ *trademark* — used for a fine lightweight dress fabric in twill weave with a silk or rayon warp and a worsted or cotton filling

**lan·seh** *also* **lan·sa** \ˈlan(t)sə\ *or* **lan·sat** \-sət\ *n* -s [of Indonesian origin; akin to Malay *langsat* lanseh] **1 :** the edible yellow berry of an East Indian tree (*Lansium domesticum*) of the family Meliaceae **2 :** the tree that bears the lanseh

**lans·ford·ite** \ˈlan(t)sfə(r),dīt, -anzf-\ *n* -s [G *lansfordit*, fr. *Lansford*, Pa., its locality + G *-it* -ite] **:** a mineral $MgCO_3.5H_2O$ composed of a hydrous basic carbonate of magnesium like paraffin when first taken out of the ground but altering to nesquehonite on exposure

**lan·sing** \ˈlan(t)siŋ, ˈlaan-, ˈlain-, -sēŋ\ *adj, usu cap* [fr. *Lansing*, Mich.] **:** of or from Lansing, the capital of Michigan ⟨a *Lansing* product⟩ **:** of the kind or style prevalent in Lansing

**lansing virus** *also* **lansing strain** *n, usu cap L* **:** a strain of the virus causing poliomyelitis that is pathogenic for monkeys and rodents and has been extensively used in study of the disease

**lanson** *var of* LANZON

**lans·que·net** \ˈlan(t)skə,net, -anzk-, -kəˈnā\ *n* -s [F, modif. of G *landsknecht*, fr. MHG *landsknecht*, fr. *lands* (gen. of *lant* land, country, province, fr. OHG) + *kneht* boy, youth, foot soldier, fr. OHG, boy, youth, military follower — more at LAND, KNIGHT] **1 :** a German foot soldier in foreign service in the 15th, 16th, and 17th centuries **:** a mercenary foot soldier **2 :** a card game similar to faro played in central Europe since the 15th century or before

**lant** \ˈlant\ *n* -s [back-formation fr. *lants* (taken as pl.), alter. of *launce*, *lance*] **:** SAND LAUNCE

**lan·ta·ka** *or* **lan·ta·ca** \ˌläntəˈkä\ *n* -s [Tag *lantakà*] **:** a Philippine piece of artillery like a culverin

**lan·ta·na** \lanˈtanə\ *n* [NL, fr. ML or NL, viburnum, fr. It dial. (Switzerland and northern Italy)] **1** *cap* **:** a genus of tropical sometimes half-climbing shrubs (family Verbenaceae) having umbellate heads of small bright-colored flowers and juicy drupaceous fruit — see RED SAGE **2** -s **:** any plant of the genus *Lantana*

**lanterloo** *n* [F *lanturelu*, *lanturlu* piffle — more at LOO] *obs* **:** LOO

¹**lan·tern** *R* ˈlantərn, ˈlaan-, ˈlain-, *–R* -tən *also* -tᵊn\ *n* -s *often attrib* [ME *lanterne*, fr. MF, fr. L *lanterna*, fr. Gk *lamptēr* stand for holding a torch, lantern, fr. *lampein* to give light, shine — more at LAMP] **1 :** a protective enclosure for a light with transparent openings and often a supporting frame or carrying handle **:** a portable lamp **2 :** a giver of light ⟨~ of science⟩ **3 a** *obs* **:** LIGHTHOUSE **b :** the chamber in a lighthouse that contains the light **c :** a structure with glazed or open sides raised above an opening in a roof to light or ventilate the interior space below **:** MONITOR 5 **d :** a small tower or cupola or one stage of a cupola **4 a :** a foundry lamp **b :** CORE BARREL **c :** LANTERN PINION **5 :** ARISTOTLE'S LANTERN **6 :** PROJECTOR 2b

lanterns 1: *1* barn, *2* bull's-eye

²**lantern** \"\ *vt* -ED/-ING/-S **1 :** to furnish with a lantern ⟨~ a lighthouse⟩ ⟨~ a fishing boat⟩ **:** light the way of with a lantern **2** [F *lanterner*, fr. *lanterne* lantern, street lamp] **:** to put to death by hanging to a street lamppost

**lantern clock** *n* **1 :** a clock designed to be mounted in a wall and having its driving weights together with their supporting cords and the greater part of the pendulum outside of the case **2 :** a brass pendulum or foliot shelf clock of the 17th century whose chief features are a dome formed by a bell and open fretwork connecting the bell and dial

**lantern fish** *n* **1 :** any of numerous small mostly deep-sea fishes constituting the family Myctophidae that have a large mouth and large eyes and usu. numerous luminous spots or glands upon the body **2 :** a fish of the order Iniomi

**lantern flounder** *n* **:** ²MEGRIM a

**lantern fly** *n* **:** any of certain usu. large and brightly colored insects that are chiefly of the genera *Laternaria* and *Fulgora* of the family Fulgoridae and that have the front of the head prolonged into a large hollow vesicle formerly supposed to be luminous; *broadly* **:** an insect of the superfamily Fulgoroidea

**lantern gurnard** *n* **:** a European gurnard (*Trigla obscura*) having a brilliant silvery band along the sides

**lantern jaw** *n* **1 :** an undershot jaw **2 lantern jaws** *pl* **:** long thin jaws

**lantern–jawed** \ˈ══ˌ═\ *adj* **:** having a lantern jaw

**lanternleaf** \ˈ══,═\ *n* [alter. of *Lenten leaf*] **:** CREEPING CROWFOOT

**lantern light** *n* **1 :** a transparent pane in a lantern **2 :** a skylight raised above the roof level

**lan·tern·man** \ˈ══,man, -,mən\ *n, pl* **lanternmen :** a man who carries a lantern; *specif* **:** NIGHTMAN 1

**lantern pinion** *n* **:** a gear pinion having cylindrical bars instead of teeth inserted at their ends in two parallel disks — called also *trundle*

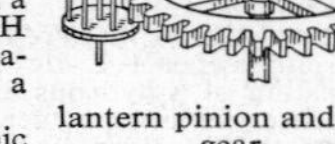
lantern pinion and spur gear

**lantern ring** *n* **:** a packing ring for shaft or piston-rod glands having a cross section resembling the letter H

**lantern shell** *n* **:** a translucent marine bivalve shell of *Laternula* or a related genus

**lantern slide** *n* **:** a photographic transparency adapted for projection in a slide projector

**lantern sprat** *n* **:** the common sprat when infested with a phosphorescent lernaean parasite (*Lerneonema monilaris*)

**lan·tha·na** \'lan(t)thənə\ *n* -s [NL, fr. *lanthanum* + *-a*] **:** lanthanum oxide $La_2O_3$ obtained as a white powder

**lan·tha·nide** \-thə,nīd, -,nəd\ *n* -s [ISV *lanthan-* (fr. NL *lanthanum*) + *-ide*] **:** a chemical element of the lanthanide series — called also *lanthanon;* symbol *Ln*

**lanthanide contraction** *n* **:** the decrease in size (as of radii of atoms or ions or of atomic volumes) with increasing atomic number of the metals of the lanthanide series

**lanthanide series** *n* **:** the group of rare-earth metals often including lanthanum and sometimes yttrium — compare PERIODIC TABLE

**lan·tha·nite** \-,nīt\ *n* -s [G *lanthanit*, fr. NL *lanthanum* + G *-it* -ite] **:** a mineral $(La,Ce)_2(CO_3)_3.8H_2O$ composed of hydrous lanthanum carbonate occurring in white crystals or earthy

**lan·tha·non** \-,nän, -,nən\ *n* -s [NL, alter. of *lantha*] **:** LANTHANIDE

**lan·tha·no·tus** \,==ˈnōd·əs\ *n, cap* [NL, fr. Gk *lanthanein* to escape notice + *ōt-, ous* ear — more at LATENT, EAR] **:** a genus of stout-bodied pleurodont lizards including a single species (*L. borneensis*) of Borneo

**lan·tha·num** \'lan(t)thənəm\ *n* -s [NL, fr. Gk *lanthanein* to escape notice] **:** a white soft malleable trivalent metallic element that tarnishes readily in moist air and forms colorless compounds, that occurs in rare-earth minerals and is usu. included in the rare-earth group, and that is one of the major components of misch metal — symbol *La;* see ELEMENT table

**lan·thi·o·nine** \lan'thīə,nēn, -,nən\ *n* -s [*lan-* + *thion-* + *-ine*] **:** an amino acid $S[CH_2CH(NH_2)COOH]_2$ obtained esp. by the action of alkali on wool, hair, or cystine

**lan·tho·pine** \'lan(t)thə,pēn, -,pən\ *n* -s [ISV *lanth-* (fr. Gk *lanthanein*) + *opium* + *-ine;* orig. formed as G *lanthopin*] **:** a crystalline alkaloid $C_{23}H_{25}NO_4$ found in opium

**lant·horn** \'lant,hȯrn, -ō(ə)n, *or like* LANTERN\ *n* -s [by folk= etymology (influence of [1]*horn*, of which the sides were formerly made) fr. *lantern*] *chiefly Brit* **:** LANTERN

**lants** *pl of* LANT

**lantskip** *obs var of* LANDSCAPE

**lan·tum** \'lantəm\ *n* -s [origin unknown] **:** a large hurdy= gurdy

**la·nu·gi·nous** \lə'n(y)üjənəs\ *also* **la·nu·gi·nose** \-jə,nōs\ *adj* [L *lanuginosus*, fr. *lanugin-*, *lanugo* + *-osus* -ous, -ose] **:** covered with down or fine soft hair **:** DOWNY — **la·nu·gi·nous·ness** *n* -ES

**la·nu·go** \lə'n(y)ü(,)gō\ *n* -s [L, down — more at WOOL] **:** a dense cottony or downy growth; *specif* **:** the soft woolly hair that covers the human fetus and that of some other mammals; *also* **:** hair of this type persisting after birth; DOWN

**la·nu·vi·an** \lə'n(y)üvēən\ *n* -s *cap* [*Lanuvium*, city in ancient Latium, Italy + E *-an*] **:** the language of ancient Lanuvium that was closely related to Latin

**lanx** \'laŋ(k)s, -ā-\ *n, pl* **lan·ces** \'lan,sēz, 'läŋ,kās\ [L — more at BALANCE] **:** an ancient Roman platter usu. of metal

**lan·yard** *also* **lan·iard** \'lanyə(r)d\ *n* -s [ME *lanyer*, fr. MF *laniere*, fr. OF *lasniere*, fr. *lasne* strap, thong, noose, prob. modif. (influenced by *laz* snare, noose) of a word of Gmc origin; akin to OHG *nestila*, *nestilo* bow, band, shoelace, OS *nestila* string, hair band, OE *net* — more at LACE, NET] **1** *obs* **:** THONG, STRAP **2 a :** a piece of rope or line for fastening something in ships; *esp* **:** one of the pieces passing through deadeyes and used to extend shrouds or stays **b :** a line for raising and lowering flags and pennants **3 a :** a cord worn around the neck by sailors to which is usu. attached a knife — called also *knife lanyard* **b :** a cord worn by members of a military unit cited for distinction as a symbol of the unit citation **c :** a strong cord worn about the neck or shoulder and attached to a pistol **4 :** a strong cord with a hook at one end used in firing cannon

**lanyard knot** *n* **:** STOPPER KNOT

**lan·zon** \län'zōn, -'sōn\ *or* **lanson** \-'sōn\ *n, pl* **lanzo·nes** \-näs\ *or* **lanso·nes** \-näs\ [PhilSp *lanzón*, *lansón*] **:** LANSEH

[1]**lao** \'laů\ *n, pl* **lao** *or* **laos** *cap* **1 a :** a Buddhist people living in Laos and adjacent parts of northeastern Thailand and constituting an important branch of the Tai race **b :** a member of such people **2 :** the Thai language of the Lao people

[2]**lao** \"\ *also* **lao·tian** \(')lā'ōshən, 'laůshən\ *adj, usu cap* [*Laotian* fr. [1]*Lao* + connective *-t-* + E *-ian*] **:** of or relating to the Lao people

**la·oc·o·on** \lā'äkə,wän\ *n* -s *often cap* [after *Laocoon*, ancient Greek priest of Apollo (fr. Gk *Laokoōn*) who is portrayed in a 1st cent. B.C. sculpture in a heroic struggle against two giant serpents] **:** one that struggles heroically with crushing or baffling difficulties ⟨a man engaged in a *Laocoon* struggle with his imagination —Robert Lynd⟩ ⟨gives the impression of being . . . forced into ~ attitudes —Graham Greene⟩

**lao·dah** *also* **low·dah** \'laů'dä\ *n* -s [Chin (Pek) *lao*[3] *ta*[4], fr. *lao*[3] old + *ta*[4] great] **:** the skipper of a Chinese craft

[1]**la·od·i·ce·an** \(,)lā,ädə'sēən\ *adj, usu cap* [*Laodicea*, ancient city in Asia Minor (fr. L, fr. Gk *Laodikeia*) + E *-an*] **1 :** of or relating to ancient Laodicea, a city of Asia Minor and site of an early Christian church **2 :** lukewarm or indifferent in religion or politics

[2]**laodicean** \"\ *n* -s *usu cap* **1 :** a native or inhabitant of ancient Laodicea; *esp* **:** a member of the Laodicean church **2 :** one that is lukewarm or indifferent

**la·od·i·ce·an·ism** \(,)=,==ˈsēə,nizəm\ *n* -s *usu cap* **:** indifference in religion or politics

**laoighis** \'lāsh, 'lēsh\ *adj, usu cap* [fr. *Laoighis* county, Ireland] **:** of or from County Laoighis, Ireland **:** of the kind or style prevalent in County Laoighis

**laos** \'laůs, 'lā,äs *sometimes* 'lāəs, *chiefly Brit* 'laůz\ *adj, usu cap* [fr. *Laos*, kingdom in Indochina] **:** of or from the kingdom of Laos **:** of the kind or style prevalent in Laos

**lao·tian** \lā'ōshən, 'laůshən\ *n* -s *cap* [[1]*Lao* + connective *-t-* + E *-ian*] **:** one of the Lao people

[1]**lap** \'lap\ *n* -s [ME *lappe*, fr. OE *læppa;* akin to OFris *lappa* flap, OS *lappo* lappet, OHG *lappa* flap, lappet, ON *leppr* rag, L *labi* to glide, slide — more at SLEEP] **1 a :** a loose panel or free-hanging flap esp. of a garment — called also *lappet* **b** *archaic* **:** the skirt of a coat or dress ⟨with the ~ of my coat cast over my face —Sir Walter Scott⟩ **c :** the front edges of a jacket or coat that come together in a double layer when closed **2 a** *obs* **:** a loose or pendent bodily organ (as a lobe of the liver or the lungs) **b :** a pendent protrusion of the body — usu. used in combination ⟨*earlap*⟩ ⟨*dewlap*⟩ **3 a** (1) **:** the clothing that lies on the knees, thighs, and lower part of the trunk when one sits down (2) **:** the front part of the lower trunk and thighs of a seated person ⟨sit on grandpa's ~⟩ **b :** an environment of nurture ⟨reared in the ~ of luxury⟩ **c :** a concave surface resembling that of a lap ⟨a green lake sparkling in the ~ of a pine-clad mountain —C.B.Davis⟩ **4** *obs* **a :** a fold of a garment used as a repository; *specif* **:** a chest fold (as of a toga) used as a pocket **b :** BOSOM ⟨brought back again into the ~ of the Romish Church —Edward Bowles⟩ **5 :** responsible custody **:** CHARGE, CONTROL ⟨going to drop the whole thing in your ~ —Hamilton Basso⟩ ⟨the outcome of this experiment is in the ~ of the gods⟩ ⟨the gold of Asia Minor was poured into the ~ of the pre-Hellenes —Edward Clodd⟩

[2]**lap** \"\ *vb* **lapped; lapped; lapping; laps** [ME *lappen*, fr. *lappe*, n.] *vt* **1 a** (1) **:** to fold over or around something **:** WIND ⟨~ a bandage around the wrist⟩ (2) **:** to enclose in a cover or binding **:** WRAP ⟨~ the wrist in a bandage⟩ **b :** to envelop entirely **:** SURROUND, SWATHE ⟨life flowed smoothly on *lapping* him in a changeless amber vacuum —A.J.Shirren⟩ ⟨no pains had been spared . . . to ~ them in tasteful and simple luxury —Lucius Beebe⟩ **2 :** to fold over esp. into layers: as **a :** to convert (cotton, wool, flax, or other fiber) into a lap **b** (1) **:** to fold (paper pulp) into a lap (2) **:** to fold (paper) for packaging by laying one set of sheets halfway along another set and rolling each overlapping end over each overlapped end **3 :** to hold protectively in or as if in the lap **:** CUDDLE, NESTLE ⟨legs that were intended to . . . ~ her children —A.R.Foff⟩ ⟨hills . . . fruitful valleys *lapped* in them —Thomas Carlyle⟩ **4 a :** to place over or next to so as to partially or wholly cover **:** OVERLAP ⟨~ shingles in laying a roof⟩ **b :** to unite (as beams or timbers) so as to preserve the same breadth and depth throughout — compare [4]SCARF 1 **5 a :** to dimension, smooth, or polish (as a metal surface or body) to a high degree of refinement or accuracy with a lap or loose abrasive material ⟨*lapping* is an abrading process for refining the surface finish and geometrical accuracy of flat, cylindrical, and spherical surfaces —K.B.Lewis⟩ ⟨bearing surfaces are ground, *lapped*, and honed to a precision mirror finish —Joseph Heitner⟩ **b :** to work two surfaces together with or without abrasives until a very close fit is produced — often used with *in* ⟨the valve is hand *lapped* in its seat with very light pressure and just for long enough to be sure valve is perfectly tight in its seat —H.F.Blanchard & Ralph Ritchen⟩ **6 a :** to lead (an opponent) by one or more circuits of a racecourse ⟨the champion *lapped* him at the mile⟩ **b :** to complete the circuit of ⟨*lapped* the course in 3 minutes 8 seconds —*N.Y. Herald Tribune*⟩ **~** *vi* **1 :** FOLD, WIND ⟨crowds . . . *lapped* around the corner —*Time*⟩ **2 a :** to project beyond or spread over ⟨long enough to ~ 1″ over the toepiece —*Amer. Girl*⟩ ⟨ranches *lapped* a few miles over the eastern bank of the Sacramento —Julian Dana⟩ **b :** to lie partly over or alongside of something or of one another ⟨formation flying so tight that the wings ~⟩ ⟨the edges of the coat ~ deeply⟩ **c :** to use newly received funds to cover up a previous shortage **:** KITE **3 :** to traverse a course ⟨the experimental racer *lapped* at unprecedented speed⟩

[3]**lap** \"\ *n* -s *often attrib* **1 a :** the amount by which one object overlaps or projects beyond another: as (1) **:** the distance one course of shingle or slate roofing extends over the second one below (2) **:** the part that overlaps to form a seam or joint (as the beveled ends joining sections of an endless belt) (3) **:** the distance that a steam-engine slide valve in its middle position has to move to begin to open the steam or exhaust port (4) **:** the distance one steel plate overlaps another (as in the shell plating of a ship) — compare LAPSTRAKE **b :** the part of an object that overlaps another ⟨the front ~ of a winter coat should be at least six inches wide⟩ **2 :** a smoothing and polishing tool commonly in the form of a piece of wood, leather, felt, or soft metal used with or without an embedded abrasive **3 :** a doubling or layering of a flexible substance: as **a :** a fleecy sheet or layer of combed fibers (as of cotton, wool, or flax) usu. wrapped on a cylinder and ready to be spun **b :** a sheet of wet paper pulp from a wet machine folded into convenient size for handling and shipping **c :** a surface defect in steel or glass caused by the folding over on itself of a part of the molten material and the failure of the surfaces to unite **d :** a defect in veneering resulting from misplacement of the sheets of veneer so that one overlaps the other rather than forming a smooth butt joint **4 a :** one circuit around a racecourse **b :** one round of play (as in a game of mancala) **c :** one segment of a larger unit (as a journey or time cycle) ⟨the next thousand-mile ~ of our journey —Wendell Willkie⟩ ⟨it was the last ~ of term —Mavis Gallant⟩ ⟨the last ~ of a long all= day operation —John Muggeridge⟩ **d :** one complete turn (as of a rope around a drum) **5 :** points won in excess of the number necessary to win a card game and applied to the score of the next game

[4]**lap** \"\ *vb* **lapped; lapped; lapping; laps** [ME *lapen*, *lappen*, fr. OE *lapian;* akin to OHG *laffan* to lick, Icel *lepja* to lap, L *lambere* to lick, Gk *laphyssein* to devour, gulp down, Arm *lap'el* to lick] *vi* **1 :** to scoop up food or drink with the tip of the tongue ⟨uncover, dogs, and ~ —Shak.⟩ **2 a :** to make a gentle intermittent splashing sound ⟨waves *lapped* at their feet —Laura Krey⟩ ⟨the *lapping* of the quiet water —Mary Webb⟩ **b :** to move in little waves **:** WASH ⟨when the last wavelet of some old receding ocean *lapped* over them —C.E.W. Bean⟩ ⟨a changing crowd *lapped* up against the front of the garage —Scott Fitzgerald⟩ **~** *vt* **1 :** to scoop up (food or drink) with the tongue ⟨held her kitten to ~ milk —Anne D. Sedgwick⟩ — often used with *up* **2 :** to flow or splash against in little waves ⟨the foundations of the city's buildings have been *lapped* by tides for centuries and many have been badly eroded —Arnaldo Cortesi⟩

[5]**lap** \"\ *n* -s [ME *lappe* taste, fr. *lapen*, *lappen*, v.] **1 a :** an act of lapping ⟨the cat took a ~ or two at the saucer⟩ **b :** as much as can be carried to the mouth by one scoop of the tongue **:** LICK, TASTE ⟨saw a pink tongue shoot out . . . and have a ~ of her soup —*Newsweek*⟩ **2 a :** a thin or weak beverage or food ⟨hounds should be fed . . . some light broth or ~ in the morning —F.M.Ware⟩ **b** *obs* **:** LIQUOR **3 :** a gentle splashing sound ⟨the hollow ~ of the sea at the foot of the cliff —G.G.Carter⟩

[6]**lap** \"\ *now chiefly dial past of* LEAP

[7]**lap** \"\ *n, pl* **lap** *or* **laps** [alter. of *lop*] **:** a treetop left in the woods after logging **:** [1]LOP

**la·pa·cho** \lə'pä(,)chō\ *n* -s [Sp, of AmerInd (prob. Argentine) origin] **:** any of several tropical American timber trees of the genera *Tabebuia* and *Tecoma*

**la·pa·chol** \lə'pä,chȯl, -chōl\ *n* -s [ISV *lapach-* (fr. NL *lapacho*) + *-ol;* orig. formed in F] **:** a yellow crystalline coloring matter $C_{15}H_{14}O_3$ derived from alpha-naphthoquinone and found in the grain of lapacho and similar woods

**la·pac·tic** \lə'paktik\ *adj* [Gk *lapaktikos*, fr. (assumed) Gk *lapaktos* (verbal of Gk *lapassein* to empty) + Gk *-ikos* -ic; akin to Gk *leptos* thin, weak — more at LEPER] **:** CATHARTIC, LAXATIVE

**lap·a·ge·ria** \,lapə'jirēə\ *n* [NL, fr. Marie Joséphine Rose Tascher de *la Pagerie* (maiden name of Joséphine de Beauharnais) †1814 wife of Napoleon Bonaparte + NL *-ia*] **1** *cap* **:** a genus of Chilean vines (family Liliaceae) having trumpet-shaped flowers — see CHILE-BELLS **2** -s **:** any plant of the genus *Lapageria*

**lap·an** \'lapən\ *n* -s [prob. alter. of *lapin*] **:** the meat of a castrated rabbit

**lap·a·rot·o·my** \,lapə'räd·əmē\ *n* -ES [ISV *laparo-* (fr. Gk *lapara* flank, fr. *laparos* slack, loose) + *-tomy;* akin to Gk *leptos* thin, weak] **:** surgical section of the abdominal wall (as for diagnosis or further surgery)

**la paz** \lə'paz, -paa(ə)z; -päl̩z, -päl̩, |s\ *adj, usu cap L&P* [fr. *La Paz*, city in western Bolivia, capital of Bolivia] **:** of or from La Paz, the administrative capital of Bolivia **:** of the kind or style prevalent in La Paz

**lapboard** \'=,=\ *n* **:** a board used on the lap as a substitute for a table or desk ⟨wrote his first drafts in longhand on a ~⟩ ⟨commuters playing cards on a ~⟩

**lap child** *or* **lap baby** *n, South & Midland* **:** a baby not yet able to walk

**lap dissolve** *n* [[3]*lap*] **:** DISSOLVE

**lapdog** \'=,=\ *n* **:** a small pet dog suitable for holding in the lap

**lap dovetail** *n* **:** a dovetail joint in which the recesses in one piece are cut only part way through so that part of the thickness of one board overlaps the end of the other

**la·pel** \lə'pel *sometimes* la'-\ *n* -s [[1]*lap* + *-el*] **:** a turned-back facing usu. wide and pointed at the top and tapering to nothing at the bottom that is usu. one of a pair along the front edges of a jacket, dress, or coat and extends from the collar or neckline to or toward the waistline

**la·pel·er** \-lə(r)\ *n* -s **:** one that makes or sews lapels

**la·pelled** \-ld\ *adj* **1 :** having lapels **2 :** turned back as lapels

**lap·ey·rou·sia** \,lapə'rüz(h)ēə\ *n* [NL, irreg. fr. Jean François de Galaup de *La Pérouse* †1788 Fr. sailor and explorer + NL *-ia*] **1** *cap* **:** a genus of southern African bulbous herbs (family Iridaceae) having blue or red flowers with a slender perianth tube and stamens inserted on the throat **2** -s **:** any plant of the genus *Lapeyrousia*

**lap·ful** \'lap,fůl\ *n* -s **:** as much as the lap can contain

**la·phyg·ma** \lə'figmə\ [NL, fr. Gk, greedy attack, fr. *laphyssein* to devour, gulp down — more at LAP] *syn of* SPODOPTERA

**lap·i·dar·i·an** \,lapə'da(a)rēən\ *adj* [L *lapidarius* of stone + E *-an*] **1 :** of, relating to, or inscribed on stone ⟨a ~ record⟩ **2 :** LAPIDARY 2 ⟨ornate ~ phrases —*New Republic*⟩

**lap·i·darist** \'==dərəst, -,der-\ *n* -s [prob. fr. [1]*lapidary* + *-ist*] **:** LAPIDARY 2

[1]**lap·i·dary** \-,derē, -ri\ *n* -ES [ME *lapidarie*, fr. L *lapidarius*, fr. *lapidarius*, adj.] **1 a :** a cutter, polisher, or engraver of precious stones other than diamonds **b :** the art of cutting gems ⟨an evening course in ~ —*Minerals Yearbook*⟩ **2 :** a connoisseur of precious stones and the art of cutting them ⟨the ~ is often called upon to ascertain the nature of rough gem minerals —F.J.Sperisen⟩

[2]**lapidary** \"\ *adj* [L *lapidarius* of stone, fr. *lapid-*, *lapis* stone + *-arius* -ary; akin to Gk *lepas* crag] **1 a :** LAPIDARIAN 1 ⟨his face is lean, leathery, but not ~ —Harvey Breit⟩ **b :** of or relating to precious stones or the art of cutting them ⟨the ring is of no ~ value — Lord Byron⟩ **2 :** having the elegance and precision associated with inscriptions on stone ⟨his poetry . . . alternates between the ample elegiac and the ~ epigram —Charles Weir⟩ ⟨the more ~ and terse this subject the better it is suited for symphonic elaboration —P.H.Lang⟩

**lap·i·date** \-,dāt\ *vt* -ED/-ING/-S [L *lapidatus*, past part. of *lapidare* to stone, fr. *lapid-*, *lapis* stone] *archaic* **:** to pelt or kill with stones

**lap·i·da·tion** \,==ˈdāshən\ *n* -s [L *lapidation-*, *lapidatio* action of stoning, fr. *lapidatus* + *-ion-*, *-io* -ion] **1 :** the penalty of stoning to death ⟨adultery . . . would be punished by ~ —Sir Richard Burton⟩ **2 :** an act of pelting with stones

**la·pid·e·ous** \lə'pidēəs\ *adj* [L *lapideus*, fr. *lapid-*, *lapis* stone + *-eus* -eous] **:** of the nature of stone **:** STONY

**lap·i·des·cent** \,lapə'des°nt\ *adj* [L *lapidescent-*, *lapidescens*, pres. part. of *lapidescere* to petrify, fr. *lapid-*, *lapis* stone] *archaic* **:** tending to petrify **:** PETRIFYING

**lap·i·dic·o·lous** \,==ˈdikələs\ *adj* [ISV *lapidi-* (fr. L *lapid-*, *lapis*) + *-colous*] **:** living under a stone — used esp. of an insect

**lap·i·dif·ic** \-'difik\ *also* **lap·i·dif·i·cal** \-fəkəl\ *adj* [*lapidific* prob. fr. (assumed) NL *lapidificus*, fr. L *lapidi-* (fr. *lapid-*, *lapis*) + *-ficus* -fic; *lapidifical* prob. fr. (assumed) NL *lapidificus* + E *-al*] *archaic* **:** LAPIDESCENT

**la·pid·i·fi·ca·tion** \lə,pidəfə'kāshən\ *n* -s [prob. fr. (assumed) NL *lapidification-*, *lapidificatio*, fr. ML *lapidificatus* (past part. of *lapidificare*) + L *-ion-*, *-io* -ion] **:** the act or process of lapidifying **:** FOSSILIZATION, PETRIFACTION

**la·pid·i·fy** \=ˈ==,fī\ *vb* **lapidified; lapidified; lapidifying; lapidifies** [F *lapidifier*, fr. ML *lapidificare*, fr. L *lapidi-* (fr. *lapid-*, *lapis*) + *-ficare* -fy] *archaic* **:** to convert into stone or stony material **:** PETRIFY

**lap·i·dist** \'lapədəst\ *n* -s [L *lapid-*, *lapis* stone + E *-ist*] **:** LAPIDARY 1a, 2

**la·pies** \lə'pēz\ *n pl* [modif. of F dial. (Swiss) *lapiaz*, *lapiez*, fr. (assumed) VL *lapida* stone, alter. of L *lapid-*, *lapis*] **:** grooves and ridges formed on a rock surface by solution of limestone

**la·pil·lo** \lə'pi(,)lō\ *n* -s [It, fr. L *lapillus*] **:** lava in the form of lapilli

**la·pil·lus** \-,ləs\ *n, pl* **lapil·li** \-,lī, -(,)lē\ [L, small stone, dim. of *lapis* stone] **1 :** a stony or glassy fragment of lava ¼ to 1½ inches in diameter thrown out in a volcanic eruption **:** volcanic cinder — usu. used in pl. ⟨showers of ashes and *lapilli* —Norman Douglas⟩ **2 :** OTOLITH

**lap·in** \'lapən\ *n* -s [F, rabbit, perh. of Iberian origin; akin to the source of L *lepus* hare] **:** RABBIT; *specif* **:** a castrated male rabbit

**lap·in·ized** *also* **lap·in·ised** \'lapə,nīzd\ *adj* [*lapin* + *-ize*, *-ise* + *-ed*] **:** attenuated by passage through rabbits ⟨a ~ virus⟩

**lapis la·zu·li** \,lapəs'lazə(,)lē, ¦läp-, -azhə- *also* -ə,lī *or* ¦lapə-'slāzə(,)lē\ *also* **lapis** *n* [ME, fr. ML, fr. L *lapis* stone + ML *lazuli*, gen. of *lazulum* lapis lazuli, fr. Ar *lāzaward* — more at AZURE] **1 :** a semiprecious stone usu. of a rich azure blue color that is essentially a lazurite but contains hauynite, sodalite, and other minerals, occurs usu. in small rounded masses frequently showing spangles of iron pyrites, and is probably the sapphire of the ancients **2 :** LAPIS LAZULI BLUE

**lapis lazuli blue** *n* **:** a moderate blue that is redder and duller than average copen and redder and deeper than azurite blue, dresden blue, or pompadour

**lapis lazuli ware** *n* **:** blue Wedgwood pebbleware veined with gold

**lap joint** *n* **:** a joint made by overlapping two ends or edges and fastening them together — compare BUTT JOINT — **lap-jointed** \'=¦==\ *adj*

**la·place's equation** \lə'plä¦səz-, -plal\ *n, usu cap L* [after Pierre Simon de Laplace †1827 Fr. astronomer and mathematician] **:** the equation $\frac{\partial^2 u}{\partial x^2}+\frac{\partial^2 u}{\partial y^2}+\frac{\partial^2 u}{\partial z^2}=0$ often written $\nabla^2 u=0$ in which $x$, $y$, and $z$ are the rectangular Cartesian coordinates of a point in space and $u$ is a function of those coordinates

**laplace station** *n, usu cap L* **:** a geodetic station at which coincident triangulation and astronomic longitude and azimuth determinations are made

**la·plac·ian** \lə'pläsēən, -las-; -lāshən\ *or* **laplacian operator** *n* -s *usu cap L* [Pierre Simon de *Laplace* †1827 + E *-ian*] **:** the differential operator $\nabla^2$ that yields the left member of Laplace's equation

**lap·land** \'lap,land, -lənd\ *adj, usu cap* [fr. *Lapland*, region of northern Norway, northern Sweden, northern Finland, and the northwestern U.S.S.R.] **:** of or from Lapland **:** of the kind or style prevalent in Lapland

**lapland cornel** *n, usu cap L* **:** a low herblike cornel (*Cornus suecica*) found in northern regions of Eurasia and No. America and having dark violet flowers

**lap·land·er** \-də(r)\ *n, cap* **:** LAPP

**lapland longspur** *n, usu cap 1st L* **:** a longspur (*Calcarius lapponicus*) native to Europe and Asia but found also in No. America

**lapland pine** *n, usu cap L* **:** a Scotch pine (*Pinus sylvestris lapponica*) of narrow pyramidal habit

**lapland rosebay** *or* **lapland rhododendron** *n, usu cap L* **:** a dwarf shrub (*Rhododendron lapponicum*) of the mountainous region of eastern No. America having scurfy branches, thick scurfy leaves, and purple flowers and forming extensive depressed mats esp. in arctic and subarctic regions

**lap-lap** \'la,plap\ *n* -s [origin unknown] **:** a loincloth worn by So. Pacific islanders

**la pla·ta** \lə'pläd·ə\ *adj, usu cap L&P* [fr. *La Plata*, city in eastern Argentina] **:** of or from the city of La Plata, Argentina **:** of the kind or style prevalent in La Plata

**lap-love** \'=,=\ *n* **:** FIELD BINDWEED

**lap man** *n* **:** a worker who removes pulp sheets from wet= machine press rolls and folds them into laps

**lapo-lapo** \¦läpō¦lä,pō\ *or* **la·pu·la·pu** \¦läpü¦lä(,)pü\ *n* -s [Tag *lapulapo*] **:** any of certain Philippine groupers; *esp* **:** a grouper (*Cephalopholis argus*) related to the coney and brilliantly marked with iridescent blue

**la·por·tea** \lə'pȯrd·ēə\ *n, cap* [NL, fr. *Laporte*, 19th cent. person otherwise unidentified] **:** a genus of perennial chiefly tropical stinging herbs or trees (family Urticaceae) having large serrate leaves and axillary stipules — see AUSTRALIAN NETTLE TREE, WOODNETTLE

**lapp** \'lap\ *n* -s *cap* [Sw] **1 :** a member of a people of northern Scandinavia, Finland, and the Kola peninsula of northern Russia who are typically nomadic herders of reindeer, fishermen, and hunters of sea mammals **:** LAPLANDER **2 a :** any one of the closely related Finno-Ugric languages spoken by the Lapps **b :** the Lapp languages taken as a group

[1]**lap·pa** \'lapə\ [NL, fr. L, burr] *syn of* ARCTIUM

[2]**lappa** \"\ *n* -s [NL *Lappa*] **:** the root of the great bur used as a diuretic and alterative

**lappa clover** *n* [*lappa* prob. modif. of NL *lappaceum* (specific epithet of *Trifolium lappaceum*), fr. L, neut. of *lappaceus* burrlike, fr. *lappa* burr + *-aceus* -aceous] **:** a Eurasian clover (*Trifolium lappaceum*) with lavender-rose colored flowers that is grown as a forage and hay crop in some parts of the U.S.

**lap·page** \'lapij\ *n* -s **:** the amount by which one surface overlaps another

**lapped** *past of* LAP

**lapped seam** *var of* LAP SEAM

[1]**lap·per** \'lapə(r)\ *n* -s [[4]*lap* + *-er*] **:** one that laps food or drink with the tongue

[2]**lapper** \"\ *n* -s [[2]*lap* + *-er*] **1 a :** one that wraps or folds **b :** one that converts fiber into laps **2 a :** one that dimensions,

smooths, or polishes with a lap **b :** 3LAP 2 **c :** a textile worker who handles laps

**3lapper** \"\ *vb* -ED/-ING/-S [alter. of 1*lopper*] *chiefly Scot* : COAGULATE, CLOT, CURDLE — used esp. of milk

**lap·pet** \'lapət\ *n* -S [1*lap* + -*et*] **1 a :** 1LAP 1a **b** (1) **:** a fold or flap on headgear ⟨simple cap with upturned ~ —George Eliot⟩; *specif* **:** one of a pair of streamers on a woman's headdress usu. hanging down on either side of the face (2) **:** INFULA **c :** LAPEL **2 a** *archaic* **:** 1LAP 2 **b :** a lateral extension of the shell of the living chamber of an ammonoid cephalopod **3 :** a flat overlapping or free-hanging piece (as a roofing tile or a keyhole guard) **4 :** LAPPET MOTH **5 a :** a loom attachment consisting of one or more needlebars with pendent needles carrying a series of floating warp threads to be introduced into the body of the fabric **b :** a lightweight patterned material (as dotted swiss) woven with the aid of a lappet attachment and used chiefly for curtains and dresses

**lappet caterpillar** *n* **:** the stout more or less flattened hairy larva of a lappet moth

**lap·pet·ed** \'lapəd·əd\ *adj* **:** having lappets — used esp. of headgear

**lappet loom** *n* **:** a loom for lappet weaving

**lappet moth** *n* [so called fr. the small lobes at the sides of the body of the larva] **:** any of several stout-bodied medium-sized hairy moths of the family Lasiocampidae — see LAPPET CATERPILLAR

**lappet weaving** *n* **:** machine embroidery by the use of a lappet attachment — see LAPPET 5a

**lap·pic** \'lapik\ *adj, usu cap* **:** of or relating to Lapland or the Lapps

**lapping** *n* -S [ME *lappinge*, gerund of *lappen* to lap, wrap] **1 :** WRAPPING, BINDING; *specif* **:** the protective wrapping of the middle of a bowstring **2 :** OVERLAPPING; *specif* **:** a covering of a current cash shortage by deferring the deposit of funds received until a later date

**1lapp·ish** \'lapish\ *adj, usu cap* [*lapp* + -*ish*] **:** LAPPIC

**2lappish** *n, pl* **lappish** *usu cap* **:** LAPP

**lap plate** *n* [3*lap*] **:** a strap for a butt joint

**lap·pu·la** \'lapyələ\ *n, cap* [NL, fr. L *lappa* burr + -*ula*] **:** a large genus of rough-pubescent herbs (family Boraginaceae) found in temperate regions having small flowers in terminal racemes and nutlets armed with barbed prickles — see STICKSEED

**lap–rivet** \'=,==\ *vt* **:** to rivet together (plates) with the ends or edges overlapping

**lap robe** *n* **:** a covering (as a blanket) for the legs, lap, and feet esp. of a passenger in a car or carriage — compare BUFFALO ROBE

**laps** *pl of* LAP, *pres 3d sing of* LAP

**laps·able** *or* **laps·ible** \'lapsəbəl\ *adj* **:** liable to lapse

**lap·sa·na** \'lapsənə\ *n, cap* [NL, fr. L, charlock, fr. Gk *lapsanē, lampsanē*] **:** a genus of Old World herbs (family Compositae) having pinnatifid leaves and yellow-rayed flower heads — see NIPPLEWORT

**lap·sang sou·chong** \¦lap,saŋ'sü,ch|ȯŋ, -ü,sh|, -ü,j|, |äŋ\ *n, usu cap L* **:** a fine grade of souchong with a characteristic smoky flavor

**1lapse** \'laps\ *n* -S [L *lapsus* fault, error, fall, slide, fr. *lapsus*, past part. of *labi* to glide, slide — more at SLEEP] **1 a :** an accidental mistake in fact or departure from an accepted norm **:** trivial fault **:** SLIP, ERROR ⟨~ of memory⟩ ⟨~ of taste⟩ ⟨the performances show this great pianist at the height of his powers, whatever rhythmical or technical ~*s* they may contain —Edward Sackville-West⟩ **b :** a temporary deviation ⟨~ from consciousness⟩ ⟨~ from respectability⟩ ⟨writes well, despite occasional ~*s* into polysyllabic humor —*Geog. Jour.*⟩ **2 a :** FALL; *specif* **:** a decrease of temperature, pressure, or value of other meteorological element as the height increases — see LAPSE RATE **b :** LOSS, LOWERING, DECLINE, DROP ⟨a sudden ~ of confidence —Josephine Johnson⟩ ⟨~ in the supply of college graduates during the war years —M.L. Kastens⟩ ⟨~ from grace⟩ **3 a** (1) **:** the termination or failure of a right or privilege through neglect to exercise it within some limit of time or through failure of some contingency — compare EXPIRY (2) **:** *Eng eccl law* **:** the transfer of the right to present or collate a rector to a vacant benefice from one having the first right and neglecting to exercise it to one having a secondary right (3) **:** termination of coverage (as by life insurance) for nonpayment of premiums **b :** an interruption or discontinuance ⟨~ of a custom⟩ ⟨resumed dividends after a ~ during the depression —P.J. O'Brien⟩ ⟨masters narrative ~*s* with great skill —C.C.Rister⟩ **4 a :** a yielding to temptation or inclination **:** transitory disregard of moral principles **:** FOLLY ⟨his laxity of conduct, his moral ~*s* —S.H.Adams⟩ **b :** an abandonment of religious faith or principles **:** APOSTASY, BACKSLIDE ⟨prior to Adam's ~ —R.W.Murray⟩ **5 a** *archaic* **:** a continuous flow or gentle downward glide (as of water) ⟨down comes the stream, a ~ of living amethyst —Thomas Aird⟩ **b :** a continuous passage or an elapsed period of time **:** COURSE, INTERVAL ⟨a transaction involving a considerable ~ of time because the shares could not be sold until the state debt was paid —W.P.Webb⟩ ⟨except for a ~ of two years when he studied abroad, he has taught continuously since graduation⟩ **syn** see ERROR

**2lapse** \"\ *vb* -ED/-ING/-S *vi* **1 a :** to fall into error or folly **:** depart from an accepted standard ⟨~*s* into addiction again at the first temptation —*Time*⟩ ⟨purchases . . . where his discrimination *lapsed* —Basil Taylor⟩; *specif* **:** BACKSLIDE ⟨in their view Constantinople had *lapsed* into heresy —R.M. French⟩ **b :** to sink or slip involuntarily **:** SUBSIDE, RELAPSE ⟨murmurs good morning . . . and ~*s* into silence —Gertrude Samuels⟩ ⟨some *lapsed* into reading and others into sleep —Earle Birney⟩ ⟨why does starry-eyed youth ~ into flabby middle-aged vacuity —Douglas Bush⟩ ⟨the moment his attention is relaxed . . . he will ~ into bad Shakespearean verse —T.S.Eliot⟩ **2 :** to go out of existence **:** fall into decay or disuse **:** DISAPPEAR, TERMINATE ⟨the nest-building impulse . . . ~*s* when the eggs are laid —E.A.Armstrong⟩ ⟨could think of no rejoinder . . . and our conversation *lapsed* —Maurice Cranston⟩ ⟨a relationship may be allowed to ~, but it can never be dissolved —G.M.Foster⟩ ⟨this series of experiments seems to have *lapsed* around 1910 —Frank Denman⟩ **3 :** to fall or pass from one proprietor to another or from the original destination by the omission, negligence, or failure of some one (as a patron or legatee) ⟨a legacy ~*s* when it fails to vest⟩ ⟨an insurance policy ~*s* with forfeiture of value from nonpayment of a premium when due⟩ **4 a** *of time* **:** to run its course **:** PASS ⟨the whole fund might be lost . . . by the *lapsing* of the time allowed —A.D.White⟩ **b :** to glide past ⟨saw the washed pavement *lapsing* beneath my feet —L.P.Smith⟩ **c :** to glide gently along ⟨lolled with their lovers by *lapsing* brooks —W.H.Auden⟩ ⟨barges *lapsing* on its tranquil tide —C.C.Clarke⟩ **~** *vt* **1** *obs* **:** LOSE, FORFEIT ⟨a vestry cannot ~ their right of presentation —William Byrd⟩ **2 :** to make ineffective by failing to meet the requirements of **:** let slip **:** NULLIFY ⟨*lapsed* his policy⟩ ⟨the high percentage of patients *lapsing* therapy —*Jour. Amer. Med. Assoc.*⟩

**lap seam** *also* **lapped seam** *n* **:** a seam in which the edges overlap; *esp* **:** a seam in leather or cloth made by extending a cut or folded edge over a cut edge to the width of the seam allowance and stitching in place

**1lapsed** *adj* [fr. past part. of 2*lapse*] **1 :** surrendered or nullified because of failure to meet stipulated obligations **:** FORFEITED, VOID ⟨dispose of the realm as a ~ fief —G.C.Sellery⟩ ⟨the widow gets no insurance because of a ~ policy⟩ **2 :** guilty of error or defection **:** FALLEN; *specif* **:** APOSTATE ⟨the deliberately ~ Catholic cannot be such without mortal sin —D.J.Corrigan⟩ **3 :** dropped out of sight or use **:** VANISHED ⟨now in the moonlight, and now ~ in shade —Lord Byron⟩ ⟨the ~ custom of an annual dinner —*John Bull*⟩

**2lapsed** *n pl* **:** early Christians deserting the faith because of persecution ⟨in Rome the bishop . . . was prepared to permit the restoration of the ~ —K.S.Latourette⟩

**laps·er** \'lapsə(r)\ *n* -S **:** one that lapses

**lapse rate** *n* **:** the rate of change of any meteorological element with increase of height; *specif* **:** the rate of decrease of temperature with increase of height — called also *vertical gradient*

**lap shaver** *n* [1*lap* + *shaver*; fr. the former practice of holding the leather on a board in the lap while shaving it] **:** a machine for shaving leather to a specified thickness

**lap siding** *n* [3*lap*] **1 :** building siding consisting of beveled boards wider and longer than clapboards — compare DROP SIDING **2 :** an arrangement of two railroad sidings at a station in such a way that the turnout of one overlaps that of the other

**lap stick** *n* [*lap* prob. short for 2*lapidary*] **:** DOP STICK

**lapstone** \'=,=\ *n* **:** a stone or iron plate which is held in the lap and on which a shoemaker hammers leather

**1lapstrake** *also* **lapstreak** \'=,=\ *adj* [3*lap* + *strake* or *streak*] **1 :** having overlapping strakes **:** CLINKER-BUILT — usu. used of a boat ⟨~ dinghy⟩ **2 :** characterized by the lapping of each strake on the outside of the one beneath it ⟨~ construction⟩

**2lapstrake** *also* **lapstreak** \"\ *n* **:** a boat of lapstrake construction

**lapstraked** *also* **lapstreaked** \'=,=\ *adj* [3*lap* + *strake* or *streak* + -*ed*] **:** LAPSTRAKE

**lap·strak·er** *also* **lap·streak·er** \-kə(r)\ *n* -S [1*lapstrake, lapstreak* + -*er*] **:** LAPSTRAKE

**lap·sus** \'lapsəs\ *n, pl* **lapsus** [L — more at LAPSE] **:** 1LAPSE 1a

**lap table** *n* **:** LAPBOARD

**lapulapu** *var of* LAPO-LAPO

**lap up** *vt* **1 :** to respond to enthusiastically or accept eagerly ⟨she simply *lapped up* admiration —Helen Howe⟩ ⟨readiness to *lap up* the latest sensation —Herbert Brucker⟩ **2 :** DRINK ⟨sat there . . . *lapping up* the wonderful Japanese beer —J.A. Michener⟩

**la·pu·tan** \lə'pyütᵊn\ *adj, usu cap* [*Laputa*, imaginary flying island in Swift's *Gulliver's Travels* whose inhabitants engage in a great variety of impractical projects + E -*an*] **:** ABSURD, VISIONARY

**lap–weld** \'=¦=\ *vt* [3*lap* + *weld*, v.] **:** to join by welding along overlapping edges or seams

**lap weld** \'=,=\ *n* [fr. *lap-weld*] **:** a joint made by lap-welding

**lap winding** *n* **:** a drum winding for generator and motor armatures in which each coil or set of windings overlaps the next so that there are as many armature paths as there are field-magnet poles

**lap·wing** \'la,pwiŋ\ *n* [ME *lapwinge*, by folk etymology (influence of ME *winge* wing) fr. *lappewinke*, by folk etymology (influence of ME *lappen* to lap, wrap) fr. OE *hlēapewince*; akin to OE *hlēapan* to leap and to OE *wincian* to wink, blink, *wancol* unsteady, wavering — more at LEAP, WINK] **1 :** an abundant crested plover (*Vanellus vanellus* syn. *V. cristatus*) of Europe, Asia, and northern Africa with upperparts and crest bronzy green, throat and breast black, and sides of the head and neck and most of the underparts white that is noted for its slow irregular flapping flight and its shrill wailing cry **2 :** any of several related plovers

**lapwing gull** *n* **:** a black-headed gull (*Larus ridibundus*)

**laq·ue·ar** \'lakwēər, -ē,är\ *n, pl* **laquear·ia** \,lakwē'a(a)rēə\ [L; akin to L *lacus* lake, basin — more at LAKE] **:** COFFER 4a

**laque·us** \'lakwēəs, 'lak-\ *n, pl* **laquei** \-ē,ī, -ē,ē\ [L, noose, snare — more at DELIGHT] **:** LEMNISCUS 2

**lar** \'lär\ *n* [L — more at LARVA] **1** *pl* **lares** \'la,rēz, 'la(a)(,)rēz, 'lä,rās\ *often cap* **:** a tutelary god or spirit of the ancient Romans associated with a particular locality (as a field or the home) sometimes conceived as a beneficent ancestral spirit or as the equivalent for the dead of the genius of the living **2** *also* **lar gibbon** -S [NL (specific epithet of *Hylobates lar*), fr. L] **:** a Malayan gibbon (*Hylobates lar*) with white hands and feet

**lar·a·mide** \'larə,mīd, -,məd\ *adj, usu cap* [irreg. fr. *Laramie* mountains, southeastern Wyoming and northern Colorado] **:** of or relating to the mountain-making movements near the opening of the Cenozoic era — see GEOLOGIC TIME table

**lar·a·mie** \-,mē\ *adj, usu cap* [fr. *Laramie*, county in Wyoming] **:** of, relating to, or constituting a division of the American Upper Cretaceous — see GEOLOGIC TIME table

**la·rar·i·um** \lə'ra(a)rēəm\ *n, pl* **larar·ia** \-ēə\ [LL, fr. L *lar* + -*arium*] **:** the shrine of the lares in an ancient Roman home

**larb** \'lärb\ *n* -S [origin unknown] **:** a bearberry (*Arctostaphylos uva-ursi*)

**1lar·board** \'lärbərd, 'lȧbəd\ *n* [alter. (influenced by *starboard*) of ME *ladeborde, latheborde, latebord*, perh. fr. *laden* to load + *bord* ship's side — more at LADE, BOARD] **:** the left-hand side of a ship to one on board facing toward the bow **:** PORT — opposed to *starboard*

**2larboard** \"\ *adj* **:** PORT ⟨the ~ side of a ship⟩

**lar·bo·lins** *also* **lar·bow·lines** \-bələnz\ *n pl* [perh. irreg. fr. 1*larboard* + -*lings*, pl. of -*ling*, n. suffix] *archaic* **:** PORT WATCH

**lar·ce·ner** \'lärs(ᵊ)nə(r), 'lȧs-\ *n* -S [*larceny* + -*er*] **:** LARCENIST

**lar·ce·nist** \-nəst\ *n* -S [*larceny* + -*ist*] **:** one who commits larceny

**lar·ce·nous** \-nəs\ *adj* [*larceny* + -*ous*] **1 :** having the character of or constituting larceny ⟨a ~ act⟩ **2 :** committing larceny **:** THIEVISH ⟨~ rascals⟩ — **lar·ce·nous·ly** *adv*

**lar·ce·ny** \-nē,-ni\ *n* -ES [ME, fr. MF *larcin* theft (fr. L *latrocinium* robbery, fr. *latron-, latro* mercenary soldier, brigand) + ME -*y*, -*ie* -y — more at LATRON] **1** *common law* **:** the unlawful taking and carrying away of personal property without the consent of its lawful possessor whereby every part of the property stolen is removed however slightly from its former position and is at least momentarily in the complete possession of the thief and with intent to steal or to deprive the rightful owner of his property permanently — compare EMBEZZLEMENT; see AGGRAVATED LARCENY, GRAND LARCENY, PETTY LARCENY, SIMPLE LARCENY **2 :** any of various statutory offenses whereby property is obtained by embezzlement, trick, false pretenses, fraud, breach of trust, or theft

**larch** \'lärch, 'lȧch\ *n* -ES [prob. fr. G *lärche*, fr. MHG *larche, lerche*, fr. (assumed) OHG *larihha, lericha*, fr. L *laric-, larix*] **1 a :** a tree of the genus *Larix* — see EUROPEAN LARCH, TAMARACK **b :** any of several other trees of the family Pinaceae: as (1) **:** NOBLE FIR (2) **:** AMABILIS FIR (3) **:** CORSICAN PINE (4) **:** GOLDEN LARCH **2 :** the wood of a larch esp. belonging to the genera *Larix* or *Abies*

**larch agaric** *n* **:** AGARIC 3

**larch canker** *n* **:** a destructive disease of the larch and to a lesser extent of fir and pine caused by an ascomycetous fungus (*Dasyscypha willkommii*) that produces flattened depressed cankers on the twigs and branches

**larch casebearer** *n* **:** a casebearer that is the larva of a minute moth (*Coleophora laricella*), that lives in a case made of a hollowed silk-lined leaf, and that mines in the leaves of larches sometimes causing severe defoliation

**larch·en** \'lärchən, 'lȧch-\ *adj* **:** being a larch **:** made up of larches ⟨a ~ wood⟩

**larch fir** *n* **:** lumber consisting of a mixture of Douglas fir and western larch

**larch pine** *n* **:** CORSICAN PINE

**larch sawfly** *n* **:** a very destructive red-and-black sawfly (*Pristiphora erichsonii*) of No. America and Europe whose whitish larva often defoliates the larch

**larch turpentine** *n* **:** VENICE TURPENTINE

**1lard** \'lärd, 'lȧd\ *vt* -ED/-ING/-S [ME *larden*, fr. MF *larder*, fr. OF, fr. *lart, lard*, n.] **1 a :** to insert fattening into (lean meat) before cooking; *broadly* **:** to dress (meat) for cooking by inserting or covering with something (as strips of fat) ⟨~*ing* a boned chicken⟩ ⟨a hare ~*ed* with truffles⟩ **b :** to cover or soil with grease ⟨age-blackened time-*larded* beams⟩ **2 :** to mix or garnish with something esp. by way of improvement, decorative finish, or show **:** BEDECK, STREW, INTERLARD ⟨speeches ~*ed* with compliments⟩ **3** *obs* **:** to make rich with or as if with fat **:** ENRICH

**2lard** \"\ *n* -S [ME, fr. MF, fr. OF *lart, lard*, fr. L *lardum, laridum*; akin to L *laetus* glad, *largus* abundant, generous, Gk *larinos* fat] **1** *archaic* **:** fatty tissue of the hog **:** fat pork **2 :** a soft white solid or semisolid fat obtained by rendering fatty tissue of the hog — see LEAF LARD

**lar·da·ce·in** \lär'dāsēən, lȧ'd-\ *n* -S [ISV *lardaceous* + -*in*] **:** 2AMYLOID 3

**lar·da·ceous** \(')=¦dāshəs\ *adj* [prob. fr. (assumed) NL *lardaceus*, fr. L *lardum* fat pork + -*aceus* -aceous] **1 :** resembling lard ⟨a ~ mass⟩ **2 :** AMYLOID 2 ⟨~ degeneration⟩

**lar·der** \'lärdər, 'lȧdə(r\ *n* -S [ME, fr. MF *lardier*, fr. OF, fr. *lart, lard* + -*ier*, n. suffix denoting a place (fr. L -*arium*)] **1 a :** a place (as a pantry) where meat and other foodstuffs are stored **b :** a store of food **:** food in stock or available **2** *Brit* **:** a collection of unwanted animals (as various predators) killed by a gamekeeper and hung up to act in the manner of a scarecrow

**larder beetle** *n* **:** a dark brown or nearly black beetle (*Dermestes lardarius*) that is about ¼ inch long and has a bristly larva which feeds on dried animal products (as meats, skins, feathers)

**lar·de·rel·lite** \,lärdə'reˌlīt\ *n* -S [F. de *Larderel* †1925 Ital. mineowner + E -*ite*] **:** a mineral $(NH_4)_2B_{10}O_{16}.5H_2O$(?) consisting of a hydrous ammonium borate and occurring as a white crystalline powder

**lar·der·er** \'lärdərər, 'lȧdərə(r\ *n* -S [ME *larderere*, fr. *larder* + -*ere* -*er*] *archaic* **:** one in charge of a larder

**lar·di·ner** \-d(ᵊ)nə(r)\ *n* -S [ME, larder, larderer, fr. AF, larderer, irreg. fr. OF *lardier* larder] **1 :** LARDER 1a **2** *archaic* **:** LARDERER, STEWARD

**larding needle** *n* **:** a large needle with a hollow split end that is used for inserting lardoons into meat

**lar·di·zab·a·la·ce·ae** \,lärdə,zabə'lāsē,ē\ *n pl, cap* [NL, fr. *Lardizabala*, type genus (fr. Miguel *Lardizábal* y Uribe, 18th cent. Mex. statesman) + -*aceae*] **:** a family of chiefly woody vines (order Ranales) with leaves usu. digitate and baccate fruit — **lar·di·zab·a·la·ceous** \¦==¦==¦lāshəs\ *adj*

**lard oil** *n* **:** an oil consisting chiefly of olein that is expressed from lard and used esp. as a lubricant, cutting oil, or illuminant

**lar·doon** \(')lär¦dün, (')lȧ¦d-\ *also* **lar·don** \'=,dän\ *n* -S [F *lardon* piece of fat pork, fr. OF, fr. *lart, lard*] **:** a strip of material (as of salt pork) for insertion into meat in larding

**lardry** *n* -ES [MF *larderie*, fr. *lard* (fr. OF *lart, lard*) + -*erie* -ery] *obs* **:** LARDER 1a

**lard stearin** *n* **:** the solid residue left after the expression of lard oil

**lard stone** *n* **:** STEATITE

**lard type** *n* **:** a type of hog adapted to converting feed (as corn) into fat — compare MEAT TYPE

**lardworm** \'=,=\ *n* **:** KIDNEY WORM

**lardy** \'lärdē, 'lȧdē, -di\ *adj* -ER/-EST [2*lard* + -*y*] **1 :** containing or resembling lard **:** of the character or consistency of lard ⟨a white ~ skin⟩ ⟨a heavy ~ cake⟩ **2 :** fat or tending to become fat esp. to excess ⟨~ hogs⟩

**lardy–dardy** \¦lärdē¦därdē, ¦lȧdē¦dȧdē, -di...di\ *adj* [imit. (of an affected manner of speech)] *slang* **:** languidly and affectedly dandyish — compare LA-DI-DA

**lares** *pl of* LAR

**lares and penates** *n pl* **:** one's most valued personal or household effects ⟨those *lares and penates* which a householder, driven from his city home, cannot bring himself to leave behind —Jerome Weidman⟩

**lar·ga·men·te** \,lärgə'mentē\ *adv* (*or adj*) [It, slowly, broadly fr. *largo* slow, broad, fr. L *largus* abundant, generous] **:** with slowness and breadth — used as a direction in music

**lar·gan·do** \lär'gän(,)dō\ *adj* (*or adv*) [It, making slow, widening, verbal of *largare* to make slow, widen, fr. L, to widen, loosen, fr. L *largus* abundant, generous] **:** ALLARGANDO

**1large** \'lärj, 'lȧj\ *adj* -ER/-EST [ME, fr. OF, fr. L *largus* abundant, generous — more at LARD] **1** *obs* **:** liberal in giving or expending **:** GENEROUS, PRODIGAL, LAVISH **2** *obs* **a :** ample in quantity **:** ABUNDANT **b :** ample in extent **:** ROOMY, CAPACIOUS **c :** ample in breadth **:** BROAD, WIDE **d** *of a measure or period* **:** completely fulfilled **:** being as great as or greater than called for **3 :** having more than usual power, capacity, range, or scope **:** COMPREHENSIVE ⟨~ liberty⟩ ⟨a ~ treatment of a subject⟩ ⟨a ~ sympathy⟩ ⟨having a ~ discretion in settling such subjects⟩ ⟨taking the ~ view⟩ **4 a :** exceeding most other things of like kind in bulk, capacity, quantity, superficial dimensions, or number of constituent units **:** of considerable magnitude **:** BIG — opposed to *small* ⟨a ~ horse⟩ ⟨a ~ expenditure⟩; usu. replaced by *great* in qualifying linear dimensions ⟨a ~ mountain of great height⟩ **b :** dealing in great numbers or quantities **:** extensive in scope ⟨a ~ importer⟩ ⟨problems of ~ businesses⟩ **c** (1) **:** GREAT 1c (2) *of a taxon* **:** including more than an average number of kinds of plants or animals ⟨a ~ family represented by over 200 species in No. America alone⟩ **5 a** *obs, of language or expression* **:** marked by or tending toward vulgarity **:** COARSE, GROSS, IMPROPER **b** *obs* **:** easy and unrestrained in conduct **:** LAX, UNINHIBITED **c** *archaic* **:** involving few restrictions **:** permitting considerable liberty (as of action or conscience) **6** *archaic* **a** *of an utterance* **:** full and lengthy **:** copious in words **:** PROLIX **b** *of a person* **:** tending to be frequent, lengthy, or diffuse in writing or speech **:** given to prolixity **7** *of a wind* **:** blowing from a desirable direction with respect to a ship's course **:** FAVORABLE **8 :** POMPOUS, EXTRAVAGANT, BOASTFUL ⟨~ talk⟩

**2large** \"\ *adv* [ME, fr. *large*, adj.] **1** *obs* **:** AMPLY, FULLY, LIBERALLY, FREELY **2 a :** with the wind abaft the beam ⟨a ship sailing ~⟩ **b :** at a distance **:** wide of something (as a course, the shore, a mark) **3 :** POMPOUSLY, EXTRAVAGANTLY, BOASTFULLY ⟨talks ~ but works not at all⟩

**3large** \"\ *n* -S [ME, fr. *large*, adj.] **1** *obs* **:** LIBERALITY, GENEROSITY, BOUNTY **2 :** LIBERTY, FREEDOM — now used only in the phrase *at large* **3 :** a size of paperboard 24 inches by 19 inches **4 :** the longest note in mensural notation, equal to two longs in imperfect time or three in perfect time — called also *double long, maxim* — **at large** *adv* **1 :** without restraint or confinement ⟨cattle grazing *at large*⟩ ⟨remained *at large* after conviction pending an appeal to the higher court⟩ **2 :** to the full extent **:** at length **:** fully and often diffusely ⟨discussed the matter *at large*⟩ **3** *archaic* **:** without final settlement, completing, or perfecting **4 a :** in a general or indefinite way **:** without precise limits ⟨arrangements made *at large*⟩ **b :** without particular aim or plan **:** at random **5** *obs* **:** so as to be or spread over a large area **6 :** as a whole **:** in general without regard to particularities ⟨society *at large* suffers from crime as sharply as the individual victim⟩ **7 :** by or as the representative of the whole of an area having political subdivisions rather than a particular district or other subdivision ⟨a member elected *at large*⟩ — **at–large :** chosen by or representing the whole of an area (as a state or a city) having political subdivisions rather than a particular district or other subdivision — usu. used in combination with a preceding noun ⟨in the Republican convention each state has four delegates-*at-large* —W.S.Sayre⟩ ⟨a congressman-*at-large*⟩ — **in large** *or* **in the large** *adv* **:** on a large scale **:** in general

**4large** \"\ *vi* -ED/-ING/-S [1*large*] *of a wind* **:** to shift so as to blow abaft the beam

**large–billed water thrush** \'=,=-\ *n* **:** LOUISIANA WATER THRUSH

**large black** *n, usu cap L&B* **1 :** a British breed of black lop-eared bacon-type swine **2 :** an animal of the Large Black breed

**large bond** *n* **:** a bond having a par value of over $1000 — compare BABY BOND

**large brown bat** *n* **:** BIG BROWN BAT

**large buckeye** *n* **:** SWEET BUCKEYE

**large calorie** *n* **:** CALORIE b(1)

**large cane** *n* **:** GIANT CANE

**large–cone pine** *also* **large–coned pine** \'=,=-\ *n* **:** COULTER PINE

**large coralroot** *n* **:** a widely distributed and highly variable No. American coralroot (*Corallorhiza maculata*) that grows in dry woodlands and usu. has a whitish perianth spotted with red or purple

**large crabgrass** *n* **:** a common annual crabgrass (*Digitaria sanguinalis*) that is native to Europe but a naturalized weed in much of No. America

**large cranberry** *n* **:** AMERICAN CRANBERRY

**large crested tern** *n* **:** an Oriental tern (*Thalasseus bergii*) with a black cap produced into a prominent crest

**large–eyed** \'=¦=\ *adj* **1 :** having large eyes ⟨a *large-eyed* shrimp⟩ or a large eye ⟨*large-eyed* darning needles⟩ **2 a :** having the eyes wide open in or as if in interest, curiosity, or amazement ⟨gave a shy *large-eyed* glance⟩ **b :** of a kind or degree to make the eyes open wide ⟨waiting in *large-eyed* wonder⟩

**large–flowered bellwort** \'=,=-\ *n* **:** a slender woodland herb (*Uvularia grandiflora*) of eastern No. America with perfoliate leaves and lemon-yellow bell-shaped flowers

**large–flowered dogwood** *n* **:** a tall arborescent dogwood (*Cornus nuttallii*) of upland areas of the Pacific coast having the flower cluster subtended by long white or rosy bracts up to three inches long

**large–flowered everlasting** *n* **:** PEARLY EVERLASTING

**large-flowered wake-robin** *n* : GREAT WHITE TRILLIUM

**large-handed** \ˈ=ˌ==\ *adj* **1** *obs* : GRASPING, RAPACIOUS **2** : OPENHANDED, LIBERAL

**largehearted** \ˈ=ˌ==\ *adj* : having a generous disposition : SYMPATHETIC, CHARITABLE, KINDLY ⟨a ~ humane person —H.E.Starr⟩

**large intestine** *n* : the posterior division of the vertebrate intestine being wider and shorter than the small intestine, typically divided into cecum, colon, and rectum, and concerned esp. with the dehydration of digestive residues into feces

**largeish** *var of* LARGISH

**large knot** *n* : a sound knot in lumber that is not less than 1½ inches in diameter

**large-leaved aster** \ˈ=ˌ=-\ *n* : a common No. American woodland herb (*Aster macrophyllus*) with large cordate basal leaves and lavender or violet flowers

**large-leaved magnolia** *or* **large-leaved cucumber tree** *n* : a large spreading shrub or medium-sized tree (*Magnolia macrophylla*) of the southern U.S. with long oblong silky leaves and large white purple-centered flowers

**large·ly** *adv* [ME, fr. ¹*large* + *-ly*, adv. suffix] : in a large manner: as **a** : to a large extent : EXTENSIVELY, ABUNDANTLY **b** : in a general or wide sense : on a large scale : GENERALLY, COMPREHENSIVELY **c** : POMPOUSLY **d** *obs* : at length : FULLY, FREELY, LOOSELY, WIDELY

**large-minded** \ˈ=ˌ==\ *adj* : liberal in ideas : characterized by breadth of view : not narrow in mind or outlook ⟨*large-minded* men, thinkers as well as statesmen —James Bryce⟩

**large mononuclear leukocyte** *n* : MONOCYTE

**largemouth black bass** \ˈ=ˌ=-\ *also* **largemouthed black bass** *or* **largemouth bass** *or* **largemouthed bass** *or* **large-mouth** *n* : a wide-ranging and rather large black bass (*Micropterus salmoides*) chiefly of warm sluggish waters that is blackish green above and lighter or whitish below with the angle of the jaw falling behind the eye — compare SMALLMOUTH BLACK BASS

**large-mouthed bowel worm** *n* : BOWEL WORM

**larg·en** \ˈlärjən, ˈlàj-\ *vb* -ED/-ING/-S *archaic* : ENLARGE

**large·ness** *n* -ES [ME *largenesse* magnitude, liberality, fr. ¹*large* + *-nesse* -ness] : the quality or state of being large: as **a** : large size : MAGNITUDE, BULK, BIGNESS, EXTENSIVENESS **b** : large scope or range : COMPREHENSIVENESS, BREADTH **c** : LIBERALITY **d** *obs* : DIFFUSENESS, PROLIXITY **e** : POMPOUSNESS

**large order** *n* : something difficult to attain or accomplish ⟨got the planting done without outside help; a *large order* for three boys in their early teens⟩

**large paper edition** *n* : an edition of a book printed with wider margins and often better quality paper and binding than the regular edition : a deluxe edition

**large pole** *n* : a forest tree with a diameter of from 8 to 12 inches

**large post** *n* : a size of paper 16½ inches by 21 inches

**larger** *comparative of* LARGE

**larger duckweed** *n* : GREAT DUCKWEED

**larges** *pres 3d sing of* LARGE

**large-scale** \ˈ=ˈ=\ *adj* [fr. the phrase *large scale*] : large in comparison with others of the same general class: as **a** : involving great numbers or quantities : having wide scope or extensive proportions ⟨a *large-scale* attack on polio⟩ ⟨*large-scale* preparations for war⟩ **b** *of a map* : having a scale (as one inch to a mile) that permits the plotting of much detail with comparatively great exactness — compare SMALL-SCALE

**large-souled** \ˈ=ˈ=\ *adj* : LARGEHEARTED

**lar·gess** *or* **lar·gesse** \lärˈjes, lä'-, ˈ=ˌ=\ *n, pl* **largess·es** [ME *largesse*, fr. OF *largece, largesse*, fr. *large* generous — more at LARGE] **1** *obs* : LIBERALITY, GENEROSITY **2** : liberal giving or assistance esp. when accompanied by condescension from a superior to an inferior or from one of higher rank or status to one of lower ⟨nor can we make other people like us by a one-sided ~ —S.F.Bemis⟩ ⟨obtained his post through his old teacher's ~⟩ **3** : something given: as **a** : a free gift usu. given in connection with some auspicious event ⟨there was given after the coronation a ~ to every man of a silver penny and a measure of wheat⟩ or traditional occasion ⟨coins for the harvest home ~⟩ **b** : gratuities given (as for service) esp. when excessive or ostentatious : large tips ⟨scattering ~ at every stopping place⟩ **c** : aid, support, or other valuables received as or as if as a gift or through the benevolence of another ⟨dependent for her livelihood on the ~ of a moody lover —Jean Stafford⟩ ⟨living on government ~⟩ **4** : an innate quality (as of mind or spirit) ⟨from some ~ of feeling —Nancy Cardozo⟩ ⟨a writer of imaginative ~ —Irving Howe⟩ ⟨his generosity of spirit, an absolutely natural ~ —Harvey Breit⟩ **5** *obs* : LIBERTY, FREEDOM, LEAVE

**largest** *superlative of* LARGE

**large-toothed aspen** *or* **large tooth aspen** \ˈ=ˌ=-\ *n* : a No. American tree (*Populus grandidentata*) with coarse-toothed leaves and soft wood

**large tupelo** *n* : TUPELO GUM

**large twayblade** *n* : an orchid (*Liparis liliifolia*) of eastern No. America with lustrous elliptical to nearly ovate leaves, angled scape, and terminal raceme of 5 to 40 purple and green or wholly green flowers

**large water grass** *n* : DALLIS GRASS

**large white** *n* **1** *usu cap L&W* **a** : a British breed of large long-bodied white bacon-type swine **b** : an animal of the Large White breed — see YORKSHIRE 1 **2** : CABBAGE BUTTERFLY b

**large yellow ladyslipper** *n* : a lady's slipper (*Cypripedium calceolus pubescens*) of mesophytic woodlands of eastern and central No. America that has slightly fragrant greenish yellow and often purple-marked flowers

¹**lar·ghet·to** \lärˈged·(ˌ)ō\ *adv (or adj)* [It, somewhat slow, fr. *largo* slow, broad] : in a somewhat slow manner — used as a direction in music

²**larghetto** \"\ *n* -S : a larghetto movement

**lar·ghis·si·mo** \-ˈgisəˌmō, -ˈgis-\ *adv (or adj)* [It, very slow, very broad, fr. L *largissimus* very abundant, most abundant, superl. of *largus*] : in as slow a manner as possible — used as a direction in music

**lar gibbon** *n* : LAR 2

**larging** *pres part of* LARGE

**larg·ish** *also* **large·ish** \ˈlärjish, ˈlàj-, -jēsh\ *adj* : rather large

**lar·gi·tion** \lärˈjishən\ *n* -S [L *largition-, largitio*, fr. *largitus* (past part. of *largiri* to lavish, bestow, fr. *largus* abundant, generous) + *-ion-, -io* -ion] **1** *obs* : bestowal of largess **2** : GIFT, GRATUITY — **lar·gi·tion·al** \(ˈ)=ˈjishənᵊl, -shnəl\ *adj*

¹**lar·go** \ˈlär(ˌ)gō, ˈlà(-\ *adv (or adj)* [It, slow, broad, fr. L *largus* abundant, generous — more at LARD] : in a very slow and broad manner — used as a direction in music

²**largo** \"\ *n* -S [It, fr. *largo*, adj.] : a largo movement

**la·ri** \ˈlaˌrī\ *n pl, cap* [NL, fr. LL, pl. of *larus* gull — more at LARUS] : a suborder of Charadriiformes that includes the gulls, terns, jaegers, and skimmers

¹**lar·i·at** \ˈlarēət *also* ˈler-, *usu* -əd·+V\ *n* -S [AmerSp *la reata* the lasso, fr. Sp *la* the (fem. of *el*, def. art., the, fr. L *ille* that one, that, alter. — influenced by L *is* he — of *ollus*) + AmerSp *reata* lasso, fr. Sp, rope used to keep animals in single file, fr. *reatar* to tie in single file, tie again, fr. *re-* (fr. L) + *atar* to tie, fasten, fr. L *aptare* to put on, fit, fr. *aptus* fit, suitable; L *ollus* akin to L *uls* beyond — more at ALL, ITERATE, APT] : a long light but strong rope usu. of hemp or strips of hide used with a running noose for catching livestock or with or without the noose for picketing grazing animals — compare LASSO

²**lar·i·at** \-ē̇ə]t, -ē,a], *usu* ]d·+V\ *vt* -ED/-ING/-S *West* : to secure, catch, or equip with a lariat ⟨~*ed* saddles⟩

**lariat loop** *n* : a small circular loop which is formed at one end of a lariat by knotting and through which the other end of the lariat is passed when preparing a running noose or lasso

**lar·ick** \ˈlarik\ *n* -S [L *laric-, larix*] *chiefly Scot* : LARCH

**lar·id** \ˈlarəd\ *n* -S [NL *Laridae*] : a bird of the family Laridae

**lar·i·dae** \-rəˌdē\ *n pl, cap* [NL, fr. *Larus*, type genus + *-idae*] : a family (suborder Lari) including the gulls and terns and sometimes the jaegers — compare STERCORARIIDAE

**la·ri·go** \ˈlärəˌgō\ *n* -S [perh. modif. of Sp *látigo* latigo] : a ring at each end of the cinch of a western saddle through which the latigos pass

**lar·i·got** \ˈlarəˌgō\ *n* -S [F] **1** : FLAGEOLET 1 **2** : NINETEENTH



**la·ri·idae** \ləˈrīəˌdē\ [NL, fr. *Laria* (a prior but largely disused equivalent of *Bruchus*) (prob. fr. L *lar* + NL *-ia*) + *-idae* — more at LARVA] *syn of* BRUCHIDAE

**la·rin** \ˈlärən\ *or* **la·ri** *also* **lar·ree** \ˈlärē\ *n* -S [Per *lārī*] : a piece of silver wire doubled over and sometimes twisted into the form of a fishhook that was formerly used as money in parts of Asia

**lar·ine** \ˈla(ə)ˌrīn, -ˌrən\ *adj* [NL *Larinae* subfamily containing the gulls, fr. *Larus*, type genus + *-inae*] : of or relating to gulls esp. as distinguished from terns

**la·rith·mic** \ləˈrith̲mik, -th-\ *adj* [back-formation fr. *larithmics*] : of or relating to larithmics

**la·rith·mics** \-ks\ *n pl but sing in constr* [Gk *laos* people + *arithmos* number + E *-ics* — more at ARITHMO-] : the scientific study of the quantitative aspects of population

**lar·ix** \ˈla(ə)rəks\ *n* [NL, fr. L, larch] **1** *cap* : a genus of trees (family Pinaceae) that are widely distributed in the north temperate zone and have deciduous foliage in clusters of acicular leaves of different lengths on short lateral spurs or scattered singly on the terminal shoots, solitary staminate flowers, and persistent cone scales — compare PSEUDOLARIX **2** -ES : a tree of the genus *Larix*

¹**lark** \ˈlärk, ˈlàk\ *n* -S [ME *larke*, fr. OE *lāwerce*; akin to OHG *lērihha* lark, ON *lævirki*] **1** : any of numerous singing birds of the family Alaudidae mostly of Europe, Asia, and northern Africa; *esp* : SKYLARK 1 — compare HORNED LARK **2** : any of various usu. ground-living birds of families other than Alaudidae — usu. used in combination ⟨meadow*lark*⟩ ⟨tit*lark*⟩ **3** : a grayish yellow that is duller than chamois, redder and slightly darker than crash, and redder and slightly less strong than old ivory **4 a** : POET ⟨my fellow ~*s* —Vachel Lindsay⟩ **b** : SINGER

²**lark** \"\ *vi* -ED/-ING/-S : to catch or hunt larks ⟨~*ing* with birdlime⟩

³**lark** \"\ *vb* -ED/-ING/-S [prob. alter. of ³*lake*] *vi* **1** : to behave sportively or mischievously : engage in harmless pranks : FROLIC ⟨~*ing* all day in the hills⟩ ⟨boys ~*ing* about after school⟩ **2** : to ride across country or over obstacles ~ *vt* : to make sport of : TEASE

⁴**lark** \"\ *n* -S **1 a** : a merry adventure : FROLIC, ROMP : a bit of harmless amusing mischief : PRANK **b** : something not taken or intended to be taken very seriously ⟨if an officer comes . . . to make inspection he is usually on a ~ —T.R. Fisher⟩ **2** *slang Brit* : a course of action or way of life

**lark bunting** *n* : a large finch (*Calamospiza melanocorys*) of the plains of the western U.S. that has the male black with a large white wing patch

**lark-colored** \ˈ=ˈ==\ *adj* : of a sandy brown like that of the European larks

¹**lark·er** \ˈlärkər, ˈlàkə(r\ *n* -S [¹*lark* + *-er*] : a catcher of larks

²**larker** \"\ *n* -S [³*lark* + *-er*] : one that engages in a lark or in larking

**lark finch** *n* : LARK SPARROW

**lark-heel** *in sense 1* ˈ=ˌ=, *in sense 2* ˈ=ˈ=\ *or* **lark's-heel** \ˈ=ˌ=\ *n, pl* **lark-heels** *or* **lark's-heels** **1** : LARKSPUR **2** : a long heel sometimes seen in Negroes

**lark-heeled** \ˈ=ˈ=\ *adj, of a bird* : having the claw of the hind toe long and straight ⟨a *lark-heeled* cuckoo⟩

**lark·i·ness** \ˈlärkēnəs, ˈlàk-, -kin-\ *n* -ES [*larky* + *-ness*] : light-hearted gaiety : SPORTIVENESS

**larking** *adj* [fr. pres. part. of ³*lark*] : dashing and gay : GIDDY, FROLICSOME — **lark·ing·ly** *adv*

**lark·ish** \ˈlärkish, ˈlàk-, -kēsh\ *adj* [⁴*lark* + *-ish*] : gaily mischievous : FROLICSOME ⟨a ~ mood⟩ — **lark·ish·ly** *adv* — **lark·ish·ness** *n* -ES

**lark plover** *n* : SEED SNIPE

**lark's-claw** \ˈ=ˌ=\ *n, pl* **lark's-claws** [*lark's* (gen. of ¹*lark*) + *claw*] : LARKSPUR

**lark's head** *n* [*lark's* (gen. of ¹*lark*) + *head*] : a hitch made by passing the bight of a line through a ring or around an object and then passing the two ends through the bight

lark's head

**lark·some** \ˈlärksəm, ˈlàk-\ *adj* [⁴*lark* + *-some*] : marked by or inclined toward sportive or mischievous behavior : FROLICSOME, PLAYFUL ⟨the melodrama had not been produced for ~ purposes —*London Daily News*⟩ ⟨a moderately ~ fellow —E.J.Kahn⟩

**lark sparrow** *n* : a sparrow (*Chondestes grammacus*) that is abundant in the Mississippi valley, is streaked above and white below with the head varied with black, grayish white, and chestnut, and is represented in the western U.S. by a paler bird which forms a distinct subspecies (*C. grammacus strigatus*)

**larkspur** \ˈ=ˌ=\ *n* [¹*lark* + *spur*; fr. the shape of the calyx] **1 a** : a plant of the genus *Delphinium*; *esp* : a cultivated annual plant of this genus — compare DELPHINIUM 2 **b** : the dried ripe seeds of a European larkspur (*Delphinium ajacis*) from which an acetic tincture is sometimes prepared for use against ectoparasites (as lice) **2** : a moderate greenish blue that is bluer and paler than average peacock and greener and slightly deeper than Brittany

larkspur

**larky** \ˈlärkē, ˈlàkē, -ki\ *adj* -ER/-EST [⁴*lark* + *-y*] : ready for a lark : giddy and frolicsome : SPORTIVE

**lar·mier** \ˈlärmēˌā, -mˌyā\ *n* -S [F, fr. MF, fr. *larme* tear] : DRIP 4

**lar·mor frequency** \ˈlärˌmȯ(ə)r-\ *n, usu cap L* [after Sir Joseph *Larmor* †1942 Brit. mathematician] : the frequency of Larmor precession

**larmor precession** *n, usu cap L* : the precession of a particle having magnetic moment (as an atom when spinning in a magnetic field)

**larmor's theorem** *n, usu cap L* **1** : a statement in physics: the only sensible effect of a magnetic field upon the motions of atomic electrons is the Larmor precession **2** : a statement in physics: in an enclosure traversed by thermal radiation uniformly in all directions the radiation pressure is equal to one third of the radiant energy per unit volume

**lar·moy·ant** \(ˈ)lärˈmȯiənt *or as F*\ *adj* [F, pres. part. of *larmoyer* to be tearful, snivel, fr. OF *larmoier* to weep, shed tears, fr. *larme* tear, fr. L *lacrima* — more at TEAR] : LACHRYMOSE

**lar·nau·di·an** \(ˈ)lärˈnōdēən\ *adj, usu cap* [*Larnaud*, locality in Jura mountains, eastern France + E *-ian*] : of, relating to, or being a late bronze age period in Europe

**lar·nax** \ˈlärˌnaks\ *n, pl* **lar·na·kes** \-ˌnəˌkēz\ [Gk, perh. alter. of (assumed) Gk *narnax* (whence LGk *narnax* chest); akin to OE *nearu* narrow — more at NARROW] : a chest usu. of terra cotta and often ornamented that was used in ancient Greece esp. as a sepulchral chest

**larn·ite** \ˈlärˌnīt\ *n* -S [*Larne*, city in northern Ireland, its locality + E *-ite*] : a mineral $\beta$-$Ca_2SiO_4$ consisting of the unstable beta form of calcium silicate

**lar·oid** \ˈla(ə)ˌrȯid\ *adj* [NL *Larus* + E *-oid*] : resembling or relating to gulls : like or like that of members of the genus *Larus*

**laron** *n* -S [MF *larron*, fr. L *latron-, latro* mercenary soldier, brigand — more at LATRON] *obs* : ROBBER

**lar·over** \ˈlaˌrōvə(r)\ *var of* ¹LAYOVER

**lar·rea** \ˈlarēə, -räə\ *n* [NL, fr. J. A. H. de *Larrea*, 18th cent. Span. patron of science] **1** *cap* : a small genus of American xerophytic shrubs (family Zygophyllaceae) including the creosote bush **2** -S : a shrub of the genus *Larrea*

**larree** *var of* LARIN

**lar·ri·dae** \ˈlarəˌdē\ *n pl, cap* [NL, fr. *Larra*, type genus + *-idae*] : a family of stocky medium-sized large-eyed digger wasps that nest in sandy soil

**lar·ri·gan** \ˈlarəgən\ *n* -S [origin unknown] : an oil-tanned moccasin with legs that is used esp. by lumbermen and trappers

¹**lar·ri·kin** \ˈlarəkən\ *n* -S [origin unknown] *chiefly Austral* : a noisy disorderly fellow : HOODLUM, ROWDY

²**larrikin** \"\ *adj, chiefly Austral* : BOISTEROUS, ROWDY, DISORDERLY

**lar·ri·kin·ism** \-kəˌnizəm\ *n* -S *chiefly Austral* : larrikin behavior

¹**lar·rup** \ˈlarəp *also* ˈler-\ *vb* -ED/-ING/-S [perh. imit.] *vt* **1** *dial* : to flog soundly : BEAT, WHIP **2** *dial* : to defeat decisively ⟨~*ed* the senator in the farm counties⟩ ~ *vi, dial* : to slouch or move in a heavy awkward fashion : progress in a noisy bumbling manner

²**larrup** \"\ *n* -S *dial* : BLOW : something (as a switch) for dealing blows

**larruping** *adv (or adj)* [fr. pres. part. of ¹*larrup*] *dial* : in a way or of a kind to beat others : of notable quality or size : VERY ⟨~ good baked ham⟩

¹**lar·ry** \ˈlarē\ *n* -ES [perh. fr. *Larry*, nickname for the name *Lawrence*] **1** : a long-handled hoe usu. with a perforated blade that is used esp. for mixing mortar **2** : thin sloppy mortar : GROUT

²**larry** \"\ *vt* -ED/-ING/-ES : to fill in with grout sometimes with bricks or spalls in it : GROUT

³**larry** \"\ *n* -ES [prob. alter. of ¹*lurry*] *dial Eng* : CONFUSION, EXCITEMENT, NOISE

⁴**larry** \"\ *n* -ES [alter. of *lorry*] **1** : a small usu. motor-driven car with a drop bottom used for hauling slate or rock from the tipple to the dump of a mine **2** : a hand-pushed or motor-driven car with a hopper that is used for weighing or measuring and distributing bulk materials and is suspended between overhead tracks or carried on rails — called also *weigh larry*

**lar·ry·man** *also* **lar·ri·man** \ˈlarēmən\ *n, pl* **larrymen** *also* **larrimen** [⁴*larry* + *man*] : an operator of a larry

**lars** *pl of* LAR

**lar·sen·ite** \ˈlärsᵊnˌīt\ *n* -S [Esper S. *Larsen* *b*1879 Am. geologist + E *-ite*] : a mineral $PbZnSiO_4$ consisting of a lead and zinc silicate occurring at Franklin, N.J., in colorless orthorhombic prisms

**lar·um** \ˈla(ə)rəm, -er-, -är-, -àr-\ *n* -S [short for *alarum*] : ALARM

**lar·us** \ˈla(ə)rəs\ *n, cap* [NL, fr. LL, gull, fr. Gk *laros*; perh. akin to L *lamentum* lament — more at LAMENT] : a large cosmopolitan genus of gulls comprising many of the better-known gulls and being the type of the family Laridae — see BONAPARTE'S GULL, GLAUCOUS GULL, HERRING GULL, LAUGHING GULL

**lar·va** \ˈlärvə, ˈlàvə\ *n, pl* **lar·vae** \-(ˌ)vē, -ˌvī\ *also* **larvas** [L, evil spirit, specter, mask; akin to L *lar* tutelary god, lar and perh. to L *lascivus* wanton — more at LUST] **1 a** *obs* : a disembodied spirit : GHOST **b** : an ancient Roman specter or apparition; *esp* : a malevolent spirit **c** : a supernatural monster — used chiefly in medieval occultism **2** [NL, fr. L] **a** : the immature, wingless, and often vermiform feeding form that hatches from the egg of a holometabolous insect, increases in size, undergoes other minor changes while passing through several molts, and is finally transformed into a pupa or chrysalis from which the adult ultimately emerges — see CATERPILLAR, GRUB, MAGGOT **b** : NYMPH 3 **c** : the early form of any animal that at birth or hatching is fundamentally unlike its parent and must pass through more or less of a metamorphosis before assuming the adult characters — used of later states than *embryo*

**lar·va·cea** \lärˈvāshēə\ *n pl, cap* [NL, fr. *larva* + *-acea*] : an order of small free-swimming pelagic tunicates constituting *Appendicularia* and related genera, having a permanent caudal appendage supported by a notochord, being usu. hermaphroditic, and lacking a metamorphosis

**larvacide** *var of* LARVICIDE

**lar·vae·vo·rid** \lärˈvēvərəd\ *adj or n* [NL *Larvaevoridae*] : TACHINID

**lar·vae·vor·i·dae** \ˌlärvəˈvōrəˌdē\ [NL, fr. *Larvaevora* (a prior but largely disused equivalent of *Tachina*) (fr. NL *larvae* — pl. of *larva* — + *-vora*) + *-idae*] *syn of* TACHINIDAE

**lar·val** \ˈlärvəl, ˈlàv-\ *adj* [L *larvalis*, fr. *larva* + *-alis* -al] **1** : of or relating to a spectral larva **2** [NL *larvalis*, fr. *larva* + L *-alis* -al] **a** : of, relating to, typical of, or being an animal larva ⟨the ~ eye⟩ ⟨~ crayfishes⟩ **b** : immature of its kind ⟨~ societies⟩ ⟨~ hopes and fears⟩

**lar·va·lia** \lärˈvālēə\ [NL, fr. neut. pl. of *larvalis* larval] *syn of* LARVACEA

**larva mi·grans** \-ˈmīˌgranz\ *n, pl* **larvae migran·tes** \-ˌmīˈgranˌtēz\ [NL, lit., migrating larva] : CREEPING ERUPTION

**larva of de·sor** \-dəˈzȯ(ə)r, -ˈdāˌz-\ *usu cap D* [prob. fr. the name *Desor*] : a pilidium (as of certain nemerteans) that is modified for creeping

**lar·var·i·um** \lärˈva(a)rēəm\ *n, pl* **larvar·ia** \-ēə\ *also* **larvariums** [NL, fr. *larva* + *-arium*] **1** : a nest or shelter made and occupied by the larvae of some insects **2** : a container for the rearing of insect larvae

**lar·vate** \ˈlärˌvāt\ *or* **lar·vat·ed** \-ād·əd\ *adj* [*larvate* fr. NL *larvatus*, fr. L *larva* mask + *-atus* -ate; *larvated* prob. fr. L *larva* mask + E *-ate* + *-ed*] : covered or concealed by or as if by a mask

**larve** \ˈlärv\ *n* -S [F, fr. L *larva*] *archaic* : LARVA

**larvi-** *comb form* [NL, fr. *larva*] : larva : larval ⟨*larvi*colous⟩ ⟨*larvi*form⟩ *larvi*gerous⟩

**lar·vi·cid·al** \ˌlärvəˈsīdᵊl\ *adj* : of, relating to, or being a larvicide

¹**lar·vi·cide** *also* **lar·va·cide** \ˈlärvəˌsīd\ *n* -S [*larvi-* or *larva* + *-cide*] : an insecticide or other pesticide used for killing larvae — compare ADULTICIDE

²**lar·vi·cide** \"\ *vt* -ED/-ING/-S : to treat with a larvicide ⟨effects of DDT mosquito *larviciding* on wildlife —*Public Health Reports*⟩

**lar·vic·o·lous** \(ˈ)lärˈvikələs\ *adj* [*larvi-* + *-colous*] : living in the body of a larva — used esp. of a parasitoid insect

**lar·vik·ite** \ˈlärviˌkīt\ *or* **laur·vik·ite** \ˈlau̇(ə)r-\ *n* -S [G *larvikit*, fr. *Larvik*, Norway, its locality + G *-it* -ite] : an alkali-syenite rock composed chiefly of cryptoperthite or anorthoclase in rhombic crystals and widely used as an ornamental building stone

**lar·vip·a·rous** \(ˈ)lärˈvipərəs\ *adj* [prob. fr. (assumed) NL *larviparus*, fr. NL *larvi-* + L *-parus* -parous] : bearing and bringing forth young that are larvae — used esp. of specialized two-winged flies and some mollusks; compare OVIPAROUS, VIVIPAROUS

**lar·vi·phag·ic** \ˌlärvəˈfajik\ *adj* [*larvi-* + *-phagic* (fr. *-phagy* + *-ic*)] : LARVIVOROUS

**lar·vi·pos·it** \ˈlärvəˌpäzət, ˌ==ˈ==\ *vi* -ED/-ING/-S [*larvi-* + *posit*] : to deposit living larvae instead of eggs — compare OVIPOSIT

**lar·vi·po·si·tion** \ˌlärvəpəˈzishən\ *n* : the act of larvipositing

**lar·viv·o·rous** \(ˈ)lärˈvivərəs\ *adj* [prob. fr. (assumed) NL *larvivorus*, fr. NL *larvi-* + L *-vorus* -vorous] : feeding upon larvae esp. of insects ⟨~ fishes⟩

**lar·vule** \ˈlär(ˌ)vyül\ *n* -S [*larva* + *-ule*] : the earliest larval stage of an ephemerid insect in which the respiratory, circulatory, and nerve systems do not appear to be developed

**laryng-** *or* **laryngo-** *comb form* [NL *laryng-* & LL *laryngo-*, fr. Gk *laryng-, laryngo-*, fr. *larynǵ-, larynx*] **1** : larynx ⟨*laryn*gopathy⟩ ⟨*laryng*itis⟩ **2 a** : laryngeal and ⟨*laryngo*pharyngeal⟩ **b** : laryngeal : of the larynx ⟨*laryngo*vestibulitis⟩

¹**la·ryn·ge·al** \ləˈrinj(ē)əl, ˌlarənˈjēəl\ *adj* [NL *laryngeus* laryngeal (fr. *laryng-* + L *-eus* -eous) + E *-al*] **1** : of, relating to, or used on the larynx ⟨~ forceps⟩ **2** *also* **la·ryn·gal** \ləˈriŋgəl\ [*laryngal* ISV *laryng-* + *-al*] *phonetics* : produced by or with constriction of the larynx ⟨~ articulation of sounds⟩ — **la·ryn·ge·al·ly** \ləˈrinj(ē)əlē, ˌlarənˈjēə-, -li\ *adv*

²**laryngeal** \"\ *n* -S **1** : a laryngeal part (as a nerve or artery) **2** *also* **laryngal** **a** : a laryngeal sound **b** : any of a set of several (as three or four) phonemes reconstructed for Proto-Indo-European chiefly on indirect evidence

**laryngeal artery** *n* : either of two arteries supplying blood to the larynx: **a** : an artery derived from the inferior thyroid artery — called also *inferior laryngeal artery* **b** : an artery derived from the superior thyroid artery — called also *superior laryngeal artery*

**la·ryn·ge·al·ization** \ləˌrinj(ē)ələˈzāshən, ˌlarənˌjēə-, -ˌlīˈz-\ *n* -S : articulation with laryngeal modification

**la·ryn·ge·al·ize** \ləˈrinj(ē)əˌlīz, ˌlarənˈjēə-\ *vt* -ED/-ING/-S : to articulate (as a vowel) with laryngeal modification

**laryngeal nerve** *n* **:** either of two branches of the vagus nerve supplying the larynx

**laryngeal pouch** *also* **laryngeal sac** *or* **laryngeal saccule** *n* **:** a saccular expansion of the lateral wall cavity of the larynx between the true and false vocal cords that is greatly developed in certain monkeys (as the orang)

**la·ryn·ge·at·ing** \lə'rinjē,ād·iŋ\ *n* -s [*larynge-* (as in *laryngeal*) + *-ate* + *-ing*] **:** contraction and relaxation of laryngeal musculature unaccompanied by phonation **:** subvocal speech

**lar·yn·gec·to·mee** \,larən̊'jektə'mē\ *n* -s [*laryngectomy* + *-ee*] **:** a person who has undergone laryngectomy

**lar·yn·gec·to·mize** \,==ˈ==,mīz\ *vt* -ED/-ING/-S [*laryngectomy* + *-ize*] **:** to subject (a person) to laryngectomy

**lar·yn·gec·to·my** \-,mē\ *n* -ES [NL *laryngectomia,* fr. *laryng-* + *-ectomia* -ectomy] **:** surgical removal of all or part of the larynx

**la·ryn·gic** \lə'rinjik\ *adj* [NL *laryngicus,* fr. *laryng-* + L *-icus* -ic] **:** LARYNGEAL

**lar·yn·gis·mus** \,larən'jizməs\ *n, pl* **laryngis·mi** \-,mī\ [NL, fr. *laryng-* + L *-ismus* -ism] **:** LARYNGOSPASM

**laryngismus stri·du·lus** \-'strijələs\ *n, pl* **laryngismi stridu·li** \-,lī\ [NL, lit., stridulous laryngismus] **:** a sudden spasm of the larynx that occurs in children and esp. in rickets and is marked by difficult breathing with prolonged noisy inspiration — compare LARYNGOSPASM

[1]**lar·yn·git·ic** \¦==¦jid·ik\ *adj* [*laryngitis* + *-ic*] **:** of, relating to, or characteristic of laryngitis **:** affected with laryngitis

[2]**laryngitic** *n* -s **:** an individual suffering from laryngitis

**lar·yn·gi·tis** \,larən'jīd·əs, -ītəs *also* ,ler-\ *n, pl* **laryngit·i·des** \-'jid·ə,dēz, -jitə-\ [NL, fr. *laryng-* + *-itis*] **:** inflammation of the larynx

**laryngo-** — see LARYNG-

**la·ryn·go·fissure** \lə¦riŋgō+\ *n* [ISV *laryng-* + *fissure*] **:** surgical opening of the larynx by an incision through the thyroid cartilage esp. for the removal of a tumor

**la·ryn·go·log·i·cal** \lə¦riŋgə¦läjəkəl\ *or* **la·ryn·go·log·ic** \-jik\ *adj* [*laryngological* fr. *laryngology* + *-ical; laryngologic* ISV *laryngology* + *-ic*] **:** of or relating to laryngology

**lar·yn·gol·o·gist** \,larən'gäləjəst\ *n* -s [ISV *laryngology* + *-ist*] **:** a physician specializing in laryngology

**lar·yn·gol·o·gy** \-jē\ *n* -ES [ISV *laryng-* + *-logy*] **:** a branch of medical science dealing with the study and treatment of diseases of the larynx and nasopharynx

**la·ryn·go·pharyngeal** \lə¦riŋgō+\ *adj* **:** of or common to both larynx and pharynx

**la·ryn·go·pharynx** \"+\ *n* [NL, fr. *laryng-* + *pharynx*] **:** the lower part of the pharynx lying behind or adjacent to the larynx — compare NASOPHARYNX

**la·ryn·go·phone** \=ˈ=gə,fōn\ *n* [ISV *laryng-* + *-phone*] **:** a communication-system transmitter in which the vibration-receiving diaphragm is strapped to the throat over the larynx from which it receives speech vibrations directly

**la·ryn·go·scope** \-,skōp\ *n* [ISV *laryng-* + *-scope*] **:** an instrument or apparatus for examining the interior of the larynx — **la·ryn·go·scop·ic** \¦==¦skäpik\ *or* **la·ryn·go·scop·i·cal** \-pəkəl\ *adj* — **la·ryn·go·scop·i·cal·ly** \-ək(ə)lē\ *adv* — **lar·yn·gos·co·py** \,larən'gäskəpē\ *n* -ES

**la·ryn·go·spasm** \lə'riŋgə+,-\ *n* [ISV *laryng-* + *spasm*] **:** spasmodic closure of the larynx — compare LARYNGISMUS STRIDULUS

**la·ryn·go·tracheal** \=¦=(,)gō+\ *adj* [ISV *laryng-* + *tracheal*] **:** of or common to the larynx and trachea

**la·ryn·go·tracheitis** \"+\ *n* [NL, fr. *laryng-* + *trache-* + *-itis*] **:** inflammation of both larynx and trachea — see INFECTIOUS LARYNGOTRACHEITIS

**la·ryn·go·tracheobronchitis** \"+\ *n* [NL, fr. *laryng-* + *trache-* + *bronch-* + *-itis*] **:** inflammation of the larynx, trachea, and bronchi; *specif* **:** an acute severe infection of these parts marked by swelling of the tissues and excessive secretion of mucus leading to more or less complete obstruction of the respiratory passages

**lar·ynx** \'lariŋ(k)s, -rēŋ- *also* 'ler-, *substand* 'lärniks *or* 'lán- *or* -nēks\ *n, pl* **la·ryn·ges** \lə'rin(,)jēz\ *also* **larynxes** [NL *laryng-, larynx,* fr. Gk; prob. akin to MHG *slurken* to swallow, Sw dial. *slurka* to lap up, L *lurco* glutton] **:** the modified upper part of the respiratory passage of air-breathing vertebrates bounded above by the glottis and continuous below with the trachea and having a complex cartilaginous or bony skeleton capable of limited motion through the action of associated muscles and in man, most other mammals, and a few lower forms a set of elastic vocal cords that play a major role in sound production and speech — compare SYRINX

**las** *pl of* LA

**la·sa·gna** \lə'zänyə, lä'- *or* **la·sa·gne** \", -(,)yā\ *n, pl* **lasa·gne** \-(,)yā\ [*lasagna* fr. It, fr. (assumed) VL *lasania,* fr. L *lasanum* cooking pot, fr. Gk *lasana* (pl.) trivet, *lasanon* (sing.) chamber pot; *lasagne* fr. It, pl. of *lasagna;* perh. akin to Skt *radhyati* he cooks] **1 :** broad flat noodles **2 :** lasagna baked and served usu. with a tomato, cheese, and meat sauce

**las·car** \'laskə(r)\ *also* **lash·kar** \-shk-\ *n* -s [Hindi *lashkar* army, fr. Per, fr. Ar *al-'askar* the army; E *lascar, lashkar* influenced in meaning by Hindi *lashkarī* soldier, sailor, fr. *lashkar*] **1 :** an East Indian sailor **2 :** an East Indian army servant **3 :** an East Indian native artilleryman of a low grade in the British Army

**las·cive** \lə'sēv\ *adj* [F *lascif,* fr. L *lascivus*] **:** LASCIVIOUS ⟨licentious violet and ~ rose —Wallace Stevens⟩

**las·civ·i·ous** \lə'sivēəs, la'-\ *adj* [L *lascivia* wantonness (fr. *lascivus* wanton + *-ia* -y) + E *-ous* — more at LUST] **1 :** inclined to lechery **:** LEWD, LUSTFUL ⟨flaunted the adulteries of ~ women —H.O.Taylor⟩ **2 :** tending to arouse sexual desire **:** LIBIDINOUS, SALACIOUS ⟨suggestive, even ~ poses —*Amer. Bk. Publishers Council*⟩ ⟨pleasant, ~ verses —*Times Lit. Supp.*⟩ — **las·civ·i·ous·ly** *adv* — **las·civ·i·ous·ness** *n* -ES

**la·ser** \'lāzə(r)\ *n* -s [*light amplification by stimulated emission of radiation*] **:** a device that utilizes the natural oscillations of atoms for amplifying or generating electromagnetic waves in the region of the spectrum from the ultraviolet to the far-infrared including the visible region

**las·er·piti·um** \,lasə(r)'pishēəm, ,lazə-, -pid·ē-\ *n, cap* [NL, alter. of L *lasserpicium,* a plant] **:** an Old World genus of perennial herbs (family Umbelliferae) with compound umbels of flowers and 8-winged fruits

[1]**lash** \'lash, -aa(ə)-,-ai-\ *vb* -ED/-ING/-ES [ME *lashen* to throw quickly, strike with a lash, move violently, prob. partly of imit. origin and partly fr. *lashe,* n.] *vi* **1 a :** to move violently or suddenly **:** DASH, RUSH, FLY ⟨~*ed* out eastward with the agility for which he was dreaded —Emil Lengyel⟩ ⟨~ through the brilliant sunlight of a wide arena —P.B.Martin⟩ **b** *of a horse* **:** KICK — used with *out* ⟨~*ed* out . . . at the cursing men behind us —Kenneth Roberts⟩ **c :** BEAT, POUR ⟨the rain ~*ed* against the windowpanes —J.C.Powys⟩ ⟨hail ~*ed* down mercilessly⟩ **2 a :** to strike with or as if with a whip ⟨~*ing* about him with a stout staff⟩ ⟨it had ~*ed* across a human skull —Helen Nielsen⟩ ⟨the final plunge of a wave ~*es* against the opposing land —P.S.Welch⟩ ⟨~*ed* back at the enemy —S.E. Morison & H.S.Commager⟩ **b :** to make a sudden darting, sinuous, or striking movement like the lash of a whip ⟨the snake ~*ed* and curled —William Beebe⟩ **3 :** to make a verbal assault or riposte **:** engage in biting criticism or censure ⟨~*ing* at the bullet-headed commander —J.A.Michener⟩ ⟨uses . . . newspaper ads to ~ back —*Printers' Ink*⟩ — usu. used with *out* ⟨the author ~*es* out at Fascism —J.L.LaMonte⟩ ⟨~*ed* out on the rare occasions when he was aroused —Green Peyton⟩ **4** *now chiefly dial Brit* **:** to spend money recklessly — usu. used with *out* ~ *vt* **1 a** (1) **:** to throw quickly or impetuously **:** FLING, DASH ⟨the frightened mare ~*ed* up her heels⟩ (2) **:** to move violently ⟨the kitten . . . ~*ed* its angry tail —Ethel Wilson⟩ ⟨~*ed* her feather fan to and fro —Elizabeth Bowen⟩ **b :** POUR, EMIT — usu. used with *out* ⟨~ out some 34,000,000 copies of newspapers a week —*English Digest*⟩ **2 a** (1) **:** to strike with a lash **:** WHIP, SCOURGE ⟨penitents ~*ing* themselves till the blood came⟩ (2) **:** to strike forcibly and quickly esp. in a succession of blows **:** beat upon ⟨the whale ~*ed* the sea⟩ ⟨light ~*ed* my eyes —Wirt Williams⟩ ⟨rain ~*es* the windows⟩ ⟨the wind ~*ed* the waves into destructive fury⟩ **b** (1) **:** to assail or castigate with nonphysical means ⟨the jealousy, the hatred, the terror which ~ our souls —A.L.Guerard⟩; *esp* **:** to assail with stinging, biting, or satirical words ⟨~*ed* the vices of the time⟩ (2) **:** to goad, incite, or excite to some action or into some state **:** DRIVE ⟨~*es* him into murder —G.B.Shaw⟩ ⟨~*ed* itself into a passion against Spain —Dexter Perkins⟩ ⟨easy to ~ them into fury —J.A.Froude⟩ (3) **:** to cause to lash ⟨a rising wind was ~*ing* the rain against the windows —Val Mulkerus⟩ **3** *dial chiefly Brit* **:** to spend recklessly **:** THROW ⟨prepared to ~ the money around —Edward Sheehy⟩

[2]**lash** \"\ *n* -ES [ME *lashe,* prob. fr. *lashen,* v., to throw quickly, move violently] **1 a** (1) **:** a stroke with a whip or with anything slender, pliant, and tough ⟨received ten ~*es*⟩ (2) **:** the flexible part of a whip; *specif* **:** the piece (as of whipcord) forming its end ⟨twenty feet long from butt to ~ —H.L. Davis⟩ (3) **:** something used for whipping **:** WHIP ⟨used the ~ on kids who trespassed on his property —Ronald Sercombe⟩ (4) **:** punishment by flogging ⟨provides fines, jail terms, and the ~ for any incitement to violation —H.S.Warner⟩ **b :** a sudden swinging blow **:** a sweeping stroke ⟨felt the ~ of his hand on her cheek⟩ **c :** a pelting driving onslaught (as of wind or rain) ⟨has to stand up to the ~ of a north wind —*Monsanto Mag.*⟩ ⟨the bitter ~ of the rain —T.B.Costain⟩ **2 :** a sharp or stinging blow of a nonphysical kind ⟨under the ~ of competition —C.F.Wittke⟩ ⟨the ~ of public opinion —Robert Trumbull⟩ ⟨give him another ~ with my tongue —Michael McLaverty⟩ **3 :** EYELASH **4 :** a cord or group of strings for lifting simultaneously certain warp yarns to form a figure in weaving **5 :** BACKLASH 1b

[3]**lash** \"\ *vt* -ED/-ING/-ES [ME *lasschen* to lace, fr. MF *lachier, lacier* — more at LACE] **:** to bind with a rope, cord, thong, or chain so as to fasten ⟨~ something to a spar⟩ ⟨~ a pack⟩ — **lash a hammock :** to roll a hammock up usu. lengthwise with the bedding inside and bind it

**lash cleat** *n* [[3]*lash* + *cleat*] **:** a small metal hook screwed into the frame of a theatrical flat for attaching a lash line

**lashed** \¦lasht, -aa(ə)-,-ai-\ *adj* [[2]*lash* + *-ed*] **:** having eyelashes usu. of a specified kind — used chiefly in combination ⟨that long-*lashed* teen-age floozy —James Stern⟩

**lash·er** \'lashə(r), -aash-,-aish-\ *n* -s **1 :** one that lashes or whips **2** *dial chiefly Eng* **a :** the water rushing through a weir **b :** WEIR **c :** a pool receiving the water from a weir

**La·shi** \'läshē\ *n, pl* **lashi** *or* **lashis** *usu cap* **1 :** a people of Tibeto-Burman affiliations related to the Lisu and inhabiting the frontier region between northern Yunnan and Burma **2 :** a member of the Lashi people

**lashing** *n* -s [fr. gerund of [3]*lash*] **:** something (as a rope, wire, or chain) used for binding, wrapping, or fastening

**lash·ing·ly** *adv* [*lashing* (pres. part. of [1]*lash*) + *-ly*] **:** in a lashing manner

**lash·ings** \'lashiŋz, -aash-,-aish-, -shēŋz,-shənz\ *also* **lash·ins** \-shənz\ *n pl* [fr. *lashings,* pl. of *lashing,* gerund of [1]*lash*] *chiefly Brit* **:** a great plenty **:** ABUNDANCE ⟨a porcelain bath with ~ of hot water —Agatha Christie⟩ ⟨~ of chocolate and other light snacks —D.L.Busk⟩

**lash·kar** \'ləshkə(r), 'lash-\ *adj, usu cap* [fr. *Lashkar,* city in north central India] **:** of or from the city of Lashkar, India **:** of the kind or style prevalent in Lashkar

**lash·less** \'lashləs, -aash-,-aish-\ *adj* **:** having no eyelashes

**lash line** *n* [[3]*lash* + *line*] **:** a light rope usu. of sash cord used for fastening flats together in setting up stage scenery

**lash·orn** \'la,shȯrn\ *n* -s [origin unknown] *Midland* **:** FRASER FIR

**lash rope** *n, chiefly West* **:** a rope used for lashing a pack (as on a packsaddle)

**lash-up** \'=,=\ *n* [fr. the phrase *lash up,* fr. [3]*lash* + *up*] **1 :** something improvised esp. in an emergency **:** MAKESHIFT, CONTRAPTION, CONTRIVANCE ⟨crammed with an ingenious time-bomb *lash-up*—*Time*⟩ **2 :** SETUP, OUTFIT ⟨sounded as if he knew the *lash-up* well enough —Nard Jones⟩ ⟨man, Lieutenant, you got a real *lash-up* here —Gordon Webber⟩

**la·si·o·cam·pa** \,lāzēō'kampə, ,lasē-\ *n, cap* [NL, fr. *lasio-* (fr. Gk *lasios* shaggy) + *-campa;* akin to Gk *lēnos* wool — more at WOOL] **:** the type genus of the family Lasiocampidae

[1]**la·si·o·cam·pid** \,===ˈ=pəd\ *adj* [NL *Lasiocampidae*] **:** of or relating to the Lasiocampidae

[2]**lasiocampid** \"\ *n* -s **:** a moth of the family Lasiocampidae

**la·si·o·cam·pi·dae** \,===ˈ=pə,dē\ *n pl, cap* [NL, fr. *Lasiocampa,* type genus + *-idae*] **:** a family of moths including the tent caterpillars, eggars, and lappet moths and being of medium size, stout-bodied and usu. tan or grayish, with pectinate antennae in both sexes

**la·si·o·rhi·nus** \,===ˈrīnəs\ *n, cap* [NL, fr. *lasio-* (fr. Gk *lasios* shaggy) + *-rhinus* — more at WOOL] **:** a genus containing solely the hairy-nosed wombat

**lasi·urus** \,==ˈyürəs\ *n, cap* [NL, fr. Gk *lasios* shaggy + NL *-urus*] **:** a genus of bats (family Vespertilionidae) including the red bat — compare NYCTERIS

**la·si·us** \'lās(h)ēəs\ *n, cap* [NL, fr. Gk *lasios* shaggy] **:** a genus of ants containing some of the brown and black ants of No. America and Europe that form large colonies nesting in the ground

[1]**lask** \'lask\ *n* -s [perh. alter. of [4]*lax*] *now dial Eng* **:** DIARRHEA

[2]**lask** \"\ *vi* -ED/-ING/-S [origin unknown] *archaic* **:** to sail with wind abeam or on the quarter

**las·ket** \'laskət\ *n* -s [perh. alter. (influenced by [1]*gasket*) of [1]*latchet*] **:** LATCHING

**las pal·mas** \lä'spälməs\ *adj, usu cap L&P* [fr. *Las Palmas,* Canary islands, Spain] **:** of or from the city of Las Palmas in the Canary islands, Spain **:** of the kind or style prevalent in Las Palmas

**las·pey·re·sia** \,laspə'rēzh(ē)ə\ *n, cap* [NL, prob. fr. Jacob H. *Laspeyres fl*1805 Ger. zoologist + NL *-ia*] **:** a genus of olethreutid moths containing many pests (as the pea moth)

**la spe·zia** \lä'spetsēə\ *adj, usu cap L&S* [fr. *La Spezia,* seaport in northwest Italy] **:** of or from the city of La Spezia, Italy **:** of the kind or style prevalent in La Spezia

**las·pring** \'laspriŋ\ *n, pl* **laspring** *or* **lasprings** [alter. of earlier *last-spring,* by folk etymology (influence of [2]*last* and *spring,* n.) fr. earlier *lakspynke,* fr. [1]*lax* + *pink* (salmon parr)] *dial Brit* **:** a young salmon

**lasque** \'lask\ *n* -s [perh. fr. Per *lashk* bit, piece] **:** a flat thin diamond usu. cut from an inferior stone and used esp. in Hindu work

**lass** \'las, -aa(ə)-,-ai-\ *n* -ES [ME *las, lasce*] **1 a :** young woman **:** GIRL ⟨the story of a small French ~ —*New Yorker*⟩ **b :** SWEETHEART ⟨the young hero of the story . . . and his ~ —Mary Ross⟩ **2** *chiefly Scot* **:** MAIDSERVANT

**las·sie** \'lasē, -aas-,-ais-, -si\ *n* -s [*lass* + *-ie*] **:** LASS, GIRL

**las·sik** \'lasik\ *n, pl* **lassik** *or* **lassiks** *usu cap* **1 :** an Athapaskan people of northwestern California **2 :** a member of the Lassik people

**las·si·tude** \'lasə,tüd, -aas-, -ə-,tyüd\ *n* -s [MF, fr. L *lassitudo,* fr. *lassus* weary — more at LET] **1 :** a condition of weariness or debility **:** FATIGUE ⟨when the walk is over, ~ recommends rest —William Cowper⟩ ⟨chronic ~ typically accompanies this disease⟩ **2 :** a condition of listlessness or indifference **:** LANGUOR ⟨surrendered to an overpowering ~, an extreme desire simply to sit and dream —Alan Moorehead⟩ ⟨succumbed to the ~ that pervades most of our prisons —Frank O'Leary⟩ ⟨sink in an indifference and ~ —John Galsworthy⟩

**lasslorn** \'=,=\ *adj* **:** forsaken by one's sweetheart ⟨broom groves, whose shadow the dismissed bachelor loves, being lasslorn —Shak.⟩

[1]**las·so** \'la(,)sō, 'laa-, -'sü, '=(,)sü\ *also* **las·soo** \='sü, '=-(,)sü\ *n, pl* **lassos** *or* **lassoes** *also* **lassoos** [Sp *lazo,* fr. L *laqueus* noose, snare — more at DELIGHT] **:** a rope or long thong of leather with a running noose that is used esp. for catching horses and cattle — compare LARIAT

[2]**lasso** \"\ *also* **lassoo** \"\ *vt* -ED/-ING/-ES **:** to catch with or as if with a lasso

lasso

**lasso cell** *n* **:** ADHESIVE CELL

**las·sock** \'lasək\ *n* -s [*lass* + *-ock*] *Scot* **:** a little girl **:** LASSIE

**las·so·er** *pronunc at* LASSO +ə(r)\ *n* -s **:** one that lassoes ⟨most skillful ~ —*Arctic*⟩

**lass-rope** \'las,=\ *n* [*lass-* (fr. [1]*lasso*) + *rope*] **:** LARIAT

**las·sú** \'lä(,)shü\ *n* -s [Hung] **:** the slow introductory section of a csardas or Hungarian rhapsody — contrasted with *friss*

[1]**last** \'last, -aa(ə)-,-ai-,-ȧ-\ *vb* -ED/-ING/-S [ME *lasten,* fr. OE *lǣstan* to last, follow, perform; akin to OHG *leisten* to perform, Goth *laistjan* to follow; denominative fr. the root of OE *lāst* footprint — more at [6]LAST] *vi* **1 :** to continue in time **:** go on ⟨the meeting ~*ed* till late in the evening⟩ ⟨winter ~*s* from December to March —*Amer. Guide Series: Nev.*⟩ **2 a** (1) **:** to continue in pristine, fresh, or unimpaired condition **:** go on or remain without loss of quality or effectiveness **:** SURVIVE, ENDURE ⟨that paint job will ~ a long time⟩ ⟨it is a book that will ~ —K.S.Latourette⟩ (2) **:** to continue to be available ⟨half price while they ~⟩ **b :** to manage to continue (as in a particular status, position, course of action) **:** stick it out **:** hold out ⟨once I ~*ed* without them for seven weeks —Monica Sheridan⟩ ⟨he won't ~; he'll quit before the week's out⟩ **c :** to continue to live ⟨he will not ~ very much longer —James Dennis⟩ ⟨couldn't have ~*ed* . . . five minutes —Lyle Saxon⟩ ~ *vt* **1 :** to continue in existence or action as long as or longer than **:** SUSTAIN, SURVIVE, ENDURE ⟨if, of course, he ~*ed* the war —Wirt Williams⟩ — often used with *out* ⟨cattle which could ~ out the drives —S.E.Fletcher⟩ ⟨could not ~ out the apprenticeship —Whitcomb Crichton⟩ **2 :** to suffice for the needs of ⟨on these two courses is golf to ~ you a lifetime —Judson Philips⟩ **syn** see CONTINUE

[2]**last** \"\ *adj* [ME *last, latst,* fr. OE *latost;* akin to OHG *lezzisto* last, ON *latastr* slowest; superl. of the adjective represented by OE *læt* late, slow — more at LATE] **1 a :** being, occurring, or coming after all others in time, place, or order of succession **:** following all the rest ⟨the ~ one out will please shut the door⟩ ⟨the ~ two days of the month⟩ ⟨was saying some ~ word to her —Scott Fitzgerald⟩ — sometimes used with an ordinal number to indicate position before the extreme end of a series ⟨the second ~ paragraph on the page⟩ **b :** being the only remaining ⟨the ~ stronghold of Atlantic salmon in the United States —Pete Barrett⟩ **2 :** of or relating to the terminal stage or point (as of life) **:** FINAL ⟨buried with impressive ~ rites⟩ ⟨comforted his ~ hours⟩; *specif* **:** administered to one dying — used of the sacraments of penance, viaticum, and extreme unction **3 :** next before the present **:** most recent **:** LATEST ⟨~ week⟩ ⟨his ~ book⟩ **4 a** (1) **:** lowest in rank or degree ⟨dead ~ in the five-paper Chicago field —*Newsweek*⟩ (2) **:** lowest in quality **:** WORST ⟨thieving is the ~ crime —Augusta Gregory⟩ **b :** farthest of all from a specified quality or condition **:** most unlikely ⟨all good men, and the ~ to condone any form of vice —Norman Douglas⟩ **5 a :** CONCLUSIVE, DEFINITIVE ⟨the ~ explanation of all rational belief in concrete matters —Father Zeno⟩ **b :** highest in degree **:** EXTREME, UTMOST, SUPREME ⟨exposed to the ~ term of contempt —Malcolm Cowley⟩ ⟨the ~ enduringness is reserved . . . for those odd chaps who discover things like the Pythagorean theorem —Clifton Fadiman⟩ **c :** SINGLE — used as an intensive ⟨every ~ square inch of good land —James Reach⟩ ⟨every ~ thing was the best of its kind —Frances G. Patton⟩

**syn** LATEST, CONCLUDING, FINAL, TERMINAL, ULTIMATE, EVENTUAL: LAST designates that which comes at the end of a series; it may imply that no more will follow or it may simply indicate that which has most recently occurred or been in existence ⟨the *last* page of the book⟩ ⟨the *last* days of his life⟩ ⟨his *last* book was successful and he is planning another⟩ ⟨that's my *last* duchess painted on the wall —Robert Browning⟩ LATEST, superlative of *late,* is often used in preference to LAST to indicate the most recent in situations in which *late* is unlikely to mean tardy or delayed ⟨his *latest* book⟩ ⟨the *latest* news⟩ ⟨the *latest* fashion in dresses⟩ CONCLUDING describes that which brings something to a conclusion ⟨repeating his main points in his *concluding* remarks⟩ FINAL emphasizes definite, decisive closing or ending of a series or process ⟨a *final* examination⟩ ⟨a *final* decree of divorce⟩ ⟨while sacrifices accepted as *final* emerged as nothing more than rehearsals for greater sacrifices to come —M.W.Straight⟩ ⟨judgment that is *final,* that settles a matter —John Dewey⟩ TERMINAL may indicate a limit or stopping point or mark beyond which a thing does not continue ⟨a soldier on *terminal* leave⟩ ⟨the *terminal* r of bar and car⟩ ⟨a disease in its *terminal* stages⟩ ULTIMATE describes a last element, stage, or event that is the outcome of a long process, often the most remote or the most important development ⟨the earth's refrigeration and the *ultimate* collapse of our solar system —L.P.Smith⟩ ⟨the word came into English from French but its *ultimate* source is Arabic⟩ ⟨control or occupation by Nazi forces of any islands of the Atlantic would jeopardize the immediate safety of portions of North and South America, and of the island possessions of the United States, and the *ultimate* safety of the continental United States itself —F.D.Roosevelt⟩ EVENTUAL while lacking implications of finality in sequence, indicates inevitability or probability of future occurrence even if after a very long period, or the actual fact of occurrence often after a very long period ⟨the belief that science shows man to be only an accident and an incident in a cosmic order that is moving toward *eventual* lifeless rest —C.C.Walcutt⟩ ⟨the *eventual* emergence of a science of grammar had been prepared for by generations of curious inquiry and practical endeavor —Benjamin Farrington⟩

— **on one's last legs :** at or near the end of one's resources **:** on the verge of failure, exhaustion, or ruin ⟨the old car was *on its last legs*⟩

[3]**last** \"\ *adv* [ME, fr. OE *latost;* akin to OHG *lazzōst,* adv., last; adverb fr. the superlative adjective represented by OE *latost,* adj. — more at [2]LAST] **1 :** after all others in time, place, or succession **:** at the end ⟨~ came the foot soldiers and supply trains⟩ ⟨ranks ~ in my estimation⟩ **2 :** on the most recent occasion **:** most lately ⟨saw him ~ in New York⟩ **3 :** in conclusion **:** FINALLY ⟨~, I wish to consider the economic outlook⟩

[4]**last** \"\ *n* -s [ME *last, latst,* fr. *last, latst,* adj. — more at [2]LAST] **:** something that is last: as **a :** the end of life **:** time of dying ⟨her pen was busy to the ~ —F.L.Pattee⟩ **b :** the last-mentioned person or thing ⟨these ~ could be scattered in case of a threatened air raid —Elmer Davis⟩ **c :** a last look, pronouncement, or other action ⟨looked his ~ on the old homestead⟩ ⟨I've spoken my ~ on that subject⟩ **d :** the last part **:** CONCLUSION, END ⟨would not hear the ~ of his story⟩ ⟨fought gamely to the ~⟩ ⟨remained in enemy hands until the very ~ —C.E.Black & E.C.Helmreich⟩ ⟨came home the ~ of March⟩ **e :** final appearance or mention ⟨hated to see the ~ of her —Ellen Glasgow⟩ ⟨knew he would never hear the ~ of that mistake⟩ **f :** one that ranks lowest ⟨would inevitably come in an inglorious ~ —Osbert Lancaster⟩ **g :** the final one ⟨the ~ of the tests was held today⟩ **h :** the score awarded for winning the final trick in certain card games (as pinochle) — **at last** *or* **at long last** *adv* **:** at the end of a certain period **:** after delay **:** FINALLY ⟨*at long last* returned to America —Dixon Wecter⟩ ⟨*at last* you've come home⟩

[5]**last** \"\ *n* -s [ME, unit of weight, load, fr. OE *hlæst* load; akin to MD *last* load, OHG *hlast;* derivative fr. the root of OE *hladan* to load — more at LADE] **:** any of several greatly varying units of weight, capacity, or quantity: as **a :** a unit of weight equal to about 4000 pounds **b :** an English unit of capacity for grain equal to 10 quarters or 80 bushels **c :** a unit of quantity for herring equal to 13,200, 10,000, or 20,000 fish

[6]**last** \"\ *n* -s [ME *laste,* fr. OE *lǣste,* fr. *lāst* footprint; akin to OHG *leist* shoemaker's last, ON *leistr* sock, Goth *laists* footprint, L *lira* furrow, track — more at LEARN] **:** a wooden or metal form which is shaped like the human foot and over which a shoe is shaped or repaired

three-way last

[7]**last** \"\ *vb* -ED/-ING/-S *vt* **:** to shape with a last **:** fasten or fit to a last ⟨~ a shoe⟩ ~ *vi* **:** to perform the operation of shaping with a last

**last·age** \-tij\ *n* -s [ME *lestage* tax levied on traders at fairs or markets, ballast of a ship, fr. MF *lastage, lestage* ballast of a ship, lastage, fr. *laster* to ballast (fr. OFris *hlesta* to load & MD *lasten* to load; akin to each other and both descended fr. a prehistoric denominative fr. the root of OE *hlæst* load) + *-age*] **:** a port duty for the privilege of loading a ship

**last clear chance** *n* **:** a doctrine in English and American law of negligence: contributory negligence of the plaintiff will not bar his action if the defendant had a clear chance of avoiding inflicting injury had he exercised due care

**last day** *n, often cap L&D* **:** JUDGMENT DAY 1a
**last ditch** *n* [²*last* + *ditch*] **:** a place of final defense **:** the last resort ⟨the journals of opinion are about the *last ditch* for the individualist —H.L.Smith b. 1906⟩ ⟨likely to fight acculturation to the *last ditch* —Ralph Linton⟩
**last-ditch** \ˈ=ˌ=\ *adj* [*last ditch*] **1 :** fought or conducted from the last ditch **:** waged with desperation and uncompromising spirit ⟨a *last-ditch* fight to block ratification —Leo Egan⟩ ⟨*last-ditch* resistance⟩ **2 :** made in a final effort to avert disaster ⟨it was a *last-ditch* gamble —Noel Houston⟩ ⟨a *last-ditch* effort to pare expenses —T.M.Pryor⟩
**last-ditch·er** \ˈ=ˈdichə(r)\ *n* [*last ditch* + *-er*] **:** a person ready to fight to the end **:** an irreconcilable combatant
**lasted** *past of* LAST
**last·er** \ˈlastə(r), -aas-, -ais-, -ȧs-\ *n* -S [⁶*last* + *-er*] **1 :** a workman who stretches shoe uppers around lasts **:** an operator of a lasting machine **2 :** a tool for stretching leather on a last
**Las·tex** \ˈlaˌsteks\ *trademark* — used for an elastic yarn consisting of a core of latex thread wound with threads of cotton, rayon, nylon, or silk and used to give a one-way or two-way stretch to fabrics and garments
**last gospel** *n, often cap L&G* **:** the liturgical gospel usu. John 1:1–14 recited by the celebrant following the close of the Mass in Roman Catholic churches, of the Divine Liturgy in Armenian churches, and of the Holy Communion service in many Episcopal churches
**last hand** *n, obs* **:** the finishing touches **:** the final polish
**last heir** *n* **:** the person (as a lord or the sovereign) to whom in English law lands escheat for want of an heir
**last in, first out** *adj* **:** being or relating to a method of valuing inventories by which items from the last lot received are assumed to be used or sold first and all requisitions are priced at the cost per item of the lot last stocked — compare FIRST IN, FIRST OUT
**¹last·ing** \ˈlastiŋ, -aas-,-ais-, -ȧs-, -tēŋ\ *adj* [ME, alter. of *lastende*, pres. part. of *lasten* to last] **:** existing or continuing a long while **:** ENDURING, DURABLE, ABIDING ⟨left a ~ mark on foreign policy —Blair Bolles⟩ ⟨a book of ~ significance⟩ — **last·ing·ly** *adv* — **last·ing·ness** *n* -ES
**²lasting** \"\ *n* -S [ME, gerund of *lasten* to last] **1** *archaic* **:** CONTINUANCE, DURATION **:** durable quality; *specif* **:** long life ⟨one of the great precepts of health and ~ —Francis Bacon⟩ **2** [¹*lasting*] **:** a sturdy cotton or worsted cloth in twill or satin weave made in narrow widths for use esp. in the shoe and luggage trades
**last judgment** *n, usu cap L&J* [ME *last juggement*, fr. ²*last* + *juggement* judgment] **:** the final judgment of mankind before God at the end of the world ⟨a moral perfection which will secure their acceptance at the *Last Judgment* —C.H.Dodd⟩ ⟨Muhammad's . . . doctrine of the *Last Judgment* —H.A.R. Gibb⟩
**last·ly** *adv* [ME *lestely*, fr. *leste, last* last + *-ly*] **:** in the last place **:** in conclusion **:** at the end ⟨~, we try to develop in them a realization —K.G.Marten⟩
**last mile** *n* **:** the walk of a condemned person to the place of execution ⟨like the shaving of the head before the *last mile* —Saul Levitt⟩
**last minute** *n* [²*last* + *minute*] **:** the moment or interval of time just before some usu. climactic, decisive, or disastrous event or development ⟨help came to the garrison at the *last minute*⟩
**last-minute** \ˈ=ˌ=ˈ=\ *adj* [*last minute*] **:** made or occurring at the last minute ⟨*last-minute* plans for preventing the war —T.B.Costain⟩ ⟨*last-minute* amendments⟩
**last name** *n* **:** SURNAME 2a — contrasted with *first name*
**last·ness** \-s(t)nəs\ *n* -ES **:** the condition of being last
**last post** *n* **:** a bugle call in the British Army equivalent to taps
**lasts** *pres 3d sing of* LAST, *pl of* LAST
**last straw** *n* **:** the last of a series (as of events, indignities, or burdens) that brings one beyond the ultimate point of endurance and causes a defeat, downfall, or breakdown ⟨that remark was the *last straw*⟩
**last supper** *n, usu cap L&S* **:** a representation usu. in painting (as that of Leonardo da Vinci in Milan) of the supper partaken of by Christ and his disciples on the night of his betrayal
**last word** *n* **1 :** the final remark in a controversy or other verbal exchange ⟨always manages to get in the *last word*⟩ **2 a :** power, right, or act of final decision **:** final judgment or say ⟨the *last word* lies with Asia and Africa —A.J.Toynbee⟩ ⟨under our proposal the civilians have the *last word* in everything —A.H.Vandenberg †1951⟩ **b :** authoritative statement or treatment **:** definitive work ⟨surely be the *last word* on the subject for many years⟩ **3 :** one that is the most advanced, up-to-date, or currently fashionable exemplar of its kind **:** ACME ⟨a character who was the *last word* in exquisite vice —Daniel George⟩ ⟨the *last word* in fireproof construction —G.F.T.Ryall⟩ ⟨absolutely the *last word* in schools —*Newsweek*⟩
**lasty** \ˈlastē\ *adj* [¹*last* + *-y*] *chiefly dial* **:** DURABLE, LASTING
**la·sya** \ˈläsyə, -sēə\ *n* -S [Skt *lāsya*, fr. *lāsayati* she dances; akin to Skt *lasati* he plays — more at LUST] **:** the lyric and feminine dance type of India — contrasted with *tandava*
**¹lat** \ˈlat\ *dial var of* LET
**²lat** \ˈlät\ *n* -S [Hindi *lāṭ, lāṭh*, alter. (influenced by Skt *lakuṭa, laguḍa* stick, club) of Skt *yaṣṭi* pillar, stick, club] **:** a separate column or pillar in some Buddhist buildings in India corresponding to the Greek stela but usu. larger
**³lat** \ˈlät\ *n, pl* **lats** \-ts\ *or* **la·ti** \ˈlä(ˌ)tē\ [Latvian *lats*, fr. *Latvija* Latvia] **1 :** the basic unit of monetary value of Latvia from 1922 to 1940 **2 :** a coin representing one lat
**lat** *abbr* **1** latent **2** lateral **3** latitude
**LAT** *abbr* local apparent time
**la·tah** \ˈläd·ə\ *n* -S [Malay] **:** a neurotic condition marked by automatic obedience, echolalia, and echopraxia observed esp. among Malays
**lat·a·kia** \ˌlad·əˈkēə\ *n* -S [fr. *Latakia*, seaport in Syria] **:** a superior aromatic Turkish smoking tobacco
**la·tania** \ləˈtānēə, -tan-\ *n, cap* [NL, fr. F *latanier* + NL *-ia*] **:** a small genus of fan palms of the Mascarene islands and the adjacent coast — see CHINESE FAN PALM
**latania scale** *n* **:** a widespread scale (*Aspidiotus lataniae*) esp. damaging to avocado and to greenhouse plants
**la·ta·nier** \ləˈtan(ˌ)yā\ *n* -S [F, prob. fr. Island Carib *alátani*] **1 :** any of various fan palms of the southern U.S. and the Caribbean region **2 :** the leaf of a latanier used in craftwork (as basketry)
**la·tax** \ˈlāˌtaks\ [NL, fr. Gk, a water quadruped, prob. the beaver; prob. akin to Gk *latax* last remnant of a cup of wine — more at LATEX] *syn of* ENHYDRA
**¹latch** \ˈlach\ *vb* -ED/-ING/-ES [ME *lachen, lacchen*, fr. OE *læccan*; akin to Gk *lambanein, lazesthai* to take, grasp] *vi* **1 a** (1) **:** to lay hold esp. with the hands or arms **:** GRASP, SEIZE, GRAPPLE ⟨searching for crevices to ~ upon —Norman Mailer⟩ — usu. used with *on* or *onto* ⟨tractors ~ on to remains of derrick and drilling tools —*Irish Digest*⟩ ⟨~*ed* onto a . . . pass —*New Yorker*⟩ (2) **:** to gain or come into possession **:** get hold — usu. used with *on* or *onto* ⟨had ~*ed* on to 444,000 shares —*Newsweek*⟩ ⟨can I ~ on to some of your dough —C.O.Gorham⟩ ⟨knew that he had ~*ed* on to a good thing —Philip Hamburger⟩ (3) **:** to keep firm possession or grasp **:** HOLD — usu. used with *on* or *onto* ⟨you ought to know enough to ~ onto your gear —John Hersey⟩ **b :** to gain understanding or comprehension **:** TUMBLE — usu. used with *on* ⟨slow . . . in ~*ing* on to the notion that her husband's work is important —John McCarten⟩ **c :** to associate oneself closely or intimately **:** attach oneself — used with *on* or *onto* ⟨I'd think he'd ~ onto a girl like that —W.C.Fridley⟩ ⟨nobody's ~*ing* onto me —Saul Levitt⟩ ⟨~*ed* onto this racket right under his nose —Harold Robbins⟩ **2** *dial Eng* **:** ALIGHT ~ *vt, dial Brit* **:** CATCH, GET, RECEIVE
**²latch** \"\ *n* -ES [ME *lache, lacche*, fr. *lachen, lacchen*, v.] **1 :** a device that holds something in place by entering a notch or cavity; *specif* **:** the catch which holds a door or gate when closed even if not bolted **2** *now dial Eng* **:** a loop or noose that fastens or holds **:** SNARE **3 :** the hinged piece of a knitting-machine needle that holds the engaged loop in position while the needle is penetrating another loop
**³latch** \"\ *vb* -ED/-ING/-ES *vt* **:** to catch or fasten by means of a latch ⟨~ the door⟩ ~ *vi* **:** to latch itself **:** shut so that the latch catches ⟨will the door ~⟩
**⁴latch** \"\ *var of* ¹LETCH
**latch bolt** *n* [²*latch*] **:** a bevel-headed self-acting spring bolt
**¹latch·et** \ˈlachət\ *n* -S [ME *lachet*, fr. MF *lachet, lacet* shoestring, string for lacing up a garment, fr. *laz* noose, snare (fr. L *laqueus*) + *-et* — more at DELIGHT] **1** *obs* **:** THONG, LOOP **2 :** a narrow strap, thong, or lace esp. of leather by which a shoe or sandal is fastened upon the foot
**²latchet** \"\ *n* -S [origin unknown] *Austral* **:** a flying gurnard or a closely related fish
**latching** *n* -S [fr. gerund of ¹*latch*] **:** an eye formed on the headrope of a bonnet by which it is attached to the foot of a sail — called also *lasket*; usu. used in pl.
**latchkey** \ˈ=ˌ=\ *n* **1 :** a key used to lift or pull back a latch of a door **2 :** a front door key
**latch needle** *n* **:** a fine steel needle for machine knitting that has a butt at one end and at the other a short hook closed by a latch — see KNITTING NEEDLE
**latch pin** *n* [²*latch*] *Midland* **:** SAFETY PIN
**latchstring** \ˈ=ˌ=\ *n* **:** a string on a latch that may be left hanging outside the door to permit the raising of the latch from the outside or drawn inside to prevent intrusion
**latd** *abbr* latitude
**¹late** \ˈlāt, *usu* -ād·+V\ *adj* **lat·er** \ˈlād·ə(r), -ātə-\ **lat·est** \-ād·əst, -ātə-\ [ME, late, slow, fr. OE *læt*; akin to OFris *let* late, OS *lat* lazy, OHG *laz* slow, ON *latr* slow, lazy, Goth *lats* lazy, OE *lǣtan* to let, allow, leave, cause — more at LET] **1** *now dial* **a :** SLOW, SLUGGISH **b :** TEDIOUS **2 a** (1) **:** coming or doing after the due, usual, or proper time **:** not early ⟨the train is ~⟩ ⟨spring is very ~ this year⟩ ⟨there were only a few ~ customers left —Vicki Baum⟩ ⟨~ fruits⟩ ⟨sells a million copies to a large and ~ audience —J.D.Hart⟩ (2) **:** of, relating to, or given or imposed because of tardiness ⟨kept on receiving ~ marks⟩ ⟨had to pay a ~ penalty⟩ **b** (1) **:** of or relating to an advanced stage in point of time or development **:** ADVANCED ⟨the decline of trade under the ~ empire —D.W. McConnell⟩ ⟨few men have remained good fellows till so ~ an age —Robert Lynd⟩; *specif* **:** far advanced toward the close of the day or night ⟨keeps very ~ hours⟩ (2) **:** coming or occurring at an advanced stage (as of life or a period) ⟨rich old man captured . . . in a ~ marriage —William Howell⟩ ⟨the comparatively ~ peopling of the Plains —Edward Sapir⟩ **c :** continuing or doing until an advanced hour ⟨looking in on one of the ~ nightclubs —Erle Stanley Gardner⟩ ⟨a ~ sleeper⟩ **3 a :** living not long ago but not now **:** comparatively recently deceased **b :** being something or holding some position or relationship recently but not now ⟨memorial week will be observed at his ~ home —*Springfield (Mass.) Daily News*⟩ ⟨formal peace between the ~ belligerents —*Foreign Policy Bull.*⟩ ⟨do not love any of their ~ enemies —*Dublin Sunday Independent*⟩ **c :** made, appearing, or happening just previous to the present time **:** RECENT ⟨many ~ students of society —Roger Burlingame⟩ ⟨missions which have been performed in ~ combat —H.H.Arnold & I.C.Eaker⟩ **syn** see LAST, TARDY
**²late** \"\ *adv* -ER/-EST [ME, fr. OE, fr. *læt*, adj.] **1 a :** after the usual or proper time or the time appointed **:** after delay ⟨came ~ to work⟩ **b :** at or to a distant or advanced point in time **:** far into the night, day, week, or other period ⟨don't sit up ~⟩ ⟨the decision was reached ~ in 1951⟩ ⟨I'll see you *later* on⟩ **2 :** not long ago **:** LATELY, RECENTLY ⟨a socialite, ~ of London and now of New York⟩ — **of late** *adv* **:** LATELY, RECENTLY ⟨have not seen him *of late*⟩ ⟨*of late* he has not been able to make his rounds⟩
**late blight** *n* **:** a blight of plants in which symptoms appear late in the growing season: as **a :** a disease of solanaceous plants and esp. of the potato and tomato caused by a fungus (*Phytophthora infestans*) and characterized by decay of leaves, stems, and in the potato also of tubers **b :** a leaf spot disease of celery caused by a fungus (*Septoria apii* or *S. apii-graveolentis*) — see CELERY BLIGHT
**late·bra** \ˈlad·əbrə; ləˈtēbrə, -teb-\ *n* -S [NL, fr. L, hiding place, fr. *latēre* to lie hidden] **:** a flask-shaped mass of white yolk extending from the blastodisc of a bird's egg to the center of the yellow yolk
**latecomer** \ˈ=ˌ=ˌ=\ *n* **:** one that arrives late **:** a recent arrival ⟨a ~ in the struggle —Galbraith Welch⟩ ⟨a comparative ~ into jazz music —Deems Taylor⟩
**late cut** *n* **:** a cut made at a ball in cricket when it is near the batsman's wicket
**lat·ed** \ˈlād·əd\ *adj* [¹*late* + *-ed*] **:** BELATED
**late egyptian** *n, cap L&E* **1 :** DEMOTIC EGYPTIAN **2 :** NEW EGYPTIAN
**¹la·teen** \ləˈtēn, laˈ-\ *adj* [F *latine* (in the term *voile latine* lateen sail), fr. MF (in *voile latine*), fem. of *latin*, lit., Latin, fr. L *latinus* — more at LATIN] **:** being or relating to a rig used esp. on the north coast of Africa and in adjacent waters and characterized by a triangular sail extended by a long spar that is slung to a mast
**²lateen** \"\ *n* -S **1** *also* **la·teen·er** \-nə(r)\ **:** a lateen-rigged ship **2 :** a lateen sail
**late greek** *n, cap L&G* **:** the Greek language as used in the 3d to 6th centuries
**late latin** *n, cap both Ls* **:** the Latin language as used by the early church fathers through the 6th century and by other writers from the 3d to the 6th centuries inclusive

lateen 2

**late·ly** *adv* [ME, fr. ¹*late* + *-ly*] **:** not long ago **:** RECENTLY ⟨died as ~ as September of last year⟩ ⟨have not seen many of them ~⟩
**late-magmatic** \ˈ=ˌ=ˈ=ˌ=\ *adj* **:** relating to rocks or minerals that crystallize during the later stages of the cooling period of a magma ⟨*late-magmatic* reactions⟩
**lat·en** \ˈlātᵊn\ *vb* **latened; latened; latening** \-t(ᵊ)niŋ\ **latens :** to make or become late ⟨time is ~*ing*⟩
**la·ten·cy** \ˈlātᵊnsē, -si\ *n* -ES [¹*latent* + *-cy*] **1 a :** the quality or state of being latent **:** dormant condition ⟨sprung from ~ into expression —H.B.Alexander⟩ **b :** something that is latent ⟨writers who know how to evoke these *latencies* —E.C.Lindeman⟩ **2 :** the state or period of living and developing in a host without producing symptoms — used of an infective agent or disease **3** *or* **latency period :** a stage of personality development variously explained as cultural or biological in origin which extends from about the age of five to the beginning of puberty and during which sexual urges often appear to lie dormant ⟨children in ~ —G.S.Blum⟩ **4 :** REACTION TIME ⟨the ~ of the reflex wink . . . is notably short —R.S.Woodworth⟩
**la tène** \läˈten, -tān\ *adj, usu cap L&T* [fr. *La Tène*, shallows at the east end of Lake of Neuchâtel, Switzerland, site of discovery of Iron-Age remains] **:** of or relating to the later period of the Iron Age in Europe assumed to date from 500 B.C. to A.D. 1 — compare HALLSTATT
**late·ness** *n* -ES [ME *latnesse*, fr. OE *lætnes* slowness, fr. *læt* late, slow + *-nes* -ness — more at LATE] **:** the quality or state of being late ⟨the ~ of his arrival⟩ ⟨the ~ of the season⟩
**la·ten·si·fi·ca·tion** \lāˌten(t)səfəˈkāshən\ *n* -S [blend of ¹*latent* and *intensification*] *photog* **:** intensification of a latent photographic image by chemical treatment or prolonged uniform exposure to light of low intensity after the initial exposure
**la·ten·si·fy** \=ˈ=ˌ=ˌfī\ *vt* -ED/-ING/-S [fr. *latensification*, after E *intensification: intensify*] **:** to subject to latensification
**¹la·tent** \ˈlātᵊnt\ *adj* [L *latent-, latens*, pres. part. of *latēre* to lie hidden; akin to OHG *luog* den, lair, ON *lōmr* deceit, Gk *lanthanein* to escape notice, OSlav *lajati* to lie in wait for] **1 a :** existing in hidden, dormant, or repressed form but usu. capable of being evoked, expressed, or brought to light **:** existing in posse **:** not manifest **:** POTENTIAL ⟨the perennial vitality ~ in tradition —J.L.Lowes⟩ ⟨the heat ~ in firewood —Laurence Binyon⟩ ⟨a small fraction of his ~ capacities —Quincy Howe⟩ ⟨in the first innovations the germs of all subsequent improvements were ~ —Henry Orenstein⟩ ⟨his sinister qualities, formerly ~, quickened into life —Thomas Hardy⟩ ⟨all the ~ brutality, degradation and stupidity of a small American mining or industrial town —H.F.West⟩ ⟨the ~ meaning of dreams —G.S.Blum⟩ ⟨the vast resources said to be ~ in the desert —*Atlantic*⟩ **b :** present or capable of living or developing in a host without producing visible symptoms of disease ⟨some of the lily mosaics may survive for years as ~ viruses in insusceptible strains⟩ ⟨a ~ virus of the red raspberry that is highly destructive to blackcaps⟩ ⟨a ~ infection⟩ **c** *of a fingerprint* **:** obtained at the scene of a crime and usu. scarcely visible but capable of being developed for study ⟨use a reading glass or common magnifying glass to search for ~ prints —D.K.Fitch⟩ **2 :** CONCEALED, DISGUISED

**syn** DORMANT, QUIESCENT, POTENTIAL, ABEYANT, and IN ABEYANCE: LATENT applies to that which is submerged and not clearly apparent or certainly present to any but a most searching examination but may emerge and develop with effect and significance ⟨the heat *latent* in coal —G.B.Shaw⟩ ⟨a *latent* tenderness which breaks out at last in the story of Griseldis —J.R.Green⟩ ⟨the *latent* uneasiness in Darnay's mind was roused to vigorous life by this letter —Charles Dickens⟩ ⟨the theological passage of arms, which brought out all her *latent* antagonism to the prejudiced young pietist —Israel Zangwill⟩ DORMANT indicates that which is quite inactive, as though sleeping, but which may be awakened later into significant activity or effect ⟨though this strength pervaded every action of his, it seemed but the advertisement of a greater strength that lurked within, that lay *dormant* and no more than stirred from time to time, but which might arouse, at any moment, terrible and compelling —Jack London⟩ ⟨that haunting fear of being drowned in a confined space which lies *dormant* in the mind of most seamen —F.W.Crofts⟩ ⟨the purchasing power of workers newly employed revived demands *dormant* for many years and stimulated a gigantic outpouring of goods —Oscar Handlin⟩ QUIESCENT stresses the fact of inactivity at the time in question, without necessary implications of causes or of past or future activity ⟨a flare-up in the now *quiescent* struggle between the two Chinas —*New Republic*⟩ ⟨somewhat *quiescent* during the winter, the city takes on a new tempo with the coming of summer —*Amer. Guide Series: Mich.*⟩ ⟨simple insects, which we shall have to call collembolas, were difficult to capture. They leaped with agility many times their own length, and when *quiescent* looked like bits of fungus —William Beebe⟩ POTENTIAL applies to that which does not at the time under consideration have being, essence, character, or effect as indicated but which is likely in time to have that being or effect ⟨thousands of people in rural districts who constitute a *potential* labor supply for new factories —*Amer. Guide Series: Va.*⟩ ⟨yet such figures can be misleading in that they indicate *potential* rather than actual strength —D.W.Mitchell⟩ ⟨if narcotic addiction is to be eliminated, the *potential* addicts must be reached before they are exposed —D.W.Maurer & V.H.Vogel⟩ ABEYANT and the more common IN ABEYANCE indicate the fact of current inactivity, of not being used, implemented, caused, or allowed to function at the time under consideration ⟨a lurking and *abeyant* fear —Edith Wharton⟩ ⟨until all danger of counterrevolution should have been removed, personal rights and liberties would have to be kept strictly *in abeyance* —F.A.Ogg & Harold Zink⟩ ⟨the union has put its strike threat *in abeyance* and evidently will stay on the job as long as government possession lasts —*N.Y.Times*⟩

**²latent** \"\ *n* -S **:** a latent fingerprint ⟨compared the prints with those of the ~*s* —Erle Stanley Gardner⟩
**latent ambiguity** *n* **:** an uncertainty which does not appear upon the face of a legal instrument but arises from evidence aliunde **:** an uncertainty not involved in words themselves but arising from outside matters — opposed to *patent ambiguity*
**latent bud** *n* **:** a bud often concealed that may remain dormant indefinitely but under certain conditions develops into a shoot
**latent content** *n* **:** the underlying meaning of a dream exposed by interpretation of the dreamwork
**latent defect** *n* **:** an unknown defect (as in a title to real property) not discoverable by such inspection or test as the law reasonably requires under all the circumstances
**latent heat** *n* **:** thermal energy absorbed or evolved in a process (as fusion or vaporization) other than change of temperature — compare SENSIBLE HEAT
**latent image** *n* **:** an invisible image produced by an effect of light on matter (as silver halide or halides) which can be rendered visible by the subsequent process of photographic development
**latent learning** *n* **:** learning that occurs prior to the introduction and acquisition of a reward
**la·tent·ly** *adv* **:** in a latent manner
**latent mosaic** *n* **:** a latent virus disease that produces a mottling or mosaic
**latent period** *n* **1 :** LATENCY 2 **2 :** REACTION TIME; *specif* **:** the time interval between establishment of excitation and the beginning of identifiable reaction in an effector organ — called also *true latent period*
**latent strabismus** *n* **:** a tendency to squint controllable by muscular effort
**latent virus disease** *n* **:** a moderately virulent but highly infective virus disease esp. common in potatoes that often show no visible external symptoms although the yield is significantly reduced
**later** *comparative of* LATE
**later-** *or* **lateri-** *or* **latero-** *comb form* [L *later-*, fr. *later-, latus*] **1 :** side ⟨*later*ad⟩ **:** sidewise ⟨*lateri*grade⟩ **2 :** lateral and ⟨*latero*-anterior⟩
**-la·ter** \ləd·ə(r), lətə-\ *n comb form* -S [alter. of ME *-latrer*, fr. MF *-latre* -later (fr. LL *-latres*, fr. Gk *-latrēs*) + ME *-er*; akin to Gk *latron* pay, hire — more at LATHE] **:** one who worships or shows fanatical devotion ⟨biblio*later*⟩
**lat·er·ad** \ˈlad·əˌrad\ *adv* [*later-* + *-ad*] *anat* **:** toward the side
**¹lat·er·al** \ˈlad·ərəl, -atərəl, -a·trəl\ *adj* [L *lateralis*, fr. *later-, latus* side + *-alis* -al; prob. akin to L *latus* wide — more at LATITUDE] **1 a :** of or relating to the side **:** situated on, directed toward, or coming from the side ⟨the ~ branches of a tree⟩ ⟨a ~ view⟩ **b** *obs* (1) **:** being, acting, or moving side by side (2) *of winds* **:** blowing from the same general direction **c :** being to the right or left of a true course ⟨~ deviation⟩ **2 a** (1) *of a body part* **:** lying at or extending toward the right or left side **:** lying away from the median axis of the body ⟨the lungs are ~ to the heart⟩ (2) **:** being a body part so situated ⟨the ~ branch of the axillary artery⟩ **b** *bot* **:** relating to, characteristic of, or borne upon the side of any organ or of the axis ⟨a ~ bud⟩ — compare BASILAR, MEDIAN, TERMINAL **c** (1) **:** situated to one side of and parallel to a main vein or mine working ⟨a ~ vein or drift⟩ (2) **:** being or relating to any horizontal underground workings as contrasted with shafts, raises, and winzes ⟨~ development⟩ **3 :** having or characterized by a stocky thickset body-build and a short broad face ⟨babies of the ~ type⟩ — opposed to *linear* **4 :** produced with the tongue forming an occlusion at some point along its longitudinally middle line but with an opening at one or both sides ⟨\l\ and \lʸ\ are ~⟩
**²lateral** \"\ *n* -S **:** something having a lateral situation, growth, or extension: as **a :** a side ditch or conduit (as in an irrigation, drainage, sewer, gas, or water system) — compare MAIN **b :** a side branch from an electrical wiring or conduit system **c :** a drift to one side of and parallel to a main drift or haulage way **d :** a lateral pass in football **e :** a lateral tooth, scale, or other body part **f :** a lateral sound
**³lateral** \"\ *vb* -ED/-ING/-S [²*lateral*] *vi* **:** to throw a lateral pass ~ *vt* **:** to throw laterally
**lateral column** *n* **:** the column of the spinal cord between the dorsal and ventral roots of the spinal nerves
**lateral conjugation** *n* **:** sexual union between neighboring cells of the same filament of an alga — compare SCALARIFORM CONJUGATION
**lateral-cut** \ˈ=(=)=ˈ=\ *adj, of a phonograph record* **:** having the undulations cut by a stylus vibrating parallel to the record face
**lateral disc** *n* **:** a disc record produced by lateral recording
**lateral ethmoid** *n* **:** ECTETHMOID
**lateral fin** *n* **:** one of the paired fins of a fish
**lateral fissure** *n* **:** a deep fissure of the lateral aspect of each cerebral hemisphere that divides the temporal from the parietal and frontal lobes
**lat·er·al·i·ty** \ˌlad·əˈraləd·ē\ *n* -ES **:** preference in use of homologous parts on one lateral half of the body over those on the other **:** dominance in function of one of a pair of lateral homologous parts ⟨studies of the ~ of individuals in the performance of different tasks —K.C.Garrison⟩
**lat·er·al·iza·tion** \ˌlad·ərələˈzāshən, ˌla·trəl-, -ˌlīˈz-\ *n* -S **:** the action or an instance of lateralizing
**lat·er·al·ize** \ˈ=(=)=ˌlīz\ *vt* -ED/-ING/-S **:** to direct to or localize on one side **:** make lateral
**lateral lemniscus** *n* **:** a band of nerve fibers passing between the cochlear nuclei and the inferior colliculus and thalamus
**lateral line** *n* **1 a :** a longitudinal line along each side of the

body of most fishes that is usu. distinguished by modified and often differently colored scales and marks the position and orifices of the lateral line organ **b :** a narrow longitudinal tract in either side of the body wall of various oligochaete worms that is made up of the cell bodies of the circular muscle layer — see FISH illustration **2 :** LATERAL LINE ORGAN 1

**lateral line organ** *n* **1 :** a system of epithelial mucus-secreting tubes in the sides of most fishes, supplied at intervals with sensory endings and considered to be responsive to low frequency vibrations **2 :** one of the sensory end organs of the lateral line organ

**lat·er·al·ly** \'ladərəlē, 'latərə-, 'la·trə-, -li\ *adv* **:** by, to, or from the side **:** SIDEWAYS ⟨will work its way often for many miles, upward or ~ —*Oil*⟩

**lateral meristem** *n* **:** a meristem (as the cambium and cork cambium) that is arranged parallel to the sides of an organ and that is responsible for increase in diameter of the organ — compare APICAL MERISTEM, INTERCALARY MERISTEM

**lateral moraine** *n* **:** a moraine deposited by a glacier at its side

**lat·er·al·most** *pronunc at* 1LATERAL + ,mōst\ *adj* [1*lateral* + *-most*] **:** farthest to the side

**lateral pass** *n* **:** a pass in football thrown parallel to the line of scrimmage or obliquely to the rear

**lateral planation** *n* **:** the reduction of the land in interstream areas to a plane by the lateral erosion of streams

**lateral plate** *n* **:** an unsegmented sheet of mesoderm on each side of the vertebrate embryo from which develops the coelom and its linings

**lateral recording** *n* **1 :** a recording process in which the cutting stylus produces a groove that remains constant in depth but undulates from side to side in accordance with the sound being recorded **2 :** a disc record produced by lateral recording

**lateral sinus** *n* **:** TRANSVERSE SINUS

**lateral tooth** *n* **:** a tooth situated before or behind the middle of the hinge in a bivalve shell — compare CARDINAL TOOTH

**lateral vein** *n* **:** either of a pair of large veins running in the lateral body walls of elasmobranchs and various other low vertebrates and opening in front into the ducts of Cuvier

**lateral ventricle** *n* **:** the internal cavity of each cerebral hemisphere consisting in man of a central body and three cornua, an anterior curving forward and outward, a posterior curving backward and inward, and an inferior curving downward

**later·an** \'lā·trən, 'letərən\ *Scot var of* LECTERN

**later-day** \¦==¦=\ *adj* **:** LATTER-DAY ⟨in *later-day* tenements, constructional details vary —J.J.McCarthy⟩ ⟨burst upon the outraged *later-day* Victorians like verbal bombshells —J.G. Fletcher⟩

**lateri-** — see LATER-

1**lat·eri·grade** \'lad·ərə,grād\ *adj* [ISV *lateri-* + *-grade*] **:** running sidewise or characterized by such running ⟨~ locomotion⟩

2**laterigrade** \"\ *n* -s **:** a laterigrade animal (as a crab spider of the family Thomisidae)

**lat·er·ite** \'lad·ə,rīt\ *n* -s [L *later* brick, tile + E *-ite;* prob. akin to L *latus* wide — more at LATITUDE] **1 :** a residual product of rock decay that is red in color and has a high content in the oxides of iron and hydroxide of aluminum and a low proportion of silica **2 a :** a zonal group of red soils developed in hot humid climates that show intense weathering and chemical change and leaching away of bases and silica leaving aluminum and iron hydroxides **b :** a crusted soil of this group or a horizon in such soil developed through restricted drainage; *esp* **:** a mottled quartzite clay which hardens on exposure to air — **lat·er·it·ic** \¦==¦rid·ik\ *adj*

**lat·er·i·tious** *or* **lat·er·i·ceous** \¦lad·ə¦rishəs\ *adj* [L *latericius, lateritius* made of brick, fr. *later* brick + *-icius, -itius* -itious] **:** BRICK-RED **:** resembling brick **:** of the color of red brick

**lat·er·i·za·tion** \,lad·ərə'zāshən, -,rī'z-\ *n* -s [*laterite* + *-ization*] **:** the process of conversion of rock to laterite

**lat·er·nar·ia** \,lad·ə(r)'na(a)rēə\ *n, cap* [NL, fr. LL *laterna* lantern (alter. of L *lanterna*) + NL *-aria* — more at LANTERN] **:** a large genus of lantern flies

**la·ter·nu·la** \lə'tərnyələ\ *n, cap* [NL, fr. LL *laterna* + L *-ula*] **:** a genus of marine bivalve mollusks (suborder Anatinacea) comprising the lantern shells

**latero-** — see LATER-

**la·tes** \'lā,tēz\ *n, cap* [NL, irreg. fr. Gk *latos* Nile perch] **:** a genus of large percoid fishes of fresh and brackish water including the Nile perch and the begti

1**lat·est** \'lād·əst, -ātə-\ *adj* [fr. superl. of 1*late*] *archaic* **:** LAST ⟨my ~ breath was spent in blessing her —Alfred Tennyson⟩ — **at latest** *or* **at the latest** *adv* **:** at a time not later than specified ⟨be there by 10 *at the latest*⟩

2**latest** \"\ *n* -s **:** the most recent or currently fashionable style **:** the most recent development ⟨a display of the very ~ in spring outfits⟩ ⟨the ~ in fire-fighting equipment⟩

**late·wake** \'lāt·,wāk\ *dial Brit var of* LYKEWAKE

**lateward** *adv (or adj)* [ME, fr. 1*late* + *-ward*] *obs* **:** LATE, BACKWARD

**latewood** \'=,=\ *n* **:** SUMMERWOOD

1**la·tex** \'lā,teks\ *n, pl* **lat·i·ces** \'lad·ə,sēz, 'læd-·\ *or* **latexes** *often attrib* [NL *latic-, latex,* fr. L, fluid, prob. fr. Gk *latag-, latax* last remnant of a cup of wine; akin to OHG *letto* clay, ON *lethja* mud, W *llaid*] **1 :** a milky usu. white fluid of variable composition that is usu. made up of various gum resins, fats, or waxes and often a complex mixture of other substances frequently including poisonous compounds, that is found in or produced by cells of plants esp. of the Asclepiadaceae but also of the Apocynaceae, Sapotaceae, Euphorbiaceae, Papaveraceae, Moraceae, and Compositae, and that yields rubber, gutta-percha, chicle, and balata as its chief commercial products ⟨~ pillows⟩ ⟨~ foundation garments⟩ — see RUBBER **2 :** any of various emulsions in water of a synthetic rubber or plastic obtained by polymerization and used chiefly in paint and other coatings (as for paper) and adhesives ⟨GR-S ~⟩

2**latex** \"\ *vt* -ED/-ING/-ES **:** to treat (as a textile material) with a latex

**latex foam** *or* **latex foam rubber** *n* **:** FOAM RUBBER

**la·tex·osis** \,lā,tek'sōsəs\ *n* -ES [NL, fr. *latex* + *-osis*] **:** abnormal exudation of latex (as in certain diseases of various latex-producing plants)

**latex paint** *n* **:** a paint whose binder consists of a latex that is usu. a synthetic resin polymerized in water phase — compare EMULSION PAINT

1**lath** \'lath, -aa(ə)-, -á-\ *n, pl* **laths** \-thz, -ths\ *also* **lath** *often attrib* [ME *lat, latte, lath, lathe,* fr. OE *lætt;* akin to MD *lat, latte* lath, OHG & ON *latta* lath, W *llath* yard (measure of length)] **1 a :** a thin narrow strip of wood used (as by nailing to rafters, ceiling joists, studding) in making a groundwork (as for slates, tiles, plaster) or in constructing a light framework (as a trellis) **b :** a building material in sheets (as expanded or otherwise perforated metal, stiffened wire cloth, gypsum) used as a base for plaster **c :** a small angle iron used to support the covering of an iron roof **d :** a quantity of laths **:** LATHING ⟨built with ~ and plaster⟩ **e :** a thin narrow strip of wood used for any purpose **f :** FOREPOLE **2 a :** someone or something that is long, thin, and narrow ⟨a ~ like you, to hoist a hulk like me —W.W.Gibson⟩ **b :** TOBACCO STICK **c :** a thin or narrow and usu. small aggregate of rock or mineral ⟨the biotite is in ~s ranging up to several millimeters in length —*Jour. of Geol.*⟩

2**lath** \"\ *vt* -ED/-ING/-S **:** to cover or line with laths

**lath brick** *n* **:** a long slender brick used esp. in making the floor on which malt is placed in the drying kiln — compare PAMENT

1**lathe** \'lāth\ *vt* [ME *lathen* to invite, fr. OE *lathian* — more at LURE] *archaic* **:** to invite esp. to a wedding or funeral

2**lathe** \"\ *n* -s [ME, fr. OE *læth;* akin to ON *láth* landed property, OE *unlǣd, unlǣde* poor, miserable, Goth *unleds* poor, Gk *latron* pay, hire, Skt *rāti* generous] **:** one of the administrative divisions each containing several hundreds into which Kent, England, is divided

3**lathe** \"\ *n* -s [ME, fr. ON *hlatha;* akin to ON *hlatha* to load — more at LADE] *now dial Brit* **:** GRANARY, BARN

4**lathe** \"\ *n* -s [prob. fr. ME *lath* supporting stand, prob. of Scand origin; akin to Dan *-lad* supporting structure (as in *drejelad* lathe, *savelad* saw bench), Norw dial. *la, lad* small wall, pile, Sw dial. *lad* folding table, lay of a loom; akin to ON *hlatha* to load] **1 :** a machine in which work is rotated about a horizontal axis and shaped by a fixed cutting, boring, or drilling tool while being held in a chuck, faceplate, or mandrel or between centers in headstock and tailstock **2 :** 7LAY 1

5**lathe** \"\ *vt* -ED/-ING/-S **:** to cut or shape with a lathe

**lathe·man** \'lāthmən\ *n, pl* **lathemen :** a lathe operator

1**lath·er** \'lathə(r) *sometimes chiefly Brit* 'lāth-\ *n* -s [fr. (assumed) ME *lather,* fr. OE *lēathor;* akin to ON *lauthr* froth, OE *lēah* lye — more at LYE] **1 a :** a foam or froth consisting of extremely small bubbles formed when soap or some other detergent is agitated with or in water **b :** foam or froth from profuse sweating (as on a horse) **:** a condition of sweating profusely ⟨worked himself into a ~⟩ **2 :** a highly agitated or overwrought state **:** DITHER ⟨in a ~ of nervous apprehension —Walter O'Meara⟩ ⟨why is she in such a ~ to get money —J.B.Benefield⟩ ⟨in a ~ of hurry to get everything finished at once —G.W.Brace⟩

2**lather** \"\ *vb* **lathered; lathered; lathering** \-th(ə)riŋ\ **lathers** [ME *latheren,* alter. (influenced by — assumed — ME *lather,* n.) of *letheren, litheren,* fr. OE *lethran, līthran;* akin to ON *leythra* to wash; denominative fr. the root of OE *lēathor,* n.] *vt* **1 :** to spread lather over ⟨~ the face⟩ **2 :** to beat severely **:** FLOG ⟨will ~ your hide —*Ballad Book*⟩ **3 :** EXCITE, AGITATE — usu. used with *up* ⟨used to ~ up the floor clerk to the point of frenzy —*Sat. Eve. Post*⟩ ~ *vi* **:** to form a lather or a froth like lather ⟨good soap ~s profusely and quickly —*Danceland*⟩

3**lath·er** \'lathə(r), -aath-, -áth-\ *n* -s [2*lath* + *-er*] **:** a person who makes laths or puts up laths as a base for plaster or fireproofing material

4**lath·er** \'lāthə(r)\ *n* -s [5*lathe* + *-er*] **:** a person who works a lathe

**lath·er·er** \'lathərə(r), -áth-\ *n* -s **:** one that lathers

**latherwort** \'==,=\ *n* **:** SOAPWORT

**lath·ery** \'lath(ə)rē, -áth-, -ri\ *adj* [1*lather* + *-y*] **:** covered with or as if with lather

**lathes** *pl of* LATHE, *pres 3d sing of* LATHE

**lathework** *n* **:** machine engraving; *specif* **:** the part of the design of a stamp or currency note that is engraved by machine

**lathhouse** \'=,=\ *n* **:** a structure made chiefly of laths or slats spaced so as to reduce excessive sunlight while permitting moderate air circulation and used for growing plants that require some shade and protection from strong winds

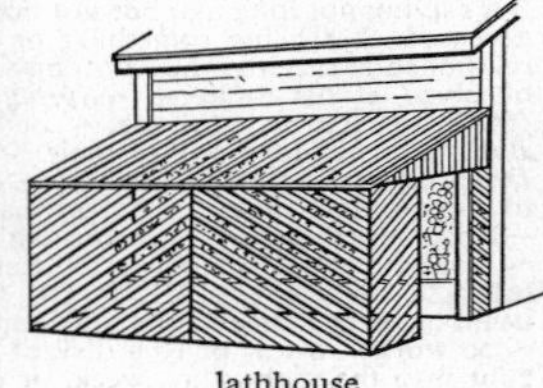

lathhouse

**la·thi** *also* **la·thee** \'lä(,)tē\ *n* -s [Hindi *lāṭhī,* fem. of *lāṭh* — more at LAT] **:** a heavy stick often of bamboo bound with iron used in India as a weapon esp. by police (as in dispersing a crowd or quelling a riot)

**lath·ing** \'lathiŋ, -aath-,-áth-, -thēŋ\ *n* -s [fr. gerund of 2*lath*] **1 :** the action or process of placing laths **2 :** a quantity or an installation of laths **:** LATHS

**lathing hatchet** *n* **:** a hatchet for trimming and nailing laths having a long thin blade and a head that is crosshatched with grooves

**lathing nail** *n* **:** LATH NAIL

**lath nail** *n* [ME *lathnail,* fr. 1*lath* + *nail*] **:** a slender nail for fastening laths

**lath·raea** \la'thrēə\ *n, cap* [NL, fr. Gk *lathraios* secret; akin to Gk *lanthanein* to escape notice — more at LATENT] **:** a genus of parasitic plants (family Orobanchaceae) having scaly leaves, small flowers, and explosively splitting capsules

**lath·ri·di·idae** \,lathrə'dīə,dē\ *n pl, cap* [NL, fr. *Lathridius,* type genus (fr. Gk *lathridios* secret) + *-idae;* fr. the small size of beetles belonging to this genus; akin to Gk *lanthanein*] **:** a family of small widely distributed light brown to dark brown beetles that have the wings fringed with short hair and feed chiefly on fungi

**laths** *pl of* LATH, *pres 3d sing of* LATH

**lath screen** *n* **:** a screen made chiefly of laths or slats spaced so as to reduce excessive sunlight while permitting moderate air circulation that is frequently placed over hotbeds or cold frames to provide some shade and protection from strong winds

**lathy** \'lathē, -aath-,-áth-, -thi\ *adj* -ER/-EST [1*lath* + *-y*] **:** being like a lath **:** long and slender **:** THIN ⟨a tall, thin, and ~ man —John Shandon⟩

**lathyarn** \'=,=\ *n* **:** a single tarred or untarred yarn put up in stranded form or with many ends

**lath·y·rism** \'lathə,rizəm\ *n* -s [ISV *lathyr-* (fr. NL *Lathyrus*) + *-ism*] **:** poisoning produced by the use as food of the seeds of certain plants of the genus *Lathyrus* and characterized by spastic paralysis of the legs

**lath·y·rus** \-rəs\ *n* [NL, fr. Gk *lathyros* chickling — more at LENTIL] **1** *cap* **:** a genus of plants (family Leguminosae) including many peas and vetchlings and differing from members of the genus *Pisum* in having the style not sulcate — see EVERLASTING PEA, SWEET PEA **2** -ES **:** any plant of the genus *Lathyrus*

1**lati** *pl of* LAT

2**la·ti** \'läd·ē\ *n* -s *usu cap* **:** a language spoken by a small group of hill people on the Vietnam-China border that was formerly held to constitute an independent language family but is now assigned to the Kadai group

**lati-** *comb form* [ME, fr. L, fr. *latus* — more at LATITUDE] **:** wide **:** broad ⟨*lati*rostral⟩

**latices** *pl of* LATEX

**lat·i·cif·er·ous** \¦lad·ə¦sif(ə)rəs\ *adj* [ISV *latici-* (fr. NL *latic-, latex* latex) + *-ferous*] **:** containing, bearing, or secreting latex

**la·ti·fon·do** \,läd·ə'fōn(,)dō\ *n, pl* **latifon·di** \-(,)dē\ [It, fr. L *latifundium*] **:** a latifundium in modern Italy

**lat·i·fun·di·ary** \,lad·ə'fəndē,erē\ *adj* [*latifundium* + *-ary*] **:** of or relating to the system of landownership through latifundia

**la·ti·fun·dio** \,läd·ə'fündē,ō, -fün-\ *n* -s [Sp, fr. L *latifundium*] **:** a latifundium in Spain or Latin America

**la·ti·fun·dis·mo** \,==='diz(,)mō\ *n* -s [AmerSp, fr. Sp *latifundio* + *-ismo* -ism] **:** the system of great landed estates in Latin America

**la·ti·fun·dis·ta** \-istə\ *n* -s [AmerSp, fr. Sp *latifundio* + *-ista* -ist] **:** the owner of a latifundio

**lat·i·fun·di·um** \,lad·ə'fəndēəm\ *n, pl* **latifun·dia** \-ēə\ [L, fr. *lati-* + *-fundium* (fr. *fundus* piece of landed property, bottom) — more at BOTTOM] **:** a great landed estate (as in ancient Italy or in eastern Europe before World War I) often held by an absentee owner and typically employing servile or semiservile labor and primitive agricultural techniques ⟨changed a region of *latifundia* into one of peasant proprietors —David Mitrany⟩

**la·ti·go** \'läd·ə,gō, 'lad-·\ *n, pl* **latigos** *also* **latigoes** [Sp *látigo*] *chiefly West* **:** a long strap on a saddletree to tighten and fasten the cinch

**latigo leather** *n* **:** a cattlehide leather tanned with a combination of alum and gambier and used esp. for halters, cinches, and saddle strings

**latigo strap** *n, chiefly West* **:** LATIGO

**lat·i·me·ria** \,lad·ə'mirēə\ *n* [NL, fr. Marjorie E. D. Courtenay-*Latimer* b1907 So. African museum director + NL *-ia*] **1** *cap* **:** a genus of living coelacanth fishes that is the type of the family Latimeriidae **2** -s **:** any fish of the genus *Latimeria*

**lat·i·me·ri·idae** \,==mə'rīə,dē\ *n pl, cap* [NL, fr. *Latimeria,* type genus + *-idae*] **:** a family of living deep-sea coelacanth fishes currently known only from the southern African genus *Latimeria* and the Malagasy genus *Malania* and having their nearest relatives among fishes that became extinct in the Mesozoic

1**lat·in** \'lat°n *also* -ad·ən *or* -atən\ *adj, usu cap* [ME, fr. OE, fr. L *Latinus,* fr. *Latium,* ancient country of Italy having Rome as its principal city from the 5th century B.C. + L *-inus* -ine] **1 :** of or relating to Latium or the Latins (sense 2) ⟨the Latin language⟩ **2 a :** of, relating to, or composed in Latin ⟨*Latin* grammar⟩ ⟨the *Latin* idiom⟩ **b :** ROMANCE ⟨the modern *Latin* tongues⟩ **3 :** of or relating to that portion of the Christian church that employs the Latin rite in its services **4 a :** of or relating to the peoples, nationalities, or countries whose chief or official languages are Romance ⟨the sister *Latin* nations have drawn closer —Thomas Okey⟩; *specif* **:** LATIN-AMERICAN ⟨make increasing amounts of U. S. dollar exchange available to the *Latin* countries —R.J. Alexander⟩ **b :** relating to the collective psychology or temper held to be characteristic of such peoples ⟨lively, one-legged . . . , very *Latin* in temperament —Rosemary Benét⟩ ⟨a way that is characteristically *Latin* —M.S.Dworkin⟩ ⟨in him they see a *Latin* disdain —W.L.Sullivan⟩ ⟨don't think I'm being complicated and *Latin* —Louis Bromfield⟩ **5 :** of, relating to, or characteristic of the Latin alphabet

2**latin** \"\ *n* -s *cap* [in sense 1, fr. ME, fr. OE, fr. L *Latinum,* fr. *latinum,* neut. of *latinus,* adj.; in other senses, fr. ME, user of the Latin language, fr. L *Latinus,* n., inhabitant of Latium, fr. *latinus,* adj.] **1 :** the Italic language of ancient Latium and of Rome and until modern times the dominant language of school, church, and state in western Europe **2 :** a member of the people of ancient Latium **3 :** a member of that portion of the Christian church that employs the Latin rite in its services **4 :** a member of one of the Latin peoples ⟨though a *Latin,* he disliked the French —Brand Blanshard⟩; *specif* **:** LATIN AMERICAN ⟨grouping of *Latins* on one side and North Americans on the other —S.P.Brewer⟩ **5 :** the Latin alphabet

3**latin** \"\ *vt* -ED/-ING/-S *often cap* **:** to translate into Latin

**latin alphabet** *n, usu cap L* **:** an alphabet that was adapted from the early form of the Etruscan alphabet for writing Latin, that had orig. 20 or 21 letters but in the classical Latin period 23 and from the Medieval Latin period 26, and that has also come to be used often with minor modifications for writing numerous other languages including English so that it is now the most extensively used of all the world's alphabets — called also *Roman alphabet*

**latin-american** \¦===¦===\ *adj, usu cap L&A* [fr. *Latin America,* those parts of America colonized by the Spanish and Portuguese + E *-an,* adj. suffix] **:** of or relating to the countries of No., Central, and So. America excluding French Canada whose chief or official languages are Romance languages

**latin american** *n, cap L&A* [fr. *Latin America* + E *-an,* n. suffix] **:** a native or inhabitant of Latin America

**lat·in·ate** \'lat°n,āt\ *adj, often cap* **:** of, relating to, resembling, or derived from Latin ⟨a preference for *Latinate* terms —R.M. Weaver⟩ ⟨attempted to make English grammar less *Latinate* —J.H.Sledd & G.J.Kolb⟩ ⟨the prose of the opening chapters is somewhat stiff and ~ —Richard Church⟩

**latin cross** *n, usu cap L* **1 :** a figure of a cross having a long upright shaft and a shorter crossbar traversing it above the middle **2 :** CRUX IMMISSA 1

Latin cross 1

**lat·in·er** \'lat°nə(r)\ *n* -s *usu cap* **:** a Latin scholar

**latin grammar school** *or* **latin school** *n, usu cap L* [*latin grammar school* fr. *latin grammar* (fr. 1*latin* + *grammar*) + *school; latin school* fr. 2*latin* + *school*] **:** GRAMMAR SCHOOL 1a

**la·tin·i·an** \la'tinēən, lə'-\ *n* -s *usu cap* **:** a division of the Italic languages that is commonly restricted to the ancient languages Latin, Lanuvian, and Faliscan, but is occas. used to include the modern Romance languages — see INDO-EUROPEAN LANGUAGES table

**la·tin·ic** \la'tinik, lə'-\ *adj, usu cap* **:** relating or related to the Latin language or the Latin peoples

**lat·in·ism** \'lat°n,izəm\ *n* -s *usu cap* [ML *latinismus,* fr. L *latinus* Latin + *-ismus* -ism — more at LATIN] **1 a :** a word, phrase, or inflection characteristic of Latin; *esp* **:** one appearing in the context of another language **b :** a word, phrase, grammatical construction, or inflection derived from or imitative of Latin **c :** a mode of speech or writing imitative or suggestive of Latin models **2 :** Latin quality, character, or mode of thought ⟨the self-assertive *Latinism* of the French ruling classes —Emil Lengyel⟩

**lat·in·ist** \-t°nəst\ *n* -s *usu cap* [ML *latinista,* fr. L *latinus* Latin + *-ista* -ist] **1 :** a person esp. skilled or informed in the Latin language or classical Latin literature or civilization **:** a specialist in the Latin language and culture **2 :** one who favors or propagates the Latin language or introduces Latin elements into another language

**la·tin·i·ty** \la'tinəd·ē, lə'-\ *n* -ES *often cap* [L *latinitat-, latinitas,* fr. *latinus* Latin + *-itat-, -itas* -ity] **1 a :** manner of speaking or writing Latin **:** LATIN ⟨the eccentric ~ of which he was master —F.M.Stenton⟩ **b :** knowledge of Latin ⟨today's youth has no *Latinity* —S.H.Adams⟩ **2 :** Latin quality, character, or traits **:** LATINISM ⟨the conflict between ~ and teutonism —Brewton Berry⟩ **3 :** the status or right of a person having the jus Latii

**lat·in·ization** \,lat°nə'zāshən, -°n,ī'z-\ *n* -s *sometimes cap* **:** the act, process, result, or an instance of latinizing ⟨this ~ of English —Frederick Bodmer⟩

**lat·in·ize** \'lat°n,īz\ *vb* -ED/-ING/-S *often cap* [LL *latinizare,* fr. L *latinus* Latin + *-izare* -ize] *vt* **1 a** *obs* **:** to translate into Latin **b :** to give a Latin form to (a word or phrase of another language) ⟨*latinized* Greek words⟩ **c :** to make latinate esp. by the use of Latin loan words ⟨the diction may be plain or heavily *latinized* —Douglas Bush⟩ **d :** ROMANIZE 2a **2 :** to make Latin or Italian in doctrine, ideas, or traits; *specif* **:** to cause to resemble the Roman Catholic Church ⟨~ the Church of England⟩ ~ *vi* **1 :** to use Latinisms in writing or speech **2 :** to come under the influence of the Romans or of the Roman Catholic Church

**la·ti·no** \la'tē(,)nō, lə'-\ *n* -s *often cap* [AmerSp, fr. Sp *latino,* adj., Latin, fr. L *latinus*] **:** LATIN AMERICAN

**latin right** *n, cap L* **:** JUS LATII

**latin rite** *n, cap L* **1 :** forms of Christian worship and liturgy utilizing Latin in their expression and employed predominantly in the Roman Catholic Church of the West **2 :** the part of the Roman Catholic Church that employs Latin liturgies

**latin square** *n, often cap L* **:** one of a set of square arrays resembling determinants in which no element occurs twice in the same column or row and by means of which statistical investigations may be planned and carried out

**lat·in·xua** \'lat°n,(h)wä\ *n* -s *usu cap* [irreg. fr. 1*latin*] **:** a system for romanization of the Chinese language utilizing an alphabet of 28 romanized characters based on Chinese phonetic principles

**lation** *n* -s [L *lation-, latio* action of bringing or proposing, fr. *latus* (used as past part. of *ferre* to carry) + *-ion-, -io* -ion — more at TOLERATE] *obs* **:** LOCOMOTION

**lati·plantar** \¦lad·ə+\ *adj* [*lati-* + *plantar*] **:** having the hinder part of the tarsus rounded ⟨~ birds⟩ — opposed to *acutiplantar*

**lati·rostral** *also* **lati·rostrate** \"+\ *adj* [*lati-* + *rostral* or *rostrate*] **:** having a broad beak

**lat·i·rus** \'lad·ərəs\ *n, cap* [NL, perh. modif. of Gk *lathyros* chickling — more at LENTIL] **:** a genus of band shells having a prolongation of the margin of the aperture resembling a horn

**latis** *pl of* LATI

**lat·ish** \'lād·|ish, -āt|, |ēsh\ *adj (or adv)* **:** somewhat late ⟨it was ~ when we showed up —A.B.Guthrie⟩ ⟨I get up ~ —O.W.Holmes †1935⟩

**la·tis·si·mus dor·si** \lə¦tisəməs'dȯ(ə)r,sī\ *n, pl* **latissi·mi dorsi** \-,mī'd-\ [NL, lit., broadest (muscle) of the back] **:** a broad flat superficial muscle of the lower part of the back that draws the arm backward and downward and rotates it inward

**la·tite** \'lā,tīt\ *n* -s [*Latium,* Italy + E *-ite* — more at LATIN] **:** a lava intermediate between andesite and trachyte that is the extrusive equivalent of monzonite

**lat·i·tude** \'lad·ə,tüd, -atə-, -ə-,tyüd\ *n* -s [ME, fr. L *latitudin-, latitudo,* fr. *latus* wide + *-tudin-, -tudo* -tude; akin to OSlav *postilati* to spread, Arm *lain* wide] **1 a** *archaic* **:** extent or distance from side to side **:** BREADTH **b** (1) **:** angular distance from some specified circle or plane of reference; *specif* **:** angular distance north or south from the earth's equator measured through 90 degrees with the length of a degree varying from 68.704 statute miles at the equator to 69.407 at the poles because of the flattened figure of the earth — compare

ASTRONOMICAL LATITUDE, CELESTIAL LATITUDE, GALACTIC LATITUDE, GEOMAGNETIC LATITUDE (2) **:** a region or locality as marked by its latitude — usu. used in pl. ⟨silences them earlier than the sun of our ~*s* —Richard Semon⟩ **c** (1) **:** the projection on the meridian of a given course in a plane survey equal to the length of the course multiplied by the cosine of its bearing (2) **:** the distance of a point in a survey from a specified east-west line of reference **2 a** *archaic* (1) **:** EXTENT, AMPLITUDE ⟨indulged himself in the utmost possible ~ of sail —T.L.Peacock⟩ (2) **:** SCOPE, RANGE **b** (1) **:** the range of exposures within which a film or plate will produce a negative or positive of satisfactory quality (2) **:** the permissible variation from the recommended development time without noticeable change of image contrast **3 :** freedom of action or decision esp. in selecting from a variety of courses or opinions **:** permitted or tolerated range or variety of action or opinion ⟨in foreign affairs alone he allowed himself a certain ~ —John Buchan⟩ ⟨took action to restrict the ~ of the chairman in determining the course of the committee's action —*N.Y. Times*⟩ ⟨allow him greater ~ in expressing his opinions —*Current Biog.*⟩

**latitude effect** *n* **:** the variation of any physical quantity with latitude; *specif* **:** an increase of cosmic-ray intensity with magnetic latitude esp. at high altitudes

**lat·i·tu·di·nal** \¦==¦tüd(ᵊ)nəl, -¦tyü-\ *adj* [L *latitudin-, latitudo* latitude + E *-al*] **:** of or relating to latitude and esp. to geographical latitude **:** in the direction of latitude — **lat·i·tu·di·nal·ly** \-d(ᵊ)nəlē, -li\ *adv*

**¹lat·i·tu·di·nar·i·an** \¦==,tüdᵊn¦erēən, ¦==·¦tyü-, -ᵊn¦a(a)r-, -ᵊn¦ār-\ *n* -S [L *latitudin-, latitudo* latitude + E *-arian* (as in *trinitarian*)] **1 :** a person who is broad and liberal in his standards of belief and conduct **:** one who displays freedom in thinking esp. in religious matters **2** *often cap* **:** a member of the Church of England who favors freedom and difference of opinion respecting government, worship, or doctrine within the church

**²latitudinarian** \"\ *adj* **:** not insisting on strict conformity to a particular standard, norm, or formula **:** TOLERANT ⟨eligible under the ~ policy of admissions —C.W.Ferguson⟩; *specif* **:** tolerant of variations in opinion or doctrine ⟨~ theology⟩

**lat·i·tu·di·nar·i·an·ism** \==,==¦==ə,nizəm\ *n* -S **:** a latitudinarian system or condition **:** latitudinarian beliefs or doctrines ⟨a broad, liberal ~ in theology —F.S.Mead⟩

**lat·i·tu·di·nous** \¦=¦tüdᵊnəs, ¦==·¦tyü-\ *adj* [L *latitudin-, latitudo* + E *-ous*] **:** having latitude or breadth esp. of thought or interpretation

**la·tium** \'lāsh(ē)əm, 'läd·ē,ùm, -d·ēəm\ *n* -S *usu cap* [LL, fr. *Latium*, Italy — more at LATIN] **:** JUS LATII

**¹la·tive** \'läd·iv\ *adj* [L *latus* (used as past part. of *ferre* to carry) + E *-ive* — more at TOLERATE] **:** being or relating to a grammatical case that denotes motion as far as or up to ⟨a ~ suffix⟩

**²lative** \"\ *n* -S **:** the lative case or a word in it

**lat·ke** \'lätkə\ *n, pl* **lat·kes** \-əs, -əz\ [Yiddish, fr. Russ *latka*, a pastry, prob. fr. (assumed) obs. Russ *oladka*, dim. of ORuss *oladiya* flat cake of leavened wheat dough, prob. fr. (assumed) MGk *eladion* oil cake, fr. Gk *elaion* olive oil, fr. *elaia* olive — more at OLIVE] **:** GRIDDLE CAKE; *esp* **:** one made from grated raw potato

**lat·o·sol** \'lad·ə,säl, -sōl\ *n* -S *sometimes cap* [*lato-* (irreg. fr. L *later* brick) + *-sol* (as in *podsol*, var. of *podzol*) — more at LATERITE] **:** leached red and yellow tropical soils — usu. used in pl. ⟨true *Latosols* . . . are found only in the tropics —F.E.Bear⟩ — **lat·o·sol·ic** \¦==¦säl̇ik\ *adj, sometimes cap*

**la·trant** \'lā·trənt\ *adj* [L *latrant-, latrans*, pres. part. of *latrare* to bark — more at LAMENT] *archaic* **:** BARKING, SNARLING, COMPLAINING

**la·tra·tion** \lə'trāshən\ *n* -S [L *latratus* (past part. of *latrare* to bark) + E *-ion*] *archaic* **:** the act or an instance of barking

**la·tria** \lə'trīə\ *n* -S [ML, fr. LL, service, worship, fr. Gk *latreia*; akin to Gk *latron* pay, hire — more at LATHE] *Roman Catholicism* **:** the supreme homage that is given to God alone — distinguished from *dulia* and *hyperdulia*

**lat·ri·dae** \'la·trə,dē\ [NL, fr. *Latris*, type genus + *-idae*] *syn of* LATRIDIDAE

**la·trid·i·dae** \lə'tridə,dē\ *n pl, cap* [NL, fr. *Latrid-, Latris*, type genus (irreg. fr. Gk *latris* maidservant) + *-idae*; akin to Gk *latron* pay, hire] **:** a small family of marine percoid fishes of Australia and New Zealand known as trumpeters

**la·trine** \lə'trēn\ *n* -S [F (usually in pl. *latrines*), fr. L *latrina*, contr. of *lavatrina*, fr. *lavere* to wash — more at LYE] **:** a receptacle (as a pit in the earth or a water closet) for use in defecation and urination or a room (as in a barracks or hospital) or enclosure (as in a camp) containing such a receptacle **:** TOILET

**latrine fly** *n* **:** a small housefly (*Fannia scalaris*) that breeds in excrement and occas. causes myiasis in man

**lat·ro·dec·tism** \,la·trə'dek,tizəm\ *n* -S [ISV *latrodect-* (fr. NL *Latrodectus*) + *-ism*] **:** poisoning due to the bite of a spider of the genus *Latrodectus*

**lat·ro·dec·tus** \-ktəs\ *n, cap* [NL] **:** a genus of nearly cosmopolitan arachnomorph spiders (family Theridiidae) that include all the well-known venomous spiders, that are of medium size and dark or black in color and often marked with red, and that have a large globular usu. glossy abdomen and long and wiry legs

**la·tron** \'lā·trən\ *n* -S [L *latron-, latro* mercenary soldier, brigand; akin to Gk *latron* pay, hire — more at LATHE] *archaic* **:** BRIGAND

**-la·try** \lə·trē, -ri\ *n comb form* -ES [ME *-latrie*, fr. OF, fr. LL *-latria*, fr. Gk *latreia* service, worship; akin to Gk *latron* pay, hire] **:** worship of or fanatical devotion to a (specified) object ⟨heliolatry⟩

**lats** *pl of* LAT

**lat·ten** *or* **lat·tin** \'latᵊn\ *n* -S [ME *latoun, laton*, fr. MF *laton, leton*, fr. OProv, fr. Ar *lāṭūn*, of Turkic origin; akin to Turk *altın* gold] **1 :** an alloy of or resembling brass hammered into thin sheets formerly much used for church utensils — called also *black latten* **2 a :** iron plate covered with tin **:** sheet tin **b** (1) **:** metal in thin sheets ⟨gold ~⟩ (2) **lattens** *pl* **:** metal sheets between $\frac{1}{64}$ and a little less than $\frac{1}{32}$ of an inch in thickness

**lat·ter** \'lad·ə(r), -atə-\ *adj* [ME, fr. OE *lætra* slower; akin to MHG *lazzer* slower, ON *latari*; compar. of the adjective represented by OE *læt* late, slow — more at LATE] **1 a :** belonging to a subsequent time or period **:** coming after something else **:** LATER ⟨the ~ stages of a process⟩ ⟨promises to deal with ~ events in a second volume⟩ ⟨how spiritless, how fallen upon meager ~ days —D.C.Peattie⟩ **b** (1) **:** belonging or relating to the end (as of life or the world) **:** LAST, FINAL ⟨in his ~ years threw his printing press into the sea —Mabel Dolmetsch⟩ ⟨remind worshipers of . . . their own ~ end —G.G.Coulton⟩ ⟨proclaimed these were the ~ days, with God's judgment drawing nigh⟩ (2) **:** belonging to the second half of the two divisions of a period ⟨indicates composition in the ~ months of 1813 —K.N.Cameron⟩; *specif* **:** SECOND ⟨during the ~ half of the nineteenth century —F.L.Allen⟩ **c :** RECENT, PRESENT ⟨the human race in these ~ days —G.M.Trevelyan⟩ **2 :** being the last named of two or more mentioned or understood things ⟨the novel . . . grows out of the epic as a reaction against the ~ —Leon Livingstone⟩ ⟨the drum, the rattle, and the flute, the ~ reserved wholly for love songs —*Amer. Guide Series: Minn.*⟩

**latter-day** \¦==¦=\ *adj* **1 :** of a later or subsequent time or period ⟨these *latter-day* prospectors were unsuccessful —*Amer. Guide Series: Wash.*⟩ **2 :** of present or recent times ⟨considers most amusingly the *latter-day* state of eastern potentates —*Times Lit. Supp.*⟩ ⟨the complex modern documents of *latter-day* corporation finance —T.J.Grayson⟩

**latter-day saint** *n, usu cap L&S, often cap D* **:** a member of a religious body that traces its origin back to Joseph Smith who in 1830 announced that he had discovered buried golden tablets and translated their hieroglyphics into the Book of Mormon considered by his followers as a new revelation from God equal with but not supplanting the Bible **:** MORMON

**latter lammas** *n, usu cap 2d L* [so called ironically fr. the fact that there is only one Lammas in a year] **:** a day that will never come

**lat·ter·ly** *adv* **1 :** at a subsequent time **:** LATER ⟨had been a salesman . . . and ~ a guide to anglers and hunters —Margaret K.Zieman⟩ ⟨had a school and, ~ at any rate, a Roman Catholic chapel —D.B.Forrester⟩ **2 :** of late **:** RECENTLY ⟨~, they have given to it more than its due place —J.G.Edwards⟩ ⟨buys food and drink . . . and, ~, quite a lot of beer —John Hyslop⟩

**lattermath** \'==,=\ *n* [*latter* + *math* (mowing)] *now dial Eng* **:** AFTERMATH

**¹lat·tice** \'lad·əs, -atəs\ *n* -S *often attrib* [ME *latis*, fr. MF *lattis*, fr. *latte* lath, fr. OF, prob. of Gmc origin; akin to OHG *latta* lath — more at LATH] **1 a :** a framework or structure of wood or metal made by crossing laths or other thin strips so as to form a network ⟨the ~ of a window⟩ **b :** a window, door, or gate having a lattice **c :** a representation or imitation of a lattice **d :** a lattice used as the sign of an alehouse **2 a :** a system of small intersecting diagonal or zigzag bars or angles that rigidly connect two parallel parts of a structural member **b :** a rectangle cut up into equal small rectangles by parallels to the sides **c :** a regular geometrical arrangement of points or objects over an area or in space: as (1) **:** SPACE LATTICE (2) **:** a geometrical arrangement of fissionable material in a nuclear reactor **3 :** something resembling a lattice: as **a** (1) **:** narrow strips of pastry laid over a pie in lattice fashion (2) **:** potato slices perforated in cutting to resemble latticework ⟨~ potatoes⟩ **b :** a decorative openwork (as of interwoven strips of leather on a shoe) **c :** a vestigial sieve plate with indefinite outlines and perforations minute or lacking

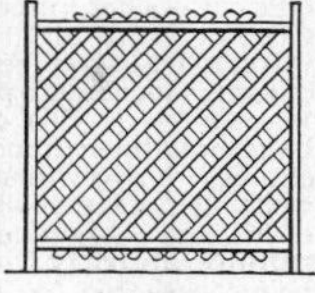

lattice 1a

**²lattice** \"\ *vt* -ED/-ING/-S [ME *lattizen*, fr. *latis* lattice] **1 :** to make a lattice of **:** give the appearance of a lattice to ⟨neatly arranged in strips that *latticed* his baldness —Pearl Kazin⟩ **2 :** to close or enclose (as an opening) with or as if with latticework ⟨~ a window⟩

**lattice bar** *n* **:** one of the diagonal connecting bars in a lattice (sense 2a)

**lattice constant** *n* **:** one of the geometrical constants of a crystal lattice: as **a :** the distance between identical points at two of the corners of the unit cell **b :** the angle between two edges of the cell

**lat·ticed** \-st\ *adj* **1 :** furnished with a lattice or latticework ⟨the huge, ~ iron door —Donn Byrne⟩ ⟨from the ~ shelves looked down an imposing array of eighteenth-century quartos —John Buchan⟩ **2 :** marked or arranged so as to represent or suggest a lattice; *specif* **:** CLATHRATE ⟨a ~ leaf⟩

**lattice girder** *or* **lattice beam** *or* **lattice frame** *n* **:** a girder with top and bottom flanges connected by a latticework web

**latticelike** \'==,=\ *adj* **:** like or resembling a lattice

**lattice plant** *or* **latticeleaf** \'==,=\ *n* [so called fr. the veined, skeletonized leaves] **:** a plant of the genus *Aponogeton*; *esp* **:** a plant (*A. fenestralis*) of Madagascar

**lattice shell** *n* **:** an oval shell (family Cancellariidae) with short spire and moderately large aperture

**lattice truss** *n* **:** a truss having its upper and lower chords so connected by diagonal members as to resemble latticework

**latticewise** \'==,=\ *adv* **:** in the manner of a lattice

**latticework** \'==,=\ *n* [ME *latise werk*, fr. *latise, latis* lattice + *werk* work] *n* **:** a lattice or work made of lattices **:** an assemblage of lattices

**latticing** *n* -S **:** LATTICE, LATTICEWORK ⟨the ~ of a lattice girder⟩

**lat·ti·ci·nio** \,lad·ə'chēn(,)yō\ *n, pl* **latti·ci·ni** \-ē(,)nē\ [It, dairy product, cheese, butter, fr. LL *lacticinium*, fr. L *lact-, lac* milk — more at GALAXY] **:** a glass or glassware containing milk-white canes or threads and made principally in Murano near Venice

**lattin** *var of* LATTEN

**latuka** *usu cap, var of* LOTUKO

**la·tus rec·tum** \,lad·əs'rektəm, ¦läd-, ¦läd-\ *n* [NL, lit., straight side] **:** the chord of a conic section through a focus and parallel to a directrix

**lat·via** \'latvēə\ *adj, usu cap* [fr. *Latvia*, country in northern Europe] **:** of or from Latvia **:** of the kind or style prevalent in Latvia **:** LATVIAN

**¹lat·vi·an** \-ēən\ *adj, usu cap* [*Latvia* + E *-an*, adj. suffix] **:** of or relating to Latvia, the country of the Letts on the Baltic

**²latvian** \"\ *n* -S *cap* [*Latvia* + E *-an*, n. suffix] **1 :** a native or inhabitant of Latvia **2 :** the Baltic language of the Latvian people

**la·uan** \lə'wän\ *n* -S [Tag *lawaan*] **:** any of various Philippine timbers (as from trees of the genera *Shorea* and *Parashorea*) that are light yellow to reddish brown or brown, moderately close-grained, and rather stringy, and of moderate strength and durability, and that include some which enter commerce as Philippine mahogany

**laub·mann·ite** \'laùbmə,nīt\ *n* -S [Heinrich *Laubmann*, 20th cent. Ger. mineralogist + E *-ite*] **:** a mineral $Fe_3Fe_6(PO_4)_4(OH)_{12}$ consisting of a basic phosphate of ferrous and ferric iron

**lauch** \'läk\ *Scot var of* LAUGH

**¹laud** \'lȯd\ *n* -S [ME *laudes* (pl.), fr. MF or ML; MF *laudes* (pl.), fr. ML *laudes* (pl.), fr L, pl. of *laud-, laus* praise; akin to OE *lēoth* song, OHG *liod* song, ON *ljōth* stanza, Goth *liuthon* to sing praises] **1 lauds** *pl but sing or pl in constr, often cap* **:** a religious service that constitutes the second or with matins the first of the canonical hours and that is usu. sung at dawn in monastic houses **2** [ME *laude* (influenced in meaning by L *laud-, laus* praise), fr. *laudes* (pl.)] **:** public acclaim **:** PRAISE ⟨his chief employment being the ~ of his dead love —W.H.Dixon⟩ — now used chiefly in hymns ⟨all glory, ~ and honor to Thee —J.M.Neale⟩ **3 :** a hymn of praise

**²laud** \"\ *vt* -ED/-ING/-S [L *laudare*, fr. *laud-, laus* praise] **:** to sing the praises of **:** ACCLAIM, EXTOL ⟨we ~ and magnify Thy glorious name —*Bk. of Com. Prayer*⟩ ⟨editors and publishers are to be ~ed for their accomplishment —J.A.Mourant⟩

**³la·ud** \lä'üd\ *n* -S [Sp *laúd*, fr. OSp *alaút*, fr. Ar *al-'ūd* the wood, fr. *al* the + *'ūd* wood] **1 :** LUTE **2 :** CITTERN

**laud·abil·i·ty** \,lȯdə'bilad·ē, -lətē, -i\ *n* [LL *laudabilitat-, laudabilitas*, fr. L *laudabilis* laudable + *-itat-, -itas* -ity] **:** the quality or state of being worthy of praise **:** PRAISEWORTHINESS

**laud·able** \'lȯdəbəl\ *adj* [ME, fr. L *laudabilis*, fr. *laudare* to laud, praise + *-abilis* -able] **1 :** worthy of praise **:** COMMENDABLE ⟨showed ~ courtesy in the face of provocation⟩ ⟨originality, a ~ characteristic in any textbook —L.L.Snyder⟩ **2** *archaic* **:** of a normal or salutary nature **:** HEALTHY — **laud·ably** \-blē,-bli\ *adv*

**laud·able·ness** *n* -ES **:** LAUDABILITY

**laudable pus** *n* **:** pus discharged freely (as from a wound) and formerly supposed to facilitate the elimination of unhealthy humors from the injured body

**lau·dan·i·dine** \lȯ'danə,dēn, -anədən\ *n* -S [ISV *laudan*ine + *-idine*] **:** a crystalline levorotatory alkaloid $C_{20}H_{25}NO_4$ obtained from opium or by resolution of laudanine into its optically active forms; *levo*-laudanine

**lau·da·nine** \'lȯdᵊn,ēn, -ᵊnən\ *n* -S [ISV *laudanum* + *-ine*; orig. formed as G *laudanin*] **:** a poisonous crystalline optically inactive alkaloid $C_{20}H_{25}NO_4$ obtained from opium

**lau·dan·o·sine** \lȯ'danə,sēn, -sən\ *n* -S [G *laudanosin*, irreg. fr. *laudanin* laudanine] **:** a poisonous crystalline alkaloid $C_{21}H_{27}NO_4$ obtained from opium; the methyl ether of dextrorotatory laudanine

**lau·da·num** \'lȯdᵊnəm\ *n* -S [NL] **1** *obs* **:** any of various opium preparations esp. compounded from alchemists **2 :** a tincture of opium

**lau·da·tion** \lȯ'dāshən\ *n* -S [ME *laudacion*, fr. L *laudation-, laudatio*, fr. *laudatus* (past part. of *laudare* to laud, praise) + *-ion-, -io* -ion] **:** an act or instance of praising **:** EULOGY

**laud·a·tive** \'lȯdəd·iv\ *adj* [L *laudativus*, fr. *laudatus* + *-ivus* -ive] **:** LAUDATORY

**lau·da·tor** \'lȯ,dād·ər, ='==, laù'dä,tȯ(ə)r\ *n* -S [L, fr. *laudatus* + *-or*] **:** one that lauds or eulogizes

**lau·da·to·ri·ly** \¦lȯdə¦tȯrəlē, -tȯr-, -li\ *adv* **:** in a laudatory manner

**lau·da·to·ry** \'lȯdə,tȯrē, -tȯr-, -ri\ *adj* [LL *laudatorius*, fr. L *laudatus* + *-orius* -ory] **:** of, relating to, or containing praise **:** COMMENDATORY, EULOGISTIC

**¹laud·ian** *also* **laud·ean** \'lȯdēən\ *adj, usu cap* [William *Laud* †1645 Eng. prelate, archbishop of Canterbury + E *-ian* or *-ean*] **:** of, relating to, characteristic of, or supporting Archbishop Laud in his repudiation of Roman Catholicism, affirmation of the continuity of the Church of England with the primitive church, and support of the divine right of kings and bishops

**²laud·ian** \"\ *n* -S *usu cap* **:** a supporter of Archbishop Laud or his doctrines

**laud·ian·ism** \-,nizəm\ *n* -S *usu cap* **:** the principles and practices established by Archbishop Laud and his supporters

**laud·num bunches** \'lȯdnəm-\ *n pl but usu sing in constr, usu cap L&B* [origin unknown] **1 :** a morris dance with corner figures, leaps, and capers **2 :** the music for Laudnum Bunches

**lauds** *pl of* LAUD, *pres 3d sing of* LAUD

**laue·gram** \'laùə,gram\ *n, usu cap* [Max von *Laue* b1879 Ger. physicist + E *-gram*] **:** LAUE PATTERN

**laue pattern** \'laùə-\ *or* **laue photograph** *n, usu cap L* **:** a photographic record of the diffraction pattern formed when a beam of X rays passes through a thin crystal plate

**laue spot** *n, usu cap L* **:** a spot corresponding to maximum X ray intensity in the Laue pattern of a crystal

**¹laugh** \'laf, -aa(ə)-, -ai-, -á-, -ä-\ *vb* -ED/-ING/-S [ME *laughen*, fr. OE *hliehhan, hlehhan, hlæhan*; akin to OHG *lachēn* to laugh, ON *hlæja*, Goth *hlahjan* to laugh, OE *hlōwan* to moo — more at LOW] *vi* **1 a :** to give audible expression to an emotion (as mirth, joy, derision, embarrassment, or fright) by the expulsion of air from the lungs resulting in sounds ranging from an explosive guffaw to a muffled titter and usu. accompanied by movements of the mouth or facial muscles and a lighting up of the eyes ⟨~*ing* loudly at a funny clown⟩ ⟨others . . . read for the sake of sarcastically ~*ing* —Aldous Huxley⟩ **b :** to find amusement or pleasure in something **:** enjoy oneself ⟨~ at the memory of an embarrassing encounter⟩ **c :** to become amused or derisive ⟨her eyes ~*ed*⟩ ⟨he was ~*ing* I knew though his face was . . . grave —George Meredith⟩ — often used with *at* ⟨a very skeptical public ~*ed* at our early efforts —Graenum Berger⟩ **2 a :** to produce the sound or appearance of laughter ⟨~*ing* voice⟩ ⟨~*ing* brook⟩ ⟨a cypress tree that ~*ed* with all its leaves —Ruth Tomalin⟩ **b :** to be of a kind that inspires joy ⟨the blue sky of Autumn ~*s* above —Amy Lowell⟩ ~ *vt* **1 :** to bring to a specified state by laughing ⟨eat and drink . . . and ~ themselves fat —John Trapp⟩ ⟨this book ~*s* the littlest child into . . . manners —*N. Y. Herald Tribune*⟩ ⟨~*ed* aside academic rules —C.V. Woodward⟩ ⟨~ him to scorn⟩ ⟨~*ed* away the popular taste for bombast —Van Wyck Brooks⟩ ⟨a less able speaker would have been ~*ed* off the stage —J.D.Hicks⟩ **2 :** to utter laughingly ⟨~*s* her consent⟩ — **laugh in one's sleeve** *or* **laugh up one's sleeve** *also* **laugh in one's beard :** to become inwardly elated **:** congratulate oneself secretly (as on having successfully played a trick on someone) — **laugh on the wrong side of one's mouth :** CRY — **laugh out of court :** to eliminate from serious consideration by ridicule ⟨their flimsy arguments are *laughed out of court* —V.L.Parrington⟩ ⟨they went far towards *laughing* him *out of court* —J.F.Dobie⟩

**²laugh** \"\ *n* -S **1 a :** an act or instance of laughing ⟨the appealing look passed into a smile and the smile into a ~ —Thomas Hughes⟩ ⟨the ~, however wry, goes deeper and hurts more than the snarl —Dudley Fitts⟩ ⟨the longest pause . . . followed by the longest ~ ever heard on radio —Goodman Ace⟩ **b** *archaic* **:** a disposition to laughter **:** HILARITY ⟨full of ~, and must give it some vent —John Crowne⟩ **c :** something that resembles a laugh ⟨rejoiced to see the first ~ of the fire —Leigh Hunt⟩ ⟨heard the ~ of a loon⟩ **2 a :** a cause for derision or merriment **:** JOKE, ADVANTAGE ⟨the ~ of the twenties was my confident insistence that I would defeat Jack Dempsey —Gene Tunney⟩ ⟨a book with a ~ on page one —Bennett Cerf⟩ ⟨had the ~ on him then —David Fairchild⟩ ⟨rack their poor brains to get the ~ of us —George Meredith⟩ **b :** an expression of scorn or mockery **:** JEER ⟨he failed to make good and they gave him the ~⟩ ⟨even in the most straitlaced societies the ~ was against the husband —Edith Wharton⟩ **3 laughs** *pl* **:** a means of entertainment **:** DIVERSION, SPORT ⟨girl mobsters beating up other girls simply for ~*s* —*Newsweek*⟩ ⟨when others might ridicule or overplay it for ~*s*, he can write breezily of a zealous nun —John Farrelly⟩

**laugh·able** \-fəbəl\ *adj* **:** giving rise to mirth or derision **:** COMICAL, ABSURD ⟨antique finery, which would have been ~ on another woman —W.H.Hudson †1922⟩

**syn** RISIBLE, FUNNY, DROLL, COMICAL, COMIC, FARCICAL, RIDICULOUS, LUDICROUS: LAUGHABLE is a general term describing that which intentionally or unintentionally occasions laughter either benign or derisive ⟨considered it a *laughable* affair, and was continually bobbing his head out the galley door to make jocose remarks —Jack London⟩ ⟨the lower classes aped the rigid decorum of their "betters" with *laughable* results —Harrison Smith⟩ RISIBLE is a close synonym for LAUGHABLE, also lacking special connotation ⟨has some *risible* material that she delivers well —*New Yorker*⟩ FUNNY describes that which occasions laughter esp. through obvious peculiarity or absurdity ⟨where a *funny* little happy-go-lucky, native-managed railway runs to Jodhpore —Rudyard Kipling⟩ ⟨children thought he was a very *funny* old Chinaman, as children always think anything old and strange is *funny* —John Steinbeck⟩ DROLL indicates laughable qualities arising from either odd quaintness or arch waggishness ⟨a serious child with a *droll* adult expression⟩ ⟨are apt to take on a *droll* sly humor, especially those "tall tales" of exaggeration —*Amer. Guide Series: N. C.*⟩ COMICAL describes that which elicits spontaneous hilarity ⟨the abrupt transition of her features from assured pride to ludicrous astonishment and alarm was *comical* enough to have sent into wild uncharitable laughter any creature less humane —Arnold Bennett⟩ ⟨gave his figure a *comical* air of having been loosely and inaccurately strung together from a selection of stuffed bags of cloth —Leslie Charteris⟩ COMIC is sometimes a close synonym of COMICAL but may differ from it in applying to that which calls for a degree of reflection and occasions more thoughtful mirth ⟨people laugh at absurdities that are very far from being *comic* —Joseph Conrad⟩ FARCICAL applies to that which is so extravagant or extreme as to provoke laughter or derision ⟨the cases described in the preceding pages are mainly *farcical* in their extravagance —Aldous Huxley⟩ ⟨almost *farcical* to suppose that Henry, as a Norman prince, could not talk his own language to his Norman bride —William Empson⟩ RIDICULOUS describes that which is derided as vain or inappropriate ⟨to be always harping on nationality is to convert what should be a recognition of natural conditions into a *ridiculous* pride in one's own oddities —George Santayana⟩ ⟨formed a humorous compound consisting of 168 letters, a thing that would be *ridiculous* rather than funny in English —E.S.McCartney⟩ LUDICROUS indicates that which is so absurd or preposterous that it excites both laughter and scorn ⟨enacted a scene as *ludicrous* as it was pitiable —Charles Kingsley⟩ ⟨had friendships, one after another, so violent as to be often *ludicrous* —Hilaire Belloc⟩

**laugh·able·ness** *n* -ES **:** the quality or state of being laughable

**laugh·ably** \-fəblē, -li\ *adv* **:** in a laughable manner ⟨the plane itself looks almost ~ archaic —*Irish Digest*⟩

**laugh·er** \-fə(r)\ *n* -S [ME, fr. *laughen* to laugh + *-er*] **:** one that laughs

**¹laughing** *n* -S [ME, gerund of *laughen* to laugh] **:** the act or process of emitting a laugh ⟨a sound of ~ came from down the corridor⟩ ⟨~ exercises the diaphragm as well as the risorius⟩

**²laughing** *adj* [in sense 1, fr. gerund of ¹*laugh*; in sense 2, fr. pres. part. of ¹*laugh*] **1 :** LAUGHABLE ⟨this is no ~ matter⟩ **2 :** expressing or seeming to express mirth or good humor **:** MERRY, JOCULAR ⟨~ girl⟩ ⟨~ mood⟩ ⟨looking for an ouzel's nest along . . . a ~ stream —D.C.Peattie⟩ — **laugh·ing·ly** *adv*

**laughing bird** *n* [*laughing* fr. pres. part. of ¹*laugh*] *dial Eng* **:** GREEN WOODPECKER

**laughing falcon** *n* **:** a So. American falcon (*Herpetotheres cachinnans*)

**laughing frog** *n* **:** an edible European frog (*Rana ridibunda*)

**laughing gas** *n* [*laughing* fr. gerund of ¹*laugh*] **:** NITROUS OXIDE

**laughing goose** *n* [*laughing* fr. pres. part. of ¹*laugh*] **:** WHITE-FRONTED GOOSE

**laughing gull** *n* **1 :** a black-headed gull (*Larus ridibundus*) **2 :** an American gull (*Larus atricilla*)
**laughing hyena** *n* **:** SPOTTED HYENA
**laughing jackass** *n* **1 :** KOOKABURRA **2 :** LAUGHING OWL **3 :** an orchid (*Arethusa bulbosa*)
**laughing muscle** *n* [*laughing* fr. gerund of [1]*laugh*] **:** RISORIUS
**laughing owl** *n* [*laughing* fr. pres. part. of [1]*laugh*] **:** a reddish-brown owl (*Sceloglaux albifacies*) of New Zealand that is almost extinct
**laughingstock** \'⸗⸗,⸗\ *n* [*laughing* (fr. gerund of [1]*laugh*) + *stock*] **:** an object of ridicule **:** BUTT ⟨his ineptitude with a power mower made him the ~ of the neighborhood⟩
**laughing thrush** *n* [*laughing* fr. pres. part. of [1]*laugh*] **:** any of several Asiatic singing birds; *esp* **:** a bird of the genus *Garrulax* often kept as a cage bird
**laugh off** *vt* **:** to treat with ridicule or contempt **:** ignore or dismiss as absurd ⟨officials *laugh off* these reports as nonsense —L.E.Davies⟩ ⟨you can't *laugh off* a royal commission —Alan Villiers⟩
**laughs** *pres 3d sing of* LAUGH, *pl of* LAUGH
**laugh·some** \'⸗səm\ *adj, archaic* **:** provocative of or addicted to laughter **:** MERRY
[1]**laugh·ter** \'laftə(r), -aaf-,-aif-,-áf-,-äf-\ *n* -s [ME, fr. OE *hleahtor;* akin to OHG *lahtar* laughter, ON *hlātr;* derivative fr. the root of OE *hliehhan* to laugh — more at LAUGH] **1 a :** a sound of or as if of laughing ⟨~ rippled through the room⟩ ⟨after the scream came hideous ~⟩ ⟨the glowing gully rang with a kookaburra's ~ —Rex Ingamells⟩ ⟨there is ~ in its waters —Robert Gibbings⟩ **b :** an inclination to laugh **:** EXUBERANCE, AMUSEMENT ⟨the ~ in him has turned the scale —Walter Lippmann⟩ ⟨the capacity for civilized enjoyment, for leisure and ~ —Bertrand Russell⟩ **2 :** [2]LAUGH 1a ⟨the three ~s broke forth together —Dorothy M. Richardson⟩ **3** *archaic* **:** a cause of merriment ⟨would be argument for a week, ~ for a month —Shak.⟩
[2]**laugh·ter** \'laftə(r), 'lätə-, 'lōtə-\ *n* -s [of Scand origin; akin to ON *lātr* place where animals lay their young; akin to ON *leggja* to lay — more at LAY] *dial Brit* **:** a clutch of eggs
**laugh·ter·less** \'laftə(r)ləs, -aaf-,-aif-,-áf-,-äf-\ *adj* **:** of a grim or mirthless nature **:** SERIOUS
**lau·ha·la** \lau̇'hälə, *attrib* (')⸗;⸗⸗\ *n* -s [Hawaiian, fr. *lau* leaf + *hala* pandanus] **1 :** TEXTILE SCREW PINE **2 a :** dried pandanus leaves used as a material for weaving ⟨a handbag of ~⟩ **b :** a Polynesian mat woven of dried pandanus leaves
**lau·ia** \lau̇'ēə\ *n* -s [Hawaiian] *Hawaii* **:** PARROT FISH
**lau·lau** \'lau̇,lau̇\ *n* -s [Hawaiian] *Hawaii* **:** meat and fish (as pork and salmon) wrapped in leaves (as taro or ti) and baked or steamed
**lau·mont·ite** *also* **lau·mon·ite** *or* **lo·mon·ite** \lō'män(t),īt\ *n* -s [*laumontite, laumonite* alter. of *lomonite*, irreg. fr. F. P. N. G. de *Laumont* †1834 Fr. mineralogist + E *-ite*] **:** a white monoclinic mineral $CaAl_2Si_4O_{12}.4H_2O$ consisting of a hydrous calcium and aluminum silicate and having a vitreous luster that upon exposure to the air loses water, becomes opaque, and crumbles
**launce** *also* **lance** \'lȯn(t)s, -ä-, -a-, -aa(ə)-, -ai-, -á-\ *n* -s [prob. fr. [1]*lance*] **:** SAND LAUNCE
[1]**launch** \'lȯnch, -ä-, -á-, *dial* -a-, -aa(ə)-, -ai-\ *vb* -ED/-ING/-ES [ME *launchen*, fr. ONF *lancher*, fr. LL *lanceare* to handle a lance, pierce with a lance — more at LANCE] *vt* **1 a :** to dart or throw forward ⟨~*ed* a looping right to the jaw⟩ ⟨suddenly ~*ed* himself from between his guards . . . and vanished into the rocks and heather, still handcuffed —Philip Rooney⟩ **b :** to throw or propel with force **:** FLING, SHOOT ⟨finding another stone, I raised and was about to ~ it —W.H.Hudson †1922⟩ ⟨~ an arrow at a target⟩; *specif* **:** to release or catapult (a self-propelling object) from a ramp, rack, or other device ⟨~ a torpedo⟩ ⟨~ a carrier plane⟩ ⟨~ a rocket⟩ ⟨~ a satellite⟩ **c :** COMMENCE ⟨~ a hostile action⟩ **:** commit (as troops) to battle ⟨~*ed* his cavalry against them —Tom Wintringham⟩ **d :** to direct (as abuse or criticism) against ⟨~*ed* a determined attack on academic criticism —C.I.Glicksberg⟩ ⟨~*ed* a fresh anathema against him —R.W.Southern⟩ ⟨~*ed* a . . . protest against the political power of the well-to-do —J.D.Hicks⟩ **2** *obs* **:** LANCE 1, 2 **3 a :** to put or cause to slide into the water **:** set afloat ⟨~ a canoe⟩ ⟨~ a battleship⟩ ⟨~ a lifeboat⟩ **b** (1) **:** to give (a person) a start ⟨~ a daughter in society⟩ ⟨~ a son in business⟩ ⟨~*ed* their peoples on the path of war and conquest —Sir Winston Churchill⟩ (2) **:** EMBARK ⟨she ~*ed* herself on her nursing career⟩ ⟨his massive task begins and he ~*es* himself upon it —Ira Wolfert⟩ ⟨he was now well ~*ed* on a speech of his own —Waldo Frank⟩ ⟨pipeline companies now are ~*ed* on a . . . construction and expansion program —*Trends*⟩ **c** (1) **:** to originate or set in motion **:** put into operation **:** INITIATE, INTRODUCE ⟨~ an enterprise⟩ ⟨~ a program⟩ ⟨~ a fund drive⟩ ⟨~ a new product⟩ (2) **:** to get off to a good start **:** gain public acceptance for ⟨a literary dinner to ~ the book —*Newsweek*⟩ **d :** to cast forth or send out ⟨~*ed* himself upon the intellectual currents of the age —H.O.Taylor⟩ ⟨~ a first-class minstrel company on the road —C.F. Wittke⟩ ⟨a young pair ~*ed* their first invitations in the third person —Edith Wharton⟩ **4** *obs* **:** to hoist (as a yard) or push out (as capstan bars) — used of equipment on sailing ships ~ *vi* **1 a :** to spring forward **:** take off ⟨a junco had ~*ed* off a chinquapin twig —W.V.T.Clark⟩ ⟨the catapult snagged and the plane overturned before it could ~⟩ **b** (1) **:** to throw oneself energetically **:** PLUNGE ⟨~ into a brilliant harangue⟩ ⟨~*ed* into a vigorously rhythmic, sharply accentuated playing of the . . . prelude —Irving Kolodin⟩ (2) **:** to speak out critically **:** LASH ⟨listened . . . politely for ten minutes and then ~*ed* out —H.J.Laski⟩ **2 a** *archaic* **:** to slide down the ways **:** become launched ⟨the *Resolution* now in the dock ~*es* on Tuesday —*London Gazette*⟩ **b :** to set out **:** GO ⟨one of the party . . . had ~*ed* off by himself —*Appalachia*⟩ **c :** to make a start **:** COMMENCE ⟨had ~*ed* on his hour of study —Hallam Tennyson⟩ ⟨~ upon the production of films —Jean Begeman⟩; *specif* **:** to go into business
[2]**launch** \"\ *n* -ES [ME *launche*, fr. *launchen*, v.] **:** LAUNCHING ⟨may hold up a ~ for days —H.H.Martin⟩ ⟨after ~ it could shift targets —Clay Blair⟩
[3]**launch** \"\ *n* -ES [Sp or Pg; Sp *lancha*, fr. Pg, fr. Malay *lancharan*, fr. *lanchar* effortless speed] **1** *archaic* **:** a large often sloop-rigged ship's boat of relatively shallow draft designed to carry men and stores and often fitted with a light gun in the bow **2 :** a small open or half-decked motorboat used commercially or as a pleasure craft in harbors and coastal waters
**launch·able** \-chəbəl\ *adj* **:** capable of being launched
**launch·er** \-chə(r)\ *n* -s **:** one that launches: as **a :** a device for firing a grenade from a rifle **b :** a device for launching a rocket or rocket shell; *specif* **:** ROCKET LAUNCHER **c :** CATAPULT
**launching** *n* -s **1 a :** an act or instance of initiating (as a program or enterprise) ⟨a major project . . . is the ~ of a series of books of poetry —F.W.Boardman⟩ ⟨the ~ of . . . Nashville's third television station —*Retailing Daily*⟩ **b :** an act or instance of public introduction **:** PRESENTATION ⟨a coming-out ball and other social ~s —*Irish Digest*⟩ ⟨ideas emerge not only from Paris ~s but also New York designers' concepts —*Women's Wear Daily*⟩ **2 a :** the act or process of placing a boat in the water **b :** WAY 13a **c :** a ceremony accompanying the launching of a ship **3 :** the act or process of releasing a self-propelled object from a ramp, rack, or other device ⟨the pads may get more of a workout for satellite ~s —*Newsweek*⟩
**launching pad** *n* **:** a nonflammable platform from which a rocket or guided missile can be launched
**launching ways** \'⸗⸗,⸗\ *or* **launchways** \'⸗,⸗\ *n pl but sing or pl in constr* **:** WAY 13a
**launch·man** \-chmən\ *n, pl* **launchmen :** an operator of a motor launch
**laund** \'lȯnd\ *n* -s [ME *launde*, fr. MF *lande* heath, of Celt origin; akin to OIr *land* open space — more at LAND] *archaic* **:** an open usu. grassy area among trees **:** GLADE ⟨through this ~ anon the deer will come —Shak.⟩
[1]**laun·der** \'lȯndə(r), 'län-, 'lan-, *dial* 'lan- *or* 'laan-\ *n* -s [ME *lander, launder* launderer, laundress, alter. of *lavender*, fr. MF *lavandier* (masc.) male launderer, *lavandiere* (fem.) laundress, fr. ML *lavandarius* (masc.) male launderer, *lavandaria* (fem.) laundress, fr. L *lavandus* that needs to be washed (gerundive of *lavare* to wash) + *-arius, -aria* -ary — more at LYE] **:** a conduit or trough for water and other liquids: as **a :** a box conduit conveying middlings or tailings suspended in water in ore dressing **b :** a refractory trough conveying molten metal **c :** a usu. movable wooden trough into which water is run or pumped while engineering construction work is carried on
[2]**launder** \"\ *vb* **laundered; laundered; laundering** \-d(ə)riŋ\ **launders** [obs. *launder* launderer, laundress, fr. ME *lander, launder*] *vt* **1 a :** to wash (as clothes) in water ⟨nylon shorts are easy to ~⟩ ⟨his only towel and he had ~*ed* it himself —Katharine N. Burt⟩ **b :** to wash and iron ⟨put on a freshly ~*ed* shirt⟩ **2 a :** to remove dirt or impurities from **:** CLEANSE ⟨the cat ~*s* her kittens with her tongue⟩ ⟨a dust-collecting device for ~*ing* air⟩ ⟨~ greasy tools with supersonic sound waves⟩ **b :** to free from flaws or objectionable matter **:** PURIFY, CENSOR ⟨succeeded pretty well in ~*ing* the grammar —H.R. Warfel⟩ ~ *vi* **1 a :** to wash or wash and iron clothing or household linens ⟨cooks, cleans, ~*s*, and does other household chores⟩ **b :** to withstand washing and ironing ⟨this fabric ~*s* well⟩ **2 :** SLUICE ⟨water . . . which his colleague has ~*ed* out of his ears —Maurice Collis⟩
**laun·der·abil·i·ty** \-d(ə)rə'bilәd·ē\ *n* **:** the quality or state of being washable ⟨~ is a major factor in choosing a summer dress⟩
**laun·der·able** \'⸗d(ə)rəbəl\ *adj* **:** capable of being washed
**laun·der·er** \-dərə(r)\ *n* -s [ME, fr. *lander, launder* launderer, laundress + *-er*] **:** one that launders
**laun·der·ette** \,⸗də;ret\ *n* -s [fr. *Launderette*, a service mark] **:** a commercial establishment in which automatic washing machines are installed for the use of individual customers
**laundering** *n* -s **:** the act or process of washing or cleansing ⟨cotton dresses, faded from many ~*s* —Hamilton Basso⟩ ⟨the coal undergoes another ~ as it passes over screens for final sizing —*Amer. Guide Series: Pa.*⟩
**launder man** *n* [[1]*launder*] **:** a worker who cleans and repairs launders
**Laun·der-Om·e·ter** \,⸗⸗'rämәd·ә(r)\ *trademark* — used for a machine with rotating containers for testing the colorfastness of dyed cloth to washing solutions or the efficiency of washing solutions in cleansing soiled cloth
**laun·dress** \'⸗drəs\ *n* -ES [obs. E *launder* launderer, laundress (fr. ME *lander, launder*) + E *-ess*] **:** a woman who does household laundry
**Laun·dro·mat** \'⸗drə,mat\ *trademark* — used for an electric washing machine
**laun·dry** \'lȯndrē, 'län-,'lan-, *dial* 'lan-,'laan-\ *n* -ES *often attrib* [obs. E *launder* launderer, laundress + E *-y*] **1 a** *obs* **:** LAUNDERING **b :** a collection of clothes or household linens to be laundered ⟨a truck picks up the ~ once a week⟩ **2 a :** a room or area set aside for doing the family wash **b :** a commercial establishment where laundering is done
**laundry·man** \-mən, -,man\ *n, pl* **laundrymen 1 :** one who works at laundering (as in a commercial laundry, home, factory, camp, or institution) **2 :** an institutional or industrial worker who prepares soiled articles for delivery to the laundry and checks and takes care of them upon their return **3 :** the driver of a laundry truck
**laundry soap** *n* **:** soap (as rosin soap) for the laundry
**laundry tray** *or* **laundry tub** *n* **:** a fixed tub (as of slate, earthenware, soapstone, enameled iron, or porcelain) with running water and drainpipe for washing clothes and other household linens — called also *set tub*

laundry tray

**laundrywoman** \'⸗⸗,⸗⸗\ *n, pl* **laundrywomen :** LAUNDRESS
**lau·ned·das** \lau̇'nedәs\ *n pl but sing in constr* [Sardinian] **:** a Sardinian triple clarinet
**laur-** *or* **lauro-** *comb form* [ISV, fr. NL *Laurus* — more at LAURUS] **1 :** laurel ⟨*lauric* acid⟩ **2 :** lauric acid ⟨*lauramide*⟩ ⟨*lauromitrile*⟩
**lau·ra** \'lävrə\ *n* -s [LGk, fr. Gk, lane, alley; akin to OIr *lie* stone, Gk *laas* stone, Alb *lerë* rock, rockfall] **:** a monastery of the Eastern Church orig. consisting of a number of monks living a communal life yet inhabiting separate cells grouped around a church
**lau·ra·ce·ae** \lȯ'rāsē,ē\ *n pl, cap* [NL, fr. *Laurus*, type genus + *-aceae*] **:** a family of shrubs and trees (order Ranales) having flowering with definite stamens in several series of three, more or less united sepals, no petals, and a single pistil — **lau·ra·ceous** \(')lȯ'rāshəs\ *adj*
**laur·aldehyde** \(')lȯr, (')lär+\ *n* **:** a fragrant crystalline compound $C_{11}H_{23}CHO$ found in some essential oils (as from needles of the silver fir of Europe) and used in perfumes
**lau·rate** \'lȯ,rāt, 'lä,-\ *n* -s [ISV *laur-* + *-ate*] **:** a salt or ester of lauric acid
[1]**lau·re·ate** \'lȯrēət,'lär-, *usu* -ēd·+V\ *adj* [ME *laureat*, fr. L *laureatus* crowned with laurel, fr. *laurea* laurel wreath (fr. fem. of *laureus* of laurel, fr. *laurus* laurel + *-eus* -eous) + *-atus* -ate — more at LAUREL] **1 a :** of an excellence esp. in poetry worthy of the laurel wreath **b :** of or relating to a prizewinner ⟨at the ~ concert Sunday night —*N. Y. Times*⟩ ⟨~ pension⟩ ⟨Nobel ~ geneticist —*Newsweek*⟩ **2** *archaic* **:** of, relating to, or resembling laurel ⟨to grace by youthful brow the ~ wreath . . . she brings —Thomas Gray⟩ **3 :** crowned or decked with laurel ⟨~ head of Caesar⟩ ⟨strew the ~ hearse —John Milton⟩
[2]**laureate** \"\ *n* -s **1 :** a recipient of an honor or award for preeminence in his field ⟨Nobel ~ in physics⟩; *specif* **:** POET LAUREATE ⟨~ John Masefield's special ode —*College English*⟩ **2 :** one that praises **:** EULOGIST ⟨the ~ of a dying society —Martin Turnell⟩ ⟨dry and amusing ~ of Cape Cod —Carl Van Doren⟩
[3]**lau·re·ate** \-ē,āt, *usu* -ād·+V\ *vt* -ED/-ING/-S **1 :** to crown with or as if with a laurel wreath as a mark of honor or achievement; *specif* **:** to confer a European university degree upon ⟨privileges which made the member of one university a citizen of all others . . . whether he was *laureated* in Paris or Bologna —J.H.Burton⟩ **2 :** to appoint to the office of poet laureate
**laureated** *adj* **:** LAUREATE 3
**lau·re·ate·ship** \-rēət,ship\ *n* **:** the office of poet laureate
**lau·re·a·tion** \,lȯrē'āshən, ,lär-\ *n* -s [[3]*laureate* + *-ion*] **1 :** an act of crowning with or as if with laurel as a mark of honor or achievement **2** *archaic* **:** the conferring of an academic degree ⟨the right of ~ conceded to the University of Vienna by Maximilian I —William Hamilton †1856⟩
[1]**lau·rel** \'lȯrəl, 'lär-\ *n* -s [ME *lorel, lorer, laurer*, fr. OF *lorier*, fr. *lor* laurel, fr. L *laurus* — more at DAPHNE] **1 a :** a tree or shrub of the genus *Laurus; specif* **:** a tree (*Laurus nobilis*) bearing foliage used by the ancient Greeks to crown victors in the Pythian games — called also *bay, bay laurel, bay tree* **b :** the leaves of the laurel that yield a fragrant oil — compare BAY LEAF **2 a :** a branch or wreath of laurel awarded as a token of victory or preeminence **b** (1) **:** a recognition of superior achievement **:** mark of public esteem **:** HONOR ⟨added one more ~ to his growing collection today when he was voted the . . . most valuable player —*Springfield (Mass.) Union*⟩ — usu. used in pl. ⟨his technique . . . sufficed to win him such ~*s* as few architects have enjoyed —C.H.Whitaker⟩ (2) **laurels** *pl but sing or pl in constr* **:** CHAMPIONSHIP, REPUTATION ⟨won the regional ~*s* and went on to the finals⟩ ⟨after winning the title he decided to rest on his ~*s* and retire from the ring⟩ ⟨enthusiastic critical acclaim for the newcomer is forcing older actors to look to their ~*s*⟩ **3 a :** a British gold coin bearing a laureate head of a monarch **:** UNITE **b :** a unit of value corresponding to one of these coins ⟨a half-*laurel*⟩ **4 :** a tree or shrub that resembles the laurel: as **a :** CHERRY LAUREL **b :** SPURGE LAUREL **c :** any of several plants of the heath family: as (1) **:** MOUNTAIN LAUREL (2) **:** BIG LAUREL **d :** MADRONA **e :** CALIFORNIA LAUREL **f :** any of several tropical American trees of the genera *Cordia, Sebesten*, and *Magnolia* **g :** OLEANDER **h :** any of several New Zealand and Australian evergreen trees of the genera *Cryptocarya, Pittosporum, Corynocarpus*, and *Likea* **5 :** a variable color averaging a dark grayish green that is bluer than average ivy, bluer and duller than Persian green, and yellower and paler than hemlock green — compare LAUREL GREEN

European laurel

[2]**laurel** \"\ *vt* **laureled** *or* **laurelled; laureled** *or* **laurelled; laureling** *or* **laurelling; laurels :** to deck or crown with or as if with laurel
**laurel bay** *n* [ME *lorel baye*, fr. *lorel* laurel + *baye* bay] **1** *obs* **:** the laurel berry **2 :** LAUREL 1a **3 :** EVERGREEN MAGNOLIA
**laurel camphor** *n* **:** dextrorotatory camphor
**laurel cherry** *n* **:** CHERRY LAUREL 2
**laureled** *or* **laurelled** *adj* **1 :** crowned or decked with laurel **:** LAUREATE **2 :** recognized publicly for excellence or achievement **:** PRAISED, HONORED
**laurel family** *n* **:** LAURACEAE
**laurel green** *n* **1 :** a variable color averaging a moderate green that is yellower and duller than sea green (sense 1a) and bluer and less strong than myrtle (sense 3a) **2 :** a light olive
**laurel-leaved willow** \'⸗⸗,⸗⸗-\ *n* **:** BAY WILLOW 1
**laurel magnolia** *n* **:** EVERGREEN MAGNOLIA
**laurel oak** *n* **1 :** either of two American oaks with glossy leaves resembling those of the European laurel: **a :** a large oak (*Quercus laurifolia*) of the southeastern U.S. with a rather smooth dark brown bark, nearly evergreen leaves, and a small acorn with a shallow cup — called also *pin oak* **b :** SHINGLE OAK 1 **2 :** a moderate reddish brown that is yellower than roan and yellower and slightly lighter and stronger than mahogany — called also *acajou*
**laurel pink** *n* **:** a deep pink to moderate red that is bluer and less strong than rose dorée or watermelon
**laurel sumac** *n* **:** an aromatic Californian shrub (*Rhus laurina*) having paniculate flowers and whitish fruit
**laurel-tree** \'⸗⸗,⸗\ *n* [ME *lorel tre* laurel, fr. *lorel* laurel + *tre, tree* tree] **:** RED BAY
**laurelwood** \'⸗⸗,⸗\ *n* **:** DAGAME
**lau·ren·cia** \lȯ'ren(t)sēə, -nchə\ *n, cap* [NL, fr. M. de la *Laurencie*, 19th cent. Fr. naturalist + NL *-ia*] **:** a genus of mostly flattened leathery red algae (family Rhodomelaceae) — see PEPPER DULSE
**lau·ren·tian** \lȯ'rench(ē)ən\ *adj, usu cap* [L *Laurentius* Lawrence (in sense 1 representing the St. Lawrence river, southern Quebec and southeast Ontario, Canada, and in sense 2 representing D. H. Lawrence †1930 Eng. novelist) + E *-an*] **1 a :** of, relating to, or near the St. Lawrence river ⟨*Laurentian* hills⟩ **b :** of or relating to mountain-making movements of the Archeozoic era — see GEOLOGIC TIME table **2 :** of or relating to D. H. Lawrence
**lau·ren·tide** \'lȯrən,tīd, 'lär-\ *adj, usu cap* [irreg. fr. L *Laurentius* Lawrence (representing the St. Lawrence river)] **:** of or relating to the region of the St. Lawrence river
**laurent's acid** \-änz-\ *n, usu cap L* [after Auguste *Laurent* †1853 Fr. chemist] **:** a crystalline naphthylaminesulfonic acid $H_2NC_{10}H_6SO_3H$ made by sulfonating alpha-naphthylamine and used as an intermediate for azo dyes; 5-amino-1-naphthalenesulfonic acid
**lau·rer's canal** \'lau̇(r)ərz-, 'lau̇rəz-\ *n, usu cap L* [after Johann Friedrich *Laurer* †1873 Ger. pharmacologist] **:** a muscular duct passing from the dorsal surface to join the oviduct between the ovary and vitelline duct in some trematode worms
**lau·ric acid** \'lȯ|rik-, 'lä|\ *n* [*lauric* ISV *laur-* + *-ic*] **:** a crystalline fatty acid $CH_3(CH_2)_{10}COOH$ occurring in the form of its glycerol esters in the berries of the European laurel (*Laurus nobilis*) and esp. in coconut oil and palm-kernel oil and used often as obtained from coconut oil in mixtures with other fatty acids in making chiefly metallic soaps, esters, and lauryl alcohol
**lau·rin** \'lȯrən, 'lär-\ *n* -s [ISV *laur-* + *-in*] **:** a glycerol ester of lauric acid; *esp* **:** TRILAURIN
**lau·ri·nox·y·lon** \,lȯrə'näksə,län, ,lär-\ *n* -s [NL, fr. *laurino-* (fr. L *laurinus* of laurel, fr. *laurus* laurel + *-inus* -ine) + *-xylon*] **:** a fossil dicotyledonous wood resembling that of the existing genus *Laurus*
**lau·ri·on·ite** \'lȯrēə,nīt, 'lärē-, 'lävrē-\ *n* -s [G *laurionit*, fr. *Laurion*, Greece, its locality + G *-it* -ite] **:** a basic lead chloride $Pb(OH)Cl$ found in prismatic crystals at Laurion, Greece
**lau·rite** \'lȯ,rīt, 'lä,-\ *n* -s [G *laurit*, prob. fr. the name *Laura* + G *-it* -ite] **:** a mineral $RuS_2$ consisting of an iron-black ruthenium sulfide often containing osmium and found in minute crystals or grains
**lau·rit·sen electroscope** \'lau̇|rətsən-, 'lȯ|, 'lä|\ *n, usu cap L* [after Charles C. *Lauritsen b*1892 and Thomas *Lauritsen b*1915 Am. physicists born in Denmark, who designed it] **:** an electroscope in which the sensitive element is a quartz fiber used in precise measurements of ionizing radiation
**lauro-** — see LAUR-
**lau·ro·cer·a·sus** \,lȯrō'serəsəs, ,lär-\ *n, cap* [NL, fr. *laur-* + L *cerasus* cherry tree — more at CHERRY] *in some classifications* **:** a genus of trees and shrubs that occur in warm or tropical regions, that include the European cherry laurel and related plants with alternate usu. evergreen leaves and pentamerous white flowers in racemes, and that are now commonly included in the genus *Prunus*
**lau·ro·yl** \'lȯrə,wil, 'lär-\ *or* **lau·ryl** \-rəl\ *n* -s [ISV *laur-* + *-yl*] **:** the radical $CH_3(CH_2)_{10}CO$— of lauric acid
**lau·rus** \'lȯrəs, 'lär-\ *n, cap* [NL, fr. L, laurel — more at DAPHNE] **:** a genus of trees (family Lauraceae) having alternate entire leaves and small tetramerous involucrate flowers succeeded by fruits that are ovoid berries — see [1]LAUREL 1a
**lau·rus·tine** \'lȯrə,stīn, 'lär-, -tēn\ *n* -s [NL *laurustinus*, fr. L *laurus* laurel + *tinus* a plant, prob. fr. the base of *tinus*; akin to OE *thīnan* to become moist, OSlav *tina* mud, OE *thawian* to thaw — more at THAW] **:** a European shrub (*Viburnum tinus*) widely cultivated for its evergreen leaves and white or pink fragrant flowers
**lau·rus·ti·nus** *or* **lau·res·ti·nus** \,⸗⸗'stīnəs, -tēn-\ *n* -ES [NL] **:** LAURUSTINE
**laur·vik·ite** \'lau̇rvi,kīt\ *var of* LARVIKITE
**lau·ryl** \'lȯrəl, 'lär-\ *n* -s [ISV *laur-* + *-yl*] **1 :** normal dodecyl **2 :** a mixture of alkyl radicals derived from commercial lauryl alcohol — compare SODIUM LAURYL SULFATE
**lauryl alcohol** *n* **1 :** a crystalline compound $CH_3(CH_2)_{10}CH_2OH$ made by reduction of ethyl laurate; normal dodecyl alcohol **2 :** a liquid mixture containing lauryl alcohol and other alcohols that is produced commercially by reduction of coconut oil, the fatty acids from coconut oil, or their esters and is used esp. in making anionic detergents
**lau·sanne** \lō'zän, -zan\ *adj, usu cap* [fr. *Lausanne* Switzerland] **:** of or from the city of Lausanne, Switzerland **:** of the kind or style prevalent in Lausanne
**lau·sen·ite** \'lȯsᵊn,īt, 'lau̇zᵊn-\ *n* -s [Carl *Lausen*, 20th cent. Am. mining engineer + E *-ite*] **:** a mineral $Fe_2(SO_4)_3.6H_2O$ consisting of a hydrous ferric sulfate — called also *rogersite*
**lau·ta·rite** \'lau̇də,rīt\ *n* -s [G *lautarit*, fr. Oficina *Lautaro*, Chile, its locality + G *-it* -ite] **:** a mineral $Ca(IO_3)_2$ consisting of calcium iodate and occurring in prismatic crystals
[1]**lau·ter** \'lau̇d·ər\ *adj* [G, clear, pure, fr. OHG *hlūtar* pure — more at CLYSTER] **1 :** CLEAR ⟨~ mash⟩ **2 :** CLARIFIED ⟨~ beer⟩
[2]**lauter** \"\ *vt* -ED/-ING/-S **:** to treat (mash) in a lauter tub **:** FILTER
**lauter tub** *or* **lauter tun** *n* **:** a large tank containing a slotted or perforated false bottom for filtering the clear liquid wort from the residual grain in the mash in brewing
**lau·tite** \'lau̇,tīt\ *n* -s [G *lautit*, fr. *Lauta*, Germany, its locality + G *-it* -ite] **:** a mineral CuAsSp consisting of a sulfide and arsenide of copper possibly related to arsenopyrite
**laut·ver·schie·bung** \'lau̇tfer,shē(,)bu̇ŋ\ *n, pl* **lautverschie·bung·en** \-ŋən\ [G, fr. *laut* sound + *verschiebung* shift] **:** CONSONANT SHIFT
**lav** *abbr or n* -s lavatory

**la·va** \'lävə, 'la|, 'lå|\ *n* -s *often attrib* [It, fr. It dial. (Naples), lava, torrent of floodwater, fr. L *labes* fall; akin to L *labi* to glide, slide — more at SLEEP] **1 a :** fluid rock that issues from a volcano or from a fissure in the earth's surface, that consists of mineral matter dissolved in mineral matter at high temperatures, and that is more fluid when at higher temperatures and when basic rather than acid — compare MAGMA **b :** any of several solid materials (as obsidian, pumice) resulting from the cooling of lava under different conditions ⟨black ~s⟩ ⟨a ~ bed⟩ ⟨~ plateaus of vast dimensions —O.D.Von Engeln⟩ **2 :** a nearly neutral slightly brownish black that is lighter than African

**la·va·bo** \lə'vä(,)bō, *chiefly Brit* -vā(-\ *n* -s [L, I shall wash, 1st pers. sing. fut. indic. of *lavare* to wash — more at LYE] **1** *often cap* **a :** a ceremonial cleansing in certain Christian churches in which the celebrant liturgically washes his hands after touching the Host in the offertory and repeats in the Roman rite Psalms 25:6 (DV) beginning *Lavabo* **b :** a basin used in this ceremonial washing **2 a :** a washbasin and a tank with a spigot that are both fastened to a wall **b :** a decorative wall basin and water container that is sometimes used for flowers

**lava cone** *n* **:** a volcanic cone composed predominantly of lava flows

**lava flow** *n* **:** a stream or sheet of molten or solidified lava

**¹la·vage** \lə'väzh, -vȧzh\ *n* -s [F, action of washing, fr. MF, fr. *laver* to wash (fr. L *lavare*) + *-age*] **:** WASHING; *esp* **:** the therapeutic washing out of an organ

**²lavage** \"\ *vt* -ED/-ING/-S **:** to wash (a lesion) or wash out (an organ) therapeutically

**la·va·la·va** \,lävə'lävə\ *n* [Samoan, clothing] **:** a rectangular cloth worn like a kilt or skirt by men, women, and children in Polynesia and esp. in Samoa that is now usu. of a bright cotton print often with white or yellow floral designs on a red or blue background

**lava·liere** *or* **lava·lier** *also* **laval·liere** \,lavə'li(ə)r, ,läv-\ *n* -s [F *lavallière* necktie with a large bow, prob. fr. Françoise Louise de la Baume Le Blanc, Duchesse de *La Vallière* †1710 mistress of Louis XIV] **1 :** a pendant ornament on a fine chain that is worn as a necklace **2 :** something suggesting a lavaliere (as a spot of white on the neck of a cat)

**la·van·din** \lə'vandən\ *n* -s [perh. fr. F, irreg. fr. NL *Lavandula*] **:** a hybrid lavender (*Lavandula hybrida*) cultivated for its essential oil esp. in France

**lavandin oil** *n* **:** a fragrant yellowish essential oil obtained from the flowers of lavandin and used in soaps and perfumes

**la·van·du·la** \lə'vanjələ\ *n, cap* [NL, fr. ML *lavandula, lavendula* marjoram, lavender — more at LAVENDER] **:** a genus of Eurasian herbs or shrubs (family Labiatae) having small spicate flowers with a tubular 5-toothed calyx — see LAVENDER

**la·van·du·lol** \-,lȯl, -,lōl\ *n* -s [ISV *lavandul-* (fr. NL *Lavandula*) + *-ol*] **:** a liquid terpenoid alcohol $C_{10}H_{17}OH$ occurring in lavender oil from France

**la·van·ga** \lə'vaŋgə\ *n* -s [modif. of Skt *lavaṅgalatā*, fr. *lavaṅga* clove tree + *latā* creeper] **:** a spiny woody vine (*Luvunga scandens*) of the family Rutaceae that is native to southeastern Asia and is used as a stock for citrus grafts

**lav·a·ret** \,lavə'ret, '==,rət\ *n* -s [F, fr. LL *levaricinus*] **:** a central European whitefish (*Coregonus lavaretus*) found in mountain lakes

**la·vash** \'lä,väsh\ *n* -ES [Arm] **:** a large thin crisp unleavened wafer with a rough surface from air bubbles

**lava soil** *n* **:** soil derived from lava ⟨rich *lava soils* —W.G.East⟩

**La·va·te·ra** \,lävə'tirə, lə'väd·ərə\ *n, cap* [NL, fr. J. R. *Lavater*, 17th cent. Swiss physician and naturalist] **:** a genus of herbs, shrubs, and trees (family Malvaceae) with large flowers subtended by an epicalyx of 6 to 10 bractlets

**la·va·tion** \lā'vāshən, lə'-\ *n* -s [L *lavation-, lavatio*, fr. *lavatus* (past part. of *lavare* to wash) + *-ion-, -io* -ion] **:** WASHING, CLEANSING, LAVAGE — **la·va·tion·al** \-shən°l, -shnəl\ *adj*

**lav·a·to·ri·al** \,lavə'tōrēəl, -tȯr-\ *adj* **:** LAVATORY

**¹lav·a·to·ry** \'lavə,tōre, -tȯr-, -ri\ *n* -ES [ME *lavatorie*, fr. ML *lavatorium*, fr. L *lavatus* (past part. of *lavare* to wash) + *-orium*] **1 :** a basin or other vessel for washing: as **a :** PISCINA **b :** a water basin in a sacristy **2 :** a ritual washing of the hands by a celebrant of the Eucharist **:** LAVABO 1a **3 :** a place for washing: as **a :** a room with conveniences for washing the hands and face and usu. with one or more toilets **b :** a fixed bowl or basin with running water and drainpipe for washing the hands and face **c :** a place, trough, or tub in which bodies are washed before burial **4 :** WATER CLOSET, TOILET

wall-hung lavatory 3b

**²lavatory** \"\ *adj* **:** of, related to, or characteristic of washing

**¹lave** \'lāv\ *n* -s [ME (northern dial.), fr. OE *lāf*; akin to OHG *leiba* remainder, ON *leifar* (pl.) remnants, Goth *laiba* remnant; derivative fr. the root of OE *belīfan* to remain, be left over — more at LEAVE] *now dial* **:** something that is left or remains **:** RESIDUE, REMAINDER ⟨he aye did as the ~ did —J.G.Lockhart⟩

**²lave** \"\ *vb* -ED/-ING/-S [ME *laven*, fr. OE *lafian*; akin to MD *laven* to refresh, soak, OHG *labōn* to refresh, wash; all fr. a prehistoric WGmc word borrowed fr. L *lavare* to wash — more at LYE] *vt* **1 :** to wash or flow along or against **:** WASH, BATHE ⟨*laved* her injured foot in the cold stream —W.H.Hudson †1922⟩ ⟨baptism is performed by *laving* the candidate's head —George Stimpson⟩ ⟨all stuffed into a whole long loaf of bread and *laved* generously with oil —R.B.Gehman⟩ **2 :** POUR **3** *obs* **:** to dip or scoop up or out (as with a ladle) **:** LADE, BAIL ~ *vi, archaic* **:** to wash oneself **:** BATHE ⟨in her chaste current oft the goddess ~s —Alexander Pope⟩

**³lave** \"\ *dial var of* LEAVE

**la·veer** \lə'vi(ə)r\ *vi* [D *laveren*, fr. MD *laveren, loveren*, fr. MF *louvier*, fr. *lof* side of a ship toward the wind — more at LUFF] *archaic* **:** to beat against the wind in sailing **:** TACK

**lavement** *n* -s [F, fr. OF, action of washing, fr. *laver* to wash (fr. L *lavare*) + *-ment*] *obs* **:** ENEMA, LAVAGE

**¹lav·en·der** \'lavəndə(r)\ *n* -s [ME *lavendre*, fr. AF, fr. ML *lavandula, lavendula, livendula* marjoram, lavender, perh. irreg. fr. L *lividus* livid — more at LIVID] **1 a :** a Mediterranean mint (*Lavandula officinalis*) that is widely cultivated for its narrow aromatic leaves and spikes of lilac-purple flowers which are dried and used in sachets — called also *English lavender*; see LAVENDER OIL **b :** any of several other plants of the genus *Lavandula* used similarly to English lavender but often considered inferior — see SPIKE LAVENDER **2 :** a variable color averaging a pale purple that is bluer and deeper than wistaria (sense 2a), flossflower blue, or mauvette and bluer, darker, and slightly stronger than phlox pink

**²lavender** \"\ *vt* **lavendered; lavendered; lavendering** \-d(ə)riŋ\ **lavenders :** to sprinkle or perfume with lavender

**lavender blue** *n* **:** a light to brilliant purplish blue

**lavender cotton** *n* **:** a branching shrub (*Santolina chamaecyparissus*) of the Mediterranean region with strong-scented foliage

**lavender gray** *n* **:** a light bluish gray that is darker and slightly redder than sky gray or chicory

**lavender mist** *n* **:** a pale purple that is paler than average lavender, bluer and duller than wistaria (sense 2a), and bluer, stronger, and slightly lighter than flossflower blue

**lavender oil** *n* **:** a colorless to yellowish aromatic essential oil obtained from the flowers of several species of lavender (as *Lavandula officinalis* in France) and used chiefly as a perfume and also in medicine as a stimulant

**lavender thrift** *n* **:** SEA LAVENDER 1

**lavender water** *n* **:** a perfume consisting primarily of an alcoholic solution of lavender oil

**la·ven·du·la** \lə'venjələ\ *syn of* LAVANDULA

**lave net** *n* [perh. fr. ²*lave* + *net*] **:** a fishnet used in shallow estuaries in Great Britain

**lavenite** *var of* LAAVENITE

**la ven·ta** \lə'ventə\ *adj, usu cap L&V* [fr. *La Venta*, village in southeastern Mexico, site of the finds] **:** of or relating to a culture of southeastern Mexico of about 500 B.C. to A.D. 600 characterized by huge stone realistic figures and carved jade figurines and ornaments

**¹la·ver** \'lāvə(r)\ *n* -s [ME, alter. (influenced by *-er*) of *lavour*, fr. MF *lavoir, lavouer*, prob. fr. ML *lavatorium* — more at LAVATORY] **1** *archaic* **:** a vessel, trough, or cistern for washing **:** BASIN 1a **2** *archaic* **:** something that cleanses physically or spiritually ⟨with ~s pure and cleansing herbs wash off the clotted gore —John Milton⟩ ⟨Christ's ~ hath refreshing power —John Keble⟩ **3 a :** a large brazen vessel near the Mosaic tabernacle and in Solomon's temple where priests washed their hands and feet **b :** one of several vessels in Solomon's temple in which the offerings for burnt sacrifices were washed **4** *archaic* **:** the basin of a fountain

**²laver** \"\ *n* -s [NL, fr. L, a water plant] **1 :** any of several seaweeds: as **a :** RED LAVER **b :** SEA LETTUCE **2 :** AMANORI

**lav·er·a·nia** \,lavə'rānyə\ *n, cap* [NL, fr. Charles L. A. *Laveran* †1922 Fr. physician + NL *-ia*] *in some classifications* **:** a genus of malaria parasites (family Plasmodiidae) that is now usu. included in the genus *Plasmodium*

**lav·er·ock** *or* **lav·rock** \'lav(ə)rək\ *n* [ME *laverok*, fr. OE *lāwerce* — more at LARK] *chiefly Scot* **:** LARK

**laverwort** \'==,=\ *n* [²*laver* + *wort*] **:** ²LAVER

**la·vette** \la'vet\ *n* -s [prob. fr. *lavatory* + *-ette*] **:** LAVATORY 3a

**¹lav·ish** \'lavish, -vēsh\ *n* -ES [ME *lavas*, fr. MF *lavasse, lavache* downpour of rain, fr. *laver* to wash, fr. L *lavare* — more at LYE] *now dial* **:** an unstinted outpouring **:** ABUNDANCE, PROFUSION ⟨he'll maybe see trouble and a ~ of it too —Elizabeth M. Roberts⟩

**²lavish** \"\ *adj, sometimes* -ER/-EST [ME *lavas*, fr. *lavas*, n.] **1 :** expending or bestowing profusely **:** PRODIGAL ⟨the war redistributed national wealth with a ~ and careless hand —Allan Nevins & H.S.Commager⟩ ⟨peculiarly ~ of endearments to his second son —D.H.Lawrence⟩ ⟨remarkably ~ with invective —H.J.Muller⟩ **2 a** *archaic* **:** unrestrained in speech **:** EFFUSIVE ⟨the ~ tongue shall honest truths impart —George Crabbe †1832⟩ **b** *obs* **:** unrestrained in conduct or disposition **:** IMPETUOUS, WILD ⟨when rage and hot blood are his counselors, when means and ~ manners meet together —Shak.⟩ **3 :** expended or produced in abundance **:** characterized by profusion or excess **:** UNSTINTED ⟨a country in which there is ~ consumption and no production —G.B.Shaw⟩ ⟨the ~ attentions of his mother —George Meredith⟩ ⟨bearing a sandwich board on which his name was inscribed in ~ capitals —Max Beerbohm⟩ **syn** see PROFUSE

**³lavish** \", *chiefly in pres part* -vəsh\ *vt* -ED/-ING/-ES **:** to expend or bestow with profusion **:** use with prodigality **:** SQUANDER ⟨the princes of the Renascence ~*ed* upon private luxury . . . enormous amounts of money —Lewis Mumford⟩ ⟨~*ed* his great talents on paltry themes —C.H.Sykes⟩

**lav·ish·ly** \-vəshlē, -vēsh-, -li\ *adv* **:** in a lavish manner ⟨both volumes are ~ illustrated —S.E.Morison⟩ ⟨the candidates found their halting utterances ~ reported —John Buchan⟩

**lav·ish·ment** \-vishmənt, -vēsh-\ *n* -s **:** the action of lavishing

**lav·ish·ness** *n* -ES **1 :** a lavish quality **:** ABUNDANCE ⟨marveling at the ~ of the green world about him —Ferdinan Moltke-Hansen⟩ **2 :** a lavish manner or propensity **:** EXTRAVAGANCE, PRODIGALITY ⟨granted with special ~ to the medical profession —Richard Watts⟩

**la·vol·ta** \lə'vōltə, -väl-\ *n* -s [It *la volta* the lavolta, the turn, fr. *la* the (fem. of *il*, def. art., the, fr. L *ille* that one, that) + *volta* lavolta, turn, fr. *voltare* to turn, fr. (assumed) VL *volvitare*, freq. of L *volvere* to roll — more at LARIAT, VOLUBLE] **:** an early French couple dance characterized by pivoting and making high springs or bounds

**lav·rov·ite** *or* **lav·roff·ite** \'lavrə,vīt, -rə,fīt\ *n* -s [Russ *lavrovit*, fr. N. von *Lavrov*, 19th cent. Russ. scientist + Russ *-it* -ite] **:** a mineral consisting of a pyroxene colored green by vanadium

**lavs** *pl of* LAV

**¹law** \'lȯ\ *n* -s [ME (northern dial.), fr. OE *hlāw, hlǣw*; akin to OHG *hlēo* grave mound, Goth *hlaiw* tomb, L *clivus* hill, *-clinare* to incline — more at LEAN] *dial Brit* **:** a conical hill or mound — usu. used in place names ⟨Berwick ~⟩

**²law** \"\ *n* -s *often attrib* [ME *lawe*, fr. OE *lagu*, of Scand origin; akin to ON *lög* law, pl. of *lag* layer, due place, order; akin to OE *orlæg* fate, OS *gilagu*, OHG *urlag* fate, ON *liggja* to lie — more at LIE] **1 a** (1) **:** a binding custom or practice of a community **:** a rule or mode of conduct or action that is prescribed or formally recognized as binding by a supreme controlling authority or is made obligatory by a sanction (as an edict, decree, rescript, order, ordinance, statute, resolution, rule, judicial decision, or usage) made, recognized, or enforced by the controlling authority (2) **:** the whole body of such customs, practices, or rules constituting the organic rule prescribing the nature and conditions of existence of a state or other organized community (3) **:** COMMON LAW 1,2 — see MARTIAL LAW, MILITARY LAW, PRIVATE LAW, PUBLIC LAW, ROMAN LAW **b** (1) **:** the control or regulation brought about by the existence or enforcement of such law ⟨preserved ~ and order in the town⟩ (2) **:** the action of laws considered as a means of redressing wrongs **:** trial or remedial justice under or by the laws of the land **:** judicial remedy; *also* **:** court action **:** LITIGATION ⟨developed the habit of going to ~ for the slightest provocation —H.A.Overstreet⟩ (3) **:** a law enforcement agent or agency ⟨when he found that goods had been stolen he called in the ~⟩ ⟨put out a guard to watch for the ~ while they robbed the store⟩ **c** (1) **:** a rule, order, or injunction that it is advisable or obligatory to follow or observe ⟨a ~ of self-preservation⟩ (2) **:** a rule or custom of conduct ⟨taking a walk every evening was one of his personal ~s⟩ **d :** something consonant or compatible with established law or enforceable by such law ⟨the decrees were judged not to be ~ and so were rescinded⟩ **e :** CONTROL, AUTHORITY ⟨the child submits to no ~⟩ **f :** a rule or generalization (esp. of established law) as opposed to a fact ⟨a question of ~, not a question of fact⟩ **2** *usu cap* **a :** divine teaching or instruction; *esp* **:** a divine commandment or a revelation of the will of God **b :** the whole body of God's commandments or revelations **:** the will of God **c** *obs* **:** a religion or religious system **d :** a religious dispensation **3 :** a rule of construction or procedure (as in art, a craft, or games) conforming to the conditions of success **:** PRINCIPLE ⟨the ~s of poetry⟩ ⟨the ~s of architecture⟩ ⟨a ~ of courtesy⟩ **4 :** a rule of right living or good conduct esp. when conceived as having the sanction of God's will, of conscience or the moral nature, or of natural justice **:** MORAL LAW **5 a :** the whole body of laws relating to one subject or emanating from one source usu. including the writings on them and the judicial proceedings under them ⟨insurance ~⟩ ⟨criminal ~⟩ ⟨probate ~⟩ — compare ADJECTIVE LAW, CIVIL LAW, COMMERCIAL LAW, DECISIONAL LAW, EQUITY, LAW MERCHANT, STATUTORY LAW, SUBSTANTIVE LAW **b :** a rule or a body of rules or prescriptions for conduct to be observed in a particular place or under particular circumstances ⟨the ~ of the house⟩ **6 a :** the legal profession — usu. used with *the* **b :** law as a department of knowledge **:** legal science **:** JURISPRUDENCE **c :** legal learning or knowledge ⟨a man with much history and letters but little ~⟩ **7** *obs* **:** MERCY, INDULGENCE **8 :** an allowance of time or distance given to a weaker competitor in sports or to a hare or fox before the hounds are released in hunting **9 a :** a statement of an order or relation of phenomena that so far as is known is invariable under the given conditions ⟨a ~ of thermodynamics⟩ ⟨the ~s of chemistry⟩ — often used in combination with the name of the discoverer of the order or relation ⟨Boyle's ~⟩ ⟨Gresham's ~⟩ **b :** a relation proved or assumed to be true between or among mathematical expressions **c :** the observed regularity of nature

**syn** RULE, CANON, PRECEPT, REGULATION, ORDINANCE: each of these terms indicates a principle governing action or procedure. LAW implies issuance and imposition of that principle as binding and obligatory by an ultimate sovereign authority ⟨the *laws* of our federal government⟩ In physical sciences LAW suggests a principle or assertion formulated on the basis of conclusive evidence or tests and presumably universally valid ⟨when this formula first dawned on the mind of Newton, it was a scientific conjecture; when it was tested and proved to conform to facts, it became an accepted scientific *law* —P.E.More⟩ LAW may refer to that which is unwritten or uncodified but universally accepted ⟨the common *law* of England⟩ RULE, often interchangeable with LAW in ordinary uses, may be used in more personal, individual, or specific situations with somewhat less inexorability and power implied ⟨so many handsome girls are unmarried, and so many of the other sort wedded, that there is no possibility of establishing a *rule* —W.M. Thackeray⟩ ⟨ritual is not easy compliance with usage; it is strict compliance with detailed and punctilious *rule* —W.G. Sumner⟩ ⟨the *rules* of stud poker are drawn up to accord with the laws of chance⟩ CANON in nonreligious use may suggest a principle of treatment or judgment in intellectual and creative activities that is generally accepted as a valid guide or test ⟨the Aristotelian *canon* that the "nature" of a thing must be sought in its completed development, its final form —W.R.Inge⟩ ⟨prefer the particular to the general, the definite to the vague — as a *canon* of rhetoric —A.T.Quiller-Couch⟩ More than other words in this group PRECEPT is likely to suggest something that is advisory and nonobligatory ⟨the Old Bailey, at that date, was a choice illustration of the *precept* that "whatever is is right" —Charles Dickens⟩ ⟨the one child to whom the "spare-the-rod" *precept* did not apply —Margaret Deland⟩ REGULATION suggests directives for a detail of procedure or conduct applying within an organization and established with executive or administrative authority ⟨regular scholarships are awarded in accordance with the following *regulations* set up by the Committee on Scholarships —*Official Register of Harvard Univ.*⟩ ⟨a colonel not on flying status was by *regulation* ineligible for most Air Force commands —J.G.Cozzens⟩ ORDINANCE suggests an obligatory order, direction, or injunction governing some detail of conduct and issued and enforced by a limited and not sovereign agency, for instance a municipal government or a county or shire governing board ⟨an *ordinance* about parking on Main Street⟩ ⟨the new *ordinance* about delinquent property taxes⟩ **syn** see in addition PRINCIPLE — **have the law on :** to institute legal proceedings against

**³law** \"\ *vb* -ED/-ING/-S [ME *lawen*, fr. *lawe*, n.] *vi* **:** to go to law ~ *vt* **1** *chiefly dial* **:** to sue or prosecute at law ⟨I won't go to the sheriff and I won't ~ you; I'll shoot you —Luke Short⟩ **2 :** to mutilate (an animal) so as to prevent mischief **:** EXPEDITATE

**⁴law** \"\ *now dial var of* LOW

**⁵law** \"\ *interj* [partly alter. of ²*la*, partly euphemism for *Lord*] *now dial* — used esp. to express surprise

**la·wa** \'lä(,)wä\ *n, pl* **lawa** *or* **lawas** *usu cap* **1 a :** the Wa of the Shan plateau in Burma **b :** a member of such people **2 a :** one of two related ethnic groups of Mon-Khmer-speaking people of Thailand that live near Chiengmai and the Korat plateau respectively **b :** a people of Thailand living in the Kanburi province **c :** a member of one of these three peoples

**law-abiding** \'==,==\ *adj* **:** abiding by or obedient to the law — **law-abid·ing·ness** *n* -ES

**law agent** *n, Scots law* **:** LAWYER, SOLICITOR

**law binding** *n* **:** a plain book binding made in light brown calf, sheep, or buckram with leather backbone and used on lawbooks

**lawbook** \'=,=\ *n* **:** a book containing or dealing with laws, legal subjects, or cases adjudicated

**law-borrow** \'=,bä(,)rō\ *or* **law-burrow** \'=,bə(,)rō\ *n* [ME (Sc) *law borow*, fr. ME *law, lawe* law + *borow, borwe* something deposited as security, pledge — more at LAW, BORROW] *Scots law* **:** a cautionary or security measure designed to keep the peace; *also* **:** the process necessary to put such a measure into effect — usu. used in pl.

**lawbreaker** \'=,==\ *n* [ME *lawbreker*, fr. *law, lawe* law + *breker* breaker] **:** one who violates the law

**lawbreaking** \'=,==\ *n* **:** the act of violating the law

**law buckram** *n* **:** BUCKRAM 2a

**law calf** *n* **:** a fine grade of light brown calfskin for binding lawbooks

**law clerk** *n* **:** a student of law or a lawyer studying law or working under the supervision of a lawyer or judge in order to learn law or gain experience, often for little or no pay

**lawcourt** \'=,=\ *n* **:** ¹COURT 3; *esp* **:** COURT OF LAW

**law day** *n* [ME *lawe day*, fr. *lawe* law + *day*] **1** *obs* **:** a day in which a court is or is to be in session; *also* **:** the session of such a court **2 :** a day named in a bond or mortgage for the payment of the money secured by it

**law french** *n, cap F* **:** the form of Anglo-French used in England in judicial proceedings, pleadings, and lawbooks from medieval times to the 17th century

**law·ful** \'lȯfəl\ *adj* [ME *lawful*, fr. *lawe* law + *-ful*] **1 a :** conformable to law **:** allowed or permitted by law **:** enforceable in a court of law **:** LEGITIMATE **b :** constituted, authorized, or established by law **:** RIGHTFUL ⟨the ~ owner⟩ ⟨a ~ day to hold court⟩ **2 :** LAW-ABIDING ⟨made his appeal to all ~ citizens against the criminals⟩

**syn** LAWFUL, LEGAL, LEGITIMATE, and LICIT can mean, in common, sanctioned by law. LAWFUL implies law of any kind and often comes close to PERMISSIBLE ⟨a *lawful* king⟩ ⟨a *lawful* husband⟩ ⟨found that there is nothing fortuitous about color mixtures but, on the contrary, that they are entirely regular and *lawful* in operation —F.A.Geldard⟩ ⟨the behavior of organisms is plainly *lawful*, the business of science is still to determine how they arrive —H.J.Muller⟩ ⟨that was the only sense in which ambition was *lawful* for a Christian: ambition for the work and not for self —Bruce Marshall⟩ ⟨the time has come when, if ever, it is *lawful* for me to doubt as it is imperative for you to affirm —O.W.Holmes †1935⟩ LEGAL usu. implies the law of the statute books or the courts, often applying more to what is not contrary to that law than to what is allowable by the terms of it ⟨a *legal* resident of the state⟩ ⟨*legal* ownership of property⟩ ⟨*legal* control of crime⟩ ⟨*legal* dishonesty in business⟩ LEGITIMATE now implies not only recognition by law but acceptance by custom, tradition, the rules of inference, a sense of fitness or rightness, or standards of authenticity ⟨the difference between crooked dealing and *legitimate* profiting⟩ ⟨in the light of the parallels which I have adduced the hypothesis appears *legitimate*, if not probable —J.G.Frazer⟩ ⟨a short novel of what might be called *legitimate* adventure —E.L.Acken⟩ ⟨both toy and *legitimate* wooden shoes are manufactured —Loyal Durand⟩ ⟨*legitimate* to claim that much of our truly wonderful prodigality of talent is due to the work of gifted teachers —J.A.Michener⟩ ⟨this *legitimate* contrast to be made between China and western Europe —E.R.Hughes⟩ ⟨the problem of selling books is met through the industry's most *legitimate* channels, namely the bookstores —A. A. Van Duym⟩ LICIT usu. implies strict conformity to law in the way something (esp. what is specifically regulated by law) is performed, executed, or carried on ⟨the state is given its right to determine what is *licit* and illicit for property owners in the use of their possessions —*Commonweal*⟩ ⟨extremely difficult to disentangle truth from falsehood, and far more reliance must be placed on personal and private sources of information than would be *licit* if these barriers did not exist —E.S.Skillin⟩ ⟨the biggest dealer in ivory, both *licit* and illicit, in the town —Stuart Cloete⟩ ⟨a wife's *licit* love⟩

**lawful age** *n* **:** the age specified by law for entering into a particular relationship or engaging in a particular transaction; *specif* **:** the age at which one normally attains to full legal rights and responsibilities

**law·ful·ly** \-f(ə)lē, -li\ *adv* [ME *lawefully*, fr. *laweful* + *-ly*] **:** in a lawful manner

**lawful money** *n* [ME *laweful moneye*, fr. *laweful* + *moneye* money] **1 a :** any money whether coin or currency that may by the laws of a country be circulated as a medium of exchange — compare LEGAL TENDER **b :** any money recognized in a community as a medium of exchange **2 :** money (as bank reserves) designated as acceptable for a particular purpose

**law·ful·ness** \-fəlnəs\ *n* -ES [ME *lahfulnesse*, fr. *lahful, laweful* lawful + *-nesse* -ness] **:** the quality or state of being lawful **:** LEGALITY

**lawful rate** *n* **:** a rate for interstate or intrastate traffic established and published in accord with the laws, rules, and regulations prescribed by interstate and state commissions — called also *legal rate*

**lawgiver** \'=,==\ *n* [ME *lawe givere*, fr. *lawe* law + *givere* giver] **:** one that makes, enacts, or transmits a law or system of laws ⟨the scientific ~s —Douglas Bush⟩; *esp* **:** LEGISLATOR a ⟨the prophet was both teacher and ~⟩

**law-hand** \'=,=\ *n* **:** a special style of handwriting used in engrossing old legal documents in England

**¹law·ing** \'lȯiŋ\ *n* -s [ME, gerund of *lawen* to go to law — more at LAW] **1 :** LITIGATION **2** *obs* **:** EXPEDITATION

**²lawing** \"\ *n* -s [obs. Sc *law* charge to be paid (fr. ME — north dial. — *lagh*, fr. ON *lag* market price, tax, layer, due place, order) + E *-ing* — more at LAW] *chiefly Scot* **:** a bill for food or drink (as at a tavern) ⟨paid my ~ —*Kinmont Willie*⟩

**lawk** \'lȯk\ *or* **lawks** \-ks\ *interj* [euphemism for *Lord*] *dial Brit* — used to express surprise

**law lamb** *n* **:** a grade of light-brown sheepskin made from the younger and finer-grained skins and used on lawbooks

**law latin** *n, cap 2d L* **:** the Low Latin containing latinized English and old French words that is used in English law

**law·less** \'lȯlə̇s\ *adj* [ME *lawelees*, fr. *lawe* law + *-lees* -less] **1 a :** being without law **:** having no laws **:** not regulated by law ⟨the ~ desert⟩ ⟨thought is anarchic and ~ —Bertrand Russell⟩ **b :** not based on law ⟨the ~ dictates of the conqueror⟩ **2** *archaic* **:** exempt from the operation of law **3 a :** not restrained or controlled by consideration for a law (as of morality or decency) **:** UNRULY, DISORDERLY ⟨the frontier . . . produced a ~ class of Indian traders —H.E.Davis⟩ **b :** ILLEGAL ⟨engaging in ~ activity until the police finally caught him⟩ — **law·less·ly** *adv* — **law·less·ness** *n* -ES

**lawlike** \'=,=\ *adj* **:** being like the law (as in methods, principles, or terminology)

**law list** *n* **:** a publication compiling the names and addresses of those engaged in the practice of law and information of interest to the law profession often including the courts, court calendars, lawyers engaged in specialized fields (as admiralty or patent law), public officers, stenographers, handwriting experts, private investigators, or abstracts of law **:** a legal directory

**law lord** *n* **:** a member of the British House of Lords who by appointment as a lord of appeal in ordinary or as lord chancellor or by possession of eminent legal experience usu. obtained by having held high judicial office is qualified to participate in the proceedings of the House as a court of last resort ⟨no appeal can be decided by the House unless at least three *law lords* . . . are present at the hearing —Edward Jenks⟩

**lawmaker** \'=,==\ *n* [ME *lawe maker*, fr. *lawe* law + *maker*, *makere* maker] **:** one that makes laws **:** LEGISLATOR, LAWGIVER ⟨several bills . . . held over from the last session will be considered by the ~*s* —*Publishers' Weekly*⟩ ⟨the wise man and ~ of Athens —J.A.Macy⟩

**law·man** \'lȯmən\ *n, pl* **lawmen** [trans. of OE *lageman*, fr. *lage-* (fr. *lagu* law) + *man*] **1 :** an hereditary official acting chiefly as a doomster in boroughs of medieval England formerly under Danish rule ⟨the *lawmen* of Lincoln were holders of heritable franchises —F.W.Maitland⟩ **2** [²*law* + *man*] **:** a law enforcement officer (as a sheriff or policeman) ⟨the killing of a ~ is not taken lightly in the Texas border country —Caddo Cameron⟩

**law merchant** *n, pl* **laws merchant** [ME *lawe marchaund* (trans. of ML *lex mercatoria*), fr. *lawe* law + *marchaund*, *marchant*, adj., merchant] **1 :** the legal rules formerly applied to cases arising in commercial transactions esp. by the courts of piepoudre, the staple courts, and merchant's courts **2 :** COMMERCIAL LAW

¹**lawn** \'lȯn, 'län\ *n* -S [ME, fr. *Laon*, town in northern France] **1 :** a sheer plainwoven cotton or linen fabric that is given various finishes (as semicrisp) when used for clothing **2** [so called fr. the use of the fabric lawn for the sleeves of an Anglican bishop's official dress] **:** the office or dignity of a bishop **3 a :** a lawn or silk sieve **b :** a brass or copper sieve of fine texture

²**lawn** \"\ *vt* -ED/-ING/-S **:** to screen (as pigment) through a lawn or silk screen

³**lawn** \"\ *n* -S *often attrib* [alter. of *laund*] **1** *archaic* **a :** an open space between woods **:** GLADE **b :** a level stretch on a mountainside **2 :** ground covered with grass and not tilled; *esp* **:** ground covered with fine grass kept closely mowed esp. in front of or about a house or as part of a garden or park

⁴**lawn** \"\ *vt* -ED/-ING/-S **:** to make into or like a lawn

**lawn billiards** *n pl but usu sing in constr* **:** TROCO

**lawn bowling** *n* **:** a game played on a closely cropped green with wooden balls which are rolled as close as possible to a jack — called also *bowls, bowling on the green*

**lawn chair** *n* **:** any usu. reclining chair used or designed to be used for sitting or reclining comfortably outdoors esp. on lawns or in garden areas

**lawn finish** *n* **:** a finish on paper similar to linen finish

**lawn green** *n* **:** a moderate yellow green that is greener, lighter, and stronger than average moss green, yellower and deeper than average pea green, yellower and darker than apple green (sense 1), and yellower, lighter, and stronger than spinach green

**lawnleaf** \'=,=\ *n, pl* **lawnleaves :** DICHONDRA 2

**lawn mixture** *n* **:** a mixture of grass seeds of various types intended primarily for making lawns

**lawn mower** *n* **:** a hand-operated or power-operated machine for cutting grass on lawns

**lawn mowings** *n pl* **:** clippings from a lawn that has been mowed sometimes used for mulching purposes or added to a compost pile

**lawn party** *n* **1 :** a social party held on a lawn or in a garden **:** GARDEN PARTY **2 :** an outdoor carnival or fete that usu. features games and amusements (as pony rides or fortune-telling) and booths for the selling of food or drinks or chances on prizes and that is held for the raising of money usu. for a church or some civic purpose

lawn mower

**lawn pennywort** *n* **:** a tufted and creeping Asiatic herb (*Hydrocotyle rotundifolia*) that has round cordate leaves and that is adventive in lawns of the eastern U. S.

**lawn plant** *n* **:** a So. American herb (*Lippia canescens*) prostrate and rooting at the nodes and commonly grown in drier parts of California as a substitute for lawn grasses

**lawn sleeves** *n pl but sing or pl in constr* **:** the episcopal office **:** BISHOP

**lawn tennis** *n* **:** TENNIS; *specif* **:** tennis played on a grass court — distinguished from *court tennis*

¹**lawny** \'lȯnē, 'länē, -ni\ *adj* [¹*lawn* + *-y*] **:** made of, wearing, or resembling lawn

²**lawny** \"\ *adj* [³*lawn* + *-y*] **:** having or resembling a grass lawn

**law of absorption :** a theorem in logic: to affirm that either some proposition is true or else that that proposition and some other proposition are both true is equivalent to affirming the first proposition

**law of acceleration :** a generalization in biology: the order of development of a structure or organ is directly related to its importance to the organism

**law of action and reaction :** LAW OF MOTION 3

**law of areas** *or* **law of equal areas :** KEPLER'S LAW 2

**law of averages :** BERNOULLI'S THEOREM 1

**law of boyle and mar·i·otte** \-,marē'ät\ *usu cap B & M* [after Robert *Boyle* †1691 Brit. physicist and Edme *Mariotte* †1684 Fr. physicist who independently discovered it] **:** BOYLE'S LAW

**law of causation** *or* **law of causality :** a principle in philosophy: every change in nature is produced by some cause

**law of combining volumes :** GAY-LUSSAC'S LAW

**law of conservation of energy :** CONSERVATION OF ENERGY

**law of conservation of mass :** CONSERVATION OF MASS

**law of conservation of momentum :** CONSERVATION OF MOMENTUM

**law of constant angles :** a law in crystallography: the angles between the various faces of a crystal remain unchanged throughout its growth

**law of constant proportion :** LAW OF DEFINITE PROPORTIONS

**law of constant return :** a statement in economics: an increase of the scale of production in an industry gives a proportionate increase of return or the increase in area of land cultivated requires a proportionate increase in outlay for labor or materials

**law of continuity :** a principle in philosophy: there is no break in nature and nothing passes from one state to another without passing through all the intermediate states

**law of contradiction :** a principle in logic: a thing cannot at the same time both be and not be of a specified kind (as a table and not a table) or in a specified manner (as red or not red)

**law of cosines 1 :** a law in trigonometry: the square of a side of a plane triangle equals the sum of the squares of the remaining sides minus twice the product of those sides and the cosine of the angle between them **2 :** a law in trigonometry: the cosine of an arc of a spherical triangle equals the product of the cosines of the remaining arcs plus the product of the sines of those arcs and the cosine of the angle between them

**law of definite proportions :** a statement in chemistry: every definite compound always contains the same elements in the same proportions by weight

**law of demand :** a statement in economics: the quantity of an economic good purchased will vary inversely with its price — compare INFERIOR GOOD

**law of diminishing returns :** a principle in economics: at any given stage of technological advance an increase in productive factors (as labor or capital) applied beyond a certain point fails to bring about a proportional increase in production

**law of diminishing utility :** a principle in social science: as one acquires successive units of a good, the intensity of desire for additional units declines

**law of dominance :** MENDEL'S LAW 3

**law of dulong and petit** *usu cap D & P* **:** DULONG AND PETIT'S LAW

**law of effect :** a statement in psychology: in trial-and-error learning satisfying or successful behavior is repeated whereas unsatisfying or unsuccessful behavior is not

**law of error :** the equation of the normal probability curve to which the accidental errors associated with an extended series of observations tend to conform — called also *normal law of error*

**law of excluded middle :** a principle in logic: if one of two contradictory statements is denied the other must be affirmed

**law of exponents :** one of a set of rules in algebra: exponents of numbers are added when the numbers are multiplied, subtracted when the numbers are divided, and multiplied when raised by still another exponent: $a^m \times a^n = a^{m+n}$; $a^m \div a^n = a^{m-n}$; $(a^m)^n = a^{mn}$

**law of fechner** *usu cap F* **:** WEBER-FECHNER LAW

**law office** *n* **:** an office maintained by a lawyer or a firm of lawyers for the practice of law

**law officer** *n* **:** a public official employed to administer or advise in legal matters: **a** *or* **law officer of the crown** *usu cap C* **:** the attorney general or the solicitor general of England ⟨the opinions of the *law officers of the Crown* . . . are not usually laid before Parliament —T.E.May⟩ **b :** an official of a general court-martial in the U.S. armed forces who may not vote but is charged with advising the members of the court on matters of law and who is appointed from the Judge Advocate General's Corps or from the bar of a federal court or the highest court of a state

**law of frontality :** the convention of frontality (as in Egyptian art)

**law of gravitation :** a statement in physics: any particle in the universe attracts any other particle with a force that is proportional to the product of the masses of the two particles and inversely proportional to the square of the distance between them

**law of guld·berg and waa·ge** \-'gül,bergən'vägə\ *usu cap G&W* [after Cato M. *Guldberg* †1902 Norw. chemist and mathematician and Peter *Waage* †1900 Norw. chemist, its formulators] **:** LAW OF MASS ACTION

**law of identity :** one of three principles in logic: **1 :** a statement (as "a house is a house") in which the subject and predicate are the same is true **2 :** the copula in an identity affirms an existent of which the identity is true **3 :** a statement of an identity is the expression of an abstract relation of identity symbolized by a term (as *A* in "A is A") that apparently refers in its separate instances to the subject and predicate respectively

**law of independent assortment :** MENDEL'S LAW 2

**law of inertia :** LAW OF MOTION 1

**law of large numbers :** a law in statistics: the probability that the mean of a random sample differs from the mean of the population from which the sample is drawn by more than a given amount approaches zero as the size of the sample approaches infinity

**law of mass action :** a statement in chemistry: the rate of a chemical reaction is directly proportional to the molecular concentrations of the reacting substances

**law of motion 1 :** a statement in dynamics: a body at rest remains at rest and a body in motion remains in uniform motion in a straight line unless acted upon by an external force — called also *Newton's first law of motion* **2 :** a statement in dynamics: the acceleration of a body is directly proportional to the applied force and is in the direction of the straight line in which the force acts — called also *Newton's second law of motion* **3 :** a statement in dynamics: for every force there is an equal and opposite force or reaction — called also *Newton's third law of motion*

**law of multiple proportions :** a statement in chemistry: when two elements combine in more than one proportion to form two or more compounds the weights of one element that combine with a given weight of the other element are in the ratios of small whole numbers

**law of nations** [trans. of L *jus gentium*] **1 :** JUS GENTIUM **2 :** INTERNATIONAL LAW

**law of nature 1 :** a natural instinct or a natural relation of human beings or other animals due to native character or condition **2 :** a generalized statement of natural processes; *specif* **:** one of the chief generalizations of science variously conceived as imposed upon nature by the Creator, as representing an intrinsic orderliness of nature or the necessary conformity of phenomena to reason and understanding, or as the observed regular coincidences of phenomena which are ultimate data for our knowledge **3 :** NATURAL LAW

**law of parsimony 1 :** economy of assumption in reasoning **2 :** economy of pain or effort in seeking pleasure or gain

**law of partial pressures :** a statement in physics: the component of the total pressure contributed by each ingredient in a mixture of gases or vapors is equal to the pressure that it would exert if alone in the same enclosure — called also *Dalton's law*

**law of priority :** a principle in taxonomy: the first properly published name of a species or genus takes precedence over any subsequently published — compare NOMENCLATURE, NOMEN CONSERVANDUM

**law of recapitulation :** RECAPITULATION THEORY

**law of reflection :** a statement in optics: when light falls upon a plane surface it is so reflected that the angle of reflection is equal to the angle of incidence and that the incident ray, reflected ray, and normal ray all lie in the plane of incidence

**law of refraction :** a law in physics: in the refraction of radiation at the interface between two isotropic media the incident ray and the corresponding refracted ray are coplanar with the refracting surface at the point of incidence and the ratio of the sine of the angle of incidence to the sine of the angle of refraction is equal to the refractive index

**law of segregation :** MENDEL'S LAW 1

**law of signs 1 :** a rule in algebra: the product or the quotient of two numbers of like sign is positive **2 :** a rule in algebra: the product or the quotient of two numbers of unlike sign is negative

**law of sines 1 :** a law in trigonometry: the ratio of each side of a plane triangle to the sine of the opposite angle is the same for all three sides and angles **2 :** a law in trigonometry: the ratio of the sine of each arc of a spherical triangle to the sine of the opposite angle is the same for all three arcs and angles

**law of sufficient reason :** a principle in logic: for everything that is there is a reason why it should be as it is rather than otherwise

**law of superposition :** a law in geology: where there has been no subsequent disturbance sedimentary strata were deposited in ascending order with younger beds successively overlying older beds

**law of supply and demand :** a statement in economics: the competitive price that clears the market for a commodity is determined through the interaction of offers and demands

**law of tangents :** a law in plane trigonometry: in any plane triangle the tangent of one half the difference of any two angles is to the tangent of one half their sum as the difference of the sides opposite the respective angles is to the sum of those sides

**law of the flag :** the law of the sovereign state under whose protection a ship is registered and whose flag the ship flies

**law of the jungle :** a code that dictates survival by any means possible and that is presumed to be in effect among animals in their natural state or people unrestrained by any established law or civilized personal or civic control; *also* **:** activity following this code

**law of the minimum :** a law in physiology: when a process is conditioned by several factors its rate is limited by the factor present in the minimum

**law of thermodynamics 1 :** a law in physics: CONSERVATION OF ENERGY — called also *first law of thermodynamics* **2 :** a law in physics: mechanical work can be derived from the heat in a body only when the body is able to communicate with another at a lower temperature or all actual spontaneous processes result in an increase of total entropy — called also *second law of thermodynamics* **3 :** a law in physics: at the absolute zero of temperature the entropy of any pure crystalline substance is zero and its derivative with respect to temperature is zero — called also *third law of thermodynamics*

**law of the staple :** the law merchant as administered in the staple courts

**law of thought :** any of several principles in logic: **a :** LAW OF CONTRADICTION **b :** LAW OF EXCLUDED MIDDLE **c :** LAW OF IDENTITY

**law of ti·ti·us** \-'tētsēəs\ *usu cap T* [after J. D. *Titius* †1796 Ger. mathematician] **:** BODE'S LAW

**law of transposition :** a principle in logic: transposition yields a valid inference

**law of von baer** *usu cap B* **:** VON BAER'S LAW

**law of war :** the code that governs or one of the rules that govern the rights and duties of belligerents in international war chiefly affecting prisoners, spies, traitors, private property, blockades, and rights of capture

**law of weber-fechner** *usu cap W&F* **:** WEBER-FECHNER LAW

**law proper** *n, pl* **laws proper :** POSITIVE LAW

**law·rence's goldfinch** \'lȯrənsə̇z-, 'lär-\ *n, usu cap L* [after George N. *Lawrence* †1895 Am. ornithologist] **:** a goldfinch (*Spinus lawrencei*) of southern California and northern Mexico having yellow lower parts and greenish yellow upper parts

**law·ren·cian** *or* **law·ren·tian** \(')lȯ¦renchən, (')lä¦-\ *adj, usu cap* [*lawrencian* fr. D. H. *Lawrence* †1930 Eng. novelist + E *-ian*; *lawrentian* alter. (influenced by *laurentian*) of *lawrencian*] **:** of, relating to, or befitting the writings of D. H. Lawrence ⟨has an affair with a *Lawrencian* foreman who has been dismissed from his employment —*Times Lit. Supp.*⟩

**law·renc·ite** \'lȯrən,sīt, 'lär-\ *n* -S [F, fr. J. *Lawrence* Smith †1883 Am. chemist and mineralogist + F *-ite*] **:** a mineral consisting of ferrous chloride often found in meteoric iron

**laws** *pl of* LAW, *pres 3d sing of* LAW

**law sakes** *or* **law sakes alive** *interj* [euphemism for *for the Lord's sake*] *dial* — used to express surprise or protest

**law sheep** *n* **:** a fine grade of light-brown sheepskin made from the outside of the skins and commonly used in binding lawbooks

**law skiver** *n* **:** a sheepskin skiver tanned to imitate law sheep

**laws of planetary motion :** KEPLER'S LAWS

**law·son** \'lȯs°n\ *adj, usu cap* [after Thomas W. *Lawson* †1925 Am. financier for whom furniture of this kind was designed] **:** being of or belonging to an overstuffed furniture design marked by square seat cushions, short squarish back rests, and high square or roll arms ⟨a *Lawson* sofa⟩ ⟨furniture built on *Lawson* lines⟩

**law·sone** \'lȯ,sōn\ *n* -S [*laws-* (fr. NL *Lawsonia*) + *-one*] **:** a yellow crystalline dye $C_{10}H_5O_2(OH)$ obtained esp. from leaves of Egyptian henna; 2-hydroxy-1,4-naphthoquinone

**law·so·nia** \lȯ'sōnēə\ *n, cap* [NL, fr. Isaac *Lawson* †1747 Scot. naturalist + NL *-ia*] **:** a genus of tropical Old World shrubs (family Lythraceae) having tetramerous flowers and a four-celled capsular fruit — see HENNA

**law·so·ni·ana** \(,)lȯ,sōnē'anə, -'änə,-'ānə\ *n* -S [NL (specific epithet of *Chamaecyparis lawsoniana*), fem. of *lawsonianus* of Lawson, fr. Peter *Lawson*, 19th cent. Scot. nurseryman who introduced the species into cultivation + L *-ianus* -ian] **:** PORT ORFORD CEDAR

**law·son·ite** \'lȯsə,nīt\ *n* -S [Andrew C. *Lawson* †1952 Am. geologist + E *-ite*] **:** a pale or grayish blue mineral $CaAl_2Si_2O_6(OH)_4$ in prismatic orthorhombic crystals consisting of hydrous calcium aluminum silicate

**lawson's cypress** *or* **lawson cypress** *n, usu cap L* [After Peter *Lawson*, 19th cent Scot. nurseryman] *chiefly Brit* **:** PORT ORFORD CEDAR

**law stationer** *n* **:** one that deals in paper, forms, and other stationer's supplies used by lawyers and that in Great Britain and Ireland also makes fair or engrossed copies of legal instruments

**lawsuit** \'=,=\ *n* **:** a suit in law **:** a case before a court **:** any of various technical legal proceedings (as an action, prosecution)

**law·sy** *or* **law·zy** \'lȯzē\ *interj* [euphemism for *Lordy*] *dial* — used to express surprise, astonishment, or strength of feeling

**lawter** *n* -S [of Scand origin; akin to ON *lāttr* place where animals lay their young — more at LAUGHTER] *dial Eng* **:** ²LAUGHTER

**law-way** \'=,=\ *n* **:** a custom or tradition that acts practically as a law esp. among a people

**law-worthy** \'=,==\ *adj* **:** entitled to or coming within the benefits or rules of law or legal procedure

**law·yer** \'lȯyə(r), 'lȯiə-\ *n* -S [ME *lawyere*, fr. *lawe* law + *-ere, -iere* -er] **1 :** a specialist in or a practitioner of law **:** one (as an attorney, counselor, solicitor, barrister, or advocate) whose profession is to conduct lawsuits for clients or to advise as to the prosecution or defense of lawsuits or as to legal rights and obligations in other matters **2 a :** BOWFIN **b :** the New World burbot **c :** GRAY SNAPPER **3 a** *dial Eng* **:** a bramble or the thorny stem of a brier **b :** any of various trailing brambles of New Zealand (esp. *Rubus australis*) that scramble over other growth, can be held in position by backward-pointing hooks, and sometimes attain a basal thickness of 5 to 6 inches **4 :** BLACK-NECKED STILT

**lawyer bush** *or* **lawyer cane** *n* **:** LAWYER 3b

**law·yer·ess** \-ərə̇s\ *n* -ES **:** a female lawyer

**law·yer·ing** \-riŋ\ *n* -S **:** following the profession or performing the functions of a lawyer — often used disparagingly

**lawyerlike** \'==,=\ *adj* **:** resembling or befitting a lawyer ⟨~ speech⟩

**law·yer·ly** \-lē, -li\ *adj* **:** LAWYERLIKE

**lawyer palm** *n* **:** an Australian climbing palm (*Calamus australis*) with slender prickly stems and pinnate leaves

**lawyer vine** *n* **1 :** LAWYER 3b **2 :** LAWYER PALM

¹**lax** \'laks\ *n* -ES [partly fr. Norw *laks*, fr. ON *lax;* partly fr. Sc (also obs. E) *lax*, fr. ME, fr. OE *leax;* OE *leax* akin to OHG *lahs* salmon, ON *lax*, Russ *losos'* salmon, Toch B *laks* fish] **:** SALMON

²**lax** \'laks\ *vt* -ED/-ING/-ES [ME *laxen*, fr. L *laxare*, fr. *laxus*] **:** RELAX, LOOSEN ⟨~*ed* its hold in death —G.M.Trevelyan⟩

³**lax** \"\ *adj* -ER/-EST [ME, fr. L *laxus* slack, loose, spacious — more at SLACK] **1 a** *of the bowels* **:** LOOSE, OPEN **b :** having the bowels open **2 :** not strict or stringent ⟨~ discipline⟩ ⟨~ laws⟩ **3 a :** not tense, firm, or rigid **:** SLACK, RELAXED ⟨took his ~ hand in hers —David Walden⟩ ⟨a ~ tone of voice⟩; *also* **:** EASYGOING, CARELESS ⟨a man of ~ habits⟩ **b :** having an open or loose texture ⟨a ~ fiber⟩ ⟨a ~ soil⟩ **c :** not close together **:** SCATTERED ⟨a ~ flower cluster⟩ **4** *of a speech sound* **:** produced with the muscles involved in a relatively relaxed state ⟨the vowels \i\ and \u̇\ in contrast with the vowels \ē\ and \ü\ are ~⟩ — compare TENSE **syn** see NEGLIGENT

⁴**lax** \"\ *n* -ES *now chiefly dial* **:** looseness of the bowels **:** DIARRHEA

**lax·ate** \'lak,sāt\ *vt* -ED/-ING/-S [L *laxatus*, past part. of *laxare*, fr. *laxus* slack, loose, spacious] *obs* **:** LOOSEN, RELAX

**lax·a·tion** \lak'sāshən\ *n* -S [ME *laxacion*, fr. L *laxation-*, *laxatio*, fr. *laxatus* + *-ion-*, *-io* -ion] **1 :** the act of loosening or relaxing or the state of being loosened or relaxed **2 :** a bowel movement

**1lax·a·tive** \'laksəd·|iv, -ət|\ *adj* [ME *laxatif*, fr. ML *laxativus*, fr. L *laxatus* + *-ivus* -ive] **1 :** having a tendency to loosen or relax; *specif* **:** producing bowel movements and relieving constipation **2 a** *archaic* **:** subject to looseness or free movement — used of the bowels **b :** subject to or marked by looseness of the bowels ⟨obese and ~ robins —Christopher Morley⟩ ⟨on silage alone animals are liable to become too ~ —*Successful Farming*⟩ **3 :** running freely **:** LOOSE, UNRESTRAINED ⟨a ~ tongue⟩ — **lax·a·tive·ly** \|əvlē, -li\ *adv* — **lax·a·tive·ness** \|ivnəs\ *n* -ES

**2laxative** \"\ *n* -S [ME *laxatif*, fr. *laxatif*, adj.] **:** a laxative drug **:** a mild cathartic

**lax·ism** \'lak,sizəm\ *n* -S [prob. fr. (assumed) NL *laxismus*, fr. L *laxus* slack, loose + *-ismus* -ism] **:** a viewpoint in the probabilistic controversy that in a conflict between liberty and law a slightly probable argument for liberty suffices to furnish a basis for action — compare PROBABILISM 2

**lax·ist** \-səst\ *n* -S [prob. fr. (assumed) NL *laxista*, fr. L *laxus* + *-ista* -ist] **:** a believer in laxism

**lax·i·ty** \-səd·ē, -sətē, -i\ *n* -ES [L *laxitat-, laxitas* spaciousness, fr. *laxus* slack, loose, spacious + *-itat-, -itas* -ity] **:** the quality or state of being lax: as **a :** LOOSENESS ⟨a certain ~ of bowels⟩ **b :** lack of tenseness ⟨a ~ in his grip⟩ **:** lack of strictness ⟨a ~ in discipline⟩ **c :** looseness of structure or texture ⟨a ~ in the weave of the cloth⟩ **d :** CARELESSNESS ⟨~ in handling participles —E.S.McCartney⟩

**lax·ly** *adv* **:** in a lax manner

**lax·ness** *n* -ES **:** the quality or state of being lax

**1lay** \'lā\ *vb* **laid** \'lād\ **laid; laying; lays** [ME *leyen, leggen*, fr. OE *lecgan*; akin to OHG *leggen* to lay, ON *leggja*, Goth *lagjan*; causative fr. the root of OE *licgan* to lie — more at LIE] *vt* **1 :** to bring down with force **:** beat down **:** strike prostrate ⟨a blow from a swinging club *laid* him in the dust⟩ ⟨wheat *laid* flat by the wind and rain⟩ **2 a :** to put or set down **:** place so as to lie flat **:** place carefully or gently ⟨*laid* a comforting hand on his shoulder⟩ ⟨*laid* her hat on the table⟩ **b :** to place (as in bed) for rest or sleep; *esp* **:** BURY **c :** to copulate with — not often in formal use **d :** to cause (as land) to disappear below the horizon or to seem lower and lower by moving away — opposed to *raise* **3 a :** to produce and deposit (an egg) **b :** to set (as a mine) in the ground or in water **c :** to drop (a bomb) or spread (a smoke screen) from an airplane **4** *obs* **:** to put down (as in writing, in rhyme, in Latin) **:** COUCH **5 :** to cause to be still **:** CALM, ALLAY ⟨manufacture an oil especially to ~ waves —H.A.Calahan⟩ ⟨~ the dust⟩ ⟨chased the clouds . . . and *laid* the winds —John Milton⟩; *esp* **:** to cause (a ghost or spirit) to return to the grave or lower world **6 a :** to deposit as a wager **:** BET; *also* **:** to bet on ⟨~ the favorite⟩ **b** *obs* **:** PLEDGE, MORTGAGE **7** *dial Eng* **:** to assist in childbirth **:** DELIVER **8 :** to press down smooth and even ⟨brushing to ~ the nap⟩ ⟨warp slashing ~*s* the surface fibers of the yarn, making it more compact, smoother, and stronger —*Encyc. of Chem. Technol.*⟩ **9 :** LAYER **10 a** *obs* **:** to impose a tax on **:** ASSESS **b** *obs* **:** to deal a blow to **11 a** *obs* **:** to set a watch or ambush on (a place) **b** *obs* **:** to quarter (as soldiers) upon **12 a :** to dispose over or along a surface ⟨~ a pavement⟩ ⟨~ an ocean cable⟩ or a prepared position ⟨~ a railroad track⟩ ⟨~ a sewer⟩ ⟨~ pipe to a spring⟩ **b :** to spread on a surface ⟨~ plaster⟩ ⟨~ paint⟩ **c :** to place (as brick, stone, or tile) in a wall or a pier **d :** to put (strands) in place and twist to form a rope, hawser, or cable; *also* **:** to make (as a rope, cable, cordage, yarn) by so doing — often used with *up* **13 :** to set in order for a meal ⟨~ the table⟩ ⟨places were *laid* for three people⟩ **14 a :** IMPOSE — sometimes used with *down* **b :** to place (new type) in a case — compare DISTRIBUTE **15 a :** to impose as a duty, burden, or punishment ⟨~ a tax on land⟩ ⟨his father *laid* an injunction upon him never to reveal the secret⟩ **b :** INFLICT ⟨~ blows⟩ **c :** to put or cast as a burden of reproach ⟨found someone to ~ the blame on⟩ **d :** to advance as an accusation **:** CHARGE, IMPUTE ⟨the disaster was *laid* to faulty inspection⟩ ⟨guilt for the murder was *laid* at his door despite strenuous denials⟩ **16 :** to place (something immaterial) on something ⟨~*s* stress on correct grammar⟩ ⟨*laid* special stress on cleanliness⟩ **17 :** to prepare the outlines or details of **:** CONTRIVE ⟨when they . . . slay for passion's sake, they ~ no elaborate schemes —Dorothy Sayers⟩ ⟨deep-*laid* plot⟩ ⟨must somehow form part of the pattern, or ~ the design of the book —F.A.Swinnerton⟩ **18 :** to put in place **:** put to **:** APPLY ⟨*laid* the watch to his ear⟩ ⟨~ siege to a town⟩: as **a :** to put in position for action or operation ⟨~ a fire in the fireplace⟩ ⟨~ glass for grinding⟩ ⟨dogs were *laid* on the scent⟩ ⟨the ship was *laid* alongside the pier⟩ ⟨thought it all out before ~*ing* pen to paper⟩ **b :** to adjust (a fieldpiece or machine gun) with the proper direction and elevation to obtain the desired trajectory **19 :** ANNEX, APPROPRIATE ⟨woe unto them that . . . ~ field to field —Isa 5:8 (AV)⟩ **20 :** to cause to lie in a (specified) condition ⟨so mad I'd like to ~ his head open with a liquor bottle —Earl Hamner⟩ ⟨~ waste the land⟩ ⟨employees . . . whose behavior ~ them open to blackmail —Elmer Davis⟩ ⟨seem to have *laid* the writers under certain inhibitions —V.L.Parrington⟩ **21 a :** to present for consideration **:** put forward **:** ASSERT, STATE, ALLEGE ⟨~ claim to an estate⟩ ⟨*laid* an information against the Kitchen Committee . . . for selling liquor without a license —A.P.Herbert⟩ **b :** to submit for examination and judgment ⟨*laid* his case before the commission⟩ **22 :** to place fictitiously ⟨scene is *laid* in wartime London⟩ **23 :** to line up **:** ASSEMBLE ⟨~ aft on the quarterdeck all the liberty party⟩ ~ *vi* **1 :** to produce and deposit eggs **2** *nonstand* **:** 1LIE **3 a :** WAGER, BET **b :** to assert strongly **:** PREDICT, DECLARE **4** *dial* **:** to await an opportunity **:** PLAN, PREPARE, SCHEME ⟨~*ing* for a chance to escape⟩ **5 a :** to apply oneself vigorously ⟨*laid* to his oars⟩ **b** *naut* **:** GO, COME; *esp* **:** to place oneself in a specified position ⟨~ aloft⟩ ⟨~ forward⟩ **6** *chiefly Midland, of the wind* **:** to decrease in force **:** SUBSIDE **syn** see SET — **lay aboard :** to place a ship close alongside of (a ship) for fighting or for boarding — **lay a course** *or* **lay one's course 1 :** to sail toward the point intended without tacking **2 :** to sail in a certain direction **:** HEAD — **lay a finger on :** to touch or meddle with however lightly **:** do the least violence to — **lay an egg 1 :** to fail to get a favorable response (as from an audience) **:** fall flat **:** FIZZLE **2** *slang* **:** to drop a bomb — **lay at** *now chiefly dial* **:** ATTACK, ASSAIL — **lay bare :** UNCOVER, REVEAL, DISCLOSE, EXPOSE ⟨searches out and *lays bare* every insincerity of liberal professions —V.L.Parrington⟩ — **lay by the heels 1 :** to seize and imprison **:** CAPTURE **2 :** to cause the downfall of **:** bring down **:** OVERTAKE ⟨Romanticism . . . proceeded to hold the field till it was *laid by the heels* by naturalism —Edmund Wilson⟩ — **lay eyes on :** to catch sight of **:** SEE — **lay for :** to lie in wait for **:** prepare to capture or attack **:** AMBUSH — **lay hands on 1 :** to get hold of **:** SEIZE, OBTAIN **2 :** to commit violence upon **:** handle roughly; *also* **:** to kill (oneself) ⟨feared that in his despair he might *lay hands on* himself⟩ **3 :** to ordain or bless by imposition of hands — **lay hold of :** to take hold of **:** GRASP, SEIZE ⟨*lay hold of* that rope and pull⟩ ⟨ideas difficult to *lay hold of*⟩ — **lay into :** to pitch into **:** ATTACK — **lay it on :** to do something with vigor or lavishness or extravagance: as **a :** to charge exorbitantly **b :** to be unduly severe (as in a reprimand) **c :** to exaggerate or flatter grossly — **lay one's account** *archaic* **:** EXPECT, ANTICIPATE — used with *with, on,* or *for* — **lay oneself out :** to take pains **:** try earnestly **:** do one's best ⟨*laid themselves out* to make their guest comfortable⟩ — **lay one's finger on :** to discover and point out with accuracy — **lay on the line 1 :** to advance or put up (a sum of money) in full ⟨the option was about to expire, and a million dollars had to be *laid on the line* —Marquis James⟩ **2 :** to make (as an offer or a statement) without reservations or conditions ⟨the court *laid* the proposition *on the line* that the due process clause protected freedom of speech —C.P.Curtis⟩ — **lay on the table 1 :** to remove (a parliamentary motion) from consideration indefinitely **2** *or* **lay upon the table** *Brit* **:** to put (as legislation) on the agenda — **lay on the wood :** to bat forcefully in cricket — contrasted with *sit on the splice* — **lay wait :** to lie in wait **:** AMBUSH

**2lay** \"\ *n* -S **1 :** something that lies or is laid or as if laid: as **a :** LAYER, STRATUM **b** *obs* **:** WAGER **c** *obs* **:** CHANCE, HAZARD **d** *dial Eng* **:** TAX; *esp* **:** a pecuniary tax levied by local authority **2 :** a place to lie or lodge **:** COVERT, LAIR **3 a :** line of action **:** PLAN, TACK **b :** line of business or work **:** OCCUPATION **4 a :** terms of sale or employment **:** PRICE ⟨he sold his farm at a good ~⟩ **b :** a share of the profit of a venture (as on a whaling or fishing vessel) paid wholly or partly in lieu of wages **c :** employment on shares **5 a :** a strip or layer of leather or felt laid upon or beneath another in a harness or saddle **b :** a layer or thickness of cloth; *esp* **:** a layered pile of cloth on which patterns are laid out by cutters in the garment trade **6 a :** the amount of advance of any point in a rope strand for one complete turn **b :** the nature of a fiber rope as determined by the amount of twist put into the rope, the angle of the strands in the rope, and the angle of the threads in the strands — see HARD LAY, LONG LAY, MEDIUM LAY, ORDINARY LAY, SOFT LAY **c :** the direction in which the components of a rope or cable are laid **7 :** the way in which a thing lies or is laid in relation to something else **:** position or arrangement of parts: as **a :** topographical features and situation ⟨the houses . . . took form from the ~ of the land to which they were fastened —Isa Glenn⟩ **b :** the manner in which parts of garment patterns are laid out on the cloth for cutting **c :** the direction of tool or abrasive marks on a machined surface **8 a :** the position of a sheet to be printed relative to the printing surface **b :** the plan or scheme of arrangement of the type in a case or of the keyboard of a typesetting machine **c :** the arrangement of imposed pages on the stone or of printed pages in the signature; *also* **:** a plan showing such arrangement — called also *laydown* **d :** a guide or gage to which a sheet is laid when being fed into a printing press **9 :** the plowshare of a moldboard plow **10 a :** the state of one that lays eggs **:** the capacity to lay eggs ⟨a hen just coming into ~⟩ ⟨in full ~⟩ **b :** the act of laying an egg ⟨time of ~⟩ **11 :** a partner in sexual intercourse — usu. considered vulgar

**3lay** \"\ *past of* LIE

**4lay** \"\ *n* -S [ME, fr. OF *lai*, perh. of Scand origin; akin to ON *lag* tune, meter, layer, due place, order — more at LAW] **1 :** a simple narrative poem **:** BALLAD **2 :** MELODY **:** a melody fragment **:** SONG ⟨birds chanting their cheerful ~*s*⟩

**5lay** \"\ *adj* [ME, fr. OF *lai*, fr. LL *laicus*, fr. Gk *laikos* of the people, fr. *laos* people + *-ikos* -ic] **1 :** belonging or relating to those not in holy orders **:** not of the clergy **:** not clerical **:** not ecclesiastical ⟨politics and commerce had gradually become dominant with crusaders, and the conduct of the enterprises became more completely ~ —H.O.Taylor⟩ ⟨the Vatican not interested in supporting either the ~ republicanism of France —*Times Lit. Supp.*⟩ **2 :** of or relating to members of a religious house that are occupied chiefly with domestic or manual work — distinguished from *choir* ⟨~ brothers⟩ ⟨~ sisters⟩ **3 :** not of or from a particular profession **:** not having special training or knowledge **:** UNPROFESSIONAL **:** COMMON, ORDINARY ⟨~ public⟩ ⟨~ citizen⟩ ⟨like so many other ~ writers with little actual building experience —S.H.Van Gelder⟩ ⟨~ opinion⟩ ⟨~ vocabulary⟩ **syn** see PROFANE

**6lay** \"\ *dial Brit var of* 1LEA

**7lay** \"\ *n* -S [alter. of 4*lathe*] **1 :** a section of a loom that oscillates and carries the reed, shuttle boxes, and batten during the process of beating up; *specif* **:** the batten of a loom that beats up the newly laid filling **2** *Scot* **:** 4LATHE 1

**lay abbot** *n* **:** a layman holding title to an abbey and its revenues

**lay about** *vi* **1 :** to strike in all directions **:** hit out at random **2 :** to take steps in preparation **:** seek means **:** go about

**la·ya·ná** \,lāyə¦nä, ¦līə-\ *n, pl* **layaná** *or* **layanás** *usu cap* [Sp, of AmerInd origin] **1 :** an Arawakan people living opposite the mouth of the Apa river in Paraguay **2 :** a member of the Layaná people

**lay analyst** *n* **:** a psychoanalyst who is not a physician

**lay aside** *vt* [ME *leyen aside*, fr. *leyen* to lay + *aside*] **1 :** to put out of use or consideration **:** DISCARD, ABANDON, SHELVE ⟨plans for a new school have been *laid aside*⟩ ⟨time to *lay* old prejudices *aside* and grudges⟩ ⟨*laid aside* his pose of indifference⟩ **2 :** to set aside for special or future use **:** RESERVE, SAVE ⟨able to *lay* a few dollars *aside* each week⟩

**lay away** *vt* [ME *leyen away*, fr. *leyen* to lay + *away*] **1 :** to lay aside **2 :** to store for preservation or future use **3 :** to spread (hides) flat in tanning liquor **4 :** BURY, INTER **5 a :** to put (specified cards) in the crib in cribbage **b :** to bury (specified cards or cards worth a specified number of points) in pinochle ⟨*lay* two kings *away*⟩ ⟨*laid away* 18 points⟩

**layaway** \'==,=\ *n* -S [*lay away*] **1 :** the liquor or pit of liquor in which hides are laid away in tanning **2 :** an article of merchandise reserved for future delivery to a customer who pays a deposit and agrees to complete payment when the article is called for at a later date

**layback** \'=,=\ *n* -S [fr. the phrase *lay back*] **1 :** a combination of a receding nose and undershot jaw in certain animals (as a bulldog) **2 :** a rock-climbing maneuver in which a climber maintains his balance in a nearly horizontal position by pulling strongly against an underhold or sidehold **3 :** the backward inclination of an oarsman's body at the completion of the power phase of a stroke

**lay baptism** *n* **:** baptism administered by a member of the laity usu. under the stress of necessity (as because of the unavailability of a clergyman)

**lay bone** *n* [1*lay*] **:** either of the pubic bones of a hen

**layboy** \'=,=\ *n* [1*lay* + *boy*; prob. fr. the fact that this work was formerly done by a boy] **:** a device that stacks and jogs into even piles sheets of pulp or paper received from cutters, ruling machines, paper machines, and printing presses — called also *jogger*

**lay by** *vt* **1 :** to lay aside **:** put away **:** DISCARD **2 :** to store for future use **:** SAVE **3 a** *South & Midland* **:** to cultivate (as corn) for the last time **b :** to store (a crop) after harvesting **4 :** to lay to (a ship) ~ *vi* **:** to lay to **:** hold in the wind **:** PAUSE

**lay-by** \'=,=\ *n* -S [*lay by*] **1 :** a portion of a stream or canal widened so that boats may lie up or pass each other **2 :** a siding for empty cars (as at a mine) **3** *Brit* **:** a branch from or a widening of a road to permit vehicles to stop without obstructing traffic **4 :** LAYAWAY 2

**lay chalice** *n* **:** communion for the laity under the species of wine as well as of bread

**lay clerk** *n* **:** a member of a choir in an Anglican cathedral or collegiate church

**lay communion** *n* **:** the state of being in communion with the church as a layman; *specif* **:** the condition of Roman Catholic clerics reduced to lay status

**lay cord** *n* [1*lay*] **:** the loop of cord around the crossbar of a bookbinder's hand-sewing frame to which the sewing cord is fastened

**lay corporation** *n* **:** a corporation composed of laymen and organized for other than spiritual purposes — contrasted with *ecclesiastical corporation*

**lay day** *n* [prob. fr. 1*lay*] **1 :** one of the days allowed by the charter party for loading or unloading a vessel — compare DEMURRAGE **2 :** a day of delay in port

**lay deacon** *n* **:** one in deacon's orders who engages in secular occupations

**lay down** *vt* **1 :** to put aside or give up (something borne) **:** SURRENDER ⟨called on them to *lay* their arms *down*⟩ ⟨*laid down* his kingly power⟩ **2** *obs* **:** to put down as a wager, stake, or payment **3 a :** to construct or put in place the foundation or main framework or features of ⟨inherited tendencies . . . do not operate as they do in birds or ants to *lay down* inexorably his whole way of life —Ruth Benedict⟩ **b :** ESTABLISH, PRESCRIBE ⟨*lays down* common codes for reporting so that all countries understand each other's messages —J.M.Stagg⟩ ⟨scale *laid down* for a map⟩ **c :** to assert or command dogmatically **:** expound or state positively ⟨*lay down* the law⟩ ⟨it may be *laid down* as a maxim, that wherever a great deal can be made by the use of money —Adam Smith⟩ **d :** to lay off (sense 1) **4 :** to plant or sow (a field) with a crop; *also* **:** to plant (a crop) ⟨had already *laid* his melons *down*⟩ **5** *archaic* **:** to cause (a ship) to lie on the side — used of the wind or sea **6** *archaic* **:** to lay embroidery on **7 a :** to store or put in a supply of (as wine) in a cellar **b :** to pack for aging ⟨*lay down* sauerkraut⟩ or preservation ⟨*lay down* eggs in waterglass⟩ **8 :** to deliver (merchandise) at a specified destination **9 a :** MELD **b :** to lead or play (a card) in bridge ~ *vi* **1 :** to lie down **2 :** to meld as many matched sets as one has in rummy

**lay-down** \'=,=\ *adj* [*lay down*] *of a collar* **:** turned over

**laydown** \"\ *n* -S [*lay down*] **1 :** the arrangement of piles of book sections in sequence preparatory to gathering — called also *layout* **2 :** LAY 8c **3 :** a declarer's hand in bridge that is so easily able to fulfill his contract that he might or does expose it and claim the required number of tricks

**lay elder** *n* [5*lay*] **:** 3ELDER 4b

**1lay·er** \'lā(ə)r, 'le(ə)r, 'leə\ *n* -S [ME *leyer, legger*, fr. *leyen, leggen* to lay + *-er*] **1 :** one that lays: as **a** *obs* **:** MASON **b :** one whose work is laying something — usu. used in combination ⟨brick*layer*⟩ **c :** a hen that lays or is kept to lay eggs **d :** one who lays odds **:** BOOKMAKER **e :** a machine for twisting strands in making rope **f :** a workman who removes sheets of handmade paper from the felts after pressing — called also *layerman, layman* **g :** a member of a gun crew who lays the gun **2 a :** one thickness, course, or fold laid or lying over or under another ⟨~ of bricks⟩ ⟨~ of plaster⟩ ⟨~ of paint⟩ ⟨~ of veneer⟩ ⟨several ~*s* of clothing⟩ ⟨~*s* of an onion⟩ ⟨upper ~*s* of the atmosphere⟩ **b :** STRATUM, BED ⟨~ of clay⟩ ⟨~ of sandstone⟩ ⟨fill the dish with alternate ~*s* of potatoes and cheese⟩ **c :** HORIZON 2 **d :** any of several strata of plant forms in an ecological association ⟨a moss ~ in a bog⟩ **3 a :** a branch or shoot of a plant treated to induce rooting while still attached to the parent plant (as by mounding with soil or by bending over and covering often intermittently with soil) — compare STOOL **b :** a plant prepared by layering **4 a** *dial Eng* **:** a field in which a grass and a grain crop are planted together with the grass crop growing up after the grain is harvested **b** *archaic* **:** earth suitable for cultivation **:** SOIL **c :** LEA 2b **5** *obs* **:** an artificial oyster bed **6 :** a pit of strong tanning liquor into which hides are put on coming from the handler

**2layer** \"\ *vb* -ED/-ING/-S *vt* **:** to propagate (a plant) by means of layers — see AIR LAYERING, MARCOTTAGE ~ *vi* **1 :** to separate into layers ⟨mists ~*ed* thick about him —Stewart Toland⟩ **2** *of a plant* **:** to multiply by layering; *esp* **:** to form roots where a stem comes in contact with the ground ⟨many brambles spread by ~*ing* under natural conditions⟩

**lay·er·age** \-āərij, -eər-\ *n* -S **:** the practice or art of layering plants

**layer board** *n* **:** a board support for lead roof gutters

**layer cake** *n* **:** a fancy cake that is in layers held together by a sweet filling and that is usu. covered with frosting

**lay·ered** \'lāə(r)d, ¦le(ə)rd, ¦leəd\ *adj* [1*layer* + *-ed*] **:** having layers **:** arranged in or divided into layers **:** covered in layers ⟨the earth's crust is ~⟩ ⟨a many-*layered* social structure⟩ ⟨~ relief map in eight colors⟩

**layering** *n* -S [fr. gerund of 2*layer*] **:** the shading or coloring of the areas between contour lines of a map in a manner suggestive of progressive change for emphasizing or clarifying differences in elevation

**lay·er·man** \-āə(r)mən, -eə(-\ *n, pl* **layermen** [1*layer* + *man*] **:** LAYER 1f

**layer of langhans** *usu cap 2d L* [after Theodor *Langhans* †1915 Ger. pathologist] **:** CYTOTROPHOBLAST

**layer-on** \¦=(=)¦=\ *n, pl* **layers-on** [*lay on* + *-er*] *Brit* **:** a worker who feeds a printing press by hand

**layer-out** \¦=(=)¦=\ *n, pl* **layers-out** [*lay out* + *-er*] **:** one that lays out: as **a :** one who prepares a body for burial **b :** one who lays out articles for sorting or drying **c :** one whose work is the laying out of patterns on materials for cutting

**layer's cramp** *n* **:** lameness or leg weakness of poultry in heavy lay possibly due to nerve injury or to calcium deficiency

**layer-up** \¦=(=)¦=\ *n, pl* **layers-up** [*lay up* + *-er*] **:** one that lays up: as **a :** a worker who arranges strips or folds of material (as cloth) **b :** a worker who glues sheets of veneer to make plywood

**lay·ette** \(')lā¦et\ *n* -S [F, fr. MF, small box, small drawer, fr. *laye* box, drawer (fr. MD *laeye, lade* box) + *-ette*; MD *laeye, lade* akin to MHG *lade* box, ON *hlatha* barn — more at LATHE (barn)] **1 :** a complete outfit of clothing and equipment for a newborn infant **2 :** a special web spun by some spiders for the use of the newly hatched spiderlings

**lay fee** *n* [ME, fr. 5*lay* + *fee*] **:** a fee in land held on condition of the rendering of secular as opposed to religious services — compare FRANKALMOIGN, PETER'S PENCE

**lay figure** *n* [*lay* (fr. 2*layman*) + *figure*] **1 :** a jointed model of the human body that may be put in any attitude and that is used by artists as a model for showing the disposition of drapery — compare DUMMY **2 :** one who serves the will of others without independent volition **:** a person or fictitious character of no marked individuality **:** PUPPET, DUMMY

**layfolk** \'=,=\ *n, pl in constr* [ME, fr. 5*lay* + *folk*] **:** ordinary people **:** LAYMEN ⟨decreed that no ~ should possess books of scripture —G.G.Coulton⟩

**lay·ia** \'lā(y)ə\ *n, cap* [NL, fr. George T. *Lay*, 19th cent. Eng. botanist + NL *-ia*] **:** a genus of mostly Californian annual herbs (family Compositae) having showy heads of yellow or white ray flowers — see TIDYTIPS

**lay in** *vt* **1 :** to store up **:** lay by ⟨*lay in* an ample supply of groceries⟩ **2** *archaic* **:** to assert as a claim **3 a :** to paint in roughly subject to finishing, elaboration, or addition **b :** to put (masses of color) on a canvas ⟨helped him to *lay* the background blues and browns *in*⟩ **4 a :** to heel in (a plant) **b :** 4TRAIN 2 **5** *Brit* **:** to shut down or discontinue working (a colliery or coal pit)

**laying** *pres part of* LAY

**laying duck** *n* **:** EIDER 1

**laying on of hands 1 :** a form used in consecrating to office, in the rite of confirmation, and in blessing persons and consisting in placing the hands upon the head of the person on whom the divine blessing is invoked **2 :** a Mormon rite used in conferring the Holy Ghost upon one baptized and performed only by a member of the Melchizedek priesthood **3 :** the application of a spiritual healer's hands to the patient's body

**laying press** *n* **:** LYING PRESS

**laying top** *n* **:** a conical grooved wooden block placed between the strands in laying a rope

**laylight** \'=,=\ *n* [1*lay*] **:** a glazed panel usu. set flush with the ceiling for admitting natural or artificial light

**lay·lock** \'lālək, -ā,läk\ *dial var of* LILAC

**lay lord** *n* **:** a British peer who is not a law lord

**lay low** *vt* **1 :** to bring or strike to earth **:** FELL ⟨hurricane winds are likely to *lay low* the balloon⟩ **2 :** to knock out of a fight or out of action ⟨flu had *laid* him *low*⟩ **3 :** KILL ⟨*laid low* six or seven jackdaws —Ian Niall⟩ ~ *vi* **:** to lie low

**1lay·man** \'lāmən\ *n, pl* **lay·men** \-mən *sometimes* -,men\ [ME *lay man*, fr. 5*lay* + *man*] **1 :** one of the laity as distinguished from the clergy **2 :** one not belonging to some particular profession or not expert in some branch of knowledge or art

**2layman** \"\ *n* [D *leeman, ledeman*, fr. *lee-, lede-* (fr. *lid* limb, part of the body, fr. MD *lit, let*) + *man*, fr. MD — more at LITH, MAN] *obs* **:** LAY FIGURE

**3layman** \"\ *n, pl* **laymen** [1*lay* + *man*] **:** LAYER 1f

**layne** \'lān\ *vb* -ED/-ING/-S [ME *laynen*, fr. ON *leyna* to conceal; akin to OE *lȳgnan* to deny, OHG *lougnen*, Goth *laugnjan* to deny, ON *ljūga* to lie, tell a lie — more at LIE] *vt, chiefly Scot* **:** to hold back, conceal, or disguise (information) ~ *vi, chiefly Scot* **:** to refrain from telling something

**lay off** *vt* **1 :** to mark or measure off; *specif* **:** to draw on the mold-loft floor to full dimensions the lines or outlines of (a ship and its members) **2 :** to steer (a ship) away from the shore or from a pier or another ship **3 a** *of a bookmaker* **:** to place all or part of (a bet accepted) with another bookmaker in order to reduce the risk **b :** to subscribe to or cause subscriptions to be made to (a new issue of securities offered to a corporation's stockholders) so as to reduce the liability of the issue's underwriters **4 :** to distribute (a coat of paint) evenly **5** *Midland* **:** PLAN, INTEND ⟨*laid off* to go to town the next day⟩ **6 a :** to halt or suspend operation of (as a mill or factory) **b :** to cease to employ (a worker) usu. temporarily because of slack in production and without prejudice to the worker — usu. distinguished from *fire* **7 :** to add (a card or cards) in rummy to sets already melded **8 a :** to refrain or cease from pursuing or annoying **:** let alone ⟨if you'll *lay off* me I'll promise not to do it again⟩ **b :** AVOID, SHUN, QUIT ⟨advised to *lay off* smoking and alcohol⟩ ~ *vi* **1 :** to lie off **2 a :** to stop work ⟨time to *lay off*⟩ **b :** to take time off or a rest from working ⟨*lays off* a couple of days each month⟩ or activity ⟨weekends he just likes to *lay off*⟩

**lay·off** \'=,=\ *n* -s [*lay off*] **1 a :** the act of laying off an employee or a work force **b :** OFF-SEASON, SHUTDOWN **2 a :** a period of being away from or out of work **b :** a period of being out of an activity or competition ⟨champion was badly out of condition from a long ~⟩

**lay of the land :** the disposition of circumstances which one is considering ⟨wanted to know more about the *lay of the land* before investing⟩

**lay on** *vt* **1 :** to apply to or spread on a surface ⟨*lay* a coat of paint *on*⟩ ⟨*lay on* liniment to soothe his lameness⟩ **2 :** to take on or gain (as flesh, fat) ⟨*laid* 10 pounds *on* in a month⟩ **3** *Brit* **a :** to provide for the supply of (as water, gas, electricity) ⟨a 3-room flat with gas and hot water *laid on*⟩ **b :** to provide or make arrangements for (as a convenience, entertainment, or service) ⟨stage shows and open-air dancing all *laid on* —Richard Huson⟩ **4 a :** to feed (sheets) into a printing press **b :** to place (a form) on the bed of a press ~ *vi* **:** ATTACK, BEAT ⟨seized a club and began to *lay on* for dear life⟩

**lay out** *vt* **1 :** to extend or stretch out at length: as **a :** to prepare (a corpse) for burial **b :** to knock flat or unconscious ⟨can *lay* him *out* in the first round⟩ **2 a :** to plan in detail **:** map out ⟨*lay out* an election campaign⟩ ⟨the work for tomorrow is all *laid out*⟩ **b :** to make an arrangement of (copy, illustration) for printing **c :** to set (book sections) in the right order for gathering **3 :** to mark (work) for drilling, machining, filing to specified contour and dimensions **4 :** ARRANGE, DESIGN ⟨walks, flower beds, and lawn were *laid out* in a formal pattern⟩ **5 :** DISPLAY, EXHIBIT **6** *Midland* **:** PROPOSE, PLAN, INTEND ⟨was *laying out* to look for another job⟩ **7 :** to make an expenditure of (a sum of money) **:** SPEND ~ *vi South & Midland* **:** to absent oneself (as from school) without permission

**lay·out** \'=,=\ *n* -s [*lay out*] **1 a :** the act or process of laying out or planning in detail **b :** the plan or design or arrangement of something that is laid out: as (1) **:** a plan or design to show the arrangement and general appearance of something to be produced or reproduced graphically (as by printing or photography) ⟨an artist's ~ of an advertisement⟩ ⟨a typographer's ~ of a projected book⟩ (2) **:** arrangement of matter to be reproduced; *esp* **:** the placement of negatives preparatory to plate making (as for offset or gravure printing) (3) **:** the position of men, machines, and materials within a manufacturing plant in relation to the flow of goods in process of manufacture **2 :** something that is laid out: as **a :** an area usu. of green cloth marked to indicate spaces on which may be placed bets on various contingencies (as in roulette) **b :** cards dealt (as in solitaire) into a prescribed pattern on which plays may be made **:** TABLEAU **c :** something displayed **:** SPREAD ⟨the dinner was a fine ~⟩ **d :** ESTABLISHMENT, PLACE ⟨lives in an elaborate ~ including swimming pool, private golf course, tennis court, acres of woods⟩ **3 :** LAYDOWN **4 a :** a set or collection of tools or apparatus ⟨miner's ~⟩ ⟨opium ~⟩ **b** *chiefly South & West* **:** OUTFIT, GANG **5 :** a body position used in diving, swimming, and gymnastics in which the trunk is extended, the head is back, the back is arched, and the arms are extended sideways — compare ¹¹PIKE, TUCK

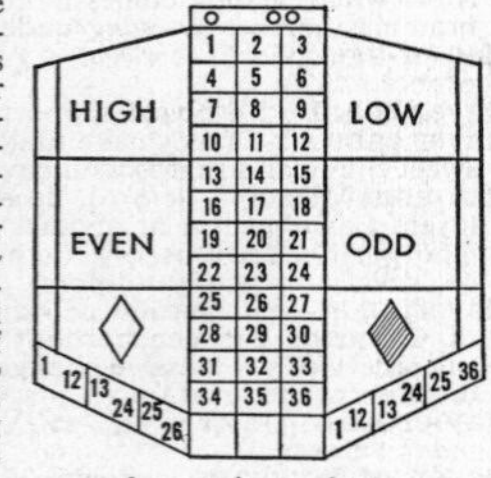

layout in roulette

**layout man** *n* **1 :** one who plans the layout of material to be printed or reproduced **2 :** a worker who marks out patterns on metal, stone, glass, textiles, or other material in preparation for such subsequent operations as cutting, bending, punching: as **a :** one who outlines on stock lumber the shape of furniture or other parts **b :** one who marks guide lines on metal parts to indicate material to be removed in machining **c :** one who uses a guiding design to prepare settings for stones on models of jewelry **d :** one who indicates by chalk lines the way in which steel plates are to be cut for use in ship or locomotive building — called also *duplicator*

**lay over** *vt* **1 :** POSTPONE ⟨voted to *lay* the measure *over* until the following meeting⟩ **2** *dial* **:** EXCEL, SURPASS ⟨it *lays over* anything else of the kind⟩ ~ *vi* **:** to lie over

**¹lay·over** \'=,==\ *n* -s [origin unknown] *dial* **:** something whose identity is intentionally concealed — used typically in the phrase *layovers to catch meddlers* as an evasive answer to a question from a child

**²layover** \"\ *n* -s [*lay over*] **:** a stay or wait for a period in a place **:** STOPOVER ⟨~ between trains⟩

**lay preacher** *n* **:** an unordained preacher

**lay race** *n* **:** the part of a lay on which the shuttle travels in weaving — called also *shuttle race*

**lay reader** *n* **:** a layman authorized by a bishop to read parts of the public service in an Anglican or Protestant Episcopal church

**lay rector** *n* **:** a layman who receives the tithes of a parish or in whom the rectory is vested

**lays** *pres 3d sing of* LAY, *pl of* LAY

**lay·san albatross** \'lī,sän-\ *n, usu cap L* [fr. *Laysan*, islet in Leeward Islands, Hawaii] **:** an albatross (*Diomedea immutabilis*) that is white with dark back and wings and is found on Laysan and adjacent islands of the Pacific ocean

**lay sermon** *n* **:** an address or essay on moral and religious questions by a layman

**layshaft** \'=,=\ *n* [prob. fr. ¹*lay*] **:** COUNTERSHAFT 2

**laystall** \'=,=\ *n, Brit* **:** a place where rubbish and dung are deposited

**lay to** *vt* [ME *leyen to*, fr. *leyen* to lay + *to*] **:** to bring (a ship) into the wind and hold stationary except for drifting ~ *vi* **1 :** to lie to **2 :** to apply or exert oneself ⟨told to get a shovel and *lay to* with the others⟩ **3 :** to deal blows **:** strike out ⟨*laying to* right and left with a club⟩

**lay underwriter** *n* **:** an underwriter of life or accident or health insurance who is without medical training

**lay up** *vt* **1 :** to save or put by for future use **:** store up **:** lay away **:** HOARD, ACCUMULATE, SAVE ⟨*lay* not *up* for yourselves treasures upon earth —Mt. 6:19 (AV)⟩ **2 a** *obs* **:** IMPRISON **b :** to disable or confine with illness or injury ⟨*laid up* with a bad knee⟩ **3 :** to take (as a ship) out of active service ⟨when you *lay* the yacht *up* it is best to remove the motor —Peter Heaton⟩ **4 a :** to leave (a field) in a specified condition ⟨*laid up* for pasture⟩ **b :** to reserve (a field) for a crop **5 a :** to set (as stones, bricks) one on top of another (as in a wall) **b :** to construct (as a wall) by laying bricks or stones ⟨the front was *laid up* in ashlar⟩ **c :** to spread (cloth) in a pile of many layers — compare LAY 5b **d :** to assemble (layers of veneer or cores) after application of the glue or adhesive in preparation for pressing and bonding plywood **6 :** to drive (a horse) in a heat of a trotting race so as neither to win nor to be distanced **7 :** to form (a hot rivet that is in position) by striking several hard blows ~ *vi* **1 :** to lie up **2 :** to shape the course of a ship ⟨time to *lay up* for home⟩

**lay–up** \'=,=\ *n* -s [*lay up*] **:** the action of laying up or the condition of being laid up: as **a :** the condition (as of a ship) of being set aside out of active service **b :** an assembly of layers of veneer or cores for pressing **c :** a jumping one-hand shot in basketball made off the backboard from close under the basket

**lay vicar** *n* **:** CLERK VICAR

**laywoman** \'=,==\ *n, pl* **laywomen :** a woman who is unordained and thus a member of the laity in distinction from the clergy

**laz** \'läz\ *or* **la·ze** \-zə\ *or* **la·zi** \-zē\ *n, pl* **laz** *or* **lazes** *or* **laze** *or* **lazi** *or* **lazis** *usu cap* **1 a :** a Muslim Kartvelian Sunnite people of Caucasia found on both sides of the Turkish-Soviet frontier **b :** a member of such people **2 :** the south Caucasic language of the Laz people

**lazar** \'lazə(r), 'lāz-\ *n* -s [ME, fr. ML *lazarus*, fr. LL *Lazarus*, beggar with sores mentioned in Lk 16:20] **:** a person afflicted with a repulsive disease; *specif* **:** LEPER

**laz·a·ret·to** \,lazə'red·(,)ō\ *or* **laz·a·ret** *also* **laz·a·rette** \,lazə'ret\ *n* -s [It dial. (Venetian) *lazareto*, alter. (influenced by It *lazzaro* leper, fr. ML *lazarus*) of *nazareto*, fr. *Santa Maria di Nazaret*, church in Venice that maintained a well-known hospital] **1** *usu lazaretto* **:** a hospital for contagious diseases **2 :** a building or a ship used for detention in quarantine **3** *usu lazaret* **:** a space in a ship between decks used as a storeroom

**lazar house** *n* **:** LAZARETTO 1; *esp* **:** a hospital for lepers

**laz·a·rist** \'lazərəst\ *n* -s *usu cap* [College of St. *Lazare*, Paris, occupied by the Vincentians from 1632 to 1792 + E *-ist*] **:** VINCENTIAN 1

**lazarlike** \'===,=\ *adj* **:** full of sores **:** LEPROUS

**laz·a·rus** \'laz(ə)rəs\ *n* -ES *often cap* [ML] **:** a diseased esp. leprous beggar **:** LAZAR

**¹laze** \'lāz\ *vb* -ED/-ING/-S [back-formation fr. ¹*lazy*] *vi* **:** to act or lie lazily ⟨*lazing* in the sun⟩ **:** LAZY, IDLE ~ *vt* **:** to pass (as time) in idleness or relaxation ⟨~ away whole days⟩

**²laze** \"\ *n* -s **:** the act or state of lazing ⟨a long ~ at the beach⟩ **:** IDLENESS, LAZINESS, RELAXATION

**la·zi·ly** \'lāzəlē, -li\ *adv* **:** in a lazy manner ⟨drifting ~ downstream in the peaceful atmosphere⟩

**la·zi·ness** \-zēnəs, -zin-\ *n* -ES **:** the quality or state of being lazy

**la·zule** \'la(,)zhül\ *n* -s [ML *lazulum* — more at LAPIS LAZULI] **:** LAPIS LAZULI

**lazuli** *n* -s [by shortening] **:** LAPIS LAZULI

**lazuli bunting** *or* **lazuli finch** *n* **:** a finch (*Passerina amoena*) of the western U.S. having the head, neck, and upper parts blue, buff on the breast, and a white belly

**laz·u·line** \'lazə,lēn, 'lazhə-, -,līn\ *adj* [*lazuli* + *-ine*] **:** of the color of lapis lazuli

**laz·u·lite** \-,līt\ *n* -s [G *lazulith*, fr. *lazu-* (fr. ML *lazulum*) + *-lith*] **:** an azure-blue mineral $(Mg,Fe)Al_2(PO_4)_2(OH)_2$ occurring in small masses or in monoclinic crystals, consisting of hydrous phosphate of aluminum, iron, and magnesium, and isomorphous with scorzalite (hardness 5–6, sp. gr. 3.06–3.12) — **laz·u·lit·ic** \,==='lid·ik\ *adj*

**laz·u·rite** \-,rīt\ *n* -s [G *lasurit*, fr. ML *lazur* lapis lazuli (fr. Ar *lāzaward*) + G *-it* -ite — more at AZURE] **:** a mineral $(Na,Ca)_8(Al,Si)_{12}O_{24}(S,SO_4)$ occurring as the chief constituent of lapis lazuli, isomorphous with sodalite, and composed of a sodium silicate containing sulfur

**¹la·zy** \'lāzē, -zi\ *adj* -ER/-EST [perh. fr. MLG *lasich* feeble, faint; akin to MHG *erleswen* to become weak, ON *lasinn* dilapidated, Goth *lasiws* weak, Bulg *loš* bad] **1 a :** disliking physical or mental exertion **:** not energetic or vigorous **:** INDOLENT, INACTIVE ⟨having to deal with a ~ slut, might feel strongly tempted to take up the nearest broomstick —G.B. Shaw⟩ ⟨gifted but ~ artist⟩ **b :** encouraging or causing inactivity or indolence ⟨~ summer day⟩ ⟨~ weather⟩ ⟨~ chair⟩ **c :** marked by lack of activity ⟨spent a ~ weekend at home⟩ ⟨~ expedient⟩ **2 :** moving slowly and without or as if without energy **:** SLUGGISH ⟨~ river⟩ ⟨spoke with a ~ articulation⟩ **3 :** not firmly erect **:** DROOPING, LAX ⟨~ corn⟩ ⟨a rabbit with ~ ears⟩ ⟨habitually ~ posture⟩ **4** *of a letter or number* **:** placed on its side ⟨~ E livestock brand⟩ ⟨~ 2 on a bank note⟩ — see BRAND illustration

**syn** LAZY, INDOLENT, SLOTHFUL, and FAINEANT can all signify not easily aroused to responsible, purposeful activity. LAZY stresses an aversion to work and a habitual tendency to idleness ⟨we were too *lazy* . . . We passed our indolent days leaving everything to somebody else —H.G.Wells⟩ ⟨the lion is by nature so essentially *lazy* that he will never do more hunting than he feels to be necessary —James Stevenson-Hamilton⟩ ⟨even when the heat is not extreme, a sudden rise may make us uncomfortable and *lazy*, as often occurs in the spring —Ellsworth Huntington⟩ INDOLENT implies a constitutional love of ease and inactivity or dislike of purposeful activity ⟨an *indolent* son sleeping away his life⟩ ⟨he was an *indolent* man, who lived only to eat, drink, and play at cards —Jane Austen⟩ ⟨life is more leisured without being essentially *indolent* —*Amer. Guide Series: Va.*⟩ SLOTHFUL suggests temperamental inactivity or slowness when action or speed is called for ⟨he would use political means to jog a *slothful* conscience and marshal its forces —V.L.Parrington⟩ ⟨waiting for the hostler's *slothful* boy to bring out the horses —*Amer. Guide Series: Va.*⟩ FAINEANT, now infrequent, implies a disposition to do nothing even under urgency ⟨in a typical statement of the *faineant* judicial philosophy he sometimes espouses, [he] refused to put judgment on so slender a foundation —E.V.Rostov⟩ ⟨to avoid all issues by electing a *faineant* mayor and city council⟩

**²lazy** \"\ *vb* -ED/-ING/-ES **:** to move or lie lazily **:** LAZE

**lazyback** \'==,=\ *n* **:** a backrest attached to a carriage seat

**lazybed** \'===,=\ *n* **1** *chiefly Brit* **:** a small plot of land tilled by hand on rocky ground **2** *chiefly Brit* **:** a plot of potatoes or other crop not tilled but covered with soil, leaves, or sawdust

**lazybird** \'===,=\ *n* **:** COWBIRD

**lazy board** *n* **:** a projecting seat for the driver placed on the left side of a freight wagon within reach of the brake

**lazybones** \'===,=\ *n pl but sing or pl in constr* **:** a lazy person

**lazy crab** *n* **:** a large sedentary crab (*Parthenope horrida*) of the East and West Indies having long heavy chelipeds and rough and spiny shell

**lazy daisy stitch** *n* **:** an embroidery stitch formed by an elongated loop held down at the free end by a small stitch

lazy daisy stitch

**lazy eight** *n* **:** an aerial maneuver in which a plane by gradual climbing, banking, and turning traces an imaginary figure eight on its side

**lazy guy** *n* **:** a guy for steadying the boom of a fore-and-aft sail

**la·zy·ish** \'lāzēish, -zi·ish\ *adj* **:** somewhat lazy

**lazy jack** *n* **1 :** a device that compensates for expansion and contraction (as in a pipe line) consisting of two linked bell cranks pivoted at the vertices of their complementary angles **2 :** an often forked line reaching from the masthead or the topping lift on each side of a fore-and-aft sail to about the middle of the boom to confine the sail when it is lowered — usu. used in pl.

**lazy painter** *n* **:** a long painter led from well forward of a boom to a boat riding to one of the guess-warps of that boom to permit hauling the boat up to a ladder

**lazy–shark** \'==,=\ *n, Africa* **:** CAT SHARK 1

**lazy squaw stitch** *n* **:** a stitch used in coiled basketwork consisting essentially of loops alternately encircling one and two coils

**lazy strap** *n* **:** a looped strap attached to the breeching of a harness through which the traces are passed to prevent sagging

**lazy su·san** \,==ˈsüzᵊn\ *n, usu cap S* [¹*lazy* + *Susan* (the name)] **1 :** MUFFIN STAND **2 :** a revolving tray placed on a dining table for serving food, condiments, relishes; *broadly* **:** any similar revolving device (as for storage shelves or display racks)

lazy susan 2

**lazy tongs** *n pl* **:** a series of jointed and pivoted bars capable of great extension used orig. for picking up something at a distance; *broadly* **:** any of various devices adjustable in similar manner

**laz·za·ro·ne** \,lazə'rōnē, ,lädzə-\ *n, pl* **lazzaro·ni** \-nē\ [It, aug. of *lazzaro* beggar, leper, fr. ML *lazarus* — more at LAZAR] **:** one of the homeless idlers of Naples who live by chance work or begging

**laz·zo** \'läd(,)zō\ *n, pl* **laz·zi** \-(,)zē\ [It, perh. fr. Sp *lazo* lasso, noose, snare, fr. L *laqueus* noose, snare — more at DELIGHT] **:** a piece of interpolated comic business or dialogue in the commedia dell'arte — compare BURLA

**lb** [L *libra*] *abbr* pound

**LB** *abbr* **1** landing barge **2** left on base **3** leg bye **4** letter box **5** light bomber **6** local board

**LBF** *abbr* lactobacillus bulgaricus factor

**LBP** *abbr* length between perpendiculars

**lbr** *abbr* **1** labor **2** lumber

**LC** *abbr* **1** label clause **2** lance corporal **3** landing craft **4** law courts **5** left center **6** letter of credit **7** level crossing **8** lightly canceled **9** line of communication **10** *often not cap* [L *loco citato*] in the place cited **11** lord chamberlain **12** lord chancellor **13** *often not cap* lower case

**l casei factor** *n, cap L* [*l* initial of *lactobacillus*] **:** LACTOBACILLUS CASEI FACTOR

**l c classification** *n, usu cap L & 1st C* **:** LIBRARY OF CONGRESS CLASSIFICATION

**LCD** *abbr* least common denominator; lowest common denominator

**lce** *abbr* lance

**LCJ** *abbr* lord chief justice

**lcl** *abbr* local

**LCL** *abbr* less-than-carload; less-than-carload lot

**LCM** *abbr* least common multiple; lowest common multiple

**LCT** *abbr* local civil time

**ld** *abbr* **1** land **2** lead **3** limited **4** load **5** lord

**LD** *abbr* **1** [L *laus Deo*] praise be to God **2** left defense **3** lethal dose **4** line of departure **5** line of duty **6** local delivery **7** long delay **8** long distance

**LDC** *abbr* lower dead center

**ldg** *abbr* **1** landing **2** leading **3** loading **4** lodging

**LDO** *abbr* limited duty officer

**ldp** *abbr* **1** ladyship **2** lordship

**ldr** *abbr* leader

**ldry** *abbr* laundry

**LDS** *abbr* **1** Latter-day Saints **2** [L *laus Deo semper*] praise to God always

**-le** \əl, ³l\ *vb suffix* **-led; -led; -ling** \(ə)liŋ, (ᵊ)l-\ **-les** [ME *-len*, fr. OE *-lian*; akin to OHG *-ilōn*, *-alōn*, verb suffixes indicating repeated action] — indicating repeated action or movement esp. of a trifling or small-scale character ⟨prattle⟩ ⟨wriggle⟩ ⟨hobble⟩

**le** *abbr* lease

**LE** *abbr* **1** labor exchange **2** leading edge **3** left end **4** low efficiency **5** low explosive **6** lupus erythematosus

**¹lea** *or* **ley** \'lē, 'lā\ *n* -s [ME *lee*, *leye*, fr. OE *lēah*; akin to OHG *lōh* thicket of shrubs, L *lucus* grove, Skt *loka* open space, world, L *lux* light — more at LIGHT] **1 :** GRASSLAND, PASTURE ⟨the lowing herd winds slowly o'er the ~ —Thomas Gray⟩ **2** *usu ley* [ME *leye*, fr. *leye*, adj.] **a :** arable land sown to grasses or clover for hay or grazing and usu. plowed and planted with other crops after two or more years **b :** a crop of grass or clover raised on cultivated land — called also *layer*

**²lea** \'lē\ *adj* [ME *leye*, fr. OE *lǣg-* (in *lǣghrycg* lea rig); akin to OE *licgan* to lie — more at LIE] **:** lying under grass **:** FALLOW, UNPLOWED

**³lea** \"\ *n* -s [ME *lee*, perh. back-formation fr. *lees* unit of measure of thread, leash (taken as a plural) — more at LEASH] **1 :** a unit of 300 yards used in counting linen yarns — compare COUNT 8 a **2 :** a unit of 120 yards of a yarn used for testing

**⁴lea** \", 'lā\ *n* -s [ME *ley*, fr. ON *lē*; akin to MLG *lē* sickle, OE *losian* to get lost, perish — more at LOSE] *dial Eng* **:** SCYTHE

**⁵lea** \'lē\ *chiefly Scot var of* LEAVE

**lea** *abbr* **1** league **2** leather **3** leave

**LEA** *abbr* local education authority

**¹leach** *var of* LEECH

**²leach** \'lēch\ *n* -ES [in sense 1, prob. alter. of ¹*letch*; in other senses, fr. ³*leach*] **1 a :** a perforated vessel to hold wood ashes through which water is passed to extract the lye **b :** a pit or tub in which ooze is made by steeping tanbark in water **2 a :** LEACHATE **b :** the saturated brine that is drained from the salt or left in the pan when the salt is drawn out **3 :** the process or an instance of leaching ⟨is about 60°F. for the last ~ —R.N.Shreve⟩

**³leach** \"\ *vb* -ED/-ING/-ES *vt* **1 a :** to subject to the action of percolating water or other liquid in order to separate the soluble components **:** LIXIVIATE ⟨~ an ore⟩ — compare EXTRACT 1e **b :** to dissolve out by the action of a percolating liquid — often used with *out* ⟨~ out alkali from ashes⟩; compare EXTRACT 1d **c** (1) **:** to remove nutritive or harmful elements from (soil) by percolation ⟨soil ~*ed* of its salts by torrential rains⟩ (2) **:** to remove (nutritive or harmful elements) from soil by percolation — often used with *out* ⟨~*ed* out the beneficial nutrients —*Harper's*⟩ ⟨~*ing* excess salt out of the soil —D.W.Israelsen⟩ **2 :** to draw out or remove as if by percolation ⟨the evil . . . is ~*ed* out of him —I.L.Salomon⟩ **:** draw out or remove something from as if by percolation ⟨the teeth of women during pregnancy are not ~*ed* of their lime salts —F.L.Hise⟩ ~ *vi* **:** to pass out or through by percolation ⟨will not ~ out of the wood with rainwater —*Monsanto Mag.*⟩

**leach·abil·i·ty** \,lēchə'biləd·ē\ *n* **:** the quality or state of being leachable ⟨experiments on the ~ of salts —*Experiment Station Record*⟩

**leach·able** \'lēchəbəl\ *adj* **:** capable of being leached

**leach·ate** \'lē,chāt\ *n* -s **:** the liquid that has percolated through soil or other medium **:** a solution obtained by leaching

**leach·er** \'lēchə(r)\ *n* -s **:** one that leaches: as **a :** a worker who makes tanning liquor by leaching — called also *leachman* **b :** a worker who leaches minerals from crushed ore **c :** a worker who leaches soda ash from black ash

**leach house** *n* **:** the part of a tannery where leaching is performed

**leaching** *n* -s **1 a :** the process or an instance of separating the soluble components from some material by percolation **b :** the process of extracting tannin by boiling ground-up bark or other vegetable tanning material in water **c :** the process or an instance of removing nutritive or harmful elements from soil by percolation **2 a :** a product of leaching ⟨swamp water, colored by the ~s of gum, cypress, maple, and juniper —*Amer. Guide Series: N.C.*⟩

**leach·man** \'lēchmən\ *n, pl* **leachmen :** LEACHER

**leach's petrel** \'lēchəz-\ *or* **leach's petrel** *n, usu cap L* [after William E. *Leach* †1836 Eng. naturalist] **:** a petrel (*Oceanodroma leucorhoa*) distinguished from the storm petrel by its larger size, forked tail, longer wings, and distinctive bounding flight

**leachy** \'lēchē\ *adj* -ER/-EST [³*leach* + *-y*] **:** permitting liquids to pass by percolation **:** not capable of retaining water **:** POROUS, PERVIOUS ⟨a ~ soil⟩

**¹lead** \'lēd\ *vb* **led** \'led\ **led** \'led\ **leading** \'lēdiŋ, -dēŋ\ **leads** \'lēdz\ [ME *leden*, fr. OE *lǣdan*; akin to OHG *leiten* to lead, ON *leitha*; causative fr. the root of OE *līthan* to go, OHG *līdan* to go, pass, ON *lītha*, Goth *-leithan*; akin to Av *raēθ-* to die, Toch A *lit-* to go away] *vt* **1 a :** to cause to go with oneself **:** take or bring with use of duress ⟨*led* the condemned man to the scaffold⟩ ⟨*led* them captives to a distant land⟩ **b** *dial Brit* (1) **:** to convey (stone, coal, or other materials) in a vehicle (2) **:** to convey (a crop) from the field (as to a place of storage) **2 a** (1) **:** to guide on a way **:** show the way to a place esp. by going with or in advance of ⟨*led* the officers to his hiding place⟩ ⟨can a blind man ~ a blind man —Lk 6: 39 (RSV)⟩ — often used in the phrase *lead the way* ⟨he *led* the way and we followed⟩ (2) **:** to serve as a passage for **:** conduct to some place or in some direction ⟨a road ~*ing* the traveler to the heart of the city⟩ (3) **:** to guide by indicating the way **:** mark out or show the way to ⟨*led* through the fog by the distant lights of the city⟩ (4) **:** to direct or draw the gaze or attention of ⟨we are *led* on from page to page —R.S.Hillyer⟩ ⟨a straight line . . . can ~ the eye in two directions only —C.W.H.Johnson⟩ **b :** to guide or conduct with the hand or by means of some physical contact or connection ⟨a third native . . . to ~ your pony —James Stevenson-Hamilton⟩ **c** (1) **:** to guide or constrain in its passage or course ⟨a rope is *led* around the curve⟩ (2) **:** to conduct or serve as the way or channel for ⟨pipes . . . *led* the water into canals —G.W. Murray⟩ **3 a :** to go through (life or some other period of time) **:** PASS, LIVE ⟨there he *led* a very peaceful existence⟩ ⟨*led* one of the most dramatic careers of criminal history —Anne Brooks⟩ **b :** to cause (another person) to pass a life of a particular kind ⟨she *led* him a dog's life⟩ ⟨such a life as that man *led* me⟩ **4 a** (1) **:** to go with usu. at the head and direct the operations of (an armed force or other expedition) ⟨*led* a cavalry group in a raid behind enemy lines⟩ ⟨*led* a safari into little-known territory⟩ (2) **:** to march in front of **:** go at the head of ⟨a tall drum major *led* the band⟩ — often used in the phrases *lead the way* ⟨*led* the way in the adoption of social legislation⟩ and *lead the van* ⟨*led* the van in solving problems susceptible of certain knowledge —G.C.Sellery⟩ (3) **:** to have the first place in ⟨~s the world in the production of steel⟩ ⟨*led* the league for the most double plays —*Current Biog.*⟩ (4) **:** to have a margin of advantage or superiority over ⟨*led* his closest opponent by 200 votes⟩ **b** (1) **:** to take a principal or directing part in **:** have charge or direction of ⟨*led* a successful campaign to suspend import duties —*Current Biog.*⟩ ⟨*led* the minority party in the senate⟩ (2) **:** to guide by performance of one's own part ⟨*led* the congregation in prayers⟩ ⟨*led* the audience in singing the national anthem⟩ (3) **:** DIRECT, CONDUCT ⟨*led* the orchestra in a poor performance of the overture⟩ (4) **:** to guide or direct in a course of study, discussion, or similar group activity ⟨~ a Sunday-school class⟩ ⟨~ a discussion group in foreign affairs⟩ **c :** to suggest to (a witness) the answer desired by putting leading questions ⟨counsel is ~*ing* this witness, putting the words in her mouth —Erle Stanley Gardner⟩ **5 a** (1) **:** to bring by reasoning, cogency, or other influence to some conclusion or condition ⟨a heart-shaped Venetian map . . . *led* him to the happy belief that the land he discovered was in eastern Asia —Tad Szulc⟩ ⟨reflection *led* him to a better understanding of the problem⟩ (2) **:** to prevail upon **:** CAUSE, INDUCE ⟨situations which can ~ an inquiring mind to engage in aesthetic thought —Hunter Mead⟩ ⟨this reasoning ~*s* him to propose the creation of a new profession —*Jour. of Accountancy*⟩ **b :** ENTICE, ALLURE ⟨*led* him into evil courses⟩ ⟨*led* him astray⟩ **6 :** to play as the first card or suit of a game, round, or trick ⟨going to ~ trumps⟩ **7 a :** to aim a weapon in front of (a moving object) ⟨~ a duck⟩ ⟨~ an airplane⟩ **b :** to pass a ball ahead of (an intended receiver) so that it can be received on the run **c :** to be in advance of in phase ⟨in a capacitive circuit the current may ~ the voltage⟩ **8 :** to direct (a blow) at an opponent in boxing **~** *vi* **1 a** (1) **:** to guide or conduct someone or something along a way ⟨you ~ and we'll follow⟩ (2) **:** to guide or direct someone in reference to action or opinion ⟨follow the truth of scholarship wherever it may ~ —*New School for Social Research Bull.*⟩ ⟨that sort of project . . . ~*s* on to new fields of endeavor —B.G.Gallagher⟩ **b** (1) **:** to serve as a passage ⟨flagstone walks ~ to the gateway —*Amer. Guide Series: La.*⟩ ⟨a narrow covered bridge ~*s* across the . . . river —*Amer. Guide Series: Vt.*⟩ ⟨short lanes that ~ to the water —C.R.Sumner⟩ (2) **:** to have a specified terminus, course, or direction **:** RUN ⟨a long valley ~*ing* up into the heart of the main range —E.E.Shipton⟩ ⟨swampy canals ~ on either side to vast bayous —Tom Marvel⟩ ⟨does the road ~ uphill all the way —O.W.Holmes †1935⟩ ⟨rang by means of a thick yellow rope which *led* down from the belfry —Grace Metalious⟩ ⟨the line ~*s* as if the whale were ahead of the boat when in reality he is right under it —M.A.Chippendale⟩ (3) **:** to serve as an entrance, channel, or connection ⟨ran to the door that *led* to the kitchen —Kenneth Roberts⟩ ⟨his eyes on the glass window ~*ing* into the reception room —Jane Woodfin⟩ **2 a :** to be first or foremost in some respect ⟨this state ~*s* in wealth and population⟩ ⟨the incumbents were ~*ing* in all races⟩ **b** (1) **:** to begin or open a passage or course of action ⟨*led* with "What a superb literal translation" —Bennett Cerf⟩ — usu. used with *off* ⟨*led* off for the southern opponents of the measure —*Current Biog.*⟩ ⟨will ~ off with a Christmas story —Richard Bissell⟩ ⟨*led* off at bat for the home team⟩ (2) **:** to play the first card of a trick, round, or game (3) **:** to direct the first of a series of blows at an opponent in boxing **3 :** to tend toward a definite result **:** EVENTUATE — used with *to* ⟨his plan need not ~ to fresh delays —Kenneth Fairfax⟩ ⟨~*s* to overgrazing and the destruction of vegetation —W.B.Fisher⟩ ⟨study ~*ing* to a bachelor of arts degree⟩ **syn** see GUIDE — **lead by the nose :** to cause to obey or follow meekly or submissively ⟨*leads* her husband *by the nose*⟩ — **lead into :** to lead so as to permit the last play to the trick to be made from (a specified hand, high card, or combination of cards) — **lead one a dance :** to subject one to irksome or exasperating experiences **:** put off or thwart one by delays or time-consuming artifices ⟨*led* her *boy friend a* fine *dance*⟩ — **lead one a merry chase :** to cause one extreme difficulty by speed or evasive tactics ⟨*led* his *pursuers a merry chase* over hill and dale⟩ — **lead one up the garden path** *also* **lead one up the garden** *Brit* **:** to pull the wool over one's eyes **:** DECEIVE, MISLEAD ⟨so you *led us up the garden path* . . . you cooked up a beautiful story —William Sansom⟩ — **lead through :** to lead so as to force a play from (a specified player, high card, or combination of cards) before one or more other players play to the table — **lead toward :** to lead so as to force one or more opponents to play before (a specified player, high card, or combination of cards)

**²lead** \ˈlēd\ *n* -s [ME *lede* action of leading, guidance, fr. *leden*, v. — more at ¹LEAD] **1 a** (1) **:** position at the front **:** VAN ⟨the bowmen were in the ~⟩ ⟨took the ~ on the dark winding road⟩ (2) **:** INITIATIVE ⟨took the ~ in fighting the measure⟩ (3) **:** the act or privilege of playing first in a card game, round, or trick ⟨your partner has the ~⟩; *also* **:** the card, suit, or piece so played ⟨his ~ was the ace⟩ (4) **:** the condition of being first to bet voluntarily in a round of a poker game **b** (1) **:** an act of directing or guiding **:** LEADERSHIP ⟨look to the president for a unifying ~ —D.W.Brogan⟩ (2) **:** EXAMPLE, PRECEDENT ⟨followed the ~ of the majority leader in voting⟩ **c** (1) **:** the condition or position of having a margin of advantage or superiority **:** the condition of being ahead ⟨this country has the ~ over all rivals in steel production⟩ ⟨took the ~ in the race from the first⟩ (2) **:** the measure or margin of such advantage or superiority ⟨enjoys a good ~ over all competitors⟩ ⟨a ~ of a boat's length⟩ **2 :** one that leads or acts as a guide: as **a :** an artificial waterway (as to a mill) **b** (1) **:** the announcement by one voice part of a musical theme to be repeated by the other parts (2) **:** a mark in a canon serving as a cue for the entrance of other parts (3) **:** the first place in change ringing **c :** the player who throws the jack and bowls first in lawn bowling or who throws the first stone in curling **d** (1) **:** LODE (2) **:** an auriferous gravel deposit in an old river bed; *esp* **:** one buried under lava **e :** a channel of water through a field or floe of ice; *esp* **:** one that is wider than a lane **f :** something serving as an indication, tip, or clue ⟨may turn up a ~ —Hamilton Basso⟩ ⟨provides ~*s* for further research in Africa —W.R.Bascom⟩ **g :** a role for a leading man or leading woman; *also* **:** one who plays such a role **h :** LEASH **i :** a length of net, supported on stakes, placed to guide fish into the pot of a pound net **j** *forestry* **:** a block or series of blocks or rollers attached to a stationary object to guide the cable by which logs are dragged **k** (1) **:** the first summary or introductory section of a news story varying in length from a sentence to several paragraphs ⟨reporters would spend hours . . . polishing up ~*s* —C.B.Jones⟩ (2) **:** a news story that is of chief importance in an edition of a newspaper and that is usu. given the most prominent display (3) **:** the first and presumably most significant item in a news broadcast **l :** the first of a series of blows delivered by one or both boxers **m :** LEADER 1a(1) **n :** a pattern of movement of a horse at a canter or gallop in which one or the other of the front feet consistently strikes the ground first **o** *Brit* **:** LEADER 1m **p :** the leading or top part in a section of a jazz band ⟨one man who blew almost all the ~ —*Metronome*⟩; *also* **:** the man who plays that part **3 a** (1) **:** the distance measured along a straight railroad track from the point of switch to the point of frog in a turnout (2) **:** a piece of track leading from a switch to a frog (3) **:** an extended track connecting either end of a yard with the main track (4) **:** the distance from the point where material is excavated to that where it is deposited in roadbed construction **b :** the distance of haul **c** (1) **:** a flexible or solid insulated conductor connected to or leading out from an electrical device (2) **:** the angle between the line joining the brushes of a continuous-current dynamo and the plane perpendicular to the undisturbed magnetic field between the poles (3) **:** the advance of the current phase in an alternating circuit beyond that of the electromotive force producing it **d** (1) **:** the width of port opening at the end of the stroke of a steam engine (2) **:** the distance measured in length of piston stroke or the corresponding angular displacement of the crank of the piston from the end of the compression stroke when ignition takes place in an internal-combustion engine **e** (1) **:** the course of a rope from end to end (2) **:** a line of fire hose extended toward a fire **f** (1) **:** the amount of axial advance of any point in the thread for a complete turn (as of a screw or worm) (2) *usu* **leed :** such rate of advance in the helical rifling of a gun barrel **g :** the distance one leads a moving target **h :** the distance from the start of one climb to the next belay point in mountaineering **i :** a position taken by a base runner off the base in the direction of the next base

**³lead** \ˈlēd\ *adj* **1 :** acting as a leader **:** going in front **:** LEADING, LEAD-OFF ⟨the ~ mule⟩ ⟨now it was the ~ cruiser's turn to leave the formation —J.A.Michener⟩ ⟨the ~ article in this month's issue⟩ **2 :** given prominent display as of first importance ⟨a ~ headline⟩ ⟨a ~ editorial⟩

**⁴lead** \ˈled\ *n* -s [ME *leed*, fr. OE *lēad*; akin to MD *lood* lead, MHG *lōt*, MIr *luaide*] **1 a :** a heavy soft malleable ductile plastic but inelastic bivalent or tetravalent metallic element that is bluish white when freshly cut but tarnishes readily in moist air to dull gray, that occurs mostly in combination (as in galena and cerussite) and usu. is extracted from its ores by smelting and refined by removal esp. of copper, silver, zinc, and bismuth, and that is used often in the form of alloys chiefly in pipes, sheaths for cables, acid-resistant linings, plates for lead-lead acid cells, solder, type metal, and shields against radioactivity and in making pigments and chemicals — symbol *Pb;* see ACTINIUM SERIES, ELEMENT table, LEAD POISONING, THORIUM SERIES, URANIUM SERIES **b :** a trait or quality suggestive of some attribute of lead; *specif* **:** SLUGGISHNESS ⟨perk up and get the ~ out of their heels —Frederick Way⟩ **2 a** *dial Eng* **:** a milk pan made of or lined with lead **b :** a plummet or mass of lead (as used in sounding at sea) — see SOUNDING LEAD **c leads** *pl, Brit* **:** a lead roof usu. flat **d leads** *pl* **:** lead framing for a pane (as in a window of latticework or stained glass) **e :** a thin strip of metal usu. lead but sometimes brass ranging from ½ to 3 points in thickness, less than type high, and used to separate lines of type; *often* **:** a 2-point lead — compare THICK LEAD, THIN LEAD, REGLET, SLUG **f :** a lead or tin socket to hold one or more needles in a knitting machine by the shanks **3 a :** GRAPHITE 1 **b :** a thin cylinder or stick of marking substance (as graphite) in or for a pencil **c :** WHITE LEAD **4 :** BULLETS, PROJECTILES ⟨let fall half a ton of ~ over our lines —P.C.Mitchell⟩ ⟨moved out to Oklahoma when ~ was still law —Whitney Balliett⟩ **5 :** a nearly neutral, slightly reddish dark gray that is lighter and slightly bluer than grebe — called also *squirrel* **6 :** TETRAETHYL LEAD

**⁵lead** \ˈled\ *vb* -ED/-ING/-S [ME *leden, leeden*, fr. *leed*, n. — more at ⁴LEAD] *vt* **1 a :** to cover or line the inside of with lead **:** clog with lead (as the grooves of a rifle with continuous firing) **b :** to weight with a piece of lead **:** attach lead to **2 a :** to fix (window glass) in position with leads **b :** to secure with melted lead (as a bolt or railing into stonework) — often used with *in* **3 :** to smooth (as the bore of a gun) with a lead lap **4 :** to place leads or other spacing material between the lines of (type matter); *also* **:** to add spacing between the lines of (as printed or photocomposed matter) — often used with *out* **5 :** to treat or mix with lead or a lead compound ⟨~*ed* zinc⟩ ⟨~*ed* gasoline⟩ **~** *vi* **1 :** to take soundings with the lead **2 :** to become coated or clogged with lead ⟨a gun barrel may ~⟩

**⁶lead** \ˈled\ *adj* [⁴*lead*] **1 :** relating to or made of lead **:** containing lead ⟨~ bullets⟩ ⟨~ pipes⟩ ⟨a ~ mine⟩ **2 :** containing lead oxide ⟨a ~ glaze⟩

**lead acetate** \ˈled-\ *n* **:** an acetate of lead: as **a :** the poisonous efflorescent soluble crystalline normal salt $Pb(C_2H_3O_2)_2 \cdot 3H_2O$ that has a slightly sweet taste, that is usu. made by reaction of lead monoxide with acetic acid, and that is used chiefly as a mordant in dyeing and printing, as a drier in paint, in the manufacture of other lead salts, and in medicine esp. formerly as an astringent — called also *sugar of lead* **b :** LEAD SUBACETATE **c :** LEAD TETRAACETATE

**lead angle** \ˈlēd-\ *n* [²*lead*] **:** the angle between the tangent to a helix or screw thread and the plane perpendicular to the helical axis

**lead arsenate** \ˈled-\ *n* **:** an arsenate of lead: as **a :** a crystalline acid salt $PbHAsO_4$ made usu. by reaction of lead monoxide with arsenic pentoxide and used as an insecticide; di-lead orthoarsenate — called also *acid lead arsenate, standard lead arsenate* **b :** a mixture of basic orthoarsenates of lead used as an insecticide esp. on sensitive plants — called also *basic lead arsenate*

**lead ash** *or* **lead ashes** \ˈled-\ *n* **:** LITHARGE 1

**lead azide** \ˈled-\ *n* **:** a crystalline explosive compound $Pb(N_3)_2$ made by reaction of sodium azide with lead acetate or lead nitrate and used as a detonating agent

**leadback** \ˈled,=\ *n* [⁴*lead*] **:** a red-backed sandpiper (*Erolia alpina pacifica*)

**lead back** \(ˈ)lēd¦=\ *vt* **:** to lead (a card) from a suit that one's partner led originally

**lead bullion** \ˈled-\ *n* **:** impure lead containing gold and silver

**lead-burn** \ˈled,=\ *vt* [back-formation fr. *lead burner*] **:** to join (two pieces of lead) by fusion (as in plumbing or roofing or joining storage-battery cells)

**lead burner** \ˈled-\ *n* [⁴*lead* + *burner*] **:** a worker who welds by lead-burning

**lead cable borer** \ˈled-\ *n* **:** a western bostrychid beetle (*Scobicia declivis*) that normally bores into hardwood but often damages telephone cables and liquor casks

**lead carbonate** \ˈled-\ *n* **:** a carbonate of lead: as **a :** the poisonous insoluble normal salt $PbCO_3$ occurring naturally as the mineral cerussite and obtained synthetically as a white crystalline powder **b :** a poisonous basic salt $Pb_3(OH)_2(CO_3)_2$ occurring naturally as the mineral hydrocerussite and obtained synthetically as a component of white lead (sense a)

**lead-chamber process** \ˈled-\ *n* **:** CHAMBER PROCESS 1

**lead chloride** \ˈled-\ *n* **:** a chloride of lead; *esp* **:** the poisonous dichloride $PbCl_2$ occurring naturally as the mineral cotunnite and obtained synthetically as insoluble white crystals

**lead chromate** \ˈled-\ *n* **:** a chromate of lead: as **a :** the poisonous normal salt $PbCrO_4$ that occurs naturally as the mineral crocoite, that is obtained synthetically as a yellow crystalline powder by precipitation from a solution of a lead compound and sodium chromate or sodium dichromate, and that is used as a pigment either alone or in admixture with other compounds **:** CHROME YELLOW **b :** a poisonous basic salt $Pb_2OCrO_4$ or a mixture of chromates containing it that is used as a reddish yellow to orange to red pigment — compare CHROME ORANGE, CHROME RED

**lead colic** \ˈled-\ *n* **:** intestinal colic associated with obstinate constipation due to chronic lead poisoning — called also *painter's colic*

**lead-collision course** \¦lēd-\ *n* **:** an interception course designed for radar-equipped rocket-armed interceptors in which an airplane closes on the target airplane on a straight-line heading which if pursued would end in collision, the rockets being fired automatically to arrive at the point of collision ahead of the interceptor — compare PURSUIT CURVE

**lead-colored bush tit** \ˈled,==-\ *n* **:** a bush tit (*Psaltriparus minimus plumbeus*) of the arid interior of No. America from Wyoming to western Texas

**lead curve** \ˈlēd-\ *n* [²*lead*] **:** the curve in the turnout interposed between the heel of a railroad switch and the frog

**lead dioxide** \ˈled-\ *n* **:** a poisonous compound $PbO_2$ that occurs naturally as the mineral plattnerite but is usu. obtained as an insoluble brown crystalline powder by oxidation (as by electrolysis) of lead monoxide or lead salts and that forms the active material of the positive plates of lead-lead acid cells and as an oxidizing agent in the dye and chemical industries

**¹lead·en** \ˈledᵊn\ *adj* [ME *leden*, fr. OE *lēaden*, fr. *lēad* lead + *-en*] **1 a :** made of lead ⟨a ~ box⟩ **b** (1) **:** of the color lead (2) **:** of the color lead gray (3) **:** dull gray **:** DUN ⟨a ~ sky⟩ ⟨of a dull ~ paleness —Anthony Trollope⟩ **2 a :** lacking value or quality **:** POOR, MEAN ⟨his golden tact and ~ taste —H.M.Reichard⟩ **b** (1) **:** oppressively heavy ⟨all their equipment had become ~ —Norman Mailer⟩ ⟨his body seemed a trifle less ~ —John Buchan⟩ **:** OPPRESSIVE ⟨a ~ silence fell —Jean Stafford⟩ (2) **:** DRAGGING, SLUGGISH ⟨had a lot of power and a lot of ~ feet —Ty Cobb⟩ **c** (1) **:** DULL, EXPRESSIONLESS, INERT ⟨the heavy ~ eyes turn on you —R.W. Emerson⟩ ⟨its hero is a ~ bore —*New Yorker*⟩ (2) **:** lacking spirit, animation, or sparkle **:** HEAVY-FOOTED, FLAT ⟨giving the music a ~ character —Arthur Berger⟩ ⟨their ironies are ~ —Charles Lee⟩ ⟨there's a rather ~ first act —*Springfield (Mass.) Union*⟩ ⟨this version . . . is full of fine shots of India . . . but the picture itself is ~ —John McCarten⟩ — **lead·en·ly** *adv* — **lead·en·ness** \-ᵊn(n)əs\ *n* -ES

**²leaden** \"\ *vt* -ED/-ING/-S **:** to make like lead ⟨the dead palace floors had ~*ed* his feet —William Sansom⟩ ⟨a brain ~*ed* with fear⟩

**leaden flycatcher** *n* **:** a small flycatcher (*Myiagra rubecula*) of Australia and New Guinea

**lead·er** \ˈlēdə(r)\ *n* -s [ME *leder, ledere*, fr. *leden* to lead + *-er, -ere* -er] **1 :** something that leads: as **a** (1) **:** a primary or terminal shoot of a plant (as a main branch of an apple tree or the terminal shoot of a spruce tree) (2) **:** the upper portion of the primary axis of a tree esp. when extending beyond the rest of the head and forming the apex **b :** a remark or question intended or likely to bring a response esp. of a particular kind **:** a leading remark or question ⟨did not respond to his tactful ~⟩ **c :** TENDON, SINEW ⟨the ~*s* in his wrists moved like baling wire —Dillon Anderson⟩ **d :** the principal wheel in machinery; *also* **:** a part to guide exactly the motion of another piece **e leaders** *pl* (1) **:** dots or hyphens (as in a table or index) to lead the eye horizontally across a space to the right word or number (2) **:** a piece of type faced with a row of dots or hyphens **f** *chiefly Brit* **:** a newspaper editorial **g :** a branch or small vein leading to a larger one in a mine **h :** a thin paper tube containing quick match to cause rapid ignition (as of fireworks) **i** (1) **:** a net, fence, or wall for leading fish into a pound, weir, or trap (2) **:** a short length of material (as silkworm gut, wire, or heavy line) used to attach the end of a fishline to a lure or hook **j :** a pipe for conducting water or other fluid to some particular place (as a rainwater pipe from a roof to a cistern or the ground or a hot-air pipe in a heating system for a building) **k :** an article of value offered at an attractive special low price to stimulate business — compare LOSS LEADER **l :** LEAD 3a(2) **m :** a short length of blank film attached to each end of a filmstrip or of a reel of motion-picture film for threading into a film mechanism **n :** a length of yarn, rope, or cloth left threaded in a machine (as a textile machine) to act as a guide for new material attached to it **o** *or* **leader stroke :** an electrical discharge that precedes the main discharge and ionizes the path through which the main discharge surges (as in a lightning stroke) **p :** something that ranks first or has a margin of advantage or precedence over others ⟨the ~*s* among major communicable diseases⟩ ⟨steel and utilities were the ~*s* in today's stock market⟩ **2 :** a person or animal that leads: as **a :** GUIDE, CONDUCTOR ⟨acted as our ~ on the hazardous climb⟩ **b** (1) **:** a person who directs and usu. accompanies an armed force **:** COMMANDER, CAPTAIN ⟨captains of war, and ~*s* of their armies —John Locke⟩ (2) **:** a person who by force of example, talents, or qualities of leadership plays a directing role, wields commanding influence, or has a following in any sphere of activity or thought ⟨the great religious ~*s* of mankind⟩ ⟨a ~ in the reform movement⟩ ⟨summoned a conference of business ~*s*⟩ **c** (1) **:** the principal officer of a British political party who usu. exercises authority over both the parliamentary party and the national party organization ⟨while the party remains in opposition the ~ of the Parliamentary Labour Party has nothing like the authority granted by the Conservative Party to its ~ —R.T.McKenzie⟩ (2) **:** a member often chosen by caucus of his party to exercise general direction of or management of a particular phase of party activities in a legislative body — usu. used with a qualifier — compare FLOOR LEADER, LEADER OF THE OPPOSITION, MAJORITY LEADER, MINORITY LEADER (3) **:** such a member exercising primary authority over the business of the whole legislative body when his party constitutes a majority in the house — usu. used in phrases including the name of the legislative body ⟨responsible to the prime minister as ~ of the House —T.E.May⟩ ⟨~ of the House of Lords⟩ ⟨the ~ of the Executive Council . . . in New Zealand —Walter Nash⟩ (4) **:** one that exercises paramount but to some degree responsible authority over a state or local party organization ⟨the ~ is seldom the titular head of the party organization —H.R.Penniman⟩ ⟨the ~ of the Connecticut Democratic party⟩ — compare ⁵BOSS 3a (5) **:** the principal member of the party elite in a totalitarian system (as fascism or nazism) endowed by official ideology with a heroic or mystical character, exercising state power with a minimum of formal constitutional restraints, and characterized by extreme use of nationalist demagogy and claims to be above narrow class or group interests ⟨the ~ manipulates the people as an artist molds clay —G.H.Sabine⟩ **d** (1) **:** CONDUCTOR 6 (2) **:** the leading performer of a musical ensemble ⟨the concertmaster is the ~ of the violin section⟩ **e :** the front or foremost person in a file or advancing body **f :** the first player in any of various games **g** (1) **:** a horse placed in advance of others (as either of a forward pair of horses or the front horse of a tandem team) (2) *Midland* **:** LEAD HORSE **h :** a person who directs a class in the Methodist Church **i :** the counsel in an English legal proceeding who is entitled to precedence over his associates or is entitled to manage a case **j** (1) **:** an adult immediately responsible for the guidance of a Girl Scout troop (2) **:** a woman who guides the activities of blue birds — compare ADVISER, GUARDIAN **k :** a skilled employee who supervises one or more groups of workers **:** STRAW BOSS, FOREMAN

**leader head** *n* **:** a box usu. of metal placed at the top of a leader to collect roof water

**lead·er·less** \-(r)ləs\ *adj* **:** being without a leader

**lead·er·man** \-(r)mən\ *n, pl* **leadermen :** a subforeman in a shipyard

**leader of the opposition :** the principal member of the opposition party in a British legislative body who is given the status of a salaried government official and an important role in organizing the business of the house ⟨one of the ministers will open the debate and he will . . . be followed by the *leader of the opposition* —Eric Taylor⟩

**leader pin** *n* **:** GUIDE PIN

**lead·er·ship** \ˈlēdə(r),ship\ *n* **1 :** the office or position of a leader ⟨forced from the ~ by younger men —*Collier's Yr. Bk.*⟩ ⟨could not have maintained that ~ without her reputation for fair play —Lewis Galantiere⟩ ⟨assumed ~ of the opposition⟩ **2 a :** the quality of a leader **:** capacity to lead ⟨could not fail to perceive that there was no ~ in him —S.H. Adams⟩ ⟨~ is that ingredient of personality which causes men to follow —H.S.Gilbertson⟩ ⟨only a few people possess the quality of ~ —J.A.Schumpeter⟩ **b :** the act or an instance of leading ⟨the essence of ~ is the successful resolution of problems —Dean Acheson⟩ ⟨true ~ . . . is enlightenment and exhortation —Max Eastman⟩ ⟨fought bravely under his ~⟩ ⟨~ molds individuals into a team —Harold Koontz & Cyril O'Donnell⟩ **c :** a group of persons who lead ⟨a ~ is one of the major functional divisions to be found in all groups —H.D.Lasswell & Abraham Kaplan⟩ ⟨the party ~ ignored the dispute —Frank Tollman⟩ ⟨recruit youth ~ in the conduct of recreation activity —*Springfield (Mass.) Union*⟩

**leader tape** *n* **:** a nonmagnetic tape of paper or plastic used in magnetic recording at the beginning or end of a reel or as a marking for the beginning of a selection within the tape

**lead glance** \ˈled-\ *n* [trans. of G *bleiglanz*] **:** GALENA

**lead glass** \ˈled-\ *n* **:** glass containing a high proportion of lead oxide and having a relatively high refractive index and high dispersion value

**lead grass** \ˈled-\ *n* [⁴*lead* + *grass;* prob. fr. its weight] **:** GLASSWORT

**lead gray** \ˈled-\ *n* **1 :** a brownish gray **2 :** a light grayish olive

**lead·hill·ite** \ˈled,hi,līt\ *n* -s [F, fr. *Leadhills*, Lanarkshire, Scotland + F *-ite*] **:** a monoclinic mineral $Pb_4(SO_4)(CO_3)_2(OH)_2$ of a yellowish or greenish white color consisting of basic sulfate and carbonate of lead

**lead horse** \ˈlēd-\ *n, dial* **:** the horse on the left side in a team of two — called also *leader*

**leadier** *comparative of* LEADY

**leadiest** *superlative of* LEADY

**¹lead-in** \ˈlē,din\ *n, pl* **lead-ins** [fr. *lead in*, v.] **:** something that leads into something else: as **a :** the part of a radio antenna that runs from the larger or main elevated portion to the transmitting or receiving set **b :** something that opens or introduces **:** something that gradually leads the eye or attention from one thing to another ⟨with a front-cover portrait serving as a *lead-in* to a five-page article —*Publishers' Weekly*⟩ ⟨a *lead-in* which can attract people who don't agree with you —P.P.Van Riper⟩; *specif* **:** that part of a radio program or a radio broadcaster's talk which leads into the commercial ⟨tuneful program *lead-ins* —*Advertising Age*⟩

**²lead-in** \"\ *adj* **:** that leads in — used esp. of an electrical conductor ⟨a *lead-in* wire⟩; see INCANDESCENT LAMP illustration

**¹leading** \ˈlēdiŋ, -dēŋ\ *n* -s [ME *leding,* fr. gerund of *leden* to lead, conduct] **1 a :** the act or an instance of conducting from one place to another ⟨proposed a ~ of the excess water to arid lands⟩ **b** (1) **:** the act or an instance of commanding or directing **:** COMMAND, LEADERSHIP ⟨entrusted the ~ of the army to the earl⟩ (2) *archaic* **:** ability to lead or command **:** AUTHORITY ⟨men of great ~ and property in the state⟩ **2 :** capacity to enlighten **:** GUIDANCE, ENLIGHTENMENT — usu. used in the phrase *men of light and leading* ⟨commissioned six men of light and ~ to settle the . . . question —Ernest Weekley⟩

**²leading** \ˈlē-\ *adj* [fr. pres. part. of ¹*lead*] **1 a :** preceding others in order of march or other movement **:** coming first ⟨the ~ boat was destroyed before it had a chance to fire⟩ **b :** ranking first or among the first in regard to influence, importance, or popularity ⟨a ~ topic of conversation⟩ ⟨the ~ ski center in this area⟩ ⟨among the ~ infectious diseases⟩ ⟨a ~ item in all the stores⟩ ⟨played a ~ part in the settlement of the colony⟩ **c :** exercising leadership in some area **:** accorded or meriting prominence as a leader ⟨a ~ citizen of the town⟩ ⟨a ~ exponent of the dance⟩ ⟨married into one of the ~ pastoral families —E.H.Collis⟩ ⟨a ~ literary critic⟩ **d :** GUIDING, DIRECTING ⟨a ~ thread in American foreign policy⟩ ⟨what are his ~ motives⟩ **e :** given prominent or most prominent display ⟨the ~ story in this morning's paper⟩ ⟨a ~ editorial⟩ **2 :** being in advance during normal rotation or motion — used esp. of an edge or side of a mechanical part **3 :** ranking immediately below a petty or noncommissioned officer in the British armed forces ⟨~ seaman⟩ ⟨~ signalman⟩ ⟨~ aircraftsman⟩ **syn** see CHIEF

**³leading** \ˈlediŋ, -dēŋ\ *n* -s [ME *leeding* action of covering or lining with lead, fr. gerund of *leden, leeden* to lead, cover or line with lead] **:** a covering or framework of lead **:** LEADWORK ⟨the ~ of a Tudor window⟩

**leading article** \ˈlē-\ *n* **1** *chiefly Brit* **:** EDITORIAL — compare LEADER 1f **2 :** the article given the most significant position or most prominent display in a periodical

**leading case** \ˈlē-\ *n* **:** a case so well reasoned and important in the rules of law determined and in the principles declared that it becomes well known and is frequently cited by courts and lawyers as not only settling the points of law ruled upon, but as of assistance in resolving new questions of law

**leading edge** \ˈlē-\ *n* **1 :** the foremost edge of an airfoil or propeller blade **2 :** the forward edge of a part on a vehicle or of something that itself moves ⟨the *leading edge* of an automobile hood⟩ ⟨the *leading edge* of an air mass⟩

**leading lady** \ˈlē-\ *n* **:** an actress who plays the leading feminine role in a play or movie

**leading light** \ˈlē-\ *n* **1 :** a light that serves as a navigational guide (as in entering or leaving port) **2 :** a prominent and influential member (as of a community or church)

**leading load** \ˈlē-\ *n* **:** CONDENSIVE LOAD

**lead·ing·ly** \ˈlē-\ *adv* **:** in a leading manner

**leading man** \ˈlē-\ *n* **:** an actor who plays the leading male role in a play or movie

**leading mark** \ˈlē-\ *n* **:** a conspicuous object (as a prominent landmark easily seen from seaward) that serves as a navigational guide (as in entering or leaving port)

**leading motive** \ˈlē-\ *n* [trans. of G *leitmotiv*] **:** a dominant motive in or leading to action; *specif* **:** a musical leitmotiv

**leading question** \ˈlē-\ *n* **:** a question so framed as to guide the person questioned in making his reply **:** LEADER

**leading rein** \ˈlē-\ *n* **:** the use of an opened-out rein in such a way as to direct the horse's head and neck to the left or right

**lead-in groove** \ˈlē,din-\ *n* **:** a blank spiral groove extending from the outer edge of a disc to the beginning of recording and having a distance of pitch that is much greater than normal

**leading stone** \ˈlē-\ *n* **:** LODESTONE

**leading strings** \ˈlē-\ *n pl* **1 :** strings by which children are sometimes supported when beginning to walk **2 :** a state of dependence or tutelage **:** GUIDANCE ⟨*leading strings* had been so willingly accepted that they were scarcely felt —E.M. Forster⟩ — usu. used in the phrase *in leading strings* ⟨no longer in *leading strings* to his wife or his wife's father —Francis Hackett⟩ ⟨passed his whole adolescence in his mother's *leading strings* —Van Wyck Brooks⟩

**leading tone** *or* **leading note** \ˈlē-\ *n* **:** the seventh musical degree of a major or minor scale — called also *subtonic*

**leading-tone seventh** *or* **leading seventh** \ˈlē-\ *n* **:** a musical seventh chord composed of the seventh, second, fourth, and sixth notes or tones of the major scale — compare TRIAD; see SEVENTH CHORD illustration

**leading truck** \ˈlē-\ *n* **:** a swiveling frame mounted on two or four wheels under the front of a locomotive to guide it around curves and help carry the weight

**leading wheel** \ˈlē-\ *n* **:** a wheel situated before the driving wheels of a locomotive

**leading wind** \ˈlē-\ *n* **:** a free or fair wind

**lead-lead acid cell** \ˈled¦led-\ *n* **:** a storage cell in which the positive plate is lead dioxide, the negative plate is spongy lead, and the electrolyte is dilute sulfuric acid

**lead·less** \ˈledləs\ *adj* **1 :** being without lead **2 :** not using lead — used of a printing process (as photocomposition)

**¹lead line** \ˈled,=\ *n* [ME *leede lyne,* fr. *leede, leed* lead + *lyne, line* line] **1 a :** SOUNDING LINE **b** *usu* **leadline :** the lower line of a gillnet having lead or other weights at intervals to keep the bottom of the net submerged — compare CORKLINE **2 :** a dark line along the gums due to deposition of lead sulfide (as in chronic exposure to lead compounds or fumes)

**²lead line** \ˈlēd,=\ *n* [²*lead* + *line*] **1 :** a wire rope with an eye at each end used to anchor the snatch block in setting a lead in logging **2 :** a line for leading a horse usu. for excercise

**¹lead·man** \ˈledmən, -,man\ *n, pl* **leadmen** [⁴*lead*] **:** SOUNDER, ¹LEADSMAN

**²lead·man** \ˈlēdmən, -,man\ *n, pl* **leadmen** [²*lead*] **:** LEADER 2k

**lead monoxide** \ˈled-\ *n* **:** a poisonous compound PbO that is obtained usu. in different yellow to brownish red forms by heating lead moderately in air and that is used chiefly in making plates for lead-lead acid cells, in compounding rubber, in glass, glazes, and vitreous enamels, and in the manufacture of other lead compounds — see LITHARGE, MASSICOT

**lead nitrate** \ˈled-\ *n* **:** a poisonous soluble crystalline salt $Pb(NO_3)_2$ obtained by reaction of lead or a lead compound with nitric acid and used chiefly in making other lead salts and in fireworks; *also* **:** any of several closely related basic salts

**lead ocher** \ˈled-\ *n* **:** MASSICOT 2

**lead off** \(ˈ)lē¦dȯf, -däf\ *vt* **:** to make a start on **:** OPEN ⟨*led off* his comments by describing details of the attack —*N.Y. Times*⟩ ⟨able to *lead off* another offensive —H.L.Merillat⟩

**leadoff** \ˈlē,d-\ *n* -s [*lead off*] **1 :** a beginning or leading action; *specif* **:** a hit made in offense in boxing **2 :** a player who leads off; *esp* **:** the player who heads the batting order or bats first in an inning in baseball

**lead-off** \ˈ=,=\ *adj* [*lead off*] **:** leading off **:** STARTING, OPENING ⟨a *lead-off* batter⟩ ⟨my *lead-off* proposal —Inez Robb⟩ ⟨the *lead-off* essay —Clifton Fadiman⟩

**lead oleate** \ˈled-\ *n* **:** a poisonous white powder or yellowish pasty mass made usu. by precipitation from solutions of a lead salt and a commercial sodium oleate and used chiefly as an additive to lubricants and as the base for a medicinal plaster or a molding wax — compare DIACHYLON

**lead on** \(ˈ)lē¦dȯn, -dän\ *vt* **:** to entice or induce to proceed in a course esp. when unwise or mistaken ⟨a more or less ignorant girl is *led on* by her irresponsible lover —H.M. Parshley⟩ ⟨*led me on* to think that he loved me⟩

**lead-out groove** \ˈlē,daůt-\ *n* [*lead-out* fr. the phrase *lead out*] **:** a blank spiral groove of coarse pitch extending from the end of a recording inward to the locked or eccentric groove near the disc center

**lead-over groove** \ˈlē,dōvə(r)-\ *n* [*lead-over* fr. the phrase *lead over*] **:** a coarse-pitch groove joining recordings of short duration to carry the pickup stylus from one recording to the next on the record

**lead oxide** \ˈled-\ *n* **:** a binary compound of lead and oxygen; *esp* **:** LEAD MONOXIDE — compare LEAD DIOXIDE, MINIUM, RED LEAD

**lead palsy** \ˈled-\ *n* **:** localized paralysis caused by lead poisoning esp. of the extensor muscles of the forearm leading to wristdrop

**lead pencil** \ˈled-\ *n* **:** a pencil of which the marking material is graphite

**lead peroxide** \ˈled-\ *n* **:** LEAD DIOXIDE — not used systematically

**lead-pipe cinch** \ˈled,=-\ *also* **lead-pipe** *n* [*lead-pipe* fr. the phrase *lead pipe* pipe made of lead, fr. ME *lede pype,* fr. *lede, leed* lead + *pype, pipe* pipe] *slang* **:** something very easy or certain ⟨ought to be a *lead-pipe cinch* to find —*Big Detective Cases*⟩ ⟨if it wasn't him it was you and that's a *lead-pipe cinch* —Nelson Algren⟩

**leadplant** \ˈled,=\ *n* **:** any of several American shrubs of the genus *Amorpha; esp* **:** a shrub (*A. canescens*) of the western U.S. having hoary pinnate leaves and dull-colored racemose flowers and in some opinions indicating the presence of lead ore

**lead poisoning** \ˈled-\ *n* **:** chronic intoxication produced by the absorption of lead into the system and characterized by anemia with stippling of red cells, severe colicky pains, a blue lead line on the gums, and local muscular paralysis (as wrist= drop) — called also *plumbism, saturnism*

**leads** *pres 3d sing of* LEAD, *pl of* LEAD

**lead screw** \ˈled-\ *n* **:** the screw that moves the tool carriage of a lathe when cutting threads — compare FEED SCREW

**lead sheet** \ˈlēd-\ *n* **:** the manuscript of a song consisting of the melody, words, and indication of the basic harmony written in simple form

**lead silicate** \ˈled-\ *n* **:** any of various salts (as the normal monosilicate $PbSiO_3$) made by reaction of lead monoxide or a lead salt with silica or a silicate and used chiefly in glass and ceramics and as pigments (as in compounding rubber) — see WHITE LEAD c

**¹leads·man** \ˈledzmən\ *n, pl* **leadsmen** [*lead's* (gen. of ⁴*lead*) + *man*] **:** a man who uses a sounding lead to determine depth of water

**²leads·man** \ˈlēdzmən\ *n, pl* **leadsmen** [*lead's* (gen. of ²*lead*) + *man*] **:** ²LEAD 2c

**lead soap** \ˈled-\ *n* **:** any of various lead salts of higher carboxylic acids (as fatty acids) esp. for use as a drier in paints and varnishes or as an additive to lubricants

**lead spar** \ˈled-\ *n* **:** CERUSSITE

**lead subacetate** \ˈled-\ *n* **:** a poisonous basic salt $Pb(C_2H_3O_2)_2.PbO$ used esp. in solution (as in Goulard's extract); basic lead acetate

**lead sulfate** \ˈled-\ *n* **:** a sulfate of lead: as **a :** the poisonous normal sulfate $PbSO_4$ occurring native as anglesite and obtained synthetically as a white crystalline powder **b :** any of several basic salts (as the monobasic sulfate $Pb_2OSO_4$ occurring naturally as lanarkite) or a mixture containing one or more of these used as a pigment — compare ²BLUE LEAD 2, WHITE LEAD b

**lead sulfide** \ˈled-\ *n* **:** a compound PbS occurring naturally as the mineral galena and obtained synthetically as a black precipitate when solutions of lead salts are exposed to hydrogen sulfide

**lead-swinger** \ˈled,swiŋə(r)\ *n* [⁴*lead* + *swinger* (one that swings); perh. fr. the belief of some sailors that the leadsman's job is an easy one] *chiefly Austral* **:** SHIRKER, SLACKER; *esp* **:** MALINGERER ⟨the sick and the lame, the halt and the *lead-swinger* —I.L.Idriess⟩

**lead tetraacetate** \ˈled-\ *n* **:** a poisonous crystalline compound $Pb(C_2H_3O_2)_4$ made usu. by reaction of red lead with glacial acetic acid and used as an oxidizing agent esp. in organic synthesis

**lead tetraethyl** \ˈled-\ *n* **:** TETRAETHYL LEAD

**lead time** \ˈlēd-\ *n* **1 :** the time interval between the conception or designing of a product and its actual production and use **2 :** the time interval between the placing of an order and delivery

**lead track** \ˈlēd-\ *n* **:** ²LEAD 3a(3)

**lead tree** \ˈled-\ *n* **1 :** lead crystallized in arborescent forms from a solution of some lead salt (as by suspending a strip of zinc in lead acetate) **2 :** a plant of the genus *Leucaena; esp* **:** a low scrubby tree (*Leucaena glauca*) prob. native to tropical America but now pantropical in distribution and often cultivated as a ground cover, for windrows or hedging, and as forage for cattle and sheep though reputedly toxic to horses and swine

**lead up** \(ˈ)lē¦dəp\ *vt, obs* **:** to lead off (a dance) **~** *vi* **1 :** to prepare the way **:** constitute the antecedents or preliminaries — used with *to* ⟨the series of events which *led up to* the former's dismissal —*Current Biog.*⟩ ⟨the first 60 pages of this book *lead up to* the revolution of 1911 —*Times Lit. Supp.*⟩ **2 :** to make a gradual or indirect approach to a topic — used with *to* ⟨would she let her have the dress? Perhaps she should have *led up* to it —Stuart Cloete⟩

**lead-up** \ˈlē,dəp\ *n* [*lead up*] **:** something that leads up to or prepares the way for something else ⟨the race will serve as a *lead-up* to the classic —*Sydney (Australia) Bull.*⟩

**lead water** \ˈled-\ *n* **:** Goulard's extract diluted with water

**leadwood** \ˈled,=\ *n* **1 :** LEATHERWOOD 1a **2 :** an African tree or shrub (*Combretum imberbe*) with pale gray bark and small pale green leaves

**lead wool** \ˈled-\ *n* **:** lead in the form of fine shreds or shavings used for calking pipe joints

**leadwork** \ˈled,=\ *n* **1 :** something made of lead **2 :** work that is done with lead

**leadwort** \ˈled,=\ *n* **1 :** a plant of the family Plumbaginaceae esp. of the genus *Plumbago; specif* **:** a plant (*P. europaea*) with lead-blue flowers **2 :** LEADPLANT

**leady** \ˈledē, -di\ *adj* -ER/-EST [ME *leedy,* fr. *leed* lead + *-y*] **:** containing or resembling lead

**¹leaf** \ˈlēf\ *n, pl* **leaves** \ˈlēvz\ [ME *leef,* fr. OE *lēaf;* akin to OHG *loub* leaf, foliage, ON *lauf,* Goth *laufs* leaf, foliage, L *liber* inner bark of a tree, pith of papyrus, book, Gk *lypē* grief, pain, Skt *lumpati* he injures, robs, Russ *lupit'* to peel, *lub* bast; basic meaning: to peel] **1 a** (1) **:** a lateral outgrowth from a stem that constitutes part of the foliage of a plant and functions primarily in food manufacture by photosynthesis, that arises in regular succession from the growing point, that consists typically of a flattened green blade which is joined to the stem by a petiole often with a pair of stipules at its base, which in cross section exhibits an outer covering of epidermal cells penetrated by stomata usu. more numerous on the lower surface, which has one or more layers of palisade cells beneath the upper epidermis and between these and the lower epidermis a mass of spongy parenchyma cells, both palisade and spongy tissue being ramified by a network of veins, and that is distinguished from a leaflet, cladophyll, or phylloclade by the presence of a bud at the juncture of petiole and stem and from a phyllode by differentiation into blade and petiole (2) **:** any of various modified leaves (as a bract, sepal, petal, or scale) that are primarily engaged in functions other than food manufacture; *esp* **:** FLORAL LEAF (3) **:** PETAL ⟨a candied rose ~⟩ **b** (1) **:** the leaves of trees or plants **:** FOLIAGE (2) **:** the leaves of any plant as an article of commerce; *specif* **:** the leaves of the tea plant **c** (1) **:** tobacco leaves; *also* **:** the leaf form of tobacco ⟨Connecticut seed ~⟩ (2) **:** raw unmanufactured tobacco (3) **:** the whole leaf **:** unstemmed tobacco (4) **:** a grade of tobacco leaves consisting of those of the best quality — distinguished from *seconds* and *lugs* **2 :** something resembling or suggestive of a leaf: as **a :** a part of a book or folded sheet containing two pages, one on each side; *also* **:** the written or printed matter on it **b** (1) **:** a side, division, or part (as of window shutters, folding doors, hydraulic gates) that slides or is hinged (2) **:** the movable parts of a table top whether hinged or separate (as in an extension table) (3) **:** one of the moving portions of a drawbridge (4) **:** LEAF SIGHT (5) **:** either flap of a hinge **c** *now chiefly dial* **:** one of the layers of fat about the kidneys of a hog; *also* **:** a similar layer of fat in other animals **d** (1) **:** a thin sheet or plate of any natural or artificial substance **:** LAMINA ⟨the *leaves* of a gill⟩ (2) **:** metal in thin layers usu. thinner than foil ⟨silver ~⟩ **e :** an ornament (as on a capital) shaped like a leaf **f** (1) **:** a tooth of a pinion (as of a gear pinion) (2) **:** one of the cylindrical pieces serving as the teeth of a lantern pinion (3) **:** one of the plates of a leaf spring **g** *dial Brit* **:** a hat brim **h :** a thin section of a filter consisting of a frame or wire screen covered by a filter medium (as cloth) — called also *filter leaf* **i :** a loop of a leaf-shaped

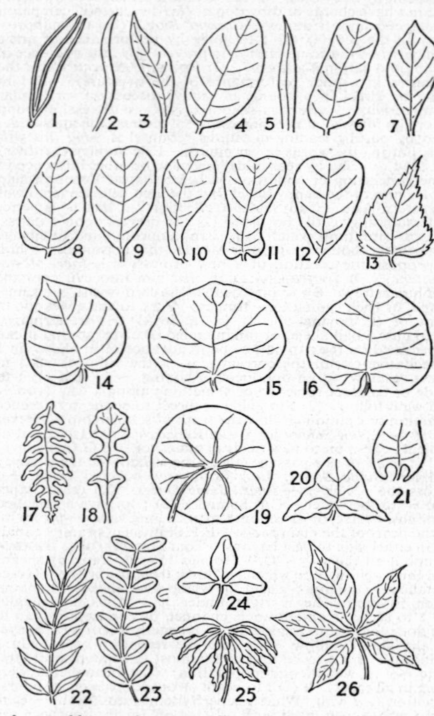


forms of leaves: *1* acerate; *2* linear; *3* lanceolate; *4* elliptic; *5* ensiform; *6* oblong; *7* oblanceolate, with acuminate tip; *8* ovate in form, with acute tip; *9* obovate; *10* spatulate; *11* pandurate; *12* cuneate; *13* deltoid; *14* cordate; *15* reniform; *16* orbiculate; *17* runcinate; *18* lyrate; *19* peltate; *20* hastate; *21* sagittate; *22* odd-pinnate; *23* abruptly pinnate; *24* palmate (trifoliolate) *25* palmate (pedate in form with margin incised) *26* palmate (quinquefoliolate)

curve **j :** HARNESS 4 **k :** isinglass dried in the form of a leaf **l :** a foundry molder's leaf-shaped trowel or tool — **in leaf :** in or with foliage ⟨lush pasture and woods *in leaf* —Thomas Wood †1950⟩

**²leaf** \"\ *vb* -ED/-ING/-S *vi* **1 :** to shoot out or produce leaves **:** LEAVE ⟨chestnuts which were just *~ing* in the spring sun —M.E.Bates⟩ — often used with *out* ⟨a fern just *~ing* out —W.V.T.Clark⟩ **2** *of metallic powder in enamel or paint* **:** to assume an overlapping arrangement like that of fish scales on a painted or coated surface **3 :** to turn over the pages — often used with *through* ⟨*~s* through the old newspaper files —Francis Russell⟩ ⟨*~ing* through the fifteen letters that had come from her —Norman Mailer⟩ **~** *vt* **:** to turn over esp. one by one ⟨*~ed* the pages —Louis Vaczek⟩ ⟨*~ed* his notes a final time —Kathryn Grondahl⟩ **:** turn over the pages of ⟨*~ing* a new novel⟩

**³leaf** \"\ *adj* **1 :** of, relating to, or in the form of a leaf ⟨~ fiber⟩ **2 :** LEAVED — used in combination ⟨clover-*leaf*⟩ ⟨cut-*leaf*⟩

**leaf·age** \ˈlēfij, -fēj\ *n* -s **1 a :** a quantity of leaves **:** LEAVES ⟨much ~ was also found in the nests —*Ecology*⟩ **b :** the leaves of plants as produced in nature **:** FOLIAGE ⟨the deep ~ of a garden —Anne D. Sedgwick⟩ ⟨crouched amongst the ~ watching them —W.H.Hudson †1922⟩ ⟨maples in ~ full —Mary Austin⟩ **2 :** the representation of foliage esp. for ornamental purposes ⟨all four legs of the table show scrolls and ~ —*Antiques*⟩

**leaf and square** *n* **:** a small plasterer's tool for modeling and ornamental work consisting of a handle with a leaf-shaped blade at one end and a rectangular blade at the other

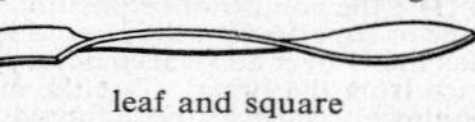

leaf and square

**leaf-and-tongue** *or* **leaf-and-dart** \¦=,=ˈ=\ *n* **:** an ornamental pattern of alternating leaves and narrow tongues or darts

**leaf beet** *n* **:** SPINACH BEET

**leaf beetle** *n* **:** a beetle of the family Chrysomelidae

**leafbird** \ˈ=,=\ *n* **:** GREEN BULBUL

**leaf bite** *n* **:** a disease of the coconut palm esp. in Jamaica caused by an imperfect fungus (*Thielaviopsis paradoxa*)

**leaf blight** *n* **:** a plant disease characterized by a general browning, death of foliage, and falling of leaves: **a :** FIRE BLIGHT 1 **b :** LEAF CAST

**leaf blister** *n* **:** any of several diseases caused by leaf-curl fungi of the genus *Taphrina:* as **a :** a disease of the pear caused by a fungus (*T. bullata*) **b :** a disease of the oak caused by a fungus (*T. coerulescens*)

**leaf-blister sawfly** *n* **:** a sawfly (*Phylacteophaga eucalypti*) whose larvae damage eucalyptus foliage in Australia

**leaf blotch** *n* **:** a plant disease esp. of fungous origin producing irregular dead or discolored areas in the leaves and distinguished from leaf spot mainly by the more indistinct or diffuse margins

**leaf-book** \ˈ=,=\ *n* **:** CODEX 2

**leafboy** \ˈ=,=\ *n* **:** a person who supplies the stringers with tobacco leaves from the baskets in which they are brought from the field in harvesting primed tobacco

**leaf bud** *n* **1 :** a bud that develops into a leafy shoot and does not produce flowers — compare FLOWER BUD, MIXED BUD **2 :** a grayish yellowish brown that is darker than deer, slightly darker than acorn, and slightly yellower than olive wood

**leaf-bud cutting** *n* **:** a cutting consisting of a segment of current season's growth with a leaf, axillary bud, and a small section of stem used in the propagation of various plants — called also *leaf mallet cutting*

**leaf bug** *n* **:** any of various bugs esp. of the families Tingidae and Miridae; *specif* **:** FOUR-LINED PLANT BUG

**leaf bundle** *n* **:** LEAF TRACE

**leaf butterfly** *n* **:** any of various butterflies that mimic leaves; *esp* **:** those constituting the nymphalid genus *Kallima* found in southern Asia and the East Indies

**leaf case moth** *n* **:** a bagworm (*Hyalarcta hübneri*) that damages leaves and fruit in Australia

**leaf cast** *n* **:** any of several diseases of conifers (as that caused by fungi of the order Hysteriales) producing a falling of the needles

**leaf chafer** *n* **:** a scarabaeid beetle that feeds as an adult on foliage of various plants

**leaf climber** *n* **:** a climbing plant that supports itself by means of its leaves which either have petioles (as in the clematis) that twist round the support or develop tendrils (as in the pea)

**leaf-climbing** \ˈ=¦=\ *adj* **:** supporting itself by means of its leaves ⟨a *leaf-climbing* plant⟩

**leaf crumpler** *n* **:** any of several small American moths or their caterpillars that form a nest by crumpling and fastening leaves together in clusters; *esp* **:** a moth (*Acrobasis indigenella*) of the family Pyralididae that feeds on the apple and related trees

**leafcup** \'⸗,⸗\ *n* **:** either of two tall coarse weedy No. American perennial composite herbs (*Polymnia uvedalia* and *P. canadensis*) that are strongly scented and have large thin opposite leaves and panicled corymbs of pale yellow or whitish flower heads
**leaf curl** *n* **:** a plant disease characterized by curling of leaves: as **a :** a disease of peaches caused by a fungus (*Taphrina deformans*) **b :** LEAF ROLL **c :** a virus disease of raspberries — called also *raspberry curl* **d :** EARLY BLIGHT a
**leaf-cushion** \'⸗,⸗⸗\ *n* **:** the remnant of the thickened leaf base remaining after abscission in some extinct plants and in various conifers (as members of the genus *Picea*)
**leaf cutter** *n* **1 :** LEAF-CUTTING ANT **2** *or* **leaf-cutter bee :** LEAF-CUTTING BEE
**leaf cutting** *n* [1*leaf* + *cutting*, n.] **:** a cutting consisting of a leaf instead of a shoot commonly used in propagating a plant (as begonia, gloxinia, African violet) — see SECTIONAL LEAF CUTTING
**leaf-cutting ant** \'⸗,⸗⸗-\ *n* [*leaf-cutting* fr. 1*leaf* + *cutting*, pres. part. of *cut*] **:** any of several chiefly tropical American ants of the genus *Atta* that cut and carry off the leaves of plants which they use in culturing various fungi for food
**leaf-cutting bee** *n* **:** any of various wild bees of the genus *Megachile* that cut rounded and oval pieces from the edges of leaves or petals to use in building their nests
**leaf disease** *n* **1 :** a disease localized in the foliage **2 :** a coffee disease caused by a rust fungus (*Hemileia vastatrix*) — called also *coffee disease*
**leaf drop** *n* **:** a premature falling of leaves (as the blighting and drooping of leaves associated with various virus diseases of the potato) — compare LEAF FALL
**leaf-drop streak** *n* **:** a phase of rugose mosaic developing soon after infection and characterized by necrotic streaks on the stem and underside of the veins of some of the leaves and by falling of the leaves from the lowest upward
**leaf-eating ladybird** \'⸗,⸗⸗-\ *n* **:** an Australian coccinellid beetle (*Epilachna 28-punctata*) whose larvae and adults damage potatoes and other plants
**leafed** \'lēft\ *adj* **:** having leaves **:** having leaves of a specified character or number — used chiefly in combination ⟨broad⸗leafed⟩ ⟨three-*leafed*⟩
**leaf·er** \'lēfə(r)\ *n* -s **:** a bindery worker who inserts leaves or sheets
**leaf·ery** \'lēf(ə)rē\ *n* -ES **:** LEAFAGE
**leaf fall** *n* **1 :** the natural separation and dropping of the leaf at the end of the growing season and over a short period in deciduous plants or intermittently throughout the year in coniferous trees — compare ABSCISSION **2 :** fallen leaves on the forest floor
**leaf fat** *n* **:** the fat that lines the abdominal cavity and encloses the kidneys of a hog and that is used in the manufacture of leaf lard and neutral lard
**leaf feeding** *n* **:** the application of nutrients to the foliage of plants
**leaf fish** *n* [so called fr. its resemblance to a floating dead leaf] **:** a small brown nandid fish (*Monocirrhus polyacanthus*) of tropical So. American freshwaters
**leaf folder** *n* **:** any of several moths whose larvae make shelter cases by folding the leaves of plants
**leaf-footed** \'⸗,⸗⸗\ *adj* **:** having leaflike expansions on the appendages **:** PHYLLOPODOUS
**leaf-footed bug** *also* **leaf-foot bug** *n* **:** a large sap-sucking bug of the genus *Leptoglossus* having leaflike expansions on its legs: as **a :** a bug (*L. oppositus*) injurious to cucumber, melon, and squash **b :** a bug (*L. phyllopus*) very injurious to orange, peach, pear, and other fruit
**leaf gap** *n* **:** a gap that surrounds a leaf trace
**leafgirl** \'⸗,⸗\ *n* **:** a girl or woman performing the work of a leafboy
**leaf gold** *n* **:** GOLD LEAF
**leaf green** *n* **1 :** CHLOROPHYLL **2 :** a variable color averaging a moderate yellow green that is greener, lighter, and stronger than average moss green, greener and deeper than average pea green, and greener and duller than apple green (sense 1) — compare FOLIAGE GREEN
**leafhopper** \'⸗,⸗⸗\ *n* **:** any of numerous small leaping homopterous insects constituting a family Cicadellidae that suck the juices of plants and on account of their abundance do considerable damage esp. to grass and fruit trees — see GRAPE LEAFHOPPER
**leafier** *comparative of* LEAFY
**leafiest** *superlative of* LEAFY
**leaf·i·ness** \'lēfēnəs, -fin-\ *n* -ES **1 :** FOLIAGE ⟨in these bits of ~ a few birds find grateful homes —John Muir †1914⟩ **2 a :** the extent to which a plant is provided with leaves **b :** the extent to which a cured legume hay has retained its leaves
**leafing** *pres part of* LEAF
**leaf insect** *n* **:** any of several insects of the family Phyllidae (order Orthoptera) in which the wings and expansions upon the legs resemble leaves in color and form and which are common in southern Asia and the East Indies
**leaf·it** \'lēfət\ *n* -s [irreg. fr. 1*leaf*] *archaic* **:** LEAFLET 1
**leaf lard** *n* **:** lard made from leaf fat into the highest quality lard
**leaf·less** \'lēfləs\ *adj* **:** being without leaves ⟨a ~ tree⟩ — **leaf·less·ness** *n* -ES
**leaf·let** \'lēflət, *usu* -əd.+V\ *n* -s **1 a :** one of the divisions of a compound leaf **b :** a small or young foliage leaf **2 a :** a leaflike organ or part; *esp* **:** the thin projecting part of the valve of a blood vessel **3 a :** a single sheet of paper unfolded or folded but not trimmed at the folds and bearing print (as an advertisement or instructions) on one or both sides **b :** a sheet of small pages folded but not stitched
**leaf lettuce** *n* **:** any of various cultivated lettuces that constitute a distinct variety (*Lactuca sativa crispa*) and are distinguished by leaves having curled, crisped, or incised margins and forming a loose rosette which does not develop into a compact head — compare HEAD LETTUCE
**leaf lichen** *n* **:** a foliaceous lichen
**leaflike** \'⸗,⸗\ *adj* **:** resembling a leaf in structure or function **:** having a broad flat thin form ⟨~ gills⟩
**leaf louse** *n* **:** APHID
**leaf mallet cutting** *n* **:** LEAF-BUD CUTTING
**leaf manna** *n* **:** LERP
**leaf meal** *n* **:** the dried and ground product of young leafy alfalfa plants used as a supplement in feeding livestock and poultry
**leaf metal** *n* **:** metal (as gold, silver, or tin) in thin leaves
**leaf miner** *n* **:** any of various small insects that in the larval stages burrow in and eat the parenchyma of leaves and mostly belong to the lepidopterous superfamily Tineoidea and the dipterous group Acalyptratae
**leaf-mining** \'⸗¦⸗⸗\ *adj* **:** being or living as a leaf miner ⟨*leaf⸗mining* beetles⟩
**leaf mold** *n* **1** *or* **leaf soil :** a compost or layer composed chiefly of decayed vegetable matter (as fallen leaves) — compare HUMUS **2 :** a mold or mildew of foliage
**leafmold** \'⸗,⸗\ *n* [*leaf mold*] **:** a dark brown that is lighter than art brown — called also *kolinsky, weathered oak*
**leaf monkey** *n* **:** any of several oriental langurs (genus *Presbytis*) — compare BANDED LEAF MONKEY, CRESTED LEAF MONKEY
**leaf mosaic** *n* **1 :** the arrangement of foliage in most plants (as in the common ivy) in such a pattern as to expose the maximum number of leaves to the direct rays of the sun with little loss of intervening space **2 :** MOSAIC 7
**leaf mustard** *n* **:** INDIAN MUSTARD
**leaf-nosed** \'⸗¦⸗\ *adj* **:** having a leaflike membrane or plate on the nose — used esp. of bats of the families Phyllostomatidae, Rhinolophidae, and Hipposideridae
**leaf-nosed snake** *n* **:** any of several small pale yellowish dark-blotched colubrid snakes (genus *Phyllorhynchus*) widely distributed at lower altitudes in southwestern No. America and having the rostral plate greatly expanded
**leaf of life :** AIR PLANT 2
**leaf plant** *n* **1 :** FOLIAGE PLANT **2 :** AIR PLANT 2
**leaf-raker** \'⸗,⸗⸗\ *n* **:** a person who engages in leaf-raking
**leaf-raking** \'⸗,⸗⸗\ *n* **:** work or a work project designed to relieve the plight of unemployed persons by providing them with gainful employment but having little or no intrinsic value ⟨we shall never again have to resort to *leaf-raking* as a way of making work for people —Henry Wallace⟩
**leaf red** *n* **:** CARTHAMUS RED
**leaf roll** *n* **1 a :** any of various plant diseases characterized by an upward rolling of the leaf margins **b :** a virus disease of the potato characterized by an upward rolling of the leaf margins, smaller tubers, and netlike necrotic areas in the phloem **2 :** potato mosaic that is characterized by a rolling upward or inward of the leaf margins
**leaf roller** *n* **:** the larva of an insect (as a tortricid moth) that makes a nest by rolling up plant leaves
**leaf rosette** *n* **:** ROSETTE 5
**leaf rust** *n* **:** a rust disease of plants and esp. of cereal grasses (as wheat or rye) primarily affecting the leaves
**leafs** *pres 3d sing of* LEAF
**leaf scald** *n* **1 :** LEAF SCORCH a **2 :** a vascular disease of sugarcane caused by a bacterium (*Bacterium albilineans*) characterized by creamy or grayish streaking and later withering of the leaves
**leaf scorch** *n* **:** an abnormal condition of foliage characterized by a burned or scorched appearance of the tissues: as **a :** a nonparasitic disease of the apple and other fruits in which there is a marginal burning of the leaves **b :** a purplish red scorch of strawberry leaves caused by a fungus (*Diplocarpon earliana*) **c :** a disease of the cherry caused by a fungus (*Gnomonia erythrostoma*)
**leaf sewer** *n* **:** a moth (family Tortricidae) or its caterpillar that makes a nest by rolling up a leaf and fastening the edges together with silk as if sewn
**leaf-shaped** \'⸗¦⸗\ *adj* **:** shaped like a leaf
**leaf sheath** *n* **1 :** SHEATH 2b **2 :** OCREA
**leaf sight** *n* **:** a hinged sight on a firearm that can be raised or folded down
**leaf spine** *n* **:** a spine (as of the barberry) developed from a leaf instead of from a branch
**leaf spot** *n* **1 :** a discolored area on a leaf caused by parasitic organisms or environmental factors; *esp* **:** one having a more or less sharp line of demarcation between it and healthy tissue — compare BLOTCH, MOSAIC **2 :** a disease characterized by discolored often circular spots on the leaves — compare ANGULAR LEAF SPOT, LEAF BLOTCH
**leaf spring** *n* **:** a spring made of superposed strips, plates, or leaves
**leafstalk** \'⸗,⸗\ *n* **:** PETIOLE
**leaf stripe** *n* **:** any of several diseases of plants causing striped discolorations on the leaves (as virus diseases of sugarcane or barley stripe)
**leaf supply** *n* **:** the one or more vascular bundles connecting the leaf with the vascular system of the branch or stem — compare TRACE
**leaf-tailed gecko** \'⸗,⸗-\ *n* **:** an Australian desert lizard (*Phyllurus platurus*) having a broad flat tail
**leaf tendril** *n* **:** a tendril developed from a part of a leaf (as of the pea)
**leaftier** *also* **leaftyer** *n* **:** a moth larva that lives in a folded leaf held together by silk strands
**leaf tobacco** *n* **:** LEAF 1c(2), 1c(3)
**leaf trace** *n* **:** a trace associated with a leaf — compare BRANCH TRACE
**leafwood** \'⸗,⸗\ *n, Brit* **:** HARDWOOD
**leafwork** \'⸗,⸗\ *n* **:** ornamental work resembling leaves
**leafworm** \'⸗,⸗\ *n* [ME *lefe-worm*, fr. OE *lēafwyrm*, fr. *lēaf* leaf + *wyrm* worm] **:** a moth larva that feeds on leaves — compare COTTON LEAFWORM
**leafy** \'lēfē, -fi\ *adj* -ER/-EST [1*leaf* + -*y*] **1 a :** furnished with or abounding in leaves **:** clothed with leaves ⟨the ~ forest⟩ ⟨the ~ month of June —S.T.Coleridge⟩ **b :** having broad⸗bladed leaves **:** BROAD-LEAVED ⟨mosses, grasses, and ~ plants⟩; *specif* **:** consisting chiefly of leaves ⟨a ~ vegetable⟩ **2 :** made or consisting of leaves ⟨a ~ bed —Lord Byron⟩ **3 :** resembling a leaf; *specif* **:** LAMINATE ⟨a ~ layer⟩
**leafy liverwort** *n* **:** a liverwort of the order Jungermanniales with a leafy gametophyte that has one ventral and two dorsal rows of leaves on the stem and is usu. epiphytic — called also *scale moss*
**leafy spurge** *n* **:** a tall perennial European herb (*Euphorbia esula*) naturalized and troublesome as a weed in the northern U. S. and Canada and having persistent rootstocks and linear to narrowly oblong leaves
**leag** \lēg\ *n* -s [origin unknown] **:** a kelp (*Laminaria cloustoni*)
1**league** \'lēg *sometimes* 'lig\ *n* -s [ME *lege*, fr. LL *leuga, leuca*, of Gaulish origin; akin to the source of OE *lēowe* league] **1 :** any of various units of distance from about 2.4 to 4.6 statute miles; *esp* **:** an English unit of about three miles — see LAND LEAGUE, MARINE LEAGUE **2 :** any of various units of land area equal to a square league (as an old Spanish unit equal to 4439 acres or 1796 hectares used in the old California surveys and an old Texas unit equal to 4428.4 acres or 1792.1 hectares)
2**league** \"\ *n* -s [ME (Sc) *ligg*, fr. MF *ligue*, fr. OIt *liga*, fr. *ligare* to bind, fr. L — more at LIGATURE] **1 a :** an agreement or covenant made between two or more nations, heads of state, or other political entities to achieve cooperatively a desired end ⟨~s are commonly made for mutual defense —Thomas Hobbes⟩ ⟨the ~ is between states of unequal quality —Sir Walter Scott⟩ **b :** an association or combination of nations or other political entities formed by such an agreement or covenant ⟨the economic and social work of the *League* of Nations —Mary E. Bradshaw⟩ ⟨the Political Committee of the Arab *League* —H.L.Hoskins⟩ ⟨Plymouth, Massachusetts Bay, Connecticut, and New Haven united in a ~ of friendship —W.S.Sayre⟩ — compare ALLIANCE, CONFEDERATION, ENTENTE **c :** an association of persons or groups united by common interests or for the achievement of common ends ⟨the organization of ~s for bowling and softball —Robert Hazel⟩ ⟨playwrights and musicians organize themselves into ~s of authors, composers, and performers —Thomas Munro⟩; *specif* **:** an association of baseball clubs — see MAJOR LEAGUE, MINOR LEAGUE **d :** an informal and often tentative compact or alliance — usu. used in the phrase *in league* ⟨privately in ~ with some particularly unsavory crooks —John Brooks⟩ ⟨entirely in ~ with her mother to embarrass me —Lloyd Alexander⟩ **2 :** a class or category of a particular quality or rank ⟨a bit out of your ~, though —Hugh Cave⟩ ⟨my sons are not in the same ~ with me when it comes to building a campfire —Hodding Carter⟩ ⟨don't make me laugh, I'm not in your ~ —Robert De Vries⟩ ⟨had no idea your folks were in that sort of ~ —Louis Auchincloss⟩
3**league** \"\ *vb* -ED/-ING/-S **:** to unite in a league **:** combine for mutual support ⟨we four were *leagued* together by a tacit treaty —C.E.Montague⟩
1**lea·guer** \-gə(r)\ *n* -s [D *leger* camp, siege, couch, lair, fr. MD; akin to OHG *legar* act of lying, bed — more at LAIR] **1 a :** a military camp: as (1) **:** the camp of a besieging army (2) **:** LAAGER **b :** SIEGE ⟨the ~ of Leningrad was broken —R.C.K.Ensor⟩ **2** *archaic* **:** a resident ambassador or agent
2**lea·guer** \"\ *vb* **leaguered; leaguered; leaguering** \-g(ə)riŋ\ **leaguers** *vi* **:** ENCAMP; *specif* **:** to form a laager ⟨at no time did a squadron ~ forward of the local infantry —J.C.Gorman⟩ ~ *vt* **:** BESIEGE, BELEAGUER ⟨the tide of war beats high around the ~*ed* walls —J.J.Roche⟩
3**leag·u·er** \"\ *n* -s [2*league* + -*er*] **:** a member of a league — usu. used with a qualifier indicating membership in a particular league ⟨12 million youth ~s —Kuo-Chan Chao⟩
4**lea·guer** \"\ *n* -s [D *ligger, legger* tun, fr. *liggen* to lie (akin to OE *licgan* to lie) & *leggen* to lay (akin to OE *lecgan* to lay) + -*er* (akin to OE -*ere* -er) — more at LIE, LAY, -ER] **:** an old Dutch unit of liquid capacity equal to about 128 imperial gallons (153.7 U. S. gallons or 5.82 hectoliters) still in use (as in the Union of So. Africa)
1**leak** \'lēk\ *vb* -ED/-ING/-S [ME *leken*, fr. ON *leka* to drip, leak; akin to OE *leccan* to moisten, OHG *zelechen* cracked by heat, leaky, OIr *legaim* I melt, dissolve, Arm *lič* swamp] *vi* **1 a :** to enter or escape through a hole, crevice, or other opening usu. by a fault or mistake ⟨the possibility of oil or exhaust fumes ~*ing* in —H.G.Armstrong⟩ ⟨if the granary be not tight, the grain will ~ out —C.H.Grandgent⟩ **b :** to let a substance (as water or gas) or light in or out through a hole, crevice, or other opening ⟨a camera bellows may ~⟩ ⟨the boat ~s⟩ ⟨the gas tank ~s⟩ **2 :** URINATE **3 :** to become known despite efforts at concealment **:** become public information **:** get out ⟨it's top secret, not a word can ~ for forty-eight hours —Louis Vaczek⟩ ⟨how it had been done would ~ across in time —Frank Ritchie⟩ — often used with *out* ⟨news of the discoveries ~*ed* out —*Amer. Guide Series: Nev.*⟩ ~ *vt* **1 a :** to permit to enter or escape through a leak ⟨camera bellows which . . . ~ light —*Eastman Kodak Monthly Abstract Bull.*⟩ ⟨hot in the train, the windows ~*ed* cinders —Lionel Trilling⟩ ⟨the little granary ~*ed* wheat —C.T.Jackson⟩ **b :** to cause to be issued as if by a leak **:** give off ⟨exquisite mosaics ~*ed* the sour stench —L.C.Douglas⟩ ⟨July night ~*ed* heat —J.T.Farrell⟩ ⟨phonographs ~*ed* . . . symphonies and string quartets —Winthrop Sargeant⟩ **2 :** to give out or pass on (as secret information) surreptitiously ⟨~*ed* information which resulted in some people making quick profits —*Springfield (Mass.) Union*⟩ ⟨~ important news to friendly newspapers⟩
2**leak** \"\ *n* -s [ME *leke*, prob. fr. ON *leki*; akin to ON *leka* to leak] **1 a :** a crack, crevice, fissure, or hole that usu. by mistake admits or lets escape (as water or light) ⟨the ship sprang a ~⟩ ⟨a camera bellows may have a light ~⟩ **b :** something that permits the admission or escape of something else usu. with prejudicial effect ⟨even the tightest precautions have some ~s —*Time*⟩ ⟨errors in change and pilfering are common ~s in the grocery business⟩ **c :** a loss of electricity or of electric current sometimes due to faulty insulation; *also* **:** the point or the path at which such loss occurs **2 :** the act, process, or an instance of leaking ⟨in the sun the outward ~ of energy is carried by radiation —Fred Hoyle⟩ ⟨through the process of premeditated ~s, the press may tell all —*New Republic*⟩ **3 :** a soft watery rot of fruits or vegetables caused by various fungi (as *Rhizopus stolonifer* or *Pythium debaryanum*) **4 :** an act of urinating — usu. used with *take* ⟨stopped to take a ~ —Saul Bellow⟩; not often in polite use
3**leak** *adj* [prob. of Scand origin; akin to ON *lekr* leaky; akin to ON *leka* to leak] *obs* **:** LEAKY
**leak·age** \'lēkij, -kēj\ *n* -s **1 a :** the act, process, or an instance of leaking ⟨fear of ~ of military understandings —F.W.D. Deakin⟩ ⟨such defects cause ~ of cement paste —J.R.Dalzell⟩ ⟨~ of body fluids from a surgical wound⟩ **b** (1) **:** loss of electricity due to a leak (2) *or* **leakage flux :** magnetic flux that does not follow a useful path (as between the pole pieces of a dynamo without passing through the armature) **2 :** an allowance of a certain rate percent for loss by leaking **3 :** something or the amount that issues or is lost through a leak ⟨in the grocery business . . . a ~ of about one percent is fairly common —Kenneth Ives⟩
**leakage inductance** *n* **:** the part of the inductance of a circuit that corresponds to the leakage flux
**leakage reactance** *n* **:** the part of the reactance of a circuit that corresponds to the leakage flux
**leak·er** \'lēkə(r)\ *n* -s **:** one that leaks: as **a :** a poultry egg with a cracked shell and broken membrane **b :** a leaky receptacle for canned goods
**leak·i·ness** \-kēnəs, -kin-\ *n* -ES **:** the condition of being leaky
**leak·less** \-kləs\ *adj* **:** being without a leak
**leak·man** \-kmən\ *n, pl* **leakmen :** a worker who looks for and repairs leaks in filled whiskey barrels
**leakproof** \'⸗;⸗\ *adj* **:** proof against leakage ⟨a ~ roof⟩
**leaky** \'lēkē, -ki\ *adj* -ER/-EST [2*leak* + -*y*] **1 a :** permitting water or other fluid (as blood) to leak in or out ⟨a ~ roof⟩ ⟨a ~ heart valve⟩ **b :** exuding large drops of water — used of butter **2** *archaic* **:** given to blabbing **:** not closemouthed
1**leal** \'lē(ə)l\ *adj* [ME *lel, leel*, fr. OF *leel, leal, leial*, fr. L *legalis* legal, of or relating to law — more at LEGAL] **1** *chiefly Scot* **:** LOYAL, TRUE ⟨~ to the core of her intrepid Scottish heart —Harry Lauder⟩ **2** *Scot* **:** free from error, inaccuracy, or falsehood **syn** see FAITHFUL
2**leal** \"\ *adv* [ME *lel, leel, lel, leel*, adj.] *Scot* **:** in a leal manner
**leal·ly** \-ē(ə)lē, -li\ *adv* [ME *lelly*, fr. *lel, leel*, adj. + -*ly*] *Scot* **:** in a leal manner
1**leam** \'lēm\ *n* -s [ME *leme*, fr. OE *lēoma*; akin to OS *liomo* gleam, radiance, ON *ljōmi* radiance, OE *lēoht* light — more at LIGHT] *chiefly Scot* **:** a gleam of light **:** RADIANCE
2**leam** \"\ *vi* -ED/-ING/-S [ME *lemen*, fr. *leme*, n.] *chiefly Scot* **:** to shine forth **:** GLEAM
3**leam** \"\ *n* -s [origin unknown] *dial Eng* **:** a drain in a fen
4**leam** \"\ *vt* -ED/-ING/-S [origin unknown] *dial Brit* **:** to take (nuts) from the husks
**leam·er** \-mə(r)\ *n* -s [4*leam* + -*er*] *dial Brit* **:** a nut fully ripe and ready to fall from the husk
1**lean** \'lēn\ *vb* **leaned**, *chiefly Brit* 'lent\ *or chiefly Brit* **leant** \'lent\ **leaned** *or chiefly Brit* **leant; leaning; leans** [ME *lenen*, fr. OE *hleonian, hlinian*; akin to OS *hlinōn* to lean, OHG *hlinēn* to lean, L *clinare* to bend, incline, Gk *klinein* to lean, Skt *śrayate* he leans on] *vi* **1 a :** to incline, deviate, or bend from a vertical position ⟨~*ed* forward to get a better look⟩ **:** be in an inclining position ⟨this fence ~s badly⟩ **b :** to incline or bend so as to receive support **:** cast one's weight by inclining or bearing down to one side ⟨~ on me as we walk⟩ ⟨~*ed* on his staff⟩ **c :** to put the weight of one's body into a stroke ⟨~*ed* into another inviting pitch —*N.Y. Times*⟩ **2** *now chiefly Scot* **:** to sit or lie down — usu. used with *down* **3 :** to rest, rely, or draw for support or inspiration — used with *on* or *upon* ⟨preferring not to ~ on his father in building a career —*Current Biog.*⟩ ⟨this room not only ~s on the past but improves on it —Edgar Kaufmann⟩ ⟨~s heavily upon certain modern clichés —R.D.Altick⟩ ⟨eastern Brazilians ~ more heavily on the sweet potato —R.H. Lowie⟩ **4 :** to incline in opinion, taste, or desire ⟨~*ed* toward a teaching career —*Current Biog.*⟩ ⟨~ to the belief that there was foul play —S.H.Adams⟩ ⟨~s toward the native dishes —A.L.Himbert⟩ ~ *vt* **1 :** to cause to lean **:** INCLINE, REST ⟨~*ed* her head upon her arm —Pearl Buck⟩ ⟨~ the board against the wall⟩ **2** *now chiefly Scot* **:** to seat or lay (oneself) — usu. used with *down* — **lean over backward :** to go to the opposite extreme in order to offset a tendency ⟨*leaning over backward* to offend no one —H.L.Smith b. 1913⟩ ⟨*leaned over backward* . . . to avoid the appearance of favoritism —*Nation*⟩
2**lean** \"\ *n* -s **:** the act or an instance of leaning **:** SLOPE, INCLINATION ⟨the ~ of a sail⟩ ⟨the wall has a decided ~⟩ ⟨body ~ is apparent only on the sharpest of curves —Walt Woron⟩
3**lean** \"\ *adj* -ER/-EST [ME *leene, lene*, fr. OE *hlǣne*] **1 a :** lacking flesh **:** not plump **:** THIN, LANK ⟨a ~ body⟩ ⟨a ~ man⟩ ⟨~ cattle⟩ **b :** having little fat or free from fat **:** chiefly or wholly of muscle ⟨eats only ~ meat⟩ **2 :** lacking richness, sufficiency, or productiveness: as **a :** lacking nutritive quality **:** MEAN, MEAGER ⟨supped on ~ fare⟩ **b :** POOR, SCANTY ⟨ample profits will produce better goods and services than ~ profits —*Report of Amer. Tel & Tel. Co.*⟩ ⟨~ material resources⟩ ⟨~ tax collections —*N.Y.Times*⟩ **c :** attended or characterized by privation, hardship, or scarcity ⟨a ~ life, that of a college professor —A.W.Long⟩ ⟨important as a source of food after a ~ winter —F.C.Lincoln⟩ ⟨came upon ~ days —Anatole Chujoy⟩ **d :** UNPRODUCTIVE, INFERTILE ⟨never ceased to love the ~ red soil —Josephine Y. Case⟩ ⟨attempts to make ~ soils yield —*Amer. Guide Series: Mich.*⟩ **e :** scantily furnished or provided **:** DEFICIENT ⟨a paper that was slim in size and ~ on news —W.A.Swanberg⟩ ⟨this year, so ~ in its new plays —John Mason Brown⟩ **f** *printing* (1) **:** not susceptible of fast and easy setting and hence unprofitable as piecework — contrasted with *phat* (2) **:** THIN, SLENDER ⟨type with a ~ face⟩ ⟨a ~ stroke in a letter⟩ **3 :** deficient in some essential or important quality or ingredient: as **a** *of clay* **:** deficient in plasticity **b** *of coal* **:** deficient in volatile matter **c** *of lime* **:** containing impurities and not slaking freely **d** (1) *of ore* **:** containing little valuable mineral (2) *of an alloy* **:** DILUTE **e :** low in combustible component — used esp. of fuel mixtures for internal-combustion engines; opposed to *rich* ⟨if the gasoline-air mixture is too ~ (too much air) excess air passes out the exhaust —Irving Frazee⟩ **f :** deficient in cementing material — used esp. of concrete and mortars **4 :** characterized by an artistically effective economy of style or expression **:** not lush **:** not verbose ⟨an orchestral suite . . . is ~, supple and sure —*New Yorker*⟩ ⟨~, compact writing that implies as much as it states —Stanley Cooperman⟩ ⟨his diction . . . is ~, his imagery precise —Herbert Read⟩ ⟨retold in ~ and forthright prose —*Word Study*⟩
**syn** SPARE, LANK, LANKY, GAUNT, RAWBONED, ANGULAR, SKINNY, SCRAWNY: LEAN stresses lack of fat and of rounded

contours ⟨a *lean* face with prominent cheekbones⟩ ⟨described as *lean* and wiry . . . six feet tall and weighs 170 pounds —*Current Biog.*⟩ SPARE may suggest an easy sinewy frame resulting from lack of excess ⟨his *spare,* not unsolid, but unobtrusive figure —John Galsworthy⟩ ⟨the *spare,* alert, and jaunty figure that one often finds in army men —Thomas Wolfe⟩ LANK may suggest tallness as well as leanness, sometimes suggesting the wiry strength of an economical build, sometimes connoting the effects of wasting away ⟨the hounds were fine beasts, they seemed *lank* and swift —Elizabeth M. Roberts⟩ ⟨meager and *lank* with fasting grown, and nothing left but skin and bone —Jonathan Swift⟩ LANKY may suggest a leanness accompanied by loose-jointed articulation or by callow awkwardness ⟨Lincoln, an awkward, *lanky* giant —Allan Nevins & H.S.Commager⟩ ⟨very tall and *lanky,* all wrists and ankles —Margaret Deland⟩ GAUNT may suggest a bony haggard leanness resulting from continued strain and undernourishment ⟨this one with the passing of the years had grown lean and *gaunt* and the rocklike bones of her face stood forth and her eyes were sunken —Pearl Buck⟩ ⟨always a very lean boy, but now he is looking positively *gaunt* —Compton Mackenzie⟩ RAWBONED describes persons not noticeably fat but stresses large often ungainly build ⟨a long, gawky, *rawboned* Yorkshireman —Rudyard Kipling⟩ ⟨tall, lean, stooping, *rawboned,* with coarse features —V.L.Parrington⟩ ANGULAR applies to leanness accompanied by a degree of graceless stiffness ⟨*angular* face and straight hair rather unattractive —Dorothy Sayers⟩ ⟨the thin, *angular* woman, with her haughty eye and her acrid mouth —Lytton Strachey⟩ SKINNY may suggest noticeable thinness resulting from inadequate food and suggesting lack of vitality ⟨the *skinniest* human being I ever saw. He had not enough flesh on his bones to make a decent-sized chicken —Robert Lynd⟩ SCRAWNY is closely synonymous with SKINNY but may suggest an underlying toughness ⟨*scrawny* kid, all legs and arms —Agatha Christie⟩ ⟨they were *scrawny* and underfed and "pinched their guts" with their belts for lack of food —*Amer. Guide Series: Tenn.*⟩

**4lean** \"\ *vt* -ED/-ING/-S [ME *lenen,* fr. OE *hlǣnian,* fr. *hlǣne,* adj.] **1 :** to make lean ⟨~*ed* down for travel —A.B.Guthrie⟩ ⟨~*ed* out by his illness —*Time*⟩; *specif* **:** to make (a fuel mixture) lean — often used with *out* **2 :** to cut the lean from (whale blubber)

**5lean** \"\ *n* -S [ME *lene,* fr. *leene, lene,* adj.] **:** the part of flesh which consists principally of muscle without the fat **:** lean meat

**lean·er** \-nə(r)\ *n* -S [1*lean* + *-er*] **:** one that leans; *specif* **:** HOBBER

**lean·ing** \-niŋ, -nēŋ\ *n* -S [ME *leninge,* fr. OE *hlinung, hlining,* fr. *hleonian, hlinian* to lean + *-ung, -ing* -ing] **1 :** the act or an instance of deviating from a vertical position **:** SLOPE ⟨detected a certain list or ~ of the tower⟩ **2 :** INCLINATION ⟨had a strong ~ toward law⟩ ⟨a reformer with radical ~*s* —Martin Gardner⟩

**syn** PROPENSITY, PROCLIVITY, PENCHANT, FLAIR: LEANING suggests a liking or attraction likely to influence although often not decisive about an eventual choice, policy, or course ⟨in spite of their antirationalistic *leanings,* the mystics of the twelfth and thirteenth centuries remained true to the established doctrines —Frank Thilly⟩ ⟨an able comedy actor with a *leaning* towards farce —E.H.Collis⟩ PROPENSITY may apply to an innate or deeply engrained longing or attraction making a certain course of action highly probable ⟨only precariously civilized and within us there is the *propensity,* persistent as the force of gravity, to revert under stress and strain, under neglect or temptation, to our first natures —Walter Lippman⟩ PROCLIVITY may apply to a strong inclination, sometimes notably individual, often to one indulged or manifested ⟨her free speech, her Continental ideas, and her *proclivity* for championing new causes even when she did not know much about them —Willa Cather⟩ ⟨despite her *proclivity* for gossip she was reticent upon family affairs —A.J.Cronin⟩ PENCHANT may indicate a decided taste for, special ability at, or strong proclivity for ⟨Americans, though in years now well in the past, had shown a *penchant* for tinkering with the money supply —J.K. Galbraith⟩ ⟨the psychiatrist does not deny that the child who rebels against his father is in many significant ways different from the same individual as a middle-aged adult who has a *penchant* for subversive theories —Edward Sapir⟩ FLAIR may refer to an instinctive ability or perception joined with innate power of discernment; it may also be a synonym for *aptitude, talent,* or *knack* ⟨good, although not quite tops, at his job until about a year before. Then something had happened to his judgment — his *flair* —Frances & Richard Lockridge⟩ ⟨as an ordinary clergyman he showed a great *flair* for organizing and the true ministry —George Bellairs⟩

**leaning tower** *n* [*leaning* fr. pres. part. of 1*lean*] **:** any of many towers which are out of the true vertical and have a visible slant (as that of Pisa, Italy, which is 16½ feet out of the perpendicular in a height of 179 feet)

**leanly** *adv* **:** in a lean manner

**lean·ness** \'lēnnəs\ *n* -ES [ME *lenenes,* fr. OE *hlǣnnes,* fr. *hlǣne* lean + *-nes* -ness] **:** the quality or state of being lean

**leans** *pres 3d sing of* LEAN, *pl of* LEAN

**leant** \'lent\ *chiefly Brit past of* LEAN

**1lean-to** \'lēn,tü\ *n* -S [ME *lenetoo,* fr. *lenen* to lean + *too, to* to] **1 :** a wing or extension of a building having a single-pitched roof typically built against and supported by the wall of a higher structure with a double-pitch or complete roof; *specif, NewEng* **:** a section of a barn often so constructed and used to house cows **2 :** a rough shelter formed by a sloping roof (as of boughs) supported typically by two uprights (as posts or trees)

lean-to 1

**2lean-to** \"\ *adj* **:** having only one slope or pitch — used of a roof

**lea oak** \'lē-\ *or* **lea's oak** *n, usu cap L* [after Thomas G. *Lea* †1844 Am. botanist] **:** a hybrid American oak (*Quercus leana*) regarded as a cross between the shingle oak (*Q. imbricaria*) and the black oak (*Q. velutina*)

**1leap** \'lēp, *dial or sometimes with reference to manege in Brit speech* 'lep\ *vb* **leaped** *also* **leapt** \'lept, *chiefly Brit* 'lēpt\ **leaped** *also* **leapt; leaping; leaps** [ME *lepen* to run, jump, leap, fr. OE *hlēapan;* akin to MD *lopen* to run, OHG *hlouffan* to run, ON *hlaupa* to jump, leap, Goth us*hlaupan* to jump up] *vi* **1 :** to run hastily or with a leaping gait **:** RUSH, BOUND ⟨~*ed* home to greet his father⟩ ⟨~*ed* into the fray⟩ **2 a (1) :** to spring free from the ground or some other supporting surface by the muscular action of the feet and legs or in some animals the tail **:** project oneself through the air **:** HOP, VAULT ⟨~*ed* high into the air⟩ ⟨~ over a fence⟩ ⟨~ down from a wall⟩ ⟨a fish ~*ed* out of the water⟩ ⟨~*ed* on a moving bus⟩ ⟨~*ed* on his horse and rode off⟩ **(2)** *chiefly Scot* **:** to dance in skipping or bounding movements **(3) :** to spring high from one foot to the other in dancing **(4) :** to rise or throw itself into or through the air **:** move precipitately or violently ⟨guns on the hillocks ~*ed* as they bellowed —Kenneth Roberts⟩ ⟨the great rocket ~*ed* skyward⟩ ⟨a tongue of flame ~*ed* down the stairway —Frank Yerby⟩ ⟨a sparkling waterfall ~*s* from a cliff —*Amer. Guide Series: Oregon*⟩ **(5) :** to rise to one's feet with a bound or other energetic movement ⟨~*ed* up and asked the chairman some pointed questions⟩ **b :** to beat high **:** THROB ⟨my heart would have ~*ed* at sight of him —Kenneth Roberts⟩ **3 a :** to pass abruptly or without transition (as from one state or topic to another) ⟨the states of Latin America have ~*ed* . . . from the ox-drawn cart to the airplane —Vera M. Dean⟩ ⟨made his face ~ into a sudden grimacing life —Bruce Mason⟩ ⟨~ irreverently from one trifling matter to another —H.A.Overstreet⟩ **b :** to increase suddenly and sharply ⟨costs on a job ~ entirely out of proportion —P.J.Adam⟩ **c :** to act or move precipitately or without careful thought or study (as in making judgments) ⟨~ to conclusions⟩ **d :** to join, enter, or intervene with eagerness or alacrity ⟨~*ed* to his absent friend's defense⟩ ⟨~*ed* into the discussion⟩ **e :** to take quick or immediate advantage **:** accept eagerly — usu. used with *at* ⟨~*ed* at the chance⟩ ~ *vt* **1 a :** to pass over by a leap ⟨~ a wall⟩ ⟨~ a ditch⟩ **b :** to pass over as if by a leap ⟨may be said to have ~*ed* the usual transitional stages —*Amer. Guide Series: Vt.*⟩ **2 :** to copulate with **:** COVER, SERVE — used of a male animal (as a stallion) **3 :** to cause to leap ⟨~ a horse across a ditch⟩ **syn** see JUMP

**2leap** \"\ *n* -S [ME *leep,* fr. OE *hlȳp;* akin to OE *hlēapan* to run, jump, leap] **1 a (1) :** an act of leaping **:** SPRING, BOUND **(2) :** a spring high into the air from one foot to the other in dancing **b (1) :** a place that is or must be leaped over or one leaped from ⟨took the ~ with great ease⟩ **(2) :** the distance covered by a leap ⟨a ~ of 10 feet⟩ **(3) :** a place in a waterfall where fish can shoot up in ascending the stream **(4) :** the sudden descent of a river to a lower level ⟨five clear ~*s* with intervening cascades —Arthur Holmes⟩ **c (1) :** an act of covering a female animal **(2)** *obs* **:** an act of coitus **2 a (1) :** a sudden passage, transition, or change (as from one state to another) ⟨made an abrupt and difficult ~ from a Latin classroom to an editorial desk —E.S.McCartney⟩ ⟨knowledge took a great ~ forward —Stuart Chase⟩ **(2) :** a choice exercised in the area of ultimate concerns **:** an existential decision ⟨a ~ of faith⟩ **b :** a skip in successive musical notes or tones **c :** a sharp or sudden increase ⟨a ~ of over 117 percent —Rex Lardner⟩ — **by leaps and bounds :** with extraordinary rapidity ⟨population is increasing *by leaps and bounds*⟩ **syn** see JUMP

**3leap** \"\ *n* -S [ME *leep* basket, fr. OE *lēap;* akin to ON *laupr* basket, OE *lēaf* leaf — more at LEAF] **1** *dial Eng* **:** a basket or box used esp. for chaff or seed **2** *dial Eng* **:** WEEL

**leap day** *n* **:** February 29, the intercalary day in the Gregorian calendar; *broadly* **:** an intercalary day in any calendar

**leap·er** \-pə(r)\ *n* -S [ME *lepere* one that leaps, one that runs, fr. OE *hlēapere* dancer, courier, fr. *hlēapan* to run, jump, leap + *-ere* -er] **:** one that leaps; *specif* **:** a circus performer who does acrobatic jumps

**1leapfrog** \'=,=\ *n* [1*leap* + *frog*] **1 :** a game in which one player bends down on all fours and another places his hands on the first player's shoulders or back and leaps over him **2 :** an act of leapfrogging ⟨aerial assaults, perhaps followed by new amphibious ~*s* —*Time*⟩

**2leapfrog** \"\ *vb* **leapfrogged; leapfrogged; leapfrogging; leapfrogs** *vi* **:** to leap or progress in or as if in the game of leapfrog: as **a :** to move from one locality to another in one or more jumps ⟨the vast majority came to our shores and then *leapfrogged* West —G.W.Pierson⟩ ⟨*leapfrogging* from city to city, lecturing —Bernard Kalb⟩ ⟨people *leapfrogged* from one suburban rim to the other⟩ **b :** to pass or go ahead of one another in turn ⟨giant trucks and midget cars *leapfrogging* along a highway⟩ ~ *vt* **1 :** to go ahead of (each other) in turn **:** leapfrog over ⟨packaging improvements and sales have been *leapfrogging* each other —*Modern Packaging*⟩ ⟨arranged to fish alternate pools, *leapfrogging* each other —Nevil Shute⟩ ⟨teams of scientists ~ each other, spurting ahead of the column to set up their instruments —*Time*⟩; *specif* **:** to advance (two military units or parts of two military units) by keeping one unit in action while moving the other unit past or through it to a position farther in front **2 :** to evade (an obstacle) by or as if by a bypass or jump ⟨demonstrated its ability to ~ defense pacts and unfriendly borders —John Bird⟩ — **leapfrogging** *n* -S

**1leap·ing** \'lēpiŋ, -pēŋ\ *n* -S [ME *leping,* fr. OE *hlēaping* dancing, fr. *hlēapan* + *-ung* -ing] **:** an act of one that leaps ⟨~ is usually done with a springboard that catapults the performer high into the air⟩

**2leaping** \"\ *adj* [ME *lepinge,* alter. (influenced by *-ing,* suffix forming gerunds) of OE *hlēapende,* fr. pres. part. of *hlēapan* to run, jump, leap] **1 :** marked by or using leaps ⟨a ~ gait⟩ ⟨~ animals⟩ **2 :** used for leaps ⟨a ~ board⟩ — **leapingly** *adv*

**leaping tuna** *n* **:** BLUEFIN TUNA

**leaping weir** *n* **:** a weir before an aqueduct or sewer intake to cause flood water to overshoot the opening

**leaps** *pres 3d sing of* LEAP, *pl of* LEAP

**leapt** *past of* LEAP

**leap year** *n* [ME *lepe yere,* fr. *lepe, leep* leap, jump + *yere, yeer* year] **1 :** one of the years in the Gregorian calendar containing the intercalary day February 29 **:** a Gregorian year of 366 days —see YEAR table **2 :** an intercalary year in any calendar

**leap-year day** *n* **:** LEAP DAY

**1lear** \'li(ə)r, -iə\ *vt* -ED/-ING/-S [ME *leren, leeren,* fr. OE *lǣran;* akin to OHG *lēren* to teach, ON *lǣra,* Goth *laisjan* to teach, OE *leornian* to learn] **1** *archaic* **:** to give instruction to **:** TEACH **2** *archaic* **:** LEARN

**2lear** \'lēr\ *n* -S [ME *lere,* fr. *leren, leeren* to teach] *Scot* **:** LORE; *esp* **:** knowledge gained through instruction

**3lear** \'li(ə)r\ *n* -S [ME *layour, lyer,* fr. MF *lieure* thickening for sauce, tie, bond, fr. LL *ligatura* tie, bond — more at LIGATURE] *archaic* **:** a thick sauce or gravy **:** a thickening for sauce or soups

**4lear** \"\ *var of* 6LEER

**5lear** *var of* LEHR

**lea rig** *n* [fr. (assumed) ME (northern dial.) *leye rig,* fr. OE *lǣghrycg,* fr. *lǣg-* fallow + *hrycg* back, ridge — more at LEA (fallow), RIDGE] *Scot* **:** a grassy ridge or piece of land **:** a ridge left unplowed in a cultivated field

**learn** \'lərn, 'lən, 'ləin *dial* 'larn *or* -'lan\ *vb* **learned** \-nd,-nt, *Brit usu* -nt\ *also* **learnt** \-nt\ **learned** *also* **learnt; learning; learns** [ME *lernen,* fr. OE *leornian;* akin to OHG *lirnēn, lernēn* to learn, *-leisa* track, L *lira* furrow, track, Russ *lekha* garden bed, furrow; basic meaning: furrow, track] *vt* **1 a :** to gain knowledge or understanding of or skill in by study, instruction, or experience **:** receive instruction in ⟨~ a language⟩ ⟨~ arithmetic⟩ ⟨~ a trade⟩ ⟨~ dancing⟩ ⟨a law which must . . . be *learnt,* but can never be taught —Havelock Ellis⟩ ⟨only just *learnt* how to enjoy life —Joyce Cary⟩ **b :** to develop an ability to or readiness for by practice, training, or repeated experience — usu. used with an infinitive ⟨~ to read⟩ **c :** to become aware **:** REALIZE ⟨he had ~*ed* that in order to do what he wanted in writing he would have to publish himself —H.S.Canby⟩ **d :** to acquire (as a skill or habit or a modification of an existing habit) through experience, practice, or exercise ⟨we ~ our responses —W.H.Kilpatrick⟩ **e :** to commit to memory **:** MEMORIZE **2 a** *now chiefly substand* **:** TEACH ⟨send the Sirocco ten times a year . . . to ~ us to be toads —F.M.Ford⟩ ⟨had to ~ myself just about . . . everything —Harold Sinclair⟩ ⟨that will ~ you to keep out of mischief⟩ ⟨I'll ~ you to have done with misspellings —Augusta Gregory⟩ **b** *obs* **:** to inform (a person) of something **3 :** to find out **:** ASCERTAIN, HEAR ⟨I ~ that he will arrive shortly⟩ ⟨what have you ~*ed* about this matter⟩ ~ *vi* **:** to acquire knowledge or skill **:** make progress in acquiring instruction or skill **:** receive instruction ⟨~*ed* fast and well when he put his mind to it⟩ ⟨evidently went to school to play, not to ~⟩ **syn** see DISCOVER

**learn·able** \-nəbəl\ *adj* **:** capable of being learned ⟨it is a ~ thing —Edmond Taylor⟩

**learned** *in sense a* -nəd *sometimes* -nd, *in sense b* -nd *or* -nt\ *adj* [ME *lerned* instructed, educated, fr. past part. of *lernen* to learn] **:** of or relating to learning: as **a (1) :** possessing or characterized by academic learning **:** ERUDITE ⟨a ~ periodical⟩ ⟨the dean was a ~ man, and loved long Latin words —W.M. Thackeray⟩ **(2) :** associated with or dedicated to learning ⟨such ~ languages as Latin and Greek⟩ ⟨a ~ society⟩ **(3) :** well informed, skilled, or practiced in a specific field ⟨both are ~ in Horace —E.T.Booth⟩ ⟨experience had made my eye ~ in the valuing of motion —Thomas De Quincey⟩ **b :** acquired by the learning process ⟨~ skills⟩ ⟨~ responses⟩ — **learned·ly** *adv* — **learned·ness** *n* -ES

**learned profession** *n* **:** one of the three professions, theology, law, and medicine, traditionally associated with extensive learning or erudition; *broadly* **:** any profession in the preparation for or practice of which academic learning is held to play an important part

**learn·er** \'lərnər; 'lənə(r, 'ləin-\ *n* -S [ME *lerner,* fr. OE *leornere,* fr. *leornian* to learn + *-ere* -er] **:** one that learns **:** STUDENT, APPRENTICE **:** a beginner in some field ⟨a slow ~⟩ ⟨a foreign ~ of English —A.S.Hornby⟩; *specif* **:** an employee being taught and trained to perform a task or fill a position requiring a degree of skill and experience through instruction that is usu. informal and of indefinite duration as distinguished from that of an apprentice

**learn·ing** \-niŋ, -nēŋ\ *n* -S *often attrib* [ME *lerning,* fr. OE *leornung,* fr. *leornian* to learn + *-ung* -ing] **1 a (1) :** the act or experience of one that learns ⟨the ~ of a trade⟩ ⟨gives . . . evidence of trial-and-error ~ in paramecia —W.N.Kellogg⟩ ⟨~ may be regarded as a property of all living organisms —R. C.Noble⟩ ⟨~ experiences⟩ **(2) :** the process of acquisition and extinction of modifications in existing knowledge, skills, habits, or action tendencies in a motivated organism through experience, practice, or exercise — compare MATURATION **b (1) :** something that is learned or taught ⟨increasing the practical value of the ~*s* —H.R.Douglass⟩ ⟨the film does provide ~*s* —Catherine M. Adler⟩; *specif* **:** a subject that is taught in school ⟨emphasize the mastery of essential ~*s* —M. B.Smith⟩ **(2)** *obs* **:** ACQUIREMENT **2 a :** knowledge or skill acquired by instruction or study **:** ERUDITION ⟨book ~⟩ ⟨a man of good education and ~ —Jonathan Swift⟩ ⟨obtuseness in perception can never be made good by any amount of ~ —John Dewey⟩ **b :** knowledge accumulated and handed down by generations of scholars **:** CULTURE ⟨~ is a sacred deposit from the experience of ages —William Hazlitt⟩ ⟨Assyrian ~ of the seventh century B.C. is well represented —H.J.J.Winter⟩ **3** *dial* **:** formal education **:** SCHOOLING **syn** see KNOWLEDGE

**learns** *pres 3d sing of* LEARN

**learnt** *past of* LEARN

**lears** *pres 3d sing of* LEAR, *pl of* LEAR

**leary** *var of* LEERY

**leas·able** \'lēsəbəl\ *adj* **:** capable of being leased

**1lease** *or* **leaze** \'lēz\ *vb* -ED/-ING/-S [ME *lesen,* fr. OE *lesan* to gather, glean; akin to OHG *lesan* to gather, select, ON *lesa* to gather, pick, Goth *lisan* to gather, Lith *lesti* to peck up] *vi, now dial Eng* **:** to glean grain ~ *vt, dial Eng* **:** to separate (as impurities from grain) by picking

**2lease** \"\ *n* -S [ME *leese, lese,* fr. OE *lǣs* open pasture (gen., dat., & acc. *lǣse, lǣswe*); perh. akin to ON *lāth* landed property — more at LATHE] *dial* **:** an open pasture or common

**3lease** \'lēs\ *n* -S [ME *les,* fr. AF, fr. *lesser,* v.] **1 :** a contract by which one conveys lands, tenements, or hereditaments for life, for a term of years, or at will or for any less interest than that of the lessor, usu. for a specified rent or compensation; *also* **:** the act of such conveyance, the instrument by which it is made, or the term for which it is made — distinguished from *license* **2 :** a piece of land or property that is leased **3 :** a continuance or opportunity of continuance esp. in vigorous existence or action usu. because of some favoring change or development **:** HOLD, TERM — often used in the phrase *lease on life* or *lease of life* ⟨criticism took on a new ~ on life —C.I. Glicksberg⟩ ⟨with the development of civilian air commerce it took on a new ~ of life —*Current Biog.*⟩ ⟨if the election yields a majority prepared to support them, the ministry is given a new ~ on life —F.A.Ogg & Harold Zink⟩ ⟨the Scottish forwards seemed to have got a new ~ of life —John Buchan⟩

**4lease** \"\ *vb* -ED/-ING/-S [AF *lesser,* fr. OF *laissier, lessier* to let loose, let go, leave, fr. L *laxare* to loosen, fr. *laxus* slack, loose, spacious — more at SLACK] *vt* **1 :** to grant or convey to another by lease **:** LET ⟨*leased* his house for the summer⟩ **2 :** to hold under a lease **:** take a lease of ⟨a tenant ~*s* his land from the owner⟩ ~ *vi* **1 :** to be under lease or be subject to lease ⟨this property ~*s* at a monthly rental of $100⟩ **2 :** to lease a property ⟨fitted to limn the genus summer renter, having *leased* to a few invaders himself —*N. Y. Times Mag.*⟩

**5lease** \"\ *n* -S [perh. alter. of 1*leash*] **1 :** a system of crossing warp threads with cords or rods alternately over and under one end or in groups to keep them in position during beaming and weaving **2 :** LASH 4

**6lease** \"\ *vt* -ED/-ING/-S **:** to make a lease in (yarn or thread)

**lease and release** *n* **1 :** a nearly obsolete common-law mode of conveyance of freehold estates by means of a lease vesting a leasehold estate in the lessee upon actual entry and a subsequent release of the reversion to the lessee, thus vesting the fee in the lessee without livery of seisin **2 :** a nearly obsolete mode of conveyance under the Statute of Uses by means of a bargain and sale for a leasehold interest conventionally for a year, which under the statute vested the leasehold estate without entry, with a subsequent release vesting the fee in the lessee without entry or livery of seisin

**leaseback** \'=,=\ *n* [fr. the phrase *lease back*] **:** the sale of property to a financial or eleemosynary institution that leases it to the vendor for a period of years at a rental that will give a return and amortize the investment — called also *sale-and-leaseback*

**leasehold** \'=,=\ *n, often attrib* **1 :** a tenure by lease **2 :** land held by lease; *specif* **:** land held as personalty under a lease for years

**leaseholder** \'=,==\ *n* **:** one having a leasehold

**leasehold insurance** *n* **:** insurance against loss to a lessee because of cancellation of a lease as a result of fire or other specified peril

**leasehold mortgage** *n* **:** a mortgage under which a leasehold interest in property secures a debt or obligation

**lease hound** *n* **:** LEASEMAN 1

**1lease-lend** \'=,=\ *n, often attrib* [4*lease* + *lend,* v.] **:** LEND-LEASE

**2lease-lend** \"\ *vt* **:** LEND-LEASE

**lease·less** \'lēsləs\ *adj* **:** not having a lease

**lease·man** \'lēsmən\ *n, pl* **leasemen 1 :** a person in the petroleum industry who negotiates with landowners for land options, oil-drilling leases, and royalties and with producers for the pooling of production in a field — called also *landman, lease hound, leaser* **2 :** a person who contacts property owners to lease sites for the erection of advertising billboards

**lease picker** *n* [5*lease*] **:** 2LEASER

**1leas·er** \-sə(r)\ *n* -S [4*lease* + *-er*] **:** LEASEMAN 1

**2leaser** *n* -S [5*lease* + *-er*] **:** a textile worker who forms a lease

**lease rod** *or* **lease stick** *n* **:** one of the usu. two rods that form and keep the lease orderly during separation of the warp threads

**lease system** *n* **:** a system of hiring out prisoners at a fixed rate per day to a contractor

**1leash** \'lēsh\ *n* -ES [ME *lees, lese, leshe,* fr. OF *laisse,* fr. *laissier* to let loose — more at LEASE] **1 a (1) :** a thong, cord, or chain attached to an animal's collar or harness or to a hawk's jess and held in the hand for the purpose of leading, checking, or controlling the bird or animal or fastened to an object to secure or tether it ⟨a puppy on a ~⟩ — often used in the phrase *in leash* or *on leash;* called also *lead* **(2) :** such an article used for leading or restraining a small child (as on a walk) **b :** CONTROL, RESTRAINT, CHECK ⟨keep the reader under a guiding ~ —Robert Humphrey⟩ — usu. used in the phrase *in leash* ⟨the plan had been devised to keep floods in ~ —*Amer. Guide Series: Texas*⟩ ⟨the same quivering emotion held in tight ~ —R.C.Carpenter⟩ **2 a :** a set of three animals (as greyhounds, foxes, bucks, or hares) **:** a brace and a half ⟨a ~ of Russian wolfhounds —*Nat'l Geographic*⟩ **b :** any set of three individuals ⟨a ~ of stalwart sons —Green Peyton⟩ **3 a :** LASH 4 **b :** 5LEASE 1

**2leash** \"\ *vt* -ED/-ING/-ES **1 :** to tie together or hold with a leash **2 :** CONTROL, RESTRAIN ⟨exhausted by the effort of keeping his emotions ~*ed* —W.R.Marsh⟩

**leas·ing** \'lēzəŋ, -ziŋ\ *n* -S [ME *lesing,* fr. OE *lēasung,* fr. *lēasian* to tell a lie (fr. *lēas* devoid, false) + *-ung* -ing — more at -LESS] *now chiefly Scot* **:** the act of lying **:** FALSEHOOD

**lea's oak** *usu cap L, var of* LEA OAK

**lea·sow** \'lezō\ *n* -S [ME *lesow, leswe,* fr. OE *lǣs* open pasture (gen., dat., & acc. *lǣse, lǣswe*) — more at LEASE] *dial Brit* **:** rough pasture land

**1least** \'lēst\ *adj* [ME *leest,* fr. OE *lǣst;* akin to OFris *lērest* least; superl. corresponding to the compar. represented by OE *lǣssa* less, smaller — more at LESS] **1 :** lowest in importance or position ⟨the ~ of my worries⟩ ⟨anyone who preached its abrogation would be ~ in the Kingdom of Heaven —M.R.Cohen⟩ **2 a :** smallest in size or degree ⟨the ~ finger of his left hand appeared to have suffered a slight sprain —Elinor Wylie⟩ **b** *now dial* **:** being the smallest or youngest child — often used in the phrase *least one* or *least un* ⟨one of the ~ uns at home gets took down —M.E.Sheppard⟩ ⟨too busy . . . to show affection for any but the ~ one —Charlie M. Simon⟩ **c :** being a member of a kind distinguished by diminutive size — used in plant or animal names **d :** smallest possible **:** SLIGHTEST ⟨the ~ noise would startle her⟩ ⟨negotiates his way with trust and the ~ violence —Robert Francis⟩ ⟨treasures every ~ indication that she may be softer than her sister —E.K.Brown⟩ ⟨the ~ means shall be used to achieve the greatest end —Robert Richman⟩ ⟨believed that the ~ government was the best government —Irving Stone⟩

**2least** \"\ *n* -S [ME *leest,* fr. OE *lǣst,* fr. *lǣst,* adj.] **1 :** something that is least **:** something of the lowest or slightest possible value, importance, or scope ⟨that's the ~ of my worries⟩ ⟨the ~ that may be said⟩ ⟨at his ~ . . . he is diverting —Robert Phelps⟩ ⟨the ~ it can then do is to lend a hand —W.H.Whyte⟩ **2 :** a game in skat in which the object is to win as few points as possible with jacks trumps and with a base value of 10 points and which is played when no player bids voluntarily — **at least** *or* **at the least** *adv* **1 :** at the lowest estimate **:** as the minimum ⟨*at least* once a year . . . my wife and I drive up into New England —Budd Schulberg⟩ **2 :** in any case **:** at any rate ⟨unknown to the outside world, *at least* until recently —N.D.Palmer & S.C.Leng⟩ — **in the least** *adv* **:** in the least degree or manner ⟨not *in the least* unfriendly⟩

[3]**least** \"\ *adv* [ME *leest,* fr. *leest,* adj.] **:** in the smallest or lowest degree ⟨the ~ important of his reasons⟩ ⟨may grant a divorce to the party ~ in fault —Morris Ploscowe⟩ ⟨the Federal government acts best when it acts ~ —Max Ascoli⟩

**least bittern** *n* **:** a small American bittern (*Ixobrychus exilis*) that is largely black above with chestnut or yellowish brown sides fading to white below

**least common denominator** *n* **:** LOWEST COMMON DENOMINATOR

**least common multiple** *n* **:** LOWEST COMMON MULTIPLE

**least flycatcher** *n* **:** a small plainly colored flycatcher (*Empidonax minimus*) common in eastern No. America

**least sandpiper** *n* **:** the smallest American sandpiper (*Erolia minutilla*) — compare STINT

**least squares** *n pl* **:** a statistical method of fitting a line or plane to a set of observational points in such a way that the sum of the squares of the distances of the points from the line or plane is a minimum ⟨a straight line was fitted to the data by means of *least squares* —*Jour. of Research*⟩ ⟨a *least squares* fit of the best straight line to the points of Fig. 1 yields a slope —*Physical Rev.*⟩

**least tern** *n* **:** a very small tern of temperate No. America and Middle America that is usu. considered to constitute a race (*Sterna albifrons antillarum*) of the little tern

**least·ways** \ˈlēs,twāz\ *adv* [¹*least* + *-ways*] *dial* **:** at least ⟨~ I'm the only one working there regular —Harold Sinclair⟩

**least weasel** *n* **:** a small weasel (*Mustela rixosa*) having a short tail without a black tip that is found from Alaska to the Alleghenies and is the smallest American weasel

**least·wise** \-wīz\ *adv* [¹*least* + *-wise*] **:** at least ⟨or ~ that the robbers be made to answer for it —George Eliot⟩

**leat** \ˈlēt\ *n* -s [perh. fr. (assumed) ME *leet,* fr. OE *gelǣt* road junction, conduit; akin to OHG *gilāz* road junction; both fr. a prehistoric WGmc compound consisting of a prefix represented by OE *ge-* (perfective, associative, and collective prefix) and a final constituent derived fr. the root of OE *lǣtan* to let, leave, allow — more at CO-, LET] *dial Eng* **:** an artificial water trench esp. leading to or from a mill

[1]**leath·er** \ˈleth̲ə(r)\ *n* -s [ME *lether,* fr. OE *lether-;* akin to OHG *leder* leather, ON *lethr-,* OIr *lethar*] **1 a :** the skin of an animal or some part of such skin tanned, tawed, or otherwise dressed for use to render it resistant to putrefaction and relatively soft and flexible when dry **b :** dressed hides ⟨a dealer in ~⟩ **2 a :** SKIN; *specif* **:** a person's skin ⟨fell and scraped a bit of ~ off⟩ **b :** the pendulous part of the ear of a dog (as a hound) — see DOG illustration **3 :** something wholly or partly made of leather: as **a** (1) **:** STRAP (2) *chiefly Irish* **:** a strap used to discipline schoolchildren ⟨hit the front desk a ferocious crack with the ~ —James Plunkett⟩ **b :** a pump washer ⟨that pump leaks at the ~*s* —Joseph Whitehill⟩ **c :** STIRRUP LEATHER ⟨riding as the Boers always ride, with long ~*s* —Stuart Cloete⟩ **d leathers** *pl* **:** leggings or breeches made of leather ⟨a number of members of the Quality, on shining horses, their ~*s* creaking beautifully —F.M.Ford⟩ **e :** any of various balls used in games: as (1) **:** CRICKET BALL (2) **:** FOOTBALL (3) **:** BASEBALL **f :** the tip of a billiard cue **g :** the leather-covered part of an oar that engages the oarlock **h :** POCKETBOOK, PURSE, WALLET ⟨maybe you can get his ~; I couldn't —J.F.Fishman⟩ **4 :** a brownish orange that is yellower, stronger, and slightly lighter than spice or gold pheasant and paler and slightly yellower than feuille morte — called also *adust, oriole, tan*

[2]**leather** \"\ *vt* -ED/-ING/-S [ME *letheren,* fr. *lether,* n.] **1 a :** to apply or supply leather to **:** bind or cover with leather **:** form into leather **b :** to form a surface like leather on (a skin or pelt) esp. by treading **2 :** to beat with a strap **:** THRASH ⟨before I ~ the answers out of you —B.T.Cleeve⟩

[3]**leather** \"\ *adj* [¹*leather*] **:** relating to, made of, or resembling leather ⟨a ~ jacket⟩

**leatherback** \ˈ==,=\ *n* **1 :** the largest existing sea turtle (*Dermochelys coriacea*) distinguished by its flexible carapace composed of a mosaic of small bones embedded in a thick leathery skin, occurring in all warm seas but most commonly in the Atlantic, measuring up to nine feet, and weighing over a thousand pounds **2** *dial* **:** a soft-shelled turtle of the family Trionychidae

**leatherbark** \ˈ==,=\ *n* **:** a tree of the genus *Dirca* or the genus *Thymelaea*

**leatherboard** \ˈ==,=\ *n* **:** an artificial leather made by a pulping and compressing process typically from scrap leather or fibrous materials (as waste paper and wood pulp)

**leather breeches** *n pl, chiefly Midland* **:** green beans dried and cooked in the pod

**leather brown** *n* **:** a moderate brown that is lighter, stronger, and slightly yellower than bay, lighter and stronger than auburn, redder, lighter, and stronger than chestnut brown, and slightly darker than marron glacé

**leather brown 5RT** *n, usu cap L&B* **:** a basic dye — see DYE table I (under *Basic Brown 2*)

**leather carp** *n* **:** a scaleless variety of the carp (sense 1) developed under domestication

**leathercloth** \ˈ==,=\ *n* **:** a cloth usu. of cotton or plastic made to imitate leather by various coating, embossing, and finishing processes

**leathercoat** \ˈ==,=\ *n* **:** a russet apple

**Leath·er·ette** \ˌleth̲əˈret\ *trademark* — used for a product that is colored, finished, and embossed in imitation of leather grains and qualities and is used esp. in bookbinding and in the manufacture of various fancy articles

**leather fern** *n* **1 :** TEN-DAY FERN **2 :** GOLDEN FERN

**leatherfish** \ˈ==,=\ *n* [so called fr. the leathery skin] **:** any of various filefishes

**leatherflower** \ˈ==,==\ *n* **1 :** any of several plants of the genus *Clematis; esp* **:** a plant (*C. viorna*) of the southeastern U.S. having large reddish purple bell-shaped flowers with leathery recurved sepals **2 :** the flower of leatherflower

**leather-hard** \ˌ==ˈ=\ *adj, of clayware* **:** partly dry and hard enough for tooling

**leatherhead** \ˈ==,=\ *n* **1 :** BLOCKHEAD, DUNCE **2** *Austral* **:** FRIARBIRD **3** [so called fr. the practice of wearing a leather cap] **:** a 19th century watchman or policeman esp. in New York City

**leather-headed** \ˌ==ˈ==\ *adj* **:** STUPID, SLOW-WITTED

**leath·er·ine** \ˌleth̲əˈrēn\ *n* -s [¹*leather* + *-ine,* n. suffix] **:** an artificial or imitation leather

**leathering** *n* -s [fr. gerund of ²*leather*] **1 :** the act or an instance of forming, applying, or furnishing with leather **2 :** a covering or furnishing of leather **3 :** a process of inserting narrow strips of leather or cloth into long-haired pelts (as fox) to improve appearance and reduce bulkiness of garments

**leath·er·ize** \ˈleth̲ə,rīz\ *vt* -ED/-ING/-S **:** to convert into leather **:** treat so as to resemble leather

**leatherjacket** \ˈ==,==\ *n* **1 a :** a filefish (family Monacanthidae) **b** *also* **leather jack :** any of several fishes (genus *Oligoplites*) of the family Carangidae having the scales reduced and embedded in the skin; *esp* **:** a common fish (*O. saurus*) of both coasts of tropical America **2 :** any of several Australian trees with very tough close smooth bark; *esp* **:** COACHWOOD 1a **3** *Austral* **:** a johnnycake pan-fried or baked in hot ashes

**leather lake** *n* **:** FEUILLE MORTE

**leatherleaf** \ˈ==,=\ *n* **1 :** a north temperate bog shrub (*Chamaedaphne calyculata*) of the family Ericaceae with evergreen coriaceous leaves and small white cylindrical flowers **2 :** LEATHERFLOWER **3 :** a stiff leathery-leaved fern (*Polypodium scouleri*) with ovate fronds parted to the midrib

**leather-lunged** \ˌ==ˈ=\ *adj* **:** having an inordinately loud voice or tending to speak in an inordinately loud manner ⟨only the *leather-lunged* representatives could make themselves heard by their colleagues —Harold Zink⟩

**leather mouse** *n* **:** ³BAT 1

**leath·ern** \ˈleth̲ə(r)n\ *adj* [ME *letherne,* fr. OE *lethern, lethren,* fr. *lether* leather + *-en,* adj. suffix] **1 :** made of leather **:** consisting of leather ⟨a ~ purse⟩ **2 :** like or suggestive of leather ⟨the ~ wings of a bat⟩

**leatherneck** \ˈ==,=\ *n, often cap* [so called fr. the leather neckband which was formerly part of the marine uniform] **:** MARINE

**Leath·er·oid** \ˈleth̲ə,rȯid\ *trademark* — used for an artificial leather consisting of chemically treated paper combined with rubber and sandarac

**leather paper** *n* **:** an imitation leather made from properly colored paper embossed with a leather grain and sometimes varnished

**leatherroot** \ˈ==,=\ *n* **:** a stout Californian purple-flowered herb (*Psoralea macrostachya*) with tough roots used as fiber by the Indians

**leather rot** *n* **:** a firm rot of strawberries caused by fungi of the genus *Phytophthora*

**leathers** *pl of* LEATHER, *pres 3d sing of* LEATHER

**leather star** *n* **:** a common brightly colored starfish (*Dermasterias imbricata*) of the western coast of No. America distinguished by a thick leathery membrane covering the surface of the body

**leather turtle** *n* **:** LEATHERBACK

**leatherware** \ˈ==,=\ *n* **:** goods made of leather

**leatherwing** \ˈ==,=\ *or* **leather-winged bat** *n* **:** ³BAT 1

**leather-winged** \ˌ==ˈ=\ *adj* **:** having wings like leather

**leatherwood** \ˈ==,=\ *n* **1 a** *also* **leatherwood bush :** a small tree or shrub (*Dirca palustris*) with tough pliant stems and small yellow flowers — called also *moosewood* **b :** a tree (*Cyrilla racemiflora*) of the southeastern U.S. and So. America **2 a :** COACHWOOD 1 **b** (1) **:** a gum-yielding tree (*Eucryphia billardieri*) of Tasmania (2) **:** the red wood of such a tree

**leatherwood fern** *n* **:** EVERGREEN WOOD FERN 1

**leatherwork** \ˈ==,=\ *n* **:** work in leather **:** something made of leather

**leatherworker** \ˈ==,==\ *n* **:** a person who works in leather: as **a :** a worker who cuts, skives, sews, and otherwise prepares leather trim for automobiles **b :** a maker of the leather parts of surgical appliances **c :** a worker who makes and repairs gun slings, straps, and similar articles

**leatherworking** \ˈ==,==\ *n* **:** the process or occupation of making things from leather

**leath·ery** \ˈleth̲(ə)rē, -ri\ *adj* [¹*leather* + *-y*] **:** of or resembling leather in appearance or consistency **:** TOUGH ⟨showing his ~ calluses —James Still⟩ ⟨the ~ old solicitor —Christopher Morley⟩ ⟨those ~ weeds, so hard to kill —Cyril Connolly⟩ ⟨her husband's dark, ~ library —Louis Auchincloss⟩

**leathery turtle** *n* **:** LEATHERBACK 1

**lea·the·sia** \lēˈthēzh(ē)ə\ *n, cap* [NL, prob. fr. the name *Leathes* + NL *-ia*] **:** a genus of brown algae of the family Corynophlaeaceae having a globose generally hollow convoluted and gelatinous thallus made up of radiating threads

**leath·wake** \ˈlēth,wāk\ *adj* [ME *lithwayke,* fr. OE *lithewāc, leothuwāc,* fr. *lith* limb, part of the body + *wāc* weak, pliant — more at LITH, WEAK] *dial Eng* **:** capable of being flexed **:** SUPPLE

[1]**leave** \ˈlēv\ *vb* **left** \ˈleft\ **left; leaving; leaves** [ME *leven,* fr. OE *lǣfan;* akin to OHG *verleiben* to leave, ON *leifa,* Goth *bilaibjan;* causative fr. the root of OE *belīfan* to remain, be left over, OHG *bilīban;* akin to L *lippus* blear-eyed, dripping, Gk *lipos* fat, lard, Skt *limpati* he smears; basic meaning: to smear with fat, make sticky] *vt* **1 a :** BEQUEATH, DEVISE ⟨*left* a fortune to his wife⟩ ⟨was *left* a substantial legacy⟩ **b** (1) **:** to have remaining after one's death or extinction ⟨*left* a widow and two children⟩ ⟨*left* many water color sketches that . . . have won for him a significant place —*Amer. Guide Series: Minn.*⟩ ⟨prehistoric peoples *left* behind material witnesses to their cultures —Brewton Berry⟩ (2) **:** to cause to remain as a trace, vestige, or effect upon removal or cessation ⟨*left* a large stain on the tablecloth⟩ ⟨a wound that would probably ~ a scar⟩ ⟨these cheerful trees would ~ a sorry gap . . . if they were to disappear —Tom Marvel⟩ (3) **:** to cause to be or remain in some specified condition ⟨the educational system under English rule *left* the Irish-speaking people illiterate in their native tongue —David Greene⟩ ⟨the incident *left* him furious⟩ ⟨the war *left* Rome exhausted —W.K.Ferguson⟩ ⟨his rhetoric ~*s* me cold⟩ ⟨*left* me in the dark as to his true intentions⟩ ⟨a plan that would ~ younger members of the staff out in the cold⟩ ⟨*left* me holding the bag⟩ **2 a** (1) **:** to permit to remain undisturbed or in the same position ⟨~ the door open⟩ ⟨cut down the infected trees, but *left* the sound ones⟩ ⟨took cash and jewelry, but *left* the stock certificates⟩ **:** permit to remain unoccupied ⟨~ room in the car for your little sister⟩ (2) **:** to refrain from or omit doing, including, or dealing with ⟨*leaving* aside for the moment matters of political strategy —Y.G.Krishnamurti⟩ ⟨much was *left* undone⟩ ⟨*left* out many points of interest⟩; *also* **:** to fail to include or take along ⟨the poor kid always gets *left* at home⟩ — often used with *out* ⟨she's always *left* out when it comes to a date or a party⟩ (3) **:** to have as a remainder in a mathematical operation ⟨4 from 7 ~*s* 3⟩ (4) **:** to have as a remainder after consuming or utilizing ⟨did away with the whole pie, *leaving* nothing for me⟩ ⟨only one ton of coal is *left*⟩ — often used with *over* ⟨give what is *left* over to the dog⟩ ⟨too hungry to ~ anything over⟩ (5) **:** to allow to remain in the possession of after taking a part away ⟨how much does that ~ you⟩ **:** YIELD ⟨the price . . . which ~*s* him 30 per cent . . . ⟩ ⟨. . . which ~*s* him much does this profit —Adam Smith⟩ (6) **:** to fall short of being satisfactory by (an indicated amount) — used chiefly in the phrase *leave much to be desired* or *leave something to be desired* ⟨his playing ~*s* much to be desired⟩ **b** (1) **:** to let be without interference **:** permit to remain subject to another's action, control, or consideration **:** COMMIT, REFER ⟨~ it to you to decide —A.A.Hill⟩ ⟨unwilling to ~ it at that —*Time*⟩ ⟨it is well to ~ much to the reader's imagination —C.E. Montague⟩ ⟨the rest being *left* to the judgment of God —Irwin Shaw⟩ (2) **:** to refrain from interfering with the control, action, or destiny of ⟨~ them to work without hampering interference —*Irish Digest*⟩ ⟨was *left* to shift for himself⟩ ⟨~ him to do it himself —M.C.A.Henniker⟩ (3) *substand* **:** LET ⟨~ him go⟩ ⟨~ him be⟩ ⟨~ him have it⟩ ⟨~ loose of the rope⟩ ⟨~ him through⟩ **3 a** (1) **:** to take leave of or withdraw oneself from whether temporarily or permanently **:** go away or depart from ⟨*left* school at an early age⟩ ⟨~ the room this minute⟩ ⟨the cold did not ~ him for weeks⟩ ⟨it was clear their zest had *left* them —T.B.Costain⟩ (2) **:** to branch off **:** diverge from ⟨the road now ~*s* the river valley and enters the hill country⟩ (3) **:** to arrive at the position of the last exterior contact with ⟨the moon ~*s* the earth's shadow in a lunar eclipse⟩ **b :** to put, place, deposit, or deliver before or in the process of departing or withdrawing ⟨the caller *left* his card⟩ ⟨~ your hat in the hall⟩ ⟨the bus *left* me off at the corner⟩ **4 a :** DESERT, ABANDON, FORSAKE ⟨her husband *left* her and she is considering a divorce⟩ **b :** to terminate association with **:** quit the service of ⟨*left* the company in May⟩ ⟨has a job waiting when he ~*s* the army⟩ **5 a** (1) **:** to give up the practice or use of or a devotion or addiction to ⟨the opium eater who cannot ~ his drug —Thomas Wolfe⟩ (2) **:** to abandon as a field of interest or activity ⟨thinking of *leaving* business for research⟩ ⟨*left* her native lakes of rural New England to write a romance of the swashbuckling seventeenth century —Carl Van Doren⟩ **b :** CEASE, DESIST, STOP ⟨the sunset had just *left* blowing —Mary Webb⟩ ~ *vi* **1** *obs* **a :** CEASE, STOP **b :** to break off (as in a narrative) **:** leave off **2 :** to set out **:** DEPART ⟨time to ~ for the station⟩ ⟨*left* for the office at eight sharp⟩ — **leave alone 1 :** to leave in solitude ⟨afraid that she would be *left alone* —Carson McCullers⟩ **2 :** to refrain from touching or disturbing ⟨*leave* that paper *alone*⟩ **3 :** to refrain from using or having to do with ⟨*leave* the beer *alone* tonight —A.P.Gaskell⟩ ⟨housewives can presumably take their soap operas or *leave* them *alone* —M.C.Faught⟩ **syn** see GO, LET, RELINQUISH, WILL

[2]**leave** \", *dial & in Brit armed services* -ēf\ *n* -s *often attrib* [ME *leve,* fr. OE *lēaf;* akin to MHG *loube* permission, OE *alȳfan* to allow — more at BELIEVE] **1 a** (1) **:** permission to do something ⟨asked ~ to read a short statement⟩ ⟨absent by ~ of the Senate on official business —*Congressional Record*⟩ ⟨came without ~ to shoot on the estate —H.E.Scudder⟩ ⟨applied for ~ to inspect it —G.B.Shaw⟩ (2) **:** LIBERTY, LICENSE — used chiefly in the phrase *take leave* ⟨the subscribers take ~ respectfully to inform the public —*Amer. Guide Series: La.*⟩ **b** (1) **:** an authorized absence or vacation from duty or employment usu. with pay ⟨canceled all ~*s*⟩ ⟨collected his ~ pay⟩ ⟨most Federal employees earn annual ~, for vacation and other purposes —*Federal Jobs Outside Continental U.S.*⟩; *also* **:** the extent, duration, or period of such allowed absence ⟨still have 2 days' ~ coming to me⟩ — often used in the phrase *on leave* ⟨a professor on sabbatical ~⟩ ⟨on ~ from his law firm for government service⟩ ⟨had left orders that he was not to be bothered while on ~⟩ (2) **:** authorized absence or vacation from military duty usu. charged to the accumulated leave to which a person is entitled under provisions of law — compare FURLOUGH, LIBERTY (3) **:** authorized absence from an institution (as a school or hospital) ⟨at home on ~ from a state hospital —*Springfield (Mass.) Daily News*⟩ ⟨~ privileges are not extended to freshmen⟩ (4) **:** LEAVE OF ABSENCE ⟨at once agreed to give the necessary ~ —F.W.Crofts⟩ ⟨don't know if I can get ~ for that long a time⟩ **2 a :** an act of leaving the presence or company of a person or of departing from a place typically with some expression of regard or farewell — usu. used in the phrase *take leave* ⟨took very courteous ~ of the ladies⟩ ⟨took his ~ about nine⟩ ⟨reluctantly took our ~ of that pleasant town⟩ **b :** an act or experience of separation or alienation — usu. used in the phrase *take leave* ⟨have you taken ~ of your senses⟩ ⟨let us take ~ of that subject and turn to another⟩ **3** [¹*leave*] **a :** the position of billiard balls after a shot is completed **b :** the pins left standing after a bowler has rolled the first ball

[3]**leave** \"\ *vi* -ED/-ING/-S [ME *leven,* fr. *leef* leaf] **:** to send out leaves **:** LEAF — often used with *out* ⟨the black locust ~*s* out later than the other shade trees —Brooks Atkinson⟩

[4]**leave** \"\ *chiefly dial var of* LIEF

**leave and license** *n* **:** a plea in defense in an action of trespass that sets up the permission of the plaintiff

**leaved** \ˈlēvd\ *adj* [ME *leved,* fr. *leef* leaf + *-ed*] **1 :** having or displaying leaves ⟨a ~ branch⟩ **2 :** having leaves of a specified character or number — usu. used in combination ⟨the palmate-*leaved* horse chestnut⟩ ⟨four-*leaved* clover⟩

**leave in** *vt* **:** to pass a bid or double made in bridge by one's partner or rarely opponent

**leavelooker** \ˈ=,==\ *n* [prob. fr. ²*leave* "license" + *looker*] **:** a municipal inspector of markets in an English town (as in Lancashire)

[1]**leav·en** \ˈlevən\ *n* -s [ME *levain,* fr. MF, fr. (assumed) VL *levamen,* fr. L *levare* to raise — more at LEVER] **1 a :** a substance (as yeast) acting or used to produce fermentation in dough or a liquid; *esp* **:** SOURDOUGH **b :** a material (as sour milk and soda or baking powder) used to produce a gas that lightens dough or batter while it is baking; *also* **:** a gas so produced (as carbon dioxide, air, or steam) **2 :** LEAVENING ⟨a few really funny stories by way of ~ —Geoffrey Boumphrey⟩ ⟨without the ~ of popular education, a landlocked region was not apt to make much progress —S.E.Morison & H.S.Commager⟩

[2]**leaven** \"\ *vt* **leavened; leavened; leavening** \-v(ə)niŋ\ **leavens** [ME *levainen,* fr. *levain,* n.] **1 a :** to cause (as dough) to ferment **b :** to make light by aerating (as with carbon dioxide by the action of yeast or baking powder) **:** RAISE 11b ⟨practically all breads, rolls, and some products like coffee cake are yeast-*leavened;* crackers, biscuits, pretzels, cookies, and the major portion of cakes are chemically ~*ed* —Oscar Skovholt⟩ **2 :** to mingle or permeate with some modifying, alleviating, or vivifying element ⟨serious poetry ~*ed* with wit —Sara H. Hay⟩ ⟨a large fund of shrewd ability ~*ed* by charm —*Current Biog.*⟩ ⟨his bitterness is ~*ed* by a mischievous humor —N.R.Nash⟩ **syn** see INFUSE

**leavening** *n* -s [fr. gerund of ²*leaven*] **1 :** a leavening agent **:** LEAVEN **2 :** a trait or element that modifies, alleviates, or vivifies ⟨with a Welsh and French ~ in her mother's background —*Current Biog.*⟩ ⟨a ~ of genuine tourists —Rex MacGall⟩

**leav·en·less** \-vənləs\ *adj* **:** having no leaven

**leave of absence 1 :** permission to be absent from duty or employment ⟨obtained a *leave of absence* from the university —*Current Biog.*⟩ **2 :** LEAVE ⟨on an informal *leave of absence* from the First National Bank —Jean Boley⟩

**leave off** *vt* **1 :** to desist from **:** break off **:** STOP ⟨*left off* thinking about himself at all —L.C.Douglas⟩ ⟨*leave off* work at five⟩ ⟨is reluctant to *leave off* arguing⟩ **2 :** to stop wearing or using **:** omit to put in the usual position ⟨warm enough to *leave* his overcoat *off*⟩ **3 :** to abandon the use of **:** give up ⟨I have *left off* all other medicines —*Farmer's Weekly (So. Africa)*⟩ ~ *vi* **:** to make an end **:** break off **:** STOP ⟨the rain . . . finally *left off* at noon —H.E.Bates⟩ ⟨starts . . . where most writers *leave off* —Burke Wilkinson⟩

**leave out** *vi* **1** *chiefly South & Midland* **:** to go away **:** set out **:** LEAVE ⟨*left out* in a buggy⟩ **2** *dial* **:** to end for the day ⟨school *leaves out* at four o'clock⟩

**leave over** *vt, Brit* **:** to cause to remain unconsumed or undone till a future time ⟨*leave* this pie *over* for tomorrow⟩ ⟨*left* the job *over* until the next week⟩

**leav·er** \ˈlēvə(r)\ *n* -s **:** one that leaves ⟨high school ~*s* aged from 16 to 18 —L.R.McColvin⟩

**lea·ver·wood** \ˈlēvə(r),wu̇d, ˈlev-\ *n* [by alter.] **:** LEATHERWOOD 1 a

**leaves** *pl of* LEAF *or of* LEAVE, *pres 3d sing of* LEAVE

**leave-taking** \ˈ=,==\ *n* [ME *leve-taking,* fr. *leve* leave + *taking,* gerund of *taken* to take] **:** a taking of leave **:** ADIEU, DEPARTURE, FAREWELL

**leav·ing** \ˈlēviŋ, -vēŋ\ *n* -s [ME *leving,* fr. gerund of *leven* to leave] **:** something left **:** REMNANT, RELIC, RESIDUE — usu. used in pl. ⟨the ~*s* of meals —*Times Lit. Supp.*⟩

**leaving certificate** *n* [*leaving* fr. gerund of ¹*leave*] *Brit* **:** SCHOOL CERTIFICATE

**leavy** \ˈlēvē\ *adj* -ER/-EST [ME *levy,* fr. *leef* leaf + *-y*] *archaic* **:** LEAFY

**leaze** *var of* LEASE

**le·bach·ia** \ləˈbäkēə, -bak-\ *n, cap* [NL, fr. *Lebach,* town in northern France + NL *-ia*] **:** a genus of Paleozoic fossil conifers differing mainly from other conifers in having hairs on the leaves

[1]**leb·a·nese** \ˌlebəˈnēz, -ēs\ *adj, usu cap* [*Lebanon,* country in southwestern Asia + E *-ese*] **1 :** of, relating to, or characteristic of Lebanon **2 :** of, relating to, or characteristic of the people of Lebanon

[2]**lebanese** \"\ *n, pl* **lebanese** *cap* **:** a native or inhabitant of Lebanon

**leb·a·non** \ˈlebənən *sometimes* -bə,nän\ *adj, usu cap* [fr. *Lebanon,* country in southwestern Asia] **:** of or from the republic of Lebanon **:** of the kind or style prevalent in Lebanon **:** LEBANESE

**lebanon cedar** *n, usu cap L* [fr. *Lebanon,* mountain range in Palestine — more at CEDAR OF LEBANON] **:** CEDAR OF LEBANON

**leb·bek** \ˈle,bek\ *n* -s [origin unknown] **1** *or* **lebbek tree :** an Old World tropical leguminous tree (*Albizzia lebbeck*) that has large leaves with 4 to 8 pinnae and 10 to 18 oblong or obovate nearly sessile leaflets and greenish yellow flowers in globose axillary heads followed by long lustrous seed pods which clatter in the wind, that is widely planted in warm regions as a shade and ornamental tree, and that yields a valuable mottled coarse-grained wood somewhat resembling mahogany —called also *koko, siris, woman's tongue tree* **2 :** the wood of the lebbek — called also *East Indian walnut*

**leb·en** *also* **leb·an** \ˈlebən\ *n* -s [Ar *laban*] **:** a liquid or semisolid food made from curdled milk by the peoples of the Levant and No. Africa — compare KOUMISS, YOGURT

**le·bens·raum** \ˈlābənz,rau̇m\ *n* -s *often cap* [G, lit., living space, fr. *leben* life, living + *raum* space] **1 :** territory that is held to be necessary for the existence or the economic self-sufficiency of a state ⟨lands . . . earmarked by the Nazis as part of their ~ —H.C.Wolfe⟩ **2 :** space required (as by a community, institution, organism, individual) for life, growth, or activity ⟨the library is badly in need of new ~ —Hollis W. Piatt⟩

**le·ber·wurst** \ˈlābər,vu̇rst\ *n* -s [G, fr. *leber* liver (fr. OHG *lebra*) + *wurst* sausage — more at LIVER, BRATWURST] **:** LIVER SAUSAGE

**leb·haft** \ˈlāp,häft\ *adj* [G, lively, fr. MHG *lebehaft* alive, fr. *leben* to live (fr. OHG *lebēn*) + *-haft* (adj. suffix) — more at LIVE] **:** VIVACE, LIVELY — used as a direction in music

**le·bis·tes** \lə'bi(,)stēz\ *n, cap* [NL, fr. Gk *lebias*, a small fish + *-istes* -ist] : a genus of So. American topminnows that includes the guppy

**leb·ku·chen** \'lāp,kükən\ *n, pl* **lebkuchen** [G, fr. MHG *lebekuoche*, fr. *lebe* loaf (akin to MHG *leib* loaf, fr. OHG *leib, hleb*) + *kuoche* cake, fr. OHG *kuocho, chuohho* — more at LOAF, CAKE] : a Christmas cookie usu. made with honey, brown sugar, almonds, candied fruit peel, and spices

**le·blanc process** \lə'blän-, -läŋk-\ *n, usu cap L* [after Nicolas *Leblanc* †1806 French chemist] : a process formerly used for manufacturing soda by treating salt with sulfuric acid, heating the resulting sodium sulfate with limestone and coal, and extracting with water the soluble sodium carbonate from the dark-colored mass formed; *also* : a similar process for manufacturing potash

**le·bran·cho** \lā'bräŋ(,)kō, -än(-\ *n* -s [AmerSp] : a common mullet (*Mugil liza*) of the Caribbean area and south to Brazil — called also *blueback mullet*

**le·ca·ni·um** \lə'kānēəm\ *n* [NL, fr. Gk *lekanion* small dish or pan, dim. of *lekanē* basin, dish, pan — more at LEKANE] **1** *cap* : a genus of naked soft-bodied somewhat hemispherical scales **2** -s : any insect of the genus *Lecanium* — called also *tortoise scale;* see PEACH SCALE

**le·ca·no·man·cy** \'lekənō,man(t)sē\ *n* -ES [Gk *lekanomanteia*, fr. *lekanē* basin + *-manteia* -mancy] : divination by inspection of water in a basin

**lec·a·no·ra** \,lekə'nōrə, -nórə\ *n* [NL, fr. Gk *lekanē* basin + *hōra* beauty, grace; fr. the form and color of the apothecium] **1** *cap* : a genus (the type of the family Lecanoraceae) of crustaceous lichens that have apothecia in which the disk is surrounded by a pale margin and that are sometimes used for dyeing or for food — see ARCHIL, MANNA LICHEN **2** -s : any lichen of the genus *Lecanora* — **lec·a·no·ra·ceous** \;lekə-(,)nō;rāshəs, -nó;-\ *adj* — **lec·a·no·rine** \;lekə;nō;rən, -nȯl, \|,rēn\ *adj* — **lec·a·no·roid** \|,rȯid\ *adj*

**lec·a·no·ra·les** \,lekə(,)nō'rā(,)lēz, -nó'-\ *n pl, cap* [NL, fr. *Lecanora* + *-ales*] *in some classifications* : an order comprising all the lichens that produce apothecia

**lec·a·no·ric acid** \;lekə;nōrik-, -nórik-\ *n* [ISV *lecanor-* (fr. NL *Lecanora*) + *-ic*] : a crystalline phenolic acid $C_{15}H_{13}O_5$-COOH obtained from lichens

**lech** \'lek\ *n* -s [W *llech* slab, slate; akin to Bret *liac'h* stone monument, OIr *lie* stone (gen. *liac*)] : a prehistoric monumental stone; *specif* : the capstone of a cromlech

**le·cha·te·lier·ite** \lə,shäd·ᵊl'i,rīt\ *n* -s [F *lechateliérite*, fr. Henry-Louis *Le Châtelier* †1936 Fr. chemist + E *-ite*] : a mineral $SiO_2$ consisting of a vitreous or glassy silica formed naturally by the melting of quartz sand as a result of lightning or occas. the heat of impact of meteorites

**le cha·te·lier's law** *or* **le chatelier's principle** \lə'shäd·ᵊl-,yāz-\ *n, usu cap 1st L & C* [after Henry-Louis *Le Châtelier*] : a statement in physics and chemistry: if the equilibrium of a system is disturbed by a change in one or more of the determining factors (as temperature, pressure, or concentration) the system tends to adjust itself to a new equilibrium by counteracting as far as possible the effect of the change

**lechayim** *or* **lechayyim** *var of* LEHAYIM

**lech·ea** \'lekēə\ *n, cap* [NL, fr. Johan *Leche* †1764 Sw. botanist] : a genus of herbs or subshrubs (family Cistaceae) having much-branched stems and minute purplish or greenish trimerous flowers — see PINWEED

**¹lech·er** \'lechə(r)\ *n* -s [ME *lechour*, fr. OF *lecheor*, fr. *lechier* to lick, live in debauchery or gluttony (of Gmc origin; akin to OHG *leckōn* to lick) + *-eor* -or — more at LICK] : a man who engages in lechery

**²lecher** \"\ *vi* -ED/-ING/-S [ME *lecheren*, fr. *lechour*, n.] : to practice lechery ⟨something better to do than drink and ~ —Agnes Repplier⟩

**lech·er·ous** \-ch(ə)rəs\ *adj* [ME, fr. MF *lechereus*, fr. OF, fr. *lecheor* + *-eus* -ous] **1** : given to lechery ⟨a ~ and self-indulgent good-for-nothing —Thomas Halton⟩ **2** : of, suggesting, or having the characteristics of a lecher ⟨well calculated to raise a ~ gleam in the . . . eye —R.S.Lanier⟩ **3** : arousing lust : sexually provocative ⟨a young girl came on with a ~ fandango —G.A.Wagner⟩ — **lech·er·ous·ly** *adv* — **lech·er·ous·ness** *n* -ES

**lech·er wires** \'lekə(r)-\ *n pl, usu cap L* [after Ernst *Lecher* †1926 Austrian physicist] : a pair of parallel wires so adjusted in length that the frequency of an electromagnetic wave may be determined from the position of the nodes and loops of the standing electromagnetic waves formed along the wires

**lech·ery** \'lech(ə)rē, -ri\ *n* -ES [ME *lecherie*, fr. OF, fr. *lechier* to lick, live in debauchery or gluttony + *-erie* -ery — more at LECHER] **1** : inordinate indulgence in sexual activity : LEWDNESS, LASCIVIOUSNESS ⟨a horrific sex prudishness which dissolved into an enervating ~ —*Times Lit. Supp.*⟩ **2** : an act of lechery ⟨his tasteless *lecheries* —*N.Y. Herald Tribune*⟩

**le·cho·sa** \lā'chōsə\ *or* **le·cho·za** \-ōzə\ *n* -s [Sp *lechosa*, fr. fem. of *lechoso* milky, fr. *leche* milk (fr. L *lact-, lac*) + *-oso* -ous (fr. L *-osus*) — more at GALAXY] : PAPAYA

**lech·ri·o·dont** \'lekrēə,dänt\ *adj* [fr. Gk *lechrios* slanting + E *-odont*] *of a salamander* : having palatal teeth only in anteriorly diverging or transverse rows on the posterior end of the vomers

**lech·ri·o·don·ta** \,==='däntə\ *n pl, cap* [NL, fr. Gk *lechrios* slanting + NL *-odonta*] *in some classifications* : a primary division of Caudata comprising salamanders that are lechriodont

**lech·u·gui·lla** *also* **lech·e·gui·lla** \,lechə'gē(y)ə\ *n* -s [MexSp, fr. Sp, wild lettuce, dim. of *lechuga* lettuce, fr. L *lactuca* — more at LETTUCE] : any of several Mexican agaves (as *Agave lecheguilla*) yielding istle fiber

**lechuguilla fever** *also* **lechuguilla poisoning** *n* : a serious intoxication occurring in sheep and goats in the southwestern U.S. as a result of their feeding on a lechuguilla (*Agave lecheguilla*) and involving necrosis of the liver and kidney accompanied by jaundice and in light-skinned animals photosensitization and dermatitis

**le·chwe** \'lēchwē\ *also* **li·chi** \-chē\ *n* -s [of Bantu origin; akin to Sesuto *letsa* lechwe] : an African antelope (*Onotragus leche*) that is somewhat smaller than the related waterbuck and is chiefly fulvous with white belly and blackish legs

**le·cid·ea** \lə'sidēə\ *n, cap* [NL, fr. Gk *lekid-, lekis*, dim. of *lekos* dish — more at BALANCE] : a large genus (the type of the family Lecideaceae) of crustose lichens found on rocks and tree trunks and distinguished by the usu. dark hypothecium — **le·cid·e·a·ceous** \lə;sidē;āshəs\ *adj* — **le·cid·e·i·form** \lə'sidēə,fȯrm\ *adj* — **le·cid·e·ine** \-ēən\ *adj* — **le·cid·i·oid** \-ē,ȯid\ *adj*

**lecith-** *or* **lecitho-** *comb form* [ISV, fr. Gk *lekith-, lekitho-*, fr. *lekithos*, prob. of non-IE origin] : yolk of an egg ⟨*lecithin*⟩ ⟨*lecitho*protein⟩

**lec·i·thal** \'lesəthəl\ *also* **lec·i·thic** \-thik, -thēk\ *adj* [*lecith-* + *-al* or *-ic*] : having a yolk — often used in combination ⟨*homolecithal*⟩ ⟨*telolecithal*⟩ — **lec·i·thal·i·ty** \,=='thaləd·ē\ *n* -ES

**lec·i·thin** \'lesəthən\ *n* -s [ISV *lecith-* + *-in*] **1** : any of several waxy hygroscopic phosphatides that are widely distributed in animals and plants (as in nervous tissue), that form colloidal solutions in water and have emulsifying, wetting, and antioxidant properties, and that are choline esters of phosphatidic acids yielding on complete hydrolysis two fatty acid molecules and one molecule each of glycerol, phosphoric acid, and choline **2** : a commercially produced mixture of phosphatides containing lecithin: as **a** : a yellow to brown waxy solid obtained from egg yolk and used chiefly in medicine — called also *ovolecithin* **b** : a brown unbleached to light yellow bleached plastic to fluid substance that is obtained in the manufacture of soybean oil and usu. contains oil and other components as well as phosphatides and that is used in foods (as margarine, chocolate, bakery products) and animal feeds, in pharmaceutical and cosmetic products, in paints and printing inks, and in gasoline, lubricating oils, and other petroleum products as an additive — called also *commercial lecithin, soybean lecithin*

**lec·i·thin·ase** \-thə,nās, -āz\ *n* -s [ISV *lecithin* + *-ase*] : any of four enzymes that hydrolyze lecithins or cephalins by attacking different ester linkages: as **a** : a crystallizable enzyme that is found esp. in many venoms and that accelerates the removal of only one of the two fatty acid units in a molecule — called also *lecithinase A, phospholipase A;* compare LYSOLECITHIN **b** : an enzyme that is found in various plant and animal extracts and in bacteria and that accelerates the removal of the remaining fatty acid unit — called also *lecithinase B, phospholipase B*

**lec·i·tho·protein** \¦lesə(,)thō+\ *n* [*lecith-* + *protein*] : any of a class of compounds of lecithin or other phosphatide with protein

**leck** \'lek\ *n* -s [origin unknown] *dial Brit* : a hard clay subsoil

**le·clan·ché cell** \lə¦klä^n¦shā-\ *n, usu cap L* [after Georges *Leclanché* †1882 French chemist] : a zinc-carbon primary cell whose exciting liquid is a solution of sal ammoniac

**le·conte's sparrow** \lə'känt(s)-\ *n, usu cap L* [after John L. *Le Conte* †1883 Am. entomologist] : a small streaked buffy and brown sparrow (*Passerherbulus caudacutus*) of the grasslands of the west-central U.S. and Canada

**le·cont·ite** \lə'känt·,īt\ *n* -s [John L. *Le Conte* + E *-ite*] : a mineral $Na(NH_4,K)SO_4 \cdot 2H_2O$ consisting of a hydrous sodium potassium ammonium sulfate found in bat guano

**le·cros·ia** \lə'krósēə\ *n, cap* [NL, fr. *Le Cros*, town in southeastern France + NL *-ia*] : a genus of fossil coniferous woody plants of the Carboniferous and Permian periods characterized by isolated erect ovoid female cones that consist of numerous sessile narrow scales each of which bears two winged seeds

**lect** *abbr* **1** lector **2** lecture, lecturer

**lec·tern** \'lektə(r)n, -,tərn, -,tən, -,təin\ *n* -s [ME *lectorne, lectrun*, alter. (influenced by ML *lectorinum, lectrinum* lectern) of *lettorne, letrune*, fr. MF *letrun, letrin*, fr. ML *lectorinum, lectrinum*, fr. LL *lector* + L *-inum* (neut. of *-inus* -ine) — more at LECTOR] **1 a** : a reading desk in a church on which the Bible is placed and from which scripture lessons are read during public worship **b** : a singing desk used in the choir of a church **2** : a desk or stand with a sloping top and usu. a ledge at the bottom of the slope designed to support a book or script in a convenient position for a reader standing before it ⟨was always standing restlessly at his ~ when his classes assembled —James Thurber⟩ ⟨spoke from an ornate ~⟩

lectern 1a

**lec·tin** \'lektən\ *n* -s [L *lectus* (past part. of *legere* to gather, select) + E *-in*] : a substance that is not known to be an antibody but that combines specifically with an antigen and produces phenomena resembling immunological reactions

**lec·tion** \'lekshən\ *n* -s [LL *lection-, lectio* — more at LESSON] **1** : a lesson or selection from sacred writings read in a church service **2** [NL *lection-, lectio*, fr. L] : a variant reading in a copy or edition of a text ⟨are offended by the obtrusion of the new ~s into the text —Thomas De Quincey⟩

**lec·tion·ary** \'lekshə,nerē, -ri\ *n* -ES [ML *lectionarium*, fr. LL *lection-, lectio* lection + *-arium* -ary] **1** : a book of lections for use in a church service **2** : a list of lections for use in a church service

**lec·ti·ster·ni·um** \,lektə'stərnēəm\ *n, pl* **lectisterniums** \-ēəmz\ *or* **lectister·nia** \-ēə\ [L, fr. *lectus* couch + *-i-* + *-sternium* (fr. *sternere* to spread) — more at LIE, STREW] : a religious rite of ancient Greece and Rome marked by the placing of images of gods on couches and the spreading of food before them

**lec·tor** \'lektə(r), -k,tō(ə)r, -ó(ə)\ *n* -s [LL, fr. L, one that reads, fr. *lectus* (past part. of *legere* to read) + *-or*] **1** : one whose chief duty is to read the lessons in a church service; *specif* : one ordained in the second lowest office of the minor orders in the Roman Catholic Church **2** [ML, fr. L] : a public lecturer at a college or university

**lec·tor·ate** \'lekt(ə)rət, -tə,rāt\ *or* **lec·tor·ship** \'lektər,ship, -k,tór,-\ *n* -s *often cap* [LL *lectoratus*, fr. *lector* lector + L *-atus* -ate] : the office or order of lector

**lec·to·type** \'lektə,tīp\ *n* [Gk *lektos* picked, chosen (fr. *legein* to gather, choose) + E *type*] : a specimen chosen as type of a species or subspecies if the author of the classification fails to designate a type

**¹lec·ture** \'lekchə(r), -kshə(r)\ *n* -s *often attrib* [ME, fr. MF, fr. L *lectura*, fr. *lectus* (past part. of *legere* to gather, select, read) + *-ura* -ure — more at LEGEND] **1** *archaic* **a** (1) : the act of reading : PERUSAL ⟨that face whose ~ shows what perfect beauty is —Philip Sidney⟩ (2) : something read or perused ⟨would limit . . . the Latin ~s to selected plays —Catherine Macaulay⟩ **b** (1) : the act of reading aloud ⟨her tongue faltered: the ~ flowed unevenly —Charlotte Brontë⟩ (2) : something read aloud ⟨then came a ~ out of some pious writer —Daniel Rock⟩ **2 a** : a discourse given before an audience esp. for instruction ⟨resources for growth . . . in books, exhibits, conferences, ~s —Gertrude H. Hildreth⟩ ⟨~ hall⟩ **b** *archaic* : a course of lectures usu. given regularly in accordance with the terms of their foundation : LECTURESHIP **3 a** : an instructional discourse given by a member of a college or university faculty ⟨are still using ~s to pass out information —Lynn White⟩ ⟨the ~ method⟩ ⟨a ~ course⟩ **b** : a college or university class; *esp* : one at which a lecture is given ⟨students . . . carrying only one subject or a short series of ~s —L.L.Bethel⟩ **c** *obs* : a private lesson ⟨attends every morning to give him a ~ upon speaking —Samuel Foote⟩ **4** *obs* : an instructive example ⟨heaven means to make one half of the species a moral ~ to the other —Edward Young⟩ **5** : a severe or formal reproof : REPRIMAND, SCOLDING ⟨was giving the rest of the family a sharp-tongued ~ —Eve Langley⟩

**²lecture** \"\ *vb* **lectured; lectured; lecturing** \-kchəriŋ, -ksh(ə)riŋ\ **lectures** *vi* : to deliver a lecture or a course of lectures ⟨found time to ~ at various colleges —J.C.Archer⟩ ~ *vt* **1** : to deliver a lecture to ⟨*lecturing* a group of tourists —Jack Goodman⟩ **2** : to reprove severely or formally : REBUKE, REPRIMAND ⟨she's always *lecturing* me —S.N.Behrman⟩ ⟨was mildly *lectured* for his part in the escapade⟩

**lecture bottle** *n* : a narrow metal cylinder about a foot long for holding a compressed gas (as hydrogen sulfide)

**lec·tur·ee** \¦lekchə¦rē, -kshə-\ *n* -s : one who listens to or receives a lecture ⟨lecturers who exercised their wits at the expense of the ~s —Vincent Sheean⟩

**lec·tur·er** \'==rə(r)\ *n* -s **1** : one that lectures; *specif* : one giving a lecture course in a college or university ⟨the best ~ on the campus⟩ **2** : a clergyman in the Church of England holding an ancient teaching and preaching office ⟨to church, where our ~ made a sorry silly sermon —Samuel Pepys⟩ **3 a** : a member of the faculty of a British college or university who ranks below a professor **b** : a member of a college or university faculty having a temporary or part-time appointment

**lec·ture·ship** \'lekchə(r),ship, -kshə-\ *n* **1** : the office or position of lecturer; *esp* : the position of lecturer in a college or university **2 a** : a course of lectures **b** : a foundation supporting a lecture or lecture series

**lec·tur·ette** \¦lekchə¦ret, -ksh-\ *n* -s : a short lecture

**lec·y·thi·da·ce·ae** \,lesəthə'dāsē,ē\ *n pl, cap* [NL, fr. *Lecythid-, Lecythis*, type genus + *-aceae*] : a family of large tropical trees (order Myrtales) having alternate leaves and large fruit with a woody epicarp — **lec·y·thi·da·ceous** \¦===¦dāshəs\ *adj*

**lec·y·this** \'lesəthəs\ *n, cap* [NL, fr. LL *lecythus*] : a genus (the type of the family Lecythidaceae) of very large So. American trees distinguished by the woody operculate capsular fruit — see SAPUCAIA; compare MONKEY POT

**lec·y·thoid** \-sə,thȯid\ *adj* [*lecythus* + *-oid*] : resembling a lecythus

**lec·y·thus** \'lesəthəs\ *or* **lek·y·thos** \'lekə,thäs\ *also* **lek·y·thus** \-kəthəs\ *n, pl* **lecy·thi** \-sə,thī\ *or* **leky·thoi** \-kə,thȯi\ [LL & Gk; LL *lecythus*, fr. Gk *lēkythos*, prob. of non-IE origin] : a cylindrical or round and squat vase used by the ancient Greeks for oils and ointments

lecythus

**led** *past of* LEAD

**-led** *past of* -LE

**led** *abbr* ledger

**led captain** *n* : an obsequious follower : SYCOPHANT, TOADY ⟨and a rich lad at school or college has his followers, tuft-hunters, *led captains* —W.M.Thackeray⟩

**le·de·bur·ite** \'lādə,bu̇,rīt\ *n* -s [G *ledeburit*, fr. Adolf *Ledebur* †1906 Ger. metallurgist + G *-it* -ite] : the cementite-austenite eutectic structure in iron-carbon alloys or commercial cast iron

**le·der·ho·sen** \'lādə(r),hōzᵊn\ *n pl* [G, fr. MHG *lederhose*, fr. *leder* leather + *hose* leg covering, trousers] : knee-length leather trousers worn esp. in Bavaria

**led farm** *n, chiefly Scot* : a farm owned and managed by a nonresident farmer

**¹ledge** \'lej\ *n* -s [ME *legge*, prob. fr. *leggen* to lay — more at LAY] **1** : a raised or projecting edge or molding added to protect or check: as **a** : a bar forming the top of a gate **b** : a strip making the raised edge of a shelf, tray, or printer's galley **c** : the side of a rabbet against which a door or window closes **d** : CHAIR RAIL **e** : BATTEN, CLEAT **2** : a narrow shelf forming the top or projecting from the side of a wall or other vertical structure ⟨~s high on two walls served as plate racks⟩ **3** : RIDGE, REEF; *esp* : one under water near the shore **4 a** : a narrow horizontal shelf formed in a rock wall or declivity **b** : rock solid enough to form a ledge : BEDROCK **5** : an architectural stringcourse, molding, or fillet **6** : an ingate for a mold **7** : a mass of rock that constitutes a valuable mineral deposit : LODE, VEIN **8 a** : an athwartships timber supporting the deck of a wooden ship from beneath **b** : COAMING

**²ledge** \"\ *vb* -ED/-ING/-S *vi* : to form a ledge ~ *vt* : to form as or supply with ledges : place on or as if on a ledge

**ledged** \-jd\ *adj* : having ledges

**ledge·less** \-jləs\ *adj* : having no ledge

**ledge·man** \-jmən\ *n, pl* **ledgemen** : BREAKER 4e

**¹ledg·er** \'lejə(r)\ *n* -s [ME *legger*, prob. fr. *leggen* to lay + *-er* — more at LAY] **1 a** *obs* : a book of permanent record : REGISTER **b** : a book containing accounts to which debits and credits resulting from business transactions are posted from books of original entry **2** : a memorial stone slab laid flat over a grave ⟨buried . . . under a black marble ~ close to the North wall —J.L.Chester⟩ **3** : a horizontal timber that is secured to the uprights of scaffolding during building construction and supports the putlogs **4** *archaic* : a resident ambassador, agent, or commissioner **5** *or* **leg·er** \"\ **a** : LEDGER BAIT **b** : LEDGER LINE **c** : LEDGER TACKLE **6** *dial Brit* : a narrow wooden strip used to secure thatch to a roof

**²ledger** \"\ *vi* -ED/-ING/-S : to fish with ledger tackle

**³ledger** *adj, obs* : lying or remaining in a place : RESIDENT, STATIONARY

**ledger bait** *n* : fishing bait rigged so that the bait lies on the bottom below the sinker

**ledger bark** *n* [after Charles *Ledger*, 19th cent. Eng. botanist in Peru] : the chief commercial cinchona bark derived from cultivated Javanese cinchonas and notably rich in quinine

**ledger blade** *n* : a stationary blade in a machine for shearing cloth

**ledger board** *n* **1** : a horizontal board forming the top rail of a simple fence or the handrail of a balustrade **2** : a flooring board in scaffolding **3** : RIBBON 2b

**ledger line** *n* **1** : a fishing line arranged so that the lead and bait rest upon the bottom **2** *also* **leger line** : a short line added above or below the staff to extend its range in musical notation

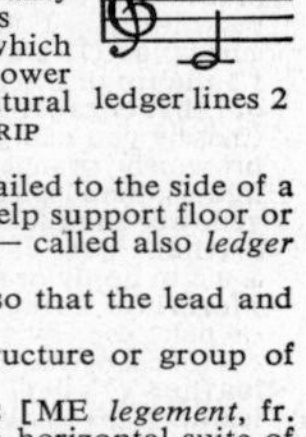

ledger lines 2

**ledger paper** *n* : a strong durable medium to heavy writing paper with good erasing quality used in business ledgers and record books

**ledger plate** *n* **1** : the shearing base over which a section of a reciprocating sickle or mower knife slides in cutting with an agricultural binder, reaper, or mower **2** : LEDGER STRIP

**ledger score** *n* : BACK SCORE 2

**ledger strip** *n* : a narrow strip of lumber nailed to the side of a girder and flush with its bottom edge to help support floor or ceiling joists notched to accommodate it — called also *ledger plate*

**ledger tackle** *n* : fishing tackle arranged so that the lead and bait rest upon the bottom

**ledg·ing** \'lejiŋ, -jēŋ\ *n* -s : a ledged structure or group of ledges : LEDGE

**ledg·ment** *or* **ledge·ment** \-jmənt\ *n* -s [ME *legement*, fr. *legge* ledge + *-ment* — more at LEDGE] : a horizontal suite of moldings (as the base moldings of a building)

**ledgy** \-jē\ *adj* -ER/-EST : abounding in ledges : consisting of a ledge or reef ⟨fields are ~ in places —E.B.White⟩

**le·dol** \'lē,dōl, -dȯl\ *n* -s [ISV *led-* (fr. NL *Ledum*) + *-ol*] : a crystalline sesquiterpenoid alcohol $C_{15}H_{25}OH$ occurring in the oil from the leaves and flowering tops of the marsh tea and in other essential oils

**le·duc effect** \lə'dük-\ *n, usu cap L* [after Sylvestre Anatole *Leduc*, 20th cent. French physicist] : RIGHI-LEDUC EFFECT

**le·dum** \'lēdəm\ *n* [NL, fr. Gk *lēdon* rockrose — more at LABDANUM] **1** *cap* : a genus of shrubs (family Ericaceae) of cold regions having a deciduous corolla of separate petals and a septicidal capsule — see LABRADOR TEA, MARSH TEA **2** -s : any plant of the genus *Ledum*

**ledum camphor** *n* : LEDOL

**¹lee** \'lē\ *n* -s [ME *le, lee*, fr. OE *hlēo, hlēow;* akin to OFris *hlī* protection, shelter, OS *hleo*, ON *hlé* protection, shelter, lee side, *hlýr* lukewarm, OHG *lāo* lukewarm, Goth *hlija* hut, tent, L *calēre* to be warm, W *clyd* warm, cozy, Skt *śarad* autumn; basic meaning: warm] **1** : protecting shelter ⟨found a place . . . where we could get a little ~ provided we anchored close enough to the shore —Peter Heaton⟩ ⟨had squatted in the ~ of a rock —Farley Mowat⟩ ⟨worked in the ~ of the great, but did great things himself —*Times Lit. Supp.*⟩ **2** : the side (as of a ship or mountain) that is sheltered from the wind and provides shelter from it ⟨the smaller vessels clung to the ~ of some high mangrove island —Marjory S. Douglas⟩ ⟨a tramp snoring under the ~ of a haystack —Nicholas Monsarrat⟩ — **by the lee** *adv* : with the sails brought aback by falling off when running free

**²lee** \"\ *adj* **1** : of or relating to the side sheltered from the wind — opposed to *weather* ⟨the rocky point . . . was in sight, broad on the ~ bow —Frederick Marryat⟩ **2 a** : located on the side away from which an advancing glacier moves ⟨~ slope⟩ — opposed to *stoss* **b** : located on the side away from which the prevailing wind blows — used of a hillside or a knob of rock

**³lee** \"\ *n* -s [ME *lie*, fr. MF, fr. ML *lia*, prob. of Celt origin; akin to OIr *lige* bed, Gaulish *legasit* he laid, W *llaid* mud — more at LIE] : the settlings of liquor (as wine) during fermentation and aging : DREGS, SEDIMENT — now used only in pl. ⟨the wine of life is drawn and the mere ~s . . . left —Shak.⟩ ⟨broken men, bond servants, "gaolbirds," the ~s and settlings of the old world —V.L.Parrington⟩

**lee·an·gle** *also* **li·an·gle** \'lē,aŋgəl\ *n* -s [native name in Australia] : a heavy weapon of the Australian aborigines with a sharp-pointed end about nine inches long bent at right angles to the shank

**leeboard** \'=,=\ *n* : either of the wood or metal planes attached outside the hull of a sailing ship or sailboat to prevent leeway

**lee-bow** \'=,=\ *vt* : to get (a tide or current) on a sailing ship's lee bow to offset a leeward course caused by the wind

**¹leech** \'lēch\ *n* -ES [ME *leche*, fr. OE *lǣce;* akin to OHG *lāhhi* physician, ON *lækn*ir, Goth *lekeis* physician, and perh. to Gk *legein* to gather, choose, speak — more at LEGEND] **1 a** *archaic* : PHYSICIAN, SURGEON ⟨make each prescribe to other as each other's ~ —Shak.⟩ ⟨presents herself as a ~ able to cure the disease —Mary D. Anderson⟩ **b** *now dial Brit* : VETERINARIAN **2** [so called fr. its former use by physicians for bleeding patients] **a** : any of numerous carnivorous or bloodsucking annelid worms constituting the class Hirudinea, having typically a flattened segmented body of lanceolate outline that is broader near the posterior end and has externally well-marked annulations which are far more numerous than the true segments, a sucker at each end of the body, a mouth within the anterior sucker, and a large stomach with capacious pouches at the sides, being hermaphroditic usu. with direct development, and occurring chiefly in fresh water although a few are marine and some tropical forms are terrestrial — see GNATHOBDELLIDA, PHARYNGOBDELLIDA, RHYNCHOBDELLIDA

**b** : an insect larva superficially resembling a leech **3** : a hanger-on who seeks advantage or gain : PARASITE ⟨the shark is there and the shark's prey; the spendthrift and the ~ that sucks him —William Cowper⟩ ⟨~*es* . . . hateful parasites feeding upon the blood of artists —Robertson Davies⟩ **syn** see PARASITE

**²leech** \"\ *vb* -ED/-ING/-ES [ME *lechen*, fr. *leche*, n.] *vt* **1 a** : to treat as a physician : CURE, HEAL ⟨cobra poison none may ~ —Rudyard Kipling⟩ **b** : to bleed by the use of leeches **2** : to fasten onto as a leech : feed on the blood or substance of : DRAIN, EXHAUST ⟨bankers who had always ~*ed* them white —D.A.Munro⟩ ~ *vi* : to attach oneself in or as if in the manner of a leech ⟨she would ~ on to him and drain the life out of him —W.L.Gresham⟩

**³leech** *or* **leach** \"\ *n* -ES [ME *lek, leche, lyche*, fr. MLG *līk* rope to which the sail is fastened; akin to MHG *geleich* joint, limb — more at LIGATURE] **1** : either vertical edge of a square sail — see SAIL illustration **2** : the after edge of a fore-and-aft sail

**leechcraft** \ˈ=,=\ *n* [ME *lechecraft*, fr. OE *lǣcecræft*, fr. *lǣce* physician + *cræft* craft — more at LEECH, CRAFT] : the art of healing : medical knowledge and skill

**leech·dom** \ˈlēchdəm\ *n* -S [ME *lechedom*, fr. OE *lǣcedōm*, fr. *lǣce* + *-dōm* -dom] *archaic* : MEDICINE

**leecheater** \ˈ=,==\ *n* **1** : CROCODILE BIRD **2** : SPUR-WINGED PLOVER

**leechee** *var of* LITCHI

**leeches** *n pl* [fr. pl. of ¹*leech* (worm); fr. the appearance of the blisters] *dial* : summer sores of the horse or mule

**leech line** *n* [³*leech*] : a line attached to the middle of the leech of a sail and used to haul the leech up to the yard

**leech rope** *n* [³*leech*] : the part of the boltrope that is sewed to the leech of a sail

**¹leed** \ˈlēd\ *n* -S [ME *lede, leden*, fr. OE *Læden, Leden* Latin, language, fr. (assumed) VL *Ladinus*, fr. L *Latinus* — more at LATIN] **1** *now Scot* : spoken or written language : SPEECH **2** *Scot* : SONG, TUNE

**²leed** *var of* LEAD

**leeds** \ˈlēdz\ *adj, usu cap* [fr. *Leeds*, England] : of or from the city of Leeds, Yorkshire, England : of the kind or style prevalent in Leeds

**lee-enfield rifle** \ˈlē'en,fēld-\ *n, usu cap L&E* [James P. *Lee* †1904 American inventor born in Scotland + *Enfield*, town near London, Eng.] : a short repeating British military rifle fed from a magazine and fitted with a knife bayonet

**lee-fang** *or* **lee-fange** \ˈlē,faŋ\ *n* -S [¹*lee* + *fang*] *Brit* : TRAVELER 3b

**lee·ful** \ˈlēfəl\ *adj* [ME *leveful*, fr. *leve* leave + *-ful* — more at LEAVE] *archaic* : LAWFUL, LICIT

**lee gauge** *n* : a position to leeward of another ship — used in the phrase *to have the lee gauge of;* compare WEATHER GAUGE

**leeg·te** \ˈlēktə\ *n* -S [Afrik, emptiness, valley, fr. *leeg* empty, fr. MD *lēdich* free, idle, empty] : LAAGTE

**lee helm** *n* : a helm kept somewhat alee to offset a sailing ship's tendency in some conditions to fall away from the wind to leeward ⟨the ship carries a *lee helm*⟩

**leek** \ˈlēk\ *n* -S [ME *lek, leek*, fr. OE *lēac* leek, onion, garlic; akin to OS *lōk* leek, OHG *louh*, ON *laukr* leek, garlic, and perh. to Gk *lygizein* to bend — more at LOCK] **1 a** : a biennial herb (*Allium porrum*) that is closely related to the garlic and onion, is known only in cultivation but believed to be derived from a wild Eurasian plant (*A. ampeloprasum*), and is commonly grown as an annual for its mildly pungent succulent linear leaves and esp. its thick cylindrical stalk consisting of blanched leafstalks and small simple bulb **b** : any of several alliums usu. with slender cylindrical bulbs — usu. used in combination ⟨sand ~⟩; see WILD LEEK **2** *or* **leek green a** : RESEDA 2a **b** : a moderate yellow green that is greener and duller than average moss green, yellower and duller than average pea green or apple green (sense 1), and yellower and less strong than spinach green — called also *porret, prasine* **3** : GREEN LEEK

**leek moth** *n* : a small European moth (*Acrolepia assectella*) having a larva that burrows in and feeds on the developing leaves of leeks and some related plants

**lee·lane** \ˈlē,lān\ *adj* [*lee* (prob. alter. of ¹*lief*) + *lane* (lone)] *Scot* : all alone — used with a possessive pronoun

**lee·lang** \ˈlē,laŋ\ *adj* [*lee-* (prob. alter. of ²*lief*) + *lang* (long)] *Scot* : LIVELONG

**¹leem** \ˈlēm\ *var of* LEAM

**²leem** \"\ *Scot var of* ¹LOOM

**¹leep** \ˈlēp\ *vt* -ED/-ING/-S [prob. of Scand origin; akin to ON *hleypa* to cause to leap, curdle, Norw *løpe, løypa* to curdle, boil or fry gently, Icel *hleypa* to curdle, put in boiling water for a short time, fry gently; causatives fr. the root of ON *hlaupa* to leap — more at LEAP] *dial Brit* : BOIL, SCALD

**²leep** \"\ *vt* -ED/-ING/-S [Hindi *līpnā*] *India* : to plaster (as a wall) with cow dung

**¹leer** *n* -S [ME *ler, lere* cheek, face, aspect, fr. OE *hlēor* cheek, face; akin to OS *hleor* cheek, MD *lier, liere*, ON *hlȳr* cheek, *hlust* ear — more at LISTEN] *obs* : COMPLEXION, ASPECT, COUNTENANCE

**²leer** \ˈli(ə)r, ˈli(ə)\ *vb* -ED/-ING/-S [prob. fr. obs. *leer* cheek, fr. ME *ler, lere*] *vi* **1** : to cast a sidelong glance : give a lascivious, knowing, or malicious look : FLEER ⟨~*ed* like the face of a trollop worn out by the passage of men and time —T.H.Raddall⟩ ⟨poured the drink, added water, and looked again at the judge, ~*ing* with a kind of comic cunning —R.P. Warren⟩ **2** *obs* : to move furtively : SLINK, SNEAK ⟨~*ed* away on the other side, as one ashamed of what he had done —John Bunyan⟩ ~ *vt* **1** : to glance with or turn (the eye) **2** : to seduce with the eye

**³leer** \"\ *n* -S : a sly, sinister, or immodest glance : a knowing or wanton look ⟨she gives the ~ of invitation —Shak.⟩ ⟨the sordid furtive ~ of the profit seeker —A.L.Guérard⟩

**⁴leer** \"\ *adj, archaic* : looking slyly, wantonly, or knowingly

**⁵leer** \"\ *adj* [ME *lere*, fr. OE *gelǣr*; akin to OS & OHG *lāri* empty; prob. derivatives fr. the stem of OE *lesan* to gather, glean — more at LEASE] **1** : EMPTY, UNLADEN **2** *dial Eng* : weak from hunger : HUNGRY

**⁶leer** \ˈlē(ə)r\ *n* -S [ME *leere*, prob. fr. OE *līra* fleshy part of the body — more at LEG] *now dial Brit* : FLANK, LOIN

**⁷leer** *var of* LEHR

**leer·fish** \ˈlir,fish\ *also* **leer·vis** \-,vis\ *n* [*leerfish* part trans. of Afrik *leervis*, fr. *leer* leather + *vis* fish; *leervis* fr. Afrik] : a leading carangid game fish (*Hypacanthus amia*) of the west coast of Africa that is bluish gray, vigorous, and often 6 feet in length — called also *garrick*

**leer·i·ly** \ˈlirəlē\ *adv* : in a leery manner

**leer·i·ness** \-rēnəs\ *n* -ES : WARINESS

**leering** *adj* : LEWD, SLY, MALICIOUS ⟨a fine ~ gusto —Wolcott Gibbs⟩ ⟨an uneasy ~ quality . . . that I find in dubious taste —Dudley Fitts⟩ ⟨she had run in fear of him, his evil ~ eye —Amy Lowell⟩ — **leer·ing·ly** *adv*

**leerman** *var of* LEHRMAN

**leer·ness** \ˈlirnəs\ *n* -ES [ME *lerenesse*, fr. OE *lǣrnes*, fr. *gelǣr* empty + *-nes* -ness] : EMPTINESS

**leer·sia** \ˈlirzēə\ *n, cap* [NL, fr. Johann D. *Leers* †1774 Ger. botanist + NL *-ia*] : a genus of perennial chiefly swamp grasses having flat roughish leaves and one-flowered spikelets — see RICE CUT-GRASS, WHITE GRAMA

**¹leery** \ˈlēri\ *adj* [⁵*leer* + *-y*] *dial Eng* : ⁵LEER

**²leery** \ˈlirē, -ri\ *adj* -ER/-EST [⁴*leer* + *-y*] **1** *archaic* : ALERT, KNOWING, WIDE-AWAKE **2** : exhibiting suspicion or doubt : DISTRUSTFUL, WARY — usu. used with *of* ⟨the local woodpeckers . . . are ~ of any sort of enclosure —*New Yorker*⟩ ⟨bookmakers were beginning to get ~ of taking his bets —Robert Rice⟩ ⟨liberalism has been singularly ~ of defining its own theoretical principles —Max Ascoli⟩

**lees** *pl of* LEE

**lee's birthday** \ˈlēz-\ *n, usu cap L&B* [after Robert E. *Lee* †1870 Am. soldier, commander in chief of the Confederate armies] : January 19 observed as a legal holiday in 10 southern states

**leese** *vb* [ME *lesen*, fr. OE *lēosan* — more at LOSE] *vt, obs* : LOSE ~ *vi, obs* : to be a loser

**lee shore** *n* **1 a** : a shore lying off a ship's leeward side and constituting a severe danger in storm ⟨a dangerous *lee shore* —F.D.Ommanney⟩ **b** : a source of peril or cause of ruin ⟨dramatizes our present course as a drift toward the *lee shore* of totalitarianism —C.E.Ayres⟩ **2** *obs* : a shore offering shelter from storm

**¹lee·some** \ˈlēsəm\ *adj* [ME *lefsum*, fr. *lef* dear + *-sum* -some — more at LIEF] *Scot* : PLEASANT, DELIGHTFUL

**²leesome** \"\ *adj* [ME *lefsum*, fr. *leve* leave + *-sum* -some — more at LEAVE] *Scot* : LAWFUL, JUST

**¹leet** *n* -S [fr. (assumed) ME, fr. OE *gelǣte*, fr. *lǣtan* to let — more at LET] *obs* : a place where roads meet or cross : INTERSECTION

**²leet** \ˈlēt\ *n* -S [ME *lete*, fr. AF *lete* or ML *leta*] **1** : COURT LEET **2** : the jurisdictional district of a court leet

**³leet** \"\ *n* -S [ME (Sc) *lite*] *chiefly Scot* : a list of candidates

**⁴leet** \"\ *n* -S [origin unknown] *dial Brit* : STACK, PILE

**⁵leet** \"\ *dial Eng var of* LIGHT

**¹leeve** \ˈlēv\ *chiefly dial var of* LIEF

**²leeve** \"\ *dial Brit var of* ¹LIVE

**lee·ward** \ˈlüə(r)d (*usual nautical pronunc*), ˈlēwə-\ *adj* [¹*lee* + *-ward*] : situated away from the wind : DOWNWIND ⟨~ side of the house —Hamlin Garland⟩ — opposed to *windward*

**²leeward** \"\ *n* -S : the lee side ⟨advisable to try to sail to ~ of your objective —H.A.Calahan⟩ — opposed to *windward*

**lee·ward·ly** \-dlē\ *adj* : tending to fall off to leeward or to make leeway — opposed to *weatherly*

**lee·ward·most** \-d,mōst *also chiefly Brit* -dməst\ *adj, archaic* : most leeward

**leeward tide** *also* **lee tide** *n* : a tide running onshore or offshore while the wind blows in the same direction and thus creating danger for small craft

**leeway** \ˈ=,=\ *n* [¹*lee* + *way*] **1 a** : off-course lateral movement of a ship when under way caused by wind or current **b** : DRIFT ANGLE **2** **2** : the measure of discrepancy between fact and standard : degree of deviation from a criterion or goal standard : margin of shortcoming in performance ⟨men had to catch up on a dreadful ~ of ignorance —A.T.Quiller-Couch⟩ **3 a** : allowable variation : TOLERANCE ⟨there can be little ~ in the size of the explosive charge —*Science Yr. Bk.*⟩ **b** : degree of freedom of action or permitted discretion : room for choice ⟨a professor of English . . . can generally enjoy more intellectual ~ than a professor of sociology —Irving Howe⟩ ⟨only an hour's ~ to catch the plane⟩ **c** : margin of safety ⟨an hour's ~ to catch the plane⟩ ⟨maintains a capital reserve to provide financial ~⟩ **syn** see ROOM

**lee wheel** *n* : the share in steering done by one or more assistants to a ship's helmsman — compare WEATHER WHEEL

**lef·se** \ˈlefsə\ *n, pl* **lef·sen** \-sən\ *or* **lefses** [Norw, fr. *lev, leiv* pancake, slice of bread, fr. ON *hleifr* loaf — more at LOAF] : a large thin potato pancake served buttered and folded

**¹left** \ˈleft\ *adj, sometimes* -ER/-EST [ME *luft, lift, left*, fr. OE *left, lyft-* (as in *lyftādl* palsy) weak; akin to MD *lucht, luft, loft* left, MLG *lucht*] **1 a** : of or relating to the hand that in most persons is weaker, to the side of the body on which it is, or to the parts of that side of the body ⟨combat men who looked at a man's ~ chest before they looked at his face —C.H.Norcross⟩ **b** : located on an observer's left or directed as his left hand would point ⟨outflanked the army's ~ wing⟩ ⟨the ~ fork of the road looked the more inviting of the two⟩ **2** *often cap* : of, adhering to, or constituted by the left esp. in politics ⟨this ~ government with a cabinet of moderate liberals —F.A.Magruder⟩ ⟨the Communists and their political ally, the *Left* Socialists —C.A.L.Rich⟩ ⟨fashionable . . . among many ~ intellectuals —Philip O'Connor⟩ ⟨the ~ religious movements . . . animated by the social gospel —G.A.Almond⟩ ⟨untiring representative of the ~*est* of left-wingers —*Glasgow Herald*⟩ ⟨in some respects they are going still ~*er* —A.A. Berle⟩ — **over the left shoulder** *or* **over the left** : not at all — used as an aside to indicate negation of what is said

**²left** \"\ *n* -S [ME *luft, lift, left*, fr. *luft, lift, left*, adj.] **1 a** : the left hand ⟨lashed out with his ~ —Gregor Felsen⟩ **b** : the location or direction lying on the left side of one's body ⟨passed a house on his ~⟩ **c** : the part (as the wing of an army) that is on the left side of an observer facing in the direction it faces **d** : the member of a pair situated or used on the left side **2 a** : LEFT FIELD **b** : a boxer's blow with the left fist ⟨broke through the American's defense repeatedly with jolts and spearing ~*s* —P.J.Cunningham⟩ **3** *often cap* **a** : the part of a legislative chamber located to the left of the presiding officer and usu. occupied in continental European and other countries having a similar political pattern by members professing a more radical political position on political issues than other members ⟨loud applause in the center and on certain benches of the ~ —D.W.S.Lidderdale⟩ ⟨in the other European countries . . . the ~ is occupied by the Communists and Socialists —Enzo Di Cocco⟩ — compare CENTER 3c, RIGHT **b** : the members of a legislative body occupying the left as a result of their political views ⟨members of the Chamber of Deputies . . . became tense; the *Left* became vociferous —A.W.Macmahon & W.R.Dittmar⟩ **4** *usu cap* **a** : individuals or groups professing views usu. characterized by opposition to and a desire to alter (as by reform or revolution) the established order esp. in politics and usu. advocating change in the name of the greater freedom or well-being of the common man ⟨the tradition of liberalism, democracy, and socialism belongs to the democratic *Left* —Simon Paynter⟩ ⟨the totalitarianism of the *Left* —Howard Rushmore⟩ ⟨his position in the literary *Left* —Paul Potts⟩ ⟨his contempt for the Right is exceeded only by his contempt for the *Left* —Bergen Evans⟩ — compare RIGHT **b** : the symbolic position occupied by persons professing such views : a radical as distinguished from a conservative position ⟨the clericalist threat from the Right drove the earlier governments of the Third Republic . . . further to the radical *Left* —*Times Lit. Supp.*⟩ ⟨after an interval of twenty or thirty years the *Left* of one period becomes the Right of the next —Barbara & Robert North⟩

**³left** \"\ *adv* [ME *luft, lift, left*, fr. *luft, lift, left*, adj.] : on or to the left ⟨questing neither ~ nor right —Rudyard Kipling⟩ ⟨as right-center governments continued to ignore reform, the people moved ~ —*New Republic*⟩

**⁴left** *past of* LEAVE

**¹left-bank** \ˈ=ˈ=\ *adj, often cap L&B* [fr. the *Left Bank* (of the Seine river), the bohemian district of Paris, France; trans. of F *Rive Gauche*] : of, relating to, or situated in the bohemian district of Paris

**²left-bank** \"\ *vb* [fr. the phrase *left bank*] *vt* : to bank (an airplane) to the left ~ *vi* : to bank to the left (as an airplane or a bird in flight)

**left bower** *n* : the jack of the other suit of the same color as the trump suit (as in euchre and five hundred)

**left-center** \ˈ=ˈ==\ *n, often cap L&C* [trans. of F *centre gauche*] : a political group or an organized party belonging to the Center but closely associated with the Left in policies and practice ⟨in Denmark . . . the Liberals represented the Right-Center and the Radicals the *Left-Center* —Barbara & Robert North⟩ — compare RIGHT-CENTER

**left face** *n* [fr. the imper. phrase *left, face*] : the act of turning 90 degrees to the left from the halted position of attention as a military maneuver — often used as a command; compare ABOUT-FACE, RIGHT FACE

**left field** *n* **1** : the part of the baseball outfield to the left facing from the plate **2** : the station of the player defending left field — see BASEBALL illustration

**left fielder** *n* : one who plays left field

**left-footed** \ˈ=ˈ==\ *adj* **1** : stronger or more adept with the left foot ⟨a *left-footed* player for the left wing, and vice-versa —C.W.Alcock⟩ **2** : AWKWARD, CLUMSY, WEAK ⟨the new version sounds *left-footed* and pathetic —J.M.Conly⟩ — **left-footed·ness** *n*

**left-hand** \ˈ=ˈ=\ *adj* [ME *lefthand*, fr. the phrase *left hand*] **1** : situated on the left : nearer the left hand than the right ⟨decided to try the *left-hand* house⟩ **2** : using or being performed with the left hand : LEFT-HANDED ⟨made a *left-hand* pitch⟩ **3 a** *of a door* : opening to the left away from one **b** *of a hinge* : fitting or designed to fit a left-hand or left-hand reverse bevel door **c** *of a lock* (1) : fitting or designed to fit on a left-hand or left-hand reverse bevel door or on a right-hand reverse bevel door if both sides of the lock operate (2) : throwing or designed to throw left **4 a** *of a turning tool* : designed to cut to the left **b** *of a thread chaser* : designed to cut a left-hand screw thread **c** *of a milling cutter* : designed to rotate clockwise **5 a** : DEVIOUS, INDIRECT, OBLIQUE ⟨his statement was verified in a *left-hand* way —Earl Brown⟩ **b** : CLUMSY **c** : SINISTER **6 a** : MORGANATIC **b** : of, relating to, united in, or born of an illicit liaison : ILLEGITIMATE ⟨never acknowledged his *left-hand* family⟩ **7** *of a rope* : LEFT-LAID **8 a** : of or relating to a division of non-Brahmanical castes in southern India formerly subjected to social and ceremonial disabilities **b** : of or relating to a division of Shaktism marked by secret orgiastic rites

**¹left-handed** \ˈ=ˈ==\ *adj* [ME *left handed*, fr. *left hand* + *-ed*] **1** : having the left hand more apt or usable than the right : preferring the left hand : SOUTHPAW ⟨a brilliant *left-handed* pitcher⟩ **2 a** : marked by clumsiness or ineptitude : AWKWARD **b** : exhibiting deviousness or indirection : OBLIQUE, UNINTENDED ⟨New England contributed to freedom of conscience only by the *left-handed* method of making martyrs to that cause —G.W.Johnson⟩ **c** *obs* : given to malevolent scheming or contriving : SINISTER, UNDERHAND **3** : marked by uncertain or ambiguous intent : BACKHANDED, DUBIOUS, DOUBLE-EDGED ⟨is not very grateful for this support, which it considers a *left-handed* compliment —J.A.C.F.Auer⟩ ⟨did the industry a *left-handed* favor —*Steelways*⟩ **4** *archaic* : portending ill : INAUSPICIOUS **5 a** : of, relating to, or born of a morganatic marriage **b** : of or relating to an illicit or informal liaison : ILLEGITIMATE ⟨though only four marriages between Frenchmen and Indians were recorded, *left-handed* marriages are known to have been frequent —*William & Mary Quarterly*⟩ **6** : LEFT-HAND 4 **7 a** : having a crystal structure that has a mirror-image relationship to another enantiomorphous structure regarded as right-handed in which the same compound can crystallize ⟨*left-handed* quartz⟩ **b** : having crystal faces that result from and may be used to characterize such a structure **c** : LEVOROTATORY **8** *of a rope* : LEFT-LAID **9** : SINISTRAL ⟨*left-handed* whelks⟩ — **left-hand·ed·ly** *adv* — **left-hand·ed·ness** *n* -ES

**²left-handed** \"\ *adv* : with the left hand : in a left-handed manner : LEFT-HANDEDLY ⟨pitched *left-handed*⟩

**left-handed rope** *or* **left-hand rope** *n* **1** : a left-laid rope in which the strands are formed of yarns with right-handed twist — called also *back-handed rope;* compare RIGHT-HANDED ROPE **2** : any left-laid rope

**left-hand·er** \ˈleft,handə(r), -aan-\ *n* **1** : a left-handed person : SOUTHPAW ⟨young *left-hander* who tossed two shutouts —*N.Y. Times*⟩ **2** : a blow struck with the left hand ⟨started in with a fine *left-hander* on his right eye —O.Henry⟩

**left-hand lady** *n* : CORNER LADY

**left-hand reverse bevel** *adj, of a cupboard or closet door* : opening to the left toward one

**left-hand rule** *n* : a rule in electricity: if the thumb and first two fingers of the left hand are arranged at right angles to each other on a conductor and the hand oriented so that the first finger points in the direction of the magnetic field and the middle finger in the direction of the electric current then the thumb will point in the direction of the force on the conductor

**left-hand screw thread** *n* : a screw thread whose helix moves upward when the screw is inserted vertically from above in a fixed mating thread and turned clockwise

**left heart** *n* : the left auricle and ventricle : the half of the heart containing oxygenated blood

**left·ish** \ˈleftish, -tēsh\ *adj* : showing leftist tendencies ⟨high-brow ~ periodical —Isaac Deutscher⟩ ⟨a ~ congressman⟩

**left·ism** \ˈlef,tizəm\ *n* -S *sometimes cap* **1** : the principles and views of the Left; *also* : the movement embodying these principles ⟨the real danger is not liberalism or ~ —*New Republic*⟩ ⟨~, British style, played an important part in the freedom movement —Christopher Rand⟩ **2** : advocacy of or adherence to the doctrines of the Left ⟨a swing from the right of the Popular Front to a ~ —James Burnham⟩ ⟨charges and taints of ~ —Lawrence Stessin⟩

**¹left·ist** \ˈleftəst\ *n* -S *often cap* [²*left* + *-ist*] **1** : a member of a group (as a political party) belonging to the Left ⟨the United Front of *Leftists* . . . obtained 25 seats —*Amer. Scholar*⟩ ⟨~*s*, encouraged by their success in Sunday's general election —*N.Y. Herald-Tribune*⟩ **2** : one that believes in or advocates principles associated with the Left : RADICAL ⟨contrary to the opinion of romanticists and ~*s* —L.L.Sharkey⟩ ⟨many . . . unaffiliated ~*s* were at one time Communists or Communist sympathizers —Granville Hicks⟩

**²leftist** \"\ *adj, often cap* **1** : of, relating to, or favoring the Left or a group belonging to the Left ⟨the *Leftist* ticket . . . would be certain of 238 of the 473 seats —*N.Y. Herald-Tribune*⟩ ⟨~ elements . . . have taken a leading part in the nationalist movements —A.H.McDonald⟩ **2** : favoring, characterized by, or based upon the principles of the Left ⟨the ~ . . . movement of this generation —Lillian Symes⟩ ⟨the present ~ attitude of the . . . administration —M.K.Hart⟩

**left-laid** \ˈ=ˈ=\ *adj, of rope* : formed of strands twisted to the left of an observer viewing them lengthwise

**left-luggage office** \ˈ=ˈ==-\ *n, Brit* : CHECKROOM

**left·ments** \ˈleftmənts\ *n pl* [⁴*left* + *-ment* + *-s*] : LEFTOVERS, REMAINDERS, RESIDUE

**left-most** \ˈleft,mōst\ *adj* : farthest on the left

**left-off** \ˈ=ˈ=\ *adj* [fr. the past part. of *leave off*] : laid aside : CAST-OFF ⟨all sent Christmas and birthday presents and parcels of *left-off* clothing —Flora Thompson⟩

**¹leftover** \ˈ=,==\ *adj* [fr. the past part. of *leave over*] : remaining as unused residue ⟨put the Thermos bottles back in, and the *leftover* lobster and things —B.A.Williams⟩ ⟨spring has been like *leftover* winter here —Janet Flanner⟩

**²leftover** \"\ *n* -S **1** : an unused or unconsumed residue: as **a** : fragments of food remaining from a meal ⟨made supper from the ~*s* from dinner —J.B.Benefield⟩ ⟨poetry in full retreat . . . all literature living on sufferance, feeding on ~*s* —H.J.Muller⟩ **b** : a dish prepared from leftovers ⟨a pretty appetizing morsel when incorporated with other ingredients for a ~ —Nancy Dixon⟩ **c** : SURPLUS ⟨bedding, cooking equipment and similar supplies presumably can be drawn from the army's ~*s* —R.A.H.Thompson⟩ **2** : an anachronistic survival : VESTIGE ⟨the forelimbs of the heavy vertical reptiles seem . . . to have become useless ~*s* —Weston LaBarre⟩ ⟨an aristocratic ~ in modern government —Mollie Panter-Downes⟩

**left rudder** *n* : a position of a ship's rudder that will turn the ship to the left — often used as a command

**left shoulder arms** *n* [fr. the imper. phrase *left shoulder, arms*] : a position in the manual of arms in which the rifle is held in the left hand with the barrel resting against the left shoulder and the muzzle inclined to the rear — often used as a command; compare RIGHT SHOULDER ARMS

**¹left stage** *n* [¹*left* + *stage*] : the half of a theatrical stage to the left of an actor facing the audience

**²left stage** *adv* (*or adj*) : toward or on the half of a theatrical stage to the left of an actor facing the audience ⟨enters *left stage*⟩ ⟨quite ignored the whole *left stage* fiasco⟩ — compare DOWNSTAGE, RIGHT STAGE, UPSTAGE

**left·ward** \ˈleftwərd\ *or* **left·wards** \-dz\ *adv* (*or adj*) [ME *leftward*, fr. *left* + *-ward*] : toward or on the left ⟨veered ~ and so missed the stalled car⟩ ⟨prevent any more legislation with a ~ tinge —*New Republic*⟩ — **left·ward·ly** *adv*

**left wing** *n* **1** : the division of a group (as a political party) that believes in or advocates leftist principles and practices ⟨the right wing and the *left wing* of his own party —R.L.Strout⟩ ⟨the leader of Labour's radical *left wing* —*N.Y. Times*⟩ ⟨the *left wing* in the needle trades —*Nation*⟩ — compare RIGHT WING **2** : LEFT 4a ⟨in the estimation of the *left wing* of American politics —*Nation*⟩

**left-wing** \ˈlef,twiŋ\ *adj* [*left wing*] : of, adhering to, or favoring the Left ⟨the history of English *left-wing* political thought —*Brit. Book News*⟩ ⟨the bulk of the *left-wing* intelligentsia —George Orwell⟩ ⟨a veteran pro-Commie . . . leader of the *left-wing* camarilla —Victor Riesel⟩

**left-wing·er** \-ŋə(r)\ *n* -S **1** : a member of a left wing ⟨the Labor *left-wingers* claim the walkout as a victory for themselves —*Irish Statesman*⟩ **2** : LEFTIST ⟨nearly all English *left-wingers*, from Laborites to Anarchists —George Orwell⟩

**lefty** \ˈleftē, -ti\ *n* -ES **1** : LEFT-HANDER **2** : a political leftist

**¹leg** \ˈleg, ˈlāg\ *n* -S *often attrib* [ME *leg, legge*, fr. ON *leggr* leg, bone; akin to OE *līra* fleshy part of the body, ON *lær* thigh, L *lacertus* muscles, upper arm, *lacerta* lizard, Gk *lax* with the foot, Skt *ṛkṣalā* foot joint of a hoofed animal] **1** : one of the appendages of an animal that are used chiefly in supporting the body and in moving from point to point esp. by walking: as **a** (1) : one of the paired limbs of a vertebrate so used ⟨bipeds like man have two ~*s;* quadrupeds have four⟩

— compare ARM, WING (2) **:** the part of such a limb between

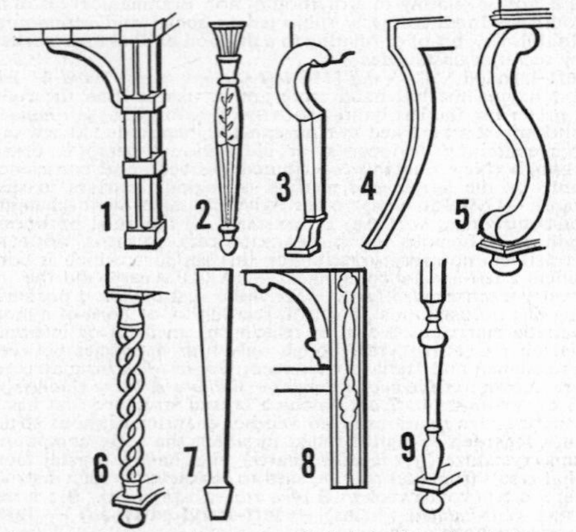


legs 2c: *1* clustered column, *2* fluted, *3* hock, *4* saber, *5* scroll, *6* spiral, *7* taper, *8* truss, *9* turned

the knee and the foot — distinguished from *thigh* **b :** one of the paired jointed segmental appendages of an arthropod; *esp* **:** one of the rather generalized appendages used in walking or crawling ⟨a typical abdominal ~ of a caterpillar consists of three parts —R.E.Snodgrass⟩ **2 :** something resembling an animal leg in form or use: as **a** (1) **:** a pole or bar serving as a support (as in a tripod) or as a prop or shore (as to a ship or building) ⟨the four ~*s* of each tower rest in large porcelain insulators —*Scientific American*⟩ (2) **:** something resembling or held to resemble such a support ⟨the third ~ upholding this tripod of international economic cooperation —Paul Bareau⟩ **b :** a contrivance or representation made to resemble or function esp. as a human leg ⟨the unfortunate man wore a wooden ~⟩ **c :** a support of a piece of furniture ⟨a chair ~⟩ ⟨the table's single pedestal . . . branched into four ~*s* —Adrian Bell⟩ **d :** a branch of a forked or jointed object (as an instrument) ⟨the ~*s* of a pair of compasses⟩ **e :** a section of rope in a knot or a bridle ⟨the ~*s* of a bowline⟩ ⟨the towing stresses will be divided between the two ~*s* of the bridle —*Manual of Seamanship*⟩ **f :** a part of a structure ⟨a starting ~ on the north side of a T-maze —*Psychological Abstracts*⟩ **g :** the part of a plant stem between the base and the point from which branches arise ⟨the bush should have a 6 to 9 in. ~, free from growth —J.H.Watt⟩ **3 :** a cut of meat: **a :** the back half of a hindquarter of lamb, mutton, or veal — compare HAM; see LAMB illustration **b :** the drumstick of a fowl **4 a :** the part of an article of clothing that covers the leg ⟨the ~*s* of trousers⟩ ⟨the ~ of a stocking⟩ **b :** the part of the upper of a boot that extends above the ankle **5 :** a bow made by drawing one leg back and bending the other **:** OBEISANCE, SCRAPE — used chiefly in the phrase *to make a leg* ⟨they . . . stood up and made a ~ respectfully in the direction of the Governor —Frank Yerby⟩ **6 :** either side of a triangle as distinguished from the base or hypotenuse **7** *Brit* **:** BLACKLEG 2 ⟨he was a horse chanter; he's a ~ now —Charles Dickens⟩ **8** *or* **leg up :** BOOST — often used in the phrase *to give a leg up* ⟨gave me my first ~ to literary standing —W.A.White⟩ ⟨the opportunity to give his profession a ~ *up* —R.E.Garis⟩ ⟨where . . . candidates need a ~ *up* toward election —L.C.Wilson⟩ **9 a :** the portion of the on side of a cricket field that lies behind the batsman and between the boundary and the extended line of the popping crease ⟨trying to force a ball to ~ —Ray Robinson⟩ **b :** a fielding position on this side in cricket; *also* **:** a player fielding in this position — see LONG LEG, SHORT LEG, SQUARE LEG; CRICKET illustration **c :** guard covering the leg stump in cricket **10 a :** the course and distance sailed by a boat on a single tack ⟨on the windward ~ —H.A.Calahan⟩ ⟨turn about on the next ~ of her zigzag course to windward —N.D.Ford⟩ **b** (1) **:** a straight-line portion of a flight pattern or air route ⟨the pilot . . . flies a crosswind ~ of half a mile —Joseph Bryan & P.G.Reed⟩ ⟨turned onto the base ~, just before landing —*Skyways*⟩ (2) **:** BEAM 2e(2) **c :** a portion of an entire trip or distance **:** STAGE ⟨another ~ of his continental journey —*Publishers' Weekly*⟩ ⟨on the homeward ~ of her . . . around-the-world tour —Anna Einarson⟩ **d :** the portion of the total distance or course that each member of a relay team must complete ⟨swam his ~ of the relay in 56 seconds flat —*N.Y. Times*⟩ **11 :** the case containing the vertical part of the belt that carries the buckets in a grain elevator **12 :** either of the two inclined sides of an anticlinal deposit **13 a :** one of several (as three) events or games necessary to be won to decide a competition ⟨gained a ~ on the trophy⟩ ⟨his horse won the first two ~*s* of the triple crown⟩ **b :** either half of a double entry in betting (as the daily double) **14 :** one of the two projecting parts of a structural-metal angle **15 a :** a branch electrical circuit **b :** a phase of a polyphase system **16 :** a branch or lateral circuit connecting a communications instrument with the main line **17 :** a road radiating from an intersection of which it forms a part ⟨location of . . . service stations in the ~*s* of interchanges —*Globe and Mail*⟩ **18 :** one of a pair of strips of material (as drapery) usu. hung parallel to the proscenium arch to mask the extreme offstage sides of a set **19 :** one link of several stations in a communications network **20 :** DIVISION 2 ⟨one ~ of the deal violates the exchange control regulations —R.F.Mikesell⟩ — **a leg to stand on :** SUPPORT; *esp* **:** a basis for one's position in a controversy — usu. used in the negative ⟨would not have *a leg to stand on* in his defiance —A.L.Hammond⟩ ⟨he had no legal *legs to stand on* —*Spectator*⟩ — **on one's last legs :** near death, extinction, or defeat ⟨looking like he was *on his last legs* —J.T.Farrell⟩ ⟨evident to any impartial observer that colonialism in Asia was *on its last legs* —*Yale Rev.*⟩ — **on one's legs** *or* **upon one's legs :** on one's feet ⟨*upon his legs*, in the House of Commons —John Almon⟩

**²leg** \"\ *vb* **legged; legged; legging; legs** *vi* **1 :** to use the legs in walking; *esp* **:** walk fast **:** RUN ⟨he . . . *legged* after him —Elgar Dolson⟩ — often used with *it* ⟨I *legged* it out to the barn —*New Yorker*⟩ **2 :** to bestir oneself for someone or something ⟨three . . . Congressmen *legged* for moving the Supreme Court —Julien Hyer⟩ **3 :** to propel a boat through a canal tunnel by moving the feet against the top or sides ⟨we've the tunnel to ~ through —C.S.Forester⟩ ~ *vt* **:** to propel (a boat) through a canal tunnel by means of the legs

**leg** *abbr* **1** legal **2** legate; legation **3** legato **4** legend **5** legislation; legislative; legislature **6** [L *legit*] he reads; [L *legunt*] they read

**¹leg·a·cy** \ˈlegəsē, -si\ *n* -ES [ME *legacie*, fr. MF or ML; MF *legacie*, fr. ML *legatia* office or jurisdiction of a legate, fr. L *legatus* (past part. of *legare* to send as a deputy, bequeath) + *-ia* -y — more at LEGATE] **1** *obs* **a :** the office, dignity, or function of a legate **b :** the business committed to a legate **:** COMMISSION 3 ⟨he came and told his ~ —George Chapman⟩ **2 :** a gift by will esp. of money or other personal property **:** BEQUEST 2 — compare CUMULATIVE 2b, DEMONSTRATIVE LEGACY, ²DEVISE, GENERAL LEGACY, MODAL, RESIDUARY LEGACY, SPECIFIC LEGACY **3 a :** something received (as from an ancestor or predecessor) resembling or suggestive of a gift by will ⟨their chief intellectual ~ to posterity —Norman Douglas⟩ ⟨men whose main ~ to us was a simple, direct . . . style —D.J.Lloyd⟩ ⟨she has left her granddaughter a rich ~ of expert knowledge —Alice Winchester⟩ **b :** something coming from the past (as from an age, event, or policy) ⟨a beautiful ~ from the age of Enlightenment —F.J.Mather⟩ ⟨one . . . ~ of the Roman domination of Europe —Harvey Graham⟩ ⟨military intervention . . . continued as a ~ of the dollar diplomacy —R.M.Lovett⟩ **4 :** a candidate for membership in an organization (as a fraternity) who is given special status because he is related to a member

**²legacy** \"\ *vt* -ED/-ING/-ES *archaic* **:** to give as a legacy

**legacy by damnation** *or* **legacy per dam·na·ti·o·nem** \-,damˌnāshēˈōˌnem\ *n, pl* **legacies by damnation** *or* **legacies per damnationem** [*legacy by damnation* trans. of L *legatum per damnationem*; *legacy per damnationem* part trans. of L *legatum per damnationem*] **:** a form in Roman law for declaring a legacy in which the heir is ordered to pay money or deliver property to the legatee in any event or pay its value

**legacy duty** *n, chiefly Brit* **:** LEGACY TAX

**legacy hunter** *n* **:** one that is attentive to old and rich persons in the hope of obtaining a legacy

**legacy tax** *n* **:** a tax levied on the privilege of passing title by will to property, esp. personal property — compare DEATH TAX, ESTATE TAX, INHERITANCE TAX

**¹le·gal** \ˈlēgəl *sometimes* ˈlig-\ *adj* [ME, fr. MF, fr. L *legalis* of or relating to law, fr. *leg-*, *lex* law (prob. orig. meaning a collection) + *-alis* -al; prob. akin to L *legere* to gather, select — more at LEGEND] **1 a :** according with the Mosaic law **b :** of, relating to, or based on the doctrine of salvation through works rather than by grace **2 :** of or relating to law ⟨may request . . . an advisory opinion on any ~ question —*U.N. Charter*⟩ ⟨the question of control was a ~ one which should not have been submitted to the jury —D.N.Edelstein⟩ ⟨~ textbooks⟩ **3 a :** deriving authority from law **:** founded upon law **:** de jure ⟨a ~ government⟩ ⟨the duly constituted and ~ successors of the ancien régime⟩ — compare LEGITIMATE, POLITICAL **b :** having a formal status derived from or as if from law often without a basis in actual fact **:** TITULAR ⟨an artificial ~ difference —F.D.Roosevelt⟩ **c :** established by law; *esp* **:** STATUTORY ⟨the ~ test of mental capacity —K.C. Masteller⟩ **4 :** conforming to or permitted by law or established rules (as of a game) **:** according to the principles of law **:** conforming to the procedures and methods prescribed by law ⟨an enterprise which is not only ~ for positivists but positively enjoined by their creed —W.P.Alston⟩ ⟨their action was made regular and ~ —J.R.Green⟩ — compare CONSTITUTIONAL **5 :** recognized or made effective by a court of law as distinguished from a court of equity **:** existing or valid in law as distinguished from equity — compare EQUITABLE 2 **6 :** of, relating to, or having the characteristics of the profession of law or of one of its members ⟨a bottle . . . that some ~ friend had sent him —J.G.Cozzens⟩ ⟨stood in ~ gravity —Hamlin Garland⟩ ⟨surprised to hear it from a ~ gentleman —Ellen Wilkinson⟩ **7 a :** created by the constructions of the law ⟨passed her life in a kind of ~ childhood —Charles Dickens⟩ ⟨a ~ fiction⟩ **b :** recognized as such by law ⟨as a ~ woman . . . she could presumably marry —Norman Ober⟩ **8 :** arising by operation of law as distinguished from that which arises by agreement or act of the parties ⟨a ~ hypothec⟩ — compare CONVENTIONAL 1a **syn** see LAWFUL

**²legal** \"\ *n* -S **1 :** a requirement or right established by law; *esp* **:** LEGAL REVERSION **2 :** a paid advertisement in a newspaper consisting of matter required by law or ordinance to be made public **3** *or* **legal investment :** a class of securities in which trustees, savings banks, and other investors regulated by law may legally invest

**legal age** *n* **:** LAWFUL AGE

**legal aid society** *or* **legal aid association** *n* **:** an organization affording counsel and representation in court to litigants unable to pay a lawyer

**legal buckram** *n* **:** ¹BUCKRAM 2b

**legal cap** *n* [*cap* fr. *-cap* (as in *foolscap*)] **:** a white writing paper for legal use that is usu. 8½ inches wide and 13 or 14 inches long and is often ruled ⟨some . . . use *legal cap* with margins ruled in red —Eva L. Connelly & T.P.Moroney⟩

**legal capacity** *n* **:** the capability and power under law of a person to occupy a particular status or relationship with another or to engage in a particular undertaking or transaction ⟨by giving the organization *legal capacity* —*Internat'l Court of Justice / Advisory Opinion*⟩ ⟨the *legal capacity* to sue⟩

**legal chemistry** *n* **:** FORENSIC CHEMISTRY

**legal duty** *n* **:** an obligation arising out of contract or law — compare LEGAL RIGHT 3

**le·gal·ese** \ˌlēgəˈlēz, -ēs *sometimes* ˌlig-\ *n* -S **:** the specialized language of the legal profession that is usu. wordy and complicated and often unintelligible to an outsider ⟨befogged far beyond the ordinary achievements of military ~ —Bernard DeVoto⟩

**legal estoppel** *n* **:** COMMON-LAW ESTOPPEL

**legal fiction** *n* **:** FICTION 4

**legal foreclosure** *n* **:** a method of foreclosure used in some states of the U.S. that is carried out by proceedings at law (as by writ of entry or of ejectment or of scire facias) rather than in equity and bars the equity of redemption

**legal fraud** *n* **:** constructive or equitable fraud for which a court of equity and sometimes a court of law will grant a remedy

**legal heir** *n* **:** HEIR AT LAW

**legal holiday** *n* **:** a holiday established by legal authority and characterized by legal restrictions on work and transaction of official business

**legal intromission** *n, Scots law* **:** intromission undertaken upon grounds recognized in law as sufficient — compare VICIOUS INTROMISSION

**le·ga·lis ho·mo** \ləˈgäləsˈhō(ˌ)mō\ *n, pl* **lega·les ho·mi·nes** \-ä(ˌ)lāsˈhōmə,nās\ [ML, lit., legal man] **:** one possessing full legal capacity under Old English law and not debarred of any of his rights in court (as to make oath, testify, and serve as a juror) by outlawry, excommunication, infamy, or disqualification **:** one within the protection of the law **:** one standing rectus in curia

**le·gal·ism** \ˈlēgə,lizəm *sometimes* ˈlig-\ *n* -S **1 :** the principles and practices characterizing the theological doctrine of strict conformity to a code of deeds and observances (as the Mosaic law) as a means of justification ⟨the first great battle which the Church had to fight was with Jewish ~ —R.C.Trench⟩ ⟨the worship of the Bible with its attending moralism, ~, and obscurantism —*Saturday Rev.*⟩ **2 a :** an often excessive reliance on legal principles and practices esp. as interpreted literally **:** an adherence to the letter as distinguished from the spirit of the law **:** an emphasis on the importance of formulated rules (as for governing conduct) ⟨a revolt against formalism and ~ . . . inspired by American pragmatic philosophy —T.I. Cook⟩ ⟨the best that can be said for ritualistic ~ is that it improves conduct —Aldous Huxley⟩ **b :** a legal term or rule often having little or no meaning in actual practice ⟨sterile ~*s* developed . . . to make war respectable —R.H.Jackson⟩ **3** *usu cap* **:** the philosophy of the Chinese Legalists ⟨the contrast between Confucianism and *Legalism* —*Times Lit. Supp.*⟩

**le·gal·ist** \-ləst\ *n* -S **1 :** one that believes in or advocates theological legalism **2 :** one that views things from a legal standpoint; *esp* **:** one that places primary and often excessive emphasis on legal principles as interpreted literally or on the formal structure of governmental institutions ⟨he condemns . . . the ~ who divorces international law from politics —R.N. Swift⟩ **3** *usu cap* **:** one of a group of thinkers flourishing in China during the 3d and 4th centuries B.C. and greatly influencing Chinese ethical and political philosophy by an advocacy of government on the basis of a fixed body of laws as distinguished from the Confucian ideal of government by moral example ⟨the authoritarianism of the *Legalists* —*Times Lit. Supp.*⟩

**le·gal·is·tic** \ˌlēgəˈlistik, -tēk *sometimes* ˌlig-\ *adj* **:** characterized by legalism ⟨the American tendency to approach foreign policy in moralistic and ~ fashion —W.G.Carleton⟩ ⟨a ~ religion⟩ ⟨no amount of ~ argument can becloud this issue —F.D.Roosevelt⟩ — **le·gal·is·ti·cal·ly** \-tək(ə)lē, -tēk-, -li\ *adv*

**le·gal·i·ty** \ləˈgaləd·ē, lēˈ-, -ətē, -i\ *n* -ES [ME *legalite*, fr. MF & ML; MF *legalité*, fr. ML *legalitat-, legalitas*, fr. L *legalis* legal + *-itat-, -itas* -ity — more at LEGAL] **1 :** attachment to or observance of law; *esp* **:** conformity to or reliance upon the letter of theological law **2 :** the quality or state of being legal **:** LAWFULNESS ⟨Supreme Court . . . upheld the ~ of such contributions —J.A.Morris b. 1904⟩ ⟨a supreme court to rule on the ~ of legislation —*Collier's Yr. Bk.*⟩ **3 legalities** *pl* **:** obligations imposed by law ⟨entrenched and protected by *legalities* —Agnes Repplier⟩

**le·gal·iza·tion** \ˌlēgələˈzāshən -lī'z- *sometimes* ˌlig-\ *n* -S **:** the act of legalizing **:** the state of being or having been legalized ⟨the ~ of the employment of the navy in enforcing the laws of trade —*Edinburgh Rev.*⟩ ⟨~ of a document to be submitted in evidence⟩

**le·gal·ize** \ˈlēgə,līz *sometimes* ˈlig-\ *vt* -ED/-ING/-S *see -ize in Explan Notes* [¹*legal* + *-ize*] **1 a :** to make legal **:** give legal validity or sanction to ⟨~ an act which without those instructions would have been a plain trespass —John Marshall⟩ ⟨the state was one of the first to ~ prizefighting —*Amer. Guide Series: La.*⟩ ⟨the . . . act ~*s* hardships which it was never the intention of Parliament to create —*Fortnightly Rev.*⟩ **b :** to authenticate a document or a signature thereon so that it may be admissible in evidence ⟨these documents should be notarized . . . and then *legalized* at the nearest consulate —Manuel Perez⟩ **2 :** to interpret or apply in a legalistic spirit ⟨you persist to ~ the gospel —J.W.Fletcher⟩

**legal jointure** *n* **:** JOINTURE 2b

**le·gal·ly** \-gəlē, -li\ *adv* **1 :** in a legal manner **:** in accordance with the law **:** LAWFULLY ⟨dissolution of a ~ valid marriage —Edward Jenks⟩ **2 :** from the point of view of law ⟨legal science can only cognize ~ —William Ebenstein⟩ ⟨~ she had no claim to the estate⟩

**legal man** *or* **legal person** *n* [trans. of ML *legalis homo*] **:** LEGALIS HOMO

**legal medicine** *n* **:** FORENSIC MEDICINE

**legal memory** *n* **:** the minimum period of time usu. prescribed by statute for a custom existing for that time to have the force of law or for conduct continued for that time to be the foundation of a legal right or title not otherwise provable — compare PRESCRIPTION, TIME IMMEMORIAL

**legal name** *n* **1 a :** the designation of a person recognized by the law as correct and sufficient and constituting under common law one given name followed by the family name and in modern times requiring or permitting one or more middle given names or initials in abbreviation thereof and upon the marriage of a female the substitution of her husband's family name for her maiden or former family name **b :** the designation of a firm or corporation similarly recognized by law **2 :** a name by which a person, firm, or corporation is actually known in a community and which discloses true identity recognized as sufficient in legal matters or proceedings

**legal officer** *n* **:** a military officer engaged chiefly in legal duties — see JUDGE ADVOCATE, JUDGE ADVOCATE GENERAL

**legal rate** *n* **:** LAWFUL RATE

**legal representative** *n* **:** a personal representative having legal status: **a :** one that represents another (as a deceased or incompetent person) **:** one that succeeds to the interest in property of a person living or corporate — compare ADMINISTRATOR, ASSIGNEE, CURATOR, EXECUTOR, GUARDIAN, HEIR, LEGATEE, RECEIVER, TRUSTEE IN BANKRUPTCY; DISTRIBUTION 1d **b :** an agent having legal status; *esp* **:** one acting under a power of attorney

**legal reserve** *n* **:** the minimum amount as determined by government standards of the deposits held by a bank or of the assets of a life insurance company required by law to be kept as reserves

**legal residence** *n* **1 :** the permanent fixed place of abode at a specific address to which one intends to return despite temporary absences or residence elsewhere **:** a domiciliary house or habitation where one intends to dwell indefinitely despite temporary absences **2 :** a domicile that may or may not constitute an actual place of abode at a specific address **3 :** DOMICILE 2c

**legal reversion** *n* **:** the period of time allowed by Scots law for a debtor to redeem his heritable property from a debt adjudged against it — called also *legal*

**legal right** *n* **1 a :** a claim recognized and delimited by law for the purpose of securing it **b :** the interest in a claim which is recognized by and protected by sanctions of law imposed by a state, which enables one to possess property or to engage in some transaction or course of conduct or to compel some other person to so engage or to refrain from some course of conduct under certain circumstances, and for the infringement of which claim the state provides a remedy in its courts of justice **2 :** the aggregate of the capacities, powers, liberties, and privileges by which a claim is secured **3 :** a capacity of asserting a legally recognized claim — compare LEGAL DUTY **4 :** a right cognizable in a common-law court as distinguished from a court having jurisdiction in equity

**legals** *pl of* LEGAL

**legal secretary** *n* **:** a government official in several British colonies performing the functions of an attorney general ⟨the governor shall appoint a person to be *legal secretary* —*Ceylon Constitution*⟩

**legal separation** *n* **:** JUDICIAL SEPARATION — not used technically

**legal-size** \ˈ≈≈ˌ≈\ *or* **legal-sized** \ˈ≈≈ˌ≈\ *adj* **1 :** of a size conforming to standards set by law ⟨the river is stocked with *legal-size* trout —E.W.Smith⟩ **2 :** of a size commonly used in the work of the legal profession ⟨a *legal-size* filing cabinet⟩ ⟨*legal-sized* paper⟩

**legal tender** *n* **1 :** the act of tendering in the performance of a contract or satisfaction of a claim the payment or service which the law prescribes or permits and at such time and place as the law prescribes or permits **2 :** currency in such amounts and denominations as the law authorizes a debtor to tender and requires a creditor to receive in payment of money obligations — compare LAWFUL MONEY

**legal term** *n* **:** either Whitsunday or Martinmas fixed by Scots law for the payment of semiannual rent or interest as distinguished from a conventional day agreed upon for such payment

**legal weight** *n* **:** the weight of goods and interior wrapping but not including the weight of the container — used esp. in foreign trade

**leg·an·tine** \ˈlegən,tēn, -n·,tīn\ *adj* [prob. fr. L *legant-, legans* (pres. part. of *legare* to send with a commission or charge, send as a deputy) + E *-ine*] **:** LEGATINE ⟨exercise his ~ functions —William Robertson †1686⟩

**leg art** *n* **:** CHEESECAKE 2 ⟨a lush display of . . . *leg art* —*Time*⟩

**¹leg·a·tary** \ˈlegə,terē\ *n* -ES [L *legatarius*, fr. *legatus* (past part. of *legare* to bequeath) + *-arius* -ary] *archaic* **:** LEGATEE ⟨the benevolence of the testator towards the ~ —George Wythe⟩

**²legatary** \"\ *adj* **:** of or relating to a legacy

**¹leg·ate** \ˈlegət, *usu* -əd·+V\ *n* -S [ME, fr. OE *legat*, fr. OF & L; OF *legat*, fr. L *legatus* ambassador, deputy, provincial governor, fr. *legatus*, past part. of *legare* to send with a commission or charge, bequeath, fr. *leg-, lex* law — more at LEGAL] **1 a :** an ecclesiastic representing the Roman Catholic pope and invested with the authority of the Holy See ⟨among the ~*s* sent by the pope —M.W.Baldwin⟩ ⟨the papal ~*s* . . . joined with the council and the representatives of the three other patriarchs —K.S.Latourette⟩ — compare APOSTOLIC DELEGATE, NUNCIO **b :** the governor of a province in the Papal States **2 :** an emissary usu. having official status (as an ambassador, delegate, or envoy) **3 a :** a deputy of a Roman general or of the governor of a Roman province **b :** a provincial governor of the Roman Empire

**²le·gate** \ləˈgāt\ *vt* -ED/-ING/-S [L *legatus*, past part.] **:** BEQUEATH 1 **syn** see WILL

**legate a la·te·re** \-ä'läd·ə,rā\ *n* [part trans. of ML *legatus a latere*, lit., legate from the side] **:** a confidential papal legate of the highest degree who is appointed esp. for a particular mission and not as a permanent representative abroad — distinguished from *nuncio*

**leg·a·tee** \ˌlegəˈtē\ *n* -S [²*legate* + *-ee*] **:** one to whom a legacy is bequeathed or to whom a devise is given ⟨the Florida decree was binding . . . on the ~ of the plaintiff —H.S.Drinker⟩ ⟨the working class . . . is the ~ of racist attitudes —W.R.Goldschmidt⟩

**leg·ate·ship** \ˈlegət,ship\ *n* **:** the dignity and office of a legate

**leg·a·tine** \ˈlegə,tēn, -,tīn, -tən\ *adj* [ML *legatinus*, fr. L *legatus* legate + *-inus* -ine] **:** of, headed by, or enacted under the authority of a legate ⟨the pope would send a ~ commission to England —F.M.Stenton⟩ ⟨a ~ constitution⟩

**le·ga·tion** \ləˈgāshən, lēˈ-\ *n* -S [ME *legacioun*, fr. MF & L; MF *legation*, fr. L *legation-, legatio*, fr. *legatus* (past part. of *legare* to send with a commission or charge, depute) + *-ion-, -io*

-ion — more at LEGATE] **1 a :** the sending forth of a legate or a diplomatic representative **b :** the charge or business entrusted to such an envoy **:** MISSION **2 :** a body of deputies sent on a mission; *specif* **:** a diplomatic mission in a foreign country headed by a minister ⟨air attachés on the staffs of our embassies and ~s —F.A.Ogg & P.O.Ray⟩ **3 :** LEGATESHIP **4 :** the official residence and office of a diplomatic minister at the seat of a foreign government ⟨troops occupied the premises of the American ~ —G.H.Stuart⟩

**leg·a·tive** \ˈlegəd·iv\ *adj* [LL *legativus*, fr. L *legatus* (past part. of *legare* to depute) + *-ivus* -ive] **:** LEGATINE

**¹le·ga·to** \lə'gä(,)tō, lā'-\ *adv (or adj)* [It, lit., tied, bound, fr. past part. of *legare* to bind, tie, fr. L *ligare* — more at LIGATURE] **1 :** in a manner that is smooth and connected between successive tones — often used as a direction in music **2 :** in a smooth and continuous manner **:** without abrupt break in movement — often used as a direction in dancing

**²legato** \"\ *n* -s **:** a smooth and connected manner of performance (as of a musical instrument); *also* **:** a passage of music so performed

**le·ga·tor** \lə'gād·ə(r)\ *n* -s [L, fr. *legatus* (past part. of *legare* to bequeath) + *-or* — more at LEGATE] **:** one who bequeaths a legacy **:** TESTATOR

**leg bail** *n* **:** FLIGHT **:** escape by flight — **give leg bail** *or* **take leg bail :** to run away **:** ESCAPE

**leg band** *n* **:** an identification tag on the leg of a bird (as a fowl or pigeon)

**leg·bar** \ˈleg,bär\ *n, usu cap* [Leghorn + barred rock] **:** a breed of autosexing domestic fowls developed by crossing brown leghorns with barred rocks

**leg before wicket** *adj* **:** having with any part of the person except the hand illegally stopped a bowled ball that would otherwise have hit the wicket ⟨to be out, *leg before wicket*⟩ ⟨to be clearly *leg before wicket*⟩ — used of a batsman in cricket

**leg boot** *n* **:** a laceless and strapless boot with the leg often extending almost to the knee

**leg–break** \ˈ=,=\ *n* **:** a bowled ball in cricket that breaks from the leg side to the off side

**leg bye** *n* **:** a bye in cricket made on a bowled ball that glances off some part of the batsman's person other than his hand

**leg drop** *n* **:** a scenery drop from which the center portion has been cut to produce two legs with a space between

**¹leg·end** \ˈlejənd\ *n* -s [ME *legende*, fr. MF & ML; MF *legende*, fr. ML *legenda*, fr. L *legendus*, gerundive of *legere* to gather, select, read; akin to Gk *legein* to collect, gather, choose, speak, *logos* word, reason, speech, account, Alb mb-*leth* I collect] **1** *obs* **a :** the story of the life of a saint **b :** a collection of such stories **c :** ACCOUNT, HISTORY ⟨those rambling letters . . . are naught else than a ~ of the cumbersome life and various fortunes of a cadet —James Howell⟩ **2 a :** LECTIONARY 1 **b :** PASSIONAL **3 a :** a story coming down from the past; *esp* **:** one handed down from early times by tradition and popularly regarded as historical although not entirely verifiable ⟨all the well-known families had their grotesque or tragic or romantic ~s —W.B.Yeats⟩ ⟨~s regarding buried treasure . . . are as numerous as they are improbable —Thomas Barbour⟩ ⟨steeped himself in the ~s of the river —Saxe Commins⟩ **b :** the total body of such stories and traditions; *esp* **:** the collective stories and traditions of a particular group (as a people or clan) ⟨a place in American ~⟩ ⟨local ~ perpetuates the tale —*Amer. Guide Series: Oregon*⟩ ⟨lives on in ~⟩ **c :** a popular myth usu. of current or recent origin ⟨the ~s they weave offer valuable clues to their nature —Julian Towster⟩ ⟨creation of a ~ about a movie star by the publicity department⟩ **d :** one around whom such stories and traditions have grown up **:** one having a special status as a result of possessing or being held to possess extraordinary qualities that are usu. partly real and partly mythical ⟨a ~ at forty-seven, as he has been for some years —Ward Morehouse⟩ ⟨had already had a resounding public career and . . . become a ~ in his own time —Vincent Sheean⟩ **e :** the subject of a legend ⟨some cartoons . . . are good enough to become ~ —Gerald Gottlieb⟩ ⟨big bonuses in prosperous times are ~ —*Newsweek*⟩ **4 a :** the wording (as an inscription, motto, or title) on an object ⟨a brass placard bore the ~ —Erle Stanley Gardner⟩ ⟨cancellation with the three-line ~ —*Stamps*⟩ ⟨the ~s on both sides of the coins —J.F.Lhotka⟩ ⟨on one side of the glass entrance is a ~ twenty feet in height —R.G.Young⟩ **b :** CAPTION 4b **c :** an explanatory list of the symbols appearing on a map or chart **d :** a statement on the label of a drug product indicating that federal law prohibits the druggist from dispensing it except on the prescription of a physician **syn** see MYTH

**²legend** \"\ *vt* -ED/-ING/-S **:** to inscribe (as a map or illustration) with a legend

**le·gen·da** \lə'jendə\ *n pl* [ML, lit., things to be read, fr. L *legenda*, neut. pl. of *legendus*, gerundive of *legere* to read, gather] **:** stories and other writings (as from a passional) to be read usu. for edification

**leg·end·ar·i·ly** \ˈlejən,derəlē\ *adv* **:** by legend **:** in a legendary manner ⟨~ successful personality —*N. Y. Herald Tribune*⟩

**¹leg·end·ary** \-derē, -ri\ *n* -ES [ML *legendarius* collection of saints' lives, fr. *legenda* legend + L *-arius* -ary — more at LEGEND] **1 :** a book containing a collection of legends; *esp* **:** one devoted to stories of the lives of saints ⟨ordered as a sign of repentance to write a ~ of good women —H.S.Bennett⟩ **2 :** a writer of legends ⟨the ancient . . . historians and more modern *legendaries* —John Spencer⟩

**²legendary** \"\ *adj* **:** of, relating to, or having the characteristics of legend or a legend **:** according to legend ⟨the ~ cry of the arctic trailblazers —Horace Sutton⟩ ⟨all that ~ and Talmudic lore which has become so familiar to us —J.R. Green⟩ ⟨~ history reported in the next generation —J.A. Froude⟩ **syn** see FICTITIOUS

**leg·end·ist** \-ndəst\ *n* -s **:** a writer of legends

**leg·end·ize** \-n,dīz\ *vt* -ED/-ING/-S **:** to endow (as a person) with a legend ⟨to be *legendized* as the father of the world's most remarkable group of brothers and sisters —J.N.Moody⟩

**leg·end·ry** \-ndrē\ *n* -ES **:** LEGENDS ⟨its heritage of romantic ~ —Aubrey Drury⟩ ⟨his place in American ~ —C.L.Carmer⟩

**leger** *var of* LEDGER

**leg·er·de·main** \ˌlejə(r)də'mān\ *n* -s [ME *lygarde-de-mayne, lechardemane*, fr. MF *leger de main* light of hand] **1 a :** SLEIGHT OF HAND **b :** the practice of magic or trickery usu. involving sleight of hand **2 :** an artful deception or display of trickery held to resemble sleight of hand ⟨a remarkable piece of diplomatic ~ —Anthony West⟩

**le·ger·i·ty** \lə'jerəd·ē\ *n* -ES [MF *legereté*, fr. OF, lightness, fr. *leger, legier* light in weight (fr. — assumed — VL *leviarius*, fr. L *levis*) + *-té* -ty — more at LIGHT (in weight)] **:** a mental or physical agility and quickness **:** NIMBLENESS ⟨the ~ of the French mind made the . . . visitor quick to comprehend his desire for solitude —Elinor Wylie⟩

**leges** *pl of* LEX

**leg·ga·da** \ˈlegədə\ *n, cap* [NL] **:** a genus of murid rodents that comprises the jungle mice and is sometimes regarded as a subgenus of *Mus*

**legged** \ˌlegəd *or* ˌläg-, *Brit usu* -gd\ *adj* [ME, fr. *leg* (n.) + *-ed*] **:** having legs ⟨a ~ table⟩ **:** having such or so many legs ⟨hairy-*legged*⟩ ⟨one-*legged*⟩ **:** so shaped in the legs ⟨bow*legged*⟩

**leg·ger** \ˈlegə(r)\ *n* -s **1 :** one who legs a canal barge through a tunnel **2 a :** a machine for knitting the legs of hosiery — compare FOOTER **b :** an operator of this machine **3 :** LEGMAN **4** [by shortening] **:** BOOTLEGGER **5 :** a butcher in a slaughter-house or packing plant who works on the legs of carcasses

**leg·gie·ra·men·te** \lə,jerə'men(,)tā\ *adv (or adj)* [It, lit., lightly, fr. *leggiero*, adj.] **:** in a light, delicate, and brisk style — used as a direction in music

**leg·gie·ro** \-e(,)rō, -i(,)-\ *adv (or adj)* [It, fr. OF *legier* light in weight — more at LEGERITY] **:** LIGHTLY, GRACEFULLY — used as a direction in music

**leg·gi·ness** \-gēnəs, -gin-\ *n* -ES **:** the quality or state of being leggy

leggings for a child

**leg·ging** *or* **leg·gin** \ˈlegən, -giŋ, -gēŋ\ *n* -s [¹*leg* + *-ing*] **:** a covering for the leg usu. of leather or cloth: **a :** a covering made in various lengths and worn for protection (as by children, industrial workers, and sportsmen) ⟨shoes topped with soft leather ~s —Jean & Franc Shor⟩ — usu. used in pl. **b :** GAITER **c :** PUTTEE ⟨the man in the field . . . in his field jacket and *leggins* —*Infantry Jour.*⟩ **d leggings** *pl* **:** ²CHAPS

**leg·ginged** *also* **leg·gined** \-nd,-ŋd\ *adj* **:** clad in leggings ⟨white-*legginged* soldiers⟩

**leg glance** *n* **:** a glance that deflects a cricket ball to the leg side

**leg guard** *n* **:** PAD 1a (3)

**leg·gy** \ˈlegē, -gi\ *adj* -ER/-EST **1 :** having conspicuous legs: as **a :** having disproportionately long legs esp. as a result of immature or faulty development ⟨a long, thin, ~, gawky boy —A.J.Beveridge⟩ ⟨using ~ . . . high-withered animals for cavalry horses —C.F.Rooks⟩ **b :** having long, well-formed, and attractive legs ⟨a girl in a red outfit . . . , lithe and ~ and of course attractive —*Commonweal*⟩ **c** (1) **:** SPINDLY — used of a plant or seedling ⟨the plants will become ~ and straggly —Helen M. Fox⟩ (2) **:** having few or no lower branches ⟨beneath old ~ shrubs —*Nature Mag.*⟩ **2 :** characterized by a display of legs ⟨~ photography⟩

**leg–harness** \ˈ=,==\ *n* [ME *legharneis*] **:** armor for the legs ⟨armed with . . . *leg-harness*, sword, spear, and dagger —P.F. Tytler⟩

**leg hit** *n* **:** a hit that sends a cricket ball to leg

**¹leg·horn** \ˈleg,hȯrn, -e,gȯ-, -ó(ə)n, ˈlegə(r)n; *with reference to fowls* ˈlegə(r)n *is usual in US &* le'gȯ(ə)n *or* lə'g- *in Brit*\ *adj, usu cap* [fr. *Leghorn*, Italy] **:** of or from the city of Leghorn, Italy **:** of the kind or style prevalent in Leghorn

**²leghorn** \"\ *n* [fr. *Leghorn*, Italy, its place of exportation] **1** -s **a :** a fine plaited straw made from an Italian wheat that is usu. cut green and bleached ⟨a terrific hat of natural ~ —Lois Long⟩ **b :** a hat or bonnet of this straw ⟨had they new hats or last year's ~s —*Atlantic*⟩ **2 a** *usu cap* **:** a Mediterranean breed of rather small hardy nonbroody domestic fowls having smooth yellow legs, white ear lobes, and rose or single combs, laying numbers of white eggs of good size, and occurring in several color varieties — see WHITE LEGHORN **b** -s *often cap* **:** any bird of this breed **3** -s **:** a pale yellow that is deeper and slightly redder than ivory, redder and deeper than cream, and redder and less strong than straw yellow

**leg·i·bil·i·ty** \ˌlejə'biləd·ē, -atē, -i\ *n* -ES **:** the quality or state of being legible ⟨the influence of typeface on the ~ of print —Helen A. Webster & M.A.Tinker⟩

**leg·i·ble** \ˈlejəbəl\ *adj* [ME *legible*, fr. LL *legibilis*, fr. L *legere* to read + *-ibilis* -able — more at LEGEND] **1 :** capable of being read or deciphered **:** distinct to the eye **:** PLAIN ⟨a handsome, supremely ~ type —Bruce Bliven b.1916⟩ ⟨small but ~ gold watches —*New Yorker*⟩ ⟨a used stamp . . . with a light but ~ cancellation —H.M.Ellis⟩ **2 :** capable of being discovered or understood by apparent marks or indications ⟨murder sweltered in his heart and was ~ upon his face —Thomas Wolfe⟩ — **leg·i·bly** \-blē, -li\ *adv*

**le·gion** \ˈlējən\ *n* -s [ME *legiun, legioun*, fr. OF *legiun, legion*, fr. L *legion-, legio*, fr. *legere* to levy, gather, read + *-ion-, -io* -ion] **1 :** the principal unit of the Roman army comprising at first 3000 but later 5000 to 6000 foot soldiers with a complement of cavalry ⟨withdrawal of the Roman ~s from Britain⟩ ⟨Caesar's ~s⟩ — compare COHORT **2 :** a large military force; *esp* **:** ARMY 1a ⟨the French Foreign *Legion*⟩ ⟨the Arab *Legion*⟩ **3 :** a very large number (as of persons or things) **:** HOST, MULTITUDE ⟨won him . . . a ~ of devoted followers —Irving Kolodin⟩ ⟨the growing ~ of nature lovers —A.F.Gustafson⟩ ⟨the tales which have made him a legendary character are ~ —Laura Gilpin⟩ **4 :** a now uncommon taxonomic category of varying rank sometimes corresponding to a superfamily and sometimes to a class **5 :** a national association of ex-servicemen ⟨the American *Legion* has championed a universal draft plan —C.W.Ferguson⟩ ⟨delegates from the various branches of the British *Legion* —*Whitaker's Almanack*⟩

**¹le·gion·ary** \-jə,nerē, -ri\ *adj* [L *legionarius*, fr. *legion-, legio* legion + *-arius* -ary] **:** of, relating to, or constituting a legion ⟨accompanied by three or four ~ soldiers —A.C.Whitehead⟩ ⟨a ~ camp⟩ ⟨~ forces⟩

**²legionary** \"\ *n* -ES **:** LEGIONNAIRE

**legionary ant** *n* **:** ARMY ANT; *specif* **:** any of several predatory ants of *Eciton* and related genera chiefly of tropical America that build no permanent nests and travel in large colonies

**le·gioned** \-jənd\ *adj* **:** formed in legions ⟨like ~ soldiers —John Keats⟩

**le·gion·naire** \ˌlējə'na(a)(ə)r, -neI, |ə\ *n* -s *often cap* [F *légionnaire*, fr. MF, fr. *legion* + *-aire* -ary] **:** a member of a legion ⟨Arab *Legionnaires* with their red scarves —Horace Sutton⟩ ⟨the American doughboy who probably still regales his fellow ~s . . . with provoking tales —*Nation*⟩

**leg–iron** \ˈ=,==\ *n* **:** a shackle for the leg ⟨no . . . handcuffs, shackles, or *leg-irons* could hold him —Walter Gibson⟩

**leg·is·late** \ˈlejə,slāt, *usu* -ād-+V\ *vb* -ED/-ING/-S [back-formation fr. *legislator*] *vi* **:** to perform the function of legislation **:** make or enact laws ⟨whether Congress has a right to investigate in fields where the Constitution forbids it to ~ —Elmer Davis⟩ ⟨allowed to ~ for themselves —J.A.Froude⟩ ~ *vt* **:** to cause, create, or bring about by legislation ⟨morality cannot be *legislated* —B.G.Gallagher⟩ ⟨proceed to ~ a better world into being —Lloyd Harrington⟩ ⟨*legislated* some of its own members into seats in a new legislature —R.M.Dawson⟩

**leg·is·la·tion** \ˌlejə'slāshən\ *n* -s [L *legis latio*, *legis latio* legal bill, action of proposing a law, fr. *legis* (gen. of *lex* law) + *lation-, latio* action of proposing — more at LEGAL, LATION] **1 :** the action of legislating **:** the making or giving of laws (as by an individual or an organized body); *specif* **:** the exercise of the power and function of making rules (as laws, ordinances, edicts) having the force of authority by virtue of their promulgation by an official organ of a state or other organization ⟨the major function of Congress is ~ —W.S.Sayre⟩ ⟨the regulation of these various . . . interests forms the principal task of modern ~ —James Madison⟩ — compare FIRST READING, REPORT STAGE, SECOND READING, THIRD READING **2 :** the enactments of a legislator or a legislative body ⟨one of the most progressive passages in German ~ —*Social Service Rev.*⟩ ⟨the ~ passed . . . by the California State Board of Education —N.P. Sacks⟩ ⟨rent-control ~ was . . . extended for another year —*Collier's Yr. Bk.*⟩ **3 :** a matter of business (as a bill or nomination) for or under consideration by a legislative body ⟨he has the power to introduce ~ . . . this proposed ~⟩

**¹leg·is·la·tive** \ˈlejə,slād·iv, |t|, |ēv *also* -slə|\ *adj* [*legislator* + *-ive*] **1 :** having the power or performing the function of legislating ⟨the ~ power may not rule by arbitrary decrees —J.H.Hallowell⟩ ⟨a national constitutional convention is clearly a ~ body —M.O.Hudson⟩ — compare ADMINISTRATIVE, EXECUTIVE, JUDICIAL **2 a :** of or relating to a legislature ⟨~ committees⟩ ⟨~ clerk⟩ ⟨~ act⟩ **:** composed of members of a legislature ⟨~ cabinet⟩ ⟨~ caucus⟩ ⟨a presession ~ conference⟩ **b :** created by a legislature esp. as distinguished from an executive or judicial body ⟨~ budget⟩ ⟨~ justice⟩ **c :** designed to assist a legislature or its members ⟨~ reference bureau⟩ ⟨~ research agency⟩ **3 :** of, concerned with, or created by legislation ⟨~ advocate⟩ ⟨~ courts⟩ ⟨~ home rule⟩

**²legislative** \"\ *n* -s **1** *obs* **:** the power and function of legislating **2 :** the body or department exercising the power and function of legislating **:** LEGISLATURE 1 ⟨the ~ cannot transfer the power of making laws to any other hands —John Locke⟩ ⟨having both the executive and the ~ of the same party —Ellen D. Ellis⟩ — compare ADMINISTRATION, EXECUTIVE, JUDICIARY

**legislative agent** *n* **:** LOBBYIST — compare LEGISLATIVE COUNSEL

**legislative assembly** *n, often cap L&A* **1 :** a bicameral legislature in an American state or territory ⟨election to the *legislative assembly* in Montana or Oregon⟩ ⟨in Puerto Rico . . . a daily record of its proceedings shall be published by the *Legislative Assembly* —G.K.Lewis⟩ **2 :** the lower house of a bicameral legislature; *esp* **:** one in a state or province of a nation that is a member of the British Commonwealth ⟨depriving the . . . government in South Australia of its absolute majority of the floor of the *Legislative Assembly* —*Australian Weekly Rev.*⟩ ⟨elected members of the *Legislative Assemblies* of the Indian States⟩ **3 :** a unicameral legislature ⟨the membership of the East African Central *Legislative Assembly* —*United Kingdom Dependencies*⟩; *esp* **:** one in a Canadian province ⟨the *Legislative Assembly* in Alberta⟩

**legislative council** *n, often cap L&C* **1 :** the upper house of a bicameral legislature: **a :** one in a British colony whose members usu. are chosen by the governor of the colony ⟨property requirements for members of the Cape Colony's *Legislative Council*⟩ ⟨the Assembly and the *Legislative Council* constitute the legislature of Bermuda⟩ **b :** the upper house of the New Zealand Parliament abolished in 1950 ⟨constitutional documents pertaining to the New Zealand *Legislative Council* —H.J.Benda⟩ **c :** one in a state or province of a nation that is a member of the British Commonwealth ⟨the *Legislative Council* of Quebec is composed of twenty-four members —R.M.Dawson⟩ ⟨in New South Wales the Labour Party twice came close to abolishing the *Legislative Council* —J.D.B.Miller⟩ **2 :** a unicameral legislature in a British colony containing the governor, official members appointed by the governor, and usu. unofficial members appointed or elected to represent the people ⟨*legislative councils* on the usual crown colony model —W.E.Simnett⟩ ⟨the normal type of colonial legislature in the modern dependent empire . . . is the *legislative council* —Martin Wight⟩ **3 :** the unicameral legislature of a territory of the U.S. ⟨the expenses of the *legislative council* of the territory of Michigan —*Niles' Register*⟩ ⟨the Virgin islands . . . are composed of two municipalities, each having a *legislative council* —W.S.Sayre⟩ **4 :** a permanent committee usu. composed of several members chosen from both houses that meets between sessions of a state legislature to study state problems and plan a legislative program ⟨the median size of *legislative councils* . . . is around 18 members —H.W.Davey⟩

**legislative counsel** *n* **:** LOBBYIST; *specif* **:** one that appears before a committee holding hearings on proposed legislation

**legislative day** *n* **:** a day during which a legislature is in session **:** a period of time that commences with the opening of a daily session and ends with adjournment for that day and that may often last more than one calendar day

**leg·is·la·tive·ly** \|əvlē\ *adv* **:** in a legislative manner **:** by legislation ⟨it was only ~ that the Lords could have to deal with this matter —*Annual Register*⟩

**leg·is·la·tor** \ˈlejə,slād·ə(r), -ātə- *sometimes* ¦==¦slād-,ó(ə)r *or* -ā,tó- *or* -ó(ə)\ *n* -s [L *legis lator*, lit., proposer of law, fr. *legis* (gen. of *lex* law) + *lator* proposer, bearer, fr. *latus* (suppletive past part. of *ferre* to carry, propose) + *-or* — more at LEGAL, TOLERATE, BEAR (to carry)] **:** one that makes laws esp. for a political unit (as a nation or state): **a :** an individual or an organized group that enacts a fundamental law (as a constitution) ⟨every form of government . . . is created by the ordinance of the ~ —C.H.McIlwain⟩ **b :** one that makes or helps to make laws and other enactments of policy as distinguished from a fundamental law ⟨the president often is termed our chief ~ —F.A.Ogg & P.O.Ray⟩ **c :** a member of a legislative body ⟨while ~s themselves . . . originate a certain number of bills, even more come from outside —F.A.Ogg & P.O.Ray⟩

**leg·is·la·to·ri·al** \ˌlejəslə¦tōrēəl, -tȯr-\ *adj* **:** LEGISLATIVE

**leg·is·la·tor·ship** \ˈ==,slād·ə(r),ship, -ātə-\ *n* **:** the position of legislator

**leg·is·la·tress** \ˌlejə¦slā·trəs\ *also* **leg·is·la·trix** \-ā·triks\ *n, pl* **legislatresses** \-trəsəz\ *also* **legislatrixes** \-ksəz\ *or* **legislatri·ces** \ˌ==ˈslā·trə,sēz, -ˌslə'trī(,)sēz\ [*legislatress* fr. *legislator* + *-ess*; *legislatrix* fr. *legislator*, after such pairs as E *executor*: *executrix*] **:** a woman who makes laws **:** a female member of a legislative body

**leg·is·la·ture** \ˈlejə,slāchə(r) *sometimes* ,==ˈ==\ *n* -s [*legislator* + *-ure*] **1 :** a body of persons having the power to legislate; *specif* **:** an organized body having the authority to make laws for a political unit and often exercising other functions (as control of the administration) ⟨the ~ in every state except Nebraska is a bicameral . . . body —F.A.Ogg & P.O.Ray⟩ ⟨the imperial parliament is historically the supreme ~ of the king's dominions —Martin Wight⟩ — compare ASSEMBLY 1a, CONGRESS 3, PARLIAMENT, SENATE **2** *obs* **:** the exercise of the power or function of legislating **:** LEGISLATION 1 ⟨inconvenient to have both the ~ and the execution in the same hands —Gilbert Burnet⟩

**le·gist** \ˈlējəst\ *n* -s [MF *legiste*, fr. ML *legista*, fr. L *leg-, lex* law + *-ista* -ist] **1 :** a specialist in law or a branch of law; *esp* **:** one learned in Roman or civil law ⟨the ~s elaborated their ideas of the royal rights with the aid of the Roman law —G.C.Sellery⟩ **2 :** a medieval law student **3** *usu cap* **:** one of a group of Chinese philosophers emphasizing penal law as the principal means of social control ⟨the *Legists* urged the full rigor of military despotism —C.P.Fitzgerald⟩ — compare CONFUCIAN

**¹le·git** \lə'jit, lē'-, *usu* -id·+V\ *n* -s [by shortening] *slang* **:** legitimate drama or theater

**²legit** \"\ *adj, slang* **:** LEGITIMATE ⟨an almost forgotten Broadway ~ house —*Variety*⟩ ⟨rehearse as though for the ~ stage —Hal March⟩ ⟨a few ~ playwrights —F.N.Karmatz⟩ ⟨a racket boy with a lot of ~ business —Harold Robbins⟩

**leg·i·tim** \ˈlejə,tim\ *n* -s [F *légitime*, fr. MF, fr. ML *legitima*, fr. L, fem. of *legitimus* legitimate] **:** the portion of an estate usu. including both real and personal property reserved to the children and sometimes other heirs upon the death of the father under Roman, civil, and Scots law — compare DEAD'S PART, REASONABLE PART

**le·git·i·ma·cy** \lə'jid·əməsē, lē'-, -itəm-, -si\ *n* -ES **:** the quality or state of being legitimate: as **a :** the legal status of kinship between a child and its natural parent usu. resulting from conception and birth in lawful wedlock and entitling the child to support by and the right to bear the surname of its lawful father together with the unrestricted right of inheritance and the maximum protection of the law — compare BASTARDY, ILLEGITIMACY **b** (1) **:** the possession of title or status as a result of acquisition by means that are or are held to be according to law and custom ⟨old-established governments do not need to produce certificates of ~ —Aldous Huxley⟩ ⟨acceptance by almost everybody . . . of the ~ of their rulers' authority —D.W.Brogan⟩ (2) **:** the right to rule possessed by a monarch as a result of strict adherence to the hereditary principle ⟨the Stuart belief in ~ —G.H.Sabine⟩ **c :** a conformity to recognized principles or accepted rules and standards ⟨the ~ of a large majority of the world's postal paper —H.M.Ellis⟩ ⟨~ of personal success —Kenneth de Courcy⟩

**¹le·git·i·mate** \-mət, *usu* -əd·+V\ *adj* [ML *legitimatus*, past part. of *legitimare* to legitimate, fr. L *legitimus* legitimate, fr. *leg-, lex* law — more at LEGAL] **1 :** lawfully begotten **:** born in wedlock **:** having full filial rights and obligations by birth ⟨a ~ child⟩ **2 :** GENUINE ⟨the ~ work of an artist⟩ ⟨many of them had ~ grievances against him —W.A.Swanberg⟩ **3 a** (1) **:** accordant with law or with established legal forms and requirements ⟨a ~ government⟩ ⟨pharmacies, hospitals, and other ~ storage places for narcotics —D.W.Maurer & V.H. Vogel⟩ (2) **:** LAW-ABIDING ⟨the ~ citizen⟩ ⟨it does not occur to the successful racketeer that he is not respectable; he is simply not ~ —D.W.Maurer⟩ **b :** ruling by or based upon the strict principle of hereditary right ⟨a ~ king⟩ ⟨a ~ monarchy⟩ **4 a :** conforming to recognized principles or accepted rules and standards ⟨~ advertising expenditure for the national advertiser —L.H.Bristol⟩ ⟨Australian notions of ~ conduct on the cricket field —D.W.Brogan⟩ **b** *of a taxon* **:** published validly and in strict accordance with the rules of the relevant international code — compare VALID **5 :** following in logical sequence **:** REASONABLE ⟨a ~ inference⟩ ⟨from this it would be ~ to conclude —B.P.Babkin⟩ **6 a :** of, relating to, or comprising a category of plays acted by live professional actors that does not include revues, burlesque, and many forms of musical comedy ⟨costs far more to produce a musical than . . . a standard ~ play —F.M.Whiting⟩ ⟨the ~ drama⟩ **b :** producing or performing in such plays ⟨does not feel that television has hurt the ~ theater as yet —Clarissa Start⟩ ⟨a ~ actor⟩ **syn** see LAWFUL

**²le·git·i·mate** \-ə,māt, *usu* -ād·+V\ *vt* -ED/-ING/-S [ML *legitimatus* (past part.)] **:** to make lawful or legal: **a** (1) **:** to give legal status or authorization to ⟨was *legitimated* by at most 58.7 percent of the voters —Kurt Glaser⟩ ⟨even to ~ vice —John Milton⟩ (2) **:** to show or affirm to be justified ⟨the untestable absolutes by which so much . . . human suffering is perennially *legitimated* —Charles Frankel⟩ **b :** to put (a bastard) in the position or state of a legitimate child before the law by legal means (as the subsequent marriage of the parents) ⟨the principle that marriage of parents should ~ prior-born children —Morris Ploscowe⟩ — compare ADOPT 1

[3]le·git·i·mate \-mət\ *n* -s [¹*legitimate*] **1 :** one having a legitimate status ⟨~*s* and natural children —*Dublin Univ. Mag.*⟩ **2 :** legitimate drama or theater — usu. used with *the*
**le·git·i·mate·ly** *adv* **:** in a legitimate manner **:** according to law or rules **:** LEGALLY, PROPERLY ⟨in a position to see, quite ~, what appeared to be an official dispatch —Elmer Davis⟩ ⟨an obscure region on which curiosity is ~ focused —*Geog. Jour.*⟩
**le·git·i·mate·ness** *n* -ES **:** the quality or state of being legitimate
**le·git·i·ma·tion** \lə̇ˌjid·əˈmāshən\ *n* -s [ME *legitimacioun*, fr. MF or ML; MF *legitimation*, fr. ML *legitimation-, legitimatio*, fr. *legitimatus* (past part. of *legitimare* to legitimate) + L *-ion-, -io* -ion] **1 :** the act or process of making legitimate ⟨English domestic law allowed ~ by subsequent marriage —J.H.C.Morris⟩ ⟨the ~ of money⟩ **2** *obs* **:** LEGITIMACY a
**le·git·i·ma·tize** \lə̇ˈjid·əmə,tīz, lēˈ-, -itəm-\ *vt* -ED/-ING/-s **:** LEGITIMATE ⟨American law has adopted a concept . . . that the intermarriage of parents ~*s* children —Morris Ploscowe⟩ ⟨the approbation of the men ~*s* the government —James Mackintosh⟩
**legitime** *adj* [ME, fr. MF, fr. L *legitimus* — more at LEGITIMATE] *obs* **:** LEGITIMATE
**le·git·i·mism** \lə̇ˈjid·ə,mizəm\ *n* -s *often cap* [F *légitimisme*, fr. *légitime* legitimate + *-isme* -ism] **:** adherence to the principles of political legitimacy or to a person claiming or holding authority based upon such principles ⟨international principles such as nonintervention, neutrality, and ~ —Bruce Bliven b.1889⟩ ⟨*Legitimism* has always been strong in Spain —*Blackwood's*⟩
¹**le·git·i·mist** \-məst\ *n* -s *often cap* [F *légitimiste*, fr. *légitime* legitimate + *-iste* -ist] **:** one that believes in or supports political legitimacy: as **a :** a supporter of the elder branch of the Bourbon dynasty to the crown of France — compare ORLEANIST **b :** one that supports the Alid claim of hereditary authority based on descent from Muhammad
²**legitimist** \"\ *adj* **:** of, belonging to, or supporting political legitimacy ⟨a ~ party⟩ ⟨a ~ movement⟩
**le·git·i·mize** \-ə,mīz\ *vt* -ED/-ING/-s *see -ize in Explan Notes* **:** LEGITIMATE ⟨she wouldn't marry and ~ the child —Marcia Davenport⟩ ⟨national patriotism *legitimized* war between nations —J.S.Schapiro⟩
**legits** *pl of* LEGIT
**leg·len** *or* **leg·lin** \ˈleglən\ *n* -s [perh. fr. MD *legelkijn, lagelijn* small flask, dim. of *lagel, lagele, legel, legele* flask, cask, fr. L *lagena* large flask — more at LAGENA] *Scot* **:** a milk pail ⟨the lady . . . came forth to see her maidens pass to the herds with their ~*s* —Sir Walter Scott⟩
**leg·less** \ˈlegləs\ *adj* **:** having no legs
**leg·let** \-lət\ *n* -s [¹*leg* + *-let*] **:** an ornamental band or ring for the leg ⟨these armlets and ~*s* were . . . worn for superstitious reasons —Rafael Karsten⟩
**leglike** \ˈ=,=\ *adj* **:** like a leg esp. in action or function
**leg·man** \ˈ=,man, -aa(ə)n\ *n, pl* **legmen 1 a :** a newspaperman who chiefly gathers information and sends in reports from the scene of an occurrence or from a special locale — compare BEAT MAN, REWRITE MAN **b :** REPORTER; *esp* **:** one that goes after his own information **2 :** one that assists another by gathering information or running errands and often performing subordinate administrative tasks ⟨~ for a movie columnist⟩
**leg–of–mutton** *or* **leg–o'–mutton** \ˌ;==;==\ *adj* **:** having the general shape or outline of a leg of mutton; *esp* **:** having a full upper arm and a fitted lower arm and wrist — used of the sleeve of a woman's garment
**leg–of–mutton rig** *n* **:** BERMUDA RIG
**leg–of–mutton sail** *n* **:** a triangular sail with its apex at the masthead
**le·gong** \ˈlā,gäŋ\ *n* -s *often cap* [Balinese] **:** a delicate and graceful Balinese drama dance that is performed by two young girls in sumptuous costumes
**leg–pull** \ˈ=,=\ *n* [back-formation fr. *leg-pulling*] **:** a deception or hoax usu. of a humorous character ⟨always full of jokes and *leg-pulls* —David Garnett⟩ ⟨the . . . anecdote near the end of the memoir sounds like a final *leg-pull* —Hugh Kenner⟩
**leg–puller** \ˈ=,==\ *n* **:** one that practices leg-pulls ⟨listen to the . . . redoubtable *leg-pullers* spouting their reminiscences of the wide and wonderful —*John O'London's Weekly*⟩
**leg–pulling** \ˈ=,==\ *n* -s [fr. the phrase *pull one's leg*] **:** the action of one that practices leg-pulls or an instance of such action ⟨fishermen's yarns and mutual *leg-pulling* —Sam Pollock⟩ ⟨never could stand criticism or *leg-pulling* —Paul Scott⟩
**le·grand·ite** \ləˈgran,dīt\ *n* -s [*Legrand*, name of a 20th cent. Belgian mine manager who collected the specimen + E *-ite*] **:** a mineral $Zn_{14}(OH)(AsO_4)_9 12H_2O$ consisting of a hydrous basic arsenate of zinc
**legroom** \ˈ=,=\ *n* **:** space in which to extend the legs while seated ⟨more ~ per passenger⟩ ⟨the right ~ for every driver —*Newsweek*⟩
**legs** *pl of* LEG, *pres 3d sing of* LEG
**leg show** *n* **:** a theatrical performance featuring a display of their legs by the female performers — compare BURLESQUE 3, STRIPTEASE
**leg spin** *n* **:** a spin imparted to a bowled cricket ball that tends to cause it to break from the leg side to the off side
**leg stump** *n* **:** the outside stump near the batsman in cricket — compare MIDDLE STUMP, OFF STUMP
**leg theory** *n* **:** a technique in cricket in which a concentration of fielders is placed on the leg side and the bowling aimed generally at the leg stump to tempt the batsman to make leg hits — compare BODY-LINE, OFF THEORY
**le·guan** *or* **le·guaan** \ləˈgwän\ *n* -s [prob. fr. D, fr. F *l'iguane* the iguana, fr. *le* the + *iguane* iguana, fr. Sp *iguana*] **:** a large lizard ⟨the ~ had the tortoise gripped in its jaws —W.H. Archer⟩
**leg·u·a·tia** \ˌlegyüˈāsh(ē)ə\ *n, cap* [NL, fr. François *Leguat* †1735 French Huguenot traveler + NL *-ia*] **:** a genus of fossil birds including an extinct rail (*L. gigantea*) found in the Mascarene islands
**leg·u·le·ian** \ˌlegyəˈlēən\ *n* -s [L *leguleius* pettifogger (fr. *leg-, lex* law) + E *-an* — more at LEGAL] **:** PETTIFOGGER ⟨some silly ~*s* . . . argue unawares against their own clients —Joseph Washington⟩
**leg·ume** \ˈle,gyüm, ləˈ g-, leˈ-, *in sense 1b* lāgüm\ *n, pl* **legumes** \-üm*z*,-üm\ [F *légume*, fr. MF, fr. L *legumen*, fr. *legere* to gather — more at LEGEND] **1 a :** the fruit or seed of a leguminous plant (as peas or beans) used for food **b :** a vegetable used for food — used chiefly in menus **2 :** a leguminous plant; *esp* **:** one grown as a forage or green-manure crop (as clover, alfalfa) **3 :** a dry dehiscent one-celled fruit developed from a simple superior ovary and usu. dehiscing into two valves with the seeds attached to the ventral suture **:** POD — compare FRUIT 1d, LOMENT; see FRUIT illustration
**legume inoculation** *n* **:** the inoculation of legume seeds with a specific culture of bacteria that multiply in the roots of a legume plant forming nodules where the bacteria fix atmospheric nitrogen for the nutrition of the plant
**le·gu·me·lin** \ləˈgyüməlән\ *n* -s [*legume* + *-el* + *-in*] **:** an albumin obtained from the pea and other leguminous seeds
**le·gu·men** \ləˈgyümən\ *n, pl* **legumi·na** \-mənə\ *or* **legumens** [L] **:** LEGUME
**le·gu·min** \"\ *n* -s [F *légumine*, fr. *légume* + *-ine* -in] **:** a globulin found as a characteristic constituent of the seeds of leguminous plants
**le·gu·mi·no·sae** \lə̇,gyüməˈnō(,)sē\ *n pl, cap* [NL, fr. fem. pl. of *leguminosus* leguminous] **:** a very large family of dicotyledonous plants (order Rosales) that includes herbs, shrubs, trees, and climbers usu. with highly irregular flowers, with a fruit which is a legume or loment, and commonly with root nodules containing nitrogen-fixing bacteria and that is divided into several subfamilies which in many classifications are considered separate families
**le·gu·mi·nous** \lə̇ˈgyümənəs, leˈ-\ *adj* [NL *leguminosus*, fr. L *legumin-*, *legumen* + *-osus* -ous] **1 :** of, resembling, or consisting of peas or other legumes **2 :** of or relating to the Leguminosae
¹**leg up** *n* **:** LEG 8
²**leg up** *vt* **:** CONDITION 3 e ⟨a colt . . . properly hardened and *legged up* —F.A.Wrensch⟩
**legwork** \ˈ=,=\ *n* **:** work or activity involving a preponderance of physical movement and esp. of walking from place to place: **a :** the work of a legman **b :** detailed investigation (as of a crime) **c :** the practical administration of a scheme or enterprise as distinguished from its planning
**le havre** *or* **havre** \ləˈhäv, -hàv, -vr(ᵊ), ÷-ˈhärv\ *adj, usu cap L&H* [fr. *Le Havre*, France] **:** of or from the city of Le Havre, France **:** of the kind or style prevalent in Le Havre
**le·ha·yim** *or* **le·cha·yim** *or* **le·hay·yim** *or* **le·chay·yim** \ləˈk̲äyəm, -,yēm\ *n* -s [Heb *leḥayīm*, lit., to life] **:** a traditional Jewish toast — often used interjectionally ⟨raised his glass and said "*lehayim!*"⟩
**le·hi·ite** \ˈlē,hī,īt\ *n* -s [*Lehi*, Utah, its locality + E *-ite*] **:** a mineral $(Na,K)_2Ca_5Al_8(PO_4)_8(OH)_{12}.6H_2O$(?) consisting of a hydrous basic phosphate of calcium and aluminum
**leh·mann love grass** \ˈlāmən-, ˈlē\ *or* **lehmann's love grass** *n, usu cap L* [prob. fr. the name *Lehmann*] **:** an African drought-resistant grass (*Eragrostis lehmanniana*) grown esp. in arid sections of western No. America as a hay and forage crop and for erosion control
**lehr** *also* **leer** *or* **lear** \ˈli(ə)r, ˈle(ə)r, ˈlāər\ *n* -s [G *lehr*, *leer* model, pattern, measuring instrument, fr. MHG *lēre* model, measure] **:** a long oven in which glassware is annealed as it travels through on a continuous belt
**lehr·man** *also* **leer·man** \-mən\ *n, pl* **lehrmen** *also* **leermen :** one that works at a lehr
**le·hua** \lāˈhüə\ *n* -s [Hawaiian] **1 :** a common very showy tree (*Metrosideros villosa*) of the Pacific islands having bright red corymbose flowers and a hard wood **2 :** the blossom of the lehua
¹**lei** \ˈlā(ē), -(i)\ *n* -s [Hawaiian] **:** a wreath, garland, or necklace of flowers, leaves, shells, or other materials that is a symbol of affection in Polynesia
²**lei** *pl of* LEU
¹**leib·niz·ian** *also* **leib·nitz·ian** \līpˈnitsēən -ībˈ-\ *n* -s *usu cap* [Gottfried Wilhelm von *Leibniz* †1716 Ger. philosopher and mathematician + E *-ian*] **:** a follower of Leibniz or an adherent of Leibnizianism
²**leibnizian** *also* **leibnitzian** \(ˈ)=ˈ===\ *adj, usu cap* **:** of or relating to Gottfried Wilhelm von Leibniz or his philosophy
**leib·niz·ian·ism** \=ˈ===,nizəm\ *n* -s *usu cap* **:** the philosophy of Leibniz and his followers distinguished by (1) its monadism (2) its theory of pre-established harmony (3) the viewpoint that this is the best of all possible worlds because God has chosen it out of an infinity of possible worlds for that reason and apparent evil is not a positive reality but a mere privation and (4) its proposals for a universal calculus of reasoning and scientific language, presaging symbolic logic — compare OPTIMISM 1a

lei

¹**leices·ter** \ˈlestə(r)\ *adj, usu cap* **1** [fr. *Leicester*, city in England] **:** of or from the city of Leicester, England **:** of the kind or style prevalent in Leicester **2** [fr. *Leicester*, county in England] **:** LEICESTERSHIRE
²**leicester** \"\ *n, usu cap* [fr. *Leicester*, county in England; fr. its being orig. bred there] **:** a breed of white-faced long-wool mutton-type sheep originating in England but now widely kept and having white fleece that is finer than that of most long-wool sheep
³**leicester** \"\ *or* **leicester cheese** *n* -s *usu cap L* **:** a hard cheese made of whole cow's milk resembling cheddar and Cheshire cheese
**leicester red** *n, usu cap L* **:** a variety of heavy pressed brick
**leices·ter·shire** \ˈlestər,shi(ə)r, -,shər; -tə,shiə, -,shə\ *adj, usu cap* [fr. *Leicestershire* county in England] **:** of or from the county of Leicester, England **:** of the kind or style prevalent in Leicester
**leich·hardt's pine** *also* **leichhardt's tree** \ˈlī,kä|rts-, ˈlīk,hä|\ *n, usu cap L* [prob. after F. W. Ludwig Leichhardt †1848 Ger. explorer in Australia] **:** a low-growing Australian and East Indian tree (*Sarcocephalus cordatus*) of the family Rubiaceae that has light gray-brown wood with a spongy grain and globular heads of bright yellow flowers
**lei day** *n, usu cap L&D* **:** May Day in Hawaii celebrated with pageants and prizes for the most beautiful or distinctive leis
**leif·ite** \ˈlē,fīt, ˈlā,-\ *n* -s [ISV *leif-* (fr. *Leif* Ericson *fl*1000 Norse mariner and adventurer) + *-ite*] **:** a mineral $Na_2AlSi_4O_{10}F$ consisting of a rare fluoride and silicate of sodium and aluminum and found in Narsarsuak, Greenland
**leigh·ton·ite** \ˈlāt°n,īt\ *n* -s [Tomás Rafael *Leighton b*1894 Chilean civil and mining engineer + E *-ite*] **:** a mineral $K_2Ca_2Cu(SO_4)_4.2H_2O$ consisting of a hydrous sulfate of copper, calcium, and potassium
**lein·ster** \ˈlenztə(r), -n(t)st-\ *adj, usu cap* [fr. *Leinster*, province of Ireland] **:** of or from the province of Leinster, Ireland **:** of the kind or style prevalent in Leinster
**leio-** *or* **lio-** *comb form* [NL, fr. Gk *leio-*, *leios* — more at LIME] **:** smooth ⟨*leio*cephalous⟩ ⟨*leio*phyllous⟩ ⟨*leio*dermia⟩
**lei·o·lo·pis·ma** \ˌlīəlōˈpizmə\ *n, cap* [NL, fr. *leio-* + MGk *lopisma* peel, fr. Gk *lopos*] **:** a large genus of skinks having limbs more or less reduced or even absent
**leio·myoma** \ˌ;==+\ *n, pl* **leiomyomas** *or* **leiomyomata** [NL, fr. *leio-* + *myoma*] **:** a tumor consisting of smooth muscle fibers — **leio·myomatous** \"+\ *adj*
**lei·o·my·o·sarcoma** \ˌlīō,mīō+\ *n* [NL, blend of *leiomyoma* and *sarcoma*] **:** a sarcoma composed in part of smooth muscle cells some of which are of embryonic form
**lei·o·thrix** \ˈlīō,thriks\ *n, cap* [NL, fr. *leio-* + *-thrix*] **:** a genus of hill tits (family Timaliidae) comprising the mesia and the Japanese nightingale
**lei·ot·ri·chi** \līˈä·trə,kī\ *also* **leiotri·ches** \-,kēz\ *n pl, usu cap* [NL, pl., fr. *leio-* + *-trichi*] **:** a division of mankind comprising peoples having straight smooth hair
**lei·ot·ri·chous** \(ˈ)līˈä·trəkəs\ *adj* [NL *leiotrichi* + E *-ous*] *anthrop* **:** having straight smooth hair — **lei·ot·ri·chy** \ˈ=ˈ==kē\ *n* -ES
**leiotropic** *var of* LAEOTROPIC
**lei·poa** \līˈpōə\ *n* [NL, fr. Gk *leipein* to leave + *ōion* egg; fr. the fact that it deserts its eggs] **1** *cap* **:** a genus of Australian mound-building megapodes with black, white, brown, and gray ocellated plumage that are about two feet long, have a short crest, and comprise a single species (*L. ocellata*) **2** -s **:** any bird of the genus *Leipoa*
**leip·zig** \ˈlīpsi|g, -sē|\ *also* **leip·zic** \|k\ *adj, usu cap* [fr. *Leipzig*, Germany] **:** of or from the city of Leipzig, Germany **:** of the kind or style prevalent in Leipzig
**leipzig yellow** *n, usu cap L* **:** a chrome yellow pigment
**leir** \ˈlēr\ *n* [alter. of ³*lair*] *Scot* **:** LEARNING 2a
**leis** *pl of* LEI
**leish·mania** \lēshˈmānēə, -man-\ *n* [NL, fr. Sir William B. *Leishman* †1926 Brit. medical officer + NL *-ia*] **1** *cap* **:** a genus of flagellates (family Trypanosomatidae) parasitic in the tissues of vertebrates, probably transmitted by insects in a manner comparable to trypanosomes, and occurring parasitically as a minute ovoid or spherical nonflagellated body with a definite kinetoplast and usu. an intracellular axoneme but in culture and presumably in the invertebrate host assuming the form typical of a leptomonas—see KALA AZAR, ORIENTAL SORE **2** -s **:** any organism of the genus *Leishmania*; *also* **:** any member of the family Trypanosomatidae when showing the typical intracellular leishmanial form — **leish·mani·al** \(ˈ)=ˈ===\ *adj*
**leish·ma·ni·a·sis** \ˌlēshməˈnīəsə̇s\ *also* **leish·mani·o·sis** \(,)lēsh,manēˈōsə̇s, -man-\ *n, pl* **leishmania·ses** \-ə,sēz\ *or* **leishmanio·ses** \-ō,sēz\ [NL, fr. *Leishmania* + *-iasis* or *-osis*] **:** infection with or disease caused by protozoans of the genus *Leishmania* — compare KALA AZAR; see ORIENTAL SORE
**leish·man·ic** \(ˈ)lēshˈmanik\ *adj* [NL *Leishmania* + E *-ic*] **:** LEISHMANIAL
**leish·man·i·form** \lēshˈmanə,fȯrm\ *adj* [NL *Leishmania* + E *-form*] **:** resembling a leishmania
**leish·mani·oid** \-mānē,ȯid, -man-\ *adj* [NL *Leishmania* + E *-oid*] **:** like or resembling a leishmania
¹**leis·ter** \ˈlēstə(r), ˈlis-\ *n* -s [of Scand origin; akin to ON *ljōstr* leister, Norw *ljoster*, Dan *lyster* leister, ON *ljōsta* to strike, stab, MIr *loss* tail, end, W *llost* spear, ON *lauss* loose — more at -LESS] **:** a spear armed with three or more barbed prongs for catching fish
²**leister** \"\ *vt* ED/-ING/-s **:** to spear with a leister
**leis·ter·er** \-tərə(r)\ *n* -s **:** one who catches fish with a leister
**lei·sur·able** \ˈlēzh(ə)rəbəl *also* ˈlezh- *sometimes* ˈlāzh-\ *adj* **1 :** proceeding deliberately without haste **:** LEISURELY ⟨walked at a ~ pace along the road⟩ **2 :** free from a need for haste ⟨books written in ~ hours⟩
¹**lei·sure** \ˈlēzhə(r) *also* ˈlezh- *sometimes* ˈlāzh-\ *n* -s [ME *leiser, leisere, laiser* fr. OF *leisir*, fr. *leisir*, v., to be permitted, fr. L *licēre* — more at LICENSE] **1 a :** freedom or spare time provided by the cessation of activities: as (1) **:** free time as a result of temporary exemption from work or duties ⟨did not know how to occupy his ~⟩ ⟨worked harder, for their ~ was doubled and they arrived fresh at the factory —Eric Keown⟩ ⟨~ has been gained by a vast number of people who until recently had been merely beasts of burden —H.W.Van Loon⟩ (2) **:** time at one's command that is free of engagements or responsibilities ⟨increase of ~, diminution of hustle are the ends to be sought —Bertrand Russell⟩ **b :** a period of unemployed time — often used in pl. ⟨possessed sufficient literary quality to tempt my rare ~*s* —H.J.Kaplan⟩ **2 a :** apparent effortlessness **:** EASE, LEISURELINESS ⟨its distinction and its charm lie in the ~ and grace of its style —Sara H. Hay⟩ **b** *obs* **:** calm deliberation **:** judicious care ⟨much ~ and accurateness were used in filling the tube —Henry Power⟩ **3 a :** opportunity provided by free time ⟨the settlers . . . had neither ~ nor impulse for a conscious art —*Amer. Guide Series: Minn.*⟩ ⟨the intellect should have ~ to refresh itself at the fountainhead —S.M.Crothers⟩ **b :** the duration of such opportunity **:** time left ⟨the authority of the government . . . for whose sanction there was no ~ to wait —James Mill⟩ — **at leisure** *or* **at one's leisure :** in one's own time **:** at one's convenience ⟨should live long enough to carry out my extensive plan *at leisure* —Havelock Ellis⟩ ⟨hope she won't repent *at her leisure* —Margaret Deland⟩ — **by leisure** *obs* **:** in a leisurely manner **:** SLOWLY ⟨I'll trust *by leisure* him that mocks me once; thee never —Shak.⟩ **syn** see REST
²**leisure** \"\ *adj* **1 :** UNOCCUPIED, UNEMPLOYED, LEISURED ⟨now he writes in his ~ hours —W.J.Reilly⟩ ⟨something that sounds like an enchanted picture, a picture of life as it ought to be for the ~ classes —J.J.Chapman⟩ **2** *of clothing* **:** suitable for leisure and informal occasions **:** CASUAL
**lei·sured** \-zhə(r)d\ *adj* **:** having leisure **:** characterized by leisureliness ⟨even the artist and the sculptor were not regarded . . . as ~ men —Ida Craven⟩ ⟨life is more ~ without being essentially indolent —*Amer. Guide Series: Va.*⟩ ⟨world had grown too large . . . for the constitution which a small ~ landowning class had created —J.H.Plumb⟩
**lei·sure·ful** \-zhə(r)fəl\ *adj* [ME *leiserful*, fr. *leiser* leisure + *-ful*] *archaic* **:** having leisure **:** LEISURELY
**lei·sure·less** \-ə(r)ləs\ *adj* **:** having no leisure
**lei·sure·li·ness** \-lēnə̇s, -lin-\ *n* -ES **:** the quality or state of being leisurely ⟨elegance, urbanity, a quill-pen ~ . . . are not much valued in our day —Louis Kronenberger⟩ ⟨broad streets, an almost southern ~, and fewer tall buildings than are seen in most cities —*Amer. Guide Series: Ind.*⟩
¹**lei·sure·ly** \-lē, -li\ *adv* [ME *laiserly*, fr. *laiser* leisure + *-ly*] **:** without haste **:** DELIBERATELY, SLOWLY ⟨in order to write the book I would have to visit America, travel ~, have money in my pocket —Henry Miller⟩ ⟨others shove in, at first ~ and then more and more like schoolboys —G.W.Stonier⟩
²**leisurely** \"\ *adj* **:** characterized by leisure **:** taking abundant time **:** showing deliberation ⟨this book . . . has the ~ flow of recollection and anecdote —Crane Brinton⟩ ⟨rivers that for the most part pursue a long and ~ course to the sea —Ellen Semple⟩ ⟨procuring their rifles, they opened fire in a ~ manner upon the deserters —Jack London⟩ **syn** see SLOW
**lei·sure·ness** *n* -ES **:** LEISURELINESS
**leisure–time** \ˌ;==ˌ=\ *adj* **:** taking place during time not used for gainful employment ⟨the *leisure-time* problems of the Filipino immigrant are legion —F.J.Brown & J.S.Roucek⟩
**leitch's blue** \ˈlēchə̇z-\ *n, often cap L* [prob. fr. the name *Leitch*] **1 :** CYANINE BLUE 1a **2 :** CYANINE BLUE 2
**leith·ner's blue** \ˈlītnə(r)z-\ *n, usu cap L* [perh. modif. and part trans. of G *leidener blau* Leyden blue] **1 :** COBALT BLUE 2 **2 :** COBALT BLUE 1a
**leit·mo·tiv** *or* **leit·mo·tif** \ˈlītmō,tēf\ *n* -s [G *leitmotiv*, fr. *leit-* leading (fr. *leiten* to lead, fr. OHG) + *motiv* motive fr. F *motif* — more at LEAD] **1 a :** a marked melodic phrase or figure in Wagnerian music drama expressive of or associated with a certain idea, person, or situation, and accompanying its reappearance **b :** a similar principle of construction in other music **2 :** something resembling a musical leitmotiv (as a word or phrase, an emotion, an idea) that is repeated again and again **:** a dominant recurring theme ⟨faith in the saving grace of art has become the ~ of the entire autobiography—C.J. Rolo⟩ ⟨the word "again" has become the ~ of German life —Norbert Mühlen⟩ ⟨a competent designer instinctively chooses a theme or ~ for a given structure, and allows it to influence all his choice of form and line—W.D.Teague⟩
**leit·ne·ria** \lītˈnirēə\ *n, cap* [NL, fr. Edward F. *Leitner*, 19th cent. Am. botanist + NL *-ia*] **:** a genus (coextensive with the family Leitneriaceae) including solely the corkwood (*L. floridana*) and being commonly isolated in a distinct order near Myricales
**lei·trim** \ˈlē·trəm\ *adj, usu cap* [fr. *Leitrim*, county in Ireland] **:** of or from county Leitrim, Ireland **:** of the kind or style prevalent in county Leitrim
**leix** \ˈlāsh, ˈlēsh\ *adj, usu cap* [fr. *Leix*, county in Ireland] **:** LAOIGHIS
¹**lek** \ˈlek\ *n* -s [Alb] **1 :** an Albanian monetary unit formerly equal to ⅕ Albanian franc, established as the basic unit in 1947 — see MONEY table **2 :** a coin representing one lek
²**lek** \"\ *n* -s [prob. fr. Sw, play, game, sport, fr. ON *leikr* — more at LAKE (amusement)] **:** a site to which birds (as grouse) regularly resort for purposes of sexual display and courtship
**lek·ach** \ˈlekək̲\ *n* -s [Yiddish, perh. fr. Aram *lēkhakh* to mix thoroughly] **:** a leavened honey cake
**le·kai salmon** \ləˈkī-\ *n* [origin unknown] **:** DOG SALMON 1
**lek·a·ne** \ˈlekə(,)nē\ *n, pl* **leka·nai** \-,nī\ [Gk *lekanē*, fr. *lekos* dish, pot — more at BALANCE] **1 :** a basin-shaped vessel or large bowl of ancient Greece **2 :** a late form of painted vase of southern Italy resembling a stamnos but provided with upright handles and often with a cover of elaborate form
**lekin** *var of* LIKIN
**lekythos** *also* **lekythus** *var of* LECYTHUS
**l electron** *n, cap L* **:** an electron in the L-shell of energy in an atom
**lel·wel** \ˈlel,wel\ *n* -s [origin unknown] **:** a large rufous Sudanese antelope (*Alcelaphus lelwel*)
**le·mair·eo·cereus** \ləˌmereō+\ *n, cap* [NL, fr. Charles *Lemaire* †1871 Fr. horticulturist + NL *-o-* + *Cereus*] **:** a genus of tropical American cacti usu. of tall branching habit with stout spines, funnel-shaped flowers, and globular or ovoid often edible fruit — see CHICHIPE
**leman** \ˈlemən, ˈlēm-\ *n* -s [ME *leman, lemman, lefman, leofmon*, fr. *lef, leof* lief, dear + *man, mon* man — more at LIEF, MAN] **1** *obs* **:** a sweetheart or lover of either sex **2** *archaic* **:** one who is loved illicitly; *esp* **:** MISTRESS
**le·man·ea** \ləˈmanēə\ *n, cap* [NL, fr. M. *Leman*, 18th. cent. Fr. botanist] **:** a genus of dull gray or greenish red algae (order Nemalionales) whose filaments form solid or hollow cylinders in tufts in swift waters
**leman·ry** \ˈlemənrē, ˈlēm-\ *n* -ES [ME, fr. *leman* + *-ry*] *archaic* **:** unlawful love
**le mans** \ləˈmäⁿ\ *adj, usu cap L&M* [fr. *Le Mans*, France] **:** of or from the city of Le Mans, France **:** of the kind or style prevalent in Le Mans
**leme** *var of* ¹LEAM
**le·mel** \ˈleməl\ *n* -s [alter. of earlier *limall, limmell*, fr. ME *lemaille, limail*, fr. MF *limaille*, fr. OF, fr. *limer* to file, fr. L *limare* — more at LIMATION] **:** metal filings
¹**lem·ma** \ˈlemə\ *n, pl* **lemmas** \-məz\ *or* **lemma·ta** \-məd·ə\ [L, fr. Gk *lēmma* thing received or taken, assumption, fr. root of *lambanein* to receive, take, grasp — more at LATCH] **1 a :** a preliminary or auxiliary proposition or theorem demonstrated or accepted for immediate use in a demonstration of some other proposition **b** (1) **:** the premise of a syllogism in early Greek logic (2) **:** a major premise of the Stoics **2 :** the argu-

ment or theme of a composition prefixed as a title or introduction; *also* **:** the heading or theme of a comment or note **3 :** a word or phrase glossed in a glossary

**2lemma** \"\ *n* -s [Gk, rind, husk, fr. *lepein* to peel — more at LEPER] **:** the lower of the two bracts enclosing the flower in the spikelet of grasses — called also *flowering glume*; see WILD OAT illustration

**lem·mer** \'lemə(r)\ *n* -s [origin unknown] **:** one that butchers whales — compare FLENSER

**lem·ming** \-miŋ\ *n* -s [Norw *lemming, lemende, lomund,* fr. ON *lōmundr* (assumed fr. acc. pl. *lōmundi*); akin to ON *lōmr* guillemot, *lō* curlew, Goth *lailoun* they derided, L *latrare* to bark — more at LAMENT] **:** any of several small rodents of circumpolar distribution belonging to the genera *Lemmus* and *Dicrostonyx*, being four or five inches long with a very short tail, furry feet, and small ears, usu. colored tawny yellowish varied with black and reddish, and best known for the recurrent mass migrations of a European form (*L. lemmus*) which often continue into the sea where vast numbers are drowned

**lemming mouse** *n* **1 :** any of several small rodents of the genus *Synaptomys* that are confined to northern No. America and resemble the voles (genus *Microtus*) but have a very short tail and peculiar teeth — see BOG LEMMING **2 :** any of a number of No. American voles (genus *Phenacomys*) related to the muskrat

**lemmo-** *comb form* [Gk *lemma* rind, husk + E *-o-*] **:** neurilemma ⟨*lemmo*blastic⟩ ⟨*lemmo*cyte⟩

**lem·mus** \'leməs\ *n, cap* [NL, fr. *lemmus* lemming, fr. Norw *lemming*] **:** a genus of myomorph rodents consisting of the typical lemmings

**lem·na** \'lemnə\ *n, cap* [NL, fr. Gk, a water plant] **:** a genus (the type of the family Lemnaceae) of very small aquatic herbs having simple fronds with a single root

**lem·na·ce·ae** \lem'nāsē,ē\ *n pl, cap* [NL, fr. *Lemna,* type genus + *-aceae*] **:** a family of aquatic plants (order Arales) consisting of a single flat or thickened frond bearing a root or roots below and one or two naked flowers on the upper surface — see DUCKWEED — **lem·na·ceous** \(')lem'nāshəs\ *adj*

**lem·nad** \'lem,nad\ *n* -s [NL *Lemna* + E *-ad*] **:** DUCKWEED

**1lem·ni·an** \'lemnēən\ *adj, usu cap* [L *Lemnius* Lemnian (fr. Gk *Lēmnios,* fr. *Lēmnos* Lemnos, island in the Aegean Sea) + E *-an*] **:** of or relating to the Greek island of Lemnos

**2lemnian** \"\ *n* -s *cap* **:** a native or inhabitant of Lemnos

**lemnian bole** *or* **lemnian earth** *n, usu cap L* **:** a gray to yellow or red clay obtained from Lemnos and used formerly in medicine as an adsorbent and protective

**lem·nis·cate** \lem'niskət\ *n* -s [NL *lemniscata,* fr. fem. of L *lemniscatus* with hanging ribbons, fr. *lemniscus* pendent ribbon (fr. Gk *lēmniskos*) + *-atus* -ate] *math* **:** the locus of the foot of the perpendicular from the center of a conic on its tangent

**lem·nis·cus** \-iskəs\ *n, pl* **lemnis·ci** \-i,sī, -i,skē\ [NL, fr. L, ribbon] **1 :** a form ÷ of the obelus **2 :** a band of fibers; *specif* **:** a band of nerve fibers of the second neurons in the sensory path terminating in the thalamus — called also *fillet, laqueus*; compare LATERAL LEMNISCUS, MEDIAL LEMNISCUS **3 :** either of two club-shaped organs hanging into the body cavity from the base of the proboscis in the Acanthocephala

**1lem·on** \'lemən\ *n* -s [ME *lymon,* fr. MF *limon,* fr. ML *limon-, limo,* fr. Ar *laymūn*] **1 a** (1) **:** an acid fruit that is botanically a syncarpous polycarpellary many-seeded pale yellow berry of oblong form usu. with a nipple at the apex and a yellow rind that contains the fragrant lemon oil and is often candied or preserved — compare 6LIME (2) **:** the stout thorny tree (*Citrus limon*) that bears this fruit — see CITRON **b :** any of numerous trees and shrubs of families other than Rutaceae having fruit similar to the lemon — used with a qualifying word **2 a :** LEMON YELLOW **b :** CHLOR **3 :** something (as a float for a ring buoy) shaped like a lemon **4 :** something or someone that proves to be unsatisfactory or undesirable **:** DUD, FAILURE ⟨it is quite possible that one manufacturer . . . may find that he has created an all-around ~ —*Atlantic Bull.*⟩ ⟨being stuck with a ~ on the dance floor —William Irish⟩

**2lemon** \"\ *adj* **1 :** containing lemon **:** having the flavor or scent of lemon ⟨~ tea⟩ ⟨~ bitters⟩ ⟨sipping a ~ drink⟩ **2 :** of the color lemon yellow (sense 1) ⟨the winter afternoons glowed with a hazy ~ light —Carson McCullers⟩

**lem·on·ade** \¦lemə¦nād\ *n* -s [F *limonade,* fr. *limon* lemon (fr. MF *lymon*) + *-ade*] **:** a beverage of sweetened lemon juice mixed with plain or carbonated water

**lemonade berry** *n* **:** an evergreen shrub or small tree (*Rhus integrifolia*) of southern California with simple obtuse leaves, white or pinkish flowers in dense panicles, and dark red glandular hairy fruit — called also *sourberry*

**lemonade bush** *or* **lemonade sumach** *or* **lemon bush** *n* **:** SQUAWBUSH 2

**lemonado** *n* -s [Sp *limonada*] *obs* **:** LEMONADE

**lemon balm** *n* **:** a bushy perennial Old World mint (*Melissa officinalis*) often cultivated for its fragrant lemon-flavored leaves — called also *garden balm, sweet balm*

**lemon chrome** *n* **1 a :** a pale chrome yellow pigment **b :** barium chromate used as a pigment **2 :** a brilliant yellow that is redder and deeper than butter yellow or jasmine yellow

**lemon chrome yellow** *n* **:** LIGHT CHROME YELLOW

**lemon cucumber** *n* **:** MANGO MELON

**lemon curd** *n* **:** lemon juice and rind, sugar, butter, and eggs cooked together until thick and used as a spread or tart filling

**lemon dab** *n* **:** SMEAR DAB

**lemonfish** \'==,=\ *n, South* **:** COBIA

**lemon geranium** *n* **:** a common garden pelargonium (*Pelargonium limoneum*) having lemon-scented foliage

**lemongrass** \'==,=\ *n* **:** any of several grasses of the genus *Cymbopogon:* as **a :** a grass (*C. citratus*) of robust habit that has a large compound inflorescence and is cultivated in tropical regions (as the West Indies) as a source of lemongrass oil **b :** a similar East Indian grass (*C. flexuosus*) that is also a source of lemongrass oil **c :** CITRONELLA 2

**lemongrass oil** *n* **:** a yellow to reddish brown essential oil that has an odor of lemon or verbena, is obtained esp. from either of two lemongrasses (*Cymbopogon citratus* or *C. flexuosus*), and is used chiefly as a perfume (as in soap) and as a source of the aldehyde citral

**lem·on·ish** \'lemənish\ *adj* **:** somewhat resembling a lemon

**lemonlike** \'==,=\ *adj* **:** resembling or suggestive of lemon

**lemon lily** *n* **:** a day lily (*Hemerocallis flava*) with lemon yellow flowers

**lemon mint** *n* **:** an annual horsemint (*Monarda citriodora*) with densely pubescent foliar bracts

**lemon oil** *n* **:** a fragrant yellow essential oil obtained from the peel of lemons usu. by expression and used chiefly as a flavoring agent and in perfumes

**lemon scab** *n* **:** citrus scab of the lemon

**lemon–scent** \'==,=\ *n* **:** LEMONWEED 2

**lemon–scented gum** \'==,==-\ *n* **:** a fragrant-leaved ornamental spotted gum (*Eucalyptus maculata citriodora*)

**lemon shark** *n* **:** a moderate-sized shark (*Negaprion brevirostris*) of the warm Atlantic that is yellowish brown to gray above with yellow or greenish sides and is sought for its hide and oily liver but in some areas is feared as a man-eater

**lemon sole** *n* **:** a small European sole (*Solea lascaris*); *broadly* **:** any of several other flatfishes (as a Georges Bank flounder or megrim)

**lemon thyme** *n* **:** a lemon-scented wild thyme (*Thymus serpyllum vulgaris*)

**lemon verbena** *n* **:** a small shrub (*Lippia citriodora*) of Chile and Argentina that has narrow verticillate lemon-scented leaves and is used in gardens

**lemon vine** *n* **:** BARBADOS GOOSEBERRY 1

**lemon walnut** *n* **:** BUTTERNUT 1a

**lemonweed** \'==,=\ *n* **1 :** SEA MAT **2 :** any of several lemon-scented composite herbs of the genus *Pectis* in the southwestern U.S.

**lemonwood** \'==,=\ *n* **1** *in New Zealand* **:** TARATA **2 :** a southern African evergreen tree (*Psychotria capensis*) with hard tough elastic wood used for making bows **3 :** DAGAME

**lem·ony** \'lemənē\ *adj* **:** suggestive of lemon **:** LEMON ⟨all the more palatable for the ~ taste —Christopher Morley⟩ ⟨we had cold fried chicken and . . . ~ iced tea —Jean Stafford⟩

**lemon yellow** *n* **1 a :** a variable color averaging a brilliant greenish yellow **b :** a brilliant yellow — called also *Cassel yellow, Chinese yellow* **2 :** a pigment of the color lemon yellow: as **a :** a preparation of barium chromate often mixed with zinc chromate **b :** a preparation of lead chromate with lead carbonate

**le·mo·si** \,lemə'zē, -ə'sē\ *or* **li·mo·si** \,lim-\ *n* -s *usu cap* [Catal *llemosí,* prob. fr. (assumed) VL *lemovicensis* of the Lemovices, fr. L *Lemovices,* a Gallic people inhabiting what is now the region of Limousin in west central France] **1 :** the langue d'oc in the Iberian peninsula **2 :** the written literary speech in the Catalan region before it was felt to be different from Provençal

**lem·o·vi·ces** \,lemə'vī(,)sēz\ *n pl, usu cap* [L] **:** an ancient Gallic people occupying what became the French province of Limousin

**lem·pi·ra** \lem'pirə\ *n* -s [AmerSp, after *Lempira,* Indian chief who opposed the Spanish conquest] **1 :** the basic monetary unit of Honduras — see MONEY table **2 :** a coin or note representing one lempira

**le·mur** \'lēmə(r)\ *sometimes* -,myu̇(ə)r *or* -u̇ə\ *n* [NL, fr. L *lemures,* pl., nocturnal spirits, ghosts; fr. its nocturnal habits; akin to Gk *lamia* devouring monster, *lamyros* gluttonous, Latvian *lamāt* to rail at, *lamatas* mousetrap; basic meaning: open jaws] **1** *cap* **:** the type genus of Lemuridae **2** -s **:** any of numerous arboreal chiefly nocturnal mammals formerly widespread but now largely confined to Madagascar that are related to the monkeys but are usu. regarded as constituting the distinct superfamily Lemuroidea and that resemble monkeys in general form and habits but usu. have a muzzle like a fox, large eyes, very soft woolly fur, and a tail which is sometimes rudimentary but usu. long and furry and never prehensile — see AYE-AYE, LORIS, POTTO, TARSIER

lemur 2

**lem·u·res** \'lemyə,rēz\ *n pl* [L] **:** hostile spirits of the unburied dead exorcised from homes in religious observances of early Rome — compare LAR, MANES

**1le·mu·ri·an** \lə'myu̇rēən\ *adj* [NL *Lemur* + E *-ian*] **:** lemuroid

**2lemurian** \"\ *adj, usu cap* [*Lemuria,* hypothetical former continent in the Indian ocean supposed to be now represented chiefly by Madagascar (fr. NL *Lemur*) + E *-an*] **:** MALAGASY

**lem·u·rid** \'lemyərəd, -,rid, 'lēmə-\ *adj* [NL *Lemuridae*] **:** of or relating to the Lemuridae

**2lemurid** \"\ *n* -s **:** a lemur of the family Lemuridae

**le·mu·ri·dae** \lə'myu̇rə,dē\ *n pl, cap* [NL, fr. *Lemur,* type genus + *-idae*] **:** a family comprising the typical lemurs

**le·mu·ri·form** \lə'myu̇rə,fȯrm\ *adj* [NL *Lemur* + E *-iform*] **:** of, relating to, or resembling lemurs

**le·mu·ri·for·mes** \lə,myu̇rə'fȯr,mēz\ *n pl, cap* [NL, fr. *Lemur* + *-iformes*] *in some classifications* **:** a division of Lemuroidea comprising the typical lemurs, the aye-aye, and sometimes the tree shrews

**lem·u·rine** \'lemyə,rīn, 'lēmə-\ *adj* [NL *Lemur* + E *-ine*] **:** LEMUROID

**1lem·u·roid** \-,rȯid\ *adj* [NL *Lemuroidea*] **:** of, relating to, or resembling the lemurs or the Lemuroidea

**2lemuroid** \"\ *n* -s [NL *Lemuroidea*] **:** one of the Lemuroidea

**lem·u·roi·dea** \,==='rȯidēə\ *n pl, cap* [NL, fr. *Lemur* + *-oidea*] **1** *in some classifications* **:** a suborder of Primates including lemurs, lorises, tarsiers, and living and extinct related mammals **2 :** a superfamily or other division of Primates comprising the typical lemurs

**lenape** \lə'nāpē, lə'napē, 'lenə(,)pē, lə'nap, lə'nāp\ *n, pl* **lenape** *or* **lenapes** *usu cap* [Delaware, lit., person, Indian] **:** 1DELAWARE

**le·nard rays** \'lā,närt-, lə'närd-\ *n pl, usu cap L* [after Philipp *Lenard* †1947 Ger. physicist] **:** a mixture of cathode rays that have emerged from a vacuum tube into the outside space through a window consisting of a piece of thin metal foil and rays emitted by the foil as a result of the incidence of the cathode rays

**len·ca** \'leŋkə\ *n, pl* **lenca** *or* **lencas** *usu cap* [Sp, of AmerInd origin] **1 a :** an Indian people of central Honduras and Salvador **b :** a member of such people **2 :** the Lencan language of the Lenca people

**len·can** \-kən\ *n* -s *usu cap* **:** a language family of uncertain relationships comprising the Lenca language

**1lend** \'lend\ *vb* **lent** \-nt\ **lent; lending; lends** [ME *lenden,* alter. (influenced by past *lende,* after such pairs as ME *sende* sent: *senden* to send) of *lenen,* fr. OE *lǣnan,* fr. *lǣn* loan — more at LOAN] *vt* **1 a :** to give into another's keeping for temporary use on condition that the borrower return the same or its equivalent ⟨the purser has kindly *lent* us excellent binoculars —W.R.Benét⟩ ⟨some 46 works *lent* by museums and private collectors —*Harvard Foundation Newsletter*⟩ **b :** to let out (money) for temporary use on condition that it be repaid with interest at an agreed time ⟨it is sometimes said that the capitalists who *lent* the government the money for the war deserve the hire of it —G.B.Shaw⟩ ⟨commercial banks were obliged . . . to reduce their investments in securities in order to ~ more in advances to customers —*World Economic Survey*⟩ **c :** to place (a subordinate) at the disposal of another for temporary service ⟨he was *lent* by the army to the Institute of Inter-American Affairs as a specialist —*N.Y. Times*⟩ — compare 1LOAN 2b **2 a :** to give the assistance or support of **:** ADD, AFFORD, FURNISH, PROVIDE, SUPPLY ⟨his teaching . . . had *lent* to Oxford thought much of its early originality and distinction —G.G.Coulton⟩ ⟨contributed much to the development of the cog railroad . . . ~*ing* his mechanical ability to the problems encountered —*Amer. Guide Series: N.H.*⟩ **b :** to devote the use or effort of (as a part of the body or a faculty of the mind) ⟨the young king seemed to ~ a willing ear —George Eliot⟩ ⟨~ a hand to those in charge of these schools —J.B.Conant⟩ ⟨*lent* eager attention to these hopeful projections⟩ ⟨~*s* a courteous arm to woman or child⟩ **c :** to adapt or apply (oneself or itself) **:** ACCOMMODATE, OFFER ⟨the peoples *lent* themselves to the nearest leader in their quest for salvation as a group —Francis Hackett⟩ ⟨a buggy exhibit did not ~ itself to much exciting variation —Ben Riker⟩ ⟨hypotheses which ~ themselves to the straining of facts in their support —Edward Clodd⟩ **3** *dial chiefly Brit* **:** to deal or deliver (a blow) to someone ~ *vi* **:** to make a loan

**2lend** \"\ *n* -s *dial* **:** temporary possession and use by a borrower **:** LOAN ⟨the ~ of her brass fender —Mary Lavin⟩

**lend·able** \-dəbəl\ *adj* **:** available for lending ⟨will tend to further reduce the supply of ~ funds —L.H.Olsen⟩

**lend·er** \-də(r)\ *n* -s [ME *lendare,* alter. (influenced by ME *lenden* to lend) of *lenere,* fr. OE *lǣnere,* fr. *lǣnan* to lend + *-ere* -er] **:** one that lends

**lending** *n* -s [ME *lendinge,* alter. (influenced by ME *lenden* to lend) of *lenninge, leninge,* gerund of *lenen* to lend — more at LEND] **1 :** a giving or letting out for temporary use **2 :** something lent

**lending library** *n* **1 :** RENTAL LIBRARY **2** *chiefly Brit* **a :** the lending department of a public library **b :** PUBLIC LIBRARY

**1lend–lease** \'=¦=\ *n* [after the title of the U.S. *Lend-Lease* Act (1941)] **:** the transfer of goods and services to an ally to aid in a common cause (as the winning of a war) with payment being made by a return of the original items or their use in the common cause or by a similar transfer of other goods and services ⟨*lend-lease* . . . will stand forth as the most unselfish and unsordid financial act of any country —Sir Winston Churchill⟩ ⟨the two-way *lend-lease* in ideas —*New Republic*⟩

**2lend–lease** \"\ *vt* **:** to provide by means of lend-lease ⟨have returned most of the naval craft *lend-leased* them during the war —*Christian Science Monitor*⟩

**len·du** \'len(,)dü\ *n, pl* **lendu** *or* **lendus** *usu cap* **1 a :** a people of Uganda **b :** a member of such people **2 :** a central Sudanic language of the Lendu people

**lenes** *pl of* LENIS

**leng·en·bach·ite** \'leŋən,bä,kīt\ *n* -s [*Lengenbach,* Switzerland, its locality + E *-ite*] **:** a mineral $Pb_6(Ag,Cu)_2As_4S_{13}$ consisting of a sulfide of lead, silver, copper, and arsenic

**length** \'leŋ(k)th, *chiefly in dial or substand speech* 'len(t)th\ *n, pl* **lengths** \-ths, 'leŋks\ [ME *lengthe,* fr. OE *lengthu* (akin to OFris *lenginge* length, MD *lengede, lengde,* ON *lengd*), fr. *lang, long* long + *-thu* -th — more at LONG] **1 a :** the longer of the 2 straight-line dimensions of a surface or plane or the longest of the 3 straight-line dimensions of a solid **:** extent from end to end — distinguished from *width* **b :** a distance or dimension expressed in units of linear measure ⟨a ~ of 10 inches⟩ **c :** the quality or state of being long — opposed to *shortness* ⟨weariness and boredom exaggerated the ~ of the journey⟩ **d :** WAVELENGTH **2 a :** duration or extent in time ⟨doesn't seem to prove much, considering the ~*s* of the lives of both women —Elizabeth Bishop⟩ ⟨stood weaving on his feet for the ~ of a long breath —F.B. Gipson⟩ ⟨finally the ~ of the high school was standardized . . . at four years —T.H. Briggs⟩ **b** (1) **:** relative duration of a sound (as a vowel or syllable in speech or prosody or a note in music) (2) **:** protracted duration or stress of a sound in speech, prosody, or music ⟨the long *a* gives the word *sale* its ~⟩ **c** *archaic* **:** prolixity or excess in expression ⟨there is such ~ in grief —Shak.⟩ **3 a :** distance or extent in space ⟨it would be hard, even in New England, to match Main Street for its ~ of 18th century square houses —Elizabeth Coatsworth⟩ ⟨appeared dimly white round a distant bend of the dusty road, a weary ~ behind —Haldane Macfall⟩ **b** (1) **:** the measure of something taken as a unit of distance ⟨darted across the highway scarcely two car ~*s* ahead of me⟩ ⟨kept most of his acquaintances at arm's ~⟩ (2) **:** the length of a competitor (as a horse or boat) taken as a unit in stating the margin of victory in a race ⟨he led by three ~*s* after a quarter of a mile —James Roach⟩ (3) **:** the fully extended body ⟨stretched her ~ lazily on the warm earth⟩ ⟨took a hard right on the jaw and measured his ~ on the floor⟩ **4 a** *chiefly Scot* **:** an indicated or specified distance ⟨I'll go with you the ~ to the hall⟩ **b :** the degree, limit, or extreme to which a course of action or a line of thought or discussion is carried ⟨tended to carry his policy of masterly inactivity to dangerous ~*s* —Harvey Graham⟩ ⟨even went the ~ of reading the play . . . to ascertain what it was all about —G.B.Shaw⟩ ⟨here we see the foolish ~*s* to which human malevolence will go —Norman Douglas⟩ **5 a :** a long expanse or stretch ⟨brushed her ~*s* of lustrous hair⟩ ⟨large ~*s* of seas and shores between my father and my mother lay —Shak.⟩ **b :** a piece constituting or usable as part of a whole or of a connected series **:** SEGMENT, SECTION ⟨steel bars are furnished in standard shapes and sizes, in both coils and straight ~*s* —*advt*⟩ ⟨short ~*s* of film with both ends spliced together to permit continuous repetition —W.F. Mackey⟩ **6 a :** FLUIDITY **b :** ability to yield a fluid mixture — compare OIL LENGTH **7** *archaic* **:** a 42-line portion of an actor's part **8 :** the volume of wort drawn from a quantity of malt during brewing **9 :** the holding of more than a player's proportionate share of the cards of one suit in a card game (as four or more at bridge) ⟨he had ~ in trumps⟩ **10 a :** the distance an esp. well pitched ball in cricket travels before hitting the ground ⟨bowled a good ~⟩ ⟨pitched the ball a fraction short of a ~ —Ray Robinson⟩ **b :** the distance to be shot in archery **11 :** the vertical dimension of an article of clothing esp. with reference to the part of the body it reaches or its height above the floor ⟨stockings are made in three ~*s*⟩ ⟨evening dresses in short and long ~*s*⟩ ⟨knee-*length* pants⟩ ⟨a hip-*length* jacket⟩ ⟨a floor-*length* gown⟩ — **at length** *adv* **1 :** COMPREHENSIVELY, FULLY ⟨an important clash of principles which have to be debated *at length* —*London Calling*⟩ **2 :** at last **:** FINALLY ⟨events looked forward to with trepidation, when *at length* they occur, often fall flat —George Santayana⟩

**length–breadth index** *n* **:** CRANIAL INDEX

**length·en** \-thən\ *vb* **lengthened; lengthened; lengthening** \-th(ə)niŋ\ **lengthens** *vt* **1 :** to extend in length **:** make longer **:** ELONGATE, PROLONG, PROTRACT ⟨~*ed* their skirts halfway to their shoe tops —Mary Austin⟩ ⟨overhauls and renewals which would undoubtedly have ~*ed* her life —F.W. Crofts⟩ **2 a** *obs* **:** to eke out (provisions) **:** STRETCH **b :** to increase by diluting ⟨standing by the counter ~*ing* out a short supply of wine —Charles Dickens⟩ ~ *vi* **:** to grow longer ⟨fall ~*ed* out into winter —Laura Krey⟩ ⟨faces ~*ed* as the news became more certain⟩ **syn** see EXTEND

**length·en·er** \-th(ə)nə(r)\ *n* -s **:** one that lengthens

**length·ful** \-thfəl\ *adj* [*length* + *-ful*] *archaic* **:** LONG

**length–height index** *n* **1 :** the ratio of the auricular height of the head to its length **2 :** the ratio of the distance between basion and bregma on the skull to its length

**length·i·ly** \-thəlē, -li\ *adv* **:** in a lengthy or prolix manner

**length·i·ness** \-thēnəs, -thin-\ *n* -ES **:** the quality or state of being lengthy **:** PROLIXITY

**length·ways** \-th,wāz\ *adv* **:** LENGTHWISE

**1lengthwise** \'=,=\ *adv* [*length* + *-wise*] **:** in the direction of the length **:** LONGITUDINALLY ⟨opened his newspaper, folded it ~ —Nathaniel Benchley⟩

**2lengthwise** \"\ *adj* **:** moving, placed, or directed on or toward the long axis ⟨tiers of planks had been fashioned into ~ seats —Agnes M. Cleaveland⟩

**lengthy** \-the̅, -thi\ *adj* -ER/-EST **1 a :** protracted excessively or tediously **:** OVERLONG — used of written or spoken expression ⟨~ and histrionic discussions —*N.Y. Times*⟩ **b :** unduly copious **:** PROLIX — used of a speaker or writer ⟨must not be ~⟩ **2 :** EXTENDED, LONG ⟨no very ~ journey was involved —Allan Fraser⟩ ⟨twirled his ~ key chain —Don Davis⟩ ⟨a ~ debate⟩

**len·gua** \'leŋgwə\ *n, pl* **lengua** *or* **lenguas** *usu cap* [Sp, lit., tongue, fr. L *lingua*; fr. its custom of wearing labrets — more at TONGUE] **1 a :** a group of Amerind peoples of Gran Chaco, Paraguay, including the Macá and Mascoi **b :** a member of any such people **2 :** a language of a Lengua people

**le·nien·cy** \'lēnēənsē, 'lēnyən-, -si *sometimes* 'len-\ *or* **lenience** \-ən(t)s\ *n, pl* **leniencies** *or* **leniences :** a lenient disposition or practice **:** MERCY ⟨had the ~ of the unprincipled —Francis Hackett⟩

**le·nient** \-ənt\ *adj* [L *lenient-, leniens,* pres. part. of *lenire* to soften, fr. *lenis* soft, mild; akin to Latvian *lēns* mild, slow, lazy, OSlav *lěnŭ* — more at LET (to permit)] **1** *archaic* **:** relieving pain (as a medicine) or stress (as soothing influence) **:** ASSUASIVE, EMOLLIENT **2 :** of mild and tolerant disposition or effect **:** INDULGENT, MERCIFUL ⟨strict legality was mitigated by his ~ understanding⟩ ⟨contiguous states were attracting capital and enterprise through ~ laws —Broadus Mitchell⟩ **syn** see FORBEARING, SOFT

**le·nient·ly** *adv* **:** in a lenient manner

**leni·fy** \'lenə,fī, 'lēn-\ *vt* -ED/-ING/-ES [MF or LL; MF *lenifier,* fr. LL *lenificare,* fr. L *lenis* soft, mild + *-ficare* -fy] *archaic* **:** ALLEVIATE, ASSUAGE, MITIGATE, SOFTEN

**leni–lenape** *or* **lenni–lenape** \¦lenē *pronunc at* LENAPE\ *n, usu cap both Ls* [Delaware, lit., real person, fr. *leni, lenni* real + *lenape* person, Indian] **:** 1DELAWARE

**len·in·grad** \'lenən,grad, -raa(ə)d\ *adj, usu cap* [fr. *Leningrad,* U.S.S.R.] **:** of or from the city of Leningrad, U.S.S.R. **:** of the kind or style prevalent in Leningrad

**len·in·grad·er** \-də(r)\ *n* -s *cap* [*Leningrad,* U.S.S.R. + E *-er*] **:** a native or resident of Leningrad

**len·in·ism** \'lenə,nizəm\ *n* -s *usu cap* [Nikolai *Lenin* (real name, Vladimir Ilich Ulyanov) †1924 Russ. Communist leader + E *-ism*] **:** the political, economic, and social principles and policies advocated by Lenin; *esp* **:** the theory and practice of communism developed by or associated with Lenin ⟨the application of the principles of *Leninism* to an entirely new situation —D.J.Dallin⟩ ⟨appreciate *Leninism* as an organizational technique —B.I.Schwartz⟩ ⟨the . . . development of Marxism through *Leninism* and Stalinism —Francis Conklin⟩ — compare BOLSHEVISM, MARXISM, MARXISM-LENINISM, STALINISM

**1len·in·ist** \'lenənəst\ *n* -s *usu cap* [Nikolai *Lenin* + E *-ist*] **:** a follower of Lenin **:** an adherent of Leninism ⟨our party has always been a party of *Leninists* —*Russian Information & Rev.*⟩ ⟨a *Leninist* . . . on the question of power —Lucjan Blit⟩

**2leninist** \"\ *adj, usu cap* **:** of, relating to, or having the characteristics of Leninism or Leninists ⟨the *Leninist* form of communism —*Brit. Book News*⟩ ⟨backing a party with *Leninist* organization —M.F.Lindsay⟩

**len·in·ite** \'lenə,nīt\ *adj or n, usu cap* [Nikolai *Lenin* + E *-ite*] **:** LENINIST

**1le·nis** \'lēnəs, 'lān-\ *adj* [NL, fr. LL, smooth (of breathing, as in LL *spiritus lenis*) fr. L, soft, smooth, mild — more at LENIENT] *of one of two homorganic consonants* **:** produced with more lax articulation and weaker expiration — opposed to *fortis* ⟨\d\ in *doe* is ~, \t\ in *toe* is fortis⟩

**2lenis** \"\ *n, pl* **le·nes** \'lē(,)nēz, 'lā(,)nās\ [NL, fr. LL, adj., smooth] **1 :** a lenis consonant **2 :** SMOOTH BREATHING

**le·nite** \lə'nīt, lē'-\ *vb* -ED/-ING/-S [back-formation fr. *lenition*] *vt* : to transform by lenition ~ *vi* : to undergo lenition
**le·nit·ic** \-'nid·ik\ *adj* [L *lenitas* mildness + E *-ic*] : LENTIC
**le·ni·tion** \-'nishən\ *n* -S [L *lenitus* (past. part. of *lenire* to soften) + E *-ion;* intended as trans. of G *lenierung*] **1** : the change from fortis to lenis articulation **2** : the replacement of a consonant in a Celtic language by a phonetically related consonant requiring less energy of articulation (as voiceless \k\ by voiced \g\ or stopped \k\ by continuant \k\)
**¹len·i·tive** \'lenəd·iv\ *adj* [MF *lenitif,* fr. ML *lenitivus,* fr. L *lenitus* (past part. of *lenire* to soften, alleviate) + *-ivus* -ive — more at LENIENT] **1** : alleviating pain or acrimony : ASSUASIVE, MITIGATING, SOOTHING ⟨this is not a ~ novel —John Barkham⟩ **2** *obs* : of mild or lenient disposition : GENTLE
**²lenitive** \"\ *n* -S **1** *archaic* : a soothing medicine or application **2** : a means of mitigation or alleviation : PALLIATIVE ⟨the gentle ~ of sleep —Elinor Wylie⟩
**len·i·ty** \-nəd·ē\ *n* -ES [L *lenitat-, lenitas,* fr. *lenis* soft, mild + *-itat-, -itas* -ity] : the quality or state of being lenient : MILDNESS, GENTLENESS, LENIENCY **syn** see MERCY
**len·ni·lite** \'lenᵊl,īt\ *n* -S [*Lenni* Mills, Pa., its locality + E *-lite*] : a mineral consisting of a vermiculite
**len·no·ace·ae** \,lenə'wāsē,ē\ *n pl, cap* [NL, fr. *Lennoa,* type genus + *-aceae*] : a family of fleshy parasitic herbs (order Ericales) that are natives of California and Mexico and that lack green foliage, have small flowers in a head or compact thyrse and 5 to 10 stamens, and produce a 2-celled capsular fruit — **len·no·aceous** \,lenə'wāshəs\ *adj*
**len·now** \'le(,)nō\ *adj* [origin unknown] *dial chiefly Eng* : LIMP
**le·no** \'lē(,)nō\ *n* -S [perh. fr. F *linon* linen fabric, lawn, fr. MF *lin* flax, linen, fr. L *linum* — more at LINEN] **1** *also* **leno weave** : an open weave in which pairs of warp yarns cross one another and thereby lock the filling yarn in position **2** : a fabric made with a leno weave; *esp* : MARQUISETTE
**¹lens** \'lenz\ *n, pl* **lenses** *except sense 6* [NL, fr. L, lentil (plant); fr. its shape — more at LENTIL] **1 a** *also* **lense** \"\ : a piece of glass or other transparent substance that has two opposite regular surfaces either both curved or one curved and the other plane and that is commonly used in an optical instrument (as a camera, microscope, eyeglasses) to form an image by focusing rays of light — see CONVERGING LENS, DIVERGING LENS; CAMERA illustration **b** : a combination of two or more simple lenses — see OPTICAL SYSTEM **c** : a piece of plane colorless glass or colored or polarizing glass used (as in safety goggles or sunglasses) to protect the eye from dust or glare **2** : a device for directing or focusing radiation other than light (as sound waves, radio microwaves, electrons) ⟨a revolutionary metal ~ capable of focusing radio waves —*Mech. Engineering*⟩ **3** : a medium that focuses or clarifies ⟨this artist . . . is the ~ through which the 16th century can be examined microscopically and understood —F.H.Taylor⟩ **4** *also* **lense** : something shaped like a double-convex optical lens: as **a** : LENTIL 2 ⟨a ~ of ore⟩ ⟨a ~ of sandstone⟩ **b** : a deposit of archaeological material (as ashes or shells) that has a lens-shaped cross section on excavation **5** *also* **lense** : a highly transparent biconvex lens-shaped or nearly spherical body in the eye that focuses light rays entering the eye typically onto the retina, in the vertebrate lying immediately behind the pupil and being made up of slender curved rod-shaped ectodermal cells in concentric lamellae surrounded by a tenuous mesoblastic capsule and through a peripheral suspensory ligament continuous with the ciliary muscle contraction of which relaxes the ligament allowing the lens to become more spherical and thereby altering its focal length — compare ACCOMMODATION; see EYE illustration **6** *cap* [NL, fr. L, lentil] : a genus of small erect or partly climbing herbs with pinnate leaves, small inconspicuous whitish flowers, and small flattened pods — see LENTIL

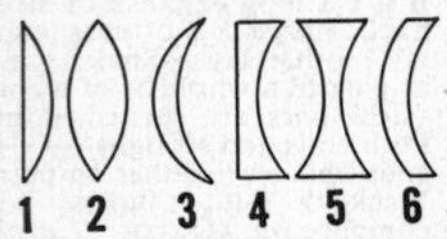

lens 1a: *1* plano-convex, *2* biconvex, *3* converging meniscus, *4* plano-concave, *5* biconcave, *6* diverging meniscus

**²lens** \"\ *vb* -ED/-ING/-ES *vi* : to deposit or form a geologic lens ~ *vt* : to take a picture of : PHOTOGRAPH; *esp* : to make a motion picture of
**³lens** \"\ [NL, fr. L, lentil] *syn of* ENTADA
**len·sat·ic compass** \(')len¦zad·ik-\ *n* [¹*lens* + *-atic* (as in *quadratic*)] : a magnetic compass having a magnifying lens for reading the compass scale
**lens board** *n* : a removable panel support for a camera lens usu. equipped with iris diaphragm and shutter mounted in the lens barrel
**lens cell** *n* : a cell whose function is assumed to be light sensitivity that is found in the epidermis of leaves and other organs
**lensed** \'lenzd\ *adj* [¹*lens* + *-ed*] : provided with a lens
**lens hood** *n* : a shade for excluding stray light from a camera lens
**lens·less** \'lenzləs\ *adj* : having no lens
**lenslike** \'=,=\ *adj* : having the shape or function of a lens
**lens louse** *n, pl* **lens lice** : a person overeager to get into a news photograph or one who seeks undue prominence before a television or motion picture camera
**lens·man** \-zmən\ *n, pl* **lensmen** : PHOTOGRAPHER, CAMERAMAN ⟨it was common to see a Leatherneck ~ wield a .45 automatic pistol in one hand and a 16 mm. camera in the other —Sam Jaffe⟩
**lens mount** *n* : the housing containing the components of a lens
**lens paper** *or* **lens tissue** *n* : a soft nonabrasive lintless tissue paper used for wiping and wrapping lenses
**lens placode** *n* : an ectodermal placode from which the lens of the embryonic eye develops
**lens turret** *n* : a device that can be rotated to allow the user of a photographic or television camera his choice of two or more lenses of different focal length
**¹lent** *past of* LEND
**²lent** \'lent\ *n* -S *usu cap* [ME *lente, lenten, leinte* springtime, Lent, fr. OE *lengten, længten, lencten;* akin to OS *lentin* spring, MD *lente, lenten, lentin,* OHG *lengizin, lenzin;* all fr. a prehistoric WGmc compound whose constituents are represented respectively by E *long* and Goth *-tein-* in *sinteins* daily; akin to Skt *dina* day, L *dies* — more at DEITY] **1 a** : a period of penitence and fasting observed on the 40 weekdays from Ash Wednesday to Easter in the Roman Catholic and some other churches of Western Christianity : QUADRAGESIMA **b** : a somewhat longer Lent observed in Eastern Orthodox churches — compare XEROPHAGY **2** : a period of fasting ordained by any religion
**³lent** \"\ *n* -S [ME *lente,* fr. *lent,* past part. of *lenden* to lend — more at LEND] *dial Brit* : LOAN
**⁴lent** \"\ *adj* [ME *lente,* fr. MF *lent,* fr. OF, fr. L *lentus* slow, calm, flexible — more at LITHE] **1** *obs* : SLOW — used esp. of a fever or a fire **2** *archaic* : LENTO
**len·ta·men·te** \,lentə'men·(,)tā\ *adv (or adj)* [It, lit., slowly, fr. *lento,* adj., slow, fr. L *lentus*] : SLOWLY — used as a direction in music
**len·tan·do** \len·'tän(,)dō\ *adv (or adj)* [It, lit., becoming slower, fr. L *lentandus,* gerundive of *lentare* to lengthen in time, make flexible, fr. *lentus* slow, flexible] : in a retarding manner — used as a direction in music
**lent corn** *or* **lent grain** *n, usu cap L* [²*lent*] *dial Eng* : grain sown in Lent
**lent·en** \'lentᵊn, -ntən\ *adj, often cap* [ME *lenten, leinten,* fr. OE *lengten, læncten, lencten* of spring, Lenten, fr. *lencten, lengten* Lent, springtime — more at LENT] **1** : of or relating to Lent **2** : suitable to Lent : suggestive of fasting or abstinence : MEAGER, SOMBER, SPARE ⟨a somewhat rigorous and *Lenten* manner in which to pass the happy festival of Easter —Elinor Wylie⟩ **3** : MEATLESS ⟨~ soup⟩
**lenten lily** *n, usu cap 1st L* : DAFFODIL
**lenten pie** *n, usu cap L* : meatless pie
**len·tib·u·lar·i·a·ce·ae** \(,)len·,tibyə,la(a)rē'āsē,ē\ *n pl, cap* [NL, fr. *Lentibularia,* type genus (prob. irreg. fr. L *lent-, lens* lentil + *tubulus* small tube, dim. of *tubus* tube) + *-aceae* — more at LENTIL, TUBE] : a family of insectivorous aquatic or bog herbs (order Polemoniales) having irregular flowers and capsular fruits — see BLADDERWORT, PINGUICULA, UTRICULARIA — **len·tib·u·lar·i·a·ceous** \(¦)=¦==,==¦āshəs\ *adj*
**len·tic** \'lentik\ *adj* [L *lentus* slow, calm, sluggish + E *-ic*] : of, relating to, or living in still waters (as lakes, ponds, swamps) — compare LOTIC
**len·ti·cel** \'lentə,sel\ *n* -S [NL *lenticella,* lit., small lentil, dim. of *lent-, lens* lentil] : a pore that is common in the stems of woody plants, is usu. opposite a stoma, is composed chiefly of loosely packed unsuberized cells produced by a phellogen, and is the path of exchange of gases between the atmosphere and the stem tissues
**len·ti·cel·late** \,lentə¦selət\ *adj* [NL *lenticellatus,* fr. *lenticella* lenticel + L *-atus* -ate] : having or producing lenticels
**len·ti·cle** \'lentəkəl\ *n* -S [L *lenticula* lentil (plant, seed)] : a geological lens of moderate extent : LENTIL
**len·tic·u·la** \len·'tikyələ\ *n, pl* **lenticulas** \-ləz\ *or* **lenticulae** \-,lē\ [L, freckly eruption, freckles, lentil, dim. of *lent-, lens* lentil — more at LENTIL] **1** *med* : FRECKLE **2** [NL, dim. of *lent-, lens* lens] : a small optical lens
**len·tic·u·lar** \(')=¦==lə(r)\ *adj* [L *lenticularis,* fr. *lenticula* lentil + *-aris* -ar] **1** : like a lentil in size or form : having the shape of a double-convex lens ⟨a ~ cloud⟩ ⟨a ~ truss⟩ **2** : of or relating to a lens **3** : of, relating to, mediated by, or indicating the lenticular nucleus **4** *photog* **a** : LENTICULATED ⟨~ film⟩ **b** : utilizing lenticules ⟨a ~ photographic process⟩ — **len·tic·u·lar·ly** *adv*
**lenticular ganglion** *n* : CILIARY GANGLION
**len·tic·u·lar·is** \(,)len·,tikyə'la(a)rəs\ *adj* [L, lenticular] : shaped like a lens — used of clouds
**lenticular nucleus** *n* : the larger and external nucleus of the corpus striatum including the outer reddish putamen and two inner pale yellow globular masses constituting the globus pallidus
**¹len·tic·u·late** \(')=¦==lət, -,lāt\ *adj* [LL *lenticulatus* like a lentil in form, fr. L *lenticula* lentil + *-atus* -ate] : having lenticels
**²len·tic·u·late** \-,lāt\ *vt* -ED/-ING/-S [*lenticule* + *-ate*] *photog* : to provide with lenticules (as by embossing, molding, or coating) ⟨*lenticulated* film⟩
**len·tic·u·la·tion** \(,)=,==¦lāshən\ *n* -S **1** : the process of lenticulating **2** : LENTICULE 3
**len·ti·cule** \'lentə,kyül\ *n* -S [L *lenticula*] **1** *med* : FRECKLE **2** [influenced in meaning by NL *lent-, lens*] **a** small geological lentil **3** [influenced in meaning by NL *lent-, lens*] : any of the minute lenses produced (as by embossing) on the base side of a photographic film, serving to record elements of two or more photographic images, and used in stereoscopic or color photography
**len·ti·form** \-,fȯrm\ *adj* [L *lent-, lens* lentil + E *-iform*] : LENTICULAR
**len·tig·i·nous** \(')len·tijənəs\ *also* **len·tig·i·nose** \-,nōs\ *adj* [L *lentiginosus,* fr. *lentigin-, lentigo* lentigo + *-osus* -ous] : of or relating to lentigo : FRECKLED
**len·ti·go** \len·'tī(,)gō, -tē(-\ *n, pl* **len·tig·i·nes** \-tijə,nēz\ [L, fr. *lent-, lens* lentil] **1** : a small melanotic spot in the skin, the pigmentation being unrelated to exposure to sunlight and the lesion potentially malignant; *esp* : NEVUS — compare FRECKLE **2** : FRECKLE
**len·til** \'lentᵊl\ *n* -S [ME, fr. OF *lentille,* fr. L *lenticula,* dim. of *lent-, lens;* akin to Gk *lathyros* chickling, *lathyris* caper spurge] **1 a** : a widely cultivated Eurasian annual plant (*Lens culinaris*) grown for its flattened seeds that are cooked like peas or beans and are also ground into meal and for its leafy stalks that are used as fodder **b** : the seed of the lentil **2** : a thin-edged geological stratum of limited extent enclosed by strata of different material
**len·tile** \'lentᵊl\ *archaic var of* LENTIL
**lentil tare** *n* : SLENDER VETCH
**len·tisc** *or* **len·tisk** \'len·,tisk, =ˈ=\ *n* -S [ME *lentisk,* fr. L *lentiscus*] : LENTISCUS
**len·tis·cus** \len·'tiskəs\ *n, pl* **lentiscus·es** \-iskəsəz\ *or* **lentis·ci** \-i,sī, -i(,)skē\ [L] **1** : MASTIC TREE **2** : a preparation of mastic leaves
**len·tis·si·mo** \len·'tisə,mō\ *adv (or adj)* [It, lit., very slow, fr. L *lentissimus,* superl. of *lentus* slow] : in a very slow manner — used as a direction in music
**len·ti·tude** \'lentə,tüd, -ə·,tyüd\ *n* -S [F or L; F, fr. L *lentitudo,* fr. *lentus* flexible, slow + *-tudo* -tude — more at LITHE] *archaic* : SLOWNESS, SLUGGISHNESS
**lent lily** *or* **lent rose** *n, usu cap Lent* [²*lent*] **1** *dial chiefly Eng* : DAFFODIL **2** : MADONNA LILY
**len·to** \'len·(,)tō\ *adv (or adj)* [It, adv., fr. *lento,* adj., slow, fr. L *lentus*] : in a slow manner — used as a direction in music
**¹len·toid** \'len·,tȯid\ *adj* [NL *lent-, lens* lens + E *-oid*] : shaped like a lens ⟨a ~ gem⟩ ⟨~ bodies in the retina⟩
**²lentoid** \"\ *n* -S : a lens-shaped structure
**len·tor** \'len·,tȯ(ə)r\ *n* -S [L, fr. *lentus* sticky, flexible, slow + *-or*] **1** *archaic* : VISCIDITY — used of the blood **2** *archaic* : SLOWNESS
**len·zi·tes** \'lenzə,tēz\ *n, cap* [NL, fr. H. O. *Lenz* 19th cent. Ger. botanist + L *-ites* -ite] : a genus of bracket fungi (family Polyporaceae) having the hymenium of frequently interconnected plates resembling gills and including a fungus (*L. sepiaria*) that causes a dry rot of timber
**lenz's law** \'len(t)səz-, -nzəz-\ *n, usu cap 1st L* [after H. F. E. *Lenz* †1865 Ger. physicist, its formulator] : a law in physics: the electromotive force due to electromagnetic induction tends to produce a current in such direction that the reaction of the current with the inducing flux opposes whatever change is responsible for the induction
**leo** \'lē(,)ō\ *n* -S *usu cap* [L, lit., lion — more at LION] : the fifth sign of the zodiac — see SIGN table, ZODIAC illustration
**le·od·i·ce** \lē'ädə(,)sē\ *n, cap* [NL, prob. irreg. fr. Gk *Laodikē* Laodice, a proper name] : a genus (the type of the family Leodicidae) of polychaete worms that includes the largest known polychaetes
**¹le·od·i·cid** \-,səd, -,sid\ *adj* [NL *Leodicidae*] : of or relating to the Leodicidae
**²leodicid** \"\ *n* -S : a worm of the family Leodicidae
**le·o·dic·i·dae** \,lēə'disə,dē\ *n pl, cap* [NL, fr. *Leodice,* type genus + *-idae*] : a family of polychaete worms related to the Nereidae
**le·o·nar·desque** \¦lāə¦när¦desk\ *adj, usu cap* [*Leonardo* da Vinci †1519 Florentine painter, sculptor, architect, engineer, and scientist + E *-esque*] : of, relating to, or suggesting Leonardo or the subjects or style of his paintings
**le·o·nar·di·an** \¦lāə¦närdēən\ *adj, usu cap* [*Leonard* Mountain, Brewster co., Tex. + E *-ian*] : of or relating to a subdivision of the Permian following the Wolfcamp and preceding the Guadalupian —see GEOLOGIC TIME table
**le·on·ci·to** \,lāən'sē(,)tō\ *n* -S [Sp *león* lion (fr. L *leon-, leo*) + *-cito* (dim. suffix)] : LION MONKEY
**le·o·nese** \¦lāə¦nēz, ¦lēə-, -ēs\ *n, pl* **leonese** *cap* [Sp *leonés,* fr. *León,* region and ancient kingdom of Spain + Sp *-és* (adj. & n. suffix), fr. (assumed) VL *-esis* — more at -ESE] **1** : a native of León **2** : the Spanish dialect spoken in León
**le·on·har·dite** \,lāən'här,dīt\ *n* -S [G *leonhardit,* fr. Karl C. von *Leonhard* †1862 Ger. mineralogist + G *-it* -ite] : a laumontite altered by loss of water
**¹le·o·nine** \'lēə,nīn, -,nən\ *adj* [ME, fr. L *leoninus,* fr. *leon-, leo* lion + *-inus* -ine — more at LION] **1** : resembling or suggesting that of a lion ⟨a ~ head and shoulders —Albert Spalding⟩ ⟨evoked the ~ rage of the master —F.J.Mather⟩ **2** : of or relating to a lion
**²leonine** \"\ *adj, usu cap* [ML *Leoninus,* fr. *Leon-, Leo* Pope Leo IV †855 + L *-inus* -ine] : of or relating to Pope Leo IV ⟨thenceforth known as the *Leonine* city, it contained St. Peter's —M.W.Baldwin⟩
**³leonine** \"\ *adj, usu cap* [NL *Leoninus,* fr. *Leon-, Leo* Pope Leo XIII †1903 + L *-inus* -ine] : of or relating to Pope Leo XIII ⟨the translation . . . is from the Latin of the *Leonine* edition —W.L.Farrell⟩
**leonine partnership** *n* [trans. of L *leonina societas*] : a partnership in which one partner is made liable for the losses but is not entitled to share in the profits and which is usu. regarded as not legally permissible
**leonine rhyme** *n* [prob. trans. of F *rime léonine,* fr. MF] : internal rhyme used in leonine verse
**le·o·nines** \'lēə,nīnz, -,nənz\ *n pl* : LEONINE VERSE
**leonine verse** *n* [prob. fr. F *léonin,* fr. MF, fr. OF] **1** : Latin verse in which the last word in the line rhymes with the word just before the middle caesura (as in "gloria factorum temere conceditus horum") **2** : English verse in which the end of the line rhymes with a sound occurring near the middle of the line (as in Tennyson's "the long light shakes across the lakes")
**le·o·nite** \'lēə,nīt\ *n* -S [G *leonit,* fr. *Leo* Strippelmann 19th cent. Ger. director of salt works + connective *-n-* + G *-it* -ite] : a mineral $K_2Mg(SO_4)_2.4H_2O$ consisting of a hydrous magnesium potassium sulfate occurring in monoclinic crystals
**le·o·no·tis** \,==ˈnōd·əs\ *n, cap* [NL, fr. Gk *leōn* lion + *ōt-, ous* ear — more at LION, EAR] : a small genus of tropical herbs or low shrubs (family Labiatae) of southern Africa with whorls of showy very irregular red, yellow, or white flowers — see DAGGA 2
**le·on·ti·a·sis** \,lēən·'tīəsəs\ *n, pl* **leontia·ses** \-ə,sēz\ [NL, fr. Gk *leontiasis* early stage of elephantiasis, fr. *leont-, leōn* lion + *-iasis*] **1** : leprosy affecting the flesh of the face and giving it a leonine appearance **2** *or* **leontiasis ossea** : an overgrowth of the bones in the head producing enlargement and distortion of the face
**le·on·to·ce·bus** \lē¦äntə'sēbəs\ *n, cap* [NL, fr. Gk *leont-, leōn* lion + NL *Cebus*] : a genus of So. American marmosets comprising the tamarins
**le·on·to·don** \lē'äntə,dän\ *n, cap* [NL, fr. Gk *leont-, leōn* lion + NL *-odon*] : a genus of Old World weedy herbs (family Compositae) having pinnatifid leaves, solitary heads of mostly yellow ray flowers, and achemes with a plumose pappus — see FALL DANDELION
**le·on·to·po·di·um** \=,==ˈpōdēəm\ *n, cap* [NL, fr. L *leontopodion,* a plant, lion's-foot, fr. Gk, fr. *leont-, leōn* lion + *-podion* -podium] : a small genus of herbs (family Compositae) that are natives of mountainous regions of Eurasia and So. America and have small discoid flower heads much exceeded by the white woolly black-tipped bracts
**le·o·nu·rus** \,lēə'n(y)ürəs\ *n, cap* [NL, fr. Gk *leōn* lion + NL *-urus*] : a genus of stout Old World herbs (family Labiatae) having cut-lobed leaves, close whorls of axillary flowers and angled nutlets — see MOTHERWORT
**leop·ard** \'lepə(r)d\ *n* -S *often attrib* [ME *leupard, leopard, lepard,* fr. OF *lepart, leupart, liepart,* fr. LL *leopardus,* fr. Gk *leōn* lion + *pardos* pard — more at LION, PARD] **1 a** : a large strong cat (*Felis pardus*) of southern Asia and Africa that is usu. tawny or buff with black spots arranged in broken rings or rosettes, is somewhat arboreal, and often lies in ambush for its prey that consists of most animals small or weak enough for it to overcome — called also *panther* **b** : any of several other cats closely resembling a leopard — usu. used with a qualifying word ⟨hunting ~⟩ **2 a** (1) : a heraldic representation of a lion passant guardant (2) : a heraldic representation of a lion guardant **b** : a heraldic representation of a leopard **3** : a leopard that is a symbol of unchangeableness ⟨can the Ethiopian change his skin or the ~ his spots? —Jer 13:23 (RSV)⟩ **4** : the fur or pelt of a leopard

leopard 1a

**leopard cat** *n* **1** : a small spotted cat (*Felis bengalensis*) of southern Asia and Malaysia **2** : OCELOT
**leop·ard·ess** \'lepə(r)dəs\ *n* -ES : a female leopard
**leopard flower** *n* : BLACKBERRY LILY
**leopard frog** *n* **1** : a common American frog (*Rana pipiens*) that is bright green with large black white-margined blotches on the back **2** : a frog (*Rana sphenocephala*) of the southeastern U. S. similar to the leopard frog
**leop·ard·ine** \'lepə(r),dēn\ *n* -S [*leopard* + *-ine*] : rabbit fur processed to simulate leopard
**leopard lily** *n* **1** : a Californian lily (*Lilium pardalinum*) with mottled orange flowers **2** : a plant (*Lachenalia pendula*) of southern Africa with spotted flowers **3** : a plant of the genus *Sansevieria* **4** : BLACKBERRY LILY
**leopard lizard** *n* : a large blotched and barred iguanid lizard (*Crotaphytus wislizenii* syn. *Gambelia wislizenii*) of Mexico and the western U. S.
**leopard man** *n, pl* **leopard men** : a member of a West African native secret society that practices clawing its victims to death for ritual or cannibalistic purposes
**leopard moth** *n* : a large European moth (*Zeuzera pyrina*) that has white wings thickly spotted with black, bores in fruit and shade trees in its larval stage, and is now abundant in eastern No. America
**leopard of england** *usu cap E* : LION OF ENGLAND
**leopard plant** *n* : an herb (*Ligularia kaempferi*) native to Japan; *esp* : the ornamental form of the leopard plant (*L. k. aureomaculata*)
**leopard's-bane** \'==,=\ *n, pl* **leopard's-banes** **1** *also* **leopardbane** \'==,=\ : a plant of the genus *Doronicum* **2** : a perennial herb (*Arnica cucanlis*) with a glandular stem and sessile or short-based leaves **3** : HERB PARIS
**leopard seal** *n* : a spotted antarctic seal (*Hydrurga leptonyx*) occas. encountered on the south coasts of Australia and New Zealand — called also *sea leopard*
**leopard's face** *n, pl* **leopard's faces** *or* **leopards' faces** : a heraldic representation of the head of a leopard affronté without any of the neck showing — compare LION'S FACE
**leopard shark** *n* : any of several sharks more or less mottled or blotched with black on a lighter ground: as **a** : a small widely distributed Pacific cat shark (*Triakis semifasciata*) of commercial importance as a food fish in California **b** : TIGER SHARK **c** : a sluggish mollusk-eating Indo-Pacific shark (*Stegostoma fasciatum*)
**leopard's head** *n, pl* **leopard's heads** *or* **leopards' heads** **1** : LEOPARD'S FACE **2 a** : a heraldic representation of the head and neck of a leopard affronté **b** : a heraldic representation of the head and neck of a leopard in profile
**leopard-skin chief** \'==,=-\ *n* : a mediator or arbitrator who settles disputes and feuds among the Nuer
**leopard snake** *n* : a widely distributed European spotted colubrid snake (*Elaphe situla*) closely related and similar in habits to the American corn snake
**leopard squirrel** *n* : THIRTEEN-LINED GROUND SQUIRREL
**leopard tortoise** *n* : a large black yellow-spotted African land tortoise (*Geochelone pardalis*) often attaining a shell length of 20 inches and weighing more than 50 pounds
**leopard tree** *n* : an Australian tree (*Flindersia maculosa*) whose bark splits off in irregular pieces thereby giving the trunk a spotted appearance — called also *leopardwood*
**leopardwood** \'==,=\ *n* **1 a** : LETTERWOOD **b** : a tree yielding such wood **2 a** : leopard tree wood **b** : LEOPARD TREE
**le·o·pol·din·ia** \,lēə,pōl'dinēə\ *n, cap* [NL, fr. Maria *Leopoldina* †1826 wife of Dom Pedro I of Brazil + NL *-ia*] : a small genus of very large pinnate-leaved palms mostly confined to the Amazon valley including some (as *L. piassaba*) that yield a piassava fiber
**le·o·pold·ite** \'==,dīt\ *n* -S [G *leopoldit,* fr. *Leopoldshall,* town in Germany (now part of Stassfurt), its locality + G *-it* -ite] : SYLVITE
**lé·o·pold·ville** \'lēə,pōl(d),vil\ *adj, usu cap* [fr. *Léopoldville,* Congo] : of or from Léopoldville, capital of Congo : of the kind or style prevalent in Léopoldville
**le·o·tard** \'lēə,tärd\ *n* -S [after Jules *Léotard,* 19th cent. Fr. aerial gymnast] **1** : a close-fitting garment for the torso that sometimes has long sleeves, a high neck, or ankle-length legs and that is worn for practice or performance by dancers, acrobats, and aerialists — often used in pl. **2** : TIGHTS — often used in pl.

leotard 1

**¹lep·a·did** \'lepədəd, -,did\ *adj* [NL *Lepadidae*] : of or relating to the Lepadidae
**²lepadid** \"\ *n* -S : a barnacle of the family Lepadidae
**le·pad·i·dae** \lə'padə,dē\ *n pl, cap* [NL, fr. *Lepad-, Lepas,*

type genus + *-idae*] : a family of goose barnacles typified by the genus *Lepas*

**lepas** \ˈlepəs, ˈlēˌpas\ *n, cap* [NL, fr. L, limpet, fr. Gk] : a widely distributed genus (the type of the family Lepadidae) of goose barnacles

**lep·cha** \ˈlepchə\ *n, pl* **lepcha** *or* **lepchas** *usu cap* **1 a** : a Mongoloid people of Sikkim, India **b** : a member of such people **2** : the Tibeto-Burman language of the Lepcha people

**lep·er** \ˈlepə(r)\ *n* -s [ME, fr. ME *leper, lepre* leprosy, fr. OF *lepre, liepre,* fr. LL *lepra* (L *leprae*, pl.), fr. Gk *lepra*, fr. *lepein* to peel; akin to OE *læfer* rush, reed, *lōf* fillet, band, OHG *leber* rush, L *lepidus* agreeable, charming, nice, Russ *lepen'* small piece, *lepest* tatter, petal, *lapot'* bast shoe] **1** : a person affected with leprosy **2** : a person shunned for moral or social reasons ⟨to be an artist is to be a moral ~, an economic misfit, a social liability —Henry Miller⟩ ⟨afraid to join the society of the pious . . . I looked upon myself as a ~ —Robert Nesbit⟩

**le·pe·ro** \ˈlepəˌrō\ *n* -s [AmerSp *lépero*] : a Mexican of low social and economic standing ⟨half-naked ~*s* who roamed the streets and begged —T.E.Sanford⟩

**leper's squint** *or* **leper window** *n* : a small window in the exterior wall of some medieval churches through which lepers are believed to have viewed the service being conducted at the altar

**lep·id** \ˈlepəd\ *adj* [L *lepidus*] *archaic* : evoking amusement or pleasure : WITTY ⟨as for the joyous and ~ consul, he jokes upon neutral flags and frauds —Sydney Smith⟩ ⟨~ fables —*Edinburgh Rev.*⟩

**lepid-** *or* **lepido-** *comb form* [NL, fr. Gk, fr. *lepid-, lepis,* fr. *lepein* to peel] : flake : scale ⟨*Lepidoptera*⟩

**lep·i·dine** \ˈlepəˌdēn, -dən\ *n* -s [NL *Lepidium* + E *-ine*] : an oily nitrogenous base $C_{10}H_9N$ found in coal tar and obtained esp. by the distillation of cinchonine; 4-METHYL-QUINOLINE

**le·pid·i·um** \ləˈpidēəm\ *n, cap* [NL, fr. L, a plant, dittander, pepperwort, fr. Gk *lepidion,* dim. of *lepid-, lepis* scale, flake] : a genus of herbs of the family Cruciferae having a rounded fruit with a notch or depression at its summit — see CANARY GRASS 2, GARDEN CRESS

**lep·i·do·blas·tic** \ˌlepədōˈblastik\ *adj* [ISV *lepid-* + *-blastic;* orig. formed as G *lepidoblastisch*] : relating to a texture in a metamorphic rock corresponding to the scaly texture of an igneous rock

**lep·i·do·car·pa·ce·ae** \ˌ===ˌkärˈpāsēˌē\ *n pl, cap* [NL, fr. *Lepidocarpon*, type genus + *-aceae*] *in some classifications* : a family of plants that is coextensive with the genus *Lepidocarpon* and comprises plants believed to have been arborescent lycopsids with male and female fructifications on separate plants or in separate cones

**lep·i·do·car·pon** \ˌ===ˈkärˌpän\ *n, cap* [NL, fr. *lepid-* + *-carpon* (fr. Gk *karpos* fruit) — more at HARVEST] : a form genus of Carboniferous fossil lycopsid plants (order Lepidodendrales) known from strobili with heterosporous megasporangia containing a single mature seedlike megaspore and three abortive megaspores that is sometimes considered to be on the ancestral line of true seed plants

**lep·i·do·cro·cite** \-ˈkrōˌsīt\ *n* -s [G *lepidokrokit,* fr. *lepid-* + Gk *krokē* thread + G *-it* -ite] : a ruby red to reddish brown mineral FeO(OH) consisting of an iron oxide hydroxide that is an important constituent of some iron ores and often occurs with goethite

**lep·i·do·den·dra·ce·ae** \-ˌdenˈdrāsēˌē\ *n pl, cap* [NL, fr. *Lepidodendron*, type genus + *-aceae*] : a family of fossil pteridophytic plants (order Lepidodendrales) that are characterized by conspicuous spirally arranged leaf scars on the trunk

**lep·i·do·den·dra·les** \-ˌdenˈdrā(ˌ)lēz\ *n pl, cap* [NL, fr. *Lepidodendron* + *-ales*] : an order of arborescent fossil plants (class Lycopodineae) arising during the Lower Devonian, being a conspicuous floral element throughout the Carboniferous, and being characterized by dichotomous branching both in the formation of the crown and of the thick spreading rootlike supports — see LEPIDODENDRACEAE

**lep·i·do·den·drid** \-ˈdendrəd\ *n* -s [NL *Lepidodendron* + E *-id*] : a plant or fossil of *Lepidodendron* or a related genus

**lep·i·do·den·droid** \ˌ===ˌdrȯid\ *adj* [NL *Lepidodendron* + E *-oid*] : resembling or related to the lepidodendrids

**lep·i·do·den·dron** \ˌ===ˈdrən\ *n, cap* [NL, fr. *lepid-* + *-dendron*] **1** : a genus (the type of the family Lepidodendraceae) of fossil trees having closely set slender or subulate leaves and resembling modern club mosses in their fructification — see LEPIDOSTROBUS **2** -s : any tree of the genus *Lepidodendron*

**lep·i·doi·dei** \ˌlepəˈdȯidēˌī\ *n pl, cap* [NL, fr. *lepid-* + *-oidei*] *in some classifications* : a group of extinct ganoid fishes

**le·pid·o·lite** \ləˈpidᵊlˌīt, ˈlepədōˌlīt\ *n* -s [G *lepidolith,* fr. *lepid-* + *-lith*] : a mineral of somewhat variable composition typically $K(Li, Al)_3(Si, Al)_4O_{10}(F, OH)_2$ that consists of a mica containing lithium and usu. occurs in rose-colored masses made up of small scales

**lep·i·do·mel·ane** \ˌlepədōˈmeˌlān\ *n* -s [G *lepidomelan,* fr. *lepid-* + *-melane*] : a mineral $K_2(Fe, Mg)_{4-6}(Si, Al, Fe)_8O_{20}(OH)_4$ consisting of a mica that is a biotite containing ferric iron

**lep·i·do·phloi·os** \-ˈflȯiˌäs\ *n, cap* [NL, fr. *lepid-* + Gk *phloios* bark — more at PHLOEM] : a form genus of fossil plants of the family Lepidodendraceae consisting of stems with overlapping or imbricated scars

**lep·i·do·phyl·lous** \ˌ===ˈfiləs\ *adj* [*lepid-* + *-phyllous*] : having scaly leaves

**lep·i·do·phyl·lum** \ˌ===ˈfiləm\ *n, cap* [NL, fr. *lepid-* + *-phyllum*] : a form genus of lepidodendroid fossils based on leaves or parts of leaves that is now recognized to be part of *Lepidodendron*

**lep·i·do·phyte** \ˈ===ˌfīt\ *n* -s [ISV *lepid-* + *-phyte*] : a Paleozoic fern — **lep·i·do·phyt·ic** \ˌ===ˈfid·ik\ *adj*

**lep·i·dop·ter** \ˌlepəˈdäptə(r), ˈ==ˌ==\ *n* -s [NL *Lepidoptera*] : an insect of the order Lepidoptera

**lep·i·dop·tera** \ˌ==ˈ=t(ə)rə\ *n pl, cap* [NL, fr. *lepid-* + *-ptera*] : a large order of insects comprising the butterflies and moths whose adult forms have four broad or lanceolate wings usu. covered with minute overlapping often brightly colored scales, have a long tubular proboscis composed of the maxillae and usu. capable of being coiled spirally between the labial palpi, have mandibles wanting or very rudimentary, and feed chiefly on the nectar of flowers, whose caterpillar larvae have well-developed mandibles, feed chiefly on leaves to which they frequently do great damage, and undergo a complete metamorphosis, and whose pupae in the more advanced families are completely obtected and are frequently enclosed in a cocoon composed partly of silk secreted by glands opening on the larval labium — **lep·i·dop·te·ral** \ˌ==ˈ=t(ə)rəl\ *adj* — **lep·i·dop·te·ran** \-rən\ *n or adj* — **lep·i·dop·te·rid** \-rəd\ *n* -s

**lep·i·dop·ter·ist** \ˌ==ˈ=tərəst\ *n* -s [NL *Lepidoptera* + E *-ist*] : a specialist in lepidopterology

**lep·i·dop·te·ro·log·i·cal** \ˌ==ˌ=tərəˈläjəkəl\ *adj* : of or relating to lepidopterology

**lep·i·dop·ter·ol·o·gist** \ˌ==ˌ=təˈräləjəst\ *n* -s : LEPIDOPTERIST

**lep·i·dop·ter·ol·o·gy** \-jē\ *n* -ES [ISV *lepidopter-* (fr. NL *Lepidoptera*) + *-o-* + *-logy*] : a branch of entomology dealing with the Lepidoptera

**lep·i·dop·te·ron** \ˌ==ˈ=t(ə)rən, -təˌrän\ *n, pl* **lepidoptera** \-t(ə)rə\ [NL, sing. of *Lepidoptera*] : an insect of the order Lepidoptera

**lep·i·dop·ter·ous** \ˌ==ˈ=t(ə)rəs\ *adj* [NL *Lepidoptera* + E *-ous*] : of, relating to, or having the characteristics of the Lepidoptera

**lep·i·dos·a·phes** \ˌlepəˈdäsəˌfēz\ *n, cap* [NL, fr. *lepid-* + Gk *saphēs* clear, distinct] : a genus of destructive armored scales including the oystershell scale

**¹lep·i·do·sau·ria** \ˌlepədōˈsȯrēə\ *n pl, cap* [NL, fr. *lepid-* + *-sauria*] : a subclass of fossil and recent reptiles first appearing in the early Permian, comprising reptiles with two temporal openings and a scaly skin, and including modern lizards, snakes, and tuataras — **lep·i·do·sau·ri·an** \ˌ===ˈ=rēən\ *adj or n*

**²lepidosauria** \"\ [NL, fr. *lepid-* + *-sauria*] *syn of* SQUAMATA

**lep·i·do·si·ren** \ˌ===+\ *n* [NL, fr. *lepid-* + *Siren*] **1** *cap* : a genus of eel-shaped dipnoan fishes containing a single species (*Lepidosiren paradoxa*) inhabiting the swamps of the Amazon and La Plata rivers and their tributaries and with the related *Protopterus* constituting a family (Lepidosirenidae) **2** -s : any fish of the genus *Lepidosiren* or of the family Lepidosirenidae — **lep·i·do·sirenoid** \ˌ===+\ *adj or n*

**lep·i·do·sis** \ˌlepəˈdōsəs\ *n, pl* **lepido·ses** \-ōˌsēz\ [NL, fr. *lepid-* + *-osis*] **1** : a scaly skin disease (as ichthyosis) **2** : the arrangement and character of the scales or shields of an animal

**lep·i·do·some** \ˈlepədəˌsōm, ləˈpid-\ *n* -s [ISV *lepid-* + *-some;* orig. formed as F *lépidosome*] : GOLGI BODY

**lep·i·do·sper·ma** \ˌlepədōˈspərmə\ *n, cap* [NL, fr. *lepid-* + *-sperma*] : a large genus of sedges of the family Cyperaceae having imbricated subdistichous floral scales — see SWORD SEDGE

**lep·i·do·sper·mae** \-ˌmē\ *n pl, cap* [NL, fr. *lepid-* + *-spermae*] *in some classifications* : a class of fossil pteridosperms resembling lepidodendrons but bearing seeds instead of megaspores

**lep·i·dos·tei** \ˌlepəˈdästēˌī\ *n pl, cap* [NL, fr. *lepid-* + *-ostei* (pl. of *-osteus*)] *in some classifications* : a group or order of ganoid fishes that includes the Lepisosteidae and several related extinct families now usu. divided between the orders Cycloganoidei, Halecostomi, and Ginglymodi and that has numerous representatives in the Mesozoic and constitutes the dominant type of fish in the Jurassic

**lep·i·do·ste·idae** \ˌlepədōˈstēəˌdē\ [NL *Lepidosteus* + *-idae*] *syn of* LEPISOSTEIDAE

**lep·i·dos·te·us** \-ˈdästēəs\ [NL, fr. *lepid-* + *-osteus*] *syn of* LEPISOSTEUS

**lep·i·dos·tro·bus** \-ˈdästrəbəs\ *n* -ES [NL, fr. *lepid-* + Gk *strobos* act of whirling round — more at STROPHE] : a fossil composed of a large cluster of spirally arranged imbricated sporophylls and described orig. as belonging to a form genus of the same name but now believed to represent the fructification of a plant of the genus *Lepidodendron*

**lep·i·dote** \ˈlepəˌdōt\ *adj* [Gk *lepidōtos* scaly, fr. *lepid-, lepis* scale — more at LEPID-] : covered with scurf or scurfy scales ⟨~ rhododendrons⟩

**lep·i·do·tes** \ˌ==ˈdōd·(ˌ)ēz\ *n, cap* [NL, fr. Gk *lepidōtos* scaly] : a widely distributed genus of Mesozoic fishes of the order Cycloganoidei

**lep·i·do·trich·i·um** \ˌlepədōˈtrikēəm\ *n, pl* **lepidotrich·ia** \-ēə\ [NL, fr. *lepid-* + *trich-* + *-ium*] : one of the elongated jointed rays in the fins of certain bony fishes representing highly modified rows of scales

**lep·i·do·tus** \ˌ==ˈdōd·əs\ [NL, fr. Gk *lepidōtos* scaly] *syn of* LEPIDOTES

**lep·i·du·rus** \-ˈd(y)ùrəs\ *n, cap* [NL, fr. *lepid-* + *-urus*] : a genus of phyllopod crustaceans of the family Triopidae including a species (*L. couesi*) common in western No. America

**lepi·lemur** \ˌlepə+\ *n, cap* [NL, fr. L *lepidus* pleasing, agreeable + NL *Lemur* — more at LEPER] : a small genus of rare and little-known lemurs — see SPORTIVE LEMUR

**lep·i·o·ta** \ˌlepēˈōd·ə\ *n* [NL, fr. Gk *lepion* thin rind, scurf, dim. of *lepos* rind, husk, scale, fr. *lepein* to peel — more at LEPER] **1** *cap* : a genus of white-spored agarics having a prominent annulus and a flat expanded pileus and including several edible mushrooms (as *L. procera*) and others (as *L. morgani*) regarded as poisonous **2** -s : any fungus of the genus *Lepiota* — called also *parasol mushroom*

**-le·pis** \ləpəs\ *n comb form* [NL, fr. Gk *lepis* — more at LEPID-] : flake : scale — in generic names ⟨Bothrio*lepis*⟩ ⟨Osteo*lepis*⟩

**le·pis·ma** \ləˈpizmə\ *n, cap* [NL, fr. Gk, peel, fr. *lepizein* to peel, fr. *lepos* rind, scale + *-izein* -ize] : a genus (the type of the family Lepismatidae) of primitively wingless insects of the order Thysanura having a long flat body covered with shining scales and terminated by three long jointed styles — see SILVERFISH; compare FIREBRAT — **le·pis·mid** \-məd\ *n* -s

**¹lep·i·sos·te·id** \ˌlepəˈsästēəd\ *adj* [NL *Lepisosteidae*] : of or relating to the Lepisosteidae

**²lepisosteid** \"\ *n* -s : a fish of the family Lepisosteidae

**lep·i·sos·te·idae** \ˌ==(ˌ)säˈstēəˌdē\ *n pl, cap* [NL, fr. *Lepisosteus*, type genus + *-idae*] : a family of freshwater ganoid fishes comprising the genus *Lepisosteus*

**lep·i·sos·te·us** \ˌ==ˈsästēəs\ *n, cap* [NL, fr. Gk *lepis* scale + *-osteus*] : a genus of ganoid fishes containing the American freshwater gars

**lepo-** *comb form* [prob. fr. NL, fr. Gk *lepos* — more at LEPIOTA] : husk : rind : scale ⟨*lepo*cyte⟩ ⟨*lepo*thrix⟩

**le·po·mis** \ləˈpōməs\ *n, cap* [NL, fr. Gk *lepis* scale, flake + *-pomis* (fr. *pōma* lid, cover, operculum); akin to Gk *poimēn* herdsman, shepherd, *pōy* herd, flock — more at LEPID-, FUR] : a genus of No. American freshwater sunfishes (family Centrarchidae) that includes the bluegill and several closely related panfishes

**¹lep·o·rid** \ˈlepərəd, -ˌrid\ *adj* [NL *Leporidae*] : of or relating to the Leporidae

**²leporid** \"\ *n* -s : a mammal of the family Leporidae

**le·por·i·dae** \ləˈpȯrəˌdē\ *n pl, cap* [NL, fr. *Lepor-, Lepus,* type genus + *-idae*] : a family consisting of the hares and rabbits and with the pikas constituting the order Lagomorpha

**lep·o·ride** \ˈlepərəd, -ˌrid, -ˌrīd, -ˌrēd\ *n* -s [F *léporide,* fr. L *lepor-, lepus* hare — more at LAPIN] : BELGIAN HARE — used esp. by those who consider the Belgian hare to be a hybrid between the European rabbit and hare

**lepori·form** \ˈlepərəˌfȯrm, ləˈpȯr-\ *adj* [L *lepor-, lepus* hare + E *-iform*] : resembling a hare in form

**lep·o·ril·lus** \ˌlepəˈriləs\ *n, cap* [NL, dim. of L *lepor-, lepus* hare] : a genus of large gregarious blunt-nosed Australian rats that build community houses of sticks, grasses, and debris

**¹lep·o·rine** \ˈlepəˌrīn, -rən\ *adj* [L *leporinus,* fr. *lepor-, lepus* hare + *-inus* -ine] : of, relating to, or resembling a hare

**²leporine** \"\ *n* -s : LEPORIDE

**lep·o·spon·dyl** \ˌlepəˈspändᵊl, ˈ==ˌ==\ *n* [NL *Lepospondyli*] : an amphibian of the order, subclass, or other division Lepospondyli

**lep·o·spon·dy·li** \ˌ==ˈspändəˌlī\ *n pl, cap* [NL, fr. *lepo-* + *-spondyli*] : a taxonomic category comprising amphibians in which the centra of the vertebrae develop directly as bone without an intermediate cartilaginous stage: as **a** : an order or other division comprising the extinct Aistopoda, Microsauria, and Nectridia **b** : a subclass of Amphibia comprising the above groups together with the Caudata and Gymnophiona

**lep·o·spon·dy·lous** \ˌ==ˈ=dələs\ *adj* [*lepo-* + *spondylous*] **1** : having vertebrae enclosing the notochord each of which consists of a cylinder of bone shaped like an hourglass in longitudinal section — used esp. of some extinct stegocephalian amphibians **2** [NL *Lepospondyli* + E *-ous*] : of or relating to the Lepospondyli **3** : having the vertebral centra develop directly as bone

**lep·o·thrix** \ˈlepəˌthriks\ *n, pl* **lepothrixes** \-ksəz\ *also* **le·pot·ri·ches** \ləˈpä·trəˌkēz\ [NL, fr. *lepo-* + *-thrix*] : TRICHOMYCOSIS

**lep·per** \ˈlepə(r)\ *n* -s [*lep* + *-er*] : a horse skilled in jumping : JUMPER

**lep·py** \ˈlepē\ *n* -ES [origin unknown] *chiefly West* : a motherless calf : DOGIE

**lep·ra** \ˈleprə\ *n* -s [LL, leprosy — more at LEPER] **1** *archaic* : any of various skin diseases **2** : LEPROSY

**lepra reaction** *n* : one of the acute episodes of chills and fever, malaise, and skin eruption occurring in the chronic course of leprosy

**lep·re·chaun** *also* **lep·re·caun** *or* **lep·re·haun** \ˈleprəˌkän, -ˌkȧl, -ˌhȯl, ˌȯn *sometimes* -ˌkən *or* -ˌkən\ *n* -s [IrGael *leipreachān, luprachān,* fr. MIr *lūchorpān,* fr. *lū* small + *corpān,* dim. of *corp* body, fr. L *corpus* — more at MIDRIFF] : a mischievous elf of Irish folklore usu. conceived as a shoemaker and believed to reveal the hiding place of treasure if caught

**lep·rid** \ˈleprəd\ *n* -s [ISV *lepr-* (fr. LL *lepra* leprosy) + *-id*] : a skin lesion characteristic of neural leprosy

**lep·roid** \ˈleˌprȯid\ *adj* [LL *lepra* leprosy + E *-oid*] : resembling leprosy

**lep·rol·o·gist** \leˈpräləjəst\ *n* -s : a specialist in leprology

**lep·rol·o·gy** \-jē\ *n* -ES [LL *lepra* leprosy + E *-o-* + *-logy*] : the study of leprosy and its treatment

**lep·ro·ma** \leˈprōmə\ *n, pl* **lepromas** \-məz\ *or* **leproma·ta** \-məd·ə\ [NL, fr. LL *lepra* leprosy + NL *-oma*] : a nodular lesion of leprosy

**lep·roma·tous** \(ˈ)leˈprämәd·əs, -rōm-\ *adj* [NL *lepromat-, leproma* + E *-ous*] **1** : characterized by the formation or presence of lepromas ⟨~ leprosy⟩ **2** : relating to or exhibiting nodular leprosy ⟨cases of the ~ type⟩ ⟨a higher ~ rate⟩

**lep·ro·min** \leˈprōmən\ *n* -s [NL *leproma* + E *-in*] : an extract of human leprous tissue used in a skin test for leprosy infection

**lep·ro·sar·i·um** \ˌleprəˈsa(a)rēəm, -ser-,-sär- *sometimes* -sär-\ *n, pl* **leprosariums** *or* **leprosar·ia** \-ēə\ [ML, fr. LL *leprosus* leprous + L *-arium*] : a hospital for lepers

**lep·rose** \ˈleˌprōs\ *adj* [LL *leprosus* leprous] : SCURFY, SCALY

**lep·ro·sery** \ˈleprəˌserē, -eri\ *n* -ES [F *léproserie,* fr. L *leprosus* leprous + F *-erie* -ery] : LEPROSARIUM

**le·pro·sis** \ləˈprōsəs\ *n* -ES [NL, fr. LL *lepra* leprosy + NL *-osis*] : a disease of the sweet orange of undetermined cause that is characterized by the spotting of smooth bark and fruits and by the scaling of the bark on the larger limbs and sometimes on the trunk — called also *nailhead rust, scaly bark;* compare PSOROSIS

**lep·ro·sy** \ˈleprəsē, -si\ *n* -ES [*leprous* + *-y*] **1** : a chronic disease caused by infection with an acid-fast bacillus (*Mycobacterium leprae*) and characterized by the formation of nodules on the surface of the body and esp. on the face or by the appearance of tuberculoid macules on the skin that enlarge and spread and are accompanied by loss of sensation followed sooner or later in both types by involvement of nerves with eventual paralysis, wasting of muscle, and production of deformities and mutilations **2** : an ideological or moral influence that is felt to deteriorate sound principles or moral values ⟨cannot think of a single collective organization today . . . untainted by the ~ of nihilism —Ignazio Silone⟩ ⟨even moral ~ can be cured by divine grace —*Time*⟩ ⟨this badness is not radical . . . this ~ cannot destroy man's original grandeur —Jacques Maritain⟩

**lep·rot·ic** \(ˈ)leˈpräd·ik\ *adj* [*leprosy* + *-otic*] : of, caused by, or infected with leprosy ⟨~ lesions⟩

**lep·rous** \ˈleprəs\ *adj* [ME *leprous, leprus, lepros,* fr. LL *leprosus,* fr. *lepra* leprosy + L *-osus* -ous — more at LEPER] **1 a** : infected with leprosy **b** : of, relating to, or associated with leprosy or a leper ⟨~ neuritis⟩ **2 a** : resembling or suggestive of leprosy or a leper ⟨plates and superstructure were ~ with rust —N.R.Raine⟩ ⟨a morally ~ character with a lust for power —Sidney Hook⟩ **b** : LEPROSE — **lep·rous·ly** *adv* — **lep·rous·ness** *n* -ES

**lepry** *n* -ES [ME *leprie,* fr. *lepre* leprosy + *-ie* -y — more at LEPER] *obs* : LEPROSY

**-lep·sy** \ˌlepsē, -si\ *also* **-lep·sia** \ˈlepsēə\ *or* **-lep·sis** \-lepsəs\ *n comb form, pl* **-lepsies** \-sēz,-siz\ *also* **-lepsias** \-sēəz\ *or* **-lep·ses** \-(ˌ)sēz\ [*-lepsy* fr. MF *-lepsie,* fr. LL *-lepsia,* fr. Gk *-lēpsia,* fr. *lēpsis* act of taking hold or receiving, seizure (fr. *lēptos,* verbal of *lambanein* to take, seize) + *-ia* -y; *-lepsia,* NL, fr. LL & Gk; LL, fr. Gk *-lēpsia; -lepsis,* L, fr. Gk *-lēpsis,* fr. *lēpsis* — more at LATCH] : taking : seizure ⟨epi*lepsy*⟩ ⟨andro*lepsia*⟩

**lept-** *or* **lepto-** *comb form* [*lept-,* NL, fr. Gk *leptos,* lit., peeled, husked, fr. *lepein* to peel; *lepto-* fr. Gk, fr. *leptos* — more at LEPER] : small : weak : thin : fine ⟨*Lept*andra⟩ ⟨*lepto*logy⟩ ⟨*lepto*rrhine⟩

**lepta** *pl of* LEPTON

**¹lep·tan·dra** \lepˈtandrə\ [NL, fr. *lept-* + *-andra*] *syn of* VERONICASTRUM

**²leptandra** \"\ *n* -s *often cap* [NL *Leptandra,* genus name of *Leptandra virginica*] : CULVER'S ROOT

**lep·ta·zol** \ˈleptəˌzōl, -ˌzōl\ *n* -s [prob. fr. *lept-* + *az-* + *-ol*] : PENTYLENETETRAZOL

**lep·tene** \ˈlepˌtēn\ *also* **lep·ten·ic** \(ˈ)lepˈtenik\ *adj* [*leptene* fr. G *lepten,* fr. *lept-* + *-en* (as in G *euryen* euryene); *leptenic* fr. *leptene* + *-ic* — more at EURYENE] : having a high, a narrow, or a high narrow forehead with an upper facial index of 55 to 60 on the skull and of 53 to 57 on the living

**lep·te·ny** \ˈleptənē\ *n* -ES : the quality or state of being leptene

**lep·ti·no·tar·sa** \ˌleptənōˈtärsə\ *n, cap* [NL, fr. *lept-* + *-ino-* (fr. *-inus* -ine) + *-tarsa* (fr. *tarsus*)] : a genus of beetles of the family Chrysomelidae containing the Colorado potato beetle

**lep·tite** \ˈlepˌtīt\ *n* -s [ISV *lept-* + *-ite*] : a mineral consisting of a fine-grained leucocratic metamorphic rock that is composed essentially of quartz and feldspar sometimes along with dark minerals

**lep·to·bos** \ˈleptə+ˌ-\ *n, usu cap* [NL, fr. *lept-* + *Bos*] : an extinct polled bovine held to be an ancestor of domestic cattle

**lep·to·car·dia** \ˌleptəˈkärdēə\ [NL, fr. *lept-* + *-cardia*] *syn of* LEPTOCARDII

**lep·to·car·dii** \-dēˌī\ *n pl, cap* [NL, fr. *lept-* + *-cardii* (fr. Gk *kardia* heart) — more at HEART] *in some classifications* : a class coextensive with Cephalochorda and often considered the lowest division of Vertebrata

**lep·to·ceph·a·lid** \-ˈsefələd\ *n* -s [NL *leptocephalus* + E *-id*] : LEPTOCEPHALUS 2a

**lep·to·ceph·a·lous** \ˌ==ˈsefələs\ *also* **lep·to·ce·phal·ic** \-ˌsəˈfalik\ *adj* [NL *leptocephalus* + E *-ous* or *-ic*] **1** : of, relating to, or having the characteristics of a leptocephalus **2** [*leptocephaly* + *-ous* or *-ic*] : characterized by or exhibiting leptocephaly

**lep·to·ceph·a·lus** \ˌ==ˈsefələs\ *n* [NL, fr. *lept-* + *-cephalus*] **1** *cap, in some esp. former classifications* : a genus (the type of the family Leptocephalidae) of small pelagic fishes comprising the leptocephali when these are not larvae of other fishes **2** *pl* **lep·to·ceph·a·li** \-ˌlī\ **a** : a small-headed transparent ribbonlike pelagic first larva of various eels that lives three years in the open sea before migrating to coastal waters and gradually transforming into an elver **b** : any of various similar larvae of fishes other than eels **3** *pl* **leptocephali** [NL, fr. *lept-* + *-cephalus*] **a** : LEPTOCEPHALY **b** : an individual with leptocephaly

**lep·to·ceph·a·ly** \-lē\ *also* **lep·to·ce·pha·lia** \-ˌsəˈfālyə\ *n, pl* **leptocephalies** *also* **leptocephalias** [NL *leptocephalia,* fr. *lept-* + *cephal-* + *-ia* -y] : abnormal narrowness and tallness of the skull

**lep·to·cer·cal** \ˌ==ˈsərkəl\ *adj* [*lept-* + *-cercal*] **1** : tapering off to a long slender point — used of the tail of a fish (as a sting ray) **2** : having a leptocercal tail

**lep·to·chlorite** \ˌ==+\ *n* [ISV *lept-* + *chlorite;* prob. orig. formed as G *leptochlorit*] : a mineral consisting of any of several chlorites of indistinct crystallization — opposed to *orthochlorite*

**lep·to·clase** \ˈleptəˌklās, -āz\ *n* -s [ISV *lept-* + *-clase;* prob. orig. formed in F] : a minute crack or fracture in rock

**¹lep·to·dac·tyl** \ˌ==ˈdaktᵊl\ *adj* [NL *leptodactylus,* fr. *lept-* + *-dactylus* (fr. Gk *-daktylos* -dactylous)] : LEPTODACTYLOUS

**²leptodactyl** \"\ *n* : a bird or other animal having slender toes

**lep·to·dac·tyl·id** \ˌ==ˈ=tələd\ *adj* [NL *Leptodactylidae*] : of or relating to the Leptodactylidae

**lep·to·dac·tyl·i·dae** \ˌ==ˌdakˈtiləˌdē\ *n pl, cap* [NL, fr. *Leptodactylus,* type genus + *-idae*] *in some classifications* : a family of toothed toads that is more or less coextensive with Bufonidae

**lep·to·dac·ty·lous** \ˌ==ˈdaktələs\ *adj* [*lept-* + *-dactylous*] : having slender toes ⟨~ birds⟩

**lep·to·dac·ty·lus** \ˌ==ˈdaktələs\ *n, cap* [NL, fr. *lept-* + *-dactylus* (fr. Gk *daktylos* finger, toe)] : a genus of toothed toads that is usu. placed in the family Bufonidae and that comprises the So. American bullfrogs and related forms

**lep·to·der·mous** \ˌ==ˈdərməs\ *also* **lep·to·der·ma·tous** \-məd·əs\ *adj* [NL, fr. *lept-* + *-dermous* (as in *pachydermous*) or *-dermatous*] : having a thin skin — used esp. of the theca of a moss

**lep·tod·o·ra** \lepˈtädərə\ *n, cap* [NL, fr. *lept-* + Gk *dora* hide, fr. *derein* to skin, flay — more at TEAR (rend)] : a genus (the type of the family Leptodoridae) of freshwater entomostracans of the order Cladocera

**lep·to·form** \ˈleptəˌfȯrm\ *n* [*lept-* + *form*] : a plant rust having a telial stage that is not preceded by a resting stage — compare MICROFORM

**lep·to·kur·tic** \ˌ==ˈkərd·ik\ *adj* [*lept-* + Gk *kyrtos* bulging, convex, curved + E *-ic;* akin to L *curvus* bent, curved — more at CROWN] **1** *of a frequency distribution curve* : being more peaked than the corresponding normal distribution curve **2** *of* *a frequency distribution* : being more concentrated about the mean than the corresponding normal distribution

**lep·to·kur·to·sis** \ˌ⸗⸗ˌkərˈtōsə̇s\ *n* [NL, fr. E *leptokurtic* + NL *-osis*] : the condition of being leptokurtic

**lep·to·lep·i·dae** \ˌ⸗⸗ˈlepəˌdē\ *n pl, cap* [NL, fr. *Leptolepis*, type genus + *-idae*] : a family of primitive clupeoid fishes of the Upper Lias and Lower Cretaceous

**lep·tol·e·pis** \lepˈtäləpə̇s\ *n, cap* [NL, fr. *lept-* + *-lepis*] : a genus (the type of the family Leptolepidae) of primitive clupeoid fishes that includes numerous small thin-scaled fishes with the tail nearly homocercal

**lep·to·li·na** \ˌleptəˈlīnə, -lēnə\ *also* **leptoli·nae** \-ˌlīˌnē, -lēˌnī\ [NL] *syn of* HYDROIDA

**lep·tol·o·gy** \lepˈtäləjē\ *or* **lep·to·nol·o·gy** \ˌleptəˈnäləjē\ *n* -ES [*leptology* fr. *lept-* + *-logy*; *leptonology* fr. Gk *lepton* (neut. of *leptos* small, fine) + E *-o-* + *-logy* — more at LEPT-] : CRYSTALLOGRAPHY

**lep·to·mat·ic** \ˌ¦leptəˌmad·ik\ *adj* [*leptome* + *-atic* (after such pairs as E *symptom*: *symptomatic*)] : of or relating to the leptome

**lep·tome** \ˈlepˌtōm\ *also* **lep·tom** \-täm\ *n* -S [G *leptom*, fr. *lept-* + *-om* -ome] **1** : a part of the mestome that conducts food materials **2** : a somewhat rudimentary phloem in cryptogams

**lep·to·medusae** \ˌ¦lep(ˌ)tō+\ *n pl, cap* [NL, fr. *lept-* + *medusae* (pl. of *medusa*)] : a suborder of the order Hydroida or in some classifications a separate order of Hydrozoa comprising coelenterates in which the hydranths and the productive zooids are protected by a theca, the medusae bear gonads on the radial canals, and the lithocysts when present are of ectodermal origin — **lep·to·medusan** \"+\ *adj or n*

**lep·to·meningeal** \ˌ¦lep(ˌ)tō+\ *adj* [NL *leptomeninges* + E *-al*] : of or involving the leptomeninges ⟨~ infection⟩

**lep·to·meninges** \"+\ *n pl* [NL, fr. *lept-* + *meninges*] : the pia mater and the arachnoid

**lep·to·meningitis** \"+\ *n* [NL, fr. *lept-* + *meningitis*] : inflammation of the pia mater and the arachnoid membrane

**lep·tom·er·yx** \lepˈtäməriks\ *n, cap* [NL, fr. *lept-* + *-meryx*] : a genus of small Oligocene ruminants of western No. America distantly related to the recent chevrotains

**lep·to·mi·ta·les** \ˌlep(ˌ)tōˌmīˈtā(ˌ)lēz\ *n pl, cap* [NL, fr. *Leptomitus*, genus of water molds (fr. Gk *leptomitos* of fine threads, fr. *lepto-* lept- + *mitos* thread) + *-ales*] : an order of water molds (subclass Oomycetes) resembling the Saprolegniales but forming branching chains because of regular constrictions of the hyphae

**¹lep·tom·o·nad** \lepˈtäməˌnad\ *adj* [NL *Leptomonad-*, *Leptomonas*] : of or relating to the genus *Leptomonas*

**²leptomonad** \"\ *n* : LEPTOMONAS 2

**lep·tom·o·nas** \-ˌnəs\ *n* [NL, fr. *lept-* + *-monas*] **1** *cap* : a genus of flagellates of the family Trypanosomatidae that are parasites esp. of the digestive tract of insects and that occur as elongated flagellates with anterior flagellum and no undulating membrane but also pass through stages indistinguishable from intracellular crithidias and leishmanias **2** -ES **a** : any flagellate of the genus *Leptomonas* **b** : a flagellate of the family Trypanosomatidae when exhibiting a typical leptomonad form

**¹lep·ton** \lepˈtȯn\ *n, pl* **lep·ta** \-ˈtä\ [Gk, fr. neut. of *leptos* small — more at LEPT-] **1** : a small bronze coin of ancient Greece **2** : a small bronze Judaean coin minted until the middle of the 1st century A.D. **3** [NGk, fr. Gk] **a** : a unit of value of modern Greece equal to $1/100$ of a drachma — see MONEY table **b** : a coin representing such a lepton

**²lep·ton** \ˈlepˌtän, -ˌtən\ *n* [NL, fr. Gk, neut. of *leptos* small, fine] **1** *cap* : a genus of minute bivalve mollusks (suborder Submytilacea) with round flat thin shells **2** -S : any mollusk of the genus *Lepton*

**³lepton** \"\ *n* -S [*lept-* + *-on*] : any of a family of particles consisting of electrons, muons, and neutrinos that have one-half quantum unit of spin, obey Fermi-Dirac statistics, experience no strong interactions, and are less massive than mesons

**lep·to·necrosis** \ˌlep(ˌ)tō+\ *n* [NL, fr. E *leptome* + NL *necrosis*] : a necrosis of the phloem tissues

**lep·to·ne·ma** \ˌleptəˈnēmə\ *n* -S [NL, fr. *lept-* + *-nema*] : a chromatin thread or chromosome at leptotene : a meiotic chromosome before the beginning of synapsis — compare PACHYNEMA

**lep·to·phis** \ˈleptəfə̇s\ *n, cap* [NL, fr. *lept-* + *-ophis*] : a genus of slender harmless tree snakes of Central and So. America

**lep·to·pro·sopic** \¦⸗⸗prə¦sōpik, -säp-\ *also* **lep·to·pro·so·pous** \-sōpəs\ *adj* [G *leptoprosop* leptoprosopic (fr. *lepto-* lept- + Gk *prosōpon* face) + E *-ic* or *-ous* — more at PROSOP-] : having a long, a narrow, or a long narrow face with a facial index of 88 to 93 on the living and of 90 to 95 on the skull

**lep·to·proso·py** \ˌ⸗⸗ˈpräsəpē, -ˌprəˈsōpē\ *n* -ES : the quality or state of being leptoprosopic

**lep·top·ti·los** \lepˈtäptəˌläs\ *n, cap* [NL, fr. *lept-* + Gk *-ptilos* -feathered, -winged (fr. *ptilon* down, feather)] : a genus of storks consisting of the adjutant birds and marabous

**lep·tor·rhine** *also* **lep·to·rhine** \ˈleptəˌrīn\ *or* **lep·tor·rhin·i·an** \ˌ⸗⸗¦rinēən\ *or* **lep·tor·rhin·ic** \-¦rinik\ *adj* [*leptorrhine* & *leptorhine* prob. fr. F *leptorrhin*, fr. *lepto-* lept- + *-rrhin* -rrhine; *leptorrhinian* fr. F *leptorrhinien*, fr. *lepto-* lept- + *-rrhin* -rrhine + *-ien* -ian; *leptorrhinic* fr. *leptorrhine* + *-ic*] : having a long narrow nose with a nasal index of less than 47 on the skull or of less than 70 on the living

**lep·tor·rhi·ny** \ˈleptəˌrīnē\ *n* -ES : the quality or state of being leptorrhine

**¹lep·to·some** \-ˌsōm\ *also* **lep·to·so·mat·ic** \¦⸗⸗sō¦mad·ik\ *or* **lep·to·som·ic** \-¦sōmik\ *adj* [*leptosome* fr. G *leptosom*, fr. *lepto-* lept- + *-som* (fr. Gk *sōma* body); *leptosomatic* fr. *leptosome* + *-atic* (after E *somatic*); *leptosomic* fr. *leptosome* + *-ic* — more at -SOME (body)] : ASTHENIC 2, ECTOMORPHIC — opposed to *eurysome*

**²lep·to·some** \ˈleptəˌsōm\ *also* **lep·to·som** \-säm\ *n* -S [G *leptosom*, n. & adj.] : an ectomorphic individual

**lep·to·sper·mone** \ˌ⸗⸗ˈspərˌmōn\ *n* -S [NL *Leptospermum* + E *-one*] : a pale yellow viscous oily ketone $C_{15}H_{22}O_4$ occurring in the essential oils from various plants of the genus *Leptospermum*

**lep·to·sper·mum** \-ˌməm\ *n, cap* [NL, fr. *lept-* + *-spermum*] : a genus of Australasian shrubs or small trees of the family Myrtaceae having small rigid alternate leaves and white flowers — see TEA TREE

**lep·to·sphae·ria** \-ˈsfirēə\ *n, cap* [NL, fr. *lept-* + Gk *sphaira* sphere + NL *-ia* — more at SPHERE] : a genus of ascomycetous fungi that is commonly placed in the family Sphaeriaceae, is characterized by the production of dark ascospores with five or more septa, and includes saprophytes and a few fungi that are associated with leaf spots or rots of economic plants

**lep·to·spi·ra** \-ˈspīrə\ *n* [NL, fr. *lept-* + L *spira* coil, twist — more at SPIRE (spiral, curl)] **1** *cap* : a genus of extremely slender aerobic spirochetes (family Treponemataceae) free-living or parasitic in mammals that includes a number of important pathogens (as *L. icterohaemorrhagiae* of Weil's disease or *L. canicola* of canicola fever) **2** *pl* **leptospira** \"\ *also* **leptospiras** \-rəz\ *or* **leptospi·rae** \-ˌrē\ : any spirochete of the genus *Leptospira*

**lep·to·spi·ral** \¦⸗⸗¦⸗rəl\ *adj* [NL *leptospira* + E *-al*] : of, due to, or involving leptospira ⟨~ infection⟩ ⟨~ disease⟩

**leptospiral jaundice** *n* : WEIL'S DISEASE

**lep·to·spi·ro·sis** \ˌ⸗⸗ˌspīˈrōsə̇s\ *n, pl* **leptospiro·ses** \-ˌōˌsēz\ [NL, fr. *Leptospira* + *-osis*] : any of several diseases of man and domestic animals (as cattle and dogs) caused by infection with spirochetes of the genus *Leptospira* — see STUTTGART DISEASE, WEIL'S DISEASE; compare CANICOLA FEVER

**lep·to·spo·ran·gi·a·tae** \ˌlep(ˌ)tōspəˌranjēˈāˌtī, -ˈäˌtē\ *n pl, cap* [NL, fr. fem. pl. of *leptosporangiatus*, adj.] *in some classifications* : a group comprising all the orders of ferns in which sporangium formation is leptosporangiate — compare EUSPORANGIATAE

**lep·to·spo·ran·gi·ate** \¦⸗(ˌ)⸗spə¦ranjēə̇t, -ēˌāt\ *adj* [NL *leptosporangiatus*, fr. *lept-* + *sporangium* + L *-atus* -ate] : having each sporangium formed from a single epidermal cell ⟨~ ferns⟩ — opposed to EUSPORANGIATE

**lep·to·staph·y·line** \¦leptə¦stafəˌlīn, -ˌlən\ *adj* [*lept-* + Gk *staphylē* uvula + E *-ine*] : having a palate which is narrow and high with a palatal index of less than 80 on the skull

**lep·to·staph·y·li·ny** \ˌ⸗⸗ˈ⸗⸗ˌlīnē\ *n* -ES [ISV *leptostaphyline* + *-y*] : the quality or state of being leptostaphyline

**lep·tos·tra·ca** \lepˈtästrəkə\ *n pl, cap* [NL, fr. *lept-* + *-ostraca*] : a division of Malacostraca including the Phyllocarida, the Nebaliacea, and various fossil forms that are regarded as intermediate between the typical malacostracans and the lower crustaceans although classed among the former — see NEBALIA — **lep·tos·tra·can** \(ˈ)⸗¦⸗kən\ *adj & n* — **lep·tos·tra·cous** \(ˈ)⸗¦⸗kəs\ *adj*

**lep·to·stro·ma·ta·ce·ae** \ˌleptəˌstrōməˈtāsēˌē\ *n pl, cap* [NL, fr. *Leptostromat-*, *Leptostroma*, type genus (fr. *lept-* + *stroma*) + *-aceae*] : a family of imperfect fungi of the order Sphaeropsidales having more or less dimidiate shield-shaped black pycnidia

**lep·to·tene** \ˈleptəˌtēn\ *n* -S [ISV *lept-* + *-tene*; orig. formed as F *leptotène*] : a stage of the meiotic prophase immediately preceding synapsis in which the chromosomes appear as fine discrete threads — compare PACHYTENE — **lep·to·tenic** \¦⸗⸗¦tēnik, -¦ten-\ *adj*

**lep·to·thermal** \¦leptə+\ *adj* [*lept-* + *thermal*] : of or relating to a portion of the hydrothermal sequence of ore deposits that lies between mesothermal and epithermal

**lep·to·thrix** \ˈ⸗⸗ˌthriks\ *n* [NL, fr. *lept-* + *-thrix*] **1** *cap* : a genus of sheathed filamentous bacteria (family Chlamydobacteriaceae) that are unbranched or exhibit false branching, that multiply by division or by motile swarmers, and that have the sheath encrusted with ferric hydroxide — see LEPTOTRICHIA **2** *pl* **lep·to·trich·ia** \ˌ⸗⸗ˈtrikēə\ *also* **lep·tot·ri·ches** \lepˈtä·trəˌkēz\ : a bacterium of the genus *Leptothrix*

**lep·to·trich·ia** \ˌ⸗⸗ˈtrikēə\ *n, cap* [NL, fr. *Leptotrich-*, *Leptothrix* + *-ia*] : a genus of long filamentous typically oral bacteria that are often placed among the actinomycetes but have sometimes been included in the genus *Leptothrix*, or divided among several other genera

**lep·to·typhlops** \¦leptə+\ *n, cap* [NL, fr. *lept-* + *Typhlops*, genus of snakes — more at TYPHLOPIDAE] : a genus (the type of the family Leptotyphlopidae) of small burrowing vermiform snakes of Africa, southwestern Asia, and the warmer parts of America

**lep·tus** \ˈleptəs\ *n* [NL, fr. Gk *leptos* small, thin — more at LEPT-] **1** *pl* **leptuses** \-təsəz\ *also* **lep·ti** \-ˌtī, -(ˌ)tē\ *often cap* : any of several 6-legged larval mites — often used as a generic name; compare CYSTICERCUS 1 **2** *cap* : a genus of predaceous mites (family Erythraeidae) that are parasitic as larvae on insects

**lepus** \ˈlepəs, ˈlēp-\ *n, cap* [NL, fr. L, hare — more at LAPIN] : a genus (the type of the family Leporidae) comprising the typical hares

**lere** \ˈlēr\ *vb* [ME *leeren*, *leren*, fr. OE *lǣran* to teach; akin to OS *lērian* to teach, OHG *lēren*, Goth *laisjan*; causative fr. the root of E *lore*] *archaic Scot* : LEARN

**ler·naea** \ˌlərˈnēə\ *n, cap* [NL, fr. L, fem. of *Lernaeus* Lernaean] : a genus (the type of the family Lernaeidae) of copepod crustaceans that in some stages are parasitic usu. externally on fishes — **ler·nae·i·form** \-ēəˌfȯrm\ *or* **ler·nae·oid** \-ēˌȯid\ *adj*

**¹ler·nae·an** *also* **ler·ne·an** \ˌlərˈnēən\ *adj* [L *Lernaeus* of Lerna near ancient Argos (fr. Gk *Lernaios*, fr. *Lernē* Lerna) + E *-an*] **1** *usu cap* : of or relating to Lerna, a lake or swamp near Argos **2** [NL *Lernaea* + E *-an*] : of or relating to the lernaeans

**²lernaean** \"\ *n* -S : a crustacean of the genus *Lernaea*

**le·rot** \(ˈ)läˌrō\ *n* -S [F *lérot*, fr. MF, fr. *loir*, fr. L *glir-*, *glis* dormouse] : any of several dormice of a genus (*Eliomys*) of southern Europe and northern Africa

**lerp** \ˈlərp\ *also* **laap** \ˈläp\ *n* -S [native name in Australia, lit., sweet] : a sweet waxy secretion found in Australia and Tasmania on the leaves of eucalyptus trees that is produced as a protection by the young of jumping plant lice of *Spondyliaspis* and related genera and is eaten by aborigines

**lerp insect** *n* : JUMPING PLANT LOUSE

**ler·ret** \ˈlerə̇t\ *n* -S [origin unknown] : an open boat with two sails and 2, 4, or 6 oars that is used in the English channel

**ler·wa** \ˈlərwə\ *n, cap* [NL, fr. Nepali *larwā* snow partridge; akin to Skt *laṭvā*, *laṭvākā*, *laḍvākā*, a bird] : a genus constituted by the snow partridge

**-les** *pres 3d sing of* -LE

**LES** *abbr* local excitatory state

**¹les·bi·an** \ˈlezbēən\ *adj, often cap* [L *Lesbius* of Lesbos (fr. Gk *Lesbios*, fr. *Lesbos*, island in the Aegean Sea) + E *-an*] **1** : of or relating to Lesbos (now Mytilene) **2** [so called fr. the reputed sensuality of the Lesbian people and literature] : highly sensual : EROTIC ⟨~ novels⟩ **3** [so called fr. the reputed homosexual band associated with Sappho *fl ab* 600 B.C. Greek lyric poet of Lesbos] : of or relating to homosexual relations between females

**²lesbian** \"\ *n* -S *often cap* **1** : an Aeolic dialect of ancient Greek used in Lesbos **2** : a female homosexual

**les·bi·an·ism** \-ˌnizəm\ *n* -S : lesbian love : SAPPHISM

**les·che** \ˈle(ˌ)skē\ *n* -S [Gk *leschē*; akin to Gk *lechos* bed — more at LIE] : a social gathering place of classical antiquity

**lese majesty** *or* **lèse ma·jes·té** \ˈlēzˈmajə̇stē, -ti\ *n, pl* **lese majesties** *or* **lèse majestés** [*lese majesty* part trans. of MF *lese majesté*, *leze majesté*, fr. L *laesa majestas*, lit., injured majesty; *lèse majesté* fr. F, fr. MF] **1 a** (1) : a crime (as high treason) committed against a sovereign power ⟨people convicted of *lèse majesté* —*Hartford (Conn.) Courant*⟩ (2) : an offense violating the dignity of a ruler as the representative of a sovereign power ⟨so did *lèse majesté* against Stalin surpass all other crimes —Georg Mann⟩ **b** : a detraction from the dignity or importance of a constituted authority ⟨*lèse majesté* toward the Church —*New Yorker*⟩ ⟨time has so mellowed Strachey's *lèse majesté* that his biography has been accepted . . . as a human portrait of the great Queen —*Time*⟩ ⟨to belittle the Hong Kong and Shanghai Bank has always been almost *lèse majesté* here —Christopher Rand⟩ **2** : an affront to position or authority : INDIGNITY, OUTRAGE ⟨some varlet put a parking ticket on the . . . car, which is *lèse majestè*, and the whole town had to prostrate itself —Claudia Cassidy⟩ ⟨any criticism of it is . . . *lese majesty* —Hunter Mead⟩

**lesghian** *usu cap, var of* LEZGHIAN

**le·sion** \ˈlēzhən\ *n* -S [ME *lesioun*, fr. MF *lesion*, fr. OF, fr. LL *laesion-*, *laesio*, fr. L, verbal attack, fr. *laesus* (past part. of *laedere* to injure, hurt) + *-ion-*, *-io* -ion] **1 a** : INJURY, IMPAIRMENT, FLAW ⟨looking for . . . ~s, for bubbles in the gutta-percha —*London Times*⟩ ⟨crime . . . has become the symptom of a radical ~ in the stamina of humanity —M.D.Zabel⟩ **b** : an abnormal change in structure of an organ or part due to injury or disease; *esp* : one that is circumscribed and well defined **2** *civil & Scots law* : loss from another's failure to fulfill a contract : injury arising from failure to receive the full equivalent of what was bargained for in a commutative contract **syn** see WOUND

**les·ke·ace·ae** \ˌleskēˈāsēˌē\ *n pl, cap* [NL, fr. *Leskea*, type genus (fr. Nathaniel G. *Leske* †1786 Ger. naturalist) + *-aceae*] : a family of pleurocarpous mosses (order Hypnobryales) that grow on trees and rocks, are typified by the genus *Leskea*, and are characterized by papillose, rounded, or rhomboid leaves and mostly erect capsules — **les·ke·aceous** \¦⸗⸗¦āshəs\ *adj*

**les·leya** \ˈleslēə, ˈlezl-, ⸗ˈ⸗⸗\ *n, cap* [NL, fr. J. P. *Lesley* †1903 Am. geologist] : a genus of fossil plants of Carboniferous age and uncertain affinities that resemble ferns

**les·ley·ite** \ˈleslēˌīt, -ezl-\ *n* -S [John *Lesley*, Jr., 19th cent. Am. on whose farm it was found + E *-ite*] : a mineral approximately $K_2Al_{8\frac{2}{3}}Si_4O_{20}(OH)_4$ consisting of a brittle mica that is related to margarite but contains potassium

**le·so·tho** \ləˈsō(ˌ)tō\ *adj, usu cap* [fr. *Lesotho*, country in southern Africa] : of or from the country of Lesotho : of the kind or style prevalent in Lesotho

**les·pe·de·za** \ˌlespəˈdēzə\ *n* [NL, irreg. (by misreading of the surname) fr. V. M. de *Zespedes fl*1785 Span. governor of East Florida] **1** *cap* : a genus of herbaceous or shrubby plants (family Leguminosae) having exstipulate leaves, often both apetalous fertile and papilionaceous sterile flowers, and one-jointed one-seeded pods covered by the calyx, some members of which are widely used for forage, soil improvement, and esp. hay in the southern U.S. — see BICOLOR LESPEDEZA, KOREAN LESPEDEZA, SERICEA LESPEDEZA **2** -S : any plant of the genus *Lespedeza*

**les·que·rel·la** \ˌleskəˈrelə, ˌlāk-\ *n, cap* [NL, fr. Leo *Lesquereux* †1889 Swiss paleobotanist in U.S. + NL *-ella*] : a genus of low annual or perennial American herbs (family Cruciferae) having stellate pubescence, simple leaves, yellow racemose flowers, and inflated pods — see BLADDERPOD

**¹less** \ˈles\ *adj* **less·er** \ˈlesə(r)\ **least** \ˈlēst\ [ME *lasse*, *las*, *less*, *lesse*, partly fr. OE *lǣs*, adv. & n. and partly fr. *lǣssa*, adj.; akin to OS & OFris *lēs* less, MHG *lin* tepid, faint, OHG *bilinnan* to cease, ON *linr* soft, gentle, weak, *linna* to cease, *læ* fraud, treason, bane, Goth *aflinnan* to go away, MIr *léine* shirt, *lian* soft, Gk *liazesthai* to bend, recoil, sink, *limos* hunger, *liaros* warm, soft, gentle, Lith *liesas* thin] **1** : of a more limited number : FEWER ⟨~ operating miles of railway track —*N.Y. Times*⟩ ⟨~ than two years later —C.S.Forester⟩ ⟨the subcommittee shall consist of not ~ than three nor more than five members⟩ ⟨the more watch officers, the ~ watches —Wirt Williams⟩ ⟨~ family ties than a wild thing in the woods —H.L. Mencken⟩ **2 a** : of humbler rank : LOWLIER ⟨no ~ a person than Winston Churchill —A.A.Hill⟩ **b** *obs* : of a lower quality : INFERIOR ⟨hope to joy is little ~ in joy than hope enjoyed —Shak.⟩ **3** *archaic* : younger or of diminished magnitude : MINOR ⟨Dr. Franklin the ~ —T.B.Macaulay⟩ ⟨the tyrant of ~ Asia —Josuah Sylvester⟩ ⟨barons . . . upward we call the greater nobility, the others beneath them the ~ nobility —John Selden⟩ **4 a** : of reduced size, extent, or degree : SMALLER, SLIGHTER ⟨the much ~ subordination of the individual to the social community than of the cell or organ to the animal body —Julian Huxley⟩ **b** : more limited in quantity or amount ⟨after 1764 Adams devoted even ~ time than formerly to making a living —C.L.Becker⟩

**²less** \"\ *adv* [ME *lesse*, *lasse*, *less*, fr. OE *lǣs*] **1** : to a lesser extent or degree ⟨doubtful cases . . . are bound to come up in regard to the ~ investigated languages —A.L.Kroeber⟩ ⟨was ~ angry than perplexed —Jean Stafford⟩ ⟨coccinellids . . . were common during April and May and ~ so in June —*Jour. of Economic Entomology*⟩ ⟨the more they were exposed to the campaign . . . the ~ voters changed their positions —R.M. Goldman⟩ ⟨Italian is no ~ a mother tongue for her than English —Irving Kolodin⟩ **2** : more emphatically not ⟨they were not attacking the churches, still ~ religion as such —Elmer Davis⟩ — **less than** *adv* : by no means : far from : not at all ⟨the road . . . was something *less than* smooth —M.W.Fishwick⟩ ⟨America's friends abroad would be *less than* candid if they did not report the fact —Barbara Ward⟩

**³less** \"\ *prep* [ME *las*, *lesse*, fr. OE *lǣs*, prep., adv., & n.] **1** : diminished by : with the subtraction of : MINUS ⟨the weight so found, ~ the weight of the sieve, shall be considered to be the drained weight —*Definitions & Standards for Food*⟩ **2** : with the exception of : EXCLUDING ⟨appeared originally, ~ some stitchwork, in the *New Yorker* —John Lardner⟩

**⁴less** \"\ *n, pl* **less** [ME *lesse*, *lasse*, fr. OE *lǣsse* (fr. *lǣssa*, adj.), *lǣs*] **1 a** : a smaller portion or quantity ⟨no ~ than 97 million dollars has been added —J.B.Conant⟩ ⟨the radio towers were askew and ~ of them protruded above the snow —*Geog. School Bull.*⟩ **b** : something not as consequential or elaborate ⟨people have been sent to Siberia for ~ —*Time*⟩ ⟨hewed to the current architectural concept that "~ is more"⟩ **2** : something inferior to that with which it is compared ⟨of two evils choose the ~⟩ **3** *obs* : one that is of inferior rank ⟨nemesis . . . doth raze the great and raise the ~ —Samuel Daniel⟩

**⁵less** \"\ *pron* [ME *lesse*, *lasse*, pron. & adj., fr. OE *lǣsse* (fr. *lǣssa*, adj.)] **1** : something smaller or below average ⟨can not honorably do ~⟩ **2** *pl in constr* : fewer persons or things ⟨~ were available than he had hoped⟩

**⁶less** \"\ *conj* [ME, fr. earlier *lasse than*, *lesse than*, fr. *lasse*, *lesse* (adv.) + *than*] *now dial* : UNLESS

**-less** \lə̇s\ *adj suffix* [ME *-les*, *-lesse*, fr. OE *-lēas*, fr. *lēas* devoid, false; akin to OS *lōs* loose, false, MD *los* loose, OHG *lōs*, ON *lauss* loose, Goth *laus* empty, OE *losian* to get lost, perish — more at LOSE] **1** : destitute of : not having : free from ⟨wit*less*⟩ ⟨child*less*⟩ ⟨father*less*⟩ ⟨doubt*less*⟩ **2** : beyond the range of — in adjectives formed from nouns of action ⟨count*less*⟩ **3** : unable or lacking power to be acted on or to act (in a specified way) — in adjectives formed from verbs ⟨resist*less*⟩ ⟨daunt*less*⟩ ⟨quench*less*⟩ ⟨tire*less*⟩ ⟨fade*less*⟩ ⟨cease*less*⟩

**less and less** *adv (or adj)* : to a progressively smaller size or extent ⟨watched his figure grow *less and less* in the dim grey light —O.E.Rölvaag⟩ ⟨a world that . . . has been *less and less* governed by reason —Lewis Mumford⟩

**lesse** *obs var of* LESS

**les·see** \(ˈ)leˈsē\ *n* -S [ME, fr. AF, fr. *lessé*, past part. of *lesser* to lease — more at LEASE (let)] **1** : one taking possession of real estate under a lease, esp. a written lease : a tenant of a leasehold estate **2** : a bailee under bailment agreement providing a rental for personal property

**¹less·en** \ˈlesᵊn\ *vb* **lessened**; **lessened**; **lessening** \-s(ᵊ)niŋ\ **lessens** [ME *lessenen*, fr. *lesse*, adj., less + *-nen* -en] *vi* **1** : to shrink in size, number, or degree : DECREASE ⟨as transportation improves, distances seem to ~⟩ ⟨with the tightening of border restrictions, the stream of refugees ~s⟩ ⟨the medicine begins to take effect and symptoms ~⟩ ⟨attacks on academic freedom seem to have ~ed —F.M.Hechinger⟩ **2** *archaic* : to become smaller to the perception as distance increases ⟨the white sail is ~ing from his view —Robert Southey⟩ ⟨distant warblings ~ on my ear —Thomas Gray⟩ ~ *vt* **1** : to reduce in size, extent, or degree : make smaller ⟨~s the chain length of the cellulose —G.S.Hotte⟩ ⟨~ the gap between income and outgo —E.B. George⟩ ⟨the use of chlordane ~s beetle damage⟩ ⟨grammatical errors . . . ~ the respect of the reader —Milton Hall⟩ ⟨international conferences help to ~ tensions between nations⟩ **2 a** *archaic* : MINIMIZE, MITIGATE, DISPARAGE ⟨not that I endeavor to ~ . . . my offense —John Milton⟩ ⟨far from wishing to ~ the merit of this . . . benevolent action —Junius⟩ **b** *obs* : to lower in status or dignity : DEGRADE ⟨the making of new lords ~s all the rest —John Selden⟩ **syn** see DECREASE

**²lessen** \"\ *conj* [contr. of *less than*, fr. ME *lesse than* — more at LESS (conj.)] *dial* : UNLESS

**lessening** *n* -S [ME, fr. gerund of *lessenen* to lessen] : REDUCTION, DIMINUTION ⟨~ or complete elimination of government controls —*Annual Report Continental Steel Corp.*⟩ ⟨a marked ~ of redness and swelling —*Better Homes & Gardens*⟩

**¹less·er** \ˈlesə(r)\ *adj* [ME *lasser*, *lesser*, comp. of *lasse*, *less* less] **1** : of less size, quality, or significance : SMALLER : INFERIOR ⟨~ rivers⟩ ⟨~ men⟩ ⟨~ works⟩ **2** *in plant or animal names* : of a size less than that of similar forms

**²lesser** \"\ *adv* : ²LESS 1 ⟨never a man in Christendom can ~ hide his love . . . than he —Shak.⟩ — now used chiefly with an adjective to form the comparative ⟨works of *lesser*-known composers —*Music Lovers' Encyc.*⟩

**lesser adjutant** *n* : an Asiatic stork (*Leptoptilus javanicus*)

**lesser alcaic** *n, usu cap A* : an Alcaic with four iambic feet

**lesser archilochian** *n, usu cap A* : ARCHILOCHIAN b

**lesser asclepiad** *n, usu cap A* : ASCLEPIAD

**lesser bindweed** *n* : FIELD BINDWEED

**lesser black-backed gull** *n* : a European black-backed gull (*Larus fuscus graellsi*)

**lesser broomrape** *n* : CLOVER BROOMRAPE

**lesser bulb fly** *n* : a small syrphid fly (*Eumerus tuberculatus*) having a grayish to yellowish larva that bores in and destroys the bulbs of various plants (as narcissus, onion, iris)

**lesser butcher-bird** *n, Eng* : BEARDED TIT

**lesser celandine** *n* : a perennial herb (*Ranunculus ficaria*) that is native to Europe but naturalized locally in many areas, has more or less heart-shaped leaves, yellow flowers resembling buttercups, and tuberous roots which have been used as a poultice for the relief of piles — called also *pilewort*

**lesser centaury** *n* : a common European glabrous annual centaury (*Centaurium minus*) with flowers in dense cymes

**lesser chimpanzee** *n* : a small chimpanzee (*Pan paniscus* or *Pan satyrus paniscus*) found locally south of the Congo river in the Belgian Congo

**lesser civet** *n* : RASSE

**lesser clover leaf weevil** *n* : a small green to blue-green weevil (*Hypera nigrirostris*) with a shiny black head and beak and a larva that feeds in the developing head of clover

**lesser cornstalk borer** *n* : a crambid moth (*Elasmopalpus lignosellus*) with a slender greenish larva that burrows in the stalk of Indian corn and various other plants near the ground level and is esp. destructive in warmer parts of the New World

**lesser covert** *n* : one of the last of the secondary coverts of a bird

**lesser crested tern** *n* **:** a large Oriental tern (*Thalasseus bengalensis*)

**lesser curlew** *n* **:** WHIMBREL

**lesser curvature** *n* **:** the short border of the stomach primitively ventral but in man turned to the right

**lesser duckweed** *n* **:** an Old World duckweed (*Lemna minor*) that is widely naturalized in No. America

**lesser emerald bird of paradise :** a bird of paradise (*Paradisea minor*) with brilliant plumes formerly used on hats

**lesser finner** *n* **:** LESSER RORQUAL

**lesser grain borer** *n* **:** a small cosmopolitan bostrychid beetle (*Rhizopertha dominica*) that is a serious pest of stored grain

**lesser housefly** *n* **:** a fly (*Fannia canicularis*) that is smaller than the housefly — called also *little housefly*

**lesser koodoo** *n* **:** an antelope (*Strepsiceros imberbis*) of Somaliland that is similar to but smaller than the koodoo

**lesser omentum** *n* **:** an omentum connecting the liver and stomach and supporting the hepatic vessels

**lesser peach tree borer** *n* **:** a borer that is the larva of a clearwing moth (*Synanthedon pictipes*) and that usu. attacks the forks and crotches of peach trees and other stone-fruit trees esp. in the southern U.S.

**lesser rorqual** *n* **:** the smallest species of finback (*Balaenoptera acuto-rostrata*)

**lesser scaup** *or* **lesser scaup duck** *n* **:** a common No. American diving duck (*Aythya affinis*) similar to the greater scaup but smaller and with the black head glossed with purple rather than green — called also *lake duck*

**lesser snipe** *n* **:** a jacksnipe (*Limnocryptes minima*)

**lesser snow goose** *n* **:** a snow goose (*Chen hyperborea hyperborea*) of the Pacific flyways — called also *Alaska goose, white brant*

**lesser socratic** *n, usu cap S* **:** SOCRATIC 2

**lesser spearwort** *n* **:** either of two creeping species of *Ranunculus:* **a :** an English spearwort (*R. flammula*) — called also *banewort* **b :** a spearwort of the U.S. (*R. pusillus*)

**lesser stomach worm** *n* **:** a small threadlike nematode worm (*Ostertagia ostertagi*) often present in immense numbers in the pyloric part of a sheep's stomach

**lesser yellowlegs** *n pl but sing or pl in constr* **:** a yellowlegs (*Totanus flavipes* or *Tringa flavipes*) that is about 11 inches long including the bill, is streaked brownish gray on the head, neck, breast, and upperparts, has white on the belly, and is barred on the sides and the tail — compare GREATER YELLOWLEGS

**les·ses** \ˈlesəz\ *n pl* [ME, fr. MF, fr. *lesser, lessier* to leave — more at LEASE] *archaic* **:** the dung of a beast of prey

**less·est** \ˈlesəst\ *adj* [superl. of ¹*less*] *now dial* **:** LEAST

**les·sing·ite** \ˈlesiŋ,īt\ *n* -s [Russ *lessingit*, fr. Frantz Yulievich Levinson-*Lessing*, 20th cent. Russ. professor + Russ *-it* -ite] **:** a mineral $Ca_2Ce_4Si_3O_{13}(OH)_2(?)$ consisting of a silicate of calcium and cerium

**less·ness** *n* -ES **:** the quality or state of being less **:** INFERIORITY

¹**les·son** \ˈlesᵊn\ *n* -s [ME *lessoun*, fr. OF *leçon, lecon* lesson, reading, fr. LL *lection-, lectio*, fr. L, act of reading, fr. *lectus* (past part. of *legere* to read) + *-ion-, -io* -ion — more at LEGEND] **1 :** a portion of Scripture read for instruction as part of a worship service ⟨here endeth the first ~⟩ **2 a :** a piece of instruction **:** TEACHING ⟨the ~ intended by an author —G.B. Shaw⟩ ⟨the second of the great ~s of Quakerism . . . respect for the individual —H.S.Canby⟩; *specif* **:** a reading or exercise assigned to a pupil as part of his schoolwork ⟨get out your books and study your ~s⟩ ⟨~s to be got and recited —H.C. McKown⟩ **b :** a fact, principle, or technique learned or to be learned by study or experience ⟨many revealing ~s of past experience have been overlooked —Bruce Payne⟩ ⟨the ~s of the flood also emphasize . . . that the landward side of the banks needs protection —J.A.Steers⟩ ⟨teach a horse his ~s —Ephraim Chambers⟩ **3 a :** one of the segments into which a course of instruction is divided ⟨this textbook presents the material in 20 ~s⟩; *specif* **:** a period of formal instruction devoted to a single subject and usu. lasting no more than an hour ⟨music ~⟩ ⟨French ~⟩ ⟨finished her ~s with the governess —Audrey Barker⟩ **b :** an object or event from which knowledge may be derived **:** instructive example ⟨the ~ of Coventry should be accepted by . . . every American city that is at all vulnerable to enemy air raids —*Training Manual for Auxiliary Firemen*⟩ ⟨he stands, a ~ to us in integrity —C.D.Lewis⟩; *specif* **:** a rebuke or punishment intended to forestall the repetition of an offense ⟨sent the culprit to the office and let the principal give him a ~⟩ **4 a** *obs* **:** an instrumental piece or set of pieces esp. for a keyboard instrument — compare SUITE 2b **b :** an exercise or study serving to advance musical knowledge or proficiency

²**lesson** \ˈ"\ *vt* **lessoned; lessoned; lessoning** \-s(ə)niŋ\ **lessons 1 :** to give a lesson to **:** INSTRUCT ⟨~*ed* his contemporaries in the platitudes —Clement Wood⟩ **2 :** LECTURE, REBUKE, PUNISH ⟨I'll ~ you, you madman —Mary Johnston⟩

**les·so·nia** \leˈsōnēə\ *n, cap* [NL, fr. R. P. *Lesson* †1849 Fr. naval pharmacist + NL *-ia*] **:** a genus (the type of the family Lessoniaceae) of large brown algae (order Laminariales) that resemble full-grown palm trees and occur chiefly in offshore waters of the southern Pacific

**les·sor** \ˈleˌsȯ(ə)r, -ō(ə), ˌ=ˈ=\ *n* -s [ME *lessour*, fr. AF, fr. *lesser* to lease + *-our* -or — more at LEASE (let)] **1 :** one that surrenders possession of real estate under a lease (as a written lease) **:** a grantor of a leasehold estate **2 :** a bailor under a bailment agreement providing a rental for personal property

**less–than–carload** *adj* **:** insufficient in weight to fill a freight car and therefore not qualifying for a carload rate — abbr. *LCL*

**less–than–truckload** *adj* **:** insufficient in weight to make a minimum truckload — abbr. *LTL*

¹**lest** \ˈlest\ *conj* [ME *the leste, leste, lest*, fr. OE *thȳ lǣs the*, fr. *thȳ* (instrumental of *thæt* this, that, which) + *lǣs*, adj., less + *the*, relative particle — more at THAT, LESS] **1 :** for fear that **:** so that (one) should not ⟨prefer a man who acts decisively . . . rather than one who hesitates ~ he be guilty of imprudence —C.B.Kelland⟩ **2 :** THAT — used after an expression denoting fear to introduce the cause of apprehension ⟨live in daily apprehension ~ the wholesome sons and daughters whom they commit to a college return to them as brazen fools —W.L. Sullivan⟩

²**lest** \ˈ"\ *archaic var of* LEAST

**les·to·bi·o·sis** \ˌlestō,bīˈōsəs\ *n, pl* **lestobio·ses** \-ō,sēz\ [NL, fr. Gk *lēistēs* robber + NL *-biosis;* akin to L *lucrum* gain, profit — more at LUCRE] **:** cleptobiosis in which covert thievery replaces aggressive plundering

**les·to·bi·ot·ic** \ˌ=ˌ=bīˈäd·ik\ *adj* [fr. NL *lestobiosis*, after such pairs as NL *hypnosis:* E *hypnotic*] **:** of, relating to, or marked by lestobiosis

**les·to·don** \ˈlestəˌdän\ *n* [NL, fr. Gk *lēistēs* robber + NL *-odon*] **:** a genus of large So. American Pleistocene ground sloths

**le·su** \ˈlā(ˌ)sü\ *n, pl* **lesu** *or* **lesus** *usu cap* **1 a :** a people inhabiting New Ireland **b :** a member of such people **2 :** the Austronesian language of the Lesu people

¹**let** \ˈlet, *usu* -ed·+V\ *vt* **letted; letted** *or* **let; letting; lets** [ME *letten*, fr. OE *lettan* to delay, hinder; akin to OS *lettian* to hinder, MD *letten* to hinder, OHG *lezzen* to delay, hurt, ON *letja* to hold back, Goth *latjan;* causative-denominatives fr. the stem of E *late*] *archaic* **:** HINDER, IMPEDE, PREVENT ⟨by Heaven! I'll make a ghost of him that ~s me —Shak.⟩

²**let** \ˈ"\ *n* -s [ME *lette, lett, let*, fr. *letten* to let (hinder)] **1 :** something that prevents or impedes **:** OBSTRUCTION ⟨free to inquire without ~ or hindrance —B.G.Gallagher⟩ ⟨the task of a socialist movement to challenge without ~ the moral values of society —Lloyd Harrington⟩ **2 :** a stroke, point, or service esp. in racket and net games that does not count and must be replayed

³**let** \ˈ"; *in rapid speech the* t *may be lost before* "me" & "'s"\ *vb* **let; let; letting; lets** [ME *leten, lǣten*, fr. OE *lǣtan;* akin to OFris *lēta* to let, permit, OS *lātan*, MD *laten*, OHG *lāzzan*, ON *lāta*, Goth *letan* to let, permit, Gk *lēdein* to be tired, L *lassus* weary, tired, *lenis* soft, mild, Lith *leisti* to let; basic meaning: to let go] *vt* **1 :** MAKE, CAUSE ⟨the king . . . ~ me know that when and if that story was told he would do the telling himself —John Barkham⟩ ⟨doctor, ~ me know the worst⟩ ⟨he ~ it be known that he might consider parting with his Stradivarius⟩ **2 a** *chiefly Brit* **:** RENT, LEASE ⟨she ~ him the rooms at once —Margaret Kennedy⟩ ⟨~ the premises⟩ ⟨the island is now ~ as grazings —A.A.MacGregor⟩ — often used with *off* or *out* ⟨working part of their land themselves and *letting* off the rest —Alfons Dopsch⟩ ⟨small holdings which were ~ out on long leases by the crown —Alan Edwards⟩ **b :** to award or assign esp. after asking for bids or proposals ⟨bids are opened before the contract is ~ —T.W. Arnold⟩ ⟨another contract for some 300 miles will be ~ —*Wall Street Jour.*⟩ ⟨~ one's timber rights⟩ — often used with *out* ⟨work was ~ out to be done in the homes —*Amer. Guide Series: N.H.*⟩ **3 a** *chiefly dial* **:** to allow to remain **:** leave behind ⟨I'll give him my commission, to ~ him there a month —Shak.⟩ **b** *obs* **:** to surrender completely **:** RELINQUISH ⟨to her mother Nature all her care she ~s —Edmund Spenser⟩ **4 a :** to give opportunity to or fail to prevent ⟨jagged holes . . . ~ him see the mountains —Paul Bartlett⟩ ⟨throw them together . . . and ~ dialogue and incident evolve —Richard Garnett †1906⟩ ⟨live and ~ live⟩ ⟨very particular not to ~ his beasts stray —F.D.Smith & Barbara Wilcox⟩ ⟨~s himself be pushed around —Margaret Mead⟩ **b** (1) — used in the imperative to introduce a request or proposal ⟨~ us pray⟩ ⟨~ not the reader be frightened away by a first impression —William Barrett⟩ ⟨at the outset, ~ it be acknowledged —D.C.Buchanan⟩ ⟨~ sleeping dogs lie⟩ (2) — used esp. in Ireland as an intensive auxiliary to form the second person imperative ⟨~ you go along with her, stranger —J.M.Synge⟩ **c** — used imperatively as an auxiliary to express a warning ⟨~ one drama hit the air waves with this dialogue . . . and the wires will be clogged by protests —Jessamyn West⟩ ⟨~ him set foot on my property and I'll have him arrested⟩ ⟨just ~ him try⟩ **5 :** to free from confinement **:** RELEASE, SPILL ⟨consult you about *letting* the water from the great pond —E.G.Bulwer-Lytton⟩ ⟨received no American aid . . . so he must attempt to prolong the emotion *letting* —*New Republic*⟩ ⟨fight until their blood is all ~ —Winston Churchill⟩ — used with *off* or *out* ⟨got mad and ~ off steam by kicking the dog⟩ ⟨~ out a scream⟩ **6 :** to facilitate the passage of by eliminating a restraint **:** allow to go **:** permit to enter, pass, or leave ⟨he ~ the lid back down slowly —W.F.Davis⟩ ⟨the pickets would not ~ them through⟩ ⟨who ~ the cat in⟩ ⟨the warden ~s the prisoner out⟩ ⟨~s the car into high gear —F.L.Allen⟩ ⟨~s the slack out⟩ ⟨~ himself quietly out the bedroom window⟩ ⟨~ herself down light and easy, for that chair . . . was frail —Dorothy C. Fisher⟩ **7 :** to deliver on attestation **:** ADMIT ⟨~ to bail⟩ **8** *obs* **:** to refrain or abstain from ⟨did not ~ to praise the clear unmatched red and white —Shak.⟩ **~** *vi* **1** *chiefly Brit* **:** to become rented or leased ⟨the flat ~s for £35 a month⟩ **2 :** to become awarded to a contractor ⟨blueprints of . . . projects advertised for *letting* —*U.S.Code*⟩

**syn** LET, ALLOW, PERMIT, SUFFER, LEAVE mean to refrain from preventing. LET is less formal than PERMIT or ALLOW ⟨*let* him go⟩ ⟨wanted to go but his parents would not *let* him⟩ and besides signifying, at one extreme, a positive giving of permission can, at the other, signify failure to prevent because of neglect, inability, or inaction ⟨to *let* the cold in by forgetting to close a door⟩ ⟨tremble so that he *let* the plate fall from his hands⟩ ⟨countries that *let* themselves become dependent on the labor of other countries —G.B.Shaw⟩ ALLOW and PERMIT both imply more strongly than the comparable use of LET the power or authority to prohibit or prevent or to refrain from prohibiting or preventing. ALLOW usu. implies a forbearing to prohibit; PERMIT implies a more express willing or acquiescing ⟨nothing is *permitted*, everything is *allowed*⟩ ⟨under absentee ownership the machinery was *allowed* to become obsolescent —*Amer. Guide Series: N.H.*⟩ ⟨*allow* a child to go out without his overcoat⟩ ⟨would have liked to have begun the study of art, but family finances did not *permit* this —*Current Biog.*⟩ ⟨*permits* his cattle to graze on the new pasture in such numbers that the feed is quickly used up —P.E.James⟩ SUFFER is often but rather bookishly interchangeable with ALLOW in its narrowest sense ⟨*suffer* little children to come unto me —Lk 18:16 (AV)⟩ but more usu. implies indifference or reluctance ⟨would the state *suffer* its foundation to be destroyed —Henry Adams⟩ ⟨*suffered* herself to be led to the tiny enclosure —S.E. White⟩ LEAVE when used in this sense implies strongly a noninterference ⟨*leave* them to determine their own fates⟩ ⟨the parents *left* the children free to come and go as they pleased⟩ ⟨his principle was to choose competent lieutenants, and then to *leave* them to work without hampering interference —*Irish Digest*⟩ — **let alone 1 :** to say nothing of **:** not to mention ⟨but does he have the boldness, *let alone* the skill, of his own convictions —*New Republic*⟩ ⟨no provision for the health of servants, *let alone* for their comfort —O.S.J.Gogarty⟩ **2 a :** to refrain from interfering with **:** leave undisturbed ⟨in the spring or summer, *let* nests *alone* —*Boy Scout Handbook*⟩ ⟨the government . . . promised to *let* them *alone* in part of the Everglades —Marjory S. Douglas⟩ ⟨could not *let* well enough *alone* —L.O.Coxe⟩ — often used as an imperative ⟨*let* it *alone;* you'll break it⟩ **b :** to leave to oneself ⟨the red-faced boy wanted nothing so much as to be *let alone*⟩ ⟨her mother told her to *let* the frightened kitten *alone*⟩ **3 :** to exclude from consideration ⟨the . . . party is inclined to *let* nationalization pretty well *alone* —Alzada Comstock⟩ — **let be :** to let alone **:** leave untouched — **let fly 1 :** to hurl with force **:** THROW, SHOOT ⟨warriors *let fly* their spears —Tom Marvel⟩ ⟨*let fly* two torpedoes —E.L.Beach⟩ **2 :** to release suddenly (the sheets of a sail) so as to spill wind **3 a :** to hurl an object (as a projectile) ⟨*let fly* with a tremendous pass —G.S.Halas⟩ ⟨infuriated householders have been known to *let fly* at them with shotguns —Gerald Priestland⟩ **b :** to loose an arrow **4 :** to give unrestrained expression to an emotion ⟨*let fly* with some observations that shook space enthusiasts —*Time*⟩ ⟨she was *letting fly* on the trombone —*Irish Digest*⟩ — **let go 1 a :** to cast off or drop ⟨the mooring lines are *let go* —*Lamp*⟩ ⟨more windjammers *let go* their anchors on the reef —Marjory S. Douglas⟩ **b :** to release one's hold on or break away from ⟨he *let go* the ladder and jumped —K.M.Dodson⟩ ⟨tons of riverbank *let go* . . . into the stream —S.H.Adams⟩ **c :** to cease to pay attention to **:** dismiss from one's mind ⟨had not made a career . . . of being young, but she had not *let* herself *go*, either —Hamilton Basso⟩ ⟨did the best he could, and *let* it *go* at that⟩ **d :** to dismiss from employment **:** FIRE ⟨couldn't do the work so they had to *let* him *go*⟩ **2 :** to give out **:** EMIT ⟨the great whistle *let go* a defiant blast —Frederick Way⟩ **3 a :** to abandon self-restraint **:** give uninhibited expression to impulses or emotions **:** cut loose ⟨one of those actors who are too anxious to be thought gentlemen to *let* themselves *go* —T.C.Worsley⟩ ⟨*let* himself *go* in his letters as though he were talking to his correspondent —*Atlantic*⟩ ⟨in Port Royal they *let go* with a roar after the long watches at sea —H.E.Rieseberg⟩ ⟨once home, she thought, . . . she could really *let go* —Nancy Hale⟩ **b :** to discharge matter or wind from the body **4 a :** to relax one's hold ⟨the dog had him by the throat and wouldn't *let go*⟩ **b :** to release a line or drop anchor ⟨at the command "*let go* and haul" we came smartly about on a new tack⟩ ⟨found a good anchorage in the lagoon and *let go*⟩ **5 :** to let fly ⟨*Punch let go* with a serial diatribe —*Saturday Rev.*⟩ — **let into :** to let in ⟨have large windows *let into* most of the walls —Fay King⟩ ⟨flower beds *let into* the asphalt —Elizabeth Taylor⟩ ⟨stranger walked in, asked to be *let into* the game —*Amer. Guide Series: Md.*⟩ — **let loose 1 a :** to turn loose or free from restraint **:** let go **:** LIBERATE ⟨floating mines, evidently *let loose* by French patrols —P.W. Thompson⟩ ⟨an entomologist who was *let loose* on the same small area —C.W.M.Swithinbank⟩ ⟨the rancors *let loose* by war —J.D.Hicks⟩ **b :** to give rise to **:** set off ⟨the great success of the pioneer lines *let loose* a torrent of speculative buying —O.S.Nock⟩ **2 :** to let fly ⟨I do now *let loose* my opinion —Shak.⟩ ⟨*let loose* a torrent of invective —Albert Dasnoy⟩ ⟨*let loose* a tremendous outburst of laughter —Walter O'Meara⟩ ⟨a machine gun *let loose* on the man —Mack Morriss⟩; *specif* **:** to pour down rain ⟨get the shocks into the stack before the skies *let loose* —Irving Dilliard⟩ **3 :** to throw off restraint **:** let go **:** give way ⟨the friction clutch would *let loose* at its appointed tension —F.J.Haskin⟩ — **let on 1 a :** to let know **:** DISCLOSE, REVEAL ⟨don't you *let on* I wasn't there —Ellen Glasgow⟩ **b :** to give evidence of **:** SHOW, BETRAY ⟨they went on at it without *letting on* to notice —H.L.Davis⟩ **c :** SUGGEST, IMPLY, INSINUATE ⟨tries to *let on* that the whole country is rising —Sinclair Lewis⟩ **2 :** to give the appearance of **:** PRETEND ⟨wasn't as put out as he *let on* to be —Robert Frost⟩ ⟨*let on* like he didn't hear a word they said —Vance Randolph⟩ — **let one have it :** to subject to vigorous assault ⟨hauled back and *let him have it* full in the solar plexus⟩ ⟨held her tongue until the company left and then she really *let him have it*⟩; *specif* **:** SHOOT ⟨took careful aim and *let him have it* right between the eyes⟩ ⟨the musketeers advanced to within sixty paces of the enemy and then *let them have it* —Tom Wintringham⟩ — **let slide :** to cease to pay attention to **:** let go — **let slip :** to allow to escape; *esp* **:** to impart (information) inadvertently ⟨*let slip* one day that he had once been married —Nevil Shute⟩ — **let the cat out of the bag :** to reveal hitherto undisclosed information ⟨his vacation plans were a secret but he *let the cat out of the bag* by purchasing deep-sea fishing tackle⟩

⁴**let** \ˈ"\ *n* -s [³*let*] *Brit* **1 a :** an act of leasing or renting **b :** LEASE **2 :** a rented house or apartment

**-let** \lət, *usu* -əd·+V\ *n suffix* -s [ME *-let, -lette*, fr. MF *-elet*, fr. OF, fr. *-el* + *-et* (dim. suffix)] **1 :** small one ⟨book*let*⟩ ⟨cover*let*⟩ ⟨stream*let*⟩ **2 :** article worn on — in names of articles of dress ⟨ank*let*⟩ ⟨wrist*let*⟩

**let bug** *or* **let dab** *vi* [prob. fr. ³*let* + *bug* (origin unknown) or *dab*] *Scot* **:** to disclose information — usu. used with a negative ⟨didna mean to *let bug* about it —J.J.Bell⟩

¹**letch** \ˈlech\ *n* -ES [ME *lache, leche* stream flowing through boggy land, bog (attested in place names), fr. OE *læcc, lecc*, fr. *leccan* to wet, moisten — more at LEAK] *dial Brit* **:** a muddy ditch or pool **:** BOG, SWAMP

²**letch** \ˈ"\ *n* -ES [perh. back-formation fr. *letcher*, alter. of *lecher*] **:** CRAVING ⟨full of politics and a ~ for fishing —W.A. White⟩; *specif* **:** sexual desire ⟨develops a ~ for an attractive Circassian lady —Anthony West⟩

**let down** *vt* **1 a :** to allow to descend gradually **:** LOWER ⟨*let* the wagons *down* the steep slope by means of ropes snubbed around trees —G.R.Stewart⟩ **b** (1) **:** to lengthen (a garment) by releasing a fold of material ⟨*let down* a skirt⟩ (2) **:** to reduce the amount of (a fold) so as to lengthen a garment ⟨*let* a hem *down*⟩ **c :** to release (formed milk secretion) within the udder **2 a :** to fail to support **:** desert in a moment of need **:** FORSAKE, BETRAY ⟨peasants who had *let down* the revolutionary cause —*Times Lit. Supp.*⟩ ⟨senators felt that they had been *let down* by their own administration —Harry Conn⟩ ⟨will not *let* each other *down* at the conference table any more than we did on the battlefield —R.M.Makins⟩ **b :** to fall short of the expectations of **:** go back on a promise to **:** DISAPPOINT, FAIL ⟨the plot is good but the end *lets* you *down*⟩ ⟨The White mountains wouldn't *let* me *down* —G.M. Smith⟩ ⟨had two appointments with the crown prince and *let* him *down* on both occasions —George Mikes⟩ ⟨sorry for the kid, and tried to *let* him *down* easy —Dorothy C. Fisher⟩ **3 :** to thin out **:** DILUTE: as **a :** to reduce the intensity of (a colored pigment) by the addition of colorless pigment **b :** to reduce the viscosity of (a paint or varnish) by adding thinner **4 a :** to put (a horse) out of action by having a sinew broken **b :** to hang low and straight — used of the posterior parts of an animal's body ⟨the hocks are well *let down*⟩ ⟨a sow well *let down* in the hams⟩ **c :** to reduce the weight of (an animal in show condition) **:** make less fat ⟨highly fitted cattle . . . may have to be *let down* carefully to develop into useful breeders —W.A.Cochell⟩ **~** *vi* **1 :** to slacken exertion or mental tension **:** RELAX ⟨all through the crisis she never once *let down*⟩ **2 a :** to bring an airplane down in a glide esp. as a prelude to landing it ⟨throttle back . . . until you're *letting down* about 200 feet a minute —J.N.Bell⟩ **b :** to come down gradually esp. for a landing ⟨the plane *let down* through heavy overcast —*Time*⟩

¹**letdown** \ˈ=ˌ=\ *n* [*let down*] **1 a :** a source or mood of mental depression **:** DISCOURAGEMENT, DISAPPOINTMENT ⟨the enterprise . . . has been a big ~ to those of us who had high hopes for it —E.R.Bentley⟩ ⟨the balance of the collection is a sad ~ —J.F.McComas⟩ ⟨came home . . . with a vague feeling of ~ about Italian art —R.M.Coates⟩ **b :** a slackening of effort **:** RELAXATION, DEFECTION ⟨the sudden ~ from discipline —Dixon Wecter⟩ ⟨at that time of day, a general air of ~ hung over the kitchen —Joseph Wechsberg⟩; *specif* **:** a lapse from high moral standards ⟨how hard as stone people are about other folks' ~s —Dorothy C. Fisher⟩ **2 :** a drop in amount or volume **:** DECLINE, SLUMP ⟨an amazing buying rush was resumed after a brief ~ —*N.Y.Times*⟩ ⟨the ~ in steel production . . . brought moderate declines in sales —*Newsweek*⟩ ⟨a normal seasonal decline is expected but no general business ~ is in sight⟩ **3 :** the descent of an airplane from cruising altitude to the point at which a landing approach is begun ⟨cross-country flying and instrument ~s at strange airfields —*Crowsnest*⟩ **4** *usu* **let–down** \ˈ"\ **:** a physiological response of a lactating mammal to suckling or allied stimuli whereby increased intramammary pressure forces previously secreted milk from the acini and finer tubules into the main collecting ducts whence it can be drawn through the nipple

²**letdown** \ˈ"\ *adj* **1 :** characterized by mental lassitude **:** DEPRESSED, DISPIRITED ⟨the ~ feeling that comes with emptying ashtrays after a party⟩ **2 :** of or relating to the gradual descent of an airplane ⟨~ procedure⟩ ⟨the first ~ point after Honolulu —*Sperryscope*⟩

¹**le·thal** \ˈlēthəl\ *adj* [L *lethalis, letalis*, fr. *letum* death + *-alis* -al; prob. akin to L *lenis* soft, mild — more at LET] **1** *archaic* **:** of or relating to spiritual death ⟨discoursing of sinners and their ~ end —Charles Reade⟩ **2 a :** of, relating to, or causing death ⟨the two convicted men will soon enter the ~ chamber —William Mayer⟩ ⟨in mice the mean ~ dose was more than twice as large as the mean paralyzing dose —*Science*⟩ ⟨the ~ fire that destroyed the building and all its occupants⟩ **b :** capable of causing death **:** DEADLY ⟨wished I had a gun or some ~ weapon, that I might destroy him —Bram Stoker⟩ ⟨prohibits the transportation in interstate . . . commerce of ~ munitions —*U.S.Code*⟩ ⟨the increasing quantity of ~ carbon monoxide poured into the air by the internal-combustion motor —Lewis Mumford⟩ ⟨gathering edible mushrooms . . . is a pleasant but potentially ~ pastime —*Pfizer Spectrum*⟩ **3 :** causing damage or destruction **:** DEVASTATING ⟨showed a ~ skill in his dissection of the . . . book —*Times Lit. Supp.*⟩ ⟨a ~ attack by the opposition caused him to resign⟩ ⟨used the ~ veto ten times to block action in the security council —*Time*⟩ **syn** see DEADLY

²**lethal** \ˈ"\ *n* -s **1 :** a lethal substance **2 a :** an abnormality of genetic origin causing the death of the organism possessing it usu. before maturity **b :** LETHAL GENE

**lethal gene** *or* **lethal factor** *n* [prob. trans. of F *gène létal* or *facteur létal*] **:** a gene that in some (as homozygous) conditions may prevent development or cause the death of an organism or its germ cells

**le·thal·i·ty** \lēˈthaləd·ē\ *n* -ES **:** the quality or state of being lethal **:** DEADLINESS

**le·thal·ly** \ˈlēthəlē, -li\ *adv* **:** in a deadly manner ⟨this remarkable document . . . was a ~ dull volume —R.A.Billington⟩

**le·thar·gic** \ləˈthärjik, leˈ-, -thäj-, -jēk\ *adj* [prob. fr. MF *lethargique*, fr. L *lethargicus*, fr. Gk *lēthargikos*, fr. *lēthargos* lethargy + *-ikos* -ic] **1 a :** of, relating to, or characterized by lethargy **:** SLOW-MOVING, SLUGGISH ⟨bullfrogs . . . were quite ~ after storage —A.C.Giese⟩ ⟨the market . . . was even more ~ than they indicated —*Fortune*⟩ ⟨the ~ sullen power of the ocean —Norman Mailer⟩ **b :** LISTLESS, INDIFFERENT, APATHETIC, DULL ⟨the weak and ~ government of Spain —Bernard DeVoto⟩ ⟨a ~ entrepreneur in the egg business —Roger Eddy⟩ **2 :** causing lethargy **:** SOPORIFIC ⟨yielded to the ~ music and fell asleep⟩

**syn** LETHARGIC, SLUGGISH, TORPID, COMATOSE: LETHARGIC implies a state of sleepiness or drowsiness that makes for slowness in reaction, responses, or movements and that may be constitutional, temporary, or induced by disease or injury ⟨a *lethargic* effect to compare somewhat with the effect of insulin —*Jour. of Nervous and Mental Diseases*⟩ ⟨she did look — not exactly sleepy, but *lethargic*, relaxed. All her movements were peculiarly slow —Margery Sharp⟩ ⟨a people grown *lethargic* from economic abundance —V.L.Parrington⟩ SLUGGISH describes a similar state but often implies criticism ⟨*sluggish* transportation⟩ ⟨*sluggish* pond⟩ ⟨*sluggish* digestion⟩ ⟨England has become unenterprising and *sluggish* because England has been so prosperous and comfortable —H.G. Wells⟩ ⟨we are apt to scorn our neighbor because his rate of motion is faster or more *sluggish* than our own —A.L.Guérard⟩ TORPID and COMATOSE both imply an aberration, more or less lasting, from the normal; TORPID literally implies the numb or benumbed state of a hibernating animal, but in its more common extended sense it implies a lack of energy, responsiveness, or vigor commonly associated with healthy, active individuals ⟨Oxford was *torpid* also, droning along in its eighteenth-century grooves —Van Wyck Brooks⟩ ⟨it would be a *torpid* and spiritless reader . . . who would pass by everything sensational —F.L.Mott⟩ ⟨as a reviver of the half-dead, or the merely *torpid*, Mencken's only rival . . . was Bernard Shaw —DeLancey Ferguson⟩ COMATOSE literally suggests the state of profound insensibility of a coma ⟨the almost *comatose* condition which had first intervened never developed into a fatal diabetic coma —Havelock Ellis⟩; in extended use COMATOSE implies immobility, stagnation, extreme lethargy, often due to a paralyzing external force ⟨the tradition of art remained *comatose*. Here and there a genius appeared and wrestled with the coils of convention —Clive Bell⟩

**le·thar·gi·cal·ly** \-jək(ə)lē, -jēk-, -li\ *adv* : in a lethargic manner : SLUGGISHLY, APATHETICALLY

**lethargic encephalitis** *n* : ENCEPHALITIS LETHARGICA

**leth·ar·gize** \'lethə(r),jīz\ *vt* -ED/-ING/-S *archaic* : to make lethargic : BENUMB

**¹leth·ar·gy** \'lethə(r)jē, -ji\ *n* -ES [alter. (influenced by LL *lethargia*) of ME *litargie*, fr. MF or ML; MF *litargie*, fr. ML *litargia*, *lethargia*, fr. LL *lethargia*, fr. Gk *lēthargia*, fr. *lēthargos* lethargy (fr. *lēthē* forgetfulness) + -*ia* -y] **1** *archaic* : a comatose torpor : abnormal drowsiness ⟨seized with a ~, in which he continued till Friday evening, and then expired, much lamented —*Boston Gazette*⟩ **2** : the quality or state of being lazy or indifferent : LASSITUDE, APATHY ⟨the hot moist air of the tropics spreads a feeling of ~ and indolence over everything —G.H.Reed b. 1887⟩ ⟨in spite of his urgent pleas . . . for supplies and men a disheartening ~ was displayed —J.C.Fitzpatrick⟩ ⟨an ancient people, sunk in ~ and refusing to be inspired —Joseph Frank⟩

**²lethargy** \"\ *vt* -ED/-ING/-ES *archaic* : LETHARGIZE ⟨his discernings are *lethargied* —Shak.⟩

**le·the** \'lē(,)thē\ *n* -S [L, fr. Gk *lēthē*] : OBLIVION, FORGETFULNESS ⟨severances of soul for which there is neither balm nor ~ —W.R.Greg⟩

**le·the·an** \'lēthēən, lə'th-,lē'th-\ *adj, usu cap* [L *Lethaeus* of Lethe, Lethean (fr. Gk *lēthaios*, fr. *Lēthē* Lethe, place of oblivion in the lower world, fr. *lēthē* forgetfulness) + E -*an*; akin to Gk *lanthanesthai* to forget, *lanthanein* to escape notice — more at LATENT] : of, relating to, or causing forgetfulness ⟨the *Lethean* sensuousness of Keats —Wylie Sypher⟩

**lethied** *adj* [alter. of *Lethe* + E -*ed*] *obs* : LETHEAN

**le·thif·er·ous** \(')lē¦thif(ə)rəs\ *adj* [L *lethifer*, *letifer* lethiferous (fr. *letum* death + -*fer* -ferous) + E -*ous* — more at LETHAL] *archaic* : LETHAL

**le·thoc·er·us** \lə'thäsərəs\ *n, cap* [NL, fr. *letho-* (fr. Gk *lētho-*, fr. *lēthē* forgetfulness) + -*cerus*] : a genus of very large predaceous aquatic bugs (family Belostomatidae) — compare GIANT WATER BUG

**le·thri·nus** \lə'thrīnəs\ *n, cap* [NL] : a genus (the type of the family Lethrinidae) of percoid fishes that are related to those of the family Sparidae from which they are distinguished by possession of a long scaleless snout, are widely distributed in warm southern seas, and include several important food fishes and others which are regarded as dangerously toxic

**let in** *vt* **1** : to insert or embed in (a surface) ⟨*lets in* diagonal sheathing at each corner of the house⟩ **2** : to involve or commit unfavorably ⟨the provisions . . . could still *let* us *in* for trouble —Elmer Davis⟩ ⟨smiled at all her schemes, little dreaming that . . . she was *letting* him *in* for some £20,000 —Elizabeth Montizambert⟩ **3** : to share information with or allow to participate ⟨learned a lot more . . . and I'll *let* you *in* on it —Rex Ingamells⟩

**let-in** \'≈,≈\ *adj* [*let in*] : shortened and widened by the cutting and sewing in of additional pieces — used of pelts

**let off** *vt* **1 a** : to touch off : IGNITE, EXPLODE ⟨felt like a boy who wanted to *let off* crackers —I.L.Idriess⟩ ⟨explosions produced by *letting off* small charges of dynamite backstage —W. L. Gresham⟩; *specif* : FIRE ⟨*let off* their guns at British ships —G.F.Hudson⟩ **b** : to give vent to : get off ⟨before I left I *let off* a dissent —O.W.Holmes †1935⟩ **2 a** : to release from something, esp. a penalty : PARDON, EXCUSE ⟨the offender was *let off* with a severe reprimand —Harvey Graham⟩ ⟨you have promised to sing one song . . . and I cannot *let* you *off* —W.H.Hudson †1922⟩ **b** : to release from duty ⟨had *let* the men *off* for the last quarter of the day —Mary Austin⟩ **3** : to neglect an opportunity to dismiss or score against (an opponent)

**let-off** \'≈,≈\ *n* -S [*let off*] **1** : an act or instance of letting off ⟨spend the rest of his life in gaol, and a damned lucky *let-off* it is for him —Ngaio Marsh⟩; *specif* : neglect of a chance to dismiss or score against an opponent **2 a** : a device for releasing a strand (as yarn from a warp beam) to a loom at a regulated tension **b** : the release of the cocked hammer of a gun by the sear in firing **c** : the discontinuance of contact between an escape wheel tooth and a pallet in a watch

**let on** *vi* **1 a** : to make acknowledgment : ADMIT ⟨knew what the matter was but never *let on*⟩ **b** : to reveal one's presence ⟨the others were up in the tree house all the time and didn't *let on* —Agnes N. Keith⟩ **2** : to repeat confidential information : TATTLE ⟨the jealous woman has *let on* to an old bum —Charlotte Armstrong⟩ **3** : PRETEND ⟨ain't half as sick as she *lets on* —Edna Ferber⟩

**let-on** \'≈,≈\ *n* -S [*let on*] *Scot* : SHAM

**¹let out** *vt* **1** *chiefly Brit* : to make known : REVEAL ⟨never *let out* his plans —Lord Dunsany⟩ **2 a** : to extend in dimension : LOOSEN; *esp* : to release (extra material) so as to enlarge a garment ⟨the man who *lets out* the seams in my clothing —J.A. Maxwell⟩ **b** : to cut (a pelt) in strips and reassemble into a longer narrower piece with better color and texture — compare TAPE 3 **3** *archaic* : to furnish for temporary use at a fee : LOAN ⟨*let out* their coin upon large interest —Shak.⟩ ⟨a girl who *let out* chairs for hire —J.M.Jephson & L.A.Reeve⟩ **4 a** : to release from further responsibility ⟨the old curmudgeon has found a new scapegoat and that *lets* me *out*⟩ **b** : to release from an obligation : let off ⟨Japan was to be . . . *let out* of paying reparations —*Time*⟩ **5 a** : to release from restraint : allow to gather speed ⟨*let* the car *out* a bit —Steve McNeil⟩ **b** : to let go : FIRE ⟨some workers without tenure guarantee will probably be *let out* —Henry Giniger⟩ ~ *vi* **1** : to lash out **2** : to conclude a session or performance : turn loose a group of people : break up ⟨waiting for school to *let out* —B.A.Williams⟩ ⟨after the theatres *let out*, a . . . throng trooped in for midnight supper —Robert Shaplen⟩

**²let out** \'≈,≈\ *n* -S *chiefly Irish* : a lavish entertainment

**let-out** \(')≈¦≈\ *adj* [¹*let out*] *of furs* : lengthened by letting-out

**let·o·vic·ite** \,led·ə'vi,sīt\ *n* -S [G *letovicit*, fr. *Letovice*, Czechoslovakia, its locality + G -*it* -ite] : a mineral $(NH_4)_3H(SO_4)_2$ consisting of an acid ammonium sulfate

**lets** *pres 3d sing of* LET, *pl of* LET

**let's** \(')lets, *when not followed by a pause often* (,)les *in rapid speech*\ [by contr.] : let us

**lett** \'let, *usu* -ed·+V\ *n* -S *usu cap* [G *Lette*, fr. Latvian *Latvi*] **1 a** : a people closely related to the Lithuanians and mainly inhabiting Latvia **b** : a member of such people **2** : LATVIAN 2

**let·ta·ble** \'led·əbəl, -etəb-\ *adj* [³*let* + -*able*] *chiefly Brit* : capable of being rented or leased

**letted** *past of* LET

**¹let·ter** \'led·ə(r), -etə-\ *n* -S *often attrib* [ME *lettre*, *letter*, fr. OF *lettre*, fr. L *littera*, *litera* letter, *litterae*, pl., epistle, writing, literature; perh. akin to L *linere* to daub, smear — more at LIME] **1 a** : a conventional symbol usu. written or printed representing alone or in combination a simple or compound speech sound, constituting one of the units of an alphabet, and often including the arabic numbers — compare ACROPHONY, DACTYLOLOGY, SEMAPHORE **b letters** *pl* : ALPHABET ⟨teach a child his ~s⟩ **c** *obs* : ALLITERATION ⟨I will something affect the ~, for it argues facility —Shak.⟩ **2 a** : a written or printed message intended for the perusal only of the person or organization to whom it is addressed : MISSIVE ⟨a business ~ should preferably be typed⟩ **b** : such a message enclosed in an addressed envelope and usu. sealed ⟨a table on which were several ~s — evidently this was where mail was left for those in the house —Millen Brand⟩ **c** : an official communication conferring authority or status ⟨a ~ from the admiral admits him to the naval base⟩ ⟨~ of absolution⟩, conveying information or instructions ⟨circular ~ outlining requirements for admission⟩ ⟨pastoral ~ calling upon the people to resist —W.E.McManus⟩ ⟨his contribution to the book was a ~ from New York⟩, serving as an introduction ⟨asked her minister for a ~ to the new church⟩, or attesting to length, quality, or terms of employment ⟨service ~⟩ ⟨~ of recommendation⟩ ⟨~ of appointment⟩ **d** (1) *Roman & civil law* : RESCRIPT (2) : a written communication issued from a court in attestation of an appointment or status or rights or duties ⟨parliament is summoned by the king's . . . ~ issued out of chancery —T.E.May⟩ — usu. used in pl. ⟨~s of adoption⟩ ⟨~s of citizenship⟩ **3 letters** *pl but sing or pl in constr* **a** : literary expression : LITERATURE, BELLES LETTRES ⟨a polished novel which shows British ~s at its best —*Hunting's Monthly List*⟩ ⟨good ~s have some significance in the health of the state —Ezra Pound⟩ ⟨words exist before the art of ~s —John Dewey⟩ **b** : scholarly attainment : LEARNING ⟨man of ~s⟩ ⟨more a friend of ~s than a learned man himself —R.W.Southern⟩ **4** : the outward sense or significance : literal terms ⟨rigorous insistence on the ~ of the contract —Alvin Johnson⟩ ⟨a decision dealing with human beings cannot be based on the ~ of the law alone —F.M.Hechinger⟩ — opposed to *spirit* **5 a** : a single piece of type **b** : a style of type ⟨roman ~⟩ **c** : TYPE ⟨a font of body ~⟩; *esp* : a supply of type ⟨can't set it without any ~⟩ **6** : the initial of a school or college awarded to a student for achievement usu. in athletics ⟨a rugged physique that helped him win football and basketball ~s in college —Howard Rushmore⟩ — **to the letter** *adv* : to the minutest detail : METICULOUSLY ⟨followed his instructions *to the letter*⟩ ⟨seeing his bargains carried out *to the letter* —Norman Douglas⟩

**²letter** \"\ *vb* -ED/-ING/-S *vi* **1** *archaic* : to write or carry letters ⟨our people go backwards and forwards . . . ~*ing* and messaging —Charles Dickens⟩ **2** : to win a school letter for athletic prowess ⟨as a freshman he ~*ed* in football —Tom Siler⟩ ~ *vt* **1** : to set down in letters : PRINT ⟨few painters alive can ~ a respectable caption on a portrait —P.M.Hollister⟩ — often used with *out* ⟨streamers on which are ~*ed* out the names of historic battles —Elbridge Colby⟩ **2 a** : to mark with letters : INSCRIBE ⟨~ a poster⟩ ⟨~ a squad car⟩ **b** : to append letters to ⟨numbers were ~*ed* on all the books —Helen V. Samuelson⟩ ⟨twelve companies, ~*ed* from A to M, skipping J—W.H.Baumer⟩; *specif* : to impress alphabetical letters on (a page or book cover) near the fore edge parallel to the same letters of the thumb index

**³letter** \"\ *n* -S [³*let* + -*er*] *chiefly Brit* : one that rents or leases

**letter board** *n* : a board (as a sliding shelf in a rack) used for storage of standing type

**letter book** *n* : a book in which letters or copies of letters are kept esp. to provide a running account of a business or enterprise ⟨the general's *letter books* give an intimate picture of the campaign⟩

**letter box** *n* : MAILBOX; *esp* : a box provided by the post office for the deposit of letters and other first-class mail

letter box

**lettercard** \'≈≈,≈\ *n* [prob. trans. of F *carte-lettre*] : a postcard that folds and seals like a letter sheet with the message inside

**letter carrier** *n* : MAIL CARRIER

**letter case** *n* : a usu. folding leather case for carrying letters ⟨stuffing my watch, *letter case*, loose change and handkerchief into my pockets —W.J.Locke⟩

**letter drawer** *n* : a file drawer for letters usu. having a partition that can be moved back as correspondence accumulates

**let·tered** \'led·ə(r)d, -etə-\ *adj* [ME, fr. *letter* + -*ed*] **1 a** : possessed of learning : EDUCATED ⟨spread their translations before the ~ public —G.C.Sellery⟩ **b** : of, relating to, or characterized by learning : CULTURED ⟨a man of ~ tastes —Benjamin Disraeli⟩ **2** : inscribed with or as if with letters ⟨the walls of the lower grade schoolroom were covered with . . . ~ statements —Oliver LaFarge⟩ ⟨~ tortoise⟩ **3** : consisting of letters ⟨~ cipher⟩

**let·ter·er** \'led·ərə(r), -etə-\ *n* -S : one that letters: as **a** : a commercial artist who does lettering **b** : a craftsman who paints company names or other lettering on commercial vehicles **c** : an artisan who cuts incised or raised letters and designs on monumental stones **d** : a craftsman who copies the magnified outlines of lead type as patterns for steel type

**letterer-siwe disease** \'led·ərə(r)'zēvə-\ *n, usu cap L&S* [after Erich *Letterer* b1895 Ger. pathologist and Sture A. *Siwe* b1897 pediatrician and professor in Sweden, who first described it] : an acute disease of children characterized by fever, hemorrhages, and other evidences of a disturbance in the reticuloendothelial system and by severe bone lesions esp. of the skull

**let·ter·et** \¦led·ə¦ret\ *n* -S : a short letter

**letter founder** *n* : TYPEFOUNDER

**let·ter·gae** \'letər¦gā\ *n* -S [prob. fr. ³*let* + -*er* + *gae*; fr. the phrase *let gae (the tune)* raise the tune] *Scot* : PRECENTOR

**letter hand** *n* : a style of medieval handwriting used in public letters

**letterhead** \'≈≈,≈\ *also* **letter heading** *n* **1** : a sheet of printed or engraved stationery usu. giving the name and address of the organization and the nature of the enterprise and often including the title of the sender **2** : the heading at the top of a letterhead

**lettering** *n* -S **1** : the act or process of inscribing or marking with letters ⟨taught herself ~ . . . and was promoted to the studio —*Mademoiselle*⟩; *specif* : the impressing of a title on the backbone of a book **2** : the letters or calligraphy used in an inscription ⟨anthology shows examples of modern ~ as used in contemporary advertising —*Brit. Book News*⟩ ⟨~ can be condensed, elongated, slanted . . . to fill any need —Harry Roth⟩

**lettering pen** *n* : a pen with a nib end especially shaped for forming the thick or thin strokes of letters in calligraphy and freehand lettering

lettering pens

**let·ter·less** \'led·ə(r)ləs\ *adj* **1** *archaic* : devoid of learning : ILLITERATE **2** : devoid of correspondence **3** : devoid of inscription

**letter lichen** *n* : a lichen (as a member of the genus *Graphis*) in which the apothecium assumes a form like written characters

**letter mail** *n* : first-class mail

**let·ter·man** \'≈≈,man, -,maa(ə)n, -mən\ *n, pl* **lettermen** : an athlete who has earned a letter in a school sport

**letter missive** *n, pl* **letters missive** [ME *lettres missives*, *letter missive*] : a letter from a superior authority addressed to a particular individual or group and conveying a command, recommendation, permission, or invitation

**letter of advice** : ADVICE 5a

**letter of attorney** [ME] : POWER OF ATTORNEY

**letter of credence** *or* **letters of credence** [ME *letter of credance*, prob. part trans. of ML *litterae de credentia*, *litterae credentiae*] : a formal document furnished a diplomatic agent for presentation to the government to which he is sent attesting to his power to act for his government or head of state — compare RECREDENTIAL

**letter of credit 1** : a letter addressed by a banker to a correspondent certifying that a person named therein is entitled to draw on him or his credit up to a certain sum — called also *traveler's letter of credit, circular letter of credit, circular note* **2** : a letter addressed by a banker to a person to whom credit is given authorizing him to draw on the issuing bank or on a bank in his country up to a certain sum and guaranteeing to accept the drafts if duly made — called also *commercial letter of credit, confirmed credit, confirmed letter of credit*

**letter of delegation** : a letter delegating authority esp. to collect a debt

**letter of hypothecation** : HYPOTHECATION CERTIFICATE

**letter of instruction** : a form of order dealing only with the broader phases of operations and issued by or to higher commanders for the guidance and control of a large military command

**letter of intent** : a written statement of the intention to enter into a formal agreement; *esp* : a written authorization enabling officers of the federal government in time of imperative need for war materials and supplies to order the making or furnishing of such materials and supplies before the issuance of a formal contract and providing reimbursement for the contractor's expenses if no contract is subsequently issued

**letter package** *n* : a package sent by international mail at the first-class rate

**letter paper** *n* : paper of a size suitable for writing letters

**letter-perfect** \¦≈≈¦≈≈\ *adj* : correct to the smallest detail ⟨*letter-perfect* as to the duration of notes, nuances, and phrasing —Samuel Chotzinoff⟩; *specif* : VERBATIM ⟨gave a *letter-perfect* rendition of the soliloquy⟩

**letter post** *n* : a class of mail in the United Kingdom comprising chiefly letters and postcards and corresponding to first-class mail in the U. S.

**letterpress** \'≈≈,≈\ *n* **1 a** : the process of printing direct from an inked raised surface upon which the paper is impressed — called also *printing, relief printing, typographical printing*; compare ELECTRONOGRAPHY, INTAGLIO, PLANOGRAPHY, STENCIL **b** : work done by this process **c** : a machine for letterpress printing **2** : COPYING PRESS **3** *chiefly Brit* : reading matter as distinct from pictorial illustrations : TEXT ⟨lively pencil sketches . . . dodge in and out among the ~ —*Manchester Guardian Weekly*⟩

**letter rate** *n* : the rate of postage for first-class mail

**letters** *pl of* LETTER, *pres 3d sing of* LETTER

**letters close** \-'klōs\ *n pl* [trans. of F *lettres closes*, fr. MF, trans. of ML *litterae clausae*] : letters issued by a government or sovereign to a private person in a private matter — distinguished from *letters patent*

**letters credential** *n pl* [part trans. of ML *litterae credentiales*] : LETTER OF CREDENCE

**letter sheet** *n* : a sheet of stationery that is folded and sealed with the message inside and serves as its own envelope for mailing

**lettershop** \'≈≈,≈\ *n* : an independent agency that handles secretarial and office work (as mailing, mimeographing, and bookkeeping) on a job basis

**letters of administration** : a formal written communication from a court evidencing the right of an administrator to administer the goods or estate of a deceased person

**letters of horn·ing** \-'hȯrniŋ\ [*horning* act of proclaiming a person an outlaw by blowing three blasts upon a horn, fr. *horn* (instrument) + -*ing*] *Scots law* : a process of a court directing a debtor to pay or perform according to the terms of the letters under penalty of being proclaimed an outlaw by the blowing of three blasts upon a horn

**letters of marque** *also* **letter of marque** [ME *letters of marc*, prob. part trans. of ML *litterae de marqua*] : written authority granted to a private person by a government to seize the subjects of a foreign state or their goods by way of retaliation for injuries; *specif* : a license or extraordinary commission granted by a government to a private person to fit out an armed vessel to cruise as a privateer or corsair at sea and plunder the enemy — called also *letters of marque and reprisal*

**letters of request** [ME] **1** : a written request from one government or sovereign to another to aid an injured person in seeking redress, with a promise to reciprocate **2** *Eng eccl law* : an instrument by which an inferior court waives jurisdiction over a case and requests a higher court to hear it

**letters overt** *n pl* [trans. of AF *lettres overtes*, trans. of ML *litterae patentes*] : LETTERS PATENT

**letterspace** \'≈≈,≈\ *vt* : to insert or leave a space between the letters of (a word)

**letterspacing** *n* : spacing between letterspaced characters

**letters patent** *n pl* [ME, part trans. of AF & ML; AF *lettres patentes*, trans. of ML *litterae patentes*] : written communications usu. signed and sealed from a government or sovereign of a nation conferring upon a designated person a grant (as a right, title, status, property, authority, privilege, monopoly, franchise, immunity, or exemption) that could not otherwise be enjoyed in a form readily open for inspection by all seeking confirmation of the grant conferred — distinguished from *letters close*

**letters rogatory** *n pl* : a formal written request by a court or judge to a court or judge in a foreign jurisdiction to summon and cause to be examined a specified witness within its jurisdiction and transmit his testimony for use in a pending action — compare DEDIMUS

**letters testamentary** *n pl* : a written communication from a court or officer informing an executor of his appointment and authority to execute the will of the testator

**letterweight** \'≈≈,≈\ *n* : PAPERWEIGHT

**letterwinged kite** \'≈≈,≈-\ *n* : an Australian kite (*Elanus scriptus*) with a black edging on the underwing that resembles the letter M when the bird is in flight

**letterwood** \'≈≈,≈\ *n* [trans. of F *bois de lettres*; fr. the fancied resemblance of its markings to letters of the alphabet] **1** : the mottled wood of a So. American tree (*Brosimum aubletii*) used for veneer **2** : the tree that yields letterwood

**letter writer** *n* : one that writes letters; *specif* : one whose employment is letter writing ⟨a professional *letter writer* spread his papyrus on a table under the candlelight —Alice Parmelee⟩

**let·tic** \'led·ik\ *adj, usu cap* [*Lett* + -*ic*] : ¹LETTISH

**letting** *n* -S **1** *chiefly Brit* : an act of letting or leasing **2** *chiefly Brit* : a tenement let or to be let

**letting-in** \¦≈≈¦≈\ *n* -S : the process of shortening and widening pelts by cutting in strips and stitching

**letting-out** \¦≈≈¦≈\ *n* -S : the process of lengthening pelts by cutting them in narrow diagonal strips that are nailed to a board in a stepped-down layout and stitched together to improve the marking and appearance of the fur for garments

**¹lett·ish** \'led·ish\ *adj, usu cap* [prob. fr. G *lettisch*, fr. *Lette* Lett + G -*isch* -ish] : of or relating to the Latvians or their language

**²lettish** \"\ *n* -ES *cap* : LATVIAN 2

**letto-** *comb form, usu cap* [*Lett* + -*o*-] : Lettish and ⟨*Letto-*Lithuanian parentage⟩

**let·tre bâ·tarde** \¦le·trəbə¦tärd\ *n, pl* **lettres bâtardes** \"\ [F, lit., bastard letter] **1** : a Gothic letter with the angles rounded **2** : BÂTARDE

**let·tre de ca·chet** \¦le·trədə,ka¦shā\ *n, pl* **let·tres de cachet** \"\ [F] : a letter bearing an official (as a royal) seal and usu. authorizing imprisonment without trial of a named person ⟨these leaflets . . . were simply *lettres de cachet* issued by the Ogpu for action by the Gestapo —Anthony West⟩

**let·tre de cré·ance** \¦le·trədəkrā¦äⁿs\ *n, pl* **lettres de créance** \"\ [F, fr. MF, trans. of ML *litterae credentiae*] : LETTER OF CREDENCE

**lett·som·ite** \'letsə,mīt\ *n* -S [William G. *Lettsom* †1887 Eng. mineralogist + E -*ite*] : CYANOTRICHITE

**let·tuce** \'led·əs, -etəs\ *n* -S [ME *letuse*, fr. OF *laitues*, pl. of *laitue*, fr. L *lactuca*, fr. *lact-*, *lac* milk; fr. its milky juice — more at GALAXY] **1 a** : a plant of the genus *Lactuca*; *specif* : a common garden vegetable (*L. sativa*) the succulent leaves of which are used esp. in salads — see COS LETTUCE, HEAD LETTUCE, LEAF LETTUCE **b** : any of several plants (as members of the genera *Claytonia* and *Valerianella*) having succulent foliage **2** *slang* : GREENBACKS

**lettuce aphid** *n* : an aphid (esp. *Macrosiphum barri*) that is a pest of lettuce

**lettuce bird** *n* : an American goldfinch (*Spinus tristis*)

**lettuce cabbage** *n* : CHINESE CABBAGE

**lettuce green** *n* : a variable color averaging a moderate yellow green that is greener, lighter, and stronger than average moss green or mosstone and yellower, lighter, and stronger than average pea green or spinach green

**lettuce mildew** *n* : a destructive disease of lettuce caused by a downy mildew (*Bremia lactucae*)

**lettuce opium** *n* : LACTUCARIUM

**lettuce saxifrage** *n* : a saxifrage (*Saxifraga micranthidifolia*) of the eastern U. S. having foliage that resembles lettuce

**let up** *vi* [³*let* + *up*] **1 a** : to diminish or slow down : SLACKEN, RELAX ⟨the wind's *letting up* a little⟩ ⟨not one of us should *let up* in our drive for standardizing our procedures —H.H.

Helm⟩ ⟨free to . . . *let up* and enjoy ourselves —A.L.Rowse⟩ **b :** to become idle **:** CEASE, STOP ⟨pitched horseshoes the whole evening and never *let up* until it was too dark to see⟩ ⟨took shelter under a tarred shed until the rain *let up* —Oliver LaFarge⟩ **2 :** to ease up or become less severe — used with *on* ⟨able to *let up* slightly on armament expenditures —D.M.Keezer⟩ ⟨remove some of these restrictions, *let up* a bit on people —T.P.Whitney⟩ ⟨*let up* on him — he didn't mean any harm⟩

**letup** \ˈ=,=\ *n* -s [*let up*] **1 a :** a lessening of effort or intensity **:** SLACKENING, ABATEMENT ⟨they labored without ~, forming two constantly moving lines —Hamilton Basso⟩ ⟨during the six-day ~ in ground fighting —*Wall Street Jour.*⟩; *specif* **:** a break in inclement weather ⟨the rain continued without ~ —Hilbert Schenck⟩ **b :** a reduction in quantity or quality ⟨seems to be no ~ in the flow of nature books —Dorothy H. Jenkins⟩ ⟨a major achievement to sustain without ~ . . . 100 minutes of running jokes —*Newsweek*⟩ ⟨no ~ in the billingsgate between Berlin and Moscow —H.C.Wolfe⟩ **2 :** an act or instance of relaxation **:** abandonment of restraint ⟨allowed myself the ~ of a drive in the park —O.W.Holmes †1935⟩

**leu** \ˈleü\ *n, pl* **lei** \ˈlā\ [Romanian *leu*, lit., lion, fr. L *leon-, leo* — more at LION] **1 :** the basic monetary unit of Romania — see MONEY table **2 :** a coin representing one leu

**leuc-** *or* **leuco-** *also* **leuk-** *or* **leuko-** *comb form* [NL, fr. Gk *leuk-, leuko-* white, fr. *leukos* — more at LIGHT] **1 :** white **:** colorless **:** weakly colored ⟨*leuc*augite⟩ ⟨*leuco*plast⟩ ⟨*leuko*cyte⟩ — often in names of chemical compounds derived from (as by reduction) or related to a dye or other colored compound ⟨*leuc*aurin⟩ ⟨*leuco*methylene blue⟩ **2 :** leukocyte ⟨*leuko*penia⟩ **3 :** white matter of the brain ⟨*leuco*tomy⟩

**leu·ca·den·dron** \,lükəˈdendrən\ *n, cap* [NL, fr. *leuca-* (irreg. fr. Gk *leukos* white) + *-dendron*] **:** a large genus of evergreen trees and shrubs (family Proteaceae) native to the Cape of Good Hope that have silvery white leaves and dioecious capitate flowers — see SILVER TREE

**leu·cae·na** \lüˈsēnə\ *n, cap* [NL, fr. Gk *leukainein* to make white, become white, fr. *leukos* white] **:** a small genus of tropical trees (family Leguminosae) that have pods resembling those of the acacia and 10 stamens — see LEAD TREE

**leuc·au·gite** \(ˈ)lük+\ *n* [*leuc-* + *augite*] **:** a white or grayish augite that resembles diopside

**leucemi·a** *or* **leucaemia** *var of* LEUKEMIA

**leu·cet·ta** \lüˈsed·ə\ *n, cap* [NL, irreg. fr. Gk *leukos* white] **:** a genus of calcareous sponges (order Asconosa) of leuconoid structure

**leuch** \ˈlyük\ *Scot past of* LAUGH

**leuch·ten·berg·ite** \ˈlȯiktən,bər,gīt\ *n* -s [G *leuchtenbergit*, fr. Maximilian, Duke of *Leuchtenberg* †1852 + G *-it* -ite] **:** a clinochlore that often resembles talc and contains little or no iron

**leuc·ich·thys** \lüˈkikthəs, lüˈsi-\ *n, cap* [NL, fr. *leuc-* + *-ichthys*] **:** a genus of whitefishes comprising the lake herrings and ciscoes that differ from members of the genus *Coregonus* in having a large mouth with a long and often projecting lower jaw

**leu·ci·fer** \ˈlüsəfə(r)\ *n, cap* [NL, alter. (influenced by NL *leuc-*) of L *lucifer* morning star — more at LUCIFER] **:** a genus of free-swimming slender macruran crustaceans that is sometimes made the type of a distinct family

**leu·cine** \ˈlü,sēn, -üsᵊn\ *n* -s [ISV *leuc-* + *-ine*] **:** a white crystalline amino acid $(CH_3)_2CHCH_2CH(NH_2)COOH$ that is obtained by the hydrolysis of most dietary proteins (as casein or zein) and is also made synthetically and that in its levorotatory L-form is essential in the nutrition of animals and man; α-amino-γ-methyl-valeric acid

**leu·cite** \-,sīt\ *n* -s [obs. G *leucit* (now *leuzit*), fr. *leuc-* + *-it* -ite] **:** a white or gray mineral $KAlSi_2O_6$ consisting of a potassium aluminum silicate occurring in igneous rocks (as recent lavas) usu. in trapezohedral crystals with a glassy fracture (hardness 5.5–6.0, sp. gr. 2.45–2.50) — called also *amphigene*

**leu·cit·ic** \(ˈ)lüˈsid·ik\ *adj* **:** relating to, containing, or resembling leucite

**leu·ci·tite** \ˈlüsə,tīt\ *n* -s [obs. G *leucitit* (now *leuzitit*), fr. obs. G *leucit* leucite (now *leuzit*) + G *-it* -ite] **:** a basaltic rock chiefly composed of leucite with augite, some magnetite, and no feldspar

**leu·ci·to·he·dron** \,lüsə(,)tōˈhēdrən\ *n* -s [ISV *leucite* + *-o-* + *-hedron*] **:** a trapezohedron or tetragonal trisoctahedron

**leu·ci·toid** \ˈlüsə,tȯid\ *n* -s [ISV *leucite* + *-oid*] **:** LEUCITOHEDRON

**leu·cit·o·phyre** \lüˈsīd·ə,fī(ə)r\ *n* -s [ISV *leucite* + *-o-* + *-phyre;* prob. orig. formed as G *leuzitophyr*] **:** a porphyry with leucite phenocrysts

**leu·co** \ˈlü(,)kō\ *adj* [ISV, fr. *leuc-*] **:** relating to or being a colorless or weakly colored compound derived from or related to a dye or other colored compound — compare LEUC- 1

**leuco-** — see LEUC-

**leu·co·anthocyanin** \ˌlü(,)kō+\ *n* [*leuc-* + *anthocyanin*] **:** a colorless precursor of an anthocyanin

**leuco base** *n* [ISV *leuco* + *base*] **:** a colorless or weakly colored amine that is formed by reduction of a dye (as a triphenylmethane dye) or its carbinol derivative and that on oxidation and treatment with acids usu. gives back the dye

**leucoblast** *var of* LEUKOBLAST

**leu·cob·ry·um** \lüˈkäbrēəm\ *n, cap* [NL, fr. *leuc-* + *-bryum* (fr. Gk *bryon* moss) — more at BRY-] **:** a genus of mosses that is related to *Dicranum* though sometimes made type of a separate family and is characterized by a tufted habit of growth resulting in the formation of thick cushiony masses and by great reduction in chlorophyll with many void cells resulting in a dull grayish white or greenish white coloration of the plant — see WHITE MOSS

**leu·co·chal·cite** \,lükōˈkal,sīt\ *n* -s [obs. G *leucochalcit* (now *leukochalcit*), fr. G *leuc-* + *chalc-* + *-it* -ite] **:** a mineral $Cu_2(AsO_4)(OH).H_2O(?)$ consisting of a basic arsenate of copper crystallizing in the form of white silky needles

**leu·co·choly** \ˈlükə,kälē\ *n* -ES [*leuc-* + *-choly* (as in *melancholy*)] **:** a state of feeling that accompanies preoccupation with trivial and insipid diversions ⟨~ . . . though it seldom laughs or dances, nor ever amounts to what one calls joy or pleasure, yet is a good easy sort of a state —Thomas Gray⟩

**leu·co·ci·din** \,lükəˈsīdᵊn, ˈ==,==\ *n* -s [ISV *leuc-* + *-cide* + *-in*] **:** a substance (as produced by bacteria) destroying leukocytes

**leu·co·crat·ic** \ˌlükəˈkrad·ik\ *adj* [G *leukokrat* leucocratic (fr. *leuk-* leuc- + *-krat*, fr. Gk *kratein* to rule, prevail) + E *-ic;* akin to Gk *kratos* strength — more at HARD] *of a mineral or rock* **:** having a light color — compare MELANOCRATIC, MESOCRATIC

**leu·cocri·num** \lüˈkäkrənəm, ,lükəˈkrīnəm\ *n, cap* [NL, fr. *leuc-* + Gk *krinon* lily] **:** a genus of plants (family Liliaceae) of the western U.S. having a short rootstock, leaves like those of the crocus, and large white umbellate flowers — see SAND LILY

**leucocyt-** *or* **leucocyto-** — see LEUKOCYT-

**leu·co·cyt·al** \ˌlükəˈsīd·ᵊl\ *or* **leu·co·cy·ta·ry** \-d·ərē\ *adj* **:** LEUKOCYTIC

**leucocyte** *var of* LEUKOCYTE

**leu·co·cy·the·mia** *also* **leu·co·cy·thae·mia** \,lükə,sīˈthēmēə\ *n* -s [NL, fr. *leuc-* + *cyt-* + *-emia*] **:** LEUKEMIA — **leu·co·cy·the·mic** *also* **leu·co·cy·thae·mic** \;==;==ˈ=mik\ *adj*

**leucocytoblast** *var of* LEUKOCYTOBLAST

**leucocytopoiesis** *var of* LEUKOCYTOPOIESIS

**leucocytosis** *var of* LEUKOCYTOSIS

**¹leu·co·cy·to·zo·an** \ˌlükə,sīd·əˈzōən\ *adj* [NL *Leucocytozoon* + E *-an*, adj. suffix] **:** of or relating to the genus *Leucocytozoon*

**²leucocytozoan** \"\ *n* -s [NL *Leucocytozoon* + E *-an*, n. suffix] **:** LEUCOCYTOZOON

**leu·co·cy·to·zo·on** \,==,==ˈzō,än, -ōən\ *n* [NL, fr. *leuc-* + *cyt-* + *-zoon*] **1** *cap* **:** a genus of sporozoans parasitic in birds — see HAEMOPROTEIDAE **2** *pl* **leucocytozoa** \-ōə\ **:** a member of the genus *Leucocytozoon*

**leu·co·derm** \ˈlükə,dərm\ *n* -s [*leuc-* + *-derm* (fr. Gk *derma* skin) — more at DERM-] **1 :** a person with a white or light skin **2** *usu cap* **:** a member of a hypothetical Caucasoid race

**leucoderma** *var of* LEUKODERMA

**leucoencephalitis** *var of* LEUKOENCEPHALITIS

**leuco ester** *n* **:** a water-soluble sodium salt of the sulfuric acid ester of the leuco compound of a vat dye that is applied to textiles and then oxidized in acid solution to the corresponding vat dye — compare DYE table I

**leu·co·indigo** \ˌlü(,)kō+\ *n* [ISV *leuco* + *indigo*] **:** INDIGO WHITE

**leu·co·jum** \lüˈkōjəm\ *n, cap* [NL, fr. Gk *leukoïon* stock (*Matthiola incana*), fr. *leuk-* leuc- + *ion* violet — more at VIOLET] **:** a genus of bulbous herbs (family Amaryllidaceae) that are native to the Old World, are widely cultivated for their early spring bloom, and have a regular perianth with equal segments and stamens with long filaments — see SNOWFLAKE

**leu·co·lyt·ic** \ˌlükəˈlid·ik\ *adj* [*leuc-* + *-lytic*] **:** inducing lysis of white blood cells — used of drugs and infective agents

**leu·co·ma** *also* **leu·ko·ma** \lüˈkōmə\ *n* -s [LL *leucoma*, fr. Gk *leukōma*, fr. *leuk-* leuc- + *-ōma* -oma] **:** a dense white opacity in the cornea of the eye

**leu·co·maine** \ˈlükə,mān\ *n* -s [ISV *leuc-* + *-maine* (as in *ptomaine*); orig. formed as F *leucomaïne*] **:** a basic substance normally produced in the living animal body as a decomposition product of protein matter — compare PTOMAINE

**leu·con** \ˈlü,kän\ *n* -s [NL, fr. Gk *leukon*, neut. of *leukos* white — more at LIGHT] **:** a sponge or sponge larva having a complex structure in which the flagellated layer is restricted to numerous small interstitial chambers intercalated between the incurrent and excurrent canals and the paragaster is reduced or lacking — compare ASCON, SYCON — **leu·co·noid** \ˈlükə,nȯid\ *adj or n*

**leu·co·nostoc** \ˈlükə+\ *n* [NL, fr. *leuc-* + *Nostoc*] **1** *cap* **:** a genus of saprophytic bacteria (family Lactobacillaceae) including several that are pests in sugar refineries because of the habit of forming slime in sugar solutions **2** -s **:** any bacterium of the genus *Leuconostoc*

**leucopenia** *var of* LEUKOPENIA

**leu·coph·a·nite** \lüˈkäfə,nīt\ *also* **leu·co·phane** \ˈlükə,fān\ *n* -s [*leucophanite* fr. *leucophane* (fr. Sw *leukophan*, fr. *leuk-* leuc- + *-phan* -phane) + *-ite*] **:** a mineral $(Na, Ca)_2BeSi_2(O, F, OH)_7$ consisting of a beryllium sodium calcium silicate with fluorine occurring in glassy greenish tabular crystals

**leu·co·phoe·ni·cite** \lükōˈfēnə,sīt\ *n* -s [*leuc-* + *phoenic-* (fr. Gk *phoinik-, phoinix* purple) + *-ite* — more at PHOENICIAN] **:** a mineral $Mn_7Si_3O_{12}(OH)_2$ consisting of a manganese silicate

**leu·co·phore** \ˈlükə,fō(ə)r\ *n* -s [ISV *leuc-* + *-phore*] **:** a white chromatophore — compare GUANOPHORE

**leu·co·phos·phite** \,lükəˈfä,sfīt\ *n* [*leuc-* + *phosph-* + *-ite*] **:** a mineral approximately $K_2(Fe,Al)_7(PO_4)_4(OH)_{11}.6H_2O$ consisting of a hydrous basic phosphate of potassium, iron, and aluminum

**leu·co·plast** \ˈlükə,plast\ *n* -s [ISV *leuc-* + *-plast;* orig. formed as G *leukoplast*] **:** a colorless plastid; *specif* **:** a nonpigmented plastid that occurs esp. in the cytoplasm of interior plant tissues and is capable under proper conditions of developing into a chromoplast — see AMYLOPLAST, ELAIOPLAST

**leu·co·plas·tid** \,lükəˈplastəd, ˈ==,==\ *n* [*leuc-* + *plastid*] **:** LEUCOPLAST

**leucopoiesis** *var of* LEUKOPOIESIS

**leu·cop·te·rin** \lüˈkäptərən\ *n* [ISV *leuc-* + *pterin*] **:** a crystalline alkali-soluble compound $H_2NC_6N_4(OH)_3$ that constitutes the white pigment of cabbage butterflies and other lepidoptera and wasps and is convertible into xanthopterin on reduction; 2-amino-4,6,7-trihydroxy-pteridine

**leu·co·py·rite** \,lükəˈpī,rīt\ *n* [*leuc-* + *pyrite*] **:** LOELLINGITE

**leucorrhea** *or* **leucorrhoea** *var of* LEUKORRHEA

**leu·co·ryx** \ˈlükə(,)riks\ *n, pl* **leucoryxes** *also* **leucoryx** [NL, fr. *leuc-* + Gk *oryg-, oryx* leucoryx] **:** a large chiefly pale brownish antelope of No. Africa (*Oryx leucoryx*) related to the gemsbok

**leu·co·sin** \ˈlükəsən\ *n* -s [ISV *leucos-* (fr. Gk *leukos* white) + *-in* — more at LIGHT] **:** a substance believed to be a carbohydrate occurring in the form of whitish lumps as a food reserve in many yellow-green algae of the class Chrysophyceae

**leucosis** *var of* LEUKOSIS

**leu·co·so·le·nia** \,lükəsōˈlēnēə\ *n, cap* [NL, fr. *leuc-* + Gk *sōlēn* channel, pipe + NL *-ia* — more at SYRINGE] **:** a genus (the type of the family Leucosolenidae) of small ascon sponges that grow in colonies on rocks near the seashore

**leu·co·sphe·nite** \,==ˈsfē,nīt\ *n* -s [ISV *leuc-* + *sphen-* + *-ite;* prob. orig. formed as G *leukosphenit*] **:** a mineral $Na_4BaTi_2Si_{10}O_{27}$ consisting of a sodium barium silicotitanate occurring in white wedge-shaped crystals

**leu·co·stic·te** \,==ˈstik(,)tē\ *n* [NL, fr. *leuc-* + *-sticte* (fr. Gk *stiktos* tattooed, spotted, fr. *stizein* to tattoo) — more at STICK] **1** *cap* **:** a genus consisting of the rosy finches **2** -s **:** any bird of the genus *Leucosticte*

**leucotaxine** *var of* LEUKOTAXINE

**leu·coth·o·e** \lüˈkäthə,wē\ *n* [NL, fr. L *Leucothoe*, legendary Persian princess supposed to have been changed by Apollo into a sweet-scented shrub] **1** *cap* **:** a large genus of American and Asiatic shrubs of the family Ericaceae with herbage that contains a poisonous substance similar to that found in shrubs of the genus *Kalmia* and with flowers in terminal and axillary one-sided racemes **2** -s **:** any plant of the genus *Leucothoe*

**leu·co·tome** \ˈlükə,tōm\ *n* -s [*leuc-* + *-tome*] **:** a narrow rotating blade in a cannula for use in lobotomy

**leu·cot·o·my** \lüˈkäd·əmē\ *n* -ES [ISV *leuc-* + *-tomy*] **:** LOBOTOMY

**leucotoxic** *var of* LEUKOTOXIC

**leu·cov·o·rin** \lüˈkävərən\ *n* -s [*leuco-* (fr. NL *Leuconostoc*, genus name of *Leuconostoc citrovorum*) + *-vor-* (fr. NL *citrovorum*, specific epithet of *Leuconostoc citrovorum*) + *-in* — more at LEUCONOSTOC, CITROVORUM FACTOR] **:** a crystalline synthetic acid $C_{20}H_{23}N_7O_7$ derived from folic acid and used in the form of its calcium salt esp. in treating some anemias and toxic symptoms arising from the use of folic acid antagonists; $N^5$-formyl-tetrahydro-pteroylglutamic acid — called also *folinic acid-SF*

**leu·cox·ene** \lüˈkäk,sēn\ *n* -s [G *leukoxen*, fr. *leuk-* leuc- + *-xen* -xene] **:** a mineral consisting mostly of rutile and partly of anatase or sphene occurring in some igneous rocks from the alteration of ilmenite

**leu·cyl** \ˈlüsəl\ *n* -s [ISV *leucine* + *-yl*] **:** the acid radical $(CH_3)_2CHCH_2CHNH_2CO–$ of leucine

**leud** \ˈlüd\ *n, pl* **leuds** \-dz\ *or* **leu·des** \-,dēz\ [ML *leudes* (pl.), of Gmc origin; akin to OHG *liuti* people (pl. of *liut* person, people) — more at LIBERAL] **:** a feudal tenant or vassal in the ancient Frankish kingdoms

**leugh** \ˈlyük\ *Scot past of* LAUGH

**leuk** \ˈlyük\ *chiefly Scot var of* LOOK

**leuk-** *or* **leuko-** — see LEUC-

**leuk·ane·mia** \ˌlük+\ *n* [NL, fr. *leuc-* + *anemia*] **1 :** LEUKEMIA **2 :** LEUKOSIS 2

**leu·ke·mia** *also* **leu·kae·mia** \lüˈkēmēə\ *or* **leu·ce·mia** *or* **leu·cae·mia** \" *also* -üˈsē-\ *n* -s [NL, fr. *leuc-* + *-emia*] **:** an acute or chronic disease of unknown cause in man and other warm-blooded animals that involves the blood-forming organs, is characterized by an abnormal increase in the number of leukocytes in the tissues of the body with or without a corresponding increase of those in the circulating blood, and is classified according to the type of leukocyte most prominently involved

**leu·ke·mic** *also* **leu·kae·mic** \(ˈ)lüˈkēmik, -mēk\ *adj* [*leukemia* + *-ic*] **1 :** of, relating to, or affected by leukemia ⟨~ mice⟩ **2 :** characterized by an increase in white blood cells ⟨~ blood⟩ ⟨transmissible ~ . . . diseases of fowls —*Experiment Station Record*⟩

**leu·ke·mid** \lüˈkēməd\ *n* -s [ISV *leukem-* (fr. NL *leukemia*) + *-id*] **:** a skin lesion of leukemia

**leu·ke·mo·gen** \lüˈkēməjən, -,jen\ *n* -s [*leukemia* + *-o-* + *-gen*] **:** a substance tending to induce the development of leukemia — compare CARCINOGEN

**leu·ke·mo·genesis** \lüˌkēmə+\ *n* [*leukemia* + *-o-* + *genesis*] **:** induction or production of leukemia

**leu·ke·mo·gen·ic** \=ˌ=ˌ=ˈjenik\ *adj* [*leukemia* + *-o-* + *-genic*] **:** causing or tending to induce leukemia ⟨~ effects of ionizing radiation —*Science*⟩

**leu·ke·moid** \lüˈkē,mȯid\ *adj* [*leukemia* + *-oid*] **:** resembling leukemia but not involving the same changes in the blood-forming organs ⟨a ~ reaction in malaria⟩

**leu·ker·gy** \ˈlü(,)kərjē\ *n* -ES [ISV *leuc-* + *-ergy;* prob. orig. formed as Pol *leukergia*] **:** the clumping of white blood cells that accompanies some inflammations and infections

**leu·ko·blast** *also* **leu·co·blast** \ˈlükə,blast\ *n* [ISV *leuc-* + *-blast*] **:** a developing leukocyte **:** a cellular precursor of a leukocyte

**leu·ko·blas·to·sis** \,==,blaˈstōsəs\ *n, pl* **leukoblasto·ses** \-ō,sēz\ [NL, fr. ISV *leukoblast* + NL *-osis*] **:** LEUKOSIS

**leukocyt-** *or* **leukocyto-** *also* **leucocyt-** *or* **leucocyto-** *comb form* [NL, fr. ISV *leukocyte*] **:** leukocyte ⟨*leukocyto*penia⟩ ⟨*leukocyt*osis⟩

**leu·ko·cyte** *also* **leu·co·cyte** \ˈlükə,sīt, *usu* -īd·+V\ *n* -s [ISV *leuc-* + *-cyte*] **1 :** a white or colorless nucleated cell of the blood that occurs to the number of 5000 to 10,000 in each cubic millimeter of normal human blood and that is classified into two main groups comprising (1) highly phagocytic cells with densely granular cytoplasm and complexly segmented nucleus and (2) cells with nearly clear cytoplasm and simple or kidney-shaped nucleus, including some that are immunologically active — called also respectively (1) *granulocyte* (2) *agranulocyte;* compare ERYTHROCYTE **2 :** a cell (as a histiocyte) of the tissues comparable to or identical with a leukocyte of the blood

**leu·ko·cyt·ic** *also* **leu·co·cyt·ic** \ˌ==ˈsid·ik\ *adj* **1 :** of, relating to, or involving leukocytes **2 :** characterized by an excess of leukocytes

**leu·ko·cy·to·blast** *also* **leu·co·cy·to·blast** \ˈlükə,sīd·ə,blast, ,==ˈ==,=\ *n* [*leukocyt-* + *-blast*] **:** a cellular precursor of a leukocyte — compare LYMPHOBLAST, MYELOBLAST — **leu·ko·cy·to·blas·tic** \ˌ==ˌ==ˈblastik\ *adj*

**leu·ko·cy·to·gen·e·sis** \,==ˌ==ˈjenəsəs\ *n, pl* **leukocytogene·ses** \-ə,sēz\ [NL, fr. *leukocyt-* + L *genesis*] **:** LEUKOPOIESIS

**leu·ko·cy·toid** \ˌ==ˈsīd,ȯid\ *adj* **:** resembling a leukocyte

**leu·ko·cy·toly·sin** \,lükə,sīˈtäləsən, ˌlükə,sīd·ᵊlˈīsᵊn\ *n* [ISV *leukocyt-* + *lysin*] **:** a specific lytic antibody that dissolves white blood cells

**leu·ko·cy·tol·y·sis** \,lükə,sīˈtäləsəs\ *n, pl* **leukocytolyses** \-ə,sēz\ [NL, fr. *leukocyt-* + *-lysis*] **:** destruction of leukocytes — **leu·ko·cytolytic** \ˌ==+\ *adj*

**leu·ko·cy·to·pe·nia** \,lükə,sīd·əˈpēnēə\ *n* [NL, fr. *leukocyt-* + *-penia*] **:** LEUKOPENIA

**leu·ko·cy·to·poi·e·sis** *also* **leu·co·cy·to·poi·e·sis** \-,pȯiˈēsəs\ *n, pl* **leukocytopoie·ses** *also* **leucocytopoie·ses** \-ē(,)sēz\ [NL, fr. *leukocyt-* + *-poiesis*] **:** LEUKOPOIESIS

**leu·ko·cy·to·sis** *or* **leu·co·cy·to·sis** \,lükə,sīˈtōsəs\ *n, pl* **leukocyto·ses** *or* **leucocyto·ses** \-ō,sēz\ [NL, fr. *leukocyt-* + *-osis*] **:** an increase in the number of leukocytes in the circulating blood that occurs normally (as after meals) or abnormally (as in some infections) — **leu·ko·cy·tot·ic** *or* **leu·co·cy·tot·ic** \ˌ==,=ˈtäd·ik\ *adj*

**leu·ko·der·ma** *also* **leu·co·der·ma** \,lükəˈdərmə\ *n* -s [NL, fr. *leuc-* + *-derma*] **:** a skin abnormality that is characterized by a usu. congenital lack of pigment in spots or bands and produces a patchy whiteness — compare VITILIGO

**leu·ko·encephalitis** *also* **leu·co·encephalitis** \ˌlü(,)kō+\ *n* [NL, fr. *leuc-* + *encephalitis*] **:** inflammation of the white matter of the brain — compare STAGGER 4

**leu·koly·sin** \lüˈkäləsən, ˌlükəˈlīsᵊn\ *n* -s [*leuc-* + *lysin*] **:** LEUKOCYTOLYSIN

**leukoma** *var of* LEUCOMA

**leu·kon** \ˈlü,kän\ *n* -s [NL, fr. Gk, neut. of *leukos* white — more at LIGHT] **:** a body organ consisting of the white blood cells and their precursors — compare ERYTHRON

**leuk·onych·ia** \,lükōˈnikēə\ *n* -s [NL, fr. *leuc-* + *-onychia*] **:** a white spotting, streaking, or discoloration of the fingernails caused by injury or ill health

**leu·ko·pe·nia** \,lükōˈpēnēə\ *n* -s [NL, fr. *leuc-* + *-penia*] **:** a condition in which the number of leukocytes circulating in the blood is abnormally low and which is most commonly due to a decreased production of new cells in conjunction with various infectious diseases, as a reaction to various drugs or other chemicals, or in response to irradiation — **leu·ko·pe·nic** \ˌ==ˈpēnik\ *adj*

**leu·ko·plakia** \,lükōˈplākēə, -lak-\ *n* -s [NL, fr. *leuc-* + Gk *plak-, plax* flat surface + NL *-ia* — more at PLEASE] **:** a condition commonly considered precancerous in which thickened white patches of epithelium occur on the mucous membranes esp. of the mouth, vulva, and kidney pelvis; *also* **:** one of the thickened patches — **leu·ko·plakic** \ˌ==ˈplakik\ *adj*

**leu·ko·poi·e·sis** *or* **leu·co·poi·e·sis** \,lükə,pȯiˈēsəs\ *n, pl* **leukopoie·ses** *or* **leucopoie·ses** \-ē,sēz\ [NL, fr. *leuc-* + *-poiesis*] **:** the formation of white blood cells

**leu·ko·poi·et·ic** *or* **leu·co·poi·et·ic** \ˌ==ˌ=ˈed·ik\ *adj* [*leuc-* + *-poietic*] **:** relating to, characterized by, or inducing the formation of white blood cells

**leu·kor·rhea** *also* **leu·kor·rhoea** *or* **leu·cor·rhea** *or* **leu·cor·rhoea** \,lükəˈrēə\ *n* -s [NL, fr. *leuc-* + *-rrhea*] **:** a white, yellowish, or greenish white viscid discharge from the vagina resulting from inflammation or congestion of the uterine or vaginal mucous membrane — **leu·kor·rhe·al** *also* **leu·kor·rhoe·al** *or* **leu·cor·rhe·al** *also* **leu·cor·rhoe·al** \ˌ==ˈrēəl\ *adj*

**leu·ko·sarcoma** \ˌlükō+\ *n* [NL, fr. *leuc-* + *sarcoma*] **:** lymphosarcoma accompanied by leukemia — **leu·ko·sar·comatosis** \"+\ *n*

**leu·ko·sis** *or* **leu·co·sis** \lüˈkōsəs\ *n, pl* **leuko·ses** *or* **leuco·ses** \-ō,sēz\ [NL, fr. *leuc-* + *-osis*] **1 :** LEUKEMIA **2 :** any of several poorly differentiated diseases of poultry commonly grouped as the avian leukosis complex that involve disturbed blood formation and are distinguished individually by special manifestations (as paralysis, tumor formation, leukemia, and eye damage) — see BIG LIVER DISEASE, FOWL PARALYSIS, LYMPHOMATOSIS, OSTEOPETROSIS, PEARL EYE

**leu·ko·tax·ine** *or* **leu·co·tax·ine** \ˌlükəˈtak,sēn, -,sən\ *n* -s [*leuc-* + Gk *taxis* arrangement, order (fr. *tassein, tattein* to arrange) + E *-ine* — more at TACTICS] **:** a crystalline polypeptide that is obtained from the fluid at sites of inflammation in the body and that increases the permeability of capillaries and migration of leukocytes

**leu·kot·ic** *or* **leu·cot·ic** \(ˈ)lüˈkäd·ik\ *adj* [fr. *leukosis*, after such pairs as *narcosis: narcotic*] **:** characterized by or inducing the diseased blood condition found in avian leukosis

**leu·ko·tox·ic** *or* **leu·co·tox·ic** \ˌlükəˈtäksik\ *adj* [ISV *leuc-* + *toxic*] **:** of or relating to a toxin destructive to leukocytes — **leu·ko·toxicity** \"+\ *n*

**leu·ko·toxin** \ˌ==ˈ=sən\ *n* [ISV *leuc-* + *toxin*] **:** a substance specif. destructive to leukocytes

**leu·ma** \ˈlümə\ *n* -s [G, fr. LGk *loimē* pestilence; akin to OE *læssa* less — more at LESS] **:** SHIPPING FEVER 2c

**lev** \ˈlef\ *n, pl* **le·va** \ˈlevə\ [Bulg, lit., lion, fr. OBulg *lĭvŭ*, prob. fr. OHG *lewo*, fr. L *leo* — more at LION] **1 :** the basic monetary unit of Bulgaria — see MONEY table **2 :** a coin representing one lev

**lev-** *or* **levo-** *also* **laev-** *or* **laevo-** *comb form* [F *lévo-*, fr. L *laevus* left; akin to Gk *laios* left, OSlav *lěvŭ*] **1** *usu levo- also laevo-, usu ital* **:** levorotatory — in names of chemical compounds ⟨*lev*an⟩ ⟨*levo*-limonene⟩ ⟨*levo*-tartaric acid⟩; symbol (—)- ⟨(—)-tartaric acid⟩; compare L- **2 :** left **:** on the left side **:** to the left ⟨*levo*version⟩

**lev** *abbr* levant

**le·vade** \ləˈväd\ *n* -s [G, fr. F *lever* to raise (fr. L *levare*) + *-ade* — more at LEVER] **:** a show-ring movement in which a horse raises the forequarters, brings the hindquarters under him, and balances with haunches deeply bent and forelegs drawn up

**le·val·loi·sian** \,levəˈlȯizēən, -ōizhən\ *also* **le·val·lois** \ləˈval(,)wä\ *adj, usu cap* [*levalloisian* fr. *Levallois*-Perret, suburb of Paris, France + E *-ian; levallois* fr. *Levallois*-Perret] **:** of or relating to a culture tradition overlapping the late Acheulean and early Mousterian and notable for a technique of stone-tool manufacture by the striking of flakes from a flat flint nodule

**le·val·loi·so-mousterian** \ˌlevəˌlȯi(,)zō+\ *adj, usu cap L&M* [*levalloiso-* (fr. *levalloisian*) + *mousterian*] **:** of or relating to a culture with Levalloisian and Mousterian tool traditions

**lev·an** \ˈle,van\ *n* -s [*lev-* + *-an*] **:** any of a group of sparingly soluble levorotatory polysaccharides $(C_6H_{10}O_5)_n$ composed of levulose units of the furanose type and formed esp. from sucrose solutions by the action of various bacteria (as *Bacillus subtilis* or *B. mesentericus*) — compare DEXTRAN

**lev·ance and cou·chance** \ˌlevən(t)sən'kau̇chən(t)s\ *also* **lev·an·cy and cou·chan·cy** \-vənsē...chənsē\ *n* [*levance and couchance* alter. (influenced by *-ance*) of *levancy and couchancy*, fr. *levancy* (fr. *levant* — in *levant and couchant* — + *-cy*) + *and* + *couchancy* (fr. *couchant* — in *levant and couchant* — + *-cy*)] : the state of being levant and couchant

**¹le·vant** \lə'vant\ *adj, often cap* [*Levant*, the countries of the eastern Mediterranean, fr. ME *levaunt* East, Orient, fr. MF *levant*, fr. pres. part. of *lever* to raise (*se lever* to rise), fr. L *levare*; fr. the direction of the sunrise — more at LEVER] : LEVANTINE, EASTERN

**²levant** \"\ *n* -s [*Levant*, the countries of the eastern Mediterranean] **1** : LEVANTER 2 **2** *usu cap* : LEVANT MOROCCO

**³levant** \"\ *vt* -ED/-ING/-s : to give (leather) the finish of Levant morocco

**⁴levant** *n* -s [perh. fr. Sp *levantar* to break (camp), raise, fr. OSp, to raise, irreg. fr. *levar*, fr. L *levare*] *obs* : a wager made with intent not to pay if lost

**⁵le·vant** \lə'vant\ *vi* -ED/-ING/-s *chiefly Brit* : to default a losing bet or a debt and abscond ⟨his Buddhist friend has ~*ed* after taking my name and address —Rudyard Kipling⟩

**lev·ant and cou·chant** \ˌlevəntən¦kau̇chənt\ *adj* [alter. of ME *couchant and levant*, part trans. of MF *couchant et levant* lying down and rising up, fr. *couchant* (pres. part. of *coucher* to lay down, *se coucher* to lie down) + *et* and + *levant* (pres. part. of *lever* to raise, *se lever* to rise) — more at COUCH] : rising up and lying down — used of trespassing beasts and indicating that they have been long enough on land to lie down and rise up to feed, such time being held to include a day and night at the least and being required as grounds for legal distraint

**levant cotton** *n, usu cap L* : an annual Old World cotton (*Gossypium herbaceum*) that has heart-shaped 5-lobed to 7-lobed leaves, yellow flowers with purplish centers, and small fruits with large seeds and short grayish lint and that is sometimes considered to be one of the ancestors of modern short-staple commercial cottons

**levant dollar** *n, usu cap L* [so called fr. its wide circulation in the Levant] : MARIA THERESA DOLLAR

**¹le·vant·er** \lə'vantə(r)\ *n* -s [*Levant*, the countries of the eastern Mediterranean + E *-er*] **1** *cap* : a native or inhabitant of the Levant **2** : a strong easterly Mediterranean wind ⟨the Mediterranean squadron battling its way into Valletta harbor through the high steep seas of a ~ —C.S.Forester⟩

**²levanter** \"\ *n* -s [⁵*levant* + *-er*] : one that levants to avoid paying a debt or a bet

**³levanter** \"\ *n* -s [³*levant* + *-er*] : a leather dresser who works up or imitates the grain of levant skins

**¹levan·tine** \'levən.ˌtīn, -tēn, lə'van-\ *adj, usu cap* [*Levant*, the countries of the eastern Mediterranean + E *-ine*] : of or relating to the Levant

**²levantine** \"\ *n* -s **1** *cap* : a native or inhabitant of the Levant; *esp* : a cosmopolitan descendant of Frenchmen or Italians who is often a middleman between Europeans and the indigenous peoples **2 a** : a silk fabric formerly made in the Levant **b** : a twilled cotton with a glazed finish used chiefly for linings

**levan·tin·ism** \-ˌī,nizəm, -ē,n-\ *n* -s *usu cap* : customs, interests, ideas, or attitudes characteristic of Levantine peoples

**levant morocco** *n, usu cap L* : leather from sheep, goat, or seal skins with drawn grain pattern used for bookbinding — called also *Levant*

**levant red** *n, often cap L* : TURKEY RED

**levant sponge** *or* **levantine sponge** *n, usu cap L* : TURKEY CUP SPONGE

**levant wormseed** *n, usu cap L* **1** : the buds of a European wormwood (*Artemisia cina*) used as an anthelmintic **2** : the plant bearing Levant wormseed

**levant wormseed oil** *n, usu cap L* : a yellow essential oil obtained from the flowers of Levant wormseed for use as an anthelmintic

**le·va·ri fa·ci·as** \lə'varē'fākē,as\ *n* [NL, you should cause to be levied] : a common-law writ of execution for the satisfaction of a judgment debt out of the goods and lands or profits of the lands of the judgment debtor — compare FIERI FACIAS

**lev·arterenol** \ˌlev+\ *n* [*lev-* + *arterenol*] : levorotatory norepinephrine

**le·va·tor** \lə'vād·ə(r), -vā·d-\ *n, pl* **lev·a·to·res** \ˌlevə'tōr-(ˌ)ēz\ *or* **levators** [NL, fr. ML, lever, one that levies, fr. L *levatus* (past part. of *levare* to raise) + *-or* — more at LEVER] : a muscle that serves to raise a body part — compare DEPRESSOR

**¹le·vee** \'levē, -vi; lə'vē, -'vā\ *n* -s [F *lever*, fr. MF, action of rising from bed, fr. *lever* to rise from bed, raise, fr. L *levare* to raise] **1 a** : a reception held by a person of distinction on rising from bed ⟨the Sun King had one nobleman to hand him his stockings, another his shirt, in his morning ~ —Saul Bellow⟩ **b** *Brit* : an afternoon assembly at which the king or his representative receives only men **c** : a fashionable party or reception usu. in honor of a particular person ⟨the years of ~s and parades and other suave peacetime occasions —Gladys B. Stern⟩ ⟨young ladies who were invited to ~s, as the college receptions were then called —Mary A. Allen⟩ ⟨they were dressed as if for a ~ —A.J.Liebling⟩ **2** *archaic* : the act or action of arising from or as if from bed ⟨the sun's ~ —Thomas Gray⟩ **3** *obs* : the guests gathered at a levee

**²levee** *vt* **leveed; leveed; leveeing; levees** *obs* : to court (the great or powerful) by attending or seeking entry to levees

**³lev·ee** \'levē, -vi\ *n* -s [F *levée*, fr. MF *levee* levee, action of raising, fr. OF, action of raising, fr. fem. of *levé*, past part. of *lever* to raise] **1 a** : an embankment designed to prevent flooding ⟨the Mississippi river ~s have often had to be sandbagged⟩ **b** : a river landing place : PIER, QUAY **2** : a small continuous dike or ridge of earth for confining the irrigation checks of land to be flooded **3** : the very low ridge sometimes built up by streams on their floodplains on either side of their channels **4** : a red-light district esp. in Chicago **syn** see WHARF

**⁴levee** \"\ *vt* **leveed; leveed; leveeing; levees** : to provide with a levee ⟨*leveed* the stream channel⟩ ⟨*leveed* banks⟩

**levee en masse** *var of* LEVY EN MASSE

**¹lev·el** \'levəl\ *n* -s [ME *livel, level*, fr. MF *livel*, fr. (assumed) VL *libellum*, fr. L *libella*, dim. of *libra* pound, weight, balance] **1 a** : a device for finding a horizontal line or plane by means

level 1a

of a bubble in a nonfreezing liquid (as alcohol or ether) that shows adjustment to the horizontal by movement of the bubble to the center of a glass tube that is slightly bowed up from the horizontal longitudinally **b** : a surveyor's telescope on which is mounted a sensitive bubble tube and which indicates a horizontal line of sight when the bubble is centered by means of leveling screws **c** [prob. fr. ²*level*] : a measurement of the difference of altitude of two points by means of a level ⟨take a ~⟩ **2** : horizontal state or condition : uniform altitude ⟨brings the tilted surface to a ~⟩; *esp* : equilibrium of a fluid marked by a horizontal surface of even altitude ⟨water tries to find its own ~⟩ **3** : an approximately horizontal line or surface: as **a** : such a line or surface taken as an index of altitude ⟨wall charts arranged at eye ~ —J.K.Blake⟩ ⟨we were then 400 feet beneath the ~ of the fields overhead —Andrew Finn⟩ **b** : an area of country unbroken by noticeable elevations or depressions ⟨a side-hill village, spilling from the ~ of a plateau down a sharp incline into the valley —*Amer. Guide Series: Vt.*⟩ **4** : a position in any scale of achievement, importance, significance, or value : PLANE, RANK: as **a** : a degree of artistic, intellectual, or spiritual meaning ⟨the ~ of insight is generally very high —S.E.Hyman⟩ ⟨the ~ of excellence achieved in the novel . . . provides an imposing yardstick against which the film repeatedly will be measured —Arthur Knight⟩ ⟨different ~s or orders of truth —J.W.Krutch⟩ **b** : a measure of personal worth or dignity ⟨I don't feel that it's necessary to quarrel with people. One puts himself on their ~ in that way —J.C.Powys⟩ **c** : a rank in an organization or hierarchy ⟨stipulated that the meeting should be on the ~ of foreign ministers —*N.Y. Times*⟩ ⟨had a genius for . . . using her associates at all ~s in . . . building her own career —Harrison Smith⟩ ⟨only on the provincial and state ~ had a certain regrouping taken place —*Americana Annual*⟩ ⟨handled major problems of the union on a national ~ —*Current Biog.*⟩ **d** : social standing or precedence ⟨the social ~s . . . were laid upon one's position in the university rather than money —Virginia D. Dawson & Betty D. Wilson⟩ **5 a** : a line or surface that cuts perpendicularly all plumb lines that it meets and hence would everywhere coincide with a surface of still water **b** : the plane of the horizon or a line in it **6** : an open stretch of water in a canal or river (as between two canal locks) **7** [²*level*] *obs* : the act of aiming a gun or other missile-firing weapon **8 a** : a horizontal passage in a mine intended for regular working and transportation — compare ADIT **b** : the horizontal plane containing a main level and other workings (as crosscuts and drifts) ⟨the 700-foot ~⟩ — compare DRIFT 6 **9** : a characteristic and fairly uniform concentration of a constituent of the blood or other body fluid ⟨a normal blood-sugar ~⟩ **10** : the magnitude of a quantity considered in relation to an arbitrary reference value (as volts or decibels) ⟨a scale of auditory magnitudes has been derived from loudness tests and can be used whenever the loudness ~ of a sound is known —J.C.Steinberg & W.A.Munson⟩ ⟨video signal ~ is usually referred to in terms of volts, while audio ~ is measured in volume units —H.E.Ennes⟩ **11** : ENERGY LEVEL **12 a** : a degree of ability or aptitude or measure of performance ⟨the student who has not reached an advanced ~ —A.S.Hornby⟩ ⟨they slow the game down to a tempo corresponding to their ~ of fitness —W.J.Finn⟩ **b** : a grade of mental or emotional development or maturity ⟨evidence as to ~s of personality development (e.g., anal, oral) —G.P.Murdock⟩ **13** : a plane of economic activity, prices, or production ⟨production, employment, and national income were at record peacetime ~s —*Collier's Yr. Bk.*⟩ ⟨continued high ~ of private capital investments —Fritz Sternberg⟩ **14** : a natural or fit position in relation to others — used in the phrase *one's level* ⟨the peso . . . was allowed to seek its own ~ —*Collier's Yr. Bk.*⟩ — **on the level** : bona fide : GENUINE, HONEST ⟨the deal seems to be *on the level*⟩ ⟨gained wide credit for acting always *on the level*⟩

**²level** \"\ *vb* **leveled** *or* **levelled; leveled** *or* **levelled; leveling** *or* **levelling** \-v(ə)liŋ\ **levels** [ME *levellen*, fr. *livel, level*, n. — more at ¹LEVEL] *vt* **1** : to make (a line or surface) horizontal : even off : make flat or level ⟨they are the natural highways of all nations . . . ~*ing* the ground and removing obstacles from the path of the traveler —H.D. Thoreau⟩ **2 a** : to bring to a horizontal aiming position ⟨a second sentry . . . ~*ed* his halberd at the parson's breast —Max Peacock⟩ ⟨hesitates to ~ his barrage directly —C.H. Stoddard⟩ **b** : AIM, DIRECT ⟨bitter taunts that his wife had ~*ed* at him —J.C.Powys⟩ ⟨two major criticisms have been ~*ed* at the program —*N.Y. Times*⟩ ⟨jokes, ridicule, and ill-natured gossip were ~*ed* against the daring females who succeeded in getting employment —Langston Day⟩ **3** : to bring to a common level or plane (as of rank or condition) : EQUALIZE ⟨love ~s all ranks —W.S.Gilbert⟩ ⟨social differences in the plantation country of the South were ~*ed* down to some extent after the Civil War —Hans Kurath⟩ **4 a** : to lay level with the ground : FLATTEN, RAZE ⟨a mysterious fire ~*ed* the tower —*Amer. Guide Series: Pa.*⟩ ⟨the cyclone of 1889 ~*ed* the entire city —*Amer. Guide Series: Minn.*⟩ **b** : to knock down : lay prone ⟨brought his fist up quickly under my chin and ~*ed* me backwards on the bed —Shea Murphy⟩ **5** : to make even, equal, or uniform (as in color) **6** : to alter by linguistic or phonetic leveling (sense 2) **7** : to find the heights of different points in (a piece of land) esp. with a surveyor's level : to make a contour of by means of a level — sometimes used with *over* or *up* ~ *vi* **1** : to attain or come to a level — often used with *down, out*, or *up* ⟨the deck of the *Janet* ~*ed* a little as she slowed down —Arnold Gifford⟩ ⟨the trail turned south there and ~*ed* out —W.V.T.Clark⟩ **2 a** : to aim a gun or other weapon horizontally ⟨they ~ : a volley, a smoke and the clearing of smoke —Robert Browning⟩ **b** *obs* : to direct attention or effort at an object **3** : to bring persons or things to a level ⟨your levelers wish to ~ down as far as themselves; but they cannot bear ~*ing* up to themselves —Samuel Johnson⟩ **4** : to impart color evenly or with uniform shade ⟨dyes that ~ readily⟩ **5** : to be made identical by linguistic or phonetic leveling (sense 2) **6** : to form a smooth film free of brush marks — used of paints **7** : to deal frankly and without artifice : speak candidly and openly ⟨I'll ~ with you. From you I hold back nothing —Richard Brooks⟩

**³level** \"\ *adj* [¹*level*] **1 a** : having no part higher than another : conforming to the curvature of the earth's ocean surfaces ⟨these low, ~ landscapes . . . are characteristic of the continent as a whole —*Atlas of Australian Resources*⟩ ⟨this land is so ~ that before the erection of . . . fences snow-sailing was a popular and very exciting sport —*Amer. Guide Series: Minn.*⟩ **b** : coinciding or parallel with the plane of the horizon : HORIZONTAL ⟨the bottom of the excavation must be ~ —J.R.Dalzell⟩ **2 a** : even or unvarying in height ⟨secure the advantage of a ~ temperature —*Oil*⟩ **b** : equal in advantage, progression, or standing ⟨where every democratic dream had been fulfilled, and where all men had started ~ —W.B.Yeats⟩ ⟨another rider drew ~ with the squire —T.B. Costain⟩ ⟨sitting down as a ~ member of the dairyman's household seemed at the outset an undignified proceeding —Thomas Hardy⟩ **c** : proceeding monotonously or uneventfully ⟨their ~ life is but a smoldering fire, unquenched by want, unfanned by strong desire—Oliver Goldsmith⟩ **d** (1) : PENETRATING, STEADY, UNFLINCHING, UNWAVERING ⟨she gave him a ~ look —Louis Auchincloss⟩ (2) : CALM, QUIET, UNEXCITED ⟨finished his bottle and began to speak in ~ tones and with a quiet final authority —Honor Tracy⟩ ⟨it was not in ~ and sober mood that the heir was expected but in a stew of high excitement —Francis Hackett⟩ **e** : contested on even terms : exhibiting no handicap ⟨the race was clearly ~⟩ **3** : maintaining equilibrium : BALANCED, JUST, STEADY ⟨a longtime producer, who, from seeing so many actors come and go, keeps a ~ head about them —*N.Y. Times*⟩ ⟨arrive at a justly proportioned and ~ judgment on this affair —Sir Winston Churchill⟩ **4** : distributed evenly : of a uniform shade ⟨a badly prepared fabric cannot be expected to give ~ dyeing —R.S.Horsfall & L.G.Lawrie⟩ **5 a** : uttered with stress on two or more syllables that is heavy and equal or apprehended as equal ⟨pronounced *impossible* with ~ stress⟩ ⟨~ stress is characteristic of the French language⟩ **b** : uttered at a pitch that remains the same for an entire syllable or for more than one ⟨a kind of ~ whine —Robert Browning⟩ **6** : being a surface perpendicular to all lines of force in a field of force so that no energy is transformed in moving a mass along it : EQUIPOTENTIAL **7 a** : suited to a particular plane of ability or achievement — usu. used in combination ⟨college-*level* institutes and higher-than-college-*level* academies—Joseph Alsop⟩ **b** : conducted at or proper to a particular organizational rank or status — usu. used in combination ⟨the nature and extent of top-*level* thinking with respect to planned action —J.F.H.Turton⟩ **8** : evenly matched in appearance and qualities ⟨"a nice ~ lot," said the colonel . . . as they watched the first four companies —Rudyard Kipling⟩ ⟨by only keeping white hounds and by most careful and judicious mating he obtained a ~ pack in 20 years —B.V.Fitzgerald⟩ **9** : bona fide : untainted by devious motive or intent to deceive ⟨the game is ~⟩ **10** : of or relating to the spreading out of a cost or charge in even payments over a period of time rather than making a single lump sum payment ⟨~ premium plans are offered widely by insurance companies⟩

**syn** FLAT, PLAIN, PLANE, EVEN, SMOOTH, FLUSH: LEVEL in its literal meanings is almost entirely limited to the notion of conforming to or paralleling either the curvature line of the surface of the earth or the nearly identical line horizon to horizon; its stress is on the notion of a plane through either of these lines and its connotation not so precise that no minor irregularity of surface is possible. Its suggestion is usu. a favorable one ⟨a *level* and convenient lot⟩ FLAT stresses the notion of an unbroken horizontal surface; it indicates lack of a break in surface contour and may be deprecatory ⟨*flat* uninteresting prairies⟩ No longer common, the adjective PLAIN in this sense is likely to apply to terrain and have about the same implications as the noun PLAIN. PLANE, a close cognate of PLAIN, similarly has the connotations of the noun PLAIN. In mathematical use it contrasts with *solid* or *spherical*. EVEN stresses lack of noteworthy breaks or irregularities in surfaces although it does not indicate, as SMOOTH does, complete lack of any roughnesses, ruptures, or irregularities. SMOOTH stresses a completely regular surface lacking irregularities perceptible to touch or sight, roughnesses, dents, ridges, breaks, or inept jointures. SMOOTH has no suggestion of a given plane. FLUSH may stress lack of designed breaks in an even surface, like panels, ridges, molding strips, or cornices; it may suggest the setting or embedding of one thing into another leaving an uninterrupted plane ⟨bolts set *flush*⟩ — **level best** : very best ⟨did his *level best* to make money at it —F.L.Allen⟩

**⁴level** *adv, obs* : in a level line or manner

**level-coil** *n* [by folk etymology (influence of ³*level* and ¹*coil*) fr. MF *lever le cul* to raise or remove the rump, displace from a seat] **1** *obs* : an old game in which the players at a given signal replace each other in seats amid a general scramble and tumult **2** *obs* : a noisy sport or melee

**level crossing** *n, Brit* : GRADE CROSSING

**leveled** *or* **levelled** *past of* LEVEL

**lev·el·er** *or* **lev·el·ler** \'lev(ə)lə(r)\ *n* -s **1** : one that levels: as **a** : a scraper for leveling ground ⟨large automatic ~s like the land plane —O.W.Israelsen⟩ **b** : an adjustable attachment on row-cultivating tools for leveling off ridges left by the cultivators **2 a** *usu leveller, usu cap* : one of a group of radicals arising in the Parliamentary army during the English Civil War and advocating a program of constitutional reform designed to secure equality before the law for all men esp. in political and economic rights together with religious toleration as opposed to all forms of church establishment ⟨the *Levellers* . . . objected to political privilege on the part of the nobility —G.H.Sabine⟩ **b** : one advocating or held to advocate the leveling of differences of rank, privilege, or possession among men; *esp* : one favoring the removal of political or social inequalities ⟨determined ~s of society, the Swedish dislike any sort of ostentation —*Harper's Bazaar*⟩ ⟨the republicans, the ~s, the fanatics, — all ranged themselves on the side of the new ideas —George Bancroft⟩ **c** : something that tends to reduce or eliminate differences among men ⟨for us housewives, a ration card was the great ~ —Joan Comay⟩ ⟨war has always been the great ~ —*Harper's*⟩

**level-headed** \¦==¦==\ *adj* : exhibiting balance and deliberation : COOL ⟨the more *level-headed* leaders distrusted this flamboyant orator —Desmond Ryan⟩ — **level-head·ed·ness** \==¦===\ *n*

**leveling** *or* **levelling** *n* -s [fr. gerund of ²*level*] **1** : the action of one that levels **2** : a change in the spelling or pronunciation of a word or word form or element to conform with that of a different although often related one : obliteration of a phonetic or linguistic distinction ⟨Middle English *sang* (singular) and *sungen* (plural) have both become *sang* by ~ in modern English⟩ ⟨~ of *riding* and *writing* is frequent in American speech⟩ **3** : the finding of a horizontal line, the ascertaining of differences of elevation between points on the earth's surface, or the establishing of grades (as for a railway roadbed) by use of a surveyor's level **4** : the establishment of a standard time for a job or a piecework operation by time-study computations based on the actual performance of workers in order to fix incentive pay rates or appraise workers' efficiency **5** : the formation of a smooth film free of brush marks — used of paints

**leveling rod** *n* : a graduated rod used in measuring the vertical distance between a point on the ground and the line of sight of a surveyor's level

**leveling screw** *n* : one of three or more adjusting screws for bringing an instrument or other object into level

**lev·el·ism** \'levə,lizəm\ *n* -s *archaic* : disposition or endeavor to level distinctions of rank

**lev·el·ly** \-vəl(l)ē, -)i\ *adv* : in a level manner

**lev·el·man** \'levəlmən, -,man\ *n, pl* **levelmen** : a surveyor who operates a leveling instrument

**level measure** *n* : dry measure obtained by filling a container level with the top — called also *struck measure*

**levelness** *n* -ES : the quality or state of being level

**level off** *vt* : to make smooth or even ⟨dry ingredients are heaped into the utensil, then *leveled off* with a knife —Ida B. Allen⟩ ⟨bulldozers quickly *leveled off* the site⟩ ~ *vi* **1** : to reach a constant rate or unvarying volume, total, or amount : attain equilibrium : STABILIZE ⟨populations often *level off* as they press harder on natural resources⟩ ⟨the signs are that unemployment is *leveling off* —*Wall Street Jour.*⟩ **2** : to change a flight path to horizontal after a climb, glide, or dive **3** : to approach a limit ⟨the plate current in a vacuum tube *levels off* as the applied voltage is increased⟩

**level premium** *n* : one of a series of equal installments by which the premium on an insurance policy may be paid rather than in a lump sum

**levels** *pl of* LEVEL, *pres 3d sing of* LEVEL

**level-wind** \¦==¦=\ *n* : a device for winding a fishing line evenly on a multiplying reel

**¹lever** \'levə(r), 'lēv-\ *n* -s [ME *lever, levour*, fr. OF *levier*, fr. *lever* to raise, fr. L *levare*; akin to L *levis* light, having little weight — more at LIGHT] **1 a** : a bar used for prying or dislodging something : CROWBAR **b** : any means, instrument, or agency used for achieving a purpose (as by inducing or compelling action or providing motive) : TOOL ⟨attempts to use food as a political ~ —*Time*⟩ ⟨could use the girl's action as a ~ to make her lawyer . . . turn over the letters —Erle Stanley Gardner⟩ ⟨others misuse the interview as a ~ to force the employee to resign —R.S.Brown⟩ ⟨shies away from reflection . . . and seeks out the ~s of power — and those who control them —Dwight Macdonald⟩ **2 a** : a rigid piece that transmits and modifies force or motion when forces are applied at two points and it turns about a third; *specif* : a bar of metal, wood, or other rigid substance used to exert a pressure or sustain a weight at one point of its length by the application of a force at a second and turning at a third on a fulcrum **b** : a projecting piece by which a mechanism is operated or adjusted ⟨gearshift ~⟩ ⟨to increase speed move the starting ~ to the right⟩ **3** : LEVER TUMBLER **4** : a supported or hanging position in which a gymnast's body while extended or bent at right angles at the hips is held parallel to the floor

three kinds of levers; *F* fulcrum, *P* power, *W* weight

**²lever** \"\ *vb* **levered; levered; levering** \-v(ə)riŋ\ **levers** *vi* **1** : to pry or work with or as if with a lever ⟨~*ing* at the rock —F.V.W.Mason⟩ **2** : to operate a lever ~ *vt* **1** : to pry, raise, or move with or as if with a lever ⟨~*ed* the other boot off with his bare toes —Richard Llewellyn⟩ ⟨like every alliance . . . it can be ~*ed* into action only with difficulty —A.A.Berle⟩ **2** : to operate as a lever ⟨~s the throttles back until the engines are turning out 44 inches at 2400 revolutions —Richard Thruelsen⟩

**lever action** *n* : a rifle action that is manually operated by an external lever

**lever·age** \'lev(ə)rij, 'lēv-, -rēj\ *n* -s **1 a** : the action or mechanical effect of a lever ⟨its weight is greatly aggravated by the ~ caused by its projection —*Harper's*⟩ **b :** an arrangement or system of levers **2 :** EFFECTIVENESS, POWER, INFLUENCE ⟨would have had little bargaining ~ while the blast furnaces were cold —*Christian Science Monitor*⟩ ⟨serious criticism has failed of ~ —Louis Kronenberger⟩ **3 :** the intensified speculative effect of market fluctuations on a company's common stock caused by its outstanding bonds and preferred stock on which the interest rate is fixed ⟨the majority of the large closed-end companies do have senior securities outstanding in varying amounts, and accordingly the companies have varying degrees of ~ —H.V.Prochnow⟩

**lever arm** *n* **:** the perpendicular distance from the fulcrum of a lever to the line of action of the effort or to the line of action of the weight

**lev·er·et** \'lev(ə)rət\ *n* -s [ME, fr. (assumed) MF *levret*, fr. MF *levre* hare (fr. L *lepor-*, *lepus*) + *-et* — more at LAPIN] **1 :** a hare in its first year **2** *obs* **:** MISTRESS, LIGHT-O'-LOVE

**lever·man** \'levə(r)mən, 'lēv-\ *n, pl* **levermen :** a man who operates levers or controls: as **a :** TOWERMAN ⟨a ~ on duty in the switch tower nearby was suspended soon after the accident —*N.Y. Times*⟩ **b :** a sawmill deckman **c :** a sawmill worker who controls the mechanism that transfers lumber from one set of conveyor rolls to another or from rolls to platform — called also *rollerman* **d :** an operator of a donkey engine for moving logs **e :** a member of a forging crew who handles billets during forging

**lever scales** *n pl* **:** STEELYARD

**lever shears** *n pl* **:** shears constructed on the principle of the lever — called also *alligator shears, crocodile shears*

**lever tumbler** *n* **:** an internal member of a lock usu. of flat sheet metal that is moved by a key to operate the bolt — distinguished from *pin tumbler* and *sliding tumbler*

**lever watch** *n* **:** a watch with lever escapement having a vibrating lever to connect the action of the escape wheel with that of the balance

**leverwood** \'==,=\ *n* **:** HOP HORNBEAM

**levet** *n* -s [prob. fr. It *levata* call to arms, action of raising, fr. fem. of *levato*, past part. of *levare* to raise, fr. L — more at LEVER] *obs* **:** REVEILLE

**levi·able** \'levēəbəl\ *adj* [ME *levyable*, fr. *levien* to levy + *-able*] **1 :** that may be levied ⟨the fine . . . is ~ not upon the string or succession of oaths, but upon each individual malediction —A.P.Herbert⟩ **2 :** that may be levied upon ⟨~ goods⟩

**¹le·vi·a·than** \lə'vīəthən\ *n* -s [ME, fr. LL, fr. Heb *liwyāthān*] **1 a** *often cap* **:** a sea monster often symbolizing evil in the Old Testament and in Christian literature ⟨thou didst crush the heads of ~ —Ps 74:14 (RSV)⟩ **b** (1) **:** any of various large sea animals ⟨this ~ of animals is the great Blue Whale —Weston LaBarre⟩ (2) a large oceangoing ship ⟨the modern ~ would be a commercial failure were the traveling public not willing to pay . . . for the extra speed, comfort, and luxury —W.D.Winter⟩ **c** *archaic* **:** a wealthy or powerful man **2** *or* **leviathan state** *usu cap L* [so called fr. the use of the word *Leviathan* to designate the state in the book *Leviathan* (1651) by Thomas Hobbes †1679 Eng. philosopher] **:** the political state; *esp* **:** an all-powerful state usu. held to be characterized by a vast bureaucracy and machinery of coercion and exercising totalitarian control over its citizens ⟨the oppression of *Leviathan* at its worst —*Times Lit. Supp.*⟩ ⟨the prostration of the judiciary before the Nazi *Leviathan* —Karl Loewenstein⟩ ⟨millions . . . surrendered their right of private judgment to the *Leviathan state* —Geoffrey Bruun⟩ **3 :** the largest or most massive thing of its kind **:** the monster of a class ⟨America has come to look like . . . a ~ of mechanized power —Irwin Edman⟩ ⟨published that ~ of school books —G.H.Genzmer⟩ ⟨~ shovels . . . dig their wide trench as they crawl —Frederick Simpich †1950⟩

**²leviathan** \"\ *adj* **:** of enormous size **:** MONSTROUS, VAST ⟨the ~ proportions of international scandal —Paul Murray⟩ ⟨show the volume and pressure of that ~ intelligence —Christopher Morley⟩

**leviathan stitch** *n* **:** a double cross-stitch producing an 8-pointed figure usu. worked in wool on canvas

leviathan stitch

**levied** *past of* LEVY

**levi·er** \'levēə(r)\ *n* -s **:** one that levies

**levies** *pl of* LEVY, *pres 3d sing of* LEVY

**¹lev·i·gate** \'levə,gāt\ *vt* -ED/-ING/-S [L *levigatus*, past part. of *levigare*, fr. *levis* smooth + *agere* to drive — more at LIME, AGENT] **1** *archaic* **:** to polish or make smooth **2 a :** to grind to a fine smooth powder while in moist condition ⟨by first *levigating* the zinc oxide with a small amount of glycerin a smooth paste is obtained —*Art of Compounding*⟩ **b :** to separate (fine powder) from coarser material by suspending in a liquid ⟨whiting is pure finely divided calcium carbonate prepared by wet-grinding and *levigating* natural chalk —R.N.Shreve⟩

**²lev·i·gate** \'levəgət, -və,gāt\ *adj* [L *levigatus*] *bot* **:** GLABROUS

**lev·i·ga·tion** \,levə'gāshən\ *n* -s [ME *levygacyon*, fr. L *levigation-*, *levigatio*, fr. *levigatus* + *-ion-*, *-io* -ion] **:** the action or process of smoothing or levigating

**lev·i·ga·tor** \'==,gād·ə(r)\ *n* -s **1 :** a workman who levigates (as pigments) **2 :** a levigating tool

**lev·in** \'levən\ *n* -s [ME *levene*; prob. akin to Goth *lauhmuni* lightning, *liuhath* light — more at LIGHT] *archaic* **:** LIGHTNING

**le·vin tube** *also* **le·vine tube** \lə'vēn-\ *n, usu cap L* [after Abraham Louis *Levin* †1940 Am. physician who invented it] *med* **:** a tube designed to be passed into the stomach or duodenum through the nose

**levi·rate** \'levərət, 'lēv-, -,rāt\ *n* -s *often attrib* [L *levir* husband's brother + E *-ate*; akin to OE *tācor* husband's brother, OHG *zeihhur*, Gk *daēr*, Skt *devr*] **:** the marriage of a widow by the brother or occas. the heir of her deceased husband sometimes (as among the ancient Hebrews) constituting a compulsory custom — compare JUNIOR LEVIRATE, SORORATE — **levi·rat·ic** \;==¦rad·ik\ *adj*

**Le·vi's** \'lē,vīz\ *trademark* — used for heavy blue denim pants that are reinforced at strain points with copper rivets and have close-fitting legs

**le·vis·ti·cum** \lə'vistəkəm\ *n, cap* [NL, fr. LL, lovage — more at LOVAGE] **:** a genus of European herbs (family Umbelliferae) with yellow flowers and dorsally flattened fruit — see LOVAGE

**lev·i·tate** \'levə,tāt\ *vb* -ED/-ING/-S [*levity* + *-ate*] *vi* **:** to rise or float in the air esp. in seeming defiance of gravitation (as objects at a spiritualistic seance) ~ *vt* **:** to lift, suspend, or cause to move in the air esp. in seeming defiance of gravitation ⟨*levitating* being the term used by spiritualistic mediums for causing chairs and tables to rise into the air without apparent motivation —Alva Johnston⟩ ⟨we are *levitated* between acceptance and disbelief —Sean O'Faolain⟩ **syn** see RISE

**lev·i·ta·tion** \,==¦tāshən\ *n* -s [*levity* + *-ation*] **:** a rising or lifting in the air ⟨speed and the special ~ that skates give to the human form —H.E.Clurman⟩ ⟨the use of hydrogen gas for ~ —*Manchester Guardian Weekly*⟩; *esp* **:** the rising or lifting of a person or thing by means held to be supernatural ⟨reported that he had seen manifestations of ~, had heard accordions play without being touched by human hands —M.L.Bach⟩ — **lev·i·ta·tion·al** \¦==¦tāshən°l, -shnəl\ *adj*

**lev·i·ta·tive** \'==,tād·iv\ *adj* [*levitate* + *-ive*] **:** having the ability to rise by levitation **:** marked by or relating to levitation

**lev·i·ta·tor** \'==,tād·ə(r)\ *n* -s **:** one that levitates

**le·vite** \'lē,vīt, *usu* -īd·+V\ *n* -s [ME, fr. LL *Levita*, *Levites*, fr. Gk *Leuitēs*, fr. *Leui* Levi, third son of Jacob and ancestor of the Levites (fr. Heb *Lēwī*) + *-itēs* -ite] **1** *usu cap* **:** a member of the Hebrew tribe of Levi **:** a descendant of Levi; *specif* **:** a non-Aaronic descendant of Levi assigned to assist the Levitical priests of the family of Aaron in the care of the tabernacle and later of the temple **2** *sometimes cap* **:** a Christian cleric in orders below those of priest; *specif* **:** DEACON 1

**le·vit·i·cal** \lə'vid·ə̇kəl, -it|, |ēk-\ *also* **le·vit·ic** \|ik, |ēk\ *adj, usu cap* [*levitical* fr. LL *leviticus* levitical (fr. Gk *leuitikos*, fr. *Leuitēs* Levite + *-ikos* -ic) + E *-al*; *levitic* fr. LL *leviticus*] **1 a :** of, characteristic of, or relating to the Levites **b :** qualified as a Levite **2 :** of, relating to, or characteristic of the book of Leviticus **3 a :** of or relating to Hebrew dogma or ritual ⟨*Levitical* questions⟩ **b :** PRIESTLY **4 :** AARONIC 2 — **le·vit·i·cal·ly** \|ə̇k(ə)lē, |ēk-, -li\ *adv, usu cap*

**levitical degrees** *n pl, usu cap L* **:** the degrees of kinship within which marriage is forbidden in Leviticus 18

**lev·i·ty** \'levəd·ē, -ətē, -i\ *n* -ES [L *levitat-*, *levitas* lightness in weight, frivolity, fr. *levis* light + *-itat-*, *-itas* -ity — more at LIGHT] **1 a :** excessive or unseemly frivolity **:** lack of fitting seriousness **:** TRIFLING ⟨light without ~ and serious without solemnity, always within the limits of classically disciplined form —*New Yorker*⟩ ⟨there was about him something that made ~ seem out of place —O.S.J.Gogarty⟩ **b :** lack of steadiness **:** CHANGEABLENESS, FICKLENESS, INCONSTANCY ⟨that emotional seriousness will not transform intellectual ~ —W.C.Brownell⟩ ⟨pitted its gravity and longevity against the ~ and evanescence of the brisk fire —Charles Dickens⟩ **2 a :** the quality or state of being light in weight ⟨the qualities of warmth, ~, and least resistance to the air —William Paley⟩ **b :** a positive property of lightness opposed to gravity and formerly believed to be a characteristic of some physical objects ⟨it will no longer be lightness in the sense of very little weight, but positive and active lightness; we call this ~ —George Adams & Olive Whicher⟩ ⟨substitutes for universal gravity a polarity of gravity and ~, the latter a nonmechanical . . . force apparent . . . in certain volcanic phenomena and the growth of plants —*Times Lit. Supp.*⟩

**le·vo** *or* **lae·vo** \'lē(,)vō\ *adj* [*lev-*] **:** LEVOROTATORY

**levo-** — see LEV-

**le·vo·glucosan** \¦lē(,)vō+\ *n* [*lev-* + *glucosan*] **:** a levorotatory crystalline anhydride $C_6H_{10}O_5$ of glucose that is best prepared by treating the beta form of phenyl glucoside with alkali, and that regenerates glucose on heating with water; 1,6-anhydro-β-D-glucose — compare GLUCOSAN; GLUCOSE illustration

**le·vo·gyrate** \¦lēvō+\ *or* **le·vo·gyre** \'lēvō+,-\ *adj* [*levogyrate* fr. *lev-* + *gyrate*, adj.; *levogyre* ISV *lev-* + *-gyre* (fr. L *gyrus* circular motion) — more at GYRE] **:** LEVOROTATORY

**le·vo·pimaric acid** \¦=(,)=+ . . . -\ *n* [*levopimaric* ISV *lev-* + *pimaric* (in *pimaric acid*)] **:** a crystalline levorotatory resin acid $C_{19}H_{29}COOH$ occurring esp. in oleoresins from pine trees and isomerizing readily to abietic acid on heating or treatment with acids

**le·vo·rotation** \¦lēvō+\ *n* [*lev-* + *rotation*] **:** left-handed or counterclockwise rotation — used chiefly of the plane of polarization of light; opposed to *dextrorotation;* compare OPTICAL ROTATION

**le·vo·rotatory** *or* **le·vo·rotary** \"+\ *adj* [*lev-* + *rotatory* or *rotary*] **:** turning toward the left hand or counterclockwise; *esp* **:** rotating the plane of polarization of light toward the left hand ⟨~ crystals⟩ ⟨~ sugar solutions⟩ — opposed to *dextrorotatory;* compare OPTICALLY ACTIVE

**lev·u·li·nate** \'levyələ,nāt\ *n* -s [*levulinic* (in *levulinic acid*) + *-ate*] **:** a salt of levulinic acid

**lev·u·lin·ic acid** \¦==¦linik-\ *n* [*levulinic* ISV *levulin* substance yielding levulose on hydrolysis (ISV *levul-* — fr. *levulose* — + *-in*) + *-ic*] **:** a crystalline keto acid $CH_3CO(CH_2)_2COOH$ obtained by action of dilute acids on hexoses (as levulose) and on substances (as starch or sucrose) that yield hexoses on hydrolysis

**lev·u·lose** \'==,lōs *also* -ōz\ *n* -s [ISV *lev-* + *-ule* + *-ose*] **:** levorotatory D-fructose obtained usu. by hydrolysis either of inulin from dahlia tubers or from the Jerusalem artichoke or of sucrose

**¹levy** \'levē, -vi\ *n* -ES [ME *levee*, *levy*, fr. MF *levee* levy, action of raising, fr. OF, action of raising, fr. fem. of *levé*, past part. of *lever* to raise — more at LEVER] **1 a :** the imposition or collection of an assessment, tax, tribute, or fine ⟨make a ~ on all meat, out of which to pay the running costs of the . . . organization —*Sydney* (*Australia*) *Bull.*⟩; *specif* **:** the taking of property on execution to satisfy a judgment ⟨it authorizes a ~ upon property of the witness —E.D.Dickinson⟩ **b :** an amount levied **:** IMPOST, TAX ⟨a direct food ~ was imposed —Leonard Mason⟩ **2 a :** the enlistment or conscription of men for military service **:** MUSTER ⟨the ~ of the militia, which had previously been confined to the countryside, was extended to Paris —Evelyn Cruickshanks⟩ **b :** the troops raised by a levy ⟨defeat followed by victory had transmuted green *levies* into veteran soldiers —Peter Rainier⟩ ⟨*levies*, who were eating the village out of hearth and home —Marguerite Steen⟩

**²levy** \"\ *vb* -ED/-ING/-ES [ME *leveyen*, *levien*, fr. *levee*, *levy*, n.] *vt* **1 :** to impose or collect (as a tax or tribute) by legal process or by authority **:** EXACT ⟨we cannot ~ unlimited drafts on the future to avoid bankruptcy in the present —W.R.Inge⟩ ⟨there will be no European army if the exclusive right to ~ taxes is left to individual governments —*European Federation Now*⟩ ⟨the time-honored graft that policemen usually ~ on prostitutes —Green Peyton⟩ ⟨*levied* a heavy fine for contempt of court⟩ **b :** to exact or require (as a service) by authority or power ⟨upon those did Solomon ~ a tribute of bond service unto this day —1 Kings 9:21 (AV)⟩ **2 :** to enlist or conscript for military service ⟨go ~ men and make prepare for war —Shak.⟩ ⟨the armies of the early 17th century were mercenary, rapidly *levied*, disbanded again, haphazard —Hilaire Belloc⟩ **3 :** to carry on (war) **:** MAKE, WAGE ⟨treason against the U.S. shall consist only in ~*ing* war against them, or in adhering to their enemies, giving them aid and comfort —*U.S.Constitution*⟩ ⟨only a skirmish in the general war *levied* upon social distinctions —V.L.Parrington⟩ **4** *law* **a :** to seize in satisfaction of a legal claim or judgment **b :** to carry into effect (as a writ of execution) **:** ENFORCE **c :** to arrange (a fine) in settlement of a suit to establish title to land ⟨she was also prohibited from ~*ing* a fine —Joshua Williams⟩ ~ *vi* **1 :** to seize real or personal property or subject it to attachment or execution **:** make a levy ⟨*levied* on the judgment debtor's property under an execution⟩ **2 :** to draw for provisions or resources — usu. used with *on* ⟨I have *levied* on many writers for my essential conception of American culture —Max Lerner⟩ ⟨had *levied* on their cellars to produce new offerings —A.J.Liebling⟩

**³levy** \"\ *n* -ES [by shortening & alter. fr. *eleven pence* (approximate value of the coin)] **1 :** a Spanish real — used esp. in Pennsylvania, Maryland, and Delaware **2 :** the sum of 12½ cents

**levy court** *n* **:** a body of magistrates exercising in some states (as Delaware) the functions performed in other states by county commissioners ⟨the *Levy Court* of each county shall meet at the courthouse . . . three times in every year —*Del. Revised Statutes*⟩

**levy en masse** \¦levē-, -vi- + *pronunc at* EN MASSE\ *also* **le·vée en masse** \" *or* lə¦vā-\ *or* **levy in mass** *n, pl* **levies en masse** *also* **levées en masse** *or* **levies in mass** [*levy en masse* & *levy in mass* trans. of F *levée en masse*, fr. *levée* levy + *en masse*; *levee en masse* fr. F] *international law* **:** the spontaneous act of the people of a territory not yet occupied by an enemy force of taking up arms for self-defense upon the approach of an enemy without having had time to organize in accordance with recognized rules of warfare

**le·vyn·ite** \lä'vē,nīt\ *or* **le·vyne** \lä'vēn\ *n* -s [*levynite* fr. *levyne* (irreg. fr. Armand *Lévy* †1841 Fr. mineralogist + E *-ine*) + *-ite*] **:** a white or light-colored mineral $NaCa_3Al_7Si_{11}O_{36}.15H_2O$ that occurs in rhombohedral crystals and is a hydrous calcium aluminum silicate

**¹lew** \'lü\ *adj* [ME *lew*, *lewe* lukewarm, warm, fr. OE *hlēow* warm; akin to ON *hlýr* lukewarm — more at LEE] **1** *now dial Brit* **:** having little warmth **:** LUKEWARM **2** *now dial Brit* **:** ²LEE 1

**²lew** \"\ *n* -s *now dial Brit* **:** a place of shelter **:** the side sheltered (as from the wind)

**lewd** \'lüd\ *adj* [ME *lewed*, *lewede* vulgar, base, laical, fr. OE *lǣwede* laical] **1** *obs* **a :** of, relating to, or characteristic of common and ignorant people **:** VULGAR **b :** BASE, EVIL, WICKED — used of persons and their conduct **c :** POOR, WORTHLESS — used of things **2 a :** sexually unchaste or licentious **:** DISSOLUTE, LASCIVIOUS **b :** suggestive of or tending to moral looseness **:** inciting to sensual desire or imagination **:** INDECENT, OBSCENE, SALACIOUS ⟨moralists looked upon it as a ~ distraction —Lewis Mumford⟩ ⟨loud, ~ dissonances from the . . . orchestra in the pit —*Time*⟩ ⟨the hawk stood . . . with his ~ purple tongue lolling from his open beak —Liam O'Flaherty⟩

**lewd·ly** *adv* [ME *lewedly* ignorantly, badly, fr. *lewed*, *lewede* + *-ly*] **:** in a lewd manner

**lewd·ness** *n* -ES [ME *lewednesse* ignorance, wickedness, fr. *lewed*, *lewede* + *-nesse* -ness] **:** the quality or state of being lewd

**lewd·ster** \'lüdztə(r), -dst-\ *n* -s *archaic* **:** a lewd person

**lew·is** \'lüə̇s\ *n* -ES [prob. fr. the name *Lewis*] **:** an iron dovetailed tenon that is made in sections, can be fitted into a dovetail mortise, and is used in hoisting large stones — called also *lewisson*

lewis: *1* stone, *2* mortise, *3* tenon, *4* bolt, *5* link, *6* chain to pulleys

**lewis acid** *n, usu cap L* [after Gilbert N. *Lewis* †1946 Am. chemist] **:** ²ACID 2c

**lewis base** *n, usu cap L* **:** ¹BASE 8c

**lewis bolt** *n* **:** a bolt with an enlarged head leaded into masonry as a foundation bolt or into a stone for use as a lewis

**lewis gun** *n, usu cap L* [after Isaac N. *Lewis* †1931 Am. army officer and inventor] **:** a gas-operated air-cooled machine gun fed by a drum magazine and first used in World War I ⟨dropped my stick with a clatter like a *Lewis gun* —Angus Mowat⟩

**lew·i·sia** \lü'izh(ē)ə\ *n* [NL, fr. Meriwether *Lewis* †1809 Am. explorer + NL *-ia*] **1** *cap* **:** a large genus of herbs (family Portulacaceae) of western No. America with linear woolly leaves and large pink flowers — see BITTERROOT **2** -s **:** any plant of the genus *Lewisia*

**lew·i·sian** \(')lü¦izh(ē)ən\ *adj, usu cap* [*Lewis*, northern part of the island of Lewis with Harris, Outer Hebrides + E *-ian*] **:** of, relating to, or constituting a division of the Precambrian — see GEOLOGIC TIME table

**¹lew·is·ite** \'lüə̇,sīt\ *n* -s [William J. *Lewis* †1926 Eng. mineralogist + E *-ite*] **:** a mineral consisting of a titanian romeite related to pyrochlore

**²lewisite** \"\ *n* -s [Winford Lee *Lewis* †1943 Am. chemist + E *-ite*] **:** a colorless to amber to dark brown liquid vesicant that sometimes has an odor like that of geraniums, that is made by reaction of acetylene with arsenic trichloride, and that was developed for use as a war gas but has never been so used; dichloro-2-chloro-vinyl-arsine

**lewis-langmuir theory** \¦lüə̇s'laŋ,myu̇(ə)r-\ *n, usu cap both Ls* [after Gilbert N. *Lewis* †1946 and Irving *Langmuir* †1957 Am. chemists] **:** a chemical theory of atomic structure: the atom consists of a positive nucleus surrounded by concentric cubic shells at the corners of which the electrons are located — compare OCTET

**lew·is·son** \'lüə̇sən\ *n* -s [by alter.] **:** LEWIS

**lew·is's woodpecker** \'lüə̇səz-\ *n, usu cap L* [after Meriwether *Lewis* †1809] **:** a woodpecker (*Asyndesmus lewis*) of western No. America with the upper parts greenish black, the breast and collar gray, and the face and abdomen rich red

**lew·is·ton·ite** \'lüə̇stə,nīt\ *n* -s [*Lewiston*, Utah, its locality + E *-ite*] **:** a mineral $(Ca,K,Na)_5(PO_4)_3(OH)$ consisting of a basic phosphate of calcium, potassium, and sodium

**lewth** \'lüth\ *n* -s [ME *-lewth*, fr. OE *hlēowth*, *hlȳwth*, fr. *hlēow* warm — more at LEW] *now dial Brit* **:** shelter or protection from the weather **:** WARMTH

**lew-warm** \'=¦=\ *adj* [ME, fr. *lew* + *warm*] *dial Brit* **:** LEW 1

**lex** \'leks\ *n, pl* **le·ges** \'lā(,)gās, 'lē(,)jēz\ [L *leg-*, *lex* law — more at LEGAL] **1** *Roman law* **a :** LEX PUBLICA **b :** LEX PRIVATA **2 :** LAW

**lex** *abbr* lexical; lexicon

**lex actus** *var of* LEX LOCI ACTUS

**lex com·mis·so·ria** \-,kämə'sōrēə\ *n* [L] *Roman & civil law* **:** a penalty clause for nonperformance of a contract: as **a :** a provision that a pledge shall be forfeited if a loan is not repaid **b :** a condition that money paid on a contract of sale shall be forfeited and the sale rescinded if remaining payments are defaulted

**lex do·mi·ci·lii** \-,dämə'kilē,ē\ *n* [NL, law of the domicile] **:** the law of the domicile by which the rights of persons are sometimes governed (as where a person dies leaving personal property)

**lex·eme** \'lek,sēm\ *n* -s [*lexicon* + *-eme*] **:** a meaningful speech form that is an item of the vocabulary of a language — **lex·em·ic** \(')lek¦sēmik\ *adj*

**lex fo·ri** \-'fȯr(,)ē\ *n* [NL, law of the court] **:** the law of the court in which a proceeding is brought

**lex ge·ne·ra·lis** \-,genə'rāləs\ *n* [NL, general law] *Roman & civil law* **:** a law of general application as contrasted with one applicable to a particular person

**le·xia** \lə'hēə\ *n* -s [perh. fr. obs. Sp *lexia* lye (now *lejía*), fr. L *lixiva*, fem. of *lixivus* consisting of lye — more at LIQUID] **:** a soft light-colored raisin produced chiefly in Spain and Australia from white vinifera grapes that are treated with a caustic solution and sometimes with olive oil before drying

**-lex·ia** \'leksēə\ *n comb form* -s [NL, fr. Gk *lexis* word, speech] **:** reading of (such) a kind or with (such) an impairment ⟨brady*lexia*⟩ ⟨dys*lexia*⟩

**lex·i·cal** \'leksə̇kəl, -sēk-\ *also* **lex·ic** \-sik, -sēk\ *adj* [*lexical* fr. *lexicon* + *-al*; *lexic* back-formation fr. *lexical*] **1 a :** of or relating to words or the vocabulary of a language as distinguished from its grammar and construction ⟨~ elements like *book*, *run*, and so on —Sol Saporta⟩ ⟨~ research is not so much linguistic research as research in the culture of a community —R.I.McDavid⟩ **b :** uttered with heavy stress when devoid of context or when emphatic ⟨\'and\ or \'aa(ə)nd\ is the ~ pronunciation of *and*, which in context usu. has \ə\ for vowel or no vowel at all and often has not two consonants but one, which is \n\ or by environmental assimilation \m\ or \ŋ\⟩ ⟨a distinction may be present in ~ pronunciation which disappears in connected speech —A.F.Hubbell⟩ **2 :** of or relating to a lexicon or to lexicography ⟨~ methods aim to list all the relevant forms —A.F. Parker-Rhodes⟩ — **lex·i·cal·i·ty** \,leksə'kaləd·ē, -lətē, -i\ *n* -ES — **lex·i·cal·ly** \-sə̇k(ə)lē, -sēk-, -li\ *adv*

**lexical meaning** *n* **:** the meaning of the base (as the word *play*) in a paradigm (as *plays, played, playing*) — compare GRAMMATICAL MEANING

**lex·i·cog·ra·pher** \,leksə'kägrəfə(r)\ *n* -s [LGk *lexikographos* compiler of a glossary (fr. LGk *lexikon* lexicon + Gk *-graphos* one that writes) + E *-er* — more at -GRAPHER] **:** an author or compiler of a dictionary ⟨~: . . . a harmless drudge that busies himself in tracing the original, and detailing the signification of words —Samuel Johnson⟩

**lex·i·co·graph·ic** \¦leksə̇kō¦grafik, -sēk-, -kə¦g-, -fēk\ *or* **lex·i·co·graph·i·cal** \-fə̇kəl, -fēk-\ *adj* [*lexicography* + *-ic* or *-ical*] **:** of or relating to lexicography ⟨~ methods⟩ ⟨~ history⟩ — **lex·i·co·graph·i·cal·ly** \-fə̇k(ə)lē, -fēk-, -li\ *adv*

**lex·i·cog·ra·phist** \,leksə'kägrəfə̇st\ *n* -s [*lexicography* + *-ist*] **:** LEXICOGRAPHER

**lex·i·cog·ra·phy** \-fē, -fi\ *n* -ES [fr. *lexicographer*, after such pairs as E *geographer: geography*] **1 :** the editing or making of a dictionary **2 :** the principles and practices of dictionary making ⟨a martyr, by my ~, is on all fours with a fool who risks and loses his life in any other showy but useless way —H.L. Mencken⟩

**lex·i·co·log·i·cal** \¦leksə̇kō¦läjə̇kəl, -sēk-, -kə¦l-, -jēk-\ *or* **lex·i·co·log·ic** \-jik, -jēk\ *adj* **:** of or relating to lexicology

**lex·i·col·o·gist** \,leksə'käləjə̇st\ *n* -s **:** a specialist in lexicology

**lex·i·col·o·gy** \-jē, -ji\ *n* -ES [F *lexicologie*, fr. *lexico-* (fr. LGk *lexiko-*, fr. *lexikon*) + *-logie* -logy] **:** the science of the derivation and signification of words **:** a branch of linguistics that treats of the signification and application of words

**lex·i·con** \'leksə,kän, -sə̇kən, -sēkən\ *n, pl* **lexi·ca** \-kə\ *or* **lexicons** [LGk *lexikon*, fr. neut. of *lexikos* of words, fr. Gk *lexis* word, speech (fr. *legein* to speak) + *-ikos* -ic — more at LEGEND] **1 :** a book containing an alphabetical or other systematic arrangement of the words in a language or of a considerable number of them and their definitions **:** DICTIONARY, WORDBOOK ⟨for the making of the great ~ of the Greek language —*Times Lit. Supp.*⟩ **2 :** the vocabulary of a language, of an individual speaker, of a set of documents, of a body of speech, of a subject, or of an occupational or other group ⟨in her financial ~, five cents was as valuable as five dollars —Calder Willingham⟩ ⟨the realization that Marxism is not a complete ~ of progress —*New Republic*⟩ ⟨the missile . . . will become more and more important in the whole ~ of war —H.W.Baldwin⟩ **3 :** COMPENDIUM, ACCOUNT, RECORD ⟨the ~ of human struggle, through which she had searched to decipher a meaning, dissolved for her and floated away —Helen Howe⟩ ⟨in the bright ~ of LP, I know of no other pair of standard symphonies . . . so essentially satisfying —Irving Kolodin⟩ **4 :** the total stock of morphemes in a language ⟨linguistic classifications established on the basis of ~ (as against those based on grammar) are more apt to prove right and to be demonstrable —N.A.McQuown⟩

**lex·i·con·ize** \-ˌkəˌnīz\ *vt* -ED/-ING/-S **1 :** to make a lexicon of (a language or subject) **2 :** to incorporate in a lexicon

**lex·i·co·statistic** *or* **lex·i·co·statistical** \ˌleksə(ˌ)kō+\ *adj* [*lexico-* (as in *lexicographer*) + *statistic* or *statistical*] **:** of, relating to, or involving glottochronology (sense 2)

**lex·i·co·statistics** \"+\ *n pl but sing in constr* [*lexico-* + *statistics*] **:** GLOTTOCHRONOLOGY 2

**lex·i·graph·ic** \ˌleksə¦grafik\ *or* **lex·i·graph·i·cal** \-fəkəl\ *adj* **:** of or relating to lexigraphy — **lex·i·graph·i·cal·ly** \-fək(ə)lē\ *adv*

**lex·ig·ra·phy** \lek'sigrəfē\ *n* [Gk *lexis* word + E *-graphy*] **1 :** the art or practice of defining words **2 :** a system of writing (as that of the Chinese) in which each character represents a word

**lex·i·phan·ic** \ˌleksə¦fanik\ *adj* [*Lexiphanes* (bombastic speaker in the dialogue *Lexiphanes* by Lucian, 2d cent. A.D. Greek satirist) + E *-ic*] *archaic* **:** using ostentatiously recondite words **:** BOMBASTIC, PRETENTIOUS

**lex·i·phan·i·cism** \ˌ==ˈfanəˌsizəm\ *n* -s *archaic* **:** pretentious phraseology or an instance or example of such phraseology

**lex lo·ci ac·tus** \ˌlekˌslōkēˈaktəs, -ēˈäk-\ *or* **lex actus** *n* [*lex loci actus* fr. NL, law of the place of the act; *lex actus* fr. NL, law of the act] **:** the law of the place where an act is done or a transaction takes place

**lex loci ce·le·bra·ti·o·nis** \-ˌkeləˌbrädˌēˈōnəs\ *n* [NL, law of the place of the ceremony] **:** the law of the place where a contract esp. of marriage is made

**lex loci con·trac·tus** \-ˌkən·ˈtraktəs\ *n* [NL, law of the place of the contract] **:** the law of the place where a contract is made or is to be performed

**lex loci de·lic·ti** \-dəˈliktē\ *n* [NL] **:** the law of the place of the wrong or tort

**lex loci rei si·tae** \-¦rāˈsiˌtī\ *or* **lex si·tus** \-ˈsiˌtüs\ *n* [*lex loci rei sitae* fr. NL, law of the place of the situated property; *lex situs* fr. NL, law of the site] **:** the law of the place where a property is situated

**lex loci so·lu·ti·o·nis** \-ˌsəˌlütēˈōnəs\ *n* [NL] **:** the law of the place of performance of a contract

**lex mer·ca·to·ria** \-ˌmərkəˈtōrēə\ *or* **lex mer·ca·to·rum** \-rəm\ *n* [*lex mercatoria* fr. ML, lit., mercantile law; *lex mercatorum* fr. NL, lit., law of merchants] **:** LAW MERCHANT

**lex non scrip·ta** \ˌlekˌsnänˈskriptə, -nōn-\ *n* [LL, unwritten law] **:** unwritten law; *esp* **:** the common law as distinguished from statutory law

**lex pri·va·ta** \ˌleksprəˈvädˌə\ *n* [NL, private law] *Roman law* **:** a provision (as a restriction or obligation) of a private contract — called also *lex*

**lex pu·bli·ca** \(ˈ)lekˈspüblәkə, -ˈspəb-\ *n* [ML, public law] **1** *Roman law* **:** a law passed by a popular assembly **2** *Roman law* **:** a written law

**lex sa·li·ca** \(ˈ)lek(s)ˈsaləkə\ *n, usu cap S* [ML] **:** SALIC LAW

**lex scrip·ta** \(ˈ)lek(s)ˈskriptə\ *n* [LL, written law] **:** the written or statute law

**lex ta·li·o·nis** \ˌlekˌstalēˈōnəs\ *n* [NL, law of retaliation] **:** the law of retaliation equivalent to an offense; *esp* **:** the principle of retributive justice based on the Mosaic law of "eye for eye, tooth for tooth" in Exod 21:23–25 — called also *talion*

[1]**ley** *archaic var of* LYE

[2]**ley** *var of* LEA

**ley·den blue** \ˈlīdᵊn-\ *n, often cap L* [fr. *Leiden, Leyden,* city in the southwest Netherlands] **:** COBALT BLUE

**leyden jar** *n, usu cap L* [so called fr. its having been invented in Leiden] **:** the earliest form of electrical condenser consisting essentially of a glass jar coated part way up both inside and outside with metal foil and having the inner coating connected to a conducting rod passed through the insulating stopper

**ley·dig cell** \ˈlīdig-\ *also* **ley·dig's cell** \-dig(z)-\ *n, usu cap L* [after Franz *Leydig* †1908 Ger. zoologist] **:** an interstitial cell of the testis usu. considered the chief source of testicular androgens and perhaps other hormones

**ley·dig's duct** \-digz-\ *n, usu cap L* **:** MESONEPHRIC DUCT

**ley farming** \ˈlē-,ˈlā-\ *n* [[2]*ley*] **:** the growing of grass or legumes in rotation with grain or tilled crops as a soil conservation measure

**ley pewter** \ˈlā-\ *n* [perh. fr. the name *Ley*] **:** pewter containing a relatively large percentage of lead

**ley·ton** \ˈlātᵊn\ *adj, usu cap* [fr. *Leyton,* municipal borough, northeastern suburb of London, England] **:** of or from the municipal borough of Leyton, England **:** of the kind or style prevalent in Leyton

**le·za** \ˈlēzə\ *n* -s [origin unknown] **:** the heavy hard gray to grayish brown smooth lustrous wood of an Indian tree (*Lagerstroemia tomentosa*) used for furniture, flooring, and paneling

**lez·ghi·an** *also* **les·ghi·an** \ˈlezgēən, ˈleskē-\ *n* -s *usu cap* [Russ *Lezgin,* n., Lezghian + E *-ian,* n. suffix] **1 :** a division of the peoples of the Caucasus that includes the Avars, the Lakhs, and the Kyurins **2 :** a member of the Lezghian people

**lez·gin·ka** \lezˈgiŋkə\ *n* -s [Russ, fr. *Lezgin*] **:** a courtship dance of the Caucasus mountains in which the woman moves with graceful ease while the man dances wildly about her

**lf** *abbr* **1** leaf **2** leaflet **3** lightface

**LF** *abbr* **1** ledger folio **2** left field **3** left foot **4** left forward **5** left front **6** lettering faded **7** lineal feet **8** load factor **9** lock forward **10** *often not cap* low frequency

**LFA** *abbr* local freight agent

**LFB** *abbr* left fullback

**LFC** *abbr, often not cap* low-frequency current

**LFD** *abbr* least fatal dose

**l-form** \ˈ=,=\ *n, usu cap L* **:** a filterable form of certain bacteria commonly regarded as a specialized reproductive body appearing chiefly when the environment is unfavorable and much resembling typical pleuropneumonia organisms

**lft** *abbr* leaflet

**lg** *abbr* **1** large **2** long

**LG** *abbr* **1** landing ground **2** large grain **3** left guard **4** life-guard

**lge** *abbr* large

**lgr** *abbr* **1** larger **2** longer

**lgt** *abbr* light

**lgth** *abbr* length

**LH** *abbr* **1** left hand **2** lighthouse **3** lower half **4** luteinizing hormone

**LHA** *abbr* **1** local hour angle **2** lord high admiral

**lha·sa** \ˈläsə *also* ˈlasə\ *adj, usu cap* [fr. *Lhasa,* Tibet] **:** of or from Lhasa, the capital of Tibet **:** of the kind or style prevalent in Lhasa

**lhasa ap·so** \ˌ==ˈap(ˌ)sō\ *also* **lhasa** *or* **lhasa terrier** *n, usu cap L, often cap A* [*apso* fr. Tibetan] **1 :** a Tibetan breed of small terrier lionlike in appearance with a dense coat of long hard straight hair, a heavy fall over the eyes, heavy whiskers and beard, and a well-feathered tail curled over its back **2** *pl* **lhasa apsos :** a terrier of the Lhasa apso breed

**LHB** *abbr* left halfback

**LHC** *abbr* lord high chancellor

**l-head** \ˈ=,=\ *adj, cap L* **:** having the intake and exhaust valves in compartments of the block to the same side of the cylinder head ⟨an *L-head* gasoline engine⟩

**lho·ke** \ˈlō(ˌ)kā\ *n* -s *usu cap* **:** the Tibeto-Burman language of Bhutan

**lho·ta** \ˈlōd·ə\ *n, pl* **lhota** *also* **lhotas** *usu cap* **1 :** one of several Naga peoples of the Assam-Burma frontier region **2 :** a member of the Lhota people

**LHT** *abbr* lord high treasurer

[1]**li** \ˈlē\ *n, pl* **li** *also* **lis** [Chin (Pek) *li³*] **:** any of various Chinese units of distance; *esp* **:** one equal to about ⅓ mile

[2]**li** \"\ *n* -s [Chin (Pek) *li³* propriety] **:** one of the cardinal virtues in Confucianism that consists of propriety or correct behavior as the outward expression of an inner harmony with the ethical principles of nature

[3]**li** \"\ *n, pl* **li** *or* **lis** *usu cap* [Chin (Pek) *li³*, lit., rude, rustic] **1 :** an ethnic group that is culturally a branch of the early Tai people of southern China and that forms the largest ethnic group next to the Chinese in Hainan Island in southeast China **2 :** a member of the Li people

**LI** *abbr* **1** light infantry **2** low intensity

**Li** *symbol* lithium

**li** *abbr* link

**li·a·bil·i·ty** \ˌlīəˈbiləd·ē, -lətē, -i\ *n* -ES **1 a :** the quality or state of being liable ⟨the ~ of an insurer⟩ **b :** LIKELIHOOD ⟨the ~ to take to their beds at the drop of a hat —Osbert Lancaster⟩ **2 :** something for which one is liable: as **a** (1) **:** an amount that is owed whether payable in money, other property, or services — compare ACCRUED LIABILITY, CAPITAL LIABILITY, CONTINGENT LIABILITY, CURRENT LIABILITY, FIXED LIABILITY (2) **liabilities** *pl* **:** pecuniary obligations **:** DEBTS — compare ASSET **b :** an obligation or duty which is owed by one person to another to refrain from some course of conduct injurious to the latter or to perform some act or to do something for the benefit of the latter and for breach of which the law gives a remedy to the latter (as damages, restitution, specific performance, injunction) **:** accountability and responsibility to another enforceable by legal civil or criminal sanctions **3 :** something that works as a disadvantage **:** DRAWBACK ⟨effects on the growing self of a . . . child that will be his *liabilities* instead of assets —Bingham Dai⟩ ⟨the very traits which made him a success . . . are likely to be serious *liabilities* at a later stage —P.B.Sears⟩ **syn** see DEBT

**liability insurance** *n* **:** insurance against loss resulting from liability for injury or damage to the persons or property of others

**liability limit** *n* **:** the maximum amount which a liability insurance company agrees to pay as a result of a single accident or injury to a single person

**li·a·ble** \ˈlīəbəl, *esp in sense 3* ˈlībəl\ *adj* [fr. (assumed) AF, fr. OF *lier,* to bind, tie (fr. L *ligare*) + *-able* — more at LIGATURE] **1 a :** bound or obligated according to law or equity **:** RESPONSIBLE, ANSWERABLE ⟨~ for the debts incurred by his wife⟩; *also* **:** subject to appropriation or attachment ⟨all his property is ~ to pay his debts⟩ **b** (1) **:** subject to control by — used with *to* ⟨~ to the driving laws of the state⟩ (2) **:** being in a position to incur — used with *to* ⟨~ to the death penalty⟩ ⟨those who do not vote are ~ to fines —*Americana Annual*⟩ **c** *obs* **:** belonging to ⟨all that we find . . . ~ to our crown and dignity —Shak.⟩ **2** *obs* **:** SUITABLE, FIT, APT **3 :** exposed or subject to some usu. adverse contingency or action **:** LIKELY ⟨~ to fall⟩ ⟨~ to be hurt⟩ ⟨these values are ~ to fluctuate with every change in the current market —J.A.Hobson⟩

**syn** SUBJECT, OPEN, EXPOSED, SUSCEPTIBLE, PRONE, SENSITIVE, INCIDENT: LIABLE, now rather wide in its use, may retain its original legalistic suggestion and imply the consequences of the actions of legal authority ⟨*liable* to military service⟩ ⟨*liable* to be fined⟩ or range variously between this use and employment as a very close synonym for LIKELY; however used, it often though by no means always implies that the likely development will be unpleasant ⟨*liable* to be burned at the stake for . . . heresy —Agnes Repplier⟩ ⟨a palatal semiconsonant . . . *liable* to pass into another consonant —W.J.Entwistle & W.A.Morison⟩ SUBJECT may imply a great likelihood of the development that is indicated; more than the others it may although it does not always indicate that the development has happened or must happen ⟨another mystery . . . how, *subject* to the life he describes, he was able to become a poet —Osbert Sitwell⟩ ⟨rivers and streams . . . *subject* to great floods —Bram Stoker⟩ OPEN does not stress the probability of the ensuing development that is indicated; it stresses the ease with which that development may occur and esp. the lack of shield, guard, or defense against an unpleasant development ⟨another modern tendency in education . . . perhaps somewhat more *open* to question —Bertrand Russell⟩ ⟨standing thus alone . . . *open* to all the criticism which descends on the lone operator —Bruce Catton⟩ OPEN and EXPOSED are often interchangeable but OPEN makes no necessary implication about the presence or existence of the development, simply indicating lack of defense; in some but not all uses, EXPOSED indicates actual presence of the influencing force without indication of lack of defense ⟨*exposed* to streptococcus infection⟩ SUSCEPTIBLE changes the focus of attention and suggests not a temporary situation but an inherent or essential characteristic of the person or thing involved which makes the indicated influence or development likely ⟨fell in love with her . . . was already in a highly *susceptible* state and tumbled immediately —H.S.Canby⟩ ⟨a nature . . . perhaps even less *susceptible* than other men's characters of essential change —Walter Pater⟩ PRONE suggests a more positive predisposition of the subject toward the influence or development, a predisposition which is not merely receptive to the influence or development but which invited it ⟨you may well warn me against such an evil. Human nature is so *prone* to fall into it —Jane Austen⟩ ⟨I think that girls are less *prone* than boys to punish oddity by serious physical cruelty —Bertrand Russell⟩ SENSITIVE does not suggest a predisposition toward so much as a very readily perceptive or impressionable nature likely to be influenced by stimuli that might be without effect in another situation ⟨the founding of the university by the greatest capitalist in America made it *sensitive* to charges of capitalistic influence and inclined to lean backward to avoid them —R.M.Lovett⟩ ⟨so sweet and *sensitive* that she feels influences more acutely than other people do —Bram Stoker⟩ SENSITIVE may imply that the matter being perceived and calling forth a reaction is unpleasant ⟨raised her voice to a squeaking tone that was very painful to a *sensitive* ear —Ellen Glasgow⟩ INCIDENT may be mentioned in this series only because it indicates the fact of concomitant or ensuing result and implies nothing more than the existence of this fact ⟨economic factors *incident* to the depression —J.B.Conant⟩ **syn** see in addition RESPONSIBLE

**li·a·ble·ness** *n* -ES **:** the quality or state of being liable ⟨mutability and ~ to change —Ralph Wardlaw⟩

**li·ag·o·ra** \līˈagərə\ *n, cap* [NL, after *Liagora,* a nereid, fr. Gk *Leiagorē*] **:** a genus of marine red algae (family Helminthocladiaceae) characterized by the branched cylindrical thallus and by calcification of the gelatinous matrix so that it is often brittle and of a chalky texture

**li·aise** \lēˈāz\ *vi* -ED/-ING/-S [back-formation fr. *liaison*] **1 :** to establish liaison ⟨told me to go to Bonn and ~ with the newly formed government —C.W.Thayer⟩ **2 :** to act as a liaison officer ⟨*liaising* with the next unit's guard posts —Earle Birney⟩

**li·ai·son** \ˈlēəˌzän, ˈlē(ˌ)āˌz|, lēˈāˌz| *also* ÷ˈlāə,z *or* -,s| *or* |ōn *or* |ōn *or* |ōⁿ *or* |äⁿ *or* ,=ˈ= *or* ,=(ˌ)ˈā= *or* ˈlēə|zən *or* lēˈā|zᵊn *or* ÷ˈlāə|zən *or* |sən *or* |sᵊn\ *n* -s *often attrib* [F, fr. MF, fr. *lier* to bind, tie + *-aison* -ation (fr. L *-ation-, -atio*) — more at LIABLE] **1 a :** a close bond or connection ⟨the farmers and the labor people ended up supporting the same people but without much of a ~ between them —Tilford Dudley⟩ **:** RELATIONSHIP, INTERRELATIONSHIP ⟨a proper ~ between the school and the ordinary experience of the students —*Nat'l Catholic Educational Assoc. Bull.*⟩ ⟨establish any kind of ~ with the top men who were running trade and business —H.W.Carter⟩ **b :** an illicit sexual relationship between a man and a woman **2 :** the pronunciation at the end of the first of two consecutive words the second of which begins with a vowel sound and follows without pause of a consonant sound not present in the first word in other positions (as of \z\ in French \lāzāmē\ for *les amis* by contrast to \lāpwä\ for *les pois,* or in eastern New England of \r\ in \fårōf\ for *far off* by contrast to \fåkrī\ for *far cry*) **3 a :** intercommunication established and maintained between parts of an armed force to ensure mutual understanding, unity of action, and esp. prompt and effective support by artillery and air units ⟨a ~ officer⟩ ⟨doing ~ work in the front lines⟩ **b :** any intercommunication for establishing and maintaining mutual understanding ⟨such ~ work as we have goes on between theological liberals in both groups —W.L.Sperry⟩

**liaison aircraft** *n* **:** a light airplane or helicopter used by military forces for courier and staff work behind the lines and for limited reconnaissance and artillery spotting over battle lines

**li·ana** \lēˈänə, -ˈanə\ *or* **li·ane** \-n\ *n* -s [F *liane,* fr. F dial. *liône, lieune, liane,* prob. fr. *lier* to bind, tie — more at LIABLE] **:** a climbing plant that roots in the ground with woody lianas being characteristic of tropical rain forests and herbaceous lianas of temperate regions — **li·anoid** \-ˌnȯid\ *adj*

**li·ang** \lēˈäŋ, -ˈaŋ\ *n, pl* **liang** *also* **liangs** [Chin (Pek) *liang³*] **:** an old Chinese unit of weight equal to ⅟₁₆ catty and equivalent to a little more than an ounce avoirdupois — called also *tael*

**liangle** *var of* LEEANGLE

**liao·yang** \lēˈaüˈyäŋ\ *adj, usu cap* [fr. *Liaoyang,* Manchuria] **:** of or from the city of Liaoyang, Manchuria **:** of the kind or style prevalent in Liaoyang

**li·ar** \ˈlī(ə)r, -īə\ *n* -s [ME *lier, liar,* fr. OE *lēogere,* fr. *lēogan* to lie + *-ere* -er — more at LIE] **:** one that usu. knowingly and habitually utters falsehood **:** one that lies

**liard** \lēˈär\ *n* -s [MF, after Guigues *Liard,* 15th cent. Frenchman who coined them] **:** a French coin of the 15th to the 18th centuries orig. of base silver but of copper from the time of Henry IV and worth ¼ of a sou

**liar dice** *n* **:** a poker-dice game in which a player's cast is concealed by a screen or his hands and he may bluff by announcing a better hand than he has

**liar paradox** *n* **:** a semantical paradox associated with the Cretan philosopher Epimenides (†7th cent. B.C.) and occurring when someone says "I am lying" or "I am now asserting a falsehood" which is a true statement if it is false and a false one if it is true — compare EPIMENIDEAN, RUSSELL'S PARADOX

[1]**li·as** *also* **ly·as** \ˈlīəs\ *n* -ES *often attrib* [ME *lyas,* fr. MF *liois,* prob. fr. *lie* dregs; fr. the appearance — more at LEE] **:** a kind of blue limestone found esp. in southwestern England

[2]**lias** *adj, usu cap* [fr. *Lias* oldest division of the European Jurassic system, fr. [1]*lias*] **:** of or relating to a subdivision of the European Jurassic — see GEOLOGIC TIME table

**li·as·sic** \(ˈ)līˈasik\ *adj, usu cap* [[2]*lias* + *-ic*] **:** LIAS

**li·atris** \līˈa·trəs, ˈlīə·t-\ *n* [NL] **1** *cap* **:** a genus of perennial American herbs (family Compositae) having aromatic often cormous roots, linear grassy leaves, and spikes of rose-purple or white discoid heads of perfect tubular flowers — see BLAZING STAR, BUTTON SNAKEROOT **2** -ES **:** any of several herbs of *Liatris* or the closely related genus *Trilisa* (as wild vanilla and the button snakeroot) sometimes used in medicine

**lib** \ˈlib\ *vt* **libbed; libbed; libbing; libs** [ME *libben;* akin to MD & MLG *lubben* to castrate; perh. akin to OE *lēaf* leaf — more at LEAF] *now dial Brit* **:** CASTRATE

**lib** *abbr* **1** [L *liber*] book **2** liberal **3** [L *libra*] pound **4** library; librarian

**li·bate** \ˈlībāt, =ˈ=\ *vb* -ED/-ING/-S [L *libatus,* past part. of *libare* to pour as an offering] *vt* **:** to pour out a libation or make libation to ~ *vi* **1 :** to make libation **2 :** to drink alcoholic drink ⟨sat up with three *libating* guests who would not leave⟩

**li·ba·tion** \līˈbāshən\ *n* -s [L *libation-, libatio,* fr. *libatus* (past part. of *libare* to pour as an offering) + *-ion-, -io* -ion; akin to Gk *leibein* to pour, drip, Lith *lieti* to pour] **1 :** the act of pouring a liquid (as wine) either on the ground or on a victim in a sacrifice to a deity **2 a :** a liquid (as wine) serving as a libation or poured out in or as if in the manner of a libation ⟨pours water on the ground as a ~ to Mother Earth —J.G. Frazer⟩; *also* **:** the amount of such a liquid ⟨poured . . . a generous ~ of paraffin on the embers —Mary Webb⟩ **b :** a drink (as of wine) often taken ceremoniously ⟨the copious ~s of Burgundy in which he had indulged —T.L.Peacock⟩ ⟨consuming a final ~ at the bar —F.V.W.Mason⟩ ⟨a ~ in celebration of their long marriage⟩ — **li·ba·tion·al** \-shənᵊl, -shnəl\ *adj* — **li·ba·tion·ary** \-shəˌnerē\ *adj*

**li·ba·tion·er** \-sh(ə)nə(r)\ *n* -s **:** one that pours a libation

**lib·bard** \ˈlibə(r)d\ *archaic var of* LEOPARD

**lib·bet** \ˈlibət\ *n* -s [origin unknown] *now dial Brit* **:** a torn and hanging strip **:** TATTER, RAG — usu. used in pl. ⟨torn all to ~s⟩

**li·bec·cio** \ləˈbechē,ō, -e(ˌ)chō\ *or* **li·bec·chio** \-ekē,ō, -e(ˌ)kō\ *n* -s [It, fr. colloq. Ar *labāj, labash,* fr. Gk *lib-, lips,* fr. *leibein* to pour, drip — more at LIBATION] **:** a southwest wind

[1]**li·bel** \ˈlībəl\ *n* -s [ME, fr. MF, fr. L *libellus,* dim. of *liber* book — more at LEAF] **1 a** *obs* **:** a written declaration, bill, certificate, request, or supplication **b :** the written statement made in civil law and admiralty law practice and in proceedings in ecclesiastical and occas. other courts by the plaintiff of his cause of action and the relief he seeks — compare DECLARATION **c** *Scots law* **:** the part of an indictment stating the grounds of the charge **d** *Scots law, archaic* **:** the punishment attached to an offense **2** *obs* **:** a brief piece of writing (as a little book or short treatise) **3 a** *archaic* **:** a handbill or circular esp. attacking or defaming someone **b** (1) **:** a written or oral defamatory statement or a representation or suggestion that conveys an unjustly unfavorable impression ⟨his criticism was a ~ of the writer⟩ ⟨the photograph is more a ~ than a reproduction⟩ (2) **:** a statement or representation published without just cause or excuse, expressed either in print or in writing or by pictures, effigies, or other signs and tending to expose another to public hatred, contempt, or ridicule **:** defamation of a person by means of written statements, pictures, or other visible signs **:** the publication of such writings or pictures as are of a blasphemous, treasonable, seditious, or obscene character — compare PRIVILEGED COMMUNICATION 2, SLANDER (3) **:** the act, tort, or crime of publishing such a libel

[2]**li·bel** \"\ *vb* **libeled** *or* **libelled; libeled** *or* **libelled; libeling** *or* **libelling** \-b(ə)liŋ\ **libels** *vi* **1 :** to spread defamation **:** make libelous statements — often used with *against* or *on* **2 :** to institute legal proceedings by a libel ~ *vt* **1 :** to hurt the reputation of by malicious or unfair issue of any false or harmful representation **:** issue a libel against **:** make a libelous statement or insinuation about or representation of **2 a :** to proceed against in law by filing a libel (as against a ship or goods) **b :** to allege in a libel **syn** see MALIGN

**li·bel·ant** *or* **li·bel·lant** \ˈlībələnt\ *n* -s **1 :** one that institutes a suit by a libel **2 :** one who makes or publishes a libel **:** LIBELER

**li·bel·ee** *or* **li·bel·lee** \ˌlībəˈlē\ *n* -s **:** one against whom a libel has been filed — compare DEFENDANT

**li·bel·er** *or* **li·bel·ler** \ˈlībələ(r)\ *n* -s **:** one that libels

**li·bel·ist** *or* **li·bel·list** \-ləst\ *n* -s **:** LIBELER

**li·bel·lu·la** \līˈbelyələ, ləˈ-\ *n* [NL, dim. of *libella* dragonfly, fr. L, level (instrument); fr. the horizontal position of the wings — more at LEVEL] **1** *cap* **:** a genus of large often brightly colored dragonflies usu. with dark blotches on the wings that is the type of the family Libellulidae and in older classifications includes all the dragonflies **2** -s **:** any dragonfly of the genus *Libellula* **:** SKIMMER

**li·bel·lu·li·dae** \ˌlībəˈlüləˌdē\ *n pl, cap* [NL, fr. *Libellula,* type genus + *-idae*] **:** a large family of dragonflies having the abdomen triangular in cross section and females without a well-developed ovipositor — see LIBELLULA

**li·bel·ous** *or* **li·bel·lous** \ˈlībələs\ *adj* [[1]*libel* + *-ous*] **:** constituting or including a libel **:** DEFAMATORY ⟨a ~ statement⟩ ⟨a ~ book⟩ ⟨claimed the movie was ~ —*Associated Press*⟩ ⟨a ~ portrait⟩ — **li·bel·ous·ly** *or* **li·bel·lous·ly** *adv*

**libels** *pl of* LIBEL, *pres 3d sing of* LIBEL

**li·ber** \ˈlībə(r), ˈli,be(ə)r\ *n, pl* **li·bri** \ˈli,brī, ˈli(ˌ)brē\ *or* **libers** [L, inner bark of a tree, pith of papyrus, book — more at LEAF] **1 :** BAST **2 :** a book of records (as of deeds or wills)

**li·be·ra** \ˈlēbə,rä\ *n* -s *usu cap* [L (first word of the responsory), imper. of *liberare* to set free — more at LIBERATE] **:** a Roman Catholic responsory that is sung usu. at funerals after the Mass and prior to the final prayers for the deceased

[1]**lib·er·al** \ˈlib(ə)rəl\ *adj* [ME, fr. MF, ML & L; MF, fr. ML & L; ML *liberalis* of or constituting liberal arts, fr. L, of freedom, of a freeman, noble, generous, fr. *liber* free + *-alis* -al; akin to OE *lēodan* to grow, *lēod* people, OHG *liotan* to grow, *liut* person, people, ON *lothiun* shaggy, Goth *lindan* to grow, Gk *eleutheros* free, Skt *rodhati, rohati* he climbs, grows; basic meaning: growing] **1 a :** of, belonging to, being, or consisting of liberal arts or one of the liberal arts ⟨the studies are ~, not in one of the technical fields⟩ **b** *archaic* **:** of, belonging to, or befitting a man of free birth; *also* **:** of, belonging to, or befitting one that is a gentleman in social rank **c :** of, belonging to, or befitting a free man ⟨the ~ occupations of the gentry of ancient Rome⟩ **2 a :** marked by generosity, bounteousness, openhandedness **:** not stinting ⟨a ~ giver⟩ ⟨a man of ~ nature⟩ **b :** bestowed in a generous and openhanded way **:** ABUNDANT, BOUNTIFUL, AMPLE ⟨a ~ donation⟩ ⟨a ~ quantity⟩ ⟨receiving ~ rewards for the risks they took —*Amer.*

*Guide Series: N.H.*〉 **c** : LARGE, FULL 〈possessed a ~ lip〉 〈a ~ bosom〉 **3 a** : free from restraint or check : unchecked by a sense of the decorous, the fitting, or the polite 〈possessed a ~ tongue that was always offending people〉 **b** *obs* : lacking significant moral restraints : LICENTIOUS **4 a** : not strict or rigorous 〈a ~ attitude toward one's children〉 **b** : not confined or restricted to the exact or literal 〈a ~ translation of the Greek text〉 **5 a** : not narrow in mind : BROAD-MINDED, OPEN-MINDED **b** : not bound by authoritarianism, orthodoxy, or traditional or established forms in action, attitude, or opinion 〈a man of ~ views who would not mind making significant changes in the social or economic structure if he felt it was for the best〉 〈~ in his interpretation of his duties as a governor〉 〈theologians, even the most ~, will rally to the defense of theology —A.L.Guérard〉 **c** [F *libéral*, fr. MF *liberal*] : of, favoring, or based upon the principles of liberalism 〈the ~ theory of progress —M.Q.Sibley〉 〈the issue of ~ constitutionalism —G.H.Sabine〉 〈the ~ emphasis upon the inalienable rights of the individual —J.H.Hallowell〉 〈the Prussian monarchy was not ~, but it was progressive and enterprising —Stringfellow Barr〉 — compare CONSERVATIVE, RADICAL 3a **d** *usu cap* : of, belonging to, or constituting a political party advocating or associated with the principles of political liberalism: as (1) : of or constituting a political party in the United Kingdom evolving from the Whigs and associated during the period of its status as one of the two major British parties of the 19th and early 20th centuries with ideals of individual esp. economic freedom, greater individual participation in government, and constitutional, political, and administrative reforms designed to secure these objectives 〈the English *Liberal* party was rent asunder by the explosives of modern nationalism —C.J.Friedrich〉 〈*Liberal* representation in Parliament has been reduced to a tiny handful —Henry Slesser〉 — compare CATHOLIC, CONSERVATIVE, LABOR, RADICAL 3c(1), TORY, UNIONIST, WHIG (2) : of or constituting a major political party in another member nation of the British Commonwealth 〈the Province of Quebec . . . is the stronghold of the *Liberal* party —C.E.Silcox〉 〈launched the *Liberal* government's policy in Australia's federal election campaign —A.E.Norman〉 〈*Liberal* opposition to Labor proposals in the New Zealand parliament〉 (3) : of or constituting a minor political party active chiefly in New York and associated with social reform and support of policies favorable to organized labor 〈the anticommunist stand of the founders of the *Liberal* party〉

**syn** PROGRESSIVE, ADVANCED, RADICAL agree in application to a person or thing freed from or opposed to what is established or orthodox. LIBERAL, the most general term, suggests an emancipation from convention, tradition, or dogma that extends from a belief in altering institutions to fit altering conditions to a preference for lawlessness; on the one hand it suggests a commendable pragmatism, tolerance, and broad-mindedness and on the other a highly questionable unorthodoxy, experimentalism, or positive irresponsibility 〈a *liberal* Episcopalian, preferred a non-Gothic auditorium in which the congregation could hear well, rather than merely view distant ritual —Robert Berkelman〉 〈the prevailing *liberal* movement of the time was Benthamite in its emphasis on legal and social reform, and denounced tradition as the chief obstacle to progress —Michael Polanyi〉 〈don't let us be hampered by routine and red tape and precedent, let's . . . put a *liberal* interpretation on our duties —W.S.Gilbert〉 〈if *liberal*, in respect to language, means "tolerant of change", this book is *liberal*. If it means "not strict", the book is not *liberal*, or at least not intentionally so —J.B.McMillan〉 〈the strict school of rabbis allowed divorce only on the ground of adultery; the *liberal* school, on almost any ground —J.C.Swaim〉 PROGRESSIVE implies an opposition to the reactionary or backward, a willingness to forsake past methods or beliefs in the interests of improvement or amelioration 〈one *progressive* publisher is now experimenting with plastic bindings —*Third Degree*〉 〈the party direction must be moderate and yet *progressive* and dynamic —*N.Y.Times*〉 〈the struggle . . . between the conservative and the *progressive* mind —G.G.Coulton〉 〈to *progressive* leadership — a leadership which has sought . . . to advance the lot of the average American citizen —F.D.Roosevelt〉 〈much *progressive* economic and social legislation designed to benefit the masses and to break the power of the privileged —A.C. Gordon〉 ADVANCED usu. applies to something high in a scale of development or ahead of its time often suggesting mental daring. It can favorably suggest the extremely liberal or progressive or unfavorably suggest something new and experimental to the point of foolishness or bizarreness 〈the economic interests of the *advanced* and backward peoples —J.A.Hobson〉 〈the most *advanced* nuclear weapons —V.M.Barnett〉 〈the continuing notion among many *advanced* writers that only difficult writing is good writing —F.L.Allen〉 〈to her own generation she seemed *advanced* in realism and in daring —F.L. Pattee〉 RADICAL usu. suggests extremeness to the point of a sharp break with the already established and esp. in its political application a desire to uproot and destroy; it is often interchangeable with *revolutionary* 〈*radical* innovators, challenging the authority of the past —G.C.Sellery〉 〈*radical* and experimental music —Humphrey Searle〉 〈of mild nature and inclined to oppose *radical* changes in the established order —*Amer. Guide Series: Maine*〉 〈*radical* and revolutionary views of the state〉

**syn** GENEROUS, BOUNTIFUL, BOUNTEOUS, OPENHANDED, MUNIFICENT, HANDSOME: LIBERAL suggests openhandedness and lack of close stinting in giving 〈*liberal* gifts to his nephews〉 〈a *liberal* legacy to his servant〉 〈*liberal* grants from the legislature〉 〈a *liberal* serving of pie〉 GENEROUS may suggest some pleasing personality trait like magnanimity, warmheartedness, willingness to aid, altruism, or forgetfulness of self 〈he ladled out food with such a *generous* hand that the Indians named him 'Big Spoon' —*Amer. Guide Series: Md.*〉 〈if she gave a friend a present — and this must have happened every day, for she was *generous* beyond the dreary bounds of common sense —Osbert Sitwell〉 〈such a kindly, smiling, tender, gentle, *generous* heart of her own, as won the love of everybody who came near her —W.M.Thackeray〉 BOUNTIFUL suggests lavish, abundant, and unremitting giving or providing 〈spare not now to be *bountiful*, call your poor to regale with you . . . give your gold to the hospital, let the weary be comforted, let the needy be banqueted —Alfred Tennyson〉 BOUNTEOUS has about the same suggestion as BOUNTIFUL but seems somewhat less likely to be applied to persons 〈the *bounteous* yields of cotton, alfalfa, small grains, sorghums, melons, lettuce, dates, and citrus fruits for which the state is noted —*Amer. Guide Series: Ariz.*〉 OPENHANDED suggests free and unguarded generosity; its antonym is *closefisted* 〈*openhanded* to all appeals for charity〉 MUNIFICENT may suggest princely or lordly lavishness and richness in giving 〈had been most *munificent* to his soldiers. He had doubled their ordinary pay. He had shared the spoils of his conquests with them —J.A.Froude〉 〈guaranteed by the United States government in terms of *munificent* land grants —Irving Stone〉 HANDSOME may imply either that a gift is large and impressive or that the giver is magnanimous or gracious 〈final decision to join the Allies was based on their favorable military position . . . as well as on the *handsome* prizes which she was offered —C.E.Black & E.C.Helmreich〉 〈this method of dealing with her, if not lavish, was suitable, and in fact *handsome* —Edith Wharton〉

**²liberal** \"\ *n* -s : one that is liberal: as **a** : one that is open-minded or not strict in his observance of orthodox, traditional, or established forms or ways **b** *usu cap* : a member or supporter of a Liberal party 〈Conservatives, Labourites, and *Liberals* have two whips each in the House of Lords —F.A. Ogg & Harold Zink〉 〈in Australia *Liberals* and Conservatives coalesced . . . in the face of the growth of Labour —Barbara & Robert North〉 〈a preference for the Democratic presidential nominee among *Liberals* in New York〉 〈in most European countries, the *Liberals* today are a right-wing party —A.M. Schlesinger b. 1917〉 **c** : an adherent or advocate of liberalism esp. in terms of individual rights and freedom from arbitrary authority 〈writing as a theological ~〉 〈Manchester *Liberals* . . . fought factory legislation as a cardinal sin —Louis Filler〉 〈the ~'s concern for individual or minority rights and freedoms —F.W.Coker〉 — compare PROGRESSIVE

**liberal arts** *n pl* [trans. of ML *liberales artes*] **1** : the studies comprising the trivium and quadrivium in the middle ages **2** : the studies (as language, philosophy, history, literature, abstract science) esp. in a college or university that are presumed to provide chiefly general knowledge and to develop the general intellectual capacities (as reason or judgment) as opposed to professional, vocational, or technical studies 〈a *liberal arts* curriculum〉 〈a *liberal arts* college〉; *also* : the humanities 〈studied mainly the sciences and the *liberal arts*〉 — see HUMANITY 3c

**liberal catholic** *n, cap L&C* : a person or group rejecting the authority of the Roman Catholic Church in specific matters of doctrine, discipline, or church government but accepting the body of its teachings or its forms of worship

**liberal education** *n* : education based on the liberal arts and intended to bring about the improvement, discipline, or free development of the mind or spirit — compare GENERAL EDUCATION

**lib·er·al·ism** \'lib(ə)rə,lizəm\ *n* -s **1** : the quality or state of being liberal: as **a** : lack of strictness or rigor 〈treats his children with a certain ~〉 **b** : BROAD-MINDEDNESS, OPEN-MINDEDNESS 〈an outlook marked by ~ and tolerance〉 **2** : principles, theories, or actions that are liberal: as **a** *often cap* : a movement in modern Protestantism emphasizing intellectual liberty and the spiritual and ethical content of Christianity 〈nineteenth century *Liberalism* . . . introduced historical method in the interpretation of the gospels —C.H.Moehlman〉 — compare FUNDAMENTALISM, MODERNISM **b** : a theory in economics emphasizing individual freedom from restraint esp. by government regulation in all economic activity and usu. based upon free competition, the self-regulating market, and the gold standard 〈the decline of mercantilism produced a period characterized notably by the ideas and policy of ~〉 — called also *economic liberalism*; compare CAPITALISM, COLLECTIVISM, FREE ENTERPRISE, INDIVIDUALISM, LAISSEZ-FAIRE, MERCANTILISM, SOCIALISM **c** : a political philosophy based on belief in progress, the essential goodness of man, and the autonomy of the individual and standing for tolerance and freedom for the individual from arbitrary authority in all spheres of life esp. by the protection of political and civil liberties and for government under law with the consent of the governed 〈the touchstone that enables us to recognize ~ is the question of toleration —M.R.Cohen〉 〈the classic ~ . . . derived from French rationalism and Benthamite utilitarianism —C.H.Driver〉 〈~ had always claimed to stand for the greatest social good —G.H.Sabine〉 — compare CATHOLICISM 4, COMMUNISM 2, CONSERVATISM 1b, FASCISM 2a, INDIVIDUALISM, SOCIALISM **d** *usu cap* : the principles or policies of a Liberal party 〈the individualism of British *Liberalism* —L.D.Epstein〉 〈nonconformist religion . . . was traditionally associated with political *Liberalism* —G.D.H.Cole〉 **e** : an attitude or philosophy favoring individual freedom for self-development and self-expression 〈a positive and noble impulse . . . of intellectual ~ was its immanent zeal for truth —F.C.Sell〉

**lib·er·al·ist** \-ˌləst\ *n* -s : LIBERAL

**lib·er·al·is·tic** \¦lib(ə)rə¦listik\ *also* **lib·er·al·ist** \'lib(ə)rələst\ *adj* : of or belonging to, being marked by, or tending toward liberalism 〈the ~ philosophy of the eighteenth century〉

**lib·er·al·i·ty** \ˌlibə'ralәd·ē, -lətē, -i\ *n* -ES [ME *liberalite*, fr. MF *liberalité*, fr. L *liberalitat-, liberalitas*, fr. *liberalis* liberal + *-itat-, -itas* -ity — more at LIBERAL] **1** : the quality or state of being liberal in giving, granting, or yielding : GENEROSITY 〈gifts to charity marked by a great ~〉; *also* : an instance of such liberality : a liberal gift : GRATUITY 〈almost financially ruined by his *liberalities*〉 **2** : the quality or state of being liberal in attitude or principle 〈coeducation was introduced in 1870, early evidence of the institution's ~ and vigor —*Amer. Guide Series: Mich.*〉 〈my grandmother was proud of her ~ in not objecting to his marrying into what she called 'Trade' —Bertrand Russell〉 **3** *archaic* : LIBERALS **4** : FULLNESS, AMPLENESS, BROADNESS 〈a ~ of mouth and feature〉 〈crossing areas of knowledge so as to insure a genuine ~ of awareness —J.P.Elder〉

**lib·er·al·iza·tion** \ˌlib(ə)rələ'zāshən, -ˌlī'z-\ *n* -s : the act of liberalizing or the state of being liberalized 〈the ~ of citizenship requirements —Cecil Hobbs〉 〈college entrance requirements had . . . undergone considerable ~ —Alfred Kähler〉

**lib·er·al·ize** \'lib(ə)rəˌlīz\ *vb* -ED/-ING/-S [¹*liberal* + *-ize*] *vt* **1** : to make liberal or more liberal: as **a** : to imbue with liberal ideas, principles, or attitudes 〈somewhat *liberalized* politically after he was exposed to a variety of opposing opinions〉 **b** : to alter in the direction of breaking away from orthodoxy, tradition, or an established pattern 〈~ the ritual of the church〉 〈~ a college curriculum〉 **c** : to make less strict or rigorous 〈~ the immigration laws〉 **d** : to make larger, freer, fuller, or more comprehensive (as in coverage or scope) 〈*liberalized* health and hospitalization coverage by insurance companies —*Trends*〉 〈studies to ~ the mind〉 〈an effort to ~ foreign trade —*Time*〉 **2** : to free from official control : DECONTROL ~ *vi* : to become liberal or more liberal in ideas, principles, attitudes, or affiliations

**lib·er·al·iz·er** \-zə(r)\ *n* -s : one that liberalizes

**liberal jew** *n, usu cap L&J* : REFORM JEW

**liberal judaism** *n, usu cap L&J* : REFORM JUDAISM

**lib·er·al·ly** \'lib(ə)rəlē, -li\ *adv* : in a liberal manner 〈gave ~ to charity〉 〈~ endowed with relatives〉 〈~ educated〉 〈a great esplanade ~ provided with seats —F.J.Haskin〉

**lib·er·al·ness** *n* -ES : LIBERALITY

**liberal republican** *n, usu cap L&R* : a member of a political party of dissident Republicans formed in opposition to the first Grant administration 〈the Democratic convention accepted . . . the ticket of the *Liberal Republicans* —H.R.Penniman〉

**liberal unionist** *n, usu cap L&U* : a member of a British political group seceding from the Liberals over opposition to home rule for Ireland and maintaining existence as a separate party during the late 19th century 〈the Conservatives and *Liberal Unionists* were . . . in power —G.M.Trevelyan〉

**¹liberate** *adj* [L *liberatus*, past part. of *liberare*] *obs* : LIBERATED, FREE

**²lib·er·ate** \'libəˌrāt, *usu* -ād·+V\ *vt* -ED/-ING/-S [L *liberatus*, past part. of *liberare*, fr. *liber* free — more at LIBERAL] **1 a** : to give release (as from restraint or bondage) : set at liberty : let loose : FREE 〈~ a slave〉 〈~ him from economic worry —Will Durant〉 〈*liberated* great, new, and unexpected forces —Drew Middleton〉; *specif* : to free (as a country) from control or domination by a foreign power **b** *in Hinduism & Buddhism* : to provide with salvation or grant salvation to **2** : to free from combination : SEPARATE, DISENGAGE 〈use of the acid sintering material is necessary to ~ the zinc —R.B.Fulton〉 **3** *slang* : to acquire by some legally irregular means : STEAL 〈played in Army bands . . . rarely traveled with fewer than three *liberated* pianos —*Time*〉 **syn** see FREE

**lib·er·a·tion** \ˌlibə'rāshən\ *n* -s [ME *liberacion*, fr. L *liberation-, liberatio*, fr. *liberatus* + *-ion-, -io* -ion] : the act of liberating or the state of being liberated 〈eliminated affectation and propaganda from her work . . . results of this ~ give to these poems of her last decade a variety, spontaneity, and depth —R.S.Hillyer〉 〈the slow oxidation . . . with the ~ of appreciable quantities of iodine —W.H.Dowdeswell〉 〈complete ~ of the mind from what is nonmental —Samuel Alexander〉; *specif* : the act of freeing from control or domination by a foreign power or the state of being freed from such power 〈the struggle for the ~ of France in the early 1940's —*Current Biog.*〉

**lib·er·a·tion·ism** \-shə,nizəm\ *n* -s : principles or attitudes advocating liberation; *esp* : the principles of those opposed to a state or established church and esp. in England advocating disestablishment

**lib·er·a·tion·ist** \-sh(ə)nəst\ *n* -s : one that favors or advocates liberationism

**lib·er·a·tive** \'libəˌrād·iv, -b(ə)rəd·-\ *adj* : liberating or tending toward liberation

**lib·er·a·tor** \'libəˌrād·ə(r), -ātə-\ *n* -s [L, fr. *liberatus* + *-or*] : one that liberates 〈came as a ~ against the . . . man, who for a century or two had imposed his military and economic will on these peoples —*Saturday Rev.*〉 〈the aspect not simply of an earthly ~ but of a divine redeemer —Maurice Samuel〉

**lib·er·a·to·ry** \'lib(ə)rəˌtōrē\ *adj* [L *liberatus* (past part. of *liberare* to set free) + E *-ory* — more at LIBERATE] : tending, serving, or attempting to liberate

**¹li·be·ria** \lī'birēə, -bēr-\ *adj, usu cap* [fr. *Liberia*, country in western Africa] : of or from Liberia : of the kind or style prevalent in Liberia : LIBERIAN

**²liberia** \"\ *n* -s *often cap* : a dark grayish brown that is very slightly redder and deeper than Rembrandt and slightly less strong and very slightly redder than average chocolate brown

**¹li·be·ri·an** \-rēən\ *adj, usu cap* [*Liberia*, Africa + E *-ian*] : LIBERIA

**²liberian** \"\ *n* -s *usu cap* : a native or inhabitant of Liberia

**liberian rubber** *n, usu cap L* : a low-grade resinous rubber collected in parts of tropical western Africa from a native fig tree (*Ficus vogelii*)

**libers** *pl of* LIBER

**¹lib·er·tar·i·an** \ˌlibə(r)'terēən, -ta(a)r-, -tār-\ *n* -s [¹*liberty* + *-arian*] **1** : an advocate of the doctrine of free will — contrasted with *necessitarian* **2** : one who upholds the principles of liberty; *specif* : one who upholds the principles of individual liberty of thought and action 〈private judgment and constitutional authority . . . authoritarians have left but little scope for the former, ~s would always cut down the latter to the smallest proportions —C.H.McIlwain〉

**²libertarian** \¦==¦===\ *adj* : of or belonging to a libertarian: as **a** : advocating a theory of free will 〈a ~ doctrine〉 **b** (1) : advocating or advancing liberty 〈a ~ ruler〉 (2) : based on or embodying principles of liberty 〈a ~ rule of law〉 〈the ~ tradition〉

**lib·er·tar·i·an·ism** \ˌ==¦==,nizəm\ *n* -s : the theories or practices of a libertarian 〈a new and extreme ~ arising which . . . goes almost to the length of anarchy in rejecting any state —Norman Thomas〉

**li·ber·ti·cid·al** \lə¦bərd·ə¦sīdᵊl\ *adj* [F *liberticide* + E *-al*] : LIBERTICIDE

**¹li·ber·ti·cide** \lə'bərd·əˌsīd\ *adj* [F, fr. *liberté* liberty + *-i-* + *-cide* killing (fr. *-cide*, n. comb. form) — more at LIBERTY] : destroying or tending to destroy liberty

**²liberticide** \"\ *n* -s **1** : the destruction of liberty **2** : a destroyer of liberty

**lib·er·tin·age** \'libə(r)ˌtēnij, -nēj, ˌ=='==\ *n* -s [¹*libertine* + *-age*] : libertinism esp. in religious matters or in conduct 〈his lifelong untidiness, ribald small talk, obscure ~ —Glenway Wescott〉

**¹lib·er·tine** \'libə(r)ˌtēn, ˌ=='=, *chiefly Brit* -tīn\ *n* -s [ME *libertyn*, fr. L *libertinus*, fr. *libertinus*, adj.] **1 a** *obs* : a manumitted slave : FREEDMAN **b** *usu cap* : a member of a first-century Jerusalem synagogue composed of the descendants of Jews who had been carried in captivity to Rome and later freed 〈members of the synagogue of the *Libertines* disputed with Stephen according to Acts 6: 9 (AV)〉 **2** *usu cap* **a** : one of a political party in Geneva that until its fall in 1555 championed the ancient liberties of the city against the rigor of Calvin and the French refugees — called also *Perrinist* **b** : one of a 16th century pantheistic sect in France and the Netherlands that denied the distinction between good and evil **3** : a freethinker esp. in religious matters — usu. used disparagingly **4** : one that is markedly unrestrained esp. by convention or morality; *esp* : one leading a dissolute life

**²libertine** \"\ *adj* [L *libertinus* of a freedman, fr. *libertus* freedman (fr. *liber* free) + *-inus* -ine — more at LIBERAL] : of, belonging to, or being a libertine: as **a** : freethinking in religion — usu. used disparagingly **b** *archaic* : free from restraint : UNCONTROLLED **c** (1) : showing unusual freedom from conventions or usual or standard patterns of behavior (2) : morally loose in conduct : LICENTIOUS, PROFLIGATE, DISSOLUTE

**lib·er·tin·ism** \'libə(r)ˌtēˌnizəm, ˌ=='=\ *n* -s : the quality or state of being libertine or a libertine or the principles or behavior of a libertine: **a** : licentiousness in conduct : marked disregard of conventional moral restraints **b** : freethinking in religious matters; *esp* : excessive or blameworthy freethinking of this kind **c** *archaic* : freedom from restraint : LIBERTY

**¹lib·er·ty** \'libə(r)d·ē, -)tē, -i\ *n* -ES *often attrib* [ME *liberte*, fr. MF *liberté*, fr. L *libertat-, libertas*, fr. *liber* free + *-tat-, -tas* -ty — more at LIBERAL] **1** : the quality or state of being free: **a** (1) : freedom from usu. external restraint or compulsion : the power to do as one pleases (2) : a condition of legal nonrestraint of natural powers — compare PRIVILEGE 1e **b** : exemption from subjection to the will of another claiming ownership or services — compare BONDAGE, SERFDOM, SLAVERY **c** : freedom from arbitrary or despotic control **d** : the power of choice : freedom from necessity : freedom from compulsion or constraint in the act of willing something **e** (1) : CIVIL LIBERTY (2) : POLITICAL LIBERTY (3) : INDIVIDUAL LIBERTY (4) : PERSONAL LIBERTY **2** : a figure representing a personification of liberty (as on a coin) **3 a** : a right or immunity enjoyed by prescription or by grant (as from a sovereign power) : PRIVILEGE, EXEMPTION, FRANCHISE **b** : LEAVE, PERMISSION 〈granted the boy ~ to go out〉 **c** : a place within which certain immunities are enjoyed or jurisdiction is exercised; *specif* : a district of some British cities within which the exclusive privilege or franchise of executing legal process was by royal grant vested in one or more persons exempting them from the jurisdiction of the sheriff **d** : permission to go freely within the limits 〈given the ~ of the house〉 〈allowed only the ~ of his prison cell〉 **4** : action or an action or license that goes beyond a usu. acceptable, proper, or wise limit: as **a** (1) : action or an action or privilege in or as if in violation of the laws of strict etiquette or propriety : FAMILIARITY 〈guilty of many *liberties* in his dealings with his superiors〉 〈take undue ~ with a stranger〉 (2) : an undue intimacy : an improper familiarity esp. with another's person **b** : an action that goes beyond the limits of prudence 〈took *liberties* with his health〉 **c** : action or an action that goes beyond the limits of strict accuracy or conformity (as to a rule) 〈a certain ~ in his translation〉 〈took *liberties* in the way he played the game〉 **5** : a short authorized absence from naval duty usu. for less than 48 hours — compare LEAVE **6** : a strong blue that is redder and deeper than sèvres and redder and darker than cerulean blue (sense 1b) — called also *regatta* — **at liberty 1** : FREE 〈set the prisoners *at liberty*〉 〈*at liberty* to do what one likes〉 **2** : at leisure : UNOCCUPIED, UNUSED

**²liberty** \"\ *adj, usu cap* [fr. *Liberty* and Co., drapery firm in London, England] : of, belonging to, being, or resembling a fabric manufactured by the London drapery firm of Liberty and Co. or a pattern associated with such fabric or an item made from it 〈a *Liberty* print〉 〈*Liberty* silk prints〉

**liberty bond** *n, usu cap L* : a bond of a Liberty loan

**liberty cap** *n* : a limp close-fitting conical cap resembling that given to a Roman slave upon his manumission and adopted as the cap of French revolutionists and as a symbol of liberty esp. in the U.S. before 1800 — compare BONNET ROUGE

liberty cap as worn by the French revolutionists

**liberty freighter** *n* : LIBERTY SHIP

**liberty green** *n* : a moderate yellow green that is greener and paler than average moss green and yellower and paler than average pea green or apple green (sense 1a)

**liberty hall** *n* : a place where one can do as one likes; *esp* : a house where a guest is encouraged to act with unusual freedom

**liberty horse** *n* : a circus horse that performs tricks (as wheeling, circling, running in file) in a group and without a rider

**liberty loan** *n, usu cap 1st L* : one of the five U. S. government gold bond issues authorized by acts of Congress between April 24, 1917 and March 3, 1919

**lib·er·ty·man** \'===,man\ *n, pl* **libertymen** *Brit* : a sailor having permission to go ashore

**liberty of contract** : FREEDOM OF CONTRACT

**liberty of speech** : FREEDOM OF SPEECH

**liberty of the press** : FREEDOM OF THE PRESS

**liberty pole** *n* : a tall flagstaff surmounted by a liberty cap, the flag of a republic, or other object regarded as a symbol of liberty

**liberty ship** *n, usu cap L* : a cargo ship of a type built in the U. S. during World War II

**liberty tea** *n* [so called fr. its having been used as a substitute for tea by the American colonists to evade the British tea tax] : WHORLED LOOSESTRIFE

**li·be·rum ma·ri·ta·gi·um** \ˌlēbə,ru̇m,märə'tägē,u̇m\ *n* [ML] : FRANKMARRIAGE

**li·be·rum veto** \'libərəm-\ *n* [L *liberum* (neut. of *liber* free) + E *veto* — more at LIBERAL] : a veto exercised by a single member (as of a legislative body) under rules requiring unanimous consent ⟨the anarchic potentialities of the *liberum veto* —C.J. Friedrich⟩ ⟨exercise a sort of *liberum veto* as in the Polish Diet —Max Lerner⟩

**li·beth·en·ite** \lə'bethə,nīt\ *n* -s [G *libethenit*, fr. *Libethen*, Czechoslovakia + G *-it* -ite] : an olive green orthorhombic mineral $Cu_2(PO_4)(OH)$ consisting of a basic copper phosphate and occurring in small prismatic crystals or in globular or reniform masses (hardness 4, sp. gr. 3.6–3.8)

**libi·dibi** \ˌlibē'dibē, ˌlēbē'dēbē\ *or* **libi·divi** \-'divē, -'dēvē\ *n* -s [AmerSp *libidivi*, alter. of Sp *dividivi* — more at DIVI-DIVI] : DIVI-DIVI

**li·bid·i·nal** \lə'bidᵊnəl\ *adj* [NL *libidin-*, *libido* + E *-al*] : of or belonging to the libido ⟨acting out of ~ or hostile impulses —R.M.Dorn⟩ — **li·bid·i·nal·ly** \-nəlē, -li\ *adv*

**li·bid·i·ni·za·tion** \=ˌ==ə'zāshən, -ˌī'z-\ *n* -s : the act of libidinizing or the state of being libidinized : investment with libido ⟨may lead to a ~ of sleep and may develop into a craving for sleep —Emanuel Windholz⟩

**li·bid·i·nize** \=ˈ==,īz\ *vt* -ED/-ING/-S [NL *libidin-*, *libido* + E *-ize*] : to feel toward or treat as if a source or avenue of sexual gratification : invest with libido ⟨a woman in labor suffers injury to the most highly *libidinized* organs of the body — *Diseases of the Nervous System*⟩

**li·bid·i·nous** \lə'bidᵊnəs\ *adj* [ME *lybydynous*, fr. MF *libidineus*, fr. L *libidinosus*, fr. *libidin-*, *libido* + *-osus* -ous] **1** : having or marked by lustful desires : characterized by lewdness : LUSTFUL, LASCIVIOUS ⟨indulged in ~ orgies —Samuel Putnam⟩ **2** [influenced in meaning by NL *libido*] : of or belonging to the libido ⟨the struggles against ~ temptation — *Psychological Abstracts*⟩ ⟨identification and ~ ties between individuals, the latter being reduced to forms of sexual love —Abram Kardiner⟩ — **li·bid·i·nous·ly** *adv* — **li·bid·i·nous·ness** *n* -ES

**li·bi·do** \lə'bē(,)dō *also* ÷'libə,dō *or* 'libē,dō *or* lə'bī(,)dō\ *n* -s [NL, fr. L, desire, lust, fr. *libēre* to please — more at LOVE] **1 a** : emotional or psychic energy derived from primitive biological urges and usu. goal-directed ⟨described the relation of person to person with the aid of the concept of ~, the grossest manifestation of which is sexual love —Abram Kardiner⟩ **b** : desire for sexual outlet or gratification ⟨may be prompted to take a second wife not by an excessive ~ —R.H. Loure⟩ **c** : frequency of sexual outlet ⟨during the nonbreeding season in the young ram there occurs a similar marked decline in ~ —*Nature*⟩ ⟨therapy . . . to stimulate ~ in bulls during the season of the year when sexual activity is depressed —*Veterinary Bull.*⟩ **2** : lustful desire or striving ⟨the will . . . has a strong ~ of its own —L.J.A.Mercier⟩

**lib–lab** \'lib,lab\ *n* -s *usu cap both Ls* [*Liberal-Labor*] **1** : a member of the British Liberal party in the late 19th century belonging to or supporting the trade-union movement **2** : a political liberal associated with policies favorable to organized labor

**libo·ce·drus** \ˌlībə'sēdrəs, ˌlib-\ *n*, *cap* [NL, fr. Gk *liboi* tears (fr. *leibein* to pour) + L *cedrus* cedar; fr. the resinous nature of the tree — more at LIBATION, CEDAR] : a genus of trees (family Pinaceae) having leaves that resemble those of the sequoia — see INCENSE CEDAR

**libr** *abbr* librarian

**li·bra** *in senses 1 & 2* 'lībrə *or* 'lēb-, *in sense 3* 'lēbrə *or* -ēvrə\ *n* [ME, fr. L, lit., balance, unit of weight] **1** -s *usu cap* : the 7th sign of the zodiac — see SIGN table, ZODIAC illustration **2** *pl* **li·brae** \'lī(,)brē, 'lē,brī\ [L] : an ancient Roman unit of weight equal to 327.45 grams or 0.7221 pound avoirdupois **3** -s [Sp & Pg, fr. L] **a** : any of various Spanish or Portuguese units of weight varying around 460 grams or 1.01 pounds avoirdupois **b** : the Colombian unit equal to 500 grams **c** : the Venezuelan unit equal to 1 kilogram **d** : the basic monetary unit of Peru from 1898 to 1930; *also* : a gold coin worth one libra

**li·brar·i·an** \lī'brerēən, -bra(a)r-, -brār-\ *n* -s [*library* + *-an*] **1 a** : a specialist in the care or management of a library **b** : one whose vocation is working with library books (as by cataloging) **2** : one whose special task is the management of any body of literature (as the musical scores for an orchestra)

**li·brar·i·an·ship** \-,ship\ *n* : the office or duties of a librarian

**li·brary** \'lī,brerē, -,b(r)ərē, -,brē, -ri *also* ÷-,ber- *sometimes* -,bər·ē *or* -,bər·i\ *n* -ES *often attrib* [ME *librarie*, fr. ML *librarium* & *libraria*, fr. neut. & fem. respectively of L *librarius* of books, fr. *libr-*, *liber* book + *-arius* -ary — more at LEAF] **1 a** : a room, a series or section of sections of a building, or a building itself given over to books, manuscripts, musical scores, or other literary and sometimes artistic materials (as paintings or musical recordings) usu. kept in some convenient order for use but not for sale ⟨the house contained a ~ besides the living, dining, and kitchen areas⟩ ⟨a college ~⟩ — see PUBLIC LIBRARY **b** (1) : a collection of books, manuscripts, or other literary materials kept (as in a library) for study or reading or a collection of paintings, musical scores, musical recordings, photographs, maps, or films kept for convenient use, study, or enjoyment ⟨a ~ of early American travel books⟩ ⟨a ~ of Bach recordings⟩ ⟨a private ~ of manuscript plays⟩ (2) : an institution for the custody or administration of such a collection ⟨the *Library* of Congress⟩ (3) : a collection suggesting a library (as a reference library) ⟨the most complete ~ of illustrations available in book form —*advt*⟩ ⟨a ~ of color chips —*Amer. Fabrics*⟩ **c** : RENTAL LIBRARY **d** (1) : CANON 3c ⟨the goal of going through the entire Shakespeare ~ —Lewis Funke⟩ (2) : a series of books of some similarity issued by a publisher ⟨a Hawthorne ~⟩ (3) : a series of reference materials bearing on the same matter (as programs, routines, and subroutines in digital computing) **e** : MORGUE 2a **f** : something suggesting a library esp. in being a receptacle of wide or miscellaneous information ⟨men and women . . . who are oral *libraries* for neighborhood history and gossip —*Amer. Guide Series: Tenn.*⟩ **2** *Brit* : a business established to conduct transactions for others : AGENCY; *esp* : a theater ticket agency

**library binder** *n* : one that binds and rebinds books in durable cloth for frequent use

**library binding** *n* : an esp. strong durable cloth bookbinding suitable for use by a circulating library; *also* : the production of books so bound — compare EDITION BINDING

**library buckram** *n* : a fabric used for library bindings

**library corner** *n* : a corner of a book-cover turn-in in which the surplus cloth is folded under for greater strength instead of being cut away as in ordinary binding

**library edition** *n* : a set of books uniform in size and format usu. of the works of one author

**library of congress classification** *n*, *usu cap L&1st C* : a library classification using the letters of the alphabet plus numbers for its notation — compare DECIMAL CLASSIFICATION, EXPANSIVE CLASSIFICATION

**library paste** *n* : a thick white smooth adhesive made from starch and used esp. on paper and paperboard

**library school** *n* : a school specializing in the teaching of library science

**library science** *n* : the study or the principles and practices of library care and administration or of any division of it (as bibliography or reference work)

**library steps** *n pl* : a portable set of often folding steps used to gain access to the high shelves of a library

library steps

**library van** *n* : BOOKMOBILE

**¹li·brate** \'lī,brāt, -brət\ *n* -s [ML *librata*, fr. ML *libra* English pound (fr. L, balance, libra) + L *-ata* (fem. of *-atus* -ate)] : land having a value of a pound a year

**²li·brate** \-,brāt\ *vb* -ED/-ING/-S [L *libratus*, past part. of *librare*, fr. *libra* balance] *vi* **1** : to vibrate as a balance does before resting in equilibrium **2** : to stay poised ~ *vt*, *archaic* : to cause to librate : BALANCE, WEIGH

**li·bra·tion** \lī'brāshən\ *n* -s [L *libration-*, *libratio*, fr. *libratus* + *-ion-*, *-io* -ion] **1** : the action or state of librating **2** *obs* : the act or process of weighing **3** : an oscillation in the apparent aspect of a secondary body (as a planet or a satellite) as seen from the primary object around which it revolves caused by the inclination of its axis of rotation, variations in its orbital speed, real irregularities in its rotation, or changes in the observer's position on the primary body — see LIBRATION OF THE MOON

**libration of the moon** : the combination of four libration effects that causes parts of the side of the moon turned to the earth to be alternately visible and invisible so that as much as 59 percent of the moon's entire surface can be observed from the earth

**li·bra·to·ry** \'lībrə,tōrē\ *adj* : moving like a balance as it tends to an equipoise : BALANCING

**li·bret·tist** \lə'bred·əst, -etəst\ *n* -s [F or It; F *librettiste*, fr. It *librettista*, fr. *libretto* + *-ista* -ist] : the writer of a libretto

**li·bret·to** \lə'bred·(,)ō, -e(,)t\ *n*, *pl* **libret·tos** \|ōz\ *or* **libret·ti** \|ē\ [It, dim. of *libro* book, fr. L *libr-*, *liber* — more at LEAF] **1** : the text of a work (as an opera) for the musical theater **2** : the book containing a libretto

**li·bre·ville** \'lēbrə,vēl, -vil, ,==ˈ=\ *adj*, *usu cap* [fr. *Libreville*, Gabon] : of or from Libreville, the capital of Gabon : of the kind or style prevalent in Libreville

**libri** *pl of* LIBER

**libri·form** \'lībrə,fȯrm, 'lib-\ *adj* [ISV *libri-* (fr. L *libr-*, *liber* inner bark of a tree, pith of papyrus, book) + *-form* — more at LEAF] : resembling phloem fibers

**libs** *pres 3d sing of* LIB

**li·bur·ni·an** \(')lī'bərnēən\ *adj*, *usu cap* [*Liburnia*, ancient district of Illyria (fr. L) + E *-an*] : of or belonging to Liburnia, an ancient country on the northeast coast of the Adriatic

**liburnian galley** *n*, *usu cap L* : a fast light large-sailed sharp-prowed galley invented by the Liburnian pirates

**lib·ya** \'libēə\ *adj*, *usu cap* [fr. *Libya*, country in northern Africa] : of or from Libya : of the kind or style prevalent in Libya : LIBYAN

**¹lib·y·an** \-ēən\ *adj*, *usu cap* [*Libya*, ancient territory variously conceived in northern Africa (fr. L *Libye*, *Libya*, fr. Gk *Libyē*) + E *-an*] **1** : of, relating to, or characteristic of ancient Libya **2** : of, relating to, or characteristic of the ancient Libyans **3** [*Libya*, country in northern Africa + E *-an*] : of, relating to, or characteristic of modern Libya or its people

**²libyan** \"\ *n* -s *usu cap* **1 a** : a member of any of the peoples indigenous in historical ancient times to the region immediately west of Egypt **b** : a member of any of the peoples that in historical ancient times were indigenous to No. Africa west from Egypt to the Atlantic **2** *in some ethnological classifications* : a member of a branch of the Mediterranean subrace comprising some or all of the Libyans and those peoples (as the Berbers) believed to be descended from them without substantial mixture with other stocks and also comprising the people believed to have been the principal racial stock of prehistoric Egypt and perhaps of adjoining parts of prehistoric northeastern Africa **3** : a Berber language of ancient No. Africa **4** : a native or inhabitant of modern Libya

**libyan alphabet** *n*, *usu cap L* : an alphabet of consonantal characters of simple geometric form of uncertain origin but perhaps derived in part from the Punic or neo-Punic alphabet in which several hundred inscriptions in the Libyan language are known from the late pre-Christian period and the first several centuries of the Christian era principally from what are now Tunisia and eastern Algeria — called also *Numidian alphabet*; see TIFINAGH

**libyan cat** *n*, *usu cap L* : KAFFIR CAT

**libyco–berber** \ˌlibə(,)kō+\ *n*, *usu cap L&B* [*Libyco-* (fr. L *Libycus* of Libya, fr. Gk *Libykos*, fr. *Libyē* Libya) + *Berber*] : BERBER 2

**libyo-** *comb form*, *usu cap* [*Libya*] : Libyan and ⟨*Libyo-Phoenician*⟩ ⟨*Libyo-Teutonic*⟩

**lib·y·the·idae** \ˌlibə'thēə,dē\ *n pl*, *cap* [NL, fr. *Libythea*, type genus (perh. fr. Gk *Libys* Libyan + *thea* appearance, aspect) + *-idae*] : a small family comprising the snout butterflies and often considered a subfamily of Nymphalidae

**lic** *abbr* **1** license; licensed **2** licentiate

**li·ca·nia** \lə'kānēə, lī'-\ *n*, *cap* [NL, modif. (with some letter rearrangement) of Galibi *caligni* (tree of the genus *Licania*)] : a large genus of tropical American trees (family Rosaceae) having alternate simple leaves and small panicled flowers

**li·can·ic acid** \lə'kanik-, (')lī|\ *n* [NL *Licania* + E *-ic*] : a crystalline unsaturated keto acid $C_4H_9(CH{=}CH)_3(CH_2)_4COCH_2CH_2COOH$ that in the form of the glyceride is the chief component of oiticica oil and that may be hydrogenated to stearic acid

**li·car·e·ol** \lə'ka(a)rē,ōl, lī'-, -,ōl\ *n* -s [ISV *licare-* (fr. NL *Licaria*, genus of trees of the family Lauraceae) + *-ol*] : levorotatory linalool

**lice** *pl of* LOUSE

**li·cens·able** \'līsᵊnsəbəl\ *adj* : capable of being licensed or of receiving a license ⟨licenses to import most ~ commodities from hard-currency areas —*Foreign Commerce Weekly*⟩

**¹li·cense** *or* **li·cence** \'līsᵊn(t)s\ *n* -s *see sense 5* [ME *licence*, fr. MF, fr. L *licentia*, fr. *licent-*, *licens* (pres. part. of *licēre* to be permitted, be for sale) + *-ia* -y; akin to Latvian *likt* to come to terms] **1** : permission to act ⟨go from hence without their ~ —Daniel Defoe⟩ **2 a** : unusual freedom of action permitted because of extenuating circumstances or special prerogatives ⟨in the decoration the Chinese silversmiths had been allowed the utmost ~ —Osbert Lancaster⟩ ⟨reason and common sense were given full ~ to take no notice of pedants —Stuart Hampshire⟩ ⟨had a stranger's ~ to go everywhere —Nadine Gordimer⟩ **b** (1) : excessive freedom : the abuse of liberties granted ⟨a wave of municipal reform . . . for the correction of what was regarded as ~ —Havelock Ellis⟩ ⟨Caesar's legions . . . were enjoying their victory in the ~ which is miscalled liberty —J.A.Froude⟩ ⟨freedom of the press also carries the grave responsibility that it not be turned into ~ —*Time*⟩ (2) : abusive disregard for rules of personal conduct : LICENTIOUSNESS ⟨like most women of that character and those circumstances her ~ was peculiarly unlimited —Tennessee Williams⟩ ⟨prenuptial chastity in one tribe and adolescent ~ in another —Ruth Benedict⟩ **3 a** (1) : a right or permission granted in accordance with law by a competent authority to engage in some business or occupation, to do some act, or to engage in some transaction which but for such license would be unlawful ⟨a ~ to sell liquor⟩ ⟨a marriage ~⟩ ⟨a ~ to practice medicine⟩ (2) : a document evidencing a license granted **b** : authority or permission of one having no possessory rights in land to do something on that land which would otherwise be unlawful or a trespass — distinguished from *lease* **c** : the grant by a patent holder to another of any of the rights embodied in the patent short of an assignment of a fractional interest therein and short of assigning all the rights protected by the patent **d** : the grant of some but not all of the rights embraced in a copyright **e** *Canad* : a free miner's certificate **4** : a deviation from strict fact, form, or rule utilized by an artist or writer on the assumption that it will be permitted for the sake of the advantage or effect gained ⟨permitting myself a certain ~ of treatment, the better to round out the picture —S.H.Adams⟩ ⟨has little truck with those who have taken literary ~ —D.L.Horner⟩ **5** *pl* **license** *chiefly Midland* **a** : a formal permission from local authorities **b** : a document embodying such permission ⟨get a pair o' *license* fer to marry —J.W.Riley⟩

**²license** *also* **licence** \"\ *vt* -ED/-ING/-S [ME *licencen*, fr. *licence*, n.] **1 a** : to grant or issue a license to (someone) usu. after special qualifications have been met ⟨was *licensed* and later ordained to the ministry —J.C.Brauer⟩ **b** : to permit or authorize esp. by formal license ⟨patented processes were freely *licensed* in a general effort to do everything and anything to help win the war —Marquis James⟩ **2 a** : to accord permission or consent to : ALLOW ⟨at a wedding everybody seemed *licensed* to kiss everyone else —Irwin Shaw⟩ ⟨a popular novelist may be *licensed* to draw on his imagination —A.T. Quiller-Couch⟩ ⟨an able man, *licensed* by the times to do pretty much as he pleased —J.H.Hanford⟩ **b** [MF *licencier*, fr. *licence*, n.] *archaic* : to give permission for departure to : DISMISS ⟨thus *licensed*, the chief . . . left the presence chamber —Sir Walter Scott⟩ **syn** see AUTHORIZE

**license bond** *n* : a surety bond required by law as a condition precedent to the pursuit of a specified business or profession

**li·censed** *also* **li·cenced** \-ᵊn(t)st\ *adj* **1** : having a license : permitted or authorized by license ⟨a ~ bureau of judges —Harry Lewis⟩ ⟨a ~ preacher⟩; *specif* : having a liquor license ⟨a ~ hotel⟩ **2** : permitted an unusual freedom : PRIVILEGED ⟨status of a sort of ~ amateur jester —Harvey Graham⟩

**licensed premises** *n pl but sing or pl in constr*, *Brit* : an establishment in which alcoholic beverages and tobacco are permitted to be retailed and consumed

**li·cens·ee** \ˌlīsᵊn'sē\ *n* -s : a licensed person: as **a** : a person who is on the property of another with the consent of its possessor whether by permission or invitation — compare INVITEE, TRESPASSER **b** : a person who is on the property of another with the consent of the possessor but solely for purposes in which the possessor has no business or pecuniary interest — compare GUEST 2b **c** : a person (as a fireman in the course of his duty) who is on the property of another by authority of law **d** : a person having a liquor license

**li·cense·less** \-ᵊn(t)sləs\ *adj* : having no license

**license plate** *or* **license tag** *n* : a plate or tag of metal, leather, or some other durable material attesting that a license has been secured and usu. bearing a registration number

**li·cens·er** \'līsᵊnsə(r)\ *n* -s : one that licenses

**li·cen·sor** \'līsᵊnsə(r); ,==ˈsȯ(ə)r, -ȯ(ə)\ *n* -s : one that grants a license

**li·cen·sure** \'līsᵊnshər, -,shu̇(ə)r\ *n* -s [²*license* + *-ure*] **1** : the granting of licenses esp. to practice a profession **2** : the system of granting licenses (as for professional practice) in accordance with established standards

**¹li·cen·ti·ate** \lī'senchēət, -ē,āt, *esp in sense 1b* lə's-\ *n* -s [ML *licentiatus*, fr. past part. of *licentiare* to allow, fr. L *licentia* license — more at LICENSE] **1 a** : one who has a license to practice a profession; *esp* : one who has a license granted by a university or other degree-conferring body ⟨with a year and a half off to become a ~ in canon law —*Time*⟩ **b** : an academic degree ranking below that of a doctor given by some European institutions of higher education ⟨as a part of his work toward the ~ . . . prepared a critical edition of two late 14th century commentaries —T.A.Kirby⟩ **2** : one licensed to preach in some churches (as the Presbyterian) but not yet installed as a pastor

**²licentiate** *adj* [ML *licentiatus*, past part.] **1** *obs* **a** : given permission : ALLOWED **b** : licensed to preach **2** *obs* : taking unusual liberties : DISORDERLY, UNGOVERNED ⟨only commend me the most ~ loose strayer under heaven —Thomas Nash⟩

**³li·cen·ti·ate** \-ē,āt\ *vt* -ED/-ING/-S [ML *licentiatus*, past part.] : to give liberty, permission, or scope to ⟨were *licentiated* to go a-begging —Isaac D'Israeli⟩

**li·cen·ti·ate·ship** \-ēət,ship\ *n* : the quality or state of a licentiate

**li·cen·ti·a·tion** \(,)lī,senchē'āshən\ *n* -s : the act of licensing esp. to practice medicine

**li·cen·tious** \(')lī'senchəs\ *adj* [L *licentiosus*, fr. *licentia* + *-osus* -ous] **1** : marked by the absence of legal or moral restraints : hostile or offensive to accepted standards of conduct ⟨the ~ practice . . . of making depredations upon foreign nations —Thomas Hutchinson⟩ ⟨the lying and ~ character of our newspapers —Thomas Jefferson⟩ **2** : marked by lewdness : LASCIVIOUS, UNCHASTE ⟨ribaldry . . . too well suited to the taste of a profane and ~ pit —T.B.Macaulay⟩ ⟨a more depraved ~ lot of rascals don't exist —C.B.Nordhoff & J.N. Hall⟩ **3** : marked by neglect of or disregard for strict rules of correctness ⟨verse . . . somewhat ~ in number of syllables —Henry Hallam⟩ ⟨English speech was never more syntactically ~ —Havelock Ellis⟩ — **li·cen·tious·ly** *adv*

**li·cen·tious·ness** *n* -ES : the quality or state of being licentious ⟨the utmost ~ of the press and of the stage —T.B.Macaulay⟩

**lich** \'lich\ *n* -s [ME *lich*, *lik* body, corpse, fr. OE *līc* — more at LIKE] *dial Brit* : a dead body : CORPSE — used chiefly in combination ⟨*lich*-house⟩

**lich bird** *n* : a nightjar (*Caprimulgus europaeus*)

**lichee** *var of* LITCHI

**¹li·chen** \'līkən *sometimes chiefly Brit* 'lichən\ *n* -s [L, fr. Gk *leichēn*, *lichēn*, prob. fr. *leichein* to lick — more at LICK] **1** : any of numerous complex thallophytic plants that constitute the group Lichenes, that are made up of an alga and a fungus growing in symbiotic association on various solid surfaces (as rocks or the bark of trees), that consist of a branching thallus which is not differentiated into stem and leaves but which may be crustose, fruticose, or foliaceous and which contains algal gonidia embedded in a meshwork of fungal hyphae, and that include organisms important in the weathering and breakdown of rocks and some that are sources of foods or dyes — see ASCOLICHENES, BASIDIOLICHENES; ICELAND MOSS, REINDEER MOSS; ARCHIL, LITMUS **2** : any of several skin diseases characterized by the eruption of flat papules; *esp* : LICHEN PLANUS

**²lichen** \"\ *vt* -ED/-ING/-S : to cover over with or as if with lichens ⟨they lay till all their bones were . . . ~*ed* into color with the crags —Alfred Tennyson⟩ ⟨look down upon the ~*ed* walls of this lovely building —R.M.Lockley⟩ ⟨~*ed* history, an immeasurably vast continuity —R.L.Mittenbuhler⟩

**li·che·na·les** \ˌlīkə'nā(,)lēz\ *n pl*, *cap* [NL, fr. L *lichen* + NL *-ales*] *in some esp former classifications* : an order of fungi comprising the lichens

**li·che·nes** \lī'kē(,)nēz\ *n pl*, *cap* [NL, fr. pl. of L *lichen*] : a major category of thallophytes comprising the lichens now usu. treated as an independent group more or less coordinate with Algae and Fungi — compare LICHENALES

**lichen green** *n* : a light greenish gray that is yellower, lighter, and stronger than French gray and bluer than ash gray

**li·chen·i·fi·ca·tion** \lī,kenəfə'kāshən ,līkən-\ *n* [ISV ¹*lichen* + *-i-* + *-fication*] : the process by which skin becomes hardened and leathery or lichenoid usu. as a result of chronic irritation; *also* : a patch of skin so modified

**li·chen·i·fied** \lī'kenə,fīd, 'līkən-\ *adj* [¹*lichen* + *-ify* + *-ed*] : HARDENED, LEATHERY ⟨~ eczema⟩

**li·chen·in** \'līkənən\ *n* -s [¹*lichen* + *-in*] : a gelatinous polysaccharide $(C_6H_{10}O_5)_n$ composed of glucose units and found esp. in several species of moss and lichen and in cereal grains and bulbs

**lichen is·lan·di·cus** \ˌ==,ī'slandəkəs\ *n* [NL, lit., Icelandic lichen] : ICELAND MOSS

**li·chen·ism** \'līkə,nizəm\ *n* -s : symbiosis between certain algae and fungi that produces lichens

**li·chen·ist** \-,nəst\ *n* -s : LICHENOLOGIST

**li·chen·oid** \-,nȯid\ *adj* : resembling lichen ⟨~ dermatitis⟩

**li·chen·o·log·ic** \ˌlīkənə'läjik\ *or* **li·chen·o·log·i·cal** \-jəkəl\ *adj* : of or relating to lichenology

**li·chen·ol·o·gist** \ˌlīkə'näləjəst\ *n* -s : a specialist in lichenology

**li·chen·ol·o·gy** \-jē\ *n* -ES [ISV ¹*lichen* + *-o-* + *-logy*] : the study of lichens

**li·chen·oph·a·gous** \ˌlīkə'näfəgəs\ *adj* [¹*lichen-* + *-o-* + *-phagous*] : feeding on lichens

**li·chen·op·o·ra** \ˌlīkə'näpərə\ *n*, *cap* [NL, fr. ¹*lichen* + *-o-* + *-pora*] : a genus of bryozoans (class Gymnolaemata) usu. forming small laminate colonies on shells

**li·chen·ous** \'līkənəs\ *also* **li·chen·ose** \-,nōs\ *adj* [¹*lichen* + *-ous* or *-ose*] **1 a** : of, relating to, or resembling lichens **b** : abounding in or covered with lichens ⟨a stone seat stood at one end, a fountain at the other, both ~ and crumbling —Frederic Prokosch⟩ **2** : of or relating to lichen : LICHENOID

**lichen pla·nus** \ˌ==ˈplānəs, -lān-\ *n* [NL, lit., flat lichen] : a skin disease characterized by an eruption of wide flat papules covered by a horny glazed film, marked by intense itching, and often accompanied by lesions on the oral mucosa

**lichens** *pl of* LICHEN

**li·cheny** \'līkənē\ *adj* [¹*lichen* + *-y*] : LICHENOUS 1 ⟨the bald patch . . . gleamed like a brown pebble through his ~ hair —Gerald Durrell⟩

**lich fowl** *n* : a nightjar (*Caprimulgus europaeus*)

**lich–gate** *var of* LYCH-GATE

**lich–house** \'=,=\ *n* [ME *lich hus*, fr. *lich* corpse + *hus*, *hous* house — more at LICH, HOUSE] : MORTUARY

**¹lichi** *var of* LITCHI

²lichi *var of* LECHWE

**lich owl** *n, Brit* : BARN OWL

**lich stone** *n* : a stone on which to rest a coffin at the lych-gate

**licht** \'likt\ *Scot var of* LIGHT

**lich·ten·berg figure** \'liktən,bərg-\ *n, cap L* [after Georg Christoph *Lichtenberg* †1799 Ger. physicist and writer] : a pattern of branching lines formed by fine powder (as of sulfur) dusted over an insulating surface across which an electric leakage discharge has recently taken place

**lich·tit** \'liktət\ *Scot var of* LIGHTED

**licht·ly** \-ktli\ *Scot var of* LIGHTLY

**licht·some** \-ktsəm\ *Scot var of* LIGHTSOME

**lic·it** \'lisət, *usu* -əd·+V\ *adj* [MF *licite*, fr. L *licitus*, fr. past part. of *licēre* to be permitted — more at LICENSE] : not forbidden by law : ALLOWABLE, PERMITTED **syn** see LAWFUL

**lic·i·ta·tion** \,lisə'tāshən\ *n* -s [L *licitation-*, *licitatio*, fr. *licitatus* (past part. of *licitari* to bid a price, freq. of *licēre* to be for sale) + *-ion-*, *-io* -ion — more at LICENSE] **1** : the act of offering for sale or bidding at an auction **2** : ⁷CANT 2

**lic·it·ly** *adv* : in a licit manner : LEGALLY

¹**lick** \'lik\ *vb* -ED/-ING/-S [ME *licken*, fr. OE *liccian*; akin to OS *likkon* to lick, OHG *leckōn*, ON *sleikja*, L *lingere*, Gk *leichein* to lick, Skt *leḍhi*, *reḍhi* he licks] *vt* **1 a** (1) : to draw or pass the tongue over ⟨kept trying to ~ his swollen lips with a dry tongue —Ray Duncan⟩ ⟨a few of the reporters ~*ed* their pencils nervously —*Time*⟩ ⟨~ a postage stamp⟩ (2) : to flicker or play over like a tongue : LAP ⟨a brick wall perpetually ~*ed* by smoke —Andrew Buchanan⟩ ⟨walked down to the sea where it ~*ed* the beach —Richard Sale⟩ **b** : to take into the mouth with or as if with the tongue : lap up ⟨watched the cat ~ the flecks of cream from the rim of the bowl⟩ ⟨sauntered down the street ~*ing* ice-cream cones⟩ **2 a** : to strike repeatedly esp. as a punishment : BEAT, THRASH ⟨taken her to her pa and said if he didn't ~ her, they would —Helen Eustis⟩ **b** : DEFEAT, OVERCOME : get the better of ⟨if you ~ me, you take what money I have —William Faulkner⟩ ⟨when its road-building program is completed, it will ~ one of its major problems —Mary R. Johnson⟩ ⟨a man's not ~*ed* when he's got a wife like this —Caroline Slade⟩ ⟨we've got the outfit to ~ the wilderness —S.H.Adams⟩ **3** : to give a finished appearance to ⟨carefully leveled, ~*ed*, snipped artificial lawns —John Muir †1914⟩ ~ *vi* **1** : to lap with the tongue or in the manner of a tongue ⟨the surf ~*ed* at the seawall —Isa Glenn⟩ **2** : to dart like a tongue ⟨the pain ~*ed* over . . . in short little spasms —Gordon Merrick⟩ ⟨a huge puff of smoke-fringed flame filled the doorway, ~*ing* outward toward me —Ralph Ellison⟩ **3** : to move at top speed ⟨rattled down the stony track as hard as he could ~ —T.A.Browne⟩ **syn** see CONQUER — **lick into shape** : to give proper form to : train or drill into orderly form ⟨a civilian can be *licked into shape* as a soldier by the manual of arms —Dixon Wecter⟩ — **lick one's chops** : to anticipate with relish ⟨a banker *licks his chops* over the increase in the earnings on each dollar —George Shea⟩ — **lick one's wounds** : to tend one's injuries : recover from defeat ⟨those gray silent ships which carried the war to the enemy . . . while the fleet *licked its wounds* —E.L.Beach⟩

²**lick** \"\ *n* -s **1 a** (1) : an act or instance of licking ⟨a quick ~ at the frosting bowl⟩ (2) : an amount held on the tongue ⟨the cat took a ~ of milk⟩ **b** (1) : a quick often careless application of something as if by a stroke of the tongue : a small amount of something seemingly so applied : the least bit : ⁴DAB 2 ⟨ready, down to the last ~ of paint —Mollie Panter-Downes⟩ ⟨a ~ of rain beat against the window —E.L. Thomas⟩ ⟨how long have you known I can't read a ~ —James Street⟩ (2) : a trace of some characteristic or quality ⟨has a faint ~ of the charlatan about him⟩ **c** : something that darts like a tongue ⟨the campfire played its little ~*s* of light against a tree trunk —A.B.Guthrie⟩ **2 a** (1) : a sharp hit : BLOW ⟨hit the board a hard ~ with the blunt end of an ax —Bruce Siberts⟩ (2) *dial Brit* : WHIPPING, BEATING — usu. used in pl. ⟨he was ready to take his ~*s* like a man⟩ **b** : an effective effort : CRACK 11, THRUST — usu. used in pl. ⟨treasure was often found in the last few ~*s* with the pick and shovel —W.P.Webb⟩ ⟨give the cameraman a chance to put in some heavy artistic ~*s* —John McCarten⟩ **c** : the smallest effort or act esp. of work : STROKE ⟨ain't had a ~ of work since November —Edna Ferber⟩ ⟨the truth is that neither . . . has ever done a ~ —Hamilton Basso⟩ **3 a** (1) : a place where salt is found on the surface of the earth and wild animals resort to lick it up (2) : a salt spring or a salt brook **b** : an artificial often medicated saline preparation given to sheep and cattle to lick **4** *West* : SYRUP, MOLASSES ⟨piles flapjacks before me up to my chin, with plenty of butter and ~ —F.B.Gipson⟩ **5** *in swing music* : a musical figure; *specif* : an interpolated and usu. improvised figure or flourish **6** : a strand of hair usu. fixed neatly in place ⟨slicking his dark hair . . . in immaculate shiny ~*s* —John Phillips⟩ — **lick and a promise** : a perfunctory performance of a task ⟨gives his job little more than a *lick and a promise* —Jack Iams⟩ ⟨breakfast over, I gave the house a *lick and a promise* —Kathleen Thomas⟩

**lick·er** \'likə(r)\ *n* -s [ME *lykkare*, fr. *lykken*, *licken* to lick + *-are* -er] : one that licks

**licker-in** \,likə'(r)in\ *n* -s : a drum or cylinder in a carding machine that takes the lap from the feed rollers

**lick·er·ish** \'lik(ə)rish, -rēsh\ *adj* [alter. (influenced by *-ish*) of *lickerous*] **1 a** : fond of good food : eager to taste or enjoy ⟨he drank . . . rather by way of good fellowship than from a ~ appetite —W.E.Heitland⟩ **b** : having a craving : DESIROUS ⟨their own ~ affection to gold —Jonathan Swift⟩ **2** *obs* : tempting to the appetite : DAINTY ⟨and wouldst thou seek again to trap me here with ~ baits —John Milton⟩ **3** : having or suggesting lustful desires : LECHEROUS ⟨they responded with . . . frank, ~ stares —Shelby Foote⟩ — **lick·er·ish·ly** *adv* — **lick·er·ish·ness** *n* -ES

**lickerous** *adj* [ME *likerous*, fr. (assumed) ONF, var. of OF *lechereus* — more at LECHEROUS] *obs* : LICKERISH

**lickety-split** \,likəd·ē,=\ *also* **lickety-brindle** \-;==\ *or* **lickety-cut** \-;=\ *adv* [prob. irreg. fr. ¹*lick* + *split* or *brindle* or *cut*] : with a rush : RAPIDLY ⟨you climb astride a little trolley and rattle out of the place *lickety-split* —Claudia Cassidy⟩

¹**licking** *n* -s [ME, fr. gerund of *licken* to lick — more at LICK] **1** : the act of one that licks (as by lapping with the tongue) **2 a** : a sound thrashing : a beating at the hands of another : DRUBBING ⟨when I was cornered and fought, even a ~ wasn't a hundredth as bad as I thought it would be —John Reed⟩ **b** : a severe setback : DEFEAT ⟨American industries competing with import industries took their ~ —A.H.Hansen⟩ ⟨in the long run . . . apathetic voters would take the ~ —*Time*⟩ **3** : the act or process of taking the lap from the feed roller in a carding machine by the licker-in

²**licking** *adv* [fr. pres. part. of *lick* (to hit)] *dial* : EXCEEDINGLY ⟨a ~ big frame of light wood —Eden Phillpotts⟩ ⟨eaten with a spoon . . . I only remember that it was — and is — ~ good —Della Lutes⟩

**licking disease** *or* **licking sickness** *n* : pica of cattle

**licking stone** *n* : a lick in brick form

**lick-log** \'=,=\ *n* : a felled tree in which troughs are cut and filled with salt for cattle

**lickpenny** \'=,==\ *n* [ME *lickpeny*, fr. *licken* to lick + *peny* penny] *archaic* : something that uses up money ⟨law is a ~ —Sir Walter Scott⟩

lick-log

**lick·some** \'liksəm\ *dial Eng var of* LIKESOME

**lick-spigot** *n* [¹*lick*] **1** *obs* : TAPSTER **2** *obs* : LICKSPITTLE

**lickspit** \'=,=\ *n* [¹*lick* + *spit* (spittle)] : LICKSPITTLE **syn** see PARASITE

¹**lickspittle** \'=,==\ *n* [¹*lick* + *spittle*] : an abject parasite or toady ⟨they were . . . hired hands and ~*s* —R.P.Warren⟩ **syn** see PARASITE

²**lickspittle** \"\ *vb* -ED/-ING/-S *vt* : to act servilely toward : FLATTER, TOADY ⟨*lickspittled* everyone in the hope of advancement⟩ ~ *vi* : to flatter or toady to someone in a servile manner ⟨hated to see anyone ~⟩

**lic·noph·o·ra** \lik'näfərə\ *n, cap* [NL, fr. Gk *liknon* winnowing fan + NL *-phora*] : a genus of peritrichous ciliate protozoans that have a posterior attaching disk and a very large fanlike anterior membranellar zone extending to the cytopharynx and are commensal

**lic·o·rice** *also* **li·quo·rice** \÷'lik(ə)rish, ÷ -rēsh, ÷ -rəs\ *n* -s [ME *licoris*, *licorice*, fr. OF *licorece*, *licorice*, fr. LL *liquiritia*, alter. of L *glycyrrhiza*, fr. Gk *glykyrrhiza*, fr. *glykys* sweet + *rhiza* root — more at DULCET, WORT] **1 a** *or* **licorice root** : a dried root of gummy texture and sweet rather astringent flavor that is the source of extracts used to mask unpleasant flavors (as of drugs) or to impart pleasing flavors (as to confections or tobacco) **b** : an extract of licorice commonly prepared in the form of a gummy or rubbery paste **2 a** (1) : a tall perennial leguminous herb (*Glycyrrhiza glabra*) of the Mediterranean region that has odd-pinnate leaves with ovate leaflets and stalked racemes of blue flowers and that is widely cultivated in southern Europe for its long thick sweet roots which are the source of licorice (2) : any of several other plants of the genus *Glycyrrhiza* **b** : any of various plants resembling members of the genus *Glycyrrhiza* — usu. used in combination; see INDIAN LICORICE

**licorice fern** *n* : any of several ferns of the genus *Polypodium* having rootstocks of a sweetish flavor

**licorice powder** *n* : a laxative composed of powdered senna and licorice, sulfur, fennel oil, and sugar

**licorice root** *n* **1** : LICORICE 1a **2** : WILD LICORICE 1

**licorice vine** *n* : INDIAN LICORICE

**lic·tor** \'liktər, -,tȯ(ə)r\ *n* -s [L; perh. akin to *ligare* to bind — more at LIGATURE] : a Roman officer bearing the fasces as the insignia of his office whose duties included attendance upon the chief magistrates appearing in public, clearing the way and causing due respect to be paid to them, and also the apprehension and punishment of criminals

**lic·to·ri·an** \(')lik¦tōrēən\ *adj* : of, relating to, or resembling a lictor

**lic·u·a·la** \,likyə'wälə, -wälə\ *n, cap* [NL, fr. Makassar *lekowala* (palm of the genus *Licuala*)] : a genus of tropical Asiatic dwarf fan palms having prickly petioles and large branching spikes of flowers

**lic·u·ry** *or* **lic·u·ri** \'likərē\ *n, pl* **licuries** *or* **licuris** [Pg *licuri*, *licuri*, fr. Tupi] : OURICURY

**licury wax** *n* : OURICURY WAX

¹**lid** \'lid\ *n* -s [ME, fr. OE *hlid* lid, gate, opening; akin to OFris *hlid* cover, eyelid, OHG *lit*, *hlit* cover, ON *hlith* opening, door, gate, Goth *hleithra* hut, tent, OE *hleonian*, *hlinian* to lean — more at LEAN] **1** : something that covers the opening of a hollow container (as a vessel or box) : a movable cover ⟨a trunk ~⟩ ⟨a piano ~⟩ ⟨simple pine chests with lift ~*s* —*Antiques*⟩ **2** : EYELID **3** *dial* : either cover of a book **4 a** : the operculum in mosses **b** : the cap of a pyxidium **5** *slang* : HAT ⟨in a slaphappy painter's cap that looked like an Italian officer's ~ —Saul Bellow⟩ **6** : a force that confines or represses ⟨if he doesn't clamp the ~ down hard on his feelings —Constance Foster⟩; *specif* : an official curb or check ⟨clapped a ~ on further release of information⟩ ⟨votes to clamp a four-month ~ on wages and prices —*Current History*⟩ ⟨the ~ was clamped on . . . gambling in nightclubs —*Newsweek*⟩

²**lid** \"\ *vt* **lidded; lidded; lidding; lids** : to cover with or as if with a lid ⟨the classified fruit is then *lidded* . . . ready for shipment —*Westralian Farmers Co-op Gazette*⟩ ⟨she . . . *lidded* her eyes —Wright Morris⟩

**lid cell** *n* **1** : one of the terminal cells closing the neck of an archegonium until the maturation of the egg cell **2** : the uppermost cell of the antheridium in ferns

**lid·ded** \'lidəd\ *adj* [¹*lid* + *-ed*] **1** : having a lid ⟨milk is left in a heavy ~ mug —Hamlin Garland⟩ **2** : having or covered with lids — used of the eyes chiefly in combination ⟨her blue-*lidded* eyes —Calder Willingham⟩ ⟨his weather-*lidded* eyes watched the floor —Helen Rich⟩

**lid·der** \'lidə(r)\ *n* -s : one that fastens lids to packed containers

**lid·less** \'lidləs\ *adj* **1** : having no lid ⟨a ~ container⟩ **2** : without or as if without covering by the eyelids : SLEEPLESS, WATCHFUL ⟨to an eye like mine, a ~ watcher of the public weal —Alfred Tennyson⟩

**li·do** \'lē(,)dō\ *n* -s [fr. the *Lido*, town and fashionable sea resort near Venice, Italy] **1** : a luxuriously equipped and fashionable beach resort ⟨a *Lido* for Dubliners —George Burrows⟩ **2** : a well-equipped swimming pool (as on an ocean liner)

**lid·o·caine** \'lidə,kān\ *n* -s [*acetanilid* + *o-* + *-caine*] : a crystalline compound $(CH_3)_2C_6H_3NHCOCH_2N(C_2H_5)_2$ derived from acetanilide that is used in the form of its hydrochloride as a local anesthetic

¹**lie** \'lī\ *vb* **lay** \'lā\ **lain** \'lān\ *or archaic* **lien** \'lī(ə)n\ **ly·ing** \'līiŋ\ **lies** [ME *liggen*, *ligen*, *lien*, fr. OE *licgan*; akin to OHG *ligen* to lie, ON *liggja* to lie, L *lectus* bed, Gk *lechos* bed, *lechesthai* to lie down, OIr *lige* bed, grave, OSlav *ležati* to lie] *vi* **1 a** : to be or to stay at rest in a horizontal position : be prostrate : REST, RECLINE ⟨~ motionless⟩ ⟨~ asleep⟩ ⟨~ dead⟩ ⟨~*s* in his grave⟩ **b** : to assume a horizontal position — often used with *down* **c** *archaic* : to reside temporarily : stay for the night : LODGE, SOJOURN, SLEEP **d** *archaic* : to have sexual intercourse — used with *with* **e** : to stay without moving (as in concealment) ⟨~ in wait for deer⟩ ⟨~ in ambush⟩ **f** *of a game bird* : to remain still at the approach of hunters or dogs ⟨~ close to the gun⟩ ⟨~ to a point⟩ **2 a** : to be in a helpless or defenseless state ⟨the town *lay* at the mercy of the invader⟩ ⟨*lying* in prison⟩ **b** : to remain subject — used with *under* ⟨the house *lay* under a curse⟩ ⟨*lying* under a cruel despotism⟩ **3** *of an inanimate thing* : to be or remain in a flat or horizontal position upon a broad support ⟨books *lying* on the table⟩ ⟨snow ~*s* on the fields⟩ ⟨leaves *lay* thick on the ground⟩ **4** : to have direction : STRETCH, EXTEND ⟨the route *lay* to the west⟩ ⟨thought of the empty hours that *lay* ahead⟩ ⟨the grain of the wood *lay* crosswise⟩ **5 a** : to occupy a certain relative place or position : become situated ⟨easterly oases . . . ~ close to or below sea level —W.B.Fisher⟩ ⟨the song ~*s* well within his range⟩ ⟨meadows *lying* along the river⟩ ⟨mountains *lay* between us and our goal⟩ ⟨that way madness ~*s* —Shak.⟩ **b** : to have a place in relation to something else ⟨motive that *lay* behind his actions⟩ ⟨question ~*s* outside the scope of our inquiry⟩ ⟨real reason ~*s* deeper⟩ **c** : to have an effect through mere presence, weight, or relative position ⟨remorse *lay* heavily on his conscience⟩ ⟨her years *lay* lightly upon her⟩ ⟨your time will not ~ heavy upon your hands —Jonathan Swift⟩ **d** *law* : to be sustainable or admissible : be capable of being maintained ⟨action for libel will ~ in such cases⟩ ⟨appeal usually ~*s* to the supreme or high court of the colony —W.E.Simnett⟩ **6 a** : to remain at anchor or becalmed ⟨fleet *lying* in the harbor⟩ **b** : to assume or maintain a position in relation to the wind ⟨able to ~ closer to the wind than the other yachts⟩ ⟨the more a ship is trimmed by the stern the farther she will ~ off the wind —*Manual of Seamanship*⟩ **c** : ¹LAY 5a **7** : to have place : EXIST ⟨choice *lay* between fighting or surrendering⟩ : BELONG, PERTAIN, CONSIST — used with *in* ⟨felt that his future *lay* in teaching⟩ ⟨tried with all the strength that *lay* in him⟩ **8** : REMAIN ⟨field *lying* fallow⟩ ⟨machinery *lying* idle⟩ ⟨talent *lay* hid⟩; *esp* : to remain unused ⟨unsold goods *lying* on the shelves⟩ ⟨money *lying* in the bank⟩ or uncared-for ⟨left his tools *lying* about⟩ ⟨dishes *lying* in the sink⟩ **9 a** *now dial* : to be still : SUBSIDE ⟨near dark, the wind ~*s* —G.S.Perry⟩ **b** *of wind* : to blow from a certain direction ⟨came out to see where the wind *lay*⟩ **10** *obs* : to engage in some occupation or live in a specified way — used with *at* or *about* ~ *vt* **1** *now chiefly dial* : to cause to lie : LAY **2** *of a ship* : to make headway along (as a course) — **lie low 1** : to lie prostrate, defeated, or disgraced **2** : to stay in hiding : strive to avoid notice ⟨better *lie low* until this affair blows over⟩ **3** : to bide one's time : remain secretly ready for action

²**lie** \"\ *n* -s **1** : the position or situation in which something lies ⟨~ of a golf ball⟩ ⟨~ of a ball in lawn bowling⟩ ⟨~ of the cards in a bridge deal⟩ ⟨~ of fibers in felted pulp⟩ ⟨~ of a stone in curling⟩ **2** *chiefly Brit* : topographical features and situation : SLOPE ⟨~ of the land⟩ **3** : the haunt of an animal or a fish : COVERT ⟨a fine trout ~⟩ **4** *Brit* : an act or instance of lying or resting (as in bed) ⟨I have clearly in mind the coldest ~ I have so far met —Thomas Skelton⟩; *esp* : a period of lying in bed beyond the usual time of arising ⟨why didn't you take a ~ in your bed a morning like that —Michael McLaverty⟩ **5** : the angle of the blade or clubhead with the shaft of a hockey stick or golf club

³**lie** \"\ *vb* **lied; lied; ly·ing** \'līiŋ\ **lies** [ME *ligen*, *leyen*, *lien*, fr. OE *lēogan*; akin to OHG *liogan* to lie, ON *ljūga*, Goth *liugan*, OSlav *lŭgati* to lie, Lith *lūgoti* to request] *vi* **1** : to make an untrue statement with intent to deceive : tell a lie ⟨man is the only animal . . . that habitually ~*s* —Leo Stein⟩ **2** : to create a false or misleading impression : convey an untruth ⟨unless these figures ~⟩ ⟨that thermometer must be *lying*⟩ ~ *vt* : to bring about by lying : affect in a specified way by telling lies ⟨men have been *lied* out of office⟩ ⟨managed to ~ himself out of trouble⟩

**syn** LIE, PREVARICATE, EQUIVOCATE, PALTER, FIB can mean to tell an untruth directly or indirectly. LIE is direct and blunt, imputing dishonesty ⟨children sometimes *lie* to avoid punishment⟩ ⟨the camera can cheat and *lie* with all the success and assurance of a confidence trickster —Richard Harrison⟩ PREVARICATE is commonly used to evade the insulting bluntness of LIE, but also can imply evasion of truth as by quibbling or confusing the issue ⟨he could *prevaricate* no longer, and, confessing to the gambling, told her the truth —Thomas Hardy⟩ EQUIVOCATE implies evasion by the use of words or remarks with double meanings in the hope that an incorrect one will be understood ⟨he was wholly in sympathy with Congregationalism, and had no mind to conceal or *equivocate* concerning its democratic tendencies —V.L.Parrington⟩ or by the use of talk which avoids committing one to anything. PALTER implies a falseness or unreliability in statements or dealings ⟨if insanity is not to be a defense, let us say so frankly and even brutally, but let us not mock ourselves with a definition that *palters* with reality —B.N.Cardozo⟩ FIB is often used as an innocuous equivalent of LIE but more often implies telling a trivial, insignificant, or socially necessary untruth ⟨the government admitted the laboratory, but . . . may be *fibbing* patriotically, of course —*Time*⟩

— **lie in one's throat** *or* **lie in one's teeth** : to lie flatly, maliciously, or outrageously

⁴**lie** \"\ *n* -s [ME *lige*, *leye*, *lie*, fr. OE *lyge*; akin to OHG *lugī* lie, ON *lygi*; derivatives fr. the root of E ³*lie*] **1 a** : an assertion of something known or believed by the speaker to be untrue : a deliberate misrepresenting of fact with intent to deceive ⟨his story was a tissue of ~*s*, evasions, and exaggerations⟩ ⟨his decent reticence is branded as hypocrisy, his circumlocutions are roundly called ~*s* —W.S.Maugham⟩ ⟨believes . . . that men have petty larceny forever in their hearts and ~*s* forever in their mouths —Bergen Evans⟩ ⟨any printed ~ that any notorious villain pens —Charles Dickens⟩ **b** : an untrue or inaccurate statement that may or may not be believed true by the speaker ⟨often suspected that history was mostly ~*s* anyway⟩ **2** : something that misleads or deceives ⟨his pose of humility was a ~⟩ **3** : a charge of lying ⟨threw the ~ in his face⟩

**lie-abed** \'=,=\ *n* -s : one given to rising late

**lie along** *vi* **1** *archaic* : to lie flat or at full length **2** : to careen under pressure of the wind

**lie athwart** *vi* : to ride at anchor or mooring with head to the wind across the tide

**lie back** *vi* **1** : to lean backward against a support ⟨*lay back* in his chair and dozed off⟩ **2** : to cease from strenuous effort or activity ⟨after a busy life he was content to *lie back* and take life easy⟩

**lie-back** \'=,=\ *n* [*lie back*] : LAY-BACK

**lie·be·ner·ite** \'lēb(ə)nə,rīt\ *n* -s [F *liebenerite*, fr. L. *Liebener*, 19th cent. Fr. mineralogist + F *-ite*] : a variety of pinite

**lie·ber·kühn's gland** *also* **lieberkühn's crypt** \'lēbə(r)-,k(y)ünz-, -kēnz-\ *n, usu cap L* [after Johann N. *Lieberkühn* †1756 Ger. anatomist] : any of the tubular glands of the intestinal mucous membrane

**lie·ber·mann-bur·chard reaction** \'lēbərmən'bu̇(ə)r,kärt-\ *n, usu cap L&B* [after Karl T. *Liebermann* †1914 Ger. chemist and H. *Burchard*, 19th cent. Ger. chemist] : a test for unsaturated steroids (as cholesterol) and triterpenes based on the formation of a series of colors (as pink to blue to green) with acetic anhydride in the presence of concentrated sulfuric acid

**lieb·frau·milch** \'lēp,frau̇,milk, -miu̇k\ *also* **lieb·frau·en·milch** \lēp'frau̇ən,-\ *n* -s *usu cap* [G; *liebfraumilch*, alter. of *liebfrauenmilch*, fr. *Liebfrauenstift* (lit., foundation of the Virgin Mary), religious foundation in Worms, Germany, where the wine was first produced + *milch* milk] : a white wine of the Rhenish variety from Worms in Rheinhessen, Germany; *also* : a similar wine from elsewhere in Germany often blended to approximate a standard

**lie·big condenser** \'lēbig-\ *n, usu cap L* [after Baron Justus

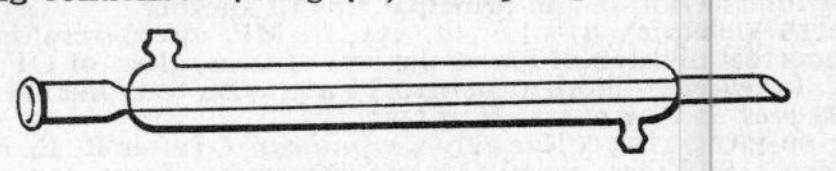

Liebig condenser

von *Liebig* †1873 Ger. chemist, who described it] : a condenser for use in distillation that consists of two tubes one inside the other with space between for circulation of water

**lie·big·ite** \'lēbi,gīt\ *n* -s [Baron Justus von *Liebig* + E *-ite*] : an apple-green mineral $Ca_2U(CO_3)_4.10H_2O$ consisting of hydrous uranium calcium carbonate and occurring as concretions or coatings

**lieb·lich** \'lēplik, -ik\ *adj* [G, pleasant, charming, attractive, fr. MHG *lieplich* friendly, affectionate, pleasure, fr. *liep* dear, beloved (fr. OHG *liob*) + *-lich* -ly — more at LIEF] : sweet in tone — used in organ-stop names ⟨~ gedeckt⟩

**lie by** *vi* **1** : to intermit activity, work, or progress : REST ⟨we *lay by* during the heat of the day⟩ ⟨the ship was forced to *lie by* for several days for repairs⟩ **2** : to be in a state or condition of disuse ⟨his dogs and guns *lay by* that season⟩

**lie-by** \'=,=\ *n* -s [*lie by*] *Brit* : a railroad siding for passing

**liech·ten·stein** \'liktən,stīn\ *adj, usu cap* [fr. *Liechtenstein*, principality in central Europe] : of or from the principality of Liechtenstein : of the kind or style prevalent in Liechtenstein

¹**lied** *past of* LIE

²**lied** \'lēt\ *n, pl* **lie·der** \'lēdə(r)\ [G, song, fr. OHG *liod* — more at LAUD] : a German folk song; *specif* : a German art song of the 19th century (as by Schubert, Hugo Wolf) in which a lyric text is set to a well-considered usu. through-composed melody and accompaniment with all three elements contributing nearly equally to the total effect

**Lie·der·kranz** \'lēdə(r),kran(t)s, -rän-\ *trademark* — used for a soft surface-ripened cheese with a somewhat strong pungent flavor and odor

**lie detector** *n* : a device using instruments to register changes in blood pressure, strength of pulse beat or respiratory movements, or increased perspiration as indicative of emotional excitement assumed to accompany lying under questioning; *esp* : KEELER POLYGRAPH

**lie down** *vi* **1** *archaic* : to go to bed for the night **2** : to lie on a bed for a brief rest : take a nap **3** *obs* : lie in **4** : to submit meekly or abjectly to defeat, disappointment, or insult ⟨they will not take this violation of their rights *lying down*⟩ **5** : to fail to perform or to neglect one's part deliberately ⟨*lie down* on the job⟩

**lie-down** \'=,=\ *n* -s [*lie down*] : a lying down or period of lying down : NAP, REST

¹**lief** \'lēf, -ēv\ *adj* -ER/-EST [ME *lef*, *leef*, *leif*, *lif*, fr. OE *lēof*; akin to OHG *liob* dear, beloved, ON *ljūfr*, Goth *liufs* dear, beloved, OE *lufu* love — more at LOVE] **1** *archaic* : DEAR, BELOVED : PRECIOUS **2** *obs* : PLEASING, AGREEABLE, ACCEPTABLE — used with dative of personal pronoun ⟨death me ~*er* were than such despite —Edmund Spenser⟩ **3** *archaic* : WILLING, GLAD

²**lief** \"\ *n* -s [ME *lef*, *leef*, *leif*, *lif*, fr. OE *lēof*, fr. *lēof*, adj.] **1** *archaic* : BELOVED, SWEETHEART **2** *obs* : DEAR — used as a title of respect in addressing a superior

³**lief** \'lē|v, 'li|, |f\ *adv* -ER/-EST [ME *lef*, *leef*, *leif*, *lif*, fr. *lef*, *leef*, *lif*, adj.] : GLADLY, WILLINGLY, FREELY — used in the phrases *had as lief*, *would as lief*, *had liefer*, or *would liefer* ⟨I had as ~ go as not⟩ ⟨far ~*er* by his dear hand had I die —Alfred Tennyson⟩ ⟨he would as ~ have the Germans as neighbors as the British —Manfred Nathan⟩ ⟨frankly, I'd just as ~ stay⟩

**lief·ly** \'lē|vlē, 'li|, |flē\ *adv* [¹*lief* + *-ly*] : WILLINGLY, GLADLY

¹**liege** \'lēj *sometimes* -ēzh\ *adj* [ME *lige*, *liege*, *lege*, fr. OF

*lige* (fr. — assumed — ML *liticus*, fr. LL *litus* serf — alter. of *laetus* — + L *-icus* -ic) & *liege*, fr. LL *laeticus*, fr. *laetus* serf (of Gmc origin; akin to OLF *leto* serf, OS *lat*, OFris *let*) + L *-icus* -ic; prob. akin to OE *lǣtan* to let — more at LET] **1 a :** having the right to feudal allegiance and service ⟨a vassal's responsibilities to his ~ lord⟩ **b :** obligated to render feudal allegiance and service ⟨a right to call on every ~ subject to render assistance —Sir Walter Scott⟩ **2 :** bound by obligations resembling those existing between a feudal lord and his vassal **:** FAITHFUL, LOYAL ⟨master of his own impulses, as a soloist should be, and not ~ to the conductor —Irving Kolodin⟩ ⟨all the ~ people of Pennsylvania —Thomas McKean⟩

**[2]liege** \"\ *n* -s [ME *lige*, *liege*, *lege*, fr. *lige*, *liege*, *lege*, adj.] **1 a :** a vassal bound to feudal service and allegiance **:** LIEGE MAN 1 **b :** a loyal subject (as in a monarchy) **2 :** a liege lord **:** a feudal superior to whom allegiance and service are due **:** a lord paramount

**[3]li·ège** *or* **li·ége** *or* **li·ege** \lē'āzh, -'ezh\ *adj*, *usu cap* [fr. *Liège*, Belgium] **:** of or from the city of Liège, Belgium **:** of the kind or style prevalent in Liège

**liege man** *n* [ME] **1 :** a vassal serving his lord under a solemn obligation and entitled to receive protection from him ⟨you shall become true *liege men* to his crown —Shak.⟩ **2 :** a devoted adherent and follower ⟨he's the *liege man* of his division commander on discipline —J.W.Bellah⟩

**liege pou·stie** \'lēj¦püstē, -paùs-\ *n* [ME *lege pouste*, fr. MF *lige poestí*, *lige pousté*, lit., liege power] **:** the state of good health requisite under Scots law to the exercise of full legal powers esp. in the transfer of property (as by deed or will) — compare DEATHBED DEED

**lieger** *archaic var of* LEDGER 4

**lie in** *vi* **:** to be in childbed **~** *vt*, *obs* **:** COST

**[1]lien** *archaic past part of* LIE

**[2]lien** \'lē(ə)n\ *n* -s [MF, band, tie, bond, fr. L *ligamen* band, tie, fr. *ligare* to bind, tie — more at LIGATURE] **1 :** a charge upon real or personal property for the satisfaction of some debt or duty ordinarily arising by operation of law **:** a right in one to control or to hold and retain or enforce a charge against the property of another until some claim of the former is paid or satisfied ⟨the owner of the cargo has a ~ on the vessel for any injury —David Davis⟩ ⟨efforts to effect a release of the federal tax ~ —J.D.Johnson⟩ **2 a :** MORTGAGE **b :** the security interest created by a mortgage ⟨the ~ of a mortgage⟩

**[3]li·en** \'līən, 'lī,en\ *n* -s [L — more at SPLEEN] **:** SPLEEN

**lien·able** \'lē(ə)nəbəl\ *adj* [[2]*lien* + *-able*] **:** capable of being subjected to or made the subject of a lien ⟨a ~ article⟩

**li·enal** \(')lī¦ēnᵊl, 'līən-\ *adj* [ISV [3]*lien* + *-al*] **:** of or relating to the spleen **:** SPLENIC

**li·en·cu·lus** \lī'eŋkyələs\ *n*, *pl* **liencu·li** \-yə,lī\ [NL, dim. of L *lien* spleen — more at SPLEEN] **:** a small accessory or supplementary spleen

**lien·ee** \(')lē¦nē, ¦lēə¦nē\ *n* -s [[2]*lien* + *-ee*] **1 :** one whose property is subject to a lien **2** *Austral* **:** LIENHOLDER

**lienholder** \'⸗(⸗),⸗⸗\ *n* **1 :** one having a valid lien **2 :** one having an inchoate lien capable of being perfected **:** a lien claimant

**lien·or** \'lē(ə)nər, (')lē¦nȯ(ə)r, ¦lēə¦n-\ *n* -s [[2]*lien* + *-or*] **1 :** LIENHOLDER **2** *Austral* **:** LIENEE 1

**li·eno·renal ligament** \¦līə(,)nō, lī¦ē(,)nō + . . .-\ *n* [[3]*lien* + *-o-* + *renal*] **:** a mesenteric fold passing from the spleen to the left kidney and affording support to the splenic artery and vein

**li·en·ter·ic** \¦līən·¦terik\ *adj* [F or L; F *lientérique*, fr. L *lientericus*, fr. Gk *leienterikos*, fr. *leienteria* + *-ikos* -ic] **:** containing or characterized by the passage of undigested or partially digested food — used of feces or diarrhea

**li·en·tery** \'līən·,terē, lī'entərē\ *n* -ES [MF or ML; MF *lienterie*, fr. ML *lienteria*, fr. Gk *leienteria*, fr. *leios* smooth + *enteron*, intestine + *-ia* -y — more at LIME, INTER-] **:** lienteric diarrhea

**lie off** *vi* **1 :** to keep a little away from the shore or another ship **2 :** to cease work for a time **:** rest during a period of exertion **3 :** to hold back in the early part of a race

**lie over** *vi* **1** *of a ship* **:** lie along **2 a :** to remain unpaid when overdue **b :** to await disposal or attention at a later time ⟨several jobs *lying over* from last week⟩

**[1]li·er** \'lī(ə)r, -īə\ *n* -s [[1]*lie* + *-er*] **:** one that lies (as in ambush)

**[2]lier** \'li(ə)r\ *archaic var of* LEHR

**-lier** *comparative of* -LY

**li·erne** \lē'ərn, -'e(ə)rn\ *n* -s [F, fr. MF, fr. *lier* to bind, tie — more at LIABLE] **:** a rib in Gothic vaulting that does not spring from the impost and is not a ridge rib but passes from one boss or intersection of the principal ribs to another

**lierre** \lē'e(ə)r\ *n* -s [F, lit., ivy, fr. MF, alter. (resulting fr. incorrect division of *l'ierre* the ivy) of *ierre*, alter. of OF *edre*, fr. L *hedera* — more at HEDERA] **:** a grayish to moderate olive

**lies** *pres 3d sing of* LIE, *pl of* LIE

**lie·se·gang ring** \'lēzə,gäŋ-\ *n*, *usu cap L* [after R. E. *Liesegang* †1947 Ger. chemist] **:** one of a series of usu. concentric bands of a precipitate that are separated by clear spaces and that are often formed in gels by periodic or rhythmic precipitation — usu. used in pl.

**-liest** *superlative of* -LY

**lie to** *vi*, *of a ship* **:** to stay as nearly stationary as feasible with head to windward ⟨*lying to* all night waiting for daylight to check their position —Stanley Rogers⟩

**lieu** \'lü\ *n* -s [MF, fr. L *locus* — more at STALL] **:** PLACE, STEAD — **in lieu** *adv* **:** INSTEAD ⟨a small monetary payment . . . is given *in lieu* —Wilfred Whitely⟩ — **in lieu of** *prep* **:** in the place of **:** instead of ⟨the mumbling cant that . . . the characters employ *in lieu of* English —John McCarten⟩ ⟨rendered three days' work . . . *in lieu of* rent —G.G.Coulton⟩ ⟨striking out the words "one year" and inserting *in lieu* there*of* the words "six months" —*U.S. Code*⟩

**lieu lands** *n pl* **:** public lands that a patentee has a right to locate and select in place of lands within the limits of a previous grant which are occupied by persons given special protection by the law

**lie up** *vi* **1 :** to stay in bed or at rest ⟨his doctor insists . . . the patient should *lie up* for 5 weeks —*Lancet*⟩ **:** keep to one's room, den, or covert ⟨the lions were *lying up* after feeding⟩ **2** *of a ship* **:** to go into or remain in a dock (as for repairs)

**lieut** *abbr*, *often cap* lieutenant

**lieu·ten·an·cy** \lü'tenənsē, -si, *Brit usu* lef't- *or* ləf't- *or esp in the navy* le't- *or* lə't-\ *n* -ES [ME *lieutenauncie*, fr. MF *lieutenancie*, fr. *lieutenant* + *-cie* -cy] **1 :** the office, rank, or commission of a lieutenant ⟨the earl . . . had recently been turned out of the ~ of the county —T.B.Macaulay⟩ ⟨jumped at a chance for a second ~ in the marines —*Time*⟩ **2** *obs* **:** a territorial unit under the jurisdiction of a lieutenant **3 :** the term of office of a lieutenant **4** *usu cap*, *obs* **:** the body of deputies to the lord lieutenant of an English county ⟨addresses from the *Lieutenancy*, grand juries, and corporations in our county —*London Gazette*⟩

**lieu·ten·ant** \-tenənt\ *n* -s [ME *lieutenaunt*, fr. MF *lieutenant*, fr. *lieu* place + *tenant* holding, fr. pres. part. of *tenir* to hold, fr. L *tenere* — more at LIEU, THIN] **1 a :** an officer representing and exercising powers on behalf of a higher official (as a king) — compare LORD LIEUTENANT **b :** a representative of or substitute for another in the performance of duty **c :** ASSISTANT 2b ⟨the president's intimate friend and most trusted ~ —*Harper's*⟩ **2 a :** a military officer — see FIRST LIEUTENANT, FLIGHT LIEUTENANT, SECOND LIEUTENANT **b :** a naval officer ranking just below a lieutenant commander and above a lieutenant junior grade **c :** a Salvation Army officer — see FIRST LIEUTENANT 2, SECOND LIEUTENANT **d :** a fire or police department officer ranking below a captain **3 :** the adult assistant leader of a Girl Guide or Ranger company and formerly of a Girl Scout troop

**lieutenant colonel** *n* **1 :** an army, marine, or air force officer ranking just below a colonel and above a major **2 :** a Salvation Army officer ranking above a brigadier and below a colonel

**lieutenant commander** *n* **:** a naval officer ranking below a commander and above a lieutenant

**lieutenant commissioner** *n* **:** a Salvation Army officer ranking above a colonel and below a commissioner

**lieutenant general** *n* [MF, lit., general lieutenant] **1 :** VICE-REGENT ⟨name the Prince of Piedmont as *lieutenant general* —*The New Republic*⟩ **2 :** an army, marine, or air force officer ranking just below a general and above a major general

**lieutenant governor** *n* **:** a deputy or subordinate governor: as **a :** an elected official serving as deputy to the governor of an American state and as his successor in case of death or removal from office and usu. presiding over the upper house of the state legislature **b :** the formal head of the government of a Canadian province appointed by the federal government as the representative of the crown and resembling the governor-general in power and function ⟨the power of the *lieutenant governors* to reserve provincial bills for the approval of the Dominion government —Alexander Brady⟩

**lieutenant junior grade** *n*, *pl* **lieutenants junior grade :** a naval officer ranking below a lieutenant and above an ensign

**lieu·ten·ant·ry** \-tenəntrē\ *n* -ES **:** LIEUTENANCY ⟨strip you out of your ~ —Shak.⟩

**lieu·ten·ant·ship** \-tenənt,ship\ *n* [ME *lieutenauntship*, fr. *lieutenaunt* + *-ship*] *archaic* **:** LIEUTENANCY 1

**lieve** \'lēv, 'liv\ *dial var of* LIEF

**lieves** \'lēvz, 'livz\ *New Eng var of* [3]LIEF

**liev·rite** \'lēv,rīt\ *n* -s [G *lievrit*, fr. C.H. Le*lièvre*, 19th cent. Fr. mineralogist + G *-it* -ite] **:** ILVAITE

**[1]life** \'līf\ *n*, *pl* **lives** \-īvz\ [ME *lif*, fr. OE *līf;* akin to OHG *līb* life, ON *līf* life, OE *libban*, *lifian* to live — more at LIVE] **1 a :** animate being **:** the quality that distinguishes a vital and functional being from a dead body or purely chemical matter ⟨~ is the immediate gift of God —William Blackstone⟩ ⟨my ability to give ~ to an animal —Mary W. Shelley⟩ — compare DEATH 1 **b :** the principle or force by which animals and plants are maintained in the performance of their functions and which distinguishes by its presence animate from inanimate matter **c** (1) **:** the state of a material complex or individual characterized by the capacity to perform certain functional activities including metabolism, growth, reproduction, and some form of responsiveness or adaptability (2) **:** a specific aspect of the process of living or performing the functions involved in living ⟨the physical and emotional ~ of a boy —Harrison Smith⟩ ⟨the cowboy's sex ~ was intermittent —D.B.Davis⟩ **2 :** the course of existence **:** the sequence of physical and mental experiences that make up the existence of an individual **:** the totality of actions and occurrences constituting an individual experience ⟨emotions provoked by particular events in his ~ —T.S.Eliot⟩ ⟨interests . . . that have occupied his ~ —F.R.Leavis⟩ ⟨children . . . are the joy of our *lives* —Agnes S. Turnbull⟩ **3 :** BIOGRAPHY 1 ⟨a shilling ~ will give you all the facts —W.H.Auden⟩ ⟨a full-length ~⟩ **4 a :** the earthly state of human existence as distinguished from the spiritual state after death ⟨all those who in this transitory ~ —*Bk. of Com. Prayer*⟩ **b :** a spiritual form of eternal existence transcending physical death ⟨he who hears my word . . . has passed from death to ~ —Jn 5:24 (RSV)⟩ ⟨his craving . . . for release into the ~ to come —Rodney Gilbert⟩ **5 a :** the duration of the earthly existence of an individual; *specif* **:** the period from birth to death ⟨his habits were such as promise a long ~ —T.B.Macaulay⟩ ⟨early in ~ he had married⟩ **b :** a specific phase of earthly existence ⟨parents . . . had more effect on your child ~ —*Glamour (Australia)*⟩; *esp* **:** the period from an event until death ⟨six senators appointed for ~⟩ **c :** a sentence of imprisonment for the remaining portion of the convict's earthly existence ⟨if found guilty . . . he could get ~ —George Quint⟩ **d :** continued existence and right to function (as in a political office) ⟨the secretary of state . . . whose ~ depends on such a fickle thing as votes —E.O.Hauser⟩ ⟨fighting for his political ~ —*N.Y. Times*⟩ **6 :** a way or manner of living; *esp* **:** one associated with an occupation, location, or time ⟨a continent where the rural ~ is predominant —P.E.James⟩ ⟨she will have a wretched ~ with this young scamp —L.C.Douglas⟩ ⟨the ~ of the colonists is visible to the eye —R.W.Hatch⟩ **7 :** someone held to be as dear to one as existence — usu. used as a term of endearment ⟨my bride, my wife, my ~ —Alfred Tennyson⟩ **8 :** something held to be essential to animate existence or to a livelihood ⟨the words that I have spoken to you are spirit and ~ —Jn 6:63 (RSV)⟩ ⟨the fishing village drew its ~ from the sea⟩ **9 :** a vital or living being; *specif* **:** PERSON ⟨many youthful *lives* miss the opportunities for education —Ernest & Pearl Beaglehole⟩ **10 :** the force or principle that animates and usu. tends to shape the development of something ⟨the ~ of the constitution . . . has been not logic but experience —F.A.Ogg & Harold Zink⟩ **11 :** energy and liveliness in action, thought, or expression **:** ANIMATION, SPIRIT ⟨gives thy gestures grace and ~ —William Wordsworth⟩ ⟨there was little ~ in her voice —Winston Churchill⟩ ⟨there is still ~ in the old conceptions of loyalty —Leslie Rees⟩ ⟨breathe ~ into books for children —Rumer Godden⟩ **12 :** the form or pattern of something as it exists in reality ⟨a drawing from the ~⟩ ⟨screen motion was a little faster and more jerky than ~ —Otis Ferguson⟩ ⟨pictures show the family to the ~ —May L. Becker⟩ **13 :** a person whose life is insured (as by a life-insurance policy); *esp* **:** one considered with regard to his prospects for a long existence ⟨an insurance doctor had pronounced him a first-class ~ —E.M.Lustgarten⟩ **14 a :** the period of duration of something held to resemble a natural organism in structure or functions ⟨throughout the ~ of the republic —C.L.Jones⟩ ⟨ended the Labour government's ~ within . . . one year —Herbert Dorn⟩ **b :** the period of time during which a material object is fit for use or the efficient performance of its functions **:** the number of times an object may be used efficiently ⟨the ~ of the road was hardly a year —*Amer. Guide Series: N.H.*⟩ ⟨the ~ of a battleship was set at twenty years —C.E.Black & E.C.Helmreich⟩ ⟨tool ~ varied greatly with the microstructure of the steels being machined —F.H.Colvin⟩ **c :** the period of existence (as of an ion) — compare HALF-LIFE **d :** the period of time during which a legal document or relationship (as a marriage) is in force and effect **e :** the period of time during which something (as a book or a play) continues to be popular ⟨making a few books tremendously popular but shortening the *lives* of all —J.D.Hart⟩ ⟨the permanent ~ of distinguished minor fiction —E.K.Brown⟩ **f :** the property (as resilience, elasticity, springiness) of an inanimate substance resembling the animate quality of a living being ⟨the ~ of a bow⟩ ⟨an elastic belt that had lost most of its ~⟩ **g :** the length of time that the usefulness or quality of a packaged product lasts before deterioration begins ⟨lengthen the ~ of packaged fresh meat cuts —V.J.Hillery⟩ ⟨shelf ~ of baked pies —Lou Bisno⟩ **15 :** living beings; *esp* **:** the living things of a particular kind, quality, or environment ⟨bird ~⟩ ⟨plant ~⟩ ⟨forest ~⟩ **16 a :** human activities: as (1) **:** the active or practical part of human existence ⟨if a student is to be prepared for ~, he must be prepared for making a living —*Bull. of Bates Coll.*⟩ (2) **:** social activities ⟨entered the ~ of the court⟩ **b :** the activity and movement characterizing the presence of living beings ⟨sidewalk cafes just now stirring to midmorning ~ —P.E.Deutschman⟩ **c :** the activities of a given sphere, area, or time ⟨economic and commercial ~ was almost wholly at a standstill —R.A.Hall b.1911⟩ ⟨~ in the Mediterranean war theater⟩ ⟨participate in local, state, and national ~ —John Lodge⟩ ⟨his private ~⟩ **17 :** one that inspires or excites spirit and vigor and is usu. held to provide a principal basis for enjoyment or success ⟨the ~ of the party⟩ ⟨he was the ~ of the enterprise⟩ **18 a :** another chance or a continued opportunity given to one likely to lose; *esp* **:** an opportunity given a batter in cricket and baseball to reach a base or to continue at bat because of a fielding error **b :** one of several turns limited in number by the rules of a game (as English pool) during which a player may continue in the game until he makes a mistake (as hitting the wrong ball or pocketing his own ball) **19** *cap*, *Christian Science* **:** [2]GOD b(6) **20 :** something resembling animate life: as **a :** continued active existence and development ⟨British Columbia's chance for a separate political ~ —R.W.Van Alstyne⟩ ⟨upon circulation . . . the ~ and prosperity of a newspaper depends —F.L.Mott⟩ **b :** a state characterized by the functioning of the mechanical parts (as of a motor) ⟨the engine coughed into ~ —B.R.Ingram⟩ **21 :** conscious existence supposed to be a quality of the soul or as the soul's nature and being — **for dear life** *adv* **:** so as to save or as if trying to save one's life **:** with might and main ⟨a giant octopus . . . was holding on *for dear life* with a dozen legs —C.L.Carmer⟩ — **on your life** *adv* **:** by all means **:** under any or all circumstances ⟨obey them *on your life* —John Buchan⟩ **:** on any account — usu. used in negative constructions ⟨have any of them appreciated one jot or one tittle of it? not *on your life* —Louis Auchincloss⟩

**[2]life** \"\ *adj* **1 :** of or relating to animate being ⟨manifestations of ~ instincts —Abram Kardiner⟩ ⟨~ processes⟩ **2 :** for or lasting throughout the duration of existence **:** LIFELONG ⟨~ income⟩ ⟨~ tenure⟩ ⟨a ~ member⟩ ⟨~ aims⟩ **3 :** using a living model ⟨a ~ class⟩ **4 :** of, relating to, or provided by life insurance ⟨a ~ policy⟩

**life-and-death** *also* **life-or-death** \¦⸗⸗¦⸗\ *adj* **:** involving or culminating in life or death **:** having vital importance as if involving life or death ⟨engaged in a *life-and-death* struggle —Fitzroy Maclean⟩ ⟨the desperate *life-and-death* battle between workers and owners —*Yale Rev.*⟩ ⟨the *life-and-death* power of the Senate Appropriations Committee —Douglass Cater⟩

**life annuity** *n* **:** an annuity payable during the lifetime of the annuitant — called also *single life annuity;* compare ANNUITY, JOINT LIFE ANNUITY, JOINT LIFE AND SURVIVOR ANNUITY

**life arrow** *n* **:** an arrow for carrying a line to a boat or ship

**life assurance** *n*, *chiefly Brit* **:** LIFE INSURANCE

**life belt** *n* **1 :** a life preserver in the form of a buoyant belt **2 :** SAFETY BELT

**lifeblood** \'⸗¦⸗\ *n* **1 :** blood regarded as the seat of vitality ⟨a gaping wound issuing ~ —Shak.⟩ **2 :** something that gives or is held to give life and energy **:** a vital or life-giving force ⟨water is the ~ of India —Chester Bowles⟩ ⟨fuel oil has come to be the ~ of their civilization —K.R.Greenfield⟩

**lifeboat** \'⸗,⸗\ *n* **1 :** a strong buoyant boat esp. designed for use in saving shipwrecked people ⟨the cart, bearing the ~, was on its way down the beach —J.C.Lincoln⟩ **2 :** a boat carried by a ship for use in emergency; *esp* **:** a quarter boat kept in readiness for lowering in an emergency ⟨the ~*s* are arranged along almost the full length of the uppermost deck —F.E.Dodman⟩

**lifeboat falls** *n pl* **:** ropes and blocks used with davits for lowering a lifeboat

**lifeboat gun** *n* **:** a gun used for shooting a lifeline to a ship in distress

**life·boat·man** \'⸗,⸗mən, -,man\ *n*, *pl* **lifeboatmen :** a member of the crew of a lifeboat

**life breath** *n* **:** the breath that sustains life ⟨giving *life breath* to the skeleton —*Spectator*⟩

**life buoy** *n* **:** a float usu. consisting of a ring of buoyant material to support persons who have fallen into the water

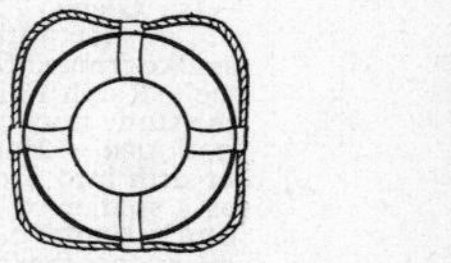

life buoy

**life car** *n* **:** a watertight boat or chamber traveling on a rope and usu. used to haul persons through surf too heavy for an open boat

**life cast** *or* **life mask** *n* **:** a cast taken from the face of a living person — compare DEATH MASK

**life cycle** *n* **1 :** the series of stages or changes in form and functional activity through which an organism passes between successive recurrences of a specified primary stage — compare NUCLEAR CYCLE **2 :** LIFE HISTORY 1a **3 :** a series of significant periods (as infancy and adolescence) through which an individual, group, or culture passes during its lifetime ⟨the *life cycle* of the family⟩ ⟨the Apache *life cycle*⟩

**life estate** *or* **life interest** *n* **:** an estate or interest in property held only during or measured by the term of the life of a specified natural person — compare LIFE TENANT, REMAINDER, REVERSION

**life everlasting** *n* **1 :** LIFE 4b **2 a :** EVERLASTING 3 **b :** PEARLY EVERLASTING **c :** ORPINE

**life expectancy** *n* **:** an expected number of years of life based on statistical probability ⟨the normal *life expectancy* in the U. S. has been raised —G.R.Cowgill⟩ ⟨the *life expectancy* of the average new book —David Dempsey⟩ — called also *expectation of life*

**life-force** \'⸗¦⸗\ *n* **:** ÉLAN VITAL ⟨freedom . . . has always been the *life-force* of western civilization —Harold Butler⟩ ⟨the conflict between the *life-force* of his characters —Arthur Miller⟩

**life-form** \'⸗,⸗\ *n* **:** the body form characterizing a kind of organism (as a species) at maturity ⟨trees are commonly the dominant *life-form* in moist cool areas⟩

**life·ful** \'līffəl\ *adj* [ME *lifful*, fr. *lif* life + *-ful* — more at LIFE] **:** full of or giving vitality ⟨~ eyes⟩

**life-giving** \'⸗,⸗⸗\ *adj* **:** giving or having power to give life and spirit **:** INVIGORATING ⟨returning the *life-giving* humus to the land —Louis Bromfield⟩ ⟨the *life-giving* streams of foreign investment by private companies —*Lamp*⟩

**[1]lifeguard** \'⸗,⸗\ *n* [[1]*life* + *guard*] **:** one that guards or protects a person's life; *specif* **:** an expert swimmer employed (as at a beach or pool) to safeguard bathers and to prevent drownings ⟨seen a ~ work over a half-drowned man —Zane Grey⟩

**[2]lifeguard** \"\ *vt* **:** to guard or protect the life of (a person) **~** *vi* **:** to serve as a lifeguard

**life guardsman** *n*, *usu cap L&G* **:** a member of a body of soldiers assigned to guard the British monarch

**life gun** *n* **:** a device used esp. in rescue work to extend a line of rope to an otherwise inaccessible place

**life history** *n* **1 a :** a history of the stages or changes through which an organism passes in its development from the egg, spore, or other primary stage until its natural death **b :** one series of these changes often constituting a life cycle **2 :** the history of an individual's development in his social environment ⟨the technique of collecting *life histories* in social research⟩ — compare CASE HISTORY 1

**lifehold** \'⸗,⸗\ *adj* **:** held for life or as a life estate

**life income policy** *n* **:** a life-insurance policy providing for a stated life income to the beneficiary beginning at the death of the insured

**life instinct** *n* **:** unconscious or biological tendencies toward maintenance and increase of organic existence

**life insurance** *n* **:** insurance providing for payment of a stipulated sum to a designated beneficiary upon death of the insured

**life jacket** *n* **:** a life preserver in the form of a sleeveless jacket **:** LIFE VEST

**lifeleaf** \'⸗,⸗\ *also* **liveleaf** \'⸗,⸗\ *n* **:** AIR PLANT 2

**life·less** \'līfləs\ *adj* [ME *lifles*, fr. OE *līflēas*, fr. *līf* life + *-lēas* -less — more at LIFE] **:** having no life: **a :** having ceased to live **:** deprived of life **:** DEAD ⟨a ~ carcass⟩ **b :** of a kind that is without life **:** INANIMATE ⟨as cold and ~ as marble —W.M.Thackeray⟩ ⟨animate the ~ clay —Mary W. Shelley⟩ **c :** lacking qualities expressive of life and vigor **:** COLORLESS, DULL ⟨a speech more ~ . . . than most of its mechanical type —S.H.Adams⟩ ⟨a ~ voice⟩ **d :** having the appearance of being dead ⟨that ~ but yet breathing creature —Anthony Trollope⟩ **e :** destitute of living beings ⟨the plain lay dark . . . and ~ —O.E.Rölvaag⟩

**life·less·ly** *adv* **:** in a lifeless manner

**life·less·ness** *n* -ES **:** the quality or state of being lifeless

**lifelike** \'⸗,⸗\ *adj* **:** like a living being or a real object **:** accurately representing or imitating real life ⟨a ~ portrait⟩ ⟨~ dialogue⟩

**life·like·ness** *n* -ES **:** the quality or state of being lifelike ⟨~ of expression⟩

**lifeline** \'⸗,⸗\ *n* **1 a :** a line to which persons may cling to save or protect their lives: as (1) **:** one stretched along the deck or from the yards of a ship — see SHIP illustration (2) **:** one attached to a ship or buoy for the use of people in the water (3) **:** one stretched through surf for the use of bathers **b :** a line attached to a diver's helmet for use chiefly in raising and lowering him in the water **c :** a rope line by which a person may be lowered to safety (as from a burning building) **2 :** something held to resemble a line used for the saving or protection of life ⟨the . . . program is the very ~ by which an alcoholic can pull himself back to a normal position in life —*Alcoholics Anonymous Grapevine*⟩ **3** *usu cap* **:** LINE OF LIFE **4 :** a land, sea, or air route regarded as indispensable to life; *esp* **:** one held necessary to supply or communicate with a usu. distant outpost or to maintain an empire ⟨severing the Mediterranean ~ of the empire —Malcolm Wheeler-Nicholson⟩

**lifelong** \'⸗¦⸗\ *adj* **:** lasting or continuing through life ⟨the ~ relations between master and slave —V.L.Parrington⟩ ⟨my ~ friend⟩ ⟨whose ~ study of Mediterranean . . . art —S.L. Faison⟩

**life·man** \'līfmən\ *n, pl* **lifemen :** one who practices lifemanship

**life·man·ship** \'==‚ship\ *n* **:** the art or practice of achieving superiority or an appearance of superiority over other people (as in conversation or business) by perplexing and demoralizing them — compare GAMESMANSHIP, ONE-UPMANSHIP

**life mask** *n* **:** LIFE CAST

**life master** *n, usu cap L&M* **:** a player of the highest rank in U.S. contract bridge tournament play ⟨develop promising players into *Life Masters* —J.P.Dunne & A.A.Ostrow⟩ — compare MASTER POINT

**life net** *n* **:** a strong net or sheet (as of canvas) held by firemen or others to catch persons jumping from burning buildings

**life-of-man** \'=‚=‚=\ *n, pl* **life-of-mans :** any of several plants found in the U.S.: as **a :** SPIKENARD 2a **b :** BUSH HONEYSUCKLE **c :** ORPINE **d :** MOUNTAIN ASH

**life of ri·ley** \-ə(v)'rīlē, -li\ *usu cap R* **:** a carefree way of living characterized by ease, comfort, and often luxury ⟨living the *life of Riley*⟩

**life-or-death** *var of* LIFE-AND-DEATH

**life peer** *n* **:** a British peer whose title is not hereditary ⟨the bill . . . calls for the creation of *life peers* — both men and women —*Associated Press*⟩

**life peerage** *n* **:** the rank or dignity of a life peer ⟨ten men who are to receive *life peerages* —T.P.Ronan⟩

**life plant** *n* **:** AIR PLANT 2

**life preserver** *n* **1 :** a device (as a life belt, life ring, or life vest) designed to save a person from drowning by buoying up the body while in water **2 :** BLACKJACK 4 ⟨beaten and bruised with *life preservers* —Charles Reade⟩

**lif·er** \'līfə(r)\ *n* -s **1 :** one sentenced to imprisonment or similar punishment for life **2 :** LIFE 5c

**life raft** *n* **:** a very buoyant raft usu. made of wood or an inflatable material and designed to be used by people forced into the water (as from a sinking ship)

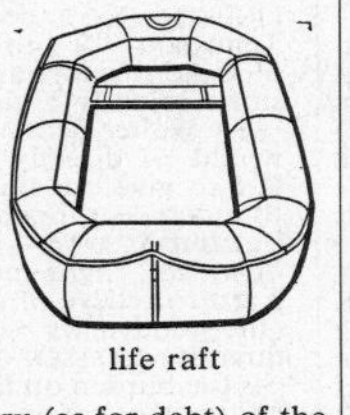

life raft

**¹liferent** \'=‚=\ *n* [ME (Sc) *lifrent*, fr. *lif* life + *rent* — more at LIFE, RENT] **:** a right in Scots law regarded either as a personal servitude or as a usufruct to use and enjoy while preserving the substance of usu. heritable property

**²liferent** \"\ *vt* **:** to grant a liferent of

**liferenter** \'=‚==\ *n* **:** a person holding a liferent

**liferent escheat** *n* **:** the forfeiture under Scots law to the superior of the annual profits from property held by liferent during the life or duration of the outlawry (as for debt) of the liferenter

**life·rent·rix** \'=‚rentriks\ *n, pl* **liferentrix·es** \-triksə̇z\ *or* **liferentri·ces** \-trə‚sēz\ [¹*liferent* + *-trix*] **:** a female liferenter

**life ring** *n* **:** a ring-shaped life preserver usu. made of cork and other buoyant materials

**liferoot** \'=‚=\ *n* **:** GOLDEN RAGWORT

**lifesaver** \'=‚==\ *n* **1 a :** one trained to save lives of drowning persons **b** *chiefly Brit* **:** LIFEGUARD **2 :** one that saves a person from a serious predicament or difficulty usu. at a critical time ⟨the fellowship income is a ~ to me —F.A.Perry⟩

**¹lifesaving** \'=‚==\ *n* [*life* + *saving*, fr. gerund of *save*] **:** the art or practice of saving or protecting lives esp. of drowning persons ⟨a course in ~⟩

**²lifesaving** \"\ *adj* **:** that engages in or is designed for lifesaving ⟨a ~ squad⟩

**life scout** *n* **:** a boy scout who has earned ten merit badges — compare EAGLE SCOUT, STAR SCOUT

**life sentence** *n* **:** LIFE 5c

**life-size** *also* **life-sized** \'=‚=\ *adj* **:** of natural size **:** equal in size to the form of a living being or an object in real life ⟨a *life-size* bronze figure of a woman —*Amer. Guide Series: N.C.*⟩ | ⟨a *life-size* London bus —*Newsweek*⟩ ⟨two *life-sized* statues of the king —*Literary Digest*⟩

**life·some** \'līfsəm\ *adj* **:** full of animation and vigor **:** SPRIGHTLY ⟨the speeches . . . are very witty and ~ —Hartley Coleridge⟩

**life space** *n* **:** the physical and psychological environment of an individual or group

**life-span** \'=‚=\ *n* **1 :** the duration of existence of an individual ⟨the effect on his *life-span* of the great pressure under which her husband works —George Lawton⟩ **2 :** the average length of life of a kind of organism or a material object esp. in a particular environment or under specified circumstances ⟨some insects whose *life-span* is no longer than a season —*Nat'l Geographic*⟩ ⟨the *life-span* of the daily political cartoon —E.W.Kenworthy⟩ ⟨the whole *life-span* of the commonwealth —*So. Atlantic Quarterly*⟩

**life-style** \'=‚=\ *n* **:** STYLE 4c(2)

**life table** *n* **:** MORTALITY TABLE

**life tenant** *n* **:** a tenant having possession (as of property) for the duration of his life — compare LIFE ESTATE, REMAINDER, REVERSION

**lifetime** \'=‚=\ *n* [ME *liftime*, fr. *lif* life + *time* — more at LIFE, TIME] **1 :** the time that a life continues **:** the duration of the existence of a living being or a thing ⟨a ~ of writing nonfiction —Stuart Chase⟩ ⟨these edifices . . . possess only a limited ~ —Osbert Sitwell⟩ ⟨during its ~ the university has absorbed several other institutions —*Amer. Guide Series: Md.*⟩ **2 a :** the duration of the existence of an ion or subatomic particle **b :** HALF-LIFE

**life tree** *n* **:** TREE OF LIFE

**life vest** *n* **:** a life preserver designed as a vestlike garment of buoyant or inflatable material — compare MAE WEST

**life·ward** \'līfwə(r)d\ *adv* **:** toward life ⟨the world had turned ~ from death —Bernard De Voto⟩

**lifeway** \'=‚=\ *n* **:** LIFE 6 ⟨the ~s of these rural New Mexicans —Ruth Underhill⟩ ⟨practices suitable to their hunting ~ —Laura Thompson⟩

life vest

**lifework** \'=‚=\ *n* **:** the entire or principal work of one's lifetime; *also* **:** a work extending over a lifetime ⟨influenced him to choose government service as a ~ —*Current Biog.*⟩ ⟨spent his last . . . years waging an exhausting literary battle to defend his ~ —*Infantry Jour.*⟩

**lif·ey** \'līfi\ *adj* [ME *lify*, fr. *lif* life + *-y*] *now chiefly Scot* **:** full of life **:** SPIRITED

**life zone** *n* **:** a biogeographic zone

**LIFO** *abbr* last in, first out

**¹lift** \'lift\ *n* -s [ME *luft, lift*, fr. OE *lyft* air, sky — more at LOFT] *now chiefly Scot* **:** HEAVENS, SKY ⟨the sweet calm moon in the midnight ~ —John Wilson †1854⟩

**²lift** \"\ *vb* -ED/-ING/-S [ME *liften*, fr. ON *lypta*; akin to MLG *lüchten* to lift, MHG *lüften*; derivative fr. the root represented by OE *lyft* air — more at LOFT] *vt* **1 a :** to raise from a lower to a higher position (as from the ground into the air) **:** move away from the pull of gravitation **:** ELEVATE 1 ⟨the elevator ~s pedestrians ninety feet up the steep face of the cliff —*Amer. Guide Series: Oregon*⟩ ⟨did not ~ his head from his book —D.M.Davin⟩ ⟨~*ed* his pen from the paper⟩ **b :** to raise in rank, condition, or position ⟨~*ed* him to national recognition⟩ ⟨millions of families . . . have been ~*ed* from poverty —F.L.Allen⟩ **c :** to raise or project above surrounding objects ⟨a . . . church building ~*s* a tall clock tower —*Amer. Guide Series: Texas*⟩ ⟨the highest of these peaks . . . ~*s* its majestic cone far into the zone of permanent snow —P.E.James⟩ **d :** to raise in rate or amount ⟨~ prices of commodities —L.C.Jauncey⟩ **2** *now chiefly dial* **:** to attend to the collection of (as a payment due) ⟨the laird ~*ed* his rent —Charles Gibbon⟩ **3** *archaic* **:** to cut up (a swan) **4 a :** to take up and remove (as a tent or camp) **b :** to put an end to (a blockade or siege) by withdrawing or causing the withdrawal of investing forces **c** (1) **:** to revoke by an authoritative act **:** RESCIND ⟨urged the . . . government to ~ the embargo on the shipment of arms —*Current Biog.*⟩ (2) **:** to revoke or confiscate usu. temporarily or for a specified time ⟨~ a passport⟩ **d :** to take (as a bus ticket) esp. in order to issue a replacement **5 :** to take from its proper place: **a :** STEAL ⟨had his pocketbook ~*ed*⟩: as (1) **:** to carry or drive off (as cattle) by theft ⟨I'll never ~ no more cattle —R.M.Daw⟩ (2) **:** PLAGIARIZE **b :** to take out of normal setting ⟨~ a word out of context⟩ ⟨the writer ~*ed* an episode from history⟩ **6** *chiefly Scot* **:** to take up and carry (a coffin) in a funeral procession **7 :** to take up from the ground: **a :** to dig (root crops) ⟨tubers should not be ~*ed* when there are blight spots on the leaves —*New Zealand Jour. of Agric.*⟩ **b :** to loosen and remove (as seedlings) from the seedbed or from a nursery ⟨don't ~ bulbs before leaves are brown —*Sydney (Australia) Bull.*⟩ **8 :** to remove by scalping ⟨~ the hair⟩ **9 :** to pay off (an obligation) ⟨~ a mortgage⟩ **10 :** to soften and swell (as a film of paint or size) **11 :** FACE-LIFT **12 :** to call in (hounds) for withdrawal from the chase or for redirection in hunting **13 a :** to shift (artillery fire) from one area to another usu. at greater range **b :** to withhold (fire) from an area ⟨~ the fire prior to the advance of the infantry —*Organized Reserve Corps Army Training Bull.*⟩ **14 :** to move from one place to another (as by an airlift) **:** TRANSPORT ⟨~*ed* the staff and students . . . to California and back —*Collier's Yr. Bk.*⟩ **15 :** to remove (a fingerprint) from a surface usu. by the use of plastics and powders **16 a :** to remove (a form) from a printing press **b :** to remove (as matter in a form) for use in another job ~ *vi* **1 a :** RISE ⟨a hundred-passenger airliner ~*s* from a New York airport —Seth Babits⟩ ⟨a blue jay ~*ed* suddenly from the rubbish heaps —Clemence Dane⟩ **b :** to appear elevated (as above surrounding objects) ⟨white church spires ~ above green valleys —Gladys Taber⟩ ⟨green mountains which ~ above the desert —*Holiday*⟩ **2 a :** to rise and disperse — used chiefly of fog or clouds **b :** to cease temporarily — used of rain ⟨the rain slackened, ~*ed*, and finally left off —H.E.Bates⟩ **3 :** WARP — used of a floor **4 :** to shake slightly — used of a sail **5 :** PICK 5 **6 :** to rise after pitching — used of a ball ⟨on such a wicket . . . the ball is liable to ~ sharply —*Calling All Cricketers*⟩ **7 :** to remain intact when raised from a supporting surface — used of printing type in a locked-up form

**syn** LIFT, RAISE, REAR, ELEVATE, HOIST, HEAVE, and BOOST can mean, in common, to move from a lower to a higher place or position. LIFT, when it does not merely apply to any moving upward or causing to rise as by picking up, can suggest both a moving upward with a certain effort or a moving upward as in aspiring ⟨*lift* a book to dust under it⟩ ⟨*lift* a log onto a truck⟩ ⟨the tall buildings *lifted* their spires above the surrounding plain⟩ RAISE can be interchanged with LIFT but often suggests strongly a bringing of something to a vertical or a high position for which it is designed or fitted ⟨*raise* a chair above his head⟩ ⟨*raise* a flag⟩ ⟨*raise* a building⟩ ⟨*raise* a civilization to eminence⟩ REAR can sometimes esp. in figurative use be interchanged with RAISE, but can also suggest a certain literal or figurative suddenness in the movement from a lower to higher position, as of something jutting ⟨*raise* children to be responsible adults⟩ ⟨*rear* children to a happy adulthood⟩ ⟨the horse *reared*, its front feet flailing high in the air⟩ ⟨the building *reared* thirty-odd stories high⟩ ELEVATE can, in a certain literary style, be interchanged with LIFT or RAISE, but generally suggests exaltation, uplifting, or enhancing ⟨*elevate* a hand and an eyebrow⟩ ⟨an instructor *elevated* to a professorship⟩ ⟨*elevate* your standards of good conduct⟩ ⟨*elevate* his thoughts⟩ HOIST usu. implies the raising aloft of something of considerable weight esp. by mechanical means ⟨lay the heavy weights on the ground and subsequently have to *hoist* them up again —C.S.Forester⟩ ⟨the boat rocked as the admiral *hoisted* his bulk inboard —A.B.Mayse⟩ ⟨it takes five power winches to *hoist* this mammoth expanse of canvas on the five 62-foot center poles of Douglas fir —*Monsanto Mag.*⟩ HEAVE suggests strain and great effort ⟨he looked like a massive, slow-footed bear as he *heaved* himself out of the car —Jean Stafford⟩ ⟨nature's way of creating a mountain peak — first the *heaving* up of some blunt monstrous bulk of rumpled rock —C.E. Montague⟩ ⟨his men *heaved* and *heaved*, but they couldn't get that anchor off the bottom —C.L.Carmer⟩ BOOST suggests lifting or assisting to move upward by a push or other help from below ⟨*boosted* him through the skylight on the new roof —*Amer. Guide Series: La.*⟩ **syn** see in addition STEAL

**— lift at** *obs* **:** to rise in or stir up hostility to **— lift one's voice** *or* **lift up one's voice :** to cry aloud **:** call out ⟨thousands . . . *lifted their voices* to demand an end to uncertainty —Julian Dana⟩

**³lift** \"\ *n* -s *often attrib* [ME, fr. *liften*, v.] **1 :** the unit or weight that may be lifted at one time **:** QUANTITY ⟨a ~ of sheet steel⟩ ⟨610,000 pounds of daily cargo ~ —*N.Y. Times*⟩ **2 a :** the action or an instance of lifting ⟨the clear ~ of a girl's voice —Cliff Farrell⟩ ⟨a ~ of her eyebrows⟩ **b :** the action or an instance of rising as if lifting something ⟨the ~ and boom of the waves —Sacheverell Sitwell⟩ ⟨the ~ and sweep of the hills to the sky —John Connell⟩ **c :** the action or habit of carrying (a part of the body) in an upright position **:** elevated carriage ⟨the proud ~ of her head⟩ **d :** the lifting up of a dancer usu. by her partner ⟨in a superb ~ at the end —*Dance Observer*⟩ — compare ELEVATION 1d **3 a :** a device for lifting: **a :** a rope leading from a masthead to the extremity of a yard below and used chiefly to raise and support the yard — see SHIP illustration **b :** a device (as a handle or knob) used to raise a window **c :** a hinged handle used on chests **d :** the part used to lift the bar in some early door latches **4 a :** an act of stealing **:** THEFT 1 **b** *obs* **:** THIEF **5 a :** the action or an instance of assistance (as in the attainment of a higher position) **b :** a ride along one's way in a vehicle going in the same direction ⟨gave her ~*s* in his car between there and the village —Elizabeth Taylor⟩ ⟨the rain-drenched couple raising their thumbs for a ~ —E.D.Radin⟩ **6** *dial Eng* **:** a gate (as in a wall or fence) that is opened by lifting **7 :** one of the layers forming the heel of a shoe — see TOP LIFT **8** *dial Eng* **:** a cut of meat usu. from the thigh **9 a :** one of a series of levels or stepped workings in a mine; *also* **:** the vertical distance apart of such workings **b :** one of a series of sections or slices successively removed from a temporary pillar in a mine **10 :** a rise in position or condition **:** a favorable advance ⟨people . . . most deserving of such a ~ in fortune —F.L.Allen⟩ ⟨another ~ in transport costs —*Sydney (Australia) Bull.*⟩ **11 :** a usu. slight rise or elevation (as of the ground) ⟨came down from the little ~ in the ground where they were standing —W.C.Williams⟩ **12 :** the distance or extent to which something (as the water in a canal lock) rises ⟨the vertical ~ of the lower lock is 25 feet —*Civil Engineering*⟩ **13 :** an apparatus or machine used for hoisting: as **a :** a set of pumps used in a mine **b :** DUMBWAITER **2 a** ~ for books in a library⟩ **c** *chiefly Brit* **:** ELEVATOR 1 ⟨heard him ring for the ~ —J.D.Beresford⟩ **d :** an apparatus for raising an automobile from the ground to a higher level (as for repair or parking) **e :** a conveyor for carrying people up or down a mountain slope ⟨three new ~*s* highlight New Hampshire's extension of ski facilities —Judith D. Beal⟩ — see ALPINE LIFT, CHAIR LIFT, SKI LIFT **f :** a mechanism for raising certain parts of farm implements above the ground ⟨a tractor with a power ~⟩ **14 a :** an elevating power or influence ⟨the great ~ of the thing . . . is what still compels in this great picture —F.J.Mather⟩ **b :** an elevation of the spirits produced by such an influence ⟨needs the ~ that the right clothes can give —*Springfield (Mass.) City Library Bull.*⟩ ⟨got a tremendous ~ from the experience —W.P.Webb⟩ ⟨a sudden ~ of excitement —Oliver La Farge⟩ **15 :** the portion of the escapement action in a timepiece in which the escape tooth imparts an impulse to the pallets **16 a :** the distance between the terminal limits of yarn or thread wound on a bobbin **b :** the traverse of a piece of mechanism in winding a bobbin **17 :** the component of the total aerodynamic force acting on an airplane or airfoil that is perpendicular to the relative wind and that for an airplane constitutes the upward force that opposes the pull of gravity **18 :** the cope of a foundry mold **19 :** a stack of brick in the kiln **20 :** a single haul of a lift net; *also* **:** the fish taken in such a haul **21 :** the amount of concrete placed at a single time in the building of a structure (as a wall, pier, abutment) **22 :** a pile of sheets (as of paper) constituting a number convenient for handling in a single printing operation ⟨when a ~ of printed sheets is removed from the press —R.W.Polk⟩ **23 a :** an organized movement of men and equipment or of supplies by some form of transportation ⟨move 1332 troops with their equipment in a single ~ —E.A. Suttles⟩ ⟨our ship carried a diverse and colorful fragment of . . . the second ~ —Gordon Merrick⟩ ⟨a food ~⟩ **b :** ¹AIRLIFT ⟨says the Korea ~ is the longest in the world —Frederick Graham⟩ ⟨how the Berlin ~ works —Charles Gardner⟩ **— on the lift** *adv (or adj), South & Midland* **:** in a weak condition (as from illness, hunger, or exposure) **:** unable to rise or stand without support

**lift·able** \'liftəbəl\ *adj* **:** capable of being lifted

**lift bridge** *n* **:** a drawbridge whose movable parts are lifted

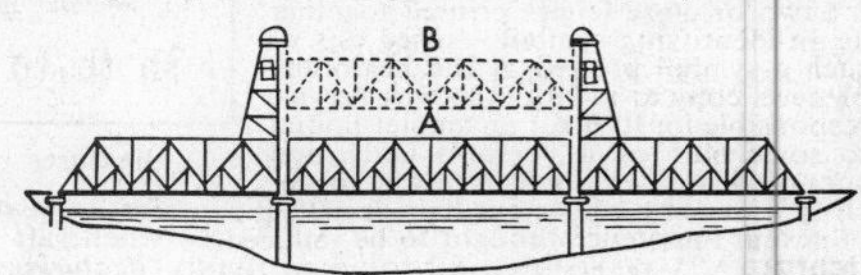


vertical lift bridge: *A* normal position, *B* raised

vertically or by rotating about a horizontal axis — compare BASCULE BRIDGE, SWING BRIDGE

**lifted** *past of* LIFT

**lifted stem turn** *n* **:** a stem turn in which the inside ski is unweighted, lifted, and set down parallel with the outside stemming ski

**lift·er** \'liftə(r)\ *n* -s **1 a :** one that lifts **b :** THIEF — see SHOPLIFTER **2 :** a machine or device for lifting: as **a :** a hoisting apparatus (as a bucket wheel in a paper mill or a device in a harvesting machine for elevating grain) **b :** a cam or other device used for lifting an engine valve **c :** a foundry tool for lifting loose sand from the mold; *also* **:** a contrivance that is attached to a cope to hold the sand together when the cope is lifted **d :** a removable handle for lifting lids in a kitchen range or stove **e :** a root-crop harvesting machine consisting essentially of a pair of spaced inclined bars that pass through the soil with low pointed ends foremost **f :** a piece in a lever-tumbler lock that moves the tumblers when the master key or skeleton key is inserted and turned exactly as they are moved by the ordinary key

**lift gate** *n* **:** an upper rear panel (as on a station wagon) that opens upward as a tailgate opens downward

**lift ground** *n* **:** a substance painted or drawn on the plate in etching to cause the acid-resistant ground coated over it to break down in water or acid exposing the painted parts to the biting action

**lifting** *pres part of* LIFT

**lifting bolt** *n* **:** an eyebolt to which a hook or other tackle is attached for lifting heavy machinery

**lift·man** \'lif(t)mən\ *n, pl* **liftmen** *chiefly Brit* **:** an elevator operator

**lift net** *n* **:** a bag or basket-shaped net designed to be fished vertically through the water (as in taking smelts)

**lift-off** \'=‚=\ *n* -s [fr. *lift off*, v.] **:** a vertical takeoff by an aircraft or a rocket missile or vehicle

**lift pump** *also* **lifting pump** *n* **:** SUCTION PUMP

**lifts** *pres 3d sing of* LIFT, *pl of* LIFT

**lift-slab** \'=‚=\ *adj* **:** of, relating to, or being a method of concrete building construction in which floor and horizontal roof slabs are cast one on top of the other usu. at ground level and then lifted to their proper heights after the concrete has developed the necessary strength

**lift truck** *n* **:** a small truck or a hand- or power-operated dolly equipped (as with a forklift or platform) for lifting and transporting loads (as about a shop or freight depot) — see FORK TRUCK

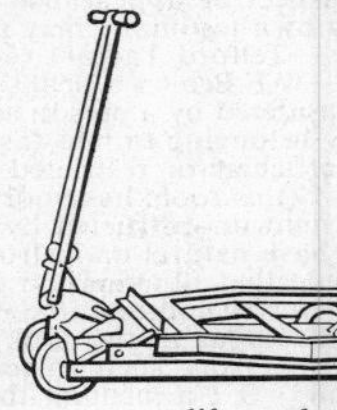

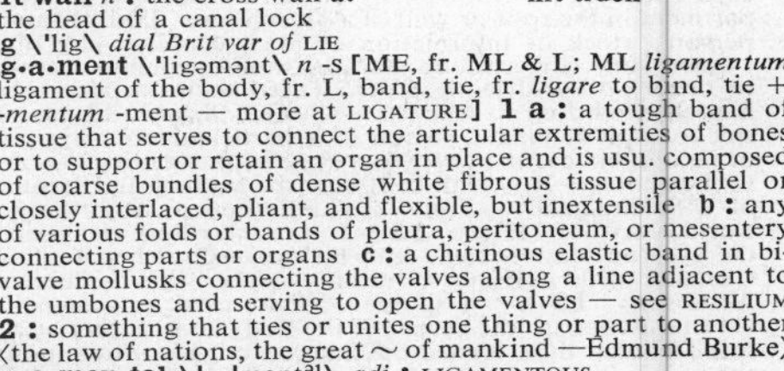

lift truck

**lift valve** *n* **:** a valve whose direction of movement is perpendicular to the plane of its seat

**lift van** *n* **:** a large strong waterproof shipping case in which household or other goods may be sealed and shipped as a unit

**lift wall** *n* **:** the cross wall at the head of a canal lock

**lig** \'lig\ *dial Brit var of* LIE

**lig·a·ment** \'ligəmənt\ *n* -s [ME, fr. ML & L; ML *ligamentum* ligament of the body, fr. L, band, tie, fr. *ligare* to bind, tie + *-mentum* -ment — more at LIGATURE] **1 a :** a tough band of tissue that serves to connect the articular extremities of bones or to support or retain an organ in place and is usu. composed of coarse bundles of dense white fibrous tissue parallel or closely interlaced, pliant, and flexible, but inextensible **b :** any of various folds or bands of pleura, peritoneum, or mesentery connecting parts or organs **c :** a chitinous elastic band in bivalve mollusks connecting the valves along a line adjacent to the umbones and serving to open the valves — see RESILIUM **2 :** something that ties or unites one thing or part to another ⟨the law of nations, the great ~ of mankind —Edmund Burke⟩

**lig·a·men·tal** \‚==ˈmentᵊl\ *adj* **:** LIGAMENTOUS

**lig·a·men·ta·ry** \-tərē\ *adj* **:** LIGAMENTOUS

**ligament of cooper** *usu cap C* [after Sir Astley P. *Cooper* †1841 Eng. surgeon] **:** COOPER'S LIGAMENT

**ligament of the ovary :** a rounded cord of fibrous and muscular tissue extending from each superior angle of the uterus to the inner extremity of the ovary of the same side

**ligament of treitz** *usu cap T* [after Wilhelm *Treitz* †1872 Austrian physician] **:** TREITZ'S MUSCLE 1

**ligament of wins·low** \-'winz(‚)lō, -'vin(t)(‚)slō\ *usu cap W* [after Jakob B. *Winslow* †1760 Dan. naturalist] **:** a ligament of the posterior surface of the knee formed by the expansion of the tendons of the semimembranosus and other muscles

**ligament of zinn** \-'zin, -'tsin\ *usu cap Z* [after Johann G. *Zinn* †1759 Ger. physician] **:** the common tendon of the inferior rectus and the internal rectus muscles of the eye

**lig·a·men·tous** \‚ligə'mentəs\ *adj* **1 :** of or relating to a ligament **2 :** forming or formed of a ligament **— lig·a·men·tous·ly** *adv*

**lig·a·men·tum** \‚==ˈmentəm\ *n, pl* **ligamen·ta** \-tə\ [ML — more at LIGAMENT] **:** LIGAMENT 1

**ligamentum fla·vum** \-'flāvəm\ *n, pl* **ligamenta fla·va** \-və\ [NL, lit., yellow ligament] **:** any of a series of ligaments of yellow elastic tissue connecting the laminae of adjacent vertebrae from the axis to the sacrum

**ligamentum nu·chae** \-'n(y)üke\ *n, pl* **ligamenta nuchae** [NL, lit., ligament of the back of the neck] **:** a median ligament of the back of the neck that is rudimentary in man but highly developed and composed of yellow elastic tissue in many quadrupeds where it assists in supporting the head

**ligan** *or* **ligen** *var of* LAGAN

**lig·and** \'ligənd, 'lig-\ *also* **ligand group** *n* -s [L *ligandus*, gerundive of *ligare* to bind, tie — more at LIGATURE] **:** a group, ion, or molecule coordinated to the central atom in a coordination complex

**li·gas** \lē'gäs\ *n* -ES [Tag *ligás*] **:** a poisonous Philippine tree (*Semecarpus perrottetii*) of the family Anacardiaceae that has hardwood and yields an illuminating resin

**li·gate** \'lī‚gāt\ *vt* -ED/-ING/-S [L *ligatus*, past part. of *ligare* to bind,tie — more at LIGATURE] **:** to tie with a ligature

**li·ga·tion** \lī'gāshən\ *n* -s [MF, fr. LL *ligation-, ligatio*, fr. L *ligatus* + *-ion-, -io* -ion] **1 :** the action of binding; *specif* **:** the surgical process of tying up a blood vessel **2 :** something that binds **:** CONNECTION, LIGATURE

**lig·a·tive** \'ligəd·iv\ *adj* [L *ligatus* + E *-ive*] *linguistics* **:** CONNECTIVE, BINDING ⟨the ~ article in Tagalog⟩

**¹lig·a·ture** \'ligəchə(r), -gə‚chu̇(ə)r, -‚u̇ə\ *n* -s [ME, fr. MF, fr. LL *ligatura* tie, bond, fr. L *ligatus* (past part. of *ligare* to bind, tie) + *-ura* -ure; akin to MLG *lik* band, MHG *geleich* joint, limb, Alb *lith* I tie] **1 a :** something that is used to bind; *specif* **:** a thread, wire, or other material used in surgery (as for tying the blood vessels) **b :** something that unites or connects **:** BOND ⟨having no ~ of race and family affection to bind them together —Horace Bushnell⟩ **2 :** the action of binding or tying ⟨the ~ of an artery⟩ **3 a** *in mensural notation* **:** a compound note form indicating a group of musical notes or tones to be sung to one syllable **b :** a flexible metal band with its adjusting screws that holds in place the reed of single reed woodwind instruments (as of a clarinet) **4 a :** a character consisting of two or more letters combined into one or joined by a tie **b :** a connecting line or stroke (as ⌣ or ⌢) used to indicate that two successive sounds are pronounced as one syllable **c :** two or more letters printed together as an identifying symbol — used esp. of such a symbol printed at the beginning of news copy to identify the wire service responsible for it **5 a :** an amulet bound to some part of a person's body and supposed to have a magic power to destroy an enemy whose cut hair or nails it contains **b :** a state of sexual impotence thought to be induced by witchcraft

fi fl ff ffi ffl
ct st ch sp
sh th tu

ligatures

**²ligature** \"\ *vt* -ED/-ING/-S **:** to tie up **:** BIND ⟨*ligaturing* the blood vessels —*Veterinary Record*⟩

**li·geance** \'līјən(t)s, 'lēj-\ *n* -s [ME *legeaunce,* fr. MF *ligeance,* fr. *lige* liege + *-ance* — more at LIEGE] **1** *archaic* **:** ALLEGIANCE **2** *now chiefly Brit* **:** the jurisdiction or territory of a liege lord or of a sovereign

**li·ger** \'līgə(r)\ *n* -s [*lion* + *tiger*] **:** a hybrid between a male lion and a female tiger — compare TIGON

**ligg** \'lig\ *now dial Brit var of* LIE

**lig·gat** *or* **lig·get** \'ligət\ *n* -s [ME *lidgate,* fr. OE *hlidgeat,* fr. *hlid* covering, door, gate + *geat* gate — more at LID, GATE] *Scot* **:** GATE; *esp* **:** SWING GATE

**lig·ger** \'ligə(r)\ *n* -s [*lig, ligg* + *-er*] **1** *dial Eng* **:** a float that usu. consists of a bundle of reeds with baited line attached for pike fishing **2** *dial Eng* **:** a footbridge (as a plank) across a ditch or drain

**¹light** \'līt, *usu* -īd·+V\ *n* -s [ME *liht, light,* fr. OE *lēoht, līht;* akin to OHG *lioht* light, ON *ljōs,* Goth *liuhath,* L *luc-, lux* light, *lucēre* to shine, Gk *leukos* white, Skt *rocate* he shines] **1 a :** something that makes vision possible ⟨God said, "Let there be ~"; and there was ~ —Gen 1:3 (RSV)⟩ **b :** the sensation aroused by stimulation of the visual pathways **:** BRIGHTNESS, LUMINOSITY ⟨that ~ we see is burning in my hall —Shak.⟩ **c :** an electromagnetic radiation in the wavelength range including infrared, visible, ultraviolet, and X rays and traveling in a vacuum with a speed of about 186,281 miles per second; *specif* **:** the part of this range that is visible to the human eye and extends approximately from a wavelength of 3900 angstroms to a wavelength of 7700 angstroms **2 a :** the light of the sun **:** DAYLIGHT ⟨was up each morning at the first ~ —Frank O'Connor⟩ **b :** DAWN **3 :** a specific material source of light: as **a :** a heavenly body ⟨as night fell the ~*s* in the sky multiplied⟩ **b :** CANDLE ⟨put a ~ in the window⟩ **c :** ELECTRIC LAMP ⟨turned on all the ~*s* in the house⟩ **4** *archaic* **:** EYESIGHT ⟨when I consider how my ~ is spent ere half my days in this dark world —John Milton⟩ **5 a :** spiritual illumination that is a divine attribute or the embodiment of divine truth ⟨the ~ shines in the darkness, and the darkness has not overcome it —Jn 1:5 (RSV)⟩ ⟨Jesus is the ~ —Eliza E. Hewitt⟩ ⟨Celestial *Light,* shine inward —John Milton⟩ **b :** INNER LIGHT **c :** ultimate truth **:** ENLIGHTENMENT ⟨reaching out and groping for a pathway to the ~ —B.N.Cardozo⟩ **d :** a doctrine or set of beliefs representing true Christianity — used esp. in Scotland in the phrases *old light* and *new light* **6 a :** open view **:** public knowledge ⟨brought to ~ languages that were hitherto practically unknown —A.V.W.Jackson⟩ **b :** a particular aspect or appearance presented to view ⟨an accused person's own testimony may put him in a very bad ~ before the jury —Telford Taylor⟩ ⟨every owner saw his dogs in the best ~ —W.F.Brown b. 1903⟩ **7 a :** a source or measure of light considered by a person as necessary for his vision and as properly belonging to him ⟨asked him not to stand in her ~⟩ **b :** a particular or restricted illumination ⟨this studio has a north ~⟩ ⟨this room has poor ~⟩ ⟨ ~ of the fire⟩ **c** (1) **:** the natural light unobstructed by a building or wall (2) **:** a legal right to have natural unobstructed light (3) **:** ANCIENT LIGHT **8 :** intellectual illumination **:** something that enlightens or informs ⟨throw considerable ~ on some of the problems that now confront us in the U.S. —J.B.Conant⟩ ⟨could proudly take his ~ from such unembarrassed conservatism —Eric Goldman⟩ **9 :** a medium through which light is admitted: as **a :** WINDOW, WINDOWPANE **b :** SKYLIGHT **c :** a glass compartment in the roof or wall of a greenhouse **10 lights** *pl* **:** a person's stock of information or ideas **:** philosophy of life **:** STANDARDS ⟨the attitude that one should worship according to one's ~*s* —Adrienne Koch⟩ ⟨tried to make him behave himself according to English ~*s* —G.B.Shaw⟩ **11 :** a conspicuous or dominant person in a particular country, place, or field of endeavor **:** LUMINARY ⟨one of the leading ~*s* of the French court —R.A.Hall b. 1911⟩ ⟨the leading and lesser ~*s* of U.S. diplomacy —*Time*⟩ ⟨some literary ~ from the book world —Arthur Miller⟩ **12 :** a particular look or aspect of the eye ⟨an ugly ~ came into his eye —Gretchen Finletter⟩ ⟨listened with a fiery ~ burning in her eyes —Sherwood Anderson⟩ **13 a :** a source of light used as a signal: as (1) **:** LIGHTHOUSE ⟨the keeper of the Eddystone *Light*⟩ (2) **:** a ship's blinker light ⟨called the flagship on the ~ to announce she was reporting for duty⟩ (3) **:** TRAFFIC SIGNAL ⟨turn left at the next ~⟩ **b :** a signal esp. of a traffic light ⟨stopped by a red ~⟩ ⟨given the green ~ to go ahead with his plan⟩ **14 :** something that gives life or individuality to a person **:** vital spark ⟨hide his ~ under a bushel⟩ ⟨the ~ of individual human character shining through these events —Leslie Rees⟩ **15 a :** a quality of animation, brilliance, or intensity ⟨a man of deep shadows and dazzling ~ —O.S.J.Gogarty⟩ ⟨almost any crowd shows higher ~*s* than this one —Katherine F. Gerould⟩ **b** (1) **:** the part of a picture that represents those objects or areas upon which the light is supposed to fall — opposed to *shade;* compare CHIAROSCURO (2) **:** the part of a work of sculpture that provides a reflecting surface for light **16 :** a flame or spark by which something (as a cigarette, cigar, or pipe) may be lighted ⟨took out a cigarette and asked him for a ~⟩ **17 :** LIGHTFACE **18 lights** *pl* **a :** FOOTLIGHTS **b :** an illuminated display of a performer's name on a theater marquee ⟨dreamed of seeing her name in ~*s*⟩ — **in the light of 1 :** from the point of view of ⟨advised his students to read the old authors and to criticize them *in the light of* their enhanced anatomical knowledge —Harvey Graham⟩ **2 :** in view of ⟨were fascinated — particularly *in the light of* his recent attack on modern poets —Harvey Breit⟩ ⟨*in the light of* the current news his argument seems well taken —R.A.Smith⟩

**²light** \"\ *adj, usu* -ER/-EST [ME *liht, light,* fr. OE *lēoht, līht;* akin to OFris *liacht* bright, OS & OHG *lioht* bright, OE *lēoht,* n., light — more at ¹LIGHT] **1 a** *archaic* **:** burning brightly **:** BLAZING — used of fire ⟨piled those ancient books together and set them all on a ~ fire —John Jortin⟩ **b :** having light **:** BRIGHT ⟨the rooms are airy and ~⟩ ⟨still ~ when he arrived⟩ **2 a :** having a high lightness of color ⟨though her hair was dark, she had ~ eyes⟩ **b :** having a light complexion ⟨~*er* than his brother⟩

**³light** \"\ *vb* **lighted** \-īd·əd, -ītəd\ *or* **lit** \'lit, *usu* -id·+V\ **lighted** *or* **lit; lighting; lights** [ME *lihten, lighten,* fr. OE *lȳhtan, lihtan, liehtan;* akin to OS *liohtian* to light, OHG *liuhten,* Goth *liuhtjan;* causative-denominative fr. the root of E ²*light*] *vi* **1** *now dial* **:** to emit light **:** be light ⟨the two candles . . . were still ~*ing* —Eamonn O'Neill⟩ **2 :** to become filled with light **:** BRIGHTEN — usu. used with *up* ⟨people ~ up when he speaks with or to them —E.K.Lindley⟩ ⟨his face *lit* up at the small triumph —W.J.McKee⟩ **3 a :** to become ignited **:** take fire ⟨the match ~*s* easily⟩ **b :** to ignite something (as a cigarette, cigar, or pipe) — usu. used with *up* ⟨a small yellow flame flickered where a smoker was ~*ing* up —A.P.Gaskell⟩ ~ *vt* **1 :** to set fire to **:** cause to burn **:** IGNITE, KINDLE ⟨*lit* a cigarette⟩ ⟨struck a match and ~*ed* the lamp —Ellen Glasgow⟩ — sometimes used with *up* ⟨~ up a cigarette⟩ **2 a :** to attend or conduct with or as with a light **:** GUIDE ⟨all our yesterdays have ~*ed* fools the way to dusty death —Shak.⟩ **b :** to give light to **:** fill with light or furnish with lights **:** ILLUMINATE ⟨the chapel . . . *lit* by a three-light east window —*Country Life*⟩ — often used with *up* ⟨~ up the sky⟩ **c :** to cause to glow **:** ANIMATE, BRIGHTEN ⟨a quick animation *lit* her face —Clarissa F. Cushman⟩ — often used with *up* ⟨one shining smile *lit* up the whole place for me —Margaret Biddle⟩ — **light a shuck** *also* **light a rag** *chiefly South & Midland* **:** to leave in haste **:** run away

**⁴light** \"\ *adj, usu* -ER/-EST [ME *liht, light,* fr. OE *lēoht, līht;* akin to OHG *līhti* light, ON *lēttr,* Goth *leihts,* L *levis* light, Gk *elachys* small, Skt *laghu, raghu* fast, light, slight] **1 a :** having little weight **:** not heavy ⟨~ enough for even a very small child to manage alone —Betty Pepis⟩ **b :** less heavy than others of its kind ⟨a ~ overcoat⟩ ⟨a ~ log⟩ **c :** designed to move swiftly or to carry a comparatively small load ⟨a ~ truck⟩ ⟨a ~ airplane⟩ **d :** being of small specific gravity **:** having relatively little weight in proportion to bulk ⟨~ as a feather⟩ ⟨aluminum is a ~ metal⟩ **e :** containing less than the legal, standard, or usual weight ⟨~ coin⟩ **2 a :** of slight extent or little importance **:** TRIVIAL ⟨shows the ~*est* incidence and intensity of infection —J.H.Fischthal⟩ ⟨attests in what ~ esteem we held the tank —S.L.A.Marshall⟩ **b :** not abundant **:** INCONSIDERABLE ⟨a ~ rain⟩ ⟨the early voting was ~⟩ ⟨trading on the commodity exchange was ~⟩ ⟨has relatively ~ traffic and few billboards —*Amer. Guide Series: Md.*⟩ ⟨a ~ breakfast⟩ **3 a** (1) **:** not oppressive **:** easily broken or disturbed ⟨a ~ and fitful sleep⟩ (2) **:** easily aroused **:** not weighed down by sleep ⟨a ~ sleeper⟩ **b :** barely moving or existing **:** exerting a minimum of force or pressure **:** GENTLE ⟨a ~ touch⟩ ⟨a ~ breeze⟩ ⟨that ~ irregular breathing —Aldous Huxley⟩ **c :** resulting from a very slight pressure **:** FAINT, INDISTINCT ⟨a ~ impression⟩ ⟨a ~ stroke of the pen⟩ ⟨the print was too ~ to read⟩ **4 a :** capable of being borne **:** easily endurable ⟨a ~ illness⟩ ⟨a ~ misfortune⟩ **b :** able to be performed with little effort **:** demanding comparatively little energy or strength ⟨contributed to the family income by doing ~ work —M.S. Kendrick⟩ **5 :** capable of moving or acting swiftly and dexterously **:** NIMBLE ⟨although her hands were old and often tremulous, they were ~ at whatever they performed —Elizabeth M. Roberts⟩ ⟨a healthy stout man in a hurry, ~ on his feet —Glenway Wescott⟩ **6** *now Scot* **:** delivered of a child — used always in the comparative **7 a :** showing a lack of seriousness **:** FRIVOLOUS, GIDDY ⟨had forfeited by his ~ conduct and his intemperate opinions —Ellen Glasgow⟩ ⟨~ stories, risky anecdotes were discouraged —Gamaliel Bradford⟩ **b :** lacking in stability or steadiness **:** FICKLE, CHANGEABLE ⟨a ~ man, in whom no person can place any confidence —W.E.H.Lecky⟩ **c :** sexually promiscuous **:** WANTON ⟨their thoughts strayed to ~ women —John Steinbeck⟩ **8 :** free from care **:** not burdened by suffering **:** BUOYANT, CHEERFUL ⟨more pleased and ~ of mind than she had been —W.M. Thackeray⟩ **9 :** intended to amuse and entertain **:** demanding little mental effort of the reader, listener, or spectator ⟨one generation's ~ reading often becomes another's heavy text —J.D.Hart⟩ ⟨standard ~ ballet music — inoffensive until it overdoes the waltz —Arthur Berger⟩ **10** *of a beverage* **a :** having a comparatively low alcoholic content ⟨~ wines and beers⟩ **b :** having a low concentration of flavoring congenerics **:** characterized by a relatively mild flavor **:** not heavy **11 a :** capable of being easily digested ⟨a ~ soup⟩ **b :** well leavened **:** not soggy or heavy ⟨~ bread⟩ **c :** full of air **:** FLUFFY ⟨well beaten eggs make a ~ omelet⟩ ⟨a ~ soufflé⟩ **12 :** lightly armed or equipped ⟨a fairly ~ cavalry, not fully armored —Tom Wintringham⟩ **13 :** easily pulverized **:** LOOSE, POROUS ⟨a ~ soil⟩ **14 a** *of the head* **:** having a sensation of lightness or instability **:** DIZZY, GIDDY, DISORDERED **b** *now dial Brit* **:** light in the head **:** LIGHT-HEADED, GIDDY ⟨he's a bit ~ since his accident⟩ **15 :** carrying a small cargo or none at all **:** not heavily burdened ⟨the ship returned ~⟩ **16 :** characterized by a relatively small capital investment and the use of relatively simple machinery and usu. devoted to the production of consumer goods ⟨moving into the ~*er* industries like furniture manufacture —Sam Pollock⟩ **17 :** not heavy or massive in construction or appearance ⟨despite its size, the building is ~ and graceful⟩ **18 a** *of a syllable* **:** UNACCENTED, WEAK — contrasted with *heavy* **b :** designating the second-strongest of the three degrees of stress recognized by some linguists ⟨the stress on the last syllable of "basketball" is ~⟩ **c** *of a vowel* **:** articulated without raising of the back of the tongue ⟨the front vowels and \ä\ are ~⟩ — compare DARK **d** *of an l sound* **:** CLEAR 2b **19** *of sound* **:** having a clear usu. soft and airy quality without heaviness ⟨afraid that she would ruin her small ~ voice if she persisted in singing heavy operatic music —*Current Biog.*⟩ **20** *of poultry* **:** losing weight — see GOING LIGHT **21 :** of, relating to, or containing atoms of normal mass or less than normal mass — used of isotopes ⟨deuterium has twice the mass of ordinary ~ hydrogen atoms⟩ **22** *of a domino* **:** having a comparatively small number of pips ⟨the 6-3 is ~*er* than the 6-6⟩ **23 :** being in debt to the pot in a poker game ⟨three chips ~⟩ **syn** see EASY

**⁵light** \"\ *adv, usu* -ER/-EST [ME *lihte, lighte, light,* fr. OE *lēohte, līhte,* fr. *lēoht, līht,* adj.] **1 :** in a light manner **:** LIGHTLY ⟨experienced campers travel ~ —*Boy Scout Handbook*⟩ — often used in combination ⟨light-clad⟩ ⟨light-loaded⟩

**⁶light** \"\ *vb* **lighted** *or* **lit; lighted** *or* **lit; lighting; lights** [ME *lihten, lighten,* fr. OE *līhtan, līohtan;* akin to OFris *līchta* to lighten, MD *lichten,* OHG *līhten;* causative-denominative fr. the root of E ⁴*light*] *vi* **1 :** to climb downward (as from a horse) **:** DISMOUNT — now usu. used with *down* ⟨every time he *lit* down from his saddle —W.F.Harris⟩ **2 :** to descend on a surface **:** fall to the ground **:** PERCH, SETTLE ⟨laying waste every foot of the field they ~*ed* in —O.E.Rölvaag⟩ **3 :** to come down suddenly **:** fall unexpectedly (as of a blow, good fortune, or bad fortune) — usu. used with *on* or *upon* ⟨when he got that far . . . Nemesis *lit* on him —Elmer Davis⟩ **4 :** to come or arrive by chance **:** HAPPEN — usu. used with *on* or *upon* ⟨~*ed* upon the lonely spot quite by accident —Lady Barker⟩ **5** *now dial Brit* **a :** to come to pass **:** occur by chance **b :** to experience good or bad fortune or success **:** FARE — often used with *on* ~ *vt* **1** *archaic* **:** to ease of a burden or load **:** LIGHTEN ⟨this weary vessel of her load —Edmund Spenser⟩ **2** *now dial Eng* **:** to deliver of a child **3 :** HAUL, MOVE ⟨~ the sail out to windward —G.S.Nares⟩ — **light into :** to attack forcefully ⟨has *lit into* the Administration's tax bill with some sparkling epithets —*Wall Street Jour.*⟩ ⟨*lit into* that food until I'd finished off the heel of the loaf —Helen Eustis⟩

**light adaptation** *n* **:** the adjustments including narrowing of the pupillary opening, decrease in visual purple, and dispersion of melanophores by which the retina of the eye is made efficient as a visual receptor under conditions of strong illumination — compare DARK ADAPTATION

**light air** *n* **:** wind having a speed of 1 to 3 miles per hour — see BEAUFORT SCALE table

**light airplane** *n* **:** LIGHTPLANE

**light–armed** \'ˌ≈\ *adj* **:** armed with light weapons

**light artillery** *n* **:** guns and howitzers of no more than 105-millimeter caliber

**light battery** *n* **:** a battery of light artillery

**light–beam pickup** *n* **:** a phonograph pickup using a beam of light to couple the stylus to a light-sensitive converting element

**lightboat** \'≈,≈\ *n* **:** LIGHTSHIP

**light bob** *n* [⁴*light* + *bob* (nickname for *Robert*)] *Brit* **:** a light infantry soldier

**light bomber** *n* **:** a bomber of relatively light weight (as under 100,000 pounds) that is designed primarily to carry a moderate bombload against tactical targets (as bridges, barracks, convoys, and supply dumps) and is used also for strafing and rocketing ground targets — compare MEDIUM BOMBER, HEAVY BOMBER

**light box** *n* **:** a device for providing a strong uniform light on a surface (as for examining negatives or transparencies)

**light bread** *n, chiefly South & Midland* **:** wheat bread in loaves made from white flour leavened with yeast

**light breeze** *n* **:** wind having a speed of 4 to 7 miles per hour — see BEAUFORT SCALE table

**light bridge** *n* **:** ¹BRIDGE 3m(1)

**light–brown apple moth** *n* **:** a variable yellow and brown tortricid moth (*Tortrix postvittana*) that damages apple leaves in Australia and New Zealand

**light brunswick green** *n, often cap B* **:** a green that is yellower and paler than holly green (sense 1), lighter, stronger, and slightly yellower than deep chrome green, and yellower, lighter, and stronger than average hunter green or middle Brunswick green — called also *royal green;* compare DEEP BRUNSWICK GREEN

**light bulb** *n* **:** INCANDESCENT LAMP

**light chrome green** *n* **:** a green that is yellower and less strong than holly green (sense 1), yellower and darker than golf green, yellower, lighter, and stronger than average hunter green, and lighter and stronger than deep or medium chrome green — called also *navy green, Windsor green;* compare DEEP CHROME GREEN

**light chrome yellow** *n* **:** a strong yellow that is slightly less strong than yolk yellow and greener and stronger than gamboge — called also *Cologne yellow, gallstone, lemon chrome yellow, oxgall, Paris yellow, ultramarine yellow, zinc yellow*

**light comedy** *n* **:** comedy characterized by delicacy and wit

**light cruiser** *n* **:** a naval cruiser whose principal armament usu. consists of 6-inch guns — compare HEAVY CRUISER

**light curve** *n* **:** a curve expressing graphically the fluctuations in light of a variable star or other astronomical body (as a planet or asteroid)

**light displacement** *n* **:** the displacement of a ship completely equipped but unladen

**light–draft** \'≈'≈\ *adj, of a ship* **:** capable of operating in shallow waters

**light due** *or* **light duty** *n* **:** a toll levied on ships in certain waters for the upkeep of lighthouses and lightships

**light–duty** \'≈'≈≈\ *adj* **1 :** designed for occasional or moderate service only — used of a tool or a machine **2 :** capable of being done by a light-duty device

**lighted** *past of* LIGHT

**¹light·en** \'līt°n\ *vb* **lightened; lightened; lightening** \-t(°)niŋ\ **lightens** [ME *lihtenen, lightenen,* fr. *liht, light,* adj., light, bright — more at LIGHT (bright)] *vt* **1 a :** to throw light on **:** make light or clear **:** ILLUMINATE ⟨a moon riding high ~*ed* their path to the beach —Ernest Beaglehole⟩ **b :** to make brighter **:** lessen the darkness of ⟨~ the picture for consumption abroad —U.T.Holmes⟩ ⟨the good news ~*ed* his gloom⟩ **2** *archaic* **:** to illuminate intellectually or spiritually **:** ENLIGHTEN ⟨have power on this dark land to ~ it —Alfred Tennyson⟩ **3 :** to make lighter (as a shade or tint) ⟨~*ed* the blue paint before applying it to the wall⟩ ~ *vi* **1 a** *archaic* **:** to shine brightly **:** glow with light ⟨her lamp ~*s* in the tower —Sir Walter Scott⟩ **b :** to grow lighter **:** BRIGHTEN ⟨her face would ~ directly you entered the room —Osbert Sitwell⟩ **2 :** to give out flashes of lightning ⟨this dreadful night that thunders, ~*s,* opens graves, and roars —Shak.⟩

**²lighten** \"\ *vb* -ED/-ING/-S [ME *lihtenen, lightenen,* fr. *liht, light,* adj., light (not heavy) — more at LIGHT (not heavy)] *vt* **1 a :** to relieve of a burden in whole or in part ⟨~*s* the ship⟩ ⟨the good news ~*ed* his mind⟩ **b :** to reduce in weight or quantity **:** LESSEN ⟨every student educated at private expense ~*s* the burden on the state —T.L.Hungate⟩ ⟨decide to ~ their holdings of rayon goods —S.B.Hunt⟩ **2 :** to make happier **:** CHEER, GLADDEN ⟨the time since I wrote last has been ~*ed* by two jolly dinners —H.J.Laski⟩ **3 :** to make less wearisome **:** ALLEVIATE ⟨no companionship to ~ his work —Robertson Davies⟩ ⟨afraid of intruding upon a sorrow that I could not ~ —Oscar Wilde⟩ ~ *vi* **1 :** to become light or less heavy **:** become less burdensome ⟨some correspondents believe censorship has ~*ed* somewhat —*N.Y. Times*⟩ ⟨as the war debt ~*ed,* economic and commercial development was rapid —*Amer. Guide Series: La.*⟩ **2 :** to become more cheerful ⟨his mood ~*ed* and brightened as he figured things out —O.E. Rölvaag⟩ **syn** see RELIEVE

**light·en·er** \-t(°)nə(r)\ *n* -s **:** one that lightens

**light engine** *n* **:** a locomotive operating without cars attached or with caboose only

**lightening** *n* -s [fr. gerund of ²*lighten*] **:** a sense of decreased weight and abdominal tension felt by a pregnant woman on descent of the fetus into the pelvic cavity prior to labor

**lightening hole** *n* **:** a hole cut in a plate or structural member of a ship to reduce its weight without reducing its strength

**light equation** *n* **:** the 498.6 seconds required by light to traverse a distance equal to the mean radius of the earth's orbit

**¹light·er** \'līd·ə(r), -ītə-\ *n* -s [ME, fr. (assumed) MD *lichter* (whence D), fr. MD *lichten* to lighten, unload + *-er* — more at LIGHT (to ease of a burden)] **:** a large usu. flat-bottomed boat or barge that is mainly used in unloading or loading ships not lying at wharves or in transporting freight around a harbor

**²lighter** \"\ *vt* -ED \-ING\ -S **:** to convey by or as if by a lighter ⟨goods have to be ~*ed* half a mile or more between ship and shore —W.R. Moore⟩ ⟨they could ~ the stuff down to Colon —D.B.Chidsey⟩

**³lighter** \"\ *n* -s [³*light* + *-er*] **1 :** one that lights or sets fire ⟨a ~ of lamps⟩ ⟨excelled as a ~ of fires —D.L.Busk⟩ ⟨a pressurized can of charcoal ~⟩ **2 :** a device for lighting a fire; *esp* **:** a mechanical or electrical device used for lighting cigarettes, cigars, or pipes

**⁴lighter** *comparative of* LIGHT

**light·er·age** \-ərij, -rēj\ *n* -s [ME, fr. *lighter* + *-age*] **1 :** a price paid for lightering **2 :** the loading, unloading, or transportation of goods by means of a lighter ⟨organized the ~ service of the harbor —Joseph Conrad⟩ **3 :** the boats engaged in lightering

**lighterage limits** *n pl* **:** the area of a harbor within which lighter service is regularly provided under certain conditions and charges

**lighterman** \'līd·ə(r)mən\ *n, pl* **lightermen :** a person employed on a lighter

**light·er–out** \'līd·ə'raůt\ *n* -s [*light out,* v. + *-er*] **:** a worker who inspects the lining of beer barrels by inserting a light through the side hole and looking through the top

**lighter–than–air** \'≈≈≈'≈\ *adj* **:** of less weight than the air displaced — used of aircraft

**lightest** *superlative of* LIGHT

**lightface** \'≈,≈\ *n* **:** a typeface or font of characters having comparatively light thin lines (as *this*) — compare BOLDFACE

**lightfaced** \'≈'≈\ *adj* **:** of or referring to lightface

**lightfast** \'≈'≈\ *adj* **:** resistant to light and esp. to sunlight; *specif* **:** colorfast to light

**light·fast·ness** *n* -ES **:** ability to resist change by light and esp. by sunlight; *specif* **:** resistance to fading or change of color by light ⟨violet shades of outstanding ~⟩ ⟨testing dyed materials for ~⟩

**light field artillery** *n* **:** LIGHT ARTILLERY

**light filter** *n* **:** COLOR FILTER

**light–fingered** \'≈'≈≈\ *adj* **1 :** adroit and skillful in stealing esp. by picking pockets **2 :** having a light and dexterous touch ⟨a *light-fingered* burglar who can crack the combination of a bank vault —Harry Hansen⟩ **:** NIMBLE ⟨the *light-fingered* thoughtfulness, the ironic lyricism of the most civilized playwright of the era —*Time*⟩ — **light–fin·gered·ness** *n* -ES

**light flux** *n* **:** LUMINOUS FLUX

**light–foot** \'≈,≈\ *adj* [ME *lightfot,* fr. *light* + *fot* foot — more at LIGHT (not heavy), FOOT] **:** LIGHT-FOOTED ⟨impressed by their *light-foot* walk and their easy carriage —John Buchan⟩

**light–footed** \'≈'≈≈\ *adj* [ME *liht fotyd,* fr. *liht, light* + *fotyd, foted,* footed fr. *fot* foot + *-ed*] **1 :** having a light and springy step ⟨a *light-footed* girl⟩ **2 :** moving gracefully and nimbly ⟨this last, incredibly *light-footed,* transparent opera —Curt Sachs⟩ — **light–foot·ed·ly** *adv* — **light–foot·ed·ness** *n*

**light·ful** \'lītfəl\ *adj* [ME *lihtful, lightful,* fr. *liht, light* + *-ful* — more at LIGHT] *archaic* **:** full of light **:** BRIGHT ⟨the hall within was ~ and airy —A.Conan Doyle⟩ — **light·ful·ness** *n*

**light–grasp** \'≈,≈\ *n* **:** the light-gathering power of a telescope

**light green SF yellowish** *or* **light green SF** *n, usu cap L&G&Y* **:** an acid triphenylmethane dye used chiefly as a biological stain and color for foods — see DYE table (under *Acid Green 5*)

**light grège** *n* **:** PIPING ROCK

**light gunmetal** *n* **:** PELICAN 4

**light–handed** \'≈'≈≈\ *adj* [ME *lyghte handyd*] **1 :** having a light or delicate hand or touch ⟨the translation . . . is very good, being *light-handed,* apparently effortless, and generally unobtrusive —*New Yorker*⟩ **2** *archaic* **:** having little to carry **3 :** SHORTHANDED — **light–hand·ed·ness** *n*

**light harness** *n* **:** a class of show or race horses

**light–headed** \'≈'≈≈\ *adj* **1 :** disordered in the head **:** DELIRIOUS **:** DIZZY ⟨so *light-headed* from no sleep that my head felt big as the sky —R.P.Warren⟩ **2 :** lacking in maturity or seriousness **:** FRIVOLOUS, HEEDLESS ⟨like the teen-agers they are, tender, graceful, *light-headed* —Walter Goodman⟩ — **light–head·ed·ly** *adv* — **light–head·ed·ness** *n* -ES

**light·heart·ed** \ˈ≈ˌ≈≈\ *adj* [ME *ligt-herted*] **1 :** free from care or anxiety **:** GAY, HIGH-SPIRITED ⟨~ and cheerful to an irrepressible degree —Merran McCulloch⟩ — opposed to *heavyhearted* **2 :** cheerfully optimistic and hopeful **:** CASUAL ⟨this ~ trust in evolution —M.R.Cohen⟩ ⟨like other old races . . . they can be ~ in the midst of misery and joke at their own expense —H.J.Forman⟩ **syn** see GLAD

**light·heart·ed·ly** *adv* **:** in a lighthearted manner ⟨~ overlooks some of the less noble but basic facts of international life —S.L.Sharp⟩ ⟨sending them out to continue the war that was so ~ entered upon —C.S.Forester⟩

**light·heart·ed·ness** *n* **:** the quality or state of being lighthearted ⟨scientists are unduly sensitive to any suspicion of ~ in serious journals —T.H.Savory⟩ ⟨smiled innocently at their ~ —Robert Hichens⟩

**light heavyweight** *n* **1** *also* **light heavy :** a boxer weighing more than 160 but not over 175 pounds **2 :** a wrestler weighing more than 174 but not over 191 pounds

**light-heeled** \ˈ≈ˌ≈\ *adj* **1** *archaic* **:** lively in walking or running **:** BRISK, NIMBLE ⟨the villain is much *lighter-heel'd* than I, I followed fast, but faster he did fly —Shak.⟩ **2** *archaic* **:** UNCHASTE, WANTON

**lighthouse** \ˈ≈ˌ≈\ *n* **:** a tower or other building equipped to guide navigators by means of a powerful light that gives a continuous or interrupted signal

lighthouse

**lighthouse keeper** \ˈ≈ˌ≈ˌ≈≈\ *n* **:** one who maintains a lighthouse and operates the light and fog signals

**light housekeeping** \(ˈ)≈ˈ≈ˌ≈≈\ *n* **1 :** domestic work restricted to the less laborious duties (as dusting or using a vacuum cleaner) **2 :** housekeeping in a room or apartment with limited facilities for cooking

**lighthouse tube** *n* **:** a triode that is shaped like a tiered lighthouse and that develops ultrahigh-frequency power — called also *megatron*

**light·ing** \ˈlīd·iŋ, -ītˌ, |ēŋ\ *n* -S [ME *lihting, lighting,* fr. OE *lihting,* fr. *lihten* to light + *-ing* — more at LIGHT (to illuminate)] **1 a :** ILLUMINATION ⟨the only ~ comes through a small window⟩ **b :** the action of setting on fire **:** IGNITION ⟨the ~ of the candle⟩ ⟨the ~ of the fire⟩ **2 :** an incidence or disposition of light (as in a painting) ⟨a good portrait except for the ~ of the hands⟩ **3 :** an artificial supply of light or the apparatus providing it

**light·ish** \ˈlīd·ish\ *adj* **:** rather light ⟨the lean, *lightish*-haired young man —Kay Boyle⟩

**lightkeeper** \ˈ≈ˌ≈≈\ *n* **:** one who is in charge of a lighthouse or lightship

**light·less** \ˈlītləs\ *adj* [ME *lihtles, lightles,* fr. OE *lēohtlēas,* fr. *lēoht* light + *-lēas* -less — more at LIGHT] **1 :** receiving no light **:** without illumination **:** DARK ⟨came up the ~ stairs —James Jones⟩ **2 :** giving no light ⟨tells us of ~ stars, "visible" only to radio antennae —*Scientific American Reader*⟩

**light·less·ness** *n* -ES **:** the quality or state of being lightless **:** DARKNESS

**light lock** *n* **:** LIGHT TRAP

**¹light·ly** *adv* [ME *lihtly, lightly,* fr. OE *lēohtlīce,* fr. *lēohtlic,* adj., light, fr. *lēoht* light + *-lic* -ly (adj. suffix) — more at LIGHT (not heavy)] **1 :** with little weight **:** with little force or pressure **:** not heavily or severely **:** BUOYANTLY, GENTLY ⟨wearing its mantle of history ~ —Richard Joseph⟩ ⟨~ kneaded to produce a fine texture —*Amer. Guide Series: N.C.*⟩ ⟨that odd superstition that the dead sleep ~ —Margery Allingham⟩ ⟨these sixty years he wears ~ —I.A.Gordon⟩ ⟨the little boat floated ~ on the sea⟩ **2 :** in a small degree or quantity **:** to no great extent or amount ⟨land ~ wooded with a varied growth —*Amer. Guide Series: La.*⟩ ⟨~ infected with the disease, recovering quite promptly —Morris Fishbein⟩ ⟨~ damaged⟩ ⟨~ fried eggs⟩ **3 :** with little effort or difficulty **:** EASILY, READILY ⟨did not get off so ~ —Jean Stafford⟩ ⟨much more deeply rooted and much less ~ resolved —Marjorie Grene⟩ **4 :** with agility **:** NIMBLY, SWIFTLY ⟨leaped ~ over the extended tongues of wagons and buggies —Sherwood Anderson⟩ **5 :** without strong cause or reason ⟨the experiment which had so nearly ended in disaster was not to be ~ repeated —J.T.McNish⟩ ⟨not a man to propose anything ~ —Bernard DeVoto⟩ **6 :** with indifference or lack of care **:** SLIGHTINGLY, UNCONCERNEDLY ⟨she says it ~ but she means it —Walter Havighurst⟩ ⟨a terrific responsibility, and one that we do not take ~ —*N. Y. Times Mag.*⟩ **7 :** without dejection **:** CHEERFULLY, GAILY ⟨an end that shall ~ and joyfully meet its translation —Walt Whitman⟩ ⟨not his words, for they were spoken ~ enough —J.E.Simmons⟩

**²light·ly** \ˈliktli\ *vt* -ED/-ING/-ES [ME (Sc) *lightlien,* fr. *lihtly, lightly* frivolous, fr. OE *lēohtlic* light] *chiefly Scot* **:** to make light of **:** treat slightingly **:** BELITTLE

**light machine gun** *n* **:** an air-cooled machine gun of not more than .30 caliber

**light marching order** *n* **:** an equipment of troops consisting of at most a canteen and haversack with arms and ammunition

**light meat** *n* **:** light-colored meat (as veal)

**light metal** *n* **:** a metal or alloy of low density (as aluminum, magnesium, titanium and beryllium, and alloys composed predominantly of one or more of these metals)

**light meter** *n* **:** a small portable illuminometer usu. of the photovoltaic type **:** EXPOSURE METER

**light-minded** \ˈ≈ˈ≈≈\ *adj* **:** lacking in moral earnestness **:** FRIVOLOUS, TRIFLING ⟨felt that it was a *light-minded* room, a room for sinning in evening clothes —Sinclair Lewis⟩ ⟨completely *light-minded* and unmoral and the events . . . are those of a racy morning tabloid —Rosemary Benét⟩

**light-mind·ed·ly** *adv* **:** in a light-minded manner

**light-mind·ed·ness** *n* **:** the quality or state of being light-minded

**¹light·ness** *n* -ES [ME *lihtnesse, lightnesse,* fr. OE *līhtnes,* fr. *lēoht, līht* bright + *-nes* -ness — more at LIGHT (bright)] **1 :** the quality or state of being illuminated **:** ILLUMINATION ⟨the ~ of the room⟩ ⟨the ~ of the sky⟩ **2 :** the attribute of object colors by which the object appears to reflect or transmit more or less of the incident light and which varies for surface colors from black as a minimum to white as a maximum and for transparent volume colors from black to colorless

**²lightness** *n* -ES [ME *lihtnesse, lightnesse,* fr. *liht, light* light + *-nesse* -ness — more at LIGHT (not heavy)] **1 :** the quality or state of being light or having little weight ⟨the primary object of the Gothic vault was its appearance of immaterial ~ —Nikolaus Pevsner⟩ ⟨the ~ of the bread⟩ **2 :** a lack of seriousness or dignity **:** LEVITY ⟨the ~ of tone with which I uttered such serious words —E.J.Goodman⟩ **3 a :** ease of movement **:** NIMBLENESS ⟨trotted up the stair with much ~ —John Brown⟩ **b :** an ease and gaiety of style or manner ⟨a charming ~ of speech —Shane Leslie⟩ ⟨a ~ of inflection that made the statement seem disarming —H.V.Gregory⟩ **4 :** an absence of heaviness or pressure ⟨a comparable feathery ~ of touch —A.M.Daintrey⟩ **5 :** GRACEFULNESS ⟨the ~ of her figure⟩

**¹light·ning** \ˈlītniŋ, -nēŋ\ *n* -S [ME *lightning, lightening,* fr. gerund of *lihtenen, lightenen* to lighten — more at LIGHTEN (illuminate)] **1** *obs* **:** the action of giving light **:** ILLUMINATION, ENLIGHTENMENT ⟨a ~ before death —Shak.⟩ **2 :** the flashing of light produced by a discharge of atmospheric electricity from one cloud to another or from a cloud to the earth; *also* **:** the discharge itself **3** *slang* **:** cheap whiskey of poor quality **4 :** a sudden stroke of good fortune; *esp* **:** a nomination or selection for high political office ⟨a multiplicity of candidates, including favorite sons hoping for real ~ to strike —*Time*⟩ **5** *often cap* **:** one of a class of racing sailboats about 19 feet in length that are sloop-rigged and have a centerboard

**²lightning** \"\ *adj* **:** moving with or having the speed and suddenness of lightning ⟨the jargon of the auctioneer as he works with ~ rapidity —*Amer. Guide Series: N.C.*⟩ ⟨the ~ speed of modern warfare —F.D.Roosevelt⟩ ⟨superb fighters, masters of the ~ raid —Seth Agnew⟩ ⟨made ~ descents on the native villages —Tom Marvel⟩

**³lightning** \"\ *vi* **lightninged; lightninged; lightning; lightnings :** to discharge a flash of lightning ⟨it is *lightning* more than ever⟩ ⟨it ~*ed* terribly last night⟩

**lightning arrester** *n* **1 :** any of various devices for protecting an electrical apparatus and its operator from injury by a momentary abnormal rise of voltage caused by lightning or other surges **2 :** a protective device usu. used in parallel with a radio set to carry accumulations of static electricity and minor lightning discharges to the ground without going through the radio set

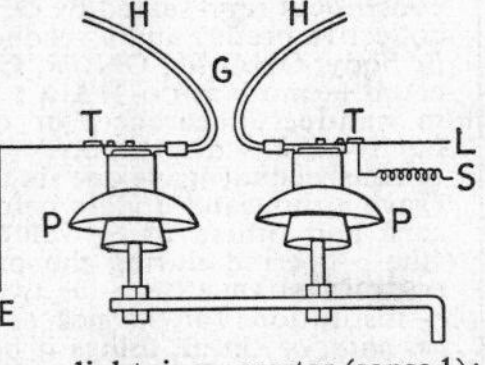


horn lightning arrester (sense 1): *G* spark gap; *H,H,* diverging horns; *P,P,* insulators; *T,T,* terminals; *E* ground; *L* line; *S* station

**lightning bug** *n* **:** FIREFLY

**lightning calculator** *n* **:** a person able to solve arithmetical problems mentally with extraordinary speed

**lightning chess** *n* **:** RAPID TRANSIT

**lightning conductor** *n* **:** a conductor leading from a lightning rod to the ground

**lightning pains** *n pl* **:** intense shooting or lancinating pains occurring in locomotor ataxia

**lightningproof** \ˈ≈≈ˌ≈\ *adj* **:** protected from lightning

**lightning rod** *n* **1 :** a metallic rod set up on a building or mast and connected with the moist earth or water below to diminish the chances of destructive effect by lightning **2 :** a person or object that serves to divert attack from another ⟨serves as the *lightning rod* for complaints by our friends and allies abroad —Dorothy Fosdick⟩

**lightning stone** *or* **lightning tube** *n* **:** FULGURITE

**lightning storm** *n* **:** THUNDERSTORM ⟨the *lightning storm* in the night had touched off the fire —Hugh Fosburgh⟩

**lightning switch** *n* **:** a switch used in an antenna circuit (as during lightning storms) to connect the antenna to the ground instead of to the radio set

**lightning war** *n* **:** a war marked by surprise and speed of movement and intended to achieve victory quickly for the attacking power — compare BLITZKRIEG

**light of the moon :** the period between the new moon and the full moon

**light oil** *n* **1 :** an oil of low specific gravity or relatively low boiling point (as below about 200° C): as **a :** a flammable product obtained by the distillation of coal tar and containing aromatic hydrocarbons, phenols, and pyridine **b :** a somewhat similar product recovered from wash oil after the scrubbing of coke-oven gas and used as a source of benzene and other aromatic hydrocarbons **c :** naphtha or other flammable petroleum distillate **2 :** a crude petroleum having a high Baumé gravity (as 30° or higher)

**light-o'-love** *also* **light-of-love** \ˈ≈ˌ≈ˈ≈\ *n, pl* **light-o'-loves** *also* **light-of-loves 1 :** a light woman **:** PROSTITUTE ⟨couldn't disapprove of me any more obviously if I were a *light-o'-love* you'd picked up on the street —B.A.Williams⟩ **2 :** LOVER, PARAMOUR

**light opera** *n* **:** opera that has a usu. gay and relatively trivial subject matter and a conventional and tuneful musical treatment — compare COMIC OPERA

**light out** *vi* [⁶*light*] **:** to leave in a hurry **:** start quickly ⟨after the spring roundup, ranch hands *light out* for the nearest cow town and a good time —S.E.Fletcher⟩

**light pillar** *n* **:** a white halo extending vertically above and below the sun or moon and caused by reflection from the upper and under surfaces of snow crystals

**lightplane** \ˈ≈ˌ≈\ *n* **:** a small and comparatively lightweight airplane; *esp* **:** a privately owned passenger airplane — called also *light airplane*

**light plot** *n* **:** a plan and complete set of instructions for lighting a stage production (as a play or opera)

**light pressure** *n* **:** the radiation pressure of light

**lightproof** \ˈ≈ˌ≈\ *adj* **:** impenetrable by light

**light quantum** *n* **:** PHOTON; *esp* **:** one of luminous radiation

**light railway** *n* **:** a railroad not properly equipped for ordinary heavy traffic: **a :** a railroad restricted to light traffic under British statutory laws **b :** a narrow-gage railroad

**light red** *n* **1 a :** a red that is lighter than moderate or grayish red **b :** a dark pink **2 :** BURNT OCHER 2 **3 :** any of various pale red or reddish orange pigments; *esp* **:** a calcined yellow ocher

**light red silver ore** *or* **light ruby silver ore** *n* **:** PROUSTITE

**light repair** *n* **:** a repair to freight cars in revenue service requiring no more than 20 man-hours of work

**light repeater** *n* **:** a device for conveying information on the condition of a railroad signal light

**lightroom** \ˈ≈ˌ≈\ *n* **:** the chamber in a lighthouse that contains the lamp

**lights** \ˈlīts\ *n pl* [ME *lihte, lihtes, lightes,* fr. *liht, light,* adj., light (not heavy) — more at LIGHT] **1** *now dial* **:** LUNGS ⟨his liver began to grow into his ~ and the doctors couldn't save him —L.P.Hartley⟩ **2 :** the lungs of a slaughtered animal

**light sails** *n pl* **:** the sails carried on a sailing ship only in light winds

**light·scot** \ˈlītˌskät\ *n* [trans. of OE *lēohtgesceot, lēohtsceot*] *Old Eng law* **:** a tax of half a penny per hide of land for church candles

**light sensitization** *n* **:** PHOTOSENSITIZATION

**lightship** \ˈ≈ˌ≈\ *n* **:** a ship that is equipped with various signaling and warning devices including a brilliant light at the masthead and that is moored off a shoal or place of dangerous navigation where a lighthouse is impracticable

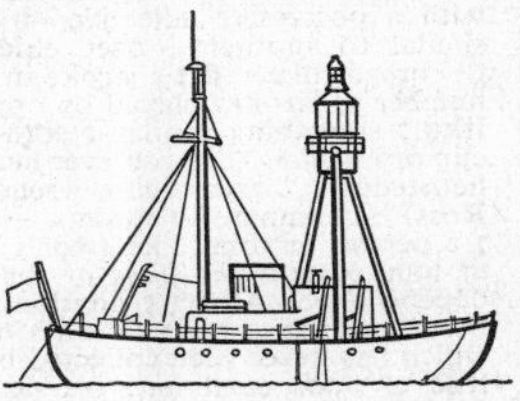

lightship

**light sickness** *n* **:** a disease of animals caused by photosensitization

**light-skirts** \ˈ≈ˌ≈\ *n pl but sing in constr* **:** a loose woman

**¹light·some** \ˈlītsəm\ *adj* [ME *lihtsum, lightsum,* fr. *liht, light* light + *-sum* -some — more at LIGHT] **1 :** marked by lightness **:** AIRY, GRACEFUL, NIMBLE ⟨too old and portly for more ~ parts —J.W.Draper⟩ ⟨walked with a ~, buoyant step —O.E.Rölvaag⟩ ⟨this talk may be . . . as ~ as the white smoke of coals in a severe campfire —J.F.Dobie⟩ **2 :** free from care **:** CHEERFUL, GAY ⟨expecting to indulge in an evening of ~ frolic —Theodore Dreiser⟩ ⟨trilling songs with a ~ heart —W.M.Thackeray⟩ **3 :** FRIVOLOUS, UNSTEADY ⟨a ~, changeable person⟩ — **light·some·ly** *adv* — **light·some·ness** *n* -ES

**²lightsome** \"\ *adj* [ME *lihtsum, lightsum,* fr. *liht, light* light + *-sum* -some — more at LIGHT (not heavy)] **1 :** giving light **:** LUMINOUS ⟨~ clouds and shining seas —P.B.Shelley⟩ **2 :** not dark or gloomy **:** well lighted **:** BRIGHT ⟨a school with spacious ~ rooms⟩ **3** *archaic* **:** CLEAR, LUCID ⟨with plain and ~ brevity —John Milton⟩ **4** *archaic* **:** light in color ⟨~ green of ivy and holly —J.R.Lowell⟩

**lights-out** \ˈ≈ˈ≈\ *n, pl* **lights-out 1 :** a command or signal (as a bell or bugle call) for putting out lights **2 :** a prescribed bedtime for persons living under discipline (as in a boarding school or army camp) ⟨the only place where he could hide to study after *lights-out* —H.H.Martin⟩ ⟨while away the hours before *lights-out* —*English Digest*⟩

**light splitter** *n* **:** BEAM SPLITTER

**light stand** *n* **:** a small stand or table on which a light is put

**light stone** *n* **:** a grayish to dark grayish yellow that is very slightly redder than golden green — called also *Portland stone*

**light-struck** \ˈ≈ˌ≈\ *adj* **:** having reference to a light-sensitive photographic material fogged by accidental exposure to light

**lighttight** \ˈ≈ˌ≈\ *adj* **:** LIGHTPROOF

**light-time** \ˈ≈ˌ≈\ *n* **:** the time required for light to travel from any specified heavenly body to the earth

**light trap** *n* **1 a :** a passageway (as for a photographic darkroom) provided with double doors, curtains, or bends to allow passage of a person while excluding light **b :** a device (as for a photographic apparatus) that allows free passage of air or movement of a sliding part but excludes light — called also *light lock* **2 :** a device for collecting or destroying insects that consists of a bright light in association with a suitable trapping or killing medium

**light valve** *n* **:** an electromagnetically operated device whose light transmission varies in accordance with an electrical quantity (as current) and that is used esp. in recording sound on motion-picture film

**light verse** *n* **:** verse that is written mainly to amuse and entertain and that is often marked by qualities of wit, elegance, and lyric beauty

**light vessel** *n* **:** LIGHTSHIP

**light wedgwood** *n, often cap W* **:** a grayish blue — distinguished from *dark Wedgwood*

**¹lightweight** \ˈ≈ˌ≈\ *n* [⁴*light* + *weight*] **1 :** one of less than average weight: as **a :** a boxer weighing more than 126 but not over 135 pounds **b :** a wrestler weighing more than 134 but not over 145 pounds **2 a :** a person lacking in strength of character or intellectual depth ⟨shows up its author as a ~ —C.J.Rolo⟩ ⟨if she hadn't been the ~, the weakling she was —Donn Byrne⟩ **b :** a person inadequately qualified for the position he fills or the duties he is charged with ⟨the muddled thinking of a ~ in diplomacy —*Times Lit. Supp.*⟩

**²lightweight** \"\ *adj* **1 :** of or relating to a lightweight ⟨a ~ bout⟩ ⟨the ~ championship⟩ **2 :** having less than average weight without fully corresponding lessening of strength, warmth, or other desirable quality ⟨~ aluminum railroad cars⟩ ⟨a ~ sweater⟩ **3 :** lacking in earnestness or profundity **:** not to be taken seriously ⟨a ~ kid who gets by on bare maintenance mentality —*Mademoiselle*⟩ ⟨~ discourses on long dead and justly forgotten court ladies —*Saturday Rev.*⟩

**lightweight aggregate** *n* **:** an aggregate for structural concrete, mortar, or plaster that weighs less than the usual rock aggregate

**light well** *n* **:** a shaft designed to admit light to the interior rooms of a building

**light wine** *n* **:** TABLE WINE

**light within** *n, pl* **lights within** *usu cap L&W* **:** INNER LIGHT

**light·wood** \ˈlītˌwu̇d, *Southern usu* ˈlīd·|əd *or* -ˌīt| *or chiefly dial* |ərd\ *n* **1** *chiefly South* **:** a dry wood that burns readily **:** KINDLING WOOD; *esp* **:** coniferous wood abounding in pitch **2 a :** an Australian acacia (*Acacia melanoxylon*) — called also *blackwood* **b :** any of several trees (as the candlewood) containing flammable volatile substances

**light-year** \ˈ≈ˌ≈\ *n* [¹*light*] **:** a unit of length in interstellar astronomy equal to the distance that light travels in one year in a vacuum or 5,878,000,000,000 miles

**light yellowwood** *n* **1 :** any of several timber trees with yellow wood: as **a** *southern Africa* **:** a podocarp (*Podocarpus thunbergii*) **b** *Austral* (1) **:** SASSAFRAS 3a(2) (2) **:** a flindersia (*Flindersia oxleyana*) (3) **:** ARBORVITAE 1 **2 :** the wood of a light yellowwood tree

**lig·ia** \ˈlijēə, lə'ljīə\ *n, cap* [NL, prob. after *Ligia,* a siren in ancient Greek mythology, fr. Gk *Ligeia*] **:** a genus of large dark-colored active terrestrial isopod crustaceans (the type of the family Ligiidae) having long antennae and uropods and living about wharves and among rocks along seacoasts — see WHARF MONKEY

**lign-** *or* **ligni-** *or* **ligno-** *comb form* [L *lign-, ligni-,* fr. *lignum* — more at LIGNEOUS] **1 :** wood ⟨*ligni*form⟩ ⟨*ligni*vorous⟩ ⟨*ligno*graphy⟩ **2** [ISV, fr. *lignin*] **:** lignin ⟨*ligno*protein⟩ ⟨*ligno*sulfonic acid⟩

**lign·al·oe** \līnˈa(ˌ)lō, ligˈ-\ *or* **lign·al·oes** \-ōz\ *n* [ME *ligne aloes,* fr. MF *lignaloe, lignaloes,* fr. ML *lignum aloes,* lit., wood of the aloe] **1 :** AGALLOCH **2 :** LINALOA

**lignaloe oil** *n* **:** LINALOE OIL

**ligne** \ˈlēnʸ\ *n* -S [F, lit., line, fr. L *linea* — more at LINE] **:** any of various units of measure: as **a :** a French unit for watch movements equal to 0.0888 inch **b :** a Swiss unit for watches equal to 0.0802 inch **c :** LINE 9a(2)

**lig·ne·ous** \ˈlignēəs\ *adj* [L *ligneus,* fr. *lignum* wood (fr. *legere* to gather) + *-eus* -eous — more at LEGEND] **:** of or resembling wood **:** WOODY

**lig·nes·cent** \(ˈ)ligˈnesᵊnt\ *adj* [*lign-* + *-escent*] **:** somewhat woody **:** tending toward woodiness

**lig·ni·fi·ca·tion** \ˌlignəfəˈkāshən\ *n* -S **:** the action or process of being or becoming lignified

**lig·ni·fy** \ˈlignəˌfī\ *vb* -ED/-ING/-ES [F *lignifier,* fr. *lign-* + *-fier* -fy] *vt* **:** to convert into wood or woody tissue ~ *vi* **:** to become wood or woody by chemical and physical changes in the cell walls that convert some or all of the constituents into lignin or lignocellulose — compare CUTICULARIZED, CUTINIZED, SUBERIZATION

**lig·nin** \ˈlignən\ *n* -S [*lign-* + *-in*] **1 :** an amorphous substance or mixture that together with cellulose forms the woody cell walls of plants and the cementing material between them and thus gives them added mechanical strength, that is a polymeric material characterized by a higher carbon content than cellulose and by propyl-benzene units, methoxyl groups, and hydroxyl groups, and that is not hydrolyzed by acids but is soluble in hot alkali and bisulfite and is readily oxidizable **2 :** any of various usu. brown products obtained from wood or woody plants by separation from cellulosic materials and often other organic materials: as **a :** a brown amorphous insoluble powder recovered from the black liquor resulting from the sulfate or soda process of making cellulosic pulp and used chiefly as a binder, filler, and extender (as in phenolic resins) — called also *alkali lignin* **b :** a brown amorphous powder recovered from sulfite liquor and composed usu. of ligninsulfonates — called also *sulfite lignin*

**ligninsulfonate** \ˌ≈≈ˈ≈≈ˌ≈\ *or* **lig·no·sulfonate** \ˌlignō+\ *n* [*lignin* or *lign-* + *sulphonate*] **:** a salt of a ligninsulfonic acid

**ligninsulfonic acid** \ˌ≈≈(ˌ)≈ˈ≈≈-\ *or* **lig·no·sulfonic acid** \ˌlignō+ . . . -\ *n* [ISV *lignin* or *lign-* + *sulfonic*] **:** any of various sulfonic acids derived from lignin; *esp* **:** those found as calcium or other soluble salts in sulfite liquor and used chiefly in tanning, as dispersing agents, and as raw materials for the manufacture of vanillin

**lig·ni·per·dous** \ˌlignəˈpərdəs\ *adj* [*lign-* + L *perdere* to destroy + E *-ous* — more at PERDITION] **:** that destroys wood ⟨a ~ insect⟩

**lig·nite** \ˈligˌnīt, *usu* -īd.+V\ *n* -S [F, fr. *lign-* + *-ite*] **:** a variety of coal intermediate between peat and bituminous coal that is of comparatively recent origin, contains much volatile matter, and is usu. brownish black; *esp* **:** such coal in which the texture of the original wood is distinct — called also *brown coal, wood coal* — **lig·nit·ic** \(ˈ)ligˈnid·|ik, -it|, |ēk\ *adj*

**lig·ni·tif·er·ous** \ˌlignəˈtif(ə)rəs\ *adj* [ISV *lignite* + *-i-* + *-ferous*] **:** containing lignite

**lig·ni·tize** \ˈlignəˌtīz\ *vt* -ED/-ING/-S [*lignite* + *-ize*] **:** to convert into lignite

**lig·no·cellulose** \ˌlignō+\ *n* [ISV *lign-* + *cellulose*] **:** any of several closely related substances constituting the essential part of woody cell walls and consisting of cellulose intimately associated with lignin — **lig·no·cellulosic** \"+\ *adj*

**lig·no·cer·ic acid** \ˌlignəˈserik-\ *n* [*lignoceric* ISV *lign-* + *cer-* + *-ic*] **:** a crystalline fatty acid $CH_3(CH_2)_{22}COOH$ found esp. in wood tar (as from beechwood) and in the form of esters in many fats, fatty oils, and waxes

**lig·no·sae** \ligˈnō(ˌ)sē\ *n pl, cap* [NL, fr. L, fem. pl. of *lignosus* woody, fr. *lign-* + *-osus* -ous] *in some classifications* **:** a phylum comprising all those plants that are fundamentally woody and remain predominantly so — compare HERBACEAE

**lig·no·tuber** \ˈlig(ˌ)nō+\ *n* [*lign-* + *tuber*] **:** BURL 2a

**lig·num** \ˈlignəm\ *n, pl* **lignums** \-mz\ *also* **lig·na** \-nə\ [NL, fr. L, wood — more at LIGNEOUS] **1 :** woody tissue **2 :** any of various trees (as lignum vitae) **3** *Austral* **:** any of various polygonaceous plants

**lignum aloes** *n pl but usu sing in constr* [ME, fr. ML, lit., wood of the aloe] **:** LIGNALOE

**lig·num vi·tae** \ˈlignəmˈvīd·|ē, -ītˌ, |ī\ *n, pl* **lignum vitaes** [NL, fr. LL, a tree, lit., wood of life] **1 :** any of several trees of the genus *Guaiacum:* as **a :** a tropical American tree (*G. officinale*) found esp. in the West Indies **b :** BASTARD LIGNUM VITAE **2 :** the wood of lignum vitae **3** *Austral* **:** any of various hardwood trees (as members of the genera *Metrosideros, Acacia, Eucalyptus,* and *Vitex*) **4 :** SANDARAC TREE 1

**lig·ro·in** *also* **lig·ro·ine** \ˈligrəwən\ *n* -S [origin unknown] **:** any of several petroleum naphtha fractions boiling usu. in the range 20° to 135°C that commonly have a specified boiling range whether narrow (as for petroleum pentane or petroleum hexane) or wide (as 40° to 75°C) and that are used chiefly as solvents

**ligul-** or **liguli-** comb form [NL [1]ligula] **1 :** ligule ⟨*ligul*ar⟩ ⟨*liguli*form⟩ : ligulate ⟨*liguli*florous⟩ **2** [NL [2]*Ligula*] **:** the genus Ligula ⟨*ligul*oid⟩

[1]**lig·u·la** \ˈligyələ\ n, pl **ligu·lae** \-yə,lē\ also **ligulas** [NL, fr. L, small tongue, small strap, spoon — more at LIGULE] **1 :** LIGULE **2 :** a band of white matter in the wall of the fourth ventricle of the brain **3 :** the distal lobed part of the labium of an insect consisting typically of a pair of median glossae and a pair of lateral paraglossae

[2]**ligula** n [NL, fr. L, small tongue, small strap, spoon] **1** cap **:** a genus of tapeworms (family Diphyllobothriidae) that lack external evidence of segmentation, are extremely short-lived intestinal parasites of fish-eating birds or rarely of man as adults, and develop almost to maturity in the body cavity of freshwater fishes **2** -s **:** a larval tapeworm developing reproductive organs and living in the body cavity of a fish

**lig·u·lar** \ˈligyələ(r)\ adj [ligul- + -ar] **:** LIGULATE

**lig·u·lar·ia** \,ligyəˈla(a)rēə\ n, cap [NL, fr. L *ligula* small tongue, small strap, spoon + NL -aria — more at LIGULE] **:** a genus of Old World herbs (family Compositae) resembling the groundsel and having the margins of the involucral bracts overlapping — see LEOPARD PLANT

**lig·u·late** \ˈligyələt, -yə,lāt\ adj [L & NL *ligula* + E -ate] **1 :** shaped like a strap — used of the narrow flat corollas of the ray flowers in a composite plant **2 :** furnished with ligules, ligulae, or ligulate corollas

**lig·u·lat·ed** \-ād·əd\ adj [L & NL *ligula* + E -ate + -ed] **:** LIGULATE

**lig·ule** \ˈli,gyül\ n -s [NL *ligula*, fr. L, spoon; akin to L *lingere* to lick — more at LICK] **1 a :** a thin appendage of a foliage leaf; esp **:** one forming a membranous projection from the top of the leaf sheath of a grass **b :** a ligulate corolla of a ray floret in a composite head **c :** a membranous scale on the leaf above the sporangium in *Selaginella* and *Isoetes* **d :** a scale associated with the ovule in *Araucaria* **2 :** a lobe like a tongue on the parapodia of an annelid

**lig·u·li·flo·rous** \ˈligyələˈflōrəs, -lȯr-\ adj [ISV ligul- + -florous] **:** having ligulate flowers

**lig·u·loid** \ˈligyə,lȯid\ adj [ligul- + -oid] **:** of or relating to the genus *Ligula*

**lig·ure** \ˈli,gyü(ə)r\ n -s [LL *ligurius*, fr. Gk *ligyrion*] **:** a precious stone that is prob. the jacinth ⟨the third row a ~, an agate, and an amethyst —Exod 28:19 (AV)⟩

[1]**li·gu·ri·an** \ləˈgyürēən\ n -s cap **1 :** a native or inhabitant of ancient Liguria **2 :** a language known from a small body of inscriptions from the area inhabited by the ancient Ligurians and generally considered as having affinities with Indo-European **3 :** a native or inhabitant of modern Liguria

[2]**ligurian** \"\ adj, usu cap **1** [*Liguria*, country in southwestern Europe + E -an] **:** of, relating to, or characteristic of ancient Liguria or its people **2** [*Liguria*, compartimento of Italy + E -an] **:** of, relating to, or characteristic of the modern Italian compartimento of Liguria or its people

**lig·u·rite** \ˈligyə,rīt\ n -s [F *ligurite*, fr. *Liguria*, compartimento of Italy + F -ite] **:** an apple-green variety of sphene

**li·gus·ti·cum** \ləˈgəstəkəm\ [NL, fr. L, lovage — more at LOVAGE] syn of LEVISTICUM

**lig·us·tra·les** \,ligəˈstrā(,)lēz\ [NL, fr. *Ligustrum*, type genus + -ales] syn of OLEALES

**li·gus·trum** \-trəm\ n, cap [NL, fr. L, privet, perh. fr. *Ligus* Ligurian] **:** a large genus of Old World shrubs (family Oleaceae) having smooth entire leaves and terminal panicles of white flowers — see PRIVET

**lig·u·us** \ˈligyüəs\ n, cap [NL] **:** a genus of large spiral pulmonate arboreal snails of Florida and the West Indies much prized by shell collectors for their polished shining shells that are banded with many colors

**lig·y·da** \ˈlijədə\ [NL, irreg. after *Ligeia*, a siren in ancient Greek mythology, fr. Gk] syn of LIGIA

**lih·yan·ic** \lēˈyanik\ or **lih·yan·i·an** \-ānēən\ or **lih·yan·ite** \-ä,nīt\ n -s usu cap [Ar *Liḥyān* + E -ic or -ian or -ite] **:** a Semitic language of western Arabia known from inscriptions of the 2d and 1st centuries B.C.

**li·ja** \ˈlē(,)hä\ n -s [Sp] **:** any of several filefishes

**lik·abil·i·ty** \,līkəˈbiləd·ē\ n **:** the quality or state of being likable

**lik·able** or **like·able** \ˈlīkəbəl\ adj **:** that can be liked or attracts liking ⟨a friendly ~ man⟩ ⟨a ~ feature of the book⟩ ⟨a gay and ~ humor —*N.Y. Times*⟩ — **lik·able·ness** n -es

[1]**like** \ˈlīk\ vb -ED/-ING/-S [ME *liken*, fr. OE *līcian*; akin to OHG *līhhēn* to please, ON *līka*, Goth *leikan*; derivative fr. the root of the second constituent of OE *gelīc* like, alike — more at [3]LIKE] vt **1** chiefly dial **:** to be suitable, pleasing, or agreeable to (a person) ⟨at first in heart it *liked* me ill —Sir Walter Scott⟩ ⟨till then, if it ~s you —Andrew Lang⟩ **2 a :** to feel attraction toward or take pleasure in **:** have a liking for ⟨which friend he ~s best⟩ **:** FAVOR ⟨~s some vegetables and dislikes others⟩ **:** ENJOY ⟨~s doing business with them⟩ **b :** to affect favorably **:** agree with **:** SUIT ⟨I like onions but they don't ~ me⟩ **:** BECOME ⟨she likes red but it doesn't ~ her⟩ — usu. used in negative constructions **3 :** to feel toward or concerning **:** REGARD — used with *how* ⟨how would you ~ to lose your job⟩ ⟨how do you ~ her new hat⟩ ⟨learning how he *liked* the new worker⟩ **4 :** to wish to have **:** WANT ⟨do not ~ anybody to touch my things —Marjorie Osterman⟩ — often used with a conditional auxiliary ⟨would ~ a drink⟩ ⟨would ~ you to do it⟩ ⟨would ~ it returned soon⟩ ⟨isn't as widely circulated as we would ~ for it to be —E.B.Atwood⟩ ⟨would ~ for you to look this over⟩ **:** INCLINE, PREFER ⟨cases in which the doctor ~s to give an injection⟩ ~ *vi* **1** obs **:** to be in a healthy condition **:** THRIVE ⟨quinces . . . will not ~ in our cold parts —William Lawson⟩ **2** now dial **:** APPROVE — used with *of* or *with* ⟨I daredn't do't; my master wouldn't ~ of it —Anne Baker⟩ **3 :** to feel inclined **:** CHOOSE ⟨had salmon almost any time he *liked* —Edison Marshall⟩ **4 :** to feel liking **:** find oneself attracted ⟨would rather ~ than criticize —E.A.Weeks⟩

**syn** LOVE, ENJOY, RELISH, FANCY, DOTE: LIKE is a general term indicating a viewing or regarding with favor and without aversion, but without great warmth of feeling ⟨*liked* inns, and farmers, and loafers on the river —H.S.Canby⟩ LOVE (opposed to *hate*) does imply ardent attachment and great warmth ⟨I *love* Henry, but I cannot *like* him; and as for taking his arm I should as soon think of taking the arm of an elm tree —R.W. Emerson⟩ ⟨they *loved* Maurice too, but more mildly. And, very temperately, they *liked* their Aunt Rome —Rose Macaulay⟩ ⟨*loved* to roam and was passionately fond of beauty both in nature and in art —H.E.Starr⟩ ENJOY suggests taking pleasure or satisfaction in possessing, using, being with, or appreciating what one likes or loves ⟨*enjoy* a finer degree of civilization than the individuals and the nations around us —Havelock Ellis⟩ ⟨seemed to *enjoy* the beautiful site of that building —Willa Cather⟩ RELISH applies to an enjoying and savoring of something that gives one peculiar satisfaction or gratification ⟨a paradox that the happiest, most vigorous, and most confident ages which the world has ever known—the Periclean and the Elizabethan—should be exactly those which created and which most *relished* the mightiest tragedies —J.W.Krutch⟩ ⟨a few hundred (not more) choice-loving connoisseurs *relish* him as the most perfect opportunist in prose —Christopher Morley⟩ FANCY may apply to a liking or a taking pleasure in something appealing to one's imagination or to one's personal tastes or whims ⟨yachts, horses, whatever he *fancied* —George Meredith⟩ ⟨would he really *fancy* a little farm somewhere inland, or would he die of the landlocked loneliness —Frank Ritchie⟩ DOTE may indicate an excessive or compulsive fondness and liking, often foolish or infatuated ⟨he *doted* on his daughter Mary; she could do no wrong —Walter Havighurst⟩ ⟨you know how servants are. They *dote* on such yarns —L.C. Douglas⟩

[2]**like** \"\ n -s **1 :** a feeling of attraction toward a person or thing **:** LIKING — usu. used in pl. ⟨has so many ~s in life—and almost as many dislikes —*Times Lit. Supp.*⟩ ⟨he now takes violent ~s to people —H.J.Laski⟩ **2 :** something that one likes ⟨black in summer is one of her ~s —*Holiday*⟩

[3]**like** \"\ adj, sometimes **liker**; sometimes **likest** [ME *lik*, *ilik*, alter. (influenced by ON *glīkr*, *līkr*) of *ilich*, fr. OE *gelīc* like, alike; akin to OHG *gilīh* like, alike, ON *glīkr*, *līkr*, Goth *galeiks*; all fr. a prehistoric Gmc compound having a first constituent represented by OE *ge-* (perfective, associative, and collective prefix) and a second constituent represented by OE *līc* body, OHG *līh*, ON *lík*, Goth *leik*; akin to Lith *lygus* like, equal — more at CO-] **1 a :** the same or nearly the same (as in nature, appearance, or quantity) ⟨members of the cat family have ~ dispositions⟩ ⟨fabrics of ~ consistency⟩ **:** equal or nearly equal ⟨gave one six blows and the other a ~ number⟩ ⟨gave a thousand dollars before and a ~ sum now⟩ ⟨his own card and others of ~ value —J.B.Pick⟩ **:** CORRESPONDING ⟨the ~ period during the preceding year⟩ **:** IDENTICAL, INDISTINGUISHABLE ⟨as ~ as two peas⟩ **:** SIMILAR ⟨hospitals and ~ institutions for the sick or disabled⟩ — formerly used with *as, unto, of* ⟨in all things it behoved him to be made ~ unto his brethren —Heb. 2:17 (AV)⟩; formerly and sometimes now used with *to, with* ⟨~ to the soft caress bestowed . . . by loving fingers —*Phoenix Flame*⟩ ⟨an old Greek was a being of ~ passions with a modern Englishman —E.A.Freeman⟩ **b :** of a form, kind, appearance, or effect resembling or suggesting — used postpositively in combination ⟨a box*like* seedpod⟩ ⟨a home*like* atmosphere⟩ ⟨a life*like* statue⟩ ⟨dog*like* existence⟩; used with a hyphen after nouns in *-ll* ⟨bell-*like*⟩ and often in nonce or infrequent compounds ⟨president-*like*⟩ ⟨opium-*like*⟩ **c :** faithful to a subject or original ⟨the finished portrait being ever so ~⟩ **2 a :** LIKELY ⟨the importance of statistics as the one discipline ~ to give accuracy of mind —H.J.Laski⟩ **b :** being about or as if about — used with the infinitive ⟨it's ~ to drive me crazy⟩ **3 :** of the kind befitting or characteristic of — used postpositively in combination ⟨a lady*like* behavior⟩ ⟨lawyer*like* argumentation⟩ — **like as we lie :** having each played an equal number of golf strokes — **something like :** something nearly or altogether as it should be

**syn** ALIKE, SIMILAR, ANALOGOUS, COMPARABLE, AKIN, PARALLEL, UNIFORM, IDENTICAL: LIKE is a general word indicating resemblance or similarity ranging from virtual identity in all characteristics to a chance resemblance in only one ⟨convincing only to himself, or to a limited circle of *like* minds —*Times Lit. Supp.*⟩ ALIKE is similar to LIKE but is less likely to be used for the chance, farfetched resemblance and is generally limited to use in a predicate or postposed situation after a compounded substantive modified ⟨their resemblance as brother and sister . . . they looked utterly *alike* —Sinclair Lewis⟩ SIMILAR often stresses the likenesses between different things, implying that differences may be overlooked or ignored for a time ⟨Virginia creeper or the deceptively *similar* poison ivy —*Amer. Guide Series: Md.*⟩ ⟨regard the attraction which illusion has for us as *similar* to that which a flame at night has for a moth —M.R. Cohen⟩ ANALOGOUS indicates presence of some likeness which makes it feasible or permissible to draw from it an analogy, a sustained or appropriate comparison ⟨the two new states would have a position *analogous* to that of British Dominions —*Manchester Guardian Weekly*⟩ ⟨quite *analogous* to the emotionalizing of Christian art is the example afforded by the evolution of the Latin hymn —H.O.Taylor⟩ COMPARABLE indicates a likeness on one point or a limited number of points which permits a limited or casual comparison or matching together ⟨the Syrians . . . with Arabian coffee, served thick and strong in tiny cups, as a national drink *comparable* to the Englishman's tea —*Amer. Guide Series: R.I.*⟩ COMPARABLE is esp. likely to be used in connection with considerations of merit, standing, rank, or power ⟨neither in military nor industrial terms is China *comparable* to the other three great powers —Vera M. Dean⟩ AKIN, limited to use in postpositive situations, indicates an essential likeness, sometimes the sort of likeness found in kinship, in common descent from an original ancestor, prototype, or ancestral stock ⟨the Mongols of Outer Mongolia . . . are *akin* to those of the neighboring Buryat-Mongol A.S.S.R. —*Foreign Affairs*⟩ ⟨real nursery tales, *akin* to Brer Rabbit —*Times Lit. Supp.*⟩ ⟨science . . . is *akin* to democracy in its faith in human intelligence and cooperative effort —H.J.Muller⟩ PARALLEL is used to indicate the fact of similarities over a course of development throughout a history or account or the fact of resemblances or likenesses permitting a setting or bracketing together as though side by side ⟨the almost *parallel* growth of the Twin Cities —*Amer. Guide Series: Minn.*⟩ ⟨*parallel* to the classic and academic Italian school was one with a more distinctive native feeling —Paul Manship⟩ ⟨*parallel* to the powers of the king were the powers of the father in the individual household —Ralph Linton⟩ UNIFORM suggests a likeness and similarity throughout, a lack of noticeable variation wherever things in question occur or operate ⟨one of the most fundamental social interests is that law shall be *uniform* and impartial —B.N.Cardozo⟩ ⟨schools . . . no longer expect all children to learn to read at a *uniform* rate —*Education Digest*⟩ IDENTICAL indicates either the fact of being the same person or thing or, in connection with things copied, reproduced, or repeated, an exact correspondence with no significant difference being involved ⟨George Eliot and Mary Ann Evans were *identical*⟩ ⟨the interests of workers and their employers were not altogether *identical* —M.R.Cohen⟩ ⟨his home life and his life as a man of letters are never *identical* —H.S.Canby⟩

[4]**like** \"\ n -s [ME *lik, like, ilik, ilike*, fr. *lik, ilik*, adj. — more at [3]LIKE] **1 a :** a person or thing similar or equal to the one referred to **:** sort of person **:** KIND ⟨made it hard for you and your ~ —C.S.Lewis⟩ **:** COUNTERPART ⟨not less talented than his French or English ~ —*New Republic*⟩ **:** EQUAL ⟨scarcely expect to hear its ~ again —A.N.Whitehead⟩ — usu. used with a possessive adjective **b** archaic **:** a person or thing similar to another — used chiefly in proverbial expressions ⟨~ breeds like⟩ **2 :** a stroke in golf that will make equal the number of strokes played by opposing players or sides — **the like :** something similar **:** SUCHLIKE ⟨fastened with a paper clip or *the like*⟩ ⟨did you ever hear *the like*⟩ ⟨taking everything he needed . . . grease gun, wrenches, and *the like* —Danforth Ross⟩ — compare ET CETERA — **the like of** or **the likes of :** a person or thing like ⟨won't take such talk from *the likes of* him⟩ ⟨upon *the likes of* them that such schools and colleges depend —F.L.Allen⟩ **:** anything to equal ⟨did you ever see *the likes of* that boy⟩ ⟨a mass of . . . information *the like of* which has never been collected before —*Times Lit. Supp.*⟩

[5]**like** \"\ adv, sometimes -ER/-EST [ME *lik, like, ilik, ilike*, fr. *lik, ilik*, adj. — more at [3]LIKE] **1** archaic **:** ALIKE, EQUALLY — used to qualify an adjective or adverb ⟨hut and palace show ~ filthily —Lord Byron⟩ **2 :** LIKELY, PROBABLY — now usu. used in the phrase *like enough* ⟨you'll try it, some day, ~ enough —Mark Twain⟩ **3 a :** in some degree or to some extent **:** RATHER — used sometimes with a hyphen as a limiting modifier after adjectives ⟨a small-*like* wagon⟩, adverbs ⟨saunter over nonchalantly ~ —Walter Karig⟩, verbs and verb-adverb phrases ⟨he shrunk up ~ and went away⟩, and sentences ⟨they were working in the field, ~⟩ **b** substand **:** sort of **:** in a way — used before and after nouns sometimes with a hyphen usu. to suggest uncertainty as to the exactness of description ⟨little sort of pictures ~ on his hat⟩ ⟨valley surrounded with ~ little mountains⟩ **c** substand **:** in a specified manner or degree — used after adjectives sometimes with a hyphen ⟨raise the children decent ~⟩ ⟨he spoke knowing-*like*⟩ **4 :** NEARLY ⟨the real rates . . . are more ~ 18 per thousand —B.K.Sandwell⟩ — **as like as not** or **like as not :** in all likelihood **:** PROBABLY ⟨*like as not*, her estimate won't be very good —S.L.Payne⟩

[6]**like** \"\ prep [ME *lik, like, ilik, ilike*, fr. *lik, ilik*, adj. & *lik, like, ilik, ilike*, adv. — more at [4]LIKE, [5]LIKE] **1 :** of the character of **: a :** typical of ⟨was ~ him to remember us at Christmas⟩ ⟨isn't that just ~ a man⟩ **b :** that compares with **:** EQUALING — usu. used in negative constructions ⟨no place ~ home⟩ ⟨no fool ~ an old fool⟩ ⟨nothing ~ a warm bath for relaxing⟩ ⟨never saw anything ~ it⟩ **c :** of a like nature with **:** comparable to — used in questions and noun clauses ⟨what is she ~⟩ ⟨learn what skiing is ~⟩ **d :** of the kind indicated by **:** of such a character as ⟨was autocratic but dictators are ~ that⟩ ⟨have great respect for a man ~ that⟩ **:** of the kind represented by ⟨keep people ~ him in line⟩ **2 :** in or after the manner of**: a :** in a manner befitting ⟨returned home ~ a dutiful son⟩ ⟨act ~ gentlemen⟩ ⟨treated him ~ a hero⟩ **b :** in the manner indicated **:** in such a manner as ⟨stop crying ~ this⟩ ⟨can't do it ~ that⟩ **c :** in what manner — used in questions and noun clauses ⟨take the wheel and see what it drives ~⟩

**3 a :** the same or similar to (as in structure, character, appearance, or effect) ⟨foxes are ~ dogs⟩ ⟨she looks ~ her sister⟩ ⟨understood the English character, so much ~ his own —W.C.Ford⟩ ⟨our notion of fair play, ~ theirs, includes the opponent —Margaret Mead⟩ **:** of a character or in a manner suggesting ⟨vitamins that are ~ candy —*Jour. Amer. Med. Assoc.*⟩ ⟨the mist is thick ~ white cotton —Vicki Baum⟩ **:** RESEMBLING, APPROACHING ⟨has done something ~ justice to its complexity —Lewis Mumford⟩ **b :** the same as or similar to that of ⟨heard sounds ~ a motor running⟩ **4 —** used correlatively with the force of *as . . . so* ⟨~ master, ~ man⟩ **5 a :** as though there would be **:** indicative of the probable occurrence of ⟨looks ~ rain⟩ ⟨looks ~ good fishing⟩ **b :** as though he, she, or it were or might be ⟨felt ~ a hypocrite⟩ ⟨looks ~ a smart boy⟩ **:** as is characteristic of or usual to ⟨sounds ~ thunder⟩ ⟨tastes ~ grape to me⟩ ⟨feeling ~ himself again⟩ **6 :** such as ⟨traditional concerns ~ law and literature —G.B.Saul⟩ **7 —** used to form intensive or ironic phrases ⟨worked ~ a house afire⟩ ⟨rub out . . . a backache ~ nobody's business —Fannie Hurst⟩ ⟨sold ~ hot cakes⟩ ⟨screamed ~ hell⟩ ⟨fight ~ the devil⟩ ⟨hurt ~ anything⟩ ⟨~ fun he did⟩ — **like a book** adv **1 :** in formal often pedantic language ⟨talks *like a book*⟩ **2 :** with complete understanding ⟨can read his mind *like a book*⟩ — **like that 1 :** of that kind **:** in that manner ⟨small towns *like that*⟩ ⟨talked *like that*⟩ **2 :** in close accord ⟨no great family in the city he's not just *like that* with —C.B.Kelland⟩

[7]**like** \"\ conj [[5]like] **1 a** archaic **:** as of or in the manner of one that is ⟨the look is vivid still nor seems ~ dead —Thomas Creech⟩ **b —** used in intensive phrases ⟨waved ~ mad⟩ ⟨dancing ~ crazy⟩ **2 :** in the same way or manner as or to the same degree or extent as ⟨impromptu programs where they ask questions much ~ I do on the air —Art Linkletter⟩ — often followed by a noun or pronoun representing an incomplete clause whose verb would be the same as that of the main clause ⟨took to figures ~ a duck to water⟩ ⟨looks ~ they can raise better tobacco —Caroline Gordon⟩ ⟨looks ~ he will get the job⟩ **3 :** as if **:** as though ⟨wore his clothes ~ he was . . . afraid of getting dirt on them —*St. Petersburg (Fla.) Independent*⟩ ⟨was ~ he'd come back from a long trip⟩ ⟨acted ~ she felt sick⟩ — used esp. with intransitive verbs of the senses ⟨sounded ~ the motor had stopped⟩ **4 :** in accordance with the way in which **:** the way that ⟨the violin now sounds ~ an old masterpiece should —*Baton*⟩ **:** in the manner that ⟨did it ~ he told me to⟩ **5 a :** of the kind that ⟨wanted a doll ~ she saw in the store window⟩ **:** such as ⟨anomalies ~ just had occurred —*New Republic*⟩ **b :** similar to ⟨it was a little ~ when the war came —Gouverneur Paulding⟩ **6 :** for example ⟨when your car gives trouble — ~ when the motor won't start⟩ ⟨things that were beginning increasingly to come up — ~ next week every rifle . . . had to be turned in —James Jones⟩

[8]**like** \"\ or **liked** \-kt\ verbal auxiliary [[3]like] now substand **:** came near **:** was near — used with the perfect infinitive sometimes in the reduced form without *have* ⟨had four quarrels and ~ to have fought one —Shak.⟩ ⟨these fellows . . . had ~ to a been whipped —Anne Royall⟩ ⟨it *liked* to killed me —John Dos Passos⟩ and sometimes in that form with a substandard past participle identical with a past tense form ⟨I *liked* to have went crazy —Stetson Kennedy⟩ ⟨so loud I ~ to fell out of bed —Helen Eustis⟩

[9]**like** vt -ED/-ING/-S [[3]like] obs **:** LIKEN ⟨~ me to the peasant boys of France —Shak.⟩

[10]**like** chiefly South & Midland var of LACK

**likeable** var of LIKABLE

**like as** conj [ME, fr. *lik*, like, adv. + *as* — more at [5]LIKE] chiefly dial **:** in the way or manner that **:** AS ⟨*like as* a father pitieth his children, so the Lord pitieth them —Ps.103:13 (AV)⟩ ⟨an eddy there . . . *like as* you'd expect —C.S.Forester⟩ — now usu. used with *if* ⟨it was . . . *like as* if the films suddenly come real —Richard Llewellyn⟩

**liked** past of LIKE

**like·li·head** \ˈlīklē,hed\ n [ME *liklihede*, fr. *likli* likely + *-hed, -hede* -hood (akin to ME *-hod, -had* -hood)] archaic **:** LIKELIHOOD

**like·li·hood** \ˈlīklē,hu̇d, -li,-\ n [ME *liklihod*, fr. *likli* likely + *-hod, -had* -hood] **1** obs **:** LIKENESS **2 :** PROBABILITY ⟨in all ~ it will rain⟩ **3** chiefly Brit **:** appearance of probable success **:** PROMISE

**like·li·ness** \-lēnəs, -lin-\ n -ES [ME *liklinesse*, fr. *likli* likely + *-nesse* -ness] **:** LIKELIHOOD

[1]**like·ly** \ˈlīklē, -li\ adj -ER/-EST [ME *likli*, fr. ON *glīkligr*, *líkligr* likely, probable, fr. *glīkr*, *līkr* like, alike + *-ligr* -ly — more at [3]LIKE] **1 :** of such a nature or so circumstanced as to make something probable ⟨any approach more ~ of success⟩ **:** in a fair way — usu. used with a following infinitive ⟨any . . . government would be subject to the same dangers and ~ to meet the same fate—Elmer Davis⟩ **2 a :** seeming to justify belief or expectation ⟨if there is failure in one quarter . . . it is a ~ sign of failure in the other —R.P.Blackmur⟩ **:** CREDIBLE ⟨a ~ story⟩ **b :** having a better chance of existing or occurring than not **:** having the character of a probability ⟨tell the road authorities of their ~ future demands —John Kemp⟩ ⟨it is ~ that modern farming methods are increasing the quantities of small animals —*Amer. Guide Series: Ark.*⟩ **3 :** apparently fit or adapted for something expressed or implied **:** SUITABLE, QUALIFIED ⟨a ~ place to fish⟩ ⟨the more ~ district for discovery of prehistoric remains —Edward Clodd⟩ ⟨thrusting their spears . . . into *likely*-looking water —Wilfred Thesiger⟩ **4 :** giving promise of success or excellence **:** PROMISING ⟨sifted . . . the universities for ~ men —*Science Digest*⟩ **5** now dial **:** AGREEABLE, HANDSOME ⟨a ~ child . . . thoroughly nice, cheerful, obliging —Frances G. Patton⟩ **syn** see PROBABLE

[2]**likely** \"\ adv [ME *likli*, fr. *likli*, adj.] **:** in all probability **:** PROBABLY ⟨a popular dance hall was more ~ her choice than his —Valentine Williams⟩ ⟨they will ~ betray themselves by loud breathing —*Scribner's*⟩ ⟨more than ~ pictures it in terms of assembly lines —*Item*⟩ — **as likely as not** or **likely as not :** as like as not

**like–minded** \ˈ=ˈ==\ adj **:** having a like disposition or purpose **:** of the same mind or habit of thought — **like–mind·ed·ly** adv — **like–mind·ed·ness** n

**lik·en** \ˈlīkən\ vb **likened; likened; likening** \-k(ə)niŋ\ **likens** [ME *liknen*, fr. *lik* like + *-nen* -en — more at [3]LIKE] vt **:** to represent as similar **:** COMPARE ⟨~ life to a pilgrimage⟩ ~ vi **:** to be or become like ⟨once knew a lady that ~ed surprisingly to you —M.A.Bianchi⟩

**like·ness** n -ES [ME *liknesse*, fr. OE *līcnes*, prob. short for *gelīcnes*, fr. *gelīc* like, alike + *-nes* -ness — more at [3]LIKE] **1 :** the quality or state of being like **:** RESEMBLANCE, SIMILARITY ⟨should have known you anywhere from your ~ to your father —Archibald Marshall⟩ ⟨the ~es that hold people together . . . are greater than the unlikenesses that would make them foes —Max Gilstrap⟩ **2 :** APPEARANCE, FORM, GUISE, SEMBLANCE, SHAPE ⟨low-hanging clouds took on the ~ of a wintry sky —H.A.Chippendale⟩ ⟨modeling . . . its gods after its own ~ —Agnes Repplier⟩ **3 :** a copy, counterpart, or portrait; usu. visual representation (as of a person) **:** COPY, EFFIGY, PORTRAIT ⟨her ~ has appeared on the cover of a . . . magazine —*Newsweek*⟩ ⟨a bronze bust . . . which is an excellent ~ —W.G. MacCallum⟩

[1]**liker** comparative of LIKE

[2]**lik·er** \ˈlīkə(r)\ n -s [[1]like + -er] **:** one that likes ⟨the ~ does not like . . . in accordance with mere tradition —George Saintsbury⟩

**likes** pres 3d sing of LIKE, pl of LIKE

**like·some** \ˈlīksəm\ adj [[1]like + -some] now dial **:** pleasing to the mind or senses **:** AGREEABLE ⟨a ~ girl⟩ ⟨seemed quite ~⟩

**likest** superlative of LIKE

**like·ways** \ˈlīk,wāz\ adv [[3]like + -ways] now dial **:** LIKEWISE ⟨~ and what a pleasure —Charles Dickens⟩

**likewise** \ˈ=,=\ adv [ME, fr. [3]like + wise, n.] **1 :** in like manner **:** SIMILARLY ⟨when the prime minister resigns, all the lords of the admiralty do ~ —*Encyc. Americana*⟩ **2 :** in addition **:** MOREOVER, BESIDES ⟨a governor who is ~ High Commissioner for the Pacific —*Colliers Yr. Bk.*⟩ **3 :** so am I or so do I — used informally to express agreement with a sentiment expressed by another ⟨would answer "*Likewise*" when someone said "Pleased to meet you"⟩

**li·kin** also **le·kin** or **li·ken** \ˈlēˈkēn\ n -s [modif. of Chin

(Pek) *li²-chin¹*, fr. *li²* one thousandth of a tael + *chin¹* money] **:** a former Chinese provincial tax at inland stations on imports or articles in transit

**lik·ing** \ˈlīkiŋ, -kēŋ\ *n* -s [ME, fr. OE *līcung* pleasure, fr. *līcian* to be pleasing to + *-ung* -ing — more at ¹LIKE] **1 :** an inclination to be pleased with a person or thing **:** favorable regard ⟨had a greater ~ for law —E.M.Coulter⟩ **:** FANCY ⟨took a ~ to the newcomer⟩ **:** PREFERENCE ⟨the ~ for independent dwellings has persisted —*Amer. Guide Series: Minn.*⟩ **:** RELISH, TASTE ⟨the hot night was not to his ~ —Irving Kolodin⟩ **2** *archaic* **:** the bent of one's desire **:** PLEASURE, WILL ⟨had married him against his ~ —Shak.⟩ **3** *archaic* **:** bodily condition **:** HEALTH ⟨their young ones are in good ~ —Job 39:4 (AV)⟩ — **on liking** *adv* **:** on condition of pleasing and being pleased ⟨his policy to engage a servant *on liking*⟩

**li·lac** \ˈlīlək, -ī,lak, -,läk\ *n* -s [obs. F *lilac* (now *lilas*), fr. Ar *laylak*, *līlak*, fr. Per *nīlak* bluish, fr. *nīl* blue, indigo, fr. Skt *nīla* dark blue] **1 a :** a plant of the genus *Syringa; esp* **:** a European shrub (*S. vulgaris*) that is often found as an escape in No. America and has cordate ovate leaves and large panicles of fragrant pink-purple flowers **b :** any of various cultivated shrubs that are derived directly or by hybridization from members of the genus *Syringa* (as *S. vulgaris*, *S. persica*, *S. josikea*, *S. emodi*, and *S. amurensis*) and have white, pink, purple, or blue flowers **2 a :** any of several Australian plants of the genus *Melia* having purple flowers; *esp* **:** CHINABERRY 2 **b :** BLUEBLOSSOM **3 a :** a variable color averaging a moderate purple that is redder and paler than heliotrope, paler than average amethyst, and bluer and paler than cobalt violet **b :** a moderate pink to light grayish red that is very slightly lighter than corinthian pink

**lilac daphne** *n* **:** a daphne (*Daphne genkwa*) of China and Korea that blooms before the leaves emerge

**li·la·ceous** \(ˈ)lī¦lāshəs\ *adj* [*lilac* + *-aceous*] **:** of or resembling the color lilac

**lilac gray** *n* **:** a light purplish gray that is less strong and very slightly redder than orchid haze

**lilac leaf miner** *n* **:** the larva of a minute gracilariid moth (*Gracilaria syringella*) that mines and rolls the leaves of the lilac

**lilac mildew** *n* **:** a powdery mildew (*Microsphaera alni*) that attacks the leaves of the lilac

**lilacthroat** \ˈ≈(,)≈,≈\ *n* **:** a metallic green So. American hummingbird (genus *Heliodoxa*) with a triangular lilac throat patch

**lil·ae·op·sis** \,lilēˈäpsə̇s\ *n, cap* [NL, fr. *Lilaea*, genus of plants belonging to the family Juncaginaceae + *-opsis*] *in some classifications* **:** a small genus of perennial creeping aquatic or marsh herbs (family Umbelliferae) with the leaves obsolete and the petioles altered into hollow cylindrical or subulate septate phyllodia and with small umbels of minute white flowers

**li·las** \lēˈlä\ *n* -ES [F, lilac] **:** LILAC 3

**lil·i·a·ce·ae** \,lilēˈāsē,ē\ *n pl, cap* [NL, fr. *Lilium*, type genus + *-aceae*] **:** a large family of monocotyledonous plants (order Liliales) characterized by a regular perianth of separate segments, dependent superior ovary, loculicidal capsular fruit, and usu. bulbous stem base

**lil·i·a·ceous** \¦≈≈¦āshəs\ *adj* [LL *liliaceus*, fr. L *lilium* lily + *-aceus* -aceous — more at LILY] **1 :** of, relating to, or resembling lilies **2 a :** of or relating to the family Liliaceae **b :** having a regular corolliform perianth similar to that of plants of the genus *Lilium*

**lil·i·a·les** \,≈≈ˈā(,)lēz\ *n pl, cap* [NL, fr. *Lilium* + *-ales*] **:** an order of monocotyledonous plants with complete, perfect, and typically trimerous flowers, a compound ovary, and seeds with an oily or fleshy endosperm — see AMARYLLIDACEAE, IRIDACEAE, LILIACEAE

**lil·ied** \ˈlilēd, -lid\ *adj* [¹*lily* + *-ed*] **1** *archaic* **:** resembling a lily in whiteness or fairness ⟨soft ~ fingers —Samuel Warren⟩ **2 :** full of or covered with lilies ⟨~ pool and grassy acres —George Eliot⟩ **3 :** bearing or decorated with the emblematic or heraldic fleur-de-lis ⟨the ~ banner of France —S.R. Gardiner⟩

**lilies** *pl of* LILY

**lil·i·i·flo·rae** \,lilē,īˈflō(,)rē, -lȯ(,)-\ [NL, fr. *lilii-* (fr. *Lilium*) + *-florae* (fr. L *flor-, flos* flower — more at BLOW (to bloom)] *syn of* LILIALES

**lil·i·um** \ˈlilēəm\ *n* [NL, fr. L, lily] **1** *cap* **:** a large genus (the type of the family Liliaceae) of herbaceous plants having scaly bulbs, whorled or scattered leaves, showy flowers with a perianth of six segments, versatile anthers, a 3-lobed stigma, and a capsular fruit — see LILY **2 -s :** any plant of the genus *Lilium*

**¹lill** \ˈlil\ *vb* -ED/-ING/-S [perh. alter. of *loll*] *vt, now dial Eng* **:** to allow (the tongue) to hang ⟨~ out their tongue like a calf —James Mabbe⟩ ~ *vi, now dial Eng* **:** to hang out **:** PROTRUDE ⟨a tongue ~*ing* out of the mouth —John Florio⟩

**²lill** \"\ *n* -s [perh. alter. of ²*lilt*] *Scot* **:** a hole of a wind instrument

**³lill** \"\ *or* **lill pin** *n* -s [*lill* perh. short for ¹*lilliputian*] **:** a very small pin

**lille** \ˈlēl, *esp before pause or consonant* -ē(ə)l\ *adj, usu cap* [fr. *Lille*, city in northern France] **:** of or from the city of Lille, France **:** of the kind or style prevalent in Lille

**lille lace** *n, usu cap 1st L* **:** a bobbin lace having a hexagonal mesh ground and simple patterns outlined with a heavy flat thread

**lil·li·an·ite** \ˈlilēə,nīt\ *n* -s [G *lillianit*, fr. *Lillian* mine, Leadville, Colo. + G *-it* -ite] **:** a mineral $Pb_3Bi_2S_6$ consisting of a steel gray sulfide of lead and bismuth

**¹lil·li·put** \ˈlilə(,)pət, -lē(,)-\ *adj, sometimes cap* [fr. *Lilliput*, imaginary country in Swift's *Gulliver's Travels* (1726) inhabited by people six inches high] **:** LILLIPUTIAN 2 ⟨these ~ frogs —John Burroughs⟩

**²lilliput** \"\ *n* -s *sometimes cap* **:** LILLIPUTIAN 2 ⟨would the Arabs show much respect for ~*s* when they seem ready to challenge giants —Hal Lehrman⟩

**¹lil·li·pu·tian** \¦≈≈¦pyüshən\ *adj, sometimes cap* [*Lilliput*, imaginary country + E *-ian*, adj. suffix] **1 :** of, relating to, or characteristic of the imaginary country Lilliput **2 :** of, relating to, or characteristic of the Lilliputians: **a :** extremely small ⟨displaying . . . all of that ~ wardrobe —Hamlin Garland⟩ **b :** SMALL-MINDED, PETTY ⟨the ~ senators —W.A. White⟩

**²lilliputian** \"\ *n* -s *often cap* [*Lilliput*, imaginary country + E *-ian*, n. suffix] **1 :** an inhabitant of the imaginary country Lilliput **2 :** one that resembles a Lilliputian: **a :** a tiny person **b :** a petty or small-minded person ⟨the ~*s* that now misrule the destiny of America —B.J.Davis⟩

**lil·loo·et** \ˈliləwə̇t, -,wet\ *n, pl* **lillooet** *or* **lillooets** *usu cap* **1 a :** a Salishan people of the Fraser river valley in British Columbia **b :** a member of such people **2 :** the language of the Lillooet people

**lil·ly-low** \ˈlili,lō\ *n* [alter. of *low* (flame)] *chiefly dial Eng* **:** a bright flame

**lil·ly·pil·ly** \ˈlilē,pilē\ *n* -ES [origin unknown] **:** a plant of the genus *Eugenia*; *esp* **:** an Australian tree (*E. smithii*) with hard fine-grained wood

**¹lilt** \ˈlilt\ *vb* -ED/-ING/-S [ME *lulten*] *vt* **1 :** to begin to sing, sound, or play **:** STRIKE — often used with *up* ⟨~ up your pipes —Allan Ramsey †1758⟩ **2 :** to sing in a lively cheerful manner ⟨~*ing* a tune to supply the lack of conversation —Emily Brontë⟩ ~ *vi* **1 :** to sing or speak in a rhythmical manner ⟨whose shrill voice I have heard this half hour ~*ing* in the . . . kitchen —Sir Walter Scott⟩ **2 a :** to move in a lively springy manner ⟨a young man . . . ~*ing* a little in his walk —Rudyard Kipling⟩ **b :** to sway gently from side to side (as in some dances)

**²lilt** \"\ *n* -s **1 :** a spirited and usu. gay song or tune ⟨a well-known rollicking Irish ~ —Samuel Lover⟩ ⟨the wordless music of a ~ —Brian George⟩ **2 :** a rhythmical swing, flow, or cadence ⟨the lines go with a ~ —R.L.Stevenson⟩ ⟨the ~ of the train as it picked up speed —John Masters⟩ **3 :** a springy movement indicative of buoyant spirits ⟨a ~ in her step⟩

**lilting** *adj* [fr. pres. part. of ¹*lilt*] **:** characterized by a rhythmical swing or cadence **:** BUOYANT ⟨the flute broke into a light ~ air —J.G.Frazer⟩ ⟨swinging down the street with an easy, ~ stride —*Longman's Mag.*⟩ — **lilt·ing·ly** *adv* — **lilt·ing·ness** *n* -ES

**lilting skip** *n* **:** a skip with sideward swaying

**¹lily** \ˈlilē, -li\ *n* -ES [ME *lilie*, fr. OE, fr. L *lilium*, of non-IE origin; akin to the source of Gk *leirion* lily] **1 a :** any of numerous erect perennial leafy-stemmed bulbous herbs that constitute the genus *Lilium*, are native to the northern hemisphere, and are widely cultivated for their showy but unscented flowers **b :** any of various other plants of the family Liliaceae that usu. have showy flowers suggesting those of plants of the genus *Lilium* — used chiefly in combination; compare DAY LILY, LILY OF THE VALLEY, MARIPOSA LILY, PLANTAIN LILY **c :** any of various plants of other families (as Amaryllidaceae, Iridaceae) of the order Liliales including several that are cultivated for their showy and often fragrant flowers — usu. used in combination; compare BUTTERFLY LILY 1, SPIDER LILY **2 :** any of various plants with showy flowers: as **a :** the scarlet anemone that grows wild in Palestine — used chiefly in biblical references **b :** WATER LILY **c :** CALLA 2 **3 :** one that resembles the lily in whiteness, fairness, purity, or fragility ⟨a virgin, a most unspotted ~ —Shak.⟩ **4 a :** the conventional or heraldic fleur-de-lis considered as the symbol of France — usu. used in pl. ⟨the golden *lilies* of France —Gilbert Parker⟩ **b** *obs* **:** the north-pointing end of a compass needle **5 :** ROYAL SPADE **6 :** a pontoon airstrip consisting of interlocked hexagonal metal drums

lily

**²lily** \"\ *adj* **:** resembling a lily in whiteness, fairness, purity, or fragility ⟨my lady's ~ hand —John Keats⟩

**lily family** *n* **:** LILIACEAE

**lily green** *n* **:** a moderate yellow green that is greener and lighter than average moss green and yellower and paler than average pea green or apple green

**lily iron** *n* **1 :** a harpoon with a detachable barbed head used esp. in swordfishing **2 :** the head of a lily iron

**lilylike** \ˈ≈≈,≈\ *adj* **:** resembling a lily ⟨~ in her stateliness and sweetness —Alfred Tennyson⟩

**lily-livered** \¦≈≈¦≈≈\ *adj* [¹*lily* + *livered*; fr. the whiteness of the lily and fr. the former belief that the choleric temperament depends on the body's producing large quantities of yellow bile] **:** lacking courage **:** COWARDLY ⟨*lily-livered* poltroons lacking even the . . . courage of a rabbit —P.G.Wodehouse⟩

**lily of the incas** *usu cap I* **:** PERUVIAN LILY

**lily of the nile** *usu cap N* [*Nile*, river in northeast Africa] **:** AGAPANTHUS 2

**lily of the valley** *n, pl* **lilies of the valley 1 :** a low perennial herb (*Convallaria majalis*) of the family Liliaceae having usu. two large oblong lanceolate leaves and a raceme of fragrant nodding bell-shaped white flowers — compare FALSE LILY OF THE VALLEY **2 :** the dried rhizome and roots of the lily of the valley used as a cardiac tonic

lily of the valley

**lily-of-the-valley shrub** \¦≈≈≈≈¦≈≈-\ *n* **:** MOUNTAIN FETTERBUSH

**lily-of-the-valley tree** *n* **1 :** SWEET PEPPERBUSH **2 :** MOUNTAIN FETTERBUSH **3 :** SOURWOOD

**lily pad** *n* **:** a floating leaf of a water lily

**lily thorn** *n* **:** PRICKLY APPLE

**lily-trotter** \ˈ≈≈,≈≈\ *n* **:** any of various birds of the family Jacanidae that have feet adapted for running on floating vegetation

**lilyturf** \ˈ≈≈,≈\ *n* **:** a plant of either of two genera (*Liriope* and *Ophiopogon*) used as an ornamental

**¹lily-white** \ˈ≈≈¦≈\ *adj* [ME *lilie-whit*, fr. *lilie* lily + *whit* white] **1 :** white as a lily **:** pure white **2 a :** designed to maintain a color line by excluding Negroes ⟨overruled the rank and file on the basis of the *lily-white* clause in the union ritual —John Beecher⟩ **b :** characterized by or favoring the exclusion of Negroes esp. from politics ⟨began to identify themselves with a *lily-white* movement which would expel Negroes from the organization —H.R.Penniman⟩ — opposed to BLACK-AND-TAN **3 :** lacking faults or imperfections **:** IRREPROACHABLE, PURE, INNOCENT ⟨will show the jury he isn't as *lily-white* as he would have them believe —George Norris⟩

**²lily-white** \"\ *n* **:** a member of a lily-white organization; *esp* **:** a member of a faction of the Republican party in the southern U.S. favoring the exclusion of Negroes from political life — opposed to *black and tan*

**lim** *abbr* limit; limited

**¹lima** \ˈlēmə\ *adj, usu cap* [fr. *Lima*, Peru] **:** of or from Lima, the capital of Peru **:** of the kind or style prevalent in Lima

**²li·ma** \ˈlīmə\ *n, cap* [NL, fr. L *lima* file; fr. the shape of the shell — more at LIME] **:** a genus of bivalve mollusks (suborder Pectinacea) that is the type of the family Limidae comprising the file shells

**³li·ma** \ˈlēmə\ *usu cap* — a communications code word for the letter *l*

**li·ma bean** \ˈlīmə-\ *also* **lima** *n* -s [fr. *Lima*, Peru] **1 a :** any of various bush or tall-growing beans that are derived from a perennial tropical American species (*Phaseolus limensis*) and that are widely cultivated for their large flat edible usu. pale green or whitish seeds **b :** SIEVA BEAN **2 :** the seed of any lima bean

**lima-bean pod borer** *n* **:** the larva of a small European pyralidid moth (*Etiella zinckenella*) introduced into No. America that bores into the green pods of many legumes including lima beans

**li·ma·cea** \lī'māshēə\ *n pl, cap* [NL, fr. *Limac-*, *Limax*, type genus + *-ea* (fr. L, neut. pl. of *-eus* -eous)] *in old classifications* **:** a natural group comprising the terrestrial slugs

**lim·a·cel** *or* **lim·a·celle** \,limə'sel\ *n* -s [F *limacelle*, fr. *limace* slug (fr. L *limac-, limax*) + *-elle* -el (fr. L *-ella*)] **:** the small internal shell of slugs of *Limax* and related genera

**li·mac·i·dae** \lī'masə,dē\ *n pl, cap* [NL, fr. *Limac-*, *Limax*, type genus + *-idae*] **:** a family of gastropod mollusks — see LIMAX

**li·mac·i·form** \-,fȯrm\ *adj* [prob. fr. (assumed) NL *limaciformis*, fr. L *limac-, limax* slug + *-iformis* -iform] **:** resembling a slug — used esp. of insect larvae

**lim·a·cine** \'limə,sīn, 'līm-, -sən\ *adj* [NL *limacinus*, fr. L *limac-, limax* slug + *-inus* -ine] **:** of, relating to, or resembling a slug

**li·ma·cod·i·dae** \,līmə'kädə,dē\ *n pl, cap* [NL, fr. *Limacodes*, included genus (fr. L *limac-, limax* slug + NL *-odes*) + *-idae*] *syn of* EUCLEIDAE

**lim·a·coid** \'limə,kȯid\ *adj* [NL *limacoides*, fr. L *limac-, limax* slug + *-oides* -oid] **:** like a slug **:** LIMACINE

**li·ma·çon** \,lēmə'sōⁿ, 'limə,sän\ *n* -s [F, lit., snail, fr. OF, dim. of *limaz* snail, slug, fr. L *limac-, limax* slug] **:** a plane curve consisting of the collection of points obtained by taking a fixed distance in both directions along a half line from a fixed point on a circle measured from its second intersection with the circle

**li·man** \lē'män\ *n* -s [Russ, fr. Turk, harbor, fr. Gk *limenion* small harbor, dim. of *limen-, limēn* harbor] **:** a bay or estuary at the mouth of a river **:** LAGOON

**li·man·da** \lə'mandə\ *n, cap* [NL, fr. F *limande* dab, fr. OF, irreg. fr. *lime* dab, file, fr. L *lima* file — more at LIME] **:** a genus of flounders that have the eyes on the right side, a humped nose, small scales, and the undersurface often brightly colored and that include certain excellent food fishes of northern temperate seas (as the rusty dab)

**li·ma·tion** \lī'māshən\ *n* -s [L *limation-, limatio*, fr. *limatus* (past part. of *limare* to file, fr. *lima* file) + *-ion-, -io* -ion] **:** FILING, POLISHING

**li·ma wood** \'lēmə-, 'līmə-\ *n, usu cap L* [fr. *Lima*, Peru] **:** a soluble red wood derived from a tree (*Caesalpinia tinctoria*) of Ecuador and Peru and used in dyeing

**¹li·max** \'lī,maks\ *n, cap* [NL *Limac-*, *Limax*, fr. L *limac-, limax* slug, fr. (assumed) Gk *leimak-*, *leimax* (whence LGk *leimak-*, *leimax* slug) — more at LIME] **:** a genus (the type of the family Limacidae) of gastropod mollusks containing typical slugs including several troublesome garden pests and formerly including most of the slugs

**²limax** \"\ *adj* **:** resembling a slug — used esp. of small amoebas that form a single broad anterior pseudopodium and flow sluggishly forward

**¹limb** \'lim\ *n* -s [ME *lim*, fr. OE; akin to ON *limr* member of the body, *lim* limb of a tree, L *limit-, limes* boundary, limit, *limus* sidelong, *limin-, limen* threshold, Gk *leimōn* meadow, *limen-, limēn* harbor, *ōlenē* elbow — more at ELL] **1** *now dial Brit* **:** an organ or member of the body **2 a :** one of the projecting paired appendages (as an arm, wing, fin, or parapodium) of an animal body made up of diverse tissues (as epithelium, muscle, and bone) derived from two or more germ layers and concerned esp. with movement and grasping but sometimes modified into sensory or sexual organs **b :** a leg or arm of a human being ⟨a froufrou of petticoats concealing their upper ~*s* —Godfrey Winn⟩ ⟨lost the use of his ~*s*⟩ ⟨artificial ~*s* — better elbows and wrists, legs capable of producing a smooth walking cadence —R.M.Yoder⟩ ⟨packed so close together in a boat already leaking that they could hardly move a ~ —B.N.Cardozo⟩ **3 :** a large primary branch of a tree ⟨the knotty ~*s* of an enormous oak —P.B.Shelley⟩ **4 :** a person that is an active member or agent ⟨choose such ~*s* of noble counsel —Shak.⟩ ⟨lame the ~*s* of the democracy —J.A.Froude⟩ ⟨~ of the law⟩ **5 :** a branch or arm of something ⟨a ~ of the sea⟩ ⟨a ~ of a cross⟩ ⟨the Stanleyville ~ is a completely detached rail segment —Tom Marvel⟩ ⟨elongation of the ~*s* of the letters —F.W.Goudy⟩ **6 :** a mischievous child **:** a young scamp ⟨his folks likely fretting themselves to prostration over him, the ungrateful ~ —Helen Eustis⟩ **7 :** either part of an archery bow from the handle to the tip ⟨upper ~⟩ ⟨lower ~⟩ **8 :** one of the two parts of an anticline or syncline on either side of the axis — **out on a limb :** in an exposed and dangerous position with little chance of retreat ⟨was not quite willing to go *out on a limb* for a little piece of paper —John Steinbeck⟩ ⟨like other venture-loving businessmen, he occasionally finds himself *out on a limb* —*Time*⟩

**²limb** \"\ *vt* -ED/-ING/-S **:** to cut or tear off the limbs of **:** DISMEMBER; *esp* **:** to cut off the limbs of (a felled tree) ⟨after being felled and ~*ed* —W.F.Driver⟩

**³limb** \"\ *n* -s [L *limbus* border — more at LIMP] **1 :** EDGE, BORDER: as **a :** the graduated margin of an arc or circle in an instrument for measuring angles **b :** the graduated staff of a leveling rod **2 :** the outer edge of the apparent disk of a celestial body or a portion of the edge ⟨the east ~ of the sun⟩ **3 a :** the expanded portion of an organ or structure: as (1) **:** the spreading upper portion of a gamosepalous calyx or a gamopetalous corolla as distinguished from the lower tubular portion (2) **:** the broad terminal portion of a petal as contrasted with the narrow basal part (3) **:** a leaf blade **b :** the margin or the terminal portion of the leaf in mosses when different in color or structure from the median or basal portion

**¹lim·ba** \'limbə\ *n, pl* **limba** *or* **limbas** *usu cap* **1 a :** a peasant people of Sierra Leone traditionally distantly affiliated with their neighbors as far afield as Fouta Djallon in French Guinea **b :** a member of such people **2 :** a West-Atlantic language of the Limba people

**²limba** \"\ *n* -s [prob. native name in West Africa] **1 :** a tall whitish-trunked West African tree (*Terminalia superba*) — called also *afara*, *korina* **2 :** the straight-grained wood of the limba tree

**lim·bal** \'limbəl\ *adj* [*limbus* + *-al*] **:** LIMBIC

**lim·bate** \'lim,bāt\ *adj* [LL *limbatus* bordered, fr. L *limbus* border + *-atus* -ate] **:** having a part of one color surrounded by an edging of another color ⟨a ~ leaf⟩

**lim·ba·tion** \lim'bāshən\ *n* -s [*limbate* + *-ion*] **:** LIMBUS

**limb bud** *n* **:** a proliferation of embryonic tissue shaped like a mound from which a limb develops

**lim·beck** *also* **lim·bec** \'lim,bek\ *n* -s [ME *lambyke*, *lembike*, modif. of MF *alambic* & ML *alembicum* — more at ALEMBIC] **:** ALEMBIC ⟨shelves filled with jars, bottles, phials and ~*s* —Josephine Pinckney⟩

**limbed** \¦limd\ *adj* [ME *-limed*, fr. *lim* limb + *-ed*] **:** having limbs; *specif* **:** having limbs of a specified character — usu. used in combination ⟨broad-*limbed*⟩ ⟨strong-*limbed*⟩

**¹lim·ber** \'limbə(r)\ *n* -s [ME *lymour*] **1** *now dial Eng* **:** the shaft of a cart, wagon, or carriage — usu. used in pl. **2 a :** a horse-drawn 2-wheeled vehicle to which a gun or caisson may be attached by means of a lunette that is slipped over a pintle and that includes a pole to which the horses are joined and an ammunition chest that serves as a seat for cannoneers **b :** a similar vehicle designed to be drawn by a tractor

**²limber** \"\ *vb* -ED/-ING/-S *vt* **:** to attach a gun or caisson to the limber preparatory to moving to a new position ~ *vi* **:** to put together the limber and the gun or caisson — usu. used with *up*

**³limber** \"\ *adj, often* -ER/-EST [origin unknown] **1 a :** capable of being shaped **:** FLEXIBLE, PLIABLE ⟨diamond necklaces . . . as ~ as a ribbon collar —*New Yorker*⟩ ⟨loosen their already ~ credit terms —*Newsweek*⟩ **b :** lacking in firmness **:** PLIANT, UNTRUSTWORTHY ⟨put me off with ~ vows —Shak.⟩ **2 a :** having a resilient and supple quality of body or movement **:** AGILE, NIMBLE ⟨with his ~ springiness and his arms dangling from half-length sleeves —W.B.Furlong⟩ **b :** having a lively and supple quality of mind or style ⟨your sharpened eye and ~*er* imagination —Edwin Denby⟩ ⟨delightfully ~ renditions —Whitney Balliett⟩ **3** *now dial* **:** FLABBY, LIMP, WEAK **syn** see SUPPLE

**⁴limber** \"\ *vb* **limbered; limbered; limbering** \-b(ə)riŋ\ **limbers** *vt* **:** to cause to become limber **:** make flexible or pliant **:** LOOSEN — often used with *up* ⟨~*ed* his mental and moral muscles —Janet Whitney⟩ ⟨for the musician to ~ up his smallest joint —J.M.Barzun⟩ ~ *vi* **:** to become limber esp. by engaging in light exercise — usu. used with *up*

**⁵limb·er** \'limə(r)\ *n* -s [²*limb* + *-er*] **:** a logger who trims limbs from felled trees — called also *brusher*, *brutter*

**limber board** *n* [*limber* (as in *limbers*) + *board*] **:** one of the movable planks used to cover the bilge-water passages on each side of a keelson — see SHIP illustration

**limber chain** *n* [*limber* (as in *limbers*) + *chain*] **:** a chain used to clean limber holes

**limber chest** *n* [¹*limber* + *chest*] **:** an ammunition box or chest on the limber

**limberham** \ˈ≈≈,≈\ *n* [³*limber* + *ham*] *archaic* **:** a supple-jointed obsequious person

**limber hole** *n* [*limber* (as in *limbers*) + *hole*] **:** a drain hole near the bottom of a frame or other structural member of a ship — see SHIP illustration

**lim·ber·ly** *adv* [³*limber* + *-ly*] **:** in a limber manner ⟨turns about ~ and marches away —Saul Bellow⟩

**limberneck** \ˈ≈≈,≈\ *n* [³*limber* + *neck*] **:** a botulism of poultry and other birds characterized by paralysis of the neck muscles and pharynx that interferes with swallowing and with raising or controlling the head — compare DUCK SICKNESS

**lim·ber·ness** *n* -ES [³*limber* + *-ness*] **:** the quality or state of being limber

**limber pine** *n* [³*limber* + *pine*] **:** a pine (*Pinus flexilis*) of the Pacific coast of No. America that has the needles in bundles of five and densely clustered at the branchlet ends and the cones with a very short stalk

**limber rope** *n* [*limber* (as in *limbers*) + *rope*] **:** a rope passing through the limbers of a ship to keep them clear of dirt

**lim·bers** \'limbə(r)z\ *n pl* [modif. of F *lumière* (sing.), fr. OF *lumiere* light, opening, fr. L *luminare* window, fr. *lumin-, lumen* light — more at LUMINARY] **:** gutters or conduits on each side of the keelson to afford a passage for water to the pump well

**lim·bic** \'limbik\ *adj* [F *limbique*, fr. *limbe* limbus (fr. NL *limbus*, fr. L, border) + *-ique* -ic] **:** of, relating to, or forming a limbus

**limbic lobe** *n* [part trans. of F *lobe limbique*] **:** the marginal medial portion of the cortex of a cerebral hemisphere

**lim·bif·er·ous** \(ˈ)lim¦bif(ə)rəs\ *adj* [prob. fr. F *limbifère* limbiferous (fr. *limbe* limbus + *-i-* + *-fère* -ferous) + E *-ous*] **:** having a border or margin

**limbing** *pres part of* LIMB

**limb·less** \'limlə̇s\ *adj* [¹*limb* + *-less*] **:** having no limbs

**limb·meal** \'limməl\ *adv* [ME *limmele*, fr. OE *limmǣlum*, fr. *lim* limb + *-mǣlum* -meal] *now dial Eng* : limb from limb : in pieces

**lim·bo** \'lim(,)bō\ *n* -s [ME, fr. ML, abl. of *limbus* limbo, fr. L, border — more at LIMP] **1** *often cap* : a region believed to exist on the border of hell as the abode of souls barred from heaven through no fault of their own (as the souls of just men who died before the coming of Christ or the souls of unbaptized infants) **2 a** : a place or state of restraint or confinement ⟨trapping travelers in an airless ~ —Sam Boal⟩ ⟨trapped by its own sense of inadequacy in a ~ of boredom —William Murray⟩ **b** : a place or state of neglect or oblivion ⟨the ~ of forgotten things⟩ ⟨vanished into the ~ of profitless products —S.H.Adams⟩ ⟨disappeared into the ~ of lost ships —E.L. Beach⟩ **c** : an intermediate or transitional place or state : a middle ground ⟨the infinitely complex pattern of business practices which occupies the ~ between competition and monopoly —S.M.Fine⟩ ⟨half-man, half-child, and yet neither, the adolescent occupies a special human ~ —*New Republic*⟩

**limbs** *pl of* LIMB, *pres 3d sing of* LIMB

**lim·bu** \'lim(,)bü\ *n, pl* **limbu** *or* **limbus** *usu cap* **1 a** : a Mongoloid people chiefly of Nepal **b** : a member of such people **2** : the Tibeto-Burman language of the Limbu people

**lim·burg·er** \'lim,bərgər, -bōgə(r, -bəigə(r\ *also* **limburger cheese** *or* **limburg cheese** *n* -s *usu cap L* [*limburger* fr. Flem, one belonging to Limburg, fr. *Limburg*, province in northeast Belgium + Flem *-er* (akin to D *-er*); *limburg* fr. *Limburg*, province in northeast Belgium] : a semisoft surface-ripened cheese that has a rind of pungent odor and a creamy-textured body of strong flavor

**lim·bus** \'limbəs\ *n* -ES [ML, fr. L, border] **1** : LIMBO **2** [NL, fr. L, border] : a border distinguished by color or structure: as **a** : a circumference or margin of a bivalve shell or of an insect wing external to the closed cells **b** : the marginal region of the cornea of the eye by which it is continuous with the sclera

**limby** \'limē\ *adj, often* -ER/-EST [[1]*limb* + *-y*] : having many or prominent limbs ⟨this figured birch tends to be ~, requiring pruning —*Jour. of Forestry*⟩

[1]**lime** \'līm\ *n* -s [ME *lim*, fr. OE *līm*; akin to OHG *līm* birdlime, ON *līm* lime (calcium oxide), L *lima* file, *linere* to smear, *levis* smooth, Gk *leios* smooth, LGk *leimak-*, *leimax* slug, Russ *slina* saliva, Skt *layate* he clings, sticks] **1** : BIRDLIME **2 a** : a caustic highly infusible solid that consists essentially of calcium oxide often together with magnesia, that is obtained usu. in the form of white to grayish lumps or pebbles by calcining limestone, seashells (as oyster or conch shells), coral, or other forms of calcium carbonate, and that is used chiefly in building (as in mortar, plaster, and brick), in agriculture, in metallurgy, in the chemical and related industries, and in the treatment of water, sewage, and trade wastes — called also *burnt lime, caustic lime, quicklime* **b** : HYDRATED LIME **c** : HYDRAULIC LIME **d** : CALCIUM — not used systematically ⟨~ nitrate⟩ ⟨carbonate of ~⟩ **3** : limestone or other form of calcium carbonate with or without magnesium carbonate **4 a** : a pit or the liquid it contains in which skins are limed **b** : the process of liming in leather manufacturing

[2]**lime** \"\ *vt* -ED/-ING/-S [ME *limen*, fr. OE *-līman*; akin to OHG *līmen* to cement, ON *līma*; denominative fr. the root of E [1]*lime*] **1** *archaic* : to bind together : CEMENT ⟨who gave his blood to ~ the stones together —Shak.⟩ **2** : to smear with a sticky substance (as birdlime) ⟨would have found twigs *limed* for him —Sir Walter Scott⟩ **3** : to entangle or catch with or as if with birdlime ⟨birds are *limed* with the sticky sap of wild fig trees smeared on splinters of bamboo —C.D.Forde⟩ ⟨*limed* soul . . . struggling to be free —Shak.⟩ **4 a** : to coat with a solution of lime and water : WHITEWASH ⟨their gaudy-hued houses and *limed* picket fences —*Time*⟩ **b** : to apply ground limestone or other forms of lime to (land) : fertilize with lime ⟨can ~ it, cross-plow it, manure it —F.D.Roosevelt⟩ **c** : to treat with lime: as (1) : to steep in a lime solution in order to remove hair (as in tanning) or to dissolve proteins (as in glue making) (2) : to add lime to in order to precipitate impurities **d** : to coat (as the inside of water pipes) with calcareous scale ⟨hard water ~s pipes⟩

[3]**lime** \"\ *adj* [[1]*lime*] : of, relating to, or containing lime or limestone

[4]**lime** \"\ *vi* -ED/-ING/-S [prob. alter. of [6]*line*] *archaic* : COPULATE ⟨how the raging lion is to ~ with the yearning unicorn —W.H.Auden⟩

[5]**lime** \"\ *n* -s [alter. of earlier *line*, fr. *lind* — more at LIND] : LINDEN 1a

[6]**lime** \"\ *n* -s [F, lime (the fruit), fr. Prov *limo*, fr. Ar *līm*] **1** : a spiny tropical tree (*Citrus aurantifolia*) with elliptic oblong narrowly winged leaves **2** : the small globose fruit of the lime that is greenish yellow when ripe and has a very acid pulp that yields a juice used as a flavoring agent and as a source of ascorbic acid — compare LEMON **3** *or* **lime yellow** : a grayish to moderate yellow — called also *justic, old justic*

**lime·ade** \'lī'mād\ *n* -s : a beverage of lime juice sweetened and mixed with plain or carbonated water

**lime anthracnose** *n* : a blighting and fruit spotting disease of the lime in the West Indies caused by a fungus (*Colletotrichum gloeosporioides*)

**lime–ash** \'=,=\ *n, dial Eng* : ashes and lime mixed for flooring

**lime·berry** \'līm- — *see* BERRY\ *n* **1** : a spiny Malayan shrub (*Triphasia trifolia*) of the family Rutaceae with small pleasantly flavored red berries **2** : the fruit of the limeberry shrub

**lime blue** *n* **1** : a blue pigment stable toward lime: as **a** : a mixture of copper hydroxide and lime that is no longer used **b** : a mixture of ultramarine or methylene blue and gypsum **2 a** : AZURITE BLUE **b** : FRENCH BLUE

**lime boil** *n* : a process (as in bleaching cotton) of boiling with water containing lime

**limeburner** \'=,==\ *n* [ME *limbrennere*, fr. *lim* lime + *brennere* burner] : one that burns limestone or shells to make lime

**limed ginger** \'līmd-\ *n* : ginger rootstocks coated with lime — called also *bleached ginger*

**limed oak** *n* : oak that has been treated with a lime paste rubbed into the grain to give it a special finish

**limed rosin** *n* : CALCIUM RESINATE

**lime glass** *n* : a glass containing a substantial proportion of lime that is used in most commercial glass products (as bottles, tumblers, and window glass)

**lime green** *n* **1** : LINDEN GREEN **2** : TILLEUL GREEN **3** : a grayish greenish yellow to light olive **4** : a variable color averaging a strong yellow green

**lime–juic·er** \'līm,jüsə(r)\ *n* [*lime juice* (noun phrase, fr. [6]*lime* + *juice*) + *-er*; fr. the use of lime juice on British ships as a beverage to prevent scurvy] **1** *Austral* : an Englishman newly arrived in Australia **2** *slang* **a** : a British ship ⟨ship aboard a British *lime-juicer* —J.C.Lincoln⟩ **b** : an English sailor ⟨*lime-juicers* beating their way aft with a belaying pin —Joseph Hergesheimer⟩ **c** : ENGLISHMAN ⟨exhibits less of that deadly stuffiness than many another *lime-juicer* —*New Republic*⟩

**limekiln** \'=,=\ *n* [ME *limkilne*, fr. *lim* lime + *kilne* kiln] : a kiln or furnace for reducing limestone or shells to lime by burning

**lime·less** \'līmləs\ *adj* : having no lime ⟨these allegedly ~ oceans —*Yale Rev.*⟩

[1]**lime·light** \'līm,līt, *usu* -īd-+V\ *n* **1 a** : a stage lighting instrument producing its illumination by means of an oxyhydrogen flame directed on a cylinder of lime and usu. equipped with a lens to concentrate the light in a beam **b** : the intense white light produced by such an instrument ⟨as the branches burn they glow with the dazzling white of ~ —M.A.Wilson⟩ **c** *Brit* : SPOTLIGHT ⟨his genial smile was spotted on everyone in turn, like a ~, with an orange slide over it, at a theatre —Osbert Sitwell⟩ **2** : the light of public attention : the center of the stage ⟨held the ~ in this period and set the pace, tone, and temper of the movie medium —Lewis Jacobs⟩ ⟨in the ~⟩

[2]**limelight** \"\ *vt* : to center attention on : SPOTLIGHT ⟨pleased and flattered . . . to be so studied, so ~*ed* —Hamlin Garland⟩

**lime·light·er** \-īd·ə(r)\ *n* [[1]*limelight* + *-er*] : one who is or wants to be in the limelight ⟨a perfect modern pantheon of ~*s* —*Saturday Rev.*⟩

**limelike** \'=,=\ *adj* : resembling the lime ⟨~ fruit⟩

**lime liniment** *n* [[1]*lime*] : CARRON OIL

**lime·man** \'līmmən\ *n, pl* **limemen** **1** : a slaughterhouse worker who removes fat and flesh from hides by washing them in clear water, soaking them in lime, and rewashing them **2** : LIMER

**lime mortar** *n* : a mortar made of lime, sand, water, and occas. a small quantity of cement

**lime myrtle** *n* : LIMEBERRY

**li·men** \'līmən\ *n* -s [L *limin-*, *limen* threshold; intended as trans. of G *schwelle* — more at LIMB] : THRESHOLD 3 ⟨make urgent the appetites and needs which are smoldering below the ~ of awareness —R.M.Lindner⟩

**li·me·ña** \lə'mānyə\ *n* -s *cap* [Sp, fem. of *limeño*] : a female native or resident of Lima, Peru

**lim·e·ni·tis** \,limə'nīd·əs\ *n, cap* [NL, fr. Gk *limenitis* harbor goddess, fem. of *limenitēs* harbor god, fr. *limen-*, *limēn* harbor + *-itēs* -ite — more at LIMB] : a holarctic genus of butterflies (family Nymphalidae) comprising mainly dark butterflies with a white wing bar but including also the two important mimics, viceroy (*L. archippus*) and red-spotted purple (*L. astyanax*)

**lime nitrogen** *n* : CALCIUM CYANAMIDE — used chiefly commercially

**li·me·ño** \lə'mān(,)yō\ *n* -s *cap* [Sp, fr. *Lima, Peru*] : a male native or resident of Lima, Peru

**lime oil** *n* : either of two essential oils obtained from limes and used chiefly as flavoring materials: **a** : an oil obtained by steam distillation of the juice of the crushed fruit **b** : a yellow oil resembling lemon oil and obtained by expression of the fresh peel of the fruit

**lime peel** *n* **1** : a variable color averaging a strong yellow green that is yellower and duller than viridine yellow and greener and darker than parrot green **2** *of textiles* : a moderate yellow green that is lighter, stronger, and slightly yellower than average moss green and yellower and stronger than average pea green

**lime pit** *n* [ME *lymepit*, fr. *lyme*, *lim* lime + *pit*] **1** : a limestone quarry **2** : a pit where lime is made **3** : a pit where lime is used (as in liming hides)

**lime putty** *n* : a cement that consists of lump lime slaked with water to the consistency of cream and left to harden by evaporation until it becomes like soft putty

**lime·quat** \'līm,kwät\ *n* -s [[6]*lime* + *kumquat*] **1** : a hybrid between the lime and the kumquat **2** : the fruit of the limequat tree

[1]**lim·er** \'līmə(r)\ *n* -s [ME, fr. MF *limier*, fr. OF *liemier*, fr. *lien* leash, band, tie + *-ier* -er — more at LIEN] *archaic* : a leash hound; *esp* : BLOODHOUND

[2]**limer** \"\ *n* -s [[2]*lime* + *-er*] **1** : one that snares birds with birdlime **2** : one that uses or applies lime; *esp* : a tannery worker who soaks hides and skins in lime solution to loosen the hair — called also *limeman*

[1]**lim·er·ick** \'lim(ə)rik, -rēk\ *adj, usu cap* [fr. *Limerick*, city and county in southwest Ireland] **1** : of or from the city of Limerick, Ireland : of the kind or style prevalent in Limerick **2** : of or from County Limerick, Ireland : of the kind or style prevalent in County Limerick

[2]**limerick** \"\ *n* -s [fr. *Limerick*, Ireland; prob. fr. its use by a group of Irish poets writing in Limerick in the 18th cent.] : a light verse form of 5 anapestic lines of which lines 1, 2, and 5 are of 3 feet and rhyme and lines 3 and 4 are of 2 feet and rhyme

[3]**limerick** \"\ *n* -s *usu cap* [fr. *Limerick*, Ireland] : a fishhook of a shape first made in Ireland — see FISHHOOK illustration

**limerick lace** *also* **limerick** *n* -s *usu cap 1st L* : a lace of Irish origin made by embroidering or darning patterns on net; *esp* : TAMBOUR LACE

[1]**limes** *pl of* LIME, *pres 3d sing of* LIME

[2]**li·mes** \'lī,mēz\ *n, pl* **lim·i·tes** \'limə,tēz\ [L *limit-*, *limes* — more at LIMB] : a boundary or line of fortifications; *specif* : one of the fortified frontiers of the ancient Roman Empire

**lime soap** *n* : an insoluble soap that is formed as a troublesome curd when ordinary soap is used in hard water but that may be specially prepared for use in lubricating greases, in waterproofing agents, and in the paint industry — compare CALCIUM STEARATE

**lime–soda feldspar** *n* : PLAGIOCLASE

**limestone** \'=,=\ *n* **1** : a rock that is chiefly formed by accumulation of organic remains (as shells or coral), that consists mainly of calcium carbonate though sometimes also containing magnesium carbonate, and that is extensively used in building, agriculture, and metallurgy and yields lime when burned — compare CALCITE, CHALK, DOLOMITE, OOLITE **2** : HAIR BROWN

**limestone sink** *n* : SINK 5b

**lime sulfur** *n* : a fungicide and insecticide containing calcium polysulfides usu. obtained by boiling sulfur with lime and water

**lime tree** *n* **1** : LINDEN 1a **2** : OGEECHEE LIME **3** : LIME

**li·met·ta oil** \lə'med·ə-\ *or* **li·mette oil** \-et-\ *n* [*limetta* fr. NL (former specific epithet or varietal epithet of the lime *Citrus aurantifolia*), prob. fr. F *limette* fr. *lime* + *-ette*; *limette* fr. F] : LIME OIL

**li·met·tin** \lə'met°n\ *n* -s [ISV *limett-* (fr. NL *limetta*) + *-in*] : CITROPTEN

[1]**lime–twig** \'=,=\ *n* [ME *lyme twig*, fr. *lyme*, *lim* lime + *twig*] **1** : a twig covered with birdlime to catch birds **2** : SNARE, TRAP ⟨called her beauty *lime-twigs* —John Donne⟩

[2]**lime–twig** \"\ *vt, archaic* : ENSNARE, CATCH ⟨allowed his mind to be *lime-twigged* and ruffled and discomposed by words —W.S.Landor⟩

**lime uranite** *n* [prob. trans. of G *kalkuranit*] : AUTUNITE

[1]**limewash** \'=,=\ *n* : a solution of lime and water used as a substitute for paint

[2]**limewash** \"\ *vt* : to cover (as walls or cupboards) with limewash : WHITEWASH

**limewater** \'=,==\ *n* **1** : an alkaline water solution of calcium hydroxide that absorbs carbon dioxide from the air forming a film of calcium carbonate on the surface of the liquid and that is used in medicine as an antacid and ingredient of external washes — compare MILK OF LIME **2** : natural water containing considerable amounts of calcium carbonate or calcium sulfate in solution

**limewood** \'=,=\ *n* : the wood of the linden tree

**limey** \'līmē, -mi\ *n* -s *often cap* [*lime-* (fr. *lime-juicer*) + *-y*] **1** *slang* : an English sailor **2** *slang* : ENGLISHMAN ⟨among us ~*s* —Maurice Ashley⟩

**lime yellow** *n* : [6]LIME 3

**lim·ia** \'limēə\ *n, cap* [NL] : a genus of West Indian topminnows including several that are sometimes kept in tropical aquariums

**li·mic·o·lae** \lī'mikə,lē\ *n pl, cap* [NL, fr. LL, pl. of *limicola* mud-dweller, fr. LL *limi-* (fr. L *limus* mud) + L *-cola* dweller, inhabitant; akin to L *linere* to smear — more at LIME, -COLOUS] **1** *in some esp former classifications* : an order or suborder of migratory birds comprising the sandpipers and related forms (family Scolopacidae) or often being made coextensive with the suborder Charadrii **2** *in some esp former classifications* : a group of Oligochaeta comprising the more aquatic and typically smaller oligochaete worms — compare TERRICOLAE

**li·mic·o·line** \-ə,līn, -,lən\ *adj* [NL *Limicolae* + E *-ine*] : shore-inhabiting : of or relating to the Limicolae

**li·mic·o·lous** \(')lī¦mikələs\ *adj* [*limi-* (fr. LL, fr. L *limus* mud) + *-colous*] : living in mud

**lim·i·dae** \'limə,dē\ *n pl, cap* [NL, fr. *Lima*, type genus + *-idae*] : a family of mollusks comprising the file shells and belonging to the suborder Pectinacea

**limier** *comparative of* LIMY

**limiest** *superlative of* LIMY

**li·min·al** \'limən°l, 'līm-\ *adj* [ISV *limin-* (fr. L *limin-*, *limen* threshold) + *-al* — more at LIMEN] **1** : of or relating to the limen ⟨~ research⟩ **2** : situated at the limen : barely perceptible ⟨observation of ~ hues is beset with difficulties —Elsie Murray⟩ **3** : having the lowest amount necessary to produce a particular effect : possessing the minimal quantity ⟨an electron must be given a certain ~ amount of energy before it can escape from the metal —Therald Moeller⟩

**lim·i·nary** \'limə,nerē\ *adj* [F *liminaire*, fr. LL *liminaris*, fr. L, of a threshold, fr. *limin-*, *limen* threshold + *-aris* -ar — more at LIMB] : placed at the beginning (as of a book) : INTRODUCTORY, PRELIMINARY ⟨~ quotations from the Greek or Latin —Gouverneur Paulding⟩

**lim·i·ness** \'līmēnəs\ *n* -ES : the quality or state of being limy

**liming** *pres part of* LIME

[1]**lim·it** \'limət, *usu* -əd·+V\ *n* -s [ME *limite*, fr. MF, fr. L *limit-*, *limes* boundary, limit — more at LIMB] **1 a** : a geographical or political boundary : BORDER, FRONTIER ⟨at the exact northern ~ of this valley —*Amer. Guide Series: Minn.*⟩ ⟨just outside the three-mile ~ —Beverly Smith⟩ — often used in pl. ⟨kept within the ~*s* of Detroit —*Amer. Guide Series: Mich.*⟩ **b lim·its** *pl* : the place or area enclosed within a boundary : BOUNDS ⟨into the ~*s* of the North they came —John Milton⟩ ⟨the first collegiate foundation in the ~*s* of the present U.S. —K.B. Murdock⟩ **2 a** : something that bounds, restrains, or confines — usu. used in pl. ⟨simple-minded because of the ~*s* to his experience —Margaret F. Richey⟩ ⟨discover the relationships of meanings within the ~*s* of his form —W.V.O'Connor⟩ ⟨cooperate within ~*s*⟩ **b** : the utmost extent : a point beyond which it is impossible to go ⟨pushed to the ~ to meet these demands —R.E.Barnaby⟩ ⟨a veteran operator who can be trusted to the ~ —Tris Coffin⟩ ⟨the sky's the ~⟩ **3** : LIMITATION ⟨the sadness is without ~ —Shak.⟩ ⟨her opportunity is practically without ~ other than the limitation of her own ability —G.W.Johnson⟩ **4** : a determining feature or differentia in logic **5** : a prescribed maximum or minimum amount, quantity, or number ⟨the store set a ~ of five pounds of coffee to a customer during the sale⟩ ⟨suggested lowering the age ~ for voting from 21 to 18⟩: as **a** : the maximum quantity of game or fish that may be taken legally in a specified period ⟨so many ducks that ~ bags are almost routine among competent hunters —Scott Young⟩ **b** (1) : a maximum established for a gambling bet, raise, or payoff ⟨playing blackjack, two cents' ~ —Hamilton Basso⟩ (2) : an agreed time for ending a card game ⟨set a ~ of 1 a.m.⟩ **6 a** : a number such that the numerical difference between it and a mathematical function will be arbitrarily small for all values of the independent variables sufficiently close to but not equal to certain prescribed numbers or sufficiently large positively or negatively ⟨the ~ of $(x^2-1) \div (x-1)$ as $x$ approaches 1 is 2⟩ **b** : a number such that if $Sn$ represents the *nth* term of an infinite sequence the numerical difference between $Sn$ and the number will be arbitrarily small for $n$ sufficiently large ⟨the ~ of the sequence ½, ⅔, ¾, . . . , $\frac{n}{n+1}$ as $n$ becomes large is 1⟩ **c** : either of the two numbers substituted in an antiderivative for the independent variable in evaluating a definite integral **7** : the maximum or minimum permissible dimension (as of a machine part or manufactured object) ⟨the plungers and cylinders of the injection system are fitted to extremely close ~*s* —William Landon⟩ **8** : something that is exasperating or intolerable : LAST STRAW — used with *the* ⟨I've seen bad weather, but this is the ~⟩ **9** : the full duration of a ball game or prizefight — used with *the* ⟨a good pitcher but he couldn't go the ~⟩ ⟨although he went the ~ he lost the fight on points⟩

[2]**limit** \"\ *vt* -ED/-ING/-S [ME *limiten*, fr. MF *limiter*, fr. L *limitare*, fr. *limit-*, *limes* boundary, limit] **1** : to assign to or within certain limits : fix, constitute, or appoint definitely : ALLOT, PRESCRIBE ⟨no end is ~*ed* to damned souls —Christopher Marlowe⟩ — now used chiefly in legal terms **2** *obs* : to assign (a duty) to someone ⟨'tis my ~*ed* service —Shak.⟩ **3 a** : to set bounds or limits to : CONFINE ⟨~*s* itself to fresh water —Richard Semon⟩ ⟨must ~ itself to functions which are consistent with the needs of collective defense —A.O.Wolfess⟩ ⟨the town is pleasantly ~*ed* —William Sansom⟩ ⟨persons whose musical experience is ~*ed* —Virgil Thomson⟩ **b** : to curtail or reduce in quantity or extent ⟨could ~ production and marketing of dairy products —*Wall Street Jour.*⟩ ⟨medical science knows how to ~ these evils —C.W.Eliot⟩ **4** *archaic* : to be or act as a boundary to ⟨a stone wall ~*s* the farm on the west⟩

**syn** RESTRICT, CIRCUMSCRIBE, CONFINE: LIMIT stresses the fact of existence of boundaries, checks to expansion, or exclusions which either are not passed over or cannot or may not be; it is a general term with less power of suggestion than others in this set ⟨the airplane has possibilities so many that fancy cannot *limit* them —B.N.Cardozo⟩ ⟨*limiting* the purposes for which public funds could be appropriated —*Americana Annual*⟩ RESTRICT may imply a narrow limitation, a more sharp and severe constriction or checking than LIMIT ⟨the decision to restrain French influence . . . and to *restrict* it to the frontiers of his own choosing —Hilaire Belloc⟩ ⟨combinations have arisen which *restrict* the very freedom that Bentham sought to attain —O.W.Holmes †1935⟩ CIRCUMSCRIBE may suggest a bounding circle, often close and narrow, preventing free outward range or activity, in other words, an encompassing restriction ⟨think that the emotional range . . . of drama is limited and *circumscribed* by verse —T.S.Eliot⟩ ⟨the Government's . . . imposition of restrictions and quotas that have *circumscribed* the conduct of publishing so radically —*Times Lit. Supp.*⟩ CONFINE is the strongest in this set in indicating bounds not to be passed; it suggests close cramping restriction, hindrance by encircling environment, or exclusion seemingly arbitrary or, at any rate, positive ⟨strong congressional leaders have always sought to *confine* the President to mere administration —Alan Barth⟩ ⟨must *confine* himself to inferior jobs allotted to his kind —Ruth Benedict⟩

**lim·it·able** \-məd·əbəl, -mətəb-\ *adj* : capable of being limited — **lim·it·able·ness** *n* -ES

**lim·i·tar·i·an** \,limə'ta(a)rēən, -ter-\ *n* -s [[1]*limit* + *-arian* (as in *trinitarian*)] : one that limits or restricts; *specif* : one who holds that Christ died only for the elect or that not all men are to be saved

**lim·i·tary** \'limə,terē, -ri\ *adj* **1** *archaic* : subject to limits : limited in capacity ⟨poor ~ creature calling himself a man of the world —Thomas DeQuincey⟩ **2** *archaic* **a** : of or relating to a boundary **b** : ENCLOSING, LIMITING ⟨imagined isles beyond the ~ ocean —R.C.Trench⟩

**lim·i·ta·tion** \,limə'tāshən\ *n* -s [ME *limitacioun*, fr. MF or L; MF *limitation*, fr. L *limitation-*, *limitatio*, fr. *limitatus* (past part. of *limitare* to limit) + *-ion-*, *-io* -ion] **1** : the action of limiting ⟨without any other express ~ or restraint —John Locke⟩ ⟨fighting to restore the doctrine of ~ to its high place among the nations —*New Republic*⟩ **2** : the quality or state of being limited ⟨itself conditioned by our inescapable human ~ —M.R.Cohen⟩ **3 a** : a restriction or restraint imposed from without (as by law, custom, or circumstances) ⟨all railroads have weight and height ~*s*, because of tunnels, bridges and so forth —*Westinghouse News*⟩ ⟨still further ~*s* on the work of the editors of the news —F.L.Mott⟩ **b** : a restrictive weakness or lack of capacity ⟨the ~*s* of the power of speech —B.N. Cardozo⟩ ⟨within the ~*s* of black and white —Hunter Mead⟩ ⟨the ~ of materials, their strength, their resistance to strain —Mary Austin⟩ **4** : a time assigned for something; *specif* : a certain period limited by statute after which actions, suits, or prosecutions cannot be brought in the courts **5 a** : the limiting or marking out of the bounds of an estate in property **b** : the creation by deed or devise of a lesser estate or estates out of a fee **c** : an exception to the usual rules for the descent of titles of nobility or honor — **lim·i·ta·tion·al** \¦==¦tāshən°l, -shnəl\ *adj*

**lim·i·ta·tive** \'limə,tād·iv, -,təd-\ *adj* [ML *limitativus*, fr. L *limitatus* + *-ivus* -ive] : serving to limit or restrict : LIMITING, RESTRICTIVE ⟨a ~ enumeration of the categories of work on which prisoners might be employed —J.S.Pictet⟩; *esp* : having reference in logic to a third quality of judgment besides affirmative and negative

**limit bid** *n* : a bid in bridge understood to mean that the bidder can barely expect to make the contract named and has no values in reserve

**limit dextrin** *n* : a nonreducing dextrin obtained by the exhaustive action of an enzyme (as beta-amylase on amylopectin or phosphorylase on glycogen) — called also *residual dextrin*

[1]**limited** *adj* [fr. past part. of [2]*limit*] **1 a** : confined within limits : restricted in extent, number, or duration ⟨the product of ~ rainfall —Samuel Van Valkenburg & Ellsworth Huntington⟩ ⟨~ markets of one thousand —V.G.F.Reynolds⟩ ⟨such enterprises should have a ~ life —Leslie Rees⟩ **b** *of a train* (1) : having a limited number of cars and making a limited number of stops in order to provide fast through service

(2) : offering superior accommodations or service and faster transportation **2 :** characterized by enforceable limitations prescribed (as by custom or a constitution) upon the scope or exercise of powers ⟨the government of the United States . . . though ~ in its powers, is supreme —John Marshall⟩ ⟨England has been great . . . under the present ~ monarchy —Edmund Burke⟩ — compare ABSOLUTE 3, CONSTITUTIONAL 4, DIVINE RIGHT 1 **3 :** narrow and unimaginative : lacking in originality of thought ⟨a thorough good sort; a bit ~; a bit thick in the head —Virginia Woolf⟩ — **lim·it·ed·ly** *adv* — **lim·it·ed·ness** *n* -ES

**²limited** *n* -s : a limited train

**limited–access highway** *n* : EXPRESSWAY

**limited atonement** *n* : a theological doctrine that the reconciliation effected between God and man by the sufferings of Jesus Christ was efficacious for some but not all men — compare GENERAL ATONEMENT

**limited company** *or* **limited–liability company** *n, Brit* : a company in which the liability of each shareholder is limited to the par value of his stock or to an amount fixed by a guarantee

**limited divorce** *n* : a divorce a mensa et thoro

**limited edition** *n* : an edition of a book or other publication limited to a specified number of copies and usu. printed in a special format

**limited fee simple** *n, pl* **limited fees simple** **1 :** a fee simple estate in land that may last forever but is limited to terminate automatically whenever certain circumstances in existence when the estate is created cease to exist : a base, qualified, or determinable fee simple estate **2 a :** a fee simple estate that is defeasible and may come to an end for any reason (as by reentry after breach of a condition subsequent upon which the estate was limited) **b :** a reversion or remainder estate in land or a conditional fee-tail estate

**limited liability** *n* **1 :** the liability of shareholders in a corporation or a limited company **2 :** a liability (as of shipowners) limited by statute or treaty

**limited owner** *n* : a person having an ownership that is not absolute or perfect (as one for a limited period)

**limited partner** *n* : a partner whose liability to creditors of the partnership is usu. limited to the amount of capital he has contributed to the partnership providing he has not held himself out to the public as a general partner and has complied with other requirements of law : SPECIAL PARTNER

**limited partnership** *n* : a partnership having one or more general partners and one or more limited partners — called also *special partnership*; compare GENERAL PARTNERSHIP

**limited payment insurance** *n* : life insurance for which premiums are collected over a limited period (as 20 years)

**limited policy** *n* : an insurance policy specif. excluding certain classes or types of loss

**limited service** *n* **1 :** a military classification for equipment not considered suitable for use in combat areas **2 :** a military classification for personnel considered not acceptable for combat service

**limited war** *n* **1 :** a war with an objective less than the total defeat of the enemy's armed forces **2 :** a war limited to a relatively small area

**lim·it·er** \'limәd·ә(r), -әtә-\ *n* -s [alter. (influenced by *-er*) of ME *limitour*, fr. *limiten* to limit + *-our* -or] : one that limits ⟨continue to rely on competition as the principal ~ of private economic power —E.S.Mason⟩: as **a :** CURRENT LIMITER **b :** an electronic device for limiting a train of electrical oscillations to a uniform prescribed amplitude

**limites** *pl of* LIMES

**limit gage** *n* : a gage that serves to determine whether the measured part is within prescribed limits of tolerance

**¹limiting** *adj* [fr. pres. part. of ²*limit*] **1 :** functioning as a limit : CONFINING, RESTRICTIVE ⟨abandoned the ~ dramatic plot —Douglas Cleverdon⟩ **2** *of a modifying word* : serving to limit the application of the modified noun without reference to quality, kind, or condition (as *this* in *this book, which* in *which book*) or to express the absence of limitation (as *any* in *any book*) — distinguished from *descriptive*

**²limiting** *n* -s [fr. gerund of ²*limit*] : the process by which an electronic signal is held within prescribed limits or by which the relationship between the outgoing and incoming signal in a device is no longer linear

**limiting factor** *n* **1 :** the factor that limits the reaction rate in any physiological process governed by many variables **2 :** the environmental factor that is of predominant importance in restricting the size of a population ⟨lack of winter browse is a *limiting factor* for many deer herds⟩

**lim·it·less** \'limәtlәs\ *adj* : having no limits : UNBOUNDED, INEXHAUSTIBLE ⟨humanity with its ~ desires —Mary Webb⟩ ⟨the view plunged into the ~ horizon —William James⟩ ⟨had a ~ war chest —Hodding Carter⟩ — **lim·it·less·ly** *adv* — **lim·it·less·ness** *n* -ES

**limit of accommodation** **1 :** AMPLITUDE OF ACCOMMODATION **2 :** RANGE OF ACCOMMODATION

**limit of liability** : the maximum amount for which an insurance company may be held liable under a given policy

**limit order** *also* **limited order** *n* : an order to buy securities at a specified maximum price or sell them at a specified minimum price

**lim·i·trophe** \'limә,trōf\ *adj* [F, fr. LL *limitrophus* set apart to furnish subsistence to troops stationed on the frontiers, irreg. fr. L *limit-, limes* boundary, limit + Gk *trophos* feeder, fr. *trephein* to nourish — more at LIMB, ATROPHY] **1 :** situated on a border or frontier : ADJACENT, NEIGHBORING ⟨disputes between ~ powers —*Contemporary Rev.*⟩ ⟨this territory is ~ to the Union —A.J.Bruwer⟩ **2 :** MARGINAL, INCIPIENT, BORDERLINE ⟨~ plasmolysis⟩

**limits** *pres 3d sing of* LIMIT, *pl of* LIMIT

**limit switch** *n* : a switch that operates as an automatic control to prevent a mechanism or process from going beyond a prescribed limit

**li·miv·o·rous** \(')lī¦miv(ә)rәs\ *adj* [prob. fr. (assumed) NL *limivorus*, fr. LL *limi-* (fr. L *limus* mud) + L *-vorus* -vorous; akin to L *linere* to smear — more at LIME] : swallowing mud for the organic matter contained in it

**lim·ma** \'limә\ *n, pl* **limma·ta** \-әd·ә\ [LL, fr. Gk *leimma* Pythagorean semitone, remnant, fr. *leipein* to leave — more at LOAN] **1** *in ancient Greek music* : a semitone in the Pythagorean scale that is less than half a whole step and is designated as the difference between a perfect fourth and two whole steps or 256/243 — called also *diesis* **2** [LGk *leimma*, fr. Gk] : a pause in Greek verse equivalent to one mora — symbol Λ, λ, ⋀

**¹lim·mer** \'limәr\ *n* -s [ME (Sc)] **1** *chiefly Scot* : a worthless unprincipled fellow : SCOUNDREL **2** *chiefly Scot* : a loose or immoral woman : PROSTITUTE

**²limmer** \"\ *adj, chiefly Scot* : SCOUNDRELLY, UNPRINCIPLED

**lim·mock** \'limәk\ *adj* [prob. alter. of ³*limber*] *dial Eng* : LIMBER, LIMP

**lim·mu** \'li(,)mü\ *n* -s [Assyr] : EPONYM 1b

**limn** \'lim\ *vt* **limned** \-md\ **limned; limning** \-m(n)iŋ\ **limns** [ME *limnen* to illuminate (a manuscript), alter. of *luminen*, modif. of MF *enluminer* to illuminate (a manuscript), light up, fr. OF, modif. (influenced by OF *en-*) of L *illuminare* to light up, illuminate, embellish — more at ILLUMINATE] **1 a :** to draw or paint upon a canvas or other flat surface ⟨not every ancestral likeness had been ~*ed* by the brush of a maestro —R.P.Warren⟩ **b :** to outline in clear sharp detail : DELINEATE ⟨sees the tanker ~*ed* in her periscope sights —E.L. Beach⟩ ⟨the sweep of the main avenues sprang forth ~*ed* in light —H.T.Desa⟩ ⟨its contours framed in a luminous aureole rather than ~*ed* —Norman Douglas⟩ **2 :** to describe or portray in symbols (as words or notes) ⟨testimony ~*ed* a desperate situation —*Time*⟩ ⟨~*s* the complete domination and degradation of the state —Murray Seasongood⟩ **syn** see REPRESENT

**limn-** *or* **limni-** *or* **limno-** *comb form* [NL, fr. Gk, pool, marshy lake, fr. *limnē*; akin to Gk *limen-, limēn* harbor — more at LIMB] : freshwater lake : pond ⟨*limni*meter⟩ ⟨*limnol*ogy⟩

**lim·naea** \lim'nēә\ *syn of* LYMNAEA

**limnaeid** *var of* LYMNAEID

**lim·nae·i·dae** \lim'nēә,dē\ *syn of* LYMNAEIDAE

**lim·nal** \'limnәl\ *adj* [*limn-* + *-al*] : of or relating to lakes

**lim·nan·tha·ce·ae** \,lim(,)nan'thāsē,ē\ *n pl, cap* [NL, fr. *Limnanthes*, type genus + *-aceae*] : a family of aquatic or marsh herbs (order Geraniales) that have pinnate leaves, long-peduncled small flowers, and polycarpellary fruit — see LIMNANTHES — **lim·nan·tha·ceous** \¦=(,)=¦thāshәs\ *adj*

**lim·nan·thes** \lim'nan,thēz, -an(t)thēz\ *n, cap* [NL, fr. *limn-* + *-anthes*] : a genus (the type of the family Limnanthaceae) of western No. American annual herbs having trimerous flowers and entire petals that are shorter than the sepals — see MEADOW-FOAM

**¹lim·neph·i·lid** \(')lim¦nefәlәd\ *adj* [NL *Limnephilidae*] : of or relating to the Limnephilidae

**²limnephilid** \"\ *n* -s [NL *Limnephilidae*] : an insect of the family Limnephilidae

**lim·ne·phil·i·dae** \,limnә'filә,dē\ *n pl, cap* [NL, fr. *Limnephilus*, type genus (fr. Gk *limnē* pool + NL *-philus*) + *-idae*] : a family of large caddis flies whose larvae live usu. in ponds or slow streams

**lim·ner** \'lim(n)ә(r)\ *n* -s [ME *lympner*, alter. (influenced by *-er*) of *limnour*, alter. of *luminour*, fr. *luminen* to illuminate (a manuscript) + *-our* -or] **1 a :** an illuminator of medieval manuscripts ⟨illustrated by sedulous ~*s* —*Times Lit. Supp.*⟩ **b :** one that draws or paints; *esp* : a self-taught itinerant artist ⟨among the last of the traveling ~*s* —Esther Forbes⟩ **2 :** one who describes or portrays (as in words) ⟨in such terms does Carlyle, the fine, vivid ~ that he is, introduce the Abbot —E.V.Lucas⟩

**lim·netic** \(')lim¦ned·ik\ *also* **lim·nic** \'limnik\ *adj* [ISV *limn-* + *-etic* or *-ic*] : of, relating to, or inhabiting the pelagic part of a body of fresh water ⟨~ worms⟩

**lim·ne·tis** \lim'nēd·әs\ *n, cap* [NL, fr. Gk *limnētis*, fem. of *limnētēs* living in marshes, fr. *limnē* marshy lake] : a genus of phyllopod crustaceans (order Conchostraca) including numerous small almost spherical forms that have only the first pair of feet in the male provided with a clasping organ

**lim·nim·e·ter** \lim'nimәd·ә(r)\ *or* **lim·nom·e·ter** \-näm-\ *n* [ISV *limn-* + *-meter*] : a sensitive form of tide gage for measuring variations of level in lakes

**-lim·ni·on** \'limnē,än, -ēәn\ *n comb form, pl* **-limnia** [NL, fr. Gk *limnion* small lake, dim. of *limnē* marshy lake] : lake water ⟨*hypo*limnion⟩

**lim·nite** \'lim,nīt\ *n* -s [G *limnit*, fr. *limn-* + *-it* -ite] : BOG IRON ORE

**limno-** — see LIMN-

**lim·no·bi·um** \lim'nōbēәm\ *n, cap* [NL, fr. Gk *limnobion*, neut. of *limnobios* living in a lake, fr. *limn-* + *bios* mode of life — more at QUICK] : a genus of American aquatic herbs (family Hydrocharitaceae) that have flowers with spathes — see FROGBIT 2

**lim·noc·ni·da** \lim'näknәdә\ *n, cap* [NL, fr. *limn-* + Gk *knidē* nettle — more at CNIDA] : a genus of small freshwater hydrozoan jellyfishes (suborder Trachomedusae) found in central Africa

**lim·nod·ri·lus** \lim'nädrәlәs\ *n, cap* [NL, fr. *limn-* + LGk *drilos* leech] : a common genus of the family Tubificidae comprising aquatic oligochaete worms of the eastern U.S.

**lim·no·graph** \'limnә,graf, -räf\ *n* [ISV *limn-* + *-graph*] : a record made on a limnimeter

**lim·no·log·i·cal** \¦limnә¦läjәkәl\ *also* **lim·no·log·ic** \-jik\ *adj* : of or relating to limnology — **lim·no·log·i·cal·ly** \-jәk(ә)lē\ *adv*

**lim·nol·o·gist** \lim'näläjәst\ *n* -s [ISV *limnology* + *-ist*] : a specialist in limnology

**lim·nol·o·gy** \-jē\ *n* -ES [ISV *limn-* + *-logy*] : the scientific study of physical, chemical, meteorological, and biological conditions in fresh waters esp. of ponds and lakes

**limnometer** *var of* LIMNIMETER

**lim·no·pi·the·cus** \,limnōpә'thēkәs, -ō'pithәkәs\ *n, cap* [NL, fr. *limn-* + *-pithecus*] : a genus of fossil nonbrachiating gibbons from the Lower Miocene of eastern Africa

**lim·no·plankton** \¦limnō+\ *n* [ISV *limn-* + *plankton*] : the plankton of fresh waters esp. of lakes — **lim·no·planktonic** \"+(,)=¦==\ *adj*

**lim·nor·chis** \lim'nȯrkәs\ *n, cap* [NL, fr. *limn-* + *Orchis*] *in some classifications* : a genus of No. American orchids closely related to *Habenaria* that have greenish or whitish flowers with an entire lip

**lim·no·ria** \,limnә'rīә\ *n* [NL, fr. Gk *Limnōreia*, one of the Nereids] **1** *cap* : a genus (the type of the family Limnoriidae) of isopod crustaceans that contains the gribble **2** -s : any isopod of the genus *Limnoria*

**lim·nos·ce·lis** \lim'näsәlәs\ *n, cap* [NL, fr. *limn-* + Gk *skelis, schelis* rib of beef; akin to Gk *skelos* leg — more at CYLINDER] : a genus of very primitive Lower Permian reptiles (order Cotylosauria) of the southwestern U.S. that are clumsily built creatures about five feet long somewhat like lizards and now thought to be very near the point of divergence between amphibians and reptiles

**limns** *pres 3d sing of* LIMN

**li·mo·do·rum** \,līmә'dōrәm\ [NL, fr. Gk *leimodōron*, a plant, perh. broomrape (genus *Orobanche*), fr. *leimo-* (fr. *leimōn* meadow) + *dōron* gift; akin to Gk *didonai* to give — more at LIMB, DATE] *syn of* CALOPOGON

**¹li·moges** \lē'mōzh, lә'-\ *adj, usu cap* [fr. *Limoges*, city in west central France] : of or from the city of Limoges, France : of the kind or style prevalent in Limoges

**²limoges** \"\ *n, usu cap* **1 :** LIMOGES ENAMEL : LIMOGES WARE **2 :** a superior variety of china — compare HAVILAND

**limoges enamel** *n, usu cap L* : enamelware in which the enamel is applied over the entire surface of the metal with the various colors being juxtaposed

**limoges ware** *n, usu cap L* **1 :** LIMOGES ENAMEL **2 :** articles of porcelain made at Limoges

**li·moid** \'lī,mȯid\ *adj* [NL *Lima* + E *-oid*] : like or relating to the genus *Lima* or the family Limidae

**¹li·mon** \lē'mō\ *n* -s [F, loess, silt, fr. OF, silt, fr. *lum, lun* mud, fr. L *limus*; akin to L *linere* to smear — more at LIME] : LOESS

**²li·mon** \'līmәn\ *n* -s [blend of ⁶*lime* and *lemon*] : a hybrid citrus fruit produced by crossing a lime and a lemon

**li·mon·cil·lo** \,lēmōn'sē(,)(y)ō\ *n* -s [AmerSp, dim. of Sp *limón* lemon, fr. Ar *laymūn*] **1 a :** any of several tropical American fruit or timber trees **b** *Puerto Rico* : BAYBERRY 1 **2** *Southwest* : any of several yellow-flowered composite plants (genus *Pectis*) with strongly lemon-scented foliage; *esp* : CHINCHWEED

**li·mon·ci·to** \-sē(,)tō\ *n* -s [PhilSp, dim. of Sp *limón* lemon] *Philippines* : LIMEBERRY

**li·mo·nene** \'limә,nēn, 'līm-\ *n* -s [ISV *limon-* (as in *limonin*) + *-ene*] : a liquid terpene hydrocarbon $C_{10}H_{16}$ that has an odor like a lemon and exists in a dextrorotatory form occurring in many essential oils (as orange, lemon, or celery-seed oil), in a levorotatory form occurring esp. in pine-needle oils, and in the racemic form dipentene; 1,8-*para*-menthadiene

**li·mo·nin** \'limәnәn, 'līm-\ *n* -s [F *limonine*, fr. *limon* lemon + *-ine* — more at LEMON] : a bitter lactone $C_{26}H_{30}O_8$ found esp. in lemon seeds, in the pulp and seeds of navel oranges, and in the bark of amur cork trees

**li·mo·nite** \'līmә,nīt\ *n* -s [G *limonit*, fr. Gk *leimōn* meadow + G *-it* -ite — more at LIMB] : a naturally occurring hydrous ferric oxide that was formerly thought to be a distinct mineral $2Fe_2O_3.3H_2O$ but that is now known to have a variable composition and to consist of a mixture of several minerals (as goethite, lepidocrocite, hematite) with or without presumably adsorbed additional water, that may in some cases be principally goethite and in other cases essentially ferric oxide gel, or that may be bog iron ore or a brown, yellow, or red ocher in which impurities are very common — **li·mo·nit·ic** \¦==¦nid·ik\ *adj*

**li·mo·nit·iza·tion** \,==,nīd·ә'zāshәn\ *n* -s : the alteration of a mineral or rock to limonite usu. by weathering

**li·mo·ni·um** \lī'mōnēәm\ *n, cap* [NL, fr. Gk *leimōnion* sea lavender, fr. *leimōn* meadow] : a genus of annual or perennial sometimes shrubby herbs (family Plumbaginaceae) with leaves usu. radical and flowers in cymose panicles or spikes and subtended by scaly bracts — see SEA LAVENDER

**li·mo·ni·us** \lī'mōnēәs\ *n, cap* [NL, prob. fr. Gk *leimōnios* of a meadow, fr. *leimōn* meadow] : a genus of click beetles whose larvae include many wireworms that are economic pests

**li·mo·sa** \lī'mōsә\ *n, cap* [NL, fr. L, fem. of *limosus* muddy, fr. *limus* mud + *-osus* -ose; akin to L *linere* to smear — more at LIME] : a genus of birds (family Scolopacidae) comprising the godwits

**li·mo·sel·la** \,līmә'selә\ *n, cap* [NL, fr. L *limosus* muddy + *-ella*] : a small genus of widely distributed aquatic herbs (family Scrophulariaceae) having stems that root at the nodes, small entire leaves, and very small solitary scapose flowers — see MUDWORT

**limosi** *usu cap, var of* LEMOSI

**li·mos·phere** \'līmә,sfi(ә)r\ *n* [*limo-* (fr. L *limus* mud) + *sphere*] : an apical body near the blepharoplast of the spermatozoid of some bryophytes comparable to the acroblast in animals

**li·mous** \'līmәs\ *adj* [ME *lymous*, fr. L *limosus*, fr. *limus* mud + *-osus* -ose] *archaic* : MUDDY, SLIMY

**lim·ou·sine** \'limә,zēn, ¦==¦=\ *n* -s [F, lit., cloak, fr. *Limousin*, region in west central France] **1 :** an automobile having an enclosed compartment seating three or more passengers and orig. a driver's seat outside and covered with a roof but later a driver's seat enclosed but separated from the passengers' compartment by a glass usu. movable partition **2 :** a small bus (as for transporting passengers to or from an airport) ⟨the wide seats in the airline's ~ were built to hold three people —J.S.Redding⟩ **3 :** a large luxurious sedan; *esp* : one for hire and seating five persons behind the driver

**¹limp** \'limp\ *vi* -ED/-ING/-S [prob. fr. ME *lympen* to fall short; akin to OE *limpan* to happen, OHG *gilimpfan* to be fitting, MHG *limpfen* to limp, OE *lemphealt* lame, MHG *lampen* to dangle, L *limbus* border, Skt *lambate* it hangs down, L *labi* to glide, slide — more at SLEEP] **1 a :** to walk lamely : HOBBLE ⟨leaning on the old-fashioned ebony cane . . . she ~*ed* across the floor —Ellen Glasgow⟩ **b :** to go unsteadily : FALTER, STUMBLE ⟨the conversation ~*ed* for some time —Henry Green⟩ ⟨this comparison admittedly ~*s* as much as any —Alfred Einstein⟩ ⟨his logic ~*s* woefully —Hudson Hoagland⟩ ⟨a deliberately ~*ing* meter and desperately forced rhymes —William DuBois⟩ **2 a :** to proceed slowly or with difficulty esp. as the result of a disabling accident or storm ⟨~*ed* into the harbor with her hold full of water —*Amer. Guide Series: Mich.*⟩ ⟨the plane ~*ed* in over the edge of the strip, its engine coughing badly —Howard Hunt⟩ **b :** to barely make headway ⟨capable of ~*ing* along, hovering around the subsistence level —R.C.Doty⟩ ⟨commerce ~*ed* toward a standstill —*Time*⟩

**²limp** \"\ *n* -s : the action of limping ⟨walked with a ~⟩

**³limp** \"\ *adj, usu* -ER/-EST [akin to ¹*limp*] **1 a :** having no defined shape : SLACK, SOFT ⟨a ~ body that seemed to have been poured into his clothes as if it were sand —Edith Sitwell⟩ ⟨letting his body go completely ~ with ecstasy —Liam O'Flaherty⟩ ⟨~ as a rag⟩ **b :** DROOPING, EXHAUSTED ⟨as a result of this protracted session he now felt fairly ~ —J.R.Parker⟩ ⟨~ with fatigue⟩ **2 :** lacking in strength or firmness : FLABBY, SPIRITLESS ⟨made a ~ gesture as if waving away all desire to know —G.K.Chesterton⟩ ⟨small, rather ~ jokes —Wolcott Gibbs⟩ ⟨a ~ young man who finds most of his enjoyment in witnessing the pains and loves of others —*New Yorker*⟩ **3 a** *of a book cover* : lined with very flexible paper rather than rigid board **b** *of a binding or a book* : having limp covers

**lim·pa** \'limpә\ *n* -s [Sw] : rye bread made with molasses or brown sugar

**limp·er** \-pә(r)\ *n* -s : one that limps

**lim·pet** \'limpәt, *usu* -әd·+V\ *n* -s [ME *lempet*, fr. OE *lempedu*, fr. ML *lampreda* limpet, lamprey — more at LAMPREY] **1 :** a marine gastropod mollusk with a low conical shell broadly open beneath that browses over rocks or timbers chiefly between tidemarks and adheres very tightly when disturbed; *specif* : a member of the families Acmaeidae and Patellidae in which the uncoiled shell apex is imperforate — compare KEYHOLE LIMPET, SLIPPER LIMPET **2 :** a person who clings tenaciously to someone or something ⟨disconcert the studio loafer and the studio ~ —Osbert Sitwell⟩ **3** *or* **limpet bomb** *or* **limpet mine** : an explosive designed to cling to the hull of a ship ⟨saboteurs stuck *limpet mines* on two gunrunning yachts —*Newsweek*⟩

**lim·pid** \'limpәd\ *adj* [F or L; F *limpide*, fr. L *limpidus*, fr. *limpa, lumpa* water — more at LYMPH] **1 a :** completely free from cloudiness or other obstacles to the passage of light ⟨the water itself is so ~ that you can get no concept of depth by peering down into it —Thomas Barbour⟩ ⟨a ~ stream, through which we see to the very bottom —Lindley Murray⟩ **b :** clear and simple in style : readily intelligible ⟨absolute simplicity of subject is matched by ~ and artless style —C.S.Kilby⟩ **2 :** absolutely serene and untroubled ⟨still shows the benign effects of a ~ childhood —*Time*⟩ ⟨my conscience ~ —Geoffrey Household⟩ **syn** see CLEAR

**lim·pid·i·ty** \lim'pidәd·ē, -әtē, -i\ *n* -ES [LL *limpiditat-, limpiditas*, fr. L *limpidus* + *-itat-, -itas* -ity] : the quality or state of being limpid ⟨its marvelous simplicity and ~, its ruthless abstinence from the pleasures of mere rhetoric —Irving Kristol⟩

**lim·pid·ly** *adv* : in a limpid manner ⟨state all this in ~ clear English —John Gillin⟩

**lim·pid·ness** *n* -ES : the quality or state of being limpid : LIMPIDITY ⟨lake waters under rock, unfathomable in ~ —George Meredith⟩

**limp·ing·ly** *adv* [*limping* (pres. part. of ¹*limp*) + *-ly*] : in a limping manner ⟨had a smattering of college German and could get along ~ —W.A.White⟩

**limping standard** *n* : a monetary system under which both gold and silver are legal tender but only one metal is given free coinage

**limp·kin** \'limpkәn\ *n* -s [¹*limp* + *-kin*] : a large brown wading bird (*Aramus pictus*) that resembles a bittern but has a longer slightly curved bill, longer neck and legs, and white stripes on head and neck — see COURLAN

**limp·ly** *adv* : in a limp manner

**limp·ness** *n* -ES : the quality or state of being limp

**limp·sy** *also* **limp·sey** \'limpsē\ *or* **lim·sy** \-msē\ *adj* [³*limp* + *-sy* (as in *tipsy*)] **1** *dial* : limp esp. from lack of physical strength : WEAK ⟨suddenly the half-frozen and lifeless body fell ~ in their hands —Walt Whitman⟩ **2** *dial* : lacking in energy : LAZY

**li·mu** \'lē(,)mü\ *n* -s [Hawaiian] *Hawaii* : a water plant; *esp* : any of more than 70 various edible seaweeds

**limu–eleele** \-,ālā'ā(,)lā\ *n* -s [Hawaiian *limu-'ele'ele*] *Hawaii* : an edible marine green alga (*Enteromorpha intestinalis*)

**limu–kohu** \-'kō(,)hü\ *n* -s [Hawaiian] *Hawaii* : an edible brown alga (*Asparagopsis sandfordiana*)

**li·mu·li·dae** \lә'myülә,dē\ *n pl, cap* [NL, fr. *Limulus*, type genus + *-idae*] : a family (order Xiphosura) comprising the king crab and various related extinct forms

**¹lim·u·loid** \'limyә,lȯid\ *adj* [NL *Limulus* + E *-oid*] : like or relating to the king crabs

**²limuloid** \"\ *n* -s : KING CRAB

**lim·u·lus** \-lәs\ *n* [NL, fr. L *limus* sidelong + *-ulus* — more at LIMB] **1** *cap* : the type genus of Limulidae comprising the king crabs or in some classifications including solely the No. American king crab **2** *pl* **limulus** \"\ *or* **limu·li** \-yә,lī\ *also* **limuluses** : KING CRAB

**limy** \'līmē, -mi\ *adj, usu* -ER/-EST [¹*lime* + *-y*] **1 :** smeared with or consisting of lime : VISCOUS **2 :** containing lime or limestone ⟨a ~ soil⟩ **3 :** resembling or having the qualities of lime

**¹lin** \'lin\ *vi* **linned; linned; linning; lins** [ME *linnen*, fr. OE *linnan*; akin to OHG *bilinnan* to cease, ON *linna* to cease, Goth *aflinnan* to go away — more at LESS] *now dial Brit* : to come to a stop : CEASE

**²lin** \"\ *dial var of* ¹LINE

**³lin** \"\ *var of* LINN

**⁴lin** \"\ *n* -s [Chin (Pek) *lin²*] : a female unicorn — used in Chinese mythology

**lin** *abbr* **1** lineal **2** linear **3** liniment

**lin·able** *also* **line·able** \'līnәbәl\ *adj* [⁴*line* + *-able*] : lying or arranged in a straight line

**li·na·ce·ae** \lī'nāsē,ē\ *n pl, cap* [NL, fr. *Linum*, type genus + *-aceae*] : a widely distributed family of herbs, shrubs, or trees (order Geraniales) having regular pentamerous flowers with the stamens twice as many as the petals and a fruit that is a capsule or a drupe — see LINUM — **li·na·ceous** \(')lī¦nāshәs\ *adj*

**lin·age** *also* **line·age** \'līnij, -nēj\ *n* -s [³*line* + *-age*] **1 :** the number of lines of printed matter or of written matter estimated in terms of the number of lines it would occupy in print **2 :** payment for literary matter at so much a line (as by newspapers or periodicals) ⟨the ~ of many magazines is about 15 cents⟩ ⟨offered him a chance to do several articles on ~⟩ **3 :** the amount of space occupied (as by advertising matter in a newspaper or periodical) usu. measured in terms of agate lines

**li·na·loe** \lə'nalōə\ *also* **li·na·loa** \-ōä\ *n* -s [MexSp *lináloe*, fr. Sp, agalloch, fr. ML *lignum aloes*, lit., wood of the aloe] **:** the wood of any of several trees of the genus *Bursera* esp. of a Mexican tree (*B. aloexylon*) that yields a perfume and is used to some extent in furniture and cabinetwork

**linaloe oil** *n* **:** any of several chemically similar essential oils used in perfumery and as sources of linalool: as **a :** a colorless or pale yellow oil obtained from linaloe or the wood of other trees of the family Burseraceae — called also *Mexican linaloe oil* **b :** BOIS DE ROSE OIL

**lin·al·o·ol** \lə'nalə,wōl, -,ōl, -,ȯl, ,linə'lül\ *also* **lin·a·lol** \'linə,lōl, -lōl\ *n* -s [ISV *linaloe* + *-ol*] **:** a fragrant liquid unsaturated tertiary alcohol $C_{10}H_{17}OH$ that occurs both free and in the form of esters in many essential oils and that exists in dextrorotatory form obtained esp. from bois de rose oil or coriander oil, in levorotatory form obtained esp. from Mexican linaloe oil and the oil from a Japanese cinnamon, and in racemic form obtained by isomerization of geraniol or synthetically all optically isomeric and all used in perfumes, soaps, and flavoring materials

**lin·a·lyl** \'linə,lil, -lēl\ *n* -s [ISV *linal-* (fr. *linalool*) + *-yl*] **:** a radical $C_{10}H_{17}$ derived from linalool by removal of the hydroxyl group

**linalyl acetate** *n* **:** a fragrant liquid ester $CH_3COOC_{10}H_{17}$ that is found esp. in bergamot oil, lavender oil, and petitgrain oil, that is also made from linalool, and that is used similarly to linalool

**lin·a·mar·in** \,linə'ma(a)rə̇n, -mer-\ *n* -s [ISV *lin-* (fr. L *linum* flax) + *amar-* (fr. L *amarus* bitter) + *-in*; orig. formed as F *linamarine* — more at LINEN, AMAROID] **:** a bitter crystalline cyanogenetic glucoside $(CH_3)_2C(CN)OC_6H_{11}O_5$ occurring esp. in flax and the lima bean and yielding acetone cyanohydrin and glucose on hydrolysis — called also *phaseolunatin*

**li·nan·thus** \lī'nan(t)thəs\ *n, cap* [NL, fr. *lin-* (fr. L *linum*) + *-anthus*] **:** a genus of delicate herbs (family Polemoniaceae) of the western U.S. having opposite usu. palmately divided leaves

**li·nar·ia** \lī'na(a)rēə, -ner-\ *n* [NL, fr. *lin-* (fr. L *linum*) + *-aria*] **1** *cap* **:** a genus of herbs and undershrubs (family Scrophulariaceae) having a personate spurred corolla — see TOADFLAX **2** -s **:** any plant or flower of the genus *Linaria*

**li·na·rite** \'līnə,rīt, lə'nä,-\ *n* -s [G *linarit*, fr. *Linares*, Spain, its locality, + G *-it* -ite] **:** a mineral $PbCu(SO_4)(OH)_2$ consisting of a basic lead copper sulfate occurring in deep blue monoclinic crystals

¹**linch** \'linch\ *or* **linch·et** \-chə̇t\ *Brit var of* ¹LYNCH

²**linch** \"\ *var of* LINGE

**linch·pin** *also* **lynch·pin** \'linch,pin\ *n* [ME *lynspin*, fr. *lyns*, *lins* linchpin (fr. OE *lynis*) + *pin*; akin to OS *lunisa* linchpin, OHG *lun*, Skt *āni* — more at ELL] **1 a :** a pin inserted in an axletree outside of the wheel to prevent the latter from slipping off **b :** a linking device (as for making a plow rig fast to a tractor) that consists essentially of a metal pin that can be fitted into sockets in the objects to be linked and usu. has some locking device to prevent shifting **2 :** something that serves to hold together the elements of a situation ⟨the ~ in the prosecution's case was a subpoenaed canceled check —Joel Sayre⟩ ⟨the ~ in this entire policy is clearly collaboration —Joseph Barnes⟩

**linch-pinned** \-pind\ *adj* **:** supplied or secured with linchpins

¹**lin·coln** \'liŋkən\ *adj, usu cap* [fr. *Lincoln*, city in Lincolnshire, England] **:** of or from the city of Lincoln, England **:** of the kind or style prevalent in Lincoln

²**lincoln** \"\ *adj, usu cap* [fr. *Lincolnshire* or *Lincoln*, county in eastern England] **:** LINCOLNSHIRE

³**lincoln** \"\ *adj, usu cap* [fr. *Lincoln*, Nebraska] **:** of or from Lincoln, the capital of Nebraska **:** of the kind or style prevalent in Lincoln

⁴**lincoln** \"\ *n* [²*lincoln*] **1** *usu cap* **:** an English breed of long-wool mutton type sheep similar to the Leicester but heavier and having a larger and bolder head with a characteristic tuft of wool on the forehead — see LINCOLN LAMB **2** *or* **lincoln longwool** -s *usu cap 1st L & often cap 2d L* **:** a sheep of the Lincoln breed

**lincoln day** *n, usu cap L&D* [after Abraham *Lincoln* †1865 16th president of the U.S.] **:** LINCOLN'S BIRTHDAY

**lin·coln·esque** \,liŋkə'nesk\ *adj, usu cap* **:** resembling or resembling that of Abraham Lincoln ⟨a *Lincolnesque* pose⟩

**lincoln green** *n* [¹*lincoln*] **1** *usu cap L* **:** a woolen of Lincoln green formerly worn by foresters **2** *often cap L* **:** a moderate olive green that is yellower and paler than forest green (sense 2), yellower, lighter, and slightly stronger than cypress and greener and slightly duller than holly green (sense 2)

**lin·coln·i·an** \(')liŋ'kōnēən\ *adj, usu cap* [Abraham *Lincoln* + E *-ian*] **:** of or relating to Abraham Lincoln or to his character or style

**lin·coln·i·ana** \liŋ,kōnē'anə, ,liŋkənē, -'änə, -'ānə *also* 'ānə\ *n pl, usu cap* **:** matter (as papers, books, letters, relics) relating to Abraham Lincoln

**lin·coln·ite** \'liŋkə,nīt\ *n* -s *usu cap* **:** a follower or adherent of Abraham Lincoln or of his policies **:** a person oriented toward or serving the Northern side in the Civil War

**lincoln lamb** *n, usu cap 1st L* [⁴*lincoln*] **1 :** a crossbred Argentine sheep developed from the Lincoln breed **2 :** the pelt of the young lamb of the Lincoln lamb commonly processed as fur

**lincoln red** *n* [²*lincoln*] **1** *or* **lincoln red shorthorn a** *usu cap L&R&S* **:** a British breed of red dual-purpose cattle that is sometimes considered a variety of the Shorthorn breed **b** *usu cap L & often cap R&S* **:** an animal of this breed **2** *often cap L* **:** CARTHAMUS RED

**lincoln rocker** *n, usu cap L* [after Abraham *Lincoln*] **:** a high-backed upholstered rocking chair with open arms that was popular in the middle of the 19th century

**lincoln's birthday** *n, usu cap L&B* [after Abraham *Lincoln* †1865 16th president of the U. S.] **:** February 12 observed as a legal holiday in many of the states of the U. S.

**lin·coln·shire** \'liŋkən,shi(ə)r, -,shiə, -,shə(r)\ *adj, usu cap* [fr. *Lincolnshire* or *Lincoln*, county in eastern England] **:** of or from the county of Lincoln, England **:** of the kind or style prevalent in Lincoln

**lincoln's sparrow** *also* **lincoln's finch** *n, usu cap L* [after Thomas *Lincoln* †1883 friend of Audubon (who named it)] **:** a small No. American sparrow (*Melospiza lincolni*) similar to the song sparrow but having a buff band on the breast

**Lin·crus·ta Wal·ton** \,lin,krəstə'wōltᵊn, -ltən\ *trademark* — used for a heavy fabric coated with thickened and colored linseed oil, stamped with decorative designs, and used to cover walls and ceilings

**linc·tus** \'liŋktəs\ *n* -ES [NL, fr. L, past part. of *lingere* to lick — more at LICK] **:** a syrupy or sticky preparation containing medicaments exerting a local action on the mucous membrane of the throat

**lind** \'lind\ *n* -s [ME *linde*, fr. OE *lind*; akin to OHG *linta* linden, ON *lind* linden, and prob. to OE *līthe* mild, gentle — more at LITHE] *archaic* **:** LINDEN 1

**lin·dack·er·ite** \lin'dakə,rīt\ *n* -s [G *lindackerit*, fr. Joseph *Lindacker*, 19th cent. Austrian chemist who analyzed it + G *-it* -ite] **:** a light green mineral $Cu_6Ni_3(AsO_4)_4(SO_4)(OH)_4.5H_2O$ consisting of a hydrous basic nickel copper sulfate and arsenate and occurring either as tabular crystals or massive

**lin·dane** \'lin,dān\ *n* -s [T. van der *Linden*, 20th cent. Du. chemist who isolated four isomers of benzene hexachloride + E *-ane*] **:** an insecticide consisting of not less than 99 percent of the gamma isomer of benzene hexachloride used esp. against agricultural pests but also in medicine (as in the treatment of scabies by application to the skin)

**lin·den** \'lindən\ *n* -s [prob. fr. (assumed) obs. E *linden*, adj., made of linden wood, fr. ME *linden*, fr. OE, fr. *lind* + *-en*] **1 :** a tree of the genus *Tilia*: as **a :** a large European tree (*T. europaea*) that is usu. thought to be a natural hybrid and is much used for ornamental and street planting — called also *European linden, lime* **b :** a tall forest tree (*T. americana* or *T. glabra*) of eastern and central No. America — called also *American linden, basswood;* see TREE illustration **2 :** the light soft fine-grained white wood of linden; *esp* **:** BASSWOOD 1b

**linden borer** *n* **:** a common spotted longicorn beetle (*Saperda vestita*) whose larva bores in the linden and whose imago eats the twigs and petioles causing the leaves to fall

**linden family** *n* **:** TILIACEAE

**linden green** *or* **linden yellow** *n* **:** a moderate greenish yellow that is greener and duller than citron yellow, redder and paler than Javel green, and paler than oil yellow

**linden looper** *also* **linden inchworm** *n* **:** a yellow black-lined looper that is the larva of a moth (*Erannis tiliaria*) of the family Geometridae and that frequently defoliates the linden

**linde process** \'lind-\ *n, usu cap L* [after Carl von *Linde* †1934 Ger. physicist] **:** a process of liquefying air or other gas by repeated compression and expansion producing cooling by the Joule-Thomson effect

**lin·der** \'lində(r)\ *n* -s [prob. of Scand origin; akin to ON *lindi* belt, girdle; akin to ON *lind* linden] *dial* **:** a woolen undershirt or vest

**lin·dera** \'lindərə\ *n, cap* [NL, fr. Johann *Linder* †1723 Swed. botanist] **:** a small genus of evergreen or deciduous shrubs (family Lauraceae) that are native to Asia and No. America and sometimes cultivated as ornamentals with small yellow flowers in nearly sessile axillary clusters — see SPICEBUSH

**lin·der·man joint** \'lində(r)mən-\ *n, usu cap L* [prob. fr. the name *Linderman*] **:** a joint used in making wooden boxes that is similar to a tongue-and-groove joint and is usu. glued

**lind·gren·ite** \'lin(d)grə,nīt\ *n* -s *often cap L* [Waldemar *Lindgren* †1939 Am. geologist + E *-ite*] **:** a mineral $Cu_3(MoO_4)_2(OH)_2$ consisting of a basic molybdate of copper

**lind·ley·an** \'lin(d)lēən\ *adj, usu cap* [John *Lindley* †1865 Eng. botanist + E *-an*] **:** of, relating to, or devised by the English botanist John Lindley ⟨the *Lindleyan* system of classification⟩

**lin·do** \'lin(,)dō\ *n* -s [Sp, pretty, fr. L *legitimus* legitimate — more at LEGITIMATE] **:** any of several bright-colored So. American tanagers

**lind·strom·ite** *or* **lind·ström·ite** \'linztrə,mīt, -n(t)st-\ *n* -s *usu cap* [Sw *lindströmit*, fr. Gustaf *Lindström* †1916 Swed. mineral analyst + Sw *-it* -ite] **:** a mineral $PbCuBi_3S_6$ consisting of a sulfide of bismuth, copper, and lead

**lind·worm** \'lin,dwərm\ *also* **lin·dorm** \-dȯrm\ *n* -s [*lindworm* part trans. of Dan & Sw *lindorm*; *lindorm* fr. Dan & Sw, fr. ON *linnormr*, fr. *linnr* serpent + *ormr* serpent; perh. akin to OE *līthe* mild, gentle — more at LITHE, WORM] **:** a fabulous monster usu. resembling a wingless wyvern

¹**lin·dy** \'lindē, -di\ *n* -ES [prob. fr. *Lindy*, nickname of Charles A. *Lindbergh* b1902 Am. aviator who made the first solo nonstop transatlantic flight in 1927] **:** a jitterbug dance originating in Harlem and later developing many local variants of tap steps, two-steps, balance, and grapevine

²**lindy** \"\ *vi* -ED/-ING/-ES **:** to dance the lindy

¹**line** \'līn\ *n* -s [ME, fr. OE *līn* — more at LINEN] **1 a** *archaic* **:** spun or woven flax **:** linen material **b** *obs* **:** linen clothing **2 a** *obs* **:** the fiber of flax **b :** long fibers of flax hackled and ready for spinning **3** *archaic* **:** a flax plant (*Linum usitatissimum*)

²**line** \"\ *vt* -ED/-ING/-S [ME *linen*, fr. ¹*line*] **1 :** to cover the inner surface of ⟨~ cloak with silk⟩ ⟨*lined* the cheese box with cheesecloth⟩ **2 :** to put something in the inside of **:** FILL, SUPPLY ⟨and then the justice, in fair round belly with good capon *lined* —Shak.⟩ **3 :** to serve as the lining of ⟨silk hangings *lined* the walls⟩ **4** *obs* **a :** to cover the outer surface of **:** PAD **b :** to place persons or things along the side of for security **:** strengthen by adding something **:** FORTIFY **5 :** to strengthen (a book) after sewing, trimming, and usu. backing by applying glue to the back and affixing lining material (as super, leather, or flannel) and paper — often used with *up* — **line one's pockets :** to take money freely esp. from questionable sources ⟨*lined his pockets* on the new school contract⟩

³**line** \"\ *n* -s [ME, partly fr. OF *ligne* (fr. L *linea*, fr. fem. of *lineus* made of flax or linen, fr. *linum* flax, linen + *-eus* -eous) & partly fr. OE *līne*; OE *līne* akin to OHG *līna* rope; derivative fr. the root of OE *līn* spun or woven flax — more at LINEN] **1 a :** THREAD, STRING, CORD, ROPE: as (1) **:** a comparatively strong slender cord — often used in combination ⟨hand*line*⟩ ⟨a hard hemp ~⟩ (2) **:** LEASH, LEAD (3) *archaic* **:** a cord or nerve of the body (4) **:** a thread of a spider's web (5) **:** CLOTHESLINE (6) **:** a rope used on shipboard (as for hauling, towing, mooring); *specif* **:** a piece of rope that has been cut from a coil for a particular use (7) **:** a rope of about 150 fathoms length that is attached to a whaling harpoon (8) **:** a single 50-fathom skein of the rope used to make up a skate of a fisherman's setline or groundline **b** (1) **:** a device for catching fish consisting of a cord (as of silk or linen) together with baited hooks, sinkers, floats, and other appurtenances — see HANDLINE (2) **:** scope for activity **:** ROPE **c :** a length of material (as cord, wire, or steel tape) that is used esp. in measuring and leveling ⟨used a ~ to level the foundation⟩ **d :** cordage as a material ⟨makes of fine linen ~⟩ ⟨only the strongest ~ will serve⟩ **e :** REIN 1 — usu. used in pl. ⟨dropped the ~s over the horse's head⟩ **f :** piping for conveying a fluid (as steam, gas, water, oil) from one location to another ⟨blew out the main ~⟩ ⟨installed a new sewage ~⟩; *broadly* **:** HOSE, PIPE **g** (1) **:** a wire or pair of wires connecting one telegraph or telephone station with another or a whole system of such wires (2) **:** the principal circuits of an electric power system **2 a** (1) **:** a row of written or printed characters or of spacing material esp. when extending across a page or column ⟨70 ~s of crabbed gothic script⟩ ⟨the last ~ on the page⟩ (2) **:** a row of type (as for printing a line) (3) **:** SLUG 2b(4), 2b(5), 2c **b :** a unit in the rhythmic structure of verse that is formed by the grouping together of a number of the smallest units of the rhythm (as syllables, stress-groups, metrical feet) according to some principle or norm supplied by the nature or a convention of that kind of verse and that constitutes a rhythmic unit intermediate between the foot and the larger structural units into which lines in turn may be composed or combined either by continuous stichic repetition in series or by arrangement in systematic patterns (as strophes or stanzas) **c :** a brief bit of writing **:** a short letter **:** NOTE ⟨dropped him a ~ confirming the date⟩ ⟨jotted down a few ~s⟩ **d lines** *pl* **:** a certificate of marriage **:** MARRIAGE LINES **e :** the words making up a part in a drama — usu. used in pl. ⟨spent four hours a day memorizing his ~s⟩ **f lines** *pl* **:** a task usu. assigned as a school punishment that consists of writing out or sometimes memorizing or translating a specified number of lines of writing (as classical verse) **3 a :** something (as a ridge, seam, furrow, band of color) that is distinct, elongated, narrow, and rather uniform in width ⟨~s of color in stratified rock⟩ ⟨growth ~s in a tree trunk⟩ **b :** a narrow crease on the visible part of the body **:** WRINKLE ⟨face seamed with ~s⟩ **c :** the course or direction of something in motion or treated as if in motion ⟨the ~ of flight of a bullet⟩ ⟨~s of flow⟩ **:** ROUTE **d** (1) **:** a real or imaginary straight line oriented in terms of at least temporarily stable points of reference or arrangement in such a line ⟨sight along the ~ from the fence corner to the blasted oak⟩ ⟨the reserves advanced to the ~ of the guns⟩ ⟨waiting in ~ for tickets⟩ (2) **:** an oriented state of harmonious agreement ⟨had to bring the doubters into ~⟩ ⟨it was difficult to get everyone into ~⟩ ⟨hardly in ~ with our policy⟩ **e :** a boundary or limit esp. of a plot of ground — usu. used in pl. ⟨had a surveyor run property ~s⟩ **f** (1) **:** the track and roadbed of a railway (2) **:** condition of track as to uniformity of direction on tangents or variation on curves **g** (1) **:** a sharp image of the slit in a spectrograph produced by light of a particular wavelength or a narrow range of wavelengths, the position of the image providing data from which the wavelength can be determined (2) **:** a similar image in a mass spectrograph whose position provides data that can be used to determine the mass of an isotope **4 a :** a course of conduct, action, or thought ⟨took a firm ~ with his nephew⟩ ⟨his decision took the ~ of duty⟩ **b :** an individual's field of intellectual, artistic, or business activity or interest ⟨modern art is his ~⟩ ⟨completely out of my ~⟩ **c :** a field of business or professional activity ⟨worked in the plumbing ~⟩ ⟨men used to want their sons to enter one of the professional ~s⟩ **d** *slang* **:** an individual's characteristic form of glib and often persuasive address ⟨had a ~ to make angels weep⟩ **5 a** (1) *obs* **:** a basis or standard by which one lives **:** rule of conduct (2) **:** a bounding restriction (as on personal conduct) **:** LIMIT, RESTRAINT ⟨really overstepped the ~ of good taste⟩ **b** *archaic* **:** position in life **:** LOT, RANK **c :** FORTUNE, CHANCE, LUCK — usu. used in the phrase *hard lines* ⟨it was hard ~s to have such a sudden setback⟩ **6 :** any of various things that are or may be considered as arranged in a row or sequence: as **a** (1) **:** a succession of ancestors or descendants of an individual **:** FAMILY, RACE, LINEAGE ⟨descended from a noble ~⟩ ⟨the sire of an evil ~⟩ (2) **:** a strain produced and maintained by selective breeding ⟨a high-fat ~ of cattle⟩ (3) **:** a chronological series **b :** a series of related positions that may be represented by a continuous line which does not intersect itself **:** CHAIN 3b ⟨a ~ of mountain peaks⟩ ⟨extended the ~ of fire towers⟩ ⟨the intricate ~ of the coast⟩ **c** (1) *obs* **:** TRENCH, RAMPART (2) **:** dispositions made to cover extended military positions and presenting a front to the enemy — usu. used in pl. (3) **:** a military formation in which the different elements are abreast of each other — contrasted with *column* (4) **lines** *pl, Brit* **:** a row or block of tents or small buildings for troops in cantonment **d :** naval ships arranged in a regular order **:** a regular ordering of ships; *esp* **:** an arrangement of ships abreast **e** (1) **:** the combatant forces of an army as distinguished from the staff corps and services of supply and in Great Britain from the household troops (2) **:** the force of a regular navy **f** (1) **:** officers of the U. S. Navy eligible for command at sea as distinguished from officers of the staff (2) **:** officers of the U. S. Army belonging to a combatant branch **g :** a rank of objects that are or are accounted to be of one kind ⟨a ~ of small houses⟩ ⟨a ~ of trees along the stream⟩ **h** (1) **:** a group of public conveyances (as buses, ships, or airplanes) plying regularly under one management over a route ⟨several stage ~s were started⟩; *broadly* **:** a system of transportation together with its equipment, routes, and appurtenances ⟨the eastern freight ~s⟩ (2) **:** the company or organization owning or conducting a transportation line **i :** a rhythmic succession of musical notes or tones ⟨a musical ~⟩ ⟨the melodic ~⟩ **j** (1) **:** an arrangement of manufacturing or assembling operations designed to permit sequential occurrence on various stages of production ⟨a carefully engineered production ~⟩ (2) **:** the personnel of an organization responsible for its stated objective (as by manning a production line) — compare STAFF (3) **:** the channel of communication within an organization **k** (1) **:** the 7 players, including center, 2 guards, 2 tackles, and 2 ends, who in offensive football play line up on or within one foot of the line of scrimmage (2) **:** the players who in defensive play line up within one yard of the line of scrimmage **l** *slang* **:** RED-LIGHT DISTRICT **7 :** a narrow elongated mark drawn or projected (as with pencil or graver): as **a** (1) **:** a circle of latitude or longitude on a map (2) **:** EQUATOR — usu. used with *the* ⟨passing the ~⟩ **b** (1) **:** STRAIGHT LINE — used esp. technically when confusion with *curve* is unlikely (2) **:** a locus of points whose coordinates depend on a single independent variable **:** CURVE 5a **:** the intersection of two surfaces **c :** a mark recording a boundary, division, or contour (as on a map) **d :** any of the horizontal parallel strokes on a music staff, on and between which the notes are placed **e :** a mark (as by pencil, brush, or graver's tool) that forms part of the formal design of a picture as distinguished from the shading or coloring **f :** a heavy horizontal line on a bridge score that divides the honor score from the trick score **g** (1) **:** a demarcation of a limit with reference to which the playing of some game (as football) or sport (as racing) is regulated — usu. used in combination; see END LINE, FREE THROW, GOAL LINE, SIDELINE; RUGBY illustration (2) **:** LINE OF SCRIMMAGE **8 a :** a defining outline **:** CONTOUR, LINEAMENT ⟨the rising ~ of the hills⟩ — often used in pl. ⟨the sleek ~s of blooded stock⟩ **b :** the general style of an artistic composition with respect to the sequence or arrangement of its outlines, contours, and other elements — usu. used in pl. **c lines** *pl* **:** the outlines of a ship from stem to stern and from keel to sheer strake whether visualized from a sectional plan or viewed directly **d :** a plan or sketch of something done or to be done **:** MODEL — usu. used in pl. ⟨brief notes on the ~s of a guidebook⟩ ⟨explained the ~s of his foreign policy⟩ **e :** the contour or lineament of a specific instrumental or voice part in music and its horizontal motion as distinguished from the overall vertical harmonic structure ⟨the soaring tenor ~⟩ ⟨the bass ~ of the harmony⟩ **f :** one of four imaginary areas on a fencer's body when confronting an opponent that is determined as being the quarter of defense and attack in a given position of the blades **g :** the style or cut of a garment ⟨a dress cut on the princess ~⟩ — often used in pl. **h :** the visible design or outline of a dancer's body **9** [trans. of F *ligne*] **a** (1) **:** a disused unit of length equal to ½ inch (2) **:** a unit of measure for buttons equal to 1/40 inch — called also *ligne* **b :** MAXWELL **c** (1) **:** AGATE LINE (2) *chiefly Brit* **:** PICA — used to indicate the size of large type ⟨288-point type is often called 24-*line* type⟩ (3) **:** the top-to-bottom or belly-to-back dimension of a text letter used as a unit to denote the relative size of a larger esp. initial letter or of a cut appearing with matter set in such text letters ⟨this 72-point ornament will be a 9-*line* initial when set with 8-point text type or a 12-*line* initial when set with 6-point text type⟩ (4) **:** one line of text type used as a unit for measuring the body size of a larger character set with it — used in combination ⟨a 3-*line* initial⟩ ⟨a 10-*line* ornament⟩ **d :** the unit of fineness of halftones expressed as the number of screen lines to the linear inch with the lower numbers (as 60-line) denoting coarse and the higher numbers (as 120-line) fine **10 a :** a stock of goods on hand and available for sale or bought for resale usu. including more than one kind of item but of varied quality and price ⟨a new store carrying a ~ of fancy groceries⟩ ⟨a new ~ of accessories⟩ ⟨a full ~ of electrical supplies⟩ **b** (1) **:** kinds of insurance available (2) **:** the amount of insurance written (as by several companies) on a single risk **c :** amount of credit available to a single borrower **11 a :** an indication (as of a trend or intention) based on insight or investigation ⟨tried to get a ~ on his brother's plans⟩ **b :** the trail of scent left by a quarry **12 a :** a complete game of 10 frames in bowling — called also *string* **b :** a hand won in gin rummy; *also* **:** the points gained by winning a hand **13 a :** a strip on a craps layout on which are placed side bets to the effect that the caster of the dice will pass — called also *pass line* **b :** FLIGHT LINE — **down the line** *adv (or adj)* **1 :** to or toward the center of town **:** DOWNTOWN **2 :** all the way **:** FULLY, COMPLETELY ⟨are prepared to back the president *down the line*⟩ — **in line :** in or into a lineal arrangement: as **a :** in a straight line **:** in or into alignment **b :** in or into a state of harmonious conformity **c :** in or into order or control — **in line for** *prep* **:** due or in a position to attain or receive ⟨*in line for* a promotion⟩ — **in line with** *prep* **:** in agreement or concordance with ⟨*in line with* our previous policy⟩ — **on the line** *adv (or adj)* **1 a :** on a level with the eye of a spectator — used of the arrangement of a picture in an exhibition **b :** in full view and at hazard ⟨put his future *on the line* when he backed this policy⟩ **2 :** on the border between two categories of a classification **3 :** IMMEDIATELY **:** without delay ⟨paid cash *on the line*⟩ **4 :** into prostitution ⟨she lost her job and went *on the line*⟩ — **on the lines of :** similar to **:** closely resembling **:** LIKE — **out of line :** not in a lineal arrangement: as **a :** not in a straight line **:** out of alignment **b :** not in a state of harmonious conformity ⟨prices and wages were badly *out of line*⟩ **c :** not in order or concord **:** badly behaved ⟨sorry if I was *out of line* last evening⟩

⁴**line** \"\ *vb* -ED/-ING/-S [ME *linen*, fr. ³*line*] *vt* **1** *archaic* **a :** to tie or make fast with a line **b** (1) **:** to measure, sound, or examine with a line (2) **:** to reach or extend like a line **2 :** to mark with a line or lines **:** deface with lines ⟨time that ~s the faces of the fair⟩ **3 :** to depict with lines **:** portray esp. in outline **:** DRAW **4 :** to place, be placed, or be in a line along **:** place or form a line or lines along ⟨pedestrians ~ the walks⟩ ⟨shabby houses *lining* mean streets⟩ **5 :** to form into a line or lines **:** bring into physical alignment, into agreement with some standard, or into concord (as with an idea) — often used with *up* ⟨*lined* up the troops to face the river⟩ ⟨*lining* up support for the candidate⟩ ⟨we will ~ up an invincible resistance⟩ **6 :** to track (wild bees) to their nest by following their line of flight **7 :** LINE OUT **8 :** to throw or hit (as a baseball) so as to cause to travel swiftly and not far above the ground ~ *vi* **1 a :** to

form a line : come together into a line — often used with *up* ⟨*lined* up and marched away⟩ **b** : to share a common boundary : ADJOIN ⟨their lands *lined* on the brook⟩ **2** : to fish with a line ⟨seining and *lining*⟩ **3** : to hit a line drive in baseball **4** : ALIGN

**[5]line** \"\ *adj* [[3]*line*] : LINEAL, LINEAR: as **a** (1) : made up of or delineated by means of lines ⟨a ~ sketch⟩ — see LINE ENGRAVING (2) : involving or consisting of line work ⟨~ copy⟩ **b** (1) : having authority and responsibility flowing in a direct unbroken line between superior and subordinate persons in an organization ⟨the machinery of policy formulation is controlled by ~ executives⟩ (2) : belonging to personnel of the line of an organization ⟨the nature of ~ authority becomes apparent from the scalar principle —Harold Koontz & Cyril O'Donnell⟩ (3) : STRAIGHT-LINE

**[6]line** \"\ *vt* -ED/-ING/-S [ME *linen*, modif. of MF *aligner* to impregnate, align — more at ALIGN] : COVER, IMPREGNATE — used of a canine male

**lin·ea** \'linēə\ *n, pl* **line·ae** \-ē,ē\ [L, line — more at LINE (cord)] : a line or linear body structure — see LINEA ALBA

**linea al·ba** \-'albə\ *n, pl* **lineae al·bae** \-l,bē\ [NL, lit., white line] : a median vertical tendinous line on the mammalian abdomen formed of fibers from the aponeuroses of the two rectus abdominus muscles and sometimes visible externally as a furrow

**lineable** *var of* LINABLE

**lineae al·bi·can·tes** \-,albə'kan·,tēz\ *n pl* [NL, lit., whitish lines] : whitish marks in the skin esp. of the abdomen and breasts that usu. follow pregnancy

**[1]lin·eage** \'linēij, -ē·ēj\ *n* -S [ME *linage*, fr. MF *linage*, *lignage*, fr. OF, fr. *ligné* line of descent, line, cord + *-age* — more at LINE (cord)] **1 a** : descent in a line from a common progenitor ⟨a person of unknown ~⟩ **b** : derivation or source of origin ⟨the characters reveal the play's ~⟩ : line of descent or tradition : BACKGROUND ⟨conceptions of ancient ~⟩ **2** : a group of persons (as a family or clan) tracing descent from a common ancestor who is regarded as its founder : a unilineal descent group — compare MAXIMAL LINEAGE, MINIMAL LINEAGE **3** : the number of lines on a score sheet that a set of bowling pins can withstand **syn** see ANCESTRY

**[2]lineage** *var of* LINAGE

**line ahead** *n, Brit* : COLUMN 4a

**[1]lin·eal** \'linēəl\ *adj* [ME, fr. LL *linealis*, fr. L *linea* line + *-alis* -al] **1** : of or relating to a line : measured on or ascertained by a line : having the direction of a line : LINEAR ⟨~ magnitude⟩ ⟨50 ~ feet of walk⟩ **2** : composed of or arranged in lines ⟨~ designs⟩ ⟨a ~ rather than a literal translation⟩ **3 a** : consisting of or being in a direct male or female line of ancestry or descent ⟨a ~ descent⟩ ⟨~ heirs⟩ ⟨a ~ ancestor⟩ — distinguished from *collateral* **b** : relating to or derived from ancestors in the direct line ⟨~ rights⟩ ⟨~ dignity⟩ : HEREDITARY ⟨a ~ feud⟩ **c** : descended in a direct line : being in a line of succession through lineage **4 a** : belonging to one lineage ⟨~ relatives⟩ **b** : of, relating to, or dealing with a lineage ⟨written in ~ terminology⟩ ⟨a ~ chief⟩ **5** : of or relating to the line or officers of the line in an army or navy — **lin·eal·i·ty** \,linē'aləd·ē\ *n* -ES — **lin·eal·ly** \'linēəlē, -li\ *adv*

**[2]lineal** \"\ *n* -S : a lineal descendant

**lineal measure** *n* : LINEAR MEASURE

**lineal promotion** *n* : promotion of an officer by seniority according to lineal rank

**lineal rank** *n* : the rank of an officer in his arm of the service — distinguished from *relative rank*

**[1]lin·ea·ment** \'linēəmənt\ *n* -S [ME *liniament*, fr. L *lineamentum*, fr. *linea* line + *-mentum* -ment] **1 a** : an outline, feature, or contour of a body or figure and esp. of a face — usu. used in pl. **b** : the distinguishing or characteristic feature of something immaterial — usu. used in pl. ⟨the ~s of Christian life⟩ **2** *archaic* : a small amount : RUDIMENT, TRACE **3** : a topographic feature; *esp* : one that is rectilinear — **lin·ea·men·tal** \¦===¦mentᵊl\ *adj*

**[2]lineament** \"\ *vt* -ED/-ING/-S : to give lineaments to : form lineaments on or in ⟨a harsh land ~*ed* by frost and wind⟩ — **lin·ea·men·ta·tion** \,===mən·'tāshən\ *n* -S

**lin·ear** \'linēə(r)\ *adj* [L *linearis*, fr. *linea* line + *-aris* -ar] **1 a** : of or relating to a line: as (1) : following a straight course : being or going in a straight direction (2) *of music* : HORIZONTAL (3) *of a unit of measure* : involving a single dimension : not square or cubic **b** : consisting of or arranged in a line: as (1) : capable of being represented by a straight line on a graph — used of a relationship between two variables such that a change in one is accompanied by a proportional change in the other ⟨the relation between urban population percentage and propensity to compete is not ~ —V.O.Key⟩ ⟨this series of samples may have been drawn from a population in which there is a ~ relation between age and height —G.W.Snedecor⟩ ⟨many sweeping systems of cosmology have been based on this ~ (directly proportionate) relationship between the distance of galaxies and their speed —*Time*⟩ (2) : having or showing a linear relationship ⟨instead of a ~ trend we find merely temporary fluctuations —P.A.Sorokin⟩ (3) *of painting* : characterized by an emphasis on line; *broadly* : having forms that are painted flat and evenly and with precise fully indicated outlines (4) : consisting of an open and usu. long straight chain of atoms ⟨a ~ molecule⟩ ⟨~ polymers⟩ **2 a** (1) : resembling a line esp. in extended length and narrow uniform width : long and slender ⟨a wire is a ~ conductor⟩ ⟨a ~ leaf⟩ — see LEAF illustration (2) : intermediate between linear and a specified characteristic — used in combination ⟨a *linear*-ensate leaf⟩ ⟨petals *linear*-obovate⟩ **b** *of a human body* : ECTOMORPHIC — opposed to *lateral* **3 a** : giving a scale reading directly proportional to the quantity measured — used of a measuring instrument **b** : being, giving, or involving a response directly proportional to the input — used esp. in connection with electronic devices ⟨the amplifier must . . . have a pronounced ~ response several octaves greater, in treble and bass, than you require in practical use —David Sarser⟩ ⟨the crystal detector is not ~, so that a given increase in rectified current does not indicate a directly proportional increase in field strength —*Radio Amateur's Handbook*⟩ **4** : of, relating to, or constituting a segmental phoneme

**linear accelerator** *n* : an accelerator in which particles are propelled in a straight line and receive successive increments of energy through the application of alternating potentials to a series of electrodes and gaps

**linear content** *n* : LENGTH

**linear differential equation** *n* : an equation of the first degree only in respect to the dependent variable or variables and their derivatives

**linear equation** *n* [prob. trans. of F *équation linéaire;* fr. the fact that every such equation in two variables in Cartesian coordinates represents a straight line] : an equation of the first degree in any number of variables

**linear function** *n* : a mathematical function in which the variables appear only in the first degree, multiplied by constants, and combined only by addition and subtraction

**lin·ear·ism** \'linēə,rizəm\ *n* -S : LINEARITY; *esp* : the condition of having linear historical continuity without significant fluctuation or deviation ⟨it is doubtful whether true ~ exists in any social process or evolution⟩

**lin·ear·is·tic** \¦===¦ristik\ *adj* : having a linear quality : characterized by linearity

**lin·ear·i·ty** \,linē'arəd·ē *also* -'er-\ *n* -ES : the quality or state of being linear: as **a** : the condition of extending along or in a line **b** : one to one correspondence between diverse and often opposed elements **c** : the faithfulness with which an output signal of an electronic reproducing system reproduces an input signal; *specif* : the faithfulness with which the shape and arrangement of the elements in a television picture reproduce the shape and arrangement of the original televised image

**lin·ear·iza·tion** \,linēərə'zāshən\ *n* -S **1** : the process of linearizing or the condition of being linear **2** : a thing made linear

**lin·ear·ize** \'===,rīz\ *vt* -ED/-ING/-S : to give a linear form to : make linear : project in linear form ⟨a heterogeneous catalyst . . . not only can ~ polyethylene —*Chem. and Engineering News*⟩

**lin·ear·ly** *adv* : in a linear manner : so as to be or appear linear

**linear measure** *n* **1** : a measurement of length **2** : a system of such measures (as the inch, foot, yard system)

**linear momentum** *n* : the momentum of translation being a vector quantity equal to the product of the mass and the velocity of the center of mass

**linear perspective** *n* : perspective projection in which an object is represented on a surface by means of lines from points of the object through the drawing surface to a common point of intersection

**linear programming** *n* : a theory of maximization of linear functions of a large number of variables subject to constraints used esp. in the administrative and economic planning of industrial and military operations

**[1]lineate** *vt* -ED/-ING/-S [ML *lineatus*, past part. of *lineare*, fr. L, to make straight, fr. *linea* line — more at LINE (cord)] **1** *obs* : to mark with lines **2** *obs* : DELINEATE

**[2]lin·eate** \'linēət, -ē,āt\ *or* **lin·eat·ed** \-ē,ād·əd\ *adj* [*lineate* fr. ML *lineatus; lineated* fr. past part. of [1]*lineate*] : marked with lines or stripes

**lin·ea·tion** \,linē'āshən\ *n* -S [ME *lineacion* outline, fr. LL *lineation-*, *lineatio*, fr. L, line, fr. *lineatus* (past part of *lineare*) + *-ion-*, *-io* -ion] **1 a** : the action of marking with lines or outlining : DELINEATION **b** : a depiction in outline **2** : an arrangement of lines : MARKINGS **3** : arrangement (as of verse) by or in lines

**lineback** \'=,=\ *n* : an animal (as some Hereford cattle) having a stripe of distinctive color along the spine

**linebacker** \'=,==\ *n* [[3]*line* + *backer*] : a football player stationed within one to four yards of the line of scrimmage and expected to make quick tackles close to the line of scrimmage on running plays and to protect against short passes

**linebacking** \'=,==\ *n* [*linebacker* + *-ing*] : the action, ability, or manner of playing linebacker on a football team

**line block** *n* : LINECUT

**line bonus** *n* : a bonus (as of 10, 20, or 25 points) scored in gin rummy for each hand won

**[1]linebred** \'=¦=\ *adj* [fr. past part. of *linebreed*] : produced by or subjected to linebreeding

**[2]linebred** \"\ *n* -S : a linebred individual

**line·breed** \'līn,brēd\ *vb* [back-formation fr. *linebreeding*] *vi* : to practice linebreeding ~ *vt* : to interbreed (animals) related within the degrees usual for linebreeding : produce by linebreeding

**line·breed·ing** \-diŋ\ *n* [[3]*line* + *breeding*] : the breeding of individuals within a particular line of descent: **a** : moderately close inbreeding (as between aunt and nephew, between cousins) **b** : any of various schemes of breeding designed to perpetuate the desirable characters of a superior animal by interbreeding its descendants — compare INBREEDING

**line camp** *n, West* : a camp for the use of employees working on the outlying parts of a large ranch

**linecasting** \'=,==\ *n* : the act or process of producing type in the form of metal slugs — called also *slugcasting*

**line chief** *n* : a noncommissioned aviation officer (as in the U.S. Air Force) who supervises the upkeep of a flight line — compare LINE CREW

**line crew** *n* : a maintenance crew on an airfield flight line

**linecut** \'=,=\ *n* : a relief printing plate made by photographing a design (as a pen-and-ink drawing composed of lines of varying thickness and sometimes grains, dots, stipples, cross-hatching) onto a plate or film and then photographing the negative onto a sensitized usu. zinc or copper plate that is then developed with the lines that will form the relief printing surface being protected with an acid resist and the rest of the plate surface being etched down; *also* : a print made from a linecut — called also *line block*, *line engraving*, *line plate*

**[1]lined** \'līnd\ *adj* [ME, fr. past part. of *linen* to line (as a cloak)] **1** : having a lining or liner **2** : depicted with a lining of a specified color — used of heraldic representations ⟨the mantling gules, ~ ermine⟩

**[2]lined** \"\ *adj* [fr. past part. of [4]*line*] **1** : marked or covered with lines **2** : depicted with a line attached to the collar — used of a heraldic representation of an animal

**line drawing** *n* : a drawing made with pen, crayon, or other pointed instrument in solid lines or solid masses as copy for linecuts

**line drive** *n* : a batted baseball hit in a nearly straight line and typically not far above the ground — called also *liner*

**line drop** *n* : a voltage drop along an electric transmission or distribution line due to the impedance of the circuit

**line engraver** *n* : one engaged in line engraving : a maker of line engravings

**line engraving** *n* **1 a** : engraving in metal in which the effects are produced by lines of different widths and closeness; *also* : a plate so engraved **b** : a picture produced by intaglio printing from such an engraving **2** : the photomechanical process by which linecuts are made; *also* : LINECUT

**line etching** *n* : LINECUT

**line fence** *n* : a fence built along the boundary or property line of a farm or ranch

**line-firing** \'=,==\ *n* : the application of a firing iron in parallel lines over the skin of a horse in cases of chronic inflammation of the tendons of the leg

**line frequency** *n* : the number of lines scanned per second by the sawtooth wave of current used in television for horizontal scanning with an electron beam — compare FRAME FREQUENCY

**line gauge** *n* : a printer's ruler with measurements in picas, usu. in other point sizes, and sometimes in inches

**line geometry** *n* : the geometry that assumes the line instead of the point as the element of space

**line graph** *n* : a graph in which points representing values of a variable for suitable values of an independent variable are connected by a broken line

**line-haul** \'=,=\ *n* : the actual transporting of items (as freight) between terminals as distinguished from pickup, delivery, and other terminal services

**line integral** *n* : the limit of the sum of products formed by dividing a given arc into *n* parts and multiplying the length of each part by the value of the function to be integrated at any point in this part, the number of parts increasing indefinitely and the length of each part approaching zero

**line·less** \'līnləs\ *adj* : free from lines : lacking a line

**line letter** *n* : a method of reproducing text matter for the blind by embossing on paper the outlines of the roman letters ⟨point systems mostly superseded *line letter* before the 20th century⟩ — compare BRAILLE

**line loss** *n* : a loss of electric energy due to heating of line wires by the current

**line·man** \'līnmən\ *n, pl* **linemen** **1** : CHAINMAN 4 **2** : one who sets up or repairs electric wire communication or power lines — called also *linesman* **3** : any football player except the quarterback in a T-formation (as a guard, tackle, end, or center) whose position is within one yard of the line of scrimmage when the ball is snapped

**lineman's loop knot** *n* : BUTTERFLY KNOT

**line measure** *n* : LINE GAUGE

**linemen's pliers** *n pl* : stout pliers with cutting edges on the jaws used esp. for cutting wire

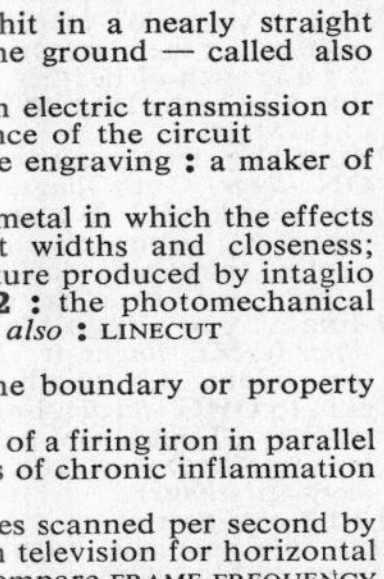

lineman's loop knot

**[1]lin·en** \'linən\ *adj* [ME, fr. OE *līnen*, fr. *līn* flax, spun or woven flax + *-en;* akin to OHG & ON *līn* flax, Goth *lein* linen cloth; all fr. a prehistoric Gmc word borrowed fr. L *linum* flax, linen, prob. of non-IE origin; akin to the source of Gk *linon* cord, flax] **1 a** : made of flax ⟨waxed ~ thread⟩ **b** : being or made of linen ⟨~ cloth⟩ ⟨a ~ blouse⟩ **2** : like that of linen ⟨a ~ finish⟩

**[2]linen** \"\ *n* -S [ME, fr. *linen*, adj.] **1 a** : cloth made of flax and noted for its strength, coolness, and luster though somewhat subject to creasing — see BUTCHER LINEN **b** : thread or yarn spun from flax **2 a** : clothing (as shirts, underwear) or household articles (as sheets, tablecloths) made or orig. made of linen cloth and now usu. of other fabrics (as cotton, rayon) ⟨washed out her ~ every evening⟩ ⟨had a good stock of ~*s*⟩ **b** *obs* : a piece bandage of linen cloth **c** *archaic* : a wrapping of linen for the dead : GRAVECLOTHES — often used in pl. **3** : LINEN PAPER

**linen closet** *n* : a closet with deep shelves and drawers for the storage of domestic linens (as towels, tablecloths, and sheets)

**linen decency** *n, obs* : commonplace and prosperous conventionality as symbolized by fine linen

**linendraper** \'==,==\ *n, chiefly Brit* : a retail dealer in yard goods

**linen finish** *n* : a finish on paper resembling the texture of linen cloth

**linenfold** \'==,=\ *n* : a carved or molded ornament (as for paneling) representing a fold or scroll of linen

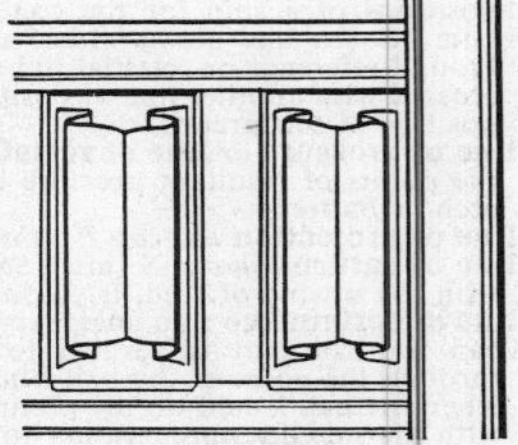

**lin·en·ized** \'linə,nīzd\ *adj* : made or finished to resemble linen cloth or weave

**linen paper** *n* **1** : paper made from linen fibers **2** : paper with a linen finish

**linen pattern** *or* **linen scroll** *n* : LINENFOLD

**linen press** *n* **1** : a large cupboard or cabinet for the storage of domestic linens **2** : a press consisting of a flat bed upon which damp linen is placed for flattening through pressure applied with a large wooden screw

linenfold

**linen tester** *n* : a small magnifier used esp. for counting threads in fabrics

**lin·eny** \'linənē\ *adj* [[2]*linen* + *-y*] : resembling linen cloth

**lineo-** *comb form* [L *linea* line — more at LINE (cord)] : line ⟨*lineo*graph⟩ : linear and ⟨*lineo*circular⟩

**line of action** **1** : the line along which a force or the resultant of any number of forces may be considered to act **2** : the locus of all points of contact between two interacting teeth of a pair of gears

**line of affection** *usu cap A* : a short horizontal line on the Mount of Mercury that runs from the percussion toward the center of the palm and that is held by palmists to indicate affection for a member of the opposite sex — see LINE OF MARRIAGE, PALMISTRY illustration

**line of apollo** *usu cap A* [after *Apollo*, Graeco-Roman god of manly beauty, of poetry and music, and of the wisdom of oracles, sometimes regarded as a sun god — more at APOLLO] : LINE OF THE SUN

**line of apsides** : the major axis of an elliptical orbit

**line of battle** : the position of troops or ships arranged for or as if for delivery of an attack or reception of a charge

**line-of-battle ship** \'=='==-\ *n* : SHIP OF THE LINE

**line of beauty** : HOGARTH'S LINE

**line of brilliancy** : LINE OF THE SUN

**line of columns** : a group of parallel columns (as of soldiers or ships) whose fronts are in a straight line

**line of communication** *or* **line of communications** : the net of land, water, and air routes connecting a field of action (as a military front) with its bases of operations and supplies

**line of credit** : LINE 10c

**line of defense** **1** : an artificial or natural barrier that can be readily employed for defense against invasion or attack (as a line of fortifications, a river, or a narrow pass) **2** : an organization of military land forces with which a nation seeks to maintain its integrity against armed aggression or invasion ⟨the standing army usu. forms a nation's first *line of defense*⟩

**line of departure** : a line which units of a military force are ordered to cross at a certain time in order to coordinate an attack

**line of destiny** *usu cap D* : LINE OF FATE

**line of distance** : the perpendicular extending from the eye to the plane of perspective and having as its foot the center of vision

**line of duty** : all that is authorized, required, or normally associated with some field of responsibility (as of a policeman, fireman, or soldier) — used esp. in connection with assessment of responsibility for or classification of sickness, injury, or death of persons subject to a line of duty ⟨it is now customary to consider any sickness or injury of a member of an armed service that is suffered while on active duty to have been incurred in the *line of duty* in the absence of personal fault or neglect or of existence of the condition prior to entry into service⟩

**line of elevation** : the prolongation of the axis of the bore when an artillery piece is laid

**line off** *vt* : to separate with or into lines : mark off ⟨*line* several columns *off*⟩

**line of fate** *usu cap F* : a line located on the center of the palm that often runs straight from the wrist to the Mount of Saturn and that is usu. held by palmists to indicate according to its direction and strength the nature and degree of a person's success in life esp. as a result of outside influences — called also *line of Destiny*, *line of Saturn;* see PALMISTRY illustration

**line officer** *n* : an officer of the line of an army or navy

**line of fire** : the flight path of a projectile fired from a gun

**line of flow** **1** : a field line of the velocity vector in a flowing fluid **2** : the path of any particle in an ensemble of particles moving under one law

**line of flux** : FIELD LINE

**line of force** : a field line in a field of force (as a magnetic field, an electric field, a gravitational field)

**line of fortune** : LINE OF THE SUN

**line of head** *usu cap H* : a line that begins on the Mount of Jupiter or at the start of the line of Life or on the Mount of Mars and runs across the palm and that is usu. held by palmists to indicate intellectual strength, temperament, and the quality and direction of talents — see PALMISTRY illustration

**line of health** *usu cap H* : LINE OF MERCURY

**line of heart** *usu cap H* : a line that runs across the palm at the base of the mounts parallel to the line of head and that is usu. held by palmists to indicate the strength and nature of a person's affections and emotional nature — called also *mensal line;* see PALMISTRY illustration

**line of induction** : a field line in a field of magnetic induction

**line of influence** *sometimes cap I* : one of a series of lines that appear on the Mount of Venus inside and parallel or perpendicular to the Life line and that are usu. held by palmists to indicate influences on a person's life from outside factors esp. by relatives or close friends

**line of intuition** *usu cap I* : a line located at the side of the hand and formed almost as a semicircle from the Mount of Mercury to the Mount of Luna that is usu. held by palmists to indicate a sensitive and impressionable nature and often a strong faculty of intuition

**line of least resistance** **1** : the shortest distance between the center of an underground charge of explosive and the open air **2** : the easiest line of conduct

**line of life** *usu cap 2d L* : a line that rises under the Mount of Jupiter and runs down the palm in an arc around the Mount of Venus and that is usu. held by palmists to indicate the duration, vitality, and events of life — see PALMISTRY illustration

**line of liver** *usu cap 2d L* : LINE OF MERCURY

**line of march** **1** : the route along which a column (as of troops) advances ⟨driver ants destroying everything along their *line of march*⟩ **2** : the arrangement of troops in column for a march

**line of marriage** *usu cap M* **1** : a relatively long line of Affection that when corroborated by the lines of Life or Fate is usu. held by palmists to indicate the event and the approximate time of marriage or sometimes a very important love affair **2** : LINE OF AFFECTION

**line of mars** *usu cap M* [after *Mars*, Roman god of war and agriculture, fr. L *Mart-*, *Mars*] : a line on the hand that rises on the lower Mount of Mars and forms an arc around the Mount of Venus inside the line of Life and that is usu. held by palmists to strengthen the line of Life and sometimes to indicate martial qualities — called also *line of Protection;* see PALMISTRY illustration

**line of mercury** *usu cap M* [after *Mercury*, Roman god of commerce, fr. L *Mercurius*] **:** a line on the hand that usu. begins on the Mount of Mercury and often runs straight down the hand to the rascettes and that is usu. held by palmists to indicate the condition of the liver and the digestive system and the presence of maladies or physical and mental qualities associated with them — called also *Hepatica, Hepatic line, line of Health, line of Liver;* see PALMISTRY illustration

**line of metal :** the line of sight passing along the upper surface of the tube of a cannon

**line of nodes :** a straight line joining the two opposite nodes of an astronomical orbit

**line of position 1 :** LINE OF SITE **2 :** a locus of all possible positions of a ship for the conditions given — see SUMNER LINE **3 :** a line along which an aircraft is known (as by ground reference or celestial fix) to be flying and which when crossed with another line of position will establish the precise position of the aircraft

**line of pressure** *or* **line of resistance :** a broken line joining the points of resultant pressure between the voussoirs of an arch or buttress

**line of protection** *usu cap P* **:** LINE OF MARS

**line of saturn** *usu cap S* [after *Saturn,* Roman god connected with the sowing of seed, fr. L *Saturnus*] **:** LINE OF FATE

**line of scrimmage :** an imaginary line for each side in American football that is parallel to the goal lines and passes through the point of the ball nearest the side's own goal line when the ball is laid on the ground with its long axis parallel with the side lines preparatory to a scrimmage

**line of sight 1** *or* **line of sighting :** a linear projection toward a target of the straight line obtained when the sights of a firearm are in perfect alignment **:** the axis of the line of vision of a sight (as of an artillery piece) or other angle-measuring instrument **2 :** LINE OF VISION **3 a :** a line from an observer's eye to a distant point (as on the celestial sphere) toward which he is looking or directing an observing instrument **b :** a line joining the earth or the sun and a distant astronomical body **4 :** the straight path between a radio transmitting antenna and receiving antenna when unobstructed by the horizon ⟨reports of receptions far beyond the *line of sight* beyond which the signals should not have gone —*Science News Letter*⟩

**line of site :** a straight line from the muzzle of an artillery piece to a target

**line of success :** LINE OF THE SUN

**line of supply :** the routes (as roads, railways, rivers) in the rear of an army by which the army is supplied

**line of the sun** *or* **line of sun** *usu cap S* **:** a line that may begin on any part of the hand but ascends the palm to the Mount of Apollo and that is usu. held by palmists to indicate possession of exceptional talents leading toward success in life — called also *line of Apollo, line of brilliancy, line of fortune, line of success;* see PALMISTRY illustration

**line of travel 1 :** WALKING LINE **2** *usu cap T* **:** a line that rises from the rascettes high into the Mount of the Moon and esp. when strengthened by other markings on the hand is usu. held by palmists to indicate restlessness and travel

**line of vision :** a straight line joining the fovea of the eye with the fixation point

**lin·eo·late** \'linēə,lāt\ *or* **lin·eo·lat·ed** \-ād·əd\ *adj* [*lineolate* fr. NL *lineolatus,* fr. L *lineola* small line (dim. of *linea* line) + *-atus* -ate; *lineolated* fr. NL *lineolatus* + E *-ed* — more at LINE (cord)] **:** marked with fine lines ⟨a ~ parrakeet⟩

**line organization** *n* **:** the part of a business organization that forms an integrated whole concerned with the production of the goods or services that are the stock in trade of the organization — often distinguished from *staff*

**line out** *vt* **1 a :** to mark (as a casting) with lines indicating material to be removed **b :** to indicate with or as if with lines **:** OUTLINE ⟨followed the route he had *lined out*⟩ **2 a :** to plant (young nursery stock) in rows or lines for growing on **b :** to arrange in an extended line ⟨*lined* his cattle *out* along the trail⟩ **3** *dial* **:** SCOLD, PUNISH, REBUKE **~** *vi* **1 :** to move rapidly usu. in a particular direction ⟨*lined out* for home without a backward glance⟩ ⟨the plane climbed and *lined out* east —W.B.Mowery⟩ **2 :** to make an out by hitting a baseball in a line drive that is caught ⟨cut into the first ball and *lined out* —Ring Lardner⟩

**line–out** \'ˌ=,=\ *n* -s [fr. the phrase *line out* "to line up, form a line"] **:** a play in rugby which is used to restart the game after the ball has gone into touch and in which the forwards of both teams form two close lines at right angles to the touchline and the ball is thrown between them

**line pattern** *n* **:** a virus disease of peach and cherry characterized by faint leaf mottling in more or less regular lines

**line plate** *n* **:** LINECUT

**¹lin·er** \'līnə(r)\ *n* -s [partly fr. ME (Sc), fr. ME *linen* to line, measure with a line, mark with a line + *-er;* partly fr. ³*line* + *-er*] **1 :** a person that makes or draws lines: as **a** *Scot* **:** an official that traces the boundaries of estates **b :** a worker that draws line detail (as in wheel dressing or ornamenting pottery ware) **c :** a writer employed at a fixed rate per line **:** PENNY-A-LINER **2 :** something with which lines are made: as **a :** a sable brush used by coach painters **b :** FITCH 2 **c :** a small grease pencil used to delineate lines in theatrical makeup **3 :** one that uses a line (as a man or a boat in fishing) — often used in combination ⟨a hand ~⟩ **4 :** something that has a position fixed with reference to or on a particular line; *esp* **:** LINE TREE **5 a** (1) **:** a ship belonging to a regular line of ships ⟨a transatlantic ~⟩ (2) **:** SHIP OF THE LINE **b :** an aircraft belonging to an airline **6 :** LINE DRIVE **7 a :** a small plant or seedling intended for lining out for further growth in the nursery row before being set out in its final growing place **b :** a plant that is to be budded in the nursery

**²liner** \"\ *n* -s [²*line* + *-er*] **1 :** one that lines something: as **a :** a worker that applies, inserts, or attaches a lining (as in or into a carton, garment, suitcase) **b :** a machine that lines up the backbones of books **2 :** something used to line or back another part: as **a :** a replaceable tube to fit inside an engine cylinder or a bushing for a bearing **b :** a facing placed between two surfaces or between a surface and some damaging agent to diminish wear, avoid overheating, or serve as reinforcement ⟨a tire ~⟩ ⟨an asbestos ~ for the kitchen range⟩ ⟨a flexible water and vapor proof drum ~⟩ **c :** a slab on which small pieces of material (as marble or tile) are fastened for grinding **d :** paper or other material that is used to cover board (as shelving or the bottom of a drawer) and often decorated **e :** a removable insert (as of glass, metal, or paper) in a container ⟨covered silver butter dish with glass ~⟩ **f :** an insert in the cover of a container that serves to make a hermetic seal between cover and container **g :** a removable and usu. warm lining for a garment (as a coat or pair of gloves) **h :** an outside ply of a combination paperboard or of a corrugated board; *also* **:** the smoother or more finished ply of a two-ply paperboard (as pasteboard) **3 :** a narrow strip of plate to fill in between a frame and an outer strake of a ship **4 :** a casing for a drilled oil well that does not extend to the surface **5 :** a supplementary or explanatory text accompanying a recording

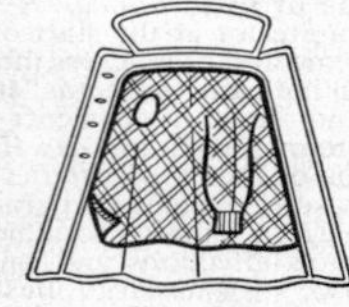
liner 2g

**linerboard** \'ˌ=,=\ *n* **:** paperboard used as a facing on corrugated or solid fiberboard

**line rider** *n* **1 :** a ranch employee who patrols boundaries, turning back stray cattle, repairing fences, and checking conditions (as of grazing or water supply) **2 :** a worker who patrols along a petroleum pipeline to inspect and make minor repairs

**liner–up** \'ˌ=ˈ=\ *n, pl* **liners–up** [²*line up* + *-er*] **:** one that lines up the backbones of books

**lines** *pl of* LINE, *pres 3d sing of* LINE

**line scale** *n* **:** a scale in front of a typewriter platen against whose vertical lines typed characters may be aligned and against whose top edge paper and typing may be straightened

**line screen** *n* **:** SCREEN 10a

**lineshaft** \'ˌ=,=\ *n* **:** a main shaft in a shop or factory usu. bearing pulleys by which machines are driven

**lineside** \'ˌ=,=\ *adj* **:** adjacent to a railway line ⟨~ equipment for handling mail⟩

**linesides** \'ˌ=,=\ *n pl but sing or pl in constr* [³*line* + *sides,* pl. of *side*] **1 a :** LARGEMOUTH BLACK BASS **b :** SPOTTED BLACK BASS **2 :** BLACK SEA BASS 1

**lines·man** \'līnzmən\ *n, pl* **linesmen** [*line's* (gen. of ³*line*) + *man*] **1 :** a soldier of the line **2 :** LINEMAN 2 **3 :** an official who assists a referee esp. in various goal and net games: as **a :** a lawn tennis official who decides whether a ball falls inside or outside of the line or lines he is assigned to watch **b :** a football official whose duties include marking the distance gained or lost in the progress of each play, observing defensive holding of eligible forward pass receivers, marking the point where the ball goes out-of-bounds, and noting violations of the scrimmage formation **c :** a soccer official who assists the referee in deciding where and when a ball is out-of-bounds and which team is entitled to a kick-in, goal kick, or corner kick **d :** a touch judge in rugby **e :** either of two volleyball officials who are stationed at diagonally opposite corners of the court to assist the referee in determining out-of-bounds balls and illegal serves **f :** either of two officials assigned esp. to determine off side violations at the zone lines and at center in professional ice hockey **4 :** LOFTSMAN; *esp* **:** one who specializes in laying down full-size line plans of ships

**line space** *n* **:** the space provided for a single line of typewriting

**line space lever** *or* **line spacer** *n* **:** the lever on a typewriter that operates the spacing ratchet and revolves the platen to a new line of writing and that is used to throw the carriage to a new line

**line spectrum** *n* **:** an optical spectrum more or less separated into sharply defined regions — used esp. of atomic spectra

**line squall** *n* **:** a squall or thunderstorm occurring along a windshift line; *also* **:** a line of squalls or thunderstorms

**line storm** *n, chiefly New Eng* **:** an equinoctial storm

**line–throwing gun** \'ˌ=,==-\ *n* **:** LYLE GUN

**line tree** *n* **:** a tree lying in a boundary line; *specif* **:** one intersected by a survey line and marked (as by blazing) for subsequent identification of a boundary point — called also *sight tree*

**¹line up** *vb* [⁴*line* + *up*] *vi* **:** to assume an orderly linear arrangement ⟨*line up* for inspection⟩ **~** *vt* **:** to put into alignment: as **a :** to put in correct adjustment for smooth running or perfect fitting **b :** to arrange in a line ⟨*line* the silverware *up*⟩ **c :** to assemble and make available ⟨*lined* a lot of support *up* for the reform candidate⟩ **d :** to check, mark, or correct the position of printed matter on (a press sheet)

**²line up** *vt* [²*line* + *up*] **:** to cover (a surface of a book's cover-board or backbone) by applying and affixing a liner

**lineup** \'ˌ=,=\ *n* -s [¹*line up*] **1 :** a line of persons arranged for inspection; *esp* **:** a muster containing suspects whose identification is sought by the police **2 a** (1) **:** a list of players who will take part in a game (as of football or baseball) and of their positions (2) **:** the players on such a list **b :** an arrangement of persons or sometimes of things usu. having a common purpose or sentiment ⟨the ~ at a ticket-office window⟩ ⟨the ~ of political factions⟩ **3 :** the condition or manner of being lined up **4 a :** the act of lining up a printed sheet **b :** a sheet that has been lined up

**lin·e·us** \'linēəs\ *n, cap* [NL, perh. irreg. fr. L *linea* line — more at LINE (cord)] **:** a genus of long slender nemertine worms (order Heteronemertea) sometimes attaining an extended length of 75 feet

**line voltage** *n* **:** the voltage of a power transmission circuit or distribution circuit up to the point of transformation or utilization

**linewalker** \'ˌ=,==\ *n* **:** a worker who patrols a petroleum line on foot to inspect and make minor repairs — compare LINE RIDER

**liney** *var of* LINY

**¹ling** \'liŋ\ *n* -s [ME *linge, lenge;* akin to D *leng* ling, G *länge,* ON *langa;* derivative fr. the root of E ¹*long*] **1 :** any of various fishes of the family Gadidae: as **a :** a large fish (*Molva molva*) of shallow seas of northern Europe and Greenland that is commonly salted and dried for food or a closely related and similarly used deep-sea fish **b :** the American burbot **c :** any of several American hakes (genus *Urophycis*) **2 :** any of various fishes belonging to families other than Gadidae: as **a :** LINGCOD **b :** a fish of the family Ophidiidae **c :** COBIA

**²ling** \"\ *n* -s [ME *lyng,* fr. ON; akin to OE ²*-ling*] **1 :** a heath plant; *esp* **:** the common Old World heather (*Calluna vulgaris*) **2 :** a growth of heather or other heaths

**³ling** \'liŋ\ *also* **ling ko** \-'kō\ *n* -s [Chin (Pek) *ling²*] **:** WATER CHESTNUT 1

**¹-ling** \liŋ, lēŋ\ *n suffix* -s [ME, fr. OE; akin to OHG *-ling,* ON *-lingr,* Goth *-lings,* OE *-ing* — more at -ING (one of a specified kind)] **1 :** one belonging to or associated with a (specified) group or condition or marked by a (specified) quality ⟨hire*ling*⟩ ⟨dar*ling*⟩ ⟨nest*ling*⟩ **2 :** young, small, or inferior one ⟨duck*ling*⟩ ⟨gos*ling*⟩ ⟨prince*ling*⟩

**²-ling** \"\ *or* **-lings** \-ŋz\ *adv suffix* [*-ling* fr. ME, fr. OE; *-lings* fr. ME *-linges,* fr. *-ling* + *-es,* gen. sing. ending of nouns (functioning adverbially, as in *nedes* needs, *alweyes* always); akin to OHG *-lingūn* -ling, OE *-lō* strap, Lith *lenkti* to bend — more at -s] **:** in (such) a direction or manner **:** to (such) an extent ⟨east*ling*⟩ — chiefly in adverbs of state or manner ⟨dark*ling*⟩ ⟨first*lings*⟩

**³-ling** *pres part of* -LE

**ling** *abbr* linguistic, linguistics

**lin·ga·la** \liŋ'gälə\ *n* -s *usu cap* **:** a Bantu language widely used in trade and public affairs in the Congo — compare TSHILUBA

**lin·gam** \'liŋgəm\ *or* **lin·ga** \-gə\ *n* -s [Skt *liṅga* (nom. *liṅgam*), lit., mark, characteristic] **1 :** a stylized phallic symbol often depicted in conjunction with the yoni, connoting maleness, vitality, and creative power, and being an emblem of the Indian god Siva **2 :** lingam and yoni

**lin·ga·yat** *also* **lin·ga·yit** \liŋ'gäyət\ *n* -s *usu cap* [Kanarese *liṅgāyata,* fr. Skt *liṅga*] **:** a member of an Indian religious sect characterized by worship of the god Siva, wearing of the lingam, denial of caste distinctions, and burial of the dead

**ling·berry** \'liŋ- — *see* BERRY\ *n* [²*ling* + *berry*] **:** MOUNTAIN CRANBERRY

**lingbird** \'ˌ=,=\ *n* [²*ling* + *bird*] *dial Eng* **:** MEADOW PIPIT

**lingcod** \'ˌ=,=\ *n* [¹*ling* + *cod*] **:** a large greenish-fleshed scorpaenid fish (*Ophiodon elongatus*) of the Pacific coast of No. America that is an important food fish closely related to the typical greenlings — called also *cultus*

**linge** \'linj\ *vt, past or past part* **linged** [origin unknown] *dial chiefly Brit* **:** STRIKE, FLOG

**¹lin·gel** *also* **lin·gle** \'liŋ(g)əl\ *n* -s [ME *liniolf,* fr. MF *ligneul,* fr. L *lineola* small line, dim. of *linea* line — more at LINE (cord)] *now Scot* **:** a shoemaker's thread

**²lingel** *also* **lingle** \"\ *n* -s [ME *lingell* leather of a horse's harness] *Scot* **:** a little thong of leather

**lin·ger** \'liŋgə(r)\ *vb* **lingered; lingered; lingering** \-g(ə)riŋ\ **lingers** [ME (northern dial.) *lengeren* to dwell, freq. of *lengen* to tarry, prolong, fr. OE *lengan* to prolong; akin to OHG *lengen* to make long, ON *lengja;* causative fr. the root of E ¹*long*] *vi* **1 :** to remain or wait long **:** be slow in parting or in quitting something **:** DELAY, LOITER, TARRY **2 a :** to remain alive although suffering or gradually dying ⟨would not have thee ~ in thy pain —Shak.⟩ ⟨the old man ~*ed* several months after his stroke⟩ **b :** to remain existent though waning in strength, importance, or influence ⟨winter ~*ed*⟩ ⟨old customs ~⟩ **3 :** to be slow to act **:** PROCRASTINATE, DAWDLE, HESITATE ⟨charged that he ~*ed* in settling the estate to increase his fees⟩ **4 :** to move slowly **:** SAUNTER ⟨~*ing* homeward⟩ **5** *now dial Eng* **:** LONG, HANKER — usu. used with *after* **~** *vt* **1** *obs* **:** to put off **:** POSTPONE, DEFER **2** *obs* **:** to make extended **:** PROTRACT, PROLONG **3 :** to spend or pass (as a period of time) slowly and often in suffering or distress — often used with *out* ⟨~ *out* several more years⟩ **syn** see STAY

**lin·ger·er** \-gərə(r)\ *n* -s **:** one that lingers

**¹lin·ge·rie** \ˌlänjəˈrā, ˌlaⁿzhə-, ˌlaⁿzhə-, ˌlanjə-, -'rē, 'ˌ=,= *also* 'ˌ=ˌrē *or* 'ˌ=ri *sometimes* ˌlōⁿzhə-; *by many, vowels other than a in the first syllable and* ē *or* i *in the last are regarded as substand*\ *n* -s [F, fr. MF, fr. *linge* linen (fr. *linge,* adj., made of linen, fr. L *lineus* made of flax or linen) + *-erie* -ery — more at LINE (cord)] **1** *archaic* **:** linen articles or garments **2 :** intimate feminine apparel (as nightwear and underwear)

**²lingerie** \"\ *adj* **:** having a frilly dainty finish or style like that characteristic of fine underwear for women ⟨a tailored black suit with a white ~ blouse⟩ ⟨sheer fabric and ~ detail⟩

**lin·ger·ing·ly** *adv* **:** in a lingering manner **:** slowly or for a prolonged period

**lingier** *comparative of* LINGY

**lingiest** *superlative of* LINGY

**ling ko** *var of* LING

**¹lin·go** \'liŋ(ˌ)gō\ *n, pl* **lingoes** *also* **lingos** [prob. fr. Prov *lengo, lingo* tongue, language, fr. L *lingua* — more at TONGUE] **:** language or speech that is thought of as strange: as **a :** foreign language esp. when of purely local or remote usage ⟨became skilled in several tribal ~*es*⟩ **b :** the special vocabulary of a particular field of interest **:** the jargon, cant, or argot of a particular interest group or class of persons ⟨seaman's ~⟩ ⟨hospital ~⟩ **c :** language or style in utterance that is characteristic of an individual ⟨the shouted invective that is the basis of her ~⟩ **syn** see DIALECT

**²lingo** *or* **lin·goe** \"\ *n, pl* **lingoes** [prob. fr. F *lingot* ingot] *weaving* **:** a metal weight attached to the bottom of cords in a jacquard harness

**lin·goa wood** \liŋ'gōə-\ *also* **lingoa** *n* -s [*lingoa* fr. native name in the Moluccas] **:** AMBOYNA 1

**ling·on·berry** \'liŋən- — *see* BERRY\ *or* **lingon** \'liŋən, 'lin-gōn\ *or* **lin·gen·berry** \'liŋən- — *see* BERRY\ *or* **lingen** *n* [*lingonberry & lingenberry* fr. Sw *lingon* mountain cranberry + E *berry; lingon & lingen* fr. Sw *lingon;* akin to ON *lyng* heather — more at LING] **:** MOUNTAIN CRANBERRY

**lin·got** \'liŋgət\ *n* -s [ME (Sc) *lingat,* fr. MF *lingot,* prob. fr. OProv, fr. *lenga* tongue, fr. L *lingua*] *archaic* **:** an ingot of metal

**lin·go·um** \liŋ'gōəm\ [NL, fr. the native name (in the Moluccas) of lingoa wood] *syn of* PTEROCARPUS

**lings** *pl of* LING

**¹-lings** *pl of* -LING

**²-lings** — see -LING

**ling·tow** \'liŋˌtō\ *n* [prob. fr. Sc *ling* line (fr. F *ligne*) + E *tow* — more at LINE (cord)] *Scot* **:** a rope used by smugglers for packing burdens

**lingu-** *or* **lingua-** *or* **lingui-** *or* **linguo-** *comb form* [L *lingu-,* fr. *lingua*] **1 :** language ⟨*lingui*potence⟩ ⟨*lingu*ist⟩ **2 :** tongue ⟨*linguo*papillitis⟩ **3 a :** produced by the tongue and in terms referring to speech sounds ⟨*linguo*dental⟩ ⟨*lingua*nasal⟩ ⟨*linguo*nasal⟩ ⟨*linguo*palatal⟩ **b :** lingual and ⟨*linguo*maxillary⟩ **4 :** lingually ⟨*linguo*distal⟩

**lin·gua** \'liŋgwə\ *n, pl* **lin·guae** \-ŋˌgwē\ [L, tongue, language] **:** a tongue or organ resembling a tongue in structure or function: as **a :** GLOSSA **b :** HYPOPHARYNX

**lin·guae·form** \'liŋgwēˌfȯrm\ *adj* [by alter. (influence of L *linguae,* gen. of *lingua* tongue)] **:** LINGUIFORM

**lingua fran·ca** \-'fraŋkə\ *n, pl* **lingua francas** \-kəz\ *or* **linguae fran·cae** \-anˌsē\ [It, lit., Frankish language] **1 :** a common language that consists of Italian mixed with French, Spanish, Greek, and Arabic and is spoken in the ports of the Mediterranean — compare SABIR **2 :** any of various hybrid or other languages that are used over a wide area as common or commercial tongues among peoples of diverse speech (as Hindustani, Swahili) — compare JARGON 2c, KOINE, PIDGIN **3 :** something (as a system of common interests or social symbols) that functions like a common language in making individuals comprehensible to one another ⟨some tradition where a *lingua franca* of symbols, dogma, style, and learning survives —Stephen Spender⟩

**lingua ge·ral** \-zhə'räl\ *n, pl* **lingua gerals** [Pg *lingua geral,* lit., general language] **:** a trade language based on Tupi and used in inland Brazil

**lin·gual** \'liŋgwəl *sometimes* -gyəw-\ *adj* [ML *lingualis,* fr. L *lingua* + *-alis* -al] **1 a :** of or relating to the tongue ⟨~ inflammation⟩ **:** resembling a tongue **b :** lying near or next to the tongue ⟨a ~ blood vessel⟩ ⟨the ~ surface of the teeth⟩ **c** *of a speech sound* **:** produced by the tongue; *sometimes* **:** dental or cerebral (sense 3a) **2 :** LINGUISTIC

**lingual artery** *n* **:** an artery arising from the external carotid between the superior thyroid and external maxillary arteries and supplying the tongue

**lingual bone** *n* **:** HYOID BONE

**lin·gua·le** \liŋ'gwa(ˌ)lē, -wā(-, -wä(-\ *n* -s [NL, fr. ML, neut. of *lingualis*] **:** the midpoint of the upper border of the mandible — compare GNATHION 1

**¹lin·gua·lis** \liŋ'gwaləs, -wäl-, -wäl-\ [ML] **:** LINGUAL

**²lingualis** \"\ *n* -ES [NL, fr. ML *lingualis,* adj.] **:** the tongue musculature **:** the intrinsic muscles of the tongue

**lin·gual·ly** \'liŋgwəlē *sometimes* -gyəw-\ *adv* **:** in a lingual manner **:** toward the tongue

**lingual nerve** *n* **:** a branch of the mandibular division of the trigeminal nerve supplying the anterior two thirds of the tongue and responding to stimuli of pressure, touch, and temperature

**lingual tonsil** *n* **:** a variable mass or group of small nodules of lymphoid tissue lying at the base of the tongue just anterior to the epiglottis

**lin·gua·ta** \liŋ'gwäd·ə, -wād·ə\ *n pl, cap* [NL, fr. LL, neut. pl. of *linguatus* tongued, eloquent, fr. L *lingua* tongue + *-atus* -ate] *in some esp former classifications* **:** a large suborder of Salientia including all toads and frogs having a tongue and separate openings for the eustachian tubes — compare AGLOSSA 1, PHANEROGLOSSA

**lin·guat·u·la** \liŋ'gwachələ\ *n, cap* [NL, fr. LL *linguatus* + NL *-ula*] **:** a genus of tongue worms that includes a cosmopolitan parasite (*L. serrata*) of the nasal and respiratory passages of various canines, sheep and goats, the horse, and occasionally man

**lin·guat·u·lid** \-ləd\ *n* -s [NL *Linguatulida*] **:** a tongue worm of the genus *Linguatula; broadly* **:** TONGUE WORM

**lin·gua·tu·li·da** \ˌliŋgwə'tüləda, -wə'tyü-\ *n pl, cap* [NL, fr. *Linguatula* + *-ida*] **:** a group of wormlike pseudosegmented parasitic animals that are considered to constitute a separate phylum, a class of Arthropoda, or esp. formerly an order of Arachnida, that lack eyes, circulatory system, and respiratory organs, that live as adults in the respiratory passages or body cavity of reptiles, birds, or mammals, and that undergo larval development in the visceral tissues of similar hosts and that comprise the tongue worms

**lin·guat·u·lo·sis** \liŋˌgwachə'lōsəs\ *n, pl* **linguatulo·ses** \-ōˌsēz\ [NL, fr. *Linguatula* + *-osis*] **:** infestation with or disease caused by tongue worms

**lin·gue** \'liŋgwā\ *n* -s [AmerSp, fr. Araucanian *ligē*] **:** a Chilean timber tree (*Persea lingue*) that is closely related to the avocado, has a bark which is a locally important source of tannin, and yields a lustrous pale brown timber esteemed for cabinetwork and joinery

**lin·guet** \'liŋˌgwet\ *n* -s [by alter.] **:** LANGUET

**lingui-** — see LINGU-

**lin·gui·form** \'liŋgwəˌfȯrm\ *adj* [*lingu-* + *-form*] **:** having the form of a tongue **:** tongue-shaped

**lin·guip·o·tence** \liŋ'gwipəd·ən(t)s\ *n* [*lingu-* + *potence*] **:** mastery of languages

**lin·guist** \'liŋgwəst\ *n* -s [L *lingu-* + E *-ist*] **1 :** a person accomplished in languages and esp. in living languages **:** one who is facile in several languages **2 :** a student of or expert in linguistics

**lin·guist·er** \-tə(r)\ *n* -s [*linguist* + *-er*] **:** INTERPRETER

**lin·guis·tic** \liŋ'gwistik, -tēk\ *also* **lin·guist·i·cal** \-təkəl, -tēk-\ *adj* [*linguist* + *-ic* or *-ical*] **1 :** of or relating to language or to the knowledge or study of languages **:** relating to linguistics or to the affinities of languages ⟨~ studies⟩ ⟨the ~ point of view⟩ **2 :** constituting language ⟨nonliterary ~ acts —Joshua Whatmough⟩

**lin·guis·ti·cal·ly** \-tək(ə)lē, -tēk-, -li\ *adv* **:** from the linguistic point of view **:** in respect to language or linguistics

**linguistic atlas** *n* **:** a publication containing or consisting of a set of maps upon which are recorded dialectal variations of pronunciation, vocabulary, inflection, and idiom — called also *dialect atlas*

**linguistic form** *n* **:** a meaningful unit of speech (as an allomorph, morpheme, word, phrase, clause, sentence) — called also *speech form*

**linguistic geographer** *n* **:** a specialist in linguistic geography

**linguistic geography** *n* **:** local or regional variations of a language or dialect as a field of study or knowledge — called also *dialect geography*

**lin·guis·ti·cian** \ˌliŋgwə'stishən\ *n* -s [*linguistic* + *-an*] **:** LINGUIST 2

**linguistic island** *n* [trans. of G *sprachinsel*] **:** SPEECH ISLAND

**lin·guis·tics** \liŋ'gwistiks, -tēks\ *n pl but usu sing in constr* **:** the study of human speech in its various aspects (as the units, nature, structure, and modification of language, languages, or a language including esp. such factors as phonetics, phonology, morphology, accent, syntax, semantics, general or philosophical grammar, and the relation between writing and speech) — called also *linguistic science, science of language;* compare PHILOLOGY

**lin·guist·ry** \'liŋgwəstrē\ *n* -ES [*linguist* + *-ry*] **:** knowledge or study of languages

**lin·gu·la** \'liŋgyələ\ *n* [NL, fr. L, small tongue, object like a tongue, fr. *lingua* tongue + *-ula* — more at TONGUE] **1** *pl* **lingu·lae** \-yə,lē\ **:** a tongue-shaped process or part: as **a :** a ridge of bone in the angle between the body and the greater wing of the sphenoid **b :** an elongated prominence of the vermiform process of the cerebellum **c :** a dependent projection of the upper lobe of the left lung **2 a** *cap* **:** the type genus of Lingulidae comprising burrowing brachiopods with very long contractile pedicles that have existed from at least Ordovician time **b** *pl* **lingulae :** any brachiopod of the genus *Lingula* — **lin·gu·lar** \-_lə(r)\ *adj*

**lin·gu·late** \'liŋgyə,lāt\ *also* **lin·gu·lat·ed** \-ād·əd\ *adj* [*lingulate* fr. L *lingulatus*, fr. *lingula* + *-atus* -ate; *lingulated* fr. L *lingulatus* + E *-ed*] **:** shaped like a tongue or a strap

**lin·gu·lel·la** \,liŋgyə'lelə\ *adj, usu cap* [fr. *Lingulella*, subdivision of the European Cambrian, fr. NL, genus of brachiopods, fr. *Lingula*, genus of burrowing brachiopods + *-ella*] **:** of or relating to a subdivision of the European Cambrian — see GEOLOGIC TIME table

[1]**lin·gu·lid** \'liŋgyələd\ *adj* [NL *Lingulidae*] **:** of or relating to Lingulidae

[2]**lingulid** \"\ *n* -S [NL *Lingulidae*] **:** a brachiopod of the family Lingulidae

**lin·gu·li·dae** \liŋ'gyülə,dē\ *n pl, cap* [NL, fr. *Lingula*, type genus + *-idae*] **:** a family of brachiopods (order Atremata) that includes the earliest recorded Lower Cambrian animal fossils and is represented by a few recent forms — see LINGULA 2

**lin·gu·lif·er·ous** \¦liŋgyə¦lif(ə)rəs\ *adj* [NL *Lingula* + E *-iferous*] **:** containing or made up of shells of brachiopods of *Lingula* or related genera ⟨~ rocks⟩

[1]**lin·gu·loid** \'liŋgyə,lȯid\ *adj* [NL *Lingula* + E *-oid*] **:** like or like that of a brachiopod of the genus *Lingula*

[2]**linguloid** \"\ *n* -S **:** a brachiopod resembling or related to those of the genus *Lingula*

[3]**linguloid** \"\ *adj* [NL *lingula* + E *-oid*] **:** LINGULATE

**linguo-** — see LINGU-

**lin·guo·version** \¦liŋgwə+\ *n* [*lingu-* + *version*] **:** displacement of a tooth to the lingual side of its proper occlusal position

[1]**lingy** \'liŋē\ *adj* -ER/-EST [[2]*ling* + *-y*] **:** covered with or abounding in heaths, esp. heather **:** HEATHY, HEATHERY

[2]**lin·gy** \'linji\ *adj* [origin unknown] *dial Eng* **:** SUPPLE, ACTIVE

**lin·hay** \'lini\ *n* -S [origin unknown] *dial chiefly Eng* **:** a shed usu. with a lean-to roof and one or more open sides

**linier** *comparative of* LINY

**liniest** *superlative of* LINY

**lin·i·ment** \'linəmənt\ *n* -S [ME *lynyment* ointment, fr. LL *linimentum*, fr. L *linere, linire* to smear + *-mentum* -ment — more at LIME] **:** a liquid or semiliquid alcoholic, oily, or saponaceous preparation of a consistency thinner than an ointment for application to the skin with friction esp. as an anodyne or a counterirritant **:** EMBROCATION

[1]**li·nin** \'līnən\ *n* -S [ISV *lin-* (fr. L *linum* flax) + *-in* — more at LINEN] **1 :** a bitter white crystallizable substance with purgative qualities obtained from the purging flax **2 :** a protein obtained from flaxseed

[2]**linin** \"\ *n* -S [ISV *lin-* (fr. L *linum* thread, flax) + *-in;* orig. formed in G] **:** the feebly-staining portion of the reticulum of the nucleus of a resting cell in which chromatin granules appear to be embedded that is variously construed as chromatin in a particular physical state or in fixed preparations as precipitated protein

[1]**lin·ing** \'līniŋ, -nēŋ\ *n* -S [ME, fr. gerund of *linen* to line (as a cloak)] **1 :** material or an arrangement of material used to line something: as **a :** a layer (as of fabric) inserted under, usu. following the lines of, and made temporarily or permanently fast to the principal material of a garment ⟨a coat with a warm fur ~⟩ — see [2]LINER 2g **b** (1) **:** the material used in reinforcing the backbone of a book (2) **:** PASTEDOWN (3) **:** a sheet of paper or other material placed immediately under a pastedown **c :** LINING LEATHER **d** *or* **lining cloth :** extra canvas sewed on a part of a sail exposed to chafing **e :** an attached or loose sheet or an applied coating on all or part of the inner surfaces of a container **2** *archaic* **:** CONTENTS **3 linings** *pl, now dial Eng* **:** UNDERCLOTHES; *esp* **:** DRAWERS **4 :** the act of providing something with a lining **:** the process of inserting a lining

[2]**lining** \"\ *n* -S [fr. gerund of [4]*line*] **1 :** an act or instance or the process of lining: **a :** the fixing of boundaries of estates in a burgh in Scotland by the lines; *also* **:** the erection or alteration of a building by permission of a dean of guild **b :** ordering in a line or lines **:** ALIGNMENT **c :** marking or tracing lines on a surface **d :** fishing with hook and line — often used in combination ⟨made his living hand-*lining*⟩ **e :** measuring or checking with a line **2 :** a product of lining; *esp* **:** ornamentation in the form of narrow lines ⟨wheels brightened with crimson ~⟩

**lining bar** *n* [[2]*lining*] **:** a crowbar the working end of which has a square section and ends in a pinch, wedge, or diamond point

**lining figure** *n* [[2]*lining*] **:** an arabic numeral that aligns with the base of a type line or printed line — called also *modern figure*

**lining leather** *n* [[1]*lining*] **:** lightweight leather for lining leather goods (as shoes, handbags)

**lining-out stock** \'⸗⸗'⸗-\ *n* [*lining-out* fr. gerund of *line out*] **:** small or seedling plants for use as liners

**lining page** *n* [[1]*lining*] **:** the exposed side of a pastedown in a book

[1]**link** \'liŋk\ *n* -S [ME, fr. OE *hlinc;* akin to OE *hlanc* lank — more at LANK] **1 a** *now dial Brit* **:** a ridge of land **:** stretch of rising ground **b links** *pl, chiefly Scot* **:** sandy level or undulating land built up along a coastline **2 links** *pl but sing or pl in constr* **a** *archaic* **:** a seaside golf course **:** a golf course built on coastal links **b :** GOLF COURSE

[2]**link** \"\ *n* -S [ME, of Scand origin; akin to ON *hlekkr* chain, link; akin to ON *hlykkr* bend, noose — more at LANK] **1 :** a connecting structure (as a loop by which something is made fast): as **a links** *pl, obs* **:** FETTERS **b** (1) **:** a single ring or division of a chain (2) **:** one of the standardized links of a surveyor's chain being 7.92 inches long and serving as a measure of length **c :** CUFF LINK **d :** BOND 3e **e :** an intermediate rod or piece for transmitting force or motion; *esp* **:** a short connecting rod with a hole or pin at each end **f :** the fusible member of a fuse designed to melt when an excessive current flows **g :** a metal unit that connects the cartridges of an automatic weapon and with them forms a feed belt **2 :** something analogous to a link of chain (as in form, function, or serial arrangement): as **a** (1) **:** one of the segments into which sausage in continuous casing is usu. constricted (as by tying) at regular intervals (2) **:** a small sausage resembling one of the links of a chain of sausage but not being part of a chain (3) **links** *pl* **:** a chain of sausages **b :** a unifying element **:** a means of connecting or communicating ⟨the letters that were the last ~ with her past⟩ ⟨love of nature forms a ~ with our pioneer ancestors⟩ **c :** a constructive part of a mechanism having at least two elements belonging to different pairs **d :** a unit in a communication system (as a radio transmitter and receiver operating together to form part of a more extensive communication system) **3 links** *pl, dial* **:** a winding of a river or watercourse; *also* **:** the ground along such a winding **4 :** a step in ballroom dancing involving weaving forward and back in the manner of the grapevine

[3]**link** \"\ *vb* -ED/-ING/-S [ME *linken*, fr. [2]*link*] *vt* **1 :** to couple or connect by or as if by a connecting element ⟨to ~ the new settlements on the Pacific with the settled east —R.H.Brown⟩ ⟨none of the subjects that ~*ed* us together could be talked about —Nevil Shute⟩ ⟨~*ing* the human heart to the life of the earth —Laurence Binyon⟩ — often used with *up* ⟨the . . . elaborate network of schools ~*ed* up with industry —A.R. Williams⟩ **2** *dial Brit* **:** to take (a person) by the arm usu. as an escort **:** walk arm in arm with **3** *chiefly Brit* **:** LOOP 3 ~ *vi* **1 :** to become coupled or connected esp. by means of a connecting element ⟨a piston ~*s* to a drive shaft by means of a connecting rod⟩ — often used with *up* ⟨the two families ~ *up* through the marriage of a daughter and son⟩ **2 :** to form a connection or association ⟨the newer company ~*ed* with several older ones in self-protection⟩; *esp* **:** to join company — often used with *up* ⟨~*ed* up with two young waitresses . . . off for the evening —Earle Birney⟩ **syn** see JOIN

[4]**link** \"\ *adj* [[2]*link*] **1 :** relating to or made of links ⟨a ~ fence⟩ ⟨~ sausage⟩ **2 :** serving to connect; *specif* **:** functioning as a linguistic connective

[5]**link** \"\ *n* -S [perh. modif. of ML *linchinus, lichinus* candle, lamp, alter. of L *lychnus*, fr. Gk *lychnos;* akin to Gk *leukos* bright, white — more at LIGHT] **1 :** a torch (as of tow and pitch) formerly used to light a person on his way through the streets **2 :** LINKBOY, LINKMAN **3** *obs* **:** a black coloring agent or blacking sometimes considered to have been lampblack

[6]**link** \"\ *vi* [origin unknown] *Scot* **:** to trip along **:** walk or move smartly and quickly

[7]**link** \"\ *adj* [Yiddish, fr. MHG *linc, lenc* left, awkward, ignorant; akin to OHG *lenka* left hand and prob. to L *languēre* to be languid — more at SLACK] **:** not devout **:** lax in respect to religious observances

**link·able** \-kəbəl\ *adj* **:** capable of being linked

**link·age** \-kij, -kēj\ *n* -S **1 :** the manner or style of being fitted together or united: as **a :** the manner in which atoms or radicals are linked in a molecule **b :** BOND 3e **2 :** the quality or state of being linked; *esp* **:** a relationship between genes that causes them to be manifested together in inheritance through concurrence of characters that they separately control, and that is usu. considered to result from the location of such genes on the same chromosome **3 a :** a system of links; *specif* **:** a system of links or bars which are jointed together and more or less constrained by having a link or links fixed and by means of which straight or approximately straight lines or other point paths may be traced **b :** the product of the magnetic flux through an electrical coil by its number of turns with the magnetic flux and the coil being connected like two links of a chain and each unit of flux threading through one turn of the coil to contribute one unit to the linkage

**linkage group** *n* **:** a group of genes that tend to be inherited as a unit

**link and pin coupler** *n* **:** an early device for coupling railroad cars consisting of a heavy metal pin inserted through a metal link

**linkboy** \'⸗,⸗\ *n* **:** an attendant formerly employed to bear a torch or other light to light the way of a person abroad in the streets at night

**linked** \'liŋkt\ *adj, of genes* **:** exhibiting genetic linkage **:** tending to be inherited together

**link·er** \'liŋkə(r)\ *n* -S **:** one that links; *esp* **:** a worker who makes or joins links by hand or machine

[1]**linking** *n* -S [fr. gerund of [3]*link*] **:** LIAISON 2

[2]**linking** *adj* [fr. pres. part. of [3]*link*] **:** being a speech sound that has an analogue in the spelling and that is pronounced before a vowel-initial word that follows without pause but not before a consonant or a pause ⟨*r*-droppers often have a ~ \r\ in *four eighths*⟩ ⟨in French there is a ~ \z\ before the *autres* of *les autres*⟩

**lin·kis·ter** *or* **link·ster** \'liŋk(ə)stə(r)\ *dial var of* LINGUISTER

**link·man** \'liŋkmən\ *n, pl* **linkmen 1 :** LINKBOY **2 :** an attendant (as at a theater) who summons vehicles and shows passengers to and from them

**link motion** *n* **:** motion imparted by a linkage (as in some steam locomotive engines to operate the slide valve); *also* **:** LINKAGE 3a

**link relative** *n* [[2]*link*] **:** the ratio usu. expressed in percent of any value of a statistical variable evaluated at equal intervals of time (as annual crop yield) to the value for the immediately preceding interval

**links** *pl of* LINK, *pres 3d sing of* LINK

**links-and-links** \¦⸗⸗¦⸗\ *also* **links-links** \'⸗,⸗\ *adj* **1 :** of, relating to, or being a circular or flat knitting machine for producing purl or fancy stitches **2 :** produced on a links-and-links machine ⟨*links-and-links* patterns⟩

**links·man** \'liŋksmən\ *n, pl* **linksmen** [*links* (pl. of [1]*link*) + *man*] **:** GOLFER

**linkup** \'⸗,⸗\ *n* -S [fr. the phrase *link up*] **1 :** establishment of contact ⟨planned a ~ with the eastern allies near the river⟩ **2 :** something that serves as a linking device or factor ⟨the new highway will provide an east-west ~⟩

**link verb** *or* **linking verb** *n* **:** a verb (as *be, become, seem, feel, grow*) that connects a predicate with a subject **:** copulative verb

**linkwork** \'⸗,⸗\ *n* **1 :** something (as a chain or a fabric of metal mesh) consisting of interlocking links **2 :** LINKAGE 3a

**link-worming** \'⸗,⸗⸗\ *n* **:** the protection of rope cables (as on a ship) with windings of chain

**linky** \'liŋki\ *adj* -ER/-EST [[1]*link* + *-y*] *Scot, of land or country* **:** resembling or made up of links

**lin·lith·gow·shire** \lin'lithgō,shi(ə)r\ *or* **lin·lith·gow** \(,)gō\ *adj, usu cap* [fr. *Linlithgowshire, Linlithgow*, county in Scotland] **:** WEST LOTHIAN

[1]**linn** *also* **lin** \'lin\ *n* -S [ME *lyn*, alter. of *linde* — more at LIND] **:** LINDEN 1

[2]**linn** *also* **lin** \"\ *n* -S [ScGael *linne* pool; akin to W *llyn* lake and perh. to Gk *plein* to sail, float — more at FLOW] **1** *chiefly Scot* **:** a pool or collection of water; *esp* **:** one below a fall of water **2** *chiefly Scot* **:** WATERFALL, CATARACT **3** *chiefly Scot* **:** a steep ravine **:** PRECIPICE

**lin·naea** \lə'nēə\ *n* [NL, fr. Carolus *Linnaeus* (Latinized form of Carl von *Linné*) †1778 Swed. botanist] **1** *cap* **:** a monotypic genus of creeping evergreen subshrubs (family Caprifoliaceae) of the northern parts of both hemispheres with small exstipulate leaves and the flowers borne in pairs at the end of elongated peduncles and having the corolla campanulate — see TWINFLOWER **2** -S **:** a plant of the genus *Linnaea*

**lin·nae·an** *or* **lin·ne·an** \-ēən\ *adj, usu cap* [prob. fr. (assumed) NL *linnaeanus*, fr. *Linnaeus* + L *-anus* -an] **:** of, relating to, or following the method of the Swedish botanist Carl von Linné who established the system of binomial nomenclature

**linnaean species** *n, usu cap L* **:** a taxonomic species distinguished on morphological grounds; *specif* **:** one of the large species delimited on broad morphological grounds by Linnaeus or another of the early naturalists — compare MACROSPECIES

**lin·nae·ite** *or* **lin·ne·ite** \lə'nē,īt\ *n* -S [G *linneit*, fr. Carl von *Linné* + G *-it* -ite] **:** a mineral $Co_3S_4$ of pale steel-gray color and metallic luster that occurs in isometric crystals and also massive and that is essentially a cobalt sulfide

**linned** *past of* LIN

**lin·ne·on** \'linē,än\ *n* -S [NL, fr. Carl von *Linné* + Gk *-on* (neuter n. & adj. suffix)] **:** MACROSPECIES

**lin·net** \'linət, *usu* -əd·+V\ *n* -S [MF *linette*, fr. *lin* flax (fr. L *linum*) + *-ette;* fr. the fact that it likes to feed on flaxseed — more at LINEN] **1 :** a common small Old World finch (*Carduelis cannabina* or *Acanthis cannabina*) having plumage that varies greatly according to age, sex, and season and is sometimes pied or nearly white **2 :** any of various finches (as of the genera *Spinus* and *Chloris*) that are closely related to the common linnet — usu. used in combination ⟨green ~⟩ ⟨pine ~⟩ **3** *chiefly West* **:** HOUSE FINCH

**linnet hole** *n* [*linnet* modif. (influenced by *linnet*) of F *lunette* small opening — more at LUNETTE] **:** one of the small holes connecting a glass-melting furnace with its arch

**lin·ney** *or* **lin·ny** \'lini\ *var of* LINHAY

**linning** *pres part of* LIN

**li·no** \'lī(,)nō\ *n* -S **1** [by shortening] *chiefly Brit* **:** LINOLEUM **2** [by shortening fr. *Linotype*] *chiefly Brit* **:** a machine for setting type

**li·no·cut** \'līnə,kət\ *n* [*lino* + *cut*] **:** a printing surface made by cutting a design on a mounted piece of linoleum; *also* **:** a print made from it — compare BLOCK PRINT

**li·nog·na·thus** \lə'nägnəthəs\ *n, cap* [NL, fr. *lino-* (fr. Gk, fr. *linon* thread, cord, flax) + *-gnathus* — more at LINEN] **:** a cosmopolitan genus of sucking lice including parasites of several domestic mammals

**li·no·le·ate** \lə'nōlē,āt\ *n* -S [ISV *linoleic* (in *linoleic acid*) + *-ate*] **:** a salt or ester of linoleic acid

**lin·o·le·ic acid** \¦linə¦lēik-, lə'nōlēik-\ *n* [*linoleic* ISV *lin-* (fr. Gk, fr. *linon* flax) + *oleic* (in *oleic acid*)] **:** a liquid unsaturated fatty acid $C_{17}H_{31}COOH$ that occurs in the form of glycerides in linseed oil, soybean oil, cottonseed oil, and other drying and semidrying oils, that is used chiefly in making salts for use as driers in paints and varnishes, and that is considered one of the fatty acids essential in animal nutrition; *cis*-9, *cis*-12-octadecadienoic acid

**li·no·le·in** \lə'nōlēən\ *n* -S [ISV *linoleic* + *-in*] **:** a glycerol ester of linoleic acid; *esp* **:** glycerol tri-linoleate

**lin·o·le·nate** \,linə'lē,nāt, -le,-\ *n* -S [*linolenic* (in *linolenic acid*) + *-ate*] **:** a salt or ester of linolenic acid

**lin·o·le·nic acid** \¦linə¦lēnik-, -lenik-\ *n* [*linolenic* ISV *linoleic* + connective *-n-* + *-ic*] **:** a liquid unsaturated fatty acid $C_{17}H_{29}COOH$ that occurs in the form of glycerides along with glycerides of linoleic acid esp. in linseed oil, perilla oil, and other drying oils and that is considered one of the fatty acids essential in animal nutrition; 9,12,15-octadeca-trien-oic acid

**lin·o·le·nin** \,⸗⸗'lēnən, -lenən\ *n* -S [*linolenic* + *-in*] **:** a glycerol ester of linolenic acid; *esp* **:** glycerol tri-linolenate

**li·no·le·um** \lə'nōlēəm *sometimes* -lyəm\ *n* -S *often attrib* [L *linum* flax + *oleum* oil — more at OIL] **1 :** a floor covering made by laying on a burlap or canvas backing a mixture of solidified linseed oil with gums, cork dust or wood flour or both, and usu. pigments **2 :** a material similar to linoleum in use and qualities but made with substitutes for the linseed oil, the filler, or both

**linoleum-block printing** *n* **:** relief printing from a carved linoleum block — compare BLOCK PRINT

**linoleum brown** *n* **:** BEESWAX 3

**linoleum knife** *n* **:** a knife with a short stiff blade ending in a sharp curved point that is used esp. for cutting and trimming linoleum

linoleum knife

**li·no·lic acid** \lə'nōlik-\ *n* [by alter.] **:** LINOLEIC ACID

**lin·on** \'linən, lē'nōⁿ\ *n* -S [F, fr. *lin* flax, linen] **:** a fine lawn of linen or cotton

**li·nop·ter·is** \lə'näptərəs\ *n, cap* [NL, fr. *lino-* (fr. Gk, fr. *linon* net, cord, flax) + *-pteris*] **:** a genus of fossil ferns abundant in the coal measures and distinguished by their reticulate venation

**li·no·type** \'līnə,tīp\ *vi* [*Linotype*] **:** to operate a Linotype machine ~ *vt* **:** to set by means of a Linotype machine

**Li·no·type** \"\ *trademark* **1** — used for a keyboard-operated typesetting machine that uses circulating matrices and produces each line of type in the form of a solid metal slug **2 :** matter produced by a Linotype machine or printing done from such matter

**li·no·typ·er** \-pə(r)\ *or* **li·no·typ·ist** \-pəst\ *n* **:** one that operates the keyboard of a Linotype machine

**li·nox·yn** \lə'näksən\ *n* -S [ISV *lin-* (fr. L *linum* flax) + *oxy-* + *-n* (fr. *-in*) — more at LINEN] **:** an elastic solid that is formed when linseed oil is oxidized and is used chiefly in cements, adhesives, and linoleum

**lins** *pres 3d sing of* LIN, *pl of* LIN

[1]**lin·sang** \'lin,saŋ\ [NL, fr. Malay, linsang] *syn of* PRIONODON

[2]**linsang** \"\ *n* -S [Malay] **1 :** any of various Asiatic viverrid mammals of *Prionodon* and related genera that resemble long-tailed cats and differ from the related civets and genets in the absence of a second upper molar **2 :** an African viverrid mammal (*Poiana poensis*) related to the Asiatic linsangs

**lin·seed** \'lin,sēd\ *n* [ME, fr. OE *līnsǣd*, fr. *līn* flax + *sǣd* seed — more at LINEN, SEED] **1 :** FLAXSEED **2 :** the common agricultural flax plant

**linseed cake** *n* **:** the residue that remains when oil is expressed or extracted from flaxseed and that is used chiefly as a cattle feed

**linseed meal** *n* **:** ground linseed or linseed cake

**linseed oil** *n* **:** a yellowish drying oil that is expressed or extracted from flaxseed, contains large proportions of glycerides of linolenic, linoleic, and oleic acids, and is used chiefly in paint and varnish, in printing ink, in linoleum — compare BLOWN OIL 1, BOILED OIL

**linseed tea** *n* **:** a demulcent tea made by infusing flaxseed

**lin·sey** \'linzē, -zi\ *n* -S [ME *lynesey, lynsy*, prob. fr. *Lynsey* Lindsey, village in Suffolk, England, where it was made] **:** LINSEY-WOOLSEY

**lin·sey-wool·sey** \'linzē'wu̇lzē, -zi . . . zi\ *n* -S *often attrib* [ME *lynsy wolsye*, prob. fr. *lynesey, lynsy* linsey + *wolsye* (fr. *wolle* wool + *-sey, -sy, -sye* — as in *lynesey, lynsy*) — more at WOOL] **1 a :** a formerly used textile of wool and linen **b :** a coarse sturdy fabric with cotton warp and woolen filling **2 :** something incongruously mingled **:** disordered or nonsensical speech or action ⟨what *linsey-woolsey* hast thou to speak to us again —Shak.⟩

**lin·stock** \'linz,täk, -n,st-\ *n* [earlier *lyntstock*, by folk etymology (influence of [1]*lint*) fr. D *lontstok*, fr. *lont* match, rag + *stok* stick; akin to OHG *stoc* stick — more at LUNT, STOCK] **:** a pointed forked staff shod with iron at the foot formerly used to hold a lighted match for firing cannon

[1]**lint** \'lint\ *n* -S [ME, perh. fr. L *linteum* linen cloth, fr. neut. of *linteus* made of linen, irreg. fr. *linum* flax, linen — more at LINEN] **1** *chiefly Scot* **:** FLAX 1 **2 a :** a soft fleecy material (as for poultices and dressings for wounds) made from linen usu. by scraping **b :** fuzz consisting usu. of fine ravelings and short fibers of yarn and fabric; *esp* **:** an accumulation of dust and fuzz on a floor **c :** fluff or fuzz of any material (as paper) **3** *dial* **:** the actual netting of a fishnet **4 a :** a fibrous coat of thickened convoluted hairs borne by the seeds of cotton plants and constituting the staple of cotton fiber after ginning — compare LINTER 1 **b** *or* **lint cotton :** virgin cotton

[2]**lint** \"\ *vi* -ED/-ING/-S **1 :** to leave lint adhering to a surface after contact **:** give off or deposit lint ⟨found that his napkin had ~*ed*⟩ **2 :** PICK *vi* 5

**lint bells** *n pl but sing or pl in constr* **:** the common agricultural flax plant

**lin·tel** \'lintᵊl\ *n* -S [ME, fr. MF, modif. of LL *limitaris* threshold (influenced in meaning by L *limin-, limen* threshold), fr. L *limitaris*, adj., constituting a boundary, fr. L *limit-, limes* boundary, limit + *-aris* -ar — more at LIMB] **:** a horizontal architectural member spanning and usu. carrying the load above an opening

lintel

**lin·teled** *or* **lin·telled** \-ᵊld\ *adj* **:** having a lintel

[1]**lin·ter** \'lintə(r)\ *n* -S [alter. of *lean-to*] **1** *chiefly NewEng* **:** a cow stable built either in or as an extension of a barn **2** *North* **:** LEAN-TO

[2]**lint·er** \"\ *n* -S [[1]*lint* + *-er*] **1 a :** a machine for removing residual fuzz from cottonseed that has been ginned **b :** a worker who operates such a machine **2 linters** *pl* **:** the fuzz of short fibers that adheres to cottonseed after ginning and is recovered and used for many purposes (as batting, padding, or a source of cellulose) that do not require long fibers

**lint·er·man** \-(r)mən\ *n, pl* **lintermen :** the operator of a linter

**linthead** \'⸗,⸗\ *n* **1** *chiefly South* **:** a cotton-mill worker **2** *chiefly South* **:** a Southern lower class white person — used disparagingly

**lin·tie** \'linti\ *n* -S [*lint-* (in *lintwhite*) + *-ie*] *chiefly Scot* **:** LINNET

**lint·less** \'lintləs\ *adj* **:** free from lint ⟨immaculately ~ corners⟩ ⟨a ~ wild cotton⟩

**lin·tol** \'lintᵊl\ *Brit var of* LINTEL

**lin·ton·ite** \'lintᵊn,īt, -tən,-\ *n* -S [Laura A. *Linton* †1915 Am. scientist + E *-ite*] **:** a green mineral that is a variety of thomsonite

**lintseed** \'⸗,⸗\ *n* **:** FLAXSEED; *esp* **:** an inferior flaxseed obtained from flax plants grown for fiber

**lint·white** \'lint,(h)wīt\ *n* [ME *lynkwhyt*, by folk etymology (influence of *whyt, whit* white) fr. OE *līnetwige*, prob. fr. *līne-* (fr. *līn* flax) + *-twige* (perh. akin to OHG *zwigōn* to pluck, OE *twig* branch, twig); prob. fr. the fact that it likes to feed on flaxseed — more at LINEN, TWIG] **:** LINNET 1

**lint-white** \ˈ≈,≈\ *adj* [¹*lint* + *white*] **1 :** of the color of dressed flax **2 :** of the color flax
**linty** \ˈlintē\ *adj* -ER/-EST [¹*lint* + *-y*] **:** like lint **:** full of or covered with lint
**li·num** \ˈlīnəm\ *n* [NL, fr. L, flax — more at LINEN] **1** *cap* **:** the type genus of Linaceae comprising herbaceous annual or perennial plants that have small sessile leaves, terminal or axillary racemes of flowers with fugacious petals, and capsular fruits — see FLAX 1 **2** -S **:** any plant of the genus *Linum; esp* **:** any plant of this genus cultivated for ornament or growing wild as distinguished from the common agricultural flax
**li·nus** \ˈlīnəs\ *n* -ES [Gk *linos*] **:** a dirge or lamentation of ancient Greece
**liny** *also* **liney** \ˈlīnē\ *adj* **linier; liniest** [³*line* + *-y*] **:** like a line or streak **:** marked with or full of lines
**lin·y·phi·idae** \,linəˈfīə,dē\ *n pl, cap* [NL, fr. *Linyphia*, type genus (fr. Gk *linyphos* linen weaver — fr. *linon* linen, cord, flax + *hyphos* web — + NL *-ia*) + *-idae* — more at LINEN, WEAVE] **:** a large family of small spiders that weave horizontal sheet webs
**linz** \ˈlin(t)s, -nz\ *adj, usu cap* [fr. *Linz*, city in northwest Austria] **:** of or from the city of Linz, Austria **:** of the kind or style prevalent in Linz
**linz·er torte** \-(t)sə(r)-, -zə(r)-\ *n, usu cap L* [G, lit., Linz torte] **:** a baked torte made of a rich pastry dough composed of chopped almonds, butter, flour, cocoa, sugar, eggs, and spices, filled with jam or preserves, and topped with a lattice — compare SACHER TORTE
**lio-** — see LEIO-
**li·on** \ˈlīən\ *n* -S *often attrib* [ME *leon, lion*, fr. OF, fr. L *leon-, leo*, fr. Gk *leōn*, prob. of non-IE origin] **1 a :** a large carnivorous chiefly nocturnal mammal (*Felis leo*) of the cat family that is now found mostly in open or rocky areas of Africa but also in southern Asia and that has a tawny body with a tufted tail and a shaggy blackish or dark brown mane in the male **b :** any of several other animals of the genus *Felis; esp* **:** COUGAR **2 :** a person felt to resemble a lion esp. in courage, ferocity, dignity, or dominance ⟨he that trusts to you, where he should find you ~s, finds you hares —*Shak.*⟩ ⟨they tame the ~s in the Army, not appease them —James Jones⟩ ⟨outsmarted the other old financial ~s —Meridel Le Sueur⟩ **3 a** *usu cap* **:** a lion that is a symbol of a country, people, or individual ⟨British *Lion*⟩ ⟨*Lion* of Judah⟩ ⟨*Lion* of St. Mark⟩ **b :** a heraldic representation of a lion rampant **4 :** any of several old coins bearing the figure of a lion (as a gold coin of Philip VI of France) — see SAINT ANDREW **5 a lions** *pl, Brit* (1) **:** the principal sights of a city or country (2) *obs* **:** the world or experience of the world **b :** a person who is a center of attention or an object of admiration, interest, or curiosity ⟨they were fountains of interesting gossip, and the ~s of the meal —Arnold Bennett⟩ ⟨one must certainly have the ~ of the moment at one's parties —Victoria Sackville-West⟩ **6 :** a light to moderate yellowish brown **7** *usu cap* **:** a member of one of the major service clubs **8 :** a cub scout of the fourth rank comprising boys at least 10 years old — **lion in the way** *also* **lion in the path :** a dangerous obstacle; *esp* **:** a danger invented or exaggerated as an excuse for inaction ⟨the indecisive man always sees a *lion in the way*⟩ — **lion's mouth :** a place or situation of great danger ⟨test pilots fly constantly into the *lion's mouth*⟩ — **lion's share :** the largest part ⟨the central government collects and spends the *lion's share* of the citizens' tax dollar —Cabell Phillips⟩ ⟨slyly sneaked the *lion's share* of buttered toast at tea —Jean Stafford⟩

lion (forepart)

**li·on·cel** \ˈlīən,sel\ *n* -S [F, fr. MF, dim. of *lion*] **:** a heraldic representation of a small lion rampant usu. as one of a group of at least three
**lion dollar** *n* [trans. of D *leeuwendaalder;* fr. the lion rampant on the obverse] **:** DOG DOLLAR
**li·on·esque** \,līəˈnesk\ *adj* **:** having the characteristics of a lion
**li·on·ess** \ˈlīənəs\ *n* -ES [ME *liones,leonesse*, fr. OF *lionesse, leonesse*, fr. *lion, leon* lion + *-esse* -ess — more at LION] **:** a female lion ⟨hardly a literary lion or ~ whom she did not ventilate —*Times Lit. Supp.*⟩
**li·on·et** \ˈlīənət, ˌ≈≈ˈnet\ *n* -S [MF, dim. of *lion*] **:** a young or small lion
**lion-fish** \ˈ≈,≈\ *n* **1 :** any of several scorpion fishes (genus *Pterois*) of the tropical Pacific brilliantly striped and barred with elongated fins and venomous dorsal spines **2 :** STONEFISH
**lionheart** \ˈ≈,≈\ *n* **:** a lionhearted person
**lionhearted** \ˈ≈ˈ≈\ *adj* **:** having a courageous heart **:** BRAVE ⟨band of ~ fighters —Stuart Cloete⟩ — **lionheartedly** *adv* — **li·on·heart·ed·ness** *n* -ES
**lion-hunter** \ˈ≈,≈,≈\ *n* **1 :** one that hunts lions esp. for sport **2 :** a person who seeks the company of celebrities ⟨included in her makeup some of the impulses of the *lion-hunter* and of the social climber —J.W.Krutch⟩
**li·on·ism** \ˈlīə,nizəm\ *n* -S **:** the practice of lionizing or the state of being lionized
**li·on·iza·tion** \līənəˈzāshən, -,nīˈ-\ *n* -S **:** the act of lionizing
**li·on·ize** \ˈ≈≈,nīz\ *vb* -ED/-ING/-S *see -ize in Explan Notes, vt* **1 :** to treat or regard as a celebrity or object of interest ⟨the opera-mad city *lionized* the new tenor⟩ **2** *Brit* **a :** to show the sights of a place to **b :** to visit or view the sights of **~** *vi* **1** *Brit* **:** to visit or view the sights **2 :** to seek the company of celebrities ⟨this tendency of human nature to ~ —A.J.Todd⟩ — **li·on·iz·er** \-zə(r)\ *n* -S
**lionlike** \ˈ≈≈,≈\ *adj* **:** resembling a lion
**lion lizard** *n* [so called fr. its crest that resembles a lion's mane] **:** BASILISK 3
**li·on·ly** *adj, archaic* **:** LIONLIKE
**lion-mask** \ˈ≈≈,≈\ *n* **:** a decorative motif consisting of a conventionalized lion's face found esp. in 18th century English furniture
**lion monkey** *or* **lion marmoset** *n* **:** any of several So. American marmosets (genus *Leontocebus*) having tufted tails and well-marked neck ruffs of long hair **:** TAMARIN — called also *leoncito*
**lion of england** *usu cap E* **:** a heraldic representation of a lion passant gardant or (as on the shield of England)
**lion-paw foot** \ˈ≈≈,≈-\ *n* **:** a foot in the form of a lion's paw found esp. in 18th century English furniture — see LION-MASK illustration
**lion's beard** *n* **:** a pasqueflower (*Pulsatilla ludoviciana*) of No. America

lion-mask with lion-paw foot

**lion's-ear** \ˈ≈≈,≈\ *n, pl* **lion's-ears 1 :** a mint of the genus *Leonotis; esp* **:** a common tropical mint (*L. nepetaefolia*) **2 :** any of various woolly-leaved So. American plants constituting two genera (*Culcitium* and *Espeletia*) of the family Compositae **3 :** MOTHERWORT 1
**lion's face** *n, pl* **lion's faces** *or* **lions' faces :** a heraldic representation of a lion's head affronté without any of the neck showing but usu. with part of the mane visible — compare LEOPARD'S FACE
**lion's foot** *n* **1 :** a plant having leaves so shaped or lobed as to suggest a lion's foot; *specif* **:** a plant of the genus *Prenanthes* (esp. *P. serpentaria*) — see GALL OF THE EARTH 1 **2 :** EDELWEISS 1
**lion's-heart** \ˈ≈≈,≈\ *n, pl* **lion's-hearts :** DRAGONHEAD
**li·on·ship** \ˈlīən,ship\ *n* **:** the quality or state of being a social lion
**lion's-mouth** \ˈ≈≈,≈\ *n, pl* **lion's-mouths 1 :** SNAPDRAGON **2 :** FOXGLOVE 1 **3 :** TOADFLAX 1
**lion's-snap** \ˈ≈≈,≈\ *n, pl* **lion's-snaps :** SNAPDRAGON
**lion's-tail** \ˈ≈≈,≈\ *n, pl* **lion's-tails 1 :** LION'S-EAR 1 **2 :** MOTHERWORT 1
**lion's-tooth** \ˈ≈≈,≈\ *or* **lion's-teeth** *n, pl* **lion's-tooths** *or* **lion's-teeth 1 :** DANDELION **2 :** FALL DANDELION
**lion-tailed** \ˈ≈≈,≈\ *adj* **:** having a tufted tail
**lion-tailed macaque** *or* **lion-tailed monkey** *n* **:** a black Indian macaque (*Macaca silenus*) that has a pale gray ruff of long hairs around the face and a tuft at the tip of the tail
**lion-tawny** \ˈ≈≈ˈ≈≈\ *adj* **:** of the color lion
**li·o·pel·mid** \,līəˈpelməd, -,mid\ *adj* [NL *Liopelmidae*] **:** of or relating to the Liopelmidae
**li·o·pel·mi·dae** \-ˈmə,dē\ *n pl, cap* [NL, fr. *Liopelma*, type genus (fr. *leio-* + Gk *pelma* sole of the foot) + *-idae* — more at FELL] **:** a family of primitive frogs with four toes on the forefeet, five on the hind feet, and no webs that includes a genus (*Liopelma*) with a single New Zealand species (*L. hamiltoni*) — see ASCAPHUS
**liou·ville's theorem** \(ˈ)lyüˈvēlz-\ *n, usu cap L* [after Joseph *Liouville* †1882 Fr. mathematician] **:** a theorem in fluid dynamics: the density of any selected part of a stream of fluid that does no work and that has no work done on it remains constant as that part moves along its stream line
¹**lip** \ˈlip\ *n* -S [ME *lippe, lip*, fr. OE *lippa;* akin to OFris *lippa* lip, OHG *leffur* & *lefs*, OSw *læpi*, Norw *lepe*, and prob. to L *labium, labrum* lip, and to L *labi* to slide, glide — more at SLEEP] **1 a :** either of the two fleshy folds which surround the orifice of the mouth in man and many other vertebrates and in man are organs of speech essential to certain articulations **b :** this part of the mouth considered as an organ of speech — used chiefly in pl. ⟨taken down from the ~s of his mother or teacher —H.E.Scudder⟩ **2** *slang* **:** saucy or impudent speech ⟨I'll have none of your ~⟩ **3 :** EMBOUCHURE **2 4 :** an edge of a wound **5 :** either of a pair of fleshy folds surrounding an orifice **6 :** a liplike anatomical part or structure: as **a :** LABIUM **b :** LABELLUM 1 **7 a :** the edge or margin of a hollow vessel or cavity (as a cup, bell, or crater) esp. if it shows a slight flare ⟨slept that night on the ~ of a dead volcano —Negley Farson⟩ — see BELL illustration **b :** an edge, rim, or margin esp. when projecting or overlapping ⟨that narrow ~ of rock on the mountain's face —N.C.McDonald⟩ ⟨on the ~ of the Plymouth beach —Sean O'Dwyer⟩ ⟨the car roared up across the ~ of the hill —Thomas Wolfe⟩: as (1) **:** the edge in a flue pipe (as in a pipe organ) across which a current of air is forced causing a wave motion in the air within the pipe that produces the tone (2) *Brit* **:** the lower part of the roof near a face in a coal mine (3) **:** the sharp cutting edge on the end of an auger, drill, or similar tool (4) **:** a projection of the top of a railhead at a joint caused by flow of metal under the action of traffic (5) **:** a low parapet erected on the downstream edge of a mill-race or dam apron to minimize scouring of the river bottom **8 :** a short open spout or drip (as on a pitcher) **9 :** the lapping of water at the margin
²**lip** \ˈ"\ *adj* **1 a** *of utterance* **:** coming from the lips only without thoughtfulness or without sincerity of intent ⟨~ comfort⟩ ⟨~ devotion⟩ ⟨~ praise⟩ ⟨~ reverence⟩ ⟨~ allegiance⟩ — compare LIP-LABOR, LIP SERVICE, LIP-WORSHIP **b** *of a person* **:** speaking or otherwise expressing oneself without thought as to the meaning of the words used or without sincerity ⟨~ comforter⟩ — compare LIP SERVER, LIP-WORSHIPER **2 :** produced with the participation of the lips or one of the lips **:** LABIAL ⟨~ consonants⟩
³**lip** \ˈ"\ *vb* **lipped; lipped; lipping; lips** *vt* **1 a :** to touch with the lips **:** put the lips to; *specif* **:** KISS ⟨a hand that kings have *lipped* and trembled kissing —*Shak.*⟩ **b :** to take into the mouth by action of the lips (as by nipping or sucking) — sometimes used with *up* **2 a :** to utter esp. in a murmuring voice **b** *slang* **:** SING **3 :** to fill in the chinks of ⟨~ a wall⟩ **4 :** to set a piece of wood in (an archer's bow) where a flaw has been cut out **5 :** to notch the edge of ⟨~ a sword⟩ **6 :** to lap against **:** LAVE ⟨the water *lipped* the shingle —R.P. Warren⟩ **7 :** to rise above (as the horizon or the top of a hill or cliff) ⟨*lipping* the rim of a long hill street —Thomas Wolfe⟩ **8 :** to form a lip on (as machine work) **9 :** to strike a golf ball so that it hits the edge of (the cup) but fails to drop in **10 :** to put (snuff) behind the lip **~** *vi* **1 a :** to flow over the lip of a container or vessel — used with *over* or *in* **b :** to have liquid flowing over the brim or edge — used with *over* **2 :** to form or take the form of a lip **3 :** to lap with a splashing noise **:** PLASH **4 :** to use the lips; *specif* **:** to adjust one's lips to the mouthpiece of a wind instrument — sometimes used with *up* **5 :** to apply the lips (as in kissing) — used with *at*
**lip-** *or* **lipo-** *comb form* [NL, fr. Gk, fr. *lipos* — more at LEAVE] **1 :** fat **:** fatty tissue **:** fatty **:** ADIP- ⟨*lipectomy*⟩ ⟨*lipocardiac*⟩ ⟨*lipocele*⟩ **2 :** lipide
**LIP** *abbr* life insurance policy
**li·pa–li·pa** \ˈlēpəˈlēpə\ *n* -S [native name in the Sulu islands] **:** a dugout with planked sides used by natives of the Sulu islands
**li·pan** \lēˈpän, li-\ *n, pl* **lipan** *or* **lipans** *usu cap* **1 a :** an Apache people of eastern New Mexico and western Texas **b :** a member of such people **2 :** the Athapaskan language of the Lipan people
**lipar-** *or* **liparo-** *comb form* [Gk, fr. *liparos*, fr. *lipos* fat — more at LEAVE] **:** fatty **:** fat ⟨*liparocele*⟩ ⟨*liparoid*⟩ ⟨*liparous*⟩
**li·par·i·an** \ləˈperēən, -pa(a)r-, -pär-\ *adj, usu cap* [*Lipari* islands, group of islands in the Tyrrhenian sea off the coast of Sicily + E *-an*] **:** of, relating to, or characteristic of the Lipari islands
¹**lip·a·rid** \ˈlipərəd, -,rid\ *adj* [NL ²*Liparidae*] **:** of or relating to the Liparididae
²**liparid** \ˈ"\ *n* -S [NL ²*Liparidae*] **:** a fish of the family Liparididae
¹**li·par·i·dae** \ləˈparə,dē\ [NL, fr. *Liparis* genus of moths (fr. Gk *liparos* fatty, shiny, bright) + *-idae* — more at LIPAR-] *syn of* LYMANTRIIDAE
²**liparidae** \ˈ"\ [NL, fr. *Liparis*, genus of scorpaenoid fishes (fr. Gk *liparos*) + *-idae*] *syn of* LIPARIDIDAE
**lip·a·rid·i·dae** \,lipəˈridə,dē\ *n pl* [NL, fr. *Liparid-, Liparis*, type genus + *-idae*] **:** a family of scorpaenoid fishes containing the sea snails
**lip·a·ris** \ˈlipərəs\ *n, cap* [NL, fr. Gk *liparos* fatty, shiny, bright — more at LIPAR-] **:** a genus of terrestrial orchids having two broad shining leaves and terminal racemes of irregular flowers — see TWAYBLADE
**lip·a·rite** \-,rīt\ *n* -S [G *liparit*, fr. *Lipari* islands + G *-it* -ite] **:** RHYOLITE
**li·pase** \ˈlī,pās, ˈli-, -āz\ *n* -S [ISV *lip-* + *-ase*] **:** any of a class of enzymes that accelerate the hydrolysis or synthesis of fats or the breakdown of lipoproteins and that occur in both animals (as in pancreatic juice) and plants (as in the castor bean) — compare ESTERASE
**lipbrush** \ˈ≈,≈\ *n* **:** a small brush for applying lipstick
**lip-deep** \ˈ≈ˈ≈\ *adj* **1 :** plunged in to or as if to the lips **2 :** no deeper than the lips **:** INSINCERE **:** SHALLOW
**li·pe·mia** *also* **li·pae·mia** \ləˈpēmēə\ *n* -S [NL, fr. *lip-* + *-emia, -aemia*] **:** the presence of an excess of fats or lipides in the blood; *specif* **:** HYPERCHOLESTEROLEMIA — **li·pe·mic** *also* **li·pae·mic** \-mik\ *adj*
**li·peu·rus** \ləˈpyürəs\ *n, cap* [NL, irreg. fr. *lip-* + *-urus*] **:** an extensive genus of bird lice that are parasites of various birds
**lip fern** *n* [so called fr. the liplike indusium] **:** a fern of the genus *Cheilanthes*
**liph·i·sti·idae** \,lifəˈstīə,dē\ *n pl, cap* [NL, fr. *Liphistius*, type genus + *-idae*] **:** a family of primitive spiders belonging to the suborder Liphistiomorphae
¹**li·phis·ti·o·morph** \ləˈfistēə,mȯrf\ *adj* [NL *Liphistiomorphae*] **:** of or relating to the Liphistiomorphae
²**liphistiomorph** \ˈ"\ *n* **:** a spider of the suborder Liphistiomorphae
**li·phis·ti·o·mor·phae** \≈,≈≈≈ˈmȯr,fē\ *n pl, cap* [NL, fr. *Liphistius*, genus of spiders + *-o-* + *-morphae*] **:** a suborder comprising the primitive spiders that retain abdominal segmentation
**lip·ide** \ˈli,pīd, -,pəd\ *or* **lip·id** \ˈlipəd\ *n* -S [ISV *lip-* + *-ide, -id;* orig. formed as F *lipide*] **:** any of a group of substances that in general are soluble in ether, chloroform, or other solvent for fats but are only sparingly soluble in water, that with proteins and carbohydrates constitute the principal structural components of living cells, and that are considered to include fats, waxes, phosphatides, cerebrosides, and related and derived compounds and sometimes steroids and carotenoids — called also *lipin, lipoid*
**lip·i·do·plast** \ˈlipədə,plast\ *also* **lip·i·do·plas·tid** \,≈≈≈+\ *n* -S [ISV *lipide* + *-o-* + *-plast* or *plastid*] **:** ELAIOPLAST
**lip·i·do·sis** \,lipəˈdōsəs\ *n, pl* **lipido·ses** \-,sēz\ [NL, fr. ISV *lipid* + NL *-osis*] **:** LIPOIDOSIS
**lip·i·do·some** \ˈlipədə,sōm\ *n* -S [ISV *lipide* + *-o-* + *-some*] **:** a fatty inclusion body of cytoplasm
**lipid pneumonia** *or* **lipoid pneumonia** *n* **:** pneumonia caused by the aspiration or absorption into the lungs of oily substances (as nose drops or mineral oil) and usu. found to be chronic
**lip·in** \ˈlipən\ *n* -S [*lip-* + *-in*] **:** LIPIDE; *esp* **:** a complex lipide (as a phosphatide or a cerebroside)
**lipizzan** *often cap, var of* LIPPIZAN
**lipizzaner** *usu cap, var of* LIPPIZANER
**lip–labor** \ˈ≈,≈≈\ *n, archaic* **:** action with the lips (as in speaking) — used esp. to designate the saying of prayers by rote or repetitively with little or no thought about their meaning
**lip·less** \ˈlipləs\ *adj* **:** having no lips
**liplike** \ˈ≈,≈\ *adj* **:** resembling a lip esp. in forming a fleshy fold or margin
**lip microphone** *n* **:** a microphone worn on the speaker's lip
¹**lipo-** — see LIP-
²**lipo-** *comb form* [F, fr. LL, fr. Gk, fr. *leipein* to leave, be lacking — more at LOAN] **1 :** lacking **:** without ⟨*lipo*graphy⟩ **2 :** leaving **:** abandoning ⟨*lipo*xenous⟩
**lip·o·blast** \ˈlipə,blast\ *n* [ISV *lip-* + *-blast*] **:** a connective-tissue cell destined to become a fat cell
**lip·o·ca·ic** \ˌ≈≈ˈkāik\ *n* -S [*lip-* + Gk *kaiein* to burn + E *-ic* — more at CAUSTIC] **:** a lipotropic preparation from the pancreas
**lip·o·chon·dri·on** \,≈≈ˈkändrēən\ *n, pl* **lipochon·dria** \-drēə\ [NL, fr. *lip-* + Gk *chondrion* granule, dim. of *chondros* grain — more at GRIND] **:** GOLGI BODY
**lip·o·chrome** \ˈ≈≈,krōm\ *n* [ISV *lip-* + *-chrome*] **:** any of the naturally occurring pigments soluble in fats or in solvents for fats; *esp* **:** CAROTENOID
**lip·o·dystrophy** \,≈≈+\ *n* [ISV *lip-* + *dystrophy*] **:** a disorder of fat metabolism esp. involving loss of fat from or deposition of fat in tissue — compare LIPOIDOSIS
**lip·o·fuscin** \"+\ *n* -S [ISV *lip-* + *fuscin*, a brown animal pigment, fr. L *fuscus* dark brown, blackish + ISV *-in* — more at DUSK] **:** any of several brown pigments that are similar to the melanins and are found in various tissues (as of the heart) in a state of exhaustion or of senility
¹**lip·o·genesis** \"+\ *n* [NL, fr. *lip-* + L *genesis*] **:** formation of fat in the living body esp. when excessive or abnormal
²**lipogenesis** \"\ *n* [NL, fr. ²*lipo-* + L *genesis*] **:** acceleration of development by the omission of certain ancestral stages — compare BRADYGENESIS, TACHYGENESIS
**li·pog·e·nous** \ləˈpäjənəs, līˈ-\ *also* **lip·o·gen·ic** \ˌlipəˈjenik, ˌlī-\ *adj* [*lip-* + *-genous, -genic*] **:** producing or tending to produce fat ⟨the ~ effect of estrogens⟩
**lip·o·gram** \ˈlipə,gram, ˈlī-\ *n* [MGk *lipogrammatos*, adj., lacking a letter, fr. Gk *lipo-* ²lipo- + *-grammatos* (fr. *grammat-, gramma* letter) — more at GRAM] **:** a writing composed of words not having a certain letter (as the *Odyssey* of Tryphiodorus which had no alpha in the first book, no beta in the second, and so on)
**lip·o·gram·mat·ic** \ˌ≈≈grəˈmad·ik\ *adj* [MGk *lipogrammatos* + E *-ic*] **:** being a lipogram **:** having the character of a lipogram
**lip·o·gram·ma·tism** \ˌ≈≈ˈgramə,tizəm\ *n* -S [MGk *lipogrammatos* + E *-ism*] **:** the practice of writing lipograms
**lip·o·gram·ma·tist** \-məd·əst\ *n* -S [MGk *lipogrammatos* + E *-ist*] **:** a writer of lipograms
**li·pog·ra·phy** \ləˈpägrəfē, lī-\ *n* -ES [²*lipo-* + *-graphy*] **:** inadvertent omission (as of a letter or syllable) in writing
**li·po·ic acid** \ləˈpōik-\ *n* [*lip-* + *-ic*] **:** any of several microbial growth factors occurring esp. in yeast and liver; *specif* **:** the crystalline alpha variety $C_7H_{13}S_2COOH$ that together with cocarboxylase and other factors is essential for the oxidation of alpha-keto acids (as pyruvic acid to acetic acid) during metabolic changes in the body; 6,8-epi-dithio-octanoic acid — compare THIOCTIC ACID
¹**lip·oid** \ˈli,pȯid, ˈlī-\ *or* **li·poi·dal** \ləˈpȯidᵊl, lī-\ *adj* [ISV *lip-* + *-oid* (adj. suffix) or *-oidal*] **:** FATLIKE
²**lipoid** \ˈ"\ *n* -S [ISV *lip-* + *-oid* (n. suffix)] **:** a fatlike substance: as **a :** a mixture extracted from biological tissue by ether **b :** LIPIDE **c :** LIPIN
**li·poid·ic** \ləˈpȯidik, lī-\ *adj* [ISV ²*lipoid* + *-ic*] **:** LIPOID
**lip·oi·do·sis** \,li,pȯiˈdōsəs, ,lī-\ *n, pl* **lipoido·ses** \-,sēz\ [NL, fr. ISV ²*lipoid* + NL *-osis*] **:** a disorder of fat metabolism esp. involving the deposition of fat in an organ (as the liver or spleen) — compare LIPODYSTROPHY
**li·pol·y·sis** \ləˈpäləsəs\ *n, pl* **lipoly·ses** \-,sēz\ [NL, fr. *lip-* + *-lysis*] **:** the hydrolysis of fat
**li·po·lyt·ic** \ˌlipəˈlid·ik, ˌlī-\ *adj* [ISV *lip-* + *-lytic*] **:** of, relating to, causing, or resulting from lipolysis ⟨lipase is a ~ enzyme⟩
**li·po·ma** \ləˈpōmə\ *n, pl* **lipo·mas** \-məz\ *or* **lipoma·ta** \-məd·ə\ [NL, fr. *lip-* + *-oma*] **:** a tumor consisting of fatty tissue — **li·pom·a·tous** \-ˈpämədəs, -pōm-\ *adj*
**li·po·ma·to·sis** \lə,pōməˈtōsəs\ *n, pl* **lipomato·ses** \-,sēz\ [NL, fr. *lipomat-, lipoma* + *-osis*] **:** any of several abnormal conditions marked by local or generalized deposits of fat or replacement of other tissue by fat; *specif* **:** the presence of multiple lipomas
**lip·o·mi·cron** \,lipəˈmī,krän, -ˈmi,k-\ *n* [NL, fr. *lip-* + *chylomicron*] **:** a chylomicron esp. in the blood of an insect
**lip·o·nys·sus** \,≈≈ˈnisəs\ [NL, fr. *lip-* + *-nyssus* (fr. Gk *nyssein, nyttein* to prick, sting) — more at NUMEN] *syn of* BDELLONYSSUS
**lip·o·phage** \ˈ≈≈,fāj\ *n* [*lip-* + *-phage*] **:** a cell (as a phagocyte) that takes up fat — **lip·o·pha·gia** \,≈≈ˈfājēə\ *n* -S — **lip·o·phag·ic** \ˌ≈≈ˈfajik\ *adj*
**lip·o·phan·er·o·sis** \,≈≈,fanəˈrōsəs\ *n* [NL, fr. *lip-* + *phaner-* + *-osis*] **:** fatty degeneration of cells involving the unmasking of cellular lipoids
**lip·o·phil·ic** \ˌ≈≈ˈfilik\ *also* **lip·o·phile** \ˈ≈≈,fīl\ *adj* [*lip-* + *-philic, -phile*] **:** relating to or having strong affinity for fats or other lipides **:** promoting the solubilization or absorption of lipides ⟨the ionic type of emulsifier is composed of an organic ~ group and a hydrophilic group —W.C.Griffin⟩ — compare HYDROPHILIC, HYDROPHOBIC, OLEOPHILIC
**lip·o·phore** \ˈ≈≈,fō(ə)r\ *n* -S [*lipochrome* + *chromatophore*] **:** a pigment cell or chromatophore containing a lipochrome pigment
**lip·o·protein** \,lipə, ,līpə+\ *n* [*lip-* + *protein*] **:** any of a class of widely distributed conjugated proteins that contain a considerable percentage of lipide and that have the solubility and mobility properties of alpha globulins or beta globulins — compare PROTEOLIPIDE
**lip·o·sarcoma** \,≈≈+\ *n* [NL, fr. *lip-* + *sarcoma*] **:** a sarcoma arising from immature fat cells of the bone marrow
**li·po·sis** \ləˈpōsəs\ *n, pl* **lipo·ses** \-,sēz\ [NL, fr. *lip-* + *-osis*] **:** OBESITY
**li·po·si·tol** \ləˈpōsə,tōl, -,tōl\ *n* -S [*lip-* + *inositol*] **:** any of several phosphatides occurring in plants (as soybeans) and in animals esp. in the brain and spinal cord and containing the meso form of inositol in combination
**lip·o·soluble** \,lipō+\ *adj* [ISV *lip-* + *soluble*] **:** soluble in fats or oils **:** FAT-SOLUBLE **:** OIL-SOLUBLE ⟨~ bismuth preparations⟩
**lip·o·some** \ˈ≈≈,sōm\ *n* -S [ISV *lip-* + *-some*] **:** one of the fatty droplets in the cytoplasm esp. of an egg
**li·po·thym·ia** \,lipəˈthimēə, ,lī-\ *or* **li·poth·y·my** \ləˈpäthəmē\ *n, pl* **lipothymias** *or* **lipothymies** [F & LL; F *lipothymie*, fr. LL *lipothymia*, fr. Gk, fr. *lipothymein* to faint (fr. *lipo-* ²lipo- + *thymos* spirit, mind, courage) + *-ia* -y — more at FUME] **:** FAINTNESS, FAINTING — **li·po·thym·i·al** \ˌlipəˈthimēəl\ *adj* — **li·po·thym·ic** \-mik\ *adj*
**lip·o·trop·ic** \ˌlipəˈträpik, ˌlī-, -trōp-\ *also* **lip·o·troph·ic** \-äfik, -ōf-\ *adj* [ISV *lip-* + *-tropic* or *-trophic*] **:** tending to prevent abnormal deposition of fats or deposition of abnormal fats or to accelerate their removal if present
**li·pot·ro·pism** \ləˈpä·trə,pizəm\ *n* [*lip-* + *-tropism*] **:** the state or tendency of being lipotropic
**lip·o·typh·la** \,lipəˈtiflə\ *n pl, cap* [NL, fr. *lip-* + *-typhla* (fr. Gk *typhlon* cecum) — more at TYPHL-] **:** a suborder of insectivores comprising the moles, hedgehogs, and true shrews and having the pubic symphysis short and the postorbital process undeveloped — compare MENOTYPHLA
**li·pox·e·nous** \ləˈpäksənəs, lī-\ *adj* [²*lipo-* + *-xenous*]

**:** abandoning the host — used of various parasitic fungi (as ergot) — **li·pox·e·ny** \-nē\ *n* -ES

**li·pox·i·dase** \-ksə,dās, -āz\ *n* -S [*lip-* + *oxidase*] **:** a crystallizable protein enzyme that catalyzes the oxidation primarily of unsaturated fatty acids or unsaturated fats by oxygen and secondarily of carotenoids to colorless substances and that occurs esp. in soybeans and cereals

**¹lipped** \'lipt\ *adj* [ME, fr. *lippe*, *lip* lip + *-ed* — more at LIP] **1 a :** having a lip **:** having a raised edge resembling a lip **b :** having a lip (of such a kind) ⟨a virgin purest ~ —John Keats⟩ **2 :** LABIATE

**²lipped** *past of* LIP

**lip·pen** \'lipən\ *vb* -ED/-ING/-S [ME *lipnien*, *lipnen*] *chiefly Scot*, *vi* **:** to have faith or trust **:** TRUST, RELY, CONFIDE — usu. used with *to* ⟨too merry a lass at times to ~ to entirely —R.L. Stevenson⟩ ~ *vt* **:** ENTRUST ⟨had done wrong in ~*ing* a boat to such a young crew —William Black⟩

**¹lip·per** \'lipər\ *vi* -ED/-ING/-S [prob. of imit. origin] *Scot* **1 :** RIPPLE **2** *of a boat* **:** to become sunk to the gunwale — used with *with*

**²lipper** \-pə(r)\ *n* -S **1 :** a slight roughness or ruffling of the sea **2 :** a light spray from small waves

**³lipper** \"\ *n* -S [²*lip* + *-er*] **1 :** an implement for making a lip on a glass vessel **2 :** one that shapes the lip of a glass or earthen vessel

**⁴lipper** \"\ *n* -S [origin unknown] **:** a thin piece of blubber used to wipe the decks of a whaler

**⁵lipper** \"\ *vt* -ED/-ING/-S **:** to wipe with a lipper — used with *up* or *off* ⟨~ up the decks⟩

**lip·per·ings** \-pəriŋz\ *n pl* [fr. pl. of *lippering*, gerund of ⁵*lipper*] **:** oil and refuse cleaned from a whaling ship's deck with a lipper **:** SLUMGULLION

**lip·pia** \'lipēə\ *n*, *cap* [NL, fr. Augustin *Lippi* †1705 French physician and traveler + NL *-ia*] **:** a large genus of tropical American herbs, shrubs, and small trees (family Verbenaceae) having small flowers in heads or spikes

**lippie** *var of* LIPPY

**lip·pi·ness** \'lipēnəs, -pin-\ *n* -ES **1 :** the state or quality of being lippy **2 :** saucy or impertinent language

**¹lip·ping** \'lipiŋ\ *n* -S [¹*lip* + *-ing*] **1 :** outgrowth of bone in liplike form at a joint margin (as in degenerative arthritis) **2 :** a piece of wood set in an archer's bow where a flaw has been cut out **3 :** EMBOUCHURE 2a

**²lipping** *pres part of* LIP

**lip·pi·tude** \'lipə,tüd, -ə-,tyüd\ *n* -S [F, fr. L *lippitudo*, fr. *lippitus* (past part. of *lippire* to be blear-eyed, fr. *lippus* blear-eyed) + *-udo* -ude — more at LEAVE] *archaic* **:** soreness or blearedness of the eyes

**lip·pi·zan** *also* **lip·iz·zan** \'lipət'sän\ *n* -S *often cap* [*Lippiza*, *Lipizza* + E *-an*] **:** LIPPIZANER 2

**lip·pi·zan·er** *also* **lip·iz·zan·er** \'lipət'sänər\ *or* **lip·pi·za·na** \-nə\ *or* **lip·piz·zan·er** \-nər\ *n* -S [*Lippizaner*, *Lipizzaner*, *Lippizzaner* fr. G, fr. *Lippiza*, *Lipizza*, *Lippizza*, stud in northwestern Yugoslavia (formerly the Austrian Imperial Stud) where the strain was developed; *Lippizana* fr. It, fr. *Lippiza*] **1** *usu cap* **:** a strain or breed of shapely spirited chiefly white horses developed by crossbreeding Spanish, Danish, Italian, and Arab stock at the Austrian Imperial Stud at Lippiza near Trieste **2** *often cap* **:** a horse of the Lippizaner strain or breed used esp. in specialty display and dressage

**lip plug** *n* **:** LABRET

**lipp·mann process** \'lipmən-\ *n*, *usu cap L* [after Gabriel *Lippmann* †1921 French physicist] **:** a method of color photography depending upon the interference of light waves and employing in the camera an extremely fine-grain photographic plate in contact with a mercury reflector

**¹lip·py** *also* **lip·pie** \'lipē, -pi\ *n*, *pl* **lippies** [*lip* (Sc var. of ³*leap*) + *-y*, *-ie*] **:** an old Scotch unit of capacity equal to ¼ Scotch peck

**²lip·py** \'lipē, -pi\ *adj*, *usu* -ER/-EST [¹*lip* + *-y*] **1 a** *of a dog* **:** having hanging lips when hanging lips are not acceptable by the standard of the breed or having lips excessively hanging by the standard of the breed **b** *of a person* **:** having an excessively prominent lip **2 :** impudent or impertinent in speech ⟨~ adolescents⟩

**lip-read** \'=,=\ *vt* **:** to understand by lipreading ⟨a surprising vocabulary of words which they could *lip-read* quite successfully —*Lancet*⟩ ~ *vi* **:** to read lips ⟨teaching the deaf child to *lip-read* and to talk —Grace Coolidge⟩

**lip-reader** \'=,==\ *n* **:** one that can understand the words or meaning of a speaker by lipreading

**lipreading** \'=,==\ *n* **:** the catching of the words or meaning of a speaker by watching the movements of his lips without hearing his voice (as by a deaf person) — compare ORAL METHOD

**lip rouge** *n* **:** rouge for the lips

**lip-rounding** \'=,==\ *n* **:** ROUNDING 1c

**lips** *pl of* LIP, *pres 3d sing of* LIP

**lipsalve** \'=,=\ *n* **:** an ointment for the lips

**lip server** *n* **:** one that practices lip service

**lip service** *n* **:** service consisting only of avowed expressions of adherence, devotion, or allegiance **:** service by words but not by deeds ⟨pay *lip service* to the principles of competitive business but . . . permit big business to deny access to scarce raw materials to independent businessmen —Henry Wallace⟩ ⟨were . . . established as accepted religions provided their followers did *lip service* to the cult of the emperor —Brooke P. Church⟩

**¹lipstick** \'=,=\ *n* [¹*lip* + *stick*] **:** a waxy solid preparation or rouge put up in stick form for use as a cosmetic on the lips; *also* **:** a stick of such a preparation with its case

**²lipstick** \"\ *vb* -ED/-ING/-S *vt* **1 :** to apply lipstick to **2 :** to form by applying lipstick ⟨she had loops ~*ed* above a rather thin upper lip —Earle Birney⟩ ~ *vi* **:** to apply lipstick

**lip stop** *n* **1 :** FLUE STOP 1 **2 :** either of the sounds \p\ and \b\

**lip strike** *n* **:** the part of a lock that makes contact with the lip of a bolt or fastener

**lip sync** *n* [*lip synch*ronization] **1 :** LIP SYNCHRONIZATION **2 :** the relationship that exists between sound and action in a sound motion picture when the two are in synchrony **3 :** sound in a sound motion picture that is perceived as proceeding from concurrent action in distinction from sound that is heard but perceived not to be proceeding from concurrent action **:** synchronous dialogue

**lip-sync** *adj* [*lip sync*] **:** of, relating to, or produced by lip synchronization or lip sync

**lip synchronization** *n* **1 :** recording of sound simultaneously with photographing of action so as to secure perfect synchrony of both (as when a motion picture is projected) **2 :** recording of sound and photographing of action at separate times but utilizing techniques designed to secure synchrony of sound and action when the two are combined — compare ⁵DUB 2

**lip-teeth** \'=;=\ *adj* **:** LABIODENTAL

**li·pu·ria** \lə'pyu̇rēə\ *n* -S [NL, fr. *lip-* + *-uria*] **:** the presence of fat in urine

**lipwork** \'=,=\ *n* **1** *obs* **:** KISSING **2 :** unthinking or insincere use of words **:** vain repetition

**lip-worship** \'=,==\ *n* **:** worship in utterance but not in deed **:** affirmation of devotion or fidelity without corresponding action

**lip-worshiper** \'=,===\ *n* **:** one that worships in utterance only **:** one affirming devotion or fidelity without corresponding action

**liq** *abbr* **1** liquid **2** liquor

**li·quate** \'lī,kwāt *also* 'li-, *usu* -ād·+V\ *vb* -ED/-ING/-S [L *liquatus*, past part. of *liquare*; akin to L *liquēre* to be fluid — more at LIQUID] *vt* **:** to cause (a metal or other substance that is more fusible than a substance with which it is combined) to separate out by the application of heat — often used with *out* ⟨*liquating* the impure metal out⟩ ~ *vi* **:** to become separated from a less fusible substance by being subjected to heat — often used with *out* ⟨metallic lead that readily ~*s* out⟩

**li·qua·tion** \lī'kwāshən, lə-, -āzhən\ *n* -S [LL *liquation-*, *liquatio*, fr. L *liquatus* + *-ion-*, *-io* -ion] **:** the process of separating a fusible substance (as a metal) from one less fusible by the application of heat

**liq·ue·fa·cient** \,likwə'fāshənt\ *n* -S [L *liquefacient-*, *liquefaciens*, pres. part. of *liquefacere* to liquefy, fr. *liquēre* to be fluid + *facere* to make — more at LIQUID, DO] **:** something that serves to liquefy or to promote liquefaction

**liq·ue·fac·tion** \,==ˈfakshən\ *n* [ME, fr. LL *liquefaction-*, *liquefactio*, fr. L *liquefactus* (past part. of *liquefacere*) + *-ion-*, *-io* -ion] **1 :** the process of making or becoming liquid **:** conversion of a solid into a liquid by heat or of a gas into a liquid by cold or pressure **2 :** the state of being liquid

**liq·ue·fac·tive** \,==ˈfaktiv\ *adj* [*liquefaction* + *-ive*] **:** relating to or causing liquefaction

**liq·ue·fi·a·ble** \,==ˈfīəbəl\ *adj* [*liquefy* + *-able*] **:** capable of being liquefied

**liquefied petroleum gas** *n* **:** a compressed gas consisting of flammable light hydrocarbons (as propane and butane) obtained esp. as a by-product in the refining of petroleum or the manufacture of natural gasoline and used chiefly as a domestic and industrial fuel, as a motor fuel, and as a raw material for chemical synthesis (as of synthetic rubber) — abbr. *LPG*; called also *bottled gas*, *LP gas*

**liq·ue·fi·er** \'likwə,fī(ə)r, -īə\ *n* -S **:** one that liquefies: as **a :** an apparatus for liquefying gases **b :** a worker who operates compressors for liquefying gases (as chlorine gas)

**liq·ue·fy** *also* **liq·ui·fy** \'likwə,fī\ *vb* -ED/-ING/-S [MF *liquefier*, modif. (influenced by MF *-fier* -fy) of L *liquefacere* — more at LIQUEFACIENT] *vt* **:** to reduce to a liquid state — used both of solids and gases ~ *vi* **:** to become liquid

**li·quesce** \li'kwes\ *vb* -ED/-ING/-S [L *liquescere*] **:** LIQUEFY

**li·ques·cence** \-ˢᵊn(t)s\ *n* -S **:** the quality or state of being liquescent

**li·ques·cent** \-ˢᵊnt\ *adj* [L *liquescent-*, *liquescens*, pres. part. of *liquescere* to become fluid, incho. of *liquēre* to be fluid — more at LIQUID] **:** being or becoming or tending to become liquid **:** MELTING

**¹li·queur** *R* li'kər, lē'-, + V -kər-; -*R* -kə̄, + V -kər- *or* -kə̄ *also* -kə̄r; -'k(y)u̇(ə)r, -u̇ə\ *n* -S [F, liquid, liquor, liqueur, fr. OF *licour*, *liqueur* liquid — more at LIQUOR] **1 :** an alcoholic beverage often used as an after-dinner drink and as a cocktail ingredient, flavored with various aromatic substances and usu. sweetened, and made chiefly by steeping and distilling the flavoring substances in spirit — compare CORDIAL **2 :** a solution of sugar and aged wine used to induce second fermentation in the production of champagne

**²liqueur** \"\ *vt* -ED/-ING/-S **:** to treat or mix with liqueur

**liqueur d'or** \-'dȯr\ *n*, *pl* **liqueurs d'or** [F, lit., gold liqueur] **:** a sweet colorless French liqueur flavored primarily with lemon and containing tiny golden flecks — compare DANZIGER GOLDWASSER

**liqueur green** *n* **:** a light to moderate greenish yellow that is greener and stronger than dyer's broom or acacia

**liqueur jaune** \-'zhōn\ *n*, *pl* **liqueurs jaunes** \"\ [F, lit., yellow liqueur] **:** a liqueur resembling yellow chartreuse

**liqueur verte** \-'vert\ *n*, *pl* **liqueurs vertes** \"\ [F, lit., green liqueur] **:** a liqueur resembling green Chartreuse

**¹liq·uid** \'likwəd\ *adj* [ME, fr. MF *liquide*, fr. L *liquidus*, fr. *liquēre* to be fluid; akin to L *lixa* water, lye, *lixivus* consisting of lye, OIr *fliuch* damp, W *gwlith* dew, *gwlyb* wet] **1 a** (1) **:** that is extremely fluid without being gaseous so as to flow freely typically in the manner of water and to have a definite volume without having a definite shape except such as is temporarily given by a container and such as is readily lost (as by an upset or overflow) and that is only slightly compressible and incapable of indefinite expansion in such a way that constituent molecules while moving with extreme ease upon each other do not tend to separate from each other in the manner characteristic of the molecules of gases ⟨water and milk and blood are ~ substances⟩ (2) **:** WATERY ⟨sailing over the ~ depths of the seas⟩ **b :** brimming with tears ⟨sorrow which made the eyes of many grow ~⟩ **2 a :** bright and clear to the vision ⟨the ~ air of a spring morning⟩ ⟨shining with a ~ luster⟩ **b** *obs* **:** clearly evident **:** MANIFEST **c** *chiefly Scots law* (1) *of an account or obligation* **:** UNDISPUTED (2) *of a debt* **:** ascertained and constituted against a debtor by a written obligation or by a court decree **3 a** (1) **:** that is smooth and musical in tone **:** that has a flowing quality entirely free of harshness or discord or abrupt breaks ⟨the ~ song of a robin in the early evening⟩ (2) **:** that is smooth and unconstrained in movement ⟨the ~ grace of a ballerina⟩ **b** *of a consonant* (1) **:** that is frictionless and capable of being prolonged like a vowel (as \l\, some varieties of \r\, and in some classifications \n\, \m\, \ŋ\) (2) **:** CONTINUANT **4 :** tending to become altered (as in form or content) **:** not fixed **:** not stable ⟨~ political agreements that were quite without real significance⟩ **5 :** that is cash or capable of being readily converted into cash ⟨~ assets⟩

**syn** FLUID**:** LIQUID implies a flow characteristic of water and implies a substance, as water, with definite volume but no definite form except that given by its container; figuratively, it is opposed to *harsh* or, sometimes, *fixed* or *rigid* ⟨its coal and *liquid* fuel —*Current Biog.*⟩ ⟨*liquid* soap⟩ ⟨the *liquid* sweetness of the thrush —H.J.Laski⟩ FLUID implies flowing of any kind and extends to gases, to highly viscous substances, or to something usu. solid but liquefied, as by heating or dissolving; figuratively, it is, more commonly than LIQUID, opposed to *rigid* or *fixed* ⟨the memory of him would become as *fluid* as water and trickle out of her mind —Ellen Glasgow⟩ ⟨a more *fluid* oil paint on canvas —*Nat'l Gallery of Art*⟩ ⟨representatives whose task it should be not to codify and embalm the laws, but to keep them *fluid* —D.C.Peattie⟩ ⟨our moral notions are always *fluid* —J.E.E.Dalberg-Acton⟩

**²liquid** \"\ *n* -S [F *liquide*, fr. MF, fr. *liquide*, adj.] **1 :** a liquid substance — compare GAS, SOLID **2 :** a liquid consonant

**liquid air** *n* **:** air in the liquid state but usu. richer in oxygen than gaseous air that is obtained as a faintly bluish transparent mobile intensely cold liquid by compressing purified air and cooling it by its own expansion to a temperature below the boiling points of its principal components nitrogen and oxygen and is used chiefly as a refrigerant and as a source of oxygen, nitrogen, and inert gases (as argon)

**liquid-air trap** *n* **:** a tube which is immersed in liquid air and through which gases are passed to have vaporous impurities removed by condensation or sublimation

**liq·uid·am·bar** \'likwə'dambə(r)\ *n* [NL, fr. L *liquidus* liquid + ML *ambar* amber — more at LIQUID, AMBER] **1 a** *cap* **:** a genus of trees (family Hamamelidaceae) with small monoecious flowers and a globose fruit composed of many woody carpels — see SWEET GUM **b** -S **:** any tree of the genus *Liquidambar* **2** *also* **liq·uid·am·ber** \"\ **:** a storax or a resin from the sweet gum

**liquid ammonia** *n* **:** a heavy liquid that has a high vapor pressure at ordinary temperatures, that causes freezing when brought into contact with the skin, that is obtained by compressing anhydrous gaseous ammonia, and that is used in refrigeration and as a solvent (as in the study of ammono compounds) and as a source of gaseous ammonia

**liq·ui·date** \'likwə,dāt, *usu* -ād·+V\ *vb* -ED/-ING/-S [LL *liquidatus*, past part. of *liquidare* to melt, fr. L *liquidus* liquid — more at LIQUID] *vt* **1 a** (1) **:** to determine by agreement or by litigation the precise amount of (indebtedness, damages, accounts) ⟨was prepared to pay the debt as soon as it was *liquidated*⟩ (2) **:** to determine the liabilities and apportion assets toward discharging the indebtedness of (as a firm that is going out of business) ⟨decided to ~ the corporation by the end of the year⟩ **b :** to settle (a debt) by payment or other adjustment or settlement ⟨made every effort to stabilize the economy by *liquidating* the national debt⟩ **2 :** to get rid of **:** dispose of ⟨any remaining doubts or objections can be easily *liquidated*⟩; *esp* **:** to get rid of by force or violence and esp. by killing ⟨ruthlessly ~*s* all opponents of the regime⟩ **3** *archaic* **:** to make clear **:** make plain **:** make unambiguous or less ambiguous ⟨time only can ~ the meaning —Alexander Hamilton⟩ **4 :** to convert (assets) into cash ⟨*liquidated* his securities⟩ ~ *vi* **1 :** to liquidate debts or damages or accounts **2 :** to determine (as of a firm that is going out of business) liabilities and to apportion assets toward discharging indebtedness

**liquidating dividend** *n* **:** a final payment to a stockholder (as by a firm that is going out of business) that is usu. a simple return of the stockholder's capital

**liq·ui·da·tion** \,likwə'dāshən\ *n* -S **1 :** the action or process of liquidating or of being liquidated **2 :** the condition of being liquidated

**liq·ui·da·tor** \'==,dād·ə(r), -ātə-\ *n* -S **:** one that liquidates; *esp* **:** an individual appointed by law to liquidate assets (as of a bankrupt company) — compare RECEIVER

**liquid bleach** *n* **:** a liquid containing bleaching agents; *esp* **:** a solution of sodium hypochlorite used for bleaching (as in laundry and textile work), disinfecting, and deodorizing — compare BLEACH LIQUOR

**liquid compass** *n* **:** a compass in which the compass card and magnets rest on a pivot in a bowl filled with liquid

**liquid crystal** *n* **:** a mesomorphic substance (as para-azoxyanisole) having observable optical anisotropy like a crystal as evidenced by double-refraction polarization but having such low viscosity as to behave mechanically like a liquid — compare CYBOTAXIS

**liquid extract** *n* **:** FLUIDEXTRACT

**liquid fire** *n* **:** a flammable liquid composition of chemicals that can be shot in a flaming stream (as against tanks or into fortified positions)

**liquid glue** *n* **:** a fluid preparation of glue (as of animal glue with a chemical liquefier in water)

**liquid gold** *n* **:** a liquid preparation (as a suspension of finely divided gold in an oil) for decorating ceramic ware with gold or gold color

**li·quid·i·ty** \li'kwidəd·ē, -ətē, -i\ *n* -ES [F or L; F *liquidité*, fr. L *liquiditat-*, *liquiditas*, fr. *liquidus* liquid + *-itat-*, *-itas* -ity — more at LIQUID] **1 :** the quality or state of being liquid **2 :** the quality or state of possessing liquid assets ⟨a bank that has progressively increased its ~⟩

**liquidity preference** *n* **:** preference for actual cash rather than for income-yielding investments; *specif* **:** this preference insofar as it affects the relationship between cash balances and interest rates

**liq·uid·ize** \'likwə,dīz\ *vt* -ED/-ING/-S **:** to cause to be liquid

**liq·uid·ly** *adv* **:** in a liquid manner ⟨laughed ~⟩ **:** like a liquid ⟨silk that rippled ~⟩

**liquid measure** *n* **1 :** a unit or series of units for measuring liquid capacity — see MEASURE table **2 :** a measure for liquids

**liq·uid·ness** *n* -ES **:** the quality or state of being liquid

**liquid oxygen** *n* **:** a pale blue transparent mobile magnetic liquid obtained by compressing gaseous oxygen and used chiefly in liquid-oxygen explosives and as the oxidizer in rocket propellants — called also *lox*

**liquid-oxygen explosive** *n* **:** a blasting explosive that consists essentially of a cartridge containing combustible material (as carbon black or lampblack) and immersed in liquid oxygen shortly before use

**liquid petrolatum** *also* **liquid paraffin** *n* **:** a transparent oily liquid obtained usu. by distilling petroleum fractions boiling between 330°C and 390°C and used chiefly in medicine for treating constipation and esp. formerly as a demulcent and solvent for nose and throat medication — called also *mineral oil*, *white mineral oil*

**liquid rosin** *n* **:** TALL OIL

**liquid sugar** *n* **:** a thick saturated solution of usu. refined cane or beet sucrose that is often partially or fully inverted to prevent crystallization

**liq·ui·dus** \'likwədəs\ *also* **liquidus curve** *n* -ES [L *liquidus* liquid — more at LIQUID] **:** a curve usu. on a temperature-composition diagram for a binary system that over a range of temperatures between the melting points of the pure components relates compositions of the liquid phase to the solid phase in equilibrium with the liquid phase and that indicates temperatures above which only the liquid phase can exist — compare SOLIDUS, SOLVUS

**liquify** *var of* LIQUEFY

**¹li·quor** \'likə(r)\ *n* -S [ME *licour*, *liquour*, fr. OF *licour*, *liqueur*, fr. L *liquor*, fr. *liquēre* to be fluid — more at LIQUID] **:** a liquid substance: as **a :** something drunk as a beverage (as water, milk, fruit juice); *esp* **:** a usu. strong distilled alcoholic beverage (as whiskey, rum) rather than a fermented one (as wine, beer) **b** (1) **:** the liquid in which meat or vegetables have been cooked **:** BROTH (2) **:** the juice of meat given off during cooking and often combined with a thickening agent and spices and served with the meat **:** GRAVY (3) **:** a dressing or sauce served with foods (4) **:** the juice contained in oysters or clams **c :** sugarcane sap that has not been crystallized to sugar **d :** a solution of a medicinal substance usu. in water — distinguished from *tincture* **e :** a solution or emulsion or suspension used or obtained in an industrial process **:** BATH 2b ⟨scouring ~ for wool⟩ ⟨dye ~⟩ ⟨waste ~*s*⟩: as (1) **:** a solution of a chemical used in digesting raw materials for cellulosic pulp ⟨soda ~⟩ — see SULFITE LIQUOR (2) **:** the liquid drained from such pulp at the end of the cook — see BLACK LIQUOR (3) **:** AMMONIA LIQUOR (4) **:** BLEACH LIQUOR (5) **:** IRON LIQUOR (6) **:** FAT LIQUOR — **in liquor :** DRUNK ⟨men *in liquor* must be handled differently at the country club —Bernard De Voto⟩

**²liquor** \"\ *vb* **liquored; liquored; liquoring** \-k(ə)riŋ\ **liquors** *vt* **1 :** to treat with a liquid substance: as **a** *archaic* (1) **:** to dress (as leather) with an oily or greasy liquid substance (2) **:** to cover or smear with a greasy or oily lubricant **b :** to steep or soak in or with a liquid (as in various industrial processes or as in the preparation of some foods) **2 :** to ply with usu. strong distilled alcoholic liquor (as whiskey, rum) — usu. used with *up* ⟨had been pretty well ~*ed* up by his friends by the time she found him⟩ ~ *vi* **:** to drink usu. strong distilled alcoholic liquor esp. in large quantities — usu. used with *up* ⟨sit down amid a lot of bottles and ~ up —Coulton Waugh⟩ ⟨after they had been ~*ed* awhile he started up his ~*ing* again —Helen Rich⟩

**li·quor am·nii** \'lī,kwȯr'amnē,ī\ *n* [NL] **:** AMNIOTIC FLUID

**liquor cabinet** *n* **:** a cabinet or closet or similar enclosure in which alcoholic beverages and the materials for mixing drinks are kept

**liquored up** *also* **liquored** *adj* **:** DRUNK ⟨a *liquored up* lumberjack, returning from a spree —H.J.Barnes⟩

**liquor head** *n* **:** DRUNKARD

**liquorice** *var of* LICORICE

**li·quor·ish** \'lik(ə)rish\ *adj* [¹*liquor* + *-ish*] **1 :** LICKERISH **2 a :** inclined to drink liquor (as whiskey, rum) **:** showing an appetite for liquor **b :** alcoholic in composition ⟨a somewhat ~ drink⟩ — **li·quor·ish·ly** *adv* — **li·quor·ish·ness** *n* -ES

**¹liquorous** *obs var of* LICKERISH

**²li·quor·ous** \'lik(ə)rəs\ *adj* [¹*liquor* + *-ous*] **1 :** LIQUORISH 2 ⟨a ~ old man⟩ ⟨a ~ beverage⟩ **2 :** that results from or resembles an intoxicated condition ⟨~ speech⟩ ⟨this rising state of ~ ecstasy —Richard Scowcroft⟩

**li·quory** \-k(ə)rē, -ri\ *adj* [¹*liquor* + *-y*] **:** marked by or given to or prompted by the drinking of strong liquor **:** BOOZY; LIQUORISH ⟨the glittering ~ boom which the heavy-spending war years had brought on —*Life*⟩ ⟨~ joy⟩

**¹li·ra** \'lirə, 'lē-\ *n* [It, fr. L *libra* balance, unit of weight] **1** *pl* **li·re** \'lē(,)rā\ *also* **li·ras** \'lirəz, 'lē-\ **a :** the basic monetary unit of Italy — see MONEY table **b :** a coin or note representing one lira **2** *pl* **li·ras** \'lirəz, 'lē\ *also* **li·re** \'lē(,)rā\ [Turk, fr. It] **:** a Turkish or Syrian pound **3** *pl* **li·roth** *or* **li·rot** \'lē,rō(h)\ *also* **li·res** \-(,)rās\ *or* **li·re** \-(,)rā\ [NHeb, fr. It] **:** the Israeli pound

**²li·ra** \'lērə\ *n* -S [It, fr. L, lyre — more at LYRE] **1 :** LYRE 1 **2 :** HURDY-GURDY 1 **3 :** a bowed stringed musical instrument dating from about the 15th century and related to the viol and having additional free strings

**³li·ra** \'līrə\ *n*, *pl* **li·ras** \-rəz\ *also* **li·rae** \-(,)rē\ [NL, fr. L, furrow — more at LEARN] **:** a ridge (as on some shells) resembling a fine thread or a hair — **li·rate** \-,rāt, -,rət\ *adj* — **li·ra·tion** \lī'rāshən\ *n* -S

**lire** \'lī(ə)r, 'lē-(-, -īə, -ēə\ *n* -S [ME, fr. OE *līra* muscle, fleshy part of the body — more at LEG] *dial Brit* **:** BRAWN, MUSCLE

**li·rel·la** \lə'relə, lī-\ *n* -S [NL, dim. of L *lira* furrow — more at LEARN] **:** an elongated apothecium in lichens that has a furrow along the middle — **li·rel·late** \-,lāt\ *adj*

**lir·i·o·den·dron** \,lirēə'dendrən\ *n* [NL, fr. Gk *leirion*, *lirion* lily + NL *-dendron* — more at LILY] **1** *cap* **:** a genus of No. American and Asiatic trees (family Magnoliaceae) with 4-lobed smooth shining leaves and large greenish yellow flowers resembling tulips — see TULIP TREE **2** -S **:** any tree of the genus *Liriodendron*

**lir·i·o·my·za** \-'mīzə\ *n*, *cap* [NL, fr. Gk *leirion*, *lirion* lily + NL *-myza*] **:** a genus of agromyzid flies having larvae that are leaf miners and that include several economically important pests of cultivated plants — see PEA LEAF MINER

**li·ri·o·pe** \lə'rīə(,)pē\ *n, cap* [NL, after *Liriope*, a nymph in Roman mythology] **:** a genus of stoloniferous scapose grass-leaved herbs (family Liliaceae) with short thick rhizomes and small whitish or blue or violet flowers in racemes or spikes and with a superior ovary — see LILYTURF

**lir·i·pipe** \'lirə,pīp\ *also* **lir·i·poop** \-,püp\ *n* [ML *liripipium*] **1 :** a very long tippet orig. an extension of the peak of a hood and later attached to a medieval chaperon or forming part of the old clerical and academic dress **2** *obs* **:** something (as a lesson, a role) to be learned

**¹lirk** \'lirk\ *n* -s [ME (northern dial.) *lerk*] *Scot* **:** WRINKLE

**²lirk** \"\ *vb* -ED/-ING/-S *Scot* **:** WRINKLE

**li·roc·o·nite** \lī'räkə,nīt\ *n* -s [F, fr. Gk *leiros* resembling a lily, delicate (fr. *leirion* lily) + *konia* powder (fr. *konis* dust) + F *-ite* — more at LILY, INCINERATE] **:** a basic hydrous aluminum copper arsenate $Cu_2Al(AsO_4)(OH)_4.4H_2O$ occurring in monoclinic crystals of a sky-blue or verdigris-green color (hardness 2–2.5, sp. gr. 2.88–2.99)

**¹lis** \'lēs\ *n, pl* **lis** *or* **lisses** [F, lit., lily, fr. OF, fr. pl. of (assumed) *lil*, fr. L *lilium* — more at LILY] **:** FLEUR-DE-LIS

**²lis** *var of* LISS

**³lis** *pl of* LI

**li·sa** \'lēsə\ *n* -s [Sp, fr. OSp *liça*] **1 :** either of two gray mullets (*Mugil cephalus* or *M. curema*) of the tropical western Atlantic highly regarded as table fishes **2** *also* **lisa fran·ce·sa** \-frän'sāsə\ [*lisa francesa* fr. Sp, lit., French lisa] **:** TENPOUNDER 1

**li·saw** \'lē,sò\ *also* **li·shaw** \,shò\ *n, pl* **lisaw** *or* **lisaws** *usu cap* **:** LISU

**lis·bon** \'lizbən\ *adj, usu cap* [fr. *Lisbon*, Portugal] **:** of or from Lisbon, the capital of Portugal **:** of the kind or style prevalent in Lisbon

**lis·e·ran purple** \'lizərən-\ *n* [*liseran* prob. by shortening & alter. fr. *alizarin*] **:** a strong reddish purple that is bluer, lighter, and stronger than average fuchsia purple and redder and paler than purple orchid or phlox purple

**lish** \'lish\ *adj* [origin unknown] *dial Brit* **:** lithe and quick **:** NIMBLE

**li·si** \'lēsē\ *n* -s [native name in the Solomon islands] **:** a Solomon islands canoe built of planks and with a high upturned stem and stern

**lisk** \'lisk\ *n* -s [ME *leske*, of Scand origin; akin to ON *ljóski* groin, OSw & ODan *liuske*; akin to OE *lēosca* groin, MLG *lēsche* groin, MD *liese* thin skin, G dial. (Switzerland) *lösch* loose, OE *losian* to get lost — more at LOSE] *dial Brit* **:** GROIN

**lis·keard·ite** \li'skär,dīt, -kȧ,d-\ *n* -s [*Liskeard*, town in Cornwall, England, its locality + E *-ite*] **:** a mineral $(Al, Fe)_3(AsO_4)(OH)_6.5H_2O$ consisting of a basic hydrous arsenate of aluminum and iron

**lisle** \'līl, *esp before pause or consonant* 'līəl\ *or* **lisle thread** *n* -s [fr. *Lisle* (now *Lille*), France, where it was first manufactured] **:** a smooth tightly twisted thread usu. made in two or more plies of long-staple cotton and used chiefly in making hosiery, underwear, and gloves

**¹lisp** \'lisp *sometimes in mockery* 'lithp\ *vb* -ED/-ING/-S [ME *wlispen, lispen*, fr. OE *-wlyspian*; akin to MD & OHG *lispen* to speak unclearly, stammer, stutter, lisp, Norw dial. *leispa*, Sw *läspa*] *vi* **1 a :** to pronounce the sibilants *s* and *z* imperfectly esp. by giving them the sound of *th* ⟨imperfect adjustment of the organs of speech causes children to ~⟩ ⟨some people ~ when they first wear an upper denture —H.E. Kessler⟩ **b :** to speak falteringly or with a lisp ⟨look you ~, and wear strange suits —Shak.⟩ ⟨children often ~ when they first learn to talk⟩ **2 :** to make a sound resembling a lisp ⟨bits of dirty newspaper *~ed* along —Elizabeth Taylor⟩ **~** *vt* **:** to utter falteringly or with a lisp ⟨at his mother's knee first *~s* his ABC's⟩ ⟨*l* is *~ed* for the *r* which the baby can't pronounce —E.C.Smith⟩ ⟨demurely lowers her eyes and *~s* a soft reply⟩

**²lisp** \"\ *n* -s **1 :** a speech defect or affectation characterized by the imperfect pronunciation of sibilants, esp. the substitution of interdental sounds **:** act of lisping ⟨spoke with an engaging ~ —Charles Dickens⟩ **2 :** a sound resembling a lisp ⟨the rhythmic ~ of sandal straps —L.C.Douglas⟩

**lis pen·dens** \'lis'pen,denz\ *n* [L] **1 :** a pending lawsuit **2 :** a written notice usu. required by law to be recorded in a public registry office of a pending lawsuit identifying the principals, the court, and the specific property in controversy **3 :** the legal doctrine that one dealing with or purchasing an interest in property involved in pending litigation with actual or constructive knowledge of the existence of that litigation is subject to all the rights of others adjudicated in that litigation

**lisp·er** \'lispə(r); *see pronunc at* LISP\ *n* -s [ME *lyspare*, fr. *lispen* to lisp + *-are* -er] **:** one that lisps

**¹lisp·ing** \-piŋ\ *n* -s [ME, fr. gerund of *lispen* to lisp] **1 :** defective pronunciation of sibilants ⟨interdental ~⟩ **2 :** ²LISP 2 ⟨the first *~s* of Greek art —Florence Simmonds⟩ ⟨low *~s* of the summer rain —H.W.Longfellow⟩

**²lisping** *adj* [fr. pres. part. of ¹*lisp*] **:** characterized by a lisp or lisping — **lisp·ing·ly** *adv*

**lis·pund** \'lispənd\ *or* **lis·pound** \-,paůnd, -,pənd\ *n* -s [LG *lispund*, fr. MLG *lispunt, livespunt*, fr. *lis, lives* Livonian + *punt* pound; akin to OHG *phunt* pound — more at POUND] **:** any of various units of weight of the Shetland and Orkney islands varying from 12 to 30 or more pounds

**liss** *or* **lis** \'lis\ *n, pl* **lisses** [IrGael *lios*, fr. MIr *liss, less*; akin to W *llys* court] **:** an ancient Irish fortification or storage place enclosed by a circular mound or trench or both

**liss-** *or* **lisso-** *comb form* [NL, fr. Gk *lissos, lispos, lisphos*; prob. akin to OE *līm* lime — more at LIME] **:** smooth ⟨*liss*encephalous⟩ ⟨*Lisso*flagellata⟩

**lis·sa·jous figure** \'lēsə,zhü-\ *also* **lissajous curve** *n, usu cap L* [after Jules A. *Lissajous* †1880 Fr. physicist] **:** any of an infinite variety of curves formed by combining two mutually perpendicular simple harmonic motions, commonly exhibited by the oscilloscope, and used in studying frequency, amplitude, and phase relations of harmonic variables

**lis·sam·phib·ia** \,li,sam'fibēə\ *n pl, cap* [NL, fr. *liss-* + *Amphibia*] **:** a primary division of smooth-skinned amphibians comprising the existing orders — compare STEGOCEPHALIA

**lis·sau·er's tract** \'li,saůə(r)z-\ *n, usu cap L* [after Heinrich *Lissauer* †1891 Ger. neurologist] **:** a slender column of white matter between the dorsal gray column and the periphery of the spinal cord

**lisse** \'lēs\ *n* -s [F *lice, lisse* heddle, warp, lisse, fr. L *licia*, pl. of *licium* thread, thrum] **:** a silk gauze used for dresses and trimmings

**lis·sen·ceph·a·la** \,li(,)sen'sefələ, ,sən-, -,sᵊn-\ *n pl, cap* [NL, fr. *liss-* + *-encephala* (fr. Gk *enkephalos* brain) — more at ENCEPHAL-] *in some classifications* **:** eutherian mammals having a brain with few or no cerebral convolutions and including the edentates, bats, insectivores, and rodents

**lis·sen·ce·phalic** \¦li¦sensə¦falik, -lēk\ *or* **lis·sen·ceph·a·lous** \-(,)sen¦sefələs, -,sən-, -,sᵊn-\ *adj* [*liss-* + *encephalic, -encephalous*] **1 :** having a smooth cerebrum without convolutions **2** [NL *Lissencephala* + E *-ic* or *-ous*] **:** of or relating to the Lissencephala — **lis·sen·ceph·a·ly** \,=(,)='sefəlē\ *n*

**lisses** *pl of* LIS

**lis·so·flagellata** \,lisō+\ *n pl, cap* [NL, fr. *liss-* + *Flagellata*] *in some esp former classifications* **:** an order or other major division of Mastigophora comprising all the flagellates that lack a protoplasmic collar — compare CHOANOFLAGELLATA — **lis·so·flagellate** \"+\ *n* -s

**¹lis·some** *also* **lis·som** \'lisəm\ *adj* [alter. of *lithesome*] **1 :** easily flexed **:** SLENDER, LITHE, LIMBER ⟨~ girl⟩ ⟨as ~ as a hazel wand —Alfred Tennyson⟩ **2 :** quick and light in action **:** NIMBLE ⟨~ grace of the cat tribe —James Stevenson-Hamilton⟩ **syn** see SUPPLE

**²lis·some** \'lisəm\ *adv* **:** in a lissome manner **:** SUPPLELY, NIMBLY ⟨*lissome*-swaying hips —Ednah P. Hayes⟩

**lis·some·ness** *n* -ES **:** the quality or state of being lissome

**lis·sot·ri·chi** \li'sä·trə,kī\ [NL, fr. *liss-* + *-trichi*] *syn of* LEIOTRICHI

**lis·sot·ri·chous** \-kəs\ *adj* [*liss-* + *-trichous*] **:** LEIOTRICHOUS

**lis·sot·ri·chy** \-kē\ *n* -ES [*liss-* + *-trichy*] **:** the racial characteristic of having straight hair

**lissu** *usu cap, var of* LISU

**¹list** \'list\ *vb* **listed** *or* **list; listed** *or* **list; listing; lists** [ME *lusten, lysten, listen*, fr. OE *lystan*; akin to OS *lustian* to desire, long for, OHG *lusten*, ON *lysta*; causative-denominatives fr. the root of E ¹*lust*] *vt* **:** to give pleasure to **:** GRATIFY, SUIT ⟨could have my being while it *~ed* me —W.J.Locke⟩ **~** *vi* **:** to have a desire or inclination **:** CHOOSE, WISH ⟨allowed that mind of mine to stray thereafter as it *~ed* —Rafael Sabatini⟩

**²list** \"\ *n* -s [ME, prob. fr. *listen*, v.] **1** *archaic* **:** INCLINATION, CRAVING, DESIRE ⟨which I have neither ~ nor leisure to recount —Thomas Fuller⟩ **2** *archaic* **:** personal inclination **:** WILL ⟨by the law of the land, and not the arbitrary ~ . . . of any man living —Edmund Hickeringill⟩

**³list** \"\ *vb* **listed** *or* **list; listed** *or* **list; listing; lists** [ME *listen*, fr. OE *hlystan* — more at LISTEN] *vi* **:** to give ear **:** LISTEN ⟨she talks and I am fain to ~ —Robert Frost⟩ **~** *vt, archaic* **:** to listen to **:** HEAR ⟨teach your ears to ~ me with more heed —Shak.⟩

**⁴list** \"\ *n* -s [ME *liste, list*, fr. OE *līste*; akin to MLG *līste* edge, border, OHG *līsta*, Alb *leth* edge, bank, border] **1 a** *obs* **:** a strip of cloth ⟨gartered with a red and blue ~ —Shak.⟩ **b :** a band or strip of any material; *esp* **:** a narrow strip of wood cut from the edge of a plank or board **c :** LISTEL **d** *archaic* **:** LISTER RIDGE **e** (1) **:** the first thin coat of tin applied in the manufacture of tin plate (2) **:** a rim of tin left on an edge of tin plate after it is coated **2 lists** *pl but sing or pl in constr* [influenced in meaning by MF *lice* lists, of Gmc origin; akin to OHG *līsta* edge, border] **a :** a tilting arena or the palisade enclosing it ⟨give proof of your knightly worth in the *~s* tomorrow —Rafael Sabatini⟩ **b :** an arena for any kind of combat ⟨entered the *~s* against the bull —Frank Yerby⟩ **c :** a controversy or field of competition ⟨enter the *~s* . . . for or against practical programs of population resettlement —Ethel Albert⟩ ⟨a thick skin and a ready wit make him a good candidate for the political *~s*⟩ ⟨one of Ireland's major industries . . . has now entered the dollar-earning *~s* —E.M.Woolf⟩ **3** *obs* **a :** a line marking a limit or extent **:** BOUNDARY ⟨the very ~, the very utmost bound of all our purposes —Shak.⟩ **b :** a railing or railed enclosure esp. used as an exercising ground ⟨a ~ to ride horses in, much frequented by the gallants in summer —John Evelyn⟩ **4 a** *chiefly Brit* **:** a strip forming the edge of a woven fabric **:** SELVAGE ⟨pieces having tightly woven *~s* which curl badly should be sewn together . . . and dyed in tubular form —C.M.Whittaker & C.C.Wilcock⟩ **b** *archaic* **:** a material resembling selvage ⟨have had ~ nailed round my doors, and stopping every crack —Mary Delany⟩ **5 :** a streak of color **:** STRIPE ⟨a hackle with a blue or dun ~ —J.E.Leisenring⟩; *specif* **:** a dark stripe along the midline of a horse's back

**⁵list** \"\ **listed** *or* **list; listed** *or* **list; listing; lists** *vt* [ME *listen*, fr. *liste, list*, n.] **1** *obs* **:** to put a border around **:** EDGE **2 :** to cut away a narrow strip (as sapwood) from the edge of ⟨staves, air-dried and *~ed* —F.P.Hankerson⟩ **3 a :** to prepare (land) for a crop or check (soil) from blowing by making ridges and furrows with a lister — compare LISTING 2 **b :** to plant (a field) with a lister

**⁶list** \"\ *n* -s [F *liste*, fr. MF, group of people, roster, fr. OIt *lista* band, stripe, row, group, roster, of Gmc origin; akin to OHG *līsta* edge, border — more at ⁴LIST] **1 a :** ROLL, ROSTER ⟨there were 109 publications . . . but the casualty ~ was long, too —*Amer. Guide Series: Wash.*⟩; *specif* **:** an official roster ⟨drawing up a ~ for . . . party nomination —Richard Scammon⟩ — compare ACTIVE LIST, BLACKLIST, RETIRED LIST **b :** INDEX, CATALOG, CHECKLIST ⟨the card catalog in a library . . . is used mainly as a finding ~ —Saul Herner⟩ ⟨the . . . disc jumped to the top of the hit ~ in ten days —R.G.Hubler⟩ ⟨the publisher added the book to his fall ~⟩ ⟨put eggs on the shopping ~⟩ ⟨check the ~ of qualifications for a job⟩ **c :** the total number to be considered or included ⟨among the essentials of true democracy, responsible citizenship comes high on the ~⟩ ⟨added spelling reform to the ~ of his interests —W.B. Shaw & E.S.Bates⟩ **2 :** a record of individual holdings of real and personal property subject to taxation ⟨tax the grand ~ a definite percentage . . . for school revenue —*Amer. Guide Series: Vt.*⟩ **3 :** the total register of securities admitted to trading on a stock exchange ⟨there were many . . . strong individual stocks in the ~ —*Springfield (Mass.) Union*⟩ **4 :** LIST PRICE ⟨set your own ~, take a big markup and still undersell the field —*Office Appliances*⟩

**⁷list** \"\ *vb* -ED/-ING/-S *vt* **1 a :** to make a list of **:** ENUMERATE ⟨~ five reasons why you enjoyed the book⟩ ⟨it is now possible . . . to ~ all the amino acids necessary —*Americana Annual*⟩ ⟨~ the specialized agencies of the United Nations⟩ **b :** to include on a list **:** REGISTER, RECORD: as (1) **:** to enter (taxable property) on an official list (2) **:** to enter (a stock or other security) in the list of those officially admitted to dealings on the exchange (3) **:** to place (property) in the hands of a real-estate agent for sale or rent (4) **:** to enter in a price list **c :** to declare to be **:** GIVE ⟨increased confidence . . . was *~ed* as a reason for the increase in spending —*Dun's Rev.*⟩ ⟨twenty-four books . . . two of them *~ed* as essential library acquisitions —Anthony Boucher⟩ **d :** to put in writing **:** SHOW ⟨the only membership he *~s* is in a professional society⟩ **2 a** *obs* **:** to put into a category **:** CLASSIFY ⟨virtues are *~ed* in the rank of invisible things —Thomas Traherne⟩ **b :** to put (oneself) down — used with *as* ⟨*~s* himself as a political liberal⟩ **3** *archaic* **:** to recruit or appoint into or as if into military service ⟨will ~ you for my soldier —Sir Walter Scott⟩ **~** *vi* **1** *archaic* **:** to enlist in or as if in the armed forces ⟨he is going to ~ with us, and be our clergyman —George Borrow⟩ **2 :** to become entered in a catalog with a selling price ⟨the wrench alone *~s* at $3 —*Industrial Equipment News*⟩

**⁸list** \"\ *vb* -ED/-ING/-S [origin unknown] *vi* **:** to lean to one side **:** CANT, TILT ⟨she *~s* steeply to port —H.W.Baldwin⟩ ⟨the trees . . . all *~ed* to leeward —Frances G. Patton⟩ **~** *vt* **:** to cause to list ⟨shift tanks and bulldozers in transport's holds, *~ing* the ships —K.M.Dodson⟩

**⁹list** \"\ *n* -s **1 :** a deviation from the vertical **:** CANT, TILT ⟨water flooding into the hold gave the ship a heavy ~ to starboard⟩ ⟨there was a faint forward ~ to his body as he walked —Lawrence Williams⟩ **2 :** a tendency to incline **:** LEANING ⟨a consistent political ~ to the left —Paul Woodring⟩

**list·able** \'listəbəl\ *adj* [⁷*list* + *-able*] **:** capable of being listed; *specif* **:** TAXABLE

**¹list·ed** \'listəd\ *adj* [ME, fr. *liste, list* edge + *-ed* — more at LIST (edge)] **1 :** striped or banded with color ⟨~ pig⟩ **2 :** planted or prepared for planting with a lister ⟨~ corn⟩ ⟨~ ground⟩ **3 :** reduced in width by having a strip removed from the edge — used of a board ⟨~ barrel staves⟩

**²listed** *adj* [fr. past part. of ⁷*list*] **:** incorporated in a list; *specif* **:** admitted to trading on a stock exchange ⟨~ securities⟩ ⟨~ stock⟩

**list·ee** \li'stē\ *n* -s [⁷*list* + *-ee*] **:** one that is included in a list

**lis·tel** \'listᵊl\ *n* -s [F, fr. It *listello*, dim. of *lista* band, stripe — more at LIST (roll)] *archit* **:** a narrow band or list **:** FILLET

**¹lis·ten** \'lisᵊn\ *vb* **listened; listened; listening** \-s(ᵊ)niŋ\ **listens** [ME *listnen*, alter. (influenced by *listen* to listen, fr. OE *hlystan*, fr. *hlyst* hearing) of OE *hlysnan*; akin to OHG *lūstrēn* to listen, ON *hlust* hearing, ear, OIr *cluas* ear, Skt *śroṣati* he hears, OE *hlūd* loud — more at LOUD] *vt, archaic* **:** to give ear to **:** HEAR ⟨lady, vouchsafe to ~ what I say —Shak.⟩ **~** *vi* **1 :** to pay attention to sound **:** perceive with the ear ⟨stood erect and quiet as if *~ing* —O.E.Rölvaag⟩ ⟨partial heart block may be determined by *~ing* with the stethoscope —H. G.Armstrong⟩ ⟨he'd ~ nervously to the gunfire —Ira Wolfert⟩ ⟨liked to follow him about and talk with him or ~ to him ask . . . devastating questions of their elders —Irwin Edman⟩ — often used in imperative ⟨~ to this from a great philosopher —Brand Blanshard⟩; used dial. with *at* ⟨~ at that mother bird —J.H.Stuart⟩ ⟨got a radio . . . we could ~ at —Vereen Bell⟩ **2 :** to hear with thoughtful attention **:** consider seriously **:** HEED ⟨have heard but not *~ed* —R.L.Shayon⟩ ⟨frame an issue to which voters would ~ —F.L.Paxson⟩ ⟨had not the slightest intention of *~ing* to the grievances of the colonies —H.E.Scudder⟩ **3 :** to be alert to catch an expected sound — usu. used with *for* ⟨*~ed* for his step in the hall⟩ **4** *slang* **:** to make an impression on a listener **:** SOUND ⟨it doesn't ~ right —Mark Reed⟩ ⟨it *~s* to me as though the wise guys had been giving him a tip to lay off —*New Republic*⟩ ⟨why do some bands ~ better than others —*Musical Enterprise*⟩

**²listen** \"\ *n* -s **:** an act of listening ⟨listened, and with each ~ the game grew clearer —Rudyard Kipling⟩

**lis·ten·able** \-s(ᵊ)nəbəl\ *adj* **:** agreeable to the ear ⟨produces highly ~ music —Norman Cousins⟩

**lis·ten·er** \-s(ᵊ)nə(r)\ *n* -s **1 :** one that listens ⟨to enjoy conversation means to be a good ~ as well as a good talker⟩ ⟨this book . . . is not intended to appeal to the musicologist nor yet to the untrained ~ —Ralph Hill⟩ ⟨dogs make good *~s* on a frontline patrol⟩ **2 :** one that sets himself to hear ⟨*~s* wrote in to congratulate the radio actor on his performance⟩; *specif* **:** AUDITOR 5

**listener-in** \'=(=)=¦=\ *n, pl* **listeners-in** [*listen in* + *-er*] **:** one that listens in **:** AUDITOR, EAVESDROPPER

**lis·ten·er·ship** \'=(=)=,ship\ *n* **:** the extent of a radio audience or the appeal of a radio program in number of listeners ⟨broadcasting in so many languages . . . it is hard even to guess at our ~ —Osmond Dowling⟩ ⟨nor were they or the company disappointed by the ~ of the program —*Advertising Age*⟩

**listen in** *vi* **1 :** to tune in to or monitor a transmission ⟨*listened in* last night to Continental stations —B.L.K. Henderson⟩ ⟨*listen in* on the submarine-bell receivers for the noises made by the propellers of passing vessels —*Scientific American*⟩ ⟨*listen in* on the enemy's communications line⟩ **2 :** to give ear to a conversation without participating in it ⟨I remember *listening in* while a foreman and his girl workers were discussing who was going to work —Sam Pollock⟩; *esp* **:** EAVESDROP ⟨*listen in* on a party line⟩ ⟨when they speak from a telephone booth in a hotel, everybody sitting in the lobby *listens in* —A.T.Weaver⟩

**¹lis·ten·ing** \'lis(ᵊ)niŋ\ *n* -s [ME *listning*, fr. gerund of *listnen* to listen] **:** the act of one that listens; *esp* **:** the monitoring of a foreign broadcast ⟨methods used internally to combat foreign ~ —Tangye Lean⟩

**²listening** *adj* [fr. pres. part. of ¹*listen*] **1 :** alert to or receptive of sound ⟨two underwater ~ stations —J.W.Cross⟩; *specif* **:** receiving radio broadcasts ⟨~ homes . . . were presumably exposed to the product's other forms of advertising —T.J. Allard⟩ **2 :** facilitating the reception of sound ⟨~ galleries⟩ ⟨wore his ~ button in his ear —William Faulkner⟩

**listening post** *n* **1 :** a center for gathering intelligence concerning an adversary ⟨a master hand at reading political riddles, with a thousand *listening posts* throughout the country —Charles Michelson⟩ ⟨establishment of normal diplomatic relations . . . will give us *listening posts* behind the bamboo curtain —N.D.Palmer⟩; *specif* **:** a concealed forward military position occupied during periods of reduced visibility for the purpose of detecting enemy activity by listening **2 :** a short-wave radio station capable of monitoring foreign broadcasts ⟨a *listening post*, whither high-powered radio sets daily brought news and views direct from all the continents —*Christian Science Monitor*⟩

**¹list·er** \'listə(r)\ *n* -s [⁷*list* + *-er*] **:** one that lists or catalogs: as **a :** ASSESSOR 2 ⟨once every four years the *~s* . . . reappraise all the real and personal property in the township —J.A. Kouwenhoven⟩ **b :** an employee of a woodworking establishment who estimates the cost of materials and labor for work done **c :** a laundry worker who itemizes the articles in bundles of soiled laundry

**²lister** \"\ *n* -s [⁵*list* + *-er*] **1 :** a double-moldboard plow that throws a ridge of earth both ways, is frequently equipped to prepare a seedbed at the bottom of the furrow by means of a small subsoiling attachment, and is used mainly in growing sorghum, corn, and cotton in the central and southern great plains where rainfall is limited — called also *middlebreaker, middle-burster, middlebuster, middlesplitter* **2** *or* **lister-planter** \'=,=,=\ **:** a lister plow with an attachment for dropping seeds into the furrow

**lis·tera** \'listərə\ *n, cap* [NL, after Martin *Lister* †1712 Eng. physician] **:** a genus of opposite-leaved orchids native to the north temperate and arctic zones and having racemose greenish flowers without spurs — see TWAYBLADE

**lis·ter bag** *also* **lys·ter bag** \'listə(r)-\ *n, usu cap L* [after Col. William J. *Lyster* †1947 Am. army medical officer] **:** a canvas water bag used esp. for supplying troops with chemically treated drinking water

**lister cultivator** *n* [²*lister*] **:** a cultivator usu. having blades designed to throw soil toward the roots of a crop, two heavy furrow balance wheels, and two wheels to hold the machine on the ridges

**¹lis·ter·el·la** \,listə'relə\ [NL, fr. Joseph *Lister* †1912 Eng. surgeon and bacteriologist + NL *-ella*] *syn of* LISTERIA

**²listerella** \"\ *n* -s **:** LISTERIA 2

**lis·ter·el·lo·sis** \,listə,re'lōsəs\ *also* **lis·te·ri·a·sis** \-'rīəsəs\ *or* **lis·te·ri·o·sis** \(,)li,stirē'ōsəs\ *n, pl* **listerelloses** *also* **listeriases** *or* **listerioses** [NL, fr. *Listerella* or *Listeria* + *-osis*] **:** a serious commonly fatal disease of a great variety of wild and domestic mammals and birds and occas. man caused by a bacterium (*Listeria monocytogenes*) and taking the form of a severe encephalitis accompanied by disordered movements usu. ending in paralysis, fever, monocytosis, and sometimes abortion — compare CIRCLING DISEASE

**lis·te·ria** \li'stirēə\ *n* [NL, fr. Joseph *Lister* + NL *-ia*] **1** *cap* **:** a genus of small gram-positive flagellated bacterial rods (family Corynebacteriaceae) of which the chief and type species (*L. monocytogenes*) causes infectious mononucleosis in man and a wide variety of infections in mammals **2** -s **:** any bacterium of the genus *Listeria* — called also *listerella*

**lis·te·ri·an** \(')li¦stirēən\ *adj, often cap* [Joseph *Lister* + E *-ian*] **:** of or relating to listerism or to Lord Lister

**lis·ter·ism** \'listə,rizəm\ *n* -s *often cap* [Joseph *Lister* + E *-ism*] **1 :** the use of an antiseptic on the field of a surgical operation **2 :** aseptic and antiseptic surgery

**lis·ter·ize** \-,rīz\ *vt* -ED/-ING/-S *often cap* [Joseph *Lister* + E *-ize*] **:** to treat by means of listerian methods

**lister ridge** *n* **:** a raised strip of ground thrown up by a lister to form a seedbed

**l'i·stes·so tem·po** \lē'ste(,)sō'tem(,)pō\ *adv* [It] **:** in the same tempo as before — used as a direction in music

**listful** *adj* [³*list* + *-ful*] *obs* **:** ATTENTIVE ⟨the shepherd swains . . . with greedy ~ ears —Edmund Spenser⟩

**¹list·ing** \'listiŋ\ *n* -s [ME, fr. *liste, list* strip, selvage + *-ing* — more at LIST (strip)] **1 :** ⁴LIST 4a **2 a :** the furrowing of soil esp. for seedbeds in which row crops are sown in the furrows **b :** the method of planting crops in a furrow with a lister **3 :** a narrow strip cut from the edge of a board

**²listing** *n* -s [fr. gerund of ⁷*list*] **1** *archaic* **:** ENLISTMENT **2 a :** an act or instance of making or including in a list or catalog; *specif* **:** the admission of securities to trading on a securities exchange **b :** ⁶LIST 1 ⟨made a ~ of the ten most intelligent animals —Charles Mulvey⟩ ⟨an important annotated ~ —*Middle East Jour.*⟩ **3 a :** an authorization to a real-estate broker to sell or rent property **b :** a broker's record of available properties **c :** a piece of property listed with a real-estate broker

**list·less** \'listləs\ *adj* [ME *listles*, fr. *list* desire + *-les* -less — more at LIST (desire)] **:** characterized by lack of inclination or impetus to exertion **:** LANGUID, SPIRITLESS ⟨~ stance⟩ ⟨~ voice⟩ ⟨a cold and ~ day of autumn —Edith Sitwell⟩ ⟨hearings . . . have been ~, seldom drawing more than two committee members —*New Republic*⟩ **syn** see LANGUID

**list·less·ly** *adv* **:** in a listless manner ⟨shook hands rather ~ —A.S.Crockett⟩

**list·less·ness** *n* -ES **:** the quality or state of being listless

**list price** *n* **:** the basic price of an item as published in a catalog, price list, or advertisement but subject to trade, quantity, and other discounts

**lists** *pres 3d sing of* LIST, *pl of* LIST

**list system** *n* **:** a system of proportional representation under which a voter chooses between party lists each containing as many names as there are representatives to be chosen and the number of candidates declared elected from each list is determined by the percentage cast for each list out of the total vote ⟨all of the *list systems* . . . give the voter little or no discretion in choosing particular candidates —H.F.Gosnell⟩ — compare HARE SYSTEM, PREFERENTIAL VOTING, SINGLE TRANSFERABLE VOTE

**li·su** *or* **lis·su** \'lē,sü\ *n, pl* **lisu** *or* **lisus** *or* **lissu** *or* **lissus**

*usu cap* **1 a :** a Tibeto-Burman people inhabiting the hilly Salween drainage in the Yunnan-Burma borderlands **b :** a member of such people **2 :** the north Lolo dialect of the Lisu people

**liszt·i·an** \'listēən\ *adj, usu cap* [Franz von *Liszt* †1886 Hungarian piano virtuoso and composer + E *-ian*] **:** of, relating to, or characteristic of Franz Liszt or his music

**1lit** \'lit\ *vt* **lited** *or* **litted; lited** *or* **litted; liting** *or* **litting; lits** [ME *liten, litten*, fr. ON *lita* to dye, fr. *litr* color — more at LITMUS] *Scot* **:** DYE

**2lit** \"\ *n* -s [ME, fr. ON *litr* color] *Scot* **:** DYE, DYESTUFF

**3lit** *adj* [fr. past part. of ³*light*] **:** LIGHTED: as **a :** ILLUMINATED ⟨a brightly ~ room⟩ **b :** IGNITED ⟨~ candle⟩ ⟨~ firecracker⟩ **c** *slang* **:** intoxicated by liquor or narcotics ⟨not exactly ~ but considerably exalted —Hans Zinsser⟩

**lit** *abbr* **1** liter **2** literal; literally **3** literary **4** literature

**lit·a·ny** \'lit(ᵊ)nē, -ni\ *n* -ES [alter. (influenced by LL *litania* litany) of ME *letanie*, fr. OF, fr. LL *litania*, fr. LGk *litaneia*, fr. Gk, entreaty, supplication, fr. *litaneuein* to entreat, supplicate, fr. *litanos* entreating, fr. *litē* supplication; akin to OE *līm* lime — more at LIME] **1 a :** a liturgical prayer consisting of a series of invocations and supplications either read or sung usu. with alternate responses by clergy and congregation **b :** a liturgical procession during which clergy and congregation sing or chant prayers **2 a :** a ritualistic repetition of prayers usu. of praise and supplication ⟨in his morning ~ he could pray to be kept from lasciviousness —Carl Van Doren⟩ **3 :** a recital or chant having the resonant or repetitive qualities associated with a litany ⟨the author recites his ~ of the great mysteries — birth, death, flood, water, sky —Sidney Alexander⟩ ⟨the shrill *litanies* of shopboys —James Joyce⟩ ⟨rehearsed her ~ of symptoms —John Dollard & N.E.Miller⟩

**li·tas** \'lē,täs\ *n, pl* **li·tai** \-,tā\ [Lith] **1 :** the basic unit of monetary value of Lithuania from 1923 to 1940 **2 :** a silver coin representing one litas

**li·tchi** \'lī(,)chē, 'lē(-\ *n* [Chin (Pek) *li⁴ chih¹*] **1** *or* **litchi nut** *or* **li·chee** *also* **lee·chee** *or* **li·chi** *or* **ly·chee** \"\ -s **:** the fruit of a Chinese tree (*Litchi chinensis*) that is about one inch in diameter and has a hard scaly outer covering and a small hard seed surrounded by white translucent watery flesh which on drying becomes firm, sweetish, and black and constitutes the edible part of the fruit **2 a** *cap* **:** a genus of Chinese trees (family Sapindaceae) with pinnate leaves and regular greenish white flowers in terminal panicles **b** -s **:** any tree of the genus *Litchi; esp* **:** a tree (*L. chinensis*) often cultivated in the Philippines, India, and elsewhere for its edible fruits

**lit clos** \lē'klō\ *n* [F, lit., enclosed bed] **:** a free-standing or built-in French bed enclosed in wooden panels

**LitD** *abbr or n* -s **:** a doctor of literature

**lit de re·pos** \-dərə'pō\ *n* [F, lit., bed of repose] **:** CHAISE LONGUE

**1lite** \'līt\ *n* -s [ME *lut, lit*, fr. OE *lȳt*, n. & adj. — more at LITTLE] *dial Eng* **:** LITTLE

**2lite** \"\ *adj* [ME *lut, lit*, fr. OE *lȳt*] *dial Eng* **:** FEW, LITTLE

**3lite** \"\ *vi* -ED/-ING/-S [ME *liten*, of Scand origin; akin to ON *hlīta* to rely on, trust; akin to OE *hleonian* to lean — more at LEAN] *dial Eng* **1 :** WAIT, EXPECT **2 :** RELY, TRUST

**-lite** *also* **-lyte** \,līt, *usu* -īd·+V\ *n comb form* [F *-lite*, alter. of *-lithe*, fr. Gk *lithos* stone] **1 a :** mineral **:** rock **:** fossil in stone ⟨cryo*lite*⟩ ⟨rhyo*lite*⟩ ⟨dendro*lite*⟩ **b :** -LITH 1b ⟨albo*lite*⟩ **2 :** -LITH 2 ⟨phlebo*lite*⟩

**li·ter** *or* **li·tre** \'lēd·ə(r), -ētə-\ *n* -s [F *litre*, alter. of *litron*, an old measure, modif. of ML *litra*, fr. Gk, a weight, a coin] **:** a metric unit of capacity equal to the volume occupied by one kilogram of water at 4° C and at the standard atmospheric pressure of 760 millimeters equivalent to 1 cubic decimeter — see METRIC SYSTEM table

**lit·er·a·cy** \'lid·ərəsē, 'litərə-, 'li·trə-, -si\ *n* -ES [*literate* + *-cy*] **1 :** the quality or state of being literate **2 :** an ability to read a short simple passage and answer questions about it

**1lit·er·al** \'lid·ərəl, 'litər-, 'li·trəl\ *adj* [ME, fr. MF, fr. ML *litteralis, literalis*, fr. L, of a letter, of writing, fr. *littera, litera* letter & *litterae, literae* epistle, writing + *-alis* -al — more at LETTER] **1 a :** according with the letter of the scriptures ⟨amillennialists recognize the need for ~ interpretation —*Bibliotheca Sacra*⟩ **b :** adhering to fact or to the ordinary construction or primary meaning of a term or expression **:** ACTUAL, OBVIOUS ⟨the need for a ~ breathing spell forces the fish to let go —L.P.Schultz⟩ ⟨a ~ solitude like a desert —G.K.Chesterton⟩ ⟨liberty in the ~ sense is impossible —B. N.Cardozo⟩ ⟨reactionary in the ~ sense of the word, but did not agree . . . how far back they wanted to go —William Petersen⟩ **c :** being without exaggeration or embellishment **:** PLAIN, UNADORNED ⟨~ prose⟩ ⟨a love of ~ truth —Robert Graves⟩ **d :** characterized by a concern mainly with facts **:** PROSAIC, UNIMAGINATIVE ⟨the opposite of a liberal education . . . is a ~ education —Sidney Hook⟩ ⟨if a painter tells a story . . . even the most ~ person will have no difficulty in understanding what the artist is trying to say —Huntington Hartford⟩ ⟨statue . . . dressed as he had been when alive, in accordance with the ~ standards of late-century monumental sculpture —J.T.Soby⟩ ⟨a ~ and academic reading of a classic score —Virgil Thomson⟩ **2 a :** of, relating to, or expressed in letters ⟨the distress signal SOS has no ~ meaning⟩ ⟨~ coefficient⟩ ⟨cryptographic codes may be either ~ or numerical⟩ **b :** resulting from the mistaken use or omission of a letter ⟨~ error⟩ **3 :** reproduced word for word **:** EXACT, VERBATIM ⟨~ translation⟩

**2literal** \"\ *n* -s **:** a small error usu. of a single letter in writing or printing ⟨in setting type, allow enough space so that a line will accommodate any ~ the proofreader may find⟩

**literal contract** *n, civil law* **:** an obligation fully evidenced by writing and binding upon the party signing and promising therein

**lit·er·al·ism** \'lid·ərə,lizəm, 'litərə,-, 'li·trə,-\ *n* -s **1 :** adherence to the explicit substance of an idea or expression ⟨Biblical ~ . . . has never realized that no historic document is self-explanatory —W.L.Sperry⟩ ⟨the book employed Marxian dialectics with ruthless ~ —Leo Gurko⟩ ⟨the spirit of legalistic ~ —J.C.Swaim⟩ **2 :** fidelity to observable fact **:** REALISM ⟨picturesque scenery painted with laborious ~ —*Amer. Guide Series: Pa.*⟩

**lit·er·al·ist** \-ləst\ *n* -s **:** one that advocates or practices literalism ⟨the ~ wants to hear cowbells in his music —H.A. Overstreet⟩; *specif* **:** ¹FUNDAMENTALIST 1 ⟨others of the early church fathers . . . were not ~s in regard to the Mosaic account of creation —V.A.Rice & F.N.Andrews⟩

**lit·er·al·is·tic** \¦===¦listik\ *adj* **:** of or relating to literalism — **lit·er·al·is·ti·cal·ly** \-tək(ə)lē\ *adv*

**lit·er·al·i·ty** \,lid·ə'raləd·ē, ,litə-, ,litrə-, -ətē, -i\ *n* -ES **:** LITERALNESS

**lit·er·al·ize** \'lid·ərə,līz, 'litərə,-, 'li·trə,-\ *vt* -ED/-ING/-S **:** to make literal ⟨disposition to ~ metaphors —R.A.Vaughan⟩

**lit·er·al·ly** \'lid·ərəlē, 'litər(ə)l-, 'li·trə-, -li\ *adv* **1 a :** in the literal sense **:** without metaphor or exaggeration **:** EXPLICITLY ⟨he can always be taken seriously; he cannot always be taken ~ —E.R.Bentley⟩ ⟨interpret the Bible figuratively as well as ~ —R.W.Murray⟩ **b :** in the literal meaning of the term **:** ACTUALLY, REALLY ⟨broke the . . . ice ~ by jointly blasting the formidable frozen barrier —Alexander Kendrick⟩ ⟨migrations of passenger pigeons . . . crossed here by the millions, ~ darkening the sky —*Amer. Guide Series: Mich.*⟩ **2 :** with exact equivalence **:** VERBATIM ⟨simultaneous interpreters translate the speaker's words ~⟩ **3 :** in effect **:** VIRTUALLY ⟨a collection of . . . devices that will ~ make your hair stand on end —Horace Sutton⟩ ⟨this boy ~ rode roughshod over the patient —L.E.Hinsie⟩

**lit·er·al·ness** \-rəlnəs\ *n* -ES **:** the quality or state of being literal

**lit·er·ar·i·ly** \¦lid·ə¦rerəlē, ¦litə¦r-,-li\ *adv* **:** in a literary manner

**lit·er·ar·i·ness** \'===,renəs, -rin-\ *n* -ES **:** the quality or state of being literary

**lit·er·ary** \'lid·ə,rerē, 'litə,r-, -ri\ *adj* [in sense 1, fr. L *littera, litera* letter + E *-ary*; in other senses, fr. F *littéraire*, fr. L *litterarius, literarius* of writing, fr. *litterae, literae* writing + *-arius* -ary — more at LETTER] **1** *archaic* **:** ¹LITERAL 2a **2 a :** of, relating to, or having the characteristics of humane learning ⟨the educational system should provide a ~ as well as a rational education —G.K.Chalmers⟩ ⟨~ institution⟩ **b :** of, relating to, or having the characteristics of literature ⟨renouncing the dogma that Latin was the ~ language of Italy, began to write in Tuscan —J.E.Sellery⟩ ⟨described his types in the grand ~ manner, with great subtlety and penetration —William Stephenson⟩ ⟨a ~ magazine may deal with . . . anything at all, so long as each article is a piece of literature —R.G.Howarth⟩ **c :** BOOKISH 2 ⟨this work is too wordy, and the dialogue has a muffled ~ flavor —T.G.Bergin⟩ **d :** of or relating to books ⟨~ agent⟩ ⟨~ manuscripts⟩ **3 a :** having a firsthand knowledge of literature **:** WELL-READ ⟨he is ~, given to quoting to himself rather long stretches of remembered lines —F.J.Hoffman⟩ **b :** of, relating to, or concerned with men of letters or with writing as a profession ⟨a new star in the ~ firmament —*Yankee*⟩ ⟨for her admirable series of ~ biographies she has chosen . . . nineteenth-century poets —Harrison Smith⟩ ⟨was rather ~ in college —Scott Fitzgerald⟩ **4** *of a painting or sculpture* **:** characterized by a primary interest in depicting an event, story, or allegory **:** ANECDOTAL

**literary apabhramsa** *n* **:** APABHRAMSA c

**lit·er·ary·ism** \-rē,izəm\ *n* -s **:** an instance of or tendency to use excessive refinement of expression in written compositions ⟨every ~ . . . fritters away a scrap of the reader's patience —Ezra Pound⟩

**literary property** *n* **1 a :** the property an author or those claiming under him has in the written product of his intellectual skill and labor either before or after general publication and either at common law or under statutory copyright **b :** the written product of an author or any copy thereof **2 :** the property an author or those claiming under him has in his work under common law prior to copyright consisting chiefly of his right to control the use, enjoyment, and disposition of such work for profit or any purpose, this right being superseded by statutory copyright and lost by dedication of such work to the public — compare COPYRIGHT

**1lit·er·ate** \'lid·ərət, 'litərət, 'li·trət, *usu* -əd·+V\ *adj* [ME *literat*, fr. L *litteratus, literatus*, adj. & n., fr. *litterae, literae* epistle, writing, literature + *-atus* -ate — more at LETTER] **1 a :** characterized by or possessed of learning **:** EDUCATED, CULTURED ⟨one of the more ~ analysts working in this area —Webster Schott⟩ ⟨citizens . . . highly ~ in economic matters —Alan Valentine⟩ ⟨the familiar magic in words and miracles in perception that are Shakespeare's . . . provide the mind with a ~ and often gusty evening —*New Republic*⟩ ⟨it is a ~ community, with several good museums and its own symphony orchestra⟩ **b :** able to read and write — opposed to *illiterate* ⟨a large percentage of the world's adult population is ~ in some language⟩ **2 a :** versed or immersed in literature or creative writing **:** LITERARY ⟨a novel . . . of the former master of satire, who nevertheless is always ~ and engrossing —Harvey Breit⟩ **b :** dealing with literature or belles lettres ⟨innovators in this form of ~ publishing —Seymour Krim⟩ **c :** well executed or technically proficient **:** POLISHED, LUCID ⟨though it is . . . always cinematically ~, the picture is longer on talk than on action —*Time*⟩ ⟨assembling doctoral findings into a ~ thesis —J.P.Elder⟩

**2literate** \"\ *n* -s [L *litteratus, literatus*] **1 a :** an educated person **b :** one who can read and write **2 :** one admitted to holy orders in the Church of England without having a university degree

**lit·er·ate·ly** *adv* **:** in a literate manner

**lit·e·ra·ti** \,lid·ə'räd·(,)ē, ,litə-, -'rä¦, ¦(,)t¦, ¦i *also* -'rä,tī\ *n pl* [It & L; It, fr. L *litterati, literati*, pl. of *litteratus, literatus*] **1 :** the educated class **:** INTELLIGENTSIA ⟨these ~ educated to admire the spirit of classical antiquity —C.J.Friedrich⟩ ⟨the Indian ~ —Selig Harrison⟩ **2 :** MEN OF LETTERS ⟨hegira of many of the ~ to Europe, where they hoped to live the creative life and produce . . . poems and novels —C.I.Glicksberg⟩; *specif* **:** AVANT-GARDE 2 ⟨professed intense scorn for its crackpot ~ and painters —S.J.Perelman⟩

**lit·e·ra·tim** \-'rād·əm, -ātəm\ *adv (or adj)* [ML, fr. L *littera, litera* letter — more at LETTER] **:** letter for letter

**lit·er·a·tion** \,lid·ə'rāshən, ,litə'-\ *n* -s [L *littera, litera* letter + E *-ation* — more at LETTER] **:** the representation of sounds or words by letters

**lit·e·ra·to** \,==ˈräd·(,)ō, -'nä¦, ¦(,)tō\ [It, fr. L *litteratus, literatus* literate — more at LITERATE] *sing of* LITERATI

**lit·er·a·tor** \'lid·ə,rād·ə(r), 'litə-, -,rātə-\ *n* -s [L *litterator, literator* grammarian, critic, fr. *litteratus, literatus* + *-or*] **1** *archaic* **:** one who engages in textual criticism or descriptive bibliography **2** [modif. of F *littérateur* — more at LITTERATEUR] **:** LITTERATEUR

**lit·er·a·ture** \'lid·ərə,chu̇(ə)r, 'litərə-, 'li·trə-, 'lid·ə(r),ch-, -,chu̇ə, -,chə(r), -rə,tyu̇-, -rə,tu̇-\ *n* -s *often attrib* [ME *litterature*, fr. L *litteratura, literatura* writing, grammar, learning, fr. *litteratus, literatus* literate + *-ura* -ure] **1** *archaic* **:** knowledge of books **:** literary culture ⟨in many things he was grotesquely ignorant; he was a man of very small ~ —W.D. Howells⟩ **2 :** the production of literary work esp. as an occupation ⟨continually dissociated himself from ~ . . . as a profession —Philip Rahv⟩ **3 a :** writings in prose or verse; *esp* **:** writings having excellence of form or expression and expressing ideas of permanent or universal interest ⟨~ stands related to man as science stands to nature —J.H.Newman⟩ ⟨our conceptions of types of character and the manifold variations of these types is due mainly to ~ —John Dewey⟩ **b :** the body of written works produced in a particular language, country, or age ⟨they speak a . . . sonorous and flexible language, and their ~ is not unworthy of their language —H. T.Buckle⟩ ⟨that superb mess of thought and observation, lust, rhetoric, and pedantry, that we call Renaissance ~ —Clive Bell⟩ **c :** the body of writings on a particular subject ⟨the ~ on field sports is a mass of technicalities held together with a sticky kind of nature loving —J.M.Barzun⟩ ⟨any scientist . . . will answer that at the beginning of an attack on any problem his first task is to look up the existing ~ —T.H.Savory⟩ **d :** leaflets, handbills, circulars, or other printed matter of any kind ⟨asked for volunteers to distribute campaign ~⟩ ⟨induced to migrate by glowing real-estate development ~ —*Amer. Guide Series: Tenn.*⟩ **4 :** the aggregate of musical compositions ⟨programs . . . representing within any one year the greatest possible breadth of musical ~ —William Schuman⟩; *specif* **:** compositions of regional or historical significance or for any particular instrument or group of instruments ⟨a cross section of the Brahms piano ~ —*Saturday Rev.*⟩

**literature search** *n* **:** the methodical investigation of all published sources for information bearing on a usu. scientific or technological subject ⟨it is in chemistry that the *literature search* has attained full stature —*New Technical Books*⟩

**lit·e·ra·tus** \,lid·ə'räd·əs, ,litə-, -rä-, -təs\ *n* -ES [L *litteratus, literatus* literate — more at LITERATE] **:** a member of the literati

**liters** *pl of* LITER

**lites** *pl of* LITE, *pres 3d sing of* LITE

**lith** \'lith\ *n* -s [ME, fr. OE; akin to MD *lit, let* limb, part of the body, OHG *lid*, ON *lithr*, Goth *lithus* limb, L *lituus* crooked staff carried by augurers, Toch A & B *lit-* to go away, fall down, OE *eln* ell — more at ELL] **1** *Scot* **:** JOINT, LIMB, MEMBER — often used in the phrase *lith and limb* **2** *Scot* **:** DIVISION, SEGMENT

**lith-** *or* **litho-** *comb form* [L, fr. Gk, fr. *lithos*] **1 :** stone ⟨*lith*anthrax⟩ ⟨*litho*phyte⟩ ⟨*litho*graph⟩ **2 :** calculus ⟨*lith*osis⟩ ⟨*lith*ology⟩ **3** [NL *lithium*] **:** lithium ⟨*lith*ic⟩; lithic ⟨*lith*emia⟩

**-lith** \,lith\ *n comb form* -s [NL *-lithus* & F *-lithe*, fr. Gk *lithos* stone] **1 a :** stone **:** structure or implement of stone ⟨cyclo*lith*⟩ ⟨mono*lith*⟩ ⟨eo*lith*⟩ **b :** artificial stone **:** cement ⟨grano*lith*⟩ **2** *med* **:** calculus ⟨angio*lith*⟩ ⟨nephro*lith*⟩ **3 :** -LITE 1a ⟨zoo*lith*⟩

**lith** *abbr* lithograph; lithography

**li·tham** \lē'thäm\ *n* -s [Ar *lithām*] **:** a strip of cloth wound round the head covering all but the eyes and worn by Tuaregs of the Sahara desert

**lith·arge** \'li,thärj, -äj-, =ˈ=\ *n* -s [ME *litarge, litharge*, fr. MF, fr. L *lithargyrus*, fr. Gk *lithargyros*, fr. *lith-* stone + *argyros* silver — more at ARGENT] **1 :** lead monoxide obtained in flake or powdered form by processes carried out at temperatures above the melting point of the oxide; *broadly* **:** LEAD MONOXIDE — compare MASSICOT 1 **2** *also* **lith·ar·gite** \-,jīt\ **:** lead monoxide occurring native in the form of red crystals — compare MASSICOT 2

**1lithe** \'līth, 'līth\ *adj* -ER/-EST [ME *lithe, lith*, fr. OE *līthe* mild, gentle; akin to OS *līthi* mild, gentle, OHG *lindi*, L *lentus* flexible, slow, W *llathr* bright, smooth, Skt *latā* vine, liana; basic meaning: flexible] **1** *chiefly Scot* **:** mild and soothing **:** GENTLE, SERENE ⟨sang the mass with ~ devotion —Bruce Marshall⟩ **2 a :** agile and lissome **:** easily flexed **:** SUPPLE, RESILIENT ⟨~ dancing girls⟩ ⟨saw the ~ mechanic's body . . . flex like a drawn bow —Waldo Frank⟩ ⟨the long palette knife, with its thin blade of ~ steel —Oscar Wilde⟩ **b :** characterized by effortless grace ⟨charming and ~ in writing —*Times Lit. Supp.*⟩ **syn** see SUPPLE

**2lithe** \'līth\ *vt* -ED/-ING/-S *dial* **:** to make thick (as broth)

**3lithe** \"\ *vb* -ED/-ING/-S [ME *lithen*, fr. ON *hlȳtha*; akin to OE *hlȳdan* to make a noise, shout, OFris *hlēda* to make a noise, OHG *hlūten* to make a noise, OE *hlūd* loud — more at LOUD] *archaic* **:** LISTEN, HEAR

**4lithe** \"\ *n* -s [perh. alter. of *lewth*] *Scot* **:** a sheltered place **:** SHELTER

**lithe·ly** *adv* [¹*lithe* + *-ly*] **:** in a supple manner **:** FLEXIBLY, RESILIENTLY

**li·the·mia** *also* **li·thae·mia** \lə'thēmēə\ *n* -s [NL, fr. *lith-* + *-emia, -aemia*] **:** a condition in which excess uric acid is present in the blood — **li·the·mic** *also* **li·thae·mic** \-mik\ *adj*

**lithe·ness** *n* -ES [ME *lithnes*, fr. *lith, lithe* lithe + *-nes* -ness — more at LITHE] **:** the quality or state of being lithe **:** SUPPLENESS, FLEXIBILITY

**lith·er** \'lith̬ə(r)\ *adj* [ME, bad, wicked, wretched, lazy, fr. OE *lȳthre* bad, wicked, wretched; akin to OE *loddere* beggar, MLG *lüder* dissolute person, *lodder* shiftless person, OHG *lottar* insignificant, empty, MHG *lieder* lich slight, insignificant, OIr *lott* whore] **1** *now dial Eng* **:** disinclined to exertion **:** SLOTHFUL, LAZY **2** *now dial Eng* **a :** easily displaced **:** YIELDING ⟨winged through the ~ sky —Shak.⟩ **b :** supple and active **:** AGILE ⟨boys . . . are made that ~ —Maxwell Gray⟩

**lith·er·ness** *n* -ES [ME *lithernesse* wickedness, laziness, fr. *lither* + *-nesse* -ness] *now dial Eng* **:** the quality or state of being lither **:** LAZINESS

**lithe·some** \'līthsəm, 'lith-\ *adj* [¹*lithe* + *-some*] **:** characterized by agile grace ⟨an altogether more ~ and none the less useful wolfhound —*Nat'l Geographic*⟩ **syn** see SUPPLE

**lithe·some·ness** *n* -ES **:** the quality or state of being lithesome

**lithi-** *or* **lithio-** *comb form* [NL *lithium*] **:** lithium ⟨*lithio*philite⟩ ⟨*lithi*ate⟩

**lith·ia** \'lithēə\ *n* -s [NL, fr. *lith-* + *-ia* (as in *magnesia*)] **1 :** lithium oxide $Li_2O$ obtained as a white crystalline substance (as by burning lithium in oxygen) **2** [NL, fr. *lithium* + *-a*] **:** LITHIASIS 1

**lithia emerald** *n* **:** HIDDENITE

**lithia mica** *n* **:** LEPIDOLITE

**li·thi·a·sis** \lə'thīəsəs\ *n, pl* **lithia·ses** \-,sēz\ [NL, fr. Gk, fr. *lith-* + *-iasis*] **1 :** the formation or presence of stony concretions in the body (as in the urinary tract and gall bladder) — usu. used in combination ⟨chole*lithiasis*⟩ ⟨nephro*lithiasis*⟩ **2 :** an abnormal development of sclerotic or grit cells in a plant (as the pear)

**lith·i·ate** \'lithē,āt, *usu* -ād·+V\ *vt* -ED/-ING/-S [*lithi-* + *-ate*] **:** to combine or impregnate with lithium or a lithium compound ⟨*lithiated* water⟩

**lithia water** *n* **:** a mineral water characterized by the presence of lithium salts (as lithium carbonate or lithium chloride)

**lith·ic** \'lithik, -ēk\ *adj* [Gk *lithikos*, fr. *lith-* + *-ikos* -ic] **1 :** of or relating to stone ⟨eruptions in which only old ~ debris is expelled —*Jour. of Geol.*⟩; *esp* **:** made of stone ⟨~ artifacts⟩ **2** [*lith-* + *-ic*] **:** of or relating to lithium — **lith·i·cal·ly** \-th̬ək(ə)lē, -ēk-, -li\ *adv*

**-lith·ic** \¦lithik, -ēk\ *adj comb form* [*lithic*] **1 :** relating to or characteristic of a (specified) stage in man's use of stone as a cultural tool ⟨Neo*lithic*⟩ ⟨pre*lithic*⟩ ⟨techno*lithic*⟩ **2** *bot* **:** stone ⟨epi*lithic*⟩

**li·thid·i·o·nite** \lə'thidēə,nīt\ *n* -s [It *litidionite*, fr. Gk *lithidion* pebble (dim. of *lithos* stone) + It *-ite*] **:** a mineral $(Cu,Na_2,K_2)Si_3O_7$ consisting of a rare silicate of alkalies and copper

**lithier** *comparative of* LITHY

**lithiest** *superlative of* LITHY

**lith·i·fi·ca·tion** \,lithəfə'kāshən\ *n* -s [fr. *lithify*, after such pairs as E *edify: edification*] **:** the conversion of unconsolidated sediments into solid rock

**lith·i·fy** \'==,fī\ *vb* -ED/-ING/-ES [*lith-* + *-ify*] *vt* **:** to change to stone **:** PETRIFY ⟨coal is carbonized and *lithified* vegetation —H.A.Meyerhoff⟩ ~ *vi* **:** to become changed into stone ⟨sands ~ into sandstones —C.M.Nevin⟩

**lithing** *pres part of* LITHE

**lith·i·oph·i·lite** \,lithē'äfə,līt\ *n* -s [*lithi-* + *phil-* + *-ite*] **:** a mineral $LiMnPO_4$ consisting of a phosphate of lithium and manganese usu. containing iron and being isomorphous with triphylite

**lith·i·oph·o·rite** \-fə,rīt\ *n* -s [G *lithiophorit*, fr. *lithi-* + *phor-* + *-it* -ite] **:** a mineral $LiMn_3Al_2O_9{\cdot}3H_2O$(?) consisting of hydrous oxide of manganese, aluminum, and lithium

**li·this·tid** \lə'thistəd, -,tid\ *adj* [NL *Lithistida*] **:** of, relating to, or resembling the Lithistida or related sponges

**li·this·ti·da** \-,stədə\ *n pl, cap* [NL, fr. (assumed) Gk *lithistos* (verbal of Gk *lithizein* to resemble a stone, fr. *lith-* + *-izein* -ize) + NL *-ida*] *in former classifications* **:** an order of sponges (class Demospongiae) comprising well-preserved fossil sponges with a massive reticulate skeleton of fused siliceous spicules

**lith·ite** \'li,thīt\ *n* -s [*lith-* + *-ite*] **:** a calcareous concretion esp. in a tentaculocyst or lithocyst

**lith·i·um** \'lithēəm\ *n* -s [NL, fr. *lith-* + *-ium*] **:** a soft silver-white univalent element of the alkali metal group that is the lightest metal known, that occurs combined in several minerals (as amblygonite, spodumene, lepidolite, zinnwaldite), in many mineral waters, and in plant ashes, that is obtained as the metal by electrolysis of fused lithium chloride, and that is used chiefly in nuclear reactions, in metallurgy for removing gases from molten metals and making light alloys, and in the manufacture of lithium compounds — symbol *Li;* see ELEMENT table

**lithium aluminum hydride** *n* **:** a white flammable solid $LiAlH_4$ soluble in ether that is made by the reaction of lithium hydride and anhydrous aluminum chloride and that is used as a reducing agent esp. for organic compounds [as a carboxylic acid (RCOOH) to an alcohol ($RCH_2OH$)]

**lithium carbonate** *n* **:** a crystalline salt $Li_2CO_3$ used chiefly in the glass and ceramic industries and in the manufacture of other lithium salts

**lithium chloride** *n* **:** a hygroscopic crystalline salt LiCl used chiefly in the manufacture of metallic lithium, in welding fluxes, and in the form of an aqueous solution for controlling humidity in air conditioning

**lithium hydride** *n* **:** a flammable crystalline solid LiH that is usu. bluish owing to traces of metallic lithium, that is made by direct union of lithium and hydrogen at high temperatures, and that is used chiefly as a source of hydrogen and in the synthesis of lithium aluminum hydride and other lithium compounds

**lithium perchlorate** *n* **:** a crystalline salt $LiClO_4$ useful as an oxidizer in solid rocket propellant systems

**1litho** \'li,thō\ *n* -s [by shortening] **1 :** LITHOGRAPH **2 :** LITHOGRAPHY

**2litho** \"\ *adj* [by shortening] **:** LITHOGRAPHIC

**3litho** \"\ *vt* -ED/-ING/-S [by shortening] **:** LITHOGRAPH

**litho-** — see LITH-

**lith·o·bi·o·mor·pha** \,lithō,bīə'mȯrfə\ *n pl, cap* [NL, fr. *lith-* + *bi-* + *-morpha*] **:** a large order of centipedes having lateral spiracles and 15 pairs of legs in the adult and 7 pairs in the newly hatched young

**li·tho·bi·us** \lə'thōbēəs\ *n, cap* [NL, fr. *lith-* + Gk *bios* life — more at QUICK] **:** a large nearly cosmopolitan genus (the type of the family Lithobiidae) of centipedes having the body composed of nine long and six short segments and living usu. under stones or logs

**lith·o·car·pus** \,lithə'kärpəs, -kȧp-\ *n, cap* [NL, fr. *lith-* + *-carpus*] **:** a large genus of chiefly Asiatic evergreen trees (family Fagaceae) differing from *Quercus* mainly in the erect staminate catkins — see OAK, TANBARK OAK

**lith·o·cho·lic acid** \¦lithə+-\ *n* [ISV *lith-* + *cholic*] **:** a crystalline bile acid $C_{23}H_{38}(OH)COOH$ found esp. in man and the ox; 3-hydroxy-cholanic acid

**lith·o·chro·my** \'lithə,krōmē\ *n* -ES [*lith-* + *-chromy*] **:** the art of painting on stone

**lith·o·clase** \'=ə,klās, -āz\ *n* -s [F, fr. *lith-* + *-clase*] **:** a natural fracture in rock

**lith·o·culture** \'lithə+,-\ *n* [*lith-* + *culture*] **:** culture of the Stone Age

**lith·o·cyst** \"+,-\ *n* [ISV *lith-* + *cyst*] **1 :** a sac containing lithites that is found in many medusae and other invertebrates and is held to be an auditory organ **2 :** a cell that includes a cystolith

**li·tho·des** \lə'thō,dēz\ *n, cap* [NL, fr. Gk *lithōdēs* resembling stone, fr. *lith-* + *-ōdēs* -ode] **:** a genus (the type of the family Lithodidae) of anomuran crabs that live in cold water toward the poles or in the deep sea

**lith·o·des·ma** \,lithə'dezmə\ *n, pl* **lithodesma·ta** \-məd·ə\ [NL, fr. *lith-* + Gk *desma* bond — more at DESMA] **:** a small shelly plate connected with the resilium in many bivalve shells

**¹lith·o·did** \'lithədəd, -,did\ *adj* [NL *Lithodes* & *Lithodidae*] **:** of or relating to the genus *Lithodes* or the family Lithodidae

**²lithodid** \"\ *n* -s **:** a crab of the genus *Lithodes* or the family Lithodidae

**li·thod·o·mous** \lə'thädəməs\ *adj* [Gk *lithodomos* mason + E *-ous*] **:** burrowing in rock

**li·thod·o·mus** \-məs\ [NL, fr. Gk *lithodomos* mason, fr. *lith-* + *-domos* (fr. *demein* to build) — more at TIMBER] *syn of* LITHOPHAGA

**lith·o·facies** \,lithə+\ *n* [NL, fr. *lith-* + *facies*] **:** a facies characterized by a particular lithologic aspect

**lith·o·gen·e·sis** \"+\ *n* [NL, fr. *lith-* + *genesis*] **1 :** the science of the formation of rocks **2 :** the formation of calculi

**li·thog·e·nous** \lə'thäjənəs\ *adj* [*lith-* + *-genous*] **:** that produces stone ⟨~ polyp⟩

**lith·o·glyph** \'lithə,glif\ *n* [Gk *lithoglyphia*, fr. *lith-* + *glyphein* to engrave, carve + *-ia* -y — more at CLEAVE (split)] **1 :** an engraving on stone **2 :** an engraved stone

**lith·o·glyp·tics** \,==+\ *n pl but usu sing in constr* [*lith-* + *glyptics*, pl. of ¹*glyptic*] **:** the art or process of engraving gems

**¹lith·o·graph** \'lithə,graf, -raa(ə)f,-raif,-râf\ *vt* -ED/-ING/-S [back-formation fr. *lithography*] **1 :** to produce, copy, or portray by lithography **2 :** to inscribe or record by inscribing on stone or ware

**²lithograph** \"\ *n* [back-formation fr. *lithography*] **:** a print made by lithography ⟨a show of drawings and ~*s* —Arnold Bennett⟩

**li·thog·ra·pher** \lə'thägrəfə(r), 'lithə,grafə(r)\ *n* -s **:** one that lithographs **:** one engaged in lithography

**lith·o·graph·ic** \,lithə'grafik, -fēk\ *adj* [*lithography* + *-ic*] **:** of, done by, or used in lithography ⟨the ~ printing⟩ ⟨the ~ principle⟩ ⟨~ paper⟩ — **lith·o·graph·i·cal·ly** \-fək(ə)lē, -fēk-,-li\ *adv*

**lithographic crayon** *n* **:** a crayon or stylus of compressed grease and coloring matter used by lithographers for drawing a design on stone or metal

**lithographic limestone** *n* **:** a fine-grained dense limestone with conchoidal fracture formerly used in lithography

**lithographic varnish** *n* **:** a heat-thickened linseed oil of various viscosities used in lithography

**li·thog·ra·phy** \lə'thägrəfē, -fi\ *n* -ES [G *lithographie*, fr. *lith-* + *-graphie* -graphy] **1 a :** the process of printing from a plane surface (as a smooth stone or metal plate) on which the image to be printed is ink-receptive and the blank area ink-repellent — compare OFFSET **b :** the art of making designs on lithographic surfaces **2 :** a planographic process **:** PLANOGRAPHY

**lith·o·gra·vure** \,lithəgrə'vyů(ə)r, -grä,v-, -üə\ *n* [*lith-* + *gravure*] **:** a process of photoengraving on stone

**lith·oid** \'li,thȯid\ *also* **li·thoi·dal** \lə'thȯidᵊl\ *adj* [*lithoid* fr. Gk *lithoeidēs*, fr. *lith-* stone + *-oeidēs* -oid; *lithoidal* fr. Gk *lithoeidēs* + E *-al*] **:** resembling a stone

**lithoing** *pres part of* LITHO

**Lith·ol** \'li,thȯl, -ōl\ *trademark* — used for any of a group of organic pigments most of which consist essentially of salts of difficultly soluble azo compounds; see DYE table I (under *Pigment Red 49, 52,* and *57*)

**lith·ol·a·paxy** \li'thälə,paksē, 'lithələ-\ *n* -ES [*lith-* + Gk *lapaxis* evacuation (fr. assumed Gk *lapaktos* — verbal of *lapassein* to empty — + *-sis*) + E *-y* — more at LAPACTIC] **:** the operation of crushing a urinary calculus in the bladder and removing the fragments

**lith·o·log·ic** \,lithə'läjik\ *also* **lith·o·log·i·cal** \-jəkəl\ *adj* **:** of or relating to lithology — **lith·o·log·i·cal·ly** \-k(ə)lē\ *adv*

**li·thol·o·gy** \lə'thäləjē, -ji\ *n* -ES [*lith-* + *-logy*] **1 :** the study of rocks **2 :** the character of a rock formation or of the rock found in a geological area or stratum expressed in terms of its structure, mineral composition, color, and texture ⟨a relation between the fossil content of a stratum and its ~ —F.J. Pettijohn⟩

**lith·o·man·cy** \'lithə,mansē\ *n* -ES [F *lithomantie*, fr. *lith-* + *-mantie* -mancy] **:** divination by stones or by charms or talismans of stone

**lith·o·marge** \-,märj, -äj\ *n* -s [*lith-* + L *marga* marl] **:** a smooth compact common kaolin

**lith·o·meteor** \,==+\ *n* [*lith-* + *meteor*] **:** a conglomeration of small solid particles (as of dust or sand) that is suspended in the atmosphere and often produces a dry haze

**lith·o·mor·phic** \'=='mȯrfik\ *adj* [*lith-* + *-morphic*] *of soils* **:** deriving color from parent material

**¹lith·on·trip·tic** \,li,thän'triptik\ *also* **lith·o·trip·tic** \,lithə;-\ *adj* [*lithontriptic* modif. (influenced by Gk *tribein* to rub) of Gk *lithōn thryptikos* stone-crushing; *lithotriptic* alter. (influenced by *lith-*) of *lithontriptic*] **:** having the quality of or used for dissolving or destroying stone in the bladder or kidneys

**²lithontriptic** \"\ *also* **lithotriptic** \"\ *n* -s **:** a lithontriptic agent

**lith·o·pe·di·on** \,lithə'pēdē,än\ *n* -s [NL, fr. *lith-* + Gk *paidion* small child, dim. of *paid-, pais* child — more at FEW] **:** a fetus calcified in the body of the mother

**li·thoph·a·ga** \lə'thäfəgə\ *n, cap* [NL, fr. *lith-* + *-phaga*] **:** a genus of elongated bivalve mollusks (family Mytilidae) comprising the date mussels that live and bore in limestone and coral — compare PHOLAS

**li·thoph·a·gous** \-gəs\ *adj* [*lith-* + *-phagous*] **:** consuming stone ⟨~ mollusks⟩

**lith·o·phane** \'lithə,fān\ *n* -s [ISV *lith-* + *-phane* (as in *diaphane*)] **:** porcelain impressed with figures that are made distinct by transmitted light (as from a lampshade) — **lith·o·phan·ic** \'=='fanik\ *adj*

**lith·o·phile** \'lithə,fīl\ *adj* [*lith-* + *-phile*] **:** tending to be concentrated in the silicate outer shell of the earth ⟨uranium is a typical ~ element —*Jour. of Geol.*⟩

**li·thoph·i·lous** \lə'thäfələs\ *adj* [ISV *lith-* + *-philous*] **:** growing or living in stony places ⟨~ plants⟩ ⟨~ insects⟩

**lith·o·photogravure** \,lithō+\ *n* [*lith-* + *photogravure*] **:** a photomechanical process in which a photolithographic transfer is made on a stone ruled with very fine lines to produce halftone effects

**lith·o·phy·sa** \,=='fīsə\ *n, pl* **lithophy·sae** \-,sē\ [NL, fr. *lith-* + Gk *physa* bubble — more at PUSTULE] **:** a spherulitic cavity often with concentric chambers that is observed in some rhyolitic lavas — **lith·o·phy·sal** \'=='=sᵊl\ *adj*

**lith·o·phyte** \'lithə,fīt\ *n* -s [F, fr. *lith-* + *-phyte*] **1** *archaic* **:** a plant or a plantlike organism having a hard stony structure or skeleton **2 :** a plant or a plantlike organism that grows on the surface of rocks — **lith·o·phyt·ic** \'=='fid·ik\ *adj*

**lith·o·pone** \'lithə,pōn\ *n* -s [ISV *lith-* + Gk *ponos* work, artifact] **:** a white pigment consisting essentially of a mixture of zinc sulfide and barium sulfate precipitated by mixing solutions of barium sulfide and zinc sulfate and used chiefly in paint, printing ink, and linoleum and as a filler in paper, rubber, and plastics — compare CADMIUM LITHOPONE

**lith·o·print** \'==+,-\ *vt* [*lith-* + *print*] **:** to print (as typewritten matter) by offset or photo-offset

**lith·o·printing** \'==+,-\ *also* **lith·o·print** \'==+,-\ *n* [*lith-* + *printing, print*] **:** photo-offset printing

**lith·ops** \'li,thäps\ *n* [NL, fr. *lith-* + *-ops*] **1** *cap* **:** a genus of stemless succulent southern African plants (family Aizoaceae) that are sometimes grown for ornament and that have the leaves in pairs forming a stonelike body with a fissure on top from which the sessile usu. solitary flower emerges **2** *pl* **lithops :** any plant of the genus *Lithops* — called also *living stone, stoneface, stone life face*

**litho purple** *n* [¹*litho*] **:** a grayish to dark purple

**lithos** *pl of* LITHO, *pres 3d sing of* LITHO

**lith·o·sere** \'lithə+,-\ *n* [*lith-* + *sere*] **:** an ecological sere originating on rock

**li·tho·si·an** \lə'thōsēən\ *adj* [NL *Lithosiidae* + E *-an*] **:** of or relating to the Lithosiidae

**li·tho·si·id** \-sēəd\ *n* -s [NL *Lithosiidae*] **:** a moth of the family Lithosiidae

**lith·o·si·idae** \,lithə'sīə,dē\ *n pl, cap* [NL, fr. *Lithosia*, type genus (fr. Gk *lithōsis* petrifaction, fr. *lithoun* to become petrified — fr. *lithos* stone — + *-sis*) + *-idae*] **:** a large family of moths closely related to the Arctiidae but lacking normal ocelli and sometimes included as a subfamily in Arctiidae

**lith·o·sol** \'lithə,säl, -ōl\ *n* -s *sometimes cap* [*lith-* + L *solum* ground, soil — more at SOLE] **:** an azonal group of shallow soils consisting of imperfectly weathered rock fragments usu. on steep mountain slopes or high plateaus

**lith·o·sper·mum** \,=='spərməm\ *n, cap* [NL, fr. Gk *lithospermon* gromwell, fr. *lith-* + *-spermon* (fr. *sperma* seed) — more at SPERM] **:** a genus of herbs (family Boraginaceae) having a regular tubular corolla and polished white stony nutlets — see CORN GROMWELL, PUCCOON

**lith·o·sphere** \'==+,-\ *n* [ISV *lith-* + *sphere*] **:** the solid part of the earth; *specif* **:** the outer part of the solid earth composed of rock essentially like that exploded at the surface and believed to be about 50 miles in thickness — compare ATMOSPHERE, HYDROSPHERE

**¹lith·o·tham·ni·oid** \,=='thamnē,ȯid\ *adj* [NL *Lithothamnion* + E *-oid*] **:** of or relating to the genus *Lithothamnion*

**²lithothamnioid** \"\ *n* -s **:** an alga of the genus *Lithothamnion*

**lith·o·tham·ni·on** \,=='=nē,än\ *n* [NL, fr. *lith-* + Gk *thamnos* bush + *-ion* (dim. suffix)] **1** *cap* **:** a genus of crustose reef-forming red algae (family Corallinaceae) that are abundant in post-Jurassic geologic strata and are represented by numerous recent forms growing chiefly on rocks and other algae **2** -s **:** any plant of the genus *Lithothamnion*

**lith·o·tome** \'==,tōm\ *n* -s [F, fr. MGk *lithotomon*, fr. Gk *lith-* + *-tomon* -tome] **1 :** a knife used for lithotomy **2** [*lith-* + *-tome*] **:** a stone so formed as to appear as if cut by art

**li·thot·o·mist** \lə'thäd·əməst, -ätə-\ *n* -s [F *lithotomiste*, fr. *lithotomie* + *-iste* -ist] **:** a specialist in lithotomy

**li·thot·o·mize** \-,mīz\ *vt* -ED/-ING/-S [*lithotomy* + *-ize*] **:** to subject to lithotomy

**li·thot·o·my** \-mē, -mi\ *n* -ES [LL *lithotomia*, fr. Gk, fr. *lithotomein* to quarry, perform a lithotomy, fr. *lith-* + *-tomein* (fr. *temnein* to cut) — more at TOME] **:** the operation of cutting into the urinary bladder for removal of a stone

**lith·o·tope** \'lithə,tōp\ *n* -s [*lith-* + *-tope*] **:** an area of relatively uniform conditions of rock deposition

**lithotriptic** *var of* LITHONTRIPTIC

**lith·o·trite** \'lithə,trīt\ *n* -s [back-formation fr. *lithotrity*] **:** an instrument for performing lithotrity

**li·thot·ri·tist** \lə'thä·trəd·əst\ *n* -s [*lithotrity* + *-ist*] **:** a specialist in lithotrity

**lith·o·tri·tor** \'lithə,trīd·ə(r)\ *n* -s [alter. (influenced by L *tritor* one that rubs) of earlier *lithotriptor*, fr. *lithotriptic* + *-or*] **:** LITHOTRITE

**li·thot·ri·ty** \lə'thä·trəd·ē\ *n* -ES [*lithotritor* + *-y*] **:** the breaking of a stone in the bladder into small pieces capable of being voided or washed out

**lith·o·type** \'lithə,tīp\ *n* [*lith-* + *type*] **1 :** a letterpress printing plate made of shellac, fine sand, tar, and linseed oil; *also* **:** an imprint made from it **2 :** an etched stone surface for printing a design in relief; *also* **:** an imprint made from it

**li·thox·yl** *or* **li·thox·yle** \lə'thäk,sil\ *also* **li·thox·y·lite** \-,sə,līt\ *n* -s [*lithoxyl, lithoxyle* fr. Sw *lithoxylon*, fr. *lith-* + Gk *xylon* wood; *lithoxylite* fr. *lithoxyl* + *-ite*] **:** petrified wood

**liths** *pl of* LITH

**-liths** *pl of* -LITH

**liths·man** \'lithsmən\ *n, pl* **lithsmen** [OE *lithsmann*, fr. ON *lithsmann-, lithsmathr* warrior, sailor, fr. *liths* (gen. of *lith* people, host) + *mann-, mathr* man; akin to ON *lītha* to go — more at LEAD] **:** a sailor in the navy during the period of the Danish kings of England

**lith·u·a·nia** \,lith(y)ə'wānēə, -nyə\ *adj, usu cap* [fr. *Lithuania*, country in eastern Europe] **:** of or from Lithuania **:** of the kind or style prevalent in Lithuania **:** LITHUANIAN

**¹lith·u·a·ni·an** \-nēən, -nyən\ *adj, usu cap* [*Lithuania* + E *-an*] **1 a :** of, relating to, or characteristic of Lithuania, a country of eastern Europe **b :** of, relating to, or characteristic of the Lithuanians **2 :** of, relating to, or characteristic of the Lithuanian language

**²lithuanian** \"\ *n* -s *cap* **1 :** a native or inhabitant of Lithuania **2 :** a Baltic language of the Lithuanian people and the official language of Lithuania — see INDO-EUROPEAN LANGUAGES table

**¹lith·u·an·ic** \-;wanik\ *adj, usu cap* [*Lithuania* + E *-ic*] **:** LITHUANIAN

**²lithuanic** \"\ *n* -s *cap* **:** LITHUANIAN 2

**lit hum** *abbr, often cap L&H* [ML *literae humaniores*] the humanities

**lith·u·ria** \lə'thyůrēə\ *n* -s [NL, fr. *lith-* + *-uria*] **:** excess of uric acid or of its salts in the urine

**lithy** \'lī*th*ē, 'lithē, -i\ *adj* -ER/-EST [ME *lethy, lithy;* akin to MHG *ledic, ledec* free, unhindered, ON *lithugr*, and perh. to OE *lith* limb — more at LITH] *now dial Eng* **:** easily bent **:** PLIABLE, SUPPLE

**lit·i·ga·ble** \'lid·əgəbəl, 'litə-\ *adj* [*litigate* + *-able*] **:** capable of being litigated

**¹lit·i·gant** \-gənt\ *adj* [L *litigant-, litigans*, pres. part. of *litigare*] **:** contending in law **:** engaged in a lawsuit ⟨the parties ~⟩

**²litigant** \"\ *n* -s **:** one engaged in a lawsuit ⟨right of ~*s* . . . to be unhampered in the quest for justice —*Jour. of the Amer. Judicature Society*⟩

**lit·i·gate** \'lid·ə,gāt, 'litə-, *usu* -ād+V\ *vb* -ED/-ING/-S [L *litigatus*, past part. of *litigare*, fr. *lit-, lis* lawsuit (fr. OL *stlit-, stlis*) + *-igare* (fr. *agere* to drive, lead, act, do); perh. akin to Gk *stellein* to set up — more at STALL, AGENT] *vi* **:** to carry on a legal contest by judicial process ⟨only states can ~ before this court —R.H.Heindel⟩ ⟨the great *litigating* public —Geoffrey Lincoln⟩ ~ *vt* **1** *archaic* **:** to enter into controversy over ⟨the point indeed has been much *litigated* —Horace Walpole⟩ **2 :** to make the subject of a lawsuit **:** contest in law **:** prosecute or defend by pleadings, evidence, and debate in a court ⟨the restraining order is being *litigated* —H.J.Ruttenberg⟩ ⟨~ the validity of a state statute —*Harvard Law Rev.*⟩

**litigated motion** *n* **:** a motion at law that can be decided only after notice to an opposing party entitled to be heard — compare EX PARTE

**lit·i·ga·tion** \,=='gāshən\ *n* -s [LL *litigation-, litigatio*, fr. L *litigatus* (past part. of *litigare*) + *-ion-, -io* -ion] **1** *archaic* **:** DISPUTE ⟨was, after some ~, obliged to consent —Henry Fielding⟩ ⟨a matter of ~ among psychologists —William James⟩ **2 a :** the act or process of litigating ⟨losses arising from ~ in a civil antitrust suit —*Wall Street Jour.*⟩ ⟨~ over an estate⟩ **b :** the practice of taking legal action ⟨my lawyer is bound by all his affections to encourage me in ~ —G.B.Shaw⟩ ⟨he enjoyed ~ —Louis Auchincloss⟩ **3 :** a controversy involving adverse parties before an executive governmental agency having quasi-judicial powers and employing quasi-judicial procedures

**lit·i·ga·tor** \'==,gād·ə(r), -ātə-\ *n* -s [L, fr. *litigatus* + *-or*] **:** one that litigates **:** LITIGANT

**li·ti·gi·os·i·ty** \lə,tijē'äsəd·ē\ *n* -ES [fr. *litigious*, after such pairs as E *ponderous: ponderosity*] **:** the quality or state of being litigious

**li·ti·gious** \lə'tijəs\ *adj* [ME, fr. MF *litigieux*, fr. L *litigiosus*, fr. *litigium* quarrel, dispute (fr. *litigare*) + *-osus* -ous] **1 a :** marked by an inclination to quarrel **:** DISPUTATIOUS, CONTENTIOUS ⟨the ~ and acrimonious spirit . . . fostered by a training in medieval logic —R.W.Southern⟩ **b :** fond of litigation **:** prone to engage in lawsuits ⟨pertinacious and ~ in collecting their alleged dues —F.D.Smith & Barbara Wilcox⟩ **2 a** *obs* **:** inviting controversy **:** DISPUTABLE ⟨an age . . . that hath almost lost piety in the chase of some ~ truths —Joseph Hall⟩ **b :** liable or subject to litigation ⟨not known to be ~ when purchased —James Muirhead⟩ **3 :** of, relating to, or marked by litigation ⟨able to trace the story of the . . . heirs through the ~ tangle of a dozen generations —J.T.Winterich⟩ — **li·ti·gious·ly** *adv* — **li·ti·gious·ness** *n* -ES

**liting** *pres part of* LIT *or of* LITE

**li·ti·o·pa** \lə'tīəpə\ *n, cap* [NL, fr. Gk *litos* plain, simple + *opē* opening, hole] **:** a genus of minute marine gastropod mollusks (suborder Taenioglossa) commonly living among seaweeds

**li·tis·con·test** \,līd·əskən'test\ *vt* [back-formation fr. *litiscontestation*] *Scots law* **:** to bring to litiscontestation

**li·tis·con·tes·ta·tion** \,==+\ *n* [ME *litiscontestacioun*, fr. MF *litiscontestation*, fr. ML *litis contestation-, litis contestatio*, lit., attestation of a lawsuit] **1 :** a legal process by which controverted issues are established and a joinder of issues arrived at **2 :** the issues involved in a law case **3 :** the statement or pleading by which a party contests a suit — **li·tis·con·tes·ta·tion·al** \'=;=,=;tāshənᵊl, -shnəl\ *adj*

**lit·mus** \'litməs\ *n* -ES [of Scand origin; akin to ON *litmosi* herbs used in dyeing, fr. *litr* color + *mosi* moss; akin to OE *wlite* face, OHG *antlizzi* face, ON *līta* to look, Goth *wlits* face, figure, *wlaiton* to spy, look, L *voltus, vultus* facial expression, appearance, face, MW *gwelet* to see — more at MOSS] **:** a coloring matter that turns red in acid solutions and blue in alkaline solutions, is obtained from several lichens (as *Roccella tinctoria, R. fuciformis*, or *Lecanora tartarea*), is usu. formed with powdered chalk or gypsum into small blue cakes, and is used as an acid-base indicator — compare ARCHIL, AZOLITMIN

**litmus milk** *n* **:** milk colored with litmus and used as a culture medium for determining acid or alkali production

**litmus paper** *n* **:** unsized paper colored red, blue, or violet by treating with an aqueous infusion of litmus for use as an acid-base indicator

**li·to·mo·soi·des** \,līd·ōmə'sȯi,dēz, ,lid-·-\ *n, cap* [NL] **:** a genus of filariid worms including a form (*L. carinii*) that is parasitic in the cotton rat and is much used in research on chemotherapy and other problems concerning human filariases

**li·top·tern** \lī'täp,tərn\ *n* -s [NL *Litopterna*] **:** one of the Litopterna

**li·top·ter·na** \,=(,)='tərnə\ *n pl, cap* [NL, fr. Gk *litos* plain, smooth + *pterna* heel] **:** an order of extinct So. American Cenozoic ungulates with one or three functional toes

**litorina** [NL, fr. L *litor-, litus* seashore + NL *-ina*] *syn of* LITTORINA

**litorinidae** [NL *Litorina* + *-idae*] *syn of* LITTORINIDAE

**li·to·tes** \'līd·ə,tēz, 'lid-; lī'tōd·ēz\ *n, pl* **litotes** [Gk *litotēs*, fr. *litos* simple, plain; akin to Gk *leios* smooth — more at LIME] **1 :** understatement in which an affirmative is expressed by the negative of the contrary (as in "He's not a bad ballplayer") — opposed to *hyperbole* **2 :** an example of litotes ⟨the ~ in this passage⟩

**lit-par-lit** \'lē,pär'lē\ *adj* [F, lit., bed-by-bed] **:** of, relating to, or having the form of foliated or fissile rock that has been intruded by many thin sheets or stringers of magma

**li·tra** \'lī·trə\ *n, pl* **li·trae** \-,trē\ [Gk] **1 :** a unit of value of ancient Sicily based on the value of a pound of bronze **2 :** a silver coin worth one litra

**¹litre** *var of* LITER

**²li·tre** \'lē·trā\ *n* -s [Sp] **:** a poisonous Chilean shrub (*Lithraea caustica*) of the family Anacardiaceae that has hardwood used in cabinetwork

**lits** *pres 3d sing of* LIT, *pl of* LIT

**lit·sea** \'litsēə\ *n, cap* [NL, fr. F *litsé* shrub of the genus *Litsea*, fr. Chin (Cant) *leĭ tsai* cherry, lit., small plum] **:** a genus of aromatic shrubs or trees (family Lauraceae) having small evergreen leaves, short racemes of flowers, and berrylike fruits — see MANGEAO

**lit·ster** \'litstər\ *n* -s [ME *litestere*, fr. *liten, litten* to dye + *-stere* -ster — more at LIT] *Scot* **:** DYER

**Litt D** *abbr or n* -s [ML *litterarum doctor*] **:** a doctor of letters

**litted** *past of* LIT

**¹lit·ten** \'litᵊn\ *n* -s [ME *lytton, letton*, fr. OE *līctūn*, fr. *līc* body, corpse + *tūn* enclosure, field, village — more at LIKE, TOWN] *dial Eng* **:** CHURCHYARD; *esp* **:** a churchyard used as a cemetery

**²litten** \"\ *adj* [*lit* (past part. of ³*light*) + *-en*] *archaic* **:** LIGHTED ⟨like a cloud of ~ gold —*Blackwood's*⟩ — often used in combination ⟨dim-*litten* chamber —William Morris⟩

**¹lit·ter** \'lid·ə(r), 'litə-\ *n* -s [ME *litere, liter* bed, litter, fr. OF *litiere*, fr. *lit* bed, fr. L *lectus* — more at LIE] **1 a :** a vehicle consisting of a usu. covered and curtained couch in which a single passenger is carried ⟨as Rome became powerful and captured many slaves, the usual conveyance in the city was a ~ carried on the shoulders of four men —Edwin Tunis⟩ **b :** a bed, stretcher, basket, or other device for carrying a sick or injured person ⟨the wounded general . . . was moved to the rear first by wagon, then by ~ —John Mason Brown⟩ **2 a :** material (as straw or hay) used esp. as bedding for animals ⟨fibrous peat is also used as . . . ~ material for bedding stock and for stable and poultry yards —J.A.DeCarlo & Maxine M. Otero⟩ **b :** the uppermost slightly decayed layer of organic matter on the forest floor ⟨rain . . . is absorbed by the spongelike mass of ~ and then seeps into the soil —*London Calling*⟩ — compare DUFF, HUMUS **3 a :** the offspring at one birth of a multiparous animal ⟨a ~ of puppies⟩ **b** *archaic* **:** an act of animal parturition ⟨the female produces from three to six young ones at a ~ —Samuel Williams⟩ **4 a :** refuse or rubbish lying scattered about ⟨the ~ of rusty cans and foul rags —Van Wyck Brooks⟩ **b :** an untidy accumulation of objects lying about ⟨an old pamphlet among the ~ of the abbot's study —J.H.Blunt⟩

Roman litter

**²litter** \"\ *vb* -ED/-ING/-S *vt* **1 a :** to supply (an animal) with material for bedding ⟨keep him warm by ~*ing* him up to the belly with fresh straw —Edward Topsell⟩ **b :** to cover (as a floor) with material for bedding ⟨a loose stable, well ~*ed* down with fresh straw —*Sporting Mag.*⟩ **2 :** to produce a litter of ⟨wolves ~*ed* their young in the deserted farmhouses —Samuel Smiles⟩ **3 a :** to strew with scattered articles ⟨the great majority ~*s* the scene with papers, boxes, cans . . . —*Phoenix Flame*⟩ **b :** to scatter about in disorder ⟨~*ed* his clothing all over the floor⟩ **c :** to lie about in disorder ⟨pieces of stuccoed tracery . . . ~*ed* the garden —Charles Lever⟩ ~ *vi* **1 :** to produce a litter ⟨a horrible desert . . . where the she wolf still ~*ed* —T.B.Macaulay⟩ **2 :** to strew litter ⟨don't ~⟩

**lit·te·rae clau·sae** \'lid·ə,rē'klȯ,zē\ *n pl* [NL] **:** LETTERS CLOSE

**litterae hu·ma·ni·o·res** \-hyü,manē'ō,rēz\ *n pl* [ML, lit., more humane letters] **:** HUMANITIES

**lit·ter·a·teur** \,lid·ərə'tər, ,litər-, +V -;tər-; -tȯ(r *also* -tů(ə)r *or* -tůə\ *n* -s [F *littérateur*, fr. L *litterator, literator* grammarian, critic — more at LITERATOR] **:** one that devotes himself to literary pursuits; *esp* **:** a professional writer ⟨a distinguished Danish ~⟩ ⟨a satire on life among the ~*s* —Carlos Baker⟩

**litterbug** \'==,=\ *n* [²*litter* + *bug*] **:** one that litters a street, park, or other public area with waste paper, trash, or garbage ⟨hand out summonses impartially to ~*s*, whether they are motorists, pedestrians, or throwers of refuse from apartment windows —Charles Grutzner⟩ ⟨don't be a ~⟩

**litter carrier** *n* **1 :** one that carries a litter **:** STRETCHER-BEARER **2 :** a box or bed with a dumping mechanism suspended from wheels on an overhead track that is used to move manure (as from a stable to a spreader)

**lit·ter·er** \'lid·ərə(r), -itə-\ *n* [²*litter* + *-er*] **:** LITTERBUG

**littermate** \'==,=\ *n* **:** a product of a multiple birth considered in relation to other members of the same litter

**lit·tery** \'lid·ərē, 'litə-, -ri\ *adj* [¹*litter* + *-y*] **1 :** of, relating to, or having the character of litter ⟨let nothing ~ nor dusty go inside the room —Emily Holt⟩ **2 :** covered with litter **:** UNTIDY ⟨he took me into his library, a rough, ~, but considerable collection —Thomas Carlyle⟩

**litting** *pres part of* LIT

[1]**lit·tle** \'lid-ᵊl, -it ᵊl *sometimes when not heavily stressed* (,)lil *esp when a vowel follows*\ *adj, in sense 1 usu* **lit·tler** \-id-ᵊlə(r), -it(ᵊ)l-\ *usu* **lit·tlest** \-id-ᵊləst, -it(ᵊ)l-\ *in senses 2 & 3 usu* **less** \'les\ *or* **less·er** \'lesə(r)\ *usu* **least** \'lēst\ [ME *lutel, litel, littel,* fr. OE *lȳtel;* akin to OE *lȳt* little, few, OS *luttil* small, miserable, OHG *luzzil* little, ON *lūta* to bow down, Goth *liuts* hypocritical, W *lludded* fatigue, Lith *liūsti* to be sad] **1 :** not big : not great: as **a** (1) : small in size : DIMINUTIVE, TINY ⟨has ~ feet⟩ (2) : short in stature ⟨a pompous ~ man⟩ (3) : that has not attained the full growth of maturity ⟨a ~ child⟩ (4) : that is viewed as tiny or as short; *esp* : that seems brief ⟨had only a ~ month to wait⟩ (5) : small in comparison with related forms — used in vernacular names (as of animals) **b :** small in number : comprising only a few individuals (as members or inhabitants) ⟨a ~ group of people⟩ ⟨a ~ herd of buffalo⟩ ⟨a ~ village⟩ **c :** small in rank or condition : lacking distinction ⟨~ magistrates much occupied with picayune matters⟩ ⟨big businessmen trampling on the ~ fellow⟩ **d :** contemptibly limited (as in scope or outlook) : PALTRY, MEAN, NARROW ⟨disgusted with the pettiness of ~ minds⟩ **e** (1) : small in a way that arouses in the speaker or writer a feeling of tenderness, pity, or sympathy (as through real or supposed defenselessness) ⟨my dear ~ mother⟩ ⟨bless your ~ heart⟩ ⟨stood there trying to warm her poor ~ hands⟩ ⟨hurt his ~ knee⟩ (2) : small or trivial in a way that amuses the speaker or writer (as by arousing a mood of playfulness or bantering) ⟨what ~ game are you up to now⟩ ⟨used to enjoy her ~ tricks⟩ ⟨a funny ~ way of smiling⟩ (3) : small in a way that arouses in the speaker or writer a feeling of exasperation or disapprobation (as through paltriness, meanness, deviousness) ⟨couldn't stand her mean ~ accusations⟩ ⟨know all about your ~ scheme⟩ **2 :** not much: as **a :** that exists only in a small amount or to a slight or limited extent or degree ⟨has ~ money⟩ ⟨have ~ space to work in⟩ ⟨~ change for the better⟩ : barely any : SCANTY ⟨have ~ hope left⟩ ⟨has ~ love for her⟩ ⟨can do it with but ~ effort⟩ **b :** short in duration : BRIEF ⟨had ~ sleep⟩ ⟨there is ~ time left⟩ **c :** that exists in or to an appreciable though not extensive amount, extent, or degree : some but not much — used with *a* ⟨fortunately I still have a ~ money left⟩ ⟨don't worry, you still have a ~ time⟩ **3 :** small in importance or interest : TRIFLING, TRIVIAL ⟨mentioned a lot of ~ points that I found not worth attention⟩ **syn** see SMALL

[2]**little** \"\ *adv* **less** \"\ **least** \"\ [ME *lutel, litel, littel,* fr. OE *lȳtel,* fr. *lȳtel,* adj.] **1 a :** to only a slight or limited extent or degree : not to any great extent or degree : only slightly : not much : not very much ⟨said ~ more than what you already know⟩ ⟨loved her ~⟩ ⟨a once popular writer who is now ~ heard from⟩ ⟨facts that were ~ known at the time⟩ **b :** not at all : not in the least — used prepositively as an emphatic negative esp. with a verb of knowing, thinking, believing, caring ⟨he ~ knows or cares what may happen⟩ **2 :** INFREQUENTLY, RARELY ⟨has been seeing her very ~⟩

[3]**little** \"\ *n* -s [ME *lutel, litel, littel,* fr. OE *lȳtel,* fr. *lȳtel,* adj.] **1 :** something not very extensive (as in amount, quantity): **a** (1) : a small amount or quantity ⟨worked hard to earn what ~ he could⟩ : not much ⟨pointed out that ~ had been accomplished⟩ (2) : only a small amount or quantity : something far short of everything : something constituting only a tiny fraction of all : practically nothing ⟨lost most of her money and has to be satisfied with ~ of what life offers⟩ ⟨remembered ~ of the past⟩ ⟨knows ~ of what has happened⟩ ⟨has learned to be happy with ~⟩ **b :** an appreciable though not extensive amount or quantity : a considerable amount or quantity — used with preceding *a* ⟨spent a lot of money but still has a ~ in the bank⟩ **2 a :** a short time ⟨after a ~ she glanced at him⟩ ⟨stepped out into the garden for a ~⟩ ⟨will be back in a ~⟩ **b :** a short distance ⟨had traveled quite far and a ~ still remained to be covered⟩ — **a little** *adv* **1 a :** for a short time ⟨remain with me *a little*⟩ **b :** for or at a short distance ⟨can walk *a little* and then catch a cab⟩ ⟨the two buildings are set *a little* apart from each other⟩ **2 :** to an appreciable though not extensive amount or degree : to a considerable though not great extent or degree : SOMEWHAT, RATHER ⟨found the play *a little* dull⟩ ⟨liked her *a little*⟩ **3 :** from time to time though not frequently : SOMETIMES, OCCASIONALLY ⟨still gets around to seeing her *a little*⟩ — **by little and little** : little by little — **in little** *adv* : on a small scale; *esp* : in miniature ⟨a painting done *in little*⟩

**little anteater** *n* : SILKY ANTEATER

**little auk** *n* : DOVEKIE 2

**little barley** *n* : an annual barley (*Hordeum pusillum*) that is native to western No. America and widespread in the southern states and in tropical America and that has flattened glumes and the lemmas of the lateral spikelets raised on pedicels

**little bittern** *n* : any of several small bitterns (genus *Ixobrychus*); *esp* : a European bittern (*I. minutus*) with dark upper parts and buffy white underparts and wing coverts

**little bitty** *adj, dial* : SMALL, TINY

**little black ant** *n* : a tiny slender glossy black ant (*Monomorium minimum*) that usu. nests out of doors and invades houses in search of food (as sweets)

**little blue heron** *n* : a small American heron (*Florida caerulea*)

**little bluestem** *n* : a forage grass (*Andropogon scoparius*) of central No. America — called also *bluejoint turkeyfoot*

**little-boys' breeches** \'≈≈,≈-\ *n pl but sing or pl in constr* : DUTCHMAN'S-BREECHES

**little brain** *n* : CEREBELLUM

**little brown bat** *n* : a small widely distributed No. American bat (*Myotis leucifugus*) having rich bronzy brown fur, flight membranes partially furred, and moderately long bluntly pointed ears

**little brown crane** *n* : a crane (*Grus canadensis canadensis*) of western No. America that is a variety of the sandhill crane distinguished by its smaller size and shorter bill

**little buckeye** *n* : RED BUCKEYE

**little bull bat** *n* : a small Central American mastiff bat (*Noctilis albinenter*)

**little bustard** *n* : a bustard (*Otis tetrax*) of Mediterranean countries

**little by little** *adv* : by small degrees or amounts : a little at a time : GRADUALLY ⟨*little by little* they got to know each other⟩ ⟨added the water *little by little*⟩

**little casino** *n* : the two of spades in the game of casino which scores one point for the player who takes the card in a trick

**little cat** *n* : a hand recognized in some poker games that consists of an eight, seven, six, five, and three, contains no pairs, is composed of two or more suits, and ranks next below a big cat

**little cherry** *or* **little cherry disease** *n* : a virus disease of sweet cherries characterized by angular pointed fruits of about half normal size which retain the brilliant red color of immaturity beyond the normal picking time

**little chief hare** *n* [trans. of Chipewyan *bucka-thrae-gga-yaze*] : a pika (*Ochotona princeps*) of No. America

**little corporal** *n* : billiards played with three balls and a small wooden pin in which caroms count as in ordinary billiards but the knocking down of the pin by the cue ball after contact with an object ball scores five points

**little-ease** \'≈≈,≈\ *n* : a place of confinement (as an extremely small prison cell) or a confining device (as a pillory) making it impossible for a prisoner to have even ordinary comfort or freedom of movement

**little englander** *n, usu cap L & E* : an Englishman opposed to territorial expansion of the British Empire and usu. anticipating the gradual voluntary secession of existing possessions therefrom

**little eng·land·ism** \-'iŋ(g)lən,dizəm *sometimes* -'eŋ(g)-\ *n, usu cap L&E* : the policies and convictions of Little Englanders

**little entrance** *n, usu cap L&E* : an entrance in the liturgy of the Eastern Church during which the book of the Gospel is brought in

**little finger** *n* : the fourth finger of the hand

**little folk** *n* : LITTLE PEOPLE

**little grebe** *n* : a common European dabchick

**little greenshank** *n* : a small sandpiper (*Totanus stagnatilis*) of eastern Asia that resembles the lesser yellowlegs

**little gull** *n* : a European black-headed gull (*Larus minutus*) that is the smallest of the true gulls

**littlehead porgy** \'≈≈,≈-\ *n* : a silvery porgy (*Calamus proridens*) of Florida and the West Indies that is brilliantly marked with violet-blue and orange

**little hours** *n pl* : the offices of prime, terce, sext, and none

**little house** *n* : PRIVY 2

**little housefly** *n* : LESSER HOUSEFLY

**little ice age** *n, often cap L&I&A* : an episode of glacial expansion whose maximum extension occurred in the 17th and 18th centuries

**little italy** *n, pl* **little italies** *usu cap L&I* : a quarter or section (as in a city) populated chiefly by Italian immigrants or by persons of Italian descent

**little joe** *n, usu cap L&J* : a throw of four in the game of craps

**little joker** *n* **1 :** JOKER 2a **2 :** a playing-card joker rated lower in scoring value than a big joker

**little king** *n* : a very small wren (*Nannus troglodytes*) that is of a dark brown color barred and mottled with black and that has a short erect tail and is common throughout Europe

**littleleaf** \'≈≈,≈\ *adj* : having little leaves — used as a qualifying epithet esp. in the vernacular names of some plants ⟨~ lilac⟩

**little leaf** \"\ *n* : a plant disorder characterized by small and often chlorotic and distorted foliage: as **a :** a zinc-deficiency disease of deciduous woody plants (as grape, peach, or pecan) **b** *usu* **little-leaf disease** : a destructive disease of southern pines (as *Pinus echinata*) of unknown cause

**little league** *n, often cap both Ls* : a commercially sponsored baseball league made up of teams whose players are boys from 8 to 12 years old — compare PONY LEAGUE

**little leaguer** *n, often cap both Ls* : one that belongs to or plays in a little league

**little locust bird** *n* : a pratincole (*Glareola nordmanni*) that resembles a long-legged swallow

**little magazine** *n* : a literary usu. noncommercial magazine typically small in format that esp. features experimental writing or other literary expression appealing to a relatively limited number of readers

**little magpie** *n* : MAGPIE LARK

**little mary** *n, often cap M, slang* : STOMACH, BELLY

**littlemouth porgy** \'≈≈,≈-\ *n* : SHEEPSHEAD PORGY

**littleneck** \'≈≈,≈\ *or* **littleneck clam** *n* [fr. *Littleneck* Bay, inlet of Long Island Sound, N.Y.] : the young of the quahog when large enough to be eaten raw

**lit·tle·ness** *n* -ES [ME *litelnesse,* fr. OE *lȳtelnes,* fr. *lȳtel* little + *-nes* -ness] **1 :** the quality or state of being little ⟨the ~ of the world in the vast emptiness of space⟩ **2 :** an act marked by littleness; *esp* : a mean or petty act ⟨a life of envy, filled with ~*es*⟩

**little office** *n, often cap L&O* : a usu. invariable office resembling but shorter than the daily canonical office and designed to honor a special saint or mystery of religion; *esp* : such an office honoring the Virgin Mary

**little one** *n* : young offspring; *esp* : CHILD

**little owl** *n* : a small squat owl (*Athene noctua*) common in Europe and having a flattened head and face, dark brown upper parts spotted and barred with white, and whitish underparts streaked with dark brown

**little peach** *n* : a virus disease of the peach tree characterized typically by a dwarfing of the fruit and delay in ripening and by yellowing of the leaves and finally by death of the tree

**little people** *n* : tiny imaginary beings (as fairies, elves, leprechauns) of folklore

**little pickerel** *n* : GRASS PICKEREL

**little piked whale** *n* : PIKED WHALE

**little potato** *n* : RHIZOCTONIA DISEASE 2

**littler** *comparative of* LITTLE

**little red fox** *n* : a small Australian fruit bat (*Pteropus scapulatus*) with short chocolate-brown fur and transparent wing membranes

**little review** *n* : LITTLE MAGAZINE; *esp* : a little magazine featuring nonfiction and critical writing

**little rock** \'≈≈,≈\ *adj, usu cap L&R* [fr. *Little Rock,* Ark.] : of or from Little Rock, the capital of Arkansas : of the kind or style prevalent in Little Rock

**little russian** *n, usu cap L&R* **1 :** UKRAINIAN **2 :** RUTHENIAN

**lit·tle's disease** \'lid-ᵊlz-, -itᵊlz-\ *n, usu cap L* [after William J. *Little* †1894 Eng. physician that described it] : SPASTIC PARALYSIS

**little sister of the poor** *usu cap L&S&P* [trans. of F *Petite Sœur des Pauvres*] *Roman Catholicism* : a member of a religious community founded in Brittany, France, about 1840 and devoted esp. to the care of old people

**little skate** *n* : a ray (*Raja erinacea*) small in size and brown above mottled with black spots that is common in American coastal waters of the Atlantic

**little slam** *n* : the winning of all tricks except one in a card game (as bridge) — called also *small slam*

**little snowball** *n* : BUTTONBUSH

**little snowy** *n* : SNOWY EGRET

**little spotted skunk** *n* : any of a number of small skunks (genus *Spilogale*) that have a coat of marbled black and white and that are common and widely distributed in the southwestern U.S. and in Mexico

**littlest** *superlative of* LITTLE

**little staggerweed** *n* : DUTCHMAN'S-BREECHES

**little stint** *n* : a small sandpiper (*Pisobia minuta*)

**little striker** *n* : LEAST TERN

**little stroke** *n* : a usu. transient blockage of one or more arteries in the cerebrum causing temporary numbness or impaired function of a part, slowed mentation, speech defects, dizziness, and nausea — called also *strokelet;* compare APOPLEXY

**little sugar pine** *n* **1 :** WESTERN WHITE PINE 1 **2 :** SUGAR PINE

**little tern** *n* : a very small cosmopolitan tern (*Sterna albifrons*)

**little theater** *n* **1 :** a small theater for legitimate productions that is designed for a relatively small group or community; *esp* : such a theater in which usu. noncommercial low-cost productions are presented that are often experimental or otherwise designed for a relatively limited audience and that have usu. small often amateur casts **2 :** drama of a kind that is best suited to production in a little theater; *esp* : drama that is usu. noncommercial and low in production costs and that is often experimental or otherwise designed for a relatively limited audience

**little toe** *n* : the outermost and smallest digit of the foot

**little tuna** *also* **little tunny** *n* : a small active pelagic tuna (*Euthynnus alletteratus*) circumtropical in distribution and widely known as a sport fish — called also *false albacore*

**little vehicle** *n, usu cap L&V* [trans. of Skt *hīnayāna*] : HINAYANA — usu. used with *the* ⟨reverted to the pure form of Buddhism known as the *Little Vehicle*⟩

**Lit·tle·way Lockstitch** \,litᵊl,wā-\ *trademark* — used for a shoe constructed by a method in which the upper and lining are attached to the insole by means of staples that do not penetrate to the upper surface of the insole and the outsole is attached to the insole by means of a lockstitch

**little whaup** *n* : WHIMBREL

**little white heron** *n* : SNOWY EGRET

**little woman** *n* : WIFE — not often in formal use

**lit·tling** \'lid-ᵊliŋ, 'lit(ᵊ)l-\ *n* -s [¹*little* + *-ing*] *Scot* : a young child or young animal

**lit·tlish** \-lish\ *adj* : somewhat little : comparatively little

[1]**lit·to·ral** \'lid-ərəl, 'litə-; ¦≈≈¦ral, -räl, -rȧl\ *adj* [L *littoralis, litoralis,* fr. *littor-, littus, litor-, litus* seashore + *-alis* -al] : of or relating to or on or near a shore esp. of the sea: **a :** of, relating to, or being the biogeographic zone that includes (1) the intertidal and eulittoral regions on a seacoast or (2) the marginal part of a body of fresh water extending downward to the limit of rooted vegetation **b :** inhabiting or growing on or near a seacoast **c :** composed of material deposited near a shore and within the zone affected by waves and coastal currents

[2]**littoral** \"\ *n* -s [It *littorale,* fr. *littorale,* adj., of the seashore, fr. L *littoralis, litoralis*] : a coastal region including both the land along the coast and the water near the coast : the shore zone between high and low watermarks

**littoral cell** *n* : one of the reticuloendothelial cells lining the sinuses of various reticular organs of the body

**littoral current** *n* : a current moving along and roughly parallel to a shore

**littoral right** *n* : the right of one owning littoral land to have access to and use of the shore and water — compare RIPARIAN RIGHT

**lit·to·ri·na** \,lid-ə'rīnə, -rēnə\ *n, cap* [NL, fr. L *littor-, littus* seashore + NL *-ina*] : the type genus of Littorinidae comprising the typical littoral marine periwinkles — **lit·to·ri·noid** \¦≈≈,nȯid\ *adj*

**lit·to·rin·i·dae** \,≈≈'rinə,dē\ *n pl, cap* [NL, fr. *Littorina,* type genus + *-idae*] : a large nearly cosmopolitan family of snails (suborder Taenioglossa) that have broad conical shells with round aperture and horny operculum, that are chiefly littoral in salt water or brackish or fresh water and are remarkably resistant to desiccation, and that feed on algae — **lit·to·ri·nid·i·an** \-,rə'nidēən\ *n* -s

**lit·tre's gland** \'lē·trəz-\ *n, usu cap L* [after Alexis *Littre* †1726 Fr. physician] : one of the mucous glands in the submucous tissue of the urethra

**lit·trow spectrograph** \'li·,trō-\ *n, usu cap L* [after Joseph Johann von *Littrow* †1840 Austrian astronomer and mathematician] : a spectrograph in which dispersion is produced by a prism backed by a reflecting metallic film so that the light traverses the prism twice

**lit·u·ate** \'lichəwət, usu -əd·+V\ *adj* [L *lituus* crooked staff carried by augurs + E *-ate* — more at LITH] *bot* : forked with the points turned slightly outward ⟨~ fruit⟩

**lit·u·ite** \-,wīt\ *n* -s [NL *Lituites*] : a fossil of the genus *Lituites*

**lit·u·i·tes** \,≈≈'wīd-,ēz\ *n, cap* [NL, fr. L *lituus* + NL *-ites*] : a genus of Ordovician nautiloid mollusks with the shell fully coiled when young but with the later increments forming a straight tube — **lit·u·i·toid** \'≈≈wə,tȯid\ *adj*

**lit·u·ol·i·dae** \,≈≈'wälə,dē\ *n pl, cap* [NL, fr. *Lituola,* type genus (dim. of L *lituus* curved staff) + *-idae*] : a family of imperforate foraminiferans that are related to those of the family Fusulinidae and have shells divided into cells and composed chiefly of sand grains cemented together

**lit up** *adj, slang* : DRUNK

**lit·u·rate** \'lichə,rāt, -,rət, usu -d·+V\ *adj* [LL *lituratus,* past part. of *liturare* to erase, fr. L *litura* smear, erasure, fr. *litus* (past part. of *linere, linire* to smear) + *-ura* -ure — more at LIME] *biol* : SPOTTED

**li·tur·gi·cal** \lə'tərjəkəl, -tə̄j-,-təij-, -jēk-\ *also* **li·tur·gic** \-jik, -jēk\ *adj* **1 a :** of, relating to, or having the characteristics of liturgy ⟨~ vestments⟩ ⟨a ~ service⟩ **b :** being in accordance with officially prescribed form : RUBRICAL ⟨ceremonies conducted in strict ~ form⟩ **2 :** using or favoring the use of liturgy ⟨a ~ Christian sect⟩ — **li·tur·gi·cal·ly** \-jək(ə)lē, -jēk-, -li\ *adv*

**lit·ur·gi·cian** \,lid-ə(r)'jishən\ *n* -s : a student of liturgics

**li·tur·gics** \lə'tərjiks, -tə̄j-, -təij-\ *n pl but usu sing in constr* **1 :** the study of liturgies; *esp* : LITURGIOLOGY 1 **2 :** a branch of practical theology concerned with the forms of worship and their practice

**li·tur·gi·o·log·i·cal** \lə¦tərjēə¦läjəkəl\ *adj* : of or relating to liturgiology or a liturgiology

**li·tur·gi·ol·o·gist** \,≈,≈≈'äləjəst\ *n* -s : a specialist in liturgiology

**li·tur·gi·ol·o·gy** \-jē\ *n* -ES [*liturgy* + *-o-* + *-logy*] **1 :** the history, doctrine, and interpretation of liturgies **2 :** a treatise on liturgies

**lit·ur·gism** \'lid-ə(r),jizəm, 'litə(-\ *n* -s : strict or excessive adherence to liturgy

**lit·ur·gist** \-jəst\ *n* -s **1 :** one who favors or adheres to a liturgy **2 :** a student or compiler of liturgies **3 :** one who leads in liturgical worship — **lit·ur·gis·tic** \¦≈≈¦jistik, -tēk\ *adj*

**lit·ur·gy** \'lid-ə(r)jē, 'litə(-, -ji\ *n* -ES [LL *liturgia,* fr. Gk *leitourgia* public service, divine service, liturgy, fr. *leit-* (fr. *leōs* people) + *-ourgia* -urgy] **1 a :** a rite or series of rites, observances, or procedures prescribed for public worship in the Christian church in accordance with authorized or standard form **b :** a Eucharistic rite or service **c :** ceremonial or ritualistic worship **2 :** a system or series of ceremonial or ritualistic actions done according to a prescribed arrangement ⟨the scoop and stretch of her fingers . . . might have been part of a witch's ~ —Richard Llewellyn⟩ **3** [Gk *leitourgia*] : a public service or office imposed upon the wealthy citizens of ancient Athens **syn** see FORM

**lit·vak** \'lit,väk, -,vək\ *n* -s *cap* [Yiddish, fr. Pol *Litwak* fr. *Litwa* Lithuania] : a Lithuanian Jew

**litz wire** \'lits-\ *n* [part trans. of G *litzendraht,* fr. *litze* braid, cord, lace + *draht* wire] : a wire composed of individually enameled copper strands braided together to reduce skin effect and consequent high-frequency resistance

**liv·a·bil·i·ty** *also* **live·a·bil·i·ty** \,livə'biləd-ē, -ətē, -i\ *n* **1 :** survival expectancy : VIABILITY — used esp. of poultry and domestic livestock ⟨breeders are coming to select for ~ as well as for high egg production —W.F.Hollander⟩ **2 :** suitability for human living — used of housing and environment ⟨your city . . . can have the power to enforce a reasonable level of ~ in all of its homes —J.W.Lund⟩ ⟨nothing a town may gain in size will compensate for loss of ~ —*Atlantic*⟩

**liv·able** *also* **live·able** \'livəbəl\ *adj* [¹*live* + *-able*] **1 :** VIABLE **2 :** suitable for living ⟨a very ~ house⟩ **3 :** BEARABLE, ENDURABLE ⟨found life scarcely ~⟩ — **liv·able·ness** *n* -ES

[1]**live** \'liv\ *vb* -ED/-ING/-S [ME *liven,* fr. OE *libban, lifian;* akin to OHG *lebēn* to live, ON *lifa,* Goth *liban,* L *caelebs* unmarried] *vi* **1 :** to be alive : have the life of an animal or plant ⟨the child *lived* and grew⟩ **2 :** to continue alive ⟨the longer I ~, I find the folly and the fraud of mankind grow more and more intolerable —Tobias Smollett⟩ ⟨*lived* to a ripe and vigorous old age⟩ ⟨had nine children of whom only five *lived*⟩ **3 :** to maintain oneself : FEED, SUBSIST ⟨*lived* on peanut-butter sandwiches and milk, but was very contented —*Current Biog.*⟩ ⟨a man must always ~ by his work —Adam Smith⟩ ⟨many of our customers *lived* on high inventories —*Monsanto Chemical Co. Annual Report*⟩ ⟨*lived* on his relatives⟩ ⟨*lived* by his wits⟩ **4 :** to conduct, direct, or pass one's life ⟨had religiously *lived* up to that standard —C.L.Jones⟩ ⟨I *lived* and cared only for science —Harrison Brown⟩ **5 :** to occupy a home : DWELL, RESIDE ⟨~*s* in the suburbs⟩ ⟨the houses in which they *lived,* the ceremonies of their courts, he cannot accurately figure to himself —Matthew Arnold⟩ **6 :** to attain eternal life or beatitude ⟨I am the resurrection and the life; he who believes in me, though he die, yet shall he ~ —Jn 11:25 (RSV)⟩ **7 :** to survive oblivion : remain in human memory or record ⟨though you die in combat gory, ye shall ~ in song and story —W.S.Gilbert⟩ ⟨and yet the past ~*s* in us all —W.R.Inge⟩ ⟨the desire of man to ~ on through his deeds, characteristic of the erection of pyramids —John Dewey⟩ **8 :** to flourish in human life or consciousness : retain effect, existence, or vigor ⟨his name cannot die while courage and honor ~ among men⟩ **9 :** to outlast storm or danger : remain afloat or operative — used of a ship or airplane ⟨the 20 to 25 Jap torpedo planes managed to ~ long enough to launch four torpedoes —Ira Wolfert⟩ **10 :** to realize the possibilities of life amply : attain fulfillment or satisfaction ⟨the boy who is mentally awake ~*s* more in a day than a dull boy does in a month —*Boy Scout Handbook*⟩ ⟨I smile when I find people cheerfully talking of "happiness" as something to be desired in life. I have *lived* —Havelock Ellis⟩ **11 :** COHABIT ⟨for 18 months she had *lived* with that Canadian colonel —Fred Majdalany⟩ ~ *vt* **1 :** to pass through or spend the duration of ⟨we do not ~ our lives unattended by divinity —*Amer. Scholar*⟩ ⟨*lived* an unforgettable hour that seemed a lifetime⟩ **2 :** ENACT, PRACTICE ⟨what other men were preaching, he *lived* —P.E.More⟩ ⟨images and ideas which can be *lived* and defended —Stephen Spender⟩ **3 :** to exhibit vigor, gusto, or enthusiasm in ⟨seized life with both hands and *lived* every minute of it —H.W.Glover⟩ **syn** see RESIDE — **live it up** : to live with gusto and usu. fast and loose ⟨*lived it up* with wine and song —*Newsweek*⟩ — **live up to** : to be equal to : compare in quality or worth with

[2]**live** \'līv\ *adj* -ER/-EST [short for *alive*] **1 :** having life : LIVING ⟨she purged a ~ eel —Robert Burton⟩ ⟨ships ~ cattle⟩ **2 :** abounding with life : VITAL, VIVID ⟨the portrait is . . . always ~ and spirited —*Times Lit. Supp.*⟩ ⟨a ~ appreciation of the role of cultural forces in history —L.A.White⟩ ⟨he saw an oldening, flaccid face with ~ eyes —Maurice Walsh⟩ **3 :** exerting force or containing energy: as **a :** AFIRE, GLOWING ⟨tossed a ~ cigarette from the car⟩ **b :** connected to electric

power ⟨a thousand-volt wire, ~ and burning with its power —Adria Langley⟩ **c :** charged with explosives and containing shot or a bullet ⟨a ~ shell⟩ ⟨~ cartridge⟩ ⟨~ ammunition⟩; *also* **:** UNDISCHARGED, UNEXPLODED ⟨a ~ bomb⟩ **d :** imparting or driven by power **:** having motion ⟨the ~ center of a lathe⟩ ⟨~ conveyor rolls⟩ **e :** charged with fissionable material ⟨the pile was built up . . . with alternating layers of ~ and dead blocks —L.R.Hafstad⟩ **4 :** living in thought or controversy **:** of continuing interest **:** open to debate **:** not settled or decided **:** UNCLOSED ⟨long-standing denominational disputes still were ~ issues —Oscar Handlin⟩ **5 :** being in a pure native state: as **a** *of a mineral* **:** NATIVE, VIRGIN **b** *of rock* **:** UNWROUGHT, UNQUARRIED **6 a :** of bright vivid color **b :** of normal brightness or luster — used of timber and lumber **7 :** highly reverberant — used of a room or enclosed space in which sound is produced — compare ANECHOIC, DEAD 10 **8 a** *of a playing card* **:** available for play because still in the hands or stock **b :** being in play ⟨a ~ ball⟩ **9** *of rubber* **:** SPRINGY, RESILIENT **10 a :** not yet printed from or plated **:** to be held for possible further or future printing — used of a printing surface **b :** not yet typeset; *also* **:** typeset but not yet proofread **c :** used for storing or holding live matter **11 a :** of or relating to a performance done without mechanical reproduction by phonograph or cinema **:** presented directly by musicians or actors in concert hall or theater or on radio or television **:** not recorded or filmed **b :** present and responsive — used of a radio or television studio audience

**liveability** *var of* LIVABILITY

**liveable** *var of* LIVABLE

**live axle** *n* **:** the driving axle of any self-propelled vehicle ⟨the usual front axle of a passenger car is a dead axle and the rear axle is a *live axle* —*Principles of Automotive Vehicles*⟩

**live-bearer** \ˈlīv+,-\ *n* **:** a fish that brings forth living young rather than eggs

**live-bearing** \ˈ=ˌ==\ *adj* **:** bringing forth living young **:** VIVIPAROUS

**live birth** *n* **:** birth in such a state that acts of life are manifested after the extrusion of the whole body — compare STILLBIRTH

**live-born** \ˈ=ˈ=\ *adj* **:** born in such a state that acts of life are manifested after the extrusion of the whole body — compare STILLBORN

**live-box** \ˈ=,=\ *n* **:** a box or pen suspended in water to keep aquatic animals alive

**¹lived** *past of* LIVE

**²lived** \ˈlīvd, ˈlivd\ *adj* [ME, fr. *lif* life + *-ed* — more at LIFE] **:** having a life of a specified kind or length — usu. used in combination ⟨short-*lived*⟩ ⟨tough-*lived*⟩

**li·ve·do** \lə'vē,dō, lī-\ *n* -s [L, fr. *livēre* to be blue — more at LIVID] **:** a bluish usu. patchy discoloration of the skin

**live down** *vt* **:** to live so as to refute, overcome, or cause to be forgotten (as a mistake, misconduct, slander) ⟨managed to *live* his youthful follies *down*⟩

**live-forever** \ˈ=ˌ==\ *n* -s **1 :** SEDUM 2 **2 :** PEARLY EVERLASTING

**live hole** *n* **:** one of the flues in a clamp of bricks

**live in** *vi* **:** to lodge in one's place of employment — used of a servant

**live·ing·ite** \ˈliviŋ,īt, ˈlīv-\ *n* -s [George D. *Liveing* †1924, Eng. chemist + E *-ite*] **:** a mineral $Pb_8As_8S_{17}$ consisting of a sulfide of arsenic and lead

**liveleaf** *var of* LIFELEAF

**livelihead** *n* [ME *livelihed, livelihede,* fr. *lively* + *-hed, -hede* (var. of *-hod, -had* -hood)] **1** *obs* **:** living presence **:** LIFE **2** *obs* **:** LIVELIHOOD

**live·li·hood** \ˈlīvlē,hu̇d, -vli-,-\ *n* [alter. (influenced by ¹*lively* & *-hood*) of ME *livlod, livelode* course of life, livelihood, fr. OE *līflād* course of life, fr. *līf* life + *lād* course, journey — more at LIFE, LODE] **1 :** means of support or subsistence ⟨even then I had a low opinion of politics as a ~ —W.A.White⟩ ⟨for almost 30 years the inhabitants . . . have obtained their ~ from granite —*Amer. Guide Series: Minn.*⟩ ⟨by canny foraging on farm gardens, the rabbit still maintains a comfortable ~ —*Amer. Guide Series: Va.*⟩ **2** *obs* **:** income-producing property **:** ESTATE, PATRIMONY **3** [¹*lively* + *-hood*] *obs* **:** LIVELINESS
**syn** see LIVING

**live·li·ly** \-lələ̄, -li\ *adv* [¹*lively* + *-ly*] **:** in a lively manner

**live-line** \ˈ=,=\ *vi* [fr. the phrase *live line*] **:** to fish by allowing the bait or lure to drift with the current on a slack line

**live·li·ness** \ˈlīvlēnəs, -lin-\ *n* -ES [ME *livelinesse,* fr. *lively* + *-nesse* -ness] **:** the quality or state of being lively

**live load** *n* **1 :** the load (as furniture and persons) to which a structure is subjected in addition to its own weight not including wind load, earthquake shocks, and such effects as the centrifugal force acting on railroad bridges located on curves, tractive effort, and impact due to sudden application of the load — compare DEAD LOAD **2 :** the weight of passengers or cargo carried by a vehicle

**¹live·long** \ˈliv,=, ˈlīv-\ *adj* [ME *lef long,* fr. *lef* dear + *long* — more at LIEF, LONG] **:** WHOLE, ENTIRE, COMPLETE — usu. used of a period of time ⟨the *livelong* day he sat in his loom, his ear filled with its monotony —George Eliot⟩

**²live·long** \ˈliv,=\ *n* -s [¹*live* + *long* (adv)] **1 :** ORPINE **2 :** PEARLY EVERLASTING

**live·ly** \ˈlīvlē, -li\ *adj, usu* -ER/-EST [ME, fr. OE *līflīc,* fr. *līf* life + *-līc* -ly — more at LIFE] **1** *obs* **:** LIVING **2 :** ANIMATED, VIVID, BRISK, KEEN, VIGOROUS ⟨is a ~ and fluent conversationalist —Arthur Knight⟩ ⟨the school's great tradition of ~ teaching —N.M.Pusey⟩ ⟨two Californians . . . were ~ entries —S.H.Adams⟩ ⟨a Glasgow journalist with a ~ mind and ready wit —Gilbert Harding⟩ **3 :** ACTIVE, INTENSE ⟨a ~ sense of the ludicrous —T.L.Peacock⟩ ⟨roused his *liveliest* disgust —John Buchan⟩ ⟨a ~ trade in farm products —H.E.Starr⟩ **4 :** BRILLIANT, FRESH, GAY ⟨the ~ charm of Florentine and Venetian artists —*Amer. Guide Series: N.Y. City*⟩ ⟨a ~, flashing wit⟩ ⟨it was moist and overgrown with mosses, ferns, creepers, and low shrubs, all of the *liveliest* green —W.H.Hudson †1922⟩ **5 :** ENLIVENING, TANGY **:** not flat **:** SPARKLING ⟨many a peer of England brews *livelier* liquor than the Muse —A.E.Housman⟩ **6 a :** quick to rebound **:** RESILIENT **b** *of a baseball* **:** capable of traveling an excessively great distance when hit ⟨the pitchers know they are throwing that ~ ball —Ted Williams⟩ **c :** riding lightly on the sea **:** responding readily to the helm ⟨a ~ boat⟩ **7 a :** full of life, movement, or incident ⟨the Detroit river . . . surface was ~ with craft of all descriptions —*Amer. Guide Series: Mich.*⟩ **b :** requiring alertness or activity because of danger or opposition ⟨enemy artillery made things ~ for a while⟩ ⟨speakers from across the aisle gave them a ~ time⟩
**syn** ANIMATED, VIVACIOUS, SPRIGHTLY, GAY: LIVELY may suggest briskness, alertness, keenness, or energy ⟨the *liveliest,* the most provocative, and the most curiously informed study of the current political situation . . . written with energy and with racy humor —H.S.Commager⟩ ⟨boomtowns, stomping dances, big talk, hope unlimited, a veritable explosion of moving, building, and moving, kept things *lively* —Russell Lord⟩ ANIMATED is close to LIVELY and may apply to the spirited, sparkling, or quite active ⟨even the hardest of his friends . . . became *animated* when he took her hand, tried to meet the gay challenge in her eyes and to reply cleverly to the droll word of greeting on her lips —Willa Cather⟩ ⟨an *animated* chatter, like the bubbles of champagne made articulate —Joseph Hergesheimer⟩ VIVACIOUS suggests a very active liveliness, often sportive, compelling, or alluring ⟨they began to laugh and play, and turn heels over head, showing themselves jolly and *vivacious* brats —Nathaniel Hawthorne⟩ ⟨remember her as very pretty and *vivacious.* I never met a girl with as much zip as she had in those days —Ring Lardner⟩ SPRIGHTLY, close to VIVACIOUS, may suggest a liveliness that is alert and spirited ⟨the thrill of his enthusiasm made him walk with an elastic step. He was *sprightly,* vigorous, fiery in his belief in success —Stephen Crane⟩ ⟨Mrs. Thomas, *sprightly* again, laughed with Dylan as they recounted old stories the day's visits had recalled, and waved greetings to friends —J.M.Brinnin⟩ GAY suggests demonstrative carefreeness, sometimes marked by merriment or exuberance ⟨three *gay* girls, overflowing with life, health, and youth; and full of spirits and mischief —Herman Melville⟩ ⟨a *gay* world with its country squires and their horses and racing, its Madeira drinking, its promenades and dancing and assemblies —V.L. Parrington⟩

**²lively** \ˈ"\ *adv, usu* -ER/-EST [ME, fr. *lively,* adj.] **:** in a lively manner ⟨now then, step ~ there⟩

**liv·en** \ˈlīvən\ *vb* **livened; livened; livening** \-v(ə)niŋ\ **livens** [²*live* + *-en*] *vt* **:** ENLIVEN — often used with *up* ~ *vi* **:** to become lively or more lively — often used with *up* — **liv·en·er** \-v(ə)nə(r)\ *n* -s

**live·ness** *n* -ES [²*live* + *-ness*] **:** the quality or state of being live; *esp* **:** the reverberant quality of a room

**live oak** *n* **:** any of several American evergreen oaks: as **a :** a medium-sized oak (*Quercus virginiana*) that is native to eastern No. America from Virginia southward to the eastern coast of Mexico, is often cultivated as a shelter and shade tree because of its rapid growth and wide-spreading shapely form, and is noted for its extremely hard tough durable wood once much used in shipbuilding **b :** any of various western No. American oaks (as canyon live oak, coast live oak, interior live oak) with evergreen foliage and hard durable wood

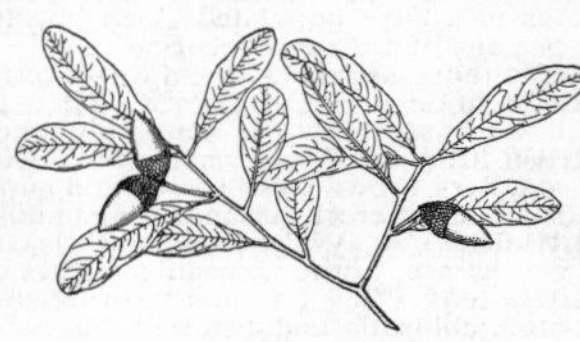
leaves and acorns of live oak

**live-oak·er** \ˈ=ˈōkə(r)\ *n* -s *South* **:** one engaged in live-oak lumbering

**live out** *vi* **:** to lodge elsewhere than where employed — used of a servant

**live parking** *n* **:** the parking of a vehicle with a driver or operator in attendance

**¹liv·er** \ˈlivə(r)\ *n* -s [ME, fr. OE *lifer;* akin to OFris *livere* liver, OHG *lebra,* ON *lifr,* and perh. to Gk *lipos* fat — more at LEAVE] **1 a :** a large very vascular glandular organ of vertebrates that secretes bile and causes important changes in many of the substances contained in the blood which passes through it (as by converting sugars into glycogen which it stores up until required and in forming urea), in man being the largest gland, from 40 to 60 ounces in weight, of a dark red color, occupying the upper right portion of the abdominal cavity immediately below the diaphragm to whose curvature its upper surface conforms, being divided by fissures into five lobes, and receiving blood both from the hepatic artery and the portal vein and returning it to the systemic circulation by the hepatic veins — see DIGESTION illustration **b :** any of various large compound glands associated with the digestive tract of invertebrate animals and prob. concerned with the secretion of digestive enzymes **2** *archaic* **:** the liver regarded as determining the quality or temper of a man ⟨hot ~s and cold purses —Shak.⟩ — compare WHITE-LIVERED **3 :** the liver of an animal (as a calf or pig) eaten as food by man **4 :** disease or disorder of the liver; *esp* **:** BILIOUSNESS ⟨had a touch of ~ —Christopher Isherwood⟩ **5** *or* **liver brown** *or* **liver maroon :** a grayish reddish brown that is redder and deeper than average taupe brown — called also *autumn oak* **6 :** a liver-colored substance (as any of several sulfur compounds) — called also *hepar*

**²liver** \ˈ"\ *adj* **:** of a dark chestnut color — used esp. of horses and dogs

**³liver** \ˈ"\ *vi* **livered; livered; livering** \-v(ə)riŋ\ **livers :** to become thick and rubbery like liver **:** GEL — used esp. of paints, varnishes, and printing inks

**⁴liver** \ˈ"\ *vt* -ED/-ING/-S [ME *liveren,* partly fr. OF *livrer,* fr. L *liberare* to free; partly short for ME *deliveren* — more at LIBERATE, DELIVER] *now dial Eng* **:** DELIVER

**⁵liver** \ˈlivə\ *n* -s [ME, fr. *liven* to live + *-er*] **1 :** one that lives esp. in a specified way ⟨my father was a good ~ —W.A. White⟩ ⟨the typical American cheap ~ abroad —Herbert Gold⟩ ⟨the grossest of evil ~s —W.J.Locke⟩ **2 :** RESIDENT

**⁶liver** *comparative of* LIVE

**liverberry** \ˈ==-— *see* BERRY\ *n* **1 :** TWISTED-STALK **2 :** the fruit of twisted-stalk

**liver cell** *n* **:** one of the secretory cells characteristic of the liver

**liv·ered** \ˈlivə(r)d\ *adj* [¹*liver* + *-ed*] **:** having a liver of a specified character — usu. used in combination ⟨lily-*livered*⟩

**liver extract** *n* **:** an extract of the water-soluble constituents of fresh mammalian liver used in treatment of anemia

**liver fluke** *n* **:** any of various trematodes (as *Fasciola hepatica*) that invade the mammalian liver — compare AMERICAN FLUKE, CHINESE LIVER FLUKE

**liver fungus** *n* **:** BEEFSTEAK FUNGUS

**liv·er·ied** \ˈliv(ə)rēd, -rid\ *adj* [*livery* + *-ed*] **:** wearing a livery

**livering** *n* -s [ME *levering,* fr. *lever, liver* liver + *-ing* — more at LIVER] *obs* **:** a pudding or sausage of liver

**liv·er·ish** \ˈliv(ə)rish\ *adj* **1 :** like liver esp. in color ⟨arabesques of a ~ bronzy hue —Mary Austin⟩ **2 a :** suffering from liver disorder **:** BILIOUS ⟨looked pretty ~ but was all right next morning⟩ ⟨was feeling ~⟩ **b :** causing biliousness ⟨and Turkish coffee which though ~ stuff he always drank —John Galsworthy⟩ **c :** seeming or acting bilious **:** CRABBED, MELANCHOLY ⟨a gloomy, ~ sort of man —P.B.Kyne⟩ — **liv·er·ish·ness** *n* -ES

**liverleaf** \ˈ==,=\ *n* **:** HEPATICA 1b

**liv·er·less** \-ləs\ *adj* **1 :** lacking a liver **2 :** deficient in liver function or in courage or temper

**liver lily** *n* **:** an iris (*Iris versicolor*) of the eastern U. S.

**liver line** *n, usu cap 1st L* **:** LINE OF MERCURY

**liver maroon** *n* **:** LIVER 5

**liver of antimony** *archaic* **:** a brown powder obtained by heating an antimony sulfide with an alkaline sulfide

**liver of sulfur :** SULFURATED POTASH

**liver oil** *n* **:** a fatty oil obtained from liver; *usu* **:** FISH-LIVER OIL

**liv·er·pool** \ˈlivə(r),pül\ *adj, usu cap* [fr. *Liverpool,* England] **1 :** of or from the city of Liverpool, England **:** of the kind or style prevalent in Liverpool **2 :** of or relating to a usu. white or cream-colored ceramic ware made in Liverpool potteries beginning in the early 18th century

**liver·pool bit** *n, usu cap L* **:** a curb bit with a straight shank

**liverpool rummy** *n, usu cap L* **:** a card game of the contract rummy group

**¹liv·er·pud·li·an** \ˌlivə(r)ˈpədlēən\ *adj, usu cap* [*Liverpudl-* (alter. — influenced by *puddle* — of *Liverpool,* England) + E *-ian*] **1 :** of, relating to, or characteristic of Liverpool, England **2 :** of, relating to, or characteristic of the people of Liverpool

**²liverpudlian** \ˈ"\ *n* -s *cap* **:** a native or inhabitant of Liverpool

**liver rot** *n* **:** a disease that is caused by liver flukes esp. in sheep and cattle and is marked by sluggishness, anemia, and wasting and by great local damage to the liver due to the presence of the worms and their by-products — compare BLACK DISEASE

**livers** *pl of* LIVER, *pres 3d sing of* LIVER

**liver sausage** *or* **liver pudding** *n* **:** a sausage consisting of cooked ground liver and lean pork trimmings seasoned with condiments and herbs and stuffed into casings and boiled or smoked

**liver spots** *n pl* **:** CHLOASMA

**liverwort** \ˈ==,=\ *n* **1 :** a bryophyte of the class Hepaticae **2 :** HEPATICA 1b

**liverwort lettuce** *n* **:** FALSE WINTERGREEN

**liv·er·wurst** *R* ˈlivə(r),wərst, -,wu̇rst, *-R* -,wōst, -,wu̇əst, *R & -R* -,wu̇st *also* -,wə(r)st *sometimes* -,wu̇sht\ *n* -s [part trans. of G *leberwurst,* fr. *leber* liver + *wurst* sausage — more at BRATWURST] **:** LIVER SAUSAGE

**¹liv·ery** \ˈliv(ə)rē, -ri\ *n* -ES [ME *livere,* fr. OF *livree,* lit., distribution, delivery, fr. fem. of *livré,* past part. of *livrer* to deliver — more at LIVER] **1** *archaic* **:** the apportioning of provisions esp. to servants or the rations so given **2 a :** the distinctive clothing or badge formerly given by a person of rank or wealth to be worn by his retainers esp. in wartime service **b :** LIVERY COLOR 1 **c liveries** *pl, in Scottish heraldry* **:** LIVERY COLOR 2a **d :** a servant's uniform ⟨a chauffeur in ~⟩ **e :** distinctive dress (as of an organization, profession, occupation) ⟨the ~ of the guild members⟩ ⟨the sisters wear a white habit and scapular with a black veil, the ~ of St. Dominic —T.P. McCarthy⟩ **:** CLOTHES, GARB, GARMENTS ⟨if he can dress his endeavors in the ~ of patriotism, . . . he can cover the scandals of his own character —J.A.Froude⟩ **f :** LIVERY COMPANY **3** *archaic* **a :** one's retainers or retinue **b :** the members of a British livery company **4 a** *obs* **:** the ration of provender given a horse **b :** the feeding, stabling, and care of horses for pay **:** BOARDING **c :** a stable keeping horses and usu. carriages for hire **d :** a concern offering vehicles of any of various kinds for rent ⟨a canoe ~⟩ ⟨an automobile ~⟩ ⟨a bicycle ~⟩ **5 a :** the act of delivering legal possession of property (as lands or tenements) — compare GRANT 3a, LIVERY OF SEIZIN **b** *Eng law* (1) **:** the delivery of the possession of lands released from a court dealing with wardships (2) **:** the writ by which such possession is obtained

**²livery** \ˈ"\ *adj* **1 :** issued as livery **2 :** constituting livery ⟨a chauffeur's visored ~ cap⟩ **3 :** kept for hire ⟨~ limousines⟩

**³livery** \ˈ"\ *adj* [¹*liver* + *-y*] **1 a :** resembling liver **b :** suggesting liver disorder **:** LIVERISH ⟨he returned a captain, unwounded, but thin and yellow, with the ~ look that confirmed the stories —Edna Ferber⟩ **2 :** HEAVY, CLINGING, GUMMY — used of soil ⟨heavy soil plows up in ~ slices in winter —F.D. Smith & Barbara Wilcox⟩

**livery color** *n* **1 :** the color or one of the colors of the clothing issued by a feudal superior to his retainers or by a person of wealth or rank to his servants **2 livery colors** *pl* **a :** the principal metal and the principal color of an escutcheon of arms often used also as the principal colors of a flag or ensign or of a personal standard as well as of the liveries of the armiger's servants **b :** the principal colors of the flag of a political unit (as a nation) sometimes not identical with its armorial colors **:** the national or civic colors

**livery company** *n* **:** any of various London craft or trade associations that are descended from medieval guilds

**livery cupboard** *n* **:** a free-standing cupboard used for the storage of food and drink esp. in the middle ages

**livery·man** \ˈ=(=)=mən\ *n, pl* **livery·men** \-mən, -,men\ **1** *archaic* **:** a liveried retainer **2 :** a freeman of the city of London entitled to wear the livery of the company to which he belongs and to enjoy other privileges (as to vote for some of the chief London municipal officials) **3 :** the keeper of a vehicle-rental service

**livery of seizin** *Eng law* **:** a now disused ceremony for conveyance of land by the symbolic transfer of a key, twig, or turf or by symbolic entry of the grantee

**livery stable** *n* **:** a stable where horses and vehicles are kept for hire and where stabling is provided

**¹lives** *pl of* LIFE, *pres 3d sing of* LIVE

**²lives** \ˈlivz\ *North var of* LIEF

**live-sawed** \ˈ=ˈ=\ *adj* **:** sawed through without being turned — used of a log

**livest** *superlative of* LIVE

**live steam** *n* **:** steam direct from a boiler and under full pressure

**livestock** \ˈ=,=\ *n* **:** animals of any kind kept or raised for use or pleasure; *esp* **:** meat and dairy cattle and draft animals — opposed to *dead stock*

**live storage** *n* **:** storage of property permitting use at will by the owner

**liv·e·tin** \ˈlivəd·ən\ *n* -s [anagram of *vitellin*] **:** a protein obtained from egg yolk

**live trap** *n* **:** a trap for catching an animal alive and uninjured

**livetrap** \ˈ=,=\ *vt* [*live trap*] **:** to capture (an animal) with a live trap (as for removal to another area for restocking)

**liveweight** \ˈ=ˈ=\ *n* **:** the weight of an animal while living

**live well** *n* **1 :** a well for keeping fish alive in a fishing boat by allowing seawater to circulate through it **2 :** LIVE-BOX

**live wire** *n* **1 :** an energized electrical conductor **2 :** an alert, active, aggressive person ⟨a *live wire,* full of American know-how —C.W.Mills⟩

**liveyere** *var of* LIVYER

**liv·id** \ˈlivəd\ *adj* [F *livide,* fr. L *lividus,* fr. *livēre* to be blue; akin to OIr *lī* color, W *lliw* color, OE *slāh* sloe, OHG *slēha* sloe, Russ *sliva* plum] **1 :** discolored by or as if by bruising **:** BLACK-AND-BLUE ⟨~ flesh⟩ **2 :** of the color lead — compare LIVID BROWN, LIVID PINK, LIVID PURPLE, LIVID VIOLET **3 :** ASHEN, PALLID, GHASTLY, GRAY ⟨as I imprinted the first kiss on her lips, they became ~ with the hue of death —Mary W. Shelley⟩ **4 :** LURID ⟨world of sideshow freaks among whom he has a large and rather ~ acquaintance —J.S.Sandoe⟩ — **li·vid·i·ty** \lə'vidəd·ē, -ətē, -i\ *n* -ES — **liv·id·ness** *n* -ES

**livid brown** *n* **:** a grayish red that is bluer and less strong than bois de rose, yellower and paler than blush rose, and bluer and duller than Pompeian red

**liv·id·ly** *adv* **:** in a livid manner

**livid pink** *n* **:** a grayish pink

**livid purple** *n* **:** a grayish reddish purple that is redder and duller than heather (sense 2a) and deeper than Campanula violet

**livid violet** *n* **:** a light grayish red that is bluer and very slightly lighter than ashes of rose

**liv·ier** \ˈlivyə(r), -vēə-\ *n* -s [prob. fr. *lives* (pl. of *life*) + *-ier*] *dial Eng* **:** the holder of a lease granted for one or more lifetimes

**¹liv·ing** \ˈliviŋ\ *adj* [ME, fr. pres. part. of *liven* to live — more at LIVE] **1 a :** having life **:** not dead ⟨all ~ things by definition have irritability and response —Weston LaBarre⟩ ⟨swore by the ~ God that he spoke truth⟩ ⟨the skin is a ~ tissue —Morris Fishbein⟩ ⟨and he stood between the dead and the ~; and the plague was stopped —Num 16: 48 (RSV)⟩ **b :** now or still having life **:** CONTEMPORARY, SURVIVING ⟨not in the memory of ~ men had such another opportunity offered⟩ ⟨the ~ orders of insects⟩ **c :** ACTIVE, EFFECTIVE, FUNCTIONING, PRODUCTIVE, VITAL ⟨the past of mankind . . . abides as a ~ reality in our present —P.E.More⟩ ⟨educators who think of the liberal-arts tradition in a ~ and creative fashion —H.D. Gideonse⟩ ⟨a suffix that continues to form new compounds remains ~ in the language⟩ **2 a :** exhibiting the life or motion of nature or its life-giving powers ⟨it was a land of high, rolling prairies, wide valleys, and sweet ~ water —F.B.Gipson⟩ ⟨drinking this champagne water is pure pleasure, so is breathing the ~ air —John Muir †1914⟩ ⟨the happy ~ sunlight —Edith Sitwell⟩ **b :** BURNING ⟨then on the ~ coals red wine they pour —John Dryden⟩ **3 :** remaining uncut or unquarried **:** NATIVE ⟨in places the track was hewn out of the ~ rock —*Geog. Jour.*⟩ **4 a :** full of life or vigor **:** LIVELY ⟨visualized anatomy as a ~ subject —H.R.Viets⟩ **b :** true to life or reality **:** VIVID ⟨no mere historical curiosity but a ~ and moving work of art —Edward Sackville-West⟩ ⟨seek through the flesh: you will not find the ~ likeness of the mind —D.C. Babcock⟩ **c :** animated by thought or purpose bearing directly on life **:** vitally inspired or relevant **:** moved or formed by significant aims ⟨a working library, a ~ library —Virginia Woolf⟩ **5 :** appropriate, designed, or adequate for living ⟨rug and wood paneling define the ~ area —Edgar Kaufmann⟩ **6 :** having or using live performers (as actors or musicians) rather than mechanical recordings ⟨baffled in the effort to detect the ~ performance from the . . . record —R.D.Darrell⟩ ⟨there would be a renaissance of the ~ theater —*Theatre Arts*⟩ **7 :** VERY — used as an intensive ⟨history . . . scares the ~ daylights out of school kids —*Nicholas County (W. Va.) News Leader*⟩ ⟨beat the ~ tar out of him⟩

**²living** \ˈ"\ *n* -s [ME, fr. gerund of *liven*] **1 :** the condition of being alive or the action of a being that has life ⟨~ in the same house became impossible⟩ ⟨the ascetic with a passion for ~ —H.S.Canby⟩ **2 :** the passing of one's life in a particular way **:** conduct or manner of life ⟨the art of ~ is thus recognized as a subject which concerns everyone —Herbert Spencer⟩ ⟨the collegiate way of ~ —J.B.Conant⟩ ⟨utter impatience with totalitarian ~ —G.P.Musselman⟩ ⟨was conspicuous for loose ~⟩ **3 a :** means of subsistence **:** LIVELIHOOD ⟨we both earn our ~s —Virginia Woolf⟩ ⟨bees, too, are here . . . getting a ~ among the blue flowers of the sea holly —Robert Lynd⟩ **b** *archaic* **:** an estate or income-producing property **c** *Brit* **:** ¹BENEFICE 1 ⟨the diaries of clergymen in quiet country ~s —*Sydney (Australia) Bull.*⟩
**syn** LIVELIHOOD, SUBSISTENCE, SUSTENANCE, MAINTENANCE, SUPPORT, KEEP, BREAD, OR BREAD AND BUTTER: LIVING is general in meaning but is now limited to use in a few idioms ⟨to make a *living* selling books⟩ ⟨to take a *living* from the soil⟩ LIVELIHOOD often applies to the wages, salary, or income from which one lives or to the profession or craft whereby one earns his wages or salary ⟨provided with a modest *livelihood*⟩ ⟨while the profession is of necessity a means of *livelihood* or of financial reward, the devoted service which it inspires is motivated by other considerations —R.M.MacIver⟩ ⟨stock raising is his *livelihood*⟩ ⟨education is a preparation for life, not merely for a

livelihood, for living not for *a* living —George Sampson⟩ SUBSISTENCE suggests living with only the barest necessities ⟨*subsistence* wages are the lowest needed to sustain life⟩ ⟨if he could raise enough corn and pork for *subsistence*, he cared for nothing more —*Amer. Guide Series: N.C.*⟩ SUSTENANCE applies to whatever sustains life; it ranges from indicating food and other necessities for bare subsistence to more liberal provision ⟨the purely *sustenance* type of farming in which the farmer merely supplies his own needs —Samuel Van Valkenburg and Ellsworth Huntington⟩ ⟨Irish parents who had come to this country in search of more *sustenance* than they could glean from the barren soil of Connemara —Russel Crouse⟩ MAINTENANCE applies to a complex of necessities like food, lodging, clothing, and cleaning or to money sufficient to provide them ⟨*maintenance* for his separated wife⟩ ⟨the hospital had advertised for a general resident doctor at $300 a month and *maintenance* —Greer Williams⟩ ⟨monthly allowances to parents for the *maintenance*, care, training, education, and advancement of the child —*Current Biog.*⟩ SUPPORT may apply to means of maintenance or to the person who provides the means ⟨his scanty wages are his parent's sole *support*⟩ KEEP is a somewhat colloquial synonym for MAINTENANCE and is applicable to animals as well as persons ⟨hired men could no longer be had for ten or fifteen dollars a month and *keep* —W.A.White⟩ BREAD and BREAD AND BUTTER are synecdoches for LIVING or SUSTENANCE ⟨give us this day our daily *bread* Mt 6: 11 (RSV)⟩ ⟨earning one's *bread and butter* at the mill⟩

**living death** *n* **:** life emptied of joys and satisfactions **:** extreme wretchedness ⟨what happened . . . at the Nazi camp adds little to the all too familiar *living-death* literature —*Time*⟩

**living fossil** *n* **:** an animal or plant (as the king crab or the gingko tree) that has remained essentially unchanged from earlier geologic times and whose near relatives are usu. extinct — compare RELICT

**living language** *n* **:** a language in use as a vernacular ⟨any world language must be a *living language* —Charlton Laird⟩

**liv·ing·ly** *adv* [ME, fr. *living* + *-ly*] **:** VITALLY, REALISTICALLY

**liv·ing·ness** *n* -ES [¹*living* + *-ness*] **:** VITALITY, VIGOR, VIVIDNESS ⟨what he likes in nature is perhaps more than anything else the mere sense of ~ —J.W.Beach⟩ ⟨his memory stored up an amazing gallery of faces and figures, and he got these down with supreme ~ —Sheldon Cheney⟩

**living newspaper** *n* **:** a theatrical presentation often using a medley of techniques (as staged and filmed episodes) to dramatize social and economic problems — compare EPIC DRAMA

**living picture** *n* **:** TABLEAU, PANTOMIME

**living pledge** *n* **:** the transfer of possession of an estate to a lender to be held by him until the debt is paid out of the rents and profits — compare MORTGAGE

**living rock** *n* **1 :** MESCAL 1 **2 :** a cactus (*Ariocarpus fissuratus*) of the southwestern U.S. and adjacent Mexico that resembles the related mescal

**living room** *n* **1 :** a room in a residence used for the common social activities of the occupants — compare DRAWING ROOM, PARLOR, SITTING ROOM **2 :** space in which to live **:** LEBENSRAUM ⟨surplus populations would demand *living room* —W.P. Webb⟩

**living space** *n* **1 :** territory needed or sought for occupation by a nation whose population is expanding **:** LEBENSRAUM ⟨countries which had the doubtful honor of being regarded as belonging to Germany's *living space* —Paul Einzig⟩ **2 :** habitable space in a dwelling ⟨only actual rooms can be called *living space* —J.R.Dalzell⟩

**living standard** *n* **:** STANDARD OF LIVING ⟨to provide a minimum *living standard* for our 150 million people —M.S.Eccles⟩

**living stone** *n* **:** LITHOPS 2

**liv·ing·ston·ite** \ˈliviŋstə‚nīt\ *n* -S [David *Livingstone* †1873 Scot. missionary and explorer + E *-ite*] **:** a mineral $HgSb_4S_7$ consisting of a lead-gray mercury antimony sulfide resembling stibnite

**living trust** *n* **:** a trust created by the transfer of property by its owner to a living or existing person to hold as trustee **:** a trust inter vivos — compare TESTAMENTARY TRUST

**living unit** *n* **:** an apartment or house for use by one family

**living wage** *n* **1 :** a subsistence wage **2 :** a wage sufficient to provide the necessities and comforts held to comprise an acceptable standard of living

**liv·i·sto·na** \‚livə'stōnə\ *n, cap* [NL, fr. *Liviston*, estate near Edinburgh, Scotland] **:** a genus of Asiatic, Malaysian, and Australian fan palms — see CHINESE FAN PALM

**¹li·vo·ni·an** \lə'vōnēən, -nyən\ *adj, usu cap* [*Livonia*, district in Latvia + E *-an*] **1 a :** of, relating to, or characteristic of Livonia **b :** of, relating to, or characteristic of the people of Livonia **2 :** of, belonging to, or in the Livonian language

**²livonian** \"\ *n* -S *cap* **1 :** a native or inhabitant of Livonia **2 :** a Finno-Ugric language of the Livonian people — see URALIC LANGUAGES table

**li·vor** \ˈlī‚vȯ(ə)r, -‚vər\ *n* -S [L, fr. *livēre* to be blue + *-or* — more at LIVID] **1** *obs* **:** MALIGNITY, SPITE **2** *archaic* **:** livid condition

**li·vrai·son** \‚lēvrā¦zōⁿ\ *n* -S [F, lit., delivery, fr. OF, fr. L *liberation-, liberatio* action of freeing — more at LIBERATION] **:** FASCICLE 2

**li·vre** \ˈlēvə(r), -vr(ᵊ), -v(rə)\ *n* -S [F, fr. L *libra* balance, unit of weight] **1 :** a former French unit of value worth a pound of silver in the reign of Charlemagne **2** *or* **livre tour·nois** \-tu̇rn'wä\ **:** the livre of Tours that from 1667 until replaced by the franc in 1795 was the only legal French livre and consisted of 20 sous of 12 deniers each

**liv·yer** \ˈlivyər\ *or* **live·yere** \(ˈ)liv¦ye(ə)r\ *n* -S [alter. of *livier*] **:** a permanent settler of northeastern Canada who lives by trapping, trading, or fishing

**li·wa** \ˈlēwə\ *n* -S [Ar *liwā'*] **:** a large administrative district in any of several Muslim countries

**lix·iv·i·al** \(ˈ)lik¦sivēəl\ *adj* [*lixivium* + *-al*] *archaic* **:** relating to or like lixivium **:** obtained by lixiviation **:** ALKALINE

**lix·iv·i·ate** \-vē‚āt, *usu* -ād.+V\ *vt* -ED/-ING/-S [*lixivium* + *-ate*] **:** to extract a soluble compound from (a solid mixture) by washing or percolation **:** LEACH

**lix·iv·i·a·tion** \(‚)=‚=ˈāshən\ *n* -S **:** the process of lixiviating **:** PERCOLATION

**lix·iv·i·ous** \(ˈ)=¦sivēəs\ *adj* [L *lixivius* made of lye, fr. *lixa* lye, water + *-ivus* -ive — more at LIQUID] *archaic* **:** LIXIVIAL

**lix·iv·i·um** \=ˈ=ēəm\ *n, pl* **lixiv·ia** \-ēə\ *or* **lixiviums** [LL, lye, fr. neut. of L *lixivius*] *archaic* **:** a solution (as lye) obtained by lixiviation

**liz·ard** \ˈlizə(r)d\ *n* -S [ME *lesard, liserd*, fr. MF *laisarde*, fr. L *lacerta* — more at LEG] **1 a :** any member of the suborder Lacertilia of the reptilian order Squamata characterized in distinction from the snakes by a fused inseparable lower jaw, a single temporal opening, two pairs of well differentiated functional limbs which may be lacking in burrowing forms, external ears, and eyes with movable lids and having a scaly or tuberculate skin, replaceable teeth that lack true sockets and are fused to the ridge of the jaw in agamid lizards and the chameleons and to the side of the jaw in most other lizards — compare ACRODONT, GILA MONSTER, PLEURODONT **b :** any relatively long-bodied reptile with legs and tapering tail (as a crocodile or dinosaur) **c :** a similarly shaped amphibian (as a newt or salamander) **2 :** a domestic greenish bronze canary with a yellow crown and scaly-appearing plumage **3 :** ALLIGATOR 6b **4** *or* **lizard green :** a moderate green that is yellower and paler than sea green (sense 1a) and lighter and slightly bluer than laurel green (sense 1) **5 :** a rope with a thimble or block spliced into one or both of the ends used as a fairlead in handling a ship's rigging **6** *usu cap* **:** ALABAMIAN — used as a nickname **7 :** leather made from lizard skin **8 :** LOUNGE LIZARD ⟨the lonely wives and the ~*s* with the thin mustaches —Willard Robertson⟩

typical lizard

**lizard bronze** *n* **:** OLD MOSS

**lizard fish** *n* **:** any of various slender marine fishes having a scaly head like that of a lizard and a large mouth and constituting the family Synodontidae

**lizard flower** *or* **lizard orchis** *n* **:** any of several European plants of the genus *Orchis*

**lizard's-tail** \ˈ==‚=\ *n, pl* **lizard's-tails :** a No. American herbaceous perennial plant (*Saururus cernuus*) with small white apetalous flowers — called also *breastweed*

lizard's-tail

**lizard's-tail family** *n* **:** SAURURACEAE

**lizardtail** \ˈ==‚=\ *n* **1 :** LIZARD'S-TAIL **2 :** a Californian white-woolly herb (*Eriophyllum stoechadifolium*) of the family Compositae with yellow flowers

**lizari** *or* **lizary** *var of* ALIZARI

**liz·zie** \ˈlizē, -zi\ *n* -S [(*tin*) *lizzie*] *slang* **:** a small and relatively inexpensive automobile

**LJ** *abbr* lord justice

**LJJ** *abbr* lords justices

**lju·blja·na** \lē¦üblē¦änə, lē'üblēə‚nä\ *adj, usu cap* [fr. *Ljubljana*, Yugoslavia] **:** of or from the city of Ljubljana, Yugoslavia **:** of the kind or style prevalent in Ljubljana

**lkg** *abbr* leakage

**lkr** *abbr* locker

**¹'ll** \(ə)l, ᵊl\ *vb* [by contr.] **:** SHALL, WILL ⟨I'*ll* leave it to you —Noel Coward⟩ ⟨you'*ll* remember —Anne Brooks⟩ ⟨when'*ll* he go⟩

**²'ll** \ᵊl\ *conj* [by contr.] **:** TILL ⟨wait'*ll* he leaves⟩

**LL** *abbr* **1** large letter **2** leased line **3** lending library **4** limited liability **5** live load **6** *often not cap* [L *loco laudato*] in the place cited **7** loose leaf **8** lord lieutenant **9** lower left

**ll** *abbr* **1** leaves **2** [L *leges*] laws **3** lines

**lla·ma** \ˈlämə, ˈyä-\ *n, pl* **llamas** *also* **llama** [Sp, fr. Quechua] **1 :** any of several wild and domesticated So. American ruminants related to the camels but smaller and without a hump; *specif* **:** the domesticated variety of the guanaco that is about three feet high at the shoulder with a coat of long coarse woolly hair varying in color from black to white and that has been used for centuries in the Andes as a beast of burden and a source of wool — compare ALPACA, VICUÑA **2 :** cloth made from the llama's hair

**llan·dei·lo** \lan'dī(‚)lō\ *adj, usu cap* [fr. *Llandeilo*, subdivision of the European Ordovician, fr. *Llandeilo*, So. Wales] **:** of or relating to a subdivision of the European Ordovician — see GEOLOGIC TIME table

**llan·do·ve·ri·an** \‚landə¦virēən\ *adj, usu cap* [fr. *Llandoverian*, subdivision of the European Silurian, fr. *Llandovery*, Wales + E *-ian*] **:** of or relating to a subdivision of the European Silurian — see GEOLOGIC TIME table

**lla·ne·ro** \lä'ne(‚)rō, yä-\ *n* -S [Sp, fr. *llano* + *-ero* -er] **:** a cowboy or herdsman in Spanish America

**lla·no** \ˈlä(‚)nō, ˈla(-, ˈyä(-\ *n, pl* **llanos** [Sp, plain, fr. L *planum*, fr. neut. of *planus* level, flat — more at FLOOR] **:** an extensive plain in Spanish America or southwestern U.S. generally with few trees — compare CAMPO

**llan·virn** \(ˈ)lan¦vi(ə)rn, -¦vərn\ *adj, usu cap* [fr. *Llanvirn*, subdivision of the European Ordovician] **:** of or relating to a subdivision of the European Ordovician — see GEOLOGIC TIME table

**lla·re·ta** \yə'rād·ə\ *n* [Sp, fr. Quechua *yareta*] **:** YARETA

**llau·tu** \ˈlau̇(‚)tü\ *n* -S [Sp *llautu, llauto*, fr. Quechua *lláutu*] **:** a fringed cord of vicuña wool worn wound about the head by ancient Peruvians as an emblem of nobility

**LLB** *abbr or n* -S [NL *legum baccalaureus*] **:** a bachelor of laws

**LLD** *abbr or n* -S [NL *legum doctor*] **:** a doctor of laws

**l level** *n, usu cap 1st L* **:** the energy level of an electron in the L-shell

**llew·el·lin setter** \lü'elən-, lə'wel\ *n, usu cap L* [after R.L. Purcell-*Llewellin*, 19th cent. Eng. dog breeder] **:** a strain of English setter noted for its field-trial performance

**LLI** *abbr* latitude and longitude indicator

**LLJJ** *abbr* lords justices

**LLM** *abbr or n* -S [NL *legum magister*] **:** a master of laws

**lloyd–geor·gian** \¦lȯid¦jȯrj(ē)ən\ *also* **lloyd–george·ite** \-ȯr‚jīt\ *adj, usu cap L&G* [David *Lloyd George* †1945 British statesman + E *-ian* or *-ite*] **:** of or associated with the statesman David Lloyd George or his policies

**lloyd's bushtit** \ˈlȯidz-\ *n, usu cap L* [fr. the name *Lloyd*] **:** a gray black-marked bushtit (*Psaltritus minimus lloydi*) of the southwestern U.S. and adjacent Mexico

**LLR** *abbr* line of least resistance

**llyn** \ˈlin\ *n* -S [W — more at LINN] **:** a lake or pool in Wales

**LM** *abbr* **1** land mine **2** long meter **3** lord mayor

**lm** *abbr* lumen

**LMD** *abbr* long meter double

**LMG** *abbr* light machine gun

**lmn** *abbr* lineman

**lmt** *abbr* limit

**LMT** *abbr* **1** length, mass, time **2** local mean time

**LMTD** *abbr* logarithmic mean temperature difference

**ln** *symbol* natural logarithm

**Ln** *symbol* lanthanide

**ln** *abbr* **1** lane **2** lien **3** loan

**LNC** *abbr* local naval commander

**LND** *abbr* limiting nose dive

**lng** *abbr* lining

**¹lo** \ˈlō\ *interj* [ME, fr. OE *lā*] — used to call attention ⟨~, all ye miserable sinners . . . hearken unto my words —Harold Fleming⟩ or to express wonder or surprise ⟨pulled aside the napkin and ~, there were roses —Gladys B. Stern⟩

**²lo** \"\ *n* -S *usu cap* [¹*lo*, taken as a proper name in the phrase *Lo, the poor Indian* in *Essay on Man* I, 99, by Alexander Pope †1744, Eng. poet] **:** a No. American Indian ⟨appeared again at the head of our train in the company of thirty or forty other *Los* —G.W.Perrie⟩

**LO** *abbr* **1** liaison officer **2** lubricating oil

**lo** *abbr* lord

**¹loa** \ˈlōə\ *n* [NL, of African origin; akin to Kongo *lowa, loba* eye worm] **1** *cap* **:** a genus of African filarial worms (family Dipetalonematidae) infecting the subcutaneous tissues and blood of man, transmitted by the bite of flies of the genus *Chrysops*, and associated with urticarial and other allergic manifestations — compare CALABAR SWELLING; see EYE WORM **2** -S **:** any worm of the genus *Loa*

**²loa** \lə'wä\ *n, pl* **loa** *or* **loas** [Haitian Creole *lwa*] **:** a Haitian voodoo cult deity of African origin

**LOA** *abbr* length over all

**loach** \ˈlōch\ *n* -ES [ME *loche, loch*, fr. MF *loche*] **:** any of a family (Cobitidae) of small Old World freshwater fishes closely related to the Cyprinidae but resembling catfishes in appearance and habits

**¹load** \ˈlōd\ *n* -S [ME *lod, lood* act of loading, load (influenced in meaning by *laden* to load), fr. OE *lād* course, way, journey, carrying, support — more at LADE, LODE] **1 :** an item or collection of things, material, animals, or passengers carried: **a :** whatever is put on a man or pack animal to be carried **:** PACK ⟨the supply men hiked their ~*s* up on their shoulders —Burgess Scott⟩ **b :** whatever is put in a ship or vehicle or airplane for conveyance **:** a collection of freight or passengers **:** CARGO ⟨one more stop before he finished delivering his ~⟩; *specif* **:** a quantity of material assembled or packed as a shipping unit sometimes with a specified character or arrangement ⟨each ~ of 50 disks is packaged in a . . . glass vial —*Modern Packaging*⟩ ⟨a car with a transverse ~⟩ **c** (1) **:** the quantity that can be or customarily is carried at one time by an often specified means of conveyance ⟨a dump truck with a full ~ of sand⟩; *specif* **:** a measured quantity of a commodity fixed for each type of carrier ⟨a ~ of plain tiles is 1000 —*Gregory's Handbook for Australian Builders*⟩ — often used in combination ⟨a boat*load* of tourists⟩ ⟨an arm*load* of bundles⟩ ⟨arrived by the jeep*load*⟩ (2) *Midland* **:** an armful esp. of firewood **d :** the mineral matter transported by a stream as visible sediment or in solution **2 a :** a mass or weight supported by something ⟨a roof sagging under its ~ of snow⟩ ⟨branches bent low by their ~ of fruit⟩ **b :** the forces to which a structure is subjected because of weights carried on the supports or the overturning moments to which a structure is subjected by wind pressure on the vertical surfaces ⟨the external forces, or ~*s*, to which a roof truss is subjected consist of the weights of materials of construction, snow, ice, and wind pressure together with the reactions developed at the supports as a result of these ~*s* —F.E.Kidder & Harry Parker⟩ ⟨the most accurate way of determining the full ~ on each tire is to weigh each axle of a fully loaded truck —*Armstrong Tires Data Bk.*⟩ — see DEAD LOAD, LIVE LOAD **c :** the amount of stress put on something ⟨the ~ on a glued joint⟩ ⟨this normal instinctive fear which adds its ~ to the burden of the nervous system —H.G.Armstrong⟩ **3 :** something borne or conveyed in a manner suggesting a material load: as **a :** something that weighs down the mind or spirits ⟨a ~ of care⟩ ⟨took a great ~ off his mind⟩ **b :** a burdensome or laborious responsibility ⟨carry his share of the ~ in a democratic society —*Bull. of Bates Coll.*⟩ ⟨his heavy ~ of day-to-day work —*N.Y.Times*⟩ **c :** the content of thought or feeling carried (as by a piece of writing) ⟨a work which has acquired an enormous ~ of sentimental values —Hunter Mead⟩ **4** *slang* **:** an intoxicating amount of liquor drunk **:** a state of intoxication ⟨he'd come in with a small ~ on, but he was never really high —Roderick Lull⟩ **5 :** a large quantity **:** LOT — usu. used in pl. ⟨a singing comedienne with . . . ~*s* of energy —*New Yorker*⟩ **6 a :** a charge or cartridge for a firearm: (1) **:** a charge of powder (2) **:** a charge of shot in a shotshell (3) **:** a fully loaded cartridge **b :** the quantity of material loaded into a device or machine at one time ⟨a washer that takes a 10 pound ~⟩ ⟨put three ~*s* through the dryer⟩ **7 :** external resistance overcome by a machine or prime mover ⟨at all ~*s* less than full capacity, the turbine operates at better efficiency with individual nozzle control — B.G.A.Skrotzki & W.A.Vopat⟩ **8 a :** power output (as of an engine, motor, power plant, or source of electric current) or power consumed (as by a device or circuit) **b :** a device or group of devices to which power is delivered **9 :** something (as a railway freight car) that contains a load ⟨a train of thirty empties and ten ~*s* —Elton Brown⟩ **:** one that is loaded **10 a** (1) **:** the amount of work that a person carries or is expected to carry ⟨workers . . . willing to adapt to work ~*s* set by time study methods —J.A.Morris b. 1918⟩ ⟨counseling duties in addition to normal teaching ~*s* —Bates Boyle⟩ ⟨patient ~ of physicians in private practice⟩ ⟨the case ~ of social workers⟩ ⟨a regular student with an academic ~ of 12 semester hours⟩ (2) **:** the amount of authorized work to be performed by a machine, a group, a department, or a factory **b :** the demand upon the operating resources of a system (as a telephone exchange, postal system, or railroad) ⟨the ~ in a refrigeration system is the name applied to the quantity of heat that must be removed per unit of time —B.H.Jennings⟩ **:** the number or quantity (as of persons, vehicles) accommodated (as by an institution, transportation system) at one time ⟨the population ~ on the land —Russell Lord⟩ ⟨care for the potential ~ of senile mental cases —*Psychological Abstracts*⟩ ⟨traffic reaching its peak ~ during rush hours⟩ **11** *slang* **:** a full view **:** EYEFUL; *also* **:** EARFUL — used in the phrase *get a load of* ⟨get a ~ of this new convertible —Bennett Cerf⟩ **12 :** BURDEN 10 ⟨the worm ~ in rats⟩ **13 :** an amount added to the selling price of an article, service, or security to represent selling or delivery expense and profit of the distributor — called also *loading*

**²load** \"\ *vb* -ED/-ING/-S [ME *loden*, fr. *lod, lood*, n.] *vt* **1 a :** to put a load in or on (a means of conveyance) **:** to fill with material, animals, or passengers to be transported ⟨had ~*ed* the moving van by noon⟩ ⟨~ the plane with cargo⟩ ⟨steamboats ~*ed* down with goods and passengers —*Amer. Guide Series: Minn.*⟩ **b :** to place in or on a means of conveyance **:** pack or stow as a load ⟨~ the freight into the car⟩ ⟨~*s* his family into the car for a ride⟩ **2 a :** to encumber or oppress with something heavy, laborious or disheartening **:** weigh down **:** BURDEN — often used with *with* ⟨a railway president . . . would not ~ himself with departmental minutiae —W.J. Cunningham⟩ ⟨a business that was ~*ed* down with debts⟩ ⟨~ human life with frustration and grief —David Cort⟩ **b :** to place as a burden or obligation **:** SADDLE — often used with *on* ⟨~ more work on him⟩ **c :** ⁴GUM *vt* 4 **d :** to play a card (as in the game of hearts) that will increase the count against (an opponent who takes the trick) **3 a :** to place or be a material weight or physical stress on ⟨grapes ~ down the vines⟩ ⟨~ the springs to the limit⟩ **b :** to increase the weight of by adding something heavy ⟨the stockwhip was . . . ~*ed* with shot at the butt —H.L.Davis⟩ **c :** to add a conditioning substance esp. a mineral salt to (something) for body or some other property: as (1) **:** to add filler to (paper) **:** FILL (2) *of textiles* **:** WEIGHT 1c ⟨silk which has been ~*ed* with . . . metallic salts —*Irish Digest*⟩ **d :** to weight (dice) to fall unfairly **e :** to pack with one-sided or prejudicial influences or assumptions or numbers **:** give a determining slant or proportion to **:** BIAS ⟨the system was heavily ~*ed* in favor of royalty, aristocracy, and priesthood —A.L.Kroeber⟩ ⟨the situation is a little ~*ed* against the male of the species —John Gould⟩ ⟨so ~*ed* his questions that a witness had to answer as desired or appear unpatriotic⟩ ⟨the jury comes in ~*ed* to soak an anarchist — Maxwell Anderson⟩ **f :** to weight (as a test or experimental situation) with factors influencing validity or outcome **g :** to charge with emotional associations or significance ⟨the sentiment that ~*s* such words as *mother*⟩ **4 a :** to supply in abundance or excess ⟨a prewar custom of ~*ing* visitors with gadgets —DeWitt Morrill⟩ ⟨an uncle . . . who, like all pawnbrokers, was ~*ed* with trumpets —E.J.Kahn⟩ ⟨their questions were ~*ed* with insinuation —Jean Stafford⟩ **:** HEAP ⟨an enameled plate that was ~*ed* high with potatoes —Liam O'Flaherty⟩ **:** PACK ⟨clearly written and ~*ed* with pictures and diagrams —*Dun's Rev.*⟩ ⟨~ up on them while the price is low⟩ **b** (1) **:** to apply (as a pigment) heavily ⟨the ~*ed* streaks of orange and cinnabar —F.J.Mather⟩ (2) **:** to color (a painting) thickly (3) **:** to make (as a color) opaque by mixing in white **c :** to put runners on (first, second, and third bases) in baseball ⟨the pitcher ~*ed* the bases by walking three batters⟩ **d :** to fill (a person) with fanciful information ⟨the pilot warmed to his opportunity, and proceeded to ~ me up in the good old-fashioned way —Mark Twain⟩ **5 a :** to put a load in (a device or piece of equipment) **:** supply with the material to be used or processed ⟨~ his corncob pipe⟩ ⟨~, unload, and reload the washer by hand⟩: as (1) **:** to place a charge or cartridge in (the chamber of a firearm) **:** assemble the components of (a cartridge) (2) **:** to transfer (germinated grain) from the working floor to dry in a kiln (3) **:** to insert photographic film in (as a holder or magazine) **:** place a holder or magazine in (as a camera or machine) **b :** to place or insert as a load in a device, machine, or container ⟨~ the cloth into a dye vat⟩ **6 a :** to increase the resistance in the working of ⟨~ a windmill for a 15-mile wind —F.E.Kidder & Harry Parker⟩ **b** (1) **:** to change (as by introducing a loading coil) the resonance frequency or wavelength of (a radio transmitter) (2) **:** to introduce (loading coils) or distribute (induction) along an electrical conductor (3) **:** to add a power-absorbing device (as a resistance or antenna) to (a telephone line) in order to reduce attenuation and distortion (4) **:** to add (as a circuit element or antenna) to a circuit to absorb power **7 :** to change (as an alcoholic drink) by adding an adulterant or drug **8 a :** to add loading to (an insurance premium) **b :** to add a sum to (as the selling price of a book or security) after profits and expenses are accounted for ⟨~*ed* prices⟩ ⟨waiters can ~ checks more deftly than any of their colleagues on the European Continent —T.H.Fielding⟩ ~ *vi* **1 :** to receive a load **:** take on cargo or passengers ⟨trucks were ~*ing* with mail at the platform in back⟩ ⟨stopped behind a school bus that was ~*ing*⟩ **2 :** ⁴GUM *vi* 2 **3 :** to put a load on or in a carrier, device, machine, or container; *specif* **:** to insert the charge or cartridge in the chamber of a firearm **4 :** to go or go in as a load **:** make one's way as a passenger ⟨the nurses were called . . . to ~ into the boat —Lonnie Coleman⟩ **:** be suitable for loading a carrier, device, or machine ⟨razor blades that ~ without handling⟩ **syn** see BURDEN — **load the dice :** to prejudice the outcome **:** place one at an advantage or disadvantage **:** present an argument one-sidedly ⟨the victim has already *loaded the dice* against himself by . . . previous actions —*Economist*⟩ ⟨a survey of labor-management relations which does not *load the dice* in favor of management —*Infantry Jour.*⟩

**³load** *var of* LODE

**load–bearing tile** \ˈ=‚==‚=\ *n* **:** tile capable of carrying superimposed loads for use in masonry construction

**load binder** *n* **:** ²BOOMER

**load chart** *n* **:** a schematic and graphic device to indicate the amount of authorized work yet to be performed by a machine, a group, or any other producing unit in a factory

**load dispatcher** *n* **:** a worker whose duty is seeing that the demand on a utility system (as for gas, electricity, or water) is continuously supplied

**load displacement** *n* : the displacement of a ship when loaded to the extent for which it was designed

**loaded** *adj* [fr. past part. of 2*load*] **1** *slang* : DRUNK ⟨celebrated by getting ~ on champagne⟩ **2** : containing an explosive charge ⟨a ~ cigar⟩ **3** *of a quadruped's shoulder* : having the upper muscles excessively developed or lumpy **4** : full to bursting with strong feeling (as anger) **5** : having a large amount of money — **loaded for bear** : supplied with all one needs for success : amply prepared ⟨learning that every outfit . . . was at full strength, sober, and *loaded for bear* —E.G.Love⟩

**loaded line** *n* : a telephone or telegraph line that has exceptionally high inductance distributed uniformly or introduced at regular intervals

**1load·en** \ˈlōdᵊn\ *dial var of* LOADED

**2loaden** \"\ *vt* [1*load* + *-en*] *now dial* : 2LOAD

**load·er** \ˈlōdə(r)\ *n* -s [ME *loder*, fr. *loden* to load + *-er* — more at LOAD] **1** : a person whose work is loading: as **a** : one who loads articles or materials to be transported into or onto the means of conveyance **b** : one who charges processing equipment with material **c** : one who fills containers or instruments with a specified quantity of material **2** : a device or machine used for loading ⟨an automatic bobbin ~⟩; *specif* : a machine (as a belt or bucket conveyor or a power scoop shovel) that picks up loose material (as snow or gravel) and loads it upon a vehicle or into a container within the same unit **3** : an attendant who loads guns for a hunter ⟨many Highland folk still look to the grouse season for some welcome ready money, by working as . . . ~s —Colin Gibson⟩

**load·er·man** \-mən\ *n, pl* **loadermen** : a logger who operates the machinery for hoisting and loading logs

**load factor** *n* **1** : the ratio of average to maximum load; *specif* : the ratio of the average load carried by a power station or system for a given period to the maximum load during that period **2** : the ratio stated as a percentage between the freight or passenger capacity of a vehicle or line and its actual utilization ⟨averaged a passenger *load factor* of about 92 percent —*Boeing Mag.*⟩

**loading** *n* -s [fr. gerund of 2*load*] **1 a** : a cargo, weight, or stress placed on something; *specif* : WING LOADING **b** : the amount of freight loaded during a specified period : SHIPMENT — usu. used in pl. ⟨quarterly ~s of inland barges averaging ten million tons⟩; *esp* : CARLOADING **2** *or* **loading charge** : LOAD 13; *specif* : an amount added to the net or pure premium of an insurance policy to provide for business expenses, future contingencies, and profits or bonuses **3** : material used to load paper, cloth, leather, or rubber : FILLER, STUFFING **4** : a cartridge or charge for a firearm consisting of particular components or characteristics **5 a** : the amount or degree to which something is or can be loaded ⟨the maximum axle ~⟩ ⟨an average ~ of 0.2 percent boric acid —*Rev. of Applied Entomology*⟩ **b** : the relative contribution of each component factor in a psychological test or in an experimental, clinical, or social situation

**loading chute** *n* : an inclined plane fenced in on each side up which cattle or other livestock can be driven for loading into trucks or other means of conveyance

**loading coil** *n* : a coil inserted in a tuned electrical circuit to increase its inductance

**loading density** *n* : the quantity of powder per unit volume of a cartridge case

**loading tool** *n* : a device for loading ammunition by hand

**load·less** \ˈlōdləs\ *adj* : having no load

**load limit** *n* : the maximum recommended or permitted weight of a vehicle determined by combining the tare weight with the load weight

**load line** *n* **1** *or* **load waterline a** : the line on the outside of a ship to which it sinks in the water when loaded or safely loaded **b** *also* **load line mark** : a mark representing the safe load line **2** : one of a set of marks graduated in accordance with international standards and required by law in most maritime countries to be cut and painted amidships on the sides of a seagoing cargo ship to indicate the greatest draft to which it can be safely loaded under various conditions (as tropical fresh water or North Atlantic winter) — see PLIMSOLL MARK

**Load·om·e·ter** \(ˈ)lōˈdäməd·ə(r)\ *trademark* — used for an instrument that records the weight borne by a wheel of a vehicle passing over it

**loads** *pl of* LOAD, *pres 3d sing of* LOAD

**loadstar** *var of* LODESTAR

**loadstone** *var of* LODESTONE

**load water plane** *n* : the horizontal plane of a ship at the load waterline — abbr. *LWP*

**1loaf** \ˈlōf\ *n, pl* **loaves** \-ōvz\ *also* **loafs** \-ōfs\ [ME *lof, laf*, fr. OE *hlāf* bread, loaf; akin to OHG *hleib, leib* bread, loaf, ON *hleifr*, Goth *hlaifs*] **1 a** : a shaped or molded mass of bread ⟨a ~ of white bread⟩ ⟨~ bread and rolls⟩ **b** : a hollowed crust of a loaf of bread with a specified filling ⟨oyster ~⟩ **2** : a regularly molded often rectangular mass ⟨a ~ of cheese⟩ ⟨dried banana *loaves*⟩: as **a** : a conical mass of sugar ⟨sugar ~⟩ **b** : a baked dish consisting usu. of a specified main ingredient (as ground meat or fish) held together with soft crumbs or eggs and a liquid (as milk or tomato sauce) ⟨beef ~⟩ ⟨salmon ~⟩ **3 a** : a thick lump or mass ⟨her dark hair piled into an overhanging ~ —William Sansom⟩ **b** *Brit* : a head of a vegetable (as cabbage) **4** *or* **loaf of bread** *slang Brit* : HEAD, MIND ⟨going to be a useful boy, so long as you use your ~ —Robert Westerby⟩

**2loaf** \"\ *vb* -ED/-ING/-S [prob. back-formation fr. 1*loafer*] *vi* : to spend time in idleness : to lounge or loiter about or along : do no work ⟨fired when he ~*ed* on the job⟩ ⟨cast the fly and ~ and dream —Henry van Dyke⟩ ⟨a place where the cows ~, usually near water, shade, or shelter —*Plan & Profit with Herefords*⟩ ⟨got up slowly from the settee in the corner and ~*ed* across the . . . lobby —Raymond Chandler⟩ ⟨the herring gull . . . ~*s* along on slow wingbeats —Brooks Atkinson⟩ ~ *vt* : to spend in idleness ⟨crowds of men who had come to ~ the evening away —Sherwood Anderson⟩—**loaf one's way** : to proceed on a course in an idle manner ⟨the bright ones *loaf their way* through and acquire habits of indolence instead of an education —*College English*⟩

**3loaf** \"\ *n* -s : a time spent at loafing ⟨went camping for a good ~⟩

**loaf cake** *n* : a cake (as a pound cake) baked in a loaf pan

**loaf cheese** *n* : process cheese molded in the form of a usu. rectangular loaf

**1loaf·er** \ˈlōfə(r)\ *n* -s [perh. short for *landloafer*, modif. of G *landläufer* vagabond, tramp, fr. *land* + *läufer* runner, walker] : one that loafs : IDLER ⟨neighborhood ~*s* tipped their chairs within reach of the cracker barrel —S.T.Williamson⟩

**2loafer** \"\ *or* **loafer wolf** *n* -s [by folk etymology fr. Sp *lobo* wolf, fr. L *lupus* — more at WOLF] : TIMBER WOLF

**Loafer** \"\ *trademark* — used for a low leather step-in shoe with an upper resembling the moccasin but with a broad flat heel

**loaf·er·ish** \ˈlōf(ə)rish\ *adj* : befitting or having the appearance of a loafer ⟨stood around in ~ indifference⟩ ⟨~ looking men standing on the street corner⟩

**loafing barn** *or* **loafing shed** *n* : a barn or shed for cattle in which they range at will on a heavy bedding of straw rather than occupy fixed stanchions

**loaf·ing·ly** *adv* : in a loafing manner

**loaf pan** *n* : a deep rectangular pan of metal or glass used for baking food in the form of loaves

**loaf sugar** *n* : refined sugar molded into loaves or small cubes or squares

**lo·a·i·a·sis** \ˌlōəˈīəsəs\ *or* **lo·i·a·sis** \lōˈī·ə-\ *n, pl* **loaia·ses** *or* **loia·ses** \-ˌsēz\ [NL, fr. *Loa* + *-iasis*] : infestation with or disease caused by an eye worm (*Loa loa*) that migrates through the subcutaneous tissue and across the cornea of the eye — compare CALABAR SWELLING

**loa loa** \ˈlōəˈlōə\ *n* [NL, fr. *Loa loa*, species of worm that causes the disease] : LOAIASIS

**1loam** \ˈlōm, ˈlüm\ *n* -s [ME *lom, lam*, fr. OE *lām*; akin to OS *lēmo* clay, mud, OHG *leimo* clay, mud, OE *līm* lime — more at LIME] **1 a** *obs* : clayey earth : CLAY **b** : a mixture composed chiefly of moistened clay (as for plastering, making bricks) **c** : a coarse strongly bonded molding sand used in founding **2** : SOIL, TOPSOIL; *specif* : a usu. fertile and humus-rich soil consisting of a friable mixture containing from 7 to 27 percent clay, 28 to 50 percent silt, and less than 52 percent sand **3** : BROCCOLI BROWN

**2loam** \"\ *vt* -ED/-ING/-S : to cover, smear, or fill with loam

**loam board** *n* : a board of definite profile used to strickle a mold in loam or to strike up its core on a core barrel

**loam·i·ness** \ˈlōmēnəs, ˈlüm-, -min-\ *n* -ES : the quality or state of being loamy

**loam·less** \ˈlōmləs, ˈlüm-\ *adj* : having no loam ⟨a ~ yard⟩

**loam mold** *n* : a foundry mold made of siliceous sand, clay, and organic matter in proper proportions and used in making iron castings

**loamy** \ˈlōmē, ˈlüm-, -mi\ *adj, usu* -ER/-EST : consisting of, like, or of the character of loam

**1loan** \ˈlōn\ *n* -s [ME *loon, lon, lan*, fr. ON *lān*; akin to OE *lǣn* loan, *lēon* to lend, OHG *lēhan* borrowed property, *līhan* to borrow, lend, ON *ljā* to lend, grant, Goth *leihwan* to lend, L *linquere* to leave, Gk *leipein* to leave, Skt *riṇakti* he leaves; basic meaning: to leave] **1 a** : money lent at interest ⟨was authorized to make ~*s* upon farm commodities —F.D.Roosevelt⟩ ⟨a bond issue is a typical form of major business ~⟩ **b** : something lent for the borrower's temporary use on condition that it or its equivalent be returned ⟨life's not our own, — 'tis but a ~ to be repaid —Charles Swain⟩ **2 a** : the grant of temporary use made by a lender ⟨able to get the ~ of a car to take them back —George Farwell⟩ **b** : the temporary duty of a person transferred by a superior to the service of another for a limited time ⟨he had been on ~ to the navy during the war, away from the campus —C.O.Gorham⟩ **3** : LOANWORD

**2loan** \"\ *vb* -ED/-ING/-S *vt* **1** : to lend (money) at interest **2** : LEND 1a ⟨~*ed* her the clothes to wear and primped her to look nice —Carson McCullers⟩ **3** : LEND 1c ⟨our pink-cheeked conducting officer . . . who had been ~*ed* by the Red Signal Corps for the trip —E.P.Snow⟩ **4** *dial* : BORROW 1 ⟨can I ~ a ladder from you for a day or so⟩ ~ *vi* : to lend money at interest ⟨in times of distress, ~ to good customers —N.S.B. Gras⟩

**3loan** \"\ *n* -s [ScGael *lōn*; akin to OIr *loun* provision] *Scot* : PROVISIONS

**4loan** \"\ *n* [ME (Sc) *lone*, alter. of *lane* — more at LANE] *dial Brit* : LOANING

**loan·able** \ˈlōnəbəl\ *adj* : that may be loaned; *esp* : available for loan at a certain time at interest ⟨~ funds⟩

**loanblend** \ˈ=,=\ *n* : a word some of whose constituents are native and others of foreign origin — called also *hybrid*

**loan crowd** *n* : a group of stock exchange members meeting to borrow or lend stocks

**lo and behold** *interj* — used to express wonder or surprise ⟨there, *lo and behold*, in the window . . . was a 'To Let' board —A.P.Herbert⟩

**loan·er** \ˈlōnə(r)\ *n* -s **1** : one that loans **2** : something lent (as in place of an article left for repair)

**loan farm** *n* [trans. of Afrik *leningsplaas*] *southern Africa* : a piece of land held from the government on payment of an annual quitrent

**loan form** *n* : a form borrowed by one language from another ⟨English *their* and *get* are *loan forms* from Old Norse⟩ — compare LOANWORD

**loan·ing** \ˈlōniŋ\ *n* -s [ME *loning*, fr. *lone* lane, loaning + *-ing* — more at LOAN] **1** *dial Brit* : a way between fields : LANE **2** *dial Brit* : an open space near a farm or village where cows are often milked : PADDOCK

**loan office** *n* : an office at which loans are negotiated or at which the accounts of loans are kept and the interest paid to the lender

**loan-out** \ˈ=,=\ *n* -s [fr. *loan out*, v.] : the loan to another motion-picture studio of a player under contract in exchange for money or the services of another player

**loan paper** *n* : a paper similar in characteristics and use to bond paper but often somewhat heavier and stronger

**loan shark** *n* : one who lends money to individuals at extortionate interest rates

**loan-shark** \ˈ=,=\ *vi* [*loan shark*] : to lend money as a loan shark

**loanshift** \ˈ=,=\ *n* : a change in the meaning of a word under the influence of another language (as when a word meaning "pedal extremity" acquires also the meaning "12-inch unit of length" under the influence of English "foot"); *also* : a word that has undergone such a change in meaning : CALQUE 1

**loan translation** *n* [trans. of G *lehnübersetzung*] : a compound, derivative, or phrase introduced into a language through translation of the constituent parts of a term in another language (as *neogrammarian* from German *junggrammatiker*, *reason of state* from French *raison d'état*) — called also *calque*

**loan value** *n* : the amount which the owner may borrow against a life insurance policy, equal to the cash value less interest to the end of the current policy year

**loanword** \ˈ=,=\ *n* [trans. of G *lehnwort*] : a word taken from another language and at least partly naturalized : a borrowed or adopted word — called also *loan*

**loas** *pl of* LOA

**lo·a·sa** \ˈlōəsə\ *n* [NL] **1** *cap* : a genus (the type of the family Loasaceae) of tropical American prickly herbs having 10 staminodia and a 3- to 5-valved capsule **2** -s : any plant or flower of the genus *Loasa*

**lo·a·sa·ce·ae** \ˌlōəˈsāsēˌē\ *n pl, cap* [NL, fr. *Loasa*, type genus + *-aceae*] : a family of mainly herbaceous bristly hairy sometimes climbing plants (order Parietales) having regular pentamerous flowers with numerous stamens — **lo·a·sa·ceous** \ˌ=ˌ=ˈsāshəs\ *adj*

**loasa family** *n* : LOASACEAE

**loath** *or* **loth** *also* **loathe** \ˈlōth, -t͟h\ *adj* [ME *loth, lath* hostile, loathsome, averse, fr. OE *lāth* hostile, loathsome; akin to OFris & OS *lēth* hated, loathsome, OHG *leid*, ON *leithr* hated, loathsome, OIr *liuss* aversion, disgust, and perh. to Gk *aleitēs* sinner] : characterized by unwillingness to do something contrary to one's tastes, likes, sympathies, or ways of thinking ⟨when he suggested a meal, I was nothing ~ —H.G. Wells⟩ — usu. used predicatively or postpositively with an infinitive ⟨seemed ~ to enter, yet drawn by some desire stronger than his reluctance —Willa Cather⟩ ⟨a spirit of camaraderie . . . that made us ~ to part —Jack Hulbert⟩ **syn** see DISINCLINED

**loathe** \ˈlōt͟h\ *vt* -ED/-ING/-S [ME *lothen*, fr. OE *lāthian*, fr. *lāth*, adj.] : to feel strong aversion for : have extreme disgust at : DETEST, ABHOR ⟨~ writing harp parts, because they mean writing out so many notes —Deems Taylor⟩ ⟨sickened of it and *loathed* it —Arnold Bennett⟩ **syn** see HATE

**loath·er** \-t͟hə(r)\ *n* -s : one that loathes something

**loath·ful** \-t͟hfəl\ *adj* [ME *lothful* hateful, loathsome, reluctant, fr. *loth* evil, harm, hatred (fr. OE *lāth*, fr. *lāth*, adj.) + *-ful*] *now Scot* : SHRINKING, RELUCTANT, BASHFUL

**loath·ing** \ˈlōt͟hiŋ, -t͟hēŋ\ *n* -s [ME *lothing*, fr. gerund of *lothen* to loathe] : a feeling of aversion, abhorrence, or detestation : extreme digust : ANTIPATHY ⟨the crew was divided between admiration and ~ —Elinor Wylie⟩

**loath·ing·ly** *adv* : in the manner of one who feels loathing

**1loath·ly** \ˈlōthlē, -th-, -li\ *adj* [ME *lothly*, fr. OE *lāthlic*, fr. *lāth* hostile, loathsome + *-līc* -ly] : LOATHSOME, REPULSIVE ⟨the ~ lady . . . changes back again into her original lovely and youthful self —Boris Ford⟩

**2loathly** \"\ *adv* [ME *lothly*, fr. OE *lāthlīce*, fr. *lāthlīc*, adj.] : UNWILLINGLY

**loath·ness** \ˈlōthnəs, -t͟h-\ *n* -ES [ME *lothnesse, lathnesse* harmfulness, unpleasantness, reluctance, fr. *loth, lath* hostile, loathsome, averse + *-nesse* -ness] : the quality or state of being loath : RELUCTANCE

**loath·some** \ˈlōthsəm, -t͟h-\ *adj* [ME *lothsum*, fr. *loth* evil, harm, hatred + *-sum* -some — more at LOATHFUL] : exciting loathing : DISGUSTING: **a** : offensive to the senses : NAUSEATING, FOUL ⟨rot with some ~ disease —W.S.Maugham⟩ **b** : repulsive to sensibility or conscience : ODIOUS, ABHORRENT ⟨what is holy and what is ~ are in like manner set aside —W.G. Sumner⟩ **syn** see OFFENSIVE

**loath·some·ly** *adv* [ME *lothsumly*, fr. *lothsum* + *-ly*] : in a loathsome manner ⟨~ ugly⟩

**loath·some·ness** *n* -ES [ME *lothsumnesse*, fr. *lothsum* + *-nesse* -ness] **1** : the quality or state of being loathsome **2** : something loathsome **3** *archaic* : LOATHING

**loathy** \ˈlōt͟hē, -th, ǀi\ *adj* [obs. *loath* evil, harm, hatred (fr. ME *loth*) + *-y* — more at LOATHFUL] : LOATHSOME ⟨~ examples of age, sickness, and death —E.W.Hopkins⟩

**loaves** *pl of* LOAF

**loaves and fishes** *n pl* [so called fr. the 5 barley loaves and 2 fishes with which Jesus miraculously fed a multitude of 5000 (John 6) that he later reproached for their greater interest in the food than in him (John 6: 26)] : material gain ⟨concentrating on how to get *loaves and fishes*, the schools . . . make out of our youngsters precisely what their parents wish them to become —B.I.Bell⟩

**1lob** \ˈläb\ *n* -s [prob. of LG or Flem origin; akin to Flem *lobbe* simpleton, LG *lubbe* coarse, awkward person, MLG *lobbe* thick underlip; akin to OE *lobbe, loppe* spider, Fris *lob, lobbe* hanging mass of fat or flesh, G dial. *loppen* to be loose, Sw dial. *lubbe* plump figure, ON *lūfa* thick hair — more at SLOBBER] **1** *now dial Brit* : a dull heavy person : LOUT ⟨a great fat ~ that had no life in him at all —Samuel Lover⟩ **2** *archaic* : a loosely hanging object **3** *dial Brit* : a large amount

**2lob** \"\ *vb* **lobbed; lobbed; lobbing; lobs** *vt* **1** *archaic* : to let hang heavily : DROOP ⟨their poor jades ~ down their heads —Shak.⟩ ⟨goggling at her grandmother with her mouth *lobbed* wetly open —Norman Lindsay⟩ **2** : to throw, hit, or propel slowly in or as if in a high arc ⟨*lobbing* hand grenades over the rock —Burtt Evans⟩ : as **a** : to return (a tennis ball) in a high arc usu. over an opposing player's head **b** : to bowl or throw (a cricket ball) underhand usu. slowly **c** (1) : to throw (a baseball) in a soft easy manner ⟨~ the ball in⟩ (2) : to hit (a baseball) in a slow high arc ⟨~ a few practice flies to the outfield⟩ **3** : COB 3 ~ *vi* **1** : to move slowly and heavily ⟨rockets . . . *lobbed* shoreward —K.M.Dodson⟩ **2** : to hit a tennis ball easily in a high arc **3** *Austral* : to arrive at a place ⟨just *lobbed* in town —R.M.Daw⟩

**3lob** \"\ *n* -s [2*lob*] **1** : a cricket ball bowled or thrown underhand usu. slowly **2** : a tennis ball hit slowly in a high arc

**4lob** \"\ *also* **lobb** *n* -s [origin unknown] **1** : a step or stair in a mine **2** : a mineral vein descending like steps

**5lob** \"\ *n* -s [origin unknown] *slang Brit* : a container for valuables; *esp* : TILL

**lob-** *or* **lobi-** *or* **lobo-** *comb form* [*lobe*] : lobe ⟨*lob*ectomy⟩ ⟨*lobi*form⟩ ⟨*lobi*gerous⟩ ⟨*lobo*tomy⟩

**lo·ba** \ˈlōbə\ *n* -s [prob. native name in the Philippines] : a Manila copal hardened somewhat by delaying collection of the resin usu. for one to three months after tapping the tree

**lo·bal** \ˈlōbəl\ *adj* [*lob-* + *-al*] : LOBED

**lo·bar** \ˈlōbə(r), -ˌbär, -ˌbä(r\ *adj* [*lob-* + *-ar*] : of or relating to a lobe : LOBATE

**lo·bar·ia** \lōˈba(a)rēə\ *n, cap* [NL, fr. *lob-* + *-aria*] : a genus of foliaceous lichens (family Stictaceae) — see LUNGWORT

**lobar pneumonia** *n* : acute pneumonia involving one or more lobes of the lung characterized by sudden onset, chill, fever, difficulty in breathing, cough, and blood-stained sputum, marked by consolidation, and normally followed by resolution and return to normal of the lung tissue

**lo·ba·ta** \lōˈbäd·ə, -ˈbād·ə\ *n pl, cap* [NL, fr. *lob-* + *-ata*] : an order of ctenophores (class Tentaculata) with the body compressed in the vertical plane and produced into two large oral lobes and four pointed processes

**lo·ba·tae** \-d·ˌē\ [NL, fr. *lob-* + L *-atae* (fem. pl. of *-atus* -ate)] *syn of* LOBATA

**lo·bate** \ˈlō,bāt, *usu* -ād.+V\ *also* **lo·bat·ed** \-ād·əd\ *adj* [*lobate* fr. NL *lobatus*, fr. *lob-* + L *-atus* -ate; *lobated* fr. NL *lobatus* + E *-ed*] **1 a** : having lobes ⟨a ~ leaf⟩ **b** : resembling a lobe ⟨a ~ tongue⟩ **2 a** *of a fish* : having the integument of the fin continued on the bases of the fin rays **b** *of a bird* : having lateral membranous flaps — **lo·bate·ly** *adv*

**lo·ba·tion** \lōˈbāshən\ *n* -s **1 a** : the quality or state of being lobed **b** : the formation of lobes or lobules **2 a** : LOBE **b** : LOBULE

**1lob·ber** \ˈläbə(r)\ *n* -s [2*lob* + *-er*] : one that lobs

**2lobber** \"\ *var of* 1LOPPER

**1lob·by** \ˈläbē, -bi\ *n* -ES [ML *lobium, lobia, laubia* covered walk, gallery, portico, of Gmc origin; akin to OHG *louba, louppea* protective roof, porch — more at LODGE] **1 a** : a corridor or hall connected with a larger room or series of rooms and used as a passageway or waiting room ⟨ignorant where the narrow *lobbies* led —Emily Brontë⟩ ⟨this ~ of many doors at the head of the windowed staircase —Elizabeth Bowen⟩ ⟨the small ~ of the post office —Willard Robertson⟩: as (1) one of the two corridors or anterooms of the British House of Commons to which members go to vote when the House divides on a motion ⟨time and again, on issues of foreign policy, Labor and Conservative MPs have gone into the same ~ —*New Republic*⟩ (2) : a large hall serving as a foyer or anteroom ⟨a hotel ~⟩ ⟨a theater ~⟩ (3) : an anteroom of a capitol **b** *archaic* : a small room or enclosure: as (1) : a small apartment on board ship (2) : a small enclosed pen for cattle (3) : a watchman's enclosure in or outside a factory **2 a** : the persons who frequent the lobbies of a legislative house to do business with the members; *specif* : persons not members of a legislative body and not holding government office who attempt to influence legislators or other public officials through personal contact **b** : a particular group of such persons representing a special interest

**2lobby** \"\ *vb* -ED/-ING/-ES *vi* **1** : to conduct activities (as engaging in personal contacts or the dissemination of information) with the objective of influencing public officials and esp. members of a legislative body with regard to legislation and other policy decisions ⟨~ for their proposals when they reached the floor of the legislature —Gladys M. Kammerer⟩ **2** : to attempt to secure a desired objective by the use of methods resembling or held to resemble those of a political lobbyist ⟨members successfully *lobbied* among the convention delegates —*New Republic*⟩ ~ *vt* **1** : to influence or attempt to influence with regard to policy decisions and esp. proposals for legislation ⟨wine, dine, and ~ the legislature —*Newsweek*⟩ **2 a** : to promote and esp. to secure the passage of (as legislation) by influencing public officials ⟨the man who *lobbied* the prohibition law through Congress —Herbert Asbury⟩ **b** : to advance or otherwise secure favorable treatment for (as a desired project) by influencing public officials before the beginning or following the completion of the legislative process

**lob·by·er** \-bēə(r)\ *n* -s : one that lobbies : LOBBYIST

**lob·by·gow** \ˈläbē,gau̇\ *n* -s [origin unknown] *slang* : an errand boy : MESSENGER

**lob·by·ism** \ˈläbē,izəm\ *n* -s : the activities of a lobbyist or the practice of lobbying

**lob·by·ist** \-əst\ *n* -s : one who lobbies; *specif* : a person employed and compensated for lobbying

**lob·by·man** \-mən\ *n, pl* **lobbymen** : one who serves as an attendant or porter in a lobby; *specif* : one employed in the lobby of a theater to take tickets and give information

**lobcock** \ˈ=,=\ *n* [1*lob* + *cock*] *now dial Eng* : a stupid blundering person : LOUT

**lobe** \ˈlōb\ *n* -s [MF, fr. LL *lobus*, fr. Gk *lobos* — more at SLEEP] **1** : a curved or rounded projection or division: as **a** : a more or less rounded projection of a body organ or part ⟨~ of the ear⟩ — see EAR illustration **b** : a division of a body organ marked off by a fissure on the surface (as of the brain, lungs, liver) **c** : a division or projection of a plant organ ⟨~ of a leaf⟩ **d** : a rounded projection or dome of a building **2 a** : a membranous flap on the sides of the toes of some birds (as the coot) **b** : a portion of a suture in a cephalopod shell that forms an angle or curve whose convexity is directed away from the orifice — opposed to *saddle* **c** : one of the longitudinal divisions of the body or one of the lateral divisions of the glabella in a trilobite **3** : a projecting part of a cam wheel or of a noncircular gear wheel in a machine **4** : a great rounded marginal projection from a continental ice sheet **5 a** : one of the inflated bags at the stern of a kite balloon that acts either as a fin or as a stabilizer **b** : one of the sections into which the envelope of a balloon is sometimes divided by the tension of the internal rigging **6** : a portion of the radiation pattern of a directional antenna representing an area of stronger transmission of radio signals

**lo·bec·to·my** \lōˈbektəmē, -mi\ *n* -ES [ISV *lobe* + *-ectomy*] : surgical removal of a lobe of an organ or gland; *specif* : excision of a lobe of a lung

**lobed** \ˈlōbd\ *adj* : having lobes : LOBATE — used chiefly of leaves

**lobe-finned fish** \'⸗,⸗-\ *also* **lobe-fin** \'⸗,⸗\ *n* : CROSSOPTERYGIAN
**lobefoot** \'⸗,⸗\ *n, pl* **lobefoots** : a bird having lobate toes; *esp* : NORTHERN PHALAROPE
**lobe·less** \'lōbləs\ *adj* : lacking lobes
**lobe·let** \-lət\ *n* -s : a small lobe
**lo·be·lia** \lō'bēlyə, -lēə\ *n* [NL, fr. Matthias de *Lobel* †1616 Flemish botanist + NL *-ia*] **1 a** *cap* : a large genus (the type of the family Lobeliaceae) of herbaceous plants of wide distribution that have the corolla tube split **b** -s : any plant or flower of this genus **2** -s : the leaves and tops of a lobelia (*L. inflata*) — see INDIAN TOBACCO **3** *or* **lobelia blue** -s : a strong violet that is bluer than clematis, bluer and paler than pansy, and bluer and stronger than royal purple (sense 2)
**lo·be·li·a·ce·ae** \lō,bēlē'āsē,ē\ *n pl, cap* [NL, fr. *Lobelia*, type genus + *-aceae*] : a family of widely distributed herbs, shrubs, or trees (order Campanulales) that are characterized by the irregular corolla and often syngenesious anthers and are esp. abundant in the Pacific islands — **lo·be·li·a·ceous** \⸗¦⸗⸗¦āshəs\ *adj*

lobelia

**lobelia family** *n* : LOBELIACEAE
**lobelia violet** *n* : a grayish purple that is redder, lighter, and stronger than telegraph blue, bluer, lighter, and stronger than mauve gray, and bluer and lighter than average rose mauve
**lo·be·line** \'lōbə,lēn, -,lən, lō'bē-\ *n* -s [NL *Lobelia* + E *-ine*] : a poisonous crystalline alkaloid $C_{22}H_{27}NO_2$ obtained from lobelia and used chiefly as a respiratory stimulant — called also *alpha-lobeline*
**lo·bel·lat·ed** \¦lōbə¦lād·əd\ *adj* [*lobe* + L *-ellus* (dim. suffix) + E *-ate* + *-ed*] : LOBULATE
**lo·bel's catchfly** \'lōbəlz-\ *n, usu cap L* [after Matthias de *Lobel* — more at LOBELIA] : a European annual herb (*Silene armeria*) with hollow stems and deep rose flowers that is adventive in eastern No. America — called also *flybane, garden catchfly, sweet william catchfly*
**lobes** *pl of* LOBE
**lobi** *pl of* LOBUS
**lobi-** — see LOB-
**lob·ing** \'lōbiŋ\ *n* -s : LOBATION
**1lo·bi·ped** \'lōbə,ped\ *adj* [ISV *lob-* + *-ped*] : having lobate toes
**2lobiped** \"\ *n* -s : LOBEFOOT
**lob·lol·ly** \'läb,lälē, -li\ *n* [prob. fr. E dial. *lob* to bubble while boiling + obs. E dial. *lolly* broth, soup] **1** *dial* **a** : a thick gruel **b** : an unsightly miry mess : MUDHOLE ⟨when the fall rains came there wouldn't be anything here but a ~ —R. P.Warren⟩ ⟨made *loblollies* by treading and treading in one spot —William Faulkner⟩ **2** *now dial* : a clownish person : LOUT **3** : LOBLOLLY PINE
**loblolly bay** *n* **1** : an ornamental evergreen shrub or small tree (*Gordonia lasianthus*) of the southern U.S. **2** : an endemic Jamaican tree (*Haemocharis haematoxylon*) of the family Theaceae
**loblolly boy** *n, archaic* : a surgeon's attendant on shipboard
**loblolly pine** *n* **1** : a tall spreading pine (*Pinus taeda*) of the central and southeastern U.S. with reddish brown fissured bark, leaves in groups of three, sessile cones having the umbones of the scales prolonged into spines, and a full bushy upper head — called also *frankincense pine* **2** : any of several shrubby to tall arboreal pines of the U.S.
**loblolly tree** *n* : a West Indian or tropical American tree having more or less leathery leaves (as *Pisonia subcordata, Cordia alba, Cupania glabra*)
**lo·bo** \'lō,bō\ *or* **lobo wolf** *n* -s [Sp *lobo* wolf — more at LOAFER] : TIMBER WOLF ⟨prepared to fight the fiercest panther or a pack of ~s —J.F.Dobie⟩
**lobo-** — see LOB-
**lo·bo·la** *or* **lo·bo·lo** \'lōbələ\ *n* -s [native name in southern Africa] : bride-price esp. among the Bantu-speaking peoples of southern Africa
**lo·bo·podium** \,lōbə+\ *or* **lo·bo·pod** \'⸗⸗,päd\ *n, pl* **lobopodia** *or* **lobopodiums** *or* **lobopods** [NL *lobopodium*, fr. *lob-* + *podium*] : a broad thick pseudopodium with a core of endoplasm
**lo·bo·sa** \lō'bōsə\ *n pl, cap* [NL, fr. *lob-* + L *-osa* (fem. of *-osus* -ous)] *in many classifications* : an order of protozoans having thick irregular pseudopodia — **lo·bose** \'lō,bōs\ *adj*
**lo·bo·ste·mon** \,lōbə'stē,män\ *n, cap* [NL, fr. *lob-* + Gk *stēmōn* warp, thread — more at STAMEN] : a genus of southern African perennial herbs or shrubs (family Boraginaceae) that have alternate, sessile, and usu. hairy leaves and white, pink, or blue infundibuliform flowers in scorpioid cymes or dense heads and are sometimes cultivated as greenhouse ornamentals
**lo·bot·o·mize** \lō'bäd·ə,mīz\ *vt* -ED/-ING/-S : to incise a lobe of the brain of
**lo·bot·o·my** \-,mē, -mi\ *n* -ES [ISV *lob-* + *-tomy*] : incision into the brain (as into the frontal lobes) to sever nerve fibers for the relief of certain mental disorders and tension — called also *leucotomy*
**lobs** *pl of* LOB, *pres 3rd sing of* LOB
**lob·scouse** \'läb,skaùs\ *n* -s [origin unknown] : a sailor's dish prepared by stewing or baking bits of meat with vegetables, hardtack, and other ingredients
**lobsided** *var of* LOPSIDED
**lob's pound** *n* [¹*lob*] **1** *dial Eng* : PRISON **2** *dial Eng* : DIFFICULTY, DISGRACE **3** : BITTERSWEET 3b — compare LOBSTER RED
**1lob·ster** \'läbztə(r), -bst-\ *n* -s *see sense 1* [ME *lopster, lobster*, fr. OE *loppestre*, fr. *loppe, lobbe* spider — more at LOB] **1** *pl also* **lobster a** : a large marine decapod crustacean of the family Homaridae commonly used for food; *esp* : a member of the genus *Homarus* including the American lobster (*H. americanus*) and the European lobster (*H. vulgaris*) of the Atlantic coasts and the very small cape lobster (*H. capensis*) of southern Africa **b** : SPINY LOBSTER **c** *Austral* : the common freshwater crayfish **2** *archaic* **a** : a British soldier — called also *boiled lobster* **b** : a uniformed police officer — called also *unboiled lobster* **3** : a person regarded with contempt: as **a** *archaic* : a man unduly responsive to female wiles : one willing to pay for female company **b** : a stupid or awkward person : LUMMOX, CLOWN **4** : BITTERSWEET 3b

American lobster

**2lobster** \"\ *vi* -ED/-ING/-S : to fish for or catch lobsters
**lobsterback** \'⸗⸗,⸗\ *n* [so called fr. the red uniforms] *archaic* : a British soldier
**lobster car** *n* : a slatted container in which live lobsters are kept under water awaiting sale or transportation
**lobster caterpillar** *or* **lobster** *n* -s : a caterpillar that has extremely long thoracic legs and two long caudal processes, rests in a grotesque position, and feeds on many trees and shrubs — see LOBSTER MOTH
**lobster claw** *n* : an incompletely dominant genetic anomaly in man marked by variable reduction of the skeleton of the extremities and cleaving of the hands and feet into two segments resembling lobster claws
**lobster crab** *n* : PORCELAIN CRAB
**lob·ster·ling** \'läbstə(r)liŋ, -bst-\ *n* -s : a young lobster
**lob·ster·man** \-mən\ *n, pl* **lobstermen** : one whose business is catching lobsters
**lobster moth** *n* : a European moth (*Stauropus fagi*) of the family Notodontidae that is the adult of the lobster caterpillar
**lobster new·burg** *or* **lobster new·burgh** \-'n(y)ü,bərg, -bōg, -əig\ *n, usu cap N* [*Newburg, Newburgh* of unknown origin] : cooked lobster meat heated usu. in a chafing dish in a sauce of cream, egg yolk, and sherry
**lobster pot** *n* : an oblong cage with slat sides and a funnel-shaped net used as a trap for catching lobsters

lobster pot (Maine)

**lobster red** *n* : a strong red that is yellower and paler than Goya, bluer, lighter, and slightly stronger than average cherry red, and yellower and deeper than geranium (sense 3a)
**lobster roll** *n* : lobster salad in a long roll
**lobster shift** *or* **lobster trick** *n* **1** : a tour of duty esp. in newspaper work that covers the late evening or early morning hours : GRAVEYARD SHIFT **2** : the skeleton staff left on duty in a newspaper office from the time one edition has gone to press until work begins on the next edition
**lobster-tail** \'⸗⸗,⸗\ *n* : jointed armor for the lower part of the body
**lobster thermidor** *n, pl* **lobsters thermidor** : a mixture of cooked lobster meat, mushrooms, cream, egg yolks, and sherry stuffed into a lobster shell with or without a covering of Parmesan cheese and oven-browned
**lobster trap** *n* : LOBSTER POT
**lob·stick** \'läbz,tik, -b,st-\ *var of* LOPSTICK
**lobtail** \'⸗,⸗\ *vi* [¹*lob* + *tail*] *of a whale* : to beat the surface of the water with the flukes
**lob·u·lar** \'läbyələ(r)\ *adj* : of, relating to, or resembling a lobule — **lob·u·lar·ly** *adv*
**lob·u·lar·ia** \,⸗⸗'la(a)rēə\ *n, cap* [NL, fr. *lobulus* + *-aria*] : a genus of Mediterranean herbs (family Cruciferae) with forked pubescence and small white flowers in racemes — see SWEET ALYSSUM
**lobular pneumonia** *n* : BRONCHOPNEUMONIA
**lob·u·late** \'läbyələt, -,lāt, *usu* -d·+V\ *also* **lob·u·lat·ed** \-,lād·əd\ *adj* : made up of, divided into, or provided with lobules
**lob·u·la·tion** \,⸗⸗'lāshən\ *n* -s **1 a** : the quality or state of being lobulate **b** : the formation of or division into lobules **2** : LOBULE
**lob·ule** \'läb(,)yül\ *n* -s [*lobe* + *-ule*] **1** : a small lobe ⟨the ~ of the ear⟩ **2** : a subdivision of a lobe; *specif* : one of the small masses of tissue of which various organs (as the liver) are built up
**lob·u·lose** \'läbyə,lōs\ *or* **lob·u·lous** \-,ləs\ *adj* : having lobules
**lob·u·lus** \-ləs\ *n, pl* **lobu·li** \-,lī\ [NL, fr. F or E *lobule*] **1 a** : LOBE **b** : LOBULE **2** : ALULA 2b
**lo·bus** \'lōbəs\ *n, pl* **lo·bi** \-,bī\ [NL, fr. Gk *lobos*] : LOBE
**-lo·bus** \ləbəs\ *n comb form* : one having a (specified) kind of lobe — in generic names ⟨Chaeno*lobus*⟩ ⟨Gono*lobus*⟩
**lobworm** \'⸗,⸗\ *n* [¹*lob* + *worm*] : LUGWORM
**loc** *abbr* **1** local **2** location **3** [L *loco*] in the place
**loca** *pl of* LOCUS
**1lo·cal** \'lōkəl\ *adj* [ME *localle*, fr. MF *local*, fr. LL *localis*, fr. L *locus* place (fr. OL *stlocus*) + *-alis* -al — more at STALL] **1** : characterized by or relating to position in space : having a definite spatial form or location ⟨a ~ body⟩ ⟨a ~ heaven and hell⟩ ⟨give to airy nothing a ~ habitation and a name —Shak.⟩ **2** : characterized by, relating to, or occupying a particular place : characteristic of or confined to a particular place : not general or widespread ⟨~ politics⟩ ⟨a ~ custom⟩ **3** : relating to what is local : not broad or general ⟨a person of ~ ideas⟩ ⟨a ~ point of view⟩ **4** : current only in a particular section of a country — used of words or expressions whether dialect or standard (as *you-all, down East, the food is all*) **5 a** : primarily serving the needs of a particular limited district, often a community or minor political subdivision ⟨all-weather ~ roads⟩ ⟨a ~ bus line⟩ **b** : applicable in or relating to such a district only ⟨~ transportation costs⟩ ⟨~ taxes⟩ **c** *of a public conveyance* : making all the stops on its run ⟨a ~ train⟩ — compare EXPRESS **d** *of an act, law, statute* : limited in operation to only part of the territory subject to the legislative power (as a town, district, county) **6** : involving or affecting only a restricted area or portion of the organism : not general ⟨a ~ ailment⟩ ⟨~ anesthesia⟩
**2local** \"\ *n* -s : a local person or thing ⟨found the ~s somewhat dour and unfriendly⟩: as **a** : a local train, elevator, or other public conveyance **b** : a local or particular branch, lodge, or chapter of an organization (as a labor union or a college fraternity) **c** : a local company or team (as of ballplayers) — usu. used in pl. ⟨the ~s play tomorrow⟩ **d** (1) : a newspaper story or item of interest mainly to readers who live in the town or city where the paper is published (2) : a radio or television program sent out from one station only **e** (1) : a stamp for paying postage within a restricted area (2) : a carrier's stamp issued by a private carrier (3) : a precanceled stamp precanceled in the city where it is used — compare BUREAU **f** *Brit* : a nearby or neighborhood pub **g** (1) : LOCAL ANESTHESIA (2) : LOCAL ANESTHETIC
**3local** \"\ *vt* **localed** *or* **localled**; **localed** *or* **localled**; **localing** *or* **localling**; **locals** *Scots law* : to impose as a local charge; *specif* : to assign to the landholders of a parish their individual shares in the payment of (the parish minister's stipend)
**local action** *n* **1** : voltaic action at an electrode of an electrolytic cell consisting of currents set up in the electrolyte between chemically different areas due to impurities on its surface **2** : a legal action that by its nature must have arisen in a particular place (as an action of trespass or replevin or one against a municipal corporation) — compare TRANSITORY ACTION
**local agent** *n* : a person or firm authorized to act as agent for one or more property insurance companies in a particular community and usu. paid by commission
**local allegiance** *n* : allegiance due to the government of a state in which an alien temporarily resides
**local anesthesia** *n* : loss of sensation in a limited and usu. superficial area esp. from the effect of a local anesthetic
**local anesthetic** *n* : an anesthetic for topical and usu. superficial application : an anesthetic intended to produce local anesthesia
**local color** *n* **1** : the color belonging to an object under normal daylight and not caused by accidental influences (as of reflection or shadow) **2** : color in writing derived from the presentation of the features and peculiarities of a particular locality and its inhabitants
**local colorist** *n* : a writer who makes much use of local color esp. as derived from the quaint or picturesque
**lo·cale** \lō'kal *sometimes* lə'- *or* -käl\ *n* -s [modif. of F *local*, fr. *local*, adj. — more at LOCAL] **1** : a place or locality esp. when viewed in relation to a particular event or characteristic ⟨the actual ~ of the crime⟩ ⟨a healthful ~ esp. helpful to asthmatics⟩ **2** : LOCATION, SITE, SITUATION ⟨the ~ and period of the story⟩ ⟨a universe that has no real ~ or date —Edmund Wilson⟩
**local freight** *n* : a freight train performing local services including picking up and setting out cars, switching, and loading and unloading less-than-carload freight at way stations
**local government** *n* **1 a** : the government of a specific local area (as a city, county, or town) constituting a subdivision of a nation, state, or other major political unit ⟨no tradition of autonomy in *local government* —J.A.Corry⟩ ⟨every state is divided into *local government* areas —F.A.Ogg & P.O.Ray⟩ **b** *or* **local self-government** : self-government in local affairs by a political subdivision as distinguished from administration of the area by the central government ⟨a law passed by the appropriate legislature may abolish *local government* —J.A. Corry⟩ ⟨customary to think of Britain as the home of *local self-government* —C.J.Friedrich⟩ — compare HOME RULE 2 **2** : the body of persons exercising the functions of government in a local territorial unit and constituting the unit as an active agency ⟨in the performance of such powers the *local government* is acting as the state's agent —J.E.Pate⟩ **3** : a branch of political science dealing with the government of local areas ⟨college-level courses in *local government*⟩
**lo·cal·ism** \'lōkə,lizəm\ *n* -s **1** : affection for a particular place : concern with local affairs : SECTIONALISM; *specif* : the tendency to place local interests above national **2** : something characteristic of a locality; *esp* : a local idiom or peculiarity of speaking or acting
**lo·cal·ist** \-,ləst\ *n* -s **1** : one that is strongly or unduly concerned with purely local matters **2** : one that attributes the origin of disease to local causes
**lo·cal·is·tic** \¦lōkə¦listik, -tēk\ *adj* : locally oriented or limited : concerned or associated with a particular locality ⟨a ~ theory of disease⟩ ⟨the colonist's ~ defense of home —W.L. Miller⟩
**lo·cal·ite** \'⸗⸗,līt\ *n* -s : a native or resident of a locality under consideration : LOCAL
**lo·cal·itis** \,⸗⸗'līd·əs\ *n* -ES [¹*local* + *-itis*] : undue concern (as on the part of a military commander) with a particular area or the problems of a particular situation resulting in failure to visualize adequately the whole of which it is a part
**lo·cal·i·ty** \lō'kaləd·ē, -ətē, -i\ *n* -ES [F *localité*, fr. LL *localitāt-, localitas*, fr. *localis* local + *-itat-, -itas* -ity — more at LOCAL] **1 a** : the fact or condition of having a location in space or time ⟨every real object has ~ as one of its attributes⟩ **b** *archaic* : restriction to a particular place : LOCALIZATION **2** : a particular spot, situation, or location: as **a** : the place from which something (as a sample of a mineral or a specimen of a plant) was obtained or is available ⟨type *localities* should be exactly specified⟩ ⟨a ~ rich in mineral springs⟩ **b** : a place having or considered in respect to a particular feature ⟨*localities* of heavy rainfall⟩ **c** : a political subdivision of a state : LOCAL GOVERNMENT **3 a** : space or place reference : orientation in respect to space ⟨a strong sense of ~⟩ **b** : a phrenological indication for the faculty of observing and recognizing places and their relative positions **4** *Scots law* **a** : the provision by a marriage contract of a liferent in lands to a wife **b** : the assignment to the landholders of a parish of their individual shares in the payment of the parish minister's stipend
**lo·cal·iz·able** \'lōkə,līzəbəl, ,⸗⸗'⸗⸗⸗\ *adj* : capable of being localized
**lo·cal·iza·tion** \,lōkələ'zāshən, -lī'-\ *n* -s : an act of localizing or the state of being localized: as **a** : the reference of a sense impression to some particular locality in the body or of a perceived object to a definite locality in space **b** : the reference of an event to a particular position in a temporal series **c** (1) : restriction (as of a lesion) to a limited area of the body (2) : restriction of functional centers (as of sight, smell, or speech) to a particular section of the brain
**lo·cal·ize** \'lōkə,līz\ *vb* -ED/-ING/-S *see -ize in Explan Notes* [¹*local* + *-ize*] *vt* **1** : to make local or orient locally: as **a** : to fix in or assign or confine to a definite place or locality ⟨hot applications helped to ~ the infection⟩ ⟨it was not hard to ~ the origins of this legend **b** to give local significance to; *esp* : to write up (a news story of more than local significance) or rewrite (a press release or wire service story) so that local significance is played up ~ *vi* : to collect or accumulate in or be restricted to a specific or limited area ⟨iodine tends to ~ in the thyroid⟩ ⟨anger *localized* sharply on the new tax⟩ ⟨the infection *localized* with the formation of a definite abscess⟩
**localized vector** *n* : a vector (as a force) requiring for its description not only its magnitude and direction but also its axis, the line along which its representative segment lies
**lo·cal·iz·er** \-zə(r)\ *n* -s : one that localizes; *esp* : a radio transmitter used in blind landing to keep an airplane aligned with the runway
**local law** *also* **local act** *n* : a law passed by a legislative body and intended to apply only to one part of the area under its jurisdiction — distinguished from *general law*; compare BYLAW
**localled** *past of* LOCAL
**localling** *pres part of* LOCAL
**lo·cal·ly** \'lōkəlē, -li\ *adv* [ME *localliche*, fr. *localle* local + *-iche* -y] **1** : in relation to position in space **2** : in relation or respect to a particular place or situation **3** : in or about an area under consideration : NEARBY ⟨much corn is grown ~⟩ **4** : in the region of origin : in the place where native or grown ⟨a fruit used ~ to flavor brandy⟩
**lo·cal·ness** *n* -ES : the quality or state of being local; *esp* : concern with local matters
**local officer** *n* : a layman in a Salvation Army corps who voluntarily undertakes part-time duties and serves without pay
**local option** *n* : the privilege or power granted by a legislature to a political subdivision (as a town) to determine by popular vote of the citizens of the subdivision whether a law on a controversial issue (as the sale of liquor or the fluoridation of the water supply) shall apply in the subdivision
**local preacher** *n* : a layman licensed by his church to preach in a specified district
**local rate** *n* : a transportation rate for a shipment that does not leave the lines of the originating carrier
**local road** *or* **local street** *n* : a way used primarily for access to adjacent property
**locals** *pl of* LOCAL, *pres 3d sing of* LOCAL
**local self-government** *n* : LOCAL GOVERNMENT 1b
**local service airline** *n* : an airline that connects cities or larger terminals with smaller communities or makes all or most stops between larger terminals — called also *feeder line*
**local time** *n* : time expressed with respect to the celestial meridian of a particular place being the same for all points along the same meridian of longitude — usu. distinguished from *standard time* and *Greenwich time*
**local union** *n* **1** : a local branch of a trade union (as a national or international union) made up of many branches **2** : a trade union that exists only in a particular locality and is not affiliated with a larger union
**lo·cant** \'lōkənt\ *n* -s [*location* + *-ant*] : the portion of a chemical name that designates the position of an atom or group in a molecule (as *β-* in *β-naphthylamine*, *m-* in *m-xylene*, *2-* in *2-butanol*, or *1-* in *glucose-1-$C^{14}$*)
**lo·car·no** \lō'kär(,)nō\ *n* -s *usu cap* [fr. the *Locarno* Pact, a series of treaties and conventions between Germany on the one hand and Belgium, France, Great Britain, Italy, Poland, and Czechoslovakia on the other, signed in Locarno, Switzerland on Dec. 1, 1925] : a nonaggression pact or other arrangement for international peace and security usu. based upon a mutual guarantee of borders by and provision for arbitration of disputes among the signatory nations ⟨proposed an Asian *Locarno* —*Christian Science Monitor*⟩ ⟨pleasant daydreams about *Locarnos* and mutual self-restraint pacts —Delmer Hubbell⟩
**lo·cat·able** \(')lō¦kād·əbəl\ *adj* : possible to locate
**lo·cate** \'lō,kāt *also* ⸗'⸗; *usu* -ād·+V\ *vb* -ED/-ING/-S [L *locatus*, past part. of *locare*, fr. *locus* place — more at STALL] *vi* **1** : to take up one's residence : establish oneself or one's business : SETTLE ⟨the company *located* north of town⟩ ⟨their parents *located* in Ohio⟩ **2** *of a Methodist minister* : to retire from clerical life or duties ~ *vt* **1** : to determine or indicate the place of : define the site or limits of (as by a survey) ⟨*locating* the lines of the property⟩ **2 a** : to set or establish in a particular spot or position : STATION ⟨*located* himself behind the screen⟩ ⟨carefully *located* the clock in the exact center of the mantel⟩ **b** : to establish in a charge or office **3 a** : to seek out and discover the position of ⟨*located* the children in the attic⟩ ⟨try to ~ the source of the sound⟩ **b** : to find the place of or assign a place to in a sequence ⟨*locating* the reigns of the pastoral kings⟩ **c** : to determine the position of (a mathematical object) ⟨~ a decimal point⟩ ⟨~ a point in a plane⟩ **4** *civil law* : to let out by a contract of location
**lo·cat·er** \-ād·ə(r)\ *n* -s : one that locates
**lo·ca·tio** \lō'kād·ē,ō\ *n* -s [L (also, location)] *Roman, civil, & Scots law* : LETTING, LEASING
**locatio con·duc·tio** \-kən'dùktē,ō\ *or* **locatio et conductio** \-,etkən-\ *n* [L, letting (and) hiring] *Roman & civil law* : a contract of letting and hiring
**lo·ca·tion** \lō'kāshən\ *n* -s [L *location-, locatio*, fr. *locatus* (past part. of *locare* to place, lease) + *-ion-, -io* -ion — more at LOCATE] **1 a** : an act or the process of locating ⟨devoted all her time to the ~ of the missing money⟩ **b** : the act or process of marking out an area of land : the surveying of a tract of land (as for settlement) **2 a** : a position or site occupied or available for occupancy (as by a building) or marked by some distinguishing feature ⟨a sheltered ~⟩ ⟨much of the charm of the house was in its ~⟩ ⟨discovered the ~ of the hiding place⟩ **b** : an area or tract of land: as (1) : a tract of land whose bounds have been officially designated (as for settlement or

'or a mining claim) (2) *Austral* : FARM, STATION (3) *Africa* : a segregated area of a town or city in which natives are required to live **c** : the center line and grade line of a railway established preparatory to its construction **d** : a place outside of a motion-picture studio where a picture or part of it is filmed — used chiefly in the phrase *on location* **3** : a letting for hire : a contract for the use of something (as a house, a vehicle, the service of a person) for hire — **lo·ca·tion·al** \-shən°l, -shnəl\ *adj* — **locationally** \-°lē, -əlē, |i\ *adv*

**locatio rei** \-'rā\ *n* [L, letting of a thing] *law* : a bailment of a chattel for use and for hire

**¹loc·a·tive** \'läkəd·iv, -ətiv\ *n* -s [L *locus* place + E *-ative* (as in *vocative*)] : the locative case or a word in that case

**²locative** \"\ *adj* [F *locatif*, fr. MF, fr. L *locatus* + MF *-if* -ive] **1** : serving or tending to locate ⟨a ~ impulse⟩ **2** [¹*locative*] : belonging to or being a grammatical case that denotes place or the place where or wherein

**lo·ca·tor** \'lō,kād·ə(r), -ātə- *also* ='==\ *n* -s [L, fr. *locatus* (past part. of *locare* to locate, lease) + *-or* — more at LOCATE] : one that locates: as **a** *civil & Scots law* : one that lets for hire — compare CONDUCTOR 4 **b** : one that locates land or a mining claim **c** : a device used to designate location (as a card or file used to show location of records) **d** : JIG 4b **e** : RADIOLOCATOR

**loc cit** \'läk'sit, 'läk-\ *abbr* [L *loco citato*] in the place cited

**lo·cel·late** \lō'se(,)lāt, -,lət\ *adj* [NL *locellus* + E *-ate*] : divided into locelli — often used in combination ⟨a bi*locellate* ovary⟩

**lo·cel·lus** \-eləs\ *n, pl* **locel·li** \-e,lī\ [NL, fr. LL, compartment, dim. of L *locus* place — more at STALL] **1** : a secondary compartment of a unilocular ovary of various legumes formed by a false partition **2** : either of the two cavities of a pollen sac

**¹loch** \'läk, 'läk\ *n* -s [ME (Sc) *louch, locht*, fr. ScGael *loch*; akin to OIr *loch* lake, pond — more at LAKE] **1** *Scot* : LAKE **2** *Scot* : a bay or arm of the sea esp. when nearly landlocked

**²loch** \'läk\ *n* -s [origin unknown] *Brit* : a fissure or void cavity in a mineral vein esp. of a lead mine

**loch·aber ax** \läk'|äbə(r)-, lä'k|, |abə(r)-\ *n, usu cap L* [fr. *Lochaber*, district in Scotland] : a weapon formerly used by Scottish Highlanders consisting of a pole with a long ax head often provided with a hook at its end

**loch·age** \'läkij\ *or* **loch·a·gus** \lä'kāgəs\ *n, pl* **lochages** \-jəz\ *or* **locha·gi** \-ā,jī\ [Gk *lochagos*, fr. *lochos* + *-agos* (fr. *agein* to lead, drive) — more at AGENT] : the commander of a lochus

**loch·an** \'läkən\ *n* -s [ScGael, dim. of *loch*] *Scot* : a small lake : POND

**loche** \'lōch\ *n* -s [F] **1** *archaic* : LOACH **2** [CanF, fr. F, loach] : the New World burbot

**lo·chet·ic** \lō'ked·ik\ *adj* [LGk *lochētikos*, fr. *lochan* to lie in wait (fr. *lochos* ambush, lochus) + *-ikos* -ic — more at LOCHUS] : lying in wait for prey — used esp. of insects

**lo·chia** \'lōkēə, 'läkēə\ *n, pl* **lochia** [NL, fr. Gk, fr. neut. pl. of *lochios* of childbirth, fr. *lochos* childbirth, ambush, lochus — more at LOCHUS] : a discharge from the uterus and vagina following delivery — **lo·chi·al** \-ēəl\ *adj*

Loch-aber ax

**loch le·ven trout** \-'levən-\ *n, usu cap both Ls* [fr. *Loch Leven*, Scotland] : a trout native to Loch Leven and other lakes of southern Scotland and northern England that is a variety (*Salmo trutta levenensis*) of the European brown trout; *broadly* : any brown trout introduced into and established in North American waters

**loch·us** \'läkəs\ *n, pl* **lochi** \-ā,kī\ [NL, fr. Gk *lochos* ambush, childbirth, lochus; akin to Gk *lechos* bed — more at LIE] : a small division of an ancient Greek army comprising about 100 to 200 men — see LOCHAGE

**lochy** \'läki\ *adj* [¹*loch* + *-y*] *Scot* : having many lakes

**loci** *pl of* LOCUS

**lo·ci·a·tion** \,lōsē'āshən\ *n* -s [*local* + *faciation*] : a subunit of an ecological faciation, one such subunit in each faciation being distinguishable from others in relative abundance of the dominant species

**¹lock** \'läk\ *n* -s [ME *lok, lokk*, fr. OE *locc*; akin to OFris & OS *lok* lock of hair, OHG *loc*, ON *lokkr* lock, L *luctari, luctare* to struggle, wrestle, *luxus* dislocated, Gk *lygos* withe, *lygizein* to bend, twist, Lith *lugnas* flexible; basic meaning: to bend] **1 a** : a tuft, tress, or ringlet of hair as it grows **b locks** *pl* : the hair of the head **c** *obs* : a tress of false or artificial hair **2** : a cohering bunch of wool, cotton, flax, or other natural fiber : TUFT, FLOCK: as **a locks** *pl* : short inferior wool obtained in small bunches (as from the legs) and not part of the coherent fleece **b** : the cotton lint contained in a single cell of a cotton boll; *also* : a cell of a cotton boll **3** : a usu. small quantity esp. of hay or straw : BUNDLE, HEAP

**²lock** \"\ *n* -s [ME *lok*, fr. OE *loc*; akin to OE *lūcan* to lock, close, OHG *loh* enclosure, prison, cave, opening, OHG *lūhhan* to close, ON *lok, loka* lock of a door, *lūka* to close, Goth *galūkan* to enclose, *usluk* opening, OE *locc* lock of hair — more at ¹LOCK] **1 a** : a fastening (as for a door, box, trunk lid, drawer) in which a bolt is secured by any of various mechanisms and can be released by inserting and turning a key or by operating a special device (as a combination, time clock, automatic release button, magnetic solenoid) **b** *obs* : HOBBLE, SHACKLE **c** : the mechanism by which the charge or cartridge of a firearm is exploded — often used in combination; see GUNLOCK, MATCHLOCK **2 a** *obs* : a movable barrier across a stream **b** *archaic* : the space of water between the piers of a bridge **c** (1) : an enclosure (as in a canal, river, or dock) with gates at each end used in raising or lowering boats as they pass from level to level (2) : AIR LOCK 1 **3 a** : a locking or fastening together : a closing of one thing upon another **b** : a group of objects (as vehicles) intricately massed together so as to impede the freedom or mobility of individual objects : a block or jam esp. of traffic **c** (1) : a hold in wrestling secured on one part of the body ⟨an arm*lock*⟩ ⟨a leg *lock*⟩ (2) *obs* : STRATAGEM, TRICK (3) *obs* : DIFFICULTY, DILEMMA **d** : plaster forced through laths to form a key **e** *archaic* : a receiver or place for receipt of stolen goods **f** *or* **lock seam** : a joint made by folding over two or more lapped edges of sheet metal **g** : the contact of a tooth of the escape wheel of a timepiece with the locking surface of the pallet; *specif* : the amount by which the escape tooth overlaps the pallet at the instant it leaves the impulse face **h** (1) : the joint at which two panels of a rail fence are locked together (2) : the triangular area in a field formed by the corner panels of a rail fence **4** [by shortening] : OARLOCK, ROWLOCK **5** : LOCK FORWARD

**³lock** \"\ *vb* -ED/-ING/-s [ME *lokken*, fr. *lok*, n.] *vt* **1** : to fasten the lock of ⟨~ the door⟩ : make fast with or as if with a lock ⟨closed and ~*ed* the box⟩ — often used with *up* ⟨don't forget to ~ up all the doors and windows⟩ ⟨~ up the house⟩ **2 a** : to fasten in or out or to make secure or inaccessible by means of or as if by means of locks : confine or shut in or out ⟨~ oneself in⟩ ⟨~ up the prisoners⟩ ⟨~*ed* their secret in her heart⟩ ⟨~*ing* the child in his arms⟩ ⟨a ship ~*ed* fast in ice⟩ **b** : to hold fast or inactive : OVERCOME, FIX ⟨a mind ~*ed* in contemplation⟩ ⟨sleep ~*ing* the tired eyelids⟩ **3** : to make fast by or as if by the interlacing or interlocking of parts ⟨~*ing* arms across the table⟩: as **a** : to make fast or rigid by the engaging of parts or the action of a restraint esp. friction ⟨~ the wheels of a carriage⟩ **b** : to hold in a close embrace ⟨~*ed* in each other's arms⟩; *also* : to grapple in combat ⟨~*ed* in a death struggle⟩ **c** : to fasten (imposed letterpress matter) securely in a chase or on the bed of a press by tightening the quoins; *also* : to attach (a curved printing plate) to the plate cylinder of a rotary press — usu. used with *up* **4** : to invest (capital) where conversion into money is not easy — usu. used with *up* ⟨had his resources ~*ed* up in the canal scheme⟩ **5 a** : to move or permit to pass (as a ship) by raising or lowering in a lock — often used with *in, out, down, up, or through* **b** : to provide (as a canal) with locks **c** : to divide off (a portion of a river) by a lock — used with *off* ~ *vi* **1** : to become locked : become fixed or fast by or as if by means of a lock ⟨the door ~*s* easily⟩ **2** : INTERLACE, INTERLOCK ⟨the sections ~ into one another⟩ **3 a** *of a vehicle* : to permit the fore wheels to swivel round with more or less freedom in turning **b** *of wheels* : to have such freedom of motion **4 a** : to build locks to facilitate navigation **b** : to go or pass by means of a lock (as in a canal) ⟨~*ed* into the new canal⟩ — **lock horns 1** *of cattle* : to engage or interlock the horns in fighting **2** *of persons* : to come into conflict ⟨will probably *lock horns* over the appointment of a new supervisor⟩

**⁴lock** \"\ *adj* : capable of being made fast : LOCKABLE

**⁵lock** \"\ *vt* -ED/-ING/-s [D *locken*, fr. MD; akin to OE *loccian* to attract, entice, OHG *lockōn, lucchen* to entice, allure, ON *lokka*, and prob. to OHG *liogan* to lie — more at LIE (tell a falsehood)] *archaic* : ALLURE, ENTICE, SEDUCE

**lock·able** \'läkəbəl\ *adj* : capable of being locked ⟨a desk with one ~ drawer⟩

**lock·age** \-kij, -kēj\ *n* -s [²*lock* + *-age*] **1 a** : an act or the process of passing something (as a boat) through a lock **b** : something passed or passing through a lock; *esp* : the quantity (as of logs) that can be locked at one time **2** : the construction of a system of locks (as in a canal); *also* : a system of locks **3** : toll paid for passing through a lock or locks (as of a canal) **4** : the vertical distance through which a boat is raised or lowered in passing through a lock or series of locks; *also* : the volume of water involved in the process

**lockaid gun** \'=,=-\ *n* [²*lock* + *aid*] : a tool consisting of a barrel with a thin vibrator blade used to force open a lock

**lock-and-block system** \'==='=-\ *n, Brit* : a railway block system in which the signals permitting a train to enter a block are locked while a train is in the block and automatically unlocked as it leaves the block

**lock bolt** *n* **1** : BOLT 2b **2 a** : a bolt or pin employing a special locking collar instead of a nut **b** : a bolt for securing an adjustable part of a machine in a desired position

**lockbox** \'=,=\ *n* : a box (as a strongbox or safe-deposit box) that locks; *esp* : a post-office box that is accessible to the renter by means of a key

**lock corner** *n* : a corner (as of a wood or metal box) secured by dovetail or other interlocking construction

**lock-down** \'=,=\ *n* [fr. *lock down*, v.] : a strip of wood with holes in the ends through which pins are driven to hold together a raft of logs

**lock·e·an** *also* **locke·i·an** *or* **lock·i·an** \'läkēən\ *adj, usu cap* [John *Locke* †1704 Eng. philosopher + E *-an, -ian*] : of or relating to John Locke or to his theories or philosophical system

**lock·e·an·ism** *also* **lock·i·anism** \-ēə,nizəm\ *n* -s *usu cap* : the philosophical system of John Locke that denies the existence of innate ideas and asserts that the mind orig. resembles a tabula rasa so that all knowledge comes from experience specif. from sense perception and from reflection upon the relations of apprehended ideas and the operations of the mind itself, maintains that the primary qualities of objects (as extension, figure, number, motion, rest) inhere in the objects independently of being perceived and that the secondary qualities (as color, sound, odor) are caused by external objects but do not resemble them, and holds that political sovereignty is based on the consent of the governed

**locked** *adj* [fr. past part. of ³*lock*] **1** : fastened or united by locking ⟨a ~ closet⟩ **2 a** : *of a joint* : held rigidly in the position assumed during complete extension ⟨struck a blow with a ~ wrist⟩ **b** *of the knee joint* : having a restricted mobility and incapable of complete extension

**locked groove** *n* : a final closed groove on a recording disc

**locked-in** \'=,=\ *adj* [fr. past part. of *lock in*] : unalterably fixed ⟨a *locked-in* finish⟩

**locked jaw** *var of* LOCKJAW

**locked jury** *n* : a jury considering a case under orders not to separate and to communicate with no one except the court or its officers

**locked-wire rope** *or* **locked-coil wire rope** *n* : a rope esp. adapted for haulage and rope transmission having a smooth cylindrical surface and made by drawing the outer wires to such shape that each one interlocks with the other so that the wires lie in concentric layers about a wire core

**lock·er** \'läkə(r)\ *n* -s [ME *lokker*, fr. *lokken* lock + *-er* — more at LOCK] **1** : a container used for safekeeping or storage and usu. capable of being locked: as **a** : a drawer, cupboard, or compartment that may be closed with a lock; *esp* : one for individual storage use ⟨gym ~*s*⟩ **b** : a chest or compartment on shipboard for compact stowage of articles of a particular class ⟨a boatswain's ~⟩ ⟨forward paint ~*s*⟩; *esp* : an enclosed storage space (as for valuable cargo) **c** *South* : LINEN CLOSET **d** : one of the compartments available for rent in a locker plant designed for storing quick-frozen foods for extended periods usu. at or below 0° F and at 80% relative humidity **2** *archaic* : a locking device **3** : one that locks: as **a** : a British customs employee in charge of a warehouse **b** : a locking device for use on a vehicle wheel

**locker paper** *n* : a flexible protective paper for wrapping food for quick-freezing and storage

**locker plant** *n* : a refrigeration and storage establishment consisting of quick-freezing equipment and storage lockers rentable for food storage

**locker room** *n* : a room devoted to storage lockers; *esp* : one in which participants in a sport have individual lockers for their clothes and special equipment and change into and out of sports costume

**locke's solution** \'läk(s)-\ *or* **locke solution** *n, usu cap L* [after Frank S. *Locke*, 19th-20th cent. Brit. physiologist] : a solution isotonic with blood plasma that contains the chlorides of sodium, potassium, and calcium and sodium bicarbonate and dextrose and is used similarly to physiological saline

**lock·et** \'läkət, *usu* -əd·+V\ *n* -s [MF *loquet* latch, fr. MD *loke* latch, bolt + MF *-et* (dim. suffix); akin to OE *loc* bolt, lock — more at LOCK] **1** *obs* : a crossbar of a window **2** : a part of a scabbard where a belt hook fastens **3** : a group of set jewels **4** : a catch or spring for fastening something (as a necklace) **5 a** : a small and often ornate case usu. of precious metal having space for a memento (as a miniature or a lock of hair) and worn typically suspended from a chain or necklace **b** : a patch of distinctive color (as white) on the throat or chest of a cat

locket 5a

**lockfast** \'=,=\ *adj* [ME (Sc) *lokfast*, fr. *lok* lock + *fast*] *Scot* : made fast by a lock

**lock forward** *n* : the middle player in the third row of the scrum in rugby

**lock-grained** \'=,=\ *adj, of lumber* : having interlaced grain

**lock handle** *also* **locking handle** *n* : a handle that can be locked in a fixed position

**lockhole** \'=,=\ *n* : KEYHOLE

**lock hospital** *n, Brit* : a hospital for the treatment of venereal diseases

**lockhouse** \'=,=\ *n* : a house for the person in charge of a canal or river lock

**lockian** *usu cap, var of* LOCKEAN

**lockier** *comparative of* LOCKY

**lockiest** *superlative of* LOCKY

**locking** *pres part of* LOCK

**locking plate** *n* : the count wheel used in one type of clock striking train — distinguished from *rack*

**locking ring** *n* : a screw collar connecting the tube and jacket of some types of guns of minor caliber

**lockjaw** \'=,=\ *also* **locked jaw** *n* : an early symptom of tetanus characterized by spasm of the jaw muscles and inability to open the jaws : TRISMUS; *broadly* : TETANUS

**lock-joint** \'=,=\ *n* : a joint in which the elements joined are interlocked (as in a dovetail joint) with or without other fastening (as glue, solder, or pinning)

**lockkeeper** \'=,==\ *n* : a person in charge of a lock (as on a canal) ⟨the ~ . . . came to the rescue with his boathook —Thomas Hughes⟩

**lockless** \'läkləs\ *adj* : having no lock ⟨a ~ cabin⟩ ⟨a long ~ stretch of water⟩

**lockmaker** \'=,==\ *n* : one that makes locks

**lockmaking** \'=,==\ *n* : the process of making locks

**lock·man** \'läkmən\ *n, pl* **lockmen** **1** *Scot* : a public executioner **2** : a coroner's summoner in the Isle of Man **3** : LOCKKEEPER, LOCKMASTER

**lockmaster** \'=,==\ *n* : a person who immediately directs the operation of a lock (as of a canal) ⟨the ~ . . . relays word to the control tower that we are ready to start our lift —J.H. Winchester⟩

**Lock-nit** \'läk,nit\ *trademark* — used for a fabric knitted with an interlocking stitch that resists runs

**locknut** \'=,=\ *n* **1** : a nut screwed down hard on another to prevent it from slacking back **2** : a nut so constructed that it locks itself when screwed up tight **3** : a nut screwed against the end of a pipe fitting to hold it securely and prevent leakage **4** : a nut used with an electrical conduit for locking it into a junction box or fitting

**lock on** *vt* : to sight and follow (a target) automatically by means of a radar beam ⟨will automatically follow, through any gyrations, the object on its screen to which it has been *locked on* —*New Republic*⟩

**lock out** *vt* **1** : to withhold employment from (a body of employees) in order to gain concessions **2** : to shut out from by or as if by a locked door ⟨meters are usually *locked out* of the system when premises are to be left vacant⟩

**¹lockout** \'=,=\ *n* -s [*lock out*] : an act of locking out or the condition of being locked out: as **a** : the withholding of employment by an employer and the whole or partial closing of his business establishment in order to gain concessions from employees — compare STRIKE **b** : involuntary closure of secure premises (as a bank vault) due to failure of an intricate time-lock device either by chance or as a result of tampering

**²lockout** \"\ *adj* : serving to prevent operation of a device or part of it ⟨the ~ circuit breaker operates when there is an excessive current flowing —Ernest Venk & William Landon⟩

**lockpick** \'=,=\ *n* : PICKLOCK

**lockpin** \'=,=\ *n* : a peg or pin that is inserted through a hole or holes and locks two parts together

**lock plate** *n* : a plate to which the several parts of the lock of some firearms are attached and by which the whole is fastened to the stock by screws

**lock rail** *n* : a horizontal stiffening member of a paneled door in or to which the lock is fixed

**lock·ram** \'läkrəm\ *n* -s [ME *lokerham*, alter. (influenced by *bukeram, bokeram* buckram) of *Locronan*, town in Brittany where it was made] **1** : a coarse plain-woven linen of French origin formerly used in England (as for clothing) **2** *or* **lock-rum** \"\ *dial* : NONSENSE

**locks** *pl of* LOCK, *pres 3d sing of* LOCK

**lock seam** *n* : LOCK 3f

**lockset** \'=,=\ *n* **1** : a complete lock system including the lock mechanism together with knobs, keys, plates, strikes, and other accessories **2** : a jig or template used to prepare a door for receiving a lock

**locks·man** \'läksmən\ *n, pl* **locksmen** **1** *Scot* : TURNKEY **2** : LOCKKEEPER

**locksmith** \'=,=\ *n* [ME *loksmith*, fr. *lok* lock + *smith* — more at LOCK, SMITH] : a worker who makes or repairs locks

**locksmithing** \'=,==\ *n* : the work or business of a locksmith

**lockspit** \'=,=\ *n* [³*lock* + *spit* (spadeful)] *Brit* : a small trench cut to indicate the line to be followed in further work (as in making a railroad or a line of fortifications)

**lockstep** \'=,=\ *n* : a mode of marching in step by a body of men (as prisoners) going one after another as closely as possible

**lock stile** *n* : the stile on the free edge of a door that receives the lock — compare LOCK RAIL

**¹lockstitch** \'=,=\ *n* [²*lock* + *stitch*] : a sewing machine stitch formed by the looping together of two threads one on each side of the material being sewn

**²lockstitch** \"\ *vt* : to sew on or together with a lockstitch ⟨~*ing* the border of the cuff⟩ ~ *vi* : to sew with a lockstitch ⟨most modern sewing machines ~⟩

**lock, stock, and barrel** *adv* [so called fr. the three principal parts of a flintlock] : WHOLLY, COMPLETELY ⟨sold his property *lock, stock, and barrel*⟩ ⟨took over the duties of his predecessor *lock, stock, and barrel*⟩

**lock strike** *n* : a metal fastening on a doorframe into which the bolt of a lock is projected to secure the door

**lock tender** *n* **1** : LOCKKEEPER **2** : a worker in charge of an air lock (as of a caisson)

**lock time** *n* : the interval between the releasing of the hammer on a firearm and the striking of the primer by the firing pin

**lock turtle** *or* **lock tortoise** *n* : BOX TORTOISE

**lockup** \'=,=\ *n* -s [fr. *lock up*, v.] **1** : an act of locking or the state of being locked ⟨~ occurs regularly at six o'clock⟩ **2** : something that is or is intended to be locked: as **a** : JAIL; *esp* : a local jail where persons are detained prior to court hearing **b** *Brit* : a shop or store without living quarters **c** *chiefly Brit* : rented storage space (as a locker or garage) that may be locked by the user **d** (1) : a credit obligation (as a renewed note) or other investment in which capital is locked up (2) : a stamp or other philatelic item bought speculatively for anticipated appreciation in value **3 a** : the operation of locking up imposed letterpress matter **b** : the quality of such locking up ⟨a secure ~ for foundry⟩

**lock washer** *n* : a washer (as a spring washer or a tooth lock washer) placed underneath a nut or screwhead to prevent loosening

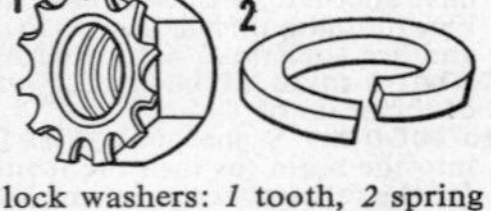

lock washers: *1* tooth, *2* spring

**lockwire** \'=,=\ *n* : wire thrust through matching holes (as in a nut and bolt) to lock parts together, the ends often being secured by a metal seal

**lockwork** \'=,=\ *n* : the mechanism on or in locks : the parts of a lock

**locky** \'läkē\ *adj* -ER/-EST : having or characterized by locks ⟨a loose ~ fleece⟩

**locn** *abbr* location

**¹lo·co** \'lō(,)kō\ *n* -s *often cap* [by shortening] : LOCOFOCO 2

**²loco** \"\ *n, pl* **locoes** *or* **locos** [MexSp, fr. Sp, adj., crazy] **1** : LOCOWEED **2** *or* **loco disease** : LOCOISM **3 a** : an animal affected by locoism **b** : a mentally disordered person

**³loco** \"\ *vt* -ED/-ING/-s **1** : to poison with locoweed **2** : to make or cause to be frenzied or crazy

**⁴loco** \"\ *adj* [Sp] *slang* : out of one's mind : FRENZIED ⟨went ~ with rage⟩ : CRAZY ⟨a ~ idea⟩

**⁵loco** \"\ *adv (or adj)* [It (*al*) *loco*, lit., at the passage] : in the register as written — used as a direction in music; compare OTTAVA

**⁶loco** \"\ *n* -s [by shortening] : LOCOMOTIVE

**loco-** *comb form* [F, fr. MF, fr. L *loco*, abl. of *locus* place — more at STALL] **1** : from place to place ⟨*locomotion*⟩ **2** : place ⟨*locodescriptive*⟩

**lo·co ci·ta·to** \'lō(,)kōsī'tā(,)tō, 'lä(,)kōsə'tä(,)tō\ *adv* [L] : in the place cited : in the passage quoted — abbr. *loc. cit.*

**lo·co·descriptive** \,lōkō+\ *adj* [*loco-* + *descriptive*] : describing a locality or a particular place

**locoed** *adj* [fr. past part. of ³*loco*] **1** *West, of an animal* : affected by locoism **2** *West, of a person* : ECCENTRIC, CRAZY, INSANE

**lo·co·fo·co** \,lōkō'fō(,)kō\ *n* -s [prob. fr. ¹*locomotive* (self-propelled) + It *foco, fuoco* fire, fr. L *focus* fireplace, hearth — more at FOCUS] **1** : a match or cigar developed during the 19th century and capable of being ignited by friction on any hard dry rough surface ⟨~*s* . . . were a decided improvement over the lucifers —*Springfield (Mass.) Union*⟩ — compare LUCIFER, SAFETY MATCH **2** *usu cap* [so called fr. a meeting of New York City Democrats on Oct. 22, 1835, to which the radical members came provided with matches to forestall a reported plot by their adversaries to disrupt the meeting by putting out the lights] **a** : a member of a radical group of New York Democrats organized in 1835 in opposition to the regular party organization ⟨editorials that, in the fashion of the northern *Locofocos*, called for . . . freedom of banking —Joseph Dorfman⟩ **b** : DEMOCRAT 2 ⟨the two great belligerents — the *Locofocos* and Whigs —*Diplomatic Correspondence of Texas*⟩

**lo·co·fo·co·ism** \-'fōkō,izəm\ *n* -s *often cap* : the principles of the Locofocos ⟨the most arrant democracy and ~ that I ever happened to hear —Nathaniel Hawthorne⟩

**lo·co·ism** \'lōkō,izəm\ *n* -s [²*loco* + *-ism*] **1** : a disease of horses, cattle, and sheep caused by chronic poisoning with locoweeds and characterized by motor and sensory nerve damage resulting in peculiarities of gait, impairment of vision, lassitude or extreme excitement, emaciation, and ultimately paralysis and death if not controlled **2 :** any of several intoxications of domestic animals (as alkali disease) that are sometimes confused with locoweed poisoning

1**lo·co·mo·bile** \¦lōkəmō¦bēl\ *adj* [F, fr. *loco-* + *mobile*] **:** having the power to move about **:** SELF-PROPELLING ⟨a ~ crane⟩ — **lo·co·mo·bil·i·ty** \ˌ≈≈≈'biləd·ē\ *n*

2**locomobile** \"\ *n* [F, fr. *locomobile*, adj.] **:** a self-propelling vehicle or engine

**lo·co·mote** \'lōkəˌmōt, ˌ≈≈'≈\ *vi* -ED/-ING/-S [back-formation fr. *locomotion*] **:** to move about ⟨*locomoting* down the road with a peculiar halting stride⟩

**lo·co·mo·tion** \ˌlōkə'mōshən\ *n* [*loco-* + *motion*] **1 :** an act or the power of moving from place to place **:** progressive movement (as of an animal body) **2 :** TRAVEL

1**lo·co·mo·tive** \¦lōkə¦mōd·|iv, -mōt|, |ēv *also* ¦əv; *by railroad men sometimes* ¦lək-\ *adj* [F, fr. MF, fr. *loco-* + LL *motivus* moving, capable of moving — more at MOTIVE] **1 a :** of or relating to locomotion ⟨the ~ faculty typical of animal life⟩ **b :** having the ability to move independently from place to place ⟨a ~ mollusk⟩ **c :** functioning in locomotion **:** LOCOMOTOR ⟨~ organs include flagella, cilia, pseudopodia, and limbs⟩ **2 a :** of or relating to travel ⟨a positive ~ mania⟩ **b :** traveling much or frequently ⟨having lately led a very ~ existence⟩ **3 :** of, relating to, or being a machine (as an engine) that moves about by operation of its own mechanism ⟨a ~ crane⟩ — **lo·co·mo·tive·ly** \|əvlē, -li\ *adv* — **lo·co·mo·tive·ness** \|ivnəs, |ēv- *also* |əv-\ *n* -ES

2**locomotive** \"\ *n* **1 a** *archaic Brit* **:** LOCOMOBILE **b :** a self-propelled vehicle or combination of self-propelled vehicles operating under a single control, running on rails, utilizing any of several forms of energy for producing motion, and used for moving railroad cars — compare DIESEL-ELECTRIC LOCOMOTIVE, ELECTRIC LOCOMOTIVE, STEAM LOCOMOTIVE, TURBINE-ELECTRIC LOCOMOTIVE, TURBINE LOCOMOTIVE **2 :** a cheer characterized by a slow beginning and a progressive increase in speed and used esp. at school and college sports events

**locomotive engineer** *n* **:** ENGINEER 4b

**lo·co·mo·tive·man** \¦≈≈¦≈≈ˌman\ *n, pl* **locomotivemen** *Brit* **:** ENGINEER 4b

**locomotive works** *n pl but sing or pl in constr* **:** a plant for building locomotives

**lo·co·mo·tiv·i·ty** \ˌlōkəmō'tivəd·ē\ *n* **:** locomotive power **:** capacity for independent movement

1**lo·co·mo·tor** \¦lōkə¦mōd·ə(r), -mōtə-\ *n* [*loco-* + L *motor* one that moves — more at MOTOR] **:** one that has power of locomotion

2**locomotor** \"\ *also* **lo·co·mo·to·ry** \¦≈≈¦mōd·ərē\ *adj* **1 :** of or relating to locomotion **:** functioning in or concerned with locomotion **:** LOCOMOTIVE 1 **2 :** affecting or involving the organs concerned with locomotion ⟨~ incoordination⟩

**locomotor ataxia** *n* **:** TABES DORSALIS

**locos** *pl of* LOCO, *pres 3d sing of* LOCO

**locoweed** \'≈≈ˌ≈\ *n* [2*loco* + *weed*] **1 :** any of several leguminous plants (genera *Astragalus* and *Oxytropis*) of western No. America that cause locoism in livestock **2 :** any of several noxious or poisonous plants other than those causing locoism: as **a** *West* (1) **:** a plant (as white snakeroot or rayless goldenrod) associated with alkali disease (2) **:** WATER HEMLOCK 1 (3) **:** any of several wild larkspurs of western No. America that are poisonous to livestock **b** *slang* **:** HEMP 1; *also* **:** MARIJUANA

1**lo·cri·an** \'lōkrēən, 'läk-\ *adj, usu cap* [*Locris*, region in the central part of ancient Greece (fr. L, fr. Gk *Lokris*) + E *-an*] **:** of or relating to Locris in ancient Greece

2**locrian** \"\ *adj, usu cap* [*Locri*, ancient city in southwestern Italy (fr. L) + E *-an*] **:** of or relating to the ancient city of Locri

**locrian mode** *n, usu cap L* [1*Locrian*] **:** an authentic ecclesiastical mode represented on the white keys of the piano by an ascending scale from B to B but not actually used because its pentachord and tetrachord comprise respectively the forbidden diminished fifth and augmented fourth — see MODE illustration

**loc·tal** *or* **lok·tal** \'läktᵊl\ *adj* [fr. *Loktal*, a trademark] **:** having, being, or fitting an 8-pin vacuum-tube base having a central guide pin with a groove that fits into a spring catch in the socket to hold the tube firmly in place

**loc·u·la·ment** \'läkyələmənt\ *n* -S [L *loculamentum* receptacle, fr. *loculus* compartment, receptacle, coffin + *mentum* -ment — more at LOCULUS] **:** LOCULUS b

**loc·u·lar** \¦läkyələ(r)\ *adj* [ISV *locul-* (fr. NL *loculus*) + *-ar*] **:** having or composed of loculi — usu. used in combination ⟨multi*locular*⟩

**loc·u·late** \-yələ̇t, -yəˌlāt\ *or* **loc·u·lat·ed** \-ˌlād·ə̇d\ *adj* [NL *loculus* + E *-ate* or *-ated* (fr. *-ate* + *-ed*)] **:** having, forming, or divided into loculi ⟨a ~ pocket of pleural fluid⟩ ⟨a ~ ovary⟩

**loc·u·la·tion** \ˌläkyə'lāshən\ *n* -S **1 :** the condition of being or the process of becoming loculate ⟨a gradual ~ of bony tissue⟩ **2 :** a group of loculi usu. isolated from surrounding structures (as by a fibrous tissue septum) ⟨the development of ~*s* in empyema⟩

**loc·ule** \'läˌkyül\ *n* -S [F, fr. L *loculus* compartment, receptacle, coffin — more at LOCULUS] **:** LOCULUS — used chiefly in botany

**loc·uled** \-ld\ *adj* **:** LOCULATE

**loc·u·li·ci·dal** \¦läkyələ¦sīdᵊl\ *adj* [NL *loculus* + E *-i-* + *-cidal*] *of a capsular fruit* **:** dehiscent longitudinally so as to bisect each loculus — compare CIRCUMSCISSILE, SEPTICIDAL; see FRUIT illustration — **loc·u·li·ci·dal·ly** \-ᵊlē\ *adv*

**loc·u·lus** \'läkyələs\ *n, pl* **locu·li** \-yəˌlī\ [NL, fr. L, compartment, receptacle, coffin, dim. of *locus* place — more at STALL] **:** a small chamber or cavity: as **a :** a recess in an ancient tomb or catacomb for the reception of a body or a funeral urn **b** (1) **:** one of the cells of the compound ovary of a plant (2) **:** the cavity of a pollen sac (3) **:** a spore-bearing chamber in the stroma of a fungus **c** (1) **:** one of the spaces between the septa of the theca of an anthozoan (2) **:** one of the chambers in the shell of a foraminifer (3) **:** an egg case (as of a mollusk) (4) **:** a sucker on a haptor **d :** a small sinus in a bone (as in the mastoid bone)

**lo·cum** \'lōkəm\ *n* -S **1** [by shortening] **:** LOCUM TENENS **2** [by shortening] **:** LOCUM TENENCY

**lo·cum·ship** \-mˌship\ *n* -S [*locum* + *-ship*] **:** LOCUM-TENENCY

**locum–te·nen·cy** \-'tēnənsē, -'tenə-\ *n* -ES [ML *locum tenentia*, fr. *locum tenent-*, *locum tenens* + L *-ia* -y] **:** the position or duties of a locum tenens

**locum te·nens** \-'tē|ˌnenz, -'te|, |nənz\ *n, pl* **locum tenen·tes** \-tə'nen·ˌtēz\ [ML, lit., one holding an office] **:** one filling an office for a time or temporarily taking the place of another **:** SUBSTITUTE, DEPUTY — used esp. of a physician or clergyman

**lo·cus** \'lōkəs\ *n, pl* **lo·ci** \'lōˌsī, -ˌsē, -ˌkē\ *also* **lo·ca** \'lōkə\ [L — more at STALL] **1 :** PLACE, LOCALITY; *esp* **:** the place connected with a particular event having legal import — used esp. in legal phrases **2** [by shortening] **:** LOCUS CLASSICUS **3** [NL, fr. L] **a :** the regular linear position occupied in a chromosome by any one gene or its allele **b :** the point in a chromosome associated with a particular hereditary character **4** [NL, fr. L] *math* **:** the collection of all points whose location is determined by some stated law

**locus clas·si·cus** \-'klasə̇kəs\ *n, pl* **lo·ci classi·ci** \-ˌsī'klasəˌsī\ [L] **:** a classical passage **:** a standard passage important for the elucidation of a word or subject

**lo·cus poe·ni·ten·ti·ae** \-ˌpenə'tenchēˌē\ *n, pl* **loci poenitentiae** [LL, lit., place of repentance] **:** an opportunity to withdraw or resile from an inchoate obligation before it is completed **:** an opportunity to change one's mind or to decide not to commit an intended crime

**locus si·gil·li** \-sə'jiˌlī\ *n, pl* **loci sigilli** [L] **:** the place of or for the seal — abbr. *L. S.*

**locus stan·di** \-'standē, -nˌdī\ *n, pl* **loci standi** [L, lit., place to stand] **:** a right to appear in a court or before any body on a given question **:** a right to be heard

**lo·cust** \'lōkəst\ *n* -S [ME, fr. L *locusta* locust, lobster; perh. akin to L *lacertus* muscle — more at LEG] **1 :** a grasshopper of the family Acrididae; *esp* **:** any of numerous migratory grasshoppers that often travel in vast swarms and strip the areas through which they pass of all vegetation **2 :** CICADA 2 **3 a** *or* **locust tree :** any of various hard-wooded trees of the family Leguminosae: as (1) **:** CAROB 1a (2) **:** a tall tree (*Robinia pseudoacacia*) of eastern No. America that has pinnately compound leaves, drooping racemes of fragrant white flowers, and strong stiff wood that is remarkably resistant to decay — called also *black locust*, *honey locust* (3) **:** COURBARIL 1 (4) **:** HONEY LOCUST 1a(1) (5) *NewZeal* **:** KOWHAI **b :** any of various trees of other families resembling a locust — used with a qualifying term ⟨bastard ~⟩ **c :** the wood of a locust tree

**lo·cus·ta** \lō'kəstə\ *n, cap* [NL, fr. L, locust] **1 :** a genus of short-horned grasshoppers including the common migratory locust of the Old World **2** *in some esp former classifications* **:** a variously limited genus of long-horned grasshoppers

**lo·cus·tal** \-tᵊl\ *adj* [NL *Locusta* + E *-al*] **:** of or relating to locusts or to the genus *Locusta*

**lo·cus·tar·i·an** \ˌlōkə'sta(a)rēən\ *n* -S [NL *Locustariae*, old name designating a group of saltatorial insects (fr. *Locusta* + L *-ariae*, fem. pl. of *-arius* -ary) + E *-an*] **:** LOCUST 1, CICADA 2

**locust bean** *n* **1 :** CAROB 1b **2 :** AFRICAN LOCUST

**locust bean gum** *n* **:** CAROB GUM

**locust bean gum powder** *or* **locust bean flour** *n* **:** CAROB FLOUR

**lo·cust·berry** \'lōkəst- — *see* BERRY\ *n* **1 :** any of several nances (genus *Byrsonima*) of extreme southern Florida and the West Indies **2 :** the acid drupe of a locustberry sometimes used as food

**locust bird** *n* **1** *India* **:** ROSE-COLORED STARLING **2** *Africa* **a :** GRACKLE **b :** WHITE STORK **c :** a pratincole (*Glareola nordmanni*)

**locust borer** *also* **locust beetle** *n* **:** a brownish black yellow-barred long-horned beetle (*Megacyllene robiniae*) whose larvae bore in the wood of the black locust tree

**locust eater** *n* **1 :** DIAL BIRD **2 :** ROSE-COLORED STARLING

**lo·cus·telle** \ˌlōkə'stel\ *n* -S [F, dim. of *locuste* locust, fr. L *locusta* — more at LOCUST] **:** GRASSHOPPER WARBLER

1**lo·cus·ti·dae** \lō'kəstəˌdē\ [NL, fr. *Locusta* + *-idae*] *syn of* ACRIDIDAE

2**locustidae** \"\ [NL, fr. *Locusta* + *-idae*] *syn of* TETTIGONIIDAE

**locust leaf miner** *n* **:** a small orange and black beetle (*Xenochalepus dorsalis*) that skeletonizes the leaves of the black and honey locust or its larva that mines within the leaves

**locustlike** \'≈≈ˌ≈\ *adj* **:** like a locust; *esp* **:** like a migratory locust in voracity, swarming habit, or numbers

**locust lobster** *n* [*locust* fr. It. *locusta* locust, lobster, fr. L — more at LOCUST] **:** a decapod crustacean of the family Scyllaridae; *esp* **:** a large edible crustacean (*Scyllarus arctus*) of the Mediterranean sea that somewhat resembles a lobster

**locust plant** *n* **:** a wild senna (*Cassia marilandica*)

**locust pod** *n* **:** CAROB 1b

**locust shrimp** *n* **:** SQUILLA 2

**locust tree** *n* **:** LOCUST 3a

**lo·cu·tion** \lō'kyüshən\ *n* -S [ME *locucioun*, fr. L *locution-*, *locutio*, fr. *locutus* (past part. of *loqui* to speak) + *-ion-*, *-io* -ion] **1 :** a particular form of expression **:** a peculiarity of phrasing; *esp* **:** a word, phrase, or expression characteristic of a region, group, or cultural level ⟨~*s* which nearly all . . . hill people use daily — *Amer. Guide Series: Ark.*⟩ **2** *obs* **:** the act of uttering **:** SPEECH ⟨and give ~ from a thousand tongues —W.L.Lewis⟩ **3 :** style of discourse **:** PHRASEOLOGY ⟨the vein of Homeric feeling and the general style of ~ . . . would be maintained —George Grote⟩

**lo·cu·tor·ship** \lō'kyüd·ə(r)ˌship\ *n* [L *locutor* speaker (fr. *locutus* + *-or*) + E *-ship*] **:** the office of spokesman

**LOD** *abbr* **1 :** line of dance **2 :** line of direction **3 :** line of duty

**lod·di·ge·sia** \ˌlädə'jēzēə\ *n, cap* [NL, fr. Conrad *Loddiges* †1826 Eng. nurseryman + NL *-ia*] **:** a genus of hummingbirds containing one species (*L. mirabilis*) of Peru in which the two outer tail feathers are very long and devoid of webs except at the ends

**lode** *also* **load** \'lōd\ *n* -S [ME *lod*, *lode*, fr. OE *lād* way, course, journey, carrying, support; akin to ON *leith* way, course, OE *līthan* to go — more at LEAD] **1** *dial Eng* **a :** COURSE, PATH, ROAD **b :** WATERWAY, CANAL; *also* **:** an open drain ⟨down that long dark ~ . . . he and his brothers skated home —Charles Kingsley⟩ **2 :** a deposit of ore: as **a :** a mineral deposit that fills a fissure in the country rock **b :** an ore deposit occurring in place within definite boundaries separating it from the adjoining rocks — called also *lead*, *vein;* compare PLACER **3 :** something that resembles a lode ⟨found a new ~ of moral strength —A.C.Fields⟩ ⟨had struck a ~ of human kindliness —Marcia Davenport⟩ ⟨his letters are an astonishingly rich ~ of information —J.M.England⟩

**lode·man·age** \'lōdmənij\ *n* -S [ME *lodmanage*, fr. *lodman* pilot (fr. OE *lādman*, fr. *lād* + *man*) + *-age*] **:** PILOTAGE

**lo·den** \'lōdᵊn\ *or* **loden cloth** *n* -S *sometimes cap L* [G *loden*, fr. OHG *lodo*, *ludo* coarse cloth] **:** a thick woolen cloth of Tyrolean origin that is heavily fulled to make it wind and water resistant and is used for outer clothing

**lode·star** *or* **load·star** \'lōdˌstär, -tȧ\ *n* [ME *lodsterre*, *lodesterre*, fr. *lod*, *lode* lode + *sterre* star — more at STAR] **1 :** a star that leads or guides; *esp* **:** POLESTAR 1 **2 :** someone or something that serves as a guiding star or as a focus of hope or attention ⟨a strangely compelling . . . human ~ whose influence half the time was unsuspected —Struthers Burt⟩ ⟨inconstancy and opportunism were the ~*s* of the day —*Saturday Rev.*⟩

**lodestone** *or* **loadstone** \'≈ˌ≈\ *n* [*lode*, *load* + *stone*] **1 :** magnetite possessing polarity **2 :** something that strongly attracts **:** MAGNET ⟨was a scholastic ~ himself, and students . . . flocked to his classes —T.S.Lovering⟩ ⟨devotion to the law — the ~ of his life —*Newsweek*⟩

1**lodge** \'läj\ *vb* -ED/-ING/-S [ME *loggen*, fr. OF *logier*, fr. *loge*, n.] *vt* **1 a :** to provide temporary quarters for **:** give a place to sleep to **:** show hospitality to ⟨there were some in which two or three hundred people . . . could without difficulty be *lodged* and fed —T.B.Macaulay⟩ **b :** to establish or settle in a place ⟨the troops *lodged* themselves in the enemy's outworks⟩ **c :** to serve as a habitation or shelter for ⟨every house was proud to ~ a knight —John Dryden⟩ **d :** to rent lodgings to **:** ACCOMMODATE 4b ⟨hoped they would ~ him for the winter⟩ **2 :** to serve as a receptacle for **:** CONTAIN ⟨a sinus *lodging* the nerve and artery of the part⟩ **3 :** to drive or track (a deer) to covert **4 :** to beat flat on the ground ⟨though bladed corn be *lodged* and trees blown down —*Shak.*⟩ **5 a :** to cause to reach an intended or a fixed position or place usu. by throwing, discharging, or thrusting ⟨two bullets were found *lodged* in the table —*Newsweek*⟩ ⟨the limit of my ambition is to ~ a few pebbles where they will be hard to get rid of —Robert Frost⟩ **b :** to deposit in passing ⟨a fish bone that was *lodged* in his throat⟩ **6 a :** to place in custody **:** INCARCERATE ⟨his scurrilities may ~ him in the pillory —H.M.Reichard⟩ ⟨just 45 days after the perpetration of the crime, every participant was securely *lodged* behind bars —D.D.Martin⟩ **b :** to deposit for safeguard or preservation ⟨agents collect the rent for the land, and ~ it in the bank —G.B.Shaw⟩ ⟨wrote a full account of our transaction and *lodged* it with a trusty man —J.H.Wheelwright⟩ **7 :** to place or vest esp. in a source, means, or agent ⟨we shall reach the best results if we ~ power in a group —B.N. Cardozo⟩ ⟨small family unit of the patriarchal type with formal authority *lodged* in the father —John Dollard⟩ **8 :** to lay or deposit before a proper authority or person **:** FILE, DELIVER ⟨the defendant then *lodged* an appeal —Priscilla Hughes⟩ ⟨fled to his solicitors to ~ his defense —Clive Arden⟩ ⟨strong protests *lodged* by a number of religious groups —B.L.Fox⟩ **9 :** to fell (a tree) so as to cause to become caught against another when falling **:** HANG UP ~ *vi* **1 a :** to occupy a place temporarily **:** stay overnight **:** SLEEP ⟨he would ~ on the cot in the spare room upstairs —Elmer Davis⟩ **b** (1) **:** to have a residence **:** DWELL, STAY ⟨~ over a bookbinder's shop —T.B.Costain⟩ (2) **:** to be a lodger ⟨the entire year of the major's *lodging* with them —Glenway Wescott⟩ **2 :** to seek covert ⟨found the place where the deer had *lodged*⟩ **3 :** to come to a rest **:** stop or settle and remain ⟨bullets pinged . . . *lodged* in the walls of houses, zipped through windows —Green Peyton⟩ ⟨could hardly have marveled more if real stars had fallen and *lodged* on his coat —Van Wyck Brooks⟩ ⟨it had *lodged* in his memory —Victor Canning⟩ **4 :** to fall or lie down — used esp. of grass or grain ⟨buckwheat . . . tends to ~ by late fall —R.E.Trippensee⟩ **syn** see RESIDE

2**lodge** \"\ *n* -S [ME *loge*, *logge*, fr. OF *loge*, of Gmc origin; akin to OHG *louba*, *louppea* sheltered roof, porch, prob. fr. *loub* leaf, foliage — more at LEAF] **1 a** *now chiefly dial* **:** a small or temporary dwelling; *esp* **:** a rude shelter or abode (as a hut, cabin, tent) **b** *obs* **:** a place of confinement or detention ⟨books of controversy . . . have always been confined in a separate ~ from the rest —Jonathan Swift⟩ **c** *dial Eng* **:** OUTBUILDING **2 a** *obs* **:** the workshop of a body of freemasons **b :** the meeting place of a branch of a fraternal organization ⟨a Masonic ~⟩ **c :** the body of members composing a branch of a fraternal organization **3 a :** a house set apart for residence in the hunting or other special season ⟨had a hunting and fishing ~ on the peak —Nard Jones⟩ **b :** an inn or resort hotel ⟨gave half-hour magic shows at mountain ~*s* and dude ranches —*Current Biog.*⟩ **c :** a recreation center of a camp or vacation spot often containing dining facilities ⟨in the evening we gathered in the main ~ —Wright Morris⟩ **4 a :** a house on an estate orig. for the use of a gamekeeper, caretaker, porter, or similar person but now often used to house guests of the owner **b :** a shelter for an employee (as a gatekeeper or porter of an institution or a factory) ⟨the beautiful fountain . . . which conceals the ~ of the attendant of the square —O.S.J.Gogarty⟩ **c :** the residence of the head of a college (as at Cambridge University) **5 :** a den or lair esp. of gregarious animals that often involves constructive work ⟨a beaver's ~⟩ ⟨a buck's ~⟩ **6** *archaic* **:** a place to put or hold something **:** a place of temporary sojourn ⟨earth is our ~, and heaven our home —Isaac Watts⟩ **7 :** a theater loge ⟨the theater lent its ~ —Robert Browning⟩ **8 a :** a dwelling, cabin, hut, or tent of the No. American Indians **:** WIGWAM — compare HOGAN, TEPEE, WICKIUP **b :** the regular occupants of a lodge **:** a family of No. American Indians ⟨a tribe of 200 ~*s* comprising about 1000 individuals⟩ **9 :** a local union; *also* **:** a branch of a national union

**lodge·able** \-jəbəl\ *adj* **:** suitable to be used for lodging ⟨~ quarters⟩

**lodged** \-jd\ *adj* **:** lying down — used of a heraldic beast of the chase

**lodgepole** \'≈ˌ≈\ *n* **:** a pole used (as by the Plains Indians of No. America) in the construction of a lodge

**lodgepole needle miner** *n* **:** the larva of a very small gelechiid moth (*Coleotechnites milleri*) that mines in the leaves of lodgepole pine in western No. America and sometimes causes extensive defoliation

**lodgepole pine** *also* **lodgepole** *n* **:** either of two pines of western No. America that have needles in pairs and short ovoid usu. asymmetric cones: **a :** a scrubby coastal pine (*Pinus contorta*) with thick deeply furrowed bark and hard strong coarse-grained medium-light wood — called also *beach pine* **b :** a taller straight pine of the interior that has thin and little-furrowed bark and soft weak fine-grained lightweight wood and that is usu. considered to be a variety (*Pinus contorta* var. *latifolia*) of the coastal lodgepole though sometimes treated as a separate species (*P. murrayana*)

**lodg·er** \'läjə(r)\ *n* -S **1** *archaic* **a :** one that lives or dwells in a place **:** INHABITANT, OCCUPANT **b :** one that passes the night in a place (as at an inn) **2 :** one that occupies a rented room in another's house **:** a person who lives in lodgings ⟨took in permanent ~*s*⟩ ⟨the eternal ~, nowhere really at home —Oscar Handlin⟩; *specif* **:** one who by agreement with the owner of housing accommodations acquires no property, interest, or possession therein but only the right in accordance with the agreement to live in and occupy a room or other designated portion therein that still remains in the owner's legal possession — compare GUEST **3 :** something that becomes fixed or lodged in a place

**lodges** *pres 3d sing of* LODGE, *pl of* LODGE

**lodg·ing** \'läjiŋ, -jēŋ\ *n* -S [ME *logging*, fr. gerund of *loggen* to lodge — more at LODGE] **1 a :** a place to live **:** DWELLING, HABITATION ⟨high wages that go at once for ~ —Marjory S. Douglas⟩ **b :** a place in which to settle or come to rest **:** LODGMENT ⟨must not allow the recklessness of despair to find any ~ in our hearts —A.E.Stevenson b.1900⟩ **2 a** (1) **:** sleeping accommodations ⟨itinerant schoolteacher who found board and ~ in the house of his pupils' parents —*Amer. Guide Series: La.*⟩ ⟨accepting a night's ~ in the barn —*Amer. Guide Series: Mich.*⟩ (2) **:** a temporary place to stay ⟨find a ~ for the night⟩ **b :** a room or rooms in the house of another used as a place of residence — usu. used in pl. ⟨bent his footsteps toward his ~*s* —Gilbert Parker⟩ **3 lodgings** *pl* **a** *obs* **:** quarters for soldiers **:** CAMP **b** *Brit* **:** the living quarters of a college or university student who is neither staying with his family nor living on campus **4 :** the act of lodging ⟨had a regard for me from the time of my first ~ in their house —Benjamin Franklin⟩

**lodging house** *n* **:** a house where lodgings are provided and let that is often somewhat arbitrarily defined for the purpose of regulation under a particular statute or ordinance

**lodging knee** *n* **:** a horizontal wooden knee for securing a deck beam to a ship's side

**lodging–room** \'≈≈ˌ≈\ *n* **:** a place for sleeping that often accommodates more than one person **:** BEDROOM ⟨we have one *lodging-room* with two single beds —Dorothy Wordsworth⟩

**lodg·ment** *or* **lodge·ment** \'läjmənt\ *n* -S [MF *logement*, fr. OF, fr. *logier* to lodge + *-ment* — more at LODGE] **1 a** *obs* **:** quarters for soldiers **b** *obs* **:** an entrenchment or other defensive work thrown up on a captured advance position as protection against attack **c** (1) **:** the occupation and holding of a position in hostile or disputed territory ⟨had a very stiff fight all day to make any ~ at all —Sir Winston Churchill⟩ (2) **:** an act resembling that of a lodgment by armed troops ⟨they were able to find ~ in corners where no monastery could have supported itself —R.W.Southern⟩ **2 a :** a place usu. a building for lodging or protecting something **:** SHELTER ⟨a hut built years ago for temporary ~ of cattlemen herding —Horace Kephart⟩ **b** (1) **:** ACCOMMODATIONS, LODGINGS ⟨found temporary ~*s* in Paris —W.H.Auden⟩ (2) *archaic* **:** accommodations provided in an inn ⟨the miserable ~ and miserable fare of a provincial inn —Washington Irving⟩ **3 a :** the act, fact, or manner of lodging **b :** a placing, depositing, or coming to rest ⟨the ~ of the balloon in the tree⟩ **4 a :** an accumulation or collection of something deposited in a place or remaining at rest ⟨the plains on both sides are covered at this season by heavy ~*s* of water —Henry Beveridge⟩ **b :** a place of rest or deposit **:** a securely established position ⟨O.K. has gained ~ in practically all civilized languages —Thomas Pyles⟩ **c :** a firm emplacement of glacial till

**lodgment area** *n* **:** an initial base of operations resulting from the consolidation of two or more beachheads or airheads

**lo·dha** \'lō(ˌ)dä\ *n, pl* **lodha** *or* **lodhas** *usu cap* [Hindi *lodhā* agriculturist] **1 :** a low caste numerous in Madhya Pradesh and Uttar Pradesh **2 :** a member of the Lodha caste

**lodh bark** \'lōd-\ *n* [Hindi *lodh*, fr. Skt *lodhra*, *rodhra;* akin to Skt *rudhira* red — more at RED] **:** the bark of an East Indian tree (*Symplocos racemosa*) that is a source of a yellow dye and is used locally as a mordant

**lod·i·cule** \'lädəˌkyül\ *n* -S [L *lodicula* coverlet, dim. of *lodic-*, *lodix* cover] *in the grass flower* **:** one of the two (rarely three) delicate membranous hyaline scales at the base of the ovary which by their swelling assist in anthesis

**lod·o·my** \'lädəmi\ *Scot var of* LAUDANUM

**lodz** \'lädz, 'lüj, 'wüj\ *adj, usu cap* [fr. *Łódź*, Poland] **:** of or from the city of Lodz, Poland **:** of the kind or style prevalent in Lodz

**loe** \'lü\ *Scot var of* LOVE

**loef·fler's syndrome** \'leflə(r)z-\ *also* **loeffler's pneumonia** *n, usu cap L* [after Wilhelm *Löffler* b1887 Swiss physician] **:** a mild pneumonitis marked by transitory pulmonary infiltration and eosinophilia and usu. considered to be basically an allergic reaction

**loel·ling·ite** *also* **löl·ling·ite** \'leliŋˌīt\ *n* -S [G *löllingit*, fr. *Lölling*, town in Austria, its locality + G *-it* -ite] **:** a mineral $FeAs_2$ consisting of a tin-white iron arsenide that is isomorphous with arsenopyrite and usu. occurs massive — called also *leucopyrite*

**loe·some** \ˈlüsəm\ *Scot var of* LOVESOME

**loess** \ˈles, ˈləs, ˈlō,es\ *also* **löss** \ˈles, ˈləs\ *n* -ES [G *löss*, alter. of *lösch*, fr. G dial. (Switzerland) *lösch*, adj., loose; akin to OHG *lōs* loose — more at -LESS] : an unstratified deposit of loam that ranges to clay at the one extreme and to fine sand at the other, is usu. of a buff or yellowish brown color, covers extensive areas in No. America, Europe, and Asia, is now generally believed to be chiefly deposited by the wind, is usu. calcareous, often contains shells, bones, and teeth of mammals as well as concretions of calcium carbonate and occas. of iron oxide, and makes an excellent soil where adequately watered

**loess·i·al** \ˈlesēəl, ˈləs-, lōˈes-\ *also* **loess·al** \-səl\ *adj* : relating to or consisting of loess

**loess·land** \ˈles,land, ˈləs,-, ˈlō,es,-\ *n* : land whose surface is of loess

**loe·we·ite** \ˈlāvə,īt\ *or* **loe·wig·ite** \-vi,gīt\ *n* -S [*loeweite* fr. G *löweit*, fr. Karl J. *Löwe* †1890 Ger. chemist + G *-it* -ite; *loewigite* fr. G *löwigit*, alter. of *löweit*] : a mineral $Na_4Mg_2(SO_4)_4.5H_2O$ consisting of hydrous magnesium sodium sulfate occurring in pale yellow cleavable masses

**L of C** *abbr* line of communications

**¹loft** \ˈlȯft *also* ˈläft\ *n* -S [ME, fr. OE, fr. ON *lopt* air, upper story; akin to OE *lyft* air, OS & OHG *luft*, Goth *luftus*] **1 a** *archaic* : the upper regions : SKY ⟨they are only birds — swifts in the ~ of the morning —Walter de la Mare⟩ **b** *obs* : the ceiling of a room **2** : a room or floor above another : an upper room or story : an attic room : ATTIC ⟨moved into a student ~ —Saul Bellow⟩ ⟨a slated cottage . . . containing a kitchen, two bedrooms and a ~ —J.M.Mogey⟩ **3 a** : a gallery in a church or hall ⟨below the organ ~ —H.S.Morrison⟩ **b** (1) : one of the upper floors of a warehouse or business building esp. when not partitioned ⟨stock clerk in a garment ~ —William DuBois⟩ (2) : a work space in an industrial or manufacturing building **c** : an upper part of a barn used esp. for storing hay : HAYLOFT ⟨climbing painfully up into the ~ to pitch down some hay —F.B.Gipson⟩ **4** : a coop or house for pigeons; *also* : a stock of pigeons **5 a** (1) : the backward slant of the face of a golf-club head (2) : HEIGHT 2b(1) ⟨won't give the ball enough ~ —Johnny Revolta⟩ **b** : the act of lofting : a lofting stroke **6** : the resilience of textile fibers esp. wool

**²loft** \"\ *vb* -ED/-ING/-S *vt* **1 a** : to place or store in a loft ⟨the remainder of the crop which was measured and ~*ed* —George Washington⟩ **b** : to house in a loft ⟨~*ed* his pigeons on the roof⟩ **2** *obs* : to build or furnish with a loft **3 a** (1) : to strike (a ball) so as to cause to rise sharply : toss usu. in an arc ⟨~*ed* a pop fly to short center field —W.B.Furlong⟩ ⟨~*ing* stones at street lights —Maxwell Griffith⟩ (2) : to cause to rise or advance : PROMOTE ⟨was ~*ed* to a new job —*Time*⟩ **b** : to shoot (a taw) in an arched course through the air **c** : to release (a bowling ball) in such a way as to cause to drop onto the alley beyond the foul line **4** : to cause (as a golf ball) to rise high into the air **5** : to lay out a full-sized working drawing of the lines and contours of (as a ship's hull or an airplane's wing) **~** *vi* **1 a** : to hit or throw a ball high into the air **b** : to rise high into the air when struck **2** : to loft a bowling ball

**loft building** *n* : a large building usu. of more than one story whose open floor space without partitions allows maximum adaptability of use (as for the display of merchandise or light manufacturing)

**loft–dried** \ˈ=,=\ *adj* : dried by hanging in a drying loft ⟨*loft-dried* writing paper⟩

**loft·er** \-tə(r)\ *n* -S : an iron golf club whose face is laid back sufficiently for lofting the ball — called also *lofting iron*

**loft·i·ly** \-tᵊlē, -tᵊli, -təl-\ *adv* : in a lofty manner ⟨bore herself still more ~ and resolved to snub him explicitly if he addressed her again —G.B.Shaw⟩

**loft·i·ness** \-tēnəs, -tin-\ *n* -ES : the quality or state of being lofty ⟨with the ~ of a patriot of old Rome —George Meredith⟩ ⟨soap imparts to silk material a bulk and ~ difficult to obtain with synthetic softening agents —H.C.Speel & H.H.Mosher⟩

**lofting** *n* -S [fr. gerund of ²*loft*] : the process of lofting an airplane or ship or a part of one

**lofting iron** *n* : LOFTER

**loft·less** \-tləs\ *adj* : having no loft

**loftly** *adv* [by alter.] *obs* : LOFTILY

**loft·man** \-tmən\ *n, pl* **loftmen 1** : a worker in a drying loft **2** : FLYMAN 2

**lofts·man** \-tsmən\ *n, pl* **loftsmen** : one who lays out to scale the lines (as of an airplane and its parts) preparatory to the making of blueprints and tools — called also *linesman*

**lofty** \-tē, -ti\ *adj* -ER/-EST [ME, fr. ¹*loft* + *-y*] **1** : having a haughty overbearing manner : characterized by arrogance and pride : SUPERCILIOUS ⟨looked down upon him with the *loftiest* contempt —Charles Dickens⟩ ⟨expected to treat this exhibition with an attitude of ~ scorn —Ralph Linton⟩ **2 a** : elevated in character and spirit : dignified of mien and bearing : elegant of speech : NOBLE, STATELY ⟨of unquestionable integrity and ~ standards of judgment —Paul Moor⟩ ⟨he was handsome, with fine, even features, a ~ brow —Aline B. Saarinen⟩ ⟨trees, or the sight of them, excites their minds to ~ thinking —W.F. Hambly⟩ **b** : elevated in station or position : SUPERIOR ⟨the bright bar or kitchen . . . where the less ~ customers of the house were in the habit of assembling —George Eliot⟩ ⟨the insignia of a particularly ~ secret society —Jean Stafford⟩ **3** : extending or rising high in the air : having great or imposing height : TOWERING ⟨a ~ perpendicular cliff —E.V.Lucas⟩ ⟨a ~ and magnificent spire —Edwin Benson⟩ **4** : having full-bodied, firm, and resilient textile fibers **5** : having little practical application or value : ESOTERIC ⟨basic precepts are not ~ abstractions far removed from matters of daily living —D.D. Eisenhower⟩ **syn** see HIGH

**¹log** \ˈlȯg *also* ˈläg\ *n* -S *often attrib* [ME *logge*, prob. of Scand origin; akin to Norw *låg* fallen tree, ON *lāg*; akin to ON *liggja* to lie — more at LIE] **1 a** : a usu. bulky piece or length of unshaped timber; *esp* : a tree trunk or a length of a trunk or branch trimmed and ready for sawing and usu. over six feet long — compare BILLET, BOLT **b** : a stick of wood cut for fuel (as in a fireplace) usu. two to three feet in length with all or part of the bark on it ⟨a birch ~⟩ **c** : a heavy piece of wood or sometimes other material attached to the leg (as of a prisoner or an animal) so as to restrain movement **d logs** *pl, slang Austral* : a jail esp. when of rude construction **2** : one of several devices (as the common one consisting of a log chip and log line) designed to gauge the speed of a ship **3** [short for *logbook*] **a** : a daily record of a ship's speed or progress or the full record of a ship's voyage including notes on the ship's position at various times and including notes on the weather and on important incidents occurring during the voyage **b** : any of various other journals or records in which are noted sequential data on the speed or progress or performance of something: (1) : a record of a flight by an airplane or of the operating history of an airplane or of a piece of its equipment or of the flying time of a pilot or other aircrew member (2) : a record of the performance of an engine or boiler or similar piece of equipment (3) : a record of the progress made in drilling an oil well including notes on formations penetrated and on the casing used and including other pertinent data (4) : a record of camera shots taken esp. in motion pictures (5) : a minute-by-minute record of what is broadcast by a radio station

**²log** \"\ *vb* **logged; logged; logging; logs** *vt* **1 a** (1) : to cut down for use as logs ⟨*logged* most of the trees in the area⟩ (2) : to cut up into logs : saw into logs ⟨*logging* the timber into 7-foot lengths⟩ **b** : to cut down the trees of (a region) and remove the felled trees from for use as logs ⟨had *logged* off most of that part of the country⟩ **2** : to make a note or record of (the speed, progress, performance, or other sequential details of something) esp. in a journal or other record of data : enter details of or about in a log ⟨*logged* the ship's speed at 10 knots⟩ **3 a** : to move (an indicated distance) or attain (an indicated speed) as noted in a log ⟨the ship *logged* 100 miles that day⟩ ⟨the plane ~*s* 600 miles an hour⟩ **b** (1) : to sail a ship or fly an airplane for (an indicated distance or an indicated period of time) ⟨asked how many hours he had *logged*⟩ (2) : to have or arrive at a record of (an indicated distance or an indicated period of time) in sailing a ship or flying an airplane : have (an indicated record) to one's credit **~** *vi* : to fell trees and cut them up into logs and transport the logs to sawmills or a place of sale

**³log** \ˈläg\ *vb* **logged; logged; logging; logs** [origin unknown] *dial Eng* : OSCILLATE, ROCK

**⁴log** \ˈlȯg *also* ˈläg\ *abbr or n* -S logarithm

**log** *abbr* **1** logic **2** logistic

**log-** *or* **logo-** *comb form* [Gk, fr. *logos* word, reason, speech, account — more at LEGEND] : word : thought : speech : discourse ⟨*logogram*⟩ ⟨*logolatry*⟩ ⟨*logomania*⟩

**-log** — see -LOGUE

**¹lo·gan** \ˈlōgən\ *n* -S [by shortening] *NewEng* : POKELOGAN

**²logan** \"\ *n* -S [by shortening] : LOGANBERRY

**³logan** *var of* LAGAN

**lo·gan·berry** \ˈlōgən- — *see* BERRY\ *n* [James H. *Logan* †1928 Am. lawyer and horticulturist + E *berry*] **1 a** : a red-fruited upright-growing dewberry regarded as a variety (*Rubus ursinus loganobaccus*) of the western dewberry or as a hybrid of the western dewberry and the red raspberry **b** : the berry borne by a loganberry **2** : PRUNE PURPLE

**lo·ga·nia** \lōˈgānēə\ *n* [NL, fr. James *Logan* †1751 Irish botanist + NL *-ia*] **1** *cap* : the type genus of the family Loganiaceae comprising Australian and New Zealand herbs and subshrubs that are sometimes cultivated for their clusters of pentamerous white to flesh-colored flowers **2** -S : any plant of the genus *Logania*

**lo·ga·ni·a·ce·ae** \lō,gānēˈāsē,ē\ *n pl, cap* [NL, fr. *Logania*, type genus + *-aceae*] : a family of herbs, shrubs, and trees (order Gentianales) distinguished by the opposite stipulate leaves and the bilocular superior ovary — **lo·ga·ni·a·ceous** \=;=ˈāshəs\ *adj*

**lo·ga·nin** \ˈlōgənən\ *n* -S [ISV *logan-* (fr. NL *Loganiaceae*, family to which nux vomica belongs) + *-in*] : a crystalline glucoside $C_{17}H_{26}O_{10}$ obtained esp. from nux vomica and the buckbean

**log·an stone** *or* **log·gan stone** \ˈlägən-\ *n* [prob. alter. of *logging*, pres. part. of ³*log*] : ROCKING STONE

**lo·gan tent** \ˈlōgən-\ *n, usu cap L* [after Sir William Edmond *Logan* †1875 Canadian geologist] : a pyramidal tent that is about seven feet wide and seven feet high and that is made roomy by a vertical back wall about two feet high

Logan tent

**¹log·a·oe·dic** \,lägəˈēdik\ *adj* [LL *logaoedicus*, fr. LGk *logaoidikos*, fr. *log-* + *aoidē* music, poetry (fr. *aeidein* to sing) + *-ikos* -ic — more at ODE] : having a metrical rhythm marked by the mixture of several meters; *specif* : having a rhythm that uses both dactyls and trochees or anapests and iambs

**²logaoedic** \"\ *n* -S : a logaoedic piece of verse

**log·a·rithm** \ˈlȯgə,rithəm *also* ˈläg-\ *n* -S [NL *logarithmus*, fr. *log-* + Gk *arithmos* number — more at ARITHMO-] : the exponent that indicates the power to which a number must be raised to produce a given number ⟨if $B^z=N$, then 2 is the ~ of *N* (to the base *B*)⟩ ⟨4 is the ~ of 16 to the base 2⟩ — abbr. *log*; see ANTILOGARITHM, COMMON LOGARITHM, NATURAL LOGARITHM; compare BASE 6d

**log·a·rith·mic** \;=;=ˈrithmik, -mēk\ *also* **log·a·rith·mi·cal** \-məkəl, -mēk-\ *adj* **1** : of, involving, or expressed in terms of a logarithm **2** : using, based on, or relating to a logarithmic scale — **log·a·rith·mi·cal·ly** \-mək(ə)lē, -mēk-, -li\ *adv*

**logarithmic curve** *n* : a graph in which the ordinate is the logarithm of the abscissa

**logarithmic decrement** *n* : the natural logarithm of the decrement for a series of exponentially damped oscillations

**logarithmic function** *n* : a function that is a logarithm

**logarithmic paper** *n* : graph paper in which actual distances on one or both axes are proportional to the logarithm of the quantities to which they correspond

**logarithmic scale** *n* : a scale on which actual distances from the origin are proportional to the logarithms of the corresponding scale numbers rather than to the numbers themselves

**logarithmic spiral** *n* : EQUIANGULAR SPIRAL

**logbook** \ˈ=,=\ *n* [¹*log* (device for gauging a ship's speed) + *book*] : LOG 3

**log chip** *also* **log ship** *n* : a thin flat usu. triangular piece of wood that is typically like a quadrant of a circle and that usu. has a radius of 5 or 6 inches and is loaded with lead on the arc so as to float point up and that is attached to a log line by cords from each corner and is tossed into the water so that the log line may run out from the log reel when the motion of a ship through the water or the velocity of a current is being gauged

**logcock** \ˈ=,=\ *n* **1** : PILEATED WOODPECKER **2** : IVORY-BILLED WOODPECKER

**log drive** *n* : DRIVE 1f

**log driver** *n* : one that guides logs in a drive downstream working with a pike pole from a river bank or a boat or on the floating logs

**log driving** *n* : the occupation of a log driver

**loge** \ˈlōzh, ˈlōj\ *n* -S [F — more at LODGE] **1 a** : a small compartment : BOOTH, STALL, ENCLOSURE ⟨the doorkeeper peered out from his ~ just inside the entrance to the building⟩ **b** : a box in a theater **2 a** : a small area (as in a room) that is partitioned off from a larger area (as by a railing) **b** : the forward section of a mezzanine or balcony in a theater when this section is in some way (as by an aisle or railing) partitioned off from the part farther back

**log fixer** *n* : ROSSER a

**log frame** *n* : a sawing machine; *specif* : one having a gang of saws for cutting a log into boards

**loggan stone** *var of* LOGAN STONE

**logged** *adj* [fr. past part. of ²*log*] **1** : made heavy or sluggish so that movement is impossible or difficult ⟨his feet . . . feeling ~ as a landed sailor's —William Sansom⟩ **2** : made sodden : soaked or permeated with something; *specif* : WATERLOGGED ⟨a graveyard of rotting ~ ships⟩ ⟨the boat still rolled and pitched, but sickishly now because it was so ~ down with water —Roy Sparkia⟩

**log·ger** \ˈlȯgə(r) *also* ˈläg-\ *n* -S [¹*log* + *-er*] **1 a** : one who is engaged in the action or business of logging — called also *lumberjack*; compare LUMBERMAN **b** : a worker who insulates petroleum pipelines and tanks and still towers against heat radiation and absorption **2** [²*log* + *-er*] : a device that automatically records data esp. about temperature or humidity or barometric pressure or other physical conditions

**log·ger·head** \ˈlȯgə(r),hed *also* ˈläg-\ *n* [prob. fr. E dial. *logger* block of wood (fr. ¹*log* + *-er*) + *head*] **1** *now chiefly dial* **a** : BLOCKHEAD, DUMBBELL **b** : HEAD; *esp* : a large cumbrous head **2** *or* **loggerhead turtle a** : any of various very large marine turtles (family Cheloniidae); *esp* : a carnivorous turtle (*Caretta caretta*) that is common in the warmer parts of the Atlantic ocean from Brazil to Cape Cod **b** : ALLIGATOR SNAPPER **c** : a snapping turtle (*Chelydra serpentina*) **3** : an iron tool consisting of a long handle terminating in a ball or bulb that is heated and used to melt tar or to heat liquids **4** : an upright piece of round timber which is fixed in a whaleboat and around which a turn of the line is taken when it is running out too fast **5** : a disease of cotton characterized by a shortening of the internodes of stems and branches **6 loggerheads** *pl but sing or pl in constr, dial Eng* : any of several herbs of the genus *Centaurea* — **at loggerheads** *adv (or adj)* : in or into a state of strong antagonistic usu. quarrelsome disagreement ⟨*at loggerheads* with the people of his village —Harold Hobson⟩ ⟨the story of an energetic subordinate *at loggerheads* with his superiors —*Times Lit. Supp.*⟩ ⟨confusions which put old friends *at loggerheads* —L.C.Douglas⟩ — **to loggerheads** *adv (or adj), archaic* : at loggerheads

**log·ger·head·ed** \;=;=ˈhedəd\ *adj, now chiefly dial* : BLOCKHEADED, STUPID

**loggerhead shrike** *n* : a shrike (*Lanius ludovicianus*) of the southeastern U.S.

**loggerhead sponge** *n* : a massive sponge (*Spheciospongia vespera*) of the West Indies and Florida that attains a weight of 700 pounds but is of little commercial importance

**log·gets** *or* **log·gats** \ˈlägəts\ *n pl but usu sing in constr* [prob. fr. ¹*log* + *-et* + *-s*] : a game formerly played in England in which players threw pieces of wood at a stake driven into the ground

**log·gia** \ˈläj(ē)ə, ˈlȯj-\ *n, pl* **loggias** \-əz\ *also* **log·gie** \-jā\ [It, fr. F *loge* — more at LODGE] : a roofed open gallery or arcade in the side of a building esp. when facing upon an open court; *specif* : such a gallery or arcade set at a height of one or more stories and not projecting from the surface of the building but forming an integral part of the building **syn** see BALCONY

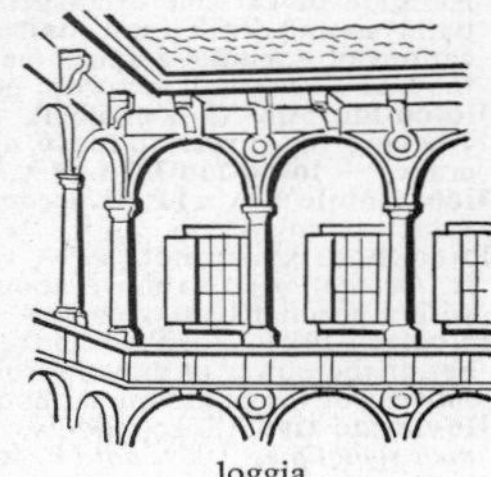

loggia

**logginess** *var of* LOGINESS

**logging** *n* -S [fr. gerund of ²*log*] : the occupation of felling trees and cutting them up into logs and transporting the logs to sawmills or to a place of sale

**logging wheel** *n* : one of a pair of large wheels from 7 to 12 feet in diameter that are used for hauling logs

**log·gish** \ˈlȯgish *also* ˈläg-\ *adj* : resembling or suggestive of a log ⟨everything was still, with that ~ inanimate thing lying there —Sheila Kaye-Smith⟩

**log glass** *n* : a small hourglass used to time the running out of a log line

**loggy** *var of* LOGY

**logia** *pl of* LOGION

**-lo·gia** \ˈlōj(ē)ə\ *n comb form* -S [L, fr. Gk — more at *-logy*] : -LOGY

**log·ic** \ˈläjik, -jēk\ *n* -S [ME *logik*, fr. MF *logique*, fr. L *logica*, fr. Gk *logikē*, fr. fem. of *logikos* of speech, argumentative, logical, fr. *logos* word, reason, speech, account + *-ikos* -ic — more at LEGEND] **1 a** (1) : a science that deals with the canons and criteria of validity in thought and demonstration and that traditionally comprises the principles of definition and classification and correct use of terms and the principles of correct predication and the principles of reasoning and demonstration : the science of the normative formal principles of reasoning : the science of correct reasoning — see FORMAL LOGIC, MATERIAL LOGIC (2) : a system of formal principles of deduction or inference (3) : semiotic or a branch of semiotic; *esp* : SYNTACTICS (4) : the formal principles of a branch of knowledge ⟨the ~ of art⟩ **b** (1) : a particular mode of argumentation or reasoning viewed as valid or faulty according to its apparent agreement with or departure from accepted principles of logic ⟨she spent quite a long time explaining the situation, but he failed to see her ~⟩ (2) : relevance or propriety (as of a quality, a procedure) judged as present or absent according to apparent conformity or lack of conformity with the dictates of logic ⟨could not understand the ~ of such a deed⟩ **c** : interrelation or connection or sequence (as of facts or events) esp. when seen by rational analysis as inevitable, necessary, or predictable ⟨by the ~ of events, anarchy leads to dictatorship⟩ **2** : something that convinces or proves or that obviates argument or makes argument useless and that is by its nature quite apart from or beyond or opposed to the use of reason as a means of arriving at decisions or settling disputes or attaining truth **3** : an exposition of or treatise on logic

**lo·gi·cal** \-jəkəl, -jēk-\ *adj* [ML *logicalis*, fr. L *logica* + *-alis* -al] **1 a** : of or relating to logic : having the nature of logic ⟨~ argumentation⟩ **b** : that agrees with accepted principles of logic : that is in harmony with sound reasoning ⟨a ~ conclusion⟩ **c** : that is in accordance with inferences reasonably drawn from preceding or surrounding or predictable facts or events or circumstances ⟨a ~ result⟩ ⟨a ~ candidate⟩ **d** : analytical and not factual or empirical : FORMAL ⟨a ~ statement⟩ ⟨a ~ expression⟩ **2** : that is capable of reasoning or that uses reason in a way that agrees with accepted principles of logic ⟨a ~ thinker⟩ — **log·i·cal·ly** \-jək(ə)lē, -jēk-, -li\ *adv* — **log·i·cal·ness** *n* -ES

**logical implication** *or* **logical entailment** *n* : IMPLICATION 2b(2)

**log·i·cal·i·ty** \,läjəˈkaləd·ē\ *n* -ES : the quality or state of being logical : logical character : LOGICALNESS

**log·i·cal·iza·tion** \,läjəkələˈzāshən\ *n* -S : the act of logicalizing or state of being logicalized

**log·i·cal·ize** \ˈläjəkə,līz\ *vt* -ED/-ING/-S : LOGICIZE

**logical positivism** *or* **logical empiricism** *n* : a philosophical movement holding that meaningful statements are either a priori and analytic or a posteriori and synthetic and that metaphysical theories are strictly meaningless or have only emotive force — compare CONFIRMABILITY THEORY, VERIFIABILITY PRINCIPLE

**logical presumption** *n* : PRESUMPTION OF FACT

**logical realism** *n* : REALISM 2a

**logical reason** *n* : DISCURSIVE REASON

**logical subject** *n* : the subject of a sentence that expresses the actual agent of an expressed or implied action (as *father* in "it is your father speaking") or that is the thing about which something is otherwise predicated (as *to do right* in "it is sometimes hard to do right") — called also *real subject*; distinguished from *grammatical subject*

**logical syntax** *n* : SYNTAX 3b

**logical truth** *n* : FORMAL TRUTH

**lo·gi·cian** \lōˈjishən, lə'-\ *n* -S [ME *logicien*, fr. MF, fr. *logique* logic + *-ien* -ian — more at LOGIC] : one that is skilled in logic

**log·i·cism** \ˈläjə,sizəm\ *n* -S [ISV *logic* + *-ism*] **1** : a philosophical system marked by special emphasis on logic **2 a** : a philosophical thesis according to which logic is an autonomous discipline that is not reducible to psychology — opposed to *psychologism* **b** : a philosophical thesis according to which mathematics is reducible to logic — compare INTUITIONISM — **log·i·cist** \-,səst\ *n* -S

**log·i·cize** \ˈläjə,sīz\ *vb* -ED/-ING/-S [*logic* + *-ize*] *vi* : to use logic : REASON ⟨incapable of *logicizing*⟩ **~** *vt* : to make logical : convert to logical form ⟨*logicized* the argument⟩

**log·ic·less** \ˈläjikləs\ *adj* : devoid of logic

**log·i·co-** *comb form* [*logical*] : logical : logical and ⟨*logico*-mathematical⟩

**log·ics** \-ks\ *n pl but usu sing in constr* : LOGIC

**¹lo·gie** \ˈlōgi\ *n* -S [by shortening] *chiefly Scot* : KILLOGIE

**²lo·gie** \ˈlōgē\ *n* -S [after David *Logie*, 19th cent. Brit. inventor] : a piece of imitation jewelry designed for use in theater productions

**logier** *comparative of* LOGY

**-logies** *pl of* -LOGY

**logiest** *superlative of* LOGY

**lo·gi·ly** \ˈlōgəlē, -li *sometimes* ˈlȯg- *or* ˈläg-\ *adv* : in a logy manner

**lo·gi·ness** *also* **log·gi·ness** \-gēnəs\ *n* -ES : the quality or state of being logy

**lo·gi·on** \ˈlōjē,än, -ōgē- ˈläg-\ *n, pl* **logia** \-ēə\ *or* **logions** [Gk, saying, oracle, dim. of *logos* word, speech — more at LEGEND] : a usu. short pointed pregnant saying or observation of a religious teacher; *esp* : one of the agrapha

**¹lo·gis·tic** \lōˈjistik, lə'-, -tēk\ *or* **lo·gis·ti·cal** \-təkəl, -tēk-\ *adj* [*logistic* prob. fr. F *logistique*, fr. ML & LL; ML *logisticus* rational, fr. LL, of computation, fr. Gk *logistikos* calculatory, rational, fr. *logistēs* calculator, reasoner (fr. *logizein* to calculate, fr. *logos* word, reason, account + *-izein* -ize) + *ikos* -ic; *logistical* fr. ML *logisticus* + *-al* — more at LEGEND] **1** : of or relating to logic or logicism **2** : of or relating to logistic or logistics **3** : of, represented by, or relating to a logistic curve — **lo·gis·ti·cal·ly** \-tək(ə)lē\ *adv*

**²logistic** \"\ *n* -S [F *logistique*, fr. Gk *logistikē*, fr. fem. of *logistikos*] **1** : the science or art of calculating esp. arithmetically **2 a** : ALGEBRA 2 **b** : SYMBOLIC LOGIC **3** : LOGISTIC CURVE

**logistic curve** *n* : a curve representing a function involving an exponential and shaped like the letter S ⟨a mass of data on growth of subhuman and human populations, of the number of governmental functions, growth of production, inventions, state laws and so on, to show that their growth and diffusion follows the *logistic curve* —P.A.Sorokin⟩

**lo·gis·ti·cian** \,lōjəˈstishən\ *n* -S : a specialist in logistic or logistics

**lo·gis·tics** \lō'jistiks, lə'-, -tēks\ *n pl but often sing in constr* [F *logistique* + E *-s* — more at LOGISTIC] **1 :** LOGISTIC 1, 2 **2 :** military science in its planning and handling and implementation of personnel (as in classification, movement, evacuation) and matériel (as in production, distribution, maintenance) and facilities (as in construction, operation, distribution) and other related factors

**log jack** *n* **1 :** HAUL-UP **2 :** a tool like a cant hook that is used to raise or hold up a log that is being sawed so as to avoid pinching the saw

**logjam** \'ˌ\ *n* **1 :** a jamming up of logs into a deadlocked jumble in a watercourse (as in a river during a drive) **2 :** the condition of being jammed into immobility : DEADLOCK, IMPASSE ⟨trying to break the ~ in negotiations⟩ : STOPPAGE, BLOCKAGE ⟨a ~ of news dispatches⟩ ⟨extended the Congressional session to clear a legislative ~⟩

**log line** *n* **:** a line that is usu. made of cord (as hemp, braided cotton twine) and that is used in gauging the speed of a ship or the velocity of a water current; *esp* **:** such a line that is divided into knots (sense 8a) and that has a log chip attached to one end and that runs out from a log reel

**¹log–log** \'ˌ\ *n, pl* **log–logs** [⁴*log*] **:** the logarithm of a logarithm

**²log–log** \"\ *adj* **1 :** involving or expressed in terms of log-logs **2 :** using, based on, or relating to a log-log scale

**log–log paper** *n* **:** logarithmic paper having logarithmic scales both horizontally and vertically — compare SEMILOGARITHMIC

**log–log scale** *n* **:** a scale on which actual distances from the origin are proportional to the log-logs of the corresponding scale numbers rather than to the numbers themselves

**log·man** \'lògmən *also* 'läg-\ *n, pl* **logmen :** LOGGER

**logo** \'lō(ˌ)gō *also* 'lä(ˌ)-\ *n* -S [by shortening] **:** LOGOTYPE

**logo-** — see LOG-

**log·o·dae·da·ly** \ˌlägə'dēdᵊlē, -'ded-\ *n* -ES [LL *logodaedalia*, fr. LGk *logodaidalia*, fr. Gk *logodaidalos* skilled in verbal legerdemain (fr. *log-* speech, word + *daidalos* skillful, ingeniously formed) + *-ia* -y — more at CONDOLE] **:** arbitrary or capricious coinage of words

**log·o·gram** \'lògəˌgram *also* 'läg-, -raa(ə)m\ *n* [*log-* + *-gram*] **:** a letter or character or symbol or sign used to represent an entire word (as *$* represents *dollar*): **a :** a graphic sign that represents a complete word or morpheme but without providing separate phonetic representation of the individual phonemes or syllables composing the word or morpheme (as *&* represents *and*) **b :** an often conventionalized picture or a symbol that represents an object not easily indicated by a simple picture ⟨in some countries, a ~ in the form of the torch of learning stands for a school —O.R.Bontrager⟩

**log·o·gram·mat·ic** \ˌlògəgrə¦mad·ik *also* ˌläg-\ *adj* [*logogram* + *-matic* (as in *grammatic*)] **:** of, relating to, or marked by the use of logograms **:** consisting of logograms — **log·o·gram·mat·i·cal·ly** \-d·ək(ə)lē\ *adv*

**log·o·graph** \'lògəˌgraf, -ràf *also* 'läg-\ *n* [*log-* + *-graph*] **:** LOGOGRAM

**lo·gog·ra·pher** \lō'gägrəfə(r)\ *n* -S [Gk *logographos* prose writer (fr. *log-* + *-graphos* writer, fr. *graphein* to write) + E *-er* — more at CARVE] **:** a prose writer in ancient Greece

**log·o·graph·ic** \ˌlògə¦grafik *also* ˌläg-\ *adj* [*logograph* + *-ic*] **:** of, relating to, or marked by the use of logographs **:** consisting of logographs **:** LOGOGRAMMATIC ⟨Japanese, which uses a combination of ~ and syllabic writing —Robert Lado⟩ — **log·o·graph·i·cal·ly** \-fək(ə)lē\ *adv*

**log·o·griph** \'lògəˌgrif *also* 'läg-\ *n* -S [*log-* + Gk *griphos* reed fish basket, riddle — more at CRIB] **:** a word puzzle (as an anagram)

**lo·go·li** \lō'gōlē\ *n, pl* **logoli** *or* **logolis** *usu cap* **1 :** one of the peoples of the Bantu Kavirondo group **2 :** a member of the Logoli people

**log·o·mach·ic** \ˌlägə¦makik\ *also* **log·o·mach·i·cal** \-akəkəl\ *adj* **:** of, relating to, or marked by a logomachy

**lo·gom·a·chist** \lō'gäməkəst\ *or* **log·o·mach** \'lägəˌmak\ *n* -S **:** one given to logomachy

**lo·gom·a·chy** \lō'gäməkē\ *n* -ES [Gk *logomachia*, fr. *log-* + *-machia* -machy] **1 a :** a dispute over or about words **b :** contention in words that are used wholly or almost wholly without real awareness of their meaning or that have little or no actual relation to reality **:** contention made up wholly or almost wholly of pure verbiage **2 :** a game of making words (as in anagrams)

**log·o·mania** \ˌlògə *also* ˌlägə+\ *n* [NL, fr. *log-* + *mania*] **:** abnormal talkativeness **:** LOGORRHEA

**log·o·pe·dia** \ˌlògə'pēdēə *also* ˌläg- *or* ˌlōg-\ *n* -S [NL, fr. *log-* + ortho*pedia*] **:** LOGOPEDICS

**log·o·pe·dic** \¦==¦pēdik\ *adj* [*log-* + ortho*pedic*] **:** of or relating to logopedics

**log·o·pe·dics** \ˌ==¦pēdiks\ *n pl but sing or pl in constr* [*log-* + ortho*pedics*] **:** the scientific study and treatment of speech defects

**log·or·rhea** \ˌlògə'rēə *also* ˌläg-\ *n* -S [NL, fr. *log-* + *-rrhea*] **:** pathologically excessive and often incoherent talkativeness — **log·o·rrhe·ic** \¦==¦rēik\ *adj*

**lo·gos** \'lōˌgäs, 'läˌgäs, 'lōˌgōs, 'lōˌgòs\ *n, pl* **lo·goi** \-gòi\ [Gk, word, reason, speech, account — more at LEGEND] **1** *often cap* **:** reason or the manifestation of reason conceived in ancient Greek philosophy as constituting the controlling principle in the universe: **a :** a moving and regulating principle in the universe together with an element in man by which according to Heraclitus this principle is perceived **b :** a cosmic governing or generating principle according to the Stoics that is immanent and active in all reality and that pervades all reality **c :** a principle that according to Philo is intermediate between ultimate or divine reality and the sensible world **2** *usu cap* **:** the actively expressed creative revelatory thought and will of God identified in the prologue of the Gospel of St. John and in various Christian doctrinal works with the second person of the Trinity

**log·o·thete** \'lògəˌthēt *also* 'läg-\ *n* -S [ML *logotheta*, fr. LGk *logothetēs*, fr. *log-* + *-thetēs* (fr. *tithenai* to set, place) — more at DO] **:** one of various functionaries (as an administrator) under the Byzantine emperors

**logo·type** \'lògəˌtīp *also* 'läg-\ *n* [*log-* + *type*] **1 :** a genotype designated subsequent to the publication of a generic name **2 a :** a single piece of type faced with two or more separate letters or figures (as *in, on, re, the, and, 1963*) — compare LIGATURE **b :** a single piece of type or a single plate faced with a term (as the name of a newspaper, an advertiser's trademark, a company name and address)

**log perch** *n* **:** a darter (*Percina caprodes*) about six inches long found in lakes and streams about Lake Superior esp. southward and eastward

**log reel** *n* **:** a usu. small wooden reel around which a log line is wound

**log·roll** \'lòˌgrōl *also* 'lä,-\ *vb* [back-formation fr. *logrolling*] *vi* **:** to take part in logrolling ~ *vt* **:** to promote or get acceptance or passage of (legislation) by logrolling ⟨~*ed* his tax bill through⟩ — **log·roll·er** \-lə(r)\ *n* -S

**log·roll·ing** \-liŋ\ *n* -S [¹*log* + *rolling*] **1 a** (1) **:** the act or process of rolling logs; *esp* **:** the act or process of rolling logs into one place to be burned when land is being cleared (2) **:** a gathering of neighbors and friends to assist each other in rolling logs into one place to be burned **b** (1) **:** the act or process of causing a floating log to rotate by treading (as in the course of a drive) (2) **:** a sport in which a person tries to retain his balance while standing on and rotating a floating log with his feet and while trying at the same time to dislodge usu. a single competitor on the same log **2 :** the exchanging of assistance or favors (as political assistance or favors); *specif* **:** the trading of votes by legislators to secure favorable action on projects of interest to each one ⟨passed by a majority obtained by ~ among a combination of interests —Joseph Dorfman⟩ ⟨~ . . . secures a certain protection for local interests —C.J.Friedrich⟩ — compare BACK SCRATCHING, PORK BARREL

**log rule** *n* **1 a :** a table showing the estimated number of board feet of lumber that can be sawed from logs of various lengths and diameters **b :** a formula by which the estimated number of board feet may be ascertained **2 :** SCALE RULE

**log run** *n* **1 :** the total merchantable product cut from softwood logs including all grades **2 :** the total merchantable product cut from hardwood logs except the lowest grade

**log runner** *n* **:** one of two small Australian oscine birds of the genus *Orthonyx* of terrestrial habits

**logs** *pl of* LOG, *pres 3d sing of* LOG

**log scale** *n* **1 :** the board-foot content of logs as determined by a log rule **2 :** SCALE RULE

**log ship** *var of* LOG CHIP

**log slate** *n* **:** a folding slate sometimes used for preliminary noting of data to be later copied into a logbook

**log slip** *n* **:** a gangway used in logging

**log tooth** *n* **:** a chain link with one or more projecting teeth used in a chain for transporting logs

**log turner** *n* **:** NIGGER 5

**lo·gu·do·rese** \ˌlōgədə¦rēz, -ēs\ *n* -S *usu cap* [It, fr. *logudorese* of Logudoro, fr. *Logudoro*, district in central Sardinia + It *-ese*] **:** the dialect of Sardinian spoken in the Logudoro district

**-logue** *or* **-log** \ˌlòg *also* ˌläg\ *n comb form* -S [ME *-loge*, *-logue*, fr. OF *-logue*, fr. L *-logus*, fr. Gk *-logos*, fr. *legein* to speak — more at LEGEND] **1 a :** discourse, talk ⟨duo*logue*⟩ **b :** performance, recital ⟨piano*logue*⟩ **2 :** student, specialist ⟨Sino*logue*⟩

**log washer** *n* **:** a mechanical trough washer for separating a material (as ore) from clay and earth

**logway** \'ˌ\ *n* **:** a gangway used in logging

**logwood** \'ˌ\ *n* **1 a** (1) **:** a tree (*Haematoxylon campechianum*) of Central America and the West Indies (2) **:** the very hard brown or brownish red heartwood of this tree that is used in preparing a dye (3) **:** a dye prepared from this heartwood as a water extract or as a solid extract obtained by evaporation or as crystals and used in dyeing various materials (as mordanted silk or wool or cotton or as leather or fur or hair) black — see DYE table I (under *Natural Black 1*); HEMATEIN, HEMATOXYLIN **b :** a tree (*Condalia obovata*) of Texas and adjacent Mexico that has spatulate entire mucronate leaves forming dense chaparral thickets and yielding a yellow dye — called also *brasil* **2 :** a blackish purple to purplish black — called also *admiral, bluewood, campeachy wood*

**logwood black** *n* **:** a rich black formed esp. on silk by mordanting with a salt of iron and dyeing with logwood

**logwood printing black** *n, often cap L&P&B* **:** a natural dye — see DYE table I (under *Natural Black 4*)

**lo·gy** *also* **log·gy** \'lōgē, -gi *sometimes* 'lòg- *or* 'läg-\ *adj*, *usu* -ER/ -EST [perh. fr. D *log* heavy, unwieldy, cumbersome + E *-y;* akin to MLG *luggich* lazy, sleepy] **1 :** marked by sluggishness and lack of vitality **:** slowed down esp. physically or mentally to a condition of dullness or numbed languidness or lethargy **:** heavily listless **:** DOPEY, GROGGY, TORPID ⟨was ~ from eating too much⟩ ⟨took a sleeping tablet and felt ~ the next morning⟩ **2 :** lacking resilience **:** not recovering quickly when stress is released **:** having low snap ⟨a ~ piece of rubber⟩

**-lo·gy** \ləjē, -ji\ *n comb form* -ES [ME *-logie*, fr. OF, fr. L *-logia*, fr. Gk, fr. *logos* word, reason, speech, account + *-ia* -y — more at LEGEND] **1 :** oral or written expression ⟨phraseo*logy*⟩ **2 :** doctrine, theory, science ⟨socio*logy*⟩ **3 :** discourse, treatise ⟨insecto*logy*⟩

**lo·han** \'lō'hän\ *n, pl* **lohan** *or* **lohans** *often cap* [Chin (Pek) *lo²-han⁴*, short for *a¹-lo²-han⁴*, fr. Skt *arhan*, nom. masc. of *arhant* — more at ARHAT] **:** ARHAT

**lo·har** \lō'här\ *n, pl* **lohar** *or* **lohars** *often cap* [Hindi *lohār*, fr. Skt *lohakāra* blacksmith, fr. *loha* copper, iron + *kāra* maker, worker, fr. *karoti* he does, makes; akin to Skt *rudhira* red — more at RED, KARMA] **:** one of a numerous Hindu caste whose usual occupation is ironworking or carpentering

**lo·hoch** *or* **lo·hock** \'lōˌhäk\ *or* **lo·och** \'lōˌäk\ *n* -S [MF *looch*, fr. Ar *la'ūq* anything licked] **:** LINCTUS

**loiasis** *var of* LOAIASIS

**loin** \'lòin\ *n* -S [ME *loyne*, fr. MF *loigne*, fr. (assumed) VL *lumbea*, fr. L *lumbus* loin; akin to OE *lendenu* loins, OHG *lentī, lentin* kidneys, loins, ON *lend* loin, OSlav *lędvije* loins] **1 a :** the part of the body of a human being or quadruped lying on each side of the spinal column between the hipbone and the false ribs — usu. used in pl.; see HORSE illustration **b :** a cut of meat (as mutton or pork) comprising this part of one or both sides of an animal carcass with the adjoining half of the vertebrae included but without the adjoining flank — see LAMB illustration **2 loins** *pl* **a :** the upper and lower abdominal regions and the region about the hips **b** (1) **:** the pubic region (2) **:** the generative organs

**loincloth** \'ˌ\ *n* **:** a cloth worn about the loins often as the sole article of clothing in warm climates esp. among primitive peoples

**loin disease** *n* **:** aphosphorosis of cattle often complicated by botulism

**loir** \'lòi(ə)r, 'lwär\ *n* -S [F, fr. L *glir-, glis*] **:** a large European dormouse (*Glis glis*)

**loi·ter** \'lòid·ə(r), -òitə-\ *vi* -ED/-ING/-S [ME *loteren, loiteren*, prob. fr. MD *loteren* to shake, wiggle, be loose (whence D *leuteren* to dawdle); prob. akin to OE *lūtian* to lurk, *lūtan* to bend, stoop, OHG *luzēn* to lurk, ON *lūta* to bow down — more at LITTLE] **1 :** to interrupt or delay an activity or an errand or a journey with or as if with aimless idle stops and pauses and purposeless distractions ⟨asked him not to ~ on the way home⟩ **:** fritter away time in the course of doing something or proceeding somewhere ⟨don't ~ on the job⟩ **:** take more time than is usual or necessary **:** be markedly or unduly slow in doing something or going somewhere **:** DAWDLE, LINGER **2 a :** to remain in or near a place in an idle or apparently idle manner **:** hang around aimlessly or as if aimlessly ⟨vagrants found ~*ing* outside the building⟩ ⟨~*ing* in the clubhouse —Furman Bisher⟩ ⟨~*ed* in the shade of the awnings —Sherwood Anderson⟩ **b :** to be unnecessarily slow in leaving **:** fitfully put off leaving **:** hang back **:** stay around without real necessity **:** lag behind ⟨a crowd of people, who ~*ed* to hear the bloodcurdling threats the prisoner shouted —Willa Cather⟩ **syn** see DELAY

**loiter away** *also* **loiter out** *vt* **:** to spend (time) in an idle aimless way **:** fritter away ⟨*loitered away* the whole afternoon⟩

**loi·ter·ing·ly** *adv* **:** in a manner that is marked by loitering **:** with loitering ⟨moved ~ down the street⟩

**loja bark** *var of* LOXA BARK

**lo·kao** \lō'kä(ˌ)ō\ *n* -S [Chin (Pek) *lu⁴ kao¹*, lit., green ointment] **:** a green dye obtained from the bark of Eurasian buckthorns (esp. *Rhamnus utilis* and *R. globosa*) — called also *Chinese green*

**loke** \'lōk\ *n* -S [perh. fr. (assumed) ME, fr. OE *loca* enclosure, stronghold; akin to OE *loc* lock on a door — more at LOCK] *dial Eng* **:** a short narrow lane often coming to a dead end **:** a private road **:** BLIND ALLEY, LANE

**lo·ke·la·ni** \ˌlōkā'länē\ *n* -S [Hawaiian, fr. *loke* rose (fr. E *rose*) + *lani* heavenly] **:** a small fragrant pink or red rose common in Hawaii

**lo·ko·no** \lō'kō(ˌ)nō\ *n* -S **:** an Arawakan language of British Guiana

**lok·shen** \'lòkshən\ *n pl but sing or pl in constr* [Yiddish (pl. of *loksh* noodle), fr. Russ dial *loksha*, of Turkic origin; akin to Uigur & Kazan Tatar *lakča* noodles, Chavash *läškä*] **:** NOODLES

**loktal** *var of* LOCTAL

**lol·i·gin·i·dae** \ˌlälə'jinəˌdē\ *n pl, cap* [NL, fr. *Loligin-*, *Loligo*, type genus + *-idae*] **:** a family of elongated cylindrical squids having the body tapering to a point and the arms partially retractile — see LOLIGO

**lo·li·go** \lō'lī(ˌ)gō\ *n, cap* [NL, fr. L *lolligo, loligo* cuttlefish] **:** a genus (the type of the family Loliginidae) including numerous somewhat flattened cylindrical squids

**lol·i·um** \'lōlēəm, 'läl-\ *n, cap* [NL, fr. L, darnel] **:** a genus of grasses characterized by two-ranked many-flowered spikelets — see DARNEL, RYEGRASS

**¹loll** \'läl *also* 'lòl *sometimes* 'lōl\ *vb* -ED/-ING/-S [ME *lollen*, prob. of imit. origin like ME *lullen* to lull — more at LULL] *vi* **1 :** to hang loosely or laxly **:** DROOP, DANGLE ⟨his head ~*ing* on his shoulders —Norman Mailer⟩ ⟨the ~*ing* stalk of every sun-weary flower —Osbert Sitwell⟩ **2 :** to recline, lean, or move in a lax, lazy, or indolent manner **:** IDLE, LOUNGE, SPRAWL ⟨jaded people ~*ing* supine in carriages —G.B.Shaw⟩ ⟨knocks off for several days and ~*s* about in pajamas at home —E.P.Snow⟩ ⟨~*ing* about the beach —Oliver Herford⟩ **3 :** *of the tongue* **:** to hang out **:** PROTRUDE ⟨their dogs . . . lay tired, with ~*ing* tongues —Adrian Bell⟩ ~ *vt* **:** to let roll out or down or back and forth **:** to let droop or dangle ⟨~*s* his tired tongue —Carl Sandburg⟩ — often used with *out* ⟨~*ed* his tongue out in derision⟩

**²loll** \"\ *n* -S *archaic* **:** act or posture of lolling

**lollapaloosa** *var of* LALLAPALOOZA

**lol·lard** \'lälə(r)d *also* 'lòl-\ *n* -S *usu cap* [ME, fr. MD *lollaert*, fr. *lollen* to mutter, mumble, doze + *-aert* -ard — more at LULL] **1 :** one of various heretics in the Netherlands in the 14th century akin to the Fraticelli and the Beghards **2 :** one of the followers of Wycliffe in England and Scotland in the 14th and 15th centuries traveling as itinerant lay preachers throughout the land, denouncing ecclesiastical and temporal abuses, and preaching a spiritual message based on a primary appeal to the Bible

**lol·lard·ism** \-(r)ˌdizəm\ *n* -S *usu cap* **:** LOLLARDY

**lol·lardy** \-ˌdē\ *also* **lol·lard·ry** \-drē\ *n* -ES *usu cap* [ME *Lollardie, Lollardrie*, fr. *Lollard* + *-ie* -y or *-rie* -ry] **:** the principles, beliefs, and practices of the Lollards

**löllingite** *var of* LOELLINGITE

**lol·ling·ly** *adv* **:** in a lolling manner **:** in a relaxed way

**lol·li·pop** *or* **lol·ly·pop** \'lälēˌpäp, -li,-\ *n* [prob. fr. ¹*loll* (to protrude the tongue) + *-i-* + *pop*] **:** a piece of hard candy to be dissolved in the mouth: **a :** a candy held in the mouth **b :** a lump of candy on the end of a stick that may be inserted in and removed from the mouth — see ALL-DAY SUCKER

**lol·lop** \'läləp\ *vi* -ED/-ING/-S [¹*loll* + *-op* (as in *wallop, gallop*)] **1** *dial Eng* **:** to loll, lounge, or move loungingly **:** SLOUCH ⟨these men, women, and children loll and ~ about —Osbert Sitwell⟩ **2 :** to proceed with a bounding or bobbing motion ⟨watching a rabbit ~ across —Adrian Bell⟩ ⟨the jeep ~*ed* and slewed in low low —Dan Wickenden⟩ ⟨the ~*ing* gait of the wolves —George Moore⟩

**lol·ly** \'lälē, -li\ *n* -ES [short for *lollipop*] **1** *Brit* **:** a piece of candy; *esp* **:** HARD CANDY **2** *also* **lolly ice :** soft ice or ice and snow that is ground down from floes or formed in turbulent seawater

**lollygag** *var of* LALLYGAG

**lo·lo** \'lō(ˌ)lō\ *n, pl* **lolo** *or* **lolos** *usu cap* [Chin (Pek) *lo² lo²*] **1 :** NOSU **2 :** the Tibeto-Burman language of the Nosu people

**¹lo·ma** \'lōmə\ *n* -S [Sp, fr. *lomo* loin, back of an animal, fr. L *lumbus* loin — more at LOIN] *chiefly Southwest* **:** a broad-topped hill

**²loma** \"\ *n, pl* **loma** *or* **lomas** *usu cap* **1 a :** a people of the border regions of Liberia, Sierra Leone, and the Republic of Guinea **b :** a member of such people **2 :** a Mande language of the Loma people

**lo·mas** \'lōˌmäs\ *or* **lomas de za·mo·ra** \-thäsä'mòrə\ *adj*, *usu cap L&Z* [fr. *Lomas* or *Lomas de Zamora*, Argentina] **:** of or from the city of Lomas, Argentina **:** of the kind or style prevalent in Lomas

**lo·ma·tia** \lō'māsh(ē)ə\ *n, cap* [NL, fr. Gk *lōmat-, lōma* hem, fringe + NL *-ia*] **:** a small genus of low-growing Chilean and Australian trees (family Proteaceae) some of which yield dyes from their sap and wood used locally for furniture — see LOMATIOL

**lo·ma·tine** \'lōmətən, -əd·ən\ *or* **lo·mat·i·nous** \lō'matᵊnəs\ *adj* [ISV *lomat-* (fr. Gk *lōmat-, lōma* hem, fringe) + *-ine*; akin to L *lorum* strap — more at LORE] **:** LOBED ⟨the ~ toes of some birds⟩

**lo·mati·ol** \lō'māshēˌòl, -ˌōl\ *n* -S [NL *Lomatia* + E *-ol*] **:** a yellow crystalline pigment $C_{15}H_{14}O_4$ that surrounds the seeds of Australian trees of the genus *Lomatia* and that is a hydroxy derivative of lapachol

**lo·ma·ti·um** \lō'māshēəm\ *n, cap* [NL, fr. Gk *lōmation* small border, dim. of *lōmat-, lōma* hem, fringe] **:** a genus of perennial herbs (family Umbelliferae) resembling parsley and having leaves that are for the most part finely and ternately compound and winged fruit that is oblong to orbicular

**¹lom·bard** \'lämˌbärd, -bàd, -ˌbə(r)d\ *n* -S *often attrib* [ME *Lumbarde*, fr. MF *lombard*, fr. OIt *lombardo*, fr. L *Langobardus, Longobardus*] **1** *cap* **a :** a member of a Teutonic people invading Italy in A.D. 568, settling in the Po Valley, and establishing a kingdom **b :** a person descended from the Teutonic Lombards; *broadly* **:** a native of the part of Italy settled by the Lombards **2 a** *usu cap* **:** a Lombard engaged in banking or moneylending; *broadly* **:** BANKER, MONEYLENDER **b** *sometimes cap* **:** the place of business of a Lombard **:** BANK, PAWNSHOP

**²lombard** \"\ *n* -S [Sp *lombarda*, fr. fem. of *lombardo* Lombard, fr. It] **:** a cannon used in the 15th and 16th centuries

**lombard architecture** *n, usu cap L* **1 :** a round-arched architecture of northern Italy that is believed to date from the 8th century **2 :** the architecture of northern Italy including the Lombard, the later Romanesque, the Gothic, and other styles

**lom·bard·esque** \¦lämˌbär¦desk, -bà¦d-, -ˌbə(r)¦d-\ *adj, usu cap* [It *lombardesco*, fr. *lombardo* + *-esco* -esque] **1 :** of or relating to a Lombard type or school **2 :** of or relating to any of several Italian Renaissance painters named Lombardi or Lombardo

**¹lom·bar·dic** \(')läm¦bärdik, -bàd-, -dēk\ *adj, usu cap* [¹*Lombard* + *-ic*] **1 :** of or relating to the Lombards or to the region of northern Italy formerly constituting the kingdom of the Lombards **2 :** belonging to or characteristic of a medieval Italian writing developed from the Roman cursive

**²lombardic** \"\ *n* -S *usu cap* **:** a Lombardic script

**lombard loan** *n, usu cap 1st L, Brit* **:** a loan on stock-exchange securities usu. made by a central bank to commercial banks

LOMBARDIC

**lombard school** *n, usu cap L* **:** any of several Renaissance schools of painting in cities (as Mantua, Milan, Padua) of northern Italy

**lom·bar·dy poplar** \'lämˌbärdē-, -bàdē-, -di-\ *n, usu cap L* [fr. *Lombardy*, district in northern Italy] **:** a poplar that is a staminate variety (*Populus nigra italica*) of the black poplar distinguished by its columnar fastigiate shape and strongly ascending branches

**lom·bro·sian** \(')läm¦brōzhən\ *adj, usu cap* [Cesare *Lombroso* †1909 Ital. physician and criminologist + E *-ian*] **:** of or relating to the doctrines of Lombroso esp. that a criminal represents a distinct anthropological type with definite physical and mental stigmata and that he is the product of heredity, atavism, and degeneracy ⟨*Lombrosian* school⟩ ⟨a *Lombrosian* approach to criminology⟩

**lo·ment** \'lōˌment\ *also* **lo·men·tum** \lō'mentəm\ *n* -S [NL *lomentum*, fr. L, cosmetic wash made fr. bean meal, fr. *lotus* (past part. of *lavare* to wash) + *-mentum* -ment — more at LYE] **:** a dry indehiscent one-celled fruit (as of the tick trefoil) that is produced from a single superior ovary and breaks transversely into numerous segments at maturity — see FRUIT illustration

**lo·mi·lo·mi** \'lōmē'lōmē\ *n* -S [Hawaiian] **:** a vigorous massage used by the Hawaiians to relieve pain and fatigue

**lomilomi salmon** *n* **:** a Hawaiian dish consisting of salmon worked with the fingers, mixed with onions, and seasoned

**lo·mi·ta** \lō'mēd·ə\ *n* -S [Sp, dim. of *loma* hill — more at LOMA] **:** a low broad hill

**lomonite** *var of* LAUMONTITE

**lon** *abbr* longitude

**lonch-** *or* **loncho-** *comb form* [NL, fr. Gk, fr. *lonchē* spearhead, lance] **:** lance ⟨*Lonch*ocarpus⟩ ⟨*Lonch*ma⟩

**lon·cho·car·pus** \ˌläŋkə'kärpəs\ *n, cap* [NL, fr. *lonch-* + *-carpus*] **:** a large genus of chiefly tropical American trees and shrubs (family Leguminosae) that have pinnate leaves and red and white flowers with the wings and keel united

**lon·chop·ter·i·dae** \ˌläŋˌkäp'terəˌdē\ *n pl, cap* [NL, fr. *Lonchoptera*, type genus (fr. *lonch-* + *-ptera*) + *-idae*] **:** a family of small two-winged flies with porrect antennae and lanceolate wings

**lon·chura** \läŋ'kyùrə\ *n* [NL, fr. *lonch-* + *-ura*] **1** *cap* **:** a large genus of weaverbirds including the well-known cowry bird **2** -S **:** any bird of *Lonchura* or a closely related genus

**lon·don** \'ləndən\ *adj, usu cap* [fr. *London*, England] **:** of or from London, the capital of England ⟨a *London* newspaper⟩ ⟨*London* church bells⟩ **:** of the kind or style prevalent in London ⟨morning came, cold, with a high, gray, *London* sky —John Galsworthy⟩

**london bridge** *n, usu cap L&B* [fr. *London Bridge*, a bridge built in 1209 across the Thames river in London, England] **:** an old singing game in which one of a line of children passing under an arch formed by uplifted arms is captured by a downward swoop of the arms at the end of the refrain

**london broil** *n, usu cap L* **:** broiled flank steak sliced diagonally across the grain

**london brown** *n, often cap L* **:** CARBUNCLE 3

**lon·don·der·ry** \ˌləndənˌderē, -ri\ *adj, usu cap* [fr. *Londonderry*, county borough in Ireland] **1 :** of or from the county borough of Londonderry, Northern Ireland **:** of the kind or style prevalent in Londonderry **2 :** of or from County Londonderry, Northern Ireland **:** of the kind or style prevalent in County Londonderry

**lon·don·er** \ˈləndənə(r)\ *n* -s *cap* [ME *londynere*, fr. *London* England + ME *-ere* -er] **:** a native or resident of London, England

**lon·don·ese** \ˌləndəˈnēz, -ēs\ *n, usu cap* [*London*, England + E *-ese*] **:** the dialect of London; *esp* **:** COCKNEY 2b

**lon·don·esque** \-ˈnesk\ *adj, usu cap* [*London*, England + E *-esque*] **:** characteristic of London

**london forces** *n pl, usu cap L* [after Fritz Wolfgang *London* †1954 Am. physicist born in Germany] **:** nonchemical interactions between atoms or molecules

**lon·don·ish** \ˈləndənish\ *adj, usu cap* [*London*, England + E *-ish*] **:** relating to or characteristic of London

**london ivy** *n, usu cap L* **:** the smoke or the thick fog of London

**lon·don·iza·tion** \ˌləndənəˈzāshən\ *n* -s *usu cap* **:** the act or process of londonizing

**lon·don·ize** \ˈləndəˌnīz\ *vt* -ED/-ING/-S *often cap* [*London*, England + E *-ize*] **1 :** to cause to acquire a quality distinctive of London or a trait distinctive of Londoners **2 :** to cause to conform to or imitate London fashions

**london particular** *n, usu cap L* **:** an extremely thick London fog

**london plane** *or* **london plane tree** *n, usu cap L* **:** a rapid-growing smoke resistant tree (*Platanus* × *acerifolia*) that is a hybrid between the Oriental plane and a common American sycamore (*P. occidentalis*) and is used for street and shade-tree planting

**london pride** *n, usu cap L* **1 :** a hardy perennial saxifrage (*Saxifraga umbrosa*) native to western Europe **2 :** SWEET WILLIAM **3 :** MALTESE CROSS 2 **4 :** SOAPWORT

**London Purple** *trademark* — used for an arsenical insecticide obtained as a by-product of the dye industry

**london rocket** *n, usu cap L* **:** a European herb (*Sisymbrium irio*) that sprang up in London after the great fire of 1666 and is occas. adventive in No. America

**london smoke** *n, often cap L* **:** a nearly neutral slightly olive black that is very slightly lighter and less neutral than Chaetura black

**lon·dony** \ˈləndənē\ *adj, usu cap* [*London*, England + E *-y*] **:** marked by or tending to suggest characteristics of London

**lone** \ˈlōn\ *adj* [ME, by shortening (resulting fr. incorrect division of *alon, alone* alone as *a lon, a lone*) of *alon, alone* — more at ALONE] **1 a :** having no company **:** LONESOME **:** SOLITARY ⟨here and there a ~ traveler could be seen walking up the winding roads —H.A.Chippendale⟩ ⟨a ~ horseman carried the mail —*Amer. Guide Series: N.H.*⟩ **b :** preferring solitude **:** disposed to isolation ⟨the hermit, the ~ soul, does not build but seeks a cave —John Dewey⟩ ⟨a ~ wolf⟩ **c :** having no husband **:** being unmarried or widowed ⟨a big city is full of ~ women⟩ **2 :** ONLY, SOLE ⟨constitutes the ~ industry of the community —*Amer. Guide Series: Vt.*⟩ ⟨the annual picnic in many companies furnishes the ~ contact with employees' families —*Dun's Rev.*⟩ ⟨the Lone Star State⟩ **3 :** situated by itself **:** ISOLATED, REMOTE ⟨the ~ oak tree against the sky —Howard Troyer⟩ ⟨this ~ outpost on the keys —*Amer. Guide Series: Fla.*⟩ **syn** see ALONE, SINGLE — **one's lone :** one's self ⟨walks by *its* wild *lone* —E.B.White⟩ ⟨if he doesn't come I couldn't live here *my lone* —Michael McLaverty⟩

**lone hand** *n* **1 a :** a hand in certain partnership card games strong enough to be played out alone by the person holding it after his partner has laid aside his own hand **b :** a person playing such a hand **2 :** a course of action, policy, or enterprise carried out by a country, group, or individual without allies or associates

**lone·li·hood** \ˈlōnlēˌhu̇d\ *n* **:** LONELINESS

**lone·li·ly** \-ləlē\ *adv* **:** in a lonely manner

**lone·li·ness** \ˈlōnlēnəs, -lin-\ *n* -ES **1 a :** the fact or condition of being alone **:** ISOLATION ⟨had become frightened by the ~ of her position in life —Sherwood Anderson⟩ ⟨the impersonality and ~ of modern mass civilization —C.B.Forcey⟩ **b :** a seclusion from others **:** a deliberately selected state of solitude **:** SEPARATENESS ⟨holding herself aloof in chosen ~ —P.E. More⟩ **2 :** a remoteness from human habitation **:** BLEAKNESS, DESOLATENESS ⟨the ~ of the spot was set off by the unbroken snow around it⟩ **3 :** a state of dejection or grief caused by the condition of being alone ⟨felt so forlorn, so helpless, filled as she was with gnawing ~ —O.E.Rölvaag⟩ ⟨often the artist has an aching sense of great ~ —J.R.Oppenheimer⟩

**lone·ly** \-lē, -li\ *adj, usu* -ER/-EST [*lone* + *-ly*] **1 a :** being without company **:** lacking companions or associates **:** LONE ⟨a ~ fisherman stood below on a tuft of gravel —Frederic Prokosch⟩ ⟨young men who brought their girls there to dance as well as ~ ones who danced with the hostesses —Edmund Wilson⟩ **b :** cut off from company or neighbors **:** SOLITARY ⟨a ~ little town far off upon the verge of Lapland night —G.D. Brown⟩ ⟨the train stopped frequently at ~ little stations —Robert Hichens⟩ **2 :** not frequented by human beings **:** DESOLATE ⟨dangerous and ~ portions of . . . coast —A.F. Harlow⟩ ⟨a ~ road⟩ **3 :** affected by loneliness **:** dejected and unhappy as a result of being alone ⟨so far from home . . . so ~ and terribly unhappy —Eric Linklater⟩ ⟨a poor sick ~ old woman —W.M.Thackeray⟩ ⟨~ for his family⟩ **4 :** producing a condition or feeling of loneliness ⟨it's a ~ thing to be a champion —G.B.Shaw⟩ **syn** see ALONE

**lone·ness** *n* -ES **:** the quality or state of being lone **:** ISOLATION ⟨space that was absolute meaninglessness and absolute cold, and absolute dark ~ —Waldo Frank⟩ ⟨to face the ~ of their days —Marsden Hartley⟩

**lon·er** \ˈlōnə(r)\ *n* -S [*lone* + *-er*] **:** one that avoids others: as **a :** a person who keeps to himself ⟨a ~ with no close friends⟩ ⟨a political ~ who joins no factions⟩ **b :** a solitary animal ⟨the black bear is elusive, speedy . . . a ~, a nomad, and harmless —E.J.Kahn⟩

**lone scout** *n* **:** a boy or girl scout who lives in a rural community that does not have a regular scout organization

**[1]lone·some** \ˈlōnsəm\ *adj* [*lone* + *-some*] **1 a :** being in a state of loneliness **:** affected by sadness or dejection as a result of lack of companionship or separation from others ⟨was ~ for the female society of my kind —W.A.White⟩ ⟨enjoyed being abroad but was ~ for his family⟩ **b :** causing a feeling of loneliness ⟨how ~ and silent the house had seemed —Gretchen Finletter⟩ **2 a :** REMOTE, UNFREQUENTED ⟨like one that on a ~ road doth walk in fear and dread —S.T.Coleridge⟩ **b :** lacking companionship **:** separated from others of its kind **:** LONE ⟨had no industries, few towns of any size, no fences, no roads, and only a ~ railroad line or two —*Newsweek*⟩ ⟨two cruisers ahead and to port of the carrier, and one ~ destroyer on her starboard —C.A.Lockwood⟩ **syn** see ALONE

**[2]lonesome** \"\ *n* -S **:** SELF ⟨be nice if we had the patch all to our *~s* —Wallace Stegner⟩ ⟨working by his ~ in the fields —Mary Webb⟩

**lone·some·ly** *adv* **:** in a lonesome manner

**lone·some·ness** *n* -ES **:** the quality or state of being lonesome

**lone star** *adj, usu cap L&S* [fr. the *Lone Star* state, nickname for Texas; fr. the single star of its flag] **:** TEXAS

**lone star tick** *n* **:** a widely distributed No. American ixodid tick (*Amblyomma americanum*) that attacks various mammals and is regarded as a potential spotted fever vector

**lone troop** *n* **:** a girl scout troop that is not under the jurisdiction of a girl scout council

**lone wolf** *n* **1 :** a wolf that hunts or prowls alone **2 :** a person who prefers to work, act, or live alone ⟨American painters are *lone wolves* who fear to lose their individuality by working together and trading ideas —Manny Farber⟩ ⟨in all things a *lone wolf*, apparently wanting no friends and seeking to influence no man —C.W.M.Hart⟩

**lone–wolf** \ˈ≈ˈ≈\ *vi* [*lone wolf*] **:** to proceed on one's own in the manner of a lone wolf **:** work, act, or live alone ⟨bade the men stay by Location No. 1 while he *lone-wolfed* it to Location No. 2 —*Infantry Jour.*⟩

**[1]long** \ˈlȯŋ *also* ˈläŋ\ *adj* **lon·ger** \-ŋgə(r)\ **lon·gest** \-ŋgəst\ [ME *long, lang*, fr. OE; akin to OHG *lang* long, ON *langr*, Goth *langs*, L *longus*, MPer *drang*, Skt *dīrgha* — more at INDULGE] **1 a :** extending for a considerable distance **:** having great length ⟨oaks in ~ and imposing avenues —*Amer. Guide Series: La.*⟩ ⟨a ~ coastline⟩ ⟨the ~ trip from New York to London was made in remarkably short time⟩ **b :** having greater length than usual ⟨a large oval man, with a ~ oiled mustache —Lawrence Durrell⟩ ⟨a ~ car⟩ ⟨~ fingers⟩ **c :** having greater height than usual **:** TALL ⟨walked over to the ~ French windows and looked out —May Sarton⟩ ⟨a ~, lean individual —F.V.W.Mason⟩ ⟨a race of ~ gaunt men —Sherwood Anderson⟩ **d :** having a greater length than breadth **:** ELONGATED ⟨a ~ skull⟩ ⟨a ~ face⟩ **e :** longer than desirable or necessary **:** too long ⟨the dress is ~ on her⟩ ⟨the column is two lines ~⟩ ⟨his first serve was ~⟩ **2 a :** having a specified length ⟨the table was six feet ~⟩ **b :** forming the chief linear dimension ⟨the ~ side of the building⟩ ⟨placed the sofa the ~ way of the room⟩ **3 a :** extending over a considerable time ⟨even after ~ experience editing has never become easy —E.S. McCartney⟩ ⟨a ~ tradition of national consciousness —Vera M. Dean⟩ ⟨a ~ friendship⟩ **b :** having a specified duration ⟨the play was two hours ~⟩ **c :** prolonged beyond the usual time **:** not interrupted ⟨drank in ~, greedy swallows —Scott Fitzgerald⟩ ⟨the occasional shutting of a door would peal in ~ reverberations —T.L.Peacock⟩ ⟨a ~ look⟩ ⟨a ~ breath⟩ ⟨the four enemies who were lifting the ~ yell as they came racing for him —W.N.Burns⟩ **4 a :** containing many items in a series ⟨a ~ and strong list of candidates was put forward —S.H.Adams⟩ ⟨the ~ series of combat operations —Mack Morriss⟩ ⟨played a ~ list of comedy and farcical roles —W.P. Eaton⟩ **b :** having a specified number of units ⟨a book 300 pages ~⟩ **c :** consisting of a greater number or amount than usual **:** LARGE ⟨this son was a man of 40 or thereabouts, was married, and had a ~ family —A.T.Quiller-Couch⟩ ⟨now reverenced as a master . . . because his prints fetch ~ prices —Clive Bell⟩ **5 a** *of a speech sound* **:** having a relatively long duration ⟨the vowel of *dark* is ~*er* than the vowel of *dock* when the *r* is not pronounced⟩ **b :** indicating the member of a pair of similarly spelled vowel or partly vowel sounds that is descended from a vowel long in duration but that now is not long in duration or does not have duration as its chief distinguishing feature ⟨~ *a* in *fate*⟩ ⟨~ *e* in *equal*⟩ ⟨~ *i* in *sign*⟩ ⟨~ *o* in *ode*⟩ ⟨~ *u* in *fuse*⟩ **c** (1) *of a syllable in Greek or Latin verse* **:** of relatively extended duration (2) *of a syllable in English verse* **:** STRESSED **6 a :** lasting too long **:** TEDIOUS ⟨a ~ lecture⟩ ⟨a ~ explanation⟩ **b :** seeming to pass slowly and heavily ⟨those ~ grim years between the fall of France and the battle of El Alamein —R.K.Dickson⟩ ⟨hung parasitically round the court in the ~ days of its poverty —A.M.Young⟩ **7 :** having the capacity to reach or extend or travel a considerable distance ⟨the ~ voice of the hounds —Thomas Wolfe⟩ ⟨a ~ northeast wind —Marjory S. Douglas⟩ ⟨a fighter with a ~ left jab⟩ ⟨hits a ~ ball⟩ ⟨~ sight⟩ **8** *of a number or unit of measure* **:** larger or longer than the standard ⟨~ mile⟩ **9 a :** extending far into the future ⟨a ~ view of the problem⟩ ⟨the thoughts of youth are ~, ~ thoughts —H.W.Longfellow⟩ **b :** extending beyond what is known or easily verified ⟨a ~ guess⟩ **c :** far off in time **:** REMOTE ⟨a ~ date⟩ **d :** payable after a considerable period ⟨a ~ note⟩ **10 :** consisting of or containing long straw ⟨~ fodder⟩ **11 :** esp. strong in or esp. well furnished with — used with *on* ⟨deficient in logic but ~ on human understanding —Stuart Chase⟩ ⟨~ on ancestry and short on cash —Clement Eaton⟩ **12** *of betting odds* **a :** marked by an unusual degree of difference between the amounts wagered on each side ⟨odds of 30 to 1 or even ~*er*⟩ **b :** of or relating to the larger amount wagered ⟨take the ~ end of the bet⟩ **13 :** subject to great odds **:** having little likelihood of success ⟨strike out for himself, be independent, take a ~ chance for a large reward —W.P.Webb⟩ **14 :** holding securities or goods in anticipation of an advance in prices ⟨~ of cotton⟩ ⟨be on the ~ side of the market⟩ **15** *of a beverage* **:** served in a tall glass **:** constituting a large measure ⟨a ~ drink⟩ **16 :** adequate in amount **:** capable of meeting consumer needs ⟨corn is in ~ supply⟩ **17** *of fractional paper sizes* **:** having a longer dimension equal to the shorter dimension of the full-size sheet ⟨~ quarto⟩ **18 a :** flowing readily **:** FLUID ⟨a ~ printing ink⟩ **b :** yielding a readily flowing mixture ⟨a ~ carbon black⟩ **19 :** TELEPHOTO — **at long last** *adv* **:** after a long wait **:** FINALLY ⟨*at long last* they sighted land⟩ — **at the longest** *adv* **:** at the outside limit of time ⟨will take two hours *at the longest*⟩ — **long in the tooth :** past one's best days **:** OLD ⟨as fighters go, he is a sere and yellowed leaf and *long in the tooth* —Gilbert Millstein⟩

**[2]long** \"\ *adv* -ER/-EST [ME *longe, lange*, fr. OE, fr. *long, lang*, adj.] **1 :** for or during a long time ⟨children know what a story or play is ~ before they know what an essay is —George Sampson⟩ ⟨a quiet picturesque resort, ~ the gathering place of artists —*Amer. Guide Series: Mich.*⟩ **2 :** at or to a long distance **:** FAR — used chiefly in combination ⟨*long*-removed⟩ ⟨*long*-traveled⟩ **3 :** for the duration of a specified period ⟨all summer ~⟩ ⟨all his life ~⟩ ⟨all day ~⟩ **4 :** at a point of time far before or after a specified moment or event ⟨~ before the discovery of America⟩ ⟨his diary was deciphered ~ after his death⟩ **5 :** after or beyond a specified time — used in the comparative ⟨didn't stay ~*er* than five o'clock⟩ ⟨the city held out ~*er* than a year under siege⟩

**[3]long** \"\ *n* -S [ME *long, lang*, fr. *long, lang*, adj.] **1 :** a long period of time ⟨expected the train before ~⟩ **2** [ME, fr. ML *longa* — more at LONGA] *in mensural notation* **:** a note that in imperfect time is one half the length of a large note and twice the length of a breve, and in perfect time is one third the length of a large note and three times the length of a breve **3 :** a long syllable **4 :** one who purchases or operates on the long side of the market — compare BULL 2a **5 :** a long signal (as in Morse code) ⟨tapped out a ~ and a short⟩ ⟨blew two ~*s* on his whistle⟩ **6 a longs** *pl* **:** long trousers ⟨was proudly wearing his first pair of ~*s*⟩ **b :** a size in men's clothing (as suits, coats, slacks) for the person who is above average in height **7 longs** *pl* **:** LONG-TERM BONDS — **the long and short** *or* **the long and the short :** the sum and substance **:** GIST **:** WHOLE

**[4]long** \"\ *vi* -ED/-ING/-S [ME *longen, langen*, fr. OE *longian, langian*; akin to OS *langōn* to long, OHG *langēn*, ON *langa*; derivative fr. the root of E [1]*long*] **:** to feel a strong desire or craving **:** wish for something intensely **:** YEARN ⟨~ for summer to come⟩ ⟨when I look at her dancing, I ~ to dance with her —Anne D. Sedgwick⟩ ⟨~*s* for the big sales that a sensational book or a novelty may seem to promise —August Frugé⟩

**syn** LONG, YEARN, HANKER, PINE, HUNGER, and THIRST mean in common to have a strong desire (for something). LONG implies wishing for something with one's whole heart ⟨however much you may *long* for a cigarette —Agnes M. Miall⟩ ⟨*long* for peace and security after war and disorder⟩ ⟨for the first time in her life she had ceased *longing*, ceased striving —Ellen Glasgow⟩ YEARN adds to LONG the idea of eagerness, tenderness, or passionateness ⟨*yearn* for something to believe in⟩ ⟨they often became homesick and *yearned* for their old associations —V.G.Heiser⟩ ⟨gazed into his faded blue eyes as if *yearning* to be understood —Joseph Conrad⟩ ⟨*yearned* for the return of a lover⟩ HANKER suggests somewhat disparagingly that one is made uneasy or restless by a desire ⟨he *hankered* after other, strange delights —Robertson Davies⟩ ⟨no *hankering* to be the founder of a new system of philosophy —M.R.Cohen⟩ ⟨all who enjoy or *hanker* after a life in the open air —*Brit. Book News*⟩ ⟨*hanker* after illicit pleasures⟩ PINE suggests a languishing or other more or less adverse physical effect from usu. fruitless longing ⟨one realizes all the pleasure of the present good; the other converts it into pain by *pining* after something better —T.L.Peacock⟩ ⟨some people *pine* for adventure, stalk it, woo it with lures —Sylvia Berkman⟩ ⟨the job he had always *pined* for —*Time*⟩ HUNGER and THIRST suggest a compelling craving ⟨could even a mother have *hungered* more acutely for the sight of a daughter? —Ellen Glasgow⟩ ⟨people *thirsting* for conquest —Julien Benda⟩ ⟨she was *thirsting* to hear the whole of the story —Winston Churchill⟩

**[5]long** \"\ *vi* -ED/-ING/-S [ME *longen*, fr. *along* (on) because (of) — more at ALONG OF] *archaic* **:** to be suitable or fitting ⟨give thee everything that ~*s* unto the daughter of a king —William Morris⟩

**long** *abbr* **1** longeron **2** longitude; longitudinal

**lon·ga** \ˈläŋgə\ *n* -S [ML, fr. fem. of L *longus* long — more at LONG] **:** LONG 2

**long account** *n* **1 :** the account of a purchaser of securities on margin **2 :** the aggregate of margin purchases in a given security or commodity or in a delivery month or of the market as a whole

**longaeval** *var of* LONGEVAL

**[1]long ago** *adv* [[2]*long* + *ago*] **:** in the distant or comparatively distant past **:** not recently ⟨*long ago* changed their nomadic way of life for a settled one⟩ ⟨left for work *long ago*⟩

**[2]long ago** *n* **:** the distant past ⟨the excitement and uncertainties of the campaign, even the triumph of the election, seem incidents of the *long ago* —*New Yorker*⟩

**long–ago** \ˈ≈≈ˈ≈\ *adj* [[1]*long ago*] **:** belonging to a time long gone ⟨those *long-ago* dresses that had made such lovely sounds —Bruce Marshall⟩

**lon·gan** \ˈläŋgən\ *or* **lun·gan** \ˈləŋ-\ *n* -S [Chin (Pek) *lung*[2] *yen*[3], lit., dragon's eye] **1 :** a pulpy fruit related to the litchi and produced by an East Indian tree (*Euphoria longana*) **2 :** a tree that bears the longan

**long–and–short–haul clause** \ˈ≈≈ˈ≈ˈ≈-\ *n* **:** a clause in U.S. laws regulating railroad rates providing that the total rate for a distance less than and included in a longer distance shall not be higher than that for the longer distance except when specially authorized by public regulatory authorities

**long–and–short work** \ˈ≈≈ˈ≈-\ *n* **:** ashlar quoins arranged alternately horizontally and vertically (as to finish off rubblework)

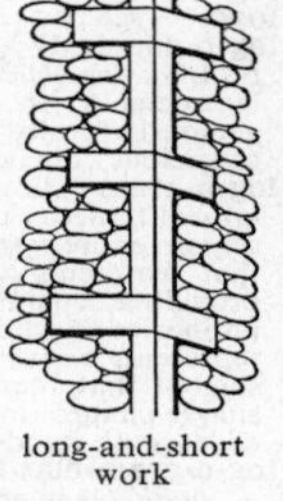
long-and-short work

**lon·ga·nim·i·ty** \ˌläŋgəˈniməd·ē\ *n* -ES [LL *longanimitas*, fr. *longanimis* long-suffering (fr. *longus* long + *animus* soul, mind, spirit) + *-itas* -ity — more at ANIMATE] **:** a disposition to bear injuries patiently **:** FORBEARANCE ⟨bears his trials with ~⟩ **syn** see PATIENCE

**lon·gan·i·mous** \läŋˈganəməs\ *adj* [LL *longanimus, longanimis*] **:** able to bear injuries patiently **:** FORBEARING

**long appoggiatura** *n* **:** a grace note that is played on the beat with half the time value taken from the principal note following it — see APPOGGIATURA illustration

**long ballot** *n* **:** BLANKET BALLOT

**long barrow** *n* **:** a neolithic burial mound of oval, wedge, or very much elongated shape — compare ROUND BARROW

**[1]long beach** *adj, usu cap L&B* [fr. *Long Beach*, Calif.] **:** of or from the city of Long Beach, Calif. ⟨the *Long Beach* harbor⟩ **:** of the kind or style prevalent in Long Beach

**[2]long beach** *n, often cap L&B* **:** a light yellowish brown that is lighter and slightly redder and stronger than khaki and paler and slightly yellower than walnut brown

**longbeak** \ˈ≈ˌ≈\ *n* **:** DOWITCHER

**longbeard** \ˈ≈ˌ≈\ *n* **1 :** a man with a long beard **2 :** BELLARMINE

**long beech fern** *n* **:** a beech fern (*Phegopteris dryopteris*)

**longbill** \ˈ≈ˌ≈\ *n* **:** a bird with a long bill (as a snipe)

**long bill** *n* **:** a bill of exchange that runs for more than 30 and often more than 60 days — compare SHORT BILL

**long–billed curlew** \ˈ≈ˌ≈-\ *n* **:** HEN CURLEW

**long–billed dowitcher** *n* **:** a rather large dowitcher (*Limnodromus griseus scolopaceus*) of western No. America that has a long bill and that breeds along the arctic coast of Alaska and winters south into Mexico

**long–billed marsh wren** *n* **:** a marsh wren (*Telmatodytes palustris palustris*) that is predominantly dark brown to blackish brown above with buffy sides and white underparts and is widely distributed in No. America east of the Rocky mountains

**longboat** \ˈ≈ˌ≈\ *n* **:** the largest boat carried by a merchant sailing ship

**long bone** *n* **:** one of the elongated bones that form the characteristic support of the vertebrate limb and consist of an essentially cylindrical shaft containing marrow and terminating at each end in an enlarged head for articulation with other bones

**longbow** \ˈ≈ˌ≈\ *n* **1 :** a wooden bow drawn by hand and usu. 5½ to 6 feet long **2 :** the great bow of medieval England that sometimes reached a length of 6 feet, 7 inches, had a drawing weight of 100 pounds, and shot a cloth-yard shaft of 37 inches

**long bowls** *n pl but sing in constr* **:** a game whose object is bowling a skittle ball along the ground for a given distance in the fewest bowls — **at long bowls :** at a distance — used of ships cannonading at a distance from their target

**long buchu** *n* **1 :** a southern African shrub (*Barosma ensata*) whose leaves furnish an adulterant of buchu **2 :** BUCHU

**long cards** *n pl* **:** cards held in bridge or whist by a player in a suit of which the other players have none

**long–case clock** *n* **:** GRANDFATHER CLOCK

**long–chain** \ˈ≈ˈ≈\ *adj* **:** having a relatively long chain of atoms (as carbon atoms) in the molecule

**long clam** *n* **1 :** SOFT-SHELL CLAM **2 :** RAZOR CLAM

**long–clawed prawn** \ˈ≈ˌ≈-\ *n* **:** RIVER PRAWN

**longcloth** \ˈ≈ˌ≈\ *n* **:** a fine bleached cotton cloth with a close plain weave and a soft finish that is used chiefly for children's wear and underwear

**long column** *n* **:** a column so slender that it will fail under longitudinal load by bending rather than by crushing and typically having a length of 20 to 30 times the diameter

**long count** *n, often cap L&C* **:** a system of dating in the Maya calendar according to the time in numbers of baktuns, katuns, tuns, uinals, and days elapsed since an arbitrary point prior to 3000 B.C. — compare SHORT COUNT

**long–crested jay** \ˈ≈ˌ≈≈-\ *n* **:** a jay (*Cyanocitta stelleri diademata*) that is a variety of the Steller's jay, is distinguished chiefly by an intensely iridescent blue abdomen and rump and bluish white streaks on the head, and is found from Wyoming to New Mexico

**long cross** *n* **:** LATIN CROSS 1

**long–cycled** *also* **long–cycle** \ˈ≈ˈ≈≈\ *adj* **:** having an aecial or uredinial stage or both intervening between the pycnial and telial stages (as certain rusts) — opposed to *short-cycled*

**long dance** *n* **:** a longways dance; *specif* **:** RINKAFADDA

**long–day** \ˈ≈ˈ≈\ *adj* **:** responding to a long photoperiod — used of plants

**[1]long–distance** \ˈ≈ˈ≈≈\ *adj* [fr. the phrase *long distance*] **1 a :** situated a long distance away ⟨a *long-distance* friend⟩ **b :** covering a long distance ⟨a *long-distance* race⟩ ⟨*long-distance* vision⟩ **2 :** of or relating to telephone communication with a distant point ⟨a *long-distance* call⟩ ⟨*long-distance* night rates⟩

**[2]long–distance** \"\ *adv* **:** by long-distance telephone ⟨called her up *long-distance*⟩

**[3]long–distance** \"\ *vt* **1 :** to make a long-distance telephone call to ⟨didn't think it was worth while *long-distancing* you in Washington —Mary Manning⟩ **2 :** to express or communicate by means of a long-distance telephone call ⟨wrote, wired or *long-distanced* their desire to move in immediately —*Life*⟩

**long distance** *n* [[1]*long-distance*] **1 :** communication by long-distance telephone ⟨decided it by *long distance*⟩ **2 :** a telephone operator or exchange that gives long-distance connections ⟨had to ask *long distance* for his number⟩

**long division** *n* **:** arithmetical division in which the several steps corresponding to the division of parts of the dividend by the divisor are indicated in detail

**long dog** *n, dial Eng* **:** GREYHOUND; *esp* **:** a greyhound mongrel

**long dozen** *n* **:** one more than a dozen **:** THIRTEEN

**long draft** *n* **:** a system of spinning yarn or drafting roving that eliminates one or more reducing or roving processes

**long–drawn–out** \ˈ≈ˈ≈ˈ≈\ *also* **long–drawn** \ˈ≈ˈ≈\ *adj* **:** extended to a great length esp. of time **:** PROTRACTED ⟨the most critical times of that *long-drawn-out* contest —Clement Attlee⟩ ⟨the *long-drawn* trials of vigilance and exertion —Mark Sullivan⟩

**[1]longe** *or* **lunge** \ˈlənj, ˈlōnzh, ˈläⁿzh, ˈlänj\ *n* -S [F *longe*, fr. OF, fr. fem. of *lonc* long, fr. L *longus* — more at LONG] **:** a long rein or strap used to lead or guide a horse in training — called also *longeing rein*

²**longe** *or* **lunge** \"\ *vt* **longed** *or* **lunged; longed** *or* **lunged; longeing** *or* **lunging; longes** *or* **lunges :** to guide or exercise (a horse) by means of a longe

³**longe** \'lənj, 'länj\ *n* -s [by shortening & alter.] **1 :** LAKE TROUT b **2 :** MUSKELLUNGE

**longear** \'ₛ,ₛ\ *n, West* **:** an unbranded calf

**long-eared** \'ₛ'ₛ\ *adj* **1 :** having long ears **2 :** ASININE **:** STUPID ⟨an evil, heavy-laden, *long-eared* age —Thomas Carlyle⟩

**long-eared bat** *n* **:** any of numerous bats having very long ears (as members of the nearly cosmopolitan genus *Plecotus* in which the ears may equal the forearm in length)

**long-eared fox** *n* **1 :** a small carnivorous mammal (*Otocyon megalotis*) of southern Africa that is related to the typical foxes but is distinguished by very large erect ears and the presence of four molars in each jaw **2 :** DESERT FOX 2

**long-eared jerboa** *n* **:** a central Asian jerboa (*Euchorentes naso*) that is ocherous or russet and has a snout like that of a pig

**long-eared owl** *n* **:** an owl of the northern hemisphere (*Asio otus*) that has conspicuous ear tufts and mottled coloration; *esp* **:** a slender long-winged and long-tailed American owl (*Asio otus wilsonianus*)

**longear sunfish** *or* **long-eared sunfish** *n* **:** a sunfish (*Lepomis megalotis*) of the central and southern U. S. that is brilliant in color with a long opercular flap

**longed** *past of* LONG

**longeing rein** *or* **lunging rein** *n* **:** LONGE

¹**longer** *comparative of* LONG

²**lon·ger** \'läŋgə(r)\ *n* -s [origin unknown] **:** a row of barrels stowed fore and aft

**lon·ge·ron** \'länjərən\ *n* -s [F, longitudinal girder, longeron, fr. *allonger* to make long — more at ALLONGE] **:** a fore-and-aft member of the framing of an airplane fuselage that is usu. continuous across a number of points of support

**long ess** *var of* LONG S

**longest** *superlative of* LONG

**lon·ge·val** *also* **lon·gae·val** \län'jēvəl\ *adj* [L *longaevus* + E *-al*] *archaic* **:** long lasting

**lon·gev·i·ty** \län'jevəd·ē, lòn-, -ətē, -i\ *n* -ES [LL *longaevitas*, fr. L *longaevus* long-lived (fr. *longus* long + *aevum* age, lifetime) + *-itas* -ity — more at LONG, AYE] **1 a :** a long duration of individual life ⟨his ~ was remarkable, considering the fact that he had been sickly as a child⟩ ⟨~ of metal parts is increased by this new process —*Report: General Motors Corp.*⟩ **b :** length of life ⟨studies in ~⟩ **2 :** long continuance **:** SENIORITY ⟨~ in office is also an asset —Stephen Parratt⟩ ⟨held a remarkable record for parliamentary ~ —*Time*⟩

**longevity pay** *n* **:** additional wages or other compensation given on the basis of length of service

**lon·ge·vous** \(ˈ)län'jēvəs\ *adj* [L *longaevus*] **:** LONG-LIVED ⟨his ~ royal grandfather —*Time*⟩

**long face** *n* **:** a facial expression of sadness or melancholy usu. affected or exaggerated ⟨go around with a *long face* feeling sorry for yourself —Gregor Felsen⟩

**long-fed** \'ₛ'ₛ\ *adj, of cattle* **:** kept on a fattening ration for a period of four or more months — compare SHORT-FED

**long field** *n* **:** the part of a cricket field near the boundary behind the bowler; *also* **:** a fielder stationed there — called also *deep field*

**longfin** \'ₛ,ₛ\ *n* **:** any of several long-finned fishes: as **a** *Austral* **:** a member of the family Serranidae **b :** ARCTIC GRAYLING **c :** ALBACORE

**long-finned tuna** *or* **long-finned tunny** \'ₛ,ₛ-\ *n* **:** ALBACORE

**longfin pompano** *n* **:** a common pompano (*Trachinotus palometa*) of the warm western Atlantic that is marked by elongated fins and tail

**long fold** *adj* **:** LONG GRAIN

**long·ford** \'lòŋfə(r)d, 'läŋ-\ *adj, usu cap* [fr. *Longford* county, Ireland] **:** of or from County Longford, Ireland **:** of the kind or style prevalent in County Longford

**long four** *n* **:** a candle weighing a quarter of a pound

**long·ful** \'lòŋfəl *also* 'läŋ-\ *adj* [¹*long* + *-ful*] *dial* **:** LENGTHY

**long game** *n* **:** the phase of golf in which distance driving is a factor of first importance — compare SHORT GAME

**long glass** *n* **:** a nautical telescope

**long grain** *adj, of paper and paperboard* **:** having the machine direction running the long way of the sheet — called also *long fold;* compare BROAD FOLD

**long green** *n, slang* **:** paper money **:** CASH ⟨the boy will have plenty of the *long green* in a couple of years —Raymond Chandler⟩

**long hair** *also* **long-haired cat** *n* **:** a domestic cat having long silky outer fur and conforming in basic characteristics to the Persian type — compare SHORTHAIR

**longhair** \'ₛ,ₛ\ *n* [back-formation fr. *long-haired*] **1 a :** a man who wears his hair long **b :** an American Indian (as a Navaho) who has not attended school ⟨the *~s* of the Southwest, if sometimes rejected for illiteracy, are sought to man jackhammers and bulldozers —Elizabeth S. Sergeant⟩ **2 a :** an artistically gifted person or one seriously interested in any of the arts; *esp* **:** a composer, performer, or lover of classical music ⟨the great and the unknown who make music in Manhattan go there — from *~s* to hot pianists, drummers, and vibraharpists —*Newsweek*⟩ **b :** an impractical or unworldly intellectual **:** a scholar remote from everyday life ⟨described the younger writers as lugubrious and timid *~s* huddling in chill academies —Irving Howe⟩ ⟨problems the hard-boiled businessmen seem willing to leave to the *~s* —H.A.Wolff⟩ ⟨books are for women and *~s* —Ellery Queen⟩

**long-haired** \'ₛ'ₛ\ *adj* **1 :** having long hair **2 :** characterized by a devotion to abstract theory and impractical ideas ⟨making the crusader seem a *long-haired* dreamer who has never met a payroll —John Lardner⟩ ⟨were called reformers, cranks, enthusiastics, *long-haired* idealists —S.V.Benet⟩ **3 :** comprising, produced by, or appealing to aesthetes, idealists, or intellectuals ⟨the advanced guard of writers, the holy few who can only appeal endlessly to a limited and *long-haired* audience —Harrison Smith⟩ ⟨playing together in informal *long-haired* jam sessions —*Newsweek*⟩ ⟨*long-haired* fiction —*Time*⟩ **4 :** of, devoted to, or having the characteristics of classical music ⟨*long-haired* pianist⟩ ⟨*long-haired* audience⟩ ⟨*long-haired* concerto⟩

**long-haired chimpanzee** *n* **:** a chimpanzee (*Pan satyrus schweinfurthii*) that has exceptionally long hair and is found in forested country north and east of the Congo river

**longhand** \'ₛ,ₛ\ *n* **:** the characters used in ordinary writing **:** HANDWRITING — compare SHORTHAND

**long handle** *n* **:** the full force of the bat in cricket ⟨the batsman used the *long handle*⟩ ⟨give the bowling the *long handle*⟩

**long haul** *n* **1 :** a long distance; *specif* **:** transportation of goods between two distant points ⟨the furniture was crated for the *long haul* between New York and Chicago⟩ **2 :** a considerable period of time — used with *the* ⟨many old wives' rules are still valid for the *long haul* from cradle to the grave —Ernestine Evans⟩ ⟨over the *long haul* there is every reason to believe that the number of college students will increase steadily —R.C. Story⟩

**longhead** \'ₛ,ₛ\ *n* **1 :** a head with a low cephalic index **2 :** a dolichocephalic person

**longheaded** \'ₛ'ₛₛ\ *adj* **1 :** having unusual foresight or wisdom **2 :** DOLICHOCEPHALIC — **long·head·ed·ly** *adv* — **long·head·ed·ness** *n* -ES

**long hop** *n* **:** a bowled ball in cricket that pitches short and takes a relatively long flight after rebounding

**longhorn** \'ₛ,ₛ\ *n* **1 :** a long-horned animal **2 a** (1) *cap* **:** an English breed of heavy beef cattle with low wide horns that is now little raised (2) *usu cap* **:** an animal of this breed **b :** any of certain practically extinct long-horned cattle of Spanish derivation formerly common in southwestern U. S. esp. in Texas **3** *or* **longhorn cheese :** mild cheddar cheese of a specified form and weight

**long-horned beetle** *also* **longhorn beetle** \'ₛ,ₛ-\ *n* **:** any of various beetles that constitute the family Cerambycidae and are usu. distinguished by their very long antennae

**long-horned grasshopper** *n* **:** any of various grasshoppers that constitute the family Tettigoniidae and are distinguished by their very long antennae — see KATYDID

**long horse** *n* **1 :** a vaulting apparatus that is similar to a side horse but has one end elongated and is placed for vaulting in the direction of its length **2 :** a gymnastic event on the long horse

long horse

**longhouse** \'ₛ,ₛ\ *n* **1 a :** a communal dwelling often over 100 feet long used by some No. American Indians (as the Iroquois) **b :** a similar dwelling used by some peoples of the Pacific **2 :** a major council of some No. American Indians (as Iroquois)

**long hundred** *n* **:** a unit of quantity for countable objects (as fish) equal to 120 objects or to some other number larger than 100

**long hundredweight** *n* **:** HUNDREDWEIGHT b — see MEASURE table

**long hunter** *n* **:** a resident of an eastern frontier settlement of late 18th century America accustomed to spending long continuous periods hunting in the mountains of Tennessee and Kentucky

**longi-** *comb form* [ME, fr. L, fr. *longus* — more at LONG] **1 :** long ⟨*longi*caudal⟩ ⟨*longi*pennate⟩ ⟨*longi*rostrine⟩ **2 :** longitudinal ⟨*longi*section⟩

**lon·gi·col·lous** \ˌlänjə'käləs\ *adj* [*longi-* + L *coll*um neck + E *-ous*] **:** having a long beak or neck ⟨a ~ perithecium⟩

**lon·gi·cone** \'länjəˌkōn\ *n* [ISV *longi-* + *cone*] **:** a long conical shell characteristic of certain cephalopods; *also* **:** an animal having such a shell — **lon·gi·con·ic** \ˌₛₛ'känik\ *adj*

¹**lon·gi·corn** \'länjəˌkòrn\ *adj* [NL *Longicornia*] **1 :** of or relating to the Cerambycidae **2** [*longi-* + *-corn*] **:** having long antennae

²**longicorn** \"\ *n* **:** LONG-HORNED BEETLE

**lon·gi·cor·nia** \ˌlänjə'kò(r)nēə\ *n pl, cap* [NL, fr. *longi-* + L *-cornia*, neut. pl. of *-cornis* -corn] *in former classifications* **:** a group of beetles coextensive with Cerambycidae

**long·ie** \'lòŋi\ *var of* LUNGIE

**long·ies** \'lòŋēz *also* 'läŋ-\ *n pl* [¹*long* + *-ie* + *-s*] **1 :** long underwear **2 :** long pants for boys

**lon·gi·fo·lene** \ˌlänjə'fōˌlēn\ *n* -s [ISV *longifol-* (fr. NL *longifolia* — specific epithet of *Pinus longifolia* — fr. *longi-* + *-folia*, fr. L *folium* leaf) + *-ene* — more at BLADE] **:** a liquid tricyclic sesquiterpene $C_{15}H_{24}$ occurring in various turpentines (as from *Pinus longifolia*, *P. ponderosa*, or *P. torreyana*)

**lon·gil·o·quence** \län'jiləkwən(t)s\ *n* [*longi-* + *-loquence* (as in *grandiloquence*)] **:** LONG-WINDEDNESS

**long·ing** \'lòŋiŋ, -ŋēŋ *also* 'läŋ-\ *n* -s [ME *longing*, *langing*, fr. OE *langung*, fr. *langian* to long + *-ung* -ing — more at LONG] **:** an eager desire esp. for something remote or unattainable **:** CRAVING ⟨this first sight of him must answer for the amassed *~s* of 20 years —Anne S. Mehdevi⟩ ⟨pined away with ~ for ancient Greece —W.A.Kaufmann⟩

**long·ing·ly** *adv* **:** in a longing manner

**long·ing·ness** *n* -ES **:** LONGING, DESIRE

**lon·ginian** \län'jinēən\ *adj, usu cap* [Dionysius Cassius *Longin*us, 3d cent. A.D. Greek philosopher and rhetorician + E *-ian*] **:** of or characteristic of Longinus ⟨the perennial dialectic between Horatian technique and *Longinian* inspiration —Harry Levin⟩

**lon·gin·qui·ty** \län'jiŋkwəd·ē\ *n* -ES [L *longinquitas*, fr. *longinquus* distant (fr. *longus* long) + *-itas* -ity — more at LONG] *archaic* **:** remoteness in space or time

**long iron** *n* **1 :** a golf iron (as a No. 1, No. 2, or No. 3 iron) that has a long shaft and relatively slight loft and is used for hitting a long relatively low ball **2 :** a shot or stroke made with a long iron — compare SHORT IRON

¹**lon·gi·ros·trine** \ˌlänjə'rästrən, -räˌstrīn\ *adj* [*longi-* + *rostr-* + *-ine*] **:** having a long jaw

²**longirostrine** \"\ *n* -s **:** a long-jawed creature; *specif* **:** one of the long-jawed primitive proboscideans of the family Gomphotheriidae

**lon·gi·section** \ˌlänjə+\ *n* [*longi-* + *section*] **:** a longitudinal section

**long·ish** \'lòŋish, -ŋēsh *also* 'läŋ-\ *adj* [¹*long* + *-ish*] **:** somewhat long **:** moderately long ⟨followed by a ~ courtship — a couple of years or more —Robert Reid⟩ ⟨some ~ hair, the mustache and Vandyke, the bohemian air —Claudia Cassidy⟩

**lon·gis·si·mus dor·si** \län'jisəməs'dòrsē\ *n* [L, lit., the longest of the back] **:** the middle and largest division of the sacrospinalis muscle

**lon·gi·tude** \'länjəˌtüd, -əˌtyüd\ *n* -s [ME, fr. L *longitudo*, fr. *longi-* + *-tudo* -tude] **1 a :** measure or distance along the longest line **:** LENGTH **b** *archaic* **:** long duration **2 a :** angular distance measured on a great circle of reference from the intersection of the adopted zero meridian with this reference circle to the similar intersection of the meridian passing through the object — used esp. in astronomy and geodesy; see CELESTIAL LONGITUDE, GALACTIC LONGITUDE **b :** the arc or portion of the earth's equator intersected between the meridian of a given place and the prime meridian (as from Greenwich, England) or sometimes from the capital of a country (as from Washington or Paris) and expressed either in degrees or in time, the length of a degree varying as the cosine of the latitude so that it is 69.65 statute miles at the equator and 53.43 miles at 40 degrees latitude ⟨the ~ of New York is 74 degrees or 4 hours 56 minutes west of Greenwich⟩

**longitude by account** *or* **longitude by dead reckoning :** the approximate longitude of a ship as calculated by dead reckoning

**longitude of node :** the angular distance of the node of a planet's or comet's orbit eastward along the ecliptic from the vernal equinox

**longitude of perihelion :** the heliocentric longitude of the perihelion point of a planet's or comet's orbit as usu. measured along the ecliptic to the orbit's node and thence along the orbit to the perihelion point

**longitude signal** *n* **:** a telegraphic or radio time signal sent out from a station whose longitude is known and received at other stations whose longitude is to be determined from the differences in local time

¹**lon·gi·tu·di·nal** \ˌlänjə'tüdᵊnəl, -ə'tyü-\ *adj* [F, fr. MF, fr. L *longitudin-*, *longitudo* longitude + MF *-al*] **1 :** of or relating to the lengthwise dimension **:** AXIAL ⟨the ~ extent of the building⟩ ⟨~ stability⟩ ⟨the ~ strength of a beam⟩ **2 a :** extending in length **:** placed or running lengthwise — opposed to *transverse* ⟨contour plowing has largely replaced ~ plowing on sloping land⟩ **b :** extending along or relating to the anteroposterior axis of a body or part ⟨a fish with yellow ~ stripes⟩ **c :** ECTOMORPHIC **3 :** extending over a period of time; *specif* **:** dealing with the growth and change of an individual or group over a period of years ⟨a ~ study of juvenile delinquents over a fiveₛ year period⟩ — **lon·gi·tu·di·nal·ly** \-ᵊnəlē, -li\ *adv*

²**longitudinal** \"\ *n* -s **1 :** a longitudinally located body part (as a sinus or nerve) **2 :** LONGERON **3 :** one of the fore-andₛ aft continuous or intercostal girders used in large merchant ships and in nearly all warships to give the required strength and stiffness

**longitudinal bulkhead** *n* **:** a bulkhead that extends fore and aft

**longitudinal crevasse** *n* **:** a crevasse roughly parallel to the direction of ice movement that forms where a glacier spreads laterally

**longitudinal fault** *n* **:** a geological fault with its strike parallel to that of the regional structure

**longitudinal framing** *n* **:** ISHERWOOD SYSTEM

**longitudinal metacenter** *n* **:** the point in a vertical line through the center of gravity of a ship where this line is intersected by a second vertical line through the center of buoyancy when the ship is inclined at a very small angle in a fore-and-aft direction

**longitudinal metacentric height** *n* **:** the distance between the center of gravity of a ship and the longitudinal metacenter

**longitudinal system** *n* **:** a method of constructing steel ships in which the required strength and stiffness in a fore-and-aft direction is obtained by working in longitudinals — compare ISHERWOOD SYSTEM

**longitudinal valley** *n* **:** a valley parallel to adjacent folds or mountain ridges **:** STRIKE VALLEY

**longitudinal wave** *n* **:** a wave (as a sound wave) in which the particles of the medium vibrate in the direction of the line of advance of the wave

**long jack** *n, usu cap J* [fr. the name *Jack*] **1 :** an Australian tree (*Flindersia oxleyana*) with smooth bark and yellow wood **2 :** the wood of the long Jack tree

**longjaw** \'ₛ,ₛ\ *or* **longjaws** *n* **1 a :** a cisco (*Leucichthys alpenae*) of Lake Huron and Lake Erie **b :** any of various other ciscoes of the Great Lakes **2 :** NEEDLEFISH

**long-jawed** \'ₛ'ₛ\ *adj* **1 :** having a long jaw **2** *of rope* **:** having lost most of its twist

**long jenny** *n* **:** a losing hazard in English billiards in which the ball is played in a corner pocket from the far end of the table — compare SHORT JENNY

**long john** *n, usu cap J* [fr. the name *John*] **:** a timber tree (*Triplaris surinamensis*) of the family Polygonaceae found along the lower Amazon and in the Guianas

**long johns** *n pl* [fr. the name *John* + *-s*] **:** long underwear

**long jump** *n, Brit* **:** BROAD JUMP

**long knife** *n, usu cap L&K* **:** BIG KNIFE

**longl** *abbr* longitudinal

¹**longleaf** \'ₛ,ₛ\ *n* **:** LONGLEAF PINE

²**longleaf** \"\ *adj* **:** made from longer leaves rather than the small tip leaves ⟨~ tea⟩

**longleaf pine** *also* **long-leaved pine** \'ₛ,ₛ-\ *n* **1 :** a large pine (*Pinus palustris*) of the southern U.S. that has very long dark green leaves, long cones, thin orange-brown bark, and gnarled twisted limbs and that is an important timber tree and the chief New World source of naval stores — called also *Georgia pine* **2 :** the rather heavy tough coarse-grained reddish orange wood of the longleaf pine — called also *southern pine*

**longleaf willow** *n* **:** any of several willows (as a sandbar willow) with slender elongated leaves

**long leg** *n* **:** a fielding position in cricket on the leg side relatively far from the batsman; *also* **:** a player fielding in this position — compare SHORT LEG; see CRICKET illustration

**long-legged bat** \'ₛ,(ₛ)-\ *n* **:** a small brown bat (*Myotis volans*) of western No. America

**long-legged duck** *n, South* **:** TREE DUCK

**longlegs** \'ₛ,ₛ\ *n pl but sing or pl in constr* **1 :** STILT **2 :** DADDY LONGLEGS

**longline** \'ₛ,ₛ\ *n* **:** a long heavy fishline with numerous baited hooks that sometimes extends for several miles and that may be used as a setline or arranged to drift with current or tide

**long-line** \'ₛ'ₛ\ *adj* **:** of or relating to long-distance communication or transportation ⟨*long-line* telephone workers⟩ ⟨*longₛline* trains⟩ ⟨*long-line* trucking⟩

**long-liner** \'ₛ,ₛₛ\ *n* [*longline* + *-er*] **:** one that fishes with a longline

**long-lining** \'ₛ,ₛₛ\ *n* **:** fishing with a longline

**long-lived** \'lòŋ'livd, -livd *also* 'läŋ-\ *adj* [ME *longe lived*, fr. *longe* long + *lived*] **1 a :** having a long life ⟨a *long-lived* man⟩ **:** typically having long life ⟨a *long-lived* family⟩ **b :** capable of having a long life by reason of constitutional peculiarities ⟨a *long-lived* tree⟩ **2 :** lasting a long time **:** ENDURING ⟨a successful textbook is *long-lived* and stays in print for several years —*Education Digest*⟩ — **long-lived·ness** *n* -ES

**long logger** *n* **:** a logger in the western American coastal fir and redwood regions

**long·ly** *adv* [ME *longly*, *langly*, fr. *long*, *lang* long + *-ly* — more at LONG] **:** at or to a considerable length **:** for a considerable distance ⟨the lawn sloping ~ up to the brick house —Ross Lockridge⟩

**long mark** *n* **:** MACRON

**long measure** *n* **:** LINEAR MEASURE

**long meter** *also* **long measure** *n* **:** a quatrain in iambic tetrameter lines with the second and fourth lines rhyming and often the first and third lines rhyming — compare BALLAD METER

**long moss** *n* **:** SPANISH MOSS

**longneck** \'ₛ,ₛ\ *n* **1** *North* **:** PINTAIL 1 **2** *Eng* **:** LITTLE BITTERN

**long-neck clam** \'ₛ,ₛ-\ *n* **:** SOFT-SHELL CLAM

**long-necked turtle** \'ₛ,ₛ-\ *n* **:** a common Australian turtle (*Chelodina longicollis*) that is distinguished by a greatly elongated neck and a peculiar garlicky odor

**long·ness** *n* -ES [ME *longnesse*, *langnesse*, fr. OE *langnes*, fr. *long*, *lang* long + *-nes* -ness] **:** the quality or state of being long

**long nine** *n* **:** a long thin cheap cigar formerly made in the U.S. and packed in barrel lots for shipment

**longnose dace** *also* **long-nosed dace** \'ₛ,ₛ-\ *n* **:** a common dace (*Rhinichthys cataractae*) that is olive green to dusky brown above with dark blotches on the sides and pale underparts and is common in clean swift streams of the central U.S.

**long-nosed cattle louse** *n* **:** a widely distributed sucking louse (*Linognathus vituli*) that feeds on cattle

**long-nosed squirrel** *n* **:** any of several Oriental squirrels that have the snout prolonged: as **a :** a member of a genus (*Dremomys*) of brightly mottled arboreal forms **b :** a short-tailed ground squirrel (genus *Rhinosciurus*) of Malaysia

**longnose gar** *also* **long-nosed gar** *n* **:** a gar (*Lepisosteus osseus*) that has a snout more than twice as long as the rest of its head and is widely distributed in rivers and lakes of the eastern and north central sections of the U.S.

**longnose sucker** *or* **long-nosed sucker** *n* **:** NORTHERN SUCKER

**long nutmeg** *n* **:** MACASSAR NUTMEG

**lon·go·bard** \'läŋgəˌbärd\ *n, pl* **longobards** \-dz\ *or* **longobar·di** \ˌₛₛ'bärˌdī, -dē\ *cap* [L *Longobardi*, *Langobardi*] **:** LOMBARD — **lon·go·bar·dic** \ˌₛₛ'bärdik\ *adj, usu cap*

**long of** *prep* [by shortening] *dial* **:** along of

**long off** *n* **:** a fielding position in cricket on the off side of the field well behind the bowler; *also* **:** a player fielding in this position — see CRICKET illustration

**long-oil** \'ₛ'ₛ\ *adj* **:** containing a relatively high proportion of drying oil to resin ⟨spar varnishes are *long-oil* varnishes⟩ — compare OIL LENGTH

**long on** *n* **:** a fielding position in cricket on the on side of the field well behind the bowler; *also* **:** a player fielding in this position — see CRICKET illustration

**long particular meter** *n* **:** an iambic hymn meter of six fourₛ foot lines to the stanza

**long pennant** *n* **:** a long narrow piece of bunting generally carried at the masthead of a government vessel in commission

**long pepper** *n* **1 a :** the fruit of an eastern Asiatic pepper (*Piper longum*) consisting of elongated spikes that are ground to produce a condiment somewhat sweeter and more aromatic but less pungent than common pepper **b :** any of several plants of the genus *Piper* (as the kava) **2 a :** a hot pepper (*Capsicum frutescens longum*) with extremely pungent slender elongated drooping red or yellow fruits that are the chief source of cayenne pepper **b :** the fruit of a long pepper

**long-period variable** *n* **:** an intrinsic variable star whose light fluctuations are fairly regular and require many months or several years to complete one cycle

**long pig** *n* **:** a human victim of a cannibal feast

**long play** *n* **:** a long-playing record

**long-playing** \'ₛ'ₛₛ\ *adj* **:** of or relating to a microgroove record having a diameter of 10 or 12 inches and turning at 33⅓ revolutions per minute

**long primer** *n* **:** an old size of type (approximately 10 point) between bourgeois and small pica — compare POINT SYSTEM

**long pull** *n* **:** LONG RUN

**long purples** *n pl* **:** MALE ORCHIS ⟨with fantastic garlands did she come of crow-flowers, nettles, daisies, and *long purples* —Shak.⟩

**long-range** \'ₛ'ₛ\ *adj* **1 :** involving or taking into account a long period of time ⟨the *long-range* inadequacy of the world's resources of coal, gas, and uranium —Farrington Daniels & R.A.Morgen⟩ ⟨a *long-range* study for development of a national postwar monetary and fiscal program —*Current Biog.*⟩ **2 a :** relating to long distances ⟨*long-range* travel⟩ **b :** designed for or fit for long distances ⟨*long-range* rockets⟩

**long rate** *n* **:** TERM RATE

**long ream** *n* **:** twenty quires of paper of 25 sheets each

**long rifle** *n* **:** KENTUCKY RIFLE

**long robe** *n* **:** the legal profession ⟨gentlemen of the *long robe*⟩

**long roll** *n* **:** a prolonged roll of the drums formerly the signal for troops to fall in immediately

**longroot** \'ₛ,ₛ\ *n* **:** PINE-BARREN SANDWORT

**long run** *n* **:** a period of time sufficiently long to permit all factors in a situation to exercise their full influence — used chiefly in the phrase *in the long run* ⟨it is obvious that in the *long run* automation will be of great benefit to us all —John Diebold⟩

**longs** *pl of* LONG, *pres 3d sing of* LONG

**long s** *also* **long ess** *n* **:** a form of the letter *s* once generally used in writing and printing but now used only for archaic effect

ſ, ſ

long s

**longs and shorts** *n pl* **:** LONG-AND-SHORT WORK

**long scale** *n* **:** GLOVER SCALE

**long·schat pine** \ˈlȯŋ,shät- *also* ˈläŋ,shät-\ *n* [*longschat* fr. ¹*long* + *shat*, n.] **:** a common pitch pine (*Pinus rigida*) of eastern No. America

**longshanks** \ˈ=,=\ *n pl but sing or pl in constr* **:** STILT

**longship** \ˈ=,=\ *n* **:** a long ship similar to a galley used by the old Northmen

**longshore** \ˈ=¦=\ *adj* [short for ¹*alongshore*] **:** of or belonging to the seacoast or a seaport ⟨the ~ herring season started with a swing —G.G.Carter⟩ ⟨~ work⟩

**longshore current** *n* **:** LITTORAL CURRENT

**long·shore·man** \ˈ=¦=mən\ *n, pl* **longshoremen** [*longshore* + *man*] **:** one who is employed at a seaport to work at the loading and unloading of ships

**long·shor·ing** *pronunc at* LONGSHORE + iŋ\ *n* -s [*longshoreman* + *-ing*] **:** the act or occupation of working as a longshoreman

**long-short story** \ˈ=¦=-\ *n* **:** a short story of more than average length **:** a prose narrative intermediate between a short story and a short novel

**long shot** *n* **1 :** an entry (as in a horse race) that seems to have little chance of winning ⟨looking over the *long shots* with his last two dollars —Tom O'Reilly⟩ ⟨a *long shot* won the race⟩ **2 :** a bet in which the chance of winning is very slight but in which one can win much more than he wagers ⟨the lure of the *long shot* is practically irresistible to the average human being —C.B.Davis⟩ **3 :** a venture or act involving great risk but promising a great reward if successful ⟨was attracted by such *long shots* as expeditions to search for buried treasure⟩ **4 :** a motion-picture shot made with the camera at a considerable distance from the scene — **by a long shot** *adv* **:** by a great deal ⟨his labors haven't ended there — not *by a long shot* —J.D.Adams⟩

**long·shucks** \ˈlȯŋ,shəks *also* ˈläŋ-\ *n pl but sing or pl in constr, also* **longshucks pine :** LOBLOLLY PINE 1

**long sight** *n* **:** HYPEROPIA

**longsighted** \ˈ=¦==\ *adj* **:** FARSIGHTED — **long·sight·ed·ness** *n* -ES

**long since** *adv* [²*long*] **1 :** LONG AGO ⟨he *long since* gave up the attempt to climb the mountain⟩ **2 :** for a long time ⟨has *long since* been recognized as a great writer⟩

**long six** *n* **:** a candle weighing a sixth of a pound

**long-sleev·er** \ˈläŋˈslēvə(r)\ *n* -s *Austral slang* **:** a large drink esp. of beer

**long smut** *n* **:** a disease of the ovaries of sorghum and millet caused by fungi of the genus *Tolyposporium*

**long·some** \ˈlȯŋsəm *also* ˈläŋ-\ *adj* [ME *longsum, langsum*, fr. OE, fr. *long, lang* long + *-sum* -some — more at LONG] **:** tediously long ⟨~ hours of overwork —William Barnes⟩ — **long·some·ly** *adv* — **long·some·ness** *n* -ES

**long splice** *n* **:** a splice without an appreciable increase of circumference that is used when the rope must run over a sheave or through a hole

**longspur** \ˈ=,=\ *n* [fr. the length of its hind claws] **:** any of several long-clawed fringillid birds chiefly of the genus *Calcarius* that inhabit the arctic regions and the Great Plains of No. America, are usu. strikingly marked with black, white, and ocher in the male, and travel in immense flocks during migration — see ALASKA LONGSPUR, CHESTNUT-COLLARED LONGSPUR, LAPLAND LONGSPUR, MCCOWN'S LONGSPUR, SMITH'S LONGSPUR

**long-spurred violet** \ˈ=¦=-\ *n* **:** a violet (*Viola rostrata*) of northeastern No. America that has lilac-purple flowers with a long slender spur

**long stack** *n, NewEng* **:** an oblong haystack with a ridged top

**long-standing** \ˈ=¦==\ *adj* **1 :** having existed for a long time ⟨aroused hope that the *long-standing* conflict between the two organizations would be ended —*Collier's Yr. Bk.*⟩ **2 :** capable of existing for a long time ⟨might . . . become a *long-standing* demonstration of how to occupy a military base —*Harper's*⟩

**long-staple** \ˈ=¦==\ *adj* **:** having relatively long fibers

**long-stemmed** \ˈ=¦=\ *adj* **1 :** having a long stem or trunk ⟨strolled on beneath the *long-stemmed* trees —George Meredith⟩ **2 :** tall and slender ⟨a *long-stemmed* redhead of breathtaking loveliness —C.J.Rolo⟩

**longstone** \ˈ=,=\ *n* **:** MENHIR

**long stop** *n* **:** a fielding position in cricket directly behind the wicketkeeper; *also* **:** a fielder occupying this position

**long-straw pine** *n* **1 :** LONGLEAF PINE **2 :** LOBLOLLY PINE

**long-sufferance** \ˈ=¦=(=)=\ *n, archaic* **:** LONG-SUFFERING **syn** see PATIENCE

¹**long-suffering** \ˈ=¦=(=)=\ *n* **:** long and patient endurance of offense ⟨it shows much *long-suffering* in you to put up with him —Thomas Hardy⟩ **syn** see PATIENCE

²**long-suffering** \ˈ=¦=(=)=\ *adj* **:** showing patience under long provocation ⟨a *long-suffering* wife abused by an evil husband —J.D.Hart⟩ — **long-suf·fer·ing·ly** *adv*

**long suit** *n* **1 a :** a holding of more than the average number of cards in a suit (as four or more cards in bridge) **b :** the suit of which one has the most cards in a hand **2 :** the activity or quality in which a person excels ⟨cooking is her *long suit*⟩

**long sweetening** *n, South & Midland* **:** sweetening in liquid form (as molasses) — compare SHORT SWEETENING

**long tackle** *n* **:** TOP BURTON

**long-tackle block** *n* **:** a block that has a long assemblage of ropes and pulleys

**longtail** \ˈ=,=\ *n* **1 a :** an animal (as a dog) that has an uncut tail **b :** GREYHOUND **2 a :** OLD-SQUAW **b :** TROPIC BIRD

**long-tailed blue** \ˈ=,=-\ *n, archaic* **:** a blue tailcoat

**long-tailed chat** *n* **:** a long-tailed yellow-breasted chat (*Icteria virens longicauda*) that is found in the Pacific coast region of the U.S.

**long-tailed cuckoo** *n* **:** KOEL

**long-tailed duck** *n* **:** OLD-SQUAW

**long-tailed jaeger** *n* **:** a relatively small and very graceful jaeger (*Stercorarius longicaudus*) that has extremely long middle tail feathers

**long-tailed mealybug** *n* **:** a mealybug (*Pseudococcus adonidum*) that is a minor pest of citrus and avocado in California and certain other regions

**long-tailed paca** *n* **:** FALSE PACA

**long-tailed pangolin** *n* **:** an African pangolin (*Manis macrura*) that has a tail nearly twice the length of its body

**long-tailed porcupine** *n* **:** a porcupine (*Trichys lipura*) of Borneo and Sumatra that has short spines and a long tail

**long-tailed shrew** *n* **:** an American shrew of the genus *Sorex*

**long-tailed skipper** *n* **:** any butterfly of the genus *Urbanus* or *Chioides* (family Hesperiidae) marked by a prolongation of the posterior margin of each hindwing which suggests a tail

**long-tailed tiger cat** *n* **:** MARGAY

**long-tailed tit** *or* **long-tailed titmouse** *n* **:** a small titmouse (*Aegithalos caudatus*) of Europe and northern Asia with a long tail and plumage largely pink and white — called also *bottle tit*

**long-tailed weasel** *n* **:** the common American weasel (*Mustela frenata*) that occurs in various races from Central America to well within the arctic circle and is distinguished from related forms by its large size and long black-tipped tail — compare ERMINE

**long-term** \ˈ=¦=\ *adj* **1 :** extending over or involving a relatively long period of time ⟨the *long-term* reconstruction of countries damaged by war —W.S.Sayre⟩ ⟨*long-term* earnest championing of American art — Aline B. Saarinen⟩ — opposed to *short-term* **2 a :** of, relating to, or constituting a financial gain, loss, operation, or obligation based on a term usu. of more than 10 years **b :** of or relating to capital assets held for more than six months

**long-term bond** *n* **:** a financial obligation that runs for at least five years and usu. for a much longer period

**long-termer** \ˈ=¦==\ *n* **:** one serving a long term esp. of imprisonment

**longtime** \ˈ=,=\ *adj* **:** LONG-STANDING ⟨a ~ friend⟩

**long·tim·er** \ˈ=¦tīmə(r)\ *n* [*long time* + *-er*] **1 :** one that has been in a place, position, or activity for a long time **:** OLD-TIMER, OLD HAND **2 :** a prisoner serving a long term **:** LONG-TERMER

**long-toed stint** \ˈ=,=-\ *n* **:** a small sandpiper (*Erolia subminuta*) that breeds in eastern Siberia and winters in southeastern Asia

**long tom** *n* [fr. *Tom*, nickname for *Thomas*] **1** *usu cap L&T* **a :** a long pivot gun formerly carried on the deck of a warship ⟨the *Long Tom* roared from his pivot and the grapeshot fell like hail —J.J.Roche⟩ **b :** a large gun having a long range used on land; *esp* **:** a U.S. 155 millimeter rifled gun used during World War II **2 a** *Eng* **:** LONG-TAILED TIT **b :** any of several Australian needlefishes **3 :** a trough for washing gold-bearing earth

**long ton** *n* **:** TON 1a — see MEASURE table

**long tongue** *n* **1 :** WRYNECK **2** *dial* **:** GOSSIP

**long·ton hall** \ˈlȯŋtən-, ˈläŋtən-\ *n, usu cap L&H* [fr. *Longton Hall*, Staffordshire, England] **:** a faintly greenish glassy English 18th century soft-paste porcelain often glazed in rich blue with decoration in opaque white enamel

**longue** \ˈlȯŋ\ *n* -s [alter. of ⁴*lunge*] **:** LAKE TROUT b

**lon·gueur** \lōŋˈgər(·)\ *n* -s [F, lit., length, fr. OF *longour*, fr. *lonc, long* long, fr. L *longus* — more at LONG] **:** a dull and tedious passage or section (as of a book, play, or musical composition) — usu. used in pl. ⟨written in a style with ~s as thick as treacle —H.J.Laski⟩ ⟨his ~s, his exactions upon the deep understanding of his performers and of his listeners —J.N.Burk⟩

**lon·gu·lite** \ˈläŋgyə,līt\ *n* -s [G *longulit*, fr. L *longulus* rather long (fr. *longus* long) + G *-it* -ite] **:** a crystallite of elongated form

**long vacation** *n, chiefly Brit* **:** the summer vacation of universities and law courts

**long view** *n* **:** an examination of or approach to a problem or situation that emphasizes the long-range factors involved ⟨the indispensable task of supplying *long views* about the problems of society —Zechariah Chafee⟩

**longwall system** \ˈ=,=-\ *n* [*longwall* fr. ¹*long* + *wall*] **:** a method of coal mining in which the working face extends entirely across the seam, the work proceeds either away from or toward the main shaft, and the roof is allowed to cave in behind the workers

¹**longways** \ˈ=,=\ *adv* [¹*long* + *-ways*] **1 :** LENGTHWISE ⟨the books lie upright, ~, or diagonally on the shelves —Stephen Spender⟩ **2** *dancing* **:** in two straight lines ⟨this number is danced ~⟩

²**longways** \"\ *or* **longways dance** *also* **longway** \ˈ=,=\ *or* **longway dance** *n* **:** a folk dance in which the basic formation is two lines of couples facing each other usu. with men on one side and women on the other — compare CONTREDANCE

**long whist** *n* **:** whist played under the rule that 10 points constitute a game

**long-winded** \ˈ=¦==\ *adj* **1 :** having the capacity to take a long sustaining breath **:** not easily subject to loss of breath ⟨men of endurance, deep-chested, *long-winded*, tough —R.W.Emerson⟩ **2 a :** tediously long in speaking or writing ⟨the most *long-winded* master of modern letters —*Time*⟩ **b :** LONG-DRAWN-OUT, TEDIOUS ⟨it begins with "in short" and proceeds to be *long-winded* —A.T.Quiller-Couch⟩ — **long-wind·ed·ly** *adv* — **long-wind·ed·ness** *n* -ES

**longwise** \ˈ=,=\ *adv* **:** LENGTHWISE

**longwood** \ˈ=,=\ *n* **:** a veneer flitch of substantial length

**long-wool** *or* **long-wooled** \ˈ=¦=\ *adj* [*long* + *wool* or *wooled*, fr. *wool* + *-ed*] **:** of or relating to a class of domestic sheep that have long but coarse wool ⟨Leicester, Cotswold, and Lincoln are breeds of *long-wool* sheep⟩

**longwool** \ˈ=,=\ *n* **:** a long-wool sheep

**long·xuyen** \ˈlau̇ŋˈswēən\ *adj, usu cap* [fr. *Longxuyen*, So. Vietnam] **:** of or from the city of Longxuyen, So. Vietnam **:** of the kind or style prevalent in Longxuyen

**long yearling** *n* **:** an animal between one and two years old esp. when nearer two than one

**long·yi** \ˈläŋ,yē\ *var of* LUNGI

**lo·nic·era** \lōˈnisərə, ,länəˈsirə\ *n, cap* [NL, after Adam *Lonicerus* (Lonitzer) †1586 Ger. botanist] **:** a genus (family Caprifoliaceae) of erect or climbing shrubs comprising the honeysuckles that have a tubular or infundibuliform corolla and fruit in the form of a berry — compare HONEYSUCKLE

**lonk** \ˈläŋk\ *n* [by shortening & alter. fr. *Lancashire*, England] **1** *usu cap* **:** an English breed of large hardy black-faced mutton type sheep **2** -s *often cap* **:** an animal of the Lonk breed

**lon·tar** \ˈläntə(r)\ *also* **lontar palm** *n* -s [Malay *lontar*, fr. Jav *ron-tal*, fr. *ron* leaf + *tal* Palmyra palm] **:** PALMYRA 1

¹**loo** \ˈlü\ *interj* [by shortening] **:** HALLOO

²**loo** \"\ *vb* -ED/-ING/-S *now dial* **:** HALLOO

³**loo** \"\ *n* -s [short for obs. E *lanterloo*, fr. F *lanturelu, lanturlu* piffle, twaddle, fr. *lanturelu, lanturlu*, meaningless syllables occurring in the refrain of a song of the early 17th century] **1 :** an ancient card game in which after contributions are made to a pool three or five cards are dealt to each player and the winner of each trick or the majority of tricks takes an agreed portion of the pool with the losing players being obligated to contribute an agreed amount to the next pool **2 :** money staked at loo **3 :** an instance of being looed

⁴**loo** \"\ *vt* -ED/-ING/-S **:** to obligate to contribute an agreed sum to a new pool at loo as a result of failing to win a trick

⁵**loo** \"\ *var of* LEW

⁶**loo** \"\ *n* -s [perh. modif. of F *lieux d'aisance*] **:** TOILET 5

**loo·by** \ˈlübē\ *n* -ES [ME *loby*; prob. akin to Flem *lobbe* simpleton — more at LOB] **:** an awkward clumsy fellow often characterized by laziness and stupidity **:** LUBBER

**looby-loo** \ˈlübēˌlü\ *n* [fr. *looby-loo*, meaningless syllables in the text of the song] **:** a singing game in which children move arms, legs, and head in accordance with the words of the song

**looch** *var of* LOHOCH

**lood** \ˈlüd\ *Scot var of* LOUD

**loo·ey** *or* **loo·ie** \ˈlüē\ *n* -s [by shortening & alter.] *slang* **:** LIEUTENANT

**loof** \ˈlüf\ *n* -s [ME *lofe*, fr. ON *lōfi* — more at GLOVE] *chiefly Scot* **:** the palm of the hand

**loofah** *var of* LUFFA

¹**look** \ˈlu̇k\ *vb* -ED/-ING/-S [ME *looken, loken*, fr. OE *lōcian*; akin to MD *loeken* to look, OS *lōcōn*] *vt* **1 :** to make sure or take care (that something is done) ⟨censor to ~ that no man lived idly —Edward Gee⟩ **2 :** to ascertain by the use of one's eyes ⟨I will ~ what time the train starts⟩ **3 a :** to exercise the power of vision upon **:** EXAMINE, OBSERVE, PERCEIVE **b** *archaic* **:** to look up ⟨if I ~*ed* a word today —John Adams⟩ **c** *dial* **:** to count (as sheep) esp. to determine whether any have strayed **4** *archaic* **:** to search for **:** SEEK ⟨at her leisure hours she ~*s* goose eggs —Samuel Johnson⟩ **5 :** EXPECT ⟨I never ~ to have a mistress that I shall love half as well —Henry Brooke⟩ **6** *dial* **:** to pick over ⟨she ~*ed* the spinach⟩ **7** *archaic* **:** to influence or bring into a place or condition by the exercise of the power of vision ⟨thou has *look'd* thyself into my grace —Shak.⟩ **8 :** to express by use of the eyes or by an expression of the countenance ⟨not an eye to ~ comfort to you —Douglas Jerrold⟩ ⟨the friar ~*ed* his surprise —Robert Brennan⟩ **9 :** to have an appearance that befits or accords with ⟨the actors . . . ~*ed* the parts they were called upon to play —*Linguaphone Mag.*⟩ ⟨he ~*ed* a typical sturdy John Bull —C.H.Driver⟩ ⟨she ~*ed* her age⟩ ~ *vi* **1 a :** to exercise the power of vision ⟨he ~*s*⟩ ⟨~ before you leap⟩ — used in the imperative as an interjection esp. to call attention ⟨~, here he comes⟩ **b :** to exercise this power in a particular direction **:** direct the eyes or one's attention upon someone or something ⟨from my elevated station I ~*ed* down —Thomas De Quincey⟩ ⟨~*ed* from one to the other —Carson McCullers⟩ ⟨~*ed* abroad for their inspiration —O. Elfrida Saunders⟩ ⟨~ at the map⟩ ⟨if we ~ at the successful serious novels of the last decade —Lionel Trilling⟩ **c :** to direct the eyes in a manner indicative of a specified feeling ⟨~*ed* sadly upon him⟩ **2 :** to have the appearance of being **:** appear to the eye **:** SEEM ⟨her . . . lips ~*ed* parched and unnatural —Ellen Glasgow⟩ ⟨his face ~*ed* almost gray —T.B.Costain⟩ ⟨it ~*s* as if . . . varnishes will meet very severe competition during the coming year —C.L. Boltz⟩ ⟨it begins to ~ as though the social scientist . . . is actually a dialectician —R.M.Weaver⟩ **3 a :** to have a specified direction **:** afford a specified outlook **:** open on or into something ⟨a village that ~*ed* across the river —Ernest Hemingway⟩ ⟨the little terrace which ~*ed* seaward —John Buchan⟩ **b :** to face or turn in a specific direction ⟨their nostrils . . . ~ downwards —T.H.Huxley⟩ **4 :** to gaze in wonder or surprise **:** STARE ⟨you should have seen them ~⟩ **5 :** to show a tendency **:** to tend or point in a specific direction ⟨the evidence ~*s* to acquittal⟩ **syn** see EXPECT, SEE — **look after 1 :** to follow with the eyes **:** look in the direction of ⟨and with dimm'd eyes *look after* him —Shak.⟩ **2** *archaic* **:** to search for **:** SEEK ⟨the knave . . . hath all those requisites in him that folly and green minds *look after* —Shak.⟩ **3 :** to attend to **:** take care of **:** see to the safety or well-being of **:** TEND ⟨sent to . . . *look after* his interests —G.C.Sellery⟩ ⟨somebody . . . who *looked after* the children —Eden Phillpotts⟩ ⟨I daresay you can *look after* yourself —Andrew Young⟩ **4 :** to busy or concern oneself with **:** pay heed to **:** CONSIDER — **look a gift horse in the mouth :** to criticize and find fault with a gift — **look alive :** to be alert or quick — usu. used in the imperative — **look at :** to hold a mental attitude toward **:** CONSIDER, REGARD, VIEW ⟨his teachings are *looked at* too narrowly by many people⟩ ⟨easy to *look at* scientists in other countries as competitors —R.L.Meier & Eugene Rabinowitch⟩ — **look black :** to express anger or hostility by the use of one's eyes **:** FROWN, SCOWL — **look down one's nose :** to view with arrogance, disdain, or disapproval — usu. used with *at* ⟨the older residents have traditionally *looked down their noses* at the newcomers —A.G.Mezerik⟩ ⟨critics who *look down their noses* at these stories —Upton Sinclair⟩ — **look for 1 :** to await with hope or anticipation ⟨tell them they may *look for* me any day —Jane W. Carlyle⟩ ⟨finality is not to be *looked for* in . . . translation —J.C.Swaim⟩ **2 :** to search for **:** SEEK ⟨we had been *looking for* a house —Dana Burnet⟩ ⟨that's where you *look for* grouse in October —Corey Ford⟩ — **look forth** [ME *loken forth*, fr. *looken, loken* to look + *forth*] **:** to look out (as from a window) ⟨the warden . . . from that old Baliol's tower *looks forth* —Sir Walter Scott⟩ — **look forward 1 :** to look into the future ⟨*looked forward* with the same ease that most people slip backward —John Mason Brown⟩ **2 a :** to look into the future with expectation (as of an event or development) ⟨*looked forward* to a hard year —J.S.Dickey⟩ ⟨*looked forward* to the time when under true Communism there would be no state —F.A. Ogg & Harold Zink⟩ **b :** to anticipate with pleasure or satisfaction ⟨they certainly *look forward* to meeting him⟩ ⟨did not *look forward* to living in the splendor of Government House —*Current Biog.*⟩ — **look here** *or* **look-a-here** — used in the imperative as an interjection to call attention and often to preface a protest, reprimand, or order — **look in the eye** *or* **look in the face :** to meet with a steady gaze as an indication of courage, confidence, or defiance — **look into 1 :** to inspect closely **:** examine carefully **:** INVESTIGATE ⟨*look into* the trade and investment opportunities —*advt*⟩ ⟨*look into* the population problem —A.L.Guérard⟩ ⟨decided to *look into* his background —Frank O'Leary⟩ **2 :** to consult (as a book) in a rapid or cursory manner ⟨*looked into* the chronicles of the middle ages —T.B.Macaulay⟩ ⟨have just *looked into* the . . . essay —O.W. Holmes †1935⟩ — **look like** *chiefly Brit* **:** to give promise of **:** show a likelihood of — used with a gerund ⟨the new age *looks like* being tougher than the old —Patrick Balfour⟩ ⟨at two months he *looked like* developing into a healthy . . . bird —*Sydney (Australia) Bull.*⟩ — **look of** *obs* **:** to direct one's gaze upon — **look on 1** *obs* **:** to regard favorably **:** ESTEEM ⟨I am not *look'd on* in the world —Shak.⟩ **2 :** to look upon ⟨people who now *look on* him as a reactionary —F.D. Roosevelt⟩ ⟨the average American . . . too often *looks on* books as furniture —John Barkham⟩ — **look the other way :** to direct one's attention away from something of which one disapproves or which one chooses to ignore — **look through 1 a :** to direct one's gaze through (as an opening or a transparent substance) ⟨we *looked through* the window⟩ ⟨the child *looked through* the screen door⟩ **b :** to see through ⟨he *looks* quite *through* the deeds of men —Shak.⟩ **c :** to gaze at as if through empty space **:** ignore haughtily or insolently ⟨the two Chinese spokesmen *looked* . . . *through* the correspondents they once knew —Peggy Durdin⟩ **2 :** to gaze over the whole of ⟨if one *looks* . . . *through* Russian history —Bernard Pares⟩; *esp* **:** to examine cursorily usu. from beginning to end ⟨the press service . . . *looked through* its files —Bruce Bliven b.1889⟩ ⟨they read or *looked through* a . . . number of weekly journals —M.K.Adler⟩ **3** *obs* **:** to be visible through ⟨that our drift *look through* our bad performance —Shak.⟩ — **look to 1 :** to direct one's attention to ⟨psychologists have tended to *look to* childhood for the sources of their troubles —D.M.Davin⟩ **2 :** to take care of **:** attend to ⟨ordered his own surgeon to *look to* the hurts of the captive —T.B.Macaulay⟩ **3 a :** to direct one's gaze at ⟨we *looked to* the sky at intervals —John Tyndall⟩ **b :** to keep watch upon ⟨constable, *look to* your prisoner —Maria Edgeworth⟩ **4 a :** to direct one's expectations to ⟨the American people *look to* the president for a unifying lead —D.W.Brogan⟩ **b :** to rely upon; *esp* **:** to count upon for something ⟨those who . . . *looked to* the printed word for inspiration —*Amer. Guide Series: N.J.*⟩ ⟨newspapers . . . no longer *look to* their subscribers as the major source of revenue —D.M.Potter⟩ **5 :** to look forward to ⟨can *look to* quiet in my old age —J.A.Froude⟩ — **look toward** *or* **look towards 1 :** to gaze or face in the direction of ⟨*looked towards* the speaker⟩ ⟨the city *looks toward* the river⟩ **2 :** to prepare for **:** ANTICIPATE ⟨*looked toward* the union of . . . some of the former provinces —C.L.Jones⟩ ⟨a definite policy *looking toward* the reduction of the number of public houses —D.W. McConnell⟩ — **look upon 1 :** to hold an opinion of **:** CONSIDER, REGARD ⟨each family *looked upon* this zone as personal property —L.S.B.Leakey⟩ ⟨generally *looks upon* a victim of airsickness as an object of ridicule —H.G.Armstrong⟩ **2 :** to direct one's gaze at **:** OBSERVE ⟨the graceful madrona . . . is beautiful to *look upon* —*Amer. Guide Series: Oregon*⟩ — **look up to :** to have a feeling of veneration or admiration for **:** regard with deference **:** RESPECT ⟨the non-Russian Slavs . . . were to *look up to* the Russians —A.M.Dragnich⟩ ⟨still *looked up to* him as their leader —T.B.Macaulay⟩

²**look** \"\ *n* -s [ME, fr. *looken* to look] **1 a :** the act of looking **:** the direction of the eyes toward something in order to see it **b :** a deliberate act of looking **:** GLANCE ⟨darted a quick ~ at me —Kenneth Roberts⟩ ⟨he was hers for a ~ or the speaking of a word —Ethel Wilson⟩ **c :** an examination of something with or as if with the eyes **:** the direction of one's attention toward something ⟨his final ~ at the present regime —J.K.Fairbank⟩ ⟨a brief ~ at the origins and development of . . . a great liberating movement —M.D.Geismar⟩ **2 a :** the appearance or expression of the countenance ⟨a round face carrying a ~ of Alpine simplicity —Osbert Sitwell⟩ ⟨wearing an ugly ~ on his face —F.B.Gipson⟩ **b :** the appearance of a person; *esp* **:** an attractive or healthy appearance — usu. used in pl. ⟨she's lost what ~*s* she ever had —Ellen Glasgow⟩ **3 :** the state or form in which something appears and which is often indicative of its nature or quality ⟨have a manufactured ~ — A.M.Young⟩ ⟨the rough-hewn rural ~ of the conventional academy —J.P.Marquand⟩ **4 :** a distance usu. encompassed by a single act of looking ⟨a long ~ of river —S.H.Holbrook⟩ **syn** see APPEARANCE

**look around** *vi* **1 :** to look in several directions **:** gaze about ⟨*looked around* in awe⟩ **2 :** to make a comprehensive examination of something (as a place or situation) **:** INVESTIGATE ⟨*looked around* before deciding which car to purchase⟩

**look back** *vi* **1 :** to turn and look at something in the direction from which one is coming or from which one's face is turned ⟨*looked back* and saw their pursuers gaining upon them⟩ **2 :** to turn one's mind or thoughts to the past **:** reflect on past events ⟨inclined to *look back* to their African origins —Oscar Handlin⟩ ⟨an era which the future will *look back* upon as another golden age —*New Englander*⟩ ⟨when I *look back* on my tolerance at the time —O.S.J.Gogarty⟩ **3 :** to show signs of retrogression or interrupted progress — usu. used in the negative ⟨from that time the industry has never *looked back* —L.D.Stamp⟩

**look down** *vb* [ME *looken doun*, fr. *looken* to look + *doun* down] *vi* **1 a :** to direct one's gaze in a downward direction esp. from an elevated position ⟨the gods *looked down* from on high⟩ ⟨*looked down* upon the servants . . . as if they had been pygmies —Jonathan Swift⟩ **b :** to become located in a position that affords a downward view ⟨the window *looks down* upon the courtyard⟩ ⟨the high plains *looked down* upon the lower areas —R.A.Billington⟩ **2 :** to assume an attitude of contempt or scorn — usu. used with *on* ⟨tended to *look down* on the other Italians —William Barrett⟩ ⟨the liberal arts colleges *looked down* on teacher training —F.M.Hechinger⟩ **~** *vt* **:** to overcome (someone) by use of the eyes ⟨never could *look* the boy *down* —Charles Dickens⟩

**look-down** \ˈ=,=\ *n* -s [*look down*] **:** the superficial appearance of paper as seen under reflected light — compare LOOK-THROUGH

**lookdown fish** \ˈ=,=-\ *also* **lookdown** *n* -s [*look down*] **:** any of several deep-bodied compressed silvery carangid fishes comprising a genus (*Argyreiosus*) widely distributed in warm seas and having high truncated foreheads

**looked** *adj* [²*look* + *-ed*] *obs* **:** LOOKING ⟨lean-*look'd* prophets whisper fearful change —Shak.⟩

**look·ee** *or* **looky** \ˈlu̇kē, -ki\ *interj* [alter. of the imperative expression *look ye*, fr. ¹*look* + *ye*] — used to call attention

**look·er** \ˈlu̇kə(r)\ *n* -s [ME *loker*, fr. *looken, loken* to look + *-er*] **1 a** *obs* **:** one (as a keeper, steward, or bailiff) that looks after or has charge of something **b** *dial* **:** HERDSMAN **2 a :** one that looks ⟨a ~ down into the wells of human loneliness —J.F.Dobie⟩ ⟨millions of free ~*s* on TV —*Time*⟩ **b** *Brit* **:** INSPECTOR — usu. used in combination ⟨cloth ~*s*⟩ ⟨glass ~⟩ **c :** one that seeks out and appraises timber **3 a :** one having features or an appearance of a specified kind ⟨she's a good ~ —S.H.Adams⟩ ⟨that skin does its best to make him a handsome ~ —*Bookman*⟩ **b :** a woman of great physical beauty or attractiveness ⟨what a ~ she is —*New Yorker*⟩

**looker-on** \ˌ=ˈ=\ *n, pl* **lookers-on** [*look on* + *-er*] **:** ONLOOKER ⟨*lookers-on* often see what familiarity obscures for the participants —Walter Moberly⟩

**look in** *vi* [ME *loken in*, fr. *looken, loken* to look + *in*] **1 :** to direct one's gaze to the interior of something ⟨children . . . *look in* at the open door —H.W.Longfellow⟩ **2 :** to enter (as a room or building) for the purpose of seeing someone **:** make a short call **:** VISIT ⟨persuaded him to *look in* for a cup of tea whenever he visited the hamlet —Flora Thompson⟩ ⟨the doctor *looked in* frequently⟩ **3 :** to watch television

**look-in** \ˈ=,=\ *n* -s [*look in*] **1 :** the action or an instance of looking in **:** a usu. brief view ⟨had a good *look-in*. Saw everything with minute care —Abanindranath Tagore⟩ ⟨gave me a curious *look-in* on peace-time labor problems —*Collier's*⟩ **2 :** a chance of success ⟨handicapped by lack of condition, he never had a *look-in* —*New Yorker*⟩ **3 :** a share in something ⟨some bargain between the rival contenders for a *look-in* at Shanghai's customs receipts —*Literary Digest*⟩

**looking** \ˈ==\ *adj* [fr. pres. part. of ¹*look*] **:** having a specified look or appearance ⟨the detergent . . . left their clothes dirty ~ —Vance Packard⟩ ⟨the most disagreeable ~ character has the tenderest heart —*Modern Language Notes*⟩ — often used in combination ⟨angry-*looking*⟩ ⟨good-*looking*⟩

**looking glass** *n* [*looking* (gerund of ¹*look*) + *glass*] **1 a :** a mirror usu. made of glass with a backing of some reflecting substance (as mercury) ⟨had first seen her face in the *looking glass* —Jean Stafford⟩ **b :** the glass used in such a mirror ⟨little pieces of *looking glass* —Leslie Thomas⟩ **2 :** something held to resemble or to perform the functions of a looking glass **:** MIRROR 1b(1)

**looking-glass plant** *n* **:** an Asiatic tree (*Heritiera littoralis*) whose leaves are silvery beneath

**look on** *vi* **:** to be a spectator **:** OBSERVE, WATCH ⟨the world *looks on* and laughs —Mark Pattison⟩

**look out** *vb* [ME *loken out*, fr. *looken, loken* to look + *out*] *vi* **1 :** to gaze from within something (as a building) to the outside **:** put one's head out of a window or similar aperture ⟨*looked out* at the window⟩ **2** *archaic* **:** to venture out **:** make a brief excursion **3 a :** to be on the lookout or the watch (as against some danger) **:** exercise vigilance **:** be on guard ⟨there's danger ahead. *Look out*⟩ — often used with following *for* ⟨the good sailor will *look out* for shoals⟩ **b :** to watch diligently (as for a person) **:** gaze about in search **:** be on the alert (as for the presence of something) — used with following *for* ⟨*look out* for some old andirons when you visit the antique shop⟩ ⟨the mole-rats . . . which I had been urged to *look out* for and to collect —Douglas Carruthers⟩ **c :** to take care or be concerned with the welfare (as of a person) — used with following *for* ⟨*look out* for the baby while I go shopping⟩ ⟨the female *looks out* for the young⟩ **4** *obs* **:** to show itself **:** APPEAR ⟨the business of this man *looks out* of him —Shak.⟩ **5 :** to have or provide an outlook ⟨the little room which *looks out* on the . . . yew hedge —Patricia Wingfield⟩ ⟨homes and churches *looking out* on the placid village green —Budd Schulberg⟩ **~** *vt, chiefly Brit* **:** to search for or find by using the eyes **:** look up ⟨I have some letters of his . . . I'll *look* them *out* —Clemence Dane⟩ ⟨discover how few words I need to *look out* —O.W.Holmes †1935⟩

**lookout** \ˈ=,=\ *n* -s *often attrib* [*look out*] **1 :** one engaged in keeping watch **:** SCOUT, WATCHMAN ⟨the ~ sang out from his perch high in the shrouds —W.P.Schramm⟩ ⟨~*s* in their towers are watching the forests —*Pomona (Calif.) Progress-Bull.*⟩ ⟨sent ~*s* . . . along the road to catch the first glimpse of the approaching delegates —Dorothy C. Fisher⟩ ⟨gambling-house ~*s* . . . pass him in without question —Joseph Mitchell⟩ **2 :** an elevated place or structure affording a wide view and often used for keeping watch **:** as **a :** CROW'S NEST 1 **b :** one used for the detection of forest fires — called also *primary lookout* **c :** BELVEDERE **3 :** the action of keeping watch **:** a careful looking or watching (as for an object or event) ⟨a sharp ~ must be kept for traffic —Cornelius Vanderbilt b. 1898⟩ ⟨keeping a keen ~ for opportunities of expanding —A.P.Ryan⟩ **4 :** a usu. distant view **:** PROSPECT ⟨the traveller feels . . . disgusted with the ugliness of the ~ —*English Illustrated Mag.*⟩ **5** *chiefly Brit* **:** a prospective condition **:** a probability for the future **:** OUTLOOK ⟨it would be a sad ~ for the Australian dramatist if there were no little theaters —Leslie Rees⟩ ⟨growing thin and wizen in a solitary prison is a poor ~ —W.S.Gilbert⟩ **6 :** a matter of care or concern to one individual as opposed to others ⟨his ~ that the message gets through, not theirs —Stuart Chase⟩ **7 :** a short wooden bracket or cantilever used to support an overhanging portion of a roof or a bay window or a balcony — **on the lookout :** in the process or state of watching ⟨*on the lookout* for thieves —L.C. Douglas⟩ ⟨those in charge will have to be continuously *on the lookout* —*Auckland (New Zealand) Weekly News*⟩ ⟨be *on the lookout* for every little flaw —Robertson Davies⟩

**look over** *vt* [ME *loken over*, fr. *looken, loken* to look + *over*] **1 :** to inspect or examine usu. in a cursory way ⟨took a stroll about the town to *look it over* —H.A.Chippendale⟩ ⟨his scripts are *looked over* for accuracy —*Saturday Rev.*⟩ **2 :** to eliminate from consideration **:** DISREGARD, OVERLOOK, PARDON ⟨I'm only a private — perhaps you'll *look over that* —*Strand*⟩

**look-over** \ˈ=,==\ *n* -s [*look over*] **:** a cursory examination or survey ⟨the table . . . was given a final *look-over* —James Reynolds⟩

**looks** *pl of* LOOK, *pres 3d sing of* LOOK

**look-see** \ˈ=,=\ *n* [²*look* + *see*, v.] **:** a general survey **:** a tour of inspection **:** INVESTIGATION ⟨my quick *look-see* at a large and complicated situation —*Survey Graphic*⟩ ⟨animals . . . will stir in their hibernation and venture out for a stretch and a *look-see* —*Science News Letter*⟩

**look-through** \ˈ=,=\ *n* -s [fr. the phrase *look through*] **:** the texture and formation of a sheet of paper when examined by transmitted light — compare LOOK-DOWN

**look up** *vb* [ME *looken up*, fr. *looken* to look + *up*] *vi* **1 :** to raise the eyes **:** turn the face upward ⟨*looked up* from his book⟩ **2 :** to cheer up **:** take courage ⟨cheer up yourself, *look up* —Shak.⟩ **3 :** to improve in prospects or condition ⟨lived on the wife's income until business *looked up* again —George Santayana⟩ ⟨chances to control the Senate are *looking up* —T.R.Ybarra⟩ **~** *vt* **1 :** to search for ⟨required to *look up* the said Indian and bring him before some one of the magistrates —*Plymouth Colonial Records*⟩ ⟨*look up* the book and send it to me⟩ **2 a :** to consult (as a reference work) in order to find out information about something ⟨if you wish to do some further reading on this . . . subject, *look up* my book —W.J.Reilly⟩ **b :** to search for in a reference work ⟨*look up* an unfamiliar word in the dictionary⟩ ⟨*look* this number *up* in the phone book⟩ **c :** to find out information about (as by consulting a reference work) ⟨seized a timetable and *looked up* the trains —Gilbert Parker⟩ **3 :** to seek out; *esp* **:** to discover the whereabouts of and make a call on **:** visit briefly ⟨if I'd known you were in the regiment . . . I'd have *looked* you *up* —James Jones⟩ ⟨I *looked up* a man in the Bureau of Internal Revenue —W.H.Upson⟩

**looky** *var of* LOOKEE

¹**loom** \ˈlüm\ *n* -s *often attrib* [ME *lome*, fr. OE *gelōma* tool, utensil; akin to MD *allame* tool] **1** *now chiefly Scot* **:** TOOL **2** *now chiefly Scot* **:** an open vessel **:** RECEPTACLE **3 :** a frame or machine for interlacing at right angles two or more sets of threads or yarns to form a cloth — compare WARP, WEFT **4 :** the art or occupation of weaving ⟨sends her for consolation to the ~ and distaff —Samuel Johnson⟩ **5** [prob. of Scand origin; akin to ON *hlummr* handle of an oar] **a :** the part of an oar which is inboard from the oarlock usu. including the handle **b :** the part of an oar between the blade and handle **6 :** flexible tubing usu. nonmetallic for protecting and insulating electric wires

²**loom** \ˈ"\ *vt* -ED/-ING/-S **:** WEAVE — **loom the web :** to mount the warp on a loom

³**loom** \ˈ"\ *adj* [origin unknown] **:** moderate in force **:** GENTLE — used of a gale

⁴**loom** \ˈ"\ *vi* -ED/-ING/-S [origin unknown] **1 a :** to come into sight esp. above the surface (as of the sea or land) in enlarged or distorted and indistinct form often as a result of atmospheric conditions ⟨the foothills were beginning to ~ ahead through the dust-haze —E.E.Shipton⟩ ⟨could avert a collision should a southbound ship ~ out of the murk ahead —R.S.Porteous⟩ ⟨the hull of the ship . . . ~*ed* up suddenly —T.B.Costain⟩ **b :** to come into view **:** make an appearance ⟨the figure of a shepherd suddenly ~*ed* before me —Robert Gibbings⟩ ⟨another merchandising consideration . . . has ~*ed* up during the last few years —*Amer. Fabrics*⟩ **c :** to take shape as an impending occurrence ⟨fit . . . for the struggle which ~*ed* ahead —Roy Lewis & Angus Maude⟩ **d :** to appear in an impressively great or exaggerated form ⟨the . . . political drives of the Italian people ~*ed* large in prose fiction —T.G.Bergin⟩ ⟨the oceans ~ large in the visions of those who specialize in geopolitics —R.E.Coker⟩ **2** *obs* **:** to move slowly up and down — used of the sea or a vessel

⁵**loom** \ˈ"\ *n* -s **1 :** the indistinct and exaggerated appearance of something (as land or a ship) seen on the horizon or through fog or darkness ⟨watching for distant sails or the first ~ of the land —Sarah O. Jewett⟩ ⟨could make out the ~ of land in the darkness —G.A.Stansfield⟩ **2 a :** a looming shadow or reflection ⟨the pale gray ~ of the stadium —J.J.Godwin⟩ ⟨turned and saw the dim ~ of the cliffs above me —William Beebe⟩ **b :** the glow in the sky created by a light whose beam is below the horizon

⁶**loom** \ˈ"\ *n* -s [of Scand origin; akin to Norw *lom* loon] **1 :** LOON **2 a :** AUK **b :** GUILLEMOT **c :** PUFFIN

**loom·ery** \ˈlümərē\ *n* -ES [⁶*loom* + *-ery*] **:** a breeding place of looms

**loomfixer** \ˈ=,==\ *n* **:** a textile worker who adjusts and repairs looms

**looming** *n* -s **:** a mirage in which images of objects below the horizon appear in distorted form

¹**loon** \ˈlün\ *n* -s [ME *loun*] **1 :** a worthless person **:** IDLER, LOUT, RASCAL **2** *chiefly Scot* **a :** a man of low station **:** MENIAL **b :** MISTRESS, HARLOT **c :** BOY, LAD ⟨the family . . . consisted of three ~*s* and a lassie —S.R.Crockett⟩ **3 a :** a crazy person **b :** SIMPLETON

²**loon** \ˈ"\ *n* -s [of Scand origin; akin to Norw *lom* loon, ON *lōmr* — more at LAMENT] **1 :** any of several fish-eating diving birds that belong to the genus *Gavia* and the order Gaviiformes and that are found in the northern part of the northern hemisphere **2 :** GREBE 1

¹**loo·ny** *or* **loo·ney** *or* **lu·ny** \ˈlünē, -ni\ *adj* **loonier** *or* **lunier**; **looniest** *or* **luniest** [*lun-* (fr. *lunatic*) + *-y*] **:** CRAZY, FOOLISH

²**loony** *or* **looney** *or* **luny** \ˈ"\ *n, pl* **loonies** *or* **looneys** *or* **lunies :** a loony person **:** LUNATIC

**loony bin** *n* **:** an insane asylum **:** MADHOUSE

¹**loop** \ˈlüp\ *n* -s [ME *loupe*; perh. akin to MD *lupen* to lie in wait, watch, peer] *archaic* **:** a small narrow opening (as in a wall) **:** LOOPHOLE ⟨massy walls . . . exhibited ~*s* for archers —Ann Radcliffe⟩

²**loop** \ˈ"\ *n* -s *often attrib* [ME *loupe*, of unknown origin] **1 a :** a fold or doubling of a line (as a thread, cord, or rope) leaving an aperture between the parts through which another line can be passed or into which a hook may be hooked **b :** such a fold of cord or ribbon serving as an ornament (as on a uniform) — see SHOULDER LOOP **c :** LOOP KNOT **2 a :** something (as a figure, course, formation, or structure) having the shape of a loop ⟨the ~ of the "a" was formed with some irregularity —F.W.Crofts⟩ ⟨saw the ~ of a river —John Buchan⟩ ⟨the driveway turns in a ~ before a fine . . . gate —*Amer. Guide Series: Va.*⟩ **b :** a turning area for cars, locomotives, or trains at the end of a railway or a street railway **c :** the portion of a lasso forming a noose ⟨the ~ settled over his prey —P.B.Kyne⟩ **d** (1) **:** a school figure in which a skater executes a semicircle followed immediately by a complete revolution around his vertical axis finishing with a second semicircle and thus tracing an oval within a larger circle while remaining on the same edge throughout (2) **:** a figure resembling a small figure eight made by following the first loop with a second one executed on the same edge of the opposite foot **e :** a surgical electrode in the form of a loop **f :** a maneuver in which an airplane starting from straight and level flight passes successively through a climb, inverted flight, a dive, and then returns to normal flight — called also *inside loop*; compare OUTSIDE LOOP **g :** a curved sand bar enclosing or nearly enclosing a body of water **h :** a road constituting a detour or an arm of a cloverleaf off a main thoroughfare ⟨graveled side ~*s* so that you can park off the highway —Mary Richards⟩ **3 :** a ring or curved piece made of some material (as wood, metal, or cloth) and used to form a fastening or a handle **:** EYE, STAPLE ⟨jeans with five belt ~*s* —*advt*⟩ **4 a :** the portion of a vibrating string, air column, or other vibrating body between two nodes **b :** the middle point of such a portion **5 :** a fingerprint in which some of the papillary ridges make a single backward turn without any twist — compare ARCH 3e, WHORL; see FINGERPRINT illustration **6** [prob. fr. the *Loop*, important business district in Chicago, Illinois] **:** the main business section or the most congested part of a city ⟨a large ~ spread over many blocks —Norman Katkov⟩ **7 :** a closed electric circuit: as **a :** one cell of a mesh or lattice **b :** a power feeder that returns to the point of origin and can thus feed in either direction **8 :** a wire usu. of platinum bent at one end into a small loop (usu. 4 millimeters in inside diameter) and used in transferring microorganisms — compare NEEDLE **9 :** an athletic conference or league **10 :** a lateral movement made by a defensive player when the ball is snapped in football **11 :** an 18-hole round of golf **12 :** LOOP ANTENNA **13 :** a portion of film or magnetic tape — **for a loop** *adv* **1 :** into a state of amazement, excitement, or confusion ⟨members of the cast were thrown *for a loop* when they caught sight of him —Cornelia O. Skinner⟩ ⟨that strange poetic touch which knocks the Japanese *for a loop* —*Time*⟩ **2 :** into a usu. sudden and unexpected reversal of fortune or a state of distress ⟨any such attempt would knock our whole economy *for a loop* —L.H.Keyserling⟩ — **on the loop** *adv (or adj)* **:** with the controller so adjusted that the motors are parallel

³**loop** \ˈ"\ *vb* -ED/-ING/-S *vi* **1 :** to form a loop ⟨the river ~*s* around the city⟩ **2 :** to move (as through the air) in loops ⟨the ring-billed gulls ~ above . . . the lake —*Amer. Guide Series: Minn.*⟩ ⟨a grenade came ~*ing* through the air —Lionel Shapiro⟩ **3 :** to execute a loop in an airplane **~** *vt* **1 a :** to place (something) within a loop **:** make a loop on or about ⟨~*ed* his finger with string⟩ ⟨lakes that ~ the town . . . like a chain of beads —*Amer. Guide Series: Minn.*⟩ **b :** to fasten with a loop ⟨the car is ~*ed* to the bag by steel cables —H.W.Baldwin⟩ — often used with *up* ⟨~ up a curtain⟩ **c :** to make a loop in or of ⟨~ a string⟩ **2 :** to furnish with loopholes **3 :** to join (two courses of loops) in knitting **4 :** to connect (electric conductors) so as to complete a loop **5 :** to cause (an airplane) to go into a loop **6 :** to cause to move esp. through the air in a course resembling or characterized by a loop ⟨~*ed* the grenade into the enemy trench⟩ ⟨~*ed* a long forward pass downfield⟩ — **loop the loop 1 :** to make a complete loop on a loop-the-loop **2 :** to perform a loop in an airplane

**loop antenna** *also* **loop aerial** *n* **:** a coil antenna usu. consisting of a single turn

**loop-back** \ˈ=,=\ *n* **:** HOOP BACK

**looped** \-pt\ *adj* [²*loop* + *-ed*] **1 :** having, formed in, or characterized by loops ⟨blend of carpet rayon and wool in a random ~ pile —*advt*⟩ **2 :** heavily intoxicated **:** DRUNK

**loop·er** \ˈlüpə(r)\ *n* -s [²*loop* + *-er*] **1 :** any of numerous usu. rather small smooth hairless caterpillars that are mostly larvae of moths of the family Geometridae, that lack prolegs on the middle segments of the body, and that move with a looping movement in which the anterior and posterior prolegs are alternately made fast and released — called also *inchworm, measuring worm, spanworm* **2 :** one that loops: as **a :** a machine that forms loops or loops things together: (1) **:** one that joins knitted edges esp. of hosiery (2) **:** one that transfers knitted loops from one knitting machine to another **b :** a worker who sews loops on garments **c :** a hosiery worker who closes toes and heels or joins ribbed tops **d :** one that hangs or ties tobacco on sticks so that it may be hung in the curing barns **e :** a ball that is pitched, hit, or thrown in a wide curve

**loop·ful** \-p,fu̇l\ *n* -s **:** the amount held in a loop; *specif* **:** the amount taken up in a standard four millimeter loop used by bacteriologists ⟨place a ~ of . . . culture on a clean slide —*Methods for Medical Laboratory Technicians*⟩

**loop hinge** *n* **:** a hinge constructed by looping two pieces of metal together (as on chests)

¹**loop·hole** \ˈlü,pōl, -üp,hōl\ *n* [¹*loop* + *hole*] **1 a :** a small opening (as in a wall or parapet) through which small arms may be discharged ⟨its attic was a fort, with ~*s* instead of windows —*Amer. Guide Series: Texas*⟩ **b :** a similar opening to admit light and air or to permit observation **2 :** an outlet or means of escape; *esp* **:** one constituted by an ambiguity or an omission in the text through which the intent of a statute, contract, or obligation may be evaded ⟨this amendment would close a ~ in the law —*U.S. Code*⟩ ⟨tax ~*s* which would cost the government . . . millions of dollars —Robert Wallace⟩

²**loophole** \ˈ"\ *vt* **:** to make loopholes in ⟨on the day of the fight this fort was extensively *loopholed* —*Scribner's*⟩

**loop in** *vt* **:** to connect (as an electric cable) in circuit

**looping snail** *n* **:** a land snail of the genus *Truncatella*

**loop jump** *n* **:** a figure skating jump in which the skater takes off from the back outside edge of one skate, makes a full turn in the air, and lands on the back outside edge of the same skate

**loop knot** *n* **:** any of several knots (as the bowline) used to form a fixed loop in a cord or rope

**loop of hen·le** \-ˈhenlē, -lə\ *usu cap H* [after F. G. J. *Henle* †1885 Ger. pathologist] **:** the part of a vertebrate nephron that lies between the proximal and distal convoluted tubules, leaves the cortex of the kidney descending into the medullary tissue, then bending back and reentering the cortex, and presumably plays a role in water resorption

**loop of retrogression :** the loop in the apparent path of a planet, asteroid, or comet caused by its retrograde motion near opposition to the sun

**loops** *pl of* LOOP, *pres 3d sing of* LOOP

**loop stitch** *n* **:** a needlework stitch (as chainstitch or lazy daisy stitch) having one or more loops as part of the design and method of working

**loop-the-loop** \ˌ=ˈ=ˈ=\ *n* [fr. the phrase *loop the loop*] **:** an amusement-park device consisting of a railway running on a largely elevated course that includes at least one portion forming an upright circle over which the passengers ride head downward

**loop winding** *n* **:** LAP WINDING

**loopy** \ˈlüpē\ *adj* -ER/-EST [²*loop* + *-y*] **1 :** having or characterized by loops ⟨the fine puff of smoke . . . floating off in a ~ ring —*Cosmopolitan*⟩ **2 a :** slightly crazy **b :** confused in one's thoughts and actions esp. as a result of mild intoxication ⟨what with the beer . . . we were all kind of ~ —Gwen Bentley⟩

**loos** *pl of* LOO, *pres 3d sing of* LOO

¹**loose** \ˈlüs\ *adj* -ER/-EST [ME *loos, lous*, fr. ON *lauss* loose, free — more at -LESS] **1 a :** not rigidly fastened or securely attached **:** lacking a firm or tight connection **:** ready to move or come apart from an attachment ⟨~ planks in a bridge⟩ ⟨sloping sides covered with . . . ~ rock —F.J.R.Rodd⟩ **b** (1) **:** lightly secured or made fast; *esp* **:** having worked partly free from attachments ⟨a ~ tooth⟩ ⟨the knife had a ~ blade⟩ ⟨~ masonry⟩ (2) **:** having relative freedom of movement or arrangement as a result of being only locally restrained or fixed ⟨~ ribbons fluttering from her hat⟩ ⟨the slamming of a ~ shutter⟩ **c :** produced freely and accompanied by raising of mucus **:** not dry or harsh **:** PRODUCTIVE ⟨a ~ cough⟩ **d :** easily altered or removed **:** not fast ⟨a ~ dye⟩ ⟨a ~ color⟩ **e :** permitting some freedom of movement — usu. used of a stable or a box stall **f :** not clinging close to the figure **:** not tight-fitting ⟨~ clothing⟩ **2 :** free from a state of confinement or restraint: **a :** free from bonds, fetters, or confining limits ⟨a ~ convict⟩ ⟨a horse ~ of his tether⟩ ⟨a lion ~ in the streets⟩ **b :** free from constraint or obligation **:** at liberty **:** not bound (as by duty or habit) ⟨if . . . your thoughts are ~ of state affairs —Joseph Addison⟩ **c :** not assigned to special use or service **:** subject to free disposal **:** having no assigned place or employment ⟨~ hours⟩ ⟨~ funds⟩ **d :** not bound together **:** not brought together in a bundle, container, or binding **:** not secured in a setting or joined in a fixed combination ⟨~ papers⟩ ⟨~ hair⟩ ⟨~ milk⟩ **e** *archaic* **:** DISCONNECTED, DETACHED, RANDOM ⟨a good deal of ~ information —Thomas Carlyle⟩ ⟨~ pages⟩ **f :** not joined to anything else ⟨a ~ line⟩ **3 :** not dense, close, or compact in structure or arrangement: as **a :** composed of particles capable of free movement ⟨~ earth⟩ ⟨the action of the tides carried away the ~ soil —*Amer. Guide Series: Maine*⟩ **b :** not in close order **:** UNSERRIED ⟨with horse and chariots ranked in ~ array —John Milton⟩ ⟨~ flocks drifting slowly from the neighboring jungle —William Beebe⟩ **c :** having wide spaces or interstices ⟨a cloth of ~ texture⟩ **d :** ³LAX 3c **e :** lacking compactness or smooth integration of build ⟨a strong, ~, round-shouldered, shuffling, shaggy fellow —Charles Dickens⟩ **4 a :** lacking in restraint or power of restraint ⟨a ~ tongue⟩ ⟨~ bowels⟩ **b :** lacking in moral restraint; *esp* **:** characterized by immorality **:** LEWD, UNCHASTE, WANTON ⟨~ writings⟩ ⟨a ~ life⟩ ⟨a ~ woman⟩ **5 a :** not tightly drawn or stretched **:** SLACK ⟨drive a pony cart with ~ reins⟩ ⟨a ~ belt⟩ ⟨~ skin⟩ **b :** having a flexible or relaxed character (as from weakness or agility) ⟨my knees ~ under me —R.L.Stevenson⟩ ⟨walked with a ~ swinging stride —E.T. Thurston⟩ **6 a :** lacking in precision, exactness, or care **:** inaccurate or indeterminate in construction **:** lacking in system or logic ⟨a ~ style⟩ ⟨~ reasoning⟩ ⟨a ~ analogy⟩ ⟨a ~ thinker⟩ **b :** lacking in rigidity (as of construction) and permitting freedom of interpretation ⟨a ~ working agreement⟩ ⟨a ~ construction of the Federal Constitution⟩ **7 :** characterized by limited cohesion between constituent elements and permitting a wide area of freedom of action ⟨a ~ federation of sovereign principalities —F.A.Ogg & Harold Zink⟩ **8 a :** not in strict accordance with the rules **:** being without special care ⟨~ practice⟩ **b :** characterized by poor quality **:** inefficient or unskilled in performance ⟨~ play⟩ **c :** having players relatively wide apart ⟨a ~ formation in football⟩ — compare TIGHT **d :** disputed as to possession **:** gone from control (as of a player or team) ⟨a ~ ball⟩ ⟨a ~ puck⟩ **9 :** LAX 4 **10 a :** expressed in or characterized by loose sentences ⟨~ style⟩ **b :** OPEN 18

²**loose** \ˈ"\ *vb* -ED/-ING/-S [ME *loosen, losen, lousen*, fr. *loos, lous*, adj. — more at ¹LOOSE] *vt* **1 a :** to let loose **:** set free **:** release from or as if from restraint ⟨the railroad had him arrested . . . but the judge *loosed* him with a warning —S.H. Adams⟩ ⟨war has again been *loosed* —Arthur Geddes⟩ ⟨the corn dance . . . should ~ downpours upon the dry country —Oliver La Farge⟩ **b :** to free (as the lips or tongue) from restraint **c :** to give absolution to ⟨whatever you ~ on earth shall be *loosed* in heaven —Mt 16:19 (RSV)⟩ **2 a :** to make loose **:** UNBIND, UNDO, UNTIE ⟨~ a knot⟩ ⟨*loosed* the laces of her shoe —B.A.Williams⟩ **b** *archaic* **:** DISSOLVE ⟨by assuming vows no pope will ~ —P.B.Shelley⟩ **3 :** to cast loose **:** DETACH ⟨*loosed* the boat from its moorings —George Eliot⟩ ⟨~ a rope⟩ **4 :** to let fly (as an arrow) **:** DISCHARGE (as a gun) **:** send forth (something) as a missile ⟨a hail of bullets and arrows was *loosed* into the flanks of the . . . advance guard —*Amer. Guide Series: Pa.*⟩ ⟨the destroyer had *loosed* a salvo of 4.7-inch shells

at her target —*Crowsnest*⟩ — often used with *off* ⟨the little boys had *loosed* off a pistol —Victoria Sackville-West⟩ **5 :** to make less rigid, tight, or strict **:** RELAX, SLACKEN ⟨the old bonds of authority have been *loosed* by the war —Bertrand Russell⟩ ⟨limbs had been *loosed* by grievous labor of combat —Alexander Pope⟩ **6** *chiefly Scot* **:** to free or obtain by payment of a fee **7** *Scots law* **:** to stop (an arrestment) from taking effect **:** WITHDRAW **~** *vi* **1 :** to let fly a missile (as an arrow) **:** discharge a gun **:** FIRE — often used with *off* ⟨almost *loosed* off at it before I saw it was a cow —Ernest Hemingway⟩ **2 :** to weigh anchor **:** set sail **3** *dial chiefly Eng* **:** to become dismissed ⟨every day when the school ~s —James Hogg⟩

**3loose** \"\ *n* -s [partly fr. *1loose* & partly fr. *2loose*] **1 :** the release of an arrow from a bow ⟨with a strong bow the ~ is easier to do well than with a weak one —A.E.Hodgkin⟩ **2** *obs* **:** the conclusion or outcome of a matter **:** ISSUE **3** *obs* **:** the state or condition of looseness; *esp* **:** freedom from or abandonment of moral restraint **4 :** loose rock or rock that may easily be loosened **5 :** open forward play in rugby — often used with *the;* contrasted with *tight* ⟨the North forwards . . . were so lively in the ~ that they neutralized the advantage gained by the visitors in the tight —*Rugger*⟩ — **give a loose to** *or* **give loose to :** to give freedom, full vent, or free rein to ⟨*gave* his usual *loose to* gaiety and mirth —Henry Fielding⟩ — **on the loose** *adv (or adj)* **1 :** in a state of freedom **:** without limits or restrictions as to movement ⟨the more warlike tribes were still *on the loose* —Oliver La Farge⟩ ⟨a dangerous animal . . . left *on the loose* —F.B.Gipson⟩ **2 :** without moral restraint (as on behavior); *esp* **:** in a state characterized by unrestrained and usu. dissolute behavior ⟨the rowdy element, . . . drunken poachers and sailors *on the loose* —*Saturday Rev.*⟩ ⟨she began shop-lifting and going *on the loose* again —Samuel Butler †1902⟩

**4loose** \"\ *adv* [*1loose*] **:** LOOSELY ⟨our manners sit more ~ upon us —Joseph Addison⟩

**loose accent** *n* **:** PIECE ACCENT

**loose-bodied** \ˈlüsˌbädēd\ *adj, of a dress* **:** hanging loosely; *specif* **:** made without stays

**loose-box** \ˈ=,=\ *n, Brit* **:** BOX STALL

**loose change** *n* **:** coins or bills of low denominations and likely to be carried loose (as in one's pocket)

**loose constructionist** *n* **:** an advocate of loose construction (as of a statute or constitution); *specif* **:** one favoring a liberal construction of the Constitution of the U.S. to give broader powers to the federal government — compare ELASTIC 4a; STRICT CONSTRUCTIONIST

**loose coupling** *n* **:** a coupling of two circuits such that any change of current in one produces relatively small change in the other

**loose cover** *n, chiefly Brit* **:** SLIPCOVER 1

**loose end** *n* **1 :** something left hanging loose **:** a fragment or piece of something remaining unused ⟨cut the *loose ends* of string after you have tied the package⟩ **2 :** a fragment of unfinished business ⟨committees will be tying up the technical *loose ends* of the . . . conference's final act —Frank Gorrell⟩ — **at loose ends** *or* **at a loose end 1 :** lacking a settled occupation or regular employment **:** uncertain of one's future course of action ⟨feeling himself *at loose ends* — no job, no immediate prospects —Dixon Wecter⟩ ⟨*at a loose end* for a time, he had been finally pitchforked into the car business —Robert Westerby⟩ **2 :** not knowing what to do with oneself **:** UNSETTLED ⟨all day long he had been *at loose ends* —Hamilton Basso⟩ ⟨being *at a loose end* that afternoon, he went to a movie⟩

**loose fit** *or* **loose fit-up** *n* **:** a fit with sufficient clearance to permit free play or in the extreme to rattle ⟨a *loose fit-up* of bearings in a groove⟩

**loose-footed** \ˈ=ˌ==\ *adj* **:** having the foot loose **:** not having or not secured to a boom — used of a sail

**loose head** *n* **:** the end player in the front line of a rugby scrum whose team is to put the ball in play

**loose-housing system** *n* **:** a system of dairy cattle management in which animals are kept at liberty in a loafing barn usu. with access to an open yard and are taken to separate areas or buildings for milking and feeding — compare MILKING PARLOR

**loose-joint butt** *n* **:** a single knuckle hinge with the pin secured in one of the halves and easily separated by sliding the pieces apart along the axis of the pin

loose-joint butt

**loose-jointed** \ˈ=ˌ==\ *adj* **1 :** having joints apparently not closely articulated **2 :** capable of or characterized by unusually free movements ⟨the easy, *loose-jointed* grace of the trained athlete —S.E.White⟩ **3 :** poorly constructed **:** CLUMSY ⟨a *loose-jointed* paragraph⟩

**loose-leaf** \ˈ=ˌ=\ *adj* **1 a :** having leaves secured in book form in a mechanical cover whose backbone may be opened for the removal, rearrangement, or replacement of leaves ⟨a *loose-leaf* notebook⟩ ⟨a *loose-leaf* ledger⟩ ⟨a *loose-leaf* encyclopedia⟩ — compare POST BINDER, RING BINDER, SPRING BINDER **b :** of, belonging to, or using articles having such leaves ⟨*loose-leaf* paper⟩ ⟨*loose-leaf* systems in bookkeeping⟩ **2 :** concerned with or used in the sale of tobacco as loose hands rather than in packed hogsheads ⟨a *loose-leaf* auction⟩ ⟨the hogshead and *loose-leaf* systems of marketing —*Experiment Station Record*⟩ ⟨make purchases . . . in the many *loose-leaf* warehouses —*Burley Tobacco Grower*⟩

**loose-lipped** \ˈ=ˌ=\ *adj* **:** LOOSE-TONGUED ⟨are not so *loose-lipped* and fond of gossip —Virginia Woolf⟩

**loose·ly** *adv* [ME *losly, losely, lousely,* fr. *loos, lous* loose + *-ly*] **:** in a loose manner ⟨lizard skulls with ~ built jaws —W.E. Swinton⟩ ⟨a union of ~ federated states⟩ ⟨these novels could be ~ grouped as mysteries —J.D.Hart⟩ ⟨played ~ with the truth —John Sparkman⟩

**loose milk** *n* **:** milk that is sold in bulk out of a large container

**loos·en** \ˈlüsᵊn\ *vb* -ED/-ING/-S [ME *losnen, loosnen,* fr. *loos, lous* loose + *-nen* -en] *vt* **1 :** to set free **:** release from restraint **:** let loose ⟨~ the tongues of the . . . prisoners —*Saturday Rev.*⟩ **2 :** to make looser **:** free from or lessen the tightness, firmness, or fixedness of ⟨~ a screw⟩ ⟨refused to ~ his control of charity funds —*Fortnight*⟩ ⟨~s social ties⟩ ⟨a liming process . . . ~s the hair —*Amer. Guide Series: Pa.*⟩ **3 :** to remove costiveness from or relax (the bowels) **4 a :** to weaken the attachment or adhesion between **:** DETACH ⟨the ivy creeping up the wall . . . does not ~ its ancient stones —Newman Smyth⟩ **b :** to separate the particles of or make less firmly packed ⟨a cultivator . . . will ~ hard-packed earth —*Monsanto Mag.*⟩ **5 :** to cause or permit to become less strict **:** relax the severity of ⟨~ the regulations governing investment in foreign countries⟩ ⟨~ discipline⟩ **~** *vi* **:** to become loose or looser ⟨even after his catastrophe his grip of his soul did not ~ —Hugh Walpole⟩ ⟨the dynastic and religious entanglements . . . have ~*ed* or disappeared —Edward Sapir⟩

**loos·en·er** \-s(ᵊ)nə(r)\ *n* -s **:** one that loosens

**loose·ness** \-snəs\ *n* -ES [ME *losenes,* fr. *loos, lous, lose* loose + *-nes* -ness] **:** the quality or state of being loose ⟨the ~ of the upper body clothing —J.H.Shaw⟩ ⟨~ of the bowels⟩ ⟨their speech may create the illusion of ~ but their behavior is straitlaced —John Mason Brown⟩ ⟨detect some vagueness and ~ in his thought —H.J.Muller⟩

**loosen up** *vi* **1 :** to become more liberal or generous with money ⟨*loosen up,* and be a big, kindly, generous human being —*Motor Print*⟩ **2 :** to become less tense or reserved **:** RELAX ⟨wanted them to *loosen up* and have a good time —Jean Boley⟩ ⟨the way you *loosen up* and forget you're a highbrow —Sinclair Lewis⟩ **~** *vt* **:** to introduce more freedom or flexibility into ⟨the private business policies which are helping to *loosen up* the economy —S.H.Slichter⟩

**loose-pin butt** *n* **:** a butt hinge with a removable pin — see BUTT HINGE illustration

**1looser** *comparative of* LOOSE

**2loos·er** \ˈlüsə(r)\ *n* -s **:** one that looses ⟨the sail ~*s* sent aloft —S.B.Luce⟩

**loose rate** *n* **:** a piece or incentive rate yielding high earnings for expenditure of effort

**looses** *pres 3d sing of* LOOSE, *pl of* LOOSE

**loose scrum** *n* **:** a scrum formed around a ball that is in play

**loose sentence** *n* **:** a usu. complex sentence in which the principal clause comes first and the latter part of which contains subordinate modifiers or trailing elements (as in "I saw him yesterday while I was walking down the street") — compare PERIODIC SENTENCE

**loose side** *n* **:** the convex face of a sheet of veneer characterized by distortion of tissue caused in cutting — compare TIGHT SIDE

**loose smut** *n* **:** a smut disease of grains in which the entire head is transformed into a dusty mass of spores with only the rachis remaining after the spores mature — compare COVERED SMUT

**loosest** *superlative of* LOOSE

**loosestrife** \ˈ=ˌ=\ *n* [*2loose* + *strife;* intended as trans. of Gk *lysimacheios* loosestrife, understood as a compound formed from Gk *lysis* action of loosing, deliverance & Gk *machē* battle, strife — more at LYSIMACHIA] **1 :** a plant of the genus *Lysimachia* (esp. *L. vulgaris*) **2 :** a plant of the genus *Lythrum; esp* **:** PURPLE LOOSESTRIFE **3 :** a plant of the genus *Steironema; esp* **:** FRINGED LOOSESTRIFE

**loosestrife family** *n* **:** LYTHRACEAE

**loose-tongued** \ˈ=ˌ=\ *adj* **:** free of speech **:** given to unrestrained talk

**loose wall** *n* **:** SEEDY TOE

**loosing** *n* -s [ME *losing, lousing,* fr. gerund of *loosen, losen, lousen* to loose] **:** the act of releasing; *specif* **:** the absolution or remission of sins ⟨a notable example of binding and ~ by the minister —G.W.Sprott⟩

**1loot** \ˈlüt\ *Scot past of* LET

**2loot** \"\ *Scot var of* LOUT

**3loot** \", *usu* -üd.+V\ *n* -s [Hindi *lūṭ,* fr. Skt *luṇṭati* he robs, plunders] **1 :** goods esp. articles of considerable value taken in war (as from the enemy or a captured city) **:** BOOTY, PLUNDER, SPOILS ⟨those who have fought solely for booty and ~ —R.E.Sherwood⟩ **2 :** something held to resemble goods of value seized in war: as **a :** anything taken by force or violence (as in a robbery) ⟨the accumulated ~ of all the sea rovers —H.E.Rieseberg⟩ **b :** illicit gains by public officials **c :** articles having or held to have great value ⟨the rich ~ of . . . wedding gifts —R.L.Shayon⟩ ⟨a rich ~ of factual material —F.L.Mott⟩ **d :** MONEY ⟨would not . . . spend all that ~ on her —Langston Hughes⟩ **3 :** the action of looting ⟨general ~ of church land —Hilaire Belloc⟩

**4loot** *vb* -ED/-ING/-S *vt* **1 a :** to plunder or sack (as a conquered city) in war **b :** to rob esp. on a large scale and usu. by violence or corruption ⟨~*ed* a bank⟩ ⟨corrupt politicians ~*ed* the nation's forest and mineral reserves⟩ **2 :** to seize and carry away by force esp. in war ⟨the enemy soldiers ~*ed* the treasures of the art museums⟩ **~** *vi* **:** to perform the action of robbing or plundering esp. in war **syn** see ROB

**5loot** \"\ *n* -s [by shortening & alter.] *slang* **:** LIEUTENANT

**loo·ten** \ˈlütᵊn\ *Scot past of* LET

**loot·er** \ˈlüd·ə(r), -ütə-\ *n* -s **:** one that loots

**loo·tie** \ˈlüd·ē\ *also* **loo·tie·wal·lah** \ˈ=ˌ=ˌwälə\ *n* -s [*lootie* fr. Hindi *lūṭī,* fr. *lūṭ; lootiewallah* fr. Hindi *lūṭīwālā,* fr. *lūṭī* + *-wālā* man — more at WALLAH] *India* **:** one that engages in looting or marauding — usu. used in pl.

**loots·man** \ˈlütsmən\ *n, pl* **lootsmans** [modif. of D *loodsmannetje,* dim. of *loodsman* pilot, fr. MD, fr. ME *lodesman,* fr. *lodes* (gen. of *lode* course) + *man* — more at LODE] **:** REMORA

**1lop** \ˈläp\ *n* -s [ME *loppe,* of unknown origin] **:** the smaller branches and twigs (as of a tree) that have been cut off **:** trimmings; *esp* **:** such parts of a tree that are not measured for timber ⟨the timber merchant who bought the trees did not wish to take away the ~ and top —H.C.W.Bouring⟩

**2lop** \"\ *vb* **lopped; lopped; lopping; lops** *vt* **1 a :** to cut off branches or twigs from (as a tree or vine) **:** remove dead parts or superfluous growth from **:** TRIM **b** *archaic* **:** to cut off the head or limbs of (a person) **2 a :** to cut (as branches or twigs) from a tree or bush — often used with *off* ⟨cut down the small tree and *lopped* the branches off —W.H.Hudson †1922⟩ **b :** to cut (the limbs or head) from a person ⟨~*s* the head of his enemy into a wine cask —Burke Wilkinson⟩ — often used with *off* ⟨the hasty decision to ~ off part of a limb —C.L.Boltz⟩ **c :** to cut (as a portion or part) from something ⟨decided to ~ the dog's tail⟩ — often used with *off* ⟨*lopped* off the border provinces of the empire⟩ **3 :** to remove esp. superfluous parts from **:** eliminate as unnecessary, superfluous, or undesirable — usu. used with *off* ⟨about 100,000 jobs . . . have been *lopped* off the federal payroll —Daniel Bell⟩ ⟨*lopped* off a billion dollars in excise revenues —*U. S. News & World Report*⟩ **~** *vi* **:** to perform the action of cutting off

**3lop** \"\ *n* -s [ME *loppe,* of Scand origin; akin to OSw *loppa* flea; perh. akin to ON *hlaupa* to jump, leap — more at LEAP] *dial Eng* **:** FLEA

**4lop** \"\ *vi* **lopped; lopped; lopping; lops** [perh. imit.] **1 :** to hang downward esp. in a loose or limp manner **:** flop or sway about loosely **:** DROOP **2 :** to move or act in a lazy and usu. slouching manner **3 :** to move with short leaps **:** BOUND ⟨a rabbit . . . *lopped* among the darkening cabbages —H.E. Bates⟩ ⟨used to ~ around in the gymnasium after badminton or handball —Dorothy Baker⟩

**5lop** \"\ *adj* [*4lop*] **:** hanging down **:** PENDENT ⟨~ ears⟩

**6lop** \"\ *n* [*5lop*] **1** *usu cap* **:** a variety or breed of domestic rabbits having very large ears that are usu. too heavy to be carried erect and fall to the side of the head **2** -s *often cap* **:** a rabbit of the Lop breed

**7lop** \"\ *n* -s [prob. imit.] **:** a condition of the sea in which the waves are short and choppy

**8lop** \"\ *vi* **lopped; lopped; lopping; lops :** to break in short choppy waves — used of the sea ⟨the tide high and *lopping* rhythmically against the side —Darrell Berrigan⟩

**LOP** *abbr* line of position

**lo·pa·rite** \ˈlōpəˌrīt\ *n* -s [Russ *loparit,* fr. *Lopar'* Lapp (prob. fr. Sw *Lappar* Lapps, pl. of *Lapp*) + *-it* -ite] **:** a perovskite containing alkalies and cerium

**lop down** *vi* **:** to sit or lie down **:** FLOP 2a ⟨thought she'd just *lop down* a few minutes on the old sofa —Harriet B. Stowe⟩

**1lope** \ˈlōp\ *n* -s [ME, alter. of *loup,* fr. ON *hlaup;* in senses 2 and 3, prob. influenced by D *loop* course, run, stride, fr. MD; ON *hlaup* akin to MD *loop,* OHG *hlouf* course; derivative fr. the root of ON *hlaupa* to jump, leap] **1** *obs* **:** LEAP **2 :** an easy natural gait of a horse resembling a canter **3 :** an easy bounding gait capable of being sustained for a considerable period ⟨the ~ of a wolf⟩

**2lope** \"\ *vb* -ED/-ING/-S [ME *lopen,* alter. of *loupen,* fr. ON *hlaupa;* in sense 2, prob. influenced by D *loopen* to run, fr. MD *lopen* — more at LEAP (v.)] *vi* **1** *obs* **:** LEAP **2 a :** to go or move at a lope ⟨the hares and rabbits *loped* away —Charles Kingsley⟩ ⟨*loped* up the trail —Donald Keith⟩ **b :** to ride at a lope **~** *vt* **:** to cause (as a horse or pony) to lope ⟨*loped* our jaded horses along at a brisk pace —Theodore Roosevelt⟩

**lop-eared** \ˈ=ˌ=\ *adj* **:** having ears that droop ⟨*lop-eared* rabbits⟩ ⟨a shaggy, mean-eyed, *lop-eared* . . . pony —C.T. Jackson⟩

**lop·er** \ˈlōpə(r)\ *n* -s **1 :** one that lopes; *esp* **:** a saddle horse having the loping gait **2 :** the vertical sliding pieces that when pulled out support the fall front of a desk or secretary

**lo·pe·zia** \lōˈpēzēə\ *n, cap* [NL, prob. fr. J. *López,* 16th cent. Span. colonial official + NL *-ia*] **:** a genus of Mexican and Central American herbs and subshrubs (family Onagraceae) having alternate leaves and small irregular mostly red racemose flowers

**lo·pez·ite** \ˈlōpəˌzīt\ *n* -s [Emiliano *López,* 20th cent. Chilean mineral collector + E *-ite*] **:** a mineral $K_2Cr_2O_7$ consisting of a dichromate of potassium and found in the nitrate deposits of Chile

**loph-** *or* **lopho-** *comb form* [NL, fr. Gk, fr. *lophos*] **:** crest **:** tuft **:** comb ⟨*lophophytosis*⟩ ⟨*Lophura*⟩

**-loph** \ˌläf\ *n comb form* -s [Gk *lophos*] **:** crest ⟨ecto*loph*⟩

**lophi-** *or* **lophio-** *comb form* [NL, fr. Gk *lophion* small crest, dim. of *lophos*] **:** small crest or tuft ⟨*Lophiodon*⟩ ⟨*Lophiomys*⟩

**lo·phi·id** \ˈlōfēəd, -ē,id\ *n* -s [NL *Lophiidae*] **:** a fish of the family Lophiidae

**lo·phi·idae** \ləˈfīə,dē\ *n pl, cap* [NL, fr. *Lophius,* type genus + *-idae*] **:** a family of large-headed marine fishes comprising the anglers and often made coextensive with a suborder Lophioidea of the order Pediculati

**lo·phine** \ˈlō,fēn, -,fən, ˈlä-\ *n* -s [prob. fr. F, fr. *loph-* + *-ine*] **:** a crystalline nitrogenous base $(C_6H_5)_3C_3HN_2$ that emits light when a solution of it in warm alcoholic potassium hydroxide absorbs oxygen; 2, 4, 5-triphenyl-imidazole

**lo·phi·o·don** \ləˈfīə,dän\ *n, cap* [NL *Lophiodont-, Lophiodon,* fr. *lophi-* + *-odont-, -odon* -odon] **:** a genus of large European Eocene perissodactyls related to the tapir

**1lo·phi·o·dont** \ˈlōfēə,dänt\ *also* **lo·phi·o·don·toid** \ˌ===-ˈdän-,tȯid\ *adj* [*lophiodont* fr. NL *Lophiodont-, Lophiodon; lophiodontoid* fr. NL *Lophiodont-, Lophiodon* + E *-oid*] **:** of or relating to the genus *Lophiodon*

**2lophiodont** \"\ *n* -s [NL *Lophiodont-, Lophiodon*] **:** an animal of the genus *Lophiodon*

**lo·phi·oi·dea** \ˌlōfēˈȯidēə\ *n pl, cap* [NL, fr. *Lophius* + *-oidea*] *in some classifications* **:** a suborder of Pediculati coextensive with the Lophiidae

**lo·phi·o·mys** \ləˈfīə,mis\ *n, cap* [NL, fr. *lophi-* + *-mys*] **:** a genus of atypical rodents of northeastern and eastern Africa having the temporal fossae of the skull bridged by plates of bone — compare CRESTED HAMSTER

**lo·phi·os·to·ma·ta·ce·ae** \ˌlōfē,ästəməˈtāsē,ē\ *n pl, cap* [NL, fr. *Lophiostomat-, Lophiostoma,* type genus (fr. *lophi-* + *-stomat-, -stoma* -stoma) + *-aceae*] **:** a family of ascomycetous fungi (order Sphaeriales) distinguished by the elongated laterally compressed opening of the perithecium

**lo·phi·us** \ˈlōfēəs\ *n, cap* [NL, fr. Gk *lophos* crest] **:** the type genus of Lophiidae

**1loph·o·branch** \ˈläfə,braŋk, ˈlōf-\ *n* -s [NL *Lophobranchii*] **:** LOPHOBRANCHIATE

**2lophobranch** \"\ *adj* [NL *Lophobranchii*] **:** LOPHOBRANCHIATE

**1loph·o·branchiate** \ˌ==+\ *adj* [NL *Lophobranchii* + E *-ate*] **:** of or relating to the Lophobranchii

**2lophobranchiate** \"\ *n* -s **:** a lophobranchiate fish

**loph·o·bran·chii** \ˌ=ˈbraŋkē,ī\ *n pl, cap* [NL, fr. *loph-* + *-branchii* (fr. Gk *branchion* gill) — more at BRANCHIA] *in some classifications* **:** an order of small teleost fishes that comprise the sea horses and pipefishes and are coextensive with the family Syngnathidae and that are sometimes considered a suborder of Thoracostei

**loph·o·dermium** \ˌ==ˈdərmēəm\ *n, cap* [NL, fr. *loph-* + *-dermium* (fr. Gk *derma* skin) — more at DERM-] **:** a genus of ascomycetous fungi (order Phacidiales) having filiform one-celled ascospores in perithecia which are finally erumpent

**1loph·o·dont** \ˈ==,dänt\ *adj* [ISV *loph-* + *-odont*] **:** having or constituting molar teeth with transverse ridges on the grinding surface ⟨~ rodents⟩ — opposed to *bunodont*

**2lophodont** \"\ *n* -s **:** an animal (as an ungulate) having lophodont teeth

**lo·phoph·o·ral** \ləˈfäf(ə)rəl\ *adj* **:** of or relating to a lophophore

**loph·o·phore** \ˈläfə,fō(ə)r, ˈlōf-\ *n* -s [*loph-* + *-phore*] **:** an organ usu. of a circular or horseshoe shape that surrounds the mouth and bears the tentacles and that serves to engulf food particles and provide a respiratory current in bryozoans, brachiopods, and a few marine worms

**lo·phoph·o·rus** \ləˈfäf(ə)rəs\ *n, cap* [NL, fr. *loph-* + *-phorus*] **:** a genus consisting of the monals

**loph·o·phyl·lid** \ˌläfəˈfiləd, ˌlōf-\ *or* **loph·o·phyl·li·did** \-lədəd, -,did\ *adj* [*lophophyllid* fr. NL *Lophophyllidium; lophophyllidid* irreg. fr. NL *Lophophyllidiidae* (family of tetracorals including the genus *Lophophyllidium*), fr. *Lophophyllidium,* type genus + *-idae*] **:** of or relating to *Lophophyllidium*

**loph·o·phyl·lid·i·um** \ˌ===fəˈlidēəm\ *n, cap* [NL, fr. *loph-* + *phyll-* + *-idium*] **:** a genus (sometimes made the type of a family Lophophyllidiidae) of tetracorals common and widely distributed in central No. American Upper Carboniferous formations

**lo·phoph·y·ton** \ləˈfäfə,tän\ [NL, fr. *loph-* + Gk *phyton* plant; fr. its occurrence as a parasite on the comb of fowls — more at PHYT-] *syn of* ACHORION

**loph·o·phytosis** \ˌläfō, ˌlōfō+\ *n* [NL, fr. *loph-* + *phytosis*] **:** favus of fowls

**lo·phor·nis** \ləˈfȯrnəs\ *n, cap* [NL, fr. *loph-* + *-ornis*] **:** a genus of hummingbirds consisting of the coquettes

**lo·phor·tyx** \-,tiks\ *n, cap* [NL, fr. *loph-* + Gk *ortyx* quail — more at OREORTYX] **:** a genus consisting of the helmet quails

**lo·phos·te·on** \ləˈfästē,än\ *n, pl* **lophos·tea** \-ēə\ *or* **lophosteons** [NL, fr. *loph-* + *-osteon*] **:** the keel-bearing part of a bird's sternum

**lo·phot·i·dae** \ləˈfäd·ə,dē\ *n pl, cap* [NL, fr. *Lophotes,* type genus (irreg. fr. Gk *lophos* crest) + *-idae*] **:** a monotypic family of elongated ribbonlike deep-sea fishes (order Allotriognathi) — compare OARFISH

**lo·phot·ri·chous** \ləˈfä·trəkəs\ *or* **lo·phot·ri·chate** \-kət\ *also* **loph·o·trich·ic** \ˌläfəˈtrikik, ˌlōf-\ *adj* [*lophotrichous* fr. *loph-* + *-trichous; lophotrichate* fr. *loph-* + *trich-* + *-ate; lophotrichic* fr. *loph-* + *trich-* + *-ic*] **:** having a tuft of flagella at one end

**-lophs** *pl of* -LOPH

**lo·phu·ra** \ləˈfyürə\ *n, cap* [NL, fr. *loph-* + *-ura*] **:** a genus of pheasants consisting of the firebacks

**lop·o·lith** \ˈläpə,lith\ *n* -s [Gk *lopos* shell, husk + E *-lith;* akin to Gk *lepein* to peel — more at LEPER] **:** a laccolith in which the base is basin-shaped instead of being horizontal

**lopped** *past of* LOP

**1lop·per** \ˈläpə(r)\ *vb* -ED/-ING/-S [ME *lopren,* of Scand origin; akin to Icel *hleypir* rennet, Norw dial. *løyper,* Sw dial. *löper,* Dan *løbe,* all fr. ON *hleypa* to cause the coagulation of, causative of *hlaupa* to undergo coagulation, jump, leap — more at LEAP] *North* **:** COAGULATE, CLOT, CURDLE — used esp. of milk

**2lopper** \"\ *n* -s [*2lop* + *-er*] **1 :** one that lops ⟨a great oak . . . spoiled of boughs by the ~'*s* ax —Thomas Jackson⟩ **2 :** pruning shears having handles about two feet long

**loppered milk** *n* [ME *lopred milk,* fr. *lopred* (past part. of *lopren*) + *milk*] *North* **:** CLABBER

**lopping** *n* -s [fr. gerund of *2lop*] **:** something cut off; *esp* **:** a branch cut from a tree or bush — usu. used in pl.

**lopping shears** *n pl* **:** pruning shears made with handles 24 to 30 inches in length and used for cutting branches of trees and shrubs

lopping shears

**1lop·py** \ˈläpē, -pi\ *adj* [ME, fr. *loppe* flea + *-y* — more at LOP (flea)] *dial Brit* **:** infested with fleas

**2loppy** \"\ *adj* [*4lop* + *-y*] **:** hanging loosely **:** LIMP

**3loppy** \"\ *adj* [*7lop* + *-y*] **:** CHOPPY — used of the sea

**lops** *pl of* LOP, *pres 3d sing of* LOP

**lopseed** \ˈ=ˌ=\ *n* [*5lop* + *seed*] **:** a perennial Asiatic herb (*Phryma leptostachya*) adventive in No. America

**lopseed family** *n* **:** PHRYMACEAE

**lopsided** \ˈ=ˌ==\ *also* **lobsided** \ˈ=ˌ=\ *adj* [*5lop* + *sided*] **1 :** leaning to one side (as from a defect of structure) ⟨looked rather ~ with three boats swung on the port side and no boat at all on the starboard side —H.A.Chippendale⟩ ⟨small, wormy, ~ apples —Joseph Mitchell⟩ **2 :** lacking in balance or symmetry **:** poorly proportioned **:** disproportionately heavy on one side ⟨~ economic development⟩ ⟨a ~ vote of 373 to 9⟩ ⟨a ~ personality⟩ — **lop·sid·ed·ly** *adv* — **lop·sid·ed·ness** *n* -ES

**lopstick** \ˈ=ˌ=\ *n* [*1lop* + *stick*] *Canad* **:** a tree with branches trimmed so that it may serve as a landmark or memorial

**loq** *abbr* loquitur

**lo·qua·cious** \lōˈkwāshəs\ *adj* [L *loquac-, loquax* loquacious (fr. *loqui* to speak) + E *-ious*] **1 a :** given to excessive talking **:** GARRULOUS ⟨the brandy made him a bit ~ —Sherwood Anderson⟩ **b :** full of excessive talk **:** WORDY ⟨the prolonged and ~ death scene —C.W.Cunnington⟩ ⟨the ~ cluttered plot —*Newsweek*⟩ **2 :** BABBLING, NOISY ⟨sometimes a ~ brook would run right through it —Christopher Rand⟩ **syn** see TALKATIVE

**lo·qua·cious·ly** *adv* **:** in a loquacious manner

**lo·qua·cious·ness** *n* -ES **:** the quality or state of being loquacious : TALKATIVENESS ⟨a ~ at times rising to eloquence —Walter Cerf⟩

**lo·quac·i·ty** \lō'kwasəd·ē, -ətē, -i\ *n* -ES [L *loquacitat-, loquacitas*, fr. *loquac-, loquax* + *-itat-, -itas* -ity] **1 :** LOQUACIOUSNESS, GARRULITY ⟨had lost his usual ~ and quaint humor —Charles Kingsley⟩ **2 :** an instance of loquacity ⟨knew what they were doing in all their ramblings and *loquacities* —C.E.Montague⟩

**lo·quat** \'lō,kwät, ˌ=ˈ=\ *n* -S [Chin (Cant) *lō-kwat*] **1 :** an Asiatic evergreen tree (*Eriobotrya japonica*) now cultivated in most tropical or subtropical regions for its fruit — called also *Japanese medlar, Japanese plum, nispero* **2 :** the fruit of the loquat used for preserves, jams, and jellies

**lo·quence** \'lōkwən(t)s\ *or* **lo·quen·cy** \-nsē\ *n, pl* **loquences** *or* **loquencies** [L *loquentia*, fr. *loquent-, loquens* + *-ia* -y] *archaic* : SPEECH, DISCOURSE

**lo·quent** \-kwənt\ *adj* [L *loquent-, loquens*, pres. part. of *loqui* to speak] *archaic* : using speech : SPEAKING — **lo·quent·ly** *adv*

**lo·qui·tur** \'läkwəd·ə(r), -ətə-\ [L, he speaks, she speaks, 3d pers. sing. pres. indic. of *loqui* to speak] : begins to speak — used as a stage direction usu. after the name of the player

**lor** \'lō(ə)r, -ó(ə)\ *substand var of* LORD

**lora** *pl of* LORUM

**lo·ral** \'lōrəl, -ȯr-\ *adj* [²*lore* + *-al*] : of or relating to a lore

**lo·ran** \'lōr,an, 'lȯ,r-, ˌ=ˈ=\ *n* -S [*long-range navigation*] : a system of long-range navigation in which pulsed signals sent out by two pairs of radio stations of known position are used by navigators to determine the geographical position of a ship or an airplane

**lor·an·dite** \'lärən,dīt\ *n* -S [Hung *lorandit*, fr. Eotvös *Loránd*, 19th cent. Hung. physicist + Hung *-it* -ite] : a cochineal red monoclinic mineral $TlAsS_2$ consisting of a thallium sulfarsenide

**lo·ran·skite** \lə'ran,skīt\ *n* -S [G *loranskit*, fr. A. M. *Loranski*, 19th cent. Russ. mine inspector + G *-it* -ite] : a mineral $(Y,Ce,Ca,Zr?)(Ta,Zr?)O_4(?)$ consisting of a black oxide of yttrium, cerium, calcium, tantalum, and zirconium

**lo·ran·tha·ce·ae** \,lō,ran'thāsē,ē, ,lȯ-\ *n pl, cap* [NL, fr. *Loranthus*, type genus + *-aceae*] : a family of parasitic or hemiparasitic shrubs or trees (order Santalales) comprising the mistletoes that are natives chiefly of tropical regions, have thick leathery mostly opposite and sometimes scaly leaves, and are attached to their hosts by haustoria

**lo·ran·thus** \lə'ran(t)thəs\ *n, cap* [NL, fr. L *lorum* strap + NL *-anthus* — more at LORE] : a very large mostly tropical genus (the type of the family Loranthaceae) of hemiparasitic plants distinguished by the baccate or drupaceous fruit

**lor·cha** \'lȯrshə\ *n* -S [Pg] : a three-masted sailing ship used in Chinese, Thai, and Philippine waters that has a hull built on a European model and rigging like that of a Chinese junk with batten lugsails

lorcha

**¹lord** \'lȯ(ə)rd, -ȯ(ə)d, *sometimes chiefly Brit* 'ləd *esp in exclamations & in the form of address "My Lord" used by lawyers in court*\ *n* -S [ME, alter. of *loverd*, fr. OE *hlāford*, fr. *hlāf* bread, loaf + *weard* keeper, guard — more at LOAF, WARD] **1 :** one having power and authority over others: **a :** a ruler by hereditary right or preeminence to whom service and obedience are due : GOVERNOR, PRINCE, SOVEREIGN ⟨~ among earls —Alfred Tennyson⟩ ⟨our late sovereign ~ —John Keats⟩ **b :** one of whom a fee or estate is held in feudal tenure : the proprietor of feudal land — compare MANOR, MESNE LORD **c :** a proprietor or owner of land or houses ⟨~ of few acres and those barren too —John Dryden⟩ — compare LANDLORD **d** *obs* : the male head of a household : a master of servants ⟨that evil servant shall say in his heart, my ~ delayeth his coming —Mt 24:48 (AV)⟩ **e :** HUSBAND ⟨my sour husband, my hardhearted ~ —Shak.⟩ **f :** one that has achieved mastery by virtue of superior strength or conquest ⟨last in the field and almost ~*s* of it —Shak.⟩ ⟨pain is a terrible ~⟩ **g :** a man who exercises leadership or great power in a particular business or occupation ⟨press ~*s*⟩ ⟨money ~*s*⟩ ⟨the ~*s* of art today —Bernard Smith⟩ ⟨a warning from the vice ~*s* . . . not to meddle in their affairs —Bosley Crowther⟩ **2** *cap* **a :** ²GOD ⟨the *Lord* will not hold him guiltless who takes his name in vain —Exod 20:7 (RSV)⟩ — often used as an interjection to express surprise or pity ⟨*Lord*, what fools these mortals be —Shak.⟩ **b :** CHRIST ⟨they have taken the *Lord* out of the tomb, and we do not know where they have laid him —Jn 20:2 (RSV)⟩ **3 :** a man of rank or high position: as **a :** a tenant in capite of the king or other feudal superior — compare BARON 1 **b :** any of various titled noblemen in Great Britain — used as a courtesy title for the younger son of a duke or marquess ⟨*Lord* Eustace Percy, younger son of a duke of Northumberland⟩ and as a mode of reference for (1) a baron ⟨*Lord* Graves, Baron of Gravesend⟩ or (2) on all but formal occasions a peer of the rank of marquess, earl, or viscount or one so styled as a courtesy title ⟨addressing the marquess of Hartington as *Lord* Hartington⟩ **c lords** *pl, usu cap* : the lords temporal and spiritual that constitute the upper house of the British Parliament ⟨only two or three bills thrown out by the *Lords* have ever been forced through by the Commons —George Orwell⟩ **4 :** a planet having controlling power or influence astrologically over a particular sign, house, or hour **5 :** a person chosen to preside over a festival — compare LORD OF MISRULE **6** *Brit* : a humpbacked person **7 :** a male harlequin duck — compare LORD-AND-LADY

**²lord** \"\ *vb* -ED/-ING/-S [ME *lorden*, fr. *lord*, n.] *vi* : to behave like a lord : act in a lordly manner : put on airs ⟨supreme the spectral creature ~*ed* —Robert Browning⟩ — usu. used with formulary *it* ⟨~*ing* it in a stucco palace —Clifton Fadiman⟩ ⟨~*ing* it around the bar —Edna Ferber⟩ ⟨the film director has ~*ed* it over the interpreter of Shakespeare —Walter Goodman⟩ **~** *vt* **1** *archaic* : to rule as lord of ⟨all the revels he had ~*ed* there —John Keats⟩ **2** *archaic* **a :** to grant the title of lord to : ENNOBLE ⟨those that hath for any services been ~*ed* —George Wither⟩ **b :** to address by the title of lord ⟨every spoken tongue should ~ you —Alfred Tennyson⟩

**lord admiral** *n* : LORD HIGH ADMIRAL

**lord advocate** *n* : the chief law officer of the crown in Scotland who in practice delegates his powers as principal prosecutor in criminal matters to the solicitor general and the four advocates-depute

**lord almoner** *n* : LORD HIGH ALMONER OF ENGLAND

**lord-and-lady** \'=ˈ==\ *n, pl* **lords-and-ladies** : HARLEQUIN DUCK

**lord baltimore cake** *n, usu cap L&B* [prob. after *Lord Baltimore* (George Calvert) †1632 Eng. proprietor in America] : a usu. gold butter cake with a filling of macaroons, nuts, and cherries and a boiled frosting — compare LADY BALTIMORE CAKE

**lord bird** *n* : HARLEQUIN DUCK

**lord chamberlain** *or* **lord chamberlain of the household** *n* : a royal officer and government official in England whose duties include the appointment of professional men and tradesmen for the court, the regulation of the royal theaters and chapels royal, and the licensing of all plays produced publicly in England

**lord chancellor** *n, pl* **lords chancellor** : a British officer of state who presides over the House of Lords in both its legislative and judicial capacities, serves as the head of the British judiciary, and is usu. a leading member of the cabinet ⟨judicial appointments are made on the advice of the *lord chancellor* —W.H.Wickwar⟩ — called also *lord high chancellor;* compare MASTER OF THE ROLLS

**lord chief justice of england** *cap E* : the presiding judge of the King's Bench Division of the High Court of Justice in England

**lord clerk register** *n* : an officer of state in Scotland who has custody of the archives

**lord commissioner** *n, pl* **lords commissioners** : a member of a board exercising the powers of a high British office of state that has been put in commission

**lord commissioner of admiralty :** one of the lords commissioners including the first lord, the sea lords, and the civil lord who perform the executive duties of the former office of lord high admiral in England

**lord commissioner of the treasury :** one of the lords commissioners who perform the duties of the former office of lord high treasurer of England — see FIRST LORD OF THE TREASURY

**lord fauntleroy** *adj, usu cap L&F* [after *Lord Fauntleroy*, boy hero of Frances Hodgson Burnett's novel *Little Lord Fauntleroy* (1886)] : resembling or suggestive of Lord Fauntleroy (as in style of clothing or haircut)

**lord great chamberlain of england** *cap E* : a hereditary great officer of state in England whose duties were orig. financial but are now mainly ceremonial

**lord harry** *n, usu cap L&H* [fr. *Harry*, nickname for the name *Henry*] : DEVIL 1

**lord high admiral** *n* : a great officer of state formerly at the head of the naval administration of Great Britain

**lord high almoner of england** *cap E* : an ecclesiastical officer of the royal household in Great Britain who distributes the royal bounty

**lord high chancellor** *n* : LORD CHANCELLOR

**lord high commissioner** *n* : a commissioner who represents the British crown at the General Assembly of the Church of Scotland

**lord high constable** *n* : a great officer of state in England now appointed only for rare occasions (as coronations)

**lord high steward** *n* : an English officer of state now appointed only for rare occasions (as a coronation or the trial of a peer)

**lord high treasurer of england** *cap E* : the former third great officer of the crown whose duties are now executed by the Treasury Board

**lord·ing** \'lȯ(ə)rdiŋ, -ȯ(ə)d-\ *n* -S [ME, alter. of *loverding*, fr. OE *hlāfording*, fr. *hlāford* lord + *-ing* — more at LORD] **1** *archaic* : LORD ⟨have a care for yourselves, ~*s* —Charles Kingsley⟩ **2** *obs* : LORDLING

**lord-in-waiting** \'=ˈ==\ *n, pl* **lords-in-waiting** : a man chosen from a noble family to serve as a personal attendant in the household of the British sovereign or of the prince of Wales

**lord justice** *or* **lord justice of appeal** *n, pl* **lords justices** *or* **lords justices of appeal** : a judge of the Court of Appeal in England

**lord justice clerk** *n, pl* **lord justice clerks** : JUSTICE CLERK

**lord justice general** *n, pl* **lord justices general** : JUSTICE GENERAL

**lord keeper of the great seal** : LORD CHANCELLOR

**lord keeper of the privy seal** : LORD PRIVY SEAL

**lord·less** \'lȯ(ə)rdləs, -ȯ(ə)d-\ *adj* [ME *lordles*, alter. of *loverdles*, fr. OE *hlāfordlēas*, fr. *hlāford* lord + *-lēas* -less] : having no lord : lacking a master

**lord·let** \-lət\ *n* -S : LORDLING

**lord lieutenancy** *n* : the office of a lord lieutenant

**lord lieutenant** *n, pl* **lords lieutenant** *or* **lord lieutenants** **1 :** an official of the crown in English counties formerly having extensive military powers and now serving as the principal justice of the peace and keeper of the county records **2 :** LORD LIEUTENANT OF IRELAND

**lord lieutenant of ireland** *cap I* : the English viceroy in Ireland before 1922

**¹lordlike** \'=,=\ *adj* [ME *lordlik*, fr. ¹*lord* + *lik* like] *archaic* : LORDLY

**²lordlike** *adv, obs* : in a manner befitting a lord

**lord·li·ly** \'lȯ(ə)rdlәlē, -ȯ(ə)d-\ *adv* : in a lordly manner

**lord·li·ness** \-lēnəs, -lin-\ *n* -ES [ME *lordlynes*, fr. ¹*lordly* + *-nes* -ness] **1 :** the quality or state of being a lord **2 a :** the manner and behavior suitable to a lord : DIGNITY **b :** an attitude of superiority toward inferiors : HAUGHTINESS

**lord·ling** \-liŋ\ *n* -S [ME, alter. of *loverdling*, fr. *loverd* lord + *-ling* — more at LORD] : a petty or insignificant lord ⟨a poor ~ of uncertain prospects —J.M.Barzun⟩

**¹lord·ly** *adj, usu* -ER/-EST [ME, alter. of *loverdlich*, fr. OE *hlāfordlic*, fr. *hlāford* lord + *-lic* -ly] **1 a :** of, relating to, or administered by a lord ⟨~ or absolute monarchy is the best and most natural government —John Hall⟩ **b :** having the characteristics of a lord : DIGNIFIED, HONORABLE ⟨more ~ than all emperors and kings condensed into one —C.H. Spurgeon⟩ ⟨its ~ and patrician detachment —Irwin Edman⟩ **c** (1) : befitting a lord : NOBLE ⟨the generous public spirit . . . responsible for this ~ gift of land —Lewis Mumford⟩ (2) : suitable for a lord : GRAND, STATELY ⟨one of the *lordliest* sites on earth —R.L.Duffus⟩ ⟨heir to a ~ fortune —Dumas Malone⟩ **2 :** having or affecting a feeling of superiority : ARROGANT, HAUGHTY, IMPERIOUS ⟨a ~ indifference to making money by his writings —Leslie Stephen⟩ ⟨a ~ nation that will not trust thee but for profit's sake —Shak.⟩ **syn** see PROUD

**²lordly** \"\ *adv* [ME, fr. *lordly*, adj.] : in a lordly manner

**lord lyon king of arms** *or* **lord lyon** : LYON KING OF ARMS

**lord marcher** *n, pl* **lords marchers** [ME *lord marchier*, fr. ¹*lord* + *marchier* marcher] : MARCHER 2

**lord mayor** *n* : the mayor of a large city esp. in the British Commonwealth

**lord of appeal in ordinary :** a life peer with eminent legal qualifications appointed to act as one of the principal members of the House of Lords in its proceedings as a court of last resort ⟨authorized the appointment of . . . nine *lords of appeal in ordinary* —F.A.Ogg & Harold Zink⟩

**lord of council and session :** a judge of the Court of Session in Scotland

**lord of erection** *Scots law* : the lord or superior of a temporal lordship created by secularization of an ecclesiastical benefice at the time of the Reformation — called also *titular*

**lord of misrule** [ME *lorde of mysrewle*] **1 :** one chosen to preside over the Christmas revels at court, in noble households, and elsewhere in England esp. in the 15th and 16th centuries — called also *Abbot of Misrule;* compare ABBOT OF UNREASON **2 :** the presiding officer of a popular festival

**lord of regality** [ME (Sc) *lord of regalite*] : one formerly granted rights of regalities by a Scottish king

**lord of session :** LORD OF COUNCIL AND SESSION

**lord of the admiralty :** LORD COMMISSIONER OF ADMIRALTY

**lord of the articles** [ME (Sc)] : one of a standing committee of the Scottish Parliament charged with the drafting and preparation of the acts or bills for laws

**lord of the ascendant :** a planet whose mansion is rising in the east

**lord of the bedchamber** **1 :** a lord in waiting in the British royal household **2 :** either of two lords in attendance in the household of the prince of Wales

**lord of the treasury :** LORD COMMISSIONER OF THE TREASURY

**lord·ol·a·try** \lȯ(ə)r'däləˌtrē, lȯ(ə)'-, -ri\ *n* -ES [¹*lord* + *-o-* + *-latry*] : adulation of a lord because of his rank or title ⟨the extent and prevalence of ~ in this country —W.M.Thackeray⟩

**lord ordinary** *n, pl* **lords ordinary** : one of the five judges constituting the Outer House of the Court of Session in Scotland

**lor·do·sis** \lȯ(ə)r'dōsəs, lȯ(ə)'-\ *n, pl* **lordo·ses** \-,sēz\ [NL, fr. Gk *lordōsis*, fr. *lordos* bent backward + *-ōsis* -osis; akin to OE *belyrtan* to deceive, MHG *lürzen* to deceive, *lerz, lurz* left, located on the left side, ScGael *lorcach* lame] **1 :** abnormally exaggerated forward curvature of the spine — opposed to *kyphosis* **2 :** the state of one affected with lordosis

**lor·dot·ic** \-'däd·ik, -ätik\ *adj* [fr. *lordosis*, after such pairs as E *hypnosis: hypnotic*] : of or relating to lordosis

**lord president** *n, pl* **lord presidents** **1 :** LORD PRESIDENT OF THE COUNCIL **2 :** the presiding officer of the Court of Session in Scotland — compare JUSTICE GENERAL

**lord president of the council :** a British officer of state who has only nominal official duties as presiding member of the Privy Council in the United Kingdom but who is often made a member of the cabinet and entrusted with special functions

**lord privy seal** *n* : a British officer of state who has only nominal official duties as custodian of the privy seal but who is often made a member of the cabinet and entrusted with special functions

**lord proprietor** *or* **lord proprietary** *n, pl* **lords proprietors** *or* **lords proprietary** : a person granted a royal charter for the establishment and government of an American colony in the 17th century

**lord provost** *n* : the chief magistrate of a large city in Scotland

**lord rector** *n* : the titular head of a Scottish university — compare CHANCELLOR 2a

**lord register** *n* : LORD CLERK REGISTER

**lords** *pl of* LORD, *pres 3d sing of* LORD

**lords-and-ladies** \'=ˈ==\ *n pl but sing or pl in constr* **1 :** CUCKOOPINT **2 :** JACK-IN-THE-PULPIT 1

**lord's day** *n, usu cap L & often cap D* [ME *Lordes day*, trans. of LL *dominica dies*, trans. of Gk *kyriakē hēmera;* fr. the Christian belief that Christ arose from the dead on Sunday] : SUNDAY ⟨nobody has ever . . . knitted a stitch in this house on the *Lord's day* —Ellen Glasgow⟩

**lord·ship** \'lȯ(ə)rd,ship, -ȯ(ə)d-\ *n* [ME, fr. OE *hlāfordscipe*, fr. *hlāford* lord + *-scipe* -ship — more at LORD] **1 a :** the rank or dignity of a lord **b :** the authority or power of a lord : DOMINION, SOVEREIGNTY ⟨the ~ of God over time —F.V. Filson⟩ ⟨this claim to racial ~ —*Times Lit. Supp.*⟩ **2 :** the domain or territory belonging to or under the jurisdiction of a lord : SEIGNIORY ⟨wandered from ~ to ~ and country to country —A.R.Wagner⟩ **3 a :** a royalty on minerals **b :** a royalty on the sales of books

**lords ordainers** *n pl* : ORDAINERS

**lord spiritual** *n, pl* **lords spiritual** [ME *lord spirituel*] : an English bishop or archbishop who is a member of the House of Lords — compare LORD TEMPORAL

**lord's room** *n* : a box for spectators of rank at the back of and overlooking the stage of an Elizabethan theater

**lord's supper** *n, usu cap L&S* [ME *Lordis sopere*, trans. of LL *dominica cena*, trans. of Gk *kyriakon deipnon*] : EUCHARIST 1a

**lord's table** *n, usu cap L & often cap T* [trans. of Gk *trapeza Kyriou*] : ALTAR 2a

**lord steward of the household :** the highest officer of the royal household of England who is a peer and privy councilor, presides at the Green Cloth, and has charge of the hall, kitchen, pantry, ewery, cellars, and almonry

**lord temporal** *n, pl* **lords temporal** [ME *lord temporel*] : a member of the House of Lords who is not an ecclesiastic ⟨in the fifteenth century the lords spiritual outnumbered the *lords temporal* —F.A.Ogg & Harold Zink⟩ — compare LORD SPIRITUAL

**lord treasurer** *n* : LORD HIGH TREASURER OF ENGLAND

**lord trier** *n, pl* **lords triers** : a member of the House of Lords sitting in judgment on a peer

**lordy** \'lȯ(ə)rdē, -ȯ(ə)dē, -di\ *interj* [¹*lord* + *-y*] — used to express surprise, astonishment, or strength of feeling

**¹lore** \'lō(ə)r, -ȯ(ə)r, -ōə, -ȯ(ə)\ *n* -S [ME, fr. OE *lār*; akin to OHG *lēra* doctrine, OE *leornian* to learn — more at LEARN] **1** *archaic* : something that is taught : LESSON, DOCTRINE, INSTRUCTION ⟨men admire virtue who follow not her ~ —John Milton⟩ ⟨we have learnt a different ~ —S.T.Coleridge⟩ **2 :** something that is learned: **a :** knowledge gained through study ⟨have plied their book diligently and know all about some one branch or another of accepted ~ —R.L.Stevenson⟩ **b :** knowledge or wisdom gained through experience ⟨learned for themselves the ~ of swift hunting in the dusk —Alan Devoe⟩ ⟨skilled in the ~ of frocks —Arnold Bennett⟩ **c :** traditional and unscientific knowledge or belief transmitted usu. by word of mouth ⟨provides ~ about words which is as pleasant as it is unreliable —Charlton Laird⟩ **3 a :** a body of knowledge relating to a particular field of learning ⟨using anatomical and physiological ~ —John Dewey⟩ ⟨basic in all modern attitudes toward earth ~ —K.F.Mather⟩ **b :** a body of traditions relating to a person, institution, or place ⟨lectured on Scottish ~ —Ashley Halsey⟩ ⟨the human and historical values in purely local ~ —John Bakeless⟩ **syn** see KNOWLEDGE

**²lore** \"\ *n* -S [NL *lorum*, fr. L, strap; akin to Gk *eulēra* reins, Arm *lar* rope, and prob. to Gk *eilein* to wind, roll — more at VOLUBLE] **1 a :** the space between the eye and bill in a bird **b :** the corresponding region in a reptile or fish **2 :** the anterior part of the gena of an insect

**¹lo·re·al** \'lōrēəl, -ȯr-\ *adj* [irreg. fr. ²*lore* + *-al*] : LORAL

**²loreal** \"\ *n* -S : a scale lying between the nasal and the eye of a snake

**lorel** *n* -S [ME, fr. *loren* (past part. of *lesen* to lose), fr. OE, past part. of *lēosan* to lose — more at LOSE] *obs* : a worthless person

**lore·lei** \'lȯrə,lī, 'lär-, 'lōr-\ *n* -S *usu cap* [after the *Lorelei*, siren of German legend said to inhabit the Lorelei rock on the right bank of the Rhine south of Koblenz and to entice boatmen to their destruction by her beauty and her singing] : SIREN 2 ⟨art is a temptation, a seduction, a *Lorelei* —H.L. Mencken⟩

**lore·less** \'lō(ə)rləs, -ȯ(ə)r-, -ōə-, -ȯ(ə)\ *adj, archaic* : lacking learning or knowledge

**lo·rentz-fitzgerald contraction** \'lȯr,en(t)s-\ *n, usu cap L&F&G* [after Hendrik A. *Lorentz* †1928 Du. physicist and George F. *FitzGerald* †1901 Irish physicist] : FITZGERALD CONTRACTION

**lorentz transformation** *n, usu cap L* : the transformation of a physical formula applicable to a phenomenon as observed by one observer so as to apply to the same phenomenon as observed by another observer in uniform motion relative to the first in accordance with the theory of relativity

**lo·renz curve** \'lȯr,en(t)s-\ *n, usu cap L* [prob. after Charlotte *Lorenz* *b*1895 Ger. statistician] : a curve formed by plotting the cumulative distribution of the amount of a variable against the cumulative frequency distribution of the individuals having the amount (as for indicating the degree of concentration of salary income among a number of individuals)

**lo·rette** \lə'ret, lō-\ *n* -S [F, fr. Notre Dame de *Lorette*, section of Paris] : a French courtesan esp. of the Second Empire period ⟨a sumptuous scene where ~*s*, actresses, respectable women . . . could satisfy their curiosity as to each other —Arnold Bennett⟩

**lorette pruning system** *n, usu cap L* [after Louis *Lorette* †1925 Fr. horticulturist who originated it] : a system of summer pruning of fruit trees to encourage the development of fruiting spurs

**lo·ret·to·ite** \lə'red·ə,wīt\ *n* -S [*Loretto*, Tennessee + E *-ite*] : a mineral $Pb_7O_6Cl_2(?)$ consisting of a lead oxychloride occurring in honey-yellow bladed aggregates (hardness 3, sp. gr. 7.6)

**lo·ret·to nun** \lə'red·(,)ō-\ *n, usu cap L* [fr. *Loreto*, city in Italy famous for its Holy House, said to have been the home of the Virgin Mary in Nazareth] : a member of a congregation of religious women founded by Mary Teresa Ball near Dublin, Ireland, in 1822 — called also *Lady of Loretto*

**l organism** *n, usu cap L* : L-FORM

**lor·gnette** \lȯr'n(y)et\ *n* -S [F, fr. *lorgner* to take a sidelong look at (fr. MF, fr. *lorgne* cross-eyed) + *-ette*] : a pair of eyeglasses or opera glasses with a handle

**lor·gnon** \lȯrn'yōⁿ\ *n* -S [F, fr. *lorgner*] : LORGNETTE ⟨aped the city lady's use of a ~ by looking through a doughnut stuck on a fork —Sinclair Lewis⟩

lorgnette

**lo·ri** \'lōrē\ *n* -S [modif. of F *loris*] : LORIS

**lo·ri·ca** \lə'rīkə\ *n, pl* **lori·cae** \-ī,sē\ [L, fr. *lorum* strap — more at LORE] **1 :** a Roman cuirass of leather or metal **2** [NL, fr. L] : a hard protective case or shell (as of a rotifer) **3** [NL, fr. L] : the cell wall or two valves of a diatom

**lor·i·car·ia** \,lȯrə'ka(a)rēə\ *n, cap* [NL, fr. LL *loricaria*, fem. of *loricarius* of a cuirass, fr. L *lorica* cuirass + *-arius* -ary] : a genus (the type of the family Loricariidae) of catfishes

**lor·i·car·i·an** \ˌ==ˈka(a)rēən\ *adj or n* [NL *Loricaria* + E *-an*] : LORICARIID

**¹lor·i·car·i·id** \-rēəd\ *adj* [NL *Loricariidae*] : of or relating to the family Loricariidae

**²loricariid** \"\ *n* -S [NL *Loricariidae*] : a catfish of the family Loricariidae

**lor·i·ca·ri·idae** \,==kə'rīə,dē\ *n pl*, [NL, fr. *Loricaria*, type genus + *-idae*] : a family of small So. American armored catfishes having the sides and back covered with angular bony plates, the air bladder with a bony capsule, and the mouth small and with thick fringed lips — **lor·i·car·i·oid** \ˌ==ˈka(a)rē,ȯid\ *adj or n*

**¹lor·i·ca·ta** \\,lȯrə'kād·ə, -ād·ə\\ *n pl, cap* [NL, fr. L, neut. pl. of *loricatus*] : any of several groups of animals with a lorica (as the armadillos or the loricate rotifers)

**²loricata** \\"\\ *n pl, cap* [NL, fr. L, neut. pl. of *loricatus*] : an order of large long-tailed reptiles (as alligators, crocodiles, gavials) having four limbs adapted to swimming or walking, a tough skin stiffened with bony plates and horny epidermal scales, teeth implanted in sockets and confined to the margins of the jaws, the quadrate bone immovably fixed to the skull, and the heart completely four-chambered

**³loricata** \\"\\ [NL, fr. L, neut. pl. of *loricatus*] *syn of* AMPHINEURA

**⁴loricata** \\"\\ [NL, fr. L, neut. pl. of *loricatus*] *syn of* PALINURA

**¹lor·i·cate** \\'lȯrə,kāt, *usu* -ād·+V\\ *vt* -ED/-ING/-S [L *loricatus*, past part. of *loricare* to arm with a cuirass, fr. *lorica* cuirass, lorica] : to enclose in or cover with a protecting substance

**²lor·i·cate** \\- kət, -,kāt, *usu* -d·+V\\ *or* **lor·i·cat·ed** \\'⸗⸗,kād·əd, -ātəd\\ *adj* [L *loricatus*] **1** : having a lorica **2** [NL *Loricata*] : of or relating to the Loricata

**³loricate** \\"\\ *n* -S [NL *Loricata*] : a loricate animal

**lor·i·ca·ti** \\,⸗⸗'kād,ī\\ [NL, fr. L, masc. pl. of *loricatus*] *syn of* ²LORICATA

**lor·i·ca·tion** \\,⸗⸗'kāshən\\ *n* -S [L *lorication-, loricatio*, fr. *loricatus* + *-ion-, -io* -ion] **1** : the quality or state of having a lorica **2** : a loricate covering

**lor·i·keet** \\'lȯrə,kēt\\ *n* -S [*lory* + *-keet* (as in *parrakeet*)] : any of numerous small arboreal usu. brush-tongued parrots that are found mostly in Australasia and that feed largely upon the nectar of flowers

**lor·i·let** \\'lȯrə,let\\ *n* -S [*lory* + *-let*] : a small short-tailed parrot of New Guinea and northern Australia that is dark green with yellow flanks and red and blue markings on the head — called also *fig parrot*

**lor·i·mer** \\'lȯrəmə(r)\\ *or* **lor·i·ner** \\-rənə(r)\\ *n* -S [ME *lorimer, loriner*, fr. OF *lormier, lorenier*, fr. *lorain* strap holding a horse's saddle (fr. LL *loramentum* harness, straps, fr. L *lorum* strap + *-mentum* -ment) + *-ier* -er] : a maker of bits, spurs, and metal mountings for bridles and saddles

**lor·i·ot** \\'lȯrēət, -ē,ō\\ *n* -S [F, fr. MF, alter. of *loriol*, fr. *l'oriol* the loriot, the oriole, fr. OF, fr. *l'* the (contr. of *le*, def. art., the, fr. L *ille* that one, that) + *oriol* loriot, oriole — more at LARIAT, ORIOLE] : the golden oriole of Europe

**lo·ris** \\'lōrəs, *in sense 1* " *or* lō'rē\\ *n* [F, perh. fr. obs. D *loeris* booby, simpleton] **1** -ES : either of two small nocturnal slow-moving lemurs: **a** : a slim-bodied lemur (*Loris gracilis*) of southern India and Ceylon — called also *slender loris* **b** : a stockier heavier-limbed lemur (*Bradicebus tardigradus*) of India and the East Indies that has a dusky dorsal stripe — called also *slow loris* **2** *cap* [NL, fr. F] : a genus (the type of the family Lorisidae) that comprises the slender loris — **lo·ri·sid** \\'lōrəsəd\\ *adj or n*

**lo·ris·i·dae** \\lə'risə,dē\\ *n pl, cap* [NL, fr. *Loris*, type genus + *-idae*] : a family of lemurs comprising the lorises and related forms (as the galagos and pottos)

**lo·ris·i·form** \\-fȯrm\\ *adj* [NL *Lorisiformes*] : resembling a loris

**lo·ris·i·for·mes** \\⸗,⸗⸗'fȯr,mēz\\ *n pl, cap* [NL, fr. *Loris* + *-iformes*] *in some classifications* : a division of Lemuroidea comprising the lorises and related forms

**lor·mery** \\'lȯrmərē\\ *n* -ES [ME *lormerie*, fr. MF, fr. OF, fr. *lormier* lorimer + *-ie* -y] *archaic* : metalware made by lorimers

**lorn** \\'lȯ(ə)rn, -ȯ(ə)n\\ *adj* [ME, fr. *loren*, past part. of *lesen* to lose] **1** *archaic* : LOST, RUINED **2 a** : left alone : ABANDONED, FORSAKEN ⟨thus to be cast out, thus ~ to die —John Keats⟩ ⟨one large brass saucepan lay ~ near the doorstep —Arnold Bennett⟩ **b** : DESOLATE, LONELY ⟨never vaunted her ~ condition —Dorothy Parker⟩ **syn** see ALONE

**lorn·ness** \\'⸗nəs\\ *n* -ES : the quality or state of being lorn

**lo·ro** \\'lōr(,)ō\\ *n* -S [AmerSp, fr. Sp, parrot, prob. fr. Carib *loro, roro*] : PARROT FISH

**lorraine cross** *n, usu cap L* : CROSS OF LORRAINE

**lor·rain·er** \\lə'rānə(r), lō'-,lō'-\\ *n* -S *usu cap* [*Lorraine*, region in western Europe + E *-er*] : a native or inhabitant of Lorraine

**lor·rain·ese** \\lə,rā'nēz, ¦lō,r-, -ēs\\ *adj, usu cap* [*Lorraine* + E *-ese*] **1** : of, relating to, or characteristic of Lorraine **2** : of, relating to, or characteristic of the people of Lorraine

**lor·ry** \\'lȯrē, 'lär-, -ri\\ *n* -ES [prob. fr. ²*lurry*] **1 a** : a large low horse-drawn wagon without sides and with a platform that slightly overhangs the four small heavy wheels **b** *Brit* : MOTORTRUCK; *esp* : one with low or open sides and sometimes a canvas cover **2** : any of various trucks running on rails: as **a** *Brit* : a light easily movable flatcar for the use of workmen on railroads **b** : LARRY

**lorry-hop** \\'⸗⸗,⸗\\ *vi, Brit* : to hitchhike esp. on lorries

**lo·rum** \\'lōrəm, 'lȯr-\\ *n, pl* **lo·ra** \\-rə\\ [NL, fr. L, strap — more at LORE] **1** : ²LORE **2 a** : a transverse piece in the proboscis of a bee in which the base of the submentum rests **b** : a similar structure in other insects **c** : an elongated sclerite in the dorsal wall of the pedicel of a spider

**lo·ry** \\'lōrē\\ *n* -ES [Malay *luri, nuri*] : any of numerous parrots of Australia, New Guinea, and the adjacent islands that belong mostly to the genera *Domicella, Trichoglossus, Chalcopsitta*, and *Eos*, often have the tongue papillose at the tip and the mandibles less toothed than in other parrots, and feed mostly on soft fruits and the nectar of flowers

**los·able** *also* **lose·able** \\'lüzəbəl\\ *adj* : capable of being lost — **los·able·ness** *n* -ES

**los angeleno** \\(,)lō,s+_-\\ *also* **los an·ge·le·an** \\(,)lō,sanjə'lēən *also* -aŋgə'l-\\ *n, cap L&A* [*los angeleno* fr. AmerSp *los angeleño*, fr. *Los Angeles*, California + Sp *-eño* (suffix added to place names to form names of inhabitants); *los angelean* fr. *Los Angeles*, California + E *-an*] : ANGELENO

**los an·ge·les** \\lō'sanjələs, -saan- *also* lō'- *or* lə'- *or* -saŋ(g)əl- *or* -saiŋ- *sometimes* -jə,lēz *or* -gə,lēz\\ *adj, usu cap L&A* : of or from the city of Los Angeles, Calif. ⟨a *Los Angeles* freeway⟩ : of the kind or style prevalent in Los Angeles

**lösch·ia** \\'lərshēə, 'lesh-\\ [NL, fr. F. *Lösch*, 19th cent. Ger. zoologist + NL *-ia*] *syn of* ENTAMOEBA

**lo·schmidt number** \\'lō,shmit-\\ *n, usu cap L* [after Joseph *Loschmidt* †1895 Austrian physicist] : the number of molecules per unit volume of an ideal gas at 0°C and a pressure of 1 atmosphere, its value for 1 cubic centimeter being about 2.7× $10^{19}$; *sometimes* : AVOGADRO NUMBER

**lose** \\'lüz\\ *vb* **lost**; **lost** \\'lȯst *also* 'läst\\ **losing**; **loses** [alter. (prob. influenced in pronunciation by ¹*loose*) of ME *losen* to lose, get lost, perish, destroy, fr. OE *losian* to get lost, perish, destroy, fr. *los* destruction; akin to OE *lēosan* to lose, OHG *forlust* destruction, ON *losa* to loosen, Goth *fralusnan* to perish, L *luere* to atone for, Gk *lyein* to unbind, release, dissolve, Skt *lunāti* he cuts off] *vt* **1** : to bring to destruction : RUIN, DESTROY ⟨what to ourselves in passion we propose, the passion ending doth our purpose ~ —Shak.⟩ — now used chiefly in passive constructions ⟨ship was *lost* on the reef⟩; *specif* : DAMN ⟨if he shall gain the whole world and ~ his own soul —Mt 16:26 (AV)⟩ **2** : to fail to keep at hand or accessible : miss from one's possession : miss from its customary or supposed place ⟨*lost* his gloves⟩ ⟨little Bopeep has *lost* her sheep⟩ **3 a** : to suffer deprivation of : part with esp. in an unforeseen or accidental manner ⟨~ a leg in an auto crash⟩ ⟨~ savings in a poor investment⟩ ⟨*lost* his job⟩ **b** : to become deprived of or lacking in (a quality) ⟨has *lost* her beauty⟩ ⟨if salt has *lost* its taste, how can its saltness be restored —Mt 5:13 (RSV)⟩ ⟨the ceremony has *lost* its original meaning⟩ **4 a** : to suffer deprivation through the death or removal of or final separation from (a person) ⟨*lost* a son in the war⟩ ⟨village *losing* its young men through emigration⟩ **b** : to fail to keep (a patient) from dying ⟨have *lost* few pneumonia cases since penicillin came into use⟩ **c** : to become deprived of the services or useful presence of (as soldiers) through death, injury, desertion, capture ⟨the victors *lost* more men than the defeated⟩ **d** : to fail to keep control of or allegiance of ⟨~ votes⟩ ⟨the sect is *losing* its younger members⟩ **5 a** : to fail to use : be unable to make proper use of : let slip by : WASTE ⟨~ time in hunting for mislaid tools⟩ : MISS ⟨hated to ~ a day's fishing⟩ ⟨*lost* no opportunity to point out faults⟩ ⟨~ the tide⟩ ⟨sarcasm was *lost* on him⟩ **b** : to fail to win, gain, or obtain ⟨~ a prize⟩ ⟨~ a hooked fish⟩ ⟨~ a contest⟩ ⟨~ a lawsuit⟩ : undergo defeat in ⟨*lost* every battle but the last⟩ **c** : to fail to catch with the senses or the mind ⟨*lost* part of what he said⟩ **6** : to cause the loss of ⟨one careless statement *lost* him the election⟩ ⟨leading from the king will ~ two tricks⟩ **7** : to fail to keep, sustain, or maintain ⟨*lost* his balance⟩ ⟨the writer seems to have *lost* his touch⟩ ⟨*lost* his temper⟩ ⟨~ interest in a game⟩ ⟨~ poise⟩ ⟨*lost* his footing on the path and fell⟩ ⟨~ caste⟩ ⟨*lost* count of the minutes⟩ **8 a** : to cause to miss one's way or bearings ⟨you could not ~ him anywhere in London⟩ ⟨soon *lost* himself in the maze of streets⟩ **b** : to make (oneself) withdrawn from immediate reality ⟨*lost* himself in daydreaming⟩ **9 a** : to wander or go astray from : miss so as not to be able to find ⟨*lost* his way⟩ ⟨the ships *lost* each other in the fog⟩ **b** : to draw away from : shake off : OUTSTRIP ⟨*lost* his pursuers⟩ **10** : to fail to keep in sight or in mind ⟨*lost* the thief in the crowded street⟩ ⟨the fielder *lost* the ball in the sun⟩ ⟨an intention that was soon *lost*⟩ **11** : to free oneself from : get rid of ⟨dieting to ~ weight⟩ ⟨~ a cold⟩ **12** : to make (itself) hidden or obscured ⟨the river ~*s* itself in the marshes⟩ ~ *vi* **1** : to undergo deprivation of something of value ⟨investors *lost* heavily⟩ or deterioration of a valuable quality ⟨the story ~*s* considerably in translation⟩ **2** : to undergo defeat : fail to win a goal or a contest ⟨able to ~ with good grace⟩ ⟨better to have loved and *lost* than never to have loved at all —Alfred Tennyson⟩ **3** *of a timepiece* : to run slow — **lose ground** : to become at a disadvantage : fall behind : fail to advance or improve — **lose one's cud** : to cease ruminating : refuse feed — **lose one's heart** : to fall in love ⟨*lost her heart* to a charming ne'er-do-well⟩

**lo·sel** \\'lōzəl\\ *n* -S [ME, fr. *losen* (past part. of *lesen* to lose), alter. of *loren* (past part. of *lesen* to lose), fr. OE, past part. of *lēosan* to lose — more at LOSE] : a worthless person

**lo·sel·ry** \\-rē\\ *n* -ES *archaic* : the character or action of a losel

**lose out** *vi* : to fail to win in competition : fail to receive an expected reward or gain ⟨afraid of *losing out* to more unscrupulous competitors⟩ ⟨*lost out* in the hurdles⟩

**los·er** \\'lüzə(r)\\ *n* -S : one that loses: as **a** : one that consistently loses or is likely to lose or is behind (as in a game or competition) ⟨a cheerful ~⟩ **b** *Brit* : LOSING HAZARD **c** : a card that may be expected to lose a trick or that does lose a trick in bridge ⟨discarded his club ~*s* on the established spades in dummy⟩ **d** : one that is convicted of a penal offense

**loses** *pres 3d sing of* LOSE

**lo·sey·ite** \\'lōzē,īt\\ *n* -S [Samuel R. *Losey* †1906? Am. mineral collector + E *-ite*] : a mineral $(Mn,Zn)_7(CO_3)_2(OH)_{10}$ composed of a basic carbonate of manganese and zinc

**¹losh** \\'läsh\\ *n* -ES *often attrib* [Russ *los'* elk; akin to OHG *elaho* elk — more at ELK] **1** : elk hide **2** : a hide dressed only with oil ⟨~ leather⟩

**²losh** \\"\\ *interj* [euphemism for *lord*] — used as a mild oath in Scots dialect

**losing** *adj* [fr. pres. part. of *lose*] : likely to result in failure or defeat ⟨~ strategy⟩ ⟨fighting a ~ battle⟩ : likely to lose : causing defeat ⟨~ cards⟩ ⟨three ~ tricks in his hand⟩

**losing hazard** *n* : the pocketing of the cue ball after it strikes an object ball in English billiards

**¹loss** \\'lȯs *also* 'läs\\ *n* -ES [ME *los*, prob. back-formation fr. *lost*, past part. of *losen* to lose, get lost, perish, destroy — more at LOST] **1 a** : the act or fact of losing : failure to keep possession : DEPRIVATION ⟨precautions against ~ or theft of property⟩ ⟨~ of a leg⟩ ⟨~ of sight⟩ ⟨~ of reputation⟩ ⟨~ of caste⟩ ⟨virtual ~ of three divisions of infantry⟩ **b** : the harm or privation resulting from losing or being separated from something or someone ⟨bore up bravely under the ~ of both parents⟩ ⟨the explosion caused a temporary ~ of hearing⟩ ⟨embittered by the ~ of his wife's affection⟩ **c** : an instance of losing ⟨his retirement was a serious ~ to the company⟩ ⟨her death was a ~ to all who knew her⟩ **d** *obs* : LACK, DEFAULT **2** : a person or thing or an amount that is lost: as **a losses** *pl* : killed, wounded, or captured soldiers **b** : power or energy wasted in a machine, apparatus, or system ⟨friction ~⟩ ⟨heat ~ due to faulty insulation⟩ **c** (1) : the power diminution of a circuit element corresponding to conversion of electric power into heat by resistance (2) : ATTENUATION **3 a** : the act or fact of failing to gain, win, obtain, or utilize ⟨~ of a battle⟩ ⟨~ of opportunity⟩ ⟨~ of a game⟩ ⟨~ of a night's sleep⟩; *specif* : an amount by which the cost of an article or service exceeds the selling price — opposed to *profit* ⟨forced to sell all the stock at a ~⟩ ⟨railroad claimed to be operating at a ~⟩ **b** : a yardage disadvantage in football that results when an offensive play ends behind the line of scrimmage **4** : decrease in amount, magnitude, or degree ⟨temperature ~⟩ ⟨~ in altitude⟩ — opposed to *gain* **5 a** : the state or fact of being destroyed or placed beyond recovery : DESTRUCTION, RUIN, PERDITION ⟨quitted all to save a world from utter ~ —John Milton⟩ ⟨~ of a ship with all hands⟩ ⟨~ of life in war⟩ **b** *obs* : a cause of ruin or destruction **6** : the amount of an insured's financial detriment due to the occurrence of a stipulated contingent event (as death, injury, destruction, or damage) in such a manner as to charge the insurer with a liability under the terms of the policy — **at a loss** : unable to determine : PUZZLED, UNCERTAIN ⟨*at a loss* for a remedy⟩ ⟨*at a loss* for words to describe the situation⟩ — **for a loss** *adv* : into a state of depression, distress, or exhaustion ⟨at times gets me down and throws me *for a loss* —Christian Gauss⟩

**²löss** *var of* LOESS

**loss-and-gain account** \\'⸗⸗'⸗-\\ *n* : INCOME ACCOUNT 2

**loss constant** *n* : an amount added to an insurance premium (as in a workmen's compensation policy) in consideration of the high loss ratio usu. sustained on small risks

**los·sen rearrangement** \\'läs'n-\\ *n, usu cap L* [prob. after Wilhelm *Lossen* †1906 Ger. chemist] : the conversion of a hydroxamic acid RCONHOH to an amine $RNH_2$, a urea $(RNH)_2CO$, a urethane $RNHCOOC_2H_5$, or a similar derivative by way of an intermediate isocyanate RNCO

**loss·er** \\'lȯsə(r) *also* 'läs-\\ *n* -S [¹*loss* + *-er*] : an element inserted into an electric circuit (as of an amplifier) for providing impedance so as to prevent resonant electric oscillation

**loss factor** *n* **1** : the ratio of the average to the maximum power loss in a circuit variably loaded over a given period **2** : the product of the dielectric constant of a capacitor dielectric by the alternating-current power factor

**loss leader** *n* : an article sold at a loss in order to draw customers

**loss·less** \\'lȯsləs *also* 'läs-\\ *adj* : being without loss : suffering no loss

**loss ratio** *n* : the ratio between insurance losses incurred and premiums earned during a given period

**loss reserve** *n* : an insurance company's reserve representing the discounted value of future payments to be made on losses which have already occurred

**lossy** \\'lȯsē *also* 'läsē\\ *adj* [¹*loss* + *-y*] **1** : of, relating to, or constituting a material capable of damping out an unwanted mode of oscillation and having little effect on a desired mode **2** : highly dissipative of electrical energy ⟨a ~ medium⟩

**lost** *adj* [fr. past part. of *lose*] **1 a** : not made use of : WASTED ⟨~ hours⟩ : MISSED ⟨~ opportunity⟩ **b** : not gained or won ⟨~ battle⟩ ⟨~ race⟩ **c** : not claimed : FORFEITED ⟨~ annuity⟩ ⟨~ option⟩ **2 a** : having wandered from the path : unable to find the way ⟨~ child⟩ **b** : no longer visible ⟨the plane was soon ~ in the distance⟩ ⟨~ in the crowd⟩ **c** : lacking assurance or self-confidence : uncertain as to direction or location : BEWILDERED ⟨felt ~ on the first day on the job⟩ : HELPLESS ⟨~ without his glasses⟩ ⟨only the intellectually ~ who ever argue —Oscar Wilde⟩ **3** : ruined or destroyed physically or morally : DAMNED ⟨~ ship⟩ ⟨~ soul⟩ : DESPERATE ⟨wild ~ manner of occasionally clasping his head in his hands —Charles Dickens⟩ ⟨crying out such ~ and terrible words —Virginia Woolf⟩ **4 a** : parted with ⟨~ limb⟩ : gone out of one's possession or control : MISLAID ⟨~ book⟩ **b** : no longer possessed ⟨~ honor⟩ ⟨~ reputation⟩ ⟨~ memory⟩ **c** : no longer known ⟨~ tunnel⟩ ⟨~ city⟩ or practiced ⟨~ art⟩ **5 a** : taken away or beyond reach or attainment : DENIED — used with *to* ⟨Asia Minor and the Balkans went the way of other regions ~ to the faith —Kemp Malone⟩ ⟨his career is ~ to history after that date⟩ **b** : HARDENED, INSENSIBLE — used with *to* ⟨~ to all sense of honor⟩ ⟨~ to shame⟩ **6** : affected by or occupied with something so as to be unaware of one's surroundings : RAPT ⟨~ in revery⟩ ⟨~ in admiration⟩ **7** *of a golf ball* : that cannot be found within five minutes

**lost ball** *n* : a bowled ball in cricket that has been hit by a batsman and cannot be found or recovered by the fielding side counting six or more runs to the batsman's credit

**lost cause** *n* : a cause that has lost all prospect of success ⟨*lost cause* of the Southern Confederacy⟩ ⟨a frequent champion of *lost causes*⟩

**lost-color process** \\'⸗¦⸗⸗-\\ *n* : a technique of pottery decoration found in Central and So. America and involving the covering of areas with wax before dipping in dye so that on subsequent firing the waxed areas lose the applied color and revert to the original color

**lost motion** *n* **1** : the lag between the motion of a driver and that of a follower in a mechanism due to yielding or looseness **2** : inefficient or poorly directed expenditure of energy or time

**lost·ness** *n* -ES : the quality or state of being lost ⟨that ~ which is the extreme product of individualism —T.L.Cook⟩

**lost river** *n* : a surface stream that flows into an underground passageway

**lost-wax process** \\'⸗¦⸗-\\ *n* [*lost-wax* trans. of F *cire perdue*] : CIRE PERDUE

**¹lot** \\'lät, *usu* -äd·+V\\ *n* -S [ME, fr. OE *hlot*; akin to OHG *luz* share of land, ON *hlutr* lot, share, *hlautr*, Goth *hlauts* lot, Lith *kliudyti* to cause to hook on, and perh. to L *claudere* to close — more at CLOSE] **1** : an object (as a piece of wood, pebble, die, straw) used as one of the counters in determining a question by the chance fall or choice of one or more of them — see SORTILEGE **2 a** : the use of lots or an equivalent process (as counting off) as a means of deciding something ⟨one was chosen by ~ to represent the group⟩ **b** : the choice resulting from such process ⟨the ~ fell on the youngest member⟩ **3 a** : something that comes to or happens to one upon whom a choice by lot has fallen : SHARE, PART, ALLOTMENT ⟨the will provided for equal ~*s* for all the children⟩ ⟨you have neither part nor ~ in this matter —Acts 8: 21 (RSV)⟩ **b** : one's way of life or one's share of worldly reward or privation determined by chance, fate, or divine providence : FORTUNE, DESTINY ⟨the ~ of man, to suffer and to die —Alexander Pope⟩ ⟨a policeman's ~ is not a happy one —W.S.Gilbert⟩ ⟨one of those women who have always been resigned to the limitations of their ~ —Nadine Gordimer⟩ **4** *obs* **a** : a customs fee : TAX, DUTY **5** *obs* **a** : a lottery prize **b** : a prizewinning lottery ticket **6 a** : an allotment or portion of land set aside for a special purpose ⟨each settler was awarded a ~⟩ ⟨pasture ~⟩ ⟨burial ~⟩ ⟨circus ~⟩ ⟨used-car ~⟩ **b** : a measured parcel of land having fixed boundaries and designated on a plot or survey ⟨farm cut up into house ~*s*⟩ ⟨building ~⟩ **c** : a parcel of land in fact used for, intended for, or appropriated to a common purpose ⟨manufacturing ~⟩ ⟨refuse ~⟩ **d** *chiefly North* : a small pasture **e** *chiefly South & Midland* : COW PEN, BARNYARD **f** : PARKING LOT **g** : a motion-picture studio and its adjoining property **7 a** : a number of units of an article ⟨stationery ~⟩ or a parcel of articles offered as one item (as in an auction sale) **b** : all the members of a present group, kind, or quantity — used with *the* ⟨one more suitcase to carry out and that is the ~⟩ ⟨when you've seen one you've seen the ~⟩ **8 a** : a number of associated persons : CREW, SET, CROWD ⟨got in with a hard-drinking poker-playing ~⟩ ⟨his wife's family were a queer and stubborn ~⟩ ⟨nothing but a ~ of busybodies⟩ ⟨not an honest man in the ~⟩ **b** : KIND, SORT ⟨stay away from him, he's a bad ~⟩ ⟨recruits were a sorry ~⟩ **9** : a considerable quantity or number : GREAT DEAL ⟨~ of money⟩ ⟨~ of trouble⟩ ⟨there are ~*s* of books on the subject⟩ — often used adverbially with *a* ⟨feels a ~ better now⟩ **syn** see FATE

**²lot** \\"\\ *vb* **lotted**; **lotted**; **lotting**; **lots** [ME *lotten*, fr. *lot*, n.] *vi* : to cast or draw lots ~ *vt* **1** : to form or divide into lots ⟨~ land⟩ ⟨~ fruit for market⟩ — often used with *out* ⟨~ out goods in parcels⟩ **2** : ALLOT, APPORTION **3** *obs* : to draw lots for — **lot on** *or* **lot upon** *now chiefly dial* : to count on : look forward to : EXPECT, PLAN

**lot** *abbr* lotion

**¹lo·ta** *or* **lo·tah** \\'lōd·ə, -ōtə\\ *n* -S [Hindi *lotā*] : a small usu. spherical water vessel of brass or copper used in India

**²lota** \\"\\ *n, cap* [NL, fr. F *lotte* burbot] : a genus of fishes (family Gadidae) consisting of the burbots

**lote** \\'lōt\\ *or* **lotebush** \\'⸗,⸗\\ *also* **lo·ti·bush** \\'lōd·ē,⸗\\ *or* **lotewood** \\'lōt·wu̇d\\ *n, pl* **lotes** *or* **lotebushes** [origin unknown] **1** a low spiny shrub (*Condalia obtusifolia*) of Mexico and southern Texas having edible fruit and roots from which a soap substitute is made — called also *Texas buckthorn* **2** : JUJUBE 2

**loth** *var of* LOATH

**lo·tha·rin·gian** \\,lōthə¦rinj(ē)ən\\ *adj, usu cap* [ML *Lotharingia* Lorraine, region in western Europe + E *-an*] : of or relating to Lorraine

**lo·thar·io** \\lō'tha(a)rē,ō, -ther-,-thār-,-thär-,-thȧr-\\ *n* -S *often cap* [after *Lothario*, seducer in the play *The Fair Penitent* (1703) by Nicholas Rowe †1718 Eng. dramatist] : a gay deceiver or seducer : LIBERTINE, RAKE

**lo·tic** \\'lōd·ik, -ōtik\\ *adj* [L *lotus* action of washing or bathing (fr. *lautus, lotus*, past part. of *lavere* to wash) + E *-ic*] : of, relating to, or living in actively moving water (as in stream currents or waves) — compare LENTIC

**lo·ti·form** \\'lōd·ə,fȯrm\\ *adj* [ISV *lotus* + *-iform*] : having the form of a lotus petal

**lo·tion** \\'lōshən\\ *n* -S [L *lotion-, lotio*, fr. *lautus, lotus* (past part. of *lavere* to wash) + *-ion-, -io* -ion — more at LYE] **1** : the act of washing : ABLUTION **2** : a liquid usu. aqueous medicinal preparation containing one or more insoluble substances and applied externally for skin disorders **3** : a liquid cosmetic preparation usu. containing alcohol and a cleansing, softening, or astringent agent and applied to the skin esp. of the face and hands ⟨hand ~⟩ ⟨after-shave ~⟩

**lo·tio ni·gra** \\'lōshē,ō'nīgrə\\ *n* [NL] : BLACK WASH 1

**lo·ti·um** \\'lōshēəm\\ *n* -S [L, urine, fr. *lautus, lotus*, past part. of *lavere* to wash] : urine formerly used as a cosmetic for the hair

**lot·ment** \\'lätmənt\\ *n* -S [²*lot* + *-ment*] *now dial* : an allotment of land

**lo·tong** \\'lō,tȯŋ\\ *or* **lu·tong** \\'lü,-\\ *n* -S [Malay *lotong*] : a common black langur (*Presbytis obscurus* or *P. maurus*) of southeastern Asia and the East Indies

**lo·toph·a·gi** \\lə'täfə,jī,lō'-\\ *n pl, sometimes cap* [L, legendary people who ate the lotus and encouraged travelers who visited them to do the same, fr. Gk *Lōtophagoi*, fr. *lōtos* lotus + *-phagoi* (pl. of *-phagos* -phagous)] : LOTUS-EATERS

**lo·toph·a·gous** \\-gəs\\ *adj* [*lotophagi* + *-ous*] : relating to or characteristic of lotus-eaters — **lo·toph·a·gous·ly** *adv*

**lo-trap** \\'lō+,-\\ *n* [alter. of *low* + *trap*] : LOW-HOUSE

**lots** \\'läts\\ *adv* [fr. pl. of ¹*lot*] : to or by a considerable number or amount : MUCH ⟨~ more fun⟩ ⟨feeling ~ better⟩

**lotted** *past of* LOT

**lot·ter** \\'läd·ə(r), -ätə-\\ *n* -S : one that separates into lots; *specif* : one that appraises merchandise to be auctioned and assembles it into salable lots

**lot·tery** \\'läd·ərē, -ätərē, -ä·trē, -ri\\ *n* -ES *often attrib* [MF *loterie*, fr. MD, fr. *lot* lot + *-erie* -ery (fr. OF); akin to OE *hlot* lot — more at *lot*] **1** : a scheme for the distribution of prizes by lot or chance; *esp* : a scheme by which prizes are distributed to the winners among those persons who have paid for a chance to win them usu. as determined by the numbers on tickets as drawn at random (as from a lottery wheel) — see DUTCH LOTTERY, INTEREST LOTTERY **2** : the occasion of selection of prizes by lot **3** : an event or affair whose outcome is or seems to be determined by chance ⟨regarded marriage as a ~⟩

**lottery bond** *n* : a bond issued by an interest lottery

**lottery wheel** *n* : a revolving drum or hollow cylinder in which lottery tickets are mixed and from which the winning numbers are drawn — called also *policy wheel*

**lotting** *pres part of* LOT

**lot·to** *also* **loto** \\'läd·,(,)ō, -ä(,)tō\\ *n* -S [F or It; F *loto*, fr. It *lotto* lotto, lottery, fr. F *lot* lot, share, fr. OF, of Gmc origin; akin to OE *hlot* lot — more at LOT] : a game played usu. for a pool with cards bearing rows of numbers in which a caller draws numbered counters from a stock and each player covers the corresponding numbers if they appear on his card, the winner being the one who first covers one complete row

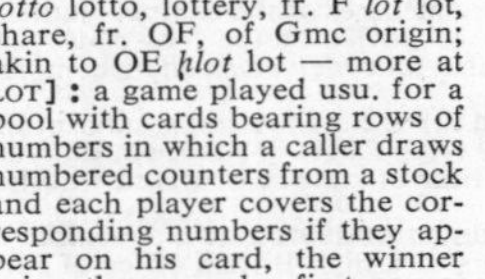

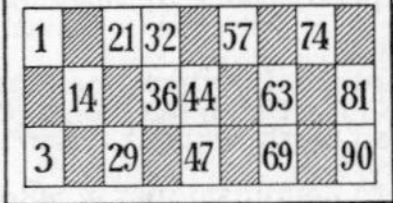

| 1 | 21 | 32 | | 57 | 74 | | | |
|---|---|---|---|---|---|---|---|---|
| | 14 | | 36 | 44 | | 63 | | 81 |
| 3 | | 29 | | 47 | | 69 | | 90 |

a card used in lotto

**lo·tu·ko** \\lə'tü(,)kō\\ *also* **la·tu·ka** \\lə'tükə\\ *n, pl* **lotuko** *or*

**lotukos** *usu cap* **1 a :** a group of Negro peoples east of the Nile in Southern Sudan **b :** a member of any of such peoples **2 :** the Nilotic language of the Lotuko peoples

**lo·tus** *also* **lo·tos** \'lōd·əs, -ōtəs\ *n* [L & Gk; L *lotus*, fr. Gk *lōtos*, fr. Heb *lōṭ* myrrh] **1** -ES **:** the fruit in legendary Greek history eaten by the Lotophagi and supposed to cause a state of dreamy content and complete forgetfulness of home and friends; *also* **:** the shrub bearing this fruit — see LOTUS TREE **2** -ES **a :** LOTUS TREE **b :** SWEET CLOVER **3** -ES **:** any of various water lilies including several represented in ancient Egyptian and Hindu art and religious symbolism: as **a :** INDIAN LOTUS; *broadly* **:** NELUMBO 2 **b :** EGYPTIAN LOTUS 1 **4** -ES **:** an ornament used in ancient decoration (as in Egyptian capitals) and generally asserted to have been suggested by the Egyptian lotus (sense 1) **5** [NL, fr. L] **a** *cap* **:** a genus of widely distributed upright herbs or subshrubs (family Leguminosae) with pinnate leaves and solitary, twin, or umbellate flowers **b** -ES **:** any plant of the genus *Lotus*

American lotus

**lotus bird** *n* **:** a jacana (*Irediparra gallinacea*) of Australia

**lotus-eater** *or* **lotos-eater** \'ˌ=ˌ==\ *n* [trans. of Gk *Lōtophagoi*] **:** one who gives himself up to indolence and daydreams ⟨a paradise for gourmets, *lotus-eaters*, and just plain tourists —T.H.Fielding⟩

**lotus eye** *n* **:** the eye (as of a Buddha) shaped or drawn in eastern art in the form of a lotus petal

**lo·tus·in** \'lōd·əsən\ *n* -S [NL *Lotus* + E *-in*] **:** a yellow crystalline cyanogenetic glucoside $C_{28}H_{31}NO_{16}$ obtained from a No. African leguminous plant (*Lotus arabicus*)

**lotus land** *n* **1 :** a place inducing dreaming and idleness **2 :** a state or an ideal marked by indolent self-indulgence and irresponsibility ⟨beguile the United States into living in a *lotus land* of isolation —M.W.Childs⟩

**lotus lily** *n* **:** WATER CHINQUAPIN

**lotus tree** *n* **:** any of several trees reputed to have furnished the lotus mentioned by the ancients: as **a :** a shrubby deciduous jujube tree (*Ziziphus lotus*) of the Mediterranean region that produces small yellow fruits **b :** a tall nettle tree (*Celtis australis*) of the same region that somewhat resembles a beech but produces a small sweet globose fruit **c :** an Asiatic persimmon (*Diospyros lotus*) that is sometimes cultivated for its small rounded yellow or purplish fruits; *also* **:** the common American persimmon (*D. virginiana*)

**louch** \'lau̇ch, 'lüch\ *vi* -ED/-ING/-S [origin unknown] *dial Brit* **:** SLOUCH

**louche** \'lüsh\ *adj* [F, lit., cross-eyed, squint-eyed, fr. L *luscus* one-eyed] **:** SQUINTING, OBLIQUE **:** DEVIOUS, PERVERSE, SINISTER ⟨you've got to keep yourself free of any suggestion of ~ behavior —Anthony West⟩

**lou·cheux** \lü'shō\ *n, pl* **loucheux** *usu cap* [F, fr. *louche*] **:** KUTCHIN 2

**¹loud** \'lau̇d\ *adj* -ER/-EST [ME, fr. OE *hlūd*; akin to OS *hlūd* loud, OHG *hlūt* loud, ON *hljōth* silence, attention, hearing, Goth *hliuma* ear, L *cluēre* to be named, be called, Gk *klytos* famous, Skt *śṛnoti* he hears] **1 a :** marked by intensity or volume of sound — opposed to *soft* ⟨where ears are willing, talk tends to be ~ and long —Aldous Huxley⟩ ⟨~ and protracted singing —John Burroughs⟩ **b :** producing a loud sound ⟨the marten was ~ beside them —David Walker⟩ **2 a :** CLAMOROUS, INSISTENT **:** NOISY, VEHEMENT, EMPHATIC ⟨giving ~ lip service . . . as a means of drowning the voice of conscience —B.G.Gallagher⟩ ⟨small but determinedly ~ groups are mistaken for vast multitudes and are causing irreparable harm —M.R.Cohen⟩ **b** *obs* **:** EVIDENT, MANIFEST, OBVIOUS — used chiefly of a lie **3 :** obtrusive or offensive in appearance or smell **:** violating taste or propriety **:** FLASHY, NOISOME, OBNOXIOUS ⟨came along in the ~*est* pinstripe suit in history —John O'Reilly⟩ ⟨a ~ fish smell which one night's hard rain hadn't even dented —Raymond Chandler⟩ ⟨he was stout, ~, red, bluff, and free from any drawback of delicacy —Charles Dickens⟩ **4 :** uttered with the normal speaking voice; *specif* **:** produced by vibration of the vocal cords ⟨~ vowels⟩ ⟨~ voiced consonants⟩ — compare ALOUD, OUT LOUD

**syn** LOUD, STENTORIAN, EARSPLITTING, HOARSE, RAUCOUS, STRIDENT, and STERTOROUS, all applying to sounds, agree in meaning great in volume or unpleasant in effect. LOUD suggests a volume above normal, sometimes suggesting vehemence or obtrusiveness ⟨a *loud* cry⟩ ⟨a *loud* blast on a trumpet⟩ ⟨*loud* demands for reform⟩ ⟨a *loud* and unpleasant person⟩ STENTORIAN, chiefly applying to voices, implies exceedingly great power and range ⟨a *stentorian* voice, husky from much bawling of orders —F. Tennyson Jesse⟩ ⟨a few words, rendered either completely inaudible or painfully *stentorian* according to the whim of the microphone —*Times Lit. Supp.*⟩ ⟨blowing his nose in *stentorian* tones —O.E. Rölvaag⟩ EARSPLITTING adds the idea of a physically oppressive loudness, esp. shrillness, as of screams or shrieks ⟨suddenly he trumpeted, an *earsplitting* sound in the close stall —W.V.T.Clark⟩ ⟨an *earsplitting* cry of terror⟩ HOARSE implies harshness, huskiness, or roughness of tone, sometimes suggesting an accompanying or causal loudness ⟨the *hoarse* growling of the mob —Kenneth Roberts⟩ ⟨voice came to my ears . . . tense and *hoarse* with an overmastering rage —Jack London⟩ ⟨the *hoarse* bellow of the bull whistle —*Amer. Guide Series: N.C.*⟩ RAUCOUS implies a loud, harsh, grating tone, esp. of voice, often implying rowdiness ⟨the voices often become *raucous* or shrill and any proper dignity of the spirit suffers —W.R.Benét⟩ ⟨music of the city, *raucous*, jazzy, witty, dramatic —Howard Hanson⟩ ⟨women . . . gathering along the platform with thin, bright, *raucous* laughter —William Faulkner⟩ ⟨the *raucous* vitality of a mining boomtown —Seth Agnew⟩ STRIDENT adds to RAUCOUS the idea of a rasping, discordant but insistent quality, esp. of voice ⟨scurrying traffic whose *strident* voice mingles whistle blasts with the hollow clang of bell buoys and the screams of softly wheeling gulls —*Amer. Guide Series: N.Y. City*⟩ ⟨a sort of a *strident*, metallic quality about her revealed in the high pitch of her voice —Claire Sterling & Max Ascoli⟩ ⟨her vocal attack often sounds *strident* and explosive —*Newsweek*⟩ STERTOROUS, usu. not applied to sounds made by the voice, suggests the loud snoring, or sounds like snoring made in breathing, esp. when it is difficult, by persons or animals in sleep, in a coma, or with marked asthmatic difficulties ⟨the *stertorous* breathing of the owl —Osbert Sitwell⟩ ⟨the horse is trembling . . . its breathing *stertorous* like groaning —William Faulkner⟩

**²loud** \"\ *adv* -ER/-EST [ME *loude*, fr. OE *hlūde*; akin to OS *hlūdo* loudly, OHG *hlūto*; derivative fr. the root of E *¹loud*] **:** with loud sound or offensive appearance, manner, or smell ⟨who screams ~*est* . . . when the dinner consists of canned tuna fish —A.C.Spectorsky⟩ ⟨Eskimo-tanned furs smell out ~, especially in a warm room —*Newsweek*⟩

**loud·en** \'lau̇dᵊn\ *vb* -ED/-ING/-S *vi* **:** to become loud **:** grow audible **:** intensify in sound ~ *vt* **:** to make loud **:** intensify the sound of

**lou·der·back** \'lau̇də(r),bak\ *n* [after George D. *Louderback* †1957 Am. geologist] **:** a tilted fault block capped by a lava flow

**loud-hailer** \'=ˌ==\ *n* **:** BULLHORN

**loud·ish** \'lau̇dish\ *adj* **:** rather loud

**loud·ly** *adv, sometimes* -ER/-EST [ME, fr. *¹loud* + *-ly*] **:** in a loud, noisy, or emphatic manner ⟨the large birds laughed so ~ that the goldfinch became annoyed —James Thurber⟩ ⟨the white man's examples . . . spoke to the Indians more ~ than words —*Amer. Guide Series: Minn.*⟩

**loudmouth** \'=ˌ=\ *n* **:** a foolish noisy person **:** BRAGGART ⟨why do you expect your children not to fall for the phony or the ~ —L. Ruth Middlebrook⟩

**loudmouthed** \'=ˌ=\ *adj* **:** given to loud and idle talk **:** noisily offensive ⟨his ~ tabloids spiel sex, crime, and the workingman's cause —*Time*⟩

**loud·ness** *n* -ES [ME *lowdenesse* quality of being loud, fr. OE *hlūdnys*, fr. *hlūd* loud + *-nys*, *-nes* -ness] **:** the attribute of a sound that determines the magnitude of the auditory sensation produced by the sound and that in a musical sound depends upon both the energy-flux density and the pitch

**loud pedal** *n* **:** DAMPER PEDAL

**loudspeaker** \'=ˌ==\ *n* **:** an electroacoustic device similar to a telephone receiver in operation but amplifying sound (as in public-address systems, radio and television receivers, and phonographs) — see CONE SPEAKER, ELECTRODYNAMIC SPEAKER

**lou·ey** *or* **lou·ie** *var of* LOOEY

**lough** \'läk\ *n* -S [ME, of Celt origin; akin to OIr *loch* lake, pond — more at LAKE] **1** *now chiefly Irish* **:** LAKE **2** *now chiefly Irish* **:** a bay or inlet of the sea

**lough·lin·ite** \'lōflə,nīt *also* 'läf-\ *n* -S [Gerald F. *Loughlin* †1946 Am. geologist + E *-ite*] **:** a mineral $Mg_2Si_2O_5.nH_2O$ consisting of a hydrous silicate of magnesium resembling asbestos

**lou·is** \'lüē\ *n, pl* **louis** [F, fr. *Louis* XIII †1643 king of France] **:** LOUIS D'OR

**louis d'or** \-'dȯr\ *n, pl* **louis d'or** [F, fr. *louis* + *d'or* of gold, golden] **1 :** a French gold coin first struck in 1640 and issued up to the Revolution **2 :** the French 20-franc gold piece issued after the Revolution

**louis heel** *n, usu cap L* [prob. after *Louis* XV †1774 king of France] **:** a French heel usu. two inches or less in height

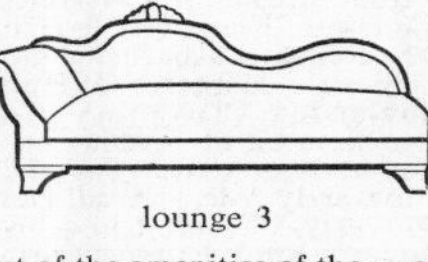

Louis heel

**lou·i·si·ana** \lü,ēzē'anə, ˌlüˌ, ˌ|ēz-, -lü'ēz-, lü'ēz-, ˌlə'wēz-, *sometimes* 'lüzē'a-\ *adj, usu cap* [fr. *Louisiana*, state in the southern U.S., fr. F *Louisiane*, former French territory extending from the Mississippi river to the Rocky mountains, fr. *Louis* XIV †1715 king of France] **:** of or from the state of Louisiana ⟨a *Louisiana* bayou⟩ **:** of the kind or style prevalent in Louisiana **:** LOUISIANIAN

**louisiana cypress** *n, usu cap L* **:** a bald cypress (*Taxodium distichum*)

**louisiana grass** *n, usu cap L* **:** CARPET GRASS 1

**louisiana heron** *n, usu cap L* **:** an American heron (*Hydranassa tricolor ruficollis*) that is slaty above and white beneath

**louisiana muskrat** *n, usu cap L* **:** an American muskrat that is restricted to the coastal marshes of Louisiana, is usu. considered to constitute a distinct subspecies, and is distinguished from the typical form by somewhat smaller size, skin with heavier leather, and hair duller and without reddish cast

**louisiana tanager** *n, usu cap L* **:** WESTERN TANAGER

**louisiana water thrush** *n, usu cap L* **:** a No. American water thrush (*Seiurus motacilla*)

**¹lou·i·si·an·i·an** \-zē'anēən\ *also* **lou·i·si·an·an** \-anən\ *n* -S *cap* [*Louisiana* + E *-an*, n. suffix] **:** a native or resident of Louisiana

**²louisianian** \"\ *also* **louisianan** \"\ *adj, usu cap* [*Louisiana* + E *-an*, adj. suffix] **1 :** of, relating to, or characteristic of the state of Louisiana **2 :** of, relating to, or characteristic of the people of Louisiana **3 :** AUSTRORIPARIAN

**lou·is qua·torze** \'lüēkə'tȯrz\ *adj, usu cap L&Q* [F *Louis Quatorze* (Louis XIV) †1715 king of France] **:** of, relating to, or having the characteristics of the reign of Louis XIV of France: as **a :** marked by imposing dignity and return to the ancient orders and details in architecture with emphasis on regularity and rich interior decoration **b :** exhibiting elaborate carving, gilding, and often inlay in furniture with Roman motifs in ornamentation and a combination of straight and curved lines in design — compare BOULLE **c :** florid and tending to rococo and rocaille in decorative art

**louis quinze** \-'kaⁿz\ *adj, usu cap L&Q* [F *Louis Quinze* (Louis XV) †1774 king of France] **:** of, relating to, or having the characteristics of the reign of Louis XV of France: as **a :** exhibiting irregularly curved lines and surfaces in interior ornamentation **b :** marked by curved lines and rich upholstery in furniture

**louis seize** \-'sez\ *adj, usu cap L&S* [F *Louis Seize* (Louis XVI) †1793 king of France] **:** of, relating to, or having the characteristics of the reign of Louis XVI of France: as **a :** approaching the antique more and more in architecture while taking on a greater lightness **b :** reverting to the straight line in decoration **c :** showing the influence of frescoes of Pompeii and Herculaneum in interior ornamentation **d :** marked by straight lines, light and simple construction, and pastoral motifs in ornamentation of furniture

**louis treize** \-'trez\ *adj, usu cap L&T* [F *Louis Treize* (Louis XIII) †1643 king of France] **:** of, relating to, or having the characteristics of the reign of Louis XIII of France: as **a :** of developed Renaissance style in architecture but retaining much Gothic picturesqueness **b :** of square and angular design in furniture

**lou·is·ville** \'lüē,vil, *esp in the South* -ēvəl\ *adj, usu cap* [fr. *Louisville*, city in north central Kentucky] **:** of or from the city of Louisville, Ky. ⟨*Louisville* officials⟩ **:** of the kind or style prevalent in Louisville

**lou·is·vill·ian** \ˌ==ˈvilyən\ *n* -S *cap* [*Louisville*, Kentucky + E *-an*] **:** a native or resident of Louisville, Kentucky

**¹louk** \'lük\ *vb* -ED/-ING/-S [ME *lowken*, *luken* to weed, pull out, fr. OE *lūcan* to pull up (a weed); akin to MLG *lūken* to pull, OHG *liochan* to pluck, pull out, ON *lok* weeds, L *lugēre* to mourn — more at LUGUBRIOUS] *dial Eng* **:** WEED

**²louk** \'lau̇k\ *vt* -ED/-ING/-S [origin unknown] *dial Eng* **:** BEAT, WHIP, STRIKE

**³louk** \"\ *n* -S *dial Eng* **:** ⁵BLOW 1a

**¹loun** \'lün\ *Scot var of* ¹LOON

**²loun** \'lau̇n\ *or* **lound** \-nd\ *chiefly Scot var of* LOWN

**¹loun·der** \'ländər\ *n* -S [origin unknown] *chiefly Scot* **:** a severe blow

**²lounder** \"\ *vb* -ED/-ING/-S *chiefly Scot* **:** to beat or thrash heavily

**¹lounge** \'lau̇nj\ *vb* -ED/-ING/-S [origin unknown] *vi* **:** to act or move idly or lazily **:** to stand, sit, or recline indolently **:** LOAF, LOLL, SAUNTER ⟨for whole days at a time he would ~ in his Windsor chair in the kitchen —George Orwell⟩ ⟨*lounged* out from the office and looked him over —S.E.White⟩ ~ *vt* **:** to pass (time) idly — usu. used with *away* ⟨returned to Rome to ~ away the remainder of his days —J.A.Froude⟩

**²lounge** \"\ *n* -S **1 :** a place for lounging: as **a :** a room in a private home or public building for informal gathering and conversation or other leisure occupations **:** LIVING ROOM, PARLOR ⟨these paints are particularly suitable for ~, dining room, and bedrooms —*Australian Home Beautiful*⟩ **:** LOBBY, WAITING ROOM ⟨had the "plush" furnishings and atmosphere and most of the amenities of the ~ of a world airport —Sam Pollock⟩ ⟨in the U.N.'s corridors and ~*s*, where the doubtful are influenced —*Time*⟩ **b :** COCKTAIL LOUNGE **c :** a room in a public building often combining lounging, smoking, and toilet facilities **d :** a room or place on a train, ship, or airplane offering club or lounging facilities ⟨had gathered her lonely charges in the ~ at the rear of the plane —Henry La Cossitt⟩ **2** *archaic* **:** a lounging gait or posture **:** SAUNTER, SLOUCH **3 :** a long couch on which one person may recline or several may sit ⟨threw herself on the ~ and buried her face in her hands —Winston Churchill⟩ — compare DAVENPORT, DAYBED, DIVAN, SOFA

lounge 3

**³lounge** \"\ *archaic var of* LUNGE

**lounge car** *n* **:** a railroad passenger car with lounging often movable seats and facilities for serving refreshments — called also *club car, club-lounge car;* compare PARLOR CAR

**lounge chair** *n* **:** EASY CHAIR

**lounge lizard** *n* **1 :** LADIES' MAN, FOP **2 :** a social parasite

**loung·er** \'lau̇njə(r)\ *n* -S **1 :** one that lounges **:** IDLER ⟨the ~*s* at the bar were beginning to show signs of leaving —Haldane Macfall⟩ **2 :** an article of clothing (as a jacket or shoes) or of furniture (as a couch) meant for comfort and leisure use

**lounge suit** *n, chiefly Brit* **:** BUSINESS SUIT

**¹lounging** *adj* [fr. pres. part. of *¹lounge*] **1 :** INDOLENT, SLACK ⟨how different is that quick springy figure from our young men's ~ style —George Meredith⟩ **2** [fr. gerund of *¹lounge*] **:** fit for leisure use or wear ⟨~ pajamas⟩ — **loung·ing·ly** *adv*

**²lounging** *n* -S [fr. gerund of *¹lounge*] **:** IDLING, SAUNTERING

**loungy** \'lau̇njē\ *adj* [*¹lounge* + *-y*] **:** suitable for lounging **:** IDLE

**¹loup** \'ləu̇p, 'lōp, 'lüp\ *vb* -ED/-ING/-S [ME *loupen* to leap — more at LOPE (v.)] *chiefly Scot* **:** LEAP, FLEE

**²loup** \"\ *n* -S [ME — more at LOPE (n.)] *chiefly Scot* **:** LEAP

**loup-cer·vier** \ˌlüser'vyā\ *n, pl* **loup-cerviers** *or* **loup cervier** [CanF, fr. F, lynx, fr. L *lupus cervarius*, lit., deer wolf, fr. *lupus* wolf + *cervarius* of deer, fr. *cervus* deer, stag + *-arius* -ary — more at HART] **:** CANADA LYNX

**loupe** \'lüp\ *n* -S [F, loupe, gem of imperfect brilliancy, fr. MF, gem of imperfect brilliancy, prob. of Gmc origin; akin to Fris *lob*, *lobbe* hanging mass of fat or flesh — more at LOB] **:** a small magnifying glass used by jewelers and watchmakers

**loup-ga·rou** \ˌlügə'rü\ *n, pl* **loups-garous** [MF, fr. OF *leu garoul*, fr. *leu* wolf (fr. L *lupus*) + *garoul*, *garulf* werewolf, of Gmc origin; akin to OE *werwulf* werewolf, OHG *werwolf* — more at WOLF, WEREWOLF] **:** WEREWOLF

**louping ill** *n* [*louping* fr. gerund of *¹loup*] **:** a tick-borne virus disease of sheep and other domestic animals and rarely man that is related to or identical with the Russian spring-summer encephalitis of man and occurs characteristically as a meningoencephalitis accompanied by muscular tremors and spasms followed by varying degrees of paralysis

**loup-the-dyke** \ˌ=ˌ=ˈ=\ *adj* [fr. the phrase *loup the dyke*, fr. *¹loup* + *the* + *dyke*] *Scot* **:** GIDDY, UNSETTLED

**lour** *var of* LOWER

**¹lourd** *n* -S [obs. *lourd*, adj., dull, stupid, fr. ME *lourde*, fr. MF *lourd*, fr. L *luridus* pale yellow, sallow — more at LURID] *obs* **:** LOUT, SOT

**²lourd** \'lu̇rd\ *adv* [alter. (influenced by *¹-ed*) of Sc *loor*, *lour*, alter. of E dial. *liever*] *Scot* **:** RATHER — used in the phrases *had lourd* and *wad lourd*

**lour·dan** \'lərdᵊn\ *var of* LURDAN

**loure** \'lu̇(ə)r\ *n* -S [F, dance in slow triple or sextuple time, bagpipe, fr. MF, bagpipe, perh. fr. ON *lūthr* trumpet] **:** a dance in slow triple or sextuple time; *also* **:** the music for such a dance

**lou·rie** \'lu̇rē\ *n* -S [Afrik *loerie*, fr. Malay *luri*, *nuri* lory] **:** any of several touracos of southern Africa

**lou·ro** \'lō(ˌ)rü\ *n* -S [Pg, lit., laurel, fr. L *laurus* — more at DAPHNE] **:** a tree of the genus *Ocotea*

**loury** *var of* LOWERY

**¹louse** \'lau̇s\ *n, pl* **lice** \'līs\ *see sense 3* [ME *lous* (pl. *lys*), fr. OE *lūs* (pl. *lȳs*); akin to OHG & ON *lūs* louse, W *llau* lice] **1 :** any of various small wingless usu. flattened insects that are parasitic on warm-blooded animals and constitute the orders Anoplura and Mallophaga — compare BIRD LOUSE, SUCKING LOUSE; BODY LOUSE, CRAB LOUSE, HEAD LOUSE **2 a :** any of various small usu. sluggish arthropods that live on various animals or plants and suck their blood or juices — usu. used in combination; compare BEE LOUSE, CARP LOUSE, FISH LOUSE, PLANT LOUSE, WHALE LOUSE **b :** any of several somewhat similar arthropods that are not parasitic — usu. used in combination; compare BOOK LOUSE, WOOD LOUSE **3** *pl* **louses :** a person regarded as extremely contemptible for parasitic or other odious low conduct **:** BASTARD, HEEL, RAT, STINKER ⟨what a beast, what a cad, what a ~ he had been —Walter Karig⟩ ⟨while all the time she was withering her inner self with ". . . you ~! You perfect ~" —Catherine Hubbell⟩

**²louse** \'lau̇s, 'lau̇z\ *vt* -ED/-ING/-S [ME *lowsyn*, fr. *lous*, *lows*, n.] **:** to pick lice from ⟨one old crone was alternately pinching a pretty child's cheeks and *lousing* her hair —I.L.Idriess⟩

**louse·berry** \'lau̇s-\ — *see* BERRY\ *n* **:** a European spindle tree (*Eronymus europaeus*) yielding berries formerly believed to repel insects

**louse fly** *n* **:** an insect of the family Hippoboscidae

**louse up** *vb* [*¹louse*] *vt* **:** to foul up **:** mess up **:** SNARL, UNDO ⟨won't play it with a partner who *louses* it *up* —John Brooks⟩ ⟨the triteness which *louses up* most novels today —Paul Engle⟩ ~ *vi* **:** to fall into confusion **:** make a mess ⟨just where any famous singer will *louse up* in any famous opera —M.M.Hunt⟩

**lousewort** \'=ˌ=\ *n* **1 :** a plant of the genus *Pedicularis* formerly reputed to cause sheep feeding upon it to be subject to vermin **:** WOOD BETONY **2 :** RATTLE 3a

**lou·si·ci·dal** \ˌlau̇sə¦sīdᵊl\ *adj* **:** louse-killing — used of an insecticide ⟨the larvicidal and ~ action of DDT —*Yr. Bk. of General Therapeutics*⟩

**lou·si·cide** \'lau̇sə,sīd\ *n* -S [*¹louse* + *-i-* + *-cide*] **:** a louse-killing insecticide **:** PEDICULICIDE ⟨DDT powder is highly effective and longer lasting than any other ~ in use —*Jour. Amer. Med. Assoc.*⟩

**lous·i·ly** \'lau̇zəlē, -li\ *adv* **:** in a lousy manner **:** MEANLY, CONTEMPTIBLY

**lous·i·ness** \-zēnəs, -zin-\ *n* -ES **1 :** PEDICULOSIS **2 :** VILENESS **3 :** a defect of silk fabric marked by fuzziness and specks caused by splitting of the fiber

**lous·ter** \'lau̇stə(r)\ *vi* -ED/-ING/-S [origin unknown] *dial Eng* **:** to bustle or scramble about **:** work actively

**lousy** \'lau̇zē, -zi\ *adj* -ER/-EST [ME, fr. *lous* louse + *-y*] **1 :** infested with or marked by the presence of lice ⟨the ragged, ~ tribesmen —T.E.Lawrence⟩ ⟨~ disease⟩ **2 a :** totally repulsive or abominable **:** CONTEMPTIBLE, FILTHY, VILE ⟨a ~ way of getting even⟩ **b :** miserably poor or inferior ⟨he believes that, contrary to the popular conception, women are ~ spies —*Infantry Jour.*⟩ ⟨forgive me for writing on this ~ paper —O.W.Holmes †1935⟩ ⟨observed that it was a ~ war, but better than no war at all —J.P.Roche⟩ — often used as an intensive ⟨get that third rocker after a ~ six months in grade —Walt Sheldon⟩ **3 :** amply supplied **:** REPLETE ⟨the concert halls . . . ~ with violinists —Virgil Thomson⟩ ⟨the avenue was ~ with pawnshops —Charles Jackson⟩ ⟨they all thought the Americans were ~ with money —Maxwell Griffith⟩ **4** *of silk* **:** fuzzy and specked because of splitting of the fiber

**¹lout** \'lau̇t, *usu* -au̇d·+V\ *vi* -ED/-ING/-S [ME *louten*, fr. OE *lūtan*; akin to ON *lūta* to bow down — more at LITTLE] **1 :** to bow in courtesy or respect ⟨I uncovered and ~*ed* as I passed —A.Conan Doyle⟩ **2 :** to bend in submission **:** YIELD ⟨have rubbed shoulders with kings and noblemen and ~*ed* to none of them —*Times Lit. Supp.*⟩

**²lout** \"\ *n* -S [perh. fr. ON *lūtr* bent down, stooped, fr. *lūta* to bow down] **:** an awkward clownish fellow **:** OAF, YOKEL ⟨married to some ~ of a shopkeeper —Frank O'Connor⟩ ⟨see that a few ~*s* don't spoil the fun for everybody —*Vancouver (Canada) Province*⟩ **syn** see BOOR

**³lout** \"\ *vt* -ED/-ING/-S **:** to treat as a lout **:** subject to contumely **:** DERIDE, SCORN ⟨I am ~*ed* by a traitor villain —Shak.⟩

**louth** \'lau̇th\ *adj, usu cap* [fr. *Louth*, county in northeast Ireland] **:** of or from County Louth, Ireland **:** of the kind or style prevalent in County Louth

**lout·ish** \'lau̇d·|ish, -au̇t|, |ēsh\ *adj* **:** resembling or suggesting a lout **:** CLOWNISH, COARSE ⟨his ~ flights of fancy —Francis Hackett⟩ — **lout·ish·ly** *adv* — **lout·ish·ness** *n* -ES

**lou·tre** \'lüd·ə(r)\ *n* -S [F, otter, fr. L *lutra*] **:** OTTER 4

**lou·troph·o·ros** \lü·'träfə,räs\ *n, pl* **loutropho·roi** \-rȯi\ [Gk, lit., carrying water for a bath, fr. *loutron* bath, water for a bath (fr. *louein* to wash) + *-phoros* — more at LYE] **:** a tall long-necked water vase with two handles used in ancient Athens for bringing water for the ceremonial bath on the eve of marriage and often buried in the grave of one dying while betrothed

**louty** \'lau̇d·ē\ *adj* -ER/-EST [*²lout* + *-y*] **:** LOUTISH

**lou·var** \'lü,vär\ *n* -S [It dial. (Calabrian & Sicilian) *lùvaru*, prob. fr. L *ruber* red — more at RED] **:** a large plump voracious scombroid fish (*Luvarus imperialis*) cosmopolitan in warm seas

**lou·ver** *or* **lou·vre** \'lüvə(r)\ *n* -S [ME *lover*, fr. MF *lovier*] **1 a :** a roof lantern or turret often with slatted apertures for escape of smoke or admission of light in a medieval building **b** *obs* **:** a dovecote resembling a louver **2 a :** an opening in wall or ceiling for ventilation or cooling provided with one or more slanted fins to exclude rain and sun and often made so that the fins may be closed at will — compare BRISE-SOLEIL **b :** a fin or shutter of a

louvers 2a

louver **3 :** a fixed or adjustable louver for cooling of an enclosed engine or motor (as of an airplane, automobile, or machine) **4 :** a finned or vaned device to deflect or control a flow of air or the radiation of light ⟨ceiling fixtures with ~s seem to diffuse and soften light⟩ ⟨electric fans are often fitted with circular ~s to direct the airstream⟩ **5 :** a closure using adjustable slanted louvers ⟨pulled the ~s in our room as tight as they'd go, but in a couple of hours the water had washed in over our shoes —Land Kaderli⟩

**lou·vered** *or* **lou·vred** \-və(r)d\ *adj* **1 :** set sloping in the manner of the boards or slats of a louver ⟨~ wooden shutters are very much a part of almost every dwelling —Harold Sinclair⟩ **2 :** furnished with louvers ⟨has . . . controlled ventilation and diffused lighting from a ~ ceiling —*Architectural Rev.*⟩

**lov·able** *also* **love·able** \'ləvəbəl\ *adj* [ME *lufabyll, luffable,* fr. *loven, luffen* to love + *-able* — more at LOVE] **:** gifted with traits and qualities that attract affection ⟨she was both likable and ~ —Oliver LaFarge⟩ — **lov·able·ness** *n* -ES — **lov·ably** \-blē, -li\ *adv*

**lov·age** \'ləvij\ *n* -s [ME *lovache,* fr. AF, modif. of LL *levisticum,* alter. of L *ligusticum,* fr. neut. of *ligusticus* Ligurian, fr. *Ligus* Ligurian] **:** any of several aromatic perennial herbs of the family Umbelliferae: as **a :** a stout branched glabrous herb (*Levisticum officinale*) that is native to southern Europe and is sometimes cultivated for its rhizomes which are used as a carminative, its stalks and foliage which are used as a potherb, a substitute for celery, or a tea, its seeds which are used for flavoring and in confectionery, and its flowering tops which yield an oil used in flavoring and perfumery — called also *sea parsley* **b :** any of several white-flowered herbs of cold and temperate regions constituting a genus (*Ligustrum*) and having large aromatic roots; *esp* **:** a coarse herb (*L. scoticum*) of rocky or marshy coasts of northwestern Europe and eastern No. America from Greenland to New York with fleshy leaves sometimes used as a potherb — called also *Scotch lovage, sea parsley*

**lovage oil** *n* **:** a yellow-brown aromatic essential oil obtained from the root or other parts of lovage and used in flavoring and in perfumery

**lov·at** \'ləvət\ *n* -s [prob. fr. *Lovat,* locality in Inverness-shire, Scotland] **:** a predominantly dusty green color mixture in fabrics (as tweeds) orig. intended to blend with the Scottish landscape

[1]**love** \'ləv\ *n* -s [ME, fr. OE *lufu;* akin to OHG *lupa* love, OE *lēof* dear, L *lubēre, libēre* to please, Skt *lubhyati* he desires] **1 a :** the attraction, desire, or affection felt for a person who arouses delight or admiration or elicits tenderness, sympathetic interest, or benevolence **b :** an assurance of love ⟨give my ~ to your father when you get home⟩ **2 a :** warm attachment, enthusiasm, or devotion (as to a pursuit or a concrete or ideal object) ⟨inherited his father's ~ of the sea —G.H. Burnham⟩ ⟨just so much instruction in Latin as would suffice to show which boys and girls had a ~ of the subject —Bertrand Russell⟩ **b :** the object of such attachment or devotion ⟨a born crusader and his ~ was language —Charlton Laird⟩ ⟨events and people are his ~, festivals, law terms, battles, licences, royalty — but especially people —G.W.Stonier⟩ ⟨automobiles are his first ~ —Hugh Humphrey⟩ **3 a :** the benevolence attributed to God as resembling a father's affection for his children **b :** men's adoration of God in gratitude or devotion **4 a :** the attraction based on sexual desire **:** the affection and tenderness felt by lovers ⟨the entrance of ~ into sex life . . . was an advance along the road of human civilization as important as the emancipation of slaves —Theodor Reik⟩ ⟨his ~ had been woven of sentiment rather than passion —Ellen Glasgow⟩ **b :** a god or personification of love (as Cupid, Amor, or Eros) or a figured representation of one (as in art or imaginative conception) ⟨on the other side a *Love* with a flaring torch and head averted —S.T.Coleridge⟩ **c :** an amorous episode **:** AMOUR, LOVE AFFAIR ⟨tremendous curiosity about her jealously guarded life and ~s —Bosley Crowther⟩ **d :** the sexual embrace **:** COPULATION ⟨many cocottes pay their coachmen either partly or wholly in ~ —Arnold Bennett⟩ **5 :** a beloved person **:** DARLING, DEAR, SWEETHEART — often used as an endearment ⟨come on, ~, let's go in and see what's doing —Lilian Balch⟩ **6** *obs* **:** a thin silk fabric formerly worn in token of mourning or a border made of this stuff **7 :** a score of zero in tennis and some other games **:** NOTHING ⟨if the server wins the first point, the score is fifteen-~ —Clement Wood & Gloria Goddard⟩ ⟨opened the match with a ~ victory on his own service —*N.Y. Times*⟩ **8** *cap, Christian Science* **:** GOD **9 :** a delightful or superb example, instance, or occurrence ⟨we had a perfect ~ of a sounding-boat —Mark Twain⟩ ⟨it's a ~, isn't it —Marguerite Steen⟩ **syn** see ATTACHMENT — **for love** *adv* **:** for pleasure **:** without stakes **:** without reward of money or material gain ⟨play cards *for love*⟩ ⟨headed the hospital's building campaign *for love*⟩ — **for love or money :** at any price **:** on any consideration — used with a negative ⟨couldn't get him to go along *for love or money*⟩ — **in love :** inspired by tender or ardent affection **:** ENAMORED, DEVOTED ⟨haven't you ever been *in love* . . . so that nothing else in the world matters at all —Louis Bromfield⟩ ⟨the ardor that makes a woman fall *in love* with a religion or an idea —Ellen Glasgow⟩ ⟨*in love* with his work, entranced by everything connected with it, grateful for his fame and fortune —*Saturday Rev.*⟩ — **of all love** *or* **of all loves** *obs* — used in entreaty

[2]**love** \"\ *vb* -ED/-ING/-s [ME *loven,* fr. OE *lufian;* akin to OHG *lubōn* to love; denominative fr. the root of E [1]*love*] *vt* **1 :** to feel affection for **:** hold dear **:** CHERISH ⟨the lonely and ailing old bachelors and widowers . . . all ~ her —G.S. Perry⟩ **2 a :** to feel a lover's passion, devotion, or tenderness for ⟨*loved* his wife devotedly —Ruth P. Randall⟩ **b :** to engage in sex play — sometimes used with *up* **c :** to copulate with **3 a :** to cherish or foster with divine love and mercy ⟨I have *loved* you with an everlasting love —Jer 31:3 (RSV)⟩ **b :** to feel reverent adoration for (God) ⟨but showing steadfast love to thousands of those who ~ me and keep my commandments —Exod 20:6 (RSV)⟩ **4 a :** to like or desire actively **:** be strongly attracted or attached to **:** delight in ⟨the sculptor must ~ the feel of stone —Leslie Rees⟩ ⟨he ~s the limelight —Eudora Welty⟩ ⟨some leading social scientists ~ their IBM machines too much —C.K.Kluckhohn⟩ **b :** to take pleasure or satisfaction in **:** LIKE — used with an infinitive as object ⟨*loved* to indulge his grief in true romantic fashion —J.W. Beach⟩ ⟨the poor folk would still ~ to emigrate to the U. S. —Frank Gorrell⟩ **5 :** FONDLE, CARESS ⟨mother nuzzled my cheek and throat and I *loved* her back⟩ **6 :** to thrive in **:** PREFER — used of plants and animals ⟨the rose ~s sunlight⟩ ⟨central Asian wild pheasants ~ impenetrable jungles —Douglas Carruthers⟩ **7** *Midland* **:** CHOOSE, PREFER, LIKE ⟨would ~ to have some lemonade⟩ ~ *vi* **:** to feel affection or experience desire ⟨the poet must learn to ~ before he can begin to hate —C.D.Lewis⟩ **syn** see LIKE

[3]**love** \"\ *usu cap* — a communications code word for the letter *l*

**loveable** *var of* LOVABLE

**love affair** *n* **1 :** a romantic attachment or episode between lovers ⟨a niece caught up in her first *love affair* —Hugh Walpole⟩ **2 :** a lively enthusiasm ⟨my *love affair* with aviation —Arthur Godfrey⟩

**love apple** *n* [prob. trans. of MF *pomme d' amour*] **:** TOMATO

**love arrow** *n* **:** [1]DART 3a

**lovebird** \'ˌ=ˌ=\ *n* **1 :** any of various small parrots that show great affection for their mates, that include esp. members of the genera *Agapornis* of Africa, *Loriculus* of Asia, and *Psittacula* of So. America, that are usu. chiefly green or delicate gray, and that are often kept as cage birds — compare BUDGERIGAR **2 :** a strong yellow green that is yellower than viridine yellow and lighter, stronger, and slightly greener than parrot green

**love child** *n* **:** an illegitimate child **:** BASTARD ⟨the uneasy tenderness of a devout churchwoman dandling her daughter's *love child* —Jan Struther⟩

[1]**loved** \'ləvd\ *adj* [ME, fr. past part. of *loven* to love] **:** held dear **:** CHERISHED ⟨death . . . deprived him of a ~ companion —W.C.Ford⟩

[2]**loved** \"\ *n, pl* **loved :** one that is loved

**love dart** *n* **:** [1]DART 3a

**love-entangle** *or* **love-entangled** \'==ˌ===\ *n* -s **1 :** LOVE-IN-A-MIST 1 **2 :** a stonecrop (*Sedum acre*) **3 :** a virgin's-bower (*Clematis vitalba*) of Europe

**love feast** *n* **:** a meal eaten in common in token of brotherly love: as **a :** [2]AGAPE 1 **b :** a modern religious service in imitation of the ancient agape **c :** a banquet, gathering, or celebration held to reconcile differences and promote good feeling or show someone affectionate honor ⟨hotel lobbies were crowded with milling politicians as the annual *love feast* of the Kansas Republicans drew near —*Emporia* (Kans.) *Gazette*⟩ ⟨the affair was a *love feast,* garnished with the floral offerings, the numberless recalls, the encores, and all the rest —*Musical America*⟩

**loveful** *adj, obs* **:** LOVABLE, LOVING

**love game** *n* **:** a game (as in tennis) won without loss of a point

**love god** *n* **:** CUPID

**love grass** *n* **:** a grass of the genus *Eragrostis* that is esp. useful for forage and for the prevention of erosion — called also *bay grass*

**love-in-a-mist** \'===ˌ=\ *n* **1 :** a European garden plant (*Nigella damascena*) having the flowers enveloped in numerous finely dissected bracts **2 :** a tropical American passionflower (*Passiflora foetida*) with finely dissected bracts **3 :** SNOW-IN-SUMMER a

**love-in-idleness** \'==ˌ==\ *n* **:** WILD PANSY

**love-in-winter** \'==ˌ==\ *n* **:** PIPSISSEWA

**love knot** *n* [ME *love knotte,* fr. [1]*love* + *knotte* knot] **:** a decorative or stylized knot sometimes used as an emblem of love — called also *lover's knot, true lover's knot*

**love·less** \'ləvləs\ *adj* [ME *loveles,* fr. [1]*love* + *-les* -less] **1 :** UNLOVING **2 :** UNLOVED **3 :** UNLOVELY — **love·less·ly** *adv*

**love·less·ness** *n* -ES **1 :** want of love for others **2 :** failure to receive the love of others **3 :** UNATTRACTIVENESS, UNLOVELINESS

**love letter** *n* **:** a letter expressing a lover's affection

**love-lies-bleeding** \'=ˌ='==\ *n* **1 :** a cultivated plant of the genus *Amaranthus* (esp. *A. caudatus*) **2 :** BLEEDING HEART 1 **3 :** PHEASANT'S-EYE 1

**love life** *n* **:** the activities, habits, and relationships centering in the affections and esp. in sexual life

**love-light** \'=ˌ=\ *n* **:** the radiance of affection ⟨and yet her eyes had that brooding *love-light* —John Galsworthy⟩

**love·li·head** \'ləvlēˌhed\ *n* [[1]*lovely* + *-head* (as in *godhead*)] **:** LOVELINESS

**love·li·ly** \-lәlē\ *adv* [ME *lovelyly,* fr. [1]*lovely* + *-ly*] **:** in a lovely manner

**love·li·ness** \'ləvlēnəs, -lin-\ *n* -ES [ME *luflynes,* fr. *lufly,* *lovely* lovely + *-nes* -ness] **:** the quality or state of being lovely **:** BEAUTY ⟨that dead first wife . . . who was all undemanding ~ —Mark Schorer⟩

**love·ling** \-liŋ\ *n* -s **:** DARLING

**lovelock** \'=ˌ=\ *n* **:** a long lock or curl of hair usu. hanging alone over the shoulder and worn esp. in the 17th and 18th centuries — compare EARLOCK

**love·lorn** \'ləvˌlȯrn, -ȯ(ə)n\ *adj* **:** bereft of love or of a lover — **love·lorn·ness** \-nnəs\ *n* -ES

[1]**love·ly** \'ləvlē, -li\ *adj, usu* -ER/-EST [ME, fr. OE *luflīc,* fr. *lufu* love + *-līc* -ly — more at LOVE] **1** *obs* **:** disposed to affectionate or amorous love **2 :** meriting love by moral or ideal worth **3 :** delightful for beauty, harmony, or grace **:** attractive because of natural charm ⟨a strange shy ~ girl —John Masefield⟩ ⟨and the stars are ~ and gleaming on the lightless heavenly floor —William Morris⟩ ⟨conservation and wise use of resources can make a wealthy people in a ~ land —H.W.Odum⟩ ⟨then we remember that harsh unflurried, that harsh unembittered laughter, and we look up the ~ lines in the book —Edmund Wilson⟩ **4 :** most pleasing **:** GRAND, SWELL ⟨a good man and a ~ preacher —Ruth Suckow⟩ ⟨if you go, the chances are you'll have a ~ time —Wolcott Gibbs⟩ **syn** see BEAUTIFUL

[2]**lovely** *adv* [ME, beautifully, affectionately, willingly, fr. OE *luflīce* affectionately, willingly, fr. *luflīc,* adj.] *obs* **:** BEAUTIFULLY

[3]**love·ly** *n* -ES [ME, beautiful one, fr. *lovely,* adj.] **1 :** a beautiful girl or woman; *esp* **:** a professional beauty (as a show girl) ⟨swept off his feet by this tempestuous young ~ —*Irish Digest*⟩ ⟨the world of impresarios, stage *lovelies,* and night club music —*Times Lit. Supp.*⟩ **2 :** a lovely object ⟨hemstitched *lovelies* that are soft, smooth, and lint-free —*Sears, Roebuck Cat.*⟩ **3 :** an outstanding or egregious example **:** BEAUTY

**lovely fir** *or* **lovely red fir** *n* **:** SILVER FIR b

**lovemaking** \'=ˌ==\ *n* [ME *love makinge,* fr. [1]*love* + *makinge* making] **1 :** wooing or courtship between lovers ⟨in his comedies . . . there is the finest ~ in the world —*Modern Language Notes*⟩ **2 :** amorous dalliance **:** SEXUAL INTERCOURSE **3 :** the courtship practices of animals ⟨idly watched the splashing and ~ of the distant ducks⟩

**love·man** \'ləvˌman\ *n, pl* **lovemans** [[2]*love* + *man*] **:** CLEAVERS

**love match** *n* **:** a marriage prompted chiefly by affection

**lovemate** \'=ˌ=\ *n* **:** LOVER

**love nest** *n* **:** a dwelling of lovers; *esp* **:** a place where illicit lovers live or meet ⟨a sordid *love nest* on a back street —Martha Gellhorn⟩

**love object** *n* **:** a person on whom affection is centered or on whom one is dependent for affection or needed help

**love parrakeet** *or* **love parrot** *n* **:** LOVEBIRD

**love-philter** \'=ˌ==\ *n* **:** PHILTER

**love-potion** \'=ˌ==\ *n* **:** PHILTER

**love-powder** \'=ˌ==\ *n* **:** a powder used as a philter

**lov·er** \'ləvə(r)\ *n* -s [ME, fr. *loven* to love + *-er*] **1 a :** a person in love ⟨a man came down to where his ~ was —J.C. Hall⟩; *esp* **:** a man in love with a girl or woman ⟨her heart went out to him as to a ~ —Sheila Kaye-Smith⟩ **b lovers** *pl* **:** two persons in love with each other ⟨he'd sit with his arm round her waist and she with her head on his shoulder just like ~s —W.S.Maugham⟩ **2 :** an affectionate or benevolent friend ⟨not an ardent denominational ecclesiastic, but a broad-souled and eager ~ of men —O.M.Buck⟩ **3 :** an enthusiastic amateur **:** DEVOTEE ⟨as a ~ of truth, the national propaganda of all the belligerent nations sickened me —Bertrand Russell⟩ ⟨a lifelong ~ of the woodcock runs and trout streams —R.W.Hatch⟩ ⟨a variety of subjects that will interest theater ~s —Henry Hewes⟩ **4 :** PARAMOUR ⟨she had chosen a bachelor girl's life, although she had children by ~s —Margaret C. Hubbard⟩

**lov·er·ing** \'ləv(ə)riŋ\ *n* -s **:** LOVEMAKING ⟨she dearly loved to see a bit of ~ going on —Mary Webb⟩

**lov·er·less** \'ləvə(r)ləs\ *adj* **:** having no lover

[1]**lov·er·ly** \-lē, -li\ *adj* [*lover* + *-ly*] **:** befitting a lover

[2]**loverly** \"\ *adv* **:** in a lover's manner

**lover's knot** *n* **:** LOVE KNOT

**lovers' lane** *n* **:** a lane or place favored by lovers for seclusion and dalliance

**lover's leap** *n* **1 :** a cliff or high point from which disappointed and despairing lovers plunge to death **2 :** the move of a man in backgammon from ace point to twelve point in one throw of the dice

**lover's-pride** \'==ˌ=\ *n, pl* **lover's-prides :** PERSICARIA

**loverwise** \'=ˌ=\ *adv* **:** in the manner of a lover

**loves** *pl of* LOVE, *pres 3d sing of* LOVE

**love scene** *n* **:** a scene between lovers (as in a play)

**love seat** *n* **:** a double chair, sofa, or settee for two persons

**love set** *n* **:** a set in tennis won without loss of a game

**love-sick** \'=ˌ=\ *adj* **1 :** languishing with love **:** YEARNING ⟨strong men behaved like *love-sick* boys before her beauty⟩ **2 :** expressing a lover's longing ⟨while the nightingales their *love-sick* ditty sing —John Dryden⟩ — **love·sick·ness** *n*

love seat (Chippendale)

**love·some** \'ləvsəm\ *adj* [ME *lovesom, lufsom,* fr. OE *lufsum,* fr. *lufu* love + *-sum* -some — more at LOVE] **1 :** CHARMING, WINSOME **:** BEAUTIFUL, LOVELY ⟨a woman young and ~, and shaped exceeding fair —William Morris⟩ **2 a :** FRIENDLY, AFFECTIONATE **b :** AMOROUS

**love song** *n* **:** a lyrical, musical, or poetic expression of love esp. of man for woman

**love spoon** *n* **:** a wooden spoon carved with double bowl by a Welsh suitor as an engagement gift for his promised bride

**love's test** *n* **:** a common everlasting (*Antennaria plantaginifolia*) of eastern No. America

**love·ston·ite** \'ləvˌstōˌnīt\ *n* -s *usu cap* [Jay *Lovestone,* 20th cent. Am. union leader expelled from the Communist party in 1929 + E *-ite*] **:** a member of a faction of the American Communist party deviating from party policy esp. on the question of accepting and working with established trade unions

**love story** *n* **:** a tale of lovers

**love vine** *n* **:** DODDER

**love wave** *n, usu cap L* [after A. E. H. *Love* †1940 Eng. mathematician] **:** a seismic disturbance consisting of horizontal transverse vibrations of the earth's crust propagated near the surface

**loveworthy** \'=ˌ==\ *adj* **:** meriting love ⟨saw how utterly ~ she was and had always been —Sheila Kaye-Smith⟩

love spoon

[1]**lovey-dovey** \'ləvē'dəvē\ *n* -s [*lovey-* (fr. [1]*love* + *-y*) + *-dovey* (fr. [1]*dove* + *-y*)] **:** SWEETHEART, PARAMOUR

[2]**lovey-dovey** \"\ *adj* **:** SENTIMENTAL, SOFT **:** SACCHARINE, MUSHY

[1]**lov·ing** \'ləviŋ, -vēŋ\ *adj* [ME *lovyng,* alter. of *lovende,* fr. OE *lufiende,* pres. part. of *lufian* to love — more at LOVE] **1 :** feeling or expressing love **:** AFFECTIONATE ⟨eyes at once critical and ~ —John Galsworthy⟩ — often used in combination ⟨a peace-*loving* people⟩ ⟨a fun-*loving* couple⟩ **2 :** marked by careful attention to detail **:** PAINSTAKING ⟨devoting ~ attention to details —*Time*⟩ ⟨the ~ protection of the liberty of the individual —Brand Blanshard⟩ — **lov·ing·ness** *n* -ES

[2]**loving** \"\ *n* -s [ME, fr. gerund of *loven* to love — more at LOVE] **:** a lover's action or attitude

**loving cup** *n* [[1]*loving* + *cup*] **1 :** a large ornamental vessel with two or more handles that is used for ceremonial drinking (as in welcome) by assembled companions **2 :** a loving cup given someone as a token of friendship or honor or presented as a trophy to the winner in sporting or other competition

**loving-kindness** \'=='==\ *n* **:** tender and benevolent affection **:** favoring mercy ⟨the cause of wisdom and *loving-kindness* in education —*Times Lit. Supp.*⟩

**lov·ing·ly** *adv* **1 :** in a loving manner **:** FONDLY, AFFECTIONATELY ⟨looked ~ into the handsome face —Israel Zangwill⟩ **2 :** with close attention to detail **:** PAINSTAKINGLY ⟨the mountain shoes so ~ made by hand —Claudia Cassidy⟩

**lo·voz·e·rite** \lō'vāzəˌrīt\ *n* -s [Russ *lovozerit,* fr. *Lovozero,* village in the Kola peninsula, northwest Russia + Russ *-it* -ite] **:** a mineral $(Na,K)_2(Mn,Ca)ZrSi_6O_{16}.3H_2O$ consisting of a hydrous silicate of alkalies, manganese, calcium, and zirconium

loving cup

[1]**low** \'lō\ *n* -s [ME, fr. OE *hlāw, hlǣw* — more at LAW] *archaic* **:** HILL, MOUND; *specif* **:** a burial mound

[2]**low** \" *sometimes* 'lü\ *vb* -ED/-ING/-s [ME *loowen,* fr. OE *hlōwan;* akin to OLF *luon, luogin* to moo, OHG *hluoen* to moo, L *calare* to call, summon, Gk *kalein* to call, Lith *kalbà* language] *vi* **1** *of cattle* **:** to make the usu. deep sustained sound characteristic of cows and other bovine animals **:** MOO **2 :** to make a sound suggestive of the lowing of cattle ⟨that's what I would say, and they would ~ with pleasure —E.L. Burdick⟩ ~ *vt* **:** to utter with a lowing sound

[3]**low** \"\ *n* -s **:** the usu. deep sustained sound characteristic of cows and other bovine animals ⟨the ~ of herds —William Wordsworth⟩

[4]**low** \'lō\ *adj* -ER/-EST [ME *low, lowe,* fr. *lah,* fr. ON *lāgr;* akin to OFris *lēch* low, MD *lage,* MHG *læge* low, flat, Russ *lezt'* to climb, and perh. to ON *liggja* to lie — more at LIE] **1 a** (1) **:** having a relatively small upward extension **:** extending upward or outward relatively little ⟨a man of ~ stature⟩ ⟨a ~ building⟩ ⟨a ~ wall⟩ ⟨~ relief⟩ (2) **:** situated, placed, or passing relatively little above the line, point, or plane with relation to which reckoning is made ⟨a ~ bridge⟩ ⟨a bird of ~ flight⟩ (3) *now chiefly dial* **:** not tall **:** SHORT ⟨a ~, fat man —Vance Randolph & G.P.Wilson⟩ ⟨about forty, ~,corpulent —Anne Royall⟩ (4) **:** having a low neck **:** DÉCOLLETÉ ⟨a ~ dress⟩; *also* **:** LOW-CUT ⟨a ~ shoe⟩ (5) **:** articulated with a wide opening between the comparatively flat tongue and the palate **:** OPEN ⟨the sounds \ä\ \a\ \a\ are ~⟩ **b** (1) **:** situated relatively below the normal level, surface, or base of measurement, or the mean elevation ⟨~ ground⟩ ⟨the ~ levels in a mine⟩ (2) **:** of or relating to the lowlands esp. near the seashore — now used chiefly in fixed phrases ⟨the *Low* Countries⟩ (3) **:** having less than or being below or farthest below the usual or normal height ⟨the water is ~ in the reservoir⟩ — compare LOW TIDE, LOW WATER (4) **:** being near the horizon ⟨the afternoon sun is ~ at four o'clock in winter⟩ **c** (1) **:** DEAD, LIFELESS — now usu. used in the phrase *lay low* ⟨keen swords and sharp arrows laid the enemy ~⟩ (2) **:** PROSTRATE — usu. used in the phrase *lay low* ⟨laid ~ for weeks by a severe illness⟩ ⟨laid him ~ with one mighty stroke of his staff⟩ (3) **:** ABASED, HUMBLED — usu. used in the phrase *bring low* ⟨added that he kept a list of all his opponents and . . . would bring them ~ —Evelyn G. Cruickshanks⟩ (4) **:** not prosperous **:** POOR, EMBARRASSED, BACKWARD ⟨sought to account for the ~ state of the higher studies in this country⟩ ⟨was ~ financially —Arthur Godfrey⟩ **d :** passing far downward ⟨a ~ swoop⟩ ⟨a ~ obeisance⟩ **2 a** (1) **:** of or relating to the lower classes **:** socially or economically humble or inferior ⟨a person of ~ birth⟩ ⟨women of ~ degree —H.M. Parshley⟩ ⟨loved by all his parishioners, high and ~⟩; *also* **:** associated with lower class status **:** IGNOBLE, PLEBEIAN ⟨these tasks become . . . too ~ to be performed by the native —B.K. Sandwell⟩ (2) **:** ranking as poor or inferior by some standard **:** INFERIOR ⟨a man of ~ intelligence⟩ ⟨results in the domination of news by ~ intellectual and moral standards —F.L.Mott⟩ ⟨groups of the population with ~ personal hygiene —E.C. Faust⟩ (3) **:** lacking dignity or elevation **:** ORDINARY, COMMONPLACE, PROSAIC ⟨distinguished between the high and the ~ style . . . the latter assigned to the realism of every day life —William Barrett⟩ ⟨have used abbreviations freely in this letter. Do you think them ~ —O.W.Holmes †1935⟩ (4) **:** characterized by burlesque, horseplay, and broad or farcical humor **:** bordering on farce ⟨~ comedy⟩ (5) **:** culturally inferior by some standard **:** little advanced in civilization ⟨savages of a ~ Negrito type —*Encyc. Americana*⟩ (6) **:** having a relatively simple organization **:** not highly developed in the scale of biological evolution ⟨~ organisms⟩ ⟨no remains of . . . ~ forms of man have been found here —S. E.Morison & H.S.Commager⟩ (7) *usu cap* **:** LOW CHURCH ⟨who was very *Low,* would forget for a moment her annoyance at the ecclesiastical lace —Osbert Lancaster⟩ **b** (1) **:** morally reprehensible **:** BASE, MEAN ⟨that was a ~ trick⟩ ⟨marked by a certain ~ cunning⟩; *also* **:** striking below the belt **:** FOUL ⟨a ~ blow⟩ (2) **:** DEGRADED, ABANDONED, DISSOLUTE, DISREPUTABLE ⟨a ~ public house —*Newsweek*⟩ ⟨intrigues with ~ women —Benjamin Franklin⟩ (3) **:** lacking in or reflecting lack of refinement or breeding **:** COARSE, VULGAR ⟨~ in her tastes and aspirations, ~ in her likes and dislikes —Joseph Furphy⟩ ⟨sporting events of a ~ type —G.M.Trevelyan⟩ ⟨scenes of would-be comedy from illiterate ~ characters —Leslie Rees⟩ ⟨that's a ~ word⟩ (4) **:** not conforming to some standard of correctness or propriety ⟨the ~ language is the everyday language —Miguel Covarrubias⟩ **c** (1) **:** lacking strength, health, or vitality **:** FEEBLE, WEAK ⟨he was very ~ —Granville Toogood⟩ ⟨a ~ pulse⟩ (2) **:** not rich or highly seasoned **:** not nourishing **:** PLAIN, SIMPLE ⟨a ~ diet⟩ (3) **:** lacking spirit or vivacity **:** DEPRESSED, DEJECTED ⟨felt too ~ even to remonstrate —Louis Auchincloss⟩ **:** marked by dejection or depression ⟨in a ~ state of mind —J.C.Lincoln⟩ ⟨better than he thought in ~ moments —*Times Lit. Supp.*⟩ **d :** UNFAVOR-

ABLE, DISPARAGING ⟨had a ~ opinion of his talents⟩ 3 : deficient, inferior, or unusually small in quantity, intensity, value, or degree: as a : less than normal : not intense : MODERATE ⟨~ barometric pressure⟩ ⟨~ speed⟩ ⟨~ visibility⟩ ⟨a ~ fever⟩ ⟨a ~ conductor of heat⟩ ⟨valleys . . . ~ in lime —Walter Bally⟩ b (1) : not loud : SOFT ⟨spoke in a very ~ voice —Katharine N. Burt⟩ (2) : depressed in musical pitch : FLAT (3) : relating to those musical notes or tones in the contra-octave esp. in singing ⟨~ G⟩ c (1) : numerically small : not high in amount ⟨the illiteracy rate is very ~⟩ ⟨a ~ number⟩ ⟨deal me a ~ card⟩ (2) : being beneath a rate, amount, or value considered normal, standard, or adequate by some criteria ⟨persons of ~ income group⟩ ⟨~ wages⟩ ⟨~ prices⟩; *specif* : CHEAP ⟨that's a very ~ price for that suit⟩ (3) : relatively small or too small : MODERATE ⟨gave me a very ~ estimate⟩ (4) : nearly exhausted : DEPLETED, SHORT ⟨left me when the coal was ~ —*New Republic*⟩ ⟨the stores being so ~ —R.L.Stevenson⟩ ⟨very ~ in pocket⟩ d : being near or not very distant from the equator ⟨the ~ northern latitudes⟩ e : being relatively near the beginning of a series of chemical compounds arranged in order of increasing molecular weight or of increasing valence of the chief constituent ⟨~*er* fatty acids⟩ — compare HIGH 1b 7 f : designed for slow or usu. the slowest speed; *specif* : giving the lowest ratio of propeller-shaft to engine-shaft speed and the highest amplification of torque ⟨~ gear⟩ g : not lively : SLOW ⟨published . . . at very ~ tempo because of lack of funds —Mortimer Graves⟩ ⟨a steady, dignified ~ dance —Anatole Chujoy⟩ 4 : very low : marking a nadir : LOWEST ⟨surely the ~ point of the entire period —Philles Nash⟩ ⟨organized religion has reached a ~ point in its history —*Humanist*⟩ **syn** see BASE

5**low** \ˈ"\ *n* -s [ME, fr. *lah*, fr. *lah*, adj. — more at 4LOW] : something that is low: as a : a piece of low-lying level ground — usu. used in pl. ⟨many ~s growing dense reedbeds —Douglas Carruthers⟩ b : LOW SPEED c (1) : the lowest card of the trump suit or the lowest trump card in play counting one point in all forms and related games (2) : the lowest number, card, or score in a game; *also* : the player having low d : a domain of low barometric pressure — compare CYCLONE 1a e : lowest prices of a movement ⟨buy stocks at the ~⟩ f : a nadir of decline or degradation ⟨whose report card marks a new ~ —Ralph Linton⟩ ⟨prestige, power, and reputation plummet to new ~s —Neal Stanford⟩ ⟨membership is at an all-time ~ —*Sydney (Australia) Bull.*⟩

6**low** \ˈ"\ *adv* -ER/-EST [ME *lowe*, fr. *lahe, lage*, fr. *lah*, adj. — more at 4LOW] 1 : in or to a low position : not on high : near the ground ⟨the village is nestled ~ in the foothills of the great range⟩ 2 : to or toward a low position : in a low direction or course ⟨aim your blows ~⟩ 3 a : in subjection, poverty, or disgrace ⟨brought ~ by misfortune⟩ b (1) : in a low or poor condition : HUMBLY, MEAGERLY ⟨on that income you must live very ~⟩ (2) : at a low rate ⟨don't value yourself too ~⟩ 4 : at a relatively low price : CHEAPLY ⟨sell wheat ~⟩ 5 a : with a low voice or sound : not loudly : SOFTLY ⟨speak ~⟩ b : with a low musical pitch or tone 6 *archaic* : LATE

7**low** *or* **lowe** \ˈ"\ *n* -s [ME, fr. ON *log, logi* flame; akin to OFris *loga* flame, MHG *lohe* flame, Goth *liuhath* light — more at LIGHT] *chiefly Scot* : FLAME, BLAZE, GLOW

8**low** *or* **lowe** \ˈ"\ *vb* [ME *lowen*, fr. ON *loga*, fr. *logi*, n.] *Scot* : FLAME, BLAZE, GLOW

9**low** \ˈlau̇\ *vb* -ED/-ING/-S [by shortening] *dial* : ALLOW

**lo·wa** \ˈlō(w)ə\ *n* -s [Hindi *lavā*] : an Indian quail of the genus *Perdicula*

**low·an** \ˈlōən\ *n* -s [native name in Australia] *Austral* : LEIPOA

**low·ance** \ˈlau̇ən(t)s\ *n* -s [short for 1*allowance*] *dial Brit* : food or drink or the equivalent in money given to a worker in addition to his wages

**low-angle fault** *n* : a geological fault with its dip less than 45 degrees

**low-back** \ˈ=¦=\ *adj, of a vowel* : uttered with the back of the tongue low in the mouth ⟨a *low-back* \ȧ\⟩

**lowball** \ˈ=ˌ=\ *n* : a form of draw poker in which the lowest-ranking poker hand wins the pot, the ace being always the lowest-ranking card, straights and flushes not counting, and the best possible hand being A, 2, 3, 4, 5 regardless of suits

**low beam** *n* : the short-range focus of a vehicle headlight that directs the light below the eye level of oncoming drivers — contrasted with *high beam*; distinguished from *parking lights*

**low-bed** \ˈ=¦=\ *or* **lowboy** \ˈ=ˌ=\ *adj, of a vehicle* : having a bed only a few inches above the roadway ⟨a *low-bed* truck⟩ ⟨a *low-bed* trailer⟩

1**lowbell** \ˈ=ˌ=\ *n* [perh. fr. 4*low* + *bell*] 1 : a small bell (as for the neck of a sheep or cow) 2 *archaic* : a bell used with a sudden casting of light to frighten, stupefy, and capture birds

2**lowbell** *vt, obs* : to frighten or capture by or as if by the use of a lowbell

**low bindweed** *n* : a feebly twining herb (*Convolvulus spithamaeus*) of eastern No. America with oval leaves and white flowers

**low birch** *n* : DWARF BIRCH

**low blood pressure** *n* : HYPOTENSION

**low blow** *n* : a blow below the belt line in boxing

**low blueberry** *n* : LOWBUSH BLUEBERRY

**lowborn** \ˈ=¦=\ *adj* : born in a low condition or rank ⟨~ rich or . . . blue-blooded poor —Clement Greenberg⟩

**lowboy** \ˈ=ˌ=\ *n* : a dressing table about three feet high with drawers and similar to but smaller than the lower part of a highboy

lowboy

**low-braced** \ˈ=¦=\ *adj, archery* : UNDERSTRUNG

**low brass** *n* 1 : brass low in zinc content 2 : brass containing about 20 percent zinc — compare HIGH BRASS

**lowbred** \ˈ=¦=\ *adj* : bred or resembling one bred in a low condition of life : characteristic or indicative of such breeding : RUDE, VULGAR ⟨a ~ man⟩

1**lowbrow** \ˈ=ˌ=\ *n* [4*low* + *brow*] : a person who does not possess or have pretensions to strong or advanced intellectual interests : one who lacks intellectual sophistication ⟨detective novels appeal to . . . highbrows as well as to ~s —W.O.Aydelotte⟩

2**lowbrow** \ˈ"\ *adj* : of, relating to, or suitable for a lowbrow ⟨a ~ book⟩ ⟨a ~ program⟩ ⟨America had two types, ~ and highbrow —W.V.O'Connor⟩

**low-browed** \ˈ=¦=\ *adj* [4*low* + *browed*] 1 : being a person with a low brow or a low forehead ⟨*low-browed* Neanderthaloids⟩ 2 : LOWBROW

**low·brow·ism** \ˈlō,brau̇,izəm\ *n* -s : the quality or state of being a lowbrow : the attitudes or traits characteristic of a lowbrow ⟨persistent ~ apparent in our slang —Sidney Baker⟩

**low-budget** \ˈ=¦=\ *adj* : suited to or made on a low budget ⟨a *low-budget* picture⟩ ⟨folk who were enjoying the *low-budget* campsites —W.L.Gresham⟩ ⟨a *low-budget* man⟩

**lowbush** \ˈ=ˌ=\ *adj* 1 : forming a very low or procumbent bush ⟨~ members of the genus *Rubus*⟩ 2 : borne on a lowbush plant ⟨tangy ~ beach plums⟩

**lowbush blackberry** *also* **low blackberry** *n* : DEWBERRY

**lowbush blueberry** *also* **low blueberry** *n* 1 : any of several low-growing No. American blueberries that are usu. considered to constitute a single highly variable species (*Vaccinium angustifolium*), have narrow serrulate leaves and sweet bluish black fruit with a heavy light blue bloom, and commonly form very large colonies by means of stolons 2 : the fruit of a lowbush blueberry

**low-central** \ˈ=¦=\ *adj* : LOW-MIXED

**low church** *adj, usu cap L&C* : tending toward or stressing the heritage of Protestant Christianity including its emphasis on the recovery of the orig. Christian gospel and personal service to its cause together with the minimization or outright rejection of sacerdotalism, sacramentarianism, and other forms of ceremonial ritualism — compare HIGH CHURCH

**low churchman** *n, usu cap L&C* : a person holding or advocating Low Church views

**low-class** \ˈ=¦=\ *adj* : LOWER-CLASS

**low comedian** *n* : a comedian that specializes in a broad type of humor

**low cornel** *n* : DWARF CORNEL a

**low-cost** \ˈ=¦=\ *adj* : obtainable at a low cost ⟨abundant and *low-cost* money —*U.S. News & World Report*⟩ ⟨*low-cost* housing⟩

**low country** *n* : a low-lying country or region; *specif* : the part of a southern state extending from the seacoast inland to the fall line

**low-country** \ˈ=¦==\ *adj* [*low country*] : of, relating to, or proceeding from a low country or region ⟨retain at least a trace of her *low-country* accent —Hamilton Basso⟩

**low cudweed** *n* : MARSH CUDWEED

**low-cut** \ˈ=¦=\ *adj* 1 : having an outline or border that is cut or shaped low as contrasted with other styles of the same article ⟨a *low-cut* neckline⟩ 2 *of a shoe* : having uppers that do not extend up as far as the ankle ⟨a *low-cut* oxford⟩

**lowdah** *var of* LAODAH

**low-down** \ˈ=¦=\ *adj* [4*low* + *down*, adv.] 1 : quite or very low ⟨there would come a shy, *low-down* little knock on the door —Flora Thompson⟩ 2 : CONTEMPTIBLE, MEAN, BASE ⟨couldn't have looked like that if he had been bad and *low-down* —Anne G. Winslow⟩ ⟨a *low-down* sneak⟩ ⟨it's right *low-down*, now, right wrong —Elizabeth M. Roberts⟩

**lowdown** \ˈ=ˌ=\ *n* -s : the actual facts : inside information : DOPE ⟨give the ~ on American life —M.D.Geismar⟩ ⟨in a position to give you folks the real ~ —Erle Stanley Gardner⟩

**low dutch** *n, cap L&D* 1 : LOW GERMAN 1 2 : a dialect of Dutch spoken in America by immigrants from the Netherlands

**lowe** *var of* LOW

**lowed** *past of* LOW

**low·ell** \ˈlōəl *also* ˈlōil\ *n* -s *usu cap* [fr. *Lowell*, city in northeast Massachusetts] : a cheap cotton cloth made in Lowell, Mass., in the 19th century

**low-end** \ˈ=¦=\ *adj* 1 : of low grade ⟨*low-end* woolens⟩ ⟨*low-end* pelts⟩ ⟨*low-end* glass ware⟩ 2 : manufacturing low grade goods esp. of cloth ⟨a *low-end* mill⟩

**low enema** *n* : an enema in which the injected material goes no higher than the rectum — compare HIGH ENEMA

1**low·er** *or* **lour** \ˈlau̇(ə)r, -au̇ə, *esp in the South* -au̇wə(r; *sometimes* ˈlō(ə)r *or* ˈlōə\ *vi* -ED/-ING/-S [ME *louren*; akin to MD *loeren* to lie in wait, watch, MHG *lūren*] 1 : to look sullen : FROWN ⟨~*ing* at the pavement —G.B.Shaw⟩ 2 a : to be dark, gloomy, and threatening ⟨the clouds ~⟩ b : to become covered with dark and threatening clouds ⟨a rising wind and ~*ing* sky⟩ c : to show threatening signs of approach ⟨dark ~s the tempest overhead —H.W.Longfellow⟩ ⟨great thunderheads ~*ing* as they came —Mary Austin⟩ 3 *archaic* : to lie in wait

2**lower** *or* **lour** \ˈ"\ *n* -s [ME *lour*, fr. *louren*, v.] : a lowering look; *also* : a lowering or gloomy sky or aspect of weather

3**low·er** \ˈlō(ə)r, -ōə\ *adj* [fr. *lower*, compar. of 4*low*] 1 : relatively low in position, amount, or degree ⟨a ~ berth⟩ ⟨a ~ estimate⟩ ⟨a ~ boiling point⟩ 2 a : being or relating to something or someone of popular or inferior origin or rank ⟨the ~ chamber of a legislative body⟩ ⟨~ officeholders⟩ b : less differentiated in structure : less highly advanced in the scale of development through evolution ⟨the ~ animals⟩ ⟨~ organisms⟩ c *also* **low** : of or relating to a phase of an educational system that must be completed before the next one is entered ⟨~ school⟩ ⟨~ division⟩ ⟨~ freshmen⟩ 3 a (1) : situated or regarded as being situated below the level of another part or place ⟨the ~ middle class⟩ ⟨the ~ settlements⟩ (2) : situated or believed to be situated beneath the surface of the earth ⟨the ~ world⟩ (3) : being the southern part of an area ⟨the center of the financial district in ~ Manhattan —*Current Biog.*⟩ ⟨the ~ South⟩ b *usu cap* : being an earlier epoch or series of the period or system named ⟨*Lower* Carboniferous⟩ ⟨*Lower* Cretaceous⟩ ⟨*Lower* Permian⟩ ⟨*Lower* Silurian⟩ — contrasted with *Upper* c : farther from the source ⟨the ~ Nile⟩ ⟨the ~ Mississippi⟩ d *usu cap* : living on lower ground, not so far inland, farther downstream, or farther south than others of the same group ⟨the *Lower* Creek⟩ 4 : more recent ⟨assigns a ~ date for this event⟩

4**lower** \ˈ"\ *vb* -ED/-ING/-S *vi* 1 : to move to a lower level : descend to a lower stage : let oneself down ⟨came and ~*ed* by her —A.B.Guthrie⟩ ⟨the river ~*ed* as rapidly as it rose⟩ 2 : to diminish or decrease in value, amount, intensity, or degree ⟨predicted that prices would gradually ~⟩ ⟨voice ~*ed* into the sound of rain —James Still⟩ 3 : to lower a boat or sail ⟨~*ed* for a bull sperm whale —H.A.Chippendale⟩ — often used with *away* ⟨as you ~ away, you can gather the jib as it comes down —Peter Heaton⟩ ~ *vt* 1 a : to let descend by its own weight : let down ⟨~ a bucket⟩ ⟨~ a sail⟩ ⟨into this the general ~*ed* his portly form —D.G.Gerahty⟩ b : to depress as to direction ⟨~ the aim of a gun⟩ c (1) : to depress the surface of (as by carving, scraping) (2) : to remove (a part) in so doing d : to reduce the height of ⟨~ a wall⟩ 2 a : to reduce in value or amount ⟨~ the price of goods⟩ ⟨~ the rate of interest⟩ b (1) : to bring down in quality, character, or reputation : DEGRADE ⟨~*ed* himself by his actions⟩ ⟨novels and tales likely to ~ taste —*Times Lit. Supp.*⟩ (2) : ABASE, HUMBLE : bring down in rank ⟨~*ed* the proud grandees and exalted the commoners⟩ c : to make less elevated as to objective ⟨~*ed* his aspirations⟩ — often used in the phrase *lower one's sights* ⟨nothing would be more fatal . . . than to ~ our sights —J.B.Conant⟩ 3 a : to move (the tongue) down away from the palate b : to replace (a sound) with an allophone or phoneme of lower tongue position ⟨\ē\ was ~*ed* to \i\ before \r\⟩ — **lower the boom** : crack down ⟨*lowered the boom* last week on congressional junketing —*Time*⟩ ⟨right pleasant about it, but he really *lowered the boom* —Maxwell Griffith⟩

5**lower** \ˈ"\ *n* -s : the lower member of a pair: as a : a lower berth b : a lower denture

**low·er·able** \ˈlō(ə)rəbəl\ *adj* : capable of being lowered

**lower angle** *n* : SECOND ANGLE

**Low·er·a·tor** \ˈlōə,rād·ə(r)\ *trademark* — used for a machine for conveying loads vertically to a lower level

**lower austral** *adj, usu cap L&A* : of, relating to, or constituting a division of the Austral Zone including the Austroriparian and Lower Sonoran subdivisions

**lower boom** *n* : a spar run out from each side of a ship at anchor to secure boats clear of the side — see SHIP illustration

**lower bridge** *n* : the lower platform of a ship's bridge having two levels

**lower case** *n* : the lower one of a pair of type cases containing small letters and usu. also figures, punctuation marks, spaces, quads — compare UPPER CASE

1**lowercase** \ˈ=¦=ˌ=\ *adj* [*lower case*] 1 *of a letter* : having as its typical form a f g or *b n i* or q z r rather than A F G or *B N I* or **Q Z R** — abbr. *lc*; compare CAPITAL 2 : set, printed, written, or otherwise rendered in lowercase letters — abbr. *lc*

2**lowercase** \ˈ"\ *n* : lowercase letters — abbr. *lc*; compare UPPERCASE

3**lowercase** \ˈ"\ *vt* : to print or set in lowercase; *also* : to change (as a capital letter) to a lowercase letter — abbr. *lc*

**lower chamber** *n* : LOWER HOUSE ⟨the House of Assembly resembles . . . the *lower chambers* in the other Dominions —Alexander Brady⟩

**lower chinook** *n, usu cap L&C* : a Chinookan language of the Clatsop and Chinook peoples

**lower class** *n* 1 : a social class occupying a position below the middle class and having the lowest status in a society: as a : a feudal and post-feudal grouping of people composed principally of laborers and peasants b : a class composed chiefly (as in England) of manual workers : WORKING CLASS c : a socioeconomic grouping (as in the U.S.) characterized chiefly by low income, lack of education, and performance of unskilled manual labor 2 **lower classes** *pl* : an aggregate of social groupings comprising subdivisions of the lower class

**lower-class** \ˈ=¦=\ *adj* [*lower class*] 1 : of or relating to the lower class 2 : belonging to or associated with the lower class and its possession of or inclination toward such characteristics as a low material standard of living, social instability, little emphasis on convention and the proprieties, and a low level of personal ambition and of aspiration esp. toward education — compare MIDDLE-CLASS, UPPER-CLASS 3 : being an inferior or low-ranking specimen of its kind : ranking low in some scale or by some standard ⟨after a couple of summers of seasoning in *lower-class* minor circuits —L.E.Davis⟩ ⟨an invitation to a *lower-class* embassy —Lillian Hellman⟩

**low·er·class·man** \ˈ=¦=ˌ=mən\ *n, pl* **lowerclassmen** [fr. the phrase *lower class* "freshman or sophomore class" + *man*] : UNDERCLASSMAN

**lower court** *n* : a court whose decisions are subject to review or to appeal to a higher court : the court that first hears or tries cases : an inferior court

**lower covert** *n* : a covert on the undersurface of the wing or tail of a bird — usu. used in pl.

**lower criticism** *n* [so called fr. its primary or foundational character as contrasted with the higher criticism which utilizes its results] : study of the Bible that aims at reconstructing the original biblical texts : TEXTUAL CRITICISM — compare HIGHER CRITICISM

**lower culmination** *n, astron* : the crossing of a circumpolar object over that part of the celestial meridian between the visible pole and the horizon

**lower deck** *n* 1 a : the lowest deck in ships with two or three decks : a deck below the main deck b : next to the lowest deck in ships with four or more decks — see DECK illustration 2 *chiefly Brit* a : the quarters of the enlisted personnel of a ship b : the enlisted personnel 3 : a deck of a newspaper headline below the top deck

**lowered** *past of* LOWER

**low·er·er** \ˈlō(ə)rə(r)\ *n* -s [4*lower* + *-er*] : one that lowers

**lower functional calculus** *n* : functional calculus in which quantification is applied only to variables of individuals or arguments — called also *functional calculus of the first order*

**lower fungus** *n* : any of numerous fungi with hyphae absent or rudimentary and nonseptate and never forming a compact tissue (as in the Phycomycetes) — compare HIGHER FUNGUS

**lower house** *n* : the popular and often the larger and more representative branch of a legislative body having two chambers ⟨the *lower house* of the Dominion Parliament is known as the House of Commons —F.A.Magruder⟩

1**low·er·ing** *also* **lour·ing** \ˈlau̇(ə)riŋ, -rēŋ *esp in the South* -au̇wər-\ *adj* [ME *louring*, fr. pres. part. of *louren* to lower, frown — more at LOWER] : dark and threatening : GLOOMY, SULLEN, FROWNING ⟨a ~ expression in her black eyes —Liam O'Flaherty⟩ ⟨it was a ~ May day —Sylvia T. Warner⟩

2**lowering** *n* -s [fr. gerund of 4*lower*] : the act or an instance of making low or lower ⟨a ~ of trade restrictions —*Current Biog.*⟩

**low·er·ing·ly** *also* **lour·ing·ly** *adv* [1*lowering* + *-ly*] : in a lowering manner : DARKLY, GLOOMILY ⟨looked at him ~⟩

**lower larynx** *n* : the syrinx of a bird

**lower limb** *n* : the edge of a celestial body that is nearest the horizon

**lower mars** *n, usu cap L&M* [3*lower* + *Mars*, Roman god of war and agriculture, fr. L *Mart-, Mars*] : a Mount located inside the line of Life beneath the Mount of Jupiter and above the Mount of Venus that when well developed is usu. held by palmists to indicate active courage and a martial spirit and sometimes an aggressive or quarrelsome nature — compare UPPER MARS; see PALMISTRY illustration

**lower mast** *n* : the lowest part of a compound mast composed of two or more poles — compare TOPMAST

**low·er·most** \ˈlō(ə)r,mōst *also chiefly Brit* -ˌmast\ *adj* : LOWEST ⟨at the ~ point of her flight —Sacheverell Sitwell⟩

**lower orders** *n pl* : LOWER CLASSES ⟨you had the marks of the *lower orders* on you —Anthony West⟩

**lower plants** *n pl* : plants (as the algae and fungi) having simple structure and reproductive processes

**lowers** *pres 3d sing of* LOWER, *pl of* LOWER

**lower sonoran** *adj, usu cap L&S* : of, relating to, or being the warmer part of the Sonoran life zone that adjoins the Tropical zone — compare UPPER SONORAN

**lower transit** *n* : the apparent crossing of a celestial body over the half of the meridian that lies between the celestial poles and contains the observer's zenith

**lower umpqua** *n, usu cap L&U* : KUITSH

**low·ery** *also* **loury** \ˈlau̇(ə)rē, -ri *esp in the South* -au̇wər-\ *adj* [2*lower* + *-y*] : CLOUDY, GLOOMY, LOWERING ⟨a ~ sky⟩

**lowest** *superlative of* LOW

**lowest common denominator** *n* 1 : the lowest common multiple of two or more denominators 2 : something (as a quality or level of taste) that typifies or is common, acceptable, or comprehensible to all or the greatest possible number of individuals ⟨the committee system . . . reduces all ideas to the *lowest common denominator* —M.W.Straight⟩ ⟨broadcasting . . . falls into the error of producing programs at the *lowest common denominator* —Franklin Dunham⟩ ⟨living together in boredom, men exhibit their *lowest common denominator* —Clement Greenberg⟩ ⟨the quest by . . . the movies and radio for *lowest common denominators* —John Collier b. 1884⟩

**lowest common multiple** *n* : the smallest common multiple of two or more numbers or the common multiple of lowest degree of two or more polynomials

**lowes·toft ware** \ˈlōz,tȯft-, -,täft-, -ˌtəft-\ *or* **lowestoft** *n* -s *usu cap L* [fr. *Lowestoft*, city in eastern England] 1 : a soft china made at Lowestoft, England from 1757 to 1802 2 : Chinese porcelain specially decorated (as with armorial bearings) for the English trade — called also *Chinese export porcelain*

**low explosive** *n* : a deflagrating or nondetonating explosive : PROPELLANT

**low-flung** \ˈ=¦=\ *adj, archaic* : very degraded : LOW-DOWN

**low franconian** *n, cap L&F* : the West Germanic language that was used by the Franks inhabiting the region around the lowest part of the Rhine and that survives into modern times as a group of Low German dialects of northwestern Germany and as one of the principal linguistic strains from which Dutch (sense 1b) has evolved — compare FRANCONIAN

**low frequency** *n* : a radio frequency in the next to lowest range of the radio spectrum — see RADIO FREQUENCY table

**low-frequency** \ˈ=¦===\ *adj* [*low frequency*] : of or relating to low frequency or a radio wave having such a frequency

**low-front** \ˈ=¦=\ *adj, of a vowel* : low and front ⟨\a\⟩

**low gallonage sprayer** *n* : CONCENTRATE SPRAYER

**low german** *n, cap L&G* [trans. of G *niederdeutsch*] 1 : the German dialects of northern Germany esp. as used since the end of the medieval period : PLATTDEUTSCH — compare HIGH GERMAN, MIDDLE LOW GERMAN, OLD SAXON 2 : the West Germanic languages other than High German — compare DUTCH

**low-grade** \ˈ=¦=\ *adj* [fr. the phrase *low grade*] 1 : being of a grade or quality rated as inferior ⟨*low-grade* materials⟩ ⟨*low-grade* minds —*English Jour.*⟩ ⟨*low-grade* ore⟩ 2 : being near the lower extreme of the range in which it may occur ⟨a *low-grade* fever is a slight fever⟩ ⟨a *low-grade* imbecile exhibits extreme deviation from normal⟩ — compare HIGH-GRADE

**low ground** *n, chiefly South* : 1BOTTOM 6 — often used in pl.

**low-headed** \ˈ=¦=\ *adj* : CHAMAECEPHALIC

**low-heat cement** *n* : a portland cement specially prepared to develop a relatively low amount of heat of hydration during the setting and hardening period

**low hop clover** *n* : a nearly prostrate European clover (*Trifolium procumbens*) with yellow flowers

**low-house** \ˈ=ˌ=\ *n* : the trap house on the right side of a skeet shooting range that projects the target from a point 3½ feet above the ground — called also *lo-trap*; compare HIGH-HOUSE

**low hurdles** *n pl but sing or pl in constr* : a track event of 220 yards or 200 meters distance with ten 2 ft. 6 in. hurdles to be surmounted — compare HIGH HURDLES, HURDLE RACE

**lowing** *pres part of* LOW

**low·ish** \ˈlōish\ *adj* : rather low ⟨an ignorant woman of ~ mentality —Rosamond Lehmann⟩ ⟨a ~ neckline —Marion Miller⟩

**low-key** \ˈ=¦=\ *adj* [fr. the phrase *low key*] 1 : of low intensity : RESTRAINED, LOW-KEYED 2 *photog* : having or producing dark tones only with little contrast ⟨a *low-key* picture⟩ — compare KEY 10d

**low-keyed** \ˈ=¦=\ *adj* : subdued or restrained in mood, treatment, or quality ⟨a *low-keyed* little movie —*Newsweek*⟩ ⟨writes a cool, *low-keyed* prose —John Woodburn⟩ ⟨a little masterpiece of *low-keyed* eloquence —*Theatre Arts*⟩

1**low·land** \ˈlōlənd, ˈlō,land, -aa(ə)nd\ *n* [4*low* + *land*] : land that is low with respect to the neighboring country : a low or level country; *specif, dial* : BOTTOM 6 — often used in pl.

2**lowland** \ˈ"\ *adj* 1 : of, relating to, or characteristic of a low-

land : inhabiting or growing in lowlands ⟨a ~ area⟩ ⟨~ speech⟩ 2 *usu cap* [fr. the *Lowlands*, southern and eastern part of Scotland] : of, relating to, or typical of the Lowlands of Scotland or the speech of that area
**low·land·er** \-də(r)\ *n* **1** : a native or inhabitant of a lowland region **2** *usu cap* : an inhabitant of the Lowlands of Scotland — compare HIGHLANDER
**lowland fir** *also* **lowland white fir** *n* : a lofty tree (*Abies grandis*) of the coast region of No. America with long curving branches, deep green leaves, and soft wood
**lowland plover** *n* : GOLDEN PLOVER
**lowland rice** *n* : rice grown on land that is flooded or irrigated — compare UPLAND RICE
**lowland scots** *n, cap L&S* : Scots spoken in the Lowlands
**low latin** *n, cap both Ls* : postclassical Latin in its later stages
**low–level** \ˈ¦=¦=\ *adj* [fr. the phrase *low level*] **1** : being on a low level (as of importance or rank) ⟨sees only *low-level* Chinese officials —*Newsweek*⟩ ⟨restricting itself to such *low-level* generalization —P.B.Rice⟩ **2** : occurring, done, or placed at a relatively low level ⟨*low-level* bombing and strafing raids⟩
**low–life** \ˈ=¦=\ *adj* [fr. the phrase *low life*] : of or relating to the world of low social life ⟨his realism turned naturally to *low-life* adventure —V.L.Parrington⟩ ⟨recalling *low-life* pictures of the old Dutch painters —Van Wyck Brooks⟩
**lowlife** \ˈ=,=\ *n, pl* **lowlifes** *also* **lowlives** [fr. the phrase *low life*] **1** : a person of low social, cultural, or economic status ⟨wanted to transcribe completely the conversation of the ~*s* —Sinclair Lewis⟩ **2** : a person of criminal or low moral character : a shady or disreputable person ⟨among the ~*s* of the underworld —J.V. Ten Eyk⟩ ⟨finds his wife has deserted him and with a dirty ~ too —Ethel Wilson⟩
**low·li·head** \ˈlōlē,hed\ *n* [ME *lowliheed*, fr. *lowli*, *lowly* + *-heed*, *-hed*, *-hede* (akin to ME *-hod*, *-had* -hood)] *archaic* : lowly state ⟨this charnel life, this ~ —Sidney Lanier⟩
**low·li·ly** \-lələ̄\ *adv* [ME *lawlyly*, fr. *lawly*, *lowly* + *-ly*] : in a lowly manner
**low·li·ness** \ˈlōlēnəs\ *n* -ES [ME *lowlinesse*, fr. *lowli*, *lowly* + *-nesse* -ness] : the quality or state of being lowly
**low–lived** \ˈlō¦līvd\ *adj* : living a low life : suggestive of a low life : MEAN, CONTEMPTIBLE ⟨a *low-lived* creature⟩ ⟨a *low-lived* trick⟩
**low–loss** \ˈ=¦=\ *adj* : having low resistance and electric power loss ⟨a *low-loss* radio condenser⟩
**¹low–low** \ˈ=ˈ=\ *adj* [⁴*low* + ⁴*low*] **1** : slower than ordinary low gear and thereby adapted to heavy loads or steep grades ⟨a *low-low* gear⟩ **2** *of tide* : lower than the normal low
**²low–low** \ˈ"\ *n* : low-low gear ⟨tried to shift into *low-low* —Hugh Fosburgh⟩
**¹low·ly** \ˈlōlē, -li\ *adv* [ME, fr. ⁴*low* + *-ly*, adv. suffix] **1** : in a lowly manner : HUMBLY, MEEKLY, MODESTLY ⟨bowed ~ before her⟩ **2** : in a low position, manner, or degree ⟨affected rams are usually ~ fertile —*Fertility of Sheep*⟩ ⟨rare records . . . ~ priced —*advt*⟩ **3** : in a low voice : not loudly
**²lowly** \ˈ"\ *adj* -ER/-EST [ME, fr. ⁴*low* + *-ly*, adj. suffix] **1 a** : humble in manner or spirit : MODEST, MODERATE, MEEK ⟨taught him to be ~ and reverent⟩ **b** : of or relating to a low social or economic rank ⟨a man of ~ birth⟩ ⟨they were too ~ to associate with me —G.B.Shaw⟩ **c** : low in the scale of biological or cultural evolution ⟨a ~ society of the present day —*Notes & Queries on Anthropology*⟩ ⟨accepted the possibility that ~ . . . animals might be generated spontaneously —S.F. Mason⟩ **d** : ranking low in some hierarchy ⟨a ~ instructor in government —Fred Rodell⟩ ⟨a ~ parish priest⟩ **e** : low in order of importance, value, or esteem ⟨need not trouble himself with the ~ business of reading and writing if he had a good scribe —G.B.Jeffery⟩ ⟨made from a ~ railroad spike —*Re-Mor-Plate*⟩ **f** : not lofty or sublime : PROSAIC, COMMONPLACE ⟨using great words on the *lowlier* subject, contrives to make them appropriate —A.T.Quiller-Couch⟩ **2** : low in position or growth : being relatively close to the ground ⟨the starvation need of air and light allotted to the ~ growths —William Beebe⟩ **syn** see HUMBLE
**low–lying** \ˈ=¦==\ *adj* **1** : having little upward extension or elevation : lying or rising relatively little above the ground or other base ⟨*low-lying* sand islands —*Amer. Guide Series: Fla.*⟩ ⟨*low-lying* hills⟩ **2** : lying below the normal level, surface, or the base of measurement or mean elevation ⟨*low-lying* haze and clouds —Alexander Forbes⟩ ⟨supplies to the *low-lying* cities of the state —*Amer. Guide Series: La.*⟩
**low mallow** *n* : DWARF MALLOW
**low mass** *n, often cap L&M* : a mass that is not sung but said in the simplest ceremonial form often without music or choir and with but one priest and one acolyte
**low–melting** \ˈ=¦==\ *adj* : melting at a relatively low temperature
**lowmen** *n pl, obs* : dice loaded to turn up low numbers
**low–minded** \ˈ=¦==\ *adj* : inclined in mind to low or unworthy things : showing a vulgar mind ⟨to my, perhaps *low-minded*, taste, they are by far the most successful pieces in the book —J.R.Hulbert⟩
**low–mixed** \ˈ=¦=\ *adj, of a vowel* : uttered (as \ä\) with the middle of the tongue low and intermediate between front and back
**low moor** *n* : a wet lowland rich in calcium and potassium and characterized by abundant moisture-loving grasses, reeds, rushes, and sedges
**¹lown** \ˈlau̇n\ *vb* -ED/-ING/-S [ME (Sc) *lownen*, of Scand origin; akin to Sw *lugna* to calm, quiet, OIcel *lygna*; derivative fr. the root of OSw *lughn*, n., calm, OIcel *logn*; akin to Goth *liuhath* light — more at LIGHT] *dial* : CALM, QUIET
**²lown** \ˈ"\ *adj* [ME (Sc) *lowne*, of Scand origin; akin to OSw *lughn*, adj., calm, Norw *logn*, OIcel *lygn*; derivative fr. the root of OSw *lughn*, n., calm, OIcel *logn*] *dial* : CALM, QUIET, STILL ⟨a ~ spring night —Maristan Chapman⟩
**³lown** \ˈ"\ *n* -S *dial* : CALM, QUIET, STILLNESS
**⁴lown** \ˈlün\ *chiefly Scot var of* ²LOON
**lownd** \ˈlau̇nd\ *dial var of* ²LOWN
**low–neck** \ˈ=,=\ *n* : a low-necked dress
**low–necked** *also* **low–neck** \ˈ=¦=\ *adj* : having a low-cut neckline
**low·ness** *n* -ES [ME *lownesse*, fr. ⁴*low* + *-nesse* -ness] : the quality or state of being low
**lowp** \ˈlau̇p, ˈlōp, ˈlüp\ *var of* ¹LOUP
**low–pass filter** *n* : an electric-circuit filter that transmits only frequencies below a prescribed frequency limit
**low pitch** *n* : DIAPASON NORMAL
**low–pitched** \ˈ=¦=\ *adj* **1** : pitched in a low key : being of low tone or dynamics ⟨a *low-pitched* voice⟩ **2** : having a low ratio of height to span ⟨a *low-pitched* roof⟩; *also* : LOW-STUDDED
**low–pressure** \ˈ=¦==\ *adj* **1 a** : having, employing, exerting, or operating under a relatively small pressure ⟨a *low-pressure* burner⟩ **b** : having or resulting from a low atmospheric pressure ⟨a *low-pressure* system⟩ ⟨a *low-pressure* storm⟩ — compare CYCLONE **2** : not strenuous, intense, or aggressive in manner or approach : EASYGOING ⟨find a wonderfully *low-pressure* feeling about the whole area —Richard Joseph⟩ ⟨*low-pressure* circulation methods —*U.S. News & World Report*⟩ ⟨a *low-pressure* and thoroughly diverting report —C.W.Morton⟩ — compare HIGH-PRESSURE
**low–quarter shoe** *n, chiefly South* : LOW SHOE
**low–rate** \ˈ=,=\ *vt, chiefly South & Midland* : BELITTLE, CENSURE, DEPRECIATE, DISPARAGE ⟨you *low-rate* me too much —Lonnie Coleman⟩ ⟨*low-rating* the achievements of his . . . friends —Lee Rogow⟩
**low relief** *n* [trans. of F *bas-relief*] : BAS-RELIEF
**¹low·rie** \ˈlau̇ri\ *n* -S [fr. *Lowrie*, nickname fr. the name *Lawrence*] *Scot* : FOX ⟨has greedy ~ been among thy sheep —David Sillar⟩
**²low·rie** \ˈlōri\ *Austral var of* LORY
**low·ry process** \ˈlau̇rē-\ *n, usu cap L* [after C. B. *Lowry*, who devised it] : an empty-cell wood-treating process involving an injection of creosote without a preliminary vacuum in excess of the amount required and removal of the excess by a quick high vacuum
**lows** *pl of* LOW, *pres 3d sing of* LOW
**low–salt diet** *n* : LOW-SODIUM DIET
**low saxon** *n, cap L&S* : the Germanic dialects of northwest Germany between the Rhine and the Elbe
**lowse** *adj* ˈlōs, *v.* ˈlōz\ *dial Brit var of* LOOSE
**low–set** \ˈ=¦=\ *adj, of an animal* : STOCKY, BLOCKY, COBBY; *specif* : having the legs short with heavily developed musculature
**low shoe** *n* : a low-cut shoe; *esp* : OXFORD
**low sick** *adj, South & Midland* : seriously ill
**low side window** *n* : a window in medieval churches that is narrow, near the ground, and out of the line of the other windows — called also *lychnoscope*
**low·sin** \ˈlōzən\ *n* -S [E dial. (northern) *lowsin*, *lowsing*, fr. pres. part. of *lowse* to loose, stop work, fr. ME *loosen*, *losen*, *lousen* to loose — more at LOOSE] *dial Brit* : an act of stopping work ⟨seen my last ~ —Charles Murray⟩
**low–slung** \ˈ=¦=\ *adj* : having relatively small upward extent : being relatively close to the ground, floor, or other base ⟨the furniture was all *low-slung* and functional —Edmund Wilson⟩ ⟨this *low-slung* modernistic building —*Women's Wear Daily*⟩ ⟨*low-slung* beef cattle —J.F.Sembower⟩; *specif* : having a low floor to facilitate loading and to maintain stability on curves at high speed ⟨made up of *low-slung* tubular cars holding 600 passengers —*Time*⟩
**low–sodium diet** *n* : a diet restricted to foods naturally low in sodium content and prepared without added salt that is used esp. in the management of certain circulatory or kidney disorders
**low speed** *n* : slow speed; *esp* : the slowest speed — used esp. of an automobile with three forward speeds
**low–spirited** \ˈ=¦===\ *adj* **1** *archaic* : lacking in ardor or in courage **2** : DEJECTED, DEPRESSED ⟨found his friend ailing and *low-spirited*⟩
**low–spir·it·ed·ness** *n* : the quality or state of being low-spirited
**low–strung** \ˈ=¦=\ *adj* : having less than a fistmele between bow and bowstring ⟨a *low-strung* bow⟩
**low–studded** \ˈ=¦==\ *adj* : furnished or built with short studs ⟨a *low-studded* house⟩
**low sunday** *n, usu cap L&S* [ME *low-sonday*, fr. ⁴*low* + *sonday* Sunday] : the Sunday following Easter
**low–temperature** \ˈ=¦=...\ *adj* : relating to or carried out at very low or relatively low temperatures ⟨*low-temperature* refrigeration⟩ ⟨*low-temperature* carbonization of coal below about 1300°F⟩
**low–tension** \ˈ=¦==\ *adj* **1** : having a low potential or voltage **2** : constructed to be used at low voltage ⟨a *low-tension* coil⟩ ⟨a *low-tension* transmission line⟩
**low–test** \ˈ=¦=\ *adj* : having a low volatility — used esp. of gasoline
**low tide** *n* : the farthest ebb of the tide : the tide at its lowest
**lowveld** \ˈ=,=\ *n* : GRASSVELD
**low voltage** *n* **1** : voltage low enough to be considered safe for indoor domestic use and typically 120 volts or less **2** : voltage below that required for normal operation
**low–warp** \ˈ=¦=\ *adj* : having the warp threads strung horizontally ⟨*low-warp* tapestry⟩
**low water** *n* **1** : a low stage of the water (as in a river or lake); *specif* : LOW TIDE **2** : a depressed, degraded, or embarrassed state ⟨the country was patently at a moral and religious *low water* —W.L.Sperry⟩ ⟨found itself in *low water* after a checkered . . . career —W.J.Thorne⟩
**low–water line** *or* **low–water mark** *n* **1** : a line or mark indicating low water **2** *usu low-water mark* : something that marks a nadir of decline or degradation ⟨the *low-water mark* of political infamy was the killing of statewide civil service —*New Orleans States*⟩
**low week** *n, usu cap L&W* : the week beginning with Low Sunday
**low wine** *n* : a weak liquor produced by the first distillation of wash : first run of the still — often used in pl.; compare FEINTS
**lowy** \ˈlōē\ *n* -ES [MF *louee*, *liuee* space of a league, fr. OF, fr. *liue* league, fr. LL *leuga* — more at LEAGUE] : BANLIEUE
**¹lox** \ˈläks\ *n* -ES [*liquid oxygen*] : LIQUID OXYGEN
**²lox** \ˈ"\ *n, pl* **lox** *or* **loxes** [Yiddish *laks*, fr. MHG *lahs* salmon, fr. OHG — more at LAX] : smoked salmon
**lox–** *or* **loxo–** *comb form* [NL, fr. Gk, fr. *loxos*; akin to MIr *lose*, OE *eln* ell — more at ELL] : oblique ⟨*loxodograph*⟩ ⟨*Loxosoma*⟩
**loxa bark** \ˈläksə-, ˈlōhə-\ *or* **lo·ja bark** \ˈlōhə-\ *n* [fr. *Loxa*, *Loja*, province in southwest Ecuador] : PALE BARK
**lox·ia** \ˈläksēə\ *n, cap* [NL, fr. *lox-* + *-ia*] : a genus constituted by the crossbill
**lox·o·clase** \ˈläksə,klās, -āz\ *n* -S [G *loxoklas*, fr. *lox-* + *-klas* -clase] : an orthoclase containing considerable sodium
**lox·o·cosm** \ˈläksə,käzəm\ *n* [ISV *lox-* + *-cosm*] : a device to show how the inclination of the earth's axis causes the day's length to vary from season to season
**lox·od·o·graph** \läkˈsädə,graf, -räf\ *n* [*lox-* + Gk *hodos* way, course + E *-graph* — more at CEDE] : an apparatus for recording a ship's course by magnetism and photography or other registering device
**¹lox·o·dont** \ˈläksə,dänt\ *also* **lox·o·don·tous** \¦==¦däntəs\ *adj* [*loxodont* fr. NL *Loxodonta*; *loxodontous* fr. NL *Loxodonta* + E *-ous*] : having shallow hollows between the ridges of the molar teeth
**²loxodont** \ˈ"\ *n* -S [NL *Loxodonta*] : an elephant with loxodont teeth
**lox·o·don·ta** \,==ˈdäntə\ *n, cap* [NL, fr. *lox-* + *-odonta*] : a genus of Elephantidae comprising the African elephants and extinct related forms
**lox·o·drome** \ˈläksə,drōm\ *n* -S [ISV, back-formation fr. *loxodromic*] : RHUMB LINE ⟨a sailor who has chosen a direction on the compass and keeps it steadily is following a ~ —Hugo Steinhaus⟩
**lox·o·drom·ic** \¦==¦drämik\ *also* **lox·o·drom·i·cal** \-mə̇kəl\ *adj* [*loxodromic* prob. fr. (assumed) NL *loxodromicus*, fr. Gk *lox-* + *drom-* + L *-icus* -ic; *loxodromical* fr. *loxodromic* + *-al*] : relating to a rhumb line or to sailing on rhumb lines — **lox·o·drom·i·cal·ly** \-mə̇k(ə)lē\ *adv*
**loxodromic curve** *n* : RHUMB LINE
**¹lox·o·loph·o·dont** \¦läksə¦läfə,dänt\ *adj* [NL *Loxolophodont-*, *Loxolophodon* genus of extinct ungulates in some classifications, fr. *lox-* + *loph-* + *-odont-*, *-odon* -odont] : having molar teeth with oblique crests connecting the anterior inner tubercle with the two outer tubercles and with the posterior inner tubercle rudimentary or absent — used esp. of several extinct ungulates
**²loxolophodont** \ˈ"\ *n* -S [NL *Loxolophodont-*, *Loxolophodon*] : a loxolophodont animal
**lox·om·ma** \läkˈsämə\ *n, cap* [NL, fr. *lox-* + *-omma*] : a genus of primitive Permian labyrinthodont amphibians (order Rhachitomi) that are commonly considered remotely ancestral to the modern salientians and are found in the coal measures of England and Bohemia
**lox·om·moid** \-sä,mȯid\ *n* -S [prob. fr. NL *Loxommoidea* (group including the genus *Loxomma*), fr. *Loxomma* + *-oidea*] : a member of the genus *Loxomma*
**lox·os·ce·les** \läkˈsäsə,lēz\ *n, cap* [NL, fr. *lox-* + Gk *-skelēs* (fr. *skelos* leg) — more at CYLINDER] : a genus of So. American spiders including a species (*L. laeta*) which is common about buildings and whose bite causes a local necrosis of tissue and sometimes systemic symptoms of poisoning
**lox·o·so·ma** \,läksəˈsōmə\ *n, cap* [NL, fr. *lox-* + *-soma*] : a genus (the type of the family Loxosomatidae) comprising solitary members of the Ectoprocta
**lox·y·gen** \ˈläksəjən, -jen\ *n* -S [*liquid oxygen*] : LIQUID OXYGEN
**loy** \ˈlȯi\ *n* -S [IrGael *láighe*; akin to Gk *lachainein* to dig] **1** : a long narrow spade used in Ireland **2** : a tool with a broad chisel point for digging post holes
**¹loyal** \ˈlȯi(ə)l ˈlȯ(i)yəl\ *adj, sometimes* -ER/-EST [MF, fr. OF *loial*, *leial*, fr. L *legalis* legal, of or relating to law — more at LEGAL] **1 a** : faithful to the lawful government or to the sovereign to whom one is subject : unswerving in allegiance ⟨the army remains ~⟩ ⟨no one can be hired until the administrator certifies that the individual is ~ to the United States —Arthur Schlesinger b. 1917⟩ ⟨there is no ~*er* subject of Her Grace than myself —J.H.Wheelwright⟩ **b** : faithful and devoted to a private person; *esp* : faithful to a person to whom fidelity is held to be due ⟨gentle, solicitous, and ~ slaves —Margaret Leech⟩ ⟨a ~ husband⟩ **2** : displaying or reflecting loyalty ⟨explained with a ~ little sob —Elinor Wylie⟩ ⟨~ utterances⟩ **3** : faithful or tenacious in adherence to a cause, ideal, practice, or custom ⟨a very ~ churchgoer⟩ ⟨~ in habits and attitudes to a vanished age —J.W.Krutch⟩ ⟨the Syrians . . . are still ~ to milk, butter, cheese, and lamb —*Amer. Guide Series: R.I.*⟩ **4** *obs* : LAWFUL, LEGITIMATE **syn** see FAITHFUL
**²loyal** \ˈ"\ *n* -S : a loyal subject or follower — usu. used in pl. ⟨those he considers to be his true-blue ~*s* —*Time*⟩
**loy·al·ism** \-ə,lizəm\ *n* -S : the principles or conduct of a loyalist : display of loyalty ⟨represents outspoken ~ —*Times Lit. Supp.*⟩
**loy·al·ist** \-ələst\ *n* -S : a person who is or remains loyal to a political cause, party, government, or sovereign: as **a** : an American opposed to separation from Great Britain during the Revolution : TORY ⟨a descendant of ~*s* who left the American colonies for Canada —*Current Biog.*⟩ **b** : an adherent to the Union cause during the Civil War esp. in a southern state **c** *usu cap* : an adherent to the constitutional republican government during the Spanish Civil War (1936–1939) ⟨rushed off to help the *Loyalists* —E.O.Hauser⟩
**loy·al·ly** \-əlē, -əli\ *adv* : in a loyal manner
**loy·al·ness** \-(ə)lnəs\ *n* -ES : the quality or state of being loyal
**loyal opposition** *n* : a minority party esp. in a legislative body whose opposition to the party in power is constructive, responsible, and bounded by loyalty to fundamental interests and principles ⟨a well-fortified minority will tend to improve . . . legislative debate and can become a genuine *loyal opposition* —*Amer. State Legislatures*⟩; *specif* : the minority party in the British parliament — often used in the phrase *His Majesty's loyal opposition*
**loy·al·ty** \ˈlȯi(ə)ltē, ˈlȯ(i)yəl- -ti\ *n* -ES *often attrib* [ME *loyaltee*, fr. MF *loialté*, fr. OF *loialté*, *leialté*, *lealté*, fr. *loial*, *leial* loyal + *-té* -ty] : the quality, state, or an instance of being loyal : fidelity or tenacious adherence (as to a government, principle, practice, or custom) ⟨~ is . . . essentially personal and moral, based on individual choice . . . and may find expression in a dozen forms —Francis Biddle⟩ ⟨why these products had failed to build brand ~ —Vance Packard⟩ ⟨~ is the absence of subversive tendencies or liaisons —L.A.Huston⟩ ⟨~ is . . . agreement with the party platform and program —E.S.Griffith⟩ ⟨~ to friends⟩ ⟨a ~ check⟩ **syn** see FIDELITY
**loyalty board** *n* : a board (as of a government agency) established and authorized to inquire into the loyalty to the government of the U.S. of persons employed or considered for employment by the U.S. government or by international organizations of which the U.S. is a member and to make usu. advisory determinations in such cases
**loyalty oath** *n* : a usu. mandatory oath affirming the loyalty of its taker (as to a sovereign, government, or party principles) ⟨ruled the Genevese . . . with the help of *loyalty oaths* and the gibbet —*Times Lit. Supp.*⟩ ⟨the *loyalty oath* will be abandoned at the next Democratic convention —*Newsweek*⟩; *esp* : an oath often required of public employees or applicants for public employment in the U.S. typically affirming that the signer upholds the U.S. or state constitutions and is not knowingly a member of any of a number of organizations held to be subversive
**loy·o·lite** \lȯiˈō,līt, lō(i)ˈyō,-, ˈlȯiə,-, ˈlō(i)yə,-\ *n* -S *usu cap* [Saint Ignatius of *Loyola* †1556 Span. ecclesiastic who founded the Jesuit order + E *-ite*] : JESUIT
**lo·zen** \ˈlōzᵊn, ˈläz-\ *n* -S [modif. of MF *losange*, fr. OF, diamond-shaped heraldic figure] *Scot* : a lozenge-shaped window pane
**¹loz·enge** \ˈläz|ᵊnj, |ənj *sometimes* ˈlō| *or* |s|\ *n* -S [ME *losenge*, fr. MF *losange*, fr. OF, diamond-shaped heraldic figure] **1** : a figure with four equal sides and two acute and two obtuse angles : DIAMOND, RHOMBUS **2** : something having the form of a lozenge: as **a** (1) : a small flat lozenge-shaped candy; *esp* : one made from sugar and gum, variously flavored, and sometimes medicated ⟨took a throat ~ for his cough⟩ (2) : PASTILLE **b** : a diamond-shaped decorative element or motif **c** (1) : a diamond-shaped heraldic figure usu. with the upper and lower angles slightly acute (2) : a diamond-shaped escutcheon now commonly used only by women **d** (1) : one of the diamond-shaped facets on a cut gem (2) : a cut with lozenge-shaped outline

lozenge 2c(1)

**²lozenge** \ˈ"\ *adj* : marked with or composed of a lozenge : LOZENGED
**lozenged** \-jd\ *or* **lozenge–shaped** \¦==¦=\ *adj* : shaped like a lozenge
**lozenge file** *n* : a die-sinker's small file with a lozenge-shaped cross section and teeth on all four faces
**lozenge molding** *n* : a molding used in Norman architecture characterized by lozenge-shaped ornaments
**loz·eng·er** \-jə(r)\ *n* -S [by alter.] *dial* : LOZENGE 2a
**lozengewise** \ˈ==,=\ *adv* : in the shape of a lozenge : so as to form a lozenge or a lozenge pattern
**loz·engy** \-jē\ *adj* [MF *losengié*, fr. OF, fr. *losenge*, *losange* diamond-shaped heraldic figure] *heraldry* : divided into lozenge-shaped compartments
**lo·zi** \ˈlōzē\ *n, pl* **lozi** *or* **lozis** *usu cap* **1 a** : a Bantu-speaking people in Northern Rhodesia known for their woodcarving — called also *Barotse* **b** : a member of such people **2** : a Bantu language of the Lozi people that is closely related to Sotho and is used as a lingua franca in Barotseland
**lp** *abbr* **1** ladyship **2** lordship
**LP** \ˈelˈpē\ *trademark* — used for a microgroove phonograph record ordinarily having a diameter of 10 or 12 inches, turning at 33⅓ revolutions per minute, and requiring a playing time of about 10 to 30 minutes
**LP** *abbr* **1** landplane **2** large paper; large post **3** liquefied petroleum **4** long picot **5** long primer **6** lord provost **7** loss of pay **8** low-pass **9** low point **10** low pressure
**LPF** *abbr* leukocytosis-promoting factor
**LPG** *abbr* liquefied petroleum gas
**lp gas** *n, usu cap L&P & sometimes cap G* [*liquefied petroleum gas*] : LIQUEFIED PETROLEUM GAS
**LPM** *abbr* long particular meter
**LPP** *abbr* large paper proofs
**LPS** *abbr* lord privy seal
**LPW** *abbr* lumens per watt
**lr** *abbr* lira
**LR** *abbr* **1** large ring **2** left rear **3** living room **4** lock rail **5** log run **6** long range **7** lower right
**lrg** *abbr* large
**LRRP** *abbr, often not cap* lowest required radiated power
**LS** *abbr* **1** landing ship **2** land service **3** leading seaman **4** left side **5** legal scroll **6** letter signed **7** library science **8** listed securities **9** local sunset **10** [L *locus sigilli*] the place of the seal **11** longitudinal section **12** long shot **13** loudspeaker **14** low speed **15** lump sum
**l's** *or* **ls** *pl of* L
**LSC** *abbr, often not cap* [L *loco supra citato*] in the place cited above
**lsd** *abbr* leased
**LSD** *abbr* **1** landing ship dock **2** *often not cap* [L *librae, solidi, denarii*] pounds, shillings, pence **3** lysergic acid diethylamide
**LSD 25** *n* : LYSERGIC ACID DIETHYLAMIDE
**l–shaped** \ˈ=,=\ *adj, cap L* : having the shape of a capital L
**l–shell** \ˈ=,=\ *n, usu cap L* : the second innermost shell of electrons surrounding an atomic nucleus — compare K-SHELL, M-SHELL
**LSM** *abbr* landing ship medium
**LSO** *abbr* landing signal officer
**l square** *n, cap L* : a carpenter's square
**LSR** *abbr* local sunrise
**LSS** *abbr* **1** lifesaving service **2** lifesaving station
**LST** *abbr* **1** landing ship tank **2** local sidereal time **3** local standard time
**lt** *abbr* **1** *often cap* lieutenant **2** light
**LT** *abbr* **1** landed terms **2** left tackle **3** legal tender **4** letter telegram **5** line telegraphy **6** local time **7** long ton **8** low tension
**LTA** *abbr* lighter than air
**ltd** *abbr, often cap* limited
**ltg** *abbr* lightning
**ltge** *abbr* lighterage
**lthr** *abbr* leather
**LTI** *abbr* light transmission index

**LTL** *abbr* less-than-truckload
**ltng** *abbr* lightning
**ltr** *abbr* **1** letter **2** lighter
**lu** \ˈlü\ *n, pl* **lu** *usu cap* **:** a Tai ethnic group inhabiting chiefly the extreme southwest part of Yunnan province in southern China and adhering to a Buddhist religion
**lu** *abbr* lumen
**Lu** *symbol* lutetium
**lu·ah** *or* **lu·ach** \lü,äk\ *n, pl* **lu·hoth** *or* **lu·hot** *or* **lu·choth** *or* **lu·chot** \lü ˈkōt(h)\ [Heb *lūaḥ*, lit., board, tablet (pl. *lūḥōt*)] **:** JEWISH CALENDAR
**lu·au** \ˈlüˈau̇, ˈ=,=\ *n* -s [Hawaiian *lu'au*] **1 :** a feast with Hawaiian food and usu. Hawaiian entertainment **2 :** cooked young taro leaves usu. with coconut cream and chicken or octopus
**lub** *abbr* lubricant; lubricating
**lu·ba** \ˈlübə\ *n, pl* **luba** *or* **lubas** *usu cap* **1 a :** an African Negro people of southern Belgian Congo **b :** a member of such people **2 :** any of numerous Bantu languages spoken in Belgian Congo; *esp* **:** TSHILUBA
**[1]lub·ber** \ˈləbə(r)\ *n* -s [ME *lobre, lobur*, prob. of Scand origin; akin to Sw dial. *lubber* fat lazy fellow, *lubbe* plump figure — more at LOB] **1** *also* **lub·bard** \ˈləbə(r)d\ **:** a big clumsy fellow; *esp* **:** a worthless idler **2 :** a clumsy or unskilled seaman — compare LANDLUBBER
**[2]lubber** \"\ *vi* **lubbered; lubbered; lubbering** \-b(ə)riŋ\ **lubbers :** to act in a lubberly manner esp. when managing a boat
**[3]lubber** \"\ *adj* **1** *also* **lub·bard** \ˈləbə(r)d\ **:** LUBBERLY **2 :** [3]BLUBBER ⟨his thick ~ lips were drawn heavily downward —Hall Caine⟩
**lubber fiend** *n* **:** a helpful goblin that does household chores at night
**lubber grasshopper** *n* **:** either of two very large stout clumsy short-winged No. American grasshoppers: **a :** a grasshopper (*Romalea microptera*) of the southeastern U.S. **b :** a grasshopper (*Brachystola magna*) of the southwestern U.S. and adjacent Mexico
**lubberland** \ˈ==,=\ *n* **:** COCKAIGNE
**lubber line** *also* **lubber's line** *or* **lubber mark** *or* **lubber's point** *n* **:** a fixed line on the compass or other directional indicator of a ship or airplane that is aligned with the longitudinal axis of the ship or plane
**lub·ber·li·ness** \ˈləbə(r)lēnəs, -lin-\ *n* -ES **:** the quality or state of being lubberly
**[1]lub·ber·ly** *adj* [[1]*lubber* + *-ly*] **1 a :** resembling or having the characteristics of a lubber **:** CLUMSY, LAZY, LOUTISH, STUPID ⟨emerged a ~ mediocrity —C.J.Rolo⟩ **b :** not seamanlike ⟨of all landlubbers, the most ~ —Herman Melville⟩ **2 :** appropriate to or fit for a lubber ⟨unfit for anything but some ~ shoreside pursuit —LaSelle Gilman⟩ **3** *of a ship* **a :** handled ineptly **b :** not shipshape
**[2]lubberly** \"\ *adv* **:** in a lubberly manner
**lubber's hole** *n* **:** a hole in a ship's top near the mast through which one may go farther aloft without going over the rim by the futtock shrouds
**lube** \ˈlüb\ *n* -s [short for *lubricating oil*] **:** a lube oil or other lubricant
**lü·beck** *or* **lu·beck** *or* **lue·beck** \ˈlü,bek\ *adj, usu cap* [fr. *Lübeck*, city in northern Germany] **:** of or from the city of Lübeck, Germany **:** of the kind or style prevalent in Lübeck
**lube oil** *n* [short for *lubricating oil*] **:** a lubricating oil obtained from petroleum
**lu·blin** \ˈlüblən\ *adj, usu cap* [fr. *Lublin*, city in eastern Poland] **:** of or from the city of Lublin, Poland **:** of the kind or style prevalent in Lublin
**lu·bra** \ˈlübrə\ *n* -s [native name in Tasmania] **:** an aboriginal girl or woman of Australia
**lu·bric** \ˈlübrik\ *or* **lu·bri·cal** \-brəkəl\ *adj* [*lubric* fr. MF *lubrique*, fr. L *lubricus*; *lubrical* fr. L *lubricus* + *-al*] *archaic* **:** LUBRICIOUS
**[1]lu·bri·cant** \ˈlübrəkənt\ *adj* [L *lubricant-, lubricans*, pres. part. of *lubricare* to lubricate, fr. *lubricus* slippery — more at SLEEVE] **:** serving to lubricate
**[2]lubricant** \"\ *n* -s **1 :** a substance capable of reducing friction, heat, and wear when introduced as a film between solid surfaces (as oil or grease for metal bearings, graphite for sprocket chains, soap or paraffin for wood surfaces, cutting compound for lathe tools); *esp* **:** such a substance interposed between moving parts of machinery — compare CUTTING FLUID **2 :** an emulsion, oil, or dressing applied to fibers and yarns to make processing easier and less damaging **3 :** something that lessens or prevents friction or difficulty ⟨a man who believed in the smile as a social ~ —Margery Allingham⟩ ⟨a kind of literary ~, that will ease the reading along —Dudley Fitts⟩
**lu·bri·cate** \-,kāt, *usu* -ād.+V\ *vb* -ED/-ING/-S [L *lubricatus*, past part. of *lubricare*] *vt* **1 :** to make smooth, slippery, or oily in motion, action, or appearance ⟨this small amount of chemical ~*s* the wax crystals —Desmond Reilly⟩ ⟨in drilling an oil well, mud is used to ~ the cutting bit —*Westinghouse News*⟩ **2 :** to apply a lubricant to **:** treat with a lubricant ⟨~ the bearings⟩ ⟨~ the economic system with a sufficiency of purchasing power —Hugh Dalton⟩ ⟨~ the skin with cold cream⟩ **3** *slang* **:** to ply with drink ⟨*lubricated* them with continuous champagne —Horace Sutton⟩ **4** *slang* **:** BRIBE ⟨*lubricated* a dishonest official⟩ ~ *vi* **1 :** to act as a lubricant ⟨oil ~*s* efficiently most of the time⟩ **2** *slang* **:** to drink or get drunk ⟨the *lubricating* kept right on, not so badly, but more than anyone could carry —Ethel Merman⟩
**lubricating oil** *n* **:** an oil (as a petroleum distillate or a fatty oil) used as a lubricant
**lu·bri·ca·tion** \,=ˈkāshən\ *n* -s **:** the act or process of lubricating or the state of being lubricated
**lu·bri·ca·tive** \ˈ==,kād.iv\ *adj* **:** acting or capable of acting as a lubricant
**lu·bri·ca·tor** \-,kād.ə(r), -ātə-\ *n* -s **:** one that lubricates: as **a :** GREASER, OILER **b :** LUBRICANT **c :** an oil container or other device for applying a lubricant
**lu·bri·ca·to·ry** \-,kə,tōr, *chiefly Brit* ˌ==ˈkātəri *or* -ā·tri\ *adj* [*lubricate* + *-ory*] **:** serving to lubricate
**lu·bri·cious** \lüˈbrishəs\ *or* **lu·bri·cous** \ˈlübrəkəs\ *adj* [*lubricious* alter. (influenced by *-ious*) of *lubricous*, fr. ML *lubricus*, fr. L, slippery] **1 a :** marked by wantonness **:** LECHEROUS ⟨eluding the *lubricous* embraces of her wealthy employer —*Amer. Mercury*⟩ ⟨some *lubricous* fellows . . . who made companions of these serving maids —E.L.Masters⟩ **b :** sexually stimulating **:** SALACIOUS ⟨a little ~ book . . . on a bed table by a pink-shaded lamp —Graham Greene⟩ ⟨exploited in full ~ detail by the metropolitan tabloids —John Woodburn⟩ **2** [influenced in meaning by L *lubricus*] **a :** having a smooth or slippery quality ⟨the skin of the cephalopods is thin and *lubricous* —R.B.Todd⟩ **b :** marked by uncertainty or instability **:** ELUSIVE, SHIFTY ⟨how ~ a friend and changeable a partisan —Robert Ferguson⟩ — **lu·bri·cious·ly** *adv*
**lu·bric·i·ty** \lüˈbrisəd.ē, -ətē, -i\ *n* -ES [MF *lubricité* lasciviousness, slipperiness, fr. ML & LL; ML *lubricitat-, lubricitas* lasciviousness, fr. LL, slipperiness, instability, fr. L *lubricus* slippery + *-itat-, -itas* -ity] **1 a :** LASCIVIOUSNESS, SENSUALITY ⟨a life of futile ~ —*Dial*⟩ **b :** something that stimulates to lewdness; *specif* **:** PORNOGRAPHY ⟨laws have been singularly ineffectual in eradicating ~ —*Christian Science Monitor*⟩ **2 a :** freedom from friction **:** SLIPPERINESS, SMOOTHNESS ⟨the scented ~ of soap —Sydney Smith⟩ **b :** a property that lessens friction ⟨the ~ of oil⟩ **3 :** INSTABILITY ⟨the ~ of fortune⟩
**lu·bri·fy** \ˈlübrə,fī\ *vt* -ED/-ING/-S [F *lubrifier*, fr. MF, fr. L *lubricus* + MF *-fier* -fy] *archaic* **:** LUBRICATE
**lu·bri·to·ri·um** \,=ˈtōrēəm, -tȯr-\ *n* -s [*lubri-* (as in *lubricate*) + *-torium* (as in *sanatorium*)] **:** a station or room for lubricating motor vehicles
**lu·can** *or* **lu·kan** \ˈlükən\ *adj, usu cap* [*lucan* fr. LL *lucanus*, fr. *Lucas* Luke, the Evangelist regarded as the author of the third Gospel in the New Testament (fr. Gk *Loukas*) + L *-anus* -an; *lukan* fr. *Luke* + E *-an*] **:** of, relating to, or having the characteristics of the Evangelist Luke or the Gospel ascribed to him
**[1]lu·ca·nid** \lüˈkanəd\ *adj* [NL *Lucanidae*] **:** of or relating to the Lucanidae
**[2]lucanid** \"\ *n* -s [NL *Lucanidae*] **:** a beetle of the family Lucanidae
**lu·can·i·dae** \=ˈkanə,dē\ *n pl, cap* [NL, fr. *Lucanus*, type genus + *-idae*] **:** a family of insects comprising the stag beetles
**lu·ca·nus** \=ˈkānəs\ *n, cap* [NL, perh. fr. LL, daylight, fr. L *luc-, lux* light + *-anus* -an — more at LIGHT] **:** a genus (the type of the family Lucanidae) of beetles
**lu·carne** \lüˈkärn, -kȧn\ *n* -s [alter. (influenced by F *lucarne* dormer window, fr. MF, alter. — influenced by MF *luiserne, luserne* lantern, fr. L *lucerna* lamp — of *lucanne*) of earlier *lucane*, fr. MF *lucanne*, fr. OF, fr. (assumed) OFrk *lūkinna*, fr. *lūk* something that closes (akin to MD *luke* something that closes, fence) + *-inna*, dim. suffix; akin to OE *lūcan* to close — more at LOCK] **:** DORMER WINDOW
**lu·cayo** \lüˈkī(,)ō, -kā(-\ *also* **lu·cayan** \-kāən, -kīən\ *n, pl* **lucayo** *or* **lucayos** *also* **lucayan** *or* **lucayans** *usu cap* [*Lucayo* fr. AmerSp, fr. Arawak; *Lucayan* fr. AmerSp *Lucayo* + E *-an*] **1 a :** an extinct aboriginal Arawakan tribe of the Bahamas **b :** a member of such tribe **2 :** the language of the Lucayo people
**luce** \ˈlüs\ *n* -s [ME, fr. MF *lus*, fr. LL *lucius*] **1 :** a pike esp. when full grown **2 :** a heraldic representation of a pike
**lu·cen·cy** \ˈlüsᵊnsē, -nsi\ *n* -ES [*lucent* + *-cy*] **:** the quality or state of being lucent **:** LUMINOSITY ⟨a color . . . with the ~ of porcelain —John Hersey⟩
**lu·cent** \-sᵊnt\ *adj* [L *lucent-, lucens*, pres. part. of *lucēre* to shine — more at LIGHT] **1 :** glowing with light **:** LUMINOUS, RADIANT ⟨the sun's ~ orb —John Milton⟩ **2 :** marked by clarity or translucence **:** CLEAR ⟨watches the underwater world . . . through the ~ membrane —*Time*⟩ ⟨reveal his ~ style —*Amer. Guide Series: Ind.*⟩ **syn** see BRIGHT
**lu·cent·ly** *adv* **:** in a lucent manner
**lucern** *n* -s [prob. modif. of G *lüchsern* of a lynx, fr. *luchs* lynx, fr. OHG *luhs* — more at LYNX] *obs* **:** LYNX
**lu·cer·nal** \(ˈ)lüˈsərnᵊl, -ˈsə̄n-, -ˈsəin-\ *adj* [L *lucerna* lamp + E *-al*] **:** of or relating to a lamp ⟨~ microscope⟩
**lu·cer·nar·ia** \,lüsərˈna(a)rēə\ *n, cap* [NL, fr. L *lucerna* lamp + NL *-aria*] **:** a widely distributed genus (the type of the family Lucernariidae) of north Atlantic littoral sessile or creeping scyphozoan jellyfishes that have a bell-shaped body prolonged at the margin into eight lobes each with a group of short tentacles — **lu·cer·nar·i·an** \ˌ==ˈna(a)rēən\ *adj or n*
**lu·cer·na·ri·da** \,lü(,)sərnəˈrīdə\ *also* **lu·cer·nar·i·id·ea** \,lüsər,na(a)rēˈidēə\ [NL, fr. *Lucernaria* + *-ida* or *-idea*] *syn of* STAUROMEDUSAE
**lu·cerne** *also* **lu·cern** \lüˈsərn, -sə̄n,-səin\ *n* -s [F *luzerne*, fr. Prov *luserno*, prob. fr. OProv *luzerna* lamp, fr. L *lucerna*; prob. fr. the shiny seeds; akin to L *lucēre* to shine — more at LIGHT] *chiefly Brit* **:** ALFALFA
**lucerne flea** *n* **:** a springtail (*Sminthurus viridis*) that damages alfalfa esp. in Australia
**luces** *pl of* LUX
**luchot** *or* **luchoth** *pl of* LUAH
**lu·chu·an** \lüˈchüən\ *n* -s *cap* [fr. *Luchu* islands (Ryukyu islands), southwest of Kyushu, Japan + E *-an*] **:** a native of the Ryukyu islands related to the Japanese but with a Malayan or Ainu admixture
**luci-** *comb form* [L, fr. *luc-, lux* — more at LIGHT] **:** light ⟨*lucimeter*⟩
**lu·ci·an·ic** \,lüshēˈanik\ *adj, usu cap L* [*Lucian*, 2d cent. A.D. Greek satirist and wit + E *-ic*] **:** of, relating to, or resembling Lucian or his writings ⟨interrogative, ironical, *Lucianic* scepticism —Douglas Bush⟩
**lu·ci·ble** \ˈlüsəbəl\ *adj* [L *lucibilis*, fr. L *lucēre* to shine + *-ibilis* -able] *archaic* **:** LUCENT
**lu·cid** \ˈlüsəd\ *adj* [L *lucidus*; akin to L *lucēre* to shine — more at LIGHT] **1 a :** suffused with light **:** BRIGHT, LUMINOUS, RADIANT ⟨satellites burning in a ~ ring —William Wordsworth⟩ ⟨wrap the hills from feet to flank in ~ haze —J.A. Symonds⟩ ⟨the lamps . . . seemed dim in that ~ twilight —C.P. Snow⟩ **b :** penetrated with light **:** TRANSLUCENT ⟨descended into the valleys to bathe in ~ streams —Elinor Wylie⟩ ⟨rain hit on the windshield, the fine ~ drops moving back slowly —H.D. Skidmore⟩ **2 :** having, manifesting, or marked by full use of one's faculties **:** ORIENTED, RATIONAL, SANE ⟨seemed to recover himself, for a ~ gleam came into his eyes —Jack London⟩ ⟨his ~ hours —W.M.Thackeray⟩ **3 :** clear to the understanding **:** readily intelligible **:** lacking ambiguity ⟨his style is ~ and he always makes his meaning clear —A.S.Hornby⟩ ⟨far more persuasive and ~ as a speaker than as a writer —A.J.Toynbee⟩ ⟨the ~ exactness of the epithets —J.L.Lowes⟩ **syn** see CLEAR
**lu·ci·da** \ˈlüsədə\ *n, pl* **luci·dae** \-,dē\ [NL, fr. L, fem. of *lucidus* lucid] **:** the brightest star of a constellation or other group
**lucid interval** *n* [trans. of ML *lucidum intervallum*] **1 :** a temporary period of rationality between periods of insanity or delirium **2 :** a period of calm or normal activity between periods of confusion
**lu·cid·i·ty** \lüˈsidəd.ē, -ətē, -i\ *n* -ES [LL *luciditat-, luciditas* brightness, L *lucidus* + *-itat-, -itas* -ity] **1 :** the quality or state of being lucid esp. in thought or style ⟨combined idealistic turbulence with ~ of expression —Maurice Edelman⟩ ⟨clearness in the narrow sense — the thin ~ of what passes at times for scientific statement —C.E.Montague⟩ **2 :** the presumed state of being able to perceive the truth directly and instantaneously **:** CLAIRVOYANCE ⟨just before one dies there comes a strange ~ —Robert Graves⟩ ⟨when the spirit is drawn to ~ by the immediacy of death —Graham Greene⟩
**lu·cid·ly** *adv* **:** in a lucid manner **:** CLEARLY ⟨the outstanding scientist who is also able to write ~ for the layman —James Stokley⟩
**lu·cid·ness** *n* -ES **:** LUCIDITY
**lucies** *pl of* LUCY
**lucifee** *var of* LUCIVEE
**[1]lu·ci·fer** \ˈlüsəfə(r)\ *n* -s [ME *lucifer* morning star & *Lucifer* fallen rebel archangel, devil, fr. OE, fr. L *lucifer* morning star, fr. *lucifer*, adj., light-bearing (prob. trans. of Gk *phōsphoros* light-bearing, morning star), fr. *luci-* + *-fer* (adj. comb. form) — more at -FER] **1** *usu cap* **:** DEVIL **2** *usu cap* **:** a person resembling Lucifer esp. in evil or pride ⟨the background of the local *Lucifer* was eminently respectable —M.D.Geismar⟩ ⟨a true man, and proud as a *Lucifer* —Thomas Hardy⟩ **3** *also* **lucifer match :** a friction match having as active substances antimony sulphide and potassium chlorate ⟨holding up a lighted ~ to a gas fixture on the wall —R.P.Warren⟩
**[2]lucifer** \"\ *n, cap* [NL, fr. L, morning star] *syn of* LEUCIFER
**lu·cif·er·ase** \lüˈsifə,rās, -āz\ *n* -s [ISV *luciferin* + *-ase*] **:** an enzyme that is associated with luciferin and that catalyzes its oxidation
**lucifer hummingbird** *n, usu cap L* [*lucifer* fr. NL (specific epithet of *Calothorax lucifer*), fr. L] **:** a bronze green fork-tailed hummingbird (*Calothorax lucifer*) of southwestern No. America that has a purple gorget in the male
**[1]lu·ci·fe·ri·an** \ˌlüsəˈfirēən\ *n* -s *usu cap* [*Lucifer* †A.D.371? bishop of Cagliari, Sardinia + E *-an*, n. suffix] **:** an adherent of a schismatic sect of the early Christian church advocating a rigorous attitude toward repentant Arians
**[2]luciferian** \"\ *adj, usu cap* [*Lucifer* †A.D.371? + E *-an*, adj. suffix] **:** of or relating to the Luciferians of the early Christian church
**[3]luciferian** \"\ *adj, usu cap* [ML *luciferianus*, fr. *Lucifer* the devil, Satan (fr. L *lucifer* morning star) + L *-ianus* -an] **:** of, relating to, or having the quality of evil or pride attributed to Lucifer **:** DEVILISH, SATANIC ⟨gave him at times a certain *Luciferian*, a dreadful, but an heroic aspect —Hervey Allen⟩
**[4]luciferian** \"\ *n* -s *usu cap* [[1]*lucifer* + *-an*] **:** a member of a 19th century party of Satan worshipers believed to hold black masses
**lu·cif·er·in** \lüˈsifərən\ *n* -s [ISV *lucifer-* (fr. L *lucifer* light-bearing) + *-in*] **:** a pigment believed to be related to the flavin pigments that is found in luminescent organisms (as fireflies) and that furnishes practically heatless light in undergoing oxidation promoted by luciferase
**lu·cif·er·ous** \-f(ə)rəs\ *adj* [L *lucifer* light-bearing + E *-ous*] **1** *archaic* **:** bringing or giving light **2** *archaic* **:** affording insight **:** ILLUMINATING
**lu·cif·ic** \-fik\ *adj* [LL *lucificus*, fr. L *luci-* + *-ficus* -fic] *archaic* **:** producing light
**lu·ci·form** \ˈlüsə,fȯrm\ *adj* [ML *luciformis*, fr. L *luci-* + *-formis* -form] **:** of, relating to, or having the characteristics of light **:** LUMINOUS
**lu·cif·u·gous** \lüˈsifyəgəs\ *also* **lu·cif·u·gal** \-gəl\ *adj* [*lucifugous* fr. L *lucifugus*, fr. *luci-* + *-fugus* (fr. *fugere* to flee); *lucifugal* fr. L *lucifugus* + E *-al* — more at FUGITIVE] **:** avoiding light ⟨a ~ creature of the darkness —Anatole Broyard⟩
**lu·ci·gen** \ˈlüsəjən\ *n* -s [*luci-* + *-gen*] **:** a lamp or torch giving a bright light by burning a spray of oil mixed with hot air
**lu·cil·ia** \lüˈsilēə\ *n, cap* [NL] **:** a genus of blowflies comprising the greenbottle flies
**[1]lu·ci·na** \lüˈsīnə\ *n* -s *usu cap* [*Lucina*, Roman goddess of childbirth] *archaic* **:** MIDWIFE
**[2]lucina** \"\ *n* [NL, prob. fr. L *Lucina*, Roman goddess of childbirth] **1** *cap* **:** a genus (the type of the family Lucinidae) of chiefly tropical edible bivalve mollusks having a white orbicular shell and a very long cylindrical foot that is sometimes placed with related forms in a superfamily (Lucinacea) of the order Eulamellibranchia **2** -s **:** any mollusk of the genus *Lucina* — **lu·cine** \ˈlü,sīn, -,sən\ *n* -s — **lu·ci·noid** \ˈlüsə,nȯid\ *adj*
**lu·cio·per·ca** \,lüs(h)ēōˈpərkə\ *n, cap* [NL *lucio-* (fr. LL *lucius* pike) + L *perca* perch — more at PERCH] **:** a genus of usu. large freshwater fishes (family Percidae) including several Old World pike perches that are excellent food fishes — see FOGAS, ZANDER
**Lu·cite** \ˈlü,sīt\ *trademark* — used for an acrylic resin or plastic consisting essentially of polymerized methyl methacrylate
**lu·ci·vee** \ˈlüsə,vē\ *n* -s [modif. of CanF *loup-cervier* — more at LOUP-CERVIER] *NewEng* **:** CANADA LYNX
**[1]luck** \ˈlək\ *n* -s [ME *lucke*, fr. MD *luc*; akin to MLG *lucke* luck, MHG *gelücke*] **1 a :** a purposeless, unpredictable, and uncontrollable force that shapes events favorably or unfavorably for an individual, group, or cause **:** FATE, FORTUNE ⟨~ is still a factor in the growth of nations as well as men —Samuel Van Valkenburg & Ellsworth Huntington⟩ **b :** a chance combination of circumstances or conditions operating for or against the individual **:** ACCIDENT ⟨seems less an act of divine providence than plain bad ~ —*Time*⟩ ⟨the ~ of the cards was against him —W.P.Webb⟩ ⟨the ~ of the hunt was with some of these teams —C.W.Nimitz⟩ **c :** customary or characteristic fortune as evidenced by a series of successes or mishaps ⟨his hard ~ followed him throughout his life⟩ ⟨it was his ~ to go through the war without a scratch⟩ ⟨just our ~ to get a fellow like that —James Hilton⟩ **2 a :** good fortune **:** favoring chance ⟨through a combination of ~ and hard work he rose to the top⟩ **b :** favorable outcome **:** SUCCESS ⟨having no ~ at all with the . . . operator on the other end of the line —R.M.Blough⟩ ⟨admired a lilac in his backyard and said I had no ~ with them —Nell G. Ahern⟩ ⟨his purchase of the Nicaragua right of way had better ~ —F.L.Paxson⟩ **3 :** something believed to bring good luck **:** CHARM ⟨jutting from her topmast was a bunch of heather, which was the ship's ~ —G.G.Carter⟩ **syn** see CHANCE — **down on one's luck :** badly off as a result of a series of unlucky chances ⟨a model who is desperately *down on her luck*, professionally and otherwise —*Theatre Arts*⟩ — **in luck :** FORTUNATE, LUCKY — **out of luck :** UNLUCKY
**[2]luck** \"\ *vb* -ED/-ING/-S [ME *lukken* to chance, happen, fr. *lucke*, n.] *vi* **1 :** to prosper or succeed esp. through chance or good fortune ⟨~*ed* out on the exam⟩ **:** happen or come upon something desirable through good fortune ⟨~*ed* into a really valuable find⟩ — usu. used with *out, on*, or *into* **2 :** to take action relying on one's luck — usu. used with *out* or *through* ⟨just ~ through without any plan or policy⟩ ~ *vt* **:** to carry out (an action) relying on one's luck **:** VENTURE, RISK — often used with *it* ⟨~ it through⟩ ⟨~ it out⟩
**luck·en** \ˈləkən\ *adj* [ME (Sc) *lukkin*, fr. past part. of *luken, louken* to lock, fasten, fr. OE *lūcan* to lock — more at LOCK] *Scot* **:** CLOSED, LOCKED
**lucken gowan** *n, chiefly Scot* **:** GLOBEFLOWER
**luck·i·ly** \ˈləkəlē, -li\ *adv* **:** in a lucky manner **:** by good luck **:** FORTUNATELY ⟨~ the man . . . was available —D.L.Busk⟩
**luck·i·ness** \-kēnəs, -kin-\ *n* -ES **:** the quality or state of being lucky
**luck·less** \ˈləkləs\ *adj* **:** being without luck **:** generally unfortunate or unlucky **:** suffering extreme ill-fortune ⟨the resting place of some ~ wanderer —*Amer. Guide Series: Calif.*⟩ ⟨the ~ enlisted man who has to go in and slug hand to hand —P.J. Searles⟩ ⟨the ~ candidate was a picture of depression —S.H. Adams⟩ **syn** see UNLUCKY
**luck·less·ly** *adv* **:** in a luckless manner **:** UNFORTUNATELY
**luck·less·ness** *n* -ES **:** the quality or state of being luckless
**luck·now** \ˈlək,nau̇\ *adj, usu cap* [fr. *Lucknow*, city in northern India] **:** of or from the city of Lucknow, India **:** of the kind or style prevalent in Lucknow
**luckpenny** \ˈ=,==\ *also* **luck money** *n, Brit* **:** a small sum or piece of money passed back from the seller to the purchaser after a bargain has been made ⟨bargaining and clutching after their ~ —Augusta Gregory⟩
**[1]lucky** \ˈləkē, -ki\ *adj, often* -ER/-EST [[1]*luck* + *-y*] **1 :** having luck **:** meeting with success **:** generally enjoying good fortune ⟨~ enough to get quarters in the town's most imposing edifice —Marquis James⟩ ⟨~ in having a lingo that hadn't yet settled into a literary language —Harold Rosenberg⟩ ⟨those who are poorer, weaker, less ~ than oneself —J.C.Powys⟩ **2 :** producing or resulting in good by chance **:** conducive to success **:** FAVORABLE ⟨a ~ sudden combination of chance mutations —Theodosius Dobzhansky⟩ ⟨regard a book-club choice as a ~ accident —John Baker⟩ ⟨a ~ hour⟩ **3 :** having a quality believed to produce good luck ⟨considered a ~ dish to eat —*Amer. Guide Series: La.*⟩ ⟨~ coin⟩ ⟨~ star⟩ **4** *chiefly Scot* **:** FULL, OVERFULL, AMPLE
**syn** LUCKY, FORTUNATE, HAPPY, and PROVIDENTIAL can all signify meeting with a success that is unforeseen or is not the direct result of merit and can also apply to an action producing or something resulting from such success. LUCKY stresses almost exclusively the agency of chance ⟨the *lucky* winner of a grand prize in a lottery⟩ ⟨a *lucky* turn of the cards⟩ ⟨the *lucky* day on which one wins a prize⟩ ⟨a *lucky* ten dollars found in the rubbish heap⟩ FORTUNATE, often interchangeable with but occurring less in speech than LUCKY, often implies less a positive luck than an encouraging absence of common, pervasive mischance or the unexpected presence of extremely favorable circumstances, sometimes even suggesting the active intervention of a higher power ⟨a *fortunate* turn of the cards⟩ ⟨a business *fortunate* in its location⟩ ⟨the *fortunate* day on which he made a good marriage⟩ ⟨the *fortunate* winner of a scholarship⟩ HAPPY, in this connection, can signify being or bringing good fortune and a consequent joy ⟨the *happy* faculty of learning from experience⟩ ⟨the *happy* results of hard work⟩ ⟨a *happy* choice of employees⟩ PROVIDENTIAL, often interchangeable with LUCKY or FORTUNATE, more often implies a good fortune resulting from the help or interference of providence ⟨it was certainly most *providential* that I looked up at that instant, as the monster would probably, in less than a minute, have seized and dragged me into the river —William Bartram⟩ ⟨a *providential* investment bringing good returns when most needed⟩
**[2]lucky** \"\ *adv, Scot* **:** GENEROUSLY **:** TOO ⟨it's ~ long⟩
**[3]lucky** \"\ *n* -ES **1 a :** something that is lucky **b :** something kept to bring luck **2** *slang Brit* **:** ESCAPE, GETAWAY
**[4]lucky** *or* **luck·ie** \"\ *n, pl* **luckies** [prob. fr. [1]*lucky*] *Scot* **:** an old woman; *specif* **:** GRANNY
**lucky bag** *n* **1 :** GRAB BAG **2 :** a locker or compartment on a warship where stray articles are stowed until claimed or disposed of
**lucky bone** *n* **1** *dial* **:** WISHBONE **2** *dial* **:** BONE; *esp* **:** one from the head of a sheep or hog worn or carried to bring good luck
**lucky dad** *n, Scot* **:** GRANDFATHER
**lucky dip** *n, Brit* **:** GRAB BAG ⟨there were *lucky dips* . . . into which small hands were plunged —W.J.MacQueen-Pope⟩
**lucky minnie** *n, Scot* **:** GRANDMOTHER
**lucky stone** *n* **:** a stone held to bring good luck (as a perforated pebble or an otolith of a fish)
**lu·come window** \ˈlükəm-\ *n* [obs. E *lucome* dormer window (alter. of earlier *lucane*) + E *window* — more at LUCARNE] **:** a wide gable-end window in early American houses
**lu·cra·tive** \ˈlükrəd.iv, -ətiv\ *adj* [ME *lucratif*, fr. MF, fr. L *lucrativus*, fr. *lucratus* (past part. of *lucrari* to gain, fr. *lucrum* gain, profit) + *-ivus* -ive] **1 a :** producing wealth **:** MONEY-MAKING, PROFITABLE ⟨~ literature meant novels and nothing else —G.B.Shaw⟩ ⟨a ~ business⟩ ⟨a ~ property⟩ **b :** worthwhile as a military target ⟨many ~ artillery targets —*Infantry*

*Army Reserve Training Bull.*〉 〈a ~ target for an atom bomb —R.W.Stokley〉 **2** *archaic* **:** having or marked by a love of gain **:** AVARICIOUS, GREEDY **3** *Roman & civil law* **:** acquired, received, or had without burdensome conditions 〈a ~ title〉 〈~ ownership〉 — **lu·cra·tive·ly** \-əvlē, -li\ *adv* — **lu·cra·tive·ness** \-ivnəs\ *n* -ES

**lucrative interest** *n* **:** interest representing the creditor's possible profits from his having the use of his own money

**lucrative succession** *n, Scots law* **:** the succession of an heir who has during the lifetime of the ancestor accepted without adequate consideration any part of the estate which he would otherwise have inherited

**lu·cre** \'lükə(r)\ *n* -S [ME, fr. L *lucrum;* akin to OE *lēan* reward, OHG *lōn,* ON *laun* (pl.) rewards, Goth *laun* reward, OIr *lōg* reward, price, Gk *leia* booty, prey, Skt *lotra* booty] **1 a :** monetary gain **:** PROFIT, REWARD **b :** MONEY 〈set aside some ~ for shopping and souvenirs —Winston Brebner〉 **2** *archaic* **:** the process of gaining **:** ACQUISITION — used esp. in the phrase *lucre of gain*

**lu·cre·tian** \lü'krēshən\ *adj, usu cap* [T. *Lucretius* Carus †55 B.C. Roman philosophical poet + E *-an*] **:** of, relating to, or having the characteristics of Lucretius or the Epicurean philosophic system expounded by him 〈dry, steely, *Lucretian* aloofness —*Modern Philology*〉

**lu·crum ces·sans** \'lükrəm'se,sanz\ *n* [*lucrum cessans* fr. ML, ceasing profit; *lucrum interceptum* fr. NL, intercepted profit] **1** *or* **lucrum in·ter·cep·tum** \-,intə(r)'septəm\ *Roman & canon law* **:** the interest or damages awarded for loss of reasonably expected profits or for loss of use of property **2** *Scots law* **:** damages for loss of expected gain or profits as distinguished from an actual loss

**luctation** *n* -S [L *luctation-, luctatio,* fr. *luctatus* (past part. of *luctari* to struggle) + *-ion-, -io* -ion — more at LOCK] *obs* **:** ENDEAVOR, STRUGGLE

**luc·tif·er·ous** \(')lək'tif(ə)rəs\ *adj* [L *luctifer* mournful (fr. *luctus* sorrow + *-fer* -ferous) + E *-ous*] *archaic* **:** bearing sorrow **:** MOURNFUL

**luctual** *adj* [L *luctus* sorrow (fr. *luctus,* past part. of *lugēre* to mourn) + E *-al* — more at LUGUBRIOUS] *obs* **:** SAD, SORROWFUL

**lu·cu·brate** \'lük(y)ə,brāt\ *vi* -ED/-ING/-S [L *lucubratus,* past part. of *lucubrare* to work by lamplight, compose by night; akin to L *lucēre* to shine — more at LIGHT] **:** to discourse learnedly in writing **:** EXPATIATE 〈~ in various scholarly journals〉 — compare ELUCUBRATE — **lu·cu·bra·tor** \-brād·ə(r), -ātə-\ *n* -S

**lu·cu·bra·tion** \,==ˈbrāshən\ *n* -S [L *lucubration-, lucubratio* study or composition at night, fr. *lucubratus* + *-ion-, -io* -ion] **1 :** the act of lucubrating **:** laborious study **:** MEDITATION 〈after long ~ I have hit upon such an expedient —Oliver Goldsmith〉 **2 :** the product of study or meditation as expressed in speech or writing **:** weighty or pretentious statement of ideas 〈bring his moldy and moth-eaten ~*s* before the public —Nathaniel Hawthorne〉 〈his oratorical ~*s* on the subject of age —*New Republic*〉

**lucubratory** *adj* [L *lucubratorius* connected with study at night, fr. *lucubratus* + *-orius* -ory] *obs* **:** laboriously thought out or expressed

**lu·cu·lent** \lükyələnt\ *adj* [ME, fr. L *luculentus,* fr. *luc-, lux* light — more at LIGHT] **1** *archaic* **:** emitting light **:** BRILLIANT, SHINING 〈a ~ flame —John Evelyn〉 **2 :** transparently clear in thought or expression **:** CONVINCING, EVIDENT 〈a ~ oration —Robert Burton〉 〈so ~ a commentary —J.G.Lockhart〉 **3** *obs* **:** ILLUSTRIOUS, RESPLENDENT 〈most debonair and ~ lady —Ben Jonson〉 — **lu·cu·lent·ly** *adv*

**lu·cul·lan** \lü'kələn\ *or* **lu·cul·li·an** \-lēən\ *adj, usu cap* [L *lucullanus, lucullianus,* fr. Lucius Licinius *Lucullus,* 1st cent. B.C. Roman general, patron of learning, and epicure + L *-anus, -ianus* -an] **1 :** of or relating to Lucullus **2 :** LAVISH, LUXURIOUS — used esp. of food 〈cornflakes or shredded wheat with bananas or fresh sliced peaches, thought by us to be a *Lucullan* treat —Mary McCarthy〉

**lucullan marble** *n, usu cap L* [trans. of L *marmor luculleum;* prob. fr. its being especially liked by Lucullus] **:** LUCULLITE

**lu·cul·lite** \-,līt\ *n* -S [G *lucullit* lucullite (fr. L *lucullanus* Lucullan) + E *-ite*] **:** an Egyptian marble colored black by carbon

**¹lu·cu·ma** \'lük(y)əmə\ [NL, fr. Sp *lúcuma* eggfruit] *syn of* POUTERIA

**²lucuma** \"\ *n* -S [Sp *lúcuma* eggfruit, fr. Quechua *lúcuma, lucma*] **:** a plant or fruit of the genus *Pouteria* **:** EGGFRUIT

**lu·cu·mi** \,lükə'mē\ *n, pl* **lucumi** *or* **lucumies** *usu cap* **1 a :** a group of people in Cuba who are members of a secret society of African origin **b :** a member of such a group **2 :** the secret language used by the Lucumi derived from Yoruba

**lu·cus a non lu·cen·do** \'lükə,sä,nänlü'sen,dō\ [NL, a grove from not being light; fr. the practice ascribed to ancient Roman etymologists of deriving words from their semantic opposites, as *lucus* ("grove") from *lucēre* ("to shine, be light") because a grove is not light] **:** an illogical explanation or absurd derivation **:** NON SEQUITUR 〈the whole discussion may seem a *lucus a non lucendo* for all the light it throws upon the effect of the classics on mediaeval literature —H.O.Taylor〉

**lu·cy** \'lüsē, -si\ *n* -ES [LL *lucius*] **:** LUCE 2

**lucy light** *n, usu cap 1st L* [after St. *Lucy* †A.D.303 virgin and martyr of Syracuse in Sicily whose feast day is December 13] **:** December 13 Old Style, the shortest day — called also *St. Lucy's day;* contrasted with *Barnaby bright*

**lucy sto·ner** \-stōnə(r)\ *n, pl* **lucy stoners** *usu cap L&S* [*Lucy Stone* †1893 Am. woman suffragist + E *-er*] **:** a female advocate of women's rights; *esp* **:** a married woman who uses her maiden name as a surname 〈the *Lucy Stoners* and women's rights fighters of her own class at college —Mary McCarthy〉

**ludd·ism** \'lə,dizəm\ *also* **ludd·it·ism** \-,dīd·,izəm\ *n* -S *usu cap* [*luddism* fr. Ned *Ludd* fl1779 half-witted Leicestershire workman who destroyed stocking frames + E *-ism; ludditism* fr. *luddite* + *-ism*] **:** the beliefs or practices of the Luddites

**ludd·ite** \'lə,dīt\ *n* -S *usu cap* [Ned *Ludd* + E *-ite*] **:** a member of a group of early 19th century English workmen engaged in attempting to prevent the use of laborsaving machinery by destroying it

**ludefisk** *or* **ludfisk** *var of* LUTEFISK

**lu·der·ick** \'lüd(ə)rik\ *n* -S [native name in Gippsland, Australia] **:** a silvery gray Australian percoid food fish (*Girella tricuspidata*) of shallow coastal seas and estuaries and tidal rivers — called also *black bream, blackfish*

**lü·ders' line** *also* **lue·ders' line** \'lü(d)ə(r)z-, 'lē(\ *n, usu cap 1st L* [after W. *Lüders* fl1859 Ger. scientist, its discoverer] **:** a line or any of a definite system of line markings appearing on the smooth surface of tough material (as metal) strained beyond its elastic limit and caused by flow of the material

**lu·dhi·a·na** \,lüdē'änə\ *adj, usu cap* [fr. *Ludhiana,* city in northwest India] **:** of or from the city of Ludhiana, India **:** of the kind or style prevalent in Ludhiana

**lu·dib·ri·ous** \lü'dibrēəs\ *adj* [L *ludibriosus* derisive, fr. *ludibrium* derision (fr. *ludus* play) + *-osus* -ose] **1** *obs* **:** RIDICULOUS **2** *archaic* **:** MOCKING, SCORNFUL

**ludicro-** *comb form* [L *ludicrus* + E *-o-*] **:** ludicrous and 〈*ludicro*pathetic〉 〈*ludicro*serious〉 〈*ludicro*splenetic〉

**lu·di·crous** \'lüdəkrəs\ *adj* [L *ludicrus,* fr. *ludus* game, play, sport; akin to L *ludere* to play, Gk *loidoros* abusive] **1** *archaic* **:** relating to, characterized by, or designed for play or amusement **:** not serious **:** FRIVOLOUS, JOKING 〈the most attractive of all ~ compositions —Samuel Johnson〉 **2 a :** amusing or laughable through obvious absurdity, incongruity, exaggeration, or eccentricity 〈an unchangeable grin that gave still more ~ effect to the comic alarm and sorrow of their features —Nathaniel Hawthorne〉 **b :** meriting derisive laughter or scorn as absurdly inept, false, or foolish 〈common sense making transparently clear what was ~ in every fallacy —Edgar Johnson〉 〈how ~ it was to leave the substance of power in a single ruler —*Times Lit. Supp.*〉 〈this act of ~ cruelty —Edmund Burke〉 **syn** see LAUGHABLE

**lu·di·crous·ly** *adv* **:** in a ludicrous manner **:** ABSURDLY, RIDICULOUSLY

**lu·di·crous·ness** *n* -ES **:** the quality or state of being ludicrous

**lu·di·fi·ca·tion** \,lüdəfə'kāshən\ *n* -S [L *ludification-, ludificatio,* fr. *ludificatus* (past part. of *ludificare* to deceive, make sport of, fr. *ludus* game, play, sport + *-ficare* -fy) + *-ion-, -io* -ion] **:** an act of deception or mockery

**lud·lam·ite** \'lədlə,mīt\ *n* -S [Henry *Ludlam* †1880 Eng. mineralogist + E *-ite*] **:** a mineral $(Fe, Mg, Mn)_3(PO_4)_2.4H_2O$ that is a hydrous iron phosphate with magnesium and manganese replacing some of the iron and that occurs in small green transparent monoclinic crystals

**lud·lo·vi·an** \,ləd'lōvēən\ *adj, usu cap* [fr. *Ludlovian,* subdivision of the European Silurian, fr. ML *Ludlovia* (Ludlow), Shropshire, England + E *-an*] **:** of or relating to a subdivision of the European Silurian — see GEOLOGIC TIME table

**Lud·low** \'ləd,lō\ *trademark* — used for a machine that casts type and material slugs from matrices set by hand in a special stick

**lu·do** \'lü,dō\ *n* -S [L, I play, 1st pers. sing. pres. indic. of *ludere* to play] **:** a form of pachisi played chiefly in the British Isles

**lud·wig·ia** \ləd'wigēə\ *also* **lud·vig·ia** \-'vig-\ *n, cap* [NL, fr. Christian G. *Ludwig* †1773 Ger. botanist + NL *-ia*] **:** a genus of perennial herbs (family Onagraceae) chiefly of tropical or warm regions that have 4-parted flowers and a short capsular fruit

**lud·wig·ite** \'ləd,wi,gīt\ *n* -S [G *ludwigit,* fr. Ernst *Ludwig* †1915 Austrian chemist + G *-it* -ite] **:** a mineral $(Mg, Fe)_2FeBO_5$ consisting of an iron magnesium borate occurring in fibrous masses of a blackish green color

**lud·wig's angina** \ lüd(,)vigz-\ *n, usu cap L* [after Wilhelm F. von *Ludwig* †1865 Ger. physician] **:** an acute streptococcal or sometimes staphylococcal infection of the deep tissues of the floor of the mouth and adjoining parts of the neck and lower jaw marked by severe rapid swelling that may close the respiratory passage and accompanied by chills and fever

**lud·wigs·ha·fen** \'lüd(,)vigz,häfən, ,=(,)='==\ *adj, usu cap* [fr. *Ludwigshafen* am Rhein, city in southwest Germany] **:** of or from the city of Ludwigshafen am Rhein, Germany **:** of the kind or style prevalent in Ludwigshafen am Rhein

**luebeck** *usu cap, var of* LÜBECK

**lue·ne·burg·ite** \'lünə,bər,gīt\ *n* -S [G *lüneburgit,* fr. *Lüneburg,* Germany, its locality + G *-it* -ite] **:** a mineral $Mg_3B_2(OH)_6(PO_4)_2.6H_2O$ consisting of a hydrous basic phosphate of magnesium and boron

**lu·er syringe** \'lüə(r)-\ *n, usu cap L* [after *Luer* †1883 Fr. instrument maker] **:** a glass syringe with a glass piston that has the apposing surfaces ground and that is used esp. for hypodermic injection

**lu·es** \'lü,ēz\ *n, pl* **lues** [NL, fr. L, plague; akin to Gk *lyein* to unbind, release, dissolve — more at LOSE] **:** SYPHILIS

**lu·et·ic** \lü'ed·ik\ *adj* [fr. *lues,* after such pairs as E *herpes: herpetic*] **:** SYPHILITIC — **lu·et·i·cal·ly** \-ək(ə)lē\ *adv*

**luf·bery** *also* **luf·ber·ry** \'ləf,berē, -bərē, -ri\ *vi* -ED/-ING/-S [after Raoul G. V. *Lufbery* †1918 Am. aviator] **:** to go into or fly in a Lufbery circle

**lufbery circle** *also* **lufberry circle** *n, usu cap L* **:** a military flying formation or maneuver in which two or more airplanes follow each other closely in circular line or ascending spiral

**¹luff** \'ləf\ *n* -S [ME *luff, loff,* fr. MF *lof,* prob. fr. (assumed) MD *loef* (whence D *loef*); akin to MLG *lōf* side of a ship toward the wind, ON *lōfi* palm of the hand — more at GLOVE] **1 a** *obs* **:** the side of a ship toward the wind **b :** the act of sailing a ship closer to the wind **c :** the forward edge of a fore-and-aft sail **d** *archaic* **:** the fullest and roundest part of a ship's bow **e :** LUFF TACKLE **2 :** a radial or in-and-out movement of the load being carried by a crane produced by raising or lowering the jib

**²luff** \"\ *vb* -ED/-ING/-S [ME *loven,* fr. *luff, loff,* n.] *vi* **1 :** to turn the head of a ship toward the wind **:** sail nearer the wind — often used with *up* **2 :** to move the jib of a crane in and out ~ *vt* **1 :** to sail on the windward side of in yacht-racing **2 :** to move (the jib of a crane) in and out

**³luff** \"\ *n* -S [by shortening & alter.] *slang* **:** LIEUTENANT

**luf·fa** \'ləfə\ *n* [NL, fr. Ar *lūf*] **1** *cap* **:** a genus of tropical climbing herbs (family Cucurbitaceae) with white flowers and large fruits **2** *or* **loo·fah** \'lüfə\ -S **a :** a plant of the genus *Luffa* **b :** the fruit of such a plant **:** DISHCLOTH GOURD **3** *or* **loofah** -S **:** the fibrous skeleton of the luffa fruit used as a sponge — called also *vegetable sponge*

**luff tackle** *n* [¹*luff*] **:** a tackle that has a single and a double block with the standing part of the fall fixed to the single block thus multiplying the power three or four times according as the single or the double block is movable — see TACKLE illustration

**luff upon luff :** a luff tackle on the fall of another

**luft·mensch** \'lüft,mench\ *n, pl* **luftmensch·en** \-chən\ [Yiddish *luftmentsh,* fr. *luft* air (fr. MHG, fr. OHG) + *mentsh* person, human being, fr. MHG *mensch, mensche,* fr. OHG *mennisco;* akin to OFris *mānniska* person, human being, MD *mensche,* OS *mennisco;* all fr. a prehistoric WGmc noun derived from the adjective represented by OE *mennisc* human, ON *mennskr,* Goth *mannisks;* all fr. a prehistoric Gmc compound whose first constituent is represented by OE *man, mann* man and whose second constituent is represented by OE *-isc* -ish — more at LOFT, MAN] **:** an impractical contemplative person having no definite trade, business, or income **:** DREAMER 〈the ~ who personifies the quixotic, speculative principle in Jewish life —Irving Howe〉

**¹lug** \'ləg, *dial* 'lüg\ *n* -S [ME *lugge*] **1** *dial Eng* **:** ROD, POLE **2** *now dial Eng* **a :** a varying measure of length usu. 16½ feet **b :** a square lug

**²lug** \"\ *vb* **lugged; lugged; lugging; lugs** [ME *luggen,* prob. of Scand origin; akin to Norw *lugge* to pull by the hair, Sw *lugga* to pull by the hair, Norw & Sw *lugg* tuft of hair] *vt* **1 a** *now chiefly dial* (1) **:** to give a pull to (as the ear or hair) (2) **:** to pull esp. by the ear or hair **b :** to pull with force **:** DRAG 〈*lugged* the little wretch . . . out of the room —Samuel Butler †1902〉 〈*lugged* the feed trough out into the open —Marjorie K. Rawlings〉 **2 :** to carry with great effort 〈*lugged* those boxes all over the city till they seemed full of marble —Dan Browne〉 〈preferred to ~ his own suitcase —Horace Sutton〉 **3 :** to bring in or introduce in a ponderous or forced manner 〈~ a story into the conversation〉 ~ *vi* **1 a :** to pull with effort **:** TUG **b** *of a horse* **:** to bear down on the bit **2 :** to move heavily or by jerks 〈printers' rollers ~ when sticky〉 **3** *of a racehorse* **:** to swerve from the course toward or away from the inside rail 〈kept *lugging* in toward the rails —G.F.T.Ryall〉 **4** *archaic* **a :** to draw one's sword **b :** to take out one's money or purse

**³lug** \'ləg\ *n* -S **1** *archaic* **a :** an act of lugging **b :** something that is lugged **2 :** a box or basket holding 25 to 40 pounds of fruit or vegetables; *specif* **:** a box having an inside width of 13½ inches, an outside length of 17½ inches, and a depth of from 4¼ to 7¾ inches **3 lugs** *pl* **:** superior airs **:** affectations of importance 〈no ~*s* about him . . . nothing hoity-toity —Louis Auchincloss〉 〈the way these doctors and profs and preachers put on ~*s* about being "professional men" —Sinclair Lewis〉 **4 :** LUGSAIL **5** *slang* **:** an exaction of money **:** a political assessment — used in the phrase *put the lug on* 〈put the ~ on state employees —*Newsweek*〉

**⁴lug** \'ləg, *dial* 'lüg\ *n* -S [ME (Sc) *lugge,* perh. fr. ME *luggen,* v.] **1** *Scot* **:** the earflap of a cap or bonnet **2** *now chiefly dial* **:** EAR 〈I got ears . . . first-class ~*s* —C.B.Kelland〉 〈a great clout in the ~ —J.M.Synge〉 **3 :** something that projects like an ear: as **a :** a projection or handle by which something may be grasped or carried **b :** a projection on a casting to which a bolt or other part may be fitted **c :** a leather loop on a harness saddle through which the shaft passes **d :** a projection or ridge on the rim of a wheel (as of a tractor) or on a rubber tire to increase traction **4 :** a small projecting part of a larger member; *esp* **:** the part of a windowsill or doorsill that tails into the masonry on each side of the opening **5 :** a fitting of copper or brass to which electrical wires are soldered or connected **6 :** a rounded nut that covers the end of a bolt (as for holding an automobile wheel in place) **7 lugs** *pl* **:** a poor grade of tobacco leaves from the lower part of the stem of the plant — compare LEAF 1c(4) **8** *slang* **a :** a heavy clumsy fellow **:** BLOCKHEAD, GOOD-FOR-NOTHING 〈cuff the daylights out of a moronic ~ —James Wallace〉 **b :** an ordinary commonplace person 〈walk among the people, just another ~ —Stephen Longstreet〉 〈just another poor ~ who'd cracked up and was talking to himself —*Scribner's*〉

**⁵lug** \'ləg\ *n* -S [origin unknown] **:** LUGWORM

**lu·gan·da** \lü'gandə, -gän-\ *n, usu cap* **:** GANDA 2

**lug·ba·ra** \lüg'bärə\ *n, pl* **lugbara** *or* **lugbaras** *usu cap* **1 a :** a people living along the border of Uganda and the Belgian Congo **b :** a member of such people **2 :** a Central Sudanic language of the Lugbara people

**lug bolt** *n* [⁴*lug*] **1 :** a bolt terminating in a long flat extension or hook instead of a head — called also *strap bolt* **2 :** a bolt for fastening a lug

**lug brick** *n* [⁴*lug*] **:** paving brick having lugs on one side and one end to control the space between adjacent bricks when laid in a pavement

**lug chair** *n* [⁴*lug*] *Brit* **:** WING CHAIR

**¹luge** \'lüzh\ *n* -S [F, fr. F dial. (Savoy & Switzerland)] **:** a small sled used for coasting esp. in Switzerland

**²luge** \"\ *vi* -ED/-ING/-S **:** to coast on a luge — **lug·er** \-zhə(r)\ *n* -S

**lug foresail** *n* [perh. fr. ⁴*lug*] **:** a foresail without a boom

**lug·gage** \'ləgij, -gēj\ *n* -S *often attrib* [²*lug* + *-age*] **1 :** something that is lugged; *esp* **:** the belongings that a traveler carries with him 〈his only ~ what he could carry in a red plaid cotton handkerchief —*Amer. Guide Series: Minn.*〉 〈brought as part of their ~ toasting irons, waffle irons, and gridirons —M.R. Werner〉 **2 a :** suitcases, traveling bags, and other articles containing a traveler's belongings **:** BAGGAGE 〈both running-boards were piled with traps and ~ —D.L.Sharp〉 〈stowing space under the beds for hand ~ —Horace Sutton〉 **b :** empty suitcases and other containers for a traveler's belongings esp. as offered for sale 〈a shop that sells fine ~〉

**lug·gage·less** \-ləs\ *adj* **:** having no luggage

**luggage tan** *n* **:** a variable color averaging a strong brown that is yellower, lighter, and slightly less strong than average russet, yellower and paler than rust, and yellower, stronger, and slightly lighter than gold brown

**luggage van** *n, Brit* **:** BAGGAGE CAR

**lug·gar** *also* **lug·ger** \'ləgə(r)\ *n* -S [Hindi *lagar, lagur*] **:** any of several large Asiatic falcons of dull brown color; *esp* **:** a gyrfalcon (*Falco jugger*) of India that somewhat resembles the American prairie falcon

**lugged** \'ləgd\ *adj* [ME (Sc) *lwgyt* having earflaps, fr. *lugge* earflap + *-yt,* alter. of ME *-ed,* adj. suffix — more at LUG] **:** having lugs

**¹lug·ger** \'ləgə(r)\ *n* -S [²*lug* + *-er*] **:** one that lugs: as **a :** a worker in a slaughterhouse or meat-packing establishment who carries meat to and from various processing operations **b :** an agricultural worker who carries containers filled with farm products from the field to a central point **c** *slang* **:** a person employed by a gambling house to bring players to it

**²lugger** \"\ *n* -S [*lug-* (fr. *lugsail*) + *-er*] **:** a small fishing or coasting boat that carries one or more lugsails and that has two or three masts with or without jibs or topsails

**lug·gie** \'ləgi\ *n* -S [⁴*lug* + *-ie*] *chiefly Scot* **:** a small wooden pail or dish with a handle

**lugging** *pres part of* LUG

**lug hook** *n* [prob. fr. ²*lug*] **:** a device consisting of a pair of pointed dogs pivoted at the middle of a short bar for carrying small logs or railroad ties

lug hook

**lu·gol's solution** \'lü,gälz-\ *n, usu cap L* [after J. G. A. *Lugol* †1851 Fr. physician] **:** a deep brown aqueous solution that has an odor of iodine, that contains approximately 5 grams of iodine and 10 grams of potassium iodide in 100 milliliters, and that is used chiefly in medicine for the internal administration of iodine and esp. in veterinary practice as a disinfectant; *also* **:** any of several similar solutions (as an aqueous or alcoholic solution containing iodine and potassium iodide for use as a microscopic stain)

**lug pole** *n* [¹*lug*] **:** a pole on which a kettle is hung in a fireplace

**lugs** *pres 3d sing of* LUG, *pl of* LUG

**lug·sail** \'ləgsəl (*usual nautical pronunc*), -,sāl\ *n* [perh. fr. ⁴*lug* + *sail*] **:** a four-sided sail bent to a yard that hangs more or less obliquely on a mast slung at about a third or quarter of its length from the forward end and hoisted and lowered with the sail — called also *lug;* compare BALANCE LUGSAIL, DIPPING LUG, SPLIT LUG, STANDING LUG

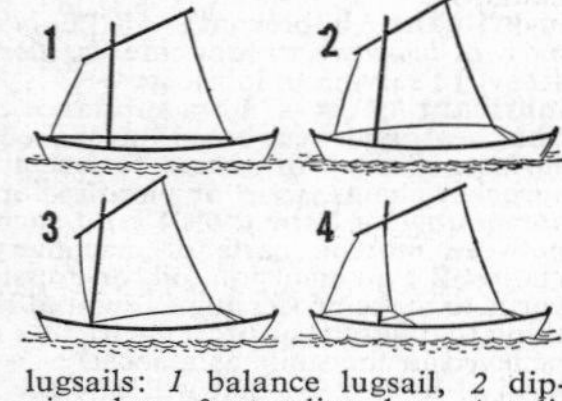


lugsails: *1* balance lugsail, *2* dipping lug, *3* standing lug, *4* split lug

**lug sole** *n* [⁴*lug*] **:** a thick rubber sole that has deep indentations in a pattern designed to provide good footing and is used on sport and work shoes

**lu·gu·bri·os·i·ty** \lə,gübrē'äsəd·ē, lü-,-ətē,-i\ *n* -ES [fr. *lugubrious,* after such pairs as E *curious: curiosity*] **:** the quality or state of being lugubrious

**lu·gu·bri·ous** \=ˈ=brēəs\ *adj* [L *lugubris* lugubrious, connected with mourning (fr. *lugēre* to mourn) + E *-ous;* akin to Gk *lygros* mournful, Skt *rujati* he breaks, hurts] **1 :** expressive of, marked by, or giving rise to grief or sorrow **:** MOURNFUL 〈~ notices on the passing of old friends —*Time*〉 〈a ~ place which filled me with dread —Henry Miller〉 **2 :** disposed to gloom **:** DISMAL 〈a certain ~ element in English taste —Bernard Leach〉 — **lu·gu·bri·ous·ly** *adv* — **lu·gu·bri·ous·ness** *n* -ES

**lugworm** \'=,=\ *n* [⁵*lug* + *worm*] **:** any of several large marine polychaetous annelids (genus *Arenicola*) that have a row of tufted gills along each side of the back, burrow in sandy beaches between tide marks in America and Europe, and are used for bait

**LUHF** *abbr, often not cap* lowest useful high frequency

**luhot** *or* **luhoth** *pl of* LUAH

**luian** *usu cap, var of* LUWIAN

**lu·id·ia** \lə'widēə\ *n, cap* [NL] **:** a large genus of chiefly tropical active starfishes (order Phanerozonia) with long slender rather flabby rays — see MUD-STAR

**lui-haai** \'lā,hī\ *n* -S [Afrik, fr. *lui* lazy (fr. D, fr. MD *loy, loey*) + *haai* shark, fr. D, fr. MD *haey* — more at HAYE] **:** a small blunt-snouted striped shark (*Poroderma africanum*) of the East African coast — called also *striped dogfish*

**lu·i·se·ño** \,lüē'sān(,)yō\ *n, pl* **luiseño** *or* **luiseños** *usu cap* [AmerSp, fr. San *Luis* Rey de Francia, mission in California + Sp *-eño* (suffix added to place names to form names of inhabitants)] **1 a :** a Shoshonean people of southwestern California **b :** a member of such people **2 :** the language of the Luiseño people

**lu·jau·vrite** \'lü,yaův,rīt\ *or* **lu·jaur·ite** \-aů,rīt\ *n* -S [G *luijaurit,* fr. *Luijaur Urt, Lujavr Urt,* Lapland, its locality + G *-it* -ite] **:** a melanocratic nepheline-syenite rock

**lukan** *usu cap, var of* LUCAN

**luk·ban** \lük'bän\ *n* -S [Tag *lukbán*] **:** SHADDOCK

**luke** \'lük\ *adj* [ME *luke, lewk;* akin to OE *hlēow* warm — more at LEW] *archaic* **:** LUKEWARM

**lukewarm** \'=ˈ=\ *adj* [ME, fr. *luke* + *warm*] **1 :** moderately warm **:** neither cold nor hot **:** TEPID 〈~ water〉 〈~ food〉 **2 :** lacking in real conviction **:** not wholly committed to a cause or belief **:** HALFHEARTED, INDIFFERENT 〈seemed ~ or capable of a divided allegiance —Hilaire Belloc〉 〈although he never openly repudiated a protectionist policy he soon grew ~ in its support —V.L.Parrington〉 — **luke·warm·ly** *adv* — **luke·warm·ness** *n* -ES

**luke·warm·ish** \'=ˈ==\ *adj* **:** somewhat lukewarm

**lukewarmth** \'=ˈ=\ *n* **:** LUKEWARMNESS

**lu·ki·ko** \lü'kē(,)kō\ *n* -S *usu cap* [native name in Uganda] **:** a native legislative and judicial council in various African provinces

**lu·lab** *or* **lu·lav** *also* **lu·lov** \'lü,läv, -,ləv\ *n, pl* **lu·la·bim** *or* **lu·la·vim** \,lülə'vēm\ *or* **lu·labs** *or* **lu·lavs** \'lü,lävz, -,ləvz\ *also* **lu·lo·vim** \lü'lōvim, -vēm\ *or* **lu·lovs** [Heb *lūlābh* branch] **:** the traditional festive palm branch that is carried and waved during the festival of Sukkoth — compare ETHROG

**lu·le** \'lü(,)lā\ *n, pl* **lule** *or* **lules** *usu cap* **1 :** a group of peoples of northern Argentina **2 :** a member of any of the Lule peoples

**[1]lull** \'ləl\ *vb* -ED/-ING/-S [ME *lullen;* prob. of imit. origin like MLG *lollen* to lull, MD *lollen* to mumble, doze, Latvian *leluot* to rock a child, Skt *lolati* he moves to and fro] *vt* **1 a :** to make quiet : cause to sleep or rest peacefully : SOOTHE ⟨sat ~*ing* the child —George Eliot⟩ ⟨~*ed* him to sleep with an interminable canticle —Rudyard Kipling⟩ **b :** to bring to a state of comparative calm ⟨~*ed* the raging seas⟩ **2 :** to induce a false sense of security and well-being in : cause to relax one's vigilance : lessen tension in ⟨~ them into an apathetic sense of security —Raymond Holden⟩ ⟨~ the group into contentment —Oscar Handlin⟩ ⟨~*ed* our minds with things we wanted to see again —H.D.Skidmore⟩ ~ *vi* **:** to diminish in force or intensity : SUBSIDE, ABATE ⟨the afternoon breeze ~*ed* and finally dropped off altogether —O.E.Rölvaag⟩ ⟨this conversation would ~ for awhile —Richard Church⟩ **syn** see CALM

**[2]lull** \"\ *n* -S **1** *archaic* **:** something that lulls or soothes; *specif* **:** LULLABY **2 a :** a temporary cessation or lessening of the wind or of a storm ⟨a ~ in the rain⟩ **b :** a period of intensified quiet ⟨the ~ before the storm⟩ ⟨a dark still summer ~ —Kay Boyle⟩ **3 :** a temporary drop in activity ⟨the business ~ will end by midyear —*Look*⟩ ⟨when a ~ comes in the creative activity —Ralph Linton⟩ **4 :** a relaxed or dazed state of mind

**[3]lull** \"\ *n* -S [LG *lull;* akin to D *lul* mouth of a pump, baby bottle, D *lullen* to suck, prattle (fr. MD *lollen* to mumble, doze)] **:** a tube through which blubber is passed to tubs in the hold of a whaling ship

**[1]lull·a·by** \'lələ,bī\ *n* -ES [obs. E *lulla, lullay, lully,* interj. used to lull a child (fr. ME, prob. fr. *lullen* to lull) + E *bye,* interj.] **1 :** a soothing refrain; *specif* **:** a song to quiet children or lull them to sleep **2** *obs* **:** GOOD-NIGHT

**[2]lullaby** \"\ *vt* -ED/-ING/-ES **:** to soothe or quiet with or as if with a lullaby ⟨the rhythm of motion *lullabied* his brain —Tom Hopkinson⟩

**lull·er** \'lələ(r)\ *n* -S **:** one that lulls

**lul·li·an** \'lələn\ *adj, usu cap* [Raymond *Lully* †1315 Catalan ecclesiastic and scholastic philosopher + E *-an*] **:** of or relating to Lully or the teachings in which he combated the separation of faith and reason and endeavored to demonstrate the exclusive truth of Christianity

**lull·i·loo** \'lələ,lü\ *vi* -ED/-ING/-S [imit.] **:** to shout joyously in the manner of various African peoples ⟨~*ed* with cries of joy —Sir Richard Burton⟩

**lull·ing·ly** *adv* **:** in a lulling manner

**[1]lu·lu** \'lü,lü\ *n* -S [prob. fr. *Lulu,* nickname fr. the name *Louise*] *slang* **:** a person or thing remarkable or wonderful : STANDOUT ⟨his first idea was a ~ —Frederic Wakeman⟩ ⟨a really low class here that is a ~ —August Hollingshead⟩ ⟨a ~ of a mistake⟩ ⟨told you this ~ of a story and made a total donkey out of you —Calder Willingham⟩

**[2]lulu** \"\ *n* -S [Samoan *lūlu*] **:** a Samoan barn owl

**lu·lu·ai** \,lülə'wī\ *n* -S [native name in eastern New Guinea] **:** a village headman or chief in New Guinea

**lu·lu·bae·an** \,lü,lü'bēən\ *n* -S *cap* **1 :** one of several early peoples who intruded into Assyria and introduced their dialects into the area **2 :** a member of the Lulubaean people

**lum** \'ləm\ *n* -S [origin unknown] *chiefly Scot* **:** CHIMNEY

**lumb-** *or* **lumbo-** *comb form* [L *lumb-,* fr. *lumbus* — more at LOIN] **1 :** loin ⟨*lumbo*dynia⟩ **2 :** lumbar and ⟨*lumbo*sacral⟩

**lum·ba·go** \,ləm'bā,gō\ *n* -S [L, fr. *lumbus* loin] **:** muscular rheumatism involving the lumbar muscles and usu. accompanied by pain

**lum·bang** \lüm'bäŋ\ *n* -S [Tag *lumbáng*] **1 :** CANDLENUT **2 :** a tree (*Aleurites trisperma*) of the Philippine islands whose nuts yield a valuable oil

**lumbang oil** *n* **:** CANDLENUT OIL

**lum·bar** \'ləmbə(r), -,bär, -,bȧ(r\ *adj* [NL *lumbaris,* fr. L *lumbus* loin + *-aris* -ar] **1 :** of, relating to, or near the loins or the group of vertebrae lying between the thoracic vertebrae and the sacrum **2 :** of, relating to, or indicating the region of the abdomen lying on either side of the umbilical region and above the corresponding inguinal — see ABDOMINAL REGION illustration

**lumbar artery** *n* **:** any artery of the four or five pairs arising from the back of the aorta opposite the lumbar vertebrae and supplying the muscles of the loins, the skin of the sides of the abdomen, and the spinal cord

**lumbar ganglion** *n* **:** one of the small ganglia of the lumbar part of the sympathetic nerves

**lum·bar·i·za·tion** \,ləmbərə'zāshən, -,rī'-\ *n* -S **:** a condition marked by fusion of the first sacral and last lumbar vertebrae

**lumbar nerve** *n* **:** one of the five pairs of the spinal nerves of the lumbar region in man one of which passes out below each lumbar vertebra and the upper four of which unite by connecting branches into a lumbar plexus

**lumbar puncture** *n* **:** a spinal puncture in the lumbar region

**lumbar vein** *n* **:** any vein of the four pairs collecting blood from the muscles and integument of the loins, the walls of the abdomen, and adjacent parts and emptying into the vena cava

**lumbar vertebra** *n* **:** one of the vertebrae situated between the thoracic vertebrae above and the sacrum below that in man are five in number

**lum·ba·yao** *also* **lum·ba·yau** \,lu̇mbä'yaů\ *n* -S [Bisayan *lumbayaw*] **:** a Philippine timber tree (*Tarrietia javanica*) whose wood is one of those sold as Philippine mahogany

**[1]lum·ber** \'ləmbə(r)\ *vi* **lumbered; lumbered; lumbering** \-b(ə)riŋ\ **lumbers** [ME *lomeren;* prob. akin to Sw dial. *loma* to walk with slow and heavy steps, ME *lame* — more at LAME] **1 :** to move heavily or clumsily : move as if burdened ⟨the airplane . . . now proceeded to ~ slowly along —Noel Coward⟩ ⟨~*ed* a little in his walk —Kenneth Roberts⟩ ⟨the story ~*s* to a permanent standstill shortly after it begins —*New Yorker*⟩ **2** [prob. imit.] **:** to make a rumbling sound

**[2]lumber** \"\ *n* -S [perh. alter. of [1]*lombard;* fr. the use of pawnshops as storehouses of disused property] **1 a :** surplus or disused articles (as furniture) that are stored away : things cumbrous, bulky, or useless **b :** something superfluous, without value, or needlessly cumbersome ⟨get rid of the useless ~ that blocks our highways of thought —John Dewey⟩ ⟨this ~ of facts, conjectures, alternate possibilities —J.G.Cozzens⟩ ⟨useless words . . . dropped as worthless linguistic ~ —T.D. Weldon⟩ **2 a :** timber or logs esp. after being prepared for the market — compare ROUGH LUMBER, SHIPLAP, SURFACED LUMBER, WORKED LUMBER **b :** one of several structural materials prepared in a form similar to lumber ⟨insulating ~⟩ ⟨metal ~⟩ **3 :** superfluous flesh — used esp. of a dog

**[3]lumber** \"\ *vb* **lumbered; lumbered; lumbering** \-b(ə)riŋ\ **lumbers** *vt* **1 :** to cover or fill with or as if with lumber : clutter up : burden unnecessarily : ENCUMBER ⟨the constitution . . . was ~*ed* with obsolete provisions —*Americana Annual*⟩ ⟨did not wish to ~ his mind with the rubbish that most men seemed to rejoice in —Van Wyck Brooks⟩ **2 :** to heap together in disorder ⟨all those things ~*ed* in the closet⟩ **3 :** to log and saw the timber of ⟨this . . . valley was ~*ed,* hard, in 1915 —R.M.Neal⟩ ~ *vi* **1 :** to cut logs in the forest : saw logs into lumber for the market ⟨colonists were squatting on their land, ~*ing* in their woods —*Amer. Guide Series: Md.*⟩ **2 :** to become stored away and useless ⟨another large box to ~ with the odd and the antiquated —Peter Maggs⟩

**[4]lumber** \"\ *adj* **1 :** of, made of, or containing lumber ⟨~ pile⟩ **2 :** dealing in lumber ⟨~ business⟩ ⟨~ camp⟩

**lumber-core** \'==,=\ *adj* **:** involving the use of or having a central layer of substantial lumber ⟨plywood of *lumber-core* construction⟩

**lum·ber·dar** \,ləmbə(r)'där, -dȧ(r\ *n* -S [Hindi *lambardār,* fr. *lambar* rank (fr. E *number*) + *-dār* holder — more at BHUMIDAR] **:** a village headman in India

**lum·ber·er** \'ləmbərə(r)\ *n* -S [[3]*lumber* + *-er*] **:** one employed in lumbering

**[1]lumbering** *adj* [fr. pres. part. of [1]*lumber*] **1 :** ponderous and graceless in appearance ⟨the enormous ~ palaces of commerce —Edith Sitwell⟩ ⟨the ~ deal table — Charles Dickens⟩ **2 a :** slow-moving : having a heavy gait : CLUMSY, CUMBERSOME ⟨the big ~ two-wheel carts piled high with supplies —Green Peyton⟩ ⟨the ~, swag-bellied trot of an old milker —F.D.Davison⟩ **b :** DULL, SLOW-WITTED ⟨could always outwit his ~ brain —Liam O'Flaherty⟩ **3 :** lacking in grace, subtlety, or fluency of expression ⟨~ and irregular hexameters —Gilbert Highet⟩ ⟨cutting through involved ~ sentences —S.T.Williamson⟩ **syn** see AWKWARD

**[2]lumbering** *n* -S [fr. gerund of [3]*lumber*] **:** the business of cutting or getting timber or logs from the forest for lumber, of processing it for sale, and of marketing it

**lum·ber·ing·ly** *adv* [[1]*lumbering* + *-ly*] **:** in a lumbering manner ⟨pursued her ~, but she was agile as a monkey —Booth Tarkington⟩

**lum·ber·ing·ness** *n* -ES **:** the quality or state of being lumbering

**lumberjack** \'==,=\ *n* [[2]*lumber* + *jack* (man)] **1 a :** LOGGER **b :** a worker who piles lumber in a yard or shed **2 :** a tripod or other stand usu. surmounted by a spike and used as a fulcrum in raising boards to the tops of lumber piles

**lumber jacket** *n* **:** one of the various jackets adapted from those worn by lumbermen and usu. made hip-length and single-breasted with a waistband and patch pockets

**lumber kiln** *n* **:** a room in which timber or lumber is dried by artificial heat

**lum·ber·less** \'ləmbə(r)ləs\ *adj* **:** having no lumber

**lum·ber·ly** *adj* [[1]*lumber* + *-ly*] **:** LUMBERING

**lum·ber·man** \'==mən\ *n, pl* **lumbermen :** one who is engaged in lumbering esp. in a supervisory or managerial capacity — compare LOGGER

**lumbermen's overs** *n pl* **:** thick felt boots combined with heavy rubber arctics worn esp. by lumbermen

lumbermen's overs

**lumber room** *n* **1 :** a room in which unused furniture and other discarded articles are kept : STOREROOM **2 :** something resembling a lumber room ⟨go through life . . . filling the *lumber room* of their minds with odds and ends of a grudge here, a jealousy there —J.L. Liebman⟩

**lum·ber·some** \'ləmbə(r)səm\ *adj* [[1]*lumber* + *-some*] **:** CUMBERSOME ⟨a massive ~ grizzly —*Scribner's*⟩

**lumber wagon** *n, chiefly North* **:** a long springless box wagon for miscellaneous hauling esp. in farm work

**lumberyard** \'==,=\ *n* **:** a yard where a stock of lumber is kept for sale

**lumbo-** — see LUMB-

**lum·bo·dorsal fascia** \¦ləm(,)bō+-\ *n* [*lumbodorsal* fr. *lumb-* + *dorsal*] **:** a large fascial band on each side of the back extending from the iliac crest and the sacrum to the ribs and the intermuscular septa of the muscles of the neck, adhering medially to the vertebral spines, and continuing laterally with the aponeuroses of certain of the abdominal muscles

**lum·bo·sacral** \"+\ *adj* [*lumb-* + *sacral*] **:** relating to the lumbar and sacral regions or parts; *specif* **:** indicating a ligament connecting the last lumbar vertebra and the sacrum

**lum·bri·cal** \'ləmbrəkəl\ *adj* [NL *lumbricalis,* fr. L *lumbricus* earthworm + *-alis* -al] **:** being one of or constituting the lumbricales

**lum·bri·ca·lis** \,ləmbrə'kāləs\ *n, pl* **lumbrica·les** \-,lēz\ [NL, fr. *lumbricalis* lumbrical] **:** one of the four small muscles in the palm of the hand that arises from and is accessory to one of the deep flexor tendons and is inserted at the base of the digit to which the tendon passes; *also* **:** one of four similar muscles in the sole of the foot

**[1]lum·bri·cid** \'ləmbrəsəd, -,sid\ *adj* [NL *Lumbricidae*] **:** of or relating to the Lumbricidae or earthworms

**[2]lumbricid** \"\ *n* -S [NL *Lumbricidae*] **:** one of the Lumbricidae : EARTHWORM

**lum·bric·i·dae** \,='brisə,dē\ *n pl, cap* [NL, fr. *Lumbricus,* type genus + *-idae*] **:** a family of segmented worms (order Oligochaeta) containing most of the earthworms of Eurasia and No. America and including important genera (as *Lumbricus, Allolobophora,* and *Eisenia*) — see EARTHWORM

**lum·bric·i·form** \-,fȯrm\ *adj* [NL *Lumbricus* + E *-iform*] **:** resembling an earthworm : VERMIFORM

**lum·bri·ci·na** \,ləmbrə'sīnə, -sēnə\ *n pl, cap* [NL, fr. *Lumbricus* + *-ina*] *in former classifications* **:** a division of oligochaete worms approximately equal to Neoligochaeta

**lum·bri·cine** \'ləmbrə,sēn, -sən\ *adj* [NL *Lumbricina*] **:** having an arrangement of setae resembling that in *Lumbricus* — used of an oligochaete worm that has eight bristles per segment usu. arranged in pairs — compare PERICHAETINE

**[1]lum·bri·coid** \-,kȯid\ *adj* [NL *lumbricoides* (specific epithet of the roundworm *Ascaris lumbricoides*), fr. L *lumbricus* earthworm + *-oides* -oid] **:** resembling an earthworm

**[2]lumbricoid** \"\ *n* -S **:** a creature (as an ascarid) that resembles an earthworm

**lum·bri·co·mor·pha** \,ləmbrəkə'mȯrfə\ *n pl, cap* [NL, fr. *lumbrico-* (fr. *Lumbricus*) + *-morpha*] *in former classifications* **:** a division of oligochaete worms approximately equal to Neoligochaeta

**lum·bri·cu·li·dae** \,=='kyülə,dē\ *n pl, cap* [NL, fr. *Lumbriculus,* type genus (fr. L *lumbricus* earthworm + NL *-ulus*) + *-idae*] **:** a family of small usu. reddish aquatic oligochaete worms somewhat resembling the Lumbricidae

**lum·bri·cus** \'ləmbrəkəs\ *n, cap* [NL, fr. L, earthworm, intestinal worm] **1 :** a genus of earthworms that is the type of the family Lumbricidae **2** -ES **:** EARTHWORM

**lum·brous** \'ləmbrəs\ *adj* [[1]*lumber* + *-ous*] **:** LUMBERING

**lume** \'lüm, 'lēm\ *Scot var of* [1]LOOM

**lu·men** \'lümən\ *n, pl* **lu·mi·na** \-mənə\ *also* **lumens** [NL *lumin-, lumen,* fr. L, light, air well, opening] **1 :** the cavity or passageway of a tubular organ ⟨the ~ of a blood vessel or the intestine⟩ **2 :** the space enclosed by the walls of a cell and in a living cell occupied by the protoplast **3 :** the bore of a tube (as of a hollow needle or catheter) **4 :** a unit of luminous flux equal to the light emitted in a unit solid angle by a uniform point source of one candle

**lumen-hour** \'==,=\ *n* **:** a unit of luminous energy equal to a lumen of luminous flux acting for one hour

**lum hat** *n, Scot* **:** STOVEPIPE HAT

**lumi-** *prefix* [irreg. fr. L *lumin-, lumen* light] **:** formed by irradiation ⟨*lumi*chrome⟩ ⟨*lumi*sterol⟩

**lu·mi·chrome** \'lümə,krōm\ *n* [*lumi-* + *-chrome*] **:** a blue fluorescent crystalline compound $C_{12}H_{10}N_4O_2$ that is a derivative of alloxazine, that is formed from riboflavin by ultraviolet irradiation in neutral or acid solution or by the action of microorganisms (as *Pseudomonas riboflavina*), and that is found in the urine and milk of ruminants

**lu·miere blue** \¦lüm¦e¦e(ə)r-, (')lüm¦ye\ *n* [*lumiere* fr. F *lumière* light, fr. LL *luminaria* lamps, pl. of *luminare* lamp] **:** a light bluish green that is darker than average aqua green (sense 1), bluer and paler than average turquoise green, and bluer, lighter, and stronger than robin's-egg blue (sense 2)

**lumiere green** *n* [*lumiere* fr. F *lumière* light] **:** SKY GREEN

**lu·mi·flavin** \,lümə+\ *n* [*lumi-* + *flavin*] **:** a yellow-green fluorescent crystalline compound $C_{13}H_{12}N_4O_2$ that is a derivative of isoalloxazine and that is formed from riboflavin by ultraviolet irradiation in alkaline solution

**lumin-** *or* **lumini-** *or* **lumino-** *comb form* [ME *lumin-,* fr. L *lumin-, lumen* light] **1 :** light ⟨*lumini*ferous⟩ ⟨*lumino*meter⟩ **2 :** lumen ⟨*lumin*al⟩ **3 :** luminescence ⟨*lumin*ol⟩

**lu·mi·naire** \¦lümə¦na(a)(ə)r, -ne(, |ə\ *n* -S [F, lighting, lights, fr. LL *luminaria* lamps, pl. of *luminare* lamp] **:** a complete lighting unit including lamp, shade, reflector, fixture, and other accessories

**lu·mi·nal** *also* **lu·me·nal** \'lümənᵊl\ *adj* [*lumin-* + *-al*] **:** of or relating to a lumen

**Luminal** \'lümə,nal, -,nȯl, -mənᵊl\ *trademark* — used for phenobarbital

**lu·mi·nance** \-nən(t)s\ *n* -S [*lumin-* + *-ance*] **1 :** the quality or state of being luminous **2 :** the luminous intensity of a surface in a given direction per unit of projected area ⟨as the word *reflectance* refers to the effective physical reflectance of a surface for a given quality of light, so the word ~ refers to the effectiveness of a given light on the eye, regardless of its origin —R.M.Evans⟩ ⟨the photographic quantities that are of interest to the photographer are ~ of the object photographed and illuminance of the sensitive plate or film —A.R.Greenleaf⟩

**lu·mi·nar·ism** \-nə,rizəm\ *n* -S [*luminarist* + *-ism*] **1 :** the concern with or skill in the portrayal of effects of light and shade in painting — compare PLEINAIRISM **2** *often cap* **:** LUMINISM 2

**lu·mi·nar·ist** \-,rəst\ *n* -S [F *luminariste,* fr. *luminaire* lighting, lights + *-iste* -ist] **1 :** an artist who is esp. concerned with the effects of light and the portrayal of them in painting : an artist skilled in the rendition of effects of light and shade **2** *often cap* **:** LUMINIST 2

**[1]lu·mi·nary** \'lümə,nerē, -ri\ *n* -ES [ME *luminarye,* fr. MF & LL; MF *luminaire* lighting, lights, fr. LL *luminaria* lamps, pl. of *luminare* lamp, fr. L, window, fr. *lumin-, lumen* light; akin to L *lucēre* to shine — more at LIGHT] **1 :** one that is an inspiration to others : one who has achieved success in his chosen field : LEADING LIGHT ⟨played host to a huge gathering of international *luminaries* —Edmund Stevens⟩ ⟨staff will . . . consist of the *luminaries* in the field and be doing the most significant research —Alfred Friendly⟩ **2 :** an artificial light : ILLUMINATION ⟨lighting of the big new structure with mercury-vapor *luminaries* on lofty standards —*Motor Transportation in the West*⟩ **3 :** a body that gives light; *esp* **:** one of the heavenly bodies ⟨as *luminaries* . . . the total amount of light they afford during the night is far inferior to that afforded by our single moon —H.P.Wilkins⟩

**[2]luminary** \"\ *adj* [*lumin-* + *-ary*] **:** of, relating to, or characterized by light ⟨at an unearthly height one ~ clock against the sky —Robert Frost⟩

**lu·mi·nate** \-,nāt\ *vt* -ED/-ING/-S [L *luminatus,* past part. of *luminare* to illuminate, light up, fr. *lumin-, lumen* light] **:** ILLUMINATE — **lu·mi·na·tion** \,=='nāshən\ *n* -S

**lu·mine** \'lümən\ *vt* -ED/-ING/-S [ME *luminen* to illuminate (a manuscript) — more at LIMN] **:** ILLUMINE ⟨a smile of joy *lumined* his wrinkled features —J.F.Cooper⟩

**lu·mi·nesce** \,lümə'nes\ *vi* -ED/-ING/-S [back-formation fr. *luminescent*] **:** to exhibit luminescence

**lu·mi·nes·cence** \-sᵊn(t)s\ *n* -S [ISV *lumin-* + *-escence;* orig. formed as G *lumineszenz*] **1 :** an emission of light that is not ascribable directly to incandescence and therefore occurs at low temperatures, that is produced by physiological processes (as in the firefly), by chemical action, by friction, by electrical action (as the glow of gases in vacuum tubes when subjected to electric oscillations of high frequency or as the glow of certain bodies when subjected to cathode rays), by certain bodies while crystallizing, by suddenly and moderately heating certain bodies previously exposed to light or to cathode rays, or by exposure to light, or that occurs in radioactivity — compare FLUORESCENCE, PHOSPHORESCENCE **2 :** the light produced by luminescence

**lu·mi·nes·cent** \¦==¦nesᵊnt\ *adj* [ISV *lumin-* + *-escent*] **:** relating to, exhibiting, or adapted for the production of luminescence

**luminescent paint** *n* **:** LUMINOUS PAINT

**lumini-** — see LUMIN-

**lu·mi·nif·er·ous** \¦==¦nif(ə)rəs\ *adj* [*lumin-* + *-ferous*] **:** transmitting, producing, or yielding light

**lu·mi·nism** \'lümə,nizəm\ *n* -S [*luminist* + *-ism*] **1 :** LUMINARISM 1 **2** *often cap* **:** any of several schools of artists active in France in the second half of the 19th century esp. concerned with effects of light and technical problems involved in rendering them — compare DIVISIONISM, IMPRESSIONISM, NEO-IMPRESSIONISM, POINTILLISM

**lu·mi·nist** \-,nəst\ *n* -S [F *luministe,* fr. L *lumin-, lumen* light + F *-iste* -ist] **1 :** LUMINARIST 1 **2** *often cap* **:** an adherent or follower of a theory, method, or practice of luminism (sense 2)

**lumino-** — see LUMIN-

**lu·mi·nol** \-,nōl, -,nȯl, -,nōl\ *n* -S [*lumin-* + *-ol*] **:** an almost white to yellow crystalline compound $C_8H_7N_3O_2$ that gives a brilliant bluish luminescence when it is treated in alkaline solution with an oxidizing agent (as hydrogen peroxide) and that is used in chemical analysis (as in testing for blood spots); 5-amino-2,3-dihydro-1,4-phthalazine-dione

**lu·mi·nom·e·ter** \,=='nämədə(r)\ *n* [*lumin-* + *-meter*] **:** ILLUMINOMETER

**lu·mi·no·phor** \'lümənə,fō(ə)r\ *n* -S [ISV *lumin-* + *-phore*] **:** a luminescent substance : PHOSPHOR

**lu·mi·no·scope** \-,skōp\ *n* [ISV *lumin-* + *-scope*] **:** an instrument used for detecting rare metals in the soil by means of ultraviolet light and developed in the U.S.S.R.

**lu·mi·nos·i·ty** \,=='näsəd·ē, -ətē, -i\ *n* -ES [fr. *luminous,* after such pairs as E *curious: curiosity*] **1 a :** the quality or state of being luminous ⟨the rare few . . . who give to accurate reporting the ~ of poetry —D.C.Peattie⟩ **b :** something luminous ⟨mind is a constant ~ —John Dewey⟩ **2 a :** the relative quantity of light **b :** BRIGHTNESS 2a **3 :** the quantity of radiation emitted by a star or other celestial source usu. expressed in terms of the sun's intensity or in centimeter-gram-second units **4 :** the luminous efficiency of radiant energy : the ratio of light to heat in radiant energy — used in psychophysics

**luminosity curve** *n* **:** a curve expressing the product of relative spectral energy distribution by visibility

**lu·mi·nous** \'lümənəs\ *adj* [ME, fr. L *luminosus* full of light, fr. *lumin-, lumen* light + *-osus* -ose — more at LUMINARY] **1 a :** emitting or seeming to emit a steady suffused light that is reflected or produced from within ⟨the sole elements of the cosmos would seem to be ~ objects — the nebula, the stars, the planets —Lincoln La Paz⟩ ⟨he had recourse to the ~ dial of his watch —Elizabeth Bowen⟩ ⟨his eyes were ~ . . . they blazed like mortal stars —Elinor Wylie⟩ ⟨there was his face, serene, ~, often smiling —A.N.Whitehead⟩ **b :** bright and shining : CLEAR, TRANSLUCENT ⟨feeling for ~ effect that her early landscapes show —F.E.Hyslop⟩ ⟨every note in her huge range is perfect, ~, and golden —Robert Evett⟩ ⟨few foresaw the ~ future of the young man —C.G.Bowers⟩ **c :** yellow, flaring, and illuminating ⟨such a flame is also ~ —R.H. Wright⟩ **2 :** bathed in or exposed to steady light : ILLUMINATED ⟨shed a faintly ~ glow upon the upturned still face —Djuna Barnes⟩ ⟨stretched out on their backs lazily inviting the ~ American weather —Thomas Wolfe⟩ ⟨gazing up into the foliage . . . ~ with the bright sunlight —W.H.Hudson †1922⟩ **3 a :** enlightened and intelligent : edifying and inspiring ⟨full of ~ ideas of statesmanship —Samuel Alexander⟩ ⟨her own fine and ~ genius —J.P.Bishop⟩ ⟨the ~ moment when men's imaginations see alike —Lillian Smith⟩ ⟨the splendor of a profound and ~ intellect —Gertrude Atherton⟩ **b :** very easily understood : clearly intelligible ⟨convert the new situation from the obscure into the clear and ~ —John Dewey⟩ ⟨his prose is simple and ~ . . . and his text is based on wide reading —Howard M. Jones⟩ **syn** see BRIGHT

**luminous efficiency** *n* **:** the ratio of the total luminous flux radiated by any source to the total radiant flux from that source commonly expressed in lumens per watt

**luminous energy** *n* **:** energy transferred by or in the form of visible radiation — compare RADIANT ENERGY

**luminous flux** *n* **:** radiant flux in the visible-wavelength range usu. expressed in lumens instead of watts — called also *light flux*

**luminous-flux density** *n* **:** the luminous energy in a beam of light passing a unit normal section per unit time — called also *intensity of light*

**luminous intensity** *n* **:** a quantity used to specify the light-giving power of a source (as a lamp) and usu. expressed in candles ⟨a point source whose *luminous intensity* is one candle emits one lumen of luminous flux per steradian of solid angle⟩

**lu·mi·nous·ly** *adv* **:** in a luminous manner ⟨this unshakable determination, so ~ apparent in him —Robert Cutler⟩ ⟨told the facts ~ for all of us⟩

**luminous moss** *n* **:** an acrocarpous moss (*Schistostega osmundacea*) occurring in caves and dark holes in the woods and glowing by reflected light

**lu·mi·nous·ness** *n* -ES **:** LUMINOSITY

**luminous paint** *n* **:** a paint containing a phosphor (as zinc sulfide activated with copper) and so able to glow in the dark either for a time after exposure to ultraviolet radiation or indefinitely by excitation with a radioactive material (as radium) if one has been incorporated with the phosphor

**lu·mis·ter·ol** \lü'mistə,rōl, -ōl\ *n* [*lumi-* + *sterol*] **:** a crystalline compound stereoisomeric with ergosterol from which it is formed by ultraviolet irradiation as an intermediate product in the production of tachysterol and vitamin $D_2$

**lum·me** *or* **lum·my** \'ləmē, -mi\ *interj* [contr. of *love me* (in the exclamation *Lord love me!*)] *Brit* — used to express surprise, interest, or approval

**lum·mi** \'ləmē, -mi\ *n, pl* **lummi** *or* **lummis** *usu cap* **1 a :** a Salishan people of northwestern Washington **b :** a member of such people **2 :** the language of the Lummi people

**lum·mox** \'ləməks\ *n* -ES [origin unknown] **:** a heavy, ungainly, and often stupid or lazy person

**lum·my** \'ləmē, -mi\ *adj* -ER/-EST [prob. fr. *lumme*] *slang Brit* **:** FIRST-RATE

¹**lump** \'ləmp\ *n* -S [ME; prob. akin to obs. D *lompe* piece, lump, D *lomp* rag, MHG *lumpe* rag, and perh. to MHG *lampen* to dangle — more at LIMP] **1 a** (1) **:** a compact mass usu. of indefinite size and shape ⟨a queer ~ of a house —Thomas Hardy⟩ ⟨a ~ of coal⟩ ⟨a ~ of sugar⟩ ⟨it is a ridge, a high and uneven ~ of land —Norman Cousins⟩ (2) **:** the amount of clay or dough needed for one vessel or one baking ⟨all men's honors lie like one ~ before him to be fashioned —Shak.⟩ **b :** something resembling a lump ⟨everything is technique which is not the ~ of experience itself —Mark Schorer⟩ ⟨everybody has a ~ of loneliness —R.H.Newman⟩ **2 a** *obs* **:** an aggregation of things **:** CLUMP **b :** a great amount or quantity ⟨a really nice ~ of salvage money —R.S.Porteous⟩ **c :** a vast mass or majority ⟨few candidates ever started with such a ~ who did not get the nomination —R.L.Strout⟩ ⟨the great ~ of radio listeners . . . let it run all day —*Atlantic*⟩ **3 :** PROTUBERANCE, SWELLING, BUMP 2a ⟨came to with nothing more than a ~ on his head⟩ **4 :** a thickset heavy person; *specif* **:** one who is stupid or dull ⟨a hearty ~ of a lad —Robertson Davies⟩ **5** *Brit* **:** a wave raised when a body of water is cut up by the wind **6** *Brit* **:** a length of gray goods **7 lumps** *pl* **a :** BEATINGS ⟨he'd taken enough ~s —John & Ward Hawkins⟩ ⟨on the back waterways the single small craft takes its ~s —A.W.Baum⟩ **b :** COMEUPPANCE ⟨self-appointed specialists on women are given their ~s —Brendan Gill⟩ ⟨the good guys . . . were as usual giving the bad guys their ~s —*Time*⟩ — **by the lump** *or* **in the lump** *adv* **:** as a whole ⟨taken *in the lump*, the . . . team ran well and up to form —*Manchester Guardian Weekly*⟩ — **in a lump** *or* **in one lump** *adv* **:** all at one time ⟨not a set which is apt to be bought *in one lump* —J.S.Wilson b. 1913⟩ — **lump in one's throat :** a constriction of the throat usu. caused by emotion ⟨seemed to be a *lump in my throat* almost all the time —Kenneth Roberts⟩

²**lump** \"\ *vb* -ED/-ING/-S *vt* **1 :** to throw into a mass **:** group or unite in a body or sum without discrimination **:** consider as a whole without distinction of the parts ⟨the town harbor is all the northeast coast's little fishing caves . . . ~*ed* together —Charles Rawlings⟩ ⟨promise that you won't ~ me with all the rest in there —Louis Auchincloss⟩ ⟨~ men together according to degrees of orthodoxy —Barbara Ward⟩ **2 a :** to make into lumps **:** HILL ⟨plowed fields, one of which was ~*ed* up for melon planting —C.A.Murray⟩ **b :** to make lumps on or in ⟨his pockets and the front of the shirt were ~*ed* . . . with various articles —Vincent McHugh⟩ **3 :** to move noisily and clumsily **:** sit heavily ⟨~*ed* his huge bulk down opposite —G. G.Carter⟩ **4 :** LOAD ⟨did not hesitate to ~ coal at Newcastle —I.L.Idriess⟩ ~ *vi* **1 :** to become formed into lumps ⟨the cushion ~*ed* up into uncomfortable hard wads⟩ **2 :** to move oneself usu. noisily and clumsily **:** sit down heavily ⟨would loll and ~ on the sofa —Harold Nicolson⟩

³**lump** \"\ *adj* **:** consisting of one whole **:** not divided into parts ⟨pay by agreement a yearly ~ sum —G.G.Coulton⟩ ⟨300 dollars coming to you in a ~ check —Edmund Schiddel⟩

⁴**lump** \'ləmp, 'lümp\ *vt* -ED/-ING/-S [perh. fr. obs. D *lompen* to beat, prob. fr. *lompe* lump] *dial Eng* **:** to beat severely **:** THRASH

⁵**lump** \ ləmp\ *vt* -ED/-ING/-S [origin unknown] **:** to put up with or get used to ⟨if you don't like it you can ~ it —W.S. Maugham⟩

**lump coal** *n* **:** bituminous coal in the large lumps remaining after a single screening that is often designated by the size of the mesh over which it passes and by which the minimum size lump is determined ⟨¾-inch *lump coal*⟩ ⟨2-inch *lump coal*⟩

**lum·pen** \'lu̇mpən, 'ləm-\ *adj* [G *lumpen-* (in *lumpenproletariat* degraded and contemptible section of the proletariat), fr. *lump* contemptible person & *lumpen* rag, fr. MHG *lumpe* rag] **:** of, relating to, or being an amorphous group of dispossessed and uprooted individuals set off by their inferior status from the economic and social class with which they are identified ⟨exclusion of the rootless ~ proletariat from a leading role in the revolutions —*Amer. Polit. Sci. Rev.*⟩ ⟨the new unemployed intelligentsia . . . will not become ~ intellectuals —Daniel Bell⟩

¹**lump·er** \'ləmpə(r)\ *vi* -ED/-ING/-S [prob. alter. (influenced by ¹*lump*) of ¹*lumber*] *dial Eng* **:** to walk awkwardly **:** STUMBLE ⟨they ~*ed* straight into the night —Thomas Hardy⟩

²**lumper** \"\ *n* -S [²*lump* + *-er*] **1 a :** a laborer employed to handle freight (as in loading a ship) **b :** one who unloads fish from a commercial fishing boat **2** *chiefly Irish* **:** a large kind of potato **3 :** a taxonomist who regards organisms as recognizably divided into relatively large complex readily separated units which may include much variability within their bounds — compare SPLITTER **4 :** a textile worker; *specif* **:** one who tends a cotton opener **5 :** a worker in a quarry or a stonecutting establishment who assists with the hoisting of blocks of stone

**lumpfish** \'‚=‚=\ *n* [obs. E *lump* lumpfish (prob. fr. D *lomp* blenny, loach, fr. MD *lompe* cod) + E *fish*; prob. akin to obs. D *lompe* piece, lump] **:** a soft thick clumsy marine fish (*Cyclopterus lumpus*) of both coasts of the northern No. Atlantic whose color is usu. translucent sea green but sometimes purplish above or in the males brilliant red and yellow — compare CYCLOPTERIDAE

**lump·i·ly** \'ləmpəlē, -li\ *adv* **:** in a lumpy manner **:** with lumps ⟨the cereal had been cooked a bit ~⟩

**lump·i·ness** \-pēnəs, -pin-\ *n* -ES **:** the quality or state of being lumpy

**lump·ing·ly** *adv* [*lumping* (pres. part. of ²*lump*) + *-ly*] **:** with heavy movements **:** CLUMSILY

**lump·ish** \'ləmpish\ *adj* [ME *lumpisch*, fr. ¹*lump* + *-isch*, *-ish* -ish] **1 :** being stupid or sluggish in speech or action ⟨the long frontier struggles added courage . . . a doggedness which was never ~ —John Buchan⟩ ⟨the hitherto ~ girl pleaded with real inspiration —Victoria Sackville-West⟩ **2** *obs* **:** being low in spirits **:** DEJECTED ⟨she is ~, heavy, melancholy —Shak.⟩ **3 :** having a heavy appearance **:** awkward and clumsy of movement ⟨the great bulk of them . . . were joyless matrons and their ~ daughters —Alistair Cooke⟩ ⟨the prime beef cow, with the ~ awkward Brahma and the Shorthorn —Green Peyton⟩ **4 :** LUMPY 1 ⟨her heavy riding jacket was ~ across her square solid shoulders —H.E.Bates⟩ **5 a :** having or producing a dull heavy often unpleasant sound or tone ⟨lifeless and ~ as the bagpipes drowsy drone —Robert Lloyd⟩ **b :** having a tedious pedantic style of writing **:** BORING ⟨written in "translator's English" of a peculiarly ~ kind —Howard M. Jones⟩ ⟨the novels therefore . . . are ~ and dull —Virginia Woolf⟩ — **lump·ish·ly** *adv* — **lump·ish·ness** *n* -ES

**lump·kin** \'ləm(p)kən\ *n* -S [after Tony *Lumpkin*, ignorant young man in the comedy *She Stoops to Conquer* (1773) by Oliver Goldsmith †1774 Brit. author] **:** a clumsy often stupid person **:** a blundering fool

**lump lime** *n* **:** quicklime in lumps as it comes from vertical kilns in calcining limestone

¹**lumps** \'ləmps\ *n pl but sing in constr* [fr. pl. of ¹*lump*] **:** a disease of canaries that is marked by development of multiple cystic tumors from the feather follicles and is probably of genetic origin

²**lumps** *pres 3d sing of* LUMP

**lumpsucker** \'‚=‚=‚=\ *n* [obs. E *lump* lumpfish + E *sucker*] **:** a fish of the family Cyclopteridae

**lump–sum** \'‚=‚=\ *adj* [fr. the phrase *lump sum*] **:** consisting of a single sum of money ⟨has made generous *lump-sum* settlements —O.J.Hale⟩ ⟨purchased or acquired . . . for a *lump-sum* price —*Jour. of Accountancy*⟩

**lumpy** \'ləmpē, -pi\ *adj* -ER/-EST [¹*lump* + *-y*] **1 a :** filled with lumps ⟨unfortunately the gravy was ~⟩ **b** (1) **:** covered with lumps **:** characterized by a rough surface ⟨severe acne which had left his skin ~ —Norman Mailer⟩ ⟨over the somewhat ~ plain abundantly dotted with pine and juniper —Gladys A. Reichard⟩ (2) **:** characterized by choppy waves ⟨fishing and sailing on the ~ waters —F.J.Mather⟩ **2 :** having a thickset clumsy appearance ⟨the ~ man with bowed head —J.T.Soby⟩ **3 :** characterized by a thick cut — used esp. of a gem **4 a :** LUMPISH 5a ⟨his solos tended to come out in an unaccustomed series of ~ almost blatant phrases —Whitney Balliett⟩ **b :** uneven and often crude in style ⟨peppered with short ~ tracts on rural education —*New Yorker*⟩ ⟨a ~ drawing of two hands —A.J.Liebling⟩

**lumpy crab** *n* **:** a small stoutly built red crab (*Xanthias taylori*) with rough tuberculated carapace and chelae that is common between the tide lines along the California coast

**lumpy jaw** *also* **lump jaw** *n* **:** ACTINOMYCOSIS; *esp* **:** actinomycosis of the head in cattle

**lumpy skin disease** *n* **:** a highly infectious disease of African cattle that is marked by mild fever, loss of condition, and the development of inflammatory nodules in the skin and mucous membranes tending to become necrotic and ulcerous, is prob. due to a filterable virus, and may be transmitted by insects

**lumpy wool** *n* **:** an exudative dermatitis of sheep marked by crusting and matting of the wool that is due to an actinomycete (*Actinomyces dermatonomus* or *Nocardia dermatonomus*)

**lu·mut** \'lü,müt\ *n pl* [native name in Guam] **:** seaweeds used as food in Guam

¹**luna** *n* -S [ME, fr. ML, fr. L, moon — more at LUNAR] *obs* **:** silver as used in alchemy

²**lu·na** \'lünə\ *n* -S [Hawaiian, lit., high, above] *Hawaii* **:** FOREMAN; *esp* **:** a foreman of a plantation

**lu·na·cy** \'lünəsē, -si\ *n* -ES [*lunatic* + *-cy*] **1 a :** insanity interrupted by lucid intervals that was formerly supposed to be influenced by the changes of the moon ⟨grating so harshly all his days of quiet with turbulent and dangerous ~ —Shak.⟩ **b :** any form of insanity; *also* **:** the state of being a lunatic ⟨if they examined him for ~, they'd have him in a straitjacket in two minutes —Irwin Shaw⟩ **c :** insanity amounting to lack of capacity or of responsibility in the eyes of the law but in some states not including idiocy **2 a :** wild foolishness **:** extravagant folly ⟨the Florida boom was also the first ~ to feel the full power of the press agent —Alva Johnston⟩ **b :** ABSURDITY, STUPIDITY ⟨the ~ of the . . . partisan political debate over Far Eastern policy —H.R.Isaacs⟩ ⟨the economic ~ of a divided national structure —Emrys Hughes⟩ **c :** gay madness **:** GIDDINESS ⟨for handsome ~ . . . a cap with white ostrich spilling over the face —Lois Long⟩ **syn** see INSANITY

**lu·na moth** \'lünə-\ *also* **luna** *n* -S *often cap L* [NL *luna* (specific epithet of *Actias luna*), fr. L, moon] **:** a large American moth (*Actias luna*) that has long extensions like tails on the hind wings which are mainly light green with a transparent spot surrounded by rings of light yellow, blue, and black and has a larva which feeds esp. on walnut, hickory, maple, and sweet gum and spins a thin papery cocoon before pupating

**luna park** *n, usu cap L&P* [fr. *Luna Park*, Coney Island, Brooklyn, N.Y., noted for its illumination] **:** a place felt to resemble the amusement center Luna Park ⟨the entire yard is illuminated by floodlights like a *Luna Park* —*Nat'l Geographic*⟩

**lu·nar** \'lünə(r), -‚när, -‚nȧ(r\ *adj* [L *lunaris*, fr. *luna* moon + *-aris* -ar; akin to OSlav *luna* moon, MIr *lūan* moon, L *lucēre* to shine — more at LIGHT] **1 a :** of, taking place on, or relating to the moon ⟨~ craters⟩ ⟨a direct ~ hit —Edwin Diamond⟩ **:** resembling the surface of the moon ⟨the odd ~ landscape of the great glacier —John Hunt⟩ ⟨his imagery is cold and ~, shadows on sand —Kathleen Raine⟩ **b :** ORBED, CRESCENT, LUNATE ⟨who grasps the struggling heifer's ~ horns —Alexander Pope⟩ **c :** measured by the moon's revolutions ⟨~ month⟩ **2** [¹*luna* + *-ar*] **:** relating to or containing silver

**lunar appulse** *n* **:** PENUMBRAL LUNAR ECLIPSE

**lunar bone** *n* [trans. of NL *os lunare*] **:** LUNATUM

**lunar caustic** *n* **:** silver nitrate esp. when fused, toughened (as by addition of hydrochloric acid or potassium nitrate), and molded into sticks or small cones for use in medicine as a caustic

**lunar cycle** *n* **:** METONIC CYCLE

**lunar day** *n* **1 :** the rotation period of the moon on its axis equal to the sidereal month of about 27⅓ days **2 :** the interval of about 24 hours and 50 minutes of sidereal time between successive transits of the moon across the meridian of any fixed observer

**lunar dial** *n* **:** a dial for showing the hour of night by the shadow of a gnomon in moonlight

**lunar distance** *n* **:** the angular distance from the moon to a planet or star used to determine longitudes at sea

**lu·nare** \lü'na(a)rē, -närē\ *n, pl* **lunar·ia** \-na(a)rēə, -ärēə\ [NL, fr. L, neut. of *lunaris* lunar] **:** LUNATUM

**lunar eclipse** *n* **:** an eclipse in which the moon near the full phase passes partially or wholly through the umbra of the earth's shadow — see ECLIPSE illustration

**lunar ecliptic limit** *n* **:** a distance along the ecliptic averaging about 11 degrees on each side of either of the moon's nodes within which the sun must be at full moon in order for a lunar eclipse to occur

**lunar equation** *n* **:** the correction of the epacts by +1 every 300 years 7 times in succession and then by +1 after the next 400 years made because of the error in the lunar cycle in relation to the Gregorian calendar — compare SOLAR EQUATION

**lu·nar·ia** \lü'na(a)rēə\ *n* [NL, fr. LL, henbane, fr. L *luna* moon + *-aria* (fem. sing. of *-arius* -ary)] **1** *cap* **:** a genus of herbs (family Cruciferae) having cordate leaves and broad siliques **2** -S **:** any plant of the genus *Lunaria* — called also *honesty, satinpod*

**lu·nar·i·an** \lü'na(a)rēən\ *n* -S *usu cap* [*lunar* + *-an*, n. suffix] **1 :** a supposed inhabitant of the moon **2 :** an authority on lunar astronomy **3** *usu cap* **:** one that has a well-developed Mount of the Moon bulging outward toward the center of the palm and that is usu. held by palmists to be characterized by imagination, desire for travel, and idealism ⟨the *Lunarian* is not often seen in pure development —W.G. Benham †1944⟩

²**lunarian** \"\ *adj* [*lunar* + *-an*, adj. suffix] **:** of, relating to, or existing on the moon

**lunar inequality** *n* **1 :** one of many variations in the moon's motion from a true ellipse caused by the perturbation of the sun or the planets **2 :** one of the nearly inappreciable fluctuations of the magnetic needle from its mean position due apparently to the moon

**lu·nar·i·um** \lü'na(a)rēəm, -'ner-,-när-\ *n* -S [NL, fr. L *luna* + NL *-arium*] **:** a device for illustrating the motion and phases of the moon

**lunar letter** *n* **:** MOON LETTER

**lunar mansion** *n* **:** any of the 28 ancient astronomical and astrological divisions of the ecliptic each of which contains the moon on successive days

**lunar month** *n* **: 1 :** SIDEREAL MONTH **2 :** SYNODIC MONTH

**lunar sigma** *n* **:** the Greek letter sigma in the form C

**lunar star** *n* **:** a star whose geocentric distances from the moon are given in nautical almanacs and are used in computing longitudes

**lunar tables** *n pl* **1 :** mathematical tables for computing the moon's position at any past or future time **2 :** tables used in navigation for correcting an observed lunar distance on account of refraction and parallax

**lunar theory** *n* **:** the theory of the moon's motion as deduced from the law of gravitation with its many perturbations

**lunar tide** *n* **:** the part of a terrestrial tide due to the mutual attraction between earth and moon

¹**lu·na·ry** \'lünərē, -ri\ *n* -ES [ME *lunarie*, a plant, fr. LL *lunaria* henbane] **1 :** HONESTY 3 **2 :** a moonwort (*Botrychium lunaria*)

²**lunary** \"\ *adj* [modif. (influenced by E *-ary*) of Sp *lunar* or L *lunaris*; Sp *lunar* fr. L *lunaris* — more at LUNAR] **:** LUNAR 1a ⟨drawn up the spectre of a planet from the limbo of ~ souls —E.A.Poe⟩

**lunar year** *n* **:** a period of 12 lunar months

**lunas** *pl of* LUNA

¹**lu·nate** \'lü‚nāt, -nət, *usu* -d·+V\ *also* **lu·nat·ed** \-‚nād·əd\ *adj* [*lunate* fr. L *lunatus*, past part of *lunare* to bend in a crescent, fr. *luna* moon; *lunated* fr. L *lunatus* + E *-ed*] **:** shaped like a crescent

²**lunate** \"\ *n* -S **:** an ancient crescent-shaped stone implement

**lunate bone** *n* [prob. trans. of (assumed) NL *os lunatum*] **:** LUNATUM

**lu·nate·ly** *adv* **:** in the shape of a crescent

¹**lu·na·tic** \'lünə‚tik\ *also* **lu·nat·i·cal** \(')lü¦nad·əkəl\ *adj* [*lunatic* fr. ME *lunatik*, fr. OF or LL; OF *lunatique*, fr. LL *lunaticus*, fr. L *luna* moon; *lunatical* fr. *lunatic* + *-al* — more at LUNAR] **1 a** *obs* **:** affected with lunacy **b :** having or controlled by an unsound mind **:** MAD **c :** designed for the treatment or care of insane persons ⟨~ asylum⟩ **2 a :** wildly foolish **:** given to or marked by extravagant folly ⟨pure fantasy unrelated to reality is dangerous, ~, and irresponsible —Rex Warner⟩ ⟨consuming with ~ speed the assets of the earth —Herbert Agar⟩ **b :** gaily mad **:** GIDDY ⟨performed . . . with wonderful precision and ~ brightness —*New Yorker*⟩ ⟨the light ~ touch which she uses to satirize fur fashion shows and torch singers —Virginia Forbes⟩ **3** *of a horse* **:** MOON-BLIND

²**lunatic** \"\ *n* -S [ME *lunatik*, fr. *lunatik*, adj.] **1 a :** a person affected with lunacy or of unsound mind **b :** one who is wildly eccentric **:** one capable of crazy actions or extravagances **:** CRACKPOT ⟨all sorts of political ~s whom no one would dream of taking seriously —G.B.Shaw⟩ ⟨he is a ~ when it comes to fishing⟩ **2 :** a person whose abnormal mental condition renders him incapable or irresponsible before the law (as an insane person or one non compos mentis)

**lu·nat·i·cal·ly** \lü'nad·ək(ə)lē, -natə-, -li\ *adv* **:** in a lunatic manner

**lunatic fringe** *n* **:** the members of a group (as a political or social movement) espousing extreme, eccentric, or fanatical views **:** an extreme or wild group on the periphery of a larger group or of a movement ⟨he's . . . a true liberal but he has not been associated with the *lunatic fringe* of radical experimentation —John Dos Passos⟩ ⟨the *lunatic fringe* in American thought —H.J.Laski⟩

**lu·na·tion** \lü'nāshən\ *n* -S [ME *lunacioun*, fr. ML *lunation-*, *lunatio*, fr. L *luna* moon + *-ation-*, *-atio* -ation] **:** the period of time averaging 29 days, 12 hours, 44 minutes, and 2.8 seconds elapsing between two successive new moons **:** SYNODIC MONTH

**lu·na·tum** \lü'nād·əm\ *n, pl* **luna·ta** \-ād·ə\ [NL, fr. L, neut. of *lunatus* lunate] **1 :** the second bone on the radial side of the proximal series of the carpus **2** *in certain amphibia* **:** a carpal bone probably representing the radiale

¹**lunch** \'lənch\ *n* -ES *often attrib* [prob. short for ¹*luncheon*] **1** *archaic* **:** a piece of food **2 a :** a light meal usu. in the middle of the day **:** LUNCHEON **b :** a light meal taken at any time of the day or night at a selected place ⟨midnight ~⟩ ⟨picnic ~⟩ **c :** the regular midday meal when the principal meal is eaten in the evening **3 :** food prepared for lunch **4 :** a place where food is cooked and sold **:** LUNCHROOM ⟨dairy ~⟩

²**lunch** \"\ *vb* -ED/-ING/-ES *vi* **:** to eat lunch ⟨~*ed* at a restaurant⟩ ~ *vt* **:** to provide lunch for ⟨insisted on ~*ing* them before they left⟩

¹**lunch·eon** \'lənchən\ *n* -S *often attrib* [perh. alter. of *nuncheon*] **1** *archaic* **:** a piece of food **:** CHUNK ⟨cramming a huge ~ of piecrust into his mouth —Sir Walter Scott⟩ **2 a :** a light meal at midday **:** LUNCH ⟨school over, we hurried home to a cold ~ —Lyman Abbott⟩ **b :** a light meal of more formal character usu. for a group of people in a public dining room (as at a club meeting or a business meeting) ⟨a handful of university press people . . . habitually attended the annual ~s —*Saturday Rev.*⟩

²**luncheon** \"\ *vi* -ED/-ING/-S **:** to eat luncheon

**luncheon bar** *n, Brit* **:** SNACK BAR ⟨standing at the little *luncheon bar* like a wilderness —John Galsworthy⟩

**lunch·eon·ette** \‚lənchə¦net, *usu* -ed·+V\ *n* -S **:** a place where light lunches are sold

**lun·cheon·less** \'lənchənləs\ *adj* **:** having no luncheon

**luncheon meat** *n* **:** ready-to-eat meat molded (as in a loaf) and packaged by a packing house

**lunch·er** \'lənchə(r)\ *n* -S **:** one that lunches ⟨looking around at the bustling ~s —Dawn Powell⟩

**lunch·less** \'lənchləs\ *adj* **:** having no lunch ⟨so anxious to be on time, they had been waiting ~ —*Cleveland (Ohio) Plain Dealer*⟩

**lunchroom** \'‚=‚=\ *n* **:** a small restaurant specializing in food ready to serve or quickly prepared

**lunchtime** \'‚=‚=\ *n* **:** a time for eating lunch ⟨worked for a living and had a regular ~ —Frederick Skerry⟩

**lunch wagon** *also* **lunch cart** *n* **:** DINER 2b

**lun·da** \'lündə, 'lün-\ *n, pl* **lunda** *or* **lundas** *usu cap* **1 a** (1) **:** a Bantu-speaking people along the Congo-Angola border (2) **:** any of the affiliates of the historical Lunda Empire (as the peoples of Balovale District in Northern Rhodesia) **b :** a member of one of the Lunda peoples **2 :** one of the Bantu languages of the Lunda peoples

**lun·den·si·an** \(')lən¦densēən\ *adj, usu cap* [prob. fr. (assumed) NL *lundensis* of or relating to Lund (fr. *Lund*, city in southwest Sweden) + E *-an*] **:** of or relating to a 20th century school of theological thought associated with the faculty at the University of Lund in Sweden and characterized by emphasis on Agape as the heart of the Christian message

**lun·dy·foot** \'ləndē‚fu̇t\ *n, usu cap* [after *Lundy Foot* *fl*1776 Irish tobacconist] **:** a variety of snuff

¹**lune** \'lün\ *n* -S [ME *loyne*, *lune*, fr. MF *loigne*, *longe*, fr. OF *longe*, fr. *lonc* long, fr. L *longus* — more at LONG] **:** a hawk's leash

²**lune** \"\ *n* -S [L *luna* moon — more at LUNAR] **1 :** the part of a plane surface bounded by two intersecting circular arcs or of a spherical surface bounded by two great circles **2 :** something in the shape of a half-moon

**lunes** \'lünz\ *n pl* [F, pl. of *lune* crazy whim, fr. MF, crazy whim, moon, fr. L *luna* moon] **:** fits of lunacy or frenzy **:** crazy or unreasonable whims ⟨these dangerous, unsafe *lunes* of the king —Shak.⟩

**lu·nette** \lü'net\ *n* -S [in sense 1, prob. fr. (assumed) MF *lunette* (whence F *lunette* horseshoe having the front semicircular part only), lit., small object resembling a full moon or a crescent moon, fr. OF *lunete* small object resembling a full moon or a crescent moon, reflecting part of a circular mirror, fr. *lune* moon (fr. L *luna*) + *-ete* -ette; in other senses, fr. F *lunette* small opening, *lunettes* (pl.) blinders for a horse, spectacles, fr. OF *lunete*] **1 :** a horseshoe having the front semicircular part only **2 a :** an opening in a vault esp. for a window **b :** the surface at the upper part of a wall that is partly surrounded by a vault which the wall intersects and that is often filled by a window, by several windows, or by mural painting **3 :** a blinder esp. for a vicious horse **4 a lunettes** *pl* **:** SPECTACLES **b :** a convexo-concave lens for spectacles **5 :** a fieldwork consisting of two faces forming a salient angle and two parallel flanks — compare REDAN **6 a :** the figure or shape of a crescent moon ⟨peered through the ~s made by the screen wipers —Margery Allingham⟩ **b :** an ornament of crescent shape ⟨a gold ~ set with diamonds⟩ **7 :** a watch crystal having a curved top glass streamlined to allow clearance to the watch hands **8 :** a gold or gilt clip or a crystal case of crescent shape used to hold the Host upright in the monstrance **9 :** a ring in the trail plate of a towed vehicle (as a gun carriage) that is used to attach the towed vehicle to the limber **10 :** a small open frame with a glass bottom carried by divers **11 :** a broad low somewhat crescentic mound of loamy or sandy material formed by the wind

¹**lung** \'ləŋ\ *n* -S [ME *lunge*, fr. OE *lungen*; akin to OHG *lungun* lung, ON *lungu* (pl.) lungs, Goth *leihts* light — more at LIGHT] **1 a :** one of the usu. two compound saccular organs that constitute the basic respiratory organ of air-breathing vertebrates, that arise from the ventral wall of the embryonic alimentary canal, each developing into a somewhat conical sac surrounded by a serous membrane continuous with the pleura, depending from the bronchus by which it is continuous with the pharynx and from the pulmonary artery and vein, being suspended in and normally occupying the entire lateral parts of the thorax, and consisting essentially of an inverted tree of intricately branched bronchioles that communicate with thin-walled terminal alveoli swathed in a network of delicate capillaries between which and the air inspired into the alveoli the actual gaseous exchange of respiration takes place, and that in man are somewhat flattened with a broad base resting against the diaphragm that closes the thoracic cavity posteriorly and have the right lung divided into three lobes and the left into two lobes **b :** any of various respiratory organs of invertebrates — compare BOOK LUNG **2 :** something that supplies air for breathing: as **a** *Brit* **:** an open space in or near a city ⟨area of hill and moor which serves like a giant ~ the great urban populations —Gerald Nethercot⟩ **b :** a device for enabling individuals abandoning a submarine to rise to the surface **c :** a mechanical device for regularly introducing fresh air into and withdrawing stale air

from the lung : RESPIRATOR — see IRON LUNG
²lung \'lůŋ\ n -s [Chin (Pek) lung²] : DRAGON 3c
**lungan** var of LONGAN
**lung book** n : BOOK LUNG; esp : the functional laminated part of a book lung
¹**lunge** \'lənj\ vb -ED/-ING/-S [by shortening & alter. fr. obs. allonge to make a thrust with a sword, fr. F allonger to extend (an arm), make long, fr. OF alongier to make long — more at ALLONGE] vt **1** archaic : to deliver (as a kick or thrust) suddenly — often used with out ⟨lunged out a kick —W.M. Thackeray⟩ **2** : to cause to make or move with a lunge : thrust or push with a lunge ⟨strode mightily through, waving his free arm, lunging his portfolio —Katherine A. Porter⟩ ~ vi **1 a** : to make a thrust or pass with a foil **b** : to tackle an opponent in field hockey **2** : to make a forceful forward movement : PLUNGE, SURGE ⟨lunged forward and opened the door for her —J.P.Marquand⟩ ⟨lunged in with a heavy black iron tray —Katherine Mansfield⟩
²**lunge** \"\ n -s **1 a** : a sudden thrust or pass (as with a sword or foil) **b** : a one-handed tackling stroke in field hockey **2** : the act of plunging forward : a forceful often abrupt movement ahead : SURGE ⟨she made a ~ at a door —Elizabeth Bowen⟩ ⟨clattering ~ from the electric shovel —George Farwell⟩ ⟨feeling the long easy ~ of the ship —Vincent McHugh⟩ ⟨no one can read a page . . . without feeling its ~, its force —John Mason Brown⟩ **3** : a movement for position in gymnastics or dancing in which one foot is advanced as far as possible with the knee bent and directly over the instep while the other foot remains stationary
³**lunge** var of LONGE
⁴**lunge** \'lənj\ n -s [short for muskellunge] **1** : LAKE TROUT b **2** : MUSKELLUNGE
**lunged** \'ləŋd\ adj [¹lung + -ed] **1** : having lungs : PULMONATE **2** : having lungs of a specified kind or number ⟨deep-lunged⟩ ⟨one-lunged⟩
**lun·geous** \'lənjəs, 'lün-\ adj [prob. fr. ¹lunge + -ous] dial Eng : rough and violent; also : ILL-TEMPERED
¹**lung·er** \'lənjə(r)\ n -s [¹lunge + -er] **1** : one that lunges **2** : a safety belt that is equipped with side swivels and rope handles which may be held by two assistants or suspended from the ceiling to give support to a gymnast when learning aerial stunts and that is sometimes equipped with ball bearings so that lateral rotation within the belt is possible
²**lung·er** \'ləŋə(r)\ n -s [¹lung + -er] : one suffering from a chronic disease of the lungs; esp : one that is tubercular
**lunger disease** n : a chronic progressive pneumonia of sheep consistently fatal and of unknown etiology
**lung fever** n : PNEUMONIA
**lungfish** \'=,=\ n : a fish of the order Dipneusti or Cladistia that breathes by a modified lunglike air bladder as well as gills — see CERATODUS; compare LEPIDOSIREN, PROTOPTERUS
**lung fluke** n : a fluke invading the lungs; esp : an Old World form (Paragonimus westermanii or P. kellicotti) attacking man and producing lesions that are comparable to those of tuberculosis and that are acquired by eating inadequately cooked freshwater crustaceans which act as intermediate hosts
**lung·ful** \'ləŋ,fůl\ n, pl **lungfuls** or **lungs·ful** \-ŋ,fůlz, -ŋz,fůl\ : the amount of air in the lungs at one time ⟨climb up . . . for even deeper lungsful of fresh air —Joyce M. Batten⟩
**lun·gi** or **lun·gyi** \'lůŋgē, |njē\ also **lon·gyi** \'lä|, 'lȯ|\ n -s [Hindi luṅgī, fr. Per] **1** : a usu. cotton cloth used esp. in India, Pakistan, and Burma for articles of clothing (as sarongs, skirts, and turbans) **2** : a piece of cotton cloth usu. 2½ yards long worn folded about the body and tied at the waist by men in southern India
**lung·ie** \'ləŋi\ n -s [Norw langve, langvi, lomvi, fr. ON langvē, fr. langr long + -vē, a bird; akin to OHG wīo kite and perh. to ON veithr hunt, hunting, fishing — more at LONG, GAIN] Scot : MURRE
**lunging rein** n [lunging fr. gerund of ²longe] : LONGE
**lungis** n -ES [MF longis slow-moving person, tall awkward person (influenced in meaning by MF long, fr. L longus), fr. LL Longinus, Roman soldier who according to an apocryphal gospel (Gospel of Nicodemus 7:8) pierced Christ's side with a spear during the crucifixion — more at LONG] obs : a dull lazy fellow : LOUT
**lung·less** \'ləŋləs\ adj : having no lungs
**lung lichen** or **lung moss** n : LUNGWORT 3
**lunglike** \'=,=\ adj : resembling a lung esp. in function
**lungoor** var of LANGUR
**lung plague** n : contagious pleuropneumonia of cattle
**lungs** pl of LUNG
**lung sickness** n : LUNG PLAGUE
**lungworm** \'=,=\ n : any of various nematodes that infest the lungs and air passages of mammals: as **a** : a member of the genus Dictyocaulus **b** : the swine lungworm (Metastrongylus elongatus) that causes bronchitis and serves as an intermediate host of the swine-influenza virus
**lungworm disease** n : HOOSE 2
**lungwort** \'=,=\ n [ME lungwurt, fr. OE lungenwyrt, fr. lungen lung + wyrt wort — more at LUNG, WORT] **1** : any of several plants once thought helpful in pulmonary diseases: as **a** : BLACK HELLEBORE **b** : MULLEIN **c** : WALL HAWKWEED **2 a** : a European herb (Pulmonaria officinalis) with hispid leaves and small blue flowers **b** : VIRGINIA COWSLIP **3** : a widely distributed lichen (Lobaria pulmonaria) formerly used in the treatment of bronchitis and now to some extent in perfumes and in tanning extracts
**lungy** \'ləŋē, -ŋi\ adj [¹lung + -y] slang : CONSUMPTIVE
**lu·ni·solar** \'lünə+\ adj [L luna moon + E -i- + solar — more at LUNAR] : relating or attributed to the moon and the sun jointly or to the mutual relations of sun and moon
**lunisolar period** n : a period of 532 years at the end of which in the Julian calendar the new and full moons and the eclipses recur on the same days of the week, month, and year as in the previous period
**lunisolar precession** n : the principal component of the precession of the equinoxes due to the joint action of moon and sun
**lu·ni·tidal interval** \"+-\ n : the interval between the transit of the moon and the time of the lunar high tide next following
**lun·ker** \'ləŋkə(r)\ n -s [origin unknown] : something large of its kind — used esp. of a fish ⟨a ~ bass⟩
**lunk·head** \'ləŋk,=\ also **lunk** n -s [lunkhead prob. fr. lunk- (alter. of ¹lump) + head; lunk short for lunkhead] : a dull-witted person : DOLT ⟨these . . . ~s couldn't come up to Shakespeare —Mark Twain⟩ — **lunk·headed** \'=;==\ adj
**lu·noid** \'lü,nȯid\ adj [L luna moon + E -oid] : LUNATE
¹**lunt** \'lənt\ n -s [D lont match, rag; akin to MLG lunte match, wick] **1** chiefly Scot : SLOW MATCH; also : LINK, TORCH **2** chiefly Scot : SMOKE; also : hot vapor
²**lunt** \"\ vb -ED/-ING/-S vt **1** chiefly Scot : to smoke tobacco in (a pipe) **2** chiefly Scot : to set fire to : light up : KINDLE ~ vi **1** chiefly Scot : to emit smoke **2** chiefly Scot : to catch fire
**lu·nu·la** \'lünyələ\ n, pl **lunu·lae** \-,lē\ [NL, fr. L, crescent-shaped ornament worn by a woman, fr. luna moon + -ula] **1** : LUNULE **2** [L] : one of various crescent-shaped ornaments usu. of bronze, copper, or silver found in archaeological sites of the early Bronze Age
**lu·nu·lar** \-lə(r)\ adj [ISV lunula + -ar] : of or relating to a lunule : LUNULATE
**lu·nu·lar·ia** \,=='la(a)rēə\ n, cap [NL, fr. L lunula + NL -aria] : a genus of liverworts (family Marchantiaceae) with crescent-shaped gemma cups
**lu·nu·late** \'lünyə,lāt, -lət, usu -d·+V\ also **lu·nu·lat·ed** \-,lād·əd\ adj [lunulate fr. NL lunulatus, fr. L lunula + -atus -ate; lunulated fr. NL lunulatus + E -ed] : resembling a small crescent ⟨a ~ process⟩ : having crescent-shaped markings ⟨~ markings on a bug⟩
**lu·nule** \'lün(,)yül\ n -s [NL lunula] : a body part that suggests a crescent: as **a** [F, fr. L lunula] : the whitish mark at the base of a fingernail **b** : an impressed or modified area in front of the beak on the outside of many bivalve shells **c** : a small area above the antennae on the front of some of the true flies **d** : the crescentic untracked border of a semilunar valve **e** : one of the openings in the test of the keyhole urchins
**lu·nu·let** \'lünyələt\ n -s [NL lunula + E -et] : LUNULA
**lu·nu·mi·del·la** \,lünyəmə'delə\ n -s [Sinhalese luṇu-midella, fr. luṇu salt + midella (any of various species of Barringtonia)] **1** : a tree (Melia dubia) of Asia, Africa, and Australasia having reddish white wood similar to toon **2** : the wood of the lunumidella tree
**luny** var of LOONY
**lun·yie** \'lün(y)i\ Scot var of LOIN
**lu·nyo·ro** \lün'yōrō\ n, pl **lunyoro** or **lunyoros** usu cap : NYORO
**luo** or **lu·oh** also **lwo** \'lü'wō\ n, pl **luo** or **luos** or **luoh** or **luohs** usu cap **1 a** : a scattered pastoral people along various tributaries of the Nile and on the eastern shore of Lake Victoria **b** : a member of such people **2** : a Nilotic language of the Luo people
**lu·or·a·wet·lan** \lə,wȯrə'wetlən\ n -s usu cap : a language family of the extreme northeast of Asia comprising Chukchi, Koryak, and Kamchadal — see PALEOSIBERIAN
**lu·pa·nar** \lü'pānə(r)\ n -s [L, fr. L lupa prostitute, she-wolf, fem. of lupus wolf — more at WOLF] : BROTHEL
**lu·pa·nine** \'lüpə,nēn, -,nən\ n -s [lupan- (irreg. fr. lupine) + -ine] : a bitter crystalline poisonous alkaloid $C_{15}H_{24}N_2O$ found in various lupines
**lu·pe** \'lü(,)pā\ n -s [Samoan] : a Polynesian fruit pigeon (Globicera pacifica)
**lu·pe·ol** \'lüpē,ȯl, -ōl\ n -s [ISV lupe- (irreg. fr. lupine) + -ol; prob. orig. formed in G] : a crystalline triterpenoid alcohol $C_{30}H_{49}OH$ found esp. in yellow lupine, gutta-percha and balata, and shea butter
**lu·per·ca·lia** \,lüpə(r)'kālēə, -ālyə\ n -s usu cap [L, fr. neut. pl. of lupercalis of or relating to the Luperci, fr. luperci + -alis -al] : an ancient Roman festival celebrated February 15 to ensure fertility for the people, fields, and flocks — **lu·per·ca·lian** \;==;kālēən, -lyən\ adj
**lu·per·ci** \lü'pər,sī\ n pl, usu cap [L, prob. fr. lupus wolf] : priests of the cult of the ancient Roman rural god Faunus whose festival was the Lupercalia
**lu·pet·i·dine** \lü'ped·ə,dēn, -dən\ n -s [ISV lu- (fr. lutidine) + -pe- + -tidine (fr. lutidine)] : any of the dimethyl derivatives $(CH_3)_2C_5H_8NH$ of piperidine all of which are colorless alkaline liquids
**lu·pi·form** \'lüpə,fȯrm\ adj [lupus + -iform] : resembling lupus
**lu·pine** or **lu·pin** \'lüpən\ n -s [ME lupine, fr. L lupinus, lupinum, fr. lupinus, adj.] **1 a** : a plant of the genus Lupinus **b** : the seed of a lupine plant (as of the lupine L. albus) used as food from earliest times **2** : a light purplish blue that is bluer and paler than average periwinkle and bluer than zenith
²**lu·pine** \-,pīn, -pən\ adj [L lupinus, fr. lupus wolf + -inus -ine] : of, relating to, or resembling a wolf : WOLFISH ⟨his death touched off a ~ scuffle for succession —Time⟩
**lupine maggot** n : the maggot of a two-winged fly (Hylemya lupini) that develops in and damages the stem of lupines esp. in the southeastern U.S.
**lu·pin·ine** \'lüpə,nēn, -,nən\ n -s [ISV ¹lupine + -ine] : a crystalline weakly poisonous alkaloid $C_{10}H_{19}NO$ found esp. in lupines
**lu·pi·no·sis** \,==='nōsəs\ n -ES [NL, fr. L lupinus, lupinum lupine + NL -osis] : acute liver atrophy of cattle and other mammals due to poisoning by ingestion of various lupines
**lu·pi·nus** \lü'pīnəs\ n, cap [NL, fr. L, lupine] : a genus of herbs (family Leguminosae) with digitate or unifoliolate leaves and white, yellow, blue, or purple flowers in long racemes
**lu·pis** \lü'pēs\ n -ES [Cebuan] Philippines : the finest quality of abaca used for delicate fabrics
**lu·poid** \'lü,pȯid\ adj [ISV lupus + -oid] : LUPIFORM
**lu·pous** \'lüpəs\ adj [lupus + -ous] : of, relating to, or affected with lupus
**lu·pu·lic acid** \lə'pyülik-\ or **lu·pu·lin·ic acid** \,lüpyə¦linik-\ n [lupulic fr. lupul- (fr. lupulin) + -ic; lupulinic fr. lupulin + -ic] : either of two acidic compounds obtained from lupulin: **a** : HUMULONE **b** : LUPULONE
**lu·pu·lin** \'lüpyələn\ n -s [lupul- (fr. NL lupulus — specific epithet of the hop plant Humulus lupulus — fr. L lupus hop plant, wolf + -ulus) + -in] : a fine yellow resinous powder on the strobiles of hops that contains humulone and lupulone
**lu·pu·line** \,līn, -lən\ or **lu·pu·li·nous** \,==;=līnəs\ adj [prob. fr. (assumed) NL lupulinus, fr. NL lupulus + L -inus -ine] : resembling a cluster of hops
**lu·pu·lone** \'lüpyə,lōn\ or **lu·pu·lon** \-,län\ n -s [ISV lupul- (fr. NL lupulus) + -one] : a bitter crystalline antibiotic $C_{26}H_{38}O_4$ that is obtained from lupulin and is effective against fungi and various bacteria
**lu·pus** \'lüpəs\ n -ES [ML, fr. L, wolf — more at WOLF] : any of several diseases characterized by skin lesions; esp : LUPUS VULGARIS
**lupus er·y·thema·to·sus** \-,erə,thēmə'tōsəs, -them-\ n [NL, lit., erythematous lupus] : a slowly progressive systemic disease of unknown origin marked by degenerative changes of collagenous tissues with erythematous skin lesions, arthritic changes, lesions of internal organs, and wasting and by fever, leukemia, and endocarditis
**lupus vul·ga·ris** \-,vəl'ga(a)rəs\ n [NL, lit., common lupus] : tuberculous disease of the skin marked by formation of soft brownish nodules with ulceration and scarring
¹**lur** \'lů(ə)r\ n, pl **lur** or **lurs** usu cap **1** : a chiefly nomadic Muslim people of undetermined ethnological origin inhabiting a wild part of the Zagros mountains of Iran — see PERSIAN 1b **2** : a member of the Lur people
²**lur** \"\ n, pl **lur** or **lurs** usu cap : ALUR
³**lur** \'lů(ə)r\ or **lu·re** \-ürə\ n, pl **lurs** \-ü(ə)rz\ also **lu·ren** \-ürən\ [Dan & Sw & Norw lur, fr. ON lūthr trumpet] : a large bronze roughly S-shaped trumpet of the Bronze Age in Scandinavian countries ⟨the oldest metal musical instruments of Europe are the signal horns called ~s —Science News Letter⟩

lur

¹**lurch** \'lərch, -ōch, -əich\ vb -ED/-ING/-ES [ME lorchen, prob. alter. of lurken to lurk — more at LURK] vi **1** dial chiefly Eng : to loiter about a place furtively : PROWL, SNEAK ⟨~ about the place looking sinister —Anthony Carson⟩ **2** obs : CHEAT, STEAL ~ vt **1** obs : to obtain by fraud or stealth : FILCH, STEAL ⟨put lately into many men's heads . . . his own ambitious ends to ~ a crown —John Milton⟩ **2** archaic : to do out of something : CHEAT, ROB ⟨in the brunt of seventeen battles . . . he ~ed all swords of the garland —Shak.⟩
²**lurch** \"\ n -ES archaic : an act of lurching or a state of watchful readiness ⟨the enemy of human happiness, always lying at ~ to make prey of the young —J.P.Kennedy †1870⟩
³**lurch** \"\ n -ES [MF lourche, n., a game & lourche, adj., deceived, prob. of Gmc origin; akin to MHG lerz, lurz left, located on the left side, lürzen to deceive — more at LORDOSIS] **1** obs : an act or instance of cheating : FRAUD **2** obs **a** : an act or instance of discomfiture : SETBACK, ROUT **b** : one's sphere of control : POWER ⟨David, when he had Saul in his ~, might . . . have cut off his head —Thomas Goodwin⟩ **3 a** : a decisive defeat in which a player wins a game by more than twice his opponent's score; specif : a defeat in which a player wins a cribbage game before his opponent has progressed halfway toward the goal — compare GAMMON, RUBICON **b** : an old game that may have resembled backgammon — **in the lurch** adv (or adj) **1** obs : in a defenseless position : at a disadvantage ⟨he took me in the lurch —Thomas D'Urfey⟩ **2** : in a vulnerable, difficult, or embarrassing position without support — used with leave ⟨at the peak of the noonday rush the cashier stalked out and left him in the lurch⟩ ⟨the U.S. cannot . . . leave the British in the lurch in their struggle against this exhibition of nationalism —Neal Stanford⟩ ⟨died just like that, and . . . left me in the lurch —F.N. Souza⟩
⁴**lurch** \"\ vt -ED/-ING/-ES **1** : to defeat by a lurch (as in cribbage) — compare SKUNK **2** archaic : to leave in the lurch : DISAPPOINT, DESERT ⟨fortune . . . hath ~ed generals in her time —Sporting Mag.⟩
⁵**lurch** \"\ n -ES [origin unknown] **1 a** : a sudden roll of a ship to one side (as in heavy weather) **b** : an act or instance of swaying or tipping ⟨a sudden ~ of the vehicle threw the two men together —John Morrison⟩ ⟨felt a great ~ of joy —Marcia Davenport⟩ **c** : a gait characterized by a sway or stagger ⟨walk with the same slow, complacent ~ —Rebecca West⟩ **2** : BENT, DRIFT, INCLINATION, TENDENCY, URGE ⟨showed a decided ~ toward a solitary life⟩
⁶**lurch** \"\ vi -ED/-ING/-ES **1 a** : to roll or tip abruptly : CANT, PITCH ⟨the schooner ~ed in the uneasy chop —Kenneth Roberts⟩ ⟨ramshackle outbuildings, ~ing rose arches —Elizabeth Taylor⟩ ⟨the glen seemed to ~ forward and become a defile —John Buchan⟩ **b** : to move with a series of lurches : CAREEN, SWAY ⟨landing craft ~ed toward shore —Time⟩ ⟨international group . . . ~ed for days over lunar roads to watch the sacred right of franchise exercised —Punch⟩ ⟨she slouched off . . . the cub ~ing along contentedly beside her —C.G.D.Roberts⟩ **2 a** : to move unsteadily or in a series of stops and starts : STAGGER ⟨a visiting . . . celebrity, somewhat bemused by whiskey, ~ed across the room —Ian Bevan⟩ ⟨horses ~ing in deep mud —Adrian Bell⟩ **b** : to give a sudden or involuntary movement : JERK, LUNGE ⟨rubbed the sleep out of his eyes and ~ed upright —Julian Dana⟩ ⟨~ed forward with a bullet in his head —E.V.Burkholder⟩ ⟨the pain ~ed in him —Ernest Hemingway⟩ **3** : to move in an awkward or uncertain fashion : BLUNDER, STUMBLE ⟨we're not all . . . ~ing along on mere instinct —Anne D. Sedgwick⟩ ⟨Congress ~ed toward adjournment —Time⟩
**lurch·er** \-chə(r)\ n -s [¹lurch + -er] **1** archaic : a petty thief : PILFERER **2** obs : GLUTTON **3 a** archaic : LURKER, SPY **b** Austral : a street loiterer : HOODLUM **4** Brit : a mongrel dog; esp : a cross between a greyhound and a collie often used by poachers
**lurch·ing·ly** adv [lurching (pres. part. of ⁶lurch) + -ly] : in a lurching manner : JERKILY, SWAYINGLY
**lur·dane** \'lərdᵊn\ n -s [ME lurdan, fr. MF lourdin dullard, fr. lourd dull, stupid — more at LOURD] archaic : an idle or lubberly fellow
¹**lure** \'lů(ə)r, -üə\ n -s [ME, enticement, falconer's lure, fr. MF loire, loirre falconer's lure, fr. OF, of Gmc origin; akin to MLG lōder bait, MHG luoder; akin to OE lathian to invite, OHG ladōn, ON latha, Goth lathon to call, invite, and perh. to Gk laimos wanton, impudent, greedy] **1** : a bunch of feathers roughly resembling a bird, attached to a long cord, often baited with raw meat, and used by a falconer to recall a hawk **2 a** : an alluring prospect : inducement to pleasure or gain : ENTICEMENT, INCENTIVE ⟨~ of adventure⟩ ⟨~ of a pleasant climate⟩ ⟨threw out all the ~s of her beauty . . . to make a prize of his heart —T.L.Peacock⟩ ⟨prohibited all inheritance taxes . . . as a ~ to wealthy settlers —C.P.Curtis⟩ ⟨textbooks . . . designed as ~s to learning —Sloan Wilson⟩ **b** (1) : drawing power : APPEAL, ATTRACTION ⟨a situation that has, in itself, an intense and universal ~ —Louis Kronenberger⟩ ⟨salmon . . . have for him a quite irresistible ~ —J.E.Sayers⟩ ⟨the high-pitched song of fine thin glass, the ~ of its translucent depths —Martin James⟩ ⟨the sets and costumes lack ~ —Time⟩ (2) archaic : a blandishment used in an attempt to gain control ⟨time stoops to no man's ~ —A.C.Swinburne⟩ **3** : a heraldic figure of two wings joined with the tips downward with a leash attached ⟨a pair of wings inverted conjoined in ~ or —E.E.Reynolds⟩ **4 a** : a device or decoy for attracting animals to capture ⟨uses about three kinds of ~s, one being oil catnip which actually makes a bobcat . . . easy to get in a trap —Fur-Fish-Game⟩; specif : live or artificial bait used for catching fish ⟨fishermen casting every kind of ~ you've ever seen —Stewart Beach⟩ — compare ⁵FLY 4 **b** : TRAP, SNARE ⟨this flamboyant role . . . is a ~ and pitfall for an ambitious singing actress —Douglas Watt⟩ ⟨party leaders sought to . . . set a special ~ for the state's support —U.S. News & World Report⟩ **c** : a structure resembling a tassel on the head of pediculate fishes that is often luminous and is used to attract prey

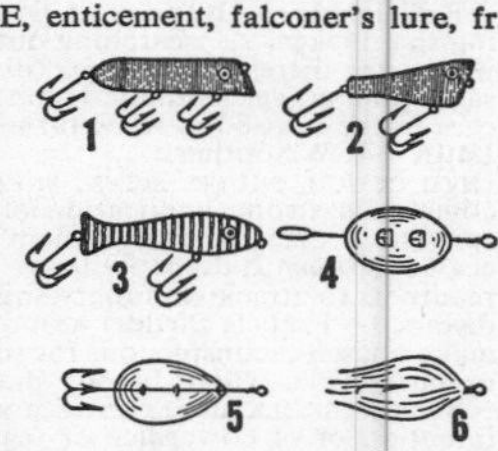

lures for fishing: *1* wiggler, *2* plunker, *3* minnow, *4* spinner, *5* spoon, *6* bucktail

²**lure** \"\ vb -ED/-ING/-S [ME luren, fr. MF loirier, fr. OF, loire, loirre, n.] vt **1** archaic **a** : to recall (a hawk) by means of a lure **b** : to call (as a hawk) to the lure ⟨O for a falconer's voice to ~ this tercel-gentle back again —Shak.⟩ **2** : to tempt with a promise of pleasure or gain : ALLURE, ATTRACT, ENTICE, INVITE ⟨don't let money ~ you into a job you don't like —W.J.Reilly⟩ ⟨the magic of a full moon had lured me from my laboratory —William Beebe⟩ ⟨lured able . . . men to his staffs —W.T.Ridder⟩ ⟨raised almost half a million dollars to ~ new industries to their town —T.E.Murphy⟩ — often used with on or onward ⟨knowledge . . . keeps luring him on —H.A. Overstreet⟩ ⟨towering cliffs . . . challenge him, ~ him onward —G.I.Bell⟩ ~ vi **1** archaic : to call a hawk to the lure **2** obs : to call loudly : HALLOO
**syn** ENTICE, INVEIGLE, DECOY, TEMPT, SEDUCE: LURE may mean to draw into danger, evil, or difficulty by ruse or wiles ⟨it was not money that lured the adolescent husbandman to the cities, but the gay life —H.L.Mencken⟩ ⟨lured into the imperfect world of coarse uncompleted passion —Oscar Wilde⟩ or merely to offer an inducement ⟨salt mines, which lured the Celts to settle on prehistoric encampments —Claudia Cassidy⟩ ENTICE may suggest artful coaxing ⟨she appeared to be playing with the bird, possibly amusing herself by trying to entice it on to her hand —W.H.Hudson †1922⟩ ⟨the fellow — for all his gentle voice — was a deceiver; enticing people to follow him about and listen to his prattle —L.C.Douglas⟩ INVEIGLE may mean persuading one against his will or better judgment ⟨I hope to be able to call and see you there, instead of inveigling you into these surreptitious meetings, even although they have the charm of secrecy —William Black⟩ DECOY means to lead into danger or entrap by artifice ⟨the islanders had been living in relative opulence from the wreckage of ships which they had skillfully decoyed to destruction on the reefs —Thomas Barbour⟩ TEMPT means to arouse a desire sometimes contrary to one's conscience or better judgment ⟨"I was forgetting," she said. "I am forbidden tea. I mustn't drink it." She looked at the cup, tremendously tempted. She longed for tea. An occasional transgression could not harm her —Arnold Bennett⟩ ⟨seated bolt upright in a chair that would have tempted a good-humored person to recline —G.B.Shaw⟩ SEDUCE means to lead astray, usu. from propriety, duty, or morality ⟨the hideous beast whose craft had seduced me into murder —E.A.Poe⟩ ⟨watching the seditious crew of "Congress men" seducing the colonials into unnatural rebellion against the best of kings and fathers —V.L.Parrington⟩ or to delude ⟨words when used with the gift of magic can seduce a reader into belief that has no roots in reality —Rose Feld⟩
³**lure** \"\ n -s [short for velure] : a heated pad for lustering felt hats
⁴**lure** \"\ vt -ED/-ING/-S : to rub (felt) with a lure
**lure·ment** \-mənt\ n -s [²lure + -ment] : ALLUREMENT
**luren** pl of LUR
¹**lur·er** \'lů(ə)rə(r)\ n -s [³lure + -er] : a worker who rubs felt hats with a lure
²**lurer** \"\ n -s [²lure + -er] : one that lures
**lu·ri** \'lůrē\ n, pl **luri** or **luris** usu cap : ALUR
**lu·rid** \'lůrəd\ adj [L luridus pale yellow, sallow; prob. akin to L lutum dyer's rocket, yellow] **1 a** : wan and ghastly pale in appearance : LIVID ⟨transfigured to death by the ~ waxworks —Sara H. Hay⟩ ⟨the leaves . . . shone ~, livid — they looked as if dipped in sea water —Virginia Woolf⟩ ⟨lights around the two effigies threw them up into ~ distinctness —Thomas Hardy⟩ **b** archaic : dingy brown or yellowish brown — used of a plant **c** : of any of several light or medium grayish colors ranging in hue from yellow to orange **2** : shining with the red glow of fire seen through smoke or cloud : suffused with red ⟨~ flames of burning chateaux —C.A. & Mary Beard⟩ ⟨the sun, shining through the smoke . . . seemed blood-red, and threw an unfamiliar ~ light upon everything —H.G.Wells⟩ **3 a** : causing horror or revulsion : HIDEOUS, GRUESOME ⟨~ examples of debauchery and vice —Liam O'Flaherty⟩ ⟨the tabloids gave all the ~ details of floating wreckage and dismembered bodies⟩ **b** : highly colored : EXTRAVAGANT, GAUDY, SENSATIONAL ⟨~ emotionalism and tear-jerking nos-

talgia —Leslie Rees⟩ ⟨his readings of standard symphonic works seemed ~ and supercharged —Douglas Watt⟩ ⟨~ as any melodrama —S.H.Holbrook⟩ ⟨paperbacks in the usual ~ covers —T.R.Fyvel⟩

**lu·rid·ly** *adv* : in a lurid manner ⟨somewhat ~ described as the sun-blistered, almost uninhabitable refuge of men and women of mystery —Raymond Holden⟩

**lu·rid·ness** *n* -ES : the quality or state of being lurid

**lur·ing·ly** *adv* [*luring* (pres. part. of ²*lure*) + *-ly*] : in an enticing manner

¹**lurk** \ˈlərk, -ə̄k, -əik\ *vi* -ED/-ING/-S [ME *lurken*; akin to Norw *lurke* to move slowly, sneak away, MHG *lūren* to lie in wait, watch — more at LOWER] **1 a** : to lie in ambush : PROWL, SKULK ⟨guerrillas ~ in the mountains⟩ ⟨unlicensed traders *~ing* along the shore —R.A.Billington⟩ ⟨below the surface ~ little beasts of prey —Alice Duncan-Kemp⟩ **b** : to move furtively or inconspicuously : SNEAK, STEAL ⟨shall I ~ about this country like a thief —Henry Fielding⟩ ⟨cook *~s* down before daylight to scour her pots and pans —W.M.Thackeray⟩ **c** : to be constantly present or persist in staying : REMAIN, LINGER ⟨melancholy that *~s* in the eyes of cripples —Ellen Glasgow⟩ ⟨bass which ~ among the cypress knees —*Amer. Guide Series: Tenn.*⟩ ⟨the excitement of the first act still *~ing* in the air —Richard Fletcher⟩ **2 a** : to be hidden but capable of being discovered : be potentially present ⟨wants what he sees, not what may be *~ing* in the future —Gertrude Atherton⟩ ⟨in the play *~ed* a wholesome plea for freedom —Leslie Rees⟩ ⟨the obviously genuine humor which *~ed* behind his utterances —Alvin Redman⟩; *specif* : to constitute a latent threat ⟨malaria *~ed* in the marshy lands —*Amer. Guide Series: Va.*⟩ ⟨these prisoners represent sinister influences that will ~ in the world long after their bodies have returned to dust —R.H.Jackson⟩ **b** : to remain out of sight : lie hidden ⟨beating the thickets . . . searching out some spring calves he knew were *~ing* there —P.B.Kyne⟩ ⟨diamonds were said to ~ in the sand and gravel —Emily Hahn⟩ ⟨treasures . . . might have *~ed* in the next book to be turned from Greek or Arabic into Latin —R.W.Southern⟩

**syn** COUCH, SKULK, SLINK, SNEAK: these five words have in common a strong implication of furtive action. LURK often suggests a place of concealment ⟨mountain defiles that concealed *lurking* Indians —*Amer. Guide Series: Oregon*⟩ or a readiness to attack ⟨a hungry shark that was *lurking* at a little distance —Francis Birtles⟩ COUCH (archaic in this sense) is to make oneself inconspicuous for some reason ⟨no vast obscurity or misty vale, where bloody murder . . . can *couch* for fear —Shak.⟩ SKULK usu. carries a strong implication of sinister intention or of cowardice or fear ⟨coyotes *skulking* near the cattle —Zane Grey⟩ ⟨eludes his pursuers and *skulks* off through the swamp —*Amer. Guide Series: Ark.*⟩ ⟨to be eternally conscious of enemies on every side; to *skulk* behind hedges; to hide in holes and corners —Kenneth Roberts⟩ SLINK implies cautious movement to evade observation ⟨a cat *slunk*, a padding shadow, across the white space —Ruth Park⟩ ⟨his way of *slinking* round a corner like a fox —Edith Sitwell⟩ ⟨Hagen *slunk* down the dark stairs, past a sound of snoring —Berton Roueché⟩ SNEAK may add a suggestion of deliberate intent to enter or leave a place or position by sly, indirect, usu. underhanded methods ⟨I *sneak* out of the house and go to a Dairy Company's tea shop —Arnold Bennett⟩ ⟨had to *sneak* into his old laboratory at night with a key he still keeps —D.C. Peattie⟩ ⟨typhoid fever . . . *sneaks* in when sanitation fails —Justina Hill⟩

²**lurk** \"\ *n* -S *slang Brit* : a method of fraud : a trick esp. of a beggar or swindler

**lurk·er** \-kə(r)\ *n* -S [ME, fr. *lurken* to lurk + *-er*] **1** : one that lurks **2** : a rowboat used by English pilchard fishermen

**lurk·ing** *adj* **1** : CONCEALED, LATENT ⟨~ danger⟩ ⟨examples of what the nature reporter with the ~ camera may capture —Walt Disney⟩ ⟨~ smile⟩ ⟨search for ~ ambiguities, latent meanings —C.I.Glicksberg⟩ **2** : PERSISTENT, LINGERING ⟨a ~ skepticism in the breast of the public teacher —Isaac Taylor⟩ ⟨was now far too important . . . to have any ~ regrets —Elinor Wylie⟩ — **lurk·ing·ly** *adv*

¹**lur·ry** \ˈlərē\ *n* -ES [by shortening & alter. fr. *liripipe*] *now dial Eng* **1** : something repeated by rote (as a formula or canting speech) ⟨turn prayer into a kind of ~ —John Milton⟩ **2** : a jumble of sounds : TUMULT

²**lurry** \"\ *vb* -ED/-ING/-ES [origin unknown] *dial Eng* : DRAG

³**lurry** \"\ *dial Brit var of* LORRY

**lurs** *pl of* LUR

¹**lu·sa·tian** \lüˈsāshən\ *n* -S *usu cap* [*Lusatia*, former region in eastern Germany between the Elbe and the Oder + E *-an*, *n suffix*] **1** : a native or inhabitant of Lusatia **2** : WENDISH

²**lusatian** \"\ *adj* [*Lusatia* + E *-an*, *adj* suffix] : of or relating to the language or people of Lusatia

**lu·scin·ia** \lüˈsinēə\ *n, cap* [NL, fr. L, nightingale] : a genus consisting of the nightingales

**lus·cious** \ˈləshəs\ *adj* [ME *lucius, licius*, perh. by shortening & alter. fr. *delicious*] **1 a** : having a delicious taste or smell : juicy and sweet : TOOTHSOME, AROMATIC ⟨pears, peaches, and grapes as large, as photogenic, and as ~ —*Better Homes & Gardens*⟩ ⟨~ steaks smothered in onions —Howard Taubman⟩ ⟨pastries and cakes, each more ~ than the other —Anna A. Coombs⟩ ⟨go on producing ~ green fodder even when all other forms of pasture have long since burned up —Henry Wynmalen⟩ **b** *archaic* : excessively sweet : CLOYING ⟨the last cup . . . is by no means improved by the ~ lump of half-dissolved sugar usu. found at the bottom of it —Sir Walter Scott⟩ **2** : having sensual appeal : arousing sexual desire : VOLUPTUOUS, SEDUCTIVE ⟨goddesses, whose round ~ legs and bare feet dangle fetchingly from the clouds —Mary McCarthy⟩ ⟨a picture of a ~ girl getting her dress ripped off by a gunman —F.L.Allen⟩ **3** : richly luxurious or highly appealing to the senses ⟨a ~ quilted silk eiderdown on the bed —Christopher Isherwood⟩ ⟨~ beauty of tone —Winthrop Sargeant⟩ ⟨the ~ poetry of the garden scene —Arthur Knight⟩; *specif* : excessively ornate : FLORID ⟨rich and ~ phrases, thick with imagery —Ruth Park⟩ ⟨arrangement . . . too ~ to be thoroughly in key with the master's style —Harold Rogers⟩ **syn** see DELIGHTFUL

**lus·cious·ly** *adv* : in a luscious manner

**lus·cious·ness** *n* -ES : the quality or state of being luscious

¹**lush** \ˈləsh\ *adj* -ER/-EST [ME *lusch* lax, soft, tender, prob. alter. of *lasche* soft, watery, fr. MF, lax, slack, indolent — more at LACHES] **1 a** : vigorously growing : producing an abundance of juicy green foliage : SUCCULENT, LUXURIANT ⟨~ grass⟩ ⟨~ crops flourished in the rich virgin soil —L.H.Beck⟩ ⟨a ~ and flowery growth of sky-blue delphinium —Louis Bromfield⟩ **b** : characterized by or capable of supporting flourishing vegetation : GREEN, FERTILE ⟨a country of ~ pastures and frequent rain —Henry Williamson⟩ ⟨gray cliffs ~ with tropical verdure —David Fairchild⟩ ⟨~ land where farm ground sells at top prices —G.P.Musselman⟩ **2 a** : displaying sturdy vigor or intensity : LUSTY, THRIVING ⟨the ~ growth of bureaucracy in . . . collective farms —John Fischer⟩ ⟨the ~ idealism of the prewar period —F.B.Millett⟩ ⟨pictures of ~ organic communities —R.E.Coker⟩ **b** : characterized by abundance : GENEROUS, PLENTIFUL ⟨~ appropriations⟩ ⟨~ campaign contributions —Fulton Lewis⟩ ⟨an increasingly ~ supply of aids and suggestions —V.M.Rogers⟩ **c** : characterized by or offering great financial gain : PROSPEROUS, PROFITABLE ⟨the ~ profit level of the war years —Gardner Jackson⟩ ⟨able-bodied men . . . hired away by the ~ war industries —R.E.Outman⟩ ⟨firms might lose out on ~ contracts —*Wall Street Jour.*⟩ **3** : LUSCIOUS: as **a** : AROMATIC, SAVORY, DELICIOUS ⟨a perfume that smells fruity and ~ —*New Yorker*⟩ ⟨made a ~ lattice-topped pie —Myrl C. Boyle⟩ **b** : appealing to the senses : SENSUOUS ⟨this pleasant morning . . . with summer languor —Ben Hecht⟩ ⟨using full, ~ orchestras for his accompaniments —*Metronome Yearbook*⟩ ⟨the cop's nasty voice . . . turned ~ with respect —David Driscoll⟩; *specif* : VOLUPTUOUS ⟨a ~ blonde with honey-colored hair —S.J.Perelman⟩ **c** : richly ornate : LUXURIOUS, OPULENT, SUMPTUOUS ⟨stayed at the Waldorf and had a ~ time —Frances Crane⟩ ⟨cars of ~ design —Alan Moorehead⟩ ⟨business and industrial worlds provide equally ~ salaries —Jeanne K. Beaty⟩ ⟨~, imaginative descriptions of the pageantry in the daily life of the Vatican —Richard McLaughlin⟩; *esp* : excessively ornate ⟨a restrained realism which makes other passages seem ~ —Richard Plant⟩ ⟨~ overelaboration and rampant colorism —Wilder Hobson⟩ ⟨sincere and moving despite their ~ sentimentality —*Musical Digest*⟩ **syn** see PROFUSE

²**lush** \"\ *n* -ES [origin unknown] **1** *slang* : intoxicating liquor : DRINK ⟨a good fellow that loveth his ~ —Charles Lever⟩ **2** : an habitual heavy drinker : DRUNKARD, ALCOHOLIC ⟨a lazy ~ with an inordinate appetite for alcohol —Henry Von Rhau⟩ ⟨it becomes the policeman's lot to drive the *~es* home —A.C. Spectorsky⟩

³**lush** \"\ *vb* -ED/-ING/-ES *vi*, *slang* : to indulge in liquor : DRINK — often used with *up* ⟨*~ing* up on some autumnal nut-brown ale —Douglass Wallop⟩ ~ *vt* **1** *slang* : to drink up (liquor) ⟨shouldn't ~ champagne on an empty stomach —D.G.Gerahty⟩ — often used with *up* **2** *slang* : to ply with liquor — often used with *up* ⟨~ themselves up with dry martinis and large whiskeys —*Blackwood's*⟩

**lush·burg** \ˈləsh,bərg\ *n* -S [ME *lussheburgh*, fr. *Luxemburg*, medieval county and duchy in western Europe] : a lightweight imitation of the English silver penny imported from Luxemburg in the reign of Edward III

**lu·shei** *also* **lu·shai** \(ˈ)lüˈshā\ *n, pl* **lushei** *or* **lusheis** *usu cap* **1 a** : a nomadic Chin or Kuki people of southern Assam **b** : a member of such people **2** : the Tibeto-Burman language of the Lushei people

**lush·er** \ˈləshə(r)\ *n* -S *slang* : DRUNKARD, SOT

**lush·ings** \ˈləshənz, ˈlüsh-, -shiŋz\ *n pl* [prob. alter. of *lashings*] *dial Brit* : PLENTY, ABUNDANCE ⟨you can have both grub and liquor here in ~ —Hume Nisbet⟩

**lush·ly** *adv* : in a lush manner : EXTRAVAGANTLY, LUXURIANTLY

**lush·ness** *n* -ES : the quality or state of being lush : EXTRAVAGANCE, LUXURIANCE

**lush worker** *n, slang* : one that robs drunks

**lushy** \ˈləshē, -shi\ *adj* -ER/-EST : LUSH

**lu·si·an** \ˈlüsēən\ *n* -S *cap* [by shortening] : LUSITANIAN

¹**lu·si·ta·nian** \ˌlüsəˈtānēən, -nyən\ *n* -S *cap* [*Lusitania*, ancient region corresponding approximately to the greater part of modern Portugal and the Spanish provinces of Salamanca and Cáceres + E *-an*, n. suffix] **1** : a native or inhabitant of Lusitania **2** : PORTUGUESE

²**lusitanian** \"\ *adj, usu cap* [*Lusitania* + E *-an*, adj. suffix] **1** : of, relating to, or characteristic of a region of the Iberian peninsula formerly known as Lusitania and almost coinciding with modern Portugal **2** : PORTUGUESE

**lu·si·ta·no-american** \ˌlüsəˌtā(ˌ)nō+\ *n, cap L&A* [*Lusitano*-Portuguese, Portuguese and (fr. NL, fr. L *lusitanus* Lusitanian, fr. *Lusitania*) + *American*] : a Brazilian wholly or partly of Portuguese descent

**lusk·ish** \ˈləskish\ *adj* [obs. E *lusk* sluggard (fr. ME, fr. *lusken* to lie hid, be lazy) + E *-ish*] *archaic* : somewhat lazy : SLUGGISH — **luskishness** *n* -ES *archaic*

**luso-** *comb form, usu cap* [Pg, fr. *lusitano* Portuguese, fr. L *lusitanus* Lusitanian] : Portuguese and ⟨*Luso*-Brazilian⟩

**lu·so·ry** \ˈlüs(ə)rē, -üz-, -ri\ *adj* [L *lusorius*, fr. *lusus* (past part. of *ludere* to play) + *-orius* -ory — more at LUDICROUS] *archaic* **1** : used in play **2** : composed in a playful style

¹**lust** \ˈləst\ *n* -S [ME, fr. OE; akin to OHG *lust* pleasure, desire, ON *losti* sexual desire, Goth *lustus* desire, L *lascivus* wanton, playful, Gk *lilaiesthai* to yearn, Skt *laṣati* he yearns, *lasati* he plays] **1** *obs* **a** : PLEASURE, GRATIFICATION, DELIGHT ⟨gazing upon the Greeks with little ~ —Shak.⟩ **b** : personal inclination : WISH, WHIM ⟨when I am hence, I'll answer to my ~ —Shak.⟩ **c** : VIGOR, FERTILITY ⟨the increasing ~ of the earth or of the plant —Francis Bacon⟩ **2** : sexual desire esp. of a violent self-indulgent character : LECHERY, LASCIVIOUSNESS ⟨love comforteth, like sunshine after rain, but ~'s effect is tempest after sun —Shak.⟩ ⟨two lonely people . . . drawn together by the nature of their ~s (not love) —James Stern⟩ **3 a** : an intense longing : CRAVING ⟨an unquenchable ~ to dominate —B.I.Bell⟩ ⟨an insatiable ~ for land —P.W.Gates⟩ ⟨extremest commercialism and the *~s* of a great city —Robert Russell⟩ ⟨the sea . . . instilling in the restless spirit a ~ for adventure —George Theotokas⟩ **b** : EAGERNESS, ENTHUSIASM ⟨restore your vigor and ~ for living —*Nat'l Geographic*⟩ ⟨was candor incarnate, with a ~ for iconoclasm —W.A.White⟩ **syn** see DESIRE

²**lust** \"\ *vb* -ED/-ING/-S [ME *lusten*, fr. *lust*, n.] *vi* : to have an intense desire or need : have a desire as a ruling passion : CRAVE, LONG, YEARN ⟨his bulky body *~ed* for sleep with every muscle and nerve —S.V.Benét⟩ — often used with *after* ⟨scented . . . a chance of return to the old detective work that his soul *~ed* after —Rudyard Kipling⟩; *specif* : to have a sexual urge ~ *vt, obs* : to make a choice of : PLEASE ⟨I kings create . . . and, whom I ~, do heap with glory —Edmund Spenser⟩

¹**lus·ter** *or* **lus·tre** \ˈləstə(r)\ *n* -S [ME *lustre*, fr. L *lustrum* — more at LUSTRUM] : LUSTRUM 2

²**luster** *or* **lustre** \"\ *n* -S [MF *lustre*, fr. OIt *lustro*, fr. *lustrare* to brighten, fr. L; akin to L *lucēre* to shine — more at LIGHT] **1 a** : a glow of reflected light : GLOSS, SHEEN ⟨pearl with a beautiful ~⟩ ⟨~ of an enameled surface⟩ ⟨the highest . . . ~ always points to the straight, smooth hairs which are especially apparent in goat hair, such as mohair —Werner Von Bergen⟩; *specif* : the appearance of the surface of a mineral as affected by or dependent upon peculiarities of its reflecting qualities ⟨the ~ of minerals can be divided into two types, metallic and nonmetallic —C.S.Hurlbut⟩ ⟨the ~ of micas is splendent, on cleavage faces sometimes pearly —L.V.Pirsson⟩ **b** : a coating or substance that gives luster to a surface ⟨old glass sometimes acquires an iridescent ~ due to weathering⟩ ⟨*~s* are overglaze colors of metallic oxides in an oily medium —D.W.Olson⟩ **2 a** : a glow of light from within : LUMINOSITY, SHINE ⟨~ of the stars⟩ ⟨Blue Grotto of the magical ~ —Claudia Cassidy⟩ **b** : an inner beauty : RADIANCE ⟨one of those figures of spirit and light that leave an unforgettable ~ in the mind —Gordon Webber⟩ **3 a** : BRILLIANCE, DISTINCTION, RENOWN ⟨many Metropolitan stars were on hand to add ~ to the season —Ann M. Lingg⟩ ⟨his ~, after all, derives not merely from the victories . . . but also from the nobility with which he invested the Arab world —H.M.Sachar⟩ **b** *obs* : a distinction that imparts luster ⟨knighthood, which is . . . a ~ to a family —Thomas Habington⟩ **4 a** : a glass pendant used esp. to ornament a candlestick or chandelier **b** : a decorative object (as a chandelier) hung with glass pendants **5 a** *chiefly Brit* : a fabric with cotton warp and a filling of luster wool, mohair, or alpaca **b** : LUSTER WOOL **6** : LUSTERWARE

luster 4b

³**luster** *or* **lustre** \"\ *vb* **lustered** *or* **lustred**; **lustered** *or* **lustred**; **lustering** *or* **lustring** \-t(ə)riŋ\ **lusters** *or* **lustres** *vi* : to have luster : become lustrous : GLINT, GLEAM ⟨their feathers *~ed* in the moonlight as they passed —*Westminster Gazette*⟩ ~ *vt* **1** : to give luster or distinction to ⟨names that have *~ed* American literature —W.R.Benét⟩ **2** : to coat or treat with a substance that imparts luster ⟨*~ed* Majolica was first made by the Arabs and Saracens —Ernst Rosenthal⟩ ⟨*~ed* cotton is . . . weaker than cotton mercerized without tension —G.S.Fraps⟩

⁴**lust·er** \ˈləstə(r)\ *n* -S [²*lust* + *-er*] : one that lusts

⁵**luster** *n* -S [L *lustrum* cave, bog — more at POLLUTE] *obs* : CAVE

**luster blue** *n* : a moderate blue that is redder and duller than average copen and redder and deeper than azurite blue or Dresden blue

**lus·ter·er** \ˈləstərə(r)\ *n* -S : one that lusters textiles

**lus·ter·less** \ˈləstə(r)ləs\ *adj* : lacking luster : DULL ⟨hair that is dry and ~ —Morris Fishbein⟩ ⟨a lifeless, ~, and spiritless conformity —*New Republic*⟩

**lusterware** \ˈ==,=\ *n* : pottery decorated by applying to the glaze metallic compounds which become iridescent metallic films in the process of firing — called also *luster pottery*

**luster wool** *n* : coarse glossy wool from long-wool sheep (as Lincoln and Leicester) — called also *braid wool*

**lust·ful** \ˈləstfəl\ *adj* **1** : full of lust : excited or characterized by lust : having or expressing powerful unsatisfied desire or craving ⟨~ of power⟩ ⟨looked with ~ eyes upon butter, bread, and pancakes, but eschewed them —W.A.White⟩; *esp* : LECHEROUS, LIBIDINOUS ⟨a sensuous grace that roused his ~ nature⟩ **2** *archaic* : full of vigor or enthusiasm : LUSTY

**lust·ful·ly** \-fəlē, -li\ *adv* : in a lustful manner

**lust·ful·ness** *n* -ES : the quality or state of being lustful

**lustick** *adj (or adv)* [D *lustig*, fr. MD *lustich* — more at LUSTY] *obs* : LUSTY, MERRY

**lustier** *comparative of* LUSTY

**lustiest** *superlative of* LUSTY

**lust·i·head** \ˈləstē,hed\ *n* -S [ME *lustyheed*, fr. *lusty* + *-heed*, *-hed*, *-hede* -hood (akin to ME *-hod*, *-had* -hood)] *archaic* : LUSTIHOOD

**lust·i·hood** \-,hu̇d\ *n* -S [*lusty* + *-hood*] **1** : vigor of body or spirit : ROBUSTNESS ⟨to view the panorama of freedom-in-controversy, to hear the pleasing sounds of its ~ —*New Yorker*⟩ **2** : sexual inclination or capacity ⟨marveled that one hour should bring together such loveliness as hers and his ~ —J.P.Bishop⟩

**lust·i·ly** \ˈləstəlē, -li\ *adv* [ME, fr. *lusty* + *-ly*] : in a lusty manner : VIGOROUSLY, ENTHUSIASTICALLY

**lust·i·ness** \-tēnəs, -tin-\ *n* -ES [ME *lustinesse*, fr. *lusty* + *-nesse* -ness] : the quality or state of being lusty : VIGOR, ENTHUSIASM

**lusting** *pres part of* LUST

**lust·less** \ˈləstləs\ *adj* [ME *lustles*, fr. ¹*lust* + *-les* -less] *obs* : lacking vigor : LISTLESS, FLACCID ⟨in his ~ limbs . . . a shaking fever reigned continually —Edmund Spenser⟩

**lust·ly** *adj* : LUSTFUL

**lus·tral** \ˈləstrəl\ *adj* [L *lustralis*, fr. *lustrum* + *-alis* -al] **1** : of, relating to, or used for purification ⟨~ water⟩ ⟨congregating at this spot and hour for their ~ summer rites —Norman Douglas⟩ **2** *archaic* : of or relating to a lustrum : QUINQUENNIAL

**lus·trate** \ˈlə,strāt, *usu* -ād.+V\ *vt* -ED/-ING/-S [L *lustratus*, past part. of *lustrare* to lustrate, brighten, fr. *lustrum*] : to cleanse or purify by lustration

**lus·tra·tion** \(ˌ)ləˈstrāshən\ *n* -S [L *lustration-*, *lustratio*, fr. *lustratus* + *-ion-*, *-io* -ion] **1 a** : a purificatory ceremony performed as a preliminary to entering a holy place, as a means of removing bloodguiltiness, on the occasion of a birth, marriage, or death, or as a means of ceremonially cleansing a house, a city, army, or a whole people on some special occasion ⟨~ with water is a prominent feature in Babylonian cult —W.L. Wardle⟩ **b** : an act or instance of cleansing esp. by moral or spiritual purification ⟨the ~ of penitents —Lawrence Durrell⟩ ⟨the Deluge as a type of the world's ~ —F.W.Farrar⟩ **c** : an act of washing : ABLUTION ⟨had not lost the . . . habit of personal ~ —D.W.Bone⟩ **2** *archaic* : a tour of inspection : SURVEY ⟨have made a last ~ of all my walks and haunts, and taken a long farewell —Francis Jeffrey⟩

**lus·tra·to·ry** \ˈləstrə,tōrē\ *adj* : LUSTRAL 1

**lustre** *var of* LUSTER

**lustrical** *adj* [L *lustricus* lustral (fr. *lustrum* + *-icus* -ic) + E *-al*] *obs* : LUSTRAL

¹**lus·tring** \ˈləstriŋ\ *n* -S [modif. (influenced by *-ing*) of It *lustrino* — more at LUTESTRING] : LUTESTRING

²**lustring** *n* -S [fr. gerund of ³*luster*] : a finishing process (as calendering) for giving yarns and cloth a glossy surface or appearance

**lus·trous** \ˈləstrəs\ *adj* [²*luster* + *-ous*] **1** : having a gloss or shine : GLEAMING, LUMINOUS ⟨Siamese silk in ~ colors —*New Yorker*⟩ ⟨the ~ flame within the opal —Owen Wister⟩ ⟨her eyes were ~ in her pale face —A.J.Cronin⟩ **2** : shining or radiant through qualities of character or in reputation : BRILLIANT, GLAMOROUS, ILLUSTRIOUS ⟨set a ~ example for others to follow —Russell Grenfell⟩ ⟨verse . . . both ~ and deep —Mark Van Doren⟩ ⟨~ actors of the period —H.W. Wind⟩ ⟨it would be hard . . . to make the waterfront saloon setting of "Anna Christie" ~ —John Mason Brown⟩ **syn** see BRIGHT

**lus·trous·ly** *adv* : in a lustrous manner

**lus·trous·ness** *n* -ES : the quality or state of being lustrous

**lus·trum** \ˈləstrəm\ *n, pl* **lus·trums** \-trəmz\ *or* **lus·tra** \-trə\ [L; akin to L *lucēre* to shine — more at LIGHT] **1 a** : a purification of the whole Roman people made in ancient times after the census which was taken every five years **b** : the Roman census **2** : a period of five years : QUINQUENNIUM ⟨from 1797–1802 they shared a ~ of sympathy and love —George Mallaby⟩

**lusts** *pl of* LUST, *pres 3d sing of* LUST

**lusty** \ˈləstē, -ti\ *adj* -ER/-EST [ME; akin to MD *lustich* pleasant, merry, MHG *lustic* pleasant, merry, ON *lostigr* willing, ready; all fr. a prehistoric NGmc-WGmc adjective derived from the noun represented by OE *lust* pleasure with the suffix represented by OE *-ig* -y — more at LUST, -Y] **1** *archaic* : MERRY, JOYOUS **2** : LUSTFUL ⟨had his moments of ~ passion —Winthrop Sargeant⟩ ⟨~ greed in their veins —*Amer. Guide Series: Mich.*⟩ ⟨with the ~ appetite of a buccaneer —Nancy Hale⟩ **3** : full of vitality : ROBUST, FLOURISHING ⟨his six brothers were tall and healthy and ~ —Walter Macken⟩ ⟨when the missing chemicals were replaced, the cane planters began to get ~ crops —Marjory S. Douglas⟩ ⟨a ~ young city sprawling on the lake front —P.W.Gates⟩ ⟨progressive spirit of the ~ young Whig party —V.L.Parrington⟩ **4 a** : full of strength : POWERFUL ⟨it was such a ~ shock that it unsettled another rock up the mountain —Burtt Evans⟩ ⟨a tart, ~ wine of the country —John Kobler⟩ ⟨a ~ factor in the wage-price spiral —H.A.Wolff⟩ **b** : unusually large in size : CORPULENT, MASSIVE ⟨a huge florid figure of a ~ man —Erle Stanley Gardner⟩ ⟨this ~ veteran of some 700 years is 19 feet in circumference —J.A.M.Muir⟩ **5** : full of energy or activity : FORCEFUL, VIGOROUS ⟨hammers the piano in a ~, untrained way —Donita Ferguson⟩ ⟨people poured forth to give him ~ cheers —Allan Nevins & H.S.Commager⟩ ⟨the ~ days of Elizabethan England swarm to life —*N.Y. Times*⟩ ⟨in the tradition of the great satirists, the ~ haters —H.R.Hays⟩ **syn** see VIGOROUS

**lu·sus** \ˈlüsəs\ *n* -ES [NL, fr. L, game, fr. *lusus*, past part. of *ludere* to play — more at LUDICROUS] : a deviation from the normal : FREAK; *esp* : SPORT 6

**lu·ta·ceous** \(ˈ)lüˈtāshəs\ *adj* [L *lutum* mud + E *-aceous*] : formed from or having the fine texture of mud : CLAYEY — used of conglomerate rock

**lu·ta·nist** *also* **lu·te·nist** \ˈlüt(ᵊ)nəst\ *n* -S [ML *lutanista*, fr. *lutana* lute (prob. fr. MF *lut, leut*) + *-ista* -ist] : one who plays a lute

¹**lute** \ˈlüt, *usu* -üd.+V\ *n* -S *often attrib* [ME, fr. MF *lut, leut*, fr. OProv *laut*, fr. Ar *al-ʽūd* the oud, fr. *al* the + *ʽūd* oud] **1** : a stringed musical instrument of Oriental origin that has a large pear-shaped body and a neck with a fretted fingerboard having from 6 to 13 pairs of strings tuned by pegs set in the head and is played by plucking the strings with the fingers **2** : a harpsichord stop

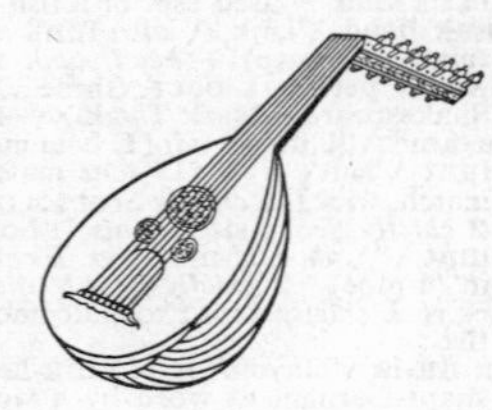

lute

²**lute** \"\ *vb* -ED/-ING/-S *vi* **1** : to play a lute **2** : to sound like a lute ~ *vt* : to play on a lute : express by means of a lute

³**lute** \"\ *n* -S [ME, fr. L *lutum* mud, clay — more at POLLUTE] **1** : a substance (as cement or clay) for packing a joint or coating a porous surface to produce imperviousness to gas or liquid **2** : a packing ring (as of rubber for a fruit jar) **3** : SEAL 2c(2)

⁴**lute** \"\ *vt* -ED/-ING/-S [ME *luten*, fr. L *lutare*, fr. *lutum* mud, clay] **1** : to seal or cover with lute ⟨~ a pipe joint⟩ ⟨*luted* his boat with grafting wax —R.L.Cook⟩; *specif* : to fill (a crevice in half-dry ceramic ware) with wet clay **2** : to fasten with lute ⟨in the neck of the steel cylinder . . . there was *luted* a vertical glass tube —P.G.Tait⟩

⁵**lute** \"\ *n* -S [D *loet*] **1** : a straight-edged piece of wood for striking off superfluous clay from a brick mold **2** : a usu. wooden implement resembling a rake without teeth used in leveling off freshly poured concrete

⁶**lute** \"\ *vt* -ED/-ING/-S : to level off (freshly poured concrete) with a lute

**lute-** *or* **luteo-** *comb form* [NL *luteum* (in *corpus luteum*), fr. L, neut. of *luteus* yellowish, luteous] : corpus luteum ⟨*lute*al⟩ ⟨*luteo*trophic⟩

**lu·te·al** \'lüd-ēəl, 'lüt-ē-\ *adj* [*lute-* + *-al*] **:** of, relating to, or involving the corpus luteum

**lutecium** *var of* LUTETIUM

**lu·te·fisk** \'lüd-ə,fisk, 'lütə-\ *or* **lut·fisk** \'lüt,f-\ *also* **lu·de·fisk** \'lüdə-\ *or* **lud·fisk** \'lüd,f-\ *n* -s [*lutefisk* fr. Norw, fr. *lute* to wash in lye solution + *fisk* fish; *lutfisk* fr. Sw, fr. *luta* to wash in lye solution + *fisk* fish; *ludefisk* & *ludfisk* fr. Dan *ludefisk*, fr. *lude* to wash in lye solution + *fisk* fish; Norw *lute*, Sw *luta*, Dan *lude* akin to ON *laug* bath, hot spring; Norw & Sw & Dan *fisk* fr. ON *fiskr* fish — more at LYE, FISH] **:** stockfish that has been soaked in lye water, skinned, boned, and boiled

**lu·te·in** \'lüd-ēən, 'lüt-ē-\ *n* -s [NL *luteum* (in *corpus luteum*) + E *-in*] **1 :** a red-orange crystalline carotenoid alcohol $C_{40}H_{54}(OH)_2$ occurring esp. in plants usu. with carotenes and chlorophylls but also in animal fat, egg yolk, and corpus luteum; a dihydroxy-α-carotene — called also *xanthophyll* **2 :** a preparation (as a hormone) from corpus luteum

**lu·te·in·ization** \,==ənə'zāshən, -,nī'z-\ *n* -s [ISV *lutein* + *-ization*] **:** the process of luteinizing

**lu·te·in·ize** \'==ə,nīz\ *vb* -ED/-ING/-S [ISV *lutein* + *-ize*] *vt* **:** to cause the production of corpora lutea in ~ *vi* **:** to undergo transformation into corpus luteum

**luteinizing hormone** *n* **:** a hormone of protein-carbohydrate composition that is obtained from the anterior lobe of the pituitary gland and that in the female stimulates the development of corpora lutea and together with follicle-stimulating hormone the secretion of progesterone and in the male the development of interstitial tissue in the testis and the secretion of testosterone — abbr. *LH;* called also *interstitial-cell-stimulating hormone*

**lutenist** *var of* LUTANIST

**lu·teo** \'lüd-ē,ō, 'lüte-\ *adj* [*luteo-*] **:** of, relating to, or being a series of coordination complexes (as of cobalt or chromium) ⟨~ chromic salts⟩ — compare LUTEO- 2

**luteo-** *comb form* [ISV, fr. L *luteus* yellowish, luteous] **1 :** yellowish **:** yellowish and ⟨*luteo*fuscous⟩ ⟨*luteo*virescent⟩ **2 :** being one of a series of coordination complexes (as of cobalt or chromium) that contain six molecules of ammonia or their equivalent and that in most cases are yellow ⟨*luteo*cobaltic chloride $[Co(NH_3)_6]Cl_3$⟩

**lu·teo·fulvous** \¦lüd-ēō+\ *adj* [*luteo-* + *fulvous*] **:** tawny yellow

**lu·teo·fuscous** \"+\ *adj* [*luteo-* + *fuscous*] **:** dusky or blackish yellow

**lu·te·o·lin** \'lüd-ēələn, 'lüte-, -,lin\ *n* -s [ISV *luteol-* (fr. NL *luteola* — specific epithet of the dyer's rocket *Reseda luteola* — fr. L, fem. of *luteolus* yellowish) + *-in*] **:** a yellow crystalline pigment $C_{15}H_{10}O_6$ occurring usu. as a glycoside in many plants (as dyer's rocket); a tetrahydroxy-flavone

**lu·te·o·lous** \lü'tēələs\ *adj* [L *luteolus*, fr. *luteus* yellowish, luteous] *biol* **:** slightly yellow **:** YELLOWISH

**lu·te·o·ma** \,lüd-ē'ōmə\ *n, pl* **luteo·mas** \-məz\ *or* **luteoma·ta** \-məd-ə\ [NL, fr. *lute-* + *-oma*] **:** an ovarian tumor derived from corpus luteum

**lu·teo·rufescent** \¦lüd-ēō+\ *adj* [*luteo-* + *rufescent*] **:** reddish yellow

**lu·teo·trophic** \¦lüd-ēə¦träfik, -rōf-\ *or* **lu·teo·trop·ic** \-¦träpik\ *adj* [*lute-* + *-trophic* or *-tropic*] **:** acting on the corpora lutea

**lu·teo·trophin** \,===trōfən, -räf-\ *or* **lu·teotro·pin** \-rōpən\ *or* **luteotrophic hormone** *n* -s [*luteotrophin, luteotropin* fr. *luteotrophic, luteotropic* + *-in*] **:** LACTOGENIC HORMONE

**lu·te·ous** \'lüd-ēəs, 'lüte-\ *adj* [L *luteus*, fr. *lutum* dyer's rocket, yellow + *-eus* -eous — more at LURID] **:** of any of several colors averaging light to moderate greenish yellow

**lu·teo·virescent** \¦lüd-ēō+\ *adj* [*luteo-* + *virescent*] **:** greenish yellow

**lut·er** \'lüd-ə(r), 'lütə-\ *n* -s [⁴*lute* + *-er*] **:** one that applies lutes; *specif* **:** a worker who seals coke-oven doors with lute — called also *dauber, paster*

**lutes** *pl of* LUTE, *pres 3d sing of* LUTE

**lu·tes·cent** \(')lü¦tes³nt\ *adj* [L *luteus* yellowish, luteous + E *-escent*] **:** YELLOWISH

**lutescent warbler** *n* **:** ORANGE-CROWNED WARBLER

**lute stern** *n* [perh. fr. ¹*lute*] **:** a transom stern particularly adapted for landing on beaches used on small fishing boats in the south of England

**lute·string** \'lüt,striŋ\ *n* [by folk etymology fr. It *lustrino* sequin, glossy fabric, fr. *lustro* luster — more at LUSTER] **:** a plain glossy silk formerly much used for women's dresses and ribbons

**lu·te·tium** *also* **lu·te·cium** \lü'tesh(ē)əm\ *n* -s [*lutetium* fr. NL, fr. L *Lutetia*, town in Gaul (now Paris) + NL *-ium*; *lutecium* fr. NL, fr. F *Lutèce* (fr. L *Lutetia*) + NL *-ium*] **:** a trivalent metallic element of the rare-earth group usu. associated with ytterbium in the purification steps leading to its isolation — symbol *Lu;* see ELEMENT table

**lutfisk** *var of* LUTEFISK

**luth** \'lüth\ *n* -s [F, lit., lute, fr. MF *lut, leut* — more at LUTE] **:** LEATHERBACK

¹**lu·ther·an** \'lüth(ə)rən, -thərn\ *n* -s *usu cap* [Martin *Luther* †1546 Ger. religious reformer + E *-an*, n. suffix] **:** a follower or adherent of Luther or of the doctrines and practices of the Lutheran Church

²**lutheran** \"\ *adj, usu cap* [Martin *Luther* + E *-an*, adj. suffix] **:** of or relating to Luther or his doctrines or to the Lutheran Church

**lu·ther·an·ism** \-th(ə)rə,nizəm\ *n* -s *cap* **:** the doctrines or religious principles taught by Luther or held by the Lutheran Church

**lutheran window** *n, usu cap L* [*Lutheran* by folk etymology (influence of ²*lutheran*) fr. earlier *lucane* — more at LUCARNE] **:** DORMER WINDOW

**lu·ther·ism** \'lüthə,rizəm\ *n* -s *usu cap* [Martin *Luther* + E *-ism*] **1 :** LUTHERANISM **2 :** something characteristic of Luther or his followers

**lu·thern** \'lüthə(r)n\ *n* -s [prob. by folk etymology (influence of ²*lutheran*) fr. earlier *lucane* — more at LUCARNE] **:** DORMER WINDOW

**lu·thi·er** \'lüd-ē(ə)(r)\ *n* -s [F, fr. *luth* lute (fr. MF *lut, leut*) + *-ier* -er — more at LUTE] **1 :** a lute maker **2 :** a maker of stringed instruments (as violins)

**lu·ti·an·i·dae** \,lüshē'anə,dē, ,lüt**ē**-\ *syn of* LUTJANIDAE

**lu·ti·dine** \'lüd-ə,dēn, -dən\ *n* -s [approximate anagram of *toluidine*] **:** any of the dimethyl derivatives $C_5H_3(CH_3)_2N$ of pyridine that are usu. associated with pyridine and the picolines in the bases of coal tar and that are obtained also in gas liquor

**lu·ti·din·ic acid** \¦==¦dinik-\ *n* [*lutidinic* ISV *lutidine* + *-ic*] **:** a crystalline acid $C_5H_3N(COOH)_2$ that is isomeric with quinolinic acid and cinchomeronic acid and is made by oxidizing one of the lutidines; 2,4-pyridine-dicarboxylic acid

**luting** *n* -s [fr. gerund of ⁴*lute*] **:** ³LUTE

**lut·ist** \'lüd-əst, -ütəst\ *n* -s **1 :** a lute player **2 :** a maker of lutes

¹**lu·tjanid** \lü'chānəd, -an-\ *adj* [NL *Lutjanidae*] **:** of or relating to the Lutjanidae

²**lutjanid** \"\ *n* -s [NL *Lutjanidae*] **:** a member of the Lutjanidae

**lu·tjan·i·dae** \-'chanə,dē\ *n pl, cap* [NL, fr. *Lutjanus*, type genus + *-idae*] **:** a large family of active carnivorous marine percoid fishes chiefly of rocks and reefs along tropic shores that includes a number of important food fishes — compare SNAPPER

**lu·tja·nus** \-'chānəs\ *n, cap* [NL, prob. fr. Malay dial. *lutjang*, a fish] **:** a genus of marine percoid fishes that is the type of the family Lutjanidae and includes both important food fishes and a few highly toxic forms

**lu·ton** \'lüt³n\ *adj, usu cap* [fr. *Luton*, city in southeast central England] **:** of or from the city of Luton, Bedfordshire, England **:** of the kind or style prevalent in Luton

**lutong** *var of* LOTONG

**lu·tra** \'lü·trə\ *n, cap* [NL, fr. L *lutra, lytra* otter] **:** a genus (family Mustelidae) comprising the common otters of Europe and America

**lu·trar·ia** \lü'tra(a)rēə\ *n, cap* [NL, fr. L *lutra* otter + NL *-aria*] **:** a genus of edible clams (family Mactridae) related to the surf clams — see OTTER SHELL

**lu·tre·o·la** \lü'trēələ\ *n, cap* [NL, dim. of L *lutra* otter] *in some classifications* **:** a genus of Mustelidae that comprises the minks and is usu. included as a subgenus in *Mustela*

**lu·trine** \'lü,trīn, 'lü·trən\ *adj* [ML *lutrinus*, fr. L *lutra* otter + *-inus* -ine] **:** of or relating to the otters

**lu·tu·am·i·an** \,lüd-ə'wamēən\ *n, pl* **lutuamian** *or* **lutuamians** *usu cap* **1 a :** an Indian people of Oregon and northern California **b :** a member of such people **2 :** a language family of Oregon comprising Klamath and Modoc

**lutulent** *adj* [L *lutulentus*, fr. *lutum* mud + *-ulentus* -ulent — more at POLLUTE] *obs* **:** TURBID

**lutz** \'lùts\ *n* -ES *usu cap* [prob. irreg. fr. Gustave *Lussi* b1898 Swiss figure skater, its inventor] **:** a figure-skating jump in which the skater makes his takeoff from the back outside edge of one skate, rotates counterclockwise, and lands on the back outside edge of the other skate

**lu·var·i·dae** \lü'varə,dē\ *n pl, cap* [NL, fr. *Luvarus*, type genus (fr. It dial. *lùvaru* louvar) + *-idae* — more at LOUVAR] **:** a family of scombroid fishes comprising the louvar

**lu·wi** \'lü(,)wē\ *n, pl* **luwi** *or* **luwis** *usu cap* **1 :** an ancient people of the southern coast of Asia Minor **2 :** a member of the Luwi people

¹**lu·wi·an** \'lüwēən\ *also* **lu·ian** \'lüyən\ *or* **lu·vi·an** \-üvēən\ *adj, usu cap* [*Luwi* + E *-an*, adj. suffix] **1 :** of, relating to, or characteristic of the Luwi or their country (Luya) **2 :** of, relating to, or characteristic of the Luwian language

²**luwian** \"\ *n* -s *usu cap* **:** the Anatolian language of the Luwi people known chiefly from the Hittite documents — see INDO-EUROPEAN LANGUAGES table

¹**lux** *vt* -ED/-ING/-ES [F *luxer*, fr. L *luxare*] *obs* **:** LUXATE

²**lux** \'ləks\ *n, pl* **lux** *or* **luxes** [L, light — more at LIGHT] **:** a unit of illumination equal to the direct illumination on a surface that is everywhere one meter from a uniform point source of one candle **:** a unit of illumination that is equal to one lumen per square meter

**lux·ate** \'ləkˌsāt, *usu* -ād·+V\ *vt* -ED/-ING/-S [L *luxatus*, past part. of *luxare*, fr. *luxus* dislocated — more at LOCK (of hair)] **:** to throw out of place or joint **:** DISPLACE, DISLOCATE ⟨the . . . fractured and *luxated* teeth were removed —*Dental Abstracts*⟩ ⟨a *luxated* patella⟩

**lux·a·tion** \ˌlək'sāshən\ *n* -s [LL *luxation-, luxatio*, fr. L *luxatus* + *-ion-, -io* -ion] **:** the act of luxating or state of being luxated **:** DISPLACEMENT, DISLOCATION

**luxe** \'lѳks\ *n* -s [L *luxus* — more at LUXURY] **:** the quality or state of being sumptuous **:** LUXURY, ELEGANCE ⟨furs and Edwardian ~ —Cyril Connolly⟩ — compare DELUXE

**lux·em·bourg** *or* **lux·em·burg** \'lùksəm,bůrg, -bùəg *also* 'lük- *or* -,bərg *or* -,bōg *or* -,bəig; 'ləksəm,bərg, -bōg,-bəig *also* -bůrg *or* -bùəg\ *adj, usu cap* [*Luxembourg, Luxemburg*, city and grand duchy in western Europe] **:** of or from the grand duchy of Luxembourg or the city of Luxembourg, its capital **:** of the kind or style prevalent in Luxembourg **:** LUXEMBOURGIAN

**lux·em·bourg·er** *or* **lux·em·burg·er** \-gə(r)\ *n* -s *cap* **:** a native or inhabitant of the duchy of Luxembourg

¹**lux·em·bourg·i·an** *or* **lux·em·burg·i·an** \¦==¦=gēən\ *adj, usu cap* **1 :** of, relating to, or characteristic of Luxembourg **2 :** of, relating to, or characteristic of the people of Luxembourg

²**luxembourgian** \"\ *n* -s *cap* **:** the Germanic speech of Luxembourg

**luxmeter** \'=,==\ *also* **lux·om·e·ter** \lək'sämәd-ə(r)\ *n* [*luxmeter* ISV *lux* + *-meter; luxometer* fr. *lux* + *-o-* + *-meter*] **:** an illuminometer giving its indications in luxes

**lux·u·ri·ance** \(,)ləg'zhůrēən(t)s, (,)lək'shůr-\ *n* -s [fr. *luxuriant*, after such pairs as E *assistant: assistance*] **:** the quality or state of being luxuriant **:** RICHNESS, PROLIFERATION

**lux·u·ri·an·cy** \-nsē, -si\ *n* -ES [*luxuriant* + *-cy*] *archaic* **:** LUXURIANCE

**lux·u·ri·ant** \-nt\ *adj* [L *luxuriant-, luxurians*, pres. part. of *luxuriare* to luxuriate] **1 a :** yielding or capable of yielding abundance **:** FRUITFUL, PRODUCTIVE ⟨placid undulating ~ country —J.C.Powys⟩ **b :** characterized by abundant growth **:** LUSH, FLOURISHING ⟨this damp and mild climate makes possible the most ~ forest growth —C.D.Forde⟩ ⟨*Canna indica* was planted and it flourished, growing a most ~ crop —Edward Samuel⟩ ⟨regular features, ~ side-whiskers and mustache —F. L.Hise⟩ **2 a :** exuberantly rich and varied **:** PROLIFIC, INVENTIVE ⟨all the ~ human life that pours out upon a traveler who knocks on many doors —J.T.Flexner⟩ ⟨a ~ mythology has . . . populated the universe with explanatory spirits —S.C.Pepper⟩ ⟨~ and vital imagery —Eunice Glenn⟩ **b :** excessively elaborate **:** FLORID ⟨a master of ~ prose . . . too often entangled in his own metaphors —Nicolas Slonimsky⟩ **3 :** characterized by luxury **:** LUXURIOUS, ELEGANT ⟨gay companies in ~ restaurants —Theodore Dreiser⟩ **syn** see PROFUSE

**lux·u·ri·ant·ly** *adv* **:** in a luxuriant manner

**lux·u·ri·ate** \-rē,āt, *usu* -ād·+V\ *vi* -ED/-ING/-S [L *luxuriatus*, past part. of *luxuriare*, fr. *luxuria* luxury] **1 a :** to grow profusely **:** FLOURISH, THRIVE ⟨in the nearby conservatory ~ tropical plants —Aubrey Drury⟩ **b :** to develop extensively **:** PROLIFERATE, EXPAND ⟨this globe . . . that ~*s* into a million forms of riotously breeding life —Will Durant⟩ ⟨around these ~*s* a free and unsymmetrical, yet ordered decoration of spiral curves —O. Elfrida Saunders⟩ ⟨the art department . . . had *luxuriated* as an easy refuge for the football player and the dilettante —F.H.Taylor⟩ **2 a :** to abandon oneself to pleasure **:** live luxuriously **:** indulge oneself ⟨we have taken a very charming little cottage . . . for the whole summer and I am going to ~ there in wanton splendor —H.J.Laski⟩ ⟨gives few interviews . . . ~*s* in no autographing parties —J.K. Hutchens⟩ **b :** to find enjoyment **:** take delight **:** REVEL ⟨was *luxuriating* in a good cigar —B.L.K.Henderson⟩ ⟨*luxuriated* in the admiration and intellectual comradeship of newfound friends —W.R.Parker⟩ ⟨tried to ~ in his own self-pity —Hanama Tasaki⟩

**lux·u·ri·ous** \-,əs\ *adj* [ME, fr. MF *luxurieux*, fr. L *luxuriosus*, fr. *luxuria* luxury, excess + *-osus* -ose] **1 :** of, relating to, or expressive of esp. unrestrained gratification of the senses ⟨gave a cautious sniff, and then a ~ one —Jan Struther⟩ ⟨the bottomland corn . . . rustled thickly, a ~, arousing sound —Max Steele⟩ ⟨that sense of tears in mortal things, that sort of ~ melancholy —Norman Birkett⟩; *often* **:** LECHEROUS, SENSUAL, VOLUPTUOUS ⟨a peep show presenting the choicest erotic fantasies evolved in the course of the most ~ civilizations —*Saturday Rev.*⟩ **2 a :** pleasure loving **:** fond of luxury or self-indulgence **:** SYBARITIC ⟨a ~ nobility having regard neither for toil nor for temperance —J.D.Hart⟩ ⟨a sophisticate who defends his ~ tastes and his simple conviction that the best is quite good enough for him —R.A.Cordell⟩ **b :** characterized by opulence, sumptuousness, or rich abundance ⟨imagined . . . her husband installed in a ~ suite of rooms —W.S. Maugham⟩ ⟨~ privileges which seem to be reserved for . . . officials —H.S.Canby⟩ ⟨never before . . . has the work been led so suavely, so powerfully, or with so ~ a sound —Virgil Thomson⟩ ⟨a ~ cargo of wine, olive oil, and candied tropic fruits —Elinor Wylie⟩; *specif* **:** excessively ornate ⟨a ~ piece of late romantic writing, heavily orchestrated —Edward Sackville-West & Desmond Shawe-Taylor⟩ **3 :** LUXURIANT ⟨~ vegetation⟩ ⟨tossed his ~ black mane —Eleanor Clark⟩

**syn** LUXURIOUS, SUMPTUOUS, and OPULENT can apply to something obviously or ostentatiously rich or magnificent. LUXURIOUS implies choice and costly and is often used to refer to that which provides unusual physical ease and gratification ⟨a *luxurious* home with every comfort⟩ ⟨a mass of gorgeous upholstery and a labyrinth of *luxurious* architecture —G.K. Chesterton⟩ ⟨the place is *luxurious*, with gay cabañas on the shore of a lake, with fencing and riding teachers, beautiful flower gardens, and various recreational facilities —*Amer. Guide Series: Maine*⟩ ⟨lighting a cigarette and stretching out his legs in *luxurious* contentment —J.C.Powys⟩ ⟨evenings of *luxurious* quiet after toil —Adrian Bell⟩ SUMPTUOUS implies extravagantly rich, splendid, or luxurious ⟨a velvet gown, *sumptuous* and wine-purple, with a white ruff that stood up . . . high and stiff —Edmund Wilson⟩ ⟨*sumptuous* as the processional colors of the forest —Elinor Wylie⟩ ⟨a *sumptuous* breakfast of hot cakes, fresh eggs and coffee and prime cold venison —Walter O'Meara⟩ OPULENT stresses an extreme richness or sometimes a flaunting luxuriousness ⟨the *opulent* court of an Indian rajah⟩ ⟨*opulent* color, used mainly in pictures of nudes and still life —Eric Newton⟩ ⟨wild *opulent* growth —Duncan Phillips⟩ ⟨the table spread with *opulent* hospitality . . . the baked ham at one end and the saddle of roast mutton at the other, with fried chicken, oysters, crabs, sweet potatoes, jellies, custards —V.L.Parrington⟩ **syn** see in addition SENSUOUS

**lux·u·ri·ous·ly** *adv* **:** in a luxurious manner

**lux·u·ri·ous·ness** *n* -ES **:** the quality or state of being luxurious

¹**lux·u·ry** \'ləksh(ə)rē, 'ləgzh-, -ri\ *n* -ES [ME *luxurie*, fr. MF, fr. L *luxuria* luxury, excess; akin to L *luxus* luxury, excess, and prob. to L *luxus* dislocated — more at LOCK (of hair)] **1** *archaic* **:** LECHERY, LUST ⟨stained with adulterous ~ —John Marston⟩ **2 a :** an habitually sumptuous environment or way of life ⟨princes of the Renascence lavished upon private ~ . . . enormous amounts of money —Lewis Mumford⟩ **b :** an elegant appointment or material aid to the achievement of luxury ⟨the sharp gaze of a woman . . . condemned the details of this chamber that imitated every ~ —Arnold Bennett⟩ **c :** a nonessential item or service that contributes to luxurious living **:** an indulgence in ornament or convenience beyond the indispensable minimum **:** EXTRAVAGANCE ⟨expensive shotguns and other *luxuries* —Thomas Munro⟩ ⟨sent her off . . . in a taxi, which was evidently a ~ for her: she protested about the expense —Edmund Wilson⟩ ⟨allowing no money to be wasted on whims and *luxuries* until necessities have been thoroughly served —G.B.Shaw⟩ **3 :** a means or source of pleasurable experience or personal satisfaction **:** COMFORT, SELF-INDULGENCE ⟨dropping into a plush-covered armchair, a ~ she seldom allowed herself —L.P.Hartley⟩ ⟨for the rich and titled, snobbery is not a superfluous ~, but a necessity —Aldous Huxley⟩ ⟨the Senate is small and can afford the ~ of very loose rules —D.W.Brogan⟩ ⟨Western European states . . . could no longer afford the ~ of full independence and freedom of action in foreign affairs —F.L.Schuman⟩ **4 :** LUXURIOUSNESS ⟨a period of ~, when racecourses, wine cellars, and balls reached their apogee —*Amer. Guide Series: Va.*⟩ ⟨nobody wants to banish ~ of language from the theater —Kenneth Tynan⟩ ⟨the fabrics . . . lacked richness and ~ of handling —E.I.Cohen⟩

²**luxury** \"\ *adj* **:** of or relating to luxury or luxuries or catering to luxurious tastes **:** SUMPTUOUS, NONESSENTIAL ⟨~ liner⟩ ⟨~ resort⟩ ⟨~ goods⟩ ⟨laughter, a ~ reflex, is without survival value —Isaac Rosenfeld⟩

**luxury consumption** *n* **:** the absorption of nitrogen or potash from the soil by a crop in excess of crop needs

**lux·us** \'ləksəs\ *n* -ES [L, luxury, excess] **:** SUPERFLUITY

**luzern** *obs var of* LUCERNE

**lu·zu·la** \'lüzyələ\ *n, cap* [NL, fr. It *luzziola, lucciola* (in *erba luzziola, erba lucciola* adder's-tongue)] **:** a genus of perennial herbs (family Juncaceae) resembling grass or rushes and having leaves and young stems frequently hairy and flowers crowded, umbeled, or in spikes — see WOOD RUSH

**lv** *abbr* **1** lava **2** leave

**LV** *abbr* **1** legal volt **2** licensed victualer **3** light vessel **4** low voltage

**lve** *abbr* leave

**lvov** \lə'vōf\ *adj, usu cap* [fr. *Lvov*, city in western Ukraine, U.S.S.R.] **:** of or from the city of Lvov, U.S.S.R. **:** of the kind or style prevalent in Lvov

**lvs** *abbr* leaves

**LW** *abbr* **1** left wing **2** long wave **3** low water

**LWB** *abbr* long wheelbase

**lwe·na** \lə'wānə\ *n, pl* **lwena** *or* **lwenas** *usu cap* **1 a :** a people of Angola and the Kabompo district of Northern Rhodesia **b :** a member of such people **2 :** a Bantu language of the Lwena people

**LWL** *abbr* **1** length at waterline **2** load waterline

**LWM** *abbr* low-water mark

¹**lwo** *or* **lwoo** \lə'wō\ *n* -s *usu cap* **:** a division of the Nilotic languages including Shilluk, Acholi, Alur, Lango, and Luo

²**lwo** *usu cap, var of* LUO

**LWP** *abbr* load water plane

**lx** *abbr* lux

**LXX** [fr. the Roman numeral for 70] *symbol* Septuagint

**ly** *abbr* langley

¹**-ly** \lē,li\ *adj suffix, usu* -ER/-EST [ME *-lich, -ly, -li*, fr. OE *-līc*, -lic; akin to OFris & OS *-lik*, MD *-lijc*, OHG *-līh, -lih*, ON *-ligr*; all fr. a Gmc noun represented by OE *līc* body, corpse — more at LIKE] **1 :** like in appearance, manner, or nature **:** having the characteristics of ⟨queen*ly*⟩ ⟨father*ly*⟩ ⟨woman*ly*⟩ **2 :** expressing regular recurrence in stated units of time **:** every ⟨hour*ly*⟩ ⟨dai*ly*⟩ ⟨week*ly*⟩

²**-ly** \"; *in -l(e)ly words pronunciation of only one l is usual if the nucleus of the next-to-the-last syllable is an unstressed vowel or a syllabic* l, *less frequent if the nucleus is a stressed vowel*\ *adv suffix, usu* -ER/-EST [ME *-liche, -ly, -li*, fr. OE *-līce, -lice*, fr. *-līc, -lic* (adj. suffix)] **1 :** in a (specified) manner ⟨slow*ly*⟩ **:** in the manner of a ⟨soldier*ly*⟩ **:** from a (specified) standpoint

**ly·all·pur** \'lī(ə)l,pù(ə)r, ,==¹=\ *adj, usu cap* [fr. *Lyallpur*, Pakistan] **:** of or from the city of Lyallpur, Pakistan **:** of the kind or style prevalent in Lyallpur

**ly·am** \'līəm\ *n* -s [ME *lyame, lyeme*, fr. MF *liem* leash, bond, fr. L *ligamen* band, tie — more at LIEN] *archaic* **:** LEASH

**lyam–hound** \'==,=\ *n, archaic* **:** BLOODHOUND

**ly·art** \'līərt\ *also* **ly·ard** \-rd\ *adj* [ME, fr. MF *liart*, fr. OF] **1** *chiefly Scot* **:** streaked with gray **2** *chiefly Scot* **:** VARIEGATED

**lyas** *var of* LIAS

**lyc-** *or* **lyco-** *comb form* [NL, fr. Gk *lyk-, lyko-*, fr. *lykos* — more at WOLF] **:** wolf ⟨*Lyco*podium⟩

**ly·cae·na** \lī'sēnə\ *n, cap* [NL, fr. Gk *lykaina*, fem. of *lykos* wolf] **:** a genus (the type of the family Lycaenidae) comprising small slender butterflies with the upper surface of the wings usu. metallic blue, green, or copper and the undersurface dull or cryptic

¹**ly·cae·nid** \-nəd\ *adj* [NL *Lycaenidae*] **:** of or relating to the family Lycaenidae

²**lycaenid** \"\ *n* -s **:** a butterfly of the family Lycaenidae

**ly·cae·ni·dae** \-nə,dē\ *n pl, cap* [NL, fr. *Lycaena*, type genus + *-idae*] **:** a family of small often brilliantly colored butterflies having the forelegs short in the male and including the blues, coppers, and hairstreaks

**ly·can·thrope** \'līkən,thrōp; lī'kan(t)thrəp, -n,thrōp\ *n* -s [NL *lycanthropus*, fr. Gk *lykanthrōpos* werewolf, fr. *lyk-* + *anthrōpos* man, human being — more at ANTHROP-] **1 :** a person displaying lycanthropy **2 :** WEREWOLF

**ly·can·throp·ic** \¦līkən¦thräpik\ *adj* **:** of or relating to lycanthropy

**ly·can·thro·pist** \lī'kan(t)thrəpəst\ *n* -s **:** LYCANTHROPE

**ly·can·thro·pous** \(')=¦==pəs\ *adj* **:** LYCANTHROPIC

**ly·can·thro·py** \-pē\ *n* -ES [NL *lycanthropia*, fr. Gk *lykanthrōpia*, fr. *lykanthrōpos* werewolf + *-ia* -y] **1 :** a delusion that one has become or has assumed the characteristics of a wolf or other predatory animal **2 :** the assumption of the form and characteristics of a wolf held to be possible through the practice of witchcraft or magic

**ly·ca·on** \lī'kāən, -ā,än\ *n, cap* [NL, fr. L, mythological king of Arcadia who was transformed into a wolf, fr. Gk *Lykaōn*] **:** a genus of animals containing the African hunting dog

**ly·cée** \(')lē¦sā\ *n* -s [F, fr. MF, lyceum, fr. L *Lyceum*] **:** a state-maintained secondary school esp. in France that prepares students for the university

**ly·ce·um** \(')lī¦sēəm, 'lī,sēəm\ *n* -s *often attrib* [L *Lyceum*, gymnasium near ancient Athens where Aristotle taught, fr. Gk *Lykeion*, fr. neut. of *Lykeios*, epithet of Apollo whose temple was nearby] **1 :** a place for holding lectures or public discussions **2 a :** an institution or movement providing public lectures, concerts, and entertainments and generally furthering education **b :** a local branch of such a lyceum **3 :** a secondary school in continental Europe; *specif* **:** LYCÉE **4** *Brit* **:** a bombastic and outmoded theatrical style

**lychee** *var of* LITCHI

**lych–gate** *or* **lich–gate** \'lich,=\ *n* [ME *lycheyate*, fr. *lyche, lich* lich + *yate* gate] **:** a roofed gate in a churchyard under which a bier rests during the initial part of the burial service

lych-gate

**lych·nis** \'liknəs\ *n* [NL, fr. L, a red flower, fr. Gk; akin to

Gk *lychnos* lamp, *leukos* bright, white — more at LIGHT] **1** *cap* **:** a large genus of herbs (family Caryophyllaceae) having sepals united into a tube or cup, usu. 5 styles, and fruit in the form of a capsule with 5 or 10 teeth — compare SILENE **2** -ES **:** any plant of the genus *Lychnis*

**lych·no·scope** \ˈliknə,skōp\ *n* [Gk *lychnos* lamp + E *-scope*] **:** LOW SIDE WINDOW — **lych·no·scop·ic** \;==ˈskäpik\ *adj*

[1]**ly·cian** \ˈlish(ē)ən *sometimes* ˈlisēən\ *adj, usu cap* [L *Lycius*, adj. & n., Lycian (fr. Gk *Lykios*, fr. *Lykia* Lycia, ancient district in Asia Minor) + E *-an*] **1 :** of, relating to, or characteristic of ancient Lycia, a region of southern Asia Minor **2 :** of, relating to, or characteristic of the people of Lycia

[2]**lycian** \"\ *n* -S *usu cap* [L *Lycius*, n., Lycian + E *-an*] **1 :** a native or inhabitant of ancient Lycia **2 :** an Anatolian language known from a small body of inscriptions from southwestern Asia Minor dating from the 5th and 4th centuries B.C. — see INDO-EUROPEAN LANGUAGES table

[1]**lycid** \ˈlīsəd, ˈlis-\ *adj* [NL *Lycidae*] **:** of or relating to the family Lycidae

[2]**lycid** \"\ *n* -S **:** a beetle of the family Lycidae

**lyc·i·dae** \ˈlisə,dē\ *n pl, cap* [NL, fr. *Lycus*, type genus (fr. Gk *lykos* wolf) + *-idae* — more at WOLF] **:** a family of soft-bodied mainly tropical beetles that are usu. marked with a bold pattern of orange or brown and black, have disagreeable qualities to many predators, and are mimicked by numerous edible insects

**lyci·um** \ˈlis(h)ēəm\ *n, cap* [NL, fr. Gk *lykion*, a thorn from Lycia, fr. neut. of *Lykios* Lycian] **:** a genus of shrubs or trees (family Solanaceae) having simple leaves and tubular campanulate flowers — see MATRIMONY VINE

**lyco-** — see LYC-

**ly·cod·i·dae** \līˈkädə,dē\ *n pl, cap* [NL, fr. *Lycodes*, type genus (fr. Gk *lykōdēs* wolflike, fr. *lyk-* lyc- + *-ōdēs* -ode) + *-idae*] *syn of* ZOARCIDAE

**ly·co·pene** \ˈlīkə,pēn\ *n* -S [ISV *lycop-* (fr. NL *Lycopersicon*) + *-ene*; orig. formed as G *lycopen*] **:** a red crystalline open-chain unsaturated hydrocarbon $C_{40}H_{56}$ that is the coloring matter of the tomato and many berries and other fruits and is isomeric with carotene

**ly·co·per·da·ce·ae** \,līkō(,)pərˈdāsē,ē\ *n pl, cap* [NL, fr. *Lycoperdon*, type genus + *-aceae*] **:** a family of fungi (order Lycoperdales) comprising the puffballs and having a spherical fruiting body with a flexible peridium of two or three layers enclosing a chambered gleba that appears solid and white when young and at maturity is filled with masses of powdery dark spores

**ly·co·per·da·les** \-ˈā(,)lēz\ *n pl, cap* [NL, fr. *Lycoperdon*, genus of fungi + *-ales*] **:** a small order of basidiomycetes comprising the puffballs, earthstars, and sometimes a few other closely related fungi and having a fleshy often globose fruiting body filled at maturity with a mass of dustlike spores

**ly·co·per·doid** \;==ˈpər,dȯid\ *adj* [NL *Lycoperdon* + E *-oid*] **:** of, relating to, or resembling the genus *Lycoperdon*

**ly·co·per·don** \,==ˈ=,dän\ *n, cap* [NL, fr. *lyc-* + Gk *perdesthai* to break wind — more at FART] **:** a genus of fungi (family Lycoperdaceae) whose fruiting body tapers toward a base consisting of spongy mycelium

**lycoperdon nut** *n* **:** a subterranean fungus (*Elaphomyces cervinus*) resembling a puffball — compare HART'S TRUFFLE

**ly·co·per·si·con** \-ˈpərsə,kän\ *n, cap* [NL, irreg. fr. Gk *lykopersion*, an Egyptian plant] **:** a genus of So. American herbs (family Solanaceae) having anthers projected into sharp or narrow sterile tips — see TOMATO

**ly·co·per·si·cum** \-sȯkəm\ [NL, fr. *Lycopersicon*] *syn of* LYCOPERSICON

**ly·co·phore** \ˈlīkə,fō(ə)r\ *n* -S [prob. fr. *lyc-* + *-phore*] **:** DECACANTH

**ly·co·pod** \-,päd\ *n* -S [NL *Lycopodium*] **:** a plant of the genus *Lycopodium* or of the order Lycopodiales

**ly·co·po·di·a·ce·ae** \,==,pōdēˈāsē,ē\ *n pl, cap* [NL, fr. *Lycopodium*, type genus + *-aceae*] **:** a family of plants (order Lycopodiales) characterized by leaves without ligules, variably rounded strobili, and homosporous reproduction — compare CLUB MOSS

**ly·co·po·di·a·les** \-ˈā(,)lēz\ *n pl, cap* [NL, fr. *Lycopodium*, genus of plants + *-ales*] **:** an order of plants (subdivision Lycopsida) coextensive with the family Lycopodiaceae or extended to include also Selaginellaceae and Isoetaceae

**ly·co·po·din·e·ae** \,līkəpōˈdinē,ē\ *n pl, cap* [NL, fr. *Lycopodium*, genus of plants + *-ineae*] **:** a class of plants coextensive with the subdivision Lycopsida

**ly·co·po·di·tes** \,līkəpōˈdī(,)ēz\ *n, cap* [NL, fr. *Lycopodium* + *-ites*] **:** a genus of fossil plants that resemble present-day lycopods

**ly·co·po·di·um** \,līkəˈpōdēəm\ *n* [NL, fr. *lyc-* + *-podium*] **1** *cap* **:** a large genus (the type of the family Lycopodiaceae) of erect or creeping plants that have evergreen one-nerved leaves in four to many ranks and are often used in Christmas decorations — see CLUB MOSS, GROUND FIR, GROUND PINE **2** *or* **lycopodium powder :** a fine yellowish flammable powder composed of the spores of a club moss (as *Lycopodium clavatum*) and used as a dusting powder for the skin and for the surface of hand-rolled pills and as a component of fireworks and flashlight powders

[1]**ly·cop·sid** \(ˈ)līˈkäpsəd\ *adj* [NL *Lycopsida*] **:** of or relating to the Lycopsida

[2]**lycopsid** \"\ *n* -S [NL *Lycopsida*] **:** a plant of the subdivision Lycopsida

**ly·cop·si·da** \līˈkäpsədə\ *n pl, cap* [NL, fr. L *lycopsis*, a plant + NL *-ida*] **:** a subdivision of Tracheophyta coextensive with the class Lycopodineae comprising vascular plants (as the club mosses and related forms) with small leaves, sessile and adaxial sporangia, and no leaf gaps in the primary vascular cylinder — compare PSILOPSIDA, PTEROPSIDA, SPHENOPSIDA

**ly·cop·sis** \-səs\ *n, cap* [NL, fr. L, a plant, bugloss, fr. Gk *lykopsis*, prob. fr. *lyk-* lyc- + *-opsis*] **:** a genus of bristly herbs (family Boraginaceae) with small blue flowers in terminal scorpioid racemes — see BUGLOSS

**ly·co·pus** \ˈlīkəpəs\ *n, cap* [NL, fr. *lyc-* + *-pus*] **:** a small genus of nonaromatic mints having two stamens in each flower — see BUGLEWEED, WATER HOREHOUND

**ly·co·rine** \līˈkōrən, ˈlīkə,rīn\ *n* -S [NL *Lycoris*, genus of plants (fr. L, a woman's name) + E *-ine*] **:** a poisonous crystalline alkaloid $C_{16}H_{17}NO_4$ found in the bulbs of the common daffodil and several other amaryllids

**ly·co·sa** \līˈkōsə\ *n, cap* [NL, fr. L *lycos*, a spider, fr. Gk *lykos*, lit., wolf — more at WOLF] **:** a genus (the type of the family Lycosidae) of spiders including the wolf spiders

[1]**ly·co·sid** \-səd\ *adj* [NL *Lycosidae*] **:** of or relating to the family Lycosidae

[2]**lycosid** \"\ *n* -S [NL *Lycosidae*] **:** a spider of the family Lycosidae

**ly·cosi·dae** \līˈkōsə,dē, -ˈkäs-\ *n pl, cap* [NL, fr. *Lycosa*, type genus + *-idae*] **:** a cosmopolitan family of relatively large active ground spiders that catch their prey by pursuit rather than in a web

[1]**lyc·tid** \ˈliktəd\ *adj* [NL *Lyctidae*] **:** of or relating to the family Lyctidae

[2]**lyctid** \"\ *n* -S [NL *Lyctidae*] **:** a beetle of the family Lyctidae

**lyc·ti·dae** \-tə,dē\ *n pl, cap* [NL, fr. *Lyctus*, type genus + *-idae*] **:** a family of small elongate wood-boring beetles — see POWDER-POST BEETLE

**lyc·tus** \-təs\ *n* [NL, fr. L, ancient city in Crete, fr. Gk *Lyktos*] **1** *cap* **:** the type genus of the family Lyctidae **2** -ES **:** any beetle of the genus *Lyctus*

**lydd·ite** \ˈli,dīt\ *n* -S [*Lydd*, England, near which it was first tested + E *-ite*] **:** a high explosive composed chiefly of picric acid

**ly·del·la** \līˈdelə\ *n, cap* [NL, fr. *Lyda*, genus of flies (fr. L *Lydus* Lydian, fr. Gk *Lydos*) + *-ella*] **:** a genus of small tachinid flies including one (*L. stabulans grisescens*) of importance in the biological control of the European corn borer

**lyd·ga·tian line** \(ˈ)lidˈgāshən-\ *n, usu cap 1st L* [John *Lydgate* †*ab*1451 Eng. poet + E *-ian*] **:** BROKEN-BACKED LINE

[1]**lyd·i·an** \ˈlidēən\ *adj, usu cap* [L *Lydius* Lydian (fr. Gk *Lydios*, fr. *Lydia*, ancient country in Asia Minor) + E *-an*] **1 a :** of, relating to, or characteristic of Lydia, an ancient country of western Asia Minor **b :** of, relating to, or characteristic of the people of Lydia **2 :** of, relating to, or characteristic of the music of Lydia ⟨soft *Lydian* airs —John Milton⟩

[2]**lydian** \"\ *n* -S *cap* [L *Lydius*, adj., Lydian + E *-an*] **1 :** a native or inhabitant of ancient Lydia **2 :** an Anatolian language known from a small body of inscriptions from western Asia Minor dating from the 4th century B.C. or earlier — see INDO-EUROPEAN LANGUAGES table

**lydian mode** *n, usu cap L* [trans. of Gk *Harmonia Lydia*] **1 :** a Greek mode consisting of two disjunct tetrachords represented on the white keys of the piano by a descending diatonic scale from C to C — see GREEK MODE illustration **2** [trans. of ML *modus Lydius*] **:** an authentic ecclesiastical mode represented on the white keys of the piano by an ascending diatonic scale from F to F — see MODE illustration

**lydian stone** *n, usu cap L* [trans. of L *Lapis Lydius*, trans. of Gk *Lydia lithos*] **:** TOUCHSTONE

**lydian tetrachord** *n, usu cap L* **:** a descending tetrachord in ancient Greek music consisting of a half step followed by two whole steps

**lyd·ite** \ˈli,dīt\ *n* -S [G *lydit*, fr. *Lydien* Lydia + G *-it* -ite] **:** TOUCHSTONE

[1]**lye** \ˈlī\ *n* -S [ME *lye, leye, lie*, fr. OE *lēag, lēah*; akin to MD *lōghe* lye, OHG *louga* lye, ON *laug* bath, hot spring, L *lavare, lavere* to wash, bathe, OIr *lūaith* ashes, Gk *louein* to wash, Arm *loganam* I bathe] **1 a :** a strong alkaline liquor that contains chiefly potassium carbonate obtained by leaching wood ashes with water and that has been used esp. in soapmaking and washing **b :** a strong alkaline solution (as of sodium hydroxide or potassium hydroxide) ⟨caustic ~⟩ — compare [2]CAUSTIC 1 **2 :** a solution obtained by lixiviation **3 :** a solid caustic — called also *concentrated lye*

[2]**lye** \"\ *vt* **lyed; lyed; lying; lyes :** to treat with lye

**lye hominy** *n* **:** hominy prepared from kernels of grain that have been soaked in lye to remove the hulls

**lyeng** \lēˈeŋ\ *n, pl* **lyeng** *or* **lyengs** *usu cap* **1 :** a Naga people chiefly in an area northwest of Manipur valley **2 :** a member of the Lyeng people

**lye-peeled** \ˈ=,=\ *adj* **:** subjected to lye peeling

**lye peeling** *n* **:** the process of removing the peels of fruits and vegetables by immersion in a lye solution

**ly·ery** \ˈlīəri\ *adj* [*lyer*, alter. of *lire* + *-y*] *dial Eng* **:** having little fat in the flesh — used of cattle

[1]**ly·gae·id** \(ˈ)līˈjēəd\ *adj* [NL *Lygaeidae*] **:** of or relating to the family Lygaeidae

[2]**lygaeid** \"\ *n* -S [NL *Lygaeidae*] **:** a true bug of the family Lygaeidae

**ly·gae·idae** \līˈjēə,dē\ *n pl, cap* [NL, fr. *Lygaeus*, type genus (fr. Gk *lygaios* shadowy) + *-idae*] **:** an extensive family of plant-sucking often brilliantly colored true bugs — see CHINCH BUG

**ly·ge·um** \līˈjēəm\ *n, cap* [NL, fr. Gk *lygos* flexible twig, withe — more at LOCK (tuft of hair)] **:** a genus of grasses having two or three one-flowered spikelets that unite to form a hard false fruit — see ESPARTO

**ly·gi·nop·te·ris** \,lījəˈnäptərəs\ *n, cap* [NL, fr. Gk *lyginos* of withe (fr. *lygos* withe + *-inos* -ine) + NL *-pteris*] **:** a genus of Carboniferous seed ferns having a stem with mesarch siphonostele, large accumulation of pith, and marked development of secondary wood

**ly·go·des·mia** \,līgəˈdezmēə\ *n, cap* [NL, fr. Gk *lygo-* (fr. *lygos* withe) + *desmos* band, bond, *desmē* bundle + NL *-ia* — more at DESM-] **:** a genus of wiry-stemmed No. American weedy herbs (family Compositae) — see SKELETON WEED 2

**ly·go·di·um** \līˈgōdēəm\ *n, cap* [NL, fr. Gk *lygōdēs* like a willow (fr. *lygos* willow, withe) + NL *-ium*] **:** a genus of mostly tropical ferns (family Schizaeaceae) characterized by twining fronds that have mostly opposite pairs of pinnae below and sporophylls above — see CLIMBING FERN

**ly·go·so·ma** \,līgəˈsōmə\ *n, cap* [NL, fr. Gk *lygo-* (fr. *lygos* withe) + NL *-soma*] **:** a genus of scincoid lizards having a slender form with limbs reduced or lacking

**ly·gus** \ˈlīgəs\ *n* [NL] **1** *cap* **:** a large genus of small plant-sucking mirid bugs some of which are vectors of virus diseases of plants **2** -ES **:** LYGUS BUG

**lygus bug** *n* **:** a bug of the genus *Lygus* (as the tarnished plant bug)

[1]**lying** *pres part of* LIE *or of* LYE

[2]**lying** *adj* [ME *leghynge*, fr. pres. part. of *leghen, leyen* to lie — more at LIE] **1 :** given to falsehood ⟨a ~ witness⟩ **2 :** calculated to mislead **:** FALSE, UNTRUE ⟨a whole world of false conceptions and ~ sentimentality —Harrison Smith⟩ ⟨silly newspapers and magazines for the circulation of ~ advertisements —G.B.Shaw⟩ **syn** see DISHONEST

**lying-in** \;==ˈ=\ *n, pl* **lyings-in** *or* **lying-ins** [ME *lynge yn*, fr. *lyynge, liynge*, gerund of *lien, ligen* to lie + *yn, in* in (adv.) — more at LIE, IN] **:** the state attending and consequent to childbirth **:** CONFINEMENT, PARTURITION

**ly·ing·ly** *adv* [ME *leeiyngli*, fr. *leeiyyng, leghynge* lying + *-li* -ly] **:** in a lying manner **:** FALSELY

**lying press** *n* **:** a press in which sheets or books are held by lateral pressure for various bookbinding operations — called also *laying press*

**lyke·wake** \ˈlī,kwāk\ *n* [ME *lych wake*, fr. *lych, lich* lich + *wake*] *now chiefly Scot* **:** the night watch kept over a corpse — compare [2]WAKE 3a

**lyle gun** \ˈlī(ə)l-\ *n, usu cap L* [after David A. *Lyle* †1937 Am. officer, U. S. Army, its inventor] **1 :** a mounted gun that resembles a small brass cannon and is used to fire a projectile attached to a line of rope to an extreme range of about 700 yards in rescue operations at sea **2 :** a firing device that resembles a short shotgun and is used to propel a weight attached to a line of rope in rescue operations at sea or on land (as in fire fighting) — called also *line-throwing gun*

**lym** *n* -S [ME *lyam*, fr. *lyame, lyeme* leash — more at LYAM] *obs* **:** BLOODHOUND

**ly·man·tria** \līˈman·trēə\ *n, cap* [NL, fr. Gk *lymantēr* destroyer + NL *-ia*] **:** the type genus of Lymantriidae

[1]**ly·man·tri·id** \-ēəd\ *adj* [NL *Lymantriidae*] **:** of or relating to the family Lymantriidae

[2]**lymantriid** \"\ *n* -S [NL *Lymantriidae*] **:** a moth of the family Lymantriidae

**ly·man·tri·idae** \,līmən·ˈtrīə,dē\ *n pl, cap* [NL, fr. *Lymantria*, type genus + *-idae*] **:** a family of moths comprising certain typical tussock moths and having larvae that are distinguished by a dense coat of often urticating hairs and that include many destructive pests which attack trees and other economic plants

**lyme** \ˈlīm\ *var of* LYAM

**lyme grass** \"-\ *n* [prob. fr. obs. E *lyme* birdlime (fr. ME *lyme, lim* birdlime) + E *grass* — more at LIME] **:** a grass of the genus *Elymus*

**lyme-hound** \ˈ=,=\ *var of* LYAM-HOUND

**lym·naea** \limˈnēə, ˈ===\ *n, cap* [NL, irreg. fr. Gk *limnaios* of the marsh, fr. *limnē* marsh, pool — more at LIMN-] **:** a genus of snails formerly almost coextensive with the family Lymnaeidae but now comprising comparatively few species of dextrally coiled freshwater snails that include some of importance as intermediate hosts of flukes of medical or veterinary interest — compare FOSSARIA, GALBA

[1]**lym·nae·id** \-ēəd\ *adj* [NL *Lymnaeidae*] **:** of or relating to the family Lymnaeidae

[2]**lymnaeid** \"\ *n* -S [NL *Lymnaeidae*] **:** a snail of the family Lymnaeidae

**lym·nae·idae** \limˈnēə,dē\ *n pl, cap* [NL, fr. *Lymnaea*, type genus + *-idae*] **:** a family of thin-shelled air-breathing freshwater snails (suborder Basommatophora) that have an elongate ovoidal shell with a large opening and a simple lip and that include numerous species important as intermediate hosts of trematode worms

**lymph** \ˈlim(p)f\ *n, pl* **lymphs** \-m(p)fs, -mps\ [L *lympha*, alter. of earlier *limpa, lumpa*, modif. of Gk *nymphē* nymph — more at NUPTIAL] **1** *archaic* **:** a spring or stream of water **:** pure clear water ⟨dips her shining ankles in the ~ —E.R.B.Lytton⟩ ⟨receive the baptismal ~ —George Borrow⟩ **2** *archaic* **:** the sap of plants ⟨that moved the pure and subtle ~ through the . . . veins of leaf and flower —William Cowper⟩ **3** [NL, fr. L, water] **:** a pale coagulable fluid that bathes the tissues, passes into lymphatic channels and ducts, and is discharged into the blood by way of the thoracic duct, and that consists of a liquid portion resembling blood plasma, numerous white blood cells, and normally no red blood cells — compare CEREBROSPINAL FLUID, CHYLE

**lymph-** *or* **lympho-** *comb form* [NL *lympha*] **1 :** lymph ⟨*lympho*genic⟩ **2 :** lymphatic tissue ⟨*lymph*enteritis⟩ **3 :** lymphocytes ⟨*lympho*protease⟩ ⟨*lympho*taxis⟩

**lym·phad** \ˈlim,fad\ *n* -S [ScGael *long-fhada*, fr. *long* ship + *fada* long] **1 :** a small one-masted galley **2 :** a heraldic representation of a lymphad

lymphad 2

**lym·pha·den** \ˈlim(p)fə,den\ *n* -S [NL, fr. *lymph-* + Gk *adēn* gland — more at ADEN-] **:** LYMPH GLAND

**lymph·ad·e·ni·tis** \,lim,fadᵊnˈīdəs, ,lim(p)fə,deˈnī-\ *n* -ES [NL, fr. *lymphaden* + *-itis*] **:** inflammation of lymph glands

**lym·phad·e·noid** \(ˈ)limˈfadᵊn,ȯid, ˈlim(p)fəˈde,nȯid\ *adj* [NL *lymphaden* + E *-oid*] **:** resembling or having the properties of a lymph gland

**lymph·ad·e·no·ma** \,lim,fadᵊnˈōmə, ,lim(p)fə,deˈnō-\ *n, pl* **lymphadenomas** \-məz\ *or* **lymphadenoma·ta** \-mədə\ [NL, fr. *lymphaden* + *-oma*] **1 :** LYMPHOMA **2 :** HODGKIN'S DISEASE

**lymph·ad·e·nop·a·thy** \-ᵊnˈäpəthē, -eˈnä-\ *n* [NL *lymphaden* + E *-o-* + *-pathy*] **:** abnormal enlargement of lymph glands

**lymph·ad·e·no·sis** \-ᵊnˈōsəs, -eˈnō-\ *n, pl* **lymphadeno·ses** \-ō,sēz\ [NL, fr. *lymphaden* + *-osis*] **:** any of certain abnormalities or diseases affecting the lymphatic system: as **a :** leukosis involving lymphatic tissues **b :** LYMPHATIC LEUKEMIA **c :** INFECTIOUS MONONUCLEOSIS

**lymphangi-** *or* **lymphangio-** *comb form* [NL, fr. *lymphangion* lymphatic vessel, fr. *lymph-* + Gk *angeion* vessel, blood vessel — more at ANGI-] **:** lymphatic vessels ⟨*lymphangi*ectasis⟩ ⟨*lymphangio*logy⟩

**lym·phan·gi·al** \(ˈ)limˈfanjēəl\ *adj* [*lymphangi-* + *-al*] **:** of or relating to the lymphatic vessels

**lym·phan·gi·o·ma** \,lim,fanjēˈōmə\ *n, pl* **lymphangiomas** \-məz\ *or* **lymphangioma·ta** \-mədə\ [NL, fr. *lymphangi-* + *-oma*] **:** a tumor formed of dilated lymphatic vessels — compare ANGIOMA — **lym·phan·gi·om·a·tous** \(;)=;==ˈämədəs, -ˈōm-\ *adj*

**lym·phan·gi·tis** \,lim,fanˈjīdəs\ *n, pl* **lymphangit·i·des** \-ˈjidə,dēz\ [NL, fr. *lymphangi-* + *-itis*] **:** inflammation of the lymphatic vessels

**lymphangitis ep·i·zo·ot·i·ca** \-,epəzəˈwädəkə\ *n* [NL] **:** EPIZOOTIC LYMPHANGITIS

**lymphangitis ul·ce·ro·sa** \-,əl(t)səˈrōsə\ *n* [NL] **:** PSEUDOGLANDERS

[1]**lym·phat·ic** \(ˈ)limˈfad·ik, -atˈ, ˈēk\ *adj* [L *lymphaticus* frantic, frenzied, fr. *lympha, lumpa* water, water goddess, modif. of Gk *nymphē* nymph, water goddess; influenced by Gk *nympholēptos* frenzied, caught by nymphs — more at NUPTIAL, NYMPHOLEPT] **1 a :** of, relating to, or produced by lymph, lymphoid tissue, or lymphocytes ⟨~ nodules⟩ ⟨~ infiltration⟩ **b :** conveying lymph ⟨a ~ channel⟩ **2** *or* **lym·phat·i·cal** \|əkəl, |ēk-\ *archaic* **:** FRENZIED **3 a** *of a person* **:** having a dull pallid complexion and slack often puffy tissues suggestive of or accompanied by a lymphatic temperament **b** *of a temperament* **:** characterized by lack of energy and indisposition to physical or mental exertion ⟨a beautiful and stupid woman of ~ type —E.C.Bentley⟩ ⟨the bacon hog is less ~ and more active and animated —A.L.Anderson⟩ — **lym·phat·i·cal·ly** \|ək(ə)lē, |ēk-, -li\ *adv*

[2]**lymphatic** \"\ *n* -S **1** *or* **lymphatical** *archaic* **:** LUNATIC **2 :** a vessel that contains or conveys lymph, that originates as an interfibrillar or intercellular cleft or space in a tissue or organ, and that if small has no distinct walls or walls composed only of endothelial cells and if large resembles a vein in structure — see THORACIC DUCT

**lymphatic leukemia** *n* **:** leukemia marked by proliferation of lymphoid tissue, abnormal increase of leukocytes in the circulating blood, and enlargement of lymph nodes

**lym·pha·tism** \ˈlim(p)fə,tizəm\ *n* -S [ISV *lymphat-* (fr. [1]*lymphatic*) + *-ism*] **1 :** lymphatic temperament **2 :** STATUS LYMPHATICUS

**lymphato-** *comb form* [ISV *lymphat-* (fr. [1]*lymphatic*) + *-o-*] **:** lymphatic tissue ⟨*lymphato*lysin⟩ ⟨*lymphato*lysis⟩

**lymph cell** *also* **lymph corpuscle** *n* **:** a cell in lymph; *specif* **:** LYMPHOCYTE

**lymph·ede·ma** *also* **lymph·oe·de·ma** \ˈlim(p)f+\ *n* [NL, fr. *lymph-* + *edema* or *oedema*] **:** edema due to faulty lymphatic drainage

**lymph follicle** *n* **:** LYMPH GLAND; *esp* **:** LYMPH NODULE

**lymph gland** *or* **lymph node** *n* **:** one of the rounded masses of lymphoid tissue surrounded by a capsule of connective tissue that occur in various parts of the body in the course of the lymphatic vessels and that consist of a reticulum of connective tissue fibers in the meshes of which are contained numerous small round cells each having a large round deeply staining nucleus and when carried off by the lymph flowing through the gland becoming a lymphocyte

**lymph heart** *n* **:** a contractile muscular expansion of a lymphatic vessel that serves to drive the lymph toward the veins (as in some amphibians)

**lymph nodule** *n* **:** a small simple lymph gland

**lympho-** — see LYMPH-

**lym·pho·blast** \ˈlim(p)fə,blast\ *n* [ISV *lymph-* + *-blast*] **1 :** a cell giving rise to lymphocytes **2 :** a primitive undifferentiated hemocyte — used only by those who consider that all blood cells have a common origin; compare MYELOBLAST — **lym·pho·blas·tic** \;==ˈblastik\ *adj*

**lym·pho·blas·to·ma** \,==,blaˈstōmə\ *n, pl* **lymphoblastomas** \-məz\ *or* **lymphoblastoma·ta** \-mədə\ [NL, fr. ISV *lymphoblast* + NL *-oma*] **:** any of several diseases of lymph glands marked by the formation of tumorous masses composed of mature or immature lymphocytes

**lym·pho·blas·to·sis** \-ˈōsəs\ *n, pl* **lymphoblasto·ses** \-ō,sēz\ [NL, fr. ISV *lymphoblast* + NL *-osis*] **:** the presence of lymphoblasts in the peripheral blood (as in acute lymphatic leukemia or infectious mononucleosis)

**lym·pho·cys·tis disease** \;lim(p)fəˈsistəs-\ *n* [NL *lymphocystis*, fr. *lymph-* + Gk *kystis* bladder, pouch — more at CYST] **:** a skin disease of the walleye that is characterized by ulceration and the formation of irregular pinkish lumps in skin and fins and is usu. held to be of virus origin

**lym·pho·cyte** \ˈlim(p)fə,sīt\ *n* -S [ISV *lymph-* + *-cyte*] **:** a colorless weakly motile cell produced in lymphoid tissue that is the typical cellular element of lymph and constitutes 20 to 30 percent of the leukocytes of normal human blood where it occurs either as the small lymphocyte of about 0.01 millimeter in diameter with large round deeply staining nucleus and narrow rim of clear cytoplasm or as the less common large lymphocyte that is regarded by some as an immature stage of the small one — **lym·pho·cyt·ic** \;==ˈsid·ik\ *adj*

**lymphocytic choriomeningitis** *n* **:** an acute virus disease characterized by fever, nausea and vomiting, headache, stiff neck, and slow pulse, marked by the presence of numerous lymphocytes in the cerebrospinal fluid, and transmitted esp. by rodents and bloodsucking insects

**lym·pho·cy·to·genesis** \,lim(p)fə,sīd·ə+\ *n* [NL, fr. ISV *lymphocyte* + NL *-o-* + L *genesis*] **:** LYMPHOPOIESIS

**lym·pho·cy·to·ma** \,==,sīˈtōmə\ *n, pl* **lymphocytomas** \-məz\ *or* **lymphocytoma·ta** \-mədə\ [NL, fr. ISV *lymphocyte* + NL *-oma*] **1 :** a tumor in which lymphocytes are the dominant cellular elements **2 :** LYMPHOCYTOMATOSIS

**lym·pho·cy·to·ma·to·sis** \-,tōməˈtōsəs\ *n, pl* **lymphocytomato·ses** \-ō,sēz\ [NL, fr. *lymphocytomat-, lymphocytoma* + *-osis*] **:** an abnormal condition characterized by the formation of lymphocytomas; *specif* **:** a neoplastic disease of the common fowl marked by lymphocytoma formation and extensive lymphocytic infiltration of the tissues that is commonly regarded as a manifestation of the avian leukosis complex but may be an independent infective process

**lym·pho·cy·to·pe·nia** \-,sīd·əˈpēnēə\ *n* -S [NL, fr. ISV *lymphocyte* + NL *-o-* + *-penia*] **:** a decrease in the normal number of lymphocytes in the circulating blood

**lym·pho·cy·to·poiesis** \,lim(p)fə,sīd·ə+\ *n, pl* **lymphocytopoieses** [NL, fr. ISV *lymphocyte* + NL *-o-* + *-poiesis*] **:** formation of lymphocytes usu. in the lymph glands

**lym·pho·cy·to·sis** \-,sīˈtōsəs\ *n, pl* **lymphocyto·ses** \-ō,sēz\ [NL, fr. ISV *lymphocyte* + NL *-osis*] **:** increase in the number of lymphocytes in the blood usu. associated with chronic inflammations and some infectious diseases (as tuberculosis and syphilis) — compare GRANULOCYTOSIS, MONOCYTOSIS

**lym·pho·cy·tot·ic** \ˌ⸗⸗ˌsīˈtäd·ik\ *adj* [fr. NL *lymphocytosis*, after such pairs as NL *hypnosis*: E *hypnotic*] **:** of or relating to lymphocytosis

**lymphoedema** *var of* LYMPHEDEMA

**lym·phog·e·nous** \(ˈ)limˈfäjənəs\ *also* **lym·pho·gen·ic** \ˌlim(p)fəˈjenik\ *adj* [*lymph-* + *-genous* or *-genic*] **1 :** producing lymph or lymphocytes **2 :** arising or resulting from lymphocytes or lymphatics ⟨a ~ spread of infection⟩

**lym·pho·granuloma** \ˌlim(p)fə+\ *n, pl* **lymphogranulomas** *or* **lymphogranulomata** [NL, fr. *lymph-* + *granuloma*] **1 :** a granuloma or a nodular swelling of a lymph node **2 :** a contagious venereal virus disease marked by swelling and ulceration of lymphatic tissues in the iliac and inguinal regions — called also *lymphogranuloma in·gui·nale* \-ˌiŋgwəˈna(ˌ)lē, -ä(-, -ä(-\, *lymphogranuloma ve·ne·re·um* \-vəˈnirēəm\

**lym·pho·gran·u·lo·ma·to·sis** \ˌlim(p)fəˌgranyəˌlōməˈtōsəs\ *n, pl* **lymphogranulomato·ses** \-ōˌsēz\ [NL, fr. *lymphogranulomat-*, *lymphogranuloma* + *-osis*] **1 :** the development of benign (as in sarcoidosis) or malignant (as in Hodgkin's disease) lymphogranulomas in various parts of the body **2 :** a condition characterized by lymphogranulomas

**lymph·oid** \ˈlimˌfȯid\ *adj* [ISV *lymph-* + *-oid*] **1 :** of, relating to, or resembling lymph **2 :** of, relating to, or resembling the tissue characteristic of the lymph glands

**lymphoid cell** *n* **:** the characteristic lymphocyte-producing cell of the lymph glands

**lym·phoid·o·cyte** \limˈfȯidəˌsīt\ *n* -s [ISV *lymphoid* + *-o-* + *-cyte*] **:** HEMOCYTOBLAST

**lym·pho·ma** \limˈfōmə\ *n, pl* **lymphomas** \-məz\ *or* **lympho·ma·ta** \-məd·ə\ [NL, fr. *lymph-* + *-oma*] **:** a tumor of lymphoid tissue — **lym·phoma·tous** \(ˈ)limˈfäməd·əs, -fōm-\ *adj*

**lym·pho·ma·toid** \limˈfōməˌtȯid\ *adj* [NL *lymphomat-*, *lymphoma* + E *-oid*] **:** characterized by or resembling lymphomas ⟨a ~ tumor⟩

**lym·pho·ma·to·sis** \(ˌ)limˌfōməˈtōsəs\ *n, pl* **lymphomato·ses** \-ōˌsēz\ [NL, fr. *lymphomat-*, *lymphoma* + *-osis*] **:** the presence of multiple lymphomas in the body; *specif* **:** a phase of the avian leukosis complex in which the viscera are infiltrated with lymphocytes and lymphomas are widely distributed in the various organs — called also *visceral lymphomatosis;* see NEUROLYMPHOMATOSIS

**lym·pho·ma·tot·ic** \(ˌ)⸗ˌ⸗⸗ˈtäd·ik\ *adj* [fr. NL *lymphomatosis*, after such pairs as NL *hypnosis*: E *hypnotic*] **:** of or relating to lymphomatosis

**lym·pho·path·ia ve·ne·re·um** \ˌlim(p)fəˈpathēəvəˈnirēəm\ *n* [NL, lit., venereal lymph disease] **:** LYMPHOGRANULOMA 2

**lym·pho·pe·nia** \-ˈpēnēə\ *n* -s [NL, fr. *lymph-* + *-penia*] **:** reduction in the number of lymphocytes circulating in the blood of man or animals

**lym·pho·poi·e·sis** \-ˌpȯiˈēsəs\ *n, pl* **lymphopoie·ses** \-ēˌsēz\ [NL, fr. *lymph-* + *-poiesis*] **:** the formation of lymphocytes or lymphatic tissue

**lym·pho·poi·et·ic** \ˌ⸗⸗ˌpȯiˈed·ik\ *adj* [ISV *lymph-* + *-poietic*] **:** of or relating to lymphopoiesis

**lym·pho·sarcoma** \ˌlim(p)(ˌ)fō+\ *n* [NL, fr. *lymph-* + *sarcoma*] **:** a malignant lymphoma tending to metastasize freely esp. along the regional lymphatic drainage

**lym·pho·spo·rid·i·o·sis** \ˈ"+spəˌridēˈōsəs\ *n, pl* **lympho·sporidio·ses** \-ōˌsēz\ [NL, fr. *lymph-* + *sporidium* + *-osis*] **:** EPIZOOTIC LYMPHANGITIS

**lymph·ous** \ˈlim(p)fəs\ *adj* [*lymph* + *-ous*] **:** resembling lymph

**lymphs** *pl of* LYMPH

**lymph sac** *n* **:** an extensive dorsal subcutaneous space that opens into a lymph heart of a frog or toad

**lymph-vascular** \ˈ⸗ˌ⸗⸗⸗\ *adj* [*lymph*atic + *vascular*] **:** of, relating to, or containing lymphatic vessels

**lyn** *or* **lynn** *var of* ²LINN

**lyn·ce·an** \(ˈ)linˈsēən, ˈlin(t)sē-\ *adj* [L *lync-*, *lynx* + E *-an;* prob. influenced by L *Lynceus* of Lynceus, sharp-sighted, fr. Gk *Lynkeios*, fr. *Lynkeus*, mythological member of the Argonauts who was famous for his sharpness of sight] **1 :** of or relating to a lynx **2 :** SHARP-SIGHTED

**¹lynch** \ˈlinch\ *or* **lyn·chet** \ˈlinchət\ *n, pl* **lynches** *or* **lyn·chets** [*lynch* alter. of *linch*, alter. of ¹*link;* *lynchet* alter. of *linch* + *-et*] **1** *Brit* **:** a terrace or ridge on the face of a down **2** *Brit* **:** a ridge or strip of unplowed land forming a boundary between fields

**²lynch** \ˈlinch\ *vt* -ED/-ING/-ES [prob. after Charles *Lynch*] **1 a** *archaic* **:** to beat or otherwise do physical violence to by mob action ⟨had been ~*ed*, tarred and feathered, and sent down the Missouri on a frail raft —*Lawrence (Kansas) Republican*⟩ **b :** to hang or otherwise kill by mob action in punishment of a presumed crime or offense ⟨had recently been ~*ed* by burning —S.C.Webster⟩ **2 :** to subject to scorn, defamation, or ridicule by violent attack in speech or writing ⟨practices through which individuals are ~*ed* by label —G.B. Oxnam⟩ ⟨liberalism . . . had not been condemned in the court of human reason, but ~*ed* outside of it —M.R.Cohen⟩ — **lynch·er** \-chə(r)\ *n* -s

**lynching** *n* -s **1 a :** the act of a mob or group that lynches **b :** an instance of this act **2 :** LYNCH LAW

**lynch law** *n* [prob. after Charles *Lynch* †1796 Am. planter and justice of the peace; fr. his presiding over an extralegal court to suppress Tory activity in Virginia during the Revolution] **:** the act or practice by a self-constituted court of condemning a person and usu. inflicting death upon him for a presumed crime or offense without due process of law

**lynchpin** *var of* LINCHPIN

**lyn·cine** \ˈlinˌsīn\ *adj* [L *lync-*, *lynx* + E *-ine*] **:** of or relating to a lynx **:** LYNCEAN

**lynn·ha·ven** \linˈhāvən\ *n* [fr. *Lynnhaven*, Va.] **:** a large oyster typically from Virginia or Maryland waters — compare BLUEPOINT

**lynx** \ˈliŋ(k)s\ *n* [L, fr. Gk; fr. its light color or its sharp sight; akin to OE *lox* lynx, OHG *luhs*, MD *los*, Lith *lušis* lynx, Skt *rušat* light, Gk *leukos* white, bright — more at LIGHT] **1 a** *pl* **lynx** *or* **lynxes :** any of various wildcats that have relatively long legs, a short stubby tail, and often tufted ears and that yield a valuable fur varying in color from pale grayish buff to black-spotted tawny: as (1) **:** the common lynx (*Lynx lynx*) of northern Europe and Asia (2) **:** BAY LYNX (3) **:** CANADA LYNX (4) **:** SPOTTED LYNX **b** *cap* [NL, fr. L] **:** the genus of Felidae or subgenus of *Felis* comprising these animals **2** *pl* **lynx** *or* **lynxes :** the fur or pelt of a lynx

lynx 1a(1)

**lynx cat** *n* **1 :** a pale grayish very slightly spotted lynx (*Lynx uinta*) of the intermountain region of the western U.S. and southern British Columbia **2** *Southwest* **:** BAY LYNX

**lynx-eyed** \ˈ⸗ˌ⸗\ *adj* **:** SHARP-SIGHTED ⟨*lynx-eyed* for scandal or for romance —Donn Byrne⟩

**lynxlike** \ˈ⸗ˌ⸗\ *adj* **:** resembling a lynx esp. in alertness ⟨his movements active and supple with a ~ gait —F.H.Lyon⟩

**lyo-** *comb form* [prob. fr. NL, fr. Gk *lyein* to loose, dissolve, release + NL *-o-* — more at LOSE] **1 :** lacking **:** rudimentary in ⟨*Lyomeri*⟩ **2 :** looseness **:** dispersion ⟨*lyophilic*⟩ ⟨*lyophobic*⟩

**ly·om·eri** \līˈäməˌrī\ *n pl, cap* [NL, fr. *lyo-* + *-meri* (fr. Gk *meros* part) — more at MERIT] **:** a small order of fragile soft-bodied deep-sea fishes with large mouth and minute eyes — see GULPER, PELICAN FISH

**ly·om·er·ous** \(ˈ)līˈämərəs\ *adj* [NL *Lyomeri* + E *-ous*] **:** of or relating to the Lyomeri

**ly·on bean** \ˈlīən-\ *n, usu cap L* [after William S. *Lyon* †1916 Am. botanist] **:** a tropical Asian plant (*Stizolobium niveum*) grown in the southern U.S. and elsewhere for forage

**lyon court** \ˈ"-\ *n, usu cap L&C* [*lyon*, obs. var. of ¹*lion*] **:** a lawcourt and administrative office in Scotland that is headed by the Lord Lyon King of Arms, has jurisdiction over the bearing and display of armorial ensigns, and maintains the public registers of Scottish armorial bearings and genealogies — called also *Court of the Lord Lyon*

**ly·o·ne·tia** \ˌlīəˈnēsh(ē)ə\ *n, cap* [NL, fr. Pierre *Lyonet* (also, *Lyonnet*) †1789 Dutch entomologist + NL *-ia*] **:** a genus (the type of the family Lyonetiidae) of moths

**¹ly·o·netid** \ˌ⸗⸗ˈnēd·əd\ *adj* [NL *Lyonetiidae*] **:** of or relating to the family Lyonetiidae

**²lyonetid** \ˈ"\ *n* -s **:** a moth of the family Lyonetiidae

**ly·o·ne·ti·idae** \ˌlīənəˈtīəˌdē\ *n pl, cap* [NL, *Lyonetia*, type genus + NL *-idae*] **:** a family of very small tineoid lepidopters whose larvae are leaf miners

**ly·on herald** \ˈlīən-\ *n, usu cap L&H* [ME (Sc. dial.) *leon heraud*, fr. *leon* lion + *heraud* herald; fr. the representation of a lion on the royal shield — more at LION, HERALD] **1 :** the chief of the royal heralds in medieval and 16th century Scotland **2 :** LYON KING OF ARMS

**ly·o·nia** \līˈōnēə\ *n, cap* [NL, fr. John *Lyon* †*ab*1818 Scot. gardener and collector of American plants + NL *-ia*] **:** a genus of upright shrubs (family Ericaceae) that have white or pinkish flowers in axillary or terminal clusters with urceolate or cylindric corolla, anthers opening by terminal pores, and a capsular many-seeded fruit

**ly·on king of arms** \ˈlīən-\ *also* **lyon** *n, pl* **lyon kings of arms** *also* **lyons** *usu cap L&K&A* [*lyon*, obs. var. of ¹*lion*] **:** the chief officer of arms in Scotland who sits as judge in Lyon Court, grants patents of arms, supervises the Scottish heralds and pursuivants in the preparation and conduct of state, public, and royal ceremonial, and is also controller of the royal messengers-at-arms

**ly·on·naise** \ˌlīəˈnāz, ˌ⸗⸗ˈ⸗\ *adj* [F (*à la*) *lyonnaise* in the manner of Lyons, fr. fem. of *lyonnais* of Lyons, fr. *Lyon*, Lyons, France] **:** prepared or seasoned with onions and sometimes parsley ⟨~ potatoes⟩ ⟨potatoes ~⟩

**lyon office** *n, usu cap L&O* [*lyon*, obs. var. of ¹*lion*] **:** the administrative and clerical section of the Lyon Court in Scotland

**ly·ons** \(ˈ)lēˈōⁿ, ˈlīənz\ *or* **lyon** \(ˈ)lēˈōⁿ, *F* lyōⁿ\ *adj, usu cap* [fr. *Lyons* (F *Lyon*), France] **:** of or from the city of Lyons, France ⟨*Lyons* silk⟩ **:** of the kind or style prevalent in Lyons

**lyons blue** *n, often cap L* **:** a strong blue that is redder and deeper than Sèvres, redder and darker than cerulean blue (sense 1b), and slightly greener and lighter than liberty

**¹ly·o·phile** \ˈlīəˌfīl\ *adj* [ISV *lyo-* + *-phile*] **1 :** LYOPHILIC **2** *also* **ly·o·phil** \-ˌfil\ **:** of, relating to, or obtained by lyophilization ⟨~ process⟩

**²lyophile** \ˈ"\ *vt* -ED/-ING/-S **:** LYOPHILIZE

**ly·o·phil·ic** \ˌ⸗⸗ˈfilik\ *adj* [*lyo-* + *-philic*] **:** of, relating to, or having a strong affinity between a dispersed phase and the liquid in which it is dispersed ⟨~ colloidal systems such as rubber and benzene are not easily coagulated⟩ — opposed to *lyophobic;* compare HYDROPHILIC

**ly·oph·i·li·za·tion** \(ˌ)līˌäfələˈzāshən, -fəˌlīˈz-\ *n* -s [ISV *lyophilize* + *-ation*] **:** the process of lyophilizing or the state of being lyophilized

**ly·oph·i·lize** \līˈäfəˌlīz\ *vt* -ED/-ING/-S [ISV *lyophil-* (fr. ¹*lyophile*) + *-ize*] **:** to dry (as tissue, blood, or serum) in a frozen state under high vacuum esp. for preservation **:** FREEZE-DRY

**ly·o·pho·bic** \ˌ⸗⸗ˈfōbik *also* -ˈfäb-\ *also* **ly·o·phobe** \ˈ⸗⸗ˌfōb\ *adj* [*lyophobic* fr. *lyo-* + *-phobic;* *lyophobe*, ISV *lyo-* + *-phobe*] **:** of, relating to, or having a lack of strong affinity between a dispersed phase and the liquid in which it is dispersed ⟨~ systems such as colloidal metals in water are easily coagulated⟩ — opposed to *lyophilic;* compare HYDROPHOBIC

**ly·o·po·ma** \ˌlīəˈpōmə\ [NL, fr. *lyo-* + Gk *pōma* lid, operculum] *syn of* INARTICULATA

**ly·o·po·ma·ta** \ˌlīəˈpōməd·ə\ [NL, fr. *lyo-* + *-pomata* (fr. Gk *pōmat-*, *pōma* lid, operculum) — more at POMACENTRIDAE] *syn of* INARTICULATA

**ly·o·trop·ic** \ˌlīəˈträpik\ *adj* [*lyo-* + *-tropic*] **:** relating to or dependent on the forces existing between components in a solution and not on their properties as individuals

**lyotropic series** *n* **:** HOFMEISTER SERIES

**ly·ra** \ˈlīrə\ *n* -s [L, lyre, fr. Gk] **1 a :** ²LIRA **b :** a glockenspiel with a lyre-shaped frame **2** *also* **lyre** \ˈlī(ə)r, ˈlīə\ [NL *lyra*, fr. L] **:** a triangular area of the ventral surface of the corpus callosum between the posterior pillars of the fornix

**lyrachord** *var of* LYRICHORD

**ly·rate** \ˈlīˌrā|t, -ˌrə|, *usu* |d·+V\ *also* **ly·rat·ed** \ˈlīˌrād·əd, -ātəd\ *adj* **:** having or suggesting the shape of a lyre ⟨a ~ leaf⟩ ⟨the bird's ~ tail⟩ — see LEAF illustration — **ly·rate·ly** *adv*

**lyraway** \ˈ⸗ˌ⸗\ *adv* [*lyra* + *-way*] **:** according to the lute tablature instead of musical notation ⟨play ~ on the viola da gamba⟩

**lyre** \ˈlī(ə)r, ˈlīə\ *n* -s [ME *lire*, fr. OF, fr. L *lyra*, fr. Gk] **1 a :** a stringed musical instrument of the harp class used by the ancient Greeks esp. to accompany song and recitation and made with a hollow body and two curved arms that are joined at the top by a yoke and four to ten strings that are struck with a plectrum — compare CITHARA, LIRA **b :** a musical instrument or device resembling the lyre **2 :** MUSIC LYRE

**lyre-back** \ˈ⸗ˌ⸗\ *n* **:** a decorative motif in the form of a lyre used esp. in the splat of American chairs of the late 18th and early 19th centuries

**lyre bat** *n* **:** a small long-eared bat (*Lyroderma lyra*) of eastern Asia

**lyrebird** \ˈ⸗ˌ⸗\ *n* **:** either of two Australian passerine birds of the genus *Menura;* *esp* **:** a bird (*M. novaehollandiae*) of New South Wales that is about the size of a grouse, is generally brown in color with rufous color on the throat, wings, tail coverts, and tail, and is distinguished in the male by 16 very long tail feathers spread out during courtship in the shape of a lyre

lyrebird

**lyre crab** *n* **:** TOAD CRAB

**lyreflower** \ˈ⸗ˌ⸗\ *n* **:** BLEEDING HEART 1

**lyre-guitar** \ˈ⸗ˌ⸗\ *n* **:** a guitar with six strings

**lyre·man** \ˈ⸗mən\ *n* -s [*lyre* + *man*] **:** DOG-DAY CICADA

**lyre pheasant** *n* **:** LYREBIRD

**lyre snake** *n* **:** a weakly venomous colubrid snake (*Trimorphodon lambda*) that has posterior grooved poison fangs in the upper jaw and a lyre-shaped blotch on the nape of the neck and is found in desert areas of southwestern No. America

**lyretail** \ˈ⸗ˌ⸗\ *n* **:** LYREBIRD

**lyre-tailed** \ˈ⸗ˈ⸗\ *adj* **:** having a lyrate tail

**lyre-tailed nightjar** *n* **:** a So. American goatsucker (*Hydropsalis brasiliana*) having a lyrate tail that it opens and shuts while in flight

**lyre turtle** *n* **:** LEATHERBACK 1

**¹lyr·ic** \ˈlirik, -rēk\ *adj* [MF or L; MF *lyrique*, fr. L *lyricus*, fr. Gk *lyrikos*, fr. *lyra* lyre + *-ikos* -ic] **1 :** of or relating to a lyre or harp **2** *of verse* **a :** suitable to sing to the lyre **b :** suitable for being set to music and sung **:** MELODIC **3 a :** characterized by or expressive of direct usu. intense personal emotion ⟨for the ~ writer virtue depends upon the intensity with which the personal vision is rendered —R.P.Warren⟩ ⟨a ~ and tender dance —*Dance Observer*⟩ ⟨a ~ and personal response to life —A.M.Mizener⟩ **b :** rhapsodic and unrestrained in manner or style ⟨publish ~ prose saying how gay an occasion it was —Katherine A. Porter⟩ ⟨the ~ typewriters of literary ghosts —Merriman Smith⟩ ⟨exploded with ~ wrath —*Time*⟩ **4 :** *of a singing voice* **:** having a relatively light, pure, melodic quality ⟨~ soprano⟩ ⟨~ tenor⟩ — compare COLORATURA, DRAMATIC

**²lyric** \ˈ"\ *n* -s [MF or L; MF *lyrique*, fr. L *lyricum*, fr. neut. of *lyricus* adj.] **1 a :** a lyric composition ⟨a tender and gay little ~ which she had sung to crowded drawing rooms —S.H. Adams⟩; *specif* **:** a lyric poem ⟨a third ~ of twenty lines —Malcolm Cowley⟩ **b lyrics** *pl* **:** the words of a popular song or musical-comedy number ⟨rereading the ~s slowly and savoring the ingenious metrical tricks that make these songs unique —William Zinsser⟩ **2** [MF *lyrique*, fr. L *lyricus*, fr. Gk *lyrikos*, fr. *lyrikos*, adj.] *archaic* **:** a lyric poet

**lyr·i·cal** \-rəkəl, -rēk-\ *adj* **:** LYRIC — **lyr·i·cal·ly** \-rək(ə)lē, -rēk-, -li\ *adv* — **lyr·i·cal·ness** \-kəlnəs\ *n* -ES

**lyric caesura** *n* **:** a feminine caesura that follows an unstressed syllable required by the meter (as in Housman's "they cease not fighting ‖ east and west") — contrasted with *epic caesura*

**lyric drama** *n* **:** OPERA

**lyri·chord** *also* **lyra·chord** \ˈlirəˌkȯrd, ˈlīr-\ *n* [*lyrichord* fr. *lyre* + harpsi*chord;* *lyrachord*, alter. (influenced by E *lyra*) of *lyrichord*] **:** a harpsichord having its strings sounded by revolving wheels instead of being plucked

**lyr·i·cism** \ˈlirəˌsizəm\ *n* -s **1 a :** the quality or state of being lyric **:** SONGFULNESS ⟨the magical union of sound and hush that is ~ at its most subtle best —David Morton⟩ ⟨~ teaches ideas to dance instead of plodding along —Peter Viereck⟩ **b :** a personal direct intense style or quality in poetry or the other arts ⟨reminds us with quiet ~ of life itself —Irwin Edman⟩ **2 :** unrestrained enthusiasm **:** exaggeration of style or feeling ⟨the sort of author who inspires ~ or invective —*Time*⟩ ⟨the extravagance of their claims and the ~ of their expression —*Times Lit. Supp.*⟩ ⟨pages of a rather hysterical ~ about the dead child —Aldous Huxley⟩

**lyr·i·cist** \-ˌsəst\ *n* -s **:** a writer of lyrics

**lyr·i·cize** \-ˌsīz\ *vb* -ED/-ING/-S *vi* **1 :** to write or sing lyrics **2 :** to write in a lyric style ~ *vt* **:** to treat in a lyric manner ⟨making a revel of life and *lyricizing* death, hardship, and villainy —W.J.Fisher⟩

**lyric theater** *n* **1 :** OPERA HOUSE **2 :** a theatrical production involving music; *esp* **:** OPERA

**ly·ri·form** \ˈlīrəˌfȯrm\ *adj* [F *lyriforme*, fr. *lyre* (fr. MF *lire*) + *-iforme* -iform] **:** shaped like a lyre

**lyriform organ** *n* **:** a cuticular groove that is connected with a nerve ending in many spiders, often occurs in groups on the legs and sternum, and is thought to be an organ of hearing

**lyr·ism** \ˈliˌrizəm\ *n* -s [¹*lyric* + *-ism*] **:** LYRICISM

**lyr·ist** *in sense 1* ˈlīrəst, *in sense 2* ˈlir-\ *n* -s [L *lyristes*, fr. Gk *lyristēs*, fr. *lyra* lyre + *-istēs* -ist] **1 :** a player on the lyre **2** [¹*lyric* + *-ist*] **:** LYRICIST

**ly·ru·rus** \līˈrůrəs\ *n, cap* [NL, fr. Gk *lyra* lyre + NL *-urus*] **:** a genus of birds including the black grouse

**lys-** *or* **lysi-** *or* **lyso-** *comb form* [NL, fr. Gk *lys-*, *lysi-* loosening, dissolution, fr. *lysis*, fr. *lyein* to loosen, dissolve + *-sis* — more at LOSE] **1 :** loosening or dissolution or decomposition ⟨*lysi*genous⟩ ⟨*lys*in⟩ **2** *usu* **lyso-** [ISV *lys*in + *-o-*] **:** lysin ⟨*lyso*gen⟩

**ly·sate** \ˈlīˌsāt\ *n* -s [ISV *lys-* (fr. NL *lysis*) + *-ate*] **:** the product resulting from lysis

**lyse** \ˈlīs, -īz\ *vb* -ED/-ING/-S [irreg. fr. *lysis*] *vt* **:** to cause to undergo lysis **:** produce lysis in ~ *vi* **:** to undergo lysis

**-lyse** *or* **-lyze** \ˌlīz\ *vb suffix* -ED/-ING/-S [ISV, prob. irreg. fr. NL *-lysis* + ISV *-ise* or *-ize*] **:** to produce lysis (sense 2) ⟨cata*lyze*⟩ ⟨hydro*lyze*⟩

**ly·sen·ko·ism** \ləˈseŋ(ˌ)kōˌizəm\ *n* -s *usu cap* [Trofim Denisovich *Lysenko* *b*1898 Russ. geneticist + E *-ism*] **:** a biological doctrine asserting the fundamental influence of somatic and environmental factors on heredity in contradiction of orthodox genetics

**ly·ser·gic acid** \ləˈsərjik-, (ˈ)līˈ|\ *n* [*lys-* + *ergot* + *-ic*] **:** a crystalline tetracyclic acid $C_{15}H_{15}N_2COOH$ obtained from ergotic alkaloids by hydrolysis

**lysergic acid di·eth·yl·amide** \-ˌdīˈethələˌmīd\ *n* [*lysergic acid* + *diethyl* + *amide*] **:** a crystalline compound $C_{15}H_{15}N_2$-$CON(C_2H_5)_2$ that causes psychotic symptoms similar to those of schizophrenia

**ly·si·gen·ic** \ˌlīsəˈjenik\ *also* **ly·si·ge·net·ic** \-jəˈned·ik\ *adj* [*lys-* + *-genic* or *-genetic*] **:** LYSIGENOUS

**ly·sig·e·nous** \(ˈ)līˈsijənəs\ *adj* [*lys-* + *-genous*] **:** formed by the breaking down of adjoining cells — used esp. of some intercellular spaces; compare SCHIZOGENOUS — **ly·sig·e·nous·ly** *adv*

**ly·si·lo·ma** \ˌlīsəˈlōmə\ *n, cap* [NL, fr. *lys-* + Gk *lōma* border, fringe; fr. the fact that in ripening the sides of the pod are loosened; akin to L *lorum* strap — more at LORE] **:** a small genus of tropical American trees (family Leguminosae) with pinnate leaves, few stamens, and a flat straight pod — see SABICU

**ly·si·mach·ia** \ˌlīsəˈmakēə\ *n, cap* [NL, fr. L, a plant, fr. Gk *lysimacheios* loosestrife, fr. *Lysimachos* Lysimachus *fl* 5th or 4th cent.B.C. Greek doctor] **:** a widely distributed genus of herbs (family Primulaceae) with leafy stems, leaves opposite or whorled, and yellow flowers — see LOOSESTRIFE 1, MONEYWORT

**ly·sim·e·ter** \līˈsiməd·ə(r)\ *n* [ISV *lys-* + *meter*] **:** a device for measuring the percolation of water through soils and determining the soluble constituents removed in the drainage

**ly·sin** \ˈlīsᵊn\ *n* -s [ISV *lys-* + *-in*] **:** any of various substances capable of causing lysis; *esp* **:** an antibody that is capable of causing the specific disintegration or solution of red blood cells or microorganisms

**ly·sine** \ˈlīˌsēn\ *n* -s [ISV *lys-* + *-ine;* prob. orig. formed as G *lysin*] **:** a crystalline basic amino acid $H_2N(CH_2)_4CH(NH_2)$-$COOH$ that is obtained in its dextrorotatory L form by hydrolysis of many proteins (as from blood), by fermentation, or by synthesis and resolution of the racemic form and that is essential in the nutrition of animals and man; α, ε-diamino-caproic acid

**ly·sis** \ˈlīsəs\ *n, pl* **ly·ses** \-īˌsēz\ [NL, fr. Gk, act of loosing, loosening, dissolution, remission of fever — more at LYS-] **1 :** the gradual decline of a disease process **:** DEFERVESCENCE; *specif* **:** the gradual lowering of fever — compare CRISIS **2 :** a process of disintegration or dissolution (as of bacteria or blood cells)

**-ly·sis** \ləsəs\ *n comb form, pl* **-lyses** \ləˌsēz\ [NL, fr. L & Gk; L, loosening, fr. Gk, fr. *lysis*] **1 :** decomposition ⟨electro*lysis*⟩ ⟨hydro*lysis*⟩ ⟨pyro*lysis*⟩ **2 :** destruction **:** disintegration **:** dissolution — esp. of material associated with living organisms ⟨bio*lysis*⟩ ⟨auto*lysis*⟩ ⟨proteo*lysis*⟩ **3 a :** relief or reduction ⟨neuro*lysis*⟩ **b :** detachment (as in the surgical operation of freeing from adhesions) ⟨cardio*lysis*⟩ ⟨gastro*lysis*⟩ **c :** paralysis ⟨glosso*lysis*⟩

**lyso-** — see LYS-

**ly·so·gen** \ˈlīsəjən, -ˌjen\ *n* -s [*lys-* + *-gen*] **:** an antigen that stimulates the production of lysins

**ly·so·genesis** \ˌlīsə+\ *n* [NL, fr. *lys-* + L *genesis*] **:** the production of lysins or of the phenomenon of lysis

**ly·so·genetic** \ˌ⸗⸗+\ *adj* [fr. NL *lysogenesis*, after L *genesis*: E *genetic*] **:** of or relating to lysogenesis

**ly·so·gen·ic** \ˌlīsəˈjenik\ *adj* [*lys-* + *-genic*] *of bacteria* **:** carrying a bacteriophage capable of lysing other bacteria — **ly·so·ge·nic·i·ty** \ˌ⸗⸗jəˈnisəd·ē, -ətē, -ī\ *n* -ES

**Ly·sol** \ˈlīˌsȯl, -ˌsōl\ *trademark* — used for a disinfectant consisting of a brown emulsified solution containing cresols

**ly·so·lecithin** \ˌlīsō+\ *n* [*lys-* + *lecithin*] **:** a hemolytic substance formed from a lecithin by the removal of one fatty acid unit per molecule by enzymatic hydrolysis esp. with lecithinase A or bacterial toxins

**ly·so·zyme** \ˈlīsəˌzīm\ *n* -s [*lys-* + *-zyme*] **:** a basic protein that is present in egg white and in biological secretions (as tears, saliva, and the latex of some plants) and that functions as a mucolytic enzyme and is capable of attacking the capsules of various bacteria

**lys·sa** \ˈlisə\ *n* -s [NL, fr. Gk, rage, madness, rabies in dogs; akin to Gk *leukos* white — more at LIGHT] **:** RABIES, HYDROPHOBIA

**lys·sa·ci·na** \ˌlisəˈsīnə\ *n pl, cap* [NL, fr. Gk *lyssa* madness + *akis* barb, spicule, needle + NL *-ina* — more at ACIDANTHERA] *in some classifications* **:** an order of Hyalospongiae comprising those members of the Hexasterophora with spicules separate or incompletely fused — compare DICTYONINA — **lys·sa·cine** \ˈ⸗⸗ˌsīn\ *adj or n*

**lys·sic** \ˈlisik\ *adj* [NL *lyssa* + E *-ic*] **:** of or relating to rabies **:** HYDROPHOBIC

**lyster bag** *usu cap L, var of* LISTER BAG

**ly·syl** \ˈlīsəl\ *n* -s [*lysine* + *-yl*] **:** the acid radical $H_2N(CH_2)_4$-$CH(NH_2)CO$- of lysine

**¹-lyte** \ˌlīt, *usu* -īd·+V\ *n comb form* -s [Gk *lytos* that may be untied, soluble, verbal of *lyein* to loosen, dissolve — more at LOSE] **:** a substance capable of undergoing lysis (sense 2) ⟨electro*lyte*⟩ ⟨hydro*lyte*⟩

**²-lyte** — see -LITE

**lythe** \ˈlīth\ *n, pl* **lythe** *or* **lythes** [origin unknown] *Brit* **:** any of several food fishes; *esp* **:** POLLACK

**ly·thra·ce·ae** \līˈthrāsēˌē\ *n pl, cap* [NL, fr. *Lythrum*, type genus + *-aceae*] **:** a family of herbs, shrubs, and trees (order Myrtales) having flowers with crumpled corolla, a hypanthium, and often unequal stamens — **ly·thra·ceous** \(ˈ)līˈthrāshəs\ *adj*

**ly·thra·les** \lī'thrā(,)lēz\ [NL, fr. *Lythrum* + *-ales*] *syn of* MYRTALES

**ly·thrum** \'līthrəm\ *n, cap* [NL, fr. Gk *lythron* gore; fr. the color of the flowers; akin to L *lutum* mud — more at POLLUTE] **:** a genus (the type of the family Lythraceae) of herbs and subshrubs having purple or rose-pink flowers with 4 to 8 petals and a 2-celled capsule — see LOOSESTRIFE 2

**lyt·ic** \'lid·|ik, 'lit|, |ēk\ *adj* [Gk *lytikos* able to loose, fr. *lytos* soluble, that may be untied + *-ikos* -ic] **:** of or relating to lysis or a lysin **:** productive of or effecting lysis esp. of cells

**-lyt·ic** \¦==\ *adj suffix* [Gk *lytikos* able to loose] **:** of, relating to, or effecting lysis (sense 2) ⟨electro*lytic*⟩ ⟨hydro*lytic*⟩

**lyt·ta** \'lid·ə\ *n* [L, fr. Gk, fr. *lytta, lyssa* madness, rabies — more at LYSSA] **1** *pl* **lyttae :** a fibrous and cartilaginous rod lying within the longitudinal axis of the tongue in many carnivorous mammals (as the dog) **2** *cap* [NL, fr. L] **:** a widespread genus of blister beetles (family Meloidae) containing the Spanish fly — compare CANTHARIS

**lyx-** *or* **lyxo-** *comb form* [*lyxose*] **1 :** related to lyxose ⟨*lyxo*flavin⟩ **2** *usu* **lyxo-**, *usu ital* **:** having the stereochemical arrangement of atoms or groups found in lyxose ⟨D-*lyxo*-3=hexulose⟩

**lyx·o·flavin** \¦liksə+\ *n* [*lyx-* + *flavin*] **:** a yellow crystalline compound $C_{17}H_{20}N_4O_6$ isolated from heart muscle and stereoisomeric with riboflavin but derived from lyxose

**lyx·ose** \'lik,sōs, -ōz\ *n* -s [anagram of *xylose*] **:** a crystalline aldose sugar $HOCH_2(CHOH)_3CHO$ that is the epimer of xylose and is made by degradation of galactose methods

**-lyze** — see -LYSE

**LZ** *abbr* landing zone

**[1]m** \'em\ *n, pl* **m's** *or* **ms** \'emz\ *often cap, often attrib* **1 a :** the 13th letter of the English alphabet **b :** an instance of this letter printed, written, or otherwise represented **c :** a speech counterpart of orthographic *m* (as *m* in *mimic, small, comfort*, or French *muet*) **2 :** 1000 — see NUMBER table **3 :** a printer's type, a stamp, or some other instrument for reproducing the letter *m* **4 :** someone or something arbitrarily or conveniently designated *m* esp. as the 12th or when j is used for the 10th the 13th in order or class **5 :** something having the shape of the capital letter M **6 a :** EM 2 **b :** PICA **7 :** an antigen of human blood that shares a common genetic locus with the N antigen — **have an M under one's girdle** *obs* **:** to show courtesy by using the title Mr., Mrs., or Miss

**[2]m** *abbr, often cap* **1** Mach **2** [L *magister*] master **3** magistrate **4** magnetic **5** maiden **6** maiden over **7** mail **8** [F *main*] hand **9** majesty **10** make **11** male **12** [L *manipulus*] handful **13** [It *mano*] hand **14** manual **15** March **16** mare **17** maritime **18** mark **19** marker **20** marquis **21** married **22** martyr **23** masculine **24** mass **25** master **26** mate **27** maxwell **28** May **29** mean **30** measure **31** mechanical **32** medical **33** [L *medicinae*] of medicine **34** medium **35** mega- **36** melts at **37** member **38** memorandum **39** meridian **40** [L *meridies*] noon **41** metal **42** meter **43** metropolitan **44** [It *mezzo*] half **45** micro- **46** middle **47** mil **48** mile **49** military **50** mill **51** [L *mille*] thousand **52** milli- **53** million **54** mine **55** minim **56** minor **57** minute **58** [L *misce*] mix **59** miscellaneous **60** mist **61** [L *mistura*] mixture **62** model **63** modulus **64** molar; mole **65** molecular weight **66** moment **67** Monday **68** monoplane **69** monsieur **70** monsoon **71** month **72** moon **73** morning **74** morphine **75** mortar **76** mortgage **77** [L *mortis*] of death **78** mother **79** motor **80** mountain **81** mucoid **82** mud **83** muscle **84** mustard gas **85** muster **86** myopia

**[3]m** *symbol, cap* **1 a** place for the insertion of a given name of a bridegroom (as in a ceremonial statement) or of a male person — compare [3]N 1 **b** place for the insertion of two or more usu. given names of a person — compare NN **2** *ital* mutual inductance **3** metal — used esp. of a univalent cation; see BASE 8a, GENERAL FORMULA

**m-** \¦med·ə, -etə\ *abbr* meta-

**[1]'m** \m\ *vb* [by contr.] **:** AM ⟨I'*m* going⟩

**[2]'m** _im, _ēm\ *pron* [by contr.] **:** HIM ⟨show'*m* the way to the fairgrounds⟩

**[3]'m** *after "yes"* əm, *after "no"* m\ *n* -s [by contr.] **:** MADAM ⟨yes'*m*⟩

**ma** \'mä, 'mȯ, 'mȧ, 'ma, 'maa\ *n* -s [short for *mama*] **:** MOTHER

**mA** *abbr* milliangstrom

**ma** *abbr* **1** major **2** milliampere

**MA** \(')e¦mā\ *abbr or n* -s Master of Arts

**MA** *abbr, often not cap* **1** mental age **2** meter angle **3** middle ages **4** military academy **5** military attaché **6** military aviator **7** mill annealed **8** mountain artillery **9** my account

**maa** \'ma, 'maa, 'mä, 'mȧ\ *n or vi* [imit.] **:** BAA

**MAA** *abbr* master-at-arms

**ma'a·ba·ra** \¦mäbə¦rä\ *n, pl* **ma'aba·rot** *or* **ma'aba·roth** \-rōt(h), -ōs\ [NHeb *maʻbārāh*, fr. Heb, crossing, ferry] **:** a transitional settlement or village for immigrants in Israel

**maal** *sometimes cap, var of* MÅL

**ma'am** *also* **mam** *or* **ma'm** \¦mam, -aa(ə)-, -ä-, -ȧ- *sometimes* ¦məm; *in some areas where both* -ä- *and* -a- *or* -aa(ə)- *occur* -ä- *is substand or dial; after "yes" often* _əm; *often* _məm *by British servants*\ *n* -s [by contr.] **:** MADAM 1

**ma'amselle** *n* -s [modif. of F *mademoiselle* — more at MADEMOISELLE] **:** MADEMOISELLE

**maanhaar–jackal** \¦män,här+\ *n* [part trans. of Afrik *maanhaarjakkals*, fr. *maanhaar* mane (fr. *maan* mane + *haar* hair) + *jakkals* jackal] **:** AARDWOLF

**maar** \'mär\ *n* -s [G] **:** a volcanic crater that is produced by explosion in an area of low relief, is generally more or less circular, and often contains a lake, pond, or marsh

**maa·rad** \'mä,rad\ *n* -s [origin unknown] **:** a brownish long=staple cotton developed in Egypt from American pima cotton

**maa·rib** *or* **maa·riv** \'märiv, 'mäər-,'mīr-\ *n, pl* **maa·ri·bim** *or* **maa·ri·vim** \¦mäə(,)rē¦vēm\ [Heb *maʻărībh* bringing evening] **:** the daily evening liturgy of the Jews — compare MINHAH, SHAHARITH

**maas·bank·er** \'mäs,baŋkə(r)\ *n* [Afrik, fr. *maas* net, mesh + *bank* bank, shoal, shelf + *-er*] **:** a horse mackerel (*Trachurus trachurus*) that is an important commercial food fish in southern Africa

**MAB** *abbr* medical advisory board

**[1]ma·ba** \'mäbə\ *n, cap* [NL, fr. Tongan & Fijian, a tree of the genus Maba] **:** a widely distributed genus of tropical trees and shrubs (family Ebenaceae) having dioecious trimerous flowers and very hard wood resembling ebony

**[2]maba** \"\ *n* -s *usu cap* **:** one of a mixed negroid people of Muslim culture who in the 17th century established the powerful sultanate of Wadai east of Lake Chad — compare KANURI

**MABA** *abbr* meta-aminobenzoic acid

**mabe** \'māb\ *n* -s [origin unknown] **:** a cultured pearl that is essentially hemispherical in form

**ma·bi** \(')mä¦bē\ *n* -s [AmerSp *mabí*] **1 :** a nakedwood (*Colubrina reclinata*) with orange-brown bark and dark brown heartwood tinged with yellow **2 :** a beverage prepared from the bark of the mabi

**ma·bo·lo** \mə'bō(,)lō\ *n* -s [PhilSp, fr. Tag *mabulo*] **:** CAMAGON

**ma·bu·ya** \mə'büyə\ *n* [NL, fr. AmerSp, lizard of the genus Mabuya] **1** *cap* **:** a genus of insectivorous lizards (family Scincidae) common about houses in Central and So. America **2** -s **:** a lizard of the genus *Mabuya*

**mab·yer** \'mabyə(r)\ *n* -s [Corn *mabyar*, fr. *map, mob* son, boy + *yar* hen] *Cornwall* **:** a young hen **:** PULLET

**[1]mac** *var of* MACK

**[2]mac** \'mak\ *n* -s *usu cap* [fr. *Mac-, Mc-*, common patronymic prefix in many Scotch and Irish surnames] **:** FELLOW — used informally to address a man whose name is unknown ⟨look, *Mac*, I don't hear a word you're saying —Maritta Wolff⟩

**[3]mac** *or* **mack** \"\ *n* -s [by shortening] **1** *Brit* **:** MACKINTOSH **2 :** MACKINAW

**mac** *abbr* **1** macadam **2** macerate

**MAC** *abbr, sometimes not cap* **1** maximum allowable concentration **2** model airplane club

**ma·cá** \mə'kä\ *n, pl* **macá** *or* **macás** *usu cap* [Sp, of AmerInd origin] **1 a :** a people or group of peoples of the Gran Chaco in Paraguay and Argentina **b :** a member of such people or group of peoples **2 :** the language of the Macá people

**ma·caa·sim** *or* **ma·kaa·sim** \mə'kä,sēm\ *n* -s [Tag *makaasim*, perh. fr. *asim* sourness] **1 :** any of several chiefly Philippine hardwood trees of the genus *Eugenia* **2 :** the hard heavy fine-grained durable wood of a macaasim tree

**ma·ca·bi** \¦mäkə¦bē\ *n* -s [Sp *macabí*] **1 :** a bonefish (*Albula vulpes*) **2 :** TENPOUNDER 1

**ma·ca·bre** *also* **ma·ca·ber** \mə'käb(rə), -kȧb(-, *chiefly before a pause* -brᵊ, *chiefly before a vowel following without pause* -br (*br beginning the syllable to which the following vowel belongs*); *sometimes-* bə(r)\ *adj* [F, fr. (*danse*) *macabre* dance of death, fr. MF (*danse*) *macabré*, (*danse de*) *Macabré*, fr. *Macchabées* Maccabees, 2d–1st cent. B.C. Jewish patriots; prob. fr. their being associated with death because of a passage in 2 Macc (12:43–46) that is important in the development of the concepts of purgatory and prayers for the dead] **1 :** concerned with death or having death as a subject **:** comprising or including a personalized representation of death ⟨German baroque poems containing ~ blazons, describing . . . the parts of the dead body —Leo Spitzer⟩ — compare DANSE MACABRE **2 :** concerned with or dwelling unduly on the grim, grisly, or gruesome **:** designed to produce an effect of horror ⟨a ~ presentation of a tragic story⟩ — often used absolutely ⟨a writer specializing in the ~⟩ **3 :** tending to produce horror in a beholder **:** HORRIBLE, DISTRESSING, UNPLEASANT ⟨this ~ procession of starving peasants⟩ ⟨government couldn't resist the ~ impulse to set down a huge, modern atomic establishment . . . in such an old-time, idyllic spot —Conrad Richter⟩ — **ma·ca·bre·ly** \-b(rə)lē *sometimes* -bə(r)lē\ *adv*

**ma·ca·ca** \mə'käkə\ *n, cap* [NL, fr. Pg, female monkey, fem. of *macaco* monkey] **:** a genus of Old World monkeys consisting of the macaques

**ma·ca·ca·hu·ba** *or* **ma·ca·ca·uba** \mə,käkə'(h)übə\ *n* -s [Pg *Macacaúba*, fr. Tupi] **:** QUIRA

**ma·ca·co** \mə'kä(,)kō\ *n* -s [Pg, fr. a native word in Africa] **1 :** any of various Old World monkeys or lemurs or New World monkeys **2** *obs* **:** MACAQUE

**ma·ca·cus** \mə'kākəs, -käk-\ [NL, fr. Pg *macaco* monkey] *syn of* MACACA

**mac·ad·am** \mə'kadəm\ *n* -s [after John L. *McAdam* †1836 Brit. engineer] **1 :** macadamized roadway or pavement **2 :** the broken stone used in macadamizing

**mac·a·damia** \,makə'dāmēə, -dam-\ *n* [NL, fr. John *Macadam* †1865 Australian chemist born in Scotland + NL *-ia*] **1** *cap* **:** a small genus of Australian evergreen trees (family Proteaceae) including one (*M. ternifolia*) that is widely cultivated in warm regions for its edible nut **2** -s **a** *or* **macadamia tree :** any tree of the genus *Macadamia* **b :** MACADAMIA NUT

**macadamia nut** *n* **:** the hard-shelled nut of the macadamia tree somewhat resembling a filbert and eaten raw or roasted — called also *Queensland nut*

**mac·ad·am·iza·tion** \mə,kadəmə̇'zāshən, -də,mī'z-\ *n* -s **:** the act or process of macadamizing

**mac·ad·am·ize** \mə'kadə,mīz\ *vt* -ED/-ING/-S [*macadam* + *-ize*] **:** to construct or finish (a road) by compacting into a solid mass a layer of small broken stone on a convex well=drained roadbed using fine stone dust and water as a cement or now usu. cement grout or bituminous material as a binder

**macadam road** *n* **:** MACADAM 1; *esp* **:** a road surfaced with a bituminous binder

**ma·ca·na** \mə'känə\ *n* -s [Sp, fr. Taino] **:** a wooden weapon or agricultural tool widely employed by the Indians of So. America and the Antilles, usu. made like a flattened club or sword, and sometimes edged or headed with stone

**mac·a·nese** \¦makə¦nēz, -ēs\ *n, pl* **macanese** *usu cap* [*Macao*, Portuguese colony on the southeastern end of Macao island at the mouth of the Pearl river in southeastern China + E *-nese* (as in *Japanese*)] **:** one of a population of Portuguese-Chinese stock who live in Macao on the coast of southern China

**[1]ma·cao** \mə'kau̇\ *adj, usu cap* [fr. *Macao* city & colony, China] **:** of or from the city or colony of Macao, China **:** of the kind or style prevalent in Macao

**[2]macao** \"\ *n* -s [fr. *Macao* colony] **:** a card game like baccarat except that only one card is dealt to each player

**ma·caque** \mə'kak, -käk\ *n* -s [F, fr. Pg *macaco* — more at MACACO] **:** any of numerous short-tailed Old World monkeys of *Macaca* and related genera having distinct ischial callosities and usu. tufted eyebrows and being found chiefly in southern Asia and the East Indies but including some that range northward into northern China and Japan and others (as the Barbary ape) that extend into northwest Africa and the tip of Europe; *esp* **:** RHESUS

**macaranduba** *var of* MASSARANDUBA

**mac·a·rize** \'makə,rīz\ *vt* -ED/-ING/-S [Gk *makarizein*, fr. *makar, makarios* blessed, happy + *-izein* -ize] **:** to pronounce happy or blessed **:** FELICITATE, LAUD

**mac·a·ro·ni** \,makə'rōnē, -ni\ *n, pl* **macaronis** *or* **macaronies** [It dial. (Naples) *maccarone* dumpling, small cake, macaroni] **1 :** an alimentary paste composed chiefly of semolina dried in the form of slender tubes or small fancy shapes ⟨~ shells⟩ ⟨elbow ~⟩; *esp* **:** tubular alimentary paste having a diameter of .11 to .27 inches — distinguished from *spaghetti;* compare VERMICELLI **2 a :** a member of a class of traveled young Englishmen of the late 18th and early 19th centuries that affected foreign ways **b :** a precious affected young man **:** EXQUISITE, FOP, DANDY ⟨spruce ~*s*, and pretty to see, tidy and dapper and gallant —J.W.Palmer⟩ **c** *or* **macaroni penguin :** ROCK HOPPER **3** *chiefly Austral* **:** something droll or extravagant **:** foolish chatter **:** NONSENSE **4** *slang* **:** ITALIAN

**[1]mac·a·ron·ic** \¦makə¦ränik\ *adj* [NL *macaronicus*, fr. It. dial. *maccarone* dumpling, macaroni (regarded as coarse peasant fare) + L *-icus* -ic] **1** *archaic* **:** having the characteristics of a jumble or medley **:** MIXED ⟨will look on the architecture . . . as belonging to the ~ order —James Dallaway⟩ **2 a :** characterized by a mixture of vernacular words with Latin words or with non-Latin words having Latin endings ⟨many carols are ~ and in them Latin and English . . . are often combined with a syntactical accuracy —E.K.Chambers⟩ **b :** characterized by a mixture of two languages — **mac·a·ron·i·cal·ly** \-nə̇k(ə)lē\ *adv*

**[2]macaronic** \"\ *n* -s **:** macaronic composition or language **:** a confused mixed-up piece of writing

**mac·a·ro·nism** \,makə'rō,nizəm\ *n* -s [*macaroni* + *-ism*] **:** FOPPISHNESS

**macaroni wheat** *n* **:** DURUM WHEAT

**mac·a·roon** \¦makə¦rün\ *n* -s [F *macaron*, fr. It dial. (Naples) *maccarone* dumpling, small cake, macaroni] **1 :** a small cake composed chiefly of the white of eggs, sugar, and ground almonds or almond paste or coconut **2** *obs* **:** MACARONI 1

**ma·cart·ney** \mə̇'kärtnē\ *n* -s *usu cap* [after George, 1st Earl *Macartney* †1806 Brit. diplomat] **1 :** FIREBACK 1 **2 :** MACARTNEY ROSE

**macartney rose** *n, usu cap M* [after George, 1st Earl *Macartney*] **:** a tall-growing rambling Chinese evergreen rose (*Rosa bracteata*) that has hairy branches, strong hooked prickles, and large solitary fragrant white flowers above prominent bracts and that has been introduced into and naturalized in warmer parts of Europe and America

**macassar** *usu cap, var of* MAKASSAR

**macassar agar-agar** *n, usu cap M* [fr. *Macassar* (Makassar) city on southwestern Celebes Island, and strait between Celebes and Borneo, Indonesia] **:** an East Indian agar-agar derived from seaweeds of the genus *Eucheuma* (esp. E. muricatum)

**macassar ebony** *also* **macassar** *n* -s **:** EBONY 1; *esp* **:** the ornately streaked and mottled wood of an East Indian ebony tree (*Diospyros macassar*)

**macassarese** *usu cap, var of* MAKASSARESE

**macassar mace** *n, usu cap 1st M* **:** mace derived from Macassar nutmeg

**macassar nutmeg** *n, usu cap M* **:** the seed of an East Indian tree (*Myristica argentea*) that is sometimes used as an adulterant of or substitute for nutmegs — called also *long nutmeg*

**macassar oil** *n, often cap M* **:** a soft fat obtained from seeds of the kusam and used in cooking, in illumination, and as a hair dressing; *also* **:** any of several similar oils or oily preparations used as hair dressings

**ma·cau·lay·an** \mə'kȯlēən\ *adj, usu cap* [Thomas Babington *Macaulay,* 1st Baron *Macaulay* †1859 English writer and statesman + E *-an*] **:** of, relating to, or resembling the English writer Macaulay ⟨a *Macaulayan* style⟩

**ma·cau·lay·ism** \-ē,izəm\ *n* -s *usu cap* [Thomas B. *Macaulay* + E *-ism*] **:** a Macaulayan style or turn of phrase

**ma·caw** \mə'kȯ\ *n* -s [Pg *macau,* prob fr. *macaúba* macaw palm, on the fruit of which they feed] **:** any of numerous parrots of *Ara* and related genera that are now confined to So. and Central America but were formerly also represented in the West Indies, include some of the largest of parrots, and have a very long tail, a naked space around the eyes, a strong hooked bill with which they crack hard nuts, a harsh voice, and brilliantly and contrastingly colored plumage

**ma·ca·wood** \mə'kä,wu̇d, -kȯ,w-\ *n* [*macacahuba* + *wood*] **:** QUIRA

**macaw palm** *or* **macaw tree** *n* [Pg *macaúba,* fr. Tupi *macahiba, macahuba*] **:** any of several So. American palms of the genus *Acrocomia* with nuts that yield a violet-scented oil used in perfumery and in some cases nutritious edible oils

**mc·bur·ney's point** \mə̇k'bərnēz-, mə|\ *n, usu cap M&B* [after Charles *McBurney* †1913 Am. surgeon] **:** a point on the abdominal wall between the right anterior superior iliac spine and the umbilicus where most pain is elicited by pressure in acute appendicitis

**mac·ca·be·an** *also* **mac·ca·bae·an** \¦makə¦bēən\ *adj, usu cap* **1** [Judas *Maccabaeus,* 2d cent. B.C. Jewish patriot + E *-an*] **:** of or relating to Judas Maccabaeus **2** [*Maccabees* or *Maccabaei* 2d–1st cent. B.C. family of Jewish patriots + E *-an*] **:** of or relating to the Maccabees

**mac·ca·bee** \'makə,bē\ *n, pl* **maccabees** *usu cap* [after *Maccabees,* 2d–1st cent. B.C. family of Jewish patriots] **:** a member of any of various fraternal orders — see KNIGHT OF THE MACCABEES

**mac·ca·boy** \'makə,bȯi\ *also* **mac·ca·baw** \-bȯ\ *or* **ma·cou·ba** \mə'küba\ *n* -s [modif. of F *macouba,* fr. *Macouba,* district in Martinique where it is made] **:** a snuff from Martinique

**mac·ca crab** \'makə-\ *n* [*macca* of unknown origin] *Jamaica* **:** DECORATOR CRAB

**mc·car·thy·ism** \mə'kärthē,izəm *sometimes* -rd·ē-\ *n* -s *usu cap M&2dC* [Joseph R. *McCarthy* †1957 Am. politician + E *-ism*] **:** a political attitude of the mid-twentieth century closely allied to know-nothingism and characterized chiefly by opposition to elements held to be subversive and by the use of tactics involving personal attacks on individuals by means of widely publicized indiscriminate allegations esp. on the basis of unsubstantiated charges

**mc·car·thy·ite** \-ē,īt\ *also* **mc·car·thy·ist** \-ēəst\ *n* -s *usu cap M&2dC* [Joseph R. *McCarthy* + E *-ite* or *-ist*] **:** a person approving of or practicing McCarthyism

**mc·cart·ney rose** \mə'kärtnē-\ *or* **mccartney's rose** *n, usu cap M & 2d C* [after George, 1st Earl *Macartney* †1806 Brit. diplomat] **:** MACARTNEY ROSE

**mc·car·ty** \mə'kärd·ē\ *n* -ES *usu cap M & 2d C* [by folk etymology (influence of the name McCarty) of MexSp *mecate* — more at MECATE] *West* **:** MECATE

**mac·chi** \'mäkē\ *n* -s [It *macchia*] **:** MAQUIS 1

**mac·chia** \'mäkēə\ *n, pl* **mac·chie** \-ē,ā\ [It — more at MAQUIS] **:** MAQUIS 1

**mc·clel·lan saddle** \mə'klelən-\ *also* **mcclellan** *n, usu cap M & 2d C* [after George B. *McClellan* †1885 Am. army officer] **:** a saddle with moderately high leather-covered pommel and cantle developed during the Civil War and long used by the cavalry of the U. S. Army

**mac·cles·field** \'makəlz,fēld, -l,sf-\ *n, usu cap* [fr. *Macclesfield,* England, where it was originally made] **:** a silk with small allover patterns used esp. for neckties

**mc·clin·tock's tables** \mə'klintəks-\ *n pl, usu cap M & 2d T* [after Emory *McClintock* †1916 Am. mathematician and actuary] **:** tables of mortality among annuitants based on the experience of 15 American insurance companies and published in 1896

**mac·co** \'ma(,)kō\ *archaic var of* ²MACAO

**mc·cown's longspur** *also* **mc·cown's bunting** \mə'kau̇nz-\ *n, usu cap M & 2d C* [after John P. *McCown,* 19th cent. Am. army officer] **:** a brownish gray longspur (*Rhynchophanes mccowni*) of central No. America with black markings on head, back, and throat and predominantly white underparts

**mc·coy** \mə'kȯi\ *n* -s, *usu cap M & 2d C* [alter. (influenced by the name *McCoy*) of Sc *Mackay* (in *the real Mackay* the true chief of the Mackay clan — a position often a matter of dispute between the two branches of the clan)] **:** the real or genuine thing **:** something that is neither an imitation nor an inferior substitute — used with the definite article

**mac·cus** \'makəs, 'mak-\ *n, pl* **mac·ci** \-k(,)kē, -ak,sī\ [L, prob. fr. Oscan] **:** a stock character of Roman comedy representing a stupid greedy country fellow

**mc·dou·gall furnace** \mək'dügəl-\ *n, usu cap M&D* [after *McDougall,* 19th cent. Brit. engineer] **:** a roasting furnace consisting of a vertical cylindrical shaft containing several superposed hearths over which ore entering at the top is made to pass consecutively by mechanical rabbles rotating around a central shaft

¹**mace** \'mās\ *n* -s [ME, fr. MF, fr. (assumed) VL *mattia;* akin to L *mateola* mallet, OHG *medela* plow, Skt *matya* harrow] **1 a :** a heavy staff or club made wholly or partly of metal, often spiked, and used esp. in the middle ages for breaking armor **b :** a club used as an offensive weapon ⟨a policeman's ~⟩ **2 :** a staff borne by, carried before, or placed near a magistrate or other dignitary as an ensign of his authority **3 :** MACE-BEARER **4 :** a knobbed mallet used by curriers in dressing leather to make it supple **5 a :** a rod with a flat wooden head formerly used in billiards instead of a cue **b :** a similar rod used in bagatelle

mace 2

²**mace** \"\ *vt* -ED/-ING/-s **:** to strike with or as if with a mace ⟨the boxer *maced* his opponent with a left hook⟩

³**mace** *n* -s [ME *mace, macis,* fr. MF *maci, macis,* fr. L *macir* reddish rind of an Indian root, fr. Gk *makir, makeir*] **1 :** a fragrant and highly aromatic spice consisting of the dried arillode of the nutmeg **2 :** the dried arillode of various other nutmeg trees used as spice — usu. used with a qualifying term ⟨Bombay ~⟩

⁴**mace** \"\ *n, pl* **mace** [Malay *mas, ĕmas* mace, gold, fr. Skt *māṣa* bean, weight] **1** *archaic* **:** a small gold coin of Malaysia **2 :** a Chinese unit of weight and a corresponding unit of value equal to one tenth of a tael

⁵**mace** \"\ *n* -s [origin unknown] **1** *or* **mace·man** \-smən\ *pl* **macemen** *slang* **:** SWINDLER **2** *slang* **:** SWINDLING

⁶**mace** \"\ *vt,* -ED/-ING/-s *slang* **:** CHEAT, SWINDLE; *esp* **:** to force political contributions from (public employees)

**mace-bearer** \'ₛ,ₛₛ\ *n* **:** an officer who carries a mace (as before a dignitary); *esp* **:** the sergeant at arms of the British House of Commons

**mace butter** *n* [³*mace*] **:** NUTMEG BUTTER

**ma·cé·doine** \¦masə¦dwän, -,sä¦-\ *n* -s [F, fr. *Macédoine* Macedonia (perh. in allusion to the mixture of races there)] **1 a :** a mixture of fruits or vegetables cut in pieces and dressed and served as a salad or cocktail in a jellied dessert or in a sauce or garnish **b :** a dish having a garnish of macédoine ⟨a chicken ~⟩ **2 :** a confused mixture **:** MEDLEY

¹**mac·e·do·nian** \¦masə¦dōnēən\ *adj, usu cap* [*Macedonia,* region in the central Balkan peninsula + E *-an*] **:** belonging or relating to Macedonia

²**macedonian** \"\ *n* -s *cap* **1 :** a native or inhabitant of ancient Macedonia **2 a :** a native or inhabitant of modern Macedonia **b :** one that is of Macedonian descent **3 :** the Slavic language of the modern Macedonian people **4 :** the language of ancient Macedonia of uncertain affinity but generally assumed to be Indo-European

³**macedonian** \"\ *n, usu cap* [*Macedonius,* 4th cent. bishop of Constantinople and patriarch of the Eastern Church + E *-an*] **:** a follower of the bishop Macedonius, who held the Holy Ghost to be a creature like the angels and a servant and minister of the Father and the Son

**macedonian cry** *or* **macedonian call** *n, usu cap M* [¹*Macedonian;* fr. the vision of St. Paul at Troas (Acts 16:9) wherein a man appealed to him to go to Macedonia to help the people there] **:** an outcry for help

**macedonian-persian** \¦ₛₛ¦ₛₛ¦ₛₛ¦ₛₛ\ *adj, usu cap M&P* **:** relating to or involving both Macedonia and Persia

**macedonian pine** *n, usu cap M* **:** BALKAN PINE

**mac·e·don·ic** \¦masə¦dänik\ *adj, usu cap* [L *Macedonicus,* fr. Gk *Makedonikos,* fr. *Makedonia* Macedonia + *-ikos* -ic] **:** MACEDONIAN

**mace-head** \'ₛ,ₛ\ *n* **:** MATTOIR

**ma·ceió** \¦masā¦ō\ *adj, usu cap* [fr. *Maceió,* Brazil] **:** of or from the city of Maceió, Brazil **:** of the kind or style prevalent in Maceió

**ma·cel·lum** \mə'seləm\ *n, pl* **macel·la** \-lə\ [L, fr. Gk *makellon* enclosure, meat market, market, fr. Heb *mikhlāh* enclosure, pen] **:** an ancient Roman market or market building; *esp* **:** a meat market

**mace oil** *n* **1 :** an essential oil obtained by distillation from mace and similar in properties to nutmeg oil **2 a :** NUTMEG OIL **a b :** NUTMEG BUTTER

**mac·er** \'māsə(r)\ *n* -s [ME, fr. *mace* + *-er*] **:** MACE-BEARER; *specif* **:** a court officer in Scotland charged with keeping order, executing warrants, and similar duties

**mac·er·al** \'masə,ral\ *n* -s [prob. fr. L *macer* soft, weak + E *-al*] **:** a fragment of plant debris in coal

¹**mac·er·ate** \'masə,rāt, *usu* -ād.+V\ *vb* -ED/-ING/-s [L *maceratus,* past part. of *macerare* to soften, fr. *macer* soft, weak — more at MEAGER] *vt* **1 :** to cause (the body or its flesh) to waste away by or as if by excessive fasting **2 a :** to cause (solid matter) to become soft or separated into constituent elements by steeping in fluid ⟨flax *macerated* in water⟩ ⟨fibrous food *macerating* in the cow's rumen⟩ **b :** to cause (a solid object) to soften and fray as if long soaked in water ⟨a mallet with ends *macerated* by pounding⟩ ~ *vi* **:** to soften and wear away esp. as a result of being wetted or steeped

²**mac·er·ate** \'masərət\ *n* -s **:** a product of macerating **:** something prepared by maceration ⟨examining the chromosomes in a liver ~⟩ — compare HOMOGENATE

**mac·er·a·tion** \,masə'rāshən\ *n* -s [L *maceration-, maceratio,* fr. *maceratus* + *-ion-, -io* -ion] **1 :** an act or the process of macerating something: **a :** a process of extracting fragrant oils that is similar to enfleurage but differs in the use of hot fat in which the flower petals are immersed **b :** the extraction of a drug by allowing it to stand in contact with a solvent **2 :** the condition of being macerated ⟨the fetus was recovered in an advanced state of ~⟩

**mac·er·a·tive** \'masə,rād·iv\ *adj* **:** characterized or accompanied by maceration ⟨~ degeneration of tissue⟩

**mac·er·a·tor** \-ād·ə(r)\ *n* -s **:** one that macerates; *esp* **:** an apparatus for converting paper or fibrous matter into pulp

**maces** *pl of* MACE, *pres 3d sing of* MACE

**mac·far·lane** \mək'färlən\ *n* -s *often cap M & sometimes cap F* [prob fr. the name *MacFarlane*] **:** a heavy caped overcoat with slit sides

macfarlane

**mac·gil·li·vray's warbler** \mə'gilə,vrāz-\ *n, usu cap M* [after William *MacGillivray* †1852 Scot. naturalist] **:** a warbler (*Oporornis tolmiei*) of western No. America that is similar and closely related to the eastern mourning warbler

**mc·gov·ern·ite** \mə'gəvə(r),nīt\ *n* -s *often cap M&G* [J.J. *McGovern* †1915 Am. mine foreman + E *-ite*] **:** a mineral $Mn_5(AsO_3)_2SiO_3(OH)_2$ consisting of a basic silicate and arsenite of manganese that is found at Sterling Hill, N.J.

**mach** *n* -s *usu cap* [by shortening] **:** MACH NUMBER

**mach** *abbr* machine; machinery; machinist

**mach·ae·rid·ia** \,makə'ridēə\ *n pl, cap* [NL, fr. L *machaera* sword, dagger (fr. Gk *machaira*) + NL *-idia*] **:** a small group of Ordovician and Devonian animal fossils that are wormlike and bilaterally symmetrical but enclosed by plates suggesting those of echinoderms, are considered structurally comparable to the dipleurula and ancestral to modern echinoderms, being then made a class of Echinodermata, or are regarded as aberrant barnacles and included among the Cirripedia

**ma·chae·ro·dus** \mə'kirədəs, -ker-\ *syn of* MACHAIRODUS

**mach·air** *or* **mach·ar** \'makər\ *n* -s [ScGael *machair* & IrGael *machaire*] *Scot & Irish* **:** a flat or low-lying plain or field

¹**ma·chai·ro·dont** \mə'kīrə,dänt\ *also* **ma·chae·ro·dont** \-kir-,ker-\ *adj* [*machairodont,* fr. Gk *machaira* sword, dagger + E *-odont; machaerodont,* fr. L *machaera* sword, dagger (fr. Gk *machaira*) + E *-odont*] **:** of or relating to the genus *Machairodus* **:** like a saber-toothed tiger **:** SABER-TOOTHED

²**machairodont** \"\ *also* **machaerodont** \"\ *n* -s **:** a member of the genus *Machairodus* **:** SABER-TOOTHED TIGER

**ma·chai·ro·dus** \-,dəs\ *n, cap* [NL, fr. Gk *machaira* sword, dagger + NL *-odus*] **:** a genus of extinct felid mammals distinguished by extreme development of the canine teeth, comprising the saber-tooth tigers, and usu. considered to constitute a subfamily of Felidae or in some classifications a distinct family

**ma·chan** *or* **ma·chaan** \mə'chän\ *n* -s [Hindi *macān* platform, scaffold, fr. Skt *mañca*] *India* **:** a platform (as in a tree) used for observation in tiger hunting

**ma·chan·cha** \mə'chänchə\ *n* -s [AmerSp] **:** a venomous Peruvian snake (*Bothrops barnetti*) related to the fer-de-lance

**mach angle** \'mäk-, 'mak-\ *n, usu cap M* [after Ernst *Mach* †1916 Austrian physicist and philosopher] **:** half of the vertex angle of a Mach cone whose sine is the ratio of the speed of sound to the speed of a moving body

**mach cone** *n, usu cap M* [after Ernst *Mach*] **:** the conical pressure wave front produced by a body moving at a speed greater than that of sound

**mache** *n* -s [by shortening and alter.] **:** PAPIER-MÂCHÉ

**ma·cheer** \mə'chi(ə)r\ *n* -s [modif. of Sp *mochila* — more at *mochila*] *West* **:** MOCHILA

**ma·chete** \mə'shed|ē, -'che| *sometimes* -shā| *or* -chā| *or* -shet

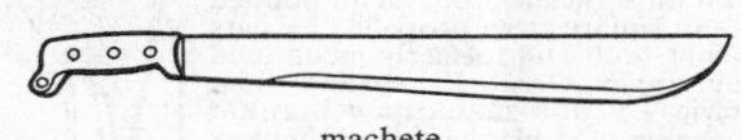

machete

*or* +V -shed·\ *n* -s [Sp *machete*] **1** *also* **ma·chette** \-shet, +V -ed·\ *or* **match·et** \'machət, +V -əd·\ **:** a large heavy knife usu. made with a blade resembling a broadsword often two or three feet in length and used esp. in So. America and the West Indies for cutting cane and clearing paths **2 :** a small four-stringed Portuguese guitar that is the forerunner of the ukulele

¹**ma·chi** \'mächē\ *n* -s [Jap, town, city] **:** a Japanese town or commercial center; *esp* **:** the lowest administrative division which is coordinate with the purely rural mura

²**machi** \"\ *n* -s [AmerSp, fr. Araucan *machi, mache*] **:** an Araucanian shaman, usu. female

**mach·i·a·vel** \'makēə,vel *sometimes* ¦mäk- *or* ¦mak-\ *n* -s *usu cap* [after Niccolò *Machiavelli* †1527 Italian statesman and political philosopher] **:** MACHIAVELLIAN

¹**mach·i·a·vel·li·an** \¦ₛₛₛ¦velēən, -lyən\ *adj, usu cap* [Niccolò *Machiavelli* + E *-an*] **1 :** of or relating to Machiavelli or his political theory (as the doctrine that any means however lawless or unscrupulous may be justifiably employed by a ruler in order to establish and maintain a strong central government) **2 :** resembling or suggesting the principles of conduct laid down by Machiavelli **:** characterized by political cunning, duplicity, or bad faith

²**machiavellian** *n* -s *usu cap* **:** an adherent to the political doctrine of Machiavelli **:** a person characterized by Machiavellian behavior esp. in political matters

**mach·i·a·vel·li·an·ism** \,ₛₛₛ'velēə,nizəm, -lyə,n-\ *n* -s *usu cap* **:** the political doctrine of Machiavelli

**mach·i·a·vel·li·an·ist** \-,nəst\ *n* -s *usu cap* **:** MACHIAVELLIAN

**mach·i·a·vel·li·an·ly** \¦ₛₛₛ¦velēənlē, -lyə-, -li\ *adv, usu cap* **:** in a Machiavellian manner

**mach·i·a·vel·lic** \¦ₛₛₛ¦velik, -lēk\ *adj, usu cap* [Niccolò *Machiavelli* + E *-ic*] **:** MACHIAVELLIAN

**mach·i·a·vel·lism** \-¦ve,lizəm\ *n* -s *usu cap* [Niccolò *Machiavelli* + E *-ism*] **:** MACHIAVELLIANISM

**ma·chic·o·late** \mə'chikə,lāt, ma'-\ *vt* -ED/-ING/-s [ML *machicolatus,* past part. of *machicolare,* fr. OF *machicoller,* fr. *machicoleis* machicolation, fr. *macher* to crush (of imit. origin) + *col* neck, fr. L *collum* — more at COLLAR] **:** to furnish (as a turret) with machicolations

**ma·chic·o·la·tion** \mə,chikə'lāshən, (,)ma,ch-\ *n* -s **1 a :** an opening between the corbels that support a projecting parapet or in the floor of a gallery or the roof of a portal for shooting or dropping missiles upon assailants attacking below **b :** a parapet containing such openings — see BATTLEMENT illustration **2 :** a construction imitating medieval machicolation

**ma·chi·co·tage** \¦mashəkō¦täzh\ *n* -s [F, fr. *machicoter* to embellish plain song (fr. *machicot,* a former choir official in the chapter of Notre Dame in Paris, France) + F *-age*] **:** the embellishment of the solo part of plain song by the insertion of ornaments between the authentic tones

**ma·chi·cou·lis** \¦mäshə(,)kü¦lē, ¦mash-, ₛₛₛ'külē\ *n, pl* **ma·chi·cou·lis** \-lē(z)\ *or* **machicou·lises** \-lēz\ [F *mâchicoulis, mâchecoulis,* fr. MF *machecoulis, machecoulis,* alter. of OF *machicoleis* — more at MACHICOLATE] **:** MACHICOLATION

**-machies** *pl of* -MACHY

**ma·chi·guen·ga** \,mächə'geŋgə\ *n, pl* **machiguenga** *or* **machiguengas** *usu cap* [Sp, of AmerInd origin] **1 a :** an Arawakan people of southern Peru **b :** a member of such people **2 :** the language of the Machiguenga people

**ma·chi·la** *also* **ma·chil·la** \mə'shēlə\ *n* -s [Pg, perh. fr. Tamil *macil, mañcil* stage in a journey, fr. Hindi *manzil,* fr. Ar] **:** a hammock slung on a pole used for carrying passengers in many parts of Africa

**ma·chil·i·dae** \mə'kilə,dē\ *n pl, cap* [NL, fr. *Machilis,* type genus + *-idae*] **:** a cosmopolitan family of primitive insects (order Thysanura) with dorsally convex body, contiguous compound eyes, and three ocelli

**ma·chi·lis** \mə'kiləs, 'makəl-\ *n, cap* [NL] **:** an Old World genus of very primitive insects that is the type of the family Machilidae

**machilla** *var of* MOCHILA

**ma·chin** \mə'chēn\ *n* -s [Tag *matsing*] **:** a grayish brown long-tailed macaque (*Macaca philippinensis*) of the Philippines

**ma·chin·abil·i·ty** \mə,shēnə'biləd·ē, -lətē, -i\ *n* **:** the quality or state of being machinable

**ma·chin·able** *also* **ma·chine·able** \mə'shēnəbəl\ *adj* **:** capable of or suitable for being machined

**machi·nal** \mə'shēnᵊl, 'makən-\ *adj* [L *machinalis,* fr. *machina* machine + *-alis* -al] *archaic* **:** of or relating to machines **:** MECHANICAL

**mach·i·nate** \'makə,nāt, ÷'mashə-, ÷'maash-, ÷'maish-, *usu* -ād.+V\ *vb* -ED/-ING/-s [L *machinatus,* past part. of *machinari,* fr. *machina* machine, plan, trick, artifice — more at MACHINE] *vi* **:** PLOT, SCHEME, CONTRIVE ~ *vt* **:** to scheme or contrive to bring (something undesirable) about **:** plan to do (something harmful) **:** PLOT

**mach·i·na·tion** \,ₛₛ'nāshən\ *n* -s [L *machination-, machinatio,* fr. *machinatus* + *-ion-, -io* -ion] **1 :** an act or instance of machinating **2 :** a scheming or crafty action, subtle maneuver, or artful design intended to accomplish some end; *esp* **:** one regarded as evil or reprehensible — usu. used in pl. ⟨thwart the vast insidious ~s of some baffled fiend —George Santayana⟩ **3** *obs* **:** use or construction of machinery; *also* **:** a mechanical appliance **syn** see PLOT

**mach·i·na·tor** \'ₛₛ,nād·ə(r), -ātə-\ *n* -s [L, fr. *machinatus* + *-or*] **:** one that machinates **:** a plotter or artful schemer

¹**ma·chine** \mə'shēn\ *n* -s [MF, fr. L *machina,* fr. Gk (Dor dial.) *machana* (Attic *mēchanē*), fr. (Dor dial.) *machos* means, expedient (Attic *mēchos*) — more at MAY] **1 a** *archaic* **:** a structure or constructed thing whether material or immaterial **:** ERECTION, HANDIWORK **b** (1) *archaic* **:** SHIP, BOAT (2) **:** CONVEYANCE, VEHICLE ⟨brought his ~ to a halt with a flourish⟩ **c** *obs* **:** APPLIANCE, DEVICE **d** *archaic* **:** a military engine (as a siege tower or catapult) **e :** any of various apparatuses formerly used in the production of theatrical stage effects **f** (1) **:** an assemblage of parts that are usu. solid bodies but include in some cases fluid bodies or electricity in conductors and that transmit forces, motion, and energy one to another in some predetermined manner and to some desired end (as for sewing a seam, printing a newspaper, hoisting a load, or maintaining an electric current) (2) **:** an instrument (as a lever) designed to transmit or modify the application of power, force, or motion (3) **:** a mechanical device of the particular kind relevant or under consideration ⟨run up the seams on the ~⟩ (4) *Brit* **:** a power-driven printing press ⟨in the printing office the hand press is spoken of as the "press" and the machine press as the "~" —John Southward⟩ **2 a :** a living organism or one of its functional systems ⟨the intricate hearing ~ of the bat⟩ **:** bodily mechanism — used esp. when the whole is thought of as a system of more or less mechanically interacting parts ⟨disease alters the balance of the human ~⟩ **b :** a person or organization that acts like a machine esp. in responding automatically and without intelligence or feeling or as though responding mechanically to activating stimuli ⟨thought of the lower animals as mere ~s without sense or sensibility⟩ ⟨making ~s of men⟩ **c** (1) **:** a combination of persons acting together (as for a common end) together with the agencies they use ⟨the entire social ~⟩ ⟨building a powerful war ~⟩ (2) **:** a highly organized group that, under the leadership of a boss or a small clique, controls the policies and activities of a political party esp. for private rather than for public ends **3 :** a literary device or contrivance (as a supernatural agency) introduced for dramatic effect; *also* **:** an agency so introduced

**syn** MACHINE, ENGINE, APPARATUS, APPLIANCE signify, in common, a device, often complex, for doing work beyond human physical or mental limitations or faster than human hand or mind. MACHINE applies to a construction or organization whose parts are so connected and interrelated that it can be set in motion and perform work as a unit ⟨those most practical *machines* of our modern life, the dynamo and the telephone —Havelock Ellis⟩ ⟨calculators, billers, duplicators, and other business *machines*⟩ ⟨the finest *machine* in the world is useless without a motor to drive it —C.C.Furnas⟩ ⟨was by no means a cold and calculating thinking *machine* —W.L.Sperry⟩ Although in an earlier and still common use ENGINE can signify any device or contrivance to multiply force or speed ⟨metal-wheeled chariots . . . soon appeared as the newest and most powerful *engines* of war —R.W.Murray⟩ ⟨television, our newest and potentially greatest *engine* of enlightenment —Gilbert Seldes⟩ more generally ENGINE applies to a particular kind of machine, usu. one which turns one form of physical power into another more useful, sometimes, however, applying to both a power-generating unit and the total working unit moved by the power unit ⟨gasoline *engines*⟩ ⟨airplane *engines*⟩ ⟨these *engines* were built to pump out mines —C.F.Kettering & Allen Orth⟩ ⟨a fire *engine*⟩ ⟨a steam *engine* pulling a hundred cars⟩ APPARATUS is more general than the other words, applying to any more or less complicated mechanism or unit of organization for effecting a given work, whose parts may be many or few, delicate or crude ⟨*apparatus* (heavy generators, transformers, etc)—*Time*⟩ ⟨substances such as glass, crystal, and flint are linked with *apparatuses* of one kind or another (compasses, barometers, spectrums, and hourglasses) —Louise Bogan⟩ ⟨a table . . . covered with his writing *apparatus* —Osbert Sitwell⟩ ⟨a professional historical journal . . . equipped with an *apparatus* of footnotes —*Times Lit. Supp.*⟩ ⟨the pipes, fixtures, and other *apparatus* inside buildings for bringing in the water supply and removing the liquid and water-borne wastes —*Water & Sewage Control Engineering*⟩ APPLIANCE is often interchangeable with APPARATUS but usu. designates a simple useful machine the power for which can be supplied readily, commonly, therefore, suggesting the electrical appliance ⟨sometimes a bow is drawn with the assistance of the feet, or of a ring-handled dagger, or other *appliance* —*Notes & Queries on Anthropology*⟩ ⟨among those *appliances* reflecting the greatest sales increases were driers and freezers —*Dun's Rev.*⟩ ⟨vacuum cleaners and home *appliances*⟩

**²machine** \"\ *vb* -ED/-ING/-S *vt* **1 :** to subject to or produce or finish by the action of machinery: as **a :** to turn, shape, plane, mill, or otherwise reduce or finish (as a metal blank or casting) by machine-operated cutting tools **b** *Brit* **:** to print with a power-driven press **2 :** to fashion as if by machinery **:** cause to conform to a fixed pattern **:** STANDARDIZE **~** *vi* **:** to be machinable ⟨brass ~s easily⟩

**ma·chine·able** \-nəbəl\ *var of* MACHINABLE

**machine bolt** *n* **:** a metal rod with a usu. square or hexagonal wrench head at one end and threads at the other that is commonly available in a size range of from ¼ inch to 3 inches in diameter — see BOLT illustration

**machine buff** *n* **:** a cut of leather from which a thin layer of the grain surface has been removed leaving a portion of the grain and which is used esp. for upholstery

**machine calender** *n* **:** a calender stack with all metal rolls placed in the line of flow of the paper between the driers and the winder — compare SUPERCALENDER

**machine cannon** *n* **:** MACHINE GUN; *esp* **:** one using projectiles larger than used in small arms

**machine carbine** *n* **:** an automatic carbine **:** SUBMACHINE GUN

**machine chest** *n* **:** the chest that in papermaking holds the stock coming from the jordan and ready to go to the paper machine

**machine-coated** \=¦=¦==\ *adj, of paper* **:** coated on a paper machine as an integral part of the papermaking operation and not on a separate machine

**machined** *adj* **:** made or finished by or as if by machine

**machine direction** *n* **:** the direction in which the stock flows onto the paper machine wire **:** the circumferential direction of a roll of paper; *also* **:** the corresponding dimension of a sheet cut from it — called also *grain, grain direction;* compare CROSS DIRECTION

**machine-dried** \=¦=¦=\ *adj, of paper* **:** completely dried by contact with steam-heated drums

**machine file** *n* **:** a file with the tang replaced by a round shank designed to be clamped in the chuck of a power-driven machine

**machine finish** *n* **:** a moderately smooth finish applied to book and cover papers by passing them through the calender rolls of a paper machine — abbr *M.F.*

**machine-glazed** \=¦=¦=\ *adj, of paper* **:** given a high finish on one side only by drying the web in continuous contact with a highly polished heated cylinder (as of a Yankee machine) — abbr. *M.G.*

**machine gun** *n* **:** an automatic gun firing small-arms ammunition that has a cooling device which permits delivery of sustained fire for relatively long periods and a highly stable mount which permits fire over masks and friendly troops — compare AUTOMATIC RIFLE

**machine-gun** \=¦=¦=\ *vb* [*machine gun*] *vt* **:** to shoot at or kill with a machine gun **~** *vi* **:** to fire a machine gun

**machine gunner** *n* **:** a member of a crew that serves a machine gun **:** an operator of a machine gun

**machine-hour** \=¦=¦=\ *n* **:** the operation of one machine for one hour used as a basis for cost finding and for determining operating effectiveness

**ma·chine·less** \mə'shēnləs\ *adj* **:** lacking or done without machines; *esp, of a permanent wave* **:** prepared without use of curlers attached to a heating unit **:** COLD-WAVED

**machinelike** \=ˈ=,=\ *adj* **:** resembling a machine esp. in precise regularity of action or stereotyped uniformity of product

**ma·chine·ly** \mə'shēnlē\ *adv* **:** as if by a machine

**machine-made** \=¦=¦=\ *adj* **1 :** made by machinery — distinguished from *handmade* **2 :** STEREOTYPED, MECHANICAL

**ma·chine·man** \mə'shēnmən, -n,man\ *n, pl* **machinemen :** one who operates or tends a machine: as **a** *Brit* **:** PRESSMAN **b :** an operator of a rock drill

**machine manager** *or* **machine minder** *n, Brit* **:** PRESSMAN

**machine operator** *n* **:** a worker assigned to or skilled in the operation of a particular kind or class of industrial machine — sometimes distinguished from *machinist*

**machine pistol** *n* **:** a light inexpensive submachine gun

**machine rest** *n*: a fixed support for holding a firearm while it is fired (as for determining the accuracy of the weapon or checking ammunition loadings)

**machine rifle** *n* **:** AUTOMATIC RIFLE

**machine room** *n, Brit* **:** a printing pressroom

**ma·chin·ery** \mə'shēn(ə)rē, -ri\ *n* -ES [¹*machine* + *-ery*] **1 :** machines as a functioning unit: as **a** *obs* **:** a setup of machines for producing theatrical stage effects **b** (1) **:** the constituent parts of a machine or instrument **:** WORKS ⟨a fine watch with precise and delicate ~⟩ (2) **:** equipment, stock, or range of machines ⟨the ~ at the mill⟩ ⟨modern textile ~⟩ **c** *archaic* **:** the machines introduced into a literary work (as a poem) **2 a :** the means and appliances by which something is kept in action or a desired result is obtained ⟨the ~ of the human body⟩ ⟨the ~ of communications⟩ **b :** the system of instrumentalities and organized activities by means of which an organization functions or a social or other process is carried on ⟨the complex ~ of modern society⟩ ⟨the ~ of negotiation⟩; *esp* **:** the apparatus of government ⟨the United Nations set up ~ for mediation⟩ **syn** see EQUIPMENT

**machine screw** *n* **:** a screw with slotted head or socket head used for holding metal parts together

**machine shop** *n* **:** a workshop in which work is machined to size and assembled

**machine steel** *also* **machinery steel** *n* **:** steel of a grade suitable for the working parts of machines — distinguished from *tool steel*

**machine tap** *n* **:** a tap operated by machinery

**machine telegraphy** *n* **:** a system of telegraphy employing an automatic transmitter **:** automatic telegraphy

**machine tender** *n* **:** the working supervisor of a papermaking machine

**machine tool** *n* **:** a usu. power-driven machine designed for shaping solid work by tooling either by removing material (as in a lathe or milling machine) or by subjecting to deformation (as in a punch press) ⟨the *machine tool* industry⟩ ⟨heavy-duty *machine tools*⟩

**machine-tooled** \=¦=¦=\ *adj* **:** made or finished with or as if with a machine tool **:** finely and precisely finished or shaped ⟨a *machine-tooled* accuracy of statement⟩

**machining** *n* -s **1 :** an act or instance of running a machine (as a sewing machine or printing press) **2 :** machine work

**ma·chin·ism** \mə'shē,nizəm\ *n* -s [¹*machine* + *-ism*] **:** preoccupation with or dependence on machines (as in economics or politics)

**ma·chin·ist** \-nəst\ *n* -s [prob. fr. F *machiniste*, fr. *machine* + *-iste* -ist] **1 a** (1) *archaic* **:** an inventor or builder of machines (2) **:** a worker who fabricates, assembles, or repairs machinery **b :** a craftsman skilled in the use of machine tools — sometimes distinguished from *machine operator* **c :** MACHINE OPERATOR **2** *archaic* **:** a person in charge of the mechanical aspects of a theatrical production (as lighting, technical machines, and handling of scenery) **3 :** a member of a political machine **4 a :** MACHINIST'S MATE **b :** a warrant officer (as in the U.S. Navy) whose specialty is supervision of the operation, maintenance, and repair of machinery and engines

**machinist's hammer** *n* **:** a cross-peen, ball-peen, or straight-peen hammer

**machinist's mate** *n* **:** a petty officer in the engineer's department of the U. S. Navy

**ma·chin·ize** \mə'shē,nīz\ *vt* -ED/-ING/-S [¹*machine* + *-ize*] **:** to make like a machine **:** convert or organize into a machine ⟨the *machinizing* of party politics⟩

**ma·chi·no·fac·ture** \mə'shēnō,fakchə(r), -ksh-\ *n* -s [¹*machine* + *-o-* + *-facture* (as in *manufacture*)] **1 :** making or building by means of machines **2 :** a product of machine activity

**mach·ism** \'mä,kizəm, -k̟-\ *n* -s *usu cap* [Ernst *Mach* †1916 Austrian physicist and philosopher + E *-ism*] **:** the theories of the physicist and philosopher Mach; *specif* **:** his empiriocriticism

**mach·me·ter** *pronunc at* MACH NUMBER+,mēd·ə(r)\ *n, usu cap* [*mach* + *-meter*] **:** an airspeed indicator calibrated to read Mach number directly

**mach number** \'mäk-, 'mȧk- *sometimes chiefly Brit* 'mak-\ *n, usu cap M* [after Ernst *Mach*] **:** a number representing the ratio of the speed of a body to the speed of sound in the surrounding atmosphere ⟨for subsonic speeds the *Mach number* is less than 1 (as 0.80) and for supersonic speeds it is greater than 1 (as 1.31 or 5)⟩

**macho·polyp** *or* **macho·zooid** \¦makō+\ *n* [Gk *machē* battle, fight + *-o-* E *polyp* or *zooid* — more at -MACHY] **:** a defensive zooid of a hydroid colony, having an abundance of stinging organs but no mouth

**ma·chree** \mə'krē\ *n* -s [IrGael *mo chroidhe* my heart, my dear] *Irish* **:** my dear

**macht·po·li·tik** \'mäkt,pōlē,tēk, -äkt-\ *n* -s [G, fr. *macht* power (fr. OHG *maht*) + *politik* politics, fr. F *politique* — more at MIGHT, POLITICS] **:** POWER POLITICS; *specif* **:** a doctrine in political theory advocating the use of power and esp. of physical force by a political state in the attainment of its objectives ⟨an internationalism based on realpolitik and ~ —*New Republic*⟩ — compare REALPOLITIK

**mach wave** *n, usu cap M* [after Ernst *Mach* †1916 Austrian physicist and philosopher] **:** the envelope of wave fronts propagated from an infinitesimal disturbance in a supersonic flow field

**-ma·chy** \məkē, -ki\ *n comb form* -ES [Gk *-machia*, fr. *machē* battle, fight (fr. *machesthai* to battle, fight) + *-ia* -y] **:** warfare **:** contest between or by means of ⟨*logomachy*⟩

**machy** *abbr* machinery

**machzor** *var of* MAHZOR

**m acid** *n, usu cap M* **:** a crystalline sulfonic acid $NH_2C_{10}H_5(OH)SO_3H$ made by alkaline fusion of a disulfonic acid of alpha-naphthylamine and used as a dye intermediate; 5-amino-1-naphthol-3-sulfonic acid

**ma·ci·gno** \mə'chēn(,)yō\ *n* -s [It, millstone, flysch, fr. (assumed) VL *machineus*, fr. L *machina* machine — more at MACHINE] **:** FLYSCH

**ma·ci·len·cy** \'masələnsē\ *also* **mac·i·lence** \-n(t)s\ *n, pl* **macilencies** *also* **macilenc·es :** macilent condition; *esp* **:** leanness of body

**mac·i·lent** \-nt\ *adj* [L *macilentus*, fr. *macies* leanness — more at EMACIATE] **:** THIN, EMACIATED, LEAN

**macing** *pres part of* MACE

**mc·in·tire** \'makən,tī(ə)r\ *n* -s *usu cap M&I* [after Samuel *McIntyre* †1811 Am. architect and woodcarver] **:** a style of late 18th and early 19th century American furniture and interior architecture distinguished by the discreet use of carving esp. on vertical elements and the employment of rich veneering

**macintosh** *var of* MACKINTOSH

**¹mack** *interj* [perh. euphemism for (*Saint*) *Mary*] *obs* — used as a mild oath

**²mack** \'mak\ *n* -s [prob. modif. of F *maquereau*, fr. OF *makerel* — more at MACKEREL] *slang* **:** PIMP ⟨accomplished courtesans were attended by their . . . ~s — Herbert Asbury⟩

**³mack** *var of* MAC

**mackallow** *n* -s [ScGael *macaladh* fostering after being weaned] *obs Scot* **:** goods held in trust by a foster parent for a child

**mc·kay** \mə'kā\ *adj, usu cap M&K* [after Gordon *McKay* †1903 Am. inventor and industrialist] **:** of, relating to, or used in the McKay process

**mack·ay·ite** \'makē,īt\ *n* -s [John W. *MacKay* †1902 Am. miner and financier + E *-ite*] **:** a mineral $Fe_2(TeO_3)_3.nH_2O$(?) consisting of a hydrous tellurite of iron

**mc·kay process** \mə'kā-\ *n, usu cap M&K* [after Gordon *McKay*] **:** a process of shoe manufacture in which the outsole is sewn to the insole, the needle going through outsole, shoe upper, lining, and insole and forming a chain stitch

**¹mack·er·el** \'mak(ə)rəl\ *n, pl* **mackerel** *or* **mackerels** [ME *makerel*, fr. OF, prob. fr. *makerel* pimp, modif. of MD *makelaer* go-between, broker, pimp, fr. *makelen* to act as go-between, broker or pimp (fr. *maken* to make, do) + *-aer* -er; fr. the belief that mackerel act as pimps for the herring in the schools they accompany — more at MAKE] **1 a :** a fish (*Scomber scombrus*) of the No. Atlantic that is green above with dark blue bars and silvery below, reaches a length of about 18 inches, and in both Europe and America is one of the most important food fishes, being caught chiefly when it leaves the high seas and approaches the coasts in great schools to spawn — see BLINKER, SPIKE, TINKER **b :** a fish of the suborder Scombroidea; *esp* **:** a comparatively small member of this group as distinguished from a bonito or tuna **2 :** any of various fishes more or less resembling members of the Scombroidea — usu. used with a qualifying term ⟨snake ~⟩ ⟨horse ~⟩ ⟨Atka ~⟩

**²mackerel** \"\ *adj* **:** TICKED — used esp. of a coat pattern of tabby cats in which the dark bars are not solid

**³mackerel** *n* -s [ME *makerel*, fr. MF — more at ¹MACKEREL] *obs* **:** PIMP

**mackerel-back** \'=(=)=,=\ *or* **mackerel-backed sky** \'=(=)=,=-\ *n* **:** MACKEREL SKY

**mackerel bait** *n* **:** jellyfish and other small oceanic creatures on which mackerel feed

**mackerel bird** *n* **1** *Brit* **:** WRYNECK **2** *Brit* **:** a young kittiwake

**mackerel breeze** *or* **mackerel gale** *n* **:** a wind that ruffles the water and is held to favor the catching of mackerel with hook and line

**mackerel cock** *n, Irish* **:** MANX SHEARWATER

**mack·er·el·er** \'mak(ə)rələ(r)\ *n* -s **:** a fisherman or boat engaged in mackerel fishing

**mackerel goose** *n* **:** PHALAROPE

**mackerel gull** *n* **:** TERN

**mack·er·el·ing** \'mak(ə)rəliŋ\ *n* -s **:** mackerel fishing

**mackerel midge** *n* **:** the young of various rocklings

**mackerel scad** *also* **mackerel shad** *n* **:** any of several small carangid fishes of a cosmopolitan genus (*Decapterus*); *esp* **:** a common western Atlantic fish (*D. macarellus*) that is of a silvery color and plumbeous below

**mackerel scale** *n* **:** any of the somewhat angular cloudlets forming one variety of mackerel sky

**mackerel shark** *n* **:** a shark of the family Lamnidae esp. of the genus *Isurus*; *specif* **:** PORBEAGLE — see BONITO SHARK

**mackerel sky** *n* **:** a sky covered with rows of altocumulus or cirrocumulus clouds resembling the patterns on a mackerel's back

**mackerel tuna** *n* **:** LITTLE TUNA

**mack·ie line** \'makē-\ *n, usu cap M* [after Alexander *Mackie*, 19th cent. scientist] **:** a light outline at the edge of dense or dark parts of a photographic image caused by a retardation of development in the edge area — compare ADJACENCY EFFECT

**mack·i·naw** \'makə,nȯ\ *n* -s *sometimes cap* [fr. *Mackinaw* City, Michigan, formerly the site of an important trading post] **1** *or* **mackinaw boat :** a flat-bottomed boat with pointed prow and square stern propelled by oars or sails or both and formerly much used on the upper Great Lakes and their tributaries **2** *also* **mackinaw blanket :** a heavy woolen blanket in solid colors or stripes formerly distributed by the U.S. government to the Indians **3 a** *also* **mackinaw cloth :** a heavy single or double cloth of wool or wool and other fibers often with face and back of different colors or with a plaid design and usu. heavily napped and felted for warmth **b** *also* **mackinaw coat :** a short usu. double-breasted and belted coat or jacket of mackinaw or similar heavy fabric — called also *blanket-coat* **4** *usu* **mackinaw trout :** LAKE TROUT b

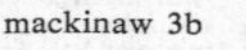
mackinaw 3b

**mack·i·nawed** \-ȯd\ *adj* **:** dressed in a mackinaw

**mc·kin·ley·ism** \mə'kinlē,izəm\ *n* -s *usu cap 1st M&K* [William *McKinley* †1901, 25th president of the U.S.] **:** the political policies advocated by or associated with William McKinley

**mack·in·tosh** *also* **mac·in·tosh** \'makən,täsh\ *n* -ES [after Charles *Macintosh* †1843 Scot. chemist and inventor] **1** *chiefly Brit* **:** RAINCOAT **2 :** a lightweight waterproof fabric orig. of rubberized cotton

**mack·in·toshed** \-sht\ *adj* **:** dressed in a mackintosh

**mack·in·tosh·ite** \-ä,shīt\ *n* -s [James B. *Mackintosh* †1891 Am. chemist + E *-ite*] **:** an altered metamict uranothorite

**¹mack·le** \'makəl\ *n* -s [F *macule*, spot, stain, mackle, fr. L *macula* spot, stain] **:** a blur or double impression on a printed sheet

**²mackle** \"\ *vb* -ED/-ING/-S **:** BLUR

**mack's cement** \'mak(s)-\ *n, usu cap M* [after L. *Mack*, 19th cent. scientist] **:** a cementing material made by the complete dehydration of gypsum and the addition of a small percentage of calcined sodium sulfate and potassium sulfate

**ma·cle** \'makəl\ *n* -s [F, wide-meshed net, mascle, macle, fr. OF, mesh, lozenge voided — more at MASCLE] **1 :** CHIASTOLITE **2 a :** a twinned crystal **b :** a flat often triangular diamond that is usu. a twinned crystal **3 :** a dark or discolored spot (as in a mineral specimen)

**mac·leaya** \mə'klāə\ *n, cap* [NL, after Alexander *MacLeay* †1848 Brit. entomologist and colonial statesman] **:** a genus of Asiatic herbs (family Papaveraceae) with pinnately lobed glaucous leaves and tall showy panicles of cream-colored apetalous flowers — see PLUME POPPY

**ma·cled** \'makəld\ *adj* **1** *of a mineral* **:** marked like chiastolite **2** *of a crystal* **:** having a twin structure **3 :** SPOTTED — used chiefly of minerals

**mc·leod** \mə'klau̇d\ *or* **mcleod tool** *n* -s [fr. the name *McLeod*] **:** a combination hoe and rake used esp. by the U.S. Forest Service in fire fighting

**mcleod gauge** *n, usu cap M&L* [after Herbert *McLeod* †1923 Eng. chemist] **:** a sensitive instrument for measuring the pressure of a highly rarefied gas by compressing a portion of the gas in a closed capillary tube and applying Boyle's law

**ma·clu·ra** \mə'klu̇rə\ *n* -s [NL, after William *Maclure* †1840 Am. geologist] **:** OSAGE ORANGE

**ma·clu·rin** \-rən\ *n* -s [ISV *maclur-* (fr. NL *Maclura*) + *-in*; orig. formed in G] **:** a light yellow crystalline pigment $C_6H_3(OH)_2COC_6H_2(OH)_3$ found esp. in old fustic **:** a pentahydroxy-benzophenone

**ma·clu·rite** \-ū,rīt\ *n, cap* [NL, after William *Maclure*] **:** a genus of Ordovician gastropod mollusks known from their usu. large flat spiral shells

**mac·nab cypress** \mək'nab-\ *also* **macnab's cypress** *n, usu cap M & often cap N* [after James *MacNab* †1878 Scot. botanist] **:** a bushy evergreen tree (*Cupressus macnabiana*) of the Pacific coast of No. America

**ma·co** \'mä(,)kō\ *n* -s [after *Maho* or *Mako* Bey, 19th cent. Egyptian official] **:** EGYPTIAN COTTON — used esp. of the natural undyed state ⟨black hose with ~ feet⟩

**ma·cock** *or* **may·cock** \'mā,käk\ *n* -s [fr. *mawcawk, mahawk* (in some Algonquian language of Virginia)] **:** an inferior melon or other cucurbit formerly cultivated by the Indians of eastern No. America

**ma·con** \mä'kōⁿ\ *n* -s *usu cap* [F *mâcon*, fr. *Mâcon*, France] **:** a still Burgundy wine that is made in the department of Saône-et-Loire, France, in both a red variety and a white variety

**ma·con·ite** \'mākə,nīt\ *n* -s [*Macon* county, Georgia + E *-ite*] **:** a vermiculite from No. Carolina

**macouba** *n* -s **:** MACCABOY

**ma·coun wild-rye** *also* **macoun rye grass** \mə'kün-\ *n, usu cap M* [fr. the name *Macoun*] **:** a native perennial forage grass (*Elymus macounii*) of western No. America

**macoute** *obs var of* MACUTA

**mac·quar·ie perch** \mə'kwärē-\ *n* [after Lachlan *MacQuarie* †1824 British army officer and governor of New South Wales, Australia] **:** a locally important food fish (*Macquaria australasica*) of the family Serranidae that is reddish brown above and yellow below and is restricted to the upper reaches of the Murray river system of Australia

**macquarie pine** *n, usu cap M* [after Lachlan *MacQuarie*] **:** HUON PINE

**mac·que·reau** \¦makə¦rō\ *n, pl* **macque·reaux** \-ō(z)\ [F *maquereau*, fr. OF *makerel* — more at MACKEREL] **:** PIMP, PROCURER

**macr-** *or* **macro-** *comb form* [F & L, fr. Gk *makr-, makro-* long, fr. *makros* — more at MEAGER] **1 :** long ⟨*macro*biotic⟩ ⟨*macro*diagonal⟩ **2 :** large ⟨*macr*ergate⟩ ⟨*macro*molecule⟩ ⟨*macro*gamete⟩ ⟨*macro*mastia⟩ ⟨*macro*gnathism⟩ ⟨*macro*podia⟩ — often used to contrast with *micr-* **3 :** macrodiagonal ⟨*macro*dome⟩ **4 :** including and more comprehensive than ⟨*Macro*-Khoisan⟩ — used of a language group

**mac·ra·can·tho·rhyn·chi·a·sis** \,makrə,kan(t)thə(,)riŋ'kīəsəs\ *n* -ES [NL, fr. *Macracanthorhynchus* + *-iasis*] **:** infestation with or disease caused by an acanthocephalid worm of the genus *Macracanthorhynchus*

**mac·ra·can·tho·rhyn·chus** \-'riŋkəs\ *n, cap* [NL, fr. *macr-* + *acanth-* + *-rhynchus*] **:** a genus of Acanthocephala that includes the common acanthocephalan of swine

**mac·rad·e·nous** \(')ma'krad°nəs\ *adj* [*macr-* + *aden-* + *-ous*] **:** having large glands

**ma·cra·me** \¦makrə¦mā, mə'krämē\ *n* -s [F or It; F *macramé*, fr. It *macramè*, fr. Turk *makrama, mahrama* napkin, kerchief, face towel, fr. Ar *migramah* embroidered veil] **1 :** a coarse lace or decorative fringe made by knotting threads or cords in a geometrical pattern — see MACRAME KNOT **2** *also* **macrame cord :** cord for or suitable for making macrame

**macrame knot** *n* **:** an ornate knot often used in making macrame

macrame knot

**mac·ran·drous** \(')ma'krandrəs\ *adj* [*macr-* + *-androus*] **:** having oogonia and antheridia borne on the same plant or on plants of similar size and form — used of green algae of the family Oedogoniaceae; compare NANNANDROUS

**mac·rau·che·nia** \,ma,krȯ'kēnēə\ *n, cap* [NL, fr. Gk *makrauchēn* long-necked (fr. *makr-* macr- + *auchēn* neck) + NL *-ia*] **:** a genus (the type of the family Macraucheniidae) of long-necked three-toed Pleistocene mammals (order Litopterna) of So. America that had a complete dentition of 44 teeth without a diastema and with pitted incisors like those of the horse, the external nostrils far back, cervical vertebrae resembling those of camels, and other characters suggesting rhinoceroses

**mac·ren·ce·phal·ic** \¦ma,kr+\ *also* **mac·ren·ceph·a·lous** \¦ma,kr+\ *adj* [*macr-* + *encephalic* or *encephalous*] **:** having a large or long brain case

**mac·ro** \'ma(,)krō\ *adj* [*macr-*] **1 :** large, thick, or excessively developed ⟨~ layer of the cerebral cortex⟩ ⟨the book as the ~ unit of thought —Eugene Garfield⟩ **2 :** of or involving large quantities **:** intended for use with large quantities ⟨a ~ procedure in analysis⟩ ⟨carrying out a test on a ~ scale⟩ **:** GROSS ⟨the ~ appearance of a specimen⟩

**mac·ro·analysis** \¦ma(,)krō+\ *n* [ISV *macr-* + *analysis*] **:** chemical analysis not on a small or minute scale **:** qualitative or quantitative analysis dealing with quantities usu. of the order of grams — opposed to *microanalysis*

**macro-axis** \"+\ *n* [*macr-* + *axis*] **:** the longer lateral axis of an orthorhombic or triclinic crystal

**mac·rob·del·la** \,ma,kräb'delə\ *n, cap* [NL, fr. *macr-* + *-bdella*] **:** a genus of large active aquatic blood-sucking leeches resembling and closely related to the Old World medicinal leech

**mac·ro·bi·an** \(')ma'krōbēən\ *adj* [Gk *makrobios* (fr. *makr-* macr- + *bios* life) + E *-an* — more at QUICK] **:** LONG-LIVED

**mac·ro·bi·o·sis** \,makrō,bī'ōsəs\ *n* -ES [NL, fr. LGk *makrobiōsis*, fr. *makr-* macr- + *-biōsis* -biosis] **:** LONGEVITY

**mac·ro·bi·ot·ic** \¦makrō,bī¦äd·ik *also* -bē-\ *adj* [Gk *makrobiotos* long-lived (fr. *makr-* macr- + *-biotos*, fr. *bios* life) + E *-ic*] **:** LONG-LIVED; *esp, of a seed* **:** surviving in the dormant state for many years — compare MESOBIOTIC

**mac·ro·bi·ot·ics** \\ˌ==(ˌ)=ˈäd·iks\\ *n pl but sing or pl in constr* **:** the art of prolonging life
**mac·ro·bi·o·tus** \\ˌmakrəˈbīəd·əs\\ *n, cap* [NL, fr. Gk *makrobiotos*] **:** a genus of bear animalcules having the body naked, transparent, and containing numerous fat globules that resemble enormous blood corpuscles
**mac·ro·blast** \\ˈmakrə,blast\\ *n* [ISV *macr-* + *-blast*] **1 :** MEGALOBLAST **2 :** an erythroblast destined to produce macrocytes
**mac·ro·brachium** \\ˌmakrō+\\ *n, cap* [NL, fr. *macr-* + *brachium*] **:** a genus of large stout chiefly tropical shrimps including one (*M. jamaicenæ*) that occurs in freshwaters of Florida and the Gulf coast to Brazil and sometimes attains a length of 17 inches and a weight of over 3 pounds
**mac·ro·car·pa** \\ˌmakrəˈkärpə\\ *n* -s [NL *macrocarpa* (specific epithet of *Cupressus macrocarpa*), fr. *macr-* + *-carpa* (fr. Gk *karpos* fruit) — more at HARVEST] **:** a New Zealand evergreen shrub or tree (*Cupressus macrocarpa*) that is used for hedges and that sometimes causes abortion in cattle that browse on it
**mac·ro·cen·trus** \\ˌmakrōˈsen·trəs\\ *n, cap* [NL, fr. Gk *makrokentros* with a long sting, fr. *makr-* macr- + *kentron* sting — more at CENTER] **:** a genus of polyembryonic braconid wasps which are larval parasites of other insects and some of which are important in the biological control of noxious pests (as the oriental peach moth)
**mac·ro·ceph·a·lous** \\ˌmakrō¦sefələs\\ *or* **mac·ro·ce·phal·ic** \\-ˌsəˈfalik\\ *adj* [F *macrocéphale* (fr. Gk *makrokephalos* having a long head, fr. *makro-* macr- + *-kephalos* -cephalous) + E *-ous* or *-ic*] **1 a :** having an exceptionally large head ⟨a ~ idiot⟩ **b** *of a cranium* **:** exceptionally or abnormally large **2** *of a dicotyledonous embryo* **:** having the cotyledons consolidated
**¹mac·ro·ceph·a·lus** \\ˌ==ˈsefələs\\ [NL, fr. Gk *makrokephalos* having a long head] *syn of* PHACOCHOERUS
**²macrocephalus** \\"\\ *n, pl* **macrocepha·li** \\-ˌlī\\ [NL, fr. Gk *makrokephalos* having a long head] **:** a macrocephalous person or skull
**mac·ro·ceph·a·ly** \\-ˌlē\\ *n* -ES [F *macrocéphalie*, fr. *macrocéphale* + *-ie* -y] **:** the quality or state of being macrocephalous
**mac·ro·chaeta** \\ˌmakrō+\\ *n, pl* **macrochaetae** [NL, fr. *macr-* + *-chaeta*] **:** any of various large bristles occurring on the bodies of insects that are used as a basis for classification — distinguished from *microchaeta*
**mac·ro·chei·ra** \\ˌmakrōˈkīrə\\ *n, cap* [NL, fr. Gk *makrocheir* long-armed, fr. *makr-* macr- + *cheir* hand — more at CHIR-] **:** a genus of deep sea spider crabs (family Majidae) consisting of the giant crab of Japan
**mac·roch·e·lys** \\məˈkräkələs\\ *n, cap* [NL, fr. *macr-* + Gk *chelys* tortoise — more at CHELYS] **:** a genus of turtles consisting of the alligator snapper
**mac·ro·chemical** \\ˌmakrō+\\ *adj* [*macr-* + *chemical*] **:** of, relating to, or using the methods of macrochemistry — **mac·ro·chemically** \\"+\\ *adv*
**mac·ro·chemistry** \\"+\\ *n* [*macr-* + *chemistry*] **:** chemistry studied or applied without the use of the microscope or of microanalysis — contrasted with *microchemistry*
**mac·ro·chi·res** \\ˌmakrōˈkī(ˌ)rēz\\ *n pl, cap* [NL, fr. Gk *makrocheir* long-armed] *in some classifications* **:** a group of birds including the swifts and hummingbirds and sometimes also the goatsuckers
**mac·ro·chiroptera** \\ˌmakrō+\\ [NL, fr. *macr-* + *Chiroptera*] *syn of* MEGACHIROPTERA
**mac·ro·cinematography** \\"+\\ *n* [*macr-* + *cinematography*] **:** photomacrography in which the product is a motion picture
**mac·ro·climate** \\"+\\ *n* [*macr-* + *climate*] **:** the overall climate of a region usu. a large geographic area — distinguished from *microclimate* — **mac·ro·climatic** \\"+\\ *adj*
**mac·ro·conidium** \\"+\\ *n, pl* **macroconidia** [NL, fr. *macr-* + *conidium*] **:** a large usu. multinucleate conidium of a fungus — compare MICROCONIDIUM
**mac·ro·conjugant** \\"+\\ *n* [*macr-* + *conjugant*] **:** the larger member of a pair of conjugating protozoans of unequal size
**mac·ro·cosm** \\ˈmakrə,käzəm\\ *n* -s [F *macrocosme*, fr. ML *macrocosmos*, *macrocosmus*, fr. *macr-* + Gk *kosmos* order, universe] **1 :** the great world **:** the universe in its entirety — contrasted with *microcosm* **2 :** a complex regarded as a whole world in itself ⟨to consider the state as the ~ of the family⟩ ⟨the great ~ of pain —Henry Miller⟩
**mac·ro·cos·mic** \\ˌ==¦käzmik\\ *adj* **:** of, relating to, or constituting a macrocosm — **mac·ro·cos·mi·cal·ly** \\-mək(ə)lē\\ *adv*
**mac·ro·cosmos** \\¦makrə+\\ *n* [ML — more at MACROCOSM] **:** MACROCOSM
**mac·ro·cranial** \\¦makrō+\\ *adj* [*macr-* + *cranial*] **:** having a large or long skull
**mac·ro·crystalline** \\"+\\ *adj* [*macr-* + *crystalline*] **:** consisting of or having crystals large enough to be determined by the eye or a simple lens
**mac·ro·cyclic** \\"+\\ *adj* [*macr-* + *cyclic*] **1** *of an organic chemical* **:** containing a ring structure of large size consisting usu. of 15 or more atoms **2** *of a rust fungus* **:** having one or more binuclear spores in addition to teliospores and sporidia **:** having a long or complex life cycle
**mac·ro·cyst** \\ˈmakrō,sist\\ *n* [ISV *macr-* + *cyst*] **:** a large spore case or cyst; *esp* **:** a young encysted resting plasmodium of a slime mold — compare MICROCYST
**mac·ro·cys·tis** \\ˌmakrōˈsistəs\\ *n* [NL, fr. *macr-* + *-cystis*] **1** *cap* **:** a genus of brown algae (family Laminariaceae) that are often very large and consist of a slender stipe with pinnate fronds and floats — see GIANT KELP **2** *pl* **macrocystis :** any plant of the genus *Macrocystis*
**mac·ro·cyte** \\ˈmakrō,sīt\\ *n* -s [ISV *macr-* + *-cyte*] **:** an exceptionally large red blood cell occurring chiefly in anemias (as pernicious anemia)
**mac·ro·cyt·ic** \\¦makrō¦sid·ik\\ *adj* **:** of or relating to macrocytes; *specif, of an anemia* **:** characterized by macrocytes in the blood ⟨pernicious anemia is a ~ anemia⟩
**mac·ro·cy·to·sis** \\ˌmakrō,sīˈtōsəs\\ *n, pl* **macrocyto·ses** \\-ō,sēz\\ [NL, fr. ISV *macrocyte* + NL *-osis*] **:** the occurrence of macrocytes in the blood
**mac·ro·diagonal** \\¦makrō+\\ *n* [*macr-* + *diagonal*] **:** MACRO=AXIS
**mac·ro·dome** \\ˈmakrə,dōm\\ *n* [*macr-* + *dome*] **:** the dome of a crystal having planes parallel to the longer lateral axis — compare BRACHYDOME, CLINODOME
**mac·ro·dont** \\-ˌdänt\\ *adj* [ISV *macr-* + *-odont*] **:** having large teeth usu. with a dental index of over 44 — **mac·ro·don·tia** \\ˌmakrəˈdänch(ē)ə\\ *or* **mac·ro·don·tism** \\ˈmakrə,dän,tizəm\\ *n* -s
**mac·ro·economic** \\¦makrō+\\ *adj* [*macr-* + *economic*] **:** of, relating to, or based on macroeconomics ⟨~ decisions⟩
**mac·ro·economics** \\"+\\ *n pl but usu sing in constr* [*macr-* + *economics*] **:** study of the economic system as a whole esp. with reference to its general level of output and income and the interrelations among sectors of the economy—opposed to *microeconomics*
**mac·ro·element** \\"+\\ *n* [*macr-* + *element*] **:** MACRONUTRIENT
**mac·ro·ergate** \\"+\\ *also* **mac·rer·gate** \\(ˈ)ma¦krər,gāt\\ *n* [ISV *macr-* + *ergate*] **:** a member of a caste of atypically large worker ants
**mac·ro·etch** \\ˈmakrō,ech\\ *vt* [*macr-* + *etch*] **:** to etch (metal) for examination with the naked eye
**mac·ro·evolution** \\¦ma(ˌ)krō+\\ *n* [*macr-* + *evolution*] **:** evolutionary change involving relatively large and complex steps (as transformation of one species to another) — distinguished from *microevolution;* compare SALTATORY EVOLUTION — **macroevolutionary** *adj*
**mac·ro·fauna** \\¦makrō+\\ *n* [NL, fr. *macr-* + *fauna*] **1 :** a large or widely distributed fauna **:** the fauna of a macrohabitat **2 :** animals large enough to be seen by the naked eye ⟨the ~ of a sewage filtration bed⟩ — compare MESOFAUNA, MICROFAUNA — **mac·ro·faunal** \\"+\\ *adj*
**mac·ro·flora** \\"+\\ *n* [NL, fr. *macr-* + *flora*] **1 :** a large or widely distributed flora **:** the flora of a macrohabitat **2 :** plants large enough to be seen by the naked eye ⟨the ~ of a coral reef⟩
**mac·ro·fossil** \\¦makrō+\\ *n* [*macr-* + *fossil*] **:** a fossil large enough to be observed by direct inspection — compare MICROFOSSIL
**mac·ro·gamete** \\¦ma(ˌ)krō+\\ *n* [ISV *macr-* + *gamete*] **:** the larger and usu. female gamete of a heterogamous organism — compare MICROGAMETE
**mac·ro·gametocyte** \\"+\\ *n* **:** a gametocyte producing macrogametes
**mac·rog·a·my** \\məˈkrägəmē\\ *n* -ES [*macr-* + *-gamy*] **1 :** HOLOGAMY **2 :** syngamy between fully developed vegetative cells (as in certain protozoa or algae) — compare MICROGAMY
**mac·roglia** \\(ˈ)ma¦kräglēə, ¦makrə¦glīə\\ *n* -s [NL, fr. *macr-* + *neuroglia*] **:** neuroglia made up of astrocytes — **mac·rogli·al** \\-ēəl, -īəl\\ *adj*
**mac·ro·glos·sia** \\ˌmakrōˈgläsēə, -lȯs-\\ *n* -s [NL, fr. *macr-* + *-glossia*] **:** pathological and commonly congenital enlargement of the tongue
**mac·ro·graph** \\ˈmakrə,graf, -ràf\\ *n* [*macr-* + *-graph*] **:** a usu. photographic graphic reproduction of an object that may be slightly reduced, of natural size, or magnified up to a limit of about 10 diameters
**mac·ro·graph·ic** \\¦makrə¦grafik\\ *adj* **:** of, relating to, being, or involved in macrography
**mac·rog·ra·phy** \\məˈkrägrəfē\\ *n* -ES [*macr-* + *-graphy*] **1 a :** a tendency to write unusually large **b :** unusually large writing **2 :** examination or study with the naked eye — opposed to *micrography* **3 :** the art or process of making macrographs
**mac·ro·habitat** \\¦makrō+\\ *n* [*macr-* + *habitat*] **:** a habitat of sufficient extent to present considerable variation of environment, contain varied ecological niches, and support a large and usu. complex flora and fauna
**mac·ro·lecithal** \\¦makrō+\\ *adj* [*macr-* + *lecithal*] **:** MEGALECITHAL
**mac·ro·lepidoptera** \\"+\\ *n pl, cap* [NL, fr. *macr-* + *Lepidoptera*] *in some esp former classifications* **:** a major division of Lepidoptera comprising the butterflies and the noctuid, bombycid, sphingid, and geometrid moths together with certain related moths and including most of the large lepidopters and none of the minute forms — now usu. used descriptively without taxonomic implications and then often not capitalized; compare MICROLEPIDOPTERA — **mac·ro·lepidopterous** \\"+\\ *adj*
**mac·ro·linguistics** \\"+\\ *n* [*macr-* + *linguistics*] **:** the study of phenomena connected in any way with language
**mac·rol·o·gy** \\məˈkräləjē\\ *n* -ES [L *macrologia*, fr. Gk *makrologia*, fr. *makrologein* to use many words, fr. *makr-* macr- + *-logein* (fr. *logos* word, speech) + *-ia* -y — more at LEGEND] **:** PLEONASM 1
**mac·ro·mania** \\¦makrō+\\ *n* [NL, fr. *macr-* + *mania*] **:** a delusion that things (as parts of the patient's body) are larger than they really are — **mac·ro·maniacal** \\"+\\ *adj*
**mac·ro·mas·tia** \\ˌmakrōˈmastēə\\ *n* -s [NL, fr. *macr-* + *-mastia*] **:** excessive development of the mammary glands
**mac·ro·mere** \\ˈmakrō,mi(ə)r\\ *n* -s [*macr-* + *-mere*] **:** any of the large blastomeres of the vegetative hemisphere of an embryo that result from the unequal segmentation of a telolecithal egg — opposed to *micromere;* see BLASTULA illustration
**mac·ro·mesentery** \\¦makrō+\\ *n* [*macr-* + *mesentery*] **:** PROTOCNEME
**mac·ro·method** \\"+\\ *n* [*macr-* + *method*] **:** a method (as of analysis) not involving the use of very small quantities of material — opposed to *micromethod*
**mac·ro·molecular** \\"+\\ *adj* [ISV *macr-* + *molecular*] **:** of or relating to a macromolecule **:** consisting of or characterized by macromolecules ⟨~ compounds⟩
**mac·ro·molecule** \\"+\\ *n* [ISV *macr-* + *molecule*] **:** a very large molecule (as of a protein, cellulose, rubber, or other natural or synthetic high polymer) ⟨possess more reliable information on the structure of atoms and small molecules than on the structure of colloidal particles and ~s —*Physics Today*⟩ ⟨~s with a diameter of about 100 A (=$10^{-5}$ mm) . . . can be seen in electron micrographs —Felix Haurowitz⟩
**macro–moth** \\ˈmakrō,-\\ *n* [*macr-* + *moth*] **:** a moth belonging to the Macrolepidoptera
**mac·ro·mutant** \\¦makrō+\\ *n* [*macr-* + *mutant*] **:** an organism that has undergone macromutation
**mac·ro·mutation** \\"+\\ *n* [*macr-* + *mutation*] **:** complex mutation involving concurrent alteration of numerous characters — compare MACROEVOLUTION — **mac·ro·mutational** \\"+\\ *adj*
**macron** \\ˈmā¦,krän, ¦,krən *also* ˈma¦\\ *n* -s [Gk *makron*, neut. of *makros* long — more at MEAGER] **:** a mark ¯ placed over a vowel to indicate that the vowel is long or placed over a syllable or used alone to indicate a stressed or long syllable in a foot of verse
**mac·ro·nuclear** \\¦ma(ˌ)krō+\\ *adj* [*macronucleus* + *-ar*] **:** of or relating to a macronucleus
**mac·ro·nucleate** *also* **mac·ro·nucleated** \\"+\\ *adj* [NL *macronucleus* + E *-ate* or *-ated* (fr. *-ate* + *-ed*)] **:** having a macronucleus
**mac·ro·nucleus** \\"+\\ *n* [NL, fr. *macr-* + *nucleus*] **:** a relatively large densely staining nucleus that is believed to exert a controlling influence over the trophic activities of most ciliated protozoans — distinguished from *micronucleus*
**mac·ro·nutrient** \\"+\\ *n* [*macr-* + *nutrient*] **:** a chemical element (as potassium, calcium, magnesium, nitrogen, phosphorus, sulfur) of which relatively large quantities are essential to the growth and welfare of a plant — called also *macroelement, major element;* compare MICRONUTRIENT
**mac·ro·phage** \\ˈmakrə,fāj\\ *n* -s [F, fr. *macr-* + *-phage*] **:** a large phagocyte; *specif* **:** HISTIOCYTE — **mac·ro·phag·ic** \\¦makrə¦fajik\\ *adj*
**macrophagic system** *n* **:** RETICULOENDOTHELIAL SYSTEM
**mac·roph·a·gous** \\(ˈ)ma¦kräfəgəs\\ *adj* [*macr-* + *-phagous*] **:** feeding on relatively large particulate matter — compare MICROPHAGOUS
**mac·ro·phoma** \\¦makrə+\\ *n, cap* [NL, fr. *macr-* + *Phoma*] *in some classifications* **:** a genus of imperfect fungi with large pycniospores that is now usu. included in *Sphaeropsis*
**mac·ro·photograph** \\¦makrō+\\ *n* [*macr-* + *photograph*] **:** PHOTOMACROGRAPH
**mac·ro·photography** \\"+\\ *n* [ISV *macr-* + *photography*] **:** PHOTOMACROGRAPHY
**mac·ro·phyl·lous** \\¦makrō¦filəs\\ *adj* [*macr-* + *-phyllous*] **:** having large or elongated leaves with usu. many veins or a much-branched main vein — compare MICROPHYLLOUS
**mac·ro·phylogeny** \\¦ma(ˌ)krō+\\ *n* [*macr-* + *phylogeny*] **:** an assumed rapid differentiation of major systematic categories through complex reorganization and mutation of the genes
**mac·ro·physics** \\¦makrō+\\ *n pl but sing or pl in constr* [ISV *macr-* + *physics*] **:** the part of physics that deals with bodies large enough to be directly and individually observed and measured
**mac·ro·phyte** \\ˈmakrə,fīt\\ *n* -s [*macr-* + *-phyte*] **:** a member of the macroscopic plant life esp. of a body of water — **mac·ro·phyt·ic** \\¦makrə¦fid·ik\\ *adj*
**mac·ro·pinacoid** \\¦makrō+\\ *n* [ISV *macr-* + *pinacoid*] **:** a pinacoid having faces parallel to the longer lateral and the vertical axis — **mac·ro·pinacoidal** \\"+\\ *adj*
**mac·ro·plankton** \\"+\\ *n* [ISV *macr-* + *plankton*] **:** macroscopic plankton comprising the larger planktonic organisms (as jellyfish, crustaceans, sargassums) — **mac·ro·planktonic** \\"+\\ *adj*
**¹ma·crop·o·did** \\məˈkräpədəd\\ *adj* [NL *Macropodidae*] **:** of or relating to the Macropodidae
**²macropodid** \\"\\ *n* -s **:** a macropodid animal **:** KANGAROO, WALLABY
**mac·ro·pod·i·dae** \\ˌmakrəˈpädə,dē\\ *n pl, cap* [NL, fr. *Macropod-, Macropus*, type genus + *-idae*] **:** a family of diprotodont marsupial mammals comprising the kangaroos, wallabies, and rat kangaroos that are all saltatory animals with long hind limbs and weakly developed forelimbs and are typically inoffensive terrestrial herbivores
**mac·rop·o·dous** \\(ˈ)ma¦kräpədəs\\ *also* **mac·rop·o·dal** \\-dᵊl\\ *adj* [*macr-* + *-podous* or *podal*] **1** *of a plant embryo* **:** having an enlarged or elongated hypocotyl **2** *of a plant or plant part* **:** having a long stem or stalk ⟨a ~ leaf⟩
**mac·ro·pol·y·cyte** \\ˌmakrōˈpälə,sīt\\ *n* -s [*macr-* + *poly-* + *-cyte*] **:** an exceptionally large neutrophil with a much=lobulated nucleus that appears in the blood in pernicious anemia
**mac·ro·pore** \\ˈmakrə,pō(ə)r\\ *n* [*macr-* + *pore*] **:** a pore (as in coal) of comparatively large size; *esp* **:** a pore in soil of such size that water drains from it by gravity and is not held by capillary action — **mac·ro·porosity** \\¦ma(ˌ)krō+\\ *n* — **mac·ropo·rous** \\¦makrə¦pōrəs, (ˈ)ma¦kräpərəs\\ *adj*
**mac·ro·prism** \\ˈmakrō+,-\\ *n* [*macr-* + *prism*] **:** a crystal prism that makes a relatively great intercept on the macro-axis
**mac·ro·procedure** \\¦makrō+\\ *n* [*macr-* + *procedure*] **:** a procedure (as for analysis) not involving the use of very small quantities of material — opposed to *microprocedure*
**mac·rop·sia** \\məˈkräpsēə\\ *also* **mac·rop·sy** \\ˈma,kräpsē\\ *n, pl* **macropsias** *also* **macropsies** [NL *macropsia*, fr. *macr-* + *-opsia*] **:** a condition of the eye in which objects appear to be unnaturally large — opposed to *micropsia*
**ma·crop·sis** \\məˈkräpsəs\\ *n, cap* [NL, fr. *macr-* + *-opsis*] **:** a genus (the type of the family Macropsidae) of leafhoppers that includes the plum leafhopper
**mac·rop·ter·ous** \\(ˈ)ma¦kräptərəs\\ *adj* [Gk *makropteros* having long wings, fr. *makr-* macr- + *-pteros* -pterous] **1 :** having long or large wings—used of birds or insects **2 :** having large or long fins — used of fishes — **mac·rop·tery** \\-tərē\\ *n*
**mac·rop·tic** \\(ˈ)ma¦kräptik\\ *adj* [*macr-* + *optic*] **:** affected with macropsia
**mac·ro·pus** \\ˈmakrəpəs\\ *n, cap* [NL, fr. *macr-* + *-pus*] **:** the type genus of Macropodidae comprising the typical kangaroos and wallabies
**mac·ro·pyg·ia** \\ˌmakrōˈpijēə\\ *n, cap* [NL, fr. *macr-* + *-pygia*] **:** a large genus of long-tailed pigeons that resemble cuckoos — see CUCKOO DOVE
**mac·ro·pyramid** \\¦makrō+\\ *n* [*macr-* + *pyramid*] **:** a crystal pyramid that corresponds to the analogous macroprism
**mac·ro·rham·pho·si·dae** \\ˌmakrō,ramˈfōsə,dē, -ōzə-\\ *n pl, cap* [NL, fr. *Macrorhamphosus*, type genus + *-idae*] **:** a family of long-snouted fishes (order Solenichthyes) consisting of the bellows fishes
**mac·ro·rham·pho·sus** \\-ōsəs,-ōzəs\\ *n, cap* [NL, fr. *macr-* + *rhamph-* + L *-osus* -ous] **:** the type genus of Macrorhamphosidae
**mac·ro·rhi·nus** \\ˌmakrōˈrīnəs\\ [NL, fr. *macr-* + *-rhinus*] *syn of* MIROUNGA
**mac·ro·sce·lid·i·dae** \\ˌmakrōsəˈlidə,dē\\ *n pl, cap* [NL, fr. *Macroscelides*, type genus (fr. *macr-* + *scel-* + L *-ides*, patronymic suffix) + *-idae* — more at -IDE] **:** a family of African insectivores comprising the elephant shrews and constituting sometimes with the addition of the Tupaiidae a suborder (Menotyphla) of Insectivora
**mac·ro·scian** \\(ˈ)ma¦kräsh(ē)ən\\ *adj* [Gk *makroskios* (fr. *makr-* macr- + *-skios*, fr. *skia* shadow) + E *-an* — more at SHINE] **:** having or casting a long shadow ⟨that ~ day which I had dreaded for so long —Osbert Sitwell⟩
**mac·ro·sclereid** \\¦makrō+\\ *n* [*macr-* + *sclereid*] **:** one of the columnar sclereids that often form an outer layer in various fruits and seeds and occur also in the stems of some xerophytes — called also *rod cell;* compare OSTEOSCLEREID
**mac·ro·scop·ic** \\¦makrə¦skäpik, -pēk\\ *also* **mac·ro·scop·i·cal** \\-pəkəl, -pēk-\\ *adj* [ISV *macr-* + *-scopic*, *-scopical*] **1 :** large enough to be observed by the naked eye — opposed to *microscopic* **2 :** being in the large or taken in the large **:** considered in terms of large units or elements ⟨a ~ equation⟩ **3 :** MEGASCOPIC 2a — **macroscopically** *adv*
**mac·ro·segment** \\¦makrō+\\ *n* [*macr-* + *segment*] **:** a continuum of speech between two perceptible pauses
**mac·ro·seism** \\ˈmakrō,sīzəm *sometimes* -sez- *or* -sāz- *or* -sēz-\\ *n* [ISV *macr-* + *-seism*] **:** a severe or major earthquake — compare MICROSEISM — **mac·ro·seis·mic** \\¦makrō¦sī¦zmik *also* ¦sm- *sometimes* -¦se¦ *or* -¦sā¦ *or* -¦sē¦\\ *adj*
**mac·ro·seismograph** \\¦makrō+\\ *n* [*macroseism* + *-o-* + *-graph*] **:** a seismograph specially adapted for recording large earthquakes
**mac·ro·si·phum** \\ˌmakrōˈsīfəm\\ *n, cap* [NL, fr. *macr-* + Gk *siphōn* tube — more at SIPHON] **:** a genus of large often pink or green aphids including a number of economically important plant pests some of which are vectors of virus diseases (as mosaic) — see ENGLISH GRAIN APHID, PEA APHID, ROSE APHID
**mac·ros·mat·ic** \\¦ma,kr+¸-\\ *also* **macro–osmatic** \\¦ma(,)krō+\\ *adj* [*macr-* + *osmatic*] **:** having the sense or organs of smell highly developed ⟨dogs are ~ animals⟩
**mac·ro·so·mat·ic** \\¦makrəsō¦mad·ik\\ *or* **mac·ro·so·ma·tous** \\-rə¦sōməd·əs\\ *adj* [*macr-* + *somatic* or *-somatous*] **:** having a usu. abnormally large body
**mac·ro·so·mia** \\ˌmakrəˈsōmēə\\ *n* -s [NL, fr. *macr-* + *-somia*] **:** GIGANTISM
**mac·ro·species** \\¦makrō+\\ *n* [*macr-* + *species*] **:** a large and usu. polymorphic biological species markedly discontinuous from its congeners **:** a polytypic species — compare LINNAEAN SPECIES, MICROSPECIES
**mac·ro·splanchnic** \\"+\\ *adj* [ISV *macr-* + *splanchnic;* orig. formed as It *macrosplancnico*] **:** ENDOMORPHIC 2 — opposed to *microsplanchnic;* compare NORMOSPLANCHNIC
**mac·ro·spo·range** \\¦makrōspə¦ranj, -krə¦spōr,anj\\ *n* [NL *macrosporangium*] **:** MEGASPORANGIUM
**mac·ro·sporangium** \\¦makrō+\\ *n* [NL, fr. *macr-* + *sporangium*] **:** MEGASPORANGIUM
**mac·ro·spore** \\ˈmakrə,spō(ə)r\\ *n* [*macr-* + *spore*] **1 :** MEGASPORE a **2 :** the larger of two forms of spores produced by certain protozoans (as radiolarians) — **mac·ro·spo·ric** \\¦makrə¦spōrik\\ *adj*
**mac·ro·spo·ri·um** \\ˌmakrəˈspōrēəm\\ *n, cap* [NL, fr. *macr-* + *-sporium*] *in some classifications* **:** a genus of imperfect fungi that are sometimes included in the genus *Alternaria* but that differ from members of that genus in having the dark greenish brown muriform spores borne singly rather than in chains
**mac·ro·sporophyll** *also* **mac·ro·sporophyl** \\¦makrə+\\ *n* -s [*macr-* + *sporophyll, sporophyl*] **:** MEGASPOROPHYLL
**mac·ro·stachya** \\ˌmakrōˈstakēə, -tāk-\\ *n, cap* [NL, fr. *macr-* + *Stachys*] **:** a form genus of Paleozoic fossil plants based on strobiles that are now regarded as fructifications of plants of the genus *Calamites*
**mac·ros·te·les** \\məˈkrästə,lēz\\ *n, cap* [NL, fr. *macr-* + *-steles* (perh. fr. Gk *stēlē* stela)] **:** a genus of leafhoppers some of which transmit virus diseases to plants — see SIX-SPOTTED LEAFHOPPER
**mac·ro·sto·mia** \\ˌmakrəˈstōmēə\\ *n* -s [NL, fr. *macr-* + *-stomia*] **1 :** the condition of having an abnormally large mouth **2** *also* **mac·ros·to·mus** \\məˈkrästəməs\\ *pl* **macrosto·mi** \\-tə,mī, -,mē\\ **:** an abnormally large mouth
**mac·ro·structural** \\¦makrō+\\ *adj* **:** of or relating to macrostructure
**mac·ro·structure** \\"+\\ *n* [ISV *macr-* + *structure*] **:** the structure (as of metal, a body part, or the soil) revealed by visual examination with little or no magnification
**mac·ro·sty·lous** \\¦makrō¦stīləs\\ *adj* [*macr-* + *-stylous*] *of a flower* **:** having long styles; *specif* **:** having long styles and short stamens — compare MESOSTYLOUS, MICROSTYLOUS
**mac·ro·sudanic** \\¦makrō+\\ *n, cap* [*macr-* + *Sudanic*] **:** CHARI-NILE
**mac·ro·taxonomy** \\¦ma(ˌ)krō+\\ *n* [*macr-* + *taxonomy*] **:** taxonomy of larger biologic units (as family, order, class)
**mac·ro·there** \\ˈmakrō,thi(ə)r\\ *n* -s [NL *Macrotherium*] **:** a member of the genus *Macrotherium*
**mac·ro·the·ri·um** \\ˌmakrōˈthirēəm\\ *n, cap* [NL, fr. *macr-* + *-therium*] **:** a widely distributed genus of Miocene and Pliocene chalicotheres (order Perissodactyla) formerly supposed to be generalized edentates — compare CHALICOTHERIIDAE
**mac·ro·therm** \\ˈmakrō,thərm\\ *n* -s [*macr-* + *-therm*] **:** MEGATHERM
**mac·ro·tia** \\məˈkrōsh(ē)ə, -ōd·ēə\\ *n* -s [NL, fr. Gk *macr-* + Gk *ōt-, ous* ear + NL *-ia* — more at EAR] **:** excessive largeness of the ears
**mac·ro·tome** \\ˈmakrə,tōm\\ *n* [*macr-* + *-tome*] **:** an apparatus for making large sections of anatomical specimens
**mac·ro·tous** \\(ˈ)ma¦krōd·əs\\ *adj* [*macr-* + Gk *ōt, ous* ear + E *-ous*] **:** having large ears
**mac·ro·trich·i·um** \\ˌmakrōˈtrikēəm\\ *n, pl* **macrotrich·ia** \\-ēə\\ [NL, fr. *macr-* + Gk *trich-, thrix* hair + NL *-ium* — more at TRICHINA] **:** one of the larger hairs found esp. along the veins of the wings of various insects — compare MICROTRICHIUM
**macroura** *syn of* MACRURA
**mac·ro·za·mia** \\ˌmakrōˈzāmēə\\ *n* [NL, fr. *macr-* + Gk (Dor dial.) *zamia* loss (Attic *zēmia*)] **1** *cap* **:** a genus of Australian cycads with erect trunks, pinnate leaves, large cones, and in

some forms edible nuts **2** -s **:** any tree of the genus *Macrozamia*

**mac·ro·zoospore** \ˈmakrə+\ *n* [*macr-* + *zoospore*] **:** one of the larger zoospores produced by algae (as members of the genus *Ulothrix*) that bear zoospores of markedly different size — compare MICROZOOSPORE

**ma·cru·ra** \məˈkrürə\ *n pl, cap* [NL, fr. *macr-* + *-ura*] *in some classifications* **:** a suborder of Decapoda comprising crustaceans (as shrimps, lobsters, prawns) with well-developed abdomens — compare BRACHYURA — **ma·cru·ral** \-ürəl\ *adj* — **ma·cru·ran** \-ürən\ *adj or n* — **ma·cru·roid** \-ü,rȯid\ *adj*

**ma·cru·ri·dae** \-ürə,dē\ *n pl, cap* [NL, fr. *Macrurus*, type genus + *-idae*] **:** a family of fishes (order Anacanthini) comprising the grenadiers

**macru·rous** \(ˈ)maˈkrürəs, məˈk-\ *adj* [*macr-* + *-urous*] **1 :** having a long tail **2** [NL *Macrura* + E *-ous*] **:** of or relating to the Macrura

**ma·cru·rus** \məˈkrürəs\ *n, cap* [NL, fr. *macr-* + *-urus*] **:** the type genus of Macruridae

**mac·ta·tion** \makˈtāshən\ *n* -s [LL *mactation-, mactatio*, fr. L *mactatus* (past part. of *mactare* to honor, sacrifice, slay, slaughter, fr. *mactus* worshiped, honored) + *-ion-, -io* -ion] **:** an act of killing; *esp* **:** the ritual slaughter of a sacrificial victim

**mac·tra** \ˈmaktrə\ *n, cap* [NL, fr. Gk *maktra* kneading trough, fr. *massein* to knead — more at MINGLE] **:** the type genus of Mactridae formerly including most members of the family but now restricted to a few somewhat triangular, usu. thin-shelled surf clams — **mac·troid** \-,trȯid\ *adj*

**mac·tri·dae** \-rə,dē\ *n pl, cap* [NL, fr. *Mactra*, type genus + *-idae*] **:** a widely distributed family of marine clams (suborder Tellinacea) that have closely fitting or slightly gapping shells with two cardinal teeth in each valve and fused ensheathed siphons of equal length and that comprise the surf clams — compare LUTRARIA, MACTRA, SPISULA

**macu** *also* **maku** \mäˈkü, məˈ-\ *n, pl* **macú** *or* **macús** *usu cap* [Pg, of AmerInd origin] **1 a :** a Puinavean people of northwestern Amazonas, Brazil **b :** a member of such people **2 :** the language of the Macú people

**ma·cu·ca** \məˈkükə\ *n* -s [Pg, fr. Tupi] **:** any of several So. American tinamous (esp. *Tinamus major*)

**macul-** *or* **maculo-** *also* **maculi-** *comb form* [ME *macul-*, fr. L, fr. *macula*] **1 :** spot **:** blotch ⟨*maculation*⟩ ⟨*maculiform*⟩ **2 :** spotted and **:** macular and ⟨*maculopetechial* lesions⟩ ⟨*macul*oanesthetic⟩

**mac·u·la** \ˈmakyələ\ *n, pl* **macu·lae** \-,lē\ *also* **maculas** [L] **1 :** BLOTCH, SPOT, STAIN; *esp* **:** MACULE 2 **2 :** any of various anatomical structures having the form of a spot differentiated from surrounding tissues: as **a :** MACULA ACUSTICA **b :** MACULA LUTEA — see EYE illustration

**macula acu·sti·ca** \-əˈküstəkə\ *n, pl* **maculae acusti·cae** \-tə,sē\ [NL, lit., acoustic spot] **:** either of two small areas of sensory hair cells in the ear located (1) in the saccule and (2) in the utricle that are covered with gelatinous material on which are located crystals or concretions of calcium carbonate and that are associated with the perception of equilibrium — called also respectively (1) *macula sacculi*, (2) *macula utriculi*

**mac·u·la·cy** \ˈmakyələsē\ *n* -ES [*maculate* + *-cy*] **:** a smirched, unclean, bespotted state

**macula lu·tea** \-ˈlüdēə\ *n, pl* **maculae lute·ae** \-ē,ē\ [NL, lit., yellow spot] **:** a small yellowish area lying slightly lateral to the center of the retina that constitutes the region of maximum visual acuity and is made up almost wholly of retinal cones

**mac·u·lar** \ˈmakyələ(r)\ *adj* [*macula* + *-ar*] **1 a :** of or relating to a spot or spots **b** [NL *macula* (*lutea*) + E *-ar*] **:** mediated by the macula lutea ⟨~ vision⟩ **2 :** marked with a spot or spots **:** SPOTTY

**¹mac·u·late** \-,lāt\ *vt* -ED/-ING/-S [ME *maculaten*, fr. L *maculatus*, past part. of *maculare*, fr. *macula* spot] **1** *archaic* **:** SPOT, SPECKLE **2** *archaic* **:** BESMIRCH, DEFILE

**²mac·u·late** \-lət\ *or* **mac·u·lat·ed** \-,lād·əd\ *adj* [*maculate* fr. L *maculatus*, past part.; *maculated* fr. L *maculatus* + E *-ed*] **1 :** marked with spots **:** BLOTCHED **2 :** BESMIRCHED, DEFILED, IMPURE

**mac·u·la·tion** \,makyəˈlāshən\ *n* -s [ME *maculacion*, fr. L *maculation-, maculatio*, fr. *maculatus* + *-ion-, -io* -ion] **1** *archaic* **:** the act of spotting or staining or the condition of being spotted or stained **2 a :** SPOT, STAIN, BLEMISH ⟨indurated ~s on the cheeks⟩ **b :** the system or arrangement of spots and markings on an animal or plant

**mac·u·la·ture** \ˈmakyələ,chü(ə)r\ *n* -s [F, fr. L *maculatus* + F *-ure*] **:** an impression made from an intaglio engraved plate to remove ink from the recessed areas

**mac·ule** \ˈma(,)kyül\ *n* -s [F, fr. L *macula*] **1 :** MACULA 2 **2 :** a patch of skin exhibiting altered coloration but usu. not elevated above the general surface that forms a characteristic feature of various diseases (as smallpox)

**mac·u·lic·o·lous** \,makyəˈlikələs\ *also* **macu·li·cole** \ˈmakyələ,kōl, məˈkyülə,-\ *adj* [*macul-* + *-colous* or *-cole*] *of a fungus* **:** having pycnidia produced in localized masses so as to form definite spots on a host plant

**maculo-** *see* MACUL-

**mac·u·lo·papular** \,makyə(,)lō+\ *adj* [*macul-* + *papular*] *of a skin lesion* **:** combining the characteristics of macules and papules — **mac·u·lo·papule** \"+\ *n*

**mac·u·lose** \ˈmakyə,lōs\ *adj* [L *maculosus*, fr. *macula* spot + *-osus* -ose] **:** SPOTTED

**ma·cum·ba** \məˈkümbə\ *n* -s [Pg] **1 :** a Brazilian fetishistic ritual or cult that is largely of African origin and combines sorcery with dancing, drumming, and chanting **2 :** the Brazilian popular music or dance based upon macumba

**ma·cu·pa** \məˈküpə\ *n* -s [Sp, fr. Tag & Bisayan] **1** *Philippines* **:** OTAHEITE APPLE **2** *Philippines* **:** the heavy red wood of the otaheite apple tree

**ma·cu·shi** \məˈküshē\ *or* **ma·cu·si** \-üsē\ *also* **ma·ku·shi** *or* **ma·ku·si** *n pl* **macushi** *or* **macushis** *or* **macusi** *or* **macusis** *usu cap* **1 a :** a Cariban people of Brazil and British Guiana **b :** a member of such people **2 :** the language of the Macushi people

**ma·cush·la** \məˈküshlə, -kùsh-, -(,)lä\ *n* -s [IrGael *mo chuisle*, lit., my vein, my blood] *Irish* **:** DARLING — used usu. as a noun of address

**ma·cu·ta** *also* **ma·cu·te** \məˈküd·ə\ *n* -s [Pg *macuta*, fr. Kimbundu *mukuta*, fr. Kongo *nkuta* cloth] **1 :** an old west African unit of value **2 :** an old copper coin equal to 50 reis issued by Portugal for its African colonies; *also* **:** a corresponding unit of value **3 :** a 5-centavo coin of Angola issued in 1927; *also* **:** a corresponding unit of value ⟨4-*macuta* coins⟩

**¹mad** \ˈmad, -aa(ə)-, -ai-\ *adj* **madder; maddest** [ME *medd*, *madd*, fr. OE *gemǣd*, *gemǣded*, past part. of (assumed) *gemǣdan* to make silly or mad, fr. *gemād* silly, mad; akin to OS *gimēd* foolish, crazy, OHG *gimeit* foolish, crazy, ON *meitha* to hurt, mutilate, Goth *gamaidans*, acc. pl., crippled, wounded, OIr *māel* bald, dull, W *moel* bald, Skt *methati* he hurts; basic meaning: chop, chop off] **1 a :** disordered in mind **:** CRAZY, INSANE ⟨the man was ~ and had berserk fits of superhuman strength and rage —Charles Kingsley⟩ **b :** arising from, indicative of, or marked by mental disorder ⟨no lunatic in a ~ fit, but a sane man fighting for his soul —Bram Stoker⟩ **2 a :** completely unrestrained by reason and judgment **:** utterly foolish **:** SENSELESS ⟨she's ~ . . . to throw away money and position for some hole-and-corner existence with a good-looking lawyer's clerk —Clara Morris⟩ **b :** arising from or indicative of a lack of reason and judgment **:** RASH ⟨was so astounded by this ~ project on the part of her husband . . . that she had not a word to say —William Black⟩ **c :** incapable of being explained, interpreted, or accounted for **:** ILLOGICAL ⟨facts which fairly shriek for explanation; for without an explanation they're ~, irrational, utterly incredible —W.H.Wright⟩ **3 a :** carried away by intense anger **:** ENRAGED, FURIOUS ⟨was so ~ . . . that I thought I could shoot the man —Liam O'Flaherty⟩ **b :** keenly displeased **:** ANGRY, IRKED ⟨looked ~ for a second but then . . . began to laugh —Robert Lowry⟩ ⟨~ as a wet hen⟩ **4 a :** carried away by enthusiasm, infatuation, or desire ⟨men were ~ for her and any girl liked men's attentions —Barnaby Conrad⟩ ⟨was not fundamentally ~ about a home and kids —Rex Ingamells⟩ ⟨the students were all perfectly ~ on highbrow music —Arnold Bennett⟩ **b :** arising from or marked by intense enthusiasm, infatuation, or desire ⟨a nation . . . engaged in the ~ pursuit of wealth —*Saturday Rev.*⟩ ⟨has been having a ~ vogue in Europe and is constantly written about —*New Yorker*⟩ **5 :** affected with rabies **:** RABID ⟨a ~ dog⟩ **6 :** marked by wild or irresponsible gaiety and merriment **:** HILARIOUS ⟨of their childhood, of the ~ pranks they played —Winston Churchill⟩ **7 a :** intensely excited, distraught, or frantic ⟨driving him ~ with jealousy —Edmund Wilson⟩ **b :** arising from or indicative of intense excitement or distress ⟨tried to reach it in a ~ resolve to claw into the wood with my nails —Jack London⟩ **8 :** marked by intense and often chaotic activity **:** WILD, FURIOUS ⟨a ~ scramble for the sides of the ship —A.C.Whitehead⟩ **syn** see ANGRY

**²mad** \"\ *vb* **madded; madded; madding; mads** [ME *madden*, fr. *medd*, *madd*, adj.] *vi, archaic* **:** to act in an insane or furious manner **:** RAGE ~ *vt* **:** to make mad: **a** *archaic* **:** to make insane **b :** to make angry **:** EXASPERATE

**³mad** \"\ *n* -s [¹*mad*] **1 :** ANGER, FURY ⟨the fight had taken all the ~ out of me —H.E.Giles⟩ **2 :** a fit or mood of angry temper ⟨had worked up a ~ before he bayoneted the corporal —R.O.Bowen⟩ ⟨still had a bit of a ~ on —William Forrest⟩

**MAD** *abbr* magnetic airborne detector

**¹mad·a·gas·can** \,madəˈgaskən, -gaas-\ *adj, usu cap* [*Madagascar*, island in the Indian ocean southeast of Africa + E *-an*] **1 :** of, relating to, or characteristic of Madagascar **2 :** of, relating to, or characteristic of the people of Madagascar

**²madagascan** \"\ *n* -s *cap* **:** a native or inhabitant of Madagascar

**mad·a·gas·car** \-kə(r)\ *adj, usu cap* [fr. *Madagascar*, island in the Indian ocean] **1 :** of or from Madagascar **:** of the kind or style prevalent in Madagascar **2 :** MALAGASY

**madagascar bean** *n, usu cap M* **1 :** HYACINTH BEAN **2 :** LIMA BEAN

**madagascar cat** *n, usu cap M* **:** a small lemur (*Lemur catta*) having the tail barred with black

**mad·a·gas·car·i·an** \ˌ⁼⁼ˌ⁼ˈska(a)rēən\ *adj, usu cap* [*Madagascar* island + E *-ian*] **:** MALAGASY

**madagascar jasmine** *n, usu cap M* **:** a twining vine (*Stephanotis floribunda*) native to Madagascar that is used as an ornamental in warm regions and in greenhouses and has thick dark green waxy leaves and waxy white flowers in clusters along the stem

**madagascar periwinkle** *n, usu cap M* **:** PERIWINKLE 1c

**madagascar rubber vine** *or* **madagascar rubber** *n, usu cap M* **:** a woody vine (*Cryptostegia madagascariensis*) with large whitish or pink flowers that is native to Madagascar and is grown in the tropics as an ornamental and for its milky juice that yields rubber

**¹mad·am** \ˈmadəm\ *n, pl* **madams** \-əmz\ *or* **mes·dames** \(ˈ)māˈdäm, -dam, -daa(ə)m, -dȧm\ *see numbered senses* [ME *madam*, *madame*, fr. OF *ma dame*, lit., my lady] **1 :** LADY — used as a form of respectful or polite address formerly to a woman of rank or position but now to any woman ⟨~, I swear I use no art at all —Shak.⟩ ⟨right this way, ~⟩ **2 :** MISTRESS 2 — used as a conventional title of courtesy formerly with the given name but now usu. with the surname ⟨how did thy master part with *Madam* Julia —Shak.⟩ ⟨with one accord lament for *Madam* Blaize —Oliver Goldsmith⟩ **3** *pl* **madams**, *archaic* **:** a woman affecting ostentatious refinement ⟨was far too pampered a ~ —Thomas Hood †1845⟩ **4** *pl* **madams a** *obs* **:** PROSTITUTE ⟨a gentleman who mistook a kept ~ for a lady —*Gentleman's Mag.*⟩ **b :** the female head of a house of prostitution **:** BAWD ⟨the hard-bitten ~ of the house where the prostitute works —Brendan Gill⟩ **5** *pl* **madams :** the female head of a household **:** WIFE ⟨every once in a while the ~ and I will order a book that we've read about —H.S.Truman⟩

**²madam** \"\ *vt* -ED/-ING/-S *archaic* **:** to address as madam ⟨they ~ each other with genteel petulance —*Examiner*⟩

**ma·dame** \(ˈ)maˈdam, -daa(ə)m *also* məˈd- *sometimes* məˈdäm *or* -ˈdȧm; *before a surname* " *or* ˈmadəm\ *n, pl* **mes·dames** \(ˈ)māˈdäm, -dam, -daa(ə)m, -dȧm\ *or* **madames** *see numbered senses* [F, fr. OF *ma dame*, lit., my lady] **1** *pl* **madames**, *archaic* **:** a French married woman ⟨would tell you which ~ loved a monsieur —Ben Jonson⟩ **2 :** a female member of the French royal family; *specif* **:** the eldest daughter of the French king or of the dauphin **3** *pl* **mesdames :** MISTRESS — used as a title that is prefixed to the surname of a woman who is not of English-speaking nationality or that is assumed by a professional woman (as a musician) esp. to imply European antecedents **4** *pl* **madames :** MADAM 4b ⟨the wrong side of the tracks, among coal miners and ~s of sporting houses —Heath Bowman⟩

**ma'·dan** \ˈmäˌdän\ *n, pl* **ma'dan** *or* **ma'dans** *usu cap* **1 :** an Arab people inhabiting the marshland below Baghdad along the Tigris and Euphrates rivers **2 :** a member of the Ma'dan people

**mad·a·pol·lam** *or* **mad·a·pol·am** \,madəˈpäləm\ *n* -s [fr. *Madapollam*, suburb of Narsapur, India, where it was originally made] **:** a soft plain cotton now woven in various weights in England

**mad apple** *n* **1 :** EGGPLANT **2 :** THORN APPLE 2 **3 :** DEAD SEA APPLE

**madar** *var of* MUDAR

**mad·a·ro·sis** \,madəˈrōsəs\ *n, pl* **madaro·ses** \-ō,sēz\ [NL, fr. Gk *madarōsis* baldness, madarosis, fr. *madaroun* to make bald (fr. *madaros* wet, bald) + *-sis*; akin to Gk *madan* to be wet, be bald — more at MEAT] **:** loss of the eyelashes or of the hair of the eyebrows

**mad·a·rot·ic** \,madəˈräd·ik\ *adj* [fr. NL *madarosis*, after such pairs as NL *hypnosis*: E *hypnotic*] **:** of, related to, or affected with madarosis

**¹madbrain** \ˈ⁼,⁼\ *n* [¹*mad* + *brain*] *archaic* **:** one who is madbrained

**²madbrain** *adj, obs* **:** MAD-BRAINED

**mad-brained** \ˈ⁼ˈbrānd\ *adj* **:** marked by hotheadedness **:** RASH

**¹madcap** \ˈ⁼,⁼\ *n* [¹*mad* + *cap*] **:** one who is madcap

**²madcap** \"\ *adj* **:** marked by impulsiveness, recklessness, or rashness ⟨the ~ girl ran up to her mother —W.M.Thackeray⟩ ⟨the venture was a sound proposition . . . no ~ haphazard scheme —*Irish Digest*⟩

**madded** *past of* MAD

**mad·den** \ˈmadᵊn, ˈmaad-,ˈmaid-\ *vb* **maddened; maddened; maddening** \-d(ᵊ)niŋ\ **maddens** [¹*mad* + *-en*] *vi* **:** to become or act as if mad ⟨whole populations ~*ing* to avenge the cause —H.H.Milman⟩ ~ *vt* **1 :** to drive mad **:** CRAZE ⟨guards do not have time to wrestle with bathers ~*ed* by fear —Charles Price⟩ **2 :** to make intensely angry **:** ENRAGE ⟨~*ed* statesmen and diplomats by his tactlessness and his colossal cheek —Roger Pippett⟩

**maddening** *adj* [fr. pres. part. of *madden*] **1 :** tending to craze ⟨~ pain . . . can rarely be alleviated but by opium —J.M. Good⟩ **2 a :** tending to infuriate ⟨was facing a horrible death . . . a ~ waste of life —Upton Sinclair⟩ **b :** tending to vex **:** IRRITATING ⟨the ceaseless tinny tumult of the jukebox was ~ —John McNulty⟩ — **mad·den·ing·ly** *adv* — **mad·den·ing·ness** *n* -ES

**¹mad·der** \ˈmadə(r)\ *n* -s [ME *madder*, *mader*, fr. OE *mædere*; akin to MD *mēde* madder, OHG *matara*, ON *mathra* madder, and perh. to Pol *modry* dark blue, Czech *modrý* blue] **1 :** any of several herbs of the genus *Rubia*; *esp* **:** a Eurasian herb (*Rubia tinctorum*) with verticillate leaves and small yellowish panicled flowers succeeded by berries **2 a :** the root of the madder plant used formerly in dyeing chiefly because of its content of alizarin in the form of the glycoside ruberythric acid **b :** a dye prepared from this root but later replaced by synthetic alizarin — compare GARANCINE, TURKEY RED 1a

**²mad·der** \", ˈmaad-,ˈmaid-\ *comparative of* MAD

**³mad·der** \ˈmadə(r)\ *or* **meth·er** \ˈmethə-\ *n* -s [IrGael *meadar* churn, madder] **:** a square wooden drinking cup used in Ireland

branch of madder

**madder bleach** *n* **:** a method of bleaching cotton goods in order to secure a pure white ground for printing by boiling several times with alkalis and then using bleach powder

**madder blue** *n* **:** a grayish violet to grayish purple

**madder brown** *n* **:** CASTILIAN BROWN

**madder carmine** *n* **:** a moderate red to purplish red that is very slightly bluer and less strong than pomegranate purple

**madder crimson** *n* **:** a vivid red that is bluer and deeper than apple red, yellower and stronger than carmine, bluer and darker than Castilian red or pimento, and bluer and deeper than scarlet — called also *crimson madder*

**madder family** *n* **:** RUBIACEAE

**madder indian red** *n, often cap I* **:** TUSCAN RED

**madder lake** *n* **1 :** MADDER ROSE **2 a :** a purplish red pigment prepared formerly from madder and usu. alum **b :** a cherry red pigment prepared from alizarin and usu. a compound of aluminum — see DYE table (under *Pigment Red 83*)

**madder orange** *n* **:** a strong orange that is lighter and stronger than pumpkin, redder than cadmium orange, and lighter and stronger than mandarin orange — called also *orange madder*

**madder pink** *n* **:** MADDER ROSE

**madder purple** *n* **:** a moderate to dark red

**madder red** *n* **:** ENGLISH RED

**madder rose** *n* **:** a strong purplish red that is redder than average bright rose — called also *casino pink, madder lake, madder pink, pink madder, rose madder*

**madder scarlet** *n* **:** a strong yellowish pink that is darker and much redder than salmon pink, redder and deeper than melon, and redder than peach red — called also *scarlet madder*

**madder violet** *n* **:** a dark purple that is bluer, lighter, and stronger than average prune, bluer and less strong than mulberry (sense 2a), and bluer and lighter than plum (sense 6b) — called also *eveque, old helio*

**madderwort** \ˈ⁼⁼,⁼\ *n* **:** a plant of the family Rubiaceae

**madder yellow** *n* **:** DUTCH PINK 3

**maddest** *superlative of* MAD

**mad·ding** \ˈmadiŋ, ˈmaad-,ˈmaid-, -dēŋ\ *adj* [fr. pres. part. of ²*mad*] **1 :** acting as if mad **:** FRENZIED, RAVING ⟨far from the ~ crowd's ignoble strife —Thomas Gray⟩ **2 :** inciting to madness **:** MADDENING ⟨her courage and loyalty balanced ~ defects —Anne Green⟩

**mad·dish** \-dish,-dēsh\ *adj* [¹*mad* + *-ish*] **1** *obs* **:** acting like a madman **2 :** somewhat mad

**mad·dle** \-dᵊl\ *vb* -ED/-ING/-S [irreg. fr. ¹*mad*] *vi, dial Eng* **:** to go mad ~ *vt, dial Eng* **:** CRAZE, CONFUSE

**mad-dog skullcap** *or* **mad-dog weed** *n* **:** an American mint (*Scutellaria lateriflora*) that yields a resinoid used esp. formerly as a tonic and antispasmodic — called also *blue pimpernel, blue skullcap*; see SCUTELLARIN

**mad·dox rod** \ˈmadəks-\ *n, usu cap M* [after Ernest E. *Maddox* †1933 Brit. ophthalmologist] **:** a transparent cylindrical glass rod or one of a series of such rods placed one above another for use in testing the eyes for heterophoria

**made** *adj* [ME *mad*, fr. past part. of *maken* to make — more at MAKE] **1 a :** artificially produced by a manufacturing process ⟨bought a few ~ goods — rope and nails —G.W.Brace⟩ **b :** artificially produced by excavation, grading, or filling ⟨the successive beds of ~ ground —T.H.Huxley⟩ **c :** INVENTED, FICTITIOUS ⟨reads like a ~ story —J.H.Newman⟩ **2 :** assured of success ⟨now am I a ~ man forever —Christopher Marlowe⟩ **3 :** fully trained — used esp. of a horse or dog ⟨a regular supply of ~ Argentine ponies at a moderate price —John Board⟩ **4 :** specially fitted, designed, or adapted ⟨a situation ~ for misunderstanding —Broadus Mitchell⟩

**made-beaver** \ˈ⁼ˌ⁼⁼\ *n* **1 :** a unit of value equivalent to the value of one beaver skin used in the early days of the Canadian fur trade **2 :** a token representing the value of a made-beaver — called also *beaver*

**made dish** *n* **:** a dish of food prepared from several ingredients (as meat, vegetables, and herbs) ⟨this beef casserole is a tasty *made dish*⟩

**mad·e·fac·tion** \,madəˈfakshən\ *n* [LL *madefaction-, madefactio*, fr. L *madefactus* (past part. of *madefacere*) + *-ion-, -io* -ion] *obs* **:** WETTING ⟨to all ~ there is required an imbibition —Francis Bacon⟩

**madefy** *vt* -ED/-ING/-ES [ME *madifien*, fr. MF *madefier*, fr. L *madefacere*, fr. *madēre* to be wet + *facere* to make, do — more at MEAT, DO] *obs* **:** WET, MOISTEN

**¹ma·dei·ra** \məˈdirə *sometimes* -derə\ *n* -s *usu cap* [Pg, fr. *Madeira* islands] **1 :** an amber-colored dessert wine of Madeira — compare BUAL, MALMSEY, SERCIAL **2 :** a wine similar to Madeira

**²madeira** \"\ *adj, usu cap* [fr. *Madeira*, island group in the eastern Atlantic ocean off the coast of Morocco] **:** of, relating to, or characteristic of the Madeira islands or their inhabitants

**³madeira** \"\ *n* -s *usu cap* [modif. (influenced by ¹*madeira*) of Sp *madera* wood, fr. L *materia* wood, material, matter — more at MATTER] **1 :** MAHOGANY 1a(1)&3a **2** *also* **madeira nut :** ENGLISH WALNUT 1

**madeira chair** *n, usu cap M* **:** a wickerwork chair orig. made in Madeira

**madeira embroidery** *n, usu cap M* **:** an eyelet and cutwork embroidery usu. having floral designs in white on white linen

**madeira mahogany** *n, usu cap 1st M* **:** canary wood from Madeira

**¹ma·dei·ran** \məˈdirən *sometimes* -der-\ *adj, usu cap* [*Madeira* islands + E *-an*] **:** MADEIRA

**²madeiran** \"\ *n* -s *usu cap* **:** a native or inhabitant of the Madeira islands

**madeira roach** *or* **madeira cockroach** *n, usu cap M* **:** a large cockroach (*Leucophaea maderae*) that is widely distributed in warm regions

**madeira vine** *n, usu cap M* **:** a vine (*Boussingaultia baselloides*) with shining entire leaves and small white flowers

**madeira-vine family** *n, usu cap M* **:** BASELLACEAE

**madeira wood** *n, usu cap M* [³*madeira*] **1 :** MAHOGANY 1a(1), 3a **2 :** WHITE IRONWOOD 1b

**mad·e·leine** \ˈmadᵊlən, ˌmadᵊlˈān\ *n* -s [F, prob. after *Madeleine* Paulmier, 19th cent. Fr. pastry cook] **:** a small rich cake baked in a tin shaped like a shell

**made mast** *n* **:** a mast composed of several longitudinal pieces held together by iron bands at intervals of about 3 feet

**ma·de·moi·selle** \ˌmadəməˈzel *also* ˌmadəmwəˈz- *or* ˌma(ə)d-mwəˈz- *or* ˌma(ə)d(ˌ)mwäˈz- *or* ˌma(ə)d-məˈz- *or* (ˈ)ma(ə)mˈz- *or* ˌma(ə)mwäˈz- *or* ˌmadəmˈz-\ *n, pl* **mademoiselles** \-lz\ *or* **mes·de·moi·selles** \ˌmādəməˈzel, -dəmwəˈ-, -dmwəˈ-, -d(ˌ)mwäˈ-, -dməˈ-\ [F, fr. OF *ma damoisele*, lit., my (young) lady] **1 a :** an unmarried French woman ⟨attractive ~*s* in national costume . . . serve twenty-nine varieties of wine —*Scots Mag.*⟩ **b :** a French governess or nurse ⟨was spending the summer in a chalet . . . with her four children, her sister, a ~, and a cook —Maddy Vegtel⟩ **2 :** a female member of the French royal family: **a :** the eldest daughter of the king's eldest brother **b :** the eldest daughter of the king **c :** the highest-ranking unmarried princess of the blood royal **3 :** MISS — often used as a title prefixed to the name of an unmarried woman who is not of English-speaking nationality **4 :** any of several silvery marine fishes with a strong second anal spine that form a genus (*Bairdiella*) of the family Sciaenidae; *esp* **:** a fish (*B. chrysura*) of the southern U.S.

**made-over** \ˈ⁼ˈ⁼⁼\ *adj* [fr. past part. of *make over*] **:** fashioned again **:** REMADE, REMODELED ⟨hostels range from *made-over* barns to comparatively luxurious houses —*Life*⟩

**made-to-measure** \ˈ⁼⁼ˈ⁼⁼\ *adj* **:** fashioned to measurements specifically required ⟨one may have one's personal idiosyncrasies built into the *made-to-measure* garment —S.D. Barney⟩

**made-to-order** \ˈ⁼⁼ˈ⁼⁼\ *adj* **1 :** produced to supply a special or an individual demand **:** made in addition to the regular stock or line; *specif* **:** MADE-TO-MEASURE ⟨*made-to-order* footgear —Edna Ferber⟩ — opposed to *ready-made* **2 :** fashioned or created in or as if in accordance with or as if with a preconceived plan ⟨in a few years Bonn will be a spick-and-span *made-to-order* capital —Joseph Wechsberg⟩

**made-up** \ˈ⁼ˈ⁼\ *adj* [fr. past part. of *make up*] **1** *obs* **:** CONSUMMATE, COMPLETE ⟨remain assured that he's a *made-up* villain —Shak.⟩ **2 :** marked by the use of makeup ⟨applied a small handkerchief carefully to her *made-up* eyelashes —Dorothy Sayers⟩ **3 :** fancifully conceived or falsely devised ⟨the style . . . seemed to be too formal, too *made-up*, insuffi-

ciently spontaneous —Aldous Huxley⟩ **4 a :** fully manufactured ⟨a *made-up* garment consists of more than one class of fabric —S.D.Barney⟩ **b** *of a necktie* **:** made with a permanently tied bow ⟨swallowed his pride and used a *made-up* tie —J.M.Barrie⟩ **5 :** firmly resolved **:** DECIDED ⟨an audience with stubbornly *made-up* minds —*Progressive Labor World*⟩
**made–work** \ˈ=,=\ *n* **:** work designed to provide employment as distinguished from work that is inherently necessary or permanently valuable ⟨heavy government spending, *made-work*, and an unbalanced budget —John Fischer⟩
**madge** \ˈmaj\ *n* -S [prob. fr. *Madge*, nickname for *Margaret*] **1 :** BARN OWL **2** *dial Brit* **:** MAGPIE
**ma·dhab** \məˈdab\ *n* -S [Ar *madhhab* opinion] **:** a school of Muslim jurisprudence
**mad–headed** \ˈ=ˈ==\ *adj* **:** MAD-BRAINED
**madhouse** \ˈ=,=\ *n* **1 :** a house where insane persons are detained and treated **:** an insane asylum **2 :** a place or scene of bewildering uproar or confusion ⟨how before we bought a television . . . the place used to be a ~ —Bennett Cerf⟩
**ma·dhu·ca** \məˈdükə\ *n* [NL, fr. Skt *madhūka* mahua — more at MAHUA] **1** *cap* **:** a genus of East Indian trees (family Sapotaceae) several of which yield valuable oils and timber — see ILLUPI, MAHUA **2** -S **:** any tree of the genus *Madhuca*
**mad·hya·mi·ka** \mäd(h)yəmikə\ *n* -S *usu cap* [Skt *mādhyamika*, fr. *madhyama* middle, superlative of *madhya* middle — more at MID] **1** *or* **madhyamaka :** one of the two major philosophical systems of Mahayana Buddhism holding against both realism and nihilism that ultimate reality has no definable characteristic and is beyond both knowing and being — compare YOGACARA **2 :** an adherent of Madhyamika
**ma·di** \ˈmädē\ *n, pl* **madi** *or* **madis** *usu cap* **1 a :** a Negro people of the upper Nile region north of Lake Albert **b :** a member of such people **2 :** a central Sudanic language of the Madi people
**ma·dia** \ˈmädēə\ *n, cap* [NL, fr. Sp *madia, madi*, a Chilean species of *Madia*, fr. Araucan *Madi*] **:** a genus of sticky herbs (family Compositae) having heads with deeply grooved bracts investing the achenes — see MELOSA, TARWEED
**madia oil** *n* **:** an oil made from the seeds of the melosa and used as a substitute for olive oil
**mad·id** \ˈmadəd\ *adj* [L *madidus*, fr. *madēre* to be wet — more at MEAT] **:** WET, MOIST ⟨his large deep blue eye, ~ and yet piercing —Benjamin Disraeli⟩
**mad·i·son** \ˈmadəsən\ *adj, usu cap* [fr. *Madison*, Wis.] **:** of or from Madison, the capital of Wisconsin ⟨*Madison* shoppers⟩ **:** of the kind or style prevalent in Madison
**madison avenue** *adj, usu cap M&A* [fr. *Madison avenue*, New York city, the center of the Amer. advertising business] **:** of, relating to, or having the characteristics of the American advertising industry ⟨taking full advantage of modern *Madison Avenue* advertising techniques —*Newsweek*⟩ ⟨dress more conservative than *Madison Avenue* junior executives —Robert Sylvester⟩
**¹mad·i·so·ni·an** \ˌmadəˈsōnēən\ *adj, usu cap* [James *Madison* †1812, 4th U.S. president + E *-ian*] **:** of or relating to James Madison or to his political principles
**²madisonian** \ˈ"\ *n* -S *usu cap* **:** a follower of James Madison **:** an adherent of the political principles of Madison ⟨persons who at that time were staunch Federalists and since that time have been staunch . . . *Madisonians* —*Annals of 14th Congress*⟩
**³madisonian** \ˈ"\ *n* -S *cap* [*Madison*, Wis. + E *-ian*] **:** a native or resident of Madison, Wisconsin
**mad itch** *n* **:** PSEUDORABIES
**mad·ling** \ˈmadliŋ\ *n* -S [¹*mad* + *-ling*] **:** a mad person **:** DOTARD, FOOL, SIMPLETON
**mad·ly** *adv* [ME, fr. *medd, madd, mad* mad + *-ly* — more at MAD] **:** in a mad manner: as **a :** in an insane manner ⟨drew his sword and rushed ~ on the justiciary —J.R.Green⟩ **b :** in a foolish or rash manner ⟨the help of that single power he had ~ rejected —T.B.Macaulay⟩ **c :** in a vigorous or energetic manner ⟨worked ~ throwing the boxes in at the door of the express car —Sherwood Anderson⟩ **d :** to an excessive or extreme degree ⟨finds herself ~ in love with a young American —B.R.Redman⟩ ⟨boasts a pedigree that is almost ~ aristocratic —Francis Steegmuller⟩
**mad·man** \ˈmad,man, ˈmaad-,ˈmaid-, -,mən, -,maa(ə)n\ *n, pl* **madmen** [ME *madd man*] **1 :** a man who is insane **:** LUNATIC ⟨there are *madmen* . . . in whom it is difficult to find any trace of hallucination —Henry Maudsley⟩ **2 :** a man who is rash or foolish ⟨the casual skill with which these *madmen* diced with danger —J.E.Macdonnell⟩
**mad money** *n* **:** carfare carried by a girl on a date to provide a means of escaping her escort in the event of unwanted familiarities; *broadly* **:** a small sum carried by a woman for emergency use
**mad·nep** \ˈ=,nep\ *n* -S [¹*mad* + E dial. *nep, neep* turnip, parsnip, fr. ME *nepe* — more at NEEP] **1** *obs* **:** COW PARSNIP **2 :** WILD PARSNIP
**mad·ness** *n* -ES [ME *maddnesse*, fr. *madd* mad + *-nesse* -ness — more at MAD] **1 :** the quality or state of being mad: as **a :** INSANITY ⟨undergoes a period of ~ in a mental hospital —W.E.Allen⟩ **b :** extreme folly **:** RASHNESS ⟨to grant such a demand would be strategic ~ —H.W.Baldwin⟩ **c :** intense anger **:** RAGE ⟨his editorials . . . often goaded the opposition to ~ —W.E.Smith⟩ **d :** complete involvement in or concern with the pursuit of an object or activity ⟨trivial by-products of her age's industrial ~ —Sherwood Anderson⟩ **e :** ECSTASY, ENTHUSIASM ⟨poetry has nothing to do with reasoning but is a sort of divine ~ —Irving Babbitt⟩ **2 :** any of several ailments of animals (as dogs) marked by frenzied or irrational behavior; *specif* **:** RABIES
**¹ma·don·na** \məˈdänə\ *n* -S [It, fr. OIt *ma donna*, lit., my lady] **1** *archaic* **:** LADY — used as a form of respectful or polite address ⟨good ~, why mournest thou —Shak.⟩ **2** *obs* **:** an Italian woman **3 :** a picture, statue, or other representation of the Virgin Mary ⟨artisans readying the giant religious floats with their jeweled life-sized ~*s* —Barnaby Conrad⟩
**²madonna** \ˈ"\ *adj* **:** of, relating to, or being a woman's hair style in which the hair is pulled back smoothly from a middle part
**madonna lily** *n, usu cap M* **:** a white lily (*Lilium candidum*) with bell-shaped to broad funnel-shaped flowers formerly extensively forced for spring blooming — called also *Annunciation lily, Lent lily*; compare BERMUDA LILY
**ma·do·qua** \məˈdōkwə\ *n* [Amharic *mēdaqwa*] **1** -S **:** ROYAL ANTELOPE **2** *cap* **:** a genus comprising some small antelopes of eastern and northeastern Africa
**mador** *n* -S [L, moisture, fr. *madēre* to be wet + *-or* — more at MEAT] *obs* **:** SWEAT
**ma·drague** \məˈdräg\ *n* -S [F, fr. Prov *madrago*, fr. Ar *mazrabah*] **:** a large fishpound or a seine used to capture tuna in the Mediterranean
**¹ma·dras** \məˈdras, -räs, -raa(ə)s, -rás; ˈmadrəs, ˈmaad-\ *adj, usu cap* [fr. *Madras*, India] **:** of or from the city of Madras, India **:** of the kind or style prevalent in Madras
**²madras** \ˈ"\ *n* -ES *sometimes cap, often attrib* **1 a** (1) **:** a fine plain-woven shirting and dress fabric usu. of cotton with small usu. woven designs (as stripes, checks) in bright colors or in white (2) **:** a light open usu. cotton fabric that has a heavy usu. woven design and that is used for curtains and draperies **b :** MADRAS HANDKERCHIEF **2 :** SUNN
**ma·dra·sah** *or* **ma·dra·sa** \məˈdrasə\ *n* -S [Ar *madrasah*, lit., place of study] **:** a Muslim school or college or university
**madras gram** *n, usu cap M* **:** HORSE GRAM
**madras handkerchief** *n, sometimes cap M* **:** a large usu. cotton kerchief in bright usu. solid colors that is often worn as a turban
**madras hemp** *n, usu cap M* **:** SUNN
**ma·dra·si** *also* **ma·dras·si** *pronunc at* ¹MADRAS + ē\ *n, pl* **madrasi** *or* **madrasis** [Hindi *madrasī*] **1** *usu cap* **:** a native or inhabitant of Madras in the subcontinent of India **2** *sometimes cap* **:** a native hired usu. as an unskilled laborer in the subcontinent of India
**mad·re·po·ra** \ˌmadrəˈpōrə, məˈdrepərə\ *n* [NL, fr. It, madrepore — more at MADREPORE] *syn of* ACROPORA
**mad·re·po·rar·ia** \ˌmadrəpəˈra(a)rēə, ˌmə,drep-\ *n pl, cap* [NL, fr. *Madrepora* + *-aria*] **:** an extensive order of Anthozoa including most species that produce stony corals and that resemble the actiniarians in the general structure of the soft parts but that usu. form colonies and always have an ectodermal calcareous skeleton — **mad·re·po·rar·i·an** \ˌmadrəpəˈra(a)rēən, mə¦drep-\ *adj or n*
**mad·re·pore** \ˈmadrə,pō(ə)r\ *n* [F *madrépore*, fr. It *madrepora*, fr. *madre* mother (fr. L *mater*) + *-pora* (fr. *poro* pore, fr. L *porus*) — more at MOTHER, PORE] **:** any of various stony reef-building corals (order Madreporaria) of tropical seas that assume a variety of branching, encrusting, or massive forms and that include the staghorn corals, the brain corals, and the mushroom corals
**¹mad·re·po·ri·an** \ˌmadrəˈpōrēən\ *adj* [*madrepore* + *-ian*] **:** MADREPORIC
**²madreporian** \ˈ"\ *n* -S **:** MADREPORE
**mad·re·por·ic** \ˌmadrəˈpórik\ *also* **mad·re·po·rit·ic** \-pəˈridik, mə¦drep-\ *adj* **:** of, relating to, or like a madrepore or a madreporite
**madreporic body** *or* **madreporic plate** *or* **madreporic tubercle** *n* **:** MADREPORITE
**mad·re·por·i·form** \ˌmadrəˈpórə,fórm\ *adj* [ISV *madrepore* + *-iform*] **:** resembling a madrepore
**mad·re·por·ite** \ˈmadrə,pō,rīt, məˈdrepə,rīt\ *n* -S [ISV *madrepore* + *-ite*] **:** a perforated or porous body that is situated at the distal end of the stone canal in echinoderms and that may be internal or inconspicuously buried in the body wall (as in holothurians) or may be a conspicuous convex plate on the dorsal side of the body (as in many starfishes)
**ma·drid** \məˈdrid\ *adj, usu cap* [fr. *Madrid*, Spain] **:** of or from Madrid, the capital of Spain **:** of the kind or style prevalent in Madrid
**madrid sweet clover** *n, usu cap M* **:** a biennial sweet clover native to Spain and introduced for use as a forage and hay crop in the southern U. S.
**mad·ri·gal** \ˈmadrəgəl, ˈmaad-,-rēg-\ *n* -S [It *madrigale*, fr. ML *matricale*, fr. neut. of (assumed) ML *matricalis* simple, fr. LL, of the womb — more at MATRIC] **1 :** a medieval short lyrical poem esp. of love **2 a :** a polyphonic part-song originating in the 14th century that has parts for three or more voices and is marked by the use of a secular text and a freely imitative style and counterpoint and that in its later development esp. in the 16th and 17th centuries is often marked by a distinct melody in the upper voice and by being designed for accompaniment by strings that either double or replace one or more of the voice parts — compare MOTET **b :** a part-song of any kind; *esp* **:** GLEE
**mad·ri·gal·er** *also* **mad·ri·gal·ler** \-lə(r)\ *n* -S **:** MADRIGALIST
**mad·ri·gal·esque** \ˈ==gə¦lesk\ *adj* [F, fr. It *madrigalesco*, fr. *madrigale* + *-esco* -esque] **:** relating to or having the characteristics of a madrigal
**mad·ri·galian** \ˈ==ˈgalēən, -gāl-, -lyən\ *adj* [*madrigal* + *-ian*] **:** of or relating to madrigals
**mad·ri·gal·ist** \ˈ==,gələst\ *n* -S **:** a composer of madrigals
**ma·drih** *or* **ma·drich** \mäˈdrik\ *n, pl* **madri·him** *or* **madri·chim** \,mädriˈkēm\ [NHeb *madhrīkh*, fr. Heb, guide, leader] **:** a leader or teacher in Israeli youth groups
**madri·le·ña** \ˌmadrəˈlānyə, ˌmäthr-\ *n* -S *often cap* [Sp, fem. of *madrileño*] **:** a female native or resident of Madrid, Spain
**¹mad·ri·lene** \ˈmadrə,lēn, ˌ==ˈ=\ *n* -S *cap* [Sp *madrileño*] **:** MADRILENIAN
**²ma·dri·lene** \ˈmadrə,len, -lān\ *n* -S [F (*consommé*) *madrilène*, lit., Madrid consommé] **:** a consommé flavored with tomato and served hot or cold
**¹mad·ri·le·nian** \ˌmadrə¦lēnēən, -nyən\ *adj, usu cap* [Sp *madrileño* of Madrid (fr. *Madrid*) + E *-ian*] **:** of or from Madrid, Spain **:** of the kind or style prevalent in Madrid
**²madrilenian** \ˈ"\ *n* -S *cap* **:** a native or resident of Madrid, Spain
**madri·le·ño** \ˌmadrəˈlān(,)yō, ˌmäthr-\ *n* -S *often cap* [Sp, fr. *Madrid*, Spain] **:** a native or resident of Madrid, Spain **:** MADRILENIAN
**ma·dro·na** *or* **ma·dro·ne** *or* **ma·dro·ño** \məˈdrōnə\ *n* -S [Sp & MexSp *madroño*] **1 :** a plant of the genus *Arbutus*: **a :** an evergreen tree or shrub (*A. menziesii*) of the Pacific coast of No. America that has a smooth bark and thick shining leaves and edible red berries **b :** a tree or shrub (*A. xalapensis*) of the Mexican border **2 :** DAGAME **3 :** STRAWBERRY TREE 1
**madrona apple** *n* **:** one of the red berries borne by the madrona
**mads** *pres 3d sing of* MAD, *pl of* MAD
**mad staggers** *n pl* **:** STAGGERS
**madstone** \ˈ=,=\ *n* **:** a stony concretion (as a hair ball taken from the stomach of a deer) supposed to counteract the poisonous effects of the bite of an animal (as one affected with rabies)
**madtom** \ˈ=,=\ *n* -S [¹*mad* + *tom* (cat)] **:** any of several small freshwater catfishes (family Ameiuridae) that are widely distributed in the central and eastern U.S. and have poisonous pectoral spines capable of inflicting painful wounds
**mad·u·ra** \ˈmajərə\ *adj, usu cap* [fr. *Madura*, India] **:** of or from the city of Madura, India **:** of the kind or style prevalent in Madura
**madura foot** *n, usu cap M* **:** maduromycosis of the foot
**madu·rese** \ˌmadəˈrēz, ¦maja-, mə¦dü-, -ēs\ *n, pl* **madurese** *usu cap* [*Madura* + E *-ese*] **1 a :** an Indonesian people inhabiting Madura and adjacent regions on Java **b :** a member of the Madurese people **2 :** the Austronesian language of the Madurese people
**ma·du·ro** \məˈdü(,)rō\ *n* -S [Sp, fr. *maduro* ripe, mature, fr. L *maturus* — more at MATURE] **:** a dark-colored relatively strong cigar
**mad·u·ro·mycosis** \ˌmajə(,)rō+\ *n* [NL, fr. *Madura*, India + NL *-o-* + *mycosis*] **:** a destructive chronic disease usu. restricted to the feet, marked by swelling and deformity resulting from the formation of granulomatous nodules drained by sinuses connecting with the exterior, and caused esp. by an aerobic form of actinomycetes and sometimes by true fungi — compare NOCARDIOSIS
**madweed** \ˈ=,=\ *n* **:** MAD-DOG SKULLCAP
**madwoman** \ˈ=,==\ *n, pl* **madwomen :** an insane woman
**madwort** \ˈ=,=\ *n* **1 :** a cress of the genus *Lobularia* **2 :** GERMAN MADWORT **3 :** GOLD OF PLEASURE **4 :** a plant of the genus *Alyssum*
**madzoon** *var of* MATZOON
**¹mae** \ˈmā\ *adj, adv, or n* [ME (northern dial.) *ma*, fr. OE *mā* — more at MORE] *Scot* **:** MORE
**²mae** \ˈma, ˈmaa, ˈmā\ *Scot var of* BAA
**maeander** *var of* MEANDER
**mae·an·dra** \mēˈandrə\ *n, cap* [NL, fr. L *maeander, maeandrus* twist, winding — more at MEANDER] **:** a large genus of massive reef-building corals including many brain corals — **mae·an·droid** \ˈ=ˈ=,dróid\ *adj*
**mae·an·drine** \-,drin, -ˈdrən\ *adj* [NL Maeandra + E *-ine*] **:** of or relating to the genus *Maeandra* — **mae·an·drin·i·form** \¦=(,)=ˈdrinə,fórm\ *adj* — **mae·an·dri·noid** \ˈ=ˈdrə,nóid\ *adj*
**mae·ce·nas** \məˈsēnəs, mē-ˈ *also* mīˈ-\ *n* -ES *usu cap* [L, after Gaius *Maecenas* †8 B.C. Roman statesman and patron of literature] **:** a generous benefactor; *esp* **:** a munificent patron of literature or art ⟨opera has never really paid its way anywhere, but in Europe government subventions have replaced the . . . vanished *Maecenases* —James Hinton⟩
**mae·ce·nas·ship** \-nəs,ship\ *n, usu cap* **:** the status of being a Maecenas
**mae·ce·na·tism** \-nə,tizəm\ *n* -S *usu cap* [Gaius *Maecenat-*, *Maecenas* + E *-ism*] **:** PATRONAGE
**maeg·bote** *or* **maeg·bot** *also* **mag·bote** \ˈmag,bōt\ *n* -S [OE *mǣgbōt*, fr. *mǣg* kinsman, relative + *bōt* compensation; akin to OS & OHG *māg* kinsman, ON *māgr* relative by marriage, Goth *megs* son-in-law, Gk *periēmektein* to be unwilling, Lith *mėgti* to like; basic meaning: friendly — more at BOOT] *Anglo-Saxon law* **:** compensation paid to the kinsmen of a man slain
**mael·strom** \ˈmālztrəm, -lst- *also* -lz,träm *or* -l,sträm\ *n* -S [obs. D (now *maalstroom*), fr. *malen* to grind, turn (fr. MD) + *strom* stream, fr. MD *strōm*; akin to OHG *malan* to grind, and to OHG *stroum, strōm* stream — more at MEAL, STREAM] **1 :** a powerful often destructive water current that usu. moves in a circular direction with extreme rapidity sucking in objects within a given radius **:** WHIRLPOOL ⟨tried to shoot the canoe across a stretch of treacherous ~ —*Harper's*⟩ **2 :** something resembling a maelstrom ⟨the ancient taboos were gone, lost in the ~ of war —Coulton Waugh⟩ ⟨childhood playmates in the country . . . later separated in the ~ of city life —J.D.Hart⟩ ⟨couldn't fuse his thoughts out of the ~ of thinking —Herbert Elliston⟩
**mael·zel's metronome** \ˈmeltsəlz-\ *n, usu cap 1st M* [after Johann N. *Maelzel* (Mälzel) †1838 Ger. musician, its inventor] **:** METRONOME
**maen** \ˈmān\ *Scot var of* MOAN
**mae·nad** *also* **me·nad** \ˈmē,nad\ *n* -S [L *maenad-, maenas*, fr. Gk *mainad-, mainas*, lit., madwoman, fr. *mainesthai* to be mad; akin to Gk *menos* spirit — more at MIND] **1 a :** a woman participating in the orgiastic Dionysian rites **:** BACCHANTE **b :** a frenzied female dancer **2 :** an unnaturally excited or distraught woman ⟨a figure scarcely human, a tragic *Maenad* —R.L.Stevenson⟩ — **mae·nad·ic** \mēˈnadik\ *adj*
**mae·nad·ism** \ˈ=,na,dizəm\ *n* -S **:** the practices of the maenads
**mae·ni·dae** \ˈmēnə,dē\ *n pl, cap* [NL, fr. *Maena*, type genus (fr. L, a kind of small sea fish, fr. Gk *mainē*) + *-idae*] **:** a small family of slender percoid marine fishes including the picarels
**mae·o·ni·an** \(ˈ)mēˈōnēən\ *adj, usu cap* [*Maeonia*, ancient country in Asia Minor (fr. L, fr. Gk *Maionia*) + E *-an*] **:** of or relating to ancient Maeonia afterward called Lydia and reputed to be the birthplace of Homer
**maerl** \ˈmer(ə)l, mäˈer-\ *n* -S [F *maërl, maërle*, fr. Bret *merl, maërl* marl, mearl, fr. MF *marle* marl — more at MARL] **:** lime-producing red seaweeds principally of the genus *Lithothamnion* used esp. in France to reduce acidity of the soil
**¹mae·sto·so** \mīˈstō(,)sō, ,mäsˈs-, -)zō\ *adj* (*or adv*) [It, majestic, fr. *maestà* majesty (fr. L *majestat-, majestas*) + *-oso* -ous — more at MAJESTY] **:** majestic and stately and usu. moderate in tempo — used as a direction in music
**²maestoso** \ˈ"\ *n* -S **:** a composition or movement in the maestoso style or tempo
**maestral** *obs var of* MISTRAL
**mae·stro** \ˈmī(,)strō *sometimes* mäˈe(-\ *n, pl* **maestros** \-rōz\ *or* **mae·stri** \-rē\ [It, lit., master, fr. L *magister* — more at MASTER] **:** one who is accomplished in a specialized field; *esp* **:** a master or teacher of an art (as music) ⟨when the ~ was active as one of the world's more famous operatic conductors —Claudia Cassidy⟩ ⟨contributors include some ~*s* in the delightful art of the spoof or parody —*Atlantic*⟩ ⟨that did not always mean that the ~ himself had actually painted the picture —H.W.Van Loon⟩
**maestro di cap·pel·la** \-dēkəˈpelə\ *n* [It] **:** CHOIRMASTER
**maestro–sastre** \ˈmīstrō¦sästrē\ *n* [Sp, fr. *maestro* master + *sastre* tailor] **:** MASTER-TAILOR
**mae·ter·linck·ian** \ˌmāt|ə(r)¦liŋkēən, ¦mel, |tə- *sometimes* ˈmä| *or* ˈma| *or* ˈmå|\ *adj, usu cap* [Maurice *Maeterlinck* †1949 Belgian poet, dramatist, and essayist + E *-ian*] **:** of, characteristic of, or resembling Maeterlinck or his writings ⟨writing a symbolic *Maeterlinckian* drama —Agnes Repplier⟩
**mae west** \ˈmāˈwest\ *n, usu cap M&W* [after *Mae West* b1892 Am. actress noted for her full figure] **:** a yellow life jacket inflatable by means of two cartridges of carbon dioxide that is worn by fliers in flights over water
**maf·fick** \ˈmafik, -fēk, *esp in pres part* -fək\ *vi* -ED/-ING/-S [back-formation fr. *Mafeking*, town in Union of So. Africa (used attrib. in such phrases as *Mafeking night*), site of a siege by the Boers during the Boer war that was relieved by British troops on May 17, 1900; fr. the rejoicing that the lifting of the siege caused in England] **:** to celebrate with boisterous rejoicings and hilarious behavior ⟨the reaction to better news caused a ~*ing* such as has rarely been seen—Nancy Mitford⟩
**maf·fle** \ˈmafəl\ *vb* -ED/-ING/-S [ME *mafflen*, prob. of imit. origin] *vi, now dial Eng* **:** to speak indistinctly **:** MUMBLE, STAMMER ~ *vt, now dial Eng* **:** to cause to become confused or bewildered
**ma·fia** *or* **maf·fia** \ˈmäfēə, ˈmaf-\ *n* -S *usu cap* [fr. *Mafia, Maffia*, a secret criminal society of Sicily, fr. It, fr. It dial. (Sicily) *mafia* boldness, bluster, swagger, prob. fr. Ar *mahyah* boasting] **1 :** a secret society of political terrorists ⟨browbeaten into joining this industrial *Mafia* —Benjamin Stolberg⟩ ⟨charges of a Soviet *Mafia* operating in Europe⟩ **2 :** a secret organization composed chiefly of criminal elements and usu. held to control racketeering, peddling of narcotics, gambling, and other illicit activities throughout the world ⟨the *Mafia* . . . concentrated on gambling, prostitution, and blackmail rackets among Italian immigrants, but prohibition brought an eruption of activity on a national scale —Stanley Frank⟩
**maf·ic** \ˈmafik\ *adj* [*magnesium* + L *ferrum* + E *-ic* — more at FARRIER] **:** of or relating to a group of minerals characterized by magnesium and iron and usu. by their dark color
**maf·ite** \-,fīt\ *n* -S [*mafic* + *-ite*] **:** a mafic mineral
**ma·foo** *also* **ma·fu** \ˈmäˈfü\ *n* -S [Chin (Pek) *ma³ fu¹* groom, fr. *ma³* horse + *fu¹* laborer] **:** a Chinese stable boy or groom
**maf·tir** \ˈmäf,ti(ə)r, ˈ=ˈ=\ *n* -S [Heb *maphṭīr* one that dismisses] **:** the reader of the Haftarah
**ma·fura** *or* **ma·fur·ra** \məˈfərə\ *n* -S [of Bantu origin; akin to Sotho & Ronga *mafura*, lit., fat, oil] **:** an East African tree (*Trichilia emetica*) having capsular fruit whose seeds yield a fatty substance resembling cocoa butter that is used for soap and candles
**¹mag** \ˈmag, -aa(ə)g, -aig\ *n* -S [short for *magpie*] **1** *dial Eng* **:** the European magpie **2 :** *now dial Brit* **:** TALK, CHATTER
**²mag** \ˈ"\ *vi* **magged; magged; magging; mags** *dial Brit* **:** to talk incessantly **:** CHATTER ⟨always *magging* about progress —John Morrison⟩
**³mag** \ˈ"\ *n* -S [origin unknown] *dial Brit* **:** HALFPENNY
**⁴mag** \ˈmag, -aa(ə)g, -aig\ *n* -S [by shortening] *slang* **:** MAGAZINE ⟨liked the plots and intrigues of the mystery ~*s* —*Newsweek*⟩
**⁵mag** \ˈ"\ *n* -S [by shortening] *slang* **:** MAGNETO ⟨all that's needed is to take the ~ out and give it a wipe —Agatha Christie⟩
**mag** *abbr* **1** magazine **2** magnet; magnetic; magnetism **3** magneto **4** magnitude
**ma·ga** \ˈmägə\ *n* -S [Skt] **:** a member of the priestly caste among the Sauras of India
**ma·ga·dhi** \ˈmägədē\ *n* -S *cap* **:** the Prakrit language of Magadha
**ma·ga·dis** \ˈmagədəs\ *n* -ES [Gk, of non-IE origin] **:** an ancient Greek musical instrument having twenty strings and the capability of being played in octaves
**ma·ga·dize** \-,dīz\ *vi* -ED/-ING/-S [Gk *magadizein*, fr. *magadis* + *-izein* -ize] **1 :** to sing or play in octaves ⟨the Greek practice of *magadizing*, in which . . . lay the fundamental principle of polyphony —H.E.Wooldridge⟩ **2 :** to play on the magadis
**ma·ga·hat** \ˈmägə¦hät\ *n, pl* **magahat** *or* **magahats** *usu cap* [native name in southern Negros] **1 :** a Bisayan people inhabiting the hills of southern Negros, Philippine islands **2 :** a member of the Magahat people
**ma·ga·hi** \ˈmägəhē\ *n* -S *cap* **:** an Indic dialect of west Bihar
**ma·ga·li** \məˈgälē\ *n, pl* **magali** *or* **magalis** *usu cap* **:** one of the numerous more isolated peoples of Arabia
**ma·ga·ni** \məˈgänē\ *n* -S *often cap* [native name in the Philippines] **:** a class of warriors of Mindanao — called also *bagani*
**¹mag·a·zine** \ˌmagəˈzēn, ˈmaig-\ *n* -S [MF, fr. OProv, fr. Ar *makhāzin*, pl. of *makhzan* storehouse, fr. *khazana* to store up] **1 a :** a place where goods or supplies are stored **:** WAREHOUSE ⟨each hamlet . . . possesses a ~ inside which families deposit all their provisions —H.T.Norris⟩ ⟨in the compting rooms and fur ~*s* of the concern —Walter O'Meara⟩ **b** *archaic* **:** a country or district esp. rich in natural resources or produce ⟨set down in a perfect ~ of fruit and vegetables, grain and wine —Leitch Ritchie⟩ **c** *archaic* **:** a city viewed as a marketing center ⟨islands . . . are now converted into complete ~*s* for all kinds of European goods —*Gentleman's Mag.*⟩ **2 a :** a place to store ammunition: as (1) **:** a building in which ammunition and explosives are kept on a military installation (2) **:** a compartment of a ship used to store ammunition and explosives **b** *archaic* **:** something resembling a place to store ammunition ⟨stored his ~ of malice with weapons equally sharp —Samuel Johnson⟩ **3 a :** the contents stored in a magazine: as (1) **:** an accumulation of munitions of war ⟨a large ~ of darts and arrows —Edward Gibbon⟩ (2) **:** a stock or store of provisions or goods ⟨~ of flesh, milk, butter, and cheese —Daniel Defoe⟩ **b :** something resembling the contents of a magazine ⟨truth becomes . . . a new weapon in the ~ of power —R.W.Emerson⟩ **4 a** (1) **:** a periodical that usu. contains a miscellaneous collection of articles, stories, poems, and pictures and is directed at the general reading public (2) **:** a periodical containing special material directed at a group having a particular hobby, interest, or profession (as education,

photography, or medicine) or at a particular age group (as children, teen-agers) ⟨alumni ~⟩ — compare LITTLE MAGAZINE **b :** a special section of a newspaper usu. appearing on Sunday ⟨seek a much wider audience for the paper . . . through an enlarged ~ —Bruce Bliven b. 1889⟩ **5 :** a supply chamber: as **a :** a holder that is incorporated in or attachable to a gun and that contains cartridges to be fed into the gun chamber by the operation of the piece — see CLIP e **b :** a lighttight chamber containing plates, sheet film, or rollable film for use in or on a camera or containing both feed and take-up spools for film for use in or on a motion-picture camera or projector **c :** the chambers to hold circulating matrices in a typesetting machine

**2magazine** \"\ *vt* -ED/-ING/-S *archaic* **:** to store in or as if in a magazine **:** store up for use

**mag·a·zine·let** \ˌ==ˈ=lət\ *n* -S **:** a small periodical

**mag·a·zin·er** \ˌ==ˈzēnə(r)\ *n* -S **:** MAGAZINIST

**magazine safety** *n* **:** a safety mechanism on an automatic pistol that makes firing impossible unless the magazine is in the weapon

**mag·a·zin·ish** \ˈ==ˈzēnish\ *adj* **:** characteristic of magazine writing **:** somewhat superficial or shallow ⟨the book seems too slick, too ~⟩

**mag·a·zin·ist** \-nəst\ *n* -S **:** one who writes for or edits a magazine ⟨usually the newspaper journalist rather than the ~ . . . has published his drama-filled memoirs —R.E.Wolseley⟩

**mag·a·ziny** \-nē\ *adj* **:** MAGAZINISH

**mag·da·len** \ˈmagdələn\ *or* **mag·da·lene** \-ˌlēn\ *n* -S *often cap* [after Mary *Magdalen* or *Magdalene*, woman whom Jesus healed of evil spirits (Lk 8:2), considered identical with a reformed prostitute (Lk 7:36 ff.)] **1 :** a reformed prostitute **2 :** a house of refuge or reformatory for prostitutes

**1mag·da·le·nian** \ˈmagdəˈlēnēən, -nyən\ *adj, usu cap* [F *Magdalénien*, fr. *Magdalen-* (fr. *La Madeleine*, rock shelter on the Vézère river in southwestern France, the type station of Magdalenian culture) + F *-ien* -ian] **:** of or belonging to a late Paleolithic period characterized by implements of flint (as scrapers, gravers, saws, and knives) and of bone and ivory (as borers, needles, harpoons, and hooks), carving, and polychrome painting in caves of southern France and northern Spain

**2magdalenian** \"\ *n* -S *usu cap* **:** one of a late Paleolithic people producing a distinct culture

**mag·de·burg** \ˈmägdəˌbu̇rg, ˈmagdəˌbərg\ *adj, usu cap* [fr. *Magdeburg*, Germany] **:** of or from the city of Magdeburg, Germany **:** of the kind or style prevalent in Magdeburg

**magdeburg hemisphere** *n, usu cap M* **:** either of a pair of hemispherical cups forming when placed together a cavity from which the air can be withdrawn by an air pump and used to illustrate the pressure of air

Magdeburg hemispheres

**mage** \ˈmāj\ *n* -S [ME, fr. L *magus* — more at MAGIC] **1 :** MAGICIAN **2 :** MAGUS

**1ma·gel·lan** \məˈjelən\ *adj, usu cap* [fr. the Straits of *Magellan*, strait between the southern tip of the mainland of So. America and the Tierra del Fuego archipelago that connects the Atlantic and Pacific oceans] **:** MAGELLANIC

**2magellan** \"\ *n* -S *usu cap* [after Ferdinand *Magellan* (Pg Fernando de Magalhães) †1521 Port. navigator who led the first expedition to circumnavigate the globe] **:** a world traveler ⟨a modern *Magellan* can leave . . . in a giant clipper of the air —*Saturday Rev.*⟩

**magellan barberry** *n, usu cap M* **:** a So. American evergreen shrub (*Berberis buxifolia*) with grooved slender branchlets, entire leaves, orange-yellow flowers, and dark purple fruit that is grown for ornament

**mag·el·lan·ic** \ˈmajəˈlanik\ *adj, usu cap* [Straits of *Magellan* + E *-ic*] **:** of, relating to, or characteristic of the Straits of Magellan or that general area of the southern hemisphere

**magellanic cloud** *n, usu cap M&C* **:** either of the two nearest galaxies to the Milky Way system located within 25 degrees of the south celestial pole and appearing as conspicuous patches of light resembling detached portions of the Milky Way but actually more than 200,000 light-years distant

**ma·gen da·vid** \mäˈgän(ˌ)däˈvēd, ˈmȯgənˈdȯvəd *sometimes* ˈmägənˈdävəd\ *also* **mo·gen da·vid** \ˈmȯgənˈdȯvəd\ *n, pl* **magen davids** *also* **mogen davids** *usu cap M&D* [Heb *māghēn Dāwīdh*, lit., shield of David, fr. *Dāwīdh* David †*ab*973B.C. king of Judah and Israel] **:** a figure in the shape of a six-pointed star formed by two intersecting equilateral triangles and widely used as a symbol of Judaism — called also *Shield of David, Star of David*

**ma·gen·ta** \məˈjentə\ *n* -S [fr. *Magenta*, town in northern Italy, site of a battle between the Austrian and the Franco-Sardinian armies on June 4, 1859; fr. its having been discovered shortly after the battle and fr. the red color of fuchsine, reminiscent of the blood spilled at Magenta] **1 :** FUCHSINE **2 a :** a deep purplish red that is bluer and stronger than American beauty, bluer, lighter, and stronger than hollyhock, and bluer and deeper than Harvard crimson (sense 2); *specif* **:** one of the subtractive primaries **b :** FUCHSIA RED **c** *of textiles* **:** a dark to deep purplish red that is redder and slightly darker than Indian lake

**magenta rose** *n* **:** a moderate purplish red that is bluer and deeper than average rose or solferino, redder and deeper than violine pink, and bluer and duller than average fuchsia rose

**mag·er·ful** \ˈmagərfəl\ *adj* [prob. by alter.] *Scot* **:** MASTERFUL

**1magged** *past of* MAG

**2magged** \ˈmagd, -aa(ə)gd, -aigd\ *adj* [prob. fr. E dial., tired, exhausted, of unknown origin] **:** WORN, FRAYED ⟨a ~ rope⟩

**mag·gid** \ˈmägid\ *n, pl* **mag·gid·im** \mäˈgēdəm, -ēm\ [Heb *maggīdh* narrator] **:** an itinerant Jewish preacher whose discourse on a biblical text is usu. embellished by parables drawn from the rabbinical commentaries and from Jewish folklore and is often delivered in a chant

**mag·gie's drawers** \ˈmagēz-, ˈmaigēz-\ *n pl, usu cap M* [fr. *Maggie*, nickname for *Margaret*] **1** *slang* **:** the red flag waved across the target by a marker on the target range when a shot has completely missed the target **2** *slang* **:** a miss when scoring targets

**magging** *pres part of* MAG

**mag·gio·re** \mäˈjō(ˌ)rā\ *adj* [It, lit., greater, fr. L *major* — more at MAJOR] **:** MAJOR 7

**1mag·got** \ˈmagət, ˈmaig-, *usu* -əd·+V\ *n* -S [ME *mathek, maddock, magotte* worm, grub, maggot, of Scand origin; akin to ON *mathkr* maggot, worm; akin to OE & Goth *matha* maggot, worm, OHG *mado* maggot, MLG *maddik* earthworm, and perh. to Arm *matʻil* louse] **1 a :** a soft-bodied legless grub that is the larva of various dipterous insects (as the housefly), that lacks a head capsule, has posterior complex respiratory apertures, and develops usu. in decaying organic matter or as a parasite in plants or animals — see MYIASIS **b :** something resembling a maggot ⟨a dead city spored with the ~*s* of helmeted figures —Bernard Frizell⟩ **2 a :** a sudden usu. eccentric idea **:** WHIM ⟨got some ~ in her head about being loved for her own sake —D.C.Murray⟩ **b :** a fixed idea **:** OBSESSION ⟨a decent and civilized lieutenant whose personal ~ was to spend the war in magnificent action —John McCarten⟩ **3 :** an old English country dance tune usu. coupled with someone's name ⟨My Lady Winwood's *Maggot*⟩

**2maggot** \"\ *n* -S [short for *maggotpie*] *dial Eng* **:** MAGPIE

**maggot-pated** *adj, obs* **:** having little sense **:** SILLY

**maggotpie** *n* [prob. fr. *Magote* (nickname for *Margaret*) + *pie* (magpie)] *obs* **:** MAGPIE

**mag·got·ry** \ˈmagətrē\ *n* -ES **:** stupid absurdity ⟨seemed somehow to come from all the . . . uncountable small ~ of the earth —Thomas Wolfe⟩

**maggot snipe** *n* **:** TURNSTONE

**mag·goty** \ˈmagəti\ *adj* **1 :** infested with maggots ⟨five small sacks of ~ apricots —Josephine Johnson⟩ **2** *chiefly Brit* **:** filled with absurd whims **:** FREAKISH

**magh** \ˈmäg\ *n* -S *usu cap* [Skt *māgha*] **:** a month of the Hindu year — see MONTH table

**mag·hem·ite** \magˈheˌmīt, ˈmagəˌm-\ *n* -S [*mag*netite + *hem*atite + *-ite*] **:** a magnetic mineral consisting of ferric oxide and constituting a member of the magnetite series

**ma·ghre·bi** *or* **ma·ghri·bi** \ˈməgrəbē\ *n, pl* **maghrebi** *or* **maghrebis** *or* **maghribi** *cap* [Ar *maghribīy*, lit., western] **1 :** a native or inhabitant of the Maghreb, a region including northwestern Africa, esp. Morocco, Algeria, and Tunis, and formerly also Moorish Spain **2 :** the Arabic dialect spoken in western No. Africa

**ma·ghreb·i·an** \məˈgrebēən\ *or* **ma·ghrib·i·an** \-grib-\ *adj, usu cap* [*Maghreb, Maghrib* northwestern Africa and Spain + E *-ian*] **1 :** of, relating to, or characteristic of the Maghreb **2 :** of, relating to, or characteristic of the people of the Maghreb

**maghzen** *var of* MAKHZAN

**magi** *pl of* MAGUS

**1ma·gi·an** \ˈmājēən\ *n* -S *usu cap* [L *magus* + E *-ian* — more at MAGUS] **:** MAGUS

**2magian** \"\ *adj* **1** *usu cap* **:** of or relating to the Magi **2 :** MAGICAL

**ma·gi·an·ism** \-əˌnizəm\ *n* -S *usu cap* **:** the beliefs and practices of the Magi

**1mag·ic** \ˈmajik, -jēk\ *n* -S [ME *magik*, fr. MF *magique*, fr. L *magice*, fr. Gk *magikē*, fr. fem. of *magikos*, adj.] **1 a :** the use of means (as ceremonies, charms, spells) that are believed to have supernatural power to cause a supernatural being to produce or prevent a particular result (as rain, death, healing) considered not obtainable by natural means and that also include the arts of divination, incantation, sympathetic magic, and thaumaturgy **:** control of natural forces by the typically direct action of rites, objects, materials, or words considered supernaturally potent **b magics** *pl* **:** magic beliefs or practices **:** CHARM 1b ⟨in their crafts, their dances, their rituals of harvest, their local ~*s* for comfort and ease —Waldo Frank⟩ ⟨masters of poems and small ~*s* who could make . . . spells and runes —Leah B. Drake⟩ **2 a :** an extraordinary power or influence seemingly from a supernatural source ⟨a thinker who proposed to test men and measures by the ~ of sincerity —V.L.Parrington⟩ ⟨he was our leader and our ~ —Ralph Ellison⟩ ⟨our dynamic economy that uses so completely the ~ of mass production —P.M.Mazur⟩ **b :** something that seems to cast a spell or to give an effect of otherworldliness **:** ENCHANTMENT ⟨all the mystery, ~ and romance which belong to royalty alone —J.E.P.Grigg⟩ ⟨the lake with its gray melancholy, its brooding ~ of an untouched world —Anita Leslie⟩ ⟨the right word gives us a sense of mystery and ~ —C.S.Kilby⟩ **3 :** the art of producing unusual illusions by legerdemain ⟨entertained with acts of jugglery and ~⟩

**syn** WITCHCRAFT, WITCHERY, WIZARDRY, SORCERY, THAUMATURGY, ALCHEMY: MAGIC applies to any supernatural power or art or to any natural power or art seeming to have miraculous results; it is often used in connection with effecting a result or influencing a tendency ⟨*magic*, the attempt of man to govern the forces of nature directly, by means of a special lore —C.S.Coon⟩ ⟨*magic* may be loosely defined as an endeavor through utterance of set words, or the performance of set acts, to control or bend the powers of the world to man's will —J.B.Noss⟩ ⟨words when used with the gift of *magic* can seduce a reader into belief that has no roots in reality —Rose Feld⟩ WITCHCRAFT and WITCHERY, often applicable to deeds of women rather than men, apply to doings of witches, the former suggesting use, usu. malevolent, of spells, enchantments, and guile, the latter suggesting enchanting allure ⟨thus with *witchcraft* I am crowned and wrapped in marvels round and round —Elinor Wylie⟩ ⟨the *witchery* of the soft blue sky —William Wordsworth⟩ ⟨the *witchery* of legend and romance —Ben Riker⟩ WIZARDRY, usu. used of men's acts or accomplishments, suggests power to enchant with or as if with supernatural skill, power, or craft ⟨the *wizardry* of my past wonder, the enchantment of romance —John Galsworthy⟩ ⟨the museum staff's *wizardry* at exhibit making —W.C.Fitzgibbon⟩ SORCERY suggests use of incantation, charm, or spell to produce an effect, often harmful ⟨there was a highly institutionalized means of covert aggression at the disposal of the Indians. This was *sorcery* —A.I. Hallowell⟩ ⟨the storyteller's *sorcery* of catapulting historical datum into dramatic detail —Frederic Morton⟩ THAUMATURGY is applicable to any performance of miracles, esp. by incantation ⟨who see *thaumaturgy* in all that Jesus did —Matthew Arnold⟩ ALCHEMY may apply to transmutation of substances according to the secret laws of early chemical inquiry or to similar processes ⟨called *alchemy*, an attempt to transmute other metals into gold, to discover the elixir of life —Rumer Godden⟩ ⟨the *alchemy* of moonlight turned all the jungle to perfect growth, growth at rest —William Beebe⟩

**2magic** \"\ *adj* [ME *magik*, fr. MF *magique*, fr. L *magicus*, fr. Gk *magikos*, fr. *magos* magus, wizard, sorcerer (of Iranian origin; akin to OPer *magush* sorcerer) + *-ikos* -ic] **1 :** of or relating to the occult **:** supposedly having supernatural properties or powers ⟨the witch doctor is there to give them some ~ medicine to drink —J.G.Frazer⟩ ⟨engravings on harpoons and awls . . . may have been ~ signs, protective against adverse influence —Hugo Obermaler⟩ **2 a :** having unusually distinctive qualities resembling the supernatural **:** producing startling and amazing effects ⟨with this ~ piece of paper, was free to go as I could —W.G.Shepherd⟩ ⟨the popular impression that a ~ method has been invented for mastering a strange language in six weeks —F.N.Robinson⟩ ⟨a man who really had the ~ touch —Leonard Bernstein⟩ **b :** giving a feeling of enchantment ⟨it was the most ~ moment of the day . . . full of meaning and loveliness —Olive Johnson⟩

**3magic** \", *esp in pres part* -jək\ *vt* **magicked; magicked; magicking; magics :** to affect or influence by or as if by magic **:** BEWITCH ⟨the light of those autumn days was *magicked* —Hervey Allen⟩ ⟨had *magicked* them free of their prison —Pamela Frankau⟩

**mag·i·cal** \-jəkəl, -jēk-\ *adj* [1*magic* + *-al*] **1 :** MAGIC 1 ⟨~ techniques take over . . . in order to ensure the success of the enterprise —O.G.Simmons⟩ **2 :** resembling magic **:** having an effect like magic **:** produced by or as if by magic ⟨that ~ hush that comes before the start of every performance of a play —Marc Connelly⟩ ⟨the ~ transformation of egg into omelet —Walter O'Meara⟩ ⟨the disappearance in the fall of the common chimney swift is so sudden as to seem almost ~ —Roy Bedichek⟩ ⟨writes with a ~ simplicity which leaves one amazed —Marvin Lowenthal⟩

**mag·i·cal·ly** \-k(ə)lē, -li\ *adv* **:** in the manner of magic **:** by or as if by magic ⟨England was ~ small, the channel to be taken in a stride —Thomas Wolfe⟩

**magic carpet** *n* **:** a legendary rug or carpet capable of transporting one who stood on it to any place desired

**magic circle** *n* **1 :** a circle drawn by a magician about any person or place protecting it from demons raised by incantations **2** *also* **magic cube :** an arrangement of numbers in rings and radial ranks in a circle or in a number of cubes forming a larger perfect cube devised on the principle of the magic square to add up to the same number along different ranks or diagonals

**Magic Eye** *trademark* — used for a small cathode-ray tube with a controlled beam used as an indicator of maximum response in tuning a radio receiver

**ma·gi·cian** \məˈjishən\ *n* -S [ME *magicien*, fr. MF, fr. *magique* magic + *-ien* -ian — more at MAGIC] **1 :** one skilled in magic; *esp* **:** one who uses charms, incantations, and spells ⟨the village ~ is called in to secure the safety and fertility of a garden —C.D.Forde⟩ — compare SORCERER **2 :** one who entertains an audience by tricks of illusion and sleight of hand **3 :** one whose skill or art seems to be magical ⟨both loved music, and this boy . . . was a ~ with his instrument —Willa Cather⟩ ⟨authors . . . are word ~*s;* they do strange things with human emotions —Allan McMahan⟩

**magic lantern** *n* **:** an early form of optical projector of still pictures using a transparent slide

**magic music** *n* **:** a game in which a player is guided in finding a hidden object by music whose volume is increased or decreased according as he moves nearer or farther away

**mag·i·co-religious** \ˈmajəˌkō+\ *adj* [2*magic* + *-o-* + *religious*] **:** of, belonging to, or having the character of a body of magical practices intended to cause a supernatural being to produce or prevent a specific result (as an increase of the crops)

**magic realism** *n* [trans. of G *magischer realismus*] **:** the meticulous and realistic painting of fantastic images

**magic square** *n* **:** a square containing a number of integers so arranged that the sum of the numbers in each row, column, and diagonal is always the same

| 4 | 9 | 2 |
|---|---|---|
| 3 | 5 | 7 |
| 8 | 1 | 6 |

| 6 | 3 | 10 | 15 |
|---|---|---|---|
| 9 | 16 | 5 | 4 |
| 7 | 2 | 11 | 14 |
| 12 | 13 | 8 | 1 |

magic squares

**magic tree** *n* **:** a showy-flowered Peruvian shrub (*Cantua buxifolia*) of the family Polemoniaceae used in Europe for ornament

**magilp** *var of* MEGILP

**ma·gin·da·nao** \məˈgindəˈnau̇\ *also* **ma·gin·da·naw** \-ˈnȯ\ *n, pl* **magindanao** *or* **magindanaos** *also* **magindanaw** *or* **magindanaws** *usu cap* **1 a :** a Moro people inhabiting central Mindanao, Philippines **b :** a member of such people **2 :** the Austronesian language of the Magindanao people being closely related to or a dialect of Maranao

**ma·gi·not line** \ˈmazhəˌnō, -ajə-\ *n, usu cap M&L* [fr. the *Maginot Line* (trans. of F *ligne Maginot*), a series of fortifications on the northeastern frontier of France begun in 1927, after André *Maginot* †1932 Fr. politician who was minister of war when the fortifications were begun] **:** a defensive barrier or entrenched position that gives a false sense of security ⟨hiding behind a *Maginot Line* of atomic bombs —L.A. DuBridge⟩ ⟨maintain prestige by withdrawing behind a *Maginot Line* of social caste⟩

**ma·gis·ter** \məˈjistə(r)\ *n* -S [L — more at MASTER] **:** a master or teacher in ancient Rome or at a medieval university

**1mag·is·te·ri·al** \ˈmajəˈstirēəl\ *adj* [LL *magisterialis* of authority, fr. L *magisterium* + *-alis* -al] **1 a** (1) **:** of, relating to, or having the characteristics of a master or teacher **:** AUTHORITATIVE ⟨a ~ survey of the evolution of man as a social animal —*Times Lit. Supp.*⟩ ⟨bespeak a sort of ~ attitude toward language which has been lost in the intervening centuries —R.M.Weaver⟩ (2) **:** marked by a dignified or sedate manner or aspect ⟨modeled on the British reviews . . . it imitated their ~ air —Van Wyck Brooks⟩ ⟨the dark ~ tone of academic eating places —Emily Coleman⟩ (3) **:** marked by a pompous or overbearing manner or aspect ⟨was ~ in petty rebuke —V.L.Parrington⟩ ⟨the ~ condescension found in so much biography these days —*Times Lit. Supp.*⟩ **b :** of, relating to, or required for a master's degree ⟨the student submitting a novel or a book of poems as his ~ thesis —Malcolm Cowley⟩ **2** *obs* **:** of, relating to, or having the characteristics of a master designer or workman **3** *obs* **:** of or relating to a magistery **4 :** of or relating to a magistrate, his office, or his duties **:** administered or conducted by a magistrate **:** holding the office of a magistrate

**2magisterial** *n* -S *obs* **:** MAGISTERY

**magisterial district** *n* **:** an administrative county division in Kentucky, Virginia, and West Virginia

**mag·is·te·ri·al·ly** \ˈmajəˈstirēəlē, -li\ *adv* **1 a :** with an authoritative manner because of knowledge and experience **:** MASTERFULLY ⟨could assert that light is corpuscular . . . so ~ that astronomical expeditions could be organized —Alvin Johnson⟩ **b :** with a lordly air **:** DICTATORIALLY ⟨it will not do to say ~, "Take the child away!" —J.L.Lowes⟩ **2 :** in the position or with the authority of a magistrate

**magisterialness** *n* -ES *obs* **:** the quality or state of being magisterial

**mag·is·te·ri·um** \ˌmajəˈstirēəm\ *n* -S [ML] **1** *obs* **:** MAGISTERY **2** *Roman Catholicism* **:** the church's teaching power or function

**mag·is·tery** \ˈ==ˌsterē\ *n* -ES [ML *magisterium*, fr. L, office of a supervisor, office of tutor or guardian, instruction, fr. *magister* master — more at MASTER] **1 :** a principle of nature having transmuting or curative powers **:** PHILOSOPHERS' STONE ⟨he that hath water turned to ashes, hath the *Magistery*, and the true Philosophers' stone —James Howell⟩ **2** *obs* **:** MASTERSHIP, AUTHORITY **3** *obs* **a :** PRECIPITATE 1 **b :** any of various white precipitates from metallic solutions ⟨a white precipitate of bismuth subnitrate was formerly known as ~ of bismuth⟩

**mag·is·tra·cy** \ˈ==strəsē, -si\ *n* -ES [*magistra*te + *-cy*] **1 :** the quality or state of being a magistrate **2 :** the office of a magistrate **:** magisterial power and dignity ⟨outlaws who . . . set at defiance the justice and ~ of the country —Sir Walter Scott⟩ **3 :** the collective body of magistrates ⟨escorted with great pomp . . . by the ~ of the city —T.B.Macaulay⟩

**1mag·is·tral** \-strəl\ *adj* [LL *magistralis*, fr. L *magistr-*, *magister* + *-alis* -al] **1 :** of, relating to, or characteristic of a master **:** AUTHORITATIVE, MAGISTERIAL 1a ⟨the ~ order, accuracy, and clarity of the physical sciences themselves —Lewis Mumford⟩ ⟨she has the dignity, the ~ presence, of an heroic figure of tragedy —*New Republic*⟩ **2 a :** concocted or prescribed by a physician to meet the needs of a particular case — opposed to *officinal* **b** *obs* **:** EFFECTUAL, SOVEREIGN

**2magistral** \"\ *n* -S *obs* **:** a sovereign medicine

**mag·is·tral·i·ty** \ˌ==ˈstraləd·ē\ *n* -ES [NL *magistralitas*, fr. LL *magistralis* + L *-itas* -ity] **:** magistral quality, position, or character

**mag·is·tral·ly** \ˈ==strəlē\ *adv* **:** in a magistral manner ⟨his summing up . . . is ~ succinct —Mary W. Hess⟩

**mag·is·trand** \ˈ==ˌstrand\ *n* -S [ML *magistrandus*, gerundive of *magistrare* to grant a master's degree, fr. ML (*artium*) *magister* master of arts — more at MASTER] *Scot* **:** a fourth and final year student in a university who will receive a master of arts degree — used officially at Aberdeen

**mag·is·trate** \-ˌstrāt, -ˌstrət, *usu* -d·+V\ *n* -S [ME *magistrat*, fr. L *magistratus*, fr. *magistr-*, *magister* master + *-atus* -ate — more at MASTER] **:** a public official entrusted with administration of the laws: as **a :** a principal official exercising governmental esp. executive powers over a major political unit (as a nation) ⟨the president of the federal council . . . and the vice-president are the first ~*s* of the confederation —*Statesman's Yr. Bk.*⟩ **b :** a local official exercising administrative and often judicial functions ⟨the ~ in South Africa is . . . the senior representative of the government in his district —Leo Marquard⟩ **c :** a local judiciary official having limited original jurisdiction esp. in criminal cases: (1) **:** JUSTICE OF THE PEACE (2) **:** the judge of a police court

**mag·is·trate·ship** \-ˌship\ *n* **:** the office of a magistrate; *also* **:** the tenure in office of a magistrate

**magistratic** *obs var of* MAGISTRATICAL

**mag·is·trat·i·cal** \ˈmajəˈstrad·əkəl\ *adj* **:** MAGISTERIAL 4 — **mag·is·trat·i·cal·ly** \-ək(ə)lē\ *adv*

**mag·is·tra·ture** \ˈ==ˌstrāchər, -ˌstrəˌchu̇(ə)r\ *n* -S [F, fr. MF, fr. *magistrat* office of a magistrate (fr. L *magistratus*) + *-ure*] **:** MAGISTRACY

**mag·le·mo·se** \ˈmagləˌmōsə, ˈmau̇l-,ˈmägl-\ *adj, usu cap* [fr. *Maglemose*, locality on the western coast of Sjælland, Denmark, type station of Maglemosian culture] **:** MAGLEMOSIAN

**mag·le·mo·sian** *or* **mag·le·mo·sean** \ˈ==ˈmōsēən, -ōshən, -ōzhən\ *adj, usu cap* [*Maglemose*, Denmark + E *-ian, -an*] **:** of or belonging to a Mesolithic culture of northern Europe characterized by bone and stone implements

**mag·ma** \ˈmagmə, ˈmaig-\ *n* -S [in sense 1, fr. L, fr. Gk; in other senses, NL, fr. L; akin to Gk *massein* to knead — more at MINGLE] **1** *archaic* **:** DREGS, SEDIMENT **2 a :** a crude mixture of mineral or organic matter in the state of a thin paste **b :** something resembling magma ⟨melt back into the primitive ~ of confusion . . . the best and sharpest instruments which the mind has forged —D.C.Williams⟩ **3 a :** molten rock material that is liquid or pasty originating within the earth **:** the molten material or mass from which an igneous rock results by cooling and crystallization — compare LAVA **b :** the glassy base of an eruptive rock **4 :** a suspension of a large amount of precipitated material in a small volume of a watery vehicle ⟨bismuth ~ is commonly known as milk of bismuth⟩ **5 :** a mass of raw sugar and syrup obtained in sugar refining by mixing — compare MASSECUITE

**magma chamber** *n* **:** the underground space usu. deep below the earth's surface occupied by magma that may ascend from it to or toward the surface

**mag·mat·ic** \(ˈ)magˈmad·ik, (ˈ)maig-\ *adj* [ISV *magmat-* (fr. NL *magmat-*, *magma*) + *-ic*] **:** of, relating to, or derived from magma ⟨water may fall originally as rain, or it may be ~ water from the bowels of the earth which ascends to the surface as the steam of volcanoes or in hot springs —*Nat'l Geographic*⟩ — compare METEORIC

**magn** *abbr* **1** magnetic; magnetism **2** magneto

**mag·na** \ˈmagnə, ˈmaig-, ˈmäg-, ˈmȧg-\ *n* -S [*magna* (*cum* *laude*)] **:** a college or university degree magna cum laude; *also* **:** a person receiving such a degree

**mag·na char·ta** *or* **mag·na car·ta** \ˌmagnə ˈkär|də, ˌmaig-, -kȧ|, |tə\ *n, pl* **magna chartas** *or* **magna cartas** *usu cap M&C* [fr. *Magna Charta* or *Magna Carta*, a charter of rights granted by King John of England on June 15, 1215, fr. ML, lit., great charter] **:** a statement of principles that is embodied in a document (as an agreement or legislative act) and usu. establishes procedures or guarantees rights ⟨the original Wagner Act was the *Magna Charta* of labor —A.F.Whitney⟩ ⟨these Articles of Capitulation were regarded by . . . the colonists as their *Magna Charta* —*Times Lit. Supp.*⟩

**mag·na cum laude** \ˈmagnə, ˌmaig-, ˌmäg-, ˌmäg- +\ *adv* (*or adj*) [L, with great praise] **:** with great distinction — used as a mark of meritorious achievement in the academic requirements for graduation from school or college; compare CUM LAUDE, SUMMA CUM LAUDE

**mag·na·flux** \ˈmagnəˌfləks, ˈmaig-\ *vt* **:** to test by the Magnaflux method ⟨~ all spindle blades —*Electrical World*⟩

**Mag·na·flux** \"\ *trademark* — used for a method of testing a ferrous metal for defects by magnetizing the material and observing the patterns assumed by iron powder applied either dry or in liquid suspension

**mag·na·nim·i·ty** \ˌmagnəˈniməd·ē, ˌmaig-, -mətē, -i\ *n* -ES [ME *magnanimite*, fr. MF *magnanimité*, fr. L *magnanimitat-, magnanimitas*, fr. *magnanimus* + *-itat-, -itas* -ity] **1 a :** a loftiness of spirit enabling one to sustain danger and trouble with tranquillity, firmness, and courage ⟨can bear whatever happens with manlike ~ —James Harris⟩ ⟨was not wanting in a sense of the ~ of warriors —Walter Pater⟩ **b** *archaic* **:** a loftiness of ambition and outlook ⟨that ~ of soul which delights in bold enterprises —William Robertson †1793⟩ **2 a :** a nobility of feeling that is superior to meanness, pettiness, or jealousy and that disdains revenge or retaliation **:** generosity of mind ⟨nothing pays richer dividends than ~ —W.E.Binkley⟩ ⟨an opportunity for ~ . . . to unite a country that seems at times to be hopelessly divided —M.W.Childs⟩ ⟨~, which was her chosen attitude, was often a strain to her —Mary Austin⟩ **b :** an instance of magnanimity — usu. used in pl. ⟨all her thoughts may like the linnet be . . . dispensing round their *magnanimities* of sound —W.B.Yeats⟩

**mag·nan·i·mous** \(ˈ)magˈnanəməs, (ˈ)maig-\ *adj* [L *magnanimus*, fr. *magnus* great + *animus* spirit — more at MUCH, ANIMATE] **1 :** showing or suggesting a lofty and courageous spirit ⟨the irreproachable lives and ~ sufferings of their followers —Joseph Addison⟩ **2 :** showing or suggesting nobility of feeling and generosity of mind **:** incapable of meanness or pettiness **:** FORGIVING ⟨even his enemies admitted that he was ~ to the point of knight-errantry —G.K.Chesterton⟩ ⟨too sincere for dissimulation, too ~ for resentment —Ellen Glasgow⟩ — **magnan·i·mous·ly** *adv* — **mag·nan·i·mous·ness** *n* -ES

**mag·nate** \ˈmagˌnāt, ˈmaig-, -ˌnə̇|, *usu* |d.+V\ *n* -S [ME *magnates*, pl., fr. LL, fr. L *magnus* great — more at MUCH] **1 a :** a person of rank **:** NOBLEMAN, PEER ⟨the king surrounded by his ~*s* was enthroned —L.G.W.Legg⟩ **b :** a person of influence or distinction ⟨the county ~*s* and the peasants who farmed their land —Sam Pollock⟩ ⟨a smart little luncheon party at which my grandfather was entertaining an important local ~ —Osbert Lancaster⟩ **2 :** a person prominent in the management of a large industry or enterprise ⟨a tobacco ~ who had crashed in competition —*Times Lit. Supp.*⟩ ⟨a ~ of the first order in the world of industry and commerce —Ernest Barker⟩

**mag·nate·ship** \-ˌship\ *n* **:** the status or position of a magnate

**magnes** *n* -ES [ME, fr. L, fr. Gk *Magnēs* (*lithos*), lit., stone from Magnesia] **1** *obs* **:** MAGNET **2** *obs* **:** magnetic power

**mag·ne·sia** \magˈnēshə, maig-, -ēzh\ *sometimes* |ēə\ *n* -S [ME, fr. ML, fr. Gk *magnēsia*, any of several ores and amalgams, fr. fem. of *Magnēs* of Magnesia, ancient city in Asia Minor] **1** *obs* **:** an ingredient of the philosophers' stone sometimes described as a plasmic saltish fluid or gum composed of the four elements **2** *archaic* **:** MANGANESE **3 a :** a white highly infusible solid consisting of magnesium oxide MgO that occurs naturally as periclase, is obtained in various forms (as a light bulky slightly alkaline reactive powder or a heavier refractory solid) usu. by calcining magnesite or a basic magnesium carbonate or magnesium hydroxide, and that is used chiefly in making firebrick and other refractories, in magnesium oxychloride cements, insulation, fertilizers, and rubber, and in medicine and pharmacy esp. as an antacid and mild laxative **b :** MAGNESIUM — not used systematically ⟨carbonate of ~⟩ ⟨citrate of ~⟩ **4 :** MAGNESIUM CARBONATE — not used systematically

**magnesia al·ba** \-ˈalbə\ *n* [NL, lit., white magnesia] **:** MAGNESIUM CARBONATE b

**magnesia cement** *n* **:** MAGNESIUM OXYCHLORIDE CEMENT

**mag·ne·sial** \ə̇ˈnēsh(ē)əl, -zh(ē)əl\ *adj* **:** MAGNESIAN

**magnesia magma** *n* **:** MILK OF MAGNESIA

**mag·ne·sian** \|ən| *sometimes* |ēən\ *adj* [*magnesia* & *magnesium* + *-an*] **:** of, relating to, or characterized by magnesia or magnesium ⟨the British ~ limes are slow-slaking —A.D.Cowper⟩

**magnesian limestone** *n* **:** DOLOMITE

**mag·ne·sic** \ə̇ˈnēsik\ *adj* [ISV *magnes-* (fr. NL *magnesium*) + *-ic*] **:** of, relating to, or containing magnesium ⟨natural ~ waters⟩

**magnesio-** *comb form* [ISV, fr. NL *magnesium*] **:** magnesium ⟨*magnesio*chromite⟩

**mag·ne·sio·chromite** \magˈnēsh|(ˌ)ō, maig-, -ēzh| *sometimes* |ē(ˌ)ō+\ *n* [*magnesio-* + *chromite*] **:** a mineral $MgCr_2O_4$ consisting of an oxide of magnesium and chromium isomorphous with chromite — called also *magnochromite*

**mag·ne·sio·copiapite** \"+\ *n* [*magnesio-* + *copiapite*] **:** a mineral $MgFe_4(SO_4)_6(OH)_2.20H_2O$ consisting of a hydrous basic sulfate of magnesium and iron and isomorphous with copiapite and cuprocopiapite

**mag·ne·sio·ferrite** \"+\ *n* [*magnesio-* + *ferrite*] **:** a magnetic usu. black mineral $MgFe_2O_4$ consisting of an oxide of magnesium and iron and constituting a member of the magnetite series — called also *magnoferrite*

**mag·ne·site** \ˈmagnəˌsīt\ *n* -S [F *magnésite*, fr. NL *magnesium* + F *-ite*] **:** a mineral $MgCO_3$ that consists of magnesium carbonate, that is isomorphous with siderite and calcite, and that is used chiefly in making refractories and magnesia

**mag·ne·sium** \magˈnēzēəm, maig- *also* -zhəm\ *n* -S [NL, fr. ML *magnesia* + NL *-ium*] **:** a silver-white light malleable ductile bivalent metallic element that occurs abundantly in nature but always in combination in minerals (as magnesite, dolomite, carnallite, olivine, spinel), in sea and mineral waters, and in animals and plants (as in bones and seeds and in the form of chlorophyll in the green parts of plants), that is obtained chiefly by electrolysis of fused salts containing magnesium chloride or by thermal reduction of magnesia, that is used in unalloyed form in metallurgical and chemical processes and also (as in the form of powder, flakes, or ribbons) in photography, signaling, and pyrotechny because of the intense white light it produces on burning to form magnesia, and that is used structurally esp. in the form of light alloys (as in airplanes) — symbol *Mg*; compare ALKALINE-EARTH METAL

**magnesium bomb** *n* **:** an incendiary bomb made with a light magnesium case and a cone of Thermit powder that burns fiercely when detonated, ignites the magnesium case, and maintains a temperature of over 3000°F for 10 minutes

**magnesium carbonate** *n* **:** a carbonate of magnesium: as **a :** the very white crystalline normal salt $MgCO_3$ that occurs naturally as magnesite and also in the form of dolomite, is prepared artificially by precipitation usu. as the trihydrate $MgCO_3.3H_2O$, and is used chiefly in paint and printing ink, as a filler (as in paper and rubber), as an addition to table salt to prevent caking, and in medicine and pharmacy **b :** a crystalline hydrated basic salt obtained by precipitation (as by heating a solution or suspension of the trihydrate) and used in thermal insulation and for many of the same purposes as normal salt

**magnesium chloride** *n* **:** a bitter deliquescent crystalline salt $MgCl_2$ that usu. crystallizes with six molecules of water, that occurs in seawaters, natural brines, and salt deposits, that is obtained by recovery from seawater, brines, or carnallite or by chlorination of magnesia, and that is used chiefly in producing magnesium metal and magnesium oxychloride cements and as a fireproofing agent

**magnesium-chlorophoenicite** *n* **:** a mineral $(Mg,Mn)_5(AsO_4)(OH)_7$ consisting of a basic arsenate of magnesium usu. with manganese

**magnesium citrate** *n* **:** a crystalline salt used in the form of a lemon-flavored acidulous effervescent solution as a saline cathartic

**magnesium fluoride** *n* **:** a crystalline salt $MgF_2$ occurring naturally as sellaite but also made synthetically and used chiefly as a flux and as a coating for optical glass to cut down reflection

**magnesium hydroxide** *n* **:** a slightly alkaline crystalline compound $Mg(OH)_2$ that occurs naturally as brucite, is obtained by hydration of magnesia or by precipitation (as from seawater by lime in the production of magnesium chloride) as a white difficultly soluble powder, and is used chiefly in medicine

**magnesium nitrate** *n* **:** a very soluble deliquescent crystalline oxidizing salt $Mg(NO_3)_2.6H_2O$ used chiefly in catalysts and fireworks

**magnesium oxide** *n* **:** MAGNESIA 3a

**magnesium oxychloride cement** *n* **:** a cement that is used only for interior work (as floors in hospitals and public buildings), is made by adding in proper proportions a strong solution of magnesium chloride to magnesia, and when used with small stones, wood flour, or cork sets to a hard mass in a short time and takes a high polish

**magnesium perchlorate** *n* **:** a deliquescent crystalline explosive salt $Mg(ClO_4)_2$ used as a drying agent

**magnesium silicate** *n* **:** any of various silicates of magnesium: as **a :** a tetrasilicate $Mg_3Si_4O_{10}(OH)_2$ found in nature as talc from which it is obtained usu. in fibrous or micaceous forms for use chiefly as a filler or extender (as in paints) **b :** a trisilicate approximately $Mg_2Si_3O_8.n\ H_2O$ obtained by precipitation as a white powder and used chiefly in medicine as a gastric antacid adsorbent and coating (as in the treatment of ulcers)

**magnesium sulfate** *n* **:** any of several sulfates of magnesium; *esp* **:** the normal salt $MgSO_4$ occurring in nature as the hydrates kieserite and epsomite and also as double salts (as langbeinite) — see EPSOM SALTS

**mag·net** \ˈmagnə̇t, ˈmaig-, *usu* -əd·+V\ *n* -S [ME *magnete*, fr. MF, fr. L *magnet-, magnes*, fr. Gk *Magnēs* (*lithos*), *Magnētis* (*lithos*), lit., stone of Magnesia, ancient city in Asia Minor] **1 a :** a variety or a piece of magnetite or magnetic iron ore having naturally the property of attracting iron **:** LODESTONE — called also *natural magnet* **b :** a body having the property of attracting iron and producing a magnetic field external to itself; *specif* **:** a mass of iron, steel, or alloy that has this property artificially imparted, that usu. has two poles of opposite nature situated near its ends so that when brought close to a similar body the unlike poles attract each other while the like poles repel each other, and that in the form of a bar or needle (as a compass needle) suspended so that it may rotate freely around a vertical axis assumes a direction nearly north and south — compare BAR MAGNET, ELECTROMAGNET, FIELD MAGNET, NORTH POLE, SOUTH POLE **2 :** something that attracts ⟨this new steel plant has also acted as a ~ in attracting . . . new industrial development to the region —J.L.Street b. 1902⟩ ⟨the pot-bellied stove is a ~ for the tellers of tall stories —*Amer. Guide Series: N.H.*⟩

magnet 1b

**magnet-** *or* **magneto-** *comb form* [ˈmagnetic] **1 :** magnetic force ⟨*magneto*meter⟩ **2 :** magnetism **:** magnetic ⟨*magneto*electric⟩ **3 :** magnetoelectric ⟨*magneto*telegraph⟩

ˡ**mag·net·ic** \(ˈ)magˈned·|ik, (ˈ)maig-, -et|, |ēk *sometimes* məgˈn-\ *adj* [F & LL; F *magnétique*, fr. LL *magneticus*, fr. L *magnet-, magnes* magnet + *-icus* -ic] **1 a :** of or relating to a magnet or to magnetism **b :** possessing the ability or power to attract **:** endowed with extraordinary charm **:** ARRESTING, CAPTIVATING ⟨so ~ a man —W.A.White⟩ ⟨an idea so ~ that he cannot divest himself of it —W.P.Webb⟩ **2 a :** of, relating to, or characterized by the earth's magnetism **b :** referred to magnetic north as a reference line ⟨a course of 71° ~ corrected for wind —*Pilots' Radio Handbook*⟩ **3 :** magnetized or capable of being magnetized **:** capable of being attracted by a magnet ⟨~ chips of steel produced by a tool⟩ ⟨a ~ alloy⟩ **4 :** actuated by magnetic attraction **5 :** having, susceptible to, or induced by animal magnetism ⟨as if he had been in a ~ slumber —Charles Dickens⟩

²**magnetic** *n* -S *obs* **:** MAGNET

**mag·net·i·cal** \(ˈ)magˈned·ə̇kəl, (ˈ)maig-, -et|, |ēk- *sometimes* məgˈn-\ *adj* [LL *magneticus* + E *-al*] *archaic* **:** MAGNETIC

**mag·net·i·cal·ly** \-ə̇k(ə)lē, -ēk-, -li\ *adv* **:** in a magnetic manner **:** by the use of magnetism ⟨her dark eyes shone ~ in the light of the chandeliers —Hudson Strode⟩ ⟨~ attracted to the city —Robert Moses⟩

**magnetic amplifier** *n* **:** a device in which an alternating current in the secondary is modulated by variations of core reluctance due to varying a direct current in the primary so that the secondary modulations may be of much greater amplitude than the primary and thus make the device an amplifier

**magnetic amplitude** *n* **:** AMPLITUDE 3b

**magnetic axis** *n* **:** the straight line joining the two poles of a magnet (as the magnetic poles of the earth)

**magnetic bearing** *n* **:** a bearing relative to magnetic north

**magnetic blowout** *n* **:** extinction of an electric arc when deflected by a magnetic field

**magnetic brake** *n* **:** a friction brake controlled by means of an electromagnet

**magnetic chart** *n* **:** a chart showing the magnetic declination, inclination, or intensity over a given geographical area

**magnetic chuck** *n* **:** a chuck in which the workpiece is held by magnetic forces

**magnetic circuit** *n* **:** a closed path followed by magnetic flux (as through the field magnet and armature of a dynamo)

**magnetic clutch** *n* **1 :** a clutch in which the coupling is between solid parts drawn together by electromagnetic force **2 :** MAGNETIC FLUID CLUTCH

**magnetic compass** *n* **:** COMPASS 4a; *broadly* **:** a compass whose operation depends upon an element that senses the earth's magnetic field

**magnetic cooling** *n* **:** application of the magnetocaloric effect to the attainment of low temperatures

**magnetic course** *n* **:** the course on which an airplane is intended to be flown that is measured from magnetic north and that is the true course as laid out on the chart

**magnetic cutter** *n* **:** a cutting head in recording phonograph records that uses attraction and repulsion of pieces of magnetized metal to swing the cutting stylus

**magnetic damping** *n* **:** mechanical damping produced by the reaction of a magnetic field with eddy currents due to relative motion of conductor and field

**magnetic declination** *or* **magnetic deviation** *n* **:** DECLINATION 6

**magnetic dip** *n* **:** DIP 3b

**magnetic elements** *n pl* **:** the magnetic declination, the magnetic dip, and the magnetic intensity or one of its components at any point on the earth's surface

**magnetic equator** *n* **:** ACLINIC LINE — compare GEOMAGNETIC EQUATOR

**magnetic field** *n* **:** a region subject to the influence of magnetism that is manifested by the mechanical forces that it exerts upon electricity moving across it and upon the poles of magnets placed in it

**magnetic fluid** *n* **1 :** a hypothetical fluid formerly assumed to account for magnetic phenomena **2 :** a mixture of finely divided iron with oil or other suitable liquid that is characterized by its marked increase in viscosity when subjected to a strong magnetic field — compare MAGNETIC FLUID CLUTCH

**magnetic fluid clutch** *n* **:** a fluid clutch in which the coupling fluid consists of finely divided ferromagnetic material suspended in oil or other liquid and is rendered practically solid when subjected to a strong magnetic field between the driving and the driven surfaces

**magnetic flux** *n* **:** the product of the average component of magnetic induction perpendicular to any given surface in a magnetic field by the area of that surface usu. expressed in maxwells or webers

**magnetic flux density** *n* **:** MAGNETIC INDUCTION 2

**magnetic focusing** *n* **:** the converging of a stream of electrons by means of a suitable magnetic field — compare MAGNETIC LENS

**magnetic force** *n* **1 :** the mechanical force exerted by a magnetic field upon a magnetic pole placed in it **2 :** MAGNETIZING FORCE **3 :** MAGNETIC INTENSITY

**magnetic head** *n* **:** an electromagnet used in magnetic recording for converting electrical signals into a magnetic record on tape or wire, converting a magnetic recording into electrical signals, or erasing a magnetic recording

**magnetic heading** *n* **:** the heading measured clockwise from magnetic north

**magnetic hysteresis** *n* **:** HYSTERESIS 1c

**mag·ne·ti·cian** \ˌmagnəˈtishən, ˌmaig-\ *n* -S **:** MAGNETIST; *esp* **:** one skilled in making magnetic measurements (as of rocks)

**magnetic inclination** *n* **:** DIP 3b

**magnetic induction** *n* **1 :** induction of magnetism in a body when it is in a magnetic field or in the magnetic flux set up by a magnetomotive force — symbol *B* **2 :** the product of the magnetic permeability of a medium by the intensity of magnetic field in it — called also *magnetic flux density*

**magnetic intensity** *n* **:** a vector quantity pertaining to the condition at any point under magnetic influence (as of a magnet, an electric current, or an electromagnetic wave) measured by the force exerted in a vacuum upon a free unit north pole placed at the point in question — called also *magnetic force*

**magnetic iron** *or* **magnetic iron ore** *n* **:** MAGNETITE

**magnetic lag** *n* **:** the failure of the magnetization in a magnetic substance to keep up with the magnetizing force as it varies

**magnetic latitude** *n* **1 :** the angle whose tangent is one half the tangent of the magnetic dip at any given point **2 :** GEOMAGNETIC LATITUDE

**magnetic lens** *n* **:** an electron lens that focuses electron beams by means of a magnetic field

**magnetic memory** *n* **1 :** the deviation of a body from normal behavior under magnetization due to its previous magnetic history **2 :** magnetic retentivity

**magnetic meridian** *n* **:** a line on the earth's surface approximating a great circle passing through the north and south magnetic poles

**magnetic mine** *n* **:** a naval mine designed to explode by the magnetic effect caused by the hull of a passing metal ship

**magnetic moment** *n* **:** the vector whose vector product by the intensity of the ambient magnetic field gives the resulting mechanical moment or torque — used of a magnet, a current-bearing electric circuit, or a magnetic dipole

**magnetic needle** *n* **:** a bar magnet or a set of bar magnets so suspended as to indicate the direction of the magnetic field in which it is placed; *esp* **:** such a magnet that is slender and pointed at the ends and used as a compass

**magnetic north** *n* **:** the northerly direction of the magnetic meridian at any given point distinguished from the true or geographic north

**magnetic oxide** *or* **magnetic oxide of iron** *n* **:** FERROSOFERRIC OXIDE

**magnetic parallel** *n* **:** ISOCLINIC LINE

**magnetic permeability** *n* **:** PERMEABILITY 4

**magnetic pickup** *n* **:** a phonograph pickup using the stylus vibration to move a piece of metal in a magnetic field and generating an electrical voltage in a coil of wire

**magnetic pole** *n* **1 :** one of the poles of a magnet **2 :** either of two nonstationary regions on the earth which sometimes move many miles in a day, toward which the isogonic lines converge, and at which the dip is plus or minus 90 degrees

**magnetic potential** *n* **:** the scalar quantity characteristic of a point in a magnetic field whose negative gradient equals the intensity or strength of the magnetic field and which represents the work required to bring a unit north pole from a point infinitely remote up to the point in question

**magnetic potentiometer** *n* **:** an instrument for measuring differences of magnetic potential between points in a magnetic field

**magnetic printing** *n* **:** the transfer in magnetic recording of a recorded signal from a position on the recording medium to a nearby position on the same or another medium due to proximity

**magnetic profile** *n* **:** a profile usu. at right angles to the geologic structure showing magnetic anomalies revealed by a geophysical survey

**magnetic pyrites** *n* **:** PYRRHOTITE

**magnetic quantum number** *n* **:** an integer that expresses the quantized angular momentum of an atom or molecule spinning in a magnetic field as a multiple of $h/2\pi$, when $h$ is the Planck constant

**magnetic recorder** *n* **:** a device for carrying out magnetic recording or a device that is usu. incorporated with it for reproducing magnetically recorded sound by moving the magnetized material so that it induces a current which when amplified actuates a loudspeaker

**magnetic recording** *n* **:** the process of recording sound, data (as for a computer), or a television program by producing varying local magnetization of a moving tape, wire, or disc

**magnetic reproducer** *n* **:** a device for reproducing material recorded on a magnetic tape, wire, or disc

**magnetic resonance** *n* **1 :** the response of electrons, atoms, molecules, or nuclei to certain discrete radiation frequencies as a result of space quantization in a magnetic field **2 :** the operating principle of the cyclotron and similar accelerators in which ions and particles are accelerated at every half revolution by an electric field in resonance with the revolving frequency of the ions or particles

**magnetic rigidity** *n* **:** a measure of the momentum of an electric particle moving normally across a magnetic field (as in a cyclotron) equal to the product of the radius of curvature by the intensity of the field

**mag·net·ics** \magˈned·|iks, maig-, -et|, |ēks\ *n pl but sing in constr* **:** the science of magnetism

**magnetic shell** *n* **:** a theoretical layer or shell so magnetized that one surface is entirely of north and the other of south polarity with the lines of induction extending through the thickness of the layer

**magnetic shielding** *n* **:** protection from the influence of an external magnetic field

**magnetic sound** *n* **:** sound recorded magnetically instead of photographically on a motion-picture film

**magnetic storm** *n* **:** a marked temporary disturbance of the earth's magnetic field held to be related to sunspots

**magnetic survey** *n* **:** a determination made by means of magnetic surveying

**magnetic surveying** *n* **:** the process of determining the magnetic elements at various points on the earth's surface including local variations (as for making isomagnetic charts or as a means of prospecting for ore)

**magnetic susceptibility** *n* **:** SUSCEPTIBILITY 3a

**magnetic tape** *n* **:** a ribbon of thin paper or plastic coated with fine magnetic iron oxide powder mixed with a binder, made usu. ¼ inch in width and about two thousandths of an inch in thickness, and used in magnetic recording

**magnetic tape recorder** *n* **:** TAPE RECORDER

**magnetic valve** *n* **:** a valve operated electromagnetically usu. by a solenoid whose axis is perpendicular to the valve seat

**magnetic variation** *n* **:** DECLINATION 6

**magnetic viscosity** *n* **:** a property of magnetizable substances because of which a certain time is required for the magnetization to reach an equilibrium value under a given magnetizing force

**magnetic wire** *n* **:** a thin wire (as of stainless steel) used in magnetic recording

**magnetic wire recorder** *n* **:** WIRE RECORDER

**mag·net·ism** \ˈmagnəˌtizəm, ˈmaig-\ *n* -S [NL *magnetismus*, fr. L *magnet-, magnes* magnet + *-ismus* -ism — more at MAGNET] **1 a :** a class of physical phenomena that includes the attraction for iron observed in lodestone and a magnet, that is believed to be inseparably associated with moving electricity, that is exhibited by both magnets and electric currents, and that is characterized by fields of force in which both magnets and electric currents experience mechanical forces — compare DIAMAGNETISM, PARAMAGNETISM, TERRESTRIAL MAGNETISM **b :** a science that deals with magnetic phenomena **2 a :** ability to attract **:** a power to charm ⟨the ~ and the glamorous oratorical gifts that make him a hero to so many —Woodrow Wyatt⟩ ⟨a personal ~ that made him irresistible —A.E.Wier⟩ ⟨the ~ of America was in her free institutions —R.J.Purcell⟩ ⟨the ~ of courage and devotion —Ambrose Bierce⟩ **3** [F or G; F *magnétisme*, fr. G *magnetismus*] : ANIMAL MAGNETISM

**mag·net·ist** \-,tə̇st\ *n* -S [*magnet* + *-ist*] : one who studies magnetism

**mag·net·ite** \-,tīt\ *n* -S [G *magnetit*, fr. *magnet* + *-it* -ite] : a black isometric mineral of the spinel group consisting of ferrosoferric oxide and constituting an important iron ore that is strongly attracted by a magnet and sometimes possesses polarity — called also *magnetic iron;* see LODESTONE

**magnetite series** *n* : a series of isomorphous minerals in the spinel group consisting of magnetite, magnesioferrite, franklinite, jacobsite, trevorite, and maghemite

**mag·net·it·ic** \¦==¦tid·ik\ *adj* : containing magnetite

**mag·net·iz·abil·i·ty** \,==,tīzə'bilәd·ē, -әtē, -i\ *n* : the quality or state of being magnetizable

**mag·net·iz·able** \¦==¦tīzəbəl\ *adj* : capable of being magnetized

**mag·ne·ti·za·tion** \,=nəd·ə'zāshən, -nətə'z-, -nə,tī'z-\ *n* -S **1** : a magnetizing or state of being magnetized; *also* : degree to which a body is magnetized **2** : intensity of magnetic force measured by magnetic moment per unit of volume

**magnetization curve** *n* : a graph representing changes in the condition of a magnetizable substance with magnetizing force *H* as abscissa and either magnetization *I* or induction *B* as ordinate

**mag·ne·tize** \'magnə,tīz, 'maig-\ *vb* -ED/-ING/-S *see -ize in Explan Notes* [F or G; F *magnétiser*, fr. G *magnetisieren*, fr. *magnet* + *-isieren* -ize] *vt* **1** : to bring under the influence of animal magnetism ⟨*magnetized* by her husband into the state termed clairvoyance —Horace Greeley⟩ **2** : to attract like a magnet : exert a powerful influence upon : CAPTIVATE, CHARM ⟨cities which don't expect to ~ visitors don't build coliseums —Robert Moses⟩ ⟨with his patrician air and his flashing wit . . . he *magnetized* the crowd —Van Wyck Brooks⟩ ⟨that dauntless company of moderns whose spirits have been *magnetized* by . . . polar exploration —John Mason Brown⟩ **3** : to communicate magnetic properties to : convert into a magnet ⟨~ a needle⟩ ~ *vi* : to become magnetized ⟨are advantageous because they will not ~ —W.F.Cloud⟩

**mag·net·iz·er** \-,tīzə(r)\ *n* -S : one that magnetizes

**magnetizing current** *n* : a current that magnetizes or energizes a magnetic core : EXCITING CURRENT

**magnetizing force** *n* : magnetic intensity applied to points within a magnetizable substance — called also *magnetic force*

**mag·ne·to** \mag'nēd·(,)ō, maig-, -ē(,)tō\ *n* -S [short for *magnetoelectric machine*] : a magnetoelectric machine; *esp* : an alternator with permanent magnets used to generate the current for the ignition in an internal-combustion engine or for ringing a telephone bell

magneto: *1* permanent magnet, *2* pole pieces, *3* armature core, *4* armature shaft, *5* armature winding, *6* slip ring, *7* collector brush

**mag·ne·to-** *in pronunciations below*, =¦== mag¦nēd·(,)ō or maig- or -¦nē(,)tō or -¦ned·(,)ō or -¦ne(,)tō or -,tə\ — see MAGNET-

**mag·ne·to·caloric effect** \=¦==+-\ *n* [*magnet-* + *caloric*] : a reversible change in the temperature of a thermally insulated magnetizable substance in a magnetic field of varying intensity with the temperature rising or falling according as the field intensity is increased or decreased

**mag·ne·to·chemical** \"+\ *adj* [*magnet-* + *chemical*] : of or relating to magnetochemistry

**mag·ne·to·chemistry** \=¦==+\ *n* [ISV *magnet-* + *chemistry*] : a branch of science that deals with the relation of magnetism to chemical phenomena

**mag·ne·toelastic** \=¦==+\ *adj* [*magnet-* + *elastic*] : relating to magnetoelasticity

**mag·ne·to·elasticity** \=,==+\ *n* [*magnet-* + *elasticity*] : the effect of elastic strain upon the magnetization of a ferromagnetic elastic material (as when the magnetization of a steel spring varies as it vibrates) — compare MAGNETOSTRICTION

**mag·ne·to·electric** \=¦==+\ *adj* [*magnet-* + *electric*] : relating to or characterized by electromotive forces developed by magnetic means ⟨~ induction⟩

**mag·ne·to·generator** \=,==+\ *n* [*magnet-* + *generator*] : MAGNETO

**mag·ne·to·gram** \=¦==,gram\ *n* [*magnet-* + *-gram*] : an automatic record of magnetic phenomena made by a magnetograph

**mag·ne·to·graph** \-,graf\ *n* [*magnet-* + *-graph*] **1** : an automatic instrument for recording (as by photography) states and variations of a terrestrial magnetic element **2** : MAGNETOGRAM — **mag·ne·to·graph·ic** \=¦==¦grafik\ *adj*

**mag·ne·to·hydrodynamic** \=¦==+\ *adj* [*magnet-* + *hydrodynamic*] : of or relating to phenomena arising from the motion of electrically conducting fluids in the presence of electric and magnetic fields

**mag·ne·to·hydrodynamics** \"+\ *n pl but sing in constr* : a branch of physics that deals with magnetohydrodynamic phenomena

**mag·ne·to·ionic** \=¦==+\ *adj* [*magnet-* + *ionic*] : of or relating to the joint effect of atmospheric ionization and the earth's magnetic field upon the propagation of electromagnetic waves

**mag·ne·to·mechanical ratio** \"+-\ *n* [*magnet-* + *mechanical*] : GYROMAGNETIC RATIO

**mag·ne·tom·e·ter** \,magnə'täməd·ə(r), ,maig-, -mətə-\ *n* [*magnet-* + *-meter*] : an instrument for measuring magnetic intensity, esp. of the earth's magnetic field

**mag·ne·to·metric** \¦=== *at* MAGNETO- +\ *adj* [*magnet-* + *-metric*] : of or relating to the magnetometer or magnetometry

**mag·ne·tom·e·try** \,magnə'tämətrē, ,maig-, -ri\ *n* -ES [ISV *magnet-* + *-metry*] : a science of measuring the intensity of magnetic fields and of determining the direction of lines of force; *also* : use of the magnetometer

**mag·ne·to·motive force** \=¦== *at* MAGNETO- +-\ *n* [*magnet-* + *motive*] : a force that is the cause of a flux of magnetic induction and is the total of the magnetic potential differences along the entire length of a magnetic line of force or is the line integral between two points or around a circuit of the intensity of the magnetic field

**mag·ne·ton** \'magnə,tän, 'maig-\ *n* -S [ISV *magnet-* + *-on*; orig. formed as F *magnéton*] : a unit of the quantized magnetic moment of a particle (as an atom) — see BOHR MAGNETON, NUCLEAR MAGNETON

**magneto-optic** \=¦==¦==\ *also* **magneto-optical** \=¦==¦===\ *adj* [*magnet-* + *optic, optical*] : relating to the influence of a magnetic field upon light (as in the Faraday effect and the Kerr effect)

**magneto-optics** \=,==¦==\ *n pl but sing in constr* : a branch of physics dealing with the influence of a magnetic field upon light

**mag·ne·to·phone** \=¦== *at* MAGNETO- +,fōn\ *also* **mag·ne·to·phon** \"+,fän\ *n* [G *magnetophon*, fr. *magnet-* + *-phon* -phone] : a German magnetic recorder using a plastic ribbon coated or impregnated with magnetic iron oxide

**mag·ne·to·photophoresis** \=,==+\ *n* [NL, fr. *magnet-* + *photophoresis*] : photophoresis under the influence of a magnetic field

**mag·ne·to·plumbite** \"+\ *n* [*magnet-* + L *plumbum* lead + E *-ite* — more at PLUMB] : a mineral $(Pb, Mn)(Fe, Mn, Ti)_6O_{10}$(?) consisting of an oxide of ferric iron with lead, manganese, and titanium occurring in acute black metallic hexagonal pyramids

**mag·ne·to·resistance** \"+\ *n* [*magnet-* + *resistance*] : the change in electrical resistance due to the presence of a magnetic field — **mag·ne·to·resistive** \=¦==+\ *adj*

**mag·ne·to·static** \=¦==+\ *adj* [ISV *magnet-* + *static*] : of, being, or relating to a stationary magnetic field

**mag·ne·to·statics** \=,==+\ *n pl but sing in constr* : a branch of physics that deals with magnetostatic properties — compare ELECTROSTATICS

**mag·ne·to·striction** \"+\ *n* [ISV *magnet-* + *-striction* (as in *constriction*)] : the change in the dimensions of a ferromagnetic body caused by a change in its state of magnetization

**magnetostriction oscillator** *also* **magnetostrictive oscillator** *n* : an electric oscillator in which the frequency is controlled by the mechanical vibrations induced in a body by magnetostriction

**mag·ne·to·strictive** \=¦==¦striktiv\ *adj* [ISV *magnetostriction* + *-ive*] : relating to, operated by, or using magnetostriction ⟨a ~ vibrator⟩

**mag·ne·tron** \'magnə,trän, 'maig-\ *n* -S [blend of *magnet* and *-tron*] : a diode vacuum tube in which the flow of electrons is controlled by an externally applied magnetic field to generate power at microwave frequencies

**magnets** *pl of* MAGNET

**mag·ni·fi·able** \¦magnə¦fīəbəl, ¦maig-\ *adj* : capable of being magnified

**mag·nif·ic** \mag'nifik, maig-, -fēk *sometimes* məg-\ *also* **mag·nif·i·cal** \-fə̇kəl, -fēk-\ *adj* [MF *magnifique*, fr. L *magnificus* — more at MAGNIFICENCE] **1** *obs* : having renown : ILLUSTRIOUS **2** : MAGNIFICENT 2a **3** *obs* : intending to impress or extol : HIGH-SOUNDING ⟨those ~ odes and hymns —John Milton⟩ **4 a** : imposing in size or splendor : EXALTED **b** : showing pomposity ⟨commenced the conversation in the most ~ style —S.T.Coleridge⟩ **5** *obs* : royally generous : MUNIFICENT — **mag·nif·i·cal·ly** \-fə̇k(ə)lē, -fēk-, -li\ *adv*

**mag·nif·i·cat** \mag'nifə̇,ka\|t, maig-, -fē,k-, *sometimes* məg- or -kä\| *or* -kȧ\|; män'yifə̇,kä\|, män . . . kä\|, -yēf-, -fē,k; *usu* \|d·+V\ *n* -S [fr. the *Magnificat*, a canticle sung at vespers in the Roman Catholic Church, fr. ME, fr. L, magnifies (3d sing pres. indic. of *magnificare* to magnify, extol), in *magnificat anima mea Dominum* my soul magnifies the Lord, the first words of the canticle, derived fr. Luke 1:46 ff.] : a song or hymn of praise ⟨a thrush was pouring forth a ~ to the spring —Rafael Sabatini⟩

**magnificate** *vt* -ED/-ING/-S [L *magnificatus*, past part. of *magnificare* — more at MAGNIFY] *obs* : MAGNIFY ⟨~ the church with triumphal pomp and ceremony —Andrew Marvell⟩

**mag·ni·fi·ca·tion** \,magnəfə̇'kāshən, ,maig-\ *n* -S [LL *magnification-, magnificatio*, fr. L *magnificatus* + *-ion-, -io* -ion] **1** : the act or process of magnifying: as **a** : the act of enlarging with praise : LAUDATION ⟨next to the glorification of himself, his mission was the ~ of his country —*Quarterly Rev.*⟩ **b** : the apparent enlargement or reduction of an object by an optical instrument, being the ratio of the dimensions of an image formed by the instrument to the corresponding dimensions of the object — compare ANGULAR MAGNIFICATION, DIAMETER 1c **2** : the quality or state of being magnified

**mag·nif·i·cence** \mag'nifəsən(t)s, maig-, məg-\ *n* -S [ME, fr. MF, fr. L *magnificentia*, fr. *magnificus* noble, splendid, magnificent (fr. *magnus* great + *-i-* + *-ficus* -fic) + *-entia* -ence — more at MUCH] **1** — used as a title of respect applied to kings and other distinguished persons ⟨your *Magnificence* has blood on your hands —Samuel Shellabarger⟩ **2** *archaic* : the virtue recognized in medieval ethics of unostentatious liberality in expenditures of money **3 a** : lavish display in one's surroundings or appointments : SPLENDOR, SUMPTUOUSNESS ⟨easily impressed by ~ —Arnold Bennett⟩ ⟨the wooden ~ of Georgian columns —Thomas Wolfe⟩ ⟨no greater ~ than a Greek robe of virgin white —Elinor Wylie⟩ **b** *obs* : a brilliant ceremony **4** *obs* : greatness of reputation ⟨and for the heavens' wide circuit, let it speak the Maker's high ~ —John Milton⟩ **5** : spectacular beauty : GRANDEUR, SPLENDOR ⟨a sublimely awful scene of power and ~, a world of mountains piled upon mountains —Mark Van Doren⟩ ⟨spring had descended in full force . . . with a gentle ~ —Horace Sutton⟩ **6** : nobleness of expression

**mag·nif·i·cen·cy** \-nsē\ *n* -ES [L *magnificentia*] **1** *obs* : MAGNIFICENCE **2** *archaic* : something magnificent — usu. used in pl. ⟨it deserves to be mentioned among the rare *magnificencies* of ancient Rome —Richard Lassels⟩

[1]**mag·nif·i·cent** \-nt\ *adj* [L *magnificent-* (in *magnificentior* more magnificent — irreg. compar. of *magnificus* — , back-formation fr. *magnificentia* magnificence)] **1 a** : great in deed or exalted in place : characterized by wonderful or splendid achievements — now used only as an epithet applied to former famous rulers ⟨Lorenzo the *Magnificent*⟩ **b** : having dignity and stateliness : displaying ceremonial pomp ⟨after them came the nobility in their coronation robes which was a most ~ sight —*Saturday Rev.*⟩ **2 a** : characterized by lavish display : exhibiting sumptuousness : BRILLIANT ⟨the ~ pavilion with its painted ceilings, flamboyant gilt decorations, and extravagant chandeliers —S.P.B.Mais⟩ ⟨~ red damask hangings round the chancel and choir —George Santayana⟩ **b** : characterized by ostentatious expenditure : EXTRAVAGANT ⟨the ~ luncheon bill was reverently borne in, on silver —Sinclair Lewis⟩ ⟨offered his brother . . . a ~ bribe, nothing less than the half of his kingdom —C.S.Forester⟩ **3** : strikingly beautiful : superb of form or shape : SPLENDID ⟨heavily built man with a ~ pair of shoulders —Robert Graves⟩ ⟨a ~ dapple-gray horse, with glossy hair —Virginia Woolf⟩ ⟨from the road there was a ~ view of the country lying to the south —Sherwood Anderson⟩ **4** : impressive to the imagination : INSPIRING, NOBLE ⟨a ~ illustration of the public's instinct for the quality of a leader —F.D.Roosevelt⟩ ⟨admonished all to know the truth for the ~ purpose of becoming free —Philip Wylie⟩ **5** : exceptionally fine ⟨valley crops were ~ that year —Julian Dana⟩ ⟨a really ~ soup —Gordon Sager⟩ ⟨our frontiers have turned out some ~ people —Russell Lord⟩ **syn** see GRAND

[2]**magnificent** \"\ *n* -S : one who is eminent ⟨seen escorting two ~*s* of literary New York —Thomas Beer⟩

**magnificent bird of paradise** : a showy bird of paradise (*Ptiloris magnificus*) of northern Australia and New Guinea with the male having a golden yellow nape, a blood red patch on the back, and shining blackish green on the breast

**magnificent frigate bird** *n* : a frigate bird (*Fregata magnificens*) that is widespread in tropical American waters and throughout the Caribbean

**mag·nif·i·cent·ly** *adv* : in a magnificent manner : GRANDLY, IMPRESSIVELY ⟨behaved so simply and ~ —C.L.Carmer⟩ ⟨an age . . . ~ confident in the future —S.C.Burchell⟩

**mag·nif·i·cent·ness** *n* -ES : the quality or state of being magnificent

**mag·nif·i·co** \mag'nifə,kō\ *n, pl* **magnificoes** *or* **magnificos** [It, fr. *magnifico*, adj., magnificent, fr. L *magnificus* — more at MAGNIFICENCE] **1** : a nobleman of Venice **2 a** : a person of importance, high position, or distinguished appearance and manner ⟨pithy character sketches of the whole gallery of Victorian ~*es* —*Newsweek*⟩ **b** : something superlative of its kind ⟨a pudding . . . is considered by Russians to be the supreme ~ of all national desserts —Alexandra Kropotkin⟩

**mag·ni·fi·er** \'magnə,fī(ə)r, 'maig-, -fīə\ *n* -S : one that magnifies; *specif* : a lens or combination of lenses

**mag·ni·fy** \-,fī\ *vb* -ED/-ING/-S [ME *magnifien*, fr. MF *magnifier*, fr. L *magnificare*, fr. *magnificus* noble, splendid, magnificent — more at MAGNIFICENCE] *vt* **1 a** : to praise highly : EXTOL, LAUD ⟨while they *magnified* the art, they often belittled the artist —Havelock Ellis⟩ ⟨history, in every country, is so taught as to ~ that country —Bertrand Russell⟩ **b** : to increase the importance of : cause to be held in greater esteem or respect ⟨on that day the Lord *magnified* Joshua in the sight of all Israel —Jos 4:14 (NCE)⟩ **2 a** : to make greater : add to : INTENSIFY, HEIGHTEN ⟨real drama . . . will use ugliness to ~ beauty —Alan Mickle⟩ ⟨felt her every weakness *magnified* and revealed in the fine mirror —Ethel Wilson⟩ **b** : to give a distorted view of : EXAGGERATE ⟨a simple mistake in judgment was often *magnified* to the proportions of a major crime —B.F.Fairless⟩ ⟨*magnified* the peril —Arnold Bennett⟩ ⟨material comfort and ease was *magnified* in contrast with the pains and risk of experimental creation —John Dewey⟩ **3** : to enlarge in fact or in appearance ⟨the microscope *magnified* the object 100 diameters⟩ ~ *vi* **1** : to have the power of causing objects to appear larger than they are : to increase the apparent dimensions of objects ⟨a glass that *magnifies* greatly⟩ **2** *now dial Brit* : to have importance : MATTER, SIGNIFY **syn** see EXALT — **magnify oneself against** : to oppose with pride ⟨if indeed you *magnify yourselves against* me and make my humiliation an argument against me —Job 19:5 (RSV)⟩

**magnifying glass** *n* : a lens that magnifies the apparent dimensions of objects seen through it

**magnifying power** *n* : magnification esp. as applied to visual instruments

**mag·nil·o·quence** \mag'niləkwən(t)s, maig-\ *n* -S [L *magniloquentia*, fr. *magniloquus* magniloquent (fr. *magnus* great + *-i-* + *-loquus*, fr. *loqui* to speak) + *-entia* -ence — more at MUCH] : the quality or state of being magniloquent ⟨an air of ~ hardly suited to the simple rusticity of its theme —John McCarten⟩

**mag·nil·o·quent** \-nt\ *adj* [back-formation fr. *magniloquence*] : characterized by a high-flown often bombastic style, manner, or quality esp. in language : GRANDILOQUENT : OSTENTATIOUS ⟨continues his comic oration . . . bent on the choice of ~ phrase —E.K.Brown⟩ — **mag·nil·o·quent·ly** *adv*

**mag·ni·to·gorsk** \mag¦nēd·ə,gȯrsk\ *adj, usu cap* [fr. *Magnitogorsk*, U.S.S.R.] : of or from the city of Magnitogorsk, U.S.S.R. : of the kind or style prevalent in Magnitogorsk

**mag·ni·tude** \'magnə,tüd, 'maig-, -nə-,tyüd\ *n* -S [ME, fr. L *magnitudo*, fr. *magnus* great + *-i-* + *-tudo* -tude — more at MUCH] **1** *obs* : greatness of character or position : NOBILITY **2 a** (1) : greatness of size or extent : VASTNESS ⟨cannot wage a war of such ~ . . . without inaugurating a new epoch —A.N. Whitehead⟩ ⟨the ~ of his literary output —H.W.H.Knott⟩ ⟨the ~ of the shift away from centralized planning of all economic activity —Harry Schwartz⟩ (2) : SIZE 3a(1) ⟨negative accelerations of any considerable ~ in aircraft are seldom encountered —H.G.Armstrong⟩ ⟨able to operate only over distances of very small ~ —G.W.Gray b. 1886⟩ (3) : QUANTITY, NUMBER ⟨the savings in amounts of metal . . . will be of dramatically significant ~*s* —*Amer. Fabrics*⟩ **b** : VOLUME, LOUDNESS ⟨the ~ of the total sound made . . . was astounding —William Beebe⟩ **3** : the importance, quality, or caliber of something ⟨a seaside curiosity of the first ~ —Charles Gordon⟩ ⟨disappointing work by a writer of first ~ —Richard Plant⟩ ⟨this is no bad test of the stature, or rather the ~, of a poet —David Daiches⟩ ⟨this court can be insensible neither to the ~ nor delicacy of this question —John Marshall⟩ **4** : a number representing the intrinsic or apparent brightness of a celestial body on a logarithmic scale in which a difference of one unit corresponds to the multiplication or division of the brightness of light by 2.512+ and a difference of five units corresponds to the multiplication or division by 100 ⟨a star of ~ 3.0 is approximately 2.512 times brighter than a star of ~ 4.0⟩ ⟨a star of ~ 1.0 is 100 times brighter than one of ~ 6.0⟩ — compare ABSOLUTE MAGNITUDE, APPARENT MAGNITUDE, VISUAL MAGNITUDE **5** : a number assigned to a quantity by means of which the quantity may be compared with other quantities of the same class **6** : the amount of energy released at the source of an earthquake or indicated by the intensity of an earthquake at one place and usu. represented by a number on an arbitrary scale **syn** see SIZE

**mag·ni·tu·di·nous** \¦==¦tüdənəs, -¦tyü-\ *adj* [L *magnitudin-*, *magnitudo* magnitude + E *-ous*] : having magnitude

**mag·no-** *in pronunciations below*, ¦== ¦mag(,)nō *or* ¦maig(,)nō *or* -,nə\ *comb form* [ISV, fr. *magnesia* & NL *magnesium*] **1** : magnesia (*magnochromite*) **2** : magnesium (*magnoferrite*) (*magnophorite*)

**mag·no·chromite** \,== *at* MAGNO- +\ *n* [G *magnochromit*, fr. *magno-* + *chromit* chromite] : MAGNESIOCHROMITE

**mag·no·ferrite** \"+\ *n* [G *magnoferrit*, fr. *magno-* + *ferrit* ferrite] : MAGNESIOFERRITE

[1]**mag·no·lia** \mag'nōlyə, maig-\ *n* [NL, fr. Pierre *Magnol* †1715 French botanist + NL *-ia*] **1** *cap* : a genus (the type of the family Magnoliaceae) of No. American and Asian shrubs and trees that have entire evergreen or deciduous leaves and usu. showy white, yellow, rose, or purple flowers appearing in early spring often before the leaves, having many ovoid pistils borne on a sessile receptacle, and being followed by a follicular fruit **2** -S : any tree or shrub of the genus *Magnolia* **3** -S : TULIP TREE 1 **4** -S : the dried bark of any plant of the genus *Magnolia* (esp. *M. virginiana*) used in folk medicine

[2]**magnolia** \"\ *adj, sometimes cap* [so called fr. the traditional popularity of magnolia trees on old southern plantations] : of, relating to, or resembling the South of pre-Civil War days ⟨smile at the sentimentalities of the ~ tradition —W.S. White⟩

**mag·no·li·a·ce·ae** \=,nōlē'āsē,ē\ *n pl, cap* [NL, fr. *Magnolia*, type genus + *-aceae*] : a family of shrubs and trees (order Ranales), having bisexual flowers, stamens arranged spirally, and numerous simple pistils spirally arranged on an elongated axis — **mag·no·li·a·ceous** \(,)=¦==¦āshəs\ *adj*

**magnolia warbler** *n* : a No. American warbler (*Dendroica magnolia*)

**mag·noph·o·rite** \mag'näfə,rīt\ *n* -S [*magno-* + *phor-* + *-ite*] : a mineral $NaKCaMg_5Si_8O_{23}OH$ of the amphibole group consisting of silicate of sodium, potassium, calcium, and magnesium

[1]**mag·num** \'magnəm, 'maig-\ *n* -S [L, neut. of *magnus* great — more at MUCH] **1** : a large wine bottle holding about ⅖ of a gallon **2** [fr. *Magnum*, a trademark] : a magnum cartridge or firearm

[2]**magnum** \"\ *adj* : high-powered due to a larger case and larger powder charge than other cartridges of approximately the same caliber — used of cartridges and of weapons designed to use the cartridges

**magnum opus** *n* [L] : a great work; *esp* : a literary or artistic work of importance : the greatest achievement of an artist ⟨a golden opportunity to finish his *magnum opus* under the conditions of leisure —Saxe Commins⟩

**mag·nus effect** \'magnəs-, 'maignəs-\ *n, usu cap M* [after Heinrich G. *Magnus* †1870 Ger. chemist and physicist] : the sideways thrust on a rotating cylinder placed with its axis perpendicular to a current of air which has been utilized to propel ships and in aviation as a lift — compare ROTOR SHIP

**magnus hitch** *n* [*magnus* of unknown origin] : a rolling hitch that is similar in form to a clove hitch and is used to hitch a rope or line to a larger rope or to a spar

magnus hitch

**ma·got** \mə'gō, ma'-, mä'-\ *n* -S [F, fr. MF, fr. *magog*, *magot* deformed creature, fr. *Magog*, a nation represented in the NT as one that will be deceived by Satan (Rev 20:8), fr. *Magog*, described in the OT as a land from which the people under their king Gog wished to set forth to destroy Jerusalem (Ezek 38 & 39)] **1** : BARBARY APE **2** : a small grotesque figure of Chinese or Japanese style or workmanship

[1]**mag·pie** \'mag,pī, 'maig-\ *n* [*Mag* (nickname for *Margaret*) + *pie* (magpie)] **1** : any of numerous birds of *Pica* and several other genera of the family Corvidae that are closely related to the jays but have a long graduated tail and usu. black-and-white plumage: as **a** : the common European magpie (*Pica pica*) **b** : a closely similar American magpie (*P. pica hudsonia*) of the Rocky Mountain region **c** : YELLOW-BILLED MAGPIE **2** : any of various other birds having black-and-white plumage suggesting the true magpies: as **a** : either of two piping crows (*Gymnorhina tibicen* and *G. leuconota*) of Australia **b** : a piping crow (*G. hyperleuca*) or a closely related shrike (*Strepera fuliginosa*) of Tasmania **3** : one who chatters endlessly or foolishly **4** : the black-and-white ceremonial dress of an Anglican bishop

[2]**magpie** \"\ *adj* **1** : pied like a magpie **2 a** : having characteristics or traits resembling those attributed to the magpie; *esp* : addicted to indiscriminate collecting ⟨have on occasions been thankful for her ~ ways —L.A.G.Strong⟩ **b** : HODGEPODGE ⟨~ collection of bric-a-brac —Louis Bromfield⟩ ⟨his eye roved uneasily over the ~ litter of his room —C.D.Lewis⟩

[3]**magpie** \"\ *vt* **magpied; magpied; magpieing; magpies** : to garner up like a magpie : pilfer and hoard ⟨those memories . . . have been *magpied* together from glittering little trivia —Basil Marriott⟩ ⟨admits *magpieing* ideas from others and using them later as his own⟩

**magpie diver** *n* : SMEW

**magpie finch** *n* : a small mannikin of variegated color; *esp* : the African mannikin (*Lonchura cucullata*)

**magpie goose** *n* **:** a black-and-white Australian swan goose (*Anseranas semipalmata*)
**magpie lark** *n* **:** a black-and-white passerine bird (*Grallina cyanoleuca*) of Australia of uncertain affinities
**magpie moth** *n* **:** either of two black-and-white moths: **a :** a European geometrid moth (*Abraxas grossulariata*) whose larva feeds on currant and gooseberry bushes **b :** any of several Australian and New Zealand moths of the genus *Nyctemera* having hairy larvae that feed on many plants
**magpie robin** *n* **:** any of several varicolored Asiatic singing birds of the genus *Copsychus; esp* **:** a bird (*C. saularis*) ranging from India to the Philippines
**magpie shrike** *n* **1 :** a So. American black-and-white tanager (*Cissopis leveriana*) **2 :** any of several Australian crow shrikes
**mags** *pl of* MAG, *pres 3d sing of* MAG
**mags·man** \ˈmagzmən\ *n, pl* **magsmen** [¹*mag* + *man*] *slang chiefly Brit* **:** SWINDLER
**ma·gua·ri** \məˈgwärē\ *n* -s [Pg *maguari, maguarí,* fr. Tupi] **:** a So. American varicolored stork (*Euxenura galatea*)
**ma·guey** \məˈgā, ˈmag‚wā\ *n* -s [Sp, fr. Taino] **1 a :** any of various fleshy-leaved agaves: as (1) **:** a Mexican agave (as *Agave atrovirens*) that is used as a source of pulque (2) *Philippines* **:** the agave (*A. cantala*) that yields cantala (3) **:** the common century plant (*A. americana*) **b :** a plant of the closely related genus *Furcraea* **2 a :** any of several hard fibers derived from magueys; *esp* **:** CANTALA **b** *or* **maguey rope** *chiefly West* **:** a rope of maguey fiber or horsehair
**maguey worm** *n* **:** AGAVEWORM
**ma·gus** \ˈmāgəs\ *n, pl* **ma·gi** \ˈmā‚jī *sometimes* ˈma‚-\ [ME, fr. L, fr. Gk *magos* — more at MAGIC] **1 :** a member of a hereditary priestly class among the ancient Medes and Persians whose doctrines included belief in astrology **:** a Zoroastrian priest; *specif, usu cap* **:** one of the traditionally three wise men from the East who according to the Gospel of Matthew paid homage to the infant Jesus **2 :** an adept in occult arts **:** MAGICIAN, SORCERER
¹**magyar** \ˈma|g‚y|är, ˈmai|, ˈmä|, ˈmå|, |ä(r *also* |gy|ə(r) *or* (*with no* ˈmai| *variant*)·|(‚)j| *or* |d(‚)y|\ *n* -s *cap* [Hung] **1 :** a member of the dominant ethnic group of Hungary — compare HUN, HUNGARIAN **2 :** the language of the Magyars that is Finno-Ugric in affiliation — see URALIC LANGUAGES table
²**magyar** \"\ *adj, usu cap* **:** of or relating to the Magyars or Magyar **:** HUNGARIAN
**magyar·ization** \‚=(‚)=rəˈzāshən, -‚rīˈz-\ *n* -s *usu cap* **1 :** the act or process of being magyarized ⟨the hard fight against *Magyarization* —J.S.Roucek⟩ **2 :** the quality or state of being magyarized ⟨bring about the *Magyarization* of the non-Magyar elements —W.J.Ehrenpreis⟩
**magyar·ize** \ˈ=(‚)=‚rīz\ *vt* -ED/-ING/-S *often cap* **1 a :** to make Magyar in quality, traits, or culture **b :** to bring under the control of Magyars **2 :** to modify or alter (a word) to conform to language characteristics distinctive of Magyar
**mah** *abbr* mahogany
¹**maha** *usu cap, var of* OMAHA
²**ma·ha** \ˈmä(‚)hä, ˈmähə\ *n* -s [Sinhalese *maha* large, great, fr. Skt *mahat*] **1 :** a Ceylonese langur (*Presbytis ursina*) **2 :** SAMBAR
**mahagua** *var of* MAJAGUA
**ma·ha·jan** *or* **ma·ha·jun** \məˈhäjən\ *n* -s [Hindi *mahājan,* fr. Skt *mahājana,* lit., great person, fr. *mahat* great + *jana* people, person — more at MUCH, KIN] *India* **:** MONEYLENDER
¹**ma·hal** \məˈhäl\ *n* -s [Ar *mahall* place] **1** *India* **a :** SUMMER HOUSE **b :** a private apartment or lodging **2 a :** a territorial division in India **b :** a division of a farm or hunting preserve in India
²**mahal** \"\ *n* -s [prob. after *Mahal,* name of a fine grade of Persian carpet] **:** NEW COCOA
**ma·hal·a** \məˈhalə\ *n* -s [Yokuts *mokel* women] *West* **:** SQUAW
**mahala mat** *n* [so called fr. its use by squaws for making mats] **:** a prostrate much-matted shrub (*Ceanothus prostratus*) of the Pacific coast of the U. S.
**ma·ha·leb** \ˈmä(h)ə‚leb\ *also* **mahaleb cherry** *n* -s [Ar *mahlab*] **:** a small slender European cherry (*Prunus mahaleb*) that has pure white fragrant flowers in racemes and small inferior fruits from which a dye and a cordial are sometimes made and that is grown for use as an understock in grafting cultivated cherries — called also *St. Lucie cherry*
**ma·hant** \məˈhənt\ *n* -s [Hindi *mahant,* fr. Prakrit *mahanta-,* fr. Skt *mahat* great] *India* **:** a religious superior **:** ELDER
**ma·ha·ra·ja** *or* **ma·ha·ra·jah** \‚mä(h)əˈräjə, -räzhə\ *n* -s [Skt *mahārāja,* fr. *mahat* great + *rājan* king — more at RAJA] **:** a Hindu prince ranking above a raja; *esp* **:** a ruler of one of the principal native states of India
**ma·ha·ra·ni** *or* **ma·ha·ra·nee** \‚mä(h)əˈränē\ *n* -s [Hindi *mahārānī,* fr. *mahā* great (fr. Skt *mahat*) + *rānī* queen — more at RANI] **1 :** the wife of a maharaja **2 :** a Hindu princess ranking above a rani; *esp* **:** a sovereign princess of one of the principal native states of India
**ma·ha·rash·tri** \məˈhäˈräsh(‚)trē\ *n* -s *cap* [Skt *Mahārāṣṭrī* — more at MARATHI] **:** the Prakrit language of the region of Maharashtra in western India
**ma·ha·san·ghi·ka** \məˈhäˈsəŋgəkə\ *n* -s *usu cap* [Skt *mahāsāṃghika,* masc. pl., name of a Buddhist school] **:** an adherent of an early Buddhist sect from which Mahayana Buddhism developed
**mahaseer** *also* **mahasir** *var of* MAHSEER
**ma·hat·ma** \məˈhätmə, -hat-\ *n* -s [Skt *mahātman,* lit., great-souled, wise, fr. *mahat* great + *ātman* soul — more at MUCH, ATMAN] **1 :** a person held worthy of reverence for high-mindedness, wisdom, and selflessness **2 :** one of a class of Indian and Tibetan sages held by Theosophists to possess superior knowledge and powers **3 :** a person of great prestige in some field of endeavor ⟨a kind of ~ of music —Ward Morehouse⟩
**ma·ha·ya·na** \‚mä(h)əˈyänə\ *n* -s *cap* [Skt *mahāyāna* the great vehicle, fr. *mahat* great + *yāna* vehicle — more at HINAYANA] **:** a branch of Buddhism made up of various syncretistic sects that are found chiefly in Tibet, Nepal, China, and Japan, have vernacular scriptures based on a Sanskrit canon, believe in a god or gods, and usu. teach the bodhisattva ideal of compassion and universal salvation — called also *Great Vehicle;* compare HINAYANA, LAMAISM
**mah·di** \ˈmädē\ *n* -s *usu cap* [Ar *mahdīy* rightly or divinely guided] **1 :** a messianic guide who according to Muslim tradition will appear prior to the last day and lead the community of the faithful to salvation **2 :** a Muslim leader who assumes a messianic role
**mah·dism** \ˈmä‚dizəm\ *n* -s *usu cap* **:** belief in or devotion to a Mahdi
**mah·dist** \-‚dəst\ *n* -s *usu cap* **:** an adherent of Mahdism
**ma·hi·can** *or* **mo·hi·can** \məˈhēkən, mōˈ-\ *n, pl* **mahican** *or* **mahicans** *or* **mohican** *or* **mohicans** *usu cap* [Mahican, lit., wolf] **1 a :** an Indian people of the upper Hudson river valley and eastward into the valley of the Housatonic **b :** a member of such people **2 :** an Algonquian language of the Mahican people
**ma·hi·ma·hi** \ˈmähēˈmähē\ *n, pl* **mahimahi** [Hawaiian, Tahitian, & Marquesan] *Hawaii* **:** DOLPHIN 2
**mah-jong** \(ˈ)mä|jȯŋ, -|zh|, |äŋ\ *vi* -ED/-ING/-S **:** to win a Mah-Jongg game
**Mah–Jongg** \"\ *trademark* — used for a game of Chinese origin usu. played by 4 persons with 144 tiles that are drawn and discarded until one player secures a winning hand of 4 sets of 3 tiles and a pair
**mahlstick** *var of* MAULSTICK
**ma·hoe** \məˈhō\ *n* -s [F *mahot, maho,* fr. Taino *maho*] **1** *also* **ma·ho** \"\ **:** any of various chiefly tropical trees with strong bast fibers: as **a** (1) **:** MAJAGUA (2) **:** PORTIA TREE **b :** any of several trees of the family Thymelaeaceae; *esp* **:** a West Indian tree (*Daphnopsis caribaea*) **c :** any of several trees of the genus *Sterculia; esp* **:** a So. American tree (*S. pruriens*) that yields a pale brown lustrous straight-grained wood **2** *also* **maho :** the wood or fiber of a mahoe **3** [Maori] **:** a small shrubby New Zealand tree (*Melicytus ramiflorus*) of the family Violaceae with dark green alternate leaves and few-seeded purple berries — called also *whitey wood*
**ma·hog·a·nize** \məˈhägə‚nīz\ *vt* -ED/-ING/-S *see -ize in Explan Notes* **:** to cause to resemble mahogany usu. by staining ⟨a *mahoganized* cabinet⟩
**ma·hog·a·ny** \-nē, -ni\ *n* -ES *often attrib* [origin unknown] **1 :** the wood of any of various chiefly tropical trees of the family Meliaceae: **a** (1) **:** the durable yellowish brown to reddish brown usu. moderately hard and heavy wood of a West Indian tree (*Swietenia mahogani*) that is readily worked, takes a high polish when dressed, can be cut to show numerous striking figures because of its well differentiated structural elements and overlapping grain, and is widely used for cabinetwork and fine finish work — called also *Cuban mahogany, Dominican mahogany* (2) **:** the similar wood of any other tree of the genus *Swietenia* — called also *Honduras mahogany* **b :** any of several African woods more or less similar to New World mahogany: (1) **:** the rather hard heavy usu. odorless wood of trees of the genus *Khaya* — called also *African mahogany* (2) **:** the rather lightweight cedar-scented wood of trees of the genus *Entandrophragma* that varies in color from pinkish to deep reddish brown — called also *African scented mahogany, cedar mahogany, sapele mahogany* **2 :** any of various woods resembling or substituted for mahogany obtained from trees of the family Meliaceae — not used technically without a qualifying term; see PHILIPPINE MAHOGANY **3** *also* **mahogany tree a :** a tree of the genus *Swietenia; esp* **:** a West Indian tree (*S. mahogani*) **b :** an African tree of the family Meliaceae that yields mahogany **c :** a tree not belonging to the family Meliaceae that yields mahogany **4 a :** TABLE ⟨ranged around the ~ are union and company representatives —Lawrence Galton⟩; *esp* **:** DINING TABLE ⟨other families did not welcome us to their ~ —W.M.Thackeray⟩ **b :** COUNTER 4b, BAR 5a ⟨every interval sees twenty orchestral players with their elbows on the ~ —Charles Reid⟩ **5** *also* **mahogany brown** *or* **mahogany red :** a moderate reddish brown that is yellower and slightly darker and less strong than roan, less strong than oxblood, redder and deeper than russet tan, and redder and slightly deeper than rustic brown **6 a** *dial Eng* **:** a Cornish drink made of gin and treacle **b :** a strong drink made of brandy and water
**mahogany acid** *n* **:** any of several dark-colored oil-soluble mixtures of sulfonic acid derivatives of petroleum that are obtained as by-products in refining white oils with sulfuric acid or made as primary products by sulfonation of petroleum distillates and are used as such or in the form of salts chiefly as emulsifying agents, as rust-proofing agents, and as additives to lubricants
**mahogany bean** *n* **:** POD MAHOGANY
**mahogany birch** *n* **:** SWEET BIRCH
**mahogany family** *n* **:** MELIACEAE
**mahogany gum** *n* **:** any of various eucalypts; *specif* **:** JARRAH
**mahogany rot** *n* **1 :** the tuber-rotting phase of late blight; *broadly* **:** LATE BLIGHT **2** *also* **mahogany browning :** a physiological disease of potato tuber due to long exposure to low temperature
**mahogany snapper** *n* **:** a small brown West Indian snapper (*Lutanus mahogoni*)
**mahogany soap** *n* **:** a salt of a mahogany acid; *esp* **:** a sodium salt of such an acid
**ma·ho·li** \məˈhōlē\ *n* -s [Tswana *mogwêlê*] **:** MOHOLI LEMUR
**ma·ho·nia** \məˈhōnēə\ *n* [NL, fr. Bernard McMahon †1816 Am. botanist + NL *-ia*] **1** *cap* **:** a genus of No. American and Asiatic shrubs of the family Berberidaceae that have unarmed branches and pinnate leaves and are sometimes included in the genus *Berberis* — see AGARITA, OREGON GRAPE **2** -s **:** any shrub of the genus *Mahonia*
**ma·hon stock** \məˈhōn-\ *n, usu cap M* [fr. *Mahón,* Minorca, Spain] **:** VIRGINIA STOCK
**mahos** *pl of* MAHO
**ma·hout** \məˈhau̇t\ *n* -s [Hindi *mahāwat, mahāut,* fr. Skt *mahāmātra* of great eminence, fr. *mahat* great + *mātra* measure, fr. *māti* he measures — more at MUCH, MEASURE] **:** a keeper and driver of an elephant
**mahratta** *or* **mahratti** *usu cap, var of* MARATHA
**mah·ri** \ˈmärē\ *also* **mah·ra** \-rə\ *n, pl* **mahri** *or* **mahris** *also* **mahra** *or* **mahras** *cap* [Ar *mahrīy* or *mahrah*] **1 :** a native or inhabitant of Mahra in southeastern Arabia **2 :** the Semitic language of the Mahri people
**mah·seer** *also* **mah·sir** \ˈmä‚si(ə)r\ *or* **mah·sur** \-‚sə(r)\ *or* **ma·ha·seer** *or* **ma·ha·sir** \məˈhä‚si(ə)r\ *n, pl* **mahseer** [Hindi *mahāsir,* prob. fr. Skt *mahat* big, great + *śiras* head — more at CEREBRAL] **:** a large Indian freshwater cyprinid food and sport fish (*Barbus mosal*)
**mah·sud** \mäˈsüd\ *n* -s *usu cap* **:** a member of a people of northwestern West Pakistan related to the Wazir
**mah·ua** \ˈmä(h)wə\ *or* **moh·wa** \ˈmō(w)ə\ *n* -s [Hindi *mahūā,* fr. Skt *madhūka,* fr. *madhu* sweet, honey, mead — more at MEAD] **:** any of several East Indian trees of the genus *Madhuca* (esp. *M. latifolia* or *M. indica*) with honey-filled flowers that are used for food and in preparing an intoxicating drink — compare ILLUPI
**mahua butter** *var of* MOWRAH BUTTER
**ma·huang** \ˈmäˈhwäŋ\ *n* -s [Chin (Pek) *ma²* huang²] **:** any of several Chinese plants of the genus *Ephedra* (esp. *E. sinica*) yielding ephedrine
**mah·zor** *or* **mach·zor** \mäkˈzō(ə)r, ˈmäkzə(r)\ *n, pl* **mahzorim** *or* **machzo·rim** \‚mäkzōˈrēm\ *or* **mahzors** *or* **machzors** [Heb *maḥăzōr,* lit., cycle] **:** a Hebrew prayer book containing the Jewish liturgy for festivals — compare SIDDUR
**mai** \ˈmī\ *n* -s [Jap] **:** a slow Japanese folk or theater dance featuring hand gestures — distinguished from *odori*
**ma·ia** \ˈmā(y)ə, ˈmīə\ [NL, fr. L, a large crab, fr. Gk] *syn of* MAJA
**ma·ian·the·mum** \mā'(y)an(t)thəməm, mīˈa-\ *n, cap* [NL, fr. L *maius* May + NL *-anthemum* — more at MAY (month)] **:** a genus of perennial herbs (family Liliaceae) having slender rhizomes and an erect stem bearing a few leaves and a terminal raceme of small white flowers — see FALSE LILY OF THE VALLEY
¹**maid** \ˈmād\ *n* -s [ME *maide,* short for *maiden*] **1 a :** an unmarried girl or woman esp. when young **:** VIRGIN **b** *obs* **:** a male virgin **2 a :** a girl or woman employed to do domestic work in a home, hotel, tourist court, or institution **b :** CHARWOMAN 2 **3** *Brit* **:** a young ray or skate
²**maid** \"\ *vb* -ED/-ING/-S **1 :** to attend as bridesmaid **2 :** to serve as maid
**mai·dan** *also* **mei·dan** \mīˈdän\ *n* -s [Hindi *maidān,* fr. Ar] **:** an Asiatic or African parade ground or esplanade
¹**maid·en** \ˈmādᵊn\ *n* -s [ME, fr. OE *mǣden, mægden,* fr. *mægth, mægeth;* akin to OS *magath* maiden, OE *mago, magu* son, man, servant, MD *maget, maecht* maiden, OHG *magad* maiden, ON *mögr* son, youth, *mær* maiden, Goth *magus* boy, child, *magaths* virgin, OIr *mug* serf, *macc* son, Latvian *mač* small] **1 :** MAID, VIRGIN ⟨supposedly a place for the ~s of that era to catch a beau —Frances H. Eliot⟩ **2** *obs* **:** MAIDSERVANT **3** *archaic* **:** a former Scottish beheading device resembling the guillotine **4** *Scot* **:** HARVEST DOLL **5 :** MAIDEN OVER **6 :** a mare, stallion, or gelding that has never won a race **7 :** *chiefly Brit* **:** WHIP 3a
²**maiden** \"\ *adj* [ME, fr. *maiden,* n.] **1** *of a girl or woman* **a :** UNMARRIED ⟨~ aunt⟩ **b :** VIRGIN **2 :** of, relating to, or befitting a maiden ⟨~ innocence⟩ ⟨~ loveliness⟩ **3 :** FIRST, EARLIEST ⟨convulses his audience with his ~ speech —*Brit. Book News*⟩ ⟨her ~ voyage —H.A.Chippendale⟩ **4 a :** INTACT, FRESH, UNTAKEN, UNTRIED, UNUSED ⟨records were of any and all manufacture . . . some were ~; none had been played more than six times —C.G.Burke⟩ ⟨the ~ city (as it was named from its successful resistance to the siege) —Sam Pollock⟩ **b :** of or relating to a horse that has never won a race ⟨yesterday she shed her ~ certificate when she won the sixth race —*Johannesburg Sunday Express*⟩ **c** *Eng law* **:** of or relating to an assize or session without cases to be tried or formerly one resulting in no sentence of death **5** *of a female animal* **a :** never yet mated **b :** never having borne young **syn** see YOUTHFUL
**maiden cane** *n* **:** a grass (*Panicum hemitomon*) of moist or low coastal areas of the southern U.S. that is propagated by extensively creeping rootstocks
**maiden duck** *n, Brit* **:** SHOVELER
**maidenhair** \ˈ==‚=\ *or* **maidenhair fern** *n* [*maidenhair* fr. ME *maidenheer,* fr. *maiden* + *heer* hair; intended as trans. of LL *capillus Veneris,* lit., Venus's hair] **:** a fern of the genus *Adiantum:* as **a :** VENUSHAIR **b :** a palmately branched No. American fern (*A. pedatum*) with fronds having divergent recurved branches borne on a lustrous reddish or blackish stipe
**maidenhair spleenwort** *n* **:** a rock-inhabiting small fern (*Asplenium trichomanes*) of the north temperate zone and Hawaii with slender pinnate black-stiped fronds
**maidenhair tree** *n* **:** GINKGO
**maidenhair-tree family** *n* **:** GINKGOACEAE
**maidenhair-vine** \ˈ==‚=‚=\ *n* **:** WIRE PLANT
**maidenhead** \ˈ==‚=\ *n* [ME *maidenhed, maidenhede,* fr. ¹*maiden* + *-hed, -hede* -hood (akin to ME *-hod, -had* -hood)] **1 :** the quality or state of being a maiden **:** intact virginity **:** unused or uncontaminated condition **:** FRESHNESS, PURITY ⟨pious pledges to safeguard the ~ of scholarship —William Manchester⟩ **2** *obs* **:** the first stage or first use of something **3 :** HYMEN
**maidenhead spoon** *n* [obs. E *maidenhead* ornamental representation of the head of the Virgin Mary (fr. ME *maidenhed,* fr. ¹*maiden* + *hed* head) + E *spoon*] **:** a 16th century silver or silver-gilt spoon with handle terminating in a bust of the Virgin Mary
**maid·en·hood** \ˈmādᵊn‚hu̇d\ *n* [ME *maidenhod,* fr. OE *mægdenhād,* fr. *mægden* maiden + *-hād* -hood] **1 :** the quality or state of being a maid or virgin **:** GIRLHOOD ⟨thoughts and emotions of maturing youth and ~ —H.A.Overstreet⟩ **2** *obs* **:** intact virginity
**maid·en·ish** \-ᵊnish\ *adj* **1 :** of or resembling a girl **:** GIRLISH **2 :** OLD-MAIDISH ⟨a short, fair, rather ~ woman —Saul Bellow⟩
**maid·en·ism** \-ᵊn‚izəm\ *n* -s **:** a girlish trait or mannerism
**maiden lady** *n* **:** an unmarried and usu. middle-aged woman
**maid·en·li·ness** \-ᵊnlēnəs, -lin-\ *n* -ES [¹*maidenly* + *-ness*] **:** conduct or traits befitting a maiden ⟨though she heard the remembered voice, her ~ had not permitted that she should show herself —Arnold Bennett⟩
¹**maid·en·ly** \-ᵊnlē, -li\ *adj* [ME] **:** of, resembling, or suitable to a maiden **:** GENTLE, MODEST, TIMID, VIRGINAL
²**maidenly** \"\ *adv, archaic* **:** in a maidenly manner
**maiden name** *n* **:** the surname of a woman before she is married
**maiden oak** *n* **:** DURMAST
**maiden over** *n* **:** a cricket over in which no runs are scored from hits
**maiden pink** *n* **:** a low-growing stoloniferous Eurasian pink (*Dianthus deltoides*) having single crimson-eyed flowers
**maiden plum** *n* **:** a West Indian guao (*Comocladia integrifolia*) with edible purplish drupes
**maidens** *pl of* MAIDEN
**maiden's–blush** \ˈ==‚=\ *n, pl* **maiden's–blushes 1** *Austral* **:** a pink-flowered timber tree (*Echinocarpus australis*) of the family Tiliaceae **2** *Austral* **:** a timber tree (*Euroschinus falcatus*) of the family Anacardiaceae
**maidenship** *n, obs* **:** the rank or standing of a maiden
**maid·hood** \ˈmād‚hu̇d\ *n* [ME *maidhod,* fr. OE *mægthād,* fr. *mægth* maiden + *-hād* -hood — more at MAIDEN] **1 :** MAIDENHOOD **2 :** the status or occupation of a maidservant
**maiding** *pres part of* MAID
**maid–in–waiting** \ˈ=ˈ=ˈ==\ *n, pl* **maids–in–waiting :** a young woman of a queen's or princess's household appointed to wait upon or attend her
**maid·ish** \ˈmādish\ *adj* **:** MAIDENISH ⟨you would think a small ~ mind had pored over the task —Audrey Barker⟩ — **maid·ish·ness** *n* -ES
**maid of all work 1 :** a domestic who does general housework **2 :** a person or thing put to a wide variety of uses ⟨the prime minister is the general *maid of all work* in the cabinet —H.J. Laski⟩ ⟨a patrol boat is a sort of *maid of all work,* ready to do anything —A.P.Herbert⟩
**maid of honor 1 :** an unmarried lady usu. of noble birth whose duty it is to attend a queen or a princess **2 :** a bride's principal unmarried wedding attendant — distinguished from *matron of honor;* compare BRIDESMAID **3 :** a pastry of puff paste filled with a rich custard flavored with almond paste and lemon
**mai·dou** \mīˈdü\ *n* -s [native name in Burma and Indochina] **:** a tree (*Pterocarpus pedatus*) of Burma and Indochina whose wood resembles amboyna but is of coarser figure and darker brown
**maids** *pl of* MAID, *pres 3d sing of* MAID
**maidservant** \ˈ=‚==\ *n* **:** a female servant
**maid's–hair** \ˈ=‚=\ *n, pl* **maid's–hairs :** YELLOW BEDSTRAW
**mai·du** \ˈmī(‚)dü\ *n, pl* **maidu** *or* **maidus** *usu cap* [Maidu, lit., person, man] **1 a :** an Indian people of the Feather and American river valleys of California **b :** a member of such people **2 :** a Pujunan language of the Maidu people **3 :** PUJUNAN
**maidy** \ˈmādē\ *n* -ES **:** a little maid
**ma·ieu·tic** \māˈyüd·ik, mīˈ-, -üt|, |ēk\ *adj* [Gk *maieutikos,* lit., of midwifery, fr. (assumed) *maieutos* (verbal of *maieuesthai* to act as midwife, fr. *maia* midwife) + *-ikos* -ic; akin to Gk *mētēr* mother — more at MOTHER] **:** of or relating to the dialectic method practiced by Socrates in order to elicit and clarify the ideas of others
¹**mai·gre** \ˈmāgrə, *F* mægr(ᵊ)\ *or* **meeg-** *or* **-g(rə)** *adj* [F, maigre, meager, fr. MF — more at MEAGER] **1 :** being a day on which the eating of flesh is forbidden by the Roman Catholic Church **2 :** constituting a food that contains no flesh nor juices of flesh and so may be eaten on maigre days
²**mai·gre** \"\ *or* **mai·ger** \-gə(r)\ *also* **mea·gre** \ˈmēgə(r)\ *n, pl* **maigres** \-grəz, *F* -gr(ᵊ)\ *or* -g(rə)z\ *or* **maigers** \-gə(r)z\ [F *maigre,* fr. MF, perh. fr. *maigre,* adj.] **1 :** a large European marine food fish (*Sciaena aquila*) **2 :** a member of the percoid family Sciaenidae **:** CROAKER 2, DRUM 5 — called also *bar*
**maiid** *var of* MAJID
**mai·idae** \ˈmā(y)ə‚dē, ˈmīə-\ [NL, fr. *Maia,* type genus + *-idae*] *syn of* MAJIDAE
**maik** \ˈmāk\ *Scot var of* MAKE
¹**mail** \ˈmāl\ *n* -s [ME *maill, male,* fr. OE *māl* terms, agreement, pay, fr. ON *māl* speech, language, agreement; akin to OE *mǣl* speech, conversation, *mæthel* assembly, OS & OHG *mahal* assembly, judgment, Goth *mathl* meeting place, market, OE *mōt* meeting — more at MEET] *now chiefly Scot* **:** PAYMENT, RENT, TRIBUTE, TAX
²**mail** \ˈmāl, *esp before pause or consonant* -āəl\ *n* -s *often attrib* [ME *male,* fr. OF, of Gmc origin; akin to MD *māle* bag, traveling bag, OHG *malaha, malha* wallet, bag] **1** *chiefly Scot* **:** BAG, WALLET, TRAVELING BAG **2 a :** the bags of letters and the other postal matter conveyed under public authority from one post office to another **b :** the postal matter consigned at one time to or from one person or one post office or conveyed by a particular train, airplane, or ship ⟨the ~ for the city⟩ ⟨the doctor's ~ was late that day⟩ ⟨the letter just made the 7 o'clock ~⟩ **c :** a conveyance that transports mail ⟨the train was a fast ~⟩ **3** *or* **mails** *pl* **a :** a nation's postal system — compare POST 3 **b :** postal matter collectively ⟨in colonial days newspapers were not considered part of the ~s⟩
³**mail** \"\ *vb* -ED/-ING/-S [²*mail*] *vt* **:** to send by mail ⟨~ a letter home⟩ ~ *vi* **:** to send postal matter by mail ⟨many advertisers ~ to carefully chosen lists of prospects⟩
⁴**mail** \"\ *n* -s [ME *maile, maille,* fr. MF, fr. OF, fr. L *macula* spot, mesh of a net] **1 a** *obs* **:** a ring or plate constituting the basic unit of the medieval warrior's defensive armor **b :** armor made of metal links or plates — compare CHAIN MAIL, PLATE ARMOR **2 a :** the hard enclosing covering of various animals (as of a tortoise or a lobster) **b** *archaic* **:** the full-grown breast feathers esp. of a hawk **3 :** a metal or glass eye in a heddle through which the thread of the warp passes
⁵**mail** \"\ *vt* -ED/-ING/-S **:** to arm with mail
⁶**mail** \"\ *vt* -ED/-ING/-S [perh. fr. ²*mail* or ⁴*mail*] **1** *obs* **:** ENVELOP **2 :** to wrap up (a hawk) **:** BIND
⁷**mail** *n* -s [F, mall, maul, fr. MF, hammer, maul — more at MAUL] *obs* **:** MALL
⁸**mail** \ˈmāl\ *Scot var of* MOLE
**mail·abil·i·ty** \‚māləˈbiləd·ē\ *n* **:** the quality or state of being mailable
**mail·able** \ˈmāləbəl\ *adj* [³*mail* + *-able*] **:** adapted for mailing **:** legally admissible as mail
**mailbag** \ˈ=‚=\ *n* **1 :** a letter carrier's shoulder bag **2 :** a pouch used in the shipment of mail

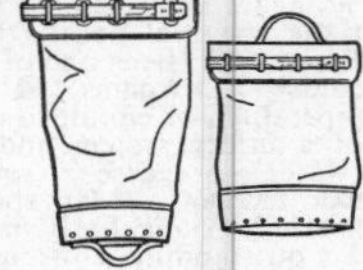
mailbags 2

**mailbox** \ˈ=‚=\ *n* **1 :** a public box for deposit of outgoing mail **2 :** a box at or near a dwelling for the occupants' mail — see BOX illustration
**mail carrier** *n* **1 :** one that carries mail between post offices **2 :** one that delivers mail along an established route

**mail-cheeked** \ˈ≈¦chēkt\ *adj* [⁴*mail* + *-cheeked* (fr. ¹*cheek* + *-ed*)] **:** having the sides of the head armored — used esp. of a fish of the order Scleroparei

**mailclad** \ˈ≈¦≈\ *adj* **:** protected by or as if by a coat of mail

**mail clerk** *n* **1 :** one who does clerical work (as selling stamps or sorting or canceling mail) in a post office **2 :** a mail sorter on a railway mail car **3 :** an employee who handles mail in a private or government establishment that is not part of the post-office department

**mail crane** *n* **:** a crane or arm at trackside in a railroad station for pouches of mail consigned to or left by moving trains

**mail drop** *n* **1 a :** a receptacle for mail esp. at the place of delivery **b :** a slot (as in a chute) for deposit of mail **2 :** an address used by an agent who transmits secret communications (as for an espionage apparatus)

**ma·i·le** \ˈmä,ēlā\ *n* -s [Hawaiian] **:** a Pacific island vine (*Alyxia olivaeformis*) of the family Apocynaceae with fragrant leaves and bark that are used for decoration and in Hawaii for leis

**mailed** \ˈmā(ə)ld\ *adj* [ME, fr. *maile* mail (armor) + *-ed*] **1 :** protected or armed with mail **2 :** protected by an outer covering (as of scales or plates) ⟨a ~ fish⟩

**mailed catfish** *n* **:** ARMORED CATFISH

**mailed fist** *n* [trans. of G *gepanzerte faust*] **:** armed or overbearing force **:** POWER, VIOLENCE ⟨this was my first experience with a *mailed fist* clothed in the kid glove —G.B.Oxnam⟩

**mail edition** *n* **:** an early-morning edition of a metropolitan newspaper for out-of-city distribution — compare CITY EDITION

¹**mail·er** \ˈmālər\ *n* -s [ME *mailler*, fr. *maill* mail (rent) + *-er*] *Scot* **:** a cotter who pays rent

²**mail·er** \ˈmālə(r)\ *n* -s [²*mail* & ³*mail* + *-er*] **1 a :** a user of the mails ⟨a wide variety of mechanical equipment is in use by large ~*s*⟩ **b :** one who addresses and otherwise prepares material that is to be mailed **2** *archaic* **:** a boat that carries mail **3 :** MAILING MACHINE **4 a :** a container (as a paperboard tube) for mailing something in **b :** an advertising leaflet for enclosure with letter mail

**mail flag** *n* **:** a flag displayed by a ship carrying mail

¹**mail·ing** \ˈmāliŋ\ *n* -s [ME *mailling*, fr. *maill* mail (rent) + *-ing*] **1** *Scot* **:** a rented farm **2** *Scot* **:** the rent paid for a farm

²**mailing** *n* -s [fr. gerund of ³*mail*] **1 :** the act of sending by mail ⟨on the day of ~ he had not appeared⟩ **2 :** the mail dispatched at one time by a sender ⟨large ~*s* which once took weeks now can be made ready for the post office overnight —*Dun's Rev.*⟩ **3 :** something sent by mail ⟨over a million domestic postcards, circulars, parcels, and other ~*s* reached the Dead Letter Office —*Canada Yr. Bk.*⟩

**mailing machine** *n* **:** any of various machines that help prepare mail (as by stamping, addressing, or weighing)

**mailing piece** *n* **:** a piece of advertising matter (as a form letter, leaflet, or catalog) for distribution by mail

**maill** \ˈmāl\ *var of* ¹MAIL

**mail·less** \ˈmālləs\ *adj* **:** not armored with mail

**mail·lot** \maˈyō\ *n* -s [F, lit., swaddling cloth, fr. MF, prob. alter. of *maillol*, fr. *maille* laced band, mesh, mail — more at MAIL (armor)] **1 :** tights for dancers, acrobats, or gymnasts **2 :** JERSEY 2 **3 :** a woman's one-piece usu. strapless bathing suit

maillot 3

**mail·man** \ˈmā(ə)l,man, -aa(ə)n\ *n, pl* **mail·men :** MAIL CARRIER

**mail messenger** *n* **:** one who works for the post-office department under contract transporting mail between a post office and a postal transportation terminal (as at an airfield or railroad station)

**mail order** *n* **:** an order for goods that is received and filled by mail

**mail-order house** *n* **:** a retail establishment whose business is conducted by mail

**mail-rider** \ˈ≈,≈≈\ *n* **:** a horseback rider who carries mail

**mails** *pl of* MAIL, *pres 3d sing of* MAIL

**mail shell** *n* [⁴*mail*] **:** CHITON

¹**maim** \ˈmām\ *vt* -ED/-ING/-S [ME *maynen, maymen, maynhen, mayhaymen*, fr. OF *mahaignier, maynier*, prob. of Gmc origin; akin to MHG *meidem, meiden* gelding, Goth *gamaidans*, acc. pl., crippled — more at MAD] **1 :** to commit the felony of mayhem upon **2 :** to wound seriously **:** MUTILATE, DISABLE, DISFIGURE ⟨he was a puritan, ~*ed* by the narrow orthodoxy of his childhood —Douglas Stewart⟩

**syn** MAIM, CRIPPLE, MUTILATE, BATTER, MANGLE apply, in common, to an injuring (of a body or an object) so severe as to leave permanent or lasting effects. MAIM implies the loss or destruction of the usefulness of a limb or member ⟨an arm hanging useless, *maimed* in a car accident⟩ CRIPPLE usu. implies the loss of an arm or leg or the serious impairment of its use but can apply to any injury seriously impairing normal mobility or functioning ⟨a boy *crippled* by the loss of a leg⟩ ⟨hands *crippled* by arthritis⟩ ⟨a battleship, *crippled* by cruisers the night before, lay smoking and floundering within sight —Ira Wolfert⟩ MUTILATE implies the cutting, esp. cutting off, or the removal of a part essential to completeness and lessening the perfection, beauty, or pleasing wholeness of the thing ⟨looking exactly like a company of dolls a cruel child had *mutilated*, snapping a foot off here, tearing out a leg here, and battering the face of a third —Richard Jefferies⟩ ⟨never *mutilate* a book by tearing out pages or removing illustrations —L.R.McColvin⟩ BATTER and MANGLE do not suggest loss, as of a limb, but rather an injuring which disfigures, usu. excessively, BATTER implying a pounding or harsh beating, MANGLE implying a tearing, twisting, or hacking ⟨a procession of *battered* automobiles —Oscar Handlin⟩ ⟨to bring up cannon and *batter* the forts into surrender —P.G.Mackesy⟩ ⟨people who have disregarded the warnings and been *mangled* by sharks —V.G.Heiser⟩ ⟨a smashed truck and *mangled* driver —G.R.Stewart⟩ ⟨his face and head were frightfully *mangled* with long cuts, evidently made by an axe —A.F.Harlow⟩

²**maim** *n* -s [ME *maheym, mayme, mayne*, fr. MF *mahaing, mahaim*, fr. OF, fr. *mahaignier*, v.] **1** *obs* **:** the loss of a limb or member of the body or of the use of it **:** serious physical injury ⟨the beggars . . . look upon their ~*s* as . . . purses, which will always give them money —J.R.Lowell⟩ **2** *obs* **:** a serious defect or mutilation **:** a major lack

³**maim** \ˈmām\ *adj, archaic* **:** MAIMED

**maimed** \-md\ *adj* [ME *maymed, mayned*, fr. past part. of *maymen, maynen* to maim] **:** CRIPPLED, MUTILATED ⟨the ~ right hand twisted and clutched —P.B.Kyne⟩ — **maimed·ness** *n* -ES

**maim·er** \-mə(r)\ *n* -s **:** one that maims ⟨a worse killer and ~ than . . . botulism, typhoid, and trichinosis —Jeff McDermid⟩

**mai·mon** \mīˈmōn\ *n* -s [It *maimone*, fr. Ar *maymūn*, fr. Gk *mimō* ape] **:** MANDRILL

¹**mai·mon·i·de·an** \mī¦mänəˈdēən\ *adj, often cap* [*Maimonides* (Moses ben Maimon) †1204 Jewish philosopher + E *-an*] **:** of or relating to Moses Maimonides

²**maimonidean** \"\ *n* -s *usu cap* **:** a follower of Moses Maimonides

**mai·mul** \(ˈ)mī¦mül\ *n, pl* **maimul** *usu cap* **:** a member of a Muslim caste of net workers and fishermen in the Bengal area

¹**main** \ˈmān\ *n* -s [ME, fr. OE *mægen*; akin to OS & OHG *magan, megin* strength, main part, ON *magn, megin* strength, *mega* to be able — more at MAY] **1 :** physical strength **:** POWER — used in the phrase *with might and main* **2 a** [by shortening] **:** MAINLAND **b** [short for obs. E *main sea*, fr. ²*main* + *sea*] **:** HIGH SEA **3** [²*main*] **:** the chief or principal part **:** the essential point ⟨the ~ of the lady's history —Robert Browning⟩ ⟨he is one of those writers who, in the ~, leave me cold —J.D.Adams⟩ **4** *obs* **:** END, PURPOSE, OBJECT **5 :** a pipe, duct, or circuit to or from which lead tributary branches of a utility system and which carries their combined flow ⟨water ~⟩ ⟨gas ~⟩ ⟨sewer ~⟩ ⟨electric ~⟩ — compare BUS BAR, LATERAL **6** [by shortening] **a :** MAINMAST **b :** MAINSAIL

²**main** \"\ *adj* [ME *mayn*, fr. OE *mægen-*, fr. *mægen*, n.] **1 :** outstanding, conspicuous, or first in any respect **:** GREAT, PREEMINENT **:** PRINCIPAL ⟨the ~ office is located in New York⟩ ⟨just inside the solid-glass ~ doors —Sylvia Gray⟩ ⟨the ~ reason that any businessman can understand —*Wall Street Jour.*⟩ **2** *now chiefly dial* **:** large in amount, effect, or extent **:** GREAT **3 a** *obs* **:** having or manifesting great strength or power **:** MIGHTY ⟨soaring on ~ wing —John Milton⟩ **b :** fully exerted **:** SHEER ⟨keep her in bed by ~ force —Edna Ferber⟩ **4** *obs* **:** of or relating to wide reaches or expanse (as of sea or land) **5 :** connected with or located near the mainmast or mainsail **6 :** expressing the chief predication in a complex sentence ⟨~ clause⟩ ⟨~ predicate⟩ ⟨~ verb⟩ **syn** see CHIEF

³**main** \"\ *n* -s [prob. fr. ²*main*] **1 a :** a number exceeding four and not exceeding nine called by the caster in the game of hazard before throwing **b :** LINE 13a **2 a :** an archery match **b** *archaic* **:** a boxing match **c** *archaic* **:** a lawn bowling match **3 :** a cockfight series consisting of an odd number of matches ⟨got himself a fighting cock . . . and was making himself a little money in the chicken ~*s* —Erskine Caldwell⟩

⁴**main** \"\ *adv* [prob. fr. ²*main*] *now dial* **:** VERY, EXTREMELY ⟨it was ~ hot —R.L.Stevenson⟩

**main battery** *n* **:** the guns of heaviest caliber on a warship

**main brace** *n* [ME *mayne brase*, fr. *mayne, mayn* main + *brase, brace* brace — more at BRACE] **1 :** the brace attached to a sailing ship's main yard **2 :** the brace that transmits the load most directly from one of its terminal joints to the other

**main chance** *n* **:** the chance that seems to promise most advantage ⟨one eye on heaven and one on the *main chance* —W.M.Thackeray⟩

**main couple** *n* **:** the principal truss in a roof

**main course** *n* **:** the mainsail of a square-rigged ship

**main crop** *n* **:** a fruit or vegetable crop gathered in the prevailing season as distinguished from an early or late harvest

**main deck** *n* **:** the principal deck of a ship: **a :** the highest complete deck on a naval vessel extending the full length and width of the ship **b :** the deck next below the upper or the shelter deck on a merchant ship usu. located at the end of the transverse framing; *often* **:** the uppermost continuous deck so constructed that it is possible to close securely all openings — see DECK illustration, SHIP illustration

**main drain** *n* **:** the principal lengthwise pipe of a ship's bilge drainage system

**main droite** \manⁿdrwät\ *adv (or adj)* [F, lit., right hand, fr. *main* hand (fr. L *manus*) + *droite*, fem. of *droit* right, direct, straight, fr. L *directus* direct, straight — more at MANUAL, DIRECT (adj.)] **:** with the right hand — used as a direction in keyboard music; abbr. *M.D.*

**maine** \ˈmān\ *adj, usu cap* [fr. *Maine*, state in the northeastern U.S., prob. fr. F, historical region of France] **:** of or from the state of Maine **:** of the kind or style prevalent in Maine

**maine cat** *n, usu cap M, chiefly NewEng* **:** ANGORA CAT

**main·er** \-nə(r)\ *n* -s *cap* [*Maine* state + E *-er*] **:** a native or resident of the state of Maine

**main gauche** \manⁿgōsh\ *adv (or adj)* [F, lit., left hand, fr. *main* hand + *gauche* left — more at GAUCHE] **:** with the left hand — used as a direction in keyboard music; abbr. *M.G.*

**main guard** *n* **1 :** the keep of a castle **2 a :** the principal guard of a garrison **b** *Brit* **:** the building or barrack in which a main guard is lodged **3 :** the chief guard of an army from which all other guards are detached — not now used technically **4 :** a support of an outpost

**main guy** *n* **1** [²*main* + *guy* (rope)] **:** the principal guy rope of a circus tent **2** [²*main* + *guy* (person)] **:** CHIEF, LEADER

**main hatch** *n* **:** a ship's principal hatch usu. just forward of the mainmast

**main·ite** \ˈmā,nīt\ *n* -s *cap* [*Maine* state + E *-ite*] **:** MAINER

**main·land** \ˈmān,land, -aa(ə)nd, -lənd\ *n* [ME *mayn land*, fr. *mayn* main + *land*] **:** a continuous body of land constituting the chief part of a country or continent

**main·land·er** \-də(r)\ *n* -s **:** a dweller on the mainland ⟨any ~ — Hawaii's term for a resident of continental United States — will find its stores . . . stocked with the latest mainland fashions —Jack Teehan⟩

**main line** *n* **1 :** a principal highway or railroad line or the chief artery of a branching system **2** *slang* **a :** a principal vein ⟨a shot of heroin in the *main line*⟩ **b :** the injection of a narcotic into a principal vein ⟨still cool and stepping dainty off my last *main line* —Herbert Gold⟩

**main·line** \ˈmān,līn\ *vi* [*main line*] *slang* **:** to inject a narcotic drug (as heroin) into a principal vein — **mainliner** \-īnə(r)\ *n* -s *slang*

**mainly** *adv* [ME *mainliche, maynly*, fr. *main, mayn*, adj., main + *-liche, -ly* -ly] **1** *obs* **:** in a strong or forceful manner **2 :** in the principal respect **:** for the most part **:** CHIEFLY **3** *now dial Eng* **:** very much **:** VERY, EXCEEDINGLY

**main·mast** \ˈmānməst (*usual nautical pronunc*), -n,mast, -,maa(ə)st, -,mȧst\ *n* **:** a sailing ship's principal mast usu. second from the bow — see SHIP illustration

**main·our** \ˈmānə(r)\ *or* **man·ner** \ˈmanə(r)\ *n* -s [ME *manor*, fr. AF *mainoure, meinoure*, fr. OF *manuevre, manœuvre* manual labor — more at MANEUVER] *Old Eng law* **:** something stolen found on the thief's person or in his immediate possession — **with the mainour** *or* **in the mainour** *adv (or adj)* **:** in the act **:** FLAGRANTE DELICTO, RED-HANDED

**main·per·na·ble** \ˈmānpə(r)nəbəl\ *adj* [ME, fr. AF *meinpernable*, fr. *mainprendre* + *-able*] **:** capable of being mainprised

**main·per·nor** \-pə(r)nə(r)\ *n* -s [ME *meinpernour*, fr. AF, fr. *mainprendre* (v.) + *-our* -or] **:** one who gives an undertaking of mainprise

¹**main·prise** \ˈmān,prīz\ *n* -s [ME *meinprise*, fr. AF, fr. *mainprendre* to accept surety, fr. OF *main* hand (fr. L *manus*) + *prendre* (past part. *pris*) to take — more at MANUAL, PRIZE (act of capturing)] **:** an undertaking given to a magistrate or court that even without having an accused in custody one will be liable for the appearance of the accused on a fixed day to defend any and all charges to be brought against him — compare BAIL

²**mainprise** \"\ *vt* -ED/-ING/-S [ME *mainprisen, meinprisen*, fr. AF *meinprise*, n.] **:** to release or procure the release of on mainprise

**main·pri·sor** \-zə(r)\ *n* -s [ME *mainprisour*, fr. *mainprisen* (v.) + *-our* -or] **:** MAINPERNOR

¹**mains** \ˈmānz\ *n pl but sing in constr* [short for *domains*, pl. of *domain*] *dial Brit* **:** the home farm of a manor

²**mains** \"\ *adj* [fr. *mains*, pl. of ¹*main*] **:** of or relating to electric power mains ⟨~ voltage⟩ ⟨~ frequency⟩

**main·sail** \ˈmānsəl (*usual nautical pronunc*), -n,sāl\ *n* [ME *mayne saile*, fr. *mayne, mayn* main + *saile, sail* sail] **:** the principal sail on the mainmast — compare MAIN COURSE; see SAIL illustration

**main sequence** *n* **:** the broad band of the spectrum-luminosity diagram which contains the great majority of stars and the sun and for which the absolute visual magnitudes range from about −3 for stars of spectral type B to 12 for stars of spectral type M

**main shaft** *n* **:** a principal drive shaft (as in a machine shop or in a motor vehicle) — distinguished from *countershaft*

**mainsheet** \ˈ≈,≈\ *n* [ME *mayne shete*, fr. *mayne, mayn*, adj., main + *shete* sheet] **:** a rope by which the mainsail is trimmed and secured — see SHIP illustration

**mainspring** \ˈ≈,≈\ *n* **1 :** the chief spring in a mechanism; *esp* **:** the coiled driving spring of a watch or clock **2 :** the chief or most powerful motive, agent, or cause ⟨the ~ was useful common sense —Van Wyck Brooks⟩

**mainstay** \ˈ≈,≈\ *n* [ME *mayne stay*, fr. *mayne, mayn* main + *stay*] **1 :** a ship's stay extending from the maintop forward usu. to the foot of the foremast — see SHIP illustration **2 :** a chief support **:** principal reliance ⟨she has been a ~ of several small luncheon clubs —Robert Rice⟩ ⟨cotton is the ~ of the surrounding country —*Amer. Guide Series: La.*⟩

**main stem** *n* **:** a main trunk or channel: as **a :** the main course of a river or stream ⟨apt to miss this offshoot to the left because the *main stem* to the creek went straight ahead through the trees —N.C.McDonald⟩ **b :** the main line of a railroad **c :** the main street of a city or town **d :** BIG TIME 2 ⟨much of his career has been off the musical *main stem* —*Time*⟩

**mainstream** \ˈ≈,≈\ *n* **:** the prevailing current or direction of activity or influence ⟨the ~ of medieval learning in the universities passed by the alchemists —S.F.Mason⟩ ⟨within the ~ of the western democratic tradition —Max Beloff⟩

**main street** *adj, usu cap M&S* [²*main* + *street* (n.); influenced in meaning by *Main Street* (1920), novel by Sinclair Lewis †1951 Am. novelist and playwright that portrays materialistic provincialism as a characteristic of American life in a small town] **:** of or relating to the mediocre, materialistic, or drab aspects of average U.S. town and city life ⟨the popularity of the *Main Street* theme —*Nation*⟩

**main street·er** \-,strēd·ə(r)\ *n, usu cap M&S* **:** a representative of Main Street attitudes ⟨with millions of other native *Main Streeters* in the army, I used to wonder how it would be to get back on Main Street in my own little town —Dale Kramer⟩

**maint** \ˈmānt\ *adj* [F, fr. OProv *mant, maint*] *archaic* **:** MANY

**maint** *abbr* maintenance

**main·tain** \(ˈ)mān¦tān, mən-\ *vt* -ED/-ING/-S [ME *maintenen, maintenen*, fr. OF *maintenir*, fr. ML *manutenēre*, fr. L *manu tenēre* to know for certain, lit., to hold in the hand, fr. *manu* (abl. of *manus* hand) + *tenēre* to hold — more at MANUAL, THIN] **1 :** to keep in a state of repair, efficiency, or validity **:** preserve from failure or decline ⟨exercise . . . sufficient to ~ bodily and mental vigor —H.G.Armstrong⟩ **2 a :** to sustain against opposition or danger **:** back up **:** DEFEND, UPHOLD ⟨only fast ironclad cruisers could ~ the position of the Union against other naval powers —H.K.Beale⟩ **b :** to uphold in argument **:** contend for ⟨~*s* his logical position⟩ **3 :** to persevere in **:** carry on **:** keep up **:** CONTINUE ⟨members of the . . . tribe ~ native customs with ceremonial dances —*N.Y. Times*⟩ ⟨the husband could be certain of ~*ing* a certain standard of living —*Saturday Rev.*⟩ ⟨in addition to ~*ing* his news schedule he served as a fire warden —*Current Biog.*⟩ **4 :** to provide for **:** bear the expense of **:** SUPPORT ⟨the lady of beauty is ~*ed* as the pampered wife of a wealthy man —Lucy Crockett⟩ ⟨two homes, with 145 beds, are ~*ed* for the aged and indigent —*Americana Annual*⟩ **5 :** to affirm in or as if in argument **:** ASSERT, DECLARE ⟨~*ed* that this government was untrustworthy —*Collier's Yr. Bk.*⟩ ⟨was ~*ing* . . . that "modern society could hardly look worse" —*Saturday Rev.*⟩ **6 :** to assist (a party to legal action) so as to commit maintenance

**syn** ASSERT, DEFEND, VINDICATE, JUSTIFY: MAINTAIN indicates firm, convinced, persistent upholding of something as true, just, valid, or acceptable ⟨*maintain* that the whole educational scheme of our schools and colleges should be recast, and that a much larger portion of it should be devoted to modern languages and to history —R.B.Merriman⟩ ⟨stubbornly *maintained* his views in any argument even to insisting upon certain observations which subsequently were shown to be practically impossible —Witmer Stone⟩ ASSERT may indicate a setting forth of something as true, valid, or existent with or without aggressive determination to convince and to silence opposition ⟨that rigid sect which *asserts* that all real science is precise measurement —Havelock Ellis⟩ ⟨in Elizabethan drama, the critic is rash who will *assert* boldly that any play is by a single hand —T.S.Eliot⟩ ⟨what I content myself with *asserting* here you can scarcely deny —A.T.Quiller-Couch⟩ DEFEND may apply to a stating as true in the face of attack, objection, or disbelief, often as a calm apologist without the aggressiveness suggested by ASSERT ⟨*defended* his action by saying it was the best and quickest way —S.H.Holbrook⟩ ⟨called upon to *defend* his action against Russian charges that undesirable persons remained in office —*Current Biog.*⟩ VINDICATE suggests an adducing with force, cogency, logic, truth, or evidence that overwhelms doubt, hesitancy, denial, or opposition ⟨the aesthetic apologies by which artists and art critics *vindicate* artistic activity —Bernard Smith⟩ ⟨have all *vindicated* ourselves and received responsible positions —John Dos Passos⟩ JUSTIFY indicates an appeal to a standard of law or right or to an accepted rule or measure to show the truth, validity, or propriety of something ⟨*justified* the right of revolution not upon the ground of hostile acts of the people but upon usurpations of authority upon the part of those to whom such authority has been delegated —W.S.Myers⟩ ⟨*justified* his seizure of power on the grounds of an alleged conspiracy by the government to control the elections —*Americana Annual*⟩

**main·tain·able** \-tānəbəl\ *adj* [ME *maintenable*, fr. *mayntenen, maintenen*, v. + *-able*] **:** capable of being maintained

**maintained school** *n* **:** a publicly supported elementary or secondary school in Great Britain

**main·tain·er** \-nə(r)\ *n* -s [alter. (influenced by E *-er*) of ME *mayntenour*, fr. AF, fr. *maintenir*, v. + *-our* -or] **1 :** one that maintains **2 :** MAINTAINOR

**maintaining power** *n* **:** a device supplying a driving force for maintaining a watch or clock in operation during winding

**main·tain·or** \mān·ˈtānə(r)\ *n* -s [ME *meyntenour*, fr. AF *meyntenour, maintenour* maintainer] **:** one guilty of maintenance

¹**main·te·nance** \ˈmānt(ə)nən(t)s, -tᵊnən-\ *n* -s [ME *meyntenaunce, maintenaunce*, fr. MF *maintenance* act of maintaining, fr. OF, fr. *maintenir*, v. + *-ance*] **1** *obs* **:** BEARING, DEPORTMENT ⟨lustier ~ than I did look for —*Shak.*⟩ **2 a :** the act of providing means of support for someone ⟨the small man looked to his neighboring lord for a protection and ~ which the state could not give —W.C.Dickinson⟩ **b :** the provisions, supplies, or funds needed to live on **:** means of sustenance ⟨at least half of them are living parasitically on the other half instead of producing ~ for themselves —G.B.Shaw⟩ **3 a** [ME *meyntenaunce, maynteynaunce*, fr. AF *mayntenaunce*, fr. OF *maintenance* act of maintaining, protection] **:** an officious or unlawful intermeddling in a cause depending between others by assisting either party with money or means with which to carry it on — see CHAMPERTY **b :** the right of a seaman to food and quarters **4 :** the labor of keeping something (as buildings or equipment) in a state of repair or efficiency **:** CARE, UPKEEP ⟨the mere ~ of the fences . . . gives much to do —Richard Jefferies⟩ **5 a :** the upholding or defense of an attitude, opinion, or cause ⟨the ~ of this belief was not rational —Abram Kardiner⟩ **b :** the action of preserving or supporting (as a condition or institution) ⟨will facilitate the ~ of peace —C.L.Jones⟩ **syn** see LIVING

²**maintenance** \"\ *adj* **:** designed or adequate to maintain a living body in a stable condition without providing reserves for growth, functional change, or healing effect ⟨established the experimental animals on a ~ ration for calcium⟩ ⟨the patient may often be kept going indefinitely on a ~ ration of digitalis⟩

**maintenance bond** *n* **:** a contract of insurance against loss from lack of durability of construction work

**maintenance man** *n* **:** a worker who keeps buildings, shops, or equipment in good repair

**maintenance of membership :** a stipulation of some labor union contracts requiring persons who are members when the contract is adopted or who join during its life to pay dues until its expiration on penalty of discharge but not requiring nonmembers to join

**maintenance of way :** the upkeep and repair of a railroad's fixed property (as track and bridges)

**main·top** \ˈ≈,≈\ *n* [ME *mayne toppe*, fr. *mayne, mayn*, adj., main + *toppe* top (platform)] **:** a platform about the head of the mainmast of a square-rigged ship — see SHIP illustration

**main·top·man** \ˈ≈,≈mən\ *n, pl* **maintopmen :** a mariner assigned to duty on a ship's mainmast or maintop

**main-topmast** \mān-ˈtäpməst (*usual nautical pronunc*), -p,mast, -,maa(ə)st\ *n* [ME *mane toppe maste*, fr. *mane, mayne, mayn* main + *toppe maste* topmast] **:** a ship's mainmast spar between the mainmast itself and the main-topgallant mast — see SHIP illustration

**main topsail schooner** *n* **:** a schooner carrying a square fore-topsail and topgallant sail

**main track** *n* **:** a track on which railroad trains travel from city to city — compare SIDING 3

**main-truck** \ˈ≈,≈\ *n* [²*main* + *truck*] **:** the truck of a ship's mainmast

**main wales** *n* **:** two or more strakes of the thickest planking lying at the widest part of a wooden ship's hull and extending its entire length and supporting the main deck

**main yard** *n* [ME *mayne yerde*, fr. *mayne, mayn*, adj., main + *yerde* yard] **:** the yard on which a ship's mainsail is extended

**mainz** \ˈmīn(t)s\ *adj, usu cap* [fr. *Mainz*, Germany] **:** of or from the city of Mainz, Germany **:** of the kind or style prevalent in Mainz

**mai·oi·dea** \mäˈöidēə, mīˈ-\ [NL, fr. *Maia*, genus of crabs + *-oidea*] *syn of* OXYRHYNCHA

**maiolica** *var of* MAJOLICA

**mai·pu·re** \mīˈpü(,)rā\ *n, pl* **maipure** *or* **maipures** *usu cap* [AmerSp *maipure, maipuru*, of AmerInd origin] **1 a :** an

Arawakan people of the upper Orinoco in Venezuela **b :** a member of such people **2 :** the language of the Maipure people
**mair** \ˈmar\ *chiefly Scot var of* MORE
**ma·i·re** \ˈmīˌrē,rā\ *n* -s [Maori] **:** any of several New Zealand trees with dense heavy wood: as **a :** a New Zealand tree of the genus *Olea* — usu. used with a descriptive qualifier; compare BLACK MAIRE, WHITE MAIRE **b :** a small light-barked tree (*Eugenia maire*) with white flowers followed by red berries **c :** a small and often shrubby tree (*Mida myrtifolia*) that is related to the Asiatic sandalwood and has glossy glabrous usu. alternate leaves and small brownish green flowers in axillary clusters followed by small red drupes
**mais** *pl of* MAI
**mai·son–dieu** \ˌmāˌzōⁿˈdyə̄\ *n, pl* **maisons–dieu** \"\ [ME *mesondieu, masondewe*, fr. MF *meson-Dieu, maison-Dieu*, fr. OF, fr. *maison* house + *Dieu* God (fr. L *deus* god) — more at DEITY] **:** HOSTEL, HOSPITAL
**mai·son·nette** *also* **mai·son·nette** \ˌmāzōˈnet\ *n* -s [F *maisonnette*, fr. OF, dim. of *maison* house, fr. L *mansion-, mansio* dwelling, habitation — more at MANSION] **1 :** a small house **2 :** an apartment often of two stories
**maist** \ˈmāst\ *dial Brit var of* MOST
**mais·ter** \ˈmāstə(r)\ *now dial var of* MASTER
**maist·ly** *dial var of* MOSTLY
**maistry** *obs var of* MASTERY
**mai·thi·li** \ˈmīd·əlē\ *n* -s *usu cap* **1 :** an Indic dialect of north Bihar **2 :** a cursive script derived from Devanagari
**maî·tre d'** \ˌmād·ə(r)ˈdē *also* -ā·trəˈdē\ *n, pl* **maître d's** [by shortening] **:** MAÎTRE D'HÔTEL
**maî·tre d'armes** \ˌmā·trəˈdärm, mātˈd-\ *n, pl* **maîtres d'armes** [F, lit., master of arms] **:** a teacher of fencing
**maî·tre d'hô·tel** \ˌmā·trə(ˌ)dōˈtel, ˌmāt(ˌ)d-\ *n, pl* **maîtres d'hôtel** [F, lit., master of house, fr. MF *maistre d'ostel*] **1 a :** a head steward (as of a great house or a hotel) **:** MAJORDOMO **b :** HEADWAITER **2** *or* **maître d'hôtel butter :** a sauce of melted butter, chopped parsley, salt, pepper, and lemon juice
**maize** \ˈmāz\ *n* -s [Sp *maiz*, fr. Taino *mahiz, mays*] **1 :** INDIAN CORN **2** *or* **maize yellow :** a variable color averaging a light yellow that is redder and duller than jasmine or chrome lemon and redder and very slightly darker than popcorn **3 :** MILO
**maize billbug** *n* **:** a weevil (*Sphenophorus maidis*) sometimes destructive to corn
**maizebird** \ˈ=,=\ *n* **:** REDWING BLACKBIRD
**maize dance** *n* **:** an American Indian ritual dance in supplication or in thanksgiving for a successful maize harvest
**maize mildew** *n* **:** a downy mildew (*Sclerospora maydis*) attacking Indian corn
**maize oil** *n* **:** CORN OIL
**maiz·er** \ˈmāzə(r)\ *or* **maize thief** *n, pl* **maizers** *or* **maize thieves :** REDWING BLACKBIRD
**maize smut** *n* **:** BOIL SMUT
**maj** *abbr* **1** major **2** majority
**¹ma·ja** \ˈmä(ˌ)hä\ *n* -s [Sp, fem. of *majo*] **:** a Spanish belle of the lower class — compare MAJO
**²ma·ja** \ˈmājə\ *n, cap* [NL, fr. L *maia*, a large crab, fr. Gk] **:** a nearly cosmopolitan genus of crabs that is the type of the family Majidae
**ma·ja·gua** *or* **ma·ha·gua** \məˈhägwə\ *n* -s [AmerSp (also, *demajagua, damajagua*), fr. Taino] **:** either of two malvaceous trees that are often considered variant forms of a single species: **a :** an irregularly spreading or shrubby tree (*Hibiscus tiliaceus*) that is widely distributed along tropical shores, yields a light tough wood used esp. for canoe outriggers and a fibrous bast used for cordage and caulking, and is often cultivated for ornament or for its useful products — called also *balibago, purau* **b :** an erect forest tree (*H. elatus*) of the West Indian uplands yielding a moderately dense timber with the heartwood variegated in purple, metallic blue, and olive that is in demand esp. for cabinetwork and gunstocks — called also *blue mahoe*
**ma·jes·tic** \məˈjestik, -tēk\ *also* **ma·jes·ti·cal** \-təkəl, -tēk-\ *adj* [*majesty* + *-ic* or *-ical*] **:** having, exhibiting, or marked by majesty or dominion **:** IMPERIAL, REGAL **syn** see GRAND
**ma·jes·ti·cal·ly** \-tək(ə)lē, -tēk-, -li\ *adv* **:** in a majestic manner
**maj·es·ty** \ˈmajəstē, -ti\ *n* -ES [ME *maieste, magestee*, fr. OF *majesté*, fr. LL *majestat-, majestas*, fr. L, sovereign power, dignity, authority, fr. a base akin to L *major* greater (compar. of *magnus* great) + *-tat-, -tas* -ty — more at MUCH] **1 a** *cap* **:** the sovereign greatness, authority, or dominion of God ⟨seated at the right hand of the throne of the *Majesty* in heaven —Heb 8:1 (RSV)⟩ **b :** sovereign power, authority, or dignity **:** kingly greatness ⟨the kingdom of truth is a threat to every historical ~ —Reinhold Niebuhr⟩ ⟨a tyrannous sun, whose ~ was almost insupportable, lorded it over the world —James Stephens⟩ **c :** the person of a sovereign ⟨and watching, one knew that ~ had passed⟩ **2** [ME *mageste*, fr. MF or ML; MF *majesté*, fr. ML *majestat-, majestas*, fr. L] — used with *your* in addressing reigning sovereigns and their consorts and with *his, her,* or *their* as a periphrastic designation of these ⟨he had pleaded with her ~ to let him study the art of war in the tented field —A.B.Feldman⟩ ⟨Your *Majesty*⟩ ⟨Their *Majesties* of England —Frank Yerby⟩ **3** [MF *maiesté*, fr. ML *majestat-, majestas*] **:** a representation in graphic or plastic art of God the Father, of Christ, of the Virgin, or of the three persons of the Trinity enthroned in glory **4 a :** royal dignity, bearing, or aspect **:** STATELINESS ⟨there is a ~ that surrounds a president in Soviet eyes —M.W.Straight⟩ **b :** august or commanding power, effect, or appearance **:** GRANDEUR ⟨the luminous band of the Milky Way that stretches in quiet ~ all around the sky —B.J.Bok⟩ ⟨stood up straight, in all the ~ of his giant stature —Liam O'Flaherty⟩ ⟨this link between mortals and forces shaping their lives was the mighty concern which gave a kind of ~ to . . . his plays —John Mason Brown⟩ **5 :** greatness or splendor of quality or character ⟨at his best in sudden ~ of phrase —Virginia Woolf⟩ ⟨nightingales disturbed the ~ of great nights —F.M.Ford⟩
**¹majid** \ˈmajəd, ˈmaj-\ *also* **mai·id** \ˈmā(y)əd, ˈmīəd\ *adj* [NL *Majidae* or *Maiidae*] **:** of or relating to the Majidae
**²majid** \"\ *also* **maiid** \"\ *n* -s **:** a crab of the family Majidae **:** a typical spider crab
**maji·dae** \ˈmajəˌdē, ˈmaj-\ *n pl, cap* [NL, fr. *Maja*, type genus + *-idae*] **:** a large family of oxyrhynchan crabs that includes most of the spider crabs
**maj·lis** *or* **mej·lis** *also* **maj·les** *or* **mej·liss** \majˈlis, mej-, -les\ *n* -ES [Per *majlis* assembly, council, fr. Ar] **:** a council, assembly, or tribunal in No. Africa or southwestern Asia; *specif* **:** a house of parliament (as in Iran or Iraq) **:** PARLIAMENT
**ma·jo** \ˈmä(ˌ)hō\ *n* -s [Sp] **:** a Spanish dandy of the lower class — compare MAJA
**ma·jol·i·ca** *also* **ma·iol·i·ca** \məˈjäləkə *sometimes* -ˈyäl-\ *n* -s [It *maiolica*, fr. ML *Majolica* Majorca, largest of the Balearic islands, Spain, where this ware was made, alter. of LL *Majorica*] **:** earthenware covered with an opaque tin glaze and decorated on the glaze before firing with color oxides; *esp* **:** early Italian ware of this type
**majolica blue** *n, often cap M* **1 :** a dark blue that is redder and duller than Flemish blue or Peking blue and less strong and very slightly greener than Japan blue **2** *of textiles* **:** a moderate blue that is greener and duller than average copen or Dresden blue and redder and duller than pompadour
**majolica earth** *n, often cap M* **:** INDIAN RED 2b
**ma·joon** \məˈjün\ *n* -s [Hindi *ma'jūn*, lit., kneaded, fr. Ar] **:** an East Indian narcotic confection that is made of hemp leaves, henbane, datura seeds, poppy seeds, honey, and ghee and that produces effects like those of hashish and opium — called also *bhang*
**¹ma·jor** \ˈmājə(r)\ *adj* [ME *majour*, fr. L *major* larger, greater, compar. of *magnus* large, great — more at MUCH] **1 :** greater in dignity, rank, importance, or interest **:** SUPERIOR ⟨regarded him as one of the ~ poets of his generation —Douglas Cleverdon⟩ ⟨the minor and ~ arts are flourishing —*Saturday Rev.*⟩ **2 :** greater in number, quantity, or extent **:** LARGER ⟨output of salt showed marked increases by all of the ~ . . . producing countries —*Americana Annual*⟩ ⟨the ~ part of this work was undertaken by him —H.W.H.Knott⟩ **3 :** of full legal age ⟨~ children⟩ **4 :** notable or conspicuous in effect or scope **:** CONSIDERABLE, PRINCIPAL — compare NEGLIGIBLE ⟨on a ~ military offensive —*Collier's Yr. Bk.*⟩ ⟨so that no single country produced any of the ~ weapons exclusively in its own territory —Denis Healey⟩ **5 :** involving grave risk **:** SERIOUS ⟨a ~ illness⟩ ⟨a ~ operative procedure⟩ **6 a :** of or relating to a subject of academic study chosen as a field of specialization **b :** of or relating to a secondary-school course requiring a maximum of classroom hours **7 a** *of a scale* **:** having half steps between the third and fourth and the seventh and eighth degrees **b** *of a key* **:** based (as in its harmonic relations) on such a scale — opposed to *minor*; used after the name of a keynote ⟨sonata in C *major*⟩ ⟨the F-*major* symphony⟩ **c** *of an interval* (1) **:** greater by a half step than minor **:** of a size equal to the distance between the keynote and a (specified) degree of the major scale — used of the second, third, sixth, and seventh — compare PERFECT (2) **:** greater by a comma — used of one whole step in an untempered scale compared with another ⟨C–D is a ~ step, greater than the minor step D–E⟩ — compare TEMPERAMENT **d** *of a mode in mensurable music* **:** having the large divided into longs
**²major** \"\ *n* -s [ML, fr. L, adj.] **1** *archaic* **:** MAJOR PREMISE **2 :** a person of full legal age **3 a :** one that is superior in rank, importance, station, or performance ⟨minor poets are legion; the ~s are few and far between⟩ **b :** one of the larger or more important members or units of a kind or group ⟨night baseball in the ~s is here to stay —John Drebinger⟩ ⟨much effort is made to "standardize" movies . . . the ~s possess a near monopoly —R.A.Brady⟩ **c :** MAJOR SUIT ⟨there is a laydown grand slam in either ~ —Florence Osborn⟩ **4** [prob. fr. F, fr. ML, magnate, chief] **:** an army, marine, or air-force officer ranking just below a lieutenant colonel and above a captain **5 :** a Salvation Army officer ranking above a senior captain and below a senior major **6 a :** a subject of academic study chosen as a field of specialization ⟨took English literature as his ~⟩ **b :** a student specializing in such a field ⟨he is a history ~⟩
**³major** \"\ *vi* -ED/-ING/-s **:** to pursue an academic major ⟨~*ing* in history at the university —John Dos Passos⟩
**major air command** *n* **:** any of the principal subdivisions of the U.S. Air Force that are directly responsible to air force headquarters — compare AIR COMMAND
**ma·jo·ra·na** \ˌmäjəˈränə\ *n, cap* [NL] **:** a genus of herbs (family Labiatae) that is sometimes included in the genus *Origanum* but is distinguished by having the flowers in verticels arranged in dense continuous spikes or heads
**ma·jor·a·tion** \ˌmājəˈrāshən\ *n* -s [ML *majoration-, majoratio*, fr. *majoratus* (past part. of *majorare* to increase, fr. L *major*, adj.) + L *-ion-, -io* -ion] **:** ENLARGEMENT, INCREASE
**major axis** *n* **:** the axis passing through the foci of an ellipse
**major bass** *n* **1 :** a 32-foot bourdon organ pipe **2 :** a 16-foot pedal open diapason organ pipe
**¹ma·jor·can** \məˈjȯrkən\ *adj, usu cap* [*Majorca* island, Spain + E *-an*] **1 :** of, relating to, or characteristic of the Balearic island of Majorca, Spain **2 :** of, relating to, or characteristic of the people of Majorca
**²majorcan** \"\ *n* -s *cap* **:** a native or inhabitant of Majorca
**major canon** *n* **:** a resident canon of a cathedral or collegiate church receiving a stipend — compare HONORARY CANON, MINOR CANON
**major diameter** *n* **:** the largest diameter of a screw thread measured at the crest of a male thread and at the root of a female thread
**ma·jor–do·mo** \ˌmājə(r)ˈdō(ˌ)mō\ *n* -s [Sp *mayordomo* or obs. It *maiordomo*, fr. ML *major domus*, lit., chief of the house, fr. *major*, n. + L *domus*, gen. of *domus* house — more at TIMBER] **1 :** a man having charge of a great household (as a royal or princely establishment) **:** a head steward or palace official **2 :** BUTLER, STEWARD **3** *Southwest* **:** MAYORDOMO
**major element** *n* **:** MACRONUTRIENT
**ma·jor·ette** \ˌmājəˈret\ *n* -s [by shortening] **:** DRUM MAJORETTE
**major excommunication** *n, Roman Catholicism* **:** absolute exclusion of a person from the church and in extreme cases even from social intercourse with church members — distinguished from *minor excommunication*
**major feria** *n* **:** GREATER FERIA 1
**major flute** *n* **:** an open flute stop of large scale usu. of 8-foot pitch in a pipe organ
**major form class** *n* **:** any one of the parts of speech of traditional grammar (as noun, verb, or preposition)
**major general** *n* [prob. fr. F *major général*, fr. *major* (officer) + *général*, adj., general] **:** an army, marine, or air-force officer ranking just below a lieutenant general and above a brigadier general
**¹ma·jor·i·tarian** \məˌjȯrəˈta(a)rēən, -järə-, -ter-, -tär-\ *adj* [*majority* + *-arian* (as in *humanitarian*)] **:** of, characterized by, or believing in majoritarianism ⟨~ politics⟩ ⟨~ principle⟩ ⟨~ party system⟩
**²majoritarian** \"\ *n* -s **:** one that believes in or advocates majoritarianism ⟨a ~ . . . holds the many more likely to be in possession of reason and truth than the few —*Va. Quarterly Rev.*⟩
**ma·jor·i·tar·i·an·ism** \-ēəˌnizəm\ *n* -s **:** the philosophy or practice according to which the decisions of an organized group should be made by a numerical majority of its members ⟨combine ~ with philosophies that are essentially aristocratic —J.R.Pennock⟩ ⟨an unchecked ~ can sweep a dictator to power during a transient mob hysteria —Peter Viereck⟩
**¹ma·jor·i·ty** \məˈjȯrəd·ē, -ˈjär-, -ətē, -i\ *n* -ES [MF *majorité*, fr. ML *majoritat-, majoritas*, fr. L *major*, adj. + *-itat-, -itas* -ity] **1** *obs* **:** the quality or state of being greater **:** SUPERIORITY ⟨whose . . . great name in arms holds from all soldiers chief ~ and military title capital —Shak.⟩ **2 :** the status of being of full legal age ⟨graduated . . . before he had attained his ~ —W.L.Burrage⟩ **3 a :** a number greater than half of a total ⟨the ~ of the human race is still today on the sidelines, watching and wondering —A.J.Toynbee⟩ — distinguished from *plurality* **b :** the excess of such a greater number over the remainder of the total **:** EDGE, MARGIN ⟨resulted in giving him a ~ of 98 out of a total of 504 votes cast —Joseph Schafer⟩ **c :** the preponderant quantity or share ⟨the ~ of the wool used in the U. S. is imported —F.J.Soday⟩ **4 :** all dead persons ⟨the end comes: he joins the ~ —W.H.Auden⟩ **5 :** the group or party whose votes preponderate **6** [prob. fr. F *majorité*, fr. *major* (officer) + *-ité* -ity] **:** the military office, rank, or commission of a major ⟨*majorities* and colonelcies were thick as June blackberries —Dixon Wecter⟩
**²majority** \"\ *adj* **:** of, relating to, or constituting a majority ⟨each committee is therefore composed of ~ and minority members —F.A.Ogg & P.O.Ray⟩
**majority leader** *n* **:** the leader of the majority party in a legislative body ⟨appointment as *majority leader* of the Senate⟩ — compare MINORITY LEADER
**majority rule** *n* **:** a political principle providing that a majority usu. constituted by fifty percent plus one of the members of a politically organized group shall have the power to make decisions binding upon the whole group ⟨democratic doctrines of political equality and *majority rule* —C.V.Shields⟩
**ma·jor·ize** \ˈmājəˌrīz\ *vi* -ED/-ING/-s *rugby* **:** to convert a try
**major key** *n* **:** a key or tonality in the major mode
**major league** *n* **1 a :** a league of highest classification in U.S. professional baseball **b :** a league of major importance in any of various other sports (as basketball or ice hockey) **2 :** BIG LEAGUE 2 ⟨a petty blackmailer going up to the *major leagues* —Gordon & Mildred Gordon⟩
**major mitch·ell** \ˌ==ˈmichəl\ *n, usu cap both Ms* [after *Major* Sir Thomas *Mitchell* †1855 Brit. explorer in Australia] *Austral* **:** PINK COCKATOO
**major order** *n* **1 :** any of three orders in the Roman Catholic Church: **a :** PRIESTHOOD **b :** DIACONATE **c :** SUBDIACONATE — compare MINOR ORDER **2 :** any of three orders in the Eastern Church or the Anglican Church: **a :** EPISCOPATE **b :** PRIESTHOOD **c :** DIACONATE
**major party** *n* **:** a political party whose electoral strength is sufficiently great to permit it to win control of a government usu. with comparative regularity and when defeated to constitute the principal opposition to the party in power ⟨caused splinter parties to form from both of the *major parties* —D.D. McKean⟩ — compare MINOR PARTY, THIRD PARTY
**major penalty** *n* **:** a five-minute suspension of a player in ice hockey with no substitute allowed — compare MINOR PENALTY
**major piece** *n* **:** a queen or rook in chess — compare MINOR PIECE
**major planet** *n* **:** any of the four largest planets of the solar system ⟨Jupiter, Saturn, Uranus, and Neptune are the *major planets*⟩ — compare ASTEROID, TERRESTRIAL PLANET
**major premise** *n* **:** the premise of a syllogism containing the major term
**major prophet** *n* **:** the author of one of the three chief prophetic books of the Old Testament ⟨Ezekiel, Isaiah, and Jeremiah are usually ranked as the *major prophets* of the Hebrews⟩
**major seminary** *n* **:** SEMINARY 2b(2)
**major seventh chord** *n* **:** a chord consisting of a major triad and a major seventh — see SEVENTH CHORD illustration
**ma·jor·ship** \ˈmājə(r)ˌship\ *n* -s [²*major* + *-ship*] *archaic* **:** MAJORITY 6
**major suit** *n* **:** either of two bridge suits of superior scoring value: **a :** SPADES **b :** HEARTS — compare MINOR SUIT
**major surgery** *n* **:** surgery involving a risk to the life of the patient; *specif* **:** an operation upon an organ within the cranium, chest, abdomen, or pelvic cavity — compare MINOR SURGERY
**major tenace** *n* **:** ace and queen of a suit held in one hand in some card games (as bridge) — compare MINOR TENACE
**major term** *n* **:** the term of a syllogism constituting the predicate of the conclusion
**major triad** *n* **1 :** a musical triad whose frequencies are in the proportions 4:5:6 **2 :** a musical triad consisting of a fundamental tone with its major third and perfect fifth — see TRIAD illustration
**ma·jus·cu·lar** \məˈjəskyələ(r)\ *adj* **:** of, relating to, or resembling a majuscule
**¹majus·cule** \ˈmajəˌskyül, məˈjə-\ *adj* [F, fr. L *majusculus* rather large, fr. *majus-*, stem of *major* larger, greater — more at MAJOR (adj.)] **:** written in or in the size or style of majuscules ⟨~ script⟩
**²majuscule** \"\ *n* -s [F, n. & adj.] **:** a large letter (as a capital or uncial) — compare MINUSCULE
**ma·jus la·ti·um** \ˌmä(ˌ)yüˈslād·ēˌüm\ *n, usu cap L* [L, lit., greater Latium, fr. *majus* greater (neut. of *major*) + *Latium*, ancient country of Italy] **:** the right of Roman citizenship granted to the holder of a magistracy in a territorial unit outside Rome and to his wife, children, and parents — compare JUS LATII, MINUS LATIUM
**mak** \ˈmak\ *Scot var of* MAKE
**makaasim** *var of* MACAASIM
**mak·able** \ˈmākəbəl\ *adj* **:** capable of being made ⟨~ contract in bridge⟩
**ma·kah** \ˈmä(ˌ)kä\ *n, pl* **makah** *or* **makahs** *usu cap* **1 a :** an Indian people forming a subdivision of the Nootka **b :** a member of such people **2 :** the dialect of the Makah people
**ma·ka·hi·ki** \ˌmäkəˈhēkē\ *n* -s [Hawaiian] **:** a period of several months which was celebrated each fall in ancient Hawaii with athletic contests, religious rites, and payment of tribute to chiefs and during which all warfare was tabooed
**ma·kai** \mäˈkī\ *adv (or adj)* [Hawaiian, fr. *ma* toward + *kai* sea] *Hawaii* **:** toward the sea **:** SEAWARD
**ma·kai·ra** \məˈkīrə\ *n, cap* [NL, perh. fr. Gk, fem. of *makar* blessed] **:** a genus of large active marine fishes (family Istiophoridae) comprising the marlins
**mak·ar** \ˈmakər\ *n* -s [ME *maker*, maker, poet — more at MAKER] *chiefly Scot* **:** POET
**ma·ka·ra** \ˈməkərə\ *n* -s [Skt] **:** a water monster of Hindu religious myth that is represented in religious art as having the body of a crocodile and head of an antelope and as being the steed of Varuna and the emblem of Kamadeva
**ma·kas·sar** *or* **ma·cas·sar** \məˈkasə(r), -aas-\ *n, pl* **makassar** *or* **makassars** *or* **macassar** *or* **macassars** *usu cap* [fr. *Makassar* (*Macassar*), city on southwestern Celebes island, and strait between Celebes and Borneo, Indonesia] **1 :** MAKASSARESE **2 :** the Austronesian language of the Makassarese people
**ma·kas·sar·ese** *also* **ma·cas·sar·ese** \məˌkasəˈrēz, -aas-, -ēs\ *n, pl* **makassarese** *also* **macassarese** *usu cap* [*Makassar* (*Macassar*), city and strait, + E *-ese*] **1 :** an Indonesian people living in and around the port of Makassar in the southwestern part of Celebes **2 :** a member of the Makassarese people
**ma·ka·tea** \ˌmäkəˈtāə\ *n* -s [Tuamotu] **:** a broad uplifted coral reef surrounding an island in the south Pacific
**¹make** \ˈmāk\ *vb* **made** \ˈmād\ **made; making; makes** [ME *maken*, fr. OE *macian*; akin to OFris *makia* to build, make, MD *maken* to make, do, OHG *mahhōn* to join, prepare, do, make, MIr *maistrid* he butters, W *maeddu* to conquer, Gk *magēnai* to be kneaded, OSlav *mazati* to anoint; basic meaning: to knead, press] *vt* **1 a** *obs* **:** BEHAVE, ACT — used with *it* and an adverb or adjective complement **b :** to seem to begin (an action) **:** BEGIN ⟨*made* to go⟩ **2 a** *archaic* **:** to bring about — used with *that* **b :** to cause to happen to or be experienced by someone ⟨~ us some sport⟩ ⟨~ trouble for him⟩ **c :** to cause to exist, occur, or appear **:** bring to pass **:** CREATE, CAUSE ⟨God *made* heaven and earth⟩ ⟨~ a disturbance⟩ ⟨his entrance *made* a sensation⟩ ⟨*making* a fuss over nothing⟩ ⟨~ mischief⟩ **d :** to give rise to **:** favor the growth or occurrence of ⟨good fences ~ good neighbors —Robert Frost⟩ ⟨lending money is a good way to ~ enemies⟩ ⟨haste ~*s* waste⟩ **e :** to fit, intend, or destine by or as if by creating ⟨laws were *made* for men, not men for laws⟩ ⟨ham and eggs were *made* for each other⟩ ⟨was never *made* to be an actor⟩ **f** *chiefly South & Midland* **:** to plant and raise (a crop) ⟨*made* a crop of oats⟩ **3** *obs* **:** to give birth to **4 a :** to bring (a material thing) into being by forming, shaping, or altering material **:** FASHION, MANUFACTURE ⟨~ a gun⟩ ⟨~ a suit of clothes⟩ ⟨~ a toy⟩ ⟨~ bricks without straw⟩ ⟨~ a railing out of water pipes⟩ **b :** COMPOSE, WRITE ⟨~ verses⟩ ⟨~ a sonnet⟩ ⟨~ an epigram⟩ **c :** to lay out and construct ⟨~ a road⟩ ⟨~ a park⟩ **5 :** to frame or formulate in the mind **:** form as a result of calculation or design ⟨~ plans for vacation⟩ ⟨~ a diagram⟩ **6 :** to put together from components or ingredients **:** CONSTITUTE ⟨~ bread with whole wheat flour⟩ ⟨house *made* of stone⟩ ⟨a chance to show the stuff he is *made* of⟩ **7 a :** to compute or estimate to be **:** find by calculation to be ⟨I ~ it 23 miles to the border from here⟩ **b :** to form and hold in the mind ⟨~ no doubt that he is guilty⟩ ⟨*made* no scruple of joining the enterprise⟩ **8 a :** to lay and set alight (a fire) **b :** to set in order ⟨~ beds⟩ **:** FIX, PREPARE ⟨~ coffee⟩ ⟨~ dinner⟩ ⟨~ camp⟩ **c :** to shuffle (a deck of cards) in preparation for the next deal **9 a** *dial* **:** to cure (as fish) by smoking or drying **b :** to cause (hay) to be cut and cured **10 a :** to cause to be or become **:** put in a certain state or condition ⟨trying to ~ the matter clear to everyone⟩ ⟨was *made* leader of the expedition⟩ ⟨*made* him sorry he had spoken so quickly⟩ ⟨*made* the scene real for us⟩ ⟨*made* himself useful around the place⟩ **b :** APPOINT, ORDAIN ⟨*made* him bishop⟩ ⟨*made* him a member of his cabinet⟩ **11 a :** ENACT, ESTABLISH ⟨~ laws⟩ ⟨~ a rule⟩ **b :** to execute in an appropriate manner **:** draw up ⟨~ a will⟩ ⟨~ a deed of transfer⟩ **c :** SET, NAME ⟨~ a price for the lot⟩ ⟨~ spades trumps⟩ **d :** to cause (an occurrence in time or the hour of the day) to be announced, indicated, or observed ⟨~ eight o'clock by striking eight bells⟩ ⟨~ sunset by hauling down the colors with ceremonies⟩ **12** *chiefly Brit* **:** to train to a requisite standard of efficiency ⟨~ a horse⟩ ⟨~ a falcon⟩ **13 a** *now dial* **:** to make fast **:** SHUT, BAR ⟨at this time the doors are *made* against you —Shak.⟩ **b :** to take possession of (a point) in backgammon by occupying with two or more men **c** (1) **:** to cause (an electric circuit) to be completed or closed (2) **:** to bring about (a contact) **d** (1) **:** to convert (a split) into a spare in bowling ⟨*made* the 3-10 split⟩ (2) **:** to score (a spare) by means of a split in bowling ⟨~ a spare by getting the 3-10 split⟩ **14** *obs* **a :** BRING ⟨have they *made* you to this —Ben Jonson⟩ **b :** PUT ⟨dangerous to ~ them hence —Ben Jonson⟩ **15 a :** to conclude as to the nature or meaning of something ⟨hardly knew what to ~ of his actions⟩ **b :** to regard as being **:** think to be ⟨not the fool some ~ him⟩ **16 a :** to carry out (an action indicated or implied by the object) **:** PERFORM ⟨~ war⟩ ⟨time to ~ a move⟩ ⟨~ an incision⟩ ⟨~ a promise⟩ ⟨~ amends⟩ ⟨~ a speech⟩ ⟨~ music⟩ ⟨~ apologies⟩ ⟨*made* a crackling noise⟩ ⟨*made* plans to go away⟩ ⟨~ preparations for the trip⟩ ⟨~ a bid⟩ **b :** to perform with a bodily movement ⟨~ a bow⟩ ⟨~ a jump⟩ ⟨~ a sweeping gesture⟩ **c :** to achieve by traversing **:** TRAVERSE ⟨~ a long detour⟩ ⟨mailman *making* his rounds⟩ **17 a :** to produce as a result of action, effort, or behavior with respect to something ⟨~ a mess of the job⟩ ⟨managed to ~ a joke of his losses⟩

⟨must be *made* an example of⟩ ⟨*made* a practice of getting up early⟩ — often used with *of it* ⟨tried to ~ a thorough job of it⟩ ⟨decided to ~ a night of it⟩ **b :** EAT ⟨*made* a good breakfast⟩ ⟨*made* a hasty lunch of soup and a sandwich⟩ **c** (1) *archaic* **:** to turn into another language by translation ⟨*making* these two authors English —John Dryden⟩ (2) *obs* **:** INTERPRET **18 :** to cause to act in a certain way **:** COMPEL — used with infinitive without *to* ⟨*made* him return the money⟩ but with *to* in passive constr. ⟨*made* to see the error of his ways⟩ **19 :** to cause or assure the success or prosperity of ⟨the night that either ~*s* me or fordoes me quite —Shak.⟩ ⟨anyone he takes a liking to is *made*⟩ **20 a :** to amount to in significance ⟨~*s* a great difference⟩ ⟨~*s* no matter⟩ ⟨doesn't ~ good sense⟩ **b :** to form the essential being of **:** be sufficient to constitute ⟨clothes ~ the man⟩ ⟨stone walls do not a prison ~ —Richard Lovelace⟩ **c :** to form by an assembling of individuals ⟨~ a quorum⟩ ⟨two more ~*s* an even dozen⟩ **:** EQUAL ⟨twice two ~*s* four⟩ ⟨two nickels ~ a dime⟩ **d :** to count as ⟨~ a fourth at bridge⟩ ⟨that ~*s* the third time he has failed⟩ **21 a :** to be or be capable of being changed or fashioned into ⟨rags ~ the best paper⟩ ⟨oak ~*s* good flooring⟩ **b :** to develop into **:** be or become useful as **:** serve as ⟨she will ~ a fine wife⟩ ⟨worried men ~ poor soldiers⟩ ⟨a collie ~*s* a good watchdog⟩ ⟨rabbit ~*s* a good stew⟩ ⟨*made* a very good witness⟩ **c :** FORM 6b **22 a :** REACH, ATTAIN, ACHIEVE ⟨tried to ~ the airfield with one motor failing⟩ ⟨*made* an average of 200 miles a day⟩ ⟨can ~ 80 miles per hour⟩ ⟨a story that *made* the front page⟩ ⟨~ a home run⟩ — often used with *it* ⟨you will never ~ it to the other shore in this weather⟩ **b :** to gain the rank of ⟨*made* corporal after a few months⟩ **c :** to gain a place on ⟨*made* the varsity soccer team⟩ **23 :** to gain (as money) by working, trading, or dealing ⟨~ a living⟩ ⟨~ a profit⟩ ⟨*made* his fortune in railroads⟩ **24 a :** to act so as to win or acquire ⟨~ acquaintances in his new job⟩ ⟨~*s* friends easily⟩ **b** *dial* **:** STEAL **c :** to score (points) in a game or sport **25 a :** to fulfill (a contract) in a card game **:** win (a specified number of points, tricks) at cards ⟨~ two spades⟩ **b :** to win a trick with (a card) **26 a :** to get sight of **:** make out ⟨*made* an enemy cruiser coming on astern⟩ **b :** to visit in the course of a journey **:** include in a route or itinerary ⟨intended to ~ Paris on the way to Vienna⟩ **c :** CATCH ⟨in time to ~ the morning train⟩ **d** *slang* **:** RECOGNIZE, IDENTIFY ⟨afraid the cops would ~ him from his fingerprints⟩ **27 :** to persuade to consent to sexual intercourse ⟨nine to one he would ~ her on the first try —Mary McCarthy⟩ ~ *vi* **1** *archaic* **:** to compose poetry **2 a :** BEHAVE, ACT ⟨*made* as though he were angry⟩ ⟨don't ~ as if you didn't hear me⟩ **b :** to begin or seem to begin a certain action ⟨*made* as though to hand it to me⟩ ⟨he *made* as though he would have gone further —Lk 24:28 (AV)⟩ **c :** to act so as to be or to seem to be — used with adj. complement ⟨~ merry⟩ ⟨*made* fast to the dock⟩ ⟨*made* ready to depart⟩ **d** *slang* **:** to play a part **:** do an imitation ⟨~ like a bird⟩ ⟨~ like a detective⟩ **3 :** to set out **:** PROCEED, HEAD ⟨last seen *making* for the river⟩ ⟨*made* after the fox⟩ **4 :** to increase in height or size ⟨the tide is *making* now⟩ ⟨water was *making* fast in forward bilges⟩ ⟨light was *making* in the east⟩ **5** *now dial* **:** to concern or busy oneself **:** INTERFERE — used in the phrase *to meddle or make* ⟨I'll neither meddle nor *make* with them further —Charlotte Brontë⟩ **6 :** to reach or extend in a certain direction ⟨the forest ~*s* up nearly to the snow line⟩ **7 :** to have weight or effect **:** TELL ⟨courtesy ~*s* for safer driving⟩ ⟨ignored evidence that *made* against his theory⟩ **8 :** to undergo manufacture or processing ⟨bolts are *making* in this shop⟩ ⟨hay ~*s* better in small heaps⟩ **9 :** *of ore in a mine* **:** APPEAR, OCCUR ⟨the ore ~*s* at the intersection of a vein by a cross fissure⟩

**syn** MAKE, FORM, SHAPE, FASHION, FABRICATE, MANUFACTURE, and FORGE can mean in common to cause something to come into being. MAKE can comprise any such action whether by an intelligent or blind agency and resulting in either material or immaterial existence ⟨*make* a boat⟩ ⟨*make* a treaty⟩ ⟨*make* a choice⟩ ⟨*make* friends⟩ ⟨*make* an impression⟩ FORM suggests a definite outline, structure, or plan ⟨*form* a figure out of clay⟩ ⟨*form* a plan⟩ ⟨*form* a league of states⟩ ⟨*form* character by training⟩ SHAPE suggests an outside agency impressing a particular form upon something ⟨a blacksmith *shapes* horseshoes out of metal⟩ ⟨*shape* a boat out of a block of wood⟩ ⟨*shape* a shoe on a last⟩ ⟨*shape* a good career out of a few talents⟩ FASHION suggests both an intelligent agency and a certain inventive power or ingenuity ⟨*fashion* a cabinet out of orange crates⟩ ⟨*fashion* a work of art out of odds and ends of scrap wood, paint, and pieces of metal⟩ FABRICATE stresses a uniting of parts or materials in a whole, often according to a standardized pattern, often with skill in construction, and in figurative extension often suggesting the imaginative constructing of a falsehood ⟨*fabricate* doors and windows for a series of identical houses⟩ ⟨*fabricate* a temporary scaffolding out of tree branches to buttress a wall⟩ ⟨*fabricate* a cock-and-bull story for the press⟩ MANUFACTURE stresses the making of something by labor, usu. by machinery, now applying to any making using raw materials and a fixed process, often extending to connote laborious, mechanical construction as opposed to skillful creation ⟨*manufacture* a pair of shoes⟩ ⟨*manufacture* airplane parts⟩ ⟨*manufacture* standard plots for a series of cheap novels⟩ FORGE still can suggest the smithy or the making of something by sudden strong uniting of elements under intense heat ⟨*forge* a chain⟩ ⟨*forged* a novel out of his own intense suffering⟩ More often, however, it implies a devising with a certain effort to give the appearance of truth or reality, extending in this use to comprise counterfeiting of documents in handwriting ⟨*forge* a lie to avoid punishment⟩ ⟨*forge* a signature on a check⟩

—**make a bag** *of a pregnant animal* **:** to undergo enlargement of the udder prior to parturition — **make a clean breast :** to make a full disclosure or confession ⟨decided to *make a clean breast* of his part in the affair⟩ — **make a dent in :** to produce an inconsiderable effect upon ⟨his gambling losses hardly *made a dent in* his huge fortune⟩ ⟨unable even to *make a dent in* his complacency⟩ — **make a face :** to express or betray a feeling (as of disgust, chagrin) or an attitude (as of defiance, derision) by distorting one's features **:** GRIMACE — **make a leg :** to bow and scrape — **make a long arm :** to extend the arm **:** reach out **:** exert oneself — **make a long nose :** to thumb one's nose — **make a market :** to provide bids and offers for a security so as to make it possible for buyers or sellers to deal without undue price fluctuations — **make a mouth :** to accustom a colt to the bit — **make a play for :** to attempt to capture ⟨*make a play for* the tourist trade with performances of native dances —*Time*⟩ — **make away with 1 :** to carry off **2 :** SPEND, DISSIPATE **3 :** DESTROY, KILL **4 :** CONSUME, EAT ⟨*made away with* the whole pie⟩ — **make believe :** PRETEND, FEIGN — **make bold :** VENTURE, DARE ⟨*made bold* to predict a successful trip to outer space⟩ — **make bones :** to show hesitation, uncertainty, or scruple ⟨*makes* no *bones* about his dislike of his in-laws⟩ ⟨how silly to *make bones* of trifles —Virginia Woolf⟩ — **make book 1 :** to accept bets at calculated odds on all the entrants in a race or contest **:** lay odds **2 :** to make a business of accepting bets — **make default :** to fail in a legal obligation (as appearing and answering in a legal proceeding or at a trial) — **make do :** to get along or manage with the means at hand however inadequate or unsatisfactory ⟨must still *make do* with temporary expedients —Walter Moberly⟩ — **make ends meet :** to live within one's income — **make even :** to typeset (a piece of copy) so that the last word ends a full line **:** to reach a point in correcting set type where the reset matter either ends a paragraph or ends a line with a word that ended a line in the old setting — **make foul water :** to sail in such shallow water that the ship's keel stirs the mud at the bottom — **make free 1 :** to adopt an unduly intimate or familiar manner ⟨if he *makes free* stop him⟩ **2 :** to help oneself without restraint ⟨my roommate *makes free* with my neckties⟩ — **make fun of :** to make an object of amusement or laughter **:** RIDICULE, MOCK — **make game** *of a hunting dog* **:** to sniff about eagerly at the scent of game — **make good :** to make valid or complete ⟨*made good* his escape⟩: as **a :** to make up or compensate for (a deficiency) ⟨*make good* previous neglect of his child⟩ **b :** INDEMNIFY ⟨the insurance company *made good* the loss⟩ **c :** to carry out (a promise or prediction) **:** FULFILL **d :** PROVE, VERIFY ⟨*make good* a charge⟩ **e :** to prove to be capable and efficient ⟨*made good* in his first job⟩ **:** justify by success a course of action or an expectation **:** SUCCEED ⟨the play *made good* at the box office — **make haste :** HASTEN, HURRY ⟨members of the committee *make haste* to tell her how glad they are —Agnes M. Miall⟩ — **make hay :** to make use of offered opportunity esp. in gaining an early advantage — **make hay of :** to throw into disorder **:** DEMOLISH, OVERTHROW ⟨new evidence *makes hay of* the accepted theory⟩ — **make head 1 :** to make progress esp. against resistance **2 :** to rise in armed revolt **3 :** to build up pressure (as in a steam boiler) — **make heavy weather :** to experience difficulty in making progress **:** FLOUNDER, LABOR ⟨*made heavy weather* with his algebra⟩ — **make hole :** to drill an oil well — **make light of :** to treat as of little account — **make love 1 :** WOO, COURT **2 a :** NECK, PET **b :** to engage in sexual intercourse — **make much of 1 :** to treat as of importance **:** EXPLOIT **2 :** to treat with obvious affection or special consideration **:** fuss over **:** FLATTER, PET — **make of** *or* **make over** *dial* **:** to praise lavishly **:** show much affection for ⟨I like to be *made of*⟩ ⟨paused to *make over* the baby⟩ ⟨felt loved and *made over*⟩ — **make one's law** *Old Eng law* **:** to adduce the sworn statements of compurgators to clear oneself of a charge — **make one's mark :** to achieve success or fame ⟨*made his mark* as a literary critic —Eric Partridge⟩ — **make one's number :** to signal the number by which the ship is designated on a register — **make one's peace :** to reconcile oneself **:** come to terms ⟨*making his peace* with his mother and promising to fight no more —William Du Bois⟩ ⟨the worker . . . fulfills himself by *making his peace* with the system —W.N. Whyte⟩ — **make one's way :** ADVANCE; *specif* **:** to gain standing in a trade, profession, or other means of livelihood ⟨world in which these youngsters have to live and *make their way* —Robert Reid⟩ — **make places** *of two bells* **:** to make a particular shift of position in successive changes in change ringing so as to allow a third bell to be struck successively before, between, and after them — **make play with 1 :** use vigorously or effectively ⟨*making play with* political issues in comedy⟩ **2 :** to act brilliantly or showily in using **:** make an effect with ⟨*makes* great *play with* fashionable critical terms⟩ — **make public :** DISCLOSE — **make ready :** to prepare and adjust the form and press for printing — **make sail 1 a :** to raise or spread sail **b :** to set additional sail **2 :** to set out on a voyage — **make shift :** to try to get along or succeed under difficulties or with inferior means — **make something of :** to start a fight or a quarrel over **:** show resentment concerning **:** CHALLENGE ⟨I said you cheated — do you want to *make something of* it⟩ — **make strange** *now dial* **:** to act in an unfriendly or surprised manner ⟨*make strange* of a request⟩ — **make sure 1** *obs* **:** BETROTH **2 :** to reach or attain certainty ⟨telephoned to *make sure* of the time⟩ **3 :** to expect strongly **:** be certain or convinced ⟨we *made sure* you were not coming today⟩ — **make the best of 1 :** to use or dispose of to the best advantage ⟨could never *make the best of* his opportunities⟩ **2 :** to regard or treat (something unsatisfactory or unfavorable) as favorably as possible ⟨*make the best of* a bad bargain⟩ — **make the blood boil :** to arouse anger or indignation — **make the fur fly 1 :** to take part in a cat-and-dog fight **2 :** to cause a lively disturbance **3 :** to hustle about in doing a temporary job (as cleaning a room) — **make the grade 1** *of a person* **:** to make good **:** SUCCEED **2** *of a thing* **:** to come up to some standard **:** win acceptance — **make the most of :** to show or use to the best advantage ⟨wanted to *make the most of* his first vacation in three years⟩ — **make time 1 :** to travel at a certain rate of speed ⟨*make* fast *time*⟩ **2 :** to go quickly **3 :** to make progress toward winning favor or sexual acceptance **:** FLIRT, WOO ⟨trying to *make time* with the waitress⟩ — **make tracks 1 :** to proceed at a walk or run **2 :** to go in a hurry **:** run away **:** FLEE — **make use of :** to put to use **:** USE, EMPLOY — **make water 1** *of a boat* **:** LEAK **2 :** URINATE — **make way 1 :** to open or give room for passing or entering **:** yield passage **:** fall back or move aside **2 :** to make progress — **make weight** *of a boxer* **:** to lose sufficient weight to remain eligible for a specified weight division — **make with** *slang* **:** PRODUCE, PERFORM — usu. used with *the* and in place of the idiomatic or normal verb ⟨start *making with* the answers⟩ ⟨let's not *make with* the jokes⟩ ⟨*making with* the tears⟩ ⟨*make with* the boyish charm⟩

**2make** \\"\\ *n* -s [ME *mak, maken,* fr. *maken,* v.] **1 a :** the manner or style in which a thing is composed or constructed ⟨needed a tool of a heavier ~⟩; *esp* **:** the quality or perfection of cutting of a gem **b :** the origin of a manufactured article ⟨an automobile of a well-known ~⟩ **2 :** the physical, mental, or moral constitution of a person ⟨had the look and ~ of a prizefighter⟩ ⟨men of his ~ are rare⟩ **3 a :** the act of producing or manufacturing ⟨the ~ cycle in the production of a fuel gas⟩ **b :** the actual yield or amount produced (as by an oil well or a mine) over a specified period **:** OUTPUT **4 :** the declaration of trumps in the game of bridge-whist **5 :** the closing or completing of an electric circuit **6 :** act of shuffling; *also* **:** turn to shuffle ⟨it's your ~ while your partner deals⟩ **7** *slang* **:** a military promotion or appointment ⟨list of ~*s*⟩ — **on the make** *adv (or adj)* **1 :** in the process of forming, growing, or improving **2 :** in quest of a higher social or financial status **:** in an aggressively and alertly opportunistic frame of mind **3 :** in search of sexual adventure

**3make** \\"\\ *n* -s [ME *make, mak,* fr. OE ge*maca* — more at MATCH] **1** *now dial Brit* **:** EQUAL, MATCH **2** *now dial Brit* **:** one who is a companion or mate; *esp* **:** SPOUSE

**4make** \\"\\ *n* -s [origin unknown] *dial Brit* **:** HALFPENNY

**make and mend** *n, Brit* **:** a period (as an afternoon) given the hands on a ship for work on their clothing or as a period of leisure without set duties **:** HALF-HOLIDAY ⟨*make and mends* were granted in celebration of the royal birthday⟩

**make·bate** \\'māk,bāt\\ *n* -s [1*make* + obs. *bate* strife, discord, fr. ME, fr. *baten* to contend, argue, beat the wings — more at BATE] *archaic* **:** one that excites contentions and quarrels

**1make-believe** *also* **make-belief** \\'=(=),=\\ *n* -s **1 :** a pretending to believe (as in the play of children) **:** a mere pretense **:** FICTION ⟨*make-believe* of the theater⟩ **2 :** one who makes believe **:** PRETENDER

**2make-believe** \\"\\ *adj* [fr. the phrase *make believe*] **:** FEIGNED ⟨lived in a private *make-believe* world⟩ **:** INSINCERE ⟨*make-believe* friendship⟩

**1make-do** \\'=,=\\ *adj* [fr. the phrase *make do*] **:** MAKESHIFT, IMPROVISED, TEMPORARY ⟨*make-do* airfield⟩ ⟨*make-do* policy⟩

**2make-do** \\"\\ *n* -s **:** something that is made use of or made to serve instead of something better or more suitable ⟨housing had the flimsy quality of wartime *make-do* —Robert Zimmerman⟩

**make down** *vi, dial* **:** RAIN, SNOW ~ *vt* **:** to prepare (a folding berth) for night occupancy

**make-down** \\'=,=\\ *n* -s [*make down*] **:** the arrangement of sleeping space (as in a pullman car) to accommodate a given number of passengers

**ma·ke·ev·ka** \\mə'kā(y)əfkə\\ *adj, usu cap* [fr. *Makeevka,* U.S.S.R.] **:** of or from the city of Makeevka, U.S.S.R. **:** of the kind or style prevalent in Makeevka

**makefast** \\'=,=\\ *n* -s [fr. the phrase *make fast*] **:** something to which a boat is fastened (as a buoy or a post)

**make-game** \\'=,=\\ *n* [fr. the phrase *make game (of)*] *archaic* **:** an object of ridicule **:** LAUGHINGSTOCK

**make·ham's law** \\'mākəmz-\\ *n, usu cap M* [after William *Makeham,* 19th cent. Brit. mathematician] **:** an actuarial rule: the mortality risk of a person at any age over 20 is equal to a constant plus a simple exponential function of the age

**make-hawk** \\'=,=\\ *n* **:** a trained hawk used to teach inexperienced ones their work

**make·less** \\'mākləs\\ *adj* [ME, fr. *make, mak* match + *-less* — more at MAKE (match)] *now dial* **:** having no mate or match

**make off** *vi* **:** to run away **:** DEPART, ESCAPE ⟨in time to see him *making off* down the road⟩ ⟨ate breakfast and *made off* for work⟩ — **make off with :** to take away **:** carry off ⟨*made off with* first prize⟩ **:** GRAB, STEAL ⟨*made off with* the whole herd of cattle⟩

**make-or-break** \\¦==¦=\\ *adj* **:** allowing of no mean between full success and complete disaster ⟨*make-or-break* attempt⟩

**make out** *vt* **1 :** to draw up or prepare in writing ⟨*make out* a list⟩ **:** fill in (as a printed form) by writing ⟨*make* the check *out* to me⟩ **2** *now chiefly dial* **:** ACCOMPLISH, ACHIEVE **3** *obs* **:** to count as or complete (a total) **4** *now chiefly dial* **:** to make shift **:** MANAGE **:** try successfully ⟨*made out* to accomplish the voyage —Washington Irving⟩ **5 :** to find or grasp the meaning of ⟨trying to *make* the blurred writing *out*⟩ **:** UNDERSTAND, INTERPRET ⟨tried to *make out* what had actually happened⟩ **6 a :** DEMONSTRATE, ESTABLISH ⟨a good case can be *made out* in his defense⟩ ⟨malicious intent was clearly *made out* in this case⟩ **b :** to form an idea or opinion about **:** CONCLUDE ⟨how on earth do you *make* that *out*⟩ **7 :** to represent as being ⟨not the villain he is often *made out*⟩ **:** pretend to be true ⟨*made out* that he had been working all morning⟩ **8 :** to represent or delineate in detail ⟨every feature of the landscape faithfully *made out*⟩ **9 :** to see and identify with effort or difficulty **:** DISCERN ⟨you can just *make* it *out* from this hill⟩ **10** *dial* **:** INTEND, PLAN ⟨*make out* to go to town tomorrow⟩ ~ *vi* **1** *now dial Brit* **:** to go or get out **:** ESCAPE **2 a :** SUCCEED, THRIVE ⟨*made out* very well as a salesman⟩ **b :** to get along ⟨how are you *making out* in your new apartment⟩ **c :** to make shift ⟨*make out* with patched gear . . . and still get the job done —F.B.Gipson⟩

**make over** *vt* **1 :** to transfer the title of (property) **:** CONVEY, ASSIGN ⟨*made* his estate *over* to his brother⟩ **2 a :** REMAKE, REMODEL, RENOVATE ⟨*made over* her mother's dress for herself⟩ ⟨*made* the entire house *over*⟩ **b :** to alter the character of **:** REFORM ⟨what good ever came of trying to *make* anyone *over* —Ellen Glasgow⟩ **c :** to change the text or arrangement of (a printed page)

**make-over** \\'=,==\\ *n* -s [*make over*] **:** something that is made over or made afresh: as **a :** an altered or restyled garment **b :** revised or fresh news copy for a new edition of a newspaper

**make-peace** \\'=,=\\ *n* [fr. the phrase *make peace*] **:** PEACEMAKER

**mak·er** \\'mākə(r)\\ *n* -s [ME, fr. *maken* to make + *-er* — more at MAKE] **:** one that makes: as **a** *usu cap* **:** 2GOD ⟨calling loudly on his *Maker*⟩ **b** *archaic* **:** one that writes verses **:** POET **c :** a person who makes a promissory note **d :** a declarer in bridge **e :** a tool used in calking ships' plates to close up the joint after splitting the edge of the overlapping plate **f :** MANUFACTURER ⟨~ of auto parts⟩

**makeready** \\'=,==\\ *n* -ES [fr. the phrase *make ready*] **:** final preparation and adjustment (as of a form and press for printing, a die for stamping, bindery machinery for folding); *also* **:** material (as underlays and overlays) used in making ready

**maker's mark** *n* **:** the hallmark on a piece of English gold, silver, or plate denoting the person or firm responsible for its production

**maker-up** \\'=='=\\ *n, pl* **makers-up** [*make up* + *-er*] **:** one that makes up **:** as **a :** one who arranges set type in form for printing **b** *chiefly Brit* **:** an assembler or packer of manufactured goods **c** *chiefly Brit* **:** a garment maker or manufacturer

**makes** *pres 3d sing of* MAKE, *pl of* MAKE

**1make·shift** \\'māk,shift\\ *n* [fr. the phrase *make shift*] **1** *obs* **:** a shifty person **2 :** a temporary expedient **:** SUBSTITUTE **3 :** the act or practice of making shift ⟨reduced to ~ and petty economizing⟩ **syn** see RESOURCE

**2makeshift** \\"\\ *also* **make·shifty** \\-tē\\ *adj* **1 :** SHIFTY **2 :** serving as makeshift **:** characterized by makeshift ⟨~ living arrangement⟩ ⟨~ government policy⟩ — **make·shift·ness** \\-f(t)nəs\\ *n* -ES

**make up** *vt* **1 a :** to draw up in complete form **:** COMPILE **b :** INVENT ⟨*make up* a plot⟩ ⟨story was partly true and partly *made up*⟩ **:** IMPROVISE ⟨*made* new verses *up* as he went along⟩ **c :** to set (an account) in order **:** BALANCE **2 a** *obs* **:** BUILD, CONSTRUCT **b :** to produce or complete by fitting together or assembling ⟨*make up* a suit⟩ ⟨*make up* a train of cars⟩ **c :** to arrange type matter into (columns or pages) for a book or newspaper **d :** to put together from ingredients **:** COMPOUND, MIX ⟨*make up* a fresh batch of dough⟩ ⟨*make up* a bottle of cough medicine⟩ **e :** to lay and light (a fire) **3 :** to form into **:** wrap or fasten up ⟨*make* the books *up* into a parcel⟩ ⟨separate mailbags are *made up* for each city on the route⟩ **4 a :** to set in order **:** PREPARE ⟨*make* a bed *up* in the guest room⟩ **:** ARRANGE ⟨*make up* a room⟩ **b :** to shuffle (a deck) for dealing **5 a :** to make good (a deficiency) ⟨add water to *make up* the difference⟩ ⟨*make up* sleep⟩ **b :** to act so as to correct (an omission) or remove (a deficiency in the record) ⟨*make up* a history examination⟩ **:** compensate for ⟨time taken off must be *made up* by overtime⟩ **c :** REPRINT, REPLACE ⟨*make* imperfect copies or sheets *up*⟩ **6 a** *of parts or quantities* **:** to combine to produce (a sum or a whole) **b :** CONSTITUTE, COMPOSE ⟨a party largely *made up* of peasants and artisans⟩ ⟨all the things that go to *make up* a national culture⟩ **7 :** SETTLE, DECIDE ⟨*made up* his mind to sell the house⟩ ⟨*make up* a quarrel⟩ ⟨glad that he has *made* it *up* with his family⟩ **8 a :** to prepare (as an actor) in physical appearance for a role ⟨came in *made up* as an Egyptian queen⟩ **b :** to apply cosmetics to ⟨no time to *make up* her face⟩ **9 :** to get (an animal) into condition for marketing ~ *vi* **1 :** to become reconciled **:** become friends again ⟨kiss and *make up*⟩ **2 a :** ADVANCE, APPROACH ⟨rapidly *making up* to the pier⟩ **b :** GATHER, RISE ⟨black clouds were *making up* in the east⟩ ⟨a storm seems to be *making up*⟩ **3 a :** to act ingratiatingly or flatteringly **:** curry favor ⟨*made up* to his aunt for a new bicycle⟩ **b :** to make love **:** make advances **:** COURT ⟨suspected of *making up* to his housekeeper⟩ **4 :** COMPENSATE ⟨hurried to *make up* for lost time⟩ **:** PAY, ATONE ⟨tried to *make up* for his neglect⟩ **5 :** to apply cosmetics ⟨began to *make up* at the age of thirteen⟩

**makeup** \\'=,=\\ *n* -s [*make up*] **1 a :** the way in which the parts or ingredients of something are put together **:** COMPOSITION ⟨chemical ~ of a cleaning fluid⟩ ⟨the present ~ of the cabinet favors big business⟩ **b :** innate character or personality **:** physical, mental, and moral constitution ⟨defeat was attributed to certain defects in the national ~⟩ **2 :** an invented story **:** FICTION, LIE ⟨came down here to . . . try and show that the blessed miracle was a ~ —G.B.Shaw⟩ **3 a :** the act or the operation of making up ⟨a compositor working on ~⟩ **b :** the arrangement of printed matter ⟨a book in attractive ~ and binding⟩ **c :** reprinted or replacement matter **4 a :** cosmetics (as lipstick, face powder, mascara, eye shadow) used to color and beautify the face or the features ⟨evening ~⟩; *also* **:** a cosmetic applied to other parts of the body ⟨leg ~ for a tanned appearance⟩ **b :** the total of cosmetics, wigs, facial and body padding, and other items often strongly applied or emphasized for projection beyond bright lighting that give an actor or actress the appearance of the character being portrayed; *also* **:** a similar application of cosmetics for persons appearing on television or making other public appearances **c :** the act or process of applying cosmetics ⟨classes in ~ for models⟩ **d :** the appearance resulting from applying cosmetics ⟨her ~ had a natural look⟩ **5 a :** COMPENSATION, REPLACEMENT; *specif* **:** material added in a manufacturing process to replace material that has been used up ⟨a daily ~ of fresh acid⟩ **b :** the screw thread at the end of a pipe for the attachment of fittings **6 :** a special examination in which a student may make up for absence or failure at a regular examination

**makeup clerk** \\'=,=-\\ *n* **:** one who prepares insurance claims for investigation and adjustment

**makeup man** *n* **1 :** a compositor or editorial worker that makes up **2 :** one who applies makeup to actors **3 :** a worker who fills orders or requisitions **4 :** a worker who prepares ingredients for such products as plastic coating solutions, artificial leather, or ice cream

**makeup pay** *n* **:** an amount paid to a piece-rated or incentive worker to bring his earnings up to a guaranteed minimum

**makeup rule** *n* [*make up*] **:** a steel rule with projecting top used (as in making up) to push apart lines of type

**makeup water** *n* [*make up*] **:** water supplied (as to a steam boiler) to compensate for loss by evaporation and leakage

**makeweight** \\'=,=\\ *n* **1 a :** something thrown into a scale to bring the weight to a desired value **b :** a thing or a person of little worth or independent value thrown into a gap or empty place to fill out a whole ⟨some of the stories in the collection are mere ~*s*⟩ **2 :** COUNTERWEIGHT, COUNTERPOISE ⟨America's power as a ~ in the international scales —J.R. Chamberlain⟩

**make-work** \\'=,=\\ *n* [fr. the phrase *make work*] **:** work devised chiefly to provide for the employment of labor ⟨older men have jobs which are *make-work* because no one can bring himself to discharge them —David Riesman⟩

**ma·khor·ka** \\mə'kórkə\\ *n* -s [Russ] **:** a coarse tobacco (*Nicotiana rustica*) grown esp. in the Ukraine

**makh·zan** or **makh·zen** also **magh·zen** \'makzən\ n -s [Ar *makhzan*] : the native Moroccan government; *collectively* : privileged peoples from whom Moroccan state officials are recruited

**maki** \'makē, 'mäkē\ n -s [F, prob. fr. Malagasy *máky*] : LEMUR

**ma·ki·mo·no** \ˌmäkəˈmō(ˌ)nō, ˌmak-, -mōnə\ n -s [Jap, fr. *maki* scroll, roll + *mono* thing] : a picture, pictured story, or writing mounted on paper and usu. rolled in a scroll — compare KAKEMONO

¹**mak·ing** \'mākiŋ, -kēŋ\ n -s [ME, fr. OE *macung*, fr. *macian* to make + *-ung* -ing — more at MAKE] **1 a** : the act or process of forming, causing, manufacturing, or coming into being ⟨a mind given to image-*making*⟩ ⟨laws already made or in the ~⟩ ⟨landed in a situation not of his own ~⟩ **b** : ORIGINATION, GROWTH ⟨when the modern age of science and technology was in the ~⟩ **2** : a process or means of advancement or success ⟨misfortune was the ~ of him⟩ **3** : something that is made: as **a** : a quantity produced at one time : BATCH ⟨~ of bread⟩ **b makings** *pl* : the slack and dirt produced in coal mining **4 a** : POTENTIALITY ⟨he had the ~ of a hero⟩ — often used in pl. ⟨has the ~s of a fine ballplayer⟩ **b makings** *pl* : the material from which something is to be made ⟨the ~s for a new suit⟩; *specif* : paper and tobacco for cigarettes

²**making** \"\ adj [fr. pres. part. of ¹*make*] **1** : that makes — often used in combination ⟨contact-*making* parts of a switch⟩ **2** : required to be made to specification ⟨a ~ order for goods not carried in stock⟩

**making iron** n : a chisel-shaped tool used by caulkers of ships to finish the seams after the oakum has been driven in

**making-up day** \'==ˈ=-\ n [fr. pres. part. of *make up*] : the first day of settlement on which contango agreements are made on the London stock exchange

**making-up price** n : the price at which stock is carried over on an account from one settlement to another on the London stock exchange

**ma·ki·ri·ta·re** \məˌkērēˈtärē\ n, pl **makiritare** or **makiritares** *usu cap* **1 a** : a Cariban people of Venezuela **b** : a member of such people **2** : the language of the Makiritare people

**mak·luk** \'makˌlək\ n -s [Esk *makliok, muklok*] : a large seal; *specif* : BEARDED SEAL

**ma·ko** \'mä(ˌ)kō\ or **mako shark** n -s [Maori *mako*] : any of several sharks of the genus *Isurus*: as **a** : BONITO SHARK **b** : a large vigorous shark (*I. oxyrhynchus*) of the Atlantic that is held to be dangerous to man but is highly esteemed as a sport fish

**ma·ko·ma·ko** \'mäkōˌmä(ˌ)kō, 'məkəˌmək\ or **ma·ko** \'mä-(ˌ)kō\ n -s [Maori] **1** : a New Zealand tree (*Aristotelia racemosa*) of the family Elaeocarpaceae having a small red berry that turns black at maturity and is used for making wine — called also *wineberry* **2** : the New Zealand bellbird

**ma·kon·de** \məˈkōn(ˌ)dā\ n, pl **makonde** or **makondes** *usu cap* **1 a** : a Bantu-speaking people of southeastern Tanganyika Territory and northern Mozambique known esp. for their sculptured masks **b** : a member of such people **2** : KONDE 3

**ma·ko·pa** \məˈkōpə\ n -s [Tag & Bikol] : the Otaheite apple or its wood

**ma·ko·re** \ˌmäkəˈrā\ n -s [native name in southern Africa] : a large tree of southern Africa (*Mimusops leckellii*) that yields a wood resembling cherry but having a pronounced black mottle — called also *cherry mahogany*

**mak·ro·skel·ic** \ˌmakrəˈskelik\ adj [Gk *makro-* macr- + *skelos* leg + E *-ic* — more at CYLINDER] : having long legs in proportion to the trunk with a skelic index of 95 to 100

**maku** *usu cap, var of* MACÚ

**ma·kua** also **ma·kwa** \məˈkwä\ n, pl **makua** or **makuas** *usu cap* **1 a** : a Bantu-speaking people of Portuguese East Africa **b** : a member of such people **2** : a Bantu language of the Makua people

**makushi** or **makusi** *usu cap, var of* MACUSHI

**ma·ku·tu** \'mäkü,tü\ n -s [Maori] *NewZeal* : a magic spell : CURSE, SORCERY

¹**mal** \'mäl, -a-, -à-\ n -s [F & It; F *mal*, fr. OF, fr. *mal*, adv., badly; It *mal, male*, fr. *male*, adv., badly; OF *mal* badly & It *male* badly fr. L *male*, fr. *malus* bad] : DISEASE, SICKNESS — used chiefly in combination ⟨~ de mer⟩ ⟨petit ~⟩

²**mâl** or **maal** n -s *sometimes cap* [Norw *mål*, lit., speech, fr. ON *māl*] : LANDSMÅL

¹**mal-** *comb form* [ME, fr. MF *mal*, adj., bad & *mal*, adv., badly; MF *mal* bad, fr. OF, fr. L *malus*; MF *mal* badly, fr. OF, fr. L *male*, fr. *malus* bad — more at SMALL] **1 a** : bad : evil ⟨*malpractice*⟩ **b** : badly : evilly ⟨*malodorous*⟩ **2 a** : irregular : abnormal ⟨*malformation*⟩ **b** : irregularly : abnormally ⟨*malformed*⟩ **3 a** : poor : inadequate ⟨*maladjustment*⟩ **b** : poorly : inadequately ⟨*malnourished*⟩

²**mal-** or **malo-** *comb form* [ISV, fr. *malic* (in *malic acid*)] : malic acid ⟨*malamide*⟩ ⟨*malonitrile*⟩

¹**mala** *pl of* MALUM

²**ma·la** \'mālə\ n, pl **ma·lae** \-(ˌ)lē\ [NL, fr. L, jaw, cheek — more at MAXILLA] **1** : a single lobe of the maxilla of an insect **2 a** : the grinding surface of a mandible of an insect **b** : the third segment of a mandible of some myriapods

**ma·la·ano·nang** \məˌläˈnōˌnäŋ\ n -s [Tag] : a Philippine timber tree (*Shorea malaanonan*) with light yellow wood

¹**mal·a·bar** \ˈmaləˌbär, -bá(r\ adj, *usu cap* [fr. *Malabar*, coast of southwestern India] : of or from the Malabar coast : of the kind or style prevalent in Malabar

²**malabar** n -s **1** *cap* : a native or inhabitant of the Malabar coast of southwestern India **2** *often cap* : ²BAY 2

**malabar almond** n, *usu cap M* **1** : a tropical Asian evergreen tree (*Terminalia catappa*) that is widely grown in warm regions for ornament and for the edible kernel of the seed of its drupaceous fruit — called also *country almond, Indian almond* **2** : the edible almond-shaped kernel of the seed of the Malabar almond

**malabar nightshade** or **malabar spinach** n, *usu cap M* : a plant of the genus *Basella*; *esp* : an Asiatic climbing plant (*B. alba*) with fleshy shining leaves and small white racemose flowers that is grown in the tropics as a potherb and in temperate regions as an ornamental vine

**malabar nut** n, *usu cap M* **1** : an East Indian shrub (*Adhatoda vasica*) of the family Acanthaceae having leaves, root, and seed that are used as a source of an antipyretic and antispasmodic **2** : the seed of the Malabar nut

**malabar rat** n, *usu cap M* : BANDICOOT 1

**malabar squirrel** n, *usu cap M* : a giant squirrel (*Ratufa indica malabarica*) of southern India

**mal·a·bath·rum** \ˌmaləˈbathrəm\ n -s [L *malabathrum, malobathrum*, fr. Gk *malabathron*, modif. of Skt *tamālapattra* garcinia leaf, fr. *tamāla* garcinia (perh. fr. *tamas* darkness) + *pattra* leaf, wing, feather; akin to Skt *patati* he flies — more at TEMERITY, FEATHER] **1** : the leaf of a plant (*Cinnamomum malabathrum*) used esp. in making a perfumed ointment **2** : an ointment prepared from malabathrum

**mal·absorption** \ˌmal+\ n [¹*mal-* + *absorption*] : faulty absorption of nutrient materials from the alimentary canal

**malac** *abbr* malacology

**malac-** or **malaco-** *comb form* [L *malac-*, fr. Gk *malak-, malako-*, fr. *malakos*; akin to MIr *malcad* decay, Russ *molchat'* to be silent, L *molere* to grind — more at MEAL] : soft ⟨*malacoid*⟩ ⟨*malacophyllous*⟩

¹**mal·a·can·thid** \ˌmaləˈkan(t)thəd\ adj [NL *Malacanthidae*] : of or relating to the Malacanthidae

²**malacanthid** \"\ n -s [NL *Malacanthidae*] : a fish of the family Malacanthidae

**mal·a·can·thi·dae** \ˌ==ˈkan(t)thəˌdē\ n pl, *cap* [NL, fr. *Malacanthus*, type genus + *-idae*] : a family of long compressed to fusiform short-headed marine percoid fishes that are often brightly colored and that include excellent food fishes

**mal·a·can·thus** \-thəs\ n, *cap* [NL, irreg. fr. *malac-* + *-acanthus*] : the type genus of the family Malacanthidae

**ma·lac·ca cane** \məˈlakə-\ also **malacca** n -s *often cap* [fr. *Malacca*, city and settlement in Malaya] : an often mottled cane obtained from an Asiatic rattan palm (*Calamus rotang*) and used esp. for walking sticks and umbrella handles

**ma·lac·can** \-kən\ adj, *usu cap* [*Malacca*, Malay Peninsula + E *-an*] : of or relating to Malacca on the Malay peninsula

**malacca weasel** n, *usu cap M* : RASSE

**ma·la·ce·ae** \məˈlāsēˌē\ n pl, *cap* [NL, fr. *Malus*, type genus + *-aceae*] *in some classifications* : a family of shrubs and trees comprising members of the family Rosaceae (as the apple, quince, pear) that have the carpels united and adnate to the calyx tube

**mal·a·chite** \'maləˌkīt\ n -s [alter. of earlier *melochite*, fr. ME *melochites*, fr. L *molochites*, prob. fr. Gk *molochitēs*, fr. *molochē, malachē* mallow + *-itēs* -ite — more at MALLOW] : a mineral $Cu_2CO_3(OH)_2$ consisting of a green basic carbonate of copper that is an ore of copper and is used to make ornamental objects (as vases) — compare AZURITE

**malachite green** n **1 a** : a pigment made of ground malachite **b** : a similar pigment made synthetically **2** *sometimes cap M&G* : a triphenylmethane basic dye prepared from benzaldehyde and dimethylaniline and used chiefly in coloring paper bluish green, in making organic pigments, in industrial and biological stains, and also in medicine as an antiseptic — called also *Victoria green*; see DYE table I (under *Basic Green 4, Pigment Green 4, Solvent Green 1*) **3** *also* **malachite** : a moderate yellowish green that is greener, stronger, and slightly lighter than tarragon, lighter and stronger than average almond green, and deeper and slightly yellower than verdigris — called also *Bremen green, copper green, green verditer, Hungarian green, iris green, mineral green, mountain green, Olympian green, shale green, Tyrolese green, verditer green*

**ma·la·cia** \məˈlāsh(ē)ə\ n -s [NL, fr. Gk *malakia* softness, fr. *malakos* soft + *-ia*] : abnormal softening of a tissue — often used in combination ⟨osteo*malacia*⟩

**mal·a·cich·thy·es** \ˌmaləˈsikthēˌēz\ n pl, *cap* [NL, fr. *malac-* + Gk *ichthyes* (pl. of *ichthys* fish) — more at ICHTHUS] : a small order of fishes including solely the family Icosteidae and being of uncertain systematic relations though possibly a specialized or degenerate offshoot of Percoidea

**mal·a·clem·ys** \-ˈkleməs\ n, *cap* [NL, irreg. fr. *malac-* + *-clemys* (fr. Gk *klemmys* tortoise)] : a genus of moderate-sized No. American edible terrapins (family Testudinidae) comprising the diamondback terrapins

**malaco-** — see MALAC-

**mal·a·cob·del·la** \ˌmaləˌkäbˈdelə\ n, *cap* [NL, fr. *malac-* + *-bdella*] : a genus of broad nemertean worms (order Bdellonemertea) that resemble leeches and are commensal in the gill cavity of clams and other mollusks

¹**mal·a·cob·del·lid** \ˌ==ˌ=ˈdeləd\ adj [NL *Malacobdella* + E *-id*, adj. suffix] : of or relating to the genus *Malacobdella*

²**malacobdellid** \"\ n -s [NL *Malacobdella* + E *-id*, n. suffix] : a worm of the genus *Malacobdella*

**mal·a·co·cotylea** \ˌmalə(ˌ)kō+\ n [NL, fr. *malac-* + *-cotylea* (fr. Gk *kotylē* cup, anything hollow) — more at KETTLE] *syn of* DIGENEA

**mal·a·coid** \'maləˌkȯid\ adj [*malac-* + *-oid*] **1** *of a living body* : having a soft or mucilaginous structure or texture ⟨the ~ plasmodia of slime molds⟩ **2** : of, relating to, or resembling malacia ⟨~ alteration of bone⟩

**ma·la·co·lite** \'maləkəˌlīt\ n -s [F *malacolithe*, fr. *malac-* + *-lithe* -lite] : DIOPSIDE; *esp* : a pale translucent diopside

**mal·a·co·log·i·cal** \ˌ===ˈläjəkəl\ adj : of or relating to malacology

**mal·a·col·o·gist** \ˌ==ˈkäləjəst\ n -s : a specialist in malacology

**mal·a·col·o·gy** \-jē\ n -ES [F *malacologie*, contr. of *malacozoologie*, fr. *malacozoo-* (fr. NL *Malacozoa* zoological group in some classifications including soft-bodied animals such as the mollusks, fr. *malac-* + *-zoa*) + *-logie* -logy] : a branch of zoology dealing with mollusks — compare CONCHOLOGY

**mal·a·con** \'maləˌkän\ also **mal·a·cone** \-ˌkōn\ or **mal·a·kon** \-ˌkän\ n -s [G *malakon*, fr. Gk, neut. of *malakos* soft] : a brown altered form of zircon

**mal·a·coph·i·lous** \ˌ==ˈkäfələs\ adj [*malaco-* mollusk (fr. *malacology*) + *-philous*] : adapted to pollination by snails — used esp. of the flowers of some arums; compare ANEMOPHILOUS, ENTOMOPHILOUS

**mal·a·co·phyl·lous** \ˌ==(ˌ)kōˈfiləs\ adj [prob. fr. (assumed) NL *malacophyllus*, fr. NL *malac-* + *-phyllus* -phyllous] : having soft or fleshy leaves ⟨~ xerophytes⟩

**mal·a·cop·o·da** \ˌ==ˈkäpədə\ [NL, fr. *malac-* + *-poda*] *syn of* ONYCHOPHORA

¹**mal·a·cop·te·ryg·i·an** \ˌmaləˌkäptəˈrij(ē)ən\ adj [NL *Malacopterygii* + E *-an*, adj. suffix] : of or relating to the Malacopterygii

²**malacopterygian** \"\ n -s [NL *Malacopterygii* + E *-an*, n. suffix] : a teleost fish of the division Malacopterygii

**mal·a·cop·te·ryg·ii** \-ˌrijēˌī\ n pl, *cap* [NL, fr. *malac-* + *-pterygii*] *in some classifications* : an extensive division of teleost fishes having soft fin rays — **mal·a·cop·te·ryg·ious** \-ˈrij(ē)əs\ adj

**mal·a·co·so·ma** \ˌmalə(ˌ)kōˈsōmə\ n, *cap* [NL, fr. *malac-* + *-soma*] : a genus of moths (family Lasiocampidae) including the common tent caterpillars

**mal·a·cos·tra·ca** \ˌmaləˈkästrəkə\ n pl, *cap* [NL, fr. Gk *malakostraka*, neut. pl. of *malakostrakos* soft-shelled, fr. *malak-* malac- + *-ostrakos* (fr. *ostrakon* shell) — more at OYSTER] : a major subclass of Crustacea including most of the well-known marine, freshwater, and terrestrial members of the group (as lobsters, crabs, shrimps, sow bugs, beach fleas) — **mal·a·cos·tra·can** \ˌ==ˈkästrəkən\ adj or n — **mal·a·cos·tra·cous** \-kəs\ adj

**mal·a·cotic** \ˌ==ˈkädˌik\ adj [*malacia* + *-otic*] *of a tooth* : exhibiting malacia : SOFT

**mal·adaptation** \ˌmal+\ n [¹*mal-* + *adaptation*] : poor or inadequate adaptation ⟨a secular, urban civilization . . . exposing the individuals to many more shocks and rebuffs, and to frequent feelings of ~ —*Social Thought From Lore To Science*⟩

**mal·adapted** \"+\ adj [¹*mal-* + *adapted*] : unsuited or poorly suited by nature, character, or design to a particular use, purpose, or situation ⟨their buildings were empty classic shells, woefully ~ to the functions they serve —Lewis Mumford⟩

**mal·adaptive** \"+\ adj [¹*mal-* + *adaptive*] **1** : marked by poor or inadequate adaptation ⟨cultures have . . . disappeared from the stage of history in consequence of ~ practices —G.P. Murdock⟩ **2** : not conducive to adaptation ⟨so long as destructive, unconscious motivations persist, ~ behavior will plague the person —L.R.Wolberg⟩

**mal·a·dive** \'malədiv\ adj [MF *maladif*, fr. OF, fr. *malade* sick + *-if* -ive] **1** : of, relating to, or affected by illness or disease : SICKLY, FEEBLE ⟨a ~ condition⟩ ⟨her ~step⟩ **2** : marked by or expressive of moral weakness or unwholesomeness ⟨a ~ apology⟩ ⟨~ poetry⟩

**mal·adjusted** \ˌmal+\ adj [¹*mal-* + *adjusted*] : poorly or inadequately adjusted; *specif* : lacking harmony with one's environment from failure to reach a satisfactory adjustment between one's desires and the conditions of one's life ⟨~ persons⟩ ⟨the ~ child⟩

**mal·adjustive** \"+\ adj [¹*mal-* + *adjustive*] : not conducive to adjustment ⟨~ behavior⟩

**mal·adjustment** \"+\ n [¹*mal-* + *adjustment*] : poor, faulty, or inadequate adjustment: as **a** : failure (of a mechanical part) to assume the proper, exact, or conforming position for adequate functioning ⟨the clutch is subject to . . . ~s upon use —Joseph Heitner⟩ **b** : a state of disharmony, imbalance, or disequilibrium ⟨~ between the customs of the East and the innovations of the West —*Orient Bk. World*⟩ ⟨~ between urban standards and rural poverty —Peter Scott⟩ ⟨~ in production and consumption with attendant unemployment, poverty, and waste —J.A.Hobson⟩ **c** : lack of harmony between the individual and his environment from failure to reach a satisfactory adjustment between one's desires and the conditions of one's life ⟨emotional ~s⟩ ⟨sexual ~⟩ ⟨symptoms of ~ . . . in early childhood —*Psychological Abstracts*⟩ **d** : an irregularity or anomaly resulting from economic instability ⟨~s . . . of the world wheat industry —A.F.Vass⟩ ⟨~s and inequities in wage rates —H.S.Truman⟩

**mal·administer** \"+\ vt [¹*mal-* + *administer*] : to administer improperly, poorly, or inefficiently ⟨~ the public relief program⟩

**mal·administration** \"+\ n [¹*mal-* + *administration*] : incompetent or corrupt administration; *specif* : inefficiency or corruption in public office ⟨awake to the dangers and disgrace of the existing ~ —J.A.Froude⟩ ⟨charging the mayor with ~⟩

**mal·a·droit** \ˌmaləˈdrȯit\ adj [F, fr. MF, fr. *mal* badly + *adroit* — more at MAL-, ADROIT] **1** : marked by a lack of dexterity or skill : CLUMSY ⟨a ~ movement of my hand . . . caused the car to swerve —C.H.Whiteley⟩ ⟨a ~ translation⟩ **2** : revealing a lack of perception, judgment, or finesse : TACTLESS, INEPT, BUNGLING ⟨embittered by ~ introductions —Sara H. Hay⟩ ⟨~ propaganda⟩ **syn** see AWKWARD

**mal·a·droit·ly** adv : in a maladroit manner ⟨groping ~ for solutions —*New Republic*⟩

**mal·a·droit·ness** n : the quality or state of being maladroit ⟨the ~ of some . . . gifts —Graham Greene⟩

**mal·a·dy** \'malədē, -di\ n -ES [ME *maladie*, fr. OF, fr. *malade* sick (fr. L *male habitus* undernourished, feeble, fr. *male* badly + *habitus*, past part. of *habēre* to have, hold) + *-ie* -y — more at MAL-, GIVE] **1** : a disease, distemper, disorder, or indisposition of the animal body proceeding from impaired or defective functions ⟨told by his physicians that he had a fatal ~ —Willa Cather⟩ **2** : an unwholesome or disordered state or condition ⟨some deep ~ of the soul —Van Wyck Brooks⟩ ⟨analyze the nature and the causes of the ~ from which the nation suffers —Reinhold Niebuhr⟩ ⟨the critical ~ of our age —Louis Kronenberger⟩

**malae** *pl of* MALA

¹**mala fide** \ˌmāləˈfīdē, ˌmäləˈfē(ˌ)dā\ adv [LL, in bad faith] : with or in bad faith : falsely and maliciously ⟨the debates . . . are reported *mala fide* —T.E.May⟩

²**mala fide** \"\ adj **1 a** : acting with intent to deceive or defraud ⟨a *mala fide* agent⟩ **b** : holding by a title known to lack legal sanction ⟨a *mala fide* possessor⟩ ⟨*mala fide* settlers . . . swore they had established residence —R.G.Lillard⟩ **2** : SPECIOUS, INSINCERE ⟨a *mala fide* proposal⟩

**mala fi·des** \ˌmāləˈfīˌdēz, ˌmäləˈfēˌdās\ n [LL, bad faith] : bad faith : purpose to deceive or defraud ⟨the *mala fides* of the company is generally a question for the jury —Ira Carlisle⟩

¹**mal·a·ga** or **má·la·ga** \'maləgə\ adj, *usu cap* [fr. *Málaga*, city in southern Spain] : of or from the city of Málaga, Spain : of the kind or style prevalent in Málaga

²**malaga** \"\ n -s **1** *usu cap* **a** : any of several aromatic usu. sweet white or red dessert wines made in the province of Málaga, Spain **b** : a similar wine made elsewhere (as in California) that is a deep amber-colored blend of juices from several kinds of grapes **2** *often cap* : a dark red to deep reddish brown

**malaga red** n, *often cap M* : OXBLOOD — distinguished from *Malaga* 2

¹**mal·a·gasy** \ˌmaləˈgasē\ n, pl **malagasy** also **malagasies** *cap* **1 a** : a people of Madagascar thought to be descended from Bantu-speaking, Malayan, and Arab peoples **b** : a member of such people **c** : a native or inhabitant of Madagascar or of the Malagasy Republic : MADAGASCAN **2** : the Austronesian language of the Malagasy people

²**malagasy** \"\ adj, *usu cap* **1 a** : of, relating to, or characteristic of the Malagasy **b** : of, relating to, or characteristic of the Malagasy Republic **2** : of, relating to, or being a biogeographic region or subregion that includes Madagascar and adjacent islands and is esp. characterized by the presence of various lemurs and by numerous mammals and birds different from those of the African mainland

**mala·gue·na** \ˌmaləˈgānyə, ˌmäl-, ÷ -gwā-; *there is no* w *in the Spanish pronunc*\ n -s [Sp *malagueña*, fr. fem. of *malagueño* of or relating to Málaga, fr. *Málaga*, city in southern Spain] **1** : a folk tune native to Málaga which is similar to a fandango and to which stanzas of four octosyllabic verses are sung **2** : a Spanish couple dance similar to a fandango

**malagueta pepper** or **malaguetta pepper** also **malagetta pepper** *var of* MELEGUETA PEPPER

**mal·a·hack** \'maləˌhak\ vt [prob. fr. ¹*mal-* + connective *-a-* + *hack*] *dial* : to cut or carve awkwardly

**mala in se** *pl of* MALUM IN SE

**mal·aise** \(')maˈlāz\ or **mal·ease** \(')maˈlēz\ n -s [*malaise* fr. F, fr. OF, fr. *mal* bad + *aise* comfort; *malease* alter. (influenced by *ease*) of *malaise* — more at MAL-, EASE] **1** : a sense of physical ill-being : an indefinite feeling of generalized debility or lack of health often indicative of or accompanying the onset of an illness ⟨marked ~ and prostration are not features of the common cold in adults —Yale Kneeland⟩ ⟨menstruation . . . gives rise to a characteristic ~ in some women —*Jour. Amer. Med. Assoc.*⟩ **2** : a vague sense of mental or moral ill-being or uneasiness ⟨without being able to analyze the source of his ~, he felt that something ominous was impending —S.N.Behrman⟩ ⟨the symptoms of his generation's ~ —Janet Flanner⟩

**malakon** *var of* MALACON

**malakostraca** or **malakostraka** *syn of* MALACOSTRACA

**ma·lam·bo** \məˈlam(ˌ)bō\ n -s [AmerSp & Pg, malambo tree] : the yellowish aromatic bark of a So. American shrub (*Croton malambo*) used in medicine and perfumery

**mal·a·mute** or **mal·e·mute** \ˈmaləˌmyüt\ n -s *sometimes cap* [after *Malemute, Malemiut*, Alaskan Eskimo people that developed the breed] : a sled dog of northern No. America; *esp* : ALASKAN MALAMUTE

**mal·an·ders** or **mal·len·ders** \ˈmaləndə(r)z\ n pl but *usu sing in constr* [ME *malawnder* (sing.) sore on a horse's knee, fr. MF *malandre*, fr. L *malandria* sore on a horse's neck] : a chronic eczema occurring usu. on the posterior or flexion surface of the knee of a horse's foreleg — compare SALLENDERS

**ma·lan·ga** \məˈläŋgə\ n -s [AmerSp, prob. fr. Kongo, pl. of *elanga* water lily] **1** : TARO **2** : YAUTIA

**ma·la·nia** \məˈlānēə\ n, *cap* [NL, fr. Daniel F. *Malan* †1959 So. African political leader + NL *-ia*] : a genus of living coelacanth fishes represented by a single specimen taken in shallow water north of Madagascar — compare LATIMERIA

**ma·la·pa·ho** \ˌmäləˈpä(ˌ)hō\ n -s [Tag *malapahò*] **1** : any of several Philippine trees of the genus *Dipterocarpus* **2 a** : wood, resin, or fiber of a malapaho tree

¹**mal·a·pert** \ˌmaləˈpərt\ adj [ME, fr. MF, unskillful, ill-taught, fr. *mal* badly + *apert* able, skillful, modif. (influenced by L *ad-*) of L *expertus* expert — more at MAL-, EXPERT] : impudently bold : SAUCY ⟨untutored lad, thou art too ~ —Shak.⟩ ⟨returning the woman's stare with a look of ~ challenge —Llewelyn Powys⟩ — **mal·a·pert·ness** n

²**malapert** \"\ n -s : a malapert person ⟨the ~ knew well enough I laughed at her —Richard Steele⟩

**ma·la prax·is** \ˌmāləˈpraksəs\ n [NL, bad practice] : MALPRACTICE

**mala prohibita** *pl of* MALUM PROHIBITUM

¹**mal·a·prop** \ˈmaləˌpräp\ n -s [after Mrs. *Malaprop*, character noted for her misuse of words in the comedy *The Rivals* (1775) by Richard B. Sheridan †1816 Irish dramatist, fr. E *malapropos*] : MALAPROPISM

²**malaprop** \"\ or **mal·a·prop·i·an** \ˌ==ˈpräpēən, -ˈprōp-\ adj : marked by the use of malapropisms ⟨a ~ use of words —Alexander Bain⟩ ⟨the ~ adolescent . . . pries at him with personal questions ("Was your wife a lymphomaniac?") —*Time*⟩

**mal·a·prop·ism** \ˈ==ˌpräˌpizəm\ n -s [¹*malaprop* + *-ism*] **1** : a usu. humorous misapplication of a word or phrase; *specif* : a blundering use of a word that sounds somewhat like the one intended but is ludicrously wrong in the context **2** : an example of malapropism (as in "an allegory on the banks of the Nile" or "if I reprehend anything in this world, it is the use of my oracular tongue and a nice derangement of epitaphs") ⟨renowned for her ~s —John Galsworthy⟩

¹**mal·ap·ro·pos** \ˌmaˌlaprəˈpō, =ˈ==ˌ=\ adv [F *mal à propos*, lit., not to the purpose, inappropriate] : in an inappropriate or irrelevant manner : UNSEASONABLY, INOPPORTUNELY ⟨listening distractedly, answering ~ —P.L.Fermor⟩

²**malapropos** \"\ adj : INAPPROPRIATE, INOPPORTUNE

**mal·ap·te·ru·rus** \ˌmaləptəˈrürəs\ n, *cap* [NL, irreg. fr. *malac-* + *pter-* + *-urus*] : a genus consisting of the electric catfish

¹**ma·lar** \ˈmālə(r)\ adj [NL *malaris*, fr. L *mala* jaw, cheek + *-aris* -ar — more at MAXILLA] **1** : of or relating to the cheek or the side of the head **2** : indicating the zygomatic bone

²**malar** \"\ n -s : ZYGOMATIC BONE

**malari-** or **malario-** *comb form* [*malaria*] : malaria ⟨*malarioid*⟩ ⟨*malariometry*⟩

**ma·lar·ia** \məˈlerēə, -la(ə)r-, -ˈlār-\ n -s [It, fr. *mala aria* bad air, fr. *mala* (fem. of *malo* bad, fr. L *malus*) + *aria* air — more at SMALL, ARIA] **1** *archaic* **a** : air infected with a noxious substance capable of causing disease; *esp* : an unhealthy exhalation from marshy soils : MIASMA **b** : a febrile disease believed to be caused by air infected with such noxious exhalations —

often used with *the* ⟨a horrid thing called the ~ —Horace Walpole⟩ **2 a :** an acute or chronic disease caused by the presence of sporozoan parasites (genus *Plasmodium*) in the red blood cells, transmitted from infected man to uninfected man by the bite of anopheline mosquitoes, and characterized by periodic attacks of chills and fever that coincide with mass destruction of blood cells and the release of toxic substances by the parasite at the end of each reproductive cycle ⟨~ remains the greatest single cause of debilitation and death throughout the world —*Jour. Amer. Med. Assoc.*⟩ — see FALCIPARUM MALARIA, VIVAX MALARIA **b :** any of various more or less similar diseases of birds and mammals caused by blood protozoans — see BIRD MALARIA

**ma·lar·i·ae** \mə'lerē,ē\ *n* -s [NL (specific epithet of *Plasmodium malariae*), gen. of *malaria*, fr. It] **:** the quartan malaria parasite (*Plasmodium malariae*) ⟨~ infection⟩

**malariae malaria** *n* **:** malaria caused by a malaria parasite (*Plasmodium malariae*) and marked by recurrence of paroxysms at 72-hour intervals — called also *quartan malaria*

**malaria germ** *n* **:** MALARIA PARASITE

**¹ma·lar·i·al** \mə'lerēəl, -la(a)r-, -lār-\ *also* **ma·lar·i·an** \-rēən\ *adj* [*malaria* + *-al* or *-an*] **:** of, relating to, infected by, or resembling malaria ⟨~ fever⟩ ⟨~ conditions in areas newly occupied by troops —*Atlantic*⟩

**²malarial** \"\ *n* -s **:** one infected with malaria

**malarial cachexia** *n* **:** a generalized state of debility that is marked by anemia, jaundice, splenomegaly, and emaciation and results from long-continued chronic malarial infection

**malarial catarrhal fever** *n* **1 :** heartwater of sheep **2 :** ICTEROHEMATURIA

**malarial fever** *n* **1 :** malaria of man **2 a :** INFECTIOUS ANEMIA **b :** TEXAS FEVER

**ma·lar·i·al·ize** \mə'lerēə,līz, -la(a)r-, -lār-\ *vt* -ED/-ING/-S **:** to infect with malaria for the purpose of inducing fever in the treatment of some diseases

**malarial mosquito** *or* **malaria mosquito** *n* **:** a mosquito that transmits the malaria parasite — compare ANOPHELES

**malaria parasite** *n* **:** a protozoan of the sporozoan genus *Plasmodium* being transmitted to man or to certain other mammals or birds by the bite of a mosquito in which its sexual reproduction takes place, multiplying asexually in the vertebrate host by schizogony in the red blood cells or in certain tissue cells, causing destruction of red blood cells and the febrile disease malaria, or producing gametocytes by sporogony that if taken up by a suitable mosquito initiate a new sexual cycle — compare MEROZOITE, OOKINETE, PHANEROZOITE, SCHIZONT, SPOROZOITE

**ma·lar·i·oid** \mə'lerē,ȯid, -la(a)r-, -lār-\ *adj* [*malari-* + *-oid*] **:** resembling malaria

**ma·lar·i·ol·o·gist** \=,==ˈäləjəst\ *n* -s **:** a specialist in the study, treatment, or prevention of malaria

**ma·lar·i·ol·o·gy** \-jē\ *n* -ES [ISV *malari-* + *-logy*] **:** the scientific study of malaria

**ma·lar·io·met·ric** \mə¦lerēə¦me·trik, -la(a)r-, -lār-\ *adj* **:** of or relating to malariometry

**ma·lar·i·om·e·try** \=,==ˈämə·trē\ *n* -ES [*malari-* + *-metry*] **:** the determination of the endemic level of malarial infection in an area or a population

**ma·lar·io·therapy** \=¦=rēə+\ *n* [ISV *malari-* + *therapy*] **:** the treatment of disease by raising the body temperature through infecting the patient with malaria

**ma·lar·i·ous** \mə'lerēəs, -la(a)r-, -lār-\ *adj* [*malaria* + *-ous*] **:** full of or infected with malaria ⟨~ regions⟩ ⟨a ~ patient⟩ ⟨the highly ~ jungles of Burma or New Guinea —*Atlantic*⟩

**ma·lar·key** *also* **ma·lar·ky** \mə'lärkē, -lākē, -ki\ *n, pl* **malarkeys** *also* **malarkies** [origin unknown] **:** insincere or pretentious talk or writing designed to impress one and usu. to distract attention from ulterior motives or actual conditions **:** NONSENSE ⟨column after column of . . . unmitigated ~ —Polly Adler⟩ ⟨masters of ~ for the masses —*Time*⟩

**malar point** *n* **:** the most prominent point on the zygomatic bone — see CRANIOMETRY illustration

**malars** *pl of* MALAR

**mal·assimilation** \¦mal+\ *n* [¹*mal-* + *assimilation*] **:** MALABSORPTION

**malate** \'ma,lāt, 'mā,-\ *n* -s [F, fr. *mal-* ²mal- + *-ate*] **:** a salt or ester of malic acid

**mal·a·thi·on** \,malə'thī,än *sometimes* mə'lāthēən\ *n* [fr. *Malathion*, a trademark] **:** a thiophosphate insecticide $C_{10}H_{19}O_6PS_2$ that has a lower mammalian toxicity than parathion and is also a valuable acaricide

**mal·a·vogue** \,malə'vōg\ *vt* [origin unknown] *dial chiefly Irish* **:** to treat or punish severely

**ma·la·wi** \mə'läwē\ *adj, usu cap* [fr. *Malawi*, country in southeastern Africa] **:** of or from the country of Malawi **:** of the kind or style prevalent in Malawi —**ma·la·wi·an** \-ēən\ *n* -s *cap* [*Malawi*, Africa + E *-an*] **:** a native or inhabitant of Malawi — **malawian** *adj, usu cap*

**ma·lax** \'mā,laks, mə'l-\ *vt* -ED/-ING/-ES [ME *malaxen*, fr. L *malaxare* to soften, fr. Gk *malaxai*, aor. infin. of *malassein*, fr. *malakos* soft — more at MALAC-] **:** MALAXATE

**malax·age** \'mā,laksij, mə'l-\ *n* -s [F, fr. *malaxer* to malaxate, knead (fr. L *malaxare*) + *-age*] **:** the act or process of softening a material (as clay) by moistening and working it

**malax·ate** \'malək,sāt, mə'lak-\ *vt* -ED/-ING/-S [L *malaxatus*, past part. of *malaxare*] **:** to soften and incorporate (as plaster, clay, or drug ingredients of pills) by rubbing, kneading, or rolling, and with a thinner substance

**malax·a·tion** \,malək'sāshən, mə,lak's-\ *n* -s [LL *malaxation-*, *malaxatio* act of softening, fr. L *malaxatus* + *-ion-*, *-io* -ion] **1 :** the act or process of reducing to a soft mass by malaxating **2 :** the process by which parasitic and predatory hymenoptera chew their victims previous to feeding by the adult or larvae

**mal·ax·a·tor** \'malək,sād·ə(r)\ *n* -s [*malaxate* + *-or*] **:** one that malaxates; *esp* **:** a machine or mill for grinding, kneading, or stirring into a pasty mass

**ma·lax·er·man** \mə'laksə(r)mən\ *n, pl* **malaxermen** [*malaxer-* (fr. *malax* + *-er*) + *man*] **:** one that mixes fireclay

**ma·lax·is** \mə'laksəs\ *n, cap* [NL, fr. Gk, act of softening, fr. *malassein* to soften] **:** a genus of terrestrial orchids with solid tubers that produce simple stems bearing one or few leaves and a raceme of tiny mostly greenish flowers — see GREEN ADDER'S-MOUTH

**¹ma·lay** \mə'lā, 'mā,lā\ *n* [obs. D *Malayo* (now *Maleier*) fr. Malay *Mĕlayu*] **1** *-s cap* **:** a member of a people of the Malay peninsula, eastern Sumatra, parts of Borneo, and some small adjacent islands **2** *-s cap* **:** the Austronesian language of the Malays widely used as a trade language **3 a** *usu cap* **:** an Asiatic breed of tall upright exhibition game fowls with walnut comb and small wattles, very long legs, naked face and throat, and distinctive mahogany red and black plumage **b** *-s often cap* **:** any bird of the Malay breed

**²malay** \"\ *adj, usu cap* **1 a :** of, relating to, or characteristic of Malaya **b :** of, relating to, or characteristic of Malaysia **2 :** of, relating to, or characteristic of the Malays **3 :** of, relating to, or characteristic of the Malay language

**ma·laya** \mə'lāə *also* (')mā¦l- *sometimes* -āyə\ *adj, usu cap* [fr. *Malaya*, federation of states in the southern part of the Malay peninsula] **:** of or from Malaya **:** of the kind or style prevalent in Malaya **:** MALAYAN

**mal·a·ya·lam** \,malə'yäləm\ *n* -s *usu cap* **1 :** the Dravidian language of Kerala, southern India, closely related to Tamil **2 :** the script normally used in writing Malayalam

**mal·a·ya·li** \-lē\ *n, pl* **malayalis** \-lēz\ *or* **malaya·lim** \-ləm\ *usu cap* **1 :** a Malayalam-speaking inhabitant of the Malabar coast of India **2 :** MALAYALAM

**¹ma·lay·an** \mə'lāən, (')mā¦l- *sometimes* -āyən\ *n* -s *cap* [¹*Malay* + E *-an*, n. suffix] **1 :** a native or inhabitant of Malaya **2 :** DEUTERO-MALAY

**²malayan** \"\ *adj, usu cap* [¹*Malay* + E *-an*, adj. suffix] **1 :** of, relating to, or characteristic of the Malays **2 :** of, relating to, or constituting the subdivision of the biogeographic Oriental region that includes the Malay peninsula, the Philippines, and the Indo-Malayan archipelago to Wallace's line

**malayan bear** *or* **malay bear** *n, usu cap M* **:** SUN BEAR

**malayan forge** *n, usu cap M* **:** a hand-operated forge with a vertical double piston bellows used esp. in Malaysia

**malay apple** *n, usu cap M* **1 :** the edible fruit of a tree (*Eugenia malaccensis*) of Asia and Polynesia **2 :** the tree that bears Malay apples

**malay camphor** *n, usu cap M* **:** BORNEO CAMPHOR

**ma·lay·ic** \-ā(y)ik\ *adj, usu cap* [¹*malay* + *-ic*] **:** MALAYAN

**malayo-** *comb form, usu cap* [²*malay* + *-o-*] **:** Malayan and ⟨*Malayo*-Indonesian⟩

**¹ma·layo-indonesian** \mə¦lā(,)ō, (¦)mā¦l-+\ *adj, usu cap M&I* **1 :** of, relating to, or characteristic of both the Malays and the Indonesians **2 :** AUSTRONESIAN

**²malayo-indonesian** \"\ *n, cap M&I* **:** a member of the Malay people of Indonesia

**¹ma·layo-polynesian** \mə¦lā(,)ō, (¦)mā¦l-+\ *adj, usu cap M&P* **1 :** of, relating to, or characteristic of both the Malays and the Polynesians **2 :** AUSTRONESIAN

**²malayo-polynesian** \"\ *n, cap M&P* **1 :** a member of the Malay people of Polynesia **2 :** AUSTRONESIAN

**ma·lay·sia** \mə'lāzh(ē)ə, -āsh-\ *adj, usu cap* [fr. *Malaysia*, country in southeastern Asia] **:** of or from the country of Malaysia **:** of the kind or style prevalent in Malaysia

**¹ma·lay·sian** \-(ē)ən\ *adj, usu cap* [*Malaysia*, Asia + E *-an*] **1 :** of, relating to, or characteristic of Malaysia **2 :** of, relating to, or characteristic of the natives or inhabitants of Malaysia **3 :** of, relating to, or characteristic of the deutero-Malays

**²malaysian** \"\ *n* -s *cap* **1 :** a native or inhabitant of Malaysia **2 :** DEUTERO-MALAY

**malay squirrel** *n, usu cap M* **:** a squirrel (*Callosciurus prevostii*) found in the Malay peninsula that has a dark back and a lighter belly separated by broad white lateral stripes

**malay wild dog** *n, usu cap M* **:** a wild dog (*Cuon javanicus*) found in Malaysia and adjacent islands and closely related to the red dog

**mal·behavior** \¦mal+\ *n* [¹*mal-* + *behavior*] **:** behavior that is regarded as socially unacceptable ⟨few forms of ~ . . . are not in history and essence a variation or deflection of normal mechanisms —A.L.Gesell & Frances Ilg⟩

**mal·brouck** \'mal,brůk\ *n* -s [F *malbrouk*, *malbrouch*, prob. fr. *Malbrouk*, figure in an 18th century French song who was popularly identified with John Churchill, 1st Duke of Marlborough †1722 Eng. military commander] **:** a West African arboreal monkey (*Cercopithecus cynosurus*)

**mal·chus** \'malkəs\ *n* -ES [F, fr. LL *Malchus*, high priest's servant whose ear St. Peter cut off with a sword (Jn 18:10), fr. Gk *Malchos*] **:** a short sword resembling an anlace

**mal·conduct** \(¦)mal+\ *n* [¹*mal-* + *conduct*] **:** bad conduct; *esp* **:** dishonesty in managing public affairs ⟨must be convicted of ~ before he can be removed —Gouverneur Morris⟩

**mal·conformation** \¦=+\ *n* [¹*mal-* + *conformation*] **:** imperfect or abnormal formation ⟨the inherent ~ of the Carlovingian Empire —F.T.Palgrave⟩; *esp* **:** disproportion between bodily structures ⟨~ of head and shoulders⟩

**mal·construction** \"+\ *n* [¹*mal-* + *construction*] **:** poor or faulty construction

**¹mal·content** \"+\ *n* [MF, fr. *malcontent*, adj.] **1 :** a discontented person: **a :** one who bears a grudge from a sense of grievance or thwarted ambition ⟨lord of folded arms . . . liege of all loiterers and ~s —Shak.⟩ ⟨every peevish, moody ~ —Nicholas Rowe⟩ ⟨in the drama of the early 17th century . . . the ~ is the man who has been unable to achieve an "advancement" commensurate with his abilities —H.B.Parkes⟩ ⟨~s . . . bitter and almost choking with self-pity —E.W.Griffiths⟩ **b :** one who is disaffected with an established order or government or in active opposition to it **:** REBEL ⟨harebrained scheme of a small group of ~s —William Plutte⟩ **2 :** *archaic* **:** DISCONTENT ⟨the ~ of Job —Sir Thomas Browne⟩

**²malcontent** \"\ *adj* [MF, fr. OF, fr. *mal* badly + *content* — more at MAL-, CONTENT] **:** marked by a restless, moody, or bitter dissatisfaction with the existing state of affairs **:** DISCONTENTED ⟨you stand pensive, as half ~ —Shak.⟩ ⟨~ satire —*New Republic*⟩; *specif* **:** disaffected with an established order or government ⟨a ~ group of political exiles⟩

**mal·contented** \"+\ *adj* [prob. fr. MF *malcontent*, adj. + E *-ed*] **:** MALCONTENT ⟨young men who are ~, unsettled, and influenced by the more extreme racial sentiments —Michael Banton⟩ — **mal·contentedly** \"+\ *adv* — **mal·contentedness** \"+\ *n*

**¹mal·dan·id** \(')mal¦danəd\ *adj* [NL *Maldanidae*] **:** of or relating to the Maldanidae

**²maldanid** \"\ *n* -s [NL *Maldanidae*] **:** a worm of the family Maldanidae

**mal·dan·i·dae** \mal'danə,dē\ *n pl, cap* [NL, fr. *Maldane*, type genus + *-idae*] **:** a family of slender cylindrical polychaete worms having rudimentary parapodia, lacking differentiated gills, and living in sand tubes

**mal de ca·de·ras** \,maldəkə'derəs\ *n* [AmerSp, lit., disease of the hips] **:** an infectious disease of horses in So. America caused by a protozoan parasite (*Trypanosoma equinum*) in the blood and characterized by rapid emaciation, anemia, blood-colored urine, paresis, and edema

**mal del pin·to** \,mal,del'pin·(,)tō\ *n* [AmerSp, lit., disease of the spotted one] **:** PINTA

**mal de mer** \,maldə'me(ə)r\ *n* [F] **:** SEASICKNESS

**mal·development** \¦mal+\ *n* [¹*mal-* + *development*] **:** abnormal growth or development **:** DYSPLASIA

**mal di gom·ma** \,maldē'gōmə, -gämə\ *n* [It, lit., gum disease] **:** a foot rot or collar rot of citrus plants caused by a fungus (*Phytophthora parasitica*)

**mal·distribution** \"+\ *n* [¹*mal-* + *distribution*] **:** bad or faulty distribution: as **a :** undesirable inequality or unevenness of placement or apportionment (as of population, wealth, or resources) over an area or among the members of a group ⟨these islands suffer from a ~ of population —Amry Vandenbosch⟩ ⟨the ~ of wealth inherent in the profit system —*N.Y. Times*⟩ **b :** inequitable or inefficient delivery or conveyance (as of goods) to the members of a group ⟨~ of steel and its diversion to the giant affiliates of the ruling steel mills —Gunther Stein⟩

**mal·dive islands** \,mal,dīv-, -ōl-, -,div-\ *adj, usu cap M&I* [fr. *Maldive Islands*, country in Northern Indian Ocean] **:** of or relating to the Maldive Islands **:** of the kind or style prevalent in the Maldive Islands

**¹mal·div·i·an** \(')mal¦divēən, (')mōl-\ *also* **mal·di·van** \'=,dīvən, -,dəv-\ *adj, usu cap* [*Maldive* Islands, in Indian Ocean southwest of Ceylon + E *-an*, adj. suffix] **1 :** of, relating to, or characteristic of the Maldive Islands **2 :** of, relating to, or characteristic of Maldivians

**²maldivian** \"\ *also* **maldivan** \"\ *n* -s *cap* [*Maldive* Islands + E *-an*, n. suffix] **:** a native or inhabitant of the Maldive Islands

**mal·don·ite** \'mōldə,nīt\ *n* -s [*Maldon*, Victoria, Australia, its locality + E *-ite*] **:** a mineral of variable composition but approximately $Au_2Bi$ consisting of an alloy of gold and bismuth

**mal·duck** \'maldək\ *n* [prob. alter. (influenced by *duck*) of *mallemuck*] *Brit* **:** FULMAR

**¹male** \'māl, *esp before pause or consonant* -āəl\ *adj* [ME, fr. MF *male*, *masle*, adj. & n., fr. L *masculus*, adj. & n., dim. of *mas*, adj. & n., male] **1 a** (1) **:** of, relating to, or being the sex that begets young by performing the fertilizing function in generation **:** of, relating to, or being the sex that produces relatively small usu. motile gametes (as sperms, spermatozoids, spermatozoa) by which the eggs of a female are made fertile **:** exhibiting maleness ⟨a ~ animal⟩ ⟨~ sex organs⟩ — symbol ♂ (2) **:** STAMINATE; *esp* **:** having only staminate flowers and not producing fruit or seeds ⟨a ~ holly⟩ ⟨a ~ bittersweet⟩ **b** (1) **:** of, relating to, or characteristic of one that is male, esp. a man **:** VIRILE ⟨a deep ~ voice⟩ **:** having a quality (as strength, vigor, courage) associated with one that is male ⟨full of ~ energy⟩ ⟨spoke to her with ~ directness⟩ (2) **:** made up of male individuals, esp. men **:** consisting of males ⟨a ~ choir⟩ ⟨the ~ population of the city⟩ **2** *of a gem* **:** having a rich and dark coloring ⟨a ~ sapphire⟩ **3 :** MASCULINE 2b(2) **4 :** designed for fitting into a corresponding female part which is hollow ⟨a ~ hose coupling⟩ **5 :** relating to a dialect or having speech forms used only by men ⟨~ language⟩ **6 :** of, associated with, or being the formal, active, or generative principle of the cosmos — compare YANG

**syn** MALE, MASCULINE, MANLY, MANLIKE, MANNISH, MANFUL, and VIRILE all mean belonging to or like a male of the species, esp. human. MALE, opposing *female*, applies to humans, animals, or plants, and always indicates sex ⟨a *male* collie⟩ ⟨a *male* willow⟩ ⟨a *male* child⟩ ⟨a *male* chorus⟩ MASCULINE, opposing *feminine*, is sometimes interchangeable with MALE ⟨the *masculine* half of the audience⟩ and is used to distinguish grammatical gender ⟨a *masculine* noun⟩ ⟨a *masculine* inflection on an adjective⟩ but most commonly applies to qualities that seem esp. to distinguish the male from the female ⟨a very *masculine* voice⟩ ⟨the *masculine* firmness, the quiet force of his style —Henry James⟩ ⟨his *masculine* longing to command —Edith Sitwell⟩ ⟨his wife was a great *masculine* virago —Tobias Smollett⟩ MANLY, usu. opposing *boyish*, *childish*, or *effeminate*, suggests the finer qualities of a man, esp. courage, independence, and mature physical characteristics or mental firmness or forthrightness ⟨a *manly* refusal to avoid difficulties⟩ ⟨a boy's love is likely to be divided between a gun and a watch; but the more active and *manly* choose the gun —H.D.Thoreau⟩ ⟨the country, with its rugged virtues and its *manly* independence —W.G.O'Donnell⟩ ⟨a sculptor had a model so perfect in *manly* symmetry and strength —G.G.Coulton⟩ MANLIKE is often close to *human* in a general sense ⟨one of the more *manlike* apes⟩ but is generally used to suggest characteristically masculine qualities or, sometimes, foibles ⟨sturdy, sunburnt creatures, in petticoats, but otherwise *manlike* —Nathaniel Hawthorne⟩ ⟨a boy *manlike* in stature, strength, and a strong tendency to try to dominate⟩ MANNISH applies chiefly to women, or things belonging to them, that have certain manlike qualities ⟨a great many women, brave in *mannish* clothes —Louis Bromfield⟩ ⟨at one time bobbed her hair, which had made her head a little too *mannish* —Edmund Wilson⟩ MANFUL adds to MANLY a greater stress on sturdiness or resoluteness ⟨we should be shabby fellows if we spent any serious proportion of our 13,000 days in shirking or whining or sponging on the more *manful* part of mankind —C.E.Montague⟩ ⟨worked like a *manful* soldier —Charles Dickens⟩ ⟨a *manful* handling of a trying situation⟩ VIRILE, stronger than MASCULINE and opposing *impotent*, suggests qualities belonging to esp. well-developed manhood, as marked aggressiveness, masterfulness, forcefulness, or, specifically, male sexuality or procreativeness ⟨the religion is *virile*, aggressive, and growing —L.C.May⟩ ⟨the robust, *virile* Elizabethan era —Rosette Hargrove⟩ ⟨he would have preferred brutality, which was *virile*, . . . rather than this sad, sedulous defeat —Audrey Barker⟩ ⟨the *virile* story of a little man, his big wife, and his bigger bull —*Atlantic*⟩

**²male** \"\ *n* -s [ME, fr. MF *male*, *masle*, adj. & n.] **:** an individual (as a man, boy, male animal, staminate plant) that begets young **:** an individual that produces relatively small usu. motile gametes by which the eggs of a female are fertilized **:** an individual possessing the qualities of maleness **:** male individual

**³ma·le** \'mälā\ *n, pl* **ma·ler** \-lər\ *or* **male** *or* **males** *usu cap* **:** a member of a Dravidian animistic people of Bengal

**male alto** *n* **:** a male singer singing falsetto — called also *countertenor*

**malease** *var of* MALAISE

**ma·le·ate** \mə'lēət, *usu* -ēd.+V\ *n* -s [ISV *maleic* (in *maleic acid*) + *-ate*] **:** a salt or ester of maleic acid

**male bamboo** *n* **:** an East Indian bamboo grass (*Dendrocalamus strictus*) forming great clumps often 50 feet high

**maleberry** \'=- — *see* BERRY\ *n* **1 :** PEABERRY **2 :** PRIVET ANDROMEDA

**mal·e·branch·ism** \¦malə¦bran,chizəm\ *n* -s *usu cap* [F *malebranchisme*, fr. Nicolas de *Malebranche* †1715 Fr. metaphysician + F *-isme* -ism] **:** a philosophical system based on the premise that the mind cannot have knowledge of anything external to itself except through its relation to God

**mal·e·branch·ist** \-,chəst\ *n* -s *usu cap* [F *malebranchiste*, fr. Nicolas de *Malebranche* †1715 + F *-iste* -ist] **:** an advocate of or believer in Malebranchism

**mal·e·cite** *or* **mal·i·seet** \'malə,sēt, ,==ˈ=\ *n, pl* **malecite** *or* **malecites** *or* **maliseet** *or* **maliseets** *usu cap* [prob. fr. Micmac *Malisit*] **1 a :** an Indian people of New Brunswick, Canada, and of the northernmost part of northeastern Maine **b :** a member of such people **2 :** an Algonquian language of the Malecite and Passamaquoddy peoples

**malecontent** *archaic var of* MALCONTENT

**mal·e·di·cent** \¦malə¦dīsᵊnt\ *adj* [L *maledicent-*, *maledicens*, pres. part. of *maledicere* to speak evil] **1** *archaic* **:** addicted to speaking evil **2** *archaic* **:** SLANDEROUS

**¹mal·e·dict** \'malə,dikt\ *adj* [LL *maledictus* (past part. of *maledicere* to curse), fr. L, past part. of *maledicere* to speak evil] *archaic* **:** ACCURSED

**²maledict** \"\ *vt* -ED/-ING/-S [LL *maledictus* (past part. of *maledicere* to curse), fr. L, past part. of L *maledicere* to speak evil, fr. *male* badly + *dicere* to speak, say — more at MAL-, DICTION] *archaic* **:** EXECRATE, CURSE

**mal·e·dic·tion** \,malə'dikshən\ *n* [ME *malediccioun*, fr. LL *malediction-*, *maledictio*, fr. *maledictus* (past part. of *maledicere* to curse) + L *-ion-*, *-io* -ion] **:** CURSE, EXECRATION ⟨the ~s of great poets, whose hate confers an unwelcome immortality —John Buchan⟩

**mal·e·dic·tive** \¦==¦diktiv\ *adj* [²*maledict* + *-ive*] **1 :** marked by cursing **:** invoking evil **2 :** ACCURSED

**mal·e·dic·to·ry** \-t(ə)rē\ *adj* [²*maledict* + *-ory*] **:** MALEDICTIVE 1

**mal·e·fac·tion** \¦malə¦fakshən *sometimes* (')mal¦fak-\ *n* [*malefactor* + *-ion*] **:** CRIME, OFFENSE ⟨is most commonly attributed to the ~ of a maternal relative —Abram Kardiner⟩

**mal·e·fac·tor** \¦malə¦faktə(r) *sometimes* (')mal¦f- *or* -,tȯ(ə)r *or* -,tȯ(ə)\ *n* [ME *malefactour*, fr. L *malefactor*, fr. *malefactus* (past part. of *malefacere* to do evil, fr. *male* badly + *facere* to do) + *-or* — more at DO] **1 :** one who commits an offense against the law; *esp* **:** FELON **2 :** one who does ill toward another **:** EVILDOER ⟨a sinister ~ abusing his power —*Iron Age*⟩ **syn** see CRIMINAL

**mal·e·fac·tress** \-,trəs\ *n* -ES [*malefactor* + *-ess*] **:** a female malefactor

**male fern** *n* **:** a fern (*Dryopteris filix-mas*) of Europe and No. America producing an oleoresin that is used in expelling tapeworms — compare ASPIDIUM

**ma·lef·ic** \mə'lefik\ *adj* [L *maleficus*, fr. *male* badly + *-ficus* -fic] **1 :** of, having, or exerting an unfavorable or malignant influence ⟨a ~ force⟩ **:** BALEFUL **2 :** MALICIOUS

**mal·e·fice** \'maləfəs\ *n* -s [ME, fr. L *maleficium*, fr. *maleficus*] **1 :** a piece of evil sorcery **:** an evil spell or enchantment ⟨a magic power working against mysterious ~s —Joseph Conrad⟩ **2** *archaic* **:** a piece of mischief **:** an evil deed

**ma·lef·i·cence** \mə'lefəsən(t)s\ *n* -s [It *maleficenza*, fr. L *maleficentia*, fr. *maleficus* + *-entia* -ence] **1 a :** the commission of harm or evil **:** EVILDOING ⟨the punishment of ~⟩ **b :** a harmful or evil act ⟨guilty of more than one ~⟩ **2 :** the quality or state of being maleficent ⟨recognized the ~ of the plan⟩

**ma·lef·i·cent** \-nt\ *adj* [fr. *maleficence*, after such pairs as E *benevolence*: *benevolent*] **1 a :** working harm or evil **:** EVIL, BALEFUL ⟨believes that he is surrounded at every step by ~ spirits —J.G.Frazer⟩ **b :** productive of harm or evil **:** HURTFUL, INJURIOUS ⟨the man does leave his mark behind him, ineffaceable, beneficial to all, ~ to none —*Harper's*⟩ **2 a :** that commits or is disposed to commit offenses or crimes ⟨were surrounded by ~ nations⟩ **b :** having the nature of an offense or crime **:** CRIMINAL ⟨guilty of a ~ act⟩

**¹maleficiate** *adj* [ML *maleficiatus*, past part. of *maleficiare* to bewitch, injure, fr. L *maleficium* evil spell] *obs* **:** placed under an evil spell; *esp* **:** made impotent by sorcery

**²maleficiate** *vt* -ED/-ING/-S [ML *maleficiatus*, past part. of *maleficiare*] *obs* **:** to put under an evil spell; *esp* **:** to make impotent by sorcery

**male griffin** *n* **:** a griffin (sense 1 b) sometimes borne in coats of arms that is without wings and that has clusters of rays or spikes issuing from various parts of its body

**ma·le·ic acid** \mə'lēik, -lāik-\ *n* [part. fr. F *maléique* (in *acide maléique* maleic acid), alter. of *malique* malic (in *acide malique* malic acid) — more at MALIC ACID] **:** a crystalline unsaturated dicarboxylic acid HOOCCH=CHCOOH obtained usu. by catalytic oxidation of benzene or naphthalene or by dehydration of malic acid and used chiefly in making polyester resins; *cis*-butene-dioic acid — compare CIS-TRANS ISOMERISM a, FUMARIC ACID

**maleic anhydride** *n* **:** a crystalline cyclic acid anhydride $C_4H_2O_3$ that gives rise to maleic acid on reaction with water, that reacts readily with dienes in the Diels-Alder reaction, and that is used chiefly in the manufacture of alkyd and other resins and in the manufacture of modified drying oils

**maleic hydrazide** *n* **:** a crystalline cyclic hydrazide $C_4H_4N_2O_2$ made by reaction of hydrazine with maleic acid or anhydride and used to retard plant growth and the sprouting of potatoes, onions, and root crops (as carrots or beets) in storage
**male incense** *n, obs* **:** a frankincense of esp. high quality
**malekite** *usu cap, var of* MALIKITE
**male menopause** *n* **:** climacteric in the male
**malemute** *sometimes cap, var of* MALAMUTE
**male·ness** *n* -ES **:** the qualities (as of form, physiology, behavior) that distinguish an individual that produces small usu. motile gametes from one that produces eggs **:** MASCULINITY — opposed to *femaleness;* see SEX
**malengine** *n* [ME *malengin,* fr. MF, deceit, fr. OF, fr. *mal* bad + *engin* skill — more at MAL-, ENGINE] **1** *obs* **:** evil machination **2** *obs* **:** GUILE, DECEIT
**mal·en·ten·du** \ˌmälänˈtänˈdüe\ *n* -S [F, fr. *mal entendu* misunderstood, fr. *mal* badly + *entendu,* past part. of *entendre* to understand, interpret, be attentive — more at MAL-, INTEND] **:** MISUNDERSTANDING ⟨through some ~ arrived an hour late⟩
**male nutmeg** *n* **:** MACASSAR NUTMEG
**mal·eo** \ˈmalē,ō\ *n, pl* **maleo** *or* **maleos** [Galelarese (language of northern Halmahera) *mĕleo*] **:** a megapode (*Macrocephalon maleo*) of Celebes that lays its eggs in holes in sandy beaches
**male orchis** *n* **:** a Eurasian orchid (*Orchis mascula*) with showy pink or purple flowers in a loose spike
**male pronucleus** *n* **:** the nucleus that remains in a male gamete after reduction and that contains only one half of the number of chromosomes characteristic of its species — compare FEMALE PRONUCLEUS
**maler** *pl of* MALE
**males** *pl of* MALE
**males·her·bia** \ˌmaləˈzərbēə, ˌmaləsˈhər-, malˈzər-\ *n, cap* [NL, fr. Chrétien G. de Lamoignon de *Malesherbes* †1794 Fr. statesman + NL *-ia*] **:** a genus of So. American herbs or undershrubs (family Malesherbiaceae) that have capsular fruit and large yellow racemose flowers with a tubular calyx exceeding the corolla
**males·her·bi·a·ce·ae** \ˌ≈(≈)ˌ≈≈ˈāsē,ē\ *n pl, cap* [NL, fr. *Malesherbia,* type genus + *-aceae*] **:** a family of plants (order Parietales) coextensive with the genus *Malesherbia*
**male shield fern** *n* **:** MALE FERN
**male–sterile** \ˈ≈ˌ≈≈\ *adj* **:** having male gametes lacking or nonfunctional ⟨a *male-sterile* plant⟩
**ma·le·ta** \məˈlād·ə\ *n* -S [Sp, bag, purse, fr. MF *malette,* fr. OF *malete,* fr. *male* bag + *-ete* -ette — more at MAIL, -ETTE] *Southwest* **:** a usu. rawhide bag
**maletolt** *var of* MALTOLTE
**ma·lev·o·lence** \məˈlevələn(t)s\ *n* -S [MF *malivolence,* fr. L *malivolentia, malevolentia,* fr. *malivolent-, malivolens, malevolent-, malevolens* malevolent + *-ia* -y] **1 :** the quality or state of being malevolent ⟨slander that arose from pure ~⟩ **2 :** behavior marked by or indicative of intense often vicious ill will ⟨an era full of selfishness and ~⟩ **syn** see MALICE
**ma·lev·o·lent** \-lənt\ *adj* [L *malivolent-, malivolens, malevolent-, malevolens,* fr. *male* badly + *volent-, volens,* pres. part. of *velle* to will — more at MAL-, WILL] **1 :** having, showing, or indicative of intense often vicious ill will **:** filled with or marked by deep-seated spite or rancor or hatred ⟨a gossipy ~ old woman⟩ ⟨a ~ lie⟩ **2 :** productive of harm or evil **:** HURTFUL, INJURIOUS ⟨have lived ~ and criminal lives and have been despised by men and punished by society —E.G.Conklin⟩ — **ma·lev·o·lent·ly** *adv*
**malevolous** *adj* [L *malevolus,* fr. *male* badly + *-volus* (fr. *velle*)] *obs* **:** MALEVOLENT
**mal·fea·sance** \malˈfēzᵊn(t)s\ *also* **mal·fai·sance** \ˌmalfəˈzäⁿs\ *n* -S [E *ˈmal-* + obs. E *feasance* doing, execution, fr. MF *faisance,* fr. OF, fr. *fais-* (stem of *faire* to make, do, fr. L *facere*) + *-ance* — more at DO] **1 :** WRONGDOING, MISCONDUCT, MISBEHAVIOR; *specif* **:** the doing by a public officer under color of authority of his office of something that is unwarranted, that he has contracted not to do, and that is legally unjustified and positively wrongful or contrary to law — called also *malpractice;* distinguished from *misfeasance, nonfeasance* **2 :** an act or instance of wrongdoing esp. by a public officer under color of authority of his office
**mal·fea·sant** \malˈfēzᵊnt\ *n* -S [fr. *malfeasance,* after such pairs as E *assistance: assistant*] **:** one that is guilty of malfeasance
**mal·form** \ˈ≈+\ *vt* [ˈ*mal-* + *form,* v.] **:** to cause to be badly or imperfectly formed **:** cause to be formed in such a way as to deviate from the normal or usual **:** give an abnormal, anomalous, or otherwise irregular and defective formation or structure to ⟨a virus that ~*s* tobacco leaves⟩ ⟨in his chair sat a personality ~*ed* beyond decency by greed and pride —Clemence Dane⟩
**mal·formation** \ˌ≈+\ *n* [ˈ*mal-* + *formation*] **1 :** the condition of being malformed ⟨suffered from a ~ of character⟩ ⟨congenital ~⟩ **2 :** something that is malformed **:** an instance of being malformed ⟨all kinds of queer ~*s* in our physical and psychological makeup —H.A.Overstreet⟩
**mal·formed** \ˈ≈≈\ *adj* [ˈ*mal-* + *formed* (past part. of *form,* v.)] **:** formed in such a way as to deviate with undesirable or pernicious results from the normal or usual **:** having a formation or structure that is abnormal, anomalous, or otherwise irregular and defective **:** badly or imperfectly formed **:** MISSHAPEN ⟨walked with a limp that was caused by a ~ foot —F.V.W.Mason⟩
[1]**mal·function** \"+\ *vi* [ˈ*mal-* + *function,* v.] **:** to function badly or imperfectly **:** fail to operate in the normal or usual manner ⟨designed a rifle that would not ~⟩ ⟨the parachute ~*ed,* opening too late⟩ ⟨attributable to some ~*ing* of the nervous system —Edward Sapir⟩
[2]**malfunction** \"\ *n* **1 :** the action or fact of malfunctioning ⟨altitudes where ~ of the plane becomes evident⟩ **2 :** an instance of malfunctioning ⟨three ~*s* had been reported and rectified before the rocket was finally launched⟩
**mal·gache** *or* **mal·gach** *also* **mal·gash** \(ˈ)malˌgash\ *n, pl* **malgache** *or* **malgach** *or* **malgaches** *also* **malgashes** *usu cap* [F *malgache*] **:** MALAGASY
**mal·gré** \(ˈ)malˌgrā\ *prep* [F, fr. OF *maugré* — more at MAUGRE] **:** DESPITE ⟨one bar where a decent drink is to be obtained, ~ the monstrous regiment of women —R.S.Hillyer⟩
**malgré lui** \ˌ≈(≈)≈lˈwē\ *adv* [F, in spite of himself] **:** despite himself ⟨extraordinary talents, which somehow always crop out to show him at his best *malgré lui* —*Saturday Rev.*⟩
**mal·gu·zar** \ˌmälgəˈzär\ *n* -S [Hindi *mālguzār,* fr. Ar *māl* property, rent + Per *guzār* payer] **:** MALIK
**mal·heur** \maˈlər\ *n* -S [F, fr. OF *maleur,* fr. *mal* bad + *eür* fortune, fr. L *augurium* augury — more at MAL-, AUGURY] *archaic* **:** MISFORTUNE
[1]**ma·li** *also* **mal·lee** *or* **mal·lie** *or* **mal·ly** *or* **mol·ly** \ˈmälē\ *n, pl* **malis** *also* **mallees** *or* **mallies** *or* **mollies** [Hindi *mālī,* fr. Skt *mālika* gardener] **:** one belonging to a caste in the subcontinent of India whose usual occupation is gardening
[2]**mali** \"\ *adj, usu cap* [*Mali,* republic in west Africa] **:** of or from the Republic of Mali **:** of the kind or style prevalent in Mali
**ma·li·an** \ˈmälēən\ *n* -S *cap* [*Mali,* country in western Africa + E *-an*] **:** a native or inhabitant of Mali — **malian** *adj, usu cap*
**mal·ic acid** \ˈmalik, ˈmālik-\ *n* [*malic* fr. F *malique,* fr. L *malum* apple + F *-ique* -ic — more at MALUS] **:** a crystalline hydroxy dicarboxylic acid HOOCCH(OH)CHCOOH known in three optically isomeric forms; hydroxy-succinic acid: (1) the levorotatory L-form found in various plant juices (as in apples, grapes, rhubarb) and formed as an intermediate in the Krebs cycle; (2) the dextrorotatory D-form usu. obtained by resolution of the racemic form; (3) the racemic form made by hydration of maleic acid or fumaric acid
[1]**mal·ice** \ˈmaləs\ *n* -S [ME, fr. OF, fr. L *malitia,* fr. *malus* bad — more at SMALL] **1 a** (1) **:** intention or desire to harm another usu. seriously through doing something unlawful or otherwise unjustified **:** willfulness in the commission of a wrong **:** evil intention ⟨ruined her reputation and did it with ~⟩ ⟨rejoiced out of pure ~ in seeing others suffer⟩ — compare IMPLIED MALICE, MALICE AFORETHOUGHT, MALICE IN FACT (2) **:** conscious and deliberate transgression esp. of a moral code viewed as established by God accompanied by an evil intention ⟨theologians hold that the gravity of an offense against divine law depends on the degree of ~ involved⟩ (3) **:** revengeful or unfriendly feelings **:** ILL WILL, ENMITY ⟨in spite of all he has had to put up with from them, he bears them no ~⟩ **b :** sportive intention or desire to discomfit others (as by teasing or joking) **:** playful mischievousness ⟨with smiling ~ asked her where she had been⟩ **2** *obs* **a :** BADNESS; *esp* **:** WICKEDNESS **b :** HARMFULNESS
**syn** MALEVOLENCE, ILL WILL, SPITE, DESPITE, MALIGNANCY, MALIGNITY, SPLEEN, GRUDGE: MALICE may apply either to a deep-seated, often unjustified, innate desire to bring pain and suffering to others or to enjoy contemplating it or to a passing impish mischievousness not arising from a hardened vindictive nature ⟨from such persons no repentance was to be looked for. They were impelled by a *malice* or a fanaticism which clemency could not touch or reason influence —J.A. Froude⟩ ⟨she was clever, witty, brilliant, and sparkling beyond most of her kind; but possessed of many devils of *malice* and mischievousness —Rudyard Kipling⟩ MALEVOLENCE may suggest a cold deep hatred or enmity underlying wishes for evil for others ⟨their society is organized by a permanent, universal animosity and *malevolence;* sullen suspicion and resentment are their chief motives, ill will and treachery their chief virtues —H.J.Muller⟩ ILL WILL may suggest a feeling of enmity, antipathy, or resentment directed against a person or thing, often with cause; it differs from MALEVOLENCE in not implying a lasting character trait ⟨Catherine could not believe it possible that any injury or any misfortune could provoke such *ill will* against a person not connected, or, at least, not supposed to be connected with it —Jane Austen⟩ SPITE suggests petty ill will and mean envy and resentment ⟨a man full of the secret *spite* of dullness, who interrupted from time to time, and always to check or disorder thought —W.B.Yeats⟩ DESPITE, now not common, may imply more pride and disdain but less pettiness than SPITE ⟨not in *despite* but softly, as men smile about the dead —G.K.Chesterton⟩ MALIGNANCY and MALIGNITY imply deep passion and relentless driving force ⟨employed by the envy, jealousy and *malignity* of his enemies, to ruin him with the queen —Hilaire Belloc⟩ ⟨he is cruel with the cruelty of petrified feeling, to his poor heroine; he pursues her without pity or pause, as with *malignity* —Matthew Arnold⟩ ⟨blinded by *malignancy* against the class of manual worker —Cecil Sprigge⟩ SPLEEN indicates choleric ill will with wrathful release of latent spite ⟨his just fame was long obscured by partisan *spleen* —V.L.Parrington⟩ ⟨venting their *spleen* against the United States in so venomous a manner —T.R.Fyvel⟩ GRUDGE suggests cherished ill will with deep resentment at a real or imagined slight, affront, humiliation, or other cause of chagrin ⟨she had never been close to Uncle Claude and had held a *grudge* against him for ending her companionship with Ralph —Jean Stafford⟩ ⟨the secret *grudges* that the relations of men whom he had killed or dishonored bore against him —Robert Graves⟩
[2]**malice** *vt* -ED/-ING/-S *obs* **:** to regard with malice ~ *vi, obs* **:** to harbor or cherish malice
**malice aforethought** *or* **malice prepense** *n* [*malice aforethought* trans. of AF *malice purpensee; malice prepense* alter. of earlier *malice prepensed* (trans. of AF *malice purpensee*), fr. E *malice* + obs. E *prepensed* premeditated — more at PREPENSE] **:** deliberate malice **:** premeditated malice; *specif* **:** malice in fact or implied malice in the intention of one who has had sufficient time to act with premeditation in the doing of something unlawful (as in doing serious bodily harm to another person or as in murdering another person)
**mal·ice·ful** \ˈ≈≈fəl\ *adj, archaic* **:** MALICIOUS
**malice in fact** *law* **:** malice actually existing or proved by direct evidence to have existed in the intention of a person in the commission of unjustified injury or harm to another — distinguished from *implied malice*
**ma·li·cious** \məˈlishəs\ *adj* [ME, fr. OF *malicius,* fr. L *malitiosus,* fr. *malitia* malice + *-osus* -ose] **:** given to, marked by, or arising from malice ⟨took a ~ pleasure in emphasizing this point and in watching me wince —Rudyard Kipling⟩ — **ma·li·cious·ly** *adv* — **ma·li·cious·ness** *n* -ES
**malicious abandonment** *n, law* **:** desertion of one spouse by the other without just cause
**malicious mischief** *n, law* **:** willful, wanton, or reckless damage or destruction of another's property
**malicious prosecution** *n, law* **:** the bringing of a civil or criminal proceeding against another in a court of law without reasonable cause and with malicious intent
**ma·lif·er·ous** \məˈlif(ə)rəs\ *adj* [L *malum* evil (fr. *malus* bad) + E *-iferous* — more at SMALL] *archaic* **:** having an unhealthful effect **:** UNWHOLESOME
[1]**ma·lign** \məˈlīn\ *adj* [ME *maligne,* fr. MF, fr. L *malignus,* fr. *male* badly + *-ignus* (as in *benignus* benign) — more at MAL-] **1 a :** evil in nature, influence, or effect **:** INJURIOUS, BALEFUL ⟨prompted by ~ motives⟩ ⟨living in a ~ environment⟩ **b :** MALIGNANT, VIRULENT ⟨a ~ lesion⟩ **2 a :** having or showing or indicative of intense often vicious ill will **:** intensely hostile **:** MALEVOLENT ⟨gave him a ~ look⟩ **b :** desiring or taking pleasure in the sufferings of others ⟨believed in the existence of witches and ~ spirits⟩
[2]**malign** \"\ *vb* -ED/-ING/-S [ME *malignen,* fr. MF *maligner,* fr. LL *malignare, malignari,* to act maliciously, fr. L *malignus*] *vi, obs* **:** to speak, think, or act malevolently ~ *vt* **1** *obs* **a :** to regard with intense ill will or with bitter dislike or hatred **b :** RESENT, BEGRUDGE **2 :** to utter injuriously misleading or deliberately and injuriously false reports about **:** induce misunderstanding of and lower regard for by falsehood or misrepresentation ⟨gossips had ~*ed* the lady —George Meredith⟩
**syn** CALUMNIATE, ASPERSE, VILIFY, TRADUCE, DEFAME, SLANDER, LIBEL: MALIGN may suggest malevolent calculation as a motivating force and specific and subtle misrepresentations and falsehoods as instruments ⟨little doubt that Lytton Strachey and other British historians have *maligned* Ward in order to build up the fame of "Chinese" Gordon —Richard Watts⟩ The past participle may be less severe in suggestion and apply to the role of innocent reiteration in conditioning a reputation ⟨in view of Hans Heysen's studies of this *maligned* and slandered tree, its beauty is clear enough —Thomas Wood †1950⟩ CALUMNIATE involves malice against the victim, is used more often in connection with public affairs and figures, and suggests blackening of the general reputation ⟨*calumniating* him as a traitor in satisfying his ancient personal grudge⟩ ASPERSE may suggest continued attack on a reputation, sometimes by direct false accusation but often by covert depreciating insinuation ⟨one may not admire it, but one can no longer *asperse* the integrity of those who do —*Times Lit. Supp.*⟩ VILIFY may suggest a direct ranting or railing abuse without subtlety, an attempt to make vile and shameful ⟨should not be *vilified* in newspapers, for that is want of tact and waste of space —Rudyard Kipling⟩ ⟨his circumlocutions are roundly called lies, and his silence is *vilified* as treachery —W.S.Maugham⟩ TRADUCE is the least rich in connotation in this series. More than the preceding words, it may suggest success in derogation ⟨fear of this witch of the East [Cleopatra], shamelessly *traduced* by Octavian's agents, hagrode the popular mind —John Buchan⟩ DEFAME stresses actual loss of reputation brought about by malicious charges ⟨*defaming* and defacing, till she left not even Lancelot brave nor Galahad clean —Alfred Tennyson⟩ SLANDER connotes nasty maliciousness in motivation, oral utterance, frequently covert, and definite suffering or loss for the victim ⟨you would darkly *slander* him you cannot openly defame —E.G.Bulwer-Lytton⟩ ⟨he was rector until the new governor listened to some cock-and-bull story against him, and made him resign. He was the best preacher they ever had — he'd have been a bishop one day, if someone hadn't *slandered* him to the governor —R.A. W.Hughes⟩ LIBEL, more legalistic than the others in this series, is much the same as SLANDER in its connotations, except that it may imply issuance of the defamatory matter in wider and more permanent media than SLANDER. In legal or legalistic use denotations and connotations of words in this series vary in different jurisdictions
**ma·lig·nance** \məˈlignən(t)s\ *n* -S [fr. *malignant,* after such pairs as E *assistant: assistance*] **:** MALIGNANCY
**ma·lig·nan·cy** \-nənsē, -si\ *n* -ES [ˈ*malignant* + *-cy*] **1 a :** the quality or state of being malignant **b :** an instance of malignant behavior or malignant nature **2 a** *of a tumor* **:** exhibition of malignant qualities **:** VIRULENCE **b :** a malignant tumor **syn** see MALICE
[1]**ma·lig·nant** \-nənt\ *adj* [LL *malignant-, malignans,* pres. part. of *malignare, malignari* to act maliciously] **1 a** *obs* **:** REBELLIOUS, DISAFFECTED, MALCONTENT **b :** evil in nature or influence or effect **:** INJURIOUS, BALEFUL, MALIGN ⟨astrological belief in the ~ power of the stars⟩ **c :** having or showing or indicative of intense often vicious ill will **:** desiring or causing or rejoicing in the sufferings of others **:** extremely malevolent or malicious ⟨the ~ tongues of gossipers⟩ **2** *med* **:** tending to produce death or deterioration ⟨~ malaria⟩: **a** *of a tumor* **:** unencapsulated and tending to infiltrate, metastasize, and in the absence of treatment terminate fatally — opposed to *benign* **b :** severe and rapidly progressive ⟨~ hypertension⟩ **c :** of unfavorable prognosis **:** not responding favorably to treatment ⟨psychotic reactions with a ~ trend⟩ — **ma·lig·nant·ly** *adv*
[2]**malignant** \"\ *n* -S **1** *archaic* **:** one that is rebellious, disaffected, or malcontent **2** *archaic, usu cap* **:** CAVALIER 4a
**malignant catarrh** *also* **malignant catarrhal fever** *n* **1 :** a catarrhal fever of cattle apparently caused by a filterable virus and marked by acute edematous inflammation of the respiratory ahd digestive systems and sometimes of the sinuses of the head and eyes and genitourinary organs **2 :** hepatic coccidiosis of the rabbit
**malignant edema** *n* **:** inflammatory edema in infections; *specif* **:** an acute wound infection of wild and domestic animals and rarely man that is clinically indistinguishable from blackleg and that is caused by an anaerobic toxin-producing bacterium (*Clostridium septicum*) — compare BIGHEAD, BRAXY
**malignant hypertension** *n* **:** essential hypertension characterized by acute onset, severe symptoms, rapidly progressive course, and poor prognosis
**malignant jaundice** *n* **:** canine piroplasmosis
**malignant lymphoma** *n* **:** HODGKIN'S DISEASE
**malignant malaria** *n* **:** FALCIPARUM MALARIA
**malignant neutropenia** *n* **:** AGRANULOCYTOSIS
**malignant pustule** *n* **:** localized anthrax of the skin taking the form of a pimple surrounded by a zone of edema and hyperemia and tending to become necrotic and ulcerated
**malignant tumor** *n* **:** a metastatic tumor **:** CANCER
**maligned** *past of* MALIGN
**ma·lign·er** \məˈlīnə(r)\ *n* -S **:** one that maligns
**maligning** *pres part of* MALIGN
**ma·lig·ni·ty** \məˈlignəd·ē, -ətē, -i\ *n* -ES [ME *malignitee,* fr. MF *malignité,* fr. L *malignitat-, malignitas,* fr. *malignus* malign + *-itat-, -itas* -ity — more at MALIGN] **1 :** great malignancy or malice **2 :** an instance of malignant or malicious behavior or nature **syn** see MALICE
**ma·lign·ly** *adv* **:** in a malign manner
**maligns** *pres 3d sing of* MALIGN
**ma·li·hi·ni** \ˌmäləˈhēnē\ *n* -S [Hawaiian] **:** a newcomer or stranger among the people of Hawaii
**ma·lik** \ˈmälik\ *n* -S [Hindi *mālik,* fr. Ar] **1 :** a chief or leader (as in a village) in parts of the subcontinent of India **:** HEADMAN **2 :** ZAMINDAR
**ma·li·ka·na** \ˌmäləˈkänə\ *n* -S [Hindi *mālikāna,* lit., proprietary, fr. Per, fr. Ar *mālik*] **1 :** a fee paid to a malik by way of rent or duty on land **2 :** a pension or allowance granted by the government to a malik
**mal·i·ki** \ˈmaləkē\ *n* -S *usu cap* [Ar *malikīy* of or relating to Malik, fr. *Malik* ibn-Anas †A.D.795 Moslem jurist] **1 :** an orthodox school of Muslim jurisprudence predominating in No. Africa and Upper Egypt — compare HANAFI, HANBALI, SHAFIʿI **2** *or* **mal·i·kite** *or* **mal·e·kite** \ˈmalə,kīt\ [*Malik* ibn-Anas †A.D.795 + E *-ite*] **:** a follower of the Maliki school
**ma·lin·che** \məˈlinchē\ *n* -S [AmerSp, fr. Nahuatl *Malintzin* (Marina) †1550? Aztec slave mistress of Hernando Cortes] **:** a man or boy dressed as a woman in a Mexican dance drama
**ma·line** \məˈlēn\ *n* -S *sometimes cap* [F, Mechlin lace, back-formation fr. *malines,* taken as a plural] **:** MALINES 2
**ma·lines** \məˈlēn\ *n, pl* **malines** *sometimes cap* [F, fr. *Malines* (Mechelen), city in northern Belgium] **1** *or* **malines lace :** MECHLIN LACE **2 :** a fine stiff net that has a hexagonal mesh and that is made of silk or rayon (as for millinery) or hair (as for veils)
**ma·lin·ger** \məˈliŋgə(r)\ *vi* **malingered; malingered; malingering** \-g(ə)riŋ\ **malingers** [F *malingre* sickly, ailing, fr. (assumed) OF *malingre,* fr. OF *mal* badly + *haingre* thin, lean, perh. of Gmc origin; akin to MHG *hager* thin, lean; akin to Av *kasu-* little — more at MAL-] **1 :** to pretend to be ill or otherwise physically or mentally incapacitated so as to avoid duty or work ⟨a ~*ing* soldier⟩ **2 :** to deliberately induce, protract, or exaggerate actual illness or other incapacity so as to avoid duty or work **syn** see DODGE
**ma·lin·ger·er** \-gərə(r)\ *n* -S **:** one that malingers
**ma·lin·ke** \məˈliŋ(ˌ)kā\ *n, pl* **malinke** *or* **malinkes** *usu cap* **1 a :** a people of Mandingo affiliation widespread in the western part of Africa from Portuguese Guinea into the French Sudan **b :** a member of such people **2 :** a Mande language of the Malinke people
**ma·li·nois** \ˌmalənˈwä\ *n, pl* **malinois** *usu cap* [F, fr. *malinois,* adj., of, or from Malines, fr. *Malines* (Mechelen), city in northern Belgium] **:** the largely fawn-colored short-haired variety of Belgian sheepdog
**mal·i·now·skite** \ˌmaləˈnäf,skīt\ *n* -S [ISV *malinowsk-* (fr. E *Malinowski,* 19th cent. Russ. civil engineer) + *-ite*] **:** a tetrahedrite containing 13 to 16 percent of lead
**mal·integration** \ˌmal+\ *n* [ˈ*mal-* + *integration*] **:** defective integration ⟨~ of one group with another⟩ ⟨personality ~⟩
**mal·investment** \"+\ *n* [ˈ*mal-* + *investment*] **:** bad investment ⟨a ~ that nearly led to bankruptcy⟩
**maliseet** *usu cap, var of* MALECITE
**ma·lism** \ˈmä,lizəm\ *n* -S [L *malus* bad + E *-ism* — more at small] **:** the doctrine that the world is evil
**mal·i·son** \ˈmaləsən, -əzən\ *n* -S [ME *malisoun,* fr. OF *maleicun, maleïcon,* fr. LL *malediction-, maledictio* — more at MALEDICTION] **:** MALEDICTION, CURSE
**mal·kin** \ˈmȯ(l)kən, ˈmalk-, ˈmäk-\ *n* -S [ME *malkyn,* fr. *Malkyn,* feminine name, prob. fr. *Mall* (nickname fr. the name *Maria, Mary*) + *-kyn, -kin* -kin] **1** *now dial Eng* **a :** a pole with a bundle of rags at one end used for cleaning out a baker's oven **b :** a ragged effigy **:** SCARECROW **2** *now dial Brit* **a :** an untidy woman **:** SLATTERN **b** (1) **:** CAT (2) **:** HARE
**mal·kite** \ˈmal,kīt\ *n* -S *usu cap* [Syr *malkā* king + E *-ite*] **:** MELCHITE
[1]**mall** \ˈmȯl\ *var of* MAUL
[2]**mall** \ˈmȯl *also* ˈmäl *or* ˈmal\ *n* -S [by shortening & alter. (influenced in pronunciation by [1]*mall*) fr. *pall-mall*] **1 a :** the mallet used in the game of pall-mall **b :** the game of pall-mall **c :** an alley used for this game **2** [fr. *The Mall,* fashionable promenade in St. James's Park, London, that was originally a pall-mall alley] **a :** a usu. public area (typically a lane or similar strip) often set with trees or bushes or flowers and designed as a promenade for leisurely strolling or as a pedestrian walk **b :** a usu. paved or grassy strip between two roadways **:** MEDIAN STRIP ⟨a highway divided by a ~⟩
**mal·la·drite** \məˈlä,drīt, ˈmalə,d-\ *n* -S [It, fr. Alessandro *Malladra* †1944 Ital. geologist + It *-ite*] **:** a sodium fluosilicate $Na_2SiF_6$ occurring in minute hexagonal crystals in fumaroles in the crater of Vesuvius near Naples in Italy
**mal·lan·gong** \ˈmalən,gäŋ\ *n* -S [native name in Australia] **:** PLATYPUS
**mal·lard** \ˈmalə(r)d\ *n, pl* **mallard** *or* **mallards** [ME, fr. MF *malart, mallart,* fr. OF, prob. fr. *male, masle* male + *-art* -ard — more at MALE] **1 :** a common and widely distributed wild duck (*Anas platyrhynchos*) of the northern hemisphere that is a dabbler, is the source of the domestic ducks, and is distinguished in the male by a greenish black head and neck, white collar, chestnut breast, grayish brown back, purple speculum, and grayish white underparts **2** *archaic* **:** a male mallard
**mal·lard·ite** \ˈmalə(r),dīt\ *n* -S [F, fr. Ernest *Mallard* †1894 Fr. mineralogist + F *-ite*] **:** hydrous sulfate of manganese $MnSO_4.7H_2O$
**mal·le·a·bil·i·ty** \ˌmalēəˈbiləd·ē, -lyəb-, ÷-ləb-, -lətē, -i\ *n* [F *malléabilité,* fr. *malléable* malleable + *-ité* -ity] **:** the quality or state of being malleable
**mal·lea·bil·i·za·tion** \ˌ≈(≈)≈bələˈzāshən, -(ˌ)bil-, -ˌlīz-\ *n* -S [*malleabiliz-* (fr. *malleableize*) + *-ation*] **:** the process of malleableizing
**mal·lea·ble** \ˈmalēəbəl, -lyəb-, ÷-ləb-\ *adj* [ME *malliable,* fr. MF or ML; MF *malleable,* fr. ML *malleabilis,* fr. *malleare* to

hammer (fr. L *malleus* hammer) + L *-abilis* -able — more at MAUL] **1 :** capable of being extended or shaped by beating with a hammer or by the pressure of rollers ⟨most metals are ~⟩ — compare DUCTILE **2 :** capable of being formed or transformed **:** susceptible of being fashioned into a new or different form or shape **:** not rigidly fixed in condition or direction **:** plastically open to outside forces or influences **:** adaptable to other conditions or needs or uses **:** IMPRESSIONABLE ⟨finds a sort of ~ mind in front of him that he can play with as he will —John Masefield⟩ ⟨the ~ character of youth⟩ ⟨tactics that are ~ and vary with circumstances⟩ **syn** see PLASTIC

**malleable iron** *also* **malleable cast iron** *n* **:** cast iron containing usu. from 2 to 3 percent carbon and 1.5 to 0.8 percent silicon and produced by annealing white cast iron of this composition in order to convert hard brittle cementite to graphite in nodular form so that the material will have greater ductility than white iron or ordinary gray iron containing graphite in flake form

**mal·lea·ble·ize** *also* **mal·lea·blize** \-bə,līz\ *vt* -ED/-ING/-S **:** to make malleable ⟨*malleableizing* cast iron⟩

**mal·lea·ble·ness** *n* -ES **:** MALLEABILITY

**mal·le·al** \'malēəl\ *also* **mal·le·ar** \-ēə(r)\ *adj* [prob. fr. (assumed) NL *mallealis, mallearis,* fr. NL *malleus* + L *-alis* -al or *-aris* -ar — more at MALLEUS] **:** relating to the malleus

**[1]mal·le·ate** \-ē,āt\ *vt* -ED/-ING/-S [ML *malleatus,* past part. of *malleare* to hammer] **:** to beat with a hammer **:** POUND ⟨the surfaces of some fragments suggested that the clay had been poorly *malleated —Amer. Antiquity*⟩; *specif* **:** to beat or mark or dent (a metal) with a hammer in working or decorating

**[2]mal·le·ate** \-,āt, -ət\ *adj* [NL *malleatus,* fr. *malleus* + L *-atus* -ate] **:** having a malleus

**mal·le·a·tion** \,==ˈāshən\ *n* -S [ML *malleation-, malleatio,* fr. *malleatus* (past part. of *malleare* to hammer) + L *-ion-, -io* -ion] **1 :** the action of malleating or state of being malleated **2 :** a mark or dent like one made by malleating

**[1]mal·lee** \'malē\ *n* -S [*mallee* native name in Victoria, Australia] **1** *also* **mallee box :** any of several low-growing Australian eucalypts; *esp* **:** one producing several stems from the base (as *Eucalyptus dumosa* or *E. oleosa*) **2 a :** a dense brushwood or thicket formed by mallees **b :** an area covered by mallee brushwood or a mallee thicket

**[2]mallee** *var of* MALI

**mallee bird** *or* **mallee fowl** *or* **mallee hen** *n* [*[1]mallee*] **:** LEIPOA

**mal·le·in** \'malēən\ *n* -S [ISV *malle-* (fr. NL *mallei* — specific epithet of the glanders-producing bacterium *Actinobacillus mallei* —, gen. of *malleus* glanders) + *-in*] **:** a product containing toxic principles of the bacillus of glanders and used to test for the presence of infection with that organism

**mal·le·in·i·za·tion** \,==ənəˈzāshən, -,nīˈz-\ *n* -S **:** the action of malleinizing or condition of being malleinized

**mal·le·in·ize** \'==ə,nīz\ *vt* -ED/-ING/-S [ISV *mallein* + *-ize*] **:** to test with mallein

**mal·le·muck** \'malə,mək\ *also* **mol·le·mock** \'mälə,mäk\ *or* **mol·ly·mawk** \'mälē,mȯk\ *n* -S [D *mallemuk, mallemok,* fr. *mal* silly (fr. MD) + *mok* gull; akin to MLG *mal* silly and to ON *mār* gull — more at MEW] **:** one of several large oceanic birds (as the fulmar or petrel)

**mallenders** *var of* MALANDERS

**mal·leo·incudal** \¦malēō+\ *adj* [*malleo-* (fr. NL *malleus*) + *incudal*] **:** of or relating to the malleus and incus

**mal·le·o·lar** \məˈlēələ(r)\ *adj* [prob. fr. (assumed) NL *malleolaris,* fr. NL *malleolus* + L *-aris* -ar] **:** of or relating to a malleolus esp. of the ankle

**mal·le·o·lare** \mə,lēəˈla(a)rē, ,malē-, -ˈlärē\ *n* -S [NL, prob. fr. neut. of (assumed) NL *malleolaris*] **:** MALLEOLAR POINT

**malleolar point** *n* **:** the tip of the malleolus of the tibia

**mal·le·o·lus** \məˈlēələs\ *n, pl* **malleo·li** \-,lī\ [NL, fr. L, little hammer, dim. of *malleus* hammer — more at MAUL] **:** the rounded lateral projection on each bone of the leg at the ankle

**mal·leo·my·ces** \,malēəˈmī,sēz\ [NL, fr. *malleo-* (fr. *malleus* glanders) + *-myces*] *syn of* ACTINOBACILLUS

**[1]mal·let** \'malət, *usu* -əd·+V\ *n* -S [ME *maillet,* fr. MF, fr. OF, fr. *mail* maul, mallet + *-et* — more at MAUL] **:** a hammer that has a cylindrical typically barrel-shaped head of wood or of other soft material: as **a :** a tool with a large head for driving another tool (as a chisel) or for striking a surface without marring it **b** (1) **:** an implement with a long handle and large head used in the game of croquet for striking the ball (2) **:** an implement with a very long narrow handle and a rather narrow tapering light head used in the game of polo for striking the ball **c :** a light hammer with a small head used in playing a vibraphone or similar percussion instrument

mallet a

**[2]mallet** \"\ *vt* -ED/-ING/-S **:** to strike with or as if with a mallet

**[3]mallet** \"\ *also* **mallet bark** *or* **mallet wood** *n* -S [*mallet* native name in Western Australia] **1 :** any of several Australian gum trees of the genus *Eucalyptus* esp. when rich in tannin **2 :** CALIFORNIA LAUREL

**mallet cutting** *n* [*[1]mallet*] **1 :** LEAF-BUD CUTTING **2 :** a hardwood cutting of current season's growth with a heel of the previous season's growth

**mal·le·us** \'malēəs\ *n* [NL, fr. L, hammer] **1** *pl* **mal·lei** \-ē,ī\ **a :** the outermost of the three auditory ossicles of mammals consisting of a head, neck, short process, long process, and handle, the short process and handle being fastened to the tympanic membrane, and the head articulating with the head of the incus — see EAR illustration **b :** one of the hard lateral pieces of the mastax of rotifers **c :** one of the middle pair of Weberian ossicles in certain fishes **2** *cap* **:** a genus of bivalve mollusks (family Pteriidae) containing the typical hammer shells **3** -ES [NL, fr. LL, a disease of animals, prob. fr. L, hammer] **:** GLANDERS

**mallie** *var of* MALI

**mal·ling rootstock** \'mȯliŋ-\ *n, usu cap M* [fr. East *Malling* Research Station, Kent, England] **:** any of several rootstocks for fruit trees developed by the East Malling Research Station, Kent, England that are propagated vegetatively and used esp. for dwarfing apple trees — see PARADISE 6

**mal·lo·mys** \'malə,mis\ *n, cap* [NL, fr. Gk *mallos* lock of wool + NL *-mys*] **:** a genus of New Guinea giant rats often reaching a length of 2½ feet

**mal·loph·a·ga** \məˈläfəgə\ *n pl, cap* [NL, fr. Gk *mallos* lock of wool + NL *-phaga*] **:** an order of secondarily wingless insects comprising the bird lice — **mal·loph·a·gan** \-gən\ *adj or n* — **mal·loph·a·gous** \-gəs\ *adj*

**ma·llor·quin** \¦ma(l),yȯ(r)¦kēn\ *adj or n, usu cap* [Sp *mallorquín,* fr. *Mallorca* Majorca, largest of the Balearic islands off the east coast of Spain + *-ín* -ine (fr. L *-inus*)] **:** MAJORCAN

**mal·lo·seismic** \¦malō+\ *adj* [Gk *mallon* rather, more (compar. of *mala* very) + E *seismic* — more at MELIORATE] **:** of, relating to, or being a region subject to frequent destructive earthquakes

**mal·lo·tus** \məˈlōd·əs\ *n, cap* [NL, fr. Gk *mallōtos* fleecy, fr. *mallos* lock of wool] **:** a genus of tropical Asiatic and Australian trees (family Euphorbiaceae) with diclinous flowers of which the staminate ones have numerous stamens — see KAMALA

**mal·low** \'ma(,)lō, -lə; -lōw, -lō+V\ *n* -S [ME *malwe,* fr. OE *mealwe,* fr. L *malva,* of non-IE origin; akin to the source of Gk *molochē, malachē* mallow] **1 :** a plant of the family Malvaceae: as **a :** an erect or decumbent European perennial herb (*Malva sylvestris*) with axillary clusters of rosy purple flowers **b :** DWARF MALLOW **2 :** a moderate purplish red that is bluer and less strong than average rose, paler than violine pink, and bluer and paler than magenta rose or average fuchsia rose

**mallow family** *n* **:** MALVACEAE

**mallow pink** *n* **:** a moderate purplish pink to light reddish purple

**mallow purple** *n* **1** *or* **mallow red :** MALLOW 2 **2 :** MAUVE 2

**mallow rose** *n* **:** ROSE MALLOW 1

**mally** *var of* MALI

**[1]malm** \'mä|m, 'mȧ| *also* |lm\ *n* -S [ME *malme,* fr. OE *mealm-;* akin to ON *malmr* metal, ore, Goth *malma* sand, OE *melu* meal — more at MEAL] **1** *dial chiefly Eng* **a :** a soft friable chalky limestone **b :** a light clayey soil containing chalk **:** MARL **2 a :** an artificial mixture of clay and chalk used in the manufacture of bricks **b :** MALM BRICK

**[2]malm** \"\ *vt* -ED/-ING/-S **1 :** to convert (clay and chalk) into artificial malm **2 :** to cover or treat (brick earth) with artificial malm

**[3]malm** \"\ *adj, usu cap* **:** of, relating to, or constituting a subdivision of the European Jurassic — see GEOLOGIC TIME table

**mal·ma** \'malmə\ *or* **malma trout** *n* -S [*malma* native name in Kamchatka, northeast U.S.S.R.] **:** DOLLY VARDEN 2

**mal·mai·son** \¦malmə¦zōⁿ\ *n* -S *usu cap* [fr. *Malmaison,* château near Paris, France] **:** any of various tender greenhouse carnations with stiff massive growth and large fully double usu. pink flowers

**malmaison rose** *n* **:** a vivid purplish red that is redder and paler than Indiana and redder and lighter than rubellite — called also *rose malmaison*

**malm brick** *n* **:** a brick made from marl or malm

**mal·mi·gnatte** \¦malmən¦yat\ *n* -S [It *malmignatta,* fr. *mal, malo* bad (fr. L *malus*) + *mignatta* leech — more at SMALL] **:** a small black venomous spider (*Latrodectus tridecimguttatus*) of southern Europe having 13 small red spots on the abdomen

**malmö** *or* **malmo** \'mal(,)mō, -l,mər(·), -l,mə̄\ *adj, usu cap* [fr. *Malmö,* city in southwest Sweden] **:** of or from the city of Malmö, Sweden **:** of the kind or style prevalent in Malmö

**malm rubber** *n* **:** a soft malm brick that is capable of being worked into special shapes by cutting or rubbing

**malm·sey** \'mämzē\ *n* -S *often cap* [ME *malmesey,* fr. ML *Malmasia* Monemvasia, town off the coast of the southeastern Peloponnesus, Greece] **1 :** a sweet aromatic wine made from the malvasia grape and produced orig. around the town of Monemvasia and later elsewhere throughout the Mediterranean and in the Canary and Madeira islands **2 :** the sweetest variety of Madeira wine

**malmstone** \'=,=\ *or* **malm rock** *n* [*[1]malm*] **1** *dial chiefly Eng* **:** MALM **2** *dial Eng* **:** a cherty rock similar to flint used in building and paving

**malmy** \'mä|mi, 'mȧ| *also* |lmi; *in sense 2 also* 'mȯ-\ *adj* -ER/-EST [*[1]malm* + *-y*] **1** *dial Eng* **:** containing malm **:** resembling malm **2** *dial Eng* **:** SOFT, MELLOW

**mal·nourished** \(')mal+\ *adj* [*[1]mal-* + *nourished*] **1 :** exhibiting the physical and physiological results of an inadequate diet **2 :** UNDERNOURISHED

**mal·nourishment** \"+\ *n* [*[1]mal-* + *nourishment*] **:** MALNUTRITION

**mal·nutrition** \¦=+\ *n* [*[1]mal-* + *nutrition*] **:** faulty nutrition due to inadequate or unbalanced intake of nutrients or their impaired assimilation or utilization

**ma·lo** \'mälō\ *n* -S [Hawaiian] **:** a loincloth now worn by Hawaiian men only on ceremonial occasions — compare MARO

**malo-** — see [2]MAL-

**ma·lo animo** \'mā,lōˈanə,mō\ *adv* [L, with bad intent] **:** with evil or wrongful intent **:** MALICIOUSLY — used in English law esp. with respect to forgery

**mal·observation** \¦mal+\ *n* [*[1]mal-* + *observation*] **:** erroneous observation or interpretation **:** MISREADING

**ma·lo·ca** \məˈlōkə\ *n* -S [Pg, fr. AmerSp, raid, attack fr. Araucanian *malocan* to fight] **:** a large communal dwelling of some So. American Indian peoples (as in Brazil); *also* **:** the group inhabiting such a dwelling

**mal·occluded** \¦mal+\ *adj* [*[1]mal-* + *occluded*] **:** characterized by malocclusion

**mal·occlusion** \"+\ *n* [*[1]mal-* + *occlusion*] **:** improper occlusion; *esp* **:** an abnormality in the occlusal relations of teeth or dentures

**mal·odor** \(')mal+\ *n* [*[1]mal-* + *odor*] **:** an offensive odor

**[1]mal·odor·ant** \maˈlōdərənt\ *n* -S [*malodor* + *-ant*] **:** an ill-smelling substance

**[2]malodorant** \(')=¦===\ *adj* **:** MALODOROUS

**mal·odorous** \(')mal+\ *adj* [*[1]mal-* + *odorous*] **1 :** ill-smelling **:** RANK, FETID, STINKING ⟨stone castles and ~ hovels —T.B. Costain⟩ ⟨the flavor . . . like that of many ~ cheeses, is delicate —Marjorie K. Rawlings⟩ **2 :** highly improper **:** SCANDALOUS ⟨methods, questionable when not ~ —John Mason Brown⟩

**ma·lo·ji·llo** \,mäləˈhē(,)(y)ō\ *or* **ma·lo·ji·lla** \-(y)ə\ *n* -S [*malojillo* fr. AmerSp, dim. of *malojo* forage plant, fr. Sp *malhojo* waste grass, fr. *mal, malo* bad (fr. L *malus*) + *-hojo* leaf (fr. L *folium*); *malojilla* fr. AmerSp, dim. of *maloja* forage plant, fem. of *malojo* — more at SMALL, BLADE] **:** PARA GRASS

**mal·o·nate** \'malə,nāt, -nət\ *n* -S [ISV *malonic* (in *malonic acid*) + *-ate*] **:** a salt or ester of malonic acid

**ma·lo·nic acid** \məˈlōnik, -länik-\ *n* [*malonic* fr. F *malonique* (in *acide malonique* malonic acid), alter. of *malique* malic (in *acide malique* malic acid) — more at MALIC ACID] **:** a crystalline dicarboxylic acid $CH_2(COOH)_2$ obtained by oxidation of malic acid but usu. made by hydrolysis of cyanoacetic acid and used esp. in the form of its diethyl ester in organic synthesis (as of barbiturates and vitamins of the B complex)

**mal·o·nyl** \'malə,nil, -nēl\ *n* -S [ISV *malonic* (in *malonic acid*) + *-yl*] **:** the bivalent radical $CH_2(CO)_2$ of malonic acid

**malonylurea** \'==,=='==\ *n* [*malonyl* + *urea*] **:** BARBITURIC ACID

**ma·loo climber** \'mä,lü-\ *also* **maloo** *n* -S [*maloo* fr. Hindi *māl* garland, rope, fr. Skt *mālā* garland] **:** an East Indian climbing shrub (*Bauhinia vahlii*) with a tough fibrous bark that is used in rope manufacture

**mal·o·pe** \'malə(,)pē\ *n, cap* [NL, fr. L, mallow] **:** a small genus of chiefly European annual herbs (family Malvaceae) having flowers subtended by three large cordate bracts

**mal·pa·is** \,mälpäˈēs\ *n* -ES [Sp *mal país* bad country] **1** *Southwest* **:** rough country underlain by dark esp. basaltic lava **:** BADLANDS **2** *Southwest* **:** basaltic lava

**mal·pigh·ia** \malˈpigēə\ *n, cap* [NL, fr. Marcello *Malpighi* †1694 Ital. anatomist + NL *-ia*] **:** a genus of tropical American shrubs and trees (family Malpighiaceae) having a glandular calyx and drupaceous fruit — see JIQUI

**mal·pigh·i·a·ce·ae** \=,=='āsē,ē\ *n pl, cap* [NL, fr. *Malpighia,* type genus + *-aceae*] **:** a family of tropical herbs, shrubs, or trees (order Geraniales) having stinging hairs, usu. opposite leaves, and yellow or red flowers with prominently clawed petals and often winged or lobed tricarpellary fruit — **mal·pigh·i·a·ceous** \¦=,==¦āshəs\ *adj*

**mal·pigh·i·an** \(')mal¦pigēən\ *adj, usu cap* [Marcello *Malpighi* †1694 + E *-an*] **:** of, relating to, or discovered by Marcello Malpighi

**malpighian cell** *n, usu cap M* **:** PALISADE CELL

**malpighian corpuscle** *also* **malpighian body** *n, often cap M* **1 :** the part of a nephron that consists of Bowman's capsule and its included glomerulus **2** *also* **malpighian follicle :** any of the small masses of adenoid tissue formed around the branches of the splenic artery in the spleen

**malpighian layer** *n, usu cap M* **:** the deeper part of the epidermis consisting of cells whose protoplasm has not yet changed into horny material

**malpighian pyramid** *n, usu cap M* **:** any of the conical masses forming the medullary substance of the kidney, projecting as papillae into the renal pelvis, and being made up of bundles of straight uriniferous tubes that open at the apex of the pyramid

**malpighian tube** *also* **malpighian tubule** *or* **malpighian vessel** *n, usu cap M* **:** one of the group of long blind vessels opening into the posterior part of the alimentary canal in most insects and some other arthropods and functioning primarily as excretory organs

**malpighian tuft** *n, usu cap M* **:** GLOMERULUS

**mal·posed** \(')mal¦pōzd\ *adj* [fr. *malposition,* after such pairs as E *composition: composed*] **:** characterized by malposition

**mal·position** \¦mal+\ *n* [*[1]mal-* + *position*] **:** wrong or faulty position **:** MISPLACEMENT

**[1]mal·practice** \(')=+\ *n* [*[1]mal-* + *practice*] **1 a :** a dereliction from professional duty whether intentional, criminal, or merely negligent by one rendering professional services that results in injury, loss, or damage to the recipient of those services or to those entitled to rely upon them or that affects the public interest adversely **b :** the failure of one rendering professional services to exercise that degree of skill and learning commonly applied under all the circumstances in the community by the average prudent reputable member of the profession with the result of injury, loss, or damage to the recipient of those services or to those entitled to rely upon them **2 :** an injurious, negligent, or improper practice **:** MALFEASANCE, WRONGDOING ⟨cheating and fixing and other ~*s* —F.A. Wrensch⟩ ⟨bewailing some current academic ~ with the English language —D.J.Lloyd⟩

**[2]malpractice** \"\ *vi* **:** to engage in or commit malpractice ⟨the death of the boy . . . is laid at his door as a *malpracticing* doctor —Rose Feld⟩

**mal·practitioner** \¦=+\ *n* [*[1]mal-* + *practitioner*] **:** one who engages in or commits malpractice

**mal·praxis** \(')=+\ *n* [*[1]mal-* + *praxis*] **:** MALPRACTICE

**mal·presentation** \"+\ *n* [*[1]mal-* + *presentation*] **:** abnormal presentation of the fetus at birth

**mals** *pl of* MAL

**malster** *var of* MALTSTER

**[1]malt** \'mȯlt\ *n* -S *often attrib* [ME, fr. OE *mealt;* akin to OHG *malz* malt, OS & ON *malt;* derivative fr. the root of E *[1]melt*] **1 :** a material that consists of grain (as barley or oats) softened by steeping in water, allowed to germinate in order to develop the enzyme diastase which is capable of saccharifying the the starch of the material itself and of raw grain mixed with it, usu. dried in a kiln, and often ground and that is used esp. in brewing and distilling and as a nutrient and digestive — compare GREEN MALT, WORT **2 a :** MALT LIQUOR **b :** MALT WHISKEY **3 :** MALTED MILK

**[2]malt** \"\ *vb* -ED/-ING/-S [ME *malten,* fr. *malt,* n.] *vt* **1 :** to convert into malt ⟨~ barley⟩ **2 :** to make or treat with malt or malt extract ⟨~ beer⟩ ~ *vi* **1 :** to become malt **2 :** to make grain into malt

**mal·ta** \'mȯltə\ *adj, usu cap* [fr. *Malta,* island in the Mediterranean sea south of Sicily] **:** of or from the country of Malta **:** of the kind or style prevalent in Malta

**malta fever** *n, usu cap M* **:** brucellosis caused by a bacterium (*Brucella melitensis*)

**maltalent** *n* [ME, fr. MF, fr. OF, fr. *mal* bad + *talent* disposition — more at TALENT] *archaic* **:** ILL WILL, MALICE

**malta orange** *or* **maltese orange** *n, usu cap M* **:** BLOOD ORANGE

**malt·ase** \'mȯl,tās, -āz\ *n* -S [ISV *[1]malt* + *-ase*] **:** an enzyme that accelerates the hydrolysis of maltose and other alpha-glucosides to glucose and that is found in plants, animals, yeast, and bacteria **:** an alpha-glucosidase

**malted** *n* -S [fr. past part. of *[2]malt*] **:** MALTED MILK

**malted milk** *n* [*malted* fr. past part. of *[2]malt*] **1 :** milk that has been malted; *specif* **:** a soluble easily digested powder prepared from dried milk and malted cereals **2 :** a beverage made by dissolving malted milk in milk or other liquid often with ice cream and flavoring added

**malt·er** \'mȯltə(r)\ *n* -S [*[2]malt* + *-er*] *now dial Brit* **:** MALTSTER

**[1]mal·tese** \(')mȯl¦tēz, -ēs\ *n, pl* **maltese** [*Malta* + E *-ese,* n. suffix] **1** *cap* **:** a native or inhabitant of Malta **2** *cap* **:** the Semitic language of the Maltese people **3** *usu cap* **:** any of various animals or breeds of animals originating in or believed to have originated in Malta: as **a :** a breed of asses **b :** a breed of large-uddered usu. hornless milch goats **c :** a breed of white long-coated toy dogs with black nose and very dark eyes **d :** a breed of erect hen-type pigeons with a turned-up fanlike tail **e :** MALTESE CAT

**[2]maltese** \"\ *adj, usu cap* [*Malta* + E *-ese,* adj. suffix] **1 a :** of, relating to, or characteristic of Malta **b :** of, relating to, or characteristic of the people of Malta **2 :** of, relating to, or characteristic of the Maltese language

**maltese cat** *n, usu cap M* **:** a bluish gray domestic short-haired cat

**maltese cross** *n, usu cap M* **1 a :** a cross formée **b :** a cross resembling the cross formée but having the outer face of each arm indented in a V — called also *cross of eight points* **2 :** a Eurasian garden perennial (*Lychnis chalcedonica*) having scarlet or rarely white flowers in dense terminal heads — called also *scarlet lychnis* **3 a :** a star wheel with teeth shaped like a Maltese cross used with a finger stop wheel to limit the uncoiling of a watch mainspring — called also *Geneva stop* **b :** a similar device in a motion-picture projector used to advance a film one or more frames at a time

Maltese cross 1b

**maltese lace** *n, usu cap M* **:** a lace of Maltese origin: **a :** a fine bobbin lace of silk **b :** a guipure with geometric designs

**malt extract** *n* **1 :** a sugary mucilaginous substance obtained from wort **2 a :** a sweet light-brown syrupy liquid prepared by infusing malt with water and evaporating and used chiefly in medicine and foods; *also* **:** a powder made by drying this liquid **b :** a weak alcoholic preparation made like beer but darker in color and thicker in consistency

**mal·tha** \'malthə\ *also* **mal·thite** \-,thīt\ *n* -S [*maltha* fr. L, soft mixture of wax and pitch, fr. Gk *maltha, malthē;* akin to Gk *malthakos* soft; *malthite* fr. *maltha* + *-ite* — more at MILD] **:** a black viscid substance intermediate between petroleum and asphalt — called also *earth pitch, mineral tar*

**mal·the** \'mal(,)thē\ [NL, fr. Gk *malthē,* a large fish] *syn of* OGCOCEPHALUS

**mal·thi·dae** \'=thə,dē\ [NL, fr. *Malthe* + *-idae*] *syn of* OGCOCEPHALIDAE

**malthouse** \'=,=\ *n* [ME *malthous,* fr. OE *mealthūs,* fr. *mealt* malt + *hūs* house — more at MALT, HOUSE] **:** a building in which malt is made

**[1]mal·thu·sian** \malˈth(y)üzhən, ÷mȯl-, -zēən\ *n* -S *usu cap* [Thomas R. *Malthus* †1834 Eng. economist + E *-an,* n. suffix] **:** a supporter of Malthus or Malthusianism

**[2]malthusian** \(')=¦=(=)=\ *adj, usu cap* [Thomas R. *Malthus* †1834 + E *-an,* adj. suffix] **:** of or relating to Malthus or Malthusianism

**mal·thu·sian·ism** \-,nizəm\ *n* -S *usu cap* **:** the doctrines of Malthus holding esp. that population tends to increase at a faster rate than its means of subsistence and that widespread poverty and degradation of the lower classes inevitably result unless the population is preventively checked by moral restraint or positively checked esp. by disease, famine, or war

**malt·i·ness** \'mȯltēnəs, -tin-\ *n* -ES **:** the quality or state of being malty

**malt·ing** \'mȯltiŋ\ *n* -S [ME, fr. gerund of *malten* to malt — more at MALT] **1 :** the act or process of making or of becoming malt; *specif* **:** the conversion of the starches of a distillery mash from starch to fermentable sugar by the enzymes of the malt **2 :** MALTHOUSE

**malt liquor** *n* **:** a fermented liquor (as beer) made with malt

**malt·man** \'=mən\ *n, pl* **maltmen** [ME, fr. *[1]malt* + *man*] **:** MALTSTER

**mal·to** \'mal(,)tō\ *n, pl* **malto** *or* **maltos** *usu cap* **1 a :** a Dravidian people of Bengal **b :** a member of such people **2 :** the language of the Malto people

**mal·to·bionic acid** \¦mȯl(,)tō,bī¦änik-\ *n* [*maltobionic* ISV *maltobiose* maltose (ISV *[1]malt* + *-o-* + *biose*) + *-onic*] **:** MALTONIC ACID

**malt·ol** \'mȯl,tōl, -tȯl\ *n* -S [ISV *[1]malt* + *-ol*] **:** a crystalline compound $C_6H_6O_3$ derived from gamma-pyrone, found esp. in pine needles, larch bark, and chicory, and formed when streptomycin is hydrolyzed and when barley and other grains are roasted

**mal·tolte** *or* **male·tolt** \'mal,tōlt\ *n* -S [MF *maletoulte, malletoute* additional duty or tax, fr. OF *mauthoste,* fr. *mau, mal* bad + *toste, tolte, toute* pillage, tax, fr. (assumed) VL *tollita,* fem. of (assumed) VL *tollitus,* past part. of L *tollere* to lift up, take away — more at MAL-, TOLERATE] **:** an arbitrary customs duty levied by the British crown during the late medieval period in addition to the regular port charges

**mal·ton·ic acid** \(')mȯl¦tänik-\ *n* [*maltonic* ISV *[1]malt* + *-onic*] **:** a syrupy aldonic acid $C_{12}H_{22}O_{12}$ obtained from maltose — called also *maltobionic acid*

**malt·ose** \'mȯl,tōs\ *n* -S [F, fr. E *[1]malt* + F *-ose*] **:** a crystalline dextrorotatory fermentable reducing disaccharide sugar $C_{12}H_{22}O_{11}$ formed esp. from starch by the action of beta-amylase (as in saliva and malt), as an intermediate product in metabolism, and in brewing and distilling and used chiefly in foods and in biological culture media; 4-α-glucosyl-glucose — called also *malt sugar;* compare GLUCOSE illustration

**mal·treat** \(')mal+\ *vt* [F *maltraiter,* fr. MF, fr. *mal* badly + *traiter* to treat, handle, manage, fr. L *tractare* — more at MAL-, TREAT] **:** to treat ill **:** treat roughly **:** ABUSE, MISTREAT, MISUSE ⟨whenever women felt ~*ed* and humiliated —Theodor Reik⟩ ⟨a machine that had already been ~*ed* —Bryan Morgan⟩ — **mal·treater** *n* — **mal·treatment** *n*

**malts** *pl of* MALT, *pres 3d sing of* MALT
**malt shop** *n* : an ice-cream shop specializing in malted milks
**malt·ster** \'mȯltstə(r)\ *also* **mal·ster** \-lstə(r)\ *n* -s [ME *maltestere, malstere,* fr. ¹*malt* + *-stere* -ster] : a maker of malt
**malt sugar** *n* : MALTOSE
**malt vinegar** *n* : the product made by fermentation without distillation of an infusion of barley malt or cereals whose starch has been converted by malt
**malt whiskey** *n* : whiskey made from malted barley in a pot still
**maltworm** \'ˌ=ˌ=\ *n, archaic* : TIPPLER, TOPER
**malty** \'mȯltē, -ti\ *adj* -ER/-EST [¹*malt* + *-y*] **1** : containing or resembling malt **2** : addicted to malt liquor
**ma·lum** \'māləm\ *n, pl* **ma·la** \-lə\ [L, fr. neut. of *malus* bad — more at SMALL] : an offense against right or law : EVIL, WRONG
**malum in se** \-in'sā\ *n, pl* **mala in se** [NL, offense in itself] : an offense that is evil or wrong from its own nature or by the natural law irrespective of statute — compare MALUM PROHIBITUM
**malum pro·hi·bi·tum** \-prō'hibəd·əm\ *n, pl* **mala prohibi·ta** \-əd·ə\ [NL, prohibited offense] : an offense prohibited by statute but not inherently evil or wrong — compare MALUM IN SE
**malungeon** *usu cap, var of* MELUNGEON
**mal·union** \(')mal+\ *n* [¹*mal-* + *union*] : incomplete or faulty union (as of the fragments of a fractured bone)
**mal·united** \ˌ=+\ *adj* [¹*mal-* + *united*] : united in a position of abnormality or deformity — used of the fragments of a broken bone
**ma·lus** \'māləs\ *n, cap* [NL, fr. L, apple tree, fr. L *malum* apple, fr. Gk (Dor) *malon*; akin to Gk (Attic) *mēlon* apple] : a genus of trees or shrubs (family Rosaceae) of the north temperate zone sometimes included in the genus *Pyrus* but distinguished by having the soft pubescent leaves revolute or plicate in the bud, flower clusters lacking a stout central column, styles more or less joined at the base, and fruit without grit cells
**mal·va** \'malvə\ *n* [NL, fr. L, mallow — more at MALLOW] **1** *cap* : a genus of Old World herbs (family Malvaceae) having palmate leaves and tribracteate flowers with naked reniform indehiscent carpels **2** -s : a plant of the genus *Malva* — *see* COMMON MALLOW
**mal·va·ce·ae** \mal'vāsē,ē\ *n pl, cap* [NL, fr. *Malva*, type genus + *-aceae*] : a family of herbs, shrubs, and trees (order Malvales) characterized by monadelphous stamens and one-celled anthers — compare COTTON, OKRA — **mal·va·ceous** \(')=¦vāshəs\ *adj*
**mal·va·les** \mal'vā(ˌ)lēz\ *n pl, cap* [NL, fr. *Malva* + *-ales*] : an order of dicotyledonous plants characterized by volvate calyx, usu. numerous stamens, and a polycarpellary ovary
**mal·va·sia** \ˌmalvə'zēə, -'sēə\ *n* -s [It, fr. *Monemvasia*, town off the coast of the southeastern Peloponnesus, Greece] **1** : a grape that yields the wine known as malmsey **2** : MALMSEY — **mal·va·si·an** \¦=ˌ=¦=ən\ *adj*
**mal·vas·trum** \mal'vastrəm\ *n, cap* [NL, irreg. fr. L *malva* mallow] : a large genus of herbs and shrubs (family Malvaceae) characterized by red or yellow flowers and capitate stigmas — see FALSE MALLOW
**mal·ver·sa·tion** \ˌmalvə(r)'sāshən\ *n* -s [MF, fr. *malverser* + *-ation*] *civil & Scots law* : misbehavior, corruption, extortion, disloyalty, embezzlement, misappropriation, or breach of trust in an office of public trust, an agency, or a commission; *broadly* : corrupt administration
**malverse** *vi* [F *malverser*, fr. MF, fr. *mal* badly + *verser* to turn, occupy oneself, fr. L *versare* to turn, transform, fr. *versus*, past part. of *vertere* to turn — more at WORTH] *civil & Scots law, obs* : to be guilty of malversation
**mal·vi** \'malvē\ *n* -s *cap* : the Indic dialect of Malwa
**mal·vi·din** \'malvədən\ *n* -s [ISV *malv-* (fr. L *malva* mallow) + *-idin*] : an anthocyanidin widely distributed in plants esp. in the form of its glucosides malvin and oenin and also in the free form in grapes and usu. obtained as the violet-brown crystalline chloride $C_{17}H_{15}ClO_7$
**mal·vin** \'malvən\ *n* -s [ISV *malv-* (fr. L *malva*) + *-in*] : an anthocyanin pigment found esp. in the European wild mallow and in species of primrose and obtained usu. as the reddish brown chloride $C_{29}H_{35}ClO_{17}$
**mal·voi·sie** \'malvə(ˌ)zē, ˌmalvwä¦zē\ *n* -s [F, fr. MF *malvesie*, fr. *Malvesie* Monemvasia] : MALMSEY
¹**mam** \'mam\ *n* -s [of baby-talk origin — more at MAMMA] *chiefly Brit* : MOM
²**mam** *or* **ma'm** *var of* MA'AM
³**mam** \'mäm\ *n, pl* **mam** *or* **mams** *usu cap* [Sp *mame*, of AmerInd origin] **1 a** : an Indian people of southwestern Guatemala **b** : a member of such people **2** : a Mayan language of the Mam people
**MAM** *abbr* milliampere minute
**mama** *var of* MAMMA
**ma·mak** \'mäˌmäk\ *n, pl* **mamak** *or* **mamaks** *usu cap* : one of several forest peoples of Sumatra related to the Toala of Celebes
**ma·ma·loi** \ˌmäməl'wä\ *n* -s [Haitian creole *mamalwa*, fr. *mama* mother + *lwa* loa] : a voodoo priestess esp. of Haiti — compare PAPALOI
**ma·ma·mu** \'mämə(ˌ)mü\ *n* -s [Hawaiian *mamamo*] : a large-eyed Indo-Pacific porgy (*Monotaxis grandoculis*) highly esteemed as food in the Pacific islands
**ma·ma·ni** \'mämənē\ *n* -s [Hawaiian *māmane*] : a tree (*Sophora chrysophylla*) of the Hawaiian mountain regions having very hard durable wood much valued for posts and building
**ma·ma·nua** \mə'mänwə\ *n, pl* **mamanua** *or* **mamanuas** *usu cap* **1** : a negritoid or Veddoid people inhabiting northern Mindanao, Philippines **2** : a member of the Mamanua people
**mama's boy** *or* **mamma's boy** *n* : a boy or man whose behavior is unnaturally good or overcautious; *esp* : one who is delicate, unaggressive, or overdependent on others
**mam·ba** \'mämbə, 'mam-\ *n* -s [Zulu *im-amba*] : any of several tropical and southern African venomous snakes of the genus *Dendraspis* related to the cobras but lacking a dilatable hood; *esp* : a southern African snake (*D. angusticeps*) that has a light or olive-green phase and a black phase, that attains in the latter phase a length of 12 feet, and that is dreaded because of its quickness and readiness to inflict its often fatal bite
¹**mam·bo** \'mäm(ˌ)bō\ *also* **mam·bu** \-bü\ *n* -s [Haitian creole] : a Haitian voodoo priestess
²**mambo** \" *sometimes* 'mam-\ *n* -s [AmerSp, prob. fr. Haitian creole (voodoo priestess)] : a complex staccato usu. fast dance related to the rumba and of Haitian origin; *also* : the style of music for this dance
³**mambo** \"\ *vi* -ED/-ING/-S : to dance the mambo
**mam·e·lière** \ˌmaməl'ye(ə)r\ *n* -s [F, fr. MF *mameliere*, fr. *mamele* breast, nipple (fr. L *mamilla*) + *-iere* -ier — more at MAMMILLA] : one of two round steel plates or a single plate used to cover the breasts in medieval armor
**mam·e·lon** \'mamələn\ *n* -s [F, lit., nipple, fr. MF, dim. of *mamele*] : a dome-shaped protuberance or elevation: as **a** : a small rounded hill esp. of lava **b** : a fortified mound or hillock **c** : one of the three rounded protuberances on the cutting ridge of recently erupted incisor teeth
**mam·e·lu·co** \ˌmamə'lü(ˌ)kō\ *n* -s [Pg *mameluco, mamaluco*, modif. (influenced by *mameluco* Mamluk, fr. Ar *Mamlūk*) of Tupi *Mamaruca*] : a Brazilian mestizo; *specif* : the offspring of a white man and an Indian woman — compare CABOCLO
**mamey** *or* **mamie** *var of* MAMMEE
**ma·mie tay·lor** \'māmē'tālə(r)\ *n, usu cap M&T* [prob. fr. the name *Mamie Taylor*] : a drink consisting of Scotch whisky, lime juice, and ginger ale served in a tall glass with cube or crushed ice
**mamilla** *var of* MAMMILLA
**mamillaria** *syn of* MAMMILLARIA
**mamillate** *or* **mamillated** *var of* MAMMILLATE
**mam·luk** \'mamˌlük\ *or* **mam·e·luke** *also* **mam·e·luk** \-məˌ-\ *n* -s [*mamluk*, fr. Turk & Ar; Turk *memlûk*, fr. Ar *mamlūk*, lit., slave; *mameluke & mameluk*, fr. F *mameluk*, fr Ar *mamlūk*] **1** *usu cap* : a member of a former Egyptian military class orig. made up of a body of Caucasian slaves converted to Islam who gained great political power in Egypt, occupied the sultanate from 1250 to 1517, and were exterminated or dispersed in 1811 by Mehemit Ali **2** *usu mameluke, often cap* **a** : a white or yellow slave in Muslim countries **b** : a member of a body of slave soldiers
¹**mam·ma** *or* **ma·ma** \'mämə *sometimes* 'məmə, *chiefly Brit* mə'mä\ *also* **mom·ma** \'mämə\ *n* -s [of baby-talk origin like E *mam* mother, G dial. *mamme* mother, L *mamma* mother, female breast, Gk *mamma, mammē* mother, IrGael & W *mam*, Alb *mëmë*, Russ *mama*] **1** : MOTHER **2** *slang* : WOMAN, WIFE
²**mam·ma** \'mamə\ *n, pl* **mam·mae** \-aˌmē\ [L, mother, breast — more at ¹MAMMA] : a glandular organ for secreting milk characteristic of all mammals but normally rudimentary in the male : a mammary gland and its accessory parts
**mam·mal** \'maməl\ *n* -s [NL *Mammalia*] : one of the Mammalia
**mam·ma·lia** \mə'mālēə, -lyə\ *n pl, cap* [NL, fr. LL, neut. pl. of *mammalis* of the breast, fr. L *mamma* breast + *-alis* -al] : the highest class of Vertebrata comprising man and all other animals that nourish their young with milk, that have the skin usu. more or less covered with hair, that have mammary glands, a mandible articulating directly with the squamosal, a chain of small ear bones, a brain with four optic lobes, a muscular diaphragm separating the heart and lungs from the abdominal cavity, only a left aortic arch, warm blood containing red cells without nuclei except in the fetus, and embryos developing both amnion and allantois, and that except in the monotremes reproduce viviparously — compare ALLOTHERIA, EUTHERIA, METATHERIA, PROTOTHERIA, THERIA
¹**mam·ma·li·an** \-ēən, -yən\ *n* -s [NL *Mammalia* + E *-an*] : one of the Mammalia
²**mammalian** \"\ *adj* : of, relating to, or characteristic of mammals : belonging to the Mammalia
**mam·ma·lif·er·ous** \ˌmamə'lif(ə)rəs\ *adj* [NL *Mammalia* + E *-ferous*] : containing mammalian remains ⟨a ~ deposit⟩ ⟨a ~ stratum⟩
**mam·mal·i·ty** \mə'maləd·ē, ma'-\ *n* -ES [*mammal* + *-ity*] : the quality or state of being mammalian
**mam·ma·log·i·cal** \ˌmamə¦läjəkəl\ *adj* : of or relating to mammalogy
**mam·mal·o·gist** \mə'maləjəst, ma'-\ *n* -s : a specialist in mammalogy
**mam·mal·o·gy** \-jē, -ji\ *n* -ES [ISV, blend of NL *Mammalia* and ISV *-logy*] : a branch of zoology dealing with mammals
**mam·ma·plas·ty** \'maməˌplastē\ *n* -ES [²*mamma* + *-plasty*] : plastic surgery of the breast
**mam·ma·ry** \'mam(ə)rē, -ri\ *adj* [L *mamma* female breast + E *-ary* — more at MAMMA] : of, relating to, lying near, or affecting the mammae
**mammary gland** *n* : one of the large compound glands that are characteristic of mammals, are regarded as highly specialized sebaceous glands, are modified in the female to secrete milk for the nourishment of the young, are situated on the ventral aspect of the body, vary in number from 2 to 22, and usu. terminate in a nipple
**mammary pouch** *n* : the marsupium of a monotreme as distinguished from that of a marsupial
**mammary ridge** *n* : either of a pair of longitudinal ectodermal thickenings in the mammalian embryo that extend from the base of the anterior to the posterior limb buds and are the source of the mammary glands — called also *milk line*
**mamma's boy** *var of* MAMA'S BOY
**mam·mate** \'maˌmāt\ *adj* [L *mammatus*, fr. *mamma* breast + *-atus* ate] : MAMMIFEROUS
**mam·ma·to·cumulus** \məˌmād·ō, maˌmād·ō+\ *n* [NL, fr. L *mammatus* of the breast + NL *-o-* + *cumulus*] : a cumulus or cumulostratus storm cloud having breast-shaped protuberances below — called also *festoon cloud*
**mam·ma·tus** \mə'mād·əs, ma'-\ *adj* [NL, fr. L, of the breast] : of, relating to, or being a cloud whose lower surface is in the form of pouches
**mam·me** \'mämā\ *n, pl* **mamme** *or* **mammes** [It dial., pl. of *mamma*, lit., breast, fr. L; fr. the shape of the fruit — more at MAMMA] : the overwintering crop of the caprifig maturing in the spring — compare MAMMONI, PROFICHI
**mam·mea** \ma'mēə, ma'-\ *n, cap* [NL, fr. Sp *mamey* mammee — more at MAMMEE] : a genus of American and Asiatic trees (family Guttiferae) that have a valvate 2-parted calyx and 2-celled or 4-celled ovary becoming a large drupaceous fruit
**mam·mec·to·my** \mə'mektəmē, ma'-\ *n* -ES [ISV *mamm-* (fr. L *mamma* breast) + *-ectomy*] : MASTECTOMY
**mam·mee** *or* **ma·mey** *or* **mam·ie** *or* **mam·mey** \(')ma¦mē *sometimes* -¦mā, *esp attributively* 'mamē\ *n, pl* **mammees** \-ēz\ *or* **mameys** \-āz\ *or* **mam·ey·es** \mə'mā,äs\ *or* **mamies** *or* **mammeys** [Sp *mamey*, fr. Taino] **1** *also* **mammee apple** **a** : a tropical American tree (*Mammea americana*) having a globular or ovoid fruit with thick russet or reddish leathery rind and yellow or reddish juicy flesh **b** : the fruit of this tree — called also *tropical apricot* **2 a** : MARMALADE TREE **b** *also* **mammee sapota** *or* **mammee colorado** : the fruit of this tree **3** : SAPODILLA
**mam·mer** \'mamə(r)\ *vi* -ED/-ING/-S [ME *mameren, memeren*, of imit. origin] **1** *now dial Eng* : STAMMER, MUTTER **2** *now dial Eng* : WAVER, HESITATE
**mam·met** \'mamət\ *var of* MAUMET
**mammey** *var of* MAMMEE
**mammies** *pl of* MAMMY
**mam·mi·fer** \'maməfə(r)\ *n* -s [F *mammifère* adj. & n., fr. L *mamma* breast + F *-ifère* -iferous — more at MAMMA] *archaic* : MAMMAL
**mam·mif·er·ous** \mə'mif(ə)rəs, ma'-\ *adj* [F *mammifère* + E *-ous*] : having breasts : MAMMALIAN
**mam·mi·form** \'maməˌfȯrm\ *adj* [L *mamma* breast + E *-iform*] : having the form of a breast or nipple : MAMMILLARY
**mam·mil·la** *also* **ma·mil·la** \mə'milə, ma'-\ *n, pl* **mammil·lae** *also* **mamil·lae** \-iˌlē\ [L, breast, nipple, dim. of *mamma*, *mama* breast — more at MAMMA] : NIPPLE
**mam·mil·lar** \'maməl(ə)r\ *adj* [LL *mamillaris*, fr. L *mamilla* breast, nipple + *-aris* -ar] : MAMMILLARY
¹**mam·mil·lar·ia** \ˌmamə'la(a)rēə\ [NL, fr. L *mammilla* breast, nipple + NL *-aria*] *syn of* CACTUS
²**mammillaria** \"\ *n* [NL, fr. L *mammilla* + *-aria*] **1** *cap* : a genus of succulents (family Cactaceae) characterized chiefly by the nipple-shaped protuberances on their surface and formerly including many species now separated into several other genera (as *Coryphantha, Cochemia, Dolichothele*) **2** -s : any cactus of *Mammillaria* or a related genus
**mam·mil·lary** \'maməˌlerē, -ri\ *adj* [L *mammilla* breast, nipple + E *-ary* — more at MAMMILLA] **1** : of or relating to the breasts **2 a** : having the form of a rounded eminence **b** : composed of concretions shaped somewhat like breasts : studded with mammiform protuberances ⟨limonite frequently occurs in ~ masses⟩
**mammillary body** *n* : either of two small rounded eminences on the undersurface of the brain behind the tuber cinereum forming terminals of the anterior pillars of the fornix — called also *corpus albicans*
**mam·mil·late** \'maməˌlāt\ *or* **mam·mil·lat·ed** \-ād·əd\ *also* **mam·il·late** \-āt\ *or* **mam·il·lat·ed** \-ād·əd\ *adj* [LL *mammillatus, mamillatus*, fr. L *mammilla, mamilla* breast, nipple + *-atus* -ate, -ated — more at MAMMILLA] **1** : having nipples or small protuberances like nipples **2 a** : having the form of a bluntly rounded protuberance **b** *usu mammillated* : having a hummocky rock surface with many closely spaced rounded knobs or mounds formed esp. as a result of glacial erosion ⟨the mammillated surface of glaciated surface —C.A. Cotton⟩
**mam·mil·la·tion** \ˌ==¦lāshən\ *n* -s [LL *mamillatus* + E *-ion*] **1** : a mammillate or mammilliform protuberance **2** : the condition of having nipples or protuberances resembling nipples
**mam·mil·li·form** \mə'miləˌfȯrm, ma'-\ *adj* [L *mamilla* + E *-iform*] : nipple-shaped
**mam·mi·tis** \mə'mīd·əs, ma'-\ *n, pl* **mam·mit·i·des** \-mid·əˌdēz\ [NL, fr. ²*mamma* + *-itis*] : MASTITIS
¹**mam·mock** \'mamək\ *n* -s [origin unknown] **1** *now dial* : a broken piece : SHRED, SCRAP, FRAGMENT **2** *now dial* : MESS, LITTER
²**mammock** \"\ *vt* -ED/-ING/-S **1** *now dial* : to tear into fragments : MANGLE; *esp* : to break or cut (as bread or meat) into ragged pieces **2** *now dial* : to rumple or make untidy : DISARRANGE, MESS
**mam·mo·gen** \'maməjən, -ˌjen\ *n* -s [²*mamma* + *-o-* + *-gen*] : any of certain hypothetical hormonal factors that stimulate mammary development and are usu. held to be produced in the pituitary body — compare LACTOGENIC HORMONE
**mam·mo·gen·ic** \ˌmamə¦jenik\ *adj* [²*mamma* + *-o-* + *-genic*] : stimulating or inducing mammary development — **mam·mo·gen·i·cal·ly** \-nək(ə)lē\ *adv*
**mam·mon** \'mamən\ *n* -s [LL *mammona*, fr. Gk *mamōna*, fr. Aram *māmōnā* riches] *often cap* : material wealth or possessions esp. having an evil power or debasing influence : WEALTH, MONEY ⟨you cannot serve God and ~ —Mt 6:24 (RSV)⟩ ⟨materialism was in the saddle; *Mammon* ruled the hearts and minds of men —C.I.Glicksberg⟩
**mam·mo·ni** \'maməˌnē\ *n, pl* **mammoni** *or* **mammonis** [It dial., pl. of *mammone*, lit., large breast, aug. of *mamma* breast — more at MAMME] : the autumn crop of the caprifig — compare MAMME, PROFICHI
**mam·mon·ish** \'mamənish\ *adj* : actuated or prompted by a devotion to money getting or the service of mammon
**mam·mon·ism** \-əˌnizəm\ *n* -s : devotion to the pursuit of wealth : the service of mammon
**mam·mon·ist** \-nəst\ *n* -s : one devoted to the ideal or the pursuit of wealth — **mam·mon·is·tic** \ˌmamə¦nistik\ *adj*
**mam·mon·ite** \'==ˌnīt\ *n* -s : MAMMONIST — **mam·mon·it·ish** \-īd·ish\ *adj*
**mam·mon·te·us** \mə'mäntēəs, ma'-\ [NL, fr. Russ *mamont, mamot* mammoth + L *-eus* -eous] *syn of* MAMMUTHUS
**mam·mose** \'maˌmōs\ *n* -s [origin unknown] *Del. & N.J.* : a young sturgeon
¹**mam·moth** \'maməth\ *n* -s [Russ *mamot, mamont, mamant*, perh. fr. a Yakut word derived fr. Yakut *mamma* earth; fr. the belief that the mammoths burrowed in the earth like moles] **1** : any of numerous extinct elephants widely distributed in the Pleistocene and distinguished from recent elephants by having molars with cementum filling the interstices of the numerous high narrow ridges of enamel and usu. by the large size, very long upcurved tusks, and well-developed body hair — compare WOOLLY MAMMOTH **2** : something that is immense of its kind : GIANT ⟨a company that is a ~ of the industry⟩ ⟨a diesel-powered ~ of the highways⟩

mammoth (restored)

²**mammoth** \"\ *adj* **1** : resembling a mammoth in size and weight ⟨a ~ bull elephant⟩ **2** : characterized by extreme size, ponderous or preponderant weight, bulk, dimension, strength, or force : GIGANTIC ⟨the ~ hydrogen bomb explosion —*N.Y. Times*⟩ ⟨a ~ parade⟩ ⟨~ watermelons, cabbages, and tomatoes —Alan Moorehead⟩ ⟨the ~ optimism of the man —*Saturday Rev.*⟩ ⟨a ~ undertaking⟩ **syn** see HUGE
**mammoth red clover** *or* **mammoth clover** *n* : a clover (*Trifolium pratense perenne*) that is a variety of red clover, is distinguished from the typical red clover by stouter, coarser, more prolific growth and darker later-flowering heads, and is cultivated chiefly for forage
**mammoth redwood** *n* : REDWOOD 3a
**mammothrept** *n* -s [Gk *mammothreptos* child brought up by his grandmother, fr. *mammē* mother, grandmother + *-o-* + *threptos*, verbal of *trephein* to bring up, nourish — more at MAMMA, ATROPHY] *obs* : a spoiled child : INFANT
**mammoth tree** *n* : BIG TREE
**mam·mo·trop·ic** \ˌmamə¦träpik\ *adj* [ISV ²*mamma-* + *-o-* + *-tropic*] : MAMMOGENIC
**mam·mu·lar** \'mamyələ(r)\ *adj* [L *mammula* small breast (dim. of *mamma* breast) + E *-ar* — more at MAMMA] : consisting of small papillae ⟨~ excrescences⟩
**mam·mut** \'mamət\ *n, cap* [NL, fr. G, mammoth, fr. F *mammouth*, fr. Russ *mamot, mamont* — more at MAMMOTH] : the proboscidean genus comprising the mastodons and being the type and in some classifications sole genus of a family (Mammutidae) closely related to the Elephantidae
**mam·mu·thus** \'maməthəs\ *n, cap* [NL, fr. G *mammut* or F *mammouth* mammoth] : the genus of Elephantidae comprising the mammoths
**mam·my** \'mamē, -mi\ *n* -ES [alter. of ¹*mamma*] **1** : MAMMA **2 a** : a Negro woman serving as a nurse to white children esp. formerly in the Southern states ⟨in the Richmond of the 1880's a ~ still ruled over every household in which there were children —J.B.Cabell⟩ **b** : a Negro woman — often taken to be offensive
**mammy chair** *n* : a basket or chair (as of canvas) attached to a cargo boom and used to convey persons to and from boats alongside ship in an open roadstead (as on the west coast of Africa)
**mammy coot** *n* : PURPLE GALLINULE
**mammy wagon** *or* **mammy lorry** *n* : a small open-sided bus or light truck used to transport passengers or goods in West Africa
**ma·mo** \'mä(ˌ)mō\ *n* -s [Hawaiian] : any of several black Hawaiian honeycreepers that constitute a genus (*Drepanis*) of the family Drepanididae, are distinguished by yellow feathers above and below the tail which were used in choice featherwork, and are now wholly extinct
**ma·mo·na** \mə'mōnə\ *n* -s [Pg] : CASTOR-OIL PLANT
**ma·mon·ci·llo** \ˌmämən'sē(ˌ)(y)ō\ *n* -s [AmerSp, dim. of Sp *mamón* mamoncillo, prob. fr. a native name in Venezuela] : GENIP 2
**ma·mo·ty** \'mäməd·ē\ *n* -ES [Tamil *mammaṭṭi*, alter. of *manvetṭi*, fr. *man* earth + *veṭṭi* spade] : a hand tool used for digging and cultivating in southeastern Asia
**mam·pa·lon** \'mampəˌlän\ *n* -s [native name in Indonesia] : a short-tailed web-footed reddish brown viverrid mammal (*Cynogale bennettii*) of Malaysia and adjacent islands that resembles an otter in appearance and habits — called also *otter civet*
**mam·pus** \'mampəs\ *n* -ES [origin unknown] *dial Brit* : a very large number : MULTITUDE ⟨a ~ of folk were there⟩
**mams** *pl of* MAM
**mam·sell** *or* **mam'·selle** \mam'zel\ *n* -s [F *mam'selle*, contr. of *mademoiselle* — more at MADEMOISELLE] : MADEMOISELLE
**ma·mu·shi** \mə'müshē\ *n* -s [Jap] : a small venomous pit viper (*Agkistrodon blomhoffi*) that is marked with dark brown blotches on a pale gray ground, is widely distributed in the Japanese islands, and is represented by identical or closely related forms on the adjacent Asiatic mainland
**mam·zer** *also* **mom·ser** *or* **mom·zer** \'mämzə(r)\ *n* -s [LL *mamzer*, fr. Heb *mamzēr*] **1** : a child of a union not sanctioned by biblical law as interpreted by the rabbis **2** [Yiddish *mamzer*, fr. Heb *mamzēr*] : BASTARD
¹**man** \'man, -aa(ə)-, *as suffix* -ˌə-, *in exclamations* -ˌai-\ *n, pl* **men** \'men, *in compounds* -mən *or* ˌmen\ [ME, fr. OE *man, mon*; akin to OS & OHG *man* human being, man, ON *mathr*, Goth *manna*, Skt *manu* human being, man, OSlav *mǫžĭ* man, and perh. to OE *gemynd* mind — more at MIND] **1 a** : a member of the human race : a human being : PERSON — now usu. used of males except in general or indefinite applications with collective adjectives or in the pl. ⟨every ~ must do his duty⟩ ⟨all *men*, both male and female —David Hume †1776⟩ — often used interjectionally to express intensity of feeling ⟨~, what a relief⟩ ⟨~, oh ~⟩ ⟨~, can that fellow shoot baskets⟩ **b** (1) : the human race : MANKIND : human beings personified as an individual — used without an article ⟨~ is a greedy beast⟩ (2) : a bipedal primate mammal (*Homo sapiens*) that is anatomically related to the great apes but is distinguished by notable development of the brain with a resultant capacity for articulate speech and abstract reasoning, marked erectness of body carriage with corresponding alteration of muscular balance and loss of prehensile powers of the foot, and shortening of the arm with accompanying increase in thumb size and apposability, that is usu. considered to occur in a variable number of freely interbreeding races, and that is the sole recent representative of the natural family Hominidae;

## Figs 1 and 2 MUSCULAR SYSTEM OF MAN

Fig 1, FRONT VIEW. Fig 2, BACK VIEW. The sides marked A show the muscles of the first layer located immediately below the skin. Those marked B show the important muscles of the deeper layers. Where a muscle is shown in only one of the figures, that fact is indicated following the name: as, temporal (fig 1)

### Head and Neck

1 frontalis
2 occipitalis
3 temporal (fig 1)
4 orbicularis of eye
5 greater zygomaticus
6 lesser zygomaticus
7 angular head of the quadratus of upper lip (fig 1)
8 nasalis (fig 1)
9 orbicularis of mouth (fig 1)
10 triangularis of chin (fig 1)
11 quadratus of lower lip (fig 1)
12 mentalis (fig 1)
13 masseter (fig 1)
14 buccinator (fig 1)
15 anterior auricularis
16 superior auricularis
17 posterior auricularis
*a* parotid gland
18 mylohyoid (fig 1)
19 digastric
20 platysma
21 sternocleidomastoid
22 omohyoid (fig 1)
23 sternohyoid (fig 1)
24 trapezius
25 splenius of head (fig 2)
26 splenius of neck (fig 2)
27 levator of scapula (fig 2)
28 supraspinatus (fig 2)

### Trunk

29 greater pectoralis (fig 1)
30 deltoid
31 latissimus dorsi
32 anterior serratus
33 external oblique
34 rectus abdominis (fig 1)
35 umbilicus (fig 1)
36 abdominal aponeurosis (fig 1)
37 linea alba (fig 1)
38 subclavius (fig 1)
39 lesser pectoralis (fig 1)
40 posterior superior serratus (fig 1)
41 internal oblique
42 infraspinatus (fig 2)
43 lesser teres (fig 2)
44 greater teres (fig 2)
45 greater rhomboideus (fig 2)
46 lesser rhomboideus (fig 2)
*b* scapula (fig 2)
*c* 9th rib (fig 2)
*d* 10th rib (fig 2)
*e* 11th rib (fig 2)
*f* 12th rib (fig 2)
47 posterior inferior serratus (fig 2)
48 lumbodorsal fascia (fig 2)
49 sacrospinalis (fig 2)

### Upper Extremity

50 biceps of arm
51 triceps of arm
52 brachialis
53 lacertus fibrosus
54 long radial extensor of wrist
55 brachioradialis
56 radial flexor of wrist
57 long palmaris (fig 1)
58 flexor of digits (fig 1)
59 ulnar flexor of wrist
60 short palmaris
61 short radial extensor of wrist
62 long flexor of thumb (fig 1)
63 pronator quadratus (fig 1)
64 short flexor of thumb (fig 1)
65 long palmaris (cut across in fig 1)
66 first dorsal interosseus
67 first lumbricalis (fig 1)
68 fibrous sheaths of the tendons
69 adductor of the little finger
70 annular ligament of the carpus
*g* head of humerus (showing bicipital groove)
71 common extensor of digits (fig 1)
72 ulnar extensor of wrist (fig 1)
73 long extensor of thumb
*h* medial epicondyle of humerus (fig 2)
*i* lower end of radius (fig 2)
*j* lower end of ulna (fig 2)
74 tendons of extensors of thumb (fig 2)
75 adductor of thumb (fig 2)
76 tendons of extensors of digits and wrist (fig 2)
77 pronator teres (fig 2)
78 palmar aponeurosis (fig 2)

### Lower Extremity

*k* anterior superior spine of ilium (fig 1)
79 iliacus (fig 1)
80 gluteus medius
81 tensor of fascia lata
82 rectus femoris (fig 1)
83 psoas major (fig 1)
84 pectineus (fig 1)
85 sartorius
86 long adductor of thigh (fig 1)
87 great adductor of thigh
88 gracilis
89 vastus lateralis
90 vastus medialis
91 gluteus minimus (fig 1)
92 superior extremity of rectus femoris (fig 1)
93 inferior extremity of rectus femoris (fig 1)
*m* head of femur (fig 1)
94 inferior extremities of psoas and iliacus (fig 1)
95 tendon of rectus femoris
*n* patella (fig 1)
*o* head of fibula (fig 1)
*p* medial condyle of femur (fig 1)
*r* tuberosity of tibia (fig 1)
96 anterior tibialis
97 medial head of gastrocnemius (fig 1)
98 soleus
99 long extensor of digits (fig 1)
100 long peroneus
101 short peroneus (fig 1)
102 long flexor of digits (fig 1)
103 long extensor of hallux (fig 1)
104 annular ligament of ankle (fig 1)
105 short extensor of digits (fig 1)
106 abductor of hallux (fig 1)
*s* ilium
*t* greater trochanter
107 gluteus maximus (fig 2)
108 biceps of thigh (fig 2)
109 semitendinosus (fig 2)
110 semimembranosus (fig 2)
111 plantaris (fig 2)
112 lateral head of gastrocnemius (fig 1)
113 long flexor of digits (fig 2)
114 third peroneus (fig 2)
115 tendon of posterior tibialis (fig 2)
116 Achilles' tendon (fig 2)
*u* tuberosity of calcaneus
117 piriformis (fig 2)
118 superior gemellus and inferior gemellus (fig 2)
119 internal obturator (fig 2)
120 quadratus of thigh (fig 2)

## Fig 3 SKELETON OF ADULT MAN

(a few small or internal bones are omitted)

### Head

*bones of the cranium*

A top of skull showing sutures
1 frontal
2 parietal
3 squamous portion of occipital
4 greater wing of sphenoid
5 squamous portion of temporal
6 ethmoid

*bones of the external face*

7 nasal
8 lacrimal
9 vomer
10 maxilla
11 mandible
12 zygomatic

*principal features of the bones of the head*

13 coronoid process of mandible
14 condyloid process of mandible
15 styloid process of temporal
16 mastoid process
17 zygomatic arch
*a* coronal suture
*b* sphenofrontal suture
*c* sphenosquamosal suture
*d* squamous suture
*e* sphenoparietal suture
*f* lambdoid suture
*g* occipitomastoid suture
*h* sagittal suture
*i* superior temporal ridge
*k* inferior temporal ridge
*l* hyoid bone

### Chest

*bones of the breast*

18 manubrium
19 gladiolus
20 xiphoid process

*true ribs*

21 *to* 27 first to seventh ribs inclusive

*false ribs*

28 *to* 30 eighth to tenth ribs inclusive
31 *and* 32 floating ribs
*m* costal cartilage

### Trunk

*spinal column*

33 first thoracic vertebra
34 twelfth thoracic vertebra
35 fifth lumbar vertebra
36 fifth sacral vertebra
37 coccyx

### Upper Extremity

*shoulder*

38 clavicle
39 scapula

*arm*

40 humerus
41 ulna
42 radius
(*p*) bones of forearm in prone position
(*r*) same in supine position

*bones of the hand*

(43) bones of right hand (dorsal surface)
(44) bones of left hand (volar surface)
B bones of the left hand (dorsal surface)
(*s*) carpus
(*t*) metacarpus
(*u*) phalanges of thumb and fingers

*bones of the carpus*

45 lunatum
46 pisiform
47 triquetrum
48 hamatum
49 capitatum
50 navicular
51 lesser multangulum
52 greater multangulum

*bones of the metacarpus*

53 *to* 57 first to fifth metacarpal bones
I thumb
II index finger
III middle finger
IV ring finger
V little finger

*phalanges*

58 first phalanx of thumb
59 second phalanx of thumb
60 ungual tuberosity
61 first phalanx of index
62 second phalanx of index
63 third phalanx of index

### Lower Extremity

*bones and principal parts of pelvic girdle*

64 ilium
65 ischium
66 pubis
67 sacrum
68 brim of pelvis
69 pelvic cavity

*bones of the leg*

70 femur
71 patella
72 tibia
73 fibula

*bones of the feet*

(74) bones of left foot (dorsal surface)
C bones of right foot (plantar surface)
(*x*) tarsus
(*y*) metatarsus
(*z*) phalanges of toes

*bones of the tarsus*

75 talus
76 calcaneus
*w* tuberosity of calcaneus
77 cuboid
78 *to* 80 cuneiform bones
81 navicular bone

*bones of the metatarsus*

82 *to* 86 first to fifth metatarsal bones
87 sesamoid bones
VI big toe
VII *to* IX second to fourth toes
X little toe

*phalanges*

88 first phalanx of big toe
89 second phalanx of big toe
90 first phalanx of little toe
91 second phalanx of little toe
92 third phalanx of little toe

Fig. 1

Fig. 2

Fig. 3

*broadly* **:** any living or extinct member of the family Hominidae comprising recent man and various extinct Old World forms that are less advanced than recent man esp. in brain development and in erectness of body carriage but are consistently more advanced in these characteristics than any known ape — compare AFRICANTHROPUS, HOMO, PITHECANTHROPUS; FLORISBAD MAN, PEKING MAN, RHODESIAN MAN **c** (1) **:** a particular aspect or part of the human being — used with qualifiers esp. to distinguish a higher from a lower, a more spiritual or worthy from a less, or a grosser from a more ethereal aspect or part ⟨qualities that differentiate the inward and spiritual from the outward and worldly ~⟩ — see INNER MAN, OUTER MAN (2) **:** one endued with the qualities that distinguish man on the one hand from purely spiritual entities and on the other from lower animals **:** an individual having or assuming human nature or form ⟨God appearing as ~ has been a recurrent theme in human culture⟩ **2 a** (1) **:** a male human being — distinguished from *woman* ⟨the *men* considerably outnumbered the women in the new settlement⟩ (2) **:** an adult male human being — distinguished from *boy* ⟨there were seven *men* and three boys in the party⟩ (3) **:** a male human being as such and without regard to any special status (as of birth, position, or office) ⟨the king is but a ~, as I am —Shak.⟩ **b :** a male human being belonging to a particular and usu. specified category (as by birth, residence, or membership) ⟨our hope is in these English*men*⟩ ⟨an experienced ~ of business⟩ — usu. used in combination and sometimes without regard to sex when the sex of the individual is not significant to the relation indicated ⟨she is a highly skilled drafts*man*⟩ or in general applications ⟨our fellow country*men* have each done his or her bit to aid the common cause⟩ **c** (1) **:** HUSBAND ⟨I'll have to ask my ~⟩ — now chiefly dial. except in the phrase *man and wife* (2) *chiefly dial* **:** a man that is lover, suitor, or sweetheart ⟨he was her ~⟩ **d** (1) **:** one possessing in high degree the qualities considered distinctive of manhood (as courage, strength, and vigor) (2) *obs* **:** manly character or quality **:** MANLINESS **e :** a prosperous or successful person **:** a person of consequence or high estate **f :** FELLOW, CHAP — used as a mode of familiar address ⟨come, come, my ~, let's waste no more time⟩ ⟨but, my good ~, what business of yours is that⟩ **3 :** a human male that serves or is subordinate to another or others: as **a :** liege man **:** VASSAL **b** *men pl* **:** members of a military or other fighting force ⟨the guerrillas had upward of 7000 *men*⟩; *esp* **:** members of the ranks of an organized force as distinguished from officers ⟨the enemy lost heavily in officers, *men*, and matériel⟩ **c :** a man that is in personal attendance on another person (as a manservant, valet, or groom) **d** *men pl* **:** the working force (as of a factory) as distinguished from the employer and usu. the management ⟨the *men* have been on strike for several weeks⟩ **e** *Brit* **:** UNDERGRADUATE **4 :** INDIVIDUAL, ONE: as **a :** the male individual in question — used in place of a pronoun ⟨the good ~ fell ill⟩ **b :** the holder of an office or position of prominence ⟨the present ~ is much inferior to his predecessor⟩ **c :** ANYONE — used indefinitely but usu. with reference to males and replacing Old English *man* or *mon* as an indefinite pronoun ⟨a ~ cannot survive without hope⟩ **d** (1) **:** the individual one requires or has in mind — used after a possessive ⟨he's your ~⟩ (2) **:** the individual best suited or adapted (as to a particular job or responsibility) — used with the definite article ⟨he's the ~ for the job if you can get him⟩ **5 :** a ship esp. when in a particular service or under an indicated flag — used in combination **6** *obs* **:** an entity (as a supernatural being) that is not but is personified as human **7 a :** one of the pieces with which various games (as chess or checkers) are played **b :** one of the players on a team ⟨nine *men* on a side⟩ **8** *Brit* **a :** a conical heap of stones set up on a mountain top **b :** the mountain top itself ⟨Scafell *Man*⟩ **9** *Christian Science* **:** the compound idea of infinite Spirit **:** the spiritual image and likeness of God **:** the full representation of Mind — **as a man** *adv* **:** in one's character of a human being **:** as a person among people — **as one man** *adv* **:** with one accord **:** UNANIMOUSLY — **one's own man :** free from interference or control **:** INDEPENDENT — **to a man** *adv* **:** without exception

**²man** \"\ *vt* **manned; manned; manning; mans** [ME *mannen*, fr. *man*, n.] **1 a :** to supply with men **:** furnish with a sufficient force or complement of men (as for management, service, operation, defense) ⟨~ a fleet⟩ **b** *obs* **:** to furnish with inhabitants **:** POPULATE **c** *obs* **:** to furnish with servants or followers **d :** to station members of a ship's crew at (an indicated place) usu. for a particular exercise or task ⟨*manned* the rail in honor of the visiting captain⟩ ⟨~ the capstan and heave in the anchor⟩ **e :** to serve in the force or complement of ⟨workers who ~ the production lines⟩ **2** *now dial* **:** to have, gain, or use control over **:** be master of **:** MANAGE **3** *obs* **a :** to attend as a manservant **b :** ESCORT **4 :** to accustom (as a hawk) to man and the human environment **5 a :** to furnish with strength or powers of resistance **:** BRACE, FORTIFY ⟨*manned* himself to meet the shock⟩ ⟨you must ~ yourself, my boy⟩ **b :** to make courageous or manly ⟨his heartening words *manned* the frightened refugees⟩

**³man** \'mȧn, 'man, ,man\ *var of* MAUN

**⁴man** \'män, 'man\ *var of* MAUND

**⁵man** \'man\ *n, pl* **man** *or* **mans** *usu cap* [Chin (Pek) *man²*] **1 a :** a loosely defined division of the aboriginal population in China usu. comprising the tribes living in the south and southwest **b :** one of these tribes or peoples (as the Yao or Miao) **2 :** any of the primitive mountain tribes of Vietnam; *esp* **:** YAO

**man** *abbr* **1** manila **2** [L *manipulus*] handful **3** manual **4** manufacture

**¹ma·na** \'mänə\ *n* -s [of Melanesian & Polynesian origin; akin to Hawaiian & Maori *mana*] **:** impersonal supernatural force or power that may be concentrated in objects or persons and that may be inherited, acquired, or conferred

**²mana** \"\ *n* -s [Jap] **1 :** Chinese characters as used phonetically in Japanese **:** the original unabbreviated form of kana **2 :** Chinese characters as used ideographically in Japanese

**³mana** \"\ *n* -s [Heb *māneh*] **:** MINA

**man–about–town** \'==='=\ *n, pl* **men–about–town :** a man who frequents private and public urban places of resort (as clubs, theaters, and balls) **:** a worldly and socially active man

**man·a·ca** \'manəkə\ *or* **man·a·can** \-kən\ *also* **manaca root** *n* -s [Pg *manacá*, fr. Tupi] **:** the dried root of a shrub (*Brunfelsia hopeana*) of Brazil and the West Indies that has been used to treat rheumatism and syphilis — called also *vegetable mercury*

**¹man·a·cle** \'manəkəl, -nēk-\ *n* -s [ME *manicle*, fr. MF, fr. L *manicula* little hand, handle of a plow, dim. of *manus* hand — more at MANUAL] **1 :** a shackle for the hand or wrist **:** HANDCUFF **2 :** something used as a restraint (as a fetter or tether) — usu. used in pl.

**²manacle** \"\ *vt* **manacled; manacled; manacling** \-k(ə)liŋ\ **manacles** [ME *maniclen, manaclen*, fr. *manicle*, n.] **1 :** to confine (the hands) with or as if with handcuffs **2 :** to make fast or secure **:** BIND, SHACKLE, FETTER; *broadly* **:** RESTRAIN **syn** see HAMPER

**man·a·cus** \'manəkəs\ *n* [NL, modif. of D *manneken* little man — more at MANIKIN] **1** *cap* **:** a genus consisting of manakins distinguished by having the throat feathers elongated **2** -ES **:** any bird of the genus *Manacus*

**ma·na·da** \mə'nädə\ *n* -s [Sp, fr. OSp, handful of grass or grain, herd, fr. *mano* hand, fr. L *manus* — more at MANUAL] *Southwest* **:** a herd of horses; *esp* **:** a breeding band of wild horses consisting of a stallion, several mares, and young stock

**¹man·age** \'manij, -nēj, *esp in pres part* -nəj\ *vb* -ED/-ING/-S [It *maneggiare*, fr. (earlier) *maneare*, fr. *mano* hand, fr. L *manus* — more at MANUAL] *vt* **1 :** to train or handle (a horse) in graceful or studied action or stance **2 :** to control and direct **:** handle either well or ill **:** cope with **:** CONDUCT, ADMINISTER ⟨~s his skis with much grace⟩ **3 :** to make and keep (one) submissive **:** guide by careful or delicate treatment ⟨*managed* her husband in everything without his being aware of it⟩ **4 :** to treat with care **:** HUSBAND ⟨properly *managed* we've enough flour to last till spring⟩ **5 :** to work upon **:** MANIPULATE: as **a :** CULTIVATE **1 b :** ADULTERATE **c :** to adjust the ecological factors to best meet the needs and ensure the survival of (a wild animal) usu. by controlling predators and hunting and by providing shelter or supplementary food supplies **6 :** to bring about by contriving **:** succeed in doing or accomplishing ⟨don't know how I'll ~ it but I'll be there⟩ — often followed by an infinitive ⟨human life on earth cannot continue unless we ordinary men and women ~ to practice these virtues —A.J.Toynbee⟩ ~ *vi* **1** *obs, of a horse* **:** to go through his paces **2 a :** to direct or carry on business or affairs **:** SUPERVISE, ADMINISTER **b :** to admit of being carried on **3 :** to achieve one's purpose **:** get on or along **:** CONTRIVE ⟨he *managed* only by careful planning⟩ **syn** see CONDUCT

**²manage** \"\ *n* -s [It *maneggio*, fr. *maneggiare*] **1 a** *archaic* **:** the action and paces of a trained riding horse **b :** the schooling or handling of a horse or the technique of such schooling or handling **c :** a place where horses are trained and horsemanship practiced **:** a riding school **:** MANEGE 1 **d :** an exhibition or theatrical act (as in a circus) that features horses and horsemanship **2** *obs* **:** efficient handling or the action of controlling something (as a weapon or a state)

**man·age·abil·i·ty** \,manijə'bilәd·ē, -nēj-, -lәtē, -i\ *n* **:** the quality or state of being manageable

**man·age·able** \'manijəbəl, -nēj-\ *adj* [¹*manage* + *-able*] **:** capable of being managed **:** submitting to control **:** GOVERNABLE, TRACTABLE — **man·age·able·ness** *n* -ES — **man·age·ably** \-blē, -li\ *adv*

**man·aged** \-jd\ *adj* **:** subjected to management; *esp* **:** not allowed to fluctuate in accord with natural laws ⟨~ money⟩ ⟨a ~ economy⟩

**managed currency** *n* **:** a currency whose purchasing power is adjusted by the monetary authorities with the purpose of influencing business activity and prices rather than determined by a fixed relationship to gold — contrasted with *automatic currency*

**man·age·ment** \'manijmənt, -nēj-\ *n* -s [¹*manage* + *-ment*] **1 :** the act or art of managing: as **a :** more or less skilled handling of something (as a weapon, a tool, a machine) **b :** the whole system of care and treatment of a disease or a sick individual ⟨the ~ of contagious diseases⟩ **c :** the conducting or supervising of something (as a business); *esp* **:** the executive function of planning, organizing, coordinating, directing, controlling, and supervising any industrial or business project or activity with responsibility for results **2** *obs* **:** an instance or act of management **3 :** judicious use of means to accomplish an end **:** conduct directed by art or craft **:** skillful and often devious treatment **:** INTRIGUE **4 a :** the collective body of those who manage or direct any enterprise or interest **:** the board of managers **b :** employer representation in an employer-employee relationship — opposed to *labor* **5** *archaic* **:** moderation (as in conduct) from respect for the feelings of another **:** CONSIDERATION, INDULGENCE

**man·age·men·tal** \;==;ment³l\ *adj* **:** of, relating to, or constituting management

**management consultant** *n* **:** one that advises business or industrial firms in the conduct of their affairs and in devising and installing more satisfactory procedures for their use

**management engineer** *n* **:** INDUSTRIAL ENGINEER

**management engineering** *n* **:** INDUSTRIAL ENGINEERING

**management shares** *n pl, chiefly Brit* **:** corporate stock generally held by officers or directors of a company that receives no dividend until a specified amount has been paid on the common stock but that receives a large share of the residual profits — compare FOUNDERS' SHARES

**man·ag·er** \'manijə(r), -nēj-\ *n* -s **:** one that manages **:** a person that conducts, directs, or supervises something: as **a :** one that conducts business or household affairs with discreet frugality and care ⟨a very good ~, able to make a little go a long way⟩ **b :** a member of a small group of a legislative body (as a house of the British Parliament) appointed to perform some special duty **c :** a person whose work or profession is the management of a specified thing (as a business, an institution, or a particular phase or activity within a business or institution) **d :** a receiver appointed under English law by a court of equity to carry on under the court's control a business for the benefit of creditors or other beneficiaries **e** (1) **:** a person that in various professional sports (as baseball or boxing) is in overall charge of a team or athlete (2) **:** a student or other person that in collegiate sports supervises equipment and records under the direction of a coach **f :** a person appointed by elected officials to supervise the activities of a civic corporate body — see CITY MANAGER

**man·ag·er·ess** \-j(ə)rəs\ *n* -ES **:** a female manager

**man·a·ge·ri·al** \;manə'jirēəl\ *adj* **:** of, relating to, or characteristic of a manager ⟨~ qualities⟩ ⟨~ problems⟩ — **man·a·ge·ri·al·ly** \-ēəlē, -li\ *adv*

**man·a·ge·ri·al·ism** \,==='jirēə,lizəm\ *n* -s **:** the philosophy or practice of conducting the affairs of an organized group (as a nation) by planning and direction by professional managers — compare LAISSEZ-FAIRE 2

**manager plan** *n* **:** COUNCIL-MANAGER PLAN

**man·a·ger·ship** \'manijə(r),ship, -nēj-\ *n* **:** the office or function of a manager

**managery** *n* -ES [¹*manage* + *-ry*] **1** *obs* **:** MANAGEMENT **2** *obs* **:** MANEGE 1,2

**managing director** *n* **:** the chief executive in an organization (as a bank, steel works, institute) **:** an executive officer in charge of a branch or part of a business

**managing editor** *n* **:** an editor in executive and supervisory charge of all editorial activities of a newspaper or periodical

**ma·na·gua** \mə'nägwə\ *adj, usu cap* [fr. *Managua*, Nicaragua] **:** of or from Managua, the capital of Nicaragua **:** of the kind or style prevalent in Managua

**man·a·hoac** \'manə,hōk\ *n, pl* **manahoac** *or* **manahoacs** *usu cap* **1 :** a Siouan people of northern Virginia **2 :** a member of the Manahoac people

**ma·na·ism** \'mänə,izəm\ *n* -s [¹*mana* + *-ism*] **:** belief in mana

**ma·na·is·tic** \;==;istik\ *adj* **:** of, relating to, characteristic of, or exhibiting manaism

**man·ak** \'ma,nak\ *n* -s [Esk] **:** an Eskimo implement consisting of a wooden ball with sharp recurved hooks that is thrown by a long line to secure and draw ashore seals killed from a distance

**man·a·kin** \'manəkən\ *n* -s [D *manneken* little man — more at MANIKIN] **1 :** MANIKIN **2 :** any of numerous small brightcolored clamatorial birds of the family Pipridae of Central and So. America — compare MANNIKIN

**¹ma·ña·na** \mə'nyänə\ *adv* [Sp, lit., tomorrow, fr. OSp, fr. (*cras*) *mañana* early tomorrow, fr. *cras* tomorrow + *mañana* early, fr. (assumed) VL *maneana*, fr. L *mane* in the morning, prob. fr. *manis, manus* good — more at MATURE] *chiefly Southwest* **:** at an indefinite time in the future ⟨a hunter passed a broken bridge several times . . . and every time he was assured that it would be fixed ~ —A.L.Campa⟩

**²mañana** \"\ *n* -s [Sp, fr. *mañana*, adv.] **:** an indefinite time in the future ⟨the glorious ~ when behaviorists will give us an adequate theory of the creative artist —Eliseo Vivas⟩

**ma·nan·do·nite** \mə'nandə,nīt\ *n* -s [*Manandona* river, Madagascar + E *-ite*] **:** a mineral $Li_4Al_{14}B_4Si_6O_{29}(OH)_{24}$ (?) that is a basic borosilicate of lithium and aluminum

**ma·na·no·say** \,manə'nō(,)sā\ *or* **man·a·nose** \'manə,nōz\ *n* -s [prob. of Algonquian origin; akin to *man-* to gather (in some Algonquian language of Virginia)] *chiefly Midland* **:** SOFT-SHELL CLAM

**ma·nao** \mə'nä(,)ō\ *n, pl* **manao** *or* **manaos** *usu cap* [Pg, of AmerInd origin] **1 a :** an Arawakan people of northwestern Brazil **b :** a member of such people **2 :** the language of the Manao people

**man ape** *n* **1 :** GREAT APE **2 :** any of various fossil primates that are intermediate in characters between recent man and the great apes

**¹manas** *pl of* MANA

**²man·as** \'manəs, 'mәnəs\ *n* -ES [Skt, fr. *manyate* he thinks — more at MIND] **:** the faculty of mental perception that receives impressions from the senses and transmits them to the atman according to Hinduism — **ma·nas·ic** \mə'nasik\ *adj*

**ma·na·si** \;mänə;sē\ *n* -s *usu cap* **:** a dialect of Chiquitoan

**ma·nas·se·ite** \mə'nasē,īt\ *n* -s [Ernesto *Manasse* †1922 Ital. mineralogist + E *-ite*] **:** a mineral $Mg_6Al_2(OH)_{16}(CO_3).4H_2O$ that is a basic hydrous carbonate of magnesium and aluminum

**ma·nas·site** \mə'na,sīt\ *n* -s *usu cap* [*Manasseh*, elder son of Joseph (Gen 41:50–52), the eponymous ancestor of the Manassites (Josh 17) + E *-ite*] **:** a member of the Hebrew tribe of Manasseh — compare EPHRAIMITE

**man–at–arms** \'==='=\ *n, pl* **men–at–arms :** SOLDIER; *esp* **:** a heavily armed and usu. mounted soldier

**man·a·tee** *also* **man·a·ti** \'manə,tē\ *n* -s [Sp *manatí*, prob. of Cariban origin; akin to Galibi *manati, manaté* breast, teats] **:** any of several chiefly tropical aquatic herbivorous mammals that constitute a genus (*Trichechus*) of the order Sirenia and differ from the dugong esp. in having the tail broad and rounded instead of like that of a whale; *esp* **:** a formerly common American mammal (*T. latirostris* syn. *T. manatus*) of the waters of the West Indies and neighboring mainland coasts from Florida to Yucatan that is about 10 feet long, nearly black, thick-skinned, and almost free from hair and that has become rare through excessive killing for its fat and hide or for its edible flesh

**manatee grass** *n* **:** a submerged aquatic herb (*Cymodocea manatorum*) of the family Cymodoceaceae having pointed rootstocks and terete leaf blades

**man·a·tus** \'manətəs\ [NL, fr. Sp *manati* manatee] *syn of* TRICHECHUS

**ma·naus** *or* **ma·ná·os** *or* **ma·naos** \mə'naùs\ *adj, usu cap* [fr. *Manaus* or *Manáos*, Brazil] **:** of or from the city of Manaus, Brazil **:** of the kind or style prevalent in Manaus

**ma·nav·el·ins** *also* **ma·nav·il·ins** \mə'navələnz\ *n pl* [origin unknown] *slang* **:** odds and ends of food **:** LEFTOVERS; *also* **:** fancy or made dishes

**manback** \'=,=\ *n* **:** the human back esp. as a bearer of burdens

**man·bark·lak** *also* **man·bark·lac** \'man,bär,klak\ *n* -s [D *manbarklak*, fr. native name in Surinam] **1 :** any of numerous usu. large tropical American trees constituting a genus (*Eschweilera*) that is closely related to *Lecythis* and has smooth leathery leaves, brightly colored flowers in panicles or racemes, and large operculate fruits with sessile seeds often containing bitter kernels **2 :** the very hard heavy reddish brown wood of various manbarklaks that is used esp. in marine construction and valued for its resistance to borers

**man·bote** *also* **man·bot** \'man,bōt\ *n* -s [OE *manbōt*, fr. *man* + *-bōt* compensation — more at BOOT] **:** a sum paid under Old English law to a lord as compensation for killing his man; *also* **:** similar compensation paid to the relatives of a murdered man

**manc** *abbr* mancando

**man·ca·la** \män'kälə, 'mäŋkələ\ *n* -s [Ar *manqalah*, fr. *naqala* to move] **:** any of various games that are widely played in Africa and southern Asia and in areas (as parts of Oceania or of the New World) influenced by African or Asiatic cultures and that involve competition between two players in the distribution of pieces (as beans or pebbles) into rows of holes or pockets (as in a board) under various rules that permit accumulation of pieces by capture — called also *wari;* see CHUBA

**man·can·do** \(')män'kän(,)dō\ *also* **man·can·te** \-(,)tā\ *adj* (*or adv*) [*mancando* fr. It, verbal of *mancare* to lack, fr. *manco* lacking, left-handed, fr. ML *mancus* lacking in weight, fr. L, having a crippled hand, maimed, infirm, prob. fr. *manus* hand; *mancante* fr. *mancare* — more at MANUAL] **:** dying away — used as a direction in music

**manche** *or* **maunche** *or* **maunch** \'mänch\ *n, pl* **manches** *or* **maunches** [ME *manche*, fr. MF, fr. L *manica* sleeve, gauntlet, manacle, fr. *manus* hand — more at MANUAL] **1** *archaic* **:** SLEEVE 1a; *esp* **:** a hanging sleeve **2 :** a heraldic charge consisting of a sleeve with a long pendent lap worn in the 12th, 13th, and 14th centuries

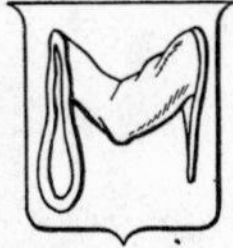

manche 2

**man·che·gan** \(')man'chāgən\ *adj, usu cap* [Sp *manchego* Manchegan (fr. *La Mancha*, region consisting of a high arid plateau in New Castile, Spain) + E *-an*] **:** of or from La Mancha **:** of the kind or style prevalent in La Mancha ⟨the *Manchegan* plain⟩ ⟨a *Manchegan* knife⟩

**¹man·ches·ter** \'man,chestə(r), 'maan-, -nchəs-\ *adj, usu cap* [fr. *Manchester*, England] **:** of or from the city of Manchester, England **:** of the kind or style prevalent in Manchester

**²manchester** \"\ *n* -s *usu cap* **1** *Brit* **:** cotton textiles ⟨*Manchester* goods⟩ ⟨a sales clerk in the *Manchester* department⟩ **2 :** MANCHESTER TERRIER

**man·ches·ter·ism** \-tə,rizəm\ *or* **manchesterdom** *n* -s *usu cap* [*Manchester* (*school*) + *-ism* or *-dom*] **:** the principles or doctrines (as laissez-faire) held by or attributed to a school of English economists

**man·ches·ter·ist** \-tərəst\ *or* **man·ches·ter·ite** \-tə,rīt\ *n* -s *usu cap* [*Manchester* (*school*) + *-ist* or *-ite*] **:** an adherent of Manchesterism

**manchester terrier** *n, usu cap M* **1 :** a breed of small lightly built short-haired black and tan terriers developed in England by interbreeding local rat-catching dogs with whippets **2 :** a dog of the Manchester terrier breed

**man·ches·tri·an** \(')man'chestrēən\ *also* **man·ches·te·rian** \;manchə'stirēən\ *adj, usu cap* [*Manchester*, England + E *-ian*] **:** ¹MANCHESTER

**man·chet** \'manchət\ *n* -s [ME] **1** *archaic* **:** wheaten bread of highest quality **2** *now chiefly dial* **:** a roll of manchet esp. when of a spindle shape with thick middle and pointed ends **:** a piece of white bread

**man–child** \'=,=\ *n, pl* **men–children** [ME] **:** a male child **:** SON

**man·chi·neel** \,manchə'nē(ə)l\ *n* -s [F *mancenille*, fr. Sp *manzanilla*, lit., small apple — more at MANZANILLA] **:** a poisonous tropical American tree (*Hippomane mancinella*) of the family Euphorbiaceae having smooth pale-brown bark, close-grained figured yellowish brown wood that is sometimes used for cabinetwork, small greenish flowers in a stiff spike, a blistering milky juice, and apple-shaped fruit

**¹man·chu** \(')man'chü, maan-\ *n, pl* **manchu** *or* **manchus** **1** *usu cap* **a :** a member of the native Mongolian race of Manchuria that is related to the Tungus, was orig. nomad but conquered China and established a Manchu dynasty on the Chinese throne in 1644, and has largely assimilated Chinese culture **b :** the Tungusic language of the Manchu people **c :** the Tungusic subfamily of the Altaic languages **2** *often cap* **:** SHERRY 2

**²manchu** \"\ *adj, usu cap* **1 :** of, relating to, or being Manchuria, its inhabitants, or their language **2** *slang, of a military law or regulation* **:** designed to require active service with troops and to prevent prolonged assignment to esp. desirable positions or locations

**manchu cherry** *n, usu cap M* **:** NANKING CHERRY

**man·chu·ria** \(')man'chùrēə, maan-\ *adj, usu cap* [fr. *Manchuria*, territory of China] **:** of or from Manchuria **:** of the kind or style prevalent in Manchuria

**¹man·chu·ri·an** \-ēən\ *adj, usu cap* [*Manchuria* + E *-an*] **1 :** of, relating to, or native to Manchuria **:** MANCHU **2 :** of, relating to, or being the subdivision of the Palaearctic region that includes Manchuria, northern and eastern China, Korea, and Japan

**²manchurian** \"\ *n* -s *cap* **:** a native or inhabitant of Manchuria **:** MANCHU

**manchurian crab** *n, usu cap M* **:** a Siberian crab (*Malus baccata mandshurica*) that produces fragrant white flowers very early in the season followed by small red crab apples

**manchurian dog** *also* **manchurian dogskin** *n, usu cap M* **:** the skin of Chinese dogs dressed and processed for use as fur

**manchurian tiger** *n, usu cap M* **:** a long-haired tiger of northeastern Asia that is often considered to constitute a distinct subspecies (*Felis tigris longipilis*) of the Asiatic tiger

**manchurian wolf** *n, usu cap M* **1 :** a wolf of northern China that is regarded as a variety of the common Old World wolf (*Canis lupus*) **2 :** MANCHURIAN DOG

**man·ci·nism** \'man(t)sə,nizəm\ *n* -s [It *mancinismo*, fr. *mancino* left-handed (fr. *manco* lacking, left-handed) + *-ismo* -ism — more at MANCANDO] **:** the condition of being lefthanded

**man·ci·pa·ble** \'man(t)səpəbəl\ *adj* [*mancipate* + *-able*] **:** subject to or capable of mancipation

**man·ci·pant** \-pənt\ *n* -s [L *mancipant-, mancipans*, pres. part. of *mancipare*] *Roman law* **:** one who transfers property by mancipation — opposed to *mancipee*

**man·ci·pate** \-sə,pāt\ *vt* -ED/-ING/-S [L *mancipatus*, past part. of *mancipare*, fr. *mancip-, manceps* purchaser, fr. *manus* hand + *-cip-, -ceps* (fr. *capere* to take) — more at MANUAL, HEAVE] **1** *obs* **:** to place in subjection or bondage **:** BIND, RESTRICT **2** *Roman law* **:** to transfer by mancipation

**man·ci·pa·tion** \ˌ==ˈpāshən\ *n* -s [L *mancipation-, mancipatio*, fr. *mancipatus* + *-ion-, -io* -ion] **1** *obs* **a** : the act of enslaving **b** : involuntary servitude : SLAVERY **2** *Roman law* **a** : an early form of ceremonial conveyance under the jus civile involving the balance scales, bronze money, a balance holder, and five citizens as witnesses in which persons and property (as Italic lands, slaves, beasts of burden, rural praedial servitudes, children under potestas, and various women) subject to the ceremony were transferred by one Roman citizen into the power and control of another — compare MANCIPIUM **b** : MANCIPATORY WILL

**man·ci·pa·to·ry** \ˈman(t)səpəˌtōrē\ *adj* : of, relating to, or involving mancipation

**mancipatory will** *n, Roman law* : an early form of will wherein a conveyance was made by the ceremony of mancipation by the owner of the family property to the buyer thereof who was charged with transferring the inheritance to an unknown heir or legatee named in a sealed document written by the testator

**man·ci·pee** \ˌman(t)səˈpē\ *n* -s [*mancipate* + *-ee*] *Roman law* : one who receives property by mancipation — opposed to *mancipant*

**man·cip·i·um** \manˈsipēəm\ *n, pl* **mancip·ia** \-ēə\ [L, fr. *mancip-, manceps* purchaser — more at MANCIPATE] **1** *Roman law* **a** (1) : the status of a freeman subject to the power and control of the head of a Roman family similar to that of a slave except that he could not be abused or killed without legal cause (2) : the power or control so exercised by such head of family over such freeman **b** : a form of quiritarian as opposed to bonitarian ownership of property common in early Roman law **c** : MANCIPATION **2** : SLAVE

**man·ci·ple** \ˈman(t)səpəl\ *n* -s [ME, fr. OF *mancipe, manciple*, fr. L *mancipium*] : a steward or purveyor esp. for a college or monastery

**man·co** \ˈmaŋ(ˌ)kō\ *n* -s [by shortening] *Scot* : CALAMANCO

**man·co·no** \ˌmäŋkəˈnō\ *n* -s [Sp *manconó*, fr. Bisayan] **1** : a Philippine timber tree (*Xanthostemon verdugonianus*) of the family Myrtaceae **2** : the heavy hard wood of the mancono

**¹man·cu·ni·an** \(ˈ)manˈkyünēən, -nyən\ *adj. usu cap* [LL *Mancunium* Manchester + E *-an*] **1** : of, relating to, or characteristic of Manchester, England **2** : of, relating to, or characteristic of the people of Manchester

**²mancunian** \"\ *n* -s *cap* : a native or resident of Manchester, England

**man·cus** \ˈmaŋkəs\ *n* -ES [OE, fr. ML *mancusus*, fr. Ar *manqūsh* engraved] : an Anglo-Saxon unit of value equal to 30 silver pence; *also* : a piece of gold or silver worth 30 pence

**-man·cy** \ˌman(t)sē, ˌmaan-, -si\ *n comb form* -ES [ME *-mancie, -mauncie*, fr. OF *-mancie*, fr. L *-mantia*, fr. Gk *manteia*, fr. *manteuesthai* to divine, prophesy + *-ia* -y; akin to Gk *mainesthai* to rage, rave — more at MIND] : divination in a (specified) manner or by means of (something specified) ⟨chiro*mancy*⟩

**¹mand** *var of* MAUND

**²mand** \ˈmand\ *n* -s [Hindi *mārnwā, marnwā*, fr. Skt *maḍaka*] : RAGGEE

**M and A** *abbr* management and administration

**¹man·dae·an** \manˈdēən\ *n* -s *usu cap* [Mandaean *mandayyā* having knowledge + E *-an*] **1** : a member of a Gnostic sect that regards John the Baptist as the Messiah and that is found in regions of the lower Tigris and Euphrates **2** : a form of Aramaic found in documents written by Mandaeans

**²man·dae·an** \(ˈ)=ˈ==\ *adj, usu cap* **1** : of, relating to, or characteristic of the Mandaeans or Mandaeanism **2** : of, relating to, or characteristic of the Mandaean language

**man·dae·an·ism** \manˈdēəˌnizəm\ *n* -s *usu cap* : the beliefs of the Mandaeans

**man·da·ic** \manˈdāik\ *n* -s *usu cap* [Mandaean *mandayyā* having knowledge + E *-ic*] : MANDAEAN 2

**man·da·la** \ˈməndələ\ *n* -s [Skt *maṇḍala* circle] : a graphic mystic symbol of the universe that is typically in the form of a circle enclosing a square and often bearing symmetrically arranged representations of deities and is used chiefly in Hinduism and Buddhism as an aid to meditation

**¹man·da·lay** \ˌmandəˌlā, -aan-\ *adj, usu cap* [fr. *Mandalay*, Burma] : of or from the city of Mandalay, Burma : of the kind or style prevalent in Mandalay

**²mandalay** \"\ *n* -s *often cap* : PILGRIM BROWN

**man·da·ment** \ˈmandəmənt\ *n* -s [L *mandare* to command + E *-ment* — more at MANDATE] : COMMAND, INJUNCTION

**¹man·da·mus** \manˈdāməs, maanˈ- *sometimes* -däm- *or* -dam- *or* -dām-\ *n* -ES [L, we enjoin, 1st pl. pres. indic. of *mandare* to enjoin — more at MANDATE] **1 a** : the mandate of the sovereign under early English law commanding a subject to perform some act or duty **b** : the prerogative writ issued under English law in the absence of any other legal remedy by the King's Bench Division of the High Court of Justice in the king's name to a public officer to enforce the performance by him of some public duty **2** : the extraordinary writ issued under constitutions and regulated by statute when there is no other adequate remedy at law, in equity, or under statute by a court of superior jurisdiction to an inferior tribunal, to a corporation, or to any person commanding the performance of some clear public duty imposed by law : a statutory extension of such a remedy

**²mandamus** \"\ *vt* -ED/-ING/-ES : to serve or coerce with a mandamus

**man·dan** \ˈmanˌdan, -ˌdən\ *n, pl* **mandan** *or* **mandans** *usu cap* **1 a** : a Siouan people ranging between the Heart and Little Missouri rivers in No. Dakota **b** : a member of such people **2** : the language of the Mandan people

**man·dant** \ˈmandənt\ *n* -s [L *mandant-, mandans*, pres. part. of *mandare* to command — more at MANDATE] : MANDATOR

**man·da·pa** \ˈməndəpə\ *or* **man·da·pam** \-pəm\ *n* -s [Skt *maṇḍapa*] : a general gathering area in an Indian temple that is comparable to the narthex of a western church

**man·dar** \mänˈdär\ *vt* -ED/-ING/-S [Sp, lit., to command, fr. L *mandare*] : to control (a bull) by aggressive action in bullfighting

**¹man·da·rin** \ˈmandərən, -aan-\ *n* -s [Pg *mandarim*, modif. (influenced by *mandar* to command, fr. L *mandare*) of Malay *mĕntĕri*, fr. Skt *mantrin* counselor, fr. *mantra* counsel; akin to Skt *manyate* he thinks — more at MANDATE, MIND] **1 a** : a public official under the Chinese Empire of any of nine superior grades that were filled by individuals from the ranks of lesser officeholders that passed examinations in Chinese literary classics **b** (1) : a pedantic official (2) : BUREAUCRAT **c** : a person of position and influence esp. in intellectual or literary circles; *often* : an elder and often traditionalist or reactionary member of such a circle **2** *cap* **a** : the primarily northern dialect of Chinese used by the court and the official classes under the Empire **b** : the chief dialect of China that is spoken in about four fifths of the country and has a southern variety centering about Nanking, a western variety centering about Chengtu, and a northern now standard variety centering about Peking **3** : a small grotesque seated image in Chinese costume with the head so fixed as to continue nodding when set in motion **4** *also* **man·da·rine** \"\ **a** *or* **mandarin tree** *or* **mandarin orange** [F *mandarine*, fr. Sp *mandarina*, prob. fr. *mandarin* mandarin, fr. Pg *mandarim*; prob. fr. the color of a mandarin's robes] (1) : a small spiny Chinese citrus tree (*Citrus reticulata*) having slender twigs and lanceolate leaves, small white flowers, and yellow to reddish orange loose-skinned fruits (2) : any of several cultivated citrus trees that are selections or hybrids of the Chinese mandarin — see SATSUMA, TANGERINE **b** *or* **mandarin orange** (1) : the fruit of a mandarin tree — called also *kid-glove orange, tangerine* (2) : a yellow or pale orange mandarin — distinguished from *tangerine* **c** *usu* **mandarine** : a sweet liqueur flavored with the dried peel of mandarin **5** : MANDARIN PORCELAIN **6 a** : MANDARIN RED **b** : MANDARIN ORANGE 2

**²mandarin** \"\ *adj* **1** : of, relating to, or typical of a mandarin ⟨~ graces⟩ **2** : resembling or styled after that of a mandarin ⟨~ styles⟩ **3** *of literary style or work* : marked by polished ornate complexity in the use of language

**man·da·rin·ate** \-əˌnāt\ *n* -s [prob. fr. F *mandarinat*, fr. *mandarin* (fr. Pg *mandarim*) + *-at* -ate] **1** : the body of mandarins : mandarins as a group or class **2** : the office or dignity of a mandarin **3** : rule by mandarins

**mandarin collar** *n* : a narrow stand-up collar usu. open in front

**mandarin duck** *n* : a brightly marked crested Asiatic duck (*Aix galericulata*) that is closely related to the New World wood duck and is often domesticated

**man·da·rin·ism** \-ˌnizəm\ *n* -s [prob. fr. F *mandarinisme*, fr. *mandarin* + *-isme* -ism] **1** : government by mandarins **2** : the character or spirit of the mandarins

**mandarin oil** *n* : a fragrant yellow essential oil expressed from the peel of mandarin oranges and used chiefly in flavoring and perfumery

**mandarin orange** *n* **1** : MANDARIN 4a, 4b **2** : a strong orange that is darker than pumpkin, redder and duller than cadmium orange, and redder and deeper than cadmium yellow

**mandarin porcelain** *n* : an oriental porcelain ware usu. with showy decorations often including figures in the costume of the mandarin

**mandarin red** *n* : a strong reddish orange that is yellower and paler than poppy or paprika and slightly redder, lighter, and stronger than fire red

**man·da·tary** \ˈmandəˌterē\ *n* -ES [LL *mandatarius*, fr. L *mandatus* + *-arius* -ary] **1** : a person to whom a legal mandate is given — distinguished from *mandator* **2** : a member nation of the League of Nations to which a mandate over territory is given

**¹man·date** \ˈmanˌdāt, -aan- *sometimes* -ndət, *usu* -d.+V\ *n* -s [MF & L; MF *mandat*, fr. L *mandatum*, fr. neut. of *mandatus*, past part. of *mandare* to commit to one's charge, order, enjoin, command, prob. irreg. fr. *manus* hand + *-dere* to put — more at MANUAL, DO] **1** [ML *mandatum*, fr. L, command, mandate] : MAUNDY **2 a** (1) : a formal order from a superior court or official to an inferior one; *esp* : the order or command that embodies the decision of a U. S. appellate court when final judgment is not entered and is sent to the court below (2) : MANDAMUS **b** *archaic* : a papal ordinance in an individual case (as preferment to a benefice) **c** (1) : a contract under Roman law by which one agrees to perform gratuitously some act for another who agrees to indemnify him (2) : a contract of agency under civil law in which one undertakes to perform some act for another whether gratuitously or for a reward; *esp* : a gratuitous bailment in which the bailee undertakes to do something in respect to the thing bailed — distinguished from *deposit* **3 a** : an authoritative command, order, or injunction : a clear instruction, authorization, or direction ⟨acting under the ~ of the statute in question⟩ **b** : the authorization to act or approval given by a constituency to its elected representative ⟨accepted the ~ of the people⟩ **4 a** : an order or commission granted by the League of Nations as mandator to a member nation as its mandatary for the establishment of a responsible government over former German colonies or other conquered territory **b** : a mandated colony or territory

**²mandate** \", *in sense 1* =ˈ=\ *vt* -ED/-ING/-S **1** *Scot* : to commit (as a sermon) to memory **2** : to administer or assign (as a colony) under a mandate

**man·da·tee** \ˌmanˌdāˈtē, -ndəˈ-\ *n* -s : one to whom a mandate is assigned

**man·da·tor** \manˈdādə(r)\ *n* -s [LL, fr. L *mandatus* + *-or*] : one that gives a mandate (as under Roman or civil law) : MANDANT — compare MANDATARY

**man·da·to·ri·ly** \ˈmandəˌtōrəlē, -aan-, -tȯr-, -li\ *adv* : so as to be mandatory : OBLIGATORILY

**¹man·da·to·ry** \-rē, -ri\ *adj* [LL *mandatorius*, fr. L *mandatus* + *-orius* -ory] : containing, constituting, or relating to a mandate; *esp* : OBLIGATORY — opposed to *directory*

**²mandatory** \"\ *n* -ES : MANDATARY; *esp* : one holding a mandate from the League of Nations

**mandatory injunction** *n* : an injunction entered at the conclusion of an equity case compelling the defendant to do some positive act or to cease to do something he has done, thereby compelling him in effect to undo it — compare PROHIBITORY INJUNCTION

**man·da·tum** \manˈdādəm\ *n, pl* **manda·ta** \-də\ [L — more at MANDATE] : MANDATE

**man-day** \ˈ=ˌ=\ *n, pl* **man-days** **1** : the labor of one man in one normal working day **2** : a unit consisting of a hypothetical average man-day

**man·da·ya** \mänˈdīyə\ *n, pl* **mandaya** *or* **mandayas** *usu cap* **1 a** : a people inhabiting southern Mindanao, Philippines **b** : a member of such people **2** : the Austronesian language of the Mandaya people

**M and B** *abbr* matched and beaded

**M and D** *abbr* medicine and duty

**man·de** \ˈmän(ˌ)dā\ *n, pl* **mande** *also* **mandes** *usu cap* **1** : MANDINGO 1, 2 **2** : a branch of the Niger-Congo language family including Malinke, Bambara, Dyula, Kono, Vai, Mende, Kpelle, Loma, Mano, and Susu spoken in French West Africa, Sierra Leone, and Liberia, with their center in the upper Niger valley — called also *Mandingo*

**man·de·ism** \manˈdēˌizəm\ *n* -s *usu cap* [F *Mandéisme*, fr. *Mandéen* Mandaean (fr. Mandaean *mandayyā* having knowledge) + *-isme* -ism] : MANDAEANISM

**mandel-** *or* **mandelo-** *comb form* [ISV, fr. *mandelic (acid)*] : mandelic acid ⟨*mandel*amide⟩ ⟨*mandelo*nitrile⟩

**man·del·ate** \ˈmandəˌlāt\ *n* -s [*mandel-* + *-ate*] : a salt or ester of mandelic acid

**man·del·ic acid** \manˈdelik-, -dēlik-\ *n* [part trans. of G *mandelsäure*, fr. *mandel* almond (fr. ML *mandala*, alter. of LL *amandula*) + *säure* acid — more at ALMOND] : a crystalline hydroxy acid $C_6H_5CH(OH)COOH$ that is known in three optically different isomeric forms, that is obtainable in the levorotatory D-form from amygdalin by hydrolysis but is usu. made in the racemic form by reaction of benzaldehyde with hydrocyanic acid and then hydrochloric acid, and that is used chiefly in the form of its salts as a bacteriostatic agent for genitourinary tract infections; phenyl-glycolic acid

**man·di·ble** \ˈmandəbəl, -aan-\ *n* -s [MF, fr. LL *mandibula*, fr. L *mandere* to chew — more at MOUTH] **1 a** : JAW 1a; *esp* : a lower jaw consisting of a single bone or completely fused bones **b** : the lower jaw with its investing soft parts — see FISH illustration **c** : either the upper or lower segment of the bill of a bird **2** : any of various invertebrate mouthparts serving to hold or bite into food materials: as **a** : either member of the anterior part of mouth appendages of an arthropod often forming strong biting jaws **b** : one of the paired corneous or calcified cutting plates on the proboscis of certain polychaete worms

**mandibul-** *or* **mandibuli-** *or* **mandibulo-** *comb form* [LL *mandibula*] : mandible : mandibular and ⟨*mandibul*ation⟩ ⟨*mandibulo*pharyngeal⟩ ⟨*mandibuli*form⟩

**man·dib·u·la** \manˈdibyələ, maan-\ *n, pl* **mandibu·lae** \-yəˌlē\ [LL] : MANDIBLE

**man·dib·u·lar** \-yələ(r)\ *adj* [LL *mandibula* + E *-ar*] : of, relating to, or located near a mandible

**mandibular angle** *n* : an angle formed by the junction at the gonion of the posterior border of the ramus and the inferior border of the body of the mandible

**mandibular arch** *n* : the first visceral arch of the vertebrate embryo

**mandibular artery** *n* : INFERIOR ALVEOLAR ARTERY

**mandibular canal** *n* : a bony canal within the mandible that gives passage to blood vessels and nerves serving the area

**mandibular nerve** *n* : a division of the trigeminal nerve that supplies sensory fibers to the mandible and its teeth and motor fibers to the muscles of mastication

**man·dib·u·lary** \-yəˌlerē\ *adj* [LL *mandibula* + E *-ary*] **1** : MANDIBULAR **2** : being or functioning like a mandible

**man·dib·u·la·ta** \manˌdibyəˈlād·ə, -ˈlād·ə-\ *n pl, cap* [NL *Mandibulata*, fr. *mandibul-* + *-ata*] *in some classifications* : a subphylum or superclass of Arthropoda comprising arthropods with mandibles on the second postoral somite and usu. preoral true antennae and including the crustaceans, myriopods, insects, and a few related forms — compare CHELICERATA, TRILOBITA

**¹man·dib·u·late** \manˈdibyələt, -yəˌlāt, *usu* -d.+V\ *adj* [*mandibul-* + *-ate*] **1 a** : having mandibles ⟨~ insects⟩ **b** *of a vertebrate* : having a lower jaw **2** [NL *Mandibulata*] : of or relating to the Mandibulata

**²man·dib·u·late** \-yəˌlāt\ *n* -s : a mandibulate animal; *esp* : one of the Mandibulata

**man·dib·u·lat·ed** \-ˌlād·əd\ *adj* [*mandibul-* + *-ate* + *-ed*] *of an arthropod* : MANDIBULATE

**man·dib·u·la·tion** \manˌdibyəˈlāshən\ *n* -s [*mandibul-* + *-ation*] : handling of nesting material by a bird with its bill

**man·dib·u·li·form** \manˈdibyələˌfȯrm\ *adj* [ISV *mandibul-* + *-form*] : having the form or function of a mandible — used esp. of the maxillae of an insect when hard and adapted for biting

**man·dil·ion** \manˈdilyən\ *n* -s [MF *mandillon*, dim. of *mandil* cloak, fr. OSp, towel, rag, horseblanket, apron, prob. fr. LGk *mandēlion, mandilion, mantēlion, mantilion* towel, napkin, fr. L *mantelium*, alter. of *mantelum*, prob. fr. *manus* hand + *-telum* (fr. *tergēre* to rub off, wipe off) — more at MANUAL, TERSE] : a loose outer garment of the 16th and 17th centuries: as **a** : a soldier's cloak usu. with hanging sleeves **b** : a servant's sleeveless garment similar to a tabard

**man·din·go** \manˈdiŋ(ˌ)gō\ *n, pl* **mandingo** *or* **mandingoes** *or* **mandingos** *usu cap* **1 a** : a people widely spread over West Africa centering in the upper Niger valley and including the Bambara, Dyula, and Malinke **b** : a member of such people **2** : the language of the Mandingo people **3** : MANDE 2

**man·din·ka** \manˈdiŋkə\ *n, pl* **mandinka** *or* **mandinkas** *usu cap* : MALINKE

**mandioc** *or* **mandioca** *var of* MANIOC

**man·dir** \ˈmənˌdir\ *n* -s [Hindi, fr. Skt *mandira*] : a Hindu temple

**mand·len** \ˈmän(d)lən\ *n pl* [Yiddish, pl. of *mandel*, lit., almond, fr. MHG — more at MANDELIC ACID] : small pieces of baked or fried dough used in soups

**man·doer** *also* **man·dor** *or* **man·dur** \(ˈ)mänˈdů(ə)r, -dȯ(ə)r\ *n* -s [D & Indonesian; D *mandoer*, fr. Indonesian *mandur*, fr. Pg *mandador*, lit., one that commands, fr. L *mandator* — more at MANDATOR] : a native foreman or overseer (as of a sugar plantation or a gang of miners) esp. in Malaysia, Java, and the Dutch East Indies

**man·do·la** \manˈdōlə\ *also* **man·do·ra** \-ōrə\ *or* **man·dore** \manˈdō(ə)r, -dȯ(-, ˈ=ˌ=\ *n* -s [*mandola, mandora* fr. It, fr. F *mandore*, modif. of LL *pandura*, a three-stringed lute; *mandore* fr. F — more at BANDORE] : a 16th and 17th century lute with a pear-shaped body that is the ancestor of the smaller mandolin of the present day

**¹man·do·lin** *also* **man·do·line** \ˌmandəˈlin, -aan-, ˈ=dᵊlən\ *n* -s [It *mandolino*, dim. of *mandola*] : a musical instrument of the lute family that has a pear-shaped body and fretted neck and from four to six pairs of strings and is played with a plectrum — see MANDOLA

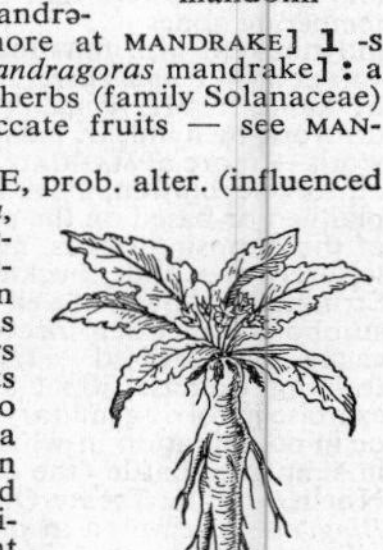
mandolin

**²mandolin** \"\ *adj* : resembling a mandolin in shape — used of rabbits with narrow forequarters and broad and deep hindquarters

**man·do·lin·ist** \-nəst\ *n* -s : a mandolin player

**man·dom** \ˈmandəm\ *n* -s [¹*man* + *-dom*] : MANKIND

**man·dor·la** \ˈmänˌdȯrˌlä\ *n* -s [It, lit., almond, fr. LL *amandula* — more at ALMOND] : a panel or contour in the shape of an almond; *usu* : an almond-shaped aureole : VESICA PISCIS ⟨Christ seated in a ~⟩

**man·drag·on** \ˈmanˌdragən\ *n* [alter. (influenced by *dragon*) of obs. *mandrag*, fr. ME *mandragge* — more at MANDRAKE] *archaic* : MANDRAKE

**man·drag·o·ra** \manˈdragərə, ˌmandrə-ˈgōrə, -aan-, -ˈgȯrə\ *n* [ME — more at MANDRAKE] **1** -s : MANDRAKE 1 **2** *cap* [NL, fr. L *mandragoras* mandrake] : a small genus of acaulescent Eurasian herbs (family Solanaceae) with campanulate flowers and baccate fruits — see MANDRAKE 1a

**man·drake** \ˈmanˌdrāk, -aan-\ *n* [ME, prob. alter. (influenced by ¹*drake*) of *mandragge, mandragora*, fr. OE *mandragora*, fr. L *mandragoras*, fr. Gk] **1 a** : an herb (*Mandragora officinarum*) of southern Europe and northern Africa that has ovate leaves, whitish or purple flowers followed by globose yellow fruits which were formerly supposed to have aphrodisiac properties, and a large forked root which has been credited with human attributes and made the subject of many superstitions **b** (1) : the root of this plant formerly used esp. to promote conception, as a cathartic, or as a narcotic and soporific (2) : a solution or draft of mandrake root (as in wine) formerly used as a narcotic (3) : a fake or substitute for this root (as one carved from the root of a bryony) **2 a** : any of several other plants; *esp* : MAYAPPLE 1 **b** : PODOPHYLLUM 2

Old World mandrake

**¹man·drel** *also* **man·dril** \ˈmandrəl\ *n* -s [prob. modif. of F *mandrin*] **1** *Brit* : a miner's pick **2 a** : a usu. tapered or cylindrical axle, spindle, or arbor that is inserted into a hole in a piece of work so as to support the work during machining **b** : a metal bar that serves as a core around which metal or other material may be cast, molded, forged, bent, or otherwise shaped **3** : any of a train of jointed units intended to be pulled through an underground duct as each joint is made to ensure perfect alignment or through a steel pipe in process of welding to ensure a smooth interior **4** : the shaft and bearings on which a tool (as a dental grinding disk or circular saw) is mounted **5** : a temporary interior support for a thin-walled tube (as a tubular steel pile to be filled later with concrete) being driven into something

**²mandrel** \"\ *vt* -ED/-ING/-S : to turn with a mandrel

**mandrel press** *n* : a press that drives mandrels into holes prepared to receive them

**man·drill** \ˈmandrəl\ *n* -s [prob. fr. ¹*man* + *drill* (baboon)] : a large fierce gregarious baboon (*Mandrillus mormon*) of western Africa with large red ischial callosities and in the male blue ridges on each side of the red-bridged nose

**man·drin** \ˈmandrən\ *n* -s [F] : a stylet for a catheter

**man·dru·ka** *also* **man·drou·ka** \manˈdrükə\ *n* -s [fr. *Mandruka (Mandrouka)*, locality near Bengasi, Libia] : a deep-water honeycomb sponge of close fiber and small root

**mands** *pl of* MAND

**M and S** *abbr* maintenance and supply

**mandt's guillemot** \ˈmänts-\ *n, usu cap M* [after Martin Wilhelm von *Mandt* †1858 Ger. physician and naturalist] : a guillemot that constitutes the northern subspecies (*Cepphus grylle mandtii*) of the black guillemot of the north Atlantic

**man·dua** \ˈmanjəwə\ *n* -s [Hindi *mārnwā, marnwā* — more at MAND] : RAGGEE

**man·du·ca·ble** \ˈmanjəkəbəl\ *adj* [LL *manducabilis*, fr. *manducare* + *-abilis* -able] *archaic* : capable of being chewed : EATABLE

**man·du·cate** \ˈmanjəˌkāt\ *vt* -ED/-ING/-S [L *manducatus*, past part. of *manducare* — more at MANGER] *archaic* : MASTICATE, CHEW, EAT

**man·du·ca·tion** \ˌ==ˈkāshən\ *n* -s [LL *manducation-, manducatio*, fr. L *manducatus* + *-ion-, -io* -ion] **1 a** *obs* : the taking of food : EATING **b** : COMMUNION 2c **2** : the act of chewing — now used chiefly of invertebrate animals

**man·du·ca·to·ry** \ˈmanjəkəˌtōrē, -tȯr-\ *adj* : relating to, employed in, or adapted for chewing ⟨the ~ apparatus of crustaceans⟩

**mandur** *var of* MANDOER

**man·dy·as** \mänˈthēəs, -ˈdē-\ *n* -ES [LL *mandya*, fr. Gk *mandya, mandyas, mandyē, mandyēs*, of non-IE origin] : an outer garment resembling a cloak or cope worn in the services of Eastern Orthodox churches

**¹mane** \ˈmān\ *n* -s [ME, fr. OE *manu*; akin to OE *mene* necklace, OHG *mana* mane, *menni* necklace, ON *mön* mane, *men* necklace, L *monile* necklace, OIr *muin-* neck, Skt *manyā*, and perh. to L *mont-, mons* mountain — more at MOUNT] **1** : the long and heavy hair growing around the neck of some mammals ⟨the lion's ~⟩ — see HORSE illustration **2** : long heavy hair on a person's head ⟨his large features and rich ~ of hair —Osbert Lancaster⟩ **3** : the full feathering on the back of the head and neck of some fancy pigeons

**2mane** \"\ *chiefly Scot var of* MOAN
**3ma·ne** \ˈmä(ˌ)nā\ *adv* [L, fr. *manis, manus* good — more at MATURE] : in the morning — used esp. in pharmacy
**man-eater** \ˈ=ˌ==\ *n* : one that has or is thought to have an appetite for human flesh: as **a** : CANNIBAL 1 **b** : a large voracious shark; *esp* : a shark (*Carcharodon carcharias*) that reaches a length of over 30 feet, is found in all warm seas, and has been known to attack and devour human beings **c** : NEWT, SALAMANDER; *esp* : HELLBENDER **d** : a lion or tiger that has acquired the habit of feeding on human flesh **e** : a man-eating crocodile: as (1) : SALT-WATER CROCODILE (2) : NILE CROCODILE
**man-eating** \ˈ=ˌ==\ *adj* : eating or having an appetite for human flesh
**man-eating shark** *n* : MAN-EATER b
**ma·ne·bach twin** \ˈmänəˌbäk-\ *n, usu cap M* [fr. *Manebach*, Thuringia, Germany] : a monoclinic twin crystal having the basal pinacoid as the twinning plane and composition face
**maned** \ˈmānd\ *adj* [1*mane* + *-ed*] **1** : having a mane **2** : CRINED
**maned rat** *n* : CRESTED HAMSTER
**maned sheep** *n* : AOUDAD
**maned wolf** *or* **maned dog** *n* : a yellowish red So. American wild dog (*Chrysocyon brachyurus*, syn. *jubatus*) with black nape, lower jaw, and feet
**man·een** \ˈmaˌnēn\ *n* -s [1*man* + *-een* (fr. IrGael *-īn*, dim. suffix)] *Irish* : a little man
**ma·nege** *also* **ma·nège** \maˈnezh, məˈn-\ *n* -s [F *manège*, fr. It *maneggio* — more at MANAGE] **1** : a school for teaching horsemanship and for training horses : a riding academy **2** : the art of horsemanship or of training horses **3** : the movements or paces of a trained horse
**maneh** *n* -s [Heb *māneh*] : MINA
**mane·less** \ˈmānləs\ *adj* : having no mane
**ma·nent** \ˈmäˌnent\ [L, they remain, 3d pl. pres. indic. of *manēre* to remain — more at MANSION] : remain on stage — used as a stage direction to specify that named characters do not leave the stage; compare EXEUNT
**ma·ne·ri·al** \məˈnirēəl\ *adj* [ML *manerium* manor (fr. OF *manoir*) + E *-al* — more at MANOR] *archaic* : MANORIAL
**ma·nes** \ˈmäˌnāz, ˈmāˌnēz\ *n pl* [L; perh. akin to L *manus* good — more at MATURE] **1** *often cap* : the spirits of the dead and gods of the lower world in ancient Roman belief — compare LEMURES **2 a** : ancestral spirits worshiped as gods **b** *sing in constr* : the spirit of a dead person regarded as an object to be venerated or appeased
**manesheet** \ˈ=ˌ=\ *n* [1*mane* + *sheet*] : a covering for the upper part of a horse's head
**man·ess** \ˈmanəs\ *n* -ES [1*man* + *-ess*] *archaic* : WOMAN
**ma·net** \ˈmäˌnet\ [L, he remains, 3d sing. pres. indic. of *manēre* to remain — more at MANSION] : remains on stage — used as a stage direction to specify that a named character does not leave the stage; compare 1EXIT
**ma·net·ti** \məˈned·ē\ *n* -s *usu cap* [after Saverio *Manetti* †1784 Ital. botanist] : a vigorous China rose (*Rosa chinensis manetti*) used chiefly as a grafting stock
**ma·net·tia** \-ēə\ *n, cap* [NL, after Saverio *Manetti*] : a genus of tropical American vines (family Rubiaceae) with showy tubular flowers that are white, yellow, or red
**manettia vine** *n* : a Brazilian vine (*Manettia bicolor*) with red and yellow flowers that is used as an ornamental in warmer temperate zones
**1ma·neu·ver** *also* **ma·noeu·vre** *or* **ma·noeu·ver** \məˈn(y)üvə(r)\ *n* -s [F *manœuvre*, fr. OF *manuevre, maneuvre* work done by hand, fr. ML *manuopera, manopera*, fr. L *manu operare* to do work by hand, fr. *manu* (abl. of *manus* hand) + *operare* to work — more at MANUAL, OPERATE] **1 a** : a military, naval, or air force evolution, movement, or change of position; *esp* : one planned or based on the position of an enemy, the relationship of the opposing forces, and factors of terrain or weather ⟨the leisurely ~s and checkmate of royal mercenary armies —Stringfellow Barr⟩ ⟨well emplaced, they sometimes proved stubborn, but when forced into an open war of ~, they were easily disorganized —Irwin Shaw⟩ **b** : an armed forces training exercise; *esp* : an extended and large-scale training exercise involving military, naval, and air force units separately or in combination in which theoretically hostile forces engage in simulated battle ⟨the eighty U.S. ships participating in the North Atlantic Treaty Organization's first naval ~ —*Current Biog.*⟩ — often used in pl. ⟨the Third Army turned in a magnificent performance at the Louisiana ~s —Green Peyton⟩ **2 a** : a movement, procedure, or method of working usu. involving skillful operation and expert physical management ⟨the simplest ~ to actuate the normal eustachian tube is to swallow —H.G.Armstrong⟩ **b** : a manipulation to accomplish a change of position; *specif* : rotational or other movement applied to a fetus within the uterus to alter its position and facilitate delivery **3 a** : an evasive movement : a change of position or shift of tactics ⟨because his area of ~ seems so small . . . his fight lacks the heroic cast —W.W.Whyte⟩ ⟨permits no room for concession or ~ —Harry Schwartz⟩ **b** : an intended and controlled variation from a straight and level flight path in the operation of an aircraft ⟨certain acrobatic ~s such as outside spins, inverted spins, outside loops, pushovers, and inverted flight —H.G.Armstrong⟩ **4 a** : a management of affairs : an action taken as one of a series of actions intended to gain a tactical end ⟨this ~ almost cost him the nomination —H.L.Mencken⟩ ⟨his stubborn and tactless ~s —A.L.Funk⟩ **b** : an adroit and clever management of affairs often using trickery and deception ⟨unable to meet the ~s of the speculative railroad wrecker —W.C.Ford⟩ **syn** see TRICK
**2maneuver** *also* **manoeuvre** *or* **manoeuver** \"\ *vb* **maneuvered**; **maneuvered**; **maneuvering** \-v(ə)riŋ\ **maneuvers** [F *manœuvrer*, fr. *manœuvre*, n.] *vi* **1 a** : to perform a movement in military, naval, or air force tactics : make changes in position in order to secure an advantage in attack or defense ⟨the regiment ~*ed* for several days before it was ready to attack⟩ **b** : to make a series of changes in direction and position for a specific purpose (as in changing course, in switching tracks, or in docking) ⟨a small freight train, having left some cars on the main line, is ~*ing* upon the siding —G.R.Stewart⟩ ⟨the ferry had to ~ in order to dock⟩ **2 a** : to use stratagems : SCHEME ⟨~*ed* successfully to get him to ask her to the dance⟩ **b** : to change ground or shift tactics : jockey for position ⟨had more freedom to ~ than has his emancipated successor —R.M.Weaver⟩ ⟨eight or ten political parties checkmated one another and ~*ed* for advantage —F.A.Ogg & Harold Zink⟩ ~ *vt* **1 a** : to change the tactical disposition of : cause to execute tactical movements ⟨large bodies of troops were ~*ed* —*Survey Graphic*⟩ **b** : to perform tactical or acrobatic evolutions with (an airplane) **2** : to manage or manipulate into or out of a position or condition ⟨~*ed* him into a car —*Time*⟩ ⟨~*ed* myself into being asked to play —Lloyd Alexander⟩ ⟨~*ed* the cork out with his thumb —Kay Boyle⟩ **3 a** : to guide or direct with adroitness and design ⟨~*ed* her guests until the talk at the table became general —Jean Stafford⟩ **b** : to bring about or secure as a result of skillful management ⟨~*ed* out of the Highway Commission the funds to build the state medical school —*Today*⟩ — **ma·neu·ver·er** \-v(ə)rə(r)\ *n* -s
**ma·neu·ver·abil·i·ty** \məˌn(y)üv(ə)rəˈbiləd·ē, -ətē, -i\ *n* **1 a** : the quality or state of being maneuverable ⟨destroy our ~ and our bargaining power —A.E.Stevenson †1965⟩ ⟨~ is an essential quality in a racing car⟩ **b** : the quality of an airplane that determines the rate at which attitude and direction of flight can be changed without loss of control **2** : the quality or state of being able to be used for maneuvering ⟨the harbor had considerable more ~ now —Russell Thacker⟩
**ma·neu·ver·able** \məˈn(y)üv(ə)rəbəl\ *adj* **1** : capable of maneuvering ⟨a ~ foreign policy⟩ **2** : capable of being maneuvered ⟨a highly ~ ship⟩
**maneuvering board** *n* : a printed compass rose with polar coordinates that is used together with parallel rulers and dividers to solve problems of relative movement of ships or airplanes such as arise in changing station in formation or mooring — called also *mooring board*
**manf** *abbr* manufacturer
**manfish** \ˈ=ˌ=\ *n, pl* **menfish** : MERMAN
**man-for-man defense** *n* : MAN-TO-MAN DEFENSE
**man·fre·da** \manˈfrēdə\ *n* [NL, prob. fr. the name *Manfred*] **1** *cap* : a genus of perennial American herbs that are closely related to and often included among those of the genus *Agave* from which they are distinguished chiefly by the bulbous stem base and annually decaying leaves — see AMOLE **2** -s : any plant of the genus *Manfreda*
**man friday** *n, pl* **men friday** *or* **men fridays** *often cap M & usu cap F* [after *Friday*, native servant of Robinson Crusoe, hero of the novel *Robinson Crusoe* (1719), by Daniel Defoe †1731 Eng. journalist and novelist] : a valued aide or employee who gives efficient and devoted service and is usu. entrusted with a wide range of tasks : RIGHT-HAND MAN ⟨the *man Friday* of the party leader is seldom a capable successor —K.R.Popper⟩
**man·ful** \ˈmanfəl\ *adj* [ME, fr. 1*man* + *-ful*] **1** : of, relating to, or befitting a man : MANLY ⟨let your recreations be ~, not sinful —George Washington⟩ **2** : having or showing courage and resolution : BRAVE, NOBLE ⟨his life has been one ~ struggle against poverty —Anthony Trollope⟩ **syn** see MALE
**man·ful·ly** \-fəlē, -li\ *adv* [ME, fr. *manful* + *-ly*] : in a manful manner : RESOLUTELY ⟨shoulder ~ the burden of teaching every freshman the elements of self-expression —H.N. Francis⟩
**man·ful·ness** *n* -ES [ME, fr. *manful* + *-ness*] : the quality or state of being manful
**man fungus** *n* : EARTHSTAR
**mang** \ˈmaŋ\ *var of* AMANG
**1man·ga** \ˈmäŋgə, ˈmaŋ-\ *n* -s [MexSp, fr. Sp, sleeve, fr. L *manica* — more at MANCHE] *Southwest* : PONCHO
**2man·ga** \ˈmaŋgə\ *n* -s [Pg — more at MANGO] : MANGO
**man·ga·bei·ra** \ˌmaŋgəˈbārə\ *n* -s [Pg, fr. *mangaba* fruit of the mangabeira, fr. Tupi *mangaba, mangahiba*] : a Brazilian vine (*Hancornia speciosa*) of the family Apocynaceae having a milky juice that yields a rubber
**mangabeira rubber** *n* : rubber obtained from the mangabeira
**man·ga·bey** \ˈmaŋgəˌbā\ *also* **man·ga·by** \-bē\ *n* -s [fr. *Mangaby*, Madagascar] : a long-tailed arboreal African monkey of the genus *Cercocebus*
**1man·ga·ian** \mäŋˈ(g)īyən, -ˈ(g)īən\ *adj, usu cap* [*Mangaia* Island, Cook islands + E *-an*] **1** : of, relating to, or characteristic of the island of Mangaia **2** : of, relating to, or characteristic of the people of Mangaia
**2mangaian** \"\ *n* -s *cap* : a native or inhabitant of Mangaia Island
**mangan-** *or* **mangano-** *also* **mangani-** *comb form* [G *mangan*, fr. F *manganèse* — more at MANGANESE] : manganese : manganese and ⟨*manganate*⟩ ⟨*manganocolumbite*⟩ ⟨*manganiferous*⟩
**man·ga·na** \mänˈgänə\ *n* -s [Sp, back-formation fr. *manganilla* trick, ruse, fr. (assumed) VL *manganella*, fr. pl. of (assumed) VL *manganellum*, dim. of LL *manganum* contrivance, device, philter, fr. Gk *manganon* mangonel, philter — more at MANGONEL] *chiefly Southwest* : a throw with a lariat designed to catch a horse by the forefeet : FOREFOOTING
**man·gan–alluaudite** \ˌmaŋgən+\ *n* [*manganese* + *alluaudite*] : a mineral $(Na,Mn)PO_4$ that consists of phosphate of manganese and sodium and is isomorphous with alluaudite
**man·gan·apatite** \"+\ *n* [G *manganapatit*, fr. *mangan* manganese + *apatit* apatite] : a dark bluish green apatite containing manganese
**man·ga·nate** \ˈmaŋgəˌnāt\ *n* -s [ISV *mangan-* + *-ate*] : any of several classes of salts containing manganese in the anion: as **a** : a salt of manganic acid obtained as a green mass usu. by fusion of manganese dioxide with an alkali — called also *manganate(VI)* **b** : MANGANITE
**man·gan·berzeliite** \ˌmaŋgən+\ *n* [G *manganberzeliit*, fr. *mangan* manganese + *berzeliit* berzeliite] : a mineral $Mn_2(Ca,Na)_3(AsO_4)_3$ that consists of arsenate of calcium, sodium, and manganese, and is isomorphous with berzeliite
**man·gan·blende** \ˈmaŋgənˌblend\ *n* [G, fr. *mangan* manganese + *blende*] : ALABANDITE
**man·gan·brucite** \ˌmaŋgən+\ *n* [Sw *manganbrucit*, fr. *mangan* manganese + *brucit* brucite] : a manganiferous brucite
**man·gan·ei·sen** \ˈmaŋgəˌnīzᵊn\ *n* -s [G, fr. *mangan* manganese + *eisen* iron, fr. OHG *īsan* — more at IRON] : an alloy of manganese and iron
**man·ga·nese** \ˈmaŋgəˌnēz, -aiŋ-, -ēs\ *n* -s *often attrib* [F *manganèse*, fr. It *manganese*, fr. *manganese* magnesia, modif. of ML *magnesia* — more at MAGNESIA] **1 a** : a black oxide of the metallic element manganese; *esp* : PYROLUSITE **b** : any of various ores of the metallic element manganese ⟨gray ~⟩ ⟨red ~⟩ **2** : a grayish white polyvalent metallic element that is ordinarily hard and brittle, resembles iron but is not magnetic, occurs in nature alloyed in meteoric iron and combined in many minerals (as pyrolusite, psilomelane, manganite, hausmannite, rhodochrosite) and as a trace element in plants and animals, is obtained in a state of high purity by electrolysis or by electric-furnace reduction of ore with aluminum or silicon or in the form of alloys (as ferromanganese or spiegeleisen) by smelting, and is used chiefly in making steel — symbol *Mn*; see ELEMENT table
**manganese black** *n* : manganese dioxide esp. when used as a pigment
**manganese brown** *n* **1** : a natural or synthetic brown oxide or hydroxide of manganese used as a pigment or produced on the fiber in dyeing **2** *or* **manganese bister** : SHERRY 2
**manganese chloride** *n* : a chloride of manganese; *esp* : MANGANOUS CHLORIDE
**manganese dioxide** *n* : a dark brown or gray-black insoluble compound $MnO_2$ found in nature as pyrolusite, made synthetically (as by decomposition of manganous nitrate or by chemical or electrolytic precipitation), and used chiefly as an oxidizing agent and a depolarizer in dry cells, in glassmaking and ceramics, as a pigment, and as a starting material for other manganese compounds (as permanganates and driers for varnishes and paints)
**manganese epidote** *n* : PIEDMONTITE
**manganese green** *n* : barium manganate $BaMnO_4$ used as a pigment — called also *Cassel green*
**manganese heptoxide** *n* : a compound $Mn_2O_7$ obtained as a dark green explosive oil by action of concentrated sulfuric acid on permanganates — called also *manganese(VII) oxide*
**manganese oxide** *n* : an oxide of manganese; *esp* : MANGANESE DIOXIDE
**manganese sesquioxide** *n* : a compound $Mn_2O_3$ obtained as a black powder by heating manganese dioxide or manganous salts in air — called also *manganese(III) oxide, manganic oxide*
**manganese spar** *n* **1** : RHODONITE **2** : RHODOCHROSITE
**manganese steel** *n* **1** : steel containing manganese **2** : HADFIELD MANGANESE STEEL
**manganese sulfate** *n* : a sulfate of manganese; *esp* : MANGANOUS SULFATE
**manganese tetroxide** *n* : a compound $Mn_3O_4$ or $MnMn_2O_4$ found in nature as hausmannite and obtained as a reddish brown powder by strongly heating manganese oxides or hydroxides in air — called also *manganomanganic oxide, red manganese oxide*
**manganese velvet brown** *n* : BURNT UMBER 2
**manganese violet** *n* : a moderate purple that is redder and duller than heliotrope (sense 4a), bluer, lighter, and stronger than average amethyst, bluer and stronger than cobalt violet, and bluer and deeper than average lilac (sense 3a) — called also *Burgundy violet, mineral violet, Nuremberg violet, permanent violet*
**man·ga·ne·sian** \ˌmaŋgəˈnēzhən, -zēən\ *adj* : of, relating to, or containing manganese
**man·gan·hedenbergite** \ˌmaŋgən-\ *n* [Sw *manganhedenbergit*, fr. *mangan* manganese + *hedenbergit* hedenbergite — more at MANGAN-] : a hedenbergite containing manganese
**mangani-** — see MANGAN-
**man·gan·ic** \manˈganik\ *adj* [ISV *mangan-* + *-ic*] : of, relating to, or derived from manganese — used esp. of compounds in which this element is trivalent and of the acid in which it is hexavalent; compare MANGANOUS
**manganic acid** *n* : an acid $H_2MnO_4$ known only in solution and esp. in the form of its salts (as potassium manganate)
**manganic hydroxide** *n* : a compound MnO(OH) occurring in nature as manganite and obtained synthetically as a brown powder by precipitation and drying; manganese oxide and hydroxide
**manganic oxide** *n* : MANGANESE SESQUIOXIDE
**man·ga·nif·er·ous** \ˌmaŋgəˈnif(ə)rəs\ *adj* [*mangan-* + *-ferous*] : containing manganese ⟨~ rocks⟩
**man·ga·nite** \ˈmaŋgəˌnīt\ *n* -s [*mangan-* + *-ite*] **1** : an ore of manganese MnO(OH) consisting of manganic hydroxide in brilliant steel-gray or iron-black orthorhombic crystals or massive — called also *gray manganese ore* **2** : any of a series of unstable salts made by reaction of manganese dioxide with a base ⟨calcium ~⟩ — called also *manganate(IV)*
**man·gan·ja** \mänˈgänjə\ *n, pl* **manganja** *or* **manganjas** *usu cap* : NYANJA
**mangano-** — see MANGAN-
**man·ga·no·calcite** \ˌmaŋgə(ˌ)nō+\ *n* [G *manganokalzit*, fr. *mangan-* + *kalzit* calcite] **1** : a rhodochrosite containing calcium **2** : a calcite containing manganese
**man·ga·no·columbite** \"+\ *n* [*mangan-* + *columbite*] : a manganiferous columbite
**man·ga·no·langbeinite** \"+\ *n* [It, fr. *mangan-* + *langbeinite*] : a mineral $K_2Mn_2(SO_4)_3$ consisting of a very rare sulfate of potassium and manganese found in lava at Vesuvius
**man·ga·no·manganic oxide** \"+ . . .-\ *n* [ISV *mangan-* + *manganic*] : MANGANESE TETROXIDE
**man·ga·no·phyl·lite** \ˌmaŋgənōˈfiˌlīt\ *n* [G *manganophyll* manganophyllite (fr. *mangan-* + *-phyll*) + E *-ite*] : a manganiferous biotite
**man·ga·no·siderite** \ˌmaŋgə(ˌ)nō+\ *n* [G *manganosiderit*, fr. *mangan-* + *siderit* siderite] : an intermediate member of the isomorphous series siderite–rhodochrosite
**man·ga·no·site** \ˌmaŋgəˈnōˌsīt, manˈganəˌ-\ *n* -s [G *manganosit*, fr. *mangan-* + connective *-s-* + *-it* -ite] : a mineral MnO consisting of manganous oxide occurring in small emerald green octahedrons that turn black on exposure (hardness 5–6, sp. gr. 5.18)
**manganoso-** *comb form* [ISV *mangan-* + *-oso-* (fr. L *-osus* -ous)] : MANGANOUS
**man·ga·no·tantalite** \ˌmaŋgə(ˌ)nō+\ *n* [G or Sw *manganotantalit*, fr. *mangan-* + *tantalit* tantalite] : a manganiferous tantalite
**man·ga·nous** \ˈmaŋgənəs, manˈganəs\ *adj* [*mangan-* + *-ous*] : of, relating to, or derived from manganese — used esp. of compounds in which this element is bivalent; compare MANGANIC
**manganous chloride** *n* : a pink deliquescent crystalline salt $MnCl_2$ used chiefly as a flux and a catalyst
**manganous hydroxide** *n* : a crystalline amphoteric compound $Mn(OH)_2$ that is found in nature as pyrochroite, that is obtained synthetically as a white precipitate by adding alkali to a solution of a manganous salt, and that rapidly turns brown in air by oxidation
**manganous oxide** *n* : an insoluble monoxide MnO of manganese found in nature as manganosite and obtained as a green easily oxidizable powder by heating other oxides of manganese in a current of hydrogen — called also *manganese(II) oxide*
**manganous sulfate** *n* : an almost white salt $MnSO_4$ that is usu. obtained as the rose-colored efflorescent crystalline tetrahydrate by treating manganese dioxide with sulfuric acid and powdered coal and that is used chiefly as a fertilizer and spray for plants
**manganous sulfide** *n* : a compound MnS found in nature as alabandite and obtained synthetically usu. as an easily oxidizable flesh-colored precipitate
**man·gan·pectolite** \ˌmaŋgən+\ *n* [G *manganpectolith*, fr. *mangan* manganese + *pectolith* pectolite] : a manganiferous pectolite
**man·gar** \ˈmaŋgə(r)\ *n, pl* **mangar** *or* **mangars** *usu cap* **1** : a people of Nepal **2** : a member of the Mangar people
**1mang·a·re·van** \ˌmäŋ(g)əˈrāvən\ *adj, usu cap* [*Mangareva* island, Gambier islands, French Oceania + E *-an*] **1 a** : of, relating to, or characteristic of the island of Mangareva or the Gambier islands **b** : of, relating to, or characteristic of the people of Mangareva or the Gambier islands **2** : of, relating to, or characteristic of the Mangarevan language
**2mangarevan** \"\ *n* -s *cap* **1** : a native or inhabitant of Mangareva or the Gambier islands **2** : the Mangarevan language — compare AUSTRONESIAN, POLYNESIAN
**mangas** *pl of* MANGA
**mang·be·tu** \mäŋˈbe(ˌ)tü\ *also* **mang·bat·tu** \-ba(-\ *or* **mangbet·tu** \-be(-\ *or* **mom·but·too** \mämˈbə(-\ *n, pl* **mangbetu** *or* **mangbetus** *usu cap* **1 a** : a people dwelling about the headwaters of the Uele in Belgian Congo and sometimes regarded as a distinctive racial type **b** : a member of such people **2** : a Central Sudanic language of the Mangbetu people
**mange** \ˈmānj\ *n* -s [ME *manjewe*, fr. MF *mangeue* appetite, itching, fr. *mangier* to eat — more at MANGER] **1** : any of various more or less severe, persistent, and contagious skin diseases that are marked esp. by eczematous inflammation and loss of hair and that affect domestic animals or sometimes man; *esp* : a skin disease caused by a minute parasitic mite of *Sarcoptes, Psoroptes, Chorioptes*, or related genera that burrows in or lives on the skin or of *Demodex* that lives in the hair follicles or sebaceous glands — see CHORIOPTIC MANGE, DEMODECTIC MANGE, PSOROPTIC MANGE, SARCOPTIC MANGE; ITCH 1b, SCABIES; compare SCAB **2** *archaic* : a constant irritating desire : ITCH
**man·ge·ao** \ˌmän(g)äˈaů\ *n* -s [Maori] : a New Zealand timber tree (*Litsea calicaris*) that has tough hard wood with dark grayish brown bark and flowers in 4- to 5-flowered umbels arranged in axillary racemes
**man·gel** \ˈmaŋgəl\ *n* -s [short for *mangel-wurzel*] : BEET; *specif* : MANGEL-WURZEL
**mangel–wurzel** \ˈ=ˌ=ˌwərzəl\ *also* **mangold–wurzel** \ˈmaŋgəl(d)w-, -ˌgōl-\ *n* -s [G *mangelwurzel* (alter. of *mangoldwurzel*) & *mangoldwurzel*, fr. *mangold* beet (fr. OHG *mānegolt*) + *wurzel* root, fr. OHG *wurzala*] **1** : a large coarse yellow to reddish orange beet extensively grown as food for cattle **2** : the fleshy so-called root of the mangel-wurzel that consists of enlarged hypocotyl and root and is less rich in sugar than either the common beet or the sugar beet
**mange mite** *n* : any of the small parasitic mites that infest the skin of animals and cause mange
**man·ger** \ˈmānjə(r)\ *n* -s [ME *manger, mangeour*, fr. MF *maingeure*, fr. *mangier* to eat, fr. L *manducare* to chew, eat, devour, fr. *manducus* glutton, fr. *mandere* to chew, eat — more at MOUTH] **1** : a trough or open box in which feed or fodder is placed for horses or cattle to eat **2** : a perforated raised floor on which an anchor chain rests in the chain locker of a ship

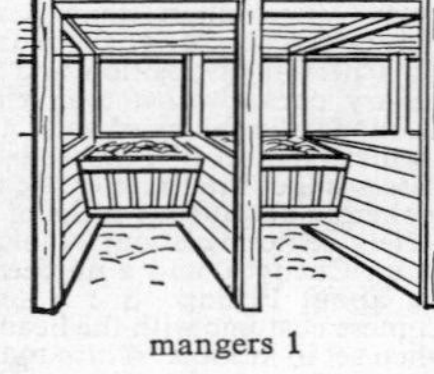
mangers 1

**manger board** *n* : a low athwartship partition aft of the hawseholes that prevents seawater from running aft on the deck of a ship
**mangey** *var of* MANGY
**man·gif·era** \manˈjif(ə)rə\ *n, cap* [NL, fr. ISV *mango* + L *-fera*, fem. of *-fer* -ferous] : a large genus of tropical Asiatic trees (family Anacardiaceae) that have coriaceous entire leaves, small paniculate flowers, and a fleshy drupaceous fruit with a fibrous mesocarp — see MANGO
**man·gi·ly** \ˈmānjəlē, -li\ *adv* : in a mangy manner
**man·gi·ness** \-jēnəs, -jin-\ *n* -ES : the quality or state of being mangy
**1man·gle** \ˈmaŋgəl, -aiŋ-\ *vt* **mangled**; **mangled**; **mangling** \-g(ə)liŋ\ **mangles** [ME *manglen*, fr. AF *mangler*, freq. of OF *mahaignier, maynier* to maim — more at MAIM] **1 a** : to cut, bruise, or hack with repeated blows or strokes : make a ragged or torn wound or series of wounds on ⟨the trees had been whittled and chewed and *mangled* with a dull ax —Wallace Stegner⟩ ⟨rocks *mangled* the feet of the animals —*Amer. Guide Series: Nev.*⟩ **b** : to destroy the shape of by a violent blow or crash ⟨the *mangled* coaches —*Associated Press*⟩ **2** : to spoil, mutilate, or make incoherent through bungling, ignorance, or deliberate falsification ⟨*mangling* a phrase out of its true context —F.L.Mott⟩ ⟨they altered the sequence, they *mangled* the text —Barbara Ward⟩ ⟨the pianist *mangled* the concerto⟩ **syn** see MAIM

**²mangle** \"\ *n* -s [Sp, fr. Taino] **1** : MANGROVE **2** : any of several trees or shrubs (as *Avicennia nitida* and *Laguncularia racemosa*) that resemble the mango

**³mangle** \"\ *n* -s [D *mangel*, fr. G, fr. MHG, dim. of *mange* mangonel, mangle, fr. L *manganum* — more at MANGONEL] **1** : a machine for ironing laundry work by passing it between heated rollers **2** : a machine for applying starch or other sizing material to textiles and then smoothing and drying them **3** : a machine resembling a hand wringer for rolling rubber latex into sheets **4** : a cylinder machine that makes stereotype molds from dry flong by impressing it on a form **5** : PADDER 3b

**⁴mangle** \"\ *vt* -ED/-ING/-S [D *mangelen*, fr. G *mangeln*, fr. *mangel*, n.] : to press or smooth (as damp linen) with a mangle

**mangle gearing** *n* : a mechanism for producing reciprocating motion consisting of a rack with teeth on both sides and around the ends or a row of pegs engaging a pinion that rotates continuously in one direction

**¹man·gler** \-g(ə)lə(r)\ *n* -s [¹*mangle* + -*er*] : one that mangles or mutilates; *specif* : a machine for chopping or mincing (as meat or sugarcane)

**²mangler** \"\ *n* -s [⁴*mangle* + -*er*] : one that smooths or presses with a mangle; *esp* : an operator of a mangle for starching and pressing cloth, mercerizing it, or giving it a finish

**man·go** \'maŋ(,)gō, -aiŋ-\ *n, pl* **mangoes** *or* **mangos** [Pg *manga*, fr. Tamil *mān-kāy*] **1 a** : a yellowish red oblong to pear-shaped tropical fruit that has a firm skin and hard central stone and is widely cultivated for its very juicy, aromatic, and pleasantly subacid pulp but in seedling and wild strains is often exceedingly fibrous and has a distinct flavor of turpentine **b** : a large evergreen tree (*Mangifera indica*) that is native to India, has alternate coriaceous leaves and small yellow or reddish flowers in branching terminal panicles, and produces mangoes and inferior grayish timber **2** *a* : any of several chiefly tropical shrubs or trees that produce edible fruits resembling mangoes — usu. used in combination; compare WILD MANGO **3 a** *chiefly Midland* : SWEET PEPPER **b** (1) : a sweet pepper stuffed (as with shredded cabbage) and pickled (2) : any of various other vegetables prepared in this manner **c** : a pickled mango melon **4** : a hummingbird of the genus *Anthracothorax*

**mango bird** *n* : an oriole (*Oriolus kundoo*) that is native to India

**man-god** \'=,=\ *n, sometimes cap M&G* **1** : one who is both human and divine **2 a** : a man who is made a god **b** : a god in human form

**mango fly** *n* : any of various tabanid flies (genus *Chrysops*) that are vectors of filarial worms

**man·gold** \'maŋgəld, -,gōld\ *n* [short for *mangold-wurzel*] : MANGEL-WURZEL

**mangold-wurzel** *var of* MANGEL-WURZEL

**mango melon** *n* : a muskmelon (*Cucumis melo chito*) that bears fruit resembling oranges and is used for pickles and preserves — called also *lemon cucumber*

**man·go·nel** \'maŋgə,nel\ *n* -s [ME *mangnel*, *mangonel*, fr. MF *mangunel*, *mangonel*, prob. fr. ML *manganellus*, dim. of *manganum* ballista, mangonel, fr. Gk *manganon* philter, ballista; akin to Gk *manganeuein* to deceive, MIr *meng* deception, ruse, Toch A *maṅk* guilt, error, Skt *mañju* beautiful; basic meaning: to beautify] : a military engine formerly used for throwing missiles (as stones or javelins)

**mangonism** *n* -s [F *mangonisme*, fr. L *mangon-*, *mango* dealer that gives a false appearance to his wares (of Gk origin; akin to *manganeuein* to deceive) + F -*isme* -ism — more at MANGONEL] *obs* : a method of training or treating plants contrary to natural conditions of growth

**mango-squash** \'=(,)=',=\ *n* : CHAYOTE

**man·go·steen** \'maŋgə,stēn\ *n* -s [Malay *mangustan*] **1 a** : the dark reddish brown fruit of an East Indian tree (*Garcinia mangostana*) with thick rind enclosing numerous carpels and juicy flesh having a flavor suggestive of both peach and pineapple **b** : a tree that bears mangosteens **2** : the pericarp of the mangosteen fruit used as an astringent

**mango weevil** *n* : a weevil (*Sternochetus mangiferae*) whose larvae feed in and destroy the seeds of mangoes

**man·grove** \'maŋ,grōv, -an,-\ *n, often attrib* [prob. fr. Pg *mangue* (fr. Sp *mangle*, fr. Taino) + E *grove*] **1** : a tropical maritime tree or shrub of the genus *Rhizophora* (esp. *R. mangle*) bearing fruit that germinates while still on the tree with the hypocotyl growing to a considerable length before detachment and having numerous prop roots that ultimately form an impenetrable mass and play an important role in land building **2** : any of various other plants that resemble the mangrove; *specif* : a tree of the genus *Avicennia* — see BLACK MANGROVE **3** *or* **mangrove cutch** : ¹CUTCH 2

**mangrove crab** *n* : any of numerous usu. small active tropical American crabs (family Grapsidae) that live in mangrove swamps climbing about the trees and sometimes feeding on their leaves

**mangrove cuckoo** *n* : a cuckoo (*Coccyzus minor*) of the West Indies and the Florida keys

**mangrove family** *n* : RHIZOPHORACEAE

**mangrove fish** *or* **mangrove skipper** *n* : MUDSKIPPER

**mangrove mullet** *n* : SEA MULLET 1a

**mangrove oyster** *n* : a small oyster (*Ostrea frons*) that grows in clumps on mangrove roots along Floridian and West Indian shores

**mangrove snapper** *n* : GRAY SNAPPER

**mangrove swamp** *also* **mangrove** *n* : a brackish-water coastal swamp of tropical and subtropical areas that is usu. dominated by shrubby halophytes and is partly inundated by tidal flow

**mangt** *abbr* management

**¹mangue** \'maŋ\ *n* -s [F] : KUSIMANSE

**²man·gue** \'mäŋ(,)gā\ *n, pl* **mangue** *or* **mangues** *usu cap* [Sp, of AmerInd origin] **1 a** : a Chorotegan people of southwestern Nicaragua **b** : a member of such people **2** : the language of the Mangue people

**man·gum terrace** \'maŋgəm-\ *n* [after P. H. *Mangum*, 19th cent. Am. farmer] : a broad low ridged terrace that is used as part of a farm's water-disposal system

**man·gun** \(,)man¦gün\ *n, pl* **mangun** *or* **manguns** *usu cap* **1** : a Tungusic people of the Amur river region in Siberia **2** : a member of the Mangun people

**man·gwe** \'maŋ(,)gwā\ *n* -s [native name in Africa] : SOUTH AFRICAN YELLOWWOOD

**man·gy** *also* **man·gey** \'mānjē, -ji\ *adj, usu* **mangier**; *usu* **mangiest** [*mange* + -*y*] **1 a** : infected with or as if with the mange ⟨a ~ dog⟩ **b** : relating to, characteristic of, or resulting from the mange ⟨a ~ appearance⟩ ⟨a ~ itch⟩ **2 a** : having many worn-out or bare spots : SEEDY, SHABBY ⟨aging but resolute, with ~ hair —W.A.White⟩ ⟨knelt on the ~ rug —Elizabeth Taylor⟩ ⟨as ~ a lawn as ever anyone paid taxes on —R.M.Yoder⟩ **b** : having a mean and wretched appearance or quality : SQUALID ⟨the meanest hotel and the *mangiest* restaurant —P.E.Deutschman⟩ **3** *obs* : CONTEMPTIBLE, MISERABLE — used as a generalized term of disapproval

**man·gyan** \män'gyän\ *n, pl* **mangyan** *or* **mangyans** *usu cap* [Tag *Mangyán*] **1 a** : any of several peoples of Mindoro, Philippines — compare HANUNÓO **b** : a member of any such peoples **2** : any of the Austronesian languages of the Mangyan peoples

**manhandle** \'=,==\ *vt* [¹*man* + *handle*] **1** : to move or manage by human force ⟨~ their car out of a ditch —*Scots Mag.*⟩ **2** : to handle roughly ⟨~ citizens who . . . failed to hang out the flag —Dixon Wecter⟩

**man-harness knot** *n* : a loop knot tied in the bight of a rope to aid in hauling

**man-hater** \'=,==\ *n* **1** : a person who hates mankind : MISANTHROPE **2** : a person who avoids the society of men

**¹man·hat·tan** \man'hat°n, maan-, mən-\ *n, pl* **manhattan** *or* **manhattans** **1** *usu cap* **a** : an Algonquian Indian people formerly inhabiting the present site of New York city **b** : a member of such people **2** *also* **manhattan cocktail** *often cap M* [fr. *Manhattan*, borough of New York city] : a cocktail consisting of Italian vermouth, rye or bourbon whiskey, and a dash or two of bitters stirred with cracked ice, strained, and served with a maraschino cherry

**²manhattan** \(')man¦hat°n, -aan-, mən'h-\ *adj, usu cap* : of or from the borough of Manhattan, New York, N.Y. ⟨a *Manhattan* skyscraper⟩ : of the kind or style prevalent in Manhattan

**manhattan clam chowder** *n, usu cap M* : chowder made of minced clams, salt pork, vegetables, esp. tomatoes, with water, and seasoned with herbs — compare NEW ENGLAND CLAM CHOWDER

**man·hat·tan·ese** \man¦hat°n¦ēz, maan-, mən-, -ēs\ *n, pl* **manhattanese** *cap, often attrib* [*Manhattan* borough + E -*ese*] **1** : a New Yorker who lives on Manhattan Island — usu. used in pl. **2** : English as spoken by the Manhattanese

**man·hat·tan·ite** \-'hat°n,īt\ *n* -s *cap* [*Manhattan* borough + E -*ite*] : a native or resident of Manhattan borough, New York, N.Y.

**manhead** \'=,=\ *n* : MANHOLE 1

**manhole** \'=,=\ *n* **1** : a hole through which a man may go; *esp* : one to gain access (as for cleaning or repair) to an underground or enclosed structure (as a sewer, electric conduit, steam boiler) — see SEPTIC TANK illustration **2** : ²SCUTTLE 1a

**man·hood** \'man,hu̇d, -aan-\ *n* [ME *manhode*, fr. *man* + -*hode* -hood] **1** : the condition of being a human being : human quality or nature ⟨make moral postulates that rest less on his scientific knowledge than on his simple ~ —Weston La Barre⟩ **2** : manly qualities : COURAGE, BRAVERY, RESOLUTION ⟨send ~ out of him in fear —G.D.Brown⟩ ⟨society everywhere is in conspiracy against the ~ of every one of its members —R.W.Emerson⟩ **3 a** : the condition of being an adult male ⟨the thing for which he had striven since ~ —Mary K. Hammond⟩ ⟨grew to ~ in a frontier town⟩ **b** : the condition of being a male as distinguished from a female ⟨has become the symbol of ~, which is socially valued —H.M.Parshley⟩ **c** : VIRILITY **d** : male genitalia **4** : MEN; *esp* : the adult males ⟨Ireland's ~ . . . were distributed among the prisons of England —O.S.J.Gogarty⟩ ⟨Britain's strength lies in her own ~, standing on her own shores —M.W. Straight⟩ **5** : mature status : MATURITY ⟨grew up to ~ under the protection of Great Britain —J.H.Underhill⟩ ⟨combat aviation has grown to ~ —H.H.Arnold & I.C. Eaker⟩

**manhood suffrage** *n* : suffrage of all male citizens not under a civil disability (as for crime or lunacy)

**man-hour** \'=¦=\ *n* : a unit of one hour's work by one man used esp. as a basis for cost finding and wages ⟨should save countless thousands of dollars and *man-hours* —*Advt*⟩

**manhunt** \'=,=\ *n* : an organized and usu. intensive hunt or search for a man esp. if charged with a crime ⟨at the time of the crime, a gigantic ~ was staged —*Springfield (Mass.) Daily News*⟩

**man hunter** *n* : one that hunts men

**ma·ni** \'mänē\ *n, pl* **mani** *or* **manis** [Sp *maní*, fr. Taino] : PEANUT

**ma·nia** \'mānēə *sometimes* -nyə\ *n* -s [ME, fr. LL, fr. Gk *mainesthai* to be mad; akin to Gk *menos* spirit — more at MIND] **1** : excitement of psychotic proportions manifested by mental and physical hyperactivity, disorganization of behavior, and elevation of mood; *specif* : the manic phase of manic-depressive psychosis **2 a** : excessive or unreasonable enthusiasm : a violent desire, passion, or partiality : CRAZE ⟨has a ~ for building and transforming —Arnold Bennett⟩ ⟨seized by a ~ for acquisition —Erico Verissimo⟩ ⟨enamel vases, for which our middle classes so long had a ~ —Albert Dasnoy⟩ ⟨letters from citizens who had the ~ of print —Winston Churchill⟩ **b** : something that is the object of a mania ⟨prizefighting, horse racing, and dog racing are national ~*s* —T.H.Fielding⟩ ⟨demobilization became the ~ of the day —Demaree Bess⟩

**syn** MANIA, DELIRIUM, FRENZY, and HYSTERIA denote in common a state of mind in which there is a loss of control over emotional, nervous, or mental processes. MANIA implies insanity, esp. when manifested as the manic phase of manic-depressive psychosis. DELIRIUM implies cerebral excitement precipitated by toxic factors in disease or drugs or occurring in the course of a prolonged mental disorder and manifest in delusions, illusions, hallucinations, incoherence, and restlessness. FRENZY usu. applies to the physical symptoms of mania or any symptoms resembling them. HYSTERIA is a functional psychic disorder simulating organic disease and is manifest in such physical symptoms as disturbances of sensation, motion, and visceral functions expressed typically as functional paralysis of a limb, nausea, emotional instability. **syn** see in addition INSANITY

**man·i·a·ble** \'manēəbəl\ *adj* [MF, fr. OF, fr. *manier* to caress, handle (fr. *main* hand, fr. L *manus*) + -*able* — more at MANUAL] **1** *obs* : capable of being handled or worked : PLIABLE **2** : MANAGEABLE, TRACTABLE ⟨some more definite and more ~ problem —Clive Bell⟩

**¹ma·ni·ac** \'mānē,ak\ *or* **ma·ni·a·cal** \mə'nīəkəl\ *adj* [*maniac* fr. LL *maniacus*, fr. Gk or LGk *maniakos*, fr. *mania*; *maniacal* fr. LL *maniacus* + E -*al*] **1 a** : affected with madness : MAD, INSANE ⟨a ~ killer⟩ **b** : indicating or suggestive of madness : characteristic of or like that of a maniac ⟨stared back from ~ little eyes —Farley Mowat⟩ ⟨~ desires to impose the national will upon other populations —Lewis Mumford⟩ ⟨that ~ glint in a housewife's scheming eye —Howard Spring⟩ **2** : characterized by ungovernable excitement or frenzy : FRANTIC, VIOLENT ⟨under the feet of a ~ mob stampeding out into the bush —Arthur Grimble⟩ — **ma·ni·a·cal·ly** \-k(ə)lē, -li\ *adv*

**²maniac** \"\ *n* -s **1** : a lunatic : MADMAN ⟨believe the crime was the work of a sex ~ —*Associated Press*⟩ **2** : a person characterized by an inordinate or ungovernable enthusiasm, passion, or partiality for something ⟨our own circle of fishing ~*s* —*Ford Times*⟩ ⟨amateur map ~*s* should revel in this book —*Scientific American*⟩

**³maniac** \"\ *n* -s [*m*athematical *a*nalyzer, *n*umerical *i*ntegrator *a*nd *c*omputer] : a high-speed electronic digital computer

**¹man·ic** \'manik, -nēk *sometimes* 'mān-\ *adj* [Gk *manikos*, fr. *mania* mania + -*ikos* -ic] **1** : affected with mania ⟨a ~ individual⟩ **2** : relating to, suggestive of, or like mania ⟨displayed a ~ excitement⟩ ⟨transitions from ~ self-assertions to painful self-doubt —Irving Howe⟩

**²manic** \"\ *n* -s : a manic individual

**¹manic-depressive** \¦==-=¦==\ *adj* [ISV *manic* + *depressive*; orig. formed as G *manisch-depressiv*] : relating to, characterized by, or exhibiting features similar to manic-depressive psychosis

**²manic-depressive** \"\ *n* : a manic-depressive individual

**manic-depressive psychosis** *or* **manic-depressive reaction** *n* : a major mental disorder manifested either by mania or by psychotic depression or by alternating mania and depression

**¹man·i·chae·an** *or* **man·i·che·an** \¦manə¦kēən\ *adj, usu cap* [LL *Manichaeus* member of the Manichean sect (fr. LGk *Manichaios*, fr. *Manichaios* Manes †ab276A.D. Persian sage who founded the sect) + E -*an*] **1** : of or relating to Manichaeism or the Manichaeans ⟨the *Manichaean* debt to Zoroastrianism⟩ **2** : characterized by or reflecting belief in Manichaeism ⟨*Manichaean* influences in Augustinian doctrines⟩ ⟨anti-Semitism of the current type . . . is a complete and irrational philosophy of life based on a *Manichaean* conception of the world —*Times Lit. Supp.*⟩

**²manichaean** *or* **manichean** \"\ *or* **man·i·chee** \'manə,kē\ *n* -s *usu cap* **1** : a member of the religious sect adhering to Manichaeism **2** : a believer in religious or philosophical dualism

**man·i·chae·ism** *or* **man·i·che·ism** \'manə,kē,izəm\ *also* **man·i·chae·an·ism** *or* **man·i·che·an·ism** \,manə'kēə,nizəm\ *or* **man·i·chee·ism** \'manə,kē,izəm\ *n* -s *usu cap* [*Manichaeus* (Manes) *or Manichaean* + E -*ism*] **1** : a syncretic religious dualism originating in Persia, widely held in the Roman empire during the third and fourth centuries A.D. and in central and eastern Asia for a longer period, and teaching as a saving wisdom given through the Hebrew prophets, Jesus, and Mani that a cosmic conflict exists between a good realm of light and an evil realm of darkness, that matter and flesh are in the realm of darkness, and that man's duty is to aid the forces of good by practicing asceticism esp. by avoiding procreation and animal food **2** : a dualistic interpretation of the world dividing it between good and evil powers or regarding matter as inherently evil

**man·i·chae·is·tic** \¦manəkē¦istik\ *adj, usu cap* [*Manichaeus* + E -*istic*] : of, relating to, or resembling Manichaeism

**ma·ni·co·ba rubber** \,mänə'sōbə-\ *n* [Pg *maniçoba* any of several trees yielding Ceará rubber, fr. Tupi *manisoba* leaf from such trees] **1** : CEARÁ RUBBER **2** *also* **manicoba** -s : any of several trees of the genus *Manihot* that yield Ceará rubber

**man·i·cole** \'manə,kōl\ *n* -s [of Arawakan origin; akin to Jucuna *manakóla* manicole, Tariána *manakóla*] : ASSAI

**¹man·i·cure** \'manə,kyu̇(ə)r, -ùə\ *n* -s *often attrib* [F, fr. L *manus* hand + -*icure* (as in *pédicure* pedicure) — more at MANUAL, PEDICURE] **1** : MANICURIST **2** : a treatment for the care of the hands and nails usu. including massage of the hand and cleaning, shaping, and polishing of the nails

**²manicure** \"\ *vt* -ED/-ING/-S **1** : to care for (hands and nails) with a manicure **2** : to trim closely and evenly ⟨wants that lawn *manicured* —Steve McNeil⟩

**man·i·cur·ist** \-ùrəst\ *n* -s : a person who gives manicure treatments

**man·i·dae** \'manə,dē\ *n pl, cap* [NL, fr. *Manis*, type genus + -*idae*] : a family of mammals that is coextensive with the order Pholidota and that includes the pangolins

**ma·ni·enie grass** \¦mänē¦nē(,)ā-\ *n* [Hawaiian *mānienie*] : BERMUDA GRASS

**ma·nière cri·blée** \mə'nyerkrē'blā\ *n* [F, lit., criblé manner] : an engraving technique orig. used in the 15th century in which round holes punched in a block or plate produce a white spotted background in the print — called also *dotted manner*

**manière noire** \-'nwär\ *n* [F, lit., black manner] : the act or process of producing an overall texture in aquatint by scratching the plate directly with a wire brush or other device or by rolling closely set parallel lines in several directions on the ground before etching

**¹man·i·fest** \'manə,fest *sometimes* |,fəst *or chiefly in southern U. S. & Brit* -ni| *or* -nē\ *adj* [ME, fr. MF or L; MF *manifeste*, fr. L *manifestus*, *manufestus*, fr. *manus* hand + -*festus* (as in *infestus* hostile) — more at MANUAL, DARE] **1 a** : capable of being readily and instantly perceived by the senses and esp. by the sight : not hidden or concealed : open to view ⟨the earth's convexity had now become strikingly ~ —E.A.Poe⟩ **b** : capable of being easily understood or recognized at once by the mind : not obscure : OBVIOUS ⟨the wisdom of the new rule was so ~ that it was accepted as a conclusive precedent —Frederick Pollock⟩ **c** : being the part or aspect of a phenomenon that is directly observable : concretely expressed in behavior : OVERT ⟨witchcraft has ~ and latent functions for the individual and for social groups —*Psychological Abstracts*⟩ **2** *obs* : bearing evident marks or signs — used with *of* **syn** see EVIDENT

**²manifest** \"\ *vb* -ED/-ING/-S [ME *manifesten*, fr. MF or L; MF *manifester*, fr. L *manifestare*, fr. *manifestus*] *vt* : to show plainly : make palpably evident or certain by showing or displaying ⟨~*ed* precisely the same bone structure as the mask of the great author —Osbert Sitwell⟩ ⟨choice ~*s* itself in society in small increments —Lewis Mumford⟩ ~ *vi* : to produce a physical disturbance indicating the presence of a ghost or spirit : APPEAR ⟨observe a number of striking phenomena which . . . were then actively ~*ing* —Hereward Carrington⟩ ⟨when the atmosphere is heavy, it is hard for the spirits to ~ —M.L.Bach⟩ **syn** see SHOW

**³manifest** \"\ *n* -s [MF or It; MF *manifeste*, fr. It *manifesto* — more at MANIFESTO] **1** : MANIFESTATION, INDICATION ⟨the Eightieth Congress had just been a ~ of Republican intentions —V.L.Albjerg⟩ **2** : MANIFESTO ⟨this ~ . . . is neither conservative nor too radical —Ernest Harms⟩ **3 a** : a list or invoice of cargo for any of several forms of transportation (as a ship or plane) usu. containing marks or indications of contents or commodity, consignee, and other pertinent information for use at terminals or a customhouse **b** : a list (as of passengers, destinations, baggage weights) in air transportation for each flight **c** : a list of cars by location, number, owners' initials, and contents in a train, accompanying the train and teletyped to yards and terminals **4** : a fast freight train usu. carrying merchandise, perishables, or livestock

**man·i·fest·able** \-təbəl\ *adj* : capable of being manifested

**man·i·fes·tant** \,manə'festənt\ *n* -s [F, fr. pres. part. of *manifester* to manifest — more at MANIFEST] : one who makes or participates in a manifestation ⟨the ~*s* paraded past the docks —J.H.Rosny⟩

**man·i·fes·ta·tion** \,manəfə'stāshən, -,fe'-\ *n* -s [ME *manifestacion*, fr. LL *manifestation-*, *manifestatio*, fr. L *manifestatus* (past part. of *manifestare* to manifest) + -*ion-*, -*io* -ion — more at MANIFEST] **1 a** : the act, process, or an instance of manifesting : DISPLAY, SHOW, EXPRESSION ⟨demanded some ~ of repentance on the part of abjured heretics⟩ ⟨love on a high level of ~ —John Dewey⟩ **b** : something that manifests or constitutes an expression of something else : a perceptible, outward, or visible expression ⟨heat and light . . . had been regarded as ~*s* of the escape of phlogiston —S.F.Mason⟩ ⟨the extent of the . . . disease cannot always be determined by its clinical ~*s* —*Encyc. Americana*⟩ ⟨violent brushwork and strident color are the ~ of a desperate intensity of vision —David Sylvester⟩ **c** : one of the forms, guises, or appearances in which an individual (as a spirit, divine being, or personality) is manifested ⟨in his West African ~ is the god of good fortune —M.J.Herskovits⟩ ⟨various ~*s* of the same god were known by different names —*History of Ukraine*⟩ ⟨dominated by four separate ~*s* of her own sick personality —William Peden⟩ ⟨another prophet, a new ~ of God —M.L. Bach⟩ **d** : an occult phenomenon ⟨the ~*s* here were of materialization —G.H.Estabrooks⟩; *specif* : MATERIALIZATION ⟨a good ghost story, with all the appropriate ~*s* —*Time Lit. Supp.*⟩ **2** : a public demonstration or display of power and purpose (as by a political party or adherents to some cause) ⟨meetings, parades, and other ~*s* —H.M.Parshley⟩

**man·i·fes·ta·tive** \¦manə¦festədiv\ *adj* [F or ML; F *manifestatif*, fr. ML *manifestativus*, fr. L *manifestatus* + -*ivus* -ive] : serving to manifest : DEMONSTRATIVE — **man·i·fes·ta·tive·ly** \-d·əvlē\ *adv*

**manifest content** *n, psychoanalysis* : the content of a dream as it is recalled by the dreamer

**manifest destiny** *n, often cap M&D* : an ordering of human history regarded as inevitable and obviously apparent that leads a people or race to expand to geographic limits held to be natural or to extend sovereignty over a usu. indefinite area ⟨a step in our *manifest destiny*, one of several acts of our territorial expansion —Lancaster Pollard⟩ ⟨a believer in *manifest destiny* in Asia —*New Republic*⟩ ⟨the *manifest destiny* school of historians —C.J.Friedrich⟩; *also* : the doctrine of or belief in such inevitable expansion ⟨that peculiar type of historical mysticism that we in America call *manifest destiny* —Donald Heiney⟩

**man·i·fest·er** \'manə,festə(r)\ *n* -s : one that manifests

**man·i·fest·ly** *adv* : in a manifest manner : PLAINLY, OBVIOUSLY ⟨from the sound of his replies, was ~ shaving —John Galsworthy⟩

**man·i·fest·ness** *n* -ES : the quality or state of being manifest

**¹man·i·fes·to** \,manə'fe(,)stō\ *n, pl* **manifestos** *or* **manifestoes** [It, fr. *manifestare* to manifest, declare, proclaim, fr. L, to manifest — more at MANIFEST] **1** *obs* : DEMONSTRATION, EVIDENCE **2** : a public declaration of intentions, motives, or views : a public statement of policy or opinion ⟨if other writers are impressed with his recipe they form a school, and perhaps issue a ~ —Susanne K. Langer⟩ ⟨gave me an opportunity to write a ~ —H.J.Laski⟩ ⟨professors signed a ~ repudiating various charges —F.L.Paxson⟩ ⟨impelled the . . . government of Russia to issue *manifestos* —F.A.Ogg & Harold Zink⟩

**²manifesto** \"\ *vi* -ED/-ING/-ES : to issue a manifesto

**¹man·i·fold** \'manə,fōld\ *adj* [ME *manifold*, *manifald*, fr. OE *manigfeald*, fr. *manig* many + -*feald* -fold — more at MANY] **1 a** : marked by diversity or variety : numerous and varied ⟨performs the ~ duties required of him —J.H.Ferguson⟩ ⟨reveal its ~ attractions for the visitor —*London Calling*⟩ ⟨~ industries put the city in line with other important industrial centers —Samuel Van Valkenburg & Ellsworth Huntington⟩ **b** : NUMEROUS, MANY ⟨brought forth fruit ~ —J.G.Edwards⟩ **2** : comprehending or uniting various features, kinds, characteristics : MULTIFARIOUS ⟨the romantic symphony, with its ~ melodic content —P.H.Lang⟩ **3** : being so in many ways : rightfully so-called for many reasons ⟨a ~ liar⟩ **4** : consisting of many of one kind combined : operating many of one kind of object ⟨a ~ bell pull⟩

**²manifold** \"\ *adv* [ME *manifold*, *manifald*, fr. *manifold*, *manifald*, adj.] : many times : a great deal ⟨will increase your blessings ~⟩

**3manifold** \"\ *n* [ME *manifold, manifald,* fr. *manifold, manifald,* adj.] **1 :** something that is manifold: as **a :** a whole uniting or consisting of many diverse elements ⟨the ~ of aspirations, passions, frustrations —Harry Slochower⟩ ⟨the unspeakably rich ~ of goings-on —Erwin Schrödinger⟩ ⟨bring into one picture the ~ of his character —John Buchan⟩ **b** [trans. of G *mannigfaltigkeit*] *Kantianism* **:** the totality of unorganized experience as it is presented in sense **c :** a metal chest with many valves by which watertight compartments, pumps, and the drains may be so connected that any or all of the pumps may be used to pump out any compartment **d :** a pipe fitting with several lateral outlets for connecting one pipe with others; *specif* **:** EXHAUST MANIFOLD **e :** AGGREGATE 5 **2** *dial chiefly Eng* **:** the third stomach of a ruminant — usu. used in pl.

manifold 1d

**4manifold** \"\ *vb* -ED/-ING/-S [¹*manifold*] *vt* **1 :** to make many or several copies of esp. by the process of manifold writing ⟨~ a letter⟩ **2 :** to make manifold **:** MULTIPLY ⟨~*ed* many times the work which could be done⟩ **3 :** to collect or distribute (a fluid) or to assemble (as sources of supply) by means of a manifold ~ *vi* **:** to make several or many copies (as of a manuscript) **:** do manifold writing

**man·i·fold·er** \-də(r)\ *n* **:** one that manifolds; *esp* **:** a contrivance for manifold writing

**man·i·fold·ly** *adv* [ME *manyfaldly,* fr. *manifold, manifald* manifold + *-ly*] **:** in a manifold manner

**man·i·fold·ness** *n* -ES **:** the quality or state of being manifold ⟨the intricacy and ~ of things —J.A.Thomson & Patrick Geddes⟩

**manifold paper** *n* **:** a lightweight paper used with carbon paper to produce multiple copies

**man·i·hot** \'manə,hät\ *n, cap* [NL, fr. F, cassava, of Tupian origin — more at MANIOC] **:** a genus of economically important herbs or shrubs (family Euphorbiaceae) orig. tropical American but now widespread in the tropics, having alternate entire or palmate leaves, apetalous monoecious flowers and 3-seeded capsular fruit — see BITTER CASSAVA, CEARÁ RUBBER, SWEET CASSAVA

**1man·i·kin** \'manəkən, -nēk-\ *n* -S [D *manneken, mannekijn,* little man, fr. MD *mannekijn,* dim. of *man;* akin to OE *man, mon* man — more at MAN] **1 :** MANNEQUIN **2 :** a little man **:** DWARF, PYGMY ⟨a bright-eyed little ~, naked like all his people —C.S.Forester⟩ **3 :** a model of the human body commonly in detachable pieces for exhibiting the parts and organs, their position, and relations

**2manikin** \"\ *adj* **:** DIMINUTIVE, DWARF, PUNY

**1ma·nila** *also* **ma·nil·la** \mə'nilə\ *adj* [fr. *Manila,* Philippines] **1** *usu cap* **:** of or from the city of Manila, Philippines **:** of the kind or style prevalent in Manila **2** [*Manila (paper)*] **a :** made of manila paper or board ⟨a ~ envelope⟩ ⟨a ~ folder⟩ ⟨~ cards⟩ **b** *usu cap* [*Manila (hemp)*] **:** made from Manila hemp ⟨*Manila* rope⟩ ⟨*Manila* yarn⟩

**2manila** \"\ *also* **manilla** *n* -S **1** [*Manila (hemp)*] **a** *sometimes cap* **:** ABACA **:** **b** *or* **manilla** \"\ [*Manila (rope)*] **:** a rope of manila **c** *or* **manilla** [*Manila (paper)*] **:** manila paper or board **2** *also* **manila cigar** *usu cap M* **:** a cigar or cheroot made of tobacco grown in the Philippines ⟨always carried on him about six or seven large *Manilas* —Osbert Sitwell⟩ **3** *usu cap* **:** MANILA COPAL **4 :** a light yellowish brown that is lighter, stronger and slightly redder than khaki, yellower and slightly darker than walnut brown, yellower and paler than cinnamon, and stronger than fallow

**manila copal** *or* **manila resin** *n, usu cap M* **:** a copal from any of several trees of the genus *Agathis* (esp. *A. alba*) usu. from the Philippines or Indonesia that varies from soft to hard depending on whether it is gathered after intentional tapping or accidental wounding of the trees and that is used chiefly in varnish — see BOEA, LOBA, MELENGKET, PONTIANAK; compare DAMMAR, KAURI

**manila elemi** *n, usu cap M* **:** an elemi obtained in the Philippines and parts of southeastern Asia from a tree (*Canarium luzonicum*)

**manila grass** *n, usu cap M* **:** a tropical Asiatic grass (*Zoisia matrella*) common in the Philippines and used more recently in America as a lawn grass

**manila hemp** *or* **manila fiber** *n, usu cap M* **:** ABACA

**manila maguey** *n* **:** CANTALA

**ma·nila·man** \-'--mən\ *n, pl* **manilamen** *cap* [*Manila,* Philippines + E *man*] **:** a native of the Philippines; *esp* **:** a sailor hailing from Manila, Philippines ⟨a nondescript crew such as lascars or *Manilamen* —Herman Melville⟩

**manila paper** *or* **manilla paper** *n, often cap M* **:** a strong and durable paper of a yellowish or buff color and smooth finish made from Manila hemp; *also* **:** a paper of similar color and finish regardless of fiber content

**manila tamarind** *n, usu cap M* **:** the edible pods of camachile

**man·il·kara** \,manəl'ka(a)rə\ *n, cap* [NL, fr. Malayan *manilkāra*] **:** a genus (family Sapotaceae) that was formerly included in *Mimusops* and comprises chiefly New World tropical timber trees some of which yield valuable gums — see BULLY TREE, MASSARANDUBA

**ma·nil·la** \mə'nē(y)ə, -ēlyə\ *n* -S [Pg *manilha* or Sp *manilla,* prob. fr. Catal *manilla,* dim. of *mà* hand, fr. L *manus* — more at MANUAL] **:** a piece of metal shaped like a horseshoe orig. mainly of copper alloys but later of iron used by some peoples of western Africa for ornamental purposes and as a medium of exchange esp. in conjunction with ceremonial exchanges

**ma·nille** \mə'nil\ *n* -S [modif. of Sp *malilla,* dim. of obs. Sp *mala* manille, fr. fem. of Sp *malo* bad, fr. L *malus* — more at SMALL] **:** the second highest trump in various card games esp. when it is a card that would have lower or the lowest rank if its suit were not trumps (as the seven of trumps in ombre or the nine of trumps in klaberjass)

**ma·ni·ni** \mə'nēnē\ *n* -S [Hawaiian] **:** CONVICT FISH; *esp* **:** a black-and-white form (*Hepatus triostegus*)

**man·i·nose** \'manə,nōz\ *var of* MANANOSAY

**man-in-the-ground** \'---,-\ *n* **:** BIGROOT

**man in the moon** [ME *mon in the mone*] **:** a fancied figure of a man or man's face suggested by the dark and bright areas of the moon

**man in the street :** an average or ordinary man **:** an average person ⟨carried Labor Party views to the *man in the street* —*Current Biog.*⟩; *specif* **:** an ordinary man without specialized knowledge of the field in question or of mediocre intellectual tastes or accomplishments ⟨simplify a message sufficiently to be understood by the *man in the street* —*Newsman*⟩ ⟨said that the *man in the street* tended to look upon book reading as a highbrow activity —*N.Y. Times*⟩

**man·i·oc** \'manē,äk *also* 'mān-\ *or* **man·i·o·ca** \,manē'ōkə\ *also* **man·di·oc** \'mandē,äk\ *or* **man·di·o·ca** \,mandē'ōkə\ *n* -S [F *manioc* & Sp & Pg *mandioca,* of Tupian origin; akin to Tupi *maniaca, manioca, mandioca* cassava, Guarani *mandióg*] **:** CASSAVA

**man·i·ple** \'manəpəl\ *n* -S [ME *manaple,* fr. ML *manipulus,* fr. L, handful, sheaf, fr. *manus* hand; fr. its having been originally held in the hand — more at MANUAL] **1 :** an ecclesiastical vestment consisting of a narrow cloth band or scarf hanging from the left arm and symbolizing the napkin that deacons of the early church used in their table ministrations **2** [L *manipulus,* fr. *manipulus* handful, sheaf; fr. the ancient Roman custom of using a pole with a handful of hay attached as a standard for a company of soldiers] **a :** a subdivision of the Roman legion consisting of either 120 or 60 men **b** *obs* **:** a small body of soldiers **:** COMPANY **3** [L *manipulus*] *archaic* **:** HANDFUL

maniple 1

**maniplies** *var of* MANYPLIES

**ma·nip·u·la·bil·i·ty** \mə,nipyələ'bilәd·ē\ *n* **:** the quality or state of being manipulable

**ma·nip·u·la·ble** \mə'nipyələbəl\ *adj* [*manipulate* + *-able*] **:** MANIPULATABLE

**ma·nip·u·lan·dum** \mə,nipyə'landəm\ *n, pl* **manipulan·da** \-də\ [NL, fr. E *manipulate* + L *-andum* (neut. of *-andus,* 1st conj. gerundive ending)] *psychol* **:** something that is or is to be manipulated ⟨the instigator and ~ of behavior, the matrix within which all action must be described —R.R.Sears⟩

**ma·nip·u·lar** \mə'nipyələ(r)\ *adj* [L *manipularis,* fr. *manipulus* maniple + *-aris* -ar] **1 :** of or relating to the ancient Roman maniple **2** [influenced in meaning by *manipulation*] **:** MANIPULATORY ⟨~ operations⟩

**ma·nip·u·lat·able** \-yə,lād·əbəl\ *adj* **:** capable of being manipulated ⟨~ variables —S.C.Dodd⟩

**ma·nip·u·late** \mə'nipyə,lāt *sometimes* -pə,-\ *vt* -ED/-ING/-S [back-formation fr. *manipulation*] **1 :** to treat, work, or operate with the hands or by mechanical means **:** handle or manage esp. with skill or dexterity ⟨was a spastic child and found it difficult to ~ a pencil —*Current Biog.*⟩ ⟨a cat was trained to ~ an electric device —J.H.Masserman⟩ ⟨~ an injured limb⟩ **2 a :** to treat or manage with the mind or intellect ⟨nature may be so *manipulated* that mathematical laws may be applied to it —M.R.Cohen⟩ ⟨if we can only quantify our material and ~ it statistically —S.L.Payne⟩ ⟨expert both in *manipulating* the dialectic processes and in applying them to theology —H.O.Taylor⟩ **b** (1) **:** to control the action or course of by management **:** utilize by controlling and managing ⟨providence has strangely *manipulated* events toward this end —Agnes S. Turnbull⟩ ⟨wealth is *manipulated* much as it is in our society —Abram Kardiner⟩ ⟨*manipulating* a situation to achieve certain advantages —F.G.Hawley⟩ (2) **:** to control, manage, or play upon by artful, unfair, or insidious means esp. to one's own advantage ⟨*manipulated* the Indians for national purposes, involving them in successive wars —H.M.Hyman⟩ ⟨knew how to ~ his weaknesses —Mary Deasy⟩ ⟨being used and *manipulated* by the knowing men around him —*New Republic*⟩ (3) **:** to force (prices) up or down by matched orders, wash sales, fictitious reports, or similar methods ⟨groups who ~ the prices —Vicki Baum⟩ **3 :** to change by artful or unfair means so as to serve one's purpose **:** tamper with **:** DOCTOR ⟨considerably *manipulated* by the suppression . . . of a number of passages —Henry Fielding⟩ ⟨suspected that the police reports were *manipulated* —Evelyn G. Cruickshanks⟩ ⟨voting lists were *manipulated* —W.O.Douglas⟩ **syn** see HANDLE

**ma·nip·u·la·tion** \-,--'lāshən\ *n* -S [F, fr. *manipule* apothecary's handful (fr. L *manipulus* handful) + *-ation* — more at MANIPLE] **1 :** the act, process, or an instance of manipulating: as **a :** the act or an instance of handling with the hands or mechanical means ⟨accidents sometimes occurred through carelessness in ~ by the drivers —O.S.Nock⟩ ⟨~ by crushing, grinding, firing —Lewis Mumford⟩ **b :** manual examination and treatment of body parts; *esp* **:** adjustment of faulty structural relationships by manual means (as in the reduction of fractures or dislocations or the breaking down of adhesions) **c :** management or handling directed toward some object ⟨it needs careful ~ to prevent its being washed away —*Amer. Guide Series: Minn.*⟩ ⟨a passion for the ~ of language as music —F.A.Swinnerton⟩ ⟨used as a tool for the description and ~ of cultural data —Ralph Linton⟩ **d :** management with use of unfair, scheming, or underhanded methods esp. for one's own advantage ⟨swing the balance of political power . . . by ~ —Paul Blanshard⟩ ⟨~ is one of the dirtiest words in the new lexicon —W.H.Whyte⟩ **e :** activity by an individual or group intended to influence the behavior of market prices **2 :** the condition of being manipulated ⟨vulnerability to psychological ~ —M.W.Straight⟩

**ma·nip·u·la·tive** \-'--,lād·iv, -,lə|, |t|, |ēv *also* |əv\ *adj* **:** of, relating to, or performed by manipulation ⟨~ practices⟩ — **ma·nip·u·la·tive·ly** \|əvlē, -li\ *adv*

**ma·nip·u·la·tor** \-,lād·ə(r), -ātə-\ *n* -S **:** one that manipulates: as **a :** a mechanical device for handling objects as desired without touching them with the hands **b :** a person engaged in activities designed to influence by artificial means the prices of stocks or commodities **c manipulators** *pl* **:** the thumb and index finger whose combined action largely controls the blade in fencing

**ma·nip·u·la·to·ry** \mə'nipyələ,tōrē, -tȯr-, -ri\ *adj* **:** MANIPULATIVE

**man·i·pur** \,manə'pu̇(ə)r, |mən-\ *n* [fr. *Manipur,* state in India] **1** *usu cap* **:** an Indian breed of small speedy ponies of mixed Mongolian and Arab ancestry **2** -S *often cap* **:** an animal of the Manipur breed

**man·i·pu·ri** \-'pu̇rē\ *n, pl* **manipuri** *or* **manipuris** *usu cap* [*Manipur* state] **1 a :** a people inhabiting the Manipur region of Assam near the Burma border **b :** a member of such people **c :** MEITHEI 2 **2 :** a dance form associated esp. with Manipur in northern India and characterized by a gentle lyrical style — compare BHARATA NATYA, KATHAK, KATHAKALI **3 :** MANIPUR

**1manis** *pl of* MANI

**2ma·nis** \'mānəs\ *n, cap* [NL, prob. fr. L *manes* spirits of the dead; fr. their nocturnal habits — more at MANES] **:** the type genus of Manidae comprising the pangolins or restricted to the five-toed Asiatic pangolin

**ma·nism** \'mä,nizəm, 'mā,-\ *n* -S [*manes* + *-ism*] **:** the worship of the spirits of deceased humans **:** ANCESTOR CULT

**ma·nis·tic** \mä'nistik, mā'-\ *adj* [*manes* + *-istic*] **:** of or relating to manism

**man·it** \'manət\ *n* -S [by shortening & alter.] **:** MAN-MINUTE

**man·i·to·ba** \,manə'tōbə\ *adj, usu cap* [fr. *Manitoba,* province of Canada] **:** of or from the province of Manitoba **:** of the kind or style prevalent in Manitoba **:** MANITOBAN

**manitoba maple** *n, usu cap 1st M* **:** BOX ELDER

**1man·i·to·ban** \-bən\ *adj, usu cap* [*Manitoba,* Canada + E *-an*] **1 :** of, relating to, or characteristic of Manitoba, Canada **2 :** of, relating to, or characteristic of the people of Manitoba

**2manitoban** \"\ *n* -S *cap* **:** a native or inhabitant of the province of Manitoba, Canada

**man·i·tou** *or* **man·i·tu** \'manə,tü\ *also* **man·i·to** \-tō\ *n* -S [of Algonquian origin; akin to Ojibwa *manito* spirit, god, Natick *manitoo,* Shawnee *maneto*] **1 a :** one of the Algonquian deities or spirits dominating the forces of nature **b :** an image or spirit of such a deity **2 :** a supernatural force or spiritual energy which gives power to spirits, deities, and natural forces

**ma·niu** \,mänē'ü\ *n* -S [AmerSp *mañiú*] **:** a Patagonian timber tree (*Saxegothaea conspicua*) of the family Taxaceae that yields wood valued for interior work

**ma·ni wall** \'mänē-\ *n* [*mani* fr. Tibetan, a prayer carved on the stones in such walls, fr. Skt *maṇi* jewel (as in *om maṇi padme hūm* Oh, the jewel on the lotus, Amen — the words of the prayer)] **:** a wall made of stones inscribed with a Lamaist prayer

**man jack** *n* **:** individual man **:** single one **:** MAN ⟨under suspicion . . . every *man jack* of us —Ngaio Marsh⟩ ⟨as good as any *man jack* —Norman Mailer⟩

**man·jak** \'man,jak\ *n* -S [Calinago] **:** asphalt found esp. on Barbados and used for making varnish and insulating electric cables and for fuel

**man·ka·to** \man'kād·ō\ *n* -S *usu cap* [fr. *Mankato,* Minn.] **:** a substage of the Wisconsin glacial stage

**man-keen** \'-,-\ *adj* [¹*man* + *keen*] **1** *dial Eng, of an animal* **:** disposed to attack human beings **:** SAVAGE **2** *dial Eng, of a woman* **:** love-smitten **:** fond of men

**man·kie** \'maŋki\ *n* -S [by shortening & alter.] *Scot* **:** CALAMANCO

**man-killer** \'-,--\ *n* [ME, fr. ¹*man* + *killer*] **:** one that kills humans

**1mankind** \(')-'-, *in sense 2* '-,-\ *n sing but sing or pl in constr* [ME, fr. ¹*man* + *kind*] **1 :** the human race **:** the totality of human beings ⟨~ speaks many languages —Leonard Bloomfield⟩ ⟨~ have agreed in admiring great talents —James Boswell⟩ **2 :** men as distinguished from women

**2mankind** *adj, obs* **:** having masculine traits **:** like a virago

**3mankind** *adj* [origin unknown] *obs* **:** FIERCE, SAVAGE, FURIOUS

**man·less** \'manləs\ *adj* **1 :** destitute of men ⟨an unaccountably ~ cocktail party —*Time*⟩ **2** *obs* **:** UNMANLY — **man·less·ly** *adv* — **man·less·ness** *n* -ES

**man·li·hood** \'manlē,hu̇d\ *n* [*manly* + *-hood*] **:** MANLINESS

**1manlike** \'-,-\ *adj* [ME, fr. *man* + *like*] **1 :** resembling man **:** having the form or nature of a man ⟨hairy ~ creatures —*Blue Bk.*⟩ **2 :** befitting or belonging to a man **:** MANLY, MANNISH, MASCULINE ⟨simple, vigorous . . . ~ passion —*Forum*⟩ **syn** see MALE

**2manlike** \"\ *adv* **:** as a man **:** MANFULLY ⟨meet the danger ~⟩

**man·like·ly** *adv* [¹*manlike* + *-ly*] **:** in the manner of a man

**man·like·ness** *n* **:** the quality or state of being like a man

**man·li·ly** \'manlәlē\ *adv* **:** in a manly manner

**man·li·ness** \-nlēnəs\ *n* -ES [ME *manlines,* fr. *manly* + *-nes* -ness] **:** the quality or state of being manly

**man·ling** \-nliŋ\ *n* -S [¹*man* + *-ling*] **:** a little man

**man lock** *n* **:** AIR LOCK 1a

**1man·ly** \'manlē, -aan-, -li\ *adj* -ER/-EST [ME, fr. *man* + *-ly* (adj. suffix)] **1 a :** having qualities appropriate to a man **:** not effeminate or timorous **:** bold, resolute, and open in conduct or bearing ⟨neither altogether coward nor brave, neither ~ nor sissified —John Reed⟩ **b** (1) **:** belonging to or appropriate in character to a man ⟨~ sports⟩ ⟨beer is a ~ drink —Giles Playfair⟩ ⟨a big booming ~ voice⟩ (2) **:** of undaunted courage **:** GALLANT, BRAVE ⟨seemed a big ~ thing to say —R.P. Warren⟩ ⟨not a very ~ thing . . . to come here and browbeat a woman —A. Conan Doyle⟩ ⟨a ~ disregard of his enemies —H.E.Scudder⟩ **2** *obs* **:** ADULT, MATURE **syn** see MALE

**2manly** *adv* [ME, fr. *man* + *-ly* (adv. suffix)] **:** in a manly manner: as **a** *obs* **:** COURAGEOUSLY **b** *obs* **:** EXCELLENTLY

**man-made** \'-'-\ *adj* **:** manufactured, created, or constructed by man ⟨*man-made* verbal systems —A.H.S.Korzybski⟩ ⟨*man-made* laws⟩; *specif* **:** SYNTHETIC ⟨*man-made* fibers⟩

**man midwife** *n, archaic* **:** ACCOUCHEUR

**man-milliner** \'-'---\ *n, pl* **man-milliners** *or* **men-milliners :** a man who makes or sells millinery

**man-minute** \'-,--\ *n* **:** a unit of measurement (as in time-motion study) consisting of the amount of work done by one worker in one minute

**mann-** *or* **manno-** *comb form* [ISV, fr. *manna*] **1 :** manna ⟨*mannite*⟩ ⟨*mannose*⟩ **2 :** related to mannose ⟨*mannan*⟩ **3 :** *manno-, usu ital* **:** having the stereochemical arrangement of atoms or groups found in mannose ⟨D-*manno*-3-hexulose⟩ ⟨*manno*-saccharic acid⟩

**man·na** \'manə\ *n* -S [ME, fr. OE, fr. LL, fr. Gk, fr. Heb *mān*] **1 a :** food miraculously supplied to the Israelites in their journey through the wilderness **b :** divinely supplied spiritual nourishment **c :** something of value that falls one's way **:** WINDFALL ⟨the seasonal ~ of flying ants and palm grubs are . . . joyfully accepted for the cooking pot —Norman Lewis⟩ ⟨onto the pavement fell a strange ~ of caramels and razors —Constantine FitzGibbon⟩ **2 a :** the sweetish dried exudation of the European flowering ash and related plants that contains mannitol as its chief constituent and has been used medicinally as a laxative and demulcent **b :** a similar product from various other plants (as a tamarisk) **3 a :** MANNA LICHEN **b :** MANNA GRASS **c :** MANNA ASH

**manna ash** *n* **:** any of several European ashes yielding manna; *esp* **:** an ash (*Fraxinus ornus*) that has flowers with sepals and greenish white petals — called also *flowering ash*

**manna grass** *n* **:** a grass of the genus *Glyceria*

**manna gum** *n* **1 :** an Australian eucalypt (*Eucalyptus viminalis*) that yields a false manna **2 :** LERP

**manna insect** *or* **manna scale** *n* **:** a scale insect (*Trabutina mannipara*) causing production of manna on the tamarisk

**manna lichen** *n* **1 :** any of several Old World lichens of the genus *Lecanora* (esp. *L. esculenta, L. affinis,* and *L. fruticulosa*) that have semicrustaceous scaly-foliose or fruticose thalli that roll up and are blown about often in large quantities over the African and Arabian deserts and are much used there for food by man and animals **2 :** a lichen (*Gyrophora esculenta*) used in Japan for food

**man·nan** \'ma,nan, -,nən\ *n* -S [ISV *mann-* + *-an*] **:** any of several polysaccharides that yield mannose on hydrolysis and occur in the cell walls of many plants (as in ivory nuts and other seeds and in the wood esp. of coniferous trees) and in micro-organisms (as yeast)

**manna sugar** *n* **:** MANNITOL

**manned** *adj* [fr. past part. of ²*man*] **:** carrying or performed by a man ⟨a ~ earth satellite is a necessary research step —H.M. Schmeck⟩ ⟨~ stellar explorations⟩ ⟨~ space flight —*Science*⟩

**man·ne·quin** \'manəkən\ *n* -S [F, fr. D *manneken, mannekijn,* little man — more at MANIKIN] **1 a :** an artist's, tailor's, or dressmaker's lay figure **b :** DUMMY 3a(1) **2 :** a woman who models clothing **:** MODEL

**1man·ner** \'manə(r)\ *n* -S [ME *manere,* fr. OF *maniere,* fr. (assumed) VL *manuaria,* fr. fem. of LL *manuarius* of the hand, fr. L *manus* hand + *-arius* -ary — more at MANUAL] **1 a :** KIND, SORT ⟨what ~ of man is he⟩ ⟨what ~ of train had borne him homeward —Ben Riker⟩ **b :** KINDS, SORTS — now used in the phrase *all manner of* ⟨observed all ~ of important people —Oscar Handlin⟩ ⟨picked up all ~ of more or less useful information —J.B.Benefield⟩ **c** *obs* **:** NATURE, CHARACTER, CONDITION — used in the phrase *the manner of* ⟨the ~ of their work and weary pain —Edmund Spenser⟩ **2 a** (1) **:** a characteristic or customary mode of acting **:** natural or normal behavior **:** HABIT, USAGE, CUSTOM ⟨stopped to speak, after the ~ of the country —Ellen Glasgow⟩ ⟨spoke to all the children, as was his ~⟩ (2) **:** the mode or method in which something is done or happens **:** a mode of procedure or way of acting **:** WAY, MODE, FASHION ⟨the ~ of entering the water . . . is important —John Tassos⟩ ⟨responded in a lively ~⟩ ⟨the ~ in which traits are transmitted⟩ ⟨in a haphazard and very far from complete ~ —R.W.Steel⟩ (3) **:** method of artistic execution or mode of presentation esp. as distinguished from the matter presented **:** STYLE, FORM ⟨examples of several earlier ~*s* —*Times Lit. Supp.*⟩ ⟨offers plenty of room for many jazz ~*s* —Wilder Hobson⟩ (4) **:** a method or style characterizing a period or phase of an artist's work ⟨a group of pictures done in his early ~⟩ (5) **:** a character that marks an artist's work as uniquely his own **:** a distinctive or personal character, quality, or tone ⟨style belongs to the age, his ~ to the poet —J.P.Bishop⟩ ⟨~ has been replaced by style —R.B.West⟩ ⟨a ~ of her own —Henry Reed b.1914⟩ **b** (1) **manners** *pl, archaic* **:** the habitual conduct or moral character of a person (2) **manners** *pl* **:** social conduct or rules of conduct as shown in the prevalent customs **:** social conditions **:** mode of life ⟨the brutal ~*s* of an age given to bear-baiting and similar amusements⟩ ⟨the novel is a study in the ~*s* of a class⟩; *specif* **:** the morality of a time as reflected in its prevalent customs or social practices ⟨the licentious ~*s* of a corrupt society⟩ (3) **manners** *pl, archaic* **:** good customs or mode of life **c** (1) **:** characteristic or distinctive bearing, air, or deportment ⟨had . . . ~ as distinct from *manners* — a certain poise, genial but always extremely self-possessed —Joyce Cary⟩ (2) **manners** *pl* **:** habitual conduct or deportment in social intercourse evaluated according to some conventional standard of politeness or civility **:** BEHAVIOR ⟨never guilty of bad ~*s*⟩ ⟨watch your ~*s*⟩ (3) **manners** *pl* **:** good manners ⟨it wouldn't have been ~*s* —Ruth Park⟩ (4) *of an animal* **:** ACTION, DEPORTMENT — usu. used in pl. ⟨the dog pointed with excellent ~*s*⟩ (5) **manners** *pl, archaic* **:** forms of courtesy or respect — usu. used in the phrase *to make one's manners* ⟨made their ~*s* to the squire —S.H.Adams⟩ (6) **:** a distinguished or stylish air ⟨taught to acquire a ~ suitable to her station⟩ **syn** see METHOD — **by any manner of means** *or* **by no manner of means :** in any or no way whatever **:** not at all ⟨are you angry with me? *By no manner of means*⟩ — **in a manner** *or* **in a manner of speaking :** so to speak **:** as it were ⟨he's *in a manner* stone dead —Horace Kephart⟩ ⟨the problem is only asleep, *in a manner of speaking*⟩ — **to the manner born 1** *obs* **:** born to follow or obey a certain practice or custom **2 :** fitted by birth, rearing, or long training or experience to occupy some post or position ⟨was *to the manner born* in the court circles of Versailles —C.G.Bowers⟩

**2manner** *var of* MAINOUR

**man·ner·able** \'manərəbəl\ *adj, dial* **:** POLITE, MANNERLY

**man·nered** \'manə(r)d\ *adj* [ME *manered,* fr. *manere* manner + *-ed*] **1 :** having manners of a specified kind — usu. used in combination ⟨well-*mannered* folk of comfortable means —Robert Shaplen⟩ **2 a** *archaic* **:** dealing with or portraying social manners or customs ⟨no hand at describing costumes, a great requisite in . . . ~ pictures —Charles Lamb⟩ **b** (1) **:** having or displaying a particular or individual manner or style ⟨delightfully ~ . . . lithographs of earlier American life —*Times Lit. Supp.*⟩ ⟨beautifully ~ without ever verging on the precious —Vernon Jarratt⟩ (2) **:** having an artificial or stilted character **:** not natural or spontaneous ⟨~, but imaginative —Dorothy Sayers⟩ ⟨find it rather cold and ~ —C.J. Rolo⟩ ⟨brief, ~ and unlifelike idiom —*Times Lit. Supp.*⟩

**man·ner·ing** \-nəriŋ\ *n* -s [¹*manner* + *-ing*] : a preliminary training (as of a colt) in manners

**man·ner·ism** \ˈmanəˌrizəm\ *n* -s [¹*manner* + *-ism*] **1 a** : exaggerated or affected emulation of or adherence to a particular style or manner : stilted or artificial quality : ARTIFICIALITY, PRECIOSITY ⟨refined almost to the point of ~ —Winthrop Sargeant⟩ ⟨avoids all tiresome ~ —Gouverneur Paulding⟩ ⟨an almost unrelieved ~ and melancholy have taken hold of mid-century poetry —Louise Bogan⟩ **b** *often cap* : an art style in late 16th century Europe characterized by spatial incongruity and excessive elongation of the human figures **2** : a characteristic mode or peculiarity of action, bearing, or treatment ⟨each of us has his own ~s in sleeping —Geoffrey Jefferson⟩ ⟨free of ~s copied from the great —David Sylvester⟩ ⟨some of the birds' curious customs and ~s —E.A.Armstrong⟩

**man·ner·ist** \-rəst\ *n* -s [¹*manner* + *-ist*] **1** : an artist whose works show a strong tendency to imitation, to obedience to the rules of a school, or to a mannerism of his own **2** *often cap* : any of the artists of late 16th century Europe practicing mannerism

**man·ner·is·tic** \ˌmanəˈristik\ *also* **man·ner·is·ti·cal** \-tə̇kəl\ *adj* : exhibiting or characterized by mannerisms; *esp, psychiatry* : characterized by stylized, individualized, often bizarre patterns or traits of behavior — **man·ner·is·ti·cal·ly** \-tə̇k(ə)lē\ *adv*

**man·ner·ize** \ˈmanəˌrīz\ *vt* -ED/-ING/-S : to make manneristic

**man·ner·less** \ˈmanə(r)lə̇s\ *adj* [ME *maner-les*, fr. *manere* manner + *-les* -less — more at MANNER] : destitute of manners : UNMANNERLY — **man·ner·less·ness** *n* -ES

**man·ner·li·ness** \-lēnə̇s, -lin-\ *n* -ES : the quality or state of being mannerly

**¹man·ner·ly** \-lē, -li\ *adj* [ME *manerly*, fr. *manere* manner + *-ly*] **1** *obs* : DECOROUS, SEEMLY, MORAL **2** : showing good manners : CIVIL, RESPECTFUL, POLITE ⟨pleasant to record that they were agreeable and ~ —A.W.Long⟩

**²mannerly** \"\ *adv* [ME *manerly*, fr. *manerly*, adj.] **1** *obs* : DECENTLY, DECOROUSLY **2** : with good manners : POLITELY, RESPECTFULLY, CIVILLY ⟨will always pull ~ over to the curb —Christopher Morley⟩

**manners** *pl of* MANNER

**man·ner·some** \ˈmanə(r)səm\ *adj* [¹*manner* + *-some*] *chiefly dial* : MANNERLY ⟨required that they be ~ and quiet —Edward Kimbrough⟩

**man·nes·mann process** \ˈmänəs,män-, ˈmanəsmən-\ *n, usu cap M* [after Reinhard M. *Mannesmann* †1922 Ger. industrialist and inventor] : a process of making seamless tubes from metal billets by piercing

**man·ness** \ˈmannə̇s\ *n* -ES : the distinctive or differential characteristics of man

**mann·heim** \ˈman,hīm, ˈmän-\ *adj, usu cap* [fr. *Mannheim*, Germany] : of or from the city of Mannheim, Germany : of the kind or style prevalent in Mannheim

**man·nich reaction** \ˈmänik-\ *n, usu cap M* [after Carl *Mannich* †1947 Ger. chemist] : the condensation typically of ammonia or a primary or secondary amine with formaldehyde and a ketone to form a beta-amino ketone

**man·nie** \ˈmanī\ *n* [¹*man* + *-ie*] **1** *chiefly Scot* : a small or undersized man **2** *chiefly Scot* : a small boy : LAD

**man·ni·kin** \ˈmanəkən\ *n* -s [D *manneken, mannekijn* — more at MANIKIN] **1** : MANIKIN **2** : any of numerous small weaverbirds (genus *Lonchura*) of Africa, Asia, and Australasia

**manning** *n* -s [fr. gerund of ²*man*] **1** : the act or action of supplying with men ⟨money destined for the equipping and ~ of the fleet —T.B.Macaulay⟩ **2** : CREW ⟨found a post for him in our ~ —*Scots Mag.*⟩

**manning table** *n* : a survey chart or inventory for scheduling manpower requirements in an industrial plant typically showing each operation with number of workers and time required, each worker classified as to job, experience, handicaps, and the minimum time for training a replacement

**man·nish** \ˈmanish, -aan-, -nesh\ *adj* [ME, fr. *man* + *-ish*] **1 a** : resembling a man as distinguished from a woman : UNWOMANLY, MASCULINE ⟨those ~ women —H.M.Parshley⟩ **b** : resembling or suggesting that of a man ⟨a ~ jacket⟩ ⟨low-heeled ~ oxfords —W.H.Wright⟩ ⟨~ pajamas⟩ ⟨a ~ hair-do⟩ **c** : peculiar to or characteristic of a man as distinguished from a woman ⟨with true ~ arrogance⟩ **2** : relating to or characteristic of an adult male as distinguished from a child **syn** see MALE

**man·nish·ness** *n* -ES : the quality or state of being mannish

**man·ni·tan** \ˈmanə,tan\ *n* -s [ISV *mannite* + *-an*] : an anhydride (as styracitol) $C_6H_{12}O_5$ of mannitol that with fatty acids forms esters useful as emulsifying agents

**man·nite** \ˈma,nīt\ *n* -s [F, fr. *mann-* + *-ite*] : MANNITOL — not used systematically

**man·ni·tol** \ˈmanə,tōl, -tōl\ *n* -s [ISV *mannite* + *-ol*] : a slightly sweet crystalline hexahydroxy alcohol $C_6H_8(OH)_6$ known in three optically isomeric forms obtainable by reduction of mannose; *esp* : the levorotatory D-form that is the principal constituent of the manna of manna ash and is found also in many other higher plants, algae, and fungi but is usu. manufactured along with sorbitol and that is used chiefly in the form of the hexanitrate and in aqueous solution for intravenous administration as a diagnostic test of kidney function

**mannitol hexanitrate** *n* : an explosive crystalline ester $C_6H_8(NO_3)_6$ made by nitration of mannitol and used in blasting caps and in medicine in admixture with a carbohydrate (as lactose) in the treatment of angina pectoris and vascular hypertension

**manno-** — see MANN-

**man·nonic acid** \məˈnänik, -ˈnōn-\ *n* [ISV *mann-* + *-one* + *-ic*] : a syrupy acid $C_5H_6(OH)_5COOH$ formed by oxidizing mannose

**man·nose** \ˈma,nōs\ *n* -s [ISV *mann-* + *-ose*] : an aldose sugar $HOCH_2(CHOH)_4CHO$ known in dextrorotatory, levorotatory, and racemic forms that are epimers of the corresponding forms of glucose; *esp* : the D-form obtained usu. by the hydrolysis of the mannan in ivory nut turnings or in impure form by treatment of D-glucose with alkali

**man·nu·ron·ic acid** \ˌmanyə¦ränik-\ *n* [ISV *mann-* + *uronic*] : an aldehyde-acid $HOOC(CHOH)_4{+}CHO$ related to mannose and obtained by hydrolysis of alginic acid

**¹ma·no** \ˈmä(,)nō\ *n* -s [Sp, lit., hand, fr. L *manus* — more at MANUAL] : a handstone used as the upper millstone for grinding maize and other grains — compare METATE

**²mano** \"\ *n, pl* **mano** *or* **manos** *usu cap* **1 a** : a Negro people inhabiting the northern tip of the central province of the Republic of Liberia, West Africa, and the adjacent territory of French West Africa to the north **b** : a member of such people **2** : a Mande language of the Mano people

**³ma·no** \məˈnō\ *n* -s [Hawaiian *mano* shark] *Hawaii* : any of several large sharks (as the man-eater)

**mano-** *comb form* [F, fr. Gk, loose, sparse, infrequent, fr. *manos* — more at MONK] : gas : vapor ⟨*manograph*⟩

**ma·no·bo** \məˈnō(,)bō\ *n, pl* **manobo** *or* **manobos** *usu cap* **1 a** : any of several closely related peoples inhabiting central Mindanao, Philippines **b** : a member of any of such peoples **2** : any of the closely related Austronesian languages of the Manobo peoples

**ma·no des·tra** \ˈmänōˈdestrə\ *n* [It] : the right hand — abbr. *M D, D M*; used as a direction in music for keyboard playing

**manoeuvre** *or* **manoeuver** *var of* MANEUVER

**man-of-all-work** \ˈ≈≈ˈ≈,≈\ *n, pl* **men-of-all-work** : a domestic employee who performs all kinds of work and services about the home

**man of god** *cap G* [ME] **1** : a godly man; *specif* : SAINT **2** : a minister or other ecclesiastic ⟨a *man of God* and unquestionably a trustworthy man —Earl Hamner⟩

**man of law** [ME] : LAWYER

**man of letters 1** : a learned man : SCHOLAR **2** : a literary man : AUTHOR, LITTÉRATEUR

**man of parts** : a talented or gifted man : a man of notable endowments or capacity ⟨no *man of parts* . . . would accept so feeble a role —H.S.Truman⟩ ⟨not in the nature of a *man of parts* to stick to the same plodding trade —Harriette Wilson⟩

**man of straw 1** : an imaginary argument of no substance advanced in order to be easily confuted or an imaginary adversary advancing such an argument ⟨seems to be looking for a *man of straw* to belabor —*Jour. of Forestry*⟩ **2** : a person usu. without means or position who is vested with some nominal or fictitious post or responsibility as a cover in proceedings of doubtful legality or to shield the real author of an action : FRONT, DUMMY ⟨a *man of straw* who appears to any summons that may be brought against the paper —F.M.Ford⟩

**man of the cloth** : a minister or other ecclesiastic

**man-of-the-earth** \ˈ≈≈≈ˈ≈\ *n, pl* **men-of-the-earth** *or* **men-of-the-earths 1** : an American morning glory (*Ipomoea pandurata*) having an enormous starchy root — called also *manroot, wild potato* **2** : a long rooted morning glory (*Ipomoea leptophylla*) of the western U. S.

**man of the house** : the chief male in a household

**man of the woods 1** [trans. of Malay *orang hutan*] : ORANGUTAN **2** *Austral* : OLD MAN 3

**man of the world 1** : a man familiar with the ways of the world and typically free from sentimentality, excessive delicacy of feelings, or illusions : a practical or worldly man of much experience ⟨his greatest vanity was that he was a *man of the world* —F.A.Swinnerton⟩ **2** : a man of the world of fashion or high life ⟨began his career as a *man of the world* at the . . . court —R.A.Hall b.1911⟩

**man-of-war** \ˈ≈≈ˈ≈\ *n, pl* **men-of-war 1** : a combatant warship of a recognized navy **2** : MAN-O'-WAR BIRD

**man-of-war fish** *n* : a small fish (*Nomeus gronovii*) of the family Nomeidae that is common in the Gulf of Mexico and that lives among the tentacles of the Portuguese man-of-war

**man·o·graph** \ˈmanə,graf, -rȧf\ *n* [ISV *mano-* + *-graph*] : an optical device for making an indicator card for high speed of an engine

**ma·noir** \maˈnwär\ *n* -s [F, fr. OF, habitation, manor — more at MANOR] : a manor house or country residence in a French-speaking country

**ma·no·le·ti·na** \mə,nōləˈtēnə\ *n* -s [Sp, fr. *Manolete* (Manuel R. Sánchez) †1947 Spanish matador + *-ina* (fr. fem. of *-ino* -ine, fr. L *-inus*)] : a right-handed pase in bullfighting in which a piece of the muleta is held by the left hand behind the back

**ma·nom·e·ter** \məˈnämə̇d·ə(r), -mətə-\ *n* [F *manomètre*, fr. *mano-* + *-mètre* -meter] **1** : an instrument for measuring the pressure of gases and vapors commonly by balancing the pressure against a column of liquid (as mercury) in a U-tube or against the elastic force of a spring or an elastic diaphragm (as in an aneroid barometer) : PRESSURE GAUGE **2** : an instrument for measuring blood pressure : SPHYGMOMANOMETER — **man·o·met·ric** \ˌmanə¦me·trik, -rēk\ *also* **man·o·met·ri·cal** \-rə̇kəl, -rēk-\ *adj* — **man·o·met·ri·cal·ly** \-rə̇k(ə)lē, -rēk-, -li\ *adv* — **ma·nom·e·try** \məˈnämə·trē\ *n* -ES

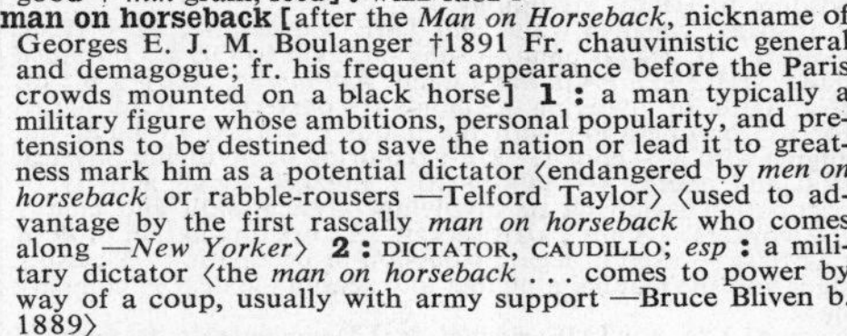
manometer 1

**manometric flame** *n* : a flame produced by a device in which pressure variations due to sound waves are communicated to the gas feeding the flame and cause it to fluctuate in height so that when viewed in a revolving mirror the image of the flame appears as a luminous band with deep serrations corresponding roughly to the sound vibrations

**ma·no·min** \ˈmänə,min\ *n* -s [Ojibway *mânomin*, fr. *mâno* good + *min* grain, seed] : WILD RICE 1

**man on horseback** [after the *Man on Horseback*, nickname of Georges E. J. M. Boulanger †1891 Fr. chauvinistic general and demagogue; fr. his frequent appearance before the Paris crowds mounted on a black horse] **1** : a man typically a military figure whose ambitions, personal popularity, and pretensions to be destined to save the nation or lead it to greatness mark him as a potential dictator ⟨endangered by *men on horseback* or rabble-rousers —Telford Taylor⟩ ⟨used to advantage by the first rascally *man on horseback* who comes along —*New Yorker*⟩ **2** : DICTATOR, CAUDILLO; *esp* : a military dictator ⟨the *man on horseback* . . . comes to power by way of a coup, usually with army support —Bruce Bliven b. 1889⟩

**man on the street** : MAN IN THE STREET

**man·op·to·scope** \maˈnäptə,skōp\ *n* [L *manus* hand + E *opt-* + *-scope* — more at MANUAL] : a device for determining ocular dominance

**man·or** \ˈmanə(r)\ *n* -s [ME *maner*, fr. OF *manoir* habitation, manor, fr. *manoir* to sojourn, dwell, fr. L *manēre* to remain, sojourn — more at MANSION] **1 a** : the house or hall of an estate : MANSION ⟨quarreled good-naturedly over the location of the ~ —Frank Yerby⟩ **b** : the house of a lord with the land belonging to it : a landed estate **2 a** (1) : a unit of English rural territorial organization; *esp* : a unit of English social, economic, and administrative organization in the middle ages consisting of an estate under a lord enjoying a variety of rights over land and tenants including the right to hold court and usu. having tenants of varying degrees of freedom and servitude and marked by a large degree of economic self-sufficiency (2) : a basically similar unit of social, economic, and administrative organization varying in specific features from region to region (as in medieval Europe) **b** : a tract of land in No. America occupied by tenants who pay a fee-farm rent to the proprietor; *specif* : a tract of land in New York granted by the king of Great Britain in colonial days either by patent or in confirmation of grants from the States-General of Holland to proprietors holding by perpetual rent in money or in kind

**man orchid** *n* : MALE ORCHIS

**manor house** *n* : the house of the lord of a manor

**ma·no·ri·al** \məˈnōrēəl, -nór-\ *adj* **1** : of or relating to a manor ⟨~ accounts⟩ ⟨~ documents⟩ ⟨~ custom⟩ **2** : based on the manor ⟨a ~ economy⟩

**manorial court** *n* : a local court held by the lord of a manor in medieval England and colonial America

**ma·no·ri·al·ism** \-ēə,lizəm\ *n* -s : a system of economic, social, and political organization based on the medieval manor — compare FEUDALISM

**ma·no·ri·al·ize** \-,līz\ *vt* -ED/-ING/-S : to cause to conform or subject to the tenure of the manorial system ⟨*manorialized* estates created by the Norman lords —F.M.Stenton⟩

**manorial system** *n* : MANORIALISM

**manos** *pl of* MANO

**ma·no si·ni·stra** \ˌmä(,)nōsə̇ˈnē(,)strä\ *n* [It] : the left hand — used as a direction in music; abbr. *MS, SM*

**man·o·stat** \ˈmanə,stat\ *n* -s [*mano-* + *-stat*] : a device for automatically maintaining a constant pressure within an enclosure — **man·o·stat·ic** \¦≈≈¦stad·ik\ *adj*

**man-o'-war bird** \ˈ≈≈ˈ≈-\ *or* **man-o'-war hawk** *n* **1** : FRIGATE BIRD **2** : SKUA **3** : ALBATROSS

**man power** *n* **1 a** : power available from or supplied by the physical effort of man **b** : a unit of power assumed to be the average rate at which a man can perform mechanical work; *sometimes* : one tenth of a horsepower **2** *usu* **manpower** \ˈ≈,≈≈\ : the strength (as of a nation, community, or industry) expressed in terms of available persons : personnel available or competent to serve : human resources ⟨requires a tremendous amount of engineering *manpower* —*Controller*⟩ ⟨the largest single supplier of educated *manpower* —T.D.Durrance⟩ ⟨*manpower* problems⟩; *specif* : the strength of a nation in terms of persons available for military service

**¹man·qué** \(ˈ)mäⁿ¦kā, -äŋ¦-\ *adj* [F, fr. past part. of *manquer* to lack, fr. It *mancare* — more at MANCANDO] : failing to achieve a desired status through the force of circumstances or some inner flaw : short of or frustrated in the fulfillment of one's aspirations : UNSUCCESSFUL — used postpositively ⟨an artist ~, now condemned to the operation of a candy store —Wolcott Gibbs⟩ ⟨already he was spoken of as the great man ~ —J.C.Smith⟩ ⟨the best writing in his book hints to me of a poet ~ —*Saturday Rev.*⟩

**²manque** \ˈmäⁿk, -äŋk\ *n* -s [F, fr. lit., lack, defect, fr. *manquer*] : the low numbers (1 to 18) in roulette when a bet is placed on them

**man·quel·ler** \ˈman,kwelə(r)\ *n* -s [ME, fr. ¹*man* + *queller* killer, fr. *quellen* to kill, quell + *-er* — more at QUELL] *archaic* : a killer of men : MURDERER, HOMICIDE

**man·rent** \ˈman,rent\ *n* [ME (Sc), alter. of *manred, manreden*, fr. OE *manrǣden*, fr. *man* + *rǣden* condition — more at MAN, KINDRED] *archaic* : HOMAGE — usu. used in the phrases *bond of manrent* or *band of manrent*

**manroot** \ˈ≈,≈\ *n* **1** : MAN-OF-THE-EARTH **2** : BIGROOT

**manrope** \ˈ≈,≈\ *n* : a side rope (as to a ship's gangway or ladder) used as a handrail

**manrope knot** *n* : a double wall knot with a double crown

manrope knot

**mans** *pres 3d sing of* MAN, *pl of* MAN

**man·sa·ka** \mänˈsäkə\ *n* -s *usu cap* : MANDAYA

**man·sard** \ˈman,särd, -sȧd\ *n* -s [F *mansarde*, after François *Mansart* (*Mansard*) †1666 Fr. architect] **1** *or* **mansard roof** : a roof having two slopes on all sides with the lower slope steeper than the upper one — compare CURB ROOF, GAMBREL ROOF **2** : the story formed by a mansard roof : GARRET

mansard 1

**manse** \ˈman(t)s, -aa(ə)n-\ *n* -s [ME *manss*, fr. ML *mansa, mansus, mansum*, fr. fem., masc. & neut. respectively of L *mansus*, past part. of *manēre* to remain, dwell — more at MANSION] **1** *archaic* : the dwelling of a householder : the house of the holder of a homestead **2** : the residence of a clergyman; *esp* : the house assigned to or occupied by a Presbyterian clergyman **3** : a hide of land

**manservant** \ˈ≈,≈≈\ *n, pl* **menservants** : a male servant: as **a** : an indentured male servant **b** : VALET

**mans·field·ite** \ˈmanz,fēl,dīt, -n(t)s,f-\ *n* -s [George R. *Mansfield* †1947 Amer. geologist + E *-ite*] : a mineral $Al(AsO_4)\cdot 2H_2O$ that consists of hydrous arsenate of aluminum and is isomorphous with scorodite

**manshift** \ˈ≈,≈\ *n* **1** : SHIFT 2b(2) **2** : a unit of work output equal to that of one man working through one shift ⟨output per ~ is an inadequate criterion of the human effort employed in raising coal —*Economist*⟩

**man·si** \ˈmänsē\ *n, pl* **mansi** *or* **mansis** *cap* [Russ, fr. Vogul *mańśi*] : VOGUL 1

**man·sion** \ˈmanchən, ˈmaan-\ *n* -s [ME *mansioun*, fr. MF *mansion*, fr. L *mansion-, mansio* act of staying or sojourning, habitation, dwelling, fr. *mansus* (past part. of *manēre* to remain, sojourn, dwell) + *-ion-, -io* -ion; akin to OIr *ainmne* patience, Gk *menein* to remain, Toch A&B *mäsk-* to be] **1 a** *obs* : the act of remaining or dwelling : STAY ⟨the solidness of the earth is for the station and ~ of living creatures —Francis Bacon⟩ **b** *archaic* : a place where one remains or dwells : ABODE ⟨on whose high branches . . . the birds of broadest wing their ~ form —Alexander Pope⟩ **2 a** *or* **mansion house** : a structure serving as a dwelling or lodging place: as (1) : the house of the lord of a manor (2) : a large imposing residence ⟨we'll build a house to last; not a ~ but a big house just the same —E.A.McCourt⟩ ⟨the governor's ~⟩ **b** : a separate apartment, compartment, lodging, or room in a large structure ⟨in my Father's house are many ~s —Jn 14:2 (RSV)⟩ **3** *obs* : a stopping or halting place : STAGE **4 a** : HOUSE 3b **b** : one of the 28 parts into which the moon's monthly course through the heavens is divided **5** [influenced in meaning by F maison, lit., house] : one of a series of permanent structures used to represent various settings (as a castle or cave) in the staging of medieval or Renaissance plays esp. in France

**man·sion·ary** \-chə,nerē\ *n* -ES [LL *mansionarius*, fr. L *mansion-, mansio* + *-arius* -ary] : SEXTON

**man·sion·ry** \-chənrē\ *n* -ES : MANSIONS

**man-size** \ˈ≈¦≈\ *or* **man-sized** \ˈ≈¦≈\ *adj* **1** : suitable for or requiring a man ⟨a *man-size* job⟩ **2** : LARGE-SCALE ⟨a *man-size* model⟩

**manslaughter** \ˈ≈,≈≈\ *n* [ME, fr. ¹*man* + *slaughter*] : the slaying of a human being; *specif* : the unlawful killing of a human being without express or implied malice

**manslayer** \ˈ≈,≈≈\ *n* [ME *manslaer, mansleer*, fr. ¹*man* + *slaer, sleer* slayer — more at SLAYER] : one who commits homicide

**man's motherwort** *n* : CASTOR-OIL PLANT

**man·so** \ˈmän(,)sō, ˈman-\ *n* -s *usu cap* [Sp, fr. *manso* tame, gentle, fr. (assumed) VL *mansus*, alter. of L *mansuetus* — more at MANSUETE] **1** : a Tanoan people of the southwestern U.S. and Mexico **2** : a member of the Manso people

**man·son·el·la** \ˌman(t)səˈnelə\ *n, cap* [NL, fr. Sir Patrick *Manson* †1922 Brit. physician and parasitologist + NL *-ella*] : a genus of filarial worms (family Dipetalonematidae) including one (*M. ozzardi*) that is common and apparently nonpathogenic in human visceral fat and mesenteries in So. and Central America

**man·so·nia** \manˈsōnēə\ *n* [NL, fr. Sir Patrick *Manson* + NL *-ia*] **1** *cap* : a widespread genus of mosquitoes which carry filarial worms and whose larvae and pupae obtain oxygen directly from plants under water **2** -s : a mosquito of the genus *Mansonia*

**man·son's disease** \ˈman(t)sᵊnz-\ *n, usu cap M* [after Sir Patrick *Manson*] : SCHISTOSOMIASIS MANSONI

**manstealing** \ˈ≈,≈≈\ *n* -s : KIDNAPPING

**manstopper** \ˈ≈,≈≈\ *n* : a bullet capable of causing a shock sufficient to stop a soldier advancing in a charge

**man·suete** \(ˈ)man¦swēt\ *adj* [ME, fr. L *mansuetus*, past part. of *mansuescere* to tame, fr. *manus* hand + *suescere* to accustom; akin to Gk *ēthos* custom — more at MANUAL, ETHICAL] *archaic* : GENTLE, TAME

**man·sue·tude** \ˈman(t)swə,tüd, -ə,tyüd\ *n* -s [ME, fr. L *mansuetudo*, fr. *mansuetus* tame + *-udo* -ude] : the quality or state of being gentle : MEEKNESS, TAMENESS ⟨his matchless knowledge of the human heart and his infinite ~ —W.J. Locke⟩

**mansura** *adj, usu cap* [fr. El Mansura, Egypt] : EL MANSURA

**man·sworn** \ˈman¦swō(ə)rn, -swó(ə)n\ *adj* [ME, fr. past part. of *mansweren* to swear falsely, fr. OE *mānswerian*, fr. *mān* crime, guilt, sin, false oath + *swerian* to swear; akin to OFris & OS *mēn* crime, guilt, false oath, OHG & ON *mein* crime, guilt, false oath, OE *mān*, adj., criminal, bad, false — more at MEAN] *now dial* : FORSWORN, PERJURED

**¹mant** \ˈmant\ *vb* -ED/-ING/-S [ScGael *mannd*, n., stammer] *chiefly Scot* : STAMMER

**²mant** \"\ *n* -s [ScGael *mannd*] *chiefly Scot* : a speech impediment : STAMMER

**³mant** *n* -s [F *mante*, fr. MF, fr. OProv *manta*, fr. (assumed) VL, blanket, cloak, alter. of LL *mantus* cloak, back-formation fr. L *mantellum*] *obs* : MANTILLA; *also* : MANTEAU

**man·ta** \ˈmantə, ˈmän-\ *n* [Sp, lit., blanket, cloak, fr. (assumed) VL, blanket, cloak] **1** -s *chiefly Southwest* : a plain cotton fabric **2** -s **a** : a square piece of cloth or blanket used in southwestern U.S. and Latin America usu. as a cloak, head covering, or shawl **b** : a piece of canvas or other heavy cloth used to cover a loaded packsaddle or to wrap loads for carrying **3 a** *also* **manta ray** -s [AmerSp, fr. Sp, blanket; fr. the method of catching the fish in traps resembling large blankets] : DEVILFISH 1 **b** *cap* [NL, fr. AmerSp] : a genus of rays containing the typical devilfishes **4 a** *pl* **manta** *or* **mantas** usu cap : an Indian people of coastal Ecuador **b** : a member of such people

**man-tailored** \ˈ≈¦≈≈\ *adj, of a woman's suit or coat* : made with the trim severe simplicity associated with men's coats and suits

**man·teau** \(ˈ)man¦tō\ *n* -s [F, fr. OF *mantel* — more at MANTLE] **1** *obs* : MANTUA **2** : a loose cloak, coat, or robe

**man·teel** \(ˈ)man¦tēl\ *n* -s [F *mantille*, fr. Sp *mantilla* — more at MANTILLA] *archaic* : a cloak or a cape worn by women

**man·te·idae** \man·ˈtēə,dē\ *n pl, cap* [NL, fr. *Mante-, Mantis*, type genus + *-idae*] : a family of carnivorous insects sometimes esp. formerly made coextensive with Manteodea but now usu. restricted to mantises with black-barred wings, a rather long pronotum, and a frontal shield that is narrow in proportion to its height

**man·tel** \ˈmantᵊl, -aan-\ *n* -s [MF *mantel, manteau* cloak, mantle, mantel — more at MANTLE] **1 a** : the beam, stone, or arch serving as a lintel to support the masonry above a fireplace ⟨a high ~ has some advantage in producing a more effectual ventilation —Thomas Tredgold⟩ **b :** the finish around a fireplace covering the front and sometimes the two sides of the chimney ⟨the skill of our craftsmen is reflected in . . . the wood ~s —*Sweet's Catalogue Service*⟩ **2 :** the usu. ornamental shelf above a fireplace ⟨stepped to the ~ and rested his elbows on it —Eudora Welty⟩

**man·te·let** \-t(ᵊ)lət, *usu* -əd.+V\ *n* -s [ME, fr. MF, dim. of *mantel, manteau* cloak] **1 :** a very short cape, cloak, or mantle **2** *or* **mant·let** \-tlət, *usu* -əd.+V\ **:** a movable shelter formerly used by besiegers as a protection when attacking ⟨they bring forward ~s and pavises and the archers muster on the skirts of the woods —Sir Walter Scott⟩

**man·tel·let·ta** \ˌmantᵊlˈed·ə\ *n* -s [It, prob. modif. of ML *mantelletum*, dim. of L *mantellum* cloak, mantle] **:** a knee-length outer garment that is sleeveless but has armholes, is open in the front but fastened at the neck, and is worn by cardinals, bishops, and other high prelates of the Roman Catholic Church

**man·tel·lo·ne** \ˌmantᵊlˈōnē\ *n* -s [It, augm. of *mantello* cloak] **:** a long purple cloak worn over the cassock by prelates of the secondary rank attached to the papal court

**mantelpiece** \ˈ=ˌ=\ *n* **1 :** a mantel with its side elements **2 :** MANTELSHELF

**mantelshelf** \ˈ=ˌ=\ *n, pl* **mantelshelves :** the part of a mantel above the fireplace that serves as a shelf ⟨standing by the hearth, one hand on the ~ —Gertrude Atherton⟩

**manteltree** \ˈ=ˌ=\ *n* [ME *mantelltree*, fr. *mantell, mantel* mantel + *tree*] **:** MANTEL 1a

**man·te·o·dea** \ˌmantēˈōdēə\ *n pl, cap* [NL, fr. *Mante-, Mantis* + *-odea*] **:** a suborder of Orthoptera often considered a separate order, comprising predaceous insects with the fore-legs specialized for seizing prey and including the mantises — see MANTEIDAE

**mant·er** \ˈmantər\ *n* -s [¹*mant* + *-er*] *chiefly Scot* **:** STAMMERER

¹**man·tic** \ˈmantik\ *n* -s [Gk *mantikē*, fr. fem. of *mantikos* prophetic] **:** the art or science of divination

²**mantic** \ˈ"\ *adj* [Gk *mantikos*, fr. *mantis* prophet, seer + *-ikos* -ic — more at MANTIS] **:** of or relating to the faculty of divination **:** PROPHETIC

**man·ti·core** \ˈmantəˌkō(ə)r\ *also* **man·ti·cho·ra** *or* **man·ti·co·ra** \ˌ==ˈkōrə\ *or* **man·ti·ger** \ˈ=tijə(r)\ *n* -s [ME *manticore, mantichora*, fr. L *mantichora*, fr. Gk *mantichōras, martichoras*, of Iranian origin; akin to OPer *martiya* man, and to OPer *khvar-* to eat, Av *khwar-*] **:** a legendary animal having the head of a man often with horns, the body of a lion, and the tail of a dragon or scorpion

¹**man·tid** \ˈmantəd\ *adj* [NL *Mantidae*] **:** of or relating to mantids

²**mantid** \ˈ"\ *n* -s **:** MANTIS 1

¹**man·ti·dae** \-təˌdē\ [NL, fr. *Mantis*, type genus + *-idae*] *syn of* MANTEIDAE

²**mantidae** \ˈ"\ [NL, fr. *Manta*, type genus + *-idae*] *syn of* MOBULIDAE

**man·tilla** \manˈtē(y)ə, -tilə\ *n* -s [Sp, dim. of *manta* blanket, cloak — more at MANTA] **1 :** a light scarf often of black lace worn over the head and shoulders esp. by Spanish and Latin American women **2 :** a short light cape or cloak

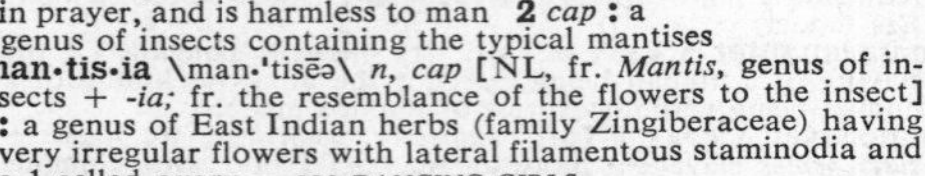

mantilla 1

**manting** *pres part of* MANT

**man·tis** \ˈmantəs, -aan-\ *n* [NL, fr. Gk, lit., prophet; fr. the posture of such insects, with the forelimbs extended as though in prayer; akin to Gk *mainesthai* to be mad — more at MANIA] **1** *pl* **mantis·es** \-təsəz\ *or* **man·tes** \-ˌtēz\ **:** an insect of *Mantis* or a related genus (suborder Manteodea) that has a long prothorax, feeds upon other insects, clasps its prey in upheld forelimbs as if in prayer, and is harmless to man **2** *cap* **:** a genus of insects containing the typical mantises

**man·tis·ia** \manˈtisēə\ *n, cap* [NL, fr. *Mantis*, genus of insects + *-ia*; fr. the resemblance of the flowers to the insect] **:** a genus of East Indian herbs (family Zingiberaceae) having very irregular flowers with lateral filamentous staminodia and a 1-celled ovary — see DANCING-GIRLS

**man·tis·pa** \manˈtispə\ *n* [NL, fr. *Mantis* + *pagana* (specific epithet of *Mantis pagana*), fr. L, fem. of *paganus* of the country — more at PAGAN] **1** *cap* **:** the type genus of Mantispidae **2** -s **:** any insect of the genus *Mantispa*

¹**man·tis·pid** \-pəd\ *adj* [NL *Mantispidae*] **:** of or relating to the Mantispidae

²**mantispid** \ˈ"\ *n* -s **:** an insect of the family Mantispidae

**man·tis·pi·dae** \-pəˌdē\ *n pl, cap* [NL, fr. *Mantispa*, type genus + *-idae*] **:** a family of insects (order Neuroptera) having the prothorax elongated and the first pair of legs developed after the manner of a mantis

**mantis prawn** *or* **mantis shrimp** *n* **:** SQUILLA

**man·tis·sa** \manˈtisə\ *n* -s [L *mantissa, mantisa*, fr. Etruscan, prob. of Celt origin; akin to OIr *mēit* size, W *maint*; akin to OIr *mār* large — more at MORE] **1** *obs* **:** an addition of little value or importance **2 :** the decimal part of a logarithm

¹**man·tle** \ˈmantᵊl, -aan-\ *n* -s [ME *mantel, mentel*; partly fr. OE *mentel*; partly fr. OF *mantel*; both fr. L *mantellum*] **1 a :** a loose sleeveless garment worn over other clothes **:** an enveloping robe or cloak ⟨brought a heavy ~ and covered her from head to foot —William Black⟩ **b :** a mantle regarded as a symbol of preeminence or authority ⟨take off the ~ of authority and drop it on younger shoulders —H.H.Arnold & I.C.Eaker⟩ **2 a :** something that covers, enfolds, or envelops ⟨the green ~ of the standing pool —*Shak.*⟩ ⟨the ~ of night made it easier for them to forget their youth —T.B.Costain⟩ **b** (1) **:** the fold or lobe or pair of lobes of the body wall in a mollusk or brachiopod lining the shell in shell-bearing forms, bearing the shell-secreting glands, and usu. forming a cavity between itself and the body proper that holds the respiratory organs (2) **:** the soft external body wall that lines the test or the shell of a tunicate or barnacle **c :** the outer wall and casing of a blast furnace above the hearth **d :** CEREBRAL CORTEX **3 :** MANTLING **4 :** the back, scapulars, and wings of a bird when distinguished from other parts of the plumage by a distinct and uniform color (as in some gulls) **5 :** a penstock for a waterwheel **6 a :** the external layers of meristematic cells in a stem apex often equivalent to the combined tunica and corpus **b :** the fungal network around an ectotrophic mycorhiza that replaces the root hairs as an absorbing system **7 a :** a lacelike hood or sheath of some refractory material that gives light by incandescence when placed over a flame **b :** a thin zone at the border of a flame **c :** HEATING MANTLE **8 a :** MANTLEROCK **b :** the part of the earth's interior beneath the lithosphere and above the central core from which it is separated by a discontinuity at a depth of about 1800 miles **9 :** MANTEL

²**mantle** \ˈ"\ *vb* **mantled; mantled; mantling** \-t(ᵊ)liŋ\ **mantles** [ME *mantellen*, fr. *mantel*, n.] *vt* **1 :** to conceal by covering **:** make obscure ⟨its venerable trunk is richly *mantled* with ivy —J.G.Strutt⟩ **2 :** to cover with or as if with a mantle ⟨the land is *mantled* with glacial deposits —W.W.Atwood b.1906⟩ **3 :** to cause to blush **:** give a glowing color to ~ *vi* **1 a** *of a hawk* **:** to spread one wing and then the other over the corresponding outstretched leg **b** *obs* **:** to spread out — used of wings **2 :** to become covered with a coating (as of scum or froth) ⟨the poison *mantled* in the cup —Alexander Pope⟩ **3 :** to spread over a surface ⟨seldom o'er a breast so fair *mantled* a plaid with modest care —Sir Walter Scott⟩ **4 :** BLUSH, COLOR ⟨her rich face *mantling* with emotion —Benjamin Disraeli⟩

**mantle cavity** *n* **:** the cavity between the mantle and the body proper of a mollusk or brachiopod in which the respiratory organs lie

**man·tled** \ˈmantᵊld, -aan-\ *adj* [¹*mantle* + *-ed*] **1 :** furnished or covered with or as if with a mantle ⟨places *mantled* with coarse, bouldery gravel —P.E.James⟩ ⟨cool, forest-*mantled* hills⟩ **2 :** ornamented with a mantling

**mantled ground squirrel** *n* **:** a common ground squirrel (*Citellus lateralis*) of western No. America that is reddish brown above with black and buff lateral stripes and resembles a large chipmunk in habits and appearance

**mantle fiber** *n* **:** one of the apparent fibers that pass between the centromeres of the chromosomes and the poles of the mitotic spindle and that appear to draw the chromosomes apart

**mantlerock** \ˈ=ˌ=\ *n* **:** unconsolidated residual or transported material that overlies or covers the solid rock in place — called also *regolith*; compare LATERITE, SAPROLITE

**mantlet** *var of* MANTELET

**mantling** *n* -s [fr. gerund of ²*mantle*] **1 :** a heraldic representation of a mantle behind and around a coat of arms — called also *lambrequin* **2 :** MANTLE 4

**man·to** \ˈmanˌtō\ *n* -s [Sp, fr. LL *mantus* — more at MANT] **1 :** a usu. black shawl worn esp. by Spanish or Latin American women as a covering for head and shoulders **2 a :** a nearly horizontal or gently inclined sheetlike body of ore — called also BLANKET DEPOSIT **b :** a pipe-shaped ore body

**man·to·dea** \manˈtōdēə\ *or* **man·toi·dea** \-ˈtȯidēə\ [NL, fr. *Mantis* + *-odea* or *-oidea*] *syn of* MANTEODEA

¹**man·toid** \ˈmanˌtȯid\ *adj* [NL *Mantoidea*] **:** of, relating to, or resembling the Manteodea

²**mantoid** \ˈ"\ *n* -s **:** MANTIS 1

**man·tol·o·gy** \manˈtäləjē\ *n* -ES [Gk *mantis* prophet + E *-o-* + *-logy* — more at MANTIS] *archaic* **:** DIVINATION

**man-to-man** \ˈ=ˌ=ˈ=\ *adj* **:** characterized by frankness and honesty ⟨their discussions had been straightforward *man-to-man* talks —J.Hendrick⟩

**man-to-man defense** *n* **:** a system of defense in various sports (as football and basketball) in which each defensive player guards a specified opponent — compare ZONE DEFENSE

**man·toux test** \(ˈ)manˈtü-\ *n, usu cap M* [after Charles *Mantoux* †1947 French physician] **:** an intracutaneous test for hypersensitivity to tuberculin and thus for past or present infection with tubercle bacilli — compare TUBERCULIN TEST

**man·tra** \ˈmantrə, ˈmən-\ *also* **man·tram** \-trəm\ *n* -s [Skt *mantra*, lit., speech, hymn, incantation, fr. *manyate* he thinks — more at MIND] **1 :** a Vedic hymn or prayer **2 :** a verbal spell, ritualistic incantation, or mystic formula used devotionally in popular Hinduism and Mahayana Buddhism

**man-trap** \ˈ=ˌ=\ *n, pl* **man-traps 1 :** a trap for catching men; *specif* **:** a trap designed to catch trespassers **2 :** something (as a carelessly built scaffold) likely to bring about injury or death to the unwary **3 :** a source of potential danger or difficulty ⟨his innocence of all the tricks and *man-traps* in the rigorous profession of politics —Herbert Agar⟩

**mants** *pres 3d sing of* MANT, *pl of* MANT

**man·tua** \ˈmanchəwə\ *n* -s [modif. (influenced by *Mantua*, Italy) of F *manteau* — more at MANTLE] **1 :** a usu. loose-fitting gown or robe worn open at the front to show the under-dress or petticoat and popular esp. with women in the 17th and 18th centuries **2** [fr. *Mantua*, Italy] **:** a silk dress fabric orig. made in Italy

**mantua-maker** \ˈ===ˌ==\ *n* **:** one that makes mantuas; *broadly* **:** DRESSMAKER

¹**man·tu·an** \ˈmanchəwən\ *n* -s *cap* [L *Mantuanus*, adj. & n., fr. *Mantua*, Italy + L *-anus* -an] **:** a native or inhabitant of Mantua, Italy

²**mantuan** \ˈ"\ *adj, usu cap* [L *Mantuanus*] **:** of or relating to the Italian city of Mantua

**man·ty** \ˈmantē\ *chiefly Scot var of* MANTUA

**man·tzu** \ˈmänt(ˌ)sü\ *or* **man·tse** \-ˌtsə\ *n, pl* **mantzu** *or* **mantzus** *or* **mantse** *or* **mantses** *usu cap* **:** ⁵MAN

**manu** \ˈmaˌnü\ *n* -s *usu cap* [Skt — more at MAN] **:** one of a series of progenitors of human beings and authors of human wisdom in Hindu mythology

¹**man·u·al** \ˈmanyə(wə)l\ *adj* [ME *manuel*, fr. MF, fr. L *manualis*, fr. *manus* hand + *-alis* -al; akin to OE & ON *mund* hand, OHG *munt*, Gk *marē* hand, Alb *marr* I take] **1 a :** of, relating to, or involving the hands ⟨~ dexterity⟩ **b :** designed for use or operation with the hands **:** worked by hand ⟨an engine with a ~ choke⟩ **2 a :** requiring or involving physical skill and energy ⟨~ labor⟩ **b :** engaged in an activity or occupation requiring or involving physical skill and energy ⟨~ workers⟩ **3** *obs* **:** AUTOGRAPH **4 :** existing in fact or deed **:** ACTUAL — used of legal possession or occupation **5 :** using signs and the manual alphabet in teaching the deaf — compare ORAL

²**manual** \ˈ"\ *n* -s [ME *manuel*, fr. LL *manuale*, fr. L, neut. of *manualis*, adj.] **1 a :** a small book capable of being carried in the hand or conveniently handled: as (1) **:** a book containing the forms of religious ceremonies used in the medieval Christian church (2) **:** a book used by underwriters and agents that gives classifications, rates, forms, and rules for writing insurance (3) **:** a book containing in concise form the principles, rules, and directions needed for the mastery of an art, science, or skill **b :** a concise treatise based on a larger work **:** HANDBOOK **2 :** the prescribed movements in the handling of a weapon or other military item during a drill or ceremony ⟨the ~ of arms⟩ ⟨the ~ of the guidon⟩ **3 :** a keyboard for the hands ⟨upper ~ of a harpsichord⟩; *specif* **:** one of the several keyboards of a pipe-organ console controlling a separate division of the instrument ⟨solo ~⟩ ⟨swell ~⟩ **4 :** PRIMARY 3a

**manual alphabet** *n* **:** an alphabet used in dactylology

**ma·nu·a·lii** \ˌmänəwəˈlēˌē\ *n* -s [Samoan, fr. *manu* bird + *alii* master] **:** a gallinule (*Porphyrio porphyrio samoensis*) of Samoa

**man·u·al·ism** \ˈmanyə(wə)ˌlizəm\ *n* -s **:** the teaching of deaf persons by the manual method

**man·u·al·ist** \-ləst\ *n* -s **1 :** one who works with the hands **2 :** one who uses or advocates the use of the manual method in teaching the deaf

**man·u·al·i·ter** \ˌmanyəˈwaləd·ə(r)\ *adv* [NL, fr. ML, by hand, fr. L *manualis* manual] **:** on the manuals only — used as a direction in organ music; compare PEDALITER

**man·u·al·ly** \ˈmanyə(wə)lē, -li\ *adv* [ME, fr. *manuel, manual* + *-ly*] **:** with or by means of the hands **:** by manual methods

**manual method** *n* **:** a method of teaching the deaf that mainly employs signs and the manual alphabet

**manual rate** *n* **:** an insurance rate based on the experience of a probable class of risks and published in a manual

**manual training** *n* **:** a course of training given in an elementary or secondary school to develop skill in using the hands and to teach practical arts (as woodworking, metalworking)

**ma·nu·an** \məˈnüən\ *adj, usu cap* [*Manua* islands, American Samoa + E *-an*] **1 :** of, relating to, or characteristic of the Manuan islands of American Samoa **2 :** of, relating to, or characteristic of the people of the Manuan islands of American Samoa

²**manuan** \ˈ"\ *n* -s *cap* **:** a native or inhabitant of the Manuan islands of American Samoa

**man·u·ary** \ˈmanyəˌwerē\ *adj* [LL *manuarius*, fr. L *manus* hand + *-arius* -ary — more at MANUAL] *archaic* **:** MANUAL

**ma·nu·bri·al** \məˈnübrēəl\ *adj* [NL *manubrium* + E *-al*] **:** of, relating to, or shaped like a manubrium

**ma·nu·bri·um** \-brēəm\ *n, pl* **manu·bria** \-ēə\ *also* **manu·briums** [NL, fr. L, handle, fr. *manus* hand] **1 :** a process or part shaped like a handle: **a** *also* **manubrium ster·ni** \-ˈstərˌnī\ **:** the cephalic segment of the sternum of man and many other mammals which is a somewhat triangular flattened bone with whose anterolateral borders the clavicles articulate **b :** a median anterior process of the sternum of a bird **c :** the process of the malleus of the ear **d :** the process bearing the mouth of a hydrozoan **:** HYPOSTOME **e :** the base of the spring of an arthropod of the order Collembola **2 :** a cylindrical cell that projects from the middle of the inner wall of each of the eight shields composing the wall of the antheridium of a stonewort and that ultimately bears the antheridial threads

**man·u·cap·tion** \ˌmanyəˈkapshən\ *n* [ML *manucaption-, manucaptio*, fr. *manucaptus* (past part. of *manucapere* to bail for, fr. L *manus* hand + *capere* to take) + L *-ion-, -io* -ion — more at MANUAL, HEAVE] **1 :** MAINPRISE **2 :** a writ for the production in court of an alleged felon **3 :** seizure in hand

**man·u·cap·tor** \-ptə(r)\ *n* [ML, fr. *manucaptus* + L *-or*] **:** MAINPERNOR

**man·u·cap·ture** \-pchə(r)\ *n* [ML *manucaptus* + E *-ure*] **:** a taking into physical possession **:** SEIZURE

**man·u·code** \ˈmanyəˌkōd\ *n* [F, fr. NL *manucodiata*, fr. Malay *manuq dewata*, lit., bird of the gods] **:** any of various birds of paradise; *esp* **:** a chiefly iridescent black or greenish bird (genus *Manucodia*) of Australia and New Guinea

¹**manucodiata** *n* -s [NL] *obs* **:** BIRD OF PARADISE

²**man·u·co·di·a·ta** \ˌmanyəˌkōdēˈäd·ə, -ˈād·ə\ [NL, fr. ¹*manucodiata*] *syn of* PARADISAEA

**man·u·duc·tion** \ˌmanyəˈdəkshən\ *n* -s [ML *manuduction-, manuductio*, fr. L *manus* hand + *duction-, ductio* action of leading, fr. *ductus* (past part. of *ducere* to lead) + *-ion-, -io* -ion — more at TOW] **1 :** the act of guiding or leading (as by the hand) ⟨the ground over which he had accepted my hurried ~ —W.E.Gladstone⟩ **2 :** something that guides or leads **:** INTRODUCTION ⟨a pleasant and scholarly ~ into alchemical byways —F.O.Taylor⟩

**man·u·duc·tive** \ˌ==ˈdəktiv\ *adj* [*manuduction* + *-ive*] **:** leading by or as if by the hand

**man·u·duc·tor** \ˈ==ˌdəktə(r)\ *n* -s [LL, fr. L *manus* hand + *ductor* leader, fr. *ductus* + *-or*] **:** DIRECTOR; *esp* **:** the director of a band or choir

**man·u·duc·to·ry** \ˌ==ˈdəkt(ə)rē\ *adj* [*manuduction* + *-ory*] **:** MANUDUCTIVE

**man·u·fac·tor** \ˌmanyəˈfaktə(r)\ *n* [LL *manufactus* made by hand + E *-or* — more at MANUFACTURE] *archaic* **:** MANUFACTURER

¹**man·u·fac·to·ry** \ˌman(y)əˈfakt(ə)rē, -ri\ *n* [LL *manufactus* + E *-ory*] **1** *archaic* **:** a product of manufacture ⟨a fleet . . . being the natural ~ of this country —Thomas Paine⟩ **2** *archaic* **:** MANUFACTURING ⟨clothed in woolens apparently of their own ~ —J.J.Henry⟩ **3 :** FACTORY 2a ⟨his father had started a match ~ in a barn —E.J.Benton⟩

²**manufactory** *adj, obs* **:** of or relating to manufacture

**man·u·fac·tur·able** \ˌ==ˈfakchərəbəl, -ksh-\ *adj* **:** capable of being manufactured ⟨aircraft, electronics, and a thousand other ~ wonders —C.M.Wilson⟩

**manufacturage** *n* -s *obs* **:** MANUFACTURE

**man·u·fac·tur·al** \ˌman(y)əˈfakchərəl, -ksh(ə)r-\ *adj* **:** of or relating to manufacture

¹**man·u·fac·ture** \ˌman(y)əˈfakchə(r), -ksh-\ *n* -s [MF, fr. LL *manufactus* made by hand (fr. L *manu* — abl. of *manus* hand — + *factus*, past part. of *facere* to make, do) + MF *-ure* — more at MANUAL, DO] **1 :** something made from raw materials by hand or by machinery ⟨hemp and tow cloth were familiar household ~s —V.S.Clark⟩ ⟨imports most ~s used by consumers or needed for internal development —D.L.Cohn⟩ **2 a :** the process or operation of making wares or other material products by hand or by machinery esp. when carried on systematically with division of labor ⟨families engaged in domestic ~ often lived and worked in one room —J.W.Krutch⟩ ⟨the ~ of furniture⟩ ⟨steel ~⟩ **b :** a productive industry using mechanical power and machinery **3** *obs* **:** a manual occupation or trade **4** *archaic* **:** FACTORY ⟨all my prospects were built on a ~ I had erected —Daniel Defoe⟩ **5 :** the act or process of making, inventing, devising, or fashioning **:** PRODUCTION, CREATION ⟨the ~ of blood goes on constantly in the human body —Morris Fishbein⟩ ⟨a true appreciation of the ~ of a movie and of a star —Horace Sutton⟩ ⟨his ideas about the ~ of this world and his hopes for his future —Rudyard Kipling⟩

²**manufacture** \ˈ"\ *vb* **manufactured; manufactured; manufacturing** \-kchəriŋ, -ksh(ə)r-\ **manufactures** [F *manufacturer*, fr. *manufacture*, n.] *vt* **1 :** to make (as raw material) into a product suitable for use ⟨the wood . . . is *manufactured* into fine cabinetwork —*Amer. Guide Series: Oregon*⟩ ⟨~ iron into steel⟩ **2 a :** to make from raw materials by hand or by machinery ⟨were *manufacturing* beautiful jewelry of gold, silver, shell, and precious stones —R.W. Murray⟩ ⟨a substitute for milk . . . *manufactured* from the soya bean —V.G.Heiser⟩ **b :** to produce according to an organized plan and with division of labor ⟨*manufacturing* 7000 cars in one day —*Amer. Guide Series: Mich.*⟩ **3 :** to make up sometimes with the intent to deceive **:** INVENT, FABRICATE ⟨the speech is evidently *manufactured* by the historian —Edward Gibbon⟩ **4 a :** to produce as if by manufacturing **:** CREATE ⟨is busy *manufacturing* a new culture —D. W.Brogan⟩ ⟨the strain of *manufacturing* conversation for at least ten minutes —Wilfred Fienburgh⟩ **b :** to produce from different and usu. less specialized materials in the living body ⟨green plants ~ carbohydrates⟩ ~ *vi* **:** to engage in manufacture **syn** see MAKE

**manufactured gas** *n* **:** a combustible gaseous mixture (as carbureted water gas or producer gas) made from coal, coke, or petroleum products for use as a fuel, illuminant, or raw material for synthesis — compare NATURAL GAS

**man·u·fac·tur·er** \ˌ==ˈfakchərə(r), -ksh(ə)rə-\ *n* -s **:** one that manufactures: as **a** *archaic* **:** a worker in a factory ⟨wages of mechanics, artificers, and ~s should be . . . higher than those of common laborers —Adam Smith⟩ **b :** an employer of workers in manufacturing **:** the owner or operator of a factory ⟨a leading automobile ~⟩ **c :** one who changes the form of a commodity or who creates a new commodity

**manufacturer's agent** *n* **:** an agent middleman operating on a contractual basis within an exclusive territory who sells for a manufacturing client noncompeting but related goods and who has limited authority over price and terms of sale

**manufacturer's joint** *n* **:** the seam where the two sides of a fiberboard container are joined by the manufacturer usu. by gluing, stitching, or taping

**manufacturing** *adj* **1 :** engaged in manufacture ⟨an important ~ city⟩ ⟨a ~ establishment⟩ **2 :** of or relating to manufacture ⟨a series of ~ projects⟩

**ma·nu for·ti** \ˌmäˌnyüˈfȯ(r)d·ˌī, -ȯ(r)ˌtī\ *adv* [L, with strong hand] **:** with such force as constitutes the crime of breaking the peace — compare VI ET ARMIS

**ma·nu·ka** \ˈmänəkə\ *n* -s [Maori] **:** either of two New Zealand woody plants that often tend to overgrow grazing land and form dense scrub: **a** NEW ZEALAND TEA TREE **b :** KANUKA

**ma·nul** \ˈmänəl\ *n* -s [Mongolian] **:** a small wildcat (*Felis manul*) of the mountains of Mongolia, Siberia, and Tibet that has soft grayish white fur marked with a few blackish transverse bands on the loins and is often held to be the source of the long-haired varieties of the domestic cat — called also *Pallas's cat*

**ma·nu·ma** \ˌmänəˈmä\ *n* -s [Samoan *manumā*, fr. *manu* bird + *mā* shame] **:** a bright-colored fruit pigeon (*Ptilinopus perousii*) of Samoa and the Fiji islands

**ma·nu·mea** \ˌmänəˈmāə\ *n* -s [Samoan] **:** TOOTH-BILLED PIGEON

**man·u·mise** \ˈmanyəˌmīz\ *vt* -ED/-ING/-s [irreg. fr. L *manumissus*, past part.] *archaic* **:** MANUMIT

**man·u·mis·sion** \ˌ==ˈmishən\ *n* [ME, fr. MF, fr. L *manumission-, manumissio*, fr. *manumissus* (past part. of *manumittere*) + *-ion-, -io* -ion] **:** the act or process of manumitting; *esp* **:** formal emancipation from slavery ⟨was true to his profession of humanitarian and liberal principles and advocated the ~ of the slaves —A.L.Harris⟩

**man·u·mit** \ˌ==ˈmit, *usu* -id.+V\ *vt* **manumitted; manumitted; manumitting; manumits** [ME *manumitten*, fr. MF *manumitter*, fr. L *manumittere*, fr. *manu* from the hand (abl. of *manus* hand) + *mittere* to send, let go — more at MANUAL, SMITE] **:** to set free **:** LIBERATE; *esp* **:** to release from slavery ⟨four million slaves had been *manumitted* by the stroke of the presidential pen —H.M.Gloster⟩ **syn** see FREE

**man·u·mit·ter** \ˌ==ˈmid·ə(r)\ *n* -s **:** one that manumits

**man·u·motive** \ˈmanyə+\ *adj* [L *manus* hand + E *motive*] *of a vehicle* **:** moved by a hand-operated mechanism

**ma·nur·able** \məˈn(y)ůrəbəl\ *adj* **:** capable of being manured

**ma·nur·age** \məˈnůrij, -ēj\ *n* -s **:** the cultivation or occupation of land

**ma·nur·ance** \-rən(t)s\ *n* -s [ME *manouraunce*, fr. *manouren* + *-aunce* -ance] **1 a** *obs* **:** the tenure, occupation, or control of land **b** *archaic* **:** the cultivation of land **2** *obs* **:** the cultivation or training of the mind

¹**ma·nure** \məˈn(y)ů(ə)r, -ůə\ *vt* -ED/-ING/-s [ME *manouren*, fr. MF *manouvrer*, lit., to do work by hand, fr. L *manu operare* — more at MANEUVER] **1** *obs* **:** to have the possession or management of (as land) **2** *archaic* **a :** to subject (land) to cultivation **:** TILL **b :** to develop (as the mind) by instruction and discipline **:** TRAIN **3 :** to apply manure to **:** enrich by the application of a fertilizing substance ⟨the fields were *manured*, the fodder was all in —Hugh MacLennan⟩

²**manure** \ˈ"\ *n* -s *often attrib* **:** material that fertilizes land; *esp* **:** refuse of stables and barnyards consisting of mammal and bird excreta with or without litter — compare FERTILIZER

**ma·nur·er** \-rə(r)\ *n* -s **:** one that manures

**manure salts** *n pl but sing or pl in constr* **:** a variable mixture of salts that contains a high percentage of chloride and from 20 to 30 percent of potash $K_2O$ and is used as a fertilizer

**ma·nu·ri·al** \mə'n(y)u̇rēəl\ *adj* **:** of, relating to, or having the characteristics of manure — **ma·nu·ri·al·ly** \-ēəlē\ *adv*

**1ma·nus** \'mānəs\ *n, pl* **manus** [NL, fr. L, hand — more at MANUAL] **1 a :** the distal segment of the forelimb of a vertebrate including the carpus and forefoot or hand **b :** the enlarged proximal part of the propodus of the chela of an arthropod **2** [L, lit., hand] *Roman law* **a :** ownership of property **b :** power over a person; *specif* **:** the power and rights of a husband and citizen over his wife in a case of marriage by coemptio, confarreation, or usus

**2manus** *pl of* MANU

**3ma·nus** \'mä,nüs\ *n, pl* **manus** *usu cap* [fr. *Manus* Island in the Admiralty islands] **1 a :** a people inhabiting Manus Island **b :** a member of such people **2 :** an Austronesian language of the Manus people

**manus chris·ti** \-'kri,stī\ *n, pl* **manus christi** *usu cap C* [ML, lit., hand of Christ] **:** a cordial made by boiling sugar usu. with rose water or violet water and formerly given to feeble persons

**1man·u·script** \'manyə,skript *sometimes* 'manə-\ *adj* [L *manu scriptus* written by hand, fr. *manu* (abl. of *manus* hand) + *scriptus*, past part. of *scribere* to write — more at MANUAL, SCRIBE] **:** written by hand or typed **:** not printed ⟨~ poems⟩ ⟨a ~ map⟩

**2manuscript** \"\ *n* -s [ML *manuscriptum*, fr. neut. of L *manu scriptus*] **1 :** a composition written before the invention or adoption of printing **b :** a handwritten copy of an ancient author or work **c :** a handwritten composition that has not been printed **2 :** a written or typewritten document as distinguished from a printed copy; *esp* **:** the copy of a writer's work from which printed copies are made **3 :** HAND 6a **4 :** writing as opposed to print **:** written documents or written characters — abbr. *MS*

**man·u·script·al** \¦==¦skriptəl\ *adj, archaic* **:** of, relating to, or existing in manuscript

**manuscript catalog** *n* **1 :** a handwritten catalog of books or other items usu. in some systematic order **2 :** a catalog of manuscripts

**man·u·scrip·tion** \,manyə'skripshən\ *n* -s [LL *manuscription-, manuscriptio*, fr. L *manus* hand + *scription-, scriptio* writing, fr. *scriptus* + *-ion-, -io* -ion] **:** writing done by hand

**manuscript ticket** *n* **:** a transportation ticket (as for theatrical troupes) sold at through rates but with stopover privileges and permitting installment payments at designated places en route

**manuscript writing** *n* **1 :** calligraphy based on the handwriting found in medieval manuscripts **2 :** writing that consists of unjoined letters made with lines and circles and that is often taught in elementary school

**ma·nu·si·na** \,mänə'sēnə\ *n* -s [Samoan, fr. *manu* bird + *sina* white] **:** a pure white tern (*Gygis alba*) of Polynesia

**ma·nu·ta·gi** \'tägē, -tänē\ *n* -s [Samoan *manutagi*, fr. *manu* bird + *tagi* cry] **:** a fruit pigeon (*Ptilinopus porphyraceus fasciatus*) of Samoa

**manutenency** *n* [ML *manutenentia*, fr. L *manus* hand + *tenentia* tenancy — more at MANUAL, TENANCY] *obs* **:** SUPPORT

**man·u·terge** \'manyə,tərj\ *or* **man·u·ter·gi·um** \,==¦tərjēəm\ *n, pl* **manu·terg·es** \'==,tərjəz\ *or* **manuter·gia** \,==¦tər-jēə\ [LL *manutergium*, fr. L *manus* hand + *-tergium* (fr. *tergēre* to wipe off, rub off) — more at TERSE] **:** a small towel used in Christian liturgies at the lavabo

**man·van·ta·ra** \man'vantərə\ *n* -s [Skt, fr. *manu* man + *antara* interval, period of time] **:** one of the 14 intervals in Hinduism that constitute a kalpa

**1man·ward** \'=wə(r)d\ *adv* [ME, fr. 1*man* + *-ward*] **:** toward man ⟨a good man, in the old . . . phrase, Godward and ~ —Sir Walter Scott⟩

**2manward** \"\ *adj* **:** directed toward man ⟨~ activities and relations —A.M.Fairbairn⟩

**manway** \'=,=\ *n* **:** a small passageway admitting a man ⟨a ~ in a coal mine⟩

**manwise** \'=,=\ *adv* [1*man* + *-wise*] **:** in the manner of men

**man–woman** \'=,==\ *n, pl* **men–women 1** *obs* **:** HERMAPHRODITE **2 :** a mannish woman

**1manx** \'maŋ(k)s, -aiŋ(-(\ *adj, usu cap* [alter. of earlier *Manisk*, fr. a Scand adj. whose first constituent is *Mana* Isle of Man in the Irish sea off the northwestern coast of England (fr. OIr), and whose second constituent is represented by ON *-iskr* -ish] **1 a :** of, relating to, or characteristic of the Isle of Man **b :** of, relating to, or characteristic of the people of the Isle of Man **2 :** of, relating to, or characteristic of the Manx language

**2manx** \"\ *n, pl* **manx** *cap* **1 :** a native or inhabitant of the Isle of Man **2 :** the Celtic language of the Manx people now almost completely displaced by English — see INDO-EUROPEAN LANGUAGES table

**manx cat** *n, usu cap M* **:** a short-haired domestic cat having the tail externally lacking though represented internally by a few rudimentary vertebrae and constituting a distinct breed

**manx·man** \'=mən, -,man,-,maa(ə)n\ *n, pl* **manxmen** \-,mən, -,men\ *cap* **:** a native or inhabitant of the Isle of Man

**manx shearwater** *n, usu cap M* **:** a small black-and-white shearwater (*Puffinus puffinus*) common in the eastern north Atlantic

**manxwoman** \'=,==\ *n, pl* **manxwomen** *cap* **:** a woman who is a native or inhabitant of the Isle of Man

**1many** \,menē, -ni *sometimes* ,mən-\ *adj* **more** \(¦)mō(ə)r, -ō(ə)r, -öə,-ȯ(ə)\ **most** \(¦)mōst\ [ME *many, mony*, many a, many, fr. OE *manig, mænig, monig*; akin to OS & OHG *manag* many a, many, ON *mangr*, Goth *managa* many, OIr *menicc* frequent, Skt *magha* gift, OSlav *mŭnogŭ* much] **1 :** consisting of or amounting to a large but indefinite number **:** not few ⟨~ people expressed fear⟩ ⟨worked hard for ~ years⟩ ⟨a country with ~ natural resources⟩ ⟨the ~ advantages of an education⟩ **2 :** one of a large but indefinite number regarded distributively — used before *a, an*, or *another* or in an inverted construction to modify a singular noun ⟨~ a man hoped for better days⟩ ⟨remained a mystery for ~ a year⟩ ⟨~ another student made the same mistake⟩ ⟨~ is the time she scolded the boy⟩ — **as many :** the same in number ⟨saw three plays in *as many* days⟩

**2many** \"\ *pron, pl in constr* [ME *many, mony* many a one, many, fr. OE *manig, mænig, monig*, fr. *manig, mænig, monig*, adj.] **:** a large number of persons or things ⟨~ are called but few are chosen —Mt 22:14 (RSV)⟩ ⟨~ of the statements are true⟩

**3many** \"\ *n, pl in constr* [1*many*] **1 :** a large but indefinite number of units or individuals ⟨a good ~ of the books were novels⟩ ⟨a great ~ of the tourists were from the East⟩ **2 :** the great majority of people **:** MASSES, MULTITUDE — often used with preceding *the* ⟨nothing but contempt for the ~⟩ **3** *obs* **:** COMPANY, HOST, RETINUE ⟨the chiefs divide and wheeling east and west before their ~ ride —John Dryden⟩ **4** *usu cap* **:** something that is manifold **:** PLURALITY ⟨philosophers have largely proclaimed the One to be reality and the *Many* to be appearance —H.M.Kallen⟩

**man·yat·ta** \mən'yad·ə\ *n* -s [native name in Kenya] *southern Africa* **:** a kraal esp. in Kenya

**man–year** \'=¦=\ *n, pl* **man–years :** the work of one man in a year composed of a standard number of working days of standard length

**1manyfold** \'=¦=\ *adj* [by alter.] **:** MANIFOLD ⟨took the form of ~ reparation, of penal and exemplary damages —Frederick Pollock & F.W.Maitland⟩

**2manyfold** \"\ *adv* [1*many* + *-fold*] **:** by many times **:** to a considerable degree or extent ⟨provision for education and health care has increased ~ —Abram Bergson⟩

**many–headed** \'==¦==\ *adj* **1 :** having many heads **2 :** of or relating to the people ⟨expelled a king in order to set up a *many-headed* tyranny —John Russell †1878⟩ — usu. used as a generalized expression of disapproval

**many·ness** \'menēnəs, -nin-\ *n* -ES **:** the quality or state of being many **:** MULTIPLICITY

**many–one** \'==¦=\ *adj, of a relation in logic* **:** constituted so that if the first term is given only one thing can be the second term whereas if the second term is given any of many things can be the first term ⟨the relation "sired-by" is *many-one* since many offspring may be sired by one animal but each offspring has only one sire⟩ — compare ONE-MANY, ONE-ONE

**manyplies** \'==,=\ *also* **mani·plies** \"\ *n pl but usu sing in constr* [1*many* + *plies*, pl. of *ply* (fold)] **:** OMASUM

**many–sided** \'==¦==\ *adj* **1 :** having many sides **:** MULTILATERAL ⟨*many-sided* figures⟩ **2 a :** having many aspects or bearings ⟨a *many-sided* topic⟩ **b :** having many interests or aptitudes ⟨*many-sided* men⟩ **syn** see VERSATILE

**many·sid·ed·ness** *n* -ES **:** the quality or state of being many-sided ⟨the loftiness and ~ of English theological thought —Leo Zander⟩

**many–valued** \'=¦==\ *adj* [trans. of G *mehrwertig*] **:** possessing three or more truth-values in place of the customary two of truth and falsehood

**man·za·na** \mən'zänə\ *n* -s [AmerSp, fr. Sp, apple, block of houses, fr. OSp *mazana, maçana* apple, fr. L (*mala*) *Matiana*, fr. *mala* apples + *Matiana*, neut. pl. of *Matianus* of Matius, fr. C. *Matius*, 1st cent. B.C. Roman writer on gastronomy + L *-anus* -an] **:** any of several units of land area used esp. in Central America that average around 1.7 acres

**man·za·ni·lla** \,manzə'nē(y)ə, -ēlyə\ *n* -s [Sp, lit., chamomile, dim. of *manzana* apple] **1 :** a pale aromatic dry sherry from the Sanlucar vineyards at the mouth of the Guadalquivir, Spain **2 a :** any of several weedy plants of the family Compositae esp. of the genera *Bidens, Stemmodontia*, and *Trixis* **b :** any of several Mexican trees or shrubs esp. of the genera *Quercus* and *Ximenia*

**man·za·ni·llo** \-ē(,)(y)ō, -ēl(,)yō\ *n* -s [Sp, dim. of *manzano* apple tree, fr. *manzana* apple] **1 :** MANCHINEEL **2 :** any of several Mexican shrubs or trees esp. of the genera *Euphorbia, Rhus*, and *Xylosma*

**man·za·ni·ta** \-ēd·ə\ *n* -s [AmerSp, dim. of *manzana* apple] **1 :** any of various California shrubs of the genus *Arctostaphylos* (esp. *A. pungens* or *A. tomentosa*) **2 :** MADRONA

**1mao·mao** \'mau̇,mau̇\ *n* -s [Samoan *ma'oma'o*] **:** a Samoan honey eater (*Gymnomyza samoensis*)

**2maomao** \"\ *n* -s [Maori] **:** a New Zealand surf fish (*Ditrema violacea*) that somewhat resembles a flounder, is typically blue in color, and is a superior food fish

**mao·ri** \'mau̇(ə)rē, -ri\ *n* **1** *pl* **maori** *or* **maoris** *usu cap* **a** (1) **:** a Polynesian people native to New Zealand (2) **:** a member of such people **b :** the Austronesian language of the Maori **2** -s **:** a brilliantly colored Australian marine percoid food fish (*Ophthalmolepis lineolatus*)

**mao·ri·an** \-rēən\ *adj, usu cap* [*Maori* + *-an*] **:** NEW ZEALAND

**maori cabbage** *n, usu cap M* **:** the wild cabbage of New Zealand

**maori hen** *n, usu cap M* **:** WEKA

**mao·ri·land·er** \-,landə(r)\ *n* -s *cap* [*Maoriland* New Zealand (fr. *Maori* + *land*) + *-er*] **:** a native or inhabitant of New Zealand

**mao·ri·tanga** \,mau̇rē'täŋə\ *n* -s *usu cap* [Maori] **1 :** the traditions and ideals and culture of the Maori people **2 :** Maori nationalism

**1map** \'map\ *n* -s [ML *mappa*, fr. L, napkin, of Sem origin; akin to Heb *mĕnaphā* fan] **1 a** (1) **:** a drawing or other representation that is usu. made on a flat surface and that shows the whole or a part of an area (as of the surface of the earth or some other planet or of the moon) and indicates the nature and relative position and size according to a chosen scale or projection of selected features or details (as countries, cities, bodies of water, mountains, deserts) — compare CHART (2) **:** a similar drawing or other representation of the celestial sphere that indicates the nature and relative position and size of stars or planets or other celestial features or phenomena **b :** something (as a significant outward appearance, a pointed or concise verbal description) that indicates or delineates or reveals by representing or showing with a clarity suggestive of that of a map ⟨thus is his cheek the ~ of days outworn —Shak.⟩ **2** *slang* **:** FACE — **put on the map :** to give great prominence of fame to (as a city, a region) **:** make widely known ⟨discovery of rich uranium deposits really *put* that section of the country *on the map*⟩ — **wipe off the map :** to utterly destroy (as a city, a region) **:** ANNIHILATE ⟨threatened a nuclear attack that would *wipe* the country *off the map*⟩

**2map** \"\ *vt* **mapped; mapped; mapping; maps 1 a :** to make a map of **:** show or establish the features or details of with clarity like that of a map ⟨~ the surface of the moon⟩ ⟨sorrow was *mapped* on her face⟩ **b :** to make a survey of or travel over for or as if for the purpose of making a map ⟨a remote section they haven't even begun to ~⟩ **c :** to place (a mathematical aggregate) in one-to-one correspondence with an aggregate ⟨a set is called denumerable if it can be *mapped* . . . onto the set of all the natural numbers —A.H.Wallace⟩ **2 :** to arrange, delineate, or plan the details of **:** show or plan in detail ⟨*mapped* a program⟩ — often used with *out* ⟨*mapping* out what he hoped to accomplish⟩

**MAP** *abbr* **1** maximum average price **2** medical aid post

**ma·pau** *also* **ma·pou** \'mä,pau̇\ *n* -s [Maori *mapau*] **:** a New Zealand tree (*Rapanea urvillei*) of the family Myrsinaceae that has reddish brown leaves and small white flowers and a light wood that is much used for fuel

**map crack** *n* **:** a minute crack (as on the surface of mortar, concrete, plaster)

**ma·ple** \'māpəl\ *n* -s *often attrib* [ME, fr. OE *mapul-*; akin to ON *mǫpurr* maple and perh. to OHG *mazzaltra* maple] **1 a** (1) **:** a tree or shrub of the genus *Acer* — see BOX ELDER, NORWAY MAPLE, SILVER MAPLE, SUGAR MAPLE, SWAMP MAPLE, SYCAMORE (2) **:** the wood of a maple tree; *esp* **:** the hard light-colored close-grained wood of the sugar maple that is used extensively for flooring, furniture, and small items (as turnings and handles) — compare BIRD'S-EYE MAPLE, CURLY 2 (3) **:** the flavor of maple sap or its products (as syrup or sugar) **b** *Austral* (1) **:** SILKY BEECH (2) **:** QUEENSLAND MAPLE (3) **:** a tree closely related to the Queensland maple **2 a :** a light brown **b :** a grayish yellow

**maple bladder–gall mite** *n* **:** an eriophyid mite (*Vasates quadripes*) producing swellings on maple leaves

**maple borer** *n* **:** an insect or insect larva that bores into maple trees

**maple cream** *or* **maple butter** *n* **:** maple syrup boiled to the concentration of soft sugar, cooled, and stirred to a creamy consistency

**maple–face** *n, obs* **:** a blotchy face

**maple family** *n* **:** ACERACEAE

**maple honey** *n* **:** maple syrup of light color boiled to a density of strained honey

**maple leaf cutter** *n* **:** the larva of a tiny incurvariid moth (*Paraclemensia acerifoliella*) that infests the leaves of maples and constructs a case of bits of leaves

**mapleleaf viburnum** \'==,=-\ *or* **maple–leaved viburnum** *n* **:** DOCKMACKIE

**maple–leaved** \¦==¦=\ *adj* **:** having leaves like those of most maples

**maplelike** \'==,=\ *adj* **:** resembling maple

**maple silkwood** *n* **:** QUEENSLAND MAPLE

**maple sugar** *n* **1 :** sugar made by boiling maple syrup to the hard sugar stage and then stirring immediately to promote crystallization **2 :** a moderate yellowish brown that is lighter and very slightly redder than Bismarck brown, lighter and slightly yellower and stronger than cinnamon brown, and redder, lighter, and slightly stronger than bronze

**maple syrup** *n* **:** syrup made by concentrating the sap of the sugar maple or various other maples

**maple worm** *n* **:** a grub that is the larva of a saturniid moth (*Anisota rubicunda*) and that defoliates maples

**ma·po** \'mä,pō\ *n* s [AmerSp] **:** a small goby (*Bathygobius soporator*) of the south Atlantic coast and the West Indies

**map·pable** \'mapəbəl\ *adj* **:** capable of being represented on or by a map

**mapped** *past of* MAP

**mappe·monde** \(')map'mōnd\ *n* -s [ME *mappemounde* map of the world, fr. MF *mappemonde*, fr. ML *mappa mundi*, fr. *mappa* map + L *mundi*, gen. of *mundus* world — more at MAP] **:** a medieval map of the world

**map·pen** \'mapən\ *adv* [contr. of *mayhappen*] *dial Eng* **:** PERHAPS, POSSIBLY, MAYBE

**map·per** \'mapə(r)\ *n* -s **1 :** CARTOGRAPHER **2 :** a fire insurance company clerk who keeps maps showing the location of buildings on which the company has written insurance and data about the coverage

**mapping** *pres part of* MAP

**map projection** *n* **:** PROJECTION 1

**maps** *pl of* MAP, *pres 3d sing of* MAP

**map turtle** *also* **map terrapin** *n* **:** a small aquatic turtle (*Graptemys geographica*) of the central and eastern U.S. that is olive-colored and marked by delicate yellow tracings

**ma·pu·che** \mə'püchē\ *n, pl* **mapuche** *or* **mapuches** *usu cap* **1 a :** an Araucanian people of southern Chile **b :** a member of such people **2 :** the language of the Mapuche people

**MAQ** *abbr* money allowance for quarters

**ma·quette** \ma'ket, mə'-\ *n* -s [F, fr. It *macchietta*, dim. of *macchia* sketch, fr. *macchiare* to sketch, blot, speckle, fr. L *maculare* to spot, stain, fr. *macula* spot] **:** a usu. small preliminary model of something designed esp. to gauge the general appearance or composition of the thing that is planned: as **a :** a wax or clay model of a contemplated piece of sculpture **b :** a model of a room and its furnishings and decorative patterns **c :** a model of a building

**ma·qui** \'mä(,)kē\ *n* -s [Sp, fr. Mapuche] **:** a Chilean shrub (*Aristotelia maqui*) of the family Elaeocarpaceae that has evergreen foliage and berries from which a wine is made

**ma·quil·lage** \¦makē¦(y)äzh, ¦mäk-\ *n* -s [F, fr. *maquiller* to make up, paint one's face + *-age*] **:** MAKEUP 4

**ma·quis** \(')ma¦kē, (')mä¦-\ *n, pl* **maquis** \-ē(z)\ [F, fr. It *macchie*, pl. of *macchia* thicket, spot, fr. L *macula* spot] **1** *also* **ma·qui** \"\ **a :** thick scrubby underbrush profuse along the shores of the Mediterranean and esp. profuse in the island of Corsica **b :** an area or zone marked by such underbrush **2** *often cap* **a :** a member of an underground movement or organization; *esp* **:** a French guerrilla fighter in World War II resisting the Nazis **b :** a band or unit of maquis

**ma·qui·sard** \¦makē¦zär(d),\ *n* -s *often cap* [F, fr. *maquis* + *-ard*] **:** MAQUIS 2

**1mar** \'mär, 'mȧ(r\ *vt* **marred; marred; marring; mars** [ME *marren*, fr. OE *mierran* to obstruct, waste; akin to OHG *merren* to obstruct, Goth *marzjan* to offend, and prob. to Skt *mr̥ṣyate* he forgets] **1 a :** to detract from the good condition or perfection or wholeness or beauty of **:** cause to be injured or damaged or defaced or blemished **:** SPOIL, IMPAIR ⟨will in no way ~ the enjoyment of your stay —Richard Joseph⟩ ⟨is too good a book to be *marred* by small defects —R.A.Smith⟩ ⟨all these gifts and qualities . . . were *marred* by prodigious faults —Virginia Woolf⟩ ⟨left a smudge that *marred* the lustrousness of the piano's polished surface⟩ ⟨the scenic beauty of this region is now *marred* by commercial signs —*Amer. Guide Series: Tenn.*⟩ **b** *archaic* **:** to inflict serious bodily harm on **:** severely disfigure **:** MUTILATE, MANGLE **c** *obs* **:** to bring to utter destruction **:** cause to be completely ruined **2** *archaic* **:** to get in the way of **:** HAMPER, IMPEDE, BLOCK **3** *obs* **:** BEWILDER, PERPLEX **syn** see INJURE

**2mar** \"\ *n* -s **:** something that mars **:** INJURY, DEFACEMENT, BLEMISH ⟨the importance of avoiding dust and ~*s* on photographic plates —*Science*⟩

**mar** *abbr* **1** marine **2** maritime **3** married

**MAR** *abbr* microanalytical reagent

**1ma·ra** \mə'rä\ *n* -s [AmerSp *mará*, perh. fr. Araucanian] **:** a long-legged long-eared rodent (*Dolichotis magellanica*) closely related to the cavies and widely distributed in southern So. America

**2mara** \'marə\ *n* -s *usu cap* [by shortening] **:** MARACAIBO 1a

**mar·a·bou** *or* **mar·a·bout** \'marə,bü\ *n* -s [F *marabout*, lit., marabout] **1 a** *or* **marabou stork :** a large stork of the genus *Leptoptilos*: as (1) **:** an African stork (*L. crumeniferus*) (2) **:** ADJUTANT BIRD **b :** a soft feathery fluffy material prepared from the long coverts of marabous or usu. from turkey feathers and used esp. for trimmings ⟨all these ladies wearing ~ —*New Yorker*⟩ **2 a :** a thrown silk usu. dyed in the gum **b :** a fabric made of this silk

**mar·a·bout** \'marə,bü(t)\ *n* -s [F, fr. Pg *marabuto*, fr. Ar *murābiṭ*] **1** *often cap* **a** Muslim monk or hermit esp. in Africa **:** Muslim ascetic **:** Muslim holy man or saint **2 :** a tomb or shrine erected to a marabout

**mar·a·bout·ism** \-ü(d·),izəm, -ü,ti-\ *n* -s *sometimes cap* **1 :** the way of life of a Muslim holy man **2 :** veneration of Muslim holy men

**ma·ra·ca** \mə'räkə, -rakə\ *n* -s [Pg *maracá*, prob. fr. Tupi] **:** a dried gourd or a rattle like a gourd containing dried seeds or pebbles that has a handle and is used as a percussion instrument often in pairs

maraca

**1mar·a·cai·bo** \¦marə¦kī(,)bō *also* ¦mer-\ *adj, usu cap* [*Maracaibo*, city in northwest Venezuela] **:** of or from the city of Maracaibo, Venezuela **:** of the kind or style prevalent in Maracaibo

**2maracaibo** \"\ *n* -s *usu cap* **1 a** *also* **maracaibo coffee :** a coffee grown in Venezuela **b :** cacao from Venezuela **2** *also* **maracaibo lignum vitae :** VERA

**maracaibo bark** *n, usu cap M* **:** an inferior variety of cinchona bark

**maracaibo boxwood** *n, usu cap M* **:** ZAPATERO 2

**mar·a·can** \'marə,kan, -kən\ *n* -s [Pg *maracanā*, prob. fr. Tupi] **:** a Brazilian macaw

**mar·a·cock** \-,käk\ *n* [fr. *maracock, maracaw* (in some Algonquian language of Virginia), fr. Carib *merecuyá*, fr. Tupi *maracuyá*] **:** MAYPOP

**ma·rae** \mə'rī\ *n, pl* **marae** *or* **maraes** [Tahitian & Maori] **1 :** a Polynesian temple enclosure used for worship or sacrifice or other religious ceremonies **2 :** a square or similar open area before a Maori tribal or family meetinghouse used for formal reception of guests or other formal functions

**marajuana** *var of* MARIHUANA

**ma·ral** \mə'räl\ *n* -s [Per *marāl*] **:** an Asiatic red deer

**ma·ran** \mə'ran\ *n* [*Marans*, town in western France] **1** *usu cap* **:** a French breed of domestic fowls that lay many large dark brown eggs **2** -s *often cap* **:** a fowl of the Maran breed

**mar·a·nao** *also* **mar·a·naw** \¦marə¦nau̇\ *n, pl* **maranao** *or* **maranaos** *also* **maranaw** *or* **maranaws** *usu cap* [Sp, fr. Maranao *Maranáw*, fr. *ranaw* lake] **1 a :** a Moro people inhabiting the area around Lake Laneo and certain parts of central Cotabato province, Mindanao, Philippines, and northern Borneo **b :** a member of such people **2 :** the Austronesian language of the Maranao people

**ma·rang** \'mä,räŋ, 'ma,raŋ\ *n* -s [Tag] **1 :** a Philippine tree (*Artocarpus odoratissima*) resembling the breadfruit **2 :** the fruit of the marang tree consisting of a mass of small seeds embedded in a white sweetish edible pulp

**ma·ra·nham jaborandi** \¦marən¦yam-, -yau̇ⁿ-\ *n, usu cap M* [*Maranhão*, state in northeast Brazil + E *jaborandi*] **:** JABORANDI 1b

**marano** *usu cap, var of* MARRANO

**ma·ran·ta** \mə'rantə\ *n* [NL, fr. Bartolomeo *Maranta* †1571 Ital. physician and botanist] **1 a** *cap* **:** a genus (the type of the family Marantaceae) of tropical American herbs with tuberous starchy roots and large sheathing leaves and regular flowers with a single petaloid filament bearing a one-celled anther **b** -s **:** any plant of the genus *Maranta* **2** -s **:** starch prepared from the rootstocks of an American arrowroot (*Maranta arundinacea*)

**mar·an·ta·ce·ae** \,marən'tāsē,ē\ *n pl, cap* [NL, fr. *Maranta*, type genus + *-aceae*] **:** a family of tropical monocotyledonous perennial herbs (order Musales) having a pronounced swelling at the junction of the petiole and leaf blade — **mar·an·ta·ceous** \¦==¦tāshəs\ *adj*

**ma·ran·tic** \mə'rantik\ *adj* [Gk *marantikos*, fr. (assumed) Gk *marantos* (verbal of Gk *marainein* to waste away) + Gk *-ikos* -ic] **:** of, relating to, or marked by marasmus **:** MARASMIC

**ma·ra·ra** \mə'rärə\ *n* -s [native name in Australia] **:** an Australian tree (*Weinmannia lachnocarpa*) of the family Escalloniaceae that is prominently buttressed at the base and has opposite compound leaves of 3-toothed leaflets and yields a light hard wood

**maras** *pl of* MARA

**ma·ras·ca** \mə'raskə\ *or* **marasca cherry** *n* -s [It *marasca*] **:** a Dalmatian bitter wild cherry (*Prunus cerasus marasca*) from the fermented juice of which maraschino liqueur is made — compare SOUR CHERRY

**mar·a·schi·no** \,marə'skē,nō, -'shē-\ *n* -s [It, fr. *marasca*] **1** *often cap* **:** a sweet liqueur made orig. in Dalmatia that is distilled from the fermented juice of the marasca and often flavored (as with bitter almonds, jasmine, or vanilla) and that is used as a cocktail ingredient, in cooking, and in preserving cherries **2** *or* **maraschino cherry** *often cap M* **a :** a usu. large cherry preserved in true or imitation maraschino **b :** MARASCA

**ma·ras·ma** \mə'razmə\ *n* -s [It, fr. LL *marasmus*] **:** MARASMUS

**ma·ras·mic** \-mik\ *adj* [*marasmus* + *-ic*] **:** of, relating to, or marked by marasmus **:** MARANTIC

**ma·ras·mi·us** \-mēəs\ *n, cap* [NL, fr. LL *marasmus*] **:** a genus of mostly small-sized white-spored mushrooms (family Agaricaceae) having a tough leathery stem and cap and lacking both ring and volva — see FAIRY RING, THREAD BLIGHT

**ma·ras·moid** \-,mȯid\ *adj* [*marasmus* + *-oid*] **:** resembling marasmus

**ma·ras·mus** \-,məs\ *n* -ES [LL, fr. Gk *marasmos*, fr. *marainein* to waste away — more at SMART] **:** progressive emaciation esp. in the young because of malnutrition due chiefly to faulty assimilation and utilization of food

**ma·ra·tha** *also* **mah·rat·ta** \mə'räd·ə, -rad·ə\ *or* **mah·rat·ti** \-d·ē\ *n, pl* **maratha** *or* **marathas** *usu cap* [Hindi *Marhaṭā*, *Marhaṭṭā* & Marathi *Marāṭhā*, fr. Skt *Mahārāṣṭra*, fr. *mahat* great + *rāṣṭra* kingdom; akin to Skt *rājan* king — more at MUCH, RAJA] **1 :** a Scytho-Dravidian people of the south central part of the subcontinent of India **2 :** a member of the Maratha people

**ma·ra·thi** \-d·ē\ *n* ²*s usu cap* [Marathi *Marāṭhī*, fr. Skt *Mahārāṣṭra*] **:** the chief Indic language of southern and eastern Bombay state

¹**mar·a·thon** \'marə,thän *also* 'mer- *sometimes* -,than\ *n* -s *sometimes cap* [*Marathon*, ancient town in east central Greece where in 490 B.C. the Greeks won a victory over the Persians of which the news was carried to Athens by a long-distance runner] **1 a :** a long-distance race: (1) **:** a footrace run on an open course of now usu. 26 miles 385 yards (2) **:** a race other than a footrace (as for swimmers, skaters) marked by esp. great length **b :** a competition in which participants vie with each other to see who can last the longest in doing something **:** a contest that tests the stamina and endurance of the contestants **:** an endurance contest ⟨a dance ~⟩ ⟨a speechmaking ~⟩ **2 :** an activity that tests or demonstrates the stamina or endurance power of the performer ⟨after a ~ of autographing some 4000 copies of the first volume of his memoirs —*Time*⟩

²**marathon** \"\ *also* **mar·a·tho·ni·an** \¦==¦thōnēən\ *or* **mar·a·thon·ic** \-¦thänik\ *adj, sometimes cap* **:** belonging to or suggestive of or suited for a marathon race or competition or other activity: **a :** marked by unusual length of time ⟨a ~ session of Congress⟩ or distance ⟨a ~ hike⟩ or extent ⟨a speech with a ~ opening sentence⟩ **b :** such as tests or demonstrates the stamina or endurance power of the performer ⟨*marathonic* lungpower —*Newsweek*⟩ ⟨besides being amused by her performance, we were stunned by the *marathonian* ebullience —Stanley Kauffmann⟩

³**marathon** \"\ *vi* -ED/-ING/-S **:** to run a marathon or take part in marathon competition or activity ⟨an exhibition of ~*ing*⟩ — **mar·a·thon·er** \-nə(r)\ *n* -s

⁴**marathon** \"\ *n* -s **:** a strong orange that is darker than pumpkin and redder and duller than cadmium orange

**ma·rat·tia** \mə'rad·ēə\ *n, cap* [NL, fr. Giovanni Francesco *Maratti* †1777 Ital. botanist + NL *-ia*] **:** the type genus of Marattiaceae comprising ferns with the sporangia in two rows forming a synangium

**ma·rat·ti·a·ce·ae** \=,==ˈāsē,ē\ *n pl, cap* [NL, fr. *Marattia*, type genus + *-aceae*] **:** a family (coextensive with the order Marattiales) of chiefly tropical eusporangiate ferns with mostly pinnate often gigantic fronds and thick stipules and abaxial sori — **ma·rat·ti·a·ceous** \=¦==¦āshəs\ *adj*

**ma·rat·ti·a·les** \=,==ˈā(,)lēz\ *n pl, cap* [NL, fr. *Marattia* + *-ales*] **:** an order of lower ferns (class Filicineae) comprising the Marattiaceae

¹**ma·raud** \mə'rȯd\ *vb* -ED/-ING/-S [F *marauder*, fr. *maraud* vagabond] *vi* **:** to roam about and make irregular sudden small-scale attacks, raids, or incursions for or as if for the sake of obtaining loot **:** rove about and pillage ⟨were told to watch out for ~*ing* bands of Indians⟩ ~ *vt* **:** to subject to marauding **:** RAID, PILLAGE — now usu. used in passive ⟨a poverty-stricken ~*ed* countryside⟩

²**maraud** \"\ *n* -s *archaic* **:** the act of marauding

**ma·raud·er** \-də(r)\ *n* -s **:** one that marauds **:** PLUNDERER

**mar·a·ve·di** \,marə'vādē\ *n* -s [Sp *maravedí*, fr. Ar *Murābiṭīn* Almoravides, Muslim dynasty of the 11th and 12th centuries in No. Africa and Spain, fr. pl. of *murābiṭ* marabout] **1 :** an old Moorish gold dinar of Spain and Morocco **2 a :** a medieval Spanish unit of value equal to 1/34 real **b :** a copper coin representing one of these units

**ma·ray** \mə'rā\ *n* -s [native name in Australia] **:** a Pacific round herring (*Etrumeus jacksoniensis*) occurring in great numbers off the coast of Australia

**marbelize** *var of* MARBLEIZE

¹**mar·ble** \'märbəl, 'måb-\ *n* -s [ME *marbel*, fr. OF *marbre*, fr. L *marmor*, fr. Gk *marmaros* marble, rock, prob. fr. *marainein* to waste away — more at SMART] **1 a :** limestone that is crystallized in varying degrees by metamorphism, that ranges from granular to compact in texture, that is white or tinted or veined or mottled with various colors (as bluish gray, red, yellow, green) or is sometimes black, that is capable of taking a usu. high polish, and that is extensively used esp. in architecture and sculpture **b :** something composed of or made from this limestone: as (1) **:** a piece (as a block, slab, shaft) of this limestone ⟨a table top of ~⟩; *esp* **:** a commemorative monument (as an inscribed tablet, pillar, shaft, or tomb) made from this limestone ⟨read the inscription on the ~⟩ (2) **:** a piece of sculpture carved from this limestone ⟨a museum with a splendid collection of ancient Greek ~*s*⟩ **c :** something resembling (as in hardness, rigidity, coldness, smoothness) or suggestive of this limestone ⟨had a heart of ~ and paid no attention to her tears⟩ **2 a :** a little ball made of a hard substance (as agate, glass, porcelain, baked clay, steel) typically ranging from about ½ inch to about 1 inch in diameter; *esp* **:** such a little ball used in various games **b marbles** *pl but sing in constr* **:** a children's game that is played with these little balls and that consists typically in trying to knock out of a certain area one or more of the balls arranged inside a circle or in a row by hitting the balls with another ball usu. propelled by the thumb **3 :** MARBLING **4 marbles** *pl, slang* **a :** elements of common sense ⟨the old man losing his ~*s* one by one —J.F.Powers⟩ ⟨persons who are born without all their ~*s* —Arthur Miller⟩ **b :** food thrown up by the stomach

²**marble** \"\ *vt* **marbled; marbled; marbling** \-b(ə)liŋ\ **marbles :** to make like marble esp. in coloration **:** MARBLEIZE **:** STREAK, BLOTCH, MOTTLE; *specif* **:** to give a veined or mottled appearance to (as paper, book edges, book end papers, tiles, glass) by staining or varying the composition of or by some other process

³**marble** \"\ *adj* **1 :** composed of or made from marble ⟨a ~ floor⟩ ⟨~ top⟩ **2 a :** resembling (as in hardness, rigidity, coldness, smoothness) or suggestive of marble ⟨had a ~ heart incapable of human warmth⟩ ⟨the still evening and the ~ calm of the lake⟩ **b :** MARBLED ⟨~ paper⟩ ⟨~ glass⟩

**marble bone** *or* **marble bone disease** *n* **:** OSTEOPETROSIS

**marble bones** *n pl but sing in constr* **:** OSTEOPETROSIS

**marble cake** *n* **:** a cake made with light and dark batter so as to have a streaked or mottled appearance suggestive of marble

**marbled** *adj* [partly fr. ¹*marble* + *-ed*, partly fr. past part. of ²*marble*] **1 a :** done in or covered with marble ⟨the ~ likeness of the emperor⟩ ⟨the ~ exterior of the building⟩ **b :** marked by an extensive use of marble as an architectural or decorative feature ⟨an ancient ~ city⟩ **2 :** having markings or a coloration that resembles or is suggestive of marble ⟨a dog with a handsome ~ coat⟩; *specif* **:** having a veined, streaked, or mottled appearance through being subjected to a process of marbling ⟨~ endpapers⟩ ⟨~ glass⟩ ⟨~ slate⟩ ⟨~ calfskin⟩ **3 :** marked by an intermixture of fat and lean ⟨a well ~ cut of meat⟩

**marbled cat** *or* **marbled tiger cat** *n* **:** a long-tailed brightly patterned cat (*Felis marmorata*) of southeastern Asia and the East Indies

**marbled godwit** *n* **:** a large American godwit (*Limosa fedoa*) that is reddish or yellowish brown in color and has a long straight or slightly upcurved bill

**marbled murrelet** *n* **:** a murrelet (*Brachyramphus marmoratus*) that is dusky and has white underparts mottled with brown and that is found from Alaska to Vancouver

**marbled polecat** *n* **:** TIGER WEASEL

**marbled sculpin** *n* **:** CABEZONE 1

**marblehearted** \'==¦==\ *adj* **:** devoid of and coldly resistant to kindness, sympathy, pity, friendliness, or affection ⟨a ~ tyrant⟩

**mar·ble·ization** \,märbələ'zāshən, ,måb-, -,lī'z-\ *n* -s **:** the process of becoming marbleized or the condition of being marbleized

**mar·ble·ize** *also* **mar·bel·ize** \'märbə,līz, 'måb-\ *vt* **marbleized** *also* **marbelized; marbleized** *also* **marbelized; marbleizing** *also* **marbelizing; marbleizes** *also* **marbelizes :** MARBLE — **mar·ble·iz·er** \-,līzə(r)\ *n* -s

**mar·bler** \-b(ə)lə(r)\ *n* -s **:** one that marbles (as paper, the edges of a book)

**marbles** *pl of* MARBLE, *pres 3d sing of* MARBLE

**marble thrush** *n* **:** MISTLE THRUSH

**marblewood** \'==,=\ *n* **1 a :** a large Asiatic tree (*Diospyros kurzii*) that has a hard mottled wood — called also *Andaman marble* **b** (1) **:** NATIVE OLIVE 1a (2) **:** an Australian timber tree of the genus *Albizzia* **2 :** the wood of a marblewood

**marbling** *n* -s [fr. gerund of ²*marble*] **1 :** the action or process of making like marble esp. in coloration **2 :** coloration or markings resembling or suggestive of marble **3 :** an intermixture of fat and lean in a cut of meat esp. when evenly distributed ⟨the quality of a cut of meat can often be judged from its degree of ~⟩

**mar·bly** \'märb(ə)lē, 'måb-, -li\ *adj, sometimes* -ER/-EST [¹*marble* + *-y*] **1 :** MARBLE 2a ⟨the ~ calm of the lake⟩ **2 :** MARBLED 1b ⟨a ~ building⟩

¹**marc** *obs var of* ³MARK

²**marc** \'märk, 'måk\ *n* -s [F, fr. MF, fr. *marchier* to trample under foot — more at MARCH] **1 a :** the residue remaining after a fruit (as grapes or olives) has been subjected to pressing — compare POMACE 1 **b :** an insoluble residue remaining after extraction of a substance (as a drug) with a solvent **2 :** a brandy that is made by distilling the skins of grapes or the pulp of apples after the wine or cider is made — called also *eau-de-vie de marc;* compare GRAPPA

**marc** *abbr* marcato

**mar·can** *or* **mar·kan** \'märkən, 'måk-\ *adj, usu cap* [*marcan* fr. LL *Marcus* Mark, evangelist traditionally regarded as author of the second gospel + E *-an*; *markan* fr. *Mark* + E *-an*] **:** of or characteristic of the Evangelist Mark or the Gospel ascribed to him ⟨carefully studied the *Marcan* text⟩

**mar·can·do** \mär'kän(,)dō\ *adv* (*or adj*) [It, verbal of *marcare* to mark, accent] **:** MARCATO

**mar·ca·site** \'märkə,sīt, ¦==ˈzēt\ *n* -s [ME *marchasite*, fr. ML *marcasita*, fr. Ar *marqashīthā*, fr. Syr *marqěshīthā*, perh. fr. Assyr *markhashītu* of or belonging to Markhashi, fr. *Markhashi*, region perhaps located in northeast Persia] **1 a :** any of several minerals with a metallic luster; *esp* **:** crystallized iron pyrites — not used technically **b :** a mineral consisting of iron disulfide $FeS_2$ having the same composition as iron pyrites and resembling it in appearance but differing from it by its orthorhombic crystallization and its lower specific gravity (4.85–4.90) — called also *white iron pyrites* **2 a :** a piece of marcasite (as crystallized iron pyrites) used in making ornaments esp. costume jewelry **b :** an ornament (as a piece of costume jewelry) made of marcasite — **mar·ca·sit·i·cal** \¦==-¦sid·əkəl\ *adj*

**mar·ca·tis·si·mo** \,märkə'tisə,mō\ *adv* (*or adj*) [It, superl. of *marcato*] **:** with very strong accentuation — used as a direction in music

**mar·ca·to** \mär'käd·(,)ō\ *adv* (*or adj*) [It, past part. of *marcare* to mark, accent, of Gmc origin; akin to OHG *marcōn* to determine the boundaries of — more at MARK] **:** with strong accentuation — used as a direction in music

¹**mar·cel** \(')mär¦sel, (')må¦s-\ *or* **marcel wave** *n* -s [after *Marcel* Grateau †1936 Fr. hairdresser] **:** a deep soft wave or series of such waves made in the hair by the use of a heated curling iron

²**marcel** \"\ *vb* **marcelled; marcelled; marcelling; marcels** *vt* **:** to make a marcel in ⟨regularly *marcelled* her hair⟩ ~ *vi* **:** to make a marcel ⟨skilled at *marcelling*⟩

**mar·cel·la** \mär'selə, må's-\ *n* -s [prob. alter. of ²*marseilles*] **:** an English cotton fabric made with a quilted or honeycomb face and used esp. for clothing, trimming, or bedspreads

**mar·cel·ler** \-lə(r)\ *n* -s **:** a hairdresser who makes marcels

**mar·ces·cence** \mär'sesᵊn(t)s\ *n* -s [fr. *marcescent*, after such pairs as E *competent: competence*] **:** the quality or state of being marcescent

¹**mar·ces·cent** \-nt\ *adj* [L *marcescent-, marcescens*, pres. part. of *marcescere* to wither, incho. fr. *marcēre* to wither; akin to MHG *mern* to dip bread in wine or water, MIr *mraich, braich* malt, and prob. to Gk *marainein* to waste away — more at SMART] *of a plant part* **:** withering without falling off ⟨~ leaves⟩

²**marcescent** \"\ *n* -s **:** a plant that has marcescent parts

**marc·gra·via** \märk'grävēə, måk'-\ *n, cap* [NL, fr. Georg *Markgraf* †1644 Ger. naturalist and traveler in So. America + NL *-ia*] **:** a genus (the type of the family Marcgraviaceae) of tropical American epiphytic woody vines that have vegetative shoots with 2-ranked closely appressed sessile leaves and flowering shoots with spreading petiolate leaves

**marc·gra·vi·a·ce·ae** \=,==ˈāsē,ē\ *n pl, cap* [NL, fr. *Marcgravia*, type genus + *-aceae*] **:** a small family of often epiphytic tropical American shrubs, trees, or vines (order Parietales) that have usu. pendulous flowers and petals united into a hood and sometimes functioning as nectaries — **marc·gra·vi·a·ceous** \(')=¦==¦āshəs\ *adj*

¹**march** \'märch, 'måch\ *n* -ES *usu cap* [ME, fr. OF *march, marz*, fr. L *martius*, fr. *martius* of Mars, fr. *Mart-, Mars*, Roman god of war and agriculture] **:** the third month of the Gregorian calendar — *abbr. Mar.;* see MONTH table

²**march** \"\ *n* -ES [ME *marche*, fr. OF, of Gmc origin; akin to OHG *marha* boundary — more at MARK] **1 a** (1) **:** a border region **:** BORDERLAND, FRONTIER (2) **:** BOUNDARY **b :** TERRITORY; *esp* **:** the territory (as a province) of an official's jurisdiction **2** *usu cap* **:** MARCH KING OF ARMS

³**march** \"\ *vi* -ED/-ING/-ES [ME *marchen*, fr. MF *marchir*, fr. OF, fr. *marche*, n.] **:** to have a contiguous location **:** have common borders or frontiers **:** lie continuously parallel or adjacent ⟨a region that ~*es* with Canada on the north and the Pacific on the west⟩ **:** lie extended ⟨mountain ranges that ~ along the horizon on every side —*Amer. Guide Series: Vt.*⟩

⁴**march** \"\, *as a command in drilling often* 'härch *or* 'håch\ *vb* -ED/-ING/-ES [MF *marcher*, *marchier* to march, trample under foot, fr. OF *marchier* to trample under foot, prob. of Gmc origin; akin to OE *mearcian* to mark, determine the boundaries of, OHG *marcōn* to determine the boundaries of — more at MARK] *vi* **1 a** (1) **:** to move along steadily with a regular measured stride; *esp* **:** to move along steadily with a rhythmic stride and in step with one or more others so moving ⟨enviously watched the column of soldiers ~*ing* smartly up the street⟩ (2) **:** to begin to move along steadily in this manner **:** begin such movement **:** set out or start marching ⟨said his troops would ~ at the crack of dawn⟩ **b :** to be in accord **:** move along in harmonious agreement **:** JIBE ⟨wherever his sympathies ~*ed* with the facts —Walter Lippmann⟩ **2 a** (1) **:** to move from one point to another usu. by walking esp. in a direct purposeful manner and without delaying ⟨heard a noise upstairs and ~*ed* up to see what was going on⟩ (2) **:** to go along **:** PROCEED, TRAVEL ⟨can ~ off to distant times and places —*Newsweek*⟩ ⟨hundreds of ships which had ~*ed* into the gulf —K.M. Dodson⟩ **b :** to make steady progress **:** move right along **:** go forward **:** move ahead **:** ADVANCE ⟨engines that ~ down the assembly line each day —A.H.Raskin⟩ ⟨forces that ~ inexorably toward greater social justice⟩ **3** *obs* **:** to have status **:** have rating **:** RANK ⟨~ in the first rank of magnificence —Robert Johnson⟩ ~ *vt* **1 a :** to cause to march ⟨~*ed* a division of foot troops forty honest miles in a day —H.H. Arnold & I.C.Eaker⟩ ⟨discipline that could ~ men past the point of exhaustion —Bruce Catton⟩ **b :** to bring or conduct somewhere esp. in a peremptory or unceremonious way or by force ⟨can remember him ~*ing* us all off from the schoolhouse —A.E.Coppard⟩ ⟨~*ed* them promptly to the jailhouse⟩ **2 :** to cover (an indicated distance or area) by marching **:** TRAVERSE ⟨~*ed* the ten remaining miles in record time⟩

⁵**march** \"\ *n* -ES [MF *marche*, fr. *marcher*, *marchier*, v.] **1 a** (1) **:** the action of marching ⟨were too tired to begin another ~⟩ (2) **:** the distance covered within a specific period of time by marching ⟨the city was at least a day's ~ away⟩ (3) **:** a regular measured stride or rhythmic step used in marching ⟨heard the ~ of the soldiers as they filed past⟩ **b** (1) **:** forward movement **:** steady advance **:** PROGRESS ⟨the ~ of time and events⟩ ⟨the ~ of science⟩; *esp* **:** forward movement of a marching unit esp. a military unit ⟨could not check the ~ of troops into their country⟩ (2) **:** direction of movement **:** COURSE ⟨did not like the current ~ of public opinion⟩ **c :** a long usu. tiring journey usu. on foot ⟨were not happy at the thought of a ~ to the top of the mountain⟩ **2 :** an instrumental or vocal composition that is in duple rhythm (as 4/4 time) or triply compound rhythm (as 6/8 time) with a strongly accentuated beat and that is designed or suitable for the accompaniment and guidance of marching **3 :** the taking of all five tricks by one side in the game of euchre — **on the march :** moving along steadily **:** ADVANCING ⟨saw that industrial improvement was *on the march*⟩ **:** MARCHING ⟨troops that were constantly *on the march*⟩ — **steal a march on** *also* **get a march on :** to get ahead of or win an advantage over esp. unexpectedly and with sly adroitness ⟨*stole a march on* his competitors by being the first to put the product on the market⟩

**march** *abbr, often cap* marchioness

**mar·chant** \'märchənt\ *archaic var of* MERCHANT

**mar·chan·tia** \mär'shantēə\ *n* [NL, fr. Nicolas *Marchant* †1678 Fr. botanist + NL *-ia*] **1** *cap* **:** the type genus of Marchantiaceae comprising liverworts that reproduce asexually by gemmae and have stalked antheridiophores **2** -s **:** any liverwort of the genus *Marchantia*

**mar·chan·ti·a·ce·ae** \=,==ˈāsē,ē\ *n pl, cap* [NL, fr. *Marchantia*, type genus + *-aceae*] **:** a family of liverworts (order Marchantiales) with prostrate usu. dichotomously branched thalli and archegonia on specialized upright branches — see MARCHANTIA — **mar·chan·ti·a·ceous** \=¦==¦āshəs\ *adj*

**mar·chan·ti·a·les** \=,==ˈā(,)lēz\ *n pl, cap* [NL, fr. *Marchantia* + *-ales*] **:** an order of Hepaticae comprising liverworts in which the gametophyte is differentiated internally into ventral storage tissue sometimes enclosing primitive conducting tissue and into a dorsal region of air chambers and in which the sporophyte has a jacket layer that is only one cell thick — see MARCHANTIACEAE

**march brown** *n, usu cap M & often cap B* **1 :** a mayfly (*Ecdyurus venosus*) mostly brown and striped with yellow **2 :** an angler's fly made to imitate the March brown mayfly

**mär·chen** \'me(ə)rkən, *G* 'meer\ *n, pl* **märchen** [G, fr. MHG *merechyn* short verse narrative, fr. *mære* report, narrative (fr. OHG *mārī, māri*, fr. *māri* famous) + *-chyn*, dim. suffix, fr. OHG *-chīn;* akin to OE *mǣre* famous, ON *mærr* famous, OE *māra* larger, more — more at MORE, -KIN] **:** TALE; *esp* **:** FOLKTALE

**march·er** \'märchə(r), 'måch-\ *n* -s [ME *marchier, marchere*, fr. *marche* border region + *-er, -ier, -ere, -iere* -er] **1 :** one that inhabits a border region **2 :** a lord enjoying royal liberties and having jurisdiction over territory in the English marches — called also *lord marcher*

**marches** *pl of* MARCH, *pres 3d sing of* MARCH

**mar·che·sa** \mär'kāzə\ *n, pl* **mar·che·se** \-(,)zā\ [It, fem. of *marchese*] **:** an Italian woman holding the rank of a marchese **:** MARCHIONESS

**mar·che·se** \-(,)zā\ *n, pl* **mar·che·si** \-(,)zē\ [It, fr. ML *marcensis*, fr. *marca* border region, of Gmc origin; akin to OHG *marha* boundary — more at MARK] **:** an Italian nobleman next in rank above a count **:** MARQUIS

**mar·chesh·van** \mär'keshvən\ *n* -s *usu cap* [Heb *marḥeshwān*] **:** HESHVAN

**mar·chet** \'märchət\ *or* **mar·che·ta** \mär'kād·ə\ *also* **merchet** \'mərchət\ *n* -s [ME *merchet*, fr. AF, fr. L *mercatus* trade, market place — more at MARKET] **:** a fee paid to a British feudal lord by his tenant for marrying off a daughter or son esp. to one outside the lord's jurisdiction or for the lord's waiving the droit du seigneur

**march fly** *n, usu cap M* **1 :** a fly of the family Bibionidae that usu. appears in early spring **2** *Austral* **:** HORSEFLY

**marching fire** *n* **:** ASSAULT FIRE

**marching flank** *n* **:** the flank of a military command farthest from the pivot when executing a change of direction

**marching orders** *n pl* **1 :** orders to set out on a march **:** orders to proceed ⟨the division got its *marching orders* one day before the attack⟩ **2 :** a notice of dismissal (as from a job) ⟨did very poor work and soon got his *marching orders*⟩

**mar·chio·ness** \'märsh(ə)nəs, 'måsh-\ *n* -ES [ML *marchionissa, marcionissa*, fr. *marchion-, marchio* marquis (fr. *marca* border region) + LL *-issa* -ess] **1 :** the wife of a marquess **2 :** a woman who holds in her own right the rank of marquess

**march king of arms** *usu cap M&K&A* [²*march*] **:** an English king of arms of the late medieval period who had jurisdiction in the west of England and in Wales and Cornwall and whose province was later divided between Clarenceux King of Arms and Norroy King of Arms

**marchland** \'=,=\ *n* **:** land in or along border regions **:** BORDERLAND

**march·man** \'=mən\ *n, pl* **marchmen** [ME *marcheman*, fr. *marche* border region + *man* — more at MARCH] **:** MARCHER 1

**march–order** \'=,==\ *vt* **:** to ready (arms or other military equipment) for marching ⟨*march-ordered* the artillery⟩

**march·pane** \'märch,pān, 'måch-\ *n* -s [It *marzapane* — more at MARZIPAN] **:** MARZIPAN

**march–past** \'=,=\ *n, pl* **march–pasts :** a filing by **:** PROCESSION ⟨reviews with relish the *march-past* of his years —*New Yorker*⟩; *specif* **:** a ceremonious procession or parade of marching units esp. of troops that file in review before inspectors or spectators

**mar·cion·ism** \'märshə,nizəm\ *n* -s *usu cap* [*Marcion*, 2d cent. A.D. Christian Gnostic + E *-ism*] **:** the doctrine of the Marcionites

**mar·cion·ite** \-,nīt\ *also* **mar·cion·ist** \-,nəst\ *n* -s *usu cap* [LL *marcionita, marcionista*, fr. *Marcion* + L *-ita* -ite or L *-ista* -ist] **:** a member of an anti-Judaic Gnostic sect that flourished from the 2d century to about the 7th century A.D.

**mar·co·man·ni** \,märkə'ma,nī\ *n pl, usu cap* [L *Marcomani, Marcomanni*] **:** an ancient Germanic people related to the Suevians

¹**mar·co·ni** \mär'kōnē, må'k-\ *adj, usu cap* [Guglielmo *Marconi* †1937 Ital. electrical engineer and inventor] **:** of or relating to the system of wireless telegraphy invented by Marconi ⟨a *Marconi* aerial⟩

²**marconi** \"\ *vt* **marconied; marconied; marconiing; marconies :** to send (a message) by wireless telegraphy

³**marconi** \"\ *adj, usu cap* [prob. so called fr. the resemblance of the complex system of struts and stays formerly characteristic of the Bermuda rig to the poles and stays used in wireless telegraphy] **:** of, relating to, or marked by a Bermuda rig ⟨a *Marconi* mainsail⟩

**mar·co·ni·gram** \-,gram\ *n* [¹*marconi* + *-gram*] **:** RADIOGRAM

**mar·co·ni·graph** \-,graf, -råf\ *n* [¹*marconi* + *-graph*] **:** apparatus used in Marconi wireless telegraphy

**marconi rig** *n, usu cap M* **:** BERMUDA RIG

**mar·co po·lo sheep** \'mär,kō'pō,lō-, 'må,k-\ *or* **marco polo's sheep** *n, usu cap M&P* [after *Marco Polo* †1324? Ital. traveler] **:** an Asiatic wild sheep with exceptionally large horns that is considered to be a variety (*Ovis ammon poli*) of the argali or to constitute a distinct species (*O. poli*)

¹**mar·cot** \'mär,kät, =ˈ=\ *vt* **marcotted; marcotted; marcotting; marcots** [F *marcotter*, fr. *marcotte*, n.] **:** to propagate (a plant) by marcottage

²**marcot** \"\ *also* **mar·cotte** \"\ *n* -s [F *marcotte*, fr. MF, prob. irreg. fr. L *mergus* layer of a plant, fr. *mergere* to dip, plunge — more at MERGE] **1 :** a branch of a plant prepared for marcottage **2 :** a new plant produced by marcottage

**mar·cot·tage** \'mär,käd·ij, =ˈ==; ,märkə'täzh\ *n* -s [F, fr. *marcotter* + *-age*] **:** air layering in which the rooting medium is bound to the plant rather than enclosed in a pot or other container; *broadly* **:** AIR LAYERING

**marcs** *pl of* MARC

**mar del pla·ta** \¦mär,del¦plād·ə\ *adj, usu cap M&P* [fr. *Mar del Plata*, city in eastern Argentina] **:** of or from the city of Mar del Plata, Argentina **:** of the kind or style prevalent in Mar del Plata

**mar·di gras** \'märdē¦grä, ¦mådē¦grå, -di,-\ *n, usu cap M&G* [F, lit., fat Tuesday] **1 a :** the last day before Lent often marked by merrymaking and feasting and in some places (as

New Orleans) by parades esp. of grotesquely costumed individuals and by masquerade balls **b :** a carnival period (as in New Orleans) preceding Lent and often lasting for many days and climaxed on the final day before Lent **2 :** a festive celebration held on or like that often held on the last day or days before Lent and marked by merrymaking and feasting

**¹mare** *n* -s [ME, fr. OE; akin to OHG & ON *mara* incubus, Croatian *mora,* and prob. to Gk *marainein* to waste away — more at SMART] *obs* **:** an evil preternatural being conceived of as causing nightmare

**²mare** \ˈma(a)|ər, ˈme|, |ə\ *n* -s [ME *mare, mere,* fr. OE *mere;* akin to OHG *merha* mare, ON *merr* mare, OE *mearh* horse, OHG *marah,* ON *marr,* W *march*] **1 :** a female horse or other equine animal esp. when fully mature or of breeding age — compare FILLY **2** *chiefly Scot* **:** ¹TRESTLE 1a

**³ma·re** \ˈmä|(ˌ)rē, ˈma(a)|, ˈmä|(ˌ)rā\ *n, pl* **ma·ria** \|rēə\ [NL, fr. L, sea — more at MARINE] **:** one of several dark areas of considerable extent on the surface of either the moon or Mars

**ma·re·ca** \məˈrēkə\ *n, cap* [NL, fr. Pg *marreca* wild duck] **:** a genus comprising the widgeons

**mare clau·sum** \-ˈklȯsəm, -ˈklau̇,su̇m\ *n* [NL, closed sea] **:** a sea or other navigable body of water that is under the jurisdiction of one nation and that is closed to other nations

**ma·re·han** \ˈmärə,hän\ *n, pl* **marehan** *or* **marehans** *usu cap* **1 :** a negroid people of Somaliland in the eastern part of Africa **2 :** a member of the Marehan people

**mare li·be·rum** \-ˈlibərəm, -ˈlēbə,ru̇m\ *n* [NL, free sea] **1 :** a sea or other navigable body of water that is open to all nations **2 :** FREEDOM OF THE SEAS

**ma·rem·ma** \məˈremə\ *n* -s [It, fr. ML *maritima* places near the sea, fr. L, neut. pl. of *maritimus* maritime — more at MARITIME] **:** swampy coastland

**mar·eng cell** \ˈmä,reŋ-\ *n, usu cap M* [*mareng* fr. Glenn L. *Martin* b1886 Am. airplane manufacturer + E *engineering*] **:** a fuel container made of airplane cloth impregnated inside and outside with a synthetic rubber that tends to seal up punctures

**ma·ren·go** \məˈreŋ(ˌ)gō\ *adj, often cap* [F, fr. *Marengo,* village in northwest Italy; prob. fr. the serving of a chicken marengo to Napoleon after his victory over the Austrians at Marengo in 1800] **:** of, consisting of, or served with a sauce made of mushrooms, tomatoes, olives, oil, and wine ⟨sautéed chicken ~⟩

**mare nos·trum** \-ˈnästrəm, -ˈnä,stru̇m\ *n* [L, our sea; fr. the fact that the Roman Empire at its greatest extent included all lands bordering on the Mediterranean] **:** a sea or other navigable body of water that belongs to a single nation or that two or more nations share by mutual agreement

**mareograph** *var of* MARIGRAPH

**mare's nest** *n, pl* **mare's nests** *or* **mares' nests 1 :** a hoax or fraud or some other nonexistent or illusory thing that seems at first to be very wonderful and full of promise but that ultimately brings ridicule on those deceived by it ⟨creating a neat little *mare's nest* in English dramatic history —R.S.Loomis⟩ ⟨spent his whole life looking for what was actually a *mare's nest*⟩ **2 :** a place, condition, or situation of great untidiness, disorder, or confusion ⟨the hold of the ship was a *mare's nest*⟩ ⟨had made a *mare's nest* of the administration⟩

**mare's tail** *n* **1** *pl* **mare's tails** *or* **mares' tails :** a cirrus cloud that has a long slender flowing appearance **2** *pl* **mare's tails a :** a common aquatic plant (*Hippuris vulgaris*) with elongated shoots clothed with dense whorls of subulate leaves **b :** HORSETAIL 2 **c :** HORSEWEED 1

**ma·rey's law** \məˈrāz-\ *n, usu cap M* [after Étienne Jules *Marey* †1904 Fr. physiologist] **:** a statement in physiology: heart rate is related inversely to arterial blood pressure

**mar·fire** \ˈmär,fī(ə)r\ *n* [perh. fr. E dial. *mar* (alter. of E ¹*mere*) + E *fire*] *dial Eng* **:** phosphorescence occurring on the sea

**marg** *abbr* margin; marginal

**mar·ga** \ˈmärgə\ *n* -s [Skt *mārga* path, fr. *mṛga* deer, gazelle] **1** *Hinduism* **:** one of several ways of approaching salvation — compare BHAKTI-MARGA **2 :** EIGHTFOLD PATH

**mar·ga·rate** \ˈmärgə,rāt\ *n* -s [ISV *margaric* (in *margaric* acid) + *-ate*] **:** a salt or ester of margaric acid

**mar·ga·ret grunt** \ˈmärg(ə)rət-\ *n* [*margaret* by folk etymology (influence of the name *Margaret*) fr. *margate*] **:** MARGATE a

**mar·gar·ic acid** \märˈgarik-, mä|, |ˈgarik-, ˈmär|garik-, ˈmä|, -rēk-\ *n* [*margaric* fr. F *margarique,* fr. *margar-* (fr. *margarine* margarin) + *-ique* -ic] **1 :** a crystalline synthetic fatty acid $CH_3(CH_2)_{15}COOH$ intermediate between palmitic acid and stearic acid — called also *heptadecanoic acid* **2 :** a mixture of palmitic acid and stearic acid obtained from various natural fats, oils, and waxes and formerly mistaken for a single acid

**mar·ga·rin** \ˈmärgərən\ *n* -s [F *margarine,* fr. Gk *margaron* pearl + F *-ine* -in] **:** a glycerol ester of margaric acid; *esp* **:** glycerol tri-margarate

**mar·ga·rine** *also* **mar·ga·rin** \ˈmärj(ə)rən, ˈmäj| *also* |ə,rēn *sometimes* -ärg| *or* -äg| *or* ,≈əˈrēn\ *n* -s [F, lit., margarin] **:** a food product that is used as a substitute for butter and made from a blend of refined oils esp. vegetable oils (as cottonseed oil, soybean oil) to which other ingredients (as salt, emulsifiers, vitamin A, vitamin D) are added and that is churned with ripened skim milk so as to have a consistency that permits ready spreading

**mar·ga·ri·ta·ceous** \ˌmärgərəˈtāshəs\ *adj* [L *margarita* pearl + E *-aceous*] **:** having a satiny iridescence like that of pearl or mother-of-pearl **:** PEARLY

**mar·ga·rite** \ˈmärgə,rīt\ *n* -s [ME, fr. MF, fr. L *margarita,* fr. Gk *margaritēs,* fr. *margaron* pearl (prob. fr. Skt *mañjara* pearl, cluster of blossoms) + *-itēs* -ite] **1** *archaic* **:** PEARL **2** [G *margarit,* fr. Gk *margaritēs* pearl] **:** a mineral $CaAl_4Si_2O_{10}(OH)_2$ consisting of a basic aluminum calcium silicate related to mica but low in silica and yielding brittle folia marked by a pearly luster **3** [F *margarite,* fr. Gk *margaritēs* pearl] **:** a primary form of rock crystallization in which globulites are arranged lineally like beads **4** [NL *Margarites*] **:** a top shell of the genus *Margarites*

**mar·ga·ri·tes** \ˌmärgəˈrī,dēz\ *n, cap* [NL, fr. Gk *margaritēs* pearl] **:** a genus of minute top shells that are widely distributed in cold northern seas and that are an important item of diet for cod and other fishes

**mar·ga·ro·des** \ˌmärgəˈrō,dēz\ *n, cap* [NL, fr. Gk *margaron* pearl + NL *-odes*] **:** a genus of scales — see GROUND PEARL

**mar·ga·ro·dite** \ˈmärgərə,dīt\ *n* -s [G *margarodit,* fr. MGk *margarōdēs* like a pearl (fr. Gk *margaron* pearl + *-ōdēs* -ode) + G *-it* -ite] **:** a pearly common mica resembling talc

**mar·gar·o·pus** \märˈgarəpəs\ *n, cap* [NL, fr. Gk *margaros* pearl oyster (fr. *margaron* pearl) + NL *-pus*] **:** a genus of ixodid ticks that in some classifications includes the cattle tick

**mar·ga·ro·san·ite** \ˌmärgəˈrōsᵊn,īt\ *n* -s [Gk *margaron* pearl + *sanis* board + E *-ite;* fr. its pearly luster and lamellar structure; prob. akin to Gk *sathē* penis, *sainein* to wag the tail, OE *thūma* thumb — more at THUMB] **:** a mineral $PbCa_2(SiO_3)_3$ consisting of a lead calcium silicate occurring in colorless lamellar masses

**mar·gate** \ˈmärgət\ *or* **margate fish** *n* -s [perh. fr. *Margate,* city in southeast England] **:** any of several grunts: as **a :** a variable usu. pearl gray fish (*Haemulon album*) of the tropical western Atlantic — called also *margaret grunt, margot fish* **b :** POMPON

**mar·gay** \ˈmär(ˌ)gā\ *n* -s [F, fr. Tupi *maracaja, maracayá*] **:** a small American spotted cat (*Felis tigrina*) resembling the ocelot and ranging from southernmost Texas to Brazil

**¹marge** \ˈmärj\ *n* -s [MF, fr. L *margin-, margo* border] *archaic* **:** EDGE, BORDER, MARGIN ⟨dogs ran howling along the water's ~ —Herman Melville⟩

**²marge** \ˈmäj\ *n* -s [by shortening & alter.] *Brit* **:** MARGARINE

**¹mar·gent** \ˈmärjənt\ *n* -s [ME *margente,* alter. of ¹*margin*] *archaic* **:** EDGE, BORDER, MARGIN

**²margent** \"\ *adj, archaic* **:** BORDERING

**¹mar·gin** \ˈmärjən, ˈmäj-\ *n* -s [ME, fr. L *margin-, margo* border — more at MARK] **1 a** (1) **:** a vertical blank column to the left or right of an area occupied or to be occupied by the main body of a printed or written text or by a group of illustrations on a page or sheet (2) **:** a straight horizontal blank area at the top or bottom of such a page or sheet (3) **:** the entire blank area running about the borders of such a page or sheet and consisting of the left and right vertical blank columns and the straight horizontal blank areas at the top and bottom **b** (1) **:** the blank border outside the printed design of a stamp; *also* **:** the portion of this border at the left or right side of the stamp or at the top or bottom (2) **:** the border of a sheet of stamps beyond the outside line of perforations; *also* **:** the portion of this border at the left or right side of the sheet or at the top or bottom **2 a :** the extreme edge of something and the area lying parallel to and immediately adjoining this edge esp. when in some way distinguished from the remaining area lying farther in **:** the outside limit and adjoining surface of something **:** boundary area **:** VERGE: as (1) **:** the boundary area extending along the edge of a body of water ⟨stood at the ~ of the lake⟩ or of a wooded section ⟨a village built at the ~ of a forest⟩ or of some other similar body or surface ⟨the melting ~s of a glacier⟩ (2) **:** the boundary area extending along the edge of a leaf of a plant (3) **:** the boundary area extending along the edge of an insect's wing **b :** the part of the momentary field of consciousness which is felt only vaguely and dimly **3 a :** the flat unmolded part of the stiles and rails of a paneled framing **b :** the cylindrical land of a drill the diameter of which determines the size of the hole **4 a :** something that is over and above what is strictly necessary and that is designed to provide for emergencies **:** a spare amount or measure or degree allowed or given for contingencies or special situations **:** a factor or group of factors making for ready opportunity or ample scope or personal choice in proceeding freely ⟨an enormous ~ of luxury in this country against which we can draw for our vital needs —Walter Lippmann⟩ ⟨the busy lawyer . . . had no ~ of time for meditation —Van Wyck Brooks⟩ **b** (1) **:** a bare minimum below which or an extreme limit beyond which something is no longer desirable or becomes impossible ⟨a joke that was on the ~ of good taste⟩ ⟨living on the ~ of respectability⟩ (2) **:** the limit below which economic activity cannot be continued under normal conditions **:** the particular condition (as with regard to the increment of return for labor or for interest on an investment) that limits the existence or continuance of an economic process other things being unchanged ⟨a ~ of production⟩ ⟨the ~ of consumption⟩ **5 a :** the difference that exists between net sales and the cost of merchandise sold and that is taken as that from which expenses must be met or profit derived or from which other obligations must be met or other advantages derived — called also *gross margin* **b :** the excess market value of collateral over the face of a loan **c** (1) **:** cash or collateral which is deposited with a broker to secure him from loss on a contract made on behalf of his principal and which may also constitute a partial payment of the purchase price (2) **:** a customer's equity if his account is terminated at prevailing market prices (3) **:** a speculative transaction in which the broker does part of the financing (4) **:** an allowance above or below a certain figure within which a purchase or sale is to be made **6 :** measure or degree of difference; *esp* **:** one by which a decision is made ⟨the vote was 54 to 34, a ~ of twenty⟩ ⟨the wide ~ between producers' and consumers' prices —*Economist*⟩ **syn** see BORDER, ROOM

**²margin** \"\ *vb* -ED/-ING/-S *vt* **1 a :** to furnish with notes in the margin of (a page or sheet) ⟨~*ing* every other page with comments and criticism⟩ **b :** to indicate or specify (as sources) by means of marginal notes ⟨historical documents from which material was drawn were carefully ~*ed* throughout the text⟩ **2 a :** to provide with an edging or border ⟨a beautifully printed page that had been ornately ~*ed*⟩ **b :** to be situated along or lie extended along so as to form a border ⟨trees ~*ing* the shore⟩ ⟨a bright band of color ~*ing* the butterfly's wings⟩ **3 :** to deposit a margin upon (as stock); *specif* **:** to hold or keep secured by depositing or adding to a margin — often used with *up* ~ *vi* **:** to deposit additional margin — usu. used with *up*

**¹mar·gin·al** \ˈmärjənᵊl, ˈmäj-\ *adj* [ML *marginalis,* fr. L *margin-, margo* border + *-alis* -al — more at MARGIN] **1 a :** written or printed in the margin of a page or sheet ⟨~ notes⟩ **b :** having notes written or printed in the margin ⟨a ~ manuscript⟩ **2 a :** of, relating to, or constituting a margin ⟨the ~ parts of an insect's wing⟩ **b** (1) **:** situated at, on, or near a margin ⟨outlying ~ territorial possessions⟩; *specif* **:** occupying the borderland of a relatively stable territorial or cultural area ⟨~ groups of aborigines⟩ (2) **:** characterized by the incorporation of habits and values from two divergent cultures and by incomplete assimilation in either ⟨the ~ cultural habits of new immigrant groups⟩ **c** (1) **:** running round a leaf parallel and near to the margin ⟨~ leaf venation⟩ (2) **:** *of a monocarpellary ovary* **:** PARIETAL **3 :** located at the fringe of consciousness ⟨~ sensations⟩ **4 a :** close to the lower limit of qualification or acceptability ⟨possesses only ~ ability⟩ **b** (1) **:** having a character or capacity fitted to yield a supply of goods which when marketed at existing price levels will barely cover the cost of production ⟨~ land⟩ ⟨~ production⟩ ⟨~ producers⟩ (2) **:** of, relating to, or concerned with a limit or margin of return or reward as measured by existing price levels that is barely sufficient to yield a profit or cover the costs of production ⟨~ profits⟩ ⟨~ sales⟩

**²marginal** \"\ *n* -s **:** something that is marginal: as **a** (1) **:** a note written or printed in a margin (2) **:** a decorative border of a page or sheet **b :** a body part (as one of the plates around the edge of the carapace of a turtle, an outer tooth in the radula of a mollusk) that is marginal in relation to another part

**marginal blight** *or* **marginal spot** *n* **:** a disease of lettuce that is caused by a bacterium (*Pseudomonas marginalis*) and is marked by a brownish discoloration along the margins of the leaves

**marginal body** *or* **marginal organ** *also* **marginal dot** *n* **:** LITHOCYST

**marginal convolution** *also* **marginal gyrus** *or* **marginal lobe** *n* **:** the convolution on the upper border of the mesial surface of the frontal lobe of each cerebral hemisphere

**marginal crevasse** *n* **:** a crevasse pointing obliquely up-valley that develops on either side of some valley glaciers

**marginal head** *n* **:** SIDEHEAD

**mar·gi·na·lia** \ˌmärjəˈnālēə, ˌmäj-, -lyə\ *n pl* [NL, fr. ML, neut. pl. of *marginalis* marginal] **1 :** marginal notes **2 :** extrinsic matters **:** nonessential items ⟨interested in both the essentials and the ~ of that science⟩

**mar·gin·al·ism** \ˈmärjənᵊl,izəm\ *n* -s **:** economic analysis that stresses use of marginal qualities in the determination of equilibrium

**mar·gin·al·ist** \-ᵊləst\ *n* -s **:** one that believes in the use of marginal analysis in economics

**mar·gin·al·i·ty** \ˌmärjəˈnaləd-ē\ *n* -ES **:** the quality or state of being marginal

**marginal lappet** *n* **:** one of a pair of delicate flaps of tissue between which lie the sense organs of jellyfishes of the order Discomedusae

**mar·gin·al·ly** \ˈmärjənᵊlē, ˈmäj-, -ᵊli\ *adv* **1 :** in a marginal manner ⟨~ qualified⟩ ⟨~ normal⟩ **2 :** in, about, or toward a margin ⟨wandering ~ through distinguished gatherings —H.G.Wells⟩

**marginal sea** *n* **:** waters adjacent to a state and under its jurisdiction and extending outward from the coast about 3½ statute miles

**marginal shield fern** *n* **:** EVERGREEN WOOD FERN 1

**marginal utility** *n* **:** the amount of additional utility provided by an additional unit of an economic good or service

**¹mar·gin·ate** \ˈmärjə,nāt\ *vb* -ED/-ING/-S [L *marginatus,* past part. of *marginare* to provide with a border, fr. *margin-, margo* border — more at MARGIN] **:** MARGIN — **mar·gin·a·tion** \ˌ≈≈ˈnāshən\ *n* -s

**²marginate** \"\ *or* **mar·gin·at·ed** \-ād·əd\ *adj* [L *marginatus*] **:** having a margin distinct in appearance or structure

**margined** *past of* MARGIN

**mar·gi·nel·la** \ˌmärjəˈnelə\ *n* [NL, fr. L *margin-, margo* border + NL *-ella*] **1** *cap* **:** the type genus of Marginellidae comprising chiefly tropical small glossy white-shelled marine snails **2** -s **:** a mollusk of the genus *Marginella* or family Marginellidae

**mar·gi·nel·li·dae** \-lə,dē\ *n pl, cap* [NL, fr. *Marginella,* type genus + *-idae*] **:** a large nearly cosmopolitan family of small marine snails (suborder Stenoglossa) with strong porcelaneous often somewhat pear-shaped shell having a long narrow aperture and a thickened outer lip — see MARGINELLA

**margining** *pres part of* MARGIN

**margin of safety :** an arithmetical index equal to the ultimate strength of a material minus the contemplated stress — compare FACTOR OF SAFETY

**margin release key** *n* **:** a key (as on a typewriter) that releases the margin stops (as for extending a line of writing)

**margins** *pl of* MARGIN, *pres 3d sing of* MARGIN

**margin shell** *n* **:** MARGINELLA 2

**margin stop** *or* **marginal stop** *n* **:** either of the stops (as on a typewriter) that limit the range of the printing and determine the width of the margins

**margin trowel** *n* **:** a small trowel having a square end for finishing angles and narrow spaces

margin trowel

**mar·go·sa** \märˈgōsə\ *n* -s [modif. of Pg *amargosa,* fem. of *amargoso* bitter, fr. (assumed) VL *amaricosus,* fr. L *amarus* bitter — more at AMAROID] **:** a large East Indian tree (*Melia azadirachta*) whose trunk exudes a tenacious gum and has a bitter bark used as a tonic and whose fruit and seeds yield a medicinal aromatic oil — compare CHINABERRY 2

**mar·got fish** \ˈmärgət-\ *n* [*margot* alter. of *margate*] **:** MARGATE

**mar·gra·vate** \ˈmärgrə,vāt\ *or* **mar·gra·vi·ate** \märˈgrāvē,āt\ *n* -s [*margravate* fr. *margrave* + *-ate; margraviate* fr. ML *margravius* margrave (fr. MD *marcgrave*) + E *-ate*] **:** the territory of a margrave

**mar·grave** \ˈmär,grāv, ˈmä,-\ *n* -s [D *markgraaf* governor of a border region, fr. MD *marcgrave;* akin to MLG *markgrēve* governor of a border region, OHG *marcgrāvo;* all fr. a prehistoric D-G compound whose constituents are akin to OHG *marha* boundary and *grāvo* count — more at MARK, BURGRAVE] **1 :** the military governor esp. of a German border province **2 :** a member of the German nobility corresponding in rank to a British marquess — **mar·gra·vi·al** \(ˈ)märˈgrāvēəl\ *adj*

**mar·gra·vine** \ˈmärgrə,vēn\ *n* -s [G *markgräfin* & D *markgravin;* G *markgräfin* fr. MHG *marcgrāvinne, marcgrævinne,* fr. *marcgrāve* margrave (akin to MD *marcgrave*); D *markgravin* fr. MD *marcgravinne,* fr. *marcgrave* margrave] **:** the wife of a margrave

**mar·gue·rite** \ˌmärg(y)əˈrēt, ˌmäg-\ *also* **marguerite daisy** *n* -s [F *marguerite,* fr. OF *margarite* daisy, pearl — more at MARGARITE] **1 a :** DAISY 1a **b :** any of various single-flowered chrysanthemums; *esp* **:** a chrysanthemum (*Chrysanthemum frutescens*) of the Canary islands **c :** any of several cultivated plants of the genus *Anthemis* **2 :** a frosted cookie made by spreading a saltine, pastry square, or other base with a mixture of whipped white of egg and boiled sugar syrup and browning in an oven

**marguerite yellow** *n, often cap M* **:** a pale yellow green that is yellower, lighter, and stronger than smoke gray or oyster gray and yellower and paler than average Nile

**mar·hesh·van** \märˈkeshvən\ *n* -s *usu cap* [Heb *marḥeshwān*] **:** HESHVAN

**¹ma·ri** *or* **mar·ri** \ˈmä(ˌ)rē\ *also* **mur·ree** \ˈmə(-\ *n, pl* **mari** *or* **maris** *or* **marri** *or* **marris** *usu cap* **1 :** a Baluchi people of Baluchistan **2 :** a member of the Mari people

**²ma·ri** \ˈmärē\ *n, pl* **mari** *or* **maris** *usu cap* **:** CHEREMIS 1

**mari-** *comb form* [L, fr. *mare* — more at MARINE] **:** sea ⟨*maricolous*⟩ ⟨*marigraph*⟩

**¹ma·ria** \məˈrēə\ *n* -s [AmerSp *maria,* perh. fr. Sp *Maria* Mary, mother of Jesus] **:** any of several shrubs and trees of tropical America; *esp* **:** a valuable timber tree (*Calophyllum longifolium*) of Panama

**²maria** *pl of* ³MARE

**ma·ri·a·chi** \ˌmärēˈächē\ *n* -s [MexSp *mariache, mariachi,* perh. modif. of F *mariage* marriage — more at MARRIAGE] **1 a :** a group of itinerant Mexican folk musicians usu. consisting of singers, guitarists, and a violinist **b :** a musician belonging to such a group **2 :** the music performed or sung by a mariachi

**ma·ri·a·lite** \məˈrēə,līt, ˈmar-\ *n* -s [G *marialith,* fr. *Maria* (latinized form of *Marie,* fr. *Marie* vom Rath, wife of Gerhard vom Rath †1888 Ger. mineralogist) + G *-lith* -lite] **:** a mineral $Na_4Al_3Si_9O_{24}Cl$ that consists of a chlorine-bearing aluminosilicate of sodium and is isomorphous with meionite — see SCAPOLITE

**¹mar·i·an** \ˈma(a)rēən, ˈmer-, ˈmār-\ *adj, usu cap* [*Mary* I (*Mary* Tudor) †1558 Queen of England + E *-an,* adj. suffix] **1 :** of or relating to Mary Tudor or her reign (1553–58) ⟨the *Marian* persecution⟩ ⟨*Marian* exiles⟩ ⟨the *Marian* bishops⟩ **2** [*Mary* (the Virgin *Mary*), mother of Jesus + E *-an,* adj. suffix] **:** of, relating to, or characterized by veneration of the Virgin Mary ⟨*Marian* songs⟩ ⟨*Marian* theology as it affects the question of Christian reunion —*British Book News*⟩

**²marian** \"\ *n* -s *usu cap* [*Mary* (the Virgin *Mary*) + E *-an,* n. suffix] **:** one who venerates or is devoted to the Virgin Mary

**ma·ri·a·nao** \ˌmärēəˈnau̇\ *adj, usu cap* [fr. *Marianao,* city in western Cuba] **:** of or from the city of Marianao, Cuba **:** of the kind or style prevalent in Marianao

**mar·i·anne** \ˌmarēˈan, ˌmer-, ˌmār-; ˌmaarēˈaa(ə)n\ *also* **mar·i·an·na** \-ˈanə\ *n* -s *usu cap* [F, fr. *Marianne,* French republican society of the 1850s with the aim of overthrowing Napoleon III, fr. the feminine name *Marianne*] **:** the French Republic personified **:** the French people

**ma·ria the·re·sa dollar** \məˈrīətəˈrēsə-, -ˈrēətəˈrē|, |zə-\ *n, usu cap M&T* [after *Maria Theresa* †1780 Archduchess of Austria and Queen of Hungary] **:** an Austrian silver dollar bearing the bust of Maria Theresa and the date 1780 used as a trade coin in the Middle East

**ma·ri·ca** \məˈrīkə\ *n* [NL, fr. L *Marica,* goddess associated with a sacred grove at Minturnae in central Italy] **1** *cap* **:** a genus of tender perennials (family Iridaceae) resembling the iris and having flowers on the side of leaflike stems **2** -s **:** a plant of the genus *Marica*

**ma·ric·o·lous** \məˈrikələs\ *adj* [*mari-* + *-colous*] **:** living in the sea ⟨strictly ~ mollusks⟩

**mar·i·co·pa** \ˌmarəˈkōpə\ *n, pl* **maricopa** *or* **maricopas** *usu cap* **1 a :** an Indian people of the Gila river valley, Arizona **b :** a member of such people **2 :** a Yuman language of the Maricopa and Halchidhoma peoples

**¹ma·rie** \ˈmäri, ˈmeri\ *n* -s *often cap* [fr. the name *Marie, Mary*] *Scot* **:** MAID OF HONOR 1 ⟨yestreen the Queen had four *Maries* —Sir Walter Scott⟩

**²ma·rie** \məˈrē\ *n* -s [by folk etymology] **:** MARLI

**ma·ri·en·gro·schen** \məˈrēən,grōshən\ *n, pl* **mariengroschen** [G, fr. *Marie* Mary, mother of Jesus + G *groschen* — more at GROSCHEN] **:** an old German silver coin bearing a representation of the Madonna and Child first issued about 1505

**maries** *pl of* MARY

**mar·i·gold** \ˈmarə,gōld, ˈmer- *sometimes* ˈma(a)rē,- *or* ˈmerē,- *or* ˈmārē,- *or* -ri,-\ *n* -s [ME *marigold, marygold,* fr. *Mary,* mother of Jesus + ME *gold*] **1 a :** POT MARIGOLD **b :** a plant of the genus *Tagetes:* as (1) **:** AFRICAN MARIGOLD (2) **:** FRENCH MARIGOLD **c :** any of numerous other yellow-flowered plants: as (1) **:** BUR MARIGOLD (2) **:** CORN MARIGOLD (3) **:** MARSH MARIGOLD **2 :** a flower of a marigold **3 a** *or* **marigold yellow :** CADMIUM ORANGE **b :** a variable color averaging a strong orange yellow that is yellower and deeper than nasturtium yellow (sense 2) and yellower and stronger than Spanish yellow

**marigold finch** *n* **:** a European goldcrest

**marigold window** *n* **:** a circular window with radial tracery **:** ROSE WINDOW, WHEEL WINDOW

**mar·i·gram** \ˈmarə,gram\ *n* [*mari-* + *-gram*] **:** an autographic record from a marigraph

**mar·i·graph** \-raf, -räf\ *or* **mar·e·o·graph** \-rēə-\ *n* [*marigraph* fr. *mari-* + *-graph; mareograph* fr. F *maréographe,* fr. *maréo-* (fr. L *mare* sea) + *-graphe* -graph — more at MARINE] **:** a self-registering tide gage — **mar·i·graph·ic** \ˌmarəˈgrafik\ *adj*

**mar·i·hua·na** *or* **mar·i·jua·na** *also* **mar·a·jua·na** \ˌmarə-ˈ(h)wänə *also* ˌmer-\ *n* -s [MexSp *mariguana, marihuana*] **1 :** a wild tobacco (*Nicotiana glauca*) **2 a :** HEMP 1 **b :** the dried leaves and flowering tops of the pistillate hemp plants that are the source of the drug cannabin and that are sometimes smoked in cigarettes with consequent action of the drug on the higher nerve centers to produce peculiar psychic disturbances — compare BHANG, GANJA, HASHISH

**ma·rim·ba** \mə'rimbə\ *n* -s [of African origin; akin to Kimbundu *marimba* xylophone, Tshiluba *madimba* xylophone, Kongo *madiumba* harmonicon] **1 :** a primitive xylophone of southern Africa and Central America with resonators beneath each bar **2 :** the modern improved form of the primitive marimba

**marimba gong** *n* **:** a marimba with metal instead of wooden bars

**mar·i·mon·da** \,marə'mändə\ *n* -s [AmerSp] **:** a So. American spider monkey (*Ateles belzebuth*)

**ma·ri·na** \mə'rēnə\ *n* -s [It & Sp, fr. fem. of *marino* of the sea, marine, fr. L *marinus*] **1 :** a seaside promenade or esplanade ⟨the houses that front the ~ —*Atlantic*⟩ **2 :** a dock or basin providing secure moorings for motorboats and yachts ⟨municipal ~*s*⟩

**¹mar·i·nade** \¦marə¦nād *also* ¦mer-\ *vt* -ED/-ING/-S [alter. (influenced by *-ade*) of *marinate*] **:** MARINATE

**²marinade** \"\ *n* -s **:** a brine or pickle usu. containing vinegar or wine, oil, spices, and herbs in which a food (as meat or fish) is soaked to enrich its flavor

**marinal** *adj* [ML *marinalis*, fr. L *marinus* marine + *-alis* -al] **1** *obs* **:** of or relating to the sea **:** MARINE **2** *obs* **:** NAUTICAL

**mar·i·nate** \'marə,nāt *also* 'mer-, *usu* -ād·+V\ *vt* -ED/-ING/-S [prob. fr. It *marinato*, past part. of *marinare* to marinate, fr. *marino* marine, fr. L *marinus*] **:** to season (as meat or fish) by steeping in a marinade ⟨~ beef⟩ ⟨*marinated* herring⟩

**ma·rind** \mə'rind\ *also* **marind-anim** \-ə,nim\ *n, pl* **marind** *or* **marinds** *usu cap* **1 a :** a Papuan people inhabiting the southern part of Netherlands New Guinea **b :** a member of such people **2 :** a language of the Marind people

**ma·rind·ese** \¦marən¦dēz, -ēs\ *n, pl* **marindese** *usu cap* **:** MARIND

**¹ma·rine** \mə'rēn\ *n* -s [ME *maryn*, fr. MF *marine*, fr. OF, fr. fem. of *marin*, adj., marine, fr. L *marinus*] **1** *obs* **a :** SEASHORE **b :** a seaside promenade **2** [F, fr. OF, seashore] **a :** the mercantile and naval shipping of a country ⟨keep our ~ in a condition commensurate to its great ends —Edmund Burke⟩ ⟨to whose direction the ~ of England was entrusted when the Spanish invaders were approaching —T.B.Macaulay⟩ **b :** seagoing ships esp. in relation to nationality or class ⟨America had the largest mercantile ~ —Richard Cobden⟩ **3** [²*marine*] **:** one of a class of soldiers serving on shipboard or in close association with a naval force (as in a landing operation); *specif* **:** a member of the Marine Corps of the U.S. or of the Royal Marine forces of Great Britain ⟨tell that to the ~*s* — the sailors won't believe it —Sir Walter Scott⟩ ⟨the United States *Marines* . . . are trained, equipped, and used as soldiers —L.G.Winans⟩ **4** [F, fr. OF, seashore] **:** an executive department (as in France) having charge of naval affairs ⟨the French Minister of *Marine*⟩ **5** [F, fr. OF, seashore] **:** a marine picture ⟨a famous exhibition of . . . ~*s* —*Atlantic*⟩

**²marine** \"\ *adj* [ME *maryne*, fr. L *marinus*, fr. *mare* sea + *-inus* -ine; akin to OE *mere* sea, pool, OHG *meri* sea, ON *marr*, Goth *marei*, OIr *muir*, OSlav *morje*] **1 a** (1) **:** of or relating to the sea ⟨~ life⟩ ⟨~ vegetation⟩ ⟨~ wonders⟩ ⟨~ and land crabs⟩ ⟨~ and continental rocks⟩ ⟨sediments . . . both terrigenous and ~ —*Jour. of Geol.*⟩ ⟨although many of the Mollusca are still ~, there are even more which live in fresh water or upon the land —W.E.Swinton⟩ (2) *of climate* **:** having characteristics (as small temperature ranges and high relative humidity) controlled primarily by oceanic winds and air masses **b :** of or relating to the navigation of the sea **:** NAUTICAL ⟨~ navigation⟩ ⟨~ chart⟩ ⟨~ engineering⟩ **c :** of or relating to the commerce of the sea **:** MARITIME 1 ⟨~ law⟩ ⟨~ risks⟩ **2** *obs* **a :** bordering on the sea **:** MARITIME 2a **b :** belonging to the seashore **3 :** of or relating to marines ⟨~ barracks⟩

**marine architect** *n* **:** one whose profession is the designing of ships

**marine barometer** *n* **:** a barometer adapted for shipboard use that has a fixed cistern and a fine capillary section in the tube to damp out oscillations of the mercury caused by the motion of the ship

**marine belt** *n* **:** MARGINAL SEA

**marine blue** *also* **marine** *n* -s **:** a moderate purplish blue that is bluer and duller than average cornflower or gentian blue and bluer and less strong than old glory blue — called also *purple navy*

**marine chronometer** *n* **:** CHRONOMETER a

**marine contract** *n* **:** MARITIME CONTRACT

**marine corps** *n* [after the U.S. *Marine Corps*] **:** a dark blue that is redder and duller than Peking blue or Flemish blue and paler than Japan blue

**marine engine** *n* **:** an engine for propelling a ship

**marine engineer** *n* **1 :** an officer charged with maintenance and operation of a ship's engines and boilers **2 :** a specialist in marine engineering

**marine engineering** *n* **:** a branch of engineering that deals with the construction and operation of the power plant and other mechanical equipment of seagoing craft, docks, and harbor installations

**marine glue** *n* **:** a water-insoluble adhesive composed usu. of a mixture of rubber and shellac and often pitch or resins

**marine green** *n* **:** a dark to dark grayish green

**marine hospital** *n* **:** one of numerous hospitals operated under the Public Health Service of the U.S. Government for the care of sick and disabled seamen

**marine iguana** *n* **:** a shore-dwelling seaweed-eating iguana (*Amblyrhynchus cristatus*) of the Galápagos islands

**marine insurance** *n* **:** insurance against loss by damage or destruction of cargo, freight, merchandise, or the means or instruments of transportation and communication whether on land, sea, or air — compare INLAND MARINE INSURANCE, OCEAN MARINE INSURANCE

**marine interest** *n* **:** interest at a legally unrestricted rate on a maritime loan — compare BOTTOMRY

**marine ivy** *n* **:** either of two vines of the southern U.S.: **a :** a simple-leaved woody vine (*Ampelopsis cordata*) with small bluish fruit **b :** a vine (*Cissus incisa*) with divided unusually heavy leaves and fleshy stems

**marine league** *n* **:** a league used as a marine unit equal to three nautical miles — called also *sea league*; compare LAND LEAGUE

**marine leg** *n* **:** an elevating conveyor that can be lowered into the hold of a ship for unloading grain

**marine oil** *n* **1 :** FISH OIL **2** *or* **marine engine oil :** a lubricating oil for marine engines

**marine perils** *n pl* **:** perils relating to or arising from or upon the high seas or navigable waters — see PERILS OF THE SEA

**mar·i·ner** \'marənə(r) *also* 'mer-\ *n* -s [ME, fr. OF *marinier*, fr. ML *marinarius*, fr. L *marinus* marine + *-arius* -ary — more at MARINE] **1 a :** one who navigates or assists in navigating a ship **:** SEAMAN, SAILOR **b :** one who is employed as a member of a ship's company, participates in the operation of or activities aboard the ship, and contributes by his labor to a safe, comfortable, and successful voyage **2 :** a senior girl scout specializing in seamanship and watercraft

**ma·ri·ne·ra** \,märə'nerə\ *n* -s [AmerSp, fr. Sp, fem. of *marinero* of the sea, marine, fr. *marino* of the sea, marine, fr. L *marinus;* fr. a wish to do honor to the Peruvian navy during a war with Chile in 1879–83] **:** a Peruvian couple dance with courtship mime and kerchief play

**marine railway** *n* **:** inclined tracks extending into the water so that a ship can be hauled up on a cradle or platform for cleaning or repairs

**marine risks** *n pl* **:** MARINE PERILS

**mariner's chronometer** *n* **:** CHRONOMETER a

**mariner's compass** *n* **:** a compass used in navigation consisting of two or more parallel magnetic needles or bundles of needles permanently attached to a compass card that is delicately pivoted and enclosed in a glass-covered box or bowl set in gimbals in the binnacle and that is read with reference to the lubber line on the front of the bowl

**marines** *pl of* MARINE

**marine soap** *n* **:** soap made usu. from coconut oil and used with seawater

**marine store** *n* **1 a :** ship supplies (as cordage, anchors, provisions) **b :** old ship material offered for sale as junk **2 :** a shop where marine stores are sold

**marine superintendent** *n* **:** an official of a steamship company charged with supervision of staff officers and crew and of matters relating to the operation of the company's ships

**marine terrace** *n* **:** a terrace formed along a seashore by the merging of wave-cut and wave-built terraces

**marine toad** *n* **:** AGUA

**marine trumpet** *n* **:** TRUMPET MARINE

**marine varnish** *n* **:** a spar varnish designed esp. for marine exposure and usu. made of tung oil and phenolic resin

**mar·in·gouin** \,marəⁿ'gwaⁿ\ *n* -s [F, fr. Tupi *marigui* mosquito] **:** BLACKFLY a

**ma·ri·nhei·ro** \,märə'nyā(,)rō\ *n* -s [Pg, fr. *marinheiro*, adj., of ships, of the sea, marine, fr. *marinho* of the sea, marine, fr. L *marinus;* fr. the use of the wood in shipbuilding] **:** any of several tropical American timber trees of the genus *Guarea*

**ma·ri·nism** \mə'rē,nizəm\ *n* -s *usu cap* [It *marinismo*, fr. Giambattista *Marini* †1625 Ital. poet + It *-ismo* -ism] **:** a florid bombastic literary style fashionable in 17th century Italy marked by extravagant metaphors, farfetched conceits, and forced antitheses — compare EUPHUISM, GONGORISM

**¹ma·ri·nist** \-ēnəst\ *n* -s *usu cap* [It *marinista*, fr. Giambattista *Marini* + It *-ista* -ist] **:** one given to Marinism ⟨disdaining the folly of the *Marinists* —Edmund Gosse⟩

**²ma·rin·ist** \mə'rēnəst\ *n* -s [²*marine* + *-ist*] **:** one who holds certain features of the earth's surface to be due to marine action rather than the action of other natural forces (as wind, rain, or frost) ⟨every line of escarpments was held by the ~*s* to be the work of sea waves —*Popular Science Monthly*⟩

**ma·ri·no·ra·ma** \mə,rēnə'ramə, -'rämə\ *n* -s [²*marine* + *-orama* (as in *panorama*)] **:** a panoramic representation of a sea view

**mar·i·o·la** \,marē'ōlə\ *n* -s [MexSp] **:** a shrub (*Parthenium incanum*) that resembles guayule and yields a rubber

**mar·i·ol·a·ter** \,ma(a)rē'äləd·ə(r), ,mer-\ *n* -s *usu cap* [fr. *mariolatry*, after E *idolatry: idolater*] **:** one that practices Mariolatry

**mar·i·ol·a·trous** \¦==¦älə·trəs\ *adj, usu cap* [*mariolatry* + *-ous*] **:** marked by Mariolatry

**mar·i·ol·a·try** \,==ˈälə·trē\ *n* -ES *usu cap* [*Mary* (the Virgin *Mary*), mother of Jesus + E *-o-* + *-latry*] **1 :** the worship of the Virgin Mary; *specif* **:** rendition to the Virgin Mary of the kind of worship held due to God alone ⟨opposed to *Mariolatry* and superstition —B.J.Kidd⟩ ⟨the tasteless excesses of *Mariolatry* —*The Rev. of Religion*⟩ **2 :** extravagant idealization of woman arising from the worship of Mary ⟨pretty conceits of *Mariolatry* —J.R.Green⟩ ⟨preaches a sort of mellowed *Mariolatry*, a humorless exaltation of woman —H.L.Mencken⟩

**mar·i·ol·o·gist** \-ləjəst\ *n* -s *usu cap* **:** one versed in Mariology

**mar·i·ol·o·gy** \-jē\ *n* -ES *usu cap* [*Mary* (the Virgin *Mary*) + E *-o-* + *-logy*] **:** doctrine or opinion about the Virgin Mary as mother of the Son of God

**mar·i·o·nette** \¦ma(a)rēə¦net, ¦mer-, *usu* -ed·+V\ *n* -s [F *marionnette*, fr. MF *maryonete*, fr. *Marion* (dim. of the name *Marie* Mary) + MF *-ete* -ette; prob. fr. the conception that a puppet resembles an image of the Virgin Mary] **1 :** a puppet moved by strings or by hand (as in a puppet show) ⟨the puppeteer makes a distinction . . . that a puppet is manipulated directly by hand, as in a Punch-and-Judy show, or sometimes with a rod or a stick from below; a ~ is manipulated by strings or wires, or occasionally by a rod, from above —A.H. Eaton⟩ **2 :** BUFFLEHEAD 2 **3 :** a mechanism that actuates the shuttle racks in a ribbon loom

**mar·i·otte bottle** \¦marē¦ät-\ *n, usu cap M* [after Edme *Mariotte* †1684 Fr. physicist] **:** an apparatus that furnishes a flow of water under a constant head equal to the height of the bottom of the adjustable vertical tube above the level of the outlet

Mariotte bottle

**mariotte's law** *n, usu cap M* **:** BOYLE'S LAW

**mar·i·po·sa** \,marə'pōsə, -ōzə\ *or* **mariposa moonfish** *n* -s [AmerSp *mariposa*, fr. Sp, butterfly, prob. fr. *Maria* Mary (the Virgin Mary) + Sp. *posar* to alight, fr. LL *pausare* to stop, rest — more at POSE] **:** OPAH

**mariposa lily** *or* **mariposa tulip** *also* **mariposa** *n* -s [prob. fr. AmerSp *mariposa*, fr. Sp, butterfly] **:** a plant of the genus *Calochortus* — compare SEGO LILY

**mar·i·po·san** \,marə'pōsᵊn, -ōzᵊn\ *n* -s *usu cap* [*Mariposa* county, central California + E *-an*] **:** a language family of the Penutian stock in California comprising a small number of languages all known as Yokuts

**mar·i·po·site** \,marə'pō,sīt\ *n* -s [*Mariposa* county, central California + E *-ite*] **:** a mineral consisting of a bright green chromium-bearing phengite

**mar·i·schal** \'märshəl\ *n* -s *often cap* [Sc, fr. ME *marshal, mareschal* marshal — more at MARSHAL] **:** a marshal of Scotland — compare EARL MARISCHAL

**¹mar·ish** \'marish\ *n* -ES [ME *mareis, marys*, fr. MF *marais, mareis*, of Gmc origin; akin to OE *mersc* marsh — more at MARSH] *archaic* **:** MARSH

**²marish** \"\ *adj, archaic* **:** MARSHY

**¹mar·ist** \'ma(a)rəst, 'mer-\ *n* -s *usu cap* [F *Mariste*, fr. *Marie* Mary (the Virgin Mary) + F *-iste* -ist] **:** a member of a Roman Catholic order founded at Lyons, France, in 1816 to do work in honor of the Virgin Mary

**²marist** \"\ *adj, usu cap* **1 :** of, relating to, or devoted to the service of the Virgin Mary **2 :** of or relating to the Marists

**ma·ri·ta** \mə'rīd·ə\ *n, pl* **mari·tae** \-d·,ē\ [NL, fr. L *marita* married woman, wife, fem. of *maritus* married man, husband] **:** a sexually mature digenetic trematode — compare METACERCARIA, PARTHENITA

**mar·i·tage** \'marəd·ij\ *also* **mar·i·ta·gi·um** \,==ˈtājēəm\ *n, pl* **maritages** \-jəz\ *also* **marita·gia** \-ēə\ [ML *maritagium*, fr. OF *mariage* maritage, marriage — more at MARRIAGE] **1 :** the property brought to a husband by a wife according to feudal custom upon her marriage **2 a :** the right of a feudal lord to dispose in marriage of the heiress, minor heir, or widow of a vassal **b** (1) **:** a payment made by a vassal in return for the lord's waiver of such right (2) **:** a fine imposed on a vassal for his violation of such right

**¹mar·i·tal** \'marəd·ᵊl, -ət·ᵊl *also* 'mer-; *chiefly Brit* mə'rīt·ᵊl\ *adj* [L *maritalis*, fr. *maritus* husband + *-alis* -al — more at MARRY] **1 :** of or relating to marriage or the marriage state **:** CONJUGAL ⟨~ relationship⟩ ⟨~ status⟩ ⟨~ happiness⟩ ⟨~ difficulties⟩ **2 :** of or relating to a husband — **mar·i·tal·ly** \-ᵊlē, -ᵊli\ *adv*

**²ma·ri·tal** \-d·ᵊl\ *adj* [*marita* + *-al*] **:** of, relating to, or being a marita

**marital deduction** *n* **1 :** a deduction according to the provisions of the U.S. Internal Revenue Code from the taxable gross estate that amounts to the value of any property interest included therein and given by will, inheritance, survivorship or otherwise by a decedent to his or her surviving spouse provided that interest is not terminable during the life of the survivor but that is limited to one half the value of the adjusted gross estate — compare COMMUNITY PROPERTY, ESTATE TAX **2 :** the right under the U.S. gift tax law to deduct one half the value of any gift by one spouse to the other and to have gifts made by the spouses to a third person treated as though made one half by each — compare COMMUNITY PROPERTY, GIFT TAX

**ma·rit·i·cid·al** \mə¦rid·ə¦sīdᵊl\ *adj* [*mariti-* (fr. L *maritus* husband & L *marita* wife) + *-cide* + *-al*] **1 :** of or relating to mariticide; *esp* **:** of or relating to the killing of a husband by his wife **2 :** of or relating to the killing by a female insect of her mate

**ma·rit·i·cide** \=ˈ==,sīd\ *n* -s [*mariti-* (fr. L *maritus* husband & L *marita* wife) + *-cide*] **1 :** one that murders or kills his or her spouse **2 :** the act of a mariticide

**maritimal** *or* **maritimate** *adj* [L *maritimus* of the sea, maritime + E *-al* or *-ate*] *obs* **:** MARITIME

**¹mar·i·time** \'marə,tīm *also* 'mer-\ *adj* [L *maritimus* of the sea, maritime, fr. *mare* sea — more at MARINE] **1 :** of or relating to navigation or commerce on the sea ⟨~ service⟩ ⟨~ power⟩ ⟨~ ancestry⟩ ⟨the national neglect of ~, as distinguished from naval, history —*Times Lit. Supp.*⟩ **2 a :** bordering on the sea ⟨a ~ province⟩ **b :** living near the seacoast ⟨~ farmers⟩ **c :** characteristic of those who live near the sea ⟨~ cultures⟩ **3 :** MARINE ⟨the kittiwakes . . . the most ~ of all gulls —Tom Weir⟩ ⟨a ~ climate⟩ **4** *archaic, of a soldier* **:** serving with a naval force **5 :** having the characteristics of a mariner ⟨he was far from having a ~ appearance —Charles Dickens⟩

**²maritime** *n* -s *obs* **:** a region or province that borders on the sea

**maritime contract** *n* **:** a contract directly relating to the navigation, business, or commerce of the sea and falling within the jurisdiction of the admiralty courts

**maritime hypothec** *also* **maritime hypothecation** *n* **:** MARITIME LIEN

**maritime insurance** *n* **:** MARINE INSURANCE

**maritime interest** *n* **:** MARINE INTEREST

**maritime law** *n* **:** law that relates to commerce and navigation on the high seas or other navigable waters and is administered by admiralty courts — compare ADMIRALTY 3

**maritime lien** *n* **:** the right of one having a recognized claim under maritime law against a ship or its cargo (as for services or supplies or for damages caused by collision) to require an admiralty court to seize the ship or other described property and enforce satisfaction of the claim — called also *tacit hypothec;* compare LIEN

**maritime loan** *n* **:** a loan or advance enforceable in a court of admiralty jurisdiction: as **a :** one giving rise to a maritime lien **b :** one secured by a bottomry or respondentia bond

**maritime perils** *n pl* **:** MARINE PERILS

**maritime pine** *n* **:** CLUSTER PINE

**mar·jo·ram** \'märjərəm, 'máj- *sometimes* -jə,ram\ *n* -s [alter. of ME *majorane*, fr. MF, fr. ML *majorana*] **:** any of various usu. fragrant and aromatic mints that constitute two genera (*Origanum* and *Majorana*) of the family Labiatae and that include several forms used as seasoning in cookery — compare SWEET MARJORAM, WILD MARJORAM

**marjoram oil** *n* **:** a yellowish essential oil obtained esp. from sweet marjoram and used chiefly in perfumes (as for soap)

**¹mark** \'märk, 'mák\ *n* -s [ME, fr. OE *mearc;* akin to OHG *marha* boundary, boundary land, ON *mörk* boundary land, forest, wilderness, Goth *marka* boundary, boundary land, L *margo* edge, border, boundary, OIr *mruig* boundary land, district, W *bro* region, Per *marz* boundary land, district] **1 a** (1) **:** ²MARCH 1 (2) [G, fr. OHG *marha* boundary, boundary land] **:** a tract of land held in common by a Germanic village community in primitive or medieval times ⟨a share in the common ~ . . . made up of the uncultivated land —Alfons Dopsch⟩; *also* **:** the community holding such a tract **b :** something placed or set up to serve as a guide or to indicate position: as (1) **:** a conspicuous object of known position serving as a guide for travelers ⟨a ~ for pilots⟩ (2) **:** something (as a line, notch, or fixed object) designed to record position (3) **:** one of the bits of leather or colored bunting placed on a sounding line at irregular but frequent intervals — compare DEEP (4) **:** PLIMSOLL MARK **c** (1) **:** something toward which a missile is directed **:** a thing aimed at **:** TARGET ⟨hit the ~ squarely in the center⟩ ⟨the officers, being on horseback, were . . . picked out as ~*s* —Benjamin Franklin⟩ (2) **:** the jack in the game of bowls; *also* **:** a proper bowling distance or position allowed for the jack (3) **:** the pit of the stomach in boxing (4) **:** a spot (as that marked by the heel of a player in making a fair catch) at which a free kick or a penalty kick is allowed in rugby football; *also* **:** a fair catch in rugby (5) **:** the starting line in a track event ⟨got off the ~ very quickly⟩ (6) **:** a position on the starting line assigned to a contestant in a track event; *also* **:** the relaxed position taken by a runner or swimmer at or slightly behind the starting line immediately prior to the position or attitude of readiness which precedes the firing of the starting gun — usu. used in pl. (7) — used as a skeet shooter's command for the release of the low-house target **d** (1) **:** an end in view **:** GOAL, OBJECT ⟨120 mph is not a hard ~ to achieve —*Ford Times*⟩ ⟨developed enough musicianship to fix his own ~*s* at which to aim —Marcia Davenport⟩ (2) **:** an object of attack, ridicule, or abuse **:** BUTT ⟨would have to explain and deny and make a general ~ of himself —Theodore Dreiser⟩ ⟨would have to go about, a ~ for the talkers —George Meredith⟩; *specif* **:** a prospective or actual victim of a confidence game or other swindle ⟨lead the ~ to her apartment —W.H.Murray⟩ ⟨the ~*s* don't know no different —W.L.Gresham⟩ (3) **:** the point desired to be made **:** the question under discussion — often used in the phrase *beside the mark* ⟨both seem curiously beside the ~ —*Times Lit. Supp.*⟩ ⟨it is beside the ~ to argue that a culture consists of something more than plastic compounds —Waldemar Kaempffert⟩ (4) **:** the actual facts or true state of affairs **:** condition of being correct or accurate ⟨was perhaps near the ~ —*Times Lit. Supp.*⟩ ⟨even the initial diagnosis was widely off the ~ —Martin Gardner⟩ (5) **:** a standard or acceptable level of performance, quality, or condition **:** NORM — usu. used in the phrase *up to the mark* ⟨weren't feeling up to the ~ lately —Michael McLaverty⟩ ⟨that's the great thing about persecution: it keeps you up to the ~ —Bruce Marshall⟩ ⟨both of these performances were very far from being up to the ~ —Claud Cockburn⟩; *also* **:** the limit of what is reasonable or acceptable ⟨wanted fifteen hundred pounds for it and I don't think that was beyond the ~ —H.J.Laski⟩ **2 a** (1) **:** something that gives evidence of something else **:** SIGN, INDICATION, TOKEN ⟨as a ~ of their change of sentiment —T.B.Costain⟩ ⟨his writings . . . bear ~*s* of haste —*Encyc. Americana*⟩ ⟨a sure ~ of the families' social position —Bernard Smith⟩ (2) **:** a narrow deep hollow on the surface of the crown of a horse's incisor tooth that gradually becomes obliterated by the wearing away of the crown and therefore is indicative of the animal's age and usu. disappears from the lower central incisors about the sixth year while traces may remain in the upper until the eleventh (3) **:** an impression or trace (as a scar or stain) made on something (4) **:** CHARACTERISTIC ⟨the ~ of every Christian —*Commonweal*⟩ (5) **:** a distinguishing characteristic or essential attribute in logic **:** DIFFERENTIA **b** (1) **:** a character usu. in the form of a cross made as a substitute for a signature by a person who cannot or is unwilling to write and often witnessed by another; *also* **:** a personal cipher used in place of a signature ⟨the symbols above the lion represent the ~ of . . . the chief sachem —Allan Forbes & R.M.Eastman⟩ (2) **:** a visible sign (as a badge or sign of honor, rank, office, or stigma) assumed by or put upon a person ⟨the vermilion ~ of marriage remained on her forehead —Nilima Devi⟩ ⟨other distinguishing ~*s* may be worn by navy men . . . who have won certain distinctions —*All Hands*⟩; *specif* **:** a small plate of gold or silver worn by a mark master Mason (3) **:** a character, device, label, brand, seal, or other sign put on an article esp. to show the maker or owner, to certify quality, or for identification **:** TRADEMARK ⟨the owner of a ~ can secure relief only where the infringer uses it on goods . . . closely resembling the owner's —*Harvard Law Rev.*⟩ (4) **:** a small heraldic bearing used or added as a distinctive sign — compare CADENCY MARK (5) **:** a written or printed symbol ⟨punctuation ~*s*⟩ (6) **:** an identifying mark (as an ear notch) cut on livestock with a knife — distinguished from *brand* ⟨every mountaineer knows his hogs by his ~ —*Amer. Guide Series: Tenn.*⟩ (7) **:** a brand on a log indicating ownership (8) **:** POSTMARK (9) *usu cap* [G *marke* mark, label, brand, fr. OHG *marha* boundary] — used with a numeral to designate a particular model of a weapon, machine, or article of equipment ⟨this nuclear power plant, known as *Mark I* —*Birmingham (Ala.) News*⟩ — abbr. *Mk* **c :** a number or other character used in registering or evaluating: as (1) **:** a symbol used by a teacher to represent his estimate of a student's work or conduct ⟨had several late ~*s* against him⟩; *esp* **:** GRADE ⟨gets excellent ~*s* at school⟩ ⟨the highest ~ in the class⟩ (2) **:** a figure registering a point or level reached or achieved ⟨within six months the population . . . topped the 500 ~ —J.D. Hillaby⟩ ⟨more than 125 have passed the half-century ~ —*Amer. Guide Series: Minn.*⟩ ⟨the 1954 figure is expected to be around that ~ —Wayne Hughes⟩; *specif* **:** RECORD ⟨the ~, almost twenty miles faster than the previous record, wasn't allowed —*Collier's Yr. Bk.*⟩ **3 a :** ATTENTION, NOTICE ⟨nothing worthy of ~ occurred in your absence⟩ **b :** IMPORTANCE, DISTINCTION ⟨might easily become a figure of ~ —H.J.Laski⟩ ⟨stands out as a man of ~ —John Bright †1889⟩ — often used in the phrase *make one's mark* ⟨has made his

~ in many ways —Milton MacKaye⟩ **c** : a lasting or strong impression : an enduring effect — usu. used in the phrase *make one's mark* ⟨had made their ~ in evolutionary history —W.E.Swinton⟩ ⟨made a ~ in western history —R.W. Southern⟩; *esp* : a strong favorable impression ⟨anxious to make a ~ with my first major book —Charles Breasted⟩ ⟨works that have made their ~ with the general public —William Murray⟩ ⟨as office boy I made such a ~ that they gave me the post of a junior clerk —W.S.Gilbert⟩ **d** : an assessment of merits : RATING ⟨would have their bad ~ against him —F.M.Ford⟩ ⟨could get higher ~s . . . for telling warm-hearted, democratic lies about the people —*New Republic*⟩ **syn** see CHARACTER, SIGN

**[2]mark** \"\ *vb* -ED/-ING/-S [ME *marken*, fr. OE *mearcian*; akin to OHG *marcōn* to determine the boundaries of, OS *markon*, ON *marka*; denominative fr. the root of E [1]*mark*] *vt* **1 a** (1) : to fix or trace the bounds or limits of : locate the boundaries of — usu. used with *out* ⟨~ out a mining claim⟩ (2) : to plot the course of : CHART, DELINEATE — usu. used with *out* ⟨some directions of social development have at least been ~*ed* out —John Dewey⟩ ⟨the course which Italy has ~*ed* out for herself —C.E.G.C.Emmott⟩ **b** : to set apart by or as if by a mark or boundary — usu. used with *off* ⟨~*ed* off their claims with tomahawks —*Amer. Guide Series: Pa.*⟩ ⟨trying to ~ off the legitimate province of an art —Edward Sapir⟩ ⟨a sign of heredity that ~*ed* them off as a race —Oscar Handlin⟩ **2 a** (1) : to designate as if by a mark : DESTINE, ASSIGN ⟨~*ed* for death by his doctors —*advt*⟩ ⟨~*ed* for greatness by his extraordinary talents and virtues⟩ ⟨~*ed* out by destiny for his place in history —Preston Slosson⟩ (2) : to make or leave a mark on ⟨his hobnails ~*ed* the floor⟩; *specif* : to affix a significant identifying mark (as a trademark or hallmark) to ⟨~ a bale of merchandise⟩ (3) : to furnish with natural marks of a specified kind ⟨wings ~*ed* with white lines⟩ (4) : to label (an article) with a sign or symbol (as for indicating price or quality) ⟨each garment is clearly ~*ed* for size and price⟩ ⟨all furs are plainly ~*ed* as to country of origin⟩ (5) : to dock and castrate (a lamb); *also* : to enumerate (the lambs of a flock) esp. by counting the tails removed during docking (6) : to enter or make notations or symbolic marks on or in (as for purposes of comment or emphasis) — usu. used with *up* ⟨~ up . . . a copy with his objections —J.G.Cozzens⟩ **b** (1) : to indicate or make note of in writing : JOT ⟨doesn't remember his exact words and nobody thought to ~ them down —Ira Wolfert⟩ ⟨~*ed* in his diary the date of his son's birth⟩ (2) : to indicate, express, or show by a mark or symbol ⟨~ an accent⟩; *also* : REGISTER, RECORD ⟨the barometer ~*ed* a continuing fall in atmospheric pressure⟩ ⟨Paris clocks ~*ed* 4:15 in the morning —C.A. Lindbergh b. 1902⟩ (3) : to make evident : SHOW, MANIFEST ⟨~*ed* his displeasure by a frown⟩ (4) : to indicate or fix (as a pivot point) in military drill or review (5) : to keep track of (the points) in a game; *also* : to keep score in (a game) ⟨~*ed* the match —*N.Y. Times*⟩ (6) : to determine the value or correctness of : score by means of marks or symbols : GRADE ⟨have you ~*ed* my paper yet⟩ (7) : to make notations on or attach symbolic marks to (as for purposes of comment or emphasis) ⟨asked him to ~ the offensive passages⟩ ⟨~*ing* up only those features of special interest to me —Joanna Jonsson⟩ **c** (1) : to be a distinguishing mark on or upon : CHARACTERIZE, DISTINGUISH ⟨high ideals ~ the work —*Encyc. Americana*⟩ ⟨stunted trees ~ the higher peaks⟩ (2) : SIGNALIZE ⟨often ~ the decisive turn in the scientific thinking —J.B.Conant⟩ ⟨may ~ a change of emphasis —*New Statesman & Nation*⟩ (3) : to identify in a particular way : BRAND, STAMP ⟨~ him as an unscrupulous politician in many eyes —Carol L. Thompson⟩ **d** : to serve as an indication of the position or course of ⟨a sign ~*ing* the city limits —*Amer. Guide Series: Mich.*⟩ **3 a** : to give attention to : take notice of : OBSERVE, NOTICE ⟨~ the change that has taken place⟩ ⟨~ my words —Walter de la Mare⟩ ⟨but ~ how certain matters are beyond us —Winston Churchill⟩ **b** : to observe and remember the spot of disappearance or taking to cover of (game) **c** *Brit* : to keep a close watch on (a member of an opposing team) so as to hamper ~ *vi* **1** : to notice or observe critically : NOTE, LOOK **2** : to observe and remember the spot where game disappeared or took cover **3** *Brit* : to play close to one's opponent and in such a position as to hamper him, prevent him from receiving the ball, or tackle him if he receives it **4** : to keep score in a game — **mark time 1** : to keep the time of a marching step (as in military drill) by moving the feet alternately without advancing **2** : to function or operate in a lackadaisical, listless, or unproductive manner : merely go through the motions of activity : fail to advance or progress : stand still ⟨the commission was just *marking time* —*Collier's Yr. Bk.*⟩ ⟨our free dynamic economy cannot *mark time* —Walter Reuther⟩ — **mark to the market** : to adjust cash deposited with a lender of securities to the prevailing market price

**[3]mark** \"\ *n* -S [ME, fr. OE *marc*, prob. of Scand origin; akin to ON *mark-*, *mörk* mark (weight); akin to OE *mearc* mark, sign; prob. fr. the marks on the bars — more at [1]MARK] **1** : any of various old European units of weight used esp. for gold and silver; *esp* : a unit equal to about 8 ounces **2** : a unit of value or a coin: **a** : an old English unit equal to 13*s* 4*d* **b** : an old Scottish unit of value equal to 13*s* 4*d* Scottish; *also* : a coin representing this unit issued by James VI and Charles II **c** : any one of various old Scandinavian or German units of value; *specif* : a unit and corresponding silver coin of the 16th century worth ½ taler **d** [G, fr. OHG *marha* boundary — more at [1]MARK] : the basic monetary unit of Germany from 1871; *also* : a coin representing this unit — see DEUTSCHE MARK, REICHSMARK **e** [Estonian, fr. G] : a unit of value used for a time in Estonia after World War I; *also* : a coin representing this unit issued 1922–26 **f** [Finn *markka*] : MARKKA **3** : a division of land in Scotland orig. of the annual value of a mark

**markan** *usu cap, var of* MARCAN

**mark degree** *n* [[1]*mark*] : the degree of a mark master Mason

**mark down** *vt* : to put a lower price on ⟨all overcoats have been *marked down* 20 percent⟩

**markdown** \ˈ=,=\ *n* -S [*mark down*] **1** : a lowering of price **2** : the amount by which an original selling price is reduced

**marked** \ˈmärkt, ˈmȧkt\ *adj* **1 a** : having a mark ⟨a ~ card⟩ ⟨a ~ coin⟩ ⟨dotted with ~ boulders and other memorials of historic interest —*Amer. Guide Series: Texas*⟩ **b** : having a mark of a specified kind — usu. used in combination ⟨a scar-*marked* lad⟩ **2** : having a distinctive or strongly pronounced character : NOTICEABLE ⟨spoke . . . with a ~ American accent —Nevil Shute⟩ ⟨a ~ feature of these occasions —*Encyc. Americana*⟩ ⟨have a ~ capacity for industrial work —*Current Biog.*⟩ ⟨found him of a very ~ physiognomy —Bram Stoker⟩ — often used in combination ⟨there is no well-*marked* nervous system —*Encyc. Americana*⟩ **3 a** : being a person on whom attention or interest is focused : enjoying fame or notoriety ⟨this small staff made the editor a ~ man —F.L.Mott⟩ **b** : being an object of attack, suspicion, or vengeance ⟨a ~ man to the British —*Amer. Guide Series: Mass.*⟩ ⟨a ~ man, guarded until recently —*Newsweek*⟩ **4** : overtly signaled by a linguistic feature ⟨in English most English nouns the plural is the ~ number⟩

**mark·ed·ly** \ˈmärkədlē, ˈmȧk-, -li\ *adv* : in a marked manner or to a marked degree : NOTICEABLY, PLAINLY

**mark·ed·ness** \-kədnəs\ *n* -ES : the quality or state of being marked; *esp* : DISTINCTIVENESS

**marked transfer** *n* : an instrument for transferring a portion of the shares of a stockholder's certificate after being certified as by a proper official on the London stock exchange

**markee** *var of* MARQUEE

**mark·er** \ˈmärkər, ˈmȧkə(r\ *n* -S **1** : a person who marks: as **a** : a person who marks game **b** : a person who keeps account of a game played (as of billiards or rackets) : SCORER; *also* : one who records the shots at target practice **c** (1) : a person who records attendance at a school or college : MONITOR (2) : a person who marks papers (as tests, compositions) for a teacher **d** : a worker who puts identifying information on articles: as (1) : a worker in a laundry or cleaning and dyeing establishment who marks articles with customer identification (2) : a worker who marks serial numbers on gun parts with a marking die (3) : a person who marks prices on merchandise **e** : a logger who marks trees for felling, felled trees for cutting into logs, or logs for identification in a drive **f** : a worker who marks outlines on leather parts of shoes as guides for such subsequent operations as cementing, punching of buttonholes, or fancy stitching **g** : a worker who pencils or chalks out a pattern on material (as cloth, wood, or metal) before it is cut; *also* : a pattern layout so made **h** : a worker who makes out merchandise tickets **2** : something that marks or is used for marking: as **a** : an implement or attachment for marking the ground to facilitate planting in rows **b** : a contrivance for marking out a tennis court **c** : any of various sewing devices for making or indicating guidelines ⟨a pin ~ for hemlines⟩ **d** (1) : a token used in gambling as a reminder (as of a bet or the next dealer) (2) : a promissory note or IOU given as evidence of a loan received or debt incurred **e** : a signal placed on each side of the rear of certain trains; *also* : a distinctive light fastened to a signal post to indicate whether the signal is permissive or absolute **f** : something (as a person, flag, stake, ship) posted at a point to indicate a position (as of a military unit, an obstacle) **g** : BOOKMARK **h** : a black or otherwise readily identifiable sheep **i** : a morphologic hereditary character used as an indicator of the presence or absence of a linked physiologic character — compare LINKAGE **j** : a geologic formation easily identified; *esp* : one used as a guide in well drilling **3 a** : an instrument connected with a switchboard that electrically selects an available trunk line and makes the necessary connections for long-distance calls **b** *or* **marker beacon** *or* **marker radio beacon** : a small transmitter of limited range used by an airplane to identify its position over a fixed spot on the earth **4** : a word, morpheme, or combination of morphemes indicating the form class or grammatical function of the linguistic form that accompanies or includes it ⟨the ~s *the* and *-ed* in *the boy* and *played*⟩

**marker bed** *n* : MARKER 2j

**[1]mar·ket** \ˈmärkət, ˈmȧk-, *usu* -əd·+V\ *n* -S *often attrib* [ME, fr. ONF, fr. L *mercatus* trade, marketplace, fr. *mercatus*, past part. of *mercari* to trade, fr. *merc-*, *merx* ware, merchandise; akin to Oscan *amiricadut* without remuneration, and perh. to Gk *marptein* to seize, Skt *mṛśati* he touches; basic meaning: to seize] **1 a** (1) : a meeting together of people at a stated time and place for the purpose of traffic (as in cattle, provisions, or wares) by private purchase and sale and usu. not by auction (2) : the people assembled at such a meeting (3) : the privilege in English law of having a public market **b** (1) : a public place (as an open space in a town or a large building) where a market is held : MARKETPLACE; *specif* : a place where provisions are sold at wholesale ⟨the city ~⟩ ⟨fish ~⟩ (2) : a retail establishment usu. of a specified kind ⟨a meat ~⟩ **2** *archaic* **a** : the act or an instance of buying and selling ⟨every man will speak of the fair as his own ~ has gone in it —Laurence Sterne⟩ **b** : an object of bargaining or dealing **c** : opportunity for buying or selling — usu. used in the phrases *lose one's market* or *overstand one's market* **3 a** : the rate or price offered for commodities : MARKET PRICE **b** : the current bid and asked price for a security or other property ⟨ask the broker for the ~ on this stock⟩ **4** : a sphere within which price-making forces operate and in which exchanges in title tend to be followed by actual movement of goods: as **a** : a geographical area of demand for commodities ⟨sell in the southern ~⟩ ⟨the world ~⟩ **b** : the course of commercial activity by which the exchange of commodities is effected : condition with respect to demand : extent of demand ⟨the ~ is dull⟩ ⟨the following prices . . . are eloquent of the declining ~ —*New Biology*⟩ **c** : a formal organized coming together of buyers and sellers of goods ⟨the stock ~⟩ ⟨the livestock ~⟩ **5** : a unit of volume in the lumber trade represented by a log 19 inches in diameter at the small end inside the bark and 13 feet long and containing approximately 200 board feet — **at the market** *adv* **1** : at the prevailing price on a stock exchange **2** : at the best price obtainable when a broker executes a customer's order — **away from the market** : with a price limit outside the prevailing range of the market on a stock exchange ⟨these orders are *away from the market* —B.E.Shultz⟩ — **in the market** *adv* (*or adj*) **1** *or* **on the market** : up for sale : available for purchase ⟨put his house *on the market*⟩ **2** : interested in buying : prepared to buy ⟨was *in the market* for a new car⟩

**[2]market** \"\ *vb* -ED/-ING/-S *vi* : to deal in a market : to go to market to buy or sell ~ *vt* **1** : to expose for sale in a market : traffic in : sell in a market **2** : SELL

**mar·ket·abil·i·ty** \ˌmärkəd·əˈbiləd·|ē, ˌmȧk-, -kətəˈbilət|, |i\ *n* : the quality or state of being marketable; *specif* : the degree to which assets can be disposed of for cash without causing a major decline in price

**mar·ket·able** \ˈmärkədəbəl, ˈmȧk-, -kətəbəl\ *adj* **1** : fit to be offered for sale in a market : being such as may be justly and lawfully sold or bought ⟨~ provisions⟩ **2** : of or relating to buying or selling ⟨~ value⟩ **3 a** : wanted by purchasers : SALABLE ⟨furs are not ~ in that country⟩ **b** : enjoying a high degree of liquidity ⟨~ securities⟩ — **mar·ket·able·ness** *n* -ES — **mar·ket·ably** \-blē\ *adv*

**marketable title** *n* : a title that conveys property and the interest therein bargained for reasonably free from all liens and encumbrances save those excepted by the bargain, that does not expose the purchaser to litigation, and that he can readily sell or offer as security to a prudent man knowing all material facts and their legal significance : merchantable title

**market analysis** *n* : a phase of marketing research conducted to determine the characteristics and extent of a market

**market basket** *n* **1 a** : a splint, veneer, or fiberboard basket of various forms and sizes usu. having wooden or wire handles and used for fruits and vegetables **b** : any of various baskets used by shoppers for carrying purchases from a market **2** : a distribution of goods purchased by consumers in a base period and used to measure changes in the cost of living

**market bleach** *n* : a method of bleaching simpler than madder bleaching for cotton cloth sold as white goods

**market cross** *n* : a cross or cross-shaped building set up where a market is held and often the scene of public business such as giving of notices or reading of warrants

**market day** *n* [ME] : a day fixed for holding a market ⟨public sales are held on *market days* —G.W.Johnson⟩

**market economy** *n* : an economy in which most goods and services are produced and distributed through the media of free markets and the price system

**mar·ke·teer** *R* ˌmärkəˈti(ə)r; *-R* ˌmȧkəˈtiə, +V -iə(r) *or* -ir\ *n* -S [[1]*market* + *-eer*] : a seller in a market : a market dealer

**mar·ket·er** \ˈmärkəd·ə(r)\ *n* -S : one who buys or sells in a market

**marketfish** \ˈ=,=\ *n* [by folk etymology fr. *margate fish*] : MARGATE

**market garden** *n* : a garden usu. comprising a relatively extensive area in which vegetables are grown for market

**market gardener** *n* : a person who operates a market garden

**market gardening** *n* : gardening for market esp. with the use of a relatively extensive area

**market hunter** *n* : a person who hunts game for a livelihood

**mar·ket·ing** \ˈmärkəd·|iŋ, ˈmȧk-, -ət|, |ēŋ\ *n* -S **1 a** : the act of selling or purchasing in a market ⟨doing all of her ~ once a week⟩ **b** : the bringing or sending of goods to market ⟨~ cooperatives⟩ **2 a** : produce for the market **b** : things purchased at a market **3** : an aggregate of functions involved in transferring title and in moving goods from producer to consumer including among others buying, selling, storing, transporting, standardizing, financing, risk bearing, and supplying market information

**marketing research** *n* : research conducted to establish the extent and location of a market or to analyze the cost of products and processes as compared with that of alternative or competitive products or processes — compare MARKET RESEARCH

**market letter** *n* : a publication usu. issued by a specialist containing market information and advice

**mar·ket·man** \ˈmärkətmən\ *n, pl* **marketmen** : a dealer in a market : MARKETER

**market order** *n* : an order to buy or sell at the best price obtainable in the market when the order is executed

**market overt** *n* -S : an open public market authorized and regulated by law at which purchasers of goods with certain exceptions acquire good title regardless of any defects in the seller's title

**marketplace** \ˈ=,=\ *n* [ME, fr. *market* + *place*] **1 a** : an open square or place in a town where markets or public sales are held **b** : MARKET ⟨aggressive competition . . . in a freely functioning ~ —Harold Fleming⟩ **c** : the world of trade or economic activity : the everyday world ⟨the depression sent him out into the ~ —J.K.Hutchens⟩ ⟨here is an educational institution that has come down . . . to the ~ —Dwayne Orton⟩ **2** : a sphere in which intangible values (as ideas) compete for acceptance ⟨the turbulent ~ of ideas —J.M. Mathes⟩ ⟨the ~ of thought —Robert Bendiner⟩

**market pot** *n* : a pot from which desilverized lead is run into pig molds in lead refining

**market price** *n* [ME *markett prise*] : a price actually given in current market dealings : a price at which the supply and demand are equal

**market research** *n* : the gathering of factual information as to consumer preferences for goods and services — compare MARKETING RESEARCH

**market-ripe** \ˈ=,=,=\ *adj* : harvested slightly immature so as to reach the market in excellent condition : not fully ripe

**markets** *pl of* MARKET, *pres 3d sing of* MARKET

**mar·ket·stead** \ˈmärkət,sted\ *n* [ME *marketstede*, fr. *market* + *stede* stead — more at STEAD] *archaic* : MARKETPLACE

**market town** *n* [ME *markettown*] : a usu. small town that has the privilege of holding at stated times a public market

**market value** *n* : a price at which both buyers and sellers are willing to do business : the market or current price

**market value clause** *n* : an insurance clause providing for payment of a loss to goods at market value rather than manufacturing cost

**mark·graf** \ˈmärk,gräf\ *n, pl* **markgraf·en** \-fən\ [G, fr. OHG *marcgrāvo* — more at MARGRAVE] : MARGRAVE 2

**mar·khor** \ˈmär,kȯ(ə)r\ *also* **mar·khoor** \-kü(ə)r\ *n, pl* **markhor** *or* **markhors** [Per *mārkhōr*, lit., snake eater, fr. *mār* snake + *-khōr* eating, consuming (fr. *khurdan* to eat, consume)] : a wild goat (*Capra falconieri*) of mountainous regions from Afghanistan to India

**mark·ing** \ˈmärkiŋ, ˈmȧk-, -kēŋ\ *n* -S [ME, fr. gerund of *marken* to mark — more at MARK] **1** : the act, process, or an instance of making, placing, or assigning a mark ⟨his ~ of pronunciation was crude —J.H.Sledd & G.J.Kolb⟩ ⟨the ~ of whales helps us to follow these movements —Robert Clarke⟩ ⟨accused his teacher of unfair ~⟩ **2 a** : a mark made ⟨~s include name and address of the consignee —*Export Packing*⟩ ⟨the ~s on this bone were made by a beaver —R.W.Murray⟩; *specif* : POSTMARK **b** : arrangement, pattern, or disposition of marks ⟨the ~ of a bird's plumage⟩

**marking felt** *n* : a felt used in papermaking to make a design (as ribs or stripes) discernible on the face of the finished paper

**marking gauge** *n* : GAUGE 2c

**marking hammer** *n* : a tool used for marking trees or logs

**marking knife** *n* : a tool for marking out wood for sawing or chiseling

**marking nut** *n* **1** : an East Indian tree (*Semecarpus anacardium*) **2** : the nut of the marking nut that yields a blackish resinous juice used for marking cotton cloth

**marking period** *n* : a part of the school year between two dates on which students' marks are sent home

**mark·ka** \ˈmärk,kä\ *n, pl* **markkaa** \"\ *or* **markkas** [Finn, fr. Sw *mark*, any of various old Scand. units of value; akin to ON *mark-*, *mörk* mark (weight) — more at MARK] **1** : the basic monetary unit of Finland — see MONEY table **2** : a coin representing one markka

**markland** \ˈ=,=\ *n* [[3]*mark* + *land*] : [3]MARK 3

**mark lodge** *n* [[1]*mark*] : an English lodge of mark master Masons

**markman** *n, pl* **markmen** [[1]*mark* + *man*] *obs* : MARKSMAN

**mark masonry** *n, usu cap 2d M* [[1]*mark*] : the institutions or work of mark lodges

**mark master mason** *n, usu cap 3d M* [[1]*mark*] **1 a** : a Freemason of the fourth degree in the order in the U. S. **b** : a Freemason of the first degree of Royal Arch Masonry in the U. S. **2 a** : a Freemason of a distinct lodge associated with the Grand Lodge of mark Masons in England **b** : a degree conferred under the authority of the Grand Chapter in Scotland

**mark of admiration** : EXCLAMATION POINT

**mark of cadency** : CADENCY MARK

**mark of exclamation** : EXCLAMATION POINT

**mark off** *vt* : to mark or scribe to correct dimensions; *esp* : to scribe (castings) for machining and fitting ~ *vi, of dyed cloth* : to bleed from darker into lighter areas

**markoff** \ˈ=,=\ *n* -S [*mark off*] : a mark on copy to indicate the beginning or ending of a galley or on a galley proof to indicate the beginning or ending of a page

**mark of interrogation** : QUESTION MARK

**mark of reference** : REFERENCE MARK

**mark of the beast** [ME *marke of the beast*, trans. of LL *character bestiae*, trans. of Gk *charagma tou thēriou*] **1** : a mark of evil **2** : a labeling as unorthodox or heretical

**mark-on** \ˈ=,=\ *n* -S [fr. *mark on*, v.] **1** : MARKUP **2** : profit margin

**mark out** *vt* **1** : to obliterate or cancel with a mark ⟨vainly tried to *mark* the defacing stain *out*⟩ **2** : MARK OFF

**mar·kov chain** *or* **mar·koff chain** \ˈmär,kȯf-\ *n, usu cap M* [after Andrei Andreevich *Markov* †1922 Russ. mathematician] : a sequence of random events in which the probabilities of transition to various future states are determined by the present state or the preceding state but not by the path by which the present is achieved

**mar·kov·ni·kov rule** \mär'kȯvnə,kȯf-\ *n, usu cap M* [after Vladimir V. *Markovnikov* †1904 Russ. chemist] : a statement in chemistry: in the addition of compounds to olefins the negative portion of the compound added (as the bromine in hydrogen bromide) becomes attached to the least hydrogenated end of the carbon-carbon double bond (as in the addition of hydrogen bromide to propylene: $CH_3CH{=}CH_2 + HBr \rightarrow CH_3CHBrCH_3$)

**mark·ry** \ˈmärkrē\ *n* -ES [by alter.] : MERCURY 2

**marks** *pl of* MARK, *pres 3d sing of* MARK

**mark sensing** *n* : actuation of the automatic punching of a card by pencil marks on the card

**marks·man** \ˈmärksmən, ˈmȧk-\ *n, pl* **marksmen** [*marks* (gen. of [1]*mark*) + *man*] **1** : one that shoots at a mark: as **a** : a person skillful or practiced at hitting a mark or target ⟨a first-class ~ with a pistol⟩ ⟨was the best ~ in the league at kicking field goals⟩ **b** : a member of the armed forces who is proficient enough in shooting to be ranked in a certain grade **2** : a person who makes his mark instead of writing his name in signing documents

**marks·man·ship** \-n,ship\ *n* : the art or skill of a marksman esp. with firearms

**marks·woman** \ˈmärk,swu̇mən\ *n, pl* **markswomen** [*marks* (gen. of [1]*mark*) + *woman*] : a woman who shoots or is skilled in shooting at a mark

**mark tooth** *n* [[1]*mark*] : an incisor tooth of a horse

**mark up** *vt* **1** : to set a higher price on : add a markup to ⟨*marked* their umbrellas *up* during the long rainy spell⟩ **2** *chiefly Brit* : to add (an item) to a store or tavern account ⟨*mark up* . . . their modest reckonings —Guy McCrone⟩

**markup** \ˈ=,=\ *n* -S [*mark up*] **1** : a raise in the price of an article ⟨extensive ~s⟩ **2** : an amount added to the cost to determine the selling price; *specif* : the gross profit to cover overhead expenses and provide net profit usu. expressed as a percentage of the selling price

**markweed** \ˈ=,=\ *n* : POISON IVY

**markworthy** \ˈ=,=,=\ *adj* [[1]*mark* + *worthy*; trans. of G *merkwürdig*] : NOTEWORTHY ⟨more ~ for its ferment of critical ideas —R.A.Hall b. 1911⟩

**[1]marl** *R* ˈmärl, *chiefly before pause or consonant* -rəl, *-R* ˈmȧl\ *n* -S [ME, fr. MF *marle*, fr. ML *margila*, dim. of L *marga*, fr. Gaulish] **1** : a loose or crumbling earthy deposit that contains a substantial amount of calcium carbonate or dolomite: as **a** : calcareous sand, silt, or clay; *also* : a deposit of unconsolidated shells **b** : a calcareous deposit in a glacial lake **2** : CLAY, EARTH ⟨a clod of wayward ~ —Shak.⟩ **3** : a brick made of marl

2marl \"\ vt -ED/-ING/-S [ME marlen, fr. marl, n.] : to overspread, manure, or dress with marl : fertilize with or as if with marl
3marl \"\ vi -ED/-ING/-S [by contr.] now dial : MARVEL
4marl \"\ n -S [by contr.] now dial : MARVEL
5marl \"\ vt -ED/-ING/-S [D marlen, back-formation fr. marling marline — more at MARLINE] : to cover or fasten with marline making a hitch at each turn to prevent unwinding
6marl \"\ n -S [by contr.] now dial Brit : 1MARBLE
7marl \"\ n -S [origin unknown] : a delicate fiber obtained from peacock feathers and used in making artificial flies
8marl \"\ n -S [native name in Australia] : a slender grayish brown bandicoot (Perameles myosura) of western Australia with a long nose and long thin ears
mar·la·ceous \(')mär¦lāshəs\ adj [1marl + -aceous] : containing or resembling marl
marl·berry \'märl- — see BERRY\ n [prob. fr. 6marl + berry] : a tropical American shrub or small tree (Ardisia paniculata) with brown wood and dark berries
marl·bor·ough \'märl,bər·|ə, 'mál-, -,bə·r|, |ō, -,bərə, chiefly Brit 'mȯl-, -,brə\ adj, usu cap [fr. Marlborough, provincial district of New Zealand] : of or from the provincial district of Marlborough, New Zealand : of the kind or style prevalent in Marlborough
marlborough foot n, usu cap M [after George Spencer, 4th duke of Marlborough †1817 Eng. politician] : a rather heavy square foot sometimes used to terminate a Marlborough leg
marlborough leg n, usu cap M [after George Spencer, 4th duke of Marlborough] : a heavy straight sometimes vertically grooved chair leg common in furniture of late Chippendale style

Marlborough foot

marled \'märld\ adj [by contr.] : MARBLED
mar·li \'märlē\ n -S [F] : an often ornamented raised border of a plate or flat dish that forms a plane nearly parallel to the bottom
1mar·lin \'märlən, 'mál-\ n -S [short for marlinspike; fr. the appearance of the beak] 1 a : any of several large oceanic game fishes (genus Makaira) of the family Istiophoridae — see BLACK MARLIN, BLUE MARLIN, SILVER MARLIN, STRIPED MARLIN, WHITE MARLIN b : SPEARFISH 2 : a synchronized swimming stunt in which the body executes a quarter turn with a full twist from a back layout position to a position at right angles to it
2marlin \"\ n -S [origin unknown] chiefly Midland : GODWIT
mar·line also mar·lin \'märlən, 'mál-\ or mar·ling \-liŋ\ n -S [marline, marlin fr. D marlijn, by folk etymology (influence of lijn line) fr. marling; marling fr. D, fr. marren, meren to tie, moor (fr. MD maren, meren) + -ling — more at MOOR] : a small usu. tarred line of two strands twisted loosely left-handed that is used for seizing and as a covering for wire rope
marlinespike also marlinspike or marlingspike \'==,=\ n 1 : an iron tool that tapers to a point and is used to separate strands of rope or wire (as in splicing) — compare FID 1b 2 a : TROPIC BIRD b : JAEGER
marlinespike hitch n : a hitch into which a marlinespike is inserted in order to draw seizing taut
marling pres part of MARL
marling hitch n : a knot that is used in series to lash long bundles (as rolled or folded awnings, hammocks, or sails)
marlinspike fish n : STRIPED MARLIN
marlin swordfish n : BLUE MARLIN

marlinespike hitch

marl·ite \'mär,līt\ n -S [1marl + -ite] : a marl resistant to the action of air — mar·lit·ic \(')mär¦lid·ik\ adj
1mar·lock \'málək\ n -S [origin unknown] dial Eng : FROLIC, PRANK
2marlock \"\ vi -ED/-ING/-S dial Eng : FROLIC, SPORT
mar·lo·vi·an \(')mär¦lōvēən\ adj, usu cap [Christopher Marlowe †1593 English dramatist + E -ian] 1 : of, relating to, or characteristic of Christopher Marlowe ⟨a Marlovian fondness for exotic names —Louis MacNeice⟩ 2 : of, relating to, or characteristic of the plays or poems of Marlowe ⟨plays of the Marlovian genre —Alan Downer⟩
marlpit \'=,=\ n [ME, fr. marl + pit] : a pit where marl is dug
marls pl of MARL, pres 3d sing of MARL
marlstone \'=,=\ n : an indurated mixture of clay materials and calcium carbonate usu. containing from 25 to 75 percent clay
1marly \'märlē\ adj, usu -ER/-EST [ME, fr. 1marl + -y] : of, relating to, or resembling marl : abounding with marl
2marly \"\ adj, usu -ER/-EST [contr. of marbly] dial Brit : MARBLED, SPOTTED
marm \'märm, 'mám\ n -S [alter. of ma'am] chiefly dial : MADAM
mar·ma·lade \'märmə,lād, 'mám- sometimes ,==¦=\ n -S [Pg marmelada quince conserve, fr. marmelo quince, fr. L melimelum, a kind of sweet apple, fr. Gk melimēlon, fr. meli honey + mēlon apple — more at MELLIFLUOUS] 1 : a soft clear translucent jelly holding in suspension pieces or slices of fruit and fruit rind ⟨orange ~⟩ 2 : MARMALADE TREE
marmalade box n : GENIPAP
marmalade cat n : a red tabby cat
marmalade tree also marmalade plum n 1 : a tropical American tree (Calocarpum zapota) that has wood like mahogany, large obovate leaves, and an egg-shaped single-seeded fruit 2 : MAMMEE
mar·ma·ri·za·tion or mar·mo·ri·za·tion \,märmərə'zāshən\ n -S : the process of being marmarized
mar·ma·rize or mar·mo·rize \'märmə,rīz\ vt -ED/-ING/-S [Gk marmaros & L marmor marble + E -ize — more at MARBLE] : to convert into marble : subject to marmarosis
mar·ma·ro·sis or mar·mo·ro·sis \,märmə'rōsəs\ n, pl marmaro·ses or marmoro·ses \-ō,sēz\ [NL, fr. Gk marmaros & L marmor marble + NL -osis] : the conversion of limestone into marble by metamorphism
mar·ma·tite \'märmə,tīt\ n -S [G marmatit, fr. Marmato, locality in Colombia + G -it -ite] : a mineral consisting of ferruginous sphalerite that is dark brown to black in color
mar·men·nill \'mär,mennətᵊl\ n -S [Icel, fr. ON, fr. marr sea + -mennill (dim. of mann-, mathr man) — more at MARINE, MAN] : MERMAN
mar·mite \'mär,mīt, (')mär¦mēt\ also mar·mit \'märmət\ n -S [F marmite] 1 a : a large metal or earthenware soup kettle with a cover b : a small individual earthenware casserole with a cover used esp. for soups — called also petite marmite 2 : the soup served in a marmite : PETITE MARMITE 1 3 : a yeast product used in extracts for flavoring meats and soups and as a dietary supplement
marmite can n : a large insulated container used to bring hot food to frontline troops
mar·mo·lite \'märmə,līt\ n -S [Gk marmairein to flash, sparkle + E -o- + -lite — more at MORN] : a thin laminated usu. pale green serpentine
mar·mo·ra·ceous \¦märmə¦rāshəs\ adj [L marmor marble + E -aceous — more at MARBLE] : of, relating to, or resembling marble
mar·mo·rate \'märmə,rāt\ or mar·mo·rat·ed \-ād·əd\ adj [marmorate fr. L marmoratus, past part. of marmorare to adorn with marble, fr. marmor marble; marmorated fr. L marmoratus + E -ed] : veined like marble : MARBLED
mar·mo·ra·tion \,==¦rāshən\ n -S [L marmoration-, marmoratio, fr. marmoratus + -ion-, -io -ion] : incrustation with marble or variegation resembling that of marble : MARBLING
mar·mo·re·al \(')mär¦mōrēəl, (')mȧ¦-, -mȯr-\ or mar·mo·re·an \-ən\ adj [L marmoreus marmoreal (fr. marmor marble) + E -al or -an] 1 : of, relating to, or resembling marble or a marble statue esp. in coldness, smoothness, or majesty : STATUESQUE ⟨art is not a ~ calm —Irwin Edman⟩ ⟨his conception of marmorean stillness —D.A.Stauffer⟩ 2 : made of marble ⟨those ~ domes —Robert Browning⟩ — mar·mo·re·al·ly \-əlē, -li\ adv
mar·mo·sa \mär'mōsə\ n, cap [NL, fr. E marmoset] : a genus comprising the New World murine opossums
mar·mo·set \'märmə,set, 'mám-, -,zet, ,==¦=, usu -ed·+V\ n -S [ME marmusette, marmozette, fr. MF marmouset, marmoset grotesque figure (prob. also "marmoset") — whence F dial. marmouset marmoset), fr. marmouser to mumble, mutter, of imit. origin] : any of numerous soft-furred So. and Central American monkeys of the family Callithricidae that have claws instead of nails on all the digits except the great toe
mar·mot \'märmət, 'mám-, usu -əd·+V\ n -S [F marmotte] 1 : a stout-bodied short-legged rodent of the genus Marmota that has coarse fur, a short bushy tail, and very small ears, lives in burrows, and hibernates in winter — see WOODCHUCK 2 : a prairie dog or one of the larger ground squirrels

European marmot

mar·mo·ta \'märməd·ə\ n, cap [NL, fr. F marmotte marmot] : a genus of large rodents (family Sciuridae) that somewhat resemble badgers and comprise the marmots
marmot squirrel n : an American ground squirrel
mar·ne·an or mar·ni·an \'märnēən\ adj, usu cap [Marne, department in France + E -an or -ian] : LA TÈNE
ma·ro \'mä(,)rō\ n -S [Tahitian & Maori] : a loincloth made of sedge or flax fiber and worn by Polynesians in New Zealand and Tahiti — compare MALO
mar·o·cain \¦marə¦kān\ n -S [F (crêpe) marocain, lit., Moroccan crepe, fr. crêpe crepe + marocain Moroccan, fr. Maroc Morocco] 1 : a dress crepe that is made with a warp of silk or rayon and a filling of other yarns and is similar to but heavier than canton crepe — called also crepe marocain 2 : MOROCCO RED
mar·o·nite \'marə,nīt\ n -S usu cap [ML Maronita, fr. Maron-, Maro, 5th cent. Syrian monk + L -ita -ite] : an Arabic-speaking member of a Uniate church chiefly in Lebanon that was established as a separate Monothelete organization in the 7th century and has retained its old Syriac liturgy and a married clergy following its union with Rome in the 12th century
ma·roo·di also ma·rou·di \mə'rüdē\ n -S [Arawak marodi] British Guiana : GUAN
maroola var of MARULA
1ma·roon \mə'rün\ n -S [modif. of AmerSp cimarrón, fr. cimarrón, adj., wild, savage, lit., living on mountaintops, fr. Sp cima top, summit, fr. L cyma young sprout of cabbage — more at CYME] 1 usu cap a : a fugitive Negro slave of the West Indies and Guiana in the 17th and 18th centuries b : a descendant of such a slave living in the West Indies and esp. in the mountains of Jamaica or in Guiana and esp. in Surinam 2 South : MAROONING PARTY 3 : a person who is marooned ⟨books suited to the life of a ~ on a desert island —T.H.Savory⟩
2maroon \"\ vb -ED/-ING/-S vt 1 : to put ashore on a desolate island or coast and leave to one's fate ⟨~ed by mutineers with only a week's supply of food⟩ 2 : to place or leave in isolation or without hope of escape ⟨~ed in Europe by the chances of war —S.H.Adams⟩ ⟨~ed more than 200 motorists and truckers in the little community for several days —Amer. Guide Series: Mich.⟩ ~ vi 1 : to escape from slavery ⟨they ~ed and fled into the hills⟩ 2 South a : PICNIC b : to camp out for some days 3 : to live in idleness ⟨~ing about the town⟩
3maroon or mar·roon \"\ n -S [F marron, lit., Spanish chestnut] 1 : a firework that consists of a pasteboard box wound with strong twine and filled with gunpowder ⟨the banging of ~s would warn us of the coming of a raid —H.G. Wells⟩ 2 a : a variable color averaging a dark red that is yellower and duller than cranberry, average garnet, or average wine and duller and slightly yellower than pomegranate — called also marron b of textiles : a dark red to purplish red that is duller than plum violet
ma·roon·er \-nə(r)\ n -S [2maroon + -er] : BUCCANEER, PIRATE
marooning party n, South : an excursion or extended picnic : a camping trip — called also maroon
ma·ro·pa \mə'rōpə\ n, pl maropa or maropas usu cap [Sp, of AmerInd origin] 1 a : a Tacanan people of northern Bolivia b : a member of such people 2 : the language of the Maropa people
mar·o·quin \'marəkən\ n -S [F, fr. Maroc Morocco] : MOROCCO
ma·ror also mo·ror \mä'rō(ə)r, -rȯ(ə)r, '=,=\ n, pl maror also moror [Heb mārōr] : the bitter herbs (as horseradish) eaten by Jews at the Passover seder to symbolize the bitterness of the Egyptian oppression of the Israelites
ma·rotte \mə'rät\ n -S [F, fr. MF, holy image, doll, dim. of the name Marie (Mary)] 1 archaic : BAUBLE 2 2 : a pet idea or notion ⟨it is a ~ of mine with which I will not trouble you —Victoria Sackville-West⟩
ma·rou·flage \¦marə¦fläzh\ n -S [F, fr. maroufler to glue canvas to a wall (fr. maroufle, a strong glue) + -age] : a process of fastening canvas to a wall with an adhesive (as white lead ground in oil)
ma·ro·vo \mə'rō(,)vō\ n, pl marovo or marovos usu cap 1 a : a people inhabiting the east side of New Georgia, Solomon Islands b : a member of such people 2 : an Austronesian language of the Marovo people
mar·plot \'mär,plät\ n [1mar + plot] 1 : one who frustrates or ruins a plan or undertaking by his meddling ⟨served by varmints, nitwits, and ~s —S.L.A.Marshall⟩ 2 : one who endangers the success of an enterprise ⟨this small ~ had discovered a great deal too much —Rudyard Kipling⟩ — mar·plot·ry \-lä·trē\ n -ES
marq abbr, often cap marquess; marquis
1marque \'märk, 'mák\ n -S [ME mark, fr. MF, fr. OProv marca, fr. marcar to mark, seize as a pledge, confiscate, fr. OIt marcare to mark — more at MARCATO] 1 obs : REPRISAL, RETALIATION 2 : LETTERS OF MARQUE
2marque \"\ n -S [F, mark, sign, band, fr. MF, fr. marquer to mark, fr. OIt marcare] : a brand or make of a product — used esp. of sport cars ⟨the radiator, while still retaining the distinctive appearance of the ~ —Grenville Manton⟩
mar·quee \mär'kē, mȧ'-\ n -S [modif. (marquise being taken as pl.) of F marquise, lit., marchioness — more at MARQUISE] 1 or mar·kee \"\ a : a large field tent formerly used by an officer of high rank ⟨during the bitter winter of 1777–78, Washington lived and worked in this flimsy ~ —Nat'l Geographic⟩ b : a large tent set up for an outdoor party, reception, or exhibition ⟨a collation and a dance in ~s on the lawn —W.S.Maugham⟩ 2 a : a permanent canopy usu. of metal and glass projecting over the entrance to a building (as a hotel) b : a similar canopy at a theater entrance usu. brightly lighted and displaying the title of the attraction and the names of the principal performers ⟨the electric sign on the ~ of the theater entrance —Burr Leyson⟩
mar·qués \mär'kās\ n, pl marque·ses \-āsəs, -āsəz\ [Sp marqués & Pg marquês, fr. OSp & OPg, fr. OProv marques, fr. marca boundary, boundary land, of Gmc origin; akin to OHG marha boundary, boundary land — more at MARK] : a marquess in Spanish and Portuguese-speaking countries
1mar·que·san \(')mär¦kāzᵊn, (')mȧ¦-, -āsᵊn\ adj, usu cap [Marquesas islands, French Oceania + E -an] 1 a : of, relating to, or characteristic of the Marquesas islands b : of, relating to, or characteristic of the Marquesans 2 : of, relating to, or characteristic of the Marquesan language
2marquesan \"\ n -S cap 1 : a Polynesian of the Marquesas islands 2 : the Austronesian language of the Marquesans
mar·quess \'märkwəs, 'mák-\ or mar·quis \", mär'kē, mȧ'-\ n, pl mar·quess·es \-kwəsəz\ or mar·quis·es \-kwəsəz\ or mar·quis \-kē(z)\ [ME markis, marquis, fr. MF marquis, alter. (influenced by OProv marques & OIt marchese marquis) of marchis, fr. marche boundary, boundary land, of Gmc origin; akin to OHG marha boundary, boundary land — more at MARQUE, MARCHESE, MARK] 1 : a nobleman of hereditary rank in Europe and Japan; specif : a member of the second grade of the peerage in Great Britain ranking below a duke and above an earl 2 obs : MARCHIONESS
mar·quess·ate or mar·quis·ate \'märkwə,zāt, -,sāt, -,zət, -,sət\ n -S [F marquisat, fr. MF, modif. (influenced by marquis) of OIt marchesato, fr. marchese + -ato -ate] 1 : the domain or territory of a marquess or marquis 2 : the rank or dignity of a marquess or marchioness
mar·que·try also mar·que·te·rie \'märkə·trē\ n, pl marquetries also marqueteries [MF marqueterie, fr. marqueter to checker, inlay (fr. marque sign, mark) + -erie -ery — more at MARQUE] 1 : a decorative process in which elaborate usu. floral patterns are formed by the insertion of pieces of wood, shell, or ivory into a wood veneer that is then applied to the surface of a piece of furniture (as a table or cabinet) ⟨the craftsman should attempt to do his own veneering and ~ —Ernest Brace⟩ 2 : an object decorated in marquetry ⟨a somewhat flamboyant piece of inlaid ~ —Agatha Christie⟩
mar·quise \mär'kēz\ n -S [F, fem. of marquis — more at MARQUESS] 1 : MARCHIONESS 2 : MARQUEE 3 a : a gem or a ring setting or bezel usu. elliptical in shape but with pointed ends — see BRILLIANT illustration b : a gem cut for use in such a setting 4 : a small upholstered sofa
mar·qui·sette \¦märk(w)ə¦zet\ n -S [marquise + -ette] : a sheer meshed fabric of leno weave that is made with variations in fiber, weight, and finishes, woven plain or with small allover designs, and is used for clothing, curtains, and mosquito nets
marquis of queens·ber·ry rules \-'kwēnz|,ber|ē- -,b(ə)r|, |i-\ n pl, usu cap M&Q [fr. the Marquis of Queensbury rules, a code of rules governing boxing matches, after Sir John Sholto Douglas, 8th Marquis of Queensbury †1900 Eng. boxing patron who supervised the code's formulation in 1867 by John G. Chambers †1883 Eng. athlete] : a code of fair play presumed to apply in any fight ⟨recognize no Marquis of Queensberry rules by which moral decorum should regulate and govern their differences —Lucius Garvin⟩
mar·qui·to \mär'kē(,)tō\ n -S [AmerSp] Southwest : a frame of ornamental tinwork of Spanish American origin
mar·ra·kech or mar·ra·kesh \mə'rä,kesh, ¦marə¦kesh\ adj, usu cap [fr. Marrakech or Marrakesh, Morocco] : of or from the city of Marrakech, Morocco : of the kind or style prevalent in Marrakech
mar·ram grass \'marəm-\ also marram n -S [of Scand origin; akin to ON maralmr, a beach grass, fr. marr sea + halmr straw — more at MARINE, HAULM] : a beach grass (Ammophila arenaria)
mar·ra·nism \mə'rä,nizəm\ or mar·ra·no·ism \-ä(,)nō,i-\ n -S : the condition or behavior of a marrano
mar·ra·no also ma·ra·no \mə'rä(,)nō\ n -S usu cap [Sp marrano, lit., pig, prob. fr. Ar maḥram something prohibited; fr. the fact that the eating of pork is outlawed by the Jewish and Muslim religions] : a Christianized Jew or Moor of medieval Spain; esp : one who accepted conversion only to escape persecution
marred past of MAR
mar·ree \'ma(,)rē\ n -S [Maori mere] : 5MERE
mar·rer \'märə(r)\ n -S [ME, fr. marren to mar + -er — more at MAR] : one that mars esp. by rendering or doing carelessly or imperfectly ⟨there are more ~s than makers of good music⟩
mar·ri \'marē\ n -S [native name in Australia] : a very large Australian red gum (Eucalyptus calophylla) having white flowers and yielding tough strong yellowish brown wood whose value as lumber is somewhat impaired by the numerous gum veins
mar·i·a·ble \'marēəbəl\ adj [ME maryable, fr. MF mariable, fr. marier to marry + -able — more at MARRY] archaic : MARRIAGEABLE
mar·riage \'marij, -rēj also 'mer-\ n -S [ME mariage, fr. MF, fr. marier to marry + -age — more at MARRY] 1 a : the state of being united to a person of the opposite sex as husband or wife b : the mutual relation of husband and wife : WEDLOCK c : the institution whereby men and women are joined in a special kind of social and legal dependence for the purpose of founding and maintaining a family — see MONOGAMY, POLYGAMY 2 : an act of marrying or the rite by which the married status is effected : WEDDING; esp : the wedding ceremony and attendant festivities or formalities — compare BEENA MARRIAGE, COEMPTIO, CONFARREATION, LEVIRATE 3 : an intimate or close union 4 : MARITAGE 5 : the combination of a king and queen of the same suit (as in pinochle) — see ROYAL MARRIAGE
mar·riage·abil·i·ty \,marijə'bilәd·ē, -rēj-, -ətē, -i also ,mer-\ n : the quality or state of being marriageable
mar·riage·able \'marijəbəl, -rēj- also 'mer-\ adj : fit for or capable of marriage: as a : of an age at which marriage is allowable b : free from any legal disability that would prohibit or nullify entry into a marriage
marriage bed n : the bed shared by a newly wed couple
marriage broker n : one whose business is marriage brokerage — compare GO-BETWEEN
marriage brokerage also marriage brokage n 1 a : the act of negotiating or arranging a marriage contract between a man and woman in return for a consideration b : the business of arranging such contracts 2 : the fee paid for the services of a marriage broker any contract for which is void at common law
marriage chest n : HOPE CHEST
marriage class n : one of the divisions within a primitive social group (as a tribe) designed to foster exogamy
marriage contract n 1 : an antenuptial contract : MARRIAGE SETTLEMENT 2 : the contractual status of marriage between husband and wife
marriage flight n : NUPTIAL FLIGHT
marriage license n : a written authorization granted by a qualified governmental official or ecclesiastic to a named man and woman to marry
marriage line n 1 usu cap M : LINE OF MARRIAGE 2 marriage lines pl but usu sing in constr, chiefly Brit : a certificate of marriage
marriage mill n : a place where it is possible to marry with a minimum of formality or delay
marriage of convenience [trans. of F mariage de convenance] : a marriage contracted rather for the advantages (as keeping an estate in a family, acquiring social position) arising out of it than because of mutual affection
marriage portion n : DOWER
marriage settlement n 1 : a settlement of property by a party to a marriage or by a third person in view and in consideration of marriage 2 : a settlement of property that benefits a husband, wife, or their issue 3 : an agreement between husband and wife fixing or waiving their respective rights in each other's property sometimes in connection with a prospective divorce or separation and providing for their children — compare JOINTURE
1married adj [ME maried, fr. past part. of marien to marry — more at MARRY] 1 a : being in the state of matrimony : WEDDED ⟨a ~ couple⟩ b : of or relating to marriage and esp. to the marriage state : CONNUBIAL ⟨~ love⟩ 2 a : UNITED, SHARED ⟨~ responsibilities⟩ ⟨our ~ voices wildly trolled —W.B. Yeats⟩ b of a piece of antique furniture : rebuilt of parts not originally from one piece c Brit, of goods for sale : available only as a unit d Brit, of a motion picture print : containing both the picture and sound record
2married n -S : a married person — usu. used in pl. and in combination ⟨the present-day young-marrieds⟩
mar·ried·ly adv : in the manner of a married couple : as if married
mar·ri·er also mar·ry·er \'marēə(r) also 'mer-\ n -S : one that marries: as a : a person that enters into the married state b : an official or clergyman who performs marriages
marries pres 3d sing of MARRY
marring pres part of MAR
marris pl of MARRI
marr·ite \'ma,rīt\ n -S [John E. Marr †1933 Eng. geologist + E -ite] : a mineral that occurs as a well-characterized substance of unknown composition in minute equant monoclinic crystals in the dolomite at Lengenbach, Valais, Switzerland
1mar·ron \'ma'rōⁿ, mə'-\ n, pl marrons \"\ [F] 1 a : SPANISH CHESTNUT 2 b marrons also marrons gla·cé pl \(,)=,=,glä'sā, ==¦=\ : chestnuts preserved in syrup flavored with vanilla 2 a : 3MAROON 2a b : 3MAROON 1
2marron \"\ n -S usu cap [F, modif. of AmerSp cimarrón — more at MAROON] : 1MAROON 1
marron glacé \see MARRON 1b\ n [F, lit., glazed Spanish chestnut] : a moderate brown that is lighter, stronger, and slightly yellower than bay, lighter and stronger than auburn, and redder, lighter, and stronger than chestnut brown — called also witchwood
marroon var of MAROON
mar·rot \'marət\ also mar·rock \-ək\ n -S [origin unknown] dial Brit : AUK, GUILLEMOT, PUFFIN

**¹mar·row** \'ma(,)rō, -,rə *also* 'mer-, often -,rəw+V\ *n* -s [ME *mergh, margh, mary, merowe, marowe,* fr. OE *mearg, mearh;* akin to OS *marg* marrow, OHG *marg, marag,* ON *mergr,* Toch A *mässunt,* Skt *majjan, majjā* marrow, OSlav *mozgŭ* brain] **1 a :** a soft highly vascular modified connective tissue that occupies the cavities and cancellous part of most bones and occurs in two forms: (1) **:** a whitish or yellowish marrow consisting chiefly of fat cells and predominating in the cavities of the long bones — called also *yellow marrow* (2) **:** a reddish marrow containing little fat, being the chief seat of red blood cell and blood granulocyte production, and occurring in the normal adult only in cancellous tissue esp. in certain flat bones — called also *red marrow* **b :** the substance of the spinal cord — called also *spinal marrow* **c** *archaic* (1) **:** PITH 1 (2) **:** the pulp of a fruit **2 :** the choicest part: as **a :** the choicest of food **:** table delicacies **b :** the seat or source of animal vigor or health **c :** the inmost, best, or essential part **:** ESSENCE **3** *chiefly Brit* **:** VEGETABLE MARROW

**²mar·row** \'marə\ *n* -s [ME *marwe, maroo, marrow*] **1** *chiefly Scot* **:** COMPANION, PARTNER **2** *chiefly Scot* **:** SPOUSE, LOVER **3** *chiefly Scot* **:** one of a pair **:** MATCH, EQUAL ⟨a pair of boots that was not ~s —J.M.Barrie⟩

**³marrow** \"\ *vb* -ED/-ING/-S [ME *marrowen,* fr. *marrow,* n.] **1** *dial Brit* **:** MATCH, EQUAL ⟨this ~s your color⟩ **2** *dial Brit* **:** MARRY

**marrow bean** *n* **:** any of several garden beans that are grown primarily as field beans for their large white seeds

**marrowbone** \'==(,)=,=\ *n* [ME *marybon,* fr. *mary* marrow + *bon* bone — more at MARROW, BONE] **1 :** a bone containing marrow esp. in sufficient quantity to be used in cookery **2 marrowbones** *pl* **:** KNEES

**marrow cabbage** *n* **:** CHOUMOELLIER

**mar·rowed** \'marōd, -rəd *also* 'mer-\ *adj* **:** having or filled with marrow

**marrowfat** \'==(,)=,=\ *n* **1** *also* **marrowfat pea :** any of several wrinkled-seeded garden peas **2 :** a tallowy product obtained by rendering bone marrow

**mar·row·ish** \'marōish, -rəwish *also* 'mer-\ *adj* **:** resembling marrow

**marrow kale** *n* **:** MARROW-STEM KALE

**mar·row·less** \'marōlǝs, -rəl- *also* 'mer-\ *adj* **:** empty of marrow

**marrow scoop** *n* **:** an 18th-century table implement often of silver with a long thin bowl suitable for removing marrow from a bone

**mar·row·sky** \mə'raůskē\ *n* -s [origin unknown] **:** SPOONERISM

**marrow squash** *n* **:** VEGETABLE MARROW

**marrow-stem kale** *also* **marrow-stemmed kale** \';=(,)=;=\ *n* **:** any of several kales with heavy foliage and thickened meaty stems that are much used for forage in areas of moderately mild winters

**mar·rowy** \'marəw|ē, -rō|, |i *also* 'mer-\ *adj* **:** full of or like marrow **:** rich or pleasing in substance **:** PITHY

**mar·rube** \mə'rüb\ *also* **mar·rub** \'marəb\ *n* -s [L *marrubium*] **:** HOREHOUND

**mar·ru·bi·in** \mə'rübēən\ *n* -s [ISV *marrubi-* (fr. NL *Marrubium*) + *-in*] **:** a bitter crystalline lactone $C_{20}H_{28}O_4$ obtained from horehound

**mar·ru·bi·um** \-ēəm\ *n, cap* [NL, fr. L, horehound] **:** a genus of Old World mints having wrinkled leaves and small white or purple flowers in dense axillary clusters — see HOREHOUND 1a

**mar·ru·cin·i·an** \,marə'sinēən\ *n* -s *usu cap* [L *Marrucini,* a people of ancient Italy + E *-an*] **:** a Sabellian dialect

**¹mar·ry** \'marē, -ri *also* 'mer-\ *vb* -ED/-ING/-ES [ME *marien,* fr. OF *marier,* fr. L *maritare,* fr. *maritus,* adj., married & *maritus,* n., husband, perh. fr. an (assumed) prehistoric word meaning "young woman" and akin to Gk *meirax* girl, boy, W *merch* daughter, girl, Skt *marya* man, young man, suitor] *vt* **1 a :** to become united in wedlock **:** constitute husband and wife according to law or custom ⟨they *married* each other soon after they met⟩ — usu. used in the passive ⟨they were *married* as mere children⟩ **b :** to dispose of (as a daughter) in wedlock **:** give in marriage — used esp. of a parent or guardian ⟨he *married* his daughter to his partner's son⟩ **c :** to take as husband or wife **:** WED ⟨he *married* the girl next door⟩ **d :** to join (persons) in wedlock **:** perform the ceremony of marriage for (a person or couple) — used of a religious or civil functionary ⟨he *married* ten couples in one week⟩ **e :** to obtain by marriage ⟨had every intention of ~*ing* wealth and security⟩ **2 :** to unite in close and usu. permanent relation: as **a** (1) **:** to join (two ropes) end to end so as to run through a block without jamming at the joint (2) **:** to place (two ropes) alongside of each other so as to be grasped and hauled on at the same time (3) **:** to join (pieces of wood) with a rope ⟨will have to use *married* wedges in launching the ship⟩ **b :** to unite two or more wines of different age, vintage, or quality either by blending or by blending and aging ~ *vi* **1 a :** to enter into the connubial state **:** take a husband or a wife **:** WED ⟨he first *married* at twenty⟩ **b :** to be a contracting party to a marriage ceremony, regardless of its validity **2 :** to enter into a close or intimate union ⟨these wines ~ well⟩ — **marry into :** to become a member of by marriage ⟨*married into* a prominent family⟩

**²marry** \"\ *interj* [ME *Marie,* after *Marie,* the Virgin Mary] *archaic* — used to express agreement or surprise esp. in answer to a question and sometimes with *come up* to express disbelief or disdain

**marryer** *var of* MARRIER

**marrying** *adj* **:** disposed to marry ⟨a ~ man⟩

**marrymuffe** *n* -s [origin unknown] *obs* **:** a coarse clothing material or a garment made of it

**marry off** *vt* **:** to dispose of in marriage **:** find a marriage partner for ⟨finally *married off* all his daughters⟩ ⟨*married* the youngest one *off* just recently⟩

**mars** \'märz, 'mȧz\ *n, usu cap* [ME, fr. *Mars,* 4th planet in order of distance from the sun, fr. L, after *Mars,* god of war and agriculture] *obs* **:** IRON — used in alchemical literature

**mar·sa·la** \mär'sälə\ *n* -s *usu cap* [fr. *Marsala,* town in Sicily] **1 :** a dark-colored wine resembling Spanish sherry that is usu. semisweet or sweet, is often classed as a dessert or appetizer wine, and is produced in western Sicily around the town of Marsala **2 :** a wine similar to Sicilian Marsala but made elsewhere (as in California)

**mars brown** *n, often cap M* [prob. fr. the planet *Mars*] **:** ARGUS BROWN

**mars·de·nia** \märz'dēnēə\ *n, cap* [NL, fr. William *Marsden* †1836 Eng. orientalist + NL *-ia*] **:** a genus of tropical woody vines (family Asclepiadaceae) having small greenish purple flowers with the crown of the corolla consisting of five flat scales united at the base to the androecium — see RANK INDIGO

**marse** *or* **marsa** *var of* MASSA

**mar·seil·lais** \mȧrseye\ *n, pl* **marseillais** *cap* [F, fr. *Marseille,* France] **:** a native or resident of Marseilles

**¹mar·seilles** *or* **mar·seille** \(')mär¦sā, (')mȧ¦-\ *adj, usu cap* [fr. *Marseilles,* France] **:** of or from the city of Marseilles, France **:** of the kind or style prevalent in Marseilles

**²mar·seilles** \mär'sā(ə)lz\ *n, pl* **marseilles** *usu cap* [fr. *Marseilles (quilting)*] **1 :** a firm reversible cotton fabric that usu. has small fancy designs and is used esp. for vests or trimmings **2 :** a heavy reversible compound fabric of cotton for bedspreads that is made with raised sometimes padded designs

**marseilles soap** *n, usu cap M* **:** soap from Marseilles orig. made from olive oil; *esp* **:** a mottled or marbled variety — compare CASTILE

**marsh** \'märsh, 'mȧsh\ *n* -ES *often attrib* [ME *mersh,* fr. OE *mersc, merisc;* akin to OFris & OS *mersk* meadowland near water, marsh, MD *mersch, maersc;* derivative fr. the root of OE *mere* sea, pool — more at MARINE] **1 :** a tract of soft wet land **:** FEN, SWAMP, MORASS; *specif* **:** such a tract of land often periodically inundated and treeless and usu. characterized by grasses, cattails, or other monocotyledons — compare BOG, LAKE, SWAMP **2** *chiefly dial* **:** a stretch of grassland **:** MEADOW

**¹mar·shal** *also* **mar·shall** \'märshəl, 'mȧsh-\ *n* -s [ME *marshal, mareschal,* fr. OF *mareschal,* of Gmc origin; akin to OHG *marahscalc* keeper of the horses, marshall, fr. *marah* horse + *scalc* servant; akin to OE *scealc* servant, OS *skalk,* Goth *skalks;* perh. akin to MHG *schel* jumping, angry, OHG *scelo* stallion, ON *skelkr* fear, Skt *śalabha* grasshopper, Lith *šuolys* gallop; basic meaning: to jump — more at MARE] **1 a** (1) **:** a high official in the household of a medieval king, prince, or noble orig. having charge of the cavalry and ranking subordinate to the constable but later usu. the chief officer in command of the military forces (2) **:** a great officer of state in various countries whose office was historically a continuation or development of the preceding but whose status came to be primarily honorary with only nominal or occasional duties — see EARL MARSHAL **b** (1) **:** any of various royal household officers of high rank charged with the arrangement of ceremonies or with other duties (2) **:** a person who arranges and directs the ceremonial aspects of any gathering **2 :** a military commander or general: as **a :** FIELD MARSHAL **b :** a general officer of the highest rank in some armies (as of France) **c :** an officer of the British Royal Air Force equivalent in rank to a field marshal in the army **3 a :** an officer having charge of prisoners: as (1) *archaic* **:** an officer of a British law court having charge of prisoners and sometimes being keeper of a prison (2) **:** KNIGHT MARSHAL (3) **:** PROVOST MARSHAL **b** (1) **:** a ministerial officer appointed for each judicial district of the U.S. to execute the process of the courts and perform various duties similar to those of a sheriff (2) **:** a law officer in some cities (as New York) of the U.S. entrusted with particular duties (as serving the process of justices' courts) **c** (1) **:** the administrative head of the police or fire department in some cities of the U.S. (2) **:** FIRE MARSHAL **4** *obs* **:** one in charge of horses esp. in respect to care of their diseases, shoeing, and grooming **:** GROOM, FARRIER

**²marshal** *also* **marshall** \"\ *vb* **marshaled** *or* **marshalled; marshaled** *or* **marshalled; marshaling** *or* **marshalling** \-sh(ə)liŋ\ **marshals** [ME *marshallen,* fr. *marshal,* n.] *vt* **1 :** to dispose (as people) in order **:** place in proper rank or position ⟨~*ing* the troops for a review⟩ ⟨~*ed* the peers to the head of the line⟩ **2 :** to arrange in order according to some planned or natural scheme ⟨carefully ~*ing* his arguments⟩: as **a :** to dispose (the parts of an heraldic composition) in due order **b** (1) **:** to fix the order of (assets) with respect to liability or availability for payment of obligations (2) **:** to fix the order of (claimants) with respect to priority of claims against a debtor's assets **c :** to assemble and dispatch (the constituent elements of a railway train) usu. in a marshaling or classification yard **3 :** to lead with ceremony **:** USHER, DIRECT ~ *vi* **:** to take form or order ⟨ideas ~*ing* neatly⟩; *esp* **:** to take one's place in a formal or ceremonious order ⟨footmen ~*ed* at the butler's heels⟩ **syn** see ORDER

**mar·shal·cy** \-lsē\ *n* -ES [ME *marshalcie,* fr. MF *mareschalcie, mareschaucie,* fr. *mareschal* + *-cie* -cy] **1 a :** the rank or position of a marshal **b** *obs* **:** the force a marshal commands **2** *obs* **:** FARRIERY

**mar·shal·er** *or* **mar·shall·er** \-sh(ə)lə(r)\ *n* -s **:** one that marshals

**mar·shal·ess** \-lǝs\ *n* -ES **:** a marshal's wife

**marshaling** *adj* **1 :** used for marshaling something (as freight cars) **2** *usu* **marshalling** *of a camp or area* **:** used for assembling troops preparatory to embarkation (as in ships or aircraft) for an operation

**mar·shall** \'märshəl\ *or* **marshall language** *n* -s *usu cap M* [fr. the *Marshall* islands in the western Pacific] **:** the Austronesian language of the Marshall islands

**mar·shall·ese** \¦märshə¦lēz, -ēs\ *n, pl* **marshallese** [*Marshall* islands + E *-ese*] **1** *cap* **:** a Micronesian native or inhabitant of the Marshall islands **2** *usu cap* **:** MARSHALL

**mar·shall·ian** \(')mär¦shalēən\ *adj, usu cap* [Alfred *Marshall* †1924 Brit. economist + E *-ian*] **:** of or relating to the economist Marshall or to his theories or followers

**mar·shal·man** \'märshəlmən\ *n, pl* **marshalmen** [¹*marshal* + *man*] **:** a man who marshals something; *esp* **:** one of the subordinates of a marshal that marches ahead to clear the way for a ceremonial procession

**marshal's court** *n, usu cap M & often cap C* **:** EARL MARSHAL'S COURT

**mar·shal·sea** \'märshəl(,)sē\ *n* -s *usu cap* [ME *marshalcie* marshalcy, marshalsea — more at MARSHALCY] **:** a former English court held before the lord steward and the knight marshal of the royal household orig. to administer justice among the sovereign's domestic servants — compare VERGE

**mar·shal·ship** \'märshəl,ship\ *n* [¹*marshal* + *-ship*] **:** MARSHALCY 1a

**marsh arrow grass** *n* **:** ARROW GRASS 1

**marshbanker** *var of* MOSSBUNKER

**marsh bass** *n* **:** LARGEMOUTH BLACK BASS

**marsh bellflower** *n* **:** a bellflower (*Campanula aparinoides*) that is common in marshes in the U. S. and has lanceolate linear leaves and small whitish flowers

**marsh bent** *or* **marsh bent grass** *n* **:** a redtop (*Agrostis alba*)

**marsh·berry** \'märsh- — *see* BERRY\ *n* **:** EUROPEAN CRANBERRY

**marsh blackbird** *n* **:** REDWING BLACKBIRD

**marsh bluebill** *n* **1 :** LESSER SCAUP **2 :** RING-NECKED DUCK

**marshbuck** \'=,=\ *n* **:** SITATUNGA

**marsh buggy** *n* **:** a motor vehicle for use in swamp lands having wheels with wide treads or large rubber tires with cleats — called also *swamp buggy*

**marsh cinquefoil** *n* **:** a shrubby cinquefoil (*Potentilla palustris*) of wet or marshy land having pinnate serrate-margined leaves and purple flowers

**marsh clematis** *n* **:** BLUE JASMINE

**marsh clover** *n* **:** BUCKBEAN

**marsh crab** *n* **:** any of various crabs of the family Grapsidae that burrow in marshy areas along the Atlantic coast from southern Florida to Brazil; *esp* **:** a crab of a common genus *Sesarma*

**marsh cress** *n* **:** an annual or biennial cress (*Rorippa islandica*) that grows in damp places, is a troublesome weed in some localities, and has leaves which are sometimes used in salads or as a potherb — called also *yellow water cress*

**marsh crocodile** *n* **:** MUGGER

**marsh crowfoot** *n* **:** CURSED CROWFOOT

**marsh cudweed** *n* **:** an annual cudweed (*Gnaphalium uliginosum*) that is a common weed of low-lying or cultivated soil — called also *mouse-ear*

**marsh cypress** *n* **:** a bald cypress (*Taxodium distichum*)

**marsh daisy** *n* **:** a thrift (*Armeria maritima*)

**marsh deer** *n* **:** a large deer (*Blastocerus dichotomus* or *Dorcelaphus dichotomus*) of Brazil and Argentina

**marsh elder** *n* **1 :** GUELDER ROSE **2 :** any of various coarse shrubby plants of the genus *Iva* that are common in moist areas (as coastal salt marshes) in eastern and central No. America — see BURWEED MARSH ELDER

**marshes** *pl of* MARSH

**marsh felwort** *n* **:** an annual herb (*Lomatogonium rotatum*) of the family Gentianaceae that occurs in marshes and wet places in Eurasia and No. America and that has narrow opposite leaves and conspicuous blue or white flowers in terminal racemes

**marsh fern** *n* **1 :** a shield fern (*Dryopteris thelypteris*) of the north temperate zone that has pinnatifid fronds with pinnae of uniform size **2 :** SAW FERN

**marsh fever** *n* **:** MALARIA

**marshfire** \'=,=\ *n* **:** IGNIS FATUUS 1

**marshfish** \'=,=\ *n* **:** BOWFIN

**marsh five-finger** *n* **:** MARSH CINQUEFOIL

**marsh fleabane** *n* **1 :** a plant of the genus *Pluchea* **2** *also* **marsh fleawort** *or* **marsh groundsel :** a groundsel (*Senecio congestus*) of northern and arctic regions that has thick hollow stems, long narrow leaves sometimes used as a potherb, and dense heads of yellow flowers

**marsh foxtail** *n* **:** a widely distributed low pale perennial grass (*Alopecurus geniculatus*) that is widely distributed in low meadows and other wet places and that has simple or sparingly branched culms which are decumbent at the base and bear slender flower spikes

**marsh frog** *n* **:** PICKEREL FROG

**marsh gas** *n* **1 :** a combustible gas resulting from vegetable decay in marshy ground and consisting chiefly of methane — compare IGNIS FATUUS 1 **2 :** METHANE

**marsh gentian** *n* **1 :** a perennial Eurasian gentian (*Gentiana pneumonanthe*) having linear leaves and sky-blue flowers with an obconic corolla tube and occurring chiefly in damp open heaths **2 :** any of several No. American gentians that occur chiefly or exclusively in wet areas

**marsh goose** *n* **1 :** GREYLAG **2 :** HUTCHINS'S GOOSE

**marsh grass** *n* **:** a coarse grass common in marshes (as members of the genus *Spartina*); *esp* **:** a grass (*S. patens*) of the salt meadows in the eastern U. S.

**marsh hare** *n* **1 :** a small hare (*Sylvilagus palustris*) that is larger than the cottontail with slender less hairy feet and is found in marshy places along the U. S. coast from No. Carolina to Florida **2 a :** MUSKRAT **b :** the flesh of the muskrat — used esp. when offered for sale for use as human food

**marsh harrier** *n* **:** a harrier (*Circus aeruginosus*) widely distributed in the Old World but now nearly exterminated in England

**marsh hawk** *n* **1 :** a widely distributed American hawk (*Circus cyaneus hudsonius*) that forms a race of the European hen harrier, frequents open or marshy regions, feeds on frogs, snakes, and other lower vertebrates, and is seldom destructive of poultry **2 :** MARSH HARRIER

**marsh hen** *n* **1 :** any of various American birds of the family Rallidae (as the king rail, the clapper rail, and the American coot) **2 :** MOORHEN **3 :** BITTERN

**marsh holy-rose** *or* **marsh holywort** \'=,==,=\ *n* **:** a small glabrous erect shrub (*Andromeda polifolia*) that spreads by creeping rhizomes, has dark green foliage and nodding pink flowers, and is widely distributed in wet areas of northern and arctic regions

**marsh horsetail** *n* **:** a highly variable and widely distributed scouring rush (*Equisetum palustre*) of wet or boggy areas of the northern hemisphere

**marshier** *comparative of* MARSHY

**marshiest** *superlative of* MARSHY

**marsh·i·ness** \'märshēnǝs\ *n* -ES **:** the quality or state of being marshy

**marsh·ite** \'mär,shīt\ *n* -s [C. W. *Marsh,* 19th cent. Australian geologist + E *-ite*] **:** a mineral that is a cuprous iodide CuI and that occurs in oil-brown isometric crystals (hardness 2.5, sp. gr. 5.6)

**marsh·land** \'märsh,land\ *n* [ME *mershland,* fr. OE *merscland,* fr. *mersc* marsh + *land* — more at MARSH, LAND] **:** a marshy district **:** MARSH — **marsh·land·er** \-də(r)\ *n*

**marshlight** \'=,=\ *n* **:** IGNIS FATUUS

**marshlike** \'=,=\ *adj* **1 :** resembling ignis fatuus **2** *of land* **:** low-lying and moist

**marsh·locks** \'märsh,läks\ *n pl but sing or pl in constr* **:** MARSH CINQUEFOIL

**marsh·mal·low** \'märsh,melō, 'mȧsh-, -mal-, -lə *often* -ləw+V\ *n* -s [ME *mershmalwe,* fr. OE *merscmealwe,* fr. *mersc* marsh + *mealwe* mallow — more at MARSH, MALLOW] **1 a :** a European perennial herb (*Althaea officinalis*) that is naturalized in the eastern U. S., has a dense velvety pubescence, ovate leaves and pink racemose flowers, and produces a mucilaginous root sometimes esp. formerly used in confectionery and in medicine **b :** ROSE MALLOW 1 **2 a :** a confection in the form of a sweetened paste made from the root of the marshmallow **b :** a confection made from corn syrup, sugar, albumen, and gelatin, beaten to a light creamy consistency, and usu. rolled in powdered sugar when partly dry

marshmallow

**marsh·mal·lowy** \-lōē, -ləwē\ *adj* **:** like marshmallow esp. in being soft and cloying

**marsh·man** \'märshmən\ *n, pl* **marshmen :** one who dwells in marshland; *esp* **:** a member of a group living and obtaining a livelihood in an area of extensive marshland

**marsh marigold** *n* **:** a plant of the genus *Caltha; esp* **:** a swamp herb (*C. palustris*) of Europe and No. America that has simple nearly orbicular leaves and bright yellow flowers resembling buttercups and that is often gathered in early spring for use as a potherb — called also *cowslip*

**marsh milkweed** *n* **:** a joe-pye weed (*Eupatorium purpureum*) with green to purplish stems and heads of white, pink, or lavender flowers

**marsh owl** *n* **:** SHORT-EARED OWL

**marsh parsley** *n* **1 :** MILK PARSLEY **2 :** TAPE GRASS

**marsh pea** *n* **:** a glabrous scrambling perennial wild pea (*Lathyrus palustris*) of damp or marshy areas in Eurasia and No. America with winged stems, lanceolate and often mucronate leaflets, and rather large pale bluish or purplish flowers

**marsh peep** *n* **:** LEAST SANDPIPER

**marsh pennywort** *n* **:** an herb of *Hydrocotyle* or the closely related genus *Centella*

**marsh pine** *n* **:** POND PINE

**marsh pink** *n* **:** any of several No. American herbs of the genus *Sabbatia* (esp. *S. stellaris*)

**marsh plover** *n* **1 :** WOODCOCK **2 :** PECTORAL SANDPIPER

**marsh pullet** *n* **:** FLORIDA GALLINULE

**marsh purslane** *n* **:** a widely distributed herb (*Ludwigia palustris*) with reddish flowers and opposite leaves that is esp. common in moist ditches

**marsh quail** *n* **:** MEADOWLARK

**marsh rabbit** *n* **:** MARSH HARE

**marsh robin** *n* **:** CHEWINK

**marsh rosemary** *n* **:** SEA LAVENDER 1

**marsh st.-john's-wort** *n, usu cap S&J* **:** a perennial glabrous marsh herb (*Hypericum virginianum*) having sessile cordate or clasping leaves and pink to mauve flowers

**marsh samphire** *n* **:** GLASSWORT

**marsh shield fern** *n* **:** MARSH FERN 1

**marsh snake** *n* **:** a common dark-bellied snake (*Denisonia signata*) of New South Wales that is related to the Australian copperhead

**marsh speedwell** *n* **:** a common blue-flowered herb (*Veronica scutellata*) of the north temperate zone

**marsh spike-grass** *n* **:** SALT GRASS a

**marsh spot** *n* **:** a manganese deficiency disease of peas characterized by black cavities or lesions in the seeds esp. on the inner surface of the cotyledons

**marsh stitchwort** *n* **:** BOG STITCHWORT

**marsh tea** *n* **:** a Eurasian bog shrub (*Ledum palustre*) that is distinguished from the closely related Labrador tea by its narrow leaves which are sometimes infused for use in killing vermin and parasites and that yields an oil from which ledol is obtained

**marsh tern** *n* **1 :** GULL-BILLED TERN **2 :** BLACK TERN

**marsh test** *n, usu cap M* [after James *Marsh* †1846 Brit. chemist] **:** a sensitive test for arsenic in which a solution to be tested is treated with hydrogen so that if arsenic is present gaseous arsine is formed and then decomposed to a black deposit of arsenic (as when the gas is passed through a heated glass tube)

**marsh tit** *also* **marsh titmouse** *n* **:** a grayish Old World titmouse (*Parus palustris*) with black cap and chin and pale underparts

**marsh treader** *n* **:** any of various extremely elongated marsh or pond-surface bugs of the family Hydrometridae

**marsh trefoil** *n* **:** BUCKBEAN

**marsh vetchling** *n* **:** MARSH PEA

**marsh violet** *n* **:** a widely distributed creeping violet (*Viola palustris*) chiefly of damp alpine and subalpine habitats that has glabrous cordate to reniform or sometimes ovate leaves, stiff stolons, and lilac purple to white and lilac flowers

**marsh warbler** *n* **:** a small brown-and-white Eurasian warbler (*Acrocephalus palustris*) with a pale eye stripe

**marshwort** \'=,=\ *n* **:** FOOL'S WATERCRESS

**marsh woundwort** *n* **:** a hairy perennial woundwort (*Stachys palustris*) that has a creeping rootstock, usu. rosy purple flowers, and a distinctly rank odor and is widely distributed in the northern hemisphere esp. in wet or waste places

**marsh wren** *n* **:** any of several American wrens (genera *Cistothorus* and *Telmatodytes*) that frequent marshes

**marshy** \'märshē\ *adj* -ER/-EST **1** *of land* **:** wet and spongy **:** like or constituting marsh ⟨a ~ field⟩ **2 :** relating to or occurring in marsh ⟨~ weeds⟩

**mar·si** \'mär,sī\ *n pl, usu cap* [L] **1 :** a people of ancient

Italy east of Rome **2 :** a Germanic people defeated by the Roman emperor Germanicus

**mar·si·an** \'märsēən\ *n* -s *usu cap* **:** the Sabellian dialect of the Italian Marsi

**mar·sil·ea** \mär'silēə\ *n, cap* [NL, after Count Luigi Ferdinando Marsigli (*Marsilius*) †1730 Ital. naturalist] **:** a widely distributed genus (the type of the family Marsileaceae) that comprises the clover ferns which are sometimes used as aquarium plants

**mar·sil·e·a·ce·ae** \mär,silē'āsē,ē\ *n pl, cap* [NL, fr. *Marsilea*, type genus + *-aceae*] **:** a family of water ferns that are heterosporous and have both microspores and megaspores in the same sporocarp — see MARSILEA — **mar·sil·e·a·ceous** \¦=¦==¦āshəs\ *adj*

**mar·sil·ia** \mär'silēə\ *syn of* MARSILEA

**mar·si·po·branch** \'märsəpō,braŋk\ *adj or n* [NL *Marsipobranchia*] **:** CYCLOSTOME

**mar·si·po·bran·chia** \,===¦braŋkēə\ *or* **mar·si·po·bran·chi·a·ta** \,===,braŋkē'ād·ə, -'äd·ə\ *or* **mar·si·po·bran·chii** \,===-'braŋkē,ī\ [NL, fr. Gk *marsipos, marsypos* pouch + *-branchia* or *Branchiata* or *-branchii* (fr. L *branchia* gill) — more at MARSUPIUM, BRANCHIA] *syn of* CYCLOSTOMI *or of* AGNATHA

**mars line** *n, usu cap M* [fr. the planet *Mars* — more at MARS] **:** LINE OF MARS

**mars orange** *n* [fr. *mars* (iron)] **1** *usu cap M* **:** an orange artist's pigment made by calcining Mars yellow **2** *often cap M* **:** a moderate reddish orange that is yellower and darker than flamingo, yellower and duller than crab apple, and very slightly redder and darker than tile red (sense 2)

**mars red** *n* [fr. *mars* (iron)] **1** *usu cap M* **:** any of various red to orange, brown, or violet artist's pigments made by calcining Mars yellow **2** *often cap M* **a :** COLCOTHAR 2 **b :** TOTEM 3

**mars·so·nia** \mär'sōnēə\ [NL, fr. T. F. *Marsson* + NL *-ia*] *syn of* MARSSONINA

**mars·so·ni·na** \,märsə'nīnə, -'nēnə\ *n, cap* [NL, fr. Theodor F. *Marsson* †1892 Ger. botanist + NL *-ina*] **:** a form genus of imperfect fungi (order Melanconiales) with hyaline one-septate spores — see RING SPOT

**mar·ster** \'märstər\ *dial var of* MASTER

**¹mar·su·pi·al** \(')mär¦süpēəl, (')mä¦-\ *adj* [NL *marsupium* + E *-al*] **1 :** having a pouch for carrying the young **2 :** of, relating to, or constituting a marsupium **3** [NL *Marsupialia*] **:** of or relating to the Marsupialia

**²marsupial** \"\ *n* -s **:** a marsupial mammal **:** one of the Marsupialia

**marsupial anteater** *n* **:** BANDED ANTEATER

**marsupial bone** *n* **:** either of a pair of small bones supporting the pouch walls in many marsupials and in monotremes

**marsupial frog** *n* **:** any of several So. American tree frogs of *Nototrema* or related genera (family Hylidae) the females of which carry the eggs and the young in a pouch on their back

**mar·su·pi·a·lia** \mär,süpē'ālēə\ *n pl, cap* [NL, fr. *marsupium* + *-alia*] **:** an order comprising the lowest existing mammals except the Monotremata and containing the kangaroos, wombats, bandicoots, opossums, and related animals that with few exceptions develop no placenta, have a pouch on the abdomen of the female containing the teats and serving to carry the young, and usu. have numerous teeth (often over 44) few or none of which are preceded by functional milk teeth, a double uterus and vagina, the scrotum located in front of the penis, and a small brain — compare DIPROTODONTIA, METATHERIA, POLYPROTODONTIA

**mar·su·pi·a·li·an** \=¦==¦ālēən\ *adj* [NL *Marsupialia* + E *-an*] **:** MARSUPIAL 3

**mar·su·pi·al·iza·tion** \mär,süpēələ'zāshən\ *n* -s **:** the operation of marsupializing; *also* **:** an instance of this operation

**mar·su·pi·al·ize** \mär'süpēə,līz\ *vt* -ED/-ING/-S [²*marsupial* + *-ize*] **:** to open (as the bladder or a cyst) and sew by the edges to the abdominal wound to permit further treatment (as of an enclosed tumor) or to discharge pathological matter (as from a hydatid cyst)

**marsupial mole** *n* **:** an Australian marsupial (*Notoryctes typhlops*) closely resembling the eutherian mole in appearance and behavior

**marsupial mouse** *also* **marsupial rat** *n* **:** any of numerous small sharp-nosed chiefly insectivorous marsupials (family Dasyuridae) that superficially resemble mice or rats — called also *pouched mouse*

**marsupial wolf** *n* **:** TASMANIAN WOLF

**mar·su·pi·on·ta** \mär,süpē'äntə\ *n pl, cap* [NL, fr. *Marsupialia* + Gk *-onta* (nom. neut. pl. participial ending)] *in some classifications* **:** a subclass of mammals coextensive with the Prototheria and Metatheria and comprising all the nonplacental mammals

**mar·su·pi·um** \mär'süpēəm\ *n, pl* **marsu·pia** \-ēə\ [NL, fr. L, purse, pouch, fr. Gk *marsipion, marsypion*, dim. of *marsipos, marsypos* pouch, perh. fr. Av *marshū* belly] **1 a** (1) **:** an abdominal pouch formed by a fold of the skin and enclosing the mammary glands of most marsupials (2) **:** INCUBATORIUM 1 **b :** an analogous structure in lower animals (as fishes or crustaceans) for enclosing or carrying eggs or young **c :** PECTEN 1a **2 :** PERIGYNIUM 1

**mars yellow** *n* [fr. *mars* (iron)] **1** *usu cap M* **:** an iron yellow artist's pigment made usu. by precipitating an iron salt with alkali and heating the product **2** *often cap M* **:** a moderate to strong orange that is yellower and darker than carrot red and darker than zinc orange or sunburst — called also *iron yellow, siderin yellow*

**¹mart** \'märt\ *n* -s [ME, fr. ScGael] **1** *chiefly Scot* **:** a beef animal fattened for slaughter **2** *chiefly Scot* **:** meat salted and stored for winter

**²mart** *n* -s [ME, after L *Mart-, Mars* Mars, ancient Roman god of war and agriculture] *obs* **:** BATTLE, CONTEST

**³mart** \'märt, 'mȧt, *usu* -d·+V\ *n* -s [ME, fr. MD *market, marct, mart*, prob. fr. ONF *market* — more at MARKET] **1** *archaic* **:** a coming together of people to buy and sell **:** FAIR 1a **2** *obs* **:** chaffering and bargaining **:** buying and selling; *also* **:** BARGAIN **3 :** MARKET

**⁴mart** \"\ *vb* -ED/-ING/-S *vi, obs* **:** MARKET ~ *vt, archaic* **:** to deal in **:** SELL

**⁵mart** \"\ *n* -s [by folk etymology (influence of ³*mart*)] *obs* **:** LETTERS OF MARQUE

**⁶mart** \'märt\ *n* -s [short for *marten*] *dial Eng* **:** MARTEN

**mart** *abbr* martyr; martyrology

**mar·ta·ban** \'märd·ə¦bän, -ban\ *n* -s [fr. *Martaban*, town in Burma] **:** a large green glazed pottery jar orig. made in lower Burma and used esp. for domestic storage (as of water or food)

**mar·ta·gon** \'märd·əgən\ *n* -s [ME, fr. Turk *martagān*, lit., turban] **:** TURK'S-CAP LILY a

**mar·tel** \'mär,tel\ *n* -s [MF *martel, marteau*, fr. LL *martellus*, alter. of L *martulus, marculus*; akin to L *malleus* hammer — more at MAUL] **:** HAMMER; *esp* **:** MARTEL-DE-FER

**martel-de-fer** \-də'fer\ *n* -s [F, lit., iron hammer] **:** a weapon like a hammer usu. with one side of the head pointed that was used esp. by horsemen in the middle ages to break armor

**mar·te·lé** \,märd·ᵊl'ā\ *adj* (*or adv*) [F, fr. It *martellato*] **:** MARTELLATO

**mar·te·line** \'märd·ᵊlən\ *n* -s [F, dim. of *marteau* hammer — more at MARTEL] **:** a small hammer with a pointed peen used by marble workers and sculptors

**¹mar·tel·la·to** \¦märd·ᵊl¦äd·(,)ō\ *adj* (*or adv*) [It, fr. past part. of *martellare* to hammer, strike, fr. *martello* hammer, fr. LL *martellus* — more at MARTEL] **:** detached and strongly accented — used as a direction to players of bowed instruments; compare DÉTACHÉ

**²martellato** \"\ *n* -s **:** martellato technique, notes, or effect

**mar·tel·lo tower** \mär'telō-\ *or* **martello** *n* -s *sometimes cap* [alter. of Cape *Mortella* in Corsica, where such a tower was captured with difficulty by a British fleet in 1794] **:** a circular masonry fort or blockhouse

**mar·tempering** \'mär+,-\ *n* -s [*martensite* + *tempering*] **:** the process of quenching steel from above the transformation temperature in a bath at about 350°F and then cooling to room temperature after the temperature has become nearly uniform with the bath

**mar·ten** \'mär|tᵊn, 'mȧ|, |d·ən, |tən\ *n, pl* **marten** *or* **martens** [ME *martryn*, fr. MF *martrine* marten fur, fr. OF, fr. fem. of *martrin* of a marten, fr. *martre* marten, of Gmc origin; akin to OE *mearth* marten, OFris *merth*, OHG *mardar*, ON *mörthr* marten; perh. akin to Lith *marti* bride, W *merch* daughter, girl — more at MARRY] **1 a** *or* **marten cat :** any of several slender-bodied carnivorous mammals (genus *Martes*) that are larger than weasels and of somewhat arboreal habits and that have a rather long tail and a coat of fine soft fur which is light-colored below and rich brown or gray above — compare AMERICAN SABLE, FISHER, PINE MARTEN, STONE MARTEN **b :** YELLOW-THROATED MARTEN **2 :** the fur or pelt of a marten

**mar·te·ni·ko** *or* **mar·ti·ni·co** \,märtᵊn'ē(,)kō\ *n* -s [native name in the Philippines] *Philippines* **:** a climbing perch (*Anabas scandens*)

**mar·te·not** \,märtᵊn'ō\ *n* -s [F, after Maurice *Martenot* *b*1898 Fr. scientist and musician] **:** ONDES MUSICALES

**mar·tens·ite** \'mär,tən,zīt\ *n* -s [Adolf *Martens* †1914 Ger. metallurgist + E *-ite*] **:** the hard constituent of which quenched steel is chiefly composed — **mar·ten·sit·ic** \¦mär,ten¦zid·ik\ *adj*

**mar·tes** \'mär,tēz\ *n, cap* [NL, fr. L, marten, of Gmc origin; akin to OHG *mard* marten — more at MARTEN] **:** a genus of carnivorous mammals (family Mustelidae) consisting of the typical martens, the sables, and the fisher

**mar·te·sia** \mär'tēzēə\ *n* [NL] **1** *cap* **:** a widely distributed genus of marine borers (family Pholadidae) burrowing in wood by means of a long elastic foot **2** -s **:** any borer of the genus *Martesia*

**martext** \'=,=\ *n* [¹*mar* + *text*] **:** a blundering preacher

**mar·tha wash·ing·ton chair** \'märthə'wȯ|shiŋtən-, -wä|\ *n, usu cap M&W* [after *Martha Washington* †1802 wife of George Washington] **:** a chair that has a high flat back, upholstery on seat and back, and open arms or none, is usu. framed in mahogany, and was orig. used in the later part of the 18th century

**martha washington geranium** *n, usu cap M&W* [after *Martha Washington*] **:** any of numerous erect hairy pelargoniums that are widely cultivated for their showy white to crimson flowers with dark blotches on the two upper petals, are commonly treated as a species (*Pelargonium domesticum*), and are prob. complex hybrids between several southern African pelargoniums — called also *Lady Washington geranium*

**martha washington table** *n, usu cap M&W* [after *Martha Washington*] **:** a usu. octagonal worktable with four slender often reeded legs, drawers under elongated sides, and a deep receptacle for sewing materials under each end

Martha Washington table

**mar tho·ma** \'mär'tōmə\ *adj, usu cap M&T* [after *Mar Thoma* (Saint Thomas), one of Christ's twelve apostles] **:** of or relating to the Mar Thoma Syrian Church of India formed in the early 19th century as an offshoot of the Syrian Orthodox Church of Malabar

**mar·tial** \'märshəl, 'mȧsh-\ *adj* [ME, fr. L *Martialis* of the god Mars, fr. *Mart-, Mars*, Roman god of war and agriculture + L *-alis* -al] **1 a :** of, relating to, or suited for war ⟨~ music⟩ **b :** belonging or relating to an army or to military life — distinguished from *civil* **c :** experienced in or inclined to war **:** WARLIKE ⟨~ men⟩ **d :** belonging or appropriate to one engaged or experienced in war or military life ⟨a ~ stride⟩ **2** *usu cap* **:** relating to or resembling Mars, the Roman god of war **3** *usu cap* **:** being or falling under the baleful astrological influence of Mars **4** *alchemy* **:** of, relating to, or like iron **:** CHALYBEATE

**martial eagle** *n* **:** a large African eagle (*Polemaetus bellicosus*) that is dusky brown above with snowy white breast speckled with brown and is often destructive to small livestock and poultry

**mar·tial·ism** \-shə,lizəm\ *n* -s **:** martial qualities

**mar·tial·ist** \-ləst\ *n* -s **:** a military man **:** one interested or skilled in warlike arts and techniques

**mar·tial·ize** \-shə,līz\ *vt* -ED/-ING/-S **:** to make martial

**martial law** *n* **1** *international law* **:** the law based on necessity or policy that is applied to all persons and property in occupied territory during invasion or occupation and is executed by the military authority of a belligerent acting directly or through civil courts; *esp* **:** such law when it is in accord with the laws and usages of war — compare MILITARY GOVERNMENT, MILITARY LAW **2 :** military rule exercised by a nation or state over its citizens or subjects in a situation where they are not legally enemies and when an emergency justifies such action

**mar·tial·ly** \-shəlē, -li\ *adv* **:** in a martial manner

**mar·tial·ness** \-shəlnəs\ *n* -ES **:** the quality or state of being martial

**¹mar·tian** \'märshən, 'mȧsh-\ *adj, often cap* [L *Mart-, Mars*, the 4th planet from the sun (fr. *stella Martis*, lit., star of Mars, after *Mars* Roman god of war and agriculture; trans. of Gk *Areōs astēr*, lit., star of Ares, Greek god of war) + E *-ian*] **:** of or relating to the planet Mars or its hypothetical inhabitants

**²martian** \"\ *n* -s *usu cap M* **1 :** a hypothetical inhabitant of the planet Mars **2 :** one that is usu. held by palmists to be characterized by qualities of aggression or resistance and sometimes an inflammable temper as a result of prominent development of Upper Mars, Lower Mars, or the Plain of Mars ⟨the *Martian* can be reasoned with . . . but never driven —W.G.Benham †1944⟩

**¹martin** *n* -s [ME, fr. the name *Martin*] *obs* **:** APE, MONKEY

**²mar·tin** \'mär|tᵊn, 'mȧ|, |d·ən, |tən\ *n* -s [MF, after Saint *Martin* †*ab*399 bishop of Tours; prob. fr. the migration of such birds around Martinmas] **1 :** a small European swallow (*Delichon urbica* syn. *Chelidon urbica*) having a moderately forked tail, bluish black head and back, and white rump and underparts **2 :** any of various swallows and flycatchers — usu. used in combination; compare PURPLE MARTIN

**³martin** \"\ *n* -s [by shortening] **:** FREEMARTIN

**¹mar·ti·net** \¦mär|tᵊn¦et, ¦mȧ|, |d·ən¦-, |tən¦-, *usu* -ed·+V\ *n* -s [ME mertinet, fr. MF *martinet*, dim. of *martin* — more at MARTIN] **1** *archaic* **:** ¹MARTIN **2 :** MARTINETA

**²martinet** \"\ *n* -s [MF, prob. dim. of the name *Martin*] **1 :** a military engine formerly used for throwing large stones **2 :** a line attached to the leech of a square sail to haul it close to the yard for furling

**³martinet** \"\ *n* -s [after Jean *Martinet*, 17th cent. Fr. army officer who devised a new system of military drill] **1 :** a system of military drill devised for the French army in the time of Louis XIV **2 a :** a strict military disciplinarian **b :** one who lays stress on a rigid adherence to the details of forms and methods

**mar·ti·ne·ta** \,märtᵊn'äd·ə, -'ēd·ə\ *n* -s [AmerSp, prob. fr. Sp *martinete* night heron, prob. after Saint Martin (San *Martin*) around whose feast day the night herons migrate; fr. the similarity of the crests of the night heron and the martineta] **:** an Argentine tinamou (*Eudromias elegans*) with a long slender crest

**mar·ti·ne·te** \,märtᵊn'äd·ā\ *n* -s [AmerSp, fr. Sp, night heron] **:** a Cuban heron that forms a variety (*Butorides virescens maculatus*) of the green heron and feeds largely on insects

**mar·ti·net·ish** \¦märtᵊn¦ed·ish\ *adj* [³*martinet* + *-ish*] **:** like or characteristic of a person who is a martinet ⟨a ~ attitude⟩ ⟨~ discipline⟩

**marting** *pres part of* MART

**mar·tin·gale** \'mär|tᵊn,gāl, 'mȧ|, |d·ən-, |tən- *sometimes* |d·iŋ,g- *or* |ti- *or* |tē-\ *n* -s [MF, perh. modif. of Ar *mirta'ah* rein] **1 :** a device for steadying a horse's head or checking its upward movement that consists essentially of a strap fastened to the girth, passing between the forelegs, and fastened to the bit or more commonly ending in two rings through which the reins pass **2** *or* **martingale guy** *or* **martingale stay a :** a lower stay of rope or chain for the jibboom or flying jibboom used to sustain the strain of the forestays and fastened to or rove through the dolphin striker — see SHIP illustration **b :** DOLPHIN STRIKER **3 :** any of several systems of betting in which a player increases his stake usu. by doubling each time he loses a bet

**martingale backrope** *n* **:** one of the stays leading from the lower end of a martingale to either bow of a sailing ship

**mar·ti·ni** \mär'tēnē, mȧ'-, -ni\ *also* **martini cocktail** *n* -s *sometimes cap M* [prob. fr. the name *Martini*] **:** a cocktail consisting of two or more parts gin to one of dry vermouth usu. stirred with ice and garnished with an olive, pearl onion, or slice of lemon peel

**¹mar·ti·ni·can** \¦märtᵊn¦ēkən\ *adj, usu cap* [*Martinique*, island in the West Indies + E *-an*] **1 :** of, relating to, or characteristic of Martinique **2 :** of, relating to, or characteristic of the Martinicans

**²martinican** \"\ *n* -s *cap* **:** a native or inhabitant of Martinique

**martinico** *var of* MARTENIKO

**mar·ti·ni·quais** \,mär,tēnə'kā\ *n, pl* **martiniquais** *cap* [F, fr. *Martinique* (island)] **:** MARTINICAN

**¹mar·ti·nique** \¦mär|tᵊn¦ēk, ¦mȧ|, |d·ən¦-, |tən¦-\ *adj, usu cap* [fr. *Martinique*, island in the West Indies] **:** of or relating to the island of Martinique, West Indies **:** of the kind or style prevalent in Martinique **:** MARTINICAN

**²martinique** \"\ *n* -s *often cap* **:** a brownish orange to light brown that is darker than caramel and very slightly yellower than sorrel

**mar·tin·ist** \'märtᵊnəst\ *n* -s *usu cap* [Martin *Luther* †1546 Ger. religious reformer] **:** a follower of Martin Luther

**mar·tin·mas** \'mär|tᵊnməs, 'mȧ|, |d·ənm-, |tənm-\ *n* -ES *usu cap* [ME *martinmasse*, fr. St. *Martin* †*ab*399 bishop of Tours + ME *masse* mass — more at MASS] **:** the feast of St. Martin occurring annually on the 11th of November

**martinmas summer** *or* **martin's summer** *n, usu cap M* **:** SAINT MARTIN'S SUMMER

**martinmas term** *n, usu cap M* **:** the first and fall term of the academic year at a Scottish university

**mar·ti·noe** \'märtᵊn,ō\ *n* -s [modif. of NL *Martynia*] **:** UNICORN PLANT

**martin process** *n, usu cap M* [after Pierre E. *Martin* †1915 Fr. engineer who invented it] **:** an open-hearth process in which steel is made from pig iron usu. charged molten by adding to it wrought iron and steel scrap

**martins** *pl of* MARTIN

**mar·tin's cement** \'märtᵊnz-\ *n, usu cap M* [fr. the name *Martin*] **:** a hard-finish gypsum plaster to which potassium carbonate has been added

**martin snipe** *n* [¹*martin*] *dial Eng* **:** GREEN SANDPIPER

**martin storm** *n* [¹*martin*; fr. its taking place about the time of the arrival of the martins in the spring] *chiefly Midland* **:** a wintry storm in spring

**mar·tite** \'mär,tīt\ *n* -s [G *martit*, fr. ML *mart-, mars* iron + G *-it* -ite — more at MARS] **:** hematite occurring in iron-black isometric pseudomorphs after magnetite (hardness 6–7)

**mar·ti·us yellow** \'märsh(ē)əs-\ *n* [after Karl A. *Martius* †1920 Ger. chemist] **1** *usu cap M, often cap Y* **:** a yellow dye that is a salt of a dinitro-alpha-naphthol and is used chiefly as a biological stain **2** *often cap M* **:** a light greenish yellow that is redder and paler than sulphur yellow (sense 2)

**mart·let** \'märtlət\ *n* -s [MF, prob. alter. of *martinet* — more at MARTINET] **1 :** ²MARTIN **1 2 :** a heraldic device consisting of a representation of a bird without visible feet and used esp. as a cadency mark to indicate a fourth son

**mart·net** \'märt,net\ *n* -s [by contr.] **:** ³MARTINET 2

**marts** *pl of* MART, *pres 3d sing of* MART

**mar·tyn·ia** \mär'tinēə\ *n* [NL, fr. John *Martyn* †1768 Eng. botanist + NL *-ia*] **1** *cap* **:** the type genus of Martyniaceae comprising annual or perennial downy and clammy herbs with a bell-shaped bladdery calyx, spreading corolla tube, and a 2-beaked capsule **2** -s **:** any plant or flower of the genus *Martynia*

**mar·tyn·i·a·ce·ae** \mär,tinē'āsē,ē\ *n pl, cap* [NL, fr. *Martynia*, type genus + *-aceae*] **:** a small family of chiefly tropical American herbs (order Polemoniales) having a racemose terminal inflorescence of zygomorphic flowers with gamopetalous corollas — **mar·tyn·i·a·ceous** \¦=¦==¦āshəs\ *adj*

**¹mar·tyr** \'mär|d·ər, 'mȧ|d·ə(r, |tə-\ *n* -s [ME *martir, marter*, fr. OE *martir, martyr*, fr. LL *martyr*, fr. Gk martyr-, *martys* witness, martyr; akin to L *memor* mindful — more at MEMORY] **1 :** one who voluntarily suffers death as the penalty of witnessing to and refusing to renounce his religion or a tenet, principle, or practice belonging to it ⟨modern-day missionary ~s⟩ **2 :** one who sacrifices his life, station, or what is of great value for the sake of principle or to sustain a cause **3 a :** a great or constant sufferer (as from disease) ⟨a ~ to rheumatism⟩ **b :** one who adopts a specious air of suffering or deprivation esp. as a means of attracting sympathy or attention

**²martyr** \"\ *vt* -ED/-ING/-S [ME *martiren, martren*, fr. OE *martyrian, martrian*, fr. *martyr, martir*, n.] **1 :** to put to death for adhering to a belief, faith, or profession (as Christianity) **:** make a martyr of **2 :** to inflict agonizing pain upon **:** TORTURE **3** *archaic* **:** to torture to death **:** kill by a cruel means **4** *obs* **:** to mutilate or disfigure with or as if with wounds

**mar·tyr·dom** \'==dəm\ *n* -s [ME *martirdom*, fr. OE *martyrdōm*, fr. *martyr* + *-dōm* -dom] **1 :** the state of being a martyr **:** the suffering of death on account of adherence to one's religious faith or to any cause ⟨early Christian ~⟩ **2 :** AFFLICTION, DISTRESS, TORMENT, TORTURE

**martyress** *n* -ES [¹*martyr* + *-ess*] *obs* **:** a female martyr

**mar·tyr·ish** \'märd·ərish\ *adj* **:** like a martyr **:** suitable to a martyr ⟨her ~ resignation —S.N.Behrman⟩

**mar·tyr·i·um** \mär'tirēəm\ *n, pl* **martyr·ia** \-ēə\ [LL, testimony, martyr's shrine, fr. LGk *martyrion* martyr's shrine, fr. Gk, testimony, fr. *martyr-, martys* witness — more at MARTYR] **1 :** a building or chamber used by the early Christians as a burial place **2 :** a place where the relics of martyrs are preserved

**mar·tyr·iza·tion** \,märd·ərə'zāshən\ *n* -s **:** the making of or condition of becoming a martyr

**mar·tyr·ize** \'märd·ə,rīz\ *vb* -ED/-ING/-S *see -ize in Explan Notes* [ME *martirizen*, fr. ML *martyrizare*, fr. LL *martyr* + L *-izare* -ize — more at MARTYR] *vt* **:** to make a martyr of: as **a :** to put to death for adhering to a faith or belief **b :** to cause great suffering to **:** TORMENT **c :** to give the appearance of being a martyr to ⟨an air of *martyrized* virtue⟩ ~ *vi* **:** to become or behave like a martyr

**mar·tyr·ly** \-d·ə(r)lē\ *adv* (*or adj*) **:** in the manner of a martyr **:** like a martyr

**mar·tyr·ol·a·try** \,märd·ə'räl·ə·trē\ *n* -ES [¹*martyr* + *-o-* + *-latry*] **:** undue exaltation or adulation of martyrs

**mar·tyr·o·log·i·cal** \¦märd·ərə¦läjəkəl\ *also* **mar·tyr·o·log·ic** \-jik\ *adj* **:** relating to martyrology or martyrs **:** registering or registered in a catalogue of martyrs

**mar·tyr·ol·o·gist** \,märd·ə'räləjəst\ *n* -s **:** a writer of or a specialist in martyrology **:** a historian of martyrs

**mar·tyr·ol·o·gy** \-jē\ *n* -ES [ML *martyrologium*, fr. LL *martyr* martyr + *-logium* (fr. Gk *-logion*, fr. *logos* word) — more at MARTYR, LEGEND] **1 :** a history or account of martyrs **:** a register of martyrs; *esp* **:** an official catalog of martyrs and saints of the Roman Catholic Church including some details of their lives and arranged by the dates of their anniversaries **2** [influenced in meaning by *-logy*] **:** a branch of ecclesiastical history that treats of the lives and sufferings of martyrs

**mar·tyry** \'märd·ərē\ *n* -ES [LL *martyrium* testimony, martyrdom, martyr's shrine — more at MARTYRIUM] **1** *obs* **:** MARTYRDOM **2 :** a chapel or shrine erected in honor of a martyr

**¹ma·ru** \'mä(,)rü\ *n* -s [Jap] **:** a Japanese ship; *esp* **:** a Japanese merchant ship

**²maru** \"\ *n, pl* **maru** *or* **marus** *usu cap* **1 :** a Tibeto-Burman people of the Nmai river region in northeastern Burma **2 :** a member of the Maru people

**ma·rua** \mə'rüə\ *also* **marua rice** *n* -s [*marua*, native name in India] **:** RAGGEE

**ma·ru·la** *also* **ma·roo·la** \mə'rülə\ *n* -s [native name in southern Africa] **1 :** a tree (*Sclerocarya caffra*) of the family Anacardiaceae that is native to the veld and low country of Africa and that has grayish mottled bark, pinnate leaves, inconspicuous flowers in sprays, and succulent fruits resembling plums which contain an edible seed and are used locally to prepare an intoxicating beverage **2** *also* **marula plum :** the fruit of the marula

**mar·um** \'ma(a)rəm\ *n* -s [L *marum, maron*, fr. Gk *maron*] **:** CAT THYME

**ma·ru·mi kumquat** \mə'rümē-\ *or* **marumi** *n* -s [Jap, fr. *maru* circle + *mi* fruit] **:** any of several round-fruited kumquats usu. considered to be derived from the natural species (*Fortunella japonica*) — compare NAGAMI KUMQUAT

**ma·ru·pa** \,märü'pä\ *n* -s [Pg *marupá*, fr. Tupi] **:** a tree (*Simarouba amara*) of northern So. America and the Amazon valley that yields a light brittle lumber locally regarded as strongly resistant to insect attack

**¹mar·vel** \'märvəl, 'mȧv-\ *n* -s [ME *merveille, mervaille, mervel,* fr. OF *merveille,* fr. LL *mirabilia* miracles, marvels, fr. neut. pl. of L *mirabilis* wonderful, marvelous, fr. *mirari* to wonder at + *-abilis* -able — more at SMILE] **1** *obs* : MIRACLE **2** : something that causes wonder or astonishment : a cause for surprise : PRODIGY ⟨with that ~ of architecture before our eyes —Martha Kean⟩ ⟨British scientists feel . . . that they could achieve ~s if they could enjoy the equipment which is available to American scientists —Bertrand Russell⟩ **3** : intense surprise or interest : ASTONISHMENT ⟨this childhood mood of ~ —*Publ's Mod. Lang. Assoc. of Amer.*⟩ **4** : HOREHOUND **syn** see WONDER — **for a marvel** *adv* : for a wonder : UNEXPECTEDLY

**²marvel** \"\ *vb* **marveled** *or* **marvelled**; **marveled** *or* **marvelled**; **marveling** *or* **marvelling** \-v(ə)liŋ\ **marvels** [ME *merveillen, mervaillen, mervelen,* fr. MF *merveillier,* fr. *merveille,* n.] *vi* : to become filled with surprise, astonishment, wonder, or amazed curiosity or perplexity ⟨~ not, my brethren, if the world hate you —1 Jn 3:13 (AV)⟩ ⟨~*ed* to see what had been done so quickly⟩ — often used with *at* ⟨~*ed* at his dexterity⟩ ⟨~*ing* at the beauty of the scene⟩ ~ *vt* **1** : to feel astonishment or perplexity at or about ⟨~*ed* that they had escaped unhurt⟩ ⟨~*ed* what it all meant⟩ **2** *obs* : to cause to marvel : ASTONISH

**³marvel** \"\ *dial var of* MARBLE

**mar·vel·ment** \'märvəlmənt\ *n* -s [*²marvel* + *-ment*] : a source or cause for wonder

**marvel-of-peru** \ˌ====ˈ=\ *n* -s *usu cap P* [fr. *Peru,* country in So. America] : FOUR-O'CLOCK

**mar·vel·ous** *or* **mar·vel·lous** \'märv(ə)ləs, 'mȧv-\ *adj* [ME *merveillous,* fr. MF *merveilleus,* fr. *merveille* marvel + *-eus* -ous — more at MARVEL] **1** : causing or being such as to cause wonder : fundamentally exceptional in character or quality ⟨the ~ directional sense of migrating birds⟩ ⟨hands with a ~ capacity for healing⟩ **2 a** : being or having the characteristics of a miracle ⟨the ~ flow of water from the stone that was struck by the prophet's rod⟩ **b** : employing or concerned with the miraculous or supernatural ⟨the Gothic revival with its stress on the ~ and bizarre⟩ **3** : of the highest kind or quality : notably superior : EXCELLENT ⟨showed a ~ coolness in the face of danger⟩ ⟨has a ~ way with children⟩ — **mar·vel·ous·ly** *or* **mar·vel·lous·ly** *adv* — **mar·vel·ous·ness** *or* **mar·vel·lous·ness** *n* -ES

**¹mar·ver** \'märvər\ *n* -s [F *marbre* marble — more at MARBLE] : a flat slab (as of metal, stone, wood) on which a gather of glass is rolled, shaped, and cooled

**²marver** \"\ *vt* -ED/-ING/-S : to roll (glass) on a marver

**mar·wa·ri** \mär'wärē\ *n* -s *usu cap* [native name in India] **1** : a member of a caste of moneylenders and merchants in India who have become the chief rivals of the Parsis as merchants and industrialists **2** : the Rajasthani dialect of Marwar

**marx·ian** \'märksēən, 'mȧk- *sometimes* -kshən\ *adj, usu cap* [Karl *Marx* †1883 Ger. political philosopher + E *-ian*] : of, developed by, or influenced by the doctrines of Marx ⟨in *Marxian* socialism . . . there is the frank acceptance of the class struggle —Jay Rumney⟩

**marx·ism** \-kˌsizəm\ *n* -s *usu cap* [Karl *Marx* + E *-ism*] : the political, economic, and social principles and policies advocated by Marx, Friedrich Engels, or their followers *esp* : a theory and practice of socialism developed by or associated with Marx and including the labor theory of value, dialectical materialism, economic determination of human actions and institutions, the class struggle as the fundamental force in history, and a belief that increasing concentration of industrial control in the capitalist class and the consequent intensification of class antagonisms and of misery among the workers will lead to a revolutionary seizure of power by and the dictatorship of the proletariat and to the establishment of a classless society — compare BOLSHEVISM, COMMUNISM, LENINISM, REVISIONISM, STALINISM, SYNDICALISM, TITOISM

**marxism-leninism** \ˈ=ˌ==ˈ==ˌ==\ *n, usu cap M&L* : a theory and practice of communism developed by or held to be developed by Lenin from the doctrines of Marx ⟨*Marxism-Leninism* is a rather flexible doctrine, imposing . . . complex problems of interpretation —F.C.Barghoorn⟩

**¹marx·ist** \'märksəst, 'mȧk-\ *n* -s *usu cap* [Karl *Marx* + E *-ist*] : a follower of Marx : an adherent of Marxism ⟨some of the keenest philosophic minds among the early Russian *Marxists* —G.L.Kline⟩

**²marxist** \"\ *adj, usu cap* : of, relating to, or having the characteristics of Marxism or Marxists ⟨the *Marxist* doctrine . . . based on the definition of all value as being created by labor —Paul Alpert⟩ ⟨forces inspired by *Marxist* thought threaten to engulf more and more of the free world —A.G.Meyer⟩

**mary** \'merē, 'mär-, 'ma(a)r-, -ri\ *n, pl* **marys** *also* **maries** *often cap* [fr. the name *Mary*] **1** *Austral & Pacific islands* : an aboriginal or native woman **2** *slang* : STOMACH, BELLY

**marybud** \'==ˌ=\ *n* [prob. fr. *Mary,* mother of Jesus + *bud*] *dial chiefly Eng* : any of various marigolds; *esp* : the common marsh marigold (*Caltha palustris*)

**mary·gold** *n* -s [ME — more at MARIGOLD] : MARIGOLD

**marygold yellow** *n* : CADMIUM ORANGE

**Mary Jane** *trademark* — used for a low-heeled broad-toed patent-leather sandal with a single-buckle ankle strap for wear esp. by young girls

**mary·knoll·er** \'merēˌnōlə(r), 'mär-, 'ma(a)r-\ *n* -s *usu cap* [*Maryknoll,* N. Y. + E *-er*] : a priest of a Roman Catholic congregation devoted to foreign missions work that was organized in 1911 with headquarters at Maryknoll, N. Y.

**¹mary·land** \'merələnd\ *adj, usu cap* [fr. *Maryland,* middle Atlantic state of the U. S., fr. Henrietta Maria (*Mary*) †1669 queen consort of Charles I of England + E *land*] : of or from the state of Maryland ⟨*Maryland* oysters⟩ : of the kind or style prevalent in Maryland

**²maryland** \"\ *or* **maryland tobacco** *n, usu cap M* : a bright tobacco that is grown in southern Maryland, air-cured, and used in cigarette and cigar manufacture

**maryland dittany** *n, usu cap M* : DITTANY 3

**mary·land·er** \-də(r), -rəˌland-\ *n* -s *cap* [*Maryland* state + E *-er*] : a native or resident of the state of Maryland

**mary·land·i·an** \-rəˌlandēən\ *adj, usu cap* [*Maryland* state + E *-ian*] : MARYLAND

**maryland pink** *also* **maryland pinkroot** *n, usu cap M* : PINKROOT a

**maryland yellowthroat** *n, usu cap M* : an American warbler (*Geothlypis trichas*) with the upper parts olive, the throat and breast yellow, and the sides of the head of the adult male black

**mary lily** *n, usu cap M* [after *Mary,* mother of Jesus] : MADONNA LILY

**mary major** *n, usu cap both Ms* [fr. the coined name *Mary Major*] : JANE DOE — used in federal pleadings

**mar·zi·pan** \'märtsəˌpän, -pan, 'märzəˌpan *sometimes* ˌ==ˈ=\ *n* -s [G, fr. It *marzapane,* a coin of the middle ages, a measure, a fancy box for confections, marzipan, fr. Ar *mawthabān,* a coin of the middle ages, lit., seated person; fr. the seated Christ on the coin] **1** : a plastic confection of crushed almonds or almond paste, sugar, and whites of eggs that is often shaped into various forms (as animals or fruits) **2** : articles of marzipan

**mas** *abbr* masculine

**MAS** *abbr* milliampere second

**ma·sa** \'mäsə\ *n* -s [Sp, mash, dough, mass, fr. L *massa* lump, mass — more at MASS] : a moist mash resulting from the grinding of corn soaked in a lime and water solution and used in preparing tortillas, tamales, and similar food

**ma·sai** \mə'sī\ *n, pl* **masai** *or* **masais** *usu cap* **1 a** : a pastoral and hunting people in Kenya and Tanganyika, east of Lake Victoria, subdivided into a number of local communities **b** : a member of such people **2** : a Nilotic language of the Masai people

**ma·sa·rid·i·dae** \ˌmasə'ridəˌdē\ *n pl, cap* [NL, fr. *Masarid-, Masaris,* type genus + *-idae*] *in some classifications* : a family of mainly tropical solitary wasps with clavate antennae now usu. treated as a subfamily of Vespidae

**masc** *abbr* masculine

**mas·cagn·ite** \ma'skanˌyēt\ *also* **mas·cagn·ine** \-nˌyēn, -nyən\ *n* -s [*mascagnite* alter. (influenced by *-ite*) of *mascagnine,* fr. G *maskagnin,* fr. Paolo *Mascagni* †1815 Ital. anatomist + G *-in* -ine] : native ammonium sulphate $(NH_4)_2SO_4$ found in volcanic districts

**mas·ca·la·ge** \ˌmäskə'lä(ˌ)hā\ *n* -s [origin unknown] : harvesting of the bark of the cork oak

**mas·cal·ly** \'maskəlē\ *adj* [by alter.] : MASCULY

**¹mas·cara** \ma'skarə *also* mə'- *or* -kerə\ *n* -s [It *mascara, maschera* mask — more at MASK] **1** : a cosmetic for coloring the eyelashes and eyebrows **2** : TUSCAN RED

**²mascara** \"\ *vt* -ED/-ING/-S : to apply mascara to : color with mascara ⟨saw the ~*ed* face —J.A.Michener⟩ ⟨the flick of a ~*ed* eyelash —Hal White⟩

**mas·ca·rene grass** \ˌmaskəˌrēn-\ *n* [*Mascarene* islands, in the Indian ocean east of Madagascar] : an Asiatic creeping perennial grass (*Zoysia tenuifolia*) introduced into the southern U. S. as a drought-resistant turf grass that has threadlike capillary leaves and flowers in a narrow compressed spike — called also *Korean velvet grass*

**mas·ca·ron** \'maskəˌrän\ *n* -s [F, fr. It *mascherone,* aug. of *maschera* mask] : MASK 1c

**mas·cle** \'maskəl\ *n* -s [ME *mascle, mascule* mesh, lozenge voided, fr. OF *macle, mascle,* of Gmc origin; akin to OHG *masca* mesh — more at MESH] **1** *heraldry* : a lozenge voided **2** : a steel plate esp. of lozenge shape used in series on 13th century armor

**mas·cled** \-kəld\ *adj* : composed of or covered with lozenge-shaped scales : having lozenge-shaped divisions

**mas·coi** \'maˌskȯi\ *n, pl* **mascoi** *or* **mascois** *usu cap* **1 a** : a people or group of peoples of the Pilcomayo river basin in Bolivia and Paraguay **b** : a member of any of such peoples **2** : the language of any of the Mascoi peoples

**mas·cot** \'maˌskät, 'maa,-, -ˌskət\ *n* -s [F *mascotte,* fr. Prov *mascoto* charm, sorcery, fr. *masco* witch, fr. ML *masca, mascha* witch, specter] **1** : a person or thing held to bring good luck; *specif* : AMULET ⟨~s made of coral, jade . . . , and silver were worn —Diana Hawthorne⟩ — compare HOODOO **2 a** : something regarded as a cherished emblem or symbol (as of a group or institution) ⟨had a mountain lion as a ~⟩ ⟨their ~ was a gamecock —F.V.W.Mason⟩ **b** *chiefly Brit* : a radiator ornament on an automobile ⟨made him adopt a fireman and his hose as a ~ for his . . . car —David Masters⟩ **3 a** : a girl or other person usu. enjoying general favor or affection adopted by a team, regiment, or other group as a cherished symbolic figure ⟨chosen ~ of the . . . football team for two years —*Amarillo (Texas) Sunday News-Globe*⟩ **b** : a small boy chosen to accompany a team to its contests, typically wearing its uniform, and usu. obliged to perform such chores as tending bats or fetching water; *specif* : the bat boy of a baseball team

**mas·cou·ten** \mə'skütᵊn,ma'-\ *n, pl* **mascouten** *or* **mascoutens** *usu cap* **1** : POTAWATOMI **2** : PEORIA

**¹mas·cu·line** \'maskyələn, 'maas-, *chiefly Brit* 'mȧs-\ *adj* [ME *masculin,* fr. MF, fr. L *masculinus,* fr. *masculus,* adj. & n., male (dim. of *mas,* adj. & n., male) + *-inus* -ine] **1** : MALE ⟨accompanied by a ~ member of her family —Joseph Hergesheimer⟩ ⟨the woman's ~ partner —C.S.Ford & F.A.Beach⟩ **2 a** : belonging to, conforming to or constituting the class of words or grammatical forms characteristically referring to males ⟨~ nouns⟩ ⟨a ~ suffix⟩ ⟨~ gender⟩ — compare FEMININE **b** (1) *of a syllable* : STRESSED, STRONG (2) *of rhyme* : occurring in stressed final syllables **3 a** : suggestive of or being in some way like a man ⟨the brazier . . . is essentially a ~ thing —Edmund Vale⟩ ⟨the worn leather armchair . . . was as ~ and durable as the benches in a railway waiting room —Walter de la Mare⟩ ⟨the mountain stands . . . ruggedly ~ in outline —*Amer. Guide Series: N. H.*⟩ **b** *of a sign of the zodiac* : having a masculine influence **c** (1) : belonging or peculiar to or used by males ⟨the poem is almost exclusively a ~ method of expression —C.W.Cunnington⟩ ⟨a sea of languishing ~ glances —Elinor Wylie⟩ ⟨had this skill as well as the ~ ones of riding and shooting —Jean Stafford⟩ (2) : consisting of, dominated by, or made by males ⟨the invasion was a purely ~ one —Seamus MacCall⟩ ⟨have created a ~ country —H.S.Commager⟩ ⟨the industry is wholly ~ —R.H.Lowie⟩ (3) : having the qualities distinctive of or appropriate to a male : VIRILE, ROBUST, MANLY ⟨a big, active, ~ creature —Margaret Deland⟩ ⟨she cannot manage ~ men —Edward Sackville-West⟩ ⟨a contagious ~ book —*Encyc. Americana*⟩ (4) : having a mannish appearance, bearing, or quality : UNWOMANLY ⟨gaunt and ~ with . . . mousey hair plastered back above her ears —Leslie Charteris⟩ (5) *obs* : POWERFUL, STRONG **syn** see MALE

**²masculine** \"\ *n* -s : something that is masculine: as **a** : a male person **b** (1) : a noun, pronoun, adjective, or inflectional form or class of the masculine gender (2) : the masculine gender

**masculine cadence** *n* : a cadence with the final chord occurring on a strong beat

**masculine caesura** *n* : a caesura that follows a stressed or long syllable

**masculine ending** *n* **1** : a grammatical ending or a suffix marking masculine forms **2** : MASCULINE CADENCE

**mas·cu·line·ly** *adv* : in a masculine manner

**mas·cu·line·ness** \-lən(n)əs\ *n* -ES : the quality or state of being masculine

**masculine protest** *n* : a tendency to compensate for feelings of inferiority or inadequacy by exaggerating one's overt aggressiveness

**mas·cu·lin·i·ty** \ˌmaskyə'linəd·ē, ˌmaas-, ˌmȧs-, -nətē, -i\ *n* -ES [F *masculinité,* fr. *masculin* masculine + *-ité* -ity] : the quality, state, or degree of being masculine ⟨measurement of ~ or femininity —*Psychological Abstracts*⟩ ⟨alternates between a polished grace and blunt ~ —Stuart Keate⟩

**mas·cu·lin·i·za·tion** \ˌ==lənə'zāshən, -ˌnī'z-\ *n* -s : the state of being masculinized

**mas·cu·lin·ize** \'==ləˌnīz\ *vt* -ED/-ING/-S [F *masculiniser,* fr. *masculin* masculine + *-iser* -ize] : to cause (a female) to take on male characters (as by the administration of an androgen)

**mas·cu·ly** *or* **mas·cu·lee** \'maskyəlē\ *adj* [*mascle* + *-y*] *heraldry* : covered with mascles

**mas·de·val·lia** \ˌmazdə'valēə\ *n, cap* [NL, fr. José *Masdevall* †1801 Span. physician + NL *-ia*] : a large genus of tropical American epiphytic orchids having flowers with sepals joined at the base into a tube and terminating in long narrow appendages

**ma·ser** \'māzə(r)\ *n* -s [*m*icrowave *a*mplification by *s*timulated *e*mission of *r*adiation] : a device that utilizes the natural oscillations of atoms or molecules for amplifying or generating electromagnetic waves in the microwave region of the spectrum

**¹mash** \'mash, -aa(ə)sh, -aish\ *n* -ES [ME, fr. OE *māsc-, māx-;* akin to MHG *meisch* mash and prob. to OE *mixen* dung, dunghill — more at MIXEN] **1 a** : crushed malt or a meal (as of rye) steeped and stirred in hot water to produce wort **b** : any fermentable mixture from which spirits or alcohol may be distilled **2** : a mixture of ground feeds used either dry or moistened for feeding poultry or other livestock — see BRAN MASH **3 a** : a mass of mixed ingredients made soft and pulpy by beating or crushing : a soft pulpy mass of something **b** : MESS, MUDDLE, MISHMASH ⟨a ~ of stale jokes, bad acting, and dull drama —John McCarten⟩

**²mash** \"\ *vb* -ED/-ING/-ES [ME *mashen,* fr. *mash,* n.] *vt* **1 a** : to convert into a mash : reduce to a soft pulpy state by beating or pressure ⟨~ apples⟩ **b** : CRUSH, SMASH ⟨~*es* his hand in an automobile accident —Anthony West⟩ ⟨~*ed* out my cigarette —J.M.Cain⟩ **c** *South & Midland* : to press or drive down esp. forcefully ⟨~ down a rivet⟩ **2** : to subject (as crushed malt) to the action of water with heating and stirring for the purpose of preparing wort **3** *dial Eng* : to make an infusion of (tea) : STEEP ~ *vi* **1** : to perform the operation of mashing malt or other grains **2** *South & Midland* : to apply pressure : press down — usu. used with *on* ⟨~*ing* suddenly on the brake pedal —William Faulkner⟩

**³mash** \"\ *dial var of* ¹MARSH

**⁴mash** \"\ *n* -ES [prob. fr. ²*mash*] : a hammer used in breaking stone or mineral

**⁵mash** \"\ *vb* -ED/-ING/-ES [prob. fr. ²*mash*] *vt* : to make amorous or flirtatious advances to : flirt with; *also* : to speak or signal to (a stranger) amorously : ACCOST ~ *vi* : to mash a person of the opposite sex

**⁶mash** \"\ *n* -ES **1** : a person who courts the affection of another or who is courted : SUITOR, SWEETHEART ⟨she's a hot-headed little virago, your ~ —Rudyard Kipling⟩ **2** : the act of mashing **3** : ²CRUSH 6 ⟨he's got an awful ~ on her⟩

**MASH** *abbr* mobile army surgical hospital

**mas·ham** \'masəm\ *n* -s *usu cap* [*Masham,* Yorkshire, northern England] : a British crossbred mutton sheep

**mashed** *adj* [fr. past part. of ⁵*mash*] : ENAMORED, STUCK ⟨couldn't get ~ on him —Mary Deasy⟩

**¹mash·er** \'mashə(r), -aash-, -aish-\ *n* -s [²*mash* + *-er*] : one that mashes: **a** : a brewery worker who mixes and cooks mash **b** : a kitchen utensil for mashing food ⟨a potato ~⟩

masher b

**²masher** \"\ *n* -s [⁵*mash* + *-er*] : a man who makes amorous advances esp. to a strange woman : WOLF, FLIRT ⟨was a born ~ —Dixon Wecter⟩ ⟨a young ~ who is forced into marriage —John McCarten⟩

**mash·gi·ah** *or* **mash·gi·ach** \mäsh'gēˌäḵ, -ēəḵ\ *n, pl* **mashgi·him** *or* **mashgi·chim** \ˌmäsh(ˌ)gē'ḵēm\ [Heb *mashgīăḥ*] : a supervisor authorized to inspect meat stores, bakeries, public kitchens, and commissaries to ensure adherence to orthodox Jewish ritual cleanliness

**mash·ie** \'mashē, -aash-, -aish-,-shi\ *n* -s [perh. fr. F *massue* club, fr. (assumed) VL *mattiuca,* fr. (assumed) VL *mattia* mace — more at MACE] : an iron golf club with a rather wide blade well laid back used for medium distances and for lofting a ball (as from a close lie or from the rough) — called also *number five iron;* see IRON illustration

**mashie iron** *n* : an iron golf club with less loft than a mashie and a longer shaft — called also *driving mashie, number four iron;* see IRON illustration

**mashie niblick** *n* : an iron golf club with a loft between those of a mashie and a niblick — called also *number six iron;* see IRON illustration

**¹mashing** *n* -s [ME, fr. gerund of *mashen* to mash, convert into a mash] **1** : the action or an act of one that mashes; *specif* : the act or process of mixing malt to produce wort or wash **2** : a quantity mashed

**²mashing** *n* -s [fr. gerund of ⁵*mash*] : the act of accosting or making amorous advances ⟨flirting and ~ are the targets of a crusade —*Associated Press*⟩

**mash·lum** \'mashləm\ *n* -s [alter. (influenced by ¹*mash*) of earlier *mesline* maslin — more at MASLIN] : a crop consisting of a mixture of a cereal and a legume

**mash note** *n* : a usu. sentimental or effusive note or letter expressing affection for the recipient ⟨blink at *mash notes* the girls send to each other —Bill Barker⟩ ⟨wrote him *mash notes* with fake names signed to them —Ring Lardner⟩

**ma·sho·na** \mə'shänə, -shōnə\ *n, pl* **mashona** *or* **mashonas** *usu cap* : SHONA

**mash·pee** *or* **mash·pi** \'mash(ˌ)pē\ *n, pl* **mashpee** *or* **mashpees** *or* **mashpi** *or* **mashpis** *usu cap* **1** : a remnant of Algonquian people from Massachusetts and Long Island living on Cape Cod **2** : a member of the Mashpee people

**mash tun** *or* **mash tub** *n* : a large vessel in which mashing is carried out

**mash weld** *n* : a spot-weld in which a number of overlapping parts (as rods) are welded in a single operation

**ma·si** \'mäsē\ *n* -s [Samoan] : fermented taro or breadfruit stored in an underground pit

**mas·jid** \'masjəd\ *n* -s [Ar] : MOSQUE

**¹mask** \'mask, 'mȧsk\ *dial Brit var of* ¹MASH, ²MASH

**²mask** \'mask, -aa(ə)-, -ai-, -ȧ-\ *n* -s [MF *masque,* fr. OIt *maschera,* prob. fr. (assumed) OIt *masca* witch (whence It dial. *masca*), fr. ML *masca, mascha* witch, specter] **1 a** (1) : a cover or partial cover for the face usu. made of cloth with openings for the eyes and used esp. for disguise at a ball or masquerade (2) : a person wearing a mask : MASKER **b** (1) : a figure of a head worn on the stage esp. by ancient Greek and Roman actors to identify the character and project the voice (2) : a grotesque false face worn at carnivals or similar merrymakings (3) : a representation of a face worn in dances and rituals among primitive peoples esp. for identification with supernatural powers or beings ⟨the fox ~s, the wolf ~s; symbols of the greatest possible power —Marjory S. Douglas⟩ **c** : an often grotesque head or face, used as an adornment (as on a keystone, on a fountain, or on furniture) **d** : a sculptured face or face and neck or a copy of a face made by means of a mold (as in plaster or wax) ⟨a death ~⟩ **2 a** (1) : a quality, trait, appearance, or posture that serves to conceal or disguise (as one's true or inner feelings or intentions) : PRETENSE, CLOAK ⟨friendship . . . is a ~ —Joseph Chiari⟩ ⟨an outward ~ of unfeelingness —Anthony Quinton⟩ ⟨a hideous ~ which conceals man's immorality —*Encyc. Americana*⟩ ⟨assumed a ~ of sullen stupidity —C.S.Forester⟩ (2) : a face suggestive of or resembling a mask in its immobility, expressionless character, or concealment of the inner personality or feelings ⟨they watched our progress with passive ~s —J.A.Michener⟩ ⟨gray-blue eyes that belied the habitual fixity of his fine olive ~ —F.J.Mather⟩ ⟨his face was a ~ that told nothing —W.S. Maugham⟩ ⟨his swarthy features stiffened into a ~ of foreboding —Walter O'Meara⟩ (3) : the side of a man's personality that is presented to the world as distinguished from his inner self : a person's public manner or outward bearing : POSE ⟨what goes on behind that ~ and behind the veil of conventional manners —P.E.More⟩ ⟨had recovered his ~, and was now polite, collected, watchful —W.H.Hudson †1922⟩ ⟨finds him a man of many ~s —E.A.Bloom⟩ ⟨according to the doctrine of the ~, a man's personality is the small portion of his inner self that he presents to the world's view —W.G. O'Donnell⟩ **b** : something that conceals from view; *specif* : a natural or artificial terrain feature which conceals a military force from view or protects it from fire **c** : a pharmaceutical masking agent **d** (1) : a translucent or opaque screen or a border design to vignette or partly to cover the sensitive surface in taking a photograph or the negative in printing, or an opaque sheet with an aperture to insert in the optical path in a motion-picture mechanism so as to modify the size, shape, or appearance of the picture (2) : an auxiliary image used to modify a photographic image (as for the purpose of improving color reproduction) **e** : a translucent or opaque border surrounding a television tube receiver screen **3** : a protective covering esp. for the face: as **a** : a gauze or wire screen worn over the face in outdoor games and in fencing : a similar protective covering used in glassworks, foundries and other industrial enterprises presenting special hazards to workers **b** : GAS MASK **c** : a device usu. covering the mouth and nose to facilitate or prevent the inhalation of a substance (as a gas, vapor, or spray) ⟨an oxygen ~⟩ **d** : a covering often of gauze-like material for the mouth and nose to prevent droplets from being dispersed into the air **e** : a cosmetic preparation esp. for the skin of the face that is applied moist, and produces a cleansing and tightening effect as it dries **f** : FRISKET 1 **4 a** : the head or face of an animal (as a fox, dog, cat) **b** : the lower lip of the nymph of a dragonfly and damselfly modified so as to form a prehensile organ

masks 1: *1* domino, *2* Greek tragedy, *3* Eskimo

**³mask** \"\ *vb* -ED/-ING/-S *vi* **1** : to take part in a masquerade : go about in a mask ⟨went ~*ing* with a group of young friends —E.P.O'Donnell⟩ **2** *obs* **a** : to assume a mask **b** : to disguise one's true character or intentions ~ *vt* **1 a** : to conceal from view (as with a screen or obstacle) ⟨trees and shrubs ~ the sandstone house —*Amer. Guide Series: Mich.*⟩ **b** : to make indistinct or imperceptible ⟨successive sounds blur and ~ each other —*Architectural Record*⟩ ⟨~s undesirable flavors —*Collier's Yr. Bk.*⟩ **c** : to cover up (as a thing, fact, state, quality, or emotion) so as to mislead concerning its true nature ⟨the lightness ~*ed* a terrible will —Edith Sitwell⟩ **2 a** : to cover for concealment or protection ⟨~*ed* before shipment with tough paper —*Plexiglass Design & Fabrication Data*⟩

**b** : to furnish with a protective mask (as a gas mask) **c** (1) : to conceal (as the position of a battery) from the enemy's sight (2) : to keep in check or on the defensive (as troops or a fortress) with part of one's force while conducting hostile operations elsewhere (3) : to prevent the delivery of fire on (a particular objective) by the interposition of a mask **d** *cookery* : to cover completely (as with thick sauce or mayonnaise) **e** (1) : to modify the size or shape of (as a photograph or an image to be photographed, printed, or projected) by means of an opaque border (2) : to modify densities of (a photographic image) selectively by means of an auxiliary image of the same subject for improving the accuracy of color reproduction **f** (1) : to prevent (an atom or group of atoms) from showing its ordinary reactions : BLOCK 1g ⟨to ~ hydroxyl in a sugar by converting it into methoxyl⟩ (2) : to modify or reduce the effect or activity of (as a process, a reaction) **g** : FLAVOR ⟨~ a pharmaceutical preparation⟩ **h** : to raise the audibility threshold of (a sound) by the simultaneous presentation of another sound **syn** see DISGUISE

**mask crab** *n* : any of various small shield-shaped crabs constituting the family Dorippidae

**masked** *adj* **1 a** : having its true character or quality concealed or disguised ⟨the ~ villainy of the man⟩ **b** : screened or concealed from view (as for protective or aesthetic reasons) ⟨a ~ battery⟩ **c** : failing to present or produce the usual symptoms : not obvious : DISGUISED, LATENT ⟨a ~ fever⟩; *specif* : affected by masking ⟨a ~ virus⟩ **2 a** : wearing or using a mask ⟨~ bandits⟩ ⟨~ dancers⟩ **b** : marked by or requiring the use of masks ⟨a ~ ball⟩

**masked bobwhite** *n* : a bobwhite of Sonora, Mexico, and nearby states having a blackish face and bright chestnut breast

**masked civet** *n* : a palm civet of a genus (*Paguma*) characterized by loss of the dorsal striped pattern

**masked crab** *n* **1** : a European crab (*Corystes cassivelaunus*) with markings on the carapace resembling a human face **2** : MASK CRAB

**masked duck** *n* : a small spiny-tailed black-faced duck (*Nomonyx dominicus*) of So. America and the West Indies

**masked hunter** *n* : a conenose (*Reduvius personatus*)

**masked quail** *n* : MASSENA QUAIL

**maskeeg** *var of* MUSKEG

**mas·ke·gon** \mə'skēgən, ma'-\ *n, pl* **maskegon** *or* **maskegons** *usu cap* [Cree *Mŭskĭgōk*, lit., of the swamp] : SWAMPY CREE

**mas·ke·lyn·ite** \'maskələ,nīt\ *n* -s [G *maskelynit*, fr. Nevil Story-*Maskelyne* †1911 Eng. mineralogist + G *-it* -ite] : a feldspar found in meteorites

**¹mask·er** \'maskə(r), -ās-\ *vt* -ED/-ING/-S [ME *maskeren, malskren;* akin to OE *malscrung* sorcery, OS *malsk* proud, Goth *untilamalsks* reckless] *now dial Eng* : to make confused or bewildered

**²masker** \"\ *n* -s [³*mask* + *-er*] **1** : a person who wears a mask; *specif* : one who appears in disguise at a masquerade **2** : a worker who places a covering over articles to protect them in handling or shipping or over parts of objects to protect them during the painting or treatment of surrounding areas

**maskery** *n* -ES [²*mask* + *-ery*] *obs* : the dress or disguise of a masker : MASQUERADE

**mask-flower** \'=,=\ *n* : a plant of the genus *Alonsoa*

**mas·kil** \'mä,skēl\ *n, pl* **maski·lim** \,mä(,)skē'lēm\ *often cap* [NHeb *maśkīl*, lit., enlightened, intellectual] : a person versed in Hebrew or Yiddish literature; *esp* : a follower or adherent of the Haskalah movement — **mas·kil·ic** \mə'skilik, mä'-\ *adj, often cap*

**¹masking** *n* -s [fr. gerund of ³*mask*] **1** : the act or an instance of taking part in a masquerade ⟨general ~ on Feb. 18, Shrove Tuesday —*N.Y. Times*⟩ **2 a** : the act or an instance of concealing or screening from view, perception, or knowledge ⟨despite ~ of part of the data by . . . some other countries —P.A.Sorokin⟩ **b** *or* **masking piece** : a piece of scenery used to screen from a theater audience any part of the stage that should not be seen **3** : a suppression of symptoms in plants (as in some virus diseases) under some environmental conditions

**²masking** *adj* [fr. pres. part. of ³*mask*] **1** : used in, appropriate to, marked by, or given to the wearing of masks ⟨~ clubs staged a festival⟩ **2** : tending to mask: as **a** : tending to conceal from view ⟨speeding down the other lane beyond the ~ truck —T.H.White b.1915⟩ **b** : being or relating to a flavoring or scenting substance used to cover or disguise an unpleasant taste or smell ⟨a ~ agent⟩

**masking paper** *n* : a paper used to cover parts of a surface that are to be kept bare when the remaining parts are painted (as with a spray gun)

**masking pat** *n* [E dial. *masking* (fr. gerund of ¹*mask*) + Sc *pat* pot, alter. of E *pot*] *Scot* : TEAPOT

**masking tape** *n* : a tape with an adhesive on one side used to cover a surface not to be painted

**maskinonge** *or* **maskalonge** *var of* MUSKELLUNGE

**mas·kins** \'maskənz, 'mäs-\ *n pl, usu cap* [¹*mass* + *-kin*] *now dial Eng* : ¹MASS — used in the phrase *by the Maskins*

**masklike** \'=,=\ *adj* : having the appearance of a mask ⟨a ~ expression⟩

**mask stop** *n* : the termination of a hoodmold when carved to bear more or less resemblance to a human face

**¹mas·lin** \'mazlən\ *n* -s [ME, fr. OE *mæslen, mæstling;* akin to MD & MHG *messinc* brass] **1** *obs* : BRASS **2** *or* **maslin kettle** *dial Eng* : a brass pot or vessel

**²maslin** \"\ *n* -s [alter. of earlier *mesline*, fr. ME *mastlioun, mestlioun*, fr. MF *mesteillon*, fr. OF, fr. (assumed) OF *mesteil* mixed grain (whence MF *mesteil*), fr. (assumed) VL *mixtilium* mixture, fr. (assumed) VL *mixtilis* mixed, constituting a mixture, fr. L *mixtus* mixed (past part. of *miscēre* to mix) + *-ilis* -ile — more at MIX] **1** *dial Brit* **a** : a mixture of different sorts of grain esp. wheat and rye or their flour or meal **b** : bread made with such flour **2** *dial Brit* : MIXTURE **3** : MASHLUM

**mas·och·ism** \'mazə,kizəm, 'mas-\ *n* -s [ISV *masoch-* (fr. Leopold von Sacher-*Masoch* †1895 Ger. novelist) + *-ism*] **1 a** : a tendency to direct aggressive or destructive impulses against one's own ego in order to reduce the anxiety attendant on anticipated inevitable punishment or to gain positive gratification through identification with a loved one who was formerly a source of pain **b** : a tendency to assume a role of submissiveness and apparently to enjoy humiliation as the outcome of feelings of worthlessness **c** : a tendency to gain or to increase sexual gratification through the acceptance of physical abuse or humiliation — compare ALGOLAGNIA **d** : a tendency to take pleasure in physical or mental suffering inflicted on one by oneself or by another or in the practice of extreme self-denial or self-punishment : a taste for suffering ⟨there's a broad streak of puritan ~ in our character —K.S.Davis⟩ **2** : the practice of masochistic tendencies ⟨it was a form of ~ . . . to condemn oneself needlessly to the tantrums of a capricious climate —Jean Stafford⟩

**mas·och·ist** \-kəst\ *n* -s [ISV *masoch-* + *-ist*] : one that is given to masochism

**mas·och·is·tic** \;==;kistik\ *adj* : relating to, marked by, or given to masochism — **mas·och·is·ti·cal·ly** \-tək(ə)lē\ *adv*

**¹ma·son** \'mās°n\ *n* -s [ME *mason, masoun*, fr. OF *maçon*, prob. of Gmc origin; akin to OE *macian* to make — more at MAKE] **1** : a skilled workman who builds with stone or similar material (as brick, concrete, artificial stone) **2** *usu cap* : FREEMASON **3 a** : MASON BEE **b** : MASON WASP

**²mason** \"\ *vt* **masoned; masoned; masoning** \-s(°)niŋ\ **masons** [ME *masownen*, fr. MF *maçonner*, fr. OF, fr. *maçon*, n.] **1** : to construct of or repair with masonry **2** : to build stonework or brickwork about, under, in, or over ⟨~ up a well⟩ ⟨~ in a boiler⟩

**mason bee** *n* : any of numerous solitary bees that construct nests of hardened mud and sand

**masoned** *adj* **1** : made or reinforced with masonry **2** *heraldry* : marked with lines of a distinct tincture representing masonry joints

**ma·son·er** \'mās(°)nə(r)\ *n* -s *now dial Eng* : MASON, BRICKLAYER

**ma·son·ic** \mə'sänik *sometimes* (')mā¦s- *or* -nēk\ *adj* **1 a** *usu cap* : of, belonging to, or connected with Freemasons or Freemasonry ⟨*Masonic* lodges⟩ **b** : suggestive of or resembling Freemasons or Freemasonry (as in display of fraternal spirit or secrecy) : like that of the Freemasons ⟨might hope for some ~ feminine support —Victoria Sackville-West⟩ ⟨comes to have a kind of ~ feeling for other diplomatists —C.J.Friedrich⟩ **2** : of or relating to masons or their work — **ma·son·i·cal·ly** \-nək(ə)lē, -nēk-, -li\ *adv*

**ma·son·ite** \'mās°n,īt\ *n* -s [Owen *Mason*, 19th cent. Am. resident of Providence, Rhode Island + E *-ite*] : a chloritoid occurring in broad dark green plates

**Ma·son·ite** \"\ *trademark* — used for a fiberboard made from steam-exploded wood fiber and used typically for insulation and for paneling

**mason jar** *n, sometimes cap M* [after John L. *Mason*, 19th cent. Am. inventor] **1** : a widemouthed glass jar with a porcelain-lined zinc screw cap sealed at cap edge and glass shoulder by a flat rubber ring **2** : any of various wide-mouth jars with a screw cap used for home canning

**ma·son·ry** \'mās°nrē, -ri\ *n* -ES [ME *masonerie*, fr. MF *maçonnerie*, fr. *maçon* mason + *-erie* -ery] **1 a** : something that is built by a mason : something constructed of the materials (as stone, brick, concrete block, tiles) used by masons; *also* : monolithic concrete when used in place of stone, brick, block, or tile masonry **b** : the art, trade, or occupation of a mason **c** : the work of a mason ⟨the ~ showed great skill and care⟩ ⟨only where economy has banished the architect do we see ~ of any merit —Clive Bell⟩ **2** *usu cap* : FREEMASONRY

**masonry cement** *n* : a cement specially prepared for use in the mortar of brick and block masonry

**masonry nail** *n* : a hardened nail with spiral flutes for fastening objects to masonry by driving into the mortar joints

**masonry saw** *n* : a saw used to cut masonry units (as brick and tile)

**mason's hammer** *n* : a hammer with a moderately heavy head sharpened at one end to a chisel edge for cutting and dressing stone

mason's hammer

**mason's level** *n* : a level longer than a carpenter's level used in laying brick and stone masonry

**mason's mark** *n* : BANKER-MARK

**mason's measure** *n* : a measure used by masons in determining quantities or volumes of masonry, no deductions being made for small openings, and corners being counted twice

**mason wasp** *n* : any of various solitary wasps (as members of the genera *Eumenes* and *Sceliphron*) that construct nests of hardened mud for their young — compare POTTER WASP

**masonwork** \'==,=\ *n* : MASONRY

**ma·soo·la** \mə'sülə\ *or* **masoola boat** *n* -s [origin unknown] : a boat made of planks sewed together with strands of coir which cross over a wadding and used for landing along the coast of Madras, India

**mas·o·rete** *or* **mas·so·rete** \'masə,rēt\ *also* **mas·o·rite** \-,rīt\ *n* -s *usu cap* [alter. (influenced by *-ete* — as in *athlete* — and by *-ite*) of earlier *massoreth*, fr. MF, fr. Heb *māsoreth* bond (dubious reading in Ezek 20: 37) (whence NHeb *massōrāh, mĕsōrāh* Masorah)] : a scholar learned in the body of textual criticism of the Hebrew Bible called the Masorah; *esp* : one of the scribes who wrote down the Masorah

**mas·o·ret·ic** *or* **mas·so·ret·ic** \;==;red·ik\ *also* **mas·o·ret·i·cal** \-d·əkəl\ *adj, usu cap* [*masorete* + *-ic* or *-ical*] : of or relating to the Masorah, a vast body of notes on the occurrence of words, features of writing, directions for pronunciation, variant sources, and other textual criticism of the Hebrew Bible, written in the margins and at the end of texts by Jewish scribes between about A.D. 600 and the middle of the 10th century

**masque** *also* **mask** \'mask, -aa(ə)-, -ai-, -á-\ *n* -s [MF *masque* mask, masquerade, fr. OIt *maschera* mask — more at MASK] **1 a** : MASQUERADE **b** *obs* : a group or company of maskers **c** : MASKER **2** : a short allegorical dramatic performance popular as court entertainment in 16th and 17th century Europe, performed by masked actors often themselves members of the court, and consisting of dumb show combined with music, dancing, and sometimes poetry culminating in a ceremonial dance participated in by the spectators

**masqu·er** \'maskə(r), 'másk-\ *n* -s [by alter. (influenced by *masque*)] : MASKER

**¹mas·quer·ade** \,maskə'rād, -aask-,-aisk-\ *n* -s [MF *mascarade, masquerade* social gathering of persons wearing masks, fr. OIt dial. *mascarada*, fr. OIt *mascara, maschera* mask + OIt dial. *-ada* -ade] **1** : an action, appearance, bearing, or mode of life that is mere outward show concealing true character or situation : a pretense of being something that one is not : CAMOUFLAGE, DISGUISE ⟨her maturity was a childish, clever ~ —Philip O'Connor⟩ ⟨traveling about in the ~ of a bon vivant —Virginia Cowles⟩ ⟨discovers under a new ~ the ancient evil —V.L.Parrington⟩ ⟨became aware of an element of ~ in the appearance of this person —Elinor Wylie⟩ **2 a** : a social gathering of persons wearing masks, often dressed in rich fantastic costumes esp. to impersonate characters from history or legend, and amusing themselves with dancing, conversation, or other diversions **b** : a costume for wear at such a gathering

**²masquerade** \"\ *vi* -ED/-ING/-S **1 a** : to disguise oneself or go about disguised so as to appear to be something that one is not ⟨wasn't the first time he'd *masqueraded* as a girl —Valentine Williams⟩ ⟨looked like a young man *masquerading* in a white wig —R.H.Davis⟩ **b** : to take part in a masquerade **2** : to pass oneself off or assume the appearance of something that one is not : POSE ⟨nonentities have too often *masqueraded* as philosophers —Richard Mayne⟩ ⟨wrong for editorial arguments to ~ as news reports —F.L.Mott⟩ ⟨exploitation *masquerading* as free enterprise —Herbert Agar⟩

**mas·quer·ad·er** \-də(r)\ *n* -s : one that masquerades; *esp* : a person taking part in a masquerade

**¹mass** \'mas, -aa(ə)s, -ais *sometimes* -ás\ *n* -ES *often cap* [ME *masse* mass, feast day, fr. OE *mæsse*, modif. of (assumed) VL *messa* mass, dismissal at the end of a religious service, fr. LL *missa*, fr. L, fem. of *missus*, past part. of *mittere* to send, dismiss — more at SMITE] **1 a** : a sequence of prayers and ceremonies constituting a commemorative sacrifice of the body and blood of Christ under the appearances of bread and wine : the Christian eucharistic rite **b** : a celebrating of the Eucharist esp. with a particular intention ⟨make a bequest for ~*es*⟩ **c** : a religious ceremony similar to or likened to the Christian mass ⟨Taoist ~*es* for the dead⟩ **2** : a setting of certain parts of the mass considered as a musical composition — compare REQUIEM

**²mass** \"\ *n* -ES [ME *masse*, fr. MF, fr. L *massa* lump, mass, fr. Gk *maza* lump, mass, barley cake; akin to Gk *massein, mattein* to knead — more at MINGLE] **1 a** (1) : a quantity of matter cohering together so as to make one body usu. of indefinite shape ⟨a ~ of dough⟩ ⟨a ~ of ore⟩ (2) : an aggregate of particles or things making one body or quantity usu. of considerable size ⟨a ~ of sand⟩ (3) : a homogeneous pasty mixture compounded for making pills, troches, and plasters ⟨blue ~⟩ (4) *obs* : UNIVERSE, EARTH **b** (1) : the extent of body of a solid object : the extent of space that an object occupies : EXPANSE, BULK ⟨the highest mountain ~ on the globe —*Encyc. Americana*⟩ ⟨lifts its bulky ~ over the tangled summits —Wynford Vaughan-Thomas⟩ (2) : massive quality or effect : MAGNITUDE, MASSIVENESS ⟨in the face of their ~ and virtuosity, what was the use of rebelling against his frequent abuse of the language —*Time*⟩ ⟨impressed me with such ~ and such vividness —F.M.Ford⟩ ⟨presented with such ~ and vehemence —Edmund Wilson⟩ (3) : the principal part : main body ⟨the great ~ of the continent is buried under an ice cap —Walter Sullivan⟩ ⟨the ~ of our imports consists of raw materials⟩ ⟨saw the dark ~ of the van —Nevil Shute⟩; *also* : an unbroken expanse of something lacking bulk, density, or solid character ⟨~*es* of color on a canvas⟩ ⟨a ~ of water⟩ ⟨dense ~*es* of smoke —George Meredith⟩ (4) : AGGREGATE, WHOLE ⟨what chiefly appeals to me is the forest seen in the ~ —Arnold Bennett⟩ ⟨men in the ~ are pretty much alike⟩; *specif* : an aggregate of related objects or items ⟨a ~ of data⟩ ⟨the ~ of such published material is too great for integral translation —Mortimer Graves⟩ (5) : concentration of combat power ⟨the principle of ~⟩ **c** (1) : the quality or appearance of considerable largeness and material density (as in a painting or architectural structure) ⟨impressive use of ~ and repetition of detail —*Amer. Guide Series: Ark.*⟩ (2) : the shape of a building considered in three-dimensional volume as opposed to silhouette or stylistic decoration **d** : the property of a body that is a measure of its inertia, that is commonly taken as a measure of the amount of material it contains, that causes a body to have weight in a gravitational field, that along with length and time constitutes one of the fundamental quantities on which all physical measurements are based, and that according to the theory of relativity increases with increasing velocity ⟨two free bodies have equal ~ if the same force gives them the same acceleration⟩ **2 a** *obs* : a sum or fund of money **b** : a large quantity, amount, or number ⟨turned out a great ~ of miscellaneous material —R.A.Hall b.1911⟩ **3 a** (1) : MAJORITY, GENERALITY ⟨the great ~ of teachers . . . use their textbooks and dictionaries —H.R.Warfel⟩ ⟨declared the ~ of mankind did not know their own best interests⟩ ⟨more human . . . than the ~ of their countrymen —E.K.Brown⟩ (2) : a large body of persons in a compact body or array : a body of persons regarded as an aggregate ⟨a ~ of spectators jammed into the hall⟩ (3) : the great body of the people as contrasted with the upper classes : ordinary people : PROLETARIAT ⟨the coupling of the elite with the ~ is the key —Percy Winner⟩ — usu. used in pl. ⟨of this . . . he felt the ~*es* to be capable —H.S.Canby⟩ **b** : a military formation in which subdivisions are separated by less than normal intervals and distances — **in mass** *adv* : en masse ⟨will fall *in mass* on some point on the . . . thin encircling line —Fletcher Pratt⟩

**³mass** \"\ *vb* -ED/-ING/-ES *vt* **1** : to form or collect into a mass : dispose in a mass : ASSEMBLE ⟨with her hair ~*ed* low on her brow —Donn Byrne⟩ ⟨eighteenth-century canvases ~*ing* a dozen gods, a hundred generals, and . . . bleeding soldiers —Sinclair Lewis⟩ **2** : to concentrate (as troops or fire) on or in a particular area ~ *vi* : to gather and form into a mass : collect in a body ⟨could see the crowd . . . ~*ing* around the gates —A.P.Gaskell⟩

**⁴mass** \"\ *adj* **1 a** : of, relating to, designed for, serving, or characteristic of the mass of the people ⟨~ psychology⟩ ⟨the modern economic phenomenon of the . . . ~ market, ~ distribution —Percy Winner⟩ ⟨~ magazines⟩ ⟨~ education⟩ ⟨~ chest X-ray surveys of healthy persons —*Jour. Amer. Med. Assoc.*⟩ ⟨~ hysteria⟩ **b** : participated in, attended by, or affecting a large number of individuals ⟨weapons of ~ destruction⟩ ⟨called for ~ demonstrations against the government⟩ ⟨airplanes made a ~ raid on the target⟩ **c** : having a large-scale character : done in large or wholesale quantities ⟨~ plantings of varicolored tulips —*Amer. Guide Series: Mich.*⟩ ⟨~ production⟩ **2** : arranged or disposed in a mass ⟨a good spot for ~ displays —*Packaging Manual for Self-Service Meats*⟩ **3** : viewed as a whole : TOTAL, AGGREGATE ⟨the ~ effect of the design is most striking⟩

**⁵mass** \"\ *n* -ES [by shortening & alter.] *now dial Eng* : MASTER

**mas·sa** \'másə, 'masə\ *or* **marse** \'márs\ *or* **mar·sa** \'másə\ *n* -s [by alter.] : MASTER — used esp. to represent southern Negro speech ⟨this Louisiana sugar planter was called ~ by a hundred Negroes —Katharine L. Bates⟩

**mass absorption coefficient** *n* : the absorption coefficient divided by the density or for a solute in solution by the density concentration

**mas·sa·chu·set** \,m|asə'chüsət, m|as'ch- *also* -üzət *sometimes* |ás- *or chiefly in substand speech* -'tü-; *usu* -əd·+V\ *or* **mas·sa·chu·setts** \-əts\ *n, pl* **massachuset** *or* **massachusets** *or* **massachusetts** *usu cap* [Massachuset *Massa-adchu-es-et*, a locality, lit., about the big hill, fr. *massa* big + *wadchu* hill + *-es*, dim. suffix + *-et*, locative suffix] **1 a** : an Indian people of the region of Massachusetts Bay **b** : a member of such people **2** : an Algonquian language of the Massachusett people

**mas·sa·chu·setts** \;==;==, (')=;=\ *adj, usu cap* [fr. *Massachusetts*, state of the northeastern U. S., fr. *Massachusetts* Bay, inlet of the Atlantic ocean on the east coast of Massachusetts, fr. *Massachusets*, pl. of *Massachuset*] : of or from the state of Massachusetts ⟨a *Massachusetts* industry⟩ : of the kind or style prevalent in Massachusetts

**massachusetts ballot** *n, usu cap M* : an Australian ballot on which the names of candidates with their party affiliations are grouped alphabetically under the title of the office they are seeking — compare INDIANA BALLOT, OFFICE-BLOCK BALLOT

**massachusetts fern** *n, usu cap M* : a delicate feathery shield fern (*Thelypteris simulata*) of the eastern U. S.

**massachusetts trust** *n, usu cap M* : an unincorporated business organization managed like and sometimes treated as a corporation (as for tax purposes) and first popular in Massachusetts in which the business capital is held in trust under a written declaration of trust publicly recorded outlining the powers and duties of the trustees and the rights of the beneficiaries and third persons, which capital or trust property is managed by the trustees for the beneficiaries who are the owners from time to time of transferable certificates resembling corporate stock evidencing an equitable interest in the trust property and the income earned by it — called also *business trust, common-law trust*

**¹mas·sa·cre** \'masəkə(r), 'maas-, -sēk-, *substand* -sə,krē\ *vt* **massacred; massacred; massacring** \-k(ə)riŋ, *substand* -sə,krēiŋ\ **massacres** [MF *massacrer*, fr. OF *macecrer*, fr. *maçacre*, n.] **1 a** : to kill by massacre : SLAUGHTER ⟨the Spaniards were neatly *massacred* —Green Peyton⟩ **b** : to murder or kill (a person) esp. with violence or cruelty **2** : MANGLE, MUTILATE ⟨some people who ordinarily ~ grammar —S.L. Payne⟩ ⟨got the knife, and *massacred* the bag —Carolyn Hannay⟩

**²massacre** \"\ *n* -s [MF, fr. OF *maçacre*] **1 a** : the act or an instance of killing a considerable number of human beings under circumstances of atrocity or cruelty : a wholesale slaughter ⟨the ~ of most of the surviving crew by natives —F.R. Dulles⟩ ⟨the Indians suffered as many ~*s* as they inflicted —R.S.Cotterill⟩ **b** : a peculiarly cruel or wanton act of murder or killing ⟨went . . . to avenge the ~ of a brother and a cousin —Elizabeth H. West⟩ **c** : a wholesale or wanton slaughter of animals ⟨a whale hunt and ~ —Brendan Maguire⟩ ⟨great ~*s* of foxes —T.B.Macaulay⟩ **2** : an act of thorough destruction : MANGLING ⟨the author's ~ of traditional federalist presuppositions —R.G.McCloskey⟩ ⟨a ~ of sense and grammar⟩

**mas·sa·crer** \-k(ə)rə(r)\ *n* -s : a person who massacres

**mass action** *n* **1** : action involving masses of people ⟨a period of *mass action* in which the individual has often felt lost —F.E. Hill⟩ ⟨by one single *mass action*, to improve the case of workers on a scale never attempted —F.D.Roosevelt⟩ ⟨concerted, public, *mass action* —Eugene Dennis⟩ **2** : uncoordinated gross motor behavior : random or nonspecific responses characteristic esp. of infants

**¹mas·sage** \mə'säzh, -säj, |j, *Brit usu* 'ma,s-\ *n* -s [F, fr. *masser* to massage (fr. Ar *massa* to stroke, strike) + *-age*] : manipulation of tissues for remedial or hygienic purposes (as by rubbing, stroking, kneading, or tapping) with the hand or other instrument (as a vibrator)

**²massage** \"\ *vt* -ED/-ING/-S : to treat by means of massage : RUB, KNEAD

**mas·sag·er** \-zhə(r), -jə-\ *n* -s : one that massages: as **a** : MASSEUR, MASSEUSE **b** : a massaging machine

**mas·sa·ge·tae** \mə'sajə,tē\ *n pl, usu cap* : an ancient Indo-European people of Russian Turkestan

**mas·sa·ran·du·ba** *also* **ma·ca·ran·du·ba** \,masərən'dübə\ *n* -s [Pg *maçaranduba*, fr. Tupi *maçarandiva*] **1** : any of various trees of the genus *Manilkara; esp* : a Brazilian forest tree (*M. excelsa*) that yields a very hard durable light red to reddish brown wood and a milky juice which is a minor source of rubber **2** : the wood of a massaranduba

**mas·sa·sau·ga** \;masə;sógə\ *or* **massasauga rattler** *n* -s [irreg. fr. *Missisauga* river, Ontario, Canada] either of two pygmy rattlers: **a** : a small rattlesnake (*Sistrurus catenatus*) widely distributed from New York across Texas into Mexico that lives chiefly in moist areas and feeds on mice and amphibians **b** : a rattlesnake (*Sistrurus miliaris*) similar to but smaller than the massasauga — called also *ground rattler*

**mass book** *n, often cap M* : MISSAL

**mass card** *n, sometimes cap M* : a card sent to inform the recipient that mass will be offered for the person or intention specified

**mass color** *n* : MASSTONE

**mass communication** *n* : communication directed to or reaching the mass of the people ⟨given full publicity in the press and other means of *mass communication* —Eugene Gressman⟩ ⟨the perils inherent in the *mass communication* media —J.L.Teller⟩

**mass defect** *n* **:** the difference between the mass of an isotope and its mass number expressed in atomic mass units and being either positive or negative ⟨the *mass defect* of the carbon isotope $_6C^{12}$, mass 12.00388, is +0.00388, while that of phosphorus $_{15}P^{31}$, isotopic mass 30.984, is −0.016⟩ — compare BINDING ENERGY, PACKING FRACTION

**mas·sé** \(ˈ)maˈsā\ *or* **massé shot** *n* -s [F *massé*, fr. *massé*, past part. of *masser* to make a massé shot, fr. *masse* maul, sledgehammer, fr. OF *mace* mace — more at MACE] **:** a shot in billiards made by elevating the cue and applying a large amount of English to the ball in order to effect an extreme draw or follow or to drive the cue ball around one object ball in order to strike another

**masse·cuite** \(ˈ)maˈskwēt\ *n* -s [F *masse cuite*, fr. *masse* mass + *cuite*, fem. of *cuit*, past part. of *cuire* to cook, fr. L *coquere* — more at MASS, COOK] **:** a dense mass of sugar crystals mixed with mother liquor obtained by evaporation — compare MAGMA 5

**massed** \ˈmast, -aa(ə)st, -aist *sometimes* -ȧst\ *adj* [fr. past part. of ³*mass*] **1 :** gathered or formed into a mass ⟨carried flame-colored . . . lilies and ~ greens —*N. Y. Herald Tribune*⟩ ⟨a staggering investment in time, in skilled labor, in ~ goods —Charlton Laird⟩ **2 :** constituting a result of massing ⟨a ~ chorus of all the clubs —*Amer. Guide Series: Texas*⟩ — **massed·ly** \-sədlē, -stlē, -li\ *adv*

**mas·se·na quail** \mə'sēnə-\ *or* **massena partridge** *n, usu cap M* [after André *Masséna* †1817 Fr. marshal] **:** any of several varieties of a crested quail (*Cyrtonyx montezumæ*) ranging from southern Arizona to Guatemala

**mass–energy equation** \ˈ=ˌ==-\ *n* **:** an equation for the interconversion of mass and energy: $E = MC^2$ where *E* is energy in ergs, *M* is mass in grams, and *C* is the velocity of light in centimeters per second — called also *Einstein equation;* compare CONSERVATION OF ENERGY, CONSERVATION OF MASS

**masses** *pl of* MASS, *pres 3d sing of* MASS

**mas·se·ter** \mə'sēd·ə(r)\ *n* -s [NL, fr. Gk *masētēr*, fr. *masasthai* to chew — more at MOUTH] **:** a large muscle that raises the lower jaw and assists in mastication and that arises from the zygomatic arch and the zygomatic process of the temporal bone and is inserted into the angle and ramus of the lower jaw — **mas·se·ter·ic** \ˌmasəˈterik\ *adj*

**mas·seur** *R* maˈsər, məˈ-, +V -ˈsər; -*R* -ˈsə, + *suffixal vowel* -ˈsər- *also* -ˈsər, + *vowel in a word following without pause* -ˈsər- *or* -ˈsə *also* -ˈsər\ *n* -s [F, fr. *masser* to massage — more at MASSAGE] **:** a man who practices massage and physiotherapy

**mas·seuse** \maˈsə(r)z, mə-, -sə̄z, -səiz, -süs, -süz\ *n* -s [F, fem. of *masseur*] **:** a female masseur

**mass house** *n, often cap M* **:** a Roman Catholic church — used formerly by Protestants

**mas·si·cot** \ˈmasəˌkät\ *n* -s [ME *masticote*, fr. MF *massicot, masticot*, fr. OIt *marzacotto, massicotto* pottery glaze] **1 :** lead monoxide obtained as a yellow powder at temperatures below the melting point of the oxide — compare LITHARGE 1 **2 :** lead monoxide occurring native in the form of yellow crystals — compare LITHARGE 2

**massier** *comparative of* MASSY

**massiest** *superlative of* MASSY

**mas·sif** \(ˈ)maˈsēf\ *n* -s [F, fr. *massif*, adj.] **1 :** a principal mountain mass **2 :** a block of the earth's crust bounded by faults or flexures and displaced as a unit without internal change **:** a large fault block of mountainous topography

**mäs·sig** \ˈmāsik\ *adj* [G, moderate, fr. OHG *māzīg*, fr. *māza* moderation + *-ig* -y; akin to OHG *mezzan* to measure — more at METE] **:** MODERATO — used as a direction in music

¹**mas·sil·i·ote** \məˈsilēˌōt, -ēət\ *or* **mas·sil·i·ot** \-ēət, -ēˌät\ *n* -s *cap* [modif. (influenced by L *Massilia*, ancient Greek colony at Marseilles, France, fr. Gk *Massalia*) of Gk *Massaliōtēs*, fr. *Massalia* + *-ōtēs* -ote] **:** a native or inhabitant of the ancient Greek colony of Massilia at Marseilles, France

²**massiliote** \"\ *or* **massiliot** \"\ *adj, usu cap* **:** of or relating to the ancient Greek colony of Massilia or to Massiliotes

**mass·i·ness** \ˈmasēnə̇s, ˈmaas-, -ais- *sometimes* -ȧs- *or* -sin-\ *n* -ES [¹*massy* + *-ness*] *archaic* **:** MASSIVENESS

**massing** *n* -s [fr. gerund of ³*mass*] **1 a :** the act or an instance of gathering or forming into a mass ⟨this ~ of troops provoked sharp protests in foreign chancelleries⟩ **b :** a massive concentration or piling up (as of words, images, or other artistic devices) for the achievement of an effect ⟨the sense of horror is . . . conjured up by sheer pressure of words and ~s of lights and scenery —N.L.Rothman⟩ **c :** the architectural relationship between the various masses or volumes of a building ⟨emphasize ~, including proportion, profile, volume relationship and contour —Sheldon Cheney⟩ **2 :** MASS ⟨above these . . . towers the magnificent ~ of the clouds —G.R.Stewart⟩ ⟨the ~ on either side of the pass —*Amer. Guide Series: N. H.*⟩

**mas·sive** \ˈmasiv, -aas-, -ais-, -sēv *also* -əv\ *adj* [ME *massiffe*, fr. MF *massif*, fr. *masse* mass + *-if* -ive — more at MASS] **1 a** (1) **:** forming or consisting of a large mass **:** having a solid bulky form **:** COMPACT, WEIGHTY, HEAVY ⟨~ rocks⟩ ⟨~ walls⟩ ⟨~, sturdy furniture —C.B.Kelsey⟩ ⟨a ~ volume of 600 pages —*Times Lit. Supp.*⟩ (2) **:** not hollow or plated **:** SOLID ⟨the sheath of his long knife, and other things about him were of ~ silver —W.H.Hudson †1922⟩ **b** (1) **:** characterized by solid agglomeration of materials (as bricks or stones piled in a wall, solid pisé or concrete) ⟨a building of ~ construction⟩ (2) **:** composed of or characterized by heavy monumental forms ⟨the ~ and pointed style of the German Gothic —Frederika Blankner⟩ **c :** having no regular form but not being necessarily without a crystalline structure ⟨~ sandstone⟩ **2 a :** having a large, solid, or heavy build ⟨faced the ~ policewoman —L.T.Shea⟩ **:** relatively or imposingly large ⟨eyebrows were very ~, almost meeting over the nose —Bram Stoker⟩ ⟨a ~ policeman's face —Ngaio Marsh⟩ ⟨the ~ jaw, and the unyielding mouth —Eric Linklater⟩ **b :** large in quantity, intensity, scope, or degree ⟨the most ~ odor I have ever known —Havelock Ellis⟩ ⟨had a sudden and ~ effect on book reading —*Publishers' Weekly*⟩ ⟨a surfeit of war and ~ injustice —John Barkham⟩ ⟨~ and instant retaliation —Elmer Davis⟩ **c** (1) **:** large in comparison to what is typical — used esp. of medical dosage or of an infective agent ⟨a ~ dose of penicillin⟩ (2) **:** extensive and severe — used of a pathologic condition ⟨a ~ hemorrhage⟩ ⟨a ~ collapse of a lung⟩ (3) **:** impressive or imposing in extent or depth, or through moral or intellectual excellence or grandeur **:** NOTABLE, MONUMENTAL ⟨~ simplicity — there's the pith of greatness in everything the man did —H.J.Laski⟩ ⟨a ~ simple man, above wile and above suspicion —Francis Hackett⟩ ⟨watched Grandmother move with a ~ dignity —Ellen Glasgow⟩ ⟨the most ~ American dramatist of his time —*Newsweek*⟩ ⟨it was this ~ figure . . . who became the master and innovator of his period —M.D.Geismar⟩

**syn** MASSIVE, MASSY, BULKY, MONUMENTAL, and SUBSTANTIAL can all mean impressively large or heavy. MASSIVE stresses bulk and solidity of construction ⟨bulky gas tanks — brown, *massive*, ugly —*Amer. Guide Series: N.Y.City*⟩ ⟨the state capitol at Austin — a *massive* pile of pink granite, bigger than the capitol at Washington —Green Peyton⟩ ⟨one of the most *massive* programs ever submitted by any president to Congress —Frank Kent⟩ MASSY, not common in spoken English, implies more ponderousness than does MASSIVE but equal solidity and strength ⟨this oak table top seems to be all of a piece, a *massy* whole —T.H.Littlefield⟩ ⟨a *massy* building of stone and orange-pink stucco —Al Hine⟩ ⟨avalanches . . . in their low *massy* thunder tones —John Muir †1914⟩ BULKY stresses size, usu. implying the occupying of a space out of proportion to the weight of an object and suggesting a consequent difficulty in the maneuvering of the object ⟨the rounded *bulky* form of a fat old lady —Lytton Strachey⟩ ⟨compartments were fitted to hold the *bulky* articles —*Amer. Guide Series: Ariz.*⟩ ⟨sitting on the floor, doubled up, *bulky* in his blue dungarees —Liam O'Flaherty⟩ MONUMENTAL suggests a great size or massiveness that is imposing ⟨this striking brick and limestone structure has *monumental* entrances flanked by chrome and frosted-glass lamps and surmounted by gilt eagles —*Amer. Guide Series: N. C.*⟩ ⟨the *monumental* six-volume work on international arbitration —L.M.Sears⟩ ⟨his commanding past, his *monumental* self-confidence —*Time*⟩ SUBSTANTIAL, though it can apply to size, stresses solidity and strength of construction, usu. implying worth, quality, or stability rather than great size or imposingness of appearance ⟨*substantial* homes for the technical employees of the two corporations —*Amer. Guide Series: Nev.*⟩ ⟨so *substantial* was the construction that a number of these buildings are standing today in a good state of preservation —*Amer. Guide Series: Ind.*⟩ ⟨this *substantial* volume, with over 700 pages of text —R.C.K.Ensor⟩

**mas·sive·ly** \-sə̇vlē, -li\ *adv* **:** in a massive manner

**mas·sive·ness** \-sivnə̇s, -sēv- *also* -səv-\ *n* -ES **:** the quality or state of being massive

**mas·siv·i·ty** \maˈsivəd·ē\ *n* -ES **:** MASSIVENESS

**mass john** \-ˈjän\ *n, usu cap M&J* [⁵*mass* + *John* (the name)] *chiefly Scot* **:** a Scotch Presbyterian minister

**mass–luminosity law** \ˈ=ˌ==ˌ===-\ *n* **:** a statement in astronomy: there is a close correlation between the luminosities or absolute magnitudes of stars and their masses so that the more massive stars are in general the more luminous

**mass man** *n* **:** an average, typical, or ordinary man **:** a prototype of the mass society esp. when regarded as lacking individuality or social responsibility, as drawing his stereotyped ideas from the mass media, and as easily manipulated by economic, social, or cultural elites

**mass medium** *n, pl* **mass media :** a medium of communication (as the newspapers, radio, motion pictures, television) that is designed to reach the mass of the people and that tends to set the standards, ideals, and aims of the masses — usu. used in pl.

**mass meeting** *n* **:** a large meeting or rally of people for discussion of a public question

**mass meristem** *n* **:** a meristem in which cell division in three or more planes results in increase in mass — compare PLATE MERISTEM, RIB MERISTEM

**mass noun** *n* **:** a noun characteristically denoting in many languages a homogeneous substance or a concept without subdivisions (as *sand, butter, beer, accuracy* distinguished from *a grain of sand, a pat of butter, a glass of beer, a degree of accuracy*), having in this usage in English only the singular form, and preceded in indefinite constructions by *some* rather than *a* or *an* — compare COUNT NOUN

**mass number** *n* **:** an integer that expresses the mass of an isotope with the mass of the most abundant oxygen isotope taken as 16 and that designates the number of nucleons in the nucleus ⟨the symbol for carbon of *mass number* 14 is $^{14}C$ or $C^{14}$⟩ — symbol *A;* compare ATOMIC MASS

**mass observation** *n, usu cap M&O* **:** an orig. and chiefly British method of ascertaining public opinion and public sentiment by study of diaries and subjective writings, private comments, and interviews on general subjects, in combination with quantitative surveys and polls

**mass of mercury** *n* **:** BLUE MASS

**mass of the catechumens** *often cap M&C* **:** the part of the mass up to the offertory when the catechumens were orig. dismissed

**mass of the faithful** *often cap M&F* **:** the part of the mass from the offertory to the end to which only the faithful were orig. admitted

**mass of the presanctified** *often cap M&P* **:** a special eucharistic service celebrated in the Latin rite on Good Friday only in which elements consecrated at a previous service are used

**massorete** *var of* MASORETE

**mas·so·therapist** \ˌma(ˌ)sō+\ *n* [*massotherapy* + *-ist*] **:** one who practices massotherapy — compare MASSEUR, MASSEUSE

**mas·so·therapy** \"+\ *n* [ISV *masso-* (fr. *massage*) + *therapy*] **:** the practice of massage for remedial or hygienic purposes

**mas·soy** *or* **mas·soi** \maˈsȯi, ˈmaˌsȯi\ *also* **massoi bark** *or* **massoy bark** *n* -s [*massoy, massoi*, native name in Papua] **:** the aromatic bark of an East Indian tree (*Massoia aromatica*) of the family Lauraceae yielding a volatile oil

**mass penny** *n, often cap M* **:** a money offering as distinguished from an offering in kind made during the mass in the medieval church

**mass priest** *n, often cap M* [ME *masseprest*, fr. OE *mæssepreōst*, fr. *mæsse* mass + *prēost* priest] **1** *obs* **a :** a secular priest as distinguished from a monk **b :** a chantry priest **2 :** a Roman Catholic priest — usu. used disparagingly

**mass–produce** \ˈ=ˌ=ˈ=\ *vt* [fr. *mass production*, after E *production: produce*] **:** to produce or manufacture in quantity; *esp* **:** to produce considerable quantities of standardized commodities with the use of machine techniques — opposed to *tailor-make*

**mass–produced** \ˌ=ˌ=ˈ=\ *adj* [fr. past part. of *mass-produce*] **:** produced in considerable quantities esp. by machinery ⟨such *mass-produced* goods as shoes, clothing, and household equipment —*Atlantic*⟩

**mass–producer** \ˈ=ˌ=ˈ=\ *n* [*mass-produce* + *-er*] **:** one that mass-produces

**mass production** *n* [²*mass*] **:** production of goods in considerable quantities esp. by machinery

**mass ratio** *n* **:** the ratio between the mass of a rocket with fuel and the mass after the fuel has been used up

**mass selection** *n* **:** selection as breeding stock of those members of a population exhibiting desirable qualities or elimination of those showing undesirable qualities **:** phenotypic selection — compare PROGENY TEST

**mass society** *n* **:** modern industrialized urbanized society **:** the society of the mass man esp. when held to be marked by anonymity, high mobility, lack of individuality, and a general dominance of impersonal relationships

**mass spectrograph** *n* **:** an apparatus for separating a stream of charged particles into a mass spectrum (as by magnetic or electric fields) usu. with photographic recording of the data and for thereby determining esp. the masses of isotopes

**mass spectrometer** *n* **:** an apparatus similar to a mass spectrograph but usu. with electrical measurement of the data for use esp. in determining abundance ratios of isotopes and in analyzing mixtures of compounds

**mass spectrum** *n* **:** the spectrum of a stream of charged particles (as electrons or nuclear particles) dispersed according to their mass

**masstone** \ˈ=ˌ=\ *n* [²*mass*] **:** the full color of a pigment or a coating — called also *mass color*

**mas·su·la** \ˈmasyələ\ *n, pl* **massu·lae** \-ˌlē\ [NL, fr. L, small mass, fr. *massa* lump, mass + *-ula* — more at MASS] **1 :** a coherent mass of pollen grains (as in certain orchids) developed from a single pollen mother cell **2 :** a hardened layer of cytoplasm formed around the maturing microspore in some heterosporous ferns (as of the genus *Azolla*)

**mass unit** *n* **:** ATOMIC MASS UNIT

**mass–wasting** \ˈ=ˌ=ˌ=\ *n* [²*mass* + *wasting*, n.] **:** the process involving movement of mantlerock that is controlled directly by gravity and that includes such gradual movements as creep and solifluction and such rapid movements as produce rockfalls, landslides, and mudflows

¹**massy** \ˈmasē, -aas-, -ais- *sometimes* -ȧs- *or* -si\ *adj* -ER/-EST [ME, fr. *masse* mass + *-y* — more at MASS] **1 a** (1) **:** not hollow or plated **:** SOLID ⟨the ~ gold frame —R.P.Warren⟩ (2) **:** having mass, weight, or thickness ⟨in the Newtonian physics a ~ particle had its location altered by other particles —Victor Lowe⟩ **b** (1) **:** bulky and heavy **:** PONDEROUS, WEIGHTY ⟨a ~ shield⟩ ⟨no reader would read such ~ volumes —G.M.Trevelyan⟩ ⟨~ beams bound together with rawhide thongs —Aubrey Drury⟩ (2) **:** composed of great blocks or masses of material ⟨a ~ wall⟩ ⟨~ battlements⟩ **c :** forming a dense mass **:** spreading densely or over a large expanse ⟨the fig tree's ~ foliage —Norman Douglas⟩ ⟨~ clouds⟩ **2 :** imposingly large in build or size ⟨saw his ~ figure striding down the street⟩ **3 :** having a massive quality **:** giving an impression of massiveness ⟨rhythms connected with a ~, frequently metallic theme —Paul Rosenfeld⟩ **syn** see MASSIVE

²**mas·sy** \ˈmasē\ *dial var of* MERCY

¹**mast** \ˈmast, -aa(ə)st, -aist, -ȧst\ *n* -s [ME, fr. OE *mæst;* akin to MD & OHG *mast*, L *malus* mast, MIr *maide* stick] **1 a :** a long pole or spar of timber or metal rising usu. vertically from the keel or deck of a ship and supporting the yards, booms, derricks, or gaffs **b :** a vertical or nearly vertical pole (as an upright post in various cranes or a structure to support an aerial) ⟨a television ~⟩ **c :** GIN POLE 2 **2 :** CAPTAIN'S MAST ⟨~ was always nasty business —K.M.Dodson⟩ — **at the mast** *or* **at mast** *adv* **:** on the main deck or quarter-deck by the mainmast where most assemblies of the crew are held for formal purposes — **before the mast** *or* **afore the mast** *adv* **1 :** forward of the foremast **2 :** as a common sailor ⟨shipped *before the mast* on a trading ship bound for the Orient⟩

²**mast** \"\ *vt* -ED/-ING/-S **:** to furnish with a mast ⟨pines . . . reserved for ~*ing* the king's navy —*Amer. Guide Series: Vt.*⟩

³**mast** \"\ *n* -s [ME, fr. OE *mæst;* akin to MD & OHG *mast* food, mast, OE *mete* food — more at MEAT] **1 :** nuts (as beechnuts and acorns) esp. as accumulated on the forest floor; *also* **:** an accumulation of such nuts used as food for hogs or other animals ⟨feed on the bountiful ~ of acorns on the wooded ridges —John Hightower⟩ **2 :** MAST BROWN

⁴**mast** \"\ *n* -s [modif. (influenced by ¹*mast*) of F *masse* billiard cue, maul, sledgehammer, fr. OF *mace* mace — more at MACE] *archaic* **:** a heavy billiard cue

**mast-** *or* **masto-** *comb form* [NL, fr. Gk, fr. *mastos* breast — more at MEAT] **1 :** breast **:** nipple **:** mammary gland ⟨*mast*itis⟩ ⟨*masto*don⟩ **2 :** mastoid and ⟨*masto*tympanic⟩

**mas·ta·ba** \ˈmastəbə\ *n* -s [Ar *maṣṭabah, miṣṭabah* stone bench] **:** an Egyptian tomb of the time of the Memphite dynasties that is oblong in shape with sloping sides and is connected with a mummy chamber in the rock beneath

**mast·age** \ˈmastij\ *n* -s *archaic* **:** MAST, NUTS; *also* **:** a right to feed animals on the mast of a tract

**mas·tax** \ˈmaˌstaks\ *n* -ES [NL, fr. Gk, mouth, jaws; akin to Gk *masasthai* to chew — more at MOUTH] **1 :** the pharynx of a rotifer usu. containing several horny pieces most commonly consisting of an incus and mallei **2 :** the lore of a bird

**mast brown** *n* [³*mast*] **:** a brownish orange that is less strong and slightly lighter than leather and yellower, lighter, and stronger than spice

**mast cell** *n* [part trans. of G *mastzelle*, fr. *mast* food, mast (fr. OHG) + *zelle* cell — more at MAST (nuts)] **1 :** a basophilic leukocyte **2 :** a cell similar to but larger than a basophilic leukocyte that is common in connective and other tissues and believed to produce heparin

**mas·tec·to·my** \maˈstektəmē, -mi\ *n* -ES [*mast-* + *-ectomy*] **:** excision or amputation of the breast

**mast·ed** \ˈmastə̇d, -aas-,-ais-,-ȧs-\ *adj* **:** having or furnished with a mast ⟨probably was so ~ when she set forth —S.E. Morison⟩ — usu. used in combination ⟨a 4-*masted* ship⟩

¹**mas·ter** \ˈmastə(r), -aas-, -ais-, -ȧs-\ *n* -s [ME *maister* master, teacher, ruler, fr. OE *mægester, magister* & OF *maistre*, both fr. L *magister;* akin to L *magnus* great, large — more at MUCH] **1 a** (1) **:** a male teacher **:** TUTOR; *esp* **:** SCHOOLMASTER ⟨watched my ~'s face pass from amiability to sternness —James Joyce⟩ (2) **:** a person qualified to teach at a medieval university (3) **:** a person who has received an academic degree higher than a bachelor's but lower than a doctor's ⟨a reception was held for the newly made ~s and doctors⟩ **b** (1) *often cap* **:** a religious leader whose doctrines one accepts **:** one who inspires devotion or reverence on the part of his disciples ⟨eighty disciples drawn from diverse faiths sat with their *Master*—M.L.Bach⟩ (2) **:** a great figure of the past (as in science, literature, or art) whose work serves as a model, ideal, or landmark for later generations **:** a figure of immense authority or generally recognized greatness ⟨one of the few valid studies of our literature on the scale of the ~s —M.D.Geismar⟩ ⟨thoughts which had already occurred to the great ~s of the past —Arturo Castiglioni⟩ ⟨music of the ~s⟩ **c :** a workman so proficient in his handicraft or trade as to be able to follow it independently and employ or supervise journeymen or apprentices; *sometimes* **:** one who has passed licensing examination and consequently is permitted to contract for services **d** (1) **:** a person who possesses mastery (as of an art or technique) **:** an artist or performer of consummate skill ⟨one of the ~s of the new poetic idiom —R.W.Southern⟩ ⟨beautiful playing by a throng of ~s —Wilder Hobson⟩ ⟨a follower of the school of English ~s —*Current Biog.*⟩ (2) *archaic* **:** a painting or statue by a master — see OLD MASTER (3) **:** an anonymous artist of distinction whose work is distinguishable from other work of his time and place by its characteristic style or quality ⟨the ~ of the St. Cecilia altarpiece⟩ **e :** a person who is highly skilled, ingenious, or dexterous in some area of activity ⟨a ~ at laying out and illustrating advertisements —W.J.Reilly⟩ ⟨a ~ at dissembling⟩ ⟨a ~ of paradox⟩ ⟨a ~ of historical technique⟩ **f :** a bridge player (as in U. S. contract bridge tournaments) eligible to play in restricted contests **2 :** an individual having control, authority, or predominance over another: as **a** (1) **:** a man having control over the actions of others **:** RULER, GOVERNOR ⟨this decisive battle left him ~ of Europe⟩ ⟨the ~s of the little state met and drafted a defiant reply⟩ (2) **:** a sovereign ruler in relation to his ministers or diplomatic agents ⟨bear this message to the king your ~⟩ **b :** one that conquers or masters or is capable of conquering or mastering another **:** VICTOR, SUPERIOR ⟨in this young, obscure challenger the champion found his ~⟩ **c** (1) **:** a person who is licensed to take complete charge of a merchant ship **:** CAPTAIN, MASTER MARINER (2) **:** a former commissioned officer (as in the U. S. and British navies) ranking next below a lieutenant and performing the duties of the present navigating officer **d** (1) **:** a person having mastery of or control over something abstract or immaterial ⟨proved himself ~ of the situation⟩ ⟨~ of his own time⟩ (2) **:** something abstract or immaterial that exercises control or mastery ⟨the doctrine that fate is the ~ of our destinies⟩ (3) **:** a possessor or owner of something inanimate ⟨~ of a stately house and broad acres⟩ (4) **:** the owner of a slave ⟨his slaves found him a kind ~⟩ or of an animal ⟨these tribesmen are ~s of vast herds of sheep⟩; *also* **:** the male person whom an animal has been trained to obey ⟨pulling his two-year-old ~ from a rain-swollen river —*Springfield (Mass.) Union*⟩ **e** (1) **:** EMPLOYER ⟨the ~ eats his meal in a separate room from the laborer —J.M.Mogey⟩; *esp* **:** the employer of a domestic or personal servant ⟨informed the caller his ~ was not at home⟩ (2) **:** the person to whom an apprentice is articled **f :** a leader (as a bellwether) of a herd of animals **g** (1) *dial* **:** HUSBAND ⟨my ~ isn't home⟩ (2) **:** the male head of a household ⟨the ~ of the house⟩ (3) **:** a woman's lover or paramour ⟨the mistress produces to the court letters from her late ~ —*Time*⟩ **h :** a man who owns or controls a pack of hounds; *esp* **:** one who leads, commands, and disciplines the field in a hunt when hounds are in full cry ⟨always refer to all persons on the hunt, other than ~s and whips, as the field —Coles Phinizy⟩ — often used in the phrase *master of hounds* or in a phrase designating a pack of hounds of a specified kind (as *master of foxhounds, master of beagles*) **i :** a supernatural being in the mythology of a primitive people, regarded as the intermediary between men and a particular species of animals, replenishing the species, and responsible for sending animals to be killed by deserving hunters ⟨success depended . . . upon a man's satisfactory relations with the superhuman ~s —*Amer. Anthropologist*⟩ **3 a** (1) *archaic* **:** MR. 1a (2) *now chiefly dial* **:** ²MISTER 2, 4 (3) **:** YOUTH, BOY — now used chiefly as a conventional title of courtesy before the name of a boy **b :** any of various members of the Scottish peerage: as (1) **:** the eldest son of a peer (as a viscount or baron) ⟨The *Master* of Ballantrae⟩ (2) **:** the heir presumptive to a peerage; *specif* **:** the eldest son of an heir apparent to an earldom **4 a** (1) **:** a presiding or administrative officer; *esp* **:** the head in an institution or society (as a college, guild, or corporation) (2) **:** an official who has custody or superintendence of a specified thing ⟨the *Master* of the Robes⟩ **b** (1) **:** any of several officers of court appointed to assist a judge (as by hearing and reporting upon matters referred to him or by recording proceedings) (2) **:** any of several clerks or recording officers of the supreme courts of England **c :** a person holding an office of authority among the Freemasons; *esp* **:** the presiding officer — called also *worshipful master* **5 a :** MASTER MATRIX **b** *or* **master copy :** a surface (as a stencil or a gelatin matrix) from which copies are printed by direct contact on a duplicating machine **c :** a master mechanism or device; *specif* **:** CASTER 1b

²**master** \"\ *vt* **mastered; mastered; mastering** \-t(ə)riŋ\ **masters** [ME *maistren*, fr. *maister*, n. — more at ¹MASTER] **1 a :** to become master of **:** bring under control **:** CONQUER, OVERCOME ⟨tried to ~ his stammer —Osbert Sitwell⟩ ⟨~*ed* his love for the wife of a neighbor —Stringfellow Barr⟩ **b :** to cause to obey **:** bend to one's will **:** SUBDUE, TAME ⟨~s his gal by knocking her down and dragging her away —M.W.Fishwick⟩ ⟨a farmer must ~ every beast on his farm —F.D.Smith &

Barbara Wilcox⟩ ⟨man has ~ed nature —P.L.Ralph⟩ **c** *obs* **:** to have or get possession of **:** OWN, POSSESS **d :** to act as master over **:** RULE, REGULATE, DIRECT **2 a :** to become skilled or proficient in the use of **:** achieve mastery or command of ⟨the telephone was an instrument he could not ~ —Osbert Sitwell⟩ ⟨~ a foreign language⟩ ⟨could not ~ the technique necessary for a concert pianist —*Current Biog.*⟩ **b :** to gain a thorough or perfect understanding, grasp, or knowledge of ⟨failed to ~ the windings of that river —Thomas Wood †1950⟩ ⟨could ~ any intricate detail of information —Robert White⟩ **c :** to work out **:** SOLVE ⟨~ a knotty problem⟩

**³master** \"\ *adj* [ME *maister*, fr. *maister*, n. — more at ¹MASTER] **1 :** being or relating to a master: as **a :** having chief authority or power **:** ruling over others **:** DOMINANT ⟨the theory of a ~ race⟩ **b :** being a master as distinguished from a journeyman and apprentice ⟨a ~ electrician⟩ ⟨a ~ plumber⟩ **c :** being a person notably or supremely proficient in something **:** consummately accomplished or skilled ⟨flute music played by a ~ minstrel —Lavinia R. Davis⟩ ⟨a ~ mathematician and craftsman —Eric Hoffer⟩ **d :** being the chief, guiding, or principal one **:** having all others subordinate to oneself **:** PRINCIPAL, CONTROLLING, RULING ⟨the fear of communism is the ~ fear —W.M.Ball⟩ ⟨anatomy and perspective are almost the ~ subjects —Reyner Banham⟩ ⟨it was the ~ design and . . . thousands of westerns would be modeled on it —Fanny K. Wister⟩ **e :** being something in a superlative degree — often used in combination ⟨a saturnine *master*-bore —D.B.W.Lewis⟩ ⟨a *master*-liar⟩ **f :** being a device or mechanism that controls the operation of another mechanism ⟨the pressure exerted by the brake fluid from the ~ cylinder acting on the rear face of the slave cylinder piston —Irving Frazee⟩ **g :** being a mechanical part or a device that establishes a dimension, weight, or other standard ⟨the use of suitable ~ gears or sample gears is necessary for reference purposes —G.F. Hessler⟩ — compare MASTER GAGE **h :** being or relating to a record (as on magnetic tape) from which duplicates or prints are intended to be made **2** *dial* **:** REMARKABLE, GREAT, NOTABLE, OUTSTANDING ⟨I've seen some ~ crops there —Adrian Bell⟩

**⁴master** \"\ *adv, chiefly dial* **:** EXCEEDINGLY, VERY ⟨a ~ long, rough road —Sarah O. Jewett⟩

**⁵master** \"\ *n* -s [¹*mast* + *-er*] **:** a ship having a specified number of masts — usu. used in combination ⟨a two-*master*⟩

**master agreement** *n* **:** a collective-bargaining agreement the terms of which apply to a number of plants or companies and which may be supplemented by local agreements not conflicting with its provisions

**master–at–arms** \'==='=\ *n, pl* **masters–at–arms :** a petty officer on a man-of-war charged with the maintenance of order, discipline, the custody of prisoners, and similar duties

**¹masterbatch** \'==,=\ *n* [³*master* + *batch*] **:** a mixture that consists of rubber or plastic with one or more compounding ingredients in definite proportions but higher concentrations than in a normal mix and that is used for convenience in compounding

**²masterbatch** \"\ *vt* **:** to mix into a masterbatch

**master bedroom** *n* **:** the principal bedroom in a house usu. occupied by the head of the household

**master builder** *n* **:** a person notably proficient in the art of building ⟨the ancient Egyptians were *master builders*⟩; *specif* **:** one who has attained proficiency in one of the building crafts and is qualified or licensed to supervise building construction

**master chief petty officer** *n* **:** a chief petty officer of the second highest rank

**master chief petty officer of the coast guard :** a petty officer of the highest enlisted rank in the coast guard — see RANK table

**master chief petty officer of the navy :** a petty officer of the highest enlisted rank in the navy — see RANK table

**master clock** *n* **:** a clock that regulates or gives movement esp. by electricity to distant clocks

**master container** *n* **:** a primary shipping container into which is packed a number of cases each carrying units of the packaged goods

**mas·ter·dom** \'mastə(r)dəm, -aas-, -ães-, -ås-\ *n* -s [ME *maisterdom*, fr. OE *mægsterdōm* function of a teacher, fr. *mægester*, *magister* master, teacher, ruler + *-dōm* -dom — more at MASTER] **:** the state or position of being master **:** MASTERY, SUPREMACY

**mastered** *past of* MASTER

**mas·ter·ful** \-fəl\ *adj* [ME *maisterful*, fr. *maister* master + *-ful* — more at MASTER] **1 a :** inclined to play the master ⟨her mother was a ~ woman —R.W.Southern⟩ ⟨no one thought of asking the ~ gentleman where his authority was —J.H.Wheelwright⟩ **b :** reflecting or suggesting an imperious or domineering character ⟨a young maid who has ~ ways —E.K.Brown⟩ ⟨his eyes were . . . enticing and ~ —Jack London⟩ **2 :** marked by the display or qualities of vigor and power **:** VIGOROUS, ENERGETIC ⟨a ~ king who put down the lawless barons of the realm⟩ ⟨an epoch of ~ national impulse —Francis Hackett⟩ **3 :** having or reflecting the technical, artistic, or intellectual skill or power of a master **:** MASTERLY ⟨the beadwork of the tribes . . . is ~ —Juan Belaieff⟩ ⟨written in ~ English —George Lenczowski⟩ ⟨a ~ speaker who can move his audiences —R.D.Robinson⟩

**syn** DOMINEERING, IMPERIOUS, PEREMPTORY, IMPERATIVE: MASTERFUL suggests a capacity for commanding, compelling, and unruffled action or an ability to lead or command through strength, force, or skill ⟨the strong, *masterful* personality of Holmes dominated the tragic scene, and all were equally puppets in his hands —A. Conan Doyle⟩ ⟨she was ever a *masterful* woman, better fitted to command than to obey —H.O.Taylor⟩ ⟨the major was a *masterful* man; and I knew that he would not give orders for nothing —Rudyard Kipling⟩ DOMINEERING suggests attempts, successful or not, or desires, fulfilled or not, to subdue others by insolent or tyrannical behavior ⟨the European nations, arrogant, *domineering*, and rapacious, have done little to recommend the name of Christianity in Asia and Africa —W.R.Inge⟩ ⟨Gourlay had to pay for his years of insolence and tyranny; all who had irked beneath his *domineering* ways got their carrying done by Wilson —G.D.Brown⟩ IMPERIOUS suggests assumption with lordly arrogance and autocratic impatience at opposition of command and domination over others ⟨he had to go. There was something final about her *imperious* courtesy — high- and-mighty, he called it —Willa Cather⟩ ⟨a second Coriolanus, a proud, *imperious* aristocrat, contemptuous, above all men living, of popular rights —J.A.Froude⟩ PEREMPTORY suggests dictatorial curtness in insisting on instant compliance with commands or wishes and impatience at delay or demur ⟨the *peremptory* tone in which money was demanded for the cost of this fruitless march, while the petitions of the Parliament were set aside till it was granted, roused the temper of the Commons —J.R.Green⟩ ⟨"I decline to listen to another word. I've heard enough." The bishop accompanied the mandate by a *peremptory* gesture with the palm of the hand —Robert Grant †1940⟩ IMPERATIVE may be a close synonym for PEREMPTORY; it may be used in reference to urgent situations calling for firm briskness ⟨"An envelope and telegram form, quick!" Overwhelmed by my *imperative* manner, he handed me the required articles —Allen Upward⟩ ⟨he heard her *imperative* voice at the telephone; he heard her summon the doctor —Ellen Glasgow⟩

**mas·ter·ful·ly** \-fəlē, -li\ *adv* [ME *maisterfully*, fr. *maisterful* masterful + *-ly*] **:** in a masterful manner

**mas·ter·ful·ness** *n* -ES **:** the quality or state of being masterful

**master gage** *n* **:** a very accurate gage used only as a standard of reference for working gages

**master gland** *n* [so called fr. the fact that it produces hormones that modify and integrate the activity of other endocrine organs] **:** PITUITARY GLAND

**master gunner** *n* **:** a warrant officer in the British artillery

**master gunnery sergeant** *n* **:** a sergeant major in the marine corps

**master–hand** \'==¦=\ *n* **1 :** the hand, ability, or agency of a master ⟨the touch of the *master-hand* . . . was conspicuously absent from the picture —Herschel Brickell⟩ **2 :** MASTER ⟨a *master-hand* at . . . fictionalized biography —*Saturday Rev.*⟩

**mas·ter·hood** \'==,hu̇d\ *n* [ME *maystyrhod*, fr. *maystyr*, *maister* master + *-hod* -hood] **:** the quality or state of being a master

**master in chancery 1 :** an officer of a court of equity appointed to assist the court (as by finding the facts in a contested case or by executing a conveyance or transfer of property owned by a defendant who has refused to convey or transfer under the decree of the court) **2 :** a public officer in Massachusetts appointed by the governor with the consent of the council to take recognizances and bail

**mastering** *pres part of* MASTER

**master key** *n* **1 :** a key made so that it will open several locks differing somewhat from each other **2 :** something of decisive or key importance in the solution of a difficulty, problem, or dispute ⟨one of the *master keys* to the outcome of the . . . struggle —*Current History*⟩ ⟨the *master key* that explained the many mysteries of recent history —Oscar Handlin⟩

**master–key** \'==,=\ *vt* [*master key*] **:** to design or fit (a series of locks) for a master key

**master leaf** *n* **:** BACK 2i

**mas·ter·less** \'==ləs\ *adj* [ME *maisterles*, fr. *maister* master + *-les* -less] **1 a :** lacking a master ⟨a ~ horse⟩ **b** *archaic* **:** being without a master or other reputable means of livelihood **:** VAGABOND, VAGRANT ⟨provided harsh punishments for sturdy vagabonds and ~ men⟩ **2** *obs* **:** UNGOVERNED, UNGOVERNABLE — **mas·ter·less·ness** *n* -ES

**masterlike** *adj* [ME *maisterlike*, fr. *maister* master + *like*] *obs* **:** MASTERFUL, MASTERLY

**mas·ter·li·ness** \'mastə(r)lēnəs, -aas-, -ais-, -ås-, -lin-\ *n* -ES **:** the quality or state of being masterly

**¹mas·ter·ly** \-lē, -li\ *adv* [ME *maisterly*, fr. *maister* master + *-ly*] **:** with the skill of a master **:** in a masterly fashion

**²masterly** \"\ *adj* [¹*master* + *-ly*] **1** *obs* **:** of or relating to a master or lord; *specif* **:** DOMINEERING **2 :** suitable to or like that of a master **:** indicating thorough knowledge or superior skill and power ⟨a ~ retreat⟩ ⟨a ~ argument⟩ ⟨~ handling of a complex topic⟩ **syn** see PROFICIENT

**mas·ter·man** \'==mən\ *n, pl* **mastermen** *dial Eng* **:** the head of a household **:** HUSBAND

**master map** *n* **:** an original usu. large-scale map which is made directly from surveys and from which other maps are derived

**master mariner** *n* [ME *maister mariner*, fr. *maister* master + *mariner*, *marinere* mariner] **1 :** a captain of a merchant ship **2 :** an experienced and skilled seaman certified to be competent to command a merchant ship

**master mason** *n* **1 :** a mason thoroughly competent in his trade and usu. in business on his own account **2** *usu cap both Ms* **a :** the third degree of Freemasonry — compare BLUE LODGE **b :** a Freemason who has been raised to the third degree

**master matrix** *n* **:** a matrix obtained by electroplating an original lacquer or wax recording of sound

**master mechanic** *n* **1 :** a foreman mechanic **2 :** a mechanic who is a thorough master of his trade

**¹mastermind** \'==¦=\ *n* [³*master* + *mind*] **1 :** a mind or person of masterly powers **:** a towering intellect ⟨the ~ of the thirteenth century —Agnes Repplier⟩ **2 :** a person who supplies the directing or creative intelligence for a project or for a group of persons undertaking a project ⟨~ of the world's first commercial jet airliner —*Newsweek*⟩

**²mastermind** \'==,=\ *vt* **:** to be the mastermind in or of **:** DIRECT, SUPERVISE, ENGINEER ⟨~*ed* . . . crimes such as warehouse burglaries —Alan Hynd⟩ ⟨~*ing* an insidious campaign to gain dominance over the world —L.M.Clucas⟩

**master of arts** *usu cap M&A* **1 :** the recipient of a master's degree that usu. signifies that the recipient has passed a certain number of courses in one of the humanities — abbr. *M.A.*, *A.M.* **2 :** the degree making one a Master of Arts — abbr. *M.A.*, *A.M.*

**master of ceremonies :** a person who determines the forms to be observed on a public occasion or superintends their observance: as **a :** a court official of high rank in charge of the reception of ambassadors and other matters of protocol **b :** an official at solemn services of the Roman Catholic Church charged with the duty of seeing that all the rites are correctly executed **c :** a person who acts as host at a formal event (as a banquet or graduation exercise) making the welcoming speech, introducing speakers, and being generally responsible for the conduct of the program **d :** a person who acts as a host for a variety program or other stage entertainment introducing other performers to the audience and usu. interspersing his introductions with jokes, songs, or other specialty acts

**master of request** *or* **master of requests :** a principal officer in the court of requests

**master of science** *usu cap M&S* **1 :** the recipient of a master's degree that usu. signifies that the recipient has passed a certain number of courses in one of the sciences or in closely related sciences — abbr. *M.S.*, *M.Sc.* **2 :** the degree making one a Master of Science — abbr. *M.S.*, *M.Sc.*

**master of the revels 1 :** an officer of the English royal household from the 15th to the 18th centuries in charge of court entertainment — see REVELS OFFICE **2 :** an officer in charge of court entertainment at a monarchical household

**master of the rolls** [ME *Maister of the Rolles*] **:** a high official of the British judiciary having custody of the records of the Court of Chancery and important patents and grants and serving usu. as presiding judge of the Court of Appeal and also as a member of the Judicial Committee of the Privy Council — compare LORD CHANCELLOR, LORD CHIEF JUSTICE OF ENGLAND

**master oscillator** *n* **:** a low-power generator of alternating current that is usu. an electron-tube apparatus the output of which is fed into an amplifier

**masterpiece** \'==,=\ *n* [prob. trans. of D *meesterstuk* or G *meisterstück*] **1 :** a piece of work attesting to a craftsman's professional skill and presented to his guild to qualify for admission to the rank of master ⟨a ~ was nothing more than a graduation piece —Virgil Thomson⟩ **2 a :** something done or made with extraordinary skill or brilliance **:** a supreme achievement ⟨a ~ of organization —O.S.Nock⟩ ⟨delicious onion sandwiches are perhaps her ~ —Jane Nickerson⟩ ⟨a ~ of ecclesiastical statesmanship —T.S.Eliot⟩ **b :** a work of art of notable excellence or brilliance **:** a supreme intellectual or artistic achievement ⟨the world's symphonic ~*s*⟩ ⟨the ~*s* of Elizabethan drama⟩ ⟨the artist may have many ~*s* —*Encyc. Americana*⟩; *specif* **:** an artist's most accomplished or climactic work marking the high point of his creativity ⟨this delay in printing what was to prove his ~ —H.S.Canby⟩ ⟨his ~ . . . scarcely fulfills one of the conditions set forth in handbooks of rhetoric —*English Jour.*⟩ **3 :** something that is a consummate example of or embodies in superlative degree some quality or trait ⟨~*s* of inept versification —*Amer. Guide Series: Mich.*⟩ ⟨his ~ of bad writing —Edmund Wilson⟩ ⟨a ~ of fence-sitting —*Amer. Guide Series: N.C.*⟩

**master plan** *n* **:** an overall plan into which the details of other specific plans are fitted **:** a plan giving overall guidance; *specif* **:** a graphic or verbal scheme for the development of a city, town, or other building project of an evolutionary nature

**masterplate** \'==,=\ *n* **:** a plate (as of metal) containing stencil letters or a design to be copied by tracing

**master point** *n* **:** a point that is permanently credited to a bridge player for winning or placing high in a tournament, the accumulation of such points forming a basis for national ranking — compare LIFE MASTER

**master policy** *n* **:** a blanket insurance policy issued to an employer providing group coverage for employees — see GROUP 1

**masterprize** *n, obs* **:** MASTERPIECE

**master–ring** \'==,=\ *n* **:** a cylindrical ring surrounding the plug in a master-keyed lock

**masters** *pl of* MASTER, *pres 3d sing of* MASTER

**master's deed** *n* **:** a deed of conveyance executed by a master in chancery in pursuance of an order of the court commanding one of the parties to make the conveyance or the master to do it in his name

**master sergeant** *n* **:** a noncommissioned officer rating in the army just below a command sergeant major and above a platoon sergeant, in the air force just below a senior master sergeant and above a technical sergeant, and in the marine corps just below a sergeant major and above a gunnery sergeant

**mas·ter·ship** \'==,ship\ *n* [ME *maistershipe*, fr. *maister* master + *-shipe* -ship] **1 :** the authority or control of a master **:** DOMINION, SUPERIORITY ⟨sent forth the warning of his ~ —William Beebe⟩ **2 a** *obs* **:** the personality of a master — used as a title of courtesy **b :** the status, office, function, or dignity of a master ⟨the competitive examination which grants the rights to a ~ —*Current Biog.*⟩ **3 :** the skill, dexterity, or knowledge of a master **:** MASTERY ⟨with authority, eloquence, and ~ —Irving Kolodin⟩

**mastersinger** \'==,==\ *n* [trans. of G *meistersinger*] **:** MEISTERSINGER

**master–slave manipulator** \'==¦=-\ *n* **:** a manipulator for very accurate remote control of duplicated operations used esp. in handling materials in nuclear laboratories

**master station** *n* **:** the transmitting station in a group of synchronized transmitters in an electronic communication system (as in radio navigation) that controls the emission of all the stations — compare SLAVE STATION

**masterstroke** \'==¦=\ *n* **:** a masterly action or achievement **:** brilliant performance or move ⟨by a ~, precisely timed, he helped to create the Republican party —W.O.Lynch⟩ ⟨a ~ of craftsmanship —F.J.Hynes⟩

**master switch** *n* **:** a switch that controls the action of relays or that makes and breaks the main supply line to a building or other installation

**master–tailor** \'==¦==\ *n* **:** a salt marsh fiddler crab (*Uca princeps*) common along the coast of western Central and So. America

**master tap** *n* **:** a tap designed to cut dies from which other screws can be threaded

**masterwork** \'==,=\ *n* **:** MASTERPIECE

**masterwort** \'==,=\ *n* **:** any of several herbaceous plants (family Umbelliferae) used esp. formerly in medicine: **a :** a coarse European plant (*Imperatoria ostruthium*) with large ternate leaves **b :** a European herb (*Astrantia major*) that has dark-colored aromatic roots and leaves mostly in a basal tuft and is sometimes cultivated for its showy compound umbels of white to rosy flowers **c :** COW PARSNIP **d :** ANGELICA 2

**mas·tery** \'mast(ə)rē, -aas-, -ais-, -ås-, -ri\ *n* -ES [ME *maistrie*, fr. OF, fr. *maistre* master + *-ie* -y — more at MASTER] **1 a :** the status, position, or authority of a master **:** CONTROL, DOMINION, SWAY ⟨a sense of ~ and power —B.N.Cardozo⟩ ⟨obtained absolute ~ of the government —J.H.Plumb⟩ ⟨little could be done to undermine that ~ —P.G.Mackesy⟩ **b :** the upper hand in a contest or competition **:** SUPERIORITY, ASCENDANCY ⟨a violent spirit in him was struggling for the ~ —Gilbert Parker⟩ **c** *archaic* **:** superior force or power **2 a** *obs* **:** a notable achievement or feat **b :** the possession or a display of skill or technique **:** freedom from flaws or imperfections ⟨cannot attain to the ~ of the great artists —Matthew Arnold⟩ ⟨greater intellectual and stylistic ~ than ever before —A.L.Locke⟩ ⟨uses . . . with absolute ~, the rhythms of actual speech —Randall Jarrell⟩ **c :** the skill or knowledge in a subject that makes one a master in it **:** COMMAND ⟨~ . . . over the difficult art —Benjamin Farrington⟩ ⟨~ of managerial techniques —W.H.Whyte⟩ ⟨a high degree of ~ in the field —*Bull. of Meharry Med. Coll.*⟩

**mast–fed** \(')=¦=\ *adj* [³*mast*] **:** fed with mast

**¹masthead** \'=,=\ *n* [¹*mast*] **1 a :** the top or head of a mast **:** the part of a mast above the hounds **b :** a sailor stationed at the masthead **2 a :** a block of matter usu. printed in the top lefthand corner of the editorial page of a newspaper or beside or near the table of contents of a periodical and consisting of the title of the publication and its address, the date of the issue, and sometimes the names of owners and editors and the subscription and advertising rates **b :** the nameplate of a newspaper or periodical

**²masthead** \"\ *vt* **1 :** to cause to go to or stand at the masthead as a punishment **2 :** to hoist (as a yard or flag) to the masthead

**masthead bombing** *n* **:** extremely low-level bombing of ships usu. with delayed-fuse bombs that explode below the waterline

**mast hoop** *n* **:** one of a number of hoops attached to the fore edge of a gaff sail which slip on the mast; *also* **:** one of the iron hoops used in making a made mast

**mast hounds** *n pl* [¹*mast*] **:** HOUNDS

**mast house** *n* **:** a small deckhouse built around a mast to serve as a support for derricks or sometimes as a winch platform and used for housing electric control equipment where electric winches are fitted

**-mas·tia** \ˌmastēə, ˌmaas-\ *n comb form* -s [NL, fr. Gk *mastos* breast + NL *-ia* — more at MEAT] **:** condition of having (such or so many) breasts or mammary glands ⟨gyneco*mastia*⟩ ⟨tetra*mastia*⟩

**mas·tic** \'mastik, -aas-, -tēk\ *n* -s [ME *mastik*, fr. L *mastiche*, fr. Gk *mastichē*; fr. its use as chewing gum; akin to Gk *mastichan* to gnash the teeth] **1** *also* **mas·tich** \"\ *or* **mas·ti·che** \-tə,kē\ **:** an aromatic resinous exudation obtained usu. in the form of yellowish to greenish lustrous transparent brittle tears from incisions in mastic trees and used chiefly in varnishes (as for protecting oil paintings and water colors) **2 :** MASTIC TREE **3 :** any of various pasty materials used as protective coatings (as for thermal insulation or waterproofing) or as cements (as for setting tile or glass): as **a :** ASPHALT MASTIC **b :** a composition of mineral matter bound by a resinous medium in a volatile solvent **4 :** an alcoholic liquor flavored with resin mastic and aniseed **5 :** a light olive brown that is lighter, stronger, and slightly redder than drab or sponge and redder and paler than average mustard tan

**mas·ti·cate** \'mastə,kāt, -aas-, -ais-, *usu* -ād.+V\ *vb* -ED/-ING/-S [LL *masticatus*, past part. of *masticare*, fr. Gk *mastichan* to gnash the teeth; akin to Gk *masasthai* to chew — more at MOUTH] *vt* **1 :** to grind or crush (as food) with or as if with the teeth and prepare for swallowing and digestion **:** CHEW **2 a :** to reduce to pulp by crushing or kneading **b :** to work (rubber) on a machine so as to make it softer and more plastic before mixing with compounding ingredients **:** break down ~ *vi* **:** to make the motions involved in masticating food **:** CHEW

**mas·ti·ca·tion** \ˌ==ˈkāshən\ *n* -s [LL *mastication-*, *masticatio*, fr. *masticatus* + L *-ion-*, *-io* -ion] **:** the act of process of masticating or the state of being masticated

**mas·ti·ca·tor** \'==,kād.ə(r)\ *n* -s [*masticate* + *-or*] **:** one that masticates: as **a :** a machine for chopping materials (as meat or rubber) into fine bits **b :** an operator of such a machine

**¹mas·ti·ca·to·ry** \'==kə,tōrē, -tȯr-, -ri, *chiefly Brit* ¦==¦kātəri *or* -ā·tri\ *adj* [*masticate* + *-ory*] **1 :** used for chewing **:** adapted to mastication ⟨~ limbs of an arthropod⟩ **2 :** of, relating to, or involving the organs of mastication ⟨~ paralysis⟩

**²masticatory** \"\ *n* -ES **:** a substance to be chewed to increase the saliva

**mastic bully** *n* **:** a tree (*Sideroxylon mastichodendron*) of Florida and the West Indies having hard wood used for shipbuilding

**mastic gum** *n* **:** MASTIC 1

**mas·tic·ic** \(')ma¦stisik\ *adj* **:** of or relating to mastic

**mas·tic·o·phis** \maˈstikəfəs, ˌmastəˈkōf-\ *n, cap* [NL, fr. *mastic-* (irreg. fr. Gk *mastig-*, *mastix* whip) + *-ophis*] **:** a common genus of harmless New World snakes (family Colubridae) comprising the whip snakes and related forms

**mastic tree** *or* **mastic shrub** *n* **1 :** a small tree (*Pistacia lentiscus*) of southern Europe that yields mastic and has leaves that are used as an adulterant of sumac **2 :** GUMBO-LIMBO 1

**mas·ti·cu·ra** \ˌmastəˈkyu̇rə\ *n, pl, cap* [NL, fr. *mastic-* (irreg. fr. Gk *mastig-*, *mastix* whip) + *-ura*] *in some classifications* **:** a division (usu. a suborder) of rays including the stingrays and having the tail long and like a whip — compare SARCURA — **mas·ti·cu·rous** \¦==¦kyu̇rəs\ *adj*

**mas·tiff** \'mastəf, -aas-, -ais-, *sometimes* -ås-\ *n* -s [ME *mastif*, modif. (influenced by ME *-if* -ive) of MF *mastin*, fr. (assumed) VL *mansuetinus*, fr. L *mansuetus* tame — more at MANSUETE] **:** a very large powerful deep-chested smooth-coated dog of a very old breed used chiefly as a watchdog and guard dog

mastiff

**mastiff bat** *n* **1 :** a member of a nearly cosmopolitan family of bats (Molossidae) having fur like plush, narrow wings, and short ridged ears with angular tips **2 :** HARELIPPED BAT

**mastig-** *or* **mastigo-** *comb form* [Gk, whip, scourge, fr. *mastig-, mastix;* perh. akin to Gk *mēnyein* to make known, inform, Russ *manit'* to beckon, entice] **:** whip **:** flagellum ⟨*Mastigo*phora⟩ ⟨*Mastig*amoeba⟩

**mas·tig·amoeba** \¦mastə̇g+\ *n, cap* [NL, fr. *mastig-* + *amoeba*] **:** the type genus of the family Mastigamoebidae

**mas·tig·amoe·bi·dae** *n pl, cap* \ˌmastə̇gə'mēbəˌdē\ [NL, fr. *Mastigamoeba*, type genus + *-idae*] **:** a family of amoeboid zooflagellates that have both pseudopods and a flagellum — see HISTOMONAS

**mas·tig·i·um** \ma'stijēəm\ *n, pl* **mastig·ia** \-jēə\ [NL, fr. Gk *mastigion* small whip, dim. of *mastig-, mastix*] **:** a defensive organ resembling a lash on the posterior parts of certain lepidopterous larvae

**mas·ti·go·bran·chia** \ˌmastə̇gō'braŋkēə\ *n, pl* **mastigo·branchi·ae** \-kēˌē\ [NL, fr. *mastig-* + *-branchia* (gill)] **:** a process of the thoracic limbs of decapod crustaceans resembling a brush and used for cleaning the gills — **mas·ti·go·bran·chi·al** \¦=≈=¦braŋkēəl\ *adj*

**mas·ti·go·neme** \'=≈=ˌnēm\ *n* -s [F *mastigonème*, fr. *mastig-* + *-nème* (fr. Gk *nēma* thread) — more at NEEDLE] **:** FLIMMER

**mas·ti·goph·o·ra** \ˌ==ˈgäf(ə)rə\ *n pl, cap* [NL, fr. *mastig-* + *-phora*] **:** a class of Protozoa comprising organisms characterized by possession of flagella and including the subclasses Phytomastigina and Zoomastigina — **mas·ti·goph·o·rous** \¦==¦gäf(ə)rəs\ *adj*

**1mas·ti·goph·o·ran** \¦==¦gäf(ə)rən\ *adj* [NL *Mastigophora* + E *-an*, adj. suffix] **:** of or relating to the Mastigophora

**2mastigophoran** \"\ *n* -s [NL *Mastigophora* + E *-an*, n. suffix] **:** a flagellate of the class Mastigophora

**mas·ti·go·phor·ic** \¦==gō¦fȯrik\ *adj* [NL *Mastigophora* + E *-ic*] **:** bearing a flagellum

**mas·ti·go·proc·tus** \ˌ=≈='präktəs\ *n, cap* [NL, fr. *mastig-* + *-proctus*] **:** a genus containing the giant whip scorpion

**mas·tig·o·pus** \ma'stigəpəs\ *n* -ES [NL, fr. *mastig-* + *-pus*] **:** a final larva of some shrimps and prawns that is very like the adult in form

**mas·tigo·some** \ma'stigəˌsōm, 'mastə̇gōˌ-\ *n* -s [*mastig-* + *-some*] **:** BASAL GRANULE

**mas·ti·gote** \'mastə̇ˌgōt\ *adj* [irreg. fr. *mastig-*] **:** having a flagellum

**mas·ti·gure** \'==ˌgyu̇(ə)r\ *n* -s [NL *Mastigura* (syn. of *Uromastix*), fr. *mastig-* + *-ura*] **:** any of the large spiny-tailed herbivorous agamid lizards (genus *Uromastix*) of southern Asia and northern Africa

**mas·ti·ka** \'mastə̇kə\ *n* -s [prob. fr. Turk, lit., mastic (sense 1), fr. Gk *mastichē* — more at MASTIC] **:** MASTIC 4

**masting** *n* -s **:** the masts of a ship

**mas·tit·ic** \(')ma¦stid·ik\ *adj* [*mastit*is + *-ic*] **:** of, relating to, or associated with mastitis ⟨~ milk⟩

**mas·ti·tis** \ma'stīd·ə̇s\ *n, pl* **mastit·i·des** \-'stid·əˌdēz\ [NL, fr. *mast-* + *-itis*] **:** inflammation of the breast or udder usu. caused by infection — see BLUE BAG, GARGET, SUMMER MASTITIS; compare BOVINE MASTITIS, CAKED BREAST

**-mas·tix** \¦mastiks\ *n comb form* [Gk *mastig-, mastix* whip, scourge] **1** -ES **:** attacker of a (specified) person or thing ⟨Latino*mastix*⟩ **2** [NL, fr. Gk *mastig-, mastix*] **a :** one having (such) a whip — in generic names in zoology ⟨Uro*mastix*⟩ **b :** one having (such) a flagellum or (such or so many) flagella — in generic names in zoology ⟨Chilo*mastix*⟩

**mast·less** \'mastlə̇s, -aas-, -ais-, -ȧs-\ *adj* [1*mast*] **:** having no mast ⟨a ~ ship⟩

**masto-** — see MAST-

**mas·to·cyte** \'mastəˌsīt\ *n* -s [*masto-* (fr. G *mast* food, mast, fr. OHG) + *-cyte;* intended as trans. of G *mastzelle* mast cell — more at MAST (nuts)] **:** MAST CELL

**1mas·to·don** \'mastəˌdän, 'maas-, -ˌdən\ *n* -s [NL *Mastodont-, Mastodon* (syn. of *Mammut*), fr. *mast-* + *-odont-, -odon* -odon; fr. the nipple-shaped projections on the molar teeth] **1 :** any of numerous extinct mammals esp. of the genus *Mammut* that greatly resemble elephants, differ from the mammoths and existing elephants chiefly in the form of the molar teeth, have sometimes small tusks in the lower jaw besides those in the upper jaw, and are widely distributed in Oligocene to late Pleistocene formations **2 :** someone or something of gigantic size or unusually large size **:** GIANT ⟨military vehicles from little jeeps to six-wheel armored ~*s* —Gelett Burgess⟩ ⟨the ~*s* in the ring sweated their way into the next match —J.K. Hutchins⟩ — **mas·to·don·ic** \¦==¦dänik\ *adj*

**2mastodon** \"\ [NL *Mastodont-, Mastodon*] *syn of* MAMMUT

**3mastodon** \"\ *adj* [1*mastodon*] **:** MAMMOTH ⟨this is the time of the ~ movie —*Newsweek*⟩

**mas·to·don·sau·rus** \ˌ==ˌdän'sȯrəs\ *n, cap* [NL, fr. *Mastodon* + *-saurus*] **:** a genus of Old World Triassic amphibians containing the largest known labyrinthodonts with the skull over four feet long and having at the front of the lower jaw a pair of short tusks that close into openings piercing the premaxillae

**1mas·to·dont** \'==ˌdänt\ *adj* [NL *Mastodont-, Mastodon*] **1 :** having or being teeth like a mastodon's **2 :** of or relating to the mastodons

**2mastodont** \"\ *n* -s [NL *Mastodont-, Mastodon*] **:** MASTODON — **mas·to·don·tic** \¦==¦däntik\ *adj*

**mas·to·don·ti·dae** \ˌ=='däntəˌdē\ [NL, fr. *Mastodont-, Mastodon* + *-idae*] *syn of* MAMMUTIDAE — see MAMMUT

**mas·to·don·toid** \¦==¦dänˌtȯid\ *adj* [NL *Mastodont-, Mastodon* + E *-oid*] **:** like a mastodon

**mas·to·dyn·ia** \ˌ=='dinēə\ *n* -s [NL, fr. *mast-* + *-odynia*] **:** pain in the breast

**1mas·toid** \'maˌstȯid, 'maaˌ-\ *adj* [NL *mastoides*, fr. Gk *mastoeidēs*, fr. *mastos* breast + *-oeidēs* -oid — more at MEAT] **1 a :** resembling a nipple or breast; *specif* **:** being a process of the temporal bone behind the ear, well developed and of somewhat conical form in adult man but inconspicuous in children **b :** being any of several bony elements (as the pterotic bone) occupying a similar position in the skull of various lower vertebrates **2 :** of, relating to, in the region of, or affecting the mastoid process

**2mastoid** \"\ *n* -s **1 :** a mastoid bone or process **2 a :** MASTOIDITIS ⟨recovering from a severe ~⟩ — not used technically **b :** an operation for the relief of mastoiditis

**mas·toi·dal** \(')=¦stȯidᵊl\ *also* **mas·toi·de·al** \-dēəl\ *or* **mas·toi·de·an** \-dēən\ *adj* [*mastoidal* fr. 2*mastoid* + *-al; mastoideal, mastoidean* fr. NL *mastoideus*, adj., mastoid (fr. *mastoides* + L *-eus* -eous) + E *-al* or *-an*] **:** MASTOID

**mas·toi·da·le** \ˌmaˌstȯi'da(ˌ)lē, -dā-, -dä-\ *n* -s [NL, fr. *mastoides* + *-ale* (fr. L, neut. of *-alis* -al)] **:** the lowest point of the mastoid process — see CRANIOMETRY illustration

**mastoid antrum** *n* **:** TYMPANIC ANTRUM

**mastoid cell** *n* **:** one of the small cavities in the mastoid process that develop after birth and are filled with air

**mas·toid·ec·to·my** \ˌ=ˌstȯi'dektəmē, -mi\ *n* -ES [ISV 1*mastoid* + *-ectomy*] **:** surgical removal of the mastoid cells or of the mastoid process

**mas·toi·deo·squamous** \ma¦stȯidēō+\ *adj* [*mastoideo-* (fr. NL *mastoideus*) + *squamous*] **:** relating to the mastoid and squamous portions of the temporal bone

**mas·toid·i·tis** \ˌmaˌstȯi'dīd·ə̇s, ˌmaaˌ-\ *n, pl* **mas·toid·it·i·des** \-'did·əˌdēz\ [NL, fr. *mastoides* + *-itis*] **:** inflammation of the mastoid or esp. of the mastoid cells

**mas·toi·do·hu·mer·a·lis** \ma'stȯidōˌhyümə'ralə̇s, -rāl-, -räl-\ *n* -ES [NL, fr. *mastoido-* (fr. *mastoides*) + *humeralis* humeral, fr. *humerus* + L *-alis* -al] **:** a long superficial muscle connecting the mastoid process and humerus in many quadruped mammals

**mas·toid·ot·o·my** \ˌmaˌstȯi'däd·əmē, ˌmaaˌ-\ *n* -ES [ISV 1*mastoid* + *-o-* + *-tomy*] **:** incision of any part of the mastoid

**mas·to·mys** \'mastəˌmis\ *n* [NL, fr. *mast-* + *-mys*] **1** *cap, in some classifications* **:** a genus of rodents comprising the multimammate mice **2** *pl* **mastomys :** MULTIMAMMATE MOUSE

**mas·to·tympanic** \¦ma(ˌ)stō+\ *adj* [*mast-* + *tympanic*] **:** of, relating to, or being a bony element bounding the tympanic cavity in the skull of certain reptiles

**mast partner** *n* **:** wood planking or steel plating around a mast hole in a deck to give support to a mast

**mast step** *n* **:** a wood or steel foundation on which a mast rests

**mast table** *n* **:** a small compartment or locker built on the main deck around the base of one of the masts

**mast tree** *n* [3*mast*] **1 :** a tree that produces mast; *specif* **:** CORK OAK **2 :** an East Indian shade tree (*Polyalthia longifolia*) of the family Annonaceae

**mas·tur·bate** \'mastə(r)ˌbāt, *usu* -ād·+V\ *vb* -ED/-ING/-S [L *masturbatus*, past part. of *masturbari*, perh. fr. *manus* hand + *stuprare* to defile, deflower, fr. *stuprum* defilement, dishonor — more at MANUAL, TYPE] *vi* **:** to practice masturbation ~ *vt* **:** to practice masturbation on

**mas·tur·bat·ic** \¦==¦bad·ik\ *adj* **:** involving masturbation

**mas·tur·ba·tion** \ˌ=='bāshən\ *n* -s [prob. fr. (assumed) NL *masturbation-, masturbatio*, fr. L *masturbatus* + *-ion-, -io* -ion] **:** erotic stimulation involving the genital organs commonly resulting in orgasm and achieved by manual or other bodily contact exclusive of sexual intercourse, by instrumental manipulation, occas. by sexual fantasies, or by various combinations of these agencies — **mas·tur·ba·tion·al** \¦==¦bāshənᵊl, -shnəl\ *adj*

**mas·tur·ba·to·ry** \'==bəˌtōrē, -tȯr-, -ri\ *adj* **:** of, relating to, or involving masturbation

**mastwood** \'=ˌ=\ *n* [1*mast*] **:** a poon tree (*Calophyllum inophyllum*) — called also *kamani*

**1masty** *adj* [ME, fattened on mast, fr. 3*mast* + *-y*] *obs* **:** abounding in or fattened on mast

**2mas·ty** \'masti\ *n* -ES [ME, modif. of MF *mastin* — more at MASTIFF] *now dial Eng* **:** MASTIFF

**ma·sur birch** \'mä¦zə(r)-, 'mā¦'\ *n* [part trans. of Sw *masurbjörk*, fr. *masur* veined wood + *björk* birch; akin to OHG *masar* gnarled excrescence on a tree — more at MAZER] **:** birch with a mottled figure cut from knotty trunks and used esp. for veneers

**ma·su·ri·an** \mə'zu̇rēən, -'su̇-\ *n* -s *usu cap* [*Masuria*, region in Olsztyn department, northern Poland + E *-an*] **:** MAZURIAN

**ma·su·ri·um** \mə'zu̇rēəm, -'su̇-\ *n* -s [NL, fr. *Masuria*, region in Olsztyn department, northern Poland + NL *-ium*] **:** chemical element 43 — a name now superseded by *technetium*

**masut** *var of* MAZUT

**1mat** \'mat, *usu* -ad·+V\ *n* -s [ME, fr. OE *matt, matte, meatte*, fr. LL *matta*, of Sem origin; akin to Heb *miṭṭāh* bed, couch] **1 :** a flat relatively thin article of usu. pliant typically coarse material and rectangular, oval, or other shape that is set or laid esp. on a horizontal surface as a protection or a support or cushion, or as a decorative feature, or marker: as **a** (1) **:** a piece of coarse fabric that is typically made by weaving or plaiting straw, hemp, rope, rushes, or other similar material, and is used as a floor covering or as an article on which to sit or lie or stand (2) **:** a piece of material that is typically made of meshed metal strips or twisted wire or of corrugated or perforated rubber so as to present a roughly ridged or furrowed surface and is placed at the entrance to a building for cleaning the bottoms of one's shoes **b :** a relatively small piece of woven, knitted, or felted cloth or of leather or finely woven or plaited straw or similar material made to have an ornamental appearance and used as a decorative and protective support (as for dishes and utensils on a table set for a meal) **c :** a piece of rubber or other material on which a lawn bowler places one foot when bowling a ball **d :** a large usu. rectangular pad or cushion several inches thick that is made of sponge rubber, kapok, felt, or other similar material typically covered with canvas or plastic and is laid out over an area of a floor (as in a gymnasium) so as to protect wrestlers, tumblers, or others engaged in gymnastic activities from injuring themselves through concussions (as from falls) **2** *obs* **:** material used in making mats **:** MATTING **3 a :** a webbing of rope yarn used to protect rigging from chafing **b :** MATTRESS 2b **c :** a mesh of heavy chain, cables, or rope used to confine debris in blasting **d :** a large slab made usu. of reinforced concrete and laid on soft ground to support a heavy building **4 a :** a sack used for packing coffee or sugar **b :** the solid part of a lace design **5 :** something made up of many strands thickly intertwined or knotted so as to form a tangled often impenetrable mass ⟨a ~ of unkempt hair⟩ ⟨a ~ of rank jungle undergrowth⟩; *specif* **:** a thick interlacing growth of vegetation either free on the surface of or overlying the margin of a body of water — **go to the mat :** to engage in a hotly fought usu. verbal and ideological struggle ⟨*go to the mat* with those whose arguments do not seem to me to be sound or fair —*Christian Century*⟩ — **on the mat** *adv* (*or adj*) **:** on the carpet ⟨summoned to Washington and put *on the mat* —*Economist*⟩

**2mat** \"\ *vb* **matted; matted; matting; mats** *vt* **1 :** to provide or cover with or as if with a mat or matting: as **a :** to provide with a floor mat or similar mat ⟨the room had been well *matted*⟩ ⟨*matted* the cottage floors⟩ **b** (1) **:** to cover over with the typically coarse material used in making mats ⟨*matting* chair bottoms⟩ (2) **:** to protect (as plants) by covering up with a warm coarse material — usu. used with *up* ⟨*matted* up the bushes before the cold snap began⟩ **c :** to cover over with a tangled often impenetrable mass made up of many thickly intertwined or knotted strands ⟨the old trail had become *matted* with undergrowth⟩ ⟨ivy *matted* the walls of the ancient temple⟩ **2 a** (1) **:** to cause to be thickly intertwined or knotted so as to form a tangled often impenetrable mass ⟨the boughs of the trees were *matted* together⟩ ⟨dirt and filth *matted* their hair⟩ (2) **:** to pack down or together so as to form a dense often impenetrable mass — usu. used with *down* ⟨constant tramping over the area had *matted* down the grass⟩ **b :** to cause (soft particles) to come together and adhere so as to form a soft semisolid mass ⟨*matting* curd particles in the making of cheese⟩ **3 :** to make into a floor mat or similar mat by weaving, plaiting or other interlacing ⟨native women *matting* straw⟩ ~ *vi* **1 a :** to become thickly intertwined or knotted so as to form a tangled often impenetrable mass ⟨untended weeds will eventually ~ together⟩ **b :** to become packed down or together so as to form a dense often impenetrable mass — usu. used with *down* ⟨corduroy pile has a tendency to ~ down in areas subjected to pressure or abrasion —Dorothy S. Lyle⟩ **2 :** to come together and adhere so as to form a soft semisolid mass ⟨piling curd at the side of a cheese-making vat and allowing it to ~⟩

**3mat** *or* **matt** *or* **matte** \"\ *vt* **matted; matted; matting; mats** *or* **matts** *or* **mattes** [F *mater*, fr. OF, to defeat, overcome, fr. (assumed) VL *mattare*, fr. L *mattus* stupid, drunk] **1 :** to cause (as metals, glass, colors) to have a surface or finish or a general appearance that is without luster or gloss **:** give a dulled effect to **2** [5*mat*] **:** to provide (a picture) with a mat

**4mat** *or* **matt** *or* **matte** \"\ *adj* [F *mat*, fr. OF, defeated, overcome, fr. L *mattus* stupid, drunk; akin to L *madēre* to be wet — more at MEAT] **1 :** being without or deprived of luster or gloss **:** having a usu. smooth even surface free from shine or highlights ⟨~ metals⟩ ⟨~ colors⟩ ⟨~ glass⟩ ⟨the ~ white face of a circus clown⟩ **2 :** having a coarse rough rugose or granular surface ⟨a bacterium that forms ~ colonies on agar⟩

**5mat** *or* **matt** *or* **matte** \"\ *n* -s [F *mat* dull color, unpolished surface, fr. *mat*, adj.] **1 :** a border (as of white or gilt cardboard) that is put around a picture so as to be between the picture and its frame or so as to serve as the sole frame of the picture **2 a** (1) **:** a surface or finish (as on metals, glass, colors) that is without luster or gloss or is otherwise dulled (2) **:** a material or instrument used in producing such a surface or finish **b** *usu matte* **:** an opaque sheet or plate sometimes containing an aperture (as a keyhole) used in a motion-picture camera or printing gate to obscure a selected area of a scene during exposure **3** [by shortening] **:** MATRIX 4a

**mat** *abbr* **1** material **2** matinee **3** matins **4** maturity

**MAT** *abbr* **1** mechanical aptitude test **2** military aircraft types

**mata** *var of* MATTO

**mat·a·be·le** \ˌmad·ə'bē(ˌ)lē\ *n, pl* **matabele** *or* **matabeles** *usu cap* **:** NDEBELE

**ma·ta·can** \mə'täkən\ *also* **ma·ta·co·an** \-kəwən\ *adj, usu cap* [AmerSp *Mataco* + E *-an*] **:** of or relating to the Mataco people or their language

**ma·ta·chin** *also* **ma·ta·chine** \ˌmäd·ə'chēn, ˌma-, -'shēn\ *n* -s *see sense 1b, often attrib* [It *mattaccino*, fr. *matto* madman, fool, fr. *matto* mad, crazy, fr. L *mattus* stupid, drunk] **1 a :** a sword dancer in a fantastic costume — called also *bouffon* **b** *pl* **matachi·ni** \-ē(ˌ)nē\ [MexSp *matachín*, fr. Sp, matachin (sense 1a), fr. It *mattaccino*] **:** a member of a society of Mexican-Indian dancers who perform ritual dances **2 :** a dance performed by a matachin

**ma·ta·chi·na** \-'chēnə, -'shē-\ *n, pl* **matachina** *or* **matachinas** [MexSp, fr. Sp *matachín* matachin (sense 1a), fr. It *mattaccino*] **:** MATACHIN 1b

**1ma·ta·co** \mə'tä(ˌ)kō\ *n* -s [AmerSp] **:** APAR

**2mataco** \"\ *n, pl* **mataco** *or* **matacos** *usu cap* [AmerSp *Mataco*] **1 a :** a people of Bolivia, Paraguay, and Argentina **b :** a member of such people **2 :** the language of the Mataco people

**mat·a·dor** *also* **mat·a·dore** \'mad·əˌdō(ə)r, -ȯ(ə)r, -ōə, -ȯ(ə)\ *n* -s [Sp, fr. *matar* to kill, prob. fr. (assumed) VL *mattare* to defeat, overcome — more at MAT] **1 :** a bullfighter who has the principal role in a bullfight and who finally kills the bull with a sword thrust after goading on and tiring the bull with a series of formalized passes with a cape **2 a** (1) **:** a principal trump in some card games (as ombre) (2) **:** a jack of clubs and each other trump held in sequence with it in the game of skat **b** (1) **:** a variation of the game of dominoes in which ends of dominoes matched in play must total seven except for four dominoes that may be played at any time (2) **:** one of the four dominoes that may be played at any time in the game of matador

**mat·a·gal·pa** \¦mad·ə¦galpə\ *n, pl* **matagalpa** *or* **matagalpas** *usu cap* [AmerSp] **1 a :** a people of Nicaragua, Honduras, and San Salvador **b :** a member of such people **2 :** a language of the Matagalpa people

**mat·a·gal·pan** \-pən\ *adj, usu cap* [AmerSp *Matagalpa* + E *-an*, adj. suffix] **:** of or relating to the Matagalpa people or their language

**mat·a·go·ry** \ˌmad·ə'gōrē, -gȯr-\ *or* **mat·a·gou·ri** \-'gürē\ *n, pl* **matagories** *or* **matagouris** [modif. of Maori *tumatakuru*] **:** TUMATAKURU

**1ma·tai** \'mäd·ˌī\ *n* -s [Maori] **:** a black pine (*Podocarpus spicata*) of New Zealand and Australia

**2matai** \"\ *n, pl* **matais** *or* **matai** [Samoan] **:** a Samoan chief bearing a hereditary title who is head of an extended family or of a village

**ma·ta·jue·lo** \ˌmad·ə'(h)wā(ˌ)lō\ *n* -s [AmerSp *matejuelo*] **:** a large squirrelfish (*Holocentrus ascensionis*) of Florida and the West Indies

**ma·ta·ma·ta** \ˌmad·əmə'tä\ *n* -s [Pg *matamatá*, fr. Tupi] **1 :** a pleurodiran turtle (*Chelus fimbriata*) of Guiana and the northern part of Brazil that reaches a length of three feet, has a rough shell and a long neck with fleshy fimbriae on the neck and on the head, and produces eggs that yield an edible oil **2 :** any of several So. American trees of the genus *Eschweilera* of the family Lecythidaceae; *esp* **:** a tree yielding a heavy hard compact wood used for pilings and foundation construction

**mat·a·sa·no** \ˌmad·ə'sä(ˌ)nō\ *n* -s [AmerSp, fr. Sp *matar* to kill + *sano* healthy person, fr. *sano* healthy, fr. L *sanus* — more at MATADOR, SANE] **:** WHITE SAPOTA

**mat·ax** \'mad·ˌaks\ *n* -ES [*mat*tock + *ax*] **:** a combination ax and mattock

**mat bean** *n* [*mat* prob. by folk etymology (influence of 1*mat*) fr. Marathi *maṭh* moth bean — more at MOTH BEAN] **:** MOTH BEAN

**mat board** *n* [5*mat*] **:** paperboard used for mounting (as pictures, specimens)

**1match** \'mach\ *n* -ES [in sense 1, fr. ME *macche* match, mate, spouse, fr. OE *mæcca, gemæcca* mate, spouse; in other senses, fr. 2*match;* OE *mæcca, gemæcca* akin to OE *gemaca* companion, mate, spouse, OHG *gimahha* wife, ON *maki* match, mate, OE *macian* to make — more at MAKE] **1 a** (1) **:** one that can as an equal compete with, combat, or otherwise oppose another **:** an individual or group of individuals possessing the same qualities (as strength, courage, intelligence) in the same degree as an opposing individual or group ⟨a wrestler who finally met his ~⟩ ⟨a baseball team that appears to be a ~ for the world champions⟩ **:** one able to cope with another ⟨will be more than a ~ for her⟩ (2) **:** one that equals another in the extent of a shared quality (as of character) ⟨a figure that for heroism has no ~ in history⟩ **b** (1) **:** one that is exactly like another **:** one that forms an exact pair with another **:** an exact counterpart ⟨a lake that was almost the ~ of one he remembered from Switzerland⟩ (2) **:** one that closely resembles or harmonizes (as in appearance) with another ⟨wore a blouse that was a nice ~ for her skirt⟩ **c :** a pair made up of two individuals that are exact counterparts of each other or that closely resemble or harmonize (as in appearance) with each other ⟨a jacket and scarf that are a good ~⟩ **2 a :** a contest or game in which two or more individuals or groups of individuals oppose each other ⟨a golf ~⟩ ⟨a cricket ~⟩ **b :** a race between two horses belonging to different owners run in accordance with terms agreed upon by the owners **3** *obs* **:** AGREEMENT, COMPACT, BARGAIN **4 a** (1) **:** an agreement to enter into marriage (2) **:** a marriage union **b :** a person eligible to enter into marriage and viewed with regard to his or her advantages or disadvantages (as of social position, wealth) as a marriage partner for a prospective mate ⟨would make a good ~ for any man⟩ **5 a :** a device for fitting together two halves of a ceramics mold that consists of a knob on one half and a corresponding depression on the other **b :** a form shaped to support a pattern and made of plaster of paris or similar materials and sand or of a mixture of sand and litharge and boiled linseed oil **6 :** a condition in which two colors appear to have the same hue, saturation, and lightness

**2match** \"\ *vb* -ED/-ING/-ES [ME *macchen*, fr. *macche*, n. — more at 1MATCH] *vt* **1 a :** to encounter esp. successfully as an antagonist or competitor **:** to meet and prove to be the equal of ⟨troops whom none could ~ in battle⟩ **b** (1) **:** to set in competition or combat with or in other opposition to **:** PIT, ARRAY ⟨~*ing* his strength against his enemy's⟩ (2) **:** to provide with a competitor or adversary of equal strength, courage, or ability ⟨was ~*ed* with someone that would really put his championship to the test⟩ **c :** to set in comparison with **:** compare the quality of ⟨almost any drama ~*ed* with his seems trivial⟩ **2 a :** to join or give in marriage ⟨thought of ~*ing* her son with an heiress⟩ **b** *obs* **:** to join in close association **:** put in close proximity **3 a** (1) **:** to pair up or put in a set as possessing equal or harmonizing attributes **:** combine as being suitable or congenial ⟨~*ed* the tie and the shirt⟩ (2) **:** to cause to be proportioned to **:** make correspond **:** ADAPT, SUIT ⟨~*ed* his generosity to her love⟩ **b** (1) **:** to be the exact counterpart of **:** equal in qualities ⟨trying to find a vase to ~ the remaining one of a pair⟩ (2) **:** to resemble sufficiently to be suitably coupled with **:** be enough like to go agreeably with **:** correspond to **:** harmonize with ⟨a coat that will ~ almost anything you choose to wear⟩ **c** (1) **:** to produce or provide with an exact counterpart of or for ⟨a climate that can't be ~*ed* anywhere else in the world⟩ (2) **:** to produce or provide with a suitable or harmonious counterpart of or for ⟨wanted to ~ the period decor with some antique furniture⟩ **4 a :** to fit together or make suitable for fitting together; *specif* **:** to furnish (boards) at the edges with a tongue and groove **b :** to couple (two electric circuits) by a device (as a transformer) that by providing equality of impedance ensures maximum transfer of power from one circuit to the other **5 a :** to flip, toss, or otherwise manipulate (coins) and compare the faces so exposed either to decide something contested or as a form of gambling ⟨~*ed* a couple of quarters to see who would pay the check⟩ **b :** to go through this process with (another person) ⟨said he would ~ him for it⟩ ~ *vi* **1 a** *archaic* **:** to enter into a marriage union **:** become married **b** *obs* **:** COUPLE, MATE **2 a :** to be an exact or close counterpart **:** be a counterpart that agreeably blends or harmonizes ⟨wore a new spring coat and a hat to ~⟩ **b :** to go together agreeably by reason of being exact or close counterparts that blend or harmonize ⟨gloves that will ~ very nicely with your coat⟩

**syn** MATCH, RIVAL, EQUAL, APPROACH, TOUCH signify in common, often in negative constructions, to be or come to be equivalent to (someone or something else) or come up to or nearly up to (the standard of another or the person or thing embodying it). MATCH stresses equivalence, usually a rival or competitive equivalence ⟨we are prone to imitate the vices of those whose virtues we cannot *match* —E.S.McCartney⟩ ⟨even in truth to nature, truth to life, he cannot *match* them —Laurence Binyon⟩ ⟨the beauty of his person was *matched* by the grace and dignity of his spirit —John Buchan⟩ ⟨his belief that . . . the United States can not *match* Russia in sheer number of workers —*Current Biog.*⟩ RIVAL is often interchangeable with MATCH but usually suggests rather a coming close to or a slight falling short of equivalence, often stressing more the idea of competitive effort or comparison ⟨the bright but penniless youth whose climb to fame *rivaled* the most incredible of the Alger stories —*Amer. Guide Series: Minn.*⟩ ⟨in winter it is a ski center *rivaling* its near neighbor —E.W.Smith⟩ ⟨he *rivaled* his friend Donne in fathering children —Douglas Bush⟩ ⟨political discussions that *rival* the temperature in intensity —*Amer. Guide Series: Tenn.*⟩ EQUAL is very close to MATCH in implying a sharing of the same level or plane, especially of excellence or achievement, stressing possibly a little less the idea of competition or rivalry ⟨when he went aloft to set sail or to shorten sail he performed feats which *equaled* those of circus performers —C.S.Forester⟩ ⟨few campaigns have *equaled* that of 1828 for its license and bitter personalities —W.C.Ford⟩ ⟨the contestants rode with a maniacal fury they had never seen *equaled* before —T.B.Costain⟩ APPROACH and TOUCH are almost interchangeable, implying a coming within sight of equivalence or a near equaling and both seldom carrying the idea of competition or rivalry, APPROACH possibly suggesting a somewhat greater falling short of equivalence than TOUCH ⟨though some of Shakespeare's songs *approach* purity, there is, in fact, an alloy —Clive Bell⟩ ⟨Lincoln *approached* perfection in the field of government —W.J.Reilly⟩ ⟨a new type, destined to be frequently imitated, but seldom *approached* and never exactly reproduced —Richard Garnett †1906⟩ ⟨you have pretty girls in Scotland . . . but none to *touch* Miss Westwater —John Buchan⟩ ⟨few of the academicians . . . can *touch* Catton's ability to get the feel of a period —Laurent Le Sage⟩

**³match** \"\ *n* -ES [ME *macche, mecche,* fr. MF *meiche,* perh. modif. of L *myxa* lamp wick, fr. Gk, lamp wick, nasal mucus — more at MUCUS] **1 a** *obs* **:** the wick of a candle or lamp **b** (1) **:** a wick or cord chemically prepared to burn at a uniform rate and formerly much used in firing cannon and muskets and other firearms and in igniting a train of powder (2) **:** the material used in making such a wick or cord **2 a :** a piece of cord, cloth, or paper or a splint of wood dipped in melted sulfur so as to be able to catch fire from a spark and formerly much used to light candles or lamps or to ignite fuel or to fumigate something **b :** a piece of flammable material (as wood) having a tip treated with potassium chlorate and sugar so as to ignite when touched with sulfuric acid **3 :** a short slender piece of wood or other fairly rigid flammable material tipped with a combustible mixture that bursts into flame through friction (as by being scratched against a usu. rough or specially prepared surface) and that so ignites the piece

**match·able** \ˈmachəbəl\ *adj* **:** capable of being matched

**matchboard** \ˈ=,=\ *or* **matched board** *n* **1 :** a board (as one of those used in laying floors) that has a groove cut along one edge and a tongue along the other so as to fit snugly with the edges of similarly cut boards of identical size **2 :** one of two molding boards to which the halves of a split foundry pattern are attached with one of the molding boards forming the cope mold and the other the drag mold

**matchboarding** \ˈ=,==\ *also* **matched boarding** *n* **1 :** a quantity of matchboards **2 :** something made of matchboards

**matchbook** \ˈ=,=\ *also* **matchfolder** \ˈ=,==\ *n* **:** a small usu. paper packet or folder containing rows of paper matches

**matchbox** \ˈ=,=\ *n* **:** a box for holding matches

**matchcoat** \ˈ=,=\ *n* [prob. by folk etymology (influence of *coat*) fr. Powhatan *matshcore*] **:** a mantle or similar loose covering of fur, feathers, or usu. woolen cloth formerly extensively worn by American Indians

**matched joint** *or* **match joint** *n* **:** a line along which two matchboards are joined together

matchbooks

**matched order** *n* **:** one of two orders designed to create artificial activity in the stock market: **a :** an order placed by an individual through one broker to buy usu. at an above-market price a number of shares of stock that the individual intends to sell at once at the same price through another broker **b :** the order placed by the individual to sell stock that has been so bought

**matched siding** *n* **:** DROP SIDING

**match·er** \ˈmachə(r)\ *n* -S [²*match* + *-er*] **1** *or* **matching machine :** a machine that planes boards and that forms the tongues and grooves in matchboards **2 :** one (as an assorter) whose work is matching articles (as for size, color, fit, quality)

**matches** *pl of* MATCH, *pres 3d sing of* MATCH

**matchet** *var of* MACHETE

**match game** *n* [¹*match*] **1 :** a game played as a test of superiority (as a play-off game or a championship game) **2** [³*match*] **:** a game played with matches typically by nine players

**matching** *pres part of* MATCH

**matching test** *n* **:** an objective test consisting of two sets of items to be matched with each other for a specified attribute

**match·less** \ˈmachləs\ *adj* **:** having no equal **:** UNPARALLELED, PEERLESS ⟨her ~ beauty⟩ — **match·less·ly** *adv*

**matchlock** \ˈ=,=\ *n* **1 :** a device used in early muskets consisting of a slow-burning cord or wick held in an arm curving over a hole in the breech and capable of being lowered so as to ignite the charge with the glowing tip of the cord or wick **2 :** a musket equipped with a matchlock

**matchmake** \ˈ=,=\ *vi* [back-formation fr. *matchmaker*] **:** to bring about a marriage esp. by scheming

**matchmaker** \ˈ=,==\ *n* [¹*match* + *maker*] **:** one that arranges a match: **a :** one that brings about a marriage or is given to bringing about marriages esp. by scheming **b :** one that arranges or promotes a match (as a prizefight)

**matchmaking** \ˈ=,==\ *n* [¹*match* + *making*, gerund of ¹*make*] **1 :** the action of bringing about a marriage esp. by scheming **2 :** the action of arranging or promoting sports matches

**¹matchmark** \ˈ=,=\ *n* [¹*match* + *mark*] **:** a mark placed on the adjacent separable parts of a device to aid in the reassembling of the parts

**²matchmark** \"\ *vt* **:** to make a matchmark on

**match penalty** *n* **:** a penalty in ice hockey consisting of a fine and a decision by league officials concerning suspension of an offending player who remains eligible for play until the decision is handed down

**match plane** *n* **:** a plane having cutters for making the tongues and grooves on the edges of matchboards

**match plate** *n* **1 :** a metal plate on the opposite sides of which the halves of a split pattern are attached **2 :** one of two metal plates to which the halves of a split pattern are attached

**match play** *n* **1 :** golf competition in which the winner is the person or team winning the greater number of holes — compare MEDAL PLAY **2 :** MATCH GAME

**match point** *n* **1 :** the last point needed to win a game of tennis or handball or similar sports match **2 :** a unit used in scoring duplicate bridge or tournament bridge and consisting of 1 point awarded to a pair of partners for each other pair making a lower score in a deal and ½ point awarded to a pair of partners for each other pair making the same score in a deal

**match race** *n* **:** a race between two contestants

**match safe** *n* **:** an ornamental or watertight matchbox

**match–splint** \ˈ=,=\ *or* **match–stalk** \ˈ=,=\ *n, chiefly Brit* **:** MATCHSTICK

**¹matchstick** \ˈ=,=\ *n* **:** the slender length of wood or other fairly rigid material used in making matches

**²matchstick** *adj* **1 :** made of or as if of matchsticks **2 :** of, relating to, or constituting stick figures ⟨how to draw buildings, animals, ~ men —*British Book News*⟩

**matchweed** \ˈ=,=\ *n* [prob. fr. ³*match*] **:** any of various plants of the genus *Gutierrezia*

**matchwood** \ˈ=,=\ *n* **1 :** wood used for making matches **2 :** thin brittle jagged pieces of wood **:** SPLINTERS ⟨the hurricane smashed the village to ~⟩

**¹mate** *vt* -ED/-ING/-S [ME *maten,* fr. OF *mater* — more at MAT] **1** *obs* **:** OVERCOME, DEFEAT **2** *obs* **a :** to frustrate by bewildering **:** CONFOUND **b :** to effectively block or reduce to nothing **3** *obs* **:** DISPIRIT, DISCOMFIT, DAUNT

**²mate** \ˈmāt, *usu* -ād·+V\ *vb* -ED/-ING/-S [ME *maten,* fr. MF *mater,* fr. OF *mat,* n., checkmate, fr. Ar *māt* (in *shāh māt* — expression used in chess to tell an opponent that his king has been checkmated) — more at CHECKMATE] *vt* **:** CHECKMATE 2 ~ *vi* **:** to bring about a checkmate

**³mate** \"\ *n* -S [ME *mat,* fr. MF, fr. OF] **:** CHECKMATE 1

**⁴mate** \"\ *interj* **:** CHECKMATE

**⁵mate** \"\ *n* -S [ME, prob. fr. MLG *māt, māte;* akin to OE *gemetta* guest at one's table, OHG *gimazzo* one eating at the same table, OE *mete* food — more at MEAT] **1 a** (1) **:** one that customarily associates with another **:** one engaged in the same activity or pursuit as another **:** ASSOCIATE, COMPANION, CONFRERE ⟨denounce our teachers, criticize certain of our ~*s*, and plan some new deviation from the rules —Sidney Lovett⟩ (2) **:** a fellow workman **:** PARTNER ⟨needed help from his ~*s* to get the job done⟩ (3) **:** an assistant to a more skilled workman **:** HELPER ⟨a plumber's ~⟩ **b** *archaic* **:** one that is equal in eminence or dignity to another **:** PEER **c :** FRIEND, BUDDY, PAL, CHUM ⟨boasted to his ~*s* about his girl —Ruth Park⟩ — often used in familiar address esp. by seamen ⟨give me a light, ~⟩ **2 a :** a deck officer on a merchant ship ranking below the captain **b :** an assistant to a warrant officer (as in the U.S. Navy) ranking as a petty officer **3 :** one of a pair: as **a** (1) **:** a marriage partner **:** SPOUSE; *esp* **:** a suitable or worthy partner in marriage ⟨finally found her ~⟩ (2) **:** one of a pair of animals brought together for breeding **b :** one of a pair that are matched in one or more qualities (as size, shape, color) ⟨couldn't find the ~ for the shoe⟩ **4 :** a guiding and retaining device placed opposite the point rail in some railroad switches — **go mates :** to be or become an associate or partner ⟨saw that it would be advantageous to *go mates* with him⟩

**⁶mate** \"\ *vb* -ED/-ING/-S *vt* **1** *archaic* **:** to equal in some quality esp. strength, courage, intelligence **:** MATCH **2 a :** to put in close association **:** join closely together **:** COUPLE ⟨*mating* words with deeds⟩ **b :** to fit (mechanical parts) together ⟨the turbine shaft is *mated* to the hollow compressor shaft —*Jet Aircraft Power Systems*⟩ ⟨watched engineers ~ . . . rocket stages —A.C.Fisher⟩ **3 :** to join together as mates: as **a :** to pair for breeding — often used with *up* ⟨~*s* fox terriers⟩ ⟨*mated* up the pigeons⟩ **b :** to join in marriage **:** take or give in marriage ⟨was finally *mated* with the man she loved⟩ ~ *vi* **1 a** (1) **:** to become joined together in marriage ⟨wondering with whom she would ~⟩ (2) **:** to become associated for breeding ⟨birds *mating* in the spring⟩ **b :** COPULATE ⟨some vigorous mature rams ~ successfully with nearly 100 ewes in a season⟩ **c :** to pair animals for breeding — often used with *up* **2** *archaic* **:** to claim equality with another **3** *archaic* **:** to go about in close association with another **:** CONSORT **4 :** to become fitted or geared together properly

**⁷ma·té** *or* **ma·te** \ˈmä(,)tā\ *n* -S [F & AmerSp; F *maté,* fr. AmerSp *mate,* fr. Quechua] **1 :** a small bottle gourd used for holding the beverage maté **2 :** an aromatic beverage used chiefly in So. America and esp. in Paraguay that has stimulant properties like those of coffee and tea and that is made by steeping the dried and ground leaves and shoots of the maté plant **3 a :** a So. American holly (*Ilex paraguayensis*) whose leaves and shoots are used in making the beverage maté — called also *Paraguay tea* **b :** leaves and young shoots of this holly dried and ground for use in making the beverage maté

**⁸mate** *or* **matee** *var of* MATY

**ma·te·las·sé** \ˌmäd·ə(ˌ)lä¦sā, ˌmät(ˌ)lä-\ *n* -S [F, fr. past part. of *matelasser* to cushion as with a mattress, fr. *matelas* mattress, fr. MF, alter. of *materas,* fr. OF — more at MATTRESS] **:** a double cloth of cotton or rayon or other fibers woven on a jacquard loom and used esp. for clothing, upholstery, and bedspreads and marked by raised floral or geometric designs with a puckered or quilted appearance achieved by the interlacing of threads in the weaving or the contracting of threads in the finishing

**mate·less** \ˈmātləs\ *adj* [⁵*mate* + *-less*] **:** having no mate

**mate·ley** \ˈmātlē\ *adj* [origin unknown] **:** URDÉE

**mate·lot** \ˈmat,lō\ *n* -S [F, fr. MF, fr. MD *mattenoot,* fr. *matte* mat, bed (fr. LL *matta* mat) + *noot* companion; akin to OE *nēotan* to make use of, enjoy — more at MAT, NEAT] **1** *Brit* **:** SAILOR **2 :** a deep blue that is greener and duller than Yale blue and greener and slightly lighter than royal (sense 8b) — called also *Olympian blue*

**ma·te·lote** \ˈmad·ᵊl,ōt, -at,lōt, *F* mȧ·tlȯt\ *n* -S [F, fr. *matelot*] **1 :** a sauce made of wine, onions, seasonings, and fish stock **2 :** fish stewed in matelote

**¹ma·ter** \ˈmātə(r\ *n* -S [L — more at MOTHER] *chiefly Brit* **:** MOTHER

**²mat·er** \ˈmād·ə(r), -ātə-\ *n* -S [⁶*mate* + *-er*] **:** a worker who arranges shoes or hosiery in pairs for packing

**ma·ter·fa·mil·i·as** \ˌmād·ə(r)fəˈmilēəs\ *n* -ES [L, fr. *mater* mother + OL *familias,* gen. of *familia* household — more at FAMILY] **:** a woman that is head of a household

**¹ma·te·ri·al** \məˈtirēəl, -tēr-\ *adj* [ME *materiel, material,* fr. MF & LL; MF *materiel,* fr. LL *materialis,* fr. L *materia* matter + *-alis* -al — more at MATTER] **1 a** (1) **:** of, relating to, or consisting of matter **:** PHYSICAL ⟨the ~ universe⟩ ⟨the ~ nature of fire⟩ (2) **:** CORPOREAL, BODILY ⟨~ needs⟩ (3) **:** of, relating to, or derived from matter as the constituent of the physical universe ⟨~ forces⟩ **b** (1) **:** of or relating to the matter of a thing and not to its form ⟨the ~ aspect of being⟩ (2) **:** of or relating to the matter of reasoning and not to its form ⟨the ~ truth embodied in a premise⟩ **c :** existing only in outward manifestation and not prompted by or joined with actual intention ⟨~ heresy⟩ ⟨~ sin⟩ **2 a** (1) **:** being of real importance or great consequence **:** SUBSTANTIAL ⟨found a ~ difference between the two things⟩ ⟨a ~ point of order⟩ ⟨made a ~ correction⟩ ⟨a ~ objection⟩ (2) **:** ESSENTIAL ⟨information that is ~ to continued research⟩ (3) **:** RELEVANT, PERTINENT ⟨neglected no data that was ~⟩ **b :** requiring serious consideration by reason of having a certain or probable bearing on the proper determination of a law case or on the effect of an instrument or on some similar unsettled matter ⟨a ~ fact⟩ ⟨a ~ piece of evidence⟩ **3 a :** being of a coarse unspiritual nature **:** not lofty ⟨a grossly ~ form of love⟩ **b :** relating to or concerned esp. excessively with what is purely physical rather than intellectual or spiritual ⟨interested only in ~ progress⟩ ⟨is ~ in all his interests⟩ **4** *obs* **a :** pregnant with substance and meaning **:** SOLID, MEATY **b :** BULKY, MASSIVE **5 :** of or relating to production and distribution of goods and the social relationship of owners and laborers rather than to financial and political institutions — compare ECONOMIC INTERPRETATION OF HISTORY

**syn** PHYSICAL, CORPOREAL, PHENOMENAL, SENSIBLE, OBJECTIVE: MATERIAL describes whatever is formed of tangible matter and may be used in opposition to *spiritual, ideal, intangible;* it may have suggestions of the mundane, crass, or grasping ⟨one's *material* possessions⟩ ⟨busy with *material* affairs⟩ ⟨no veneration for property, no sense of *material* values —Willa Cather⟩ ⟨realistic and *material* rather than romantic and Utopian —V.L.Parrington⟩ PHYSICAL applies especially to things perceived by the senses, things susceptible of treatment in one way or another by the science of physics; it is opposed to *imaginary, psychical, mental,* or *spiritual* ⟨everything *physical* is measurable by weight, motion, and resistance —Thomas De Quincey⟩ ⟨athletic grounds and equipment represent a very substantial portion of Harvard's *physical* plant —*Official Register of Harvard Univ.*⟩ CORPOREAL applies to whatever is not only tangible and material but also has some sort of body ⟨we cannot compare our ideas with these *corporeal* substances —Frank Thilly⟩ ⟨"the mind" may be regarded as a living, growing "structure," even though it lacks *corporeal* tangibility —*Science*⟩ PHENOMENAL refers to what is or may be known or perceived through the senses rather than through thought, hypothesis, intuition, or reason alone ⟨her introspective bent has yielded more and more, in her recent writing, to a determination to capture the *phenomenal* world —B.R. Redman⟩ SENSIBLE may more strongly stress the idea of application to what is knowable through the senses and is opposed to *intelligible, conceptual,* or *notional* ⟨subject to this right of every riparian owner to use the water without stint, every owner is entitled to have the water come on to him without *sensible* diminution as regards quantity and *sensible* alteration as regards quality —F.D.Smith & Barbara Wilcox⟩ OBJECTIVE may stress apartness and individual essence, as reported by the senses, of something corporeal or sensible ⟨a chronic malady which, in forty years, produced no *objective* sign of disease —Douglas Hubble⟩ **syn** see in addition RELEVANT

**²material** \"\ *n* -S **1 a** (1) **:** the basic matter (as metal, wood, plastic, fiber) from which the whole or the greater part of something physical (as a machine, tool, building, fabric) is made ⟨had a good supply of all necessary ~*s*⟩ ⟨flax is the ~ used in making linen⟩ (2) **:** the finished stuff of which something physical (as an article of clothing) is made; *esp* **:** CLOTH **b** (1) **:** the whole or a notable part of the elements or constituents or substance of something physical ⟨the solid ~*s* of the mixture will settle to the bottom of the container⟩ or not physical ⟨the ~ of his character was basically good⟩ (2) **:** something (as data, observations, perceptions, ideas) that may through intellectual operation be synthesized or further elaborated or otherwise reworked into a more finished form or a new form or that may serve as the basis for arriving at fresh interpretations or judgments or conclusions ⟨found rich ~ for a definitive biography⟩ ⟨an experience that provided stimulating ~ for new evaluation of the theory⟩ (3) **:** something (as a group of specimens) used for or made the object of study and investigation ⟨museum ~⟩ **c :** matter viewed as the relatively formless basis of reality **2 a :** apparatus (as tools or other articles) necessary for doing or making something — usu. used in pl. ⟨needed writing ~*s*⟩ ⟨library ~*s*⟩ **b :** MATÉRIEL **3 :** the pieces other than the king that a chess player has available for attacking the pieces of his opponent at one or the other point of a game

**material cause** *n, Aristotelianism* **:** something out of which something is made or comes into being

**material culture** *n* **:** the totality of physical objects made by a people for the satisfaction of their needs; *esp* **:** those articles requisite for the sustenance and perpetuation of life

**material fallacy** *n* **:** a reasoning that is unsound because of an error concerning the subject matter of an argument — compare FORMAL FALLACY

**material implication** *n* **:** IMPLICATION 2b(1)

**ma·te·ri·al·ism** \məˈtirēə,lizəm, -tēr-\ *n* -S [NL *materialismus,* fr. LL *materialis* material + L *-ismus* -ism] **1 a :** a doctrine, theory, or principle according to which physical matter is the only reality and the reality through which all being and processes and phenomena can be explained — compare MENTALISM **b :** a doctrine, theory, or principle according to which the only or the highest values or objectives of living lie in material well-being and pleasure and in the furtherance of material progress **2 :** a preoccupation with or tendency to seek after or stress material things rather than intellectual or spiritual things

**¹ma·te·ri·al·ist** \-ləst\ *n* -S [NL *materialista,* fr. LL *materialis* material + L *-ista* -ist] **:** one that adheres to, advocates, or is marked by materialism

**²materialist** \"\ *adj* **:** MATERIALISTIC

**ma·te·ri·al·is·tic** \=¦===¦listik, -tēk\ *adj* [¹*materialist* + *-ic*] **:** of, relating to, or marked by materialism — **ma·te·ri·al·is·ti·cal·ly** \-tək(ə)lē, -tēk-, -li\ *adv*

**ma·te·ri·al·i·ty** \mə,tirēˈaləd·ē, -tēr-, -ətē, -i\ *n* -ES [ML *materialitat-, materialitas* quality or state of being material, fr. LL *materialis* material + L *-itat-, -itas* -ity] **1 a** *obs* **:** MATTER, SUBSTANCE **b :** something that is material or the sum of things that are material esp. physically and in an outwardly apprehensible manner ⟨has the world of ~ under control —N.R.Nash⟩ **2 :** the quality or state of being material: as **a :** the quality or state of consisting of matter **:** the quality or state of being physical ⟨the ~ of the universe⟩ **b :** the quality or state of being something requiring serious consideration by reason of being either certainly or probably vital to the proper settlement of an issue ⟨questioned the ~ of the evidence⟩

**ma·te·ri·al·ization** \=,==ələˈzāshən, -,līˈz-\ *n* -S **1 a :** the action of materializing or of becoming materialized ⟨the ~ of thought by words⟩ ⟨resulted in the ~ of their philosophy⟩ **b :** an appearance (as of a spirit) in bodily form **:** APPARITION **2 :** something that has been materialized ⟨this old feud, of which the four stout walls in front of us were still the solid ~ before bearing witness to it today —Osbert Sitwell⟩

**ma·te·ri·al·ize** \=ˈ==ə,līz\ *vb* -ED/-ING/-S *see -ize in Explan Notes, vt* **1 a :** to cause to have or represent as having material form or characteristics **:** give an outward externally apprehensible existence to **:** make perceptible to the senses **:** make material **:** OBJECTIFY ⟨*materializing* a vague idea by putting it into words⟩ ⟨heroic statues *materializing* glorious deeds⟩ **b :** to cause (as a spirit) to appear in bodily form **:** cause to be visible ⟨said she could ~ the spirits of the dead⟩ **2 :** to cause to be materialistic ⟨had been *materialized* by the cynicism that surrounded him⟩ ~ *vi* **1** *archaic* **:** to tend toward or favor materialism **2 a :** to assume bodily form **:** appear visibly ⟨asserted that she had seen the spirit of her dead grandmother ~ before her eyes⟩ **b :** to appear as if from nowhere **:** appear with mysterious suddenness ⟨squads of police *materialized* on street corners —*Time*⟩ **3 a** (1) **:** to come into actual existence **:** develop into something tangible ⟨promised him a great deal of money which never *materialized*⟩ (2) **:** to put in an appearance **:** show up **:** be on hand ⟨said they would come right away but they didn't ~⟩ **b :** to become actual fact **:** develop into something real **:** take shape ⟨what had once been a mere possibility now *materialized*⟩ **:** become fulfilled ⟨hopes that never *materialized*⟩ — **ma·te·ri·al·iz·er** \-,līzə(r)\ *n* -S

**material logic** *n* **:** logic that is valid within a certain universe of discourse or field of application because of certain peculiar properties of that universe or field — contrasted with *formal logic*

**ma·te·ri·al·ly** \məˈtirēəlē, -tēr-, -li\ *adv* [¹*material* + *-ly*] **1 a** (1) **:** with regard to matter and not to form ⟨something that is ~ false⟩ ⟨a ~ good act⟩ (2) **:** with regard to the material cause ⟨two things that differ formally but are alike ~⟩ **b :** with regard to material substance ⟨all men are ~ equal⟩ **2** *obs* **:** soundly and to the point ⟨always spoke ~ with argument and knowledge —Earl of Chesterfield⟩ **3 :** to a significant extent or degree ⟨aided ~ in the conviction of the criminal⟩ ⟨became ~ better⟩ **4 :** so far as what is material is concerned ⟨they live well ~⟩

**material·man** \=ˈ===mən\ *n, pl* **materialmen :** one who supplies materials (as in the building trades)

**materialman's lien** *n* **:** a lien on property for materials supplied — compare MECHANIC'S LIEN

**material matter** *n* **:** MATTER OF A PROPOSITION a

**material mode** *n* **:** language that ostensively makes statements about objects, properties, and relations — contrasted with *formal mode*

**ma·te·ri·al·ness** *n* -ES **:** the quality or state of being material **:** MATERIALITY

**materials** *pl of* MATERIAL

**ma·te·ria med·i·ca** \məˈtirēəˈmedəkə, -tēr-\ *n* [NL, medical matter, trans. of Gk *hylē iatrikē*] **1 :** substances used in the composition of medical remedies **:** DRUGS, MEDICINE **2 a :** a branch of medical science that treats of the sources, nature, properties, and preparation of the drugs used in medicine **b :** a treatise on this subject

**materia pri·ma** \-ˈprīmə\ *n* [NL, first matter, trans. of Gk *prōtē hylē*] **:** indeterminate matter viewed as the material cause of the universe

**¹materiate** *adj* [ML *materiatus,* past part. of *materiare* to make material] *obs* **:** composed of or involved with matter **:** MATERIAL

**²materiate** *vt* -ED/-ING/-S [ML *materiatus,* past part. of *materiare* to make material, fr. L *materia* matter — more at MATTER] *obs* **:** to provide or constitute the material of matter of **:** make material

**ma·té·ri·el** *or* **ma·te·ri·el** \mə,tirēˈel, ma,-, -tēr-\ *n* -S [F *matériel,* fr. *matériel,* adj., material, fr. MF *materiel* — more at MATERIAL] **:** the equipment, apparatus, and supplies used by an organization or institution or required in some work or enterprise; *esp* **:** military equipment, apparatus, and supplies (as guns, ammunition, clothing) — distinguished from *personnel* **syn** see EQUIPMENT

**ma·ter lec·ti·o·nis** \ˌmäd·ə(r),lektēˈōnəs\ *n, pl* **ma·tres lec·tionis** \ˈmä·,trā,sl-\ [NL, lit., mother of reading; fr. its function of enabling a person reading aloud to give an accurate rendition of a written word] **:** the alphabetic signs א (\ʔ\), ה (\h\), ו (\w\), and י (\y\) in Hebrew which assist in indicating the vocalization in an originally consonantal writing system

**¹ma·ter·nal** \məˈtərnᵊl, -tən-,-təin-\ *adj* [ME, fr. MF & ML; MF *maternel,* fr. ML *maternalis,* fr. L *maternus* of a mother, maternal (fr. *mater* mother) + *-alis* -al — more at MOTHER]

1 *of a language* **:** acquired before any other language **:** being one's mother language ⟨English is their ~ language⟩ **2 a** (1) **:** of, relating to, or being like that of a mother **:** MOTHERLY ⟨a warm ~ affection for her guest —Dorothy Sayers⟩ ⟨~ instincts⟩ ⟨~ solicitude⟩ (2) *archaic* **:** being a mother **:** considered as a mother ⟨his ~ country⟩ (3) **:** suggestive of or acting like a mother ⟨my ~ waitress advised me in the selection of my lunch —Arnold Bennett⟩ **b :** belonging to a mother ⟨glanced over the ~ shoulder⟩ **3 a :** related through a mother or on a mother's side ⟨his ~ uncle⟩ **b :** inherited or derived from a mother ⟨exhibited both ~ traits of character and physical characteristics⟩ **c :** MATRILINEAL

**²maternal** \"\ *n* -s **:** MOTHER, MATRON ⟨our frustrated young ~s —Christopher Morley⟩

**maternal inheritance** *n* **:** matroclinous inheritance; *specif* **:** inheritance of characters transmitted through the cytoplasm of the egg

**ma·ter·nal·ism** \-nᵊl,izəm\ *n* -s **:** the quality or state of having or showing maternal instincts ⟨remarkable for her benevolent ~⟩

**ma·ter·nal·is·tic** \¦==¦istik, -tēk\ *adj* **:** having or showing maternal instincts or attitudes **:** marked by maternalism ⟨~ care⟩

**ma·ter·nal·ize** \=ˈ==,īz\ *vt* -ED/-ING/-S *see -ize in Explan Notes* **:** to cause to be maternal

**ma·ter·nal·ly** \-ᵊlē, -ᵊli\ *adv* **:** in a maternal manner ⟨fussed ~ over the boy⟩

**maternal rubella** *n* **:** rubella that may occur in a pregnant woman and that is thought to cause developmental anomalies in the fetus when occurring during the first trimester

**ma·ter·ni·ty** \məˈtərnəd·ē, -tᵊn-,-tən-, -nəte, -i\ *n* -ES *often attrib* [F *maternité*, fr. MF, fr. ML *maternitat-, maternitas* quality or state of being a mother church, fr. L *maternus* of a mother, maternal + *-itat-, -itas* -ity] **1 a** (1) **:** the quality or state of being a mother **:** MOTHERHOOD (2) **:** the quality or state of being pregnant ⟨successive *maternities*⟩ **b :** the qualities belonging to or associated with motherhood **:** MOTHERLINESS, MATERNALISM **2 :** a hospital or a section of a hospital designed for the care of women immediately before and during childbirth and for the care of newborn babies **3 :** a usu. loose or adjustable garment worn during pregnancy

**maters** *pl of* MATER

**mates** *pres 3d sing of* MATE, *pl of* MATE

**mate·ship** \ˈmāt,ship\ *n* -s [⁵*mate* + *-ship*] **1 :** the quality or state of being a mate; *esp* **:** FELLOWSHIP ⟨manliness and ~ in the face of terrible danger —Leslie Rees⟩ **2 :** an Australian code of conduct that emphasizes egalitarianism and fellowship

**¹matey** \ˈmād·ē, -āte, -i\ *n* -s [⁵*mate* + *-y*, n. suffix] **1** *chiefly Brit* **:** ⁵MATE 1c **2** *Brit* **:** a dockyard workman

**²matey** \"\ *adj* [⁵*mate* + *-y*, adj. suffix] *chiefly Brit* **:** cozily familiar and informal in personal relationship **:** friendly and companionable in an easygoing way **:** CHUMMY ⟨he is not a ~ fellow . . . not always at ease in a party — William Clark⟩

**matey·ness** *n* -ES *chiefly Brit* **:** easygoing friendliness **:** CHUMMINESS

**matgrass** \ˈ=,=\ *n* **1 a :** MATWEED 1 **b :** a low tufted European grass (*Nardus stricta*) with one-flowered spikelets **c :** SPINY ROLLING GRASS **2 :** KNOTGRASS 1 **3 :** a prostrate perennial herb (*Lippia nodiflora*) of riverbanks in the southwestern U. S. that is used as a soil binder — compare FOGFRUIT

**¹math** \ˈmath, -aa(ə)th, -äth\ *n* -s [fr. (assumed) ME *math*, fr. OE *mǣth*; akin to OFris *meth* crop of hay, mowing of grass, OHG *mād*; derivative fr. the root of OE *māwan* to mow — more at MOW] *now dial Eng* **:** a mowing of a grass or hay crop; *also* **:** the crop gathered

**²math** *also* **muth** \ˈmoth\ *n* -s [Hindi *maṭh*, fr. Skt *maṭha*, lit., hut] **:** a Hindu monastery

**³math** \ˈmath, -aa(ə)th\ *n* -s [by shortening] **:** MATHEMATICS

**math** *abbr* mathematical; mathematician; mathematics

**math·e·mat·i·cal** \,mathəˈmad·ə̇kəl, -atǀ, ǀek- *sometimes* (ˈ)math¦m-\ *also* **math·e·mat·ic** \ǀik, ǀēk\ *adj* [*mathematical* fr. L *mathematicus* mathematical (fr. Gk *mathēmatikos* mathematical, scientific, fr. *mathēmat-, mathēma* learning, mathematics — fr. *mathein, manthanein* to learn — + *-ikos* -ic) + E *-al*; *mathematic* fr. L *mathematicus*] — akin to OHG *muntar* prompt, awake, ON *munda* to aim, Goth *mundon* to pay attention to, Skt *medhā* intelligence, wisdom; all fr. a prehistoric IE combination whose first constituent means "mind" and is akin to Skt *manas* mind and whose second constituent is akin to the verb represented by Skt *dadhāti* he puts, places — more at MIND, DO] **1 a :** of, relating to, or having the nature of mathematics ⟨a ~ textbook⟩ ⟨~ problems⟩ **b :** derived by or in accordance with mathematics ⟨a ~ solution to a problem⟩ **c :** designed for use in connection with mathematics ⟨slide rules and other ~ instruments⟩ **2 a :** rigorously exact **:** perfectly accurate **:** ABSOLUTE ⟨hit the ~ center of the target⟩ ⟨had been leveled off with ~ precision —T.B.Costain⟩ **b :** having an exactness or a regularity of proportions that suggests calculation by mathematics ⟨a series of ~ flower beds⟩ **c :** being beyond doubt or questioning **:** altogether positive **:** DEFINITE ⟨~ proof⟩ ⟨~ certainty⟩ **3 :** statistically possible but highly improbable **:** BARE, OUTSIDE ⟨has only a ~ chance of making the playoffs⟩ — **math·e·mat·i·cal·ly** \-ək(ə)lē, -ēk-, -li\ *adv*

**mathematical geography** *n* **:** a branch of geography that deals with the figure and motions of the earth, its seasons and tides, its measurement, and its representation on maps and charts by various methods of projection

**mathematical induction** *n* **:** INDUCTION 2b(2)

**mathematical logic** *n* **:** SYMBOLIC LOGIC

**math·e·ma·ti·cian** \,math(ə)məˈtishən\ *n* -s [MF *mathematicien*, fr. *mathematique* mathematical (fr. L *mathematicus*) + *-ien* -an, -ian] **:** a specialist or an expert in mathematics

**math·e·mat·i·ci·za·tion** \,=(=),mad·əsə̇ˈzāshən, -matə-, -,sīˈz-\ *n* -s **:** the action of mathematicizing or state of being mathematicized

**math·e·mat·i·cize** \,=(=)ˈmad·ə,sīz, -ˈmatə,-\ *vb* -ED/-ING/-S *see -ize in Explan Notes*, *vt* **:** to reduce to mathematical form or subject to mathematical treatment ⟨enables us to ~ the whole of a scientific theory —J.H.Woodger⟩ ~ *vi* **:** to make use of mathematics or mathematical treatment **:** work or reason mathematically

**mathematico-** *comb form* [NL, fr. L *mathematicus* mathematical] **:** mathematical and ⟨*mathematico*logical⟩ ⟨*mathematico*physical⟩

**math·e·mat·ics** \,mathəˈmad·ǀiks, -atǀ, ǀēks *sometimes* math-ˈma-\ *n pl but usu sing in constr, also* **math·e·mat·ic** [*mathematics* prob. fr. MF *mathematiques*, fr. pl. of *mathematique* mathematical; *mathematic* fr. ME *mathematique*, fr. L *mathematica*, fr. Gk *mathēmatikē*, fr. fem. of *mathēmatikos* mathematical, scientific — more at MATHEMATICAL] **1 :** a science that deals with the relationship and symbolism of numbers and magnitudes and that includes quantitative operations and the solution of quantitative problems — see FORMALISM 1d, INTUITIONISM 3, LOGICISM 2b **2 a :** operations or processes involved in the solution of mathematical problems ⟨a problem requiring some very complicated ~⟩ **b :** application or use of mathematics ⟨your ~ are not so good⟩

**math·e·ma·ti·za·tion** \,=(=)məd·əˈzāshən, -matə̇ˈz-; -məd-,-ˌtīˈz-, -,tīˈz-\ *n* -s [*mathematize* + *-ation*] **:** MATHEMATICIZATION

**math·e·ma·tize** \ˈ=(=)mə,tīz\ *vb* -ED/-ING/-S *see -ize in Explan Notes* [*mathemat-* (as in *mathematical, mathematics*) + *-ize*] **:** MATHEMATICIZE

**math·e·meg** \ˈmathə,meg\ *n* -s [Cree *mâthamek*] **:** a northern catfish that is a variety of the channel cat

**ma·the·sis** \məˈthēsə̇s, ˈmathəs-\ *n, pl* **matheses** [ME, fr. LL, fr. Gk *mathēsis* acquisition of knowledge, fr. *mathein, manthanein* to learn — more at MATHEMATICAL] *archaic* **:** SCIENCE, LEARNING **:** mental discipline; *esp* **:** MATHEMATICS

**mathesis uni·ver·sa·lis** \-,yünəvə(r)ˈsäləs\ *n* [NL, universal mathesis] **:** a universal mathematics or calculus; *specif* **:** a system envisaged by Leibniz as a foundation for reasoning in all of the sciences

**ma·thet·ic** \məˈthed·ik\ *adj, archaic* [fr. *mathesis*, after such pairs as E *antithesis: antithetic*] **:** of or relating to science or learning

**mathiola** *syn of* MATTHIOLA

**¹maths** *pl of* MATH

**²maths** \ˈmaths\ *n, pl* **maths** [by shortening] *Brit* **:** MATHEMATICS

**math·u·rin** *or* **math·u·rine** \ˈmathyərə̇n\ *n* -s *usu cap* [F, fr. St. *Mathurin*, 3d cent. A.D. priest to whom the Paris convent of the Trinitarian order was dedicated] **:** TRINITARIAN 1

**ma·ti·co** \məˈtē(,)kō\ *n* -s [Sp, perh. fr. *Matico*, dim. of *Mateo* Matthew (the name); perh. fr. the discovery of its styptic qualities by a soldier named Mateo] **1 :** a shrubby tropical American wild pepper (*Piper angustifolium*) with slender elongated aromatic leaves that are rich in volatile oil, gums, and tannins **2 :** the leaves of the matico used esp. formerly in medicine chiefly as a stimulant and hemostatic

**mat·ie** \ˈmad·ē\ *n* -s [modif. of D *maatjesharing*, alter. of MD *magedekenharinc*, fr. *magedekijn* maiden, virgin, girl (fr. *maget* maiden, virgin + *-kijn* -kin) + *harinc* herring — more at MAIDEN, HERRING] **:** a young fat herring with roe or milt incompletely developed

**ma·til·da** \məˈtildə\ *n* -s [prob. fr. the name *Matilda*] *slang, Austral* **:** a tramp's bundle **:** SWAG

**ma·til·dite** \-,dīt\ *n* -s [It *matildite*, fr. *Matilda*, mine near Morococha, Peru + It *-ite*] **:** a silver bismuth sulfide $AgBiS_2$ occurring in slender gray crystals (sp. gr. 6.9)

**ma·til·i·ja poppy** \məˈtilē,hä-\ *n* [*Matilija* Canyon, Ventura county, California] **:** a tall branching subshrub (*Romneya coulteri*) of California and Mexico that is sometimes cultivated in mild climates for its silvery-blue foliage and large fragrant white flowers with yellow centers

**¹mat·in** \ˈmatᵊn\ *n* -s [*matins*] *archaic* **:** AUBADE

**²matin** \"\ *adj* [*matins*] **1** *often cap* **:** of or relating to matins ⟨a ~ hymn⟩ **2 :** MATINAL ⟨the ~ clarity of the new day —T. O.Heggen⟩

**mat·in·al** \ˈmatᵊnəl\ *adj* [F, fr. OF *matinal, matinel*, fr. *matin* morning + *-al, -el* -al] **:** of or relating to morning esp. early morning ⟨the ~ chirping of birds⟩

**mat·i·nee** *or* **mat·i·née** \,matᵊnˈā\ *n* -s *often attrib* [F *matinée* morning, time of day before dinner, matinee, fr. OF *matinee* morning, fr. *matin* morning, fr. L *matutinum*, fr. neut. of *matutinus*, adj., of the morning, fr. *Matuta*, goddess of morning + L *-inus* -ine; akin to L *maturus* ripe — more at MATURE] **1 :** a performance of a production (as a play, opera, film) or the presentation of a concert or sometimes the holding of some other event in the afternoon or occas. in the morning or at midnight **2 :** a dressing gown esp. for a woman **3** *or* **matinee race :** a race (as a harness race) requiring no entrance fee and offering trophies and not money to the contestants

**matinee idol** *n* **:** an actor or other male performer widely popular among feminine audiences for his looks and charm

**mat·i·ness** \ˈmād·ēnə̇s, -ātē-, -inə̇s\ *n* -ES [by alter.] **:** MATEYNESS

**mating** *n* -s [fr. gerund of ⁶*mate*] **1 :** the act of pairing or matching esp. sexually **2 :** the period during which a seasonal-breeding animal is capable of mating

**mating group** *or* **mating isolate** *n* **:** a sexually reproducing group in which mating within the group is favored at the expense of mating outside the group

**mating type** *n* **:** a strain or clone or other isolate made up of organisms (as certain fungi or protozoans) incapable of sexual reproduction with one another but capable of such reproduction with members of other strains of the same organism and often capable of behaving as male in respect to one strain and as female in respect to another — compare MINUS, ³PLUS 5

**mat·ins** \ˈmatᵊnz\ *n pl but sometimes sing in constr, often cap* [ME *matines*, fr. OF, fr. LL *matutinae*, fr. L, fem. pl. of *matutinus*, adj., of the morning] **1 :** a liturgical night office forming with lauds the first and chief of the canonical hours and including psalms, other scriptural and patristic readings, hymns, and prayers — see NOCTURN **2 :** MORNING PRAYER

**matin song** *n* **:** AUBADE

**ma·ti·po** \ˈmäd·ə,pō\ *also* **ma·ti·pou** \-,paů\ *n* -s [Maori *matipo*] **:** MAPAU

**mat·ka** *or* **mat·kah** \ˈmatkə\ *n* -s [Russ *matka* female animal, dim. of *mat'* mother; akin to L *mater* mother — more at MOTHER] **:** a female fur seal

**matl** *abbr* material

**mat·lat·zin·ca** \,matlətˈsiŋkə\ *n, pl* **matlatzinca** *or* **matlatzincas** *usu cap* **1 a :** an Otomian people of the southern part of Mexico **b :** a member of such people **2 :** the language of the Matlatzinca people — **mat·lat·zin·can** \¦=,=¦siŋkən\ *adj, usu cap*

**mat·less** \ˈmatlə̇s\ *adj* [¹*mat*] **:** devoid of mats ⟨a ~ floor⟩

**mat·lock·ite** \ˈmatlə,kīt\ *n* -s [*Matlock*, Derbyshire, England, its locality, + E *-ite*] **:** a mineral PbFCl consisting of lead chloride and fluoride

**mat·low** \ˈmat,lō\ *n* -s [F *matelot* — more at MATELOT] *slang Brit* **:** SAILOR

**mat·man** \ˈmatmən\ *n, pl* **matmen** [¹*mat*] **1 :** WRESTLER **2 :** PITMAN 1f

**matr-** *or* **matri-** *or* **matro-** *comb form* [L *matr-, matri-*, fr. *matr-, mater* — more at MOTHER] **:** mother ⟨*matri*lineal⟩ ⟨*matro*clinous⟩ ⟨*matr*onymic⟩

**ma·tra** \ˈmä·trə\ *n* -s [Skt *mātrā*, lit., measure, fr. *māti* he measures — more at MEASURE] **:** a unit of metrical quantity equal to a short vowel in Sanskrit and other Indian languages

**mat·rass** *also* **mat·ras** *or* **mat·trass** \ˈma·trəs\ *n* -ES [F *matras* tall bottle, fr. MF, fr. *matras* arrow, fr. L *matara* javelin, fr. Gaulish; prob. akin to L *metiri* to measure — more at MEASURE] **:** a rounded glass flask with a long neck formerly used for dissolving substances by the application of heat or for distilling — called also *bolt head*

**matres lectionis** *pl of* MATER LECTIONIS

**ma·tri·arch** \ˈmā·trē,ärk, -,äk\ *n* -s [*matr-* + *-arch*] **:** a woman (as the mother of a family) having a status like that of a patriarch: as **a** (1) **:** a woman that rules often autocratically and usu. to the exclusion of male precedence over her immediate family or a larger group made up of her more remote descendants (2) **:** a woman that originates, rules over, or dominates a social group or an activity or a political entity **b :** a woman of great age and dignity

**ma·tri·ar·chal** \¦==¦ärkəl, -äk-\ *adj* **1 :** of, relating to, or having the characteristics of a matriarch or matriarchy ⟨~ authority⟩ ⟨one of those speeches, both candid and ~ which enables one to understand why the nation adored her —Milton Waldman⟩ **2 :** showing the influence of, depending on, or dominated by a matriarch or matriarchy ⟨a ~ people⟩ ⟨the ancient ~ system of government and ownership —E.A.Holt⟩ ⟨a ~ form of society⟩

**ma·tri·arch·ate** \ˈ==,är,kā|t, -,ä,k-, -,kə̇|, *usu* |d·+V\ *n* -s **1 a :** rule or domination by a matriarch **b :** something (as a social group or an activity) ruled or dominated by a matriarch **:** the realm of a matriarch **2 :** a theoretical stage or state or system in primitive society in which chief authority is held by matriarchs **3 :** MATRIARCHY 2

**ma·tri·archy** \ˈ==,ärkē, -äk-, -ki\ *n* -ES **1 :** MATRIARCHATE 1, 2 **2 :** a system of social organization in which descent is traced solely or primarily through the female line and in which inheritance of property and social prerogatives is also established in the same way

**¹matric** \ˈmā·trik, ˈma-\ *also* **matri·cal** \-rəkəl\ *adj* [*matric* fr. *matrical*, after such pairs as E *anatomical: anatomic*; *matrical* fr. LL *matricalis*, fr. L *matric-, matrix* womb, uterus + *-alis* -al — more at MATRIX] **:** of or relating to a matrix — **matrically** *adv*

**²ma·tric** \məˈtrik\ *n* -s [by shortening] *Brit* **:** MATRICULATION

**matric** *abbr* matriculated; matriculation

**mat·ri·car·ia** \,ma·trəˈka(a)rēə\ *n* [NL *Matricaria*, fr. *matricaria* feverfew, fr. L *matric-, matrix* womb, uterus + NL *-aria*; fr. the use of the feverfew in folk medicine against menstrual disorders] **1** *cap* **:** a genus of chiefly Old World weedy herbs (family Compositae) that have a strong odor, a conical receptacle, and broadly involucrate heads with white rays and yellow disk flowers — see CHAMOMILE, CORN MAYWEED **2** *pl* **matricaria** *or* **matricarias :** a plant of the genus *Matricaria*

**matricaria camphor** *n* [NL *matricaria* feverfew + E *camphor*] **:** levorotatory camphor

**mat·ri·cary** \ˈ==,kerē\ *n* -ES [NL *Matricaria*] **:** MATRICARIA 2

**matrice** *n* -s [ME *matris*, fr. L *matric-, matrix*] **:** MATRIX

**matri·cen·tric** \,ma·trə¦sen·trik, ¦mā-\ *adj* [*matr-* + *-centric*] **:** gravitating toward or centered upon the mother ⟨a ~ family pattern⟩ — compare PATRICENTRIC

**matrices** *pl of* MATRIX

**matri·ci·dal** \¦ma·trə¦sīdᵊl, ¦mā-\ *adj* **:** of or relating to a matricide

**matri·cide** \ˈ==,sīd\ *n* -s [in sense 1, fr. L *matricidium*, fr. *matri-* (fr. *matr-, mater* mother) + *-cidium* -cide (killing); in sense 2, fr. L *matricida*, fr. *matri-* + *-cida* -cide (killer) — more at MOTHER] **1 :** murder of a mother by her son or daughter **2 :** one that murders his mother

**matri·clan** \ˈmā·trə, ˈma·+,-\ *n* -s [*matr-* + *clan*] **:** a matrilineal clan — contrasted with *patriclan*

**matri·clin·ic** \¦==¦klinik\ *adj* [*matr-* + *-clinic*] **:** MATROCLINOUS

**matri·cli·nous** \-¦klīnəs\ *adj* [*matr-* + *-clinous*] **:** MATROCLINOUS

**matri·cli·ny** \ˈ==,klīnē\ *n* -ES [*matr-* + *-cliny*] **:** MATROCLINY

**ma·tric·u·la** \məˈtrikyələ\ *n* -s [LL, fr. *matric-, matrix* list (fr. L, womb, uterus) + L *-ula* — more at MATRIX] **1 :** a list or other register of the names of individuals that make up or belong to some group or category **2 :** a certificate of enrollment in a matricula — **ma·tric·u·lar** \-lə(r)\ *adj*

**ma·tric·u·lant** \-lənt\ *n* -s [ML *matriculant-, matriculans*, pres. part. of *matriculare*] **:** one that is matriculating or has recently matriculated

**¹ma·tric·u·late** \-,lāt, *usu* -ād·+V\ *vb* -ED/-ING/-S [ML *matriculatus*, past part. of *matriculare*, fr. LL *matricula*] *vt* **1 :** to admit to membership in a body, society, or institution esp. a college or university by entering the name in a register **:** ENROLL ⟨had been *matriculated* in the university⟩ **2** *obs* **:** ADOPT, NATURALIZE ~ *vi* **:** to become admitted to membership in a body, society, or institution (as a college or university) and have one's name officially registered after having previously met entrance requirements and typically after having successfully passed an entrance examination

**²matriculate** \-,lə̇t, -,lāt, *usu* -d·+V\ *n* -s [ML *matriculatus*, past part. of *matriculare*] **:** one that has been accepted into a college or university or other institution as a student or candidate for a degree

**ma·tric·u·la·tion** \=,==ˈlāshən\ *n* -s [¹*matriculate* + *-ion*] **1 :** the action of matriculating or the state of being matriculated **2 :** an examination on which matriculation or rejection of an individual depends **:** entrance examination

**ma·tric·u·la·tor** \=ˈ==,lād·ə(r)\ *n* -s [¹*matriculate* + *-or*] **:** MATRICULANT

**ma·tri·kin** \ˈmā·trə,kin\ *n* [*matr-* + *kin*] **:** maternal relatives

**matri·lateral** \¦ma·trə, ¦mā·+\ *adj* [*matr-* + *lateral*] **:** related on the mother's side **:** MATERNAL ⟨a ~ cousin⟩ — contrasted with *patrilateral* — **ma·tri·laterally** \"+\ *adv*

**matri·line** \ˈ==+,-\ *n* [*matr-* + *line*] **:** an aggregate of matrilineages

**matri·lineage** \,==+\ *n* [*matr-* + *lineage*] **:** lineage based on or tracing descent through the maternal line — contrasted with *patrilineage*

**ma·tri·lineal** \¦==+\ *adj* [*matr-* + *lineal*] **:** relating to, based on, or tracing descent through the maternal line ⟨a ~ society⟩ — contrasted with *patrilineal* — **ma·tri·lineally** \"+\ *adv*

**ma·tri·linear** \"+\ *adj* [*matr-* + *linear*] **:** MATRILINEAL — **ma·tri·linearly** \"+\ *adv*

**matri·lin·e·ate** \,==ˈlinēə̇t\ *n* -s [*matrilineal* + *-ate*] **:** MATRILINEAGE

**mat·ri·liny** \ˈma·trə,linē, -līnē\ *n* -ES [*matrilineal* + *-y*] **:** the practice of tracing descent through the mother's line — contrasted with *patriliny*

**matri·local** \¦ma·trə, ¦mā·+\ *adj* [*matr-* + *local*] **:** located at or centered around the residence of the wife's family or people ⟨a ~ village⟩ — contrasted with *patrilocal*

**matri·locality** \"+\ *n* [*matrilocal* + *-ity*] **:** residence esp. of a newly married couple with the wife's family or people — contrasted with *patrilocality*

**mat·ri·mo·ni·al** \,ma·trə¦mōnēəl, -nyəl\ *adj* [MF or L; MF, fr. L *matrimonialis*, fr. *matrimonium* marriage] **:** of or relating to matrimony **:** MARITAL, CONJUGAL ⟨the ~ bond⟩ — **mat·ri·mo·nial·ly** \-əlē, -li\ *adv*

**mat·ri·mo·ni·ous** \-nēəs\ *adj* [*matrimony* + *-ous*] *archaic* **:** MATRIMONIAL

**mat·ri·mo·ny** \ˈma·trə,mōnē, -ni, *chiefly Brit* -rəmən-\ *n* -ES [ME *matrimony, matrimoigne*, fr. MF *matremoine, matremoigne*, fr. L *matrimonium*, fr. *matr-, mater* mother — more at MOTHER] **1 a :** the union of man and woman as husband and wife **:** married state **:** married life **:** MARRIAGE **b :** this union entered into by baptized persons and so viewed by several large Christian churches as constituting one of the sacraments **2 a :** a card game played with a layout in which certain combinations of cards occur on which bets are placed **b :** a combination of a king and queen in this game

**matrimony vine** *n* **:** a shrub or vine of the genus *Lycium*; *esp* **:** an Asiatic shrub (*L. halimifolium*) with violet-purple flowers and orange-red berries

**matri·potestal** \¦ma·trē, ¦mā·+\ *adj* [*matr-* + *potestal*] **:** of, relating to, or being the power exercised by a matriarch or her blood relatives ⟨~ authority⟩ — contrasted with *patripotestal*

**matri·sib** \ˈ==+,-\ *n* [*matr-* + *sib*] **:** a matrilineal sib

**matrix** \ˈmā·triks, -rēks *sometimes* ˈma-\ *n, pl* **matri·ces** \ˈmā·trə,sēz *or* ˈma- *sometimes* ˈma·trəsēz\ *or* **matrix·es** [L, fr. *matr-, mater* mother] **1 a** *archaic* **:** UTERUS **b :** the intercellular substance of a tissue (as cartilage) **c :** the thickened epithelium at the base of a fingernail or toenail from which new nail substance develops **2 a :** something (as a surrounding or pervading substance or element) within which something else originates or takes form or develops ⟨an atmosphere of understanding and friendliness that is the ~ of peace⟩ **b :** a place or point of origin or growth **:** CRADLE ⟨viewing the East as the ~ of civilization⟩ **3 :** a mass by which something is enclosed or in which something is embedded: as **a** (1) **:** the natural material in which a fossil, metal, gem, crystal, or pebble is embedded (2) **:** GANGUE (3) **:** GROUNDMASS **b :** an external lightly staining layer presumably composed of deoxyribonucleic acid and basic proteins that is held to surround the chromonemata of a fully differentiated chromosome **4 a :** a recessed mold from which a relief surface is cast: as (1) **:** STRIKE 14 (2) **:** a brass character used in a typesetting machine; *also* **:** a comparable character used in a photocomposing machine (3) **:** a stereotype mold (4) **:** an electrotype mold **b :** a hollow in a slab designed to receive a monumental brass **c :** a hob used to form a punch from which a die for striking coins and medals is made **d :** DIE 6a(1) **e :** an engraved or inscribed die or stamp used in making the impression of a seal (as on wax or clay) **f :** an electroformed impression of a phonograph record that is used for mass-producing duplicates of the original recording — see MASTER MATRIX **5 a :** a foundation for inlaid or overlaid damascened work or for similar work **b :** the principal constituent of an alloy **c** (1) **:** a strip or band placed so as to serve as a retaining outer wall of a tooth in filling a cavity (2) **:** a metal or porcelain pattern in which an inlay is cast or fused **6 :** a material used to bind together the materials in an agglomerated mass (as a cement used in briquetting coal dust or in making concrete) **7 :** a gem stone cut from some stone (as opal or turquoise) and the surrounding natural material **8 :** the substrate on or within which a fungus grows **9 :** one of a class of rectangular arrays of mathematical elements (as the coefficients of simultaneous linear equations) that are subject to special algebraic laws ⟨a ~ combines with numbers or other *matrices*⟩ **10** *in color photography* **:** a positive photographic image that accepts dye differentially according to density and transfers the dye to make a final color print **11 a :** a propositional function in logic **b :** TRUTH TABLE

**matrix case** *n* **:** a rectangular metal box that holds the matrices in a Monotype caster — called also *diecase*

**matrix mechanics** *n pl but sing or pl in constr* **:** a quantum mechanics based upon the application of postulates connecting frequencies and intensities of spectrum lines by the use of a matrix-involving algebra

**matrix paper** *n* **:** a bulky absorbent paper suitable for use in stereotype molds — called also *flong paper*

**matro·clinal** \¦ma·trō¦klīnᵊl, ¦mā-\ *adj* [*matr-* + *-clinal*] **:** MATROCLINOUS

**matro·clin·ic** \-¦klinik\ *adj* [*matr-* + *-clinic*] **:** MATROCLINOUS

**matro·cli·nous** \-¦klīnəs\ *adj* [ISV *matr-* + *-clinous*] **:** derived or inherited from the mother or maternal line — compare MATERNAL INHERITANCE, PATROCLINOUS

**matro·cli·ny** \'==,klīnē\ *n* -ES [*matr-* + *-cliny*] **:** the quality or state of being matroclinous

**ma·tron** \'mā·trən\ *n* -S [ME *matrone*, fr. MF, fr. L *matrona*, fr. *matr-*, *mater* mother — more at MOTHER] **1 a :** a married woman usu. a mother and usu. marked by a dignified maturity of age or manner or by considerable social distinction or by some other special prestige **b** (1) **:** a woman superintendent or manager that takes care esp. of the domestic economy of a usu. public institution (as a hospital, prison) or that supervises the maintenance of order and discipline among women and children (as in a school, police station) or that holds some similar position of responsibility and trust (2) **:** a woman guard or attendant (as in a prison for women) **c** (1) **:** an attendant in a women's or children's rest room who assists patrons and keeps the room clean (2) **:** PARLORMAID 2 **d :** the presiding or chief officer in some women's organizations — compare PATRON **2 :** BROOD MATRON

**ma·tron·age** \-nij\ *n* -S **1 :** the matrons of a region or country **2 :** supervision, guardianship, or attendance by a matron **3 :** MATRONHOOD

**ma·tron·al** \-nᵊl\ *adj* [L *matronalis*, fr. *matrona* + *-alis* -al] **:** MATRONLY

**ma·tron·hood** \'mā·trən,hůd\ *n* **:** the quality or state of being a matron

**ma·tron·ize** \'mā·trə,nīz\ *vb* -ED/-ING/-S *vt* **1 :** to give the qualities of a matron to **:** cause to be a matron ⟨was *matronized* by her children and her responsibilities⟩ **2 a :** to act as a matron to or toward **:** superintend or attend in the capacity of a matron; *esp* **:** CHAPERONE ⟨offered to ~ the young people⟩ **b :** to preside as a matron over ⟨*matronizing* the reception⟩ ~ *vi* **1 :** to become a matron **2 :** to fulfill the role of a matron

**matronlike** \'==,=\ *adj* **:** MATRONLY

**ma·tron·li·ness** \'mā·trənlēnəs, -lin-\ *n* -ES **:** the quality or state of being matronly

**ma·tron·ly** *adj* **:** relating to, having the characteristics of, or suitable to a matron ⟨her ~ expression became more severe — Ellen Glasgow⟩

**matron of honor :** a bride's principal married wedding attendant — distinguished from *maid of honor;* compare BRIDESMAID

**ma·tron·ship** \'==,ship\ *n* **1 a** *archaic* **:** the rank, dignity, or personality of a matron **b :** the position or function of a matron ⟨a candidate for the ~ of the institution⟩ **2 :** MATRONHOOD

**mat·ro·nym·ic** \,ma·trə'nimik, -mēk\ *n* -S [*matr-* + *-onymic* (as in *patronymic*)] **:** a name derived from that of the mother or a maternal ancestor — contrasted with *patronymic*

**ma·tross** \mə'träs\ *n* -ES [D *matroos* sailor, fr. MF *matelots* sailors, pl. of *matelot* sailor — more at MATELOT] **:** a onetime gunner's mate (as during the American Revolution) that assisted in loading and firing and sponging guns

**mat rush** *n* [¹*mat*] **:** GREAT BULRUSH a

**mats** *pl of* MAT, *pres 3d sing of* MAT

**mat·sail** \'matsəl (*usual nautical pronunc*), -,sāl\ *n* **:** a sail made of an extremely coarse fabric (as of strands of old rope) often stiffened with laths (as of bamboo) and used typically on junks

**mat-shed** \'=,=\ *n* **:** a usu. temporary structure with walls and sometimes a roof made of overlapping pieces of coarse matting stretched over poles

**mat·ster** \'matstə(r)\ *n* -S [¹*mat* + *-ster*] **:** WRESTLER

**mat·su** \'mat(,)sü\ *n* -S [Jap] **:** a timber pine (*Pinus massoniana*) of eastern Asia that yields a valuable ornamental resinous wood

**mat·su·coc·cus** \,==='käkəs\ *n, cap* [NL, fr. Jap *matsu* + NL *-coccus*] **:** a genus of scales that includes destructive pests of forests (as pine forests)

**mat·su·ya·ma** \,mätsü¦yämə\ *adj, usu cap* [fr. *Matsuyama*, city in western Shikoku, Japan] **:** of or from the city of Matsuyama, Japan **:** of the kind or style prevalent in Matsuyama

**matt** *var of* MAT

**matta** *var of* MATTO

**mat·ta·more** \,mad·ə¦mō(ə)r\ *also* **mat·a·mo·ro** \,=='mō,rō\ *n* -S [obs. F *matamore*, fr. Ar *maṭmūrah* something buried or hidden] **:** a subterranean storehouse

**¹matte** *var of* MAT

**²mat·te** \'mä(,)tā\ *n* -S [F & AmerSp; F *maté*, fr. AmerSp *mate* — more at MATÉ] **:** MATÉ

**³matte** \'mat, *usu* -ad·+V\ *n* -S [F] **:** a crude mixture of sulfides formed in smelting sulfide ores of metals (as copper, lead, nickel)

**⁴matte** \"\ *vt* -ED/-ING/-S **:** to convert (ore) into matte

**matte box** *n* [¹*matte*] **:** a holder for positioning mattes, filters, and diffusing screens on the front of a camera

**¹matted** *adj* [in part of sense 1 & all of sense 2, fr. past part. of ²*mat;* in part of sense 1, fr. ⁵*mat* + *-ed*] **1 :** covered or provided with a mat or mats ⟨a ~ floor⟩ ⟨a ~ picture⟩ **2 a :** tangled closely together **:** having the parts adhering closely together ⟨~ hair⟩ **b :** intertangled with something specified **:** tangled full of — usu. used in combination ⟨a *leaf-matted* lawn⟩

**²matted** *adj* [fr. past part. of ³*mat*] **1 :** having a dull surface **:** UNBURNISHED, LUSTERLESS **2 :** having an evenly roughened surface — used esp. of carving on furniture

**mat·ted·ly** *adv* [¹*matted* + *-ly*] **:** in a matted manner **:** so as to be matted ⟨~ disheveled⟩

**mat·ted·ness** *n* -ES [¹*matted* + *-ness*] **:** the quality or state of being matted

**matted row system** *n* [¹*matted*] **:** a system of growing strawberries in which all runners or all runners formed before a certain date on each plant set are allowed to develop and plants are set 1½ to 2 feet apart in rows that are 3½ to 4½ feet apart

**¹mat·ter** \'mad·ə(r), -atə-\ *n* -S [ME *matere*, fr. OF *matere, matiere*, fr. L *materia* matter, subject, physical substance, wood for building, fr. *mater* mother — more at MOTHER] **1 a :** a subject (as a fact, an event or course of events, or a circumstance, situation, or question) of interest or relevance **:** an object of thought or consideration: as (1) **:** a topic under active and usu. serious or practical consideration ⟨several other ~*s* will come before the committee⟩ ⟨weighed and argued the ~ for several days before reaching a decision⟩ (2) *archaic* **:** an affair (as of business) belonging to a particular person (3) **:** something that is a subject of disagreement, strife, or litigation **:** a source or topic of contention ⟨let the ~ between us be decided on its merits⟩ ⟨the ~ in dispute is basically trivial⟩ (4) **matters** *pl, archaic* **:** personal business **:** AFFAIRS (5) **matters** *pl* **:** the events or circumstances of a particular but usu. unspecified situation, occurrence, or relation ⟨planned to discuss ~*s* with her husband soon⟩ **b** (1) *obs* **:** the substance of a branch of knowledge **:** something that forms the subject of any field (2) **:** something (as facts, information, data) that constitutes material for thought, discussion, or action ⟨for years he had been assembling the ~ for a wholly new treatment of theoretical mechanics⟩ (3) **:** the subject or substance of a writing or discourse **:** MEAT, FUNDAMENTALS ⟨a graceful style was not enough to hide a paucity of ~⟩ (4) **:** something (as information or a topic of discussion) of a particular nature or involving a particular and often specified thing or relation ⟨I have ~ of the utmost importance to impart and to your ear alone⟩ ⟨the ~ under discussion⟩; *broadly* **:** something of an indicated kind or having to do with an indicated field or situation ⟨questions involving ~*s* of faith⟩ ⟨a serious ~⟩ (5) **:** something that is to be proved (as in a court of law) — see MATTER IN DEED, MATTER IN PAIS, MATTER OF RECORD (6) *obs* **:** sensible or serious material as distinguished from nonsense or drollery **c** (1) *obs* **:** a reason or the grounds for something (as for action or being) (2) **:** a cause or source esp. of a feeling or an emotional reaction ⟨do you call this no ~ for wonder⟩ (3) **:** a circumstance or condition affecting a particular person or thing usu. unfavorably; *esp* **:** a circumstance or condition that requires or may be subject to mitigation, assuagement, or correction — used with the definite article ⟨what's the ~⟩ ⟨something the ~ with his generator⟩ **2 a :** the substance of which a physical object is composed **:** physical substance **:** MATERIAL, CONSTITUENT; *esp* **:** substance that is considered to constitute the observable universe, that together with energy is held to form the basis of objective phenomena, that includes among its properties extension, inertia, and gravitation, and that is indicated by experimental evidence to consist ultimately of elementary particles of comparatively few kinds **b :** material substance of a particular kind or for a particular purpose ⟨a viscid tarry ~⟩ ⟨dissolved out the mineral ~ with acid⟩ **c** (1) **:** material (as feces or urine) discharged or for discharge from the living body ⟨an obstruction interfering with passage of ~ from the intestine⟩ (2) **:** material discharged by suppuration **:** purulent matter **:** PUS **d :** physical substance as distinguished on the one hand from immaterial qualities and on the other from formed bodies **3 a** *obs* **:** the first product of creation **:** CHAOS **b :** the indeterminate subject of reality **:** the wholly or virtually passive element in the universe: (1) *among the Ionian nature philosophers* **:** a particular variety of primordial stuff; *specif* **:** one or more of the four elements (2) *in Anaximander* **:** APEIRON (3) *in atomism* **:** the totality of atoms (4) *in Plato* **:** something that is unlimited, formless, insensible, relatively nonexistent, but capable of being formed (5) *in Aristotle* **:** the absolutely formless substratum of all things having existence only in abstraction; *also* **:** the potential substance upon which form acts to produce realities **:** the receptive feminine principle that is a subject of change and development and has the power of resistance or implasticity by reason of which it yields only partially to the form-giving element ⟨in the Aristotelian metaphysics, the lower stages of existence are conceived as the ~ of the next higher stages, which are forms in relation to them; and so on to the end of the series —Frank Thilly⟩ — often distinguished from *form* (6) *in Plotinus* **:** the final weakest relatively qualityless indeterminate base and worthless emanation of the divine One (7) *in Descartes* **:** one of the two relative substances distinguished from spirit in being extended, entirely passive, and having the capacity for motion (8) *in Kant* **:** the sensible stuff, sensuous content, or manifold of experience **4 a :** MATTER OF A PROPOSITION **b :** MATTER OF A SYLLOGISM **5 :** a more or less definite amount, quantity, portion, or space — used chiefly in the phrase *a matter of* ⟨would you quarrel for a ~ of a dollar⟩ ⟨been a ~ of 10 years⟩ ⟨away he goes . . . a ~ of seven miles —Roger L'Estrange⟩ **6 a :** something written or printed or to be printed ⟨~ suitable for photocomposition⟩ **b :** type and other letterpress material set up for printing **c :** the text proper as distinguished from heads, illustrations, and notes or (as in a newspaper) from advertisements **7 :** material dispatched or to be dispatched by mail **:** MAIL ⟨third-class ~⟩ **8** *Christian Science* **:** the illusion that the objects perceived by the physical senses have the reality of substance ⟨Spirit is the real and eternal; ~ is the unreal and temporal —Mary B. Eddy⟩ — **for that matter** *also* **for the matter of that :** so far as that is concerned **:** as for that — **in the matter of :** in respect to **:** with regard to — **no matter :** not being of importance, consequence, or concern ⟨for all modern men *no matter* what their work —C.B.Forcey⟩ ⟨*no matter* how unpleasant some . . . might be —Carl Van Doren⟩

**²matter** \"\ *vb* -ED/-ING/-S *vi* **1 :** to be of importance **:** IMPORT, SIGNIFY ⟨it is not death that ~*s* but the fear of death —G.B.Shaw⟩ **2 :** to form or discharge pus **:** SUPPURATE ⟨a ~*ing* wound⟩ ~ *vt* **1 :** to regard as important or worthwhile **:** concern oneself about **:** care for **:** VALUE

**³matter** \"\ *n* -S [partly fr. ME *mattere* maker of mats, fr. ¹*mat* + *-ere* -er; partly fr. ³*mat* + *-er*] **:** one that mats: as **a :** a maker of mats **b :** MATTOIR

**mat·ter·ate** \-ə,rāt, *usu* -ād·+V\ *vi* -ED/-ING/-S [alter (prob. influenced by ¹*matter*) of *maturate*] *dial* **:** SUPPURATE, ²MATTER 2

**mat·ter·ful** \'==fəl\ *adj* **:** full of substance **:** containing matter of significance or interest ⟨a small but very ~ volume⟩

**mat·ter·horn** \'mad·ə(r),hȯ(ə)rn, -atə-, -ȯ(ə)n\ *n* [fr. *Matterhorn*, peak in the Pennine Alps on the Swiss-Italian border] **:** a high steep-sided sharp-pointed peak or mountain

**matter in controversy 1 :** FACT IN CONTROVERSY **2 a :** the case in controversy **:** the subject matter of litigation **:** the case with the issues of law or of fact stated **b :** the monetary value involved in a case and the pecuniary consequences to the parties involved

**matter in deed 1 :** matter to be proved by a deed or specialty **2 :** matter to be proved by any evidence — distinguished from *matter of law*

**matter in issue 1 :** FACT IN ISSUE **2 :** the ultimate fact or state of facts set forth in legal pleadings on which a verdict or finding is predicated as distinguished from the evidentiary facts offered to prove the ultimate fact or facts pleaded

**matter in pais 1 :** matter to be proved solely by the testimony of witnesses unsupported by any judicial record, deed, or other written or tangible evidence **2 :** matter giving rise to an equitable estoppel or estoppel in pais

**mat·ter·ism** \'mad·ə,rizəm, -atə-\ *n* -S **:** MATERIALISM

**mat·ter·less** \'mad·|ə(r)ləs, -at, -R *also* |ᵊl-\ *adj* **:** lacking substance or material quality

**matter of a proposition** *logic* **:** the particular content as opposed to the form (as that in which the proposition "All men are mortal" differs from "All A is B"): **a :** the subject and predicate — called also *material matter* **b :** the fact designated — called also *formal matter*

**matter of a syllogism** *logic* **1 :** the propositions of a syllogism esp. when contrasted with the form — called also *proximate matter* **2 :** the terms of a syllogism — called also *remote matter*

**matter of breviary** [trans. of MF *matiere de breviaire*] **:** something not open to question **:** something axiomatic

**matter of course :** a natural logical result or accompaniment **:** something that is to be expected with confidence

**matter-of-course** \¦===¦=\ *adj* [*matter of course*] **1 :** being such as is or may be expected or depended upon as a matter of course **2 :** regarding or assuming something to be a matter of course

**matter of fact 1 :** an actual occurrence **:** a matter that is or is demonstrable as fact **2 :** a legal matter involving primarily proof or evidence — distinguished from *matter of law*

**matter-of-fact** \¦===¦=\ *adj* [*matter of fact*] **1 :** adhering to or concerned with fact **:** not fanciful or imaginative ⟨a *matter-of-fact* account of the trip⟩ **2 :** free from show or affectation **:** PRACTICAL, COMMONPLACE ⟨a very *matter-of-fact* manner⟩ — **mat·ter-of-fact·ly** *adv* — **mat·ter-of-fact·ness** *n* -ES

**matter of law :** a legal matter involving primarily a question of law that according to the rules of law must be answered by the court in accordance with principles of law — distinguished from *matter in deed, matter of fact*

**matter of record :** matter appearing on the judicial record of a court or in a record required by law to be kept in a particular place

**matters** *pl of* MATTER, *pres 3d sing of* MATTER

**matter wave** *n* **:** DE BROGLIE WAVE

**mat·tery** \'mad·ərē, -atərē, -ri\ *adj* [ME *mattry*, fr. *matere* matter + *-y*] **:** producing or containing pus or material resembling pus ⟨eyes all ~⟩

**mattes** *pl of* MATTE, *pres 3d sing of* MATTE

**mat·teuc·cia** \,mad·ē'üch(ē)ə, mə'tü-\ [NL, fr. Carlo *Matteucci* †1868 Ital. physicist + NL *-ia*] *syn of* PTERETIS

**mat·the·an** *or* **mat·thae·an** \mə'thēən, ma'-\ *adj, usu cap* [LL *Matthaeus, Mattheus* Matthew, one of the 12 apostles traditionally regarded as author of the first gospel + E *-an*] **:** of, relating to, or characteristic of the evangelist Matthew or the gospel ascribed to him

**mat·thew walk·er knot** \¦math(,)(y)ü'wȯk·ə(r)-\ *or* **matthew walker** *n, usu cap M&W* [prob. fr. the name *Matthew Walker*] **:** a stopper knot made by sticking the end of each strand of a rope up through the bights of the next two strands

Matthew Walker knot

**mat·thi·o·la** \mə'thīələ\ *n, cap* [NL, fr. Pierandrea *Mattioli* (*Matthiolus*) †1577 Ital. physician] **:** a genus of Old World herbs and subshrubs (family Cruciferae) having long terete siliques each with numerous winged seeds — see STOCK 24a

**¹matting** *n* -S [fr. gerund of ²*mat*] **1 a :** an act of interweaving or tangling together so as to make a mat **b :** the process of becoming matted **2 a :** material for mats; *esp* **:** a fabric of or resembling matted work **b :** mats or stock of mats **3** [⁵*mat* + *-ing*] **:** an ornamental border

**²matting** *n* [fr. gerund of ³*mat*] **:** a dull lusterless surface (as on gilding, metalwork, or satin)

**³matting** *pres part of* MATT *or of* MATTE

**matting wicket** *n* **:** a cricket wicket consisting of a usu. coir or canvas mat laid over leveled ground or other smooth base

**mattins** *often cap, chiefly Brit var of* MATINS

**matt·ness** *n* -ES **:** relative flatness of finish

**mat·to** \'mäd·(,)ō, 'ma-\ *also* **mat·ta** *or* **ma·ta** \'mäd·ə, 'ma-\ *n* -S [Pg *mato, mata*, fr. L *matta* mat — more at MAT] **:** dense tropical American forest; *also* **:** reclaimed land naturally covered with such forest

**¹mat·tock** \'mad·ək, -atək\ *n* -S [ME *mattok*, fr. OE *mattuc*, prob. fr. (assumed) VL *matteuca;* akin to L *mateola* mallet — more at MACE] **:** an implement that combines the features of an adz, ax, and pick and is used for digging, grubbing, and chopping

heads of mattocks

**²mattock** \"\ *vt* -ED/-ING/-S **:** to dig or grub with a mattock — often used with *up* or *out* ⟨~*ing* out stumps⟩

**mat·toid** \'mad·,ȯid\ *n* -S [It *mattoide*, fr. *matto* mad, crazy (fr. L *mattus* stupid, drunk) + *-oide* -oid — more at MAT] **:** a borderline psychopath

**mat·toir** \(')ma·¦twär\ *n* -S [F *matoir*, fr. *mater* to cause to have a surface without luster, mat — more at MAT] **:** a coarse punch used by engravers for making a rough surface on etching ground or on the naked copper to produce an effect after printing that is very similar to stippled lines

**mat·tole** \mə'tōl\ *n, pl* **mattole** *or* **mattoles** *usu cap* **1 a :** an Athapaskan people of northwestern California **b :** a member of such people **2 :** a language of the Mattole people

**mat·to·wac·ca** \,mad·ə'wakə\ *n* -S [prob. fr. an Algonquian language of the southeastern U. S.] **:** FALL HERRING

**mattrass** *var of* MATRASS

**¹mat·tress** \'ma·trəs\ *n* -ES [ME *materas*, fr. OF, fr. Ar *maṭraḥ* place where something is thrown] **1 a :** a resilient pad for use as a resting place either alone or supported (as by springs) on a bedstead, consisting in its simplest form of a large fabric sack stuffed with resilient filling (as wool or feathers) but now being usu. a product of manufacture with carefully stabilized filling of felted cotton, hair, or sponge rubber or sometimes of an arrangement of coiled springs that is permanently covered with fabric and often consolidated by tufting **b :** an inflatable airtight sack adapted to serve as a mattress when inflated and to collapse into a small space (as for packing) when not in use **2 a** *obs* **:** a protective covering esp. for plants **:** MAT **b :** a mass of interwoven brush and poles to protect a bank from erosion **c :** a supplementary or reinforcing foundation (as of brush, stumps, logs) to distribute a heavy load over soft ground

**²mattress** \"\ *vt* -ED/-ING/-ES **:** to provide, support, or protect with a mattress or mattresses ⟨~*ed* the curve of the bank to prevent undercutting⟩

**mattress suture** *also* **mattress stitch** *n* **:** a surgical stitch in which the suture is passed back and forth through both edges of a wound, the needle each time being reinserted on the side of egress and passing through to the side of ingress, thereby simulating the manner in which the edge of a mattress is sewed

**matts** *pl of* MATT, *pres 3d sing of* MATT

**ma·tu·ra diamond** \'mäd·ərə-\ *n, usu cap M* [fr. *Matura* (Matara), town in southern Ceylon] **:** zircon that is naturally or artificially made colorless

**mat·u·rate** \'machə,rāt, *usu* -ād·+V\ *vb* -ED/-ING/-S [L *maturatus*, past part. of *maturare* to make ripe, promote suppuration of, fr. *maturus* ripe] *vt* **1** *archaic* **:** to promote suppuration of (as an abscess) **2 :** to bring to ripeness or maturity **:** cause to ripen ~ *vi* **1 :** RIPEN, MATURE **2** *archaic* **:** SUPPURATE

**mat·u·ra·tion** \,=='rāshən\ *n* -S [MF & ML; MF, fr. ML *maturation-, maturatio* process of becoming mature or ripe, fr. L *maturatus* + *-ion-, -io* -ion] **1** *archaic* **:** the formation of pus esp. in the ripening of a boil **2 a :** the process of bringing or coming to full development **:** the process of becoming mature **b** *obs* **:** the alchemical conversion of base metal to gold **c** *obs* **:** supposed development of one form of matter or being from another **d** (1) **:** the emergence of personal characteristics and behavioral phenomena through endogenous growth processes — compare LEARNING (2) **:** the achievement of intellectual maturity or emotional maturity **e :** the final stages of differentiation of cells, tissues, or organs: as (1) **:** the lignification of xylem in a higher plant (2) **:** the final phases of ripening of a seed **3 a :** the entire process by which diploid gonocytes are transformed into haploid gametes involving usu. two meiotic divisions in which reduction occurs accompanied in the female or followed in the male by physiological and structural changes fitting the resulting gamete or gametes for their future role **b :** SPERMIOGENESIS 1

**mat·u·ra·tion·al** \¦==¦rāshənᵊl, -shnəl\ *adj* **:** of, relating to, or involved in maturation ⟨~ defects⟩

**maturation division** *n* **:** a meiotic division

**maturation factor** *n* **:** VITAMIN $B_{12}$

**¹mat·u·ra·tive** \'machə,rād·iv\ *n* -S [ME *maturatif*, prob. fr. (assumed) ML *maturativus*, fr. *maturativus*, adj.] **:** medication formerly used to promote suppuration — compare LAUDABLE PUS

**²matu·ra·tive** \" *in sense 1;* *in senses 2 & 3* mə'türəd·iv *or* mə·'tyü-\ *adj* [ME *maturatif*, prob. fr. (assumed) ML *maturativus*, fr. L *maturatus* + *-ivus* -ive] **1** *archaic* **:** conducing to suppuration **2 :** conducing to ripeness or maturity **3 :** of or relating to germ-cell maturation

**¹ma·ture** \mə'tü(ə)r, mə·'tyü-, -üə *sometimes* mə'chü-\ *adj* -ER/-EST [ME, fr. L *maturus* ripe, seasonable; akin to L *mane* in the morning, *manus* good, and perh. to OIr *maith* good] **1 :** involving, based on, or arrived at after slow and careful consideration ⟨a ~ argument⟩ ⟨~ reflections⟩ ⟨a ~ plan of action⟩ **2 a :** having attained the normal peak of natural growth and development **:** fully grown and developed **:** RIPE ⟨~ fruit⟩ ⟨the ~ reproducing human being⟩ ⟨a ~ ovary⟩ **:** having undergone maturation ⟨~ germ cells⟩ **b :** having attained a final or desired state usu. after a period of ripening or processing ⟨~ paper stock⟩ ⟨full-bodied ~ wines⟩ **c :** having or expressing the mental and emotional qualities that are considered normal to an adult socially adjusted human being ⟨a ~ outlook⟩ ⟨parents were willing to be ~, to take responsibility —H.S.Canby⟩ **3 :** of or relating to a condition of full development ⟨a man of ~ years⟩ **:** characteristic of or suitable to a mature individual ⟨~ responsibilities⟩ ⟨a ~ grace⟩ **4 a** *obs* **:** taking place at the proper time **b :** having reached a set limit of time **:** DUE ⟨a note that would become ~ in 18 months⟩ **5 a** *of the topography of a surface* **:** well dissected by the erosion of running water so that slopes predominate greatly over flats **b :** belonging to the middle portion of a cycle of erosion or other change in which geologic agents are at a maximum of efficiency or the entire work to be done is about half accomplished ⟨a ~ stream⟩ ⟨~ coasts⟩

**²mature** \"\ *vb* -ED/-ING/-S [MF & L; MF *maturer*, *madurer* to make ripe, promote suppuration of, fr. L *maturare*, fr. *maturus* ripe] *vt* **1** *obs* **:** SUPPURATE **2 a :** to bring or hasten to maturity ⟨summer suns *maturing* the fruit⟩ **b :** to promote full development of **:** bring to a desired state or to completion ⟨slowly *matured* his plans⟩ **c :** to fire (pottery) to the point that develops the optimum strength; *also* **:** to fuse (a glaze) completely on pottery ~ *vi* **1 :** to advance toward maturity **:** become fully developed or ripe ⟨wine and judgment ~ with age⟩ **2** *of an obligation* **:** to become due ⟨the note ~*s* next month⟩ **3** *of pottery* **:** to undergo maturing

**syn** DEVELOP, RIPEN, AGE: MATURE indicates attaining to a fullness of growth, an emergence from an undeveloped or incomplete stage ⟨a generation of serious students, *matured* by military service and anxious to absorb the best of what the institutions have to offer —Roy Lewis & Angus Maude⟩ ⟨he *matured* the plan and attended to the details of fitting out the expedition that destroyed the privateer —C.S.Alden⟩ DEVELOP indicates the freeing, unfolding, and growing of what has been latent, potential, or suspended ⟨the kitten's hunting instinct was not yet *developed* —Bertrand Russell⟩ ⟨there *developed* a growing hostility against special privileges granted by the government —H.S.Drinker⟩ ⟨his interest in the theater, begun while he was a chemistry student, *developed* into a lifetime vocation —*Americana Annual*⟩ RIPEN indicates attainment to a full stage of development, to the nearest possible perfection of the thing involved ⟨friendship *ripening* into love⟩ ⟨at twenty-three she was still young enough to *ripen* to a maturer beauty —Ellen Glasgow⟩ ⟨he basked and *ripened* in the sun of books till he grew as mellow as a meerschaum —Van Wyck Brooks⟩ ⟨the civil law, which was in force in most of the countries of continental Europe and their colonies, was the accepted product of the *ripened* experience of many centuries of Roman jurisprudence —*Encyc. Americana*⟩ AGE may indicate approach to a period of decline or decay in reference to people; in reference to things it may suggest withholding use until the perfective effects of time may be felt ⟨he has *aged*, suddenly, as though the burden he has been carrying for years has only now begun to tell on him —Gordon Bell⟩ ⟨*age* the wine in old wooden barrels⟩ ⟨*aging* the cheese before shipping it out⟩

**ma·ture·ly** *adv* **:** in a mature manner **:** with maturity ⟨expect children to act ~⟩

**ma·ture·ment** \-mənt\ *n* -s **:** the bringing of something to a state of maturity

**ma·ture·ness** *n* -ES **:** MATURITY 2, 4

**ma·tur·er** \mə'türə(r), mə'tyü- *sometimes* mə'chü-\ *n* -s **:** one that brings something to maturity

**mat·u·res·cence** \,machə'res°n(t)s\ *n* -s [fr. *maturescent*, after such pairs as E *different: difference*] **:** MATURATION

**mat·u·res·cent** \¦==¦res°nt\ *adj* [L *maturescent-, maturescens*, pres. part. of *maturescere* to become ripe, fr. *maturus* ripe] **:** approaching maturity

**mature soil** *n* **:** a soil that has passed through the major developmental phases and become relatively stabilized esp. to the point that incorporation of organic material is approximately equal to the withdrawal of soluble material by plants

**maturing** *adj* **:** approaching a mature stage or state ⟨~ fruits⟩ ⟨~ promissory notes⟩ ⟨~ wines⟩

**ma·tur·ism** \mə'tü,rizəm, mə'tyü- *sometimes* mə'chü-\ *n* -s **:** a state characterized by full development and consequently by lack of opportunity for further growth or development ⟨the fear of economic ~⟩

**ma·tu·ri·ty** \-,rəd·ē, -ətē, -i\ *n* -ES [ME *maturite*, fr. L *maturitat-, maturitas* ripeness, fr. *maturus* ripe + *-itat-, -itas* -ity] **1** *obs* **:** due care or consideration **:** DELIBERATENESS **2 :** the quality or state of being mature **:** full development **:** RIPENESS ⟨~ of grain⟩ ⟨~ of judgment⟩ ⟨~ of wine⟩ **3** *obs* **:** prompt action or consideration **4 :** a becoming due **:** termination of the period that a note or other obligation has to run **5 :** a stage intermediate between youth and old age that is the second of the three principal stages in a cycle of erosion or of other geologic change

**maturity of chances :** a system of betting in gambling games based on an assumption that observable past events influence the expected result of the next event

**maturity race** *n* **:** a race exclusively for 4-year-old horses

**ma·tu·ti·nal** \mə'tüt°nəl, mə'tyü-; ¦machə¦tīn°l\ *adj* [LL *matutinalis*, fr. L *matutinus* of the morning + *-alis* -al — more at MATINEE] **:** of, relating to, or occurring in the morning **:** EARLY — **ma·tu·ti·nal·ly** \-əlē, -°lē\ *adv*

**mat·u·tine** \'machə,tīn\ *adj* [ME *matutyne* of the morning, fr. L *matutinus*] **1** *archaic* **:** MATUTINAL **2** *of a star* **:** rising in or just before the dawn — **mat·u·tine·ly** *adv, archaic*

**matweed** \'=,=\ *n* [¹*mat*] **1 :** any of several maritime grasses (as *Ammophila arenaria, Spartina stricta* and *Lygeum spartum*) **2 :** MATGRASS b

**maty** \'mād·ē\ *also* **mate** \'māt\ *or* **matee** \'mād·ē\ *n* -ES [origin unknown] **:** a native servant in India; *esp* **:** an assistant servant

**mat·zah** *also* **mat·za** \'mätsə\ *n, pl* **mat·zoth** \-(,)tsōt(h), -ōs\ *or* **mat·zahs** \-,tsəz, -əs\ *or* **mat·zot** \-(,)tsōt, -ōs\ *also* **matzas** [Heb *maṣṣāh*] **:** MATZO

**mat·zo** *or* **mat·zoh** \'mätsə, -(,)tsō *also* -(,)tsō\ *n, pl* **mat·zoth** \-(,)tsōt(h), -ōs, *or* **mat·zos** \-,tsəz, -əs; -(,)tsōz, -ōs\ *or* **mat·zot** \-(,)tsōt, -ōs\ [Yiddish *matse*, fr. Heb *maṣṣāh*] **1 :** unleavened bread eaten at the Passover — often used in the pl. with either sing. or pl. construction **2 :** a wafer of matzo

**mat·zoon** *also* **mad·zoon** \(')mät¦sün, -äd¦zün\ *n* -s [Arm *madzun*; akin to L *madēre* to be wet — more at MEAT] **:** a fermented milk food resembling yogurt

**mau·bey** \'mōbē\ *n* -s [origin unknown] **:** a bitter drink prepared from the bark of a West Indian tree

**mau·cher·ite** \'maùchə,rīt\ *n* -s [G *maucherit*, fr. Wilhelm *Maucher* †1930 Ger. mineral dealer + G *-it* -ite] **:** a mineral $Ni_{11}As_8$ consisting of a nickel arsenide

**maud** \'mōd\ *n* -s [prob. fr. the name *Maud*] **1 :** a gray and black plaid worn in southern Scotland **2 :** a double fabric or a blanket or shawl with design like that of a maud plaid

**maud·lin** \'mōdlən\ *adj* [fr. *Maudlin* Mary Magdalene, woman whom Jesus healed of evil spirits (Lk 8:2), fr. ME *Maudeleyn*, fr. OF *Madelaine*, fr. LL *Magdalene*, fr. Gk *Magdalēnē*; fr. the practice of representing Mary Magdalene in paintings as a penitent sinner with eyes swollen and red with weeping] **1** *archaic* **:** TEARFUL, WEEPING, LACHRYMOSE **2 :** tearfully or weakly emotional **:** effusively sentimental ⟨~ eloquence⟩ ⟨a ~ poet⟩ ⟨~ expressions of regret⟩ **3 :** drunk enough to be emotionally silly **:** FUDDLED ⟨a mob of ~ rummies . . . sing hymns —Joseph Mitchell⟩ **syn** see SENTIMENTAL

**maud·lin·ism** \-lə,nizəm\ *n* -s **:** maudlin display or behavior or a tendency toward it ⟨a eulogy marked by ~⟩

**maud·lin·ly** *adv* **:** in a maudlin manner

**mau·ger** \'mōgə(r)\ *adj* [perh. fr. G *mager* thin, lean, fr. OHG *magar* — more at MEAGER] *dial* **:** THIN, EMACIATED, PUNY

**maught** *or* **maucht** \'mōkt, 'mäkt\ *n* -s [ME, of Scand origin; akin to ON *māttr* might, strength — more at MIGHT] *Scot* **:** MIGHT, STRENGTH, ABILITY

**mau·gra·bee** \'mōgrə,bē\ *or* **mau·gra·bin** \-bin\ *n* -s *usu cap* [Ar *maghribīy* western, North African] *archaic* **:** an African Moor

¹**mau·gre** *also* **mau·ger** \'mōgə(r)\ *prep* [ME *maugre*, fr. OF *maugré*, fr. *maugré*, n.] *archaic* **:** in spite of **:** NOTWITHSTANDING

²**maugre** *also* **mauger** *n* -s [ME *maugre*, fr. OF *maugré* displeasure, fr. *mau, mal* bad + *gré* will, pleasure, fr. L *gratum*, neut. of *gratus* beloved, dear, agreeable — more at MAL-, GRACE] *obs* **:** ILL WILL **:** SPITE — often used as a mild imprecation

**mauk** \'mōk\ *var of* MAWK

**ma·u·ka** \mä'ükə\ *adv (or adj)* [Hawaiian, fr. *ma* towards + *uka* uplands, upward] *Hawaii* **:** toward the mountains **:** INLAND, UPLAND

**mau·kin** \'mō,kin\ *or* **maul·kin** \'mōl,-\ *var of* MALKIN

¹**maul** *also* **mall** *or* **mawl** \'mōl\ *n* -s [ME *malle, mell*, fr. OF *mail* hammer, maul, fr. L *malleus* hammer; akin to L *molere* to grind — more at MEAL] **1 a :** a weapon in the form of a heavy club often with a metal-studded head **:** MACE **b :** a heavy hammer often with a wooden head; *esp* **:** one (as a beetle, mallet, or sledge) used for driving wedges or piles **2** *obs* **:** a determined or irresistible foe **3** [²*maul*] **a** (1) *or* **maul in goal :** a play formerly used in rugby and American football in which an attacking player who had carried the ball across the goal line was prevented from touching it down for a score by a defending player (2) **:** LOOSE SCRUM **b :** a rough or rowdy brawl ⟨the toughs charged the gentry and . . . the battle became a heavy ~ —Bruce Marshall⟩

maul 1b

²**maul** *also* **mall** \"\ *vb* -ED/-ING/-S [ME *mallen*, fr. OF *maillier*, fr. *mail*, n.] *vt* **1** *obs* **:** to strike or knock down with or as if with a maul **2 a :** to beat and bruise ⟨~*ed* the boy with repeated blows⟩ **b :** to injure by or as if by beating **:** beat about **:** MANGLE ⟨the heavy seas ~*ed* the boats about⟩ **c :** to handle roughly or with lack of care and consideration ⟨this blessed language of ours is so ~*ed* —*Jour. of Accountancy*⟩; *often* **:** to fondle roughly ⟨stop ~*ing* the kitten⟩ **3 :** to split (wood) with maul and wedges ⟨planned to ~ out rails for a new fence⟩ ~ *vi* **:** to engage in mauling ⟨picking and ~*ing* at the hat in his hands⟩

³**maul** \"\ *dial var of* MALLOW

**mau·la** \'maùlə\ *n, pl* **ma·wa·li** \mə'wälē\ [Ar *mawla* (pl. *mawālī*)] **:** a recent convert to Islam; *esp* **:** a non-Arab convert extended the status of a protected client by one of the Arab peoples

**mau·la·na** \maù'länə\ *n* -s [Ar *mawlānā*] **:** a learned Muslim scholar esp. in India — often used as a form of address

**maul·er** \'mōlə(r)\ *n* -s **:** one that mauls: as **a :** a splitter of rails **b** *slang* **:** FIST

**maul·ey** *or* **maul·ie** \'mōlē\ *n* -s [perh. fr. fr. ¹*maul* + *-y*] **:** HAND, FIST

**mauling** *n* -s [fr. gerund of ²*maul*] **:** rough treatment **:** hard usage **:** ABUSE ⟨the coast took a ~ from the storm⟩

**maul oak** *n* **:** CANYON LIVE OAK

**maul·stick** \'mōl,stik\ *or* **mahl·stick** \'mäl-\ *n* [part trans. of D *maalstok*, fr. obs. D *malen* to paint (fr. MD) + D *stok* stick; akin to OHG *mālōn, mālēn* to paint; derivative (influenced in meaning by the word represented by OHG *meil* spot) fr. the root of OHG *māl* time — more at MEAL, MOLE] **:** a stick used by painters as a rest for the hand while working

**maul·vi** *also* **moul·vi** \'maùlvē\ *or* **mool·vi** \'mül-\ *n, pl* **maulvies** *or* **maulvis** [Hindi *maulvī*, fr. Ar *mawlawī*] **:** a learned teacher or doctor of Islamic law — used esp. in India as a form of address for a learned Muslim who ministers to the religious needs of others

**mau·ma** \'mòmə\ *or* **mau·mer** \-mə(r)\ *dial var of* MAMMA

**mau mau** \'maù,maù\ *n, pl* **mau mau** *or* **mau maus** *usu cap both Ms* [origin unknown] **:** a member or adherent of an African terroristic and revolutionary society or movement originating among the Kikuyu people of Kenya and demanding elimination of European settlers esp. in the uplands of Kenya and restoration of control to native Africans

**mau·me·né test** \,mōmə'nā-\ *n, usu cap M* [after Edme J. *Maumené*, 19th cent. Fr. chemist] **:** a test made by determining the rise in temperature produced by adding concentrated sulfuric acid to a fatty oil under specified conditions and used for indicating the degree of unsaturation of the oil

**mau·met** \'mòmət\ *n* -s [ME, fr. OF *mahommet*, fr. *Mahommet* Muhammad †A.D. 632 Arabian prophet and founder of Islam; fr. a medieval belief that Muslims worshiped images of Muhammad] **1** *obs* **:** a false god or idol **2** *now dial Brit* **a :** an odd figure **:** PUPPET, EFFIGY, IMAGE, DOLL — used also as a generalized term of abuse or contempt **b :** SCARECROW **3** *archaic* **:** a fancy pigeon with dark eyes and white or creamy feathers

**mau·met·ry** \'mòmə·trē\ *n* -ES [ME *maumetrie*, fr. *maumet* + *-rie* -ry] **1** *obs* **:** IDOLATRY **2** *pl* **maumetries** *obs* **:** the appurtenances of idolatry **3** *usu cap, archaic* **:** MUHAMMADANISM

**maun** *also* **man** \'mán, 'mòn, mən\ *verbal auxiliary* [ME *man*, fr. ON, will, shall, 1st & 3d pers. sing. pres. indic. of *munu* — more at MUN] *chiefly Scot* **:** MUST — used with an infinitive without *to* ⟨I ~ explain to him —William Black⟩

**mau·na·loa** \'maùnə'lōə\ *n* -s [Hawaiian] **:** a leguminous vine (*Canavalia microcarpa*) that is native to the Mascarene islands, has white, lavender, pink, or reddish flowers, and is much used for leis in Hawaii

**maunch** *or* **maunche** *var of* MANCHE

¹**maund** *or* **maun** \'mòn(d), 'mänd, 'mand\ *n* -s [ME *maund* hand basket, fr. MF *mande*, fr. MD; akin to OE *mand* hand basket, MLG *mande*] **1** *now dial Brit* **:** a hand basket **:** HAMPER **2** *now dial Brit* **:** a measure, varying in quantity

²**maund** \'mònd\ *vb* [perh. fr. MF *mendier*, fr. L *mendicare* — more at MENDICANT] *archaic* **:** BEG

³**maund** \"\ *also* **man** *n* -s [Hindi *man*, fr. Skt *manā*] **:** any of various Indian units of weight; *esp* **:** a unit equal to 82.28 pounds

**maund·age** \-dij\ *n* -s [³*maund* + *-age*] **:** amount in maunds

¹**maund·er** \'mòndə(r), 'män-\ *or* **maund·er·er** \-dərə(r)\ *n* -s [*maunder* fr. ²*maund* + *-er*; *maunderer* prob. fr. obs. E *maunder* to beg (fr. ¹*maunder*) + E *-er*] *archaic* **:** BEGGAR

²**maunder** \"\ *vi* **maundered; maundered; maundering** \-d(ə)riŋ\ **maunders** [prob. imit.] **1** *now dial Brit* **:** GRUMBLE **2 :** to move or progress slowly and uncertainly without definite aim or course **:** ramble idly **3 :** to speak indistinctly or disconnectedly **:** talk without order or evident purpose

**maund·er·er** \-d(ə)rə(r)\ *n* -s **:** one that maunders

**maund·er·ing·ly** *adv* **:** in a maundering manner **:** UNCERTAINLY, DISCONNECTEDLY

**maun·dy** \'mòndē, 'män-, -di\ *n* -ES *often attrib* [ME *maunde*, fr. OF *mandé*, fr. L *mandatum* command, order; fr. the words spoken by Jesus to his disciples after washing their feet at the Last Supper, "a new commandment I give unto you, that ye love one another" (Jn 13:34 AV) — more at MANDATE] **1 :** a ceremony of washing the feet of the poor on Maundy Thursday **2 a :** alms distributed in connection with the maundy ceremony or on Maundy Thursday **b :** MAUNDY MONEY **3** *obs* **:** FEAST

**maundy coins** *n pl* **:** MAUNDY MONEY

**maundy money** *n* **:** one-penny, twopenny, threepenny, and fourpenny silver coins esp. minted for distribution to the poor by the British sovereign on Maundy Thursday

**maundy thursday** *n, usu cap M&T* **:** the Thursday in Holy Week being the day before Good Friday and the third day before Easter

**maun·na** \'mán(n)ə, 'mòn-\ [*maun* + *na*] *Scot* **:** must not

**maupe** \'mòp\ *var of* MAWP

**mau·pok method** \'maù,päk-\ *n* [Esk *maupok*, lit., he waits] **:** an Eskimo method of hunting seals by waiting for them at breathing holes in the ice in order to spear them

**maur** \'mä(r)\ *dial var of* MORE

**mau·ran·dia** \mò'randēə\ *n* [NL, fr. Catharina Pancratia *Maurandy*, 18th cent. Span. botanist + NL *-ia*] **1** *cap* **:** a genus of slender twining herbs (family Scrophulariaceae) of Mexico and southwestern U.S. having flowers with a bell-shaped corolla that is gibbous at the base **2** -s **:** a plant of the genus *Maurandia*

**mau·ran·dya** \"\ *syn of* MAURANDIA

**mau·rer's dot** \'maùrə(r)z-\ *n, usu cap M* [after Georg *Maurer* b.1909 Ger. physician in Sumatra] **:** one of the coarse granulations present in red blood cells invaded by the falciparum malaria parasite

**mauresque** *often cap, var of* MORESQUE

¹**mau·re·ta·ni·an** \,mòrə¦tānēən, ¦mär-, -nyən\ *adj, usu cap* [*Mauretania*, ancient country in northern Africa + E *-an*, adj. suffix] **1 :** of, relating to, or characteristic of ancient Mauretania **2 :** of, relating to, or characteristic of the people of ancient Mauretania

²**mauretanian** \"\ *n* -s *cap* **1 :** a native or inhabitant of ancient Mauretania **2 :** MOOR

**mau·ri·cio** \maù'rēsē,ō\ *n* -s [AmerSp] **:** a large Puerto Rican magnolia (*Magnolia splendens*) that yields high-grade lumber and an essential oil but is now becoming rare

**mau·rist** \'mòrəst\ *n* -s *usu cap* [Saint *Maurus* †A.D. 584 Fr. monk and disciple of Saint Benedict + E *-ist*] *Roman Catholicism* **:** a member of the Congregation of St. Maur, an amalgamation of French Benedictine houses that was founded in 1618, became noted for its literary productivity, and lasted until the French Revolution

¹**mau·ri·ta·ni·an** \,mòrə¦tānēən, ¦mär-, -nyən\ *adj, usu cap* [*Mauritania*, country in western Africa + E *-an*] **1 :** of, relating to, or characteristic of Mauritania **2 :** of, relating to, or characteristic of the people of Mauritania

²**mauritanian** \"\ *n* -s *cap* **:** a native or inhabitant of Mauritania

**mau·ri·tia** \mò'rishēə\ *n, cap* [NL, fr. Count Joan *Mauritz* van Nassau-Siegen †1679 Du. general and administrator + NL *-ia*] **:** a genus of lofty So. American palms with pinnately lobed leaves, almost spineless trunks, perfectly 3-celled ovaries, and smooth seeds — see MIRITI PALM

¹**mau·ri·tian** \mò'rishən\ *adj, usu cap* [*Mauritius*, island in the Indian Ocean + E *-an*, adj. suffix] **:** of or relating to the island of Mauritius

²**mauritian** \"\ *n* -s *cap* **:** a native or inhabitant of Mauritius

**mau·ri·tius** \mò'rish(ē)əs\ *adj, usu cap* [fr. *Mauritius*, island in the Indian ocean] **:** of or from Mauritius **:** of the kind or style prevalent in Mauritius

**mauritius hemp** *also* **mauritius** *n* -ES *usu cap M* **:** a hard fiber obtained from the leaves of the giant cabuya and used chiefly for cordage and sacking; *esp* **:** this fiber as grown on the island of Mauritius

**mauritius thorn** *n, usu cap M* **:** a very thorny Indian shrub (*Caesalpinia sepiaria*) with red-striped yellow flowers that is used in tropical areas to form a stock-tight hedge — compare MULTIFLORA ROSE

**mau·rya** \'maùrē(y)ə\ *n* -s *usu cap* [Skt] **:** one of an ancient Indian people that established an empire taking in most of northern India and lasting from 321 to 184 B.C. — **mau·ry·an** \-ən\ *adj, usu cap*

**mausole** *n* -s [perh. fr. MF, fr. L *mausoleum*] *obs* **:** MAUSOLEUM

**mau·so·le·an** \¦mòsə¦lēən, -òzə-\ *adj* [*mausoleum* + *-an*] **:** like, relating to, or being a mausoleum

**mau·so·le·um** \,==¦lēəm\ *n, pl* **mausoleums** \-ēəmz\ *or* **mauso·lea** \-ēə\ [L, fr. Gk *mausōleion*, fr. *Mausōlos* Mausolus †*ab*353 B.C. ruler of Caria commemorated by a magnificent tomb at Halicarnassus] **1 a :** a magnificent tomb **b :** a tomb for more than one person **2 :** a large gloomy and usu. ornate building, room, or structure ⟨the bed, a huge and not unhandsome walnut ~ —Edna Ferber⟩

**maut** \'mòt\ *chiefly Scot var of* MALT

**mau·ther** \'mòthə(r)\ *n* -s [ME *moder* maidservant] *dial Eng* **:** a young girl; *esp* **:** an awkward clumsy wench

**mauve** \'mōv *also* 'mòv\ *n* -s [F, mallow, fr. L *malva*; fr. the color of mallow petals — more at MALLOW] **1 :** a basic violet dye derived from phenazine, obtained as the first synthetic aniline dye by oxidizing crude aniline containing toluidine, and formerly used chiefly for dyeing silk **2 :** a strong purple that is bluer and paler than monsignor — called also *mallow purple, mauveine, perkin's purple, perkin's violet*

**mauve blush** *n* **:** ATMOSPHERE 7

**mauve gray** *n* **:** a grayish purple that is redder and lighter than telegraph blue, redder and less strong than average orchid gray, and bluer and paler than average mauve taupe

**mauve·ine** \'mō¦,vēn, ¦,vən *also* 'mò¦\ *n* -s [*mauve* + *-ine*] **:** MAUVE

**mauve pink** *n* **:** a pale purplish pink that is redder and deeper than orchid tint

**mauve taupe** *n* **:** a variable color averaging a dark reddish gray that is darker and very slightly bluer than blue fox and bluer, darker, and slightly less strong than average rose taupe

**mau·vette** \mō'vet\ *n* -s [F, round-leaved geranium, fr. *mauve* mallow + *-ette*] **:** a pale purple that is redder and paler than average lavender, bluer and paler than phlox pink or wistaria (sense 2a), and bluer, lighter, and stronger than flossflower blue

**mauve wine** *n* **:** a variable color averaging a dark grayish red that is bluer and stronger than average rose brown and bluer, lighter, and stronger than average cordovan (sense 3b)

**mau·vine** \'mō¦vən, ¦,vēn *also* 'mò¦\ *adj* [*mauve* + *-ine*] **:** of the color mauve

**mauvy** \'mōvē *also* 'mòvē\ *also* **mauv·ish** \-vish\ *adj* [*mauve* + *-y* or *-ish*] **:** having a shading of mauve

**maux** \'mòks\ *n, pl* **maux** [prob. irreg. fr. *malkin*] **1** *now dial Eng* **:** a slatternly woman **2** *obs* **:** SLUT 2a

¹**mav·er·ick** \'mav(ə)rik, -rēk\ *n* -s [after Samuel A. *Maverick* †1870 Am. pioneer in Texas who did not brand his calves] **1** *West* **:** an unbranded range animal; *esp* **:** a calf on the range that is unbranded and not following its mother **2 a :** a refractory or recalcitrant member of a political party who bolts at will and sets an independent course **b :** an intellectual or a member of a social upper class or of any other group who refuses to conform and takes an unorthodox stand

²**maverick** \"\ *vt* -ED/-ING/-S **1** *West* **:** to brand and take possession of (an animal) as a maverick **2** *West* **:** to obtain by dishonest or questionable means

³**maverick** \"\ *adj* **:** being, behaving like, or typical of a maverick **:** RECALCITRANT, UNMARKED, STRAY ⟨a ~ calf⟩ ⟨~ floating mine⟩ ⟨a ~ stand on a tax bill⟩

**mav·er·ick·er** \-kə(r)\ *n* -s **:** a person that in the days of the open range made a practice of seeking out and putting his brand on maverick cattle

**ma·vis** \'māvəs\ *also* **ma·vie** \-vē\ *n, pl* **mavises** *also* **mavies** [ME *mavys*, fr. MF *mauvis*] **1 a :** SONG THRUSH **b :** MISTLE THRUSH **2 :** BROWN THRASHER

**ma·vish** \'māvish\ *dial Brit var of* MAVIS

**ma·vour·neen** *also* **ma·vour·nin** \mə'vùr,nēn\ *n* -s [IrGael *mo mhuirnīn*, fr. *mo* my (fr. OIr) + *muirnīn* darling; akin to OIr *mē* I, Gk *me* me — more at ME, AVOURNEEN] *Irish* **:** my darling

**mav·ro·daph·ne** \,mavrə'dafnē\ *n* -s [NGk *maurodaphnē*, fr. LGk *mauros* dark, black + Gk *daphnē* laurel — more at DAPHNE] **:** a sweet red Greek dessert wine

¹**maw** \'mò\ *n* -s [ME *mawe*, fr. OE *maga*; akin to OHG *mago* stomach, ON *magi* stomach, W *megin* bellows, Lith *makas* purse] **1 :** the receptacle into which food is taken by swallowing: **a :** STOMACH **b :** CROP **2 a :** the hypothetical seat or symbol of voracious appetite **b** *obs* **:** APPETITE, INCLINATION **3 a :** the throat, gullet, or jaws esp. of a voracious carnivore **b :** an opening that gapes like ravenous jaws

²**maw** \"\ *n* -s [ME (Sc), fr. ON *mār* — more at MEW] *chiefly Scot* **:** SEA GULL

³**maw** \"\ *chiefly dial Brit var of* MOW

⁴**maw** \"\ *n* -s [origin unknown] **:** an early form of spoil five

⁵**maw** *chiefly South & Midland var of* MA

⁶**maw** \'mò\ *or* **maw seed** *n* -s [*maw* short for *maw seed*, part modif., part trans. of obs. G *magsame* poppy seed, fr. MHG *magesāme*, fr. *mage* poppy (fr. OHG *mago*) + *sāme* seed; akin to OS *mago-, māho* poppy, OSw val*mughi*, Gk *mēkōn*, Russ *mak*] **:** POPPY SEED; *esp* **:** that of the opium poppy which is commonly used as food for cage birds

**mawali** *pl of* MAULA

**maw–bound** \'=,=\ *adj* [¹*maw*] *of cattle* **:** COSTIVE

**mawk** \'mòk\ *n* -s [ME *mawke*, modif. of ON *mathkr* — more at MAGGOT] *dial Brit* **:** MAGGOT

**maw·ken** \'mòkən\ *n, pl* **mawken** *or* **mawkens** *usu cap* **:** one of a primitive seafaring people located in the Mergui archipelago off the southern coast of Burma

**maw·kin** \'mò,kin\ *var of* MALKIN

**mawk·ish** \'mòkish, -kēsh\ *adj* [*mawk* + *-ish*] **1** *archaic* **:** somewhat sick or disordered **:** SQUEAMISH **2 :** having an unpleasant flavor; *usu* **:** having a faint sickly insipid taste often unpleasantly sweetish **:** CLOYING **3 :** marked by sickly sentimentality **:** falsely or puerilely sentimental **syn** see SENTIMENTAL

**mawk·ish·ly** *adv* **:** in a mawkish manner **:** so as to give a mawkish effect

**mawk·ish·ness** *n* -ES **:** the quality or state of being mawkish ⟨sincere and touching without ~ —A.L.Guérard⟩

**mawl** *var of* MAUL

**mawmouth** \'=,=\ *n* [perh. fr. ¹*maw* + *mouth*] **:** any of several voracious American freshwater fishes

**mawn** *dial var of* MAUND

**mawp** \'mòp\ *n* -s [perh. alter. of *nope*] *dial Eng* **:** BULLFINCH 1

**maw·ther** \'mòthə(r)\ *var of* MAUTHER

**mawworm** \'=,=\ *n* **1 :** a parasitic worm of the stomach or intestine; *esp* **:** a parasitic nematode **2 :** a mealymouthed sanctimonious hypocrite

¹**max** \'maks\ *n* -ES [origin unknown] *slang* **:** GIN

²**max** \"\ *n* -ES [short for *maximum*] *slang* **:** a perfect score (as in a scholastic recitation) or complete success

³**max** \"\ *vi* -ED/-ING/-ES *slang* **:** to make a perfect score or attain complete success

⁴**max** \"\ *n* -ES [native name in Yucatán] **:** a weevil (*Scyphophorus acupunctatus*) that feeds on the buds of henequen both as larva and adult

**max** *abbr* maximum

**maxill-** *or* **maxilli-** *or* **maxillo-** *comb form* [L *maxill-*, fr. *maxilla*] **1 :** maxilla ⟨*maxilli*ped⟩ **2 :** maxillary and ⟨*maxillo*facial⟩ ⟨*maxillo*zygomatic⟩

**max·il·la** \mak'silə\ *n, pl* **maxil·lae** \-i,lē, -i,lī\ *also* **maxillas** [L, dim. of *mala* jaw, cheek; perh. akin to Alb *mjekrë* chin, beard, Skt *śmaśru* beard, mustache] **1 a :** JAW 1a **b** [NL, fr. L] (1) **:** an upper jaw esp. of man or other mammals in which the bony elements are closely fused (2) **:** either of two membrane bone elements of the upper jaw lying lateral to the premaxillae and in higher vertebrates and man bearing most of the teeth — see FISH illustration **2** [NL, fr. L] **:** one of the first or second pair of mouthparts posterior to the mandibles in insects, myriopods, crustaceans, and closely related arthropods — see LABIUM 3a

**max·il·lar·ia** \,maksə'la(a)rēə\ *n* [NL, fr. L *maxilla* jaw + NL *-aria*; fr. the resemblance of part of the flower to a chin] **1** *cap* **:** a large genus of tropical American epiphytic orchids with persistent often leathery leaves and single-flowered scapes that includes several cultivated for their large brilliantly colored flowers **2** -s **:** an orchid of the genus *Maxillaria*

[1]**max·il·lary** \'maksə,lerē, -ri, *chiefly Brit* mak'silər-\ *also* **max·il·lar** \-lə(r)\ *adj* [*maxillary* fr. L *maxilla* + E *-ary; maxillar* fr. L *maxillaris*, fr. *maxilla* + *-aris* -ar] **:** of, relating to, being, or associated with a maxilla ⟨~ blood vessels⟩ ⟨a ~ element⟩

[2]**maxillary** \"\ *n* -ES **1** *or* **maxillary bone :** MAXILLA 1b(2) **2 :** a maxillary part (as a nerve or blood vessel)

**maxillary artery** *n* **:** either of two arteries of the face that are the terminal branches of the external carotid artery: **a :** an artery supplying the deep structures of the face (as the nasal cavities, palate, tonsils, and pharynx) and sending a branch to the meninges of the brain — called also *internal maxillary artery* **b :** an artery running up along the side of the face and nose — called also *external maxillary artery, facial artery*

**maxillary gland** *n* **:** one of the paired excretory organs opening at the base of the maxillae of various arthropods

**maxillary nerve** *n* **:** a sensory division of the trigeminal nerve supplying the upper jaw and its teeth, the mucous membrane of the palate, nasal cavities, pharynx, and skin areas of the middle part of the face

**maxillary palpus** *n* **:** a small several-segmented process on the outer aspect of each maxilla of an insect that is believed to have a sensory function — see INSECT illustration

**maxillary sinus** *or* **maxillary antrum** *n* **:** an air cavity in the body of the maxilla that communicates with the middle meatus of the nose — called also *antrum of Highmore*

**max·il·li·ped** \mak'silə,ped\ *or* **max·il·li·pede** \-pēd\ *n* -s [ISV *maxill-* + *-ped, -pede*] **:** one of the three pairs of appendages of crustaceans situated next behind the maxillae — **max·il·li·peda·ry** \=ˌ=ˈ=;pedərē, -pēd-\ *adj*

**maxillo-alveolar index** \mak'si(,)lō+. . .-\ *n, anthrop* **:** the ratio multiplied by 100 of the breadth of the alveolar arch to its length

**max·il·lo·palatal** *or* **max·il·lo·palatine** \mak,si(,)lō+\ *n* [*maxill-* + *palatal* or *palatine*] **:** an inwardly projecting process of the maxillary bone in the skull of birds

**max·il·lu·la** \mak'silyələ\ *n, pl* **maxillu·lae** \-,lē\ [NL, fr. *maxilla* + *-ula*] **1 :** either member of the first pair of maxillae of a crustacean **2 :** any of several lobes or appendages of an insect's mouthparts that may be homologous to the crustacean maxillula

**max·im** \'maksəm\ *n* -s [ME *maxime*, fr. MF, fr. ML *maxima*, fr. L, fem. of *maximus* greatest, largest, superl. of *magnus* great, large — more at MUCH] **1 :** a mathematical or philosophical axiom **2 a :** a general truth, fundamental principle, or rule of conduct esp. when expressed in sententious form **b :** a saying of proverbial nature **3** [prob. fr. (assumed) NL *maxima*, fr. L, fem. of *maximus* greatest, largest] *or* **max·i·ma** \-səmə\ **:** [3]LARGE 4 **4** [L *maximus* greatest, largest] **:** a large worker or soldier of an ant that has polymorphic workers — compare MINIM

**max·i·mal** \'maksəməl\ *adj* [[1]*maxim*um + *-al*] **:** most complete or effective **:** HIGHEST, GREATEST — **max·i·mal·ly** \-məlē, -li\ *adv*

**max·i·mal·ism** \-mə,lizəm\ *n* -s [*maximal*ist + *-ism*] **:** the theories or practices of maximalists

**max·i·mal·ist** \-,ləst\ *n* -s [F *maximaliste*, fr. *maximal-* (prob. fr. E *maximal*) + *-iste* -ist; intended as trans. of Russ *bol'shevik* Bolshevik] **:** one that believes in or advocates immediate and direct action to secure the whole of a program or set of goals; *specif* **:** a socialist advocating the immediate seizure of power by revolutionary means as opposed to gradual achievement of limited aims (as by the processes of parliamentary democracy) — compare GRADUALIST, MINIMALIST, REVISIONIST

**max·i·mal·ize** \-,līz\ *vt* -ED/-ING/-S **:** to increase (as a quality) to the utmost

**maximal lineage** *n* **:** a large kinship group comprising all the descendants of a remotest known ancestor with lineage being usu. traced only through ancestors of the same sex as the initial progenitor — contrasted with *minimal lineage*

**max·i·mate** \'maksə,māt\ *vt* -ED/-ING/-S [[1]*maxim*um + *-ate*] **:** MAXIMIZE

**max·i·ma·tion** \,maksə'māshən\ *n* -s [*maximate* + *-ion*] **:** the act of maximizing or the quality or state of being maximized

**max·imed** \'maksəmd\ *adj* **:** expressed in a maxim

**max·im·ist** \'maksəməst\ *n* -s **:** a maker or user of or an enthusiast over maxims

**max·im·ite** \-,mīt\ *n* -s [Hudson *Maxim* †1927 Am. inventor and explosives expert + E *-ite*] **:** a high explosive of the picric acid class formerly used in armor-piercing shells

**max·i·mi·za·tion** \,maksəmə'zāshən, -sə,mī'z-\ *n* -s **:** an act of maximizing or the state of being maximized

**max·i·mize** \'maksə,mīz\ *vb* -ED/-ING/-S *see -ize in Explan Notes* [*maxim*um + *-ize*] *vt* **1 :** to increase to the highest degree **:** bring to a maximum ⟨the importance of *maximizing* the use of locally available products⟩ ⟨must ~ educational opportunities for all⟩ **2 a :** to make the most of **:** assign a position of maximum significance or worth to ⟨*maximized* the experience of highly trained specialists⟩ ⟨~ the advantages of urban life —Lewis Mumford⟩ ⟨unwise to ~ the importance of present profits at the risk of future security⟩ **b :** to find a maximum value of (a mathematical function) **~** *vi* **:** to interpret something (as a doctrine or duty) in the broadest sense

**max·i·miz·er** \-zə(r)\ *n* -s **:** one that maximizes

[1]**max·i·mum** \'maksəməm\ *n, pl* **maximums** \-səməmz\ *or* **maxi·ma** \-səmə\ [L, neut. of *maximus* greatest, largest — more at MAXIM] **1 :** the greatest quantity or value attainable in a given case **:** the greatest value attained by a quantity that first increases and then begins to decrease **:** the highest point or degree **:** the time or period of highest, greatest, or utmost development — opposed to *minimum* **2 :** an upper limit allowed by law or other authority **3 a :** a number not less than any other number of a finite set of numbers **b :** a value of a mathematical function of one or more independent variables such that either increasing or decreasing any one of the independent variables by a sufficiently small amount results in a decrease in the function

[2]**maximum** \"\ *adj* **1 :** greatest in quantity or highest in degree attainable or attained ⟨~ pressure⟩ **2 :** relating to, marking, or determining a maximum ⟨maintaining a steady ~ line on the graph⟩

**maximum card** *n* **:** a card bearing an adhesive stamp (as a commemorative) and an enlarged picture of the same stamp issued by a government or philatelic agency for sale to collectors with cancellation of the stamp

**maximum dose** *n* **:** the largest dose of a medicine or drug consistent with safety

**maximum fee** *n* **:** a fee determined on the basis of payment at an hourly or per diem rate up to but not exceeding an agreed maximum sum for the entire task

**max·i·mum·ly** *adv* **:** to the greatest degree **:** to the utmost

**max·i·mus** \'maksəməs\ *adj* [L, greatest, largest] **:** of or being a system of ringing changes on a set of twelve bells

**maxing** *pres part of* MAX

**ma·xixe** \mə'shēsh(ə)\ *n, pl* **maxi·xes** \-ēshəz\ [Pg] **:** a ballroom dance of Brazilian origin roughly like the two-step (as in action and rhythm) — called also *Brazilian maxixe*

**max·well** \'mak,swel, -swəl\ *n* -s [after James Clerk *Maxwell* †1879 Scot. physicist] **:** the cgs electromagnetic unit of magnetic flux equal to the flux per square centimeter of normal cross section in a region where the magnetic induction is one gauss — see WEBER

**maxwell-boltz·mann law** \ˈ=(,)=ˈbōltsmən-\ *n, usu cap M&B* [after J. C. *Maxwell* and Ludwig *Boltzmann* †1906 Austrian physicist] **:** the principle involved in equipartition of energy

**maxwell disk** *n, usu cap M* **:** one of two or more radially slit and concentric disks of different colors that may be overlapped by adjustable amounts to yield the average color when rotated rapidly

**max·well·ian** \(')mak'swelēən\ *adj, usu cap* [J. C. *Maxwell* + E *-an*] **:** of, relating to, exhibiting, or constituting a Maxwellian distribution ⟨*Maxwellian* gases⟩ ⟨*Maxwellian* equilibrium⟩

**maxwellian distribution** *also* **maxwell distribution** *also* **maxwell-boltzmann distribution** *n, usu cap M&B* [after J. C. *Maxwell* and Ludwig *Boltzmann*] **:** an expression based on the theory of probability for the fractional number of molecules in a gas that are in equilibrium at a given temperature and have a specified range of velocities

**maxwell's demon** *n, usu cap M* [after J. C. Maxwell, its hypothecator] **:** a hypothetical being of intelligence but molecular order of size imagined to illustrate limitations of the second law of thermodynamics

**maxwell's rule** *n, usu cap M* **:** a principle of electromagnetism: every portion of an electric circuit carrying a current experiences such mechanical forces due to its own or to any superposed magnetic field as would cause the circuit to link with a maximum of magnetic flux

**maxwell triangle** *n, usu cap M* **:** CHROMATICITY DIAGRAM

[1]**may** \(ˈ)mā, ˌmə\ *vb, past* **might** \(ˈ)mīt, *usu* -īd.+V\ *or chiefly dial* **mought** *or* **mout** *or* **mowt** \(ˈ)maůt, (ˈ)mōt, *usu* \|d·+V\ *or archaic 2d sing* **might·est** (with *thou*) \ˈmīd·əst, -ītə-\ *pres sing & pl* **may** *or archaic 2d sing* **may·est** *or* **mayst** (with *thou*) \ˈmāəst, (ˈ)māst\ [ME, have power, am able (1st & 3d sing. pres. indic. of *mowen, mayen*, past *mighte, moghte*), fr. OE *mæg* (infin. *magan*, past *meahte, mihte*); akin to OHG *mag* have power, am able (infin. *magan, mugan*), ON *mā* (infin. *mega*), Goth *mag* have power, am able, Gk *mēchos* means, expedient, Skt *magha* gift, wealth, power] *vi, obs* **:** to have power **:** be able **~** *verbal auxiliary* **1** *archaic* **:** have the ability or competence to **:** CAN **2 a :** have permission to ⟨you ~ go now⟩ ⟨no one ~ enter without a ticket⟩ ⟨if I ~ interrupt to point out⟩ **:** have liberty to ⟨you ~ say what you please, I won't do it⟩ ⟨~ I ask why it is forbidden⟩ — used nearly interchangeably with *can* **b :** be in some degree likely to ⟨you ~ be right⟩ ⟨they ~ get here in time after all⟩ ⟨~ easily be the best play of the season⟩ — used sometimes to avoid bluntness in a question ⟨how old ~ you be⟩ or request ⟨~ I help you, or are you already being waited on⟩; compare MIGHT **3 —** used in auxiliary function to express a wish or desire esp. in prayer, imprecation, or benediction ⟨~ he reign in health⟩ ⟨~ they all be damned⟩ ⟨~ the best man win⟩ **4 —** used in auxiliary function expressing purpose or expectation ⟨I laugh that I ~ not weep⟩ ⟨flatters so that he ~ win favor⟩ or contingency ⟨he'll do his duty come what ~⟩ or concession ⟨he ~ be slow but he is thorough⟩; compare MIGHT **5 :** SHALL, MUST — used esp. in deeds, contracts, and statutes

[2]**may** \'mā\ *n* -s [ME, fr. OE *mǣg*; akin to OE *mǣg* kinsman — more at MAEGBOTE] *archaic* **:** MAIDEN

[3]**may** \"\ *n* -s [ME, fr. OF & L; OF *mai*, fr. L *maius*, fr. *Maia*, Roman goddess associated with Vulcan] **1** *usu cap* **:** the fifth month of the Gregorian calendar — see MONTH table **2** *often cap* **:** the early vigorous blooming part of human life **:** PRIME, HEYDAY **3** *usu cap* **:** the merrymaking of May Day **4 a :** green or flowering branches used for May Day decorations; *esp* **:** flowering branches of the hawthorn **b :** a plant that yields may: as (1) **:** HAWTHORN (2) *dial Eng* **:** SYCAMORE (3) **:** an evergreen rutaceous shrub (*Coleonema album*) of southern Africa with fragrant white flowers in spring — called also *Cape may* (4) **:** any of several spring-flowering spireas

[4]**may** \"\ *vi* -ED/-ING/-S *often cap* [ME *mayen*, fr. *may*, n.] **:** to take part in the festivities of May or May Day; *esp* **:** to gather flowers in May

[5]**may** \"\ *dial Eng var of* [1]MAKE

[1]**ma·ya** \'mäyə, 'māyə, 'mī(,)ä, -īə\ *n* -s [Skt *māyā*] **1 :** an extraphysical wonder-working power in the Vedas **2 a :** the illusion-creating power of a god or demon **b :** the powerful force that creates the cosmic illusion that the phenomenal world is real; *broadly* **:** MAGIC, ILLUSION

[2]**maya** \'mī(y)ə *sometimes* 'mäyə *or* 'mā(y)ə\ *n, pl* **maya** *or* **mayas** *usu cap* [Sp] **1 a :** a group of people of Yucatán, British Honduras, northern Guatemala, and the state of Tabasco, Mexico whose language is Mayan **b :** a member of such people **2 a** (1) **:** a Mayan language of the ancient Maya peoples recorded in inscriptions (2) **:** YUCATEC; *esp* **:** the older form of that language known from documents of the Spanish period **b :** a system of writing used by the preconquest Maya peoples **3 :** the language of the Maya people **4 :** a brownish orange to light brown that is redder and lighter than sorrel, redder than caramel, and very slightly darker and stronger than paloma

[3]**maya** \"\ *n* -s [Tag] **:** any of several Philippine weaverbirds of the genus *Lonchura*

[4]**maya** \"\ *n* -s [AmerSp] **:** PINGUIN

**maya arch** *n, usu cap M* [[2]*Maya*] **:** a spanning structure made by corbeling opposed surfaces **:** CORBEL ARCH

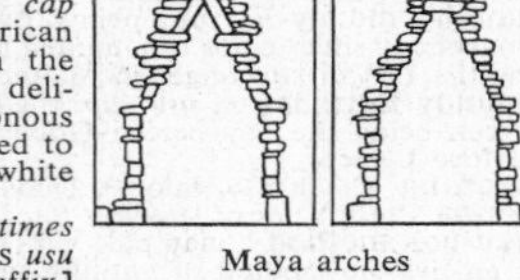

Maya arches

**ma·yaca** \mə'yakə\ *n, cap* [NL] **:** a small American genus (coextensive with the family Mayacaceae) of delicate mossy monocotyledonous bog plants that are related to the commelinas and have white or violet flowers

[1]**mayan** \'mī(y)ən *sometimes* 'mäyən *or* 'mā(y)ən\ *n* -s *usu cap* [[2]*Maya* + *-an*, n. suffix] **1 :** a language stock of Central America and Mexico consisting of Huastec, Chicomuceltec; Yucatec, Mopan; Chontal, Chol, Chorti; Tzeltal, Tzotzil, Tojolabal; Chuj; Jacaltec, Kanhobal, Motozintlec, Mam, Aguacatec, Ixil; Uspantec, Quiche, Cakchiquel, Tzutuhil; Kekchi, Pokonchi, and Pokomam **2 a :** the peoples speaking Mayan languages **b :** a member of such peoples

[2]**mayan** \"\ *adj, usu cap* [[2]*Maya* + *-an*, adj. suffix] **1 :** of, relating to, or constituting the Mayan language stock or peoples **:** of the kind or style characteristic of or used by the Mayan peoples **2 :** of or relating to Maya or the Maya **:** of the kind or style characteristic of or used by the Maya

**ma·yan·ce** \mä'yän(t)(,)sā\ *adj, usu cap* [AmerSp, fr. Sp *Maya* + *-ance* (as in *romance*, fr. L *romanice* in the Roman manner) — more at ROMANCE] **:** MAYAN

**ma·ya·pis** \mə'yäpəs\ *n* -ES [Tag] **:** any of several Philippine timber trees of the genera *Dipterocarpus* and *Shorea* some of which also yield resins

**mayapple** \'=,==\ *n, sometimes cap* **1 :** a No. American herb (*Podophyllum peltatum*) that has a poisonous rootstock and first bears a single large-lobed peltate leaf and later two similar leaves with a single large white flower at their base **2 :** the yellow egg-shaped edible but often insipid fruit of the mayapple

**may basket** *n, usu cap M* **:** a small basket holding a gift (as of flowers or candy) hung at the door of a favored person on May Day

[1]**may·be** \'mābē, -bi *sometimes* -ˈbē; *more often in dial than in stand speech* 'mebē *or* -ebi\ *adv* [ME *may be*, fr. [1]*may* + *be*, *been* to be — more at BE] **:** possibly but not surely **:** not certainly **:** PERHAPS

[2]**maybe** \"\ *n* -s **:** UNCERTAINTY, INDECISION ⟨put all the imponderables, the ifs and ~s from his mind —B.I.Kahn⟩

**may beetle** *or* **may bug** *n, often cap M* **:** JUNE BEETLE

**may·ber·ry** \'mā— — *see* BERRY\ *n, often cap* **:** an erect branching ornamental bramble (*Rubus palmatus*) with white flowers and yellow edible early-ripening fruits

**maybeso** \ˈ=;==\ *adv* [[1]*maybe* + *so*] *dial* **:** MAYBE

**maybird** \'=,=\ *n, usu cap* **:** any of various birds that tend to appear or be heard in May: as **a** *South & Midland* **:** BOBOLINK **b** *East* **:** [3]KNOT **c** *dial Eng* **:** WHIMBREL **d** *Jamaica* **:** WOOD THRUSH

**may blob** *n, usu cap M* **:** a marsh marigold (*Caltha palustris*) — often used in pl.

**maybloom** \'=,=\ *n, usu cap* **:** HAWTHORN

**may blossom** *n, usu cap M, dial Eng* **:** LILY OF THE VALLEY

**maybush** \'=,=\ *n* **:** HAWTHORN

**may butter** *n, usu cap M* **:** butter formerly prepared in May without salt and stored for medicinal use

**may cherry** *n, usu cap M* **1 :** MAYDUKE **2 :** JUNEBERRY 1

[1]**may·cock** \'mā,käk\ *n* [alter. of *maracock*] **:** MAYPOP

[2]**maycock** \"\ *n, usu cap* [[3]*may* + *cock*] **:** BLACK-BELLIED PLOVER

**may curlew** *n, usu cap M, dial Eng* **:** WHIMBREL

**may day** *n, usu cap M&D* [ME *mayday* first day of May, fr. [3]*may* + *day*] **:** the first day of May often celebrated as a springtime festival and in some countries (as the U.S.S.R.) as Labor Day

**may·day** \(ˈ)mā;dā\ *usu cap* [F *m'aider* help me] — an international radiotelephone signal word used as a distress call, to introduce a distress message, or by distress traffic

**mayden** *archaic var of* MAIDEN

**mayduke** \ˈ=;=\ *also* **mayduke cherry** *n, usu cap M* **:** an early-ripening dark red duke cherry

**mayed** *past of* MAY

**ma·yeng** \mə'yeŋ\ *n* -s [origin unknown] **:** an Indian timber tree (*Pterospermum acerifolium*) with a reddish moderately hard and heavy wood used largely for planking

**may·er** \'māə(r)\ *n* -s *sometimes cap* **:** one that goes maying

**mayest** *archaic pres 2d sing of* MAY

**mayfish** \'=,=\ *n, pl* **mayfish** *or* **mayfishes :** a common marine killifish (*Fundulus majalis*) of eastern No. America

**may·flower** \'=,==\ *n, often cap* **1 :** any of various spring-blooming plants: as **a** *Brit* (1) **:** HAWTHORN (2) **:** MARSH MARIGOLD (3) **:** CUCKOOFLOWER (4) **:** GREATER STITCHWORT (5) **:** CALLA LILY **b** (1) *chiefly New England* **:** ARBUTUS 3 (2) **:** HEPATICA (3) **:** SPRING BEAUTY (4) **:** any of several No. American anemones (5) **:** MAY APPLE **2 :** a moderate red that is yellower and paler than cerise, claret (sense 3a), or average strawberry (sense 2a) and bluer and paler than Turkey red

**may-flowering tulip** *n, usu cap M* **:** COTTAGE TULIP

**mayfly** \'=,=\ *n, sometimes cap* **1 :** a slender fragile-winged short-lived imago insect of the order Plectoptera that often emerges in multitudes in spring **2 :** an artificial angling fly that simulates an ephemerid imago

**mayfowl** \'=,=\ *n, usu cap, dial Eng* **:** WHIMBREL

**mayhap** \'=,=, =ˈ=\ *adv* [*mayhap* fr. the phrase *may hap*, fr. [1]*may* + *hap; mayhappen* fr. the phrase *may happen*, fr. [1]*may* + *happen; mayhaps* alter. of *mayhap*] **:** PERHAPS, MAYBE

**mayhappen** \'=,==, =ˈ==\ *also* **may·haps** \-haps\ *chiefly dial var of* MAYHAP

**mayhaw** \'=,=\ *n, sometimes cap* **:** a hawthorn (*Crataegus aestivalis*) of the southern U. S. that bears a juicy scarlet acid fruit often used in jellies or preserves

[1]**may·hem** \'mā,hem *also* -āəm\ *n* -s [ME *maym*, fr. AF *mahaim, mayhem* — more at MAIM] **1 a :** the malicious and permanent deprivation of another of the use of a member of his body resulting in impairment of his fighting ability and constituting a grave felony under English common law **b :** the malicious and permanent crippling, mutilation, or disfiguring of another constituting a grave felony under modern statutes but in some jurisdictions requiring a specific intent as distinguished from general malice ⟨physicians, accused . . . of sterilizing her through trickery, were ordered held for trial on charges of conspiracy to commit ~ —*Associated Press*⟩ **2 :** needless or willful damage (as in literary criticism or editorial activity)

[2]**mayhem** \"\ *vt* **mayhemed** *or* **mayhemmed; mayhemed** *or* **mayhemmed; mayheming** *or* **mayhemming; mayhems :** to commit mayhem on

**may·ing** \'mā(i)ŋ, -āeŋ\ *n* -s *sometimes cap* [ME, fr. gerund of *mayen* to may, take part in the festivities of May Day] **:** the celebrating of May Day

**may lady** *n, usu cap M, obs* **:** MAY QUEEN

**may lily** *n, sometimes cap M* **:** LILY OF THE VALLEY

**may lord** *or* **may king** *n, usu cap M, obs* **:** a youth presiding over May Day festivities

**may·nard's cuckoo** \'mānə(r)dz-\ *n, usu cap M* [after Charles J. *Maynard* †1929 Am. ornithologist] **:** a West Indian cuckoo (*Coccyzus minor maynardi*) that is the only form of the mangrove cuckoo reaching the southernmost U. S.

**mayn't** \(ˈ)mā(ə)nt\ [by contr.] **:** may not

[1]**mayo** \'mī(,)(y)ō, 'mä(,)yō\ *n, pl* **mayo** *or* **mayos** *usu cap* **1 :** a Taracahitian people of Sonora, Mexico **2 :** a member of the Mayo people

[2]**mayo** \'mā(,)ō\ *adj, usu cap* [fr. *Mayo*, county in northwest Ireland] **:** of or from County Mayo, Ireland **:** of the kind or style prevalent in County Mayo

**mayoid** \'mī,(y)ȯid, 'mä,y-\ *n* -s *usu cap* [[2]*Maya* + *-oid*] **:** a linguistic subdivision of the Mayan of Guatemala, Honduras, and the states of Chiapas, Tabasco, San Luis Potosi, Tamaulipas, and Veracruz, Mexico

**may·on·naise** \,māə'nāz, ˌ==ˈ=\ *n* -s [F, perh. irreg. fr. *Mahón*, seaport of Minorca] **1 a :** a semisolid dressing made by emulsifying a mixture of raw eggs or egg yolks, vegetable oil, and vinegar or lemon juice usu. together with salt and condiments **b :** a dish (as of fish) prepared with this dressing ⟨lobster ~⟩ **2 :** GOULASH 2a

**may·or** \'mā(ə)r, 'me(ə)r, 'māə, 'meə\ *n* -s [ME *maire*, fr. OF, fr. L *major* larger, greater — more at MAJOR] **:** the chief magistrate of a city or borough **:** the chief executive officer of a municipal corporation in the U. S. being elected by direct popular vote and serving from one to six years, having powers that vary from the merely advisory or legislative to the strongly executive with important appointments, the veto power, and sometimes preparation of the budget, and generally serving with a council but in many American cities replaced by or subordinate to a commission or city manager — used as a title or in a mode of address and to translate various foreign titles of similar municipal officials (as the French *maire* or the German *burgomaster*); see MAYOR'S COURT

[1]**ma·yo·ral** \ˈmäyəˈräl, ˈmīə-\ *n* -s [Sp, fr. *mayor* larger, greater, fr. L *major*] **:** an overseer (as of a flock, an estate, or a group of tourists) in Spain

[2]**may·or·al** \'māərəl, 'me(ə)r-\ *adj* [*mayor* + *-al*] **:** of or relating to a mayor or his office

**may·or·al·ty** \'māərəltē, 'me(ə)r-, -ti, *substand* ˌmāə'raləd·ē *or* ˌmeə'- *or* -lətē *or* -i\ *n* -ES [ME *mairaltee*, fr. MF *mairalté*, fr. OF, fr. *maire* mayor + *-al* + *-té* -ty] **1 :** the office of mayor ⟨was elected to the ~ by a large majority⟩ **2 :** the term of office as a mayor ⟨accomplished little during his ~⟩

**mayor-council** \ˈ=(=)ˈ==\ *adj* **:** of, relating to, or constituting a method of municipal government in which policy-making and administrative powers are vested in a usu. elective mayor and council — compare COUNCIL-MANAGER PLAN, STRONG MAYOR, WEAK MAYOR

**may·or·do·mo** \,mā(ə)r'dō(,)mō, ˌmeə-\ *n* -s [AmerSp, fr. Sp, majordomo — more at MAJORDOMO] *Southwest* **:** a person in charge of a group or project: as **a :** a manager of a hacienda, ranch, or estate **b :** an overseer of an irrigation system

**may·or·ess** \'māərəs, 'me(ə)r-\ *n* -ES [ME *meyresse*, fr. *meyre, maire* mayor + *-esse* -ess] **1 :** the wife or official hostess of a mayor **2 :** a woman holding the office of mayor

**mayor of the palace** [trans. of ML *mayor palatii*] **:** an official under the Frankish kings who orig. was the chief officer of the royal household, later prime minister, and under the later Merovingians practically sovereign

**mayor's court** *n* **:** a court in some cities usu. presided over by the mayor and having jurisdiction over violations of city ordinances and other petty criminal or civil matters

**may·or·ship** \'māə(r),ship, 'me(ə)r-, 'meə,-\ *n* [ME *maireshipp*, fr. *maire* mayor + *-shipp*, *-shipe* -ship] **:** the office or status of a mayor

**mayo·ru·na** \,mīə'rünə\ *n, pl* **mayoruna** *or* **mayorunas** *usu cap* **1 a :** a people of Brazil and northeastern Peru **b :** a member of such people **2 :** the language of the Mayoruna people sometimes classed as Panoan

**may pear** *n, usu cap M* **:** JUNEBERRY

**may pink** *n, usu cap M* **1 :** COTTAGE PINK **2 :** RHODORA 2

**maypole** \'=,=\ *n, often cap* **:** a tall pole in an open place and wreathed with flowers forming a center for May Day sports

**maypole dance** *n, usu cap M* **:** a folk dance in which long ribbons are woven about a Maypole by the dancers, typically as part of a May Day festivity

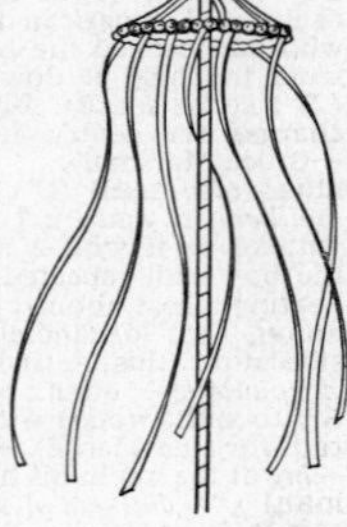

maypole

**may·pop** \'mā,päp\ *n* -s [alter. of [1]*maycock*] **1 :** a somewhat hairy climbing perennial passionflower (*Passiflora incarnata*) of the southern U. S. with large white to pale lavender flowers followed by a yellow edible but somewhat insipid berry about the size of a hen's egg **2 :** the fruit of the maypop

**may queen** *n, usu cap M* **:** a girl or young woman selected to preside over a May Day festival or other May party

**may rose** *n, usu cap M* **1 :** GUELDER ROSE **2 :** DAMASK ROSE

**mays** *pl of* MAY, *pres 3d sing of* MAY

**mayst** *archaic pres 2d sing of* MAY

**may star** *n, usu cap M* **:** STARFLOWER b

**may·ten** \(ˈ)mī¦ten\ *n* -s [Sp *maitén*, fr. Araucanian *mañtún*] **:** a Chilean evergreen tree (*maytenus boaria*) having pendulous branches, slender lanceolate leaves, and minute flowers and being cultivated as an ornamental in warm countries

**may·te·nus** \mīˈtēnəs\ *n, cap* [NL, fr. Sp *maitén*] **:** a large genus of tropical American shrubs and trees (family Celastraceae) having evergreen leaves, small axillary flowers, and leathery capsules

**maythe** \ˈmāth̲\ *n, pl* **maythes** *but sing or pl in constr* [ME, fr. OE *mægtha, magethe*] *obs* **:** any of various weedy composite plants

**maythorn** \ˈ=,=\ *n, usu cap* **:** HAWTHORN

**maytide** *or* **maytime** \ˈ=,=\ *n, usu cap* **:** the period or month of May

**may tree** *n, usu cap M* **:** HAWTHORN

**may·weed** \ˈmā,=\ *n* [*may-* (fr. *maythe*) + *weed*] **1 :** strong-scented European chamomile (*Anthemis cotula*) that is naturalized along roadsides in the U. S. and has flower heads with a yellow disk and white rays — called also *dog fennel* **2 :** FEVERFEW

**may whaup** *n, usu cap M, dial Eng* **:** WHIMBREL

**may whitewing** *n, usu cap M* **:** WHITE-WINGED SCOTER

**may wine** *n, usu cap M* [trans. of G *maiwein*] **:** a punch consisting of champagne, Moselle or Rhine wine, and claret flavored with the herb woodruff

**maywings** \ˈ=,=\ *n pl but sing or pl in constr* **:** GAYWINGS

**may-woon** \(ˈ)mī¦wün\ *n* -s [Burmese *myowun*, fr. *myo* town + *wun* official, burden] **:** a Burmese provincial governor

**¹maz-** *or* **mazo-** *comb form* [NL, fr. Gk *mazos, mastos* — more at MEAT] **:** breast ⟨*mazalgia*⟩ ⟨*mazoplasia*⟩

**²maz-** *or* **mazo-** *comb form* [NL, fr. *maza* placenta, fr. Gk, lump, mass, barley cake — more at MASS] **:** placenta ⟨*mazic*⟩ ⟨*mazopathia*⟩

**ma·zae·di·um** \məˈzēdēəm, maˈz-\ *n, pl* **mazae·dia** \-dēə\ [NL, fr. Gk *maza* lump, mass, barley cake + L *aedes* temple, house, building + NL *-ium* — more at EDIFY] **:** a fruiting body (as of some lichens) consisting of a powdery mass of free ascospores interspersed with sterile elements and enclosed in a peridium

**ma·za·gran** \¦mazə¦grän\ *n* -s [F, fr. *Mazagran*, village in northwest Algeria] **:** sweetened and usu. cold and diluted black coffee served in a glass

**ma·za·hua** \məˈzäwə\ *n, pl* **mazahua** *or* **mazahuas** *usu cap* **1 a :** an Otomian people of the states of Mexico and Michoacán, Mexico **b :** a member of such people **2 :** the language of the Mazahua people

**mazal tov** *var of* MAZEL TOV

**ma·za·ma** \məˈzämə\ *n, cap* [NL, fr. Nahuatl *maçam-*, *maçatl, mazatl* deer] **:** a genus of So. American deers (family Cervidae) comprising the brockets

**ma·zan·de·ra·ni** \¸mäzənˈdəˈränē\ *n, pl* **mazanderani** *or* **mazanderanis** *cap* **1 a :** a people of Mazanderan in northern Iran **b :** a member of such people **2 :** the Iranian language of the Mazanderani people

**ma·za·pan** \¦mäzə¦pän\ *adj, usu cap* [*Mazapan*, locality in central Mexico where remains of the culture were discovered] **:** of or belonging to a sedentary culture of Mexico centered to the northwest and west of the Valley of Mexico about A.D. 1100 and characterized by plumbate and fine orange pottery

**ma·zar** \məˈzär\ *n* -s [Ar *mazār*] **:** a Muslim shrine or enshrined tomb

**maz·ard** \ˈmazə(r)d\ *n* -s [fr. obs. E *mazard* mazer, alter. (influenced by E *-ard*) of E *mazer*] *now chiefly dial* **:** HEAD, FACE ⟨a blow on the ~⟩

**maz·a·rine** \¦mazə¦rēn, ˈmazərən\ *n* -s [perh. after Jules *Mazarin* †1661 Fr. cardinal] **1** *now usu* **ma·za·rin** \"\ **:** a deep dish often of metal; *esp* **:** one formerly used as a liner for a serving dish and usu. pierced **2 :** MAZARINE BLUE **3** *or* **mazarine hood** [perh. after Hortense Mancini, duchess of *Mazarin* †1699] **:** a hood worn by women in the 17th century

**mazarine blue** *n, often cap M* **:** a deep purplish blue that is slightly redder than hyacinth blue, redder and paler than average sapphire (sense 2a), and redder, lighter, and stronger than cyanine blue (sense 1b) — called also *bellflower, Roslyn blue*

**maz·a·tec** \¦mazə¦tek\ *or* **maz·a·teco** \¸mazəˈtā(¸)kō, -te(-\ *also* **maz·a·teca** \-ākə,-ekə\ *n, pl* **mazatec** *or* **mazatecs** *or* **mazateco** *or* **mazatecos** *usu cap* **1 a :** a people of Oaxaca, Guerrero, and Veracruz, Mexico **b :** a member of such people **2 :** the language of the Mazatec people

**maz·da·ism** \ˈmazdə,izəm\ *n* -s *usu cap* [Av *Mazdāh-* Ahura Mazda, Zoroastrian deity believed to be the source of all good + E *-ism*; akin to Skt *medhā* intelligence, wisdom — more at MATHEMATICAL] **:** ZOROASTRIANISM

**maz·dak·ite** \ˈmazdə,kīt\ *also* **maz·dak·ean** \¦mazdə¦kēən\ *n* -s [*Mazdak*, 5th cent. A.D. Persian religious reformer + E *-ite* or *-an*] **:** a member of a communistic sect that was founded late in the 5th century by Mazdak and that advocated community of property and women, simplicity in life, and abstinence from meat

**maz·da·yas·ni·an** \¸mazdəˈyäsnēən\ *n or adj, usu cap* **:** ZOROASTRIAN

**maz·de·an** \ˈmazdēən, (ˈ)mazˈd-\ *n or adj, usu cap* [Av *Mazdāh-* Ahura Mazda + E *-an*] **:** ZOROASTRIAN

**maz·door** *or* **maz·dur** \məzˈdü(ə)r\ *n* -s [Hindi *mazdūr*, fr. Per *muzdūr*] **:** an Indian laborer **:** COOLIE

**¹maze** \ˈmāz\ *vb* -ED/-ING/-S [ME *mazen, masen*, prob. fr. (assumed) OE *masian* to confuse; perh. akin to Sw *masa* to be sluggish] *vt* **1** *now chiefly dial* **:** to bring to a state of confused disorder **:** STUPEFY, DAZE **2 :** to greatly perplex **:** BEWILDER, CONFUSE ~ *vi* **:** to wander in or as if in a maze

**²maze** \"\ *n* -s [ME *maze, mase*, fr. *mazen, masen*, v.] **1 a** (1) **:** an intricate pattern of passages (as hedge-bordered paths) that ramifies and interconnects in a confusing way; *also* **:** a complicated winding path that is much longer than a corresponding direct route (2) **:** a path complicated by at least one blind alley and used in learning experiments and in intelligence tests **b :** something intricately and confusingly elaborate or complicated ⟨the ~ of inland waterways⟩ ⟨caught up in the ~ and whirl of political life⟩ ⟨the trials had become a legalistic ~ —*Collier's Yr. Bk.*⟩ **2** *now chiefly dial* **:** a state of bewilderment or amazement ⟨his mind was in a ~ —Liam O'Flaherty⟩

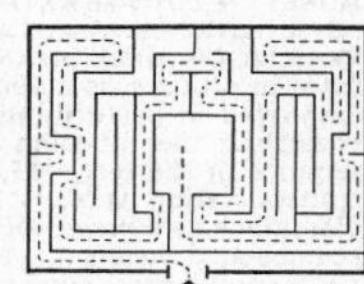

maze 1a (1)

**³maze** \"\ *n* -s [ME *meise*, fr. MF *maise* receptacle for herrings, fr. MLG *meise, mēse* barrel; akin to OHG *meisa* frame for carrying loads on the back, ON *meiss* basket, Skt *meṣa* ram, fleece] *dial Brit* **:** any of various units of quantity of fish (as herring) from 500 to 650

**mazed·ly** \ˈmāz(ə)dlē\ *adv* **:** in a stupefied or bewildered manner **:** as if utterly confused

**mazed·ness** \-zədnəs, -z(d)n-\ *n* -ES [ME *mazednesse*, fr. *mazed* (past part. of *mazen, masen* to stupefy) + *-nesse* -ness] **:** the condition of one that is mazed or behaves mazedly

**maze·ful** \ˈmāzfəl\ *adj* [*²maze* + *-ful*] *archaic* **:** CONFUSING

**ma·zel tov** *or* **ma·zal tov** \ˈmäzəl,tȯv, -tōf *also* -tōv\ *interj* [LHeb *mazzāl ṭob*, lit., good luck] — used among Jews to express congratulations

**maze·ment** \ˈmāzmənt\ *n* -s [*¹maze* + *-ment*] **1** *obs* **:** AMAZEMENT **2 :** TRANCE, STUPOR

**ma·zer** \ˈmāzə(r)\ *n* -s [ME *mazer, maser* mazer, veined wood, fr. OF *mazre, mazere*, of Gmc origin; akin to OHG *masar* gnarled excrescence on a tree, ON *mǫsurr* maple] **:** a large drinking bowl orig. of a hard wood (as maple) and often footed and silver-mounted

**mazer tree** \"-\ *n* [ME *maser-tre*, fr. *mazer, maser* + *tre*, tree] **1 :** HEDGE MAPLE **2 :** BIRD CHERRY 1

**ma·za·bi** \ˈməzəbē\ *n* -s *usu cap* [Hindi *mazhabī*, fr. Ar *madhhabīy* of or belonging to a sect, fr. *madhhab* sect] **:** an adherent of the Sikh religion of low-caste background fully assimilated into the Sikh community

**mazic** \ˈmazik, ˈmāz-\ *adj* [*²maz-* + *-ic*] **:** PLACENTAL

**maz·i·ly** \ˈmāzəlē, -li\ *adv* [*mazy* + *-ly*] **:** in a confused or obscure fashion

**mazo-** — see MAZ-

**mazo·car·pon** \¸māzōˈkär,pän, ¸maz-, -,pən\ *n, cap* [NL *mazo-* (fr. Gk, fr. *maza* lump, mass, barley cake) + *-carpon* (fr. Gk *-karpon*, neut. of *-karpos* -carpous) — more at MASS] **:** a form genus of paleozoic fossil plants orig. described from sporangia alone and now included in *Sigillariostrobus*

**ma·zoe lemon** \məˈzüˈ-\ *n* [fr. *Mazoe*, town in Southern Rhodesia] *So. Africa* **:** ROUGH LEMON

**mazo·pla·sia** \¸māzəˈplāzh(ē)ə, ¸maz-\ *n* -s [NL, fr. *¹maz-* + *-plasia*] **:** a degenerative condition of breast tissue

**ma·zo·vi·an** \məˈzōvēən\ *n* -s *usu cap* [*Mazovia*, ancient principality in Poland + E *-an*] **1 :** one of a Christian Polish community placed under the protection of the Teutonic knights early in the 13th century **2 :** the northeastern dialects of Polish

**ma·zu·ma** \məˈzümə\ *n* -s [Yiddish *mezumen*, fr. Heb *mĕzūmān, mĕzummān* fixed, appointed] *slang* **:** MONEY

**ma·zur** \ˈmä,zu̇(ə)r\ *or* **ma·zur·i·an** \məˈzu̇rēən\ *n* -s *usu cap* [*Mazur* fr. Pol; *Mazurian* fr. Pol *Mazur* + E *-an*] **1 :** a Pole of a Protestant community of southeastern Prussia **2 :** the Polish dialect of the Mazurs

**ma·zur·ka** *also* **ma·zour·ka** \məˈzər¦kə, -zu̇(ə)r¦, -zō¦, -zəi¦, -zu̇ə¦\ *n* -s [Russ *mazurka*, fr. Pol *mazurek* Mazur dance, fr. *Mazur*] **1 :** a Polish dance in moderate triple measure often of varied steps and figures but having characteristically a slide and hop to the side **2 :** music for the mazurka or in its rhythm usu. in moderate ¾ or ⅜ time and frequently with a strong accent on the second or third beat

**mazurka jump** *n* **:** a figure-skating jump in which the skater makes a vertical takeoff from the toes and bends one knee so as to cross the bent leg in front of the other in the air

**ma·zus** \ˈmāzəs\ *n* [NL, fr. Gk *mazos, mastos* breast; fr. the ridges on the lower lip of the flower — more at MEAT] **1** *cap* **:** a genus of low prostrate or creeping perennial herbs (family Scrophulariaceae) that have blue or white flowers in terminal one-sided racemes and are native to Asia and Australasia but often cultivated as ground covers or rock garden subjects **2** *pl* **mazus :** any plant of the genus *Mazus*

**ma·zut** *or* **ma·zout** *also* **ma·sut** \məˈzüt\ *n* -s [Russ *mazut*] **:** a viscous liquid residue from the distillation of Russian petroleum that is used chiefly as a fuel oil

**mazy** \ˈmāzē, -zi\ *adj* -ER/-EST [*²maze* + *-y*] **1 :** like or constituting a maze **:** confused or confusing because of intricate intertwining or overlapping ⟨a thousand rills their ~ progress take —Thomas Gray⟩ ⟨a gallant wig flowing in ~ ringlets —Norman Douglas⟩ **2** *dial Eng* **:** characterized by dizziness **:** GIDDY

**¹maz·zard** \ˈmazə(r)d\ *also* **mazzard cherry** *n* -s [origin unknown] **:** SWEET CHERRY 1; *esp* **:** wild or seedling sweet cherry used as a rootstock for grafting

**²mazzard** \"\ *var of* MAZARD

**¹maz·zi·ni·an** \(ˈ)mät¦sēnēən, -ädˈzē-\ *adj, usu cap* [Giuseppe *Mazzini* †1872 Ital. patriot + E *-an*] **:** of or relating to the Italian patriot Mazzini or his policies

**²mazzinian** \"\ *n* -s *usu cap* **:** a follower or adherent of Mazzini

**maz·zi·nist** \-sēnəst, -zē-\ *n* -s *usu cap* [Giuseppe *Mazzini* + E *-ist*] **:** MAZZINIAN

**mb** *abbr* millibar

**MB** *abbr* **1** medical board **2** medium bomber **3** motor boat **4** municipal borough **5** munitions board

**MBA** *abbr or n* -s **:** a master in business administration

**mba·lo·lo** \¸embəˈlō(¸)lō\ *n* -s [Fiji *mbololo*] **:** PALOLO

**mba·ya** \¸embəˈyä\ *n, pl* **mbaya** *or* **mbayas** *usu cap* **1 a :** a Guaicuruan people of Paraguay **b :** a member of such people **2 :** the language of the Mbaya people

**MBF** *abbr* [L *mille* thousand] thousand board feet

**MBH** *abbr* [L *mille* thousand] thousands of BTU per hour

**mbl** *abbr* mobile

**MBM** *abbr* [L *mille* thousand] thousand feet board measure

**mbo·ri** \emˈbōrē\ *n* -s [origin unknown] **:** a mild form of surra affecting camels

**MBT** *abbr* mercaptobenzothiazole

**mbun·du** \emˈbün(¸)dü\ *n, pl* **mbundu** *or* **mbundus** *usu cap* **1 :** a widespread Bantu-speaking people of Angola active in trading and known in world art circles for their wood carving esp. of miniature animal figures — called also *Ovimbundu* **2 a :** KIMBUNDU **b :** UMBUNDU

**mbu·ti** \emˈbüd·ē\ *n, pl* **mbuti** *or* **mbutis** *usu cap* **1 a :** a nomadic negroid Pygmy people of the western border of Uganda and adjacent areas to the south and west with reddish yellow skin — compare TWA **b :** a member of this people; *broadly* **:** NEGRILLO **2 :** the language of the Mbuti people

**¹MC** *abbr or n* -s **:** MASTER OF CEREMONIES, EMCEE

**²MC** *vb* **MC'd**; **MC'd**; **MC'ing**; **MC's :** EMCEE

**mc** *abbr* **1** megacycle **2** millicurie **3** millicycle

**MC** *abbr* **1** machinery certificate **2** magnetic course **3** marginal credit **4** marine corps **5** marked capacity **6** medical corps **7** medico-chirurgical **8** member of congress **9** member of council **10** metaling clause **11** meter-candle **12** metric carat **13** motor contact **14** motorcycle **15** movement control **16** multiple contact **17** my account

**MCF** *abbr* [L *mille* thousand] thousand cubic feet

**mcg** *abbr* microgram

**MCH** *abbr* mean corpuscular hemoglobin

**mcht** *abbr* merchant

**MCI** *abbr* malleable cast iron

**MCO** *abbr* mill culls out

**MCU** *abbr* medium close-up

**MCV** *abbr* mean corpuscular volume

**MCW** *abbr, often not cap* modulated continuous wave

**MD** *abbr or n* -s [L *medicinae doctor*] **:** a doctor of medicine

**MD** *abbr* **1** [F *main droite*] right hand **2** managing director **3** *often not cap* [It *mano destra*] right hand **4** medical department **5** memorandum of deposit **6** mental defective; mentally deficient **7** message dropping **8** *often not cap* months after date; month's date **9** muscular dystrophy

**Md** *symbol* mendelevium

**m-day** \ˈ=,=\ *n, usu cap M* [*m* (initial letter of *mobilization*) + *day*] **1 :** a day on which a military mobilization begins or is postulated (as in a problem in logistics) to begin **2 :** the day on which actual hostility breaks out at the commencement of a war

**MDD** *abbr* milligrams per square decimeter per day

**mde·wa·kan·ton** \¸emdēˈwōkən,tōn, ¸medəˈw-\ *n* -s **:** a portion of the eastern forest group of the Dakota people

**mdlle** *abbr, often cap* mademoiselle

**mdm** *abbr, often cap* madam

**mdme** *abbr, often cap* madame

**mdn** *abbr* midnight

**m-dog** \ˈ=,=\ *n, usu cap* [*m* (initial letter of *mine*) + *dog*] **:** a dog trained to locate buried mines

**MDR** *abbr* minimum daily requirement

**MDS** *abbr* main dressing station

**mdse** *abbr* merchandise

**mdt** *abbr* moderate

**¹me** \(ˈ)mē, ¸mi\ *pron, objective case of* I [ME, fr. OE *mē*; akin to OHG *mih* me, ON & Goth *mik*, L *me*, Gk *me*, Skt *mā*] **1 :** I: **a** (1) — used as indirect object of a verb ⟨gave ~ a book⟩ (2) — used as indirect object in some archaic or obsolete expressions (as *meseems*) and usu. written solid with the verb element of such expressions; compare METHINKS (3) — used chiefly archaically as a vague indirect object simply to suggest the concern or involvement of the one speaking or writing ⟨tie ~ up this tress instantly —Laurence Sterne⟩ and sometimes used merely to fill out a sentence and having little or no meaning ⟨he enters ~ his name in the book —Charles Lamb⟩ **b** — used as object of a preposition ⟨stand behind ~⟩ **c** — used as direct object of a verb ⟨they know ~ very well⟩ **d** — used in comparisons after *than* and *as* when the first term in the comparison is the direct or indirect object of a verb or the object of a preposition ⟨likes him better than ~⟩ ⟨would more gladly give him the money than ~⟩ ⟨would be as helpful to you as ~⟩ **e** (1) — used in absolute or elliptical constructions ⟨who, ~⟩ esp. together with a prepositional phrase, adjective, or participle ⟨I was hungry and tired, and ~ without a cent to my name⟩ ⟨~ looking like a perfect fool, she scarcely glanced in my direction⟩ (2) — used in interjectional phrases typically to express unhappiness ⟨ah ~⟩ or surprise ⟨dear ~⟩ of the one speaking or writing or to express some other state or emotion indicated by an adjective that usu. precedes ⟨poor ~⟩ ⟨unlucky ~⟩ and that occas. follows archaically ⟨~ miserable which way shall I fly infinite wrath and infinite despair —John Milton⟩ **f** — used by speakers on all educational levels and by many reputable writers though disapproved by some grammarians in the predicate after forms of *be*, in comparisons after *than* and *as* when the first term in the comparison is the subject of a verb, and in other positions where it is itself neither the subject of a verb nor the object of a verb or preposition ⟨be thou ~, impetuous one —P.B.Shelley⟩ ⟨it's ~⟩ ⟨you're as big as ~⟩ ⟨~ and my big mouth⟩ **g** — used in substandard speech and formerly also by reputable writers as the subject of a verb which it does not immediately precede or as part of the compound subject of a verb ⟨there was left surviving only ~ —Oliver Goldsmith⟩ ⟨~ and my wife never go any more⟩ **2 :** MYSELF — used reflexively as indirect object of a verb ⟨I'm going to get ~ a wife⟩, object of a preposition ⟨I don't know whether to leave it here or take it with ~⟩, or direct object of a verb ⟨if I don't respect ~, nobody else will⟩ **3** — used like the adjective *my* with a gerund by speakers and writers on all educational levels though disapproved by some grammarians ⟨disapprove of ~ being so cheerful —S.E.White⟩

**²me** \"\ *n* -s **1 :** ³I **2** *dial* **:** what belongs to me

**³me** \ˈmē, mi\ *dial var of* MY

**ME** *abbr or n* -s mechanical engineer

**ME** *abbr* **1** *often not cap* managing editor **2** marbled edges **3** maximum effort **4** medical examiner **5** metabolizable energy **6** *often not cap* milligram equivalent; milliequivalent **7** most excellent **8** Muhammadan Era **9** muzzle energy

**Me** *symbol* methyl

**MEA** *abbr* monoethanolamine

**meach** \ˈmēch\ *var of* MEECH

**mea·cock** \ˈmē,käk\ *n* -s [origin unknown] *archaic* **:** a cowardly or effeminate man ⟨I shall be compted a ~, a milksop —John Lyly⟩

**mea cul·pa** \¦māəˈku̇l(¸)pä, -ā(¸)ä'k- *sometimes* -kül- *or* ¸mēəˈkəlpə\ *n, pl* **mea culpas** [L, through my fault] **:** a formal acknowledgment of personal fault or error

**¹mead** \ˈmēd\ *n* -s [ME *mede*, fr. OE *medu*; akin to OHG *metu* mead, ON *mjǫthr*, Gk *methy* wine, Skt *madhu* sweet, honey, mead] **:** a fermented drink made of water and honey with malt, yeast, and sometimes other ingredients **:** METHEGLIN

**²mead** \"\ *n* -s [ME *mede*, fr. OE *mǣd*] *archaic* **:** MEADOW

**mead·er** \ˈmēdə(r)\ *n* -s [*²mead* + *-er*] *dial Eng* **:** MOWER

**¹mead·ow** \ˈme(¸)dō, -¸də, *often* -¸dəw+V\ *n* -s *often attrib* [ME *medwe*, fr. OE *mǣdwe*, oblique case form of *mǣd*; akin to OE *māwan* to mow — more at MOW] **1 :** land in or predominantly in grass **:** GRASSLAND: as **a :** a piece of land on which grass is grown for hay or pasture **b :** a tract of moist low-lying usu. level grassland often along a watercourse — compare ¹BOTTOM 6 **c :** an upland area covered with grass and herbs and commonly surrounded by woodland ⟨cool mountain ~s⟩ **d** *dial* **:** an open swampy or marshy area often of considerable extent ⟨the New Jersey ~s⟩ **2 :** a feeding ground for fish ⟨a cod ~⟩ **3 :** MEADOW GREEN

**²meadow** \"\ *vt* -ED/-ING/-S **1 :** to convert into grassland **:** use for the production of hay or pasture ⟨cleared and ~ed the old orchard⟩ **2 :** to pasture (livestock) on grazing land

**meadow ant** *n* **:** any of several small ants that frequent open grassy land: as **a :** an ant of the genus *Lasius* **b :** PAVEMENT ANT

**meadow barley** *n* **:** a wild barley (*Hordeum nodosum*) that is probably native to Europe but widely distributed in No. America, grows chiefly in open meadow land, and is used chiefly for forage

**meadow beauty** *n* **:** DEER GRASS 2

**meadow-beauty family** *n* **:** MELASTOMACEAE

**meadow bell** *n, Brit* **:** HAREBELL

**meadow bird** *n* **:** BOBOLINK

**meadow bright** *n, dial Eng* **:** a marsh marigold (*Caltha palustris*)

**meadowbrook** \ˈ==,=\ *n* **:** a dark to dark grayish green that is bluer and slightly lighter than marine green

**meadow brown** *n* **:** any of several satyr butterflies; *esp* **:** a British butterfly (*Maniola jurtina*) having restricted orange markings on the upper surface of the wings of the male

**meadow buttercup** *n* **1 :** TALL BUTTERCUP **2 :** a marsh marigold (*Caltha palustris*)

**meadow cabbage** *n* **:** SKUNK CABBAGE

**meadow campion** *n* **:** RAGGED ROBIN

**meadow cat's-tail grass** *also* **meadow cat's tail** *n* **:** TIMOTHY

**meadow chicken** *n* **:** SORA RAIL

**meadow chickweed** *n* **:** FIELD CHICKWEED

**meadow clary** *n* **:** a tall perennial Old World salvia (*Salvia pratensis*) that has violet-blue flowers and occurs in open grasslands and waste places

**meadow crake** *or* **meadow drake** *n* **:** CORN CRAKE

**meadow cranesbill** *n* **:** a tall perennial cranesbill (*Geranium pratense*) with paired violet-blue axillary flowers that is native to northern parts of the Old World and naturalized in No. America

**meadow crowfoot** *n* **:** BULBOUS BUTTERCUP

**meadow death camas** *n* **:** a death camas (*Zygadenus venenosus*) that grows chiefly in wet grassland

**mead·owed** \ˈme(¸)dōd, -¸dəd\ *adj* [*¹meadow* + *-ed*] **:** having meadows **:** consisting of meadowland

**meadow eelworm** *n, chiefly Brit* **:** MEADOW NEMATODE

**meadow fern** *n* **1 :** SWEET GALE **2 :** SWEET FERN

**meadow fescue** *n* **:** a tall vigorous perennial European fescue grass (*Festuca elatior*) with broad flat leaves widely cultivated in Europe and America for permanent pasture and hay

**meadow-foam** \ˈ=(¸)=,=\ *n* **:** a spreading herb (*Limnanthes douglasii*) of wet low-lying areas in the southwestern U. S. that is sometimes cultivated as an ornamental for its yellowish green lobed or parted succulent leaves and abundant showy white flowers

**meadow foxtail** *n* **:** a stout erect perennial grass (*Alopecurus pratensis*) of northern parts of the Old World that much resembles timothy, is widely cultivated for pasture and hay, and has become locally naturalized in No. America

**meadow garlic** *n* **:** a common wild onion (*Allium canadense*) of moist open land of eastern No. America

**meadow gowan** *n* **:** a marsh marigold (*Caltha palustris*)

**meadow grass** *n* [ME *medewe gras*, fr. *medewe, medwe* meadow + *gras* grass] **:** any of various grasses that thrive in the presence of abundant moisture: as **a :** a grass of the genus *Poa*; *esp* **:** KENTUCKY BLUEGRASS **b :** MEADOW FOXTAIL **c :** MANNA GRASS **d :** SKUNK GRASS

**meadow grasshopper** *n* **:** a grasshopper of the family Tettigoniidae

**meadow green** *n* **:** a dark yellowish green that is yellower and paler than holly green (sense 1), greener, lighter, and stronger than deep chrome green, and greener and lighter than average hunter green — called also *meadow*

**meadow hay** *n* **:** hay made from permanent and usu. natural grasslands

**meadow hen** *n* **1 :** AMERICAN BITTERN **2 :** AMERICAN COOT **3 a :** CLAPPER RAIL **b :** KING RAIL

**mead·ow·ing** \ˈmedōiŋ, -dəwiŋ\ *n* -s [*¹meadow* + *-ing*] **:** MEADOWLAND

**meadowland** \ˈ==,=\ *also* **meadow ground** *n* **:** land that is or is used as meadow

**meadowlark** \ˈ==,=\ *n* **1 :** any of several No. American birds of the genus *Sturnella* that are largely brown and buff above with a yellow breast marked with a black crescent and that are noted for their melodious sustained songs **2 :** ACORN 3

**mead·ow·less** \ˈmedōləs, -dəl-\ *adj* **:** lacking meadows or meadowland

**meadow lily** *n* **:** a common lily (*Lilium canadense*) of the eastern U. S. with nodding yellow or reddish flowers spotted with brown — see BULB illustration

**meadow mouse** *n* **:** any of various cricetid mice of *Microtus* and related genera; *esp* **:** a common American field mouse (*M. pennsylvanicus*)

**meadow mushroom** *n* **:** a common edible agaric (*Agaricus campestris*) occurring naturally in moist open organically rich soil and being the cultivated edible mushroom of commerce
**meadow mussel** *n* **:** an American mussel (*Volsella plicatula*) that has a ribbed shell and that is very abundant in salt marshes
**meadow nematode** *n* **:** any of numerous plant-parasitic nematode worms of *Pratylenchus* and related genera that were formerly considered to constitute a single variable species (*P. pratensis*) and that invade, migrate through, and multiply in the roots of various plants causing necrotic changes, rotting, and sloughing of tissues — compare ROOTKNOT NEMATODE
**meadow oat grass** *also* **meadow oat** *n* **:** TALL OAT GRASS
**meadow ore** *n* **:** BOG IRON ORE
**meadow parsnip** *n* **1 :** COW PARSNIP **2 :** a plant of the genus *Thaspium* **3 :** a golden alexander (*Zizia aurea*)
**meadow pea** *n* **:** a scrambling perennial Eurasian wild pea (*Lathyrus pratensis*) that has yellowish flowers and compressed seed pods and is cultivated as a forage plant
**meadow peat** *n* **:** peat formed in meadowland and predominantly from grasses and sedges
**meadow phlox** *n* **:** WILD SWEET WILLIAM 1
**meadow pine** *n* **1 :** any of several pines of the southern U. S.: as **a :** CARIBBEAN PINE **b :** LOBLOLLY PINE **2 :** a common No. American horsetail (*Equisetum arvense*) widely distributed in moist open ground
**meadow pink** *n* **1 :** RAGGED ROBIN **2 :** PURPLE-FRINGED ORCHID b
**meadow pipit** *n* **:** a common pipit (*Anthus pratensis*) that is olive brown above and largely whitish below and is widely distributed in open areas in northern and central Europe and much of Asia
**meadowpride** \'==,=\ *n* **:** AMERICAN COLUMBO 1
**meadow queen** *n* **:** MEADOWSWEET 1
**meadow rue** *n* **:** a plant of the genus *Thalictrum*
**meadow runagates** *n pl but sing or pl in constr* **:** MONEYWORT
**meadow rush** *n* **:** a perennial bulrush (*Scirpus atrovirens*) with dark brownish green spikelets and creeping rootstocks that is a troublesome weed of wet low-lying pastures of eastern No. America
**meadows** *pl of* MEADOW, *pres 3d sing of* MEADOW
**meadow saffron** *n* **:** a plant of the genus *Colchicum; esp* **:** a bulbous autumn-flowering herb (*C. autumnale*) with white, lavender and white, or purple flowers — called also *autumn crocus*
**meadow sage** *n* **:** MEADOW CLARY
**meadow salsify** *n* **:** YELLOW GOATSBEARD
**meadow saxifrage** *n* **:** a European saxifrage (*Saxifraga granulata*) having alternate leaves and white flowers with erect sepals
**meadow scabish** *n* **:** COCASH 1
**meadow snakegrass** *n* **:** STINK GRASS 1
**meadow snipe** *n* **1 :** WILSON'S SNIPE **2 :** PECTORAL SANDPIPER
**meadow soft grass** *n* **:** VELVET GRASS
**meadow sorrel** *n* **:** [1]DOCK 1
**meadow spittlebug** *n* **:** a No. American cercopid insect (*Philaenus spumarius*) that severely damages grasses and other plants
**meadowsweet** \'==,=\ *n* **1 :** a shrub of the genus *Spiraea; esp* **:** a No. American native or naturalized plant of this genus (as *S. alba* or *S. tomentosa*) **2 :** a plant of a genus (*Filipendula*) that is closely related to *Spiraea; esp* **:** a tall perennial Eurasian herb (*F. ulmaria*) that is sometimes cultivated for its single or double cymose white flowers
**meadow vetchling** *n* **:** MEADOW PEA
**meadow violet** *n* **:** a common violet (*Viola cucullata*) of wet or boggy land of eastern No. America with long-stemmed bluish violet or occasionally white or blue and white flowers
**meadow vole** *n* **:** MEADOW MOUSE
**mead·ow·wink** \'medō,wiŋk, -də,-\ *n* [perh. imit.] **:** BOBOLINK
**mead·owy** \'medōē, -dəwē, -i\ *adj* **1 :** like or like that of a meadow ⟨~ sweetness⟩ **2 :** consisting of or characterized by meadow ⟨~ shores⟩
**mea·ger** *or* **mea·gre** \'mēgə(r)\ *adj* [ME *megre*, fr. MF *maigre*, fr. L *macr-, macer;* akin to OE *mæger* lean, OHG *magar*, ON *magr* lean, Gk *makros* long, tall, Av *mas-* long] **1 :** destitute of or having little flesh **:** THIN, LEAN ⟨~ were his looks, sharp misery had worn him to the bones —Shak.⟩ **2 a :** lacking richness, fertility, strength, or comparable qualities **:** deficient in quantity or poor in quality **:** INFERIOR, INADEQUATE ⟨a ~ harvest⟩ ⟨stretching a ~ salary⟩ **b** *of verbal expression* **:** scanty in ideas **:** lacking strength of diction or sufficiency of imagery **3 :** dry and harsh to the touch ⟨chalk feels ~⟩ **4 :** MAIGRE
**syn** SCANTY, SCANT, SKIMPY, SCRIMPY, EXIGUOUS, SPARE, SPARSE: MEAGER suggests thin, pinched, slight smallness, inadequacy, barrenness, or utter lack of richness, strength, force, or fullness ⟨*meager* crops of rye, buckwheat, and potatoes scarcely provide a living for the inhabitants —Samuel Van Valkenburg & Ellsworth Huntington⟩ ⟨scientists with poor laboratories and *meager* salaries —W.A.Noyes b. 1898⟩ ⟨the child-mind is as yet too *meagre* in life-experience to confront the human enterprise —H.A.Overstreet⟩ SCANTY describes that which is barely adequate in quantity, size, extent, or degree or which only approaches adequacy ⟨the hunted wild beasts can live on *scanty* rations, going for days at a time without a mouthful —*Amer. Guide Series: Ariz.*⟩ ⟨such a *scanty* portion of light was admitted through these means that it was difficult, on first coming in, to see anything —Charles Dickens⟩ SCANT may indicate a falling or cutting short, sometimes by design, of what is desired or desirable ⟨where precipitation was too *scant* to support a solid earth covering —R.A.Billington⟩ ⟨savage people, huge in form, fierce in manner, and wearing *scant* clothing of skins —A.C.Whitehead⟩ ⟨most of the colonies gave them *scant* welcome, and many persecuted them —W.L. Sperry⟩ SKIMPY and SCRIMPY may imply niggardliness as a cause of smallness or inadequacy, the former perhaps arising from stinginess, the latter from necessitous parsimony ⟨the meal set before us upon our return to the Bear's Paw, tired and hungry, was a decidedly *skimpy* table d'hôte lunch —A.W. O'Neil⟩ ⟨the drab routine and *skimpy* meanness of the New England farm —V.L.Parrington⟩ ⟨the guests ate in silence, murmured with their food, were exceedingly well bred — more proud of their breeding than they were of the *scrimpy*, almost stingy respectability of the ménage —W.A.White⟩ EXIGUOUS describes a scanty smallness making whatever is under consideration compare most unfavorably with others of its kind ⟨in conditions the whole region, except for the river valleys that cross it, can support only a sparse and *exiguous* population who have little encouragement to cultural progress and have in fact remained backward —V.G.Childe⟩ SPARE may indicate a falling short of adequacy without, however, specific connotations, esp. depreciatory ones ⟨argument was *spare* and simple: surely the U. S. would not let a stout ally down in its hour of need —*Time*⟩ SPARSE implies thinness or lack of normal or hoped for thickness or density, with or without being therefore inadequate or insufficient ⟨the cays were little more than heaps of rock and sand, covered with coarse grass and a *sparse* growth of bush and stunted trees —C.B.Nordhoff & J.N.Hall⟩
**meager lime** *n* **:** lime containing a large amount of impurities (as 15 percent or more)
**mea·ger·ly** *adv* **:** in a meager manner **:** POORLY, INADEQUATELY ⟨very ~ represented at the conference⟩ ⟨served us grudgingly and ~⟩
**mea·ger·ness** *n* -ES **1 :** the quality or state of being meager ⟨~ of expression⟩ **2 :** something meager ⟨remembering these ~*es* and penny-pinchings⟩
[1]**meagre** \'mēgə(r)\ *vt* -ED/-ING/-S [*meager*] *archaic* **:** to make (as a person) thin
[2]**meagre** *var of* MAIGRE
**meak** \'mēk\ *n* -S [ME *meeke*] *dial Eng* **:** a long-handled bush hook **:** SCYTHE
[1]**meal** \'mēl, *esp before pause or consonant* 'mēəl\ *n* -S [ME *meel* mealtime, meal, fr. OE *mǣl* appointed time, mealtime, meal; akin to OHG *māl* time, ON *māl* measure, mealtime, Goth *mel* time, L *metiri* to measure — more at MEASURE] **1 a :** the portion of food taken at a particular time to satisfy hunger or appetite **:** REPAST **b :** an act or the time of eating a meal **2** *dial Eng* **a :** the act or time of milking **b :** the yield at a milking
[2]**meal** \"\ *vb* -ED/-ING/-S **:** EAT, FEED
[3]**meal** \"\ *n* -S [ME *mele*, fr. OE *melu;* akin to OHG *melo* meal, ON *mjöl* meal, OHG & Goth *malan* to grind, ON *mala*, L *molere* to grind, Gk *mylē* mill] **1 :** the ground seeds of a cereal grass or pulse esp. when coarsely ground and unbolted and usu. excluding flour of wheat: as **a :** OATMEAL **b** *obs* **:** the finer inner part of such ground seeds **c :** CORNMEAL **2 :** a product resembling seed meal in particle size, texture, or other quality: as **a :** a product obtained by grinding the residue remaining after removal of part of the oil from various nuts and other oily seeds — see OIL MEAL **b :** a product obtained by grinding any of various dried food products (as meat or fish) **c :** a product obtained by rapid crystallization ⟨alum ~⟩
[4]**meal** \"\ *vb* -ED/-ING/-S *vt* **1 :** to cover with meal or a mealy substance **2 :** to reduce (as the constituents of gunpowder) to powder **:** PULVERIZE ~ *vi* **:** to yield or become meal ⟨a flint corn that ~s well⟩
[5]**meal** *n* -S [ME *mele*, fr. OE *mēle* tub, bucket; akin to ON *mælir*, a measure] *obs* **:** a tub or bucket that is sometimes used as a measure
[6]**meal** \'mē(ə)l\ *n* -S [ON *mælir*, a measure; akin to ON *māl* measure, mealtime — more at [1]MEAL] **:** a variable weight used esp. formerly in the Orkney islands
[7]**meal** *vt* [perh. fr. (assumed) ME *melen*, fr. OE *-mǣlan;* akin to OHG *meilen* to stain; denominative fr. the root of OE *māl* spot, blemish — more at MOLE] *obs* **:** STAIN
[8]**meal** \'mē(ə)l\ *n* -S [ON *melr;* perh. akin to OE *melu* meal — more at [3]MEAL] *dial Eng* **:** SANDBANK, DUNE
**-meal** \,mēl, 'mē(ə)l\ *adv comb form* [ME *-mele*, fr. OE *-mǣlum*, fr. *mǣlum*, dat. pl. of *mǣl* appointed time — more at MEAL (repast)] **:** by a (specified) portion or measure at a time ⟨inchmeal⟩ ⟨piecemeal⟩
**meal·able** \'mēləbəl\ *adj* [[4]*meal*] **:** reducible to meal
**meal beetle** *n* **:** the adult of the mealworm
**meal·berry** \'mēl- — *see* BERRY\ *n* [[3]*meal*] **:** BEARBERRY 1
**meal·er** \'mēlə(r)\ *n* -S [[4]*meal*] **1 :** a wooden implement for mealing powder **2** [[1]*meal*] **:** a person rooming at one place and boarding at another
**meal·ie** \'mēlē, -li\ *n* -S [Afrik *mielie*, fr. Pg *milho* millet, Indian corn, fr. L *milium* millet — more at MILLET] **1** *Africa* **:** INDIAN CORN — usu. used in pl. ⟨the best time to plant ~*s*⟩ **2** *or* **mealie cob** *Africa* **:** an ear of Indian corn — see GREEN MEALIES
**meal·i·ness** \'mēlēnəs, -lin-\ *n* -ES **:** the quality or state of being mealy; *esp* **:** possession of a mealy texture
**meal·less** \'mēlləs\ *adj* [[1]*meal* and [3]*meal*] **:** lacking meal or a meal ⟨the gaping ~ bin⟩ ⟨sent ~ to bed⟩
**meal·man** \'mēlmən\ *n, pl* **mealmen :** a dealer in meal
**mealmonger** \'=,==\ *n* **:** MEALMAN
**meal moth** *or* **meal snout moth** *n* **:** any of several small widely distributed moths (as the Indian meal moth or the Mediterranean flour moth) having larvae that feed in milled and stored grain products; *esp* **:** a small golden brown moth (*Pyralis farinalis*) with dark and whitish markings
**meal-mouthed** \'=;=\ *adj* **:** MEALYMOUTHED 1
**meal·ock** \'mēlək\ *n* -S [origin unknown] *Scot* **:** a small piece or crumb of bread
**meal offering** *n* **:** a vegetable sacrifice among the ancient Israelites consisting of flour and salt usu. mingled with oil and frankincense
**meal pennant** *n* **:** a red pennant used (as in the U. S. Navy or on a yacht) to indicate that the crew is at a meal
**meal plum** *n* [[3]*meal*] **:** BEARBERRY 1
**meal ticket** *n* **1 :** a ticket authorizing the provision of a meal; *esp* **:** a card with a specified cash value that is sold by a restaurant at a discount, is redeemable at the face value in food, and constitutes a method of prepayment for meals **2 a :** a person that provides the living expenses of another ⟨only married her for a *meal ticket*⟩ **b :** someone or something that is the ultimate source of one's income ⟨had to nurse the old truck along because it was our *meal ticket*⟩ ⟨this toothpaste account was the real *meal ticket* of the agency⟩
**mealtide** *n* [ME *meltid*, fr. OE *mǣltīd*, fr. *mǣl* meal + *tīd* time — more at MEAL, TIDE] *obs* **:** MEALTIME
**mealtime** \'=,=\ *n* [ME *meeltime*, fr. *meel* meal + *time* — more at MEAL, TIME] **:** the time at which one takes a meal; *esp* **:** the usual time at which a meal is served ⟨knew that if he was not home by ~ he would get nothing to eat⟩
**mealworm** \'=,=\ *n* **:** the larva of various beetles of the family Tenebrionidae that infests, feeds on, and pollutes grain products (as flour and meals) but is often cultured for food for insectivorous animals, laboratory use, or as bait for fishing; *esp* **:** a pale brown to yellowish larva of a cosmopolitan beetle (*Tenebrio molitor*) — called also *yellow mealworm*
**mealy** \'mēlē, -li\ *adj* -ER/-EST [[3]*meal* + *-y*] **1 :** having the qualities of or resembling meal **:** soft, dry, and friable ⟨a ~ potato⟩ **2 :** containing or consisting of meal **:** FARINACEOUS **3 a :** covered with meal or with fine granules **:** FARINOSE, POLLINOSE ⟨a butterfly with ~ wings⟩ **b :** flecked with another color (as white or gray) ⟨a *mealy*-nosed mule⟩ **c :** SPOTTY, UNEVEN ⟨a ~ photographic negative⟩ **d** *of the complexion* **:** pale as if dusted with flour **:** PALLID, BLANCHED **4 :** tending to be obscure or affected in speech **:** MEALYMOUTHED
**mealy amazon** *n, usu cap A* **:** a large So. American parrot (*Amazona farinosa*) with the greenish upper parts of a mealy appearance
**mealy-back** \'==,=\ *n, Austral* **:** CICADA
**mealy bellwort** *n* **:** MOHAWK WEED
**mealy bird** *or* **mealy duck** *n, dial Brit* **:** an immature old-squaw duck
**mealybug** \'==,=\ *n* **:** any of numerous scales of the family Pseudococcidae that are covered with a white powdery substance and are serious pests of fruit trees and of many other cultivated plants esp. in greenhouses
**mealybug wilt** *n* **:** a wilt of the pineapple esp. destructive in Hawaii that is associated with the feeding of the pineapple mealybug
**mealymouth** \'==,=\ *n* **1 :** a mealymouthed person **2** *dial Brit* **:** WILLOW WARBLER
**mealymouthed** \'==;=\ *adj* **1 a :** unwilling to tell the truth in plain language **:** tending to cloak thoughts, ideas, or intents by the use of obscure or devious language ⟨a ~ hypocrite⟩; *often* **:** affectedly unwilling to use strong or coarse language **b** *of an utterance* **:** suitable to a mealymouthed person ⟨~ phrases⟩ **2** *of an animal* **:** having a zone of white behind a black muzzle — used esp. of cattle and horses — **mealy·mouthed·ly** \-;mau̇thədlē, -thədlē, -thtlē, -thdlē\ *adv* — **mealy·mouthed·ness** \-thədnəs, -thədn-, -th(t)n-, -th(d)n-\ *n* -ES
**mealy plum aphid** *n* **:** a pale green aphid (*Hyalopterus pruni*) with a powdery body surface that is native to Europe but widely naturalized on various fruit trees where it causes stunting and distortion of new growth and splitting and soiling of fruit
**mealy redpoll** *n* **:** a rather large pale European redpoll (*Carduelis flamea* or *Acanthis flammea*)
**mealy scale** *n* **:** MEALYBUG
**mealy starwort** *also* **mealy stargrass** *n* **:** a colicroot (*Aletris farinosa*)
**mealy tree** *n* **1 :** WAYFARING TREE 1 **2 :** ARROWWOOD 1a
**mealywing** \'==,=\ *n* **:** WHITEFLY
[1]**mean** \'mēn\ *adj* -ER/-EST [ME *mene*, fr. *imene*, fr. OE *gemǣne;* akin to OHG *gimeini* common, Goth *gamains*, L *communis;* all prob. fr. a prehistoric western IE compound whose first constituent is represented by L *com-* and whose second constituent is akin to L *munus* service, gift, Skt *mayate* he exchanges — more at CO-] **1** *now dial Brit* **:** held or done in common **2 :** destitute of distinction or eminence **:** COMMON, LOW, HUMBLE **3 :** destitute of power or acumen **:** ORDINARY, INFERIOR ⟨a man of ~ intelligence⟩ **4 :** of little value or account **:** of poor or inferior quality or status **:** worthy of little or no regard **:** SHABBY, CONTEMPTIBLE ⟨the ~*er* quarters of the town⟩ ⟨living in ~ circumstances⟩ **5 :** lacking dignity of mind **:** LOW-MINDED **:** IGNOBLE, BASE **:** destitute of honor ⟨a ~ motive⟩ **6 :** PENURIOUS, STINGY, CLOSEFISTED ⟨~ hospitality⟩ **7 a :** characterized by petty selfishness or malice **:** contemptibly disobliging or unkind ⟨a ~ surly man⟩ **b :** tending to harass or distress by reason of vexatious characteristics or conditions ⟨a ~ soil to work⟩ ⟨a ~ place to drive a car in⟩ **c** *slang* **:** of a kind to impress (as an adversary or an observer) **:** EXCELLENT, EFFECTIVE ⟨pitches a ~ curve⟩ ⟨dances a ~ tango⟩ **8 a :** lowered in self-esteem **:** ASHAMED ⟨his ready cooperation made me feel ~ for what I had said⟩ **b :** SICK, UNWELL, INDISPOSED ⟨felt thoroughly ~ with a cold⟩
[2]**mean** \"\ *adv* -ER/-EST **:** in a low, petty, or contemptible way ⟨acted ~ to us⟩ ⟨a narrow *mean*-thinking busybody⟩
[3]**mean** \"\ *vb* **meant** \'ment\ *or archaic* **meaned; meant** *or archaic* **meaned; meaning; means** [ME *menen*, fr. OE *mǣnan;* akin to OHG *meinen* to have in mind, OSlav *měniti* to mention, consider] *vt* **1 :** to have in the mind esp. as a purpose or intention **:** PURPOSE, DESIGN, INTEND ⟨houses are *meant* for use⟩ ⟨~*s* to make it difficult for you⟩ ⟨*meant* to come home early⟩ **2 :** to serve or intend to convey, show, or indicate **:** SIGNIFY, DENOTE, EXPRESS ⟨what do you ~ by such conduct⟩ ⟨these words ~ nothing to me⟩ **3 :** to have significance or importance to the extent or degree of **:** count for ⟨health ~*s* everything⟩ ⟨a happy home ~*s* much to a child⟩ ⟨music ~*s* little to me⟩ ⟨success without recognition ~*s* nothing to him⟩ ⟨her happiness *meant* the world to him⟩ **4 :** to intend for or direct to a particular individual ⟨his criticism is *meant* for all of us⟩ ⟨do you ~ this for me⟩ ~ *vi* **1 :** to have an intended purpose — used chiefly with *well* or *ill* ⟨*meant* well but seldom carried anything to a conclusion⟩ **2** *obs* **:** TALK, SPEAK, TELL **3** *obs* **:** to hold an opinion **:** THINK
**syn** MEAN, DENOTE, SIGNIFY, and IMPORT can have, in common, the sense of to convey (an idea, an interpretation, and so on) to the mind or understanding. MEAN is the most common and general in carrying the basic sense, although it can often connote evaluation or appraisal; in applying to a term it involves the term's full content ⟨to understand what foreign words *mean*⟩ ⟨what a person's actions *mean*⟩ ⟨disunion, incoherence and inconsistency *mean* failure in design —C.W.H. Johnson⟩ ⟨to understand what an obligation *means*⟩ ⟨the term "beauty" can *mean* many things⟩ DENOTE can contrast with SIGNIFY in having as its subject something that serves as an outward sign or visible indication; in application to a term it implies the limited and defined designation of a term disentangled from connotation or unessential association ⟨slumped into a chair near the doorway, his posture *denoting* complete exhaustion —L.C.Douglas⟩ ⟨that curious love of green, which . . . in nations is said to *denote* a laxity, if not a decadence of morals —Oscar Wilde⟩ ⟨the best way to show what a term *denotes* is to point at the object it stands for⟩ SIGNIFY can contrast with DENOTE in having as its subject something of a symbolic or representative character; it can also carry a stronger implication of the importance of the conveyed meaning; in application to a term it stresses the symbolic relationship between term and idea ⟨he had hopes that her demure and reticent deportment *signified* that the effervescence of youth had evaporated —Robert Grant †1940⟩ ⟨the third figure, with a background of plow handles and mining tools, *signifies* agriculture and mining —*Amer. Guide Series: Mich.*⟩ ⟨the loss of his wife *signified* more than he could ever put into words⟩ ⟨the term "bread and butter" *signifies* the material necessities of life⟩ IMPORT can carry the idea of offering for comprehension or intellectual grasp, often, however, being virtually interchangeable with SIGNIFY; in application to a term it can stress the implications involved in the term's interpretation as distinct from its denotation ⟨the radical ideas *imported* little to conservative readers except the idea of outrageous thinking⟩ ⟨though a term's denotation may be matter of fact, in its connotations the term may *import* revolution⟩ **syn** see in addition INTEND
— **mean business :** to be in earnest **:** have a sober, serious, and determined intent in respect to something
[4]**mean** \"\ *vb* -ED/-ING/-S [ME *menen*, fr. OE *mǣnan* to lament, mourn for, fr. (assumed) OE *mān* lamentation, moan — more at MOAN] *vt* **1** *now chiefly Scot* **:** to complain or lament over **:** RESENT **2** *now chiefly Scot* **:** PITY **3** *now chiefly Scot* **:** to present as a complaint ~ *vi, chiefly Scot* **:** LAMENT, COMPLAIN, BEMOAN
[5]**mean** \"\ *n* -S [ME *mene*, fr. *menen* to complain or lament over] *now chiefly Scot* **:** LAMENT, COMPLAINT
[6]**mean** \"\ *n* -S [ME *mene*, fr. MF *meien, moien*, fr. OF, fr. *meien, moien*, adj. — more at [7]MEAN] **1 a :** something (as a step, stage, connection) intervening, intermediate, or intermediary ⟨so do I wish the crown, being so far off and so I chide the ~*s* that keep me from it —Shak.⟩ **b** *or* **meane** (1) **:** the middle voice in 14th century fauxbourdon; *broadly* **:** the middle (as alto or tenor) part of a harmonized musical composition (2) **:** the alto of a consort of viols (3) **:** one of the middle strings of a viol ⟨great ~⟩ **c :** a middle point or something that is in or near a middle point **:** something that falls between extremes (as of place, time, number, rate): as (1) **:** something (as prudence, temperateness) that is intermediate between excess and deficiency and represents moderation ⟨the moral ~ is no mathematical mean between extremes, but is, in any given case, relative to persons and places —Lucius Garvin⟩ (2) *Confucianism* **:** the course of moderate action between extremes in the development of the virtues of temperance and prudence (3) *Buddhism* **:** the middle way **:** the course of moderation between asceticism and self-indulgence **d** (1) **:** a quantity of the same kind as the members of a set that in some sense is representative of them all and that is located within their range in accordance with a set rule (2) **:** the mean value of a variable between given limits (3) **:** either of the middle two terms of a proportion **2 a :** something by the use or help of which a desired end is attained or made more likely **:** an agent, tool, device, measure, plan, or policy for accomplishing or furthering a purpose — usu. used in pl. but sing. or pl. in constr. ⟨secure peace by honorable ~*s*⟩ ⟨the justification of barbarous ~*s* by holy ends —H.J.Muller⟩ ⟨~*s* . . . for keeping the prices of building materials high —T. W.Arnold⟩ ⟨a continuous belt is a ~*s* of power transmission from one shaft to another⟩ **b** *obs* **:** MEDIATOR, INTERCESSOR, GO-BETWEEN — sometimes used in pl. but sing. in constr. **c** *obs* **:** favorable condition **:** OPPORTUNITY **3 means** *pl* **:** resources (as of force or wealth) available for disposal **:** material resources in such supply as to form the basis for an economically secure and sheltered life ⟨a man of ~*s*⟩; *broadly* **:** WEALTH, MONEY **4** *obs* **:** MEANTIME
**syn** INSTRUMENT, AGENT, INSTRUMENTALITY, ORGAN, MEDIUM, VEHICLE, CHANNEL: MEAN or MEANS, the latter now the common form in all uses, is a very general term applicable to anything employed in performing or executing some end ⟨the habit of regarding the laboring class as a mere *means* to the maintenance of the rest —G.L.Dickinson⟩ ⟨the principal *means* of transportation was . . . Afghan camels —Herbert Hoover⟩ ⟨language as a *means* of social control —J.B.Carroll⟩ ⟨faith in science as a *means* . . . to knowledge and grace —F.B.Millett⟩ INSTRUMENT may suggest a certain ready applicability to the matter under consideration rather than only the bare fact of use, and with reference to people susceptibility to use or willingness to be used ⟨tariffs and immigration restriction are chief *instruments* of this economic nationalism —J.A.Hobson⟩ ⟨the American public school as an *instrument* for strengthening the spirit of national unity —J.B.Conant⟩ ⟨extremes of corruption were reached — and here again the eunuchs were sinister and convenient *instruments* —Owen and Eleanor Lattimore⟩ AGENT in reference to natural phenomena may designate an inner capability and suggest only incidentally, if that, its being used; in reference to matters personal and social it stresses being directed by another in his interest but lacks other suggestion or value notion ⟨the bee makes honey, the spider secretes a filament; you can hardly say that any of these *agents* believes —T.S.Eliot⟩ ⟨her great lords, spiritual and temporal . . . the *agents* of her will —Henry Adams⟩ ⟨an unconscious *agent* in the hands of Providence when you recalled me —Willa Cather⟩ INSTRUMENTALITY may suggest the fact of serving as an instrument but in today's English it is likely to suggest a means or agency which is a minor part of a larger entity or under the control of a subsuming organization ⟨in the American colonies, the newspapers were a major *instrumentality* throughout the entire struggle for independence —F. L.Mott⟩ ⟨governments or subdivisions or *instrumentalities* thereof —*U. S. Code*⟩ ORGAN suggests a functioning part of a larger esp. organic whole, or more specif., a means of communication, esp. a controlled or proprietary one ⟨the Council of State was a small body that met with the king three times a

week, and it was the pivotal *organ* of government —Stringfellow Barr⟩ ⟨the Journal is the *organ* of the American Medical Association⟩ MEDIUM indicates an intermediate means, esp. a means of conveyance or communication, in connection with the latter a favored or accustomed means ⟨he had now in the periodical a *medium* for his delicate poetic talent —S.T. Williams⟩ ⟨each *medium* says something that cannot be uttered as well or as completely in any other tongue —John Dewey⟩ VEHICLE likewise indicates a means of conveying or communicating; it may be more specific and tangible than MEDIUM ⟨Roosevelt's speeches were . . . the *vehicle* by which he set in motion tremendous social and moral forces —H.L. Hopkins⟩ CHANNEL suggests a course or path of transmission or communication more forcefully than a means ⟨a petition was drafted, signed by sixty-seven scientists, and sent through proper *channels* to the President of the United States —Harrison Brown⟩ **syn** see in addition AVERAGE
— **by all means** *adv* : most assuredly : without fail : CERTAINLY — **by any means** *adv* : in any way : at all — **by means of** *prep* : through the instrumentality of : by the use of as a means — **by no means** *or* **by no manner of means** *adv* : in no way : not at all : certainly not

**7mean** \ˈ"\ *adj* [ME *mene*, fr. MF *meien, moien*, fr. OF, fr. L *medianus* — more at MEDIAN] **1** : occupying a middle position : occurring between the limits or extremes: as **a** *obs* : intermediate in space **b** : intermediate in order, rank, or status ⟨the ~ term of a syllogism⟩ **c** : intermediate in time **d** : intermediate in kind or degree ⟨pursue a ~ course in politics⟩ **2** : occupying a position about midway between extremes: as **a** : near the average or norm ⟨of a ~ stature⟩ **b** : of a moderate degree of excellence : MIDDLING, MEDIOCRE **3** : serving as a means : INTERMEDIARY **4** : having an intermediate value between two extremes : AVERAGE ⟨the ~ high tide is 8 feet⟩

**8mean** *adv* [ME *meane*, fr. *meane, mene* occupying a middle position, intermediate — more at 7MEAN] **1** *obs* : MODERATELY **2** *obs* : comparatively less **3** *obs* : so as to fall between

**9mean** *vt* -ED/-ING/-S [ME *menen*, fr. *mene*, n. — more at 6MEAN] *obs* : MEDIATE

**mean calorie** *n* [7*mean*] : CALORIE c

**1me·an·der** *also* **mae·an·der** \mēˈandə(r), -ˈaan-\ *n* -S [L *maeander*, fr. Gk *maiandros*, fr. *Maiandros* (now *Menderes*), river in western Asia Minor proverbial for its winding course] **1 a** : a turn or winding of a stream **b** : a winding path or course : LABYRINTH **2** : a tortuous or intricate movement or journeying **3** : the Greek fret or key pattern originating in the period of geometric art about 1000–700 B.C. to become a permanent motif in Greek ornament

**2meander** \ˈ"\ *vb* **meandered; meandered; meandering** \-d(ə)riŋ\ **meanders** *vi* **1** : to wind or turn in a course or passage : follow an intricate course ⟨across the ceiling ~*ed* a long crack —John Galsworthy⟩ **2** : to wander aimlessly or casually and without urgent destination : RAMBLE, DRIFT ⟨~*ed* lazily through old diaries in vague search of an idea⟩ ⟨~*ing* fruitlessly from one job to another⟩ ~ *vt* **1** : to form a meander in or of : cause to meander ⟨streams ~*ing* the flat plain⟩ ⟨strolling along the ~*ed* bank⟩ **2** : to follow along the windings of (as a stream) ⟨~*ed* the lower reaches of the river⟩ **3** : to survey a meander line on or along ⟨if such streams were not ~*ed* in connection with the public survey —*U. S. Code*⟩

**meander belt** *n* : the part of a valley bottom across which a stream shifts its channel from time to time esp. in flood

**me·an·der·er** \-d(ə)rə(r)\ *n* -S : one that meanders

**me·an·der·ing·ly** *adv* : so as to form a meander : without clearcut or urgent course or aim

**meander line** *n* : a usu. irregular surveyed line that is not a boundary line; *esp* : one following the outline of a stream, lake, or swamp

**mean deviation** *n* : the average of the absolute values of the deviations from some measure of central tendency in a statistical distribution

**mean difference** *n* : the average of the absolute values of the *n*(*n*-1)/2 differences that exist between pairs in a statistical distribution of *n* elements

**mean distance** *n* : the arithmetical mean of the maximum and minimum distances of a planet, satellite, or secondary star from its primary

**me·an·dra** \mēˈandrə\ *or* **me·an·dri·na** \ˌmēənˈdrīnə\ *syn of* MAEANDRA

**me·an·drine** \mēˈanˌdrīn, -rēn, -ˌdrən\ *or* **me·an·droid** \-nˌdrȯid\ *adj* [*meandrine* ISV *meandr-* (fr. NL *Maeandra*) + *-ine*; *meandroid* fr. NL *Maeandra* + E *-oid*] *of a coral* : having a convoluted surface

**me·an·drous** \mēˈandrəs\ *adj* : WINDING, FLEXUOUS, RAMBLING

**meaned** *past of* MEAN

**1meaner** *comparative of* MEAN

**2meaner** \ˈmēnə(r)\ *n* -S [3*mean* + *-er*] : one that means

**mean error** *n* : the mean deviation of a distribution of accidental errors

**meanest** *superlative of* MEAN

**mean free path** *n* : the average distance traversed between collisions by particles (as molecules of a gas or free electrons in metal) in a system of agitated particles — called also *free path*

**mean·ie** *or* **meany** \ˈmēnē, -ni\ *n, pl* **meanies** [1*mean* + *-ie*] : an ungracious unattractive person: as **a** : a niggardly ungenerous person **b** : a harsh carping unfair critic **c** : a theatrical or literary villain

**1mean·ing** \ˈmēniŋ, -nēŋ\ *n* -S [ME *mening*, fr. gerund of *menen* to intend — more at 3MEAN] **1 a** : the thing one intends to convey by an act or esp. by language : PURPORT ⟨do not mistake my ~⟩ **b** : the thing that is conveyed or signified esp. by language : the sense in which something (as a statement) is understood : IMPORT ⟨what is its ~ to you⟩ **2** : the thing that is meant or intended : INTENT, PURPOSE, AIM, OBJECT ⟨a mischievous ~ was apparent⟩ **3** : SIGNIFICANCE ⟨a look full of ~⟩ **4 a** *or* **meaning in intension** : the logical connotation of a word or phrase : the intension of a term : what a correct definition exhibits **b** *or* **meaning in extension** : the logical denotation or extension of a term : the thing or class named by a word or substantive phrase **5** : the pattern of engrams aroused by a given stimulus

**2meaning** \ˈ"\ *adj* [fr. pres. part. of 3*mean*] **1** : exhibiting a usu. specified intent or purpose ⟨a well-*meaning* man⟩ **2** : conveying or intended to convey meaning : SIGNIFICANT ⟨a ~ smile⟩ — **mean·ing·ly** *adv* — **mean·ing·ness** *n* -ES

**mean·ing·ful** \-ŋfəl\ *adj* **1** : having a meaning or purpose : capable of being understood or interpreted : requiring or done with understanding and intent ⟨~ work⟩ ⟨~ training⟩ ⟨a ~ experience⟩ **2** : constructed according to the rules of a language or system of signs : having an assigned function in a system ⟨in a two-valued system of logic all ~ propositions are either true or false⟩ **syn** see EXPRESSIVE

**mean·ing·ful·ly** \-fəlē\ *adv* : in a meaningful manner : so as to be meaningful

**mean·ing·ful·ness** *n* -ES : the quality or state of being meaningful

**mean·ing·less** \ˈmēniŋləs, -nēŋ-\ *adj* **1** : lacking a meaning : having no significance ⟨~ jargon⟩ **2** : having no assigned function in a given language or system of signs : not formed according to the rules of construction of a system : not being a genuine element in a sign system ⟨a word group resembling a statement is either true, false, or ~⟩ ⟨the phrase "curvature of space" is ~ in Euclidean geometry⟩ — **mean·ing·less·ly** *adv* — **mean·ing·less·ness** *n* -ES

**mean life** *n* : AVERAGE LIFE

**mean line** *n* [7*mean*] : BISECTRIX

**1mean·ly** *adv* [ME *menely*, fr. *mene* occupying a middle position + *-ly* — more at MEAN] **1** *archaic* : to a moderate degree : fairly well : PASSABLY, TOLERABLY **2** *obs* : only moderately

**2mean·ly** *adv* [1*mean* + *-ly*] : in a mean manner: as **a** : in a lowly manner : POORLY, HUMBLY, PLAINLY ⟨living ~ and without ostentation⟩ **b** : in an inferior or indifferent manner : BADLY ⟨troops ~ equipped⟩ **c** : in a base or ungenerous manner or with the ascription of meanness ⟨~ threatens the deepest values of all truly traditional men —W.S.White⟩

**mean midnight** *n* : midnight by mean solar time

**mean moon** *n* [7*mean*] : a fictitious moon imagined for purposes of calculation to revolve around the earth uniformly in the same period as that of the real moon

**1mean·ness** \ˈmēnnəs\ *n* -ES [1*mean* + *-ness*] **1** : the quality or state of being mean (as in exhibiting baseness or stinginess) **2** : a mean act ⟨descend to the ~*es* of frightening children and old women —Daniel Defoe⟩

**2meanness** \ˈ"\ *n* -ES [7*mean* + *-ness*] : the quality or state of being or constituting a mean between two extremes

**mean noon** *n* : noon by mean solar time

**mean obliquity** *n* : the average angle over a long period of time between the plane of the equator of the earth or other planet and the plane of the ecliptic

**mean place** *n* : the position of a star at a given epoch (as the beginning of a year) as affected by precession of the equinoxes and proper motion — compare STAR PLACE

**mean proportional** *n* [6*mean* + *proportional*, adj.] **1** : GEOMETRIC MEAN **2** : MEAN 1d(3)

**mean reserve** *n* : the arithmetical average of the initial reserve and the terminal reserve of a policy of insurance

**means** *pl of* MEAN, *pres 3d sing of* MEAN

**mean sea level** *n* [7*mean*] : SEA LEVEL 2

**means grass** \ˈmēnz-\ *n, usu cap M* [prob. fr. the name *Means*] : JOHNSON GRASS

**mean solar day** *n* : the interval between successive transits of the lower meridian by the mean sun containing 86,400 seconds of mean solar time

**mean solar second** *n* : a cgs unit equal to 1/86,400 of a mean solar day

**mean solar time** *n* : time that is based on the motion of the mean sun and that has the mean solar second as its unit

**mean spheroid** *n* : an imaginary spheroid which is commonly assumed to be an ellipsoid of revolution but may have three unequal axes, which coincides most nearly with the actual figure of the earth at the plane of sea level, and to which trigonometrical surveys are referred

**meanspirited** \ˈ≈ˈ≈≈\ *adj* : exhibiting or characterized by meanness of spirit ⟨what is essentially vulgar and ~ in politics —J.R.Lowell⟩

**mean square** *n* : the average of the squares of a set of numbers

**mean square deviation** *n* : STANDARD DEVIATION

**means test** *n* [fr. *means*, pl. of 6*mean*] **1** : a searching examination of the financial state of an unemployed person and his resident family formerly made in Great Britain when such a person had exhausted his unemployment insurance payments in order to determine his eligibility for payments from other public funds **2** : any examination of the financial state of a person as a condition precedent to receiving social insurance, public assistance benefits, or other payments from public funds

**mean sun** *n* [7*mean*] : a fictitious sun supposed to move uniformly along the celestial equator completing crossings of the vernal equinox at intervals of a tropical year

**meant** *past of* MEAN

**me·an·tes** \mēˈan·ˌtēz\ *n pl, cap* [NL, fr. L, pl. of *meant-, means*, pres. part. of *meare* to go — more at PERMEATE] : a suborder of Caudata comprising neotenous salamanders that have horny jaw sheaths and persistent gills and lack eyelids, maxillae, and hind limbs

**1mean·time** \ˈmēn·ˌtīm\ *n* [ME *mene-time*, fr. *mene* occupying a middle position + *time* — more at MEAN] : the intervening time : INTERVAL ⟨in the ~ had satisfied his omnivorous appetite for reading in the village library —A.C.Cole⟩

**2meantime** \ˈ"\ *adv* : MEANWHILE ⟨~ he had been attentive to his other interests —H.R.Warfel⟩

**mean time** *n* [7*mean*] : MEAN SOLAR TIME

**meantime screw** *n* [*meantime* (fr. 7*mean* + *time*) + *screw*] : one of either two or four screws of precious metal set in the rim of a watch balance to regulate the speed of oscillation to very close tolerances — compare BALANCE SCREW

**meantone system** \ˈ≈,≈-\ *n* : a system of tuning keyboard instruments used before the adoption of equal temperament and based on a standard interval of a mean between a major and a minor whole tone of just intonation or one half of an acoustically pure major third

**mean value** *n* : the integral of a continuous function of one or more variables over a given range divided by the measure of the range

**1mean·while** \ˈmēn,(h)wīl\ *n* [ME *mene while*, fr. *mene* occupying a middle position + *while*] : MEANTIME ⟨were being developed in the ~ by engineers —S.I.Hayakawa⟩

**2meanwhile** \ˈ"\ *adv* [ME *menewhile*, fr. *mene while*, n.] **1** : during the intervening time : for the time being ⟨children who are crippled . . . ~ are cut off from ordinary opportunities —Martha M. Eliot⟩ **2** : at the same time ⟨~ he was becoming more and more engaged in . . . the main activity of his life —W.S.Grant⟩

**mean white** *n* : POOR WHITE — usu. used disparagingly

**meany** *var of* MEANIE

**meaow** *var of* MEOW

**1mear** *obs var of* MERE

**2mear** \ˈmēr\ *Scot var of* MARE

**mearns quail** \ˈmərnz-\ *also* **mearns's quail** \-zə̇z-\ *n, usu cap M* [after Edgar A. *Mearns* †1916 Am. naturalist] : a rather pale short-tailed quail (*Cyrtonyx montezumae*) of arid uplands of the southwestern U. S. and adjacent Mexico

**meas** *abbr* measure

**1mease** \ˈmēz\ *vt* -ED/-ING/-S [ME *mesen*, short for *amesen*, fr. MF *amaisier*, fr. (assumed) VL *admansiare*, fr. L *ad-* + (assumed) VL *mansum* house, farm, fr. L, neut. of *mansus*, past part. of *manēre* to remain — more at MANSION] *chiefly Scot* : to make calm : PACIFY, MITIGATE

**2mease** \ˈmēz\ *dial Brit var of* 3MAZE

**mea·sle** \ˈmēzəl\ *n* -S [sing. of *measles*] : a tapeworm cysticercus larva; *specif* : one found in the muscles of a domesticated mammal — compare TAENIA

**mea·sled** \ˈmēzəld\ *adj* [ME *meseled*, fr. *mesel* + *-ed*] : infected or spotted with measles — **mea·sled·ness** *n* -ES

**mea·sles** \ˈmēzəlz\ *n pl but sing or pl in constr* [ME *meseles*, pl. of *mesel* measles, spot characteristic of measles, alter. (influenced by *mesel* leper) of *masel*; akin to MD *masel* spot characteristic of measles and prob. to OHG *masar* gnarled excrescence on a tree — more at MAZER, MESEL] **1 a** : an acute contagious viral disease commencing with catarrhal symptoms, conjunctivitis, cough, and Koplik's spots on the oral mucous membrane and marked by the appearance on the third or fourth day of an eruption of distinct red circular spots which coalesce in a crescentic form, are slightly raised, and after the fourth day of the eruption gradually decline **b** : any of various other eruptive diseases (as rubella) **2** [fr. obs. E *meazel*, adj., infested with larval tapeworms in the muscles and tissues, fr. ME *mesel*, lit., leprous, fr. OF *mesel*, adj., leprous & *mesel*, n., leper — more at MESEL] : infestation with or disease caused by larval tapeworms in the muscles and tissues; *specif* : infestation of cattle and swine with cysticerci of tapeworms that as adults parasitize man — see MEASLE **3** : a disease of apple and pear trees that is of unknown cause and is characterized by roughened bark with swellings or pustules resembling pimples

**mea·sly** \ˈmēz(ə)lē, -li\ *adj* -ER/-EST [*measles* + *-y*] **1** : infected with measles **2** *of meat or an animal* **a** : infested with larval tapeworms **b** : TRICHINIZED **3 a** : BLIGHTED, POOR, INFERIOR ⟨sick and ~⟩ **b** : contemptibly small ⟨left only a ~ dime for a tip⟩ **syn** see PETTY

**mea·sur·abil·i·ty** \ˌmezh(ə)rəˈbiləd·ē, ˌmāzh-, -zhə(r)ˈ-\ *n* : the quality or state of being measurable

**mea·sur·able** \ˈmezh(ə)rəbəl, ˈmāzh-, -zhə(r)b-\ *adj* [ME *mesurable* moderate, fr. MF, fr. LL *mensurabilis* measurable, fr. *mensurare* to measure + L *-abilis* -able — more at MEASURE (v.)] **1 a** : capable of being measured ⟨such ~ factors as the amount of nitrogen in air⟩; *specif* : large or small enough to be measured ⟨only rarely found in ~ amounts⟩ ⟨a ~ distance⟩ **b** : great enough to be worth consideration : SIGNIFICANT ⟨became a ~ figure on the Parisian scene —*Times Lit. Supp.*⟩ **c** : of limited duration : not indefinite : FORESEEABLE ⟨reach its goal within the ~ future —Alan Valentine⟩ **2** *of a number* : having an exact divisor — **mea·sur·able·ness** *n* -ES

**mea·sur·ably** \-blē, -li\ *adv* [ME *mesurably* moderately, fr. *mesurable* + *-ly*] **1** : in a measure : to some extent ⟨the fear of immediate war has ~ abated —Quincy Howe⟩ **2** : to a quantitatively measurable extent ⟨radiation decreased ~⟩

**mea·sur·age** \ˈmezhərij, ˈmāzh-\ *n* -S [ME *mesurage*, fr. MF, fr. OF, fr. *mesurer* to measure + *-age* — more at MEASURE (v.)] : a toll or duty levied on a ship's cargo

**1mea·sure** \ˈmezhə(r), ˈmāzh-\ *n* -S [ME *mesure*, fr. OF, fr. L *mensura*, fr. *mensus* (past part. of *metiri* to measure) + *-ura*

MEASURES AND WEIGHTS

| UNIT | ABBR OR SYMBOL | EQUIVALENTS IN OTHER UNITS OF SAME SYSTEM | METRIC EQUIVALENT |
|---|---|---|---|
| | | length | |
| mile | mi | 5280 feet, 320 rods, 1760 yards | 1.609 kilometers |
| rod | rd | 5.50 yards, 16.5 feet | 5.029 meters |
| yard | yd | 3 feet, 36 inches | 0.914 meters |
| foot | ft *or* ′ | 12 inches, 0.333 yards | 30.480 centimeters |
| inch | in *or* ″ | 0.083 feet, 0.027 yards | 2.540 centimeters |
| | | area | |
| square mile | sq mi *or* m² | 640 acres, 102,400 square rods | 2.590 square kilometers |
| acre | a *or* ac (seldom used) | 4840 square yards, 43,560 square feet | 0.405 hectares, 4047 square meters |
| square rod | sq rd *or* rd² | 30.25 square yards, 0.006 acres | 25.293 square meters |
| square yard | sq yd *or* yd² | 1296 square inches, 9 square feet | 0.836 square meters |
| square foot | sq ft *or* ft² | 144 square inches, 0.111 square yards | 0.093 square meters |
| square inch | sq in *or* in² | 0.007 square feet, 0.00077 square yards | 6.451 square centimeters |
| | | volume | |
| cubic yard | cu yd *or* yd³ | 27 cubic feet, 46,656 cubic inches | 0.765 cubic meters |
| cubic foot | cu ft *or* ft³ | 1728 cubic inches, 0.0370 cubic yards | 0.028 cubic meters |
| cubic inch | cu in *or* in³ | 0.00058 cubic feet, 0.000021 cubic yards | 16.387 cubic centimeters |
| | | weight | |
| | | *avoirdupois* | |
| ton | tn (seldom used) | | |
| short ton | | 20 short hundredweight, 2000 pounds | 0.907 metric tons |
| long ton | | 20 long hundredweight, 2240 pounds | 1.016 metric tons |
| hundredweight | cwt | | |
| short hundredweight | | 100 pounds, 0.05 short tons | 45.359 kilograms |
| long hundredweight | | 112 pounds, 0.05 long tons | 50.802 kilograms |
| pound | lb *or* lb av *also* # | 16 ounces, 7000 grains | 0.453 kilograms |
| ounce | oz *or* oz av | 16 drams, 437.5 grains | 28.349 grams |
| dram | dr *or* dr av | 27.343 grains, 0.0625 ounces | 1.771 grams |
| grain | gr | 0.036 drams, 0.002285 ounces | 0.0648 grams |
| | | *troy* | |
| pound | lb t | 12 ounces, 240 pennyweight, 5760 grains | 0.373 kilograms |
| ounce | oz t | 20 pennyweight, 480 grains | 31.103 grams |
| pennyweight | dwt *also* pwt | 24 grains, 0.05 ounces | 1.555 grams |
| grain | gr | 0.042 pennyweight, 0.002083 ounces | 0.0648 grams |
| | | *apothecaries'* | |
| pound | lb ap | 12 ounces, 5760 grains | 0.373 kilograms |
| ounce | oz ap *or* ℥ | 8 drams, 480 grains | 31.103 grams |
| dram | dr ap *or* ʒ | 3 scruples, 60 grains | 3.887 grams |
| scruple | s ap *or* ℈ | 20 grains, 0.333 drams | 1.295 grams |
| grain | gr | 0.05 scruples, 0.002083 ounces, 0.0166 drams | 0.0648 grams |
| | | capacity | |
| | | *U.S. liquid measure* | |
| gallon | gal | 4 quarts (231 cubic inches) | 3.785 liters |
| quart | qt | 2 pints (57.75 cubic inches) | 0.946 liters |
| pint | pt | 4 gills (28.875 cubic inches) | 0.473 liters |
| gill | gi | 4 fluidounces (7.218 cubic inches) | 118.291 milliliters |
| fluidounce | fl oz *or* f ℥ | 8 fluidrams (1.804 cubic inches) | 29.573 milliliters |
| fluidram | fl dr *or* f ʒ | 60 minims (0.225 cubic inches) | 3.696 milliliters |
| minim | min *or* ♏ | 1/60 fluidram (0.003759 cubic inches) | 0.061610 milliliters |
| | | *U.S. dry measure* | |
| bushel | bu | 4 pecks (2150.42 cubic inches) | 35.238 liters |
| peck | pk | 8 quarts (537.605 cubic inches) | 8.809 liters |
| quart | qt | 2 pints (67.200 cubic inches) | 1.101 liters |
| pint | pt | ½ quart (33.600 cubic inches) | 0.550 liters |
| | | *British imperial liquid and dry measure* | |
| bushel | bu | 4 pecks (2219.36 cubic inches) | 0.036 cubic meters |
| peck | pk | 2 gallons (554.84 cubic inches) | 0.009 cubic meters |
| gallon | gal | 4 quarts (277.420 cubic inches) | 4.545 liters |
| quart | qt | 2 pints (69.355 cubic inches) | 1.136 liters |
| pint | pt | 4 gills (34.678 cubic inches) | 568.26 cubic centimeters |
| gill | gi | 5 fluidounces (8.669 cubic inches) | 142.066 cubic centimeters |
| fluidounce | fl oz *or* f ℥ | 8 fluidrams (1.7339 cubic inches) | 28.416 cubic centimeters |
| fluidram | fl dr *or* f ʒ | 60 minims (0.216734 cubic inches) | 3.5516 cubic centimeters |
| minim | min *or* ♏ | 1/60 fluidram (0.003612 cubic inches) | 0.059194 cubic centimeters |

-ure; akin to OE *mǣth* measure, Gk *metron* meter, measure, Skt *māti* he measures] **1 a :** an adequate, given, or fitting amount or degree: (1) **:** commensurate or due portion **:** QUOTA ⟨all too few of the British actresses . . . have received their ~ of remembrance —*Saturday Rev.*⟩ ⟨fill the ~ of our duty to our defective fellow citizens —B.N.Cardozo⟩ (2) **:** extent or degree that is not excessive **:** not undue portion; *also* **:** a sense of proportion or restraint **:** MODERATION, TEMPERANCE ⟨with that tactlessness, that lack of ~ that were characteristic of her, went on piling question upon rhetorical question —Aldous Huxley⟩ (3) **:** fixed or suitable proportion or limit **:** BOUNDS ⟨angry beyond ~⟩ ⟨Greek love of moderation, proportion, harmony, and due ~ —Lucius Garvin⟩ ⟨the love of God is broader than the ~ of man's mind —S.D.Harkness⟩ **b** (1) **:** the dimensions, capacity, or amount of something ascertained by measuring **:** MEASUREMENTS, SIZE ⟨a slipcover made to ~⟩ ⟨took his ~ for a coat⟩ ⟨several grades of freemen according to the ~ of their wealth —John MacNeill⟩; *specif* **:** the width of a full line of print or type usu. expressed in picas (2) **:** the limit of the distance at which a fencer can reach his opponent by lunging (3) **:** the character, ability, or magnitude of a person or thing considered as a matter of observation or judgment **:** an estimate of what is to be expected (as of a person or situation) ⟨a show tailored to the ~ of its star⟩ ⟨whoever tries to . . . size him up gives an immediate ~ of himself —Max Ascoli⟩ ⟨the ~ of their tragedy is now beyond our imagination —G.F. Kennan⟩ ⟨take the ~ of the crisis⟩ **c** (1) **:** a quantity measured out esp. in relation to a standard **:** a measured quantity of a substance or article ⟨using level ~*s* is the easiest . . . way of measuring —Bee Nilson⟩ ⟨tolerance was not dealt in the same ~ to men and women —Edith Wharton⟩ **:** a quantity measuring up to a standard ⟨whether this carton of milk contains full ~ —D.M.Turnbull⟩ ⟨a play that gives the audience short ~⟩ (2) **:** AMOUNT, EXTENT, DEGREE ⟨rooks consume an enormous quantity of grubs . . . taking a fair ~ of grain by way of reward —*Brit. Birds in Colour*⟩ ⟨giving children a greater ~ of freedom⟩ ⟨in the ~ we buy abroad, profitable markets there will attract capital —T.J.Kreps⟩ **d :** the amount or kind of treatment meted out (as in retribution) ⟨the ~ which he had dealt to others should now be meted out to him —Edith Sitwell⟩ **2 a :** an instrument (as a yardstick) or a utensil (as a graduated cup) for measuring **b** (1) **:** the customary local unit (as of volume) for a particular commodity ⟨the ~ containing two Winchester bushels —Robert Forsyth⟩ (2) **:** a quantity (as of wheat, oil, beans) measured by such a unit ⟨six ~*s* of gravel⟩ (3) **:** one of a number of equal but indeterminate measured quantities ⟨at the rate . . . of 16 ~*s* of rice for 25 of salt —H.W.Hilman⟩ **c :** something used as a standard in measuring ⟨the customary load of a donkey as a ~ of weight⟩ ⟨~*s* of time are commonly derived from some kind of human endurance —*Notes & Queries on Anthropology*⟩; *esp* **:** a standard unit of length, area, or volume (as the foot, acre, cubic inch, quart) ⟨exact weights and ~*s* maintained by a governmental bureau of standards⟩ **d :** a system of standard units of measure — usu. used with a qualifier indicating the class of the system ⟨metric ~⟩, the dimension or the kind of object or substance measured ⟨long ~⟩ ⟨board ~⟩, or the locality where the system is used ⟨British ~⟩ **3 :** the act or process of measuring ⟨settled by a ~ made by a surveyor⟩ **4 a :** something having rhythmic sound or movement ⟨extolled the jury system in stately Victorian ~*s* —*Saturday Rev.*⟩: as (1) **:** MELODY, TUNE ⟨a strong, clean wind which rushed in a droning ~ through the broom sedge —Ellen Glasgow⟩ (2) **:** a round or turn of dancing **:** DANCE (3) **:** a slow and stately dance **b :** rhythmic structure **:** measured pattern of movement **:** BEAT, CADENCE ⟨a finer language, style, and ~ than the Greek which it translates —*Times Lit. Supp.*⟩: as (1) **:** poetic rhythm measured by temporal quantity or accent; *specif* **:** METER (2) **:** musical time **c :** a division or unit (as of time or stress) in a rhythmic sequence: as (1) **:** a grouping of musical beats made by the regular recurrence of primary accents and located on the staff immediately following a vertical bar — called also *bar* (2) **:** a division of a rhythmic structure (as a poem) in terms of a quantitative relation (as temporal balance) **d :** quantitative relation (as of identity, equivalence, correspondence, or balance) among elements or parts in a rhythmic structure; *esp* **:** temporal relation or balance **5** [trans. of Gk *metron*] **a :** an exact division of a quantity ⟨6 being the greatest common ~ of 42 and 12⟩ **b :** a basis of comparison **:** DENOMINATOR ⟨no common ~ between the masses of Soviet industrial hands . . . and our own working people —E.D.Laborde⟩ **6 a** (1) **:** a standard by which something intangible is determined or regulated **:** CRITERION ⟨the ~ should not be what others are doing but what is right for the individual child —Dorothy Barclay⟩ (2) **:** a directly observable quantity from which the value of another related quantity may be obtained ⟨the ~ of an angle is the subtended arc⟩ ⟨the ~ of a quantity of electricity is the mass of silver deposited by it in electrolysis⟩ **b :** a means of measuring or indicating something that cannot be directly measured, observed, or represented **:** TEST ⟨scored low in a ~ of emotional adjustment⟩ **:** INDICATION, INDEX, YARDSTICK ⟨the tastiness . . . of such foods became a ~ of the efficiency and thrift of the family —Carol Aronovici⟩ **7 measures** *pl* **:** strata of a mineral (as coal) **8 :** an action planned or taken toward the accomplishment of a purpose **:** means to an end ⟨wore steel helmets as a safety ~⟩ ⟨apply ~*s* to prevent the spread of infection⟩ **:** STEP ⟨took strong ~*s* against the rebels⟩; *specif* **:** a proposed legislative act **:** BILL ⟨sponsored an anti-inflation ~ in the senate⟩ — **beyond measure** *adv* **:** to an extreme degree **:** ABUNDANTLY, EXCESSIVELY ⟨had happiness *beyond measure*⟩ ⟨angry *beyond measure*⟩ — **for good measure** *adv* **:** in addition to the minimum required **:** as an extra ⟨added another illustration *for good measure*⟩ — **in a measure** *adv* **:** to some degree ⟨a statement that was *in a measure* both true and false⟩

**²measure** \"\ *vb* **measured; measured; measuring** \-zh(ə)-riŋ\ **measures** [ME *mesuren*, fr. OF *mesurer*, fr. LL *mensurare*, fr. L *mensura* measure — more at ¹MEASURE] *vt* **1 a :** to choose or control (as one's words or acts) with cautious restraint **:** REGULATE, WEIGH ⟨~ his acts and words with an iron will —H.E.Scudder⟩ **b :** to regulate or adjust by a rule or standard **:** GOVERN ⟨the demand for the commodity *measuring* the amount produced⟩ ⟨~ our efforts not by what we feel like doing but by what the situation demands⟩ **2 a :** to allot or distribute as if by measure **:** deal out **:** METE — often used with *out* ⟨laws that . . . ~ out their rewards and punishments with calm indifference —P.E.More⟩ **b :** to apportion in measured amounts; *also* **:** to separate (as from a stock) or add (as to a mixture) by measure — often used with *off* or *out* ⟨~ out the ingredients carefully⟩ ⟨~ off three cups of flour⟩ and sometimes with *in* ⟨~ in the vinegar last⟩ **3 a :** to lay off, mark, or fix (a specified distance or extent) by making measurements ⟨~ three-foot intervals between the plantings⟩ ⟨~ off a half-acre plot for a house lot⟩ **b :** to lay off, mark, or fix the exact dimensions or plan of by making measurements ⟨~ out the lines for the foundations⟩ ⟨~ the course for the 200-meter race⟩ ⟨~ off the trunk into logs of 6, 12, or 18 feet⟩ **4 a :** to ascertain the quantity, mass, extent, or degree of in terms of a standard unit or fixed amount usu. by means of an instrument or container marked off in the units **:** measure the dimensions of **:** take the measurements of ⟨~ the depth, height, and width of the cabinet⟩ ⟨~ the snowfall⟩ ⟨~ the speed of the car⟩ ⟨~ the luminosity of a star⟩ ⟨~ the temperature of the oven⟩ **b :** to compute the size of (an area, object) from dimensional measurements ⟨~ the surface area⟩ **5 :** to judge or estimate the extent, strength, worth, or character of (as a quality, action, or person) ⟨~ intelligence⟩ ⟨~ the gravity of the crisis⟩ ⟨~ the value of the counseling program⟩ ⟨*measured* his opponent before announcing his candidacy⟩ ⟨~ success by salary⟩; *specif* **:** to appraise in comparison with something taken as a criterion — often used with *against* ⟨~ himself not against adults but against age-mates —Margaret Mead⟩ **6** *archaic* **:** to travel over **:** TRAVERSE ⟨the public mind had now *measured* back again the space over which it had passed between 1640 and 1660 —T.B.Macaulay⟩ **7 :** to be a means (as an instrument or standard) of measuring **:** serve as the measure of **:** INDICATE ⟨the piles of sun-bleached linen that *measured* the housewife's pride —Ruth Davidson⟩ ⟨the atomic number . . . ~*s* both the number of protons and of electrons —James Jeans⟩ **8 :** to bring into competition or contest ⟨~ his skill with his rival's in a duel⟩ **9 :** to look (a person) up and down **:** view appraisingly ⟨his eyes *measured* me for the first time —Christopher Isherwood⟩ ~ *vi* **1 :** to take or make a measurement **:** measure something ⟨the shepherd ~*s* from the time the ewes lambed —Lewis Mumford⟩ **2 :** to have a specified measurement or measurements ⟨the cloth ~*s* two yards⟩ ⟨the bedroom ~*s* 10 feet by 12⟩ **3 :** to be comparable ⟨a success that ~*s* with their aims⟩ **4 :** to admit of being measured ⟨~*s* more easily if spread on a table⟩ — **measure one's length :** to fall or lie flat ⟨tripped on a guy wire and *measured his length* on the roof —Frederick Way⟩ — **measure swords 1 :** to compare the length of swords before fighting **2 :** to fight with swords **3 :** CONTEND, CONTEST — usu. used with *with*

**mea·sured** \'mezhə(r)d, 'māzh-\ *adj* [ME *mesured*, partly fr. *mesure* measure + *-ed*, partly fr. past part. of *mesuren* to measure] **1 :** marked by due proportion ⟨the ~ beauty of classical Greek art⟩ **2 a :** RHYTHMICAL ⟨the ~ flash of the beacon⟩; *specif* **:** METRICAL ⟨the free and the ~ forms of verse⟩ **b :** slow and steady **:** DELIBERATE ⟨went about their work with ~ steps⟩ **3 :** LIMITED ⟨its fundamental poverty and ~ capacity for development —H.L.Hoskins⟩ **4 :** CALCULATED ⟨spoke with ~ insolence —*Time*⟩

**measured drawing** *n* **:** an architectural scale drawing of an existing structure

**mea·sured·ly** *adv* **:** in a measured manner or to a measured degree ⟨nodded as ~ as the jouncing taxi would permit —Hamilton Basso⟩

**measured mile** *n* **:** a distance of one mile the limits of which have been accurately measured and marked ⟨tested his mileage meter by the *measured mile*⟩

**measured music** *n* **1 :** MENSURAL MUSIC **2 :** music characterized by a pattern of regularly recurring accents — compare PLAINSONG

**mea·sured·ness** *n* -ES **:** the quality or state of being measured

**mea·sure·less** \'mezhə(r)ləs, 'māzh-\ *adj* [ME *mesureles*, fr. *mesure* measure + *-les* less] **1 :** having no observable limit **:** IMMEASURABLE, BOUNDLESS ⟨looked out at the ~ expanse of sea⟩ **2 :** very great ⟨treated them with ~ contempt⟩ — **measure·less·ly** *adv* — **mea·sure·less·ness** *n* -ES

**measure line** *n* **:** a line of known or ascertainable length put into or allowed to remain in a picture (as a linear perspective or a photograph) and often used in the determination or measurement of other lines

**mea·sure·man** \'mezhə(r)mən, 'māzh-\ *n, pl* **measuremen :** a worker whose job is measuring: as **a :** a paper mill worker who measures and inspects pulpwood to determine its value and its best uses **b :** one who measures rooms to estimate the amount of floor covering needed

**mea·sure·ment** \'mezhə(r)mənt, 'māzh-\ *n* -S **1 :** the act or process of measuring something ⟨a meter for the ~ and pricing of yard goods⟩ ⟨~ of progress in learning to read⟩ ⟨attitude ~⟩; *esp* **:** MENSURATION **2 a :** a figure expressing extent that is obtained by measuring **:** DIMENSION ⟨the room's ~*s* are 30 x 15⟩ **b :** an area, quantity, degree, or capacity obtained by measuring ⟨the ~ of the field is five acres⟩ ⟨the ~ of the jug is two quarts⟩ ⟨the temperature ~ is 72°⟩ **3 :** a system of measures **:** ¹MEASURE 2d ⟨giving serious consideration to the adoption of metric ~⟩

**measurement cargo** *also* **measurement goods** *or* **measurement freight** *n* **1 :** cargo or goods charged for carriage by bulk rather than weight **2 :** a cargo measuring less than 40 cubic feet per long ton or weighing less than 56 pounds per cubic foot

**measure of curvature :** CURVATURE 2

**measure of damage :** the method under applicable principles of law for estimating or ascertaining with reasonable certainty the damages sustained by any party in any litigation

**mea·sur·er** \'mezh(ə)rə(r), 'māzh-\ *n* -S **:** one that measures: as **a :** a worker who measures cloth before or after dyeing and finishing **b :** an operator of a hide measuring machine **c :** one who checks the size of hats **d :** a worker who measures iron or steel before and after rolling to check the measurements specified for rails, rods, or sheets **e :** a worker who takes and records measurements of garments that may change shape during cleaning or dyeing **f :** one that measures the land used for crops in order to compute the payments due contract farmers or the wages of farm laborers

**measures** *pl of* MEASURE, *pres 3d sing of* MEASURE

**measure signature** *n* **:** TIME SIGNATURE

**measure up** *vi* **1 :** to have necessary or fitting qualifications ⟨how the diets of American families *measure up* by nutrition standards —*U.S. Govt. Manual*⟩ **:** be equal — often used with *to* ⟨*measure up* to their expectations⟩ ⟨*measure up* to the demands of public office⟩ **2 :** to be equal (as in ability or achievement) — used with *to* ⟨in science and learning the Incas did not *measure up* to the Mayas —R.W.Murray⟩

**measuring** *pres part of* MEASURE

**measuring cup** *n* **:** a cup having a capacity usu. of a half pint and marked so that portions may be accurately determined

measuring cup

**measuring glass** *n* **:** a graduated medicine or dispensing glass

**measuring machine** *n* **:** a machine for measuring; *esp* **:** a machine for the accurate mechanical or optical measurement of distances on standards of length, gauges, and other parts and commonly made to measure to an accuracy of 0.0001 inch or higher

**measuring pitcher** *n* **:** a pitcher containing up to a quart and marked so that portions may be accurately determined

**measuring wheel** *n* **:** ODOMETER

**measuring worm** *n* **:** LOOPER 1

**¹meat** \'mēt, *usu* -ēd.+V\ *n* -S *often attrib* [ME *mete*, fr. OE; akin to OHG *maz* food, ON *matr*, Goth *mats* food, L *madēre* to be wet, Gk *madaros* wet, *mastos* breast, Skt *madati* it bubbles, he rejoices; basic meaning: drip, be fat] **1 a :** something eaten by man or beast for nourishment **:** FOOD ⟨and to every beast of the earth . . . I have given every green herb for ~ —Gen 1:30 (AV)⟩ ⟨it was ~ and drink to him to be the guardian of a secret —John Buchan⟩ **b :** the edible part of a nut, fruit, or egg ⟨~ of half apple showing tooth marks still fresh, not turned brown —Leslie Ford⟩ **2** *obs* **:** a particular dish prepared or served as food **3 a :** animal tissue used as food: (1) **:** FLESH 2b ⟨preferring ~ to fish⟩ (2) **:** FLESH 1b; *specif* **:** flesh of domesticated cattle, swine, sheep, and goats — distinguished esp. in legal and commercial usage from *meat by-product* and from flesh of other kinds of mammals (3) **:** the edible soft parts of any animal — usu. used with a qualifying term ⟨crab ~⟩ ⟨the dark ~ of poultry⟩ **b :** meat prepared for the table ⟨spiced ~⟩ ⟨~ loaf⟩ ⟨have another slice of ~⟩ **4** *archaic* **:** any of the usual daily meals; *esp* **:** DINNER **5 a** *archaic* **:** game animals **:** QUARRY **b :** favorite or appropriate object of pursuit **:** principal delight ⟨if you like your stories restrained and nontheatrical, this is your ~ —I.T.Marsh⟩ ⟨if a baby hippopotamus was born at the zoo, that was my ~ —St. Clair McKelway⟩ **6 :** food for thought **:** solid substance **:** MATTER ⟨this is a volume of first-rate caliber, full of ~ —H.L. Hoskins⟩ ⟨the real ~ is found in the last two chapters —*Times Lit. Supp.*⟩ ⟨to him ideas are not fleshless, misty abstractions but the meaning, the ~, and the mainspring action of men —Kathleen Sproul⟩ **7** *chiefly South & Midland* **:** PORK; *esp* **:** BACON

**²meat** \"\ *vt* -ED/-ING/-S *now dial* **:** to supply with food

**meat-** *or* **meato-** *comb form* [LL *meatus*] **:** meatus ⟨*meat*ic⟩ ⟨*meato*tomy⟩

**me·a·tal** \mē'ād·ᵊl\ *adj* [*meatus* + *-al*] **:** of, relating to, or forming a meatus

**meat ant** *n* **:** a large Australian ant (*Iridomyrmex detectus*) that is a household pest

**¹meat-ax** \'≡,≡\ *n* **1 :** CLEAVER 1a **2 :** a harsh or violent attack on a problem; *esp* **:** a rough slashing reduction of an appropriation or budget ⟨your advertising policy and budget get the *meat-ax* —Derek Brooks⟩

**²meat-ax** \"\ *vt* **:** to assail murderously **:** chop down **:** DESTROY, DEVASTATE ⟨the House has *meat-axed* the mutual security bill —*N.Y. Times*⟩

**meatball** \'≡,≡\ *n* **1 :** a small ball of chopped or ground meat often mixed with bread crumbs and vegetables and browned in a skillet **2 :** a clumsy, dull, or unattractive person ⟨it was too bad the army had sent such a ~ to be administrator —John Hersey⟩ **3 :** a pennant (as in the U.S. Navy) for battle efficiency or for an athletic championship

**meatbird** \'≡,≡\ *n* **1 :** CANADA JAY **2 :** CLARK NUTCRACKER

**meat by-product** *n* **:** a usable product other than flesh (sense 1a) obtained from slaughter animals including edible organ meats and various inedible products (as hair, bone, or fertilizer) — distinguished esp. in legal and commercial usage from *meat* 3a(2)

**meat chopper** *n* **:** MEAT GRINDER

**meatcutter** \'≡,≡≡\ *n* **:** one that cuts meat

**meat·ed** \'mēd·əd\ *adj* [¹*meat* + *-ed*] **:** having flesh or meat of a specified kind — used chiefly in combination ⟨well-*meated*⟩ ⟨lightly-*meated*⟩

**meat fly** *n* **:** FLESH FLY

**meat grinder** *n* **1 :** a device for cutting meat fine **2 :** something that reduces, pulverizes, or destroys: as **a :** a devastating military action or stratagem ⟨the American public has watched the *meat grinder* in action on the Russian front, killing millions of troops —*New Republic*⟩ **b :** a process (as an official investigation or examination) or a system that may have ruinous effect ⟨if you went into public life you often put your career and your reputation in a political *meat grinder* —*Saturday Rev.*⟩

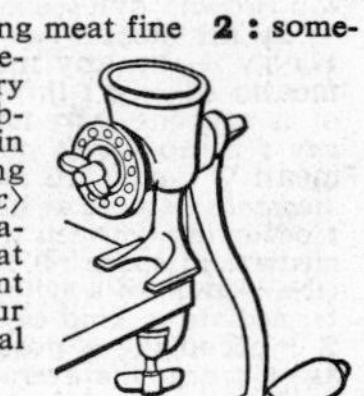
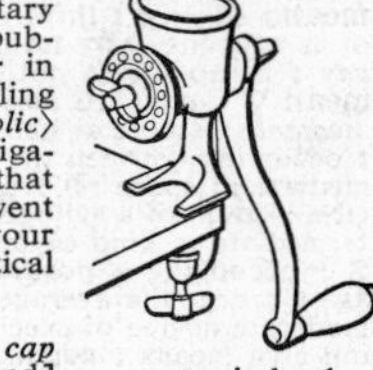
meat grinder 1

**¹meath** *obs var of* ¹MEAD

**²meath** \'mēth, 'meth\ *adj, usu cap* [fr. *Meath*, county of eastern Ireland] **:** of or from County Meath, Ireland **:** of the kind or style prevalent in County Meath

**meat hawk** *n* **:** CANADA JAY

**meathead** \'≡,≡\ *n* **:** a stupid blundering person ⟨getting letters from that ~ she's married to —W.R.Burnett⟩

**meat house** *n* **1 :** a small building for meat storage esp. on a farm **2 :** SMOKEHOUSE

**me·at·ic** \mē'ad·ik\ *adj* [*meat-* + *-ic*] *bot* **:** having intercellular spaces ⟨~ phloem⟩

**meatier** *comparative of* MEATY

**meatiest** *superlative of* MEATY

**meat·i·ly** \'mēd·ᵊlē\ *adv* **:** in a meaty manner

**meat·i·ness** \-d·ēnəs\ *n* -ES **:** the quality or state of being meaty

**meat·less** \'mētləs\ *adj* **:** having no meat or substance

**meatman** \'≡,≡\ *n, pl* **meatmen :** a vendor of meat **:** BUTCHER

**meat meal** *n* **:** a poultry feed made of cooked, dried, and ground animal tissue

**meato-** — see MEAT-

**meat offering** *n* **:** a sacrifice of food; *specif* **:** MEAL OFFERING ⟨and when any will offer a *meat offering* unto the Lord, his offering shall be of fine flour —Lev 2:1 (AV)⟩

**meat-packer** \'≡,≡≡\ *n* **:** a concern engaged in meat-packing

**meat-packing** \'≡,≡≡\ *n* **:** the wholesale meat industry including slaughtering, processing, and distribution to retailers

**meat safe** *n, Brit* **:** SAFE 1a

**meat scrap** *n* **:** a by-product of meat-packing made of bits and trimmings of meat freed from fat, dehydrated, and reduced to a meal and used as a rich source of protein in animal rations

**meat spot** *n* **:** an old discolored blood spot in a hen's egg

**meat tea** *n, Brit* **:** HIGH TEA

**meat type** *n* **:** a type of hog esp. suitable for the production of pork without excessive early fattening — compare LARD TYPE

**me·a·tus** \mē'ād·əs, -ātəs\ *n, pl* **meatuses** *or* **meatus** [LL, fr. L, passage, going, fr. *meatus*, past part. of *meare* to go — more at PERMEATE] **:** a natural body passage **:** CANAL, DUCT

**meat wagon** *n* **1** *slang* **:** AMBULANCE **2** *slang* **:** DEAD WAGON

**meatworks** \'≡,≡\ *n pl but sing or pl in constr* **1 :** SLAUGHTERHOUSE **2 :** PACKINGHOUSE

**meaty** \'mēd·ē, -ēt|, |i\ *adj* -ER/-EST **1 :** full of meat **:** FLESHY ⟨a sloping ~ jaw —Thomas Wolfe⟩ **2 :** rich in matter **:** furnishing solid food for thought or appreciation **:** SUBSTANTIAL ⟨the announcement was ~ enough as it stood —Alzada Comstock⟩ ⟨uncommonly fine voices go to work on these ~ scores —Douglas Watt⟩

**me·bos** \'mē,bäs\ *n* -ES [Afrik *mebos*, prob. fr. Jap *umeboshi* preserved plum] *Africa* **:** a confection of salted and sugared dried apricots

**mec** *or* **mech** \'mek\ *n* -S [by shortening] **:** MECHANIC

**mec-** *or* **meco-** *comb form* [ISV, fr. Gk *mēko-*, fr. *mēkos* length; akin to Gk *makros* long — more at MEAGER] **:** length **:** long ⟨*Mecodonta*⟩ ⟨*meco*meter⟩

**me·ca·te** \mə'käd·ē\ *n* -S [MexSp, fr. Nahuatl *mecatl* cord, rope] **1** *West* **:** a rope usu. of horsehair that is used for leading or tying or as hackamore reins **2 :** an old unit of land area formerly used in the Yucatan region equal to about 400 square meters or ¹⁄₁₀ acre

**¹mec·ca** *also* **mek·ka** \'mekə\ *adj, usu cap* [fr. *Mecca*, Saudi Arabia] **:** of or from Mecca, a capital of Saudi Arabia **:** of the kind or style prevalent in Mecca

**²mecca** \"\ *n* -S *often cap* [fr. *Mecca*, Saudi Arabia, birthplace of Muhammad and holy city of Islam] **1 :** a place regarded as the center of an activity or interest or as the goal of its practitioners or connoisseurs ⟨a white frame building that is the ~ of trout fishermen from all over the nation —Corey Ford⟩ ⟨he was good, good enough to play the Armistice day taps at Arlington, the *Mecca* of all army buglers —James Jones⟩ ⟨London . . . bookstores spell *Mecca* for the collector and manna for the reader —David & Marian Greenberg⟩ **2 :** TUSCAN BROWN

**mecca balsam** *n, usu cap M* **:** BALM OF GILEAD 2a

**¹mec·can** \'mekən\ *adj, usu cap* [*Mecca*, Saudi Arabia + *-an*] **1 :** of, relating to, or characteristic of the city of Mecca **2 :** of, relating to, or characteristic of the people of Mecca

**²meccan** \"\ *n* -S *cap* **:** a native or inhabitant of Mecca

**Mec·cano** \mə'ka(,)nō, me'-, -kä(-\ *trademark* — used for a steel construction set for children

**mech** *abbr* mechanic; mechanical; mechanics; mechanism; mechanized

**mechan-** *or* **mechano-** *comb form* [ME *mechan-*, fr. MF or L, fr. Gk *mēchan-*, fr. *mēchanē* machine — more at MACHINE] **:** machine ⟨*mechano*logy⟩ ⟨*mechano*morphic⟩ **:** mechanical ⟨*mechan*ize⟩ ⟨*mechano*therapy⟩ **:** mechanical and ⟨*mechano*-chemical⟩

**¹me·chan·ic** \mə'kanik, -nēk\ *adj* [prob. fr. MF *mechanique, mecanique*, adj. & n., fr. L *mechanicus*, fr. Gk *mēchanikos*, fr. *mēchanē* machine + *-ikos* -ic — more at MACHINE] **1 :** of or relating to hand work or manual skill ⟨fighting is, indeed, a ~ trade —Douglas Jerrold⟩ **2** *archaic* **a :** of or relating to laborers or artisans **b :** BASE, COARSE, VULGAR **3 a :** having or resembling the action of a machine **b :** resembling a machine in routine, dull, or involuntary performance **:** AUTOMATIC, UNINSPIRED ⟨from blank to blank a threadless way I pushed ~ feet —Emily Dickinson⟩ **4 :** agile, inventive, or resourceful like a good workman ⟨a roving artisan who lives by his ~ wits —Carl Van Doren⟩ **5 :** of, relating to, or constituting mechanistic thought or theory ⟨the dull ~ view of utility —*Fortune*⟩

**²mechanic** \"\ *n* -S [prob. fr. MF *mechanique, mecanique*] **1** *obs* **a :** manual labor or employment **b :** HANDICRAFT **2 a :** a manual worker **:** ARTISAN ⟨these Englishmen had not been ~*s* or fishermen or sailors in England —H.E.Scudder⟩ ⟨carpenters, masons, and other ~*s* —J.R.Dalzell⟩ **b :** a man skilled in the construction or operation of machines or vehicles run by machines **:** MACHINIST ⟨the machines are placed in the hands of four well-trained ~*s* who do the assembling and make the final adjustments —*Geyer's Topics*⟩ ⟨automobile ~⟩ **c** *archaic* **:** a base or vulgar fellow **:** PLEBEIAN ⟨slaves and "base ~*s*" —John Dewey⟩ **3 :** a safety belt used in practicing for a trapeze performance **4 :** a dishonest manipulator of cards, dice, or other gaming implements

**¹me·chan·i·cal** \-nəkəl, -nēk-\ *adj* [ME *mechanicall*, fr. MF or L; MF *mechanique, mecanique* (fr. L *mechanicus*) + ME *-all* -al] **1 a :** of, relating to, or concerned with machinery or tools ⟨~ design⟩ ⟨nothing is more exasperating to the farmer than to be frustrated in his plans by lack of essential supplies —*Country Life*⟩ ⟨became one of the skilled ~ superintendents of his day —Edna Yost⟩ ⟨the public had recognized the need for education in agriculture and the ~ and industrial arts —J.B.Conant⟩ **:** produced or operated by a machine or tool ⟨agitate a substance by ~ shaking⟩ ⟨a ~ saw⟩ **b :** of or relating to manual operations **2 :** of or relating to artisans, craftsmen, or machinists **3 a :** done as if by a machine **:** seeming to be uninfluenced by will or emotion **:** AUTOMATIC, INVOLUNTARY ⟨busy in a leisurely ~ way —Douglas Stewart⟩ ⟨writers . . . learned but narrow in their range of feeling, dry, ~, timid, subservient —Van Wyck Brooks⟩ **b :** absorbed in, concerned with, or devoted to technicalities or minutiae ⟨nor was capacity shown for anything above a ~ handling of the matter —H.O.Taylor⟩ **4 a :** relating to, governed by, or in accordance with mechanics ⟨the belief that the whole universe is a ~ contrivance in which nothing can happen except in absolute accordance with the eternal and unalterable laws of mechanics —M.R.Cohen⟩ ⟨one of the first applications of ~ energy in Texas manufacturing was the use of water power in pioneer sawmills and gristmills —*Amer. Guide Series: Texas*⟩ **b :** relating to the quantitative relations of force and matter as distinguished from mental, vital, and chemical ⟨the ~ pressure of a wind of about 800 miles per hour could be tolerated by the well supported body —H.G. Armstrong⟩ **5 :** relying on mechanics for theory or hypothesis ⟨~ physiologists⟩ ⟨~ determinism⟩ **6 :** AUTOMATIC ⟨a ~ stoker⟩ **7 :** caused by, resulting from, or relating to a process that involves a purely physical as opposed to a chemical change ⟨~ weathering⟩ ⟨~ erosion⟩ **8** *of pulp* **:** made from groundwood — contrasted with *chemical* **syn** see SPONTANEOUS

²**mechanical** \"\ *n* -s **1** *obs* **:** MECHANIC 2a **2** *also* **mechanical scheme :** a piece of finished copy consisting typically of type proofs, hand lettering, and art positioned and mounted for photomechanical reproduction in a letterpress, offset, or other printing plate — called also *paste-up*

**mechanical advantage** *n* **:** the advantage gained by the use of a mechanism in transmitting force; *specif* **:** the ratio of the force that performs the useful work of a machine (as a lever or a hydraulic press) to the force that is applied to the machine

**mechanical analysis** *n* **:** an analysis of soil by screening to determine its percentage composition by grain sizes

**mechanical aptitude** *n* **:** aptitude for understanding and using machines or tools

**mechanical art** *n* **:** TRADE 3a(1)

**mechanical binding** *n* **:** a binding (as for a notebook, catalog, price list) holding pages together by spiral wire, plastic combs, or metal rods

**mechanical construction** *n* **:** mathematical construction requiring means besides ruler and compass or involving figures other than straight lines and circles — opposed to *geometrical construction*

**mechanical drawing** *n* **1 :** drawing done with the aid of instruments (as square and compass) — compare FREEHAND 1 **2 :** a drawing made with instruments

**mechanical engineer** *n* **:** an engineer whose training or occupation is in mechanical engineering — abbr. *M.E.*

**mechanical engineering** *n* **:** a branch of engineering concerned primarily with the generation, transmission, and utilization of heat and mechanical power and with the production of tools, machinery, and their products

**mechanical equivalent of heat :** the value of a unit quantity of heat in terms of mechanical work units with its most probable value in cgs measure being 4.1855 x $10^7$ ergs per calorie — symbol *J*; called also *Joule's equivalent*

**mechanical heart** *n* **:** a mechanism designed to maintain the flow of blood to the tissues of the body during a surgical operation on the heart

**me·chan·i·cal·i·ty** \mə̇,kanə'kaləd·ē\ *n* -ES **:** MECHANICALNESS

**me·chan·i·cal·ize** \mə̇'kanə̇kə,līz\ *vt* -ED/-ING/-S [¹*mechanical* + *-ize*] **:** to make mechanical

**me·chan·i·cal·ly** \-nə̇k(ə)lē, -nēk-, -li\ *adv* **:** in a mechanical manner

**mechanical mixture** *n* **:** a mixture whose components are separable by mechanical means as distinguished from a chemical compound

**me·chan·i·cal·ness** *n* -ES **:** the quality or state of being mechanical ⟨was calmed by the ~ of the tasks at home —Sinclair Lewis⟩

**mechanical pencil** *n* **:** a pencil whose lead is projected by a screw or other device

**mechanical property** *n* **:** a property that involves a relationship between stress and strain or a reaction to an applied force

**mechanical refrigeration** *n* **:** the abstraction of heat by means of a working substance subjected to refrigerating thermodynamic cycles in which the energy is supplied by a mechanical compressor **:** cooling produced by a machine instead of by melting ice

**mechanical stage** *n* **:** a stage on a compound microscope equipped with a mechanical device for moving a slide lengthwise and crosswise or for registering the slide's position by vernier for future exact repositioning

**mechanical test** *n* **:** a test for determining a mechanical property

**mechanical tissue** *n* **:** tissue serving as a supporting framework in plants — compare PARENCHYMA, PROSENCHYMA

**mechanic art** *n* **:** MECHANICS 2b

**mech·a·ni·cian** \,mekə'nishən\ *n* -s [¹*mechanic* + *-ian*] **:** ARTISAN, MECHANIC, MACHINIST

**mechanico-** *comb form* [ISV, fr. L *mechanicus* mechanic, mechanical — more at MECHANIC] **1 :** mechanical ⟨*mechanico*-therapy⟩ **2 :** mechanical and ⟨*mechanico*chemical⟩

**me·chan·ics** \mə̇'kaniks, -nēks\ *n pl but sing or pl in constr* **1 :** a branch of physical science that deals with energy and forces and their relation to the equilibrium, deformation, or motion of solid, liquid, and gaseous bodies — see CELESTIAL MECHANICS, MATRIX MECHANICS, QUANTUM MECHANICS, WAVE MECHANICS; compare DYNAMICS, ENERGETICS, KINEMATICS, KINETICS, STATICS **2 a :** the practical application of mechanics to the design, construction, or operation of machines or tools or their products **b :** fabrication by any manual trade or craft — called also *mechanic art* **3 :** working structure or mechanism **:** functioning system ⟨knows the ~ of the lathe intimately⟩ ⟨the ~ of the general circulation of the atmosphere —*Climate & Man*⟩ ⟨provides an adequate ~ of meaning and value —R.P.Blackmur⟩ ⟨my enjoyment of our own parties is still dimmed by the ~ of hospitality —Doris F. Bernays⟩ ⟨liberals without much grasp of the ~ of politics —H.J.Hanham⟩ **4 :** routine procedure **:** technical details or method ⟨leaves the ~ of his agency almost solely in the hands of subordinates —*New Republic*⟩

**mechanics' institute** *n* **:** a school for adult working men formerly common in Great Britain and the U.S.

**mechanic's lien** *n* **:** a lien against a building and its site to assure payment for construction work and material — compare MATERIALMAN'S LIEN

**mech·a·nism** \'mekə,nizəm\ *n* -s [LL *mechanisma* contrivance, fr. Gk *mēchanē* machine + *-isma* -ism — more at MACHINE] **1 a :** a piece of machinery **:** a structure of working parts functioning together to produce an effect ⟨the valve ~ to operate the valve when it is in the engine block —Joseph Heitner⟩ ⟨~ of a watch⟩ **b :** a process or technique for achieving a result sometimes by cooperative effort: as (1) **:** a political practice or stratagem ⟨the ~s of peace —F.D.Roosevelt⟩ ⟨little thought is given to the real ~ of Communism —Norman Cousins⟩ ⟨the political ~s normal to a nation at war —R.A.Dahl⟩ (2) **:** a body process or function ⟨may be important in the ~ of onset of labor —J.P.Greenhill⟩ (3) **:** a creative method (as in the arts) ⟨have shown singularly little curiosity about the actual ~ of poetic inspiration —Herbert Read⟩ (4) **:** the combination of mental processes by which a result is obtained ⟨the ~ of invention⟩; *esp* **:** MECHANISM OF DEFENSE (5) **:** a systematic social or economic procedure ⟨banks provide the ~ which assures the smooth circulation of short-term credits —R.B.Westerfield⟩ **2 :** mechanical operation or action ⟨he acknowledges nothing besides matter and motion; so that all must be performed either by ~ or accident —Richard Bentley †1742⟩ **3 a :** nature or a natural process conceived as like a machine or as functioning purely in accordance with mechanical laws **b :** a philosophical doctrine that holds that natural processes and esp. the processes of life are mechanically determined and capable of complete explanation by the laws of physics and chemistry — compare TELEOLOGY, VITALISM **4 a :** the fundamental physical or chemical processes involved in or responsible for an action, reaction, or other natural phenomenon ⟨meteorologists believe that this pressure jump is the ~ responsible for storms and tornadoes —*Think*⟩ ⟨the complicated ~ that governs planets and satellites decreed that the moon should slow down —Waldemar Kaempffert⟩ **b :** a sequence of steps in a chemical reaction ⟨the most satisfactory evidence for the proposed ~ of chlorination —G.W.Wheland⟩ ⟨there are . . . many different ~s by which catalysts operate —Farrington Daniels & R.A.Alberty⟩ **5 :** an approach to language study based on an objective methodology in recording and classifying linguistic phenomena on the basis of observable forms — compare MENTALISM

**mech·a·nis·mic** \¦==¦nizmik\ *adj* **:** of, relating to, or involving mechanism

**mechanism of defense :** an unconscious mental process (as identification, projection, or repression) that enables the ego to reach compromise solutions to problems it is unable to resolve

**mech·a·nist** \'mekənə̇st\ *n* -s [*mechan-* + *-ist*] **1** *archaic* **:** MECHANIC **2 :** an adherent or practitioner of a mechanistic system; *esp* **:** an adherent of the philosophical doctrine of mechanism

**mech·a·nis·tic** \¦==¦nistik, -tēk\ *adj* **1 :** mechanically determined ⟨a ~ universe⟩ **2 a :** of, relating to, or consistent with the theory of philosophic mechanism **b :** of, relating to, or marked by a psychological mechanism **:** tending to interpret conduct in terms of theoretical mechanisms **c :** finding biological and physical causes sufficient to explain social behavior **d :** of or relating to mechanism as an approach to linguistic study **3 :** MECHANICAL — **mech·a·nis·ti·cal·ly** \-tə̇k(ə)lē, -tēk-, -li\ *adv*

**mech·a·ni·za·tion** \,mekənə̇'zāshən, -,nī'z-\ *n* -s **:** the act or process of mechanizing or the state of being mechanized

**mech·a·nize** \'mekə,nīz\ *vt* -ED/-ING/-S *see -ize in Explan Notes* [*mechan-* + *-ize*] **1 :** to give the quality or structure of a machine to: as **a** *archaic* **:** to reduce to orderly systematic method or procedure **b :** to render automatic or routine **:** impart a deadening monotony to **:** deprive of spontaneity ⟨Americans have *mechanized* their emotions and standardized their ideas —W.G.Carleton⟩ **2 a :** to equip with machinery; *esp* **:** to substitute mechanical processes for human or animal labor in ⟨shuts down marginal coal mines and ~s many of the rest, with resultant unemployment for miners —E.A.Lahey⟩ **b :** to equip (a military force) with armed and armored motor vehicles (as tanks and self-propelled cannon) — distinguished from *motorize* **c :** to provide with mechanical power ⟨*mechanized* weapons⟩ **3 a :** to produce or reproduce by machine (an effect normally or basically produced directly by man) ⟨an enormous advantage . . . over the more *mechanized* stimuli of the motion picture —Marc Connelly⟩ ⟨now music is *mechanized* in its full tonal range —Siegfried Giedion⟩ **b :** to devise or create with undue reliance on technique or mechanics ⟨fail because of an application of formula, call it *mechanized* plotting —W.T. Scott⟩

**mech·a·niz·er** \-,nīzə(r)\ *n* -s **:** one that mechanizes

**mechano-** — see MECHAN-

**mech·a·no·caloric effect** \¦mekə,nō+-\ *n* [*mechan-* + *caloric*] **:** a change of temperature by produced mechanical means; *specif* **:** a fluctuation in liquid helium II at the point where the capillary film emerges from the parent liquid — compare SUPERFLUID

**mech·a·no·mor·phic** \¦===¦mȯrfik\ *adj* [*mechan-* + *-morphic*] **:** having the form or qualities of a machine **:** described in mechanical terms ⟨a ~ God⟩ ⟨this ~ world, the City of Destruction from which we must all flee —*Saturday Rev.*⟩

**mech·a·no·mor·phism** \"+¦mȯr,fizəm\ *n* -s [*mechan-* + *-morphism* (as in *anthropomorphism*)] **:** a conception of something (as the universe or a living creature) as operating mechanically or to be fully accounted for according to the laws of physical science

**mech·a·no·therapist** \"+\ *n* **:** one who practices mechanotherapy

**mech·a·no·therapy** \"+\ *n* [ISV *mechan-* + *therapy*] **:** the treatment of disease by manual, physical, or mechanical means

**mechitarist** *usu cap, var of* MEKHITARIST

**mech·lin** \'meklə̇n\ *or* **mechlin lace** *n* -s *usu cap M* [fr. *Mechlin*, Belgium] **:** a delicate bobbin lace that is used for dresses and millinery and has floral designs outlined by a glossy cordonnet against a net ground of hexagonal mesh

**me·cho·a·can** \¦mechəwə¦kän\ *n* -s [Sp *mechoacán*, fr. *Michoacán* state, Mexico] **:** a weak jalap

**Mech·o·lyl** \'mekə,lil, -,lēl\ *trademark* — used for methacholine

**mechs** *pl of* MECH

**me·cis·to·cirrus** \mə,sistō'sirəs\ *n, cap* [NL, fr. *mecisto-* (fr. Gk *mēkistos*, superl. of *makros* long) + *cirrus* — more at MEAGER] **:** a genus of nematode worms (family Trichostrongylidae) including a common parasite (*M. digitatus*) of the abomasum of domesticated ruminants and the stomach of swine in both of which it may cause serious loss of blood and digestive disturbances esp. in young animals

**meck·e·lian bar** \me'kēlēən-\ *or* **meckelian cartilage** *or* **meckelian rod** *n, usu cap M* [Johann F. *Meckel* †1833 + E *-ian*] **:** MECKEL'S CARTILAGE

**meckelian ganglion** *n, usu cap M* [J.F.*Meckel* †1774 + E *-ian*] **:** SPHENOPALATINE GANGLION

**meck·el's cartilage** \'mekəlz-\ *n, usu cap M* [after Johann F. *Meckel* †1833 Ger. anatomist] **:** the cartilaginous axis of the mandibular arch forming no part of the jawbone but sometimes giving rise to the articular and the bones of the middle ear

**meckel's cave** *n, usu cap M* [after Johann F. *Meckel* †1774 Ger. anatomist] **:** a space beneath the dura mater lodging the gasserian ganglion

**meckel's diverticulum** *n, usu cap M* [after Johann F. *Meckel* †1774 Ger. anatomist] **:** the proximal part of the yolk stalk when persistent as a blind fibrous tube connected with the lower ileum

**meckel's ganglion** *n, usu cap M* [after Johann F. *Meckel* †1774 Ger. anatomist] **:** SPHENOPALATINE GANGLION

**meck·len·burg·ian** \¦meklən¦bərgēən\ *adj, usu cap* [*Mecklenburg*, region in northern Germany + E *-ian*] **:** WÜRMIAN

**meco-** — see MEC-

¹**me·co·dont** \'mēkə,dänt\ *adj* [NL *Mecodonta*] **:** of or relating to the Mecodonta

²**mecodont** \"\ *n* -s **:** a member of the Mecodonta

**me·co·don·ta** \,==¦däntə\ *n pl, cap* [NL, fr. *mec-* + *-odonta*] *in some classifications* **:** a primary division of Caudata comprising salamanders having the palatal teeth inserted on the inner margin of the palatine processes in posteriorly diverging longitudinal rows

**me·com·e·ter** \mə̇'kämə̇d·ə(r)\ *n* [ISV *mec-* + *-meter*] **:** an instrument for measuring a newborn child

**mecon-** *or* **mecono-** *comb form* **1 :** poppy ⟨*meconidium*⟩ ⟨*meconopsis*⟩ **2** [NL *meconium*] **:** opium ⟨*meconin*⟩ ⟨*meconology*⟩ ⟨*meconophagy*⟩

**me·con·ic acid** \mə̇'känik-, -kōn-\ *n* [Gk *mēkōnikos* of a poppy, fr. *mēkōn* + *-ikos* -ic] **:** a crystalline acid $C_7H_4O_7$ obtained from opium; 3-hydroxy-4-pyrone-2,6-dicarboxylic acid

**mec·o·nid·i·um** \,mekə'nidēəm\ *n, pl* **meconid·ia** \-dēə\ [NL, fr. Gk *mēkōn* poppy + NL *-idium*; fr. the resemblance to the seed capsule of the poppy] **:** a gonophore produced by some hydroids that resembles a medusa and remains attached by a pedicel

**mec·o·nin** \'mekənə̇n, 'mēk-\ *n* -s [F *méconine*, fr. *mécon-* + *-ine*] **:** a crystalline lactone $C_{10}H_{10}O_4$ found in opium

**me·co·ni·um** \mə̇'kōnēəm\ *n* -s [NL, fr. L, poppy juice, fr. Gk *mēkōnion*, fr. *mēkōn* poppy — more at MAW] **1 :** OPIUM **2** [L, lit., poppy juice] **a :** a dark greenish mass of desquamated cells, mucus, and bile that accumulates in the bowel during fetal life and is discharged shortly after birth **b** [NL, fr. L] **:** a mass of fecal material discharged by some insect larvae at pupation

**mec·o·nop·sis** \,mekə'näpsə̇s, ,mēk-\ *n* [NL, fr. *mecon-* + *-opsis*] **1** *cap* **:** a genus of annual or perennial chiefly Asiatic herbs (family Papaveraceae) having flowers with stigmas forming a globular mass atop the ovary **2** *pl* **meconop·ses** \-(,)sēz\ **:** any plant of the genus *Meconopsis*

**me·cop·tera** \mə̇'käptərə\ *n pl, cap* [NL, fr. *mec-* + *-ptera*] **:** an order of primitive carnivorous insects usu. having membranous heavily veined wings, a long beak with biting mouthparts at the tip, and larvae that live in soil and including the scorpion flies and hanging flies — **me·cop·ter·an** \-tərən\ *n* -s — **me·cop·ter·ous** \-t(ə)rəs\ *adj*

**mecs** *pl of* MEC

**med** *abbr* **1** medalist **2** median **3** medical; medicine **4** medieval **5** medium

**me·dad·dy-bush** \mə̇'dadē,=\ *n* [*medaddy* of unknown origin] **:** FLY HONEYSUCKLE 2

**me·dail·lon** \mādȧyōⁿ\ *n* -s [F *médaillon*, lit., medallion — more at MEDALLION] **:** a small round or oval serving of food (as a fillet or a savory)

**me·da·ka** \mə'däkə\ *n* -s [Jap] **:** a small Japanese freshwater poeciliid fish (*Oryzias latipes*) commonly occurring in flooded rice fields and usu. silvery brown in the wild but from pale yellow to deep red in aquarium strains

¹**med·al** \'medᵊl\ *n* -s [MF *medaille*, fr. OIt *medaglia*, coin worth half a denarius, medal, fr. (assumed) VL *medalia*, neut. pl. of *medalis* half, fr. LL *medialis* middle, fr. L *medius* middle, half + *-alis* -al — more at MID] **1 a :** a metal disk bearing a religious emblem or picture that represents a particular devotion or object of veneration **b** *archaic* **:** IMAGE, REPRESENTATION **2 :** a piece of metal usu. in the form of a coin with an inscription, head, or other device issued to commemorate a person, action, or event or awarded (as to a soldier) for heroic deeds or meritorious service or (as to a student) for proficiency, skill, or excellence

medal 2 : Congressional Medal of Honor, Army

²**medal** \"\ *vt* **medaled** *or* **medalled; medaled** *or* **medalled; medaling** *or* **medalling** \-d(ᵊ)liŋ\ **medals :** to honor or reward with a medal **:** to confer a medal on ⟨~*ed* by the king —W.M.Thackeray⟩

**medal bronze** *n* **:** a moderate yellowish brown to light olive brown that is duller than Isabella and very slightly yellower than clay drab — called also *calabash*

**medal chief** *n* **:** an Indian chief honored with a medal

**med·al·et** \¦medᵊl¦e|t, 'medᵊlə̇|, *usu* |d.+V\ *n* -s [¹*medal* + *-et*] **:** a small medal

**med·al·ist** *or* **med·al·list** \'medᵊlə̇st\ *n* -s [F *medailliste*, fr. It *medaglista*, fr. *medaglia* medal + *-ista* -ist — more at MEDAL] **1 :** a connoisseur or collector of medals **2 :** a designer, engraver, or maker of medals **3 a :** one awarded a medal as a prize or distinction ⟨~ of the Geological Society⟩ **b :** the low scorer in qualifying medal play in a golf tournament **c :** a recipient of a medal as a prize in competitive sports

**me·dal·lic** \mə̇'dalik\ *adj* **:** of, relating to, or shown on a medal

¹**me·dal·lion** \mə̇'dalyən, me'-\ *n* -s [F *médaillon*, fr. It *medaglione*, aug. of *medaglia* medal — more at MEDAL] **1 a :** a large medal (as for a memorial purpose) ⟨a burnished bronze ~ three inches in diameter has been issued by the . . . diamond jubilee committee —*Numismatist*⟩ **b :** any of various large ancient Greek coins ⟨a ~ of Syracuse⟩ **2 :** something resembling a large medal: as **a :** a tablet or panel in a wall or window bearing a figure shown in relief, a portrait, or an ornament **b** (1) **:** a design on a carpet or in lace (2) **:** a lace ornament in a garment **c :** a framed usu. oval or round design on a stamp or a piece of paper currency showing a portrait or denomination **3 :** a perforated design punched in the tip of a shoe

²**medallion** \"\ *vt* -ED/-ING/-S **1 :** to adorn with medallions **2 :** to make a medallion of **:** represent in a medallion

**me·dal·lion·ist** \-nə̇st\ *n* -s **:** a maker, engraver, or worker of medallions

**medal play** *n* **:** golf competition scored by total number of strokes — compare MATCH PLAY

**med·dle** \'medᵊl\ *vb* **meddled; meddled; meddling** \-d(ᵊ)liŋ\ **meddles** [ME *medelen, medlen*, fr. OF *mesler, mesdler, medler*, fr. (assumed) VL *misculare*, fr. L *miscēre* to mix — more at MIX] *vt* **1** *obs* **:** to mix together **:** COMBINE, MINGLE **2** *dial* **:** to interfere with **:** DISTURB ~ *vi* **1** *obs* **:** to engage in combat **2 a** *archaic* **:** to occupy oneself **:** DEAL — usu. used with *with* **b :** to busy oneself intrusively or officiously **:** interfere without right or propriety ⟨the driving spirit of malice which forced him to ~ in other people's lives —Carl Van Doren⟩ ⟨history and psychology can ~ too much with the meanings of art —*Times Lit. Supp.*⟩

**syn** INTERFERE, INTERMEDDLE, TAMPER: MEDDLE suggests officiously entering into something in no way one's concern, affair, or responsibility without right, permission, or request of those concerned ⟨as Minister of Finance, Chari had no business to *meddle* in political affairs —Christine Weston⟩ ⟨it is inexpedient to *meddle* with questions of State in a land where men are highly paid to work them out for you —Rudyard Kipling⟩ INTERFERE suggests taking part obtrusively and officiously in the affairs of others so as to hinder, frustrate, check, or defeat ⟨he would not allow management or labor to *interfere* with increasing production —*Collier's Yr. Bk.*⟩ ⟨when a child persistently *interferes* with other children or spoils their pleasures, the obvious penalty is banishment —Bertrand Russell⟩ INTERMEDDLE combines connotations and denotations of MEDDLE and INTERFERE ⟨a petition to parliament sets forth how all kinds of unlearned men *intermeddle* with the practice of physic —G.G.Coulton⟩ TAMPER suggests unwarranted alteration or change, ill-advised readjustment, meddlesome experimentation, or improper influence ⟨he would suddenly leave his guests and rush back to town to see that the door had not been *tampered* with —Oscar Wilde⟩ ⟨these blank notes were slipped into the note case when examiners came along and the books were *tampered* to indicate that the notes were bearing interest —W.A.White⟩ ⟨money and sex are forces too unruly for our reason; they can only be controlled by taboos with which we *tamper* at our peril —L.P.Smith⟩

**med·dler** \-d(ᵊ)lə(r)\ *n* -s [ME *medeler*, fr. *medelen, medlen* to meddle + *-er*] **:** one that meddles **:** BUSYBODY

**med·dle·some** \'medᵊlsəm\ *adj* **:** given to meddling in the affairs of others **:** officiously intrusive **syn** see IMPERTINENT

**med·dle·some·ly** *adv* **:** in a meddlesome manner

**meddlesome mat·tie** \-'mad·ē\ *n* -s *usu cap both Ms* [after *Meddlesome Matty*, subject of a poem of the same name by Ann Taylor †1866 Am. writer] **:** BUSYBODY, MEDDLER ⟨when men insist that morality is more than that, they are quickly denounced, in general correctly, as *Meddlesome Matties* —Walter Lippmann⟩

**med·dle·some·ness** *n* -ES **:** the disposition or habit of a meddler

**med·dling** \'med(ᵊ)liŋ\ *n* -s [ME *medeling, medling*, gerund of *medelen, medlen* to meddle] **:** officious interference ⟨advised against surgical ~ which would do the patient no good —Harvey Graham⟩ **:** TAMPERING

**med·dling·ly** *adv* **:** in a meddling manner

¹**mede** *obs var of* MEAD

²**mede** \'mēd\ *n* -s *usu cap* [ME, fr. L *Medus*, fr. Gk *Mēdos*] **:** a native or inhabitant of ancient Media in Persia

¹**me·dellin** *or* **me·dellín** \¦medᵊl¦ēn, 'medᵊlən, ¦mäthə¦yēn\ *adj, usu cap* [fr. *Medellín*, Colombia] **:** of or from the city of Medellín, Colombia **:** of the kind or style prevalent in Medellín

²**medellin** \"\ *n* -s *usu cap* **:** a high-grade Colombian coffee

**med·fly** \'med+,-\ *n, sometimes cap* [*Mediterranean* + *fly*] **:** MEDITERRANEAN FRUIT FLY

**medi-** *or* **medio-** *comb form* [L, fr. *medius* middle — more at MID] **1 :** medially ⟨*medio*depressed⟩ ⟨*medio*perforate⟩ **2 :** intermediate ⟨*medi*eval⟩ ⟨*medio*silicic⟩ **3 :** middle or median plane ⟨*medi*ad⟩ ⟨*medio*dorsal⟩ ⟨*medio*palatal⟩ ⟨*medio*ventral⟩

¹**media** *pl of* MEDIUM

²**me·dia** \'mēdēə\ *n, pl* **medi·ae** \-dē,ē\ [NL, fr. L, fem. of *medius*, middle — more at MID] **1 a** [so called fr. the fact

that the voice of these stops was regarded by ancient Greek grammarians as making them rougher than the voiceless unaspirated stops but smoother than the voiceless aspirated stops] **:** one of the voiced stops *β, δ, γ* in Greek — called also *medial, soft mute* **b :** a voiced unaspirated stop **c :** an unaspirated or lenis stop **2 :** the middle coat of the wall of a blood or lymph vessel, consisting chiefly of circularly arranged muscle fibers **3 :** the median vein of an insect's wing, typically having a convex anterior branch and a concave posterior branch

**me·di·a·cy** \ˈmēdēəsē, -si\ *n* -ES [¹*mediate* + *-cy*] **:** the quality or state of being mediate **:** MEDIATENESS, INTERMEDIACY — opposed to *immediacy*

**me·di·ad** \ˈmēdē,ad\ *adv* [*medi-* + *-ad*] **:** toward the median line or plane of a body or part

**mediaeval** *var of* MEDIEVAL

¹**me·di·al** \ˈmēdēəl\ *adj* [LL *medialis*, fr. L *medi-* + *-alis* -al] **1 a :** being, situated, or occurring in the middle **:** intermediate in position **:** MEDIAN **b :** extending toward the middle **2 a :** situated between the extremes of initial and final in a word or morpheme ⟨the ~ second *d* in *deeded*⟩ **b** *of a stop consonant in ancient Greek* **:** VOICED **c :** of or relating to the middle voice or a form in the middle voice **3 :** MEAN, AVERAGE

²**medial** \"\ *n* -S **1 a** (1) **:** a medial sound or letter (2) **:** a form of a letter used medially **b :** MEDIA 1 **2 :** the median vein of an insect's wing

**medial cadence** *n* **1** *in ecclesiastical modes* **:** a cadence ending on the mediant **2 :** a cadence with an inverted penultimate chord

**medial lemniscus** *n* **:** a band of nerve fibers that transmits proprioceptive impulses from the spinal cord to the thalamus

**me·di·al·ly** \ˈmēdēəlē, -li\ *adv* **:** in a medial manner or position

**medial moraine** *n* **:** a moraine in the middle of a glacier parallel to its sides that is often formed by the union of lateral moraines when two glaciers coalesce

**me·di·a·lu·na** \,mēdēəˈlünə\ *n, cap* [NL, fr. L *media luna* half-moon] **:** a genus of percoid fishes that includes the half-moon

**media man** *n* [¹*media*] **:** a worker in an advertising agency who studies, negotiates with, or selects publications or other media to carry an advertisement

¹**me·di·an** \ˈmēdēən\ *n* -S [MF *mediane*, fr. ML *mediana* (*vena*), fr. L *mediana* (fem. of *medianus* median) + *vena* vein] **1 :** a median part (as a vein, nerve, or scale) **2 :** a value in an ordered set of quantities below and above which fall an equal number of quantities ⟨the ~ of the set 19, 20, 36, is 20, that of the set 19, 20, 21, 22 is 20.5⟩ **3 a :** a line from a vertex of a triangle to the midpoint of the opposite side **b :** a line joining the midpoints of the nonparallel sides of a trapezoid **4 :** MEDIAN STRIP **syn** see AVERAGE

²**median** \"\ *adj* [MF or L; MF, fr. L *medianus*, fr. *medius* middle + *-anus* -an — more at MID] **1 :** being in the middle **:** occupying an intermediate position **:** MEDIAL ⟨was presumably of the ~ sexual type —H.S.Canby⟩ **2 :** equivalent in lightness to median gray **3 :** of, relating to, or constituting a statistical median **4 :** situated in the middle; *specif* **:** lying in a plane dividing a bilateral animal into right and left halves — used esp. of unpaired organs and parts ⟨~ fins⟩ **5** *phonetics* **:** produced without occlusion along the lengthwise middle line of the tongue — compare LATERAL — **me·di·an·ly** *adv*

³**median** \"\ *adj, usu cap* [*Media*, ancient country in southern Asia (fr. L, fr. Gk *Mēdia*) + E *-an*] **1 a :** of, relating to, or characteristic of ancient Media in Persia **b :** of, relating to, or characteristic of the people of Media **2 :** of, relating to, or characteristic of the Median language

⁴**median** \"\ *n* -S *cap* **1 :** a native or inhabitant of Media **2 :** the Iranian language of ancient Media

**median basilic vein** *or* **median cubital vein** *n* **:** a continuation of the cephalic vein of the forearm that passes obliquely toward the inner side of the arm in the bend of the elbow to join with the ulnar veins in forming the basilic vein and is often selected for venepuncture

**median gray** *n* **:** a gray having equal lightness or darkness differences from black and white as terminal members of a series of grays and for eyes adapted to a white background reflecting about 25 percent of the incident light or for eyes adapted to it reflecting about 18 percent — called also *medium gray*

**median nerve** *n* **:** a nerve that arises by two roots from the brachial plexus and passes down the middle of the front of the arm

**median plane** *n* **:** MESIAL PLANE

**median point** *n* **:** a point so placed with reference to a number of points or objects distributed over a plane surface that the sum of its distances from all the individuals is a minimum

**median segment** *n* **:** the propodeum of a hymenopterous insect

**median strip** *n* **:** a paved or planted strip of ground dividing a highway into lanes according to direction of travel

median strip

**me·di·ant** \ˈmēdēənt\ *n* -S [It *mediante*, fr. LL *mediant-, medians*, pres. part. of *mediare* to be in the middle — more at MEDIATE] **1** *in ecclesiastical modes* **:** a modulation of the authentic and the plagal modes **2 :** the third musical degree of the major or minor scale (as E in the scale of C) midway between the tonic and the dominant

**median vein** *n* **1 :** the cephalic vein in the forearm **2 :** the fourth primary vein of an insect's wing falling in the middle part of the wing

**me·di·as·ti·nal** \,mēdēəˈstīnᵊl\ *adj* [NL *mediastinum* + E *-al*] **:** of or relating to a mediastinum

**me·di·as·ti·ni·tis** \,mēdē,astəˈnīdəs\ *n, pl* **mediasti·nit·i·des** \-ˈnidə,dēz\ [NL, fr. *mediastinum* + *-itis*] **:** inflammation of the tissues of the mediastinum

**me·di·as·ti·num** \,mēdēəˈstīnəm\ *n, pl* **mediasti·na** \-nə\ [NL, fr. neut. of L *mediastinus* medial, fr. *medius* middle — more at MID] **1 :** an irregular median septum that divides the thoracic cavity into right and left halves, is formed of the opposing medial walls of the parietal pleura, and encloses between these walls all the thoracic viscera except the lungs **2 :** a mass of connective tissue at the back of the testis being continuous externally with the tunica albuginea and internally with the interlobular septa and enclosing the rete testis

¹**me·di·ate** \ˈmēdēət, *chiefly Brit* ˈmējət *or* ˈmēdyət; *usu* -əd+V\ *adj* [ME *mediat*, fr. LL *mediatus*, past part. of *mediare* to be in the middle, fr. L *medius* middle — more at MID] **1 :** occupying a middle position **:** interposed between the extremes in order of time, place, or rank **2 a** *obs* **:** fulfilling the function of an intermediary **b** *archaic* **:** serving as a means **:** INSTRUMENTAL **3 :** acting through an intervening agency **:** exhibiting indirect causation, connection, or relation ⟨the disease spreads by ~ as well as direct contact —*Veterinary Record*⟩ — **me·di·ate·ly** *adv* — **me·di·ate·ness** *n* -ES

²**me·di·ate** \ˈmēdē,āt, *usu* -ād+V\ *vb* -ED/-ING/-S [in sense 1, fr. LL *mediatus*, past part. of *mediare*; in other senses, fr. ML *mediatus*, past part. of *mediare*, fr. LL, to be in the middle] *vi* **1** *archaic* **:** to form a connecting link **:** be in the middle **:** INTERVENE **2 a :** to interpose between parties in order to reconcile them or to interpret them to each other ⟨I want to ~ between the two of you now, because if this breach continues it will be the ruin of us all —Robert Graves⟩ **b :** to negotiate a compromise of hostile or incompatible viewpoints, demands, or attitudes **:** reconcile differences ⟨critics . . . who *mediated* between extreme points of view —C.I.Glicksberg⟩ ~ *vt* **1 a :** to bring about by intervention between conflicting parties **:** effect by action as an intermediary ⟨*mediated* a settlement satisfactory to both sides⟩ **b :** to bring accord out of by action as an intermediary ⟨endeavored to ~ East-West differences on several important issues —*Collier's Yr. Bk.*⟩ ⟨had just finished *mediating* an industrial dispute —*Current Biog.*⟩ **2 a :** to act as intermediary agent in bringing, effecting, or communicating (as a gift, result, influence) **:** CONVEY ⟨individuals . . . ~ the culture to the child —Margaret Mead⟩ ⟨his sole aim was to ~ the love of God to men —W.L.Sperry⟩ **b :** to transmit or carry (as a physical process or effect) as intermediate mechanism or agency ⟨apparently the vast majority of papillae can ~ more than one sense quality —F.A.Geldard⟩

**mediate inference** *n* **:** a logical inference drawn from more than one proposition or premise — compare SYLLOGISM

**mediating** *adj* [fr. pres. part. of ²*mediate*] **:** performing a mediator's function **:** CONCILIATING, CONVEYING

**me·di·a·tion** \,mēdēˈāshən\ *n* -S [ME *mediacioun*, fr. ML *mediation-, mediatio*, fr. *mediatus* (past part. of *mediare* to mediate) + L *-ion-, -io* -ion — more at MEDIATE] **1 :** intervention between conflicting parties or viewpoints to promote reconciliation, settlement, compromise, or understanding ⟨a code . . . would not dispense with ~ between legislature and judges —B.N.Cardozo⟩ **2 :** the function or activity of an intermediate means or instrumentality of transmission ⟨attains its effects . . . through the ~ of the ideological elements in society —Max Lerner & Edwin Mims⟩ **3** *international law* **:** intercession of one power between other powers at their invitation or with their consent to conciliate differences between them **4 :** the cadence between the two reciting notes in a Gregorian psalm tone or an Anglican chant

**me·di·a·tive** \ˈ==,ā|d·iv, -,ə|, |t|, |ēv *also* |əv\ *adj* [²*mediate* + *-ive*] **:** of, relating to, or used in mediation ⟨~ efforts⟩

**me·di·a·tize** \ˈmēdēə,tīz\ *vb* -ED/-ING/-S [G *mediatisieren*, fr. *mediat* mediate (fr. LL *mediatus*, past part. of *mediare* to be in the middle) + *-isieren* -ize — more at MEDIATE] *vt* **1 :** to bring (a prince or state) down to the rank of mediate vassal from that of immediate vassal of the Holy Roman Empire **:** annex (a state) to another ⟨a *mediatized* prince —Cyril Connolly⟩ **2 :** to put into a middle or intermediate position **:** make instrumental or subordinate ~ *vi* **1 :** to act as mediator **2 :** to become a mediate vassal of the Holy Roman Empire

**me·di·a·tor** \ˈ==,ād·ə(r), -ātə-\ *n* -S [ME *mediatour*, fr. MF, fr. LL *mediator*, fr. *mediatus* + *-or*] **1 :** one that mediates; *esp* **:** one that mediates between parties at variance to reconcile them **:** INTERCESSOR ⟨for there is one God, and there is one ~ between God and men, the man Christ Jesus —1 Tim 2: 5 (RSV)⟩ **2 :** one that transmits or conveys **:** a person or agency that serves as a channel or means ⟨the Arabs as depositories and ~s of ancient thought —Leonardo Olschki⟩ **3 :** a mediating agent (as an enzyme or hormone) in a chemical reaction or biological process

**me·di·a·to·ri·al** \,mēdēəˈtōrēəl, -tȯr-\ *adj* [LL *mediatorius* (fr. *mediatus* + *-orius* -ory) + E *-al*] **:** of, relating to, or appropriate to a mediator ⟨what she wanted was some ~ wisdom —A.D.Culler⟩

**me·di·a·tor·ship** \ˈ==,ād·ə(r),ship, -ātə-\ *n* **:** the office or function of a mediator

**me·di·a·to·ry** \ˈ==ə,tōrē, -tȯr-, -ri\ *adj* [LL *mediatorius*] **:** of, relating to, or directed toward mediation ⟨~ efforts⟩

**me·di·a·tress** \ˈ==,ā·trəs\ *n* -ES [*mediator* + *-ess*] **:** a female mediator

**me·di·a·trice** \ˈ==,ā·trəs\ *n* -S [ME, fr. MF, fr. LL *mediatric-, mediatrix*, fem. of *mediator* — more at MEDIATOR] **:** MEDIATRESS

**me·di·a·trix** \ˈ==ˈā·triks, -ēks\ *n* -ES [ME, fr. LL] **:** MEDIATRESS

¹**med·ic** *or* **med·ick** \ˈmedik\ *n* -S [ME *medike*, fr. L *Medica*, fr. Gk *Mēdikē*, fr. fem. of *Mēdikos* Median, fr. *Mēdia* Media + *-ikos* -ic] **:** a plant of the genus *Medicago*

²**med·ic** \ˈmedik, -dēk\ *n* -S [L *medicus* physician, surgeon — more at MEDICAL] **:** one engaged in medical work (as a physician, a medical student, or a military corpsman)

³**medic** \"\ *adj* [L *medicus*, fr. *med-* (stem of *mederī* to heal) + *-icus* -ic — more at MEDICAL] *archaic* **:** MEDICAL

**me·di·ca·ble** \ˈmedəkəbəl, -dēk-\ *adj* [L *medicabilis*, fr. *medicare, medicari* to heal + *-abilis* -able — more at MEDICATE] **1 :** CURABLE, REMEDIABLE **2 :** having medicinal power **:** CURATIVE ⟨some ~ herb to make our grief less bitter —W.B. Yeats⟩ — **med·i·ca·bly** \-blē, -li\ *adv*

**med·i·ca·go** \,medəˈkā,gō\ *n, cap* [NL, fr. L *medica* medic + L *-ago* (as in *plantago* plantain) — more at MEDIC, PLANTAIN] **:** a genus of Old World herbs (family Leguminosae) that resemble typical clovers and have pinnately trifoliolate leaves and spirally twisted seed pods — see ALFALFA

¹**med·i·cal** \ˈmedəkəl, -dēk-\ *adj* [F or LL; F *médical*, fr. LL *medicalis*, fr. L *medicus* physician, surgeon (fr. stem of *mederī* to heal + *-icus* -ic) + *-alis* -al; akin to Gk *Mēdos*, *Mēdē*, Agamēdē, gods of healing, Av *vī-mad-* healer, physician, L *meditari* to meditate — more at METE] **1 :** of, relating to, or concerned with physicians or with the practice of medicine often as distinguished from surgery **2 :** requiring or devoted to medical treatment ⟨pneumonia is a ~ disease⟩ ⟨the ~ wards of a hospital⟩ — distinguished from *surgical* **3** *archaic* **:** MEDICINAL — **med·i·cal·ly** \-k(ə)lē, -li\ *adv*

²**medical** \"\ *n* -S **1 :** PHYSICIAN 1 **2 :** a medical examination

**medical examiner** *n* **1 :** a usu. appointed public officer who must be a person trained in medicine and whose functions are to make postmortem examinations of the bodies of persons dead by violence or suicide or under circumstances suggesting crime, to investigate the cause of their deaths, to conduct autopsies, and sometimes to initiate inquests — compare CORONER **2 :** a physician employed to make medical examinations (as of applicants for military service or for life insurance or of claimants of workmen's compensation) **3 :** a physician appointed to examine and license candidates for the practice of medicine in a political jurisdiction (as a state)

**medical geography** *n* **:** the study of the relation between geographic factors and disease

**medical jurisprudence** *n* **:** FORENSIC MEDICINE

**medical psychology** *n* **:** theories of personality and behavior not necessarily derived from academic psychology that provide a basis for psychotherapeutics in psychiatry and in general medicine

**medical record** *n* **:** a record of a person's illnesses and their treatment

¹**me·dic·a·ment** \məˈdikəmənt, meˈ-; ˈmedəkə-\ *n* -S [MF, fr. L *medicamentum*, fr. *medicare, medicari* to heal + *-mentum* -ment — more at MEDICATE] **:** a substance (as a chemical, a medicine, or an ointment) used in therapy **syn** see REMEDY

²**me·dic·a·ment** \-,ment\ *vt* -ED/-ING/-S **:** to treat with medicaments

**med·i·ca·men·tous** \,medəkəˈmentəs\ *adj* [F *médicamenteux*, fr. L *medicamentosus*, fr. *medicamentum* + *-osus* -ous] **:** functioning as or caused by a medicament ⟨~ dermatitis⟩

**med·i·cant** \ˈmedəkənt, -dēk-\ *n* -S [L *medicant-, medicans*, pres. part. of *medicare, medicari* to heal] **:** a medicinal substance

**med·i·cas·ter** \ˈmedə,kastə(r)\ *n* -S [It *medicastro*, fr. *medico* physician (fr. L *medicus*) + *-astro* -aster (fr. L *-aster*) — more at MEDICAL] **:** a medical charlatan **:** QUACK

**med·i·cate** \ˈmedə,kāt, *usu* -ād+V\ *vt* -ED/-ING/-S [L *medicatus*, past part. of *medicare, medicari* to heal, fr. *medicus* physician — more at MEDICAL] **1 :** to treat with medicine **:** provide with medical care ⟨feeds, ~s, and educates the refugee community —A.J.Liebling⟩ **2 a :** to impregnate with a medicinal substance ⟨*medicated* waters⟩ ⟨authentic Chinese wines and cordials *medicated* with snake skin and tiger bone —*Amer. Guide Series: N.Y. City*⟩ **b** *archaic* **:** to adulterate with something noxious **:** DOCTOR

**medicated candle** *n* **:** DISINFECTING CANDLE

**med·i·ca·tion** \,medəˈkāshən\ *n* -S [F or L; F *médication*, fr. L *medication-, medicatio*, fr. *medicatus* + *-ion*, *-io* -ion] **1 :** the act or process of medicating **:** treatment with a medicament **2 :** a medicinal substance **:** MEDICAMENT **syn** see REMEDY

**med·i·ca·tive** \ˈ==,kā|d·iv, -,kə|, |t|, |ēv *also* |əv\ *adj* [ML *medicativus*, fr. L *medicatus* (past part. of *medicare, medicari* to heal) + *-ivus* -ive — more at MEDICATE] **:** MEDICINAL

**med·i·ce·an** \,medəˈchēən, -dəˈsē-\ *adj, usu cap* [It *mediceo* Medicean (fr. the *Medici*, Ital. family powerful in Florence and Tuscany esp. fr. the 14th to 16th centuries) + E *-an*] **:** of or relating to the Medici family; *esp* **:** of or relating to a great Florentine library founded by Lorenzo de' Medici

**med·i·ci blue** \ˈmedə(,)chē-, -,chi-\ *n, often cap M* [after the *Medici* family] **:** a bluish gray that is darker than clair de lune, greener and duller than average dusk (sense 3a), and deeper than puritan gray

**me·dic·i·na·ble** \məˈdis(ᵊ)nəbəl, meˈ-, *archaic* ˈmed(ə)sən-\ *adj* [ME *medecinable, medicinable*, fr. MF, fr. *medeciner, mediciner* to give medicine to, heal + *-able* — more at MEDICINE] **:** MEDICINAL

¹**me·dic·i·nal** \məˈdis(ᵊ)nəl, meˈ-, *archaic* ˈmedsənᵊl *or* ˈmedəˈsīnᵊl\ *adj* [ME, fr. MF, fr. L *medicinalis*, fr. *medicina* medicine + *-alis* -al — more at MEDICINE] **1 a :** of or relating to medicine **:** tending to cure disease or relieve pain **:** used as a remedy **:** SANATIVE ⟨where a hot spring gushes forth, possessed, it is claimed, of ~ qualities —*Amer. Guide Series: Texas*⟩ **b :** having wholesome effect **:** SALUTARY ⟨a ~ phrase that he would repeat . . . in all moments of adversity —W.B. Yeats⟩ **2** *archaic* **:** MEDICAL

²**medicinal** \"\ *n* -S **:** a medicinal substance **:** MEDICINE

**medicinal leech** *n* **:** a large European freshwater gnathobdellid leech (*Hirudo medicinalis*) formerly much used by physicians for bleeding patients

**me·dic·i·nal·ly** \-nəlē, -li\ *adv* **:** with medicinal effect or aim **:** in a medicinal manner

**medicinal soft soap** *n* **:** GREEN SOAP

**medicinal wafer** *n* **:** CACHET 3

¹**med·i·cine** \ˈmedəsən, *chiefly Brit* -dsən\ *n* -S [ME *medecine, medicine*, fr. OF, fr. L *medicina*, fr. fem. of *medicinus* of a physician, medical, fr. *medicus* physician + *-inus* -ine — more at MEDICAL] **1 a :** a substance or preparation used in treating disease **b :** a person, agency, or influence that affects well-being ⟨a figure symbolic of strength and perseverance will be good ~ for the whole Western coalition —R.H.Rovere⟩ ⟨he's bad ~ —Zane Grey⟩ **2 :** the science and art dealing with the maintenance of health and the prevention, alleviation, or cure of disease; *sometimes* **:** the branch of this field concerned with the nonsurgical treatment of disease — distinguished from *obstetrics* and *surgery* **3 :** a drug or similar substance (as a potion, poison, or elixir) applied to nonmedical use **4 a :** any of various objects supposed by the No. American Indians to give control over natural or magical forces or to act as a protective or healing charm; *also* **:** magical power or a magical rite **b :** a similar object or agency among other primitive peoples **c :** a potent influence ⟨it's big ~ —Calder Willingham⟩ **syn** see REMEDY

²**medicine** \"\ *vt* -ED/-ING/-S [ME *medecinen, medicinen*, fr. MF *medeciner, mediciner*, fr. *medecine*, medicine, n.] **:** to give medicine to **:** work a medicinal effect on ⟨the mixture was smooth and palatable . . . its gracious flavor *medicined* his mind to an immediate calm —Elinor Wylie⟩

**medicine bag** *n* **:** a bag often made of the skin of an animal patron of an Amerindian people to contain an individual's medicine and worn about the person

**medicine ball** *n* **1 :** a large leather-covered ball stuffed with several pounds of soft material and used for conditioning exercises **2 :** the exercise in which a medicine ball is thrown from one person to another

**medicine bundle** *n* **:** a bundle of sacred objects used in the ceremonies of the Plains Indians

**medicine dance** *n* **:** a ceremonial dance of the Plains Indians performed to obtain supernatural assistance

**medicine dropper** *n* **:** DROPPER 4a

**medicine glass** *n* **:** a small glass vessel graduated (as in ounces, drams, or milliliters) for measuring medicine

**medicine lodge** *n* **1 :** a No. American Indian secret society devoted to the propitiation of supernatural beings **2 :** SWEATHOUSE 1

**medicine man** *n* **1 :** a priestly healer or sorcerer (as among Amerindian peoples) **:** SHAMAN **2 :** the principal of a medicine show

**me·dic·i·ner** \məˈdis(ᵊ)nə(r), ˈmed(ə)sən-\ *n* -S [ME, fr. *medicine* + *-er*] **:** PHYSICIAN ⟨for the spirit there are better ~s —Witter Bynner⟩

**medicine show** *n* **:** a traveling show using entertainers to attract a crowd among which remedies or nostrums are sold ⟨his flowing mustache, fancy vest, and heavy gold chain made him appear more like the proprietor of a traveling *medicine show* than a physician with a permanent address —Willard Robertson⟩ ⟨itinerant *medicine shows* that peddle quinine and patented cures to the farm laborers —*Amer. Guide Series: Ark.*⟩

**medicine song** *n* **:** a song sung by No. American Indians in a ceremony invoking natural or magical powers

**medicine woman** *n* **:** a female healer among No. American Indians

**medick** *var of* MEDIC

**med·i·co** \ˈmedə,kō, -dē,-\ *n* -S [It *medico* or Sp *médico*, both fr. L *medicus* — more at MEDICAL] **1 a :** a medical practitioner **:** PHYSICIAN, SURGEON **b :** a medical student **2 :** SURGEONFISH

**medico-** *comb form* [NL, fr. L *medicus* medical — more at MEDIC] **1 :** medical ⟨*medico*psychology⟩ **2 :** medical and ⟨*medico*dental⟩ ⟨*medico*botanical⟩ ⟨*medico*legal⟩

**med·i·co·legal** \,medə(,)kō, -dē(-+\ *adj* [NL *medico-legalis*, fr. *medico-* + L *legalis* legal — more at LEGAL] **:** of or relating to both medicine and law

**medics** *pl of* MEDIC

**me·di·e·ty** \məˈdīəd·ē\ *n* -ES [ME *medietee*, fr. L *medietas* — more at MOIETY] **1 :** a half or moiety esp. of an ecclesiastical benefice having more than one incumbent **2** *obs* **:** the middle or intermediate part, positon, or quality **b :** a mathematical mean

¹**me·di·e·val** *or* **me·di·ae·val** \,mēdēˈēvəl, ,med-, ,mid-; mēˈdēvəl, məd-, meˈd-\ *adj* [*medi-* + L *aevum* age + E *-al*; after NL *Medium Aevum* middle ages (the period of European history extending roughly from about A.D. 500 to about 1500)] — more at AYE] **1 :** of, relating to, or typical or suggestive of the middle ages or their art, literature, or institutions ⟨watches her daughter fulfill the ~ rites of the coronation —Marjorie Earl⟩ ⟨the town has drowsily gone its ~ way —Richard Joseph⟩ — compare ANCIENT, MODERN **2 :** ANTIQUATED, OUTMODED ⟨displayed a ~ carburetor —Nigel Dennis⟩ — **medie·val·ly** \-vəlē, -li\ *adv*

²**medieval** *or* **mediaeval** \"\ *n* -S **:** a person belonging to medieval times — usu. used in pl. ⟨the short shrift given the ~s is perhaps due to the desire to save space —H.R.Finch⟩

**medie·val·ism** \-və,lizəm\ *n* -S **:** medieval belief or practice **:** the method or spirit of the middle ages **:** devotion to the institutions, arts, and practices of the middle ages; *also* **:** a survival from the middle ages

**medie·val·ist** \-,ləst\ *n* -S **:** a specialist in medieval history and culture **:** a devotee of medievalism **:** one in sympathy with the medieval spirit or with medieval attitudes or institutions **:** a connoisseur of medieval arts — **medie·val·is·tic** \-vəˈlistik, -tēk\ *adj*

**medie·val·ize** \,==ˈēvə,līz\ *vb* -ED/-ING/-S *see -ize in Explan Notes* [*medieval* + *-ize*] *vt* **:** to make medieval **:** to give medieval quality to ~ *vi* **:** to study the middle ages or adopt their spirit or method

**medieval latin** *n, cap M&L* **:** the Latin used esp. for liturgical and literary purposes from the 7th to the 15th centuries inclusive — compare NEW LATIN

**medieval mode** *n* **:** ECCLESIASTICAL MODE

**me·di·fixed** \ˈmēdē+\ *adj* [*medi-* + *fixed*] *bot* **:** attached by the middle

**me·di·glacial** \"+\ *adj* [*medi-* + *glacial*] **:** situated between or in the midst of glaciers

**medii** *pl of* MEDIUS

**me·dim·nus** \məˈdimnəs\ *also* **me·dimn** \-ˈdim\ *n, pl* **medim·ni** \-m,nī\ [L *medimnus*, fr. Gk *medimnos* — more at METE] **:** an ancient Greek unit of capacity equal to about 1½ bushels

**me·din** *or* **me·dine** \məˈdēn\ *n* -S [MF *medin*, fr. Ar *mayyidī*] **:** MEDINO

**me·di·na** \məˈdēnə\ *n* -S [native name in northern Africa] **:** the native quarter of a North African city — compare MELLAH

**me·di·nan** \məˈdīnən\ *adj, usu cap* [*Medina*, N.Y. + E *-an*] **:** of or relating to the lowest division of the No. American Silurian — see GEOLOGIC TIME table

**me·di·na worm** \məˈdēnə-\ *n, usu cap M* [fr. *Médine*, French Sudan] **:** GUINEA WORM

¹**med·i·nese** \,medᵊnˈēz, -ēs\ *adj, usu cap* [fr. *Medina*, Saudi Arabia + E *-ese*] **1 :** of, relating to, or characteristic of Medina, Saudi Arabia **2 :** of, relating to, or characteristic of the people of Medina

²**medinese** \"\ *n, pl* **medinese** *cap* **:** a native or inhabitant of Medina

**med·i·nil·la** \,medᵊnˈilə\ *n, cap* [NL, after José de *Medinilla y Pineda* fl1820 Spanish governor of the Mariana islands] **:** a large genus of tropical Old World shrubs (family Melastomaceae) often grown for ornament and having fleshy leaves and large panicles of white or pink flowers with showy bracts

**me·di·no** \mə'dē(,)nō\ *n* -s [Ar *mayyidī*] **:** an old Egyptian bronze coin worth 1/40 of a piaster; *also* **:** a corresponding unit of value

**me·dio** \'mā(,)dyō\ *n* -s [Sp, fr. *medio*, adj., middle, half, fr. L *medius* — more at MID] **:** a coin representing one half of various Latin-American units of currency; *esp* **:** a half real

**medio-** — see MEDI-

**me·dio·brome** \'mēdēə,brōm\ *n* -s [*medi-* + *brome*, short for *bromoil*] **:** a process for altering tone values, removing distracting parts, and shifting emphasis in monochrome photographic prints by the use of oil paints

**medi·oc·ra·cy** \,mēdē'äkrəsē *sometimes* ,med- *or* -si\ *n* -ES [F *médiocratie*, blend of *médiocre* and *-cratie* -cracy] **:** rule by the mediocre ⟨the aristocracies must go, the *mediocracies* which take their place have to fade out —*Irish Statesman*⟩

**medi·o·cre** \¦mēdē¦ōkə(r) *sometimes* ¦med-\ *adj* [MF, fr. L *mediocris*, lit., halfway up a mountain, fr. *medi-* + *ocris* stony mountain; akin to Umbr *ocar*, *ukar* mountain, Gk *okris* mountaintop, edge, MIr *ochir*, *ochair* edge, L *acer* sharp — more at EDGE] **:** of a middle quality **:** of but a moderate or low degree of excellence **:** INDIFFERENT, ORDINARY ⟨a best seller is the gilded tomb of a ~ talent —L.P.Smith⟩ ⟨a ~ performance⟩ ⟨received a ~ rating⟩ ⟨~ material⟩

**medi·o·crist** \'==,ōkrəst\ *n* -s [*mediocre* + *-ist*] **:** MEDIOCRITY 3

**medi·oc·ri·ty** \,=='äkrəd·ē, -ətē, -i\ *n* -ES [ME *mediocrite*, fr. MF *mediocrité*, fr. L *mediocritat-, mediocritas*, fr. *mediocris* mediocre + *-tat-, -tas*, -ty] **1** *archaic* **:** the quality or state of being intermediate between extremes or a quality, condition, position, or degree that is intermediate: as **a :** moderation of conduct **:** avoidance of excess or extremes **:** TEMPERANCE **b :** ability or endowment in modest degree **c :** modest fortune **:** limited or less than ample means **2 :** average capacity or worth regarded as dull, uninspired, or poor **:** conspicuous lack of distinction or excellence **:** INFERIORITY ⟨not ordinary ~ this, but planned, engineered ~ — and the social engineer's jargon is the measure of it —W.H.Whyte⟩ **3 :** a person of no outstanding distinction ⟨a most intelligent middle-aged ~ —Oscar Wilde⟩ ⟨shone among the *mediocrities* who surrounded him⟩

**me·dio·palatal** \¦mēdēō+\ *adj* [*medi-* + *palatal*] **:** articulated against the middle third of the hard palate or the middle third of the palate as a whole

**¹medio·passive** \"+\ *adj* [ISV *medi-* + *passive*] **:** of, relating to, or being a form or voice of a transitive verb which by origin is of the middle voice or is reflexive and shows by its meaning that it is developing toward passive use, or is used in both middle and passive meanings, or is used only in passive meanings

**²mediopassive** \"\ *n* **:** a mediopassive voice or form

**med·i·tate** \'medə,tāt, *usu* -ād+V\ *vb* -ED/-ING/-S [L *meditatus*, past part. of *meditari* — more at METE] *vt* **1 :** to ponder or reflect on **:** muse over **:** CONSIDER, CONTEMPLATE ⟨*meditating* . . . the scholarly and political achievements of the last eight years —A.W.Levi⟩ **2 :** to plan or project in the mind **:** design in thought **:** INTEND, PURPOSE ⟨only looked at me in a curious sullen way, *meditating* revenge —Francis Yeats-Brown⟩ ⟨*meditated* a quick return —Jane Austen⟩ ~ *vi* **:** to keep the mind in a state of contemplation **:** dwell in thought **:** engage in studious reflection ⟨one would find her *meditating* on the values of poetry —H.V.Gregory⟩; *esp* **:** to practice religious contemplation **syn** see PONDER

**med·i·tat·ing·ly** *adv* **:** in a meditating manner

**med·i·ta·tion** \,medə'tāshən\ *n* -s [ME *meditacioun*, fr. MF *meditation*, fr. L *meditation-, meditatio*, fr. *meditatus* + *-ion-, -io* -ion] **1 :** a spoken or written discourse treated in a contemplative manner and intended to express its author's reflections or esp. when religious to guide others in contemplation **2 :** a private devotion or spiritual exercise consisting in deep continued reflection on a religious theme ⟨~ is very hard work —W.S.Maugham⟩ **3 :** the act of meditating **:** steady or close consecutive reflection **:** continued application of the mind ⟨enforced seclusion has given him opportunity for the ~ out of which this novel has come —Granville Hicks⟩

**med·i·ta·tive** \'==,tād·|iv, -,tət, |t|, |ēv *also* |əv\ *adj* **1 :** disposed or given to meditation ⟨there is much in them for the ~ reader —Eric Linklater⟩ **2 :** marked by, replete with, or conducive to meditation ⟨jar on the ~ silence of the morning —R.L.Stevenson⟩ — **med·i·ta·tive·ly** \-əvlē, -li\ *adv* — **med·i·ta·tive·ness** \-ivnəs, -ēv- *also* -əv-\ *n* -ES

**med·i·tat·or** \-,tād·ə(r), -ātə-\ *n* -s **:** one that meditates

**mediterrane** *also* **mediterraneal** *adj* [*mediterrane* fr. ME *mediterrayne*, fr. MF *mediterrain*, fr. L *mediterraneus*; *mediterraneal* fr. L *mediterraneus* + E *-al*] *obs* **:** INLAND, LANDLOCKED, MEDITERRANEAN

**¹med·i·ter·ra·nean** \,medətə¦rānēən, -nyən\ *adj* [in sense 1, fr. L *mediterraneus*, fr. *medi-* + *-terraneus* (fr. *terra* land); in other senses, fr. the *Mediterranean*, large inland sea enclosed by southern Europe, western Asia and northern Africa — more at TERRACE] **1 :** enclosed or nearly enclosed with land ⟨it is a sea nearly as ~ as that which lies between Africa and Europe —Waldo Frank⟩ **2** *usu cap* **a :** of, relating to, characteristic of, or situated near the Mediterranean sea **b :** of or relating to the peoples or lands about the Mediterranean sea **3** *archaic* **:** situated inland **4** *usu cap* **:** of, relating to, or being the subdivision of the Palaearctic region that includes southern Europe, Persia, Asia Minor, northern Arabia, and Africa north of the Sahara **5** *usu cap* **:** of or relating to the Mediterranean subrace or physical type of the Caucasian race characterized by medium or short stature, slender build, dolichocephaly, and dark complexion — compare ALPINE, ARMENOID, DINARIC, NORDIC

**²mediterranean** \"\ *n* -s [in sense 1, fr. *Mediterranean* sea; in sense 2, fr. ¹*Mediterranean*] **1 :** a landlocked sea **2** *usu cap* **:** a person having Mediterranean physical characteristics

**mediterranean anemia** *n, usu cap M* **:** THALASSEMIA

**mediterranean class** *n, usu cap M* **:** a group of breeds of domestic fowls mostly of Spanish or Italian origin (as the Leghorns, Minorcas, and Andalusians) typically including rather lightweight nervous fowls that produce abundant white eggs — compare ASIATIC CLASS

**mediterranean cypress** *n, usu cap M* **:** ITALIAN CYPRESS

**mediterranean fever** *n, usu cap M* **:** any of several febrile conditions often endemic in parts of the Mediterranean region; *specif* **:** human brucellosis

**mediterranean flour moth** *n, usu cap M* **:** a small largely gray and black nearly cosmopolitan moth (*Anagasta kuehniella*) having a larva that is a destructive pest of processed grain products (as flours or meals)

**mediterranean fruit fly** *n, usu cap M* **:** a two-winged fly (*Ceratitis capitata*) of the family Trypetidae that has black and white markings, is probably native to Africa but is now widely distributed, and has a larva which lives and feeds in ripening fruit

**med·i·ter·ra·ne·an·ize** \,==='rānēə,nīz\ *vt* -ED/-ING/-S *sometimes cap* [¹*Mediterranean* + *-ize*] **:** to give a Mediterranean quality to ⟨one must ~ music, regain nature, gaiety, youth, efficacy —Maurice Boucher⟩

**mediterranean release** *n, usu cap M* **:** an archery release in which arrow and bowstring are drawn with three fingers and the arrow is held between the fore and middle fingers

**mediterraneous** *adj* [L *mediterraneus* — more at MEDITERRANEAN] **1** *obs* **:** INLAND **2** *obs* **:** SUBTERRANEAN

**¹me·di·um** \'mēdēəm\ *n, pl* **mediums** \-dēəmz\ *or* **me·dia** \-dēə\ [L, fr. neut. of *medius* middle — more at MID] **1 :** something lying in a middle or intermediate position: as **a :** a middle way **:** COMPROMISE ⟨try for the happy ~⟩ **b** *archaic* **:** a mathematical mean **c :** the average, usual, or common condition or amount ⟨will be leveled off to a peacetime ~ somewhere between its present employment of 7000 and its pre-Korean War level of 2500 —*Springfield (Mass.) Daily News*⟩ **2** *archaic* **:** the middle term of a syllogism **3 :** something through or by which something is accomplished, conveyed, or carried on: as **a :** a substance (as air or ether) regarded as the means of transmission of a force or effect ⟨air is the ~ that conveys sound⟩ **b :** a condition, atmosphere, or environment in which something may function or flourish ⟨a more finely perfected ~ in which . . . feelings are at liberty —T.S.Eliot⟩ **c :** an intermediate or direct instrumentality or means ⟨affirmed that the historic church was the ~ of a continuous revelation —Stringfellow Barr⟩ ⟨cattlemen seeking a ~ to combat horse thieves —R.A.Billington⟩; *esp* **:** a channel, method, or system of communication, information, or entertainment ⟨a book needs the widest possible discussion in the reviewing *media* of the country — whether magazine, newspaper, radio, television, or public platform —*Saturday Rev.*⟩ **d** *media pl but sometimes sing in constr* **:** a vehicle (as a radio or television program or a newspaper) used to carry advertising **4 a :** a proper setting or natural environment ⟨factors involved that make this slightly contaminated water better for young goldfish than a clean ~ —W.C.Allee⟩ **b :** an appropriate occupation or means of expression **:** an activity or field in which one is at home **:** MÉTIER ⟨the work of extraction and arrangement was the true ~ of the monastic scholars —R.W.Southern⟩ **5 :** a person through whom a purpose is accomplished **:** GO-BETWEEN, AGENT, INTERMEDIARY ⟨the ~ of introduction was no doubt . . . the publisher —Richard Garnett †1906⟩ **6 :** MEDIUM OF EXCHANGE **7 :** an individual through whom other persons seek to communicate with the spirits of the dead and who is held by such persons to be a channel of communication between the earthly world of the living and a nontemporal spiritual realm of the departed — compare AUTOMATIST 2b, SPIRITUALISM **8** *pl media* **a :** any nutrient system for the artificial cultivation of bacteria or other organisms or cells that is sometimes a simple substance but more commonly a complex of inorganic and organic materials in a fluid base or one rendered more or less solid by coagulation or by the addition of gelatin or agar — called also *nutrient medium* **b :** any of many fluids or solids in which organic structures are placed (as for preservation or mounting) **9 a :** the material or technical means for artistic expression (as paint and canvas, lithographic or sculptural stone, or literary or musical form) ⟨one can't have imagination until one has a ~ by which it can be expressed —J.D.Cook⟩ ⟨as his literary ~ he has chosen a biographical form which I have ventured to describe elsewhere as that of the walkie-talkie —Ernest Newman⟩ **b :** a liquid (as oil or water) with which pigment is mixed by a painter **10 :** a size of paper usu. 23x18 in. or 22x 17½ in. **11 :** a varnish spread upon the surface or back of a photographic negative before retouching or upon the surface of a print before oil coloring **12 :** a color filter used in theatrical stage lighting **13 :** a material (as paper, cloth, or activated carbon) on which solids are deposited in chemical filtration **syn** see MEAN

**²medium** \"\ *adj* **:** intermediate in amount, quality, position, or degree **:** AVERAGE, MEAN ⟨taxation reform helpful to the low and ~ income groups followed —*Collier's Yr. Bk.*⟩ ⟨a man of ~ height⟩ ⟨bake in a ~ oven⟩ ⟨the only car in the ~ field —*advt*⟩

**medium artillery** *n* **1 :** guns of greater than 105 mm. caliber but less than 155 mm. and howitzers of greater than 105 mm. caliber up to and including 155 mm. **2 :** troops that serve medium artillery

**medium bomber** *n* **:** a bomber of intermediate weight and range designed primarily to carry big bomb loads to strategic targets — compare HEAVY BOMBER, LIGHT BOMBER

**medium chrome green** *n* **:** a green that is yellower and duller than holly green (sense 1) or golf green, yellower and less strong than average hunter green, and stronger and slightly lighter than deep chrome green

**medium chrome yellow** *n* **:** DEEP CHROME YELLOW

**medium frequency** *n* **:** a radio frequency in the range between low and high frequencies of the radio spectrum — abbr *mf*; see RADIO FREQUENCY table

**medium gray** *n* **:** MEDIAN GRAY

**me·di·um·is·tic** \¦mēdēə¦mistik\ *adj* **:** of, relating to, or having the qualities of a spiritualistic medium ⟨this moving of objects at a distance and without contact is one of the commonest happenings at a ~ séance —G.H.Estabrooks⟩

**medium-laid** \'===¦=\ *adj* **:** having the strands twisted with a tightness between that of hard-laid and that of soft-laid rope

**medium lay** *n* **:** a rope lay that combines some of the wear-resistant quality of hard lay with some of the tensile strength of soft lay — called also *regular lay*

**medium of exchange :** something commonly accepted in exchange for goods and services and recognized as representing a standard of value — see CIRCULATING MEDIUM, MONEY

**me·di·um·ship** \'mēdēəm,ship\ *n* **:** the capacity, function, or profession of a spiritualistic medium ⟨his friends had been sitting weekly about a table in the hope of spiritual manifestation and one had developed ~ —W.B.Yeats⟩

**medium shot** *n* **:** a motion-picture shot made from or as if from a distance intermediate between that of a long shot and that of a close shot and showing a moderate amount of background

**medium-term** \'===¦=\ *adj* **:** of or relating to a financial gain, loss, operation, or obligation based on a term of more than a year and usu. not more than 10 years

**me·di·us** \'mēdēəs\ *n, pl* **me·dii** \-dē,ī\ [NL, fr. L, adj., middle — more at MID] **:** the middle finger

**med·ize** \'mē,dīz\ *vb* -ED/-ING/-S *often cap* [²*Mede* + *-ize*] *vt, archaic* **:** to give a Median quality to **:** make Median ~ *vi, archaic* **:** to become Median in character **:** favor the Medes

**¹med·lar** \'medlə(r)\ *n* -s [ME *medeler*, fr. MF *meslier*, *medlier* medlar tree, fr. *mesle*, *medle* medlar (fruit), fr. L *mespilum*, *mespilus*, *mespila*, fr. Gk *mespilon*] **1 a :** a small Eurasian tree (*Mespilus germanica*) that is widely cultivated esp. in Europe **b :** the fruit of this tree resembling a crabapple and a much-used base for preserves **2 :** LOQUAT **3 a :** a small deciduous tree (*Vangueria infausta*) of southern Africa with few branches, with twigs and opposite leaves covered with velvety hairs, and with small greenish yellow flowers **b :** the globose fruit of this tree which has a leathery skin that is brown when ripe and a pithy flesh of a sweet-acid flavor

**²medlar** \"\ *n* -s [by shortening and alter.] **:** MEADOWLARK

**¹med·ley** \'medlē, -li\ *n* -s [ME *medle*, fr. MF *meslee*, *mesdlee*, *medlee*, fr. fem. of *meslé*, *mesdlé*, *medlé*, past part. of *mesler*, *mesdler*, *medler* to mix, quarrel, fight — more at MEDDLE] **1** *archaic* **:** COMBAT, MELEE **2 a** *archaic* **:** COMBINATION, MINGLING **b :** a heterogeneous mixture **:** HODGEPODGE, JUMBLE, MÉLANGE ⟨has a wood-smoke flavor along with the ~ of other tastes —Molly L. Bar-David⟩ ⟨his mind was confused with a ~ of thoughts —Wilson Collison⟩ ⟨a ~ of oil cans, empty cracker boxes, and whiskey bottles, loose spokes of cartwheels —Ellen Glasgow⟩ **3** *archaic* **:** a varicolored cloth of wool dyed in the raw **4 a** *archaic* **:** a musical composition put together of passages ill-matched in style or form **b :** a performance blending together a series of songs or other musical pieces ⟨a ~ of service songs —Virgil Thomson⟩ ⟨a piano ~⟩ **5** *archaic* **:** a literary miscellany

**²medley** \"\ *adj* [ME *medle*, fr. *medle*, n.] **1 a** *obs* **:** of a mixed color **:** MOTLEY **b** *archaic* **:** of, relating to, or consisting of medley cloth **2** *archaic* **:** of, relating to, or making up a confused or miscellaneous assemblage **:** MIXED

**³medley** \"\ *vt* **medleyed** *or* **medlied; medleyed** *or* **medlied; medleying; medleys** [¹*medley*] *archaic* **:** to make a medley of **:** MIX, MINGLE

**medley relay** *n* **1 :** a swimming relay race in which each member of a team of three or four uses a different stroke **2 :** a foot race in which each member of a relay team runs a different distance

**medo-** *comb form, usu cap* [Gk *mēdo-*, fr. *Mēdos* Mede, Median] **:** Median and ⟨*Medo*-Persian⟩ ⟨*Medo*-Scythian⟩

**mé·doc** \(')mā¦däk\ *n* -s *usu cap* [F, fr. *Médoc*, district in southwestern France] **:** a Bordeaux wine made in the Médoc district of France — compare BORDEAUX

**med·rick** \'medrik\ *n* -s [origin unknown] **:** a small gull or tern

**med·ri·na·que** \,medrən'yäkē, -rə'nä-\ *n* -s [Sp *medriñaque*] **1 :** a fiber from the sago palm in the Philippines **2 :** a cloth made from medrinaque fiber

**me·dul·la** \mə'dələ,me'-\ *n, pl* **medullas** \-ləz\ *or* **medul·lae** \-,lē\ [L; perh. akin to OE *smeoru*, *smeru* fat, grease — more at SMEAR] **1** *obs, pl medullas* **a :** the essence or pith of a matter **b :** COMPENDIUM, SUMMARY **2** *pl medullae* **a :** marrow of bone or spinal cord **b** [NL, fr. L] **:** MEDULLA OBLONGATA **3** [NL, fr. L] **a :** the inner or deep part of an organ or structure (as of a hair or kidney) **b :** the sheath of some nerve fibers **4** *pl medullae, archaic* **:** PITH **5** [NL, fr. L] **a :** the medullary layer of lichens **b :** the inner spongy layer of some fungi **c :** the central core of elongate colorless cells of the thalli of some brown algae **6** [NL, fr. L] **:** the internal portion of some protozoans

**medulla ob·lon·ga·ta** \-,ä,blȯŋ'gäd·ə\ *n, pl* **medulla oblongatas** *or* **medullae oblonga·tae** \-äd·,ē\ [NL, lit., oblong medulla] **:** the somewhat pyramidal last part of the vertebrate brain developed from the posterior portion of the rhombencephalon and continuous posteriorly with the spinal cord, enclosing the fourth ventricle, and containing nuclei associated with most of the cranial nerves, major fiber tracts and decussations that link spinal with higher centers, and various centers mediating the control of involuntary vital functions (as respiration) — see BRAIN illustration

**med·ul·lary** \,medᵊl,erē, 'mejə,le-, mə'dələrē, -ri\ *also* **me·dul·lar** \mə'dələ(r)\ *adj* [L *medullaris*, fr. *medulla* marrow + *-aris* -ar] **1 a :** of or relating to the medulla of any body part or organ **b :** containing, consisting of, or resembling marrow **c :** of or relating to the medulla oblongata or the spinal cord **d :** of, relating to, or formed of the dorsally located embryonic ectoderm destined to sink below the surface and become neural tissue **2 :** of, relating to, or composed of the pith of a plant **3 :** like marrow in consistency — used of cancers

**medullary bundle** *n* **:** a vascular bundle (as in plants of the family Umbelliferae) situated in the peripheral part of the pith of a stem and sometimes held to be an extension of a leaf trace

**medullary canal** *or* **medullary cavity** *n* **1 :** MEDULLARY GROOVE **2 :** the marrow cavity of a bone

**medullary fold** *n* **:** NEURAL FOLD

**medullary groove** *or* **medullary furrow** *n* **:** the median dorsal longitudinal groove formed in the vertebrate embryo by the medullary plate after appearance of the neural folds — called also *neural groove*

**medullary layer** *n* **:** the layer of loosely interwoven threads just below the algal layer in some lichens

**medullary nailing** *n* **:** the fixing of a fractured long bone by inserting a steel nail into the marrow cavity of the bone

**medullary plate** *n* **:** the longitudinal dorsal zone of epiblast in the early vertebrate embryo that constitutes the primordium of the neural tissue

**medullary ray** *n* **1 :** a ray of primary origin in the stele of various cryptogamous and dicotyledonous vascular plants that extends outward from the medulla often separating the vascular bundles — compare VASCULAR RAY **2 :** VASCULAR RAY

**medullary sheath** *n* **1 :** the layer of myelin surrounding a medullated nerve fiber **2 :** the outer layers of smaller usu. thick-walled cells that merge into the central pithy part of the core of many plant stems

**medullary spot** *n* **:** a small spot of irregularly arranged cells appearing as a scar in wood injured by insect boring

**medullary tube** *n* **:** NEURAL TUBE

**medullary velum** *n* **:** a thin white plate of nervous tissue forming part of the roof of the fourth ventricle

**med·ul·lat·ed** \'medᵊl,ād·əd, 'mejə,lā-, mə'dələ,lā-\ *adj* [LL *medullatus* having a marrow (fr. L *medulla* marrow + *-atus* -ate) + E *-ed* — more at MEDULLA] **1** *of a nerve fiber* **:** having a medullary sheath **2** *of other fibers* **:** having a medulla ⟨kempy wool contains many coarse ~ fibers⟩

**med·ul·la·tion** \,medᵊl'āshən, ,mejə'lā-\ *n* -s [*medulla* + *-ation*] **1 :** the formation of a medullary sheath or medulla **2 :** the condition of being medullated — used esp. of fibers but sometimes of animals (as sheep)

**me·dul·li·spinal** \mə¦dəlē+\ *adj* [*medulla* + *-i-* + *spinal*] **:** relating to the spinal cord

**me·dul·lo·blas·to·ma** \mə,dəlō,blas'tōmə\ *n, pl* **medullo-blastomas** \-məz\ *or* **medulloblastoma·ta** \-məd·ə\ [NL, fr. *medullo-* (fr. L *medulla*) + *blast-* + NL *-oma*] **:** a malignant tumor of the central nervous system arising in the cerebellum esp. in children

**medus-** *or* **medusi-** *comb form* [ISV, fr. NL *medusa*] **:** Medusa ⟨*medusi*ferous⟩ ⟨*medus*oid⟩

**me·du·sa** \mə'd(y)üsə *sometimes* -üzə\ *n, pl* **medu·sae** \-(,)sē, -(,)zē\ [NL *Medusa*, a Linnéan genus of jellyfish, after *Medusa*, one of the three Gorgons, fr. L, fr. Gk *Medousa*] **:** JELLYFISH; *esp* **:** a small hydrozoan jellyfish

**medusa bud** *n* **:** one of the buds of a hydroid destined to develop into a gonophore or medusa

**me·du·sal** \-səl, -zəl\ *adj* [*medus-* + *-al*] **:** MEDUSAN

**¹me·du·san** \-sᵊn, -zᵊn\ *adj* [*medus-* + *-an*] **:** of, relating to, or like a medusa

**²medusan** \"\ *n* -s **:** MEDUSA

**medusa's head** *n* [after *Medusa*, one of the three Gorgons, whose hair was said to have been turned into snakes] **1 :** an edible hedgehog mushroom (*Hydnum caput-medusae*) with interwoven hymenial spines **2 :** an African euphorbia (*Euphorbia caput-medusae*) with numerous drooping slender branches **3 :** a weedy rye grass (*Elymus caput-medusae*) having long bristling awns

**¹me·du·soid** \mə'd(y)ü,sȯid,-,zȯid\ *adj* [*medus-* + *-oid*] **:** like a medusa

**²medusoid** \"\ *n* -s **:** a hydroid gonophore resembling a medusa

**mee·bos** \'mē,bäs\ *var of* MEBOS

**meech** \'mēch\ *vi* -ED/-ING/-ES [ME *muchen*, *michen*, *mechen* to steal, skulk, prob. fr. ONF *muchier* to hide, lurk] **1** *now dial* **a :** to move in a furtive or cringing manner **:** SKULK, SNEAK **b :** to play truant **2** *now dial* **:** to complain in an ailing or peevish manner **:** WHINE

**meech·er** \-chə(r)\ *n* -s [ME *mucher*, *micher*, *mecher*, thief, pander, fr. *muchen*, *michen*, *mechen* + *-er*] **1** *now dial* **:** one that sneaks about or behaves dishonestly or dishonorably **:** PANDER, THIEF **2** *now dial* **:** TRUANT

**meeching** *adj* [fr. pres. part. of ¹*meech*] *now dial* **:** CRINGING, SNEAKY, WHINING ⟨not going to have you do anything that will make you feel ~ afterward —W.D.Howells⟩

**meed** \'mēd\ *n* -s [ME *med*, *meed*, fr. OE *mēd*; akin to OE *meord* recompense, reward, wage, OS *mēda*, OHG *miata*, *mieta*, Goth *mizdo*, Gk *misthos*, OSlav *mĭzda*, *mŭzda* reward, Skt *mīḍha* prize, reward, contest] **1 a** *archaic* **:** the reward or wage earned by labor, service, or merit ⟨service . . . needs a receiver as well as a giver and thrives on some small ~ of welcome or honor —Freya Stark⟩ ⟨as long as slugs abound in the garden, good carbolic acid should not lack its ~ of honor —C.E.Montague⟩ **b :** the proper prize of excellence or fine performance **:** fitting return ⟨pay my ~ of tribute to him —Edna R. Johnson⟩ ⟨the old man loves us and we give him the ~ of our admiration —*Western Folklore*⟩ ⟨might pay, to the dead impresario, the ~ of parting tears —J.B.Cabell & A.J. Hanna⟩ **c :** just desert **:** fit recompense ⟨had suffered the ~ of his inhospitable conduct —G.B.Shaw⟩ **d :** AMOUNT, PORTION ⟨the plants of the jungle won success . . . by adapting their needs to the starvation ~ of air and light —William Beebe⟩ ⟨breed their own small ~ of juvenile delinquency —Sean O'Faolain⟩ **2** *archaic* **:** bribery offered or received **:** illicit gain **3** *obs* **:** MERIT, WORTH

**¹meek** \'mēk\ *adj* -ER/-EST [ME *meoc*, *mek*, *meek*, of Scand origin; akin to ON *mjūkr* soft, gentle — more at MUCUS] **1 :** manifesting patience and long-suffering **:** enduring injury without resentment **:** MILD ⟨~ as a mouse —Langston Hughes⟩ ⟨no longer the ~, soft native girl, but a determined woman —W.S.Maugham⟩ **2 :** deficient in spirit and courage **:** SUBMISSIVE, TAME ⟨a fine, fiery blast against ~ conformity —Orville Prescott⟩ **3 :** not violent or strong **:** GENTLE, MODERATE, WEAK ⟨~ rivulet —Green Peyton⟩ **syn** see HUMBLE

**²meek** \"\ *vt* -ED/-ING/-S [ME *meoken*, *meken*, fr. *meoc*, *mek*, *meek*, adj.] **:** HUMBLE, TAME ⟨man himself, ~*ed* by his Creator, may when tamed and taught, share the divine life —Anne Fremantle⟩

**³meek** *adv* [ME *meke*, fr. *meoc*, *mek*, *meek*, adj.] *obs* **:** MEEKLY

**meek·en** \'mēkən\ *vb* -ED/-ING/-S [ME *meknen*, fr. *mek*, adj. + *-nen* -en] *vt* **:** ²MEEK ~ *vi* **:** to become meek

**meek·ly** *adv* [ME *meocliche*, *mekly*, fr. *meoc*, *mek* + *-liche*, *-ly* -ly] **:** in a meek manner

**meek·ness** *n* -ES [ME *meocnesse*, *meknesse*, fr. *meoc*, *mek* + *-nesse* -ness] **:** the quality or state of being meek **:** HUMILITY

**mee·mies** \'mēmēz, -miz\ *n pl but sing in constr* [by shortening] **:** SCREAMING MEEMIES ⟨you get the ~ when you're shut up in a tight spot —F.L.Harvey⟩

**meen** \'mēn\ *Scot var of* MOON

**meer·kat** *or* **mier·kat** \'mi(ə)r,kat\ *n* -s [Afrik *meerkat*, fr. D, a kind of monkey, fr. MD *meercatte* monkey, fr. *meer* sea + *catte* cat; fr. the fact that monkeys came to Europe from overseas] **1** : any of several mongooses; *esp* : a mongoose (*Cynictis penicillata*) of southern Africa **2** : SURICATE

**meer·schaum** \'mi(ə)rshəm, -iəsh-, -,shȯm\ *n* -s [G, a species of Alcyonacea, meerschaum, fr. *meer* sea + *schaum* froth, foam] **1** : a mineral $Mg_3Si_4O_{10}(OH)_2.4H_2O$ consisting of a hydrous magnesium silicate that is an extremely light fine soft white clayey material used for tobacco pipes and dug chiefly in Asia Minor (hardness 2–2.5, sp. gr. 2) — called also *sepiolite* **2** : a tobacco pipe made of meerschaum **3** : GRAVEL 3

**mee·rut** \'mērət, 'mir-\ *adj, usu cap* [fr. *Meerut*, India] : of or from the city of Meerut, India : of the kind or style prevalent in Meerut

**meer·wein-ponn·dorf reaction** \,me(ə)r,vīn'pän,dȯrf-\ *n, usu cap M&P* [after Hans *Meerwein* and Wolfgang *Ponndorf*, 20th cent. Ger. chemists] : the reduction of an aldehyde or ketone to the corresponding alcohol by reaction with boiling isopropyl alcohol in the presence of aluminum isopropoxide — compare OPPENAUER OXIDATION

**¹meet** \'mēt, *usu* -ēd.+V\ *vb* **met** \'met, *usu* -ed.+V\ **met; meeting; meets** [ME *meten*, fr. OE *mētan*; akin to OE & OS *mōt* meeting, assembly, OS *mōtian* to meet, OHG *muoz* meeting, ON *mæta* to meet, Goth *gamotjan* to meet, Arm *matčim* I approach] *vt* **1 a** : to come by accident into the presence of : fall in with : come upon : FIND ⟨*met* him as a stranger on a railroad journey⟩ **b** : to come near or in touch with by approach from another direction ⟨the whole delegation went to ~ them at the terminal⟩ **c** : to come into contact or conjunction with : JOIN ⟨there the brook ~*s* the river⟩ **d** : to present a sense impression to : impinge on : CATCH ⟨a brazen roar ~*s* the ear⟩ ⟨a pungent odor . . . *met* his nostrils —S.E. White⟩ **2** : to collide with : encounter as antagonist or foe : fight, cope, or grapple with : OPPOSE ⟨*met* the heavyweight contender in a successful bout⟩ **3** : to join (a person) in conversation, discussion, or social or business intercourse : enter into conference, argument, or personal dealings with **4** : to conform to the wishes or opinions of ⟨expressed willingness to ~ him on that point⟩ **5** : to discharge or pay fully : SATISFY, SETTLE ⟨could not ~ his loans —Waldo Frank⟩ ⟨did we ~ the costs —E.R.Leibert⟩ **6** : to contend successfully with : cope with : MATCH ⟨true imaginative teaching arises to ~ the situation of the moment —A.E.Wier⟩ ⟨refiners of branded gasoline *met* the offer —S.M.Loescher⟩ ⟨this problem was *met* and solved —W.D.Leggett⟩ **7** : to provide for : FILL, FULFILL ⟨natural resources . . . to ~ human needs —John Boyd Orr⟩ ⟨public and private agencies labored to ~ a critical housing shortage⟩ ⟨studied diligently to ~ the entrance requirements of his college⟩ **8** : to be introduced to or make acquainted with ⟨an attractive sister I want you to ~⟩ ~ *vi* **1 a** : to come together usu. from different directions : come face to face ⟨it was in that unpropitious place they *met*⟩ **b** : to hold a session : convene for worship, business, or other purpose : ASSEMBLE, CONGREGATE ⟨the city council will ~ soon to deal with the issue⟩ **2** : to join as contestants, opponents, or enemies ⟨the candidates *met* on many platforms to debate⟩ **3** : to form a junction or confluence : follow or enter an identical course ⟨at last the two rails *met* and the golden spikes were driven —Meridel Le Sueur⟩ **4** : to occur or appear together : UNITE ⟨many graces and many virtues ~ in her⟩

**syn** FACE, ENCOUNTER, CONFRONT: MEET, in the basic sense pertinent here, usu. implies no more than to come into the presence or company of whether by chance or design ⟨*meet* a stranger in the woods⟩ ⟨the event of my last visit to the mountain was *meeting* one of these brilliant creatures near the summit, in full song —John Burroughs⟩ ⟨as gruesome a sight as a man could *meet* in a lifetime —Marcia Davenport⟩ ⟨arrange to *meet* a friend at 2 o'clock⟩ ENCOUNTER usu. confines the meeting to one by accident or chance ⟨walked the whole of the six or seven miles . . . without *encountering* a soul —Compton Mackenzie⟩ ⟨personal reminiscences of actual incidents and people *encountered* during his 20 years of active sea life —R.W.Stallman⟩ ⟨troops moving westward by a parallel trail *encountered* the river and were delayed —*Amer. Guide Series: Fla.*⟩ ⟨this emigration *encountered* a number of obstacles —*Collier's Yr. Bk.*⟩ CONFRONT and FACE both imply a direct, usu. square, meeting in opposition. CONFRONT stresses the unavoidable, face-to-face nature of the meeting ⟨the basic question *confronting* the court —Douglass Cater⟩ ⟨the major problem *confronting* humanity —G.E.Hutchinson⟩ ⟨stared appalled at what *confronted* me —H.D.Quillin⟩ often, when the subject is personal, suggesting such a meeting resolutely entered into out of a determination to face a difficulty or settle a matter ⟨one of the most arduous tasks a conductor can *confront* —Irving Kolodin⟩ ⟨a man who can *confront* misfortune —W.S.White⟩ ⟨*confront* toil and danger —Sir Winston Churchill⟩ FACE emphasizes more the resoluteness, often courageousness, of the meeting as with something one might reasonably hesitate or dislike to meet ⟨not to avoid but to *face* the enemy⟩ ⟨the difficulties *faced* by the new government —H.C.Atyeo⟩ ⟨the government *faces* a strong storm of protest over its decision —*Current History*⟩ ⟨the ordeal he must now prepare to *face* —B.A.Williams⟩ ⟨a great many young men . . . are unwilling to *face* four years of college —*Nichols Junior College Catalogue*⟩ **syn** see in addition SATISFY

— **meet her** : to use the rudder to check the swing of a ship's head in a turn — **meet one halfway** : to make concessions to : compromise with ⟨the valley *meets him* more than *halfway* in his efforts to take the chance out of vegetable growing —*Monsanto Mag.*⟩ — **meet up with** : to encounter by chance — **meet with 1** : to come upon : FIND **2** : to join in company with **3** : to be subjected to (fortune or vicissitude) : UNDERGO, EXPERIENCE **4** *obs* : to encounter as an enemy : grapple or cope with : OPPOSE

**²meet** \"\ *n* -s **1 a** : an assembling of men and hounds for a hunt **b** : a sports meeting consisting of competitive events esp. in track and field, swimming, or gymnastics contested by individuals and often by relay or other teams **c** : a sports contest of any of various other kinds ⟨basketball ~⟩ ⟨trapshooters' ~⟩ ⟨sports car ~⟩ **d** : a festival or competition of any of various other kinds ⟨singing ~⟩ **2 a** : the passage or point of passage of two trains traveling in opposite directions **b** : the point on a single track at which one train must take a siding to permit another to pass in the opposite direction **3** *Austral* : ASSIGNATION

**³meet** \"\ *adj* [ME *mete*, fr. OE *gemǣte*; akin to OHG *māza* moderation, suitability, manner, *māzi* suitable, ON *mætr* valuable, worthy, *māt* moderation, Goth *usmet* way of life, *mitan* to measure — more at METE] **1** *archaic* : close, exact, or scant in measure or size **2** : SUITABLE, FIT, PROPER, APPROPRIATE ⟨he had been gradually growing more and more vile and ~ to be exterminated —Arnold Bennett⟩ **syn** see FIT

**⁴meet** *adv* [ME *mete*, fr. *mete*, adj.] *obs* : in a suitable manner : FITLY, SUFFICIENTLY

**meet·er** \'mēd·ə(r), -ētə-\ *n* -s : one that meets or attends a meeting

**meethelp** *also* **meethelper** *n* [³*meet* + *help*] *obs* : HELPMATE

**¹meeting** *n* -s [ME, fr. gerund of *meten* to meet — more at MEET] : an act or process of coming together: as **a** *archaic* : DUEL **b** : a chance or planned encounter ⟨his first ~ with the man in many years⟩ **c** (1) : an assembly for religious worship ⟨attended ~ on Sunday⟩ ⟨stood in the dark across the road from a Negro church where they were holding ~ —Edwin Granberry⟩ (2) *dial Eng* : a congregation of religious dissenters or their house of worship (3) : the permanent governing organization of a congregation of the Society of Friends or that of a regional group of congregations **d** : a gathering for business, social, or other purposes ⟨a ~ of the board of directors⟩ ⟨a ~ of Congress⟩ **e** : a horse or dog-racing session extending for a stated term of days at one track ⟨begins the metropolitan racing season with a 21-day ~ in April —*Amer. Guide Series: N. Y. City*⟩ **f** : CONFLUENCE, INTERSECTION, JUNCTION ⟨the ~ of two great rivers⟩ **g** : a place of meeting **h** : a joint in carpentry or masonry

**²meeting** *adj* [fr. pres. part. of ¹*meet*] **1** : that meets : marked by or used for meeting **2** *obs* : RESPONSIVE ⟨immortal verse such as the ~ soul may pierce —John Milton⟩

**meeting engagement** *n* : a collision between two advancing military forces neither of which is fully deployed for battle

**meet·ing·er** \'mēt°nə(r), -tiŋə-\ *n* -s [¹*meeting* + -*er*] *dial Eng* : a member of a nonconformist church or chapel ⟨to be a ~, you must go to chapel in all winds and weathers —Thomas Hardy⟩

**meetinghouse** \'==,=\ *n* **1** : a building used for public assembly; *esp* : the house of worship of any of various Protestant denominations **2 meetinghouses** *pl* : COLUMBINE 1a

**meeting of minds** : full agreement : CONCORD, HARMONY ⟨men . . . must make many adjustments before any *meeting of minds* is possible —Mark Starr⟩

**meeting of the minds** : assent by contracting parties to an agreement established as understood by both in the same sense as to terms, conditions, and subject matter

**meeting rail** *n* : the horizontal rail of a vertical sliding sash which meets the corresponding rail of the adjacent sash

**meeting seed** *n* [¹*meeting*] : any of various aromatic seeds or small fruits formerly chewed in an effort to stay awake during religious services

**meet·ly** *adv* : FITLY, PROPERLY, SUITABLY

**meet·ness** *n* -ES [ME *metenes*, fr. *mete* meet + -*nes* -ness — more at MEET] *archaic* : the quality or state of being meet

**meets** *pres 3d sing of* MEET, *pl of* MEET

**¹meg** \'meg\ *n* -s *usu cap* [fr. *Meg*, nickname for *Margaret*] *chiefly Scot* : WOMAN: as **a** : a country girl **b** : a coarse boisterous woman

**²meg** \"\ *n* -s [origin unknown] **1** *obs* : GUINEA **2 a** *dial Brit* : HALFPENNY **b** *slang* : a one-cent piece : PENNY

**³meg** \"\ *n* -s [by shortening] : MEGAPHONE

**⁴meg** \"\ *vb* **megged; megged; megging; megs** : MEGAPHONE

**meg** *abbr* megohm

**mega-** *or* **meg-** *comb form* [Gk, fr. *megas* large, great, strong — more at MUCH] **1 a** : great : large ⟨*mega*bacterium⟩ ⟨*mega*spore⟩ : powerful ⟨*mega*scope⟩ : of the major order ⟨*mega*diastrophism⟩ ⟨*mega*mutation⟩ : enlarged ⟨*mega*type⟩ or abnormally enlarged ⟨*mega*duodenum⟩ ⟨*mega*esophagus⟩ **b** : having a (specified) part of large size ⟨*mega*dont⟩ ⟨*mega*gnathous⟩ **c** : capable of being distinguished or identified without the aid of the microscope ⟨*mega*breccia⟩ ⟨*mega*fossil⟩ ⟨*mega*phenocryst⟩ **2** : a million of : multiplied by one million ⟨*meg*ohm⟩ ⟨*mega*lumen⟩ ⟨*meg*ampere⟩

**megacaryocyte** *var of* MEGAKARYOCYTE

**mega·ce·phal·ic** \¦megəsə¦falik\ *also* **mega·ceph·a·lous** \¦==¦sefələs\ *adj* [*mega-* + *-cephalic*, *-cephalous*] : large-headed; *specif* : having a cranial capacity in excess of the mean — **mega·ceph·a·ly** \,==¦sefəlē\ *n* -ES

**me·gac·e·ros** \mə'gasə,räs\ [NL, fr. *mega-* + *-ceros* (fr. Gk *keras* horn) — more at HORN] *syn of* MEGALOCEROS

**mega·chi·le** \,megə'kī(,)lē\ *n, cap* [NL, fr. *mega-* + *-chile* (fr. Gk *cheilos* lip) — more at GILL] : a genus (the type of the family Megachilidae) of leaf-cutting bees including some that are important pollinators of alfalfa and other legumes

**¹mega·chi·lid** \¦==¦kīləd\ *adj* [NL *Megachilidae*] : of or relating to the Megachilidae

**²megachilid** \"\ *n* -s [NL *Megachilidae*] : a bee of the family Megachilidae

**mega·chil·i·dae** \,==¦kilə,dē\ *n pl, cap* [NL, fr. *Megachile*, type genus + *-idae*] : a family of bees comprising rather large usu. dark-colored solitary leaf-cutting and mason bees — see MEGACHILE

**mega·chiroptera** \¦==+\ *n pl, cap* [NL, fr. *mega-* + *Chiroptera*] : a suborder of Chiroptera comprising the large powerful Old World fruit bats that are distinguished by smooth-crowned molars and a claw on the index finger — **mega·chiropteran** \"+\ *adj or n* — **mega·chiropterous** \"+\ *adj*

**mega·colon** \'==,=\ *n* [ISV *mega-* + *colon*] : great often congenital dilation of the colon — compare HIRSCHSPRUNG'S DISEASE

**mega·cosm** \'megə,käzəm\ *n* -s [Gk *mega-* (fr. *megas* large, great) + E *-cosm* — more at MUCH] : MACROCOSM

**mega·curie** \¦==+\ *n* [*mega-* + *curie*] : one million curies

**mega·cycle** \'==,=\ *n* [*mega-* + *cycle*] : one million cycles; *esp* : one million cycles per second used as a unit of radio frequency — abbr *mc*

**mega·der·mat·i·dae** \,==(,)dər'mad·ə,dē\ *n pl, cap* [NL, fr. *Megadermat-*, *Megaderma*, type genus (fr. *mega-* + *-derma*) + *-idae*] : a family of tropical Old World carnivorous bats with large ears united across the forehead, a large nose leaf, and no external tail — see BIG-EARED BAT, FALSE VAMPIRE BAT

**mega·der·mi·dae** \,=='dərmə,dē\ [NL, fr. *Megaderma* + *-idae*] *syn of* MEGADERMATIDAE

**mega·dont** \'==,dänt\ *adj* [irreg. fr. *mega-* + *-odont*] : MACRODONT — **mega·dont·ism** \-n,tizəm\ *n* -s — **mega·don·ty** \-ntē\ *n* -ES

**mega·dri·li** \,=='drī,lī\ *n pl, cap* [NL, fr. *mega-* + *-drili* (fr. Gk *drilos* earthworm)] *in some classifications* : a group of Oligochaeta comprising relatively large predominantly terrestrial worms that have a capillary network on the nephridium and being nearly coextensive with Neoligochaeta — compare MICRODRILI

**mega·dynamics** \¦==+\ *n pl but often sing in constr* [*mega-* + *dynamics*] : the mechanics of major earth movements

**mega·evolution** \"+\ *n* [*mega-* + *evolution*] : MACROEVOLUTION — **mega·evolutionary** \"+\ *adj*

**mega·fauna** \"+\ *n* [NL, fr. *mega-* + *fauna*] : MACROFAUNA 2 — used chiefly in paleontology — **megafaunal** *adj*

**mega·fossil** \"+\ *n* [*mega-* + *fossil*] : MACROFOSSIL

**mega·gamete** \"+\ *n* [*mega-* + *gamete*] : MACROGAMETE — used esp. in botany

**mega·gametophyte** \"+\ *n* [*mega-* + *gametophyte*] : the female gametophyte produced by a megaspore — compare MICROGAMETOPHYTE

**mega·hertz** \'==,=\ *n* [*mega-* + *hertz*] : a unit of frequency equal to one million hertz — abbr. *MHz*

**mega·karyoblast** \¦==+\ *n* [ISV *mega-* + *kary-* + *-blast*] : a large cell with large reticulate nucleus that gives rise to megakaryocytes

**mega·karyocyte** *also* **mega·caryocyte** \"+\ *n* -s [ISV *mega-* + *kary-*, *cary-* + *-cyte*] : a large cell that has a lobulated nucleus, is found esp. in the bone marrow, and is held to be the source of blood platelets — **mega·karyocytic** \"+\ *adj*

**megal-** *or* **megalo-** *comb form* [NL, fr. Gk, fr. *megal-*, *megas* large, great — more at MUCH] : large : great : of giant size ⟨*megalo*blast⟩ ⟨*megal*ops⟩ ⟨*Megalo*saurus⟩ : grand : grandiose ⟨*megalo*mania⟩ : capable of or used for enlarging ⟨*megalo*graph⟩ ⟨*megalo*scope⟩; *specif, med* : abnormally large ⟨*megalo*cardia⟩ ⟨*megalo*cornea⟩

**meg·al·ad·a·pis** \¦megəl+\ *n, cap* [NL, fr. *megal-* + *Adapis*] : a genus of Pleistocene lemurs of Madagascar

**mega·lai·ma** \,megə'līmə, -'lāmə\ *n, cap* [NL, fr. *mega-* + *-laima* (fr. Gk *laimos* throat) — more at GYMNOLAEMATA] : a genus of scansorial barbets of southeastern Asia

**mega·la·nia** \-'lānēə\ *n, cap* [NL, fr. *mega-* + *-lania* (fr. Gk *ēlainein* to wander about + NL *-ia*); fr. the terrestrial nature of such lizards] : a genus of extinct lizards related to but larger than the modern monitors and known from remains found in the Pleistocene of Queensland and the Asiatic Pliocene

**meg·a·la·trac·tus** \,==lə'traktəs\ *n, cap* [NL, fr. *megal-* + Gk *atraktos* spindle — more at TORTURE] : a genus of Australian marine snails (family Xancidae) including the largest known living gastropod

**mega·lecithal** \¦megə+\ *adj* [*mega-* + *lecithal*] *of an egg* : containing very large amounts of yolk : TELOLECITHAL, CENTROLECITHAL

**meg·aleth·o·scope** \,megə'lethə,skōp\ *n* [*mega-* + *aletho-scope*, a kind of stereoscope, fr. Gk *alētho-* (fr. *alēthēs* true) + E *-scope*] : a stereoscope having a large magnifying lens

**mega·lith** \'==,lith\ *n* -s [*mega-* + *-lith*] **1** : one of the huge undressed stones used in various types of prehistoric monuments — compare MENHIR, MONOLITH, SARSEN **2** : a prehistoric monument (as a dolmen) constructed of huge stones

**mega·lith·ic** \¦==¦lithik\ *adj* [*mega-* + *-lithic*] **1** : of prehistoric megalith construction : constructed of large undressed stones **2** : of or relating to a people who erected megaliths or to their culture

**meg·a·lo·bat·ra·chus** \,megəlō'ba·trəkəs\ *n, cap* [NL, fr. *megal-* + *-batrachus*] : a genus that consists of the giant salamander and that is sometimes included in the genus *Cryptobranchus*

**meg·a·lo·blast** \'===,blast\ *n* [ISV *megal-* + *-blast*] **1** : ERYTHROBLAST 1 **2** : a large nucleated abnormal red blood cell appearing in the blood in pernicious anemia — **meg·a·lo·blas·tic** \¦===¦blastik\ *adj*

**megaloblastic anemia** *n* : any of several anemias (as pernicious anemia) in which megaloblasts are present in the circulating blood

**meg·a·lo·ce·phal·ic** \¦===sə¦falik\ *or* **meg·a·lo·ceph·a·lous** \-¦sefələs\ *adj* [*megal-* + *-cephalic*, *-cephalous*] : MEGACEPHALIC — **meg·a·lo·ceph·a·ly** \¦===¦sefəlē\ *n* -ES

**meg·a·loc·e·ros** \,=='läsə,räs\ *n, cap* [NL, fr. Gk *megalokerōs* having large horns, fr. *megal-* + *-kerōs* (fr. *keras* horn) — more at HORN] : a genus of Pleistocene European cervid mammals including the gigantic Irish elk

**meg·a·lo·cyte** \'megəlō,sīt\ *n* -s [ISV *megal-* + *-cyte*] : MACROCYTE — **meg·a·lo·cyt·ic** \¦===¦sid·ik\ *adj*

**meg·a·lo·mania** \,megəlō, -lə *also* -gl- +\ *n* [NL, fr. *megal-* + *mania*] **1** : a mania for or for doing great or grandiose things ⟨an outburst of wildly extravagant commercial ~ —*Times Lit. Supp.*⟩ **2** : infantile feelings of omnipotence esp. when retained in later life

**¹meg·a·lo·maniac** \¦==+\ *n* [*megal-* + *maniac*] : one affected with or exhibiting megalomania

**²megalomaniac** \"\ *or* **meg·a·lo·maniacal** \"+\ *or* **meg·a·lo·manic** \"+\ *adj* : belonging to, exhibiting, or affected with megalomania ⟨a once ~ motion picture industry —Cecil Beaton⟩

**meg·al·on·yx** \,megə'läniks\ *n, cap* [NL, fr. *megal-* + *-onyx*] : a genus of large extinct Pliocene and Pleistocene edentate mammals of No. America

**meg·a·lo·pa** \,=='lōpə\ *n* -s [NL, fr. Gk *megalōpē*, fem. of *megalōpos* having large eyes, fr. *megal-* + *-ōpos* (fr. *ōps* eye) — more at EYE] : MEGALOPS

**meg·a·lop·ic** \¦==¦läpik\ *adj* [NL *megalop-*, *megalops* + E *-ic*] : of, relating to, or being a megalops

**¹meg·a·lo·pine** \'megəlō,pīn, me'galə,-\ *adj* [NL *megalop-*, *megalops* + E *-ine*] **1** : of or relating to the megalops **2** [NL *Megalop-*, *Megalops* + E *-ine*] : of or relating to the genus *Megalops*

**²megalopine** \"\ *n* -s **1** : a megalops larva **2** : a fish of the genus *Megalops*

**meg·a·lop·o·lis** \,megə'läpələs\ *n* -ES [*megal-* + *-polis*] **1** : a very large city **2** : a thickly populated region centering around a metropolis ⟨the ~ including New York City and adjacent sections of New York, New Jersey, and Connecticut⟩

**¹meg·a·lo·pol·i·tan** \¦megəlō¦pälət°n *also* -ətən *or* -əd·ən\ *adj* [fr. *megalopolis*, after such pairs as E *metropolis*: *metropolitan*] : of, relating to, or characterized by a megalopolis ⟨becoming a ~ people —B.I.Bell⟩ ⟨this immense ~ civilization —Kenneth Rexroth⟩

**²megalopolitan** \"\ *n* -s : one who lives in a megalopolis

**meg·a·lo·pol·i·tan·ism** \-°n,izəm, -ə,ni-\ *n* -s : the quality or state of being megalopolitan : megalopolitan character

**meg·a·lo·pore** \'megəlō,pō(ə)r\ *n* [ISV *megal-* + *-pore*] : one of the large pores that are found in the dorsal shell of some chitons and that lead to photosensitive organs

**meg·a·lops** \'==,läps\ *n* [NL, fr. *megal-* + *-ops*] **1** *pl* **megalops** *or* **megalopses** : a larva or larval stage following the zoea in the development of most crabs in which the legs and abdominal appendages have appeared, the abdomen is relatively long, and the eyes are large — called also *megalopa* **2** *cap* : a genus of fishes that contains several East Indian and So. Pacific species closely related to and resembling the tarpon and is sometimes made the type of a separate family but is usu. considered to form a subfamily of the Elopidae

**meg·a·lop·tera** \,=='läptərə\ *n pl, cap* [NL, fr. *megal-* + *-ptera*] : a small order of usu. large insects that are often included in Neuroptera, have ample wings with a folded anal area in the hind pair, and develop from aquatic predacious larvae — compare ALDER FLY, DOBSON FLY — **meg·a·lop·ter·an** \-tərən\ *n* -s — **meg·a·lop·ter·ous** \¦==¦t(ə)rəs\ *adj*

**meg·a·lo·pyg·i·dae** \,megəlō'pijə,dē\ *n pl, cap* [NL, fr. *Megalopyge*, type genus (fr. *megal-* + Gk *pygē* buttocks) + *-idae* — more at FOG] : a family of chiefly So. American hirsute moths having larvae with stinging hairs

**meg·a·lor·nis** \,megə'lȯrnəs\ [NL, fr. *megal-* + *-ornis*] *syn of* GRUS

**meg·a·lor·nith·i·dae** \,==='nithə,dē\ [NL, fr. *Megalornith-*, *Megalornis* + *-idae*] *syn of* GRUIDAE

**meg·a·lo·saur** \'megəlō,sȯ(ə)r\ *n* -s [NL *Megalosaurus*] : a dinosaur of the genus *Megalosaurus* or family Megalosauridae

**meg·a·lo·sau·rus** \,==='sȯrəs\ *n, cap* [NL, fr. *megal-* + *-saurus*] : a genus (the type of the family Megalosauridae) of gigantic carnivorous saurischian dinosaurs of the suborder Theropoda occurring in the European Jurassic and Lower Cretaceous

**meg·a·lo·sphere** \'===+,-\ *n* [*megal-* + *sphere*] : the large-chambered initial shell of the sexual individuals of some dimorphic foraminiferans — **meg·a·lo·spher·ic** \¦===¦sferik\ *adj*

**-meg·a·ly** \'megəlē, -li\ *also* **-me·ga·lia** \mə'gālyə\ *n comb form, pl* **-megalies** *also* **-megalias** [NL *-megalia*, fr. *megal-* + L *-ia* -y] : abnormal enlargement (of a specified part) ⟨acro*megaly*⟩ ⟨gastro*megaly*⟩ ⟨hepatospleno*megalia*⟩

**mega·mere** \'megə,mi(ə)r\ *n* -s [*mega-* + *-mere*] : MACROMERE

**mega·nephridium** \¦==+\ *n, pl* **meganephridia** [NL, fr. *mega-* + *nephridium*] : a relatively large nephridium usu. found one pair per segment in some annelid worms

**mega·neu·ra** \,==+'n(y)u̇rə\ *n pl, cap* [NL, fr. *mega-* + *-neura*] : a genus of extinct insects (order Protodonata) that includes some with a wingspread of about three feet and that is known from the Upper Carboniferous of Commentry, France

**me·gan·thro·pus** \mə'gan(t)thrəpəs, ,me,gan'thrōpəs\ *n, cap* [NL, fr. *mega-* + *-anthropus*] : a genus of large extinct primates of the Lower Pleistocene of Java known from fragmentary jawbones and held to be primitive men

**mega·nucleus** \¦megə+\ *n* [NL, fr. *mega-* + *nucleus*] : MACRONUCLEUS

**mega·parsec** \"+\ *n* [*mega-* + *parsec*] : one million parsecs

**¹mega·phone** \'megə,fōn\ *n* [*mega-* + *-phone*] **1** : a cone-shaped device used to intensify or direct the voice ⟨a cheerleader's ~⟩ ⟨power ~⟩ **2** : one that expresses or publicizes others' opinions or ideas : MOUTHPIECE ⟨making herself the ~ of his suggestions —Nigel Dennis⟩

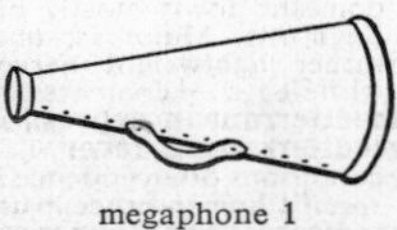

megaphone 1

**²megaphone** \"\ *vb* -ED/-ING/-S *vt* **1** : to transmit through or as if through a megaphone : publicize widely ⟨~ an announcement to the crowd⟩ ⟨wouldn't care to ~ my career —*N.Y.Sun*⟩ ⟨~ the dictator's views⟩ **2** : to address through or as if through a megaphone ⟨~ a passing ship⟩ ~ *vi* : to speak through or as if through a megaphone

**mega·phon·ic** \¦==¦fänik\ *adj* **1** : of, relating to, or transmitted by a megaphone ⟨~ messages⟩ **2** : suggestive of a megaphone or its effect ⟨a ~ voice⟩ — **mega·phon·i·cal·ly** \-nək(ə)lē\ *adv*

**mega·phon·ist** \'==,fōnəst\ *n* -s : one who uses a megaphone; *specif* : a motion-picture director

**me·gaph·y·ton** \mə'gafə,tän\ *n, cap* [NL, fr. *mega-* + Gk *phyton* plant — more at PHYT-] : a form genus of fossil tree ferns based on trunks with distichous scars

**mega·pode** \'megə,pōd\ *also* **mega·pod** \-,päd\ *n* -s [NL *Megapodiidae*] : a bird of the family Megapodiidae — called also *mound bird*

**mega·po·di·idae** \,==pə'dīə,dē\ *n pl, cap* [NL, fr. *Megapodius*, type genus + *-idae*] : a family of gallinaceous birds inhabiting Australia and neighboring islands north and east to the Philippines and Ladrones and known for their habit of heaping up a mass of vegetable debris in which their eggs are laid and hatched — compare BRUSH TURKEY, LEIPOA, MALEO

**mega·po·di·us** \,=='pōdēəs\ *n, cap* [NL, fr. *mega-* + *-podius* (fr. Gk *pod-*, *pous* foot) — more at FOOT] : a genus (the type of the family Megapodiidae) of gallinaceous birds

**me·gap·o·lis** \mə'gapələs\ *n* -ES [NL, fr. *mega-* + Gk *polis* city — more at POLICE] : MEGALOPOLIS

**mega·pol·i·tan** \,megə¦pälət°n *also* -ətən *or* -əd·ən\ *adj* [fr. *megapolis*, after such pairs as E *metropolis*: *metropolitan*] : MEGALOPOLITAN ⟨rise of the ~ city —Howard M. Jones⟩

**mega·pros·o·pous** \¦==¦präsəpəs\ *adj* [*mega-* + *prosop-* + *-ous*] : having a large face

**me·gap·tera** \mə'gaptərə\ *n, cap* [NL, fr. *mega-* + *-ptera*] **:** a cetacean genus comprising the humpback whale
**mega·rhi·nus** \,megə'rīnəs\ *n, cap* [NL, fr. *mega-* + *-rhinus*] **:** a genus of very large nonbiting American mosquitoes with a curved beak, greenish or bluish coloration, and predaceous larvae
**mega·rhyssa** \¦==+\ *n, cap* [NL, fr. *mega-* + *Rhyssa*] **:** a genus of large ichneumon flies having an extremely long slender ovipositor and including a common species (*M. lunator*) of the eastern U. S. that is a parasite of the larva of the pigeon horntail
1**me·gar·i·an** \me'ga(a)rēən, mə'-\ *also* **me·gar·e·an** \", ,megə¦rēən\ *adj, usu cap* [*megarian* fr. *Megara*, city of ancient Greece (fr. L, fr. Gk) + E *-an*; *megarean* fr. L *megareus* Megarian (fr. *Megara*) + E *-an*] **1 :** of, relating to, or characteristic of the city of Megara **2 :** of or relating to a Socratic school of philosophy established by Euclid of Megara and best known for the use of logical paradoxes and subtle arguments bordering on the specious and for holding that the good is one and is the only true being
2**megarian** \"\ *also* **megarean** \"\ *n* -s **1** *cap* **:** a native or inhabitant of Megara, Greece **2** *usu cap* **:** a member of the Megarian school of philosophy
**me·gar·ic** \me'garik, mə'-\ *adj or n, usu cap* [L *megaricus*, fr. Gk *megarikos*, fr. *Megara*, Greece + Gk *-ikos* -ic] **:** MEGARIAN
**meg·a·ron** \'megə,rän\ *n, pl* **meg·a·ra** \-rə\ [Gk, fr. *megas* large, great — more at MUCH] **1 :** the great central hall of an ancient Mycenaean house usu. containing a center hearth **2 :** CELLA
**mega·sclere** \'==+,-\ *n* [*mega-* + *sclere*] **:** a large spicule; *specif* **:** one of the skeletal spicules of a sponge — **mega·scleric** \¦==¦sklirik, -ler-\ *or* **mega·scle·rous** \-¦sklirəs, -ler-\ *adj*
**mega·sco·lec·i·dae** \,==skə'lesə,dē\ *n pl, cap* [NL, fr. *Megascolec-, Megascolex*, type genus (fr. *mega-* + Gk *skōlēk-, skōlēx* worm) + *-idae*] **:** a very large family of earthworms chiefly of the southern hemisphere containing giant forms that include an Australian species (*Megascolides australis*) held to reach a length of 11 feet
**mega·scop·ic** \¦==¦skäpik\ *adj* [*mega-* + *-scopic*] **1 :** ENLARGED, MAGNIFIED **2 a :** visible to the unaided eye **:** MACROSCOPIC — used esp. of the physical features of rocks **b :** based on or relating to observations made with the unaided eye ⟨the ~ study of rocks⟩ — **mega·scop·i·cal·ly** \-pək(ə)lē\ *adv*
**mega·se·cop·tera** \,==sə'käptərə\ *n pl, cap* [NL, prob. fr. *mega-* + Gk *sēkos* pen, fold, trunk of a tree + NL *-ptera*] **:** an order of extinct insects of the Upper Carboniferous and Permian that are related to the mayflies and dragonflies and have extremely long cerci
**mega·seism** \'megə,sīzəm *sometimes* -sez- *or* -säz- *or* -sēz-\ *n* [ISV *mega-* + *seism*] **:** a violent earthquake — **mega·seis·mic** \¦==¦sīzmik *also* |sm- *sometimes* -¦se| *or* -¦sä| *or* -¦sē|\ *adj*
**mega·sporangium** \¦==+\ *n*, [NL, fr. *mega-* + *sporangium*] **:** a sporangium that develops only megaspores (as the nucellus in a seed plant) — called also *macrosporangium;* compare MICROSPORANGIUM
**mega·spore** \'==+,-\ *n* [ISV *mega-* + *spore*] **1 :** one of the spores in heterosporous plants that give rise to female gametophytes and are generally larger than the microspores **2 :** MACROSPORE 2 — **mega·spor·ic** \¦==¦spōrik\ *adj*
**megaspore mother cell** *n* **:** a cell that produces megaspores by reduction usu. in tetrads or linear groups
**mega·sporocyte** \¦==+\ *n* [*mega-* + *sporocyte*] **:** MEGASPORE MOTHER CELL
**mega·spo·ro·gen·e·sis** \,==,spōrə'jenəsəs\ *n* [NL, fr. ISV *megaspore* + L *genesis*] **:** the formation and maturation of a megaspore — compare MICROSPOROGENESIS
**mega·sporophyll** \¦==+\ *n* [*mega-* + *sporophyll*] **:** a sporophyll that develops only megasporangia
**me·gass** \mə'gaa(ə)s, -ais-, -äs\ *or* **megasse** *n, pl* **megasses** [modif. of F *bagasse* — more at BAGASSE] **:** BAGASSE
**mega·synthetic** \¦megə+\ *adj* [*mega-* + *synthetic*] **:** forming an extensive or ponderous synthesis ⟨~ American Indian languages⟩
**mega·there** \'megə,thi(ə)r\ *n* -s [NL *Megatherium*] **:** a member of the genus *Megatherium*
**mega·the·ri·an** \¦==¦thirēən\ *adj* [NL *Megatherium* + E *-an*] **:** of, relating to, or characteristic of the genus *Megatherium* or the family Megatheriidae
**mega·the·ri·um** \,=='thirēəm\ *n, cap* [NL, fr. *mega-* + *-therium*] **:** a genus (the type of the family Megatheriidae) of ground sloths found in the Pliocene and Pleistocene of America that are often of gigantic size and are related to the sloths and anteaters, the skull and dentition resembling those of the former and the vertebrae those of the latter
**mega·therm** \'megə,thərm\ *n* [ISV *mega-* + *-therm*] **:** a plant that requires great heat combined with very abundant moisture for its successful growth — compare MESOTHERM, MICROTHERM — **mega·ther·mal** \¦==¦thərməl\ *or* **mega·ther·mic** \-mik\ *adj*
**mega·thy·mi·dae** \,=='thīmə,dē\ *n pl, cap* [NL, fr. *Megathymus*, type genus (fr. *mega-* + Gk *thymos* warty excrescence, thymus) + *-idae*] **:** a family of strong-flying No. American skipper butterflies that is often considered a subfamily of Hesperiidae — see AGAVEWORM, GIANT SKIPPER
**mega·ton** \'megə,tən, -,tän\ *n* [*mega-* + *ton*] **:** an explosive force equivalent to that of a million tons of TNT ⟨assume further that the pertinent energy release is 8 ~s —R.E.Lapp⟩ — **mega·ton·ic** \¦==¦tänik\ *adj*
**mega·tron** \'==,trän\ *n* -s [*mega-* + *-tron*] **:** LIGHTHOUSE TUBE
**mega·var** \'==+,-\ *n* [*mega-* + *var*] **:** one million volt-amperes
**mega·volt** \"+,-\ *n* [ISV *mega-* + *volt*] **:** one million volts
**mega·watt** \"+,-\ *n* [ISV *mega-* + *watt*] **:** one million watts **:** one thousand kilowatts
**mega·zooid** \"+\ *n* [*mega-* + *zooid*] **:** a relatively large stalked vegetative individual of certain higher ciliates (as *Vorticella*) — compare MICROZOOID
**mega·zoospore** \¦==+\ *n* [*mega-* + *zoospore*] **:** a large zoospore **:** MACROZOOSPORE
**megged** *past of* MEG
**megging** *pres part of* MEG
**me·gilp** *also* **ma·gilp** \mə'gilp\ *n* -s [origin unknown] **1 :** a gelatinous preparation commonly of linseed oil and mastic varnish used by artists as a vehicle for oil colors **2 :** a vehicle that facilitates a fluid application and prevents running of color
**meg·nin·ia** \meg'ninēə\ *n, cap* [NL, fr. Jean *Megnin* †1905 Fr. veterinarian + NL *-ia*] **:** a genus of analgesid mites common on the feathers of various domesticated birds
**meg·ohm** \'me,gōm\ *n* [ISV *mega-* + *ohm*] **:** one million ohms
**meg·ohm·me·ter** \-,mēd·ə(r)\ *n* [*megohm* + *-meter*] **:** an instrument for the measurement of very high electrical resistances
**meg·rel** \'megrəl\ *n, pl* **megrel** *or* **megrels** *usu cap* **:** MINGRELIAN
1**me·grim** \'mēgrəm, 'mäg-\ *n* -s [ME *migrene, migrein, migreime*, fr. MF *migraine* — more at MIGRAINE] **1 a :** MIGRAINE **b :** VERTIGO, DIZZINESS ⟨gives me the ~s to look down this way —Maxwell Anderson⟩ **2 a :** a random, furtive, or unbidden thought or feeling **:** FANCY, WHIM ⟨as though some lurking ~, some microbe of dissatisfaction with ourselves, was at work within us —John Galsworthy⟩ ⟨and with no ~ in my head of having been possessed by some great moral purpose —R.B.Cunninghame Graham⟩ **b megrims** *pl* **:** low spirits **:** DESPONDENCY, BLUES — usu. used with *the* ⟨fell victim to an attack of the combat flier's ~s —Paul Gallico⟩ **3 :** any of numerous diseases of animals marked by disturbance of equilibrium and abnormal gait and behavior — usu. used in pl.
2**megrim** \'mēgrəm\ *n* -s [origin unknown] **:** any of several small flatfishes: as **a :** a European flounder (*Arnoglossus laterna*) of the family Bothidae — called also *lantern flounder* **b :** a whiff (*Lepidorhombus megastoma*)
**megs** *pl of* MEG, *pres 3d sing of* MEG
**me·ha·ri** \mə'härē\ *n* -s [F *méhari*, fr. Ar *mahāriy*, pl. of *mahriy* of Mahrah, fr. *Mahrah*, district on the southern coast of Arabia] **:** one of a breed of swift dromedaries used chiefly as saddle animals
**me·ha·rist** *or* **me·ha·riste** \-rəst\ *n* -s [F *méhariste*, fr. *méhari* + *-iste* -ist] **:** one mounted on a mehari
**me·her·rin** \mə'herən\ *n, pl* **meherrin** *or* **meherrins** *usu cap* [fr. the *Meherrin* river] **1 a :** an Iroquoian people of the Meherrin river valley in Virginia and North Carolina **b :** a member of such people **2 :** the language of the Meherrin people
**meh·lis' gland** \'mālə̇s(əz)-\ *n, usu cap M* [fr. the name *Mehlis*] **:** one of the large unicellular glands surrounding the ootype of a flatworm and possibly playing a part in eggshell formation; *collectively* **:** the group of such glands in a worm
**meh·man·dar** \mə'män,där\ *n* -s [Per *mihmāndār*, fr. *mihmān* guest (fr. MPer *mēhmān*) + *-dār* holder — more at BHUMIDAR] **:** an official in India, Persia, or Afghanistan appointed to escort an ambassador or traveler
**meh·ri** \'mārē\ *n, pl* **mehri** *or* **mehris** *usu cap* **:** MAHRI
**meh·tar** *also* **meh·ter** \'mäd·ə(r)\ *n* -s [Per *mihtar* prince, greater, elder, fr. *mih* great (fr. MPer *meh, mas*) + *-tar*, comparative suffix (fr. MPer, fr. OPer *-tara-*)] **1 :** a groom or stable boy in Iran **2** *usu cap* **:** a member of a harijan caste of sweepers and scavengers in India
**mei·bo·mian gland** \(')mī¦bōmēən, -myən-\ *n, often cap M* [Heinrich *Meibom* †1700 Ger. physician + E *-ian*] **:** one of the long sebaceous glands of the eyelids that discharge a fatty secretion which lubricates the lids
**mei·bos** \'mē,bäs\ *var of* MEBOS
**meidan** *var of* MAIDAN
**mei·kle** \'mēkəl\ *var of* MICKLE
**meiny** \'mānē, -ni\ *n* -ES [ME *meynie* (also, household, family) — more at MENIAL] **1** *archaic* **a :** a group of attendants or followers **:** RETINUE ⟨summoned up their ~, straight took horse —Shak.⟩ **b :** a group of associates **:** BAND, COMPANY ⟨the priest of Loyola's ~ —W.H.Gardner⟩ **2** *now chiefly Scot* **:** a great number **:** MULTITUDE
**meio-** — see MI-
**meio·bar** \'mīō+,-\ *n* [ISV *mi-* + *bar*] **1 :** a region of low barometric pressure **2 :** an isobar of low pressure
**meio·cyte** \-,sīt\ *n* -s [*mi-* + *-cyte*] **:** a cell undergoing meiosis
**mei·o·nite** \'mīə,nīt\ *n* -s [F *méionite*, fr. Gk *meiōn* less + F *-ite*] **:** a mineral $Ca_4Al_6Si_6O_{24}(SO_4,CO_3,Cl_2)$ consisting of an aluminosilicate of calcium with other anions (as sulfate, carbonate, and chloride) and being isomorphous with marialite — see SCAPOLITE
**meio·phyl·ly** \'==,filē\ *n* -ES [*mi-* + *phyll-* + *-y*] **:** the suppression of one or more leaves in a whorl
**mei·o·sis** \mī'ōsəs\ *n, pl* **meioses** [NL, fr. Gk *meiōsis* diminution, fr. *meioun* to diminish (fr. *meiōn* less) + *-sis* — more at MINOR] **1 a :** representation of a thing so as to cause it to be taken as less than it really is **b :** LITOTES, UNDERSTATEMENT **2 :** the sequence of complex nuclear changes resulting in the production of cells (as gametes) with half the number of chromosomes present in the original cell and typically involving an actual reduction division in which the chromosomes without undergoing prior splitting join in pairs with homologous chromosomes of maternal and paternal origin associated and then separate so that one member of each pair enters each daughter nucleus and a second division not involving reduction — compare MATURATION, MITOSIS
**meio·stoma·tous** \¦mīō¦stämədəs, -stōm-\ *adj* [*mi-* + *-stomatous*] *of a larval nematode* **:** having the oral structures reduced or simplified as compared with related forms
**meio·stome** \'mīə,stōm\ *n* -s [*mi-* + *-stome*] **:** a meiostomatous nematode
**meio·taxy** \-,taksē\ *n* -ES [*mi-* + *-taxy*] **:** the suppression of a complete whorl of leaves or sporophylls
**mei·ot·ic** \mī'äd·ik\ *adj* [Gk *meiōtikos* lowering, diminishing, fr. *meiōtos* capable of being lowered (fr. *meioun* to lower, diminish) + *-ikos* -ic — more at MEIOSIS] **:** of, relating to, or characterized by meiosis — **mei·ot·i·cal·ly** \-ək(ə)lē\ *adv*
**meis·sen** \'mīsᵊn\ *also* **meissen china** *or* **meissen ware** *n* -s *usu cap M* [fr. *Meissen*, Saxony, Germany] **:** ceramic ware made at Meissen near Dresden; *esp* **:** a European hard-paste porcelain developed under the patronage of the king of Saxony about 1715 and used for both ornamental and table wares
**meiss·ner effect** \'mīsnə(r)-\ *n, usu cap M* [after Alexander *Meissner* †1958 Austrian radio engineer] **:** the partial or complete absence of magnetic induction in metallic substances even in a magnetic field when cooled into the superconducting state
**meissner's corpuscle** *n, usu cap M* [after Georg *Meissner* †1905 Ger. physiologist] **:** any of the small elliptical tactile end organs in hairless skin containing numerous transversely placed tactile cells and fine flattened nerve terminations
**meissner's plexus** *n, usu cap M* [after Georg *Meissner*] **:** a plexus of gangliated nerve fibers lying between the muscular and mucous coats of the intestine — compare AUERBACH'S PLEXUS
**mei·ster·ge·sang** \'mīstə(r)gə,zäŋ\ *n, pl* **meistergesän·ge** \-,zeŋə\ *often cap* [G, fr. MHG *meistersanc, meistergesanc*, fr. *meister* master + *sanc* song, singing (fr. OHG *sang*) *or gesanc* song, singing, fr. *ge-*, collective prefix (fr. OHG *gi-*) + *sanc* — more at CO-, SONG] **1 :** one of the songs of the meistersinger consisting of strophic mechanical verse usu. didactic or religious in nature and composed according to strict rules to fit a few traditional monophonic melodies **2 :** the songs of the meistersinger as a literary genre
**mei·ster·lied** \-,lēt\ *n, pl* **meisterlie·der** \-,lēdə(r)\ *often cap* [G, fr. *meister* master (fr. OHG *meistar*) + *lied* song, fr. OHG *liod* — more at LAUD] **:** MEISTERGESANG
**mei·ster·sing·er** \-,siŋə(r), -,ziŋ-\ *n, pl* **meistersinger** *or* **meistersingers** *usu cap* [G, fr. MHG, fr. *meister* master (fr. OHG *meistar*, fr. L *magister*) + *singer*, fr. *singen* to sing (fr. OHG *singan*) + *-er*, fr. OHG *-āri* -er — more at MASTER, SING] **:** a member of any of various German guilds esp. of the 15th and 16th centuries composed chiefly of middle-class workingmen and craftsmen and formed for the cultivation of poetry and music — see MEISTERGESANG
1**meith** \'mēth\ *n* -s [of Scand origin; akin to ON *mith* middle, mark, fishing banks, *mithr*, adj., middle — more at MID] **1** *Scot* **:** LANDMARK; *esp* **:** a marker serving as a guide in navigation **2** *Scot* **:** MEASURE, MEASUREMENT
2**meith** \"\ *vt* -ED/-ING/-S [of Scand origin; akin to ON *mitha* to mark, fr. *mith* mark] *Scot* **:** to mark out
**mei·thei** \'mā,thā\ *n, pl* **meithei** *or* **meitheis** *usu cap* **1 a :** a people of Manipur, India **b :** a member of such people **2 :** the Tibeto-Burman language of the Meithei people
**mejlis** *also* **mejliss** *var of* MAJLIS
**MEK** *abbr* methyl ethyl ketone
**me·ke** \'mākē\ *n* -s [Fijian] **:** a Fijian dance accompanied by singing; *also* **:** a festival of these dances
**mek·er burner** \'mekə(r)-\ *n, usu cap M* [after George *Meker*, 20th cent. chemist] **:** a laboratory gas burner that differs from a typical Bunsen burner in having a constriction in the tube and a grid at the top of the burner causing the flame of burning gas to consist of a number of short blue inner cones and a large single outer cone and to be hotter generally than the Bunsen flame
**mekh·i·tar·ist** *or* **mech·i·tar·ist** \,mekə'tärəst\ *n* -s *usu cap* [fr. Peter M. *Mekhitar* †1749 Armenian religious reformer + E *-ist*] **:** one of an Armenian order of Roman Catholic monks founded in the 18th century at Constantinople and having congregations at Venice and Vienna

Meker burner

**mekka** *usu cap, var of* MECCA
**mek·nes** *or* **mek·nès** \mek'nes\ *adj, usu cap* [fr. *Meknes* (F *Meknès*), Morocco] **:** of or from the city of Meknes, Morocco **:** of the kind or style prevalent in Meknes
1**mel** *or* **mell** \'mel\ *n* -s [L *mel* — more at MELLIFLUOUS] **:** HONEY ⟨sweet as the ~ of the bee —Samuel Bamford⟩
2**mel** \"\ *n* -s [prob. fr. *M* (1000) + *-el* (as in *bel*)] **:** a subjective unit of tone pitch equal to one thousandth of the pitch of a tone having a frequency of one thousand cycles — used esp. in audiology
1**mel-** — *see* MELA-
2**mel-** *comb form* [NL, fr. Gk *melos* — more at MELODY] **:** limb ⟨*melalgia*⟩
3**mel-** *or* **melo-** *comb form* [NL, fr. Gk *mēla* cheeks, lit., apples, pl. of *mēlon* apple] **:** cheek ⟨*melitis*⟩ ⟨*meloplasty*⟩
**me·la** \'mā(,)lä\ *n* -s [Hindi *melā*, fr. Skt *melaka, melā* meeting, assembly — more at MILITATE] **:** an Indian religious festival or fair **:** a gathering of people
**mela-** *or* **mel-** *also* **melo-** *comb form* [ISV, fr. Gk *melas* black — more at MULLET] **:** black ⟨*mela*diorite⟩ ⟨*Melo*grammataceae⟩
**me·lac·o·nite** \mə'lakə,nīt\ *n* -s [alter. (influenced by *-ite*) of earlier *melaconise*, fr. F *mélaconise*, fr. *méla-* mela- + *-conise* (fr. Gk *konis* ashes, dust) — more at INCINERATE] **:** an earthy black massive variety of tenorite
**me·la·da** \mə'lädə\ *n* -s [AmerSp, fr. Sp, fem. of *melado*, past part. of *melar* to boil sugarcane juice into syrup, fr. *miel* honey, fr. L *mel* — more at MELLIFLUOUS] **:** crude cane sugar as it comes mixed with molasses from the boiling of cane juice and prior to refining
**melaena** *var of* MELENA
**me·lai·no·type** \mə'līnə,tīp, -lān-\ *n* -s [Gk *melaino-* black, fr. *melaina*, fem. of *melas* — more at MULLET] **:** FERROTYPE 1
**mel·a·leu·ca** \,melə'lükə\ *n* [NL, fr. *mela-* + *-leuca* (fr. Gk *leukos* white); fr. the black trunk and white branches — more at LIGHT] **1** *cap* **:** a genus of Australian and East Indian shrubs and trees (family Myrtaceae) having numerous stamens in fascicles — see CAJEPUT, HONEYMYRTLE, TEA TREE 2 **2** -s **:** any plant of the genus *Melaleuca*
**mel·am** \'me,lam\ *n* -s [G, fr. *mel-* (origin unknown) + *-am* (prob. fr. NL *ammonia*)] **:** an amorphous compound $C_6H_9N_{11}$ obtained by heating ammonium thiocyanate or as a by-product in the manufacture of melamine
**me·la·med** *or* **me·lam·med** \mə'lämə̇d, me'l-, ,melə'mäd\ *n, pl* **melam·dim** \mə'lämdə̇m, me'l-\ [Heb *mĕlammēdh* teacher] **:** a teacher of Hebrew language and traditions esp. in a heder
**mel·a·mine** \'melə,mēn, -ləmən\ *n* -s [G *melamin*, fr. *melam* + *-in* -ine] **1 :** a white crystalline high-melting organic base $C_3N_3(NH_2)_3$ that is a cyclic trimer of cyanamide but is usu. made by heating dicyandiamide to high temperatures and that is used chiefly in making melamine resins; 2, 4, 6-triamino-*s*-triazine — called also *cyanuramide* **2 :** a melamine resin or a plastic made from such a resin
**melamine formaldehyde** *n* **:** a condensation product, resin, or plastic made from melamine and formaldehyde
**melamine resin** *n* **:** any of a group of thermosetting resins made from melamine and an aldehyde (as formaldehyde), characterized by resistance to heat and water and good electrical resistance, and used chiefly in molded products, laminated products, adhesives, and coatings and in treating textiles (as for improving resistance to shrinkage and creasing) and paper (as for improving wet strength)
**mel·amp·so·ra** \,meləm(p)'sōrə\ *n, cap* [NL, fr. *melan-* + Gk *psōra* scab, mange — more at PSORIASIS] **:** a genus (the type of the family Melampsoraceae) of rusts that have sessile one-celled teliospores in a single layer — see FLAX RUST
**mel·am·py·rum** \,meləm'pīrəm\ *n, cap* [NL, fr. Gk *melampyron* ball mustard, fr. *melan-* + *pyros* wheat — more at FURZE] **:** a small genus of branching annual herbs (family Scrophulariaceae) with opposite leaves and small irregular flowers with four stamens — see COWWHEAT
**melan-** *or* **melano-** *also* **melam-** *comb form* [*melan-* fr. ME, fr. MF, fr. LL, fr. Gk, fr. *melan-, melas*; *melano-* & *melam-* fr. NL, fr. Gk, fr. *melan-, melas* — more at MULLET] **1 :** black **:** dark ⟨*melan*ic⟩ ⟨*melan*in⟩ ⟨*melano*comous⟩ ⟨*Melamp*sora⟩ **2 :** melanin **:** marked by the presence of melanin ⟨*melano*gen⟩ ⟨*melan*emia⟩ ⟨*melano*sarcoma⟩
**mel·a·nau** \'melə,naů\ *also* **mil·a·nau** \'mil-\ *or* **mil·a·no** \'milə,nō\ *n, pl* **melanau** *or* **melanaus** *usu cap* **:** a member of a native people in Sarawak
**mel·an·cho·lia** \,melən'kōlēə, -lyə\ *n, pl* **melancholi·as** \-ēəz, -yəz\ *also* **melancholi·ae** \-ōlē,ē, -ōlē,ī\ [NL, fr. LL, melancholy — more at MELANCHOLY] **:** a disordered mental condition characterized by extreme depression of spirits, bodily complaints, and often hallucinations and delusions; *specif* **:** a manic-depressive psychosis **syn** see SADNESS
**mel·an·cho·li·ac** \-lē,ak\ *n* -s [NL *melancholia* + E *-ac*] **:** one affected with melancholia
1**mel·an·chol·ic** \¦melən¦kälik, -ōlēk\ *adj* [ME *melancolik*, fr. MF *melancolique*, fr. L *melancholicus*, fr. Gk *melancholikos*, fr. *melancholia* melancholy + *-ikos* -ic — more at MELANCHOLY] **1** *obs* **a :** of, relating to, being, or associated with the presence or secretion of black bile **b :** causing or constituting the melancholy that is associated with disordered secretion of black bile **2 :** given to or affected with melancholy **:** subject to depression of spirits **:** DEPRESSED **3 :** affected with, like, or relating to melancholia **4 :** tending to depress the spirits **:** SADDENING ⟨this ~ view of our future⟩ — **mel·an·chol·i·cal·ly** \-ə̇lək(ə)lē, -älēk-, -li\ *adv*
2**melancholic** \"\ *n* -s **1** *obs* **a :** MELANCHOLY **b :** a melancholy person **2 :** MELANCHOLIAC
**mel·an·chol·i·ly** \¦melən¦käləlē, -əli, *chiefly Brit* '==kələli *or* -elənk-\ *adv* **:** in a melancholy manner **:** with a show of melancholy
**mel·an·choli·ness** \¦melən¦kälēnə̇s, -əlin-, *chiefly Brit* '==kəlinə̇s *or* -elənk-\ *n* -ES **:** the quality or state of being melancholy
**mel·an·cho·lious** \¦==¦kōlyəs, -lēəs\ *adj* [ME *melancolious*, fr. MF *melancolieus*, fr. *melancolie* melancholy + *-eus* -ous — more at MELANCHOLY] **:** MELANCHOLIC
**mel·an·chol·ish** \'==,kälish\ *adj* [1*melancholy* + *-ish*] *archaic* **:** inclined to lowness of spirits
**mel·an·chol·ist** \-ləst\ *n* -s [1*melancholy* + *-ist*] **1** *archaic* **:** a person in whom black bile is the predominant humor **2 :** MELANCHOLIAC
**mel·an·chol·ize** \¦==¦kä,līz\ *vb* -ED/-ING/-S [2*melancholy* + *-ize*] *vi* **:** to indulge in melancholy ~ *vt* **:** to make melancholy or depict as melancholy
1**mel·an·choly** \'melən,kälē, -äli, *chiefly Brit* -kəli *or* -elənk-\ *n* -ES [ME *melancolie*, fr. MF *melancolie*, fr. LL *melancholia*, fr. Gk, fr. *melan-* + *cholē, cholos* gall, bile + *-ia* -y — more at GALL] **1 a** *archaic* **:** a supposed abnormal state held to be due to the presence of an excess of black bile and characterized by sullen irascibility or gloomy mental depression **b** *archaic* **:** BLACK BILE **c :** MELANCHOLIA **2** *obs* **:** a condition of sullen ill-temper **:** ANGER, IRASCIBILITY **3 a :** depression of spirits **:** gloomy mood or condition **:** DEJECTION **b :** a pensive or moody condition **:** quietly serious thoughtfulness **4** *obs* **a :** a cause of melancholy **b :** an attack of melancholy **syn** see SADNESS
2**melancholy** \"\ *adj* **1** *obs* **a :** affected with or subject to melancholy **b :** of, relating to, or caused by black bile **2** *obs* **:** ILL-NATURED, SULLEN, IRASCIBLE **3 a :** depressed in spirits **:** DEJECTED, GLOOMY, DISMAL, MOURNFUL, SAD **b :** seriously thoughtful or meditative **:** PENSIVE **4 a :** suggestive or expressive of melancholy or dejection **:** DEPRESSING ⟨~ music⟩ **b :** producing sadness **:** causing dejection **:** LAMENTABLE, AFFLICTING ⟨a ~ event⟩ **c** *obs* **:** favorable to meditation **:** SOMBER
**melancholy thistle** *n* **:** a perennial stoloniferous Old World thistle (*Circium heterophyllum*) with lanceolate finely toothed basal leaves and usu. solitary heads of reddish purple florets
1**mel·anch·tho·nian** \,melə,ŋ(k)¦thōnēən, mə¦la-, -ōnyən\ *adj, usu cap* [Philipp *Melanchthon* (Schwarzert) †1560 Ger. scholar and religious reformer + E *-ian*] **:** of or relating to the reformer Melanchthon or his theological teachings or views
2**melanchthonian** \"\ *n* -s *usu cap* **:** a follower of Melanchthon
**mel·an·co·ni·a·ce·ae** \,melən,kōnē'āsē,ē\ *n pl, cap* [NL, fr. *Melanconium*, type genus (fr. *melan-* + *-conium*, fr. *konis, konia* dust) + *-aceae* — more at INCINERATE] **:** a family of fungi coextensive with the order Melanconiales — see CORYNEUM, GLOEOSPORIUM — **mel·an·co·ni·a·ceous** \¦==,==¦āshəs\ *adj*
**mel·an·co·ni·a·les** \,==,=='ā(,)lēz\ *n pl, cap* [NL, fr. *Melanconium* + *-ales*] **:** an order of imperfect fungi that have the conidia borne in acervuli which are either immersed or erumpent and that are parasites of higher plants — see ANTHRACNOSE, MELANCONIACEAE
**-mel·ane** \'me,lān\ *n* -s *comb form* [Gk *melan-, melas* black — more at MULLET] **:** black substance **:** dark substance ⟨lepidomelane⟩
**mel·a·nel·li·dae** \,melə'nelə,dē\ *n pl, cap* [NL, fr. *Melanella*, type genus + *-idae*] **:** a family of small spiral usu. white marine gastropod mollusks (order Pectinibranchia) including a number that are parasitic on various echinoderms
**mel·ane·mia** \¦melə¦nēmēə\ *n* -s [NL, fr. *melan-* + *-emia*] **:** an abnormal condition in which the blood contains melanin

[1]**mel·a·ne·sian** \\,melə'nēzhən, -ēsh-\\ *n* -s *cap* [*Melanesia*, islands in the Pacific ocean northeast of Australia + E *-an*] **1 :** a member of the dominant native group of Melanesia who constitute a dark-skinned people with thick beards and frizzy often elaborately dressed hair and who are generally considered to be a cross between the Papuans and the Polynesians or the Malays **2 :** a language group of the Austronesian languages of Melanesia

[2]**melanesian** \\ ¦≈≈¦≈≈\\ *adj, usu cap* **:** of or relating to Melanesia, the Melanesians, or their Austronesian languages ⟨a *Melanesian* littoral fauna⟩

**melanesian pidgin** *n, usu cap M* **:** BÊCHE-DE-MER 2

**mel·a·ne·sid** \\,melə'nēsəd\\ *n* -s *usu cap* [*Melanesia* + E *-id*] **:** MELANESIAN 1

**mé·lange** *also* **me·lange** \\(')mā¦lä^n zh, -änj\\ *n* -s [F *mélange*, fr. MF *melange*, fr. *mesler, medler, meler* to mix — more at MEDDLE] **:** MIXTURE, COMMINGLING: as **a :** a mixture of heterogeneous and often incongruous elements ⟨this turgid ~ of pacification and threat⟩ ⟨the psychosis represents a bizarre ~ of behavioral normality and abnormality —Hudson Hoagland⟩ **b :** a former dress fabric of cotton and wool **c :** a yarn spun from stock printed in different colors **d :** a silken pillow lace made with a combination of Chantilly and Spanish designs **e :** a batch or sales lot of diamonds in assorted sizes **f :** coffee mixed with cream, served in a tall glass, and topped with whipped cream

**me·lan·ger** \\-zhə(r), -jə(r)\\ *n* -s **:** an operator of a melangeur

**me·lan·geur** \\,mā,lä^n 'zhər(·), -än'jər(·)\\ *n* -s [F *mélangeur*, fr. *mélanger* to mix, fr. *mélange*) + *-eur* -or] **:** a power-driven machine in which chocolate paste is mixed with sugar and flavoring and reduced to a fine smooth consistency

**me·la·nia** \\mə'lānēə, -nyə\\ [NL, fr. *melan-* + *-ia*] *syn of* THIARA

**me·la·nian** \\-ēən,-yən\\ *adj* [F *mélanien*, fr. *mélan-* melan- + *-ien* -ian] **1 :** of dark or black pigmentation **2** *usu cap* **:** belonging to a stock characterized by dark pigmentation — used of various black-skinned or brown-skinned peoples or of such peoples collectively

[1]**me·lan·ic** \\mə'lanik\\ *adj* [*melan-* + *-ic*] **1 a :** MELANOTIC **b :** MELANISTIC **2 :** MELANIAN

[2]**melanic** \\"\\ *or* **mel·a·nist** \\'melənəst\\ *n* -s **:** a melanistic individual

**mel·a·nif·er·ous** \\,melə¦nif(ə)rəs\\ *adj* [*melan-* + *-iferous*] *of a body structure* **:** containing black pigment

**mel·a·ni·idae** \\,melə'nīə,dē\\ [NL, fr. *Melania* + *-idae*] *syn of* THIARIDAE

**mel·a·nin** \\'melənən\\ *n* -s [ISV *melan-* + *-in*] **1 :** any of various dark brown or black pigments of animal or plant structures (as skin, hair, the choroid coat, or raw potato when exposed to air) **2 :** any of various pigments that are similar to the natural melanins, are obtained esp. by enzymatic oxidation of tyrosine or dopa, and are believed to be quinonoid polymers derived from indole

**melaninlike** \\'≈≈≈,≈\\ *adj* **:** resembling or chemically related to melanins

**mel·an·irid·o·some** \\,melə,nī'ridə,sōm\\ *n* -s [*melano*phore + *iridophore* + *-some*] **:** a multiple or compound chromatophore with melanophore and iridophore components that is common in teleosts

**mel·a·nism** \\'melə,nizəm\\ *n* -s [*melan-* + *-ism*] **1 a :** an unusual development of black or nearly black color in the skin or in the plumage or pelage occurring either as a characteristic of a variety or as an individual variation esp. in mammals and birds **b :** a melanistic variety or individual **2 :** the character in man of having a high degree of pigmentation in skin, eyes, and hair **3 :** a surface browning or blackening of tissues (as of wheat) due to development of pigment in the outer layers

**mel·a·nist** \\'melənəst\\ *n* -s [*melan-* + *-ist*] **:** MELANIC

**mel·a·nis·tic** \\¦melə¦nistik\\ *adj* **:** affected with or characterized by melanism **:** constituting melanism

**mel·a·nite** \\'melə,nīt\\ *n* -s [G *melanit*, fr. *melan-* + *-it* -ite] **:** a black garnet of the variety andradite — **mel·a·nit·ic** \\¦melə¦nid·ik\\ *adj*

**mel·a·ni·za·tion** \\,melənə'zāshən, -,nī'z-\\ *n* -s **:** the quality or state of being or the process of becoming melanized

**mel·a·nize** \\'melə,nīz\\ *vt* -ED/-ING/-s [ISV *melan-* + *-ize*] **1 :** to convert into or infiltrate with melanin ⟨*melanized* cell granules⟩ **2 :** to render dark or black

**melanized soil** *n* **:** a soil (as that of a mesophytic forest) that is darkened by incorporated humus

**mel·a·no** \\'melə,nō\\ *n* -s [*melan-*] **:** a melanistic individual — compare ALBINO

[1]**melano-** — see MELAN-

[2]**melano-** *comb form, usu cap* [*melanian* + *-o-*] **:** Melanian and ⟨*Melano*-Papuan⟩

**melano·blast** \\'melənō,blast, mə'lanə,-\\ *n* [ISV *melan-* + *-blast*] **:** a cell that produces melanin — **melano·blas·tic** \\¦≈≈≈¦blastik, ≈¦≈≈-\\ *adj*

**melano·blas·to·ma** \\,≈≈≈,bla'stōmə, ≈,≈≈-\\ *n, pl* **melano·blastomas** \\-məz\\ *or* **melanoblastoma·ta** \\-məd·ə\\ [NL, fr. ISV *melanoblast* + NL *-oma*] **:** a malignant tumor derived from melanoblasts

**mel·a·no·carcinoma** \\¦melə(,)nō+\\ *n* [NL, fr. *melan-* + *carcinoma*] **:** a melanoma believed to be of epithelial origin

**mel·a·no·cerite** \\¦m=lənō+\\ *n* -s [G *melanozerit*, fr. *melan-* + *zerit* cerite] **:** a mineral consisting of a complex silicate, borate, tantalate, fluoride, or other compound of cerium, yttrium, calcium, and other metals and occurring in brown or black rhombohedral crystals

**mel·a·noch·roi** \\,melə'näkrə,wī\\ *n pl, sometimes cap* [NL, fr. *melan-* + Gk *ōchroi*, nom. pl. masc. of *ōchros* pale] **:** Caucasians having dark hair and pale complexion — **mel·a·no·chro·ic** \\¦melənō¦krōik\\ *also* **mel·a·noch·roid** \\-¦nä,krȯid\\ *adj, sometimes cap*

**mel·a·noch·ro·ous** \\¦melə¦näkrəwəs\\ *adj* [Gk *melanochroos, melanochrous*, fr. *melan-* -chroos, -chrous (fr. *chroa, chroia* skin)] **:** having a dark or swarthy skin

**mel·a·noc·o·mous** \\-kəməs\\ *adj* [*melan-* + Gk *komē* hair + E *-ous*] **:** having dark or black hair

**mel·a·no·crat·ic** \\¦melənō¦krad·ik\\ *adj* [*melan-* + Gk *kratein* to be strong, rule (akin to Gk *kratos* strength) + E *-ic* — more at HARD] *of igneous rock* **:** having predominantly dark mineral constituents — compare LEUCOCRATIC, MESOCRATIC

**melano·cyte** \\'melənō,sīt, mə'lanə,-\\ *n* -s [ISV *melan-* + *-cyte*] **:** a cell producing or containing dark pigment — compare MELANOBLAST

**melano·derm** \\-,dərm\\ *n* -s [*melan-* + *-derm*] **:** a person with a dark skin; *specif* **:** a black-skinned or brown-skinned person — compare XANTHODERM

**mel·a·no·der·ma** \\,melənō'dərmə\\ *n* -s [NL, fr. *melan-* + *-derma*] **:** abnormally intense pigmentation of the skin — **mel·a·no·der·mic** \\¦≈≈≈¦mik\\ *adj*

**mel·a·no·gas·ter** \\'≈≈≈,gastə(r), ,≈≈≈'≈≈\\ *n, cap* [NL, fr. *melan-* + *-gaster*] **:** a genus of hard-skinned puffballs of the family Sclerodermataceae — see RED TRUFFLE

**mel·a·no·gen** \\'melənō,jen; mə'lanəjən, -,jen\\ *n* -s [*melan-* + *-gen*] **:** a precursor of melanin

**mel·a·no·genesis** \\,melənō+\\ *n* [NL, fr. *melan-* + L *genesis*] **:** the formation of melanin

**melanogenetic** *adj* [*melan-* + *-genetic*] **:** of or relating to melanogenesis

**mel·a·no·gen·ic** \\¦≈≈≈¦jenik\\ *adj* [*melan-* + *-genic*] **1 :** of, relating to, or characteristic of melanogenesis **2 :** producing melanin

[1]**mel·a·noid** \\'melə,nȯid\\ *adj* [ISV *melan-* + *-oid*] **1 :** characterized or darkened by melanins ⟨a ~ lesion⟩ **2 :** relating to or occurring in melanosis ⟨~ symptoms⟩

[2]**melanoid** \\"\\ *n* -s **1 :** a melanistic individual **2 :** a pigment (as one contributing esp. to the yellow color of the skin) that is a disintegration product of a melanin

**mel·a·noi·din** \\,melə'nȯid^ən\\ *n* -s [[2]*melanoid* + *-in*] **:** any of various colored substances formed from proteins or amino acids (as in the presence of glucose) — compare HUMIN b

**mel·a·no·ma** \\,melə'nōmə\\ *n, pl* **melanomas** \\-ōməz\\ *also* **melanoma·ta** \\-ōməd·ə\\ [NL, fr. *melan-* + *-oma*] **1 :** a skin tumor containing dark pigment **2 :** a tumor of high malignancy that starts in a black mole and metastasizes rapidly and widely — called also *malignant melanoma*

**mel·a·no·ma·to·sis** \\,melə,nōmə'tōsəs\\ *n, pl* **melanomato·ses** \\-ō,sēz\\ [NL, fr. *melanomat-, melanoma* + *-osis*] **:** the condition of having multiple melanomas in the body ⟨an advanced ~⟩

**mel·a·noph·i·la** \\,melə'näfələ\\ *n, cap* [NL, fr. *melan-* + *-phila*] **:** a genus of buprestid beetles that includes several destructive borers of forest trees

**melano·phore** \\'melənə,fō(ə)r, mə'lan-\\ *n* -s [*melan-* + *-phore*] **:** a chromatophore containing melanin **:** a black or brown pigment cell — **melano·phor·ic** \\¦≈≈≈¦fōrik, ≈¦≈≈-\\ *adj*

**me·lan·o·plus** \\mə'lanəpləs\\ *n, cap* [NL, fr. *melan-* + *-oplus* (fr. Gk *hoplon* tool, implement) — more at HOPLITE] **:** a large American genus containing the migratory locusts of the western U. S. and other common American grasshoppers

**mel·a·nor·rhoea** \\,melənə'rēə\\ *n, cap* [NL, fr. *melan-* + *-rrhoea*] **:** a small genus of East Indian trees (family Anacardiaceae) with simple leaves, panicled flowers, and drupaceous fruit — see BLACK-VARNISH TREE

**mel·a·no·sarcoma** \\¦melə(,)nō+\\ *n* [NL, fr. *melan-* + *sarcoma*] **:** a sarcoma that is believed to be derived from melanoblasts

**mel·a·nose** \\'melə,nōs, -ōz\\ *n* -s [F *mélanose* melanosis, melanose, fr. NL *melanosis*] **1 :** a disease of the grapevine caused by a fungus (*Septoria ampelina*) that attacks the leaves causing them to fall **2 :** a disease of citrus trees and fruits caused by an imperfect fungus (*Diaporthe citri*) that produces hard brown raised and often gummy spots in the rind of the fruit and also on twigs and leaves

**mel·a·no·sis** \\,melə'nōsəs\\ *n, pl* **melano·ses** \\-ō,sēz\\ [NL, fr. *melan-* + *-osis*] **:** a condition characterized by abnormal deposition of melanins or sometimes other pigments in the tissues of the body

**mel·a·no·sper·mous** \\¦melənō¦spərməs\\ *adj* [*melan-* + *-spermous*] *of an alga* **:** having dark olivaceous spores

**mel·a·no·stib·i·an** \\,melənō'stibēən\\ *n* -s [G, fr. *melan-* + *stibium* + *-an*] **:** a black mineral approximately $(Mn,Fe)_6Sb_2O_9$ that is an oxide of iron, manganese, and antimony

**mel·a·no·te·kite** \\-nō'tē,kīt\\ *n* -s [Sw *melanotekit*, fr. *melan-* + Gk *tēkein* to melt + Sw *-it* -ite; fr. its fusing to a black glass — more at THAW] **:** a black or dark gray mineral $Pb_2Fe_2Si_2O_9$ that is a lead iron silicate

**mel·a·not·ic** \\¦melə¦näd·ik\\ *adj* [*melan-* + *-otic*] **:** having or characterized by black pigmentation ⟨a ~ tumor⟩ ⟨a ~ race⟩

**mel·a·not·ri·chous** \\¦melə¦nä·trəkəs\\ *adj* [*melan-* + *-trichous*] **:** MELANOCOMOUS

**mel·a·no·tus** \\,melə'nōd·əs\\ *n, cap* [NL, fr. *mela-* + *-notus*] **:** a widely distributed genus of small brown elaterid beetles whose larvae include several destructive wireworms

**mel·a·nous** \\'melənəs\\ *adj* [*melan-* + *-ous*] **:** having black hair and dark brown or blackish skin — used chiefly of the darker Melanochroi

**mel·a·no·vanadite** \\¦melə(,)nō+\\ *n* -s [*melan-* + *vanadite*] **:** a mineral $Ca_2V_{10}O_{25}$ that is a complex oxide of calcium and vanadium

**me·lan·ter·ite** \\mə'lantə,rīt\\ *n* -s [G *melanterit*, fr. F *mélantérie* melanterite (fr. NL *melanteria*, fr. Gk *melantēria* pigment used for blacking shoes, fr. *melan-* + *tērein* to watch, preserve, keep + *-ia* -y) + G *-it* -ite] **:** native copperas $FeSO_4.7H_2O$ that is isomorphous with kirovite and pisanite

**mel·an·tha·ce·ae** \\,melən'thāsē,ē, ,me,lan-\\ *n pl, cap* [NL, irreg. fr. *Melanthium*, type genus + *-aceae*] *in some classifications* **:** a family of monocotyledonous plants (order Liliales) distinguished from the Liliaceae by the septicidal capsule and by the absence of bulbs — see MELANTHIUM — **mel·an·tha·ceous** \\¦≈(,)≈¦thāshəs\\ *adj*

**me·lan·thi·um** \\mə'lan(t)thēəm\\ *n, cap* [NL, fr. *mela-* + *anth-* + *-ium*; fr. the dark color of the fading perianth] **:** a small No. American genus that is sometimes made type of the family Melanthaceae or now more usu. included among the Liliaceae and that comprises perennial herbs with heavy rootstocks and erect leafy stems bearing a terminal panicle of yellowish flowers having clawed perianth segments — see BUNCHFLOWER

**mel·an·uria** \\,melə'n(y)u̇rēə\\ *n* -s [NL, fr. *melan-* + *-uria*] **:** the presence of melanins in the urine — **mel·an·uric** \\¦≈≈¦≈rik\\ *adj*

**mel·a·phyre** \\'melə,fī(ə)r\\ *n* -s [F *mélaphyre*, fr. *méla-* mela- + *-phyre*] **1 :** a porphyritic rock consisting of phenocrysts of feldspar in a dark groundmass; *broadly* **:** a porphyritic igneous rock with dark-colored aphanitic groundmass and phenocrysts of various kinds **2 :** a Mesozoic basalt

**me·las·ma** \\mə'lazmə\\ *n* -s [NL, fr. Gk, black spot, fr. *melas* black — more at MULLET] **:** a dark pigmentation of the skin (as in Addison's disease) — **me·las·mic** \\-zmik\\ *adj*

**melasses** *obs var of* MOLASSES

**me·las·si·gen·ic** \\mə¦lasə¦jenik\\ *adj* [*melasses* + *-i-* + *-genic*] **:** producing molasses **:** preventing or tending to restrict the crystallization of sugar — used esp. of certain inorganic salts

**me·las·to·ma** \\mə'lastəmə\\ *n, cap* [NL, fr. *mela-* + *-stoma*; fr. the staining property of the fruit] **:** the type genus of Melastomaceae comprising Asiatic shrubs that have coriaceous leaves and large purple flowers with several anthers of unequal lengths

**me·las·to·ma·ce·ae** \\mə,lastə'māsē,ē\\ *n pl, cap* [NL, fr. *Melastoma*, type genus + *-aceae*] **:** a family of trees, shrubs, or herbs (order Myrtales) that are characterized by opposite 3- to 9-nerved leaves, anthers with thickened connectives, and petals inserted on the throat of the calyx and that include numerous forms cultivated as ornamentals — see RHEXIA — **me·las·to·ma·ceous** \\¦≈≈¦≈¦māshəs\\ *adj*

**me·las·to·ma·ta·ce·ae** \\mə,lastəmə'tāsē,ē\\ [NL, fr. *Melastomat-, Melastoma* + *-aceae*] *syn of* MELASTOMACEAE

**mel·a·stome** \\'melə,stōm\\ *also* **me·las·to·mad** \\mə'lastə,mad\\ *n* -s [*melastome* fr. NL *Melastoma*; *melastomad* fr. NL *Melastoma* + E *-ad*] **:** a plant of the family Melastomaceae

**mel·a·tope** \\'melə,tōp\\ *n* -s [*mela-* + Gk *topos* place — more at TOPIC] **:** the point in an interference figure corresponding to the direction of an optic axis in the crystal section or grain producing the figure

**me·la·veh mal·kah** \\mə,lävə'mälkə\\ *n, pl* **melaveh malkahs** [Heb *mĕlweh malkāh*, lit., escorting the queen] **:** a traditional weekly ceremony observed chiefly by Hasidim on Saturday evening to bid farewell to the Queen Sabbath and marked by feasting, singing, dancing

**mel·a·xu·ma** \\,melə'kümə, -lək'sü-,-lə'zü-\\ *n* -s [NL, prob. irreg. (Gk χ being taken as E *x*) fr. *mela-* + Gk *chyma* fluid, fr. *chein* to pour — more at FOUND (melt)] **:** any of various plant diseases producing dark or black bark cankers; *esp* **:** a disease of the walnut caused by the imperfect fungus (*Dothiorella gregaria*)

**mel·ba** \\'melbə\\ *n* -s [after Madame Nellie *Melba* (Helen Porter Mitchell) †1931 Austral. operatic soprano] **:** fruit served with ice cream, raspberry sauce, and whipped cream ⟨ate and drank . . . sundaes, shakes, parfaits, whips, ~*s* —Elizabeth Taylor⟩ — see PÊCHE MELBA

**melba sauce** *n* [after Nellie *Melba*] **:** sauce made essentially of raspberries and sugar and served often with ice cream or whipped cream on fruit — compare PÊCHE MELBA

**melba toast** *n, sometimes cap M* [after Nellie *Melba*] **:** very thin bread toasted or rusked till crisp and well browned

**mel·bourne** \\'melbə(r)n *also* -,bōrn *or* -,bȯrn *or* -ōən *or* -ō(ə)n\\ *adj, usu cap* [fr. *Melbourne*, Australia] **:** of or from Melbourne, the capital of Victoria, Australia **:** of the kind or style prevalent in Melbourne

**mel·bur·ni·an** \\mel'bərnēən\\ *n* -s *cap* [*Melbourne*, Australia + E *-ian*] **:** a native or resident of Melbourne, Australia

**melch** \\'melch, -lsh\\ *adj* -ER/-EST [ME, prob. fr. OE *melsc* mellow; prob. akin to OE *melu* meal — more at MULCH] **1** *now dial Brit* **:** yielding easily to pressure **:** SOFT ⟨~ ground⟩ **2** *dial Brit* **:** MILD ⟨a ~ day⟩

[1]**mel·chite** *or* **mel·kite** \\'mel,kīt\\ *n* -s *usu cap* [ML *Melchita*, fr. MGk *Melchitēs*, lit., royalist, fr. Syr *malkā* king + Gk *-itēs* -ite] **1 :** a Christian in Egypt and Syria who accepted the decrees of the Council of Chalcedon in A.D. 451 against Nestorians and Monophysites **2 :** a Uniat of the Byzantine rite in Egypt, Syria, or Palestine

[2]**melchite** \\"\\ *adj, usu cap* **:** of or relating to the Melchites

**melchite alphabet** *n, usu cap M* **:** a Syriac alphabet at first uncial but becoming later cursive and the most deformed of Syriac scripts

**mel·chiz·e·dek** \\mel'kizə,dek\\ *adj, usu cap* [after *Melchizedek*, Biblical priest-king (Gen 14:18 ff.)] **:** being the greater or higher order of priesthood in the Mormon Church — compare AARONIC 2

[1]**meld** \\'meld\\ *vb* -ED/-ING/-s [G *melden* to announce, report, fr. OHG *meldōn*; akin to OE *meldian* to announce, reveal, inform on, *meld* proclamation, OS *meldon* to inform on, betray, OS & OHG *melda* betrayal, OSlav *moliti* to ask for, request, pray, Arm *malt'em* I request, Hitt *maltai, maldi* he prays; basic meaning: to pray] *vt* **:** to show or announce (a card or combination of cards that has scoring or other value in a game being played) usu. by placing face up on the table ⟨~*ing* four kings in pinochle⟩ **~** *vi* **:** to show or announce a card or combination of cards as a meld

[2]**meld** \\"\\ *n* -s **:** a card or combination of cards that is or can be melded in a card game

[3]**meld** \\"\\ *vb* -ED/-ING/-s [blend of [1]*melt* and [2]*weld*] **:** MERGE

**mel·der** \\'meld(d)ə(r)\\ *n* -s [ME *meltyre*, of Scand origin; akin to ON *meldr* flour or grain in the mill; akin to OS *maldar*, a measure for grain, OHG *maltar*; akin to OE *melu* flour — more at MEAL] *dial Brit* **:** the quantity of meal ground at one time **:** meal just ground; *also* **:** a grinding of grain

**mel·do·la's blue** \\'meldələz-\\ *or* **meldola blue** *n, usu cap M&B* [after Raphael *Meldola* †1915 Eng. chemist] **:** a basic dye — see DYE table I (under *Basic Blue 6*)

**meld out** *vi* **:** to meld the last card or cards of one's hand (as in canasta or rummy)

**me·le** \\'mā(,)lā\\ *n* -s [Hawaiian] **:** an Hawaiian song or chant

**mele·agrid·i·dae** \\,melē'gridə,dē\\ *n pl, cap* [NL, fr. *Meleagrid-, Meleagris*, type genus + *-idae*] **:** a family of large No. American birds (order Galliformes) that comprise the turkeys and a few extinct related birds and are sometimes placed in a subfamily of Phasianidae

**mele·agri·na** \\-rīnə,-rēnə\\ [NL, fr. *Meleagris*, genus of mollusks in some former classifications (fr. L, guinea fowl) + *-ina*; fr. the spotted appearance of the mollusks] *syn of* PINCTADA

**mele·agris** \\,melē'agrəs, -'ēg-\\ *n, cap* [NL, fr. L, guinea fowl, fr. Gk] **:** the type genus of Meleagrididae comprising the wild and domestic turkeys

**m electron** *n, usu cap M* **:** an electron in the M-shell

[1]**me·lee** \\'mā(,)lā, mā'lā *sometimes* mə'lā *or* 'me(,)lā\\ *n* -s [F *mêlée*, fr. OF *meslee, medlee, melee* mixture, argument, fight — more at MEDLEY] **1 :** a fight or contest between individuals mingled in a confused mass **:** a confused struggle ⟨killed in a border ~⟩ ⟨this week's wrestling card includes two team ~*s*⟩ **2 :** a cavalry exercise in which two groups of riders try to cut paper plumes off the helmets of their opponents **3 :** a confused mingling together of often incongruous elements **:** MÉLANGE ⟨pushing their . . . way through a ~ of taxis, bicycles, and people —*Atlantic*⟩ **syn** see BRAWL

[2]**melee** \\"\\ *n* -s [origin unknown] **:** a small diamond cut from a fragment of a larger stone and usu. less than one-eighth carat in weight

**mel·e·gue·ta pepper** \\¦melə¦ged·ə-, -gäd·ə-\\ *or* **mal·a·gue·ta pepper** *or* **mal·a·guet·ta pepper** *also* **mal·a·get·ta pepper** \\¦malə-\\ *n* [F & Sp; F *méléguette, maliguette*, fr. Sp *malagueta*] **:** GRAIN OF PARADISE 1

**me·le·na** *or* **me·lae·na** \\mə'lēnə\\ *n* -s [NL, fr. Gk *melaina*, fem. of *melas* black — more at MULLET] **:** the passage of dark tarry stools containing decomposing blood that is usu. an indication of bleeding in the upper part of the alimentary canal

**mel·eng·ket** \\¦meləŋ¦ket\\ *n* -s [native name in the Philippines] **:** a soft Manila copal gathered about two weeks after the trees have been tapped

**me·les** \\'mē(,)lēz\\ *n, cap* [NL, fr. L, badger, marten] **:** a genus of mustelid mammals comprising the typical Old World badgers

[1]**me·le·tian** \\mə'lēshən\\ *adj, usu cap* [*Meletius*, 4th cent. A.D. bishop of Lycopolis + E *-an*] **:** of or relating to Meletius the bishop of Lycopolis

[2]**meletian** \\"\\ *n* -s *usu cap* **:** a member or supporter of a schismatic party upholding Meletius the bishop of Lycopolis in exercising episcopal functions in the see of Alexandria early in the 4th century A.D.

[3]**meletian** \\"\\ *adj, usu cap* [*Meletius* †381 A.D. Greek ecclesiastic, bishop of Antioch + E *-an*] **:** of or relating to Meletius the bishop of Antioch in Syria

[4]**meletian** \\"\\ *n* -s *usu cap* **:** a member or supporter of a schism occasioned by dissensions over the opinions of Meletius the bishop of Antioch

**me·lets·ki** \\mə'letskē\\ *or* **me·liz·ki** \\-lit-\\ *n, pl* **meletski** *or* **meletskis** *or* **melizki** *or* **melizkis** *usu cap* **:** a member of a division of the Chulyma Tatars

**me·lez·i·tose** \\mə'lezə,tōs *also* -ōz\\ *n* -s [F *mélézitose*, fr. *mélèze* larch (fr. Prov *meleze*) + *mélitose* melitose] **:** a nonreducing trisaccharide sugar $C_{18}H_{32}O_{16}.2H_2O$ that is less sweet than sucrose, that is obtained esp. from exudations of various trees (as the larch or Douglas fir) or from honey made from such exudations, and that on partial hydrolysis yields glucose and turanose

**meli-** *comb form* [Gk *meli* — more at MELLIFLUOUS] **:** honey ⟨*meli*lite⟩

**me·lia** \\'mēlēə, -lyə\\ *n, cap* [NL, fr. Gk *melia, meliē* manna ash; fr. the resemblance of the leaves to those of the ash] **:** a genus (the type of the family Meliaceae) of East Indian and Australian deciduous trees with pinnate or bipinnate leaves resembling those of the ashes, fragrant white or lilac flowers in axillary panicles, and small drupaceous fruits containing hard bony seeds — see CHINABERRY 2, MARGOSA

**-melia** \\'mēlēə, 'mel-, -lyə\\ *n comb form* -s [NL, fr. Gk *melos* limb + NL *-ia* — more at MELODY] **:** condition of the limbs ⟨*anisomelia*⟩ ⟨*schistomelia*⟩ ⟨*ectromelia*⟩

**me·li·a·ce·ae** \\,mēlē'āsē,ē\\ *n pl, cap* [NL, fr. *Melia*, type genus + *-aceae*] **:** a family of tropical trees and shrubs (order Geraniales) that have monadelphous stamens and include various important timber and ornamental trees — see MAHOGANY, MELIA — **me·li·a·ceous** \\¦≈≈¦āshəs\\ *adj*

[1]**me·lian** \\'mēlēən, -lyən\\ *adj, usu cap* [*Melos*, one of the Cyclades islands in the southern Aegean sea + E *-ian*] **:** of or relating to the island of Melos

[2]**melian** \\"\\ *n* -s *cap* **:** a native or inhabitant of Melos

**me·li·an·tha·ce·ae** \\,mēlē,an'thāsē,ē\\ *n pl, cap* [NL, fr. *Melianthus*, type genus + *-aceae*] **:** a family of African trees and shrubs (order Sapindales) having irregular flowers and stipulate leaves — see MELIANTHUS — **me·li·an·tha·ceous** \\¦mēlē,an¦thāshəs\\ *adj*

**me·li·an·thus** \\,mēlē'an(t)thəs\\ *n, cap* [NL, fr. *meli-* + *-anthus*] **:** a small genus (the type of the family Melianthaceae) of southern African shrubs having odd-pinnate leaves and racemose flowers with unequal sepals and four stamens — see HONEYFLOWER

**mel·i·bi·ose** \\,melə'bī,ōs *also* -ōz\\ *n* -s [ISV *melitose* + *bi-* + *-ose*] **:** a disaccharide sugar $C_{12}H_{22}O_{11}$ formed by partial hydrolysis of raffinose; 6-galactosyl-glucose

[1]**mel·ic** \\'melik\\ *adj* [L *melicus*, fr. Gk *melikos*, fr. *melos* song + *-ikos* -ic — more at MELODY] **1 :** of or belonging to song **:** designed to be sung **:** LYRIC **2 :** being or relating to Greek poetry essentially lyrical and musical in character following the elegiac and iambic poetry of the 7th and 6th centuries B.C. and including monodic poetry (as in Sappho) closely akin to the modern lyric and choral poetry (as in Pindar)

[2]**melic** \\"\\ *n* -s **:** melic poetry

**mel·i·ca** \\'meləkə\\ *n, cap* [NL, fr. It *melica, meliga* sorghum, modif. (influenced by L *mel* honey) of ML (*herba*) *medica*, lit., medical herb, fr. *herba* herb + *medica*, fem. of *medicus* medical — more at MELLIFLUOUS, MEDICAL] **:** a genus of perennial mostly woodland grasses somewhat resembling *Festuca* but having lemmas 2-lobed at the apex and the upper 2 or 3 lemmas empty and forming a club-shaped mass — see MELIC GRASS

**mel·i·cer·ta** \\,melə'sərd·ə\\ *n, cap* [NL, after *Melicerta*, a sea-god, fr. L, fr. Gk *Melikertēs*] **:** a genus of rotifers (order Monogononta) that are usu. tube-living and have a conspicuous lobed corona

**mel·ic grass** \\'melik-\\ *also* **melic** *or* **melick** *n* [NL *Melica*] **:** a grass of the genus *Melica*

**mel·i·chrous** \\'meləkrəs, me'likrəwəs\\ *adj* [Gk *melichroos, melichrous*, fr. *meli* honey + *-chroos, -chrous* -chrous — more at MELLIFLUOUS] **:** of the color honey yellow

**mel·i·coc·ca** \\,melə'käkə\\ *n, cap* [NL, fr. *meli-* + Gk *-cocca* (fr. *kokkos* kermes berry)] **:** a genus of tropical American trees and shrubs (family Sapindaceae) having pinnate leaflets, abruptly tetramerous flowers with a peltate stigma, and a one-seeded or two-seeded berry

**mel·i·crate** \'melə,krāt\ *n* -s [LL *melicratum*, fr. Gk *melikraton*, fr. *meli* honey + *-kraton* (fr. *kerannynai* to mix) — more at MELLIFLUOUS, CRATER] *archaic* : a fermented or unfermented beverage of honey and water : HYDROMEL

**mel·i·lite** \'melə,līt\ *n* -s [F *mélilite*, fr. *méli-* meli- + *-lite*] : an often honey-yellow mineral $(Ca,Na_2)(Mg,Fe,Al)(Si,Al)_2O_7$ occurring in small tetragonal crystals that is a silicate of sodium, calcium, aluminum, and iron; *esp* : a member of the series consisting of an isomorphous solid-solution series between gehlenite and akermanite

**mel·i·lot** \'melə,lät\ *n* -s [ME *mellilot*, fr. MF *melilot*, fr. L *melilotos*, fr. Gk *melilōtos*, fr. *meli* honey + *lōtos* clover, melilot, lotus — more at LOTUS] : a plant of the genus *Melilotus* : SWEET CLOVER; *esp* : YELLOW SWEET CLOVER 1 — compare BLUE MELILOT

**mel·i·lo·tus** \,melə'lōd·əs\ *n* [NL, fr. L *melilotos* melilot] **1** *cap* : a genus of annual or biennial erect Old World leguminous herbs that comprise the sweet clovers, have trifoliolate leaves, small white or yellow flowers in axillary racemes, and short straight one-seeded or two-seeded pods, and are widely cultivated and naturalized as escapes **2** -s : a plant of the genus *Melilotus*

**¹meline** \'mē,līn, 'me,-\ *adj* [L *melinus*, fr. *meles* marten, badger + *-inus* -ine] : made up of or resembling badgers ⟨the ~ mammals⟩

**²meline** \"\ *adj* [Gk *mēlinos* of a quince, quince-yellow, fr. *mēlon* apple, quince] : of the color quince yellow

**mel·i·nite** \'melə,nīt\ *n* -s [F *mélinite*, fr. Gk *mēlinos* quince-yellow + F *-ite*] : a high explosive similar to lyddite

**mel·i·oi·do·sis** \,melē,ȯi'dōsəs\ *n*, *pl* **melioido·ses** \-ō,sēz\ [NL, fr. Gk *melis*, a disease of equines, prob. glanders + ISV *-oid* + NL *-osis*] : a highly fatal bacterial disease closely related to glanders that occurs naturally in rodents of southeastern Asia but is readily transmitted to other mammals and man by the rat flea or under certain conditions by dissemination of the causative bacterium (*Pseudomonas pseudomallei*) in air

**meli·o·la·les** \,melēə'lā(,)lēz, mə,līə-\ *n pl*, *cap* [NL, fr. *Meliola* genus of fungi (fr. Gk *mēlon* apple + NL *-i-* + L *-ola*, dim. suffix) + *-ales*] : an order of fungi (subclass Euascomycetes) having a stroma that resembles a perithecium and is not noticeably flattened

**me·lio·rate** \'mēlyə,rāt, -lēə-\ *vb* -ED/-ING/-S [LL *melioratus*, past part. of *meliorare*, fr. L *melior* better; akin to L *multus* much, Gk *mala* very, Umbrian *mutu* penalty, fine, Latvian *milns* very much] *vt* : to make better or more tolerable : AMELIORATE, SOFTEN ~ *vi* : to become better or more tolerable

**me·lio·ra·tion** \,mēlyə'rāshən, -lēə-\ *n* -s [LL *melioration-*, *melioratio*, fr. *melioratus* + L *-ion-*, *-io* -ion] : the quality or state of being meliorated or an act of meliorating : BETTERMENT: as **a** : lasting or major improvement of land (as by a tenant) ⟨the effect of ~s was greater on height growth of fir and on soil flora and condition —*Biol. Abstracts*⟩ **b** : the historical process by which the semantic and connotative status of a word tends to rise ⟨the emergence of *steward* from *sty-ward* is an example of ~ in action⟩ — compare PEJORATION

**me·lio·ra·tive** \'=(=)=,rād·iv, -,rəl, \|tiv, -ēv\ *adj* : tending to effect melioration : resulting in or leading toward betterment (as of status)

**me·lio·rism** \'mēlyə,rizəm, -lēə-\ *n* -s [L *melior* better + E *-ism*] : the belief or doctrine that the world tends to become better and that man has the power to aid its betterment ⟨~ seeks a compromise between both optimism and pessimism: the world is neither good nor evil, but can be improved on the condition that its parts do their best to improve it —Frank Thilly⟩ — compare DETERIORISM

**¹me·lio·rist** \-,rəst\ *n* -s [L *melior* + E *-ist*] : an advocate or adherent of meliorism

**²meliorist** \"\ *or* **me·lio·ris·tic** \¦=(=)=¦ristik\ *adj* : of or relating to meliorism

**me·lior·i·ty** \mēl'yȯrəd·ē, ,mel'ē'ȯ-\ *n* -ES [ML *melioritas*, fr. L *melior* better + *-itas* -ity — more at MELIORATE] : the quality or state of being better

**mel·i·pha·gi·dae** \,melə'fajə,dē\ *n pl*, *cap* [NL, fr. *Meliphaga*, type genus (fr. *meli-* + *-phaga*) + *-idae*] : a family of oscine birds that are almost entirely restricted to the Australian biogeographic region and have the tongue modified for taking nectar and insects from flowers — see HONEY EATER — **mel·i·phag·i·dan** \¦==¦fajədᵊn\ *adj or n*

**me·liph·a·gous** *or* **mel·liph·a·gous** \(')me¦lifəgəs\ *adj* [*meli-* + *-phagous*] : feeding or living upon honey

**mel·i·phane** \'melə,fān\ *n* -s [*meli-* + Gk *phainesthai* to appear, pass. of *phainein* to show — more at FANCY] : MELIPHANITE

**me·liph·a·nite** \mə'lifə,nīt\ *n* -s [*meliphane* + *-ite*] : a mineral occurring as a fluosilicate of sodium, calcium, and beryllium in yellow crystals

**me·lip·o·na** \mə'lipənə\ *n*, *cap* [NL, fr. *meli-* + *-pona* (fr. Gk *ponein* to toil)] : a genus of honeybees of tropical America that comprises small bees with a vestigial but functionless sting — compare STINGLESS BEE — **me·lip·o·nine** \-pə,nīn\ *adj*

**melis** \'mēləs, 'mel-\ *n* -ES [G, fr. Gk *meli* honey — more at MELLIFLUOUS] : a usu. slightly yellowish imperfectly refined sugar usu. prepared in loaf form

**me·lis·ma** \mə'lizmə\ *n*, *pl* **melisma·ta** \-zməd·ə\ [Gk, song, melody, fr. *melizein* to sing, fr. *melos* song — more at MELODY] **1** : SONG, TUNE **2** : a group of notes or tones sung to one syllable in plainsong **3** : melodic embellishment or ornamentation **4** : CADENZA

**mel·is·mat·ic** \¦meləz¦mad·ik\ *adj* [Gk *melismat-*, *melisma* + E *-ic*] *of music* : relating to or having melisma : FLORID

**mel·is·mat·ics** \-ks\ *n pl but sing or pl in constr* : the art of florid vocalization

**me·lis·sa** \mə'lisə\ *n* [NL, fr. Gk *melitta*, *melissa* bee, fr. *melit-*, *meli* honey — more at MELLIFLUOUS] **1** *cap* : a genus of Old World mints having axillary clusters of small white or yellowish flowers with a bilabiate calyx, exserted corolla, and divergent anther lobes — see BALM 3a, LEMON BALM **2** -s : a plant of the genus *Melissa*

**me·lis·sic acid** \mə'lisik-\ *n* [Gk *melissa* bee + E *-ic*] : a crystalline fatty acid $CH_3(CH_2)_{28}COOH$ found free or in the form of its ester with myricyl alcohol in beeswax and other waxes and also obtained by oxidation of myricyl alcohol — called also *triacontanoic acid*

**me·lis·syl alcohol** \-səl-\ *n* [*melissic* + *-yl*] : MYRICYL ALCOHOL

**mel·i·ten·sis** \¦melə¦ten(t)səs\ *adj* [NL (specific epithet of *Brucella melitensis*), fr. L *melitensis* of Malta, fr. *Melita* Malta, island in the Mediterranean + L *-ensis* -ese] : of, derived from, or caused by a bacterium (*Brucella melitensis*) ⟨~ proteins⟩ ⟨~ fever⟩

**mel·i·tose** \'melə,tōs *also* -ōz\ *n* -s [ISV *meli-* + connective *-t-* + *-ose*; prob. orig. formed as F *mélitose*] : RAFFINOSE

**me·lit·tia** \mə'lid·ēə\ *n*, *cap* [NL, fr. Gk *melitta*, *melissa* bee + NL *-ia*] : a large genus of chiefly tropical clearwings (family Aegeriidae) including some that mimic wasps — see SQUASH BORER

**mel·it·tol·o·gist** \,melə'täləjəst\ *n* -s [*melittology* study of bees (fr. Gk *melitta*, *melissa* bee + E *-o-* + *-logy*) + *-ist* — more at MELISSA] : an entomologist specializing in the study of bees

**mel·i·tu·ria** *or* **mel·li·tu·ria** \,melə'tu̇rēə, -lə-'tyu̇-\ *n* -s [NL, fr. Gk *melit-*, *meli* honey + *-uria*] : the presence of any sugar in the urine

**melizki** *usu cap*, *var of* MELETSKI

**melk·hout** \'mel,kōt\ *n* -s [Afrik, fr. *melk* milk + *hout* wood] : MILKWOOD d

**melkite** *usu cap*, *var of* MELCHITE

**¹mell** \'mel\ *n* -s [ME — more at MAUL] **1** *dial Brit* : a hammer or mallet esp. of wood **2** *dial Brit* **a** : the prize (as a mallet) given to the participant who places last in a contest **b** : the participant who places last in a contest

**²mell** \"\ *vt* -ED/-ING/-S [ME *mellen*, fr. *mell*, n.] *dial Brit* : to strike with a mell : BEAT

**³mell** \"\ *vb* -ED/-ING/-S [ME *mellen*, fr. MF *mesler*, *medler*, *meller* — more at MEDDLE] *vt*, *dial Brit* : MIX, MINGLE ~ *vi* **1** *now dial Brit* : to join in combat — usu. used with *with* **2** *now dial Brit* : JOIN, ASSOCIATE — usu. used with *with* ⟨~ with bad company⟩ **3** *now dial Brit* : to interest or occupy oneself ⟨~ with war —C.L.Smith⟩ : MEDDLE — usu. used with *with* or *in*

**⁴mell** \"\ *var of* MEL

**⁵mell** \"\ *n* -s [origin unknown] **1** *dial chiefly Eng* : KIRN 2 **2** *dial chiefly Eng* : HARVEST HOME 2

**mell-** *or* **melli-** *comb form* [L — more at MELLIFLUOUS] : honey : like honey ⟨*mellite*⟩ ⟨*mellisugent*⟩ ⟨*mellisonant*⟩

**mel·lah** \'melə\ *n* -s [origin unknown] : the Jewish quarter of a northern African city — compare MEDINA

**mel·lay** \mə'lā, me'lā, 'me(,)lā, 'melē\ *n* -s [ME *melle*, fr. MF *meslee*, *medlee*, *melee* mixture, quarrel, fight — more at MEDLEY] : MELEE 1, 3

**mell-doll** \'=,=\ *n* [⁵*mell*] *dial Eng* : HARVEST DOLL

**mel·le·ous** \'melēəs\ *adj* [L *melleus*, fr. *mell-* + *-eus* -eous — more at MELLIFLUOUS] : resembling or containing honey

**mel·ler** \'melə(r)\ *n* -s [by shortening and alter.] *slang* : MELODRAMA 2

**mel·lif·er·ous** \(')me¦lif(ə)rəs\ *adj* [L *mellifer* (fr. *mell-* + *-fer* -ferous) + E *-ous*] : producing or yielding honey

**mel·lif·lu·ent** \-fləwənt\ *adj* [LL *mellifluent-*, *mellifluens*, fr. L *melli-* mell- + *fluent-*, *fluens*, pres. part. of *fluere* to flow — more at FLUID] *archaic* : MELLIFLUOUS

**mel·lif·lu·ous** \(')me¦lifləwəs\ *adj* [LL *mellifluus*, fr. L *melli-* (fr. *mell-*, *mel* honey) + *-fluus* (fr. *fluere* to flow); akin to OE *milisc* sweet, mild, *mildēaw*, *melēdēaw* honeydew, OS *milidou* mildew, OHG *militou* mildew, Goth *milith* honey, Gk *melit-*, *meli*, OIr *mil*, Arm *melr*, Alb *mjal*, Hitt *milit*] **1** : flowing or sweetened with or as if with honey ⟨~ confections⟩ **2** : sweetly flowing : SMOOTH, HONEYED ⟨a ~ voice⟩ — **mel·lif·lu·ous·ly** *adv* — **mel·lif·lu·ous·ness** *n* -ES

**mel·li·lite** \'melə,līt\ *n* -s [*mell-* + *-lite*] **1** : MELILITE **2** : MELLITE

**mel·lis·o·nant** \(')me¦lisᵊnənt, mə'l-\ *adj* [*mell-* + L *sonant-*, *sonans*, pres. part. of *sonare* to sound — more at SOUND] : pleasing to the ear

**mel·li·su·gent** \¦melə¦süjənt\ *adj* [*mell-* + L *sugent-*, *sugens*, pres. part. of *sugere* to suck — more at SUCK] : feeding by sucking up honey or nectar

**mel·li·tate** \'melə,tāt\ *n* -s [*mellitic* + *-ate*] : a salt or ester of mellitic acid

**mel·lite** \'me,līt\ *n* -s [NL *mellites*, fr. *mell-* + *-ites* -ite; trans. of G *honigstein*] **1** : a honey-colored mineral $Al_2C_{12}O_{12}.18H_2O$ that is a hydrous aluminum mellitate found in brown coal and is in part a product of vegetable decomposition **2** [ISV *mell-* + *-ite*] : a medicinal preparation containing honey

**mel·lit·ic acid** \(')me¦lid·ik-, mə'l-\ *n* [*mellite* + *-ic*] : a crystalline acid $C_6(COOH)_6$ occurring in the form of its aluminum salt as the mineral mellite and also made synthetically (as by oxidation of coal or graphite); benzene-hexa-carboxylic acid

**mellituria** *var of* MELITURIA

**mel·liv·o·ra** \me'livərə, mə'l-\ *n*, *cap* [NL, fr. *mell-* + *-vora*] : a genus of mustelid mammals consisting of the ratel

**mel·liv·o·rous** \(')me¦livərəs, mə'l-\ *adj* [*mell-* + *-vorous*] : MELLIPHAGOUS

**mel·lon** *or* **mel·on** \'me,län\ *n* -s [G *mellon*, irreg. fr. *melam* + *-on* -one] : a yellow powder $C_6H_3N_9$ formed on heating various cyanogen compounds or as a by-product in the preparation of melamine

**mel·lo·phan·ic acid** \¦melə¦fanik-\ *n* [ISV *mellite* + *-o-* + Gk *phan-* (stem of *phainesthai* to appear, pass. of *phainein* to show) + ISV *-ic* — more at FANCY] : either of two isomeric acids derived from benzene: **a** : PREHNITIC ACID **b b** : a crystalline acid $C_6H_2(COOH)_4$ formed by oxidation of isodurene; 1,2,3,5-benzene-tetracarboxylic acid

**mel·lo·phone** \'melə,fōn\ *n* [¹*mellow* + *-phone*] : an althorn in circular form sometimes used as a substitute for the French horn

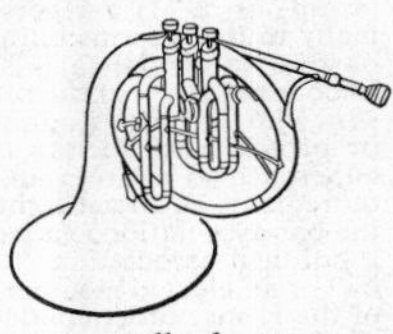

mellophone

**¹mel·low** \'me(,)lō, -lə; -ləw, -lō+V\ *adj* -ER/-EST [ME *melwe*, *melowe*] **1** : fully matured: as **a** *of a fruit* : having attained the flavor, sweetness, and softness of perfect ripeness : soft in substance and sweet in taste ⟨bit into a ~ peach⟩ **b** *of a wine* : adequately and properly aged so as to be free of harshness or acidity : mild and pleasing in flavor ⟨a ~ port⟩ **c** : having attained to softness, gentleness, or kindliness through aging and experience : freed from the rashness or harshness of youth ⟨~ wisdom⟩ ⟨the peace of ~ age⟩ **2 a** *of soil* : rich and easily worked : of soft and loamy consistency **b** (1) : free from coarseness, roughness, or harshness : rich and full but free from garishness or stridency — used esp. of sound, color, style ⟨the ~ tones of an old violin⟩ ⟨furnished the room with ~ old fabrics and richly polished woods⟩ (2) *of a speech sound* : characterized by no friction or by friction that is comparatively mild in that there is only one friction-producing component in the articulation ⟨\t\ is frictionless and ~; \th\, which has tongue-teeth friction only, is ~; but \sh\, which has both tongue-teeth and tongue-palate friction, is not⟩ — compare STRIDENT **c** *of livestock* : having a hide that is soft, sleek, and flexible to the touch **3 a** : somewhat intoxicated : warmed and relaxed by liquor **b** : relaxed and at ease : pleasantly convivial : GENIAL **4 a** *of a chemical solution* : weakened by use or materially altered in the course of time (as by bacterial action) **b** *of a process* : involving use of a mild solution to obtain mild results — **mel·low·ly** *adv* — **mel·low·ness** *n* -ES

**²mellow** \"\ *vb* -ED/-ING/-S *vt* : to make mellow ~ *vi* : to become mellow ⟨grapes ~*ing* in the sun⟩

**mellow bug** *n*, *chiefly South & Midland* : WHIRLIGIG BEETLE

**mel·lowy** \'meləwē, -lōl, \|i\ *adj* [ME *melowy*, fr. *melwe*, *meluwe* + *-y*] *archaic* : MELLOW, SOFT

**mells** *pl of* MELL, *pres 3d sing of* MELL

**mell supper** *n* : HARVEST HOME 2

**mel·ly** \'melē\ *archaic var of* MELLAY

**¹melo** \'mē(,)lō, 'me(-\ [NL, fr. LL, melon — more at MELON] *syn of* CYMBIUM

**²melo** \'me(,)lō, -lə; -ləw,-lō+V\ *n* -s [by shortening] : MELODRAMA

**¹melo-** *comb form* [F *mélo-*, fr. Gk *melo-*, fr. *melos* limb, musical phrase, melody, song — more at MELODY] : song ⟨*melo*logue⟩ ⟨*melo*mania⟩

**²melo-** — see MEL-

**mel·o·cactus** \¦melə+\ *n*, *cap* [NL, fr. LL *melo* melon + NL *Cactus*] : a genus comprising tropical American strongly ribbed globose, spheroidal, or short cylindrical cacti with a terminal woolly or spiny cap that in many classifications are divided among several other genera — see CACTUS 1

**mel·o·co·ton** \,meləkə,tōn, -tän\ *also* **mel·o·co·toon** \-tün\ *n* -s [Sp *melocotón* melocoton, peach, fr. ML *melum cotonium* quince, alter. of L *malum cotonium*, fr. *malum* apple (fr. Gk *mēlon*) + *cotonium*, *cotoneum* quince — more at QUINCE] : a peach grafted on a quince rootstock and formerly supposed to have special qualities of excellence

**me·lo·de·on** \mə'lōdēən\ *n* -s [alter. of *melodion*] **1** : AMERICAN ORGAN **2** *archaic* : MUSIC HALL

**me·lo·dia** \-ēə\ *n* -s [LL — more at MELODY] **1** : MELODY, SONG **2** : an 8-foot labial organ stop with wood pipes and tone of soft flute quality

**me·lo·di·al** \mə'lōdēəl, me'-\ *adj* : relating to melody — **me·lo·di·al·ly** \-ēəlē\ *adv*

**me·lod·ic** \-ə'lädik, me'-, -dēk\ *adj* [LL *melodicus*, fr. Gk *melōidikos*, fr. *melōidia* melody + *-ikos* -ic — more at MELODY] : relating to, containing, constituting, or made up of melody : MELODIOUS — **me·lod·i·cal·ly** \-dək(ə)lē, -dēk-, -li\ *adv*

**melodic curve** *n* : the curve described by the successive musical notes or tones of a melody

**melodic minor scale** *n* : a minor scale with the ascending intervals between the scale tones consisting of whole steps except those between two and three and seven and eight and with the descending intervals corresponding to the pattern of the natural minor scale with half steps between six and five and three and two

**me·lo·di·con** \-dəkən\ *n* -s [NL, fr. Gk *melōidikon*, neut. of *melōidikos* melodic] : a keyboard musical instrument invented about 1800 that gave its tones from tuning forks or steel bars

**me·lo·di·on** \-'lōdēən\ *n* -s [G, fr. *melodie* melody, fr. OF] **1** : a keyboard musical instrument invented in 1806 consisting of graduated metal rods sounded by contact with a revolving cylinder **2** : AMERICAN ORGAN

**me·lo·di·ous** \mə'lōdēəs, me'-\ *adj* [ME, fr. MF *melodieus*, fr. ML *melodiosus*, fr. LL *melodia* + L *-osus* -ous — more at MELODY] **1** : agreeable to the ear by a sweet succession of sounds **2** : producing or designed to produce melody ⟨a ~ instrument⟩ ⟨these ~ poets⟩ **3 a** : containing, constituting, or characterized by melody **b** : having a melody — **melodiously** *adv* — **melodiousness** *n* -ES

**mel·o·dism** \'melə,dizəm\ *n* -s : preferential use of melody

**mel·o·dist** \-,dəst\ *n* -s **1** : SINGER **2** : a composer of melodies ⟨was not a really first-rate composer, only an agreeable ~ —Arnold Bennett⟩

**mel·o·dize** \-,dīz\ *vb* -ED/-ING/-S *vt* : to make melodious : set to melody ~ *vi* : to make melody : compose a melody — **mel·o·diz·er** \-zə(r)\ *n* -s

**melo·drama** \'melə+,-\ *n* [modif. (influenced by *drama*) of F *mélodrame*, fr. *mélo-* ¹melo- + *drame* drama, fr. LL *drama* — more at DRAMA] **1 a** : a romantic sensational stage play interspersed with songs and orchestral music **b** : a recitation of a dramatic or lyric text to a musical background — compare DUODRAMA, MONODRAMA **2 a** : a play characterized by extravagant theatricality, subordination of characterization to plot, and predominance of physical action **b** : the genre of dramatic literature constituted by such plays **3** : something resembling a melodrama; *esp* : melodramatic events or behavior ⟨a monster of villainy whose life and death prove that the most lurid ~ still exists —Richard Watts⟩

**melo·dramatic** *also* **melo·dramatical** \¦melə+\ *adj* [*melodrama* + *-tic*, *-tical* (as in *dramatic*, *dramatical*)] **1** : of, relating to, or characteristic of melodrama **2** : suitable to melodrama esp. in being sensational in situation or action — **melodramatically** \"+\ *adv*

**melo·dramatics** \,melə+\ *n pl but sing or pl in constr* : melodramatic conduct or writing

**melo·dramatist** \"+\ *n* [*melodrama* + *-tist* (as in *dramatist*)] : a writer of melodramas

**melo·dramatize** \"+\ *vt* [*melodrama* + *-tize* (as in *dramatize*)] **1** : to make melodramatic ⟨*melodramatizing* a situation⟩ **2** : to make a melodrama of (as a novel)

**mel·o·drame** \'melə,dräm, -ram\ *n* -s [F *mélodrame* — more at MELODRAMA] *archaic* : MELODRAMA ⟨worn by the hero of a ~ —J.P.Kennedy †1870⟩

**¹mel·o·dy** \'melədē, -di\ *n* -ES [ME *melodie*, fr. OF, fr. LL *melodia*, fr. Gk *melōidia* chanting, singing, choral song, music, fr. *melos* limb, musical phrase, melody, song + *-ōidia* (fr. *aeidein* to sing); akin to Bret *mell* joint, articulation, Corn *mel*, W *cymal* joint, articulation, Toch A & Toch B *mälk* to fit together, Skt *marman* limb of the body — more at ODE] **1** : a sweet or agreeable succession or arrangement of sounds : musical quality : TUNEFULNESS ⟨lulled with sound of sweetest ~ —Shak.⟩ **2 a** (1) : a rhythmically organized and meaningful succession of single musical notes or tones having a definite relationship one with the other and forming an esthetic whole (2) : the melodic unit so formed **b** : a musical line as it appears on the staff when viewed horizontally — compare HARMONY, RHYTHM **c** : the chief or principal part in a harmonic composition (as the cantus firmus) **3** : something (as color in a painting) likened to or exhibiting a quality suggestive of musical melody

**²melody** \"\ *vb* -ED/-ING/-ES *vi* : to make melody : SING ~ *vt* : to make melody of

**mel·o·dy·less** \-ləs\ *adj* : lacking melody

**mel·oe** \'melə,wē\ *n* [NL] **1** *cap* : a widely distributed genus of beetles that is type of the family Meloidae and comprises the oil beetles **2** -s : OIL BEETLE

**melo·farce** \'melō+,-\ *n* [*melodrama* + *farce*] : melodrama of farcically exaggerated character

**mel·o·gram·ma·ta·ce·ae** \,melə,gramə'tāsē,ē\ *n pl*, *cap* [NL, fr. *Melogrammat-*, *Melogramma*, type genus (fr. *mela-* + Gk *grammat-*, *gramma* letter) + *-aceae* — more at GRAM] : a small family of fungi (order Sphaeriales) with perithecia sunken in pulvinate stromata and one-celled to many-celled ascospores

**mel·o·graph** \'melə,graf, -räf\ *n* [¹*melo-* + *-graph*] : a mechanical device for notating keyboard music through recording the action of the keys by stencil

**¹mel·oid** \'me,lȯid, 'meləwəd\ *adj* [NL *Meloidae*] : of or relating to the Meloidae

**²meloid** \"\ *n* -s [NL *Meloidae*] : a beetle of the family Meloidae

**me·loi·dae** \mə'lōə,dē, -lȯi,-\ *n pl*, *cap* [NL, fr. *Meloe*, type genus + *-idae*] : a widely distributed family of moderate-sized usu. rather soft-bodied cylindrical beetles that exhibit a complex hypermetamorphosis during development, are often defoliators as adults, and include some whose larvae are beneficial predators on other insects — see BLISTER BEETLE, MELOE

**me·loi·do·gyne** \mə'lȯidə,jīn, -gīn\ *n*, *cap* [NL, fr. Gk *mēlon* apple, gourd + *-oeidēs* -oid + *gynē* woman — more at QUEEN] : a genus related to *Heterodera* and comprising the typical root-knot nematodes

**mel·o·logue** \'melə,lȯg *also* -läg\ *n* -s [¹*melo-* + *-logue*] **1** : vocal and instrumental music interspersed with spoken declamation — compare MELODRAMA 1 **2** : a spoken declamation with musical accompaniment

**¹mel·o·lon·thid** \¦melə¦län(t)thəd\ *adj* [NL *Melolonthidae*] : of or relating to the Melolonthidae

**²melolonthid** \"\ *n* -s [NL *Melolonthidae*] : a beetle of the family Melolonthidae : COCKCHAFER

**mel·o·lon·thi·dae** \,melə'län(t)thə,dē\ *n pl*, *cap* [NL, fr. *Melolontha*, type genus (fr. Gk *mēlolonthē* cockchafer) + *-idae*] : a family of beetles closely related to and often included as a subfamily of Scarabaeidae — see COCKCHAFER — **mel·o·lon·thine** \¦==¦län(t)thən\ *adj*

**mel·o·lon·thoid** \¦==¦län,thȯid\ *adj* [NL *Melolonthidae* + E *-oid*] : resembling or like that of the Melolonthidae; *esp*, *of a beetle larva* : having a strongly curved body and small but definite thoracic legs

**mel·o·mane** \'melə,mān\ *adj* [F *mélomane*, fr. *mélo-* ¹melo- + *-mane* manic (back-formation fr. *manie* mania, fr. NL *mania*) — more at MANIA] : exhibiting melomania

**melo·mania** \,melə+\ *n* [NL, fr. *melo-* + *mania*] : an inordinate liking for music or melody : excessive or abnormal attraction to music

**melo·maniac** \"+\ *n* [¹*melo-* + *maniac*] **1** : a musical enthusiast : one exhibiting melomania **2** : an individual (as a person or dog) that is inordinately and abnormally affected by musical or other tones in certain ranges of sound

**¹mel·on** \'melən, *dial* 'milyən\ *n* -s *often attrib* [ME *meloun*, fr. MF *melon*, fr. LL *melon-*, *melo*, short for L *melopepon-*, *melopepo*, fr. Gk *mēlopepōn*, fr. *mēlon* apple + *pepōn*, a kind of edible gourd — more at PUMPKIN] **1 a** : either of two soft-fleshed sweet-flavored pepos that are usu. eaten raw as a fruit: (1) : MUSKMELON (2) : WATERMELON **b** *or* **melon vine** : a plant that bears melons **2** : something suggesting a musk-melon or watermelon esp. in roundness ⟨graceful ~ sleeves⟩: as **a** *archaic* : STAPHYLOMA **b** : a rounded mass of blubber found between the blowhole and the end of the nose in the grampus and several other cetaceans **c** *slang* : an abdomen that protrudes (as from fat or pregnancy) **3** : a strong yellowish pink that is redder and less strong than salmon pink, yellower and paler than peach red or madder scarlet, and redder and paler than average salmon **4 a** : a large surplus of profits available for distribution to stockholders ⟨the shareholders cut a ~ of nearly a million dollars⟩ **b** : an abundant and usu. nonrecurrent or irregular amount (as of profits or spoils) shared or available for sharing among various individuals — compare PLUM 4

**²mel·on** \'me,län\ *var of* MELLON

**³mel·on** \'melən\ *n* -s [by shortening] *Austral* : PADEMELON

**melon aphid** *n* : COTTON APHID

**melon apple** *n* : MANGO MELON

**melon beetle** *n* : either of two chrysomelid beetles (*Diabrotica vittata* and *D. duodecimpunctata*) injurious to melons

**melon cactus** *n* : a plant of the genus *Melocactus*

**melon fly** *n* **:** a small two-winged fly (*Dacus cucurbitae*) whose maggot is destructive to melons, other cucurbits, and tomatoes esp. in Hawaii
**melon foot** *n* **:** a ball foot carved with ridges
**melon fruit** *n* **:** PAPAYA
**mel·on·ge·na** \\,melən'jēnə\\ *n* [NL, fr. It dial. *melongiana, melangiana,* fr. Ar *bādhinjān* — more at BRINJAL] **1** -s **:** EGGPLANT **2 a** *cap* **:** a genus of tropical marine mollusks (family Xancidae) **b** -s **:** a mollusk of this genus; *esp* **:** a large edible Caribbean mollusk (*M. corona*) that resembles a whelk
**mel·on·gene** \\'melən,jēn\\ *n* -s [F *mélongène,* fr. NL *melongena*] *chiefly Brit* **:** EGGPLANT
**melon hole** *n* [[3]*melon*] **:** one of the shallow holes that honeycomb the soil of parts of interior Australia and are attributed esp. to the burrowing of pademelons

melon foot

**mel·on·ist** \\'melənəst\\ *n* -s **:** a melon grower
**mel·o·nite** \\'melə,nīt\\ *n* -s [*Melones* mine, Calaveras county, Calif., its locality + E *-ite*] **:** a mineral $NiTe_2$ consisting of a nickel telluride and occurring in California
**melon lo·co** \\,melən'lō(,)kō, mə,lōn-\\ *n* [MexSp *melón loco,* lit., crazy melon] **:** a rough creeping cucurbitaceous vine (*Apodanthera undulata*) of the southwestern U. S. and adjacent Mexico that has a small fruit resembling a gourd and containing seeds rich in oil
**melon louse** *n* **:** COTTON APHID
**melon pear** *n* **:** PEPINO
**melon pink** *n* **:** a vivid yellowish pink
**mel·on·ry** \\'melənrē\\ *n* -ES **:** a place for growing melons
**melon seed** *n* **:** a small wide shallow-draft sailboat with centerboard and a single-boomed spritsail that was formerly built in New Jersey for use in choppy inshore waters
**melon shell** *n* **:** any of several very large ovoid and often lustrous and richly colored gastropod mollusks constituting the genus *Cymbium* and widely distributed in the southwestern Pacific ocean — called also *bailer shell, boat shell*
**melon tree** *n* **:** PAPAYA 1
**melonworm** \\'==,=\\ *n* **:** a small caterpillar that is the larva of a white and black pyralidid moth (*Diaphania hyalinata*) and that is destructive to melons and other cucurbits by feeding on the foliage and immature fruits
**melon yellow** *n* **:** a variable color averaging a light orange yellow
**me·loph·a·gus** \\mə'läfəgəs\\ *n, cap* [NL, fr. Gk *mēlon* sheep + NL *-phagus* — more at SMALL] **:** a genus of wingless hippoboscid flies that includes the sheep ked
**mel·o·phon·ic** \\¦melə¦fänik\\ *adj* [[1]*melo-* + Gk *phōnē* sound, voice + E *-ic* — more at PHONE] **:** relating to music or to its performance
**mel·o·pho·nist** \\'melə,fōnəst, mə'läfən-\\ *n* -s [[1]*melo-* + Gk *phōnē* + E *-ist*] **:** MELODIST
**melo·piano** \\¦melō+\\ *n* [[1]*melo-* + *piano*] **:** a piano equipped with a pedal attachment for prolonging a tone at will by means of a series of rapidly striking supplementary hammers
**mel·o·plas·ty** \\'melə,plastē\\ *n* -ES [ISV [3]*mel-* + *-plasty*] **:** the restoration of a cheek by plastic surgery
**mel·o·poe·ia** \\,melə'pē(y)ə\\ *n* -s [LL, fr. Gk *melopoiia,* fr. *melopoiein* to write a lyric poem, to set to music, fr. *melo-* [1]*melo* + *poiein* to make — more at POET] **1 :** MELODY **2 :** the art or theory of inventing melody
**mel·o·po·et·ic** \\¦melōpō¦ed·ik\\ *also* **mel·o·poe·ic** \\-lə¦pēik\\ *adj* [*melopoetic* fr. [1]*melo* + *poetic; melopoeic* fr. *melopoeia* + *-ic*] **:** of, relating to, or involving melopoeia — **mel·o·po·et·i·cal·ly** \\-lōpō¦ed·ək(ə)lē\\ *adv*
[1]**melos** \\'me,läs, 'mē,-\\ *n* -ES [Gk — more at MELODY] **:** SONG, MELODY; *esp* **:** characteristic tone succession considered apart from rhythm — compare [1]MODE 7
[2]**melos** *pl of* MELO
**me·lo·sa** \\mə'lōsə\\ *n* -s [AmerSp, fr. Sp, fem. of *meloso* of honey, resembling honey, fr. LL *mellosus,* fr. L *mell-* + *-osus* -ous] **:** a So. American herb (*Madia sativa*) with glandular viscid foliage
**mel·o·spi·za** \\,melə'spīzə\\ *n, cap* [NL, fr. [1]*melo-* + Gk *spiza* chaffinch — more at FINCH] **:** a genus of birds (family Fringillidae) containing the American song sparrow and swamp sparrow
**me·lothria** \\mə'läthrēə, -lōth-\\ *n, cap* [NL, fr. Gk *mēlōthron,* a kind of white grape + NL *-ia*] **:** a genus of chiefly tropical monoecious herbaceous vines (family Cucurbitaceae) with white or yellow flowers, an elongated ovary, and a fruit resembling a typical berry that are cultivated as ornamentals
**mel·o·trope** \\'melə,trōp\\ *n* -s [[1]*melo-* + *-trope*] **:** a piano having a mechanical device for playing music from a stencil previously recorded by a melograph
**mels** *pl of* MEL
**melsh** *var of* MELCH
[1]**melt** \\'melt\\ *vb* **melted** \\-təd\\ **melted** \\"\\ *also* **mol·ten** \\'mōlt°n *also* -tən\\ **melting; melts** [ME *melten,* fr OE *meltan,* v.i., & *mieltan,* v.t., causative fr. the root of *meltan;* akin to ON *melta* to malt for brewing, to digest, Goth *gamalteins* departure, L *mollis* soft, Gk *meldein* to melt, Skt *mṛdnāti* he squeezes, rubs, L *molere* to grind — more at MEAL] *vi* **1 a :** to change from a solid to a liquid state usu. by the action of heat ⟨ice ~*ing* in the sun⟩ ⟨gold ~*s* at 1945°F⟩ **b :** to be or become extremely hot **:** run with perspiration ⟨~*ing* in heavy winter clothing⟩ **2 a :** DISSOLVE, DISINTEGRATE ⟨sugar ~*ing* in hot coffee⟩ **b :** to disappear as if dissolving **:** become dispersed, dissipated, or wholly consumed ⟨the morning fog usu. ~*s* as the sun rises in the sky⟩ ⟨their determination ~*ed* in the face of increasing hazards⟩ — often used with *away* ⟨their money ~*ed* away on unexpected expenses⟩ ⟨sometimes a tumor will ~ completely under adequate irradiation⟩ **3** *obs* **:** to become subdued, prostrated, or crushed (as by sorrow or remorse) **4 :** to become softened **:** become mild, tender, or gentle ⟨~*ed* at his kindly words⟩ **5** *archaic* **:** to become absorbed **6 :** to lose distinct individuality of outline **:** blend or blur by imperceptible degrees — usu. used with *into* ⟨the brown foothills ~*ing* into the steeper slopes⟩ ~ *vt* **1 a :** to reduce (as a metal) from a solid to a liquid state usu. by the action of heat ⟨~ wax over a flame⟩ — often used with *down* ⟨~*ed* down the family plate⟩ **b** *obs* **:** to form by melting **:** form from melted material **2 a** *archaic* **:** to cause to dissolve or disintegrate **b :** to cause to disappear or disperse ⟨the sun ~*ed* the clouds⟩ **3 a :** to make tender, gentle, or susceptible to mild influences **:** SOFTEN ⟨the child's tears ~*ed* his determination⟩ **b** *obs* **:** to take away the firmness of **:** WEAKEN, ENERVATE **4 :** to cause to merge insensibly (as colors, sounds, or outlines) **:** cause to fuse **:** BLEND **5** *slang Brit* **:** SPEND ⟨~*ing* his money⟩ **:** CASH ⟨~ a check⟩ — **melt in one's mouth :** to be of notable tenderness of texture or sometimes delicacy of flavor ⟨turns out pastry that *melts in your mouth*⟩
[2]**melt** \\"\\ *n* -s **1 a :** a melted substance **:** material in the molten state ⟨glass, being a ~ and not a crystal, has an immense range in both chemical composition and physical properties —G.F.H. Smith⟩ **b :** the mass melted at a single operation or the quantity melted during a certain period **2 a :** an act or process of melting **b :** the condition of being melted
[3]**melt** \\"\\ *also* **milt** \\'milt\\ *n* -s [ME *milte,* fr. OE; akin to OHG *milzi* spleen, ON *milti,* and prob. to OE *meltan* to melt — more at [1]MELT] **:** SPLEEN; *esp* **:** spleen of slaughtered animals for use as food ⟨use of hog ~ in mink rations⟩
**melt·abil·i·ty** \\,meltə'biləd·ē\\ *n* **:** the quality or state of being meltable
**melt·able** \\'meltəbəl\\ *adj* **:** capable of or suitable for melting
**melt·age** \\-tij\\ *n* -s **:** the act, result, or amount of melting ⟨slow ~ of ice⟩
**meltdown** \\'=,=\\ *n* -s [fr. *melt down,* v.] **:** the process or course of melting something (as scrap metal or ice cream)
[1]**melt·er** \\'meltə(r)\\ *n* -s **1 :** one (as a melting pot) that melts or is used for melting **2 :** one whose work is melting: as **a :** one who melts metal in a foundry furnace; *esp* **:** a worker in charge of the melting and purifying of scrap iron in the production of steel **b :** one who melts and molds silver or gold for use in making jewelry **c :** one who refines magnesium crystals into pure magnesium in a crucible furnace
[2]**melt·er** \\"\\ *archaic var of* MILTER
**melt·ers** \\-tə(r)z\\ *n pl but sing or pl in constr* [[1]*melt* + *-ers* (as in *glanders*)] **:** LEAK 3
**mel·teth** \\'mel,teth\\ *or* **mel·tith** \\-,tith\\ *n* -s [ME *meltid* — more at MEALTIDE] *Scot* **:** MEALTIME
**melt·ing·ly** *adv* **:** so as to melt **:** in a melting manner **:** DELICATELY, TENDERLY ⟨a ~ flavored peach⟩ ⟨gazed at him ~⟩
**melt·ing·ness** *n* -ES **:** the quality or state of being melting
**melting out** *n* -s [fr. gerund of *melt out,* v.] **:** a disease of turf grasses caused by fungi of the genus *Helminthosporium* and characterized by a bluish cast of irregularly shaped areas which later turn yellow and die out
**melting point** *n* **:** the temperature at which a solid melts **:** FREEZING POINT ⟨the *melting point* of ice is 0°C or 32°F⟩
**melting pot** *n* **1 :** a vessel (as a crucible) in which something is melted **2 a :** a place or situation where racial amalgamation and sociocultural assimilation are taking place ⟨the United States, Israel, and Brazil are great *melting pots*⟩ **b :** a population developed in such a place or situation ⟨instead of a homogeneous people a *melting pot* composed of many European nationalities⟩ **3 :** a process of blending commonly resulting in reinvigoration and novelty of concepts ⟨a *melting pot* of music —*Harper's*⟩ ⟨the architectural *melting pot* is seen in the tall Romanesque columns, the Gothic hammer-vault roofing —*Amer. Guide Series: Conn.*⟩ **4 :** DISCARD ⟨threw his original hypothesis into the *melting pot* and began anew⟩
**mel·ton** \\'melt°n *also* -tən\\ *also* **melton cloth** *n* [fr. *Melton* Mowbray, Leicestershire, England] **:** a heavy woolen fabric made usu. in twill weave and in solid colors and given a smooth hard felted finish
**melton mowbray** \\,=='mōbrē, -ō(,)brā\\ *n, usu cap both Ms* [fr. *Melton Mowbray,* England] **:** a rich English meat pie
**melts** *pres 3d sing of* MELT, *pl of* MELT
**meltwater** \\'=,==\\ *n* **:** water from melting ice and snow
**me·lun·geon** *also* **ma·lun·geon** \\mə'lənjən\\ *n* -s *usu cap* [origin unknown] **:** one of a group of people of mixed Indian, white, and Negro ancestry in the southern Appalachians esp. of eastern Tennessee
**mel·ur·sus** \\me'lərsəs\\ *n, cap* [NL, fr. L *mel* honey + *ursus* bear — more at MELLIFLUOUS, ARCTIC] **:** a genus of large Asiatic mammals (family Ursidae) consisting of the sloth bear
**-me·lus** \\-mələs\\ *n comb form, pl* **-meli** [NL, fr. Gk *melos* limb — more at MELODY] **:** one having a (specified) abnormality of the limbs ⟨*anisomelus*⟩ ⟨*ectromelus*⟩
**Mel u·sine** \\¦mel(y)ə¦sēn\\ *trademark* — used for a silky long-haired felt for hats
**mel·vie** \\'melvī\\ *vt* [prob. alter. of *melwie,* fr. ME *melw-,* stem of *mele* meal — more at MEAL] *archaic Scot* **:** to cover with meal
[1]**mem** \\'mem\\ *n* -s [Heb *mēm,* lit., water] **1 :** the 13th letter of the Hebrew alphabet — symbol מ; see ALPHABET table **2 :** the letter of the Phoenician or of any of various other Semitic alphabets corresponding to Hebrew mem
[2]**mem** \\¦mem\\ *n* -s [alter. of *ma'am*] **:** MADAM 1
**mem** *abbr* **1** member **2** memoirs **3** memoir **4** memorandum **5** memorial
**mem·ber** \\'membə(r)\\ *n* -s *often attrib* [ME *membre,* fr. OF, fr. L *membrum;* akin to Goth *mimz* flesh, OIr *mīr* bite, Gk *mēninx* membrane, *mēros* thigh, Skt *māṁsa* flesh; basic meaning: flesh] **1 a :** a bodily part or organ ⟨a lolling, impudent tongue — a truly unruly ~ —E.J.Banfield⟩ ⟨the thyroid gland . . . may be the offending ~ —H.A.Overstreet⟩; *specif* **:** a part (as a limb) that projects from the main mass of the body ⟨a man with sandy hair and large bodily ~*s* —G.S.Perry⟩ **b :** PENIS ⟨let my ~ turn to dust —William Goyen⟩ **c :** a unit of structure in a plant body ⟨a vessel ~⟩ **2 :** one who forms part of a metaphorical or metaphysical body ⟨~*s* of Christ⟩ ⟨we are ~*s* one of another —Eph 4:25 (RSV)⟩ **3 :** one of the individuals composing a society, community, association, or other group: as **a** (1) **:** a person who has been admitted usu. formally to the responsibilities and privileges of some association or joint enterprise ⟨a ~ of a law firm⟩ ⟨a ~ of the N.Y. Stock Exchange⟩ ⟨a ~ of the school's governing board⟩ (2) **:** a person who has been admitted usu. formally into some social or professional society typically requiring payment of dues, adherence to a program, or compliance with some other requirements of membership ⟨a ~ of a women's club⟩ ⟨~*s* of the bar association⟩ ⟨a paid-up ~⟩ **b :** a branch or affiliate of a political association ⟨obtained the support of all ~ states⟩ **c** (1) **:** an elected member of the British Parliament **:** a member of the House of Commons (2) **:** a member of the lower house of Congress **:** a member of the House of Representatives (3) **:** a person having membership in any of numerous legislative bodies **d** *obs* **:** a participant or associate in an action or benefit **e :** a church communicant **:** a person baptized or enrolled in a church **f :** one of the persons composing a territorial, kinship, or sociological unit ⟨~*s* of the immediate family attended the funeral⟩ ⟨alert and responsible ~*s* of their communities —*Official Register of Harvard Univ.*⟩ ⟨~*s* of the middle class⟩ ⟨~*s* of a tribe⟩ **4 :** a constituent part of a whole: as **a :** a section or district of an estate, port, or other territorial unit **b** (1) **:** a syntactic or rhythmic unit of a sentence **:** CLAUSE (2) **:** one of the propositions of a syllogism **c :** one of the elements of which a mathematical aggregate is composed **d** (1) **:** a part of a building or other structure whether constructional (as a pier or lintel) or decorative (as a molding) (2) **:** an essential part of a framed structure, a machine, or a device ⟨the design of compression ~*s* of bridge trusses —*U.S. Nat'l Bureau of Standards Annual Report*⟩ **e :** a minor stratigraphic unit of a geologic formation **f :** something belonging to a class or category ⟨*x* is a ~ of *A*⟩ ⟨a ~ of a species⟩ ⟨one who philosophizes is a ~ of the class of philosophers⟩ **syn** see PART
**member bank** *n* **:** a bank having membership in the Federal Reserve System
**mem·bered** \\'membə(r)d\\ *adj* [ME *membred,* fr. *membre* member + *-ed*] **1 :** consisting of or divided into members ⟨a ~ body⟩ **2** *heraldry* **:** depicted with legs of a specified tincture differing from that of the body — used chiefly of a bird
**mem·ber·less** \\'membə(r)ləs\\ *adj* **:** having no member ⟨the organization is still ~⟩
**mem·ber·ship** \\-),ship\\ *n* **1 :** the state or status of being a member **2 :** the body of members (as of a society) **3 :** the relation between a member of a class and the class — contrasted with *inclusion*
**membership star** *n* **:** a small gilt star worn by brownie scouts and girl scouts for each year of troop membership
[1]**mem·bra·cid** \\'membrəsəd, (')mem¦bras-\\ *adj* [NL *Membracidae*] **:** of or relating to the Membracidae
[2]**membracid** \\"\\ *n* -s [NL *Membracidae*] **:** an insect of the family Membracidae **:** TREEHOPPER
**mem·brac·i·dae** \\mem'brasə,dē\\ *n pl, cap* [NL, fr. *Membracis,* type genus (fr. Gk *membrak-, membrax* cicada) + *-idae*] **:** a large family of Homoptera consisting of the treehoppers

membership star

[1]**mem·bra·cine** \\'membrə,sīn\\ *adj* [NL *Membracis* + E *-ine*] **:** MEMBRACID
[2]**membracine** \\"\\ *n* -s **:** MEMBRACID
**mem·bral** \\'memb(ə)rəl\\ *adj* [L *membrum* member + E *-al* — more at MEMBER] **:** of, relating to, or characteristic of a member — **mem·bral·ly** \\-rəlē\\ *adv*
**membran-** *or* **membrani-** *or* **membrano-** *comb form* [*membran-* fr. MF, fr. L, fr. *membrana* skin, membrane, parchment; *membrani-* & *membrano-* fr. NL, fr. L *membrana* — more at MEMBRANE] **1 :** membrane ⟨*membranoid*⟩ ⟨*membraniferous*⟩ ⟨*Membranipora*⟩ ⟨*membranogenic*⟩ **2** *usu* **membrano- :** membranous and ⟨*membranocartilaginous*⟩ ⟨*membranonervous*⟩
**mem·bra·na** \\mem'brānə, -rānə\\ *n, pl* **membra·nae** \\-ā,nē, -ā,nī\\ [L — more at MEMBRANE] **:** MEMBRANE
**mem·bra·na·ceous** \\¦membrə¦nāshəs\\ *adj* [L *membranaceus,* fr. *membran-* + *-aceus* -aceous] **:** MEMBRANOUS — **mem·bra·na·ceous·ly** *adv*
**mem·bra·nate** \\'membrə,nāt, (')mem¦brānət\\ *adj* [*membran-* + *-ate*] **:** being, resembling, or having a membrane
**mem·brane** \\'mem,brān *sometimes* -,brən\\ *n* -s [L *membrana* skin, membrane, parchment, fr. *membrum* member — more at MEMBER] **1 :** a thin soft pliable sheet or layer esp. of animal or vegetable origin **2 :** a limiting protoplasmic surface or interface — see CELL 5 **3 :** a piece of parchment forming part of a roll ⟨the pages in the . . . ~ usually were square and had two to four columns to the page —A.T.Robertson⟩
**membrane bone** *n* **:** a bone that ossifies directly in connective tissue without previous existence as cartilage
**membrane curing** *n* **:** a method of curing concrete usu. in pavements by which a material in liquid form is sprayed over the exposed surface shortly after the concrete is finished after which the material solidifies and becomes essentially impervious and thus holds the mixing water in the concrete so that it can hydrate the cement over a period of time
**mem·braned** \\-nd\\ *adj* **:** having a membrane
**mem·brane·less** \\-nləs\\ *adj* **:** being without a membrane
**mem·bra·nel·lar** \\¦membrə¦nelə(r)\\ *adj* **:** of, relating to, or constituting a membranelle
**mem·bra·nelle** \\-l\\ *also* **mem·bra·nel·la** \\,=='nelə\\ *n, pl* **membra·nelles** \\¦==¦nelz\\ *also* **membranel·lae** \\,=='ne(,)lē, -e,lī\\ [NL *membranella,* dim. of L *membrana* membrane — more at MEMBRANE] **:** a flattened vibrating organ like a membrane comprised of a row of fused cilia in various ciliates
**membrane of cor·ti** \\-'kȯrd·ē, -ō(ə)r,tē\\ *usu cap C* [after Alfonso *Corti* †1876 Ital. anatomist] **:** a membrane overlying the organ of Corti
**membrane of descemet** *usu cap D* [after Jean *Descemet* †1810 Fr. anatomist] **:** DESCEMET'S MEMBRANE
**membrane of hen·le** \\-'henlē, -lə\\ *usu cap H* [after Friedrich G. J. *Henle* †1885 Ger. pathologist and anatomist] **:** FENESTRATED MEMBRANE
**membrane of krause** *usu cap K* **:** KRAUSE'S MEMBRANE
**mem·bra·ne·ous** \\(')mem¦brānēəs\\ *adj* [L *membraneus* of parchment, fr. *membrana* membrane, parchment + *-eus* -eous — more at MEMBRANE] **:** MEMBRANOUS
**membrani-** — see MEMBRAN-
**mem·bra·nip·o·ra** \\,membrə'nipərə\\ *n, cap* [NL, fr. *membran-* + *-pora*] **:** a genus (the type of the family Membraniporidae) of colonial encrusting bryozoans (order Cheilostomata)
**membrano-** — see MEMBRAN-
**mem·bra·noid** \\'membrə,nȯid\\ *adj* [*membran-* + *-oid*] **:** like a membrane
**mem·bra·no·phone** \\mem'brānə,fōn\\ *n* [ISV *membran-* + *-phone*] **:** a musical instrument (as a drum or kazoo) having a tightly stretched membrane as a vibrator or resonator and made to vibrate by percussion or by friction — **mem·bra·no·phon·ic** \\(¦)mem¦brānə¦fänik\\ *adj*
**mem·bra·nous** \\'membrənəs, (')mem¦brān-\\ *adj* [MF *membraneux,* fr. *membran-* + *-eux* -ous] **1 :** of, relating to, or resembling membrane ⟨a ~ lining⟩ **2 :** thin, pliable, and often somewhat transparent ⟨~ leaves⟩ **3 :** characterized or accompanied by the formation of a membrane or pseudomembrane ⟨~ croup⟩ ⟨~ gastritis⟩ — **mem·bra·nous·ly** *adv*
**membranous labyrinth** *n* **:** the sensory structures of the inner ear including the receptors of the labyrinthine sense and the cochlea — compare BONY LABYRINTH
**mem·bran·u·la** \\mem'brānyələ, -ran-\\ *also* **mem·bra·nule** \\'membrə,n(y)ül, mem'brān(,)yül\\ *n* -s [NL, fr. L, small membrane, dim. of *membrana* membrane — more at MEMBRANE] **:** a fine structure like a membranelle formed by the fusion of a few long cilia (as in the posterior ciliary ring of vorticellids)
**mem·brum** \\'membrəm\\ *n, pl* **mem·bra** \\-rə\\ [L, lit., member — more at MEMBER] **:** PENIS
**me·men·to** *also* **momento** \\mə'ment·(,)ō, -n·(,)tō\\ *n, pl* **mementos** *or* **mementoes** [ME, fr. L, remember, 2d sing. fut. imper. of *meminisse* to remember; akin to L *ment-, mens* mind — more at MIND] **1** *often cap* **:** either of two prayers in the canon of the Roman mass, one for the living and one for the dead, beginning with *memento* **2 a :** something that serves to warn or remind with regard to conduct or future events **b** *archaic* **:** REMINDER, WARNING **c** (1) **:** something that serves to remind or is a vestige (as of a past event or condition) **:** RELIC, TRACE ⟨covered with such ~*s* in several languages —Cyril Mango⟩ ⟨she was . . . a ~ of that era —Nancy Hale⟩ (2) **:** something that is kept in memory of a person or event **:** MEMORIAL, KEEPSAKE ⟨fond of carrying away ~*s* of so enjoyable an evening —Norman Douglas⟩ ⟨a state park contains ~*s* of early days —*Amer. Guide Series: Texas*⟩ **3 :** MEMORY, REMEMBRANCE ⟨the names of the streets . . . seem to fill you with terrible ~*s* —C.B.Fairbanks⟩
**memento mo·ri** \\=,=(,)='mȯr(,)ē, -r,ī\\ *n, pl* **memento mori** [L, remember that you must die] **1 :** a warning to be prepared for death ⟨that *memento mori* which it never ceases to din into the ears of the faithful —Paul Siwek⟩ **2 :** something that serves to remind of death ⟨the corpse of a bad philosophy is a powerful *memento mori* —J.H.Sledd⟩; *specif* **:** a death's head or other symbolic object used as a reminder of death ⟨two *memento mori* or mourning pieces —W.L.Warren⟩
**meml** *abbr* memorial
[1]**memo** \\'me(,)mō *sometimes* 'mē(-\\ *n* -s [by shortening] **:** MEMORANDUM
[2]**memo** \\"\\ *vt* -ED/-ING/-S **1 :** to make a memorandum of or communicate in a memorandum ⟨~*ed* what she'd have to do —Bernard Malamud⟩ **2 :** to send a memorandum to ⟨we'll ~ you in the morning —A.C.Spectorsky⟩
**mem·oir** \\'mem,wär, -wȧ(r *also* -wó(ə)r *or* -wō(ə) *sometimes* 'mēm- *or* 'mām- *or* -,mō- *or* -,mä- *or* -,má- *or* ='= *or* məm'w- *or* mə'm-\\ *n* -s [F *mémoire,* fr. *mémoire* memory, fr. L *memoria* — more at MEMORY] **1 :** an official note or report **:** MEMORANDUM, RECORD ⟨wrote a ~ on the subject for his royal master⟩ **2 a :** a history or narrative composed from or stressing personal experience and acquaintance with the events, scenes, or persons described ⟨a satirical ~ of the city of his birth —Saxe Commins⟩ — usu. used in pl. ⟨have written ~*s* of the event —Ruth McKenney⟩ **b :** an autobiographical account often anecdotal or intimate in tone whose focus of attention is usu. on the persons, events, or times known to the writer ⟨a best-selling ~ that a duke paid a fortune to keep unpublished —*N. Y. Herald Tribune*⟩ ⟨an autobiographical ~ by the dean of American literary historians —*Saturday Rev.*⟩ — usu. used in pl. ⟨in his ~*s* he describes the framework —*Amer. Guide Series: Minn.*⟩ ⟨a secret emergency fund . . . for the acquisition of just such ~*s* —S.H.Adams⟩ **c :** a biography or biographical sketch usu. based on personal acquaintance with the subject and sometimes having the character of a memorial ⟨a ~ of his brilliant pupil . . . who died early —Sarah G. Bowerman⟩ ⟨its spirit is so devout as to make it . . . more a ~ than a biography —A.J.Nock⟩ ⟨a ~ . . . by his colleague —Edmund Wilson⟩ **3 a :** an account of something regarded as noteworthy **:** a record of investigations of some subject **:** DISSERTATION, REPORT ⟨the work described and discussed in this ~ represents a first-class investigation —J.A.Steers⟩ **b memoirs** *pl* **:** the record of the proceedings of a learned society
**mem·oir·ist** \\-ärəst, -ärə-, -ȯrə-\\ *n* -s **:** a writer of a memoir
**mem·o·ra·bilia** \\,memərə'bilēə, -bēl-, -lyə\\ *n pl* [L, fr. neut. pl. of *memorabilis* memorable — more at MEMORABLE] **:** things remarkable and worthy of remembrance or record ⟨contains a . . . wealth of ~ of early Texas —*Amer. Guide Series: Texas*⟩ ⟨more than twenty trunks of ~ —R.L.Taylor⟩; *also* **:** a record of such things ⟨reads the *Memorabilia,* or summary of the closing year's events —*Amer. Guide Series: N. C.*⟩
**mem·o·ra·bil·i·ty** \\,mem(ə)rə'biləd·ē, -lətē, -ī\\ *n* **:** the quality or state of being memorable
[1]**mem·o·ra·ble** \\'mem(ə)rəbəl, 'memərb-\\ *adj* [ME, fr. L *memorabilis,* fr. *memorare* to remind (fr. *memor* mindful) + *-abilis* -able — more at MEMORY] **1 :** worthy of being remembered or noted **:** NOTABLE, DISTINGUISHED, IMPRESSIVE, SIGNIFICANT ⟨an early and ~ masterpiece —F.L.Mott⟩ ⟨considered his most ~ work —C.C.Walcutt⟩ ⟨the ~ winter of 1861⟩ ⟨the one ~ recording of the . . . sonata —Irving Kolodin⟩ **2 :** remembered or easy to remember — **mem·o·ra·ble·ness** \\-bəlnəs\\ *n* -ES — **mem·o·ra·bly** \\-blē, -bli\\ *adv*
[2]**memorable** \\"\\ *n* -s *archaic* **:** something that is memorable — usu. used in pl.
[1]**mem·o·ran·dum** \\,memə'randəm, -raan-\\ *n, pl* **memorandums** \\-dəmz\\ *or* **memoran·da** \\-də\\ [ME, fr. L, neut. of *memorandus* to be remembered, fut. pass. part. of *memorare* to remind — more at MEMORABLE] **1 a :** an informal record of something that one wishes to remember or preserve for future

use : a note to help or jog the memory : one of the notes in a diary ⟨this book . . . was assembled from his diaries, ~s, and letters —*New Yorker*⟩ **b** : MEMENTO, REMINDER **2 a** (1) : a brief or informal note in writing of some transaction or an outline of an intended instrument : an instrument drawn up in a brief and compendious form (2) : the clause beginning a record in the former Court of King's Bench in proceedings by bill (3) : MEMORANDUM OF ASSOCIATION (4) : the body of exceptions making up the clause in a marine insurance policy exempting the insurer wholly or partially from liability for loss on various articles **b** (1) : a statement by the shipper of the terms of a shipment sent with the privilege of return if not sold — used esp. in the jewelry trade (2) : the third or duplicate copy of a bill of lading **3 a** : an informal diplomatic communication; *specif* : a written statement from a department of state or a ministry of foreign affairs to an embassy or legation used esp. for routine transmissions or inquiries and never bearing a signature **b** : a usu. brief informal communication typically written for interoffice circulation on paper headed *memorandum* ⟨depend on countless *memoranda* for giving directions and for exchanging essential information —Milton Hall⟩ **c** : a routine publication by an authorized military headquarters containing directive, advisory, or informative matter

**²memorandum** \"\ *vt* -ED/-ING/-S : to make a memorandum of

**memorandum decision** *or* **memorandum opinion** *n* **1** : a brief opinion of a court or a judge announcing the result of litigation without an extended discussion of the principles involved but sometimes with the citation of precedents — compare PER CURIAM DECISION **2** : an opinion of the Tax Court of the U. S. that is ordered not to be published but that is authoritative as a precedent **3** : an opinion of a court or a judge announcing the conclusions reached on the issues of fact and of law and giving directions as to the matters to be set forth in an order, judgment, or decree to be entered **4** : an opinion of a court or a judge setting forth the conclusions reached on issues of fact and of law and containing the actual order, judgment, or decree of the court or judge

**memorandum of association** *Eng law* : a document resembling articles of association in the U. S. which in case of a company to be formed legally must be executed and filed to form the charter of the company

**mem·o·ra·tive** \ˈmeməˌrād·iv, ˈmem(ə)rəd-·\ *adj* [ME *memoratif*, fr. MF, fr. LL *memorativus*, fr. L *memoratus* (past part. of *memorare* to remind) + *-ivus* -ive — more at MEMORABLE] **1** *archaic* : COMMEMORATIVE **2** : relating to the memory ⟨powers perfected by experience . . . estimative and ~ powers —G.P.Klubertanz⟩

**¹me·mo·ri·al** \məˈmōrēəl, -mȯr-\ *adj* [ME, fr. L *memorialis*, fr. *memoria* memory + *-alis* -al — more at MEMORY] **1** : serving to preserve remembrance : COMMEMORATIVE ⟨a ~ building⟩ ⟨a ~ sketch⟩ ⟨a ~ showing of an artist's work⟩ **2** : of or relating to memory : utilizing, caused by, or done from memory ⟨the scene had been gotten by shorthand or ~ method —C.A. Greer⟩ ⟨the bad quarto . . . is a ~ reconstruction —Leo Kirschbaum⟩ ⟨~ contamination . . . of a manuscript⟩

**²memorial** \"\ *n* -S [ME, fr. LL *memoriale*, fr. L, neut. of *memorialis*, adj.] **1** *obs* : MEMORY, REMEMBRANCE, RECOLLECTION **2 a** (1) : something that serves to preserve memory or knowledge of an individual or event : RELIC, TRACE ⟨the form in which he expresses his emotion bears no ~ of any external form that may have provoked it —Clive Bell⟩ ⟨a ~ of those stormy feuds . . . is the thick oak door with its square hole —Brian Fitzgerald⟩ ⟨their bones remain . . . as ~s of a noble attempt —W.E.Swinton⟩ (2) : something that is kept to preserve the memory of a person or event : KEEPSAKE, MEMENTO ⟨carved walking stick, umbrella and best black hat still remained, sacred ~s —Rex Ingamells⟩ ⟨revive the liking for wearing ~s of the dead —Joan Evans⟩ (3) : something designed to commemorate or preserve the memory of a person or event ⟨his two-volume ~ to his father . . . was published —*Current Biog.*⟩ ⟨to visit this ~ to a former slave is a rewarding experience —Oscar Schisgall⟩ ⟨Walker *Memorial* is the student center —*Visitor's Guide to Mass. Inst. of Tech.*⟩ ⟨the mound . . . should be regarded as a ~ rather than an interment —F.M.Stanton⟩ ⟨the state's history is well recorded in 17 historic ~s —Melvin Beck⟩ ⟨established a scholarship as a ~ to his late father⟩ **b** : COMMEMORATION 2 **3 a** : RECORD, MEMOIR ⟨the text of the ~ that accompanied the map —Marjorie S. Douglas⟩ **b** : MEMORANDUM, NOTE ⟨present a long ~ to the emperor —*Times Lit. Supp.*⟩; *specif* : a legal abstract **c** (1) : a statement of facts addressed to a government or some branch of it often accompanied with a petition or remonstrance ⟨submitted a ~ to Congress —Joseph Dorfman⟩; *also* : a similar statement presented to a nongovernmental body (2) : a pleading before the Permanent Court of International Justice in which a case is set forth including facts, law, and submissions

**³memorial** \"\ *vt* -ED/-ING/-S : MEMORIALIZE

**memorial arch** *n* : TRIUMPHAL ARCH

**memorial day** *n, usu cap M&D* **1** : May 30 observed as a legal holiday in most states of the U. S. in commemoration of dead servicemen — called also *Decoration Day* **2** : CONFEDERATE MEMORIAL DAY **3** : any of several days set aside for the public commemoration of war dead

**me·mo·ri·al·ist** \-ələst\ *n* -S **1** : a person who writes or signs a memorial ⟨the ~s are not entitled to be heard —T.E.May⟩ **2** : a writer of memorials or memoirs ⟨France's amplest secret ~ —Janet Flanner⟩; *specif* : one who writes a commemorative memoir ⟨critics of the work rather than ~s of the man —*Times Lit. Supp.*⟩

**me·mo·ri·al·iza·tion** \-ˌ==ələˈzāshən, -ˌlīˈz-\ *n* -S : the act or an instance of memorializing or the state of being memorialized ⟨won . . . glamour for future ~ —J.F.Dobie⟩

**me·mo·ri·al·ize** \-ˈ==əˌlīz\ *vt* -ED/-ING/-S **1** : to address or petition by a memorial : present a memorial to ⟨~ the governors and legislatures of the several states —E.M.Carroll⟩ **2** : COMMEMORATE ⟨*memorialized* by an avenue bearing his name —David Dempsey⟩ — **me·mo·ri·al·iz·er** \-zə(r)\ *n* -S

**me·mo·ri·al·ly** \-rēəlē\ *adv* : by memory : as a memorial

**memorial mass** *n, often cap both Ms* : a Roman Catholic requiem mass offered on specif. appointed days of the year for the repose of a dead person's soul

**memorial park** *n* : CEMETERY

**memorial rose** *n* : a vigorous prostrate or trailing evergreen rose (*Rosa wichuraiana*) of eastern Asia with large fragrant white flowers in clusters of few to many

**memorial service** *n* : a commemorative service of worship held for a dead person

**memorial stamp** *n* : a commemorative stamp

**me·mo·ria tech·ni·ca** \məˈmōrēəˈteknəkə\ *n* [NL, lit., artificial memory] : an artificial aid to the memory : a mnemonic aid ⟨evidence the survival of this primitive *memoria technica* —Edward Clodd⟩

**mem·o·ried** \ˈmem(ə)rēd, -rid\ *adj* [*memory* + *-ed*] **1** : having a memory of a specified kind — usu. used in combination ⟨long-*memoried* men and women . . . were not deluded —Eden Phillpotts⟩ **2 a** : full of memories ⟨this serene and ~ village —*Amer. Guide Series: Vt.*⟩ **b** : REMEMBERED ⟨explosion of ~ happiness —Han Suyin⟩

**¹me·mo·ri·ter** \məˈmȯrəˌte(ə)r, -ˌōrəd·ə(r)\ *adv* [L, fr. *memor* mindful — more at MEMORY] : by or from memory : by heart ⟨learn ~ a series of propositions —*World Rev.*⟩

**²memoriter** \"\ *adj* : marked by emphasis on memorization ⟨there is little ~ work required —*Atlantic*⟩

**mem·o·ri·za·tion** \ˌmem(ə)rəˈzāshən, ˌmeməˌrīˈz-\ *n* -S : the act or an instance of memorizing

**mem·o·rize** \ˈmeməˌrīz\ *vb* -ED/-ING/-S [*memory* + *-ize*] *vt* **1 a** *archaic* : to commemorate in writing : RECORD, MENTION ⟨the great founders of the university are tactfully *memorized* —*Encyc. Britannica*⟩ **b** *archaic* : to cause to be remembered : COMMEMORATE ⟨entombed with a Northern spade and *memorized* with a Northern slab —H.R.Helper⟩ **c** *chiefly dial* : REMEMBER ⟨I ~ that egg —Earl Hamner⟩ ⟨wanted folk to ~ him —Stewart Toland⟩ ⟨for the first time in *memorized* history man was free to act —*Time*⟩ **2** : to commit to memory : learn by heart ⟨dread to ~ a speech for fear they will forget it —Max Eastman⟩ ~ *vi* : to learn something by heart ⟨these children can . . . ~ easily —Gertrude H. Hildreth⟩

**mem·o·riz·er** \-zə(r)\ *n* -S : one that memorizes

**mem·o·ry** \ˈmem(ə)rē, -ri\ *n* -ES [ME *memorie*, fr. MF *memorie, memoire*, fr. L *memoria*, fr. *memor* mindful + *-ia* -y; akin to OE *gemimor* well-known, *mimorian* to remember, MD *mimeren* to muse, brood, L *mora* delay, OIr *airmert* prohibition, Gk *mermēra* trouble, Skt *smarati* he remembers; basic meaning: to remember] **1 a** *archaic* : a ceremony of commemoration : a service for the dead **b** *obs* : a historical or biographical record **c** *obs* : MEMORIAL, MEMENTO **2 a** (1) : the power or process of reproducing or recalling what has been learned and retained esp. through nonconscious associative mechanisms : conscious or unconscious evocation of things past ⟨semantic reception is associated with great use of ~ —Norbert Wiener⟩ ⟨seemed lost in thought or ~ —E.A. McCourt⟩ ⟨in ~, one images or reproduces his whole state of mind on the remembered occasion —Richard Taylor⟩ (2) : this power regarded as vested in an individual : an individual's capacity for reproducing or recalling what has been learned and retained ⟨has a good ~ for faces⟩ ⟨rely on the faulty ~ of a cross section of people —S.L.Payne⟩ ⟨his ~ annoyed him . . . it did not work willingly any more —Stuart Cloete⟩ (3) : the process of reproducing or recalling what has been learned as manifested in some special way or as associated with some bodily process ⟨visual ~⟩ ⟨muscular ~⟩ **b** : persistent modification of structure or of behavior resulting from an organism's activity or from its passively acquired experience **c** (1) : the totality of what has been learned and retained esp. as evidenced by recall and recognition ⟨drew on his ~ to supply the needed names⟩ ⟨even birds and animals have an ancestral ~ —*Horizon*⟩ (2) : the function of memory regarded as a compartment or chamber in which images, perceptions, or learning are stored ⟨filling their ~ with a lumber of words —R.L.Stevenson⟩ ⟨the invisible storehouse in nothingness, called ~ —Walter Sorell & Denver Lindley⟩ ⟨retain in their ~ the preceding movements —George Balanchine⟩ ⟨a richly stored ~⟩ **3 a** (1) : commemorative remembrance ⟨a statue erected in ~ of the hero⟩ ⟨has been held in ~ in Ireland —Maxwell Nurnberg & Morris Rosenblum⟩ ⟨a local museum dedicated to the ~ of the celebrity —*Amer. Guide Series: Maine*⟩ (2) : a person or thing held in commemorative remembrance ⟨his deeds are the country's proudest *memories*⟩ **b** : the fact or condition of being remembered ⟨~ of such upheavals goes back to remote antiquity⟩ ⟨persecutions which were of recent ~ —K.S.Latourette⟩ **4 a** : a particular act of recalling something learned or experienced : the fact or a condition of recalling : REMEMBRANCE, RECOLLECTION, RECALL ⟨woke with . . . complete ~ of where she had been —Pearl Buck⟩ ⟨has no ~ of that incident⟩ ⟨recited the poem from ~⟩ **b** (1) : an image, impression, or other mental trace of someone or something known or experienced : the content of something remembered ⟨my first ~ is one of being held up to a window —George Dangerfield⟩ ⟨the ~ of his voice as distinct in her mind as it ever had been in her ear —Glenway Wescott⟩ ⟨pleasant *memories* of an Italian summer⟩ ⟨the ~ of the captain's wife had not left him —Carson McCullers⟩ ⟨*memories* of the Japanese occupation . . . created a heritage of ill will —R.H.Fifield⟩ ⟨have written down their ~ . . . of one such occasion —F.I.Cobb⟩ ⟨made the town's isolation a ~ —*Amer. Guide Series: Texas*⟩ ⟨the course is a ~ and a mark is no longer even a ghost —Norman Nathan⟩ ⟨the depression is only a bad ~⟩ (2) : the total impression or generalized image of a person preserved in remembrance, history, or tradition : posthumous opinion ⟨this ruler left behind him golden *memories*⟩ ⟨a prince of glorious ~⟩ (3) : the character, personality, or achievements of a person as preserved in remembrance ⟨the man whose ~ the Royal Irish Academy honors —Gearoid O'Sullivan⟩ ⟨his ~ recalled the most wonderful and exciting . . . adventures —R.H.Davis⟩ ⟨hates her ~ and all other women —Lucy M. Montgomery⟩ **c** : the time within which past events can be or are remembered ⟨within the ~ of living men⟩ **5** : CONCENTRATION 5 **6** : a component in an electronic computing machine into which information (as the data involved in and the instructions governing the calculations to be performed) can be inserted, stored (as in the form of magnetized spots on a special drum or tape or of charged spots on a cathode-ray tube), and automatically extracted when needed **7 a** : a capacity for showing effects recognized as the result of past treatment — used esp. of materials ⟨the wire begins to turn in the other direction corresponding to the first twisting — the ~ of the recent short-term handling has been obliterated by that of the more remote but longer lasting and therefore more impressive one —Bernhard Gross⟩ **b** : a capacity for returning to a former condition (as after being stretched) — used esp. of a material ⟨the ~ will cause the material to resume the shape it had when you purchased it —*Road Mag.*⟩

**syn** REMEMBRANCE, RECOLLECTION, REMINISCENCE, MIND, SOUVENIR: MEMORY applies both to the faculty of remembering and to what is remembered, sometimes remembered dearly or cherished ⟨a very good *memory*⟩ ⟨a *memory* training course⟩ ⟨it was the merest *memory* now, vague and a little sweet, like the remembrance of some exceptional spring day —John Galsworthy⟩ REMEMBRANCE can be the same as MEMORY but more often refers to the act of remembering and usu. to a particular act of remembering esp. something pleasant or cherished in memory, or it may apply to the state of being remembered ⟨the only moments I've lived my life to the full and that live in *remembrance* unfaded —W.W.Gibson⟩ ⟨the vivid *remembrance* of an almost identical setting one evening —Henry Miller⟩ ⟨the *remembrance* of things past —Shak.⟩ ⟨the *remembrance* of the event always brought a pang of regret⟩ RECOLLECTION is like REMEMBRANCE but carries a strong suggestion of more voluntary and sometimes effortful recalling to mind, and it may apply to the thing remembered in this way ⟨they have a tendency to forget the facts of the present in their fond *recollection* of the past —S.M.Crothers⟩ ⟨you ask me to put down a few *recollections* of your father —W.E.H. Lecky⟩ REMINISCENCE may refer to remembrance of something long past, esp. as remembered casually and accidentally; it is closely synonymous with RECOLLECTION in references to what is remembered ⟨would use all the techniques of modern psychology in his analyses of the subconscious; the phenomena of involuntary *reminiscence* fascinate him —B.M.Woodbridge⟩ ⟨the author's own *reminiscences* of childhood and youth are a good deal less pretentious and more amusing than this model —*Times Lit. Supp.*⟩ MIND in this sense commonly appears only in a few idiomatic phrases ⟨to keep in *mind*⟩ ⟨out of sight, out of *mind*⟩ SOUVENIR may still be used as a synonym of MEMORY ⟨then she carefully restored them, her mind full of *souvenirs* newly awakened —Arnold Bennett⟩

**memory book** *n* **1** : SCRAPBOOK ⟨not so much a book of memoirs as a *memory book* —*New Yorker*⟩ **2** : a small album for autographs

**mem·o·ry·less** \ˈmem(ə)rēləs, -ril-\ *adj* : devoid of memory

**memory span** *n* : the greatest amount (as the longest series of letters or digits) that can be perfectly reproduced by the subject after a single presentation by the experimenter

**memory tube** *n* : a vacuum tube (as a camera tube or electronic computer tube) that retains information for later use by having a receptive element on which an electron beam impresses signals

**memory verse** *n* : a brief passage of Scripture to be memorized in connection with a Sunday-school lesson — compare GOLDEN TEXT

**memos** *pl of* MEMO, *pres 3d sing of* MEMO

**mem·phi·an** \ˈmem(p)fēən\ *n* -S *cap* [*Memphis*, Egypt + E *-an*] **1** : MEMPHITE; *also* : EGYPTIAN **2** [*Memphis*, Tenn. + E *-an*] : a native or resident of Memphis, Tenn.

**mem·phis** \-fəs\ *adj, usu cap* [fr. *Memphis*, Tenn.] : of or from the city of Memphis, Tenn. ⟨the *Memphis* cotton market⟩ : of the kind or style prevalent in Memphis

**¹mem·phite** \ˈmemˌfīt\ *n* -S *usu cap* [L *Memphites*, fr. Gk *Memphitēs*, fr. *Memphis*, Egypt + Gk *-itēs* -ite] : a native or resident of ancient Memphis in Egypt

**²memphite** \"\ *also* **mem·phit·ic** \(ˈ)memˈfid·ik\ *adj, usu cap* [*Memphite* fr. L *Memphites*, fr. *Memphites*, n.; *Memphitic* fr. Gk *Memphitikos*, fr. *Memphitēs* + *-ikos* -ic] : of or relating to ancient Memphis, its inhabitants, or the dynasties of Egyptian kings who made it their capital

**mem·phit·ic** \memˈfid·ik\ *n* -S *usu cap* [fr. *Memphitic*, adj.] : the Coptic dialect of Memphis and vicinity

**mems** *pl of* MEM

**mem·sahib** \ˈmem+ˌ-\ *n* [Hindi *mem-ṣāhib*, fr. E ²*mem* + Hindi *ṣāhib* — more at SAHIB] : a foreign woman of the white race and some social status living in India ⟨growing up to be another nice infuriating superior English ~ —H.E.Bates⟩; *esp* : the wife of an English official or other white man of some social status in colonial India ⟨found the white ~s more violently intoxicated with . . . race poison than their men —Edmond Taylor⟩ ⟨this is a ~'s book, recalling . . . the last years of that ascendancy in India —*Times Lit. Supp.*⟩ ⟨houses designed for British officials and their ~s —Christopher Rand⟩

**men** *pl of* MAN

**men-** *or* **meno-** *comb form* [NL, fr. Gk *mēn* month — more at MOON] : menstruation ⟨*meno*pause⟩ ⟨*men*acme⟩

**me·nac·can·ite** \məˈnakəˌnīt\ *n* -S [irreg. fr. *Manaccan*, Cornwall, England + E *-ite*] : ILMENITE — **me·nac·can·it·ic** \ˌ=ˌ==ˈnid·ik\ *adj*

**¹men·ace** \ˈmenəs *also* -nis\ *n* -S [ME *manace, menasse*, fr. MF *manace, menace*, fr. L *minacia*, fr. *minac-, minax* projecting, threatening (fr. *minari* to project, threaten) + *-ia* -y — more at MOUNT] **1 a** : a show of intention to inflict harm : a threatening gesture, statement, or act ⟨~s of damnation —T.S.Eliot⟩ ⟨spitting angry ~s at her —Arnold Bennett⟩ ⟨would advance with simulated ~ —Osbert Lancaster⟩ ⟨exploding in ~s and threats of vengeance —George Meredith⟩ **b** : threatening import, character, or aspect : THREAT ⟨ominous silence of the woods held no ~ for her —Osbert Sitwell⟩ ⟨the ~ of the European war to American interests —C.B.Forcey⟩ ⟨the sky became leaden with vague ~ —Adrian Bell⟩ ⟨with a hysterical cry of ~ —C.G.D.Roberts⟩ **c** : the condition of being threatened : a threatening atmosphere or situation ⟨in the ~ and confusion of the . . . postwar period —Hans Weigel⟩ : impending evil ⟨a sense of ~, of unease, runs through their conversation —T.H.White b.1915⟩ **2 a** : someone or something that represents a threat : DANGER ⟨tuberculosis and syphilis were major ~s —T.H.Fielding⟩ ⟨the intoxicated motorist is a ~ to life and limb —Wayne Hughes⟩ ⟨the ~s of air, such as tornado and whirlwind —Osbert Sitwell⟩ **b** : a person whose actions or idiosyncrasies cause intense annoyance or discomfiture ⟨that boy's a ~⟩ ⟨her friends were beginning to find her a ~ —Guy McCrone⟩

**²menace** \"\ *vb* -ED/-ING/-S [ME *manacen, menacen*, fr. MF *manacer, menacer*, fr. *manace, menace*, n.] *vt* **1 a** : to make a show of intention to harm : make a threatening gesture, statement, or act against ⟨*menaced* him with immediate expulsion —G.B.Shaw⟩ **b** : to threaten the infliction of : offer threat of ⟨*menacing* the emperor's displeasure —S.T.Coleridge⟩ ⟨he *menaced* ruin —H.R.Trevor-Roper⟩ **2** : to represent or pose a threat to : ENDANGER ⟨the ferries were *menaced* by floating mines —P.W.Thompson⟩ ⟨mature bolls are *menaced* by the army worm —*Amer. Guide Series: Ark.*⟩ ~ *vi* : to make a threatening gesture, statement, or act ⟨the few snakes that ~ with their mouths open —C.H.Curran & Carl Kauffeld⟩ **syn** see THREATEN

**menacing** *adj* [fr. pres. part. of ²*menace*] : presenting, suggesting, or constituting a menace : THREATENING ⟨unemployment reached ~ proportions —P.E.James⟩ ⟨his all-knowing and rather ~ smile —Louis Auchincloss⟩ ⟨the prospect of a third world war is so ~ —John Strachey⟩ ⟨chamber was somber and almost ~ —Dorothy Sayers⟩ — **men·ac·ing·ly** *adv*

**men·acme** \mən, (ˈ)men+\ *n* [*men-* + *acme*] : the portion of a woman's life during which menstruation occurs

**menad** *var of* MAENAD

**men·a·di·one** \ˌmenəˈdīˌōn\ *n* -S [*methyl* + *na*phthoquinone + *-dione*] : a yellow crystalline compound $C_{11}H_8O_2$ that is usu. made by oxidation of beta-methylnaphthalene, that has the biological activity of natural vitamin K to which it is chemically related, and that is often administered in the form of a water-soluble white crystalline addition compound with sodium bisulfite; 2-methyl-1,4-naphthoquinone — called also *vitamin $K_3$*

**me·na·do·nese** \məˌnädəˈnēz, -ēs\ *n, pl* **menadonese** *cap* [*Menado* (Manado) residency in Celebes, Indonesia + E *-nese* (as in *Japanese*)] : an Indonesian native or inhabitant of Manado in northeastern Celebes

**mé·nage** \(ˈ)māˈnäzh, -ˈnazh\ *n* -S [F *ménage*, fr. OF *mesnage* dwelling house, fr. (assumed) VL *mansionaticum*, fr. L *mansion-, mansio* habitation, dwelling — more at MANSION] **1 a** : a domestic establishment : HOUSEHOLD ⟨a respectable ~ —F.A.Swinnerton⟩ ⟨an unstable ~ —Harry Levin⟩ ⟨add one or two concubines to his ~ —John Blofeld⟩ **b** : a place in which a person keeps house or that is managed like a household : QUARTERS ⟨lunch with the young men at their mess — as all communal ~s appear to be called in the East —Evelyn Waugh⟩ ⟨apartment, an eight-room ~ on the fourteenth floor —E.J.Kahn⟩ ⟨very formal, and very well kept, whereas I had expected to find myself in an entirely Bohemian ~ —George Copeland⟩ **c** : domestic management : HOUSEKEEPING ⟨accommodates our democratic ~ to the taste of the richest and most extravagant plebeian among us —W.D.Howells⟩ **2 a** : a savings club organized in some Scottish and English communities so that each member pays in a set sum each week and the total sum is paid to a different member each week **b** *dial Brit* : the selling of goods (as cloth) on installments often by an itinerant vendor

**ménage à trois** \māˌnäzhäˈtrwä\ *n* [F, lit., household of three] : an arrangement or relationship in which a married pair and the lover of one of the pair form a single household usu. with the consent or tolerance of the other married partner ⟨leaves a feeble young husband to become part of a Bohemian *ménage à trois* —*Times Lit. Supp.*⟩ ⟨a more or less harmonious *ménage à trois* —Edmund Wilson⟩

**me·nag·er·ie** \məˈnajərē, -ri *sometimes* -azhə-\ *n* -S [F *ménagerie*, fr. MF *menagerie* management of a household or a farm, place where animals are tended, fr. *menage* household + *-erie* -ery] **1 a** : a place where animals are kept and trained esp. for exhibition **b** : a collection of wild or foreign animals in cages or enclosures; *esp* : one kept for exhibition (as with a circus) **c** *obs* : AVIARY **2** : a group or collection of persons that are strange, odd, or startling or foreign to one's experience ⟨a wonderful ~ of royal hangers-on —V.S.Pritchett⟩

**me·nag·er·ist** \-rəst\ *n* -S : the proprietor or manager of a menagerie

**me·nai·on** \məˈnāˌän\ *n, pl* **me·naia** \-āə\ [MGk *mēnaion*, fr. neut. of *mēnaios* monthly, fr. Gk *mēn* month — more at MOON] *usu cap* : a collection of hymns and collects for all days of the year in the Eastern Orthodox Church arranged in calendar order and usu. divided into 12 volumes each for a different month and each containing the proper of the immovable feasts of Christ or the saints for the month; *also* : any of these volumes

**menald** \ˈmenᵊld, ˈmēn-\ *adj* [origin unknown] : SPECKLED, VARIEGATED

**me·naph·thone** \məˈnafˌthōn\ *n* -S [*methyl* + *naphtha*quin*one*] : MENADIONE

**men·ar·che** \məˈnärˌ(ˌ)kē, meˈ-\ *n* -S [NL, fr. *men-* + Gk *archē* beginning — more at ARCHI-] : the initiation of menstruation : the first menstrual period of an individual — **men·ar·che·al** *also* **men·ar·chi·al** \-ˌkēəl\ *adj*

menat

**men·as·pis** \məˈnaspəs\ *n, cap* [NL, fr. Gk *mēnē* moon + NL *-aspis* — more at MOON] : a genus of Upper Permian cartilaginous fishes (subclass Holocephali) related to the chimaeras

**me·nat** \ˈmāˌnät\ *n* -S [Egypt *mnit*] : an amulet worn in ancient Egypt to secure divine protection

**me·nav·e·lings** \məˈnavələnz, -liŋz\ *var of* MANAVELINS

**menc·ken·ese** \ˌmeŋkəˈnēz, -enk-, -ēs\ *n* -S *usu cap* [H. L. *Mencken* †1956 Amer. journalist and satirist + E *-ese*] : the peculiarly vivacious racy flamboyant and often caustic style characteristic of the journalist Mencken or a style patterned on or resembling that of Mencken ⟨difficult to read through a daily paper without finding a feature writer who employs *Menckenese* —George Mayberry⟩

**¹menc·ke·ni·an** \(ˈ)meŋ¦kēnēən, -en¦-\ *adj, usu cap* [H. L. *Mencken* + E *-ian*] : of, relating to, resembling, or suggestive of the journalist Mencken or his writings : critical of philistinism and shams and generally iconoclastic in point of view ⟨when he attacks congressmen, he is very *Menckenian* —Saul Bellow⟩ ⟨the writing is so *Menckenian* in style that it is sometimes embarrassing —Charles Angoff⟩ ⟨free of the engaging *Menckenian* slapstick —*Newsweek*⟩

**²menckenian** \"\ *n* -s *usu cap* : a disciple or imitator of the journalist Mencken ⟨the literary world was full of *Menckenians* —J.T.Farrell⟩

**¹mend** \ˈmend\ *vb* -ED/-ING/-S [ME *menden*, short for *amenden* — more at AMEND] *vt* **1 a** (1) : to improve in manners or morals : REFORM ⟨dear to their tender bosoms . . . is a bad man they are ~*ing* —George Meredith⟩ ⟨too late to ~ the nation —V.J.Ryan⟩ — usu. used in the phrases *mend one's ways* ⟨he could be counseled to ~ his ways —Ralph Linton⟩ and *mend one's manners* ⟨young man, you had better ~ your manners⟩ (2) : to remove or eliminate the defects of : set right : CORRECT ⟨~ a corrupt text⟩ (3) : to make right, improve, or remedy (a condition or state of affairs) : RECTIFY ⟨think I can do something to ~ all this —William Black⟩ ⟨an attempt was made to ~ matters by a law —C.L.Jones⟩ (4) : to improve or strengthen or consolidate by negotiation, maneuvering, or similar activity — used chiefly in the phrase *mend one's fences* ⟨spends the weekend ~*ing* political fences —E.O.Hauser⟩ ⟨went through Europe ~*ing* fences with assiduous alacrity —John Gunther⟩ **b** (1) : to put into good shape or working order again : patch up : REPAIR ⟨used to come in and ~ our car —Michael Davie⟩ ⟨the roads were never ~*ed* —Ellen Glasgow⟩ ⟨~ a torn sleeve⟩ (2) : to put in better order : READJUST — now used chiefly in the phrase *mend sail* (3) : to remove slack between a fishing rod tip and fly by flipping (the line) upcurrent so that the fly is not dragged downstream **c** : to restore to health : CURE ⟨before the bone was fully ~*ed* —*Current Biog.*⟩ ⟨learned to ~ his soul by going to sea —John Erskine †1951⟩ ⟨no sleep but one can ~ him —Herbert Gold⟩ **d** (1) : to improve the condition or quality of : make better : AMELIORATE ⟨the standards of marriage must be ~*ed* —F.S.Mitchell⟩ ⟨men who needed to ~ their fortunes —T.B.Costain⟩ (2) *obs* : to improve or better by adding to or increasing (as wages) (3) *dial* : to make up or add fuel to (a fire) (4) *obs* : to supply the deficiency or loss of : SUPPLEMENT (5) : to make more rapid : QUICKEN — usu. used in the phrase *mend one's pace* ⟨~*ed* his pace with suitable haste —Stephen Crane⟩ **2** : to make amends or atonement for : atone for — now used only in the proverb *least said, soonest mended* ~ *vi* **1** : to improve morally : REFORM — now used chiefly in the proverb *it's never too late to mend* **2** : to grow better : become corrected or improved ⟨her troubles were beginning to ~ —Ellen Glasgow⟩ ⟨depression and lack of spirit ~*ed* visibly —Arnold Nicholson⟩ **3 a** : to improve in health : get well ⟨if he ~*s* in time to play again —Rogers Whitaker⟩ ⟨after that I began to ~ —Corra Harris⟩ **b** : HEAL ⟨waited for his injury to ~ —*Amer. Guide Series: Tenn.*⟩ **4** *chiefly dial* : to rise or gain in price, weight, or other respect : INCREASE

**syn** REPAIR, PATCH, REBUILD, REMODEL: MEND, often applying to any freeing from faults or defects, usu. suggests a making of something whole or sound that has been broken, torn, or injured ⟨*mend* a sock⟩ ⟨*mend* a worn shoe sole⟩ ⟨*mend* one's ways⟩ ⟨*mend* a broken marriage⟩ REPAIR, similar to MEND and often interchangeable with it in the sense of to make whole or sound, more commonly applies to more complex things or to a more extensive damage or dilapidation ⟨*repair* a ripped coat⟩ ⟨*repair* a broken bicycle⟩ ⟨the fault which must be *repaired* swiftly —S.L.A.Marshall⟩ ⟨*repaired* the irregularities of his teeth —John Buchan⟩ ⟨constantly *repairing* an old run-down house⟩ PATCH, often PATCH UP, implies a mending of a hole, rent, or weak spot by the application of a patch but can extend to cover several ideas suggestive of this, as (in the form *patch up*) to mend or repair temporarily in an obvious, hurried, careless, or clumsy way, or to fix something up expediently ⟨*patch* a punctured tire⟩ ⟨*patch* a road with asphalt⟩ ⟨*patch up* a hole in the roof⟩ ⟨each community might make a list of its strong and weak points and go to work to *patch up* the latter —Chester Bowles⟩ ⟨*patch up* a damaged ship in order to make port⟩ ⟨*patch up* an excuse⟩ REBUILD in this comparison has a currency in industry and business to imply a more thoroughgoing repair than usual, suggesting an almost complete renewing ⟨*rebuild* old typewriters⟩ ⟨shoe *rebuilding*⟩ REMODEL implies repairing with alterations, often extensive, in the structure or design ⟨forced the owners of 6000 houses and apartment buildings to repair or *remodel* —*Time*⟩ ⟨the house was enlarged and it has been subsequently *remodeled* and modernized —*Amer. Guide Series: N. C.*⟩

**²mend** \"\ *n* -s [ME, fr. *menden*, v.] **1 mends** *pl but usu sing in constr, chiefly dial Brit* **a** : compensation or atonement for a wrong, injury, or loss : AMENDS **b** : IMPROVEMENT, CURE **2 mends** *pl, obs* : means of getting reparation : REMEDY **3 a** : an act of mending : REPAIR **b** : a mended place — **on the mend** *adv (or adj)* : in the way of improvement ⟨his health is *on the mend*⟩ ⟨business . . . continues *on the mend* —*N.Y.Times*⟩

**men·da·cious** \(ˈ)men¦dāshəs\ *adj* [L *mendac-, mendax* lying, false + E *-ious* — more at AMEND] : given to deception or falsehood ⟨a ~ person⟩ : having a false or lying character ⟨the memoirs are ~ and uninteresting —E.A.Walker⟩ **syn** see DISHONEST

**men·da·cious·ly** *adv* : in a mendacious manner

**men·da·cious·ness** *n* -ES : MENDACITY

**men·dac·i·ty** \menˈdasəd·ē, -daas-, -sətē, -i\ *n* -ES [LL *mendacitas*, fr. L *mendac-, mendax* + *-itas* -ity] : the quality or state of being mendacious : the practice or an instance of lying : FALSEHOOD ⟨blushed . . . at his own ~ —J.D.Beresford⟩ ⟨man's peculiar type of ~ —Leo Stein⟩

**men·de** \ˈmendē\ *n, pl* **mende** *or* **mendes** *usu cap* **1 a** : a politically important people of Mandingo affiliation in Sierra Leone and Liberia, West Africa **b** : a member of such people **2** : a Mande language of the Mende people

**mended** *past of* MEND

**men·de·lé·eff's law** *or* **men·de·le·ev's law** \ˌmendəˈlā(y)əfs-, -əvz-\ *n, usu cap M* [after Dmitri I. *Mendeleev* †1907 Russ. chemist] : PERIODIC LAW

**men·de·le·vi·um** \ˌmendəˈlēvēəm, -lāv-\ *n* -s [NL, fr. D. *Mendeleev* + NL *-ium*] : a radioactive element artificially produced (as by bombardment of einsteinium with high-energy alpha particles) — symbol *Md* or *Mv*; see ELEMENT table

**¹men·de·lian** \(ˈ)men¦dēlēən, -lyən\ *adj, usu cap* [Gregor J. *Mendel* †1884 Austrian botanist + E *-ian*] : of or relating to Mendel : of, relating to, or in accordance with Mendel's laws

**²mendelian** \"\ *n* -s *usu cap* : an advocate or exponent of Mendelism

**mendelian character** *n, usu cap M* : a character inherited in accordance with Mendel's laws

**mendelian factor** *or* **mendelian unit** *n, usu cap M* : GENE

**mendelian inheritance** *n, usu cap M* : PARTICULATE INHERITANCE

**men·de·lian·ism** \-ˌnizəm\ *n* -s *usu cap* : MENDELISM

**men·de·lian·ist** \-ˌnəst\ *n* -s *usu cap* : MENDELIAN

**mendelian ratio** *n, usu cap M* : the ratio of occurrence of various phenotypes in any cross involving Mendelian characters; *esp* : the 3:1 ratio shown by the second filial generation of offspring from parents differing in respect to a single character

**men·del·ism** \ˈmendəˌlizəm\ *n* -s *usu cap* [Gregor J. *Mendel* + E *-ism*] : the principles or the operations of Mendel's laws; *also* : PARTICULATE INHERITANCE

**¹men·del·ist** \-ləst\ *adj, usu cap* [Gregor J. *Mendel* + E *-ist*] : MENDELIAN

**²mendelist** \"\ *n* -s *usu cap* : MENDELIAN — **men·del·is·tic** \¦==¦listik\ *adj, usu cap*

**men·del·ize** \'==ˌlīz\ *vb* -ED/-ING/-S *sometimes cap* [Gregor J. Mendel + E *-ize*] *vi* : to conform to Mendel's laws ~ *vt* : to cause to conform to Mendel's laws

**men·del's law** \ˈmendᵊlz-\ *n, usu cap M* [after Gregor J. *Mendel*, its formulator] **1** : a principle in genetics: paired hereditary units representing alternate characters (as tallness or dwarfness) separate during the formation of gametes so that every gamete receives but one member of a pair — called also *law of segregation* **2** : a principle in genetics limited and modified as a result of the subsequent discovery of the phenomenon of linkage: the corresponding hereditary units in a pair of gametes unite in the zygote to form new combinations and recombinations according to the laws of chance — called also *law of independent combination* **3** : a principle in genetics proved subsequently to be subject to many limitations: because one of each pair of hereditary units dominates the other in expression, characters are inherited alternatively on an all or nothing basis — called also *law of independent assortment*; compare BLENDING INHERITANCE

**men·de·lye·ev·ite** \ˌmendəlˈyā(y)əˌvīt, -dəˈlā-\ *n* -s [Dmitri I. Mendeleev (*Mendelyeev*) †1907 Russ. chemist + E *-ite*] : a calcium urano-titano-niobate occurring in black isometric crystals and masses and being essentially a titanian and rare-earth-bearing betafite

**mend·er** \ˈmendə(r)\ *n* -s [ME, fr. *menden* to mend + *-er* — more at MEND] : one that mends or is used for mending; *specif* : a person whose work is mending for the purpose of repairing torn, worn, or defective parts (as of garments, textiles, parachutes, hats, straw goods, fishing nets)

**men·di·can·cy** \ˈmendəkənsē, -dēk-, -si\ *n* -ES **1** : the condition of being a beggar ⟨reduced to ~⟩ **2** : the practice or act of begging ⟨legal enactments against ~ —C.B.Fairbanks⟩

**¹men·di·cant** \-nt\ *n* -s [L *mendicant-, mendicans*, pres. part. of *mendicare* to beg, fr. *mendicus* beggar — more at AMEND] **1** : a person who begs; *esp* : one that lives by begging **2** *often cap* : a member of a mendicant order : FRIAR 1a

**²mendicant** \"\ *adj* [L *mendicant-, mendicans*, pres. part.] **1** : practicing beggary : BEGGING ⟨~ friars⟩ **2** : characteristic of a mendicant ⟨went about with a ~ air⟩

**mendicant order** *n* : any of various religious orders (as the Franciscans, Dominicans, Carmelites, or Augustinians) in which monastic life and outside religious activity are combined and in which neither personal nor community tenure of property is allowed under original regulations though less stringent regulations regarding the ownership and use of property are now usu. prevail

**men·di·cate** \-dəˌkāt\ *vb* -ED/-ING/-S [L *mendicatus*, past part. of *mendicare*] *archaic* : BEG — **men·di·ca·tion** \ˌ==ˈkāshən\ *n* -s *archaic*

**men·dic·i·ty** \menˈdisəd·ē, -sətē, -i\ *n* -ES [ME *mendicite*, fr. MF *mendicité*, fr. L *mendicitat-, mendicitas*, fr. *mendicus* indigent, beggar + *-itat-, -itas* -ity — more at AMEND] : the practice or habit of begging : the state or life of a beggar : MENDICANCY ⟨the vast increase in ~ —E.A.Peers⟩

**mending** *n* -s [ME, fr. gerund of *menden* to mend — more at MEND] **1** : an accumulation of articles (as clothing) requiring repair **2** : the act of one that mends : the process of repairing flaws or defects esp. in fabrics

**men·dip·ite** \ˈmendəˌpīt\ *n* -s [*Mendip* hills, Somersetshire, England + E *-ite*] : a mineral $Pb_3O_2Cl_2$ consisting of oxide and chloride of lead

**men·do·za** \(ˈ)men¦dōzə\ *adj, usu cap* [fr. *Mendoza*, Argentina] : of or from the city of Mendoza, Argentina : of the kind or style prevalent in Mendoza

**men·do·zite** \menˈdōˌzīt\ *n* -s [*Mendoza*, Argentina + E *-ite*] : a mineral $NaAl(SO_4)_2.11H_2O$ (?) consisting of a monoclinic hydrous sulfate of sodium and aluminum

**mends** *pl of* MEND, *pres 3d sing of* MEND

**men·e·ghi·nite** \ˌmenəˈgēˌnīt\ *n* -s [J. *Meneghini* †1889 It. mineralogist + E *-ite*] : a mineral $Pb_{13}Sb_7S_{23}$ consisting of dark lead-gray lead antimony sulfide

**me·ne·hu·ne** \ˌmenəˈhünē\ *n, pl* **menehune** *or* **menehunes** [Hawaiian] : a small mythical Polynesian being usu. pictured as a dwarf living in the mountains and working at night as a stone builder

**me·nel** \məˈnel\ *n* -s [by alter.] : MANILLE — used esp. of the nine of trumps in klaberjass

**men·e·la·us' theorem** \ˌmenə¦lāəs(əz)-\ *n, usu cap M* [after *Menelaus*, 1st cent. A.D. Greek geometer] : a theorem in geometry: if through a triangle ABC a transversal is drawn cutting the sides BC, AB, AC (produced if necessary) in the respective points p, q, r, then the product Aq×Bp×Cr is numerically equal to the product Bq×Cp×Ar

**me·ne·vian** \mə̇ˈnēvēən\ *adj, usu cap* [*Menevia*, ancient parish in Pembrokeshire, Wales (fr. LL) + E *-an*] : of or relating to the division of the European Cambrian between the Harlech and the Lingulella — see GEOLOGIC TIME table

**menfolk** *or* **menfolks** \'=,=\ *n pl* **1** : the male sex : MEN **2** : the men of a family, household, or community ⟨keep quiet when their ~ talk —Charles Angoff⟩

**meng** \ˈmeŋ\ *vb* -ED/-ING/-S [ME *mengen*, fr. OE *mengan* — more at MINGLE] *dial Brit* : MIX, MINGLE, BLEND

**men·ha·den** \(ˈ)men¦hādᵊn, mənˈh- *sometimes* -had-\ *n, pl* **menhaden** *also* **menhadens** [of Algonquian origin; prob. akin to Narraganset *munnawhatteaûg* menhaden, fr. *munnohquohteau* he fertilizes; fr. the use of menhaden as fertilizer] : a marine fish (*Brevoortia tyrannus*) of the family Clupeidae having a large head, deep compressed body, toothless jaws, and closely imbricated bluish silvery scales, attaining a length of 12 to 16 inches, and being by far the most abundant of fishes on the Atlantic coast of the U.S. where scores of millions are annually taken and used for bait or converted into oil and fertilizer — called also *mossbunker, pogy*

**menhaden oil** *n* : a drying fatty oil obtained from the body of the menhaden and used chiefly in paint, varnish, inks, and linoleum and in treating leather

**men·hir** \ˈmenˌhi(ə)r, ='=\ *n* -s [F, fr. Bret, fr. *men* stone + *hir* long; akin to W *maen* stone, Corn *mēn*, and to OIr *sīr* long — more at SINCE] : a single upright rude monolith usu. of prehistoric origin

**¹me·nial** \ˈmēnēəl, -nyəl\ *adj* [ME *meynal, meynial*, fr. *meynie* household, family, retinue (fr. OF *mesnie, meinie*, fr. — assumed — VL *mansionata*, fr. L *mansion-, mansio* dwelling, habitation + *-ata* -ate) + *-al* — more at MANSION] **1** *archaic* **a** : belonging to or constituting a retinue or train of servants : DOMESTIC ⟨stood knight and squire, and ~ train —S.T. Coleridge⟩ ⟨a ~ servant⟩ **b** : of or relating to the service of a household : appropriate to a domestic servant ⟨a few Indian women for ~ offices —W.H.Prescott⟩ **2** : of, relating to, or being work or an occupation or position not requiring special skill or not calling into play the higher intellectual powers or ranking as low in some occupational or social scale and often regarded as lacking dignity, status, or interest : LOWLY, HUMBLE ⟨those who . . . regard translation as an uninspired and ~ occupation have never practiced it —*Times Lit. Supp.*⟩ ⟨~ occupations in hotels, laundries, cigar factories —*Amer. Guide Series: N. Y.*⟩ ⟨most ~ of stations in that aristocratic old Boston world —V.L.Parrington⟩ ⟨encouraged to rise from the ~ and mechanical operations of his craft —Lewis Mumford⟩ ⟨spread from the top down to the most ~ levels of the administration —*Economist*⟩ ⟨a relatively ~ category to which volunteers without degrees . . . are generally relegated —Robert Rice⟩ ⟨~ tasks⟩ **3 a** : appropriate to a menial : SERVILE ⟨the wealthy nation they had dared speak to only in ~ tones for so long —*Atlantic*⟩ **b** : lacking interest or dignity : dull or sordid ⟨life for each man had become a ~ thing —Robert Lowry⟩

**syn** see SUBSERVIENT

**²menial** \"\ *n* -s [ME *meynal, meynial*, fr. *meynal, meynial*, adj.] : a domestic servant or retainer ⟨in the classic period the musician was generally looked upon as a ~ —A.E.Wier⟩

**me·nial·ly** \-əlē,-əli\ *adv* : in a menial manner

**mé·ni·ère's disease** *or* **ménière's syndrome** \ˌmān¦e(ə)rz, (ˈ)mān¦ye(-\ *n, usu cap M* [after Prosper *Ménière* †1862 Fr. physician] : a disorder of the membranous labyrinth of the ear that is marked by recurrent attacks of dizziness, tinnitus, and deafness, is often accompanied by nausea and vomiting, and is commonly attributed to increased pressure of the endolymphatic fluid though it is possibly of obscure allergic origin

**men·i·lite** \ˈmenᵊlˌīt\ *n* -s [F *ménilite*, fr. *Ménil*montant parish (now part of Paris), France + F *-ite*] : an impure opal in brown or dull grayish concretions

**me·nin·die clover** \məˈnindē-\ *n, usu cap M* [fr. *Menindie* county, New So. Wales, Australia] : a perennial fragrant plant (*Trigonella suavissima*) resembling clover and abundant in New South Wales

**mening-** *or* **meningo-** *also* **meningi-** *comb form* [NL, fr. *meninges*] : meninges ⟨meningococcus⟩ ⟨meningioma⟩ ⟨*meningitis*⟩ : meninges and ⟨*meningo*myelitis⟩ ⟨*meningo*vascular⟩

**me·nin·ge·al** \ˌmenənˈjēəl *sometimes* məˈninjē-\ *adj* [*meninges* + *-al*] : of, relating to, or affecting the meninges ⟨symptoms of ~ inflammation⟩

**meningeal artery** *n* : any of three arteries supplying the meninges of the brain and neighboring structures

**meninges** *pl of* MENINX

**me·nin·gi·o·ma** \mə̇ˌninjēˈōmə\ *n, pl* **meningiomas** \-məz\ *or* **meningioma·ta** \-məd·ə\ [NL, fr. *mening-* + *-oma*] : a slow-growing encapsulated tumor arising from the meninges and often causing damage by pressing upon the brain or adjacent parts

**men·in·gis·mus** \ˌmenənˈjizməs\ *also* **me·nin·gism** \məˈninˌjizəm, ˈmenən,-\ *n, pl* **men·in·gis·mi** \-ˈjizˌmī\ *also* **me·nin·gisms** \-ˌjizəmz\ [NL *meningismus*, fr. *mening-* + L *-ismus* -ism] : a state of meningeal irritation with symptoms suggesting meningitis that often occurs at the onset of acute febrile diseases esp. in children

**men·in·git·ic** \¦menən¦jid·ik\ *adj* [NL *meningitis* + E *-ic*] : of, relating to, or like that of meningitis

**men·in·gi·tis** \ˌmenənˈjīd·əs\ *n, pl* **meningit·i·des** \-jid·əˌdēz\ [NL, fr. *mening-* + *-itis*] **1** : inflammation of the meninges, esp. the pia mater and the arachnoid **2** : a disease in which inflammation of the meninges occurs and which is caused by microorganisms (as the meningococcus, the tubercle bacillus, or a pneumococcus)

**me·nin·go·cele** *also* **me·nin·go·coele** \məˈniŋgəˌsēl\ *n* -s [ISV *mening-* + *-cele, -coele*] : a protrusion of meninges through a defect in the skull or spinal column forming a cyst filled with cerebrospinal fluid

**me·nin·go·coc·ce·mia** *also* **me·nin·go·coc·cae·mia** \məˌniŋgōˌkäkˈsēmēə, -äˈkēm-\ *n* -s [NL, fr. *meningococcus* + *-emia*] : the presence of meningococci in the circulating blood

**me·nin·go·coc·cic** \=¦==¦käk(s)ik\ *also* **me·nin·go·coc·cal** \-äkəl\ *adj* [NL *meningococcus* + E *-ic* or *-al*] : having or caused by meningococci ⟨~ infection⟩ ⟨~ meningitis⟩

**me·nin·go·coc·cus** \-¦käkəs\ *n, pl* **meningococ·ci** \-äˌkī, -ä(ˌ)kē, -äkˌsī, -äk(ˌ)sē\ [NL, fr. *mening-* + *-coccus*] : a bacterium (*Neisseria meningitidis*) that causes cerebrospinal meningitis

**me·nin·go·encephalitis** \məˈniŋ(ˌ)gō+\ *n* [NL, fr. *mening-* + *encephalitis*] : inflammation of the brain and the meninges

**me·nin·go·encephalocele** \"+\ *n* [ISV *mening-* + *encephalocele*] : a protrusion of meninges and brain through a defect in the skull

**me·nin·go·encephalomyelitis** \"+\ *n* [NL, fr. *mening-* + *encephalomyelitis*] : inflammation of the meninges, brain, and spinal cord

**me·nin·go·myelocele** \mə̇¦niŋ(ˌ)gō+\ *n* [ISV *mening-* + *myelocele*] : a protrusion of meninges and spinal cord through a defect in the spinal column

**menin·ting** \məˈnintiŋ, ˈmenən·ˌt-\ *n* -s [native name in the East Indies] : an East Indian kingfisher (*Alcedo meninting*)

**meninx** \ˈmēniŋ(k)s, ˈmen-\ *n, pl* **me·nin·ges** \məˈnin(ˌ)jēz\ [NL, fr. Gk *mēninx* membrane — more at MEMBER] **1** : any of the three membranes that envelop the brain and spinal cord — compare ARACHNOID, DURA MATER, PIA MATER **2** : the solitary sheath of stout connective tissue enclosing the central nervous system of some lower vertebrates and embryos of higher forms — called also *primitive meninx*

**me·nis·co·cyte** \məˈniskəˌsīt\ *n* -s [Gk *mēniskos* crescent + E *-cyte*] : SICKLE CELL

**me·nis·co·cy·to·sis** \=ˌ==sīˈtōsəs\ *n* [NL, fr. ISV *meniscocyte* + NL *-osis*] : SICKLE CELL ANEMIA

**me·nis·coid** \məˈniˌskȯid\ *adj* [NL *meniscus* + E *-oid*] : resembling a meniscus in shape

**me·nis·co·ther·i·dae** \məˌniskəˈtherəˌdē\ *n pl, cap* [NL, fr. *Meniscotherium*, type genus (fr. Gk *mēniskos* crescent + NL *-therium*) + *-idae*] : a family of American Eocene five-toed mammals (order Condylarthra)

**me·nis·cus** \məˈniskəs\ *n, pl* **menis·ci** \-iˌskī, -iˌsī\ *also* **meniscus·es** *often attrib* [NL, fr. Gk *mēniskos*, dim. of *mēnē* moon — more at MOON] **1** : a crescent or crescent-shaped body : a crescent moon **2** : a fibrocartilage within a joint esp. of the knee **3** : a concavo-convex lens; *esp* : one of true crescent-shaped section **4** : the curved upper surface of a liquid column that is concave when the containing walls are wetted by the liquid and convex when not

A B

meniscus 4: concave meniscus of water, *A;* convex meniscus of mercury, *B*

**men·i·sper·ma·ce·ae** \ˌmenə(ˌ)spərˈmāsēˌē\ *adj, cap* [NL, fr. *Menispermum*, type genus + *-aceae*] : a family of herbaceous or woody climbers (order Ranales) having small 3-parted dioecious flowers and curved embryo — **men·i·sper·ma·ceous** \¦==(ˌ)=¦māshəs\ *adj*

**men·i·sper·mum** \ˌmenəˈspərməm\ *n, cap* [NL, fr. *meni-* (fr. Gk *mēnē* moon) + *-spermum* (fr. Gk *sperma* seed) — more at SPERM] **1** : a genus (family Menispermaceae) of climbing herbs having numerous stamens and black drupaceous fruit — see MOONSEED **2** -s : YELLOW PARILLA

**menkind** \'=,=\ *n* : MENFOLK

**¹men·nist** \ˈmenəst\ *n* -s *usu cap* [Menno Simons †1559 Frisian religious reformer + E *-ist*] : MENNONITE

**²men·nist** *adj, usu cap* : MENNONITE

**men·no·nist** \ˈmenənəst\ *n* -s *usu cap* [*Menno* Simons + connective *-n-* + E *-ist*] : MENNONITE

**¹men·no·nite** \ˈmenəˌnīt, *usu* -īd·+V\ *n* -s *usu cap* [G *Mennonit*, fr. *Menno* Simons †1559 Frisian religious reformer + connective *-n-* + G *-it* -ite] : a member of a denomination of evangelical Protestant Christians formed from the Anabaptist movement of the 16th century and noted for belief in Scriptural authority, plainness of dress, rejection of oaths, adult baptism, aloofness from the state, exercise of excommunication, restriction of marriage to members of the group, and practice of the rite of foot washing

**²mennonite** \"\ *adj, usu cap* : of or relating to the Mennonites or to their doctrines or practices

**men·no·nit·ism** \-īd·ˌizəm, -īˌti-\ *n* -s *usu cap* : the doctrines and practices of Mennonites : the Mennonite Church or movement

**me·no** \ˈmā(ˌ)nō\ *adv* [It, fr. L *minus* — more at MINUS] : LESS — used as a direction in music

**¹meno-** — see MEN-

**²meno-** *comb form* [NL, fr. Gk *menein* to remain — more at MANSION] : remaining : persisting ⟨*Menorhyncha*⟩

**men·o·dus** \ˈmenədəs\ *n, cap* [NL, fr. Gk *mēnē* moon + NL *-odus* — more at MOON] : a genus of large Lower Oligocene horned perissodactyls (family Brontotheriidae) of No. America

**me·nog·na·thous** \(ˈ)meˈnägnəthəs\ *adj* [²*meno-* + *-gnathous*] : having biting mandibles during both the larval and imaginal stages — used of various insects having a complete metamorphosis; contrasted with *metagnathous*

**me·no·lo·gion** \ˌmēnəˈlō(ˌ)yōn\ *n* -s *usu cap* [MGk *mēnologion*] : an ecclesiastical calendar and short martyrology of the Eastern Orthodox Church : an abbreviated version of the complete Menaion

**me·nol·o·gy** \məˈnäləjē, mēˈ-\ *n* -ES [MGk *mēnologion*, fr. Gk *mēn* month + *logos* word, account + *-ion*, dim. suffix — more at LEGEND] **1** : an ecclesiastical calendar of festivals celebrated in honor of particular saints and martyrs; *also* : a register of saints or outstanding religious personages **2** : MENOLOGION

**meno·metrorrhagia** \¦menō + \ *n* [NL, blend of *menorrhagia* and *metrorrhagia*] : a combination of menorrhagia and metrorrhagia

**me·nom·i·nee whitefish** \məˈnämənē-\ *n, often cap M* : a small whitefish (*Prosopium quadrilaterale*) occurring in lakes in Canada, Alaska, and parts of the northern U. S.

**me·nom·i·ni** *also* **me·nom·i·nee** \məˈnämənē\ *n, pl* **menomini** *or* **menominis** *also* **menominee** *or* **menominees** **1** *usu cap* **a** : an Indian people of the Upper Peninsula, Michigan, and northeastern Wisconsin **b** : a member of such people **c** : an Algonquian language of the Menomini people **2** *often cap* : MENOMINEE WHITEFISH

**me·no mos·so** \ˌmānōˈmȯ(s)(ˌ)sō\ *adj (or adv)* [It] : less lively : SLOWER — used as a direction in music

**men·o·pau·sal** \ˌmenəˈpȯzəl\ *adj* : of, relating to, or undergoing menopause ⟨~ disorders⟩ ⟨~ women⟩

**men·o·pause** \ˈmenə,pȯz\ *n* [F *ménopause,* fr. *méno-* men- + *pause*] **1 :** the period of natural cessation of menstruation occurring usu. between the ages of 45 and 50 — called also *change of life* **2 :** the whole group of physical and physiological alterations that occur in the menopausal woman — see CLIMACTERIC 1

**men·o·pon** \ˈmenə,pän\ *n, cap* [NL, perh. fr. ²*meno-* + Gk *ponos* pain] **:** a genus of bird lice that includes the shaft louse of poultry

**me·no·rah** \məˈnōrə, -nȯrə\ *n* -s [Heb *mĕnōrāh* candlestick] **1 :** a holy candelabrum with seven candlesticks of the ancient Jewish temple in Jerusalem **2 :** a candelabrum with any of various numbers of candlesticks used primarily in Jewish religious services

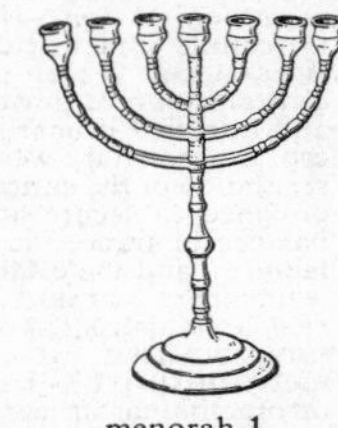

menorah 1

**men·o·rhyn·cha** \,menəˈriŋkə\ *n pl, cap* [NL, fr. ²*meno-* + *-rhyncha* (fr. Gk *rhynchos* snout)] **:** a division of insects including those which take food by suction in both the larval and adult stages — **men·o·rhyn·chous** \¦menə¦riŋkəs\ *adj*

**men·or·rha·gia** \,menəˈrāj(ē)ə\ *n* -s [NL, fr. *men-* + *-rrhagia*] **:** abnormally profuse menstrual flow — compare METRORRHAGIA — **men·or·rhag·ic** \¦menə¦rajik\ *adj*

**men·or·rhea** \,menəˈrēə\ *n* -s [NL, fr. *men-* + *-rrhea*] **:** normal menstrual flow

**men·o·typh·la** \,menəˈtiflə\ *n pl, cap* [NL, fr. ²*meno-* + *-typhla* (fr. Gk *typhlon* caecum) — more at TYPHL-] **:** a suborder of Insectivora comprising the elephant shrews and commonly the tree shrews in all of which the pubic symphysis is long and the postorbital process well developed — compare LIPOTYPHLA

**men·o·typh·lic** \¦menə¦tiflik\ *adj* [²*meno-* + *typhl-* + *-ic*] **1 :** having a cecum **2** [NL *Menotyphla* + E *-ic*] **:** of or relating to the Menotyphla

**men·sa** \ˈmen(t)sə\ *n, pl* **mensas** \-səz\ *or* **men·sae** *in sense 1* -n(,)sä, *in sense 2* -n(,)sē, -n,sī *sometimes* -n(,)sā\ [ML, fr. L, table, fr. OL, flat cake offered to the gods, perh. fr. fem. of *mensus,* past part. of *metiri* to measure — more at MEASURE] **1** *Roman Catholicism* **:** the top of the altar; *esp* **:** the top or central slab upon which the eucharistic elements are placed **2** [NL, fr. L] **:** the grinding surface of a tooth

**men·sal** \ˈmen(t)səl\ *adj* [LL *mensalis,* fr. L *mensa* table + *-alis* -al] **1 :** belonging to or used at the table **:** done or carried on at table ⟨pleasant ~ talk⟩ **2 a :** set aside for the maintenance of the table of an ancient Irish or Scotch prince or king ⟨~ land⟩ **b :** set aside for the support of a cleric of the Roman Catholic Church ⟨~ fund⟩

**mensal line** *n, usu cap M* **:** LINE OF HEART

¹**mense** \ˈmen(t)s\ *n* -s [alter. of ME *menske, mensk,* fr. ON *mennska* humanity, fr. *mennskr* human — more at LUFTMENSCH] **1** *dial Brit* **a :** mannerly or gracious behavior **:** PROPRIETY; *specif* **:** HOSPITALITY ⟨she baked a cake and butter scones for ~'s sake —H.S.Riddell⟩ **b :** a large amount or number ⟨a ~ of people⟩ **2** *dial Brit* **:** a source of honor **:** HONOR, CREDIT ⟨a ~ to the family⟩ **3** *dial Brit* **:** neatness or freshness in appearance **:** SPRUCENESS

²**mense** \"\ *vt* -ED/-ING/-S [alter. of ME *mensken,* fr. *menske, mensk,* n.] **1** *dial Brit* **:** to do honor to **:** DECORATE, GRACE **2** *dial Brit* **:** to make clean or orderly **:** dress up

**mense·ful** \-fəl\ *adj, dial Brit* **:** DECOROUS, DISCREET, CONSIDERATE; *also* **:** NEAT, TIDY

**mense·less** \-ləs\ *adj, dial Brit* **:** lacking manners, discretion, or neatness ⟨ye ~ coof —Theodore Bonnet⟩

**menservants** *pl of* MANSERVANT

**men·ses** \ˈmen(,)sēz\ *n pl but sing or pl in constr* [L, lit., months, pl. of *mensis* month — more at MOON] **:** MENSTRUATION

**men·she·vik** \ˈmenchə,vik, -,vēk\ *n, pl* **mensheviks** \-ks\ *also* **men·she·viki** \-,vikē, -,vēkē\ *usu cap* [Russ *men'shevik,* fr. *men'she* less, smaller (comp. of *malo* little, few) + *-vik* (nominal suffix); fr. their forming the minority group of the Russian Social Democratic party in 1903; akin to Russ *malyĭ* small, L *malus* bad — more at SMALL] **:** a member of the wing of the Russian Social Democratic party before and during the Russian Revolution that believed in gradualism and relied on reformist methods and an alliance with the liberal bourgeoisie to achieve socialism and that after the establishment of the Soviet government assumed an attitude of vigorous opposition to the Communist regime — compare BOLSHEVIK

**men·she·vism** \-,vizəm\ *n* -s *usu cap* [*Menshevik* + *-ism*] **:** the doctrines, tactics, or practices of the Mensheviks

**men·she·vist** \-,vəst\ *adj, usu cap* **:** of or relating to Menshevism

**men's house** *n* **:** a building in a primitive community reserved for the exclusive use of males and serving as a bachelors' dormitory, a recreational center, a cult house, or as a center for some other communal male activity

**mens rea** \ˈmenzˈrēə, -n(t)sˈrāə\ *n* [NL, lit., guilty mind] **:** the intent or state of mind accompanying an act, manifesting a purpose harmful to society, providing no justification for the act, and subjecting the perpetrator thereof to criminal punishment **:** criminal as distinguished from innocent intent

**men's room** *n* **:** a room (as in a hotel or office building) equipped with lavatories, water closets, and usu. urinals designated for the exclusive use of men

**men·stru·al** \ˈmenztr(əw)əl, -n(t)str-\ *adj* [ME *menstruall,* fr. L *menstrualis,* fr. *menstrua* menses (fr. neut. pl. of *menstruus* of a month, monthly, of menstruation, fr. *mensis* month) + *-alis* -al — more at MOON] **1 :** of or relating to menstruation **2** [L *menstrualis,* fr. *menstruus* + *-alis* -al] *archaic* **a :** occurring once a month **:** MONTHLY **b :** lasting for a month ⟨a ~ flower⟩

**menstrual cycle** *n* **:** the whole cycle of physiologic changes from the beginning of one menstrual period to the beginning of the next

**menstrual epact** *n* **:** EPACT 1b

**men·stru·ate** \ˈmenztrə,wāt, -n(t)str-, ÷-nz,trāt ÷-n(t),strāt, *usu* -ād·+V\ *vi* -ED/-ING/-S [LL *menstruatus,* past part. of *menstruari,* fr. L *menstrua* menses] **:** to undergo menstruation

**men·stru·a·tion** \,menztrəˈwāshən, ,men(t)str-, ÷menzˈtrā-, ÷men(t)ˈstrā-\ *n* -s [LL *menstruatus* + E *-ion*] **:** a discharge of blood, secretions, and tissue debris associated with necrotic changes of the uterine mucosa that recurs in nonpregnant breeding-age females of various primates at intervals of 3½ to 5 weeks (as in women typically at 4 week intervals and lasting 3 to 5 days) and that is usu. held to represent a readjustment of the uterus to the nonpregnant state following proliferative changes accompanying the preceding ovulation; *also* **:** an instance of the occurrence of this discharge **:** PERIOD

**menstruosity** *n* -ES [fr. *menstruous,* after such pairs as E *curious: curiosity*] *obs* **:** menstruous state or discharge

**men·stru·ous** \ˈmenztr(əw)əs, -n(t)str-\ *adj* [L *menstruus* of a month, monthly, of menstruation — more at MENSTRUAL] **1 :** undergoing menstruation **:** MENSTRUATING **2 :** of or relating to menstruation **:** MENSTRUAL

**men·stru·um** \ˈmenztr(əw)əm, -n(t)str-\ *n, pl* **menstruums** \-)əmz\ *or* **mens·trua** \-)ə\ [ML, lit., menses, alter. of L *menstrua;* fr. the comparison made by alchemists of a base metal in a solvent undergoing transmutation into gold with an ovum in utero undergoing development by the menstrual blood — more at MENSTRUAL] **1 :** a substance that dissolves a solid or holds it in suspension **:** SOLVENT; *specif* **:** a solvent used to extract soluble principles from drugs esp. by percolation **2 :** a universal or general solvent in which other things are dissolved or disintegrated or lose their separate identities ⟨the sea . . . has been so well named the ~ of life —W.E. Swinton⟩ ⟨one unifying ~ of all the sciences — H.M.Kallen⟩

**men·su·al** \ˈmenchəwəl\ *adj* [LL *mensualis,* irreg. fr. *mensis* month + *-alis* -al — more at MOON] **:** MONTHLY

**mensur** *abbr* mensuration

**men·su·ra·bil·i·ty** \,men(t)sərəˈbiləd·ē, -nchər-\ *n* **:** the quality or state of being mensurable

**men·su·ra·ble** \-rəbəl\ *adj* [LL *mensurabilis,* fr. *mensurare* to measure + L *-abilis* -able — more at MEASURE] **1 :** capable of being measured **:** MEASURABLE ⟨reducing to a ~ order . . . the process of life —Lewis Mumford⟩ **2 :** MENSURAL 1 — **men·su·ra·ble·ness** *n* -ES

**men·su·ral** \ˈmen(t)sərəl, ˈmenchər-\ *adj* [LL *mensuralis,* fr. L *mensura* measure + *-alis* -al — more at MEASURE] **1 :** relating to mensural music or mensural notation **2 :** of or relating to measure

**men·su·ral·ist** \-əst\ *n* -s **:** a composer of mensural music

**mensural music** *also* **mensurable music** *n* [trans. of ML *musica mensurabilis*] **:** polyphonic music originating in the 13th century with each note having a definite and exact time value — compare GREGORIAN CHANT

**mensural notation** *n* **:** a musical notation originating in the 13th century consisting of single notes (as large, breve) and ligatures each with a definitely fixed time value and thereby making possible the combination of independent voice parts that led historically to the development of counterpoint and the modern notation

**men·su·rate** \-,rāt\ *vt* -ED/-ING/-S [LL *mensuratus,* past part. of *mensurare* — more at MEASURE] **:** MEASURE

**men·su·ra·tion** \,men(t)səˈrāshən, ,menchəˈ-\ *n* -s [LL *mensuration-, mensuratio,* fr. *mensuratus,* + L *-ion-, -io* -ion] **1 :** the act, process, art, or an instance of measuring **:** MEASUREMENT ⟨problems in ~ and rudimentary astronomy —*Times Lit. Supp.*⟩ **2 :** the application of geometry to the computation of lengths, areas, or volumes from given dimensions or angles **3 :** the temporal relationships between the note values in mensural notation comparable to the different meters of the modern system ⟨customary for those reading . . . notation to deduce the ~ from the context —*Score*⟩

**men·su·ra·tion·al** \¦==¦rāshənᵊl, -shnəl\ *adj* **:** of or relating to mensuration

**men·su·ra·tive** \ˈ==,rād·iv, -,rəd-\ *adj* **:** adapted for measuring

**mens·wear** *or* **men's wear** \ˈ=,=\ *n* **1** *usu men's wear* **:** clothing for men **:** HABERDASHERY **2 :** a fabric (as worsted) suitable for men's clothing and also used for women's clothing

¹**-ment** \,mant *sometimes* ,ment\ *n suffix* -s [ME, fr. OF, fr. L *-mentum,* fr. *-men,* n. suffix + *-tum* (akin to *-tus,* past. part. ending); akin to Gk *-ma,* n. suffix — more at -ED] **1 a :** concrete result, object, or agent of a (specified) action ⟨entangle*ment*⟩ ⟨incre*ment*⟩ ⟨attach*ment*⟩ ⟨frag*ment*⟩ **b :** concrete means or instrument of a (specified) action ⟨comple*ment*⟩ ⟨nutri*ment*⟩ ⟨orna*ment*⟩ **2 a :** action, process, art, or act of a (specified) kind ⟨encircle*ment*⟩ ⟨recruit*ment*⟩ ⟨state*ment*⟩ ⟨govern*ment*⟩ ⟨develop*ment*⟩ **b :** place or object of a (specified) action ⟨escarp*ment*⟩ ⟨canton*ment*⟩ **3 :** state or condition ⟨amaze*ment*⟩ ⟨embroil*ment*⟩ ⟨fulfill*ment*⟩ ⟨involve*ment*⟩

²**-ment** *when no syllable-increasing suffix (as -ed or -ing) follows,* ,ment *also* ,mənt; *when a syllable-increasing suffix follows,* ,ment *sometimes* ,mənt\ — as final syllable in verbs corresponding to nouns of identical spelling ending in *-ment* ⟨compli*ment*⟩ ⟨imple*ment*⟩

**menta** *pl of* MENTUM

¹**men·tal** \ˈmentᵊl\ *adj* [ME, fr. MF, fr. LL *mentalis,* fr. L *ment-, mens* mind + *-alis* -al — more at MIND] **1 :** of or relating to mind: as **a :** relating to the integrated activity of an organism; *specif* **:** relating to the total emotional and intellectual response of an organism to its environment ⟨the role played by the comics in the ~ life of the children —Winfred Overholser⟩ ⟨found him in a terrible ~ state — very depressed and even panicky⟩ ⟨the ~ set of an individual⟩ **b :** of or relating to intellectual as contrasted with emotional activity **:** of or relating to the process or mode of thought or capacity for thought ⟨free from any ~ defects⟩ ⟨racial explanations of the ~ character of the Greeks —Benjamin Farrington⟩ ⟨note what ~ level you are on with that person —W.J.Reilly⟩ ⟨~ exertions⟩ **c :** of, relating to, or being intellectual as contrasted with overt physical activity ⟨~ work⟩ ⟨made swift ~ calculations⟩ **d :** occurring or experienced in the mind **:** not voiced or given other sensory expression **:** INNER ⟨~ reservations⟩ ⟨filled it for him, under ~ protest —George Meredith⟩ ⟨refusal to shape either the words or the ~ images of prayer —Frank Yerby⟩ ⟨~ anguish⟩ **e :** relating to or concerned with mind, its activity, or its products as an object of study **:** relating to or concerned with ideology **:** IDEOLOGICAL ⟨exercised a great influence on the philosophy of history, the study of jurisprudence, politics, and indeed on all the ~ sciences —Frank Thilly⟩ ⟨the whole of ~ science —William James⟩ **f :** relating to or being spirit or idea as opposed to matter **:** IMMATERIAL, SPIRITUAL, IDEAL ⟨the distinction between physical things and ~ ideas —J.W.Yolton⟩ ⟨your mind is ~, but that which you perceive with your senses is also ~ —*Encore*⟩ **2 a** (1) **:** of, relating to, or affected by mental deficiency or any of a variety of psychiatric disorders ⟨a ~ patient⟩ ⟨a ~ case⟩ (2) *chiefly Brit* **:** WACKY, CRAZY ⟨are ~ from birth . . . and every so often go quite round the bend —Rose Macaulay⟩ ⟨anyone who isn't ~ can see it's a bowl —Anthony West⟩ — often used in the phrase *go mental* ⟨was going a bit ~ from old age —Nevil Shute⟩ ⟨when people go ~ they nearly always turn against their nearest . . . relations —Rosamond Lehmann⟩ **b :** intended for or devoted to the care or treatment of persons affected by psychiatric disorders ⟨a ~ hospital⟩ ⟨the qualified psychiatric nurse in Britain is officially registered as a registered ~ nurse —*Trained Nurse & Hospital Rev.*⟩ **3 :** relating to or marked by possession or display of telepathic, mind-reading, or other occult powers ⟨set up the stage for the ~ act —W.L.Gresham⟩ ⟨the greatest ~ medium of all time —Hereward Carrington⟩

**syn** INTELLIGENT, INTELLECTUAL, CEREBRAL, PSYCHIC: MENTAL indicates a connection with or emphasis on the mind as a center of rational activity; it contrasts matters emotional or physical ⟨she writes straight from the emotions; nothing *mental* ever gets in her way —Anita Loos⟩ ⟨if from any bodily or *mental* defect the eldest son is disqualified for ruling —J.G.Frazer⟩ ⟨completed the banishment of natural appearances from the art of painting, substituting therefor a *mental* world of geometrical derivatives —F.J.Mather⟩ INTELLIGENT indicates a degree of mental power enabling a person or animal to appraise a situation and make a variety of sound or acceptable decisions; it often contrasts with *stupid* or *silly* ⟨*intelligent* self-interest should lead to a careful consideration of what the road is able to do without ruin —O.W.Holmes †1935⟩ ⟨friends who were a little more *intelligent* and would understand —John Hersey⟩ INTELLECTUAL may indicate connection with the higher powers of the mind; it may contrast with *emotional* and may suggest a noticeable scope, depth, or complexity ⟨words have an emotional and imaginative, as well as an *intellectual* context —J.L.Lowes⟩ ⟨a scientist is known not by his technical processes but by his *intellectual* processes — F.W.Peabody⟩ INTELLECTUAL may suggest an accustomed or lasting concern with higher challenges to the intellect rather than the acumen displayed in a particular decision ⟨less *intellectual* and therefore more *intelligent* in his approach —Edgar Smith⟩ CEREBRAL may suggest cold, analytic intellectual activity or inclination, to the exclusion of the emotional or sensuous ⟨wrote about Catholicism from the *cerebral* slant of the converted intelligentsia —*Book-of-the-Month Club News*⟩ PSYCHIC suggests reference to the psyche, the inner self, and guides the reader away from notions of the physical, physiological, or organic ⟨not materialist but *psychic* factors are the decisive forces of history —*Time*⟩ ⟨I don't accept the idea of *psychic* diseases analogous to mental diseases —Compton Mackenzie⟩

²**mental** \"\ *n* -s **:** a mentally disordered person ⟨no ~s had occurred for a hundred years or more —*Mag. of Fantasy & Science Fiction*⟩

³**mental** \"\ *adj* [L *mentum* chin + E *-al;* akin to W *mant* mouth, lip, L *mont-, mons* mountain — more at MOUNT] **:** of or relating to the chin, the median part of the lower jaw, or the mentum of an insect **:** GENIAL

⁴**mental** \"\ *n* -s **:** a plate, scale, or shield (of a fish or reptile) occurring in the mental area

**mental age** *n* **:** the level of a person's intellectual ability esp. as measured by an intelligence test and expressed as the numerical equivalent of the chronological age of the typical person having the same level of intellectual ability — abbr. *MA*

**mental capacity** *or* **mental competence** *n* **1 :** sufficient understanding and memory to comprehend in a general way the situation in which one finds himself and the nature, purpose, and consequence of any act or transaction into which one proposes to enter **2 :** the degree of understanding and memory the law requires to uphold the validity of or to charge one with responsibility for a particular act or transaction ⟨*mental capacity* to commit crime requires the accused to know right from wrong⟩

**mental chemistry** *n* **:** associationism by analogy with chemistry that forms mental compounds with qualities not inherent in the elements to be combined

**mental cruelty** *n* **1 :** a course of conduct by an offending spouse without physical cruelty evidencing personal indignities that wound the feelings of and show a lack of respect and affection for the complaining spouse and constituting a basis for separation **2 :** a course of conduct by an offending spouse without physical violence evidencing personal indignities calculated to endanger the mental and physical health of the complaining spouse in view of their aggravated character and the latter's sex and sensibilities and constituting a basis for divorce esp. if actual impairment results (as required in many courts)

**mental deficiency** *n* **:** failure in intellectual development resulting in social incompetence that is considered to be the result of defect in the central nervous system and to be accordingly incurable **:** FEEBLEMINDEDNESS — compare IDIOCY, IMBECILITY, MORONITY

**mental disease** *n* **:** a disease characterized esp. by mental symptoms **:** mental disorder **:** INSANITY

**mental foramen** *n* [³*mental*] **:** a foramen for the passage of blood vessels and a nerve on the outside of the lower jaw on each side near the chin

**mental hygiene** *n* **:** the science of maintaining mental health and preventing the development of psychosis, neurosis, or other personality disturbance

**mental incapacity** *or* **mental incompetence** *n* **1 :** an absence of mental capacity **2 :** an inability through mental illness or mental deficiency of any sort to carry on the everyday affairs of life or to care for one's person or property with reasonable discretion

**men·ta·lis** \menˈtāləs, -tāl-,-tal-\ *n, pl* **mentales** \-a(,)lēz, -ā(,)lēz, -ä(,)lās\ [NL, fr. L *mentum* chin + *-alis* -al — more at MENTAL] **:** a muscle that raises the chin and pushes up the lower lip

**men·tal·ism** \ˈmentᵊl,izəm\ *n* -s **1 a :** a doctrine that mind is the fundamental reality **:** BERKELEIANISM — compare IDEALISM, MATERIALISM **b :** a doctrine that distinguishes mental processes fundamentally from the accompanying brain activity **2 :** a view that conscious processes as revealed by introspection are the proper data of psychology — opposed to *behaviorism* **3 :** a hypothesis that special factors of mind must be assumed to analyze, classify, or explain some or all phenomena of language — compare MECHANISM

**men·tal·ist** \-əst\ *n* -s **1 :** an advocate of mentalism **2 :** a mind reader or fortune-teller ⟨how did the ~ know the birthdays of spectators —W.L.Gresham⟩

**men·tal·is·tic** \¦==¦istik\ *adj* **1 :** of or relating to mentalism ⟨commendably assaults ~ ways of thinking —J.R.Kantor⟩ **2 :** of or relating to mental phenomena **:** INTROSPECTIONISTIC ⟨such ~ sentences as "I remember to have seen this person before" —Arthur Pap⟩ — **men·tal·is·ti·cal·ly** \-tək(ə)lē\ *adv*

**men·tal·i·ty** \menˈtaləd·ē, -lətē, -i\ *n* -ES **1 :** mental power or capacity **:** learning ability **:** INTELLIGENCE ⟨a criminal whose ~ is low —B.N.Cardozo⟩ ⟨a man of keen ~ —S.H.Adams⟩ ⟨the ~ of apes⟩ **2 :** mode or way of thought, mental set, or disposition **:** OUTLOOK ⟨resent his Anglican curate ~ —Gordon Kent⟩ ⟨shunned attempting to depict the ~ of pregnancy — C.W.Cunnington⟩ ⟨a growing socialist ~ —A.R.Williams⟩ ⟨one of the most suggestive studies of the whole Eastern ~ — H.J.Laski⟩ ⟨the civilized Roman ~ —G.G.Coulton⟩

**men·tal·ly** \ˈmentᵊlē, -ᵊli\ *adv* **1 :** without overt motor activity or sensory expression **:** in the mind **:** in thought **:** INWARDLY ⟨work a problem out ~⟩ ⟨~ reproached himself for his weakness⟩ ⟨~ cursed him and all his works⟩ **2 :** as concerns the mind or its operations **:** as concerns capacity for thought or reasoning ⟨a ~ deficient person⟩ ⟨vigorous both physically and ~⟩ **3 :** as concerns intellectual life **:** IDEOLOGICALLY, INTELLECTUALLY ⟨a ~ stimulating atmosphere⟩ ⟨one of the most ~ provocative books of our time⟩

**mental philosophy** *n* **:** psychology, logic, and metaphysics in a single discipline or area of study or instruction ⟨a professor of *mental philosophy* and moral philosophy —*Current Biog.*⟩ — compare MORAL PHILOSOPHY, NATURAL PHILOSOPHY

**mental prominence** *or* **mental process** *or* **mental protuberance** *n* **:** the bony prominence at the front of the lower jaw forming the chin

**mental ratio** *n* **:** INTELLIGENCE QUOTIENT

**mentals** *pl of* MENTAL

**mental spine** *or* **mental tubercle** *n* [³*mental*] **:** either of two small elevations on the inner side of the symphysis of the lower jaw providing attachment for the genioglossus and geniohyoid muscles

**mental telepathist** *n* **:** MIND READER

**mental telepathy** *n* **:** MIND READING

**mental test** *n* **:** any of various standardized procedures applied to an individual in order to ascertain his ability or evaluate his behavior in comparison with other individuals or with the average of any class of individuals

**men·ta·tion** \menˈtāshən\ *n* -s [L *ment-, mens* mind + E *-ation* — more at MIND] **:** mental activity ⟨probe the innermost layers of ~ —Warren Beck⟩ ⟨~ is severely affected —*Seminar*⟩ ⟨aspects of unconscious ~ —*Times Lit. Supp.*⟩

**men·ta·wei·an** \,mentəˈwīən\ *n, pl* **mentaweian** *or* **mentaweians** *usu cap* [*Mentawei* islands off the western coast of Sumatra + E *-an*] **1 a :** an Indonesian people inhabiting the Mentawei islands **b :** a member of such people **2 :** the Austronesian language of the Mentaweian people

**mentd** *abbr* mentioned

**menth-** *or* **mentho-** *comb form* [ISV, fr. *menthol*] **:** menthol ⟨*menthone*⟩ ⟨*menthane*⟩

**men·tha** \ˈmen(t)thə\ *n, cap* [NL, fr. L, mint — more at MINT] **:** a widely distributed genus of herbs comprising the common mints (family Labiatae), having small white or pink verticillate flowers with a nearly regular corolla and four equal stamens, and yielding aromatic volatile oils — see PEPPERMINT, SPEARMINT

**men·tha·ce·ae** \menˈthāsē,ē\ *n pl, cap* [NL, fr. *Mentha,* type genus + *-aceae*] *in some classifications* **:** a family of plants coextensive with the Labiatae — **men·tha·ceous** \(ˈ)men¦thāshəs\ *adj*

**men·tha·di·ene** \,men(t)thəˈdī,ēn\ *n* -s [*menthane* + *-diene*] **:** any of several terpenes $C_{10}H_{16}$ (as dipentene, limonene, terpinolene) of which the menthanes are the tetrahydrides

**men·thane** \ˈmen,thān\ *n* -s [ISV *menth-* + *-ane*] **:** any of three isomeric liquid saturated cyclic hydrocarbons $C_{10}H_{20}$ that are hexahydro derivatives of the cymenes; *esp* **:** the para isomer that is the parent compound of many terpenoids (as carvone, menthol, terpineol) — compare STRUCTURAL FORMULA

**men·tha·nol** \ˈmen,thā,nȯl, -nōl\ *n* -s [ISV *menthane* + *-ol*] **:** a monohydroxy alcohol $C_{10}H_{19}OH$ (as menthol) derived from a menthane

**men·thene** \ˈmen,thēn\ *n* -s [ISV *menth-* (fr. NL *Mentha*) + *-ene*] **1 :** an oily unsaturated hydrocarbon $C_{10}H_{18}$ that is a tetrahydro derivative of the para isomer of cymene obtained from menthol by dehydration **2 :** any of several tetrahydro derivatives $C_{10}H_{18}$ (as carvomenthene) of the cymenes

[Structural formula: $CH_3$ (7); $CH$ (1); $H_2C$ (6), $CH_2$ (2); $H_2C$ (5), $CH_2$ (3); $CH$ (4); $CH$ (8); $H_3C$ (10), $CH_3$ (9)]

*para*-menthane (*p*-menthane)

**men·the·nol** \ˈmen,thē,nȯl, -nōl\ *n* -s [ISV *menthene* + *-ol*] **:** a monohydroxy alcohol $C_{10}H_{17}OH$ (as terpineol) derived from a menthene

**men·the·none** \ˈmen(t)thə,nōn\ *n* -s [ISV *menthene* + *-one*] **:** a monoketone $C_{10}H_{16}O$ (as pulegone) derived from a menthene

**men·thol** \ˈmen,thȯl, -thōl\ *n* -s [G, fr. NL *Mentha* + G *-ol*] **:** a secondary terpenoid alcohol $C_{10}H_{19}OH$ that is known in 12 optically isomeric forms including (1) a crystalline levorotatory form that has the odor and cooling properties of peppermint, that occurs naturally esp. in peppermint oil and Japanese mint oil as the principal constituent and is also made synthetically (as from citronellal), and that is used chiefly in medicine (as locally to relieve pain, itching, and nasal congestion) and in flavoring and (2) a crystalline racemic form made synthetically (as by reduction of thymol) and used similarly to the natural form; 3-*para*-menthanol — called also respectively (1) *levo-menthol, l-menthol, mint camphor, peppermint camphor* and (2) *dl-menthol*

**men·tho·lat·ed** \'men(t)thə,lād·əd, -ātəd\ *adj* **1 :** treated with menthol **2 :** containing or impregnated with menthol

**men·thone** \'men,thōn\ *n* -s [ISV *menth-* + *-one*] **:** a liquid ketone $C_{10}H_{18}O$ that occurs in a levorotatory form esp. in peppermint oil and pennyroyal oil and that can be made synthetically by oxidation of menthol

**men·thyl** \'men(t)thəl\ *n* -s [ISV *menth-* + *-yl*] **1 :** the univalent radical $C_{10}H_{19}$ derived from menthol by removal of the hydroxyl group; 3-*para*-menthyl **2 :** any of the univalent radicals $C_{10}H_{19}$ derived from menthane by removal of one hydrogen atom

**menti-** *comb form* [L *ment-, mens* — more at MIND] **:** mind ‹*menticide*›

**men·ti·cide** \'mentə,sīd\ *n* -s [*menti-* + *-cide*] **:** a systematic and intentional undermining of a person's conscious mind for the purpose of instilling doubt and replacing that doubt with ideas and attitudes directly inimical to his normal ideas and attitudes by subjecting him to mental and physical torture, extensive interrogation, suggestion, training, and narcotics — compare BRAINWASHING

**men·ti·cir·rhus** \,mentə'sirəs\ *n, cap* [NL, fr. *menti-* (fr. L *mentum* chin) + *-cirrhus*; fr. the appendage on the lower jaw — more at MENTAL] **:** a genus of No. American food fishes (family Sciaenidae) comprising the whitings

[1]**men·tion** \'menchən\ *n* -s [ME *mencioun*, fr. OF *mention*, fr. L *mention-, mentio*, fr. *ment-, mens* mind + *-ion-, -io* -ion — more at MIND] **1 a :** the act or an instance of citing, noting, or calling attention to someone or something esp. in a brief, casual, or incidental manner **:** reference or citation in speech or writing ‹his is the earliest ~ of obstetric forceps —Harvey Graham› ‹so obvious that we ought perhaps to pass it over with only a ~ —H.A.Overstreet› ‹the wealth of ~ and keenness of observation —W.C.Ford› ‹the mere ~ of an . . . alliance at this stage is enough to dismiss the idea —*Atlantic*› **b :** specific and usu. formal citation by name (as in a military dispatch or the report of a contest jury) in recognition of outstanding achievement or work well done ‹his service . . . from 1916 to 1918 earned him a ~ —*Sydney (Australia) Bull.*› ‹honorable ~s went to the authors of two magazine articles› ‹many will receive special ~s and special awards —Celia E. Klotz› **2** *obs* **:** INDICATION, VESTIGE, TRACE

[2]**mention** \"\ *vb* **mentioned; mentioned; mentioning** \-ch(ə)niŋ\ **mentions** [MF *mentionner*, fr. *mention*, n.] *vt* **:** to cite, note, or call attention to esp. in a brief, casual, or incidental manner **:** make mention of **:** refer to ‹had not thought of it at all until she ~*ed* it —J.P.Marquand› ‹~*ed* as a possible choice for the post of secretary-general —*Current Biog.*› ‹~*s* that the addition of alkyds improves the flexibility —H.J. Wolfe›; *specif* **:** to cite usu. formally in recognition of outstanding achievement or work well done ‹~*ed* in the dispatches —*Current Biog.*› **~** *vi, obs* **:** to make mention **:** SPEAK — usu. used with *of*

**syn** NAME, INSTANCE, SPECIFY: MENTION indicates a calling attention to, usu. by name where possible, sometimes by a brief, cursory, or incidental reference ‹I shall *mention* the accident which directed my curiosity originally into this channel —Charles Lamb› ‹intellectuals are such puritanical devils that they usually recoil with horror when prayer is *mentioned* —E.M.Forster› ‹usually the class is not directly *mentioned* in our statement; but there must be an implicit understanding, since otherwise the probability would be indeterminate —A.S. Eddington› ‹*mentioning* several minor figures in his lecture on Shakespeare› NAME implies clear mention of a name and therefore may suggest greater explicitness ‹*naming* Doe and Roe in the report and implicating their associates› INSTANCE may indicate clear explicit reference or definite emphasis as a typical example or special case ‹examples can be *instanced* from the first to the twentieth century —K.S.Latourette› ‹is it unfair to *instance* Marlowe, who died young —A.T.Quiller-Couch› ‹I have *instanced* his book because it was flagrant, not unique —Margaret Leech› SPECIFY indicates statement explicit, detailed, and specific so that misunderstanding is impossible ‹the standards *specify* the names under which these five varieties must be sold —*Americana Annual*› ‹as changes emerge from the storm of civil commotion, it is often just as hard to *specify* the exact day on which a government is born or dies —P.C.Jessup›

**men·tion·able** \-ch(ə)nəbəl\ *adj* **:** capable of being mentioned

**men·tion·er** \-ch(ə)nə(r)\ *n* -s **:** one that mentions

**mento-** *comb form* [NL, fr. L *mentum* — more at MENTAL] **:** chin **:** chin and ‹*mento*anterior› ‹*mento*condyloid›

**men·ton** \'men,tän\ *n* -s [F, chin, fr. L *mentum*] **1 :** the lowest point in the median plane of the chin **2 :** GNATHION

**men·tor** \'men,tȯ(ə)r, -ō(ə), -ntə(r)\ *n* -s [after *Mentor*, tutor of Telemachus in the Odyssey of Homer, fr. L, fr. Gk *Mentōr*] **1 :** a close, trusted, and experienced counselor or guide ‹every one of us needs a ~ who, because he is detached and disinterested, can hold up a mirror to us —P.W.Keve› ‹was much more than a ~; he supplied decisions —Hilaire Belloc› ‹has been my ~ since 1946 —Lalia P. Boone› ‹regarded by patrons . . . as a personal friend as well as fashion ~ —*N. Y. State Legislative Committee on Problems of the Aging*› **2 :** TEACHER, TUTOR, COACH ‹a writer of monographs, and a ~ of seminars —*Atlantic*› ‹although he had never accepted a pupil . . . she persuaded him to become her ~ —*Current Biog.*› ‹one of the game's most successful young ~s —*Official Basketball Guide*›

**mentor barberry** *n* **:** an upright half-evergreen barberry (*Berberis mentorensis*) used as an ornamental and having elliptic ovate subcoriaceous leaves, solitary or sparse yellowish flowers, and dark red fruit

**men·tor·ship** \-,ship\ *n* **1 :** the quality or state of being a mentor **:** the office of a mentor **2 :** the influence, guidance, or direction exerted by a mentor ‹its ~ has been mild enough —*Harper's*› ‹as it affects the power process, we call such influence ~ —H.D.Lasswell & Abraham Kaplan›

**-ments** *pl of* -MENT

**men·tum** \'mentəm\ *n, pl* **men·ta** \-tə\ [in sense 1, fr. L; in other senses, NL, fr. L — more at MENTAL] **1 :** CHIN **2 :** a projection like a chin in some orchid flowers formed by the sepals and the base of the column **3 :** a median plate of the labium of an insect — see LABIAL PALPUS **4 :** a projection below the mouth of certain mollusks

**ment·ze·lia** \men(t)'sēlēə\ *n* [NL, fr. Christian *Mentzel* †1701 Ger. physician and botanist + NL *-ia*] **1** *cap* **:** a genus of scabrous and bristly western American herbs or undershrubs (family Loasaceae) with alternate leaves, yellow or white flowers, and a one-celled ovary with numerous ovules **2** -s **a :** any plant of the genus *Mentzelia* — called also *bartonia* **b :** a plant of the related genus *Nuttallia*

**menu** \'me(,)nyü *also* 'mā(- *sometimes* -nü\ *n* -s [F, fr. *menu*, adj., small, slender, detailed, fr. L *minutus* small — more at MINUTE (adj.)] **1 a** (1) *or* **menu card :** BILL OF FARE ‹reading the ~s outside cafés —Elizabeth Taylor› (2) **:** DIET, REGIMEN ‹~s can be made up which will include a variety of foods —H.R.Litchfield & L. H. Dembo› **b :** the dishes served at a meal or the meal itself ‹serves an excellent ~› ‹the present trend is toward shorter ~s —Fannie M. Farmer› **c :** the range or variety of food consumed ‹improves his ~ with bass and bream caught within sight of his kitchen —Jackson Rivers› ‹the ~ of the rough-legged hawk —D.C.Peattie› **2 :** a program of music, drama, or other entertainment or recreation ‹the ~ was routine, the playing ditto —Virgil Thomson› ‹mastering the style of the varied ~ which the . . . company presents —Henry Hewes› ‹yachting is included in the summer fun ~ —*Springfield (Mass.) Daily News*›

**menuet** *or* **menuetto** *var of* MINUET

**me·nu·ra** \mə'n(y)ürə\ *n, cap* [NL, fr. Gk *mēnē* moon + NL *-ura* — more at MOON] **:** a genus (the type of the family Menuridae) consisting of the lyrebirds

**me·nu·rae** \-ü(,)rē\ *n pl, cap* [NL, fr. pl. of *Menura*] **:** a suborder of birds (order Passeriformes) comprising the lyrebirds and scrubbirds

**me·nus plai·sirs** \m(ə)nüplāzēr\ *n pl* [F] **:** small pleasures ‹spend her small income on her clothes and the *menus plaisirs* of the family —W.S.Maugham›

**meny·an·tha·ce·ae** \,menē,an'thāsē,ē\ *n pl, cap* [NL, fr. *Menyanthes*, type genus + *-aceae*] **:** a widely distributed family of aquatic or bog plants (order Gentianales) having basal or alternate leaves and valvate corolla lobes — **menyanthaceous** *adj*

**meny·an·thes** \,menē'an(t)(,)thēz\ *n, cap* [NL, fr. *meny-* (origin unknown) + *-anthes*] **:** a genus (the type of the family Menyanthaceae) of bog plants, having thickish creeping rootstocks and racemose flowers on a naked scape — see BUCKBEAN

**men·yie** *or* **men·zie** \'men(y)i\ *now chiefly Scot var of* MEINY

**men·zie·sia** \men'zēzh(ē)ə\ *n, cap* [NL, fr. Archibald *Menzies* †1842 Scot. botanist + NL *-ia*] **:** a genus of shrubs (family Ericaceae) of No. America and eastern Asia having small bell-shaped flowers and bluish tinged foliage — see FALSE AZALEA

**men·zies larkspur** \'menzēz-, -eŋəs-, 'miŋəs-\ *n, usu cap M* [after Archibald *Menzies*] **:** a low larkspur (*Delphinium menziesii*) of western No. America, having brownish yellow flowers with blue veins on the petals and being poisonous to stock

**menzies spruce** *n, usu cap M* [after Archibald *Menzies*] **:** SITKA SPRUCE

**meo** *usu cap, var of* MIAO

[1]**me·ow** *or* **mi·aow** *also* **mi·aou** *or* **meaow** \mē'aü\ *n* -s [imit.] **1 :** the cry of a cat **2 :** a spiteful or malicious remark ‹the ~ of the week —Walter Winchell›

[2]**meow** \"\ *vb* -ED/-ING/-S *vi* **1 :** to utter the characteristic cry of a cat **:** MEW ‹gave me that long, baffled look of which cats are capable, and immediately ~*ed* to be let out —Paul Gallico› **2 :** to make a catty remark **~** *vt* **:** to utter by or as if by meowing **:** MEW

**MEP** *abbr, often not cap* mean effective pressure

**mep·a·crine** \'mepə,krēn, -krən\ *n* -s [*methyl* + *paludism* + *acridine*] *Brit* **:** QUINACRINE

**me·per·i·dine** \mə'perə,dēn, -dən\ *n* -s [*methyl* + *piperidine*] **:** a synthetic narcotic drug $C_{15}H_{21}NO_2$ used in the form of its crystalline hydrochloride as an analgesic, sedative, and antispasmodic; ethyl 1-methyl-4-phenyl-piperidine-4-carboxylate

**me·phen·e·sin** \mə'fenəsən\ *n* -s [*methyl* + *phenol* + *cresol* + *-in*] **:** a crystalline compound $C_{10}H_{14}O_3$ used chiefly in the treatment of neuromuscular conditions; 3-*ortho*-toloxy-1,2-propane-diol

**mephis·to·phe·lian** \,mefəstə'fēlyən, ,me,fis-, mə,fis-, me,fis-, -ēlēən\ *or* **mephis·tophe·lean** \",  ,mefə,stäfə'lēən\ *adj, usu cap* [*Mephistopheles*, the devil in various versions of the Faust legend, esp. that of Johann Wolfgang von Goethe †1832 Ger. poet + E *-ian* or *-an*] **:** having a devilish character or aspect **:** SATURNINE ‹looked . . . slightly *Mephistophelian*, yet with human and lonely brown eyes —*Times Lit. Supp.*›

**me·phit·ic** \mə'fid·ik\ *also* **me·phit·i·cal** \-d·əkəl\ *adj* [F or L; F *méphitique*, fr. LL *mephiticus, mefiticus*, fr. L *mephitis, mefitis* mephitis + *-icus* -ic] **:** of, relating to, or like mephitis **:** offensive to the sense of smell **:** NOXIOUS, PESTILENTIAL ‹the ~ verdure of the Malay peninsula —Jean Stafford› ‹that purpose which is now hidden in a ~ cloud of love and romance and prudery and fastidiousness —G.B.Shaw›

**mephitic air** *or* **mephitic gas** *n* **1** *archaic* **:** CARBON DIOXIDE **2** *archaic* **:** air exhausted of oxygen and containing chiefly nitrogen

[1]**meph·i·tine** \'mefə,tēn, -ətən\ *adj* [NL *Mephitis* + E *-ine*] **:** of or relating to skunks

[2]**mephitine** \"\ *n* -s **:** SKUNK

**me·phi·tis** \mə'fīd·əs\ *n* [L *mephitis, mefitis*, fr. Oscan] **1** -ES **a :** a noxious, pestilential, or foul exhalation from the earth **b :** an offensive or poisonous smell from any source **:** STENCH **2** *cap* [NL, fr. L] **:** a genus of mammals that includes the No. American striped skunks

**mepho·barbital** \,mefō+\ *n* [*methyl* + *pho-* (fr. *phenyl*) + *barbital*] **:** a crystalline barbiturate $C_{13}H_{14}N_2O_3$ used as a sedative and in the treatment of epilepsy

**me·pro·ba·mate** \mə'prōbə,māt, ,meprō'ba,māt\ *n* -s [*methyl* + *propyl* + *dicarbamate*] **:** a bitter powder $CH_3(C_3H_7)C(CH_2OOCNH_2)_2$ that is an ester of carbamic acid and a derivative of propane-diol and is used as a tranquilizer

**meq** *abbr* milliequivalent

**mer** \'mər\ *n* -s [*-mer*] **:** a monomeric unit of a polymer

**mer** *abbr* **1** meridian **2** meridional

[1]**mer-** *comb form* [ME, fr. *mere* sea, lake, pond, fr. OE — more at MARINE] **:** sea ‹*mer*maid› ‹*mer*man› ‹*mer*woman›

[2]**mer-** *or* **mero-** *comb form* [Gk *mēr-, mēro-*, fr. *mēros* — more at MEMBER] **:** thigh ‹*mer*algia› ‹*mero*cele›

[3]**mer-** *or* **mero-** *comb form* [ISV, fr. Gk, fr. *meros* part — more at MERIT] **:** part **:** partial ‹*mer*aspis› ‹*mero*hedral› ‹*mero*sporangium›

**-mer** \(,)mə(r)\ *n comb form* -s [ISV, fr. Gk *meros* part — more at MERIT] *chem* **:** member of a (specified) class ‹iso*mer*› ‹meta*mer*› ‹poly*mer*›

**me·ral·gia** \mə'ralj(ē)ə\ *n* -s [NL, fr. [2]*mer-* + *-algia*] **:** pain esp. of a neuralgic kind in the thigh

**mer·al·lu·ride** \mə'ralyə,rīd, -rəd\ *n* -s [*mercury* + *all-* + [1]*ur-* + *-ide*] **:** a diuretic consisting of a chemical combination of an organic mercurial compound $C_9H_{16}HgN_2O_6$ and theophylline and administered chiefly by injection as an aqueous solution of its sodium salt

**mer·a·mec** \'merə,mak, -,mek\ *adj, usu cap* [fr. *Meramec* river, Mo.] **:** of or relating to the division of the Mississippian geologic period between the Osagian and the Chesterian — see GEOLOGIC TIME table

**me·ran·ti** \mə'rantē\ *n* -s [Malay *mĕranti*] **1 :** the soft weak light usu. pinkish to dark red wood of various trees of the genera *Hopea* and *Shorea* of Malaysia, Borneo, and the Philippines that is sometimes substituted for mahogany in cabinetwork, veneer, and interior finishes — compare LAUAN **2 :** a tree that yields meranti

**me·ras·pis** \mə'raspəs\ *n* -ES [NL, fr. [3]*mer-* + *aspis* shield — more at ASPID-] **:** a late larva of a trilobite in which the pygidium is beginning to form

**me·ra·tia** \mə'rāsh(ē)ə\ [NL, fr. François Victor *Mérat* †1851, Fr. physician and botanist + NL *-ia*] *syn of* CHIMONANTHUS

**me·ra·wan** \mə'räwən\ *n* -s [Malay *mĕrawan*] **:** the yellowish to brown usu. moderately heavy, hard, and durable wood of several Malayan trees of the genus *Hopea* that is used chiefly for furniture and construction work — compare MERANTI

**mer·bro·min** \,mər'brōmən\ *n* -s [*mer*curic acetate + di*bromo*-fluoresce*in*] **:** an iridescent green crystalline mercurial compound $C_{20}H_8Br_2HgNa_2O_6$ made from dibromo-fluorescein and mercuric acetate and applied topically as an antiseptic and germicide in the form of its red solution having a yellow-green fluorescence

**merc** *abbr* **1** mercantile **2** mercurial; mercury

**mer·cal·li scale** \mer'kälē-, mər\ *n, usu cap M* [after Giuseppe *Mercalli* †1914 Ital. priest and geologist] **:** an arbitrary scale of earthquake intensity ranging from I for an earthquake detected only by seismographs to XII for one causing total destruction of all buildings

**mer·cal·lite** \(,)mər'ka,līt\ *n* -s [G. *Mercalli* + E *-ite*] **:** a mineral $KHSO_4$ consisting of a bisulfate of potassium

**mer·can·tile** \'mərkən,tēl, 'mək-, 'məik-, -n,tīl *sometimes* -ntᵊl *or* -n·təl\ *adj* [F, fr. It, fr. *mercante* merchant (fr. L *mercant-, mercans*, fr. pres. part. of *mercari* to trade, deal in commodities) + *-ile* — more at MERCHANT] **1 :** of or relating to merchants or trading **:** appropriate to or characteristic of merchants **:** engaged in trade ‹the ~ North was forging ahead —Van Wyck Brooks› **2 :** of, relating to, or having the characteristics of mercantilism ‹~ system› ‹~ theories› **3 :** having or exhibiting the motives of a merchant **:** having gain as its objective **:** MERCENARY ‹preached a ~ and militant patriotism —John Buchan›

**mercantile agency** *n* **1 :** the agency of a factor who in the customary course of his business has authority binding on his principal to buy or to sell goods, to consign goods for sale, or to raise money by pledging goods **2 :** an agency that collects credit information about businesses and businessmen and furnishes it to subscribers — called also *commercial agency*

**mercantile agent** *n* **1 :** one having the powers of mercantile agency **:** FACTOR 1a **2 :** the conductor of a mercantile agency

**mercantile credit** *n* **:** credit extended by one business to another — distinguished from *consumer credit*

**mercantile law** *n* **:** the laws that govern merchants in business dealings — compare COMMERCIAL LAW, LAW MERCHANT

**mercantile marine** *n* **:** MERCHANT MARINE

**mercantile paper** *n* **:** notes, bills, and acceptances based on business activity — compare COMMERCIAL PAPER

**mer·can·til·ism** \'mərkən,tē,lizəm, 'mək-, 'məik-, -n,tī,l- *sometimes* -ntᵊl,izəm *or* -n·tə,lizəm\ *n* -s [F *mercantilisme*, fr. *mercantile* + *-isme* -ism] **1 :** the spirit, theory, or practice of mercantile pursuits **:** devotion to commercial enterprise **:** COMMERCIALISM **2 :** an economic system developing during the centralization of power accompanying the decay of feudalism and intended primarily to unify and increase the power and esp. the monetary wealth of a nation by a strict governmental regulation of the entire national economy usu. through policies designed to secure an accumulation of bullion, a favorable balance of trade, the development of agriculture and manufactures, and the establishment of foreign trading monopolies — compare AUTARKY, CAMERALISM, CAPITALISM, COMMUNISM, FREE ENTERPRISE, LAISSEZ-FAIRE, LIBERALISM, PLANNED ECONOMY, SOCIALISM

[1]**mer·can·til·ist** \-ləst\ *n* -s [*mercantile* + *-ist*] **:** an advocate or practitioner of mercantilism

[2]**mercantilist** \"\ *also* **mer·can·til·is·tic** \¦==(,)=¦listik\ *adj* **:** of or relating to the theory or practice of mercantilism ‹the monopoly chartered companies of the medieval and ~ periods —L.M.Hacker›

**mercapt-** *or* **mercapto-** *comb form* [ISV, fr. *mercaptan*] **:** derived from or related to a mercaptan ‹*mercapt*al› ‹*mercapto*ide›

**mer·cap·tal** \(,)mər'kap,tal\ *n* -s [ISV *mercapt-* + *-al*] **:** any of a class of compounds that are sulfur analogues of the acetals characterized by the group $>C(SR)_2$, that are formed by the reaction of mercaptans with aldehydes or ketones, and that in the case of the members of low molecular weight are oily liquids of unpleasant odor

**mer·cap·tan** \-,tan\ *n* -s [G, fr. Dan, fr. ML *mercurium captans*, lit., seizing mercury] **:** any of a class of compounds with the general formula RSH that are analogous to the alcohols and phenols but contain sulfur in place of oxygen and that in the case of those of low molecular weight have very disagreeable odors; *esp* **:** ETHYL MERCAPTAN — called also *thiol*; compare HYDROSULFIDE, THIOALCOHOL, THIOPHENOL

**mer·cap·tide** \-,tīd\ *n* -s [*mercapt-* + *-ide*] **:** a metallic derivative of a mercaptan

**mer·cap·to** \-,tō\ *adj* [*mercapt-*] *chem* **:** being or containing the group SH

**mer·cap·to·acetic acid** \(,)=¦==+-\ *n* [*mercapt-* + *acetic*] **:** THIOGLYCOLIC ACID

**mer·cap·to·benzothiazole** \(,)=¦==+\ *n* [*mercapt-* + *benz-* + *thiazole*] **:** a crystalline heterocyclic compound $C_7H_4NS(SH)$ made by heating aniline, sulfur, and carbon disulfide and used chiefly as an accelerator for the vulcanization of rubber — called also *2-mercaptobenzothiazole*

**mer·cap·tole** \(,)mər'kap,tōl\ *n* -s [ISV *mercapt-* + *-ole*] **:** a mercaptal formed from a ketone and analogous to a ketal

**mer·cap·tom·er·in** \(,)mər,kap'tämərən\ *n* -s [*mercapt-* + *mercury* + *-in*] **:** a mercurial diuretic related chemically to mercurophylline and administered by injection of an aqueous solution of its sodium salt $C_{16}H_{25}HgNNa_2O_6S$

**mer·cap·to·purine** \(,)=¦kaptō+\ *n* [*mercapt-* + *purine*] **:** an antimetabolite $C_5H_4N_4S$ that is a sulfur analogue of hypoxanthine and adenine, that interferes esp. with the metabolism of purine bases and the biosynthesis of nucleic acids, and that is sometimes useful in the treatment of acute leukemia esp. in children; 6-purine-thiol

**mer·cap·tu·ric acid** \¦mər,kap¦t(y)ürik-\ *n* [ISV *mercapturic*, fr. *mercapt-* + *-uric*] **:** an acid $RSCH_2CH(NHCOCH_3)COOH$ formed from cysteine and an aromatic compound (as bromobenzene) in the body and usu. excreted in the urine (as in the form of a glucuronide); an *S*-aryl derivative of *N*-acetylcysteine

**mer·ca·tor chart** \¦mər¦kād·ər-, mer'kä,tȯ(ə)r-\ *n, usu cap M* [after Gerhardus *Mercator* †1594 Flemish geographer] **:** a chart or map drawn on the Mercator projection

[1]**mer·ca·to·ri·al** \,mərkə'tōrēəl, -tȯr-\ *adj* [L *mercatorius*, fr. *mercator* merchant, fr. *mercatus* (past part. of *mercari* to trade) + *-or* — more at MERCHANT] *archaic* **:** MERCANTILE

[2]**mercatorial** \"\ *adj, usu cap* [Gerhardus *Mercator* + E *-ial*] **:** of or relating to the geographer Mercator or his method of projection ‹*Mercatorial* bearings›

**mercator projection** *n, usu cap M* [after Gerhardus *Mercator*]

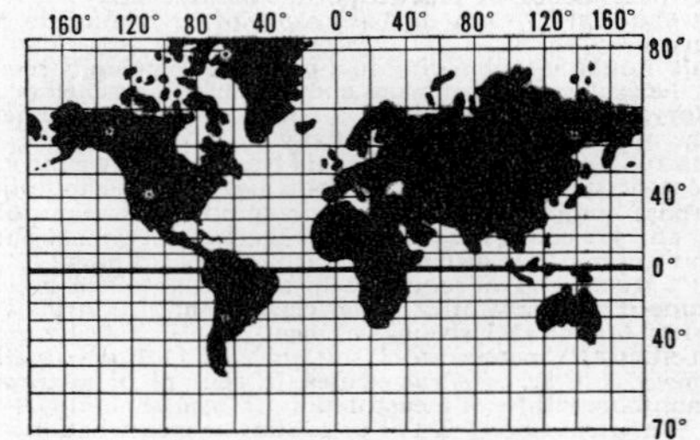


mercator projection

**:** a map projection in which the meridians are drawn parallel to each other and the parallels of latitude are straight lines whose distance from each other increases with their distance from the equator so that at all places the degrees of latitude and longitude have to each other the same ratio as on the sphere itself with resultant apparent enlargement of the polar regions but with great value in navigation since a rhumb line on a Mercator map is always a straight line

**mer·ce·dar·i·an** \,mərsə'da(a)rēən\ *n* -s *usu cap* [ML *merced-, merces* mercy (in *Ordo Beatae Mariae de Mercede* Order of Our Lady of Mercy) + E *-arian* — more at MERCY] **:** a member of the Order of Our Lady of Mercy founded at Barcelona about 1218 by St. Peter Nolasco

**mer·ce·nar·ia** \,mərsᵊn'a(a)rēə\ *n, cap* [NL, fr. L, fem. of *mercenarius* mercenary; fr. the use of the shells of *Mercenaria mercenaria* as wampum beads by American Indians — more at MERCENARY] **:** a genus of clams (family Veneridae) including the quahog

**mer·ce·nar·i·ly** \¦mərsᵊn¦erəlē, ¦mōs-, ¦məis-, -li\ *adv* **:** in a mercenary manner

**mer·ce·nar·i·ness** \'==,erēnəs, -rin-\ *n* -ES **:** the quality or state of being mercenary

[1]**mer·ce·nary** \'==,erē, -ri\ *n* -ES [ME *mercenarie*, fr. L *mercenarius, mercennarius*, adj. & n., fr. *merced-, merces* wages, reward + *-arius* -ary — more at MERCY] **1 :** one that serves merely for wages **:** HIRELING ‹half a dozen such *mercenaries* judiciously placed . . . may turn a cold audience into an enthusiastic one —A.T.Weaver› **2 :** a person paid for his work; *esp* **:** a soldier hired into foreign service ‹the kingdom was now supported . . . largely by foreign *mercenaries* and a made-to-order navy —A.L.Kroeber›

[2]**mercenary** \"\ *adj* [L *mercenarius, mercennarius*] **1 a :** serving merely for pay or gain **:** seeking sordid advantage **:** VENAL ‹abandoned their high standards and disinterested motives in favor of a ~ concern over fees —W.T. & Barbara Fitts› ‹so thoroughly ~, so frankly greedy, that there's nothing disagreeable about it —Dashiell Hammett› **b :** showing conspicuous lust for money **:** based on or marked by greed ‹if a writer's attitude toward his characters and his scene is . . . as ~ as an auctioneer's, vulgar and meretricious will his product for ever remain —Willa Cather› **2 a :** employed or engaged primarily on a wage basis — now used only of a soldier serving in the army of a country other than his own **b** *obs* **:** PAID, SALARIED **:** COMMERCIAL — used of an office or enterprise

**mer·cer** \'mərsər; 'mə̄sə(r, 'məis-\ *n* -s [ME, fr. OF *mersier, mercier* merchant, fr. *mers, merz* merchandise (fr. L *merc-, merx* ware, merchandise) + *-ier* -er — more at MARKET] *Brit* **:** a dealer in textile fabrics

**mer·cer·i·za·tion** \,ˌ=sərə'zāshən, -,rī'z-\ *n* -s **:** the act or process of mercerizing

**mer·cer·ize** \'==,rīz\ *vt* -ED/-ING/-S *see -ize in Explan Notes* [John *Mercer* †1866 English calico printer + E *-ize*] **1 :** to give (cotton yarn or cloth) luster, strength, and receptiveness to dyes by treatment under tension with caustic soda — compare CAUSTICIZE 2 **2 :** to steep (wood pulp) in a caustic soda solution during the manufacture of viscose rayon

**mer·cer·iz·er** \-,rīzə(r)\ *n* -s **1 :** a textile worker who mercerizes **2 :** a machine for mercerization

**mer·cers·burg** \'mərsərz,bərg\ *adj, usu cap* [fr. *Mercersburg*, Pa., the former site of the Theological Seminary of the German Reformed Church, where the doctrine was in part formulated] **:** of or relating to a system of American theology developed in the German Reformed Church in the middle and late 19th century and marked by Christocentrism, a Calvinist view of the Lord's Supper, and emphasis on the liturgical element in worship

**mer·cery** \'mərs(ə)rē, 'mə̄s-,'məis-, -ri\ *n* -ES [ME *mercerie*, fr. OF *merserie, mercerie*, fr. *mers, merz* merchandise + *-erie* -ery] **1** *Brit* **:** a mercer's wares or shop **2** *Brit* **:** a mercer's occupation or dealings

**merch** *abbr* merchantable

**mer·chan·dis·able** \'mərchən,dīzəbəl, 'mə̄ch-,'məich-, ,==-'===\ *adj* [²*merchandise* + *-able*] **:** MERCHANTABLE

¹**mer·chan·dise** \'==,dīz, -īs\ *n* -s [ME *marchaundise*, fr. OF *marcheandise*, fr. *marcheant* merchant — more at MERCHANT] **1 a :** the commodities or goods that are bought and sold in business **:** the wares of commerce **b** *obs* **:** an article of merchandise **2** *archaic* **:** the buying and selling of goods for profit **:** the occupation of a merchant **:** business activity

²**mer·chan·dise** *also* **mer·chan·dize** \-īz\ *vb* -ED/-ING/-S [ME *marchaundisen*, fr. *marchaundise*, n.] *vi* **:** to carry on commerce **:** TRADE, TRAFFIC ~ *vt* **1 :** to buy and sell **:** deal in **:** make merchandise of **2 :** to carry on sales promotion of **:** advertise, publicize, or present attractively or effectively — **mer·chan·dis·er** \-zə(r)\ *n* -s

**merchandise freight** *n* **:** goods in less than carload lots for expedited movement in merchandise trains

**merchandising** *n* -s [fr. gerund of ²*merchandise*] **:** sales promotion as a comprehensive function including market research, development of new products, coordination of manufacture and marketing, and effective advertising and selling

¹**mer·chant** \'mərchənt, 'mə̄ch-,'məich-\ *n* -s [ME *marchaunt, marchand, marchant*, fr. OF *marcheant*, fr. (assumed) VL *mercatant-, mercatans*, fr. pres. part. of (assumed) VL *mercatare*, fr. L *mercatus*, past part. of *mercari* to trade, deal in commodities, fr. *merc-, merx* ware, merchandise — more at MARKET] **1 a :** a buyer and seller of commodities for profit **:** TRADER **b :** the operator of a retail business **:** STOREKEEPER **2** *Scot* **:** CUSTOMER **3** *archaic* **:** FELLOW, GUY **4** *obs* **:** MERCHANTMAN **5 :** a person conspicuous for ideas or activities of a particular kind **:** PURVEYOR, SPECIALIST ⟨his guess is likely to be as accurate as that of the ~ of doom —Harrison Smith⟩ ⟨had been . . . acquiring among musical-comedy orchestrators a reputation as a speed ~ —H.W.Wind⟩

²**merchant** \"\ *adj* [ME *marchaund, marchant*, fr. *marchaunt, marchand, marchant*, n.] **1 a :** of, relating to, or used in commerce **b :** of or relating to a merchant marine **c :** having a merchant's traits or qualities **2 a :** of ordinary or standard shape or size **:** not made to special order **:** STOCK — used of metal bars and ingots ⟨~ pig iron⟩ **b :** producing metal bars or ingots in standard shapes and sizes ⟨~ mill⟩

³**merchant** \"\ *vb* -ED/-ING/-S [ME *marchaunden*, fr. MF *marchander*, fr. OF *marcheandier*, fr. *marcheant* merchant] *vi, archaic* **:** to deal or trade as a merchant ~ *vt* **:** to buy and sell **:** deal or trade in ⟨something considerably superior to what Broadway usually ~s in these days —G.J.Nathan⟩

**mer·chant·able** \-təbəl\ *adj* [ME *marchandabull*, fr. *marchaunden* + *-abull, -able* -able] **:** of commercial quality **:** acceptable to buyers **:** SALABLE ⟨it is estimated that a thousand million tons of ~ coal are in reserve —*Canadian Mining Jour.*⟩ — **mer·chant·able·ness** *n* -ES

**merchant adventurer** *n, pl* **merchant adventurers** *or* **merchants adventurers** [ME *marchaunt adventurer*] **:** a merchant who establishes foreign trading stations and carries on business ventures abroad; *esp* **:** a member of one of the former English companies of merchant adventurers operating from the 14th to the 16th centuries

**merchant banker** *n* **:** an acceptance house that also does investment banking

**merchant flag** *n* **:** a flag flown by the merchant vessels of a country that is sometimes identical with the national flag

**merchantlike** \'==,=\ *adj* **1 :** like or proper to a merchant **2** *obs* **:** MERCANTILE

**merchantly** *adj, obs* **:** of or relating to merchants

**mer·chant·man** \'==mən\ *n, pl* **merchantmen** [ME *marchand man*] **1** *archaic* **:** MERCHANT **2 :** a ship commercially operated to carry passengers or freight **:** a ship used in commerce — called also *merchant ship*

**merchant marine** *n* **1 :** the privately or publicly owned commercial vessels of a nation as distinguished from its navy **2 :** the personnel of a merchant marine

**merchant middleman** *n* **:** a middleman who takes title to goods purchased for resale

**merchant navy** *n, Brit* **:** MERCHANT MARINE

**merchant prince** *n* **:** a merchant of great wealth

**mer·chant·ry** \'mərchəntrē\ *n* -ES **:** a merchant's dealings **:** TRADE

**merchant seaman** *n* **:** a seaman employed on a merchant ship

**merchant service** *n* **:** MERCHANT MARINE

**merchant ship** *n* **:** MERCHANTMAN 2

**merchant tailor** *n* **:** a custom tailor who owns his business and supplies the fabrics he uses

**merchant venturer** *n, obs* **:** MERCHANT ADVENTURER

**merchet** *var of* MARCHET

¹**mer·cian** \'mərsh(ē)ən\ *adj, usu cap* [*Mercia*, ancient Anglian kingdom in central England + E *-an*] **1 a :** of, relating to, or characteristic of the Anglian kingdom of Mercia **b :** of, relating to, or characteristic of the Mercians **2 :** of, relating to, or constituting the Old English dialect of Mercia

²**mercian** \"\ *n* -s *cap* **1 :** a native or inhabitant of Mercia **2 :** the Old English dialect of Mercia

**mercies** *pl of* MERCY

**mer·ci·ful** \'mərsəfəl, 'mə̄s-, 'məis-, -sēf-\ *adj* [ME, fr. *merci, mercy* mercy + *-ful* — more at MERCY] **:** full of mercy **:** marked, exercising, or disposed to mercy **:** CLEMENT, COMPASSIONATE, LENIENT ⟨if tried by the manners of his age, Caesar was the most ~ of conquerors —J.A.Froude⟩ ⟨the ~ possibilities of the antibiotics — F.L.Allen⟩ **syn** see FORBEARING

**mer·ci·ful·ly** \-f(ə)lē, -li\ *adv* [ME, fr. *merciful* + *-ly*] **:** in a merciful manner **:** so as to be merciful ⟨struggles that were ~ brief⟩

**mer·ci·ful·ness** \-fəlnəs\ *n* -ES **:** the quality or state of being merciful

**mer·ci·less** \-sələs, -sə̇ləs *sometimes* -sləs\ *adj* [ME *mercyles*, fr. *merci, mercy* mercy + *-les* -less] **:** having, extending, or showing no mercy **:** CRUEL, HARSH, PITILESS, REMORSELESS ⟨turns a ~ spotlight on the precocious technicians, the spiritual sophomores, and the hairy-chested muscle men of contemporary literature —Gilbert Highet⟩ — **mer·ci·less·ly** *adv* — **mer·ci·less·ness** *n* -ES

**Mer·cu·hy·drin** \,mərkyə'hīdrən\ *trademark* — used for meralluride

**mercur-** *or* **mercuro-** *comb form* [ISV, fr. *mercury*] **:** mercury ⟨*mercuro*phylline⟩

¹**mer·cu·rate** \'mərkyərət, -,rāt, *usu* -d·+V\ *also* **mer·cu·ri·ate** \(,)mər'kyürēət, -ēāt, *usu* -d·+V\ *n* -s [*mercur-* or *mercuri-* + *-ate* (n. suffix)] **:** any of various salts containing bivalent mercury in a complex anion — compare IODOMERCURATE

²**mer·cu·rate** \'mərkyə,rāt, 'mə̄k-, 'məik-, *usu* -ād·+V\ *vt* -ED/-ING/-S [*mercur-* + *-ate* (v. suffix)] **:** to combine or treat with mercury or a mercury salt **:** introduce mercury into (as an organic compound) — **mer·cu·ra·tion** \,==='rāshən\ *n* -s

**mercuri-** *comb form* [ISV, fr. *mercury*] *chem* **:** mercuric ⟨chloro*mercuri*phenol $ClHgC_6H_4OH$⟩

¹**mer·cu·ri·al** \,mər'kyürēəl, ,mə(r)'k-, (')mə̄¦k-, (')məi¦k-\ *adj* [L *mercurialis* of the god Mercury, of the planet Mercury, fr. *Mercurius* Mercury, ancient Roman god of commerce and messenger of the gods & *Mercurius* Mercury, the 1st planet from the sun (fr. *stella Mercurii*, lit., star of Mercury, after *Mercurius*, the god Mercury; trans. of Gk *astēr tou Hermou*, lit., star of Hermes, Greek messenger of the gods) + *-alis* -al] **1** *usu cap* **:** of, relating to, or like the ancient Roman god Mercury **2 a :** of or relating to the planet Mercury **b :** born under or influenced astrologically by the planet Mercury **3 :** having qualities of eloquence, ingenuity, sharp dealing, or thievishness attributed in myth to the god Mercury and in astrology to the influence of the planet Mercury ⟨more than ~ thievishness —*Sat. Rev.*⟩ **4 :** characterized by rapid and unpredictable changeableness or by quick-wittedness **:** SPRIGHTLY, TEMPERAMENTAL, VOLATILE ⟨a deeply ~ intuitive artist —Christopher Morley⟩ ⟨~ desponds —D.C.Peattie⟩ ⟨~ twists of temperament —T.B.Costain⟩ ⟨the Japanese are ~ — high-strung, touchy, ready to fly into a rage —D.G. Haring⟩ **5** [*Mercury* + *-al*] **a :** of, relating to, containing, or consisting of mercury ⟨~ preparations⟩ **b :** caused by or exhibiting the physiological effect of the use of mercury ⟨~ sore mouth⟩ **syn** see INCONSTANT

²**mercurial** \"\ *n* -s **1** *obs* **:** a person born under Mercury or having mercurial qualities **2** [L (*herba*) *mercurialis* dog's mercury, lit., Mercurial herb] *obs* **:** GOOD-KING-HENRY **3 :** a pharmaceutical preparation or chemical compound containing mercury ⟨the diuretic action of ~s⟩

**mer·cu·ri·a·lis** \(,)mər,kyürē'alǝs, -āl-, -äl-\ *n* [NL, fr. L (*herba*) *mercurialis* dog's mercury] **1** *cap* **:** a small genus of slender herbs (family Euphorbiaceae) having opposite pinnately-veined leaves and apetalous flowers in interrupted axillary spikes — see BOYS-AND-GIRLS 2, DOG'S MERCURY **2** -ES **:** an herb (*Mercurialis annua*) formerly dried for use as a purgative, diuretic, and antisyphilitic

**mer·cu·ri·al·ism** \(,)=ˈ==ə,lizəm\ *n* -s **:** chronic poisoning with mercury (as from excessive medication or industrial contacts with the metal or its fumes) — called also *hydrargyrism*

**mercurialist** *n* -s *obs* **:** MERCURIAL 1

**mer·cu·ri·al·i·ty** \(,)=,=='aləd·ē\ *n* -ES **:** the quality or state of being mercurial **:** VOLATILITY

**mer·cu·ri·al·ly** \,mər'kyürēəlē, ,mə(r)'k-, (')mə̄¦k-, (')məi¦k-, -li\ *adv* **:** in a mercurial manner

**mercurial ointment** *n* **:** an ointment containing about 50 percent of finely divided metallic mercury incorporated with wool fat, white wax, mercury oleate, and white petrolatum — compare BLUE OINTMENT

¹**mercurian** *adj* [*Mercury* (god & planet) + E *-an*] *obs* **:** MERCURIAL

²**mer·cu·ri·an** \(,)mər'kyürēən\ *n* -s *usu cap* **1 :** one born under Mercury **2 :** one that has a well-developed Mount of Mercury and a long and large finger of Mercury and that is usu. held by palmists to be characterized by shrewdness, quickness, and energy

**mercuriate** *var of* MERCURATE

**mer·cu·ric** \,mər'kyürik, ,mə(r)'k-, (')mə̄¦k-, (')məi¦k-, -rēk\ *adj* [*mercur-* + *-ic*] **:** of, relating to, or containing mercury — used esp. of compounds in which this element is bivalent

**mercuric chloride** *n* **:** MERCURY CHLORIDE b

**mercuric cyanide** *n* **:** the mercury cyanide $Hg(CN)_2$

**mercuric iodide** *n* **:** MERCURY IODIDE b

**mercuric oxide** *n* **:** a slightly water-soluble crystalline poisonous compound HgO known in two forms (1) a yellow finely divided powder obtained usu. by precipitation from solutions of mercury chloride (sense b) and sodium hydroxide and used chiefly in medicine (as in antiseptic ointments), in antifouling paints, and in making other mercury compounds (2) a bright red coarse powder obtained by precipitation from hot solutions or by heating mercurous nitrate and used similarly to the yellow form and also in dry cells — called also *mercury(II) oxide*

**mercuric sulfide** *n* **:** an insoluble compound HgS occurring in nature as the red mineral cinnabar and the black mineral metacinnabar and also made synthetically in red and black forms — called also *mercury(II) sulfide*; see VERMILION 1a

**mer·cu·ride** \'mərkyə,rīd, -rə̇d\ *n* -s [*mercur-* + *-ide*] **:** a binary compound of mercury with a more electropositive element or radical — compare AMALGAM

**mer·cu·rize** \-,rīz\ *vt* -ED/-ING/-S [*mercur-* + *-ize*] **:** MERCURATE

**mercuro-** — see MERCUR-

**Mer·cu·ro·chrome** \(,)mər'kyürə,krōm\ *trademark* — used for merbromin

**mer·cu·ro·phyl·line** \,mərkyərō'fi,lēn, -lən\ *n* -s [*mercur-* + *theophylline*] **:** a diuretic consisting of a chemical combination of an organic mercurial compound or its sodium salt $C_{14}H_{24}HgNNaO_5$ and theophylline

**mer·cu·rous** \(')mər¦kyürəs, 'mərkyər-\ *adj* [*mercur-* + *-ous*] **:** of, relating to, or containing mercury — used esp. of compounds in which this element is regarded as univalent ⟨the ~ ion . . . is $Hg:Hg^{++}$ rather than $Hg^{+}$ —E.S.Gould⟩

**mercurous chloride** *n* **:** CALOMEL

**mercurous iodide** *n* **:** MERCURY IODIDE a

**mer·cu·ry** \'mərkyərē, 'mə̄k-, 'məik-, -k(ə)rē, -ri\ *n* -ES **1** [ME *mercurie*, fr. ML *mercurius*, fr. L *Mercurius* Mercury, ancient Roman god of commerce and messenger of the gods; prob. fr. the comparison of the mobility of the metal to the traditional fleet-footedness of the god] **a :** a heavy silver-white univalent and bivalent poisonous metallic element that is the only metal liquid at ordinary temperatures, that occurs native and in cinnabar, calomel, and a few other minerals, that is prepared usu. by roasting cinnabar and condensing the vapors, and that is used chiefly in scientific instruments (as electrical apparatus, control devices, thermometers, barometers), mercury boilers, mercury pumps, and mercury-vapor lamps — symbol *Hg*; called also *quicksilver*; see AMALGAM, ELEMENT table **b :** the mercury in a thermometer or barometer ⟨in a climate where the ~ sports around 110 the whisky should be only of the best quality —D.D.Martin⟩ **c :** pressure (as in the manifold of an engine) measured in inches or millimeters of mercury ⟨pulling between forty-seven and fifty inches of ~ —J.M. Redding & H.I.Leyshon⟩ **d :** a pharmaceutical preparation containing the metal mercury or a compound of it **e** *often cap, obs* **:** mercurial quality **:** brilliance, inconstancy, or volatility of mood or attitude **f :** the principle of liquidity and volatility in alchemy **2** [ME *mercurie* fr. *Mercurie* the god *Mercury*, fr. L *Mercurius*; after L (*herba*) *mercurialis* dog's mercury] **:** any of several plants: as **a :** a plant of the genus *Mercurialis*; *esp* **:** DOG'S MERCURY **b :** GOOD-KING-HENRY **c :** POISON IVY **3** [after *Mercury*, messenger of the gods, fr. ME *Mercurie*] **a** *often cap, archaic* **:** a bearer of messages or news or a conductor of travelers **b** *usu cap, obs* (1) **:** a statue of Mercury (2) **:** SIGNPOST (3) **:** HERM **c** *usu cap, obs* **:** a hawker of pamphlets

**mercury arc** *n* **:** an electric discharge through mercury vapor in a glass or quartz tube emitting a blue-green light rich in actinic and ultraviolet rays and used for various purposes (as for water sterilization, in photography, and in a rectifier)

**mercury-arc lamp** *n* **:** MERCURY-VAPOR LAMP

**mercury-arc rectifier** *n* **:** an alternating-current rectifier consisting of a mercury arc esp. designed to utilize its rectifying action, one electrode being a pool of mercury with current flowing only during that part of the cycle in which the mercury acts as the cathode

**mercury bichloride** *n* **:** MERCURY CHLORIDE b — not used systematically

**mercury chloride** *n* **:** a chloride of mercury: as **a :** CALOMEL **b :** a heavy transparent crystalline poisonous compound $HgCl_2$ made usu. by heating mercury with gaseous chlorine or by subliming a mixture of mercury sulfate and common salt and used chiefly as a disinfectant and fungicide, in making other mercury compounds, and in photography — called also *corrosive sublimate, mercuric chloride, mercury(II) chloride*

**mercury cyanide** *n* **:** a cyanide of mercury; *esp* **:** the crystalline poisonous mercuric compound $Hg(CN)_2$ made usu. by reaction of mercuric oxide with hydrocyanic acid and used chiefly in medicine

**mercury fulminate** *n* **:** a crystalline compound $Hg(ONC)_2$ that when dry explodes violently on percussion or heating, that is usu. made by reaction of mercury, alcohol, and nitric acid, and that is used in blasting caps, percussion caps, and detonators — called also *fulminating mercury*

**mercury glass** *n* **:** thin glass blown with double walls and sealed after silvering of the enclosed surface of the inner wall to produce an ornamental ware — called also *silvered glass*

**mercury iodide** *n* **:** either of two iodides of mercury: **a :** a yellow amorphous powder $Hg_2I_2$ that turns greenish on exposure to light — called also *mercurous iodide* **b :** a red crystalline poisonous salt $HgI_2$ that changes to a yellow crystalline modification when heated above 126° C and that is used chiefly in medicine — called also *mercuric iodide*

**mercury lamp** *n* **:** MERCURY-VAPOR LAMP

**mercury line** *n, usu cap M* [after *Mercury*, Roman god of commerce, fr. L *Mercurius*] **:** LINE OF MERCURY

**mercury oxide** *n* **:** an oxide of mercury; *esp* **:** MERCURIC OXIDE

**mercury red** *n* **:** vermilion or a color resembling it

**mercury's staff** *n, usu cap M* **:** CADUCEUS 2

**mercury sulfide** *n* **:** a sulfide of mercury; *esp* **:** MERCURIC SULFIDE

**mercury switch** *n* **:** a switch in which an electric circuit is closed and opened by tilting a reservoir of liquid mercury

**mercury thiocyanate** *n* **:** a thiocyanate of mercury; *esp* **:** the crystalline poisonous mercuric compound $Hg(SCN)_2$ made by precipitation and used chiefly in fireworks — see PHARAOH'S SERPENT

**mercury-vapor lamp** \'===¦==-\ *n* **:** a gas-discharge lamp in which the gaseous medium is mercury vapor

**mercury weed** *n* **:** THREE-SEEDED MERCURY

**mer·cy** \'mərsē, 'mə̄s-, 'məis-, -si\ *n* -ES [ME *merci, mercy*, fr. OF *mercit, merci*, fr. ML *merced-, merces*, fr. L, price paid for something, wages, reward, recompense, fr. *merc-, merx* ware, merchandise — more at MARKET] **1 a :** compassion or forbearance shown to an offender or subject **:** clemency or kindness extended to someone instead of strictness or severity **:** LENIENCY ⟨the illusion of omniscience . . . brings endless inhumanity when it leads us to shut the gates of ~ —M.R. Cohen⟩; *esp* **:** the mercy of God to man ⟨showing ~ unto thousands of them that love me and keep my commandments —Exod 20:6 (AV)⟩ **b :** a sentence of imprisonment rather than of death imposed in clemency on a person convicted of first-degree murder **2 a :** a blessing regarded as an act of divine favor or compassion ⟨seemed oblivious of all the many *mercies* of his daily life⟩ **b :** a fortunate event or circumstance ⟨the more open ground was a ~ —Fred Majdalany⟩ **3 :** relief of distress **:** compassion shown to victims of misfortune ⟨seek ways of performing acts of kindness and ~ abroad —Vera M. Dean⟩

**syn** CLEMENCY, LENITY, CHARITY, GRACE: MERCY, a word of much emotional force and hence one applicable to extreme situations, indicates a kindly refraining from inflicting punishment or pain, often a refraining brought about by genuinely felt compassion and sympathy, or a general disposition toward these latter characteristics ⟨earthly power doth then show likest God's when *mercy* season justice —Shak.⟩ ⟨the quality of brutality was not isolated in the Japanese, nor was the quality of *mercy* unknown to them —Agnes N. Keith⟩ CLEMENCY, a less emotionally colored word, indicates a tendency to be mild and compassionate, to administer or direct moderate punishment or treatment rather than drastically severe ⟨*clemency* . . . is the standing policy of constitutional governments, as severity is of despotism —Henry Hallam⟩ ⟨Cicero had prophesied so positively that Caesar would throw off the mask of *clemency* . . . that he was disappointed to find him persevere in the same gentleness —J.A.Froude⟩ LENITY may suggest absence of severity, may connote a clemency uninterrupted and unvaried and verging onto softness and careless leniency ⟨whether this indulgence comes from the wisdom and *lenity* of the government —Tobias Smollett⟩ ⟨not to be expected that they would show much *lenity* to one . . . regarded as the chief of the Rye House Plot —T.B.Macaulay⟩ CHARITY indicates clemency of judgment, a disposition to judge mildly or tolerantly ⟨marriage had begun where it so often ends happily, in *charity* of mind —Ellen Glasgow⟩ In other, more common uses it suggests a benevolent good will arising from a feeling of love of others ⟨with malice toward none, with *charity* for all —Abraham Lincoln⟩ In older usage GRACE may combine the associations of CLEMENCY and CHARITY ⟨his eyes upraised to sue for *grace* —William Wordsworth⟩ — **at the mercy of :** wholly in the power of ⟨their lives are *at the mercy of* the conqueror —John Locke⟩ ⟨farming was a risky business, *at the mercy of* weather, pests, limited markets —*Printers' Ink*⟩

**mercy seat** *n* [fr. *mercy seat*, gold covering over the ark of the covenant in the Bible (Exod 25:17); trans. of G *gnadenstuhl*, trans. of Heb *kappōreth*] **:** the throne of God regarded as a place of divine access, communion, or propitiation

**merd** *n* -s [ME, fr. MF *merde*, fr. L *merda* — more at IMMERD] *obs* **:** DUNG

**mer·di·vo·rous** \(')mər¦divərəs\ *adj* [L *merda* excrement + E *-i-* + *-vorous*] **:** COPROPHAGOUS

¹**mere** \'mi(ə)r, -iə\ *n* -s [ME, fr. OE — more at MARINE] **1** *obs* **a :** SEA **b :** an arm of the sea **:** CREEK, INLET **2 :** a sheet of standing water **:** LAKE, POOL ⟨had seen several boats on an inland ~ —*Yale Rev.*⟩ **3 :** FEN, MARSH

²**mere** \"\ *n* -s [ME, fr. OE *mǣre, gemǣre* — more at MUNITION] *archaic* **:** BOUNDARY **:** a mark or line defining a boundary **:** LANDMARK, LIMIT

³**mere** \"\ *vb* -ED/-ING/-S *vt, archaic* **:** to mark the boundaries of ~ *vi, obs* **:** to abut on

⁴**mere** \"\ *adj* -ER/-EST [ME, fr. L *merus* pure, bare — more at MORN] **1 a :** done or invoked without assistance or support — used chiefly in legal contexts in the phrases *mere motion, mere will* **b** *law* **:** having theoretical or legal but not practical reality ⟨~ right⟩ **2** *obs* **:** fully realized or developed **:** ABSOLUTE, TOTAL, UNDIMINISHED **3 :** exclusive of or considered apart from anything else **:** BARE ⟨if he does not want us to accept his theory of the good on his ~ authority, he needs to give us some rational ground for it —M.R.Cohen⟩ ⟨something above ~ politics —D.W.Brogan⟩ **4 :** having no admixture **:** PURE, UNDILUTED ⟨~ genius —Stanislaus Joyce⟩

⁵**mere** \'merē\ *n* -s [Maori] **1** *Austral* **:** a Maori war club **2** *Austral* **:** a miniature Maori war club fashioned of greenstone and worn as an ornament

⁶**mere** \'mi(ə)r, -iə\ *n* -s [*-mere*] *zool* **:** SEGMENT, METAMERE

**-mere** \,mi(ə)r, -iə\ *n comb form* -s [F *-mère*, fr. Gk *meros* part — more at MERIT] **1** *biol* **:** part **:** segment ⟨arthro*mere*⟩ ⟨cyto*mere*⟩ **2** *chem* **:** -MER ⟨iso*mere*⟩

¹**mer·e·dith·i·an** \,merə'dithēən\ *adj, usu cap* [George *Meredith* †1909 Eng. novelist & poet + E *-ian*] **:** of, relating to, or characteristic of George Meredith or his writings

²**meredithian** \"\ *n* -s *usu cap* **:** a follower of George Meredith or an enthusiast for his works, his style, or his attitudes

**mer·els** \'merəlz\ *n pl but sing in constr* [ME, pl. of *merel*, counter in the game of merels, fr. MF *merel, marel* counter, token, fr. OF; akin to OF *merele, marele* counter] **:** ²MORRIS

**mere·ly** *adv* [⁴*mere* + *-ly*] **1** *obs* **:** without admixture **:** PURELY **2 :** to the full extent **:** ENTIRELY, QUITE, WHOLLY ⟨it becomes surprising that . . . one could have been so ~ engrossed —Oliver La Farge⟩ **3 :** no more than **:** BARELY, ONLY, SIMPLY, SOLELY ⟨went past the bounds of bohemianism to the verge of the ~ sordid —*New Yorker*⟩

**me·ren·gue** \mə'reŋ(,)gā\ *also* **mé·ringue** \mā'raŋ\ *n* -s [AmerSp *merengue* & Haitian Creole *méringue*] **:** a popular Dominican and Haitian ballroom dance with a limping step

**me·re·ol·o·gy** \,mirē'äləjē\ *n* -ES [irreg. fr. ³*mer-* + *-logy*] *logic* **:** a theory of extended individuals in their relationships of part to whole and of overlapping — compare CALCULUS OF INDIVIDUALS

**meres·man** \'mi(ə)rzmən\ *n, pl* **meresmen** [*meres* (gen. of ²*mere*) + *man*] *archaic* **:** a parish officer named to ascertain boundaries

**mere·stone** \'mi(ə)r,stōn\ *n* [ME *merstane*, fr. OE *mǣrstān*, fr. *mǣre* ²boundary + *stān* stone — more at MUNITION, STONE] *archaic* **:** a stone indicating a boundary **:** LANDMARK

**mer·e·tri·cious** \,merə¦trishəs\ *adj* [L *meretricius*, fr. *meretric-, meretrix*] **1 :** of or relating to a prostitute **:** having a harlot's traits ⟨the Pennsylvania court . . . did not believe that there was a common-law marriage here, but merely a ~ relationship —Morris Ploscowe⟩ **2 :** exhibiting synthetic or spurious attractions **:** based on pretense or insincerity

: cheaply ornamental ⟨what counts in a boat is design and seaworthiness, not the ~ attractions of newness —*New Yorker*⟩ ⟨might have had fortune from the beginning if she had been willing to appear in ~ plays —E.C.Wagenknecht⟩ **syn** see GAUDY

**mer·e·tri·cious·ly** *adv* : in a meretricious manner

**mer·e·tri·cious·ness** *n* -ES : the quality or state of being meretricious

**mer·e·trix** \ˈmerə(ˌ)·triks\ *n, pl* **meretri·ces** \ˌmerəˈtrī(ˌ)sēz\ [L, fr. *merēre* to earn, gain — more at MERIT] : PROSTITUTE ⟨with my lamentable visits to the Ring at Blackfriars, or to my ~ in Holland Park —Cyril Connolly⟩

**mer·folk** \ˈmər, ˈmə̄+,-\ *n pl* [ˡ*mer-* + *folk*] : a legendary people of the sea having human head, trunk, and arms and the tail of a fish — compare MERMAID, MERMAN

**mer·gan·ser** \(ˌ)mərˈgan(t)sər, ˈ=ˌ==\ *n* -S [NL, fr. L *mergus* diver (waterfowl) + *anser* goose — more at MERGUS, GOOSE] : any of various diving ducks of *Mergus* and related genera that constitute a distinct subfamily of Anatidae, have a slender bill hooked at the end and serrated along the margins, usu. a crested head, a long broad tail, and short somewhat clumsy wings, feed almost entirely on fish, and are considered inferior as food for man — see AMERICAN MERGANSER, GOOSANDER, HOODED MERGANSER, RED-BREASTED MERGANSER, SMEW; see BILL illustration

**merge** \ˈmərj, ˈmōj,ˈməij\ *vb* -ED/-ING/-S [L *mergere*; akin to Skt *majjati* he dives, Lith *mazgoti* to wash] *vt* **1** *obs* : to plunge or engulf in a medium that wholly surrounds or absorbs : IMMERSE **2** : to cause to be legally absorbed, sunk, or extinguished by merger **3** : to cause to combine, unite, or coalesce ⟨planned to ~ the two companies⟩ **4** : to blend gradually : alter by transitional stages : blunt or destroy the distinctness of ⟨individuality and uniqueness are *merged* and blurred —Norman Kelman⟩ ~ *vi* **1** : to become legally absorbed or extinguished by merger **2** : to become combined into one ⟨the two banks *merged* to form an institution that dwarfed its nearest competitor⟩ **3** : to blend or come together without abrupt change : lose identity by absorption or intermingling : pass gradually ⟨long slopes of alluvial material spread out from the base of the mountains and ~ into a plain —Samuel Van Valkenburg & Ellsworth Huntington⟩ ⟨two streams of traffic *merging* to form the base of a gigantic Y⟩ **syn** see MIX

**mer·gence** \ˈmərjən(t)s, ˈmōj-, ˈməij-\ *n* -S : the act or process of merging or the condition of being merged ⟨~ of colored blues and white crooning, itself a Negro derivative, reflects racial integration —H.F.Mooney⟩

**merg·er** \-jə(r)\ *n* -S [*merge* + *-er* (as in *waiver*)] **1** *law* **a** : the absorption of an estate, a contract, or an interest in another, of a minor offense in a greater, or of an obligation into a judgment **b** (1) *common law* : the vesting of a lesser estate and a greater one or a higher security, obligation, or interest and a lower one in one person in the same right without an intermediate estate (2) *equity* : the vesting in one person of two interests in the same right but subject to separate treatment according to equitable demands **2 a** : absorption by a corporation of one or more others — distinguished from *consolidation;* see AMALGAMATION **b** : any of various other methods of combining two or more business concerns **3** : the combination of two or more groups (as political organizations, churches, or government departments) on any of various terms or conditions **4** : MERGENCE

**mergh** \ˈmerk\ *Scot var of* ¹MARROW

**merging** *n* -S [fr. gerund of *merge*] : the act or process of blending, combining, joining, or uniting

**mer·gus** \ˈmərgəs\ *n, cap* [NL, fr. L, diver (waterfowl), fr. *mergere* to dip, plunge — more at MERGE] : a genus of highly aquatic diving ducks including several typical mergansers having males that are brightly marked and develop an eclipse plumage

**meri-** *comb form* [F *méri-*, fr. Gk *meris* part — more at MERIT] : part : partial ⟨*mericlinous*⟩ ⟨*meriquinone*⟩ ⟨*meristele*⟩

**mer·i·ah khond** \ˈmerēə-\ *n, usu cap M&K* : a member of a Khond people of eastern India formerly engaging in human sacrifices

**-mer·ic** \ˌmerik, -rēk, *when there is a related noun form in "-mere"* ˈmer- *or* ˈmir-\ *adj comb form* [ISV ³*mer-* + *-ic*] **1** *biol* : having (such) parts or segments ⟨*cytomeric*⟩ **2** [ISV *-mer* + *-ic*] *chem* : having a (specified) association of substances in compounds ⟨*polymeric*⟩ ⟨*tautomeric*⟩

**mer·i·carp** \ˈmerəˌkärp\ *n* -S [F *méricarpe*, fr. *méri-* + *-carpe* -carp] : one of the two carpels that resemble achenes and form the schizocarp of an umbelliferous plant

**mer·i·cli·nal** \ˌmerəˈklīnᵊl\ *or* **mer·i·cli·nous** \-nəs\ *adj* [*meri-* + *-clinal, -clinous*] *of a plant chimera* : incompletely periclinal : having tissue of one kind incompletely surrounded by tissue of another kind

**mé·ri·da** \ˈmerədə\ *adj, usu cap* [fr. *Mérida*, Mexico] : of or from the city of Mérida, Mexico : of the kind or style prevalent in Mérida

**-mer·ide** \ˌməˌrīd, -ˌrəd\ *n comb form* -S [ISV *-mer* + *-ide*] : -MER ⟨*isomeride*⟩ ⟨*polymeride*⟩

¹**me·rid·i·an** \məˈridēən\ *n* -S [ME *meridien, meridian*, fr. MF *meridien*, fr. *meridien*, adj.] **1 a** *obs* : the hour of noon : MIDDAY **b** *Scot* : a midday dram **2** : a great circle of the celestial sphere passing through its poles and the zenith of a given place **3 a** *archaic* : the highest apparent point reached in the heavens by the sun or a star **b** : a high point (as of development or prosperity) ⟨the problem of the unmarried don after he had passed the ~ —H.J.Laski⟩ **4 a** (1) : a great circle on the surface of the earth passing through the poles and any given place (2) : the half of such a circle included between the poles with a plane coinciding with that of the astronomical meridian of the place — see PRIME MERIDIAN **b** : a representation of such a circle or half circle on a map or globe : any of a series of lines drawn at intervals due north and south or in the direction of the poles and numbered according to the degrees of longitude ⟨the 90th ~ east of Greenwich⟩ **c** : a graduated circle (as of brass) in which a globe is suspended and revolves **5** *archaic* : special tastes, capacities, or conditions ⟨suited the ~ of the . . . servants' hall —Washington Irving⟩ **6** : *or* **meridian curve** : the curve formed by the intersection of a surface of revolution and a plane passing through the axis of revolution **7** : a line or circle (as on the globular shell of some sea urchins) resembling a meridian of longitude

²**meridian** \"\ *adj* [ME *meridien*, fr. MF, fr. L *meridianus*, fr. *meridies* noon, south (fr. *meri-* — alter. of *medius* mid — + *dies* day) + *-anus* -an — more at MID, DEITY] **1** : being at or relating to midday : belonging to or passing through the highest point attained by a heavenly body in its diurnal course **2** : of or relating to a meridian **3 a** : of or relating to a high point, crest, or culmination ⟨the Roman people had arrived at their ~ glory —C.G.Bowers⟩ **b** *obs* : supremely excellent : CONSUMMATE, EXTREME

**meridian altitude** *n* **1** : the arc of the meridian intercepted between a celestial body at meridian transit and the south point of the horizon **2** : the altitude of a celestial body when it is on an observer's meridian

**meridian angle** *n* : the angle between the upper branch of the celestial meridian of an observer and the hour circle of a celestial object measured either westward or eastward from zero to 180 degrees — compare HOUR ANGLE

**meridian circle** *n* : an astronomical transit instrument having its vertical circle very accurately graduated for precise measurements of declination

**meridian day** *n* : the day on which a ship in the Pacific crosses the international date line losing a day going east and adding one going west

**meridian instrument** *n* : an astronomical transit instrument or meridian circle

**meridian line** *n* : a line running accurately north and south through any given point on or near the earth's surface

**meridian mark** *n* : a fixed mark due north or south of a meridian instrument to aid in adjusting or finding its azimuth error

**meridian passage** *n* : the passage of a celestial body across an observer's meridian

**meridian sailing** *n* : sailing north or south — opposed to *parallel sailing*

**mé·ri·di·enne** \məˌridēˈen\ *n* -S [F, lit., midday nap, fr. fem. of *méridien* meridian, of midday, fr. OF *meridien* — more at MERIDIAN] : a short sofa of the French Empire period having one arm higher than the other

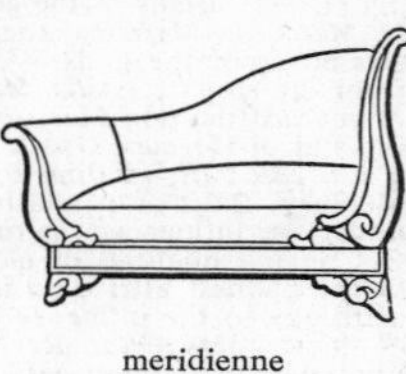

meridienne

**me·rid·i·on** \məˈridēˌän\ *n, cap* [NL, fr. Gk, dim. of *merid-, meris* part, portion — more at MERIT] : a genus (coextensive with the family Meridionaceae) of freshwater pennate diatoms having cuneate cells arranged in flat, fan-shaped, or spiral colonies and often causing odors in public water supplies

¹**me·rid·i·o·nal** \=ˈ=ēənᵊl\ *adj* [ME, fr. MF *meridionel*, fr. LL *meridionalis*, irreg. fr. L *meridies* noon, south + *-alis* -al — more at MERIDIAN] **1** : of, relating to, or situated in the south : having a southern aspect : SOUTHERN, SOUTHERLY ⟨should attract ~ travelers weary of the big-business aspects of Continental tourism —Dore Ashton⟩ **2** : of, relating to, or characteristic of people living in the south esp. of France ⟨welcomed him with ~ hospitality, and filled his leisure hours with the noisy boisterous fun of Provence —Dorothy C. Fisher⟩ **3** *obs* **a** : of or relating to the position of the sun at noon **b** : of, relating to, or characteristic of noon or midday **4 a** : of or relating to a meridian : following a north-south direction ⟨a ~ circulation which transports poleward the excess energy received at tropical latitudes —Harry Wexler⟩ **b** : marked with lines in the plane of the axis **5** *of a map* : having a meridian as the vertical axis and bounded by the circle of a meridian — **me·rid·i·o·nal·ly** \-nᵊlē\ *adv*

²**meridional** \"\ *n* -S : an inhabitant of southern Europe and esp. southern France ⟨a typical ~ —Rosemary Benet⟩

**meridional difference of latitude** *or* **meridional distance** : the difference of the meridional parts for any two latitudes

**meridionality** *n* -ES *obs* : the quality or state of being meridional or on the meridian : position in the south

**meridional part** *n* : the linear length of one minute of longitude on a Mercator chart

**meridional projection** *n* : a projection of a sphere on a plane parallel to a meridian plane through the point of projection

**me·rim·di·an** *or* **me·rim·de·an** \məˈrimdēən\ *adj, usu cap* [*Merimdeh*, ruins on the western branch of the Nile in the Delta west of Ashmun, Egypt + E *-an*] : of or relating to an early Neolithic Egyptian culture of about 5000–4000 B.C. characterized by agriculture, animal husbandry, pottery, working in gold and silver, loom-weaving, coiled basketry, pit houses, and boats made of bundles of papyrus

**mé·ri·mée's yellow** \ˌmerēˌmāz-\ *n, usu cap M* [prob. after Jean-François *Mérimée* †1836 French painter and chemist] : a permanent yellow pigment prepared by fusing lead monoxide and ammonium chloride with a little bismuth antimonate — called also *antimony yellow*

**mering** *pres part of* MERE

¹**me·ringue** \məˈraŋ, -raiŋ\ *n* -S [F] **1** : a mixture of beaten egg whites and powdered sugar baked at low temperature and used as a topping (as on pies, puddings) **2** : a shell made of meringue and filled with fruit or ice cream

²**méringue** *var of* MERENGUE

**me·ringu·er** \məˈraŋə(r), -raiŋ-\ *n* -S : one that mixes or spreads meringue

**me·ri·no** \məˈrē(ˌ)nō\ *n* [Sp] **1 a** *usu cap* : a breed of fine-wooled white sheep originating in Spain, widely popular esp. on the ranges of America and Australia, and excelling all others in weight and quality of fleece although not ranking high as a mutton producer **b** *also* **merino sheep** -S *usu cap M* : a sheep of the Merino breed **2** -S **a** : a soft clothing fabric resembling cashmere, orig. of merino wool and now of any fine wool or wool and cotton **b** : a garment of this fabric; *esp* : a merino dress or loose dressing gown **3** -S : a fine wool and cotton yarn used for hosiery and knitwear

**mer·i·on bluegrass** \ˈmerēən-\ *n, usu cap M* [prob. fr. the name *Merion*] : a strain of Kentucky bluegrass that is low growing, rapid spreading, and resistant to leaf spot

**me·ri·o·nes** \məˈrīəˌnēz\ *n, cap* [NL, fr. Gk *mēria* thigh bones, fr. *mēros* thigh; fr. the formation of the hind legs — more at MEMBER] : a genus of gerbils

**mer·i·on·eth·shire** \ˌmerēˈänəth,shi(ə)r, -ˌshiə, -ˌshə(r)\ *or* **merioneth** *adj, usu cap* [fr. *Merionethshire* or *Merioneth* county, Wales] : of or from the county of Merioneth, Wales : of the kind or style prevalent in Merioneth

**meri·quinone** \ˌmerə+\ *n* [*meri-* + *quinone*] : a compound (as quinhydrone) that is partly quinonoid and partly benzenoid — compare SEMIQUINONE

**meri·quinonoid** \"+\ *or* **meri·quinoid** \"+\ *adj* [ISV *meri-* + *quinonoid* or *quinoid;* orig. formed as G *meriquinonoid*] : partly quinonoid : having the properties of a meriquinone — compare HEMIQUINONOID

**-mer·is** \ˌmərəs\ *n comb form* [NL, fr. Gk *meris* part — more at MERIT] : one having a (specified) part — in generic names ⟨*Piptomeris*⟩

**mer·i·sis** \ˈmerəsəs\ *n, pl* **merises** [NL, fr. *meri-* + *-sis*] *biol* : GROWTH; *specif* : growth by increase in cell number — compare AUXESIS

¹**mer·ism** \ˈmeˌrizəm\ *n* -S [³*mer-* + *-ism*] *biol* : a repetition of homologous parts — compare METAMERISM

²**merism** \"\ *n* -S [Gk *merismos*, lit., division, fr. *merizein* to divide, fr. *mer-* ³*mer-* + *-izein* -ize] : a synecdoche in which a totality is expressed by two contrasting parts ⟨*old and young, thick and thin, near and far* are typical ~*s*⟩

**-mer·ism** \ˌməˌrizəm\ *n comb form* -S [ISV *-mer* + *-ism*] **1** : possession of a (specified) association of substances in chemical compounds ⟨*isomerism*⟩ ⟨*tautomerism*⟩ **2** [ISV ³*mer-* + *-ism*] : possession of (such or so many) parts

**mer·is·mat·ic** \ˌmerəzˈmad·ik\ *adj* [Gk *merismat-, merisma* part (fr. *merizein* to divide) + E *-ic*] **1** *bot* : MERISTEMATIC **2** *zool* : dividing by formation of internal partitions

**me·ris·moid** \məˈrizˌmȯid\ *or* **me·ris·ma·toid** \-zməˌtȯid\ *adj* [Gk *merisma* part, division + E *-oid*] *of a fungus* : having a branched pileus

**meri·stele** \ˈmerə+\ *n* [ISV *meri-* + *stele*] : one of the units of vascular tissue in a polystele — **meri·stelic** \"+\ *adj*

**meri·stem** \ˈmerəˌstem\ *n* -S [Gk *meristos* divided, divisible (fr. *merizein* to divide) + E *-em* (as in *system*)] : a formative plant tissue made up typically of small essentially isodiametric cells lacking prominent vacuoles and capable of an indefinite number of divisions and giving rise to initiating cells that remain meristematic and to derivatives that undergo differentiation to produce the various tissues and organs of the plant, all postembryonic growth depending ultimately on the proliferation of meristematic cells — compare CAMBIUM

**meri·ste·mat·ic** \ˌ==stəˈmad·ik\ *adj* [*meristem* + *-atic* (as in *systematic*)] : consisting of or having the qualities of meristem — **meri·ste·mat·i·cal·ly** \-ək(ə)lē\ *adv*

**me·ris·tic** \məˈristik\ *adj* [Gk *meristos* divided, divisible + E *-ic* — more at MERISTEM] **1** : of, relating to, or divided into segments (as metameres) ⟨~ changes⟩ ⟨~ organization of body structures⟩ **2** : characterized by or involving modification in number or in geometrical relation of body parts ⟨~ variation⟩ ⟨~ characters⟩ — **me·ris·ti·cal·ly** \-tək(ə)lē\ *adv*

**meri·stog·e·nous** \ˌmerəˈstäjənəs\ *adj* [Gk *meristos* divided, divisible + E *-genous*] : arising from a single hyphal cell or a group of adjacent hyphal cells by repeated cross and longitudinal divisions (as in the development of certain pycnidia) — compare SYMPHOGENOUS

¹**mer·it** \ˈmerət, *usu* -əd·+V\ *n* -S [ME *merite, merit*, fr. OF *merite*, fr. L *meritum*, fr. neut. of *meritus*, past part. of *merēre, merēri* to earn, deserve, merit; akin to Gk *meros* & *meris* part, share, *moros* fate, lot, L *mora* delay — more at MEMORY] **1 a** *obs* : reward or punishment earned or deserved : just deserts **b** : one's character regarded as the basis of his deserts : laudable or blameworthy traits or actions ⟨opinions of his ~ vary⟩ **c** : a praiseworthy quality : VIRTUE ⟨but originality, as it is one of the highest, is also one of the rarest, of ~*s* —E.A. Poe⟩ **d** : worth or excellence in quality or performance : character or conduct deserving reward, honor, or esteem ⟨she is handsome no longer, and she never had any other ~ —W.M. Thackeray⟩ ⟨composed a number of works of ~ —H.E.Starr⟩ **2** : spiritual credit or stored moral surplusage regarded as earned by performance of righteous acts and as ensuring future benefits ⟨"she has acquired ~," returned the lama. "Peradventure it was a nun" —Rudyard Kipling⟩ ⟨had thereby added to a surplus of ~ already enriched by what Christ had done —K.S.Latourette⟩ **3 a merits** *pl* : the intrinsic rights and wrongs of a legal case as determined by matters of substance in distinction from matters of form : the strict legal rights of the parties as distinguished from considerations depending on practice or jurisdiction ⟨the plaintiff . . . is entitled to have its claim decided here on its ~*s* —T.M.Maddes⟩ **b** : legal significance, standing, or importance ⟨the contention is without ~ —E.B.Denny⟩ **syn** see DUE, EXCELLENCE

²**merit** \"\ *vb* -ED/-ING/-S [MF *meriter*, fr. *merite*, n.] *vt* **1** *obs* : REWARD, REQUITE **2 a** : to be worthy of or entitled or liable to : EARN ⟨~*ed* the large sale which they obtained —E.S.Bates⟩ ⟨the man who owned both the lump and the abdomen ~*ed* as much consideration as either —Harvey Graham⟩ ⟨~ the penalty of expulsion —Virginia Murphy⟩ **b** : to have a claim on (divine mercy or reward) ⟨the supernatural life which Christ ~*ed* for us —J.J.Maher⟩ ~ *vi* **1** *obs* : to gain merit : acquire favor : be entitled to reward or honor ⟨if in my poor death fair France may ~ —Francis Beaumont & John Fletcher⟩ **2** : to be or become deserving of good or ill **syn** see DESERVE

**mer·it·able** \ˈmerəd·əbəl, -ətəb-\ *adj* [ME, fr. MF *merite, merit* merit + *-able* — more at MERIT] : MERITORIOUS

**merited** *adj* : that is properly earned or deserved ⟨often sharp in ~ criticism —G.L.Hendrickson⟩ ⟨a ~ success⟩ — **mer·it·ed·ly** *adv*

**meriter** *n* -S *obs* : one that merits

**mer·it·less** \ˈ==ləs\ *adj* : lacking merit : WORTHLESS

**meritmonger** \ˈ==ˌ==\ *n, archaic* : one who expects salvation as a recompense for good works

**mer·i·to·ri·ous** \ˌmerəˈtōrēəs, -tȯr-\ *adj* [ME, fr. ML *meritorius*, fr. L, that brings in money, fr. *meritus* (past part. of *merēre* to earn) + *-orius* -ory — more at MERIT] **1** : serving to win divine favor, blessing, or reward ⟨it is ~ to believe what cannot be demonstrated —Frank Thilly⟩ **2** : worthy of reward, gratitude, honor, or esteem ⟨made up for his lack of talent by ~ industry —W.M.Thackeray⟩ **3** *obs* : DESERVING — used with *of* — **mer·i·to·ri·ous·ly** *adv* — **mer·i·to·ri·ous·ness** *n* -ES

**meritorious consideration** *n* : GOOD CONSIDERATION

**merit rating** *n* **1** : computation of an insurance premium for a particular risk on the basis of its individual loss-causing characteristics — see EXPERIENCE RATING **2** : the rating of an employee by systematic evaluation of his proficiency in a job

**merits** *pl of* MERIT, *pres 3d sing of* MERIT

**merit system** *n* : the system of appointing employees to office in the civil service and of promoting them for competency only ⟨advocates of the *merit system* always concede that policy-determining posts should be political —D.D.McKean⟩ — opposed to *spoils system*

**merk** \ˈmerk\ *chiefly Scot var of* ³MARK 2b

**mer·kel-ran·vier corpuscle** \ˈmer\|kəl\|rä\|ⁿvyā-, ˈmər\| *n, usu cap M&R* [after Friedrich S. *Merkel* †1919 Ger. anatomist & Louis A. *Ranvier* †1922 Fr. histologist] : MERKEL'S CELL

**merkel's cell** *or* **merkel's corpuscle** *or* **merkel's disc** *n, usu cap M* [after Friedrich S. *Merkel*] : a touch receptor of the deep layers of the skin consisting of a flattened or cupped body associated peripherally with a large modified epithelial cell and centrally with an efferent nerve fiber

**mer·ker grass** \ˈmərkə(r)-\ *n, usu cap M* [prob. fr. the name *Merker*] : NAPIER GRASS

**mer·kin** \ˈmərkən\ *n* -S [origin unknown] **1** *obs* : the hair of the female genitalia **2** : false hair for the female genitalia

**merl** *or* **merle** \ˈmər(-ə)l\ *n* -S [MF *merle*, fr. L *merulus, merula*, fr. (assumed) *misula;* akin to OE *ōsle* blackbird, OHG *amsla, amsala*, W *mwyalchen*] : BLACKBIRD 1a

**merle** \"\ *n* -S [origin unknown] **1** : a bluish gray color of the coats of some dogs **2** : AUSTRALIAN CATTLE DOG

**mer·lin** \ˈmərlən\ *n* -S [ME *meriloun*, fr. AF *merilun*, fr. OF *esmerillon*, aug. of *esmeril*, of Gmc origin; akin to MD *smerle, smeerle* merlin, OHG *smerlo, smiril*, ON *smyrill*] **1** : a small European falcon (*Falco aesalon*) related to the American pigeon hawk **2** : PIGEON HAWK a

**mer·lin's-grass** \ˈmərlənz+,-\ *n, pl* **merlin's-grasses** *usu cap M* [prob. after *Merlin*, legendary 5th cent. Welsh wizard] : a common European quillwort (*Isoetes lacustris*)

**mer·lon** \ˈmərlən\ *n* -S [F, fr. It *merlone*, aug. of *merlo* battlement, fr. ML *merulus*, fr. L, blackbird — more at MERL] **1** : one of the solid intervals between embrasures of a battlemented parapet — see BATTLEMENT illustration **2** *archaic* : a part of a warship's bulwark resembling a merlon

**mer·luc·ci·us** \mərˈlüchēəs\ *n, cap* [NL, fr. ML *merlutius, merlucius* hake, fr. L *merula*, a sea fish, blackbird — more at MERL] : a genus of fishes related to the cods and included with them in Gadidae or now often isolated in a separate family — see HAKE

**mer·maid** \ˈmər, ˈmə̄+,-\ *n* [ME *mermaide*, fr. ¹*mer-* + *maide* maid — more at MAID] **1 a** : a fabled marine creature usu. represented as having the head, trunk, and arms of a woman and a lower part like the tail of a fish ⟨I have heard the ~*s* singing, each to each —T.S. Eliot⟩ — compare NIX **b** : a girl swimmer ⟨sat by the pool . . . and watched the ~*s* in the seventy-six-degree November sun —Horace Sutton⟩ **2** : a representation of a mermaid usu. holding a mirror in one hand and a comb in the other esp. as a heraldic emblem or the sign of an inn or tavern **3** *obs* **a** : SIREN 1 a **b** : HARLOT **4** : a grayish yellow green that is yellower and paler than average sage green or palmetto and yellower and darker than celadon **5** : SIRENOMELUS **6** : SIRENIAN; *esp* : MANATEE

mermaid 2

**mer·maiden** \"+,\ *n* [ME, fr. ¹*mer-* + *maiden*] : MERMAID 1

**mermaid's-hair** \ˈ=ˌ=ˌ=\ *n, pl* **mermaid's-hairs** : a common filamentous marine blue-green alga (*Lyngbya majuscula*) growing in long matted tufts on eelgrass and on larger algae

**mermaid's purse** *n* : the dark horny or leathery egg case of various skates or other elasmobranch fishes

**mermaid weed** *n* : any aquatic herb of the genus *Proserpinaca*

**mer·man** \ˈmərˌman, ˈmə̄ˌm-, -ˌmaa(ə)n, -ˌmən\ *n, pl* **mermen** [¹*mer-* + *man*] **1** : a fabled marine male creature usu. represented as having the head, trunk, and arms of a man and a lower part like the tail of a fish — called also *manfish;* compare MERMAID **2** : a male swimmer

**mer·mis** \ˈmərməs\ *n, cap* [NL, fr. Gk, cord, string, thread; akin to ON *merth* fish trap, OSw *mærthi* fish trap, MIr *braige, braiga* captive, Gk *brochos* noose, OSlav *mrěža* net; basic meaning: to plait, tie] : a genus (the type of the family Mermithidae) of very slender nematode worms that as adults live in damp earth often appearing on the ground in great numbers after rains and as larvae live in the bodies of insects

**mer·mith·ergate** \ˌmərməth+\ *n* [NL *Mermith-, Mermis* + E *ergate*] : a worker ant hypertrophied and altered in bodily form by parasitic nematodes — compare MERMITHIZED

¹**mer·mi·thid** \ˈmərməthəd\ *adj* [NL *Mermithidae*] : of or relating to the Mermithidae

²**mermithid** \"\ *n* -S : a worm of the family Mermithidae

**mer·mith·i·dae** \(ˌ)mərˈmithəˌdē\ *n pl, cap* [NL, fr. *Mermith-, Mermis*, type genus + *-idae*] : a family of elongated round-headed nematode worms (order Enoplida) having the digestive tract nonfunctional in the adult — see MERMIS

**mer·mi·thi·za·tion** \ˌ=məthəˈzāshən, -ˌthīˈz-\ *n* -S [NL *Mermithidae* + E *-ization*] : mermithid infestation

**mer·mi·thized** \ˈ==ˌthīzd\ *adj* [NL *Mermithidae* + E *-ize* + *-ed*] : infested with mermithid worms — used esp. of ants

**me·ro** \ˈmā(ˌ)rō\ *n* -S [Sp] : any of several large groupers or jewfishes of warm seas

**mero-** — see MER-

**mero·blas·tic** \ˌmerəˈblastik\ *adj* [ISV ³*mer-* + *-blastic*] *of an egg* : undergoing incomplete cleavage as a result of the presence of an impeding mass of yolk material : lacking cleavage planes that divide the whole egg into distinct and separate blastomeres — opposed to *holoblastic* — **mero·blas·ti·cal·ly** \-tək(ə)lē\ *adv*

**me·roc·er·ite** \mə'räsə,rīt\ *n* -s [³*mer-* + Gk *keras* horn, antenna + E *-ite* — more at HORN] **:** the fourth segment of the antenna of a crustacean — **me·roc·er·it·ic** \¦==¦rid·ik\ *adj*

**mer·o·crine** \'merəkrən, -ə,krīn\ *adj* [ISV ³*mer-* + *-crine* (fr. Gk *krinein* to separate) — more at CERTAIN] **:** producing a secretion that is discharged without major damage to the secreting cells; *also* **:** produced by a merocrine gland — compare HOLOCRINE

**mer·o·cyanine** \¦==+\ *or* **merocyanine dye** *n* [³*mer-* + *cyanine*] **:** any of a class of polymethine dyes that are used like the cyanine dyes as sensitizers in photography but differ from the cyanine dyes in containing an acidic heterocyclic nucleus (as rhodanine or pyrazolone) linked to a basic heterocyclic nucleus (as quinoline or benzothiazole) and in not being ionized

**me·rog·a·my** \mə'rägəmē\ *n* -ES [ISV ³*mer-* + *-gamy*] **:** MICROGAMY

**mero·genesis** \¦merə+\ *n* [NL, fr. ³*mer-* + *genesis*] **:** the production of segmental parts **:** SEGMENTATION

**mero·genetic** \"+\ *or* **mer·o·genic** \"+¦jenik\ *adj* [³*mer-* + *-genetic*] **:** of or relating to merogenesis **:** exhibiting merogenesis **:** SEGMENTED

**me·rog·na·thite** \mə'rägnə,thīt\ *n* [³*mer-* + *gnathite*] **:** the fourth segment of a crustacean gnathite

**mer·o·gon** \'merə,gän\ *also* **mer·o·gone** \-gōn\ *n* -s [ISV, back-formation from *merogony*] **:** a product of merogony

**mer·o·gon·ic** \¦==¦gänik\ *or* **me·rog·o·nous** \mə'rägənəs\ *adj* [*merogony* + *-ic* or *-ous*] **:** of, relating to, or induced by merogony

**me·rog·o·ny** \mə'rägənē\ *n* -ES [ISV ³*mer-* + *-gony*; orig. formed as F *mérogonie*] **:** development of an embryo by a process that is genetically equivalent to male parthenogenesis and that involves segmentation and differentiation of an egg or egg fragment deprived of its own nucleus but having a functional male nucleus introduced

**mer·o·he·dral** \¦merə¦hēdrəl *sometimes chiefly Brit* -¦hed-\ *or* **mer·o·he·dric** \-drik\ *adj* [³*mer-* + *-hedral* or *-hedric* (fr. Gk *hedra* seat + E *-ic*)] **:** marked by merohedrism

**mer·o·he·drism** \¦==¦hē,drizəm, -'he,-\ *n* -s [³*mer-* + Gk *hedra* seat + E *-ism*] **:** the conditioning of a crystal due to symmetrical suppression of half or three fourths of the faces of the holohedral form

**mero·is·tic** \¦merə¦wistik\ *adj* [³*mer-* + Gk *ōion* egg + E *-istic* — more at EGG] **:** producing nutritive cells as well as eggs from oocytes — used of the ovaries of various insects

**mero·it·ic** \¦merə¦wid·ik\ *n, usu cap* [*Meroë*, ancient city and kingdom in northern Sudan + E *-itic*] **1 :** a language of northern Sudan of unknown relationship known from inscriptions from the period 700 B.C. to A.D. 350 **2 :** a script derived from Egyptian hieroglyphics in which the Meroitic language was written

**mer·o·mic·tic** \¦merə¦miktik\ *adj* [ISV ³*mer-* + *-mict-* (fr. Gk *miktos* mixed, verbal of *mignynai* to mix) + *-ic* — more at MIX] *of a lake* **:** undergoing incomplete circulation at the fall overturn — compare HOLOMICTIC

**mer·o·mix·is** \-¦miksəs\ *n, pl* **meromix·es** \-k,sēz\ [NL, fr. ³*mer-* + *-mixis*] **:** the condition of being meromictic

**mero·mor·phic function** \¦merə¦mȯrfik-, -¦mō(ə)f-\ *n* [*meromorphic* fr. ³*mer-* + *-morphic*] **:** a function of a complex variable that is regular in a region except for a finite number of points at which it has infinity for limit

**mero·my·ar·i·an** \¦merō,mī¦a(a)rēən\ *also* **mero·my·ar·i·al** \-ēəl\ *adj* [³*mer-* + Gk *mys* muscle, mouse + E *-arian* or *-arial* — more at MOUSE] **:** having few cells in each quadrant of a cross section — used of the arrangement of muscle cells in a nematode worm — **mero·my·ar·i·ty** \¦==,mī'arəd·ē\ *n* -ES

**me·ro·pia** \mə'rōpēə\ *n* -s [NL, fr. ³*mer-* + *-opia*] **:** partial blindness

**me·rop·i·dae** \=¦räpə,dē\ *n pl, cap* [NL, fr. *Merop-*, *Merops*, type genus + *-idae*] **:** a family of chiefly tropical usu. brightly colored gregarious birds that nest in holes in the ground and constitute a distinct suborder of Coraciiformes — see BEE-EATER, MEROPS

**mer·o·plankton** \¦merə+\ *n* [NL, fr. ³*mer-* + *plankton*] **:** the portion of the plankton found only a part of the time at or near the surface — **mer·o·planktonic** \"+\ *adj*

**me·rop·o·dite** \mə'räpə,dīt\ *n* -s [³*mer-* + *podite*] **:** the segment fourth from the base of some limbs of crustaceans (as the ambulatory limbs of decapods) — **me·rop·o·dit·ic** \¦==¦did·ik\ *adj*

**merops** \'me,räps, 'mē,-\ *n, cap* [NL, fr. Gk *merops* bee-eater] **:** the type genus of Meropidae comprising various Old World bee-eaters

**me·ros** \'mē,räs\ *n* -ES [NL, fr. Gk *mēros* thigh — more at MEMBER] **:** the plain surface between the channels of a triglyph

**mer·o·so·ma·ta** \¦merə'sōməd·ə\ *n, cap* [NL, fr. ³*mer-* + *-somata*] *in some classifications* **:** a group consisting of those compound ascidians that have zooids with the body divided into regions (as thorax and abdomen)

**mer·o·spo·ran·gi·um** \¦==+\ *n* [NL, fr. ³*mer-* + *sporangium*] **:** one of the cylindrical outgrowths developing from the swollen sporangium tip in various fungi of the order Mucorales and having contents that divide to form a series of sporangiospores like a chain and simulate conidia upon breakdown of the sporangium wall

**mer·o·spore** \'==,spō(ə)r\ *n* [³*mer-* + *-spore*] **:** a sporangiospore formed from a merosporangium

**mer·o·sto·ma·ta** \,==¦stōməd·ə\ *n pl, cap* [NL, fr. ²*mer-* + *-stomata*] *in some classifications* **:** a class or other category of chelicerate arthropods including the Xiphosura and Eurypterida and sometimes made a subdivision of Arachnida

**mer·o·stomatous** \¦==¦stäməd·əs, -stōm-\ *also* **me·ros·to·mous** \mə'rästəməs\ *adj* [NL *Merostomata* + E *-ous*] **:** of or relating to the Merostomata

**mer·o·stome** \'merə,stōm\ *n* -s [NL *Merostomata*] **:** an arthropod of the class Merostomata

**mer·o·symmetrical** \¦==+\ *adj* [³*mer-* + *symmetrical*] **:** MEROHEDRAL

**mer·o·symmetry** \"+\ *n* [³*mer-* + *symmetry*] **:** MEROHEDRISM

**mer·o·systematic** \"+\ *adj* [³*mer-* + *systematic*] **:** MEROHEDRAL

**me·rot·o·mize** \mə'räd·ə,mīz\ *vt* -ED/-ING/-S [*merotomy* + *-ize*] **:** to divide into parts

**me·rot·o·my** \-mē\ *n* -ES [ISV ³*mer-* + *-tomy*; orig. formed as F *mérotomie*] **:** division into parts

**me·rot·ro·py** \mə'rä·trəpē\ *n* -ES [ISV ³*mer-* + *-tropy*] **:** TAUTOMERISM

**-mer·ous** \,mərəs\ *adj comb form* [NL *-merus*, fr. Gk *-merēs*, fr. *meros* part — more at MERIT] **:** having (such or so many) parts ⟨*homomerous*⟩ ⟨*pentamerous*⟩ ⟨*6-merous*⟩

**¹mer·o·vin·gian** \¦merə¦vinj(ē)ən\ *adj, usu cap* [F *mérovingien*, fr. ML *Merovingi* Merovingians (after *Merovaeus* — Merowig — †458 Frankish king, founder of the dynasty) + F *-ien* -ian] **1 :** of or relating to the first Frankish dynasty reigning from about A.D. 500 to A.D. 751 **2 :** of or relating to a narrow intricate court hand developed from the Roman cursive and found in Gaul from the 7th century

**²merovingian** \"\ *n* -s *usu cap* **:** a member of the Merovingian dynasty

**me·rox·ene** \mə'räk,sēn\ *n* -s [G *meroxen*, fr. NL (*Astrites*) *meroxenus*; NL *meroxenus* fr. ³*mer-* + Gk *xenos* stranger, guest] **:** a mineral consisting of a biotite

**mer·o·zoa** \,merə'zōə\ [NL, fr. ³*mer-* + *-zoa*] *syn of* CESTODA

**mer·o·zo·ite** \-'zō,īt\ *n* -s [ISV ³*mer-* + Gk *zōion* animal + ISV *-ite* — more at ZO-] **:** a small amoeboid trophozoite that is produced by schizogony in some sporozoans and that is capable of initiating either a new asexual or a sexual cycle of development

**mer·peo·ple** \'mər, 'mə+,-\ *n pl* [¹*mer-* + *people*] **:** MERFOLK

**mer·rie** \'merē, -ri\ *archaic var of* MERRY

**mer·ri·ly** \'merəlē, -li\ *adv* [ME *murily, mirily, merily*, fr. *mury, miry, mery* merry + *-ly*] **:** in a merry manner **:** GAILY

**mer·ri·ment** \-rēmənt, -rim-\ *n* -s [¹*merry* + *-ment*] **1** *obs* **:** something that causes mirth **:** JEST, PRANK; *esp* **:** a brief comic presentation **2 a :** lighthearted gaiety or fun-making **:** laughing enjoyment **:** HILARITY, JUBILATION ⟨no one has painted the riotous ~ of a country fair . . . with such zest —Laurence Binyon⟩ ⟨it was now her turn to be overcome with ~ —Owen Wister⟩ **b :** a gay celebration or party **:** ENTERTAINMENT, FESTIVITY ⟨in the course of this million-dollar ~, the host passed out fifty-dollar bills to one and all —R.L. Taylor⟩ ⟨special ~ such as dances, parades, feasts of regional delicacies and similar gaiety —R. E. Meyer⟩

**mer·ri·ness** \-rēnəs, -rin-\ *n* -ES [ME *mirines, merines*, fr. *mury, miry, mery* merry + *-nes* -ness] **:** the quality or state of being merry **:** MIRTH

**¹mer·ry** \'merē, -ri\ *adj* -ER/-EST [ME *mury, miry, mery*, fr. OE *myrge, mirge, merge*; akin to OHG *murg, murgi* short, Goth *gamaurgjan* to shorten — more at BRIEF] **1** *archaic* **:** giving pleasure or causing happiness **:** AGREEABLE, AMUSING, DELIGHTFUL, SWEET **2 a :** full of gaiety or high spirits **:** marked by animation or vivacity **:** CHEERFUL, HILARIOUS, JOYOUS, LAUGHING, MIRTHFUL ⟨happy as the ~ whistle of a schoolboy —John Burroughs⟩ ⟨spun yarns that are still ~ reading —*Amer. Guide Series: Va.*⟩ ⟨the windows were alight; signs of ~ life within —George Meredith⟩ **b** *obs* **:** HAPPY **c :** elated with drink **:** HIGH ⟨became ~ and befuddled —George Woodbury⟩ **d** *archaic* **:** MOCKING, TEASING **3 :** marked by festive celebration and rejoicing ⟨a ~ holiday time⟩ **4** *of a dog* **:** snappy and attractive in action **:** ALERT, QUICK — used also of the tail **5 :** BRISK, INTENSE, SHARP ⟨a major factor in keeping industrial wheels turning at a ~ clip —*Spokane (Wash.) Spokesman-Rev.*⟩ — often used as an intensive ⟨gave him ~ hell⟩

**syn** BLITHE, JOCUND, JOVIAL, JOLLY: MERRY suggests gay, cheerful, or joyous, uninhibited enjoyment ⟨very kind *merry* young people, disposed to take things as gaily as they might —W.M.Thackeray⟩ ⟨the song of the *merry* encounter of some clerk or cavalier with a mocking or complaisant shepherdess —H.O.Taylor⟩ BLITHE suggests a fresh lightheartedness lastingly glad, buoyant, and debonair ⟨then they both laughed together, and heard their own laughter returning in the echoes, and laughed again at the response, so that the ancient and solemn grove became full of merriment for these two *blithe* spirits —Nathaniel Hawthorne⟩ ⟨a *blithe* tale, and a pleasant solvent of anxiety and gloom —Amy Loveman⟩ JOCUND may suggest a habit of exhilaration, elation, good humor, cheer, or beaming complaisance ⟨this they appeared to regard rather as a *jocund* form of sport than a serious employment, and often the professor's arid chuckle echoed upon the chime of Shiloh's fiery laughter —Elinor Wylie⟩ ⟨the great rumbling, roaring, *jocund* tornado of a man, all masculine save sometimes a catlike glint, hardly a twinkle, in his merry eyes —W.A.White⟩ JOVIAL describes the convivially jolly, taking a high pleasure in good fellowship ⟨a *jovial*, full-stomached, portly government servant with a marvelous capacity for making bad puns in English —Rudyard Kipling⟩ ⟨as he roamed with his companions about Assisi singing *jovial* choruses and himself the leader of the frolic —H.O. Taylor⟩ JOLLY may suggest the abundant high spirits that go with laughing, bantering, and jesting ⟨the most colorful restaurants are those that cater to Swedish patronage, and here is often a *jolly* crowd made up mostly of workingmen with their wives or girls, with here and there a professor from the university, all sharing with gusto the beer, the lutefisk, and the occasional outburst of song —*Amer. Guide Series: Minn.*⟩ ⟨ebullient, *jolly*, big-bosomed hoydens, very clearly neither maids nor wives —W.B.Adams⟩

**²merry** \"\ *n* -ES [modif. of F *merise* (taken as pl.), prob. blend of *amer* bitter (fr. L *amarus*) and *cerise* cherry — more at AMAROID, CERISE] **:** GEAN 1b

**merry-an·drew** \¦==¦an(,)drü\ *n* -s *often cap M&A* [¹*merry* + the name *Andrew*] **:** one that clowns publicly **:** BUFFOON, MOUNTEBANK ⟨a *merry-andrew*, frivolous, vain, far too free and familiar —Van Wyck Brooks⟩

**merrybell** \'==,=\ *n* **:** BELLWORT 2 — usu. used in pl.

**merry-go-round** \'==(,)=,=\ *n* -s **1 a :** a contrivance commonly found at amusement parks and carnivals that consists of a circular platform having seats often in the form of horses or other animals and rotating around a fixed center usu. to calliope music — called also *carrousel* **b :** a children's playground device that revolves about a fixed center

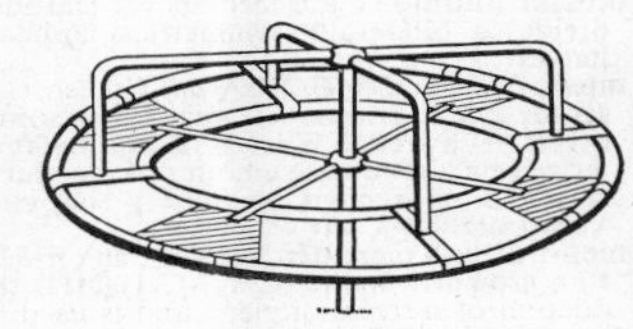

merry-go-round 1b

**2 :** a busy rapid round **:** WHIRL ⟨the high-pressure *merry-go-round* of big business administration —*Advertising Age*⟩ ⟨the weary *merry-go-round* of the commuting train —Scott Fitzgerald⟩ ⟨the familiar *merry-go-round* of fashion with its rapid alternations of season —Edward Sapir⟩

**mer·ry·ing** \'merēiŋ\ *n* -s [¹*merry* + *-ing*] *archaic* **:** FESTIVITY

**¹merrymake** \'==,=\ *n* [fr. the phrase *make merry*] *archaic* **:** MERRYMAKING

**²merrymake** \"\ *vi, archaic* **:** to make merry **:** be festive

**merrymaker** \'==,==\ *n* **:** one that shares in festivity or gaiety **:** REVELLER

**merrymaking** \'==,==\ *n* **1 :** gay or festive activity **:** CONVIVIALITY, MERRIMENT **2 :** a convivial occasion **:** FESTIVITY, PARTY

**mer·ry·man** \'==mən\ *n, pl* **merrymen** *archaic* **:** BUFFOON, JESTER

**merry-meeting** \'==,==\ *n, archaic* **:** a festive gathering

**merry night** *n, dial Eng* **:** an evening of entertainment and dancing

**merrythought** \'==,=\ *n, chiefly Brit* **:** WISHBONE

**merrywing** \'==,=\ *n* **1 :** BUFFLEHEAD **2 :** GOLDENEYE 1

**mers** *pl of* MER

**-mers** *pl of* -MER

**mer·sal·yl** \(,)mər'sa,lil, -,lēl\ *also* **mersalyl sodium** *n* -s [*mercury* + *salicyl*] **:** an organic mercurial $C_{13}H_{16}HgNNaO_6$ administered by injection in combination with theophylline as a diuretic

**merse** \'mərs\ *chiefly Scot var of* MARSH

**mer·ten·sia** \(,)mər'tench(ē)ə, -n(t)sēə\ *n, cap* [NL, fr. Franz K *Mertens*, †1831 Ger. botanist + NL *-ia*] **:** a large genus of herbs (family Boraginaceae) of temperate regions with funnel-shaped blue or purple flowers — see VIRGINIA COWSLIP

**Mer·thi·o·late** \(,)mər'thīə,lāt, -,lət\ *trademark* — used for thimerosal

**mer·u·la** \'mer(y)ələ\ [NL, fr. L, blackbird — more at MERL] *syn of* TURDUS

**me·ru·li·us** \mə'rülēəs\ *n, cap* [NL, fr. L *merula* blackbird; fr. the black color of the fungus] **:** a genus of fungi (family Polyporaceae) having resupinate sporophores on which the hymenium forms reticulate or sinuous folds — see HOUSE FUNGUS

**me·rus** \'mi(ə)rəs\ *n* -ES [NL, fr. Gk *mēros* thigh — more at MEMBER] **:** MEROPODITE; *esp* **:** the meropodite of a chela constituting the enlarged palm of the hand

**-me·rus** \,mərəs\ *n comb form* [NL, fr. Gk *mēros* thigh] **:** animal or insect having a (specified) type of thigh — in generic names in entomology ⟨*Tomicomerus*⟩ ⟨*Symmerus*⟩

**mer·win·ite** \'mərwə,nīt\ *n* -s [Herbert E. *Merwin* b1878 Am. petrologist + E *-ite*] **:** a mineral $MgCa_3(SiO_4)_2$ consisting of a calcium magnesium silicate with monoclinic crystals

**mer·woman** \'mər, 'mə+,-\ *n, pl* **merwomen** [¹*mer-* + *woman*] **:** MERMAID

**-mery** \,mərē, -ri\ *n comb form* -ES [ISV ³*mer-* + *-y*] **:** possession of (such or so many) parts ⟨*gonomery*⟩ ⟨*metamery*⟩

**mer·yc·hip·pus** \,merē'kipəs\ *n, cap* [NL, fr. Gk *mērykasthai* to ruminate + NL *-hippus*] **:** an American genus of extinct Miocene horses

**mer·yc·oi·do·don** \,=='kȯidə,dän\ *n, cap* [NL, fr. Gk *mērykasthai* to ruminate + NL *-oides* -oid + *-odon*] **:** a genus (the type of the family Merycoidodontidae) of Oligocene four-toed artiodactyls of the size of a peccary and the form of a swine that are regarded as probably archaic ruminants living in No. America from the Eocene to the early Pliocene

**mer·yc·o·pot·a·mus** \-¦kō'päd·əməs\ *n, cap* [NL, fr. Gk *mērykasthai* + NL *-o-* + *potamos* river — more at HIPPOPOTAMUS] **:** a genus of Asiatic Pliocene and Pleistocene artiodactyls related to the genus *Anthracotherium* and sometimes made the type of a distinct family

**-mer·yx** \,məriks\ *n comb form* [NL, fr. Gk *mēryx*, a ruminating fish, fr. *mērykasthai* to ruminate] **:** ruminant — chiefly in generic names of extinct ruminating mammals ⟨*leptomeryx*⟩

**MEs** *pl of* ME

**mes-** *or* **meso-** *comb form* [L, fr. Gk, fr. *mesos* — more at MID] **1 a :** in the middle **:** intermediate (as in position, size, type, time, degree) ⟨*mesoderm*⟩ ⟨*mesodont*⟩ ⟨*mesonephroma*⟩ ⟨*mesoplankton*⟩ ⟨*mesoprosopic*⟩ ⟨*Mesozoa*⟩ ⟨*mesocarp*⟩ **b :** mesentery or membrane supporting a (specified) part ⟨*mesocaecum*⟩ ⟨*mesocolon*⟩ ⟨*mesarchium*⟩ **c :** mesoderm **:** mesodermal and ⟨*mesameboid*⟩ **2** *meso-* **:** a reduction product of a porphyrin or other pyrrole derivative in which one or more vinyl groups have been hydrogenated to ethyl ⟨*mesohemin*⟩ ⟨*mesobilirubin*⟩ **3 :** an inorganic acid regarded as an intermediate hydrated form ⟨*dimesoperiodic* acid $H_4I_2O_9$⟩ **4** *meso-, usu ital* **a :** an optical isomer whose inactivity is attributed to the molecule's being internally compensated ⟨*meso-tartaric acid*⟩ **b :** a middle position or group esp. in a cyclic compound ⟨*meso-chloro-anthracene* is 9-chloro-anthracene⟩ ⟨*meso-phenyl-imidazole* is 2-phenyl-imidazole⟩ — abbr. *ms* or *μ* **5 :** of late Paleozoic or of Mesozoic age — in names of igneous rocks

**me·sa** \'māsə *sometimes* -āzə\ *n* -s [Sp, lit., table, fr. L *mensa*] **1 a :** a usu. isolated hill or mountain having abrupt or steeply sloping sides and a level top that is composed of a resistant nearly horizontal stratum of rock and is usu. greater in area than that of a butte **:** a small isolated plateau **b :** a broad terrace (as along a river) with an abrupt slope or escarpment on one side **:** BENCH **2 :** CARTOUCHE 6

**me·sa·bite** \mə'sä,bīt\ *n* -s [*Mesabi* range, Minn. + E *-ite*] **:** an ocherous goethite

**mes·acon·ic acid** \¦me¦zə¦kānik-, ¦mē¦, ¦sə¦\ *n* [prob. fr. ISV *mes-* + *citraconic acid*] **:** a crystalline unsaturated acid HOOCCH=C(CH₃)COOH made by thermal isomerization of citraconic acid; methyl-fumaric acid

**mesad** \'me,zad, 'mē, ¦,sad\ *also* **mesi·ad** \¦,zē,ad, ¦sē-\ *adv* [*mesad* fr. *mesal* + *-ad* (adv. suffix); *mesiad* fr. *mesial* + *-ad*] **:** toward or on the side toward the mesial plane

**mes·ade·nia** \,me¦zə'dēnēə, ,mē¦, ¦sə-\ *n, cap* [NL, fr. *mes-* + Gk *aden-*, *adēn* gland + NL *-ia*; fr. the central projection of the receptacle — more at ADEN-] *in some classifications* **:** a separate genus comprising the New World members of the genus *Cacalia*

**mes·ade·ni·um** \-nēəm\ *n, pl* **mesade·nia** \-nēə\ [NL, fr. *mes-* + Gk *aden-*, *adēn* gland + NL *-ium*] **:** one of the accessory glands of mesodermal origin of male insects — compare ECTADENIUM

**mesa dropseed** *n* **:** a tufted perennial No. American grass (*Sporobolus flexuosus*) having spreading or reflexed branches and usu. lead-colored spikelets

**mesal** *var of* MESIAL

**més·al·liance** \¦mā,zal¦yäⁿs; ,māzə'līən(t)s, ,mezə-, ,mesə-\ *n, pl* **mésal·liances** \-äⁿs(əz), -ənsəz\ [F, fr. *més-* mis- + *alliance* (fr. MF *alliance*, *aliance*)] **:** a marriage with a person of inferior social position **:** MISALLIANCE

**mes·ameboid** \¦me¦z, ¦mē¦, ¦s + \ *n* -s [*mes-* + *ameboid* (adj.)] **:** a primitive amoeboid mesodermal cell that gives rise to the blood cells of the embryo **:** HEMATOBLAST

**mé·sange** \mā'zäⁿzh\ *n, pl* **mé·sanges** \-zh(əz)\ [F, titmouse, fr. MF, fr. OF *mesenge*, *masenghe*, of Gmc origin; akin to OHG *meisa* titmouse — more at TITMOUSE] **:** a pale green that is bluer and duller than celadon gray or spray green — called also *titmouse blue*

**mes·aortitis** \¦me¦z, ¦mē¦, ¦s + \ *n* -ES [NL, fr. *mes-* + *aorta* + *-itis*] **:** inflammation of the middle layer of the aorta

**¹mes·a·ra·ic** \¦mezə¦rāik, -esə-\ *adj* [alter. (influenced by Gk *mesaraikos*) of ME *miserak*, fr. MF *mesaraique*, fr. Gk *mesaraikos*, fr. *mesaraion* mesentery (fr. *mes-* mid, in the middle — fr. *mesos* — + *araia* belly, fr. fem. of *araios* thin, slender) + *-ikos* -ic — more at MID] *archaic* **:** MESENTERIC

**²mesaraic** \"\ *n* -s *archaic* **:** one of the mesenteric veins

**mes·arch** \'me¦,zärk, 'mē¦, ¦,sä-\ *adj* [*mes-* + *-arch*] **1 :** having metaxylem developed both internal and external to the protoxylem **2 :** originating in a mesic habitat — used of an ecological succession; compare HYDRARCH, XERARCH

**mes·arteritis** \¦me¦z, ¦mē¦, ¦s + \ *n* [NL, fr. *mes-* + *arteri-* + *-itis*] **:** inflammation of the middle layer of an artery

**mesati-** *comb form* [Gk *mesatos* midmost, irreg. superl. of *mesos* mid, in the middle] **:** of medium or intermediate proportion

**me·sati·ce·phal·ic** \mə¦zad·əsə¦falik, mə¦sa-\ *also* **me·sati·ceph·a·lous** \-d·ə¦sefələs\ *adj* [*mesaticephalism* + *-ic* or *-ous*] **:** having a head of medium proportion with a cephalic index of 76 to 81

**me·sati·ceph·a·lism** \=,=='sefə,lizəm\ *or* **me·sati·ceph·a·ly** \-fəlē\ *n* [*mesaticephalism* fr. *mesati-* (fr. Gk *mesatos* midmost, irreg. superl. of *mesos* mid, in the middle) + *-cephalism*; *mesaticephaly*, ISV *mesati-* + *-cephaly*] **:** the quality or state of being mesaticephalic

**me·sat·i·pel·lic** \=¦==¦pelik\ *adj* [*mesati-* + *-pellic* (fr. Gk *pella* wooden bowl + E *-ic*) — more at PELVIS] **:** having a pelvis of moderate size with a pelvic index of 90 to 95 — **me·sat·i·pel·ly** \='==,pelē\ *n* -ES

**me·sati·skelic** \=¦==+\ *adj* [*mesati-* + *skelic*] **:** having limbs of moderate length in proportion to the trunk with a skelic index of 85 to 90

**mes·ax·o·nia** \,me¦,zak'sōnēə, ,mē¦, ¦,sa-\ [NL, fr. *mes-* + Gk *axōn* axis + NL *-ia* — more at AXIS] *syn of* PERISSODACTYLA

**mes·ax·on·ic** \¦==¦sänik\ *adj* **1** [*mes-* + Gk *axōn* axis + E *-ic*] **:** having the axis of the foot formed by the middle digit **2** [NL *Mesaxonia* + E *-ic*] **:** of or relating to the Perissodactyla

**mes·cal** *also* **mez·cal** \(')me'skal, mə's-\ *n* -s [Sp *mescal*, *mezcal*, *mexcal*, fr. Nahuatl *mexcalli* mescal (liquor), fr. *metl* maguey + *xcalli*, short for *ixcalli* stew, decoction] **1 :** a small cactus (*Lophophora williamsii*) with rounded stems covered with jointed tubercles that is used as a stimulant and antispasmodic esp. among the Mexican Indians who also employ it as a mild intoxicant in various ceremonies — see MESCAL BUTTON, PEYOTE **2 a :** a usu. colorless Mexican liquor distilled esp. from the central leaves of maguey plants after they have been roasted and fermented — compare SOTOL, TEQUILA; see PULQUE **b :** a plant from which mescal is produced; *esp* **:** MAGUEY

**mescal bean** *n* **1 :** MESCAL BUTTON **2 a :** a leguminous shrub or small tree (*Sophora secundiflora*) with alternate pinnate leaves often poisonous to livestock, flowers in dense one-sided racemes, and bright red narcotic seeds that resemble beans — called also *coral bean* **b :** a seed of this plant

**mescal button** *n* **:** one of the dried disklike tops of the mescal

**mes·ca·lero** \,meskə'le(,)rō\ *n, pl* **mescalero** *or* **mescaleros** *usu cap* [AmerSp, fr. Sp *mescal*, *mezcal*, *mexcal* mescal] **1 a :** an Apache people formerly ranging esp. through western and central Texas and eastern New Mexico **b :** a member of such people **2 :** the language of the Mescalero people

**mes·ca·line** *also* **mez·ca·line** \'meskə,lēn, -,lən\ *n* -s [*mescal* + *-ine*] **:** a crystalline alkaloid $C_{11}H_{17}NO_3$ that is the chief active principle in mescal buttons, produces hallucinations when administered, and is useful in experimental psychiatry for producing the symptoms of catalepsy; 3,4,5-trimethoxy-phenyl-ethylamine

**mes·calism** \'me'skä,lizəm, mə'-; 'meskə,l-\ *n* -s **:** addiction to mescal

**mescal maguey** *n* **1 :** MESCAL 2b **2 :** a fiber obtained from a Mexican plant (*Agave pseudotequilana*)

**¹meschant** *adj* [ME *mischaunt*, fr. MF *meschant*, fr. OF *meschant*, *mescheant* unlucky, miserable, fr. pres. part. of *mescheoir* to be unlucky, fr. *mes-* mis- + *cheoir* to happen, befall, fall — more at CHUTE] *obs* **:** WICKED, BASE — **meschantly** *adv, obs*

**²meschant** *n* -s *obs* **:** SCOUNDREL, WRETCH

**mesdames** *pl of* MADAM *or of* MADAME

**mesdemoiselles** *pl of* MADEMOISELLE

**mes·ectoderm** \(')me¦z, (')mē¦, ¦s + \ *n* [*mesoderm* + *ectoderm*] **:** an embryonic blastomere or cell layer not yet differentiated into mesoderm and ectoderm but destined to give rise to both — **mes·ectodermal** *adj* — **mes·ectodermic** \¦me¦z, ¦mē¦, ¦s + \ *adj*

**me·seems** \mə'sēmz, mē'-\ *vb impersonal, past 3d sing* **me-**

**seemed** \-ēmd\ *pres 3d sing* **meseems** [*me* + *seems*, 3d sing. pres. indic. of *seem*] *archaic* **:** it seems to me ⟨~ that here is much discourtesy —Alfred Tennyson⟩

**mesel** *n* -s [ME, loathsome person, leper, fr. OF, leper, fr. ML *misellus*, fr. L, wretch, fr. *misellus*, adj., miserable, fr. *miser* miserable] *obs* **:** a loathsome person

**me·self** \mə̇, mē+\ *pron* [ME, fr. OE *meself*, fr. *me* + *seolf*, *self* self — more at SELF] *now dial* **:** MYSELF

**me·sem** \mə̇ˈzem\ *n* -s [by shortening] *Africa* **:** MESEMBRYANTHEMUM

**me·sem·bry·an·the·mum** \mə̇ˌzembrēˈan(t)thəməm\ *n* [NL, fr. Gk *mesēmbria* midday, noon (fr. *mes-* + *hēmera* day) + NL *-anthemum* — more at HEMERA] **1** *cap* **:** a genus of chiefly southern African herbs or subshrubs (family Aizoaceae) having fleshy leaves and flowers with a gamosepalous calyx and a capsular fruit **2** -s **:** any plant of the genus *Mesembryanthemum*

**mes·encephalic** \ˌ(ˌ)me|z, (ˌ)mē|, |s +\ *adj* [NL *mesencephalon* + E *-ic*] **:** of or relating to the midbrain

**mes·encephalon** \ˌme|z, ˌmē|, |s +\ *n* [NL, fr. *mes-* + *encephalon*] **:** the middle division of the brain **:** MIDBRAIN

**me·sen·chy·ma** \mə̇ˈzeŋkəmə, me|, |ˈse-\ *n* -s [NL, fr. *mes-* + *-enchyma*] **:** MESENCHYME

**mes·en·chy·mal** \-məl; ˌme|zᵊnˌkīməl, ˌmē|, |sᵊn-\ *adj* [ISV *mesenchyme* + *-al*] **:** of, relating to, or being mesenchyme

**mes·en·chym·a·tous** \ˌme|zᵊnˈkimədəs, ˌmē|, |sᵊn-\ *adj* [NL *mesenchymat-*, *mesenchyma* + E *-ous*] **:** resembling or consisting of mesenchyme

**mes·en·chyme** \ˈme|zᵊnˌkīm, ˈmē|, |sᵊn-\ *also* **mesen·chym** \-ˌkim; məˈzeŋkə̇m, -ˈse-\ *n* -s [G *mesenchym*, fr. *mes-* + *-enchym* -enchyme] **:** a loosely organized mesodermal connective tissue comprising all the mesoblast except the mesothelium and the structures derived from it and giving rise to such structures as connective tissues, blood lymphatics, bone, and cartilage

**mes·endoderm** *also* **mes·entoderm** \(ˈ)me|z, (ˈ)mē|, |s +\ *n* [*mesoderm* + *endoderm* or *entoderm*] **:** an embryonic blastomere or cell layer not yet differentiated into mesoderm and endoderm but destined to give rise to both

**mesene** \ˈme|ˌzēn, ˈmē|, |ˌsēn\ *adj* [G *mesen*, fr. *mes-* + *-en* as in *euryen* euryene — more at EURYENE] **:** having a forehead of moderate proportions with an upper facial index of 48 to 53 on the living or of 50 to 55 on the skull — **meseny** \-nē\ *n* -ES

**me·sen·na** \məˈzenə, -ˈse-\ *also* **mu·sen·na** \myüˈ-\ *or* **mous·sena** \müˈ-\ *n* -s [Amharic *mĕsanna*] **:** the bark of an Ethiopian tree (*Albizzia anthelmintica*) used to expel tapeworms

**mes·en·te·ri·al** \ˌmesᵊnˈtirēəl, -ezᵊn-\ *adj* [NL *mesenterium* mesentery + E *-al*] **:** MESENTERIC; *specif* **:** indicating certain threadlike glandular organs attached to the inner edge of the mesenteries of anthozoans

**mes·en·ter·ic** \-ˈterik\ *adj* [F *mésentérique*, fr. MF *mesenterique*, fr. *mesentere* mesentery + *-ique* -ic] **:** of, relating to, or located in or near a mesentery

**mesenteric artery** *n* [trans. of F *artère mésentérique*] **:** an artery passing between the two layers of the mesentery to the intestine; *specif* **:** either a superior artery in man arising from the upper part of the aorta and distributed to the greater part of the small intestine, the cecum, and the colon or an inferior artery in man arising near the lower end of the aorta and distributed to the remainder of the large intestine

**mesenteric gland** *n* **:** one of the lymphatic glands of the mesentery

**mesenteric plexus** *n* **:** either of two sympathetic plexuses lying mostly in the mesentery in close proximity to and distributed to the same structures as the corresponding mesenteric arteries

**mesenteric vein** *n* [trans. of F *veine mésentérique*] **:** a branch of the portal vein leading from the intestine between the two layers of mesentery; *specif* **:** either a superior vein in man or an inferior vein in man corresponding to the two mesenteric arteries

**mes·en·teri·o·lum** \ˌ==ˌterēˈōləm, -ˌtəˈrīələm\ *n*, *pl* **mesenterio·la** \-lə\ [NL, dim. of *mesenterium* mesentery] **:** MESOAPPENDIX

**mes·en·ter·i·tis** \ˌ==ˌteˈrīd·ə̇s, -ˌtəˈr-\ *n* -ES [NL, fr. *mesenterium* mesentery + *-itis*] **:** inflammation of the mesentery

**mes·enteron** \(ˈ)me|z, (ˈ)mē|, |s +\ *n*, *pl* **mesentera** [NL, fr. *mes-* + *enteron*] **1 :** the part of the alimentary canal that is developed from the archenteron and is lined with hypoblast — compare PROCTODAEUM, STOMODAEUM **2 :** the central gastric cavity of an actinozoan as distinguished from the spaces between the mesenteries — compare METENTERON — **mes·en·ter·on·ic** \(ˌ)ˌme|ˌzentəˈränik, (ˌ)mē|, |se-\ *adj*

**mes·en·tery** \ˈmesᵊnˌterē, -ezᵊn-\ *n* -ES [NL *mesenterium*, fr. MF & Gk; MF *mesentere*, fr. Gk *mesenterion*, *mesenteron*, fr. *mes-* + *enteron* intestine] **1 a :** the membranes or one of the membranes that consist of a double fold of the peritoneum and enclosed tissues and that in a vertebrate animal invest the intestines and their appendages, connect them with the dorsal wall of the abdominal cavity, and serve to retain the organs in position and to support and convey to them blood vessels, nerves, and lymphatics; *specif* **:** these membranes connected with the jejunum and ileum in man — compare MESOCECUM, MESOCOLON, MESOGASTRIUM, MESORECTUM **b :** any comparable fold of membrane supporting a viscus (as the heart or an ovary) that is not a part of the digestive tract **c :** a membranous or muscular fold or septum connecting the intestine and body wall in an invertebrate **2 :** one of the radial muscular partitions extending inward from the wall of the digestive cavity of actinozoans

**mes·epimeron** \ˌme|z, ˌmē|, |s +\ *n* [NL, fr. *mes-* + *epimeron*] **:** the epimeron of the mesothorax of an insect

**mes·episternum** \"+\ *n* [NL, fr. *mes-* + *episternum*] **:** the episternum of the mesothorax of an insect

**mes·epithelium** \"+\ *n* [NL, fr. *mes-* + *epithelium*] **:** MESOTHELIUM

**me·se·ta** \məˈsād·ə, māˈ-\ *n* -s [Sp, dim. of *mesa*] **1 :** a small mesa **2 :** an extensive upland or plateau often with an uneven surface and forming the central physical feature of a region ⟨the Spanish ~⟩

**¹mes·ethmoid** \(ˈ)me|z, (ˈ)mē|, |s +\ *adj* [*mes-* + *ethmoid*, adj.] **:** located in the middle of the ethmoid region **:** being or relating to a median cartilaginous or bony element of the ethmoidal region that generally forms the greater part of the nasal septum

**²mesethmoid** \"\ *n* [*mes-* + *ethmoid*, n.] **:** a mesethmoid bone or cartilage

**¹mesh** \ˈmesh\ *n* -ES *often attrib* [prob. fr. obs. D *maesche*, *masche*, fr. MD *maessce*; akin to OE *masc*, *max*, *mǣscre* mesh, OS & OHG *masca*, ON *mǫskvi* mesh, Lith *mazgas* knot, *megsti* to weave nets, knot] **1 :** one of the openings between the threads or cords of a net; *also* **:** one of the similar spaces in any network ⟨the ~*es* of a sieve⟩ ⟨lock joint holds each ~ in true alignment —*Amer. Fence Catalog*⟩ ⟨steel ~ used for reinforcing concrete —*Dict. of Occupations*⟩ — often used to designate a size of screen or of the material passed by a screen in terms of the number of such openings per linear inch ⟨the ~ of the bolting wire —*Correspondence Course in Flour Milling*⟩ ⟨a 60-*mesh* screen⟩ ⟨30-*mesh* granulated zinc⟩ **2 a :** the cords, threads, or wires that produce the open spaces in a net or screen **:** the fabric of a net ⟨built a ramp out of wire ~ —W.B.Huie⟩ — often used in pl. ⟨a net with almost invisible ~*es*⟩ **b :** a woven, knit, or knotted fabric that has an open texture with evenly spaced small holes ⟨~ hose⟩ ⟨a ~ handbag⟩; *specif* **:** the net background fabric of many laces **c :** an arrangement of interlocking metal links used esp. for jewelry ⟨~ bracelet⟩ **d :** a flexible netting of fine wire used in surgery esp. in the repair of large hernias and other body defects **3 a :** an interlocking or intertwining arrangement or construction **:** NETWORK, WEB ⟨a ~ of narrow streets —John Buchan⟩ ⟨the ~ of irrigation canals —*Amer. Guide Series: Oregon*⟩ **b :** something that catches and holds or involves **:** TOILS, SNARE — usu. used in pl. ⟨took to panhandling, got detained in the ~*es* of the big city —Dixon Wecter⟩ ⟨diplomacy caught in its own ~*es*⟩ **c :** an intricate or inscrutable system or combination ⟨fixed in the ~ of the divine purpose —V.L.Parrington⟩ ⟨book is a gigantic dense ~ of complicated relations —Edmund Wilson⟩ ⟨a ~ of circumstance⟩ **4 :** working contact (as of the teeth of gear wheels or of a slide fastener) — used esp. in the phrases *in mesh* and *out of mesh* **5 :** a closed figure produced by joining electrical components in series ⟨~ connection⟩

**²mesh** \"\ *vb* -ED/-ING/-ES *vt* **1 a :** to catch in a mesh **:** NET ⟨nets . . . of such a mesh size that the fish are ~*ed* —*Australian Fisheries*⟩ **b :** ENMESH, ENTANGLE ⟨the unseen anchor ~*ed* in rock or bar —Spencer Brown⟩ ⟨become ~*ed* in thought⟩ **2 a :** to provide with a mesh **b :** to cause to resemble network ⟨the city was ~*ed* in haze —*New Yorker*⟩ ⟨trees ~*ed* with sunlight⟩ **3 a :** to come into or be in working contact esp. by the fitting together of teeth **:** ENGAGE **b :** to cause to come into working contact esp. by the fitting together of teeth ⟨noiselessly he ~*ed* the gears —C.B.Kelland⟩ **c :** to coordinate closely (as in a satisfactory working arrangement) **:** INTERLOCK ⟨the idea is to ~ the know-how and experience of the regulars with the enthusiasm of the amateur volunteers —Raymond Moley⟩ **:** fit together properly ⟨learn to ~ layouts —*Mademoiselle*⟩ ~ *vi* **1 :** to become entangled in or as if in meshes ⟨the fish will not ~ today⟩ **2 :** to be in or come into proper working contact — used esp. of gears or other toothed working parts ⟨wooden-cogged wheels ~*ing* at an angle —A.L.Kroeber⟩ ⟨a slide fastener that will not ~⟩ **3 :** to combine or fit together intricately, properly, or harmoniously **:** ACCORD, COORDINATE, HARMONIZE ⟨making the operations of the mind ~ with physical actuality —Aram Vartanian⟩ ⟨my plans are ~*ing* together smoothly —C.A.Lindbergh b. 1902⟩ ⟨two themes that do not quite ~ when they meet —Lisle Bell⟩ ⟨an integrating and ~*ing* of personalities —D.L.Cohn⟩

**³mesh** \"\ *dial var of* MARSH

**⁴mesh** \"\ *dial var of* MASH

**me·shech** \ˈmēˌshek\ *n pl*, *usu cap* [Heb *mĕshĕkh*] **:** MOSCHI

**¹meshed** \ˈmesht\ *adj* [*¹mesh* + *-ed*] **1 :** having meshes ⟨~ tissues⟩ **2 :** resembling meshes or network **:** RETICULATE, TANGLED ⟨a ~ road system⟩ **3 :** fitting together and interacting **:** ENGAGED — used of toothed working parts ⟨~ gears⟩

**²me·shed** \məˈshed\ *adj*, *usu cap* [fr. *Meshed*, Iran] **:** of or from the city of Meshed, Iran **:** of the kind or style prevalent in Meshed

**mesh knot** *n* **:** SHEET BEND

**meshrabiyeh** *var of* MOUCHARABY

**me·shug·ga** *or* **me·shu·ga** *or* **me·shug·ge** *or* **me·shu·ge** \məˈshügə\ *adj* [*meshugga* or *meshuga* fr. Heb *mĕshuggā'*; *meshugge* or *meshuge* fr. Yiddish *meshuge*, fr. Heb *mĕshuggā'*] **:** mentally unbalanced **:** CRAZY

**me·shug·gaas** *or* **me·shu·gaas** \mə(ˌ)shüˈgäs\ *n*, *pl* **meshug·gaas·en** *or* **meshugaas·en** \-ˈäsᵊn\ [Yiddish *meshugaas*, fr. Heb *mĕshuggā'*, adj.] **:** NONSENSE, FOOLISHNESS

**me·shul·lah** *or* **me·shu·lah** *or* **me·shul·lach** *or* **me·shu·lach** \məˈshüˌläk, -shü,-\ *n*, *pl* **meshulla·him** *or* **meshula·him** *or* **meshulla·chim** *or* **meshula·chim** \ˌ=,=ˈläkə̇m, -(ˌ)kēm\ [Heb *mĕshūllāh*, lit., one who is sent] **:** an accredited itinerant collector sent out to raise funds esp. for the maintenance of orthodox Jewish religious and charitable institutions in Palestine — compare HALUKKAH

**me·shum·mad** \məˈshüˌmäd\ *n*, *pl* **meshumma·dim** \ˌ=,=(ˌ)mäˈdēm\ [Heb *mĕshummādh*, lit., one who is destroyed] **:** an apostate from Judaism

**meshwork** \ˈ=,=\ *n* **:** MESHES, NETWORK ⟨a complicated vascular ~ —*Biol. Abstracts*⟩

**meshy** \ˈmeshē\ *adj* -ER/-EST **:** composed of meshes **:** NETTED

**me·sia** \ˈmēsh(ē)ə\ *n* -s [NL *Mesia*, genus of birds] **:** an Asiatic hill tit (*Leiothrix argentauris*) with the crown black, the ear coverts silvery gray, a red bar across the wing, and the remaining plumage yellow and olive green

**mesiad** *var of* MESAD

**mesial** \ˈmezēəl, ˈmē|, |sē-; ˈmēzhəl, -ēsh-\ *also* **mesal** \|zəl, |səl\ *adj* [*mes-* + *-ial* or *-al*] **1 :** MIDDLE, MEDIAN ⟨the ~ aspect of the metacarpal head⟩ **2 :** lying in, being in the region of, or directed toward the mesial plane ⟨the heart is ~ to the lungs⟩ — opposed to *distal* — **mesi·al·ly** \-əlē\ *also* **mesal·ly** \-əlē\ *adv*

**mesial plane** *n* **:** the median vertical longitudinal plane that divides a bilaterally symmetrical animal into right and left halves

**mesic** \ˈme|zik, ˈmē|, |sik\ *adj* [in sense 1, fr. *meson* + *-ic*; in senses 2 & 3, fr. *mes-* + *-ic*] **1 :** MESONIC ⟨the radii of the ~ orbits —Lawrence Wilets⟩ **2** *of a habitat* **:** having or characterized by a moderate amount of moisture **:** neither hydric nor xeric **3** *of a plant or flora* **:** MESOPHYTIC — **mesi·cal·ly** \|zə̇k(ə)lē, |sə̇-\ *adv*

**mes·i·dine** \ˈmezəˌdēn, -esə-, -ˌdə̇n\ *n* -s [ISV *mesityl* + *-idine*] **:** an aromatic amine $(CH_3)_3C_6H_2NH_2$ that is obtained by reduction of nitro-mesitylene and is used as a dye intermediate

**me·si·lla** \məˈsē(y)ə, -ˈzē-\ *n* -s [Sp, dim. of *mesa*] *Southwest* **:** a small mesa

**mesio-** *comb form* [*mesial* + *-o-*] **:** mesial and ⟨*mesio*buccal⟩ ⟨*mesio*labial⟩ ⟨*mesio*occlusal⟩

**mesio·clu·sion** \ˌmezēōˈklüzhən, ˌmē|, |sē-\ *also* **mesio-occlusion** \ˌme|zē(ˌ)ō, ˌmē|, |sē- +\ *n* [*mesio-* + *occlusion* or *occlusion*] **:** malocclusion characterized by mesial displacement of one or more of the lower teeth

**me·si·tes** \məˈsīd·(ˌ)ēz\ [NL, fr. Gk *mesitēs* mediator, fr. *mesos* middle, mid + *-ites* -ite — more at MID] *syn of* MESITORNIS

**mes·i·tite** \ˈmezəˌtīt, -esə-\ *or* **mes·i·tine** \-ˌtēn, -ˌtən\ *also* **mesitine spar** *n* -s [*mesitite* fr. G *mesitit*, fr. earlier *mesitinspath* mesitine spar (fr. Gk *mesitēs* mediator + G *-in* -ine + *spath*, *spat* spar) + *-it* -ite; *mesitine* fr. G *mesitin*, short for *mesitinspath*; *mesitine spar*, trans. of G *mesitinspath*; fr. its being intermediate between magnesite and siderite] **:** ferroan magnesite

**mes·it·or·nis** \ˌ==ˈtȯrnə̇s\ *n*, *cap* [NL, fr. Gk *mesitēs* + NL *-ornis*] **:** a genus that consists of two species (*M. variegata* and *M. unicolor*) of Madagascan birds related to the rails but resembling thrushes and that with the monotypic genus *Monias* forms the family Mesitornithidae

**mes·it·or·nith·i·dae** \-ˌtȯrˈnithəˌdē\ *n pl*, *cap* [NL, fr. *Mesitornith-*, *Mesitornis*, type genus + *-idae*] **:** a small family (coextensive with the suborder Mesitornithides of the order Gruiformes) of Madagascan birds

**mes·i·tyl** \ˈ==ˌtil\ *n* -s [Gk *mesitēs* mediator + E *-yl*] **1 :** a hypothetical radical $C_3H_5$ of which mesityl oxide was once regarded as the oxide and acetone as the hydroxide **2 :** either of two univalent radicals $C_9H_{11}$ derived from mesitylene by removal of one hydrogen atom: **a :** the substituted phenyl radical $(CH_3)_3C_6H_2$— **b :** the substituted benzyl radical $(CH_3)_2C_6H_3CH_2$—; 3,5-dimethyl-benzyl — called also *alpha-mesityl*

**me·sit·y·lene** \məˈsid·ᵊlˌēn\ *n* -s [*mesityl* + *-ene*] **:** an oily hydrocarbon $C_6H_3(CH_3)_3$ occurring in coal tar and petroleum and also made synthetically (as by distilling acetone with sulfuric acid); 1,3,5-trimethylbenzene

**mesityl oxide** *n* **:** a fragrant liquid ketone $(CH_3)_2C{=}CHCOCH_3$ obtained by the dehydration of diacetone alcohol and used as a solvent and an intermediate in organic synthesis

**meslin** \ˈmezlə̇n\ *dial Brit var of* ²MASLIN

**mes·mer·ic** \(ˈ)mezˈmerik, -esˈm-\ *adj* **1 :** of, relating to, or induced by mesmerism **:** that mesmerizes ⟨~ trance —E.A. Poe⟩ ⟨by his strange ~ powers held the listeners in the hollow of his hand —Agnes S. Turnbull⟩ **2 :** FASCINATING, IRRESISTIBLE ⟨a ~, warm charm that emanated from her person —Mary McCarthy⟩ — **mes·mer·i·cal·ly** \-rə̇k(ə)lē\ *adv*

**mes·mer·ism** \ˈmezməˌrizəm, -esm-\ *n* -s [F. A. Mesmer †1815 Austrian physician + E *-ism*] **1 :** hypnotic induction by Mesmer's method believed to involve animal magnetism; *broadly* **:** HYPNOTISM **2 a :** a state induced by hypnotic induction esp. by Mesmer's method **b :** hypnotic appeal **:** intense fascination

**mes·mer·ist** \-ˌrə̇st\ *n* -s **:** one who practices mesmerism

**mes·mer·iza·tion** \ˌ==rə̇ˈzāshən, -ˌrīˈz-\ *n* -s **1 :** the act of mesmerizing **2 :** the state of being mesmerized

**mes·mer·ize** \ˈ==ˌrīz\ *vt* -ED/-ING/-S *see -ize in Explan Notes* [*mesmerism* + *-ize*] **1 :** to hypnotize esp. by Mesmer's method **2 :** SPELLBIND, FASCINATE — usu. used as a past participle ⟨his *mesmerized* immersion in small-town snobbery —C.J.Rolo⟩ ⟨*mesmerized*, the skipper . . . stands at his periscope watching for the success or failure of his approach —E.L.Beach⟩

**mes·mer·iz·er** \-zə(r)\ *n* -s **:** one that mesmerizes **:** HYPNOTIST

**mes·nal·ty** \ˈmēnᵊltē\ *also* **mes·nal·i·ty** \mēˈnaləd·ē\ *n* -ES [*mesnalty* prob. fr. AF *mesnalté* (attested as *mesnatty*, *mesnattie*), fr. *mesne*, n. + *-alté* as in *comunalté* commonalty; *mesnality*, alter. (influenced by *-ity*) of *mesnalty*] **:** the estate or condition of a mesne lord

**¹mesne** \ˈmēn\ *adj* [AF, alter. of MF *meien* occupying a middle position — more at MEAN] *law* **:** MIDDLE, INTERVENING; *specif* **:** intermediate in time of occurrence or performance ⟨~ assignment⟩ ⟨~ encumbrance⟩

**²mesne** \"\ *n* -s **1** *archaic* **:** something that falls between extremes **2** [AF, fr. *mesne*, adj.] **:** MESNE LORD

**mesne lord** *n* [trans. of AF *seignior mesne*, *seignor mesne*] *Eng law* **:** a lord who holds land of a superior and is tenant to the superior but lord to his own tenant

**mesne process** *n* **:** all process issued after the commencement by original writ or any modern substitute therefor and before the termination of a lawsuit by a writ of execution

**meso** \ˈme|(ˌ)zō, ˈmē|, |(ˌ)sō\ *adj* [*mes-*] *of a molecule or compound* **:** optically inactive because internally compensated

**meso-** — see MES-

**meso·american** \ˌme|(ˌ)zō, ˌmē|, |(ˌ)sō +\ *adj*, *usu cap* [*Mesoamerica*, region extending from north central No. America to Nicaragua (fr. Sp *Mesoamérica*, fr. *meso-* mes- + *América* America) + E *-an*] **:** of, relating to, or characteristic of Mesoamerica or of the people of Mesoamerica ⟨general problems of *Mesoamerican* prehistory —*Amer. Antiquity*⟩ ⟨the classic period, which saw the full flowering of *Mesoamerican* civilization in Guatemala, Honduras, El Salvador, and Mexico —A.V. Kidder⟩ — compare CENTRAL AMERICAN, MIDDLE AMERICAN

**meso·appendiceal** \"+\ *adj* [NL *mesoappendic-*, *mesoappendix* + E *-eal* (after *appendiceal*)] **:** of or relating to the mesoappendix

**meso·appendix** \"+\ *n* [NL, fr. *mes-* + *appendix*] **:** the mesentery of the vermiform appendix

**meso·benthos** \"+\ *n* [NL, fr. *mes-* + *benthos*] **:** the fauna and flora of the sea bottom between 100 and 500 fathoms

**meso·biotic** \"+\ *adj* [*mes-* + *-biotic*] *of a seed* **:** surviving in the dormant state for a relatively long period usu. between 3 and 15 years — compare MACROBIOTIC, MICROBIOTIC

**meso·blast** \ˈme|zō, ˈmē|, |sō + ,-\ *n* [*mes-* + *-blast*] **:** the middle germ layer of an embryo; *also* **:** the undifferentiated presumptive mesoderm that makes up this layer

**meso·blastema** \ˌ==+\ *n* -s [NL, fr. *mes-* + *blastema*] **:** MESOBLAST — **meso·blastemic** \"+\ *adj*

**meso·blas·tic** \ˌ=ˈ=blastik\ *adj* [*mesoblast* + *-ic*] **:** relating to, derived from, or made up of mesoblast

**meso·car·dia** \ˌme|zōˈkärdēə, ˌmē|, |sō-\ *n* -s [NL, fr. *mes-* + *-cardia*] **:** abnormal location of the heart in the central part of the thorax

**meso·car·di·um** \-dēəm\ *n* -s [NL, fr. *mes-* + *-cardium*] **1 :** the transitory mesentery of the embryonic heart **2 :** the portion of the epicardium enclosing the blood vessels that join the heart

**meso·carp** \ˈ==ˌkärp\ *n* -s [*mes-* + *-carp*] **:** the middle layer of a pericarp — compare ENDOCARP

**meso·cecum** \ˌme|zō, ˌmē|, |sō +\ *n* [NL, fr. *mes-* + *cecum*] **:** the fold of peritoneum attached to the cecum

**meso·cen·trous** \"+ ˈsen·trəs\ *adj* [*mes-* + *centr-* + *-ous*] **:** having a median center of ossification

**meso·ceph·al** \ˌ=ˈ=sefəl\ *n* -s [NL *mesocephalus*, fr. *mes-* + *-cephalus*] **:** a mesaticephalic person

**meso·ce·phal·ic** \ˌ==səˈfalik\ *adj* [*mes-* + *-cephalic*] **1 :** MESATICEPHALIC **2** [F *mésocéphalique*, fr. *mésocéphale* mesencephalon (fr. *méso-* mes- + Gk *kephalē* head) + *-ique* -ic — more at CEPHALIC] **:** MESENCEPHALIC

**meso·ceph·a·ly** \ˌ==ˈsefəlē\ *n* -ES [ISV *mesocephalic* + *-y*] **:** the quality or state of being mesocephalic

**meso·ces·toi·des** \ˌ==seˈstȯi(ˌ)dēz\ *n*, *cap* [NL, fr. *mes-* + L *cestus* girdle + *-oides* -oid — more at CESTUS] **:** a genus (the type of the family Mesocestoididae) of atypical unarmed cyclophyllidean tapeworms having the adults parasitic in mammals and birds and a slender threadlike contractile larva free in cavities or encysted in tissues of mammals, birds, and sometimes reptiles

**meso·chon·dri·um** \ˌme|zōˈkändrēəm, ˌmē|, |sō-\ *n*, *pl* **meso·chon·dria** \-ēə\ [NL, fr. *mes-* + *chondr-* + *-ium*] **:** the matrix of cartilage

**meso·chro·ic** \ˌ==ˈkrōik\ *adj* [*mes-* + *-chroic*] **:** having a complexion intermediate between light and dark

**mesocne·mic** \ˌme|zōˈnēmik, ˌmē|, |sōˈn-, |ˌzäkˈn-, |ˌsäkˈn-\ *adj* [*mes-* + *-cnemic*] *of a shinbone* **:** rounded with a platycnemic index of 63 to 70

**meso·coele** *also* **meso·coel** *or* **meso·cele** \ˈme|zōˌsēl, ˈmē|, |sō-\ *or* **meso·coe·lia** \ˌ==ˈsēlēə\ *n* -s [*mesocoele* or *mesocele* fr. *mes-* + *-coele*; *mesocoel*, alter. of *mesocoele*; *mesocoelia*, NL, fr. *mes-* + *coelia*] **:** the ventricle of the mesencephalon — **meso·coe·li·an** \ˌ==ˈsēlēən\ *adj* — **meso·coe·lic** \-lik\ *adj*

**meso·colon** \ˌ==+\ *n* [NL, fr. Gk *mesokōlon*, fr. *meso-* mes- + *kōlon* colon — more at COLON (intestine)] **:** a mesentery joining the colon to the dorsal abdominal wall

**meso·conch** \ˈ==+,-\ *also* **meso·chonchic** \ˌ==+\ *adj* [*mesoconch* fr. *mes-* + *-conch* (fr. L *concha* conch, shell); *mesoconchic* fr. *mesoconch* + *-ic* — more at CONCH] **:** having the orbits moderately rounded with an orbital index of 83 to 89 — **meso·con·chy** \ˈ==ˌkäŋkē\ *n*

**¹meso·coracoid** \ˌ==+\ *adj* [*mes-* + *coracoid*, adj.] **:** of or relating to a median element of the coracoid arch in some teleost fishes

**²mesocoracoid** \"\ *n* [*mes-* + *coracoid*, n.] **:** a mesocoracoid bone

**meso·cot·yl** \ˈme|zō,käd·ᵊl, ˈmē|, |sō-\ *n* [*mes-* + *-cotyl*] **:** an elongated portion of the axis between the cotyledon and the coleoptile of a grass seedling

**me·soc·ra·cy** \məˈzäkrəsē, -ˈsä-\ *n* -ES [*mes-* + *-cracy*] **:** government by the middle classes

**meso·cranial** \ˌme|zō, ˌmē|, |sō+\ *adj* [prob. fr. G *mesokran* mesocranial (fr. *meso-* mes- + Gk *kranion* cranium) + E *-ial* — more at CRANIUM] **:** having a skull of medium proportions with a cranial index of 75–80

**meso·cra·ny** \ˈ==ˌkrānē\ *n* -ES [ISV *mesocranial* + *-y*] **:** the quality or state of being mesocranial

**meso·crat·ic** \ˌ==ˈkrad·ik\ *adj* [*mes-* + *-cratic* (as in *leucocratic*)] *of igneous rock* **:** having nearly equal dark and light mineral constituents ⟨a ~ diorite⟩ — compare LEUCOCRATIC, MELANOCRATIC

**mesode** \ˈme|ˌzōd, ˈmē|, |ˌsōd\ *n* [Gk *mesōidos*, fr. *mes-* + *ōidē* song — more at ODE] *in the Greek choral dance* **:** a portion of a choral ode between a strophe and its antistrophe — **mes·od·ic** \məˈzädik, -ˈsä-\ *adj*

**meso·derm** \ˈme|zəˌdərm, ˈmē|, |sə-\ *n* [ISV *mes-* + *-derm*] **:** the middle of the three primary germ layers of an embryo being the source of bone, muscle, connective tissue, inner layer of the skin, and other adult structures **:** MESOBLAST; *broadly* **:** tissue wherever located that is derived from this germ layer — **meso·der·mal** \ˌ==ˈdərməl\ *or* **meso·der·mic** \-mik\ *adj*

**meso·des·ma** \ˌme|zōˈdezmə, ˌmē|, |sō-\ *n*, *cap* [NL, fr. *mes-* + Gk *desma* band, bond — more at DESMA] **:** a genus of marine bivalves (suborder Tellinacea) living mostly in the sand in shallow water

**meso·dont** \ˈ==ˌdänt\ *adj* [*mes-* + *-odont*] **:** having medium-sized teeth — **meso·don·ty** \-tē\ *n* -ES

**meso·duodenum** \ˌ==+\ *n* [NL, fr. *mes-* + E *duodenum*] **:** the mesentery of the duodenum usu. not persisting in adult life in man and other mammals in which the developing intestine undergoes a counterclockwise rotation

**me·soe·nas** \məˈzēnəs, -ˈsē-\ [NL, fr. *mes-* + Gk *oinas* wild pigeon] *syn of* MESITORNIS

**mes·oe·nat·i·dae** \ˌmezəˈnad·əˌdē, -esə-\ [NL, fr. *Mesoenat-*, *Mesoenas*, type genus + *-idae*] *syn of* MESITORNITHIDAE

**meso-esophagus** \ˌme|zō, ˌmē|, |sō+\ *n* [NL, fr. *mes-* + E *esophagus*] **:** the transitory mesentery of the embryonic esophagus that is later modified into the mediastinum

**meso·fauna** \"+\ *n* [NL, fr. *mes-* + *fauna*] **:** animals of intermediate size ranging from those barely visible with a hand lens to forms (as worms, mollusks, and arthropods) that are several centimeters in length — compare MACROFAUNA, MICROFAUNA

**meso·furca** \"+\ *n*, *pl* **mesofurcae** [NL, fr. *mes-* + *furca*] **:** the middle apodeme of the thorax of an insect projecting upward from the sternum into the body cavity — **meso·furcal** \"+\ *adj*

**meso·gaster** \ˈ==+,-\ *n* [NL, fr. *mes-* + *-gaster*] **:** MESOGASTRIUM

**meso·gastric** \ˌ==+\ *adj* [NL *mesogastrium* + E *-ic*] **1 :** of or relating to the mesogastrium **2 :** of or relating to the middle gastric lobe of a crab's carapace

**meso·gas·tri·um** \ˌ==ˈgastrēəm\ *n, pl* **mesogas·tria** \-ēə\ [NL, fr. *mes-* + *gastr-* + *-ium*] **1** : a ventral mesentery of the embryonic stomach that persists as the falciform ligament and the lesser omentum **2** : a dorsal mesentery of the embryonic stomach that gives rise to ligaments between the stomach and spleen and the spleen and kidney

**meso·gastropoda** \ˌme\|zō, ˌmē\|, \|sō+\ [NL, fr. *mes-* + *Gastropoda*] *syn of* TAENIOGLOSSA

**meso·glea** *or* **meso·gloea** \"+\ *n* [NL, fr. *mes-* + LGk *gloia* glue — more at GLOEA] : a gelatinous substance between the endoderm and ectoderm of sponges or coelenterates — **meso·gloeal** \"+\ *adj*

**meso·gnathion** \"+\ *n* [NL, fr. *mes-* + *gnathion*] : the lateral part of the premaxilla bearing the lateral incisor tooth on each side

**me·sog·na·thous** \məˈzägnəthəs, meˈ-,mēˈ-, -ˈsä-\ *also* **me·sognath·ic** \ˌme\|za(g)ˈnathik, ˌmē\|, \|sə-\ *adj* **1** [*mes-* + *-gnathous* or *gnathic*] : having the jaws of medium size and slightly projecting with a gnathic index of 98 to 103 **2** [NL *mesognathion* + E *-ous* or *-ic*] : of or relating to the mesognathion

**me·sog·na·thy** \məˈzägnəthē, meˈ-,mēˈ-, -ˈsä-\ *n* -ES [ISV *mesognathous* + *-y*] : the state of being mesognathous : mesognathous character

**meso·gyrate** \ˌme\|zō, ˌmē\|, \|sō+\ *adj* [*mes-* + *gyrate*] : curving toward the center — used esp. of the umbones of a bivalve; compare PROSOGYRATE

**meso·hippus** \"+\ *n, cap* [NL, fr. *mes-* + *-hippus*] : a genus of No. American Oligocene 3-toed horses probably not on the direct ancestral line of the modern horses — see EQUIDAE illustration

**meso·kur·tic** \ˌ==ˈkərd·ik\ *adj* [*mes-* + Gk *kyrtos* bulging, convex, curved + E *-ic*; akin to L *curvus* bent, curved — more at CROWN] : closely resembling a normal frequency distribution : neither leptokurtic nor platykurtic

**meso·lecithal** \ˌme\|zō, ˌmē\|, \|sō+\ *adj* [*mes-* + *-lecithal* (as in *centrolecithal*)] : CENTROLECITHAL

**meso·lim·net·ic** \ˌ==ˌlimˈned·ik\ *adj* [NL *mesolimnion* + E *-etic*] : of or relating to a thermocline

**meso·lim·ni·on** \-ˈlimnēˌän, -ēən\ *n, pl* **mesolim·nia** \-ēə\ [NL, fr. *mes-* + *-limnion*] : THERMOCLINE

**meso·lite** \ˈ==ˌlīt\ *n* -S [G *mesolith*, fr. *meso-* mes- + *-lith*] : a zeolitic mineral $Na_2Ca_2Al_6Si_9O_{30}.8H_2O$ consisting of hydrous aluminosilicate of sodium and calcium

**meso·lith·ic** \ˌ==ˈlithik\ *adj, usu cap* [ISV *meso-* mes- + *-lithic*] : of or relating to a transitional period of the Stone Age between the Paleolithic and the Neolithic characterized by the appearance of the dog as the first domestic animal, of the bow and arrow, and of pottery and represented by several cultures of Europe — see ASTURIAN, AZILIAN, CAMPIGNIAN, ERTEBOLLE, MAGLEMOSIAN, TARDENOISIAN

**mesome** \ˈme\|ˌzōm, ˈmē\|, \|ˌsōm\ *n* -S [*mes-* + *telome*] : an internode between two forkings that was orig. a telome but was relegated to an internodal position by the growth of a new telome

**meso·mere** \ˈme\|zō,mi(ə)r, ˈmē\|, \|sō-\ *n* -S [*mes-* + *-mere*] **1** : a primitive segment : a mesoblastic somite **2** : a blastomere of medium size

**meso·mer·ic** \ˌ==ˈmerik, -mir-\ *adj* [*mesomerism* + *-ic*] : of or relating to the resonance of a molecule, ion, or radical

**me·som·er·ism** \məˈzäməˌrizəm, -ˈsä-\ *n* [*mes-* + *-merism*] : RESONANCE 5

**meso·me·tri·al** \ˌme\|zōˈmē·trēəl, \|sō-\ *or* **meso·me·tric** \-rik\ *adj* [*mesometrial* fr. NL *mesometrium* + E *-al*; *mesometric* fr. NL *mesometrium* + E *-ic*] : of or relating to the mesometrium

**meso·me·tri·al·ly** \-rēəlē\ *adv* : oriented or facing away from the mesometrium

**meso·me·tri·um** \ˌ==ˈ=trēəm\ *n, pl* **mesome·tria** \-ēə\ [NL, fr. *mes-* + Gk *mētra* womb + NL *-ium* — more at METRA] : a mesentery supporting the oviduct or uterus

**meso·mitosis** \ˌme\|zō, ˌmē\|, \|sō+\ *n* [NL, fr. *mes-* + *mitosis*] : nuclear division of essentially mitotic character that takes place within the intact nuclear membrane (as in various protozoa) — compare METAMITOSIS, PROMITOSIS

**meso·morph** \ˈ==ˌmȯrf\ *n* -S [*mes-* + *-morph*] **1 a** : an intermediate or average type of human body — distinguished from *hypomorph* and *hypermorph* **b** : a mesomorphic body or person — see MESOMORPHIC 2 **2** : a plant having typically mesomorphic morphology; *esp* : MESOPHYTE

**meso·mor·phic** \ˌ==ˈmȯrfik\ *adj* **1** *also* **meso·mor·phous** \-fəs\ [*mesomorphic* fr. *mes-* + *-morphic*; *mesomorphous* fr. *mesomorphic* + *-ous*] : relating to, existing in, or being an intermediate state (as of a semicrystalline condition characteristic of liquid crystals) — see NEMATIC, SMECTIC **2** [*mesomorph* + *-ic*] : characterized by predominance of the structures (as bone, muscle, and connective tissue) developed from the mesodermal layer of the embryo : of the muscular or athletic type of body-build — compare ECTOMORPHIC, ENDOMORPHIC **3** [*mesomorph* + *-ic*] : typical of a mesomorph ⟨~ leaves⟩

**meso·mor·phism** \ˌ==ˈ=ˌfizəm\ *n* -S [*mesomorphic* + *-ism*] : the quality or state of being mesomorphic

**meso·mor·phy** \ˈ==ˌ=fē\ *n* -ES [*mes-* + *-morphy*] **1** : mesomorphic build or type **2** : mesomorphic quality (as of a plant)

**meso·my·o·di** \ˌme\|zō,mīˈō,dī, ˌmē\|, \|sō-\ *n pl, cap* [NL, fr. *mes-* + *-myodi* (fr. Gk *myōdēs* muscular, fr. *mys* mouse, muscle) — more at MOUSE] *in some classifications* : a group of passerine birds nearly equivalent to Clamatores having the syringeal muscles attached to the middle of the bronchial half rings — compare ACROMYODI — **meso·my·o·di·an** \ˌ==ˌ=ˈōdēən\ *adj or n* — **meso·my·o·dous** \-dəs\ *adj*

**meson** \ˈme\|ˌzän, ˈmē\|, ˈmā\|, ˌzᵊn, \|ˌsän, \|ˌsᵊn\ *n* -S [ISV *mes-* + *-on*] : an unstable nuclear particle that was first observed in cosmic rays, that has a mass typically between that of the electron and the proton, that is either positively or negatively charged or neutral, and that occurs in more than one variety — called also *mesotron*; see MU-MESON, PI-MESON — **me·son·ic** \(ˈ)me\|ˈzänik, (ˈ)mē\|, (ˈ)mā\|, \|ˈsä-\ *adj*

**meso·nemertini** \ˌme\|(ˌ)zō, ˌmē\|, \|(ˌ)sō+\ *n pl, cap* [NL, fr. *mes-* + *Nemertini*] *in some classifications* : an order of nemertea comprising the members of Palaeonemertea that have the mouth far behind the anterior end of the body

**meso·neph·ric** \ˌme\|zōˈnefrik, ˌmē\|, \|sō-\ *adj* [*mes-* + *nephr-* + *-ic*] : of or relating to the mesonephros

**mesonephric duct** *n* : the efferent duct of the embryonic mesonephros persisting as a functional ureter in females and as a urinogenital duct in males of lower vertebrates in which the mesonephros is the definitive kidney and as the genital duct in males of higher forms — called also *wolffian duct*

**meso·nephridium** \ˌme\|(ˌ)zō, ˌmē\|, \|(ˌ)sō+\ *n* [NL, fr. *mes-* + *nephridium*] : a nephridium of mesodermal origin

**meso·nephros** *also* **meso·nephron** \ˌme\|zō, ˌmē\|, \|sō+\ *n, pl* **mesonephroi** *also* **mesonephra** [NL, fr. *mes-* + *-nephros*] : one of the middle of the three pairs of embryonic renal organs of vertebrates persisting as the definitive kidney in fishes and amphibians — called also *wolffian body*; compare METANEPHROS

**meso·notal** \"+\ *adj* [NL *mesonotum* + E *-al*] : of or relating to the mesonotum

**meso·notum** \"+\ *n* [NL, fr. *mes-* + Gk *nōton* back — more at NATES] : the dorsal portion of the mesothoracic integument of insects

**mes·onych·i·dae** \ˌme\|zōˈnikəˌdē, ˌmē\|, \|sō-\ *n pl, cap* [NL, fr. *Mesonych-, Mesonyx*, type genus + *-idae*] : a family of extinct creodont carnivorous mammals from the Paleocene and Eocene of No. America and Europe

**mes·onyx** \ˈ==ˌniks\ *n, cap* [NL, fr. *mes-* + *-onyx*] : a genus (the type of the family Mesonychidae) of extinct creodont carnivorous mammals

**meso·ontomorph** \ˌme\|zōˈäntəˌmȯrf, ˌmē\|, \|sō-\ *n* [*mes-* + *onto-* + *-morph*] : a body type characterized by a thickset robust powerful build; *also* : an individual of this type — opposed to *hyperontomorph*

**meso·pause** \ˈme\|zə,pȯz, ˈmē\|, \|sə-\ *n* [*mes-* + *pause*] : the transition zone between the mesosphere and the exosphere

**meso·perrhenic acid** \ˌ==+...-\ *n* [*mes-* + *perrhenic*] : PERRHENIC ACID b

**meso·phase** \ˈ==ˌfāz\ *n* [*mes-* + *phase*] : a mesomorphic phase

**meso·phile** \-ˌfīl\ *also* **meso·phil** \-ˌfil\ *n* -S [prob. fr. *mesophile*, adj.] : an organism growing at a moderate temperature (as bacteria that grow best at about the temperature of the human body) — compare PSYCHROPHILE, THERMOPHILE

**meso·phil·ic** \ˌ==ˈfilik\ *also* **meso·phile** \ˈ==ˌfīl\ *or* **me·soph·i·lous** \məˈzäfələs, (ˈ)meˈ\|, (ˈ)mē\|, \|sä-\ *adj* [prob. fr. G *mesophil* mesophilic (fr. *meso-* mes- + *-phil* -phile) + E *-ic* or *-ous*] : growing or thriving best in an intermediate environment (as in one of moderate temperature)

**meso·phragma** \ˌme\|zō, ˌmē\|, \|sō+\ *n* [NL, fr. *mes-* + *phragma*] **1** : a phragma of the mesothorax in various insects **2** : a process of the endosternite forming an arch over the sternal canal in some crustaceans — **meso·phragmal** \"+\ *adj*

**me·soph·ry·on** \məˈzäfrēən, -ˈsä-, -ēˌän\ *n, pl* **mesoph·rya** \-ēə\ [Gk, fr. *mes-* + *ophrys* eyebrow — more at BROW] : GLABELLA 1

**meso·phyll** \ˈme\|zō,fil, ˈmē\|, \|sō-\ *n* -S [NL *mesophyllum*] : the parenchyma between epidermal layers of a foliage leaf — **meso·phyl·lic** \ˌ==ˈfilik\ *or* **meso·phyl·lous** \-ləs\ *adj*

**meso·phyllum** \ˌme\|zō, ˌmē\|, \|sō+\ *n* [NL, fr. *mes-* + *-phyllum*] : MESOPHYLL

**meso·phyte** \ˈ==ˌfīt\ *n* -S [ISV *mes-* + *-phyte*] : a plant that grows under medium conditions of moisture — compare HYDROPHYTE, XEROPHYTE

**meso·phyt·ic** \ˌ==ˈfid·ik\ *adj* [ISV *mesophyte* + *-ic*] **1** *of a plant* : growing in or adapted to moderately moist environment **2** *of a habitat* : moderately moist

**me·sop·ic** \(ˈ)meˈz\|äpik, (ˈ)mē\|-, -\|s\|, \|ōp-\ *adj* [*mes-* + Gk *ōp-*, *ōps* face, eye + E *-ic* — more at EYE] : having a face on which the root of the nose and central line of the face project moderately

**meso·plankton** \ˌme\|zō, ˌmē\|, \|sō+\ *n* [ISV *mes-* + *plankton*] **1** : the plankton of middle depths below the penetration of photosynthetically effective light **2** : NET PLANKTON — **meso·planktonic** \"+\ *adj*

**meso·plas·tral** \ˌ==ˈplastrəl\ *adj* [*mesoplastron* + *-al*] : of or relating to a mesoplastron

**meso·plastron** \"+\ *n* [*mes-* + *plastron*] : one of a pair of bones in the plastron of various pleurodiran turtles situated one on each side between the hyoplastron and hypoplastron

**meso·pleural** \"+\ *adj* [NL *mesopleuron* + E *-al*] : of or relating to a mesopleuron

**meso·pleuron** \"+\ *n* [NL, fr. *mes-* + *pleuron*] : a pleuron of the mesothorax of an insect

**me·sop·lo·don** \məˈzäpləˌdän\ *n, cap* [NL, fr. *mes-* + Gk *hoplon* weapon + NL *-odon* — more at HOPLITE] : a genus of nearly cosmopolitan small-toothed whales — **me·sop·lo·dont** \-nt\ *adj*

**meso·po·di·al** \ˌme\|zəˈpōdēəl, ˌmē\|, \|sə-\ *adj* [NL *mesopodium* + E *-al*] : of or relating to the mesopodium

**meso·po·di·um** \-dēəm\ *n* [NL, fr. *mes-* + *podium*] : the middle portion of the foot of a mollusk — compare PROPODIUM

**mes·o·po·ta·mia** \ˌmesəpəˈtāmēə, -āmyə\ *n* -S [Gk, fr. fem. of *mesopotamios* between rivers, fr. *meso-* mes- + *potamos* river; akin to Gk *piptein* to fall — more at FEATHER] : a region between rivers

**[1]mes·o·po·ta·mian** \ˌ===ˈtāmēən, -myən\ *adj* **1** *usu cap* [*Mesopotamia*, region in southwest Asia between the Tigris and Euphrates rivers (fr. Gk) + E *-an*] : of, relating to, or characteristic of Mesopotamia ⟨*Mesopotamian* architecture⟩ — compare IRAQI **2** [Gk *mesopotamia* + E *-an*] : of, relating to, or characteristic of a mesopotamia

**[2]mesopotamian** \"\ *n* -S *cap* : a native or inhabitant of Mesopotamia — compare IRAQI

**meso·prescutum** \ˌme\|zō, ˌmē\|, \|sō+\ *n* [NL, fr. *mes-* + *prescutum*] : the prescutum of the mesothorax of an insect

**meso·pro·sopic** \ˌ==prəˈsōpik, -säp-\ *adj* [ISV *mes-* + *prosop-* + *-ic*] : having a face of average width with a facial index of 84 to 88 on the living or 85 to 90 on the skull — **meso·proso·py** \ˌ==ˈpräsəpē, -prəˈsōpē\ *n* -ES

**mesop·te·ryg·i·um** \ˌme\|zäptəˈrijēəm, ˌmē\|, \|sä-\ *n* [NL, fr. *mes-* + Gk *pterygion* fin, lit., small wing — more at PTERYGIUM] : the middle one of the three principal basal cartilages in the pectoral fins of various fishes (as the sharks and rays) — compare BASIPTERYGIUM

**[1]meso·pterygoid** \ˌme\|(ˌ)zō, ˌmē\|, \|(ˌ)sō+\ *adj* [*mes-* + *pterygoid*, adj.] : oriented with respect to the pterygoids; *specif* : being or relating to a part or a process of the pterygoid bone of a bird, to a distinct pterygoid element of a bony fish articulating in front with the palatine, behind with the metapterygoid, and laterally with the pterygoid, or to the space in a mammal between the pterygoids of opposite sides

**[2]mesopterygoid** \"\ *n* [*mes-* + *pterygoid*, n.] : a mesopterygoid part (as a bone)

**mesop·tile** \(ˈ)meˈzäptəl, (ˈ)mē\|, \|ˈsä-\ *n* -S [*mes-* + *-ptile*] : one of the second set of down feathers in a bird having two sets

**me·sor·chi·um** \məˈzȯ(r)kēəm, -ˈsȯ-\ *n, pl* **mesor·chia** \-ēə\ [NL, fr. *mes-* + *orchi-* + *-ium*] : the fold of peritoneum that attaches the testis to the dorsal wall in the fetus

**meso·rectum** \ˌme\|zō, ˌmē\|, \|sō+\ *n* [NL, fr. *mes-* + *rectum*] : the mesentery that supports the rectum

**mes·oreodon** \(ˌ)me\|z, (ˌ)mē\|, \|s+\ *n, cap* [NL, fr. *mes-* + *Oreodon*] : a genus of extinct artiodactyls (family Merycoidodontidae) from the Miocene of No. America

**mesor·rhinal** *or* **meso·rhinal** \ˌme\|zō, ˌmē\|, \|sō+\ *adj* **1** [NL *mesorrhinium*, *mesorhinium* + E *-al*] : of or relating to the mesorrhinium **2** [*mes-* + *rhinal*] : situated between the nostrils

**[1]mesor·rhine** \ˈ==ˌrīn\ *also* **mesor·rhin·ic** \ˌ==ˈrinik\ *or* **mesorhine** *adj* [*mesorrhine* or *mesorhine* fr. *mes-* + *-rrhine* or *-rhine*; *mesorrhinic* fr. *mesorrhine* + *-ic*] : having a nose of moderate size with a nasal index of 47 to 51 on the skull or of 70 to 85 on the living — **mesor·rhi·ny** \ˈ==ˌrīnē\ *n*

**[2]mesorrhine** *also* **mesorhine** \"\ *n* -S : a mesorrhine individual

**mesor·rhin·i·um** *or* **meso·rhin·i·um** \ˌ==ˈrinēəm\ *n, pl* **mesorrhin·ia** *or* **mesorhin·ia** \-ēə\ [NL, fr. *mes-* + *rhin-* + *-ium*] : the part of the base of the upper mandible of a bird that lies between the nostrils

**meso·salpinx** \ˌme\|zō, ˌmē\|, \|sō+\ *n* [NL, fr. *mes-* + *salpinx*] : a fold of the broad ligament investing and supporting the fallopian tube

**meso·saprobe** \"+\ *n* -S [ISV *mes-* + *saprobe*; prob. orig. formed as G *mesosaprobie*] : a mesosaprobic organism

**meso·saprobic** \"+\ *adj* [ISV *mes-* + *saprobic*; prob. orig. formed as G *mesosaprobisch*] : living in or being a moderately oxygenated environment in which considerable organic material and bacteria are present — compare KATHAROBIC, OLIGOSAPROBIC, SAPROBIC

**meso·saur** \ˈme\|zō,sȯ(ə)r, ˈmē\|, \|sō-\ *n* -S [NL *Mesosaurus*] : an extinct aquatic reptile of the genus *Mesosaurus*

**meso·sau·ria** \ˌ==ˈsȯrēə\ *n pl, cap* [NL, fr. *mes-* + *-sauria*] : an order of primitive aquatic and probably web-footed reptiles from the Permian of So. America and Africa that are distinguished by an elongate head with the nostrils near the eyes and are sometimes included in Pelycosauria as a suborder

**meso·sau·rus** \-rəs\ *n, cap* [NL, fr. *mes-* + *-saurus*] : a genus of small aquatic presumably fish-eating Permian reptiles of So. America and southern Africa

**meso·scapula** \ˌme\|zō, ˌmē\|, \|sō+\ *n* [NL, fr. *mes-* + *scapula*] : the spine of the scapula regarded as a distinct element — **meso·scapular** \"+\ *adj*

**meso·scutal** \"+\ *adj* [NL *mesoscutum* + E *-al*] : of or relating to the mesoscutum

**meso·scutellar** \"+\ *adj* [NL *mesoscutellum* + E *-ar*] : of or relating to the mesoscutellum

**meso·scutellum** \"+\ *n* [NL, fr. *mes-* + *scutellum*] : the scutellum of the mesothorax of insects

**meso·scutum** \"+\ *n* [NL, fr. *mes-* + *scutum*] : the scutum of the mesothorax of an insect

**meso·seismal** \"+\ *adj* [*mes-* + *seismal*] : of or relating to the center of an area of earthquake disturbance

**meso·seme** \ˈme\|zō,sēm, ˈmē\|, \|sō-\ *adj* [F *mésosème*, fr. *méso-* mes- + Gk *sēma* sign, mark — more at SEMANTICS] : MESOCONCH

**meso·sere** \-ˌsi(ə)r\ *n* [*mes-* + *sere*] : an ecological sere originating in a mesic habitat or initiated by mesophytes

**meso·sigmoid** \ˌme\|zō, ˌmē\|, \|sō+\ *n* [*mes-* + *sigmoid*] : the mesentery of the sigmoid part of the descending colon

**meso·soma** \"+\ *n, pl* **mesosomata** [NL, fr. *mes-* + *-soma*] : the middle region of the body of various invertebrates esp. when this cannot readily be analyzed into its primitive segmentation (as in most mollusks and in arachnids) — **meso·somatic** \"+\ *adj*

**meso·some** \ˈ==+ˌsōm\ *n* -S **1** [NL *mesosoma*] : MESOSOMA **2** [*mes-* + *-some* (body)] : the intromittent organ of a dipterous insect : AEDEAGUS

**meso·so·mic** \ˌ==+ˈsōmik\ *adj* [in sense 1, fr. NL *mesosoma* + E *-ic*; in sense 2, fr. *mesosome* + *-ic*; in sense 3, fr. *mes-* + *-somic* (as in *leptosomic*)] **1** : of or relating to the mesosoma **2** : of or relating to a mesosome **3** : having intermediate or average body-build

**meso·sphere** \ˈme\|zō, ˈmē\|, \|sō+,-\ *n* [*mes-* + *-sphere*] : a layer of the atmosphere extending from the top of the stratosphere to an altitude of about 50 miles — **mesospheric** *adj*

**meso·spore** \"+,-\ *also* **meso·spo·ri·um** \ˌ==ˈspōrēəm\ *n, pl* **mesospores** \-z\ *or* **mesospo·ria** \-ōrēə\ [*mesospore* fr. *mes-* + *-spore*; *mesosporium* fr. NL, fr. *mes-* + *-sporium*] **1** : the middle coat of a spore that has three coats **2** : a one-celled spore found among the compound teliospores of some rusts (as members of the genus *Puccinia*)

**meso·staph·y·line** \ˌme\|zōˈstafəˌlīn, ˌmē\|, \|sō-\ *adj* [*mes-* + Gk *staphylē* uvula + E *-ine* — more at STAPHYL-] : having a palate of moderate size with a palatal index of 80 to 85 — **meso·staph·y·li·ny** \-nē\ *n* -ES

**meso·sternum** \ˌme\|zō, ˌmē\|, \|sō+\ *n, pl* **mesosterna** [NL, fr. *mes-* + *sternum*] **1** : GLADIOLUS 3 **2** : the ventral piece of the mesothorax in insects

**me·sos·to·ma** \məˈzästəmə, -ˈsä-\ *n, cap* [NL, fr. *mes-* + *-stoma*] : a cosmopolitan genus of large transparent freshwater rhabdocoelous turbellarians — **me·sos·to·mid** \-məd\ *n* -S

**meso·style** \ˈme\|zō, ˈmē\|, \|sō+,-\ *n* [*mes-* + *style* (cusp)] : the small cusp between the metacone and paracone of a molar

**meso·sty·lous** \ˌ==ˈstīləs\ *adj* [*mes-* + *-stylous*] *of a flower* : having styles of intermediate length — compare MACROSTYLOUS, MICROSTYLOUS

**meso·su·chia** \ˌ==ˈsükēə\ *n pl, cap* [NL, fr. *mes-* + Gk *souchos* crocodile + NL *-ia*] *in some classifications* : a suborder of Loricata comprising variable and more or less archaic reptiles of the Jurassic and Lower Cretaceous — **meso·su·chi·an** \ˌ==ˈkēən\ *adj or n*

**meso·tae·ni·a·ce·ae** \ˌ==ˌtēnēˈāsēˌē\ *n pl, cap* [NL, fr. *Mesotaenium*, type genus (fr. *mes-* + *-taenium* — fr. L *taenia* ribbon, band, fillet) + *-aceae* — more at TAENIA] : a family of unicellular or colonial green algae (order Zygnematales) comprising the saccoderm desmids and differing from the Desmidiaceae in having the cell wall in a single piece and without pores — see DESMIDIALES

**meso·tarsal** \ˌme\|zō, ˌmē\|, \|sō+\ *adj* [*mes-* + *tarsal*] : of or relating to the median plane of the tarsus

**meso·the·lae** \ˌ==ˈthē(ˌ)lē\ [NL, fr. *mes-* + Gk *thēlē* nipple — more at FEMININE] *syn of* LIPHISTIOMORPHAE

**meso·the·li·al** \ˌ==ˈthēlēəl\ *adj* [NL *mesothelium* + E *-al*] : of or relating to mesothelium

**meso·the·li·o·ma** \ˌ==ˌthēlēˈōmə\ *n, pl* **mesothe·liomas** \-məz\ *or* **mesothelioma·ta** \-məd·ə\ [NL, fr. *mesothelium* + *-oma*] : a tumor derived from mesothelial tissue (as that lining the peritoneum or pleura)

**meso·the·li·um** \-ˈthēlēəm\ *n, pl* **mesothe·lia** \-lēə\ [NL, fr. *mes-* + *epithelium*] : epithelium that is derived from mesoderm, that in vertebrate embryos lines the primordial body cavity, and that gives rise to the epithelium of the peritoneum, pericardium, and pleurae, the striated muscles, the heart muscle, the epithelium of the urogenital organs except the bladder and urethra, and several minor structures

**meso·therm** \ˈ==ˌthərm\ *n* -S [ISV *mes-* + *-therm*; prob. orig. formed as F *mésotherme*] : a plant that requires a moderate degree of heat for successful growth — compare MEGATHERM, MICROTHERM

**meso·ther·mal** \ˌ==ˈthərməl\ *adj* **1** [*mes-* + *thermal*] : deposited from warm waters at intermediate depth under conditions in the medium ranges of temperature and pressure — used of mineral veins and ore deposits; compare EPITHERMAL, HYPOTHERMAL **2** [*mesotherm* + *-al*] : of, relating to, or living as a mesotherm

**me·soth·e·sis** \məˈzäthəsəs, -ˈsä-\ *n, pl* **mesothe·ses** \-thəˌsēz\ [NL, fr. *mes-* + Gk *thesis* setting, position — more at THESIS] : a mediating agency or principle

**meso·thet·ic** \ˌme\|zōˈthed·ik, ˌmē\|, \|sə-\ *adj* [*mes-* + Gk *thetikos* of placing, fr. *thetos* (verbal of *tithenai* to place) + *-ikos* -ic — more at DO] : being in a middle position : INTERMEDIATE

**meso·thoracic** \ˌ==+\ *adj* [NL *mesothorac-*, *mesothorax* + E *-ic*] : of or relating to the mesothorax

**meso·thorax** \ˌ==+\ *n* [NL, fr. *mes-* + *thorax*] : the middle of the three segments of the thorax of an insect — see INSECT illustration

**meso·thorium** \ˌme\|zō, ˌmē\|, \|sō+\ *n* [NL, fr. *mes-* + *thorium*] : either of two radioactive products intermediate between thorium and radiothorium in the thorium series or a mixture of the two products obtained usu. from thorium minerals (as monazite sand) and used as a substitute for radium esp. in luminous paints: **a** : an isotope of radium — called also *mesothorium 1*; symbol $MsTh_1$ or $Ra^{228}$ **b** : an isotope of actinium — called also *mesothorium 2*; symbol $MsTh_2$ or $Ac^{228}$

**meso·tonic system** \"+ . . . -\ *n* [*mes-* + *tonic*] : MEANTONE SYSTEM

**meso·troch** \ˈme\|zəˌträk, ˈmē\|, \|sə-\ *n* -S [*mes-* + *-troch*] : a band of ciliated cells surrounding the middle of the body of a larval marine annelid — **me·sot·ro·chal** \məˈzä·trəkəl, -ˈsä-\ *or* **me·sot·ro·chous** \-kəs\ *adj*

**me·sot·ro·cha** \məˈzä·trəkə, -ˈsä-\ *n, pl* **mesotro·chae** \-ˌkē\ *also* **mesotrochas** [NL, fr. *mes-* + *-trocha*] : a mesotrochal larva

**meso·tron** \ˈme\|zə,trän, ˈmē\|, \|sə-\ *n* -S [*mes-* + *electron*] : MESON — **meso·tron·ic** \ˌ==ˈtränik\ *adj*

**meso·troph** \ˈ==ˌträf\ *n* -S [back-formation fr. *mesotrophic*] : a mesotrophic organism

**meso·troph·ic** \ˌ==ˈträfik\ *adj* [*mes-* + *-trophic*] : requiring either a single amino acid or ammonia and an organic acid as a source of metabolic nitrogen — compare METATROPHIC — **meso·trophy** \ˌ==ˈträfē\ *n* -ES

**meso·trop·ic** \ˌ==ˈträpik\ *adj* [*mes-* + *-tropic*] : turned or directed toward or located in the median plane of a cavity

**mes·ovarium** \ˌme\|z, ˌmē\|, \|s+\ *n, pl* **mesovaria** [NL, fr. *mes-* + *ovarium*] : the mesentery uniting the ovary with the body wall

**meso·ve·li·id** \ˌme\|zōˈvēlēəd, ˌmē\|, \|sō-\ *n* -S [NL *Mesoveliidae*] : WATER TREADER

**meso·ve·li·idae** \-vəˈlīəˌdē\ *n pl, cap* [NL, fr. *Mesovelia*, type genus (fr. *mes-* + L *velum* veil, sail + NL *-ia*) + *-idae*] : a small widely distributed family of semiaquatic hemipterous insects that inhabit the surface of freshwater or the ground near water

**meso·ventral** \ˌme\|zō, ˌmē\|, \|sō+\ *adj* [*mes-* + *ventral*] : median and ventral — **meso·ventrally** \"+\ *adv*

**mes·ox·al·ic acid** \ˌme\|ˌzäkˈsalik-, ˌmē\|, \|ˌsäkˈsalik-\ *n* [*mes-* + *oxalic acid*] : a crystalline acid $CO(COOH)_2$ or $C(OH)_2$-$(COOH)_2$ made esp. by oxidation of amino-malonic acid

**mes·ox·a·lyl** \məˈzäksəlˌil, -ˈsä-\ *n* [ISV *mesoxalic* + *-yl*] : the bivalent radical $CO(CO)_2$ or $C(OH)_2(CO)_2$ of mesoxalic acid

**mes·ox·a·lyl·urea** \ˌ=ˌ===ˈ(y)u̇rēə\ *n* [NL, fr. ISV *mesoxalyl* + NL *urea*] : ALLOXAN

**meso·zoa** \ˌme\|zəˈzōə, ˌmē\|, \|sə-\ *n pl, cap* [NL, fr. *mes-* + *-zoa*] : a group of small wormlike parasitic animals that are typically comparable to a stereoblastula with an outer layer of somatic cells and an inner mass of reproductive cells and are often regarded as intermediate in organization between Protozoa and Metazoa though perhaps being degenerate descendants of more highly organized forms — see DICYEMIDA, ORTHONECTIDA — **meso·zo·an** \ˌ==ˈzōən\ *adj*

**[1]meso·zo·ic** \ˌ==ˈzōik\ *adj, usu cap* [*mes-* + *-zoic*] : of or relating to a grand division of geological history that includes the entire interval of time between the Permian and the Tertiary and is marked by the dinosaurs, marine and flying reptiles, ganoid fishes, cycads, and evergreen trees — see GEOLOGIC TIME table

**[2]mesozoic** \"\ *n* -S *usu cap* : the Mesozoic era or system of rocks

**mes·pi·lus** \ˈmespələs\ *n, cap* [NL, fr. L, medlar — more at MEDLAR] **:** a genus of Eurasian trees (family Rosaceae) having large solitary flowers, leafy calyx lobes, and a pomaceous fruit with an open top and five easily detached stones — see MEDLAR

**mes·qui·tal** \ˌmeskəˈtal\ *n* -s [Sp *mezquital*, fr. *mezquite* mesquite] **1** *Southwest* **:** an area on which mesquite is the dominant plant form **2** *Southwest* **:** a thicket of mesquite ⟨take the saddle off her and hide it in a ~ —J.F.Dobie⟩ — called also *mesquite;* compare CHAPARRAL 2

**mes·quite** *also* **mes·quit** *or* **mez·quit** *or* **mez·quite** \məˈskēt, meˈ-, *usu* -ēd.+V\ *n* -s [Sp *mezquite, mesquite*, fr. Nahuatl *mizquitl*] **1 :** a plant of the genus *Prosopis:* as **a :** a spiny deep-rooted tree or shrub (*P. juliflora*) of the southwestern U. S. and Mexico that bears pods which are rich in sugar and important as a livestock feed, that tends to form extensive thickets, and that is often the only woody vegetation on large areas — called also *algarroba* **b :** SCREW BEAN 2 **2 :** MESQUITAL

**mesquite bean** *n* **:** the pod of a mesquite (*Prosopis juliflora*) or its seed used for food by southwestern Indians — compare ALGARROBA 4

**mesquite grass** *n* **:** any of various pasture grasses (as *Bouteloua oligostachya* and other members of the genus *Bouteloua*) found associated with mesquite in the southwestern U.S.

**mesquite gum** *n* **:** a gum that is obtained from mesquite pods, resembles gum arabic, and yields L-arabinose on hydrolysis

**mes·ro·pi·an alphabet** \(ˈ)mesˈrōpēən-\ *n, usu cap M* [*Mesrob* †A.D.439 Armenian bishop and scholar, its reputed inventor + E *-an*] **:** ARMENIAN ALPHABET

[1]**mess** \ˈmes\ *n* -ES *often attrib* [ME *mes*, fr. OF, fr. LL *missus* course at a meal, fr. *missus*, past part. of *mittere* to put, place, fr. L, to send] **1 :** a quantity of food: **a** *archaic* **:** food set on a table at one time **:** COURSE **b :** a prepared dish (as of soft or pulpy food) ⟨a ~ of milk, made by crumbling bread into it —G.E.Fussell⟩ **:** a mixture of ingredients cooked or eaten together ⟨a curious savory ~ of sweetbreads and chicken liver —Margery Allingham⟩ ⟨took a lot of cheese, a lot of hardtack, and a lot of bully beef, ground them up together, and then baked the ~ —*N.Y. Times*⟩ **c :** sufficient quantity (of a specified kind of food) for a dish or a meal ⟨picking a little ~ of red raspberries for her breakfast —Jean Stafford⟩ ⟨a ~ of string beans any time you wanted it —G.S.Perry⟩ **:** CATCH ⟨a ~ of trout⟩ **d** *dial* **:** the milk given by a cow at one milking **2 :** a quantity of any soft, moist, smeary, or pulpy substance often of an unpleasant nature ⟨cannot bear to be reminded that under the skin there is blood, ~, and entrails —F.R.Leavis⟩ **3 a** [ME *messe*, fr. *mes* course] **:** one of the small groups (as of four) into which companies at banquets were formerly divided for being served — now used only of parties of benchers or students in the Inns of Court **b :** a group of persons (as of military personnel) who regularly take their meals together ⟨every officer serving with a unit . . . is obliged to belong to a ~ —S.G.Maurice⟩ **c :** a meal so taken **d** (1) **:** a place (as a room or tent) where food or sometimes drink is served ⟨fresh fruit was a rarity in marine ~es —H.L. Merillat⟩ ⟨were at the wine ~ —Frederic Wakeman⟩ ⟨the field ~ is open —John Masters⟩ (2) **:** quarters comprising both kitchen and dining areas ⟨~ building⟩ ⟨~ steward⟩ ⟨~ officer⟩ **4** *dial* **:** AMOUNT, NUMBER ⟨a little ~ of eggs —Elizabeth M. Roberts⟩ ⟨substitute father to a ~ of newly orphaned children —*Newsweek*⟩ **:** a large quantity ⟨a ~ of preaching ain't going to alter her over —Sarah O. Jewett⟩ ⟨a big ~ of people⟩ **5 a :** a confused, untidy, dirty, unpleasant, or offensive state or condition **:** HODGEPODGE, JUMBLE, MUSS ⟨clear away the ~ left by the guests —Sherwood Anderson⟩ ⟨the apartment was a ~ — floors unswept —John & Ward Hawkins⟩ ⟨the falling tide had left us well caught in a great ~ of shoals —D.B.Putnam⟩ **b :** a disordered or unsavory situation, state, or condition resulting from misunderstanding, blundering, or misconduct ⟨the ~ he is making of his life —Carl Binger⟩ ⟨viewed realistically, the past is merely a series of ~es —E.M.Forster⟩ — often used with *in* or *into* ⟨get himself in a ~⟩

[2]**mess** \"\ *vb* -ED/-ING/-ES [ME *messen*, fr. *mes*, n.] *vt* **1** *now dial Brit* **:** to portion out (food) **:** deal out (as a meal) **:** SERVE **2 :** to assign to a mess ⟨personnel will be ~ed in the building —*Crowsnest*⟩ ⟨quarter and ~ them together at some distance from their places of normal duty —*Infantry Jour.*⟩ **3 a :** to make dirty or untidy **:** DISARRANGE ⟨his clothes are all ~ed⟩ — often used with *up* ⟨without getting ~ed up in the mud of the highroad —Richard Joseph⟩ **b :** to mix up **:** BOTCH, BUNGLE, MUDDLE ⟨unless his chance came in extraordinarily lucky guise, he would probably ~ it —*Scribner's*⟩ ⟨the schedule of appointments, carelessly ~ed for the day —Helen Howe⟩ — often used with *up* ⟨a variety of state standards ~es up national contracts —*N.Y. Times*⟩ ⟨when something happens that ~es up the girl's life —Evelyn M. Duvall⟩ **c :** DAMAGE, SPOIL — usu. used with *up* ⟨a frost which would have ~ed up the outdoor peaches —Nigel Balchin⟩ **d :** to interfere with — used with *up* ⟨magnetic storms that ~ up communications —*Time*⟩ **e :** to handle roughly **:** rough up **:** MANHANDLE — used with *up* ~ *vi* **1 :** to prepare food for and serve messes **2 :** to take meals with a mess **:** belong to a mess ⟨had marched and ~ed together through the war —Dixon Wecter⟩ ⟨granted the privilege of ~ing away from the naval activity —*Naval Reservist*⟩ ⟨will ~ only twice a day aboard ship —Alan Surgal⟩ ⟨~ together by tribes —C.S.Coon⟩ **3 :** to make a mess **:** DABBLE ⟨stop ~ing and eat your breakfast⟩ **4 a :** PUTTER, TINKER, TRIFLE, PLAY ⟨~es with motors in his spare time⟩ ⟨child ~ing with his fork and spoon⟩ **b :** to become involved esp. voluntarily **:** INTERFERE, MEDDLE — usu. used with *in* or *with* ⟨~ing in other people's affairs⟩ **c :** to act toward someone in a rough or annoying manner **:** TEASE — usu. used with *with* ⟨if he ever ~es with me any more —James Jones⟩ **d :** to become mixed up or confused **:** BLUNDER — usu. used with *up* ⟨her own life ~es up —H.C.Webster⟩

[3]**mess** \"\ *dial Brit var of* [1]MASS

**mess about** *vi, chiefly Brit* **:** to mess around ⟨those who like *messing about* in boats in quiet waters —S.P.B.Mais⟩ ⟨no *messing about* and wasting time —Arnold Bennett⟩

**mes·sa di vo·ce** \ˌmäsədēˈvō(ˌ)chā, ˌmes-\ *n, pl* **mes·se di voce** \-(ˌ)säd-\ [It, lit., placing of the voice] **:** the singing of a gradual crescendo and decrescendo on a long sustained tone — used of a vocal technique originating in 18th century bel canto

[1]**mes·sage** \ˈmesij, -sēj\ *n* -s [ME, fr. OF, fr. ML *missaticum*, fr. L *missus* (past part. of *mittere* to send) + *-aticum* -age — more at SMITE] **1 :** a charge, service, or function of a messenger **:** MISSION ⟨murmuring her lesson to herself like a child sent on a ~ —Francis Hackett⟩ ⟨the girl will go on a ~ to the shop —Cahir Healy⟩ **2 :** a written or oral communication or other transmitted information sent by messenger or by some other means (as by signals) **3 a :** a divinely inspired or revealed communication (as of a prophet) **:** an inspired utterance **:** EVANGEL **b :** the basic teachings of a religious revelation ⟨the reader becomes aware of some subordinate aims which have left their mark on the form of the ~ —*Interpreter's Bible*⟩; *also* **:** an interpretation of such a revelation ⟨had preached a rather shallow ~ —J.C.Brauer⟩ **c :** a sermon or homiletical discourse forming part of a worship service or other religious meeting ⟨the pastor brought the ~⟩ **d :** a discourse or statement made to a gathering and intended esp. to inspire, encourage, or greet ⟨gave an appropriate blessing and also a ~ of goodwill for the absent members —Joseph Hitrec⟩ **4 :** an official communication (as from a sovereign to a parliament or from a chief executive to a legislature) often not made in person but delivered by messenger and read by an authorized person ⟨the presidential ~ has grown from a formal requirement of the Constitution to a recognized and influential source of legislative action —W.S. Sayre⟩ ⟨the ~s the president must work on are the State of the Union address, the budget, and the economic report —*N.Y. Times*⟩ **5 a :** a principle or basic purpose signified in one's life or lifework **:** a meaning (as of a work of art) that communicates itself **:** IMPORT, SIGNIFICANCE ⟨the ~ of a fine symphony or string quartet —Winthrop Sargeant⟩ ⟨the role of a work of art is to communicate its ~ to the spectator —Ladislas Segy⟩ **b :** an underlying or pervasive theme or idea intended to inspire, urge, advise, warn, or enlighten ⟨the ~ of a movie dealing with juvenile delinquency⟩ ⟨calls her novels fables with a ~ —W.S Campbell⟩ ⟨small size and population permits an energetic candidate to carry his ~ personally throughout the state —Douglass Cater⟩ **6 :** a group of words used to advertise or notify ⟨postcards with advertising ~s —*Nat'l Stamp News*⟩ ⟨the ~ of a radio commercial⟩ **7 :** a communication held to originate with a departed spirit, to be transmitted by a medium, and to be intended for a living person **8 a :** the substance of a telephone call **b :** the contents of a telegram, cablegram, or radiogram **9 :** a unit of information that is received by a sensory organ, is transmitted centrally in the nervous system, and functions as a stimulus ⟨certain definite and fixed ~s will be sent to the brain by the vestibular sense acting in coordination with sight and muscle sense —H.G.Armstrong⟩

[2]**message** \"\, *esp in pres part* -səj\ *vb* -ED/-ING/-S *vt* **:** to send as a message or by messenger ⟨the commander . . . *messaged* "well done" to his pilots —*Associated Press*⟩ ⟨the bill is *messaged* back to the house of origination, which house may then vote either to concur or nonconcur in the amendments —Rhoten Smith⟩ **:** order or instruct by message ⟨*messaged* the other PT to follow us into the attack —Dave Richardson⟩ ~ *vi* **:** to communicate by message ⟨after much *messaging* back and forth over the secret radio —Richard Thruelsen & Elliott Arnold⟩

**message stick** *n* **:** a carved stick serving as a mnemonic device and means of indentification for messengers among some primitive peoples (as in Australia and Africa)

**mes·sa·lian** \məˈsālyən, -lēən\ *n* -s *usu cap* [LGk *Messalianoi, Massalianoi*, pl., fr. Syr *mešallěyānē*, lit., those who pray] **:** EUCHITE 1

**mes·sa·line** \ˌmesəˈlēn\ *n* -s [F] **:** a lightweight silk dress fabric having a warp satin weave and characterized by a soft hand and high luster

**mes·san** \ˈmesᵊn\ *n* -s [ScGael *measan*, fr. MIr *messán, mesán*, dim. of *mess, mes* fosterling — more at MESTOME] *chiefly Scot* **:** LAPDOG

**mess and mell** *var of* MESS OR MELL

[1]**mes·sa·pi·an** \məˈsāpēən\ *or* **mes·sap·ic** \-ˈsapik, -sap-\ *adj, usu cap* [L *Messapii* + E *-an* or *-ic*] **1 :** of, relating to, or characteristic of the Messapii **2 :** of, relating to, or characteristic of the Messapian language or the alphabet in which it was written

[2]**messapian** \"\ *or* **messapic** \"\ *n* -s *cap* **1 :** one of the Messapii **2 :** the ancient language of Messapia sometimes classed as Illyrian

**mes·sa·pii** \-ˈsāpē,ī\ *n pl, cap* [L, fr. Gk *Messapioi*] **:** a people of Messapia, an ancient country of southeastern Italy

**mess around** *vi* **1 a :** DABBLE, PUTTER ⟨small boys and girls who like to *mess around* with paints —*New Yorker*⟩ **:** to work according to one's whim or mood ⟨busy *messing around* with cameras under water, in the air —Marya Mannes⟩ **b :** to waste time **:** DAWDLE, IDLE ⟨*mess around* on the beach most of the summer⟩ **2 :** INTERFERE, INTRUDE **3 a :** ASSOCIATE ⟨don't *mess around* with admirals much —K.M.Dodson⟩ **b :** FLIRT, PHILANDER ⟨reckon he *messes around* with some lady friend —Erskine Caldwell⟩ ~ *vt* **:** to treat roughly **:** MANHANDLE ⟨the hoodlums *messed* him *around* considerably⟩

**mess beef** *n* **:** barreled salt beef consisting of about 80 pounds of assorted cuts

**messboy** \ˈ≈,≈\ *n* **:** one who takes care of the crew's messroom on a ship and waits on the tables

**mess call** *n* [[1]mess] **:** a bugle call for meals

**messcook** \ˈ≈,≈\ *n* **:** MESSMAN

**messdeck** \ˈ≈,≈\ *n, Brit* **:** mess quarters on a ship

**messed** *past of* MESS

**messe di voce** *pl of* **messa di voce**

**mes·sen·ger** \ˈmesᵊnjə(r)\ *n* -s [ME *messager, messangere, messengere*, fr. OF *messagier*, fr. *message*, fr. ML *missaticum*, fr. L *missus*, past part. of *mittere* to send — more at SMITE] **1 :** one who bears a message or does an errand **:** COURIER, EMISSARY, ENVOY: as **a** *archaic* **:** one who prepares the way **:** FORERUNNER, HARBINGER ⟨behold, I send my ~ to prepare the way before me —Mal 3:1 (RSV)⟩ **b :** a dispatch bearer (as for an official or a government body or in military service) ⟨queen's ~⟩ ⟨city ~⟩ ⟨~s, orderlies, and any other soldiers —F.V.W.Mason⟩ **c :** one employed by a business concern to do errands within or outside the establishment ⟨bank ~s empty the boxes once a week —L.H.Olsen⟩ **d** (1) **:** a postal employee who delivers special-delivery mail (2) **:** MAIL MESSENGER **e :** a delegate to a religious convention or meeting; *esp* **:** one sent from a local church within a denomination that adheres to a congregational polity **f :** a character esp. in a classical Greek play who comes onstage to make known an action that has occurred offstage ⟨all theatergoers now must have watched for the entrance of the breathless ~, who knows the result —John Masefield⟩ **2 a :** a rope or chain passed round a capstan and having its two ends lashed together to form an endless rope or chain **b :** a light line used in hauling a heavier line (as between ships) **c :** a device sliding on a line for operating a trip (as to release a target or close a net) **d :** MESSENGER CABLE

**messenger-at-arms** \ˈ≈≈≈≈ˈ≈\ *n*, **messengers-at-arms :** an officer appointed by the Lyon king of arms and charged with executing summonses and warrants

**messenger buoy** *n* **:** a buoy that can be released by personnel inside a sunken submarine to aid rescue efforts

**messenger cable** *or* **messenger wire** *n* **:** a usu. steel cable supporting a telephone cable or other wires conducting electricity

**messes** *pl of* MESS, *pres 3d sing of* MESS

**mes·set** \ˈmesət\ *n* -s [prob. alter. (influenced by *-et*) of *messan*] *dial Brit* **:** LAPDOG

**mess hall** *n* **1 :** a dining room in which mess is served **2 :** a building (as in an army camp) serving chiefly as a dining hall

**mess house** *n, West* **:** MESS HALL

**mes·si·ah** \məˈsīə\ *n* -s [Heb *māshīaḥ* & Aram *mĕshīḥā* anointed, Messiah] **1 a :** an expected deliverer or savior **b** *usu cap* **:** the expected king and deliverer of the Jews **2 :** one accepted as or claiming to be a leader destined to bring about a desired state or condition ⟨security, which the political ~s promise —Vardis Fisher⟩ ⟨our self-appointed moral ~s —Asher Moore⟩

**mes·si·ah·ship** \-,ship\ n, *sometimes cap* **:** the office, condition, profession, or state of being a messiah ⟨the mission and ~ of Jesus —*Interpreter's Bible*⟩

**mes·si·an·ic** \ˌmesēˈanik, -nēk\ *adj* [fr. (assumed) NL *Messianicus*, fr. LL *Messias* + L *-anicus* (as in L *Romanicus* Romanic)] **1** *often cap* **:** of, relating to, or being a messiah; as **a :** of or relating to the Messiah expected by the Hebrews **b :** of or relating to Jesus Christ as the Messiah **2** *sometimes cap* **:** of or relating to a nativistic religious cult (as one whose prophet professes salvation of the native population and destruction of foreign culture and influence) ⟨the ~ element common to the present sect and nonliterate nativistic efforts —L.C.May⟩ **3** *sometimes cap* **:** mystically idealistic in a manner suggestive of messiahship and often in an aggressive or crusading spirit ⟨sustained by a ~ hope of social perfection —T.E.Utley⟩ ⟨a ~ sense of historic mission —Edmond Taylor⟩ — **mes·si·an·i·cal·ly** \-nək(ə)lē, -nēk-, -li\ *adv, sometimes cap*

**mes·si·a·nism** \məˈsīə,nizəm\ *n* -s *often cap* [*messianic* + *-ism*] **1 :** belief in a messiah; *specif* **:** an ideological movement or system of ideas that teaches the salvation of mankind through the enthroning of a messiah that may be an individual, a class, or an idea **2 :** the vocation of a messiah

**mes·si·a·nist** \-.nəst\ *n* -s *often cap* **:** an advocate of messianism

**mes·si·as** \-ˈīəs\ *n* -ES *cap* [ME, fr. LL, fr. Gk, fr. Aram *mĕshīḥā*] **:** MESSIAH 1 ⟨I know that *Messias* cometh, which is called Christ —Jn 4:25 (AV)⟩

**messieurs** *pl of* MONSIEUR

**mess·i·ly** \ˈmesəlē, -li\ *adv* **:** in a messy manner

**messin** *var of* MESSAN

**mes·si·na** \məˈsēnə\ *adj, usu cap* [fr. *Messina*, Italy] **:** of or from the city of Messina, Italy, in Sicily **:** of the kind or style prevalent in Messina

**mes·si·nese** \ˌmesəˈnēz, -ēs\ *n, pl* **messinese** *cap* [It, fr. *Messina* (fr. L & Gk; L *Messana*, fr. Gk *Messana, Messēnē*) + *-ese*] **:** a native or inhabitant of Messina, Italy, in Sicily

**mess·i·ness** \ˈmesēnəs, -sin-\ *n* -ES **:** the quality or state of being messy ⟨there is a certain ~ in the analysis in that he is forced from the start to assume multiple values —A.A.Hill⟩

**mess jacket** *n* **:** a man's semiformal tailless jacket for social or service wear, reaching just below the waistline, and worn open at the front with a vest or cummerbund — called also *monkey jacket, shell jacket*

mess jacket

**mess kit** *or* **mess gear** *n* **1 :** the cooking and table utensils of a mess together with the receptacle in which they are packed for transportation **2 :** a soldier's or camper's kit for cooking or holding food at mess

**mess·man** \ˈmesmən\ *n, pl* **messmen :** a navy enlisted man on temporary duty in the sailors' or officers' dining quarters who serves the food and clears the tables

**messmate** \ˈ≈,≈\ *n* **1 :** an associate in a mess (as on a ship) **2 :** any of several Australian eucalypts (as *Eucalyptus amygdalina* and *E. obliqua*) **3 :** COMMENSAL 2

**mess of pottage** [ME *mes of potage;* fr. allusion to Esau's selling of his birthright to his twin brother Jacob for a mess of pottage (Gen 25:29–34)] **:** something valueless or trivial or of inferior value — used esp. of something accepted instead of a rightful thing of far greater value ⟨suspense is the *mess of pottage* for which the Shakespearean birthright has been sold —E.R.Bentley⟩

**mess or mell** *vi, Scot* **:** to have familiar intercourse **:** ASSOCIATE — used with *with*

**mess pork** *n* **:** barreled salt pork made from shoulders and sides of lightweight hogs cut in pieces of about 4 pounds each

**messroom** \ˈ≈,≈\ *n* **:** a room (as on a ship) used for a mess **:** DINING ROOM

**messrs.** *pl of* MR.

**mess·tin** \ˈ≈,≈\ *n* **:** an oval-shaped metal utensil having a bail and forming part of a soldier's mess equipment

**mess traps** *n pl, Brit* **:** MESS KIT

**mes·suage** \ˈmeswij\ *n* -s [ME, fr. AF, prob. alter. of OF *mesnage* — more at MÉNAGE] *law* **:** a dwelling house with the adjacent buildings and curtilage and the adjoining lands used in connection with the household

**mess-up** \ˈ≈,≈\ *n* -s [fr. the phrase *mess up*] **:** a confused or disordered situation or condition **:** MIX-UP, MUDDLE

**messy** \ˈmesē, -si\ *adj* -ER/-EST [[1]*mess* + *-y*] **1 :** in a confused, disordered, or dirty state or condition **:** UNTIDY ⟨a ~ room⟩ ⟨those ~ herbaceous borders —Osbert Lancaster⟩ **2 :** that causes or is likely to cause a confused, disordered, or dirty state or condition ⟨a ~ pen⟩ ⟨the ~ business of infant feeding —*New Yorker*⟩ **3 :** lacking neatness or precision **:** CARELESS, SLOVENLY ⟨~ thinking⟩ ⟨~ legislation⟩ ⟨cannot simply eliminate attitudes, emotions, values, desires, multiple and ~ meanings —H.J.Muller⟩ **4 :** unpleasantly or tryingly difficult of execution or settlement ⟨a ~ job⟩ ⟨~ lawsuits⟩ ⟨a ~ traffic problem⟩ ⟨scandal, crime, and ~ disasters sell newspapers —A.J.Liebling⟩ **5 :** effusive or sentimental to an excessive or embarrassing degree ⟨~ introductions⟩ ⟨the ~ rhetorical violence of the other speakers —Robert Lowell⟩ ⟨a certain ~ generosity of manner —Louis Auchincloss⟩

**mes·ta** \ˈmestə\ *n* -s [prob. fr. Hindi] **:** KENAF

**mes·te·ño** \məˈstān(ˌ)yō\ *n* -s [Sp, adj., wild, stray — more at MUSTANG] *West* **:** a horse or cow sometimes branded that has escaped from the owner and is running wild; *also* **:** any wild horse — compare MUSTANG

**mes·ti·za** \meˈstēzə, məˈ-\ *n* -s [Sp, fem. of *mestizo*] **:** a female mestizo

**mes·ti·za·tion** \ˌmestəˈzāshən\ *n* -s [*mestizo* + *-ation*] **:** the process or state of race mixture

**mes·ti·zo** \meˈstē(ˌ)zō, məˈ-\ *n, pl* **mestizos** *also* **mestizoes** [Sp, fr. *mestizo*, adj., mixed, fr. LL *misticius, mixticius*, fr. L *mixtus*, past part. of *miscēre* to mix, mingle — more at MIX] **1 :** MIXED-BLOOD: **a :** a person of mixed European and non-Caucasian stock; *specif* **:** one of European (as Spanish or Portuguese) and American Indian ancestry **b** *Philippines* **:** a person of foreign (as Chinese) and native ancestry **2 :** a completely acculturated Central or So. American Indian

[1]**me·sto** \ˈme(ˌ)stō\ *adj* [It, fr. L *maestus* dejected, sad; akin to L *maerēre* to mourn, be sad] **:** sad and pensive — used as a direction in music

[2]**mesto** \"\ *n* -s **:** a musical composition of sad and pensive character

**mes·tome** \ˈme,stōm\ *also* **mes·tom** \-täm\ *n* -s [G *mestom*, fr. Gk *mestos* full + G *-om* -ome; akin to Gk *medea, mezea, mēdea*, pl., male genitals, MIr *mess* acorns, W *mes*, pl., acorns, and perh. to MIr *mess* fosterling] *of a vascular plant* **:** the conducting tissues comprising leptome and hadrome — compare STEREOME

**me·sua** \ˈmeshəwə\ *n, cap* [NL, fr. Johannes *Mesuë* (Ar *Yūḥanna ibn-Māsawayh*) †857 Persian Christian physician in the service of the Caliph] **:** a genus of tropical Asiatic trees (family Guttiferae) having large solitary flowers with a 2-celled ovary — see ROSE CHESTNUT

**me·su·ran·ic** \ˌmeshəˈranik\ *adj* [*mes-* + *uran-* + *-ic*] **:** having an upper alveolar arch index of between 110 and 115 — **me·su·rany** \(ˈ)≈≈,ranē\ *n* -ES

**mes·vin·ian** \(ˈ)mesˈvinēən\ *adj, usu cap* [F *mesvinien*, fr. *Mesvin*, Belgium + F *-ien* -an] **:** of or relating to a middle paleolithic culture of Belgium contemporaneous with Levalloisian and Clactonian

**mesyl** \ˈmesəl, ˈmēs-\ *n* -s [*methane* + *sulfonyl*] **:** the univalent radical $CH_3SO_2$– of methane-sulfonic acid; methylsulfonyl

**me·sym·ni·on** \məˈsimnē,än, -ēən\ *n* -s [Gk, fr. *mes-* + *hymnos* hymn] *classical prosody* **:** a short colon or rhythmic series interpolated in a stanza

**met** *past of* MEET

**met** *abbr* **1** metal **2** metallurgical; metallurgy **3** metaphor; metaphorical **4** metaphysical; metaphysics **5** meteorological; meteorology **6** metronome **7** metropolitan

**meta** \ˈmed·ə, -etə\ *adj* [*meta-*] **:** relating to, characterized by, or being two positions in the benzene ring that are separated by one carbon atom — compare META- 4 b

**meta-** *in pronunciations below*, ˈ≈≈=med·ə *or* ˈmetə\ *or* **met-** *prefix* [NL & ML, fr. LL or Gk; LL, fr. Gk, fr. *meta* between, with, after; akin to OE *mid, mith* with, OS *mid, midi*, OHG *mit, miti* with, ON *meth* with, between, Goth *mith* with, and perh. to OE *midd* mid — more at MID] **1 a :** occurring later **:** in succession to **:** after ⟨*meta*chronism⟩ ⟨*meta*biosis⟩ ⟨*meta*genesis⟩ ⟨*meta*infective⟩ **b :** situated behind **:** posterior ⟨*meta*pore⟩ ⟨*meta*nephron⟩ **c :** later or more highly organized or specialized form of ⟨*Metazoa*⟩ ⟨*meta*phyte⟩ **d :** with **:** occurring with ⟨*meta*cinnabar⟩ **2 a** [MF & L; MF, fr. L, fr. Gk, fr. *meta*] **:** change in **:** transformation of ⟨*meta*morphosis⟩ ⟨*meta*plasia⟩ **b :** produced by metamorphism ⟨*meta*diorite⟩ ⟨*meta*sediment⟩ **3 a** [ME, fr. ML, fr. Gk *meta* after, as used in *ta meta ta physika* the (works) after the physics — more at METAPHYSICS] **:** beyond **:** transcending ⟨*meta*physics⟩ ⟨*meta*psychosis⟩ ⟨*meta*geometry⟩ ⟨*meta*biological⟩ ⟨*met*empirics⟩ **b :** of a higher logical type — in nouns formed from names of disciplines and designating new but related disciplines such as can deal critically with the nature, structure, or behavior of the original ones ⟨*meta*language⟩ ⟨*meta*theory⟩ ⟨*meta*system⟩ **4** [ISV, fr. Gk, with, after, fr. *meta*] **a :** one that is isomeric with, polymeric with, or otherwise closely related to ⟨*meta*ldehyde⟩ — in names of chemical compounds — compare [1]PARA- 2a **b** (1) **:** relation of two positions in the benzene ring that are separated by one carbon atom (2) *meta-, usu ital* **:** derivative that has two substituting groups occupying such positions — abbr. *m-* ⟨*meta*-xylene or *m*-xylene is 1,3-dimethyl-benzene; compare ORTH- 3b, [1]PARA- 2b **c :** regarded as derived from (the ortho acid) by loss of water (as of one molecule of water from each molecule of acid) — in names of inorganic acids ⟨*meta*phosphoric acid⟩; compare ORTH- 3a, PYR- 2a **d :** derived from by removal or loss of some or all of the contained water — in names of minerals ⟨*meta*autunite⟩ ⟨*meta*halloysite⟩

**meta-autunite** \ˈ≈≈ *at* META-+\ *n* [*meta-* + *autunite*] **:** a mineral consisting of a partially dehydrated autunite

**me·tab·a·sis** \məˈtabəsəs\ *n, pl* **metaba·ses** \-bə,sēz\ [Gk, fr. *metabainein* to change, fr. *meta-* + *bainein* to go, move — more at COME] **1 :** a shift from one subject, point, or division in a discourse to another; *specif* **:** the rhetorical device used to

effect such a shift **2 :** a medical change (as of disease, symptoms, or treatment)
**meta·biological** \¦≠ *at* META-+\ *adj* **:** of or relating to metabiology
**meta·biology** \"+\ *n* [*meta-* + *biology*] **:** a system of knowledge or belief built around biological principles ⟨a faith which complied with the first condition of all religions that have ever taken hold of humanity: namely, that it must be . . . a science of ~ —G.B.Shaw⟩
**meta·bi·o·sis** \,≠≠,bī'ōsəs\ *n* [NL, fr. *meta-* + *-biosis*] **:** a mode of life in which one organism so depends on another that it cannot flourish unless the latter precedes and influences the environment favorably
**meta·bi·ot·ic** \¦≠≠,bī¦äd·ik, -ät\, [ēk *also* ,bē¦ä-\ *adj* [*meta-* + *-biotic*] **:** of, relating to, or marked by metabiosis — **meta·bi·ot·i·cal·ly** \¦ək(ə)lē, [ēk- *also* -li\ *adv*
**meta·bisulfite** \¦≠≠+\ *n* [ISV *meta-* + *bisulfite*] **:** a salt containing the bivalent anion $S_2O_5^{--}$ obtained by heating a bisulfite — called also *pyrosulfite*
**me·tab·o·la** \mə'tabələ\ *n pl, cap* [NL, fr. neut. pl. of Gk *metabolos* changeable, fr. *metaballein* to change, fr. *meta-* + *ballein* to throw — more at DEVIL] *in some classifications* **:** a division of Insecta comprising insects that undergo a metamorphosis
**me·tab·o·le** \-(,)lē\ *also* **me·tab·o·la** \-lə\ *n* -s [NL, fr. Gk *metabolē* change, fr. *metaballein*, v.] **1 :** METABASIS 2 **2 :** METAMORPHOSIS 2a
**meta·bo·li·an** \,med·ə'bōlēən\ *n* -s **:** an insect of the division Metabola
**meta·bol·ic** \¦≠≠ *at* META- +¦bälik, -lēk\ *also* **meta·bol·i·cal** \-lәkəl, -lēk-\ *adj* [*metabolic* fr. G *metabolisch*, fr. Gk *metabolikos* changing, fr. *metabolē* change + *-ikos* -ic; *metabolical* fr. *metabolic* + *-al*] **1 :** of, relating to, or worked by metabolism ⟨our feelings as well as our physical acts have an essentially ~ pattern —Susanne K. Langer⟩ **2 a :** undergoing metamorphosis **:** changeable in form **b** [NL *Metabola* + E *-ic* or *-ical*] **:** of or relating to the Metabola **3 :** VEGETATIVE 1a — used esp. of a cell nucleus that is not dividing; compare RESTING NUCLEUS — **meta·bol·i·cal·ly** \-lək(ə)lē, -lēk-, -li\ *adv*
**metabolic heat** *n* **:** ANIMAL HEAT
**metabolic movement** *n* **:** EUGLENOID MOVEMENT
**metabolic water** *n* **:** water produced by living cells as a by-product of oxidative metabolism; *sometimes* **:** water produced in plants as a consequence of respiration as distinguished from water of the transpiration stream
**me·tab·o·lism** \mə'tabə,lizəm\ *n* -s [ISV *metabol-* (fr. Gk *metabolē* change) + *-ism*] **1 a :** the sum of the processes concerned in the building up of protoplasm and its destruction incidental to life **:** the chemical changes in living cells by which energy is provided for the vital processes and activities and new material is assimilated to repair the waste ⟨basal ~⟩ ⟨methods of determining body and tissue ~ —*Bull. of the Univ. of Ky.*⟩ — see ANABOLISM, CATABOLISM; compare ASSIMILATION, FOOD 1a, NUTRITION, SECRETION **b :** the sum of the processes by which a particular substance is handled (as by assimilation and incorporation or by detoxification and excretion) in the living body ⟨the ~ of iodine in the thyroid⟩ ⟨vanadium ~ of tunicates⟩ **c :** the sum of the metabolic activities taking place in a particular habitat or environment ⟨the ~ of a lake⟩ ⟨complex processes of historical ~ involving the whole range of man's cultural, social, and economic existence —Walter Abell⟩ **2 :** METAMORPHOSIS 2 a — usu. used in combination ⟨*ametabolism*⟩ ⟨*holometabolism*⟩
**me·tab·o·lite** \-,līt\ *n* -s [*metabolism* + *-ite*] **1 :** a product of metabolism: **a :** a metabolic waste usu. more or less toxic to the organism producing it **:** EXCRETION **b :** a product of one metabolic process that is essential to another such process in the same organism **c :** a metabolic waste of one organism that is markedly toxic to another **:** ANTIBIOTIC **2 :** a substance essential to the metabolism of a particular organism or to a particular metabolic process
**me·tab·o·liz·a·bil·i·ty** \≠,≠≠,līzə'biləd·ē, -ətē, -i\ *n* **:** the quality or state of being metabolizable
**me·tab·o·liz·able** \≠¦≠≠¦līzəbəl\ *adj* [*metabolize* + *-able*] **1** *of a nutrient* **:** capable of being utilized in metabolism **2** *of energy* **:** producible or produced by metabolic processes
**me·tab·o·lize** \≠'≠≠,līz\ *vb* -ED/-ING/-S *see -ize in Explan Notes* [*metabolism* + *-ize*] *vt* **:** to subject (as a chemical substance) to metabolism ~ *vi* **:** to perform metabolism
**me·tab·o·lous** \-ləs\ *adj* [Gk *metabolos* changeable + E *-ous* — more at METABOLA] **:** METABOLIC 2
**me·tab·o·ly** \-lē\ *n* -ES [Gk *metabolē*, *metabolia* change, fr. *metaballein* to change] **:** METAMORPHOSIS
**meta·borate** \¦≠≠ *at* META-+\ *n* [ISV *metabor-* (in *metaboric acid*) + *-ate*] **:** a salt or ester of a metaboric acid
**meta·boric acid** \¦≠≠+-\ *n* [*metaboric* ISV *meta-* + *boric*] **:** an acid $HBO_2$ or $(HBO_2)_n$ formed as a glassy amorphous solid by heating orthoboric acid but usu. obtained in the form of its salts
**meta·branchial** \"+\ *adj* [*meta-* + *branchial*] **:** of or relating to a posterior lobe of the carapace of a crab
**meta·can·tho·ceph·a·la** \,≠≠,kan(t)thə'sefələ\ *n pl, cap* [NL, fr. *meta-* + *Acanthocephala*] *in some classifications* **:** a class of Acanthocephala comprising the orders Archiacanthocephala and Palaeacanthocephala
**¹meta·car·pal** \¦≠≠¦kärpəl\ *adj* [NL *metacarpus* + E *-al*] **:** of or relating to the metacarpus
**²metacarpal** \"\ *n* **:** a metacarpal bone **:** any of the long bones that separate the carpus from the phalanges of the hand — see BAT illustration
**meta·car·pa·le** \,≠≠+\ *n* [NL, fr. *metacarpus* + *-ale* (fr. neut. of L *-alis* -al, adj. suffix)] **:** METACARPAL
**meta·car·po·phalangeal** \¦≠≠¦kärpə+\ *adj* [*metacarpo-* (fr. NL *metacarpus*) + *phalangeal*] **:** of, relating to, or involving both the metacarpus and the phalanges
**meta·carpus** \¦≠≠+\ *n* [NL, fr. *meta-* + *carpus*] **:** the part of the hand or forefoot between the carpus and the phalanges that contains five more or less elongated bones when all the digits are present but is modified in many animals by the loss or reduction of some bones or the fusing of adjacent bones — compare CANNON BONE, SPLINT BONE
**meta·center** \'≠≠+,-\ *n* [F *métacentre*, fr. *méta-* meta- + *centre* center] **:** the point of intersection of the vertical through the center of buoyancy of a floating body with the vertical through the new center of buoyancy when the body is displaced however little
**meta·centric** \¦≠≠+\ *adj* **1 :** of or relating to the metacenter **2** [*meta-* + *-centric*] *of a chromosome* **:** having two equal arms because of the median position of the centromere — compare TELOCENTRIC — **meta·centricity** \,≠≠+\ *n*


metacenter: *1* center of gravity, *2* center of buoyancy, *3* new center of buoyancy when boat is displaced, *4* point of intersection

**metacentric height** *n* **:** the distance of the metacenter above the center of gravity of a floating body
**meta·cercaria** \¦≠≠+\ *n* [NL, fr. *meta-* + *cercaria*] **:** a late larva of a digenetic trematode that is tailless and encysted and usu. constitutes the form which is infective for the definitive host — compare ADOLESCARIA, CERCARIA, MARITA
**meta·cestode** \"+\ *n* -s [*meta-* + *cestode*] **:** a stage of a tapeworm occurring in an intermediate host **:** a larval tapeworm
**meta·chemic** \"+\ *or* **meta·chemical** \"+\ *adj* [*metachemistry* + *-ic* or *-ical*] **:** of or relating to metachemistry
**meta·chemistry** \"+\ *n* [*meta-* + *chemistry*] **1 :** chemistry beyond the bounds of chemistry proper (as in a nonmaterial sphere) **:** highly speculative chemistry **2 :** a branch of chemistry that deals with substances (as molecules in activated metastable states) capable of releasing abnormally large amounts of energy in comparison with their mass
**meta·chla·myd·e·ae** \,≠≠klə'midē,ē\ *n pl, cap* [NL, fr. *meta-* + *-chlamydeae* (fr. Gk *chlamyd-*, *chlamys* cloak, mantle)] **:** a group of Dicotyledoneae comprising plants in which the petals of the flowers are united — compare ARCHICHLAMYDEAE — **meta·chla·myd·e·ous** \¦≠≠+\ *adj*
**meta·chro·ma·sia** \,≠≠krō'māzh(ē)ə\ *or* **meta·chro·ma·sy** \-'krōməsē\ *or* **meta·chro·ma·sis** \-əsəs\ *n, pl* **metachromasias** *or* **metachromasies** *or* **metachromasises** [NL *metachromasia* or *metachromasis*, fr. *meta-* + *-chromasia* or *-chromasis* (perh. alter. of *-chromasia*); *metachromasy*, ISV, fr. NL *metachromasia* or *metachromasis*] **1 :** the property of various tissues of staining in a different color (as when treatment with a blue aniline dye makes a cellular element red) **2 :** the property of various biologic stains that permits a single dye to stain different tissue elements in different colors
**meta·chromatic** \¦≠≠+\ *adj* [NL *metachromasia* + E *-atic* (as in *chromatic*)] **:** of or relating to metachromasia ⟨vivid ~ color changes were noted —D.J.Hamerman⟩
**meta·chromatin** \,≠≠+\ *n* [ISV *metachromatic* + *-in*] **1 :** VOLUTIN **2 :** a granular densely staining material in plant cell vacuoles that may be identical with volutin — **meta·chromatinic** \¦≠≠+\ *adj*
**meta·chromatism** \,≠≠+\ *n* [*meta-* + Gk *chrōmat-*, *chrōma* color + E *-ism* — more at CHROMATIC] **:** change of color; *specif* **:** a change of color due to a change in physical conditions (as in the temperature of a body)
**¹meta·chrome** \'≠≠,krōm\ *n* [ISV *meta-* + *-chrome* (n. suffix); orig. formed as F *métachrome*] **:** a metachromatic granule
**²metachrome** \"\ *adj, often cap* [ISV *meta-* + *-chrome* (adj. suffix)] **1 :** being any of a series of mordant azo dyes — see DYE table I (under *Mordant*) **2 :** relating to a one-bath method of dyeing by applying a chromium mordant and a dye simultaneously
**³metachrome** \"\ *vt* **:** to dye by the metachrome method
**metachronism** *n* -s [ML *metachronismus* chronological error, fr. Gk *metachronios*, *metachronos* out of date, anachronistic (fr. *meta-* after — fr. *meta* — + *chronos* time) + L *-ismus* -ism — more at META-] *obs* **:** an error in chronology committed by placing an event after its real date — compare PARACHRONISM
**me·tach·ro·nous** \mə'takrənəs\ *adj* [*meta-* + *-chronous*] *of a geological surface* **:** composed of several parts formed or developed at various times
**meta·chro·sis** \,≠≠ *at* META- + 'krōsəs\ *n, pl* **metachro·ses** \-,sēz\ [NL, fr. *meta-* + Gk *chrōsis* coloring, fr. *chrōs* color — more at CHROMATIC] **:** the power of some animals (as many fishes and reptiles) to change color voluntarily by the expansion of special pigment cells
**meta·cinnabar** \"+\ *also* **meta·cin·na·bar·ite** \,≠≠+'sinəbə,rīt\ *n* [*metacinnabar* fr. *meta-* + *cinnabar*; *metacinnabarite*, ISV *meta-* + *cinnabar* + *-ite*; orig. formed as G *metacinnabarit*] **:** a mineral HgS that consists of a native black mercuric sulfide and is polymorphous with cinnabar
**met·ac·neme** \'me,tak,nēm\ *n* -s [NL, fr. *meta-* + Gk *knēmē* leg, shin] **:** a mesentery of any of the various secondary sets developed in most zoantharians
**meta·cone** \'≠≠ *at* META- +,-\ *n* [*meta-* + *cone*] **:** the posterior of the three cusps of a primitive upper molar **:** the posteroexternal cusp in higher forms
**meta·co·nid** \,≠≠'kōnəd\ *n* -s [*meta-* + *con-* + *-id*] **:** the cusp of a lower molar corresponding to a metacone
**meta·co·nule** \"+'kōn(,)yül\ *n* -s [*meta-* + *con-* + *-ule*] **:** the posterior intermediate cusp of a mammalian upper molar between the hypocone and the metacone
**meta·coracoid** \¦≠≠+\ *n* [*meta-* + *coracoid*] **:** one of the two elements forming the coracoid process
**meta·cresol** \"+\ *n* [*meta-* + *cresol*] **:** the meta isomer of cresol — written systematically with ital. *meta-* or *m-*
**meta·cro·mi·on** \"+krōmē,än, -,ən\ *n* [NL, fr. *meta-* + *acromion*] **:** a process projecting backward and downward from the acromion of the scapula of some mammals
**meta·cryptozoite** \¦≠≠+\ *n* [*meta-* + *cryptozoite*] **:** a member of a second or subsequent generation of tissue-dwelling forms of a malaria parasite derived from the sporozoite without intervening generations of blood parasites — compare CRYPTOZOITE
**meta·cryst** \'≠≠,krist\ *n* -s [*meta-* + phenocryst] **:** a crystal of a secondary mineral embedded in metamorphic rock — called also *porphyroblast*
**meta·cyclic** \¦≠≠+\ *adj* [*meta-* + *cyclic*] *of a trypanosome* **:** broad and stocky, produced in an intermediate host, and infective for the definitive host
**me·tad** \mə'täd\ *or* **metad rat** *n* -s [Telugu dial. *mettād*] **:** a small field rat (*Millardia meltada*)
**meta·discoidal** \"+\ *adj* [*meta-* + *discoidal*] *of a placenta* **:** orig. diffuse but becoming discoidal (as in man and some apes)
**meta·dyne** \'≠≠,dīn\ *n* [*meta-* + *-dyne* (fr. Gk *dynamis* power) — more at DYNAMIC] **:** a direct-current generator used as an exciter and voltage control for larger machines
**metaestrus** *var of* METESTRUS
**meta·ethical** \¦≠≠ *at* META-+\ *adj* **:** of or relating to metaethics
**meta·ethics** \"+\ *n pl but usu sing in constr* [*meta-* + *ethics*] **:** a discipline dealing with the foundations of ethics specif. with the nature of normative utterances and ethical justification
**meta·galactic** \"+\ *adj* [ISV *meta-* + *galactic*] **:** of or relating to the metagalaxy
**meta·galaxy** \"+\ *n* [ISV *meta-* + *galaxy*] **:** the entire system of galaxies **:** UNIVERSE
**meta·gastric** \"+\ *adj* [*meta-* + *gastric*] **:** of or relating to the two posterior gastric lobes of the carapace of a crab
**met·age** \'mēd·ij, -ēt|, |ēj\ *n* -s [¹*mete* + *-age*] **1 :** the official measuring of contents or weight (as of coal or grain) **2 :** the charge for metage
**meta·gelatin** *also* **meta·gelatine** \¦≠≠ *at* META- +\ *n* [ISV *meta-* + *gelatin* or *gelatine*] **:** gelatin so modified by heat or acids that it remains fluid
**meta·genesis** \"+\ *n* [NL, fr. *meta-* after (fr. Gk *meta*) + L *genesis* — more at META-] **:** ALTERNATION OF GENERATIONS; *esp* **:** regular alternation of a sexual and an asexual generation
**meta·genetic** \"+\ *adj* [*meta-* + *genetic*] **:** of, relating to, or produced by metagenesis — **meta·genetically** \"+\ *adv*
**meta·gen·ic** \¦≠≠¦jenik\ *adj* [NL *metagenesis* + E *-ic*] **:** METAGENETIC
**me·tag·na·thous** \mə'tagnəthəs\ *adj* [*meta-* + *-gnathous*] **1** *of a bird* **:** having the tips of the mandibles crossed **2** *of an insect* **:** having biting mandibles in the larval stage and sucking mouth parts when adult — contrasted with *menognathous*
**me·tag·no·my** \-nəmē\ *n* -ES [F *métagnomie*, fr. *méta-* meta- + *-gnomie* -gnomy] **:** DIVINATION ⟨recent investigations . . . incline the student of psychic research toward a decidedly antispiritist explanation of ~ —H.H.U.Cross⟩
**meta·gon·i·mus** \,med·ə'gänəməs\ *n, cap* [NL, fr. *meta-* + Gk *gonimos* productive, creative — more at GONIMOBLAST] **:** a genus of small intestinal flukes (family Heterophyidae) that includes a species common in man, dog, and cat in parts of eastern Asia as a result of the eating of raw fish containing the larva
**me·tag·ra·phy** \mə'tagrəfē\ *n* -ES [*meta-* + *-graphy*] **:** TRANSLITERATION
**meta·grob·o·lize** \,med·ə'gräbə,līz\ *also* **meta·grab·o·lize** \-rab-\ *vt* -ED/-ING/-S [obs. F *metagraboulizer*, *matagraboliser*, fr. MF *matagraboliser*, *matagroboliser*] **:** PUZZLE, MYSTIFY ⟨all this duncical nonsense has my brains *metagrobolized* —*Wall Street Jour.*⟩
**meta·halloysite** \¦≠≠ *at* META-+\ *n* [*meta-* + *halloysite*] **:** a mineral consisting of a partially dehydrated halloysite
**meta·hewettite** \"+\ *n* [*meta-* + *hewettite*] **:** a mineral resembling hewettite but differing slightly from it in its behavior during hydration
**meta·hohmannite** \"+\ *n* [*meta-* + *hohmannite*] **:** a mineral consisting of a partially dehydrated hohmannite
**me·tai** \mə'tī\ *n, pl* **metai** *or* **metais** *usu cap* **1 :** a people of the Manipure valley of Assam in India **2 :** a member of the Metai people
**meta·igneous** \¦≠≠ *at* META-+\ *adj* [*meta-* + *igneous*] **:** of, relating to, or being metamorphosed igneous rock
**meta·kamacite** \"+\ *n* [*meta-* + *kamacite*] **:** a mineral $\alpha_2$-(Fe,Ni) consisting of an unstable distorted body-centered cubic alloy of iron and about six percent nickel occurring in meteorites
**meta·ken·trin** \,≠≠+'ken·trən\ *n* -s [*meta-* + Gk *kentron* sharp point, goad + E *-in* — more at CENTER] **:** LUTEINIZING HORMONE
**meta·ki·ne·sis** \,≠≠+\ *n* [NL, fr. *meta-* + *-kinesis*] **1 a :** METAPHASE **b :** PROMETAPHASE **2 :** dance movement with psychical overtones
**meta·kinetic** \"+\ *adj* **:** of, relating to, or characterized by metakinesis
**¹met·al** \'med·ᵊl, -etᵊl\ *n* -s *often attrib* [ME, fr. OF *metal*, *metail*, fr. L *metallum* metal, mine, fr. Gk *metallon* mine (later, metal); prob. akin to Gk *metallan* to search after, inquire about] **1 a :** any of a large group of substances (as gold, bronze, steel) that typically show a characteristic luster, are good conductors of electricity and heat, are opaque, can be fused, and are usu. malleable or ductile — compare ALLOY **b :** any such substance without reference to special character ⟨a piece of ~⟩ **c :** one of more than three fourths of the known chemical elements that exhibit typical metallic properties and that except for rubidium, cesium, gallium, and mercury are crystalline solids at or near room temperature **:** an element that in general is characterized chemically by the ability to form cations by loss of one or more electrons from each atom and to form basic oxides and hydroxides — compare METALLOID 2b **2 :** something that is made of metal: as **a :** SWORD ⟨draw this ~ from my side —Shak.⟩ **b** (1) **:** the barrel of a gun; *specif* **:** the surface of the barrel between the two sights (2) **:** the aggregate mass or power of guns or armament ⟨the British ship, more than twice as powerful in men and ~, struck her colors —Edward Breck⟩ **c metals** *pl, Brit* **:** the rails of a railroad ⟨a night train roared along the ~s —Rudyard Kipling⟩ ⟨one coach . . . had left the ~s —F.A.Swinnerton⟩ **3 :** either of the heraldic tinctures or and argent **4 :** METTLE ⟨showed his ~ in dealing with such austere diplomats —Claude Pepper⟩ **5 :** the material usu. earthy substance out of which a person or thing is made ⟨here's ~ more attractive —Shak.⟩ ⟨the ~ of which American character has been built —F.D.Roosevelt⟩ **6 a :** the basic material of glass; *esp* **:** glass in its molten state **b :** the regulus in copper smelting containing about 60 percent of copper — called also *blue metal* **7 a :** ore from which a metal is derived **b :** country rock as distinguished from coal — used esp. in coal mining **8 a :** a specific metallic alloy used in an art or trade ⟨roofer's ~ of the cheapest kind⟩ **b** (1) **:** printing type metal ⟨~ rule is softer than brass rule⟩ (2) **:** set type matter ⟨the book is now in ~⟩ ⟨alterations made in the ~⟩ **9** *Brit* **:** ROAD METAL
**²metal** \"\ *vt* **metaled** *or* **metalled**; **metaled** *or* **metalled**; **metaling** *or* **metalling** \'med·ᵊliŋ, -et(ᵊ)l-\ **metals 1 :** to cover or furnish with metal ⟨~ a ship's bottom⟩ **2** *Brit* **:** to provide with road metal: **a :** MACADAMIZE, HARD-SURFACE ⟨a bright ~*ed* road —Laurence Irving⟩ **b :** BALLAST 4a
**metal** *abbr* metallurgical; metallurgy
**metal age** *or* **metallurgic age** *n, usu cap M&A* **:** the period of the Bronze Age and the Iron Age
**meta·language** \'≠≠ *at* META-+,-\ *n* [*meta-* + *language*] **:** a language used to express data about or discuss another language — compare OBJECT LANGUAGE
**met·al·ate** \'med·ᵊl,āt, -etᵊl-, *usu* -ād.+V\ *vt* -ED/-ING/-S [back-formation fr. *metalation*] **:** to bring about metalation in
**met·al·a·tion** \,≠≠'āshən\ *n* -s [¹*metal* + *-ation*] **:** the process of attaching a metal atom to a carbon atom of an organic molecule
**meta·law** \'med·ə+,-\ *n* [*meta-* + *law*] **:** law that governs the correlative rights and duties of intelligent beings on earth and those intelligent beings that may be found in outer space and that is based on the postulate that those on earth must treat the others as they desire to be treated
**metal cloth** *n* **:** LAMÉ
**metal coloring** *n* **:** BRONZING 1
**metalcraft** \'≠≠,≠\ *n* **:** the art of executing artistic designs in metal (as in repoussé work, chasing, inlaying)
**met·al·de·hyde** \mə'taldə,hīd, me'-\ *n* [*meta-* + *aldehyde*] **:** a crystalline compound $(CH_3CHO)_4$ that is a tetramer of acetaldehyde formed by cold acidic treatment of acetaldehyde and that is used as a solid fuel for portable stoves and as a lure and poison for snails — compare PARALDEHYDE
**meta·lep·sis** \,med·ᵊl'epsəs\ *n, pl* **metalep·ses** \-,sēz\ [L, fr. Gk *metalēpsis*, lit., alteration, participation, fr. *metalambanein* to exchange, participate in, fr. *meta-* + *lambanein* to take — more at LATCH] **:** a figure of speech consisting in the substitution by metonymy of one figurative sense for another
**meta·lep·tic** \,med·ᵊl¦eptik\ *also* **meta·lep·ti·cal** \-təkəl\ *adj* [Gk *metalēptikos*, fr. (assumed) *metalēptos* (verbal of *metalambanein* to have a share of, exchange) + *-ikos* -ic, -ical] **:** of or relating to metalepsis — **meta·lep·ti·cal·ly** \-k(ə)lē\ *adv*
**met·al·er** *or* **met·al·ler** \'med·ᵊlə(r), -etᵊl-\ *n* -s **:** one that places metal sheets on sized work
**meta·lim·net·ic** \¦med·ə(,)lim¦ned·ik\ *adj* [NL *metalimnion* + E *-etic*] **:** of or relating to a thermocline
**meta·lim·ni·on** \,≠≠'limnē,än, -,ən\ *n, pl* **metalim·nia** \-nēə\ [NL, fr. *meta-* + *-limnion*] **:** THERMOCLINE
**metaling** *or* **metalling** *n* -s [fr. gerund of ²*metal*] *Brit* **:** road metal for a road or railroad
**meta·linguistic** \¦≠≠ *at* META- +\ *adj* [*meta-* + *linguistic*] **1 :** of or relating to a metalanguage ⟨~ expressions⟩ **2 :** belonging to metalinguistics ⟨~ analysis⟩
**meta·linguistics** \"+\ *n pl but sing in constr* [*meta-* + *linguistics*] **:** a branch of linguistics that deals with the relation of language to the rest of culture-determined behavior
**met·al·ist** *or* **met·al·list** \,med·ᵊləst, -etᵊl-\ *n* -s **:** a worker in metals
**metalize** *var of* METALLIZE
**metal·kase brick** \'≠≠,kās-\ *n* [¹*metal* + *-kase* (alter. of *case*)] **:** magnesite or magnesite-chrome brick provided with thin steel casings
**metall-** *or* **metallo-** *comb form* [L or Gk; L *metallum*, fr. Gk *metallon* mine (later, metal) — more at METAL] **1 :** metal ⟨*metallurgy*⟩ ⟨*metallography*⟩ **2 :** containing a metal atom or ion in the molecule ⟨*metalloflavoprotein*⟩
**metal leaf** *n* **:** thin metal sheet
**met·al·le·i·ty** \,med·ᵊl'ēəd·ē, -ētē, -i\ *n* -ES [prob. fr. F *métalléité*, fr. (assumed) VL *metalleus* of metal (fr. L *metallum* metal) + F *-ité* -ity] **:** METALLICITY
**metalli-** *comb form* [L, fr. *metallum*] **:** metal ⟨*metalliform*⟩ ⟨*metallify*⟩
**me·tal·lic** *also* **me·tal·ic** \mə'talik, -lēk\ *adj* [F or L; F *métallique*, fr. L *metallicus*, fr. Gk *metallikos* metallic, of mines, fr. *metallon* mine, metal + *-ikos* -ic — more at METAL] **1 a :** of, relating to, or being a metal ⟨a ~ element⟩ ⟨metals and alloys form a distinct subdivision of the solid state of matter known as the ~ state —Marian Balicki⟩ **b :** made of or containing a metal ⟨~ salts⟩ ⟨~ ceiling⟩ **c :** having properties of a metal ⟨a ~ substance⟩; *esp* **:** exhibiting the characteristic properties of a metal in the free elemental state ⟨~ lead⟩ ⟨~ selenium⟩ **2 :** yielding metal **:** METALLIFEROUS **3 :** resembling metal: **a** *of a color* **:** having reflective and iridescent properties similar to those of a freshly cut surface of a metal ⟨~ gray finish⟩ ⟨the birds were . . . a brilliant ~ green and black —John Seago⟩ **b** *of a taste sensation* **:** resembling that produced by various metals esp. in mildly acrid unpleasant quality ⟨the tea had a ~ taste⟩ **c** *of a sound* **:** SHARP, HARSH, GRATING ⟨~ voice⟩ ⟨~ laughter⟩ ⟨the monotonous, ~ note of the bellbird —Llewelyn Powys⟩ **d** *of a literary style* **:** STARK ⟨minor poets . . . better employed in being brittle and bright and ~ than in being soft and opulently luscious —Elinor Wylie⟩ **e** *of a person* **:** cold, sharp, and hard **:** MECHANICAL ⟨hard-boiled businessmen, ~ women —Jacques Maritain⟩ — **me·tal·li·cal·ly** \-lək(ə)lē, -lēk-, -li\ *adv*
**metallic bond** *n* **:** the chemical bond typical of the metallic state and characterized by mobile valence electrons that hold the atoms together usu. in crystal lattices and are responsible for the good electrical and heat conductivity of metals
**metallic brown** *n* **1 :** any of various light reddish brown to dark purplish brown pigments that are made by calcining limonite or siderite ores and contain about 50 percent or more of ferric oxide **2 :** MINERAL BROWN
**metallic cartridge** *n* **:** a cartridge with a metal case — used esp. to distinguish a fixed load from a loose powder-and-ball load or a paper cartridge
**metallic glaze** *n* **:** a glaze with a metallic film on its surface formed as a result of the reduction of a metallic oxide by the kiln fire
**metallic gray** *n* **:** GRANITE 4
**met·al·lic·i·ty** \,med·ᵊl'isəd·ē\ *n* -ES **:** the quality or state of being metallic
**me·tal·li·cize** \mə'talə,sīz\ *vt* -ED/-ING/-S **:** to make (as a

telephone line) fully metallic by adding another wire in place of a ground return

**metallic luster** *n* **:** a luster characteristic of metals in a compact state and shown also by other substances (as a mineral or dye)

**metallic oxide** *n* **:** an oxide of a metal

**metallic paint** *n* **1 :** a paint in which the pigment is chiefly iron oxide and which is used for painting metal surfaces **2 :** a paint in which the pigment is a metal (as bronze powder)

**metallic paper** *n* **1 :** paper so coated (as with lime, whiting, and size) that marks made on it with a metal point are indelible **2 :** paper coated with finely flaked metal to give the effect of a metallic surface **3 :** paper to which a metallic foil has been laminated — called also *foil, foil paper*

**metallic red** *n* **:** a pigment similar to metallic brown but containing a higher percentage of ferric oxide

**me·tal·lics** \mə'taliks, -lēks\ *n pl* **:** metallic substances

**metallic soap** *n* **:** a salt of a monocarboxylic acid (as a higher fatty acid, resin acid, naphthenic acid) and usu. a bivalent or trivalent metal (as calcium, cobalt, zinc, copper, lead, aluminum) that typically is insoluble in water but soluble in benzene and that is used chiefly in lubricants or driers, in thickening, waterproofing, or flatting, or in fungicides

**met·al·lif·er·ous** \ˌmed·ᵊlˈif(ə)rəs, -etᵊl-\ *adj* [L *metallifer* metalliferous (fr. *metalli-* metal — fr. *metallum* — + *-fer* -ferous) + E *-ous*] **:** yielding or containing metal ⟨~ veins⟩ ⟨~ deposits⟩ ⟨a ~ compound whose very existence is still a geological enigma —J.D.Hillaby⟩

**metallike** \'==,=\ *adj* **:** resembling a metal in properties **:** METALLIC 1b

**met·al·line** \'med·ᵊl,īn, -,ēn, -ən\ *adj* [ME *mettaline*, fr. MF or ML; MF *metaline*, fr. ML *metallinus* made of metal, fr. L *metallum* metal + *-inus* -ine] **1 :** METALLIC 1 **2 :** impregnated with metallic substances ⟨~ water⟩

**metalling** *var of* METALING

**metallist** *var of* METALIST

**met·al·li·za·tion** *also* **met·al·i·za·tion** \ˌmed·ᵊlə'zāshən, -etᵊl-, -ᵊl,ī'z-\ *n* -s **:** the process of metallizing

**met·al·lize** *also* **met·al·ize** \'med·ᵊl,īz, -etᵊl-\ *vt* -ED/-ING/-S [¹*metal* + *-ize*] **1 :** to treat with a metal: as **a :** to coat with a metal (as by spraying) ⟨~ filament lamps⟩ **b :** to impregnate with metal or a metallic compound **2 :** to combine (as an azo dye) with a metal

**metallo-** — see METALL-

**me·tal·lo·genetic** \mə¦taləjə¦ned·ik\ *also* **me·tal·lo·genic** \-¦jenik\ *adj* [*metall-* + *-genetic* or *-genic*] **:** relating to the origin of ores

**me·tal·lo·graph** \='==,graf\ *n* [*metall-* + *-graph*] **1 :** a metallurgical microscope equipped with a camera **2 :** a photomicrograph, microradiograph, or electronmicrograph of a metallic surface

**met·al·log·ra·pher** \ˌmed·ᵊl'ägrəfə(r), -etᵊl-\ *also* **met·al·log·ra·phist** \-fəst\ *n* -s [*metallography* + *-er* or *-ist*] **:** one that specializes in the visual study of the structure of metals and alloys

**me·tal·lo·graph·ic** \mə¦talə¦grafik\ *also* **me·tal·lo·graph·i·cal** \-fəkəl\ *adj* [F *métallographique*, fr. *métallographie*, n. + *-ique* -ic, -ical] **:** of, relating to, or produced by means of metallography ⟨~ examination of sheet copper⟩ — **me·tal·lo·graph·i·cal·ly** \-fək(ə)lē\ *adv*

**met·al·log·ra·phy** \ˌmed·ᵊl'ägrəfē, -etᵊl-, -fi\ *n* -ES [F *métallographie*, fr. *métallo-* metall- + *-graphie* -graphy] **:** a study of the structure of metals and alloys; *esp* **:** study of such structure with the microscope

¹**met·al·loid** \'med·ᵊl,òid, -etᵊl-\ *n* -s [*metall-* + *-oid*] **1** *archaic* **:** an alkali metal (as sodium) or an alkaline-earth metal (as calcium) **2 a :** NONMETAL **b :** a nonmetal (as carbon or nitrogen) that can combine with a metal to form an alloy ⟨low ~ steel (almost pure iron) —*Steelways*⟩ **c :** an element (as boron, silicon, arsenic, or tellurium) intermediate in properties between the typical metals and nonmetals — compare SEMICONDUCTOR

²**metalloid** \"\ *also* **met·al·loi·dal** \¦==¦òidᵊl\ *adj* [*metalloid* fr. *metalloid*, n.; *metalloidal* fr. *metalloid* + *-al*] **1 :** resembling a metal **2 :** of, relating to, or being a metalloid

**metallo-organic** \mə¦talō+\ *also* **me·tal·lor·gan·ic** \mə¦tal, ¦med·ᵊl+\ *adj* [ISV *metall-* + *organic*] *of an organic compound* **:** containing a metal in the molecule; *esp* **:** ORGANOMETALLIC

**me·tal·lo·phone** \mə'talə,fōn\ *n* [ISV *metall-* + *-phone*] **:** a percussion musical instrument of definite pitch consisting of a series of graduated metal bars that are struck by hammers either manually or by a mechanical arrangement controlled from a keyboard

**me·tal·lo·porphyrin** \mə,talō+\ *n* [*metall-* + *porphyrin*] **:** a compound (as heme) formed from a porphyrin and a metal ion

**me·tal·lo·scope** \mə'talə,skōp\ *n* [*metall-* + *-scope*] **:** an instrument for examining metal

**met·al·los·co·py** \ˌmed·ᵊl'äskəpē\ *n* -ES [*metall-* + *-scopy*] **:** the act or process of examining metal with a metalloscope

**met·al·lur·gi·cal** \¦med·ᵊl¦ərjəkəl, -etᵊl-, -'əj-, -əij-, -jēk-\ *also* **met·al·lur·gic** \-jik, -jēk\ *adj* **:** of or relating to metallurgy — **met·al·lur·gi·cal·ly** \-jək(ə)lē, -jēk-, -li\ *adv*

**met·al·lur·gist** \'med·ᵊl,ərjəst, -etᵊl-, -əj-, -əij- *chiefly Brit* mə'talə(r)jəst\ *n* -s [NL *metallurgia* + E *-ist*] **:** a specialist in the science or application of metallurgy

**met·al·lur·gy** \-jē, -ji\ *n* -ES [NL *metallurgia*, fr. Gk *metallourgein* to work a mine (fr. *metallon* mine, metal + *ergon* work) + *-ia* -y — more at METAL, WORK] **:** a science and technology that deals with the extraction of metals from their ores, refining them, and preparing them for use and includes processes (as alloying, rolling, and heat-treating) and the study of the structure and properties of metals

**metal man** *n* **:** a worker who melts used type metal and casts it for reuse

**metalmark** \'==,=\ *n* [so called fr. the metallic spots or lines on its wings] **:** a butterfly of the family Riodinidae

**meta·log·ic** \¦med·ᵊl¦äjik, -d·ə¦lä-\ *n* [ML *Metalogicus*, title of a work on logic by John of Salisbury †1180 Eng. ecclesiastical leader and classical scholar] **:** a branch of analytic philosophy that deals with the critical examination of the basic concepts of logic abstracted from any meaning given them in the systems studied ⟨the ~ which grounds or justifies the logical system as a whole —R.L.Barber⟩

**meta·log·i·cal** \-jəkəl\ *adj* **1 a :** of or relating to metalogic ⟨~ investigations⟩ **b :** SYNTACTICAL **2 :** passing beyond the scope of logic ⟨not only in poetry are such ~ meanings found —Philip Wheelwright⟩ — **meta·logically** \-k(ə)lē, -li\ *adv*

**meta·loph** \'med·ə,läf\ *n* -s [*meta-* + *-loph*] **:** a crest on a lophodont molar extending from the ectoloph to the hypocone

**metal-organic** \¦==,=¦==\ *adj* **:** ORGANOMETALLIC

**metals** *pl of* METAL, *pres 3d sing of* METAL

**metalsmith** \'==,=\ *n* [¹*metal* + *smith*] **:** one skilled in metalworking

**metalware** \'==,=\ *n* **:** work or ware of metal; *esp* **:** metal utensils for household use ⟨table . . . loaded with a lot of shiny hotel ~ —John Dos Passos⟩

**metalwork** \'==,=\ *n* [¹*metal* + *work*] **:** a product of metalworking ⟨fine glass and ~ for export trade —Frances Rogers & Alice Beard⟩ ⟨sheet ~⟩ ⟨bench ~⟩

**metalworker** \'==,==\ *n* **:** one that is employed in metalworking

**metalworking** \'==,==\ *n* -s **:** the act or process of shaping things out of metal ⟨primitive ~⟩

**metalworks** \'==,=\ *n pl but usu sing in constr* [¹*metal* + *works*] **:** a workshop or factory where metal is treated, forged, or otherwise shaped

**meta·mathematical** \¦== *at* META- +\ *adj* [*meta-* + *mathematical*] **:** of or relating to metamathematics

**meta·mathematician** \"+\ *n* **:** a specialist in metamathematics

**metamathematics** \"+\ *n pl but usu sing in constr* [*meta-* + *mathematics*] **:** the philosophy of mathematics; *esp* **:** the logical syntax of mathematics ⟨~ . . . is the analysis of such mathematical concepts as "function", "variable", "real number" —Arthur Pap⟩

**meta·mer** \'med·əmə(r)\ *n* -s [*meta-* + *isomer*] **1 :** a chemical compound that is metameric with one or more others **2 :** either of two colors that appear identical to the eye but have different spectral composition

**meta·mere** \-,mi(ə)r\ *n* -s [ISV *meta-* + *-mere*] **:** any of a linear series of primitively similar segments into which the body of a higher invertebrate or vertebrate is divisible and which are usu. clearly distinguishable in the embryo, identifiable in somewhat modified form in various invertebrates (as annelid worms), and detectable in the adult higher vertebrate only in specialized segmentally arranged structures (as cranial and spinal nerves or vertebrae) **:** SOMITE — see ANTIMERE

**meta·mer·ic** \¦==¦merik\ *adj* [*meta-* + *mer-* (part) + *-ic*] **1 :** relating to or exhibiting chemical metamerism **:** ISOMERIC **2 a :** of, relating to, or exhibiting bodily metamerism ⟨a ~ animal⟩ **b :** of, relating to, or occurring in a metamere **:** SEGMENTAL ⟨~ arrangement of blood vessels⟩ — **meta·mer·i·cal·ly** \-rək(ə)lē\ *adv*

**me·tam·er·ism** \mə'tamə,rizəm\ *n* -s **1 :** isomerism esp. of chemical compounds of the same type (as butylamine and methyl-propyl-amine) **2 :** the condition of having or the stage of evolutionary development characterized by a body made up of metameres that is usu. held to be an essential prelude to the differentiation of the more highly organized animals (as arthropods and vertebrates) through the disproportionate development and elaboration of some segments together with the coalescence, reduction, or loss of others

**met·a·mer·ization** \ˌmed·əmərə'zāshən, mə,tamər-, -,rī'z-\ *n* -s [ISV *metamer-* (fr. *metamere*) + *-ization*] **:** the formation or differentiation of metameres

**me·tam·er·ized** \mə'tamə,rīzd, 'med·əmə,r-\ *adj* [*metamere* + *-ize* + *-ed*] **:** divided into metameres ⟨a ~ embryo⟩

**me·tam·er·ous** \mə'tamərəs\ *adj* [*metamerism* + *-ous*] **:** METAMERIC

**me·tam·ery** \-rē\ *n* -ES [*meta-* + *-mery*] **:** METAMERISM

**meta·mict** \'med·ə,mikt\ *adj* [*meta-* + Gk *miktos* mixed, compounded, verbal of *mignynai, meignynai* to mix — more at MIX] *of a mineral* **:** amorphous because of the disruption of the crystal structure by radiation from contained or nearby radioactive atoms

**meta·mitosis** \¦== *at* META- +\ *n* [NL, fr. *meta-* + *mitosis*] **:** mitosis involving both nuclear and cytoplasmic activities **:** EUMITOSIS

**meta·mor·phic** \¦==¦mòrfik, -ô(ə)f-\ *adj* [*metamorphosis* + *-ic*] **1 :** of or relating to metamorphosis ⟨a ~ stage⟩ **2** *of a rock* **:** of, relating to, or produced by metamorphism ⟨~ granite⟩

**meta·mor·phism** \¦==¦=,fizəm\ *n* -s [*metamorphosis* + *-ism*] **1 :** METAMORPHOSIS **2 :** a change in the constitution of rock; *specif* **:** a pronounced change usu. effected by action of pressure, heat, and water that results in a more compact and more highly crystalline condition of the rock — compare ANAMORPHISM 2, EPIGENESIS 2, KATAMORPHISM

**meta·mor·phize** \,==¦=,fīz\ *vt* -ED/-ING/-S [L *metamorphosis* + E *-ize*] **:** METAMORPHOSE

¹**meta·mor·phose** \-,fōz, -ōs\ *vb* -ED/-ING/-S [prob. fr. MF *metamorphoser*, fr. *metamorphose*, n.] *vt* **1 a :** to change into a different physical form; *esp* **:** to effect such a change in, by, or as if by supernatural means ⟨men were by the force of that herb *metamorphosed* into swine —Richard Steele⟩ **b :** to change strikingly the appearance or character of **:** TRANSFORM ⟨you are so *metamorphosed* I can hardly think you my master —Shak.⟩ ⟨*metamorphosing* the most familiar things and endowing them with a sense of mystery —J.B.D.Cotter⟩ **2 :** to cause (rock) to undergo metamorphism ⟨the rocks had been baked and thereby *metamorphosed* —Arthur Holmes⟩ ~ *vi* **1 :** to undergo biological metamorphosis ⟨a tadpole ~*s* into a frog⟩ **2 :** to undergo a transformation ⟨the little song . . . later *metamorphosed* into one of the noblest chorales —P.L. Miller⟩ ⟨many humans never ~ into moral manhood —Weston La Barre⟩ **syn** see TRANSFORM

²**met·a·mor·phose** \-,fōs\ *n* -s [prob. fr. MF *metamorphose*, fr. L *metamorphosis*] *archaic* **:** METAMORPHOSIS

**meta·mor·pho·sis** \,==¦mô(r)fəsəs *sometimes* -,mô(r)'fōs-\ *n* [L, fr. Gk *metamorphōsis*, fr. *metamorphoun* to transform, fr. *meta-* change, transformation (fr. *meta* with, between, after) + *morphē* form — more at META-, FORM] **1 a :** change of physical form or substance; *esp* **:** such a change brought about by or as if by supernatural means ⟨the ~ of men into animals⟩ **b :** a striking alteration (as in appearance, character, or circumstances) ⟨~ of the old house which he had inherited —Claud Phillimore⟩ ⟨the prospect of facing his . . . family and guests in this new ~ —David Walden⟩ **2 a :** a marked and more or less abrupt change in the form or structure of an animal during postembryonic development (as when the larva of an insect becomes a pupa or a tadpole changes into a frog) ⟨~ of a butterfly⟩ — compare EPIMORPHOSIS **b :** the sum of the various modifications whether phylogenetic or primarily ontogenetic through which a primitive plant structure may pass in the course of its development **c** *archaic* **:** evolutionary change or modification of form over the centuries **3 a :** transformation of one kind of tissue into another ⟨~ of cartilage into bone⟩ **b :** tissue degeneration marked by conversion of tissues or structures into other material ⟨fatty ~ of the liver⟩ **4 a :** a chemical change (as oxidation, reduction, hydrolysis, substitution) **b :** a changing of a chemical compound into an isomeric form **5 :** a transformation of a musical figure or idea into a rhythmically or melodically altered repetition of the original ⟨its continuity . . . relies upon the ~ of themes rather than the use of the leitmotiv —Norman Demuth⟩

**meta·mor·phot·ic** \¦==,=¦fäd·ik\ *adj* [*metamorphosis* + *-otic* (as in *narcotic*)] **:** METAMORPHIC

**meta·myelocyte** \¦==+\ *n* [ISV *meta-* + *myelocyte*] **:** a granulocyte that is the least mature present in normal blood and is distinguished by typical cytoplasmic granulation in combination with a simple kidney-shaped nucleus

**met·amyn·o·don** \,med·ə'minə,dän\ *n, cap* [NL, fr. *meta-* + *Amynodon*] **:** a genus of hornless rhinoceroses from the Oligocene of No. America and Asia

**met·analysis** \¦med·+\ *n* [*meta-* + *analysis*] **:** the analysis of words or groups of words into new elements (as *an apron* for *a napron*) — called also *affix-clipping*

**meta·nauplius** \¦== *at* META- + \ *n* [NL, fr. *meta-* + *nauplius*] **:** a crustacean larva of the stage after the nauplius that has about seven pairs of appendages

**met·an·dric** \mə'tandrik\ *adj* [*meta-* + *-andric* (as in *holandric*)] *of an annelid worm* **:** retaining only the posterior pair of the primitive two pairs of testes — compare HOLANDRIC, PROANDRIC

**meta·nemertini** \¦== *at* META- +\ *n pl, cap* [NL, fr. *meta-* + *Nemertini*] *in some classifications* **:** an order of Nemertea comprising forms in which the brain and lateral nerves lie within the somatic musculature

**meta·nephric** \"+\ *also* **meta·nephritic** \"+\ *adj* [*metanephric* fr. *meta-* + *nephr-* + *-ic*; *metanephritic* fr. *meta-* + *nephritic*] **:** of or relating to the metanephros

**meta·ne·phrid·i·al** \"+\ *adj* [NL *metanephridium* + E *-al*] **:** of, relating to, or having metanephridia

**meta·nephridium** \"+\ *n* [NL, fr. *meta-* + *nephridium*] **:** a nephridium that originates in a ciliated coelomic funnel — compare PROTONEPHRIDIUM

**meta·neph·ro·gen·ic** \¦==¦nefrə¦jenik\ *adj* [NL *metanephros* + E *-genic*] **:** producing the metanephroi

**meta·neph·ros** \,==¦ne,fräs\ *also* **meta·neph·ron** \-,frän\ *n, pl* **metaneph·roi** \-,fròi\ *also* **metaneph·ra** \-,frə\ [NL, fr. *meta-* situated behind (fr. Gk *meta* after) + *-nephros* — more at META-] **:** one of the posterior of the three pairs of embryonic renal organs developed in higher vertebrates persisting in the adult as the definitive kidney — compare MESONEPHROS

**meta·nepionic** \¦==+\ *adj* [*meta-* + *nepionic*] **:** of, relating to, or being the median of the three nepionic stages in the development of an individual **:** late nepionic

**met·a·nil·ic acid** \¦med·ə¦nilik-\ *n* [ISV *meta-* + *sulfanilic acid*] **:** a crystalline sulfonic acid $H_2NC_6H_4SO_3H$ that is isomeric with sulfanilic acid, is made by sulfonating nitrobenzene and then reducing, and is used as an intermediate for azo dyes; *meta*-amino-benzenesulfonic acid

**met·a·nil yellow** \'med·ə,nil-\ *n, often cap M&Y* [ISV *metanil*, fr. *metanilic (acid)*] **:** a yellow azo dye made from diazotized metanilic acid and diphenylamine — see DYE table I (under *Acid Yellow 36*)

**meta·noia** \,med·ə'nòi(y)ə\ *n* -s [Gk, fr. *metanoein* to change one's mind, repent, be converted (fr. *meta-* + *noein* to perceive, think) + *-ia* -y; akin to Gk *noos, nous* mind] **:** a fundamental transformation of mind or character; *specif* **:** a spiritual conversion

**meta·no·tal** \¦==¦nōdᵊl\ *adj* [NL *metanotum* + E *-al*] **:** of, relating to, or situated on the metanotum

**meta·no·tum** \,==¦nōd·əm\ *n* [NL, fr. *meta-* + Gk *nōton* back — more at NATES] **:** the dorsal portion of the metathoracic integument of an insect

**meta·nym** \'med·ə,nim\ *n* -s [*meta-* + *-onym*] **:** a generic name rejected because based on a type species congeneric with the type of a previously published genus

**metaperiodic acid** *n* [*meta-* + *periodic*] **:** PERIODIC ACID b

**metaperrhenic acid** *n* [*meta-* + *perrhenic*] **:** PERRHENIC ACID a

**metaph** *abbr* **1** metaphor; metaphorical **2** metaphysical; metaphysics

**meta·phase** \'med·ə+,-\ *n* [ISV *meta-* + *phase*; orig. formed in G] **:** the stage of mitosis preceding the anaphase

**metaphase plate** *n* **:** the equatorial plane of the spindle with the chromosomes as oriented therein during metaphase

**Met·a·phen** \'med·əfən\ *trademark* — used for nitromersol

**meta·phloem** \¦== *at* META- +\ *n* [*meta-* + *phloem*] **:** the later-formed part of the primary phloem that consists of mature phloem elements and is differentiated mainly after elongation of the axis has ceased — compare PROTOPHLOEM

**met·a·phone** \'==,fōn\ *n* [*meta-* + *-phone*] **:** a free allophonic variant chosen in preference to another because regarded as more suitable to the style of speech being used

**met·a·phon·ic** \¦==¦fänik\ *adj* [*meta-* + *-phonic*] **:** of or relating to umlaut **:** cognate in a manner explainable in terms of metaphony

**me·taph·o·ny** \mə'tafənē, me'-\ *n* -ES [ISV *meta-* + *-phony*] **:** UMLAUT

**met·a·phor** \'med·ə,fô(ə)r, 'metə-, -ô(ə) *also* -,fə(r) *sometimes* -,fō(ə)r *or* -ōə\ *n* -s [MF or L; MF *metaphore*, fr. L *metaphora*, fr. Gk, fr. *metapherein* to transfer, change, fr. *meta-* + *pherein* to bear — more at BEAR] **:** a figure of speech in which a word or phrase denoting one kind of object or action is used in place of another to suggest a likeness or analogy between them (as in *the ship plows the seas* or in *a volley of oaths*) **:** an implied comparison (as in *a marble brow*) in contrast to the explicit comparison of the simile (as in *a brow white as marble*) — compare TROPE

**met·a·phor·i·cal** \¦==¦fòrəkəl, -¦fär-, -rēk-\ *also* **met·a·phor·ic** \-rik, -rēk\ *adj* [*metaphorical* fr. ML *metaphoricus* metaphorical (fr. Gk *metaphorikos*, fr. *metaphora* metaphor + *-ikos* -ic) + E *-al*; *metaphoric* fr. ML *metaphoricus*] **:** of, relating to, characteristic of, or comprising a metaphor ⟨a ~ expression⟩ — **met·a·phor·i·cal·ly** \-rək(ə)lē, -rēk-, -li\ *adv* — **met·a·phor·i·cal·ness** \-kəlnəs\ *n* -ES

**met·a·phor·ist** \'==,fòrəst, -,fər-\ *n* -s **:** one who makes metaphors

**meta·phor·ize** \-,fə,rīz, -,fō,-\ *vb* -ED/-ING/-S [F *métaphoriser*, fr. *métaphore* metaphor + *-iser* -ize] *vt* **:** to express metaphorically ~ *vi* **:** to make metaphors

**meta·phosphate** \¦== *at* META- +\ *n* [ISV *metaphosph-* (fr. *metaphosphoric acid*) + *-ate*] **1 :** a salt or ester of a metaphosphoric acid — see SODIUM METAPHOSPHATE, TETRAMETAPHOSPHATE, TRIMETAPHOSPHATE **2 :** any of various usu. glassy phosphates approximating a metaphosphate in composition — see SODIUM PHOSPHATE GLASS

**meta·phosphoric acid** \"+-\ *n* [*meta-* + *phosphoric acid*] **:** an acid $HPO_3$ or $(HPO_3)_n$ formed by heating orthophosphoric acid but usu. obtained in the form of salts

¹**met·a·phrase** \'med·ə,frāz\ *n* [NL *metaphrasis*, fr. Gk, fr. *metaphrazein* to translate (fr. *meta-* + *phrazein* to point out, show, tell) + *-sis*] **1** *archaic* **:** a translation esp. in verse **:** PARAPHRASE **2 :** a literal translation from one language into another — opposed to *paraphrase*

²**metaphrase** \"\ *vt* **1 :** to make a metaphrase of **2** *archaic* **:** to render into verse **3 :** to alter the wording of

**me·taph·ra·sis** \mə'tafrəsəs, me'-\ *n* -ES [NL] **:** METAPHRASE

**met·a·phrast** \'med·ə,frast\ *n* -s [MGk *metaphrastēs*, fr. Gk *metaphrazein* to translate] **:** TRANSLATOR; *specif* **:** one who turns verse into a different meter or prose into verse — **met·a·phras·tic** \¦==¦frastik\ *or* **met·a·phras·ti·cal** \-təkəl\ *adj* — **met·a·phras·ti·cal·ly** \-k(ə)lē\ *adv*

**me·taph·y·se·al** \mə¦tafə¦sēəl, -¦zēəl *also* ¦med·ə¦fizē-\ *adj* [NL *metaphysis* + E *-eal* (as in *apophyseal*)] **:** of or relating to a metaphysis ⟨~ decalcification⟩

¹**meta·phys·ic** \¦== *at* META- + ¦fizik, -ēk\ *n* -s [ME *methaphesik, metaphesyk*, fr. ML *metaphysica*, fem. sing. & neut. pl. — more at METAPHYSICS] **1 a :** METAPHYSICS ⟨the most fantastic speculations of the later German ~ —Josiah Royce⟩ ⟨~ did not mean much to him —*Times Lit. Supp.*⟩ **b :** a particular system or theory of metaphysics ⟨this view of nature and man's place in nature is a ~ —W.H.Sheldon⟩ ⟨the three possible monistic ~*s*: materialism, idealism, and neutral monism —J.W.Smith⟩ **2 :** the system of first principles or philosophy underlying a particular study or subject of inquiry ⟨each injustice . . . rationalizes the claims it embodies by sheltering under a half-examined ~ of values —H.J.Laski⟩ ⟨the ~ of his love poems —George Haines⟩

²**metaphysic** \"\ *adj* [ML *metaphysicus*, after Gk *Ta meta ta Physika* (a work by Aristotle), lit., the (work) after the *Physics* (a work by Aristotle)] **:** METAPHYSICAL

**meta·phys·i·cal** \-zəkəl, -zēk-\ *adj* [ME, fr. ML *metaphysicalis*, fr. *metaphysica* metaphysics + L *-alis* -al] **1 :** of, relating to, or based on metaphysics ⟨~ truth⟩ ⟨the ~ assumption⟩ ⟨idealism which still remained ~ although no longer explicitly theistic —Emil Brunner⟩ **2 a :** of or relating to what is conceived as transcendent, supersensible, or transcendental ⟨fleeing from experience to a ~ realm —John Dewey⟩ **b :** PRETERNATURAL ⟨fate and ~ aid doth seem to have thee crown'd —Shak.⟩ **c** *archaic* **:** IMAGINARY, FANCIFUL ⟨those ~ persons . . . John Doe and Richard Roe —Sir Walter Scott⟩ **3 a :** showing an inclination toward or addiction to metaphysics ⟨a ~ man⟩ ⟨his ~ talent —Harriet B. Stowe⟩ **b :** highly abstract or abstruse ⟨~ reasoning⟩ ⟨the prohibition of ~ questions —*Social Research*⟩ **4 a :** synthetic a priori ⟨a ~ judgment⟩ **b :** neither analytic nor subject to empirical verification ⟨the view . . . that ~ statements are not, as scientific statements are, descriptions of real features of fact, but, at best, expressions of attitudes about which rational argument is impossible —W.H.Walsh⟩ **5 :** of, relating to, or producing metaphysical poetry ⟨~ school⟩ ⟨~ poem⟩ ⟨~ poet⟩

**meta·phys·i·cal·ly** \-zək(ə)lē, -zēk-, -li\ *adv* **1 :** in the manner of metaphysics or of a metaphysician ⟨the assimilation of men to machines, whatever may be thought of it ~, is hardly likely to give us a just standard of values —Bertrand Russell⟩ **2 :** in the mode of a metaphysical reality or existence ⟨the universal was more real ~, than the particular —John Dewey⟩

**metaphysical poetry** *n* **:** highly intellectualized poetry marked by bold and ingenious conceits, incongruous imagery, complexity and subtlety of thought, frequent use of paradox, and often by deliberate harshness or rigidity of expression

**metaphysical truth** *n* **:** the truth of ultimate reality as partly or wholly transcendent of perceived actuality and experience

**meta·physician** \,==+\ *n* [prob. fr. MF *metaphysicien*, fr. *metaphysique* metaphysics (fr. ML *metaphysica*) + *-ien* -an] **:** one who is versed in or advocates metaphysics ⟨the ~ . . . is trying to provide for all possible classes of facts rather than to predict which will be actualized —Charles Hartshorne⟩ ⟨every significant artist is a ~, a propounder of beauty-truths and form-theories —Aldous Huxley⟩ ⟨the ~ of history pretends that every scene is what it is by virtue of its role in the play as a whole —Kurt Riezler⟩

**meta·phys·i·cize** \,==¦fizə,sīz\ *vi* -ED/-ING/-S [¹*metaphysic* + *-ize*] **:** to engage in metaphysical speculation

**meta·phys·ics** \¦==¦fiziks, -zēks\ *n pl but usu sing in constr* [pl. of ¹*metaphysic*; rendering of ML *metaphysica*, neut. pl., fr. Gk (*ta*) *meta* (*ta*) *physika* the (works) after the physics, the things after those relating to external nature; fr. the fact that this section of the collected works of Aristotle †322 B.C. Greek philosopher was reputedly so designated by the editor, Andronicus of Rhodes *fl* 1st cent. B.C. Greek philosopher in Rome, because it came after the physics] **1 a** (1) **:** a division of philosophy that includes ontology and cosmology ⟨~ . . . treats of the relations obtaining between the underlying reality and its manifestations —Fred Sommers⟩ ⟨~ . . . analyzes the generic traits manifested by existences of any kind —J.H. Randall⟩ ⟨~, or the attempt to conceive the world as a whole by means of thought, has been developed, from the first, by the union and conflict of two very different human impulses, the one urging men towards mysticism, the other urging them towards science —Bertrand Russell⟩ (2) : ontology and epistemology ⟨~ as a philosophic discipline . . . concerned with the nature of the real only so far as that problem is amenable to the reflective method —C.I.Lewis⟩ (3) : ONTOLOGY **b** (1) : something that deals with what is beyond the physical or the experiential (2) : the more abstruse philosophical sciences ⟨the mathematics and the ~, fall to them as you find your stomach serves you —Shak.⟩ **2** : METAPHYSIC 2b ⟨differentiates between a theory of esthetic experience and a ~ of beauty —J.G.Brennan⟩ ⟨each language . . . conceals a unique ~ —B.L.Whorf⟩ ⟨erected a ~ on this fundamental antagonism of vitality or "Life" . . . and what he calls "Spirit" —V.C.Aldrich⟩ **3** : the Christian Science system of mental healing

**me·taph·y·sis** \mə̇'tafəsə̇s\ *n, pl* **metaphy·ses** \-əˌsēz\ [NL, fr. *meta-* + *-physis* (as in NL *apophysis*)] : the transitional zone at which the diaphysis and epiphysis of a bone come together

**meta·phyte** \'== *at* META- + ˌfīt\ *n* -s [ISV *meta-* + *-phyte;* orig. formed as G *metaphyt*] : a multicellular plant — compare PROTOPHYTE — **meta·phyt·ic** \¦==¦fid·ik\ *adj*

**meta·pla·sia** \ˌ=='plāzh(ē)ə\ *n* -s [NL, fr. *meta-* + *-plasia*] **1** : transformation of one tissue into another ⟨~ of cartilage into bone⟩ **2** : abnormal replacement of cells of one type by cells of another

**meta·plasm** \'==ˌplazəm\ *n* -s **1** [L *metaplasmus,* lit., transformation, fr. Gk *metaplasmos,* fr. *metaplassein* to remold, fr. *meta-* + *plassein* to mold — more at PLASTER] : alteration of regular verbal, grammatical, or rhetorical structure usu. by transposition of the letters or syllables of a word or of the words in a sentence **2** [ISV *meta-* + *-plasm;* orig. formed as G *metaplasma*] : material consisting of lifeless derivatives of protoplasm (as cell walls, starch grains) — **meta·plas·mic** \¦==¦plazmik\ *adj*

**meta·plast** \'==ˌplast\ *n* -s [*meta-* + *-plast*] : a metaplasmic body

**meta·plastic** \¦==+\ *adj* [*meta-* + *-plastic*] **1** : relating to or produced by metaplasia **2** : of or relating to metaplasm

**meta·pleural** \"+\ *adj* [NL *metapleur*on + E *-al*] : of or relating to a metapleuron

**meta·pleuron** \¦==+\ *n, pl* **metapleura** \"+\ [NL, fr. *meta-* + *pleuron*] : a pleuron of the metathorax of an insect

**meta·pneumonic** \"+\ *adj* [*meta-* + *pneumonic*] : secondary to pneumonia

**met·ap·neus·tic** \¦meˌtap¦n(y)üstik\ *adj* [*meta-* + Gk *pneustikos* of or for breathing, fr. (assumed) Gk *pneustos* (verbal of Gk *pnein* to breathe) + Gk *-ikos* -ic — more at SNEEZE] *of an insect larva* : breathing through a single pair of posterior or anal spiracles

**meta·po·di·al** \¦== *at* META- + ¦pōdēəl\ *n* -s [NL *metapodi*um metatarsus (fr. *meta-* + *-podium*) + E *-al* (n. suffix, fr. *-al,* adj. suffix)] : a metacarpal or metatarsal bone

**meta·po·di·a·le** \ˌ==ˌpōdē'ā(ˌ)lē\ *n, pl* **metapodia·lia** \-ālēə\ [NL, fr. *metapodium* metatarsus + L *-ale* (fr. neut. of *-alis* -al, adj. suffix)] : METAPODIAL

**meta·po·di·um** \ˌ=='pōdēəm\ *n, pl* **metapo·dia** \-dēə\ [NL, fr. *meta-* + *-podium*] : the posterior division of the foot in mollusks

**meta·political** \¦== *at* META- +\ *adj* : of or relating to metapolitics

**meta·politician** \"+\ *n* [*metapolitic*s + *-an*] : one who engages in abstract political theorizing

**meta·politics** \"+\ *n pl but sing in constr* [*meta-* + *politics*] : theoretical or philosophical political science

**meta·poph·y·sis** \ˌmed·ə'päfəsə̇s\ *n* [NL, fr. *meta-* + *apophysis*] : a tubercle projecting from the anterior articular process of a vertebra esp. in the lumbar region

**meta·postscutellar** \¦== *at* META- +\ *adj* [NL *metapostscutell*um + E *-ar*] : of or relating to the metapostscutellum

**meta·postscutellum** \"+\ *n* [NL, fr. *meta-* + *postscutellum*] : the postnotum of the metathorax of an insect

**meta·prescutal** \¦==+\ *adj* [NL *metaprescut*um + E *-al*] : of or relating to the metaprescutum

**meta·prescutum** \"+\ *n* [NL, fr. *meta-* + *prescutum*] : the prescutum of the metathorax of an insect

**meta·protein** \"+\ *n* [*meta-* + *protein*] : any of various products derived from proteins through the action of acids or alkalies by which the solubility and sometimes the composition of the proteins is changed — compare ALBUMINATE

**meta·psychic** \¦==+\ *or* **meta·psychical** \"+\ *adj* [*metapsychic* fr. F *métapsychique,* fr. *méta-* meta- + *psychique* psychic, fr. Gk *psychikos* of the soul, of life; *metapsychical* fr. F *métapsychique* + E *-al* — more at PSYCHIC] : of or relating to phenomena (as mediumistic) outside the range of orthodox psychology ⟨the existence of telepathic phenomena, as well as other ~ phenomena, is not accepted by most biologists and physicians —Alexis Carrel⟩

**meta·psychological** \"+\ *adj* : of or relating to metapsychology

**meta·psychology** \¦==+\ *n* [ISV *meta-* + *psychology*] : a theory that aims to supplement the facts and empirical laws of psychology by speculations on the connection of mental and physical processes or on the place of mind in the universe; *specif* : the aspect of Freud's theory that aims to supplement his treatment of the conscious and unconscious and of the motivation of behavior by a theory of memories as charges of physical energy and of emotion as a process of discharge

**me·tap·ter·yg·i·um** \mə̇¦taptə¦rijēəm\ *n, pl* **metapteryg·ia** \-jēə\ [NL, fr. *meta-* + Gk *pterygion* fin, lit., small wing — more at PTERYGIUM] : the posterior of the three principal basal cartilages in the pectoral fins of some fishes (as sharks and rays) — compare BASIPTERYGIUM

[1]**met·ap·ter·y·goid** \¦meˌtap¦terəˌgȯid\ *adj* [*meta-* + *pterygoid* (n.)] : situated behind the pterygoid

[2]**metapterygoid** \"\ *n* [*meta-* + *pterygoid*] : a metapterygoid part (as a bone)

**meta·rossite** \¦== *at* META- +\ *n* [*meta-* + *rossite*] : a mineral consisting of a hydrous calcium vanadate — compare ROSSITE

**met·ar·rhi·zi·um** \ˌmed·ə'rīzēəm\ *n, cap* [NL, fr. *meta-* + Gk *rhizion* small root, dim. of *rhiza* root — more at WORT (herb)] : a genus of imperfect fungi (family Moniliaceae) closely related to *Penicillium* and of interest chiefly in biological control of various insects — see GREEN MUSCARDINE

**met·ar·te·ri·ole** \ˌmed·ˌär'tirēˌōl\ *n* [*meta-* + *arteriole*] : a delicate blood vessel held to connect some arteries and veins and distinguished from a true capillary by the presence of smooth muscle in its walls

**meta·science** \¦== *at* META- +\ *n* [*meta-* + *science*] : a theory or science of science

**meta·scientific** \"+\ *adj* [*meta-* + *scientific*] : of, relating to, or based on metascience ⟨the richness of ~ speculation —L.S.Feuer⟩

**meta·scope** \'==ˌskōp\ *n* [*meta-* + *-scope*] **1** : a telescope that produces on a fluorescent screen by means of infrared light visible images of objects in total darkness **2** : a device designed to locate the source of infrared rays by converting them to visible light

**meta·scutal** \¦==¦skyüd·ᵊl\ *adj* [NL *metascut*um + E *-al*] : of or relating to the metascutum

**meta·scutellar** \"+\ *adj* [NL *metascutell*um + E *-ar*] : of or relating to the metascutellum

**meta·scutellum** \"+\ *n* [NL, fr. *meta-* + *scutellum*] : the scutellum of the metathorax of an insect

**meta·scutum** \"+\ *n* [NL, fr. *meta-* + *scutum*] : the scutum of the metathorax of an insect

**meta·sediment** \"+\ *n* [*meta-* + *sediment*] : a metamorphic rock of sedimentary origin — **meta·sedimentary** \"+\ *adj*

**meta·sequoia** \¦==+\ *n* [NL, fr. *meta-* + *Sequoia*] **1** *cap* : a genus of deciduous coniferous trees (family Pinaceae) comprising both fossil and living forms and having opposite arrangement of leaves, buds, and branches and only flat needlelike leaves **2** : any tree or fossil of the genus *Metasequoia; esp* : DAWN REDWOOD

**meta·sideronatrite** \"+\ *n* [*meta-* + *sideronatrite*] : a mineral $Na_4Fe_2(SO_4)_4(OH)_2.3H_2O$, consisting of a basic hydrous sulfate of sodium and iron that differs from sideronatrite only in the amount of water

**meta·silicate** \"+\ *n* [ISV *meta-* + *silicate*] **1** : a silicate containing the anion $SiO_3^{--}$ or $(SiO_3)_n^{2n-}$ in which the ratio of silicon to oxygen is 1 to 3 **2** : INOSILICATE

**meta·silicic acid** \¦==+-\ *n* [ISV *meta-* + *silicic acid*] : a hypothetical acid $H_2SiO_3$ or $(H_2SiO_3)_n$ from which the metasilicates may be regarded as derived

**meta·so·ma** \ˌ=='sōmə\ *n* [NL, fr. *meta-* + *-soma*] : the hind region of the body of some invertebrates; *esp* : such a region that cannot be readily analyzed into its primitive segmentation (as in some mollusks and arachnids) — **meta·so·mal** \¦==¦sōməl\ *adj*

**meta·somatic** \¦==+\ *adj* **1** [*metasomat*ism + *-ic*] : of or relating to metasomatism **2** [NL *metasomat-, metasoma* + E *-ic*] : of or relating to a metasoma

**meta·so·ma·tism** \ˌ=='sōməˌtizəm\ *n* -s [*meta-* + Gk *sōmat-, sōma* body + E *-ism* — more at -SOME (body)] : metamorphism that usu. involves important changes in the chemical composition as well as in the mineral composition and texture of rock

**meta·so·ma·to·sis** \ˌ==ˌsōmə'tōsə̇s\ *n, pl* **metasomato·ses** \-ōˌsēz\ [NL, fr. *meta-* + Gk *sōmat-, sōma* body + NL *-osis*] **1** : METENSOMATOSIS **2** : METASOMATISM

**meta·some** \'==ˌsōm\ *n* -s **1** [NL *metasoma*] : METASOMA **2** [*meta-* + *-some*] : the replacing mineral where one mineral grows in size at the expense of another

**meta·stability** \¦==+\ *n* : the quality or state of being metastable

**meta·stable** \"+\ *adj* [ISV *meta-* + *stable*] : marked by only a slight margin of stability — used esp. in chemistry and physics ⟨a supercooled liquid is ~⟩ ⟨many of the processes in the atmosphere are . . . ~: a slight action may initiate a very large-scale process —Roger Revelle⟩ ⟨life is fleeting, ~, a thing of delicate equilibrium of easily decomposed compounds —C.C. Furnas⟩

**metastable state** *n* : a state of precarious stability; *specif* : such a state of an atom which though excited cannot emit radiation without a further supply of energy

**me·tas·ta·sis** \mə̇'tastəsə̇s, -'taas-\ *n, pl* **metastases** [NL, fr. LL, transition, fr. Gk, fr. *methistanai* to change, fr. *meta-* + *histanai* to cause to stand, place — more at STAND] : change of position, state, or form: **a** (1) : transfer of a disease-producing agency (as cells or bacteria) from an original site of disease to another part of the body with development of a similar lesion in the new location ⟨~ in the lung usually occurs by way of the blood stream —J.B.Amberson⟩ ⟨*metastases* of breast cancer to bone —*Medical Physics*⟩ — compare CANCER, IMPLANTATION (2) : a secondary growth resulting from such transfer of cells of a malignant tumor **b** : METABOLISM 1 **c** : a paramorphic change in rock (as recrystallization of limestone or devitrification of glassy rock)

**me·tas·ta·size** \-ˌsīz\ *vi* -ED/-ING/-S [NL *metastas*is + E *-ize*] : to spread by metastasis — used chiefly of malignant tumors ⟨the lesion already had *metastasized* beyond the larynx before a diagnosis of carcinoma was made —*Amer. Practitioner*⟩

**meta·static** \¦== *at* META- +\ *adj* [fr. NL *metastasis,* after such pairs as LL *hypostasis:* E *hypostatic*] : of, relating to, or caused by metastasis ⟨~ lung cancer⟩ ⟨~ lesions⟩

**meta·sternal** \"+\ *adj* [NL *metastern*um + E *-al*] : of or relating to the metasternum

**meta·sternum** \"+\ *n* [NL, fr. *meta-* + *sternum*] **1** : the ventral plate of the metathorax of an insect **2** : XIPHISTERNUM

**meta·sthenic** \¦== *at* META- + ¦sthenik, -thēn-\ *adj* [*meta-* + Gk *sthen*os strength + E *-ic* — more at ASTHEN-] : strong in the hinder part of the body

**me·tas·to·ma** \mə̇'tastəmə, -'taas-\ *n, pl* **meta·sto·ma·ta** \ˌmed·ə'stōməd·ə\ [NL, fr. *meta-* + Gk *stoma* mouth — more at STOMACH] : a median platelike process behind the mouth in crustaceans and related arthropods

**meta·stome** \'== *at* META- + ˌstōm\ *n* -s [NL *metastoma*] : METASTOMA

**meta·strengite** \¦==+\ *n* [*meta-* + *strengite*] : a mineral $FePO_4.2H_2O$ that consists of a hydrous phosphate of iron and is polymorphous with strengite and prob. isomorphous with metavariscite

**meta·strongyle** \"+\ *n* [NL *Metastrongylus*] : METASTRONGYLID

[1]**meta·strongylid** \¦==+\ *adj* [NL *Metastrongylidae*] : of or relating to the family Metastrongylidae

[2]**metastrongylid** \"\ *n* -s [NL *Metastrongylidae*] : a nematode worm of the family Metastrongylidae

**meta·stron·gyl·i·dae** \¦==ˌsträn'jiləˌdē\ *n pl, cap* [NL, fr. *Metastrongylus,* type genus + *-idae*] : a large family of parasitic strongyloid nematode worms — see DICTYOCAULUS, METASTRONGYLUS, PROTOSTRONGYLUS

**meta·strongylus** \¦==+\ *n, cap* [NL, fr. *meta-* + *Strongylus*] : a genus (the type of the family Metastrongylidae) of slender threadlike nematode worms that parasitize as adults the lungs and sometimes other organs of mammals and as larvae various earthworms

**meta·style** \'==+ˌ-\ *n* [*meta-* + *style* (cusp)] : a cusp posterior to the metacone of a molar tooth

**meta·syndesis** \¦==+\ *n* [NL, fr. *meta-* + *syndesis*] : TELOSYNAPSIS

[1]**meta·tarsal** \¦==+\ *adj* [NL *metatars*us + E *-al*] : of or relating to the metatarsus — **meta·tar·sal·ly** \-səlē\ *adv*

[2]**metatarsal** \"\ *n* -s : a metatarsal bone

**meta·tarsale** \¦==+\ *n, pl* **metatarsalia** [NL, fr. *metatarsus* + L *-ale* (n. suffix, fr. neut. of *-alis* -al, adj. suffix)] : METATARSAL

**meta·tar·sal·gia** \ˌ==ˌtär'saljēə\ *n* -s [NL, fr. *metatarsus* + *-algia*] : a cramping burning pain below and between the metatarsal bones where they join the toe bones — called also *Morton's toe*

**meta·tar·so·phalangeal** \¦==¦tärˌsō+\ *adj* [*metatarso-* (fr. NL *metatarsus*) + *phalangeal*] : of, relating to, or involving both the metatarsus and the phalanges

**meta·tarsus** \¦==+\ *n* [NL, fr. *meta-* + *tarsus*] **1** : the part of the foot in man or of the hind foot in quadrupeds that is between the tarsus and phalanges, contains when all the digits are present five more or less elongated bones but is modified in many animals with loss or reduction of some bones or fusing of others, and forms in man the instep, in horses and cattle the part of the hind leg from the hock to the fetlock joint, and in birds the tarso-metatarsus **2 a** : the proximal segment of the tarsus of an insect **b** : the tarsus of the posterior pair of legs of an insect **c** : the proximal segment of the foot of a spider

**me·ta·te** \mə'täd·ē\ *n* -s [Sp, fr. Nahuatl *metlatl*] : a stone with a concave upper surface used as the nether millstone for grinding maize and other grains ⟨each woman in turn rose and knelt at the ~ and ground some of the corn grains —Gertrude Diamant⟩ — compare MANO

**meta·thalamus** \¦== *at* META-+\ *n* [NL, fr. *meta-* + *thalamus*] : the part of the diencephalon that contains the geniculate bodies

**meta·thenardite** \"+\ *n* [*meta-* + *thenardite*] : a mineral consisting of a high-temperature polymorph of thenardite occurring in fumaroles on Martinique Island

**meta·theory** \"+\ *n* [*meta-* + *theory*] : a theory concerned with the investigation, analysis, or description of theory itself ⟨if we investigate, analyze, and describe a language $L_1$ . . . the sum total of what can be known about $L_1$ and said in $L_2$ may be called the ~ of $L_1$ —Rudolf Carnap⟩

**meta·the·ria** \ˌ=='thirēə\ *n pl, cap* [NL, fr. *meta-* + *-theria*] **1** : a hypothetical group ancestral to placental mammals postulated to have reached a stage of development equivalent to that of the marsupials **2** *in some classifications* : a group coextensive with Marsupialia

[1]**meta·the·ri·an** \¦med·ə¦thirēən\ *adj* [NL *Metatheria* + E *-an*] : of or relating to the Metatheria

[2]**metatherian** \"\ *n* -s : a mammal of the group Metatheria

**me·tath·e·sis** \mə̇'tathəsə̇s\ *n, pl* **metathe·ses** \-ˌsēz\ [LL transposition of letters, fr. Gk, fr. *metatithenai* to transpose, fr. *meta-* + *tithenai* to place, set — more at DO] **1** : a change of place or condition : REVERSAL; *specif* : transposition of two phonemes in a word (as in Old English *wæsp, wæps*) **2** : DOUBLE DECOMPOSITION

**me·tath·e·size** \-ˌsīz\ *vb* -ED/-ING/-S [*metathes*is + *-ize*] *vi* : to undergo metathesis ~ *vt* : to subject to metathesis

**me·tath·e·tely** \mə̇'tathəˌtelē\ *n* -ES [Gk *metathet*os changed, changeable (verbal of *metatithenai* to transpose, change) + *tel*os end, completion, maturity + E *-y* — more at WHEEL] **1** : retardation of development in insect larvae without retardation of growth (as that resulting from the presence of various parasitic worms) **2** : HYSTEROTELY

**meta·thet·i·cal** \¦med·ə¦thed·ə̇kəl\ *also* **meta·thet·ic** \-¦thed·ik\ *adj* [LGk *metathetikos* able to change, fr. Gk *metathet*os changed, changeable + *-ikos* -ic, -ical] : of or relating to metathesis — **meta·thet·i·cal·ly** \-ə̇k(ə)lē\ *adv*

**me·tath·e·tize** \mə̇'tathəˌtīz\ *vb* -ED/-ING/-S [*metathet*ical + *-ize*] : METATHESIZE

**meta·thoracic** \¦== *at* META-+\ *adj* [NL *metathorac-, metathorax* + E *-ic*] : of or relating to the metathorax

**meta·thorax** \"+\ *n* [NL, fr. *meta-* + *thorax*] : the posterior segment of the thorax in an insect — see INSECT illustration

**meta·torbernite** \"+\ *n* [*meta-* + *torbernite*] : a mineral $Cu(UO_2)_2(PO_4)_2.8H_2O$ consisting of a hydrous phosphate of copper and uranium containing less water than torbernite

**meta·tracheal** \¦==+\ *adj* [*meta-* + *tracheal*] : arranged in bands or laminae mostly having no association with vessels or vascular tracheids ⟨~ parenchyma⟩ — compare APOTRACHEAL, PARATRACHEAL, VASICENTRIC

**meta·troph** \'==ˌträf, -rȯf\ *n* -s [back-formation fr. *metatrophic*] : a metatrophic organism

**meta·trophic** \¦==¦träfik, -rōf-\ *adj* [*meta-* + *-trophic*] : requiring complex organic sources of carbon and nitrogen for metabolic synthesis : HETEROTROPHIC — compare MESOTROPHIC — **metat·ro·phy** \mə̇'ta·trəfē\ *n* -ES

**meta·tungstate** \¦== *at* META- +\ *n* [ISV *metatungst-* (fr. *metatungstic acid*) + *-ate*] : a salt of metatungstic acid

**meta·tungstic acid** \¦==+-\ *n* [ISV *meta-* + *tungstic acid*] : a yellow crystalline acid $H_8W_{12}O_{40}.xH_2O$ or $H_6[H_2(W_3O_{10})_4].24H_2O$ soluble in water

**meta·type** \'==+ˌ-\ *n* [*meta-* + *type*] : a topotype or homeotype determined by the original author of its species — **meta·typ·ic** \¦==¦tipik\ *adj*

**meta–uranopilite** \¦==+\ *n* : a mineral $(UO_2)_6(SO_6)(OH)_{10}.5H_2O$ consisting of a hydrous basic sulfate of uranyl with less water than uranopilite

**meta·vanadate** \"+\ *n* [ISV *metavanad-* (fr. *metavanadic acid*) + *-ate*] : a salt or ester of metavanadic acid

**meta·vanadic acid** \¦==+-\ *n* [ISV *meta-* + *vanadic acid*] : an acid $HVO_3$ or $H_4V_4O_{12}$ obtained by precipitation from a solution of vanadium pentoxide in water

**meta·variscite** \¦==+\ *n* [*meta-* + *variscite*] : a mineral $AlPO_6.2H_2O$ that consists of a hydrous phosphate of aluminum and is polymorphous with variscite and isomorphous with metastrengite

**meta·vauxite** \"+\ *n* [*meta-* + *vauxite*] : a mineral $FeAl_2(PO_4)_2(OH)_2.8H_2O$ consisting of a hydrous iron aluminum phosphate derived by alteration from vauxite

**meta·voltine** \"+\ *n* -s [ISV *meta-* + *volt-* (fr. *voltaite*) + *-ine*] : a mineral $(K, Na, Fe)_5Fe_3(SO_4)_6(OH)_2.9H_2O$(?) consisting of a basic hydrous sulfate of iron, sodium, and potassium

**meta·xenia** \"+\ *n* [NL, fr. *meta-* + *xenia*] : the effect of a pollen parent on the developing maternal tissues of a seed or fruit outside the embryo and endosperm due to hormones produced by the embryo and endosperm after double fertilization — compare CARPOXENIA, XENIA

**me·tax·ite** \mə̇'takˌsīt\ *n* -s [G *metaxit,* fr. LGk *metaxa* raw silk + G *-it* -ite] : a mineral consisting of a fibrous serpentine

**meta·xylem** \¦== *at* META- +\ *n* [ISV *meta-* + *xylem*] : the part of the primary xylem that differentiates after the protoxylem and is typically distinguished by broader tracheids and vessels with pitted or reticulate walls

**mé·ta·yage** \¦med·ə¦yäzh, ¦mād·-\ *n* -s [F, irreg. fr. *métayer* + *-age*] : the métayer system of farming land

**mé·ta·yer** \-¦yā\ *n* -s [F, fr. MF, fr. OF *meteer, meiteier,* fr. LL *medietat-, medietas* half + OF *-ier* -er — more at MOIETY] : one that cultivates land for a share of its yield usu. receiving stock, tools, and seed from the landlord

**meta·zeunerite** \¦== *at* META- +\ *n* [*meta-* + *zeunerite*] : a mineral $Cu(UO_2)_2(AsO_4)_2.8H_2O$ consisting of a hydrous arsenate of copper and uranium with less water than zeunerite

**meta·zoa** \ˌmed·ə'zōə\ *n pl, cap* [NL, fr. *meta-* + *-zoa*] : a group that comprises all animals having the body when adult composed of numerous cells differentiated into tissues and organs and usu. a digestive cavity lined with specialized cells and that is used usu. to include the Coelenterata and all higher animals but sometimes is extended to include the Parazoa and Mesozoa — compare PROTOZOA

**meta·zo·al** \¦==¦zōəl\ *or* **meta·zo·ic** \-ik\ *adj* [NL *Metazoa* + E *-al* or *-ic*] : METAZOAN

[1]**meta·zo·an** \-ən\ *adj* [NL *Metazoa* + E *-an*] : of or relating to the Metazoa

[2]**metazoan** \"\ *n* -s : one of the Metazoa

**met·a·zoea** *also* **meta·zoaea** \¦==+\ *n* [NL, fr. *meta-* + *zoea* or *zoaea*] : a larva of various higher crustaceans intermediate between the zoea and the megalops

**meta·zo·on** \ˌ=='zōˌän\ *n, pl* **meta·zoa** \-ōə\ [NL, sing. of *Metazoa*] : one of the Metazoa

**met·calfe bean** \'metˌkaf-, -ˌkəf-, -ˌkȧf\ *n, usu cap M* [after J. K. *Metcalfe* who introduced it to the southwestern U. S. in the late 19th cent.] **1** : a prostrate perennial bean (*Phaseolus metcalfei*) of the southwestern U. S. and adjacent Mexico that is sometimes cultivated for forage **2** : the flat circular brownish black seed of the Metcalfe bean

[1]**mete** \'mēt, *usu* -ēd·+V\ *vt* -ED/-ING/-S [ME *meten,* fr. OE *metan;* akin to OS *metan* to measure, OFris *meta,* MD *meten,* OHG *mezzan* to measure, ON *meta* to value, Goth *mitan* to measure, L *modus* measure, moderation, manner, *meditari* to meditate, *modestus* moderate, modest, *moderari* to moderate, OIr *midiur* I judge, Gk *medesthai* to be mindful of, *medimnos* grain measure; basic meaning: to measure] **1** *archaic* **a** : to find the quantity, dimensions, or capacity of by any rule or standard : MEASURE ⟨~*s* the thin air and weighs the flying sound —George Crabbe†1832⟩ **b** : to determine the value of : APPRAISE ⟨a pattern or a measure . . . by which his Grace must ~ the lives of others —Shak.⟩ **2** : to assign by measure : deal out : ALLOT, APPORTION — usu. used with *out* ⟨~ out punishment⟩ ⟨so has my portion been *meted* out to me —Oscar Wilde⟩

[2]**mete** \"\ *n* -s : MEASURE ⟨sprinkled sugar over it with neither ~ nor measure —Della Lutes⟩

[3]**mete** \"\ *n* -s [AF, fr. L *meta* goal, boundary] : BOUNDARY — now used chiefly in the phrase *metes and bounds*

**met·empiric** \¦med·+\ *n* [*meta-* + *empiric* (adj. & n.)] **1** : METEMPIRICS **2** : METEMPIRICIST

**met·empirical** \"+\ *adj* [*meta-* + *empirical*] : of, relating to, or advocating metempirics — **met·empirically** \"+\ *adv*

**met·empiricism** \ˌmed·+\ *n* [*metempiric* + *-ism*] : METEMPIRICS

**met·empiricist** \"+\ *n* [*meta-* + *empiricist*] : one who advocates or practices metempirics

**met·empirics** \"+\ *n pl but sing in constr* [pl. of *metempiric*] : the study of concepts and relationships conceived as beyond and yet related to knowledge gained empirically ⟨~ sweeps out of this region in search of the otherness of things —G.H. Lewes⟩

**met·em·psy·chic** \¦med·ˌem¦sīkik, -d·ə̇m-\ *or* **metem·psy·cho·sic** \mə¦tem(p)sə̇¦kōsik, ¦medə̇ˌemˌsī¦k-, -d·ə̇mˌsī¦k-, -ōzik\ *also* **metem·psy·cho·si·cal** \-ōsə̇kəl, -ōzə̇-\ *adj* [*metempsychic* fr. LL *metempsych*osis + E *-ic; metempsychosic* or *metempsichosical* fr. LL *metempsychos*is + E *-ic* or *-ical*] : of or relating to metempsychosis

**me·tem·psy·chose** \mə'tem(p)sə̇ˌkōs, ˌmed·ə̇m'sīˌk-, -ōz\ *also* **metem·psy·cho·size** \məˌtem(p)sə̇'kōˌsīz, ˌmed·ə̇mˌsī'k-\ *vt* -ED/-ING/-S [*metempsychose,* back-formation fr. LL *metempsychosis; metempsychosize* fr. LL *metempsychos*is + E *-ize*] : to translate or transfer (as the soul) from one body to another

**metem·psy·cho·sis** \məˌtem(p)sə̇'kōsə̇s, ˌmed·ˌemˌsī'k-, -d·ə̇mˌsī'k-\ *n* [LL, fr. Gk *metempsychōsis,* fr. *metempsychousthai* to undergo metempsychosis, fr. *meta-* + *empsychos* animate, fr. *em-* en- + *psychē* soul, spirit] : the passing of the soul at death into another body either human or animal : transmigration of souls ⟨could remember all the previous lives in his *metempsychoses* —Erwin Schrödinger⟩ — contrasted with *metensomatosis*

**met·encephalic** \¦med·+\ *adj* [NL *metencephalon* + E *-ic*] : of or relating to the metencephalon

**met·encephalon** \ˌmed·+\ *n* [NL, fr. *meta-* + *encephalon*] **1 a** : the anterior segment of the rhombencephalon **b** : the cerebellum and pons that evolve from this segment **2** : MYELENCEPHALON b — used only when the anterior segment is designated *epencephalon*

**met·en·so·ma·to·sis** \ˌmed·ˌen,sōmə'tōsəs\ *n, pl* **metensomatoses** [LL, fr. LGk *metensōmatōsis*, fr. Gk *meta-* + *en-* + *sōmat-, sōma* body + *-ōsis* -osis — more at -SOME (body)] : the migration into one body of different souls — contrasted with *metempsychosis*

**met·en·ter·on** *n* [NL, fr. *meta-* + *enteron*] **1** : the alimentary canal modified in any manner from the primitive archenteron **2** : one of the radial digestive chambers of an anthozoan — compare MESENTERON — **met·en·ter·on·ic** \⸗¦⸗⸗¦ränik\ *adj*

**me·teo·graph** \'mēd·ēə,graf, -rāf\ *n* [*meteo-* (fr. ¹*meteor*) + *-graph*] : METEOROGRAPH

¹**me·te·or** \'mēd·ēə(r), -ētē-, -ē,ȯ(ə)r, -ō(ə)\ *n* -s [ME, fr. MF *meteore*, fr. ML *meteorum*, fr. Gk *meteōron* astronomical phenomenon, thing in the heaven above, fr. neut. of *meteōros* high in air, raised off the ground, fr. *meta-* + *-eōros* (akin to Gk *aeirein* to lift, raise, *aiora* suspension) — more at AORTA] **1** : a phenomenon or appearance in the atmosphere (as lightning, whirlwind, rainbow, snowfall) ⟨all day the hoary ~ fell —J.G.Whittier⟩ ⟨the ~ of the ocean air shall sweep the clouds no more —O.W.Holmes †1894⟩ **2 a** : a streak of light in the night sky produced by the passage through the earth's atmosphere of one of the countless small particles of solid matter in the solar system **b** : the small particle itself or any physical phenomenon associated with it

²**meteor** \"\ *adj* : METEORIC 3

**meteor-** *or* **meteoro-** *comb form* [MF or Gk; MF, fr. Gk *meteōr-* high in air (fr. *meteōros*), *meteōro-* astronomical phenomenon, thing in the heaven above, fr. *meteōron*] **1** : meteor ⟨*meteoroid*⟩ **2** : weather and climate ⟨*meteorobiology*⟩

**meteor** *abbr* meteorological; meteorology

**meteor crater** *also* **meteorite crater** *n* : a depression in the earth's surface produced by the impact of a large meteorite

**meteor echo** *n* : a radar echo from the ionized cylinder of air made by the passage of a meteor through the atmosphere

**me·te·or·ic** \¦mēd·ē¦ȯrik, -ētē-, -¦är-, -ēk\ *adj* [ML *meteoricus* elevated, fr. L *meteorus* high, exalted (fr. Gk *meteōros*) + *-icus* -ic — more at METEOR] **1 a** : of, relating to, or dependent on the earth's atmosphere ⟨~ phenomena⟩ ⟨~ flowers⟩ **b** : derived from the earth's atmosphere — used esp. of water ⟨water precipitated from the atmosphere, ~ water, which falls as rain or snow —P.G.Worcester⟩ — compare CONNATE 5, MAGMATIC **2** [¹*meteor* + *-ic*] : of, relating to or composed of meteors ⟨~ shower⟩ **3** : resembling a meteor in brilliance, rapidity, or short duration ⟨a young executive whose rise in his company has been ~ —*Modern Industry*⟩ ⟨the ~ rise, temporary supremacy, and abrupt fall of this liberal coalition —P.R.Levin⟩ ⟨the brief ~ career of a Negro jazz musician —Jerome Stone⟩ — **me·te·or·i·cal·ly** \-rək(ə)lē, -rēk-, -li\ *adv*

**meteoric iron** *n* : iron of meteoric origin — compare METEORITE

**meteoric paper** *n* : a paperlike substance consisting of the dried remains of filamentous green algae found floating in the air

**me·te·or·ism** \'mēd·ēə,rizəm, -ētē-\ *n* -s [F *météorisme*, fr. MF, fr. Gk *meteōrismos*, lit., act of lifting, fr. *meteōrizein* to lift, fr. *meteōr-* high in air, exalted (fr. *meteōros*) + *-izein* -ize] : gaseous distention of the stomach or intestine : TYMPANITES, BLOAT 2

**me·te·or·ist** \-rəst\ *n* -s : a specialist in the study of meteors

**me·te·or·it·al** \¦⸗⸗¦rīd·ᵊl\ *adj* [*meteorite* + *-al*] : METEORITIC

**me·te·or·ite** \'mēd·ēə,rīt, -ētē-\ *n* -s [¹*meteor* + *-ite*] : a solid particle from interplanetary space that survives the destructive effects of a flight through the earth's atmosphere and falls to the ground in one or more pieces

**me·te·or·it·ic** \¦⸗⸗⸗¦rid·ik\ *or* **me·te·or·it·i·cal** \-əkəl\ *adj* : of, relating to, or caused by meteorites ⟨~ crater⟩ ⟨~ hypothesis⟩

**me·te·or·it·i·cist** \ˌ⸗⸗⸗'rid·əsəst\ *n* -s : a specialist in meteoritics

**me·te·or·it·ics** \-'rid·iks\ *n pl but sing in constr* [*meteorite* + *-ics*] : a science that deals with meteors and meteorites

**me·te·o·ro·biology** \¦mēd·ēə(ˌ)rō+\ *n* [*meteor-* + *biology*] : a science that deals with the effects of weather and climate on living beings

**me·te·or·o·gram** \ˌmēd·ē'ȯrə,gram\ *n* [ISV *meteor-* + *-gram*] : a record made by a meteorograph

**me·te·or·o·graph** \-,graf, -rāf\ *n* [*meteor-* + *-graph*] : an autographic apparatus for recording simultaneously several meteorologic elements (as air pressure, temperature, moisture) — **me·te·or·o·graph·ic** \¦⸗⸗¦⸗⸗¦grafik\ *adj* — **me·te·o·rog·ra·phy** \ˌmēd·ēə'rägrəfē\ *n* -ES

**me·te·or·oid** \'mēd·ēə,rȯid\ *n* -s [¹*meteor* + *-oid*] **1** : a meteor revolving around the sun **2** : a meteor particle itself without relation to the phenomena it produces when entering the earth's atmosphere

**me·te·or·o·lite** \ˌmēd·ē'ȯrə,līt\ *also* **me·te·or·o·lithe** \-lith\ *n* -s [partly fr. *meteor-* + *-lite* and partly fr. F *météorolithe*, fr. *météoro-* meteor- + *-lithe* -lith] : METEORITE — **me·te·or·o·lit·ic** \¦⸗⸗¦⸗⸗¦lid·ik\ *adj*

**me·te·oro·log·i·cal** \¦mēd·|ē,ȯrə¦läjəkəl, -ēt|, |ē,är-, |ēər-, ÷ |ər(ə)¦l-, ÷ |ēər¦l-, -jēk-\ *also* **me·te·oro·log·ic** \-jik, -jēk\ *adj* [*meteorological* fr. MF *meteorologique* meteorological (fr. Gk *meteōrologikos*, fr. *meteōrologia* meteorology + *-ikos* -ic) or Gk *meteōrologikos* + E *-al; meteorologic* fr. F *météorologique* (fr. MF *meteorologique*) or Gk *meteōrologikos*] : of or relating to meteorology ⟨~ chart⟩ ⟨~ report⟩ ⟨~ factors⟩ — **me·te·oro·log·i·cal·ly** \-jək(ə)lē, -jēk-, -li\ *adv*

**meteorological element** *n* : any of the subjects of meteorological observation (as temperature, relative humidity, or barometric pressure)

**meteorological tide** *n* : tidal constituents resulting from variations in somewhat periodically recurring weather conditions

**me·te·o·rol·o·gist** \ˌmēd·|ēə'räləjəst, -ēt|, ÷ |ə'r-\ *n* -s [Gk *meteōrologos* meteorologist (fr. *meteōro-* meteor- + *-logos* -logue) + E *-ist*] : a specialist in meteorology

**me·te·o·rol·o·gy** \-jē, -ji\ *n* -ES [F or Gk; F *météorologie*, fr. MF, fr. Gk *meteōrologia*, fr. *meteōro-* astronomical phenomenon, thing in the heaven above (fr. *meteōron*) + *-logia* -logy — more at METEOR] **1 a** : a science that deals with the atmosphere and its phenomena (as variations of heat, moisture, or winds) — compare CLIMATOLOGY **b** : a science that deals with weather and weather forecasting **2** : the atmospheric phenomena and weather of a region ⟨the ~ of the Gulf of Mexico⟩

**me·te·o·rous** \'mēd·ēərəs, mə'tē-\ *adj* [¹*meteor* + *-ous*] : METEORIC ⟨~ pleasures which dance before us and are dissipated —Samuel Johnson⟩

**meteors** *pl of* METEOR

**meteor shower** *also* **meteoric shower** *n* : the phenomenon observed when members of a meteor swarm encounter the earth's atmosphere and their luminous paths appear to diverge from a single point or radiant in the sky

**meteor swarm** *n* : a group of meteoroids that have closely similar orbits around the sun — see METEOR SHOWER

**meteor trail** *n* **1** : a bright streak in the sky of very short duration caused by the shining of a meteor during its passage through the atmosphere **2** : the track of a meteor

**meteor train** *n* : a persistent glow sometimes left by a meteor after the meteor trail has faded out and caused by luminous matter left in the meteoroid's wake

**met·epimeral** \¦med·+\ *adj* [NL *metepimeron* + E *-al*] : of or relating to a metepimeron

**met·epimeron** \ˌ⸗+\ *n* [NL, fr. *meta-* + *epimeron*] : the epimeron of the metathorax of an insect

**met·episternal** \¦⸗+\ *adj* [NL *metepisternum* + E *-al*] : of or relating to a metepisternum

**met·episternum** \ˌ⸗+\ *n* [NL, fr. *meta-* + *episternum*] : the episternum of the metathorax of an insect

¹**me·ter** \'mēd·ə(r), -ētə-\ *n* -s *see -er in Explan Notes* [ME *meter, metre*, fr. OE & MF; OE *mēter*, fr. L *metrum*, fr. Gk *metron* meter, measure; MF *metre*, fr. OF, fr. L *metrum* — more at MEASURE] **1 a** : systematically arranged and measured rhythm in verse ⟨the only strict antithesis to prose is ~ —William Wordsworth⟩: (1) : rhythm that continuously repeats a single basic pattern or rhythmic system ⟨iambic ~⟩ ⟨dactylic ~⟩ — compare CADENCE (2) : rhythm characterized by the regular recurrence of a systematic arrangement of such basic patterns or systems into larger figures ⟨a verse with sapphic ~⟩ **b** : a measure or unit of metrical verse : METRON — usu. used in combination ⟨*dimeter*⟩ ⟨*pentameter*⟩; compare FOOT **c** : a fixed metrical pattern : verse form ⟨the heroic couplet was a favorite ~ of the neoclassic poets⟩ **d** *archaic* : a metrical composition : VERSE ⟨a pebble of the brook warbled out these ~s meet —William Blake⟩ **e** : rhythm in verse **2 a** : the part of rhythmical structure concerned with the division of a musical composition into measures by means of regularly recurring accents with each measure consisting of a uniform number of beats or time units the first of which has the strongest accent **b** : the distribution of long and short notes or tones within measures : TIME **syn** see RHYTHM

²**meter** \"\ *vb* **metered; metered; metering** \-əriŋ *also* 'mē·triŋ\ **meters** *see -er in Explan Notes* [ME *metren*, fr. *metre, meter*, n.] *vi* : to engage in poetic composition : VERSIFY ~ *vt* **1** : to put into meter : give metrical form to **2** : to analyze metrically : SCAN ⟨expansion of the liquid after it is ~ed —E.E.Reed⟩

³**meter** \"\ *n* -s [ME, fr. *meten* to mete, measure + *-er* — more at METE] : one that measures; *esp* : an official measurer of commodities

⁴**meter** \"\ *n* -s *see -er in Explan Notes* [F *mètre*, fr. Gk *metron* measure] : the basic metric unit of length that is equal to the distance between two lines on a platinum-iridium bar kept at the International Bureau of Weights and Measures near Paris, is approximately equal to 39.37 inches, and is equal to 1,650,763.73 wavelengths of the orange-red light of excited krypton of mass number 86 — see METRIC SYSTEM table

⁵**meter** \"\ *n* -s *often attrib* [*-meter*] **1 a** : an instrument for measuring and recording the amount of something (as water, gas, electricity) as it flows **b** : a device (as a valve in a carburetor) that regulates the flow of a fluid **2 a** : an instrument for measuring and usu. recording distance, time, weight, speed, or intensity **b** : an instrument for measuring and recording the amount of a commodity or service consumed: as (1) : PARKING METER (2) : POSTAGE METER **3 a** : the impression made by a postage meter on a piece of mail **b** : a philatelic cover bearing such an impression

⁶**meter** \"\ *vb* **metered; metered; metering** \-əriŋ *also* 'mē·triŋ\ **meters** *vt* **1** : to measure by means of a meter ⟨water . . . is ~ed and charged for —Tom Marvel⟩ **2** : to supply (fuel, oil, or other fluid) in a measured or regulated amount ⟨fuel is then ~ed to the engine by the idle adjusting needle —H.F.Blanchard & Ralph Ritchen⟩ **3 a** : to print postal indicia on by means of a postage meter **b** : to imprint a revenue stamp on by means of a machine similar to a postage meter ~ *vi* : to meter a fluid (as fuel or oil) ⟨the drilled opening in the ~ing jet controls the amount of fuel that can pass through the main fuel supply system —William Landon⟩ ⟨a ~ing pump for molasses⟩

**-me·ter** \məd·ə(r), mətə-, *esp in words in which a letter other than "o" precedes the "m", alternatively or only* ˌmēd·ə(r) *or* ˌmētə-\ *n comb form* -s [F *-mètre*, fr. Gk *metron* measure — more at MEASURE] : instrument or means for measuring ⟨*barometer*⟩ ⟨*calorimeter*⟩ ⟨*voltameter*⟩

**meter angle** *n* [⁴*meter*] : the angle between the visual axes and the median plane when the eyes are focused on a point at a distance of one meter in that plane

**meter bar** *n* [⁴*meter*] : a metal bar on which a meter length has been marked to serve as the standard length of a meter

**meter boat** *n* [⁴*meter*] : a racing sloop designed to the international rule of measurement expressed in meters

**meter cancellation** *n* [⁵*meter*] : an impression on mail by a postage meter indicating the amount of postage paid and usu. the place and date of mailing — compare CANCELLATION 2

**meter-candle** \'⸗⸗¦⸗⸗\ *n* [⁴*meter*] : LUX

**meter-candle-second** \'⸗⸗¦⸗⸗¦⸗⸗\ *n* : a unit of exposure to light equivalent to an illumination of one lux for one second

**metered mail** *n* [fr. *metered*, past part. of ⁶*meter*] : prepaid mail requiring no postage stamps but marked by an electrical machine that is set and controlled by the post office

**meter impression** *n* [⁵*meter*] : the postal indicia printed on a piece of mail by a postage meter — called also *postage impression*

**meter-kilogram** \'⸗⸗¦⸗⸗,⸗\ *n* [⁴*meter*] : KILOGRAM-METER

**meter-kilogram-second** \'⸗⸗¦⸗⸗,⸗¦⸗⸗\ *adj* : of, relating to, or being a system of units based on the meter as the unit of length, the kilogram as the unit of mass, and the mean solar second as the unit of time — abbr. *mks*

**meter mail** *n* [⁵*meter*] : mail bearing a meter impression

**meter·man** \'⸗⸗mən\ *n, pl* **metermen** [⁵*meter* + *man*] : a man trained to read and adjust meters (as gas meters)

**meter mark** *n* [⁵*meter*] : METER IMPRESSION

**meter postage** *n* [⁵*meter*] **1** : postage paid through use of a postage meter **2** : METER STAMP

**meter rate** *n* [⁵*meter*] : a utility service rate (as for water, gas, electricity) based on the number of units a customer consumes as measured by a meter

**meters** *pl of* METER, *pres 3d sing of* METER

**meter slogan** *n* [⁵*meter*] : an advertising slogan on metered mail imprinted along with the postal indicia

**meter stamp** *n* [⁵*meter*] : postal indicia printed by a postage meter

**meterstick** \'⸗⸗,⸗\ *n* [⁴*meter* + *stick*] : a measuring stick that is one meter long and is usu. marked off in centimeters and millimeters

**metes** *pres 3d sing of* METE, *pl of* METE

**metes and bounds** *n pl* [trans. of AF *metes et boundes*] **1** : the boundaries or limits of a tract of land; *specif* : the boundaries of land established by reference to natural or artificial monuments along it (as a stream, ditch, fence, road) as distinguished from those established by beginning at a fixed starting point and running therefrom by stated compass courses and stated distances — compare BUTTS AND BOUNDS **2** : established limits ⟨rules formulated by the Supreme Court in setting the *metes and bounds* of freedom of religion —E.S. Newman⟩

**met·estrous** *or* **met·oestrous** \(ˈ)med·+\ *adj* [NL *metestrus, metoestrus* + E *-ous*] : of or relating to metestrus

**met·estrus** *or* **met·oestrus** \(ˈ)med·+\ *also* **met·aestrus** \"\ *or* **met·estrum** *or* **met·oestrum** \(ˈ)med·+\ *n* [NL, fr. *meta-* + *estrus* or *oestrus* or *estrum* or *oestrum*] : the period of regression that follows estrus in the mammalian sexual cycle

**metewand** \'⸗,⸗\ *or* **meteyard** \'⸗,⸗\ *n* [ME *metwande* or *met yerde*, fr. *meten* to mete, measure + *wande* wand or *yerde* yard — more at METE] : a measuring rod

**metgl** *abbr* meteorological

**meth-** *or* **metho-** *comb form* [ISV, fr. *methyl*] : methyl ⟨*methacrylic*⟩ ⟨*methobromide*⟩

**meth** *abbr* **1** method **2** methylated

**metha·choline** \¦methə+\ *n* [*meth-* + *acetylcholine*] : a parasympathomimetic drug $[(CH_3)_3NCH_2CH(CH_3)OOCCH_3]OH$ administered in the form of its crystalline chloride or bromide; acetyl-β-methyl-choline

**meth·acrylate** \(ˈ)meth +\ *n* [ISV *methacryl-* (fr. *methacrylic acid*) + *-ate*] **1** : a salt or ester of methacrylic acid **2** *or* **methacrylate resin** *or* **methacrylate plastic** : an acrylic resin or acrylic plastic made by polymerization of a derivative of methacrylic acid; *esp* : METHYL METHACRYLATE 2

**meth·acrylic acid** \¦meth+-\ *n* [ISV *meth-* + *acrylic*] : an unsaturated liquid or crystalline acid $CH_2{=}C(CH_3)COOH$ that is isomeric with crotonic acid, that occurs in Roman chamomile oil but is usu. obtained by reaction of acetone cyanohydrin and sulfuric acid, and that resembles acrylic acid in ease of polymerization; α-methyl-acrylic acid

**metha·done** \'methə,dōn\ *also* **metha·don** \-,dän\ *n* -s [*dimethylamino-* + *diphenyl* + *heptanone*] : a narcotic drug $C_2H_5COC(C_6H_5)_2CH_2CH(CH_3)N(CH_3)_2$ administered usu. in the form of its bitter crystalline hydrochloride for the relief of pain; 6-dimethylamino-4,4-diphenyl-3-heptanone; *also* : the hydrochloride or other salt of this compound

**meth·allyl** \(ˈ)meth+\ *n* [*meth-* + *allyl*] : the beta- or 2-methyl-allyl radical $CH_2{=}C(CH_3)CH_2{-}$

**meth·amphetamine** \¦⸗+\ *n* [*meth-* + *amphetamine*] : an amine $C_6H_5CH_2CH(CH_3)NHCH_3$ used in the form of its crystalline hydrochloride as a stimulant for the central nervous system and in the treatment of obesity; *dextro-N-α-dimethylphenethyl-amine* — called also *deoxyephedrine*

**meth·a·nal** \'methə,nal\ *n* -s [ISV *methane* + *-al*] : FORMALDEHYDE

**meth·a·na·tion** \ˌmethə'nāshən\ *n* -s [*methane* + *-ation*] : METHANIZATION

**meth·ane** \'me,thān\ *n* -s [ISV *meth-* + *-ane*] : a colorless odorless flammable gaseous saturated hydrocarbon $CH_4$ that is lighter than air and forms explosive mixtures with air or oxygen, that occurs naturally as a product of decomposition of organic matter in marshes and mines and esp. in natural gas and is formed also in the carbonization of coal, and that is used chiefly as a fuel and as a raw material in the manufacture of carbon black and in chemical synthesis — see FIREDAMP; compare MARSH GAS

**methane series** *n* : the homologous series of saturated open-chain hydrocarbons $C_nH_{2n+2}$ of which methane is the first and lowest member followed by ethane, propane, the butanes, the pentanes, the hexanes, and higher members — called also *paraffin series;* compare ¹PARAFFIN 2

**meth·a·ni·za·tion** \ˌmethənə'zāshən, -ˌnī'z-\ *n* -s : the process of methanizing

**meth·a·nize** \'⸗⸗,nīz\ *vt* -ED/-ING/-S [*methane* + *-ize*] : to convert (as a mixture of carbon monoxide and hydrogen) to methane

**methano-** *comb form* [ISV, fr. *methane*] : methylene as a bridging group — in names of polycyclic chemical compounds ⟨1,4-*methanonaphthalene*⟩

**meth·a·no·ic acid** \¦methə¦nōik-\ *n* [ISV *methanal* + *-o-* + *-ic*] : FORMIC ACID

**meth·a·nol** \'methə,nōl, -nȯl\ *n* -s [ISV *methane* + *-ol*] : a light volatile pungent flammable poisonous liquid alcohol $CH_3OH$ formed in the destructive distillation of wood but now usu. made synthetically (as by catalytic reaction of carbon monoxide and hydrogen under pressure) and used chiefly as a solvent, antifreeze, denaturant for ethyl alcohol, and raw material in the synthesis of formaldehyde and other chemicals — called also *methyl alcohol, wood alcohol;* see CARBINOL, PYROLIGNEOUS ACID

**meth·a·no·lic** \¦⸗⸗¦nōlik, -näl-\ *adj* : containing methanol usu. as solvent

**meth·a·nol·y·sis** \ˌ⸗⸗'näləsəs\ *n* [NL, irreg. fr. ISV *methanol* + NL *-lysis*] : alcoholysis with methanol

**meth·a·no·mon·a·da·ce·ae** \¦methə(ˌ)nō,mänə'dāsē,ē\ *n pl, cap* [NL, fr. *Methanomonad-, Methanomonas*, type genus (fr. ISV *methane* + NL *-o-* + *-monad-, -monas*) + *-aceae*] : a family of gram-negative rod-shaped soil and water bacteria (order Pseudomonadales) that obtain energy by oxidizing simple carbon and hydrogen compounds and are often motile by means of polar flagella

**meth·an·the·line** \meˈthan(t)thə,lēn, -l,lən\ *n* -s [*meth-* + *xanthene* carboxylate + *-ine*] : an anticholinergic drug usu. administered in the form of its crystalline bromide $C_{21}H_{26}BrNO_3$ in the treatment of peptic ulcers

**me·theg·lin** \mə'theglən\ *n* -s [W *meddyglyn*, fr. *meddyg* physician (fr. L *medicus*) + *llyn* liquor, lake — more at MEDICAL, LINN] : a beverage usu. made of fermented honey and water and often spiced or medicated : MEAD

**met·hem·albumin** \¦met,hēm+\ *n* [*meta-* + *hem-* + *albumin*] : an albumin complex with hematin found in plasma during diseases (as blackwater fever) that are associated with extensive hemolysis

**met·hemoglobin** \(ˌ)met+\ *n* [ISV *meta-* + *hemoglobin*] : a soluble brown crystalline basic pigment that is found in normal blood in much smaller amounts than hemoglobin, that is formed from blood, hemoglobin, or oxyhemoglobin by oxidation (as by ozone, peroxide, ferricyanide, permanganate), and that differs from hemoglobin in containing ferric iron instead of ferrous iron and in being unable to combine reversibly with molecular oxygen — called also *ferrihemoglobin, hemiglobin*

**met·hemoglobinemia** \¦met+\ *n* -s [NL, fr. ISV *methemoglobin* + NL *-emia*] : the presence of methemoglobin in the blood due to conversion of part of the hemoglobin to this inactive form

**met·hemoglobinuria** \"+\ *n* -s [NL, fr. ISV *methemoglobin* + NL *-uria*] : the presence of methemoglobin in the urine

**me·the·na·mine** \mə'thēnə,mēn, -then-, -ˌmən\ *n* [*methene* + *amine*] : hexamethylenetetramine used as a urinary antiseptic

**meth·ene** \'me,thēn\ *n* -s [ISV *meth-* + *-ene*] **1** : METHYLENE **2** : a complex unsaturated derivative of methane of the general formula $R{-}CH{=}R'$ ⟨di-pyrryl-*methene* $HNC_4H_3{-}CH{=}C_4H_3N$⟩

**meth·e·nyl** \'methə,nil\ *n* -s [ISV *methene* + *-yl*] : METHYLIDYNE

**mether** *var of* MADDER

**me·thex·is** \mə'theksəs\ *n* -ES [Gk, fr. *metechein* to share in, fr. *meta-* + *echein* to have — more at SCHEME] : PARTICIPATION 2

**meth·ide** \'me,thīd\ *n* -s [*meth-* + *-ide*] **1** : a binary compound of methyl usu. with a metal ⟨mercuric ~ $Hg(CH_3)_2$⟩ **2** : a compound that contains a methylene group as part of a quinonoid structure and that is formed as an intermediate in the condensation of a phenol and formaldehyde to yield a resin ⟨quinone ~ $O{=}C_6H_4{=}CH_2$⟩

**me·thig·lum** \mə'thigləm\ *dial var of* METHEGLIN

**meth·ine** \'me,thēn, -ˌthən\ *n* -s [ISV *meth-* + *-ine*] : METHYLIDYNE — used esp. in names of classes of cyanine dyes and other polymethine dyes

**methine basic orange G** *n, usu cap M&B&O* : a basic dye — see DYE table I (under *Basic Orange 21*)

**methine basic yellow 3G** *n, usu cap M&B&Y* : a basic dye — see DYE table I (under *Basic Yellow 11*)

**me·thinks** \mə'thiŋ(k)s, mē'-\ *vb impersonal, past 3d sing* **me·thought** \-'thȯt\ *pres 3d sing* **methinks** [ME *me thinketh*, fr. OE *mē thyncth*, fr. *mē* (suppletive dat. of *ic* I) + *thyncth*, 3d sing. pres. indic. of *thyncan* to seem — more at ME, THINK] *archaic* : it seems to me ⟨~ that I have heard them echo back —William Wordsworth⟩ ⟨*methought* a star came down from heaven —P.B.Shelley⟩

**meth·io·dal sodium** \mə'thīə,dal\ *n* [*methiodal* fr. *meth-* + *iod-* + *-al*] : a crystalline salt $CH_2ISO_3Na$ used as a radiopaque contrast medium in intravenous urography; sodium iodo-methane-sulfonate

**meth·iodide** \məth+\ *n* [*meth-* + *iodide*] : a compound with methyl iodide

**meth·ion·ic acid** \¦methī¦änik-\ *n* [*methionic* fr. *meth-* + *thionic*] : a deliquescent crystalline acid $CH_2(SO_3H)_2$ formed from acetylene or acetamide by the action of fuming sulfuric acid; methane-disulfonic acid

**me·thi·o·nine** \mə'thīə,nēn, -ˌnən\ *n* [ISV *me-* (fr. *methyl*) blend of *meth-* + *thion-* + *-ine*] : a crystalline essential amino acid $CH_3SCH_2CH_2CH(NH_2)COOH$ that occurs in the L-form as a constituent of many proteins (as casein and egg albumin), that is important esp. as a source of sulfur for the biosynthesis of cystine and as a source of methyl groups for transmethylation reactions (as in the biosynthesis of choline, creatine, and adrenaline), that is prepared synthetically in the racemic DL-form, and that is used as a dietary supplement for humans and their domestic mammals and poultry and in the treatment of fatty infiltration of the liver; α-amino-γ-methyl-mercapto-butyric acid

**metho-** — see METH-

**metho·bromide** \¦methō+\ *n* [*meth-* + *bromide*] : a compound with methyl bromide

**meth·od** \'methəd\ *n* -s [MF or L; MF *methode*, fr. L *methodus*, fr. Gk *methodos*, fr. *meta-* + *hodos* way — more at CEDE] **1** : a procedure or process for attaining an object: as **a** *obs* : the medical system of the methodists **b** (1) : a systematic procedure, technique, or set of rules employed in philosophical inquiry : a particular approach to problems of truth or knowledge ⟨the pragmatic ~ tries to interpret each notion by tracing its respective practical consequences —William James⟩ ⟨the dialectical ~ assumes the primacy of matter⟩ ⟨the ~ of the positivists applied to philosophy the procedures of the natural sciences⟩ (2) : a discipline or system sometimes considered a branch of logic that deals with the principles applicable to inquiry into or exposition of some subject (3) : a systematic procedure, technique, or mode of inquiry employed by or proper to a particular science, art, or discipline : METHODOLOGY ⟨the historical ~⟩ ⟨the ~ of logic⟩ ⟨exploring the broadest possibilities of iconographic ~ —Harry Bober⟩ (4) **:** a systematic plan followed in presenting material for instruction ⟨the lecture ~⟩ ⟨a course in ~s⟩ (5) **:** a particular way of viewing, organizing, and giving shape and significance to artistic materials ⟨hadn't found his ~, but he had definitely found his theme —Graham Greene⟩ ⟨~ . . . can be determined only from the work as a whole —M.K.Spears⟩ ⟨~ and sensibility ought never . . . to be kept long separate —R.P. Blackmur⟩ **c** (1) **:** a way, technique, or process of or for doing something ⟨there are three ~s of touring Britain by car —Richard Joseph⟩ ⟨found their respective working ~s congenial —*Current Biog.*⟩ ⟨often slow in their business ~s —T.R.Ybarra⟩ ⟨to whom she owed her excellent ~ —*Opera News*⟩ (2) **:** a body of skills or techniques ⟨deeply professional, learned in the art of the novel, heavily armed with ~ —J.D.Scott b.1917⟩ **2 a :** orderly arrangement, development, or classification **:** PLAN, DESIGN ⟨the book is completely lacking in ~⟩ **b** *obs* (1) **:** a methodical exposition (2) **:** a table of contents (3) **:** an arrangement that follows a plan or design **c :** orderliness and regularity or habitual practice of them in action ⟨thrift was as much in her nature as ~ —Sylvia T. Warner⟩ ⟨time enough to do everything if only you used ~ —Angela Thirkell⟩

**syn** METHOD, MODE, MANNER, WAY, FASHION, and SYSTEM can all indicate the means used or the procedure followed in doing a given kind of work or achieving a given end. METHOD can apply to any plan or procedure but usu. implies an orderly, logical, effective plan or procedure, connoting also regularity ⟨the crude *methods* of trial and error —Henry Suzzallo⟩ ⟨the *method* of this book is to present a series of successive scenes of English life —G.M.Trevelyan⟩ ⟨Marx's doctrine is not a system of scientific truths, it merely represents a *method* — one possible approach to social and historical reflection —Paolo Milano⟩ ⟨surely not to leave to fitful chance the things that *method* and system and science should order and adjust —B.N. Cardozo⟩ MODE, sometimes interchangeable with METHOD, seldom implies order or logic, suggesting rather custom, tradition, or personal preference ⟨a rational *mode* of dealing with the insane —W.R.Inge⟩ ⟨this intuition is essentially an aesthetic *mode* of apprehension —H.J.Muller⟩ ⟨the *mode* of reproduction of plants and animals, however, is fundamentally identical —*Encyc. Americana*⟩ MANNER usu. suggests a personal or peculiar course or procedure, often interchanging with MODE in this sense ⟨the *manner* by which the present pattern of land ownership in this country has evolved —A.F.Gustafson⟩ ⟨it is not consistent with his *manner* of writing Latin —G.C. Sellery⟩ ⟨bearing loaves of sweet bread and of cornbread made with yeast in the Portuguese *manner* —Dana Burnet⟩ WAY is general and interchangeable with METHOD, MODE, or MANNER ⟨a special *way* to raise orchids⟩ ⟨the *way* the machine works⟩ ⟨the town's *way* of life⟩ ⟨one's *way* of tying his tie⟩ FASHION, in this comparison, may be distinguished from WAY in often suggesting a more superficial origin or source as in a mere fashion or ephemeral style ⟨was so popular that his subjects took to wearing monocles, in his *fashion* —*Time*⟩ ⟨Harvard has stoutly and successfully resisted the *fashion* by which the grounds of an American college have come to be known as a campus —*Official Register of Harvard Univ.*⟩ ⟨who were poor in a *fashion* unknown to North America —Herbert Agar⟩ SYSTEM suggests a fully developed, often carefully formulated method, usu. emphasizing the idea of rational orderliness ⟨every new discovery claims to form an addition to the *system* of science as transmitted from the past —Michael Polanyi⟩ ⟨behavior which is not in accord with the individual's *system* elicits responses of fear —Ralph Linton⟩ ⟨an earnest plea for radical reformation of the *system* of assessment and taxation —C.A.Duniway⟩

**¹me·thod·ic** \mə'thädik, me'-, -dēk\ *adj* [MF *methodique*, fr. L *methodicus*, fr. Gk *methodikos*, fr. *methodos* + *-ikos* -ic] **1** *obs* **:** METHODICAL 2 **2 :** done or acting with method **:** of or relating to method **:** METHODICAL, SYSTEMATIC ⟨~ religious exercise —Cecil Sprigge⟩ ⟨an attitude of ~ doubt⟩

**²methodic** \"\ *n* -s **:** METHODIST 2

**me·thod·i·cal** \-dəkəl, -dēk-\ *adj* [MF *methodique* + E *-al*] **1 a :** arranged with regard to method **:** characterized by method or orderliness **:** disposed or performed with method or order ⟨~ arrangement⟩ **b :** habitually proceeding according to method **:** SYSTEMATIC ⟨in habits he was regular and ~ —A.W.Long⟩ **2 :** of, relating to, or constituting an ancient school of physicians — compare ¹METHODIST **3 :** of or relating to method ⟨meeting these ~ demands, it provides a theory of change —K.R.Popper⟩ **syn** see ORDERLY

**me·thod·i·cal·ly** \-k(ə)lē, -li\ *adv* **:** in a methodical manner **:** SYSTEMATICALLY ⟨chewing slowly and ~ —J.E.Macdonnell⟩

**me·thod·i·cal·ness** \-kəlnəs\ *n* -ES **:** the quality or state of being methodical

**methodies** *pl of* METHODY

**meth·od·ism** \'methə,dizəm\ *n* -s **1** *cap* **:** the doctrines, polity, and worship peculiar to Methodists **2 :** methodical procedure **:** excessive devotion to methods

**¹meth·od·ist** \-,dəst\ *n* -s [*method* + *-ist*] **1 a :** a person devoted to some method or laying great stress on method ⟨the ~s are many and the men of vision very few —J.H.Randall⟩ **b** *archaic* **:** SYSTEMATIST 2 **2 :** a member of an ancient school of physicians basing its proceedings on theory and reasoning rather than observation of the patient's state and concentrating its attention esp. on the pores, an acute disease being indicative of their contraction and chronic disease being associated with their relaxation **3** *usu cap* **:** a member or adherent of a denomination of trinitarian Protestant Christians starting as a revival within the Church of England but later separating from that church, adopting a modified episcopacy as its form of polity in America, and emphasizing an Arminian rather than a Calvinist theology in the area of doctrine

**²methodist** \"\ *adj, usu cap* **:** of or relating to the Methodists or Methodism

**meth·od·is·tic** \¦==¦distik\ *adj, usu cap* **:** of, relating to, or characteristic of Methodists or Methodism **:** resembling a Methodist or Methodism ⟨the government was *Methodistic* —F.S. Mead⟩ — **meth·od·is·ti·cal** \-tәkəl\ *adj, usu cap* — **meth·od·is·ti·cal·ly** \-k(ə)lē\ *adv, usu cap*

**meth·od·ization** \,methədə'zāshən, -,dī'z-\ *n* -s **:** the act or process of methodizing or the state of being methodized

**meth·od·ize** \'==,dīz\ *vb* -ED/-ING/-S [*method* + *-ize*] *vt* **1 :** to reduce to method **:** arrange in an orderly manner **:** SYSTEMATIZE ⟨developed specialized procedures . . . and *methodized* them —S.E.Hyman⟩ **2** *often cap* **:** to turn or make Methodist ~ *vi, often cap* **:** to talk or act as a Methodist **:** incline to Methodism **syn** see ORDER

**meth·od·less** \-,dləs\ *adj* **:** lacking order or method

**method of agreement :** a method of scientific induction devised by J. S. Mill according to which if two or more instances of a phenomenon under investigation have only a single circumstance in common the circumstance in which all the instances agree is the cause or effect of the phenomenon

**method of concomitant variations :** a method of scientific induction devised by J. S. Mill according to which a phenomenon varying in any way whenever another phenomenon varies in some particular way is a cause or effect of that phenomenon or is related to it through some fact of causation

**method of difference :** a method of scientific induction devised by J. S. Mill according to which if an instance in which the phenomenon under investigation occurs and an instance in which it does not occur have each circumstance except one in common, that one occurring only in the former, the circumstance in which the two instances differ is the effect or cause or necessary part of the cause of the phenomenon — compare INDIRECT METHOD OF DIFFERENCE

**method of exclusion :** a method in scientific induction which proceeds by the progressive exclusion of the nonessential antecedents by comparison of cases to find the essential residue or real cause; *also* **:** a method that proceeds to the determination of the true principle by successive elimination as false of all the possible or plausible hypotheses except that one

**method of least squares :** LEAST SQUARES

**method of residues :** a method of scientific induction devised by J. S. Mill according to which if one subtracts from a phenomenon the part known by previous inductions to be the effect of certain antecedents the remaining part of the phenomenon is the effect of the remaining antecedents

**meth·od·o·logical** \¦methədə+\ *adj* **:** of or relating to method or methodology **:** of or relating to a guiding approach, procedure, or the working concepts or premises employed ⟨rejected the ~ axioms of the Greeks — the superiority of the heavenly bodies, the circularity of their bodies —S.F.Mason⟩ ⟨~ doubt is . . . an essential for scientific progress —L.J. McGinley⟩ ⟨in spite of its ~ attractiveness —G.D.Wiebe⟩ ⟨a useful enough ~ principle to begin with —Edward Sapir⟩ —

**meth·od·o·logically** \"+\ *adv*

**meth·od·ol·o·gist** \,methə'däləjəst\ *n* -s **:** a person who treats method as an object of study or who is greatly concerned with method ⟨a controversy which . . . has split not only logicians and ~s —Alfred Schutz⟩

**meth·od·ol·o·gy** \-jē, -ji\ *n* -ES [NL *methodologia*, fr. L *methodus* method + *-o-* + *-logia* -logy — more at METHOD] **1 a :** a body of methods, procedures, working concepts, rules, and postulates employed by a science, art, or discipline ⟨the limitation of science arises from a feature of its ~ —Henry Margenau⟩ ⟨the statistical ~ is perhaps the most useful tool for controlling quality —N.C.Brown⟩ ⟨applying the . . . ~ of geology and soil science to the practical problems of mineral exploration —H.T.U.Smith⟩ **b :** the processes, techniques, or approaches employed in the solution of a problem or in doing something **:** a particular procedure or set of procedures ⟨attempts to teach students a ~ of reading — Hargis Westerfield⟩ ⟨the first stage of the research has been devoted to the development of a ~ —*Amer. Anthrop. Assoc. Bull.*⟩ ⟨the ~ of this study is outlined —*Jour. Amer. Med. Assoc.*⟩ **c :** the theoretical foundations of a philosophical doctrine **:** the basic premises, postulates, and concepts of a philosophy ⟨the ~ of Aristotelianism⟩ ⟨the ~ of dialectical materialism⟩ ⟨these *methodologies* . . . are so divergent as to render futile any effort at reconciliation —Murray Krieger⟩ **2 :** a science or the study of method ⟨graduate schools of education . . . are wholeheartedly devoted to ~ —M.B.Smith⟩; *specif* **:** a branch of logic that analyzes the principles or procedures that should guide inquiry in a particular field

**methods** *pl of* METHOD

**methods engineer** *n* **:** a person qualified by training, skill, or experience to engage in methods engineering

**methods engineering** *n* **1 :** a branch of industrial engineering specializing in the analysis of methods and the improvement and standardization of methods, equipment, and working conditions **2 :** the work of one who engages in the analysis, improvement, and standardization of industrial methods, equipment, and working conditions

**methods man** *n* **:** a clerical technician

**meth·ody** \'methədē, -di\ *n* -ES *usu cap* [by shortening & alteration] *dial* **:** METHODIST

**meth·one** \'me,thōn\ *n* -s [*meth-* + *-one*] **:** DIMEDON

**me·th·o·ni·um** \mə'thōnēəm\ *n* -s [NL, fr. *meth-* + *-onium*] **:** any of several bivalent doubled substituted ammonium ions (as decamethonium or hexamethonium) in which the two quaternary nitrogen atoms are separated by a polymethylene chain ⟨~ salts⟩

**metho·sulfate** \¦methō+\ *n* [*meth-* + *sulfate*] **:** a compound with methyl sulfate

**methought** *past 3d sing of* METHINKS

**methoughts** *obs var of* METHOUGHT

**meth·oxide** \(')meth+\ *n* [*meth-* + *oxide*] **:** a binary compound of methoxyl; *esp* **:** a base formed from methanol by replacement of the hydroxyl hydrogen with a metal ⟨sodium ~ $NaOCH_3$⟩

**me·thoxy** \mə'thäksē, me'-\ *adj* [*methoxy-*] **:** relating to or containing methoxyl

**methoxy-** *comb form* [ISV, fr. *methoxyl*] **:** containing methoxyl — in names of chemical compounds ⟨*methoxy*acetophenone⟩

**me·thoxy·carbonyl** \=¦==+\ *n* [*methoxy-* + *carbonyl*] **:** CARBOMETHOXYL

**me·thoxy·chlor** \=¦==,klō(ə)r\ *n* -s [*methoxy-* + *trichloro*ethane] **:** a crystalline insecticide $(CH_3OC_6H_4)_2CHCCl_3$ said to be faster acting and less toxic to warm-blooded animals than DDT — called also *methoxy DDT*

**meth·ox·yl** \mə'thäksəl, me'-\ *n* [*meth-* + *ox-* + *-yl*] **:** a univalent radical $CH_3O$— composed of methyl united with oxygen

**me·thu·se·lah** \mə'th(y)üz(ə)lə *also* -üs(-\ *n* -s *usu cap* [after *Methuselah*, Biblical patriarch represented as having lived 969 years (Gen 5:27)] **1 :** a person of great age ⟨one of the other *Methuselahs*, reminded . . . of his own aches and miseries —Mary McCarthy⟩ **2 :** an oversize wine bottle holding about six and a half quarts

**meth·yl** \'methəl, *chiefly by Brit chemists* 'mē,thīl\ *n* -s [G *methyl* & F *méthyle*, back-formation fr. ISV *methylene*] **:** an alkyl radical $CH_3$ derived from methane by removal of one hydrogen atom that is known usu. in combination in many compounds but is also isolated momentarily in the free state as a gaseous fragmentation product of the pyrolysis of organic compounds

**methyl acetate** *n* **:** a volatile flammable fragrant liquid ester $CH_3COOCH_3$ made from methanol and acetic acid and used chiefly as a solvent (as for nitrocellulose and cellulose acetate)

**methyl acetone** *n* **:** a flammable mixture of solvents consisting usu. of about one half acetone and one half methyl acetate and methanol

**meth·yl·acetylene** \¦methəl+\ *n* [ISV *methyl* + *acetylene*] **:** an unpleasant-smelling gaseous hydrocarbon $CH_3C{\equiv}CH$ that burns with a smoky flame — called also *allylene*

**meth·yl·al** \,methə'lal, '==,=\ *n* -s [ISV *methyl* + *-al*] **1 :** a volatile flammable liquid acetal $CH_2(OCH_3)_2$ that has a pleasant ethereal odor, is made by reaction of formaldehyde and methanol or by partial oxidation of methanol, and is used chiefly as a solvent and in organic synthesis — called also *formal* **2 :** FORMAL 2

**methyl alcohol** *n* **:** the first in the series of simple aliphatic alcohols **:** METHANOL

**meth·yl·amine** \¦methələ¦mēn, -thə¦lamən\ *n* [ISV *methyl* + *amine*] **1 :** a flammable explosive gaseous base $CH_3NH_2$ that has a strong ammoniacal odor, that is very soluble in water, and that is usu. made from methanol and ammonia and used chiefly in organic synthesis — called also *monomethylamine* **2 :** an amine containing methyl attached to amino nitrogen — see DIMETHYLAMINE, TRIMETHYLAMINE

**meth·yl·aminophenol** \¦methəl+\ *n* [ISV *methyl* + *aminophenol*] **:** a poisonous crystalline compound $CH_3NHC_6H_4OH$ used chiefly in the form of its sulfate as a photographic developer — called also *methyl-p-aminophenol, para-methylaminophenol*

**meth·yl·aniline** \"+\ *n* [ISV *methyl* + *aniline*] **:** a methyl derivative of aniline; *esp* **:** a colorless oily secondary amine $C_6H_5NHCH_3$ made usu. by heating aniline hydrochloride with methanol — compare TOLUIDINE

**methyl anthranilate** *n* **:** a fragrant liquid ester $NH_2C_6H_4COOCH_3$ found in various essential oils (as neroli oil) and in grape juice and used in perfumes and flavoring materials

**¹meth·yl·ate** \'methə,lāt, -,lət\ *n* -s [*methyl* + *-ate* (n. suffix)] **:** METHOXIDE

**²meth·yl·ate** \-,lāt, *usu* -ād·+V\ *vt* -ED/-ING/-S [*methyl* + *-ate* (v. suffix)] **1 :** to impregnate or mix with methanol **2 :** to introduce the methyl group into (a compound) — **meth·yl·a·tion** \,=='lāshən\ *n* -s — **meth·yl·a·tor** \'==,lād·ə(r), -ātə-\ *n* -s

**methylated spirit** *or* **methylated spirits** *n* **:** alcohol (sense 3) denatured with methanol

**meth·yl·benzene** \¦methəl+\ *n* [ISV *methyl* + *benzene*] **:** TOLUENE

**methyl bromide** *n* **:** a poisonous gaseous compound $CH_3Br$ used chiefly as a fumigant against rodents, worms, and insects; bromo-methane

**methyl cellulose** *n* **:** any of various tasteless gummy substances that are made by methylating cellulose, have the property of swelling in water, and are used chiefly as emulsifiers, adhesives, and thickeners and in medicine as bulk laxatives

**methyl chavicol** *n* **:** ESTRAGOLE

**methyl chloride** *n* **:** a sweet-smelling gaseous compound $CH_3Cl$ made usu. by the action of hydrochloric acid on methanol and used chiefly as a refrigerant and methylating agent — called also *chloromethane*

**meth·yl·cholanthrene** \¦methəl+\ *n* [ISV *methyl* + *cholanthrene*] **:** a potent carcinogenic hydrocarbon $C_{21}H_{16}$ obtained as yellow crystals from certain bile acids and cholesterol and also synthetically

**methyl cotton blue** *also* **methyl blue** *n, often cap M&C&B* **:** an acid triphenylmethane dye used chiefly in writing ink and as a biological stain — see DYE table I (under *Acid Blue 93*)

**methyl cyanide** *n* **:** ACETONITRILE

**meth·yl·dihydromorphinone** \¦methəl+\ *n* [*methyl* + *dihydr-* + *morphine* + *-one*] **:** METOPON

**meth·yl·ene** \'methə,lēn\ *n* -s [F *méthylène*, fr. Gk *methy* wine + *hylē* wood + *-ēnē* (fem. patronymic suffix) — more at MEAD] **:** a bivalent hydrocarbon radical $CH_2$= or —$CH_2$— derived from methane by removal of two hydrogen atoms — compare POLYMETHYLENE

**methylene azure** *n, sometimes cap M&A* **:** a dye obtained by oxidation of methylene blue and used in biological stains

**methylene blue** *n, sometimes cap M&B* **:** a basic dye of the thiazine class used as a biological stain, as an antidote esp. in cyanide poisoning, as an oxidation-reduction indicator, and in a test for the bacterial content of milk — see DYE table I (under *Basic Blue 9*)

**methylene chloride** *n* **:** a low-boiling nonflammable liquid $CH_2Cl_2$ used chiefly as a solvent, paint remover, refrigerant, and propellant in aerosols; dichloro-methane

**methylenedioxy-** *comb form* [*methylene* + *dioxy-*] **:** containing the group —$OCH_2O$— — in names of organic compounds ⟨*methylenedioxy*benzaldehyde⟩

**methylene green** *n, sometimes cap M&G* **:** a basic dye obtained by nitrating methylene blue — see DYE table I (under *Basic Green 5*)

**methylene iodide** *n* **:** a yellowish liquid compound $CH_2I_2$ remarkable for its high specific gravity (3.325 at 20° C) and high index of refraction that make it useful in separating minerals and determining specific gravities and indexes of refraction — called also *diiodomethane*

**methylene violet 3R** *n, usu cap M&V* **:** a basic dye — see DYE table I (under *Basic Violet 5*)

**meth·yl·en·imine** \¦methə¦lenə,mēn, -,mən\ *n* [ISV *methylene* + *imine*] **:** a hypothetical compound $CH_2{=}NH$ known in the form of derivatives — called also *azomethine*

**methyl ester** *n* **:** an ester that yields methanol on hydrolysis ⟨*methyl esters* of carboxylic acids⟩

**methyl ether** *n* **1 :** a flammable easily condensable gas $(CH_3)_2O$ that has an agreeable odor and is usu. obtained by heating methanol with sulfuric acid — called also *dimethyl ether* **2 :** an ether in which one of the radicals united to oxygen is methyl ⟨the *methyl ether* of benzyl alcohol⟩

**methyl ethyl ketone** *n* **:** a flammable liquid compound $CH_3COC_2H_5$ resembling acetone made usu. by dehydrogenation of secondary butyl alcohol and used chiefly as a solvent — called also *2-butanone*

**methylethylpyridine** \¦=¦==¦==,=\ *n* [*methyl* + *ethyl* + *pyridine*] **:** a liquid base $C_5H_3N(CH_3)(C_2H_5)$ that has a penetrating odor, is usu. made by catalytic reaction of paraldehyde with ammonia, and is used chiefly in organic synthesis (as of nicotinic acid) — called also *aldehyde collidine, aldehydine, collidine, 2-methyl-5-ethylpyridine*

**meth·yl·glyoxal** \¦methəl+\ *n* [ISV *methyl* + *glyoxal*] **:** PYRUVALDEHYDE

**methyl green** *n* **:** a basic triphenylmethane dye made by adding methyl chloride to crystal violet and used chiefly as a biological stain

**methyl heptine carbonate** *n* **:** an oily ester $CH_3(CH_2)_4C{\equiv}CCOOCH_3$ that has a strong odor like violets and is used in perfumes and cosmetics; methyl 2-octyn-oate — not used systematically

**me·thyl·ic** \(')me¦thilik\ *adj* [ISV *methyl* + *-ic*] **:** of, relating to, or containing methyl ⟨the ~ content⟩

**me·thyl·i·dyne** \me'thilə,dīn\ *n* -s [*meth-* + *-ylidyne*] **:** the trivalent radical HC≡ or =CH— derived from methane — called also *methenyl, methine*

**methyl iodide** *n* **:** a volatile pungent flammable heavy liquid compound $CH_3I$ that turns brown on exposure to light, that causes burning on contact with the skin and is poisonous on inhalation of the vapor, and that is made usu. by interaction of methanol, red phosphorus, and iodine and used chiefly in organic synthesis; iodo-methane

**methyl isobutyl ketone** *n* **:** a pleasant-smelling flammable liquid compound $CH_3COCH_2CH(CH_3)_2$ made usu. by catalytic hydrogenation of mesityl oxide and used chiefly as a solvent; 4-methyl-2-pentanone

**methyl methacrylate** *n* **1 :** a volatile flammable liquid ester $CH_2{=}C(CH_3)COOCH_3$ that polymerizes readily (as in the presence of a peroxide) **2** *or* **methyl methacrylate resin :** an acrylic resin made by polymerization of monomeric methyl methacrylate

**meth·yl·morphine** \¦methəl+\ *n* [ISV *methyl* + *morphine*] **:** CODEINE

**meth·yl·naphthalene** \"+\ *n* [*methyl* + *naphthalene*] **:** either of two isomeric hydrocarbons $C_{10}H_7CH_3$ occurring in coal tar and petroleum: **a :** an oily liquid used as a reference fuel in determining the cetane number — called also *alpha-* or *1-methylnaphthalene* **b :** a crystalline solid used chiefly in organic synthesis (as of menadione) — called also *beta-* or *2-methylnaphthalene*

**methyl naphthyl ketone** *n* **:** ACETONAPHTHONE

**meth·yl·ol** \'methə,lȯl, -lōl\ *n* -s [*methyl* + *-ol*] **:** HYDROXYMETHYL — used esp. in naming compounds in which hydroxymethyl is attached to nitrogen

**methylolurea** \¦==,==¦=\ *n* [*methylol* + *urea*] **:** either of two compounds formed as the first stage in making urea-formaldehyde resins: **a :** a crystalline compound $H_2NCONHCH_2OH$ obtainable from one mole each of urea and formaldehyde and used esp. for impregnating wood with which it forms hard resins — called also *monomethylolurea* **b :** DIMETHYLOLUREA

**methyl orange** *n, sometimes cap M&O* **:** a basic azo dye $(CH_3)_2NC_6H_4N{=}NC_6H_4SO_3Na$ which is made by coupling diazotized sulfanilic acid with dimethylaniline, is used chiefly as an acid-base indicator, and whose dilute solution is yellow when neutral and pink when acid — see DYE table I (under *Acid Orange 52*); compare HELIANTHIN

**meth·yl·para·ben** \,methəl'parə,ben\ *n* [*methyl* + *para*-hydroxybenzoic (acid)] **:** a crystalline compound $HOC_6H_4COOCH_3$ used as a preservative (as in pharmaceutical ointments and cosmetic creams and lotions); the methyl ester of *para*hydroxybenzoic acid

**meth·yl·pentose** \¦methəl+\ *n* [*methyl* + *pentose*] **:** a methyl derivative of a pentose **:** a deoxy-hexose; *esp* **:** such a derivative $CH_3(CHOH)_4CHO$ with a terminal methyl group on the carbon chain (as in fucose or rhamnose)

**methyl phthalate** *n* **:** a methyl ester of phthalic acid; *esp* **:** DIMETHYL PHTHALATE

**meth·yl·propene** \¦methəl+\ *n* [*methyl* + *propene*] **:** ISOBUTYLENE — used in the system of nomenclature adopted by the Internat. Union of Pure and Applied Chemistry

**methyl propyl ketone** *n* **:** PENTANONE a

**methyl red** *n, sometimes cap M&R* **:** a basic azo dye $(CH_3)_2NC_6H_4N{=}C_6H_4COOH$ used similarly to methyl orange as an acid-base indicator

**meth·yl·rosaniline chloride** \¦methəl+-\ *n* [*methyl* + *rosaniline*] **:** CRYSTAL VIOLET

**methyl rubber** *n* **:** a synthetic rubber made in Germany during World War I by polymerization of dimethyl-butadiene

**methyls** *pl of* METHYL

**methyl salicylate** *n* **:** a liquid ester $HOC_6H_4COOCH_3$ that has a strong odor of wintergreen, that is the principal constituent of wintergreen oil and sweet-birch oil but is usu. made synthetically, and that is used chiefly as a flavoring material, in perfumes, and in medicine as a counterirritant — called also *sweet-birch oil, wintergreen oil*

**methyl sulfate** *n* **:** a methyl ester of sulfuric acid; *esp* **:** the poisonous liquid dimethyl ester $(CH_3)_2SO_4$ used as a methylating agent

**meth·yl·testosterone** \¦methəl+\ *n* [*methyl* + *testosterone*] **:** a synthetically prepared crystalline compound $C_{20}H_{30}O_2$ administered orally in cases of male sex hormone deficiency

**meth·yl·thiouracil** \"+\ *n* -s [*methyl* + *thiouracil*] **:** a crystalline compound $C_5H_6N_2OS$ used in the suppression of hyperactivity of the thyroid — called also *6-methyl-2-thiouracil*

**methyl violet** *n, often cap M&V* **:** any of several basic dyes that are methyl derivatives of pararosaniline: as **a** *or* **methyl violet B :** a dye consisting essentially of pentamethyl-pararosaniline chloride and used chiefly in making organic pigments (as for printing inks) and as a biological stain — called also *gentian violet;* see DYE table I (under *Basic Violet 1, Pigment Violet 3,* and *Solvent Violet 8*) **b :** CRYSTAL VIOLET

**methyl yellow** *n* **:** OIL YELLOW 1b

**met·ic** \ˈmed·ik\ *n* -s [Gk *metoikos,* fr. *meta-* + *oikos* house — more at VICINITY] **:** an alien resident of an ancient Greek city who had some civil privileges

**me·tic·u·los·i·ty** \mə̇,tikyəˈläsəd·ē\ *n* -ES [fr. *meticulous,* after such pairs as E *curious: curiosity*] **:** the quality or state of being meticulous **:** METICULOUSNESS

**me·tic·u·lous** \ˈ=ˈ==ləs\ *adj* [L *meticulosus,* fr. *metus* fear + *-iculosus* (as in *periculosus* dangerous)] **1** *obs* **:** TIMID, FEARFUL **2 :** marked by extreme painstaking care in the consideration or treatment of details: **a :** unduly fussy esp. through fear of error or censure ⟨if I seem rather ~ in my examination of this question —*World Report*⟩ ⟨in their work, they were rigid and overzealous, ~, overconscientious, inelastic —Harold Rosen & H.E.Kiene⟩ ⟨no longer interpret contracts with ~ adherence to the letter when in conflict with the spirit —B.N. Cardozo⟩ **b :** commendably thorough or precise **:** STRICT ⟨that fullness and ~ documentation which the scholar requires —G.W.Allen⟩ ⟨a ~ scholar, who has mastered the documents of the age —Reinhold Niebuhr⟩ ⟨using ~ intravascular injection techniques —N.M.Pusey⟩ ⟨had observed a ~ neutrality —Sir Winston Churchill⟩ ⟨a ~ regard for law and usage —C.G.Bowers⟩ **syn** see CAREFUL

**me·tic·u·lous·ly** *adv* **:** in a meticulous manner **:** with meticulousness ⟨behaved ~ toward the extremely suspicious government —Richard Watts⟩ ⟨the escape was planned ~ and executed boldly —Edmond Taylor⟩

**me·tic·u·lous·ness** *n* -ES **:** the quality of being meticulous ⟨dressed with almost stiff ~ —Harriet La Barre⟩ ⟨this ~ which prevents fields of knowledge from spilling over into each other —Dallas Finn⟩ ⟨the artist's ~, that fine intuitive eye for detail and relevance and comparisons —*Times Lit. Supp.*⟩

**mé·tier** \(ˈ)māˌtyā, (ˈ)me-‐\ *n* -s [F, fr. OF *mestier,* fr. (assumed) VL *misterium,* alter. of L *ministerium* work, occupation, ministry — more at MINISTRY] **1 :** VOCATION, TRADE, BUSINESS ⟨to be a sailor, this is a lonely ~ —*Lamp*⟩ ⟨blue sweatshirt, with grease from the truck and the stains of his ~ marked on it —Kay Boyle⟩ ⟨the ~ of the engineer or the practical scientist —Bernard Wall⟩ **2 a :** a special line of activity ⟨exploration was at that time the principal ~ of British geography —O.J.R.Howarth⟩ **b :** an area of activity in which one is most expert, successful, or happy **:** FORTE ⟨his ~ seems to be rather the stage fabrication of rough-and-tumble popular entertainment —G.J.Nathan⟩ ⟨political oratory is not my ~ —Francis Younghusband⟩ **3 :** the special techniques characteristic of an art or vocation **:** MODE, METHOD ⟨new writers who have something to say and try to say it with sincerity and a grasp of the ~ of the novelist —*Nation*⟩

**me·tif** \māˈtēf\ *n, pl* **metifs** \"', -fs\ *sometimes cap* [F *métif,* alter. of *métis*] **:** MÉTIS

**meting** *pres part of* METE

**mé·tis** \māˈtē(s)\ *n, pl* **métis** \", -tēz\ *sometimes cap* [F (prob. influenced in meaning by Sp *mestizo*), fr. MF *metis* mongrel, of parents of different nations, fr. LL *misticius, mixticius* mixed — more at MESTIZO] **:** one that is of mixed blood: **a :** HALF-BREED; *specif* **:** one of French and Indian ancestry **b :** a crossbred animal (as a horse or a sheep)

**mé·tisse** \māˈtēs\ *n, pl* **métisses** \", -ēsəz\ [F, fem. of *métis*] **:** a female half-breed — compare MÉTIS

**met·myoglobin** \(ˌ)met+\ *n* [*meta-* + *myoglobin*] **:** a reddish brown crystalline pigment that is formed by oxidation of myoglobin

**METO** *abbr* maximum except take-off

**met·obelus** \(ˈ)med·+\ *n, pl* **metobeli** [NL, fr. *meta-* + *obelus*] **:** a symbol variously written (as by:) and used in ancient manuscripts (as of the Septuagint) to mark the end of a suspected or spurious passage — compare OBELUS

**metoestrus** *or* **metoestrum** *var of* METESTRUS

**Me·tol** \ˈmeˌtȯl, -tōl\ *trademark* — used for a photographic developer

**me·ton·ic cycle** \məˈtänik-\ *n, usu cap M* [*Meton,* 5th cent. B.C. Greek astronomer + E *-ic*] **:** a period of 19 years after the lapse of which the phases of the moon return to a particular date in the calendar year: **a :** one of the 19-year periods reckoning from June 27, 432 B.C., that were used in determining lengths of years and the placing of the intercalary month in the ancient Greek calendar **b :** one of the 19-year periods reckoning from 1 B.C. that are used in determining the date of Easter in the Gregorian calendar

**met·o·nym** \ˈmed·əˌnim\ *n* -s [back-formation fr. *metonymy*] **:** a word used in metonymy

**met·o·nym·ic** \ˌ==ˈnimik\ *or* **met·o·nym·i·cal** \-mə̇kəl\ *adj* [*metonymic* fr. Gk *metōnymikos,* fr. *metōnymia* metonymy + *-ikos* -ic; *metonymical* fr. Gk *metōnymikos* + E *-al*] **:** of, relating to, or involving metonymy **:** used in metonymy — **met·o·nym·i·cal·ly** \-mə̇k(ə)lē\ *adv*

**me·ton·y·my** \mə̇ˈtänəmē, meˈ-, -əmi\ *n* -ES [L *metonymia,* fr. Gk *metōnymia,* fr. *meta-* + *-ōnymia* -onymy] **:** a figure of speech that consists in using the name of one thing for that of something else with which it is associated (as in "spent the evening reading *Shakespeare*", "lands belonging to the *crown*", "demanded action by *City Hall*", "ogling the heavily mascaraed *skirt* at the next table") **:** use of one word for another that it may be expected to suggest — compare TROPE

**¹me-too** \ˈ=ˈ=\ *adj* [fr. the phrase *me too*] **:** marked by similarity to or acceptance of something (as a political policy) that has proved successful or persuasive when promoted by an opponent or rival ⟨conducted a *me-too* campaign⟩ ⟨*me-too* candidates⟩ ⟨has been in the forefront of . . . the *me-too* faction —*N.Y.Times*⟩

**²me-too** \"\ *vt* -ED/-ING/-S **:** to agree with or adopt a successful or persuasive practice or policy of (a rival) ⟨*me-too* the president⟩

**me-too·er** \ˈ=ˈ=ə(r)\ *n* -s **:** one that adopts a me-too policy or principle

**me-too·ism** \ˈ=ˈ=ˌizəm\ *n* -s **:** the policies or principles of a me-tooer

**met·ope** \ˈmed·ˌōp, -eˌtōp\ *n, pl* **metopes** \-ps\ *also* **met·o·pae** \-d·əˌpē\ [Gk *metopē,* fr. *meta-* + *opē* opening, hole; akin to Gk *osse* (fr. *okye*) two eyes — more at EYE] **:** the space between two triglyphs of a Doric frieze often adorned with carved work

**me·top·ic** \meˈtäpik\ *adj* [Gk *metōpikos,* fr. *metōpon* forehead + *-ikos* -ic] **:** of or relating to the forehead **:** FRONTAL; *esp* **:** of, relating to, or being a suture uniting the frontal bones in the fetus and sometimes persistent after birth

**met·o·pi·idae** \ˌmed·əˈpīəˌdē\ [NL, fr. *Metopia,* type genus (fr. Gk *metōpion* forehead) + *-idae*] *syn of* SARCOPHAGIDAE

**me·to·pi·on** \məˈtōpēən\ *n* -s [NL, fr. Gk *metōpion* forehead, dim. of *metōpon,* fr. *meta-* + *-ōpon* (fr. *ōp-, ōps* face, eye) — more at EYE] **:** a point situated midway between the frontal eminences of the skull — see CRANIOMETRY illustration

**met·o·pism** \ˈmed·əˌpizəm\ *n* -s [ISV *metop-* (fr. Gk *metōpon* forehead) + *-ism*] **:** the condition of having a persistent metopic suture

**me·to·pi·um** \məˈtōpēəm\ *n* -s [NL, fr. *Metopium,* genus of trees including the black poison, fr. L, juice from a species of *Ferula,* fr. Gk *metōpion,* dim. of *metōpon,* a species of *Ferula,* prob. fr. *metōpon* forehead] **:** BLACK POISON

**met·o·poc·e·ros** \ˌmed·əˈpäsərəs\ *n, cap* [NL, fr. Gk *metōpon* forehead + *keras* horn — more at METOPION, HORN] **:** a genus of Iguanidae containing the rhinoceros iguana

**met·o·pon** \ˈmed·əˌpän\ *n* -s [*met*hyldihydromorphin*one*] **:** a narcotic drug $C_{18}H_{21}NO_3$ derived from morphine that is usu. administered by mouth in the form of its crystalline hydrochloride and that is more effective than morphine in its analgesic action

**met·o·pos·co·py** \ˌmed·əˈpäskəpē\ *n* -ES [Gk *metōposkopos* observing the forehead (fr. *metōpon* forehead + *skopos* watcher) + E *-y* — more at METOPION, SCOPE] **1 :** the art of reading character or telling fortunes from the markings of the forehead **2 :** PHYSIOGNOMY

**me·tox·e·nous** \məˈtäksənəs\ *adj* [irreg. fr. *meta-* + Gk *xenos* stranger, guest + E *-ous*] **:** HETEROECIOUS — **me·tox·e·ny** \-nē\ *n* -ES

**metr-** *or* **metro-** *comb form* [NL, fr. Gk *mētr-,* fr. *mētra*] **1 :** uterus ⟨*metritis*⟩ ⟨*metro*fibroma⟩ ⟨*metrotome*⟩ **2 :** pith ⟨*Metrosideros*⟩ ⟨*Metroxylon*⟩

**¹me·tra** \ˈmē·trə\ *n, pl* **me·trae** \-ēˌtrē\ [NL, fr. Gk *mētra,* fr. *mētr-, mētēr* mother — more at MOTHER] **:** UTERUS 1

**²metra** *pl of* METRON *or of* METRUM

**-me·tra** \ˈmē·trə\ *n comb form* -s [NL, fr. Gk *mētra* womb] **:** a (specified) condition of the uterus ⟨hemato*metra*⟩ ⟨hydro*metra*⟩

**me·tra·term** \ˈmē·trə+,-\ *n* [*metra* + L *term*inus boundary, limit, end — more at TERM] **:** the distal muscular portion of the uterus of a flatworm

**Met·ra·zol** \ˈme·trəˌzōl, -ōl\ *trademark* — used for pentylenetetrazol

**me·tre** \ˈmēd·ə(r), -ētə-\ *chiefly Brit var of* METER

**metreme** \ˈme·ˌtrēm, ˈmē-‐\ *n* -s [prob. fr. F *métrème,* fr. *mètre* meter + *-ème* -eme — more at METER] **:** the minimal unit of metrical structure **:** FOOT

**met·ri·al** \ˈmē·trēəl\ *adj* [NL *metra* + E *-ial*] **:** of or relating to the uterus — often used in combination ⟨endo*metrial*⟩

**¹met·ric** \ˈme·trik, -rēk\ *n* -s [in sense 1, fr. Gk *metrikē,* fr. fem. of *metrikos;* in other senses, fr. *metric* (var. of *metrical*)] **1 :** the part of prosody that deals with metrical structure ⟨the analytical study of ~ —T.S.Eliot⟩ — often used in pl. but sing. or pl. in constr. ⟨classical ~s⟩ **2 :** a standard of measurement ⟨its scale or ~ is determined by a definition —E.H.Hutten⟩ ⟨it is fairly certain that no ~ exists that can be applied directly to happiness —*Scientific Monthly*⟩ — often used in pl. but sing. or pl. in constr. ⟨an integrated system of photography, interpretation, and ~s —G.T.McNeil⟩ ⟨the ~s of his trade —C.S. Spooner⟩ **3** *math* **:** a means of specifying values of a variable or positions of a point ⟨Euclidean ~⟩ ⟨Riemannian ~⟩

**²met·ric** \"\ *or* **met·ri·cal** \-rə̇kəl, -rēk-\ *adj* [*metric* fr. F *métrique,* fr. *mètre* meter + *-ique* -ic; *metrical* fr. F *métrique* + E *-al* — more at METER] **:** based on the meter as a standard of measurement **:** of or measured in terms belonging to the metric system ⟨~ equivalents⟩ — **met·ri·cal·ly** \-rə̇k(ə)lē, -rēk-, -li\ *adv*

**-met·ric** \ˈme·trik, -rēk\ *or* **-met·ri·cal** \-rə̇kəl, -rēk-\ *adj comb form* [*-metric* fr. F *-métrique,* fr. *métrique* metrical, fr. L *metricus; -metrical* fr. F *-métrique* + E *-al* — more at METRICAL] **1 :** of, employing, or obtained by (such) a meter ⟨baro*metric*⟩ ⟨helio*metric*⟩ **2 :** of or relating to (such) an art, process, or science of measuring ⟨chrono*metric*⟩ ⟨geo*metric*⟩ ⟨psycho*metric*⟩

**met·ri·cal** \ˈme·trə̇kəl, -rēk-\ *or* **met·ric** \-rik, -rēk\ *adj* [*metrical* fr. L *metricus* (fr. Gk *metrikos,* fr. *metron* measure, meter + *-ikos* -ic) + E *-al; metric* fr. L *metricus* — more at MEASURE] **1 :** of, determined by, or in meter ⟨sent his mind ticking in a vague ~ rhythm —Joseph Hitrec⟩ ⟨anything ~ is rhythmical, but not all rhythms may be successfully reduced to meter —D.A.Stauffer⟩ ⟨even very irregular poems, which are generally included in anthologies as ~ rather than free verse —Evelyn H. Scholl⟩ ⟨not a ~ romanticist —Jonathan Daniels⟩ ⟨~ accent⟩ **2 :** used in, involving, or relating to measurement ⟨the ~ properties of space —James Jeans⟩ ⟨science is nothing if it is not ~ —T.H.Savory⟩ **3** [¹*metric*] *math* **:** relating to or capable of being defined by a metric — **met·ri·cal·ly** \-rə̇k(ə)lē, -rēk-, -li\ *adv*

**metrical signature** *n* **:** TIME SIGNATURE

**metric carat** *n* **:** CARAT 1b

**metric centner** *n* **:** a centner of 220.46 pounds or 100 kilograms — called also *double centner*

**metric geometry** *n* **:** geometry that postulates a method of determining the distance between any two of its points and thence determines the size of geometrical magnitudes (as lengths, areas, volumes, angles)

**metric horsepower** *n* **:** a horsepower unit equal to 75 kilogram-meters per second

**metric hundredweight** *n* **:** a unit of weight equal to 50 kilograms or 110.23 pounds

**me·tri·cian** \meˈtrishən, mə̇ˈ-\ *n* -s [F *métricien,* fr. *mètre* (poetic) meter (fr. MF *metre*) + *-icien* -ician — more at METER] **:** a composer in or student of meter **:** METRIST

**met·ri·cism** \ˈme·trəˌsizəm\ *n* -s **:** the character or property of being metric or having a tendency to metricity

**met·ri·cist** \-ˌsə̇st\ *n* -s **:** METRIST

**me·tric·i·ty** \meˈtrisəd·ē, mə̇ˈ-\ *n* -ES **:** the character or property of being metrical or having meter

**met·ri·cize** \ˈme·trəˌsīz\ *vt* -ED/-ING/-S **:** to make metrical

**metric system** *n* **:** a decimal system of weights and measures orig. based entirely on the meter with the unit of capacity equal to the cubic decimeter and the unit of mass equal to one cubic centimeter of water at its maximum density but now having these units based on the kilogram

**metric ton** *n* **:** a unit of mass and weight equal to 1000 kilograms or 2,204.6 pounds avoirdupois — abbr. *MT;* see METRIC SYSTEM table

**me·trid·i·um** \məˈtridēəm\ *n, cap* [NL, fr. Gk *mētridios* having a womb, fruitful, fr. *mētra* womb — more at METRA] **:** a genus of sea anemones

**-metries** *pl of* -METRY

**met·ri·fi·ca·tion** \ˌme·trəfəˈkāshən\ *n* -s [ML *metrificatus* (past part. of *metrificare*) + E *-ion*] **:** composition in metrical form **:** VERSIFICATION

**met·ri·fy** \ˈ==ˌfī\ *vt* -ED/-ING/-ES [MF *metrifier,* fr. ML *metrificare,* fr. L *metrum* meter + *-ificare* -ify — more at METER] **:** to compose in or put into meter **:** make a metrical version of

**metring** *var of* METERING

**met·rio·cra·nic** \ˌme·trēōˈkrānik\ *adj* [G *metriokran* metriocranic (fr. Gk *metrios* moderate — fr. *metron* measure — + *kranion* skull) + E *-ic* — more at MEASURE, CRANIUM] **:** having a skull of moderate height in proportion to its width with a breadth-height index of 92 to 98 — **met·rio·cra·ny** \ˈ===ˌ=nē\ *n* -ES

**met·rio·metopic** \ˈ===+\ *adj* [Gk *metrios* + E *metopic*] **:** having a forehead moderately wide in relation to the brain case — **met·rio·met·o·py** \ˌ===ˈmed·əpē\ *n* -ES

**metrist** \ˈme·trə̇st, ˈmē-‐\ *n* -s [ML *metrista,* fr. L *metrum* meter + *-ista* -ist — more at METER] **1 :** a maker of verses **2 :** one skillful in handling meter **3 :** a student of meter or metrics

**me·tri·tis** \məˈtrīd·ə̇s\ *n* -ES [NL, fr. *metr-* + *-itis*] **:** inflammation of the uterus

**-me·tri·um** \ˈmē·trēəm\ *n comb form, pl* **-me·tria** \-trēə\ [NL, fr. *metr-* + *-ium*] **:** part or layer of the uterus ⟨endo*metrium*⟩ ⟨myo*metrium*⟩

**¹met·ro** \ˈme·(ˌ)trō\ *n* -s [F *métro,* short for *métropolitain,* fr. (*chemin de fer*) *métropolitain* metropolitan railway] **:** SUBWAY

**²metro** \"\ *usu cap* — a communications code word for the letter *m*

**metro-** — see METR-

**met·ro·logical** \ˌme·trə+\ *adj* **:** of or relating to metrology ⟨~ services and laboratories —E.C.Crittenden⟩ — **met·ro·logically** \"+\ *adv*

**me·trol·o·gist** \məˈträləjə̇st\ *n* -s **:** one who specializes in metrology

**me·trol·o·gy** \-jē\ *n* -ES [F *métrologie,* fr. Gk *metrologia* theory of ratios, fr. *metron* measure + *-logia* -logy — more at MEASURE] **1 :** the science of weights and measures **:** the science of measurement **2 :** a system of weights and measures

**met·ro·mania** \ˌme·trō+\ *n* [NL, fr. Gk *metron* measure, meter + NL *mania*] **:** a mania for writing verses

**met·ron** \ˈme·ˌträn\ *n, pl* **met·ra** \-ˌtrə\ [Gk, measure, meter — more at METER] **:** the minimal unit of measure in classical Greek verse constituting in certain meters (as the iambic, trochaic, anapestic, and the lyric forms of dactylic) a syzygy of two feet, in others (as hexameters of epic verse) a dipody and where necessary for analysis in the case of spondaic series a single foot, and in compound meters (as the ionic and choriambic) a foot of four syllables

**met·ro·nome** \ˈme·trəˌnōm\ *n* -s [Gk *metron* measure, meter + *nomos* law — more at NIMBLE] **:** an instrument that emits an audible repetitive tap regulated to mark rhythm (as for music, marching, sports, or industrial repetition)

metronome

**met·ro·nom·ic** \ˌ==ˈnämik\ *also* **met·ro·nom·i·cal** \-mə̇kəl\ *adj* **1 :** of or relating to a metronome or the marking of time with it **2 :** mechanically regular (as in tempo) ⟨an exactitude of rhythm that gets dangerously close to the ~ —Neville Cardus⟩ ⟨correct attitudes, ~ meters, dull rhymes —*Publ's Mod. Lang. Assoc. of Amer.*⟩ ⟨the plane rose and fell with ~ monotony as we flew —Sumner Welles⟩ — **met·ro·nom·i·cal·ly** \-mə̇k(ə)lē\ *adv*

**metronomic mark** *or* **metronome mark** *n* **:** a mark at the beginning of a piece of music to show its tempo according to the metronome

**met·ro·nym·ic** \ˌmē·trəˈnimik, ˌme-‐\ *n* -s [MGk *mētrōnymikos,* adj., named after one's mother, fr. Gk *mētr-, mētēr* mother + *onyma, onoma* name + *-ikos* -ic — more at MOTHER, NAME] **:** MATRONYMIC

**me·tron·y·my** \məˈtrānəmē\ *n* -ES [back-formation fr. *metronymic*] **:** the custom of using matronymics

**met·ro·pole** \ˈme·trəˌpōl\ *n* -s [F *métropole,* fr. LL *metropolis*] **1 :** a chief town **:** METROPOLIS **2 :** a metropolitan see **:** METROPOLIS **3 :** a Salvation Army hostel **4 :** MOTHER COUNTRY — compare METROPOLIS 2

**me·trop·o·lis** \məˈträp(ə)lə̇s, meˈ-\ *n* -ES [LL, mother city, fr. Gk *mētropolis,* fr. *mētr-, mētēr* mother + *-o-* + *polis* city — more at MOTHER, POLICE] **1 :** a metropolitan see **2 :** the

## METRIC SYSTEM

LENGTH

| unit | abbreviation | number of meters | approximate U.S. equivalent |
|---|---|---|---|
| myriameter | mym | 10,000 | 6.2 miles |
| kilometer | km | 1,000 | 0.62 mile |
| hectometer | hm | 100 | 109.36 yards |
| decameter | dkm | 10 | 32.81 feet |
| meter | m | 1 | 39.37 inches |
| decimeter | dm | 0.1 | 3.94 inches |
| centimeter | cm | 0.01 | 0.39 inch |
| millimeter | mm | 0.001 | 0.04 inch |

AREA

| unit | abbreviation | number of square meters | approximate U.S. equivalent |
|---|---|---|---|
| square kilometer | sq km *or* km² | 1,000,000 | 0.3861 square mile |
| hectare | ha | 10,000 | 2.47 acres |
| are | a | 100 | 119.60 square yards |
| centare | ca | 1 | 10.76 square feet |
| square centimeter | sq cm *or* cm² | 0.0001 | 0.155 square inch |

VOLUME

| unit | abbreviation | number of cubic meters | approximate U.S. equivalent |
|---|---|---|---|
| decastere | dks | 10 | 13.10 cubic yards |
| stere | s | 1 | 1.31 cubic yards |
| decistere | ds | 0.10 | 3.53 cubic feet |
| cubic centimeter | cu cm *or* cm³ *also* cc | 0.000001 | 0.061 cubic inch |

CAPACITY

| unit | abbreviation | number of liters | approximate U.S. equivalent: *cubic* | *dry* | *liquid* |
|---|---|---|---|---|---|
| kiloliter | kl | 1,000 | 1.31 cubic yards | | |
| hectoliter | hl | 100 | 3.53 cubic feet | 2.84 bushels | |
| decaliter | dkl | 10 | 0.35 cubic foot | 1.14 pecks | 2.64 gallons |
| liter | l | 1 | 61.02 cubic inches | 0.908 quart | 1.057 quarts |
| deciliter | dl | 0.10 | 6.1 cubic inches | 0.18 pint | 0.21 pint |
| centiliter | cl | 0.01 | 0.6 cubic inch | | 0.338 fluidounce |
| milliliter | ml | 0.001 | 0.06 cubic inch | | 0.27 fluidram |

MASS AND WEIGHT

| unit | abbreviation | number of grams | approximate U.S. equivalent |
|---|---|---|---|
| metric ton | MT *or* t | 1,000,000 | 1.1 tons |
| quintal | q | 100,000 | 220.46 pounds |
| kilogram | kg | 1,000 | 2.2046 pounds |
| hectogram | hg | 100 | 3.527 ounces |
| decagram | dkg | 10 | 0.353 ounce |
| gram | g *or* gm | 1 | 0.035 ounce |
| decigram | dg | 0.10 | 1.543 grains |
| centigram | cg | 0.01 | 0.154 grain |
| milligram | mg | 0.001 | 0.015 grain |

mother city or state of a colony (as of ancient Greece) : MOTHER COUNTRY **3 a** : the chief town or city of a country or other land area : CAPITAL ⟨the ~ of the valley⟩ **b** : a city regarded as the center of a particular activity ⟨a lumber ~⟩ ⟨a cattle ~⟩ **c** : CITY; *esp* : an important city ⟨the world's great ~*es* —P.E. James⟩ ⟨the boom spirit which saw in every village a future ~ —G.R.Stewart⟩ **4** : a region where a particular kind of organism (as a variety or species) is most abundant

**1met·ro·pol·i·tan** \ˌme·trəˌpälətᵊn *also* -ətən *or* -əd·ən\ *n* -s [ME, fr. LL *metropolitanus*, fr. *metropolitanus*, adj.] **1** : the head of an ecclesiastical province: **a** : the head of an ecclesiastical province of the Eastern Orthodox Church who has his headquarters in a large city **b** : an archbishop of the Roman Catholic Church who presides over at least one suffragan see **c** : an archbishop of the Church of England **2** : one who lives in or has manners, customs, or ideas characteristic of a metropolis ⟨modern apartment-dwelling ~ —R.M.Weaver⟩

**2metropolitan** \"\ *adj* [LL *metropolitanus*, fr. *metropolita*, *metropolites* metropolite + L -*anus* -an — more at METROPOLITE] **1** : of or befitting a metropolitan or his see : being an ecclesiastical metropolitan ⟨~ authority⟩ ⟨~ bishops⟩ **2** : of, relating to, characteristic of, or constituting a city that is a metropolis ⟨~ markets⟩ ⟨~ newspapers⟩ **3** : evincing characteristics (as urbane manners or cosmopolitan ideas) regarded as typical of residents of a great city : not provincial ⟨our instinctive desire to be ~ rather than parochial, to be "in the know" rather than to be ignorant of the very latest idiom — G.W.Sherburn⟩ **4** : of, relating to, or constituting a mother country ⟨various ~ nations⟩ ⟨~ currency⟩ ⟨~ military forces⟩ ⟨~ France⟩ ⟨there was upon the Witwatersrand very largely the same crowd of ~ miners —C.W.de Kiewiet⟩ **5** : of, relating to, or constituting a region including a city and the densely populated surrounding areas that are socially and economically integrated with it ⟨~ area⟩ ⟨~ district⟩

**met·ro·pol·i·tan·ate** \-ˌāt\ *n* -s : the see or office of a metropolitan bishop

**metropolitan borough** *n* : any of the 28 administrative divisions that with the City of London form the County of London

**metropolitan cross** *n* : CROSS-STAFF 1

**met·ro·pol·i·tan·ism** \ˌ==ˈ===ˌizəm\ *n* -s : the condition of being metropolitan : metropolitan character

**met·ro·pol·i·tan·ize** \-ˌīz\ *vt* -ED/-ING/-S : to make metropolitan

**metropolitan round** *n*, *often cap M* : a round in archery consisting for men of 30 arrows fired successively at 100 yards, 80 yards, 60 yards, 50 yards, and 40 yards and for women of 30 arrows fired successively at 60 yards, 50 yards, 40 yards, and 30 yards

**met·ro·pol·i·tan·ship** \ˌ==ˈ===ˌship\ *n* : METROPOLITANATE

**me·trop·o·lite** \məˈträpəˌlīt, meˈ-\ *n* -s [LL *metropolita*, *metropolites*, fr. LGk *mētropolitēs*, fr. *mētropolis* + -*itēs* -ite — more at METROPOLIS] **1** : METROPOLITAN 1 **2** : a resident of a metropolis ⟨most ~*s* feel at home only in their own block —Frederic Morton⟩

**met·ro·political** \ˌme·trō+\ *adj* [LL *metropoliticus* (fr. LGk *mētropolitikos*, fr. *mētropolitēs* metropolite + -*ikos* -ic) + E -*al*] **1** : METROPOLITAN 1 ⟨~ courts⟩ **2** *obs* : METROPOLITAN 2 — **met·ro·politically** \"+\ *adv*

**me·trop·o·ly** \məˈträpəlē, meˈ-\ *n* -ES [F *métropolie*, fr. *métropole* + -*ie* -y] : METROPOLITANATE

**metror·rha·gia** \ˌmē·trəˈrāj(ē)ə, ˌme·-\ *n* -s [NL, fr. *metr-* + -*rrhagia*] : profuse bleeding from the uterus esp. between menstrual periods — compare MENORRHAGIA — **metror·rhag·ic** \ˌ==ˈrajik\ *adj*

**metro·si·de·ros** \ˌ==səˈdirəs\ *n*, *cap* [NL, fr. *metr-* + Gk *sidēros* iron] : a genus of trees, shrubs, and vines (family Myrtaceae) chiefly of the Pacific islands that have hard dense heavy wood and large flowers borne in 2-forked or 3-forked cymes — see LEHUA, LIGNUM VITAE 3

**me·trox·y·lon** \məˈträksəˌlän\ *n*, *cap* [NL, fr. *metr-* + -*xylon*] : a genus of Indo-Malayan pinnate-leaved palms that flower and fruit once and then die — see SAGO PALM 1a

**met·rum** \ˈme·trəm\ *n*, *pl* **met·ra** \-rə\ [L, fr. Gk *metron* meter, measure — more at MEASURE] : METRON

**-me·try** \ˌmə·trē, -ri\ *n comb form* -ES [ME -*metrie*, fr. MF, fr. L -*metria*, fr. Gk, fr. *metrein* to measure (fr. *metron* measure) + -*ia* -y — more at MEASURE] : art, process, or science of measuring (something specified) ⟨chrono*metry*⟩ ⟨hygro*metry*⟩ ⟨hyper*metry*⟩ ⟨photo*metry*⟩ ⟨psycho*metry*⟩

**met·ter·nich·i·an** \ˌmed·ə(r)ˈnikēən\ *adj*, *usu cap* [Prince Klemens W. N. L. von *Metternich* †1859 Austrian statesman and diplomatist + E -*ian*] : of or like Metternich or his reactionary political ideas or diplomatic policies

**1met·tle** \ˈmed·ᵊl, -etᵊl\ *n* -s [ME *metel* metal, mettle — more at METAL] **1** *archaic* : METAL **2** : quality of temperament or disposition : SPIRIT, SPIRITEDNESS, TEMPER ⟨a girl of ~ —Norman MacCaig⟩ ⟨but that poetry might be of finer ~ than prose he never apparently dreamed —S.T.Williams⟩ **3** : qualities (as ardor, courage, and stamina) and abilities in relation to a given situation ⟨those who try their ~ against the sea —Walter Hayward⟩ ⟨trucks had proved their ~ in army transport —*Pioneer & Pacemaker*⟩ ⟨spoke in Spanish later on, but at first tried my ~ by using only Yaqui —E.H.Spicer⟩ **syn** see COURAGE — **on one's mettle** *also* **upon one's mettle** : in a state of being challenged or aroused to make one's best efforts ⟨the family business failed and put him *on his mettle* as a writer —Van Wyck Brooks⟩ ⟨putting both major parties *on their mettle* —John Lodge⟩

**2mettle** \"\ *adj*, *archaic Scot* : SPIRITED, METTLESOME ⟨an honest and a ~ gentleman —R.L.Stevenson⟩

**met·tled** \ˈmed·ᵊld, -etᵊld\ *adj* **1** *obs* : METTLESOME **2** : having (such) a mettle — usu. used in combination ⟨muddy-*mettled*⟩ ⟨high-*mettled*⟩

**met·tle·some** \ˈmed·ᵊlsəm, -etᵊl-\ *adj* : full of mettle : SPIRITED, HIGH-SPIRITED ⟨a ~ dramatic performer —Lee Rogow⟩ ⟨one of the watch, a ~ fellow who fought like a wildcat —T.B. Costain⟩ ⟨a ~ horse⟩ ⟨a ~ blend of nervous fancy and impromptu characterization —James Kelly⟩ ⟨~ intellectual climate —John Cheever⟩

**mett sausage** \ˈmet-\ *n* [part trans. of G *mettwurst*] : METTWURST

**mett·wurst** \ˈmetˌ=\ *n* -s [G, fr. LG *mettworst*, fr. MLG, fr. *mett* meat, pork + *worst* sausage; akin to OHG *maz* food — more at MEAT, WURST] : a sausage of lean beef and salt pork seasoned, dried, and smoked

**met·u·la** \ˈmechələ\ *n*, *pl* **metu·lae** \-ˌlē\ [NL, fr. L, small cone or pyramid, dim. of *meta* cone, pyramid, boundary mark; perh. akin to ON *meithr* tree, MIr *methas* boundary district, Skt *methī* post, L *munire* to fortify — more at MUNITION] : one of the outermost branches of a conidiophore from which flask-shaped phialides radiate (as in molds of the genera *Aspergillus* and *Penicillium*)

**me·tur·ge·man** \məˈtərgəmən\ *n*, *pl* **meturgemans** [Heb & Aram *mĕthurgĕmān*, *mĕthargĕmān*] : a religious official of the early Hebrew synagogue who orally translated the Scriptures from Hebrew into the vernacular

**met·wand** \ˈmetˌwänd\ *var of* **METEWAND**

**Met·y·caine** \ˈmed·əˌkān\ *trademark* — used for hydrochloride of piperocaine

**metzograph** *var of* MEZZOGRAPH

**meu·bles** \mœbl(ᵊ), -b(lə)\ *n pl* [F, fr. MF, fr. pl. of *meuble* movable goods, fr. OF, fr. *meuble* movable, fr. L *mobilis* — more at MOBILE] : a class of property under French law that consists essentially of movables — compare IMMEUBLES

**me·um** \ˈmēəm\ *n*, *cap* [NL, fr. L, spicknel, fr. Gk *mēon*] : a genus of European aromatic perennial herbs (family Umbelliferae) with flowers in compound umbels — see SPICKNEL

**meu·nière** \ˌmə(r)nˈye(ə)r, mən-\ *adj* [F (*à la*) *meunière*, lit., in the manner of a miller's wife; F *meunière* miller's wife, fem. of *meunier* miller, fr. L *molinarius*, fr. *molina* mill + -*arius* -ary — more at MILL] : cooked in or served with browned butter

**1meuse** \ˈmyüs, -üz\ *n* -s [MF *muce*, *musse*, fr. *mucer*, *musser* to hide, conceal] **1** : a gap or hole (as in a hedge or wall) through which a wild animal is accustomed to pass **2** : something resembling a meuse in affording a means of escape : LOOPHOLE

**2meuse** \"\ *vi* -ED/-ING/-S : to go through a meuse

**meute** \ˈmyüt\ *n* -s [by alter.] : 4MEW 1

**MEV** *abbr*, *often not cap* million electron volts

**mev·a·lon·ic acid** \ˌmevəˌlänik-\ *n* [*me*thyl + *val*erolact*one* + -*ic*] : a branched dihydroxy acid ($HO_2C_5H_9COOH$) that is obtained by extraction of dried distillers' solubles with organic solvents or made synthetically and that is changed by enzymes in acid solution into squalene; 3,5-dihydroxy-3-methyl-valeric acid

**1mew** \ˈmyü\ *also* **mew gull** *n* -s [ME, fr. OE *mǣw*; akin to OS *mēw* gull, MD *meeuw*, ON *mār*; prob. of imit origin] : GULL; *esp* : the common European gull (*Larus canus*)

**2mew** \"\ *vb* -ED/-ING/-S [ME *mewen*, of imit. origin] *vi* **1** : MEOW 1 **2** : to make the natural noise of a gull ⟨gulls now swooped and ~*ed* round the ship —Ngaio Marsh⟩ ~ *vt* : to utter by mewing : MEOW ⟨~*ing* pitiful cries⟩

**3mew** \"\ *n* -s : MEOW ⟨gave a quick consolatory ~ of understanding —Hortense Calisher⟩

**4mew** \"\ *n* -s [ME *muwe*, *mewe*, fr. MF *mue*, fr. *muer* to molt — more at 6MEW] **1** : a cage for hawks esp. while molting **2 a** : a coop or cage for fattening animals; *esp* : a pen for fattening fowls **b** *dial chiefly Eng* : a breeding cage (as for canaries) **3 a** *obs* : CONFINEMENT : a place of confinement **b** : a secret place : a place of retirement : HIDEAWAY ⟨I've been three weeks shut within my ~ —Robert Browning⟩ **4 mews** *pl but usu sing in constr*, *chiefly Brit* **a** (1) : STABLES; *esp* : a range of stables usu. with carriage houses and living quarters built around a yard, court, or street (2) : living quarters or housing developed from such stables **b** : the court or street upon which such stables or the dwellings developed from them open : ALLEY, BACK STREET **c** : a row or group of garages

**5mew** \"\ *vt* -ED/-ING/-S [ME *muwen*, *mewen*, fr. *muwe mewe*, n.] **1 a** *obs* : to shut in or coop up for fattening — used esp. of fowl **b** : to shut or lock in : CONFINE — often used with *up* ⟨better . . . than sitting ~*ed* in a stuffy bedroom with a prayer book —Virginia Woolf⟩ ⟨a group of men ~*ed* up for years in a draughty barrack —Noel Coward⟩ **2** : to put or keep (a hawk) in a mew esp. in molting time

**6mew** \"\ *vb* -ED/-ING/-S [ME *muwen*, fr. MF *muer* to molt, change, fr. L *mutare* to change — more at MISS] *vt* **1** : to cast off (feathers) : MOLT **2** *obs* : to bring about a change in (as color or coat) : SHED **3 a** : to get rid of (the horns) : CAST — used of a stag **b** : to shed the horns from (the head) ~ *vi* **1** : to cast the feathers : MOLT **2** : to shed or cast horns

**7mew** \"\ *dial Brit var of* MOW

**me·ward** \ˈmēwə(r)d\ *adv* [*me* + -*ward*] : toward me ⟨for her hands have no kindness ~ —Ezra Pound⟩

**me·wa·ri** \maˈwärē\ *n* -s *usu cap* : the Rajasthani dialect of Mewar

**mew·er** \ˈmyüə(r)\ *n* -s : one that mews

**1mewl** \ˈmyül\ *vi* -ED/-ING/-S [imit.] **1** : to cry weakly like a child : make whimpering sounds : WHINE **2** : MEOW

**2mewl** \"\ *n* -s : the act or sound of mewling

**mewl·er** \-lə(r)\ *n* -s : one that mewls

**1mex** \ˈmeks\ *adj*, *usu cap* [by shortening] : MEXICAN ⟨get my feet all mixed up in these *Mex* dances —Edwin Corle⟩ ⟨offering him for sale for ten *Mex* dollars —Richard Hallet⟩ ⟨cost four dollars *Mex*⟩

**2mex** \"\ *n*, *pl* **mex** *or* **mexes** [by shortening] **1** *cap* : MEXICAN ⟨some *Mex* he'd never seen before was behind the bar —Oakley Hall⟩ — often used disparagingly **2** *often cap* : MEXICAN DOLLAR ⟨paper money was so plentiful that . . . a ~ was the smallest that would buy anything —Upton Sinclair⟩

**me·xi·ca** \ˈme,kä, ˈmāh-\ *n* -s *usu cap* [Sp *méxica*, prob. fr. Nahuatl *Mexictli*, an Aztec war god] : NAHUATL

**1mex·i·can** \ˈmeksəkən, -sēk-\ *adj*, *usu cap* [Sp *mexicano*, *mejicano*, fr. *México*, *Méjico* Mexico, country in southern No. America + Sp -*ano* -an] **1 a** : of, relating to, or characteristic of Mexico **b** : of, relating to, or characteristic of the people of Mexico **2** : of, relating to, or characteristic of the Mexican language **3** : CENTRAL AMERICAN 2

**2mexican** \"\ *n* -s **1** *cap* **a** : a native or inhabitant of Mexico **b** : a person of Mexican descent **c** *Southwest* : a person of mixed Spanish and Indian descent **2 a** *usu cap* : NAHUATL **b** *cap* : Spanish as spoken in Mexico **3** *usu cap* : MEXICAN DOLLAR **4** *often cap* : FRENCH YELLOW

**mexican asphalt** *n*, *usu cap M* : the residuum obtained from the distillation of Mexican petroleum

**mexican bamboo** *n*, *usu cap M* : JAPANESE KNOTWEED

**mexican bean beetle** *n*, *usu cap M* : a spotted ladybug (*Epilachna varivestis*) that feeds on the leaves of various kinds of beans and is now an important pest in the U. S.

**mexican blue oak** *n*, *usu cap M* : an evergreen oak (*Quercus oblongifolia*) of the southwestern U.S. and adjacent Mexico that grows chiefly in dry sunny regions, varies from a thicket-forming shrub to a tall tree, and produces an annual crop of edible acorns which are locally important as wildlife food

**mexican breadfruit** *n*, *usu cap M* : a ceriman (*Monstera deliciosa*)

**mexican broomroot** *n*, *usu cap M* : BROOMROOT

**mexican buckeye** *n*, *usu cap M* : BUCKEYE 1c

**mexican cedar** *n*, *usu cap M* : SPANISH CEDAR

**mexican chicken bug** *n*, *usu cap M* : ADOBE BUG

**mexican clover** *n*, *usu cap M* : a tropical American herb (*Richardia scabra*) sometimes cultivated as a forage plant

**mexican cypress** *n*, *usu cap M* : an evergreen tree (*Cupressus lusitanicas*) cultivated for its spreading habit and drooping branchlets

**mexican devil-weed** \-ˈ==ˌ=\ *n*, *usu cap M* : a large aster (*Aster spinosus*) having almost leafless often spiny stems and linear or subulate leaves and occurring as a weed in the southern and western U.S.

**mexican dollar** *n*, *usu cap M* : a Mexican silver peso

**mexican eagle** *n*, *usu cap M* : AUDUBON'S CARACARA

**mexican elm** *n*, *usu cap M* : a tropical American elm (*Ulmus mexicana*) that has heavy hard strong wood and is native to Mexico and Central America

**mexican fever** *n*, *usu cap M* : TEXAS FEVER

**mexican fiber** *n*, *usu cap M* : ISTLE b

**mexican fire plant** *n*, *usu cap M* **1** : a showy poinsettia (*Poinsettia heterophylla*) found from the southern U.S. to Peru **2** *also* **mexican fireweed** : SUMMER CYPRESS

**mexican fruit fly** *n*, *usu cap M* : a small trypetid fly (*Anastrepha ludens*) having a maggot that feeds in and damages various fruits (as citruses and mangoes)

**mexican hairless** *n* **1** *usu cap M&H* : an old breed of dogs of unknown origin that are found in Mexico, are of about the size of a fox terrier, and are hairless except for a tuft on the skull and a fuzz on the lower half of the long tail **2** *usu cap M* : a dog of the Mexican Hairless breed

**mexican hog** *n*, *usu cap M* : PECCARY

**mex·i·can·ism** \ˈmeksəkəˌnizəm, -sēk-\ *n* -s *usu cap* [Sp *mexicanismo*, *mejicanismo*, fr. *mexicano*, *mejicano* Mexican + -*ismo* -ism — more at MEXICAN] : a word, phrase, or mode of expression distinctive of Spanish as spoken in Mexico ⟨language seasoned with *Mexicanisms*⟩

**mex·i·can·ist** \-nəst\ *n* -s *usu cap* : an authority on the history or civilization of Mexico

**mex·i·can·ization** \ˌ==kənəˈzāshən, -ˌnīˈz-\ *n* -s *usu cap* **1** : the action of mexicanizing **2** : the state (in industry or farming) of having or being supplied with a large number of Mexican personnel or laborers ⟨the *Mexicanization* of farm work in the southwest⟩

**mex·i·can·ize** \ˈ==kəˌnīz\ *vt* -ED/-ING/-S *often cap* [*1mexican* + -*ize*] : to make Mexican in quality, traits, customs, or modes of conduct

**mexican jumping bean** *n*, *usu cap M* : JUMPING BEAN

**me·xi·ca·no** \ˌmehēˈkä(ˌ)nō, ˌmāh-\ *n* -s [Sp *mexicano*, *mejicano* — more at MEXICAN] **1** *cap* : MEXICAN 1 **2** *usu cap* : NAHUATL

**mexican onyx** *n*, *usu cap M* : ALABASTER 1

**mexican orange** *n*, *usu cap M* : a round-headed evergreen Mexican shrub (*Choisya ternata*) of the family Rutaceae that has opposite trifoliolate leaves with entire obovate leaflets stippled with pellucid dots and fragrant white pentamerous flowers in axillary and terminal cymes and that is widely cultivated in mild and moderate climates as a hedge or specimen plant

**mexican persimmon** *n*, *usu cap M* : a persimmon tree (*Diospyros texana*) of Texas and Mexico having small cuneate leaves and black fruit

**mexican pinon** *also* **mexican pinon pine** *n*, *usu cap M* : a bush or low tree (*Pinus cembroides*) of the southern U.S. and Mexico having usu. three needles in each fascicle and globular cones

**mexican poppy** *n*, *usu cap M* : PRICKLY POPPY

**mexican red** *n*, *often cap M* : RAW SIENNA 2

**mexican rose** *n*, *usu cap M* : a portulaca (*Portulaca grandiflora*)

**mexican rubber** *n*, *usu cap M* : GUAYULE

**mexican scammony** *n*, *usu cap M* : IPOMOEA 3

**mexican sisal** *n*, *usu cap M* : HENEQUEN 1

**mexican skipjack** *n*, *usu cap M* : FRIGATE MACKEREL

**mexican snapper** *n*, *usu cap M* : RED SNAPPER a

**mexican spanish** *n*, *cap M&S* : the Spanish used in Mexico

**mexican standoff** *n*, *usu cap M* : DRAW 3b, DEADLOCK

**mexican star** *or* **mexican star-of-bethlehem** *n*, *usu cap M&B* : FROST FLOWER 1a

**mexican stud** *n*, *usu cap M* : a variety of five-card stud poker in which all cards are dealt face down but each player must turn up one card before a round of betting begins

**mexican sunflower** *n*, *usu cap M* : TITHONIA 2

**mexican tea** *n*, *usu cap M* : a rank-scented tropical American pigweed (*Chenopodium ambrosioides*)

**mexican tiger** *n*, *usu cap M* : JAGUAR

**mexican tulip poppy** *n*, *usu cap M* : GOLDEN CUP 2

**mexican weed** *n*, *usu cap M* : BIRDEYE

**mexican whisk** *n*, *usu cap M* : BROOMROOT

**mexican white pine** *n*, *usu cap M* : AYACAHUITE

**mex·i·co** \ˈmeksəˌkō, -sē,-\ *adj*, *usu cap* [fr. *Mexico*, country in southern No. America] **1** : of or from Mexico : of the kind or style prevalent in Mexico **2** *or* **mexico city** *usu cap M&C* [fr. *Mexico City*, Mexico] : of or from Mexico City, the capital of Mexico : of the kind or style prevalent in Mexico City

**mey·er·hoff·er·ite** \ˈmī(ə)rˌhäfəˌrīt\ *n* -s [Wilhelm *Meyerhoffer* †1906 Ger. chemist + E -*ite*] : a mineral $Ca_2B_6O_{11}.7H_2O$ consisting of a hydrous calcium borate

**1mezcal** *var of* MESCAL

**2mez·cal** \ˈmeˈskäl, məˈs-\ *n* -s [AmerSp (El Salvador) *mescal*, *mezcal*, *mexcal*, fr. Sp, mescal] : MEXICAN ELM

**mezcaline** *var of* MESCALINE

**me·zere·on** \məˈzirēən, -zer-\ *n* -s [ME *mizerion*, fr. ML *mezereon*, fr. Ar *māzariyūn*, fr. Per] **1** : a small European shrub (*Daphne mezereum*) with fragrant lilac purple flowers that appear before the leaves, an acrid bark used in medicine, and a scarlet fruit sometimes used as an adulterant of black pepper **2** : MEZEREUM

**mezereon family** *n* : THYMELAEACEAE

**me·zere·um** \-ēəm\ *n* -s [NL, alter. of ML *mezereon*] **1** : MEZEREON 1 **2** : the dried bark of mezereon or other European shrubs (genus *Daphne*) used externally as a vesicatory and irritant

**mezquit** *or* **mezquite** *var of* MESQUITE

**me·zu·zah** *or* **me·zu·za** \məˈzu̇zə\ *n*, *pl* **me·zu·zoth** *or* **me·zu·zot** \-ˌzōt(h)\ *or* **mezuzahs** *or* **mezuzas** [Heb *mĕzūzāh*, lit., doorpost] : a piece of parchment inscribed on one side with the scriptural passages Deut 6:4–9 and 11:13–21 written in 22 lines and on the other with the name Shaddai, rolled up in a scroll, and placed in a small wooden, metal, or glass case or tube that is affixed to the doorpost of some Jewish homes as a symbol of Jewishness and a reminder of faith in God

**mez·za majolica** \ˌmetsə-, -edzə-,-ezə-\ *n* [It *mezza maiòlica*, lit., half majolica] : early Italian earthenware resembling majolica but whitened with a clay slip under a lead glaze and partly decorated in sgraffito

**mez·za·nine** \ˈmezᵊnˌēn\ *also* **mezzanine floor** *or* **mezzanine story** *n* -s [F, fr. It *mezzanino*, fr. *mezzano* middle, intermediate (fr. L *medianus*) + -*ino* (dim. suffix) — more at MEDIAN] **1 a** : a low-ceilinged story between two main stories of a building; *esp* : an intermediate or fractional story that projects in the form of a balcony over the ground story **b** (1) : the lowest balcony in a theater (2) : the first few rows of such a balcony **2** : a flooring laid over a floor to bring it up to a desired height or level **3** *Brit* : the floor beneath the stage of a theater from which trapdoors and other pieces of stage machinery are worked

**mezza or·ches·tra** \-ˈȯrˌkestrə, -ˈȯrkəstrə\ *adv* [It, lit., half orchestra] : with but half the orchestra

**1mez·za vo·ce** \ˌmetsəˈvō(ˌ)chā, -edzə-\ *adv* (*or adj*) [It, lit., half voice] : with medium or half volume of tone — used as a direction in music

**2mezza voce** \"\ *n* : a medium or half volume of tone ⟨the quality of her voice in *mezza voce* was warm and expressive — Winthrop Sargeant⟩

**mez·zo** \ˈmet(ˌ)sō, -ed(ˌ)zō, -e(ˌ)zō\ *n* -s [by shortening] **1** : MEZZO-SOPRANO **2** : MEZZOTINT

**mezzo forte** \ˈ=(ˌ)=ˈ=(ˌ)=\ *adj* (*or adv*) [It] : moderately loud — used as a direction in music

**mezzo-forte** \"\ *n* [*mezzo forte*] : a moderately loud tone ⟨one of those quiet atmospheric moods that never rise above a *mezzo-forte* —Julian Herbage⟩

**mez·zo·graph** *also* **metzo·graph** \ˈmetsəˌgraf, -räf\ *n* [It *mezzo* half (fr. L *medius* middle) + E -*graph* (as in *photograph*) — more at MID] : a halftone made with a grain screen and having a grained surface instead of crossline screen dots

**mezzo legato** *adv* (*or adj*) [It, lit., half legato] : in a manner intermediate between legato and staccato — used as a direction in music

**mezzo piano** *adj* (*or adv*) [It] : moderately soft — used as a direction in music

**mezzo-re·lie·vo** *or* **mezzo-ri·lie·vo** \ˈ=(ˌ)=rēˈlē(ˌ)vō, -rēlˈyā-, -yē\ *n*, *pl* **mezzo-relievos** \-vōz\ *or* **mezzo-rilie·vi** \-rēlˈyā(ˌ)vē, -ye-\ [It *mezzorilievo*, fr. *mezzo* half + *rilievo* relief — more at RELIEF] : sculptural relief that is intermediate in degree of projection between bas-relief and high relief with approximately half of the natural circumference of the modeled form projecting from the surrounding surface

**mezzo-soprano** \ˈ=(ˌ)=+\ *n* [It *mezzosoprano*, fr. *mezzo* half + *soprano* — more at SOPRANO] : a woman's voice of medium compass (as a to f″) between that of the soprano and contralto; *also* : a singer having a voice of such compass

**mezzo-soprano clef** *n* : the C clef placed on the second line of the staff

**1mez·zo·tint** \ˈ==ˌ=\ *also* **mez·zo·tin·to** \ˌ==ˈtin·(ˌ)tō\ *n* -s [modif. of It *mezzatinta*, fr. *mezza* (fem. of *mezzo* half) + *tinta* tint — more at TINT] **1** *archaic* : DEMITINT **2 a** : a manner of engraving on copper or steel by working on a surface previously roughened with a rocker or cradle and removing the roughness in places by burnishing to produce the requisite light and shade **b** : an engraving produced in this manner

**2mezzotint** \"\ *also* **mezzotinto** \"\ *vt* -ED/-ING/-S : to engrave in or represent as if in mezzotint

**mez·zo·tint·er** \ˈ=ˌ=ˌtintə(r)\ *n* : one skilled in mezzotint

**mf** *abbr* **1** manufacture **2** microfarad **3** millifarad

**MF** *abbr* **1** machine finish **2** *often not cap* medium frequency **3** *often not cap* mezzo forte **4** mill finish **5** motor freight

**MFBM** *abbr* [L *mille* thousand] thousand feet board measure

**mfd** *abbr* **1** manufactured **2** microfarad

**mfg** *abbr* manufacturing

**MFH** *abbr* master of foxhounds

**MFN** *abbr* most favored nation

**MFP** *abbr* mean free path

**mfr** *abbr* manufacture; manufacturer

**mg** *abbr* **1** margin **2** meaning **3** milligram **4** morning

**MG** *abbr* **1** machine-glazed **2** machine gun **3** [F *main gauche*] left hand **4** major general **5** make good **6** military government **7** mill glazed **8** mixed grain **9** motor generator

**Mg** *symbol* magnesium

**MGB** *abbr* motor gunboat

**MGC** *abbr* machine-gun company; machine-gun corps

**MGD** *abbr*, *often not cap* million gallons per day

**mgm** *abbr* milligram

**MGO** *abbr* military government officer

**mgr** *abbr* **1** manager **2** monseigneur **3** monsignor

**mgrm** *abbr* milligram

**mgt** *abbr* management

**mh** *abbr* millihenry

**MH** *abbr* **1** magnetic heading **2** maleic hydrazide **3** most honorable

**MHCP** *abbr*, *often not cap* mean horizontal candlepower

**MHD** *abbr* minimum hemolytic dose

**mho** \ˈmō\ *n* -s [backward spelling of *ohm*] : the practical unit of conductance equal to the reciprocal of the ohm

**mho·me·ter** \'ˌ=ˌmēd·ə(r), -ētə-\ *n* [*mho* + *-meter*] **:** an instrument for measuring conductance
**mhorr** *var of* MOHR
**MHSCP** *abbr* mean hemispherical candlepower
**MHT** *abbr* mean high tide
**MHW** *abbr* mean high water
**MHWN** *abbr* mean high water neaps
**MHWS** *abbr* mean high water springs
**MHz** *abbr* megahertz
**mi** \'mē\ *n* -s [ML, fr. L *mira* wonders, a word sung to this note in a medieval hymn to St. John the Baptist] **1 :** the third tone of the diatonic scale in solmization **2 :** the tone *E* in the fixed-do system
**mi-** *or* **mio-** *also* **meio-** *comb form* [prob. fr. NL *meio-*, fr. Gk, fr. *meiōn* — more at MINOR] **1 a :** less ⟨*Mio*cene⟩ **:** smaller ⟨*Mio*hippus⟩ **b :** slightly ⟨*mi*concave⟩ **2 :** fewer ⟨*meio*phylly⟩
**mi** *abbr* **1** mile **2** mill **3** minor **4** minute
**MI** *abbr* **1** malleable iron **2** medical inspection **3** memorial inscription **4** metabolic index **5** military intelligence
**MIA** *abbr* missing in action
**mi·ac·i·dae** \mīˈasəˌdē\ *n pl, cap* [NL, fr. *Miacis*, type genus + *-idae*] **:** a family of primitive generalized carnivorous mammals widely distributed from the Palaeocene through the lower Oligocene, sometimes classed with the creodonts, but probably being early ancestral types of the Fissipeda
**mi·a·cis** \ˈmīəsə̇s, mīˈas-\ *n, cap* [NL] **:** the type genus of Miacidae comprising short-legged long-tailed arboreal carnivores comparable in form to the civets and prob. ancestral to *Cynodictis*
**¹mi·ami** \mīˈamē, -amə\ *n, pl* **miami** *or* **miamis** *usu cap* **1 a :** an Indian people of northern Indiana **b :** a member of such people **2 :** a dialect of the Illinois language
**²miami** \"\ *adj, usu cap* [fr. *Miami*, city in southeast Florida] **:** of or from the city of Miami, Fla. ⟨*Miami* hotels⟩ **:** of the kind or style prevalent in Miami
**mia-mia** \ˈmīəˌmīə\ *n* -s [native name in Australia] **:** a rude usu. temporary hut of the Australian aborigines
**mi·am·i·an** \mīˈamēən\ *n* -s *cap* [*Miami*, Florida + E *-an*] **:** a native or resident of Miami, Fla.
**mi·a·na bug** \ˈmēəˌnä-\ *n, often cap M* [fr. *Mianeh*, town in Azerbaijan, Iran] **:** CHICKEN TICK; *also* **:** a closely related Asiatic tick (*Argas mianensis*) that has been implicated as a vector of relapsing fever
**mi·ang** \mēˈäŋ\ *n* -s [Thai] **:** a wild tea (*Thea sinensis*) of Thailand
**mi·ao** *also* **meo** *or* **maeo** \mēˈau̇\ *n, pl* **miao** *or* **miaos** *usu cap* [Chin (Pek) *Miao²*] **1 a :** an aboriginal people of China inhabiting southwestern China and the northern parts of Vietnam, Laos, and Thailand **b :** a member of such people **2 :** a language of the Miao people
**miao-tse** *also* **miao-tze** *or* **miao-tzu** \mēˈau̇dzə\ *n, pl* **miao-tse** *or* **miao-tses** *usu cap* [Chin (Pek) *Miao²-tzu³*, fr. *Miao²* + *tzu³* son, child] **:** MIAO
**miaow** *also* **miaou** *var of* MEOW
**mi·ao-yao** \mēˌau̇ˈyau̇\ *n, usu cap M&Y* **:** a language group containing the Miao and Yao languages of uncertain wider relationship
**mi·ar·gy·rite** \(ˌ)mīˈärjəˌrīt\ *n* [G *miargyrit*, fr. *mi-* + *argyr-* + *-it* -ite] **:** a mineral $AgSbS_2$ consisting of a silver antimony sulfide and occurring in iron-black to steel-gray crystals or masses whose powder is cherry red
**mi·a·ro·lit·ic** \ˌmēəroˈlid·ik\ *adj* [ISV *miaro-* (fr. It dial. *miarolo* granite with small cavities) + *-litic*] **1** *of igneous rock* **:** characterized by irregular cavities into which well-formed crystals project ⟨~ structure⟩ ⟨~ granites⟩ **2** *of a cavity* **:** having an irregular form into which such crystals project
**mi·as** \ˈmīəs\ *n* -ES [Iban *mayas*] **:** ORANGUTAN
**mi·as·ma** \mīˈazmə, mē'-\ *also* **mi·asm** \ˈmīˌazəm\ *n, pl* **mias·mas** \mīˈazməz, mē'-\ *or* **mias·ma·ta** \=ˈ=məd·ə\ *also* **miasms** [NL *miasma*, fr. Gk, defilement; akin to Gk *miainein* to defile — more at MOLE] **1 :** a vaporous exhalation (as of a marshy region or of putrescent matter) formerly believed to contain a substance causing disease (as malaria) ⟨the ~*s* of Matto Grosso —Jean Stafford⟩; *broadly* **:** a heavy vaporous emanation or atmosphere ⟨a ~ of tobacco smoke⟩ ⟨seems to be more than a scent that emanates from the hops: it is almost a visible ~, sweet yet agreeably acrid —Jan Struther⟩ **2 :** a pervasive influence or atmosphere that tends to deplete or corrupt ⟨abandoned its task in a ~ of words —J.K.Galbraith⟩ ⟨from its pages flow that same ~ of dread suspense, that same air of dissolution, decay, and death —Margaret B. Hexter⟩
**mi·as·mal** \(ˈ)mīˈazməl, (ˈ)mē¦-\ *adj* [*miasma* + *-al*] **:** MIASMIC ⟨blinding flashes of newspaper cameras and the ~ air of the closed, unventilated room —C.M.Smith⟩
**mi·as·mat·ic** \ˌmīəzˈmad·ik, ˌmēə-\ *adj* [F *miasmatique*, fr. NL *miasmat-*, *miasma* + F *-ique* -ic] **:** MIASMIC ⟨the ~ northern and northeastern coast —*Encyc. Americana*⟩
**mi·as·mic** \(ˈ)mī¦azmik, (ˈ)mē¦-\ *adj* [*miasma* + *-ic*] **1 :** of, relating to, or like a miasma **:** caused by miasma **:** producing a miasma **:** characterized by miasma ⟨rubber plantations of the ~ jungle —Robert Littell⟩ **2 :** foully contagious **:** NOXIOUS, MEPHITIC ⟨a clamorous square mile of plants and pens that spread a ~ stench —*Newsweek*⟩
**mi·as·tor** \mīˈastə(r)\ *n, cap* [NL, fr. Gk *miastōr* one that defiles; akin to Gk *miainein* to defile] **:** a genus of flies (family Cecidomyiidae) that are remarkable for their parthenogenetic and paedogenetic reproduction by which the larva on hatching from the egg develops internally a brood of similar larvae that on escaping may repeat the process for several generations before pupation and development of mature individuals
**mi·aul** \mēˈau̇l, -ˈōl\ *vi* -ED/-ING/-S [F *miauler*, of imit. origin] **1 :** MEW, MEOW **2 :** CATERWAUL
**mib** \ˈmib\ *n* -s [prob. by shortening & alter. fr. *marble*] **1** *dial* **:** MIG **2 mibs** *pl but sing in constr, dial* **:** the game of marbles
**mi·ca** \ˈmīkə\ *n* -s *often attrib* [NL (prob. influenced by L *micare* to flash, sparkle), fr. L *mica* grain, crumb; akin to Gk *mikros* small, short — more at DIMICATION, MICR-] **:** any of a group of minerals that crystallize in forms apparently orthorhombic or hexagonal but really monoclinic and characterized by highly perfect cleavage, readily separating into very thin somewhat elastic leaves, that are all silicates although differing widely in composition and varying in color from colorless, pale brown, or yellow to green or black, that are prominent constituents of many igneous and metamorphic rocks, and that form a division including the brittle micas and chlorites as well as the micas proper — see BIOTITE, LEPIDOLITE, LEPIDOMELANE, MUSCOVITE, PARAGONITE, PHLOGOPITE, ZINNWALDITE; compare DAMOURITE
**mi·ca·ceous** \(ˈ)mī¦kāshəs\ *adj* [prob. fr. (assumed) NL *micaceus*, fr. NL *mica* + L *-aceus* -aceous] **1 :** consisting of or containing mica ⟨~ sandstone⟩ **2 :** resembling mica (as in foliation or luster)
**micaceous iron ore** *n* **:** hematite having a micaceous structure
**micalike** \ˈ==ˌ=\ *adj* **:** resembling mica
**Mi·car·ta** \mīˈkärd·ə\ *trademark* — used for any of various laminated products made by bonding layers of paper or cloth with a resin under heat and pressure and used in the form of sheets, rods, tubes, or other molded shapes
**mi·caw·ber** \məˈkȯbə(r)\ *n* -s *usu cap* [fr. Wilkins *Micawber*, character in the novel *David Copperfield* (1849–50) by Charles Dickens †1870 Eng. author] **:** an improvident person who lives in expectation of an upturn in his fortunes
**mi·caw·ber·ish** \-b(ə)rish\ *adj, usu cap* **:** of, relating to, or characteristic of a Micawber (as in being habitually expectant of an upturn in one's fortunes) ⟨home production continued to lag, but the Government went on its *Micawberish* way, waiting for something to turn up —*Economist*⟩
**mi·caw·ber·ism** \-bəˌrizəm\ *n* -s *usu cap* **:** the improvident state or habitually optimistic point of view of a Micawber
**mice** [ME *mys*, fr. OE *mȳs*] *pl of* MOUSE
**mi·cel·lar** \(ˈ)mī¦selə(r), mə¦-\ *adj* [ISV *micelle* + *-ar*] **:** of, relating to, or characterized by a micelle or micelles — **mi·cel·lar·ly** *adv*
**micellar theory** *or* **micellar hypothesis** *n* **:** a theory in cytology: protoplasm and some of its products (as the plant cell wall) exist primarily as or are largely made up of micelles
**mi·celle** \mīˈsel, mə'-\ *also* **mi·cel·la** \-elə\ *or* **mi·cell** \-el\ *n, pl* **micelles** \-lz\ *also* **mi·cel·lae** \-ˌlē\ *or* **micells** [NL *micella*, fr. L *mica* crumb + *-ella*] **:** a unit of structure built up from polymeric molecules or ions: as **a :** an ordered region in a natural or synthetic fiber (as of cellulose, silk, or viscose rayon) — compare CRYSTALLITE 2, FIBRIL **b :** a highly associated particle of a colloidal solution ⟨colloidal ~*s* of soaps and detergents —J.W.McBain⟩ **c :** an organic colloidal particle ranging in size from one micron to one millimicron and found in coal and some shales
**mice pink** *n* **:** DEPTFORD PINK
**mich** \ˈmich, ˈmēch\ *var of* MEECH
**mich·ael·mas** \ˈmikəlməs\ *n* -ES *usu cap* [ME *mychelmesse*, fr. OE *Michaeles mæsse*, fr. *Michaeles* (gen. of *Michael*, archangel identified as patron of the Jewish nation in Dan 10:21 and as leader in a war against the devil in Rev 12:7–9) + OE *mæsse* mass, feast day — more at MASS] **:** the feast of the archangel Michael that is a church festival celebrated on September 29 and is one of the four quarter days in England
**michaelmas blackbird** *n, usu cap M* **:** RING OUZEL
**michaelmas daisy** *n, usu cap M* **1 :** any of several wild asters; *esp* **:** one blooming about Michaelmas **2 :** any of various hybrid asters developed from the heath aster, the New England aster, and other asters of No. America
**michaelmas term** *n, usu cap M* **1 :** the term from November 2 to 25 during which the superior courts of England were formerly open — compare EASTER TERM, HILARY TERM, TRINITY TERM **2 :** the first or fall term of the academic year lasting from the beginning of October until Christmas — used at British universities
**michaelmastide** \ˈ===ˌ=\ *n, usu cap* **:** the season of Michaelmas
**mi·chael reaction** \ˈmīkəl-\ *or* **michael condensation** *n, usu cap M* [after Arthur *Michael* †1942 Am. chemist] **:** the addition of a sodium enolate (as the sodium derivative of ethyl malonate) to the double bond of an alpha,beta-unsaturated ester (as ethyl cinnamate) or ketone
**mi·chel·an·ge·lesque** \ˌmīkə¦lanjə¦lesk\ *adj, usu cap* [*Michelangelo* Buonarroti †1564 Ital. sculptor, painter, architect, and poet + E *-esque*] **:** characteristic of or resembling Michelangelo or his work which is preeminent for grandeur of conception, dramatic action, and technical mastery of execution ⟨*Michelangelesque* statuary⟩
**mi·che·lia** \mīˈkēlēə, -lyə\ *n* [NL, fr. Piero Antonio *Micheli* †1737 Ital. botanist + NL *-ia*] **1** *cap* **:** a genus of Asiatic shrubs and trees (family Magnoliaceae) having introrse anthers and the pistil-bearing receptacle stalked within the flower — see BANANA SHRUB, CHAMPAC **2** -s **:** any plant of the genus *Michelia*
**mi·chel·son-mor·ley experiment** \ˌmīkəlsən¦mȯrlē-\ *n, usu cap both Ms* [after Albert A. *Michelson* †1931 Am. physicist and Edward W. *Morley* †1923 Am. chemist and physicist] **:** an experiment that shows that the two parts of a divided ray of light travel at the same speed over paths perpendicular to each other (as over east-west and north-south paths) and that leads to the deductions that the motion of the earth through space has no effect upon the velocity of light and the absolute motion of the earth is not measurable
**mich·er** \ˈmichə(r), ˈmēch-\ *var of* MEECHER
**¹mich·i·gan** \ˈmishə̇gən, -shēg-\ *adj, usu cap* [fr. *Michigan*, state in the north central U.S., fr. Lake *Michigan*, of Algonquian origin; akin to Fox *mešikami* large lake] **:** of or from the state of Michigan ⟨the *Michigan* automotive industry⟩ **:** of the kind or style prevalent in Michigan **:** MICHIGANIAN
**²michigan** \"\ *n* -s *usu cap* [fr. *Michigan*, state in the north central U.S.] **:** a card game in which players put chips on a layout of ace, king, queen, and jack of different suits taken from another pack, in which all cards are dealt out with an extra hand that may be taken by the dealer or sold by him to the highest bidder, in which starting with the lowest card of a suit in the hand of the player who selects and starts the suit each suit is played in sequence until it has been stopped, in which a player who plays a card matching a card of the layout takes all the chips on that card, and in which the player who first plays the last of his cards wins the deal — called also *boodle, Chicago, Newmarket, stops*
**michigan bankroll** *n, usu cap M, slang* **:** a roll of paper money consisting of a bill of large denomination on the outside of small-denomination or counterfeit bills
**mich·i·gan·der** \ˌmishə¦gandə(r), -gaan-\ *n* -s *cap* [fr. *Michigander* (derogatory nickname of Lewis Cass †1866 Am. lawyer and political figure), blend of *Michigan* and E *gander*] **:** a native or resident of Michigan
**michigan grayling** *n, usu cap M* **:** a fish that is a variety (*Thymallus signifer tricolor*) of the arctic grayling and that occurs only in northern Michigan
**¹mich·i·ga·ni·an** \ˌmishə¦gānēən, -gan-\ *n* -s *cap* [*Michigan* + E *-an*, n. suffix] **:** MICHIGANDER
**²michiganian** \"\ *adj, usu cap* [*Michigan* + E *-an*, adj. suffix] **1 :** of, relating to, or characteristic of the state of Michigan **2 :** of, relating to, or characteristic of the people of Michigan
**mich·i·gan·ite** \ˈmishə̇gəˌnīt, -shēg-\ *n* -s *cap* [*Michigan* + E *-ite*] **:** MICHIGANDER
**michigan rummy** *n, usu cap M* **:** a form of five hundred rum in which melding is a completed game
**mich·ing** \ˈmichiŋ, ˈmēch-\ *var of* MEECHING
**mich·ler's ketone** \ˈmiklə(r)z-\ *n, usu cap M* [after Wilhelm T. *Michler* †1889 Ger. chemist] **:** a crystalline amino ketone $[(CH_3)_2NC_6H_4]_2CO$ made by treating dimethylaniline with phosgene and used in the manufacture of triphenylmethane dyes
**micht** \ˈmikt\ *Scot var of* MIGHT
**mich·tam** \ˈmikˌtam\ *usu cap* [Heb *mikhtām*] — used in the Bible in the headings of Psalm 16 and Psalms 56 to 60 (AV) possibly to suggest atonement
**mi·chu·rin·ism** \məˈchu̇rəˌnizəm\ *n* -s *usu cap* [Ivan V. *Michurin* †1935 Russ. horticulturist + E *-ism*] **:** LYSENKOISM — **mi·chu·rin·ist** \-ˌnə̇st\ *or* **mi·chu·rin·ite** \-ˌnīt\ *adj or n, usu cap*
**¹mick** \ˈmik\ *also* **mike** \ˈmīk\ *n* -s *sometimes cap* [prob. fr. *Mick, Mike*, nicknames fr. the name *Michael*] **:** IRISHMAN — often taken to be offensive
**²mick** \ˈmik\ *n* -s [origin unknown] *Austral* **:** the head of a penny
**mick·ery** \ˈmik(ə)rē\ *n* -ES [origin unknown] *Austral* **:** ²SOAK 2
**mick·ey** *also* **micky** \ˈmikē, -ki\ *n, pl* **mickeys** *also* **mickies** [prob. fr. *Mickey*, nickname fr. the name *Michael*] **1** *sometimes cap* **:** IRISHMAN — often taken to be offensive **2** *pl usu mickies* **:** POTATO 2a(2) ⟨roast *mickies* in the gutter fires —Joseph Mitchell⟩ **3** *usu cap* **:** MICKEY FINN ⟨as soon slip you a *Mickey* as look at you —Merle Miller⟩
**mickey finn** \-ˈfin\ *n, usu cap M&F* [prob. fr. the name *Mickey Finn*] **1 :** a drink of liquor doctored with a drastic purgative or a stupefying drug **2 :** an anglers' streamer fly with silver body and red and yellow wings
**¹mick·le** \ˈmikəl\ *adj* -ER/-EST [ME *mikel, muchel*, fr. OE *micel, mycel* — more at MUCH] *chiefly Scot* **:** GREAT, MUCH
**²mickle** \"\ *adv* [ME *mikel, muchel*, fr. OE *micel, mycel* (fr. accus. sing. neut. of *micel, mycel*, adj.) and *micle, mycle* (fr. instrumental sing. neut. of *micel, mycel*, adj.) and *miclum, myclum* (fr. dat. pl. of *micel, mycel*, adj.)] *chiefly Scot* **:** to a great degree
**³mickle** \"\ *n* -s [ME *mikel*, fr. *mikel, muchel*, adj.] *chiefly Scot* **:** a great amount or sum
**mick·le·mote** \-ˌmōt\ *or* **mick·le·gemote** \ˌ==+\ *n* -s *usu cap* [OE *mycel gemōt*, fr. *mycel* large, great + *gemōt* gemot — more at GEMOT] **:** the great council under an Anglo-Saxon king — compare GEMOT, WITENAGEMOT
**mickle-mouthed** \ˈ==¦=\ *adj, Scot* **:** having a big mouth
**mic·mac** \ˈmikˌmak\ *n, pl* **micmac** *or* **micmacs** *usu cap* [Micmac *Migmac*, lit., allies] **1 a :** an Indian people of the Maritime Provinces and Newfoundland, Canada **b :** a member of such people **2 :** an Algonquian language of the Micmac people
**¹mi·co** \ˈmē(ˌ)kō\ *n* -s [Muskogee *miko*] **:** a Muskogean chief
**²mico** \"\ *n* -s [Sp, of Cariban origin; akin to Galibi *méku* marmoset] **:** MARMOSET; *esp* **:** a black-tailed marmoset (*Callithrix melanurus*) of tropical So. America
**mi·concave** \(ˈ)mī+\ *adj* [*mi-* + *concave*] **:** slightly curved — used esp. of a type of crystal commonly used in open-faced watches
**mi·co·nia** \mīˈkōnēə\ *n, cap* [NL, fr. Francisco *Micó* (*Micón*) 16th cent. Span. physician and botanist + NL *-ia*] **:** a large genus of tropical American shrubs or trees (family Melastomaceae) with small flowers in showy terminal inflorescences
**mi con·tra fa** \ˌmēˌkän·trəˈfä, -kōn-, -kȯn-\ *n* [ML, lit., mi against fa] **:** TRITONE — used in early contrapuntal music as an expression of caution to the musician against the use of dangerous intervals
**mi·co·qui·an** \mēˈkōkēən\ *also* **mi·coque·an** \", -ōkən\ *adj, usu cap* [La *Micoque*, site near Les Eyzies, commune in southwest central France, where remains of the culture were found + E *-an*] **:** of or relating to a late Acheulean culture of England and southern France characterized by biface hand axes having very narrow points and thin cross section and by a developed flake industry
**micr-** *or* **micro-** *comb form* [ME *micro-*, fr. L, fr. Gk *mikr-, mikro-*, fr. *mikros, smikros* small, short; akin to OE *smēalīc* careful, exquisite, OHG *smāhi* small, low, ON *smār* small, and perh. to OE *smītan* to smear — more at SMITE] **1 a :** small **:** minute **:** petty ⟨*micro*cyst⟩ — often used to contrast with *macr-* **b :** enlarging **:** magnifying or amplifying — in names of instruments ⟨*micro*phone⟩ ⟨*micro*scope⟩ **c :** used for small or minute size, quantities, intensities, or variations ⟨*micro*barograph⟩ ⟨*micro*calorimeter⟩ ⟨*micro*graph⟩ **d :** minutely ⟨*micro*level⟩ **2 :** one millionth part of (a specified unit) ⟨*micro*second⟩ — esp. in terms used in the metric system ⟨*micro*gram⟩ and in electricity ⟨*micro*farad⟩ ⟨*micr*ohm⟩ **3 :** microscopic: as **a :** dealing with, employing, or used in microscopy ⟨*micro*paleontology⟩ ⟨*micro*tome⟩ **b :** revealed by or having its structure discernible only by microscopical examination ⟨*micro*fossil⟩ **c :** prepared for microscopical examination ⟨*micro*section⟩ **4 :** abnormally small ⟨*micro*dactylous⟩ — chiefly in nouns denoting a condition of a specified part of the body ⟨*micro*gnathia⟩ **5 :** of, involving, or for very small or minute quantities of material **:** on a small or minute scale of chemical operation **:** microchemical **:** microanalytical ⟨*micro*balance⟩ ⟨*micro*sublimation⟩ — compare SEMIMICRO-, ULTRAMICRO- **6 :** of very fine grain — in names of rocks ⟨*micro*granite⟩ **7 :** of or relating to a small area ⟨*micro*climate⟩ ⟨*micro*economics⟩ ⟨*micro*habitat⟩ **8 :** microphotographed or microfilmed ⟨*micro*copy⟩ **:** employed in or relating to microphotographing or microfilming ⟨*micro*reader⟩
**micra** *pl of* MICRON
**mi·cra·ner** \ˈmīkrəˌne(ə)r, mīˈkrānər\ *n* -s [NL, fr. *micr-* + Gk *anēr* man, male animal — more at ANDR-] **:** a male ant of unusually small stature
**mi·cras·ter** \mīˈkrastə(r)\ *n, cap* [NL, fr. *micr-* + *-aster*] **:** a genus of extinct heart urchins (order Exocycloida) with ambulacral furrows arranged in a small star on the upper surface
**mi·cren·ceph·a·lon** \ˌmīˌkr+\ *n, pl* **micrencephala** [NL, fr. *micr-* + *encephalon*] **:** CEREBELLUM
**mi·cren·ceph·a·lous** \ˌmīˌkrenˈsefələs\ *adj* [*micr-* + *-encephalous*] **:** having an abnormally small brain
**mi·cren·ceph·a·ly** \-lē\ *n* -ES [NL *micrencephalia*, fr. *micr-* + *-encephalia* -encephaly] **:** the condition of having an abnormally small brain
**mi·crer·gate** \mīˈkrərˌgāt\ *also* **mi·cro·er·gate** \ˌmīkrōˈərˌ-\ *n* -s [*micr-* + Gk *ergatēs* worker — more at ERGAT-] **:** a member of a caste of small workers among various ants
**mi·cri·nite** \ˈmīkrəˌnīt\ *n* -s [*micr-* + *-inite* (as in *fusinite*)] **:** an opaque structureless material that is the dominant constituent of durain
**¹mi·cro** \ˈmīˌkrō\ *n* -s [NL *micro-* (as in *Microlepidoptera*)] **:** a very small moth
**²micro** \"\ *adj* [*micr-*] **:** small or minute in size **:** MICROSCOPIC ⟨the chemistry of ~ quantities of transuranium and radioactive materials —*Chem. & Engineering News*⟩ ⟨placed in a ~ fractionating apparatus —*Jour. of Biological Chem.*⟩ ⟨whether the pests be plants or animals, macro or ~ in size —R.N. Shreve⟩ — see MACR-
**micro-** — see MICR-
**mi·cro·aerophile** \¦mīkrō+\ *n* -s [*microaero-* (fr. *micr-* + *aer-*) + *-phile*] **:** an organism requiring very little free oxygen
**mi·cro·aero·phil·ic** \¦==(=)¦filik\ *also* **mi·cro·aerophile** \¦==+\ *or* **mi·cro·aer·oph·i·lous** \"+=(=)¦räfələs\ *adj* [*microaerophilic* fr. *microaerophile*, n. + *-ic*; *microaerophile*, *microaerophilous* fr. *microaero-* + *-phile* or *-philous*] **:** requiring very little free oxygen — **mi·cro·aero·phil·i·cal·ly** \"+¦=(=)¦filək(ə)lē\ *adv*
**mi·cro·ammeter** \¦==+\ *n* [*micr-* + *ammeter*] **:** an instrument for measuring electric current in microamperes — compare AMMETER
**mi·cro·ampere** \"+\ *n* [ISV *micr-* + *ampere*] **:** one millionth of an ampere
**mi·cro·analysis** \¦=(ˌ)=+\ *n* [ISV *micr-* + *analysis*] **:** chemical analysis on a small or minute scale that usu. requires special, very sensitive, or small-scale apparatus **:** qualitative or quantitative analysis dealing with quantities usu. of the order of milligrams (as in the vicinity of 1 mg.) or smaller — opposed to *macroanalysis*; compare CHEMICAL MICROSCOPY, SEMIMICROANALYSIS, ULTRAMICROANALYSIS — **mi·cro·analyst** \¦==+\ *n* — **mi·cro·analytic** \"+\ *or* **mi·cro·analytical** \"+\ *adj*
**mi·cro·anatomy** \¦=(ˌ)=+\ *n* [*micr-* + *anatomy*] **:** HISTOLOGY
**mi·cro·atoll** \¦==+\ *n* [*micr-* + *atoll*] **:** a coralline growth resembling a miniature atoll
**mi·cro·bacterium** \¦=(ˌ)=+\ *n* [NL, fr. *micr-* + *bacterium*] **1** *cap* **:** a genus of minute nonmotile gram-positive thermoduric lactobacteria that are common in dairy products and the mammalian intestinal tract **2** *pl* **microbacteria :** any of numerous minute heat-resistant bacteria; *specif* **:** one of the genus *Microbacterium*
**mi·cro·bal** \(ˈ)mī¦krōbəl\ *adj* [*microbe* + *-al*] **:** MICROBIAL
**mi·cro·balance** \¦mīkrō+\ *n* [ISV *micr-* + *balance*] **:** a balance designed to measure very small weights with great precision
**mi·cro·bar** \ˈmīkrə+ˌ-\ *n* [*micr-* + *bar*] **:** a unit of pressure equal to one dyne per square centimeter — used esp. in acoustics and meteorology
**mi·cro·barograph** \¦mīkrō+\ *n* [ISV *micr-* + *barograph*] **:** a barograph for recording small and rapid changes
**mi·crobe** \ˈmīˌkrōb\ *n* -s [ISV *micr-* + *-be* (fr. Gk *bios* mode of life); orig. formed in F — more at QUICK] **:** a very minute organism **:** MICROORGANISM, GERM — used esp. of pathogenic bacteria **syn** see MICROORGANISM
**mi·crobe·less** \-ləs\ *adj* **:** being without microbes **:** free from microbes
**mi·cro·bi·al** \(ˈ)mī¦krōbēəl\ *adj* [*microbe* + *-ial*] **:** being of or between microbes ⟨~ physiology⟩ ⟨~ antagonism⟩ **:** done by or by the use of microbes ⟨~ fermentation⟩ ⟨~ warfare⟩ **:** developed from microbes ⟨~ purification of milk⟩ **:** involving microbes ⟨the ~ concept of infection⟩ **:** that are microbes ⟨~ enemies of man⟩
**mi·cro·bi·an** \-bēən\ *or* **mi·cro·bic** \-ˈkrōbik, -ˈkräb-\ *adj* [*microbian* ISV *microbe* + *-an*; *microbic* fr. *microbe* + *-ic*] **:** MICROBIAL
**mi·cro·bi·ci·dal** \mī¦krōbə¦sīdᵊl\ *adj* [*microbe* + *-i-* + *-cidal*] **:** destructive to microbes
**mi·cro·bi·cide** \=ˈkrōbəˌsīd\ *n* -s [ISV *microbe* + *-i-* + *-cide*] **:** an agent that destroys microbes
**mi·cro·biological** \¦mīkrō+\ *also* **mi·cro·biologic** \"+\ *adj* [*microbiological* fr. *microbiology* + *-ical*; *microbiologic* ISV *microbiology* + *-ic*] **:** of or relating to microbiology — **mi·cro·biologically** \"+\ *adv*
**mi·cro·biologist** \¦=(ˌ)=+\ *n* [ISV *microbiology* + *-ist*] **:** a specialist in microbiology
**mi·cro·biology** \"+\ *n* [ISV *micr-* + *biology*] **:** a branch of biology dealing esp. with microscopic forms of life (as bacteria, protozoa, viruses, and fungi)
**mi·cro·bi·on** \mīˈkrōbēˌän\ *n, pl* **micro·bia** \-bēə\ [NL, fr. F *microbe* — more at MICROBE] **:** MICROBE
**mi·cro·bi·o·sis** \ˌmīkrōˌbīˈōsə̇s\ *n* -ES [NL, fr. *microbion* + *-osis*] **:** infection by microbes
**mi·cro·biota** \¦mīkrō+\ *n* [NL, fr. *micr-* + *biota*] **:** the microscopic flora and fauna of a region
**mi·cro·biotic** \"+\ *adj* [NL *microbiota* + E *-ic*] **1 :** of, relating to, or constituting a microbiota **2** [*micr-* + *-biotic*] *of a seed* **:** surviving in the dormant state for a relatively brief period usu. not exceeding three years — compare MACROBIOTIC, MESOBIOTIC
**mi·cro·bism** \ˈmīˌkrōˌbizəm\ *n* -s [ISV *microbe* + *-ism*] **:** the state of being infested with microbes

**mi·cro·bi·um** \mī'krōbēəm\ *n* -s [NL, fr. F *microbe*] : MICROBE

**mi·cro·blast** \'mīkrō,blast\ *n* -s [ISV *micr-* + *-blast*] : an erythroblast destined to produce an atypically small erythrocyte

**mi·cro·burette** or **mi·cro·buret** \¦mī(,)krō+\ *n* [*micr-* + *burette*] : a burette (as one with a capacity of 10 milliliters or less) for use esp. in microanalysis

**mi·cro·burner** \¦==+\ *n* [*micr-* + *burner*] : a burner giving a very small flame for use esp. in microanalysis

**mi·cro·bus** \'mīkrō,bəs\ *n* [AmerSp *microbús*, fr. *micr-* + *-bús* (fr. Sp *autobús* motor bus, fr. F *autobus*, fr. *auto-* — fr. *automobile* — + *-bus* — fr. *omnibus*) — more at OMNIBUS] : a small motor bus

**mi·cro·calorimeter** \¦mīkrō+\ *n* [*micr-* + *calorimeter*] : an instrument for measuring very small quantities of heat — **mi·cro·calorimetric** \"+\ *adj* — **mi·cro·calorimetry** \"+\ *n*

**mi·cro·camera** \"+\ *n* [*micr-* + *camera*] : a camera used for photomicrography

**Mi·cro·card** \'mīkrō,kärd\ *trademark* — used for a sensitized card approximately 3 in. x 5 in. on which printed matter is reproduced photographically in greatly reduced form

**mi·cro·cebus** \"+\ *n, cap* [NL, fr. *micr-* + Gk *kēbos* long-tailed monkey — more at CEBUS] : a genus of Madagascar lemurs consisting of the dwarf lemurs

**mi·cro·centrosome** \"+\ *n* [ISV *micr-* + *centrosome*] : CENTRIOLE 1

**mi·cro·centrum** \"+\ *n* [NL, fr. *micr-* + L *centrum* center — more at CENTER] : a centrosome or a group of centrioles functioning as a centrosome — compare CENTRAL APPARATUS

[1]**mi·cro·cephalic** \¦=(,)=+\ *also* **mi·cro·ceph·a·lous** \¦==¦sefələs\ *adj* [*microcephalic* prob. fr. NL *microcephalus* microcephalous + E *-ic; microcephalous* fr. NL *microcephalus*, fr. Gk *mikrokephalos* having a small head, fr. *mikr-* micr- + *-kephalos* -cephalous] : having a small head; *specif* : having an abnormally small head — **mi·cro·ceph·a·lism** \,==¦sefə,lizəm\ *n* -s

[2]**mi·cro·cephalic** \¦=(,)=+\ *n* -s : an individual with an abnormally small head

**mi·cro·ceph·a·lus** \,=='sefələs\ *n, pl* **microcepha·li** \-,lī\ [NL, fr. Gk *mikrokephalos* having a small head] : MICROCEPHALY; *also* : a microcephalic individual

**mi·cro·ceph·a·ly** \-,lē, -li\ *n* -ES [NL *microcephalia*, fr. *microcephalus* microcephalous + *-ia*] : a condition of abnormal smallness of head usu. associated with mental defects

**mi·cro·cer·a·tous** \¦==¦serədəs\ *adj* [*micr-* + *cerat-* + *-ous*] : having short antennae ⟨a ~ insect⟩

**mi·cro·cer·cous** \¦==¦sərkəs\ *adj* [*micr-* + *cerc-* + *-ous*] *of a cercaria* : having a short broad tail

[1]**mi·cro·chae·ta** \,=='kēd·ə\ *n, cap* [NL, fr. *micr-* + *-chaeta*] : a genus of earthworms of which one southern African form (*M. rappi*) reaches a length of five feet

[2]**microchaeta** \"\ *n, pl* **microchae·tae** \-ēd·(,)ē\ [NL, fr. *micr-* + *chaeta*] : a small bristle on the body of some insects (as many two-winged flies) — distinguished from *macrochaeta*

**mi·cro·chemical** \¦==+\ *adj* [ISV *micr-* + *chemical*] : of, relating to, or using the methods of microchemistry

**mi·cro·chemistry** \"+\ *n* [ISV *micr-* + *chemistry*] : chemistry dealing with the manipulation of very small quantities for purposes of preparation, characterization, or analysis — contrasted with *macrochemistry*

**mi·cro·chiroptera** \¦=(,)=+\ *n pl, cap* [NL, fr. *micr-* + *Chiroptera*] : a suborder of Chiroptera including all bats except the fruit bats — **mi·cro·chiropteran** \"+\ *adj or n* — **mi·cro·chiropterous** \"+\ *adj*

**mi·cro·chronometer** \"+\ *n* [ISV *micr-* + *chronometer*] : an instrument for measuring very small intervals of time : CHRONOSCOPE

**mi·cro·cinematographic** \¦==+\ *adj* [ISV *micr-* + *cinematographic*] : made by means of or relating to cinephotomicrography

**mi·cro·cinematography** \"+\ *also* **mi·cro·kinematography** \"+\ *n* [ISV *micr-* + *cinematography*] : CINEPHOTOMICROGRAPHY

**mi·cro·citrus** \"+\ *n, cap* [NL, fr. *micr-* + *Citrus*] : a small genus of Australian shrubs or trees (family Rutaceae) having fingerlike fruit

**mi·cro·climate** \"+\ *n* [ISV *micr-* + *climate*] : the local climate of a given site or habitat varying in size from a tiny crevice to a large land area but being usu. characterized by considerable uniformity of climate over the site involved and relatively local as compared with its enveloping macroclimate from which it differs because of local climatic factors (as elevation and exposure)

**mi·cro·climatic** \"+\ *adj* [*microclimate* + *-ic*] : of or relating to a microclimate

**mi·cro·climatologic** \"+\ or **mi·cro·climatological** \"+\ *adj* [*microclimatology* + *-ic* or *-ical*] : of or relating to microclimatology

**mi·cro·climatology** \"+\ *n* [ISV *microclimate* + *-o-* + *-logy*; orig. formed as G *mikroklimatologie*] : the study of microclimates : climatology of restricted areas

**mi·cro·cline** \'mīkrə,klīn\ *n* -s [G *mikroklin*, fr. *mikr-* micr- + *-klin* (fr. Gk *klinein* to lean) — more at LEAN] : a mineral of the feldspar group that is like orthoclase in composition but is triclinic though approaching orthoclase in crystal habit and crystal angles and that is white to pale yellow, red, or green in color

**microcline green** *n* : a very pale green that is yellower, lighter, and slightly less strong than tourmaline, bluer and duller than emerald tint, and bluer and slightly stronger than celadon tint

**mi·cro·coccaceae** \¦mī,krō+\ *n pl, cap* [NL, fr. *Micrococcus*, type genus + *-aceae*] : a family of heterotrophic spherical or elliptical eubacteria that usu. lack endospores, divide in two or three planes forming pairs, tetrads, or masses of cells, prefer an aerobic environment, and produce yellow, orange, or red pigment and that include pathogenic toxin-producing forms (as *Staphylococcus aureus* syn. *Micrococcus pyogenes* var. *aureus*) as well as numerous harmless commensals and saprophytes

**mi·cro·coc·cus** \,=='käkəs\ *n* [NL, fr. *micr-* + *-coccus*] **1** *cap* : a large genus (the type of the family Micrococcaceae) of spherical bacteria occurring in plates or irregular groups rather than in packets or chains and now usu. including numerous forms formerly placed in the genus *Staphylococcus* **2** *pl* **micrococci** : a small spherical bacterium; *esp* : a member of the genus *Micrococcus*

**mi·cro·coleoptera** \¦==+\ *n pl* [NL, fr. *micr-* + *Coleoptera*] : the smaller beetles

**mi·cro·colony** \"+\ *n* [*micr-* + *colony*] : a minute colony; *specif* : a minute colony made up of L-forms

**mi·cro·colorimeter** \"+\ *n* [*micr-* + *colorimeter*] : a colorimeter designed for use with small quantities of material — **mi·cro·colorimetric** \"+\ *adj* — **mi·cro·colorimetry** \"+\ *n*

**mi·cro·community** \¦=(,)=+\ *n* [*micr-* + *community*] : the community occupying a microhabitat

**mi·cro·conidial** \"+\ *adj* [*microconidium* + *-al*] : of or relating to a microconidium

**mi·cro·conidium** \"+\ *n* [NL, fr. *micr-* + *conidium*] : a small conidium as contrasted with a larger conidium both frequently being produced by the same species and differing often in shape (as in members of the genus *Fusarium*) — compare MACROCONIDIUM

**mi·cro·conjugant** \¦==+\ *n* [*micr-* + *conjugant*] : the smaller member of a pair of conjugating protozoans or anisogamous gametes

**mi·cro·con·o·don** \¦=='känə,dän\ *n, cap* [NL, fr. *micr-* + [2]*con-* + *-odon*] : a genus of small American Triassic reptiles (order Ictidosauria) long believed to be one of the most ancient mammals

**mi·cro·constituent** \¦=(,)=+\ *n* [*micr-* + *constituent*] : a microscopic constituent ⟨~s in high-temperature alloys⟩

**mi·cro·copier** \¦==+\ *n* [[2]*microcopy* + *-er*] : an apparatus for making microcopies

[1]**mi·cro·copy** \"+\ *n* [ISV *micr-* + *copy*, n.] : a photographic copy in which printed or other graphic matter is reduced in size (as on microfilm)

[2]**microcopy** \"\ [ISV, fr. [1]*microcopy*] *vt* : to reproduce by means of a microcopy ~ *vi* : to make microcopies

**mi·cro·cosm** \'mīkrə,käzəm\ *n* -s [ME *microcosme, mycrocossmos, microcosmus*, fr. ML *microcosmus*, alter. (influenced by L *micro-* micr-) of Gk *mikros kosmos*, fr. *mikros* small + *kosmos* order, universe — more at MICR-] **1** : a little world : a miniature universe ⟨the ~ of the atom grows constantly richer in content and interest —*Scientific American Reader*⟩ **2** : man or human nature believed to be an epitome of the world or the universe ⟨man is a ~, not in the natural sense, but in the historical sense, a compendium of universal history —*Encore*⟩ — contrasted with *macrocosm* **3** : a community, institution, or other unity believed to be an epitome of a larger unity (as a nation or the world) ⟨a set of characters, from all levels of the town's ~ —Anthony Boucher⟩ ⟨the boardinghouse was a ~ of a larger world —Van Wyck Brooks⟩ ⟨poetry is a discovery of ~s, of representative worlds —C.S.Kilby⟩ ⟨when the battle is a ~ of the entire conflict —T.C.Chubb⟩ ⟨a sunken ship is a ~ of the civilization that launched it —A.C.Clarke⟩ — **in microcosm** : in miniature ⟨the camp became a city *in microcosm*⟩

**mi·cro·cos·mic** \¦mīkrō¦käzmik, -mēk\ *adj* [NL *microcosmicus*, fr. ML *microcosmus* microcosm + L *-icus* -ic] : of, relating to, or characteristic of a microcosm ⟨the ~ world of business —*Amer. Fabrics*⟩ — **mi·cro·cos·mi·cal·ly** \-mək(ə)lē, -mēk-, -li\ *adv*

**microcosmic salt** *n* [trans. of NL *sal microcosmicus*; fr. the fact that it was originally obtained from human urine] : a white crystalline salt $NaNH_4HPO_4.4H_2O$ that is obtained by mixing solutions of sodium phosphate and ammonium phosphate or chloride, that is changed to a sodium phosphate glass on heating, and that is used as a flux like borax in beads for testing for metallic oxides and salts; sodium ammonium hydrogen phosphate

**mi·cro·cosmos** \¦==+\ *n* [ME *mycrocossmos*] **1** : MICROCOSM ⟨a little world of life, a ~ of great intimacy —William Beebe⟩ ⟨the ~ of the atomic nuclei —*Science News Letter*⟩ **2** : the world below the threshold of visibility by the naked eye

**mi·cro·cos·mus** \,=='käzməs\ *n, cap* [NL, fr. ML, microcosm] : a widely distributed genus of large simple ascidians including a Mediterranean form (*M. sulcatus*) that is sometimes used for food in southern Europe

**mi·cro·cra·nous** \¦=='krānəs\ *adj* [*micr-* + *cran-* (fr. *cranium*) + *-ous*] : having a skull of small volume or capacity

**mi·cro·crustacean** \¦==+\ *n* [*micr-* + *crustacean*] : a minute crustacean

**mi·cro·crystal** \"+\ *n* [ISV *micr-* + *crystal*] : a crystal visible only under the microscope

**mi·cro·crystalline** \"+\ *adj* [ISV *micr-* + *crystalline*] : of or relating to crystallinity that is visible only under the microscope ⟨was able to show that the halides are always ~ —C.E.K. Mees⟩ ⟨chalcedony . . . is a natural, ~ fibrous silica —F.J. Pettijohn⟩ — **mi·cro·crystallinity** \"+\ *n*

**microcrystalline wax** *n* : any of various plastic materials that are obtained from petroleum (as by refining of tank bottoms from crude oil or by removal with a solvent of oil from crude petrolatum), that differ in general from paraffin waxes in having higher melting points and viscosities and much finer and less distinct crystals, and that are used chiefly in laminated paper and similar products, in coatings and liners, in adhesives and sealing compositions, and in polishes — compare PETROLEUM WAX

**mi·cro·curie** \¦==+\ *n* [*micr-* + *curie*] : one millionth of a curie

**mi·cro·cyclic** \"+\ *adj* [*micr-* + *cyclic*] : SHORT-CYCLED

**mi·cro·cy·pri·ni** \,=(,)==sə'prī,nī, -rē,nī\ *n pl, cap* [NL, fr. *micr-* + L *cyprini*, pl. of *cyprinus* carp — more at CYPRINUS] : an order or other division of small teleost fishes resembling but somewhat more advanced than the Haplomi and including the killifishes and topminnows and various related families of chiefly freshwater and brackish-water fishes

**mi·cro·cyst** \'mīkrə+,-\ *n* [ISV *micr-* + *cyst*] **1 a** : a small cyst or spore (as a chlamydospore or a resting cell formed from a slime-mold swarm spore) — compare MACROCYST **b** : a minute resistant body in some higher bacteria that is thought to be a haploid spore **2** : a very small pathological cyst; *esp* : one arising from another cyst

**mi·cro·cys·tis** \,=='sistəs\ *n, cap* [NL, fr. *micr-* + *-cystis*] : a genus of unicellular blue-green algae (family Chroococcaceae) forming irregularly shaped colonies within a common gelatinous envelope and including at least one species (*M. aeruginosa*) that is poisonous and may become abundant and troublesome in lakes esp. where much organic matter is present

**mi·cro·cyte** \'mīkrə,sīt\ *n* -s [ISV *micr-* + *-cyte*] : a red blood cell of exceptionally small size present esp. in some anemias

**mi·cro·cy·the·mia** \,mī(,)krōsī'thēmēə\ *also* **mi·cro·cy·te·mia** \-'tē-\ *n* -s [NL, fr. ISV *microcyte* + NL *-emia*] : the presence of abnormally small red blood cells in the blood — **mi·cro·cy·the·mic** \¦==¦thēmik\ *adj*

**mi·cro·cyt·ic** \¦==¦sid·ik\ *adj* [ISV *microcyte* + *-ic*] : of, relating to, or characterized by the presence of microcytes

**microcytic anemia** *n* : anemia characterized by the presence of microcytes in the blood

**mi·cro·cy·to·sis** \,==sī'tōsəs\ *n, pl* **microcyto·ses** \-,sēz\ [NL, fr. ISV *microcyte* + NL *-osis*] : decrease in the size of red blood cells

**mi·cro·densitometer** \¦==+\ *n* [*micr-* + *densitometer*] : a densitometer for measuring the density of very small areas of a photographic plate or film — **mi·cro·densitometry** \"+\ *n*

**mi·cro·determination** \¦=(,)=+\ *n* [*micr-* + *determination*] : determination by microanalysis or by the microscope

**mi·cro·dissection** \"+\ *n* [*micr-* + *dissection*] : dissection under the microscope; *specif* : dissection of cells or tissues by means of fine needles operated through a precise system of levers

**mi·cro·distillation** \¦==+\ *n* [*micr-* + *distillation*] : the distillation of minute quantities of material

**mi·cro·dont** \'mīkrə,dänt\ *adj* [ISV *micr-* + *-odont*] : having small teeth — **mi·cro·dont·ism** \-n,tizəm\ *n* -s — **mi·cro·don·tous** \¦==¦däntəs\ *adj* — **mi·cro·don·ty** \'==,däntē\ *n* -ES

**mi·cro·drawing** \¦mīkrō+\ *n* [*micr-* + *drawing*] : a drawing made to exhibit microscopic structures or other very small details

**mi·cro·dri·li** \,=='drī,lī\ *n pl, cap* [NL, fr. *micr-* + *-drili* (fr. Gk *drilos* earthworm)] *in some classifications* : a group of Oligochaeta that comprises slender elongated predominantly aquatic worms lacking a capillary network on the nephridium and that is nearly coexistensive with Archioligochaeta — compare MEGADRILI

**mi·cro·drop** \'mīkrə+, \ *n* [*micr-* + *drop*] : a very small drop or minute droplet (as 0.1 to 0.01 of a drop)

**mi·cro·economics** \¦mīkrō+\ *n pl but usu sing in constr* [*micr-* + *economics*] : a study of economics in terms of individual areas of activity (as a firm, household, prices) — opposed to *macroeconomics*

**mi·cro·electrode** \¦=(,)=+\ *n* [*micr-* + *electrode*] : a minute electrode or one used in microelectrolysis

**mi·cro·electrolysis** \"+\ *n* [*micr-* + *electrolysis*] : electrolysis on a very small scale using small quantities of material — **mi·cro·electrolytic** \"+\ *adj*

**mi·cro·electrophoresis** \"+\ *n* [*micr-* + *electrophoresis*] : electrophoresis in which the movement of single particles is observed in a microscope or ultramicroscope — **mi·cro·elec·trophoretic** \"+\ *adj*

**mi·cro·element** \¦==+\ *n* [*micr-* + *element*] : TRACE ELEMENT

**mi·cro·environment** \¦=(,)=+\ *n* [*micr-* + *environment*] : MICROHABITAT

**microergate** *var of* MICRERGATE

**mi·cro·estimation** \¦mīkrō+\ *n* [*micr-* + *estimation*] : estimation (as by microanalysis) involving minute quantities of material : MICRODETERMINATION

**mi·cro·evolution** \"+\ *n* [*micr-* + *evolution*] : evolutionary change resulting from selective accumulation of minute variations held by many biologists to be chiefly responsible for evolutionary differentiation — distinguished from *macroevolution* — **mi·cro·evolutionary** \"+\ *adj*

**mi·cro·examination** \¦=(,)=+\ *n* [*micr-* + *examination*] : examination by means of the microscope

**mi·cro·facsimile** \"+\ *n* [*micr-* + *facsimile*] : MICROCOPY

**mi·cro·farad** \¦==+\ *n* [ISV *micr-* + *farad*] : one millionth of a farad

**mi·cro·fauna** \"+\ *n* [NL, fr. *micr-* + *fauna*] **1** : a small or strictly localized fauna : the fauna of a microhabitat **2** : minute animals; *esp* : those invisible to the naked eye ⟨the soil ~⟩ — compare MACROFAUNA, MESOFAUNA — **mi·cro·faunal** \"+\ *adj*

**micro-feeder** \"+\ *n* [*micr-* + *feeder*] : a microphagous organism

**mi·cro·fibril** \"+\ *n* [ISV *micr-* + *fibril*] : a fine fibril; *esp* : one of the submicroscopic elongated bundles of cellulose of the plant cell wall

**mi·cro·fiche** \'mīkrō,fēsh\ *n* -s [F, fr. *micr-* + *fiche* index card, slip of paper, peg, fr. OF, point, fr. *ficher, fichier* to drive in, pin, fasten — more at FICHU] : a sheet of microfilm; *esp* : one containing several rows of images

**mi·cro·fil·a·re·mia** *also* **mi·cro·fil·a·rae·mia** \,==,filə'rēmēə\ *n* -s [NL, fr. *microfilaria* + *-emia*] : the presence of microfilariae in the blood of one affected with some forms of filariasis

**mi·cro·filaria** \¦=(,)=+\ *n* [NL, fr. *micr-* + *filaria*] : a minute larval filaria

[1]**mi·cro·film** \'mīkrə+,-\ *n* [ISV *micr-* + *film*] : a film often in the form of a strip 16 millimeters or 35 millimeters wide bearing a photographic record on a reduced scale of printed or other graphic matter (as for storage or transmission in small space) that is enlarged for reading or viewing

[2]**microfilm** \"\ *vt* : to photograph on microfilm ~ *vi* : to take microfilms

**mi·cro·filmer** \"+\ *n* : one that microfilms; *esp* : an apparatus for producing microfilms

**mi·cro·fine** \¦mīkrō+\ *adj* [*micr-* + *fine*] : consisting of or being particles of minute size : MICROCRYSTALLINE ⟨~ dusting sulfur⟩

**mi·cro·flash** \"+\ *adj* [*micr-* + *flash*] : producing or produced by means of a high-intensity light flash of extremely short duration ⟨a ~ lamp⟩ ⟨a ~ picture⟩

**mi·cro·flora** \"+\ *n* [NL, fr. *micr-* + *flora*] **1** : a small or strictly localized flora : the flora of a microhabitat **2** : minute plants; *esp* : those invisible to the naked eye ⟨aquatic ~⟩ — **mi·cro·floral** \"+\ *adj*

**mi·cro·form** \'mīkrə,fȯrm\ *n* [*micr-* + *form*] **1** : MICROORGANISM **2** : a rust which lacks aecia, uredinia, and usu. pycnia and in which the teliospores undergo a resting stage prior to germination — compare LEPTOFORM

**mi·cro·fossil** \¦mīkrō+\ *n* [*micr-* + *fossil*] : a fossil whether a fragment of a larger organism or the entire remains of a minute organism that can be studied only microscopically — compare MACROFOSSIL

**mi·cro·gadus** \"+\ *n, cap* [NL, fr. *micr-* + *Gadus*] : a genus of gadoid fishes consisting of the tomcods

**mi·cro·gamete** \¦=(,)=+\ *n* [ISV *micr-* + *gamete*] : the smaller or male gamete of an organism or species producing differentiated gametes — compare MACROGAMETE

**mi·cro·gametocyte** \"+\ *n* [ISV *micr-* + *gametocyte*] : a gametocyte producing microgametes

**mi·cro·gametophyte** \"+\ *n* [*micr-* + *gametophyte*] : the male gametophyte produced by a microspore — compare MEGAGAMETOPHYTE

**mi·crog·a·my** \mī'krägəmē\ *n* -ES [*micr-* + *-gamy*] : syngamy between gametes much smaller than the vegetative cells occurring in protozoans and various algae — compare MACROGAMY

**mi·cro·gas·ter** \,mīkrō'gastə(r)\ *n, cap* [NL, fr. *micr-* + *-gaster*] : a genus of small braconid wasps whose larvae are parasitic on various caterpillars

**mi·cro·geographic** \¦==+\ *also* **mi·cro·geographical** \"+\ *adj* [*micr-* + *geographic*] : geographically localized : involving or concerned with strict geographic localization ⟨~ diversification⟩ ⟨microgeographical researches⟩ — **mi·cro·geography** \¦=(,)=+\ *n*

**microgeographic race** *n* : a highly localized and distinguishably differentiated population within a natural species

**mi·crog·lia** \mī'krägleə\ *n* -s [NL, fr. *micr-* + *-glia*] : a sustentacular and presumably phagocytic tissue element scattered through the central nervous system and made up of small cells that resemble lymphocytes and are now usu. considered to be of mesodermal origin and to arise from cells of the blood vessels — compare NEUROGLIA — **mi·crog·li·al** \(')=¦==əl\ *adj*

**mi·cro·gnathia** \,mīkrō'nāthēə, -nath-, -,kräg'n-\ *n* -s [NL, fr. *micr-* + *gnath-* + *-ia*] : abnormal shortening of one or both jaws

**mi·cro·graft** \'mīkrə+,-\ *n* [*micr-* + *graft*, n.] : a composite plant produced by micrografting

**mi·cro·grafting** \¦==+\ *n* -s [*micr-* + *grafting*, gerund of *graft*, v.] : the operation of engrafting a weak plant (as a hybrid embryo) on a related but more vigorous stock

**mi·cro·gram** \'==+,-\ *n* [ISV *micr-* + *gram*] **1** : one millionth of a gram **2** [*micr-* + *-gram*] : MICROGRAPH 2

**mi·cro·granite** \¦==+\ *n* [ISV *micr-* + *granite*; orig. formed as G *mikrogranit*] : an igneous rock composed of minute crystals of quartz and alkalic feldspar

**mi·cro·granular** \"+\ *adj* [*micr-* + *granular*] : minutely granular ⟨~ dolomite⟩

[1]**mi·cro·graph** \'mīkrə,graf, -raf\ *n* [ISV *micr-* + *-graph*] **1** : an instrument for executing minute writing or engraving **2** : a graphic reproduction of the image of an object or part of an object formed by a microscope **3** : an instrument for measuring minute movements by the magnified record of movements of a diaphragm

[2]**micrograph** \"\ *vt* : to make a micrograph of — **mi·crog·ra·pher** \mī'krägrəfə(r)\ *n* -s

**mi·cro·graph·ic** \¦mīkrə¦grafik\ *adj* [ISV *micrography*, *micrograph* + *-ic*] **1** : of or relating to micrography **2** : relating to or disclosed by micrographs or by the making of micrographs — **mi·cro·graph·i·cal·ly** \-fək(ə)lē\ *adv*

**mi·crog·ra·phy** \mī'krägrəfē, -fi\ *n* -ES [*micr-* + *-graphy*] **1** : examination or study with the microscope : MICROSCOPY — opposed to *macrography* **2** : the art or process of producing micrographs

**mi·cro·groove** \'mīkrə+,-\ *n* [*micr-* + *groove*] : a minute closely spaced V-shaped groove used on long-playing and extended-play phonograph records

**mi·cro·gyne** \-,jīn\ *n* -s [ISV *micr-* + *-gyne*] : a dwarf female ant

**mi·cro·habitat** \¦mīkrō+\ *n* [*micr-* + *habitat*] : a small usu. distinctly specialized and effectively isolated habitat (as a decaying stump, a pat of dung, or the rhizosphere of a plant)

**mi·cro·hardness** \"+\ *n* [*micr-* + *hardness*] : hardness of a substance (as an alloy) measured by an indenter (as a diamond point) that penetrates microscopic areas

**mi·cro·henry** \"+\ *n* [*micr-* + *henry*] : one millionth of a henry

**mi·crohm** \'mī,krōm\ *n* [ISV *micr-* + *ohm*] : one millionth of an ohm

**mi·crohm·me·ter** \'mī,krōm,mēd·ə(r)\ *n* [ISV *microhm* + *-meter*] : a sensitive ohmmeter for measuring very small resistances

[1]**mi·cro·hydra** \¦mīkrō+\ [NL, fr. *micr-* + *hydra*] *syn of* CRASPEDACUSTA

[2]**microhydra** \"\ *n* [NL, fr. [1]*Microhydra*] : a minute freshwater hydroid without tentacles that is the polyp of medusae of the genus *Craspedacusta*

[1]**mi·cro·hy·lid** \-¦hīləd\ *adj* [NL *Microhylidae*] : of or relating to the Microhylidae

[2]**microhylid** \"\ *n* [NL *Microhylidae*] : one of the Microhylidae

**mi·cro·hy·li·dae** \,=='hīlə,dē\ *n pl, cap* [NL, fr. *Microhyla*, type genus (fr. *micr-* + *Hyla*) + *-idae*] *in some classifications* : a family of chiefly tropical frogs closely related to the Brevicipitidae to which they are more commonly assigned

**mi·cro·hymenopteron** \¦==+\ *n* [NL, fr. *micr-* + *Hymenopteron*] : any of numerous minute and often parasitoid insects of the order Hymenoptera — used chiefly in pl. as if a taxon and then capitalized — **mi·cro·hymenopterous** \"+\ *adj*

**mi·cro·inch** \"+,-\ *n* [*micr-* + *inch*] : a unit of length equal to one millionth of an inch

**mi·cro·incineration** \¦=(,)=+\ *n* [*micr-* + *incineration*] : a technique employing high temperatures (as 600–650°C) for driving off the organic constituents of cells or tissue fragments leaving the inorganic matter for chemical identification

**mi·cro·injection** \"+\ *n* [*micr-* + *injection*] : injection under the microscope; *specif* : injection into cells or tissues by means of a fine mechanically controlled capillary tube

**microkinematography** *var of* MICROCINEMATOGRAPHY

**mi·cro·lecithal** \¦mīkrō+\ *adj* [*micr-* + *lecithal*] : having little yolk : ALECITHAL ⟨echinoderm eggs are ~⟩

**mi·cro·lepidoptera** \"+\ *n pl, cap* [NL, fr. *micr-* + *Lepidoptera*] *in some classifications* : a major division of Lepidoptera comprising the smaller moths and a few closely related larger moths (as of the families Tineidae, Tortricidae, Pyralididae, Psychidae, and Eucleidae) — usu. used descriptively without taxonomic implications and often uncapitalized; compare MACROLEPIDOPTERA — **mi·cro·lepidopterous** \"+\ *adj*

**mi·cro·lepidopterist** \"+\ *n* [NL *Microlepidoptera* + E *-ist*] : a student of the Microlepidoptera

**mi·cro·level** \"+\ *vt* [*micr-* + *level*] : to bring (an elevator) close to an exact level by automatic means

**mi·cro·lite** \ˈmīkrəˌlīt\ *n* -S [*micr-* + *-lite*] **1** : a mineral $(Na,Ca)_2Ta_2O_6(O,OH,F)$ that consists of an oxide of sodium, calcium, and tantalum with small amounts of fluorine and hydroxyl and that is isomorphous with pyrochlore **2** [G *mikrolith*, fr. *mikr-* micr- + *-lith* -lite] : a minute crystal that is visible only under the microscope and usu. affects polarized light : MICROCRYSTAL — **mi·cro·lit·ic** \¦=¦lid·ik\ *adj*

**mi·cro·liter** \¦mīkrō+\ *n* [ISV *micr-* + *liter*] : a unit of capacity equal to one millionth of a liter

**mi·cro·lith** \ˈmīkrəˌlith\ *n* -S [ISV *micr-* + *-lith*] : a tiny blade tool of the late Paleolithic usu. in the form of a triangle or other geometric figure and often set in a bone or wooden haft

**mi·cro·lith·ic** \¦=¦lithik\ *adj* [*microlith* + *-ic*] **1** : being or resembling a microlith **2** : of or relating to the people who produced microliths

**mi·cro·logical** \-ˌläjəkəl\ *or* **mi·cro·log·ic** \-jik\ *adj* [*micrological* fr. *micrology* + *-ical*; *micrologic* ISV *micrology* + *-ic*] : of or relating to micrology

**mi·crol·o·gist** \mīˈkräləjəst\ *n* -S [²*micrology* + *-ist*] : a specialist in micrology

¹**mi·crol·o·gy** \-jē, -ji\ *n* -ES [Gk *mikrologia*, fr. *mikr-* micr- + *-logia* (fr. *logos* speech) — more at LEGEND] : attention to petty items or differences

²**micrology** \"\ *n* -ES [*micr-* + *-logy*] : a science dealing with the handling and preparation of microscopic objects for study

**mi·cro·lux** \ˈmīkrə+,-\ *n* [*micr-* + *lux*] : one millionth of a lux

**mi·cro·manipulation** \¦mī(ˌ)krō+\ *n* [ISV *micr-* + *manipulation*] : the technique or practice of microdissection and microinjection — compare MICRURGY

**mi·cro·manipulator** \"+\ *n* [ISV *micr-* + *manipulator*] : an instrument for micromanipulation

**mi·cro·manometer** \"+\ *n* [ISV *micr-* + *manometer*] : a manometer specially designed to measure minute differences of pressure

**mi·cro·mas·tia** \ˌ==ˈmastēə\ *n* -S [NL, fr. *micr-* + *-mastia*] : postpubertal immaturity and abnormal smallness of the breasts

**mi·cro·me·lia** \-ˈmēlēə\ *n* -S [NL, fr. *micr-* + *-melia*] : a condition characterized by abnormally small and imperfectly developed extremities — **mi·cro·melic** \¦==¦melik, -mēl-\ *adj*

**mi·cro·membrane** \¦==+\ *n* [*micr-* + *membrane*] : a very thin semipermeable membrane

**mi·cro·mer·al** \¦mīkrə¦mirəl\ *or* **mi·cro·mer·ic** \-¦merik, -¦mir-\ *adj* [*micromere* + *-al* or *-ic*] : of or relating to a micromere

**mi·cro·mere** \ˈmīkrəˌmi(ə)r\ *n* -S [ISV *micr-* + *-mere*] : one of the smaller blastomeres resulting from the unequal segmentation of an egg — opposed to *macromere*; see BLASTULA illustration

**mi·cro·me·ria** \ˌ==ˈmirēə\ *n, cap* [NL, fr. *micr-* + Gk *meros* part, portion + NL *-ia* — more at MERIT] : a large genus of fragrant chiefly Old World herbs (family Labiatae) having a calyx chiefly 13-veined, a small corolla barely exserted, and four unequal anthers — see YERBA BUENA

**mi·cro·me·rit·ics** \ˌ=(ˌ)krōməˈrid·iks\ *n pl but sing in constr* [prob. fr. *micr-* + *mer-* (fr. Gk *meros* part) + *-ite* + *-ics*] : a science that treats of small particles and that is applied esp. in soil physics

**mi·cro·mesentery** \¦mīkrō+\ *n* [*micr-* + *mesentery*] : an incomplete secondary mesentery in an anthozoan

**mi·cro·meteorite** \"+\ *n* [*micr-* + *meteorite*] : a meteorite so small that it penetrates through the earth's atmosphere without becoming intensely heated and hence without disintegration

**mi·cro·meteorological** \"+\ *adj* : of or relating to micrometeorology

**mi·cro·meteorology** \"+\ *n* [*micr-* + *meteorology*] : the study of the meteorological characteristics of a local site that is usu. small and often is confined to a shallow layer of air next to the ground

¹**mi·crom·e·ter** \mīˈkräməd·ə(r), -ətə-\ *n* [F *micromètre*, fr. *micr-* + *-mètre* -meter] **1** : an instrument used with a telescope or microscope for measuring minute distances or the apparent diameters of objects which subtend minute angles **2** : MICROMETER CALIPER

²**micrometer** \"\ *vt* : to measure by means of a micrometer

³**mi·cro·me·ter** \ˈmīkrōˌmēd·ə(r), -krə-, -ētə-\ *n* [ISV *micr-* + *meter*] : a unit of length equal to one millionth of a meter

**micrometer caliper** *n* : a caliper for making precise measurements having a spindle moved by a finely threaded screw

**micrometer eyepiece** *n* : an eyepiece fitted with a filar micrometer the lines of which are in the focal plane of the eyepiece and so coincide with the objective image when the microscope or telescope is in focus — called also *ocular micrometer*

micrometer caliper: *1* anvil, *2* spindle, *3* frame, *4* sleeve, *5* thimble

**micrometer microscope** *n* : a microscope fitted with a micrometer eyepiece

**mi·cro·method** \¦mīkrō+\ *n* [*micr-* + *method*] : a method (as of microanalysis) involving very small quantities of material or the use of the microscope — opposed to *macromethod*

**mi·cro·metrical** \"+\ *also* **mi·cro·metric** \"+\ *adj* [*micrometrical* fr. *micrometer* + *-ical*; *micrometric* ISV *micrometer* + *-ic*] : relating to or made by a micrometer — **mi·cro·metrically** \"+\ *adv*

**mi·crom·e·try** \mīˈkräməˌtrē, -ri\ *n* -ES [ISV *micr-* + *-metry*] : measurement with a micrometer

**mi·cro·mho** \ˈmīkrə+,-\ *n* [*micr-* + *mho*] : one millionth of a mho

**mi·cro·microfarad** \¦mīkrō+\ *n* [*micr-* + *microfarad*] : one millionth of a microfarad

**mi·cro·micron** \"+\ *n* [*micr-* + *micron*] : one millionth of a micron

**mi·cro·millimeter** \"+\ *n* [ISV *micr-* + *millimeter*] : one millionth of a millimeter — called also *millimicron*

**mi·cro·modification** \"+\ *n* [*micr-* + *modification*] : a modification of a method or procedure for use on a small scale (as in microanalysis)

**mi·cro·mole** \ˈmīkrə+,-\ *n* [*micr-* + *mole*] : one millionth of a mole

**mi·cro·motion** \¦mīkrō+\ *n* [*micr-* + *motion*] : the technique in time and motion study of making a pictorial elapsed-time study of the elements or subdivisions of an operation by means of a high-speed motion-picture camera and a specialized timing device

**mi·cro·mount** \ˈmīkrə+,-\ *n* [*micr-* + *mount*] : a small often beautifully crystallized mineral specimen usu. suitable only for examination with a microscope

**mi·cro·mutation** \¦mī(ˌ)krō+\ *n* [*micr-* + *mutation*] : a small-scale or highly localized mutation; *esp* : one involving alteration at a single gene locus

**mi·cro·mycete** \¦==ˈmīˌsēt, -ˌmīˈsēt\ *n* [ISV *micr-* + *-mycete*] : a fungus (as a rust) that does not produce a large fleshy fruiting body

**mi·cro·mys** \ˈmīkrəˌmis\ *n, cap* [NL, fr. *micr-* + *-mys*] : a genus of myomorph rodents comprising the tiny Old World harvest mice

**mi·cron** \ˈmīˌkrän *sometimes* ˈmi- *or* ˌkrən\ *n, pl* **microns** \-nz\ *also* **mi·cra** \-krə\ [NL, fr. Gk *mikron*, neut. of *mikros* small — more at MICR-] **1** : a unit of length equal to one thousandth of a millimeter or about 0.000039 inch — symbol $\mu$ **2** : a unit of low pressure (as in a vacuum tube) equal to the pressure of a column of mercury one micron high

**mi·cro·needle** \¦mīkrō+\ *n* [*micr-* + *needle*] : a needle for micromanipulation

**mi·cro·nephridium** \¦=(ˌ)=+\ *n* [NL, fr. *micr-* + *nephridium*] : a small nephridium usu. numerous in each segment of various annelid worms

¹**mi·cro·ne·sian** \¦mīkrə¦nēzhən *also* -ēsh| *or* -ēzē|\ *adj, usu cap* [ISV, fr. NL *Micronesia*, islands of the western Pacific ocean east of the Philippines + ISV *-an*, adj. suffix] **1 a** : of, relating to, or characteristic of Micronesia **b** : of, relating to, or characteristic of the Micronesians **2** : of, relating to, or characteristic of the Micronesian languages

²**micronesian** \"\ *n* -S *cap* [ISV, fr. ¹*micronesian*] **1** : a native or inhabitant of Micronesia **2** : a group of Austronesian languages spoken in the Micronesian islands

**mi·cron·ize** \ˈmīkrəˌnīz\ *vt* [*micron* + *-ize*] : to pulverize extremely fine; *esp* : to pulverize into particles a few microns in diameter ⟨*micronized* graphite⟩ ⟨*micronized* penicillin⟩

**mi·cro·nuclear** \¦mīkrō+\ *adj* [*micronucleus* + *-ar*] : of or relating to a micronucleus

**mi·cro·nucleate** \"+\ *adj* [*micronucleus* + *-ate*] : having a micronucleus

**mi·cro·nucleus** \"+\ *n* [NL, fr. *micr-* + *nucleus*] : a minute nucleus; *specif* : one regarded as primarily concerned with reproductive and genetic functions in most ciliated protozoans — distinguished from *macronucleus*

¹**mi·cro·nutrient** \"+\ *n* [*micr-* + *nutrient*] **1** : TRACE ELEMENT **2** : an organic compound (as a vitamin) essential in minute amounts only to the growth and welfare of an animal — compare MACRONUTRIENT

²**micronutrient** \"\ *adj* : of, relating to, or being a micronutrient ⟨~ deficiency⟩ : required for nutrition only in minute amounts ⟨~ elements such as manganese and zinc —*Science*⟩

**mi·cro·organic** \"+\ *adj* [*micr-* + *organic*] : of, relating to, or characteristic of microorganisms

**mi·cro·organism** \"+\ *n* [ISV *micr-* + *organism*] : an organism of microscopic or ultramicroscopic size — used esp. of bacteria and protozoa ⟨soil-inhabiting ~*s* —S.A.Waksman⟩

**syn** GERM, MICROBE, BACTERIUM, BACILLUS, VIRUS, PATHOGEN: MICROORGANISM is the general term for any organism of microscopic or ultramicroscopic size. GERM and MICROBE are early nonscientific synonyms for MICROORGANISM. GERM often refers to microorganisms regarded as a source or origin (as of a disease) ⟨typhus *germs*⟩ It is often used to indicate a rudimentary beginning or embryo capable of evolving or developing ⟨*germs* of the doctrine of which he is the founder may be traced to much earlier, even ancient periods —*Encyc. Americana*⟩ MICROBE may be somewhat more awesome than GERM and is rarely used with pleasing suggestion ⟨the late stage of true invasion of the tissues around the brain and spinal cord by the deadly *microbes* —F.G.Slaughter⟩ BACTERIUM is now the common scientific designation for a large group of microscopic plants with single-celled or acellular bodies of various forms that affect the life of man in various ways. BACTERIA is sometimes used to designate rod-shaped bacteria that do not form endospores and is contrasted with BACILLUS in its narrow sense. BACILLUS in science refers to any straight rod-shaped bacterium or to any straight aerobic rod-shaped bacterium that forms endospores; popularly it refers to various disease-causing bacteria ⟨the *bacilli* of diphtheria⟩ VIRUS technically indicates a submicroscopic infective agent sometimes considered as composed of complex protein molecules capable of growth in living cells ⟨polio *virus*⟩ VIRUS is applicable to any dread, insidious, inexorable agent ⟨right in claiming that the *virus* of Pan-Germanism and Nazism was present in the speeches —*Times Lit. Supp.*⟩ PATHOGEN is applicable to any living agent that causes disease (as a bacterium, virus, fungus, or worm); it stresses this aspect and implies nothing about relative size, being freely applied to agencies that are not microorganisms ⟨many *pathogens* attack a vigorous host most readily —*Science*⟩

**mi·cro·organismal** \"+\ *adj* : MICROORGANIC

**mi·cro·paleontological** \"+\ *also* **mi·cro·paleontologic** \"+\ *adj* [*micropaleontology* + *-ical* or *-ic*] : of or relating to micropaleontology

**mi·cro·paleontologist** \"+\ *n* [*micropaleontology* + *-ist*] : a paleontologist specializing in the identification and study of microfossils

**mi·cro·paleontology** \"+\ *n* [ISV *micr-* + *paleontology*] : the study of microfossils

**mi·cro·pantograph** \"+\ *n* [*micr-* + *pantograph*] : a pantograph that produces microscopic copies

**mi·cro·parasite** \"+\ *n* [*micr-* + *parasite*] : a parasitic microorganism — **mi·cro·parasitic** \"+\ *adj*

**mi·cro·pedology** \¦=(ˌ)=+\ *n* [*micr-* + *pedology*] : a science dealing with the microscopic phenomena of soils

**mi·cro·pegmatite** \¦==+\ *n* [*micr-* + *pegmatite*] : microcrystalline graphic granite — **mi·cro·pegmatitic** \"+\ *adj*

**mi·cro·perthite** \"+\ *n* [G *mikroperthit*, fr. *mikr-* micr- + *perthit* perthite, fr. E *perthite*] : a perthite the structure of which can be discerned only with the microscope — compare CRYPTOPERTHITE — **mi·cro·perthitic** \"+\ *adj*

**mi·cro·phage** \ˈmīkrəˌfāj\ *n* -S [ISV *micr-* + *-phage*; orig. formed in F] : a small phagocyte; *specif* : a polymorphonuclear leukocyte

**mi·croph·a·gous** \(ˈ)mīˈkräfəgəs\ *adj* [*micr-* + *-phagous*] : feeding on minute particles (as bacteria) ⟨~ ciliates⟩ ⟨~ habit⟩ — compare MACROPHAGOUS — **mi·croph·a·gy** \=ˈ==jē\ *n* -ES

**mi·cro·pha·kia** \ˌmīkrōˈfākēə\ *n* -S [NL, fr. *micr-* + *phac-* + *-ia*] : abnormal smallness of the lens of the eye

¹**mi·cro·phone** \ˈmīkrəˌfōn\ *n* [ISV *micr-* + *-phone*] : an instrument whereby sound waves are caused to generate or modulate an electric current usu. for the purpose of transmitting or recording speech or music

²**microphone** \"\ *vt* : to transmit by microphone

**mi·cro·phon·ic** \¦==¦fänik\ *adj* [¹*microphone* + *-ic*] **1** : of or relating to a microphone : serving to intensify sounds **2** : having the effect of a microphone because of faulty construction or design — used of amplifier tubes or other circuit elements **3** : of or relating to microphonics of the cochlea

**mi·cro·phon·ics** \ˌ==ˈfäniks\ *n pl but sing in constr* [¹*microphone* + *-ics*] **1** : a science treating of the microphone or of the means of increasing the intensity of low or weak sounds **2** : noises in a loudspeaker resulting from unwanted variations of current in the circuit or mechanical movement of tubes or other parts **3** *often* **microphonic** [*micr-* + *phon-* + *-ics* or *-ic*] : an electrical potential arising in the cochlea when the mechanical energy of a sound stimulus is transformed to electrical energy as the action potential of the transmitting nerve

**mi·cro·phon·ing** \¦==ˌfōniŋ\ *n* -S [¹*microphone* + *-ing*] : the positioning of microphones or performers so as to produce desired effects in sound reproduction

¹**mi·cro·photograph** \¦mīkrō+\ *n* [ISV *micr-* + *photograph*] **1** : a small photograph that is normally magnified for reading or viewing : MICROCOPY **2** : PHOTOMICROGRAPH — not used technically — **mi·cro·photographic** \"+\ *adj* — **mi·cro·photography** \¦=(ˌ)=+\ *n*

²**microphotograph** \"\ *vt* : to make a microphotograph of

¹**mi·cro·photometer** \¦mī(ˌ)krō+\ *n* [ISV *micr-* + *photometer*] : an instrument for measuring the amount of light transmitted or reflected by small areas or for measuring the relative densities of spectrum lines on a photographic plate — **mi·cro·photometric** \¦==+\ *adj* — **mi·cro·photometrically** \"+\ *adv* — **mi·cro·photometry** \¦=(ˌ)=+\ *n*

²**microphotometer** \"\ *vt* : to measure or examine with a microphotometer

**mi·croph·thal·mia** \ˌmīˌkräfˈthalmēə, ÷-kräp¦th-\ *n* -S [NL, fr. *micr-* + *ophthalmia*] : abnormal smallness of the eye usu. occurring as a congenital anomaly

**mi·croph·thal·mic** \¦=¦=¦=mik\ *adj* [*microphthalmia* + *-ic*] : exhibiting microphthalmia : having small eyes

**mi·croph·thal·mus** \ˌ=ˌ=ˈ=məs\ *or* **mi·croph·thal·mos** \-məs, -ˌmäs\ *n, pl* **microphthal·mi** \-ˌmī\ *or* **microphthalmoi** \-ˌmȯi\ [*microphthalmus* fr. NL, fr. *micr-* + *-ophthalmus*; *microphthalmos* fr. NL, fr. *micr-* + Gk *ophthalmos* eye] : MICROPHTHALMIA

**mi·cro·phyll** \ˈmīkrəˌfil\ *n* -S [ISV *micr-* + *-phyll*] **1** : a small leaf **2** : a plant (as a xerophyte) having small leaves

**mi·cro·phyl·lous** \¦==¦filəs\ *adj* [*micr-* + *-phyllous*] **1** : having small leaves ⟨the ~ plants of desert regions⟩ **2** : having leaves with a single unbranched vein ⟨a ~ lycopod⟩ — compare MACROPHYLLOUS

**mi·cro·physical** \¦mīkrō+\ *adj* [fr. *microphysics*, after E *physics*: *physical*] : of or relating to microphysics ⟨events in the ~ world —*Time*⟩

**mi·cro·physics** \"+\ *n pl but sing in constr* [*micr-* + *physics*] : the physics of molecules, atoms, and elementary particles

**mi·cro·phyte** \ˈmīkrəˌfīt\ *n* -S [ISV *micr-* + *-phyte*; prob. orig. formed in F] : a minute plant: as **a** : BACTERIUM **b** : a dwarfed plant occurring under unfavorable environmental conditions and consisting typically of an abbreviated stem, a single reduced leaf, and a single minute floral unit — **mi·cro·phyt·ic** \¦=¦fid·ik\ *adj*

**mi·cro·pipette** *or* **mi·cro·pipet** \¦mī(ˌ)krō+\ *n* [*micr-* + *pipette*] **1** : a pipette for the measurement or transferring of very small volumes **2** : a small and extremely fine-pointed pipette used in microdissection and microinjection

**mi·cro·plankton** \¦==+\ *n* [ISV *micr-* + *plankton*] : microscopic plankton; *esp* : NANNOPLANKTON

**mi·crop·o·dal** \(ˈ)mīˈkräpədᵊl\ *also* **mi·crop·o·dous** \-dəs\ *adj* [*micropodal* fr. NL *micropodus* + E *-al*; *micropodous* fr. NL *micropodus*, fr. *micr-* + *-podus* -podous] : having abnormally small feet

**mi·cro·pod·i·dae** \ˌmīkrōˈpädəˌdē\ [NL, fr. *Micropod-*, *Micropus* + *-idae* — more at MICROPUS] *syn of* APODIDAE

**mi·cro·pod·i·for·mes** \ˌmīkrəˌpädəˈfȯrˌmēz\ [NL, fr. *Micropod-*, *Micropus* + *-iformes*] *syn of* APODIFORMES

**mi·cro·polariscope** \¦mī(ˌ)krō+\ *n* [*micr-* + *polariscope*] : a microscope with polarizer and analyzer attached (as for use in crystallography)

**mi·cro·pore** \ˈmīkrə+,-\ *n* [ISV *micr-* + *pore*] **1** : one of the small pores in the shell of some chitons **2** : a very fine pore (as one not easily visible to the naked eye)

**mi·cro·porosity** \¦mī(ˌ)krō+\ *n* [*micr-* + *porosity*] : extremely fine porosity (as in metal castings)

**mi·cro·porous** \¦==+\ *adj* [*micr-* + *porous*] : full of or characterized by very fine pores ⟨~ synthetic rubber⟩

**mi·cro·potentiometer** \¦=(ˌ)=+\ *n* [*micr-* + *potentiometer*] : a potentiometer for the accurate measurement of potential differences of only a few microvolts

¹**mi·cro·print** \ˈmīkrə+,-\ *n* [*micr-* + *print*] : a photographic or photomechanical print of printed or other graphic matter in reduced size usu. viewed with an enlarging device

²**microprint** \"\ *vt* : to make a microprint of ⟨material ~*ed* on cards⟩

**mi·cro·procedure** \¦mīkrō+\ *n* [*micr-* + *procedure*] : a procedure (as for microanalysis) involving very small quantities of material — opposed to *macroprocedure*

**mi·cro·projection** \"+\ *n* [*micr-* + *projection*] : the process of projecting microscope images on a screen by means of a microprojector

**mi·cro·projector** \"+\ *n* [*micr-* + *projector*] : a projector utilizing a compound microscope for projecting on a screen a greatly enlarged image of a microscopic object

**mi·crop·sia** \mīˈkräpsēə\ *also* **mi·crop·sy** \ˈ=ˌ=sē\ *n, pl* **micropsias** *also* **micropsies** [NL *micropsia*, fr. *micr-* + *-opsia*] : a pathological condition in which objects appear to be smaller than they are in reality — opposed to *macropsia*

**mi·crop·ter·ism** \=ˈ=təˌrizəm\ *n* -S [*micropterous* + *-ism*] : the state or condition of being micropterous

**mi·crop·ter·ous** \(ˈ)mīˈkräpt(ə)rəs\ *adj* [prob. fr. (assumed) NL *micropterus*, fr. NL *micr-* + *-pterus* -pterous] : having small or rudimentary wings or fins

**mi·crop·ter·us** \=ˈ=tərəs\ *n, cap* [NL, fr. *micr-* + *-pterus*; fr. the fact that the specimen on which the name was based had a mutilated dorsal fin and the author of the name consequently believed its fins were small] : a genus of sunfishes (family Centrarchidae) to which the American freshwater black basses belong

¹**mi·crop·ter·y·gid** \ˌmī(ˌ)krä¦pterəjəd\ *adj* [NL *Micropterygidae*] : of or relating to the Micropterygidae

²**micropterygid** \"\ *n* -S : a moth of the family Micropterygidae

**mi·crop·te·ryg·i·dae** \=ˌ=təˈrijəˌdē\ *n pl, cap* [NL, fr. *Micropteryg-*, *Micropteryx*, type genus (fr. *micr-* + *-pteryg-*, *-pteryx*) + *-idae* — more at -PTERYX] : a family of tiny very primitive moths sometimes made a separate order Zeugloptera that have functional mandibles

**mi·crop·tic** \(ˈ)mīˈkräptik\ *adj* [*micr-* + *optic*] : of, relating to, or affected with micropsia

**mi·cro·puccinia** \¦mī(ˌ)krō+\ *n* -S *usu cap P* [NL, fr. *micr-* + *Puccinia*] : a parasitic fungus of the genus *Puccinia* producing only teliospores

**mi·cro·pus** \mīˈkrōpəs\ [NL, fr. MGk *mikropod-*, *mikropous* having small feet, fr. Gk *mikr-* micr- + *pod-*, *pous* foot — more at FOOT] *syn of* APUS

**mi·cro·py·lar** \¦mīkrə¦pīlə(r)\ *adj* [ISV *micropyle* + *-ar*] : of, relating to, or adjacent to a micropyle ⟨eggs . . . somewhat flattened with a conical ~ knob —E.O.Essig⟩

**mi·cro·pyle** \ˈ==ˌpīl\ *n* -S [ISV *micr-* + *-pyle* (fr. Gk *pylē* gate); prob. orig. formed in F — more at PYLON] **1 a** : a differentiated area of surface in many eggs through which a sperm enters **b** : an opening in various spores through which enclosed protoplasts escape **2** : a minute opening in the integument of an ovule of a seed plant through which the pollen tube normally penetrates to the embryo sac and which often persists in the seed as an opening or superficial scar — called also *foramen*

**mi·cro·pyrometer** \¦mī(ˌ)krō+\ *n* [*micr-* + *pyrometer*] : an instrument used for the optical determination of the temperature or emissivity of microscopic glowing bodies and having a minute glow lamp mounted in the eyepiece of a microscope so that the image of the filament is superimposed upon that of the observed glowing particle

**mi·cro·radiograph** \¦==+\ *n* [*micr-* + *radiograph*] : an X-ray photograph showing the minute internal structure (as of a metal or wood in thin section) — **mi·cro·radiographic** \"+\ *adj* — **mi·cro·radiography** \"+\ *n*

**mi·cro·reader** \"+\ *n* [*micr-* + *reader*] : an apparatus that gives an enlarged image of a microphotograph suitable for reading or viewing

**mi·cro·relief** \¦=(ˌ)=+\ *n* [*micr-* + *relief*] : slight irregularities of a land surface causing variations in elevation amounting to no more than a few feet

**mi·cro·reproduction** \¦==+\ *n* [*micr-* + *reproduction*] **1** : microphotographic reproduction **2** : MICROCOPY

**mi·cro·respirometer** \"+\ *n* [*micr-* + *respirometer*] : an apparatus for the quantitative study of the respiratory activity of minute amounts of living material (as individual cells or protozoans) — **mi·cro·respirometry** \"+\ *n*

**mi·cro·rhabdus** \"+\ *n* [NL, fr. *micr-* + *rhabdus*] : a rod-shaped sponge spicule

**mi·cro·rho·pi·as** \ˌ==ˈrōpēəs\ *n, cap* [NL, perh. irreg. fr. *micr-* + Gk *rhōpeia* bushes] : a genus of typical ant wrens

**mi·cro·saur** \ˈmīkrəˌsȯ(ə)r\ *n* -S [NL *Microsauria*] : one of the Microsauria

**mi·cro·sau·ria** \ˌ==ˈsȯrēə\ *n pl, cap* [NL, fr. *micr-* + *-sauria*] **1** : an order of extinct amphibians (suborder Lepospondyli) of the Pennsylvanian and Lower Permian that resemble salamanders, are sometimes considered ancestral to modern apodal and caudate amphibians, or are placed among the primitive reptiles **2** *in some classifications* : an order or other group of amphibians equivalent to Lepospondyli (sense a)

**mi·cro·scale** \ˈmīkrə+,-\ *n* [*micr-* + *scale*] : a grade, standard, or extent suited to the handling of minute quantities or measurements — often used with *on* ⟨development of clinical methods on a ~ —*Postwar Research in Mellon Inst.*⟩

**mi·cro·sclere** \"+,-\ *n* [*micr-* + *sclere*] : a minute sponge spicule usu. supporting a single cell — **mi·cro·scleric** \¦==+\ *or* **mi·cro·sclerous** \"+\ *adj*

**mi·cro·scolex** \ˌ==ˈskōˌleks\ *n, cap* [NL, fr. *micr-* + *-scolex*] : a genus of earthworms containing a species (*M. phosphoreus*) native to So. America but now widely distributed that is sometimes highly luminescent and gives a greenish yellow light resembling that of a glowworm

**¹mi·cro·scope** \'mīkrə,skōp\ *n* [NL *microscopium*, fr. *micr-* + *-scopium* -scope] **1 :** an optical instrument consisting of a lens or combination of lenses for making enlarged images of minute objects; *esp* **:** COMPOUND MICROSCOPE — see PHASE MICROSCOPE, POLARIZING MICROSCOPE, ULTRAMICROSCOPE **2 :** an instrument using radiations other than light (as electrons, ultraviolet, or X rays) for making enlarged images of minute objects ⟨electron ~⟩

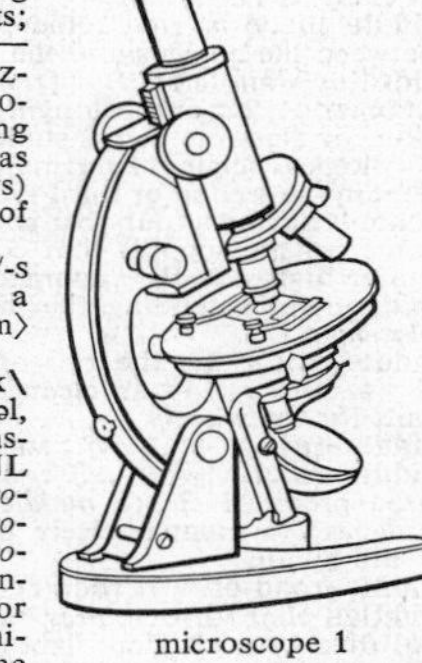
microscope 1

**²microscope** \"\ *vt* -ED/-ING/-S **1 :** to look at with or as if with a microscope ⟨~ a new program⟩ **2 :** MAGNIFY ⟨~ a minor failing⟩

**mi·cro·scop·ic** \¦==¦skäpik, -pēk\ *or* **mi·cro·scop·i·cal** \-pəkəl, -pēk-\ *adj* [*microscopic* fr. (assumed) NL *microscopicus*, fr. NL *microscopium* + L *icus* -ic; *microscopical* fr. (assumed) NL *microscopicus* + E *-al*] **1 a** *usu microscopical* **:** of, relating to, or conducted with the microscope or microscopy ⟨*microscopical* examination⟩ **b :** attainable by use of the microscope ⟨~ accuracy⟩ **2 :** resembling a microscope **:** able to see very minute objects ⟨the ~ eye of the engraver —*Amer. Guide Series: N.J.*⟩ **3 a :** so small or fine as to be invisible or not clearly distinguished without the use of a microscope ⟨~ plants⟩ ⟨~ crystallization⟩ — often distinguished from *submicroscopic* and *ultramicroscopic;* opposed to *macroscopic* **b :** very small or fine ⟨a ~ dog⟩ ⟨no matter how ~ his wage —Irving Stone⟩ ⟨~ division of labor —P.M.Mazur⟩ **c :** extremely accurate or meticulous ⟨examined the object with ~ care⟩ **syn** see SMALL

**mi·cro·scop·i·cal·ly** \-pək(ə)lē, -li\ *adv* **1 :** by means of the microscope ⟨a fact that can be demonstrated ~⟩ **2 :** to a microscopic degree ⟨took great care to get the surface ~ level —G.R.Gilbert⟩ ⟨contribute ~ to the appreciation of art —Vincent Starrett⟩ **3 :** in a microscopic manner **:** with extreme accuracy or meticulousness ⟨studying ~ the statistics of trade and industry —G.G.Coulton⟩ ⟨his past returns were scrutinized ~ —R.G.Hubler⟩

**microscopic anatomy** *n* **:** HISTOLOGY

**mi·cros·co·pist** \mī'kräskəpəst, 'mīkrə,skōpəst\ *n* -S [ISV ¹*microscope* + *-ist*] **:** a specialist in microscopy

**mi·cros·co·py** \-pē, -pi\ *n* -ES [¹*microscope* + *-y*] **:** the use of the microscope **:** investigation with the microscope

**mi·cro·second** \¦mīkrō+\ *n* [ISV *micr-* + *second*] **:** a unit of time equal to one millionth of a second

**mi·cro·section** \"+\ *n* [*micr-* + *section*] **:** a thin section (as of rock or of animal or vegetable tissue) prepared for microscopic examination

**mi·cro·seism** \'mīkrə,sīzəm *sometimes* -sez- *or* -säz- *or* -sēz-\ *n* -S [ISV *micr-* + *-seism*] **:** a feeble rhythmically recurring earth tremor that is not directly perceptible, that is detected only by means of specially constructed apparatus, and that is caused by an earthquake or by a storm at sea — compare MACROSEISM — **mi·cro·seis·mic** \¦==¦sī¦zmik *also* ¦sm- *sometimes* -¦se¦ *or* -¦sä¦ *or* -¦sē¦\ *adj*

**mi·cro·seismograph** \¦mīkrō+\ *n* [ISV *microseism* + *-o-* + *-graph*] **:** MICROSEISMOMETER

**mi·cro·seismology** \¦=(,)=+\ *n* [*microseism* + *-o-* + *-logy*] **:** a science dealing with microseisms

**mi·cro·seismometer** \"+\ *n* [*microseism* + *-o-* + *-meter*] **:** a seismometer for measuring microseisms — **mi·cro·seis·mometry** \"+\ *n*

**mi·cro·septum** \¦==+\ *n* [NL, fr. *micr-* + *septum*] **:** a narrow or imperfect mesentery in anthozoans

**mi·cro·ser·al** \¦==¦sirəl\ *adj* [*microsere* + *-al*] **:** of or relating to a microsere

**mi·cro·sere** \¦==+,-\ *n* [*micr-* + *sere*] **:** the sere of a microhabitat usu. terminating by the loss of identity of the habitat and without the development of a climax

**mi·cro·sheet** \"+,-\ *n* [*micr-* + *sheet*] **:** MICROFICHE

**mi·cro·slide** \"+,-\ *n* [*micr-* + *slide*] **:** a slip of glass on which a preparation is mounted for microscopic examination

**mi·cros·mat·ic** \¦mī,kräz¦mad·ik\ *adj* [*micr-* + *osmatic*] **:** having the sense of smell feebly developed ⟨man may be considered a ~ animal⟩

**mi·cro·sociology** \¦mīkrō+\ *n* [*micr-* + *sociology*] **:** the study of small systems of social behavior

**mi·cro·so·ma** \,mīkrə'sōmə\ *n, pl* **microsoma·ta** \-məd·ə\ [NL, fr. G *mikrosom*] **:** MICROSOME

**mi·cro·som·al** \¦==¦sōməl\ *adj* [*microsome* + *-al*] **:** of or relating to microsomes

**mi·cro·so·ma·tous** \¦==¦sōməd·əs\ *adj* [*micr-* + *-somatous*] **:** having a small body **:** DWARFISH

**mi·cro·some** \'mīkrə,sōm\ *n* -S [G *mikrosom*, fr. *mikr-* micr- + *-som* -some] **:** a minute protoplasmic granule; *esp* **:** one of the phospholipide-nucleoprotein complexes that are a regular constituent of cytoplasm and are sometimes held to be precursors of the mitochondria — **mi·cro·so·mi·al** \¦==¦sōmēəl\ *or* **mi·cro·so·mic** \-mik\ *adj*

**mi·cro·sorex** \¦mīkrō+\ *n, cap* [NL, fr. *micr-* + *Sorex*] **:** a genus formerly considered a subgenus of *Sorex* comprising the pygmy shrews

**mi·cro·species** \"+\ *n, pl* **microspecies** [*micr-* + *species*] **:** a small usu. localized population slightly but effectively differentiated from related forms — compare MACROSPECIES

**mi·cro·spectrophotometer** \"+\ *n* [*micr-* + *spectrophotometer*] **:** a spectrophotometer adapted to the examination of light transmitted by very small specimens (as a single organic cell) — **mi·cro·spectrophotometric** \"+\ *adj* — **mi·cro·spectrophotometry** \"+\ *n*

**mi·cro·spectroscope** \"+\ *n* [*micr-* + *spectroscope*] **:** a spectroscope arranged for attachment to a microscope for observation of the spectrum of light from minute portions of an object — **mi·cro·spectroscopic** \"+\ *adj* — **mi·cro·spectros·copy** \"+\ *n*

**mi·cro·sper·mae** \,==¦spər(,)mē\ [NL, fr. *micr-* + *-spermae*] *syn of* ORCHIDALES

**mi·cro·sper·mop·ter·is** \-(,)spər'mäptərəs\ *n, cap* [NL, fr. *micr-* + *sperm-* + *-pteris*] **:** a genus of Carboniferous seed ferns exhibiting features in common with the genera *Lyginopteris* and *Heterangium* and being of special interest because of the evidence it provides concerning the origin of seed plants from the Psilophytales

**mi·cro·sphae·ra** \-'sfirə\ *n, cap* [NL, fr. *micr-* + *-sphaera*] **:** a genus of powdery mildews (family Erysiphaceae) having several asci in each perithecium and the appendages once or more dichotomously branched — see LILAC MILDEW

**mi·cro·sphere** \'mīkrə,-\ *n* [*micr-* + *sphere*] **:** a very small primordial shell of the asexual individuals of various dimorphic Foraminifera — **mi·cro·spher·ic** \-¦sfirik, -fer-\ *adj*

**mi·cro·splanchnic** \¦mīkrō+\ *adj* [ISV *micr-* + *splanchnic;* orig. formed as It *microsplancnico*] **:** ECTOMORPHIC — opposed to *macrosplanchnic;* compare NORMOSPLANCHNIC

**mi·cro·spo·range** \¦mīkrōspə¦ranj, -krə¦spōr,anj\ *n* [NL *microsporangium*] **:** MICROSPORANGIUM

**mi·cro·sporangium** \¦mīkrō+\ *n* [NL, fr. *micr-* + *sporangium*] **:** a sporangium bearing microspores (as the pollen sac of the anther in a seed plant) — compare MEGASPORANGIUM

**mi·cro·spore** \'mīkrə+,-\ *n* [ISV *micr-* + *spore*] **1 :** one of the spores of a heterosporous plant (as the pollen grain of a seed plant) that gives rise to male gametophytes and that is generally smaller than the megaspore **2 :** the smaller of two forms of spores produced by various protozoans (as Radiolaria) — **mi·cro·spor·ic** \¦==¦spōrik\ *or* **mi·cro·spor·ous** \¦==¦spōrəs,(')mī¦kräspərəs\ *adj*

**mi·cro·spo·rid·ia** \,mīkrəspə'ridēə\ *n pl, cap* [NL, fr. *micr-* + *-sporidia*] **:** an order of Cnidosporidia comprising protozoan parasites of arthropods and fishes that typically invade and destroy host cells — see NOSEMA — **mi·cro·spo·rid·i·an** \¦===¦ridēən\ *adj or n*

**mi·cro·spo·ri·di·da** \,==,spə'ridədə\ [NL, fr. *micr-* + *sporidium* + *-ida*] *syn of* MICROSPORIDIA

**mi·cro·spo·ro·cyte** \,=='spōrə,sīt\ *n* [*microspore* + *-o-* + *-cyte*] **:** a microspore mother cell

**mi·cro·spo·ro·gen·e·sis** \,==,==+\ *n* [NL, fr. *microsporo-* (fr. ISV *microspore*) + L *genesis*] **:** the formation and maturation of a microspore — compare MEGASPOROGENESIS

**mi·cros·po·ron** \mī'kräspə,rän\ *syn of* MICROSPORUM

**mi·cro·sporophyll** \¦mīkrō+\ *n* [*micr-* + *sporophyll*] **:** a sporophyll (as a stamen) bearing microsporangia

**mi·cro·spo·ro·sis** \,mīkrə,spə'rōsəs\ *n, pl* **microsporo·ses** \-,sēz\ [NL, fr. *Microsporum* + *-osis*] **:** ringworm caused by fungi of the genus *Microsporum* — compare TINEA CAPITIS

**mi·cros·po·rum** \mī'kräspərəm\ *n, cap* [NL, fr. *micr-* + *-sporum* (fr. Gk *spora* seed) — more at SPORE] **:** a genus of fungi (family Moniliaceae) producing both small, nearly oval single-celled spores and large spindle-shaped multicellular spores with a usu. rough outer wall — see RINGWORM

**mi·cro·sthene** \'mīkrəs,thēn\ *n* -S [NL *Microsthenes*] **:** one of the Microsthenes

**mi·cros·the·nes** \mī'krästhə(,)nēz\ *n pl, cap* [NL, fr. *micr-* + *-sthenes* (fr. Gk *sthenos* strength) — more at ASTHEN-] *in former classifications* **:** a division of eutherian mammals approximately equal to the orders Insectivora, Chiroptera, Rodentia, and Edentata — **microsthenic** *adj*

**mi·cro·stoma·tous** \¦mīkrə¦stäməd·əs, -stōm-\ *adj* [*micr-* + *-stomatous*] **:** having a small mouth ⟨a ~ shell⟩

**mi·cro·stome** \'mīkrə,stōm\ *n* -S [*micr-* + *-stome*] **:** a small orifice

**mi·cro·sto·mia** \,==¦stōmēə\ *also* **mi·cros·to·mus** \mī'krästəməs\ *n, pl* **microstomi·as** \-tōmēəz\ *also* **microsto·mi** \-tə,mī\ [NL, fr. *micr-* + *-stomia* or *-stomus*] **:** an abnormally small mouth

**mi·cros·to·mous** \(')mī¦krästəməs\ *adj* [*micr-* + *-stomous*] **:** MICROSTOMATOUS

**mi·cro·strongyle** \¦mīkrō+\ *n* [*micr-* + *strongyle*] **:** a microsclere having the form of a strongyle

**mi·cro·structural** \"+\ *adj* **:** of or relating to microstructure

**mi·cro·structure** \"+\ *n* [ISV *micr-* + *structure*] **:** the structure of a material (as an alloy or other crystalline mass) on a minute scale as revealed by the microscope or other means

**mi·cro·sty·lous** \¦==¦stīləs\ *adj* [*micr-* + *-stylous*] *of a flower* **:** having short styles; *specif* **:** having short styles and long filaments — compare MACROSTYLOUS, MESOSTYLOUS

**mi·cro·sublimation** \"+\ *n* [*micr-* + *sublimation*] **:** sublimation of a minute quantity of a material for microscopic examination

**mi·cro·switch** \'mīkrə+,-\ *n* [*micr-* + *switch*] **:** a small and highly sensitive switch in which minute motion establishes contact and which is used esp. in automatic-control devices

**mi·cro·symbiote** \¦mīkrō+\ *n* [*micr-* + *symbiote*] **:** a microorganism living in symbiosis with a more advanced organism ⟨the ~s of many insects⟩ — compare MYCETOCYTE

**mi·cro·technic** \"+\ *or* **mi·cro·technique** \"+\ *n* [ISV *micr-* + *technic* or *technique*] **:** microscopic technic **:** MICROLOGY

**mi·cro·text** \'mīkrə+,-\ *n* [*micr-* + *text*] **:** a microfilmed or microphotographed text

**mi·cro·thel·y·phon·i·da** \,mīkrō,thelē'fänədə\ *n pl, cap* [NL, fr. *micr-* + *Thelyphonus* genus of whip scorpions + *-ida* — more at THELYPHONIDAE] **:** an order of Arachnida including minute arthropods with a whiplash at the tip of the abdomen

**mi·cro·therm** \'mīkrə,thərm\ *n* [ISV *micr-* + *-therm*] **:** a plant requiring a mean annual temperature between 0° and 14° C for full growth — compare MEGATHERM, MESOTHERM — **mi·cro·ther·mic** \¦==¦thərmik\ *adj*

**mi·cro·thermal** \¦==+\ *adj* [*micr-* + *thermal*] **:** of, involving, or relating to very small quantities of heat or changes of temperature ⟨~ measurements⟩

**mi·cro·thorax** \¦mīkrō+\ *n* [NL, fr. *micr-* + *thorax*] **:** a membranous section in the neck region of an insect consisting of a number of small sclerites

**mi·cro·thy·ri·a·ce·ae** \,mīkrə,thīrē'āsē,ē\ *n pl, cap* [NL, fr. *Microthyrium*, type genus (fr. *micr-* + Gk *thyrion*, dim. of *thyra* door) + *-aceae* — more at DOOR] **:** a family of ascomycetous fungi (order Microthyriales) with shield-shaped or radiate perithecia

**mi·cro·thy·ri·a·les** \-'ā(,)lēz\ *n pl, cap* [NL, fr. *Microthyrium* + *-ales*] **:** an order of fungi (subclass Euascomycetes) that have peltate fructifications and develop asci on ascogenous hyphae arising from the pseudoparenchymatous stroma

**mi·crot·i·dae** \mī'kräd·ə,dē\ [NL, fr. *Microtus* + *-idae*] *syn of* CRICETIDAE

**mi·cro·time** \'mīkrə+,-\ *n* [*micr-* + *time*] **:** a very short interval of time (as 0.01 millionth of a second) ⟨~ photography⟩

**mi·cro·titration** \¦mī(,)krō+\ *n* [*micr-* + *titration*] **:** microanalytical titration

**¹mi·cro·tome** \'mīkrə,tōm\ *n* -S [ISV *micr-* + *-tome*] **:** an instrument for cutting sections (as of organic tissues) for microscopic examination

**²microtome** \"\ *vt* -ED/-ING/-S **:** to cut in sections with a microtome

**mi·cro·tomic** \¦==¦tämik\ *also* **mi·cro·tom·i·cal** \-məkəl\ *adj* [*microtome* + *-ic* or *-ical*] **:** of or relating to the microtome or microtomy **:** that cuts thin slices

**mi·crot·o·my** \mī'kräd·əmē\ *n* -ES [*microtome* + *-y*] **:** the technique of using the microtome or of preparing with its aid objects for microscopic study

**mi·cro·ton·al** \¦mīkrə¦tōnᵊl\ *adj* [*microtone* + *-al*] **:** relating to or characterized by music containing microtones — **mi·cro·ton·al·ly** \-ᵊlē\ *adv*

**mi·cro·to·nal·i·ty** \-tō'naləd·ē\ *n* [*microtonal* + *-ity*] **:** the quality or state of being microtonal

**mi·cro·tone** \'mīkrə+,-\ *n* [*micr-* + *tone*] **:** a musical interval smaller than a half tone

**mi·cro·trich·i·um** \,==¦trikēəm\ *n, pl* **microtrich·ia** \-ēə\ [NL, fr. *micr-* + Gk *trich-, thrix* hair + NL *-ium* — more at TRICHINA] **:** one of the minute fixed hairs on the integument (as the wings) of various insects — compare MACROTRICHIUM

**mi·cro·tron** \'mīkrə,trän\ *n* -S [*micr-* + *-tron*] **:** a device for accelerating electrons in the same manner as the cyclotron accelerates heavier particles

**mi·cro·tus** \mī'krōd·əs\ *n, cap* [NL, fr. *micr-* + *-otus* (fr. Gk *ōt-, ous* ear) — more at EAR] **:** a genus of myomorph rodents (family Cricetidae) comprising the voles of the northern hemisphere

**mi·cro·tylote** \¦mīkrō+\ *n* [*micr-* + *tylote*] **:** a microsclere having the form of a tylote

**mi·cro·type** \'mīkrə+,-\ *n* [*micr-* + *type*] **:** MICROSPECIES — **mi·cro·typical** \¦==+\ *adj*

**mi·cro·volt** \"+,-\ *n* [ISV *micr-* + *volt*] **:** one millionth of a volt

**mi·cro·watt** \"+,-\ *n* [*micr-* + *watt*] **:** one millionth of a watt

**¹mi·cro·wave** \"+,-\ *n* [*micr-* + *wave*] **:** a very short electromagnetic wave: as **a :** a wave of less than ten meters in wavelength **b :** a wave between 100 centimeters and one centimeter in wavelength

**²microwave** \"\ *vt* **:** to transmit by means of microwaves

**microwave relay** *n* **:** a combination of receiving, amplifying, and transmitting equipment that is used to pick up, amplify, and retransmit a microwave signal

**microwave spectroscope** *n* **:** an apparatus for observing and measuring the absorption of different substances for microwaves as a function of wavelength and thus obtaining the microwave spectra of the substances — **microwave spectroscopy** *n*

**microwave spectrum** *n* **:** an absorption spectrum in the microwave wavelength range; *esp* **:** one in the range between about 15 centimeters and 0.25 centimeters

**mi·crox·ea** \mī'kräksēə\ *n* [NL, fr. *micr-* + *oxea*] **:** a microsclere having the form of an oxea

**¹mi·cro·zo·an** \¦mīkrə¦zōən\ *or* **mi·cro·zo·ic** \-ik\ *adj* [NL *microzoa* + E *-an* or *-ic*] **:** of or relating to the microzoa

**²microzoan** \"\ *n* -S **:** MICROZOON 1

**mi·cro·zooid** \¦==+\ *n* [*micr-* + *zooid*] **:** a minute free-swimming individual supposed to be budded from the megazooid of various higher ciliates

**mi·cro·zo·on** \,==¦zō,än\ *n, pl* **micro·zoa** \-'zōə\ [NL, fr. *micr-* + *-zoon*] **1 :** a microscopic animal; *esp* **:** PROTOZOAN **2** *microzoa pl, sometimes cap* **:** microscopic animal life

**mi·cro·zoospore** \¦mīkrō+\ *n* [*micr-* + *zoospore*] **:** a small zoospore — compare MACROZOOSPORE

**mi·crur·gi·cal** \(')mī¦krərjəkəl\ *or* **mi·crur·gic** \-jik\ *adj* [*micrurgy* + *-ical* or *-ic*] **:** of or relating to micrurgy

**mi·crur·gist** \'=(,)=jəst\ *n* -S [*micrurgy* + *-ist*] **:** a specialist in micrurgy

**mi·crur·gy** \-jē\ *n* -ES [ISV *micr-* + *-urgy*] **:** MICROMANIPULATION; *broadly* **:** the practice of using minute tools in a magnified field

**mi·cru·ri·dae** \mī'krůrə,dē\ [NL, fr. *Micrurus* + *-idae*] *syn of* ELAPIDAE

**mi·cru·rus** \-rəs\ *n, cap* [NL, fr. *micr-* + *-urus*] **:** a genus of small venomous elapid snakes comprising the American coral snakes

**mic·tic** \'miktik\ *adj* [Gk *miktos* mixed (verbal of *mignynai* to mix) + E *-ic* — more at MIX] **1 :** requiring, involving, or produced by sexual reproduction or union of germ cells **:** exhibiting mixis **2 a** *of a female rotifer* **:** producing eggs that without fertilization develop into males or with fertilization form resting eggs that later develop into amictic females **b :** being or relating to the egg of such a female

**mic·tion** \-kshən\ *n* -S [LL *miction-, mictio*, fr. L *mictus* (past part. of *meiere* to urinate) + *-ion-, -io* -ion] **:** URINATION

**mic·tu·rate** \'mikchə,rāt, *usu* -ād.+V\ *vi* -ED/-ING/-S [L *micturire* + E *-ate*] **:** URINATE

**mic·tu·ri·tion** \,==¦rishən\ *n* -S [prob. fr. (assumed) NL *micturition-, micturitio*, fr. (assumed) L *micturitus* (past part. of L *micturire* to urinate, want to urinate, fr. *mictus*, past part. of *meiere* to urinate) + L *-ion-, -io* -ion — more at MIXEN] **:** URINATION

**¹mid** \'mid\ *adj* [ME *mid, midde*, fr. OE *midd, midde;* akin to OHG *mitti* mid, middle, ON *mithr*, Goth *midjis*, L *medius*, Gk *mesos*, Skt *madhya*] **1 :** being the part in the middle or midst ⟨in ~ ocean⟩ — often used in combination ⟨*mid*-August⟩ ⟨*mid*-1950s⟩ ⟨*mid*-Renaissance⟩ **2 :** occupying a middle position **:** MIDDLE 1a ⟨the ~ finger⟩ — often used in combination ⟨*mid*-incisor⟩ ⟨*mid*-pillar⟩ **3** *of a vowel* **:** articulated with the arch of the tongue midway between its highest and its lowest elevation — compare CLOSE, OPEN

**²mid** \"\ *n* -S [ME *mid, midde*, fr. *mid, midde*, adj.] *archaic* **:** MIDDLE

**³mid** \"\ *adv* [ME *mid, midde*, fr. *mid, midde*, adj.] **:** in the middle

**⁴mid** \"\ *prep* [by shortening] **:** AMID

**⁵mid** \"\ *n* -S [by shortening] **:** MIDSHIPMAN

**mid** *abbr* **1** middle **2** midland **3** midnight **4** midshipman

**MID** *abbr* **1** military intelligence department **2** military intelligence division **3** minimum infective dose

**midafternoon** \'=¦==\ *n* **:** the middle part of the afternoon

**mid-age** \'=,=\ *n* [ME *myd-age*, fr. *myd, mid, midde* mid + *age*] **:** MIDDLE AGE

**mid-aged** \'=¦=\ *adj* **:** MIDDLE-AGED

**midair** \'=¦=\ *n* **1** *obs* **:** the intermediate of the three regions into which the air was formerly distinguished including the level of the clouds **2 :** any point or region in the air not immediately adjacent to the ground or other solid or liquid surface beneath it ⟨colliding in ~⟩ ⟨hovering in ~⟩ ⟨suspended in ~⟩ ⟨sat staring at ~ —Charles Dickens⟩

**mid-american** \¦=¦===\ *adj, sometimes cap M & usu cap A* **:** of, relating to, or characteristic of the central section of the U.S. or its inhabitants

**mi·das** \'mīdəs\ [NL, after *Midas* legendary king of Phrygia whose touch turned everything to gold and whose ears were turned by Apollo into ass's ears, fr. L, fr. Gk] *syn of* LEONTOCEBUS

**midas fly** *var of* MYDAS FLY

**mi·das's-ear** \'mīdəsə¦i(ə)r\ *n, pl* **midas's-ears** *usu cap* [after King *Midas*] **:** an Old World snail (*Ellobium aurismidae*)

**midas touch** *n, usu cap M* [after King *Midas*] **:** the talent for making wealth out of any activity one turns one's hands to

**mid-back** \'=¦=\ *adj, of a vowel* **:** articulated with the tongue arched at the back midway between its highest and its lowest elevation

**midbrain** \'=,=\ *n* **1 :** the middle division of the embryonic vertebrate brain that gives rise to the corpora quadrigemina, cerebral peduncles, and tegmentum and encloses the aqueduct of Sylvius **2 :** the parts of the definitive brain that develop from the embryonic midbrain

**midcapacity** \'=¦===\ *n* **:** the pulmonary volume when the lungs are in the state of contraction characteristic of the end of a normal quiet exhalation equal to the sum of the volumes occupied by the residual air, supplemental air, and dead space

**mid-carpal** \'=¦==\ *adj* **:** being between the proximal and distal carpals — used esp. of an anatomical articulation

**mid-central** \'=¦==\ *adj, of a vowel* **:** articulated with the tongue arched in the middle midway between its highest and its lowest elevation

**mid·day** \'mid¦dā\ *n* [ME, fr. OE *middæg*, fr. *midde* mid + *dæg* day — more at MID, DAY] **1 :** the middle part of the day **:** NOON **2 :** SEXT 1

**mid·den** \'midᵊn\ *n* -S [ME *midding*, of Scand origin; akin to Dan *mødding, møgdynge* dunghill, fr. *mög* dung, muck + *dynge* heap; akin to ON *myki* dung and to ON *dyngja* manure pile — more at MUCUS, DUNG] **1 :** DUNGHILL **2 a :** an accumulation of refuse about a dwelling place **:** a refuse heap **b :** KITCHEN MIDDEN **3 :** one of the masses of highly organic soil deposited by an earthworm about its burrow; *sometimes* **:** organic debris left on the soil by various other animals

**middenhead** \'==,=\ *n, Brit* **:** the top of a dunghill

**middenstead** \'==,=\ *n* **1** *Brit* **:** the site of a dunghill **:** LAYSTALL **2** *Brit* **:** DUNGHILL

**¹mid·dest** \'midəst\ *adj* [¹*mid* + *-est*] *archaic* **:** MIDMOST

**²middest** *obs var of* MIDST

**middie** *var of* MIDDY

**¹mid·dle** \'midᵊl\ *adj* [ME *middel*, fr. OE; akin to OFris *middel* middle, OS *middil*, OHG *mittil* middle, ON *methal* among, between, OE *midde* mid — more at MID] **1 a :** equally distant (as reckoned by number, space, or other particular) from the extremes **:** MEAN ⟨lived in the ~ house in a row⟩ ⟨a ~ rank in life⟩ ⟨the ~ portion⟩ **b :** halfway between the bid and asked prices ⟨the ~ price⟩ ⟨87 ~⟩ — used of prices on the London stock exchange **2** *archaic* **:** constituting or occupying the middle ⟨through ~ empire of the freezing air —John Milton⟩ **3 a :** being at neither extreme **:** INTERMEDIATE, INTERVENING ⟨filled up the ~ space⟩ ⟨of ~ size⟩ ⟨a ~ opinion⟩ ⟨a ~ line of action⟩ **b** *archaic* **:** acting as an intermediary **4 :** of middle size or volume — now used only of wool of medium-length staple **5** *archaic* **:** being the middle part of **:** MID 1 **6 a :** constituting a division intermediate between those prior and later or upper and lower ⟨the ~ ages⟩ ⟨*Middle* Jurassic⟩ ⟨*Middle* Paleozoic⟩ **b** *usu cap* **:** constituting a period of a language or literature that is intermediate between a period called *Old* and a period called *New* or *Modern* ⟨~ English⟩ ⟨~ High German⟩ **c** *of management* **:** responsible for the administration and supervision of policies and practices — distinguished from *top* **7** *of a verb form or voice* **:** typically asserting that the person or thing represented by the grammatical subject both performs and is subjected to or affected by the action represented by the verb ⟨Greek *louomai* "I wash myself" is in the ~ voice⟩ — used esp. in the grammar of Greek and Sanskrit; compare ACTIVE **8** *of a mute in ancient Greek* **:** MEDIAL **9** *usu cap* **:** of or relating to the earliest known culture of Mexico

**²middle** \"\ *n* -S [ME *middel*, fr. OE, fr. *middel*, adj.] **1 a :** a portion or part separated by equal or approximately equal substantial distances from the ends or the opposite sides (as of a line, surface, solid) or from the limits of anything regarded as extending between two extremities (as a period of time, an event, process, or condition continuing over a certain period of time, a series, or a range or compass) ⟨the ~ of the street was unpaved⟩ ⟨apples from the ~ of the barrel⟩ ⟨rain during the ~ of April⟩ ⟨the ~ of the war⟩ ⟨a voice strong in the ~⟩ ⟨in the ~ of the social scale⟩ ⟨the beginning, ~, and end of a list —R.S.Woodworth⟩ **b :** a midpoint (as of a line), median line (as of a surface), or median plane (as of a solid) or a point (as in time or other measurable entity) midway between two limits ⟨a sheet of paper folded down the ~⟩ **c :** all except the two terminal segments or units of something consisting of a series of segments or units **:** INTERIOR ⟨remove a link from the ~ of the chain⟩ ⟨the small circle joins easily to other consonant strokes at the beginning, in the ~, or at the end of a word —*New Standard Course in Pitman Shorthand*⟩

2 : an area or space at or near the center and separated by substantial distances from the exterior limits (as of a larger area or space) : central part ⟨a small bird . . . which they release . . . in the ~ of their fields —J.G.Frazer⟩ 3 : the position of being among or surrounded by others : MIDST 2 4 : the mid-part of the human body : WAIST 5 : something intermediate between extremes ⟨in this, as in most questions of state, there is a ~ —Edmund Burke⟩ 6 a : a range of points of view held or of policies advocated or practiced (as in the realm of politics) intermediate between those points of view and policies commonly regarded as reactionary and conservative and those commonly regarded as liberal and radical b : those persons or groups (as political parties) collectively that hold points of view or advocate or practice policies that fall in such a middle 7 : the body proper of an animal; *specif* : either of the pieces forming a dressed side between the shoulder and rump or ham 8 : the large intestine of beef used as casing for bologna 9 *chiefly South* : the strip or ridge of earth left between two rows of a crop (as corn or cotton) during the growing season 10 : the middle voice of a verb or a form in this voice 11 : MIDDLE TERM 12 : MIDDLE GROUND 1 13 **middles** *pl but sometimes sing in constr* : usu. low-grade material forming the middle or internal layer or layers of pasteboard or combination board 14 : the guard covering the middle stump in cricket 15 *Canadian football* : TACKLE 16 : MIDDLE ARTICLE 17 : MIDDLEWEIGHT **syn** see CENTER — **in the middle** *adv (or adj)* : in a position between two sources of difficulty : in a tight spot ⟨whatever you do, you're sure to be caught *in the middle*⟩ — **in the middle of 1** : during ⟨interrupted *in the middle of* his speech⟩ 2 : deeply involved in : in the thick of ⟨whose father was *in the* very *middle of* the Boulangist movement —Arnold Bennett⟩

[3]**middle** \"\ *vt* **middled; middled; middling** \-d(ə)liŋ\ **middles 1** : to put in the middle 2 *naut* : to fold in the middle : DOUBLE ⟨~ a hawser⟩ ⟨~ a sail⟩ — **middle the cable** : to let out the cables of a ship having two anchors out in such a way as to have the same amount of cable to each anchor

**middle age** *n* [ME *middel age*] : the period of life between youth and old age ⟨that increasingly elastic expanse called *middle age* —Harrison Smith⟩

**middle-age** \ˈ==ˈ=\ *adj* 1 [fr. the *middle age* or the *middle ages* (trans. of NL *Medium Aevum*), the period of European history from about A.D. 500 to about 1500] : MEDIEVAL 2 [*middle age*] : MIDDLE-AGED

**middle-aged** \ˈ==ˈ=\ *adj* 1 a : being at an age beyond youth and below old age b : of, relating to, or characteristic of middle-aged persons ⟨*middle-aged* love —Michael Arlen⟩ 2 a *of a thing* : having existed longer than things of the same type and group commonly or conventionally regarded as new b : of, relating to, or characteristic of such things 3 [the *middle age* + E *-ed*] *obs* : MEDIEVAL — **mid·dle-aged·ly** \ˈ==ˈājədlē, -jd-\ *adv* — **mid·dle-aged·ness** \-jədnəs, -j(d)n-\ *n* -ES

**mid·dle-ag·er** \ˈ==ˈājə(r)\ *n* [*middle age* + *-er*] : one that is middle-aged

**mid·dle-ag·ing** \ˈ==ˈājiŋ\ *adj* [*middle age* + *-ing*] : entering upon middle age

**middle-aisle** \ˈ==ˈ=\ *vt* **middle-aisled; middle-aisled; middle-aisling; middle-aisles** [so called fr. the traditional bridal procession down the middle aisle of a church] *slang* : MARRY — usu. used with *it* ⟨are expected to *middle-aisle* it in August⟩

**middle american** *adj, usu cap M&A* [*Middle America*, the region including Mexico, Central America, and sometimes the Caribbean islands + E *-an*] : of or relating to Middle America

**middle americanist** *n, usu cap M&A* : a specialist in Middle American studies

**middle and leg** *n* : the guard covering the middle and leg stumps in cricket

**middle and off** *n* : the guard covering the middle and off stumps in cricket

**middle angle** *n* : THIRD ANGLE

**middle article** *n, Brit* : a popular or light literary essay or article of less immediate current significance than an editorial printed in or suitable for printing in a newspaper or weekly

**middle assyrian** *adj, usu cap M&A* : of, relating to, or characteristic of the middle period of the Assyrian civilization

**middle babylonian** *n, usu cap M&B* : the dialect of Akkadian used in Babylonia between 2000 and 1500 B.C.

**middle base point** *n* : the lower middle part of the field of an escutcheon — see POINT illustration

**middle belt** *n, usu cap M&B* [fr. *Middle Belt*, the central section of the area where tobacco is grown in the U. S., consisting principally of the Piedmont area of Va. and No. Car.] : a flue-cured tobacco produced in No. Carolina

**middle body** *n* : the part of a ship's body amidships having a uniform or nearly uniform cross section — compare AFTERBODY, FOREBODY

**middlebreaker** \ˈ==ˌ==\ *n* : LISTER 1

[1]**middlebrow** \ˈ==ˌ=\ *n* [[1]*middle* + *brow*] 1 : a person who is moderately but not highly cultivated ⟨Mozart is everyone's tea, pleasing to highbrows, ~s and lowbrows alike —Rose Macaulay⟩ 2 : a person who possesses or has pretensions to intellectual interests but who dislikes works of art and literature that are original or unconventional in nature or that require effort for comprehension : PHILISTINE ⟨the ~s have become more intransigent in their opposition to everything that is serious and creative in our culture —Irving Howe⟩

[2]**middlebrow** \"\ *adj* : of, relating to, characteristic of, or suitable for a middlebrow ⟨the safe and comforting patterns of ~ feeling —Irving Howe⟩ ⟨~ culture attacks distinctions as such and insinuates itself everywhere, devaluating the precious, infecting the healthy, corrupting the honest, and stultifying the wise —Clement Greenberg⟩

**middlebrowed** \ˈ==ˈ=\ *adj* : MIDDLEBROW

**mid·dle·brow·ism** \ˈmidəlˌbrau̇ˌizəm\ *n* -S : the state of mind or quality of culture characteristic of a middlebrow

**middle brunswick green** *n, often cap B* : a green that is duller and slightly yellower than holly green (sense 1), bluer, stronger, and slightly lighter than deep chrome green, yellower than average hunter green, and yellower, lighter, and stronger than deep Brunswick green

**middle-burster** \ˈ==ˌ==\ *n* : LISTER 1

**middlebuster** \ˈ==ˌ==\ *n* : LISTER 1

**middle C** *n* 1 : the musical note or tone *c′* — see PITCH illustration 2 : the key of a keyboard sounding *c′*

**middle chief point** *n* : the upper middle part of the field of an escutcheon — called also *chief point;* see POINT illustration

**middle chrome yellow** *n* : DEEP CHROME YELLOW

**middle class** *n* 1 : a social class occupying a position between the upper class and the lower class: as a : a class achieving prominence in modern times during the transition from a medieval to a modern economy and constituting a grouping of people (as artisans, independent farmers, tradesmen, and lesser officials) between the hereditary nobility on the one hand and the laborers and peasants on the other b : a class occupying a position (as in England) between the aristocracy and the working class c : a fluid heterogeneous socio-economic grouping (as in the U. S.) having a status intermediate between the upper and lower classes and composed principally of business and professional people, bureaucrats, and some farmers and skilled workers sharing common social characteristics and values 2 **middle classes** *pl* : an aggregate of social groupings that includes the upper middle class and the lower middle class

**middle-class** \ˈ==ˈ=\ *adj* [*middle class*] 1 : of or relating to the middle class ⟨his unrecognized claim to *middle-class* status —Ray Gold⟩ ⟨the traditional *middle-class* basis of American politics —Samuel Lubell⟩ ⟨*middle-class* women attach more importance to social approval —P.M.Gregory⟩ 2 : belonging to or associated with the middle class and its possession of or inclination toward a diversified social morality that includes such traits as a desire for stability and a high material standard of living, a respect for convention and the proprieties, and high ideals of education, professional competence, and personal ambition ⟨a proper air of *middle-class* gentility —Gene Baro⟩ ⟨her rebellion against *middle-class* conventions —*Current Biog.*⟩ ⟨live up to *middle-class* standards of cleanliness —T.M.Newcomb⟩ — compare LOWER-CLASS, UPPER-CLASS

**mid·dled** \ˈmidəld\ *adj* [[2]*middle* + *-ed*] *of an animal* : having a middle or middles — used with a qualifying term ⟨a trim ~ lamb⟩

**middle distance** *n* 1 : a part of a pictorial representation or scene that is between the foreground and the background — called also *middle ground;* compare PERSPECTIVE 2 : any footrace distance from 400 meters and 440 yards to and sometimes including 1500 meters and one mile

**middle dutch** *n, cap M&D* : the Dutch in use from about 1100 to about 1500 — see INDO-EUROPEAN LANGUAGES table

**middle ear** *n* : the intermediate portion of the ear of higher vertebrates consisting typically of a small air-filled membrane-lined chamber in the temporal bone continuous with the nasopharynx through the eustachian tube, separated from the external ear by the tympanic membrane and from the inner ear by fenestrae, and containing a chain of three ossicles that extends from the tympanic membrane to the vestibular fenestra and transmits vibrations to the inner ear — compare INCUS, MALLEUS, STAPES

**middle-earth** \ˈ==ˌ=\ *n* [ME *middelerthe*, alter. (influenced by *erthe* earth) of *midelerde, middelert*, alter. (influenced by *middel* middle) of *middenerd*, fr. OE *middaneard*, alter. (influenced by *eard* region, dwelling-place) of *middangeard;* akin to OS *middilgard* middle-earth, OHG *mittilgart, mittingart*, ON *mithgarthr*, Goth *midjungards;* all fr. a prehistoric Gmc compound whose first constituent is akin to OE *midde* mid and whose second constituent is akin to OE *geard* yard, dwelling, land, world — more at MID, YARD] : the earth regarded as situated between the upper and lower regions or as occupying the center of the universe

**middle eastern** *adj, usu cap M&E* [*Middle East* + E *-ern* (as in *eastern*)] : of, relating to, or concerned with the Middle East — used orig. esp. of the region included in the Ottoman Empire but now usu. of southwestern Asia and northeastern Africa extending from Libya to Afghanistan or often from Morocco to Pakistan — compare FAR EASTERN, NEAR EASTERN

**middle egyptian** *n, cap M&E* : the language of Egypt under the 11th to 17th dynasties

**middle english** *n, cap M&E* : English as exhibited in manuscripts of the 12th to 15th centuries — distinguished from *Old English;* see INDO-EUROPEAN LANGUAGES table

**middle-erd** *n* [ME *midelerde, middelert* — more at MIDDLE-EARTH] *obs* : MIDDLE-EARTH

**middle-european** \ˈ==ˈ===\ *adj, usu cap M&E* [*Middle Europe* + E *-an* (as in European)] : of, relating to, or characteristic of Middle Europe — used of a vaguely defined region generally conceived of as comprising some or all of the countries east of France and west of the Soviet Union

**middle finger** *n* : the midmost of the five fingers of the hand

**middle french** *n, cap M&F* : French as exhibited in manuscripts of the 14th to 16th centuries — see INDO-EUROPEAN LANGUAGES table

**middle game** *n* : the middle phase of a board game; *specif* : the part of a chess game during which players work out combinations — compare END GAME, OPENING

**middle greek** *n, cap M&G* : the Greek language as used in the 7th to 15th centuries

middle finger

**middle ground** *n* 1 *naut* : a shoal in a fairway having a channel on either side 2 : MIDDLE DISTANCE 1 3 : a standpoint midway between extremes ⟨a *middle ground* between firmness and appeasement —*Wall Street Jour.*⟩ ⟨a characterless *middle ground* between the academic and the avant-garde —Sidney Alexander⟩

**middle-grounder** \ˈmidəlˈgrau̇ndə(r)\ *n* [*middle ground* + *-er*] : one that maintains a stand between extremes

**middlehand** \ˈ==ˌ=\ *n* [trans. of G *mittelhand*] : the second player in turn to bid in skat

**middle high german** *n, cap M&H&G* : the High German in use from 1100 to about 1500 — see INDO-EUROPEAN LANGUAGES table

**middle horde** *n, usu cap M&H* : a subdivision of the Kirghiz living chiefly in Turkestan and Tashkent

**middle indic** *n, cap M&I* : the Prakrit languages

**middle indo-aryan** *n, cap M&I&A* : PRAKRITS

**middle initial** *n* : the initial of a middle name

**middle iranian** *n, cap M&I* : the Iranian languages between the ancient and modern tongues comprising Middle Persian, Sogdian, and Sakian

**middle irish** *n, cap M&I* : the form of Irish employed between the 11th and 15th centuries — see INDO-EUROPEAN LANGUAGES table

**middle lamella** *n* : a layer of intercellular material that as seen by conventional staining and microscopic techniques lies between the apparent walls of adjacent plant cells

**middle latin** *n, cap M&L* : MEDIEVAL LATIN

**middle latitude** *n* : the latitude of the point situated midway on a north-and-south line between two parallels

**middle life** *n* 1 : MIDDLE AGE 2 *Brit* : the life lived by the middle classes

**middle low german** *n, cap M&L&G* : the Low German in use from about 1100 to about 1500 — see INDO-EUROPEAN LANGUAGES table

**mid·dle·man** \ˈmidəlˌman, -aa(ə)n\ *n, pl* **middlemen 1** *obs* : a soldier at the middle of a file 2 : one that adopts or follows a middle course 3 : an intermediary or agent between two parties (as in business dealings, management, administration, or negotiations): as a : a dealer or agent intermediate between the producer of goods and the retailer or consumer; *specif* : a person or business firm that performs functions or services in the transfer of title to goods in their flow from producers (as farmers and manufacturers) to industrial users and ultimate consumers — see AGENT MIDDLEMAN, MERCHANT MIDDLEMAN b : an intermediary between landlord and tenant (as for collection of rents or management of property) : BAILIFF c : an agent for one (as a professional entertainer or the owner of a patent or copyright) that seeks to sell services or an intangible commodity 4 : one leasing land in Ireland in large tracts and subletting it in small portions 5 : one that transmits ideas, cultural standards, or similar intangibles ⟨the perfect ~ for this new movement of ideas —Van Wyck Brooks⟩ ⟨a kind of ~ of taste between the experimenters and the general public —F.O.Matthiessen⟩ 6 : a performer in a minstrel show who occupies the middle seat

**mid·dle·man·ism** \-ˌmaˌnizəm, -ˌmaa-,-\ *n* -S : a system of using middlemen (as in business dealings)

**mid·dle·most** \ˈ==ˌmōst *also chiefly Brit* -ˌməst\ *adj* [ME *middelmast*, fr. *middel* middle + *-mast* -most] : being in the middle or nearest the middle : MIDMOST

**middle name** *n* 1 : a name between one's first name and surname; *esp* : the second of two forenames ⟨the use of *middle names* is a modern invention —Bruce Bliven b. 1889⟩ 2 : an associated or characteristic personification ⟨trouble is our *middle name* —Joseph Driscoll⟩

**middle of the road** 1 : a course of action or program for action midway between extremes 2 : a standpoint midway between extremes

**middle-of-the-road** \ˈ====ˈ=\ *adj* [*middle of the road*] 1 : following a course of action or advocating a program for action that is midway between extremes ⟨a *middle-of-the-road* government⟩ ⟨a *middle-of-the-road* candidate⟩ 2 : characterized by action or advocacy of action that is midway between extremes ⟨a *middle-of-the-road* course⟩ ⟨a *middle-of-the-road* political philosophy⟩ 3 : standing between extremes ⟨the paintings illustrated are mostly *middle-of-the-road* subject pictures —J.T.Soby⟩

**middle-of-the-road·er** \ˈ====ˈrōdə(r)\ *n* -S [*middle of the road* + *-er*] 1 : one that takes or advocates a course of action midway between extremes 2 : one that stands midway between extremes (as in opinions)

**middle oil** *n* : CARBOLIC OIL

**middle passage** *n, often cap M&P* : the middle part of the journey of a slave from Africa to America; *specif* : the trip across the Atlantic ocean ⟨half died on the way to the ships, and a quarter in the *Middle Passage* —G.S.Mitchell⟩

**middle path** *n, usu cap M&P* : the eightfold path of Buddhism regarded as a golden mean between self-indulgence and self-mortification — called also *middle way*

**middle persian** *n, cap M&P* : Persian between Old Persian and Modern Persian including chiefly Pahlavi and the language of Christian and Manichaean documents recently discovered in Chinese Turkestan

**middle piece** *n, zool* : the portion of a sperm cell that lies between the nucleus and the flagellum

**mid·dler** \ˈmidlə(r)\ *n* -S [[1]*middle* + *-er*] 1 *obs* : INTERAGENT, MEDIATOR 2 : one belonging to an intermediate group, division, or class: as a : a student in the second year class of a theological seminary having a three-year program b : a student in the second or third year class in some private secondary schools having a four-year course c : a student in a division in some private schools that corresponds approximately to the junior high school — compare MIDDLE SCHOOL 3 : a rolling-mill operator tending the middle set of rolls — called also *plateman*

**middle rail** *n* 1 : the rail of a door above the bottom rail 2 : a third rail of an electric railway when it is between the rails for the wheels

**middle-rate** \ˈ==ˈ=\ *adj* : MEDIOCRE

**middle-road** \ˈ==ˈ=\ *adj* : MIDDLE-OF-THE-ROAD — not often used predicatively ⟨a *middle-road* government⟩ ⟨*middle-road* policies⟩ ⟨a comparatively popular, *middle-road* jazz pianist —Bill Simon⟩

**middle-road·er** \ˈ==ˈrōdə(r)\ *n* -S : MIDDLE-OF-THE-ROADER

**middles** *pl of* MIDDLE, *pres 3d sing of* MIDDLE

**mid·dles·brough** \ˈmidəlzbrə\ *adj, usu cap* [fr. *Middlesbrough*, Eng.] : of or from the county borough of Middlesbrough, England : of the kind or style prevalent in Middlesbrough

**middle school** *n* 1 *obs* : a school in England intended esp. for children from middle-class families 2 : a school or a division in the school system in any of various foreign countries embracing class levels that correspond approximately to those of the American junior and senior high schools and in some countries also class levels that correspond approximately to the upper grades of the American elementary school 3 a : a division in some private schools embracing class levels that correspond approximately to those of the junior high school b : a school or a division in the school system in any of various foreign countries embracing class levels that correspond approximately to those of the American junior high school 4 : a division in some private or public schools embracing or approximately embracing the upper elementary grades

**middle scots** *n, cap M&S* 1 : the Scots language in use between the latter half of the 15th and the early decades of the 17th centuries 2 : the form of Scots spoken in central Scotland

**middle semitic** *n, cap M&S* : [2]CANAANITIC

**mid·dle·sex** \ˈmidəlˌseks\ *adj, usu cap* [fr. *Middlesex* county, Eng.] : of or from the county of Middlesex, England : of the kind or style prevalent in Middlesex

**middle-sized** \ˈ==ˈ=\ *adj* : of medium size ⟨the small and *middle-sized* powers made a little progress —*Time*⟩ — **middle-sized·ness** \ˈ==ˈsīzədnəs, -z(d)n-\ *n* -ES

**middlesplitter** \ˈ==ˌ==\ *n* : LISTER 1

**middle stone** *n* : HONEY 6

**middle stump** *n* : the stump between the leg stump and the off stump of a cricket wicket

**middle-temperature error** *n* : irregularity of rate in a watch or chronometer due to unequal progression of expansion and elasticity factors at average temperatures

**middle term** *n* : the term of a syllogism that occurs in both premises

**middle tint** *n* : a subdued or neutral tint or tone

**middletone** \ˈ==ˌ=\ *n* : HALFTONE

**middletown** \ˈ==ˌ=\ *n, usu cap* [fr. *Middletown*, arbitrary name given to a midwestern town studied in *Middletown — a Study in Contemporary American Culture* (1929) by Robert S. Lynd *b*1892 and Helen M. Lynd *b*1897 Amer. sociologists] : a community typically representative of middle-class American life and culture

**middle wall** *n* [ME *midelwalle*] : a partition wall

**middle watch** *n* : MIDWATCH

**middleway** \ˈ==ˈ=\ *adv* : MIDWAY, HALFWAY

**middle way** *n* 1 : a course of action, mode of conduct, or policy for action or conduct between two extremes: as a *usu cap M&W* : MIDDLE PATH b : a system of democratic economy between individualism and socialism 2 *obs* : the middle of one's way

**middleweight** \ˈ==ˌ=\ *n* : one of average weight: as a : a boxer weighing more than 147 but not over 160 pounds b : a wrestler weighing more than 158 but not over 174 pounds

**middle welsh** *n, cap M&W* : the Welsh in use from about 1150 to 1500

**middle west** *n, usu cap M&W* : MIDWEST

**middle western** *adj, often cap M&W* [*Middle West* + *-ern* (as in *western*)] : MIDWESTERN

**middle westerner** *n, usu cap M&W* : MIDWESTERNER

**middle white** *n* 1 *usu cap M&W* : a British breed of medium-sized white swine used esp. for production of small quick-maturing porkers — compare YORKSHIRE 2 *often cap M&W* : an animal of the Middle White breed

**middlewoman** \ˈ==ˌ==\ *n, pl* **middlewomen** *Brit* : a woman who acts as intermediary between homeworkers and a lace warehouse

[1]**mid·dling** \ˈmidliŋ, -lēŋ\ *adj* [ME (Sc) *mydlyn*, prob. fr. *mid, midde* mid + *-ling*] 1 : falling between two extremes : constituting a mean : INTERMEDIATE ⟨the extreme school of innovators had wanted a people's republic, not a national monarchy, and protested noisily against the ~ solution —Cecil Sprigge⟩ 2 : of middle, medium, or moderate size or degree ⟨the harbor was no wider than a ~ American river —Christopher Rand⟩ 3 a : of middle or medium quality : falling in a middle range of quality b : producing a yield (as of crops) or creating works (as of art or literature) falling in a middle range of quality or value ⟨the ~ lands —*Time*⟩ ⟨whether eventually I proved first-class or merely ~ — I should at least strive for consistent standards —Rex Ingamells⟩ 4 : MEDIOCRE, SECOND-RATE ⟨the ~ performance of a vulgar artist —Edmund Burke⟩ 5 *dial* a : in moderately good health b : not very well : in rather poor health 6 : of, relating to, or constituting a middle class

[2]**middling** \"\ *adv* : MODERATELY, RATHER, FAIRLY ⟨the extremely successful, the ~ successful, and the least successful —*New Yorker*⟩

[3]**middling** \"\ *n* -S 1 **middlings** *pl but sometimes sing in constr* a : the medium-sized particles separated in the sifting of ground grain b : a by-product of flour milling comprising several grades of granular particles containing different proportions of endosperm, bran, germ, and crude fiber and used as animal feed 2 a : FLITCH 1b b *or* **middling meat** *chiefly South & Midland* : SALT PORK — often used in pl. 3 : the basic grade of cotton on which market quotations are based 4 **middlings** *pl but sing or pl in constr* : a product of ore dressing intermediate between concentrate and tailings and containing enough of the valuable mineral to make re-treatment of it profitable 5 **middlings** *pl* : an inferior refined oil from petroleum

**mid·dling·ly** *adv* : INDIFFERENTLY, TOLERABLY ⟨I dare say I thought but ~ of them —Thomas Moore⟩

**middorsal** \ˈ=ˈ==\ *adj* : situated in the middle part or median line of the back

**mid·dy** *also* **mid·die** \ˈmidē, -di\ *n, pl* **middies** [by shortening and alter.] 1 : MIDSHIPMAN 2 *or* **middy blouse** : a loose overblouse with a sailor collar worn by women and children

**mi·de** *or* **mi·dé** \ˈmē(ˌ)dā\ *n* -S [Ojibwa *midē*] : MIDEWIWIN

**mid-earth** \ˈ=ˌ=\ *n* [[1]*mid* + *earth*] *archaic* : MIDDLE-EARTH

**mideastern** \ˈ=ˈ==\ *adj, usu cap* : MIDDLE EASTERN

**midevening** \ˈ=ˈ==\ *n* : the middle of the evening

middy 2

**mi·de·wi·win** \məˈdāwəˌwin\ *also* **mi·de·win** \məˈdāˌwin\ *n* -S [Ojibwa *midēwiwin*] : a once powerful secret society among the Ojibwa and neighboring Indians which aimed at the prolongation of life by herbal, magical, and ritual techniques

**midfeather** \ˈ=,==\ *n* [ˈ*mid* + *feather* (projecting strip)] **:** a longitudinal partition or division: as **a :** a brick partition wall in a salt furnace **b :** a vertical baffle in a beater or other papermaking machine of similar function **c :** a support between adjacent mine tunnels

**midfield** \ˈ=,=\ *n* **1 :** the middle portion of a field; *esp* **:** the middle portion of the field on which any of various sports (as football and lacrosse) is played **2 :** the second attack, center, and second defense of a lacrosse team

**mid·field·er** \ˈmid,fēldə(r)\ *n* **:** a member of the midfield of a lacrosse team

**mid–front** \ˈ=ˈ=\ *adj, of a vowel* **:** articulated with the tongue arched at the front midway between its highest and its lowest elevation

**midge** \ˈmij\ *n* -s [ME *migge*, fr. OE *mycg*; akin to OS *myggia* midge, OHG *mucka*, ON *mȳ* midge, Gk *myia* fly, L *musca*, OSlav *mucha*] **1 :** any of numerous tiny two-winged flies chiefly of the families Ceratopogonidae, Cecidomyiidae, and Chironomidae, many of which are capable of giving painful bites and some of which are vectors or intermediate hosts of parasites of man and various other vertebrates — compare BITING MIDGE **2 a :** a diminutive person **b :** a very small fish

**1midg·et** \ˈmijət, *usu* -əd·+V\ *n* -s [*midge* + *-et*] **1 :** BITING MIDGE, PUNKIE **2 :** a very small person; *specif* **:** a person of unusually small size who is physically well-proportioned — compare DWARF 1a **3 :** any creature or thing that is much smaller than the usual, the typical, or the average for its kind ⟨a ~ among the industries in its field⟩ ⟨all squids live in the sea, and there are many species of diverse forms and sizes from ~s to the giant squid —R.E.Coker⟩ **4 :** a member of a midget variety, type, or arbitrarily defined class: as **a :** a racing automobile of a class restricted to vehicles substantially smaller and lighter and of less piston displacement than standard automobiles **b :** MIDGET SUBMARINE

**2midget** \ˈ"\ *adj* **1 :** much smaller than the usual or the typical **:** MINIATURE, DIMINUTIVE ⟨the ~ nation of Andorra⟩ ⟨a miniature locomotive with ~ cars —W.L.Gresham⟩ **2 a :** belonging to a variety or type whose members are conspicuously smaller than what are regarded as the typical, normal, or standard or to an arbitrarily defined class in which the maximum permitted size is considerably less than the size that is usual or typical when no maximum is imposed ⟨~ beans⟩ ⟨~ racing auto⟩ ⟨a race for ~ planes⟩ **b :** of, relating to, or constituting an organization or an activity (as an organized sport) for children who are usu. the youngest eligible to belong or the smallest or lightest eligible to participate ⟨~ football⟩ ⟨*midget*-league baseball⟩

**midget golf** *n* **:** MINIATURE GOLF

**midg·et·ism** \-jəd·,izəm\ *n* -s **:** the state of being a midget

**midget submarine** *n* **:** a small submarine usu. having a crew of only two and carrying a single torpedo for use in surprise attacks

**midgrass** \ˈ=,=\ *n* **:** any of various grasses that are characterized by moderate stature, form the dominant feature of undisturbed prairie, and include the majority of economically important forage grasses of temperate regions — compare SHORTGRASS

**mid–gray** \ˈ=,=\ *n* **:** MEDIAN GRAY

**midgut** \ˈ=,=\ *n* **1 :** the middle part of the alimentary canal of a vertebrate embryo between the foregut and hindgut **2 :** the mesodermal intermediate part of the intestine of an invertebrate animal

**midheaven** \ˈ=ˈ==\ *n* **1** *archaic* **:** the point of the ecliptic on the meridian **2 :** the middle part of the sky **3 :** the midst of heaven

**1mid·i·an·ite** \ˈmidēə,nīt\ *n* -s *usu cap* [*Midian*, son of Abraham and Keturah (Gen 25:2), the eponymous ancestor of the Midianites + E *-ite*] **:** a member of an ancient northern Arabian tribe mentioned in the Bible

**2midianite** \ˈ"\ *adj, usu cap* **:** of, relating to, or characteristic of the Midianites

**mid·i·an·it·ish** \-īd·ish\ *adj, usu cap* [ˈ*Midianite* + *-ish*] **:** MIDIANITE

**mid·i·dae** \ˈmidə,dē\ [NL, fr. *Midas* + *-idae*] *syn of* CALLITHRICIDAE

**mid·i·nette** \,midᵊnˈet, ,mēdēˈnet\ *n* -s [F, prob. blend of *midi* noon (fr. OF, fr. *mi* mid, middle — fr. L *medius* — + *di* day, fr. L *dies*) and *dînette* light lunch, fr. *dîner* to dine, breakfast + *-ette*; fr. the traditional light lunches eaten at noon by the midinettes — more at MID, DEITY, DINE] **:** a Parisian shopgirl; *esp* **:** a Parisian seamstress

**midiron** \ˈ=,==\ *n* **:** an iron golf club with more loft than a driving iron and less than a mashie used typically for medium distance shots on the fairway and long approach shots from the fairway — called also *number two iron;* see IRON illustration

**mid–kidney** \ˈ=,==\ *n* **:** MESONEPHROS

**1mid·land** \ˈmidlənd, -d,land, -aa(ə)nd\ *n* [ˈ*mid* + *land*] **1 :** the interior or central region of a country (as the central counties of England or central part of the U.S.) **2** *or* **midland dialect** *usu cap M* **a :** the dialect of English spoken in the midland counties of England **b :** the dialect of English spoken in the part of the U. S. that lies between the southern boundary of Northern and a line running from central Delaware through Maryland, southwest along the Blue Ridge, east to include part of the North Carolina Piedmont, and then west through northern Georgia and Alabama and that includes parts of New Jersey and Delaware, northern Maryland, central and southern Pennsylvania, Ohio, Indiana, and Illinois, the Appalachian Mountain area, West Virginia, Kentucky, and most of Tennessee

**2midland** \ˈ"\ *adj* **1 :** being or situated in the interior country **:** distant from the coast or seashore **:** INLAND **2 a :** of, relating to, or characteristic of the midlands **b** *usu cap* **:** of, relating to, or characteristic of Midland dialect **3 :** surrounded or nearly surrounded by land **:** MEDITERRANEAN

**mid·lan·der** \-də(r)\ *n, often cap* **:** a native or inhabitant of the interior or central region of a country

**mid–latitude** \ˈ=ˈ===\ *adj* **:** of, relating to, or characteristic of the mid-latitudes

**mid–latitudes** \ˈ=ˈ==,=\ *n pl* **:** latitudes of the temperate zones or from about 30 to 60 degrees north or south of the equator

**1midleg** \ˈ=,=\ *n* [ˈ*mid* + *leg*] **:** the middle of the leg

**2midleg** \ˈ=ˈ=\ *adv* **1 :** at the middle of the leg **2 :** to the middle of the leg

**mid·lent·ing** \ˈmid,lentiŋ\ *n* -s [*Mid-Lent* (*Sunday*) + *-ing*] **:** MOTHERING

**mid–lent sunday** *n, usu cap M&L&S* [ME *mydlent Sonday*] **:** the 4th Sunday in Lent

**mid–life** \ˈ=ˈ=\ *n* **:** MIDDLE AGE

**midline** \ˈ=,=\ *n* **:** a median line; *esp* **:** the median line or median plane of the body or some part of the body

**mid·lo·thi·an** \(ˈ)midˈlōthēən, -thyən\ *adj, usu cap* [fr. *Midlothian* county, Scot.] **:** of or from the county of Midlothian, Scotland **:** of the kind or style prevalent in Midlothian

**mid–mashie** \ˈ=,==\ *n* **:** an iron golf club with less loft than a mashie iron — called also *number three iron;* see IRON illustration

**mid–mixed** \ˈ=ˈ=\ *adj, of a vowel* **:** MID-CENTRAL

**midmorn** \ˈ=ˈ=\ *n, archaic* **:** MIDMORNING

**midmorning** \ˈ=ˈ==\ *n* **:** the middle of the period from sunrise to noon or from rising to noon or from the beginning of the ordinary time of daily activities to noon ⟨the torrid ~ sun —Linton Wells⟩ ⟨the ~ coffee break⟩

**1mid·most** \ˈmid,mōst *also chiefly Brit* -,məst\ *adj* [ME *midmest*, fr. OE *midmest, midemest*, fr. *midd, midde* mid + *-mest* -most — more at MID] **1 :** being in the exact middle **:** MIDDLEMOST **2 :** the middle of **3 :** most intimate **:** INNERMOST

**2midmost** \ˈ"\ *n* [ME *midmest*, fr. *midmest*, adj.] **:** the midmost part

**3midmost** \ˈ"\ *adv* [ˈ*midmost*] **:** in the very midst or middle

**4midmost** \ˈ"\ *prep* [ˈ*midmost*] **:** in the very middle of

**midn** *abbr* **1** midnight **2** midshipman

**1midnight** \ˈ=,=\ *n* [ME *midnight, midniht*, fr. OE *midniht*, fr. *midd, midde* mid + *niht* night — more at MID, NIGHT] **1 :** the middle of the night; *specif* **:** twelve o'clock at night **2 a :** deep darkness or gloom **b :** a period of deep darkness or gloom **3** *or* **midnight blue :** a variable color averaging a blackish blue that is greener and stronger than Romany

**2midnight** \ˈ"\ *adj* **1 :** of, relating to, occurring at, like, or suggestive of midnight **2 a :** being in the middle of the night ⟨~ studies⟩ **b :** characteristic of the middle of the night ⟨~ gloom⟩

**midnight appointment** *n* **:** an appointment to political office made during the last hours of the term of office of the person in whom the right of making such appointment is vested

**midnight line** *n* **:** a hypothetical line imagined as circling the earth so as to pass over every locality exactly at midnight

**1mid·night·ly** \ˈmid,nītlē, -li\ *adv* [ˈ*midnight* + *-ly* (adv. suffix)] **:** every midnight **:** regularly at midnight

**2midnightly** \ˈ"\ *adj* [ˈ*midnight* + *-ly* (adv. suffix)] **1 :** occurring at midnight **2 :** occurring every midnight

**midnight oil** *n* **:** diligent effort expended late at night or as if late at night — compare BURN THE MIDNIGHT OIL

**midnight sun** *n* **1 :** the sun above the horizon at midnight in the arctic or antarctic summer **2 :** CHROME SCARLET

**midnoon** \ˈ=ˈ=\ *n* **:** MIDDAY, NOON

**mid off** *n, cricket* **:** a fielding position on the off side of the field nearer to the batsman than long off; *also* **:** a player fielding in this position — see CRICKET illustration

**mid on** *n, cricket* **:** a fielding position on the on side of the field nearer to the batsman than long on; *also* **:** a player fielding in this position

**midpalatal** \ˈ=ˈ===\ *adj* **:** MEDIOPALATAL

**midparent** \ˈ=,==\ *n* **:** a hypothetical single parent occupying an intermediate position between the two parents — **midparentage** \ˈ=,===\ *n* — **midparental** \,==ˈ==\ *adj*

**midpassage** \ˈ=ˈ==\ *n* **1 :** the midst of the act or state of passing **2 :** the midst of a passage

**midplane** \ˈ=,=\ *n* **:** a plane passing through something in such a way as to divide it into symmetrical halves

**midpoint** \ˈ=,=\ *n* **1 :** a point at or approximately at the center of an area or midway between the extremities of a line **2 a :** the point of time midway between the extremities of a period of time or of an event, process, or condition continuing over a given period of time **b :** a point of time assumed to be midway or approximately midway between the beginning and the probable time of termination of an event, process, or condition whose end lies at some future and not precisely determinate point of time **3 a :** a point on a line segment or an arc of a curve whose distances from the end points measured along the segment or arc are equal **b :** the arithmetic mean of the upper and lower limits of a class interval

**midportion** *n* **:** a middle part

**midrange** \ˈ=,=\ *n* **1 :** a range of medium length **2 :** the midpoint of a range (as of distance or time) **3 :** a middle portion (as of a range of musical pitch) **4 :** the arithmetic mean of the largest and smallest observations of a group

**midrange trajectory** *n* **:** the height of a bullet's trajectory measured at a point falling midway between the muzzle of the piece and the target

**mid·rash** \ˈmi,drăsh\ *n, pl* **mid·rash·im** \miˈdrăshəm, ,=drăˈshēm\ *also* **mid·rash·oth** *or* **mid·rash·ot** \,=,drăˈshōt(h)\ [Heb *midhrāsh* exposition, explanation] **1 a** *sometimes cap* **:** an ancient Jewish exposition of a passage of the Scriptures that may be either halakic or haggadic in type **b** *often cap* **:** a collection of midrashim **2** *sometimes cap* **:** Jewish religious exposition by means of midrashim **3** *usu cap* **:** the body of midrashic literature **4 :** an ancient Jewish narrative that has the form characteristic of a midrash and the purpose of setting forth or illustrating a religious teaching

**mid·rash·ic** \(ˈ)miˈdrashik\ *adj, often cap* **1 :** of, relating to, characteristic of, or constituting a midrash or the Midrash **2 :** resembling midrashim

**midrib** \ˈ=,=\ *n* **1 :** the central vein of a leaf **2 :** a dividing line, depression, or ridge analogous or similar to the midrib of a leaf

**midribbed** \ˈ=ˈ=\ *adj* **:** having a midrib

**mid·riff** \ˈmi,drif\ *n* -s [ME *midrif*, fr. OE *midhrif* (akin to OFris *midrif, midhref* midriff), fr. *midd, midde* mid + *hrif* belly, womb; akin to OFris *href, hrif* belly, OHG *href* body, lower body, womb, L *corpus* body, MIr *crī* body, Gk *prapides* diaphragm, Skt *kṛp* shape, beautiful appearance] **1 :** DIAPHRAGM 1 **2 :** the mid-region of the human torso; *esp* **:** its external ventral aspect **3 a :** a section of a woman's garment that is fitted across the midriff **b :** a woman's garment similar to a halter that exposes the midriff

**1mids** *pl of* MID

**2mids** \ˈmidz\ *n, pl* **mids** [ME *middes* — more at MIDST] **1** *now Scot* **:** MIDST, MIDDLE **2** *obs* **:** MEANS, METHOD **3** *now Scot* **:** a middle course **:** MEAN

**midsagittal** \ˈ=ˈ===\ *adj* **:** median and sagittal

**midsection** \ˈ=,==\ *n* **:** a section midway or about midway between the extremes: as **a :** MIDRIFF 2 **b :** MIDRIFF 3

**midsemester** \ˈ=ˈ===\ *n* **1 :** the end of the first half of an academic semester that is often a time for examinations and reports on students' progress — compare MIDTERM **2 :** a midsemester examination

**midship** \ˈ=,=\ *n* **1 :** the portion of a ship between the bow and the stern **2 :** the vertical line in a ship midway between the forward and aft perpendiculars

**midship beam** *n* **:** the beam in the deck in the midship section of a ship or boat

**midship bend** *n* **:** the frame in a ship or boat at the dead flat

**midship frame** *n* **:** the frame at the greatest breadth in a ship or boat

**midship line** *n* **:** the center line of the body plan of a ship or boat

**mid·ship·man** \(ˈ)midˈshipmən\ *n, pl* **midshipmen 1 a :** a naval cadet in old-time deep-waisted ships of war **b :** a commissioned officer of the lowest rank in the British navy formerly completing training at sea but now undergoing a final period of shore training **c :** a student naval officer ranking above a master chief petty officer and below a warrant officer and orig. educated principally at sea but since 1845 usu. at the Naval Academy or other college or university — see NAVAL CADET **d :** a student officer of any nation who is comparable to a British or American midshipman **2 :** any of several American toadfishes that constitute the genus *Porichthys* and have rows of luminous organs on the under surface; *esp* **:** a common fish (*P. notatus*) of the Pacific coast from Lower California to Puget Sound that is coppery brown above shading to bright yellow below and that produces a humming sound with its air bladder — called also *singing fish*

**midshipman's–butter** \(ˈ)=ˈ===\ *n, pl* **midshipman's–butters :** AVOCADO

**mid·ship·man·ship** \(ˈ)=ˈ==,ship\ *n* **:** the position of a midshipman

**midshipman's hitch** *n* **:** a hitch used esp. for mooring and lifesaving and made by tying a rolling hitch with the end of a line to the standing part

midshipman's hitch

**midshipman's nuts** *also* **midshipmen's nuts** *n pl* **:** pieces of broken sea biscuit ⟨sailors . . . pick up their broken biscuits, or *midshipman's nuts* —Herman Melville⟩

**mid·ship·mite** \ˈmid,ship,mīt\ *n* [blend of *midshipman* and *mite*] *nonstand* **:** MIDSHIPMAN; *esp* **:** a small or very young midshipman

**1mid·ships** \ˈmid,ships\ *n pl* [prob. fr. pl. of ˈ*midship*] **:** the middle part of a ship or boat

**2midships** \ˈ"\ *adv* [short for ˈ*amidships*] **1 :** AMIDSHIPS 1a **2 a :** midway between the stem and stern of the hull of a ship or boat **b :** midway between the sides of the hull of a ship or boat

**midship section** *n* **:** a drawing of the cross section of a ship amidships showing details of frames, beams, and other structural parts

**midship spoke** *n* **:** the spoke of a steering wheel that is up when the rudder is amidships

**mid–shot** \ˈ=,=\ *n* **:** MEDIUM SHOT

**mid–side** \ˈ=,=\ *n* [ME *mid side*] **:** the middle of the side

**midsole** \ˈ=,=\ *n* **:** a layer of leather, rubber, or other material placed between the insole and the outsole of a shoe

**1midst** \ˈmidzt, ˈmidst, ˈmitst\ *n* -s [ME *middest*, alter. of *middes*, back-formation fr. *amiddes* amid — more at AMID] **1 :** the interior or central part or point **:** MIDDLE, INTERIOR — preceded by *the* or occas. a possessive and now usu. only in prepositional phrases ⟨the trees in the ~ of the forest⟩ ⟨fine early houses set in the ~ of a region of fine farms —*Amer. Guide Series: N.H.*⟩ ⟨passing through the ~ of some great inland sea —Carl Van Vechten⟩ ⟨sooner or later India would seek to wipe out this enclave in its ~ —*Collier's Yr. Bk.*⟩ **2 :** position among the members of a group, company, or society — preceded by *the* or a possessive and used only in prepositional phrases ⟨a visitor in our ~⟩ ⟨dangerous criminals in their ~⟩ ⟨they saw him in their ~ like an avenging Marius —J.A.Froude⟩ ⟨why it was he should feel in the ~ of all these people so utterly detached and so lonely —Louis Bromfield⟩ ⟨missionaries in the ~ of the unbelieving —W.H. Whyte⟩ ⟨a cluster of three or four villages . . . in the ~ of irrigated rice fields —Francis Kingdon-Ward⟩ **3 a :** the condition of being figuratively surrounded ⟨grew up in the ~ of farm influences —H.W.Wiley⟩ or beset ⟨nor should he ever forget, in the ~ of his problems, that there are large if circumscribed powers that lie within himself —Weston La Barre⟩ **b :** a period of time approximately about the middle of the duration or embracing all except the extreme beginning and end of the duration (as of an event, state, or action) ⟨in the ~ of a long reign⟩ ⟨the model which he was in the ~ of building —Marcia Davenport⟩ ⟨in the ~ of life we are in death —*Bk. of Com. Prayer*⟩ **4** *obs* **:** a middle course **:** MEAN, MEDIUM **syn** see CENTER

**2midst** \ˈ"\ *adv* **1** *archaic* **:** in the middle place **2 :** in the midst

**3midst** \ˈ"\ *prep* [prob. short for *amidst*] **:** in the midst of **:** AMIDST ⟨heads down the harbor ~ the cheers —Helen Henley⟩

**1midstream** \ˈ=ˈ=\ *n* [ˈ*mid* + *stream*] **1 a :** the portion of a stream well removed from both sides ⟨keep the boat in ~⟩ ⟨the political axiom of not changing horses in ~⟩ **b :** the center line of a stream **:** a line of which the course is midway or what is considered to be midway between the sides of a stream ⟨the ~ is the boundary⟩ **2 :** the portion of a stream well removed from both source and mouth ⟨in the ~ of his career —Arthur Berger⟩ ⟨in ~ both as writer and in his profession —R.C.Beatty⟩

**2midstream** \ˈ"\ *adv* **:** in midstream

**midsummer** \ˈ=ˈ==\ *n* [ME *midsumer, midsomer*, fr. OE *midsumer*, fr. *midd, midde* mid + *sumer* summer — more at MID, SUMMER] **1 :** the middle of summer **2 :** the period about the summer solstice

**midsummer day** *n, usu cap M&D* [ME *midsomer day*, fr. OE *midsumer dæg*] **:** June 24 **:** SAINT JOHN THE BAPTIST'S DAY

**midsummer eve** *or* **midsummer night** *n, usu cap M&E&N* **:** the eve of Midsummer Day ⟨in Brittany treasure-seekers gather fern seed at midnight on *Midsummer Eve* —J.G. Frazer⟩

**midsummer madness** *n* **:** extreme folly **:** emotional extravagance and absurdity

**mid·sum·mery** \midˈsəmərē\ *adj* **:** like or characteristic of midsummer

**midterm** \ˈ=,=\ *n* **1 :** the midpoint, the approximate midpoint, or an approximate midpoint of a term of time: as **a :** the end of the first half of an academic term that is often a time for examinations and reports on students' progress **b :** a midterm examination ⟨the student who normally studies only before a ~ —Hargis Westerfield⟩ **2 :** the approximate middle of a term of office; *specif* **:** the date midway between quadrennial presidential elections when congressional and many local elections are held ⟨opposition gains at ~⟩ — compare OFF YEAR

**mid–to–four watch** \ˈ==ˈ=-\ *n* [*midnight to four*] **:** MIDWATCH

**mid–totality** \ˈ==ˈ===\ *n* **:** the middle of the period during which an eclipse is total

**midtown** \ˈ=,=\ *n* **:** a section of a city situated between other sections conventionally called *downtown* and *uptown* or between the main business section and an outlying section

**midvein** \ˈ=,=\ *n* **:** MIDRIB 1

**1mid–victorian** \ˈ=ˈ===\ *adj, often cap M & usu cap V* [ˈ*mid* + *Victorian*] **1 :** of, relating to, or characteristic of the middle period of the reign (1837–1901) of Queen Victoria ⟨*mid-Victorian* furniture⟩ **2 a :** like one of the mid-Victorian period — often used disparagingly ⟨has a *mid-Victorian* taste in art⟩ and in this use usu. stronger than *Victorian* **b :** OLD-FASHIONED, ANTIQUATED ⟨your attitude is *mid-Victorian*⟩

**2mid–victorian** \ˈ"\ *n, often cap M & cap V* **1 :** one belonging to the mid-Victorian period **2 :** one having the moral or aesthetic standards characteristic or supposedly characteristic of the mid-Victorian period

**mid–victorianism** \ˈ=====,==\ *n, often cap M & usu cap V* **:** the actual or supposed moral or aesthetic standards of the mid-Victorian period

**mid–wall column** *or* **mid–wall shaft** *n* **:** a column or shaft carrying a wall thicker than its own diameter and standing about midway between the front and back of the wall

**midwatch** \ˈ=,=\ *n* **:** a watch on a ship from midnight to 4 A.M. — called also MIDDLE WATCH, MID-TO-FOUR WATCH

**mid–water** \ˈ=,==\ *n* **:** the middle portion vertically of a body of water **:** water substantially below the surface and substantially above the bottom

**1mid·way** \ˈmid,wā\ *n* [ME, fr. OE *midweg*, fr. *midd, midde* mid + *weg* way — more at MID, WAY] **1** *obs* **:** the middle of the way or distance ⟨paths indirect, or in the ~ faint —John Milton⟩ **2** *archaic* **:** a middle way or course ⟨all good things keep the ~ of the eternal deep —R.W.Emerson⟩ **3** [fr. the *Midway* (*Plaisance*), a section of a park in Chicago which became the site of the amusement section of the Columbian Exposition of 1893] **a :** an avenue or area at a fair, exposition, carnival, or amusement park along which or in which are concessions for exhibitions of curiosities, games of chance, scenes from foreign life, merry-go-rounds and other rides, and other light amusements **b :** the amusements in a midway that constitute one of the divisions into which the attractions of a fair, exposition, or amusement park are grouped **c :** the buildings, tents, enclosures, and other structures in a midway with the exhibits and amusement devices contained in them **4 :** a place (as a street or highway) likened to a midway on account of bright lights (as of advertising signs) or of the nature of the places of business or amusement along its course

**2midway** \ˈ=ˈ=\ *adv* **:** in the middle of the way or distance **:** HALFWAY ⟨~ between reform and revolution —John Strachey⟩ ⟨~ up the mountain —Rafael Sabatini⟩ ⟨stopped ~ for a light meal⟩

**3midway** \ˈ"\ *adj* **1 a :** occupying an intermediate position **:** situated between those parts or those things or beings of the same class that are at or near the extremes ⟨the ~ air —Shak.⟩ **b :** being in the middle of the way or distance **2 :** intermediate between extremes

**4midway** \ˈ=,=\ *prep* **1 :** in the middle of **:** about halfway along **2 :** about halfway between

**midweek** \ˈ=ˈ=\ *n* **:** the middle of the week ⟨a holiday in ~⟩

**mid·week·ly** \(ˈ)midˈwēklē\ *adj* **:** occurring, appearing, or being held during the middle of the week ⟨held a ~ prayer meeting⟩

**midwest** \ˈ=ˈ=\ *n, usu cap* **1 :** regions lying somewhat to the west of a specified or implied point of orientation ⟨the farmlands of the *Midwest*⟩ **2 :** something (as people, culture, or institutions) characteristic of the Midwest ⟨the *Midwest* strongly favored the new policies⟩

**midwestern** \(ˈ)=ˈ==\ *adj, often cap* **:** of, relating to, or characteristic of the Midwest

**midwesterner** \ˈ=ˈ===\ *n, usu cap* **:** a native or resident of the Midwest

**1mid·wife** \ˈmid,wīf\ *n, pl* **mid·wives** \-īvz\ [ME *midwif*, fr. *mid* with (fr. OE) + *wif* woman, wife — more at META-, WIFE] **1 a :** a woman not qualified as a physician who assists other women in childbirth esp. habitually or as a means of livelihood **b :** an accoucheur of either sex **2 :** one that helps to produce or bring forth something ⟨thou art the ~ of my woe —Shak.⟩ ⟨what Engels had meant by describing war as the ~ of social change —E.R.Bentley⟩

**2midwife** \ˈ"\ *vt* **midwifed** \-īft\ *or* **midwived** \-īvd\ **midwifed** *or* **midwived; midwifing** \-īfiŋ\ *or* **midwiving** \-īviŋ\ **midwifes** \-īfs\ *or* **midwives** \-īvz\ **1 :** to assist in bringing (a child) to birth **2 :** to assist in producing, bringing forth, or bringing about ⟨probably the first time in history that a bank *midwived* a successful biographical novel —Irving Stone⟩

**midwife frog** *or* **midwife toad** *n* **:** OBSTETRICAL TOAD

**mid·wife·ry** \-f(ə)rē, -ri\ *n, pl* **midwiferies** [ME *medewifry,* fr. *medewif, midwif* midwife + *-ry*] **1 :** the art or act of assisting at childbirth; *also* **:** OBSTETRICS **2 :** the art, act, or process of producing or bringing forth or bringing about ⟨would have been a sorry failure but for the ~ of the director⟩

**midwing monoplane** \'=,=-\ *n* **:** a monoplane in which the wing is mounted midway between the top and bottom of the fuselage

**mid·win·ter** \'mid¦wintə(r)\ *n* [ME, fr. OE, fr. *midd, midde* mid + *winter* — more at MID, WINTER] **:** the middle of winter

**midwinter day** *n, usu cap M&D archaic* **:** CHRISTMAS

**mid·win·ter·ly** \-(r)lē\ *adj* **:** MIDWINTRY

**mid·win·try** \-n·trē\ *adj* **:** of, relating to, or characteristic of midwinter

**mid–world** \'=,=\ *n* **1** *obs* **:** MIDDLE-EARTH **2 a :** an intermediate realm ⟨neither beast nor bird, it inhabits an anomalous *mid-world* —*Saturday Rev.*⟩ **b :** a body (as of persons) occupying an intermediate position (as between two attitudes or opinions) ⟨this *mid-world* of persons, no longer hostile or indifferent to religion, though not as yet ecclesiastically or theologically minded —W.L.Sperry⟩

[1]**midyear** \'=,=\ *n* [[1]*mid* + *year*] **1 a :** the middle or middle portion of a calendar year ⟨the warm weather in ~⟩ **b :** the middle of an academic year ⟨changes of courses at ~⟩ **2 a :** a midyear examination **b midyears** *pl* **:** the set of examinations at midyear or the period of midyear examinations ⟨looking forward with apprehension to the ~s⟩

[2]**midyear** \'=¦=\ *adj* **1 :** occurring in the middle of a civil year ⟨a proposed ~ holiday⟩ **2 :** occurring in the middle of an academic year ⟨~ examinations⟩ ⟨the ~ vacation⟩

**mien** \'mēn\ *n* -s [by shortening & alter. (influenced by F *mine* appearance, perh. fr. Bret *min* beak, snout) fr. [2]*demean*] **1 :** the air or bearing of a person esp. as expressive of mood or personality **:** MANNER, EXPRESSION ⟨that ~ of a commercial traveler who has been everywhere and through everything —Arnold Bennett⟩ ⟨his ~ of settled woe —Robertson Davies⟩ ⟨usually presents a ~ of solemnity —*Current Biog.*⟩ **2 :** APPEARANCE, ASPECT ⟨dresses of fairly formal ~ —Lois Long⟩ ⟨a monster of most ferocious ~ —G.W.Johnson⟩ **3** *archaic* **:** SHOW, PRETENSE — usu. used in the phrase *make mien* ⟨foreigners who . . . made ~ to stay —F.B.Gummere⟩

**mierkat** *var of* MEERKAT

**miers·ite** \'mir,zīt\ *n* -s [Sir Henry A. *Miers* †1942 Eng. mineralogist + E *-ite*] **:** a mineral (Ag, Cu)I consisting of silver copper iodide

[1]**miff** \'mif\ *n* -s [origin unknown] **1 :** a fit of ill humor or bad temper **2 :** a petty or trivial quarrel or argument

[2]**miff** \"\ *vt* -ED/-ING/-S **:** to put into an ill humor **:** make peevish **:** OFFEND, DISPLEASE ⟨~*ed* by this refutation of his diagnosis —F.G.Slaughter⟩ ⟨~*ed* a few . . . musical sophisticates —*Time*⟩

**miffed** *adj* [fr. past part. of [2]*miff*] put out **:** OFFENDED, HURT ⟨he looks thoroughly ~ —Jacob Hay⟩ ⟨still ~ because he wasn't . . . honored with the assignment —Joseph Wechsberg⟩ ⟨~ that my arrival did not rate a more formal reception —Mohamed Mehdevi⟩

**miffy** \'mifē, -fi\ *adj* -ER/-EST **1 :** inclined to take offense **:** TOUCHY ⟨next afternoon the ~ matron was back —*Tuscaloosa (Ala.) News*⟩ **2 :** requiring favorable conditions for growth ⟨the saxifrage plants were ~⟩

**mig** *or* **migg** \'mig\ *n* -s [origin unknown] **:** a playing marble; *esp* **:** one used as an object to be shot at (as in ringer)

**mig·gle** \'migəl\ *n* -s [*mig* + *-le*] **1** *dial* **:** MIG **2 miggles** *pl but sing in constr, dial* **:** MIB 2

[1]**might** \'mīt, *usu* -īd·+V\ *archaic 2d sing* **might·est** \-īd·əst\ *or* **mightst** \-ītst\ [ME *mighte,* fr. OE *meahte, mihte;* akin to OHG *mahta, mohta* could, was able, ON *mātti,* Goth *mahta* — more at MAY] *past of* MAY — used in auxiliary function to express permission, liberty, probability, possibility in the past ⟨the king ~ do nothing without parliament's consent⟩ or a present condition contrary to fact ⟨if he were older he ~ understand⟩ or less probability or possibility than *may* ⟨~ get there before it rains⟩ ⟨~ be a good idea to wait and see⟩ or as a polite alternative to *may* ⟨~ I ask who is calling⟩ or to *ought* or *should* ⟨you ~ at least apologize⟩

[2]**might** \"\ *n* -s [ME, fr. OE *miht;* akin to OS & OHG *maht* might, power, ON *māttr,* Goth *mahts* might, OE *magan* to be able — more at MAY] **1 a (1) :** the power, authority, or collective resources wielded by an individual, group, or other entity ⟨the fading ~ of Spain⟩ ⟨the growing ~ of the middle class⟩ ⟨the ~ of three great states was arrayed against the republic⟩ ⟨sought to weaken the ~ of the barons⟩; *specif* **:** the power of such an entity given a concrete form or embodiment ⟨resisting the power of the German armed ~ —D.W.Brogan⟩ ⟨our growing ~ in the air⟩ **(2) :** power or supreme power regarded as the attribute of a divine being, as an abstraction, or as a personalized force or idea ⟨'tis ~ half-slumbering on its own right arm —John Keats⟩ **(3) :** the power or force of an inanimate, incorporeal, or intangible thing or agency ⟨the ocean's ~⟩ ⟨the ~ of winter's icy blasts⟩ ⟨the ~ of a redeeming love⟩ **b (1) :** power to effect a desired object **:** MEANS, RESOURCES, CAPACITY ⟨not zeal or goodwill were lacking, but the ~⟩ **(2) :** physical or bodily strength ⟨with a man's will and a man's ~ —Robert Browning⟩ **(3)** *archaic* **:** active property **:** VIRTUE, EFFICACY **(4) :** the power, energy, or intensity of purpose, feeling, or action of which one is capable ⟨watched a wren . . . singing with all its ~ —Stuart Chase⟩ ⟨save ourselves by the ~ of our minds —L.M.Chamberlain⟩ ⟨began to strain with all his ~ toward his own left —A.C. Whitehead⟩ ⟨ran with all his ~⟩ — often used in the intensive phrase *with might and main* ⟨were staring with ~ and main —William Black⟩ **c :** naked material power or superiority of strength regarded as the ultimate arbiter of disputes or conflicts of interest ⟨~ makes right⟩ **2** *dial* **:** a considerable amount **:** a great deal **syn** see POWER

**might and main** *adv* **:** with might and main **:** VIGOROUSLY ⟨such as any sage practical politician would strive *might and main* to avoid —G.E.G.Catlin⟩

**mightest** *archaic past 2d sing of* MAY

**might·ful** \-tfəl\ *adj* [ME, fr. *might* + *-ful*] *archaic* **:** MIGHTY

**might–have–been** \'mīd·ə(v),bin, -ītə-\ *n, pl* **might-have-beens 1 :** something that might have happened ⟨who can calculate the *might-have-beens* —W.M.Thackeray⟩ ⟨reconstructs the *might-have-beens* of English and French elections —H.C.Mansfield⟩ **2 :** a person who might have amounted to something or to more

**might·i·ly** \'mīd·ᵊlē -ītᵊl-, |ə̇l|, |i\ *adv* [ME, fr. OE *mihtiglīce,* fr. *mihtig* mighty + *-līce* -ly — more at MIGHTY] **1 :** in a mighty manner **:** EARNESTLY, VIGOROUSLY, POWERFULLY ⟨strove ~ to impress a customer with the book's merits —Bennett Cerf⟩ **2 :** to a great degree **:** very much ⟨can help you ~ in all your relations with others —W.J.Reilly⟩ ⟨~ important was the sex of a child in the imperial family —P.I.Wellman⟩

**might·i·ness** \'mīd·ēnə̇s, -ītı|, |in-\ *n* -ES [ME *mihtinesse,* fr. *mihty, mighty* + *-nesse* -ness] **1 :** the quality or state of being mighty **:** possession of might **:** POWER **2 :** HIGHNESS, EXCELLENCY — used as a title of dignity ⟨Your *Mightiness*⟩ ⟨their *High Mightinesses*⟩

**might·less** \'mītlə̇s\ *adj* [ME *mightles,* fr. *might* + *-les* -less] **:** lacking might **:** POWERLESS

**might·n't** \'mītᵊnt\ [by contr.] **:** might not

[1]**mighty** \'mīd·ē, -ītı|, |i\ *adj* -ER/-EST [ME *mihtig,* fr. *miht* might + *-ig* -y — more at MIGHT] **1 a :** having or wielding great power or authority **:** strong in material resources or social position **:** POWERFUL ⟨the mismanagement and dishonesty of those once ~ in finance —Oscar Handlin⟩ ⟨knowing the well-heeled and the ~ rather than the poor and the unimportant —John Mason Brown⟩ **b :** marked by or reflecting intellectual or artistic ability of a high order **:** immensely gifted or effective **:** GREAT, NOTABLE, EXTRAORDINARY ⟨soon recognized as the *mightiest* preacher in New England —*Amer. Guide Series: Mass.*⟩ ⟨master of a ~ line⟩ ⟨one of the *mightiest* poets of our time⟩ **c (1) :** strong in body or valor ⟨repeated the exploits of the ~ logger —*Amer. Guide Series: Wash.*⟩ ⟨this ~ man of small stature —*Boy Scout Handbook*⟩ **(2) :** exerting or made with great force **:** STRENUOUS, VIOLENT ⟨swing ~ blows to sharpen a dull bit —*Lamp*⟩ ⟨a ~ tempest⟩ ⟨a ~ thrust⟩ ⟨a ~ wind⟩ **(3) :** doing or engaging in something intensively, on a large or massive scale, or with notable success ⟨were ~ wanderers in those days —Meridel Le Sueur⟩ ⟨a ~ drinker⟩ ⟨the Egyptian cat was a ~ hunter —Agnes Repplier⟩ **(4) :** very favorable **:** HIGH ⟨has a ~ opinion of his work⟩ **d :** potent or effective in action **:** EFFICACIOUS, EFFICIENT ⟨essayed such tasks with no *mightier* tools than picks or shovels —O.S.Nock⟩ ⟨cast a ~ spell upon her⟩ ⟨the bullet was *mightier* than the ballot —Hessell Tiltman⟩ **2 :** great or imposing in size, amount, extent, or degree ⟨periods of high ideals and ~ achievement —Mary D. Anderson⟩ ⟨the great country and ~ river he had explored —Tom Marvel⟩ ⟨one of the *mightiest* ruins in the world —Kenneth Love⟩ ⟨the designer of a ~ bridge —B.N. Cardozo⟩

[2]**mighty** \"\ *adv* **:** in a great degree **:** EXTREMELY, VERY ⟨a ~ fine record⟩ ⟨~ proud of you —Gerald Beaumont⟩ ⟨a few had it ~ good —James Street⟩

[3]**mighty** \"\ *n* -ES **:** a person of might

**mig·ma·tite** \'migmə,tīt\ *n* -s [LL *migmat-, migma* mixture (fr. Gk, fr. *meignynai, mignynai* to mix) + E *-ite* — more at MIX] **:** a gneiss produced by the injection of igneous material between the laminae of a schistose formation — called also *injection gneiss*

**migniard** *adj* [F *mignard,* fr. *mignon* darling + *-ard* — more at MINION] *obs* **:** DAINTY, DELICATE, MINCING

**mig·niar·dise** \'minyə(r)də̇s\ *n* -s [F *mignardise,* fr. *mignard*] *archaic* **:** delicate fondling **:** migniard appearance or behavior

**mi·gnon** \'min,yän, *in sense 2* mēn'yōⁿ *or* 'mēn,yōⁿ\ *n* -s [F, lit., darling] **1 :** a moderate purple that is duller and slightly bluer than heliotrope (sense 4a), bluer and paler than average amethyst, bluer and less strong than manganese violet or cobalt violet, and bluer and duller than average lilac (sense 3a) **2** [by shortening] **:** FILET MIGNON

**mi·gnon·ette** \¦minyə¦net, *usu* -ed·+V\ *n* -s [F *mignonnette,* fr. obs. F, fem. of *mignonnet* dainty, fr. MF, fr. *mignon* — more at MINION] **1 :** an herb of the genus *Reseda; esp* **:** an annual (*R. odorata*) that is native to northern Africa and is widely cultivated for its long racemes of fragrant greenish yellow or greenish white flowers **2 :** a narrow bobbin lace having scattered small designs on a ground somewhat like tulle and made esp. by the French and Flemish in the 16th through the 19th centuries **3 :** *or* **mignonette green :** RESEDA 2a

mignonette

**mignonette family** *n* **:** RESEDACEAE

**mignonette pepper** *n* **:** coarsely ground pepper

**mignonette tree** *n* **:** HENNA 1

**mignonette vine** *n* **:** MADEIRA VINE

**mi·gnonne** \mēn'yōⁿ\ *adj* [F, fem. of *mignon*] **:** daintily small **:** PETITE

**mi·graine** \'mī,grān\ *n* -s [F, fr. LL *hemicrania* pain in one side of the head, fr. Gk *hēmikrania,* fr. *hēmi-* hemi- + *kranion* skull — more at CRANIUM] **1 :** a condition that is marked by recurrent usu. unilateral severe headache often accompanied by nausea and vomiting and followed by sleep, that tends to occur in more than one member of a family, and that is of uncertain origin though attacks appear to be precipitated by dilatation of intracranial blood vessels **2 :** an episode or attack of migraine ⟨suffered from ~s all her life⟩

**mi·grain·oid** \(')mī¦grā,nȯid\ *adj* **:** resembling migraine

**mi·grain·ous** \-ānəs\ *adj* **:** of, relating to, or suffering from migraine

**mi·gran·cy** \'mīgrənsē\ *n* -ES **:** the fact, condition, or phenomenon of habitual movement from one place of residence to another; *specif* **:** habitual migration from one area to another in search of seasonal work ⟨the large extent of ~ is not in doubt —Wilfred Whiteley⟩ ⟨the social and economic evils of ~⟩

**mi·grans** \'mī,granz\ *n, pl* **mi·gran·tes** \mī'gran·,tēz\ [NL, fr. L, pres. part. of *migrare* to migrate — more at MIGRATE] **:** a winged parthenogenetic viviparous female aphid produced by a fundatrigenia and serving to spread the colony either to new primary host plants or to secondary hosts

[1]**mi·grant** \'mīgrənt\ *adj* [L *migrant-, migrans,* pres. part. of *migrare* to migrate] **:** of, relating to, or being a migrant ⟨~ birds⟩ ⟨the economic and social conditions of ~ life⟩

[2]**migrant** \"\ *n* -s **:** one that migrates: as **a :** a person who moves into another area in order to find work esp. seasonal labor ⟨full of pluck—as most ~s are when they first take to the road —*Amer. Child*⟩ **b :** an animal that shifts from one habitat to another whether by chance, as a normal phase of a life cycle, or as part of a population expansion ⟨appearance of coyotes as ~s in New York⟩

**migrant shrike** *n* **:** a shrike (*Lanius ludovicianus migrans*) of central No. America that winters in the southern Mississippi valley and Texas and is distinguished by black eye bands that meet above the bill

**mi·grate** \'mī,grāt, *usu* -ād·+V\ *vb* -ED/-ING/-S [L *migratus,* past part. of *migrare;* akin to Gk *ameibein* to change, and perh. to Skt *mayate* he exchanges — more at MEAN] *vi* **:** to move from one place to another: as **a (1) :** to leave one country, region, or place in order to settle in another ⟨pretty lucky to have *migrated* to this country —Victor Boesen⟩ **(2) :** to move from one area to another in search of work (as seasonal labor) ⟨*migrating* with the alternation of crops through field after field of the West —Oscar Handlin⟩ **(3) :** TRANSFER; *specif* **:** to transfer from one college to another at a university in the British Isles ⟨designing to ~ presently to a theological college —John Buchan⟩ ⟨*migrated* to Emmanuel . . . probably to be at his elder brother's college —A.J.Shirren⟩ **b (1) :** to pass periodically from one region or climate to another for feeding or breeding ⟨birds that ~ only at night —F.A.Geldard⟩ **(2) :** to extend the habitat gradually from an old or into a new region ⟨some plants failed to ~ into their old ranges as the glaciation diminished⟩ **(3) :** to move from one site to another in a host organism esp. as part of a life cycle ⟨filiarial worms ~ within the human body⟩ **(4) :** to alter position in the course of embryologic development or other organic process ⟨one eye gradually ~s across the top the head, until both are on the same side —R.E.Coker⟩ **c (1) :** to move or undergo removal from one locality to another as a result of the operation of natural forces ⟨the dunes usually ~ inland —W.W.Atwood b. 1906⟩ **(2)** *of an atom or group* **:** to shift position within a molecule **(3)** *of an ion* **:** to move toward an electrode **(4)** *of a chemical substance* **:** to move or diffuse into an environing medium ⟨plasticizers that ~ into the adhesive film —*Product Engineering*⟩ ⟨retard the development of rancidity when oxidable oils . . . ~ into it —J.J.Aid⟩ **d :** to change locale or center of gravity **:** SHIFT ⟨the coal-mining centers . . . have *migrated* eastward —L.D. Stamp⟩ ⟨industry, having *migrated* from the manor to the craft guild of the town —Stringfellow Barr⟩ ~ *vt* **:** to cause to migrate ⟨~ a silicon atom —J.R.Goldsmith⟩

**mi·gra·tet·ic** \¦mīgrə¦ted·ik\ *adj* [prob. fr. *migrate* + *-etic*] **:** of or relating to electromigration

**mi·gra·tet·ics** \,==ˈted·iks\ *n pl but usu sing in constr* **:** ELECTRONOGRAPHY

**mi·gra·tion** \mī'grāshən\ *n* -s [F or L; F, fr. L *migration-, migratio,* fr. *migratus* (past part. of *migrare* to migrate) + *-ion-, -io* -ion — more at MIGRATE] **1 :** the act, process, or an instance of migrating: as **a (1) :** the act or an instance of moving from one country, region, or place to settle in another ⟨for the first time, the U. S. counted a net deficit by ~ —Oscar Handlin⟩ ⟨~ to the suburbs —C.B.Palmer b. 1910⟩ **(2) :** the act or an instance of moving from one area to another in search of work (as seasonal labor) ⟨the circle of their ~s reached as far north as the beet fields of Michigan —Oscar Handlin⟩ **b :** periodic movement from one region or climate to another for feeding or breeding ⟨the ~s of birds⟩ **c (1) :** a shifting of an atom or atoms from one part of the molecule to another **(2) :** a movement or drift of ions toward one or the other electrode under the influence of electromotive force **d :** an underground movement of oil, gas, or water not occasioned by artificial means **2 :** the individuals taking part in a migratory movement or those migrating during a given period — **mi·gra·tion·al** \(')mī¦grāshənᵊl, -shnəl\ *adj*

**mi·gra·tion·ist** \mī'grāsh(ə)nə̇st\ *n* -s **:** a person who assigns primary importance to migration in the diffusion of culture or the distribution of species

**migration route** *n* **:** a well-defined subdivision of a flyway

**mi·gra·tive** \'mīgrəd·iv\ *adj* [*migrate* + *-ive*] **:** MIGRATORY

**mi·gra·tor** \'mī,grād·ə(r)\ *n* -s [LL, fr. L *migratus* + *-or*] **:** one that migrates; *specif* **:** a migratory bird

**mi·gra·to·ri·al** \¦mīgrə¦tōrēəl, -tȯr-\ *adj* **:** MIGRATORY

[1]**mi·gra·to·ry** \'mīgrə,tōrē, -tȯr-, -ri\ *adj* [NL *migratorius,* fr. L *migratus* (past part. of *migrare* to migrate) + *-orius* -ory — more at MIGRATE] **1 a :** making a migration **:** moving habitually or occasionally from one region or climate to another ⟨~ birds⟩ ⟨~ tribes⟩ **b (1) :** moving in response to the demand for seasonal labor ⟨a ~ worker⟩ **(2) :** of or relating to migrant laborers ⟨the ~ shacks in the valley —Thurston Scott⟩ **2 :** ROVING, WANDERING ⟨a ~ cocktail set —Edmund Wilson⟩ ⟨a history of ~ joint pain —C.F. McKhann⟩ **3 :** of or relating to migration ⟨~ movements⟩

[2]**migratory** \"\ *n* -ES **:** MIGRATOR, MIGRANT ⟨you know how . . . all of us feel about these *migratories* —Rachel Field⟩

**migratory ant** *n* **:** ARMY ANT

**migratory divorce** *n* **:** a divorce granted to one party in a state other than that where the other party resides or is domiciled or in a state where neither party in fact resides or is domiciled

**migratory grasshopper** *n* **:** any of several migratory locusts of the genus *Melanoplus,* including serious pests of grain-growing and range areas of the central and western U.S.

**migratory locust** *n* **:** a locust that engages in group migrations; *esp* **:** a very destructive Old World locust (*Locusta migratoria*)

**migratory thrush** *n* **:** ROBIN 1c

**mi·grule** \'mī,grül\ *n* -s [*migrate* + *-ule*] **:** a disseminule by which a plant spreads into new areas **:** DIASPORE

**migs** *pl of* MIG

**miguelet** *var of* MIQUELET

**MIH** *abbr, often not cap* miles in the hour

**mih·rab** \'mērəb\ *n* -s [Ar *miḥrāb*] **:** a niche or chamber in a mosque indicating the direction of Mecca and usu. containing a copy of the Koran; *sometimes* **:** a slab only, used to indicate the direction — compare KAABA

**mi·ka·do** \mə'kä(,)dō, -kā(-\ *n* -s [Jap, fr. *mi-* (honorific prefix) + *kado* door] **1 :** an emperor of Japan — compare TENNO **2 :** a strong to vivid reddish orange

**mikado brown** *n* **:** a moderate brown that is yellower, lighter, and stronger than auburn, lighter, stronger, and slightly redder than chestnut brown, and yellower and stronger than toast brown — called also *stroller tan*

**mikado orange** *n* **1 :** a moderate orange that is yellower and stronger than honeydew, yellower, stronger, and slightly lighter than Persian orange, and stronger and slightly redder and darker than average apricot **2** *often cap M&O* **:** a direct dye — see DYE table I (under *Direct Orange 15*)

**mikado yellow G** *n, often cap M&Y* **:** a direct dye — see DYE table I (under *Direct Yellow 6*)

**mi·ka·nia** \mə'kānēə\ *n, cap* [NL, fr. J.G. *Mikan* †1814 Czech botanist + NL *-ia*] **:** a large genus of mostly tropical American herbaceous or woody vines (family Compositae) with opposite leaves and small discoid heads in panicled clusters — see CLIMBING HEMPWEED

**mi·ka·su·ki** \,mikə'sükē\ *n, pl* **mikasuki** *or* **mikasukis** *usu cap* **1 a :** a Muskogean people of northwestern Florida orig. members of the Creek Confederacy but later largely absorbed into the Seminole people **b :** a member of such people **2 :** the language of the Mikasuki people and of part of the Seminole people

[1]**mike** \'mīk\ *n* -s [origin unknown] *slang Brit* **:** an act or instance of miking — used esp. in the phrases *do a mike* and *have a mike*

[2]**mike** \"\ *vi* -ED/-ING/-S *slang Brit* **:** LOAF, LOITER

[3]**mike** *var of* MICK

[4]**mike** \'mīk\ *n* -s [by shortening & alter.] **1 :** MICROPHONE **2 :** MICROMETER CALIPER

[5]**mike** \"\ *vb* -ED/-ING/-S *vi* **:** to have a dimension indicated by a micrometer caliper ⟨the diameter ~s at 0.534 inch⟩ ~ *vt* **:** to measure with a micrometer caliper

[6]**mike** \"\ *usu cap* **—** a communications code word for the letter *m*

**mike fright** *n* [[4]*mike*] **:** intense fright or nervousness experienced by a person on having to broadcast into a microphone ⟨suffered *mike fright* and lost his voice completely —*Psychological Abstracts*⟩

**mi·kir** \'mē'ki(ə)r\ *n, pl* **mikir** *or* **mikirs** *usu cap* **1 a :** a hill people of Assam — called also *Arleng* **b :** a member of such people **2 :** the Tibeto-Burman language of the Mikir people

**mikra** *var of* MIQRA

**mik·vah** *or* **mik·veh** \'mikvə\ *n* -s [Heb *miqwāh*] **:** a ritual bath or bathing place for purification in accordance with Jewish law

**mil** \'mil\ *n* -s [L *mille* thousand — more at MILE] **1 :** a unit of length equal to 1/1000 inch or 0.0254 millimeter used esp. for the diameter of wire **2 :** a unit of angular measurement used in artillery and equal to 1/6400 of the circumference of a circle or approximately the angle subtended by one yard at 1000 yards range **3 :** a monetary unit formerly used in Palestine equal to 1/1000 pound; *also* **:** a bronze coin representing this unit

**mil** *abbr* **1** mileage **2** military **3** militia **4** millieme **5** million

**mil·acre** \'mi,lākə(r)\ *n* [*mil-* (fr. L *mille* thousand) + *acre*] **:** a plot of ground having an area of 1/1000 acre used as a test or sample area esp. for vegetational studies

**mi·la·dy** *also* **mi·la·di** \mə'lādē, mī'-, -di\ *n, pl* **miladies** *also* **miladis** [F *milady,* fr. E *my lady*] **1 :** an Englishwoman of noble or gentle birth — often used as an appellation **2 :** a woman of fashion ⟨hats designed for ~⟩

**milage** *var of* MILEAGE

[1]**mi·lan** \mə'lan, -aa(ə)n, -län\ *adj, usu cap* [fr. *Milan,* city in northern Italy] **1 :** of or from the city of Milan, Italy **:** of the kind or style prevalent in Milan **2** *of lace or needlepoint* **:** having a usu. scroll or floral pattern formed of braid or tape

[2]**milan** \"\ *n, often cap, often attrib* [fr. *Milan,* Italy] **:** a fine straw braid made from Italian wheat straw used chiefly for hats

**mil·a·naise** \¦milə¦nāz\ *adj* [F, fem. of *milanais* of Milan, fr. *Milan,* Italy] **:** garnished with spaghetti or macaroni with Parmesan cheese in a tomato sauce containing truffles and mushrooms ⟨veal cutlet ~⟩

**milanau** *or* **milano** *usu cap, var of* MELANAU

**milan cabbage** *n* **:** SAVOY CABBAGE

[1]**mil·a·nese** \,milə'nēz, -ēs\ *n, pl* **milanese** [It, fr. *Milano* Milan + It *-ese,* n. suffix] **1** *cap* **:** a native or resident of Milan, Italy **2** *cap* **:** the Italian dialect of Milan **3 :** a fine lightweight warp-knitted fabric usu. of silk, rayon, or nylon for women's wear characterized by interlocked stitches, resistance to runs, fine diagonal lines

[2]**milanese** \¦==¦=\ *adj, usu cap* [It, fr. *Milano* Milan + It *-ese,* adj. suffix] **:** of or relating to Milan, Italy or its inhabitants

**milanese mandolin** *n, usu cap 1st M* **:** a mandolin having five or six pairs of strings

**mi·lan·ji cedar** *also* **mlan·je cedar** \mə'länjē-\ *n, often cap M* [after Mt. *Milanji* or *Mlange,* Nyasaland, Africa] **:** a tall coniferous tree (*Widdringtonia whytei*) of the uplands of southern and eastern Africa that is closely related to the cypresses and much resembles a typical cedar

**mi·lar·ite** \'mēlä,rīt, 'milə,r-\ *n* -s [G *milarit,* fr. Val *Milar,* Switzerland + G *-it* -ite] **:** a mineral $K_2Ca_4Be_4Al_2Si_{24}O_{62}\cdot H_2O$ consisting of a hydrous silicate of potassium, calcium, beryllium, and aluminum occurring in glassy hexagonal crystals

**milch** \'milk, 'milch, 'milks\ *adj* [ME *milche* giving milk, fr. OE *-milce* (in *thrimilce* month of May when cows can be milked three times daily); akin to OHG *melch* giving milk, ON *mjolkr* giving milk, OE *melcan* to milk — more at MILK] **1** *of a domestic animal* **:** giving milk; *specif* **:** bred for or suitable for milk production as distinct from other uses (as meat or wool production or draft) ⟨~ goat⟩ ⟨~ camel⟩ **2** *obs* **:** flowing as if with milk **:** WEEPING ⟨would have made ~ the burning eyes of heaven —Shak.⟩

**milch cow** *n* [ME *milche cow,* fr. *milche* milch + *cow*] **1 :** a cow in milk or kept for her milk **2 :** a source of easily acquired gain ⟨the tobacco . . . industry is regarded as one of the best . . . *milch cows* of national revenue —*Canadian Horticulture & Home*⟩

**milch·er** \'milkə(r), 'milchə(r)\ *n* -s **:** a milch animal

**milch glass** *n* **:** MILK GLASS

**mil·chig** \'milkik\ *adj* [Yiddish, fr. *milch* milk (fr. MHG, fr. OHG *miluh*) + *-ig* -y (fr. MHG *-ic*, fr. OHG *-ig*) — more at MILK] *Jewish cookery* **:** made of or derived from milk or dairy products ⟨menus for ~ meals⟩

**mil·chigs** \-ks\ *n pl* **:** milk or dairy products

[1]**mild** \'mīld, *esp before pause or consonant* -ǝld\ *adj* -ER/-EST [ME *mild, milde*, fr. OE *milde;* akin to OHG *milti* kind, gracious, ON *mildr* gentle, Goth *mildi*tha affection, Gk *malthakos* soft, Skt *mardhati* it is moist, OE *melu* meal — more at MEAL] **1 a** *archaic* **:** KIND, GRACIOUS, CONSIDERATE ⟨peace on earth and mercy ~ —Charles Wesley⟩ **b :** gentle in nature or behavior **:** not harsh or vehement **:** not giving offense ⟨~ disposition⟩ ⟨~ manners⟩ **2 a :** moderate in action or sensuous effect ⟨~ drug⟩ ⟨~ cigar⟩ **:** of moderate strength or intensity **:** not sharp or bitter ⟨~ oath⟩ ⟨~ humus⟩ ⟨~ slope⟩ ⟨~ reproof⟩ **:** BLAND ⟨~ as milk⟩ ⟨~ cheese⟩ **b** *of ale or beer* **:** not strongly flavored with hops **c** *of disease* **:** not severe or dangerous **:** BENIGN ⟨~ case of whooping cough⟩ **3 a** *archaic* **:** not wild **:** TAME ⟨wild beasts . . . at his sight grew ~ —John Milton⟩ **b :** of less than normal or expected vigor, boldness, or severity ⟨~ sarcasm⟩ ⟨~ game of bridge⟩ ⟨~ punishment⟩ ⟨~ exercise⟩ **c :** characterized by absence of extremes in temperature **:** TEMPERATE ⟨~ climate⟩ **d :** not cold **:** pleasantly warm ⟨~ spring day⟩ ⟨~ spell in February⟩ **syn** see SOFT

[2]**mild** \"\ *adv, archaic* **:** MILDLY

[3]**mild** \"\ *n* -s **1** *Brit* **:** mild ale or beer **2** *usu cap* **:** coffee of fine quality **:** coffee other than Brazil — usu. used in pl.

**mild alkali** *n* **:** a weak alkali (as sodium carbonate) — distinguished from *caustic alkali*

**mild-and-bitter** \ˌ≈≈'≈≈\ *n* -s *Brit* **:** a drink consisting of a mixture of mild and bitter draft beers or ales

**mild·en** \'mīldǝn\ *vb* -ED/-ING/-s *vt* **:** to make mild or milder ⟨did what little they could to ~ their evil governments —*Foreign Affairs*⟩ ~ *vi* **:** to become mild or milder ⟨if the weather ~s, the river will thaw⟩

[1]**mil·dew** \'mil,d(y)ü\ *n* -s [ME, fr. OE *meledēaw, mildēaw;* akin to OHG *militou* honeydew; both fr. a prehistoric WGmc compound whose original first constituent, prob. represented by Goth *milith* honey, was influenced by the word represented by OE *melu* meal, and whose second constituent is represented by OE *dēaw* dew — more at MELLIFLUOUS, MEAL, DEW] **1** *obs* **:** HONEYDEW 1 **2 a :** a superficial usu. whitish growth produced on various forms of organic matter and on living plants by fungi (as of the families Erysiphaceae and Peronosporaceae) **b :** a fungus producing such growth — compare DOWNY MILDEW, [5]MOLD, POWDERY MILDEW **3 :** a discoloration (as on cloth, leather, paper) caused by parasitic fungi

[2]**mildew** \"\ *vt* -ED/-ING/-s **:** to affect with or as if with mildew ⟨prejudices that ~ attempts at social interpretation —Harlow Shapley⟩ ~ *vi* **:** to become affected with mildew ⟨prevent books from ~*ing*⟩

**mil·dew·cide** \-ü,sīd\ *n* -s **:** an agent that destroys mildew

**mildewed** *adj* [fr. past part. of [2]*mildew*] **1 :** covered with or ruined by mildew ⟨~ wheat⟩ **2 :** decaying from age or disuse **:** gone bad from keeping too long ⟨~ jokes⟩ ⟨~ notion⟩ ⟨~ old butler⟩

[1]**mildewproof** \'≈,≈,≈\ *adj* [[1]*mildew* + *proof*] **:** resistant to mildew

[2]**mildewproof** \"\ *vt* **:** to make resistant to mildew ⟨~*ing* sails⟩

**mil·dewy** \'mil,d(y)üē\ *adj* **1 :** affected with mildew **2 :** like mildew

**mildhearted** \'≈'≈≈\ *adj* [ME *mildherted*, fr. [1]*mild* + *herted* hearted] *archaic* **:** MERCIFUL

**mild·ish** \'mīldish\ *adj* **:** somewhat mild ⟨~ weather⟩ **:** somewhat lacking in sharpness or vigor ⟨~ wit⟩

**mild·ly** *adv* [ME *mildely*, fr. OE *mildelīce*, fr. *milde* mild + *-līce* -ly] **:** in a mild manner **:** to a moderate degree or extent ⟨protested ~⟩ ⟨~ successful⟩ ⟨~ cynical⟩

**mild mercurous chloride** *or* **mild mercury chloride** *n* **:** CALOMEL

**mild·ness** *n* -ES [ME *mildenesse*, fr. *milde* mild + *-nesse* -ness] **:** the quality or state of being mild ⟨surprised at the ~ of his reply⟩

**mild steel** *n* **:** low-carbon steel that contains usu. 0.05 to 0.20 percent carbon, is soft and easily worked, and is used for structural purposes

**mild streak** *n* **:** BROWN BERRY

**mile** \'mīl, *esp before pause or consonant* -ǝl\ *n, pl* **miles** *also* **mile** *often attrib* [ME, fr. OE *mīl;* akin to OHG *mīla, milla* mile; both fr. a prehistoric WGmc word borrowed fr. L *milia* miles (fr. *milia passuum*, lit., thousands of paces), pl. of *mille* mile, fr. *mille passus*, lit., thousand paces, fr. *mille* thousand + *passus*, pl. of *passus* step, pace; L *mille* thousand perh. fr. a prehistoric compound whose first constituent is represented by Gk *hen-, heis* one and whose second constituent is akin to Gk *chilioi* thousand, Skt *sahasra* — more at SAME] **1 :** any of various units of distance derived from an ancient Roman unit equal to 1620 English yards or 1482 meters: as **a :** a unit equal to 5280 ft. ⟨a distance of six ~s⟩ ⟨a ~ race⟩ — called also *statute mile;* see MEASURE table **b :** NAUTICAL MILE **2 :** a race of a mile ⟨has achieved a four minute ~⟩ **3 :** a relatively great distance or interval ⟨missed the target by a ~⟩ ⟨thoughts ~s away⟩ ⟨his guilt stuck out a ~⟩

**mile·age** *also* **mil·age** \'mīlij, -lēj\ *n* -s **1 :** an allowance for traveling expenses at a certain rate per mile **2 :** aggregate length or distance in miles: as **a :** the track of a railroad company or wire of a telegraph company **b :** the total miles traveled in a day or other period of time; *also* **:** rate of travel in miles **c :** the amount of service which something (as an automobile tire) will yield expressed in terms of miles of travel **3 :** a charge per mile (as for the use of the cars of a railroad) **4 :** USEFULNESS, ADVANTAGE, PROFIT ⟨greater press ~ from printing plates⟩ ⟨get more ~ out of school buildings by operating them all year round⟩ ⟨political ~ in promising tax cuts⟩

**mile of line** *or* **mile of road :** a unit for expressing the distance between points connected by railroad line as distinct from the amount of trackage composing the line

**milepost** \'≈,≈\ *n* **1 :** a post placed at a distance of a mile from a similar post or showing the distance in miles from a certain point **2 :** a significant point in a line of progress or development ⟨~s in the chronological development around which this brief discussion may be centered —W.B.Graves⟩

**mil·er** \'mīlǝ(r)\ *n* -s **:** a man or a horse that competes in races at the mile distance

**mi·les glo·ri·o·sus** \'mē,lāz,glōrē'ō,süs\ *n, pl* **mi·li·tes glo·ri·o·si** \'mēlǝ,tāz,glōrē'ō,sē\ [L] **:** a boastful soldier; *esp* **:** a stock comic character of this type in Roman and Renaissance comedy

[1]**mi·le·sian** \mǝ'lēzhǝn, (')mī¦l-, -ēshǝn\ *adj, usu cap* [L *milesius* Milesian (fr. Gk *milēsios*, fr. *Milētus* Miletus) + E *-an*] **1 :** of or belonging to the ancient city of Miletus, Asia Minor, or to its residents **2 :** belonging or relating to a Milesian school of nature philosophers of the 6th century B.C. who were mainly concerned with the basal stuff of which the world is made — compare ANAXIMANDRIAN, THALESIAN

[2]**milesian** \"\ *n* -s *usu cap* **1 :** a native or resident of ancient Miletus **2 :** a member of the Milesian school

[3]**milesian** \"\ *adj, usu cap* [*Milesius* (*Miledh*), mythical Spanish king whose followers are supposed to have conquered Ireland about 1300 B.C. and are regarded as the ancestors of most of the Irish + E *-an*] **:** belonging or relating to the legendary earliest Celts of Ireland; *broadly* **:** IRISH ⟨the banshee haunts only members of the high *Milesian* race —Padraic Colum⟩

[4]**milesian** \"\ *n* -s *usu cap* **:** one of a legendary early Celtic people of Ireland said to have come from Spain; *broadly* **:** IRISHMAN ⟨a true *Milesian*, pious Catholic, and descendant of King Somebody —Anthony Trollope⟩

**milesian tale** *n, usu cap M* [[1]*milesian*] **:** one of a class of short salacious tales current in Greek and Roman antiquity

[1]**milestone** \'≈,≈\ *n* **1 :** a stone serving as a milepost **2 :** a significant point in any progress or development

[2]**milestone** \"\ *vt* **:** to furnish or mark with or as if with a milestone ⟨life pathetically *milestoned* with fragments . . . frustrated hopes —W.H.Gardner⟩

milestone 1

**mile-ton** \'≈'≈\ *n* **:** TON-MILE

**mil·foil** \'mil,fȯil\ *n* -s [ME, fr. OF, fr. L *milifolium, millefolium*, fr. *mille* thousand + *folium* leaf — more at MILE, BLOW] **1 :** YARROW **2 :** WATER MILFOIL

**mil-foot** \'≈'≈\ *n* **:** a unit of electrical conducting material equal to material having a length of one foot and a cross section of one circular mil

**milia** *pl of* MILIUM

**mil·i·a·ceous** \ˌmilē¦āshǝs\ *adj* [L *miliaceus* consisting of millet, fr. *milium* millet + *-aceus* -aceous] **:** MILIARY

**mil·ia·ren·sis** \ˌmilyǝ'ren(t)sǝs\ *n, pl* **miliaren·ses** \-(t),sēz\ [LL, fr. L *mille* thousand] **:** a Byzantine silver coin introduced by Constantine the Great equal to $\frac{1}{1000}$ pound or $\frac{1}{14}$ solidus or after the reign of Justinian I $\frac{1}{12}$ solidus

**mil·i·a·ria** \ˌmilē'a(a)rēǝ, -'er-, -'ār-\ *n* -s [NL, fr. L, fem. of *miliarius* of millet] **:** an inflammatory disorder of the skin that involves the sweat glands, is characterized by redness, eruption, and burning, itching, or pricking sensations, and is associated with excessive sweating and retention of sweat in sweat glands with occluded ducts; *esp* **:** PRICKLY HEAT

**mil·i·ary** \'milē,erē, -lyǝr-, -ri\ *adj* [L *miliarius* of millet, fr. *milium* millet + *-arius* -ary — more at MILLET] **1 :** accompanied or marked by an eruption or formation of lesions the size of millet seeds **2 :** small and numerous **:** made up of many small projections ⟨~ tubercles⟩ ⟨~ granulation⟩

**miliary fever** *n* **:** an epidemic disease characterized by fever, excessive sweating, and eruption of miliary vesicles in the skin

**miliary tuberculosis** *n* **:** acute tuberculosis in which minute tubercles are formed in one or more organs of the body by tubercle bacilli usu. spread by way of the blood

**mi·lieu** \mēl'yǝ, -'yü, -'yǝ(r)\ *n, pl* **mi·lieus** \-z\ *also* **milieux** \-(z)\ [F, environment, center, midst, fr. OF, center, midst, fr. *mi* middle (fr. L *medius*) + *lieu* place, fr. L *locus* — more at MID, STALL] **1 :** ENVIRONMENT, SETTING ⟨historical ~ of a novel⟩ ⟨stylistic and dialectical speech ~s —B.H.Smeaton⟩ **2 a :** the numbers in the middle column of the layout in roulette when a bet is placed on them **b :** the numbers 13 to 24 in the roulette layout **:** the second dozen

**milieu therapy** *n* **:** the manipulation of the environment of a mental patient as an aid toward the patient's recovery

**mil·inch** \'mi,linch\ *n* [*mil-* (fr. L *mille* thousand) + *inch*] **:** a unit of length equal to $\frac{1}{1000}$ inch

**mi·li·o·la** \mǝ'līǝlǝ, ˌmilē'ōlǝ\ *n, cap* [NL, dim. of L *milium* millet; fr. the resemblance of shells of animals of this genus to millet seed] **:** a genus of Foraminifera (the type of a large family Miliolidae) including forms that have existed since the Triassic and have contributed largely to the formation of various limestones

**mil·i·o·lid** \'milēōlǝd\ *n* -s [NL *Miliolidae*, fr. *Miliola*, type genus + *-idae*] **:** a foraminiferan of the genus *Miliola* or the family Miliolidae

**mil·i·o·line** \-ō,līn, -ˌlǝn\ *adj* [NL *Miliola* + E *-ine*] **:** relating or belonging to the genus *Miliola* or the family Miliolidae

**mil·i·o·lite** \-ō,līt\ *n* -s [NL *Miliola* + E *-ite*] **:** a fossil shell of or similar to one of the genus *Miliola*

**mil·i·o·lit·ic** \ˌmilēō¦lid·ik\ *adj* [*miliolite* + *-ic*] **:** of or relating to the genus *Miliola* **:** containing miliolites

**mil·i·tance** \'milǝd·ǝn(t)s, -lǝtǝn- *also* -lǝt°n-\ *n* -s [fr. [1]*militant*, after such pairs as E *attendant: attendance*] **:** MILITANCY

**mil·i·tan·cy** \-nsē, -si\ *n* -ES [[1]*militant* + *-cy*] **:** the quality or state of being militant

[1]**mil·i·tant** \-nt\ *adj* [ME, fr. MF, fr. L *militant-, militans*, pres. part. of *militare* to engage in warfare — more at MILITATE] **1 :** engaged in warfare or conflict **:** FIGHTING ⟨~ powers⟩ **2 :** given to fighting **:** COMBATIVE **3 :** aggressively active in a cause ⟨~ suffragist⟩ ⟨~ trade unionism⟩ **4** *obs* **:** MILITARY ⟨banners ~ —William Wordsworth⟩ **syn** see AGGRESSIVE

[2]**militant** \"\ *n* -s **:** a militant person ⟨~s of the radical party⟩

**mil·i·tant·ly** *adv* **:** in a militant manner ⟨~ vociferous . . . sectarian minority —C.I.Glicksberg⟩

**mil·i·tant·ness** *n* -ES **:** the quality or state of being militant

**militar** *adj* [MF *militaire*] *obs* **:** MILITARY

**mil·i·tar·i·ly** \ˌmilǝ¦terǝlē, -li\ *adv* **:** in a military manner ⟨intervene ~⟩ **:** from a military standpoint ⟨it is ~ stupid to criticize your allies —*Short Guide to Great Britain*⟩

**mil·i·tar·i·ness** \'≈≈,terēnǝs\ *n* -ES **:** the quality or state of being military

**mil·i·ta·rism** \'milǝd·ǝ,rizǝm, -lǝtǝ,-\ *n* -s [F *militarisme*, fr. *militaire* + *-isme* -ism] **:** predominance of the military class or prevalence of their ideals **:** subordination of the civil ideals or policies of a government to the military **:** a spirit which exalts military virtues and ideals **:** a policy of aggressive military preparedness

[1]**mil·i·ta·rist** \-ˌrǝst\ *n* -s [[1]*military* + *-ist*] **1** *archaic* **:** an expert in military matters **2 :** one imbued with militarism

[2]**militarist** \"\ *adj* **:** characterized by militarism ⟨~ faction⟩ **:** dominated by military aims and ideals ⟨~ dictator⟩ — **mil·i·ta·ris·tic** \ˌmilǝd·ǝ¦ristik, -lǝtǝ¦-, -tek\ *adj* — **mil·i·ta·ris·ti·cal·ly** \-tǝk(ǝ)lē, -tek-, -li\ *adv*

**mil·i·ta·ri·za·tion** \ˌmilǝd·ǝrǝ'zāshǝn, -lǝtǝr-, -rī'-\ *n* -s **:** the act of imbuing with a military character or converting to military status ⟨~ of youth organizations⟩

**mil·i·ta·rize** \'milǝd·ǝ,rīz, -lǝtǝ,-\ *vt* -ED/-ING/-s *see -ize in Explan Notes* [F *militariser*, fr. *militaire* military + *-iser* -ize] **1 :** to arm or equip with military forces and defenses **:** prepare for military purposes ⟨a *militarized* frontier⟩ **2 :** to give (an individual or a civilian organization) a military character ⟨a merger between maintenance workers and *militarized* plant guards⟩ **:** subject to military methods ⟨~ labor⟩

[1]**mil·i·tary** \'milǝ,terē, -ri\ *adj* [MF *militaire*, fr. L *militaris*, fr. *milit-, miles* soldier + *-aris* -ar — more at MILITATE] **1 :** of or relating to soldiers, arms, or war **:** ⟨the country's ~ needs⟩ ⟨~ draft⟩ **:** belonging to, engaged in, or appropriate to the affairs of war ⟨~ parade⟩ **:** according to the methods and customs of war or of organized fighting men ⟨~ discipline⟩ — distinguished from *civil* **2 a :** performed or made by armed forces ⟨~ expedition⟩ **b :** supported by armed force ⟨~ government⟩ **3 :** of or relating to the army — distinguished from *naval*

[2]**military** \"\ *n, pl* **military** *also* **militaries** **1 :** ARMED FORCES **:** military branches of government ⟨permit the ~ to control scientific research⟩ ⟨different branches of the ~⟩ ⟨alarmed the *militaries* of both countries⟩ ⟨coronation procession overweighted by ~ though it was —*Manchester Guardian Weekly*⟩ **2 :** military persons; *esp* **:** army officers ⟨the ~ in the car gave . . . no salute as they drove off —William Sansom⟩

**military academy** *n* **1 :** a military school for the training of army officers ⟨U. S. *Military Academy* at West Point⟩ **2 :** a preparatory school for boys where the students habitually wear uniforms and follow military routine

**military band** *n* **1 :** a musical wind band attached to a military establishment **2 :** a band consisting of brass, woodwind, and percussion instruments

**military brush** *n* **:** one of a pair of hairbrushes without handles

**military college** *n* **:** a civilian college where the students habitually wear uniforms and follow military routine

**military commission** *n* **:** a court organized in time of war or suspension of the civil power to try offenses by persons (as civilians) not subject to trial by a court martial

**military crest** *n* **:** a line or position often below the topographical crest and on the slope toward the enemy from which maximum observation of the remainder of the slope can be obtained

**military engineering** *n* **:** the art and practice of designing and building offensive and defensive military works and of building and maintaining lines of military transport

**military government** *n* **:** the government established by a military commander in conquered territory to administer the military law declared by him under military authority applicable to all persons in the conquered territory and superseding any incompatible local law — compare MILITARY LAW

**military governor** *n* **:** a military officer serving as chief political executive of an area under military government ⟨German . . . actions were subject to the veto of the United States *military governor* —E.H.Litchfield⟩

**military heel** *n* **:** a woman's shoe heel like the Cuban heel but lower and thicker

military heel

**military hospital** *n* **:** a hospital for the care and treatment of sick and wounded military personnel

**mil·i·tary·ism** \'milǝ,terē,izǝm\ *n* -s **:** MILITARISM

**military law** *n* **:** law enforced by military rather than civil authority; *specif* **:** law prescribed by statute for the government of the armed forces and of the civilians accompanying them — compare MARTIAL LAW, MILITARY GOVERNMENT

**military macaw** *n* **:** a macaw (*Ara militaris*) with red and green coloring

**military march** *n* **:** a march esp. of lively tempo intended for performance by a military band

**military necessity** *n* **:** the necessity attending belligerent military operations that is held to justify all measures necessary to bring an enemy to complete submission excluding those (as cruelty, torture, poison, perfidy, wanton destruction) that are forbidden by modern laws and customs of war

**military occupation** *n* **:** control and possession of hostile territory that enables an invading nation to establish military government against an enemy or martial law against rebels or insurrectionists in its own territory

**military occupational specialty** *n* **:** the duty or related group of duties that a soldier by training, skill, and experience is best qualified to perform and that is a basis for the classification, assignment, and advancement of enlisted personnel — abbr. *MOS*

**military order** *n* **:** an association of military persons under certain rules membership in which confers some distinction

**military ordinariate** *n* **:** a body of Roman Catholic chaplains serving the military forces of a particular country and subject to the jurisdiction of an appointed bishop of that country

**military police** *n* **1 :** an organized part of an army or command that exercises the functions of police among the soldiers and those attached to the troops, arrests stragglers, takes charge of prisoners **2 :** police organized on military lines — abbr. *MP*

**military policeman** *n* **:** a member of the military police

**military press** *n* **:** PRESS 9a

**military psychology** *n* **:** the application of methods and principles of psychology to problems of military training, discipline, combat behavior

**military salvage** *n* **:** rescue of property from the enemy in time of war that gives the rescuer a right to demand a reward in the prize court

**military school** *n* **:** MILITARY ACADEMY 2

**military science** *n* **:** the known principles underlying military conflict; *specif* **:** a course in military training offered (as by a college) as part of an educational program

**military service** *n* **1 :** service in arms rendered by a feudal tenant holding by military tenure **2 :** active duty in a branch of the armed forces

**military tenure** *n* **:** feudal tenure of land on condition of performing military service — compare KNIGHT SERVICE, GRAND SERGEANTY

**military testament** *or* **military will** *n* **:** NUNCUPATIVE WILL

**military time** *n* **:** time measured in hours numbered to twenty-four (as 0100, 0800, 1600, 2300) from one midnight to the next — compare TIME illustration

**mil·i·tate** \'milǝ,tāt, *usu* -ād·+V\ *vi* -ED/-ING/-s [L *militatus*, past part. of *militare*, fr. *milit-, miles* soldier; perh. akin to Gk *homilos* assembly, Skt *melā*] **1** *obs* **a :** to serve as a soldier **:** engage in warfare **b :** to fight for a cause or a principle **2 :** to have weight or effect ⟨facts ~ against this opinion⟩ ⟨cultural unity has tended to ~ . . . in favor of political independence —G.T.Rowles⟩

**militation** *n* -s [*militate* + *-ion*] *obs* **:** CONFLICT, CONTRADICTION

**milites gloriosi** *pl of* MILES GLORIOSUS

**mi·li·tia** \mǝ'lishǝ\ *n* -s [L, military service, warfare, fr. *milit-, miles* soldier + *-ia* -y] **1** *obs* **a :** military practice or system **b :** military service **c :** ARMAMENT **2** *obs* **:** a particular military force **3 :** HOME RESERVE **4 :** the whole body of able-bodied male citizens declared by law as being subject to call to military service

**mi·li·tia·man** \-shǝmǝn\ *n, pl* **militiamen :** a member of an organized militia

**mil·i·um** \'milēǝm\ *n, pl* **mil·ia** \-ēǝ\ [ME, fr. L — more at MILLET] **1** *pl* **milia**, *obs* **:** MILLET **2** *cap* [NL, fr. L, millet] **:** a widely distributed genus of grasses having flat leaves, large compound panicles, one-flowered spikelets, and an awnless lemma — see MILLET GRASS **3** *pl* **milia** [NL, fr. L, millet] **:** a small pearly firm noninflammatory elevation of the skin (as of the face) due to retention of oil gland secretion in a gland duct blocked by a thin layer of epithelium — compare COMEDO

**mil·jee** \'mil,jē\ *n* -s [native name in Australia] **:** UMBRELLA BUSH

[1]**milk** \'milk, 'miu̇k\ *n* -s [ME, fr. OE *milc, meolc, meoluc;* akin to OHG *miluh* milk, ON *mjolk*, Goth *miluks;* all fr. a prehistoric Gmc noun prob. influenced by the prehistoric Gmc verb represented by OE *melcan* to milk but itself prob. akin to Gk *galakt-, gala* milk; OE *melcan* to milk akin to OHG *melchan*, L *mulgēre*, Gk *amelgein* to milk, Skt *mrjati* he wipes, strokes — more at GALAXY] **1 :** a white or yellowish fluid secreted by the mammary glands of female mammals for the nourishment of their young and holding in suspension fat, protein, sugar, and inorganic salts in varying proportions **2 a :** something that is mild or bland ⟨this drink goes down like ~⟩ ⟨the new general, lanky and amiable, seemed a man of ~ —A.J.Liebling⟩ **b :** something that suggests the relation of mother and child ⟨thy nature . . . too full of the ~ of human kindness —Shak.⟩ **c :** something that suggests an abundance of goodness or blessings ⟨a land flowing with ~ and honey —Josh 5:6 (RSV)⟩ ⟨drunk the ~ of Paradise —S.T.Coleridge⟩ **3 :** a liquid like milk in appearance: as **a :** the latex of a plant **b :** the juice of the coconut **c :** the contents of an unripe kernel of grain **d :** the ripe undischarged spat of an oyster **e :** MILT **f :** an emulsion made by bruising seeds **g :** a suspension of starch or other white powder in water — **in milk :** LACTATING — **in the milk** *of grain* **:** of a milky consistency because of incomplete maturity

[2]**milk** \"\ *vb* -ED/-ING/-s [ME *milken, melken*, fr. OE *milcian, meolcian*, fr. *milc, meolc, meoluc*, n.] *vt* **1 :** to press or draw milk from the breasts or udder of by the hand or by a mechanical device **:** withdraw the milk of **2 :** to draw (milk) from the breast or udder ⟨~ wholesome milk from healthy cows⟩ **3 a** *obs* **:** to suck milk from the breast ⟨love the babe that ~s me —Shak.⟩ **b :** SUCKLE — now used only of animals ⟨ewe unable to ~ her lamb⟩ **4 :** to draw something from as if by milking: as **a :** to compel or persuade to yield profit or advantage illicitly or to an unreasonable degree ⟨lawyers ~*ing* an estate⟩ **:** EXPLOIT, BLEED ⟨~ an enterprise⟩ ⟨comedian ~*ing* a joke for the last possible laugh⟩ ⟨~ a scene⟩ **b :** to draw out (as information) **:** ELICIT ⟨~ news from a source of information⟩ **c :** to draw venom from (a snake) by inducing to strike **d :** to draw (sap, turpentine) from a tree **5 :** to handle or manipulate in a manner like that of drawing milk from a teat ⟨~ blood along the tube in a blood transfusion⟩ ⟨nervously ~*ing* the fringe of the tablecloth⟩ **6 :** to put milk into ⟨cans of tea, already ~*ed* and sugared —Flora Thompson⟩ **7 :** to shuffle (cards) by drawing one from the top and one from the bottom simultaneously allowing them to fall on the table face down ~ *vi* **1 :** to draw or yield milk ⟨return in time for ~*ing*⟩ ⟨when a cow is ~*ing* heavily⟩ **2 :** to become cloudy or foggy — used with *up* ⟨weather began to ~ up⟩

[3]**milk** \"\ *adj* [[1]*milk*] **1 :** of, from, or made with milk ⟨~ chowder⟩ **:** producing or dealing with milk ⟨~ route⟩ **2 :** milk-fed ⟨~ animal⟩

**milk adder** *n* **:** MILK SNAKE

**milk-and-water** \ˌ≈≈'≈≈\ *adj* **:** lacking in vigor and richness **:** WEAK, INSIPID, WISHY-WASHY ⟨*milk-and-water* poetry⟩

**milk-and-wine lily** \'≈≈,≈-\ *n* **:** a crinum (*Crinum sanderianum*) of tropical western Africa that has narrow leaves and white flowers in umbels of three or four with lanceolate red-

banded recurved petals and that is often cultivated as an ornamental
**milk bar** *n* : a counter or a room having a counter where milk drinks and ice cream are served
**milk brother** *n* : a foster brother
**milkbush** \ˈ=,=\ *n* **1** : an Australian shrub (*Wrightia saligna*) of the family Apocynaceae **2** : a southern African spurge (*Euphorbia tirucalli*) that resembles a cactus and has milky juice which is used locally to treat syphilis **3** *West Indies* : a shrub (*Rauwolfia tetraphylla*) with milky juice
**milk chocolate** *n* : chocolate to which sugar and milk have been added in processing
**milk cistern** *n* : the space at the base of a teat or nipple into which the lactiferous ducts of a mammary gland discharge
**milk colic** *n* : pulpy kidney disease of nursing lambs and kids on pasture
**milk cow** *n* : MILCH COW
**milk dentition** *n* : the set of milk teeth
**milk·en** \ˈmilkən\ *adj, archaic* : MILKY, FOGGY
**milk·er** \ˈmilkə(r)\ *n* -S [ME, fr. *milken* to milk + *-er*] **1 a** : one that milks **b** : MILKING MACHINE **2 a** : one (as a cow) that gives milk **b** : one (as a tree) that gives a fluid resembling milk
**milker's nodules** *n pl but sing in constr* : a mild virus infection characterized by reddish blue nodules on the hands, arms, face, or neck acquired by direct contact with the udders of cows affected with cowpox
**milk fat** *n* : BUTTERFAT
**milk fever** *n* **1** : any of various febrile disorders (as puerperal fever) that follow parturition and are popularly associated with the establishment of lactation **2 a** : a disease of recently calved cows or occasionally sheep or goats that is closely related to or identical with grass tetany and caused by excessive drain on the body mineral reserves during the establishment of the milk flow **b** : ketosis of domestic animals
**milkfish** \ˈ=,=\ *n* **1** : a large active silvery herbivorous food fish (*Chanos chanos*) that is widely distributed in the warm parts of the Pacific and Indian oceans and is the sole living representative of the family Chanidae **2** : a silvery gray or dusky small-scaled percoid fish (*Parascorpis typus*) of the southern African coastal waters
**milk-float** \ˈ=,=\ *n, Brit* : a light two-wheeled horse-drawn milk cart
**milk fungus** *n* : a mushroom of the genus *Lactarius*
**milk gap** *or* **milking gap** *n, South & Midland* : an enclosure where cows are milked : COW PEN
**milk glass** *n* : opaque glass orig. milky white but later made in many colors
**milkgrass** \ˈ=,=\ *n* : CORN SALAD
**milk gravy** *n* : gravy made by thickening milk with a blend of flour and fat typically from fried salt pork
**milk hedge** *n* : MILK BUSH 2
**milk house** *n* : a building for cooling, handling, or bottling milk
**milkier** *comparative of* MILKY
**milkiest** *superlative of* MILKY
**milk ill** *n* : indigestion and scouring of young lambs associated with unclean housing
**milk·i·ly** \ˈmilkəlē\ *adv* : in a milky manner
**milk·i·ness** \-kēnəs\ *n* -ES : the quality or state of being milky
**milking** *pres part of* MILK
**milking machine** *n* : a mechanical suction apparatus for milking cows
**milking parlor** *n* : an isolated room or separate building to which cows kept on a loose-housing system are taken for milking
**milking shorthorn** *n, usu cap M&S* : a breed of Shorthorn cattle developed esp. for milk-producing qualities
**milking stool** *n* : a three-legged stool with a half-round shaped seat
**milk ipecac** *n* **1** : FLOWERING SPURGE **2** : SPREADING DOGBANE
**milk lamb** *n* : a lamb fat and ready for market before weaning : a milk-fed lamb
**milk leg** *n* **1** : postpartum thrombophlebitis of a femoral vein **2** : a chronic general swelling of the leg of a horse following an attack of lymphangitis
**milk·less** \ˈ=ləs\ *adj* : having or yielding no milk ⟨~ breasts⟩ : having no milky juice ⟨~ fungus⟩
**milklike** \ˈ=,=\ *adj* : resembling milk : MILKY

milking stool

**milk line** *n* : the line of modified glandular tissue appearing on either side of the body of a mammalian embryo between the base of the front and rear limb buds and giving rise to the mammary glands
**milk-livered** \ˈ=,==\ *adj* : COWARDLY, TIMOROUS ⟨*milk-livered* man, that bear'st a cheek for blows —Shak.⟩
**milkmaid** \ˈ=,=\ *n* : DAIRYMAID
**milk·man** \ˈ=,man, -aa(ə)n, -mən\ *n, pl* **milkmen 1** : a man who sells milk or milk products or delivers them to customers **2** : a man who milks cows
**milkman's syndrome** *n, usu cap M* [after L. A. *Milkman* b1895 Am. roentgenologist] : an abnormal condition marked by porosity of bone and tendency to spontaneous often symmetrical fractures
**milk molar** *n* : one of the deciduous molar teeth of mammals that are shed and replaced by the premolars
**milk mushroom** *n* : MILK FUNGUS
**milk·ness** *n* -ES [ME, fr. [1]*milk* + *-ness*] *chiefly Scot* : yield of milk
**milk of almonds** : ALMOND MILK
**milk of bismuth** : a thick white suspension of bismuth hydroxide and bismuth subcarbonate in water used esp. in the treatment of diarrhea
**milk of lime** : a suspension of calcium hydroxide or hydrated lime in water — compare LIMEWATER
**milk of magnesia** : a milk-white suspension of magnesium hydroxide in water used as an antacid and laxative
**milk of sulfur** : PRECIPITATED SULFUR
**milk parsley** *n* : a Eurasian herb (*Peucedanum palustre*) having an acrid milky juice
**milk pea** *n* : a leguminous plant of the genus *Galactia* (esp. *G. regularis*)
**milk plant** *n* : CAUSTIC CREEPER
**milk plasma** *n* : the fluid part of milk comprising the dissolved casein, proteins, and minerals and excluding the suspended butterfat
**milk powder** *n* : DRIED MILK
**milk punch** *n* : a mixed drink consisting of an alcoholic liquor (as rum, whiskey), milk, and sugar served iced and flavored with nutmeg
**milk purslane** *n* : any of several spurges of the genus *Euphorbia*
**milk run** *n* [so called fr. the resemblance in regularity and uneventfulness to the morning delivery of milk] : a regularly recurrent aerial bombing or search mission orig. of the early morning and expected to be without danger
**milks** *pl of* MILK, *pres 3d sing of* MILK
**milk safe** *n* : a cupboard with pierced tin panels formerly used for storing milk
**milk shake** *n* : milk and a flavoring syrup sometimes with added ice cream shaken up and down in a hand shaker or blended in an electric mixer
**milkshed** \ˈ=,=\ *n* [[1]*milk* + *shed* (divide)] : a region furnishing milk to a particular community
**milksick** \ˈ=,=\ *n* : MILK SICKNESS
**milk sickness** *n* **1** : an acute disease characterized by weakness, vomiting, and constipation and caused by eating the dairy products or meat of cattle poisoned by various plants — compare TREMBLE 3 **2** : TREMBLE 3
**milk snail** *n* : a pulmonate snail (*Helix lactea* or *Otala lactea*) with a pure white shell native to the dry parts of the Mediterranean region but introduced to several parts of the New World where it is sometimes a serious pest of cultivated plants
**milk snake** *n* : KING SNAKE; *esp* : a common harmless snake (*Lampropeltis triangulum*) that is grayish or tan with black-bordered brown blotches and an arrow-shaped occipital spot, occurs from Canada to Mexico, and is popularly believed to frequent milk houses to drink milk though in fact it preys upon the mice infesting such places
**milk·sop** \ˈ=,säp\ *n* [ME, fr. [1]*milk* + *sop*] **1** : a piece of bread sopped in milk **2** : an effeminate or unmanly man : MOLLYCODDLE ⟨that our writers are a lot of school-marmish ~*s* —*Times Lit. Supp.*⟩
**milk·sop·ping** \-piŋ\ *adj* : MILKSOPPY
**milk·sop·py** \-pē\ *adj* : resembling or of the nature of a milksop : WEAK, VAPID
**milkstone** \ˈ=,=\ *n* **1 a** : a stone (as galactite) believed to increase milk secretion **b** : any of various white stones (as a flint pebble) **2** : a hard body that forms in the bovine udder **3** : a hard deposit of milk residues that accumulates on imperfectly cleansed dairy utensils and serves as a substrate for bacteria and contributes off-flavors to milk
**milk sugar** *n* : LACTOSE
**milk thistle** *n* [ME *mylkthystel*, fr. *mylk, milk* milk + *thystel, thistel* thistle] **1** : a tall thistle (*Silybum marianum*) that has large clasping white-blotched leaves and large purple flower heads with bristly receptacles and is native to southern Europe but adventive or naturalized in No. America and many other areas **2** : MILKWEED e(2)
**milk toast** *n* : hot usu. buttered toast served in hot milk and sweetened with sugar or seasoned with salt and pepper
**milk-toast** \ˈ=,=\ *adj* [*milk toast*] : lacking in boldness or vigor : MILD, INOFFENSIVE ⟨~ policy of dealing with criminals⟩
**milk tooth** *n* : a temporary deciduous tooth of a mammal; *esp* : one of man's set of temporary deciduous teeth consisting of four incisors, two canines, and four molars in each jaw
**milk train** *n* **1** : a local train that stops at all or most points benefiting principally the dairy farmers who make daily shipments of milk **2** : a slow train making numerous stops
**milk tree** *n* : any of several trees esp. of *Brosimum, Mimusops*, and *Couma* having abundant latex; *specif* : COW TREE 1
**milk vein** *n* : a large subcutaneous vein that extends along the lower side of the abdomen of a cow and returns blood from the udder and is often supposed to be an index of milking qualities — see COW illustration
**milk vetch** *n* **1** : a bright green prostrate perennial Old World herb (*Astragalus glycyphyllos*) that has sulfur yellow flowers in dense spikes and is popularly supposed to increase the milk yield of goats **2** : any of various plants (as members of the genera *Astragalus, Geoprumnon*, and *Phaca*) that are related to the common milk vetch and that include some which are highly poisonous to livestock — compare LOCOWEED
**milk-warm** \ˈ=ˈ=\ *adj* [ME *mylke warme*, fr. *mylke, milk* milk + *warme, warm* warm] : as warm as fresh-drawn milk : LUKEWARM
**milkweed** \ˈ=,=\ *n* : any of several plants that secrete latex: as **a** : a plant of the family Asclepiadaceae; *specif* : one of the genus *Asclepias* **b** : a plant of the genus *Euphorbia* **c** : a plant of the genus *Lactuca* **d** : DOGBANE 1 **e** *Brit* (1) : MILK PARSLEY (2) : an annual sow thistle (*Sonchus oleraceus*) having leaves with soft spiny teeth
**milkweed bug** *n* : a bug feeding on milkweed; *esp* : a large black red-marked bug (*Oncopeltus fasciatus*) now cultured widely as a research organism
**milkweed butterfly** *n* : MONARCH 3
**milkweed family** *n* : ASCLEPIADACEAE
**milk well** *n* : one of the passages through the abdominal wall of a cow by which the milk veins pass into the abdomen
**milk white** *n* [ME *milc-whit*, fr. OE *meolchwīt*, fr. *meolc* milk + *hwīt* white] : a yellowish white that is less strong and slightly greener and lighter than average shell tint — compare SKIMMED-MILK WHITE
**milk willow herb** *n* **1** : either of two loosestrifes (*Lythrum salicaria* and *L. alatum*) **2** : SWAMP LOOSESTRIFE
**milkwood** \ˈ=,=\ *n* : any of several trees or shrubs having abundant latex: as **a** : a moraceous tree (*Pseudolmedia spuria*) of tropical America **b** : a tree (*Sapium laurofolium*) of Jamaica that resembles a cactus — called also *Jamaica milkwood* **c** : a West Indian poisonous shrub (*Rauwolfia canescens*) **d** : a timber tree (*Sideroxylon inerme*) of southern Africa **e** *Austral* : PAPERBARK
**milkwort** \ˈ=,=\ *n* **1** : a plant of the genus *Polygala*; *esp* : a European plant (*P. vulgaris*) formerly reputed to promote human lactation **2** : a plant of the genus *Campanula* **3** : SEA MILKWORT
**milkwort family** *n* : POLYGALACEAE
**milky** \ˈmilkē, -ki\ *adj* -ER/-EST [ME, fr. [1]*milk* + *-y*] **1** : like or suggestive of milk in color or consistency ⟨~ skin⟩ ⟨~ sap of a cactus⟩; *specif* : whitish and turbid ⟨~ water of a mountain torrent⟩ ⟨~ quartz⟩ **2** : MILD, GENTLE, TAME, SPIRITLESS, EFFEMINATE, TIMOROUS ⟨has friendship such a faint and ~ heart —Shak.⟩ **3 a** : consisting of, containing, or abounding in milk ⟨pails high foaming with a ~ flood —Alexander Pope⟩ **b** : yielding milk; *specif* : having the characteristics of a good milk producer **4** *of an oyster* : SPAWNING
**milky disease** *n* : a highly fatal disease of Japanese beetle larvae and other scarabaeid grubs due to bacilli (*Bacillus popilliae* and related species) that invade the circulation, multiply, and sporulate in great numbers to give a characteristic opaque milky look to the infected larva
**milky mangrove** *n* : BLIND-YOUR-EYES
**milky way** *n* [ME, trans. of L *via lactea*] **1** *usu cap M&W* : a broad luminous irregular band of light stretching completely around the celestial sphere, visible only at night, and caused by the light of myriads of faint stars; *specif* : MILKY WAY GALAXY **2** : GALAXY
**milky way galaxy** *also* **milky way system** *n, usu cap M&W* : the galaxy of which the sun and the solar system are a part and which contains the myriads of stars that comprise the Milky Way together with all the individual stars, clusters, bright and dark nebulosities seen in the sky
[1]**mill** \ˈmil\ *n* -S *often attrib* [ME *mille*, fr. OE *mylen*; akin to OHG *muli, mulin* mill, ON *mylna*; all fr. a prehistoric NGmc-WGmc word borrowed fr. LL *molina, molinum* mill, fr. fem. and neut. of *molinus* of a mill, of a millstone, fr. L *mola* mill, millstone + *-inus* -ine; akin to L *molere* to grind — more at MEAL] **1** : a building provided with machinery for grinding grain into flour ⟨the never-failing brook, the busy ~ —Oliver Goldsmith⟩ ⟨~ sluice⟩ ⟨the ~ cannot grind with water that is past⟩ **2 a** : a machine for grinding grain : QUERN ⟨two shall be grinding at the ~ —Mt 24:41 (RSV)⟩ **b** : a machine for crushing or comminuting some substance ⟨coffee ~⟩ ⟨bone ~⟩ ⟨curd ~⟩ **c** : machinery for the hulling, cleaning, scouring, and polishing of rice kernels **d** : a factory or a machine for reducing hay to meal suitable for poultry and other stock **3** : a machine that manufactures by the continuous repetition of some simple action ⟨operating a stamp ~⟩ ⟨a pulverizing ~⟩ **4** : a building or collection of buildings with machinery by which the processes of manufacturing are carried on ⟨textile ~⟩ ⟨fulling ~⟩ ⟨paper ~⟩ ⟨~ hands were laid off⟩ **5 a** : a screw press formerly used for stamping coins that raised and marked or serrated the edge as it struck the coin **b** : a machine for expelling juice from vegetable tissues by pressure or grinding ⟨cider ~⟩ ⟨cane ~⟩ **c** : a machine for polishing ⟨a lapidary ~⟩ **6** : an institution or office that turns out products in the manner of a factory or machine ⟨diploma ~⟩ ⟨propaganda ~⟩ **7** [[2]*mill*] **a** : a mass of people or animals moving in a circle or without clear direction ⟨turned the leaders of the stampede so as to form a ~⟩ **b** : a boxing match **c** : a folk-dance design usu. formed by two couples in which each dancer joins right or left hands with the one diagonally opposite and all move in a circle to right or left — called also *star, wagon wheel* **8** : TREADMILL **9** *Scot* : a snuffbox esp. with apparatus for pulverizing tobacco **10 a** : a slow or laborious process or routine ⟨legislative ~⟩ **b** : an experience or process that has a marked effect (as of hardening, disciplining, disillusioning) on the character or personality — usu. used in the phrase *through the mill* ⟨through the ~ of higher education⟩ **11 a** : a hardened steel roller having a design in relief used for imprinting a reversed copy of the design in a softer metal (as copper) **b** : MILLING MACHINE, MILLING CUTTER **12** : [2]MORRIS — used with *the* **13** *slang* **a** : the engine of an automobile or boat **b** : TYPEWRITER
[2]**mill** \ˈ"\ *vb* -ED/-ING/-S *vt* **1** : to subject to some operation or process in a mill : shape or finish by means of a mill or machine: as **a** : to full (cloth) in a fulling mill **b** : to grind into flour, meal, or powder **c** : to hull (seeds) by using a mill **d** : to shape or dress (as metal) by means of a rotary cutter : to make (as a key seat) with such a cutter **e** : to stamp (a coin) in a screw press **f** : to pass (soap chips) through a roller mill in the manufacture of toilet soap or soap flakes ⟨French ~*ed* soap⟩ **g** : to mix and condition (as rubber) by passing between rolls **h** : to roll (as steel) into bars **i** : to crush or grind (ore) in a mill **2** : to give a raised rim to (a coin) by a machine operation on the coin blank before striking **3** : to make frothy by churning or whipping ⟨~ chocolate⟩ **4** : to beat with the fists : THRASH, SLUG **5** : to turn or guide (as cattle) into a circular course **6 a** : to make ridges or corrugations on the edge of (a coin) by pressure against a corrugated collar at the time of striking **b** : to cut grooves or crosshatching in the metal surface of (a knob or a finger nut) to aid gripping : KNURL **7** : to saw and dress (timber) in a sawmill ~ *vi* **1** : to hit out with the fists; *esp* : to slug furiously ⟨the match was mostly rough-and-tumble ~*ing*⟩ **2 a** *of cattle* : to move or stampede in a circle **b** : to move in an eddying or disorderly mass ⟨rioters ~*ing* about in the streets⟩ ⟨crowd ~*ing* in the theater lobby⟩ **3** *of a whale* : to swim suddenly in a new direction **4** : to undergo milling or hulling ⟨seed was too wet to ~ properly⟩
[3]**mill** \ˈ"\ *vt* -ED/-ING/-S [perh. fr. [2]*mill*] *archaic* : to break into or rob (a house)
[4]**mill** \ˈ"\ *n* -S [L *mille* thousand — more at MILE] : a unit of monetary value equal to $\frac{1}{1000}$ U.S. dollar or $\frac{1}{10}$ cent
**mill** *abbr* million
**mil·la** \ˈmilə, ˈmē(y)ə\ *n, cap* [NL, fr. J. *Milla*, 18th cent. Span. horticulturist] : a small genus of tropical American cormose herbs (family Liliaceae) that are sometimes cultivated for their showy flowers — see FROST FLOWER
**mill·able** \ˈmiləbəl\ *adj* : suitable for cutting up in a sawmill ⟨acres of ~ forest⟩
**mill addition** *n* : insoluble materials added to frit before grinding in the preparation of a slip for glaze or enamel — called also *mill material*
**mill·age** \ˈmilij, -lēj\ *n* -S : a rate (as of taxation) expressed in mills per dollar
**mill agent** *n* : the responsible local executive at a mill controlled by absentee ownership
**mill bill** *n* : an adz for dressing millstones
**mill blank** *n* : a combination paperboard typically with liners of good grade and cheap filler
**millboard** \ˈ=,=\ *n* [alter. of *milled board*, fr. milled (past part. of [2]*mill*) + *board*] : strong heavy hard paperboard suitable for lining book covers and for paneling in furniture
**mill cake** *n* **1** : the incorporated materials for gunpowder in the form of a dense mass or cake **2** : oil cake obtained by milling
**mill construction** *n* : wooden building construction designed to procure the greatest possible protection against fire without actual fireproofing by disposing of the timberwork in solid masses without boxed-up hollow places and by supporting the flooring directly on girders and brick walls
**millcourse** \ˈ=,=\ *n* : MILLRACE
**milldam** \ˈ=,=\ *n* [ME *milndam*, fr. *miln, mille* mill + *dam*] : a dam to make a millpond; *also* : MILLPOND
**mill drop** *n* : a textile product of a discontinued pattern
**mil·le** \ˈmi(,)lē\ *n* -S [L — more at MILE] : THOUSAND — used chiefly in *per mille* ⟨a ratio of 1068 females per ~ males⟩
**mill edge** *n* : an edge of a sheet of paper or a book page cut by the slitting machine but not evenly trimmed
**mille-feuille** \mēlfœy\ *n, pl* **mille-feuilles** \"\ [F, fr. *mille* thousand (fr. L) + *feuille* leaf, fr. L *folia*, pl. of *folium* leaf — more at BLOW] : NAPOLEON 4
**mil·le·fi·o·ri** *also* **mil·le·fi·o·re** \,miləfēˈōrē\ *n* -S [It, fr. *mille* thousand (fr. L) + *fiori* flowers, pl. of *fiore*, fr. L *flor-, flos* flower — more at BLOW] : ornamental glass usu. of a floral pattern produced by cutting cross sections of fused bundles of glass rods of various colors and sizes and often embedding them in clear glass
**mille·fleur** *or* **mille·fleurs** \(ˈ)mēlˌflər-, -flü(ə)r\ *adj* [F *mille-fleurs*] : having an allover pattern of small flowers and plants ⟨~ tapestry⟩
**mille fleur** \ˈ"\ *n, usu cap M&F* [F *mille-fleurs*] **1** : a breed of bantam chickens with compact body, feathered shanks, and large ear muffs **2** *pl* **mille fleurs** : a bird of the Mille Fleur breed
**mille·fleurs** \ˈ"\ *n pl but sing in constr* [F *mille-fleurs*, fr. *mille* thousand (fr. L) + *fleurs* flowers, pl. of *fleur*, fr. L *flor-, flos* flower] : a perfume made from extracts of several flowers
**mille·grain** \ˈmil,grān\ *adj* [F *mille* + *grain*] *of a gem setting* : having the edge shaped into a fine beading
[1]**mil·le·nar·i·an** \,miləˈna(a)rēən\ *adj* [LL *millenarius* of a thousand + E *-an*] **1** : of or relating to 1000 years **2 a** : relating to the millennium, millenarianism, or the millenarians **b** : believing in the millennium
[2]**millenarian** \ˈ"\ *n* -S : one that believes in a millennium : CHILIAST
**mil·le·nar·ian·ism** \-,nizəm\ *n* -S : belief in the millennium of Christian prophecy
**mil·le·nar·ist** \ˈ==,nerəst\ *n* -S [[1]*millenary* + *-ist*] : MILLENARIAN
[1]**mil·le·nary** \ˈmilə,nerē, məˈlenərē, -ri\ *n* -ES [LL *millenarium* millennium, fr. neut. of *millenarius* of a thousand] **1 a** : a group of 1000 units or things **b** : 1000 years : MILLENNIUM **2** [ML *millenarius*, fr. LL *millenarius*, adj.] : MILLENARIAN **3** : a 1000th anniversary or its celebration
[2]**millenary** \ˈ"\ *adj* [LL *millenarius* of a thousand, fr. L *milleni* one thousand each (fr. *mille* thousand) + *-arius* -ary] **1 a** : relating to or consisting of 1000 (as 1000 years) **b** : being in command of 1000 men **2** : relating to the millennium or millenarians : MILLENNIAL
**mill end** *n* : a mill remnant of cloth
[1]**mil·len·ni·al** \məˈlenēəl\ *adj* [*millennium* + *-al*] **1** : relating to a millennium **2** : of, belonging to, or relating to the millennium of Christian prophecy
[2]**millennial** \ˈ"\ *n* -S : a 1000th anniversary or its celebration
**millennial church** *n, usu cap M&C* : the church of the Shakers
**millennial dawn·ist** \-ˈdȯnəst, -ˈdän-\ *n, usu cap M&D* [*Millennial Dawn* (1886), book by Charles T. Russell †1916 Am. religious leader + E *-ist*] : RUSSELLITE
**mil·len·ni·al·ism** \məˈlenēə,lizəm\ *n* -S : a doctrine that the prophecy in the book of Revelation will be fulfilled with an earthly millennium of universal peace and the triumph of righteousness
**mil·len·ni·al·ist** \-ləst\ *n* -S : MILLENARIAN
**mil·len·ni·al·ly** \-əlē, -li\ *adv* **1** : during 1000 years : in terms of thousands of years ⟨~ old customs⟩ **2** : in a manner of or suggesting the millennium
[1]**mil·len·ni·an** \-ēən\ *n* -S [*millennium* + *-an*, n. suffix] : MILLENARIAN
[2]**millennian** \ˈ"\ *adj* [*millennium* + *-an*, adj. suffix] : of or relating to a millennium
**mil·len·ni·ary** \-,erē, -ri\ *adj* [*millennium* + *-ary*] : MILLENNIAL
**mil·len·ni·um** \məˈlenēəm\ *n, pl* **millen·nia** \-ēə\ *or* **millenniums** [NL, fr. L *mille* thousand + *-ennium* (as in *biennium* period of two years) — more at BIENNIAL] **1 a** : a period of 1000 years ⟨records dating back several *millennia*⟩ **b** : a 1000th anniversary or its celebration **2 a** : the thousand years mentioned in Revelation 20 during which holiness is to be triumphant and Christ is to reign on earth **b** : a period of prevailing virtue or great happiness or perfect government or freedom from familiar ills and imperfections of human existence
**millepede** *also* **milleped** *var of* MILLIPEDE
**mil·le·po·ra** \,miləˈpōrə, məˈlepərə\ *n, cap* [NL, fr. L *mille* thousand + NL *-pora*] : a genus of corals comprising the recent millepores
**mil·le·pore** \ˈmilə,pō(ə)r\ *n* [NL *Millepora*] : any of the stony hydrozoan reef-building corals comprising the order Milleporina with the single recent genus *Millepora* and like the madrepores with which they constitute the major reef-building corals assuming a variety of branching, encrusting, or massive forms though differing from the madrepores in passing through a free-swimming medusoid stage
**mil·le·po·ri·na** \,miləpəˈrīnə, -ˈrēnə\ *n pl, cap* [NL, fr. *Millepora* + *-ina*] : an order of Hydrozoa comprising reef-building stony corals — see MILLEPORE
**mil·le·po·rite** \ˈ==,pōr,īt, ,==ˈ=,=\ *n* -S [ISV *millepore* + *-ite*] : a fossil millepore
**mill·er** \ˈmilə(r)\ *n* -S [ME *millere*, fr. *mille* mill + *-ere* -er]

**1 :** one that operates a mill; *specif* **:** one that grinds grain into flour **2 a :** any of various moths having powdery wings **b :** EAGLE RAY **c :** the male hen harrier **d** *dial Eng* **:** a young spotted flycatcher **e** *dial Eng* **:** WHITETHROAT **1 3 a :** MILLING MACHINE **b :** a tool for use in a milling machine **4 :** SOIL MILLER

**mil·ler–ab·bott tube** \'milə(r)'abət-\ *n, usu cap M&A* [after Thomas Grier *Miller* b1886 Am. physician and William Osler *Abbott* †1943 Am. physician] **:** a double-lumen balloon-tipped rubber tube used for the purpose of decompression in treating intestinal obstruction

**miller index** *n, usu cap M* [after William Hallowes *Miller* †1880 Eng. mineralogist] **:** any of a set of three numbers or letters used to indicate the position of a face or internal plane of a crystal and determined on the basis of the reciprocal of the intercept of the face or plane on the crystallographic axes

**mil·ler·ing** \'milәriŋ, -rēŋ\ *n* -s **:** the occupation or business of a miller

**mil·ler·ism** \-,rizәm\ *n* -s *usu cap* [William *Miller* †1849 Am. sectarian leader + E *-ism*] **:** the doctrines of the Millerites

**¹mil·ler·ite** \-,rīt\ *n* -s *usu cap* [William *Miller* †1849 + E *-ite*] **:** a believer in the doctrine of the American preacher William Miller who taught that the end of the world and the second coming of Christ were at hand and who specif. predicted that this would occur in 1843

**²millerite** \"\ *n* -s [G *millerit*, fr. William Hallowes *Miller* †1880 Eng. mineralogist + G *-it* -ite] **:** sulfide of nickel NiS generally occurring in capillary crystals

**miller's itch** *n* **:** GROCER'S ITCH

**miller's–thumb** \'=,=\ *n, pl* **miller's–thumbs** [ME *myllarys thowmbe*, fr. *myllarys, milleres* (gen. of *myllar, millere* miller) + *thowmbe, thombe* thumb] **1 :** any of several small freshwater spiny-finned sculpins (genus *Cottus*) of Europe (as *C. gobio*) and No. America **2** *dial Eng* **:** any of several small birds (as the goldcrest or the willow warbler)

**milles** *pl of* MILLE

**¹mil·les·i·mal** \mә'lesәmәl\ *n* -s [L *millesimus*, adj., thousandth + E *-al* (as in *decimal*, n.)] **:** THOUSANDTH

**²millesimal** \"\ *adj* [L *millesimus*, adj., thousandth (fr. *mille* thousand) + E *-al*, adj. suffix — more at MILE] **:** consisting of or concerned with thousandths ⟨~ fractions⟩ — **mil·les·i·mal·ly** \-mәlē\ *adv*

**¹mil·let** \'milәt, *usu* -әd.+V\ *n* -s [ME *milet*, fr. MF, fr. *mil* millet (fr. L *milium*) + *-et*; akin to Gk *melinē* millet and prob. to OE *melu* meal — more at MEAL] **1 :** any of various small-seeded annual cereal and forage grasses that produce abundant foliage and fibrous root systems: **a :** a grass (*Panicum miliaceum*) extensively cultivated in Europe and Asia for its grain which is used both as an article of diet for man and as a food for birds and in the U.S. sometimes grown for hay **b :** any of several grasses of genera closely related to *Panicum* (as *Echinochloa, Setaria, Pennisetum, Eleusine*, and *Sorghum*) **2 :** the seed or grain of any of these grasses

**²mil·let** \mә'let\ *n* -s [Turk, nation, people, body of coreligionists, fr. Ar *millah* religion] **:** a non-Muslim group or community in Turkey organized under a religious head of its own who also exercises civil functions of importance

**millet disease** *n* **:** a chronic disease resembling osteoporosis of the bones of horses largely fed with millet

**millet grass** *n* **1 :** a grass of the genus *Milium*; *esp* **:** a tall woodland grass (*M. effusum*) found throughout the north temperate zone **2 :** AUSTRALIAN MILLET

**millet–seed sand** \'==,=-\ *n* **:** sand that consists of smoothly rounded grains about the size of a millet seed and is generally indicative of prolonged eolian action

**mil·let·tia** \mә'led·ēә\ *n, cap* [NL, fr. Charles *Millett*, 19th cent. Eng. official in the Far East + NL *-ia*] **:** a genus of trees and shrubs (family Leguminosae) found in the Old World tropics and having showy streaked dark reddish or chocolate-colored wood

**millfeed** \'=,=\ *n* **:** the by-products (as bran, shorts, middlings) of the milling of wheat flour used for feeding livestock

**mill fever** *n* [¹*mill*] **:** BYSSINOSIS

**mill file** *n* [¹*mill* + *file*; fr. its use for filing the saws of a cotton gin] **:** a single-cut tapered or blunt file

mill files

**mill finish** *n* **:** MACHINE FINISH — abbr. *MF*

**mill head** *n* **:** the head of water employed to turn a mill wheel

**mill–headed** \'=;==\ *also* **mill–head** \'=;=\ *adj* **:** having a milled head ⟨*mill-headed* watch stem⟩

**mill hole** *n* **1 :** GLORY HOLE 4 **2 :** an excavation adjacent to mine workings to obtain waste rock for filling stopes

**millhouse** \'=,=\ *n* [ME *myllehowse*, fr. *mylle, mille* mill + *howse, hous* house] **:** a building that houses milling machinery

**milli-** *comb form* [F *milli-*, fr. L *milli-, mili-* thousand, fr. *mille* — more at MILE] **:** thousandth — esp. in terms belonging to the metric system ⟨*milli*ampere⟩ ⟨*milli*bar⟩ ⟨*milli*meter⟩

**mil·li·ammeter** \;milē+\ *n* [short for earlier *milliamperemeter* (ISV *milliampere* + *-meter*)] **:** an instrument for measuring electric currents in milliamperes — compare AMMETER

**mil·li·amp** \"+,-\ *n* [by shortening] **:** MILLIAMPERE

**mil·li·ampere** \"+\ *n* [ISV *milli-* + *ampere*] **:** one thousandth of an ampere

**mil·li·angstrom** \"+\ *n* [*milli-* + *angstrom*] **:** one thousandth of an angstrom

**mil·liard** \'mil,yärd, -lē,ärd\ *n* -s *often attrib* [F, fr. MF *miliart*, fr. *mili-* (fr. *milion*, million million) + *-ard, -art* -ard] *Brit* **:** a thousand millions — see NUMBER table

**mil·li·ary** \'milē,erē\ *adj* [L *milliarius, miliarius* consisting of a thousand, one mile long, fr. *milli-, mili-* (fr. *mille* thousand) + *-arius* -ary — more at MILE] **:** marking the distance of a mile

**mil·li·bar** \'milә+,-\ *n* [ISV *milli-* + *bar*; orig. formed in G] **:** a unit of atmospheric pressure equal to $\frac{1}{1000}$ bar or 1000 dynes per square centimeter

**mil·li·barn** \"+,-\ *n* [*milli-* + *barn*] **:** a unit of nuclear cross section equal to $\frac{1}{1000}$ barn

**mil·li·cron** \'milә,krän, -krәn\ *n* -s [*milli-* + *micron*] **:** MILLIMICRON

**mil·li·curie** \;milә+\ *n* [ISV *milli-* + *curie*] **:** one thousandth of a curie

**mil·li·darcy** \"+\ *n* [*milli-* + *darcy*] **:** a unit of porous permeability equal to $\frac{1}{1000}$ darcy

**mil·li·degree** \"+\ *n* [*milli-* + *degree*] **:** a unit of temperature equal to $\frac{1}{1000}$ degree

**mil·lieme** \(')mē(l)'yem\ *n* -s [F *millième* thousandth, fr. MF *millieme*, fr. *mille* thousand, fr. L] **1 :** a unit of value equal to one thousandth of a basic monetary unit (as in Egypt and in Libya $\frac{1}{1000}$ pound) — see MONEY table **2 :** an Egyptian or Libyan coin representing one millieme

**mil·li·equivalent** \;milē+\ *n* [*milli-* + *equivalent*] **:** one thousandth of an equivalent of a chemical element, radical, or compound

**mil·li·farad** \;milә+\ *n* [*milli-* + *farad*] **:** one thousandth of a farad

**mil·li·gal** \'milә+,-\ *n* [ISV *milli-* + *gal*] **:** a unit of acceleration equivalent to $\frac{1}{1000}$ gal or 10 microns per second per second that is approximately one millionth of normal acceleration of gravity at the earth's surface

**mil·li·gram** \'milә,gram, -aa(ә)m\ *n* [F *milligramme*, fr. *milli-* + *gramme* gram — more at GRAM] **:** a metric unit of mass and weight equal to $\frac{1}{1000}$ gram — see METRIC SYSTEM table

**milligram–hour** \;==,=\ *n* **:** a unit in which the therapeutic dosage of radium is expressed and which consists in exposure to the action of one milligram of radium for one hour

**mil·li·henry** \;milә+\ *n* [ISV *milli-* + *henry*] **:** one thousandth of a henry

**mil·li·lambert** \"+\ *n* [*milli-* + *lambert*] **:** one thousandth of a lambert

**mil·li·liter** \"+\ *n* [F *millilitre*, fr. *milli-* + *litre* liter — more at LITER] **:** a metric unit of capacity equal to $\frac{1}{1000}$ liter — see METRIC SYSTEM table

**mil·li·lux** \'==+,-\ *n* [*milli-* + *lux*] **:** one thousandth of a lux

**mil·lime** \mә'lēm\ *n* -s [modif. (influenced by F *millième* thousandth) of Ar *mallīm*, fr. F *millième* — more at MILLIEME] **1 :** a Tunisian monetary unit equal to $\frac{1}{1000}$ dinar — see MONEY table **2 :** a coin representing one millime

**mil·li·meter** \'milә,+\ *n* [F *millimètre*, fr. *milli-* + *mètre* meter — more at METER] **:** a metric unit of length equal to $\frac{1}{1000}$ meter — abbr. *mm.*; see METRIC SYSTEM table

**mil·li·met·ric** \;==me·trik\ *adj* [ISV *millimeter* + *-ic*] **:** of a magnitude measured in millimeters **:** MINUTE ⟨~ distinctions⟩

**mil·li·micron** \"+\ *n* [ISV *milli-* + *micron*] **:** a unit of length (as for light waves) equal to one thousandth of a micron or one millionth of a millimeter **:** MICROMILLIMETER — symbol $m\mu$

**mil·li·microsecond** \"+\ *n* [*milli-* + *microsecond*] **:** one thousandth of a microsecond or one billionth of a second

**mil·li·mol·ar** \;milә;mōlә(r)\ *adj* [*millimole* + *-ar*] **:** of, relating to, or containing a millimole — **mil·li·mo·lar·i·ty** \-,mә'larәd·ē\ *n*

**mil·li·mole** \'milә,mōl\ *n* [ISV *milli-* + *mole*] **:** one thousandth of a mole

**mil·line** \'mil;līn\ *n* [blend of *million* and *line*] **1 :** a unit of space and circulation equivalent to one agate line appearing in one million copies of a publication **2** *or* **milline rate :** the cost of one milline figured by multiplying the actual cost of one line by a million and dividing by the circulation

**mil·li·ner** \'milәnә(r)\ *n* -s [irreg. fr. *Milan*, city in northern Italy + E *-er*; fr. the importation of women's finery into England from Italy in the 16th century] **:** one who designs, makes, trims, or sells women's hats

**mil·li·nery** \-,nerē, -ri\ *n* -ES [*milliner* + *-y*] **1 :** the articles made or sold by milliners; *esp* **:** women's headwear **2 :** the business or work of a milliner

**milling** *n* -s [fr. gerund of ²*mill*] **:** a corrugated edge on a coin

**milling cutter** *n* **:** a rotary tool-steel cutter used in a milling machine for shaping and dressing metal surfaces

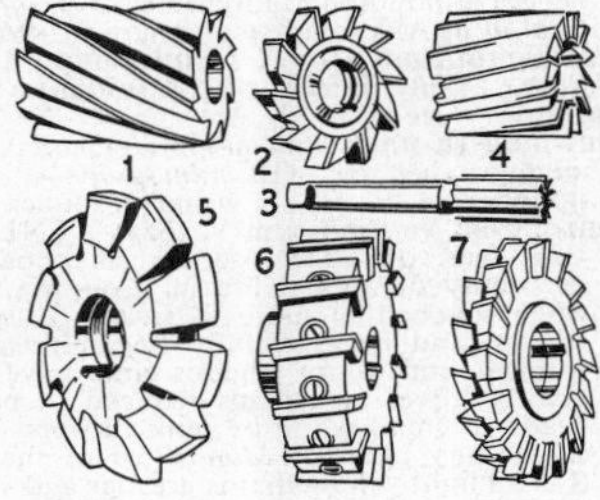

milling cutters: *1* plain, *2* side, *3* end mill, *4* spiral shell end mill, *5* gear, *6* face with inserted teeth, *7* interlocking

**milling dye** *or* **milling acid dye** *n* **:** an acid dye that is fast to fulling on wool — see DYE table I

**milling–in–transit** \'===-'==\ *n* **:** an arrangement by which a through shipment may be detained at an intermediate point usu. for the application of some manufacturing process (as conversion of wheat into flour) with or without increase of freight charge by the carrier — compare FABRICATION-IN-TRANSIT

**milling machine** *n* **:** a machine tool on which work usu. of metal secured to a carriage is shaped by being fed against rotating milling cutters — called also *miller*

**mil·li·normal** \;milә+\ *adj* [*milli-* + *normal*] **:** thousandth normal ⟨~ solution⟩

**¹mil·lion** \'milyәn\ *n, pl* **millions** *or* **million** [ME *milioun, milioun*, fr. MF *milion*, fr. OIt *milione*, aug. of *mille* thousand, fr. L — more at MILE] **1 :** 1000 thousand **:** 100,000 times 10 — see NUMBER table **2 a :** one million units or objects ⟨a total of a ~⟩ **b :** a group or set of a million **3 :** the numerable quantity symbolized by the arabic numerals 1,000,000 **4 :** a very large or indefinitely great number ⟨~*s* of mosquitoes poured into the tent⟩ **5 :** the mass of common people

**²million** \"\ *adj* **1 :** being one million in number ⟨a ~ years⟩ **2 :** being very great in number ⟨a ~ questions⟩ — usu. preceded by *a* or a numeral (as *one, four*)

**mil·lion·aire** \,milyә'na(a)(ә)r, -ne(ә)r, -na(a)ә, -neә, '==,=\ *n* -s [F *millionnaire*, fr. *million*, fr. MF *milion*] **:** one whose wealth is estimated at a million or millions (as of dollars)

**mil·lion·aire·dom** \-dәm\ *n* -s **:** the state of being a millionaire; *collectively* **:** the millionaires of a society or of the world **:** the world of the very rich

**mil·lion·air·ess** \-rәs\ *n* -ES **:** a female who is a millionaire or the wife of a millionaire

**mil·lion·air·ism** \-,rizәm\ *n* -s **:** existence or dominating influence of millionaires

**¹mil·lion·ary** \'milyә,nerē\ *adj* [¹*million* + *-ary*] **:** having a million or millions of money

**²millionary** \"\ *n* -ES **:** MILLIONAIRE

**mil·lioned** \'milyәnd\ *adj* **1 :** numbered by millions **:** INNUMERABLE **2 :** having a million or millions of money

**mil·lion·fold** \;milyәn;fōld\ *adv* [¹*million* + *-fold*] **:** by 1,000,000 times — usu. preceded by *a* or a numeral

**mil·lion·ism** \'milyә,nizәm\ *n* -s **:** MILLIONAIRISM

**mil·lions** \'milyәnz\ *also* **millions fish** *or* **million fish** *n pl but sing or pl in constr* [so called fr. the rapidity with which it reproduces] **:** GUPPY

**¹mil·lionth** \'milyәn(t)th\ *adj* **1 a :** being number one million in a countable series — see NUMBER table **b :** being one of a million equal parts into which something is divisible **2 :** constructed or drawn on a scale of one millionth of the natural size ⟨a ~ map⟩ ⟨a ~ globe⟩

**²millionth** \"\ *n, pl* **millionths** \-yәn(t)s, -yәn(t)ths\ **1 :** number one million in a countable series **2 :** the quotient of a unit divided by one million **:** one of a million equal parts of something

**mil·li·pede** *or* **mil·le·pede** \'milә,pēd\ *also* **mil·li·ped** \-ped\ *n* -s [L *millepeda*, a small crawling animal, perh. the wood louse, fr. *mille* thousand + *-peda* (fr. *ped-, pes* foot) — more at MILE, FOOT] **:** any of numerous myriopods constituting the class Diplopoda having usu. a more or less cylindrical body covered with hard integument and composed of numerous segments with two pairs of legs on most apparent segments, feeding largely on vegetable matter, and having no poison fangs — compare CENTIPEDE

**mil·li·phot** \'milә+,-\ *n* [*milli-* + *phot*] **:** one thousandth of a phot

**mil·li·poise** \"+,-\ *n* [*milli-* + *poise*] **:** one thousandth of a poise

**mil·li·roentgen** \;==+\ *n* [*milli-* + *roentgen*] **:** one thousandth of a roentgen

**mil·li·second** \"+\ *n* [ISV *milli-* + *second*] **:** one thousandth of a second

**mil·lis·ite** \'milә,sīt\ *n* -s [F. T. *Millis*, 20th cent. Am. mineral collector + E *-ite*] **:** a mineral $(Na,K)CaAl_6(PO_4)_4(OH)_9·3H_2O$ consisting of a basic hydrous phosphate of sodium, potassium, calcium, and aluminum

**mil·li·thrum** \'milә,thrәm\ *n* -s [prob. alter. of *miller's-thumb*] **:** LONG-TAILED TIT

**mil·li·volt** \'milә+,-\ *n* [ISV *milli-* + *volt*] **:** one thousandth of a volt

**mil·li·volt·me·ter** \-,mēd·ә(r), -ētә-\ *n* [ISV *millivolt* + *-meter*] **:** an instrument for measuring potential differences in millivolts

**mil·li·watt** \'milә+,-\ *n* [*milli-* + *watt*] **:** one thousandth of a watt

**millken** *n* -s [³*mill* + *ken*] *obs* **:** HOUSEBREAKER

**mill leat** *n, Brit* **:** MILLRACE

**mill·man** \'milmәn\ *n, pl* **millmen 1 :** one that owns, runs, operates, or works in a mill **2 :** one who performs all the hand-tool and machine operations in the making of furniture parts, window and door frames, or other lumber products — called also *millwright, woodworker*

**mill material** *n* **:** MILL ADDITION

**mill moth** *n, Brit* **:** MEDITERRANEAN FLOUR MOTH

**mil·lon's reagent** \(')mē;lō͞nz-\ *or* **millon reagent** *n, usu cap M* [after Eugène *Millon* †1865 Fr. chemist] **:** a solution that is usu. made by dissolving mercury in concentrated nitric acid and diluting with water and that when heated with phenolic compounds gives a red coloration used as a test esp. for tyrosine and proteins containing tyrosine

**mill outlet** *n* **:** COMPANY STORE b

**millowner** \'=,==\ *n* **:** one who owns a mill

**mill pick** *n* [ME *milnpik*, fr. *miln, mille* mill + *pik* pick] **:** MILL BILL

**millpond** \'=,=\ *n* **:** a pond produced by damming a stream to produce a head of water for operating a mill

**millpool** \'=,=\ *n* **:** MILLPOND

**millpost** \'=,=\ *n* [ME *milnepost*, fr. *milne, mille* mill + *post*] **1 :** a large post supporting a windmill **2 :** a post on which the cap of a smock mill turns

**millrace** \'=,=\ *n* [ME *milnras*, fr. *miln, mille* mill + *ras* race, current] **:** a canal in which water flows to and from a mill wheel; *also* **:** the current that drives the wheel

**mill ream** *n* **:** a 472-sheet ream of handmade or moldmade paper composed of 18 inside 24-sheet quires and 2 outside 20-sheet quires

**millrind** *or* **millrynd** \'=,=\ *n* **1 :** an iron support fixed across the hole in the upper millstone of a grist mill **2** *heraldry* **:** a conventional or stylized representation of the millrind of a millstone: as **a** *or* **millrind cross :** CROSS MOLINE **b :** a rectangle, square, or lozenge, voided or pierced, with two projections angling or curving out from the upper side and two from the lower side

millrind 2b

**mill roll** *n* **:** a roll of paper of the width made on a paper machine

**mill run** *n* **1 :** a test of the mineral contents of rock or ore by actual milling **2 :** MILLRACE **3 :** the salable lumber output of a sawmill **4 :** the common run of an article passing through a mill **5 :** something or someone average, ordinary, or mediocre ⟨an unpredictable kind of man, very different from the *mill run* of us down here —Angus Mowat⟩

**¹mill–run** \'=;=\ *adj* [*mill run*] **:** being in the state in which it comes from a run in a mill **:** ungraded and usu. uninspected ⟨*mill-run* steel⟩ ⟨*mill-run* cloth⟩

**²mill–run** \'=,=\ *vt* [*mill run*] **:** to yield (so much weight or worth of precious metal per ton of ore) at a mill run

**mill saw** *n* **:** SASH SAW

**mill scale** *n* **:** a black scale of magnetic oxide of iron formed on iron and steel when heated for rolling, forging, or other processing **:** ⁵SCALE 4a(1)

**mill's canons** \'milz-\ *or* **mill's methods** *n pl, usu cap 1st M* [after John Stuart *Mill* †1873 Eng. philosopher and economist] **:** the five canons of logical induction formulated by J. S. Mill — compare INDIRECT METHOD OF DIFFERENCE, METHOD OF AGREEMENT, METHOD OF CONCOMITANT VARIATIONS, METHOD OF DIFFERENCE, METHOD OF RESIDUES

**millsite** \'=,=\ *n* **:** a site for a mill; *specif* **:** a portion of the public lands acquired under federal law to be used for the erection of a mill or reduction plant in connection with a patent for mineral lands or rights

**mill soke** *n, Anglo-Saxon & early Eng law* **:** the duty of the tenants of land (as a manor) or of others to have their grain ground at a mill; *also* **:** the franchise of receiving the fees for such grinding — compare THIRLAGE

**mill spindle** *n* [ME *mylle spyndelle*, fr. *mylle, mille* mill + *spyndelle, spindel* spindle] **:** a vertical shaft supporting the upper millstone of a grist mill

**millstone** \'=,=\ *n* [ME *mulleston, mylneston*, fr. *mulle, mylne, mille* mill + *ston* stone] **1 :** either of two circular stones often built up of several pieces and used for grinding grain or other substance fed through a center hole in the upper stone — see MILLRIND, MILL SPINDLE **2 :** BUHRSTONE 1 **3 a :** something that grinds or crushes ⟨caught between the ~*s* of high prices and low wages⟩ **b :** a heavy or crushing burden (as of guilt)

**millstone bridge** *n* **:** MILLRIND

**mill store** *n* **:** COMPANY STORE b

**millstream** \'=,=\ *n* **1 :** a stream whose flow is utilized to run a mill **2 :** MILLRACE

**milltail** \'=,=\ *n* **:** the water that flows from a mill wheel after turning it or the channel in which the water flows

**mill tax** *n* **:** a tax of one or more tenths of a cent on each dollar of assessed valuation

**mill tooth** *n* **1** *obs* **:** MOLAR **2 :** a saw tooth having a perpendicular leading edge and a curving after edge

**mill wheel** *n* [ME *myln whele*, fr. OE *mylenhwēol*, fr. *mylen* mill + *hwēol* wheel] **:** a water wheel that drives a mill

**mill white** *n* **:** an interior white paint usu. made with a varnish or bodied oil liquid and generally drying with a glossy or semigloss appearance

**millwork** \'=,=\ *n* **1 a :** the setting up or operating of mill machinery **b :** the shafting, gearing, and other driving machinery of mills **2 :** woodwork (as doors, sashes, trim) that has been machined at a planing mill — compare CABINETWORK

**millwright** \'=,=\ *n* [ME *mylle wryte*, fr. *mylle, mille* mill + *wryte, wrighte* wright] **1 :** one whose occupation is to plan and build mills or to set up their machinery **2 :** a workman who erects the shafting, moves machinery, and cares for the mechanical equipment in a workshop, mill, or plant **3 :** MILLMAN 2

**miln** \'miln\ *now dial var of* MILL

**mil·ner** \'milnә(r)\ *n* -s [ME *mylner*, fr. *mylne, mille* mill + *-er*] **1** *dial Eng* **:** MILLER 1 **2** *dial Eng* **:** MILLMAN 1

**mi·lo** \'mī(,)lō\ *also* **milo maize** *n* -s [Sotho *maili*] **:** any of various rather small usu. early and drought-resistant grain sorghums with compact bearded heads of large yellow or whitish seeds — compare DURRA, FETERITA, KAFFIR

**milo disease** *n* **:** a root and crown rot of milo and sometimes other sorghums caused esp. by a fungus (*Periconia circinata*)

**mi·lon·ga** \mә'lȯŋgә\ *n* -s [AmerSp] **:** an Argentine ballroom dance that preceded the tango early in the 20th century

**mi·lord** \mә'lȯ(ә)r(d), mē-, -ȯ(ә)(d)\ *n* [F, fr. MF *millour, milourd*, fr. ME *my lord*] **:** an English lord or any well-to-do Englishman ⟨the ~, owner of the handsome yacht —George Eliot⟩

**mi·lo·ri blue** \mә'lȯrē-\ *n, often cap M* [after A. *Milori*, 19th cent. Fr. color maker] **:** PRUSSIAN BLUE 2

**milori green** *n, often cap M* **:** DEEP CHROME GREEN

**mil·pa** \'milpә\ *n* -s [MexSp, fr. Nahuatl, fr. *milli* cultivated plot + *pa* in, on] **1 :** a small field in Central America, Mexico, and tropical Asia cleared from the jungle, cropped for a few seasons, and then abandoned for a fresh clearing — compare SWIDDEN **2 :** a maize field in Mexico and Central America or the maize plant

**milque·toast** \'milk,tōst\ *n* -s *often cap* [after Caspar *Milquetoast*, comic strip character created by H. T. Webster †1952 Am. cartoonist, fr. *milk toast*] **:** a timid, meek, or apologetic person **:** one who is habitually afraid to assert himself **:** one readily intimidated by aggression or authority

**mil·reis** \(')mil;rās(h), -āz(h)\ *n, pl* **milreis** \"\ [Pg *mil-réis*, fr. *mil* thousand (fr. L *mille*) + *réis*, pl. of *real* — more at MILE, REAL] **1 :** a Portuguese unit of value equal before 1911 to 1000 reis; *also* **:** a coin representing this value **2 :** the basic monetary unit of Brazil until 1942; *also* **:** a coin representing this unit

**mils** *pl of* MIL

**mil·sey** *or* **mil·sie** \'milsē, -si\ *n* -s [alter. of E dial. *milk-sye*, fr. ME *mylke syhe*, fr. *mylke*, milk milk + *syhe* sieve, fr. *sien, syen* to strain — more at SIE] *chiefly Scot* **:** a milk strainer

**¹milt** *var of* MELT

**²milt** \'milt\ *also* **melt** \'melt\ *n* -s *often attrib* [prob. fr. MD *milte* milt of fish, spleen; akin to OE *milte* spleen — more at MELT] **:** the male reproductive glands of fishes in breeding condition when filled with secretion ⟨a ~ shad⟩; *also* **:** the secretion itself

**³milt** \"\ *vt* -ED/-ING/-S **:** to impregnate (roe) with milt

**milt·er** \'miltә(r)\ *n* -s [prob. fr. ²*milt* + *-er*] **:** a male fish in breeding condition

**mil·to·nia** \mil'tōnēә\ *n* [NL, fr. Charles W.W.Fitzwilliam, Viscount *Milton* †1857 Eng. statesman + NL *-ia*] **1** *cap* **:** a genus of tropical American orchids having flowers with a large unlobed labellum and flat spreading perianth — see PANSY ORCHID **2** -s **:** a plant or flower of the genus *Miltonia*

**¹mil·to·nian** \(')mil;tōnēәn\ *adj, usu cap* [John *Milton* †1674 Eng. poet + E *-an*] **:** MILTONIC

**²miltonian** \"\ *n* -s *usu cap* **:** a specialist in the life or works of John Milton

**mil·ton·ic** \='tänik\ *adj, usu cap* **1 :** characteristic of or relating to John Milton or his work ⟨a reading of those critics who have . . . ventured a comment on the *Miltonic* simile reveals a complete and far-reaching difference of opinion —L.D.Lerner⟩ **2 :** marked by sustained sublimity of style

**mil·ton·ism** \'miltə,nizəm\ *n* -s *usu cap* : a Miltonic expression

**mil·ton·ist** \-,nəst\ *n* -s *usu cap* : MILTONIAN

**mil·ton·ize** \-,nīz\ *vi* -ED/-ING/-S *sometimes cap* : to write in imitation of John Milton's poetic style ~ *vt* : to make Miltonic in style

**milty** \'miltē\ *adj* -ER/-EST [²*milt* + -*y*] : like, resembling, or full of milt ⟨~ trout⟩

**mi·lu** \'mē'lü\ *n* -s [Chin (Pek) *mi²* *lu⁴*, fr. *mi²* tailed deer + *lu⁴* deer] : PÈRE DAVID'S DEER

**mil·va·go** \mil'vä,gō\ *n, cap* [NL, irreg. fr. L *milvus* kite] : a genus of brown and white So. American caracaras

**mil·vus** \'milvəs\ *n, cap* [NL, fr. L, kite] : a genus of birds (family Falconidae) including the common European kite

**mil·wau·kee** \(')mil'wȯkē\ *adj, usu cap* [fr. *Milwaukee*, city in southeast Wisconsin] : of or from the city of Milwaukee, Wis. ⟨a *Milwaukee* industry⟩ : of the kind or style prevalent in Milwaukee

**mil·wau·kee·an** \-ēən\ *n* -s *cap* : a native or resident of Milwaukee, Wis.

**milwaukee brick** *n, often cap M* : a pale orange yellow to yellow

**milz·brand** \'milts,bränt\ *n* [G, fr. *milz* spleen (fr. OHG *milzi*) + G *brand* fire, burning, fr. OHG *brant* brand, fire — more at MILT, BRAND] : ANTHRAX 2

**mim** \'mim\ *adj* [imit.] *dial* : affectedly shy or modest : RETICENT, RETIRING : PRIM

**mim** *abbr* mimeograph

**mim-** *or* **mimo-** *comb form* [L, fr. Gk, fr. *mimos* mime] : mime : mimic ⟨*mimo*type⟩

**mim·al·lon·i·dae** \,mimə'länə,dē\ *n pl, cap* [NL, fr. *Mimallon-, Mimallo*, type genus (fr. Gk *mimallon-, mimallōn* bacchante) + *-idae*] : a family of stout hairy medium-sized diurnal American moths — see SACK-BEARER

**mi·mam·sa** \mē'mämⁿsə\ *n* -s *usu cap* [Skt *mīmāṁsā*, lit., reflection, investigation, fr. *manyate* he thinks — more at MIND] : an orthodox Hindu philosophy concerned with the interpretation of Vedic texts and literature and comprising one part dealing with the earlier writings concerned with right practice and another part dealing with the later writings concerned with right thought — called also respectively *Purva Mimamsa, Uttara Mimamsa;* compare VEDANTA

**mimbar** *var of* MINBAR

**mim·bre·ño** \mēm'brān(,)yō\ *n, pl* **mimbreño** *or* **mimbreños** *usu cap* [AmerSp, fr. *Mimbres* mountains, southwestern New Mexico + Sp *-eño* (suffix added to place names to form names of inhabitants)] **1** : an American Indian people constituting a subdivision of the Gileño **2** : a member of the Mimbreño people

**mim·bres** \'mimbrəs\ *adj, usu cap* [*Mimbres* river, southwestern New Mexico] : of or belonging to a culture in southern New Mexico characterized by dominant Anasazi traits introduced into the Mogollon culture

**¹mime** \'mīm *also* 'mēm\ *n* -s [L *mimus*, fr. Gk *mimos;* akin to Gk *mimeisthai* to imitate, represent] **1 a** : an actor in a mime **b** : one that practices the modern art of mime **2** : one (as a jester, mimic, clown, or buffoon) that performs in ways resembling or held to resemble a performer in a mime **3 a** : a Greek and Roman dramatic entertainment representing scenes from life usu. in a ridiculous manner **b** : a modern form of dramatic entertainment resembling or held to resemble the Greek and Roman mime **4** : an imitation done in or as if in a mime ⟨a perfect ~ of his performance⟩ **5** : the art of creating and portraying a character or of narration by body movement (as by realistic and symbolic gestures) ⟨the use of ~ to tell out a story is not uncommon in Polynesia —*Amer. Anthropologist*⟩ ⟨almost entirely musical on the sound track, the action being in ~ —John Huntley⟩ **6** : a performance of mime

**²mime** \"\ *vb* -ED/-ING/-S *vi* : to act as a mime : play a part with mimic gesture and action usu. without words ⟨*mimed* with all his well-known sensitiveness and power —Phyllis W. Manchester & Iris Morley⟩ ~ *vt* **1** : MIMIC ⟨his peons loyally *mimed* extreme fright —Kenneth Tynan⟩ ⟨he *mimed* outrage, batting his . . . hands together and stamping like a wrestler —A.J.Liebling⟩ **2** : to act out in the manner of a mime ⟨the warrior ~s the slaying of an enemy —H.B.Alexander⟩ ⟨dancers ~ the stories of the ancient myths while singers chant —*Atlantic*⟩

**¹mim·e·o·graph** \'mimēə,graf, -raa(ə)f, -raif, -rȧf\ *n* [fr. *Mimeograph*, a trademark] **1** : a duplicator for making many copies that consists of a frame in which the stencil is stretched and an inking roller for pressing ink through the porous lines of the stencil onto paper **2** : a copy made on a mimeograph

**²mimeograph** \"\ *vb* -ED/-ING/-S *vt* **1** : to produce with a mimeograph ⟨~ copies of a report⟩ **2** : to copy with a mimeograph ⟨~ a letter⟩ ~ *vi* : to use a mimeograph

**mim·er** \'mīmə(r) *also* 'mēm-\ *n* -s [²*mime* + *-er*] : MIME, MIMIC

**mi·me·sis** \mə'mēsəs, mī'-\ *n* -ES [LL, fr. Gk *mimēsis*, fr. *mimeisthai* to imitate] : IMITATION, MIMICRY

**mim·e·tene** \'mimə,tēn\ *also* **mi·met·e·site** \mə'med·ə,sīt, mī'-\ *n* -s [*mimetene* modif. of F *mimétèse* mimetite; *mimetesite* fr. G *mimetesit*, fr. F *mimétèse* + G *-it* -ite] : MIMETITE

**mi·met·ic** \mə'med·|ik, (')mī|m-, -et|, |ēk\ *adj* [LL *mimeticus*, fr. Gk *mimētikos*, fr. *mimētēs* imitator (fr. *mimeisthai* to imitate) + *-ikos* -ic] **1** : having an aptitude for or a tendency toward mimicry : IMITATIVE ⟨~ tendency of infancy —R.W. Hamilton⟩ **2** : of, relating to, or characterized by mimicry **3** : MIMIC 3 ⟨a whole copse of ~ fir trees was being felled —Christopher Morley⟩ **4 a** : characterized by or exhibiting biological mimicry ⟨sometimes an animal develops ~ coloring —A.M.Woodbury⟩ ⟨~ type⟩ **b** : simulating the action or effect of — usu. used in combination ⟨sympatho*mimetic* drugs⟩ ⟨adrenocortico*mimetic* activity⟩ **5** : characterized by resemblance to other forms — used of crystals ⟨a ~ growth of parallel feldspar crystals produces a comblike structure —G.E. Goodspeed⟩ **6** : representing an emotion by imitative gestures and expressions ⟨a ~ dance⟩ ⟨a ballet is a series of solo and concerted dances with ~ actions —Mark Perugini⟩ **7 a** : ONOMATOPOEIC ⟨*hiss* is a ~ word⟩ **b** : resulting from analogy — used of change in a word form

**mi·met·i·cal·ly** \|ək(ə)lē, |ēk-, -li\ *adv* : in a mimetic manner : by mime ⟨such dialogue as can be clearly expressed ~ —*Wisconsin Idea Theatre Quarterly*⟩

**mim·e·tism** \'mimə,tizəm, 'mīm-\ *n* -s [ISV *mimet-* (fr. Gk *mimētēs* imitator) + *-ism*] : MIMICRY

**mim·e·tite** \'mimə,tīt, 'mīm-\ *n* -s [G *mimetit*, fr. F *mimétèse* mimetite (fr. Gk *mimētēs* imitator, fr. *mimeisthai* to imitate) + G *-it* -ite; fr. its resemblance to pyromorphite] : a lead arsenate and chloride $Pb_5Cl(AsO_4)_3$ isomorphous with pyromorphite

**mi·mi·am·bi** \,mimē'am,bī, ,mim-\ *n pl* [L, fr. Gk *mimiamboi*, fr. *mimos* mime + *iamboi*, pl. of *iambos* iamb] : mimes in iambic or choliambic verse

**¹mim·ic** \'mimik, -mēk\ *n* -s [L *mimicus*, adj.] **1 a** : a performer in mimes : MIME 1 **b** : one that mimics (as for amusement) **2** : a cheap or servile imitator **3** : a feeble or poor imitation **4** : a usu. edible and harmless animal that escapes predation by being mistaken by potential predators for a distasteful or venomous animal

**²mimic** \"\ *adj* [L *mimicus*, fr. Gk *mimikos*, fr. *mimos* mime + *-ikos* -ic] **1 a** : of, acting as, or resembling a mime **b** : having an aptitude for or practicing mimicry **2** : befitting or having the characteristics of a mime or mimicry ⟨explained them with great detail and ~ illustration —Ernest Beaglehole⟩ **3** : constituting a copy or imitation of something, often for amusement ⟨the ~ warfare of the opera stage —Archibald Alison⟩ ⟨throwing ~ spears formed of fern stalks —Sacheverell Sitwell⟩ **4** : MIMETIC 5

**³mimic** \"\ *vb* **mimicked; mimicked; mimicking; mimics** [¹*mimic*] *vt* **1** : to copy or imitate very closely esp. in external characteristics (as voice, gesture, or manner) ⟨~s their manners with dexterity —Francis Fergusson⟩ ⟨learned Spanish by . . . *mimicking* the speech of the natives —M.B.Smith⟩ ⟨the Communist and Socialist politicians ~ Soviet policy —*Western Political Quarterly*⟩ **2** : to ridicule by imitation : make sport of by copying or imitating ⟨jumped about the platform, *mimicked* the tight, unseeing capitalists of his . . . imagination —Adria Langley⟩ **3** : to imitate by representation : represent by imitation : SIMULATE ⟨how closely he could ~ marble on paper —Charles Reade⟩ ⟨yellow cretonnes *mimicked* the sunshine that never shone through the . . . windows —Aldous Huxley⟩ **4** : to exhibit biological mimicry with : resemble by biological mimicry ~ *vi* : to perform the action of a mimic ⟨blending and gesturing, painting and *mimicking* and shedding blood —Emma Hawkridge⟩ **syn** see COPY

**mim·i·cal** \-mək*ə*l\ *adj* [²*mimic* + *-al*] : MIMIC — **mim·i·cal·ly** \-mək(ə)lē\ *adv*

**mimic gene** *n* : any of two or more nonallelic genes that have the same effect

**mim·ic·ry** \'mimikrē, -mēk-, -ri\ *n* -ES [*mimic* + *-ry*] **1** : an instance of mimicking **2 a** : the action, practice, or art of mimicking **b** : imitation less creative than mime **3** : a superficial resemblance that some organisms exhibit to other organisms or to the natural objects among which they live and thereby secure concealment, protection, or some other advantage — compare AGGRESSIVE 3a, APOSEMATIC, CRYPTIC 4

**mimic thrush** *n* : MOCKING THRUSH; *esp* : MOCKINGBIRD

**mim·i·dae** \'mimə,dē\ *n pl, cap* [NL, fr. *Mimus*, type genus + *-idae*] : a family of American passerine birds that includes the catbird, mockingbirds, and thrashers and is sometimes considered to constitute a subfamily of Troglodytidae

**mi·mine** \'mī,mīn, 'mi,, -,mən\ *adj* [NL *Miminae*, subfamily in some classifications coextensive with the Mimidae, fr. *Mimus*, type genus + *-inae*] : of or relating to the Mimidae

**miming** *pres part of* MIME

**mim·i·ny-pim·i·ny** \,mimənē'pimənē\ *adj* [prob. alter. (influenced by *mim*) of *niminy-piminy*] : absurdly nice : ridiculously delicate ⟨a *miminy-piminy* . . . young man —W.S.Gilbert⟩ : FINICAL

**mim·ma·tion** \mə'māshən\ *n* -s [Ar *mīm* (letter of the alphabet corresponding to English *m*) + E *-ation*] : the addition of a final *m* in Akkadian — compare NUNNATION

**mim-mouthed** \'≈'≈\ *or* **mim-mou'd** \'≈'müd\ *adj, chiefly Scot* : primly reticent : CLOSEMOUTHED

**mimo-** — see MIM-

**mi·mog·ra·pher** \mə'mägrəfə(r), mī'-\ *n* -s [L *mimographus* mimographer (fr. Gk *mimographos*, fr. *mim-* + *-graphos* -grapher) + E *-er*] : a writer of mimes

**mi·mo·sa** \mə'mōsə, mī'-, -ōzə\ *n* [NL, fr. L *mimus* mime + *-osa*, fem. of *-osus* -ose; fr. its apparent imitation of the sensitivity of animal life in drooping and closing its leaves when touched — more at MIME] **1** *cap* : a genus of trees, shrubs, and herbs (family Leguminosae) that are native to tropical and warm regions and have usu. bipinnate often prickly leaves sometimes reduced to phyllodes and globular heads of small white or pink flowers — see SENSITIVE PLANT **2** -s : any plant of *Mimosa* or of the related genus *Acacia* **3** -s : a light yellow that is greener and slightly less strong than average maize, greener and duller than jasmine, and greener than popcorn — called also *queen's yellow, turmeric*

**mim·o·sa·ceae** \,mimə'sāsē,ē, ,mīm-\ *n pl, cap* [NL, fr. *Mimosa*, type genus + *-aceae*] *in some classifications* : a family of plants (order Rosales) that are commonly included in the family Leguminosae and that have pinnate leaves and small regular flowers in heads or spikes — **mim·o·sa·ceous** \'≈≈'sāshəs\ *adj*

**mimosa webworm** *n* : a small brown webworm that is the larva of a silvery gray black-spotted moth (*Homadaula albizziae*) and that has recently become prominent as a defoliator of mimosa and honey locust esp. in the southeastern U.S.

**mimosa yellow** *n* : a variable color averaging a brilliant greenish yellow that is redder and paler than sulphine yellow

**mi·mo·sine** \mə'mō,sēn, mī'-, -ōsən\ *n* -s [G *mimosin*, fr. NL *Mimosa* + G *-in* -ine] : a crystalline amino acid $C_5H_3NO(OH)CH_2CH(NH_2)COOH$ that is a derivative of alanine and a hydroxy pyridone and is found esp. in the common sensitive plant and the lead tree

**mim·o·type** \'mimə,tīp\ *n* [*mim-* + *type*] : a plant or animal resembling in many respects another from which it is systematically distinct and geographically isolated ⟨the New World hummingbirds are ~s of the Old World sunbirds⟩ — **mim·o·typ·ic** \'≈≈'tipik\ *adj*

**mim·u·lus** \'mimyələs\ *n* [NL, fr. LL, comic actor, fr. L *mimus* mime + *-ulus;* prob. fr. the resemblance of the flower bud to a mask] **1** *cap* : a genus of American herbs (family Scrophulariaceae) having a tubular 5-angled calyx and an irregular 2-lipped corolla — see MONKEY FLOWER **2** -ES : any plant of the genus *Mimulus*

**mi·mus** \'mīməs\ *n, cap* [NL, fr. L, mime — more at MIME] : a genus of birds containing the mockingbirds and being the type of the family Mimidae

**-mi·mus** \"\ *n comb form* [NL, fr. L *mimus* mime] : mimic : imitator — in generic names of animals ⟨*Cetomimus*⟩

**mi·mu·sops** \mə'myü,säps\ *n, cap* [NL, fr. MGk *mimous* (gen. of *mimō* ape, prob. fr. Gk *mimeisthai* to imitate) + NL *-ops*] : a genus of Old World tropical trees (family Sapotaceae) having abundant milky juice, coriaceous leaves, and small hexamerous or octamerous flowers with as many staminodia as stamens — see BANSALAGUIN, MANILKARA

**min** \'min\ *n, pl* **min** *usu cap* [Chin (Pek) *Min³* Fukien, province in southeast China] : any of the Chinese dialects of Fukien province

**min** *abbr* **1** mineral **2** mineralogical; mineralogy **3** minim **4** minimum **5** mining **6** minister; ministry **7** minor **8** minute

**¹mi·na** \'mīnə\ *n, pl* **minas** \-əz\ *also* **mi·nae** \-ī,nē\ [L, fr. Gk *mna*, of Sem origin; akin to Heb *māneh* mina] : an ancient unit of weight of the Babylonians, Hebrews, Greeks, and others varying around one and two pounds

**²mina** \"\ *n* -s [Hindi *mainā* — more at MYNA] : MYNA; *esp* : HILL MYNA

**min·able** *or* **mine·able** \'mīnəbəl\ *adj* : capable of being mined ⟨~ coal⟩ ⟨~ graphite⟩ ⟨~ waters⟩

**mi·na·cious** \mə'nāshəs\ *adj* [L *minac-, minax* threatening + E *-ious* — more at MENACE] : of a menacing or threatening character

**¹mi·nae·an** \mə'nēən\ *adj, usu cap* [L *Minaeus* Minaean (fr. Gk *Minaios*, fr. Ar *Ma'ān, Ma'īn*) + E *-an*, adj. suffix] : of, relating to, or being an ancient kingdom of southwestern Arabia

**²minaean** \"\ *n* -s *usu cap* [L *Minaeus* Minaean + E *-an*, n. suffix] **1** : a member of the Minaean people **2** : the Semitic language of the Minaean people

**mi·na·hasa** \,mēnə'häsə\ *or* **mi·na·has·san** \-sən\ *n, pl* **minahasa** *or* **minahassans** *usu cap* **1** : an Indonesian people inhabiting the Minahasa peninsula of northeast Celebes **2** : a member of the Minahasa people

**mi·nang·ka·bau** \,mēnäŋkə'baù\ *n, pl* **minangkabau** *also* **minangkabaus** *usu cap* [Malay] **1** : an Indonesian people in central Sumatra **2** : a member of the Minangkabau people

**mi·nar** \mə'när\ *n* -s [Ar *manār*] : a tower or turret found esp. in India

**min·a·ret** \,minə'ret, *usu* -ed·+V\ *n* -s [F, fr. Turk *minare*, fr. Ar *manārah* lighthouse, lamp] **1** : a slender lofty tower attached to a mosque and surrounded by one or more projecting balconies from which the summons to prayer is cried by the muezzin **2** : a structure resembling a minaret ⟨the Town Hall . . ., an ornate cream and white building with ~s —*Amer. Guide Series: Maine*⟩

**min·a·ret·ed** \-ed·əd\ *adj* : having or characterized by minarets ⟨the great ~ . . . mosque —Robert Sherrod⟩ ⟨fanciful cities, bright colored and mildly ~ —R.M.Coates⟩

**mi·nas·rag·rite** \,mēnäs'rä,grīt\ *n* -s [*Minasragra*, near Cerro de Pasco, Peru + E *-ite*] : a hydrous acid vanadyl sulfate $(VO)_2H_2(SO_4)_3.15H_2O$ occurring as a blue efflorescent crust

**mina·tory** \'minə,tōrē, -tȯr-, -ri *also* 'mīn-\ *adj* [LL *minatorius*, fr. L *minatus* (past part. of *minari* to threaten) + *-orius* -ory — more at MOUNT] : having a menacing quality : expressive of or conveying a threat ⟨thrusting out a ~ forefinger —Lionel Hale⟩ ⟨the law was ~ and repressive —G.B.Sansom⟩ ⟨their conversation is in the decisive and ~ tone —Earl of Chesterfield⟩

**mi·nau·de·rie** \mē'nōdrē\ *n* -s [F, fr. MF, fr. (assumed) MF *minauder* to simper (whence F *minauder*) (fr. MF *mine* appearance, look) + MF *-erie* -ery — more at MIEN] : a coquettish air — usu. used in pl. ⟨the ~s of the young ladies in the ballrooms —W.M.Thackeray⟩

**minaul** *var of* MONAL

**min·a·way** \'minə,wā\ *n* -s [F *menuet* — more at MINUET] *archaic Scot* : MINUET

**min·bar** \'min,bär\ *or* **mim·bar** \-im,-\ *n* -s [Ar *minbar*] : a Muslim pulpit

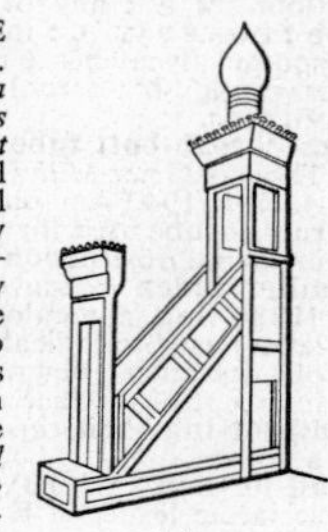

minbar

**¹mince** \'min(t)s\ *vb* -ED/-ING/-S [ME *mincen*, fr. MF *mincer, mincier*, fr. (assumed) VL *minutiare*, fr. L *minutia* smallness, minuteness, fr. *minutus* minute + *-ia* -y — more at MINUTE] *vt* **1 a** : to cut or chop into very small pieces ⟨~ ham⟩ ⟨~ glands in medical research⟩ **b** : to subdivide minutely ⟨his days . . . were *minced* into hours —Van Wyck Brooks⟩; *esp* : to damage by cutting up ⟨the director *minced* up the play⟩ **2** : to cut up (a plover) **3** : to utter or pronounce with affectation (as of refinement or elegance) : clip in pronunciation ⟨*minced* the word in the manner of the old lady⟩ ⟨who *minced* his mother tongue —Leslie Stephen⟩ **4** *archaic* : to diminish in representation : tell in part or by degrees : weaken the force of : make little of : EXTENUATE, MINIMIZE ⟨I do not ~ the truth —P.J.Bailey⟩ **5 a** : to moderate or restrain (words) within the bounds of politeness and decorum ⟨*minced* no words in stating his dislike —J.T.Farrell⟩ ⟨a typical old-school editor who never *minced* words with his enemies —*Amer. Guide Series: Pa.*⟩ **b** : EUPHEMIZE ⟨such *minced* words as *heck, darn, durn, danged* —Thomas Pyles⟩ **6** : to do or perform (something) in an affected way ~ *vi* **1** : to walk with short steps or in a prim affected manner ⟨a painted woman . . . *minced* up to them —T.B.Costain⟩ ⟨a slender, small, dapper man *minced* over the threshold —C.B. Kelland⟩ ⟨while the birds . . . ~ on the pavement at their feet —Constance Carrier⟩ **2** : to speak with affected nicety or elegance **3** : to chop food materials fine — **mince matters** *or* **mince the matter** : to speak in a restrained or subtle manner : avoid speaking frankly or bluntly — used in the negative ⟨he thought she was wrong and did not *mince matters* in telling her so⟩

**²mince** \"\ *n* -s : small bits or pieces into which something is chopped ⟨a ~ of mushrooms⟩; *specif* : MINCEMEAT

**mincemeat** \'≈,≈\ *n* [alter. of *minced meat*, fr. *minced* (past part. of ¹*mince*) + *meat*] **1** : minced meat **2** : a finely chopped and usu. cooked mixture of raisins, apples, spices, and other ingredients with or without meat and suet **3** : something felt to resemble finely chopped meat; *specif* : a state of destruction or annihilation — used in the phrase *make mincemeat of* ⟨science making ~ of the old-time religion —F.L. Allen⟩ ⟨making ~ of the inhabitants —Richard Joseph⟩

**mince pie** *also* **minced pie** *n* : a pie made of mincemeat

**minc·er** \'min(t)sə(r)\ *n* -s : one that minces ⟨a dozen golden-haired languishers and ~s —Max Peacock⟩ ⟨the bone is . . . ground in a ~ under sterile conditions —*Yr. Bk. of Orthopedics & Traumatic Surgery*⟩

**mincha** *var of* MINHAH

**min·chen** \'minchən\ *n* -s [ME *mynchoun*, fr. OE *mynecen, mynecenu*, fem. of *munuc* monk — more at MONK] *archaic* : NUN

**min·chery** \-chərē\ *n* -ES [*minchen* + *-ery*] *archaic* : NUNNERY

**min-chia** \'minjē'ä, -n'jä\ *n, pl* **min-chia** *usu cap M* [Chin (Pek) *Min²* *-chia²*, fr. *min²* people + *chia²* family] **1 a** : a people constituting a sinicized remnant of the Tai of southwest China **b** : a member of such people **2** : the language of the Min-chia people

**min·chia·te** \mēn'kyätā\ *n* -s [It] : an early form of tarok

**mincing** *adj* [fr. pres. part. of ¹*mince*] **1 a** : characterized by or expressive of affected daintiness and elegance ⟨trying to speak in a small ~ treble —George Eliot⟩ ⟨the ~ step of old-fashioned Chinese ladies —Harold Seymour⟩ **b** : affectedly dainty or delicate (as in speech, manner of walking, or behavior) ⟨a ~ lady . . . pushed a streamlined pram —Earle Birney⟩ **2** *archaic* : characterized by an attempt to minimize or extenuate ⟨those ~ names designed only to palliate wrong actions —John Doran⟩ **3** [fr. gerund of ¹*mince*] : used or designed for cutting (something) into small pieces ⟨a ~ machine⟩ ⟨a ~ knife⟩

**minc·ing·ly** *adv* : in a mincing manner ⟨the movies are bright in dialogue but ~ polite in physical action —Gilbert Seldes⟩ ⟨had to step ~ to keep from crushing bantam-size eggs —Howell Walker⟩

**min·co·pie** *also* **min·co·pi** *or* **min·kop·i** \'minkəpē\ *n* -s *usu cap* : ANDAMANESE 1

**mincy** \'min(t)sē\ *adj* -ER/-EST [¹*mince* + *-y*] *dial* : overly particular or delicate ⟨he's hard to cook for — so ~ about his food⟩

**¹mind** \'mīnd\ *n* -s *often attrib* [ME *minde, mynde*, fr. OE *gemynd;* akin to OHG *gimunt* memory, Goth *gamunds* commemoration, mention; all fr. a prehistoric Gmc compound whose first constituent is represented by OE *ge-* (perfective, associative, and collective prefix) and whose second constituent is akin to L *ment-, mens* mind, *monēre* to warn, Gk *menos* spirit, intent, *mnasthai* to remember, *mimnēskein* to remind, Skt *manas* mind, *manyate* he thinks — more at CO-] **1** : the state of remembering or being remembered : MEMORY, RECOLLECTION — used chiefly in phrases ⟨important to keep in ~ the purpose for which the council was summoned —Vernon Bartlett⟩ ⟨hunting, fishing, and other sports . . . come to ~ —E.L.Ullman⟩ ⟨rattle it off out of ~ —*Stamps*⟩ ⟨put me in ~ of an old story —E.G.Bulwer-Lytton⟩ **2** : the commemoration of a deceased person esp. by a requiem just a month or a year after the funeral — see MONTH'S MIND, YEAR'S MIND **3 a** : that which reasons : the doer of intellectual work — usu. distinguished from *will* and *emotion* ⟨formulas toward which her meditating ~ ran —R.P.Blackmur⟩ **b** (1) : an organized group of events in neural tissue occurring mediately in response to antecedent intrapsychic or extrapsychic events which it perceives, classifies, transforms, and coordinates prior to initiating action whose consequences are foreseeable to the extent of available information (2) : the aspect of a biological organism that is not organic in nature ⟨in man ~ is experienced as emotions, imagination, or will⟩ **c** : the sum total of the conscious states of an individual **d** : the sum total of the individual's adaptive activity considered as an organized whole though also capable of being split into dissociated parts ⟨as the conscious and the unconscious ~⟩ **e** : one's capacity for mental activity : one's available stock of mental and adaptive responses **4** : INCLINATION, INTENTION, DESIRE, WISH, PURPOSE — used chiefly in phrases ⟨of a ~ to listen to reason —T.B.Costain⟩ ⟨one of my crack stockmen when he has a ~ to work —Rex Ingamells⟩ ⟨anyone who was of a ~ to ransacked the floors above him —Andy Logan⟩ ⟨know one's own ~⟩ ⟨changed her ~⟩ **5** : the normal or healthy condition of the mental faculties ⟨out of his ~⟩ ⟨lost her ~⟩ **6** : the bent or fixed direction of one's thoughts, inclinations, or desires ⟨kept his ~ on one sole aim —Alfred Tennyson⟩ ⟨a wife to his ~⟩ **7** : that which one thinks regarding something : OPINION, VIEW ⟨the governor desired every member of the board would deliver his ~ —*Colonial Records of Penn.*⟩ ⟨a fool uttereth all his ~ —Prov 29:11 (AV)⟩ ⟨unwilling to speak his ~⟩ **8** : the state of one's spirits : mental disposition : cast of thought or feeling : MOOD **9 a** : a person who is the embodiment of mental qualities (as thought, feelings, or disposition) ⟨the artistic ~⟩ ⟨the scientific ~⟩ ⟨the work of . . . the world's best ~s —*advt*⟩ **b** : a group of people or the inhabitants of an area who are the embodiment of such qualities ⟨the European ~⟩ ⟨the public ~⟩ **10** : intellectual quality : mental power ⟨the works of men of ~ —Alfred Tennyson⟩ **11** *cap* **a** : DEITY 1b ⟨haunted forever by the eternal *Mind* —William Wordsworth⟩ **b** *Christian Science* : ²GOD b(6) **12 a** : the conscious element or factor in the universe that in dualistic metaphysical systems is contrasted with matter and in monistic idealistic systems is held to be the only ultimate reality : SPIRIT, NOUS, INTELLIGENCE **b** : the quality, relatedness, or temporal organization exhibited by a spatial extensity and related to it in a manner analogous to the relation of consciousness to a conscious organism **c** : the objectification of consciousness or awareness : that which attends **13** *dial* : ATTENTION — usu. used with negative ⟨don't pay him any ~⟩

**syn** INTELLECT, SOUL, PSYCHE, BRAIN, BRAINS, INTELLIGENCE, WIT (or WITS): MIND indicates the complex of man's faculties involved in perceiving, remembering, considering, evaluating, and deciding; it contrasts variously with *body, heart, soul,* and *spirit* ⟨the *mind* must have its share in deciding these important matters, not merely the emotions and desires —Rose Macaulay⟩ MIND may indicate the peculiar complex of a particular individual as differing from all others ⟨the *mind* of a dreamer joined to the temperament of a soldier —John Buchan⟩ INTELLECT, sometimes interchangeable with MIND, may focus attention on knowing and thinking powers, those by which one may know, comprehend, consider, and conclude — more coldly analytic powers independent of and discrete from willing and feeling ⟨the emotionalist steeps himself or herself in luxurious feeling and pathetic imagination, which makes no severe call upon either the will or the *intellect* —W.R.Inge⟩ ⟨now the significance of Sir Thomas Browne lies in the fact that he was at once by *intellect* a force in the forward movement and by temperament a reactionary —P.E.More⟩ SOUL, used with considerable variation in meaning and suggestion, may indicate that principle which vitalizes, directs, selects, or inspires in matters emotional and volitional as well as mental ⟨my inner existence, that consciousness which is called the *soul* —Richard Jefferies⟩ ⟨the *soul* is an intelligent, sensitive, and vital principle, a trinity which forms and moves the body predisposed to such action, as well as feels, thinks, and wills —Frank Thilly⟩ PSYCHE may refer to the totality of self composed of all attributes, powers, and activities not purely bodily or somatic but definitely including the unconscious or subconscious ⟨by the *psyche* I understand the totality of all the psychic processes, both conscious as well as unconscious; whereas by soul, I understand a definitely demarcated function-complex that is best characterized as a "personality" —H.G.Baynes⟩ BRAIN or BRAINS in the sense here considered may more forcefully than INTELLECT focus attention on powers of individual comprehension or independent thought ⟨it requires *brains* and education to follow the argument —W.R. Inge⟩ ⟨have I ever even felt inclined to write anything, until my emotions had been unduly excited, my *brain* immoderately stirred, my senses unusually quickened, or my spirit extravagantly roused? —John Galsworthy⟩ INTELLIGENCE is likely to apply specific ability to cope with problems and situations or to exhibition of the play of powers of the intellect or comparable ones ⟨has turned capable men into mere machines doing their work without *intelligence* —G.B.Shaw⟩ ⟨wild animals are not automata — they have *intelligence* if they lack intellect —J.S.Clarke⟩ WIT and WITS may refer to a mind marked by inborn capacity, strong common sense, bright perception, or ready intelligence ⟨had the *wit* to look for him at the Federation meeting —Arnold Bennett⟩ ⟨everyone had to be a jack-of-all-trades, everyone had to live by his *wits* —Van Wyck Brooks⟩ **syn** see in addition MEMORY

— **be a mind** *dial* **:** WISH, INTEND **:** be inclined — usu. used with the infinitive ⟨I'll do what *I'm a mind* to⟩ — **in two minds :** irresolute between two choices — **on one's mind :** occupying one's thoughts and often causing anxiety ⟨too many problems *on her mind*⟩

²**mind** \"\ *vb* -ED/-ING/-S [ME *minden, mynden,* fr. *minde, mynde* mind, memory — more at ¹MIND] *vt* **1 a** *chiefly dial* **:** to put (one) in mind of something **:** REMIND ⟨fight valiantly today; and yet I do thee wrong to ~ thee of it —Shak.⟩ ⟨~ the boy to perform his tasks⟩ ⟨the noise ~*ed* them of their danger⟩ **b :** to serve as a reminder of ⟨that as a sacred symbol it may dwell in her son's flesh, to ~ revengement —Edmund Spenser⟩ **2** *chiefly dial* **:** to recall and bear in mind **:** have in mind **:** REMEMBER ⟨the lads you leave will ~ you —A.E.Housman⟩ ⟨I ~ me how . . . from my Sunday coat I brushed off the burrs —J.G.Whittier⟩ ⟨I ~*ed* how easy her delicacy had been startled —R.L.Stevenson⟩ ⟨~ tomorrow's early meeting —Robert Browning⟩ **3 a :** to occupy oneself with **:** attend to (something) closely **:** direct one's attention or energies upon ⟨~*s* his own business⟩ ⟨~*s* her work and is never heard gossiping⟩ **b** *chiefly dial* **:** to have a liking for ⟨~*ed* nothing but eating and sleeping⟩ **4** *obs* **:** to remember in prayers or a will ⟨~ us when at the throne of grace —Michael Shields⟩ **5 :** to become aware of **:** NOTICE, PERCEIVE ⟨I'll fall flat. Perchance he will not ~ me —Shak.⟩ **6 a** *obs* **:** to have (something) in view **:** contemplate with the intention of taking action ⟨that noble prince began . . . to ~ the reformation of things there run amiss —Edmund Spenser⟩ **b** *chiefly dial* **:** to have as a wish, inclination, or intention **:** PURPOSE — usu. used with an infinitive phrase ⟨I ~ to tell him plainly what I think —Shak.⟩ **7 a :** to give heed to attentively in order to obey ⟨~ the instructions that are about to be issued⟩ **b :** to follow the orders or directions of **:** OBEY ⟨his aunt could not make the child ~ her⟩ ⟨~ your mother⟩ **8 a :** to be concerned or troubled about **:** become vexed or angered over ⟨I did not ~ his being a little out of humor —Richard Steele⟩ ⟨never ~ your unfortunate mistake⟩ **b :** to object to **:** DISLIKE ⟨would you ~ answering a few questions⟩ ⟨another man who does not ~ the cold —Geoffrey Boumphrey⟩ **9 :** to bear in mind and take care **:** SEE — usu. used with a clause ⟨~ that you don't forget to mail the letters⟩ ⟨~ you finish the work today⟩ ⟨~ you beat down his prices a bit —Christopher Isherwood⟩ **10 a :** to be cautious or wary about **:** be on guard against ⟨~ the broken rung on the ladder⟩ **b :** to be careful or attentive about ⟨I wish either . . . had ~*ed* what they were about —Laurence Sterne⟩ **11 :** to take care of **:** have the charge or oversight of **:** guard from harm or injury **:** watch over **:** TEND ⟨women who ~ the child for a small fee —*Social Services in Brit.*⟩ ⟨the man who ~*s* a machine in a factory —J.M. Richards⟩ ⟨the shepherd ~*s* his sheep⟩ **12 :** to regard with attention **:** treat as of consequence **:** consider or note (something) as having importance ⟨we ~ such ideas as justice and liberty; we know that they matter —H.J.Muller⟩ ⟨and this, you, from a man who voted for woman suffrage —W.A. White⟩ ~ *vi* **1** *chiefly dial* **:** REMEMBER — often used with *of, on, upon* ⟨I ~ of what he was saying last week⟩ ⟨he could ~ when that tone first crept into Pa's voice —Minnie H. Moody⟩ **2 :** to be attentive or wary **:** be on guard **3 :** to become concerned or troubled **:** feel agitated or angry **:** CARE, WORRY ⟨never ~ about the matter⟩ ⟨we thought he would be angry but he did not ~⟩ ⟨when the weather stays dry . . . nobody ~*s* about petty irritations —Hilary Phillips⟩ ⟨if nobody ~*s,* I shall go straight to bed —Nigel Balchin⟩ **4 :** to pay heed or attention; *esp* **:** OBEY ⟨a teacher must make the children ~⟩ ⟨the dog ~*s* well⟩ ⟨assigned them extra homework if they didn't ~⟩ **syn** see OBEY, REMEMBER

³**mind** \ˈmind\ *or* **minn** \ˈmin\ *n* -S [OIr *mind*] **:** a thin semioval gold plate believed to have been used by the ancient Celts as an ornament and esp. as a diadem

**mind cure** *n* **:** a method or act of healing disease (as the neuroses) by mental procedures **:** PSYCHOTHERAPY — used esp. in nonmedical practice

**mind doctor** *n* **:** PSYCHIATRIST

**mind·ed** \ˈmīndəd\ *adj* [¹*mind* + *-ed*] **1 :** having an intention, inclination, or disposition (to do something) ⟨many young couples are ~ to marry —F.S.Mitchell⟩ ⟨are further ~ to make fresh provision for the government of our colony —*Nigeria Letters Patent*⟩ ⟨was ever ~ to side with the heretic —Sidney Lovett⟩ ⟨one might query if so ~ —A.L.Kroeber⟩ **2 :** having or characterized by a mind of a specified character — usu. used in combination ⟨an open-*minded* examination —J.G.Palfrey⟩ ⟨how small-*minded* a few of them can be —H.H.Martin⟩ ⟨the hospitable and open-*minded* attitude —*Saturday Rev.*⟩ ⟨absent-*minded*⟩ **3** *obs* **:** having a specified disposition toward someone or something **4 :** having one's thoughts, tastes, or interests inclined in a specified direction (as toward a particular object) ⟨viewing by a statistically ~ . . . group yielded the following data —Walter Goodman⟩ ⟨moral religious-*minded* communities —*Amer. Guide Series: Texas*⟩ ⟨philanthropically ~ individuals and organizations —Thomas Woody⟩ ⟨to vacation-*minded* . . . buyers —Warren Winstanley⟩ ⟨a woman who is society-*minded* —H.A.Overstreet⟩ **5 :** possessing a mind ⟨predispositions of the ~ organism —H.J.McLendon⟩ **6 :** having the status of an immediate object of consciousness ⟨with us human folk there is probably little that is cognitively ~ which is not in some measure conceptualized —C.L.Morgan⟩

**mind·ed·ness** *n* -ES **:** the quality or state of being minded — usu. used in combination ⟨those who pride themselves on their tough-*mindedness* —A.G.N.Flew⟩ ⟨this word-*mindedness* . . . distinguishes writers from scholars —Malcolm Cowley⟩ ⟨the self-*mindedness* of children⟩

**min·del** \ˈmindᵊl\ *n* -S *usu cap* [*Mindel* river, southwest Bavaria, Germany] **:** the second stage of glaciation in Europe during the Pleistocene

**mindel-riss** \ˌ≈ˈ≈\ *n, usu cap M&R* **:** the second interglacial stage of the European Pleistocene between the Mindel and Riss stages of the ice advance

**mind·er** \ˈmīndə(r)\ *n* -S **1** *chiefly Brit* **:** one that minds: as **a :** one that tends or watches something — often used in combination ⟨the housewife who has to get a baby-*minder* in when she is acting as school manager —Barbara Wootton⟩ **b :** PRESSMAN 1 **2** *Brit* **:** a child entrusted to the care of a private person

**mind·ful** \ˈmīn(d)fəl\ *adj* [ME *myndeful,* fr. *minde, mynde* mind, memory + *-ful* — more at MIND] **1 a :** bearing or keeping in mind **:** AWARE — often used with *of* ⟨the whites, ~ of the vagaries of natives' directions, paid little heed —Tom Marvel⟩ ⟨~ of the unhonored dead —Thomas Gray⟩ ⟨~ that . . . this newspaper has opposed protectionism —*Wall Street Jour.*⟩ **b :** inclined to be aware (as of events occurring around one) ⟨a stirring and important book for all ~ Americans —*New Republic*⟩ **2** *obs* **:** having an intention or inclination (to do something) ⟨tired and ~ to rest —James Chetham⟩ — **mind·ful·ly** \-lē, -li\ *adv* — **mind·ful·ness** *n* -ES

**mind-healer** \ˈ≈,≈≈\ *n* **:** one who endeavors to cure physical ills by exclusively mental processes

**minding** *pres part of* MIND

**mind·less** \ˈmīndləs, *rapid* -nl-\ *adj* [ME *myndles,* fr. OE *gemyndlēas* foolish, senseless, fr. *gemynd* mind, memory + *-lēas* -less — more at MIND] **1 a :** destitute of mind or consciousness **:** characterized by or exhibiting a lack of consciousness ⟨hatred toward the sea as though it were not a ~ force but a conscious one —C.B.Nordhoff & J.N.Hall⟩ ⟨fell into a ~ sleep —Mary Austin⟩ **b :** lacking or held to be without intellectual powers **:** STUPID, UNINTELLIGENT ⟨become more than friendly with . . . a gorgeous ~ creature who teaches riding —*New Yorker*⟩ ⟨his white hair crested like a wave over his ~ face —Edith Sitwell⟩ **c :** characterized by or displaying no use of the powers of the intellect **:** UNTHINKING ⟨that deep ~ sympathy —Douglas Stewart⟩ **d :** out of one's mind **:** MAD **2 :** unattentive to **:** having no concern or interest for — usu. used with *of* ⟨empiricism . . . ~ of what has been painfully learned about Communist behavior in the past —Sidney Hook⟩ ⟨the younger men . . . dive for sixpences ~ of sharks —Joseph Crowe⟩ — **mind·less·ly** *adv* — **mind·less·ness** *n* -ES

**mind out** *vi, dial* **:** to watch out

**mind reader** *n* **:** one that professes or is held to have ability in mind reading

**mind reading** *n* **:** the art or faculty of perceiving another's thought without normal means of communication

**minds** *pres 3d sing of* MIND, *pl of* MIND

**mind-set** \ˈ≈,≈\ *n* **1 :** the direction of one's thinking ⟨our educational system has been the most powerful influence in determining the *mind-set* . . . of our youth —C.C.Morrison⟩ **2 :** a fixed state of mind

**mind's eye** *n* [ME *myndes ye,* fr. *mindes, myndes* (gen. of *minde, mynde* mind, memory) + *ye, eie, eye* eye] **:** the faculty held capable of seeing a mental vision consisting of an imaginary or recollected sight as opposed to one actually seen at the time ⟨in my *mind's eye* I could still see the fields covered with tanks, guns, and tents —G.S.Patton⟩ ⟨a hundred times, in his *mind's eye,* his car stopped at their little gate —D.D.Lloyd⟩

**mind stuff** *n* **:** the elemental material held to be the basis of reality and to consist internally of the constituent substance of mind and to appear externally in the form of matter — compare MONISM 1a

¹**mine** [ME *min,* fr. OE *mīn,* suppletive gen. of *ic* I; OE *mīn* akin to OHG *mīn* (suppletive gen. of *ih* I), ON *mīn* (suppletive gen. of *ek* I), Goth *meina* (suppletive gen. of *ik* I); all fr. a prehistoric Gmc inflectional form derived fr. the root of OE *mē* me — more at ME] *obs possessive of* ²I

²**mine** \ˈmīn\ *adj* [ME *min,* fr. OE *mīn* — more at MY] *archaic* **:** MY — used as modifier of a following noun esp. when it immediately precedes a word beginning with a vowel or *h* ⟨~ eyes⟩ ⟨~ own true love⟩ ⟨~ host⟩ ⟨~ hour is not yet come —Jn 2:4 (AV)⟩ or sometimes as a modifier of a preceding noun ⟨mother ~⟩ or as the first of two possessive adjectives modifying the same following noun ⟨~ and your ticket —Sydney Smith⟩

³**mine** \"\ *pron, sing or pl in constr* [ME *min,* fr. OE *mīn,* fr. *mīn,* adj., my — more at MY] **1 :** my one or my ones — used without a following noun as a pronoun equivalent in meaning to the adjective *my* ⟨your dog is large and ~ is small⟩ ⟨your eyes are blue and ~ are brown⟩; often used after *of* to single out one or more members of a class belonging to or connected with the one speaking or writing ⟨a friend of ~⟩ ⟨four or five books of ~⟩ or merely to identify something or someone as belonging to or connected with one speaking or writing without any implication of membership in a more extensive class ⟨those big feet of ~⟩ ⟨that preoccupied manner of ~⟩ **2 :** something belonging to me **:** what belongs to me ⟨vengeance is ~, I will repay, says the Lord —Rom 12:19 (RSV)⟩

⁴**mine** \"\ *n* -S *often attrib* [ME, fr. MF, fr. (assumed) VL *mina,* prob. of Celt origin; akin to W *mwyn* ore] **1 a** (1) **:** a pit or excavation in the earth from which mineral substances (as ores, precious stones, or coal) are taken by digging or by some other method of extraction ⟨a gold ~⟩ ⟨an asphalt ~⟩ — compare OPENCUT, QUARRY (2) **:** such a pit or excavation together with the land, buildings, and machinery belonging to it **b :** an ore deposit ⟨newly discovered ~⟩ **2** *Brit* **:** something that is mined **:** MINERAL ORE; *esp* **:** iron ore **3 a :** a subterranean passage excavated under the wall of a besieged fortress and designed to give access to the besiegers or to cause the wall to fall as a result of the removal of its foundation **b** (1) **:** a cavity or excavation in the earth under an enemy position and containing an explosive charge for destroying enemy personnel, material, or works (2) **:** the explosive charge placed in such a cavity or excavation **c :** an encased explosive anchored or floating in water or placed on or under the earth that may be detonated by contact, the passage of time, magnetic force, sound waves, or controlled means and designed to destroy or damage personnel or an object (as a boat, airplane, or vehicle) — compare ACOUSTIC 1c, AERIAL MINE, ANTIPERSONNEL, ³CONTACT 1, LAND MINE, MAGNETIC MINE, SONIC MINE **4 :** a rich source of supply **:** an abundant store from which something may be obtained in plenty ⟨this book . . . is a ~ of curious and interesting information —R.S. Churchill⟩ ⟨intellectually he was an inexhaustible ~ of sympathy —W.J.Locke⟩ ⟨the window is a favorite ~ of motives for artists to exploit —Henry Adams⟩ **5 :** a place where ore, metals, or precious stones are obtained by digging or washing the soil ⟨a placer ~⟩ **6 :** a pyrotechnic piece comprising various small fireworks (as stars) that are scattered into the air with a loud report **7 :** a gallery made by an insect esp. between the surfaces of a leaf

⁵**mine** \"\ *vb* -ED/-ING/-S [ME *minen,* fr. MF *miner,* fr. OF, fr. *mine,* n. — more at ⁴MINE] *vi* **1 :** to dig in the earth esp. for the purpose of constructing a mine under an enemy fortification ⟨they began to ~ under the castle —Richard Grafton⟩ **2 :** to dig a mine **:** to get ore, metals, coal, or precious stones out of the earth **:** to work in a mine ~ *vt* **1 a :** to dig under for the purpose of gaining access through or causing the collapse of (as the walls of an enemy fortification) **b :** to attack, ruin, or destroy by slow and secret means **:** UNDERMINE **2 a :** to get (as ore, metal, or other natural constituent) from the earth (as by digging, blasting, or pumping) ⟨to ~ oil shale⟩ ⟨to ~ ground water⟩ ⟨to ~ gold⟩ **b :** to extract from a usu. rich source of supply ⟨novels . . . from which more skillful dramatizers have been able to ~ good theatrical plays —*London Calling*⟩ **3 :** to dig or make a hollow in **:** burrow beneath the surface of ⟨a larva that ~*s* leaves⟩ **4 a :** to place an explosive charge in or under for the purpose of destroying (as an enemy fortification) **b :** to lay military mines in (as water) **:** place mines in or under (as land) **5 :** to furnish with underground passages **:** make subterranean passages under **6 a :** to dig into (as the ground) for ore or metal **b :** to process for obtaining a natural constituent ⟨~ the air for nitrogen⟩ ⟨~ sea water for magnesium⟩ **c :** to dig into (a usu. rich source of supply) for the purpose of obtaining items of use or value ⟨the many historical novels that have *mined* the rich vein of history in upstate New York —*Amer. Guide Series: N.Y.*⟩ ⟨so far *mined* only a fraction of the cultural treasures of those times —*Saturday Rev.*⟩ **7 a :** to crop (as land) repeatedly without applying fertilizer **b** *or* **mine out :** to deplete the riches or resources from (a source of supply) without making any provision for replenishment ⟨a system . . . which will increase its productivity instead of *mining* its wealth —Elspeth Huxley⟩ ⟨has . . . scholarship at last *mined out* the field —T.H.Williams⟩

**mineable** *var of* MINABLE

**minecraft** \ˈ≈,≈\ *n* **:** warships of various types whose primary mission is laying or sweeping mines ⟨commander of ~ in the Pacific Fleet —Walter Karig & Welbourn Kelley⟩

**mine detector** *n* **:** a device for locating buried or concealed mines usu. by indicating the presence of metal or by giving a signal when it is passed over something different from the ground in the vicinity

**minefield** \ˈ≈,≈\ *n* **:** an area occupied by mines anchored or sunk in water or buried in the ground for offensive or defensive purposes ⟨tanks could pass through the ~*s* and engage the enemy —Walter Nash⟩ ⟨~*s* are swept by flotillas —F.E. Dodman⟩

**minehead** \ˈ≈,≈\ *n* **:** PITHEAD

**mine inspector** *n* **:** one that checks mines to determine the safety condition of working areas, equipment, ventilation, and electricity and to detect fire and dust hazards

**minelayer** \ˈ≈,≈≈\ *n* **:** a naval vessel especially equipped for or engaged in the laying of underwater mines

**mineowner** \ˈ≈,≈≈\ *n* **:** a whole or part owner of a mine

**mine pig** *n* **:** pig iron made wholly from ore

**mine planter** *n* **:** a small ship resembling a minelayer and formerly used by the U. S. Army to lay mines as part of harbor defense operations

**min·er** \ˈmīnə(r)\ *n* -S [ME *miner, minere,* alter. (influenced by *-er, -ere* -er) of *minour,* fr. OF *mineor,* fr. *miner* to mine + *-eor* -or — more at MINE] **1 :** one that mines: as **a :** one that constructs or lays military mines; *esp* **:** a soldier having such duties **b :** one engaged in the business or occupation of getting ore, coal, precious substances, or other natural substances out of the earth **c :** a machine for automatic mining (as of coal) **d :** a worker on the construction of underground tunnels and shafts (as for roads, railways, waterways) **2 a :** any of numerous insects that in the larval state excavate galleries in the parenchyma of leaves **b :** any of several honey eaters of Australia and Tasmania (as *Myzantha melanocephala*)

**min·er·ag·ra·phy** \ˌminəˈragrəfē\ *or* **min·er·al·og·ra·phy** \ˌminərəˈlägrəfē\ *n* -ES [*mineragraphy* fr. *mineral* + *-graphy; mineralography* fr. *mineral* + *-o-* + *-graphy*] **:** the technique of studying polished surfaces of minerals with the reflecting microscope

¹**min·er·al** \ˈmin(ə)rəl\ *n* -S [ME, fr. ML *minerale,* fr. neut. of *mineralis,* adj.] **1 a :** a solid homogeneous crystalline chemical element or compound (as diamond or quartz) that results from the inorganic processes of nature and that has a characteristic crystal structure and chemical composition or range of compositions — compare METAMICT, MINERALOID **b :** any of various naturally occurring homogeneous or apparently homogeneous and usu. but not necessarily solid substances (as ore, coal, asbestos, asphalt, borax, clay, fuller's earth, pigments, precious stones, rock phosphate, salt, soapstone, sulfur, building stone, cement rock, peat, sand, gravel, slate, salts extracted from river, lake, and ocean waters, petroleum, water, natural gas, air, and gases extracted from the air) obtained for man's use usu. from the ground **c :** a synthetic substance having the chemical composition and crystalline form and other physical properties of a naturally occurring mineral ⟨compounds made in the laboratory or the smelting furnace are at best called artificial ~*s* —E.S.Dana⟩ **2** *obs* **:** MINE ⟨like some ore among a ~ of metals base —Shak.⟩ **3 :** something that is neither animal nor vegetable (as in the old general classification of things into three kingdoms: animal, vegetable, and mineral) **4 :** ORE — used esp. in the mining industry **5 :** an inorganic substance; *esp* **:** a mineral element whether in the form of an ion, compound, or complex — compare ³ASH 1b ⟨the ~*s* or the contents of the ash from the body —K.F.Maxcy⟩ **6 minerals** *pl, Brit* **:** MINERAL WATER; *esp* **:** an artificially carbonated water sometimes flavored (as ginger ale) ⟨~*s* were served . . . as well as morning coffee and afternoon teas —Sylvia T. Warner⟩

²**mineral** \"\ *adj* [ME, fr. ML *mineralis,* fr. *minera* ore, mine (fr. OF *miniere* mine, fr. *mine*) + L *-alis* -al — more at MINE] **1** *obs* **a :** of or relating to mines **b :** skilled in or well informed about mining **2 :** of or relating to minerals **:** consisting of or of the nature of a mineral ⟨~ ores⟩ **:** INORGANIC ⟨~ deposits in the water passages surrounding the valve seats —H.F. Blanchard & Ralph Ritchen⟩ **3 :** impregnated with mineral substances (as salts) ⟨~ waters⟩

**mineral acid** *n* **:** an inorganic acid ⟨the strong *mineral acids,* such as nitric, sulfuric, and hydrochloric —W.C.Tobie⟩

**mineral bister** *n* **:** SHERRY 2

**mineral black** *n* **:** a black pigment: as **a :** one made by grinding carbonaceous shale or slate **b :** a natural pigment containing graphite **c :** black iron oxide

**mineral blue** *n* **1 :** a blue pigment: as **a :** a natural pigment made by grinding the mineral azurite or a synthetic pigment of similar composition — called also *mountain blue;* compare BLUE VERDITER **b :** BREMEN BLUE 2 **c :** an iron blue usu. lightened by admixture (as with white clay) **2 a :** AZURITE BLUE **b :** ANTWERP BLUE 2

**mineral brown** *n* **1 :** any of several colors of native earths colored with iron oxide that average the color negro — called also *iron, metallic brown* **2 :** any of several pigments (as metallic brown) from natural sources

**mineral caoutchouc** *n* **:** ELATERITE

**mineral charcoal** *n* **:** a substance resembling charcoal that is interlaminated in silky fibrous layers in beds of ordinary bituminous coal — called also *mother of coal*

**mineral coal** *n* **:** COAL 3a

**mineral color** *n* **:** an inorganic pigment usu. of natural origin

**mineral dressing** *n* **:** the mechanical preparation of a mineral (as ore) either for direct use or for further processing

**mineral element** *n* **:** a chemical element usu. other than carbon, hydrogen, oxygen, or nitrogen that is a constituent of plant or animal tissue and in most cases is found in the ash remaining after incineration of the tissue ⟨specific roles of the *mineral elements* in plants —B.S.Meyer & D.B.Anderson⟩ — compare MACRONUTRIENT, TRACE ELEMENT

**mineral gray** *n* **:** a light greenish gray that is yellower, lighter, and stronger than French gray and darker than ash gray

**mineral green** *n* **1 :** a green pigment: as **a :** MALACHITE GREEN 1a **b :** SCHEELE'S GREEN **2 :** MALACHITE GREEN 3

**min·er·al·ist** \ˈmin(ə)rələst\ *n* -S [¹*mineral* + *-ist*] *archaic* **:** MINERALOGIST ⟨the mountain . . . has several of the appearances described by ~*s* —Jedidiah Morse⟩

**min·er·al·iza·tion** \ˌmin(ə)rələˈzāshən, -ˌlīˈ-\ *n* -S **1 :** the action of mineralizing **:** the state of being mineralized ⟨~ of soil nitrogen⟩ ⟨~ of bone⟩ **2 a :** the process of change or metamorphism whereby minerals are secondarily developed in a rock; *esp* **:** the formation or introduction of ore minerals into previously existing rock masses **:** METALLIZATION **b :** the state resulting from such a process of change **3 :** deposition in the cell wall of inorganic salts

**min·er·al·ize** \ˈmin(ə)rəˌlīz\ *vb* -ED/-ING/-S *vt* **1 :** to transform (a metal) into an ore **2 :** to impregnate or supply with minerals or any inorganic compound ⟨*mineralized* water⟩ ⟨~ organic matter⟩ **:** convert into mineral or inorganic form ⟨*mineralized* nitrogen in soils⟩ **3 :** PETRIFY ~ *vi* **:** to promote the formation of minerals

**min·er·al·ized** \-zd\ *adj* **:** having or characterized by a usu. abundant supply of ore ⟨the red stains that signalize ~ land —*Science Illustrated*⟩ ⟨the most richly ~ district in the world —C.O.Dunbar⟩

**min·er·al·iz·er** \-zə(r)\ *n* -S **1 :** an element that in combination with a metal forms an ore ⟨in galena sulfur is a ~⟩ **2 :** a dissolved gas or vapor (as water or fluorine) that promotes the crystallization of minerals in a molten magma, in adjacent rock, or in veins genetically related to the intrusion of the magma

**mineral jelly** *n* **:** a semisolid substance from petroleum that is similar to but cruder than petrolatum and that is used as a stabilizer in explosives

**mineral kingdom** *n* **:** the one of the three basic groups of natural objects that comprises inorganic objects — compare ANIMAL KINGDOM, PLANT KINGDOM

**mineral lands** *n pl* **:** lands usu. held by a federal government as public lands and valuable for deposits of metals and other minerals (as marble, slate, petroleum, asphalt, and guano)

**mineral lease** *n* **:** MINING LEASE

**min·er·alo·corticoid** \ˌmin(ə)rəlō+\ *n* [ISV ¹*mineral* + *-o-* + *corticoid*] **:** a corticoid (as deoxycorticosterone) that affects chiefly the electrolyte and fluid balance in the body

**min·er·al·og·i·cal** \ˌmin(ə)rə¦läjəkəl, -jēk-\ *also* **min·er·al·og·ic** \-jik, -jēk\ *adj* [*mineralogical* fr. *mineralogy* + *-ical; mineralogic* prob. fr. F *minéralogique*, fr. *minéralogie* (prob. fr. E *mineralogy*) + *-ique* -ic] **:** of or relating to mineralogy ⟨a ~ table⟩ ⟨~ chemistry⟩ ⟨~ changes⟩

**min·er·al·o·gist** \÷ˌminəˈräləjəst, -ral-\ *n* -s [prob. fr. (assumed) NL *mineralogia* mineralogy + E *-ist*] **:** a specialist in mineralogy

**mineralography** *var of* MINERAGRAPHY

**min·er·al·o·gy** \÷ˌminəˈräləjē, -ral-, -ji\ *n* -ES [prob. fr. (assumed) NL *mineralogia*, irreg. fr. ML *minerale* mineral + L *-logia* -logy] **1 :** the science of minerals that deals with their crystallography and their physical and chemical properties in general, their classification, and the ways of finding and distinguishing them **2 :** the materials of the science of mineralogy (as minerals or the attributes of minerals or mineral formations) ⟨the ~ of the Black Hills⟩ **3 :** a treatise of the science of mineralogy

**min·er·al·oid** \ˈmin(ə)rəˌlȯid\ *n* -s [ISV ¹*mineral* + *-oid*; prob. orig. formed in G] **:** an amorphous substance that would otherwise have the attributes of a mineral; *esp* **:** a metamict substance derived from a mineral — compare GEL MINERAL

**mineral oil** *n* **:** a liquid product of mineral origin that is within the viscosity limits recognized for oils (as petroleum, shale oil, or any oil obtained from them by refining); *esp* **:** LIQUID PETROLATUM — compare HYDROCARBON OIL, PARAFFIN OIL

**mineral orange** *n* **1 :** ORANGE MINERAL **2 :** FIRE RED 1

**mineral pigment** *n* **:** an inorganic pigment whether natural or synthetic — distinguished from *organic pigment*

**mineral pitch** *n* **:** ¹ASPHALT 1

**mineral pulp** *n* **:** a fibrous variety of talc used as a filler in paper manufacture

**mineral purple** *n* **1 :** a dark red pigment consisting of iron oxide **2 :** PURPLE OF CASSIUS

**mineral red** *n* **:** a grayish red that is bluer and duller than Pompeian red or bois de rose and yellower and duller than appleblossom

**mineral resin** *n* **:** any of a group of resinous usu. fossilized deposits found in various rocks **:** BITUMEN **:** ASPHALT

**mineral right** *n* **:** the legal right or title to all or to specified minerals in a given tract **:** the right to explore for and extract such minerals or to receive a royalty for them

**mineral rod** *n* **:** DIVINING ROD

**mineral rubber** *n* **1 :** any of various rubbery substances of mineral origin (as asphalt) **2 :** an artificial asphalt obtained usu. by blowing petroleum residues with air and used in compounding rubber and in insulation — compare BLOWN OIL 2

**mineral salt** *n* **1 :** a salt of an inorganic acid **2 :** a salt occurring as a mineral (as rock salt)

**mineral seal oil** *n* **:** a distillate of petroleum that boils higher than kerosine and is used as an illuminant and as a solvent oil

**mineral soil** *n* **:** a soil derived from minerals or rocks and containing little humus or organic matter

**mineral spirit** *n* **:** PETROLEUM SPIRIT

**mineral spring** *n* **:** a spring with water containing much mineral matter in solution that is usu. enough and of such kinds as to be noticeable to the taste

**mineral surveyor** *n* **:** a surveyor appointed under federal law and authorized to make official surveys of mineral lands — called also *deputy surveyor*

**mineral tallow** *n* **:** HATCHETTINE

**mineral tanning** *n* **:** the process of tanning (an animal skin) by impregnating with metallic salts — compare CHROME TANNING, TAW

**mineral tar** *n* **:** MALTHA

**mineral violet** *n* **:** MANGANESE VIOLET

**mineral water** *n* **:** water naturally or artificially impregnated with mineral salts or gases (as carbon dioxide) — compare SALINE WATER, SODA WATER 2a, SULFUR WATER

**mineral wax** *n* **:** a wax of mineral origin; *esp* **:** OZOKERITE

**mineral white** *n* **1 :** BLANC FIXE **2 :** gypsum ground and used in pigments

**mineral wool** *n* **:** any of various light-weight vitreous materials produced in the form of fibers that resemble wool fibers or glass fibers and that are used as such or after conversion into granular form, felted form (as in batts, blankets, or boards), or molded form chiefly in heat and sound insulation, in insulating cements, and as filter media: as **a :** SLAG WOOL **b :** ROCK WOOL **c :** GLASS WOOL

**mineral yellow** *n* **1 a :** YELLOW OCHER **b :** ORPIMENT 2 **2 :** CASSEL YELLOW 1

**miner's anemia** *n* **:** HOOKWORM DISEASE

**miner's asthma** *or* **miner's consumption** *n* **:** PNEUMOCONIOSIS

**miner's cramps** *n pl* **:** HEAT CRAMPS

**miner's inch** *n* **:** a unit of water flow that varies with locality; *esp* **:** a flow equal to 1.5 cubic feet per minute

**miner's phthisis** *n* **:** a disease of miners: as **a :** ANTHRACOSIS **b :** ANTHRACOSILICOSIS **c :** PNEUMOCONIOSIS

**miner's right** *n* **:** a license given to Australian miners to explore for and extract a mineral (as gold)

**miner's tent** *n* **:** a usu. triangular tent that is suspended from a tree or set up with one center pole

**miner's worm** *n* **:** the hookworm (*Ancylostoma duodenale*) that often infests miners and tunnel workers

**mine-run** \ˈ=¦=\ *n* **1 :** the unsorted product of a mine **2 :** a product of common or average grade ⟨the *mine-run* of commercial breads will fall within continued eating —Lee Anderson⟩

**min·ery** \ˈmīnərē\ *n* -ES [ML *mineria*, *minaria*, fr. OF *miniere* mine — more at MINERAL] *archaic* **:** a place where mining is carried on

**mi·nes·tra** \məˈnestrə\ *n* -s [It, fr. *minestrare* to serve minestra, dish up, fr. L *ministrare* to serve, dish up — more at MINISTER] **:** Italian vegetable soup **:** MINESTRONE

**min·e·stro·ne** \ˌminəˈstrōnē, ÷-ōn\ *n* -s [It, aug. of *minestra*] **:** a rich thick vegetable soup with dried beans, macaroni, vermicelli, or similar ingredients sometimes topped with grated cheese

**minesweeper** \ˈ=ˌ==\ *n* **:** a warship designed for sweeping or neutralizing mines

**minesweeping** \ˈ=ˌ==\ *n* **:** the action of dragging a body of water for submarine or floating mines in order to remove, neutralize, explode, or otherwise make them harmless

**mi·nette** \məˈnet\ *n* -s [G, fr. F, oolitic iron ore, fr. F *mine* ore, mine + *-ette* — more at MINE] **1 :** a dark igneous rock composed chiefly of biotite and orthoclase that occurs usu. in narrow dikes and sheets and that constitutes one of the lamprophyres **2** [F] **:** an oolitic iron ore containing as a rule 28 to 48 percent of iron and 1.5 to 2 percent of phosphorus that is plentiful in Luxemburg and Lorraine and is adapted for the basic Bessemer process

**minever** *var of* MINIVER

**mine worker** *n* **:** a workman in a mine

¹**ming** *vt* -ED/-ING/-S [ME *mingen* to mention, remind, fr. OE *myngian, myndgian, mynegian*; akin to OE *gemynd* mind, memory — more at MIND] *obs* **:** MENTION

²**ming** \ˈmiŋ\ *var of* MENG

³**ming** \ˈ"\ *adj, usu cap* [*Ming*, Chin. dynasty (1368–1644), fr. Chin (Pek) *ming²* bright, clear, luminous] **:** of, relating to, or having the characteristics of the period of the Ming dynasty and esp. the art forms developed during that period ⟨a *Ming* bowl⟩ ⟨ordinary *Ming* porcelain is apt to be heavy —Bernard Leach⟩

**minge** \ˈminj\ *n* -s [prob. alter. of *midge*] **:** MIDGE; *esp* **:** BITING MIDGE

¹**min·gle** \ˈmiŋgəl\ *vb* **mingled; mingled; mingling** \-g(ə)liŋ\ **mingles** [ME *menglen*, freq. of *mengen* to mix, mingle, fr. OE *mengan*; akin to MD *mengen* to mix, mingle, MHG *mengen* to mix, mingle, Gk *massein*, *mattein* to knead, Russ *myagkiĭ* soft] *vt* **1 :** to bring or combine together or with something else so that the components remain distinguishable in the combination **:** INTERMIX, MIX ⟨its designer . . . has *mingled* type, photographs and contemporary prints to make a book —J.K.Bettersworth⟩ ⟨these questions of . . . economic behavior clearly ~ the fields of economics and law —G.B. Hurff⟩ **2 :** to mix so that the components become physically united or form a new combination ⟨the two rivers ~ their waters to form a lake⟩ **3 :** to make or prepare by mixing ingredients **:** CONCOCT ⟨~ a sleeping draft⟩ ~ *vi* **1 :** to become combined or brought together or with something else — used esp. of things ⟨three major state highways all meet, ~, and marvellously disengage themselves —*New Yorker*⟩ ⟨beguiling byways where fact and fancy ~ —Drew Middleton⟩ ⟨apple and peach orchards along the route ~ with farms and vineyards —*Amer. Guide Series: Va.*⟩ ⟨the muddy water of the river ~s with the green of the Gulf —*Amer. Guide Series: La.*⟩ **2 a :** to associate or come in contact — used esp. of people ⟨as communication expands and races ~ —A.W.Hummel⟩ ⟨on the streets three classes ~ but do not mix —*Amer. Guide Series: Texas*⟩ ⟨he ~s only with millionaires —H.J.Laski⟩ **b :** to move about (as in a group) ⟨~ occasionally in society —Sir Walter Scott⟩ ⟨newspaper spies who were able to ~ among politicians —W.A.Swanberg⟩ **syn** see MIX

²**mingle** \ˈ"\ *n* -s **1** *archaic* **:** the action of mingling or the state of being mingled **2** *archaic* **:** something that is mingled **:** MIXTURE

¹**min·gle-man·gle** \ˈ=¦=ˌmaŋgəl\ *n* -s [redupl. of ²*mingle*] **:** a usu. confused mixture or medley **:** HODGEPODGE

²**mingle-mangle** *vt, obs* **:** to make a mingle-mangle of

**min·gle·ment** \ˈmiŋgəlmənt\ *n* -s **:** the action or an instance of mingling ⟨a close ~ of Egyptian and Babylonian culture—*Times Lit. Supp.*⟩

**min·go** \ˈmiŋ(ˌ)gō\ *n, pl* **mingoes** *or* **mingos** *usu cap* [of Algonquian origin; akin to Del *Mingwe* Iroquois, lit., stealthy, treacherous] **:** IROQUOIS 1b

**min·gre·li·an** \minˈgrēlēən, miŋˈ-\ *also* **min·grel** \ˈmiŋgrəl, ˈmiŋg-\ *n, pl* **mingrelian** *or* **mingrelians** *also* **mingrel** *or* **mingrels** *usu cap* **1 a :** a people of the Kutais region of the Caucasus related to the Georgians whose physical beauty they share **b :** a member of such people **2 :** the South Caucasic language of the Mingrelian people

**ming tree** *n* [perh. fr. *Ming*, Chin. dynasty (1368–1644) — more at MING] **1 :** a dwarfed evergreen conifer grown in a container or pot **2 :** an artificial plant patterned after bonsai and made by wiring or otherwise attaching flattened pads of prostrate alpine buckwheat (*Eriogonum ovalifolium*) left natural gray, dyed, or painted to one or more twiggy branches usu. of manzanita — called also *Peruvian cypress* **3 a :** BONSAI **b :** an ornamental arrangement patterned after the bonsai

**min·gy** \ˈminjē\ *adj* -ER/-EST [perh. blend of ¹*mean* and *stingy*] **:** STINGY, MEAN

**min·hag** \minˈhäg, ˈ=ˌ=\ *n, pl* **min·ha·gim** \minˈhäˌgēm, ˌ==ˈ=\ [Heb *minhāgh* custom] **1 :** Jewish religious custom **2 :** the form of Hebrew liturgy prevailing in a particular community **3 :** local Jewish religious practices not specified in the Talmud or medieval rabbinical codes but having authority through long observance

**min·hah** *or* **min·chah** *also* **min·ha** *or* **min·cha** \minˈkä, ˈminkə\ *n* -s [Heb *minḥāh*, lit., gift, offering] **:** a daily afternoon liturgy of the Jews — compare MAARIB, SHAHARITH

**min·i·a·ceous** \ˌminēˈāshəs\ *adj* [L *miniaceus*, fr. *minium* cinnabar, red lead + *-aceus* -aceous — more at MINIUM] **:** of the color of minium or red lead

**min·i·a·scape** \ˈminēəˌskāp\ *n* [²*miniature* + *-scape*] **:** a dish garden made with dry or other plant materials that do not require water — compare BONSAI

**min·i·ate** \ˈminēˌāt\ *vt* -ED/-ING/-S [L *miniatus*, past part. of *miniare* to color with cinnabar or red lead, fr. *minium* cinnabar, red lead] **1 :** to paint with red lead or vermilion **2 a :** to decorate (as a manuscript) with letters or the like painted red **:** RUBRICATE **b :** ILLUMINATE 4

¹**min·i·a·ture** \ˈmin(ē)əˌchu̇(ə)r, -ùə, -ˌchə(r), -nichə(r), -nēchə(r) *also* -ˌtu̇-, -ˌtyu̇- *sometimes* -nyəˌ-\ *n* -s [It *miniatura* picture on a small scale, art of manuscript illumination, fr. *miniato* (past part. of *miniare* to illuminate a manuscript) (fr. L *miniatus*, past part. of *miniare* to color with cinnabar or red lead) + *-ura* -ure] **1 :** a representation on a much reduced scale **:** a small copy or image ⟨turned the valley into a lush ~ of the Imperial Valley across the border —Marion Wilhelm⟩ ⟨a ~ of the . . . headquarters store in its capacity to meet every grade of customer —McKenzie Porter⟩ **2 :** a drawing or painting included in a book or manuscript esp. of the medieval period **:** ILLUMINATION **3 :** the art of painting miniatures **4 :** a portrait or other painting done on a very small scale (as on ivory or metal) ⟨the art of portrait ~s was orginated in England —Louise H. Burchfield⟩ **5 :** a chess problem with few (as seven or fewer) chessmen **6 :** a set or model built on a reduced scale that appears to be of normal size when photographed (as in the movies or television) **7 :** a small camera **8 :** MINIATURE SHEET **9** *also* **miniature rose :** FAIRY ROSE **10 :** a production (as in literature or music) of short length or restricted scope — **in miniature :** in a greatly diminished size, form, or scale **:** in microcosm ⟨imitating *in miniature* the elaborate programmes of the state universities —W.L.Sperry⟩ ⟨a . . . carnival which is a sort of Mardi Gras fiesta *in miniature* —Green Peyton⟩

²**miniature** \ˈ"\ *adj* **1 :** being or represented on a small scale ⟨~ reproductions⟩ ⟨a ~ book⟩ ⟨a ~ war⟩ **2 :** of or relating to still photography in which film 35 millimeters wide or smaller is used ⟨a ~ camera⟩ ⟨a ~ negative⟩ **syn** see SMALL

³**miniature** \ˈ"\ *vt* -ED/-ING/-S **:** to represent in a small compass or on a small scale ⟨this round orb . . . ~s the world —*New Monthly Mag.*⟩

**miniature golf** *n* **:** a novelty golf game played with a putter on a miniature course having tunnels, bridges, sharp corners, and other obstacles over which the ball must be guided

**miniature pink** *n* **:** a pale to grayish yellowish pink — called also *reveree*

**miniature sheet** *n* **1 :** a small sheet of postage stamps (as of 25 stamps) with gum and perforations that is printed as a souvenir and bears in the margins lettering identifying some notable event being commemorated **2 :** SOUVENIR SHEET 1 **3 :** a set of mounted postage stamps displaying all of the plate numbers (as four) from an original sheet in their correct relative positions

**min·i·a·tur·ist** \-chu̇rəst, -chər-\ *n* -s [F *miniaturiste*, fr. *miniature* picture on a small scale (fr. It *miniatura*) + *-iste* -ist] **:** a maker of miniatures

**min·i·a·tur·iza·tion** \ˌ=(=)=ˌchu̇rəˈzāshən, -ˌchər-\ *n* -s **:** the action or process of miniaturizing ⟨heat is a major problem in ~ of . . . many electrical instruments —Annesta R. Gardner⟩ ⟨the recent trend toward ~ in the . . . field of electronics —*Materials & Methods*⟩

**min·i·a·tur·ize** \ˈ=(=)=ˌchu̇ˌrīz, -ˌchəˌ-\ *vt* -ED/-ING/-S **:** to design or construct in small size esp. for economy of space or weight ⟨an all-out campaign to ~ electronic equipment —*advt*⟩

**min·i·bus** \ˈminəbəs\ *n* [prob. blend of ²*miniature* and *omnibus*] **:** a light carriage usu. having a rear door and seats for four passengers and formerly used as a cab — compare OMNIBUS

**min·i·cam** \ˈminəˌkam\ *also* **mini·camera** \ˈminə+ˌ-\ *n* -s [by shortening fr. *miniature camera*] **:** a miniature camera

**mini·car** \ˈminə+ˌ-\ *n* [²*miniature* + *car*] **:** a small automobile

**min·i·con·jou** \ˌminəˈkän(ˌ)jü\ *n, pl* **miniconjou** *or* **miniconjous** *usu cap* **:** a people of the western plains constituting a division of the Teton Dakota

**min·ié ball** \ˈminē-, -ēˌā-\ *n, sometimes cap M* [after Claude Étienne *Minié* †1879 Fr. army officer] **:** a rifle bullet having a cylindrical body, conical head, and hollow base and much used in the middle of the 19th century

**min·i·fer** \ˈminəfə(r)\ *dial var of* MINIVER

**min·i·fi·ca·tion** \ˌminəfəˈkāshən\ *n* -s [fr. *minify*, after such pairs as E *magnify: magnification*] **:** the action or process of minifying

**min·i·fy** \ˈminəˌfī\ *vt* -ED/-ING/-S [L *minimus* smallest + E *-fy*] **:** to make small or smaller **:** LESSEN

¹**min·i·kin** \ˈminəkən, -nēk-\ *n* -s [obs. D *minneken* darling, fr. MD *minnekijn*, fr. *minne* love, beloved + *-kijn* -kin; akin to OHG *minna* love, ON *minni* memory, Goth *gaminthi* remembrance, OE *gemynd* mind, memory — more at MIND] **1** *obs* **a :** a thin gut treble string of a viol or lute **b :** LUTE, VIOL **2** *obs* **:** DARLING 1a **3** *archaic* **:** a small creature **:** a diminutive or insignificant thing ⟨prepared to harry some whitebait threading the tide but . . . the ~s escaped —Hugh McCrae⟩

²**minikin** \ˈ"\ *adj* **1** *archaic* **:** dainty in manner or appearance; *esp* **:** AFFECTED 3 ⟨the pettiness, the ~ finical effect of this little man —Nathaniel Hawthorne⟩ **2 :** very small in size or form **:** DIMINUTIVE, MINIATURE, TINY ⟨the ~ little dribble that I called a canal —S.H.Adams⟩ ⟨a ~ fraction of history⟩ **3** *obs* **:** SHRILL — used of a voice ⟨one blast of thy ~ mouth —Shak.⟩

¹**min·im** \ˈminəm\ *n* -s [in sense 1, fr. ME *mynym*, fr. ML *minima*, fr. L, fem. of *minimus* smallest, least; in sense 2, fr. ML *minimus*, fr. L, smallest, least; in other senses, fr. L *minimus* smallest, least — more at MINIMUM] **1 a** (1) **:** the note in mensural notation formerly equaling one half or one third the value of the semibreve depending upon whether imperfect or perfect time respectively and constituting sometimes the shortest note in use (2) **:** HALF NOTE **b :** HALF REST **2** *usu cap* **:** a member of an austere order of mendicant hermits or friars founded in the 15th century by St. Francis of Paola **3 :** something very minute: as **a :** a creature or thing of the least size or consequence **b :** the smallest or least possible part or particle **:** JOT **4 :** a single downstroke in penmanship (as any of the three in the letter *m*) **5 :** either of two units of liquid capacity equal to ¹⁄₆₀ fluid dram: **a :** a U. S. unit equivalent to 0.003759 cubic inches — see MEASURE table **b :** a British unit equivalent to 0.003612 cubic inches — see MEASURE table **6 :** a small worker ant among ants having polymorphic workers — compare MAXIM

²**minim** \ˈ"\ *adj* **:** of the smallest size **:** MINUTE ⟨a ~ mammal which you might imprison in the finger of your glove —George Eliot⟩

³**minim** \ˈ"\ *n* -s [alter. (prob. influenced by ¹*minim*) of *minnow*] *dial* **:** a small fish; *esp* **:** MINNOW

**min·i·mal** \ˈminəməl\ *adj* [*minimum* + *-al*] **1 :** of, being, or having the character of a minimum **:** constituting the least possible in size, number, or degree **:** extremely minute ⟨a ~ charge for materials⟩ ⟨a willingness to accept ~ terms —Oscar Handlin⟩ ⟨the number required for even ~ defense —Denis Healey⟩ ⟨required . . . to enforce ~ standards —M.W. Straight⟩ **2 :** incapable of being further distinguished significantly **:** depending upon a single articulatory difference ⟨~ distinctions —Daniel Jones⟩

**min·i·mal·ist** \-ləst\ *n* -s [F *minimaliste*, fr. *minimal* (prob. fr. E) + *-iste* -ist; intended as trans. of Russ *men'shevik* Menshevik] **:** one that favors restricting something (as the functions and powers of a political organization or the achievement of a set of goals) to a minimum — compare MAXIMALIST

**minimal lineage** *n* **:** a small kinship group usu. comprising the children of one man — contrasted with *maximal lineage*; compare LINEAGE

**min·i·mal·ly** \-lē\ *adv* **:** in a minimal amount or degree ⟨the program that is to make us . . . ~ secure —Richard Parke⟩

**minimal pair** *n* **:** two spoken-language items that are identical in all constituents except one (as |ˈded: ˈdad|) and that are often used in demonstrating or testing the phonemicness of the differing constituents

**min·i·mi·za·tion** \ˌminəməˈzāshən\ *n* -s **:** the action or process of minimizing ⟨interested primarily in the ~ of governmental activity —E.E.Schattschneider⟩

**min·i·mize** \ˈminəˌmīz\ *vt* -ED/-ING/-S *see -ize in Explan Notes* [*minimum* + *-ize*] **1 :** to reduce to the smallest possible number, degree, or extent ⟨centuries of cultivation have *minimized* the distinctions between the various regions —Jacquetta & Christopher Hawkes⟩ ⟨new operating methods have helped to ~ delays —C.F.Craig⟩ **2 :** to estimate in the least possible terms, number, or proportion; *esp* **:** DEPRECIATE 2 ⟨the navy . . . was inclined to ~ its own losses —E.L.Jones⟩ ⟨will ~ and conceal the impact of this experience —*New Republic*⟩ ⟨inclined to ~ the dangers of her underwater research —*Current Biog.*⟩ **syn** see DECRY

¹**min·i·mum** \ˈminəməm\ *n, pl* **mini·ma** \-nəmə\ *also* **minimums** [L, neut. of *minimus* smallest, least, superl. fr. the root of L *minor* smaller — more at MINOR] **1** *archaic* **:** a portion (as of matter) so small as to be incapable of further division **2 :** the least quantity assignable, admissible, or possible in a given case — opposed to *maximum* ⟨economic stabilization with a ~ of government regulation —Gerhard Colm⟩ ⟨designed for a maximum of comfort and ~ of clutter —*Technical Education News*⟩ ⟨the cost per page is reduced to a ~ —*Scientific Monthly*⟩ ⟨rigid legal *minima* for bank reserves —E.W.Kemmerer⟩ **3 a :** a number not greater than any other number of a finite set of numbers **b :** a value of a mathematical function of one or more independent variables such that either increasing or decreasing any one of the independent variables by a sufficiently small amount results in an increase in the function **4 :** the lowest degree or amount of variation (as of temperature) reached or recorded **5 a :** the time of least brightness or the magnitude at this time in a variable star **b :** the time when sunspots are least numerous in the 11-year cycle **6 :** MINIM 5

²**minimum** \ˈ"\ *adj* **:** of, relating to, or constituting a minimum **:** least attainable or possible ⟨the book contains a ~ discussion of the dynamics of British politics —R.R.Hackford⟩ ⟨having achieved the highest ~ wage —H.R.Northrup⟩ ⟨types of taxation . . . administered with ~ possibility of revenue loss —Matthew Woll⟩

**minimum dose** *n* **:** the smallest dose of a medicine or drug that will produce an effect

**minimum lethal dose** *n* **:** the smallest dose experimentally found to kill any one animal of a test group

**minimum premium** *n* **:** the smallest single charge for which an insurer will write a particular policy having a specified period

**minimum rate** *n* **1 :** an insurance rate applied uniformly to all risks within a given group or class regardless of possible differences in hazards **2 :** the lowest permissible rate at which traffic may be handled by a carrier **3 :** the lowest wage rate assigned for a given task or to a given class of employees — compare MINIMUM WAGE

**minimum separable** *n* **:** the least separation at which two parallel lines are recognized by the eye as separate — compare MINIMUM VISIBLE, VISUAL ACUITY

**minimum visible** *n* **:** the least area that can be perceived as distinct by the eye — compare MINIMUM SEPARABLE, VISUAL ACUITY

**minimum wage** *n* **1 :** LIVING WAGE **2 :** a wage fixed by legal authority or by contract as the least that will provide the minimum standard of living necessary for the health, efficiency, and well-being of designated employees — compare MINIMUM RATE

**minimum weight** *n* **:** the least weight at which goods or commodities will be transported by a carrier at a specified rate usu. applied to large quantities (as barge load, carload, or truckload)

¹**min·i·mus** \ˈminəməs\ *n, pl* **mini·mi** \-nəˌmī\ [L, smallest, least] **1 :** a being of the smallest size **:** a tiny creature **2** [NL, fr. L] **:** the little finger or toe **:** the fifth digit

²**minimus** \ˈ"\ *adj* [L] **:** LEAST: as **a :** the youngest or lowest in standing of several pupils in an English public school who have the same surname **b :** SMALLEST

**mining** *n* -s [fr. gerund of ⁵*mine*] **:** the process or business of making or of working mines

**mining claim** *n* **:** a tract of land having access to a vein or lode of valuable minerals supposed to exist below and definitely located on its surface by a miner with the right to occupy and mine in the manner and under the conditions prescribed by law usu. involving discovery and the filing of legal notice

**mining engineer** *n* **:** an engineer whose training or occupation is in mining engineering

**mining engineering** *n* **:** a branch of engineering concerned primarily with the location and evaluation of mineral deposits, the survey of mining areas, the layout and equipment of mines, and the supervision of mining operations

**mining geology** *n* **:** a branch of economic geology that deals with the application of geology to mining

**mining lease** *n* **:** a legal contract for the right to work a mine and extract the mineral or other valuable deposits from it under prescribed conditions of time, price, rental, or royalties — called also *mineral lease*

**mining partnership** *n* **:** a legal partnership in which the partners agree to conduct mining operations and to share profits and losses, which is recognized in many states as having the character of an ordinary partnership except that it exists only during the existence of actual mining operations, which upon the death or bankruptcy of a partner is not dissolved, and in which upon the sale of a partner's interest his assignee becomes a partner regardless of the consent of the other partners

**¹min·ion** \ˈminyən\ *n* -s [MF *mignon* darling, fr. *mignot* dainty, wanton, fr. OF, perh. of Celt origin; akin to OIr *mīn* smooth, gentle — more at MITIGATE] **1 :** an obsequious or servile dependent **:** CREATURE 3a ⟨the inability of a dictator's ~s to tell him the truth —Reinhold Niebuhr⟩ **2 :** a piece of light artillery of about 3-inch caliber and 125 paces range used in the 16th and 17th centuries **3 :** one highly esteemed and favored **:** FAVORITE, IDOL ⟨his great charity to the poor renders him the ~ of the people —Jonas Hanway⟩ **4** [F *mignonne*, fem. of *mignon*] **:** an old size of type of approximately 7-point and between nonpareil and brevier **5 :** a subordinate (as an agent, deputy, or follower) of an individual or organization; *esp* **:** one having an official status ⟨the masters, not the ~s of the state —Russell Davenport⟩ ⟨a little fat director . . . was dispatching ~s to chivvy and silence the gaping natives —Jeremy Potter⟩ ⟨invasion of their homes by governmental ~s —*Books of the Month*⟩

**²minion** \"\ *adj* [MF *mignon*, fr. *mignot* dainty, wanton] *archaic* **:** DELICATE, DAINTY, PRETTY ⟨made . . . a downward crescent of her ~ mouth —Alfred Tennyson⟩

**³minion** *var of* MUNNION

**min·ion·ette** \ˌminyəˈnet\ *n* -s [F *mignonnette*, fr. obs. F, fem. of *mignonnet* dainty, fr. MF, fr. *mignon*] **:** an old size of type of approximately 6 ½-point and between nonpareil and minion

**miniscule** *var of* MINUSCULE

**min·ish** \ˈminish\ *vt* -ED/-ING/-ES [ME *menusen, minishen*, fr. MF *menusier, menuiser* to lessen, mince, fr. (assumed) VL *minutiare* to mince, fr. L *minutia* smallness, minuteness, fr. *minutus* minute + -*ia* -y — more at MINUTE] *archaic* **:** to make less (as in size, amount, or degree) **:** make fewer in number **:** diminish in power or influence **:** LESSEN ⟨have ~*ed* their numbers —Sir Walter Scott⟩ ⟨would not . . . ~ by a tittle the respect due to the Magistrate —J.R.Lowell⟩ ⟨without . . . muddling it up with myths which simply ~ its interest —George Saintsbury⟩

**¹min·is·ter** \ˈminəstə(r)\ *n* -s [ME *ministre*, fr. OF, fr. L *minister* servant; akin to L *minor* smaller — more at MINOR] **1 :** one that acts under the orders or authority of another **:** one employed by another for the execution of purposes **:** AGENT ⟨the angels are ~s of the divine will —H.P.Liddon⟩ ⟨a principle to which time is the ~ and not the master —P.E.More⟩ **2 a :** one duly authorized (as by ordination) to conduct Christian worship, preach the gospel, and administer the sacraments: as (1) **:** a priest who officiates at an altar in the conduct of a service of worship (as a mass) (2) **:** a deacon or subdeacon at solemn services (3) **:** a clergyman of a Protestant church (4) **:** PREACHER (5) *chiefly Eng* **:** a member of the clergy of a nonconformist church **b :** one who performs the duties of a clergyman during his customary vocation but who has never been formally licensed or ordained as a minister **3** *archaic* **:** one that waits upon or serves **:** ATTENDANT, SERVANT ⟨cooks and other inferior ~s employed in the . . . kitchens —Edward Gibbon⟩ **4 :** one exercising non-Christian clerical functions **5 a** *or* **minister-general :** the superior of one of several religious orders **b :** the assistant to the rector or the bursar of a Jesuit house **6 :** a high officer of state entrusted by the chief of state or the executive head of a government with the management of a division of governmental activities ⟨British . . . ~s who exercise the powers of government derive their formal authority from the king —J.A.Corry⟩ ⟨Canadian . . . ~s carry the political responsibility for their departments —Alexander Brady⟩ — see FOREIGN MINISTER, PRIME MINISTER; compare COMMISSAR 2 **7 a :** a diplomatic representative (as an ambassador) accredited by a sovereign or government to the court or seat of government of a foreign state ⟨shall appoint ambassadors, other public ~s and consuls —*U.S.Constitution*⟩ **b :** a diplomatic representative ranking below an ambassador and usu. accredited to states of less importance ⟨send ambassadors to most countries and ~s to the less important ones —F.A.Magruder⟩ — compare MINISTER PLENIPOTENTIARY, MINISTER RESIDENT

**²minister** \"\ *vb* **ministered; ministered; ministering** \-t(ə)riŋ\ **ministers** [ME *ministren*, fr. MF *ministrer*, fr. L *ministrare* to serve, dish up, fr. *minister* servant] *vi* **1 :** to serve or officiate in worship **:** act in the capacity of or perform the functions of a minister of religion — often used with *to* ⟨became rector of a small parish where he ~*ed* for several years⟩ ⟨after a rabbi has ~*ed* to a congregation for . . . fifteen years —B.Z.Bokser⟩ **2 :** to attend to the wants and comforts of someone **:** give aid **:** SERVE — usu. used with *to* ⟨happily he . . . had ~*ed* to this man —Louis Auchincloss⟩ ⟨during the plague he ~*ed* to the sick⟩ **3 :** to do things needful or helpful **:** be serviceable or conducive — usu. used with *to* ⟨a tract for the times . . . ~*ed* to the needs of the moment —R.W.Southern⟩ ⟨this conclusion ~*ed* to complacency —R.H.Bainton⟩ ~ *vt* **1** *archaic* **:** FURNISH, SUPPLY, AFFORD ⟨limbs . . . made to ~ delight —P.J.Bailey⟩ ⟨neither give heed to fables . . . which ~ questions —1 Tim 1:4 (AV)⟩ **2** *archaic* **:** ADMINISTER, DISPENSE ⟨I thither went to ~ the sacrament —John Wilson †1854⟩ ⟨that he might ~ the Gospel to the Gentiles —R.M. Benson⟩

**¹min·is·te·ri·al** \ˌminəˈstirēəl, -tēr-\ *adj* [LL *ministerialis*, lit., that functions as a servant, fr. L *ministerium* service (fr. *minister* servant) + -*alis* -al] **1 a :** of, being, or having the characteristics of a minister of religion ⟨those serving in a ~ capacity are trained in a Bible training school —F.S.Mead⟩ ⟨a ~ habit of mind —M.A.D.Howe⟩ **b :** of, relating to, or preparing to enter the clerical ministry ⟨examine ~ candidates —J.C.Brauer⟩ ⟨a code of ~ ethics —P.H.Furfey⟩ **2 a :** of, being, or having the characteristics of an act or duty belonging to the administration of the executive function in government and specifically prescribed by law as part of the official duties of an office **b :** of, relating to, or being an act that a person after ascertaining the existence of a specified state of facts performs in obedience to a mandate of legal authority without the exercise of personal judgment upon the propriety of the act and usu. without discretion in its performance — opposed to *judicial* ⟨action by public officials can be compelled only if the act is a purely ~ one —B.F.Tucker⟩ ⟨the controversy turns . . . on whether the function is discretionary or ~ —G.W. Folta⟩ **3 :** acting or active as an agent, instrument, or means **:** INSTRUMENTAL ⟨those uses of conversation which are ~ to intellectual culture —Thomas De Quincey⟩ **4 a :** of, relating to, or having the status of a governmental minister ⟨representatives of the political parties . . . were given ~ posts —W.S. Vucinich⟩ ⟨jobs below the ~ level —H.M.Somers⟩ ⟨promotion . . . to the office of paymaster general, a ~ appointment —*Current Biog.*⟩ **b** *often cap* **:** of, relating to, or supporting the ministry as opposed to the opposition in a parliamentary system ⟨the situation was . . . saved by a *Ministerial* crisis —*Peace Handbooks*⟩ ⟨~ benches in the House of Commons⟩ ⟨the principle of ~ responsibility under a parliamentary system —Taylor Cole⟩

**²ministerial** \"\ *n* -s [LL *ministerialis* imperial household officer, fr. *ministerialis*, adj.] **:** an administrative household officer under the feudal system

**min·is·te·ri·al·ist** \ˌ==ˈ=rēələst\ *n* -s **:** a supporter of the ministry in office ⟨enrolled himself . . . in the ranks of the ~s —G.O.Trevelyan⟩

**min·is·te·ri·al·ly** \ˌ==ˈ=rēəlē\ *adv* **:** in the manner or capacity of a minister ⟨called on to visit ~ one . . . lying on his deathbed —C.A.Johns⟩ ⟨acting judicially and ~ —*Law Times*⟩

**min·is·te·ri·um** \ˌminəˈstirēəm\ *n* -s [G, fr. L, service] **1 :** a body in the Lutheran Church: **a :** one composed of ordained ministers and charged with the examination, licensure, and ordination of candidates for the ministry and with the trial for heresy of ministers and also laymen on appeal from a church council **b :** a representative body of ministers and laymen meeting periodically to attend to the interests of the churches represented **2 :** a regional group or association of ministers in the Evangelical and Reformed Church meeting periodically for fellowship and attending to problems of common interest

**minister of music :** a director of music in a church or synagogue usu. responsible for training the choir and often for service as an organist

**minister of state** *n, pl* **ministers of state :** a British governmental official having a status between a minister and a parliamentary secretary and usu. appointed to relieve a minister of portions of his departmental work ⟨promoted *Minister of State* at the Foreign Office —Herbert Morrison⟩

**minister plenipotentiary** *n, pl* **ministers plenipotentiary :** a principal diplomatic agent ranking below an ambassador but possessing full power and authority as the representative of his government at a foreign court or seat of government — see ²ENVOY 1a; compare MINISTER 7b

**minister-president** \ˈ===ˈ=(=)=\ *n, pl* **ministers-president** *or* **minister-presidents** [trans. of G *ministerpräsident*] **:** the principal governmental minister usu. chosen by the legislature in a number of German länder and resembling a prime minister in power and status ⟨the *minister-president* . . . appoints and heads a cabinet responsible to the legislature —R.H.Wells⟩

**minister resident** *n, pl* **ministers resident 1 :** a diplomatic agent resident at a foreign court or seat of government and ranking below a minister plenipotentiary — compare MINISTER 7b **2 :** a member of the British ministry appointed to reside and handle special governmental functions in a location outside the United Kingdom ⟨a *minister resident* in West Africa was appointed to coordinate the war effort of the four dependencies —Martin Wight⟩

**ministers** *pl of* MINISTER, *pres 3d sing of* MINISTER

**minister's face** *n, dial* **:** the upper half of a hog's head with jowls, eyes, and usu. ears and nose removed

**min·is·ter·ship** \ˈminəstə(r)ˌship\ *n* **:** the office of minister

**minister without portfolio** *n, pl* **ministers without portfolios :** a member of a ministry to whom no special department is assigned

**min·is·tra·ble** \ˈminəstrəbəl\ *n* -s [F, fr. *ministrable* suitable for appointment as a cabinet minister, fr. *ministre* minister + -*able*] **:** a recurrent member of successive ministries ⟨the ~s were usually seasoned parliamentarians⟩

**¹min·is·trant** \ˈminəstrənt\ *adj* [L *ministrant-, ministrans*, pres. part. of *ministrare* to serve, dish up — more at MINISTER] **:** performing service as a minister ⟨the angels ~ sang —Bayard Taylor⟩

**²ministrant** \"\ *n* -s **:** one that ministers ⟨orgies of dissipation . . . were ~s to the clear, springing life of the imagination —Rose Macaulay⟩ ⟨~s at the altar —*Liverpool Daily Post*⟩

**min·is·tra·tion** \ˌminəˈstrāshən\ *n* -s [ME *ministracioun*, fr. L *ministration-, ministratio*, fr. *ministratus* (past part. of *ministrare* to serve, dish up) + -*ion-*, -*io* -ion] **1 :** the action of giving aid, service, or comfort ⟨under the tender ~s of this fair sister of mercy, the young warrior revived —Cedomilj Mijatovic⟩ **2 :** the action of ministering in religious matters **:** MINISTRY 2 ⟨all the baptized were to come under the disciplinary ~s of the Church —K.S.Latourette⟩ ⟨worshiping . . . under the ~s of a missionary —*Amer. Anthropologist*⟩

**min·is·tress** \ˈminəstrəs\ *n* -ES [MF *ministresse*, fr. *ministre* minister + -*esse* -ess] **:** a female minister ⟨come . . . to be ~ at London —Thomas Gray⟩ ⟨the lovely ~ of truth and good in this dark world —Mark Akenside⟩

**min·is·try** \ˈminəstrē, -ri\ *n* -ES [ME *ministerie*, fr. L *ministerium* service, fr. *minister* servant — more at MINISTER] **1 :** the action of ministering **:** the performance of any service or function for another **:** MINISTRATION ⟨the ~ of books is at least threefold —T.V.Smith⟩ ⟨the ingenuity of destruction . . . had outrun the ~ of healing —Dixon Wecter⟩ ⟨the Gospels . . . become part of the present saving ~ of the Redeemer —H.H. Farmer⟩ **2 :** the office, duties, or functions of a minister of religion ⟨prepared for the ~ —A.E.Bailey⟩ ⟨the true missionary is . . . occupied with the vital aspects of his ~ —E.A. Nida⟩ ⟨answered the call to the ~ —Wayne Hooper⟩ **3** *obs* **:** a specific kind of service **:** FUNCTION, OFFICE ⟨to sever the wheat from the tares . . . must be the angel's ~ —John Milton⟩ **4 :** the body of ordained ministers of religion **:** CLERGY ⟨insistence on a highly trained ~ —R.T.Handy⟩ **5 :** a person or thing through which something is accomplished **:** AGENCY 2, INSTRUMENTALITY ⟨heroic believers become such by the ~ of heroic pains —Austin Phelps⟩ **6 a :** the period of service of a minister of religion **b :** the total life of service of a religious figure ⟨an outline account of the ~ of our Lord —*Times Lit. Supp.*⟩ **7** *often cap* **a** (1) **:** the whole body of ministers entrusted with the government of a nation or state and from which a smaller cabinet is sometimes selected ⟨when a cabinet goes out of office, it . . . carries the entire ~ with it —F.A.Ogg & Harold Zink⟩ ⟨the crown is the supreme executive . . . in all the dominions but it acts on the advice of different *ministries* —Robert Borden⟩ ⟨a responsible ~⟩ (2) **:** the usu. smaller group of ministers constituting a cabinet **b :** the whole body of ministers or the cabinet currently holding office **8 a :** a government department presided over by a minister ⟨*ministries* of justice have been the spearhead in promoting the recurrent great codifications of Continental law —C.J.Friedrich⟩ ⟨the Communists received the three *ministries* they . . . wanted —W.S.Vucinich⟩ ⟨~ of foreign affairs⟩ ⟨~ of transport⟩ **b :** the building in which the business of a ministry is transacted ⟨whether he had noticed any other member . . . entering the ~ —C.D.Lewis⟩ **9 :** the term of office held by an individual minister or by a body of ministers ⟨the Tory ~ lasted for fifteen years⟩

**minitari** *var of* MINNETAREE

**mini·track** \ˈminəˌtrak\ *n, sometimes cap* [*mini*ature + *track*] **:** an electronic system for tracking an earth satellite or rocket by radio waves transmitted from it to a chain of ground stations

**min·i·um** \ˈminēəm\ *n* -s [ME, fr. L, cinnabar, red lead, of Iberian origin; akin to Basque *armineá* cinnabar] **1 a :** GOYA **b :** FIERY RED **2 a :** red lead oxide $Pb_3O_4$ sometimes found as a mineral but usu. prepared synthetically; tri-lead tetroxide **b :** RED LEAD

**min·i·ver** *also* **min·e·ver** \ˈminəvə(r)\ *n* -s [ME *meniver*, fr. OF *menu vair*, fr. *menu* small (fr. L *minutus*) + *vair* — more at MINUTE, VAIR] **1 :** a white or whitish fur probably from the vair and more recently from ermine or rabbit used in the medieval period esp. for the clothing of noble and wealthy persons and now chiefly for robes of state ⟨parliament robes are of crimson cloth furred with ~ —Dorothy M. Stuart⟩ **2** *dial Eng* **:** an ermine in its white winter coat

**min·i·vet** \ˈminəˌvet\ *n* -s [origin unknown] **:** any of several cuckoo shrikes that belong to the Asiatic genus *Pericrocotus* and that are brilliantly colored with the males chiefly black and scarlet and the females usu. gray and yellow

**mink** \ˈmiŋk\ *n, pl* **mink** *or* **minks** *often attrib* [ME *mynk*] **1 a :** the fur or pelt of the mink varying in color from white to dark brown ⟨an elbow-length cape of cerulean ~ —*New Yorker*⟩ **b :** an article of clothing (as a coat) made of this fur ⟨the girl was wearing a ~ —Eric Greywood⟩ **2 :** any of several slender-bodied semi-aquatic carnivorous mammals that resemble and are closely related to the weasels, comprise a subgenus of *Mustela*, and have partially webbed feet, a thick soft usu. dark brown coat, and a rather short bushy tail

mink

**mink·ery** \-kərē\ *n* -ES **:** a place where minks are bred usu. for commercial purposes

**mink frog** *n* **:** a black-spotted frog (*Rana septentrionalis*) of the northern U. S. having a strong musky odor

**minkopi** *usu cap, var of* MINCOPIE

**minn** *var of* MIND

**min·ne·ap·o·lis** \ˌminēˈap(ə)ləs\ *adj, usu cap* [fr. *Minneapolis*, city in southeast central Minnesota] **:** of or from Minneapolis, Minn. ⟨*Minneapolis* mills⟩ **:** of the kind or style prevalent in Minneapolis

**min·ne·a·pol·i·tan** \ˌminēəˈpälətᵊn, -lədən\ *n* -s *cap* [fr. *Minneapolis*, after E *metropolis: metropolitan*] **:** a native or resident of Minneapolis, Minn.

**min·ne·lied** \ˈminəˌlēt\ *n, pl* **minnelie·der** \-ēdə(r)\ *often cap* [G, fr. MHG *minneliet*, fr. *minne* love + *liet* song, fr. OHG *liod* — more at LAUD] **1 :** a song of or in the style of the minnesingers **2 :** LOVE SONG

**min·ne·sing·er** \ˈminēˌsiŋə(r), -nə,-\ *also* **min·ne·säng·er** \ˈminəˌzeŋ-\ *n, pl* **minnesingers** *also* **minnesänger** [G, fr. MHG *minnesinger, minnesenger*, fr. *minne* love (fr. OHG *minna*) + *singer* (fr. *singen* to sing — fr. OHG *singan* — + -*er*, fr. OHG -*āri* -er) or *senger* singer, fr. *sanc* song, fr. OHG *sang*) + -*er* — more at MINIKIN, SING, SONG] **:** one of a class of aristocratic German lyric poets and musicians of the 12th to the 14th centuries inspired by the French troubadors and characterized by having love and beauty as the subject of their songs — compare MEISTERSINGER

**min·ne·song** \ˈminēˌsȯŋ, -nə-, -säŋ\ *or* **min·ne·sang** \ˈminəˌzäŋ\ *n* [in sense 1, *minnesong* part trans. of G *minnelied*; in sense 1, *minnesang* alter. (influenced by G *minnesang*) of *minnesong*; in sense 2, *minnesong* part trans. of G *minnesang*; in sense 2, *minnesang* fr. G, fr. MHG *minnesanc*, fr. *minne* love + *sanc* song; singing] **1 :** a song of a minnesinger **2 :** the whole body of minnesongs constituting a musical form ⟨another characteristic shared in common by English music and German ~ —Gilbert Reaney⟩

**¹min·ne·so·ta** \ˌminəˈsōd·ə, -ōtə\ *adj, usu cap* [fr. *Minnesota*, state in the north central U. S., fr. *Minnesota* river, southern Minnesota, fr. Dakota *minisota* white water] **:** of or from the state of Minnesota ⟨a *Minnesota* lake⟩ **:** of the kind or style prevalent in Minnesota **:** MINNESOTAN

**²minnesota** \"\ *n* -s *usu cap* **:** either of two breeds of swine developed in Minnesota: **a** *or* **minnesota number one** *usu cap M&N&O* **:** a breed of red meat type swine developed by selection from crosses between Tamworths and Danish Landrace **b** *or* **minnesota number two** *usu cap M&N&T* **:** a breed of white black-spotted swine similarly developed from Large Whites and Poland Chinas

**min·ne·so·ta·ite** \ˌ==ˈsōd·əˌīt\ *n* -s [*Minnesota* (state) + E -*ite*] **:** a hydrous silicate of iron $Fe_3Si_4O_{10}(OH)_2$ probably isomorphous with talc

**¹min·ne·so·tan** \ˌminəˈsōtᵊn\ *also* **min·ne·so·ti·an** \-ōd·ēən\ *n* -s *cap* [*Minnesota* (state) + E -*an*, n. suffix] **:** a native or resident of the state of Minnesota

**²minnesotan** \ˌ==ˈ==\ *also* **minnesotian** \ˌ==ˈ===\ *adj, usu cap* [*Minnesota* (state) + E -*an*, adj. suffix] **1 :** of, relating to, or characteristic of the state of Minnesota **2 :** of, relating to, or characteristic of the people of Minnesota

**min·ne·ta·ree** \ˌminəˈtärē\ *n* -s *usu cap* [Mandan *minitari* they crossed the water] **:** HIDATSA

**min·ni** \ˈminē\ *n, pl* **minni** *or* **minnis** *usu cap* **1 :** a primitive Mongol people inhabiting the foothill region of the southern Caucasus during pre-Babylonian times — compare KASSITE **2 :** a member of the Minni people

**¹min·nie** *or* **min·ny** \ˈminī\ *n, pl* **minnies** [prob. baby-talk alter. of *mother*] *chiefly Scot* **:** MOTHER — a childish or informal term

**²min·nie** \ˈminē\ *n* -s [by shortening & alter. fr. ¹*minimum*] **1 :** a hand barely strong enough for an opening bid in bridge **2 :** the lowest possible hand that wins in lowball or high-low poker

**min·nie·bush** \ˈminēˌbu̇sh\ *n* [*minnie*- (irreg. fr. Archibald *Menzies* †1842 Scot. botanist) + *bush*] **:** a low shrub (*Menziesia pilosa*) of eastern No. America with greenish purple flowers

**min·now** \ˈmi(ˌ)nō, - nə\ *n, pl* **minnows** *also* **minnow** *often attrib* [ME *menawe*; akin to OE *myne* minnow, OHG *munewa*, a fish, Russ *men'* eelpout, and perh. to Gk *manos* sparse — more at MONK] **1 a :** a small European cyprinid fish (*Phoxinus phoxinus*) common in gravelly streams and attaining a length of about three inches maximum; *broadly* **:** any of the usu. small fishes constituting the family Cyprinidae **b :** a small killifish or topminnow — see MUDMINNOW **c :** a fish of the family Galaxiidae **2 :** a small fish not specified as a sport fish or game fish esp. in game laws **3 :** a small or insignificant person or thing **4 :** a live or artificial minnow used as bait in fishing — see LURE illustration

**min·ny** \ˈminē\ *n* -ES [by alter.] *dial* **:** MINNOW

**¹mi·no·an** \məˈnōən, (ˈ)mīˈn-\ *adj, usu cap* [L *minous* Cretan, of Minos (fr. Gk *minōios*, fr. *Minōs* Minos, legendary king of Crete) + E -*an*] **1 :** of or relating to the Bronze Age culture of Crete (3000 B.C.–1100 B.C.) and being in its latest phase virtually identical with Mycenaean — compare AEGEAN, CYCLADIC, ETEOCRETAN, HELLADIC **2 a :** of, relating to, or being the language of ancient Crete **b :** of or relating to inscriptions and documents in the Minoan language or to the hieroglyphic and esp. the linear script in which they were written — compare JAPHETIC

**²minoan** \"\ *n* -s *usu cap* **1 :** a native or inhabitant of ancient Crete **2 :** the language of the ancient Cretan civilization — compare ETEOCRETAN, MYCENAEAN

**mi·no bird** \ˈmī(ˌ)nō-\ *n* [*mino* alter. of *myna*] **:** MYNA

**mi·nom·e·ter** \məˈnäməd·ə(r), mīˈ-\ *n* [³*minute* + -*o-* + -*meter*] **:** an instrument for the detection and measurement of stray radiations from X-ray generators and radioactive materials

**¹mi·nor** \ˈmīnə(r)\ *n* -s [in sense 1, fr. ME, fr. ML, fr. L *minor*, adj.; in sense 2, fr. LL, fr. L *minor*, adj.; in other senses, fr. ²*minor*] **1 a :** the premise in logic that contains the minor term: (1) **:** the second proposition of a regular syllogism (2) **:** the categorical premise in a hypothetical syllogism **b :** MINOR TERM **2 a :** a person of either sex under full age or majority **:** one who has not attained the age at which full civil rights are accorded **:** one who in England and generally in the U.S. is under 21 years of age — compare ¹AGE 1d(2), INFANT **b :** a person in Scots law who has exceeded the age of pupillarity by being over 14 if a boy or over 12 if a girl but who has not attained the majority age of 21 years **3 :** a minor musical interval, scale, key, or mode ⟨listened . . . to the pulsating sweet ~s of the hymns —Irwin Shaw⟩ **4** *or* **minor determinant :** a mathematical determinant obtained by deleting the same number of rows and columns from the given determinant **5 a :** a minor academic course **b :** a minor academic subject ⟨degree in history with a ~ in school administration —*Current Biog.*⟩ **6 :** MINOR LEAGUE — usu. used in pl. with *the* ⟨an old pitcher retired to the ~s —Vincent McHugh⟩ **7 :** MINOR SUIT

**²minor** \"\ *adj* [ME, fr. L, smaller, less, inferior; akin to OHG *minniro* smaller, ON *minni* smaller, Goth *minniza* least, younger, inferior, L *minuere* to lessen, Gk *meiōn* less, Skt *mināti* he lessens] **1 a :** inferior in importance **:** comparatively unimportant **:** lower in standing or reputation than others of the same kind ⟨these hardy adventurers were ~ noblemen —R.A.Billington⟩ ⟨~ back roads which serve as bridle paths —*Amer. Guide Series: Mass.*⟩ ⟨a ~ poet⟩ **b :** being the less important of two things ⟨a ~ canon⟩ ⟨a ~ piece in chess⟩ **2 :** having the status of a legal minor not having reached the age of majority or full legal age ⟨~ children follow the nationality of the parents —William Samore⟩ **3** *archaic* **:** being in or constituting a numerical minority ⟨another person had the ~ vote in the election —Thomas Hutchinson⟩ **4 a** (1) *of a scale* **:** having half steps between the second and third, fifth and sixth, and sometimes seventh and eighth degrees — see HARMONIC MINOR SCALE, MELODIC MINOR SCALE, NATURAL MINOR SCALE (2) *of a key* **:** based (as in harmonic relations) on such a scale — opposed to *major*; used after the name of a keynote ⟨fugue in D ~⟩ ⟨in the key of B ~⟩ **b** *of an interval* (1) **:** less by a half step than the corresponding major interval **:** of a size equal to the distance between the keynote and a (specified) degree of the minor scale — used of the second, third, sixth, and seventh (2) **:** less by a comma — used of one whole step in an untempered scale compared with another ⟨D to E is a ~ whole step, smaller by a comma than C to D⟩ **c** *of a mode in measurable music* **:** having the long divided into breves **5 :** being the second in age or school standing of two or more boys with the same surname in an English public school ⟨Smith ~⟩ **6** *med* **:** not serious or involving risk to life ⟨a ~ illness⟩ ⟨a ~ operation⟩ — compare MAJOR **7 :** of, relating to, or being a branch of the judiciary having jurisdiction limited to a specified local area and to cases usu. involving matters of lesser importance ⟨~ courts . . . deal with such cases as breaches of the traffic laws, petty theft, and minor domestic cases —*Canadian Citizenship Series*⟩ **8 a :** of, relating to, or being an academic course usu. having fewer class hours than a major course **b :** of, relating to, or being an academic subject usu. requiring fewer courses or hours than a major subject and given secondary emphasis in a student's schedule ⟨his ~ subjects for his M.A. were plant ecology and entomology —*Current Biog.*⟩

**³minor** \"\ *vi* -ED/-ING/-S [¹*minor*] **:** to take courses in a specified field of study as one's minor ⟨will major in . . . literature and ~ in theater work —*Goucher Alumnae Quarterly*⟩

**mi·nor·ate** \'mīnə,rāt\ *vt* -ED/-ING/-S [LL *minoratus*, past part. of *minorare*, fr. L *minor* smaller] *archaic* **:** to make less in estimation or value **:** DIMINISH

**minoration** *n* -S [LL *minoration-, minoratio*, fr. *minoratus* + L *-ion-, -io* -ion] *obs* **:** DIMINUTION ⟨the excuse and ~ of our actual impieties —Jeremy Taylor⟩

**minor axis** *n* **:** the chord of an ellipse passing through the center perpendicular to the major axis

**mi·nor·ca** \mə'nȯrkə, -nȯ(ə)kə\ *n* [*Minorca*, second largest of the Balearic islands off the east coast of Spain] **1** *usu cap* **:** a breed of domestic fowls of the Mediterranean class resembling the Leghorns but larger **2** -S *often cap* **:** any bird of the Minorca breed

**minor cadence** *n* **:** a musical cadence ending on a minor chord

**¹mi·nor·can** \mə'nȯrkən, -nȯ(ə)k-\ *adj, usu cap* [*Minorca*, Balearic islands + E *-an*] **1 :** of, relating to, or characteristic of Minorca **2 :** of, relating to, or characteristic of the people of Minorca

**²minorcan** \"\ *n* -S *cap* **:** a native or resident of Minorca

**minor canon** *n* **1 :** a canon who receives no prebend **2 :** a canon in the Church of England who has no vote in the chapter to which he belongs but who receives a stipend — compare MAJOR CANON

**minor coin** *n* **:** a base-metal coin (as a nickel or cent) of a denomination smaller than the basic monetary unit — compare SUBSIDIARY COIN

**minor diameter** *n* **:** the smallest diameter of a screw thread

**minor element** *n* **:** TRACE ELEMENT

**minor excommunication** *n* **:** separation or suspension from the sacraments but not absolute exclusion from the Roman Catholic Church — distinguished from *major excommunication*

**¹mi·nor·i·ty** \mə'nȯrəd·ē, mī'-, -när-, -ətē, -i\ *n* -ES [ML *minoritat-, minoritas*, fr. L *minor* smaller + *-itat-, -itas* -ity] **1 :** the state of being a legal minor **:** the period of being under full legal age — compare INFANCY **2 a :** the smaller in number of two aggregates that together constitute a whole ⟨barred from all but a tiny ~ of cinemas —Roger Manvell⟩ ⟨ten of our presidents have had only a ~ of the popular vote behind them —F.A.Ogg & P.O.Ray⟩ **b :** the smaller in number of two groups that together constitute a larger entity ⟨only a small ~ of students is majoring in a basic subject —W.H.Whyte⟩; *specif* **:** a group (as in a legislative body) having less than the number of votes necessary for control ⟨dividing each constituency . . . into two halves, the majority to govern and the ~ to criticize —C.J.Friedrich⟩ **3** *or* **minority group :** a group characterized by a sense of separate identity and awareness of status apart from a usu. larger group of which it forms or is held to form a part: as **a :** a body of nationals of a state forming a small but appreciable part of the population of another and usu. neighboring state ⟨peasants in eastern Europe . . . wanting a guarantee that the evicted German *minorities* shall never return —A.J.Toynbee⟩ **b :** a group differing from the predominant section of a larger group in one or more characteristics (as ethnic background, language, culture, or religion) and as a result often subjected to differential treatment and esp. discrimination ⟨the constitution protects the rights of individuals and of *minorities* —Luis Muñoz Marín⟩ **c :** a group numerically smaller than other groups or a combination of other groups in a community but constituting the predominant element ⟨whites have frequently been dominant *minorities* —H.O.Dahlke⟩

**²minority** \"\ *adj* **:** of, relating to, or being a minority ⟨an advisory committee on ~ housing —*Springfield (Mass.) Union*⟩ ⟨each committee is . . . composed of majority and ~ members —F.A.Ogg & P.O.Ray⟩ ⟨~ races⟩ ⟨~ rule⟩

**minority leader** *n* **:** the leader of the minority party in a legislative body — compare MAJORITY LEADER

**minority report** *n* **:** a separate report prepared by a group constituting or representing a numerical minority (as of a committee) ⟨if any members of a committee disagree . . . they may submit a *minority report* —Alice F. Sturgis⟩ ⟨the majority and *minority reports* of this inquiry —*Current Biog.*⟩

**minor key** *n* **1 :** a musical key or tonality in the minor mode **2 :** a mood of melancholy or pathos **3 :** a restrained manner **:** a small or limited scale ⟨the high moments of social life on the farm . . . are in a decidedly *minor key* —Don Murray⟩ ⟨art in Australia . . . reflected English traditions in a *minor key* —Bernard Smith⟩

**minor league** *n* **:** a league or association of professional clubs in a particular sport (as baseball or ice hockey) other than the recognized major leagues

**minor-league** \'==;=\ *adj* [*minor league*] **1 :** of, relating to, or having the characteristics of a minor league in sports ⟨a *minor-league* baseball club⟩ **2 :** of, relating to, or being of relatively small stature or importance ⟨a *minor-league* official in one of the Hollywood studios —L.M.Uris⟩ ⟨a simple, fascinating, *minor-league* tragedy —Mel Heimer⟩ ⟨a *minor-league* hero⟩

**minor mode** *n* **1 :** the arrangement or grouping of musical notes or tones as found in the minor scale **2 :** a scale in the minor mode

**minor order** *n, often cap M&O* **1 :** the grade of acolyte, exorcist, lector, or doorkeeper in the Roman Catholic Church — compare MAJOR ORDER **2 :** the grade of subdeacon, lector, or singer in the Eastern Orthodox Church

**minor party** *n* **:** a political party whose electoral strength is so small as to prevent its gaining control of a government except in rare and exceptional circumstances — compare MAJOR PARTY, THIRD PARTY

**minor penalty** *n* **:** a two-minute suspension of a player in ice hockey with no substitute allowed — compare MAJOR PENALTY

**minor piece** *n* **:** a bishop or knight in chess — compare MAJOR PIECE

**minor planet** *n* **:** ASTEROID 1

**minor premise** *n* **:** the premise of a syllogism that contains the minor term

**minor prophets** *n pl, usu cap M&P* **1 :** the group of Old Testament prophets from Hosea to Malachi whose biblical writings are relatively brief **2 :** the books of the Bible written by the Minor Prophets

**minor seminary** *n* **:** PREPARATORY SEMINARY

**minor sentence** *n* **:** a word, phrase, or clause functioning as a sentence and having in speech an intonation characteristic of a sentence but lacking the grammatical completeness and independence of a full sentence (as *Yes, indeed*)

**minor seventh chord** *n* **:** a chord consisting of a minor triad and a minor seventh — see SEVENTH CHORD illustration

**minor socratic** *n, usu cap S* **:** SOCRATIC 2

**minor suit** *n* **:** clubs or diamonds in bridge — compare MAJOR SUIT

**minor surgery** *n* **:** surgery involving little risk to the life of the patient; *specif* **:** an operation on the superficial structures of the body or a manipulative procedure that does not involve a serious risk — compare MAJOR SURGERY

**minor tenace** *n* **:** a tenace in bridge and other card games consisting of the king and jack — compare MAJOR TENACE

**minor term** *n* **:** the term of a syllogism that forms the subject of the conclusion

**minor triad** *n* **1 :** a triad whose frequencies are in the proportions 10:12:15 **2 :** a musical triad consisting of a fundamental tone and its minor third and perfect fifth — see TRIAD illustration

**mi·not** \mē'nō\ *n* -S [MF, fr. OF, fr. *mine*, a unit of measure of volume, fr. L *hemina*, fr. Gk *hēmina*, fr. *hēmi-* hemi- — more at SEMI-] **:** any of several old French units of dry measure; *esp* **:** the Paris unit for grain equal to about 39 liters

**minsk** \'minsk\ *adj, usu cap* [fr. *Minsk*, city in western U.S.S.R.] **:** of or from the city of Minsk, U.S.S.R. **:** of the kind or style prevalent in Minsk

**min·ster** \'min(t)stə(r)\ *n* -S [ME, fr. OE *mynster*, fr. (assumed) VL *monisterium*, fr. LL *monasterium* — more at MONASTERY] **1** *obs* **:** MONASTERY **2 a** (1) **:** a church of a monastery (2) **:** a church orig. belonging to a monastery but remaining after the monastery has ceased to exist **b :** a cathedral or a church of large size or importance that has never been monastic

**minsteryard** \'=,=\ *n* **:** the close of a cathedral or other minster

**¹min·strel** \'min(t)strəl\ *n* -S *often attrib* [ME *minstrale, menestrel*, fr. OF *menestrel* minstrel, official, servant, fr. LL *ministerialis* imperial household officer — more at MINISTERIAL] **1 :** one of a class of medieval professional musical entertainers; *esp* **:** a singer of verses to the accompaniment of a harp or other instrument — compare GLEEMAN, JONGLEUR **2 :** one (as a musician or poet) felt to resemble a medieval minstrel **3 a :** one of a troupe of musical performers and comedians of a kind originating early in the 19th century in the U.S. and typically giving a program of Negro melodies, jokes, and impersonations and usu. blacked in imitation of Negroes ⟨small troupes of blackface ~*s* were among the earliest . . . traveling companies —*Amer. Guide Series: Wash.*⟩ **b :** MINSTREL SHOW ⟨the first full-scale ~ staged by the church —*Springfield (Mass.) Union*⟩

**²minstrel** \"\ *vt* -ED/-ING/-S **:** to celebrate in song esp. in the style of a minstrel

**minstrel gallery** *n* **:** a small interior balcony over the entrance doors in a church, castle, or similar public building

**minstrel show** *n* **:** a performance by blackface minstrels

**min·strel·sy** \-lsē\ *n* -ES [ME *minstralcie*, fr. MF *menestralsie*, fr. *menestral, menestrel* minstrel] **1 :** the arts and occupation of minstrels; *specif* **:** the singing and playing of a minstrel **2 :** a body of minstrels **3 :** a group of songs; *esp* **:** one of minstrel's songs

**¹mint** \'mint\ *n* -S [ME *mynt*, fr. OE *mynet;* akin to OHG *munizza* coin; both fr. a prehistoric WGmc word borrowed fr. L *moneta* mint, coin, money, fr. *Moneta*, epithet of Juno, ancient Italian goddess, wife of Jupiter; fr. the fact that the Romans coined money in the temple of Juno Moneta] **1** *obs* **:** COIN, MONEY **2 a :** a place (as a factory) where coins are made ⟨coinage by private ~*s* was born of necessity —Abraham Kosoff⟩ ⟨the abbot . . . owned the one-man ~ of that town —John Craig⟩ **b** *usu cap* **:** a government agency charged with making coins ⟨the Royal *Mint*⟩ ⟨Director of the U.S. *Mint*⟩ **3 :** a place where anything is manufactured or fabricated **:** a source of invention ⟨a man . . . that hath a ~ of phrases in his brain —Shak.⟩ **4 :** a vast sum (as of money) **:** a great amount or supply ⟨some of the scarce items cost a ~ —T.H.Fielding⟩ ⟨you save a ~ of money —*advt*⟩ ⟨he had a ~ of faith in himself —Rosalind Duforet⟩ **5** [³*mint*] **:** a coin or stamp in mint condition ⟨20th century ~*s* —*advt*⟩

**²mint** \"\ *vb* -ED/-ING/-S *vt* **1 :** to make (as coins or money) out of metal usu. by a special manufacturing process **:** create in or by the authority of a mint **:** COIN 1 ⟨a patent . . . to ~ copper coinage for Ireland —J.H.Plumb⟩ ⟨trade dollars . . . continued to be ~*ed* in proof —E.G.Bradfield⟩ ⟨Anglo-Saxon coins were ~*ed* by individuals commissioned by the rulers —C.V.Kappen⟩ **2 :** to convert (a metal) into coins ⟨this copper was to be ~*ed* into . . . 9d. pieces —R.T.Hoober⟩ ⟨the silver which was mined there was ~*ed* into coins —J.W.M.Decker⟩ **3 :** to manufacture or create as if in a mint **:** COIN 3 ⟨a phrase newly ~*ed* here —R.H.Rovere⟩ ⟨the language is freshly ~*ed* —Alfred Kreymborg⟩ ⟨new ideas . . . are ~*ed* in a few months —*Times Lit. Supp.*⟩ ~ *vi* **:** to conduct the operations of a mint **:** make coins ⟨the Romans . . . learned to ~ from the Greeks —John Craig⟩

**³mint** \"\ *adj* **1 :** of or relating to a mint **2 :** in the original condition as if fresh from a mint **:** absolutely unmarred and unused ⟨a collection of ~ and used stamps —*Nat'l Stamp News*⟩ ⟨the coins are . . . all in ~ condition —*Numismatist*⟩ ⟨his copy . . . still ~ in dust jacket, precisely as it came from the publisher —Charles Rosner⟩

**⁴mint** \"\ *n* -S *often attrib* [ME *minte*, fr. OE; akin to OHG *minza* mint; both fr. a prehistoric WGmc word borrowed fr. L *mentha, menta* mint, of non-IE origin; akin to the source of Gk *minthē* mint] **1 :** any of various aromatic plants constituting the family Labiatae; *esp* **:** a member of the genus *Mentha* — see PEPPERMINT, SPEARMINT **2 :** a soft or hard confection flavored with peppermint or spearmint and often served after dinner

**⁵mint** \"\ *vt* -ED/-ING/-S **:** to flavor or season with mint

**⁶mint** \"\ *vb* -ED/-ING/-S [ME *minten*, fr. OE *myntan;* akin to OE *gemynd* mind, memory — more at MIND] *vt* **1** *chiefly Scot* **:** INTEND, PURPOSE ⟨~*s* to go tomorrow⟩ **2** *chiefly Scot* **:** ATTEMPT, VENTURE, DARE ⟨cleave to the brisket the first man that ~*s* another stroke —Sir Walter Scott⟩ **3** *chiefly Scot* **:** INSINUATE, SUGGEST ~ *vi* **1** *chiefly Scot* **:** to make a feint **:** FEIGN ⟨don't just ~ at it; do it⟩ **2** *chiefly Scot* **:** ASPIRE — used with *at* ⟨they that ~ at a gown of gold —Sir Walter Scott⟩ **3** *chiefly Scot* **:** HINT ⟨cannot understand what we ~ at, unless we speak it out —Sir Walter Scott⟩

**⁷mint** \"\ *n* -S [ME, fr. *minten* to intend] *now chiefly Scot* **:** ATTEMPT, EFFORT ⟨make a ~ at it⟩

**mint·age** \-tij, -tēj\ *n* -S **1 a :** the action or process of minting coins ⟨a seigniorage . . . might be charged for the service of ~ —J.M.Keynes⟩ ⟨assign the varieties to their place of ~ —*Numismatist*⟩ **b :** the privilege of minting coins ⟨~ has long been a prerogative of the rulers of the country —Ludwig Von Mises⟩ **2 :** the production or fabrication of something as if by minting ⟨literary theories of modern ~ —H.J.S.Maine⟩ ⟨those achievements . . . were not of intellectual ~ —W.C. Mason⟩ **3 :** an impression or stamp resembling one placed upon a coin ⟨became stamped with the common ~ of their colleagues' manners —*London Times*⟩ **4 :** the coins produced by minting; *esp* **:** coins produced by a particular mint or minter or at a particular time ⟨the silver coinage now current . . . will be gradually replaced by the new ~ —*U.S. Treasury Report*⟩ **5 a :** the cost of manufacturing coins **b :** a charge made for coining — compare BRASSAGE

**mintbush** \'=,=\ *n* **:** any of several low shrubs of the genus *Prostanthera* and the family Labiatae having resinous opposite leaves and 2-lipped flowers

**mint camphor** *n* **:** MENTHOL

**mint charge** *n* **:** MINTAGE 5b ⟨a *mint charge* for coining gold . . . should be reimposed —John Craig⟩

**mint·er** \'mintə(r)\ *n* -S [ME *mynter*, fr. OE *mynetere;* akin to MD *munter* minter, MHG *münzære;* all fr. a prehistoric WGmc word borrowed fr. LL *monetarius* minter, fr. L *moneta* mint, coin + *-arius* -ary] **:** one that mints money ⟨pioneer gold coins of private ~*s* —Roy Hill⟩ ⟨if a ~ be convicted of striking bad money —F.M.Stenton⟩

**mint family** *n* **:** LABIATAE

**mint geranium** *n* **:** COSTMARY 1

**mint green** *n* **:** a variable color averaging a light green that is bluer and stronger than variscite green and paler and very slightly yellower than serpentine

**minting** *n* -S [fr. gerund of ²*mint*] **:** MINTAGE 4 ⟨this British ~ had lasted . . . for a century —John Craig⟩

**mint julep** *n* **:** JULEP 2b

**mintleaf** \'=,=\ *n* **1 :** a variable color averaging a strong green that is very slightly yellower than pepper green, yellower and less strong than primitive green, and yellower, lighter, and slightly stronger than viridian **2** *of textiles* **:** a strong yellowish green

**¹mintmark** \'=,=\ *n* **:** a special letter or mark placed upon a coin at the time of coinage to identify the mint

**²mintmark** \"\ *vt* **:** to place a mintmark upon (as a coin)

**mintmaster** \'=,==\ *n* **1 :** the official in charge of a mint **2** *obs* **:** one apt in or given to coining words ⟨custom, the sole ~ of current words —Thomas Fuller⟩

**min·ton ware** \'mintᵊn-\ *n, usu cap M* [after Thomas *Minton* †1836 and Herbert *Minton* †1858 Eng. pottery manufacturers] **:** ceramic tableware produced in the Minton factory in Stoke-on-Trent, Staffordshire, England

**mint par of exchange** **:** PAR 1a

**mintplace** \'=,=\ *n* **:** a place where a mint is located ⟨old German towns that were once ~*s*⟩

**mint price** *n* **:** the price at which a mint buys metal for coining ⟨a considerable difference between the market and *mint prices* of gold —Louis Infield⟩

**mintweed** \'=,=\ *n* **:** a salvia (*Salvia reflexa*) that is troublesome as a weed and stock-poisoning plant in Australia

**minty** \'mintē\ *adj* -ER/-EST [⁴*mint* + *-y*] **:** having the flavor of mint

**min·u·end** \'minyə,wend\ *n* -S [L *minuendum* something to be lessened, neut. of *minuendus*, gerundive of *minuere* to lessen — more at MINOR] **:** a quantity in mathematics from which another quantity is to be subtracted — compare SUBTRAHEND

**¹min·u·et** \,minyə'wet, *usu* -ed·+V\ *or* **men·u·et** \,men-\ *also* **min·u·et·to** \,minyə'wed·(,)ō\ *or* **men·u·et·to** \,men-\ *n* -S [*minuet, menuet* fr. F *menuet*, fr. obs. F *menuet* tiny, delicate, fr. OF, fr. *menu* small, fr. L *minutus; minuetto, menuetto* fr. It *minuetto*, fr. F *menuet;* fr. the short steps of the dance — more at MINUTE] **1 :** a slow graceful dance fashionable in 17th and 18th century France and England and consisting of forward balancing, bowing, crossing, grapevines, and toe pointing **2 :** a piece of music written for or in the rhythm and spirit of a minuet and usu. in $\frac{3}{4}$ time — compare SCHERZO **3 :** a dance movement retained from the Baroque suite and incorporated into the larger musical compositions (as symphony, sonata, quartet) of the 18th century usu. as one of the two middle movements

**²minuet** \"\ *vi* -ED/-ING/-S **:** to dance the minuet

**¹mi·nus** \'mīnəs\ *prep* [ME *mynus*, fr. L *minus*, neut. of *minor* smaller, less — more at MINOR] **1 :** diminished by **:** with the subtraction or deduction of **:** LESS ⟨seven ~ four equals three⟩ ⟨list price ~ the discount⟩ ⟨his ideas added up to Communism ~ violence —Hallam Tennyson⟩ — compare PLUS **2 :** deprived of **:** having lost **:** WANTING **:** WITHOUT ⟨came out of the army ~ a hand —Drew Middleton⟩ ⟨she met him, ~ the book, but carrying a . . . balloon —Phil Stong⟩

**²minus** \"\ *n* -ES **1 :** MINUS SIGN ⟨rendered quantitative by the use of pluses, ~*es*, and marks denoting extreme degrees of the behavior in question —F.H.Allport⟩ **2 :** a negative quantity ⟨an overdose of philosophical . . . conclusions and a ~ of historical or other data —J.B.Mason⟩ **3 :** something (as a deficiency or defect) held to resemble a negative quantity ⟨over against these advantages outside critics set a great ~ —*New Republic*⟩

**³minus** \"\ *adj* **1 a :** requiring subtraction ⟨the ~ sign⟩ **b :** algebraically negative ⟨a ~ quantity⟩ **2 :** having negative qualities or characteristics ⟨a boy . . . might live in a ~ neighborhood but not be a delinquent —Edwin Powers & Helen Witmer⟩ ⟨plus or ~ reactions to women . . . or men with beards —Jerome Frank⟩ **3 a :** reacting sexually to a morphologically indistinguishable but physiologically separable plus form — used of lower fungi in which maleness and femaleness are indeterminable as such; compare HETEROTHALLIC, MATING TYPE **b :** of, relating to, or exhibiting such a sexual character **4 :** of lesser quality than — used postpositively ⟨hesitated to give it a grade so high as C ~ —*Amer. Literature*⟩ **5 :** smaller than a specified size ⟨stocks of ~ 2-inch stone —*Pit & Quarry*⟩ ⟨all powders were ~ 200 mesh —*Amer. Jour. of Veterinary Research*⟩ **6 :** absorbing principally light of its own hue — used of subtractive color primaries

**mi·nus·cu·lar** \mə'nəskyələ(r)\ *adj* [¹*minuscule* + *-ar*] **:** MINUSCULE 2 ⟨tiny white flowers with ~ yellow centers —Victoria Lincoln⟩

**¹minus·cule** \'minə,skyül *sometimes* mə'nə- *or* 'minyə-\ *n* -S [F, n. & adj.] **1 a :** one of several styles of ancient and medieval writing developed from the cursive hand and differing from majuscule in having simplified and smaller forms — see CAROLINE MINUSCULE illustration; compare BOOK HAND, CAPITAL 2b **b :** a letter in this style **c :** a manuscript written in minuscule **2 :** a lowercase letter in printing

**²minuscule** \"\ *or* **miniscule** \'minə,-, mə'ni,-\ *adj* [F, fr. L *minusculus* rather small, fr. *minus-*, stem of *minor* smaller, less] **1 :** written in or in the size or style of minuscules ⟨adapted the Greek ~ letters into an alphabet —R.M.French⟩ ⟨~ script⟩ **2 :** very small in size or importance **:** DIMINUTIVE, INSIGNIFICANT, PETTY ⟨this ~ investment . . . paid astronomical dividends —L.S.Kuter⟩ ⟨miserable creatures on ~ salaries —John Gunther⟩ ⟨~ sculptured panels in the doors —Lewis Mumford⟩ ⟨a ~ kitchen⟩

**mi·nus la·ti·um** \,mī(,)nü'slād·ē,üm\ *n* [L, lit., lesser Latium, fr. *minus* smaller, lesser (neut. of *minor*) + *Latium*, ancient country of Italy] **:** the right of Roman citizenship conferred upon the holder of a magistracy in a territorial unit (as a colony) outside Rome but applying only to the magistrate himself as an individual and not to his children and other relatives — compare JUS LATII, MAJUS LATIUM

**minus lens** *n* **:** a lens having a virtual focus for parallel rays

**minus sight** *n* **:** FORESIGHT 5

**minus sign** *n* **1 :** a sign — used in mathematics to require subtraction (as in 8−6=2) or designate a negative quantity (as in $-10°$) — compare PLUS SIGN **2 :** a sign — used in logic to indicate exception or exclusion (as in *a*−*b* to indicate the class of A's excepting the B's) or abstraction among concepts (as in "human−rational" to indicate those attributes that man has in common with other animals)

**¹min·ute** \'minət, *usu* -əd·+V\ *n* -S *often attrib* [ME, fr. MF, fr. ML *minuta* minute, 60th part of an hour, brief note, fr. LL, 60th part of a degree, fr. L, fem. of *minutus* small — more at ³MINUTE] **1 a :** a unit of time equal to the 60th part of an hour and containing 60 seconds **b :** a point or short space of time **:** MOMENT ⟨these letters didn't get here a ~ too soon —Kenneth Roberts⟩ ⟨the train will be starting in a ~ —Florence Montgomery⟩ **c :** a particular instant of time ⟨wash . . . all sieves the ~ you are through using them —June Platt⟩ ⟨my plan is but this ~ come into my head —Charles Lamb⟩ **d :** the distance that can be traversed in a minute ⟨five ~*s* across the park . . . are Spanish-speaking slums —Irwin Edman⟩ **2** [ME, fr. LL *minuta*] *or* **minute of arc :** a unit of angular measure equal to the 60th part of a degree and containing 60 seconds of arc **3** [ML *minuta*] **a :** a usu. brief note of instructions, recommendations, or record in the form of an annotation on an existing document or of a separate memorandum **b :** an official memorandum drafted (as by an individual or a governmental agency) usu. to authorize or recommend a course of action or to analyze a particular situation ⟨the position of civil servants . . . was previously regulated by a Treasury ~ —T.E.May⟩ ⟨the governor . . . forwarded a ministerial ~, expressing alarm —Ethel Drus⟩ ⟨the whole question was reviewed . . . in a masterly ~ by the Viceroy —L.J.L.Dundas⟩ **c** (1) **:** a brief summary of events or transactions ⟨began to take their sense in ~ as right as I could —W.S.Perry⟩ ⟨unity of judgment enough to warrant a ~ of conclusion —Rufus Jones⟩ (2) **minutes** *pl* **:** a series of brief notes taken to provide a record of proceedings (as of an assembly or conference) or of transactions (as of the directors of a corporation); *specif* **:** an official record composed of such notes ⟨the ~*s* of the . . . conference are not available to the public —Vera M. Dean⟩ ⟨a complete copy of the ~*s* of the . . . presbytery —*Amer. Guide Series: Tenn.*⟩ **d :** a rough draft usu. constituting a preliminary stage of a more elaborate project ⟨the ~ of a letter . . . was submitted to the ambassador —J.L.Motley⟩ **e** (1) **:** a written statement addressed to a court under Scots law referring to some interlocutory matter (as a defect in pleading or a point of law) (2) **:** an answer to such a statement embodying the court's order and the grounds of the order **4** [LL *minutum*, fr. L, neut. of *minutus* small] *obs* **:** a very small or insignificant thing **:** a minute detail **5 :** a fixed part (as 1/12, 1/18, 1/30, 1/60) of a module — **up to the minute :** up to date in the highest degree ⟨bringing navy vessels *up to the minute* in radio equipment by replacing old sets with the newest modern apparatus —*N.Y. Times*⟩ ⟨additions calculated to give the impression of being *up to the minute* —*Saturday Rev.*⟩

**²minute** \"\ *vt* -ED/-ING/-S **1 :** to determine the minute **:** ascertain or note exactly the time, speed, or duration of **:** TIME ⟨*minuted* the speed of the train —Samuel Smiles⟩ **2 a :** to write (something) in or in the form of a minute ⟨the Empress . . . *minuted* an edict for universal tolerance —George Bancroft⟩ **b :** to make a note (as of instructions, comment, or record) on ⟨~ a dispatch⟩ **c :** to make notes or a brief summary of **:** record in the form of minutes ⟨in conversations . . . duly *minuted* on both sides —M.O.Hudson⟩ ⟨~*s* the proceedings of the meeting —James Bryce⟩

**³mi·nute** \(')mī¦n(y)üt, mə'n-, *usu* -üd·+V\ *adj, usu* -ER/-EST [L *minutus* small, minute, past part. of *minuere* to lessen — more at MINOR] **1 :** very small in size **:** TINY, INFINITESIMAL ⟨two ~, whiplike threads of protoplasm —W.E.Swinton⟩

⟨irrigation . . . could be applied only to ~ areas —P.E. James⟩ ⟨~ amounts of . . . impurities are introduced into chemically pure silicon —*Wall Street Jour.*⟩ **2 :** of very small importance or consequence : TRIFLING, PETTY ⟨the law . . . may extend to the *minutest* phases of the life of the individual —C.L.Jones⟩ ⟨small-scale . . . almost one might say ~ capitalists —J.H.Plumb⟩ ⟨explaining all the ~ happenings of the ranch —Mary Austin⟩ **3 :** marked by close attention to and meticulous exactness in the treatment of very small parts or details ⟨made a ~ scientific examination of the bullets —W.H.Wright⟩ ⟨the land is . . . cultivated with ~ care —Owen & Eleanor Lattimore⟩ ⟨a division in the tapestry so artfully constructed as to defy the *minutest* inspection —Jane Austen⟩ **syn** see CIRCUMSTANTIAL, SMALL

**minute book** *see* 1MINUTE\ *n* **1 :** a book in which written minutes or other records are entered **2 :** the official written record of the transactions of the stockholders and directors of a corporation

**minute gun** *see* 1MINUTE\ *n* **:** a discharge of a cannon repeated at intervals of a minute usu. in connection with the funeral of a general or flag officer

**minute hand** *see* 1MINUTE\ *n* **:** the long hand that marks the minutes on a watch or clock — compare SECOND HAND

1**mi·nute·ly** \(ˈ)mīˌn(y)ütlē, məˈn-, -li\ *adv* [3*minute* + *-ly*] **1 :** into very small pieces ⟨~ fragmented and scattered holdings —George Kuriyan⟩ **2 :** in a minute manner or degree : with precision : EXACTLY ⟨~ measured and studied —*Amer. Guide Series: Minn.*⟩ ⟨study their personalities and their work ~ —H.H.Arnold & I.C.Eaker⟩

2**min·ute·ly** \ˈminətlē\ *adv* [1*minute* + *-ly*, adv. suffix] **:** every minute : from minute to minute ⟨two daughters . . . played daily, hourly, ~ —Samuel Wilberforce⟩ ⟨~ proclaimed in thunder from heaven —Henry Hammond⟩

3**minutely** \"\ *adj* [1*minute* + *-ly*, adj. suffix] **:** happening every minute : CONTINUAL : UNCEASING ⟨our ~ conduct toward each other —S.T.Coleridge⟩ ⟨God's ~ providence —Henry Hammond⟩

**min·ute·man** \ˈ==ˌman, -aa(ə)n\ *n, pl* **minutemen 1 :** a member of a group of armed men pledged to take the field at a minute's notice during and immediately before the American Revolution **2 :** one who resembles a Revolutionary minuteman esp. in qualities of vigilance and readiness to take prompt action ⟨participation by political *minutemen*, excited by the issues of the day —Hubert Humphrey⟩ ⟨its vigilant lobbyists are so many *minutemen* —*Tomorrow*⟩

**minute mark** *see* 1MINUTE\ *n* **:** the mark ′ used to express chronological, geographical, or mathematical minutes

**mi·nute·ness** *pronunc at* 3MINUTE + nəs\ *n* -ES **:** the quality or state of being minute: **a :** attention to or extreme precision in small details ⟨that he would peruse with ~ and attention —F.M.Ford⟩ **b :** extreme smallness (as in size or degree) ⟨the ~ of the parts formed a great hindrance to my speed —Mary W. Shelley⟩

**minute of arc :** 1MINUTE 2

**minute pudding** *n* [1*minute*] **:** flour stirred into boiling milk

**minute repeater** *see* 1MINUTE\ *n* **:** a repeater watch that strikes minutes

**minutes** *pl of* MINUTE, *pres 3d sing of* MINUTE

**minute steak** *n* [1*minute*] **:** a small thin steak that can be quickly cooked

**minute wheel** *n* [1*minute*] **:** a wheel in the dial train of a timepiece that is driven by the cannon pinion and that drives the hour wheel by means of an attached pinion

**mi·nu·tia** \məˈn(y)üsh(ē)ə, mīˈ-\ *n, pl* **minuti·ae** \-shēˌē\ *also* **minutia** [L, smallness, fr. *minutus* small, minute + *-ia* -y — more at MINUTE] **:** a minute or precise detail : a minor particular : a petty matter : a small thing — usu. used in pl. ⟨specialized lingo and technical *minutiae* —H.B.Hough⟩ ⟨a printer caring greatly for the *minutiae* of his craft —*Countryman*⟩ ⟨even the ~ of combat cannot be ignored —H.W. Baldwin⟩

**mi·nu·tial** \məˈn(y)üshəl, (ˈ)mīˌn-\ *adj* [L *minutia* + E *-al*] *archaic* **:** of or relating to or being minutiae ⟨~ matters⟩

**mi·nu·ti·ose** \-shēˌōs\ *or* **mi·nu·ti·ous** \-shēəs\ *adj* [*minutiose* alter. (influenced by *-ose*) of *minutious*, fr. F *minutieux*, fr. *minutie* minutia (fr. L *minutia*) + *-eux* -ous] **:** attentive to or dealing with minutiae ⟨precision of ~ observation —J.A.Thomson⟩ ⟨~ and troublesome attentions —*Metropolis*⟩

**minx** \ˈmiŋks\ *n* -ES [origin unknown] **1 :** a pert girl : a saucy jade : HUSSY ⟨never make a wife out of the ~ he had seen coquetting on the opera-house stage —Marcia Davenport⟩ **2** *obs* **:** a lewd or wanton woman ⟨a couple of alluring wanton ~es —John Dryden⟩

**minx·ish** \-sish\ *adj* **:** resembling or having the character of a minx

**miny** \ˈmīnē\ *adj* [4*mine* + *-y*] *archaic* **:** of, resembling, or having the characteristics of a mine ⟨a ~ cavern⟩

**min·y·ad·i·dae** \ˌminēˈadəˌdē\ *n pl, cap* [NL, fr. *Minyad-*, *Minyas*, type genus (fr. Gk *Minyas*, legendary founder of the city Orchomenus in northwest Boeotia) + *-idae*] **:** a family of pelagic sea anemones of southern oceans

1**min·yan** \ˈminyən\ *n, pl* **min·ya·nim** \ˌminyəˈnēm\ *or* **minyans** [Heb *minyān*, lit., number, count] **:** a quorum or number necessary for conducting Jewish public worship consisting by the rules of Mishnah of not less than 10 males above the age of 13

2**min·y·an** \ˈminēən, -nyən\ *adj, usu cap* [Gk *Minyai*, ancient people of Boeotia (fr. *Minyas*, legendary founder of Orchomenus) + E *-an*] **:** of, relating to, or having the characteristics of a prehistoric Greek civilization noted for its pottery

**min·yu·lite** \ˈminyəˌlīt\ *n* -S [*Minyulo* Well, Dandaragan, Western Australia + E *-ite*] **:** a mineral $KAl_2(PO_4)_2F \cdot 4H_2O(?)$ consisting of a hydrous basic phosphate of potassium and aluminum found in Australia

**mio-** — see MI-

1**mi·o·cene** \ˈmīəˌsēn\ *also* **mi·o·cen·ic** \ˌ==ˈsenik\ *adj, usu cap* [*miocene* fr. *mi-* + *-cene*; *miocenic* prob. fr. 2*miocene* + *-ic*] **:** of, relating to, or characterizing an epoch of the Tertiary preceding the Pliocene and succeeding the Oligocene — see GEOLOGIC TIME table

2**miocene** \"\ *n* -S *usu cap* [1*miocene*] **:** the Miocene epoch or series

**mio·geosynclinal** \"+\ *adj* **:** of or relating to a miogeosyncline

**mio·geosyncline** \ˌmī(ˌ)ō+\ *n* [ISV *mi-* + *geosyncline*] **:** a comparatively stable geosyncline in which sediments accumulate without contemporaneous volcanism — compare EUGEOSYNCLINE

**mi·o·hip·pus** \ˌmīōˈhipəs\ *n, cap* [NL, fr. *mi-* + *-hippus*] **:** a genus of very small extinct horses from the Oligocene of No. America

**mio·lecithal** \ˌmīō+\ *adj* [*mi-* + *lecithal*] **:** MICROLECITHAL

**mi·o·lith·ic** \ˌmīəˈlithik\ *adj, usu cap* [*mi-* + *-lithic*] **:** MESOLITHIC

**mi·om·bo** \mīˈäm(ˌ)bō\ *n* -S [native name in East Africa] **:** a sparse open deciduous woodland characteristic of dry parts of eastern Africa

**mi·o·sis** *also* **my·o·sis** \mīˈōsəs\ *n, pl* **mio·ses** *also* **myo·ses** \-ōˌsēz\ [NL, fr. *mi-*, *my-* (fr. Gk *myein* to close, be shut, shut the eyes) + *-osis* — more at MYSTERY] **:** excessive smallness or contraction of the pupil of the eye

**mio·thermic** \ˌmīō+\ *adj* [*mi-* + *thermic*] **:** relating to or characterized by temperature conditions on the earth that now prevail as opposed to warmer or colder periods

1**mi·ot·ic** *or* **my·ot·ic** \(ˈ)mīˌädˌik\ *adj* [ISV, fr. NL *miosis*, *myosis*, after such pairs as E *narcosis*: *narcotic*] **:** relating to or characterized by miosis

2**miotic** *or* **myotic** \"\ *n* -S [ISV, fr. 1*miotic*] **:** an agent that causes contraction of the pupil of the eye

**MIP** *abbr* **1 :** marine insurance policy **2** *often not cap* **:** mean indicated pressure

**miq·ra** *also* **mik·ra** \ˈmikrə\ *n* -S [Heb *miqrā'*] **1 :** the Hebrew text of the Bible **2 :** a liturgical reading of the miqra

**mi·que·let** \ˈmikəˌlet\ *or* **mig·ue·let** \-igə,-\ *n* -S [Sp *miquelete*, *miguelete*, fr. Catal *miquelet*, prob. fr. the name *Miquel*] **1** *obs* **:** a bandit of the Pyrenees **2 a :** an irregular or partisan soldier during the Peninsular War **b :** a soldier of various Spanish local infantry regiments frequently used as escorts **3 :** a flintlock developed in Spain and distinguished by external mounting of mainspring and hammer

1**mir** \ˈmi(ə)r\ *n* -S [Russ, mir, world, peace; akin to L *mitis* soft, mild — more at MITIGATE] **:** a village community common in Russia before the collectivization of agriculture under the Communist regime and characterized by joint ownership of the land by the peasants and cultivation by individual families on a rotational basis

2**mir** \"\ *n* -S *often cap* [Per *mīr*, alter. of *amīr*, fr. Ar] **:** CHIEF, LEADER — used as a title applied esp. in India to descendants of Muhammad; compare SAYYID

**mir·a·belle** \ˌmirəˈbel\ *n* -S [F] **1 :** a small hardy European plum tree (*Prunus domestica institia*) with finely toothed leaves and small cherry-shaped fruit **2 :** the fruit of the mirabelle tree used esp. for preserves and for making a liqueur **3 :** a usu. colorless brandy distilled from the fermented juice of the mirabelle plum

**mi·ra·bi·le dic·tu** \məˈräbə(ˌ)lāˈdik(ˌ)tü, -rabə(ˌ)lēˈ-\ [L] **:** wonderful to relate ⟨has managed *mirabile dictu* to combine baby-sitting with his grandson and writing an article —F.H. Herrick⟩

**mi·rab·i·lis** \məˈrabələs\ *n, cap* [NL, fr. L, wonderful — more at MARVEL] **:** a genus of American perennial herbs (family Nyctaginaceae) having a tubular-campanulate brightly colored calyx subtended by an involucre that resembles a calyx — see FOUR-O'CLOCK

**mi·rab·i·lite** \məˈrabəˌlīt\ *n* -S [G *mirabilit*, fr. NL *mirabile* (in *sal mirabile* Glauber's salt, lit., wonderful salt) (fr. L, neut. of *mirabilis* wonderful) + G *-it* -ite] **:** a mineral $Na_2SO_4 \cdot 10H_2O$ consisting of hydrous sodium sulfate occurring as a deposit from saline lakes, playas, and springs and as an efflorescence

**mira·ble** *adj* [ME, fr. L *mirabilis*] **:** WONDERFUL

**mi·ra·cid·i·al** \ˌmīrəˈsidēəl\ *adj* [NL *miracidium* + E *-al*] **:** of or relating to a miracidium

**mi·ra·cid·i·um** \ˌ==ˈsidēəm\ *n, pl* **miracid·ia** \-ēə\ [NL, fr. Gk *meirak-*, *meirax* girl, boy + NL *-idium* — more at MARRY] **:** the free-swimming ciliated first larva of a digenetic trematode that seeks out and penetrates a suitable snail intermediate host in which it develops into a sporocyst

**mir·a·cil D** \ˈmirəˌsil-\ *n* [origin unknown] **:** a yellow crystalline compound $C_{20}H_{24}N_2OS \cdot HCl$ that is a derivative of thioxanthone and is effective in the treatment of some types of schistosomiasis

**mir·a·cle** \ˈmirəkəl, -rēk-\ *n* -S [ME, fr. OF, fr. L *miraculum*, fr. *mirari* to wonder at — more at SMILE] **1 a :** an extraordinary event taken to manifest the supernatural power of God fulfilling his purposes ⟨perform the healing ~*s* described in the Gospels⟩ **b :** an event or effect in the physical world deviating from the laws of nature **2 a :** an accomplishment or occurrence so outstanding or unusual as to seem beyond human capability or endeavor ⟨test if man can produce, through his will and faith, the ~ of peace —B.M.Baruch⟩ ⟨economic ~⟩ **b :** a wonderful thing worthy of admiration : a truly superb representative of its kind ⟨became a ~ of learning —H.O. Taylor⟩ ⟨the story is a little ~ —Willa Cather⟩ **3 :** MIRACLE PLAY **4** *Christian Science* **:** a divinely natural occurrence that must be learned humanly **syn** see WONDER — **to a miracle** *adv* **:** marvelously well ⟨I understand my part *to a miracle* —R.L. Stevenson⟩

**miracle drug** *n* **:** a drug usu. newly discovered that elicits a dramatic response in a patient's condition (as an antibiotic, sulfonamide, or hormone)

**miracle man** *n* **:** one who works or seems to work miracles

**miracle play** *n* **1 :** one of a medieval type of dramatic representation showing a sequence of episodes from the life of a wonder-working saint or martyr **2 :** a dramatic composition similar to the miracle play in character — compare 2MYSTERY 3

**mi·rac·u·lar** \məˈrakyələ(r)\ *adj* [L *miraculum* miracle + E *-ar*] **:** relating to or of the nature of a miracle

**mi·rac·u·lism** \-yəˌlizəm\ *n* -S [L *miraculum* + E *-ism*] **:** belief in miracles

**mi·rac·u·list** \-ləst\ *n* -S [L *miraculum* + E *-ist*] **:** a maker of or believer in miracles

**mi·rac·u·lize** \-yəˌlīz\ *vt* -ED/-ING/-S [L *miraculum* + E *-ize*] **:** to cause to seem to be or to treat as a miracle

**mi·rac·u·lous** \məˈrakyələs\ *adj* [MF *miraculeux*, fr. ML *miraculosus*, fr. L *miraculum* + *-osus* -ose] **1 :** of the nature of a miracle : interpreted as performed by supernatural power or effected by the direct agency of an almighty power and not by natural causes : SUPERNATURAL **2 :** resembling a miracle : possessing such unusual qualities as to seem supernatural : MARVELOUS, WONDERFUL ⟨the ~ thing about the airplane was speed —*Harper's*⟩ ⟨the book appeared to have met an almost ~ response —C.B.Forcey⟩ ⟨gave proof of a ~ memory —*Time*⟩ **3 :** working or having the power to work miracles ⟨wore a ~ medal —Jean Stafford⟩

**miraculous fruit** *or* **miraculous berry** *n* **1 :** either of two tropical African fruits that have a lingering sweetish aftertaste that causes indifferent or acid foods eaten after them to taste sweet **2 :** a plant yielding miraculous fruit: **a :** a small shrubby tree (*Synsepalum dulcificum*) of the family Sapotaceae having a fruit that is a fleshy single-seeded berry **b :** an herb (*Thaumatococcus daniellii*) of the family Marantaceae whose edible fruit is the jellylike aril surrounding the seeds

**mi·rac·u·lous·ly** *adv* **:** in a miraculous manner : by or as if by a miracle ⟨countryside through which the little train chugs its way is ~ beautiful —Arthur Knight⟩ ⟨a few parts might ~ be salvaged —Bryan Morgan⟩

**mi·rac·u·lous·ness** *n* -ES **:** the quality or state of being miraculous

**mir·a·dor** \ˌmirəˈdō(ə)r, -dȯ(ə)r\ *n* -S [Sp, fr. Catal, fr. *mirar* to look at, fr. L *mirari* to wonder at] **1 a :** WATCHTOWER **b :** a turret or a bay window, oriel window, loggia, or enclosed balcony designed to command an extensive outlook — used chiefly of Spanish architecture **2 :** ART BROWN

1**mi·rage** \məˈräzh, -räl *sometimes* ‖j\ *n* -S [F, fr. *mirer* to look at, aim at (*se mirer* to look at oneself, be reflected), fr. L *mirari* to wonder at — more at SMILE] **1 a :** an optical phenomenon that is often observed on still days over deserts or hot pavements, that has the mirrorlike appearance of a quiet lake or pool in which distant objects are seen inverted by reflection though usu. distorted, and that is due to a layer of air which has been heated and therefore rarefied by contact with the ground and which has a density distribution such as to cause rays falling obliquely upon it to curve back upward — see FATA MORGANA, LOOMING **b :** an atmospheric phenomenon in which the air appears to move in ascending waves like those above heated metal **2 :** something illusory like a mirage : something visionary and unattainable ⟨it is one to write one must have at least the ~ of an audience —F.M.Ford⟩ ⟨explorers, attracted by the ~ of a Northwest passage, pushed through the wilderness —*Amer. Guide Series: Minn.*⟩

2**mirage** \"\ *vt* -ED/-ING/-S **:** to present as a mirage ⟨on the horizon level, we could see *miraged* several small islands —*Australian Museum Mag.*⟩

**mi·ra·nya** *or* **mi·ra·nha** \məˈrānyə\ *n, pl* **miranya** *or* **miranyas** *or* **miranha** *or* **miranhas** *usu cap* **:** an Indian people of the Putumayo River region of Brazil and Colombia — often used to designate any little known people of the region

**mi·rate** \ˈmīˌrāt\ *vi* -ED/-ING/-S [prob. back-formation fr. *miration*] *Midland* **:** to feel or express surprise or admiration — used with *about, at, on, over* ⟨*mirated* at the size of the potatoes⟩

**mi·ra·tion** \mīˈrāshən\ *n* -S [prob. short for *admiration*] *chiefly South & Midland* **:** the act of mirating ⟨made a great ~ about the fish he caught⟩

**mir·bane oil** *also* **myr·bane oil** \ˈmərˌbān-\ *n* [origin unknown] **:** NITROBENZENE

**mird** \ˈmird\ *vb* -ED/-ING/-S [origin unknown] *vi, Scot* **:** to make amorous advances usu. in a light or trifling manner ~ *vt, Scot* **:** ATTEMPT

1**mire** \ˈmī(ə)r, -īə\ *n* -S [ME, fr. ON *mȳrr*; akin to OE *mōs* marsh, bog — more at MOSS] **1 a :** wet spongy earth : MARSH, SWAMP, BOG ⟨the ~ is relieved only by small stretches of open dry forest —*Saturday Rev.*⟩ **b :** something resembling a mire ⟨stuck fast in the ~ of debt —Adrian Bell⟩ ⟨wallowed continuously in an emotional ~ —Lucius Garvin⟩ ⟨sink deeper in the ~ of conflict —Joseph Alsop⟩ **2 :** heavy often deep mud, slush, or dirt ⟨played on a football field that was thick with ~⟩

2**mire** \"\ *vb* -ED/-ING/-S [ME *myren*, fr. *myre*, *mire*, n.] *vt* **1 a :** to cause to stick fast in or as if in mire : plunge or fix in mire ⟨many cattle were lost in the swamps where . . . they were *mired* down —W.M.Kollmorgen⟩ ⟨the advent of a thaw which will ~ roads and fields —*N. Y. Herald Tribune*⟩ **b :** ENTANGLE, INVOLVE ⟨the people . . . are no more *mired* in the past —Louis Kronenberger⟩ ⟨the most brilliant leadership can be *mired* in detail and confusion —Clinton Rossiter⟩ **2 :** to soil with mud, slush, or dirt ⟨my *mired* boots played havoc with the neatly sanded floor —A.T.Quiller-Couch⟩ ⟨furious because she *mired* the car⟩ ~ *vi* **:** to stick or sink in mire ⟨a road in which horses and wagons *mired* regularly —Edmund Arnold⟩

**mire crow** *n, dial Eng* **:** BLACK-HEADED GULL

**mire-drum** \ˈmī(ə)rˌdrəm\ *n* [so called fr. its booming cry] *dial Eng* **:** the European bittern (*Botaurus stellaris*)

**mire duck** *n, dial Brit* **:** MALLARD

**mire·poix** *also* **mire·pois** \mirˈpwä\ *n, pl* **mirepoix** *also* **mirepois** \"\ [F, prob. fr. Charles Pierre Gaston François de Lévis, duc de *Mirepoix* †1757 Fr. diplomat and general] **:** a foundation of ham or bacon, vegetables, herbs, and seasonings used chiefly under meat in braising

**mire-snipe** \ˈmī(ə)rˌsnīp\ *n, Scot* **:** the common European snipe (*Capella gallinago*)

**mirey** *var of* MIRY

**mir·gil** \ˈmi(ə)rgəl\ *also* **mir·ga** \mirˈgä\ *or* **mir·gal** \ˈmi(ə)rgəl\ *n* -S [Bengali *mirgala* & Oriya *mirgā*] **:** a large Indian cyprinid food or sport fish (*Cirrhina mirgala*) having a very small mouth located well under the head

1**mi·rid** \ˈmīrəd, ˈmir-\ *adj* [NL *Miridae*] **:** of or relating to the Miridae

2**mirid** \"\ *n* -S [NL *Miridae*] **:** CAPSID

**mi·ri·dae** \ˈmīrəˌdē, ˈmir-\ *n pl, cap* [NL, fr. *Miris*, type genus + *-idae*] **:** a large family of small often brightly colored leaf bugs (order Hemiptera) which feed chiefly on the juices of plants

**mi·rif·ic** \(ˈ)miˈrifik\ *also* **mi·rif·i·cal** \-fəkəl\ *adj* [*mirific* fr. MF *mirifique* marvelous, fr. L *mirificus*, fr. *mirus* wonderful + *-ficus* -fic; akin to L *mirari* to wonder at; *mirifical* fr. *mirific* + *-al*] **:** working wonders : MARVELOUS ⟨his ~ adventures —W.J.Locke⟩

**mi·ri·ki** \ˌmērēˈkē\ *n* -S [native name in Brazil] **:** WOOLLY SPIDER MONKEY

**mir·i·ness** \ˈmīrēnəs\ *n* -ES **:** the quality or state of being miry

**mir·i·ti palm** *or* **mir·i·ty palm** \ˈmirədˌē-\ *n* [*miriti*, *mirity* fr. Pg *muriti* muriti palm, miriti palm — more at MURITI PALM] **:** a lofty pinnate-leaved So. American palm (*Mauritia flexuosa*) having edible fruits and buds and yielding wine from the sap, a sago from the stem, and a cordage fiber from the leaf sheaths

**mirk** *var of* MURK

**mirky** *var of* MURKY

**mirled** \ˈmirld, ˈmər-\ *or* **mir·ly** \-li\ *adj* [*mirled* alter. of *marled*; *mirly* alter. of 2*marly*] *Scot* **:** MARBLED 2

**mir·li·goes** \ˈmərliˌgōz\ *n pl* [origin unknown] *Scot* **:** DIZZINESS, VERTIGO

**mir·li·ton** \ˈmirləˌtōⁿ\ *n* -S [F, perh. of imit. origin] **1 :** KAZOO **2 :** CHAYOTE

**mi·ro** \ˈmē(ˌ)rō\ *n* -S [Maori] **1 :** a New Zealand timber tree (*Podocarpus ferruginea*) the brown wood of which is used in interior carpentry **2** *Tahiti* **:** PORTIA TREE

**mi·roun·ga** \məˈrüŋgə\ *n, cap* [NL, fr. Australian *miouroung* elephant seal] **:** a genus of Phocidae consisting of the elephant seal

1**mir·ror** \ˈmirə(r)\ *n* -S [ME *mirour*, fr. OF *mireor*, *mireour*, fr. *mirer* to look at, fr. L *mirari* to wonder at — more at SMILE] **1 a** (1) **:** a polished or smooth substance that forms images by the reflection of light ⟨the burnished ~ of his shield⟩ ⟨the mountain reflected in the ~ of the lake⟩ (2) **:** LOOKING GLASS ⟨picked up the ~ on her dressing table⟩ **b** (1) **:** something that resembles or acts as a mirror : something which gives a true representation or in which a true image may be visualized ⟨art is a ~ whose facets reflect all kinds of current trends —Alan McCulloch⟩ ⟨each life is the ~ of many others —Malcolm Cowley⟩ ⟨the press as a ~ of public opinion —C.G.Bowers⟩ (2) **:** something esp. exemplary that may serve as a model ⟨no modern building could act as a better ~ of functional needs . . . than this seventeenth-century Spanish mission —*Liturgical Arts*⟩ **2 :** the speculum of a bird's wing **syn** see MODEL — **with mirrors** *adv* **:** by or as if by magic ⟨problem could have only been solved *with mirrors* —*Newsweek*⟩ ⟨for something done *with mirrors*, it looked pretty good —Wright Morris⟩

2**mirror** \"\ *vt* -ED/-ING/-S **1 :** to reflect or behold as in a mirror ⟨its clear waters ~*ing* the dense swamp foliage —*Amer. Guide Series: Fla.*⟩ ⟨the students' moods ~*ed* the weather —*Better Homes & Gardens*⟩ **2 :** to serve as a model for : REPRESENT ⟨a single city that ~*s* so clearly the development and character of the Scottish community —R.E.Dickinson⟩ ⟨the President ~*s* the nation —Max Ascoli⟩

**mirror canon** *n* **:** a musical canon capable of being played in retrograde or inversion as if read in a reflection of a mirror

**mirror carp** *n* **:** a fish that is a domesticated variety of the carp distinguished by few large scattered shining scales

**mir·rored** \ˈmirə(r)d\ *adj* [1*mirror* + *-ed*] **1 :** fitted with or used as a mirror ⟨buildings of ~ surfaces, expanses of plate glass, and chromium trim —*Amer. Guide Series: N.C.*⟩ **2** [fr. past part. of 2*mirror*] **:** reflected as in a mirror ⟨the brook . . . forms ~ pools of beauty —*Amer. Guide Series: Conn.*⟩

**mirror fugue** *n* **:** a musical fugue capable of being played in retrograde as if read in a mirror placed at the end of the composition or capable of being played in inversion as if read in a mirror placed underneath the music

**mirror image** *n* **:** something that has its parts so arranged as to present a reversal of the arrangement in another essentially similar thing regarded as a model or that is reversed with reference to an intervening axis or plane

**mirror-image relationship** *n* **:** the relationship of an object to its mirror image; *specif* **:** the relationship exhibited by two similar but nonsuperimposable crystals or molecular structures — see ASYMMETRIC CARBON ATOM illustration, ENANTIOMORPHISM

**mirror iron** *n* [trans. of G *spiegeleisen*] **:** SPIEGELEISEN

**mirrorlike** \ˈ==ˌ=\ *adj* **:** resembling a mirror

**mirror plate** *n* **1 :** a flat glass mirror without a frame **2 :** flat glass suitable for making mirrors

**mir·ror·scope** \ˈmirə(r)ˌskōp\ *n* [*mirror* + *-scope*] **:** an apparatus resembling a camera used in rapid field sketching or painting

**mirror writing** *n* **:** backward writing that produces manuscript resembling in slant and order of letters the reflection of ordinary writing in a mirror

**mir·rory** \ˈmirərē\ *adj* **:** of, relating to, or resembling a mirror

**mirs** *pl of* MIR

**mirth** \ˈmərth, ˈmə̄th\ *n* -S [ME *mirthe*, *myrthe*, fr. OE *myrgth*, fr. *myrge* merry + *-th* — more at MERRY] **1 :** rejoicing esp. as shown in merrymaking ⟨Christmas which . . . lights up the fireside of home with ~ —Washington Irving⟩ **2** *obs* **:** joyous sport or entertainment ⟨not amiss . . . to give a kingdom for a ~ —Shak.⟩ **3 a :** gladness or gaiety as shown by or accompanied with laughter : JOLLITY, MERRIMENT ⟨they broke into laughter, and she thought this shared ~ drew them closer —B.A.Williams⟩ **b** *obs* **:** an object of merriment ⟨he's all my exercise, my ~, my matter —Shak.⟩

**mirth·ful** \-thfəl\ *adj* [ME, fr. *mirth*, *mirthe*, *myrthe* mirth + *-ful*] **1 :** full of mirth or merriment **2 :** characterized by, expressing, or indicating, mirth — **mirth·ful·ly** \-fəlē, -li\ *adv* — **mirth·ful·ness** *n* -ES

**mirth·less** \-thləs\ *adj* [ME *myrtheles*, fr. *mirthe*, *myrthe* mirth + *-les* -less] **:** containing no gaiety or joy ⟨gave a ~ laugh —W.H.Wright⟩ — **mirth·less·ly** *adv* — **mirth·less·ness** *n* -ES

**miry** *also* **mir·ey** \ˈmīrē, -ri\ *adj* **mirier; miriest** [ME *myry*, fr. *myre*, *mire* mire + *-y*] **1 :** resembling a mire : characterized by swampy ground : BOGGY ⟨~ ground and a matted, marshy vegetation —R.L.Stevenson⟩ **2 :** characterized by heavy often deep mud or slush ⟨a ~ waste of paddy fields —George Orwell⟩ **3 :** stained or spattered with mire ⟨~ shoes⟩

**mir·za** \ˈmirzə\ *n* -S [Per *mirzā*, *mīrzā*, lit., son of a lord, fr. *mīr* lord, chief + *zā* born, son, fr. *zāda*, fr. *zādan* to be born, fr. MPer *zātan*; akin to Av *zāta-* born, L *gignere* to beget — more at MIR, KIN] **:** a common title of honor in Persia prefixed to the name of a person of distinction

**mis** \ˈmis\ *n* -ES [Afrik, fr. MD *mist, mest* — more at MIXEN] *Africa* : DUNG; *specif* : dried dung used as fuel

**¹mis-** *prefix* [partly fr. ME, fr. OE; partly fr. ME *mes-, mis-*, fr. OF *mes-*, of Gmc origin; akin to OE *mis-*; akin to OHG *missa-, missi-* mis-, OS & ON *mis-*, Goth *missa-* mis-, OE *missan* to miss — more at MISS] **1 a** : in an incorrect or improper manner : badly : mistakenly : wrongly ⟨*mis*advise⟩ ⟨*mis*classify⟩ ⟨*mis*judge⟩ ⟨*mis*cooked⟩ ⟨*mis*copied⟩ **b** : unfavorably ⟨*mis*deem⟩ **c** : in a fearful or suspicious manner ⟨*mis*doubt⟩ **2** : incorrect : improper : bad : mistaken : wrong ⟨*mis*deed⟩ ⟨*mis*impression⟩ ⟨*mis*reliance⟩ **3 a** : opposite of ⟨*mis*advantage⟩ ⟨*mis*thrift⟩ **b** : lack of ⟨*mis*adjustment⟩ ⟨*mis*ease⟩ **4** : not ⟨*mis*constitutional⟩ ⟨*mis*convenient⟩

**²mis-** *or* **miso-** *comb form* [Gk, fr. *misein* to hate & *misos* hatred] : hatred ⟨*mis*ogynic⟩ ⟨*miso*neism⟩ ⟨*miso*sophy⟩

**mis·address** \ˌmis+\ *vt* [¹*mis-* + *address*] : to address incorrectly or improperly ⟨∼*ed* the letter⟩ ⟨∼*ed* his remarks to the previous speaker instead of to the chairman⟩

**mis·adjustment** \"+\ *n* [¹*mis-* + *adjustment*] : wrong adjustment or agreement ⟨corrected the ∼ which had caused the watch to run slow⟩

**mis·adventure** \"+\ *n* [ME *mesaventure, mesadventure, misaventure*, fr. OF *mesaventure*, fr. *mesavenir* to chance badly, happen badly (fr. *mes-* ¹mis- + *avenir* to chance, happen, fr. L *advenire* to come to), after OF *avenir*: *aventure* adventure — more at ADVENE, ADVENTURE] **1 a** : calamitous misfortune : DISASTER ⟨a record of ∼ by shipwreck —*Times Lit. Supp.*⟩; *esp* : a piece of bad luck : MISHAP ⟨his marital ∼*s* (his first wife was a prostitute, his second a shrew) —G.N. Ray⟩ **b** *law* : an accident that causes serious injury or death to a human being and that does not involve negligence, wrongful purpose, or unlawful conduct ⟨a verdict of death by ∼⟩ **2** : a minor and sometimes ridiculous mishap : BLUNDER ⟨this happy-souled and sometimes uproarious book . . . belongs to the domestic ∼ school —*Time*⟩ ⟨his ∼*s* as a young immigrant in search of an unknown uncle —Wallace Markfield⟩

**misadventured** *adj, obs* : UNFORTUNATE ⟨whose ∼ piteous overthrows doth with their death bury their parents' strife —Shak.⟩

**mis·adventurous** \ˌmis +\ *adj* : UNFORTUNATE, UNLUCKY

**mis·advise** \"+\ *vt* [¹*mis-* + *advise*] : to give wrong advice to ⟨had fatally *misadvised* his countrymen —George Grote⟩

**mis·aim** \(ˈ)mis+\ *vt* [¹*mis-* + *aim*] *archaic* : to aim wrongly ⟨missing the mark of his ∼*ed* sight —Edmund Spenser⟩

**mis·aligned** \"+\ *adj* [¹*mis-* + *aligned*] : not properly aligned

**mis·alignment** \ˌ≈+\ *n* [¹*mis-* + *alignment*] : the condition of being out of line or improperly adjusted

**mis·alliance** \"+\ *n* [modif. (influenced by E ¹*mis-*) of F *mésalliance* — more at MÉSALLIANCE] **1** : an improper alliance or combination ⟨the linking of farce and tragedy is usually a ∼⟩ **2** : a marriage between persons unsuited to each other ⟨so far apart in age that marriage between them would almost certainly be a ∼⟩

**mis·ally** \"+\ *vt* [¹*mis-* + *ally*] : to ally wrongly or unsuitably

**mis·an·dry** \ˈmiˌsandrē, -aan-, -ri\ *n* -ES [Gk *misandria*, fr. *misandros* hating men (fr. *mis-* ²mis- + *-andros*, fr. *andr-, anēr* man) + *-ia* -y — more at ANDR-] : a hatred of men ⟨her bitter experiences with men led her to bring up her daughter in a spirit of ∼⟩ — opposed to *misogyny*

**mis·an·thrope** \ˈmisᵊnˌthrōp, ˈmizᵊn-\ *n* -S [Gk *misanthrōpos* hating mankind, fr. *mis-* ²mis- + *anthrōpos* man, human being — more at ANTHROP-] : one who hates or despises mankind ⟨a ∼, whose only strong emotions are those of disgust, rage, occasional sex hunger —Richard Plant⟩

**mis·an·throp·ic** \ˌ≈ˈthräpik, -pēk\ *also* **mis·an·throp·i·cal** \-pəkəl, -pēk-\ *adj* **1** : of, relating to, or characteristic of a misanthrope ⟨their ∼ natures gave a tartness to their observation and their wit —John Cournos⟩ **2** : marked by a hatred or contempt for mankind ⟨the moral corruption he saw around him made him ∼⟩ **3** : avoiding the company of others : SOLITARY ⟨a ∼ hermit⟩ ⟨claw marks fourteen feet high on a tree trunk, left there by some ∼ monarch as a warning to other bears: don't trespass here —Corey Ford⟩ **syn** see CYNICAL

**mis·an·throp·i·cal·ly** \-pək(ə)lē, -pēk-\ *adv* : in a misanthropic manner

**mis·an·thro·pism** \məˈs|an(t)thrəˌpizəm, -ˈz|, |aan-\ *n* -S : MISANTHROPY

**mis·an·thro·pist** \-ˌpəst\ *n* -S : MISANTHROPE

**mis·an·thro·pize** \-ˌpīz\ *vi* -ED/-ING/-S : to hate mankind

**mis·an·thro·py** \-ˌpē, -pi\ *n* -ES [Gk *misanthrōpia*, fr. *misanthrōpein* to be misanthropic (fr. *misanthrōpos* hating mankind) + *-ia* -y — more at MISANTHROPE] : a hatred of mankind : distrust of human nature ⟨now that he has revealed so much tenderness, we cannot talk of his ∼ —Granville Hicks⟩ — contrasted with *philanthropy*

**mis·application** \(ˌ)mis+\ *n* [¹*mis-* + *application*] **1** : the action of misapplying ⟨language develops by a felicitous ∼ of words —J.B.Greenough & G.L.Kittredge⟩ **2** : a misuse or embezzlement of usu. public money

**mis·applier** \ˌ≈+\ *n* : one that misapplies

**mis·apply** \"+\ *vt* [¹*mis-* + *apply*] **1** : to apply wrongly ⟨virtue itself turns vice, being *misapplied* —Shak.⟩ ⟨legal points in the ruling are *misapplied* to the transaction as it actually occurred —D.C.Alexander⟩ **2** : to misuse or spend (as public money) without proper authority ⟨while the handling of the relief fund was irregular . . . he could not say that any part of it had been *misapplied* or embezzled —*Ohio State Jour.*⟩

**mis·appreciate** \"+\ *vt* [¹*mis-* + *appreciate*] : to appreciate or estimate wrongly or improperly — **mis·appreciation** \"+\ *n*

**mis·apprehend** \(ˌ)mis+\ *vt* [¹*mis-* + *apprehend*] : to understand incorrectly : take the wrong meaning of ⟨the real point at issue continues to be ∼*ed* by almost everyone who writes upon the question —Richard Garnett †1906⟩

**mis·ap·pre·hend·ing·ly** *adv* : by misapprehension

**mis·apprehension** \"+\ *n* [¹*mis-* + *apprehension*] **1** : the action of misapprehending ⟨changed certain equivocal passages to prevent further ∼ of his views —S.P.Chase & J.K. Snyder⟩ **2** : the state of being misapprehended ⟨an attempt to eliminate some of the common ∼*s* and confusions which have traditionally haunted aesthetic thought —Hunter Mead⟩

**mis·apprehensive** \"+\ *adj* [¹*mis-* + *apprehensive*] : inclined to misapprehend ⟨though he seemed to listen carefully, he was inattentive and ∼⟩ — **mis·apprehensively** \"+\ *adv* — **mis·apprehensiveness** \"+\ *n*

**mis·appropriate** \ˌ≈+\ *vt* [¹*mis-* + *appropriate*] **1 a** : to apply to illegal purposes ⟨the directors *misappropriated* the company's funds for speculation⟩ **b** : to appropriate dishonestly for one's own use : EMBEZZLE ⟨*misappropriated* these funds for his own use —Hamilton Basso⟩ **2** : to appropriate wrongly or misapply in use ⟨the social scientist's techniques can be easily *misappropriated* —W.H.Whyte⟩ — **mis·appropriation** \"+\ *n*

**mis·arranged** \"+\ *adj* [¹*mis-* + *arranged*] : arranged in a wrong order or manner ⟨the books were ∼ on the shelf⟩ ⟨badly ∼ tools⟩

**mis·arrangement** \"+\ *n* [¹*mis-* + *arrangement*] : a wrong or bad arrangement ⟨the ∼ of the clothes was evidence of hurried packing⟩

**mis·array** \"+\ *n* [¹*mis-* + *array*] *archaic* : DISARRAY

**mis·ascription** \"+\ *n* [¹*mis-* + *ascription*] : a wrong ascription ⟨the ∼ of well-known writers⟩

**mis·assignment** \"+\ *n* [¹*mis-* + *assignment*] : an assignment of a person to a particular job or duty for which he is not equipped or trained ⟨psychological tests are widely used to prevent ∼ of personnel⟩

**mis·attribution** \(ˌ)≈+\ *n* [¹*mis-* + *attribution*] : a wrong attribution (as of a book or painting) ⟨collectors of old masters have been the victims of many ∼*s*⟩

**mis·be·come** \ˌmisbəˈkəm, -spə-\ *vt* [¹*mis-* + *become*] : to suit badly : to be inappropriate or unbecoming to ⟨what I have done that *misbecame* my place —Shak.⟩ ⟨such personal antagonism ∼*s* a scholar⟩

**misbecoming** *adj* [¹*mis-* + *becoming*] *archaic* : UNBECOMING

**mis·be·get** \ˌmisbəˈget, -spə-\ *vt* [ME *misbegeten*, fr. ¹*mis-* + *begeten* to beget — more at BEGET] : to beget wrongly or unlawfully

**mis·be·got·ten** \-ˈgätᵊn\ *adj* [fr. past part. of *misbeget*] **1** : unlawfully conceived : ILLEGITIMATE ⟨never acknowledged his ∼ child⟩ **2 a** : having a disreputable or improper origin : ill-conceived ⟨some of our antiquated and ∼ tax laws —R.M. Blough⟩ **b** : DEFORMED, CONTEMPTIBLE ⟨a scrawny ∼ tree⟩ ⟨a ∼ scoundrel⟩

**mis·be·had·den** \ˌmisbəˈhadᵊn, -spə-\ *Scot var of* MISBEHOLDEN

**mis·be·have** \ˌmisbəˈhāv, -spə-\ *vb* [ME *misbehaven*, fr. ¹*mis-* + *behaven* to behave — more at BEHAVE] *vt* : to conduct (oneself) badly or improperly ⟨*misbehaved* himself in school⟩ ⟨*misbehaved* herself with several men⟩ ∼ *vi* **1 a** : to behave with disregard for accepted moral standards esp. in sexual relations ⟨invited a man to her room and *misbehaved* with him —*Time*⟩ **b** : to behave with disregard for good manners or courtesy ⟨ran through the train, shouting and *misbehaving*⟩ **c** : to behave in a cowardly or unmilitary manner ⟨convicted . . . of *misbehaving* in the face of the enemy —*Associated Press*⟩ **2** : to behave in an unexpected or unwelcome way ⟨does the water you use in processing or as a raw material *misbehave* —*Chem. Engineering News*⟩ **3** : to act as if not housebroken ⟨a pigeon ∼*s* itself on his shoulder —H.J.Laski⟩ — **mis·be·hav·er** \-və(r)\ *n* -S

**mis·be·hav·ior** \-vyə(r)\ *n*, *see -or in Explan Notes* [ME *misbehaviour*, fr. ¹*mis* + *behaviour*] **1** : bad, improper, or rude behavior : ill conduct ⟨the irresponsible ∼ of a drunken driver resulted in an accident⟩ ⟨the trial court's power to hold prosecuting attorneys in contempt for ∼ in official transactions committed out of court —*Harvard Law Rev.*⟩ **2** *U. S. military law* : any conduct by a member of the armed forces before or in the presence of the enemy that does not conform to the standard of behavior established by the custom of U. S. arms for such a situation ⟨∼ before the enemy on the same day, by making an unnecessary and disorderly retreat —H.E.Scudder⟩

**mis·be·hold·en** \ˌmisbəˈhōldən, -spə-\ *adj* [¹*mis-* + *beholden*] *dial Brit* : UNBECOMING, DISOBLIGING, OFFENSIVE

**mis·be·lief** \ˌmisbəˈlēf, -spə-\ *n* [alter. of ME *misbileve, misbileave*, fr. ¹*mis-* + *beleve, beleave* belief — more at BELIEF] **1** : religious belief regarded as false or unorthodox : HERESY ⟨tried to convert him from his ∼⟩ **2** : opinion or doctrine thought to be false ⟨the ∼*s* and unscientific notions of prehistoric man⟩

**mis·be·lieve** \-ēv\ *vb* [ME *misbileven, misbeleven*, fr. ¹*mis-* + *bileven, beleven* to believe — more at BELIEVE] *vi, obs* : to hold a belief or doctrine thought to be false or unorthodox ⟨chide at him that made her ∼ —Edmund Spenser⟩ ∼ *vt, archaic* : DISBELIEVE ⟨some people . . . ∼ I was ever married —Robert Grant †1940⟩

**mis·be·liev·er** \-və(r)\ *n* : one who holds a doctrine or religious belief thought to be false : HERETIC, UNBELIEVER ⟨call me ∼, cut-throat dog —Shak.⟩

**misbelieving** *adj* : holding a belief regarded as false or heretical ⟨called for a crusade against the ∼ Saracens⟩ — **mis·be·liev·ing·ly** *adv*

**mis·be·seem** \ˌmisbəˈsēm, -spə-\ *vt* [¹*mis-* + *beseem*] : MISBECOME

**mis·be·stow** \ˌmisbəˈstō, -spə-\ *vt* [¹*mis-* + *bestow*] : to bestow wrongly ⟨had ∼*ed* her wealth on a scoundrel⟩

**mis·birth** \(ˈ)misˈbərth, -ˈspə-\ *n* [¹*mis-* + *birth*] : ABORTION

**mis·brand** \(ˈ)misˈbrand, -ˈspr-\ *vt* [¹*mis-* + *brand*] : to brand falsely or in a misleading way; *specif* : to brand (as containers of drugs or foodstuffs) in violation of statutory requirements ⟨took steps to stop the ∼*ing* of dangerous drugs⟩

**misc** *abbr* **1** miscellaneous **2** miscellany

**mis·ca** *or* **mis·ca'** \(ˈ)misˈkȯ, -ˈkä\ *Scot var of* MISCALL

**miscal** *var of* MISKAL

**mis·calculate** \(ˌ)mis+\ *vb* [¹*mis-* + *calculate*] *vt* : to calculate wrongly ⟨*miscalculated* his dive into the canal . . . and scored his chest into one mass of wounds —D.H.Lawrence⟩ ⟨*miscalculated* the state of the tide —W.F.Hambly⟩ ∼ *vi* : to make a mistake in calculation ⟨either elation or depression tends to make you ∼ when you're driving a car —*Better Homes & Gardens*⟩

**mis·calculation** \"+\ *n* [¹*mis-* + *calculation*] : a mistake in calculation : wrong calculation ⟨a glaring ∼ or oversight —J.S.Weiner⟩ ⟨an instance of political ∼ —Walter Millis⟩

**mis·calculator** \"+\ *n* : one that miscalculates

**mis·call** \(ˈ)≈+\ *vt* [ME *miscallen*, fr. ¹*mis-* + *callen* to call — more at CALL] **1** : to call by a wrong name : MISNAME ⟨a publisher whose concept of a book is the ∼*ed* "comics" —G.W. Johnson⟩ ⟨a situation which I will not ∼, which I dare not name —Edmund Burke⟩ **2** *chiefly dial* : to call by a bad name : ABUSE, REVILE ⟨you're not to ∼ . . . the best man alive —Sheila Kaye-Smith⟩ ⟨∼*ing* the wind and the cold and the wet lunch basket —Alec Robertson⟩ — **mis·caller** \"+\ *n*

**mis·carriage** \ˌmis+\ *n* [¹*mis-* + *carriage*] **1 a** : mismanagement or bad administration ⟨the immense disorganization and ∼ of life that is taking place —Lewis Mumford⟩ **b** : a blunder or failure esp. in the administration of justice ⟨these various ∼*s* cannot all be ascribed to ill fortune, since some were due to defective organization and staff work —Russell Grenfell⟩ ⟨by a grave ∼ of justice, was acquitted, though admitting the crime —A.F.Harlow⟩ **2** *archaic* : an error of behavior : MISDEED ⟨conducted themselves with such loyalty . . . as might justly wipe off all memory of former ∼*s* —Sir Walter Scott⟩ **3 a** : a failure (as of a letter) to arrive at its destination **b** : a failure (as of goods) to carry properly **4 a** : expulsion of a human fetus before it is viable esp. between the 12th and 28th weeks of gestation — compare ABORTION, PREMATURE DELIVERY **b** : abortion esp. when due to natural causes **5** *archaic* : MISCHANCE, DISASTER **syn** see FAILURE

**mis·carry** \(ˈ)mis+\ *vi* [ME *miscarien*, fr. ¹*mis-* + *carien* to carry — more at CARRY] **1** *obs* : to come to harm : become lost or destroyed : DIE, PERISH ⟨the great soldier who *miscarried* at sea —Shak.⟩ ⟨my ships have all *miscarried*, my creditors grow cruel —Shak.⟩ **2** : to suffer miscarriage : become delivered of an abortion ⟨*miscarried* several times before her first child was born⟩ **3 a** : to go wrong : fail of an effect : come to nothing ⟨an election conducted by means of paper ballots can ∼ —Allen Walker⟩ ⟨instances, all too many, in which justice has *miscarried* —B.N.Cardozo⟩ **b** : to fail in one's intention : be unsuccessful ⟨even the most gifted actor will ∼ if he neglects to take direction⟩ **4** : to fail to reach the intended destination : go to the wrong destination ⟨decided that the letter must have *miscarried*⟩

**mis·cast** \(ˈ)≈+\ *vt* [¹*mis-* + *cast*] **1** : to place in an unsuitable occupation; *esp* : to give an unsuitable acting part to ⟨a journalist without such faith is ∼ —F.L.Mott⟩ ⟨life had ∼ her in the role of wife and mother —Edna Ferber⟩ ⟨the actress who plays the lead is grotesquely ∼⟩ **2** : to make an unsuitable assignment of acting parts in ⟨the play is ∼⟩ ⟨the leading roles are ∼⟩

**mis·cege·na·tion** \məˌsejəˈnāshən *also* ˌmiˌsej- *or* ˌmisəj-\ *n* -S [L *miscēre* to mix + *genus* race + E *-ation* — more at MIX, KIN] : a mixture of races; *esp* : marriage or cohabitation between a white person and a member of another race

**mis·cel·la** \məˈselə\ *n* -S [NL, fr. L, fem. of *miscellus* mixed — more at MISCELLANEOUS] : a solution or mixture containing an extracted oil or grease ⟨∼ from soybeans obtained by extraction with a hydrocarbon solvent —P.L.Julian & H.T. Iveson⟩

**mis·cel·la·nea** \ˌmisəˈlānēə\ *n pl* [L, fr. neut. pl. of *miscellaneus*] **1** : a collection of miscellaneous writings or notes ⟨a batch of ∼ including a number of verses —*Times Lit. Supp.*⟩ **2** : a collection of miscellaneous objects ⟨the Japanese influence has been joined by early Chinese furniture and Hawaiian ∼ —T.H.Robsjohn-Gibbings⟩

**mis·cel·la·ne·i·ty** \-ˌlāˈnēəd·ē, -ətē, -i\ *n* -ES [*miscellaneous* + *-ity*] : the quality or state of being miscellaneous ⟨its appearance of ∼ in the absence of a significant general idea —Raymond Williams⟩

**mis·cel·la·neous** \ˌmisəˈlānēəs, -nyəs\ *adj* [L *miscellaneus*, fr. *miscellus* mixed, prob. fr. *miscēre* to mix — more at MIX] **1** : comprising members or items of different kinds : grouped together without system : ASSORTED : HETEROGENEOUS ⟨special areas where tiger, rhino, and ∼ smaller game were produced in abundance —Dillon Ripley⟩ ⟨did a vast amount of ∼ reading —Martin Gardner⟩ **2 a** : having various traits : dealing with or interested in unrelated topics or subjects ⟨a formal work would not have suited him; he had a ∼ talent —John Derby⟩ ⟨as a writer I was too ∼ —George Santayana⟩ **b** : lacking in unity : having the characteristics of a patchwork ⟨the French pavilion has been severely criticized . . . for being excessively ∼ —David Sylvester⟩ ⟨the large white wooden structure stands in its heroic proportions with a kind of ∼ nobility —*Amer. Guide Series: Vt.*⟩ — **mis·cel·la·neous·ly** *adv* — **mis·cel·la·neous·ness** *n* -ES

**mis·cel·la·nist** \ˈmisəˌlānəst, ˌ≈ˈ≈≈, *chiefly Brit* ˈmisələn- *or* məˈselən-\ *n* -S [*miscellany* + *-ist*] : a writer of miscellanies

**¹mis·cel·la·ny** \ˈmisəˌlānē, -ni, *chiefly Brit* ˈmisələn- *or* məˈselən-\ *n* -ES [prob. modif. of F *miscellanées*, pl., fr. L *miscellanea* — more at MISCELLANEA] **1** : a mixture of various things : HODGEPODGE : MEDLEY ⟨a ∼ of lumber, fish, dairy products —*Amer. Guide Series: Minn.*⟩ ⟨ranged along the walls were a ∼ of violin backs, viola bellies, and whole but unvarnished cellos —Joseph Wechsberg⟩ **2 a miscellanies** *pl* : separate studies or writings collected in one volume ⟨a book of ∼⟩ **b** : a collection of writings on various subjects ⟨the newspaper serves all classes of readers and must always be a highly composite ∼ —F.L.Mott⟩ ⟨its haphazard compilation leaves a doubt whether a fiction magazine, a critical journal, or a general ∼ is intended —*Times Lit. Supp.*⟩

**²miscellany** \"\ *adj* [L *miscellaneus* — more at MISCELLANEOUS] *archaic* : MISCELLANEOUS

**¹mis·chance** \(ˈ)mis(h), məs(h)+\ *n* [ME *meschaunce, mischaunce*, fr. OF *meschance, mescheance*, fr. *mes-* ¹mis- + *chance, cheance* chance — more at CHANCE] **1** : bad luck : MISFORTUNE ⟨the fears and disorders of today are a passing phase, the results of political ∼ rather than of political incompetence —*Times Lit. Supp.*⟩ **2** : a piece of bad luck : an unfortunate accident : MISHAP ⟨similar ∼*s* are frequently recorded at wrestlings —G.G.Coulton⟩

**²mischance** \"\ *vi, archaic* : to come about by mischance

**mis·chance·ful** \-fəl\ *adj* [ME *mischaunceful*, fr. *mischaunce* + *-ful*] *archaic* : UNLUCKY

**mis·chancy** \"+\ *adj* [¹*mischance* + *-y*] *dial chiefly Brit* : RISKY, UNLUCKY

**mischan·ter** \məs(h)ˈchantər, məˈsha-\ *var of* MISHANTER

**¹mis·chief** \ˈmis(h)chəf\ *n* -S [ME *meschief, mischef*, fr. OF *meschief* calamity, misfortune, fr. *mes-* ¹mis- + *chef, chief* end, head — more at CHIEF] **1** *obs* : CALAMITY : MISFORTUNE ⟨to mourn a ∼ that is past and gone is the next way to draw new ∼ on —Shak.⟩ **2 a** : a specific injury or damage caused by a person or other agency ⟨will never forget the ∼*s* they have done to us⟩ ⟨the polished floor . . . often causes ∼*s* — bruises, sprains, dislocations —Herbert Spencer⟩ **b** : harm, evil, or damage that results from a particular agency or cause ⟨one failure led to another, suspicion became general, and the ∼ was done —J.A.Todd⟩ ⟨the concealment of a truth, with its resultant false beliefs, must produce ∼ —G.B.Shaw⟩ **3** : a diseased condition : a cause of sickness ⟨the ∼ is out of your system, and all you have to do is to build your system up —John Buchan⟩ **4 a** : a cause or source of harm, evil, or irritation; *esp* : a person who causes mischief ⟨housing in rocks, of mariners the ∼ —Robert Browning⟩ ⟨he's a real ∼ to his family⟩ **b** : the aspect of a situation or the quality of a thing that produces harm or causes irritation ⟨the ∼ of snow is that it turns to slush⟩ ⟨the ∼ is that people . . . do not confine themselves to one cocktail —Arnold Bennett⟩ **5** : DEVIL ⟨an accident that played the ∼ with his plans⟩ ⟨can't see why in the ∼ you ever got mixed up with that reform gang —Willa Cather⟩ **6 a** : action or conduct that annoys or irritates without causing or meaning to cause serious harm ⟨little wretches, always up to some ∼ . . . all bedraggled from some roguery —Virginia Woolf⟩ ⟨a seasonal ritual among Rochester's youth, like today's Halloween ∼*s* —S.H.Adams⟩ **b** : MISCHIEVOUSNESS ⟨inclined to ∼ rather than malice —*Amer. Guide Series: Ariz.*⟩ ⟨a defiance, offered from sheer, youthful, wanton ∼ —Arnold Bennett⟩ **7** : DISCORD, DISSENSION ⟨has often made ∼ between husband and wife⟩ ⟨stirred up ∼ between the young people⟩ **syn** see INJURY

**²mischief** \"\ *vt* -ED/-ING/-S [ME *mischefen*, fr. *mischef*, n.] : to do harm to : INJURE ⟨that . . . tyrant that ∼*s* the world with his mines of Ophir —John Milton⟩ ⟨any of the other boys . . . they would have ∼*ed*, but they just tweaked Peter's nose —J.M.Barrie⟩

**mis·chief·ful** \-ə(f)fəl\ *adj* [¹*mischief* + *-ful*] *dial* : MISCHIEVOUS

**mischief-maker** \ˈ≈≈ˌ≈≈\ *n* : one that makes mischief : one who excites or instigates quarrels or enmity ⟨their reconciliation defeated the efforts of the *mischief-makers*⟩

**mis·chieve** \məs(h)ˈchēv\ *vt* -ED/-ING/-S [ME *mischeven*, fr. MF *meschever* to come to misfortune, fr. OF, fr. *mes-* ¹mis + *-cheves* (fr. *chef, chief* end, head) — more at CHIEF] **1** *archaic* : MISCHIEF **2** *archaic* : ABUSE, REVILE

**mis·chie·vous** \ˈmis(h)chəvəs, *chiefly in substand speech* məs(h)ˈchēvəs *or* -ˈchēvēəs\ *adj* [ME *mischevous*, fr. *mischef* + *-ous*] **1 a** : involving or productive of harm or injury : HARMFUL, INJURIOUS ⟨a thing which is excellent in moderation and only ∼ in excess —A.C.Benson⟩ ⟨this ∼ separation of the logic from the practice of science —Benjamin Farrington⟩ **b** : able to do harm or engaged in doing harm ⟨the solid foundations of church and state were threatened by ∼ men —V.L. Parrington⟩ ⟨a ∼ fanatic who was trying to destroy liberty of contract —*Times Lit. Supp.*⟩ **2 a** : capable of causing or tending to cause annoyance, trouble, or minor injury or damage to others ⟨windows broken by ∼ children⟩ ⟨the younger animals are most ∼, and I have known bags of flour ripped open and the contents scattered about —James Stevenson-Hamilton⟩ **b** : having or expressing a spirit of irresponsible fun or playfulness ⟨this same stimulating and occasionally ∼ style —W.C.Brice⟩ ⟨her eyes . . . had a sharp and ∼ glitter in them —T.B.Costain⟩ — **mis·chie·vous·ly** *adv* — **mis·chie·vous·ness** *n* -ES

**mischmasch** *var of* MISHMASH

**misch metal** \ˈmish-\ *n* [G *mischmetall*, fr. *mischen* to mix (fr. OHG *miskan*, fr. L *miscēre*) + *metall* metal, fr. MHG *metalle*, fr. L *metallum* — more at MIX, METAL] : a pyrophoric alloy that consists of a crude mixture of cerium, lanthanum, neodymium, and other rare-earth metals in the approximate ratio in which they occur in monazite sand and that is obtained usu. by electrolysis of the fused mixed chlorides of the metals

**mis·choice** \(ˈ)mis(h), məs(h)+\ *n* [¹*mis-* + *choice*] : a wrong or improper choice

**mis·choose** \"+\ *vb* [ME *mischesen*, fr. ¹*mis-* + *chesen* to choose — more at CHOOSE] *vi* : to choose wrongly ⟨∼*s* because he does not stop to think⟩ ∼ *vt* : to make a wrong choice of ⟨∼*s* the showy instead of the beautiful⟩

**misch·spra·che** \ˈmishˌshpräkə\ *n, pl* **mischspra·chen** \-kən\ *usu cap* [G, fr. *mischen* to mix + *sprache* language] : a language alleged to have arisen from a mixture of two or more previously existing languages

**mis·ci·bil·i·ty** \ˌmisəˈbiləd·ē, -ətē, -i\ *n* -ES [fr. *miscible*, after such pairs as E *possible: possibility*] : the property of being able to mix or become homogeneous

**mis·ci·ble** \ˈmisəbəl\ *adj* [ML *miscibilis*, fr. L *miscēre* to mix + *-ibilis* -ible — more at MIX] : capable of being mixed : MIXABLE; *specif* : capable of mixing in any ratio without separation of two phases — used esp. of fluids; compare COMPATIBLE 2f ⟨two ∼ liquids, such as water and alcohol, or oil and kerosene —George M. Sutheim⟩ ⟨gases are completely ∼ —F.H. Getman & Farrington Daniels⟩

**miscible oil** *n* : a hydrocarbon oil that contains emulsifiers, forms a milky emulsion with water, and is suitable for use esp. as a dormant spray

**mis·cite** \(ˈ)mis+\ *vt* [¹*mis-* + *cite*] : MISQUOTE

**miscl** *abbr* miscellaneous

**mis·classification** \(ˌ)mis+\ *n* [¹*mis-* + *classification*] : a wrong classification

**mis·color** \(ˈ)mis+\ *vt* [¹*mis-* + *color*] : to give a wrong color to : MISREPRESENT ⟨∼*ed* the facts in order to win the jury's sympathy⟩

**mis·comprehend** \(ˌ)≈+\ *vt* [¹*mis-* + *comprehend*] : to get a wrong idea of or about : MISUNDERSTAND ⟨∼*ed* the point of the lecture⟩

**mis·comprehension** \"+\ *n* [¹*mis-* + *comprehension*] : MISUNDERSTANDING

**¹mis·conceit** \ˌ≈+\ *n* [¹*mis-* + *conceit* (n.)] : MISCONCEPTION

**²misconceit** \"\ *vt* [¹*mis-* + *conceit* (v.)] : MISCONCEIVE

**mis·conceive** \"+\ *vb* [ME *misconceiven*, fr. ¹*mis-* + *conceiven* to conceive — more at CONCEIVE] *vi* : to conceive wrongly ⟨∼*s*, if he thinks acting is all fun and no work⟩ ∼ *vt* : to form a wrong idea of : mistake the meaning of ⟨*misconceived* the size of the continent⟩ ⟨*misconceived* the nature of the problem⟩ — **mis·con·ceiv·er** \-və(r)\ *n*

**mis·conception** \"+\ n [¹mis- + conception] : the act or result of misconceiving : a wrong or inaccurate conception ⟨such popular ~s as the belief that interplanetary space is of a sub-zero frigidity —J.F.McComas⟩

**¹mis·conduct** \(ˈ)=+\ n [¹mis- + conduct (n.)] 1 : mismanagement esp. of governmental or military responsibilities ⟨was charged with ~ of the war⟩ 2 : intentional wrongdoing : deliberate violation of a rule of law or standard of behavior esp. by a government official : MALFEASANCE ⟨one of his district judges has been removed from the bench . . . for official ~ —H.R.Martin⟩ ⟨indicted on two counts of bribe taking and three of ~ —Time⟩ 3 a : bad conduct : improper behavior ⟨was fined for ~ on the field⟩ b : sexual immorality; esp : ADULTERY ⟨charged her husband with ~⟩

**²mis·conduct** \¦=+\ vt [¹mis- + conduct (v.)] 1 : to manage badly : MISMANAGE ⟨~ed the expedition, losing half his supplies⟩ 2 : to behave (oneself) improperly ⟨~ed himself in office⟩

**mis·construct** \"+\ vt [¹mis- + construct] archaic : MISCONSTRUE

**mis·construction** \"+\ n [¹mis- + construction] 1 : the action of misconstruing : wrong interpretation (as of words, intentions, or actions) ⟨avowal would inevitably lead to ~ of motive —W.J.Locke⟩ ⟨~ of his words has made him seem to advocate what he opposes⟩ 2 : a bad or wrong construction ⟨this is correct in Latin, but a ~ in English⟩

**mis·construe** \¦mis=¦=, (ˈ)mis¦=+, məs'=¦=\ vt [ME misconstruen, fr. ¹mis- + construen to construe — more at CONSTRUE] 1 : to interpret wrongly : MISINTERPRET ⟨misconstrued his abruptness of manner . . . found him assertive and inflexible —Arnold Bennett⟩ ⟨the reader should be on guard against misconstruing the intention of a given passage —Carlos Baker⟩ 2 : to misinterpret the meaning or intention of ⟨~s me if he thinks I will give up my support of the plan⟩

**¹mis·content** \¦mis+\ adj [ME, fr. ¹mis- + content] archaic : DISCONTENTED

**²mis·content** \"\ vt [ME miscontenten, prob. fr. MF mescontenter, fr. mes- ¹mis- + contenter to satisfy, make content — more at CONTENT] archaic : DISPLEASE

**mis·contentment** \"+\ n [¹mis- + contentment] archaic : DISCONTENT

**mis·cook** \(ˈ)=+\ vt [¹mis- + cook] 1 : to ruin in cooking ⟨simple dishes almost impossible to ~⟩ 2 chiefly Scot : to manage badly : SPOIL

**mis·copy** \"+\ vt [¹mis- + copy] : to copy wrongly ⟨the typist miscopied the letter⟩

**mis·correct** \¦=+\ vt [¹mis- + correct] : to make a mistake in an attempt to correct ⟨"the reason I think you're silly is that — is because —" she ~ed herself —Philip Wylie⟩

**mis·counsel** \(ˈ)=+\ vt [ME misconselen, prob. fr. MF mesconseillier, fr. OF, fr. mes- ¹mis- + conseillier, conseiller to give counsel — more at COUNSEL] : to advise wrongly ⟨~ed him to refuse a job that would have suited him perfectly⟩

**¹mis·count** \"+\ vb [ME misconten, fr. MF mesconter to count falsely, cheat in counting, fr. mes- ¹mis- + conter to count — more at COUNT] vt : to count wrongly : MISCALCULATE ⟨~ed the money twice⟩ ~ vi : to make a wrong count ⟨often ~s in figuring the number of hours he has worked⟩

**²miscount** \"\ n [¹mis- + count (n.)] : a wrong count : MISCALCULATION ⟨lost the fight as a result of a ~ by the referee⟩

**mis·cre·ance** \ˈmiskrēən(t)s\ n -s [ME mescreaunce, fr. MF mescreance, fr. mes- ¹mis- + creance belief, trust, confidence — more at CREANCE] : MISBELIEF

**mis·cre·an·cy** \-nsē, -si\ n -ES 1 archaic : MISBELIEF 2 : VILLAINY ⟨embittered by the ~ of those who had cheated them⟩

**¹mis·creant** \-nt\ adj [ME miscreaunt unbelieving, fr. MF mescreant, pres. part. of mescroire to disbelieve, fr. mes- ¹mis- + croire to believe, fr. L credere — more at CREED] 1 : holding a religious faith or doctrine regarded as false : UNBELIEVING, HERETICAL ⟨either weakminded or ~ for holding that we are incapable of any rational knowledge of God —James Collins⟩ 2 : DEPRAVED, VICIOUS, VILLAINOUS ⟨a ~ gang⟩

**²miscreant** \"\ n -s [ME miscreaunt unbeliever, fr. miscreaunt, adj.] 1 : one who holds a religious faith or doctrine regarded as false : INFIDEL, HERETIC ⟨called upon to show that he is not a pagan or a ~ —Thomas DeQuincey⟩ 2 : one who behaves criminally or viciously ⟨understanding of the ~ here involved will not, of itself, necessarily solve painful administrative decisions —Group Psychotherapy⟩ syn see VILLAIN

**¹mis·create** \ˈmiskrēˌāt, ¦==¦āt\ adj [¹mis- + create (adj.)] : created or shaped badly or unnaturally ⟨a ~ monstrosity of a building⟩

**²mis·create** \(¦)=+\ vt [¹mis- + create (v.)] : to create misshapen or amiss ⟨we ~ our evils —R.W.Emerson⟩

**mis·creation** \¦=+\ n [¹mis- + creation] 1 : the action of miscreating 2 : a miscreated person or thing

**mis·creative** \(¦)=+\ adj [¹mis- + creative] : creating or shaping badly

**mis·creator** \"+\ n : one that miscreates

**mis·creed** \(ˈ)=+\ n [¹mis- + creed] archaic : a false creed

**¹mis·cue** \"+\ n [¹mis- + cue (n.)] 1 a : a faulty stroke in billiards in which the cue tip slips off the cue ball ⟨nearly ruins a billiard table with a ~ —Hamilton Basso⟩ b : an error or misplay in other games (as baseball) ⟨has learned to bottle up his anger over a strikeout or a ~ —Time⟩ 2 : MISTAKE : SLIP ⟨the slightest ~ hurtling him down six stories to the back yard —E.D.Radin⟩ ⟨a few ~s in the landing of certain units —Infantry Jour.⟩

**²miscue** \"\ vi 1 a : to make a miscue in billiards ⟨got the off-the-cushion cannon but then miscued —Billiard Player⟩ b : to make an error or mistake ⟨typical of official miscuing were the statements . . . made throughout the week —Time⟩ 2 : to miss a stage cue : to answer a wrong cue ⟨miscued and collided with an actor entering from the right⟩

**mis·date** \(ˈ)mis¦dāt, -i¦stā-\ vt [¹mis- + date] : to date wrongly ⟨carelessly misdated the letter⟩ ⟨~s several of the plays he discusses by as much as five years⟩

**¹mis·deal** \(ˈ)mis¦dē(ə)l, -i¦stē-\ vb [¹mis- + deal (v.)] vi : to deal cards incorrectly ⟨misdealt, and the cards had to be dealt again⟩ ~ vt : to deal incorrectly ⟨misdealt the hand and it had to be played over⟩

**²misdeal** \"\ n [¹mis- + deal (n.)] : a mistake in dealing cards: as a : a dealer's error that causes him to lose his turn to deal b : an irregularity in a bridge hand that requires a new deal by the same dealer

**misdealing** n : wrong conduct : false dealing ⟨exposed his ~ in the awarding of contracts⟩

**mis·deed** \(ˈ)mis¦dēd, -i¦stēd\ n [ME misdede, fr. OE misdǣd, (akin to OHG missitāt misdeed, OFris misdēde, Goth missadeths), fr. mis- ¹mis + dǣd deed — more at DEED] : a wrong deed : an immoral or criminal action ⟨the wickedness and ~s of the Borgia and his family are world-famous —R.A.Hall b.1911⟩

**mis·deem** \(ˈ)mis¦dēm, -i¦stēm\ vb [ME misdemen, fr. ¹mis- + demen to deem — more at DEEM] vt 1 archaic : to judge unfavorably : think badly of ⟨made him to ~ my loyalty —Edmund Spenser⟩ 2 a : to have a mistaken opinion of : MISJUDGE ⟨~ed the power of the opposition⟩ ⟨a gruffness that led us to ~ their true intentions⟩ b : to think or suppose wrongly ⟨but he ~s that he is wise —P.B.Shelley⟩ 3 : to mistake for something or someone else ⟨~ fantasy for reality⟩ ~ vi : to be mistaken : hold a wrong opinion ⟨careful, if I ~ not —H.F.Cary⟩

**mis·de·liv·er** \¦misdə̇¦livə(r), -stə̇-\ vt [¹mis- + deliver] : to deliver wrongly ⟨~ed the letter to the wrong address⟩ — **mis·de·liv·ery** \-v(ə)rē, -ri\ n

**¹mis·de·mean** \¦misdə̇¦mēn, -stə̇-\ vt [¹mis- + demean (v.)] archaic : to behave (oneself) badly ⟨you that best should teach us, have ~ed yourself —Shak.⟩

**²misdemean** \"\ n [¹mis- + demean (n.)] archaic : an act of misbehavior ⟨if any convict shall . . . commit any ~ —S.J. Barrows⟩

**mis·de·mean·ant** \-nənt\ n -s [¹misdemean + -ant] 1 : a person guilty of or convicted of a misdemeanor ⟨an administrator in a fairly large court handling ~s exclusively —Edmond FitzGerald⟩ 2 : a person guilty of misconduct ⟨though he has never been jailed, he is a confirmed drunkard and ~⟩

**mis·de·mean·or** \-nə(r)\ n, see -or in Explan Notes [¹mis- + demeanor] 1 : a crime less than a felony; specif : a crime that is not punishable by death or imprisonment in a state penitentiary 2 a archaic : evil conduct : MISBEHAVIOR ⟨the whole town . . . is distressed for the ~ of a few —Samuel Johnson⟩ b : an act of bad conduct : MISDEED, OFFENSE ⟨the failure of the family, a being of incalculable ~s —H.G.Wells⟩ ⟨leads to such ~s in literary criticism as the too facile relating of a writer's entire working life to an unhappy childhood —Miriam Allott⟩

**mis·de·scribe** \¦misdə̇¦skrīb, -stə̇-\ vt [¹mis- + describe] : to describe wrongly ⟨seem not so much to be describing something with which I am not acquainted as to be misdescribing something with which I am all too well acquainted —J.H. Muirhead⟩

**mis·de·scrip·tion** \-¦skripshən\ n [¹mis- + description] : an inaccurate description ⟨dangerously misleading ~ —A.G.N. Flew⟩

**mis·de·scrip·tive** \-ptiv, -tēv also -təv\ adj [¹mis- + descriptive] : serving to describe incorrectly ⟨ruled that the label was ~ and could not be used⟩

**mis·di·rect** \¦misdə̇¦rekt, -stə̇-\ vt [¹mis- + direct] 1 a : to give a wrong direction to ⟨~ed a stranger asking the way to the station⟩ b : to put a wrong direction or address on ⟨~ed the letter⟩ 2 : to charge (a jury) erroneously as to the law applicable to a case ⟨the prisoner is entitled, however, to contend that the judge ~ed the jury —Ronald Rubinstein⟩

**mis·di·rec·tion** \-kshən\ n [¹mis- + direction] 1 a : the action of misdirecting ⟨~ of the audience's attention is the secret of a magician's success⟩ b : the state of being misdirected ⟨accomplished little because of the ~ of his energies⟩ 2 a : a wrong direction ⟨gave him a ~ that wasted an hour of his time⟩ b : an error of a judge in charging a jury on a matter of law

**mis·di·vi·sion** \¦misdə̇¦vizhən, -stə̇-\ n [¹mis- + division] 1 : wrong or incorrect division (as of a word) 2 : an abnormal transverse division of a centromere that results in the formation of two telocentric chromosomes from a single metacentric chromosome

**mis·do** \(ˈ)mis¦dü, -i¦stü\ vb [ME misdon, fr. OE misdōn, fr. ¹mis- + dōn to do — more at DO] vi, obs : to do wrong ⟨not willfully ~ing, but unware misled —John Milton⟩ ~ vt : to do wrongly or improperly ⟨~ even a simple assignment⟩

**mis·do·er** \-üə(r), -ü(ə)r, -üə\ n [ME, fr. misdon to misdo + -er] : one who does wrong ⟨watching for pickpockets and other ~s —N.Y. Times⟩

**misdoing** n [ME, fr. gerund of misdon to misdo] : WRONGDOING ⟨the grievances . . . were due to the ~s of royal officers —J.G.Edwards⟩

**¹mis·doubt** \(ˈ)mis¦dau̇t, -i¦stau̇t\ vb [¹mis- + doubt (v.)] vt 1 a : to doubt the reality or truth of ⟨~ing his own executive ability —C.S.Forester⟩ — often used with a noun clause as object ⟨he took to his bed yesterday, but I ~ he is very ill —T.B.Costain⟩ b : to regard with suspicion or distrust : SUSPECT ⟨he was extremely presentable . . . you could not ~ him —George Meredith⟩ 2 chiefly dial : to be apprehensive of : suspect or fear as an evil ⟨the prisoner ~ed him to be an apparition of his own imagining —Charles Dickens⟩ ~ vi, chiefly dial : to have doubt or suspicion

**²misdoubt** \"\ n [¹mis- + doubt (n.)] : SUSPICION, DISTRUST ⟨had some ~ regarding the truth of the story⟩ ⟨could not overcome his ~⟩

**mise** \ˈmēz, ˈmīz\ n -s [MF, lit., action of putting or setting, fr. fem. of mis, past part. of mettre to put, set, fr. L mittere to send — more at SMITE] : the issue in a legal proceeding upon a writ of right; also : the writ itself

**mis·ease** \(ˈ)mis+\ n [ME meseise, misese, fr. OF mesaise, fr. mes- ¹mis- + aise comfort, ease — more at EASE] : lack of ease : DISCOMFORT, DISTRESS

**mis·educated** \(¦)=+\ adj [¹mis- + educated] : educated in the wrong way : badly educated ⟨people who have been ~ in the towns —Robert Gibbings⟩ ⟨millions were uneducated, millions more ~ —Benjamin Fine⟩

**mis·education** \"+\ n [¹mis- + education] : education regarded as wrong and harmful in purpose, content, or method ⟨~ of the public in scientific matters —Irene T. Jones⟩

**mise-en-scène** \¦mē,zäⁿ¦sen, -sän\ n, pl **mise-en-scènes** [F mise en scène, lit., (action of) putting onto the stage] 1 a : the process of putting a play or other theatrical production on the stage : the arrangement of the scenery, properties, and actors onstage ⟨the mise-en-scène suggested that nobody had had much rehearsal —Winthrop Sargeant⟩ ⟨a mise-en-scène that included eight horses galloping onstage in the last act —John Briggs⟩ b : STAGE SETTING ⟨a shabby, down-at-the-heels mise-en-scène that scarcely could be called decor —Saturday Rev.⟩ ⟨spectacle plays attempted a more realistic, three-dimensional mise-en-scène —A.N.Vardac⟩ 2 a : the physical setting of an action ⟨gaze on this ordinary house that became the mise-en-scène of an extraordinary drama —E.M.Lustgarten⟩ b : ENVIRONMENT, MILIEU ⟨the books of chivalry . . . were part of the Spanish mise-en-scène —New Yorker⟩

**mis·emphasis** \(ˈ)mis+\ n [¹mis- + emphasis] : misplaced emphasis ⟨faith has been diverted to ~ on guilt —Saturday Rev.⟩

**mis·emphasize** \"+\ vt [¹mis- + emphasize] : to give a misplaced or wrong emphasis to ⟨a theory of direction, interesting in itself, had run away with a performance and misemphasized a play —Theatre Arts⟩

**mis·employ** \¦=+\ vt [¹mis- + employ] : to use improperly ⟨~ his talents⟩ — **mis·employment** \"+\ n

**mi·senite** \mə̇ˈzē,nīt, -zä,-\ n -s [It, fr. Miseno, locality near Naples, Italy + It -ite] : a mineral $K_8H_6(SO_4)_7$ consisting of a native acid potassium sulfate

**mi·ser** \ˈmīzə(r)\ n -s [L, fr. miser wretched, miserable] 1 archaic : a wretched person ⟨~s in the hospital —Sir Walter Scott⟩ 2 : a mean grasping person; esp : a person who lives miserably in order to hoard his wealth ⟨the unenjoying ~'s treasures —S.T.Coleridge⟩ ⟨a ~ who inherited a fortune but lives in a shanty⟩

**mis·er·a·bi·lism** \ˈmizərəbə,lizəm, -iz(ə)rəb-\ n -s [L miserabilis miserable + E -ism] : a philosophy of pessimism

**¹mis·er·a·ble** \ˈmizərbəl, -z(ə)rəb-\ adj [ME, fr. MF, fr. L miserabilis wretched, pitiable, fr. miserari to lament, pity (fr. miser wretched) + -abilis -able] 1 chiefly dial Eng : STINGY, MISERLY 2 a : wretchedly deficient or meager : having little value : CONTEMPTIBLE : WORTHLESS ⟨the squalor of mean and ~ streets —Laurence Binyon⟩ ⟨a bitter sort of acorns, from which a ~ flour is ground —J.G.Frazer⟩ ⟨read the ~ newspapers which the censors plus the paper shortage permitted —Upton Sinclair⟩ b : marked by or productive of extreme discomfort or unhappiness ⟨spent a wet and ~ weekend — their medicine gone and their food running low —Amer. Guide Series: Calif.⟩ ⟨no pressure of opinion forces him to raise their ~ standard of living above the bare necessities —P.E.James⟩ 3 : existing in a state of extreme poverty or unhappiness : WRETCHED ⟨a confused, uprooted mass of ~ human beings —R.E.Crist⟩ ⟨for thousand years had been among the most ~ people on earth —Claire Sterling⟩ 4 : SHAMEFUL, DISCREDITABLE ⟨a ~ abdication of the rights of a friend —Herbert Read⟩ ⟨it's downright ~ of you to make fun of it —Robertson Davies⟩ ⟨his ~ treatment of his family⟩

syn WRETCHED: in reference to a person's feelings, MISERABLE suggests acute discomfort or distress; in reference to things it may describe what is deplorably or contemptibly poor, mean, meager, or deficient ⟨I should like him to die miserable, poor, and starving, without a friend. I hope he'll rot with some loathsome disease —W.S.Maugham⟩ ⟨the witch's cabin seemed only somewhat more miserable than that of other old women. The floor was mud, the rafters unceiled; the stars shone through the turf roof —Charles Kingsley⟩ In reference to a person's feelings or condition, wretched suggests extreme despondence and misery because of affliction, oppression, or destitution; in reference to things, it indicates extreme badness or deplorable poorness ⟨our wretched captive, shivering and cowering in the grasp of the detective —A. Conan Doyle⟩ ⟨the youth was wretched. His home life was obviously hellish —Dorothy Thompson⟩ ⟨the ruin wrought by the most wretched type of slum which seems infinitely uglier and crueller than the vilest railroad tenements —Marcia Davenport⟩

**²miserable** \"\ n -s : one who is miserable; esp : one who is extremely poor ⟨a ~ without a shirt to his back⟩

**mis·er·a·ble·ness** n -ES : the quality or state of being miserable

**mis·er·a·bly** \-blē, -li\ adv [ME, fr. ¹miserable + -ly] 1 : in a miserable manner : UNCOMFORTABLY, UNHAPPILY : WRETCHEDLY ⟨conscious that her feet were ~ wet —J.C.Powys⟩ ⟨~ eking out his existence as a hack writer —R.A.Hall b.1911⟩ 2 : MEANLY, POORLY ⟨men so ~ paid —Kenneth Roberts⟩ ⟨well fed but ~ housed⟩ 3 : in a deplorable manner or to a deplorable extent : PITIABLY ⟨tried so hard and often failed so ~ to bring order out of financial chaos —Current Biog.⟩ ⟨~ deluded by what they take to be realism —W.L.Sullivan⟩

**mi·sère** \mə̇ˈze(ə)r\ n -s [F, lit., poverty, misery, fr. MF misere — more at MISERY] : a declaration (as in the game of Boston) by which a card player engages to lose every trick

**mi·se·re·re** \,mizəˈrerē, -ˈrirē; ,mēzəˈrā(,)rā, ,mēsə-\ n -s [L, be merciful, 2d sing. pres. imp. of misereri to be merciful, fr. miser wretched, miserable; fr. the first word of the 50th Psalm in the Vulgate] 1 usu cap : a musical setting of the 50th Psalm in the Vulgate 2 : a prayer, exclamation, or speech that asks for mercy ⟨settled back to feeding him beer and cigarettes and listening to his windy ~ —Paul Moor⟩ 3 : MISERICORD 2

**mi·ser·i·cord** or **mi·ser·i·corde** \mə̇ˈzerə,kȯrd, ˈmizər-\ n -s [ME misericorde, fr. MF, lit., mercy, fr. L misericordia mercy, compassion, fr. misericord-, misericors merciful, compassionate (fr. miser + -i- + cord-, cor heart) + -ia -y — more at HEART] 1 : a thin-bladed medieval dagger used to give the coup de grace 2 : a small projection on the bottom of a hinged church seat that gives support to a standing worshiper when the seat is turned up; also : the seat itself — called also miserere 3 : a small hall in some medieval monasteries for use as a refectory by monks temporarily dispensed from monastic fast or abstinence

**mi·ser·i·cor·dia** \mə̇,zerəˈkȯrdēə, mə̇,ser-, ,mizər-\ n -s [ML, fr. L, mercy, compassion] : AMERCEMENT

**mi·ser·li·ness** \ˈmīzə(r)lēnə̇s, -lin-\ n -ES : the quality or state of being miserly

**mi·ser·ly** \-lē, -li\ adj [miser + -ly] : of, relating to, or characteristic of a miser : GRASPING, MEAN ⟨the difference between a ~ man who hoards money out of avarice and a thrifty man who saves money out of prudence —William Empson⟩ syn see STINGY

**mis·ery** \ˈmiz(ə)rē, -ri\ n -ES [ME miserie, misere, fr. MF, fr. L miseria, fr. miser wretched, miserable + -ia -y] 1 : a state of suffering and want that is the result of poverty or other external conditions ⟨the flood brought ~ to hundreds whom it made homeless⟩ ⟨living in overcrowded slums in conditions of great ~⟩ 2 : a circumstance, thing, or place that causes suffering or discomfort : CALAMITY, MISFORTUNE ⟨primitive societies in process of disappearance are therefore usu. full of maladjustments, miseries, and unsolved problems —A.L.Kroeber⟩ ⟨a thin ~ of rain, chilling and spiteful —T.H.Jones⟩ ⟨it was a terrible country . . . tamarack swamps, and spruce thickets, and windfalls, and all kinds of ~ —Henry van Dyke⟩ 3 : a state of great unhappiness and emotional distress ⟨had killed her father, cheated and shamed herself with a remorse horribly spurious, exchanged content for ~ —Arnold Bennett⟩ ⟨had ~ and loneliness in their eyes —Bruce Marshall⟩ 4 dial : PAIN, ACHE ⟨had a ~ in his back, it bothered him so much there were days when he couldn't ride —Ross Santee⟩ 5 : a wretched person or animal ⟨we want to see our weaned foals nice and round and solid, and we do not want to see any dull-coated, potbellied little miseries —Henry Wynmalen⟩ 6 : MISÈRE syn see DISTRESS

**mises** pl of MISE or of MIS

**¹mis·esteem** \¦mis+\ vt [¹mis- + esteem (v.)] : to esteem wrongly : to hold in too little regard ⟨the public ~s him, though he has done valuable scientific research⟩

**²misesteem** \"\ n [¹mis- + esteem (n.)] : a lack of esteem or respect : DISRESPECT ⟨the ~ of the newspaper press by the government —J.M.Murry⟩

**mis·estimate** \(ˈ)=+\ vt [¹mis- + estimate] : to estimate falsely : make a wrong estimate of ⟨misestimated his character and underestimated his ability⟩ — **mis·estimation** \(¦)=+\ n

**mis·evaluation** \¦=+\ n [¹mis- + evaluation] : a wrong evaluation : a false or confused view of reality ⟨lead not only to confusions and perplexities in discourse and discussion, but also to ~s in everyday life —S.I.Hayakawa⟩

**mis·explain** \"+\ vt [¹mis- + explain] : to explain badly or incorrectly ⟨argued that earlier interpreters had ~ed the text⟩

**mis·fea·sance** \misˈfēzᵊn(t)s\ n -s [MF mesfaisance, fr. mesfaisant (stem of mesfaire to do wrong, fr. mes- ¹mis- + faire to make, do, fr. L facere) + -ance — more at DO] : a wrong action : TRESPASS: as a : the performance of a lawful action in an illegal or improper manner b : wrong or improper conduct in public office — compare MALFEASANCE

**mis·fea·sor** \-zə(r)\ n -s [AF mesfesor, mesfeisour, fr. OF mesfais- (stem of mesfaire) + -or, -our -or] : one who is guilty of misfeasance or trespass

**mis·feature** \(ˈ)mis+\ n [¹mis- + feature] archaic : a bad or distorted feature

**mis·featured** \"+\ adj, archaic : having bad or distorted features

**¹mis·field** \"+\ vt [¹mis- + field] : to field (a ball) badly : FUMBLE

**²misfield** \"\ n : an error in fielding a ball (as in cricket or rugby)

**mis·file** \"+\ vt [¹mis- + file (v.)] : to file in the wrong place

**¹mis·fire** \"+\ vi [¹mis- + fire (v.)] 1 : to have the explosive or propulsive charge fail to ignite at the proper time or ignite intermittently — used of an internal-combustion engine or rocket engine 2 : to fail to fire — used of a gun or mine 3 : to miss its intended effect ⟨as criticism, this essay ~s —Stephen Spender⟩ ⟨some of it is, without doubt, magnificent, and a good deal of it ~s painfully and embarrassingly —Hollis Alpert⟩

**²misfire** \"\ n 1 a : a failure to fire b : a cartridge that fails to fire when the primer is struck by the firing pin 2 : something that misfires ⟨made the scapegoats for the ~ of the recent currency conversion —Current History⟩

**¹mis·fit** \"+\ n [¹mis- + fit (n.)] 1 : something (as an article of clothing) that fails to fit or fits badly 2 : a person who is poorly adjusted to his environment ⟨took refuge in queer and original behavior, the customary retreat of the social ~ —E.J.Simmons⟩ ⟨today's homeless youngsters are frequently tomorrow's ~s and delinquents —Alice Lake⟩

**²misfit** \"\ vb [¹mis- + fit (v.)] vt : to fail to fit or to fit badly ⟨hobbling about in shoes that misfitted him⟩ ~ vi : to be a misfit ⟨nothing could better illustrate the world of that day; and it is small wonder that the Brontë family misfitted —Times Lit. Supp.⟩

**mis·formed** \(ˈ)mis+\ adj [¹mis- + formed] : MISSHAPEN

**mis·fortunate** \"+\ adj [¹mis- + fortunate] : UNFORTUNATE ⟨not so . . . holy that I can look down on a ~ girl —Joseph Hergesheimer⟩ — **mis·fortunately** \"+\ adv

**mis·fortune** \"+\ n [¹mis- + fortune] 1 a : bad fortune : ADVERSITY ⟨it seemed to him that the tie between husband and wife, even if breakable in prosperity, should be indissoluble in ~ —Edith Wharton⟩ b : an instance of bad luck : MISHAP ⟨had the ~ to break his leg during his first season in the major leagues⟩ ⟨has the ~ to be situated between two opposing powers⟩ ⟨~s never come singly⟩ 2 dial : the bearing of an illegitimate child; also : an illegitimate child

**mis·for·tuned** \"+d\ adj : UNFORTUNATE

**mis·give** \(ˈ)mis¦giv, -i¦skiv\ vb [¹mis- + give] vt : to suggest doubt or fear to : make suspicious or apprehensive ⟨I began to dread that she might not be coming, that her heart might ~ her —Llewelyn Powys⟩ ⟨his mind misgave him that his own indiscretion had been inexcusable —Margaret Kennedy⟩ ~ vi 1 : to be fearful or apprehensive : have misgivings ⟨fetch me the handkerchief: my mind ~s —Shak.⟩ 2 chiefly Scot a : to go wrong : MISCARRY b of a gun : MISFIRE

**misgiving** n [fr. gerund of misgive] : a feeling of doubt or suspicion : a lack of confidence and trust ⟨in the midst of my anecdote a sudden ~ chilled me — had I told them about this goat before —L.P.Smith⟩ ⟨those doubts and ~s which are ever the result of a lack of decision —Theodore Dreiser⟩ syn see APPREHENSION

**mis·giv·ing·ly** adv : in a misgiving manner

**mis·go** \(ˈ)mis¦gō, -i¦skō\ vi [ME misgon, misgoon, fr. ¹mis- + gon, goon to go — more at GO] chiefly dial : to take the wrong route : go astray in conduct or action : go wrong : MISCARRY

**mis·got·ten** \(ˈ)misˈgätᵊn, -iˈskä-\ *adj* [ME *misgoten*, fr. ¹*mis-* + *goten*, past part. of *geten* to get — more at GET] **1** : ILL-GOTTEN ⟨~ treasure⟩ **2** : MISBEGOTTEN

**mis·gov·ern** \(ˈ)misˈgəvə(r)n, -iˈskə-\ *vt* [ME *misgovernen*, fr. ¹*mis-* + *governen* to govern — more at GOVERN] : to rule or govern badly ⟨if people were forbidden to ~ themselves they must be satisfied that they were being well governed —John Buchan⟩ ⟨the most ~*ed* corner of Europe —C.S. Forester⟩

**mis·gov·ern·ance** \-nən(t)s\ *n* [ME *misgovernaunce*, fr. ¹*mis-* + *governaunce* governance — more at GOVERNANCE] **1** *obs* **a** : MISCONDUCT **b** : MISUSE **2** : bad government

**mis·gov·ern·ment** \(ˈ)mis+*pronunc at* GOVERNMENT, *or* -sk- *instead of* -sg-\ *n* [¹*mis-* + *government*] : bad or corrupt government ⟨been brought into a diseased state by prolonged ~ —J.M.Synge⟩

**mis·gov·er·nor** \(ˈ)mis+*pronunc at* GOVERNOR, *or* -sk- *instead of* -sg-\ *n* [¹*mis-* + *governor*] : one who governs badly : an inept or corrupt ruler ⟨a ~ who was forced to abdicate and leave the country⟩

**misgraffed** *adj* [¹*mis-* + *graffed* (fr. past part. of *graff*)] *obs* : wrongly grafted : badly matched

**mis·growth** \(ˈ)misˈgrōth, -iˈskrō-\ *n* [¹*mis-* + *growth*] : distorted or abnormal growth

**mis·gug·gle** \(ˈ)misˈgəgəl, -iˈskə-\ *vt* [¹*mis-* + Sc *guggle*, *gruggle* to crumple, rumple, prob. fr. D *kreukelen*, fr. MD *krokelen*, fr. *kroke* wrinkle, fold; akin to OE *crycc* crutch — more at CRUTCH] *Scot* : to handle roughly or clumsily : MAUL, MAR, BUNGLE

**mis·guid·ance** \(ˈ)misˈgīdᵊn(t)s, -iˈskī-\ *n* [¹*mis-* + *guidance*] : wrong guidance : MISDIRECTION ⟨his young wife . . . being left to her own ~ —Nathaniel Hawthorne⟩

**mis·guide** \(ˈ)misˈgīd, -iˈskīd\ *vt* [¹*mis-* + *guide*] **1** *Scot* : to treat badly : SPOIL, INJURE, ABUSE **2** : to lead astray : MISDIRECT, MISLEAD ⟨see wherein we have been *misguided* in the past and so shape our future course for the better —*N.Y. Times*⟩ — **mis·guid·er** \-də(r)\ *n*

**misguided** *adj* **1** : directed by mistaken ideas, principles, or motives ⟨this ~ man who had doomed nineteen others to hardships and sufferings —J.N.Hall & C.B.Nordhoff⟩ ⟨well-meaning but ~ professors and teachers —*Irish Digest*⟩ **2** : marked by or resulting from mistaken ideas, principles, or motives : MISDIRECTED ⟨victim of her own ~ kindness —*Newsweek*⟩ ⟨~ management actions in connection with training —Bruce Payne⟩ — **mis·guid·ed·ly** *adv* — **mis·guid·ed·ness** *n* -ES

**mis·handle** \(ˈ)mis+\ *vt* [ME *mishandelen*, fr. ¹*mis-* + *handelen* to handle — more at HANDLE] **1** : to treat roughly or cruelly : MALTREAT ⟨dragged her out and *mishandled* her —Polly Adler⟩ ⟨tormented, *mishandled*, shamefully cast away peoples —Sir Winston Churchill⟩ **2** : to manage wrongly or ignorantly ⟨many of them also ~ or totally ignore some of the basic philosophic problems of materialism —Eliseo Vivas⟩ ⟨*mishandled* the car and burned out a bearing⟩

**mi·shan·ter** \məˈshantər\ *n* -S [by alter.] *chiefly Scot* : MISADVENTURE

**mis·hap** \(ˈ)mis+\ *n* [ME, fr. ¹*mis-* + *hap*] **1** *archaic* : bad luck : MISFORTUNE ⟨either my good fortune or ~, to be keenly susceptible to the influence of the atmosphere —Washington Irving⟩ **2** : an unfortunate accident ⟨any great ~, such as the rolling down of huge masses of rocks, or a landslide —W.D.Wallis⟩ ⟨directed the concert without any of the ~*s* expected of a twenty-year-old's performance —*Current Biog.*⟩

**mis·hear** \"+\ *vb* [ME *misheren*, fr. OE *mishȳran*, fr. ¹*mis-* + *hȳran* to hear — more at HEAR] *vt* : to hear wrongly ⟨he often ~*s* the southern Englishman —Sidney Baker⟩ ~ *vi* : to misunderstand what is heard ⟨if we are given a sentence pair which is distinguished by a juncture, we often ~ or are uncertain —Z.S.Harris⟩

**mi·shi·ma** \ˈmēshəmə\ *n* -S *often cap* [fr. *Mishima*, city in Honshu, Japan] : a Korean method of decorating pottery by carving the raw body and filling the cuts with clay of a different fired color

**mis·hit** \(ˈ)mis+ˈ\ *n* [¹*mis-* + *hit*] : a poor hit in cricket

**mish·mash** *also* **misch·masch** \ˈmish,mash, -,mäsh, -,maa(ə)sh, -,maish, -,mȧsh\ *n* [redupl. of ¹*mash*] : a mixture thrown together without coherence : HODGEPODGE ⟨a soggy ~ of sentimentality and half-digested social consciousness —John Woodburn⟩ ⟨a pretentious ~ of primitive rhythms, pop tunes, and sensuality —*Time*⟩

**mish·mi** \ˈmishmē\ *n*, *pl* **mishmi** *or* **mishmis** *usu cap* **1 a** : a primitive Mongoloid hill people of the upper Brahmaputra and a branch of the Naga **b** : a member of such people **2** : the Tibeto-Burman language of the Mishmi people

**mish·nah** *also* **mish·na** \ˈmishnə\ *n*, *pl* **mish·na·yoth** \,mishnäˈyōt(h)\ *usu cap* [Heb *mishnāh* instruction, oral law, fr. *shānāh* to repeat, learn] **1** : the traditional doctrine of the Jews as represented and developed chiefly in the decisions of the rabbis before A.D. 200 **2 a** : a single rabbinical tenet **b** : a collection of such tenets — **mish·na·ic** \(ˈ)mishˈnāik\ *adj*, *usu cap*

**mi·shong·no·vi** \məˈshäŋnəvē\ *n*, *pl* **mishongnovi** *or* **mishong·no·vis** *usu cap* **1 a** : a Shoshonean people of Arizona **b** : a member of such people **2** : the language of the Mishongnovi people

**mish·pa·chah** \məshˈpäkə, -pȯkə\ *or* **mish·po·cha** \-pȯkə\ *n* -S [*mishpachah* fr. Heb *mishpāhāh* family, clan; *mishpocha* fr. Yiddish *mishpokhe*, fr. Heb *mishpāhāh*] : a Jewish family or social unit including close and distant relatives ⟨invited the whole ~⟩

**mis·impression** \,mis+\ *n* [¹*mis-* + *impression*] : a mistaken impression ⟨was under a ~ as to the purpose of the meeting⟩

**mis·improve** \"+\ *vt* [¹*mis-* + *improve*] **1** : to use wrongly : make an improper use of : ABUSE ⟨has *misimproved* and wasted his talents⟩ **2** *archaic* : to make worse in an attempt to improve — **mis·improvement** \"+\ *n*

**mis·inform** \"+\ *vt* [ME *misenfourmen*, fr. ¹*mis-* + *enfourmen* to inform — more at INFORM] : to give incorrect, untrue, or misleading information to ⟨~*ed* his partner as to the extent of the firm's liabilities⟩ ⟨had been ~*ed* about the time of the meeting⟩ — **mis·information** \(,)mis+\ *n*

**mis·informative** \,mis+\ *adj* [¹*mis-* + *informative*] : serving to misinform ⟨some good common sense, some information, some ~ gossip —*New Republic*⟩

**mis·intelligence** \"+\ *n* [in sense 1, prob. fr. F *mésintelligence*, fr. MF, fr. *més-* ¹mis- + *intelligence*; in sense 2, fr. ¹*mis-* + *intelligence*] **1** : a mistaken impression : MISUNDERSTANDING ⟨a glaring ~ of the facts of the case⟩ **2** : lack of intelligence ⟨a poor showing that might have been a sign of misducation rather than ~⟩

**mis·interpret** \"+\ *vt* [¹*mis-* + *interpret*] **1** : to understand wrongly ⟨causes the pilot to ~ level ground as tipping laterally —H.G.Armstrong⟩ **2** : to give an incorrect interpretation to : explain wrongly ⟨his note on this passage ~*s* the author's meaning⟩ — **mis·interpreter** \"+\ *n*

**mis·interpretable** \"+\ *adj* : capable of being misinterpreted

**mis·interpretation** \"+\ *n* [¹*mis-* + *interpretation*] : incorrect interpretation ⟨attributed to ~ of conventional objects, to mass hysteria, or to simple hoaxes —*Current Biog.*⟩

**mis·joinder** \(ˈ)mis+\ *n* [¹*mis-* + *joinder*] : an incorrect union of parties or of causes of action in a single legal proceeding

**mis·judge** \"+\ *vb* [¹*mis-* + *judge*] *vt* **1** : to judge wrongly : have a mistaken estimation of ⟨will inject himself into his books, misread them, and so ~ them —H.A.Overstreet⟩ **2** : to have an unjust opinion of ⟨if you think him capable of such an action, you ~ him⟩ ~ *vi* : to be mistaken in judgment ⟨we have *misjudged*, and owe him an apology⟩ — **mis·judger** \"+\ *n*

**mis·judg·ing·ly** *adv* : in a misjudging manner : so as to make a misjudgment

**mis·judgment** *or* **mis·judgement** \(ˈ)mis+\ *n* [¹*mis-* + *judgment*] : incorrect or distorted judgment ⟨the accident was caused by his ~ of the sharpness of the curve⟩ ⟨his prejudices have led him into a serious ~ of his opponent⟩

**mis·kal** *also* **mis·cal** *or* **mith·kal** \məsˈkäl, mithˈkäl\ *n* -S [Turk, Per, & Ar; Turk *miskal*, fr. Per *misqāl*, fr. colloq. Ar *misqāl* (Ar *mithqāl*)] **1** : any of various units of weight of Muslim countries: as **a** : a Persian unit equal to about 71 grains **b** : a Turkish unit equal to 74.2 grains **2 a** : a silver 10-dirhem piece of Morocco **b** : a unit of value of Chinese Turkestan ⟨5, 4, 3, and 2 ~ silver coins struck 1900–11⟩

**mis·ken** \(ˈ)mis+\ *vt* [ME (Sc) *miskennen*, fr. ¹*mis-* + *kennen* to ken — more at KEN] **1** *chiefly Scot* **a** : to have incorrect ideas about : MISUNDERSTAND **b** : to have a false estimation of (oneself) **2** *chiefly Scot* : MISKNOW 1 **3** *chiefly Scot* : to pretend not to know : IGNORE

**mis·kenning** \"+\ *n* [ME, fr. ¹*mis-* + *kenning*] *old Eng law* : a mistake or variance in pleading or argument in court

**miskin** *var of* MIXEN

**mi·ski·to** \məˈskēd·(,)ō\ *n*, *pl* **miskito** *or* **miskitos** *usu cap* **1 a** : a people of the Atlantic coast of Nicaragua and Honduras **b** : a member of such people **2** : a language of the Miskito people — called also *Mosquito*

**mis·know** \(ˈ)mis+\ *vt* [ME *misknowen*, fr. ¹*mis-* + *knowen* to know — more at KNOW] **1** : to fail to recognize ⟨welcome our enemies and ~ our friends⟩ **2** : to know incorrectly : MISUNDERSTAND ⟨he who knows something quickly, often ~*s* it⟩

**mis·knowledge** \"+\ *n* [¹*mis-* + *knowledge*] : false knowledge : MISUNDERSTANDING ⟨might have augmented the already great ~ of the Arctic had I published everything I imagined I had seen —Vilhjalmur Stefansson⟩

**mis·kolc** \ˈmish,kōlts\ *adj*, *usu cap* [fr. *Miskolc*, Hungary] : of or from the city of Miskolc, Hungary : of the kind or style prevalent in Miskolc

**misky** \ˈmiskē, -ki\ *adj*, *usu* -ER/-EST [alter. of *misty*] *dial chiefly Eng* : MISTY : FOGGY

**mis·label** \(ˈ)mis+\ *vt* [¹*mis-* + *label*] : to label incorrectly or falsely ⟨charged that the company had ~*ed* its products⟩

**mis·lay** \"+\ *vt* [ME *mysse layen*, fr. *mysse-*, *mis-* ¹mis- + *layen* to lay — more at LAY] **1** : to lay, place, or set incorrectly ⟨*mislaid* the tiles so that the pattern was ruined⟩ ⟨~ the table for the usual four persons instead of six⟩ ⟨~ a stair carpet⟩ **2 a** : to put in an unremembered place ⟨~ a book⟩ ⟨~ a pair of gloves⟩ **b** : put aside : LOSE ⟨*mislaid* his principles in the drive for success⟩

**mis·lead** \"+\ *vb* [ME *misleden*, fr. OE *mislǣdan*, fr. ¹*mis-* + *lǣdan* to lead — more at LEAD] *vt* : to lead in a wrong direction or into a mistaken action or belief : DECEIVE ⟨had been much opposed by women, crossed, balked, wronged, *misled* —Francis Hackett⟩ ⟨the persons who have first deceived themselves are most effective in ~*ing* others —John Dewey⟩ ~ *vi* : to lead astray ⟨exciting as they are, they ~ —E.M. Forster⟩ **syn** see DECEIVE

**mis·leader** \"+\ *n* [ME *misleder*, fr. *misleden* + *-er*] : one that misleads ⟨have called him a ~ of youth, a debaser of traditional values and a corrupter of historical verities —C.V. Woodward⟩

**misleading** *adj* : tending to mislead : DECEIVING ⟨so vague as to be really meaningless, if not inaccurate and ~ —Havelock Ellis⟩ — **mis·lead·ing·ly** *adv* — **mis·lead·ing·ness** *n* -ES

**mis·lear** \(ˈ)misˈli(ə)r, -lēr\ *vt* [ME *misleren*, fr. OE *mislǣran*, fr. ¹*mis-* + *lǣran* to teach — more at LERE] *dial Brit* : MISLEAD

**mis·leared** \-rd\ *adj*, *chiefly Scot* : UNMANNERLY, ILL-BRED

**misled** *past of* MISLEAD

**mis·lest** \məˈslest\ *or* **mis·list** \-list\ *vt* -ED/-ING/-S [by alter. (influence of ¹*mis-*)] *dial* : MOLEST

¹**mis·like** \(ˈ)mis+\ *vt* [ME *misliken*, fr. OE *mislīcian*, fr. ¹*mis-* + *līcian* to be pleasing — more at LIKE] **1** *archaic* : to be displeasing to : DISPLEASE ⟨if my best wines ~ thy taste —T.B.Aldrich⟩ **2** : to have an aversion to : disapprove of : DISLIKE ⟨no one, least of all his father, could ~ the bearing of the youth —Francis Hackett⟩ — **mis·liker** \"+\ *n*

²**mislike** \"\ *n* : DISLIKE ⟨his ~ of pomp and ceremony⟩

**mis·line** \"+\ *vt* [¹*mis-* + *line*] : to arrange or divide (poetry) into lines incorrectly in copying or printing

**mis·lippen** \"+\ *vt* -ED/-ING/-S [¹*mis-* + *lippen*] **1** *dial Brit* : DECEIVE, DISAPPOINT **2** *dial Brit* : NEGLECT, OVERLOOK **3** *chiefly Scot* : DOUBT, SUSPECT

**mis·locate** \(ˈ)mis, ¦mis+\ *vt* [¹*mis-* + *locate*] : MISPLACE ⟨that is why his commercialized elation seems so *mislocated* —C.W.Mills⟩ — **mis·location** \¦=+\ *n*

¹**mis·luck** \(ˈ)mis+\ *n* [¹*mis-* + *luck* (n.)] *chiefly Scot* : bad luck : MISFORTUNE

²**misluck** \"\ *vi* [¹*mis-* + *luck* (v.)] *chiefly Scot* : to experience misfortune

**mis·machine** \,mis+\ *vt* [¹*mis-* + *machine*] : to machine to faulty dimensions ⟨resize a *mismachined* part⟩

**mis·made** \(ˈ)mis+\ *adj* [ME *mismad*, fr. ¹*mis-* + *mad* made — more at MADE] : badly or improperly made ⟨limping possibilities of ~ human nature —Elizabeth B. Browning⟩

**mis·manage** \"+\ *vt* [¹*mis-* + *manage*] : to manage wrongly or incompetently ⟨*mismanaging* an allowance intended for their maintenance —Margaret Kennedy⟩ ⟨a *mismanaged* household⟩ — **mis·manager** \"+\ *n*

**mis·management** \"+\ *n* [¹*mis-* + *management*] : corrupt or improper management ⟨an early history of scandal or ~ —*Amer. Guide Series: N.Y. City*⟩ ⟨the bankruptcy of the business was directly due to ~⟩

**mis·mannered** \"+\ *adj* [¹*mis-* + *mannered*] *dial Brit* : ILL-MANNERED

**mis·marriage** \"+\ *n* [¹*mis-* + *marriage*] : an unsuitable marriage ⟨the trap of poverty and ~ —G.N.Ray⟩

¹**mis·match** \"+\ *vt* [¹*mis-* + *match* (v.)] : to match wrongly or unsuitably ⟨a ~*ed* couple, who are always quarreling⟩ ⟨~*ed* him with a much better fighter⟩

²**mismatch** \"\ *n* : a faulty or unsuitable match ⟨a poor job of wallpapering, with many ~*es*⟩ ⟨the contest between the two teams was an obvious ~⟩

**mis·mate** \"+\ *vb* [¹*mis-* + *mate*] *vt* : to mate unsuitably ⟨*mismated* myself for love of you —Thomas Hardy⟩ ⟨the awful internal bleeding of *mismated* lives —*Time*⟩ ⟨a style that ~*s* Gothic and modern⟩ ~ *vi* : to become wrongly or unsuitably mated ⟨pious men who ~ with the daughters of him "who slew his brother" —*Modern Language Notes*⟩

**mis·mother** \"+\ *vt* [¹*mis-* + *mother*] *of a ewe* : to fail to own and care for (her lamb)

**mis·move** \"+\ *n* [¹*mis-* + *move*] : a wrong move : MISPLAY ⟨scared for fear he would make a ~ and there the trout would go flashing off —Helen Rich⟩

**misn** *abbr* misnumbered

**misnagid** *often cap*, *var of* MITNAGGED

**mis·name** \(ˈ)mis+\ *vt* [¹*mis-* + *name*] **1** : to call by a bad name : ABUSE ⟨let none, therefore, in our country and Commonwealth or in the outside world ~ or traduce our motives —Sir Winston Churchill⟩ **2** : to name incorrectly : MISCALL ⟨*misnamed* him a primitive painter⟩

**mis·nomed** \məˈsnōmd\ *adj* [*misnomer* + *-ed*] *archaic* : MISNOMERED

**mis·nomer** \məˈsnōmə(r)\ *n* -S [ME *misnoumer*, fr. AF *misnomer* to call by a wrong name, fr. MF *mesnommer* to call by a bad name, fr. *mes-* ¹mis- + *nommer* to name, fr. L *nominare* to name — more at NOMINATE] **1** : the misnaming of a person in a legal instrument or proceeding (as in a complaint or indictment) **2 a** : a use of a wrong name ⟨it is a ~ to call such works of fiction biographies⟩ **b** : a wrong name : an incorrect designation or term ⟨"fruit," as used to describe potatoes, is a ~ —Jackson Rivers⟩ ⟨found to his great pleasure that the name Green Lanes was no ~ for the village —Compton Mackenzie⟩

**mis·no·mered** \-(r)d\ *adj* : wrongly called or designated ⟨a patch of burned grass ~ a lawn⟩

**mi·so** \ˈmē(,)sō\ *n* -S [Jap] : a paste used in preparing soups and other foods that is made by grinding a mixture of steamed rice, cooked soybeans, and salt and fermenting it in brine

**miso-** — see MIS-

**miso·cai·nea** \,misōˈkīnēə, ,mīs-, -kān-\ *n* -S [NL, fr. ²*mis-* + *-cainea* (fr. Gk *kainos* new, recent) — more at RECENT] : an abnormal hatred of new ideas

**miso·gam·ic** \¦misō¦gamik, ¦mīs-\ *adj* [*misogamy* + *-ic*] : having a hatred of marriage

**mi·sog·a·mist** \məˈsägəməst, mīˈ-\ *n* -S [*misogamy* + *-ist*] : one who hates marriage

**mi·sog·a·my** \-mē\ *n* -ES [²*mis-* + *-gamy*] : a hatred of marriage ⟨remained a bachelor because of his ingrained ~, not for lack of opportunity to marry⟩

**miso·gyn·ic** \¦misə¦jinik, ¦mīs-\ *also* **mi·sog·y·nous** \məˈsäjənəs, mīˈ-\ *adj* [*misogyny* + *-ic* or *-ous*] : having or showing a hatred and distrust of women ⟨a ~ writer who portrays all women as scheming and selfish⟩ **syn** see CYNICAL

**mi·sog·y·nism** \məˈsäjə,nizəm, mīˈ-\ *n* -S [*misogyny* + *-ism*] : MISOGYNY

**mi·sog·y·nist** \-,nəst\ *n* -S [Gk *misogynēs* misogynist (fr. *miso-* ²mis- + *gynē* woman) + E *-ist* — more at QUEEN] : one who hates women ⟨the fulfillment of a suffragette's dream and a *misogynist's* nightmare —*Newsweek*⟩ ⟨an early and unfortunate love affair which had made of him a ~ —*Cosmopolitan*⟩ — **mi·sog·y·nis·tic** \=¦==¦nistik\ *adj*

**mi·sog·y·ny** \məˈsäjənē, mīˈ-, -ni\ *n* -ES [Gk *misogynia*, fr. *miso-* ²mis- + *gynē* woman + *-ia* -y] : a hatred of women ⟨his ~ vanished under the influence of her beauty and charm⟩ — opposed to *misandry*

**mi·sol·o·gist** \məˈsäləjəst, mīˈ-\ *n* -S : one given to misology ⟨~*s* who like to pose as hardheaded men of action⟩

**mi·sol·o·gy** \-jē\ *n* -ES [Gk *misologia*, fr. *miso-* ²mis- + *logos* word, reason, speech, account + *-ia* -y — more at LEGEND] : a dislike, distrust, or hatred of argument, reasoning, or enlightenment ⟨must keep away both from ~ . . . and from the magical attitude of those who make an idol of wisdom —K.R.Popper⟩

**miso·ne·ism** \,misəˈnē,izəm, ,mīs-\ *n* -S [It *misoneismo*, fr. *miso-* ²mis- + Gk *neos* new + It *-ismo* -ism — more at NEW] : a hatred or intolerance of something new or changed ⟨there is developed more and more as the years go on a true ~, so that the patient will positively not tolerate any change in the usual order of things —W.A.White⟩

**miso·ne·ist** \-ēəst\ *n* -S [*misoneism* + *-ist*] : one who is subject to misoneism — **miso·ne·is·tic** \¦==nē¦istik\ *adj*

**miso·pe·dia** \,misəˈpēdēə, ,mīs-\ *n* -S [NL, fr. ²*mis-* + Gk *paid-*, *pais* child + NL *-ia* — more at FEW] : a hatred of children

**miso·pe·dist** \-dəst\ *n* -S [NL *misopedia* + E *-ist*] : one who hates children

**misophobia** *var of* MYSOPHOBIA

¹**mis·order** \(ˈ)mis+\ *n* [ME, fr. ¹*mis-* + *order* (n.)] : DISORDER

²**misorder** \"\ *vt* [¹*mis-* + *order* (v.)] **1** : to put in disorder or confusion (as through mismanagement) **2** *obs* : to behave (oneself) badly

**mis·orderly** \"+\ *adj* [¹*mis-* + *orderly*] : DISORDERLY

**misos** *pl of* MISO

**mis·pel** \ˈmispəl\ *n* -S [Afrik, fr. MD *mispele*, *mespele* medlar, fr. L *mespila* — more at MEDLAR] : MEDLAR 3

**mis·perception** \¦mis+\ *n* [¹*mis-* + *perception*] : a false perception ⟨that any of the perennial human preoccupations should be mere illusion or a ~ of something else is . . . repugnant to common sense —J.V.L.Casserley⟩

**mis·perform** \"+\ *vt* [¹*mis-* + *perform*] : to perform wrongly or improperly ⟨the ship ~*ed* the maneuver and almost collided with the pier⟩ — **mis·performance** \"+\ *n*

**mis·pick** \(ˈ)mis+\ *n* [¹*mis-* + *pick* (n.)] : an improperly meshed pick in textile machinery; *also* : a defect resulting from such improper meshing

**mis·pick·el** \ˈmi,spikəl\ *n* -S [G *mispickel*, *misspickel*] : ARSENOPYRITE

**mis·place** \(ˈ)mis+\ *vt* [¹*mis-* + *place*] **1 a** : to put in a wrong place or position ⟨the sign at the western end of the bridge is *misplaced* —*Amer. Guide Series: La.*⟩ **b** : to put in an unaccustomed or forgotten place : MISLAY ⟨*misplaced* his hat⟩ ⟨*misplaced* the tickets⟩ **2** : to set (as one's hopes or confidence) on a wrong object or eventuality ⟨the barrage of good wishes with which the assembly had opened had not been *misplaced* —Guthrie Moir⟩ ⟨a sad example of trust that was *misplaced*⟩ **3** : to set aside : LOSE ⟨we are granted some insight into what has caused him to ~ his will to live —John Mason Brown⟩ ⟨this useful piece of wisdom was sadly *misplaced* in later American epochs —Van Wyck Brooks⟩ — **mis·placement** \"+\ *n*

¹**mis·play** \"+\ *n* [¹*mis-* + *play* (n.)] : a wrong or unskillful play : ERROR ⟨was charged with a ~ when he fumbled the ball⟩ ⟨one ~ caused them to lose the rubber⟩

²**misplay** \"\ *vt* [¹*mis-* + *play* (v.)] : to play wrongly or unskillfully ⟨the shortstop ~*ed* the ball and it went past him⟩ ⟨~*ed* her hand and was set two tricks⟩ ⟨~*ed* his return of service⟩

**mis·pleading** \(ˈ)mis+\ *n* [¹*mis-* + *pleading*] : an error in pleading : a wrong pleading or omission

**mis·point** \"+\ *vt* [¹*mis-* + *point*] *archaic* : to punctuate wrongly

**mis·praise** \"+\ *vb* [ME *mispraisen*, fr. ¹*mis-* + *praisen* to praise — more at PRAISE] *vt* **1** : DISPRAISE **2** : to praise wrongly ~ *vi* : to give expression to improper or unwise praise

¹**mis·print** \"+\ *vb* [¹*mis-* + *print* (v.)] *vt* : to print incorrectly ~ *vi*, *of horned game* : to walk in an uneven manner : leave irregular footprints

²**misprint** \"\ *n* : a mistake in printed matter (as a deviation from copy or a typographical error) ⟨a book full of ~*s*⟩

¹**misprise** *var of* MISPRIZE

²**mis·prise** *or* **mis·prize** \məˈsprīz\ *n* -S [MF *mespris*, fr. *mesprisier* to despise, scorn — more at MISPRIZE] : ²MISPRISION

³**misprise** *or* **misprize** \"\ *vt* -ED/-ING/-S [MF *mespris*, past part. of *mesprendre*] *obs* : MISTAKE, MISUNDERSTAND ⟨you spend your passion on a *mispris'd* mood —Shak.⟩

¹**mis·pri·sion** \məˈsprizhən\ *n* -S [ME, fr. MF *mesprison* error, wrongdoing, fr. OF, fr. *mespris*, past part. of *mesprendre* to make a mistake, do wrong, fr. *mes-* ¹mis- + *prendre* to take, fr. L *prehendere* to seize, grasp — more at GET] **1 a** : neglect or wrong performance of official duty : misconduct or maladministration by a public official : MISDEMEANOR **b** : a clerical error in a legal proceeding that can be corrected in a summary manner as distinguished from judicial error for the correction of which formal appellate or other procedure is required **c** : the active or passive concealment of treason or felony from the prosecuting authorities by one not guilty of those crimes ⟨~ of treason⟩ ⟨~ of felony⟩ **d** : a contempt against the government, the sovereign, or the courts (as lese majesty or disloyal or seditious conduct) **2** : a misunderstanding in which one thing is taken for another : MISTAKE ⟨more than ~ of the fact —Robert Browning⟩

²**misprision** \"\ *n* -S [¹*misprise* + *-ion* (as in ¹*misprision*)] : CONTEMPT, SCORN : DEPRECIATION, DISPARAGEMENT ⟨expressed his evident ~ of realism and other modern modes of literature —J.P.Bishop⟩ ⟨with a refined ~ of her country . . . lived in exile —Ellery Sedgwick⟩

**mis·priz·al** *also* **mis·pris·al** \-ˈsprīzᵊl\ *n* -S [¹*misprise* + *-al*] : ²MISPRISION ⟨a broken engagement added to her ~ of herself —Ernestine Evans⟩

¹**mis·prize** *also* **mis·prise** \məˈsprīz\ *vt* [MF *mesprisier*, fr. *mes-* ¹mis- + *prisier* to value, appraise — more at PRIZE] **1** : to hold in contempt : DESPISE ⟨do not ~ that body of just and patriotic men —S.H.Adams⟩ **2** : NEGLECT, UNDERVALUE ⟨it will acclaim foreign talent and ~ its own —W.B.Adams⟩ ⟨nor did he ~ the Spanish factor in Peru —Waldo Frank⟩ — **mis·priz·er** \-zə(r)\ *n* -S

²**misprize** *var of* MISPRISE

**mis·pronounce** \¦mis+\ *vb* [¹*mis-* + *pronounce*] *vt* **1** : to pronounce incorrectly ⟨a name almost invariably *mispronounced* by newcomers to the town⟩ ⟨had picked up a certain fluency in French, though he *mispronounced* the language ludicrously⟩ **2** : to pronounce in a way regarded as incorrect because of variations from some stated or implied criterion (as the practice of educated speakers, a regional speech assumed to be standard, spelling, or a pronunciation prescribed as correct by accepted authority) ⟨a list of words commonly *mispronounced*⟩ ⟨told him he would never be a gentleman until he stopped *mispronouncing* so many words⟩ ⟨guessed he would go to his grave *mispronouncing* "February" as "Febuary"⟩ ~ *vi* : to make a mispronunciation — **mis·pronouncer** \"+\ *n*

**mis·pronunciation** \"+\ *n* [¹*mis-* + *pronunciation*] **1** : the act of mispronouncing ⟨~ is often the result of affectation and a striving for elegance⟩ **2** : an instance of mispronouncing ⟨~ of this word is comparatively rare⟩

**mis·proud** \(ˈ)mis+\ *adj* [ME, fr. ¹*mis-* + *proud*] **:** wrongly or unreasonably proud **:** ARROGANT
**mis·punctuate** \"+\ *vt* [¹*mis-* + *punctuate*] **:** to punctuate in a way regarded as incorrect — **mis·punctuation** \(ˌ)mis+\ *n*
**mis·put** \(ˈ)mis+\ *vt* [¹*mis-* + *put*] *dial* **1 :** MISPLACE **2 :** DISCONCERT
**mis·quotation** \ˌ=+\ *n* [¹*mis-* + *quotation*] **1 :** the act of misquoting ⟨he is given to ~ and distortion of what people say⟩ **2 :** an instance of misquoting ⟨this is a flagrant ~ of what he wrote⟩
¹**mis·quote** \(ˈ)mis+\ *vb* [¹*mis-* + *quote* (v.)] *vt* **:** to quote incorrectly ⟨people commonly ~ some of the most famous lines in English poetry⟩ ~ *vi* **:** to give quotations incorrectly ⟨loves to quote, but usually ~*s*⟩ — **mis·quoter** \"+\ *n* -s
²**misquote** \"\ *n* **:** an incorrect quotation
**mis·read** \"+\ *vt* [¹*mis-* + *read*] **1 :** to read incorrectly or misinterpret in reading ⟨the driver . . . ~ an important signal —O.S.Nock⟩ ⟨suspect that this book has been ~ by a whole generation —Caroline Gordon⟩ **2 :** to interpret incorrectly ⟨totally ~ the lesson of history —Christopher Hollis⟩ ⟨Ingres' paintings still are ~ in terms of nineteenth century stereotypes —T.B.Hess⟩ — **mis·reader** \"+\ *n*
**mis·reckon** \"+\ *vi* [¹*mis-* + *reckon*] **:** to reckon wrongly **:** make an incorrect calculation ⟨unless I ~, the bill comes due tomorrow⟩
**mis·recollect** \(ˌ)mis+\ *vi* [¹*mis-* + *recollect*] **:** to recollect wrongly ⟨I put the book on the second shelf, if I do not ~⟩ — **mis·recollection** \"+\ *n*
**mis·register** \(ˈ)mis+\ *n* [¹*mis-* + *register*] *printing* **:** inaccurate register esp. of a second or subsequent color
**mis·remember** \ˌmis+\ *vb* [¹*mis-* + *remember*] *vt* **1 :** to remember incorrectly ⟨in some of the essays the facts seem to have been wrenched or ~*ed* to fit the theory —*Times Lit. Supp.*⟩ ⟨asked an expert about it, but misunderstood or ~*ed* the answer —*Time*⟩ **2** *chiefly dial* **:** FORGET ~ *vi, chiefly dial* **:** to be unable to remember
¹**mis·report** \"+\ *vt* [ME *misreporten*, fr. ¹*mis-* + *reporten* to report — more at REPORT] **1 :** to report falsely **:** to give an incorrect account of ⟨~*ed* the results of the hearing⟩ **2 :** to give an incorrect report of the words or opinions of ⟨~*ed* him as favoring the bill when he had spoken against it⟩
²**misreport** \"\ *n* [¹*mis-* + *report* (n.)] **:** a false or incorrect account
**mis·represent** \(ˌ)mis+\ *vb* [¹*mis-* + *represent*] *vt* **1 :** to represent incorrectly **:** to give a false, imperfect, or misleading representation of ⟨they all ~*ed* the past in the same prescribed way —R.B.Merriman⟩ **2 :** to serve badly or improperly as a representative of ⟨the principal lobbyists . . . were absolutely ~*ing* the membership of those societies —F.D.Roosevelt⟩ ~ *vi* **:** to make an assertion or give an impression not in accord with the facts ⟨~*s* when he says that he was driving carefully⟩ ⟨presents much from a partisan point of view; yet he never intentionally ~*s* —W.H.Allison⟩
**syn** MISREPRESENT and BELIE can mean, in common, to represent falsely. MISREPRESENT usu. implies intent, suggesting deliberate falsification, injustice, bias, or prejudice ⟨a biography completely *misrepresenting* his true character⟩ ⟨*misrepresent* a case before a jury⟩ BELIE, in this connection, implies merely to give an impression at variance with the facts ⟨nothing she saw or touched gave token of even its own reality: even her wrist watch seemed to *belie* time —Elizabeth Bowen⟩ ⟨the brevity and cheerfulness of the study *belie* the importance of its subject —*Times Lit. Supp.*⟩
**mis·representation** \"+\ *n* [¹*mis-* + *representation*] **:** an untrue, incorrect, or misleading representation (as of a fact, event, or person); *specif* **:** a representation by words or other means that under the existing circumstances amounts to an assertion not in accordance with the facts ⟨his duty to further the interest of his client does not require him to employ any sort of trickery, chicane, deceit, or ~ —H.S.Drinker⟩
¹**mis·representative** \"+\ *adj* [¹*mis-* + *representative*] **:** serving to misrepresent ⟨the production is ~ of the spirit of the play⟩
²**misrepresentative** \"\ *n* **:** one who is not a proper representative ⟨a ~ of the people of his state⟩
**mis·representer** \"+\ *n* **:** one that misrepresents ⟨a ~, or calumniator, or what they will —J.G.Lockhart⟩
**mis·route** \(ˈ)mis+\ *vt* [¹*mis-* + *route*] **:** to route incorrectly or improperly (as by a longer or more expensive route) ⟨*misrouted* freight⟩
¹**mis·rule** \"+\ *vt* [ME *misreulen*, fr. ¹*mis-* + *reulen* to rule — more at RULE] **:** to rule badly **:** MISGOVERN ⟨*misruled* and impoverished his people⟩ — **mis·ruler** \"+\ *n*
²**misrule** \(ˈ)mis+\ *n* [ME *misreule*, fr. ¹*mis-* + *reule* rule — more at RULE] **1 :** the action of misruling or the condition of being misruled ⟨not the result of a single specific grievance but a reaction to a long period of ~⟩ **2 :** a condition of disorder and confusion **:** ANARCHY ⟨the loud ~ of Chaos —John Milton⟩ ⟨in the absence of a stable government, the country fell into a state of ~⟩
**mis·run** \"+\ *n* [¹*mis-* + *run*] **:** a metal casting not fully formed
¹**miss** \ˈmis\ *vb* -ED/-ING/-ES [ME *missen*, fr. OE *missan*; akin to OHG *missan* to miss, ON *missa* to miss, be lacking, Goth *maidjan* to change, L *mutare* to change, Latvian *mituôt* to exchange, Skt *methati, mithati* he changes] *vt* **1 :** to fail to hit, reach, or make contact with ⟨~*ed* the target by a good two feet⟩ ⟨swung at the ball with great power but ~*ed* it⟩ ⟨~*ed* the step and fell to the ground⟩ ⟨~*ed* each other by seconds at the railroad station⟩ ⟨~*ed* his way⟩ **2 a :** to discover the absence or omission of ⟨~*ed* his watch almost as soon as the stranger had left⟩ ⟨cut out half of the third act knowing it would never be ~*ed*⟩ **b :** to feel the lack of **:** be unhappy because of the loss or absence of ⟨~*ed* his wife terribly⟩ ⟨~*ed* his old room and familiar surroundings⟩ **3 a :** to fail to obtain or receive ⟨ignorance ~*es* the best things in this life —W.R.Inge⟩ ⟨it is, no doubt, true that remarkable men . . . ~*ed* the presidency when contemporaries of far less ability attained it —H.J. Laski⟩ **b** *archaic* **:** to fail to do ⟨less I should ~ to bid thee a good-morrow —John Keats⟩ **4 :** ESCAPE, AVOID ⟨~*ed* being killed by a few feet⟩ ⟨just ~*ed* hitting the other car⟩ **5 a :** to leave out **:** OMIT ⟨in such a hurry that he ~*ed* his breakfast⟩ ⟨not only is there an occasional beat ~*ed* at the wrist but there is no sound over the heart —H.G.Armstrong⟩ ⟨has not ~*ed* a dividend in 39 years —*Time*⟩ **b :** to let slip **:** OVERLOOK ⟨~*ed* a bet in failing to see the possibilities of his discovery⟩ ⟨book publishers are ~*ing* a trick in not making a wider practice of including their old titles in current book lists —J. D. Adams⟩ **6 a :** to fail to perceive or understand ⟨were delighted with its merciless exposure of aristocratic attitudes but ~*ed* its attack on the businessmen and the middle class —Max Lerner⟩ ⟨to put the orthodox value on it is to expose an inappreciation of his most vital criticism, to ~ its force —F.R.Leavis⟩ ⟨~ the point⟩ **b :** to fail to see, hear, or experience ⟨~*ed* some of the softer passages⟩ ⟨a picture not to be ~*ed*⟩ ⟨though it was a frightening experience, he would not have ~*ed* it⟩ **7 :** to neglect the performance of or attendance at ⟨hasn't ~*ed* a day's work in years⟩ ⟨~*ed* school all week because of illness⟩ ⟨seldom ~*ed* a major military operation —Ed Cunningham⟩ **8 :** to be too late for ⟨~*ed* his train⟩ ⟨~*ed* his appointment by five minutes⟩ ~ *vi* **1 a :** to fail to get or secure something **:** fail to find or reach someone or something **:** fail to do something — used with *of* ⟨had very narrowly ~*ed* of success —T.B. Macaulay⟩ **2 :** to fail to hit something ⟨took three shots and ~*ed* each time⟩ ⟨took another cut at the ball but ~*ed* again⟩ **3** *archaic* **:** to be lacking or absent **4 a :** to be unsuccessful **:** FAIL — sometimes used with *out* ⟨such a fine prospect that he can't ~⟩ ⟨a play which ~*ed* on Broadway —William Barrett⟩ ⟨this is his big chance and he can't afford to ~ out⟩ **b** *dial Brit* **:** to fail to germinate or grow **c** *of a domestic animal* **:** to fail to become pregnant when bred **d :** MISFIRE — used of an internal-combustion engine **e :** to lose as caster of the dice; *specif* **:** to lose by throwing a point and then a seven rather than by throwing craps — **miss fire 1 :** to fail to go off — used of firearms **2 :** to fail to have the expected or planned result ⟨his speech was carefully planned, but it *missed fire*⟩ — **miss stays** *of a ship* **:** to fail in the attempt to go about — **miss the boat :** to blunder badly by failing to grasp an opportunity in time or by making a false judgment ⟨waiting until after the candidates are nominated is waiting until you have *missed the boat* —Marguerite J. Fisher & D.G.Bishop⟩ — **miss the bus :** to waste an opportunity **:** throw away one's chances
²**miss** \"\ *n* -ES [ME *mis, misse*, fr. *missen*, v.] **1** *chiefly dial* **:** WANT, LOSS, LACK; *also* **:** disadvantage, harm, or regret resulting from loss or deprivation **2 a :** a failure to hit something struck at or aimed at ⟨hit the nail on the head every time without a single ~⟩ ⟨hit the target five times without a ~⟩ ⟨whatever truth you contribute to the world will be one lucky shot in a thousand ~*es* —Walter Lippman⟩ **b :** a failure to attain a desired or planned result ⟨the picture is a pathetic ~ —*Time*⟩ **3 a :** MISCARRIAGE ⟨the time she thought she was going to have a baby and only had a ~ —Robert Fawcett⟩ **b** *of a domestic animal* **:** a failure to become pregnant after breeding **4 :** a deliberate avoidance of something **:** GO-BY ⟨felt so tired that she decided to give the dance a ~⟩ ⟨give dessert a ~⟩ **5 :** MISFIRE ⟨will pick up from there to a fast acceleration without a ~ —*Car Life*⟩ **6 :** an impression of a printing press when no sheet has been fed in ⟨print a ~ on the tympan as a base for makeready⟩ **7 :** MISSOUT
³**miss** \(ˌ)mis, ˌməs\ *n* -ES [short for ¹*mistress*] **1** *archaic* **a :** PROSTITUTE **b :** a kept woman **:** MISTRESS **2 a** — used as a conventional title of courtesy before the name of an unmarried woman or girl ⟨*Miss* Ann Brown⟩ ⟨*Miss* Smith⟩ or sometimes before the given name of a married woman ⟨*Miss* Mary, the wife of Mr. Green⟩ **b** — used before the name of a place (as a country, city) or of a profession or other line of activity (as a sport) or before some epithet to form a title applied to a usu. young unmarried female viewed or recognized as esp. outstanding in or as representative of the thing indicated ⟨was chosen as *Miss* America⟩ ⟨well now, *Miss* High-and-Mighty⟩ **3 :** young lady **:** GIRL — used in direct address and not followed by the given name or surname of the young woman addressed and used typically as a generalized term of conventional politeness in addressing a young woman that is a stranger ⟨may I have the menu, ~⟩ **4 :** a young unmarried woman or girl ⟨a New England ~ engaged to tutor his children —*Amer. Guide Series: Fla.*⟩ ⟨no stage-struck ~ has ever been quite so fortunate —*Irish Digest*⟩
⁴**miss** \ˈmis\ *vt* -ED/-ING/-ES **:** to address as miss
**miss** *abbr* mission; missionary
¹**mis·sal** \ˈmisəl\ *n* -S *sometimes cap* [ME *messel, missall*, fr. MF & ML; MF *messel*, fr. ML *missale*, fr. neut. of *missalis* of mass, fr. LL *missa* mass + L *-alis* -al — more at MASS] **1 :** a book containing all that is said or sung at mass during the entire year and including with the ordinary, proper, and common votive masses and supplementary prayers and masses for certain localities or orders **2 :** a book of devotions
²**missal** \"\ *adj* [ML *missalis*] *archaic* **:** of or relating to the mass or a missal
**missal initial** *also* **missal letter** *or* **missal capital** *n* **:** a decorative initial fashioned after those used in old missals
**missal stand** *n* **:** a lectern used to support a missal
**mis·say** \(ˈ)mi(s)+\ *vb* [ME *misseyen, missayen*, fr. ¹*mis-* + *seyen, sayen* to say — more at SAY] *vt* **:** to speak evil of **:** SLANDER ⟨rebuked, reviled, *missaid* thee —Alfred Tennyson⟩ ~ *vi* **:** to say something wrong or incorrect ⟨knew . . . what the press . . . would ~, misunderstand, understate, and exaggerate about him —H.S.Canby⟩

missal stand

**missed** *past of* MISS
**missed abortion** *n* **:** an intrauterine death of a fetus that is not followed by its immediate expulsion
**missed labor** *n* **:** a retention of a fetus in the uterus beyond the normal period of pregnancy
**mis·seem** \(ˈ)mi(s)+\ *vt* [ME *missemen*, fr. ¹*mis-* + *semen* to seem — more at SEEM] **:** MISBECOME
**missel thrush** *var of* MISTLE THRUSH
**mis·send** \(ˈ)mi(s)+\ *vt* [¹*mis-* + *send*] **:** to send or forward incorrectly ⟨containing what little mail was *missent* to our train —B.A.Long & W.J.Dennis⟩
¹**misses** *pres 3d sing of* MISS, *pl of* MISS
²**miss·es** \ˈmisəz\ *n pl* [fr. pl. of ³*miss*] **:** a clothing size for women and girls with average figures
**mis·set** \(ˈ)mi(s)+\ *vt* [ME *missetten*, fr. ¹*mis-* + *setten* to set — more at SET] **1 :** to set or place wrongly **:** MISPLACE **2** *Scot* **:** to put out of sorts **:** DISPLEASE
**mis·sey-moo·sey** \ˈmisēˈmüsē\ *n* -S [alter. of *moosemise*] **:** AMERICAN MOUNTAIN ASH
¹**mis·shape** \(ˈ)mis(h)+\ *vt* [ME *misshapen*, fr. ¹*mis-* + *shapen* to shape — more at SHAPE] **:** to shape badly **:** give an unnatural form to **:** DEFORM ⟨may tend seriously to ~ the cakes of butter —*Scientific American*⟩ ⟨the book that has most shaped and *misshaped* our conceptions —A.L.Kroeber⟩
²**misshape** \"\ *n* [ME, fr. ¹*mis-* + *shap, shape* shape — more at SHAPE] **:** DEFORMITY
**mis·shapen** \"+\ *adj* [ME, fr. ¹*mis-* + *shapen*, past part. of *shapen* to shape] **1 :** having an ugly or deformed shape ⟨the tree . . . dwarfed and ~ by repeated stripping of its branches —*Amer. Guide Series: N.J.*⟩ ⟨a very little oldish, spinsterish, thin, ~, stooping woman —Arnold Bennett⟩ **2 :** morally or intellectually deformed or distorted ⟨the system of representation had become so ~ that a new theory had arisen to give constitutional sanction to existing methods —V.L.Parrington⟩ ⟨~ ideas of justice⟩ — **mis·shap·en·ly** *adv* — **mis·shap·en·ness** *n* -ES
**missies** *pl of* MISSY
¹**mis·sile** \ˈmisəl *sometimes* -izəl, *chiefly Brit* -ˌīˌsīl\ *adj* [L *missilis*, fr. *missus* (past part. of *mittere* to throw, send) + *-ilis* -ile — more at SMITE] **1 :** capable of being thrown or projected to strike an object at a distance **2 :** adapted for throwing or hurling missiles
²**missile** \"\ *n* -S [L, fr. neut. of *missilis*] **1 :** a weapon or other object thrown or projected (as a stone, bullet, or artillery shell) ⟨spears are still used as ~*s* in some parts of the world⟩ ⟨open head wounds due to ~*s* —*Jour. Amer. Med. Assoc.*⟩ **2 :** a self-propelling unmanned weapon (as a rocket or a robot bomb) — compare GUIDED MISSILE
**mis·sil·eer** \ˌmisəˈli(ə)r *sometimes* -izəˈ-\ *n* -S [²*missile* + *-eer*] **:** MISSILEMAN
**mis·sile·man** *pronunc at* MISSILE + mən\ *n, pl* **missilemen :** one who helps to design, build, or operate guided missiles
**mis·sile·ry** \-lrē\ *also* **mis·sil·ry** \-isəlrē\ *n* -ES [²*missile* + *-ry*] **1 :** MISSILES; *esp* **:** GUIDED MISSILES **2 :** the science dealing with the design, manufacture, and use of guided missiles
**missing** *adj* [fr. pres. part. of ¹*miss*] **1 :** not able to be found **:** not present **:** ABSENT ⟨~ in action⟩ ⟨the ~ part of the machine⟩ ⟨an understanding of character is ~ from the book⟩ **2 :** absent without explanation from one's home or usual or expected place of resort ⟨turned up ~ in the morning and hasn't been seen since⟩ ⟨the common-law principle that anyone who has been declared a ~ person may, after seven years, be presumed dead —*Time*⟩
**missing link** *n* **1 :** an absent thing or member needed to complete a series ⟨modern technology and capital are the only major *missing links* in the underdeveloped areas —J.K.Rose⟩ **2 :** a hypothetical intermediate form between man and his presumed simian progenitors ⟨supposed by some people to be the nearest thing to the *missing link*, and thus the most primitive human being in existence —Alan Moorehead⟩ — compare APE-MAN, PREHOMINID
**missing movement** *n* **:** an offense under the U.S. Uniform Code of Military Justice that consists of missing through neglect or design the movement of a ship, aircraft, or unit with which a person is required in the course of duty to move
**mis·sio·log·i·cal** \ˌmisēəˈläjəkəl\ *adj* **:** of or relating to missiology ⟨a ~ classic⟩
**mis·si·ol·o·gy** \ˌmisēˈäləjē\ *n* -ES [¹*mission* + *-logy*] **:** the study of the church's mission esp. with respect to the nature, purpose, and methods of its missionary activity
¹**mis·sion** \ˈmishən\ *n* -S *often attrib* [NL, ML & L; NL *mission-, missio* ministry commissioned by a religious organization, fr. ML, task with which one is charged, fr. L, act of sending, fr. *missus* (past part. of *mittere* to throw, send) + *-ion-, -io* -ion — more at SMITE] **1** *obs* **:** the act or an instance of sending **2 a :** a ministry (as preaching or educational or medical work) commissioned by a church or some other religious organization for the purpose of propagating its faith or carrying on humanitarian work ⟨organized a ~ to the Indians⟩ ⟨conducted a ~ among the refugees⟩ — compare FOREIGN MISSION, HOME MISSION, RESCUE MISSION **b :** assignment to or work in a field of missionary enterprise ⟨go on ~ as an unprofessed sister⟩ **c** (1) **:** a mission institution (as a church, school, or hospital) or establishment (as a compound or a community and its lands) or a building ⟨~ hall⟩ (2) **:** a local church that is not self-supporting and that relies upon its denomination or larger religious organization for financial support **d :** the body of missionaries or the administrative organization of a missionary territory working under a church or religious organization **e missions** *pl* **:** organized missionary work ⟨the seminary's professor of ~*s*⟩ ⟨give more to local expenses than to ~*s*⟩ **f :** the administrative division of a Roman Catholic vicariate or apostolic prefecture corresponding to a parish **g :** a course of sermons and services at a particular place and time for the special purpose of quickening the faith and zeal of Christians and of converting unbelievers ⟨to conduct a preaching ~⟩ **3 :** a body of persons appointed to go somewhere to perform a service or carry on an activity: as **a :** a group of persons sent to a foreign country to conduct diplomatic or political negotiations ⟨the ill-fated Grey ~ to the United States in the latter part of 1919 —*Times Lit. Supp.*⟩ **b :** a permanent embassy or legation in a foreign country ⟨reopen diplomatic ~*s* in those countries . . . in which it had been previously authorized to establish consular offices —John Hay b. 1910⟩ **c :** a team of scientific or technical specialists sent to a foreign country (as to aid in the development of industry or natural resources) ⟨served on a ~ to help improve agricultural methods⟩ **d :** a group of leaders in culture or education unofficially representing their country in a foreign country ⟨step up the exchange of cultural ~*s*⟩ **e :** a team of military specialists sent to a foreign country to assist in the training of its armed forces ⟨military ~*s* sent by its allies have helped greatly to modernize its army⟩ **4 a :** a specific task with which a person or group is charged; *esp* **:** an assignment given to a person or group in an official capacity ⟨given the difficult and dangerous ~ of exploring the newly acquired territory⟩ ⟨by patient negotiation succeeded in his ~ of averting a strike⟩ ⟨hero of a rescue ~⟩ **b :** the chief function or responsibility of an organization or institution ⟨the Erie's principal ~, however, is freight service —*Trains*⟩ ⟨the ~ of that school was to make distant times . . . intelligible and acceptable to a society issuing from the eighteenth century —J.E.E.Dalberg-Acton⟩ **5 :** a continuing task or responsibility that one is destined or fitted to do or specially called upon to undertake **:** LIFEWORK, VOCATION ⟨took upon himself the ~ of bettering the school system⟩ ⟨his ~ was to preserve the Union⟩ ⟨gave sense and direction to a young life seeking a ~ —P.H. Vieth⟩ **6 a :** a major continuing duty assigned to a military service or command as a part of its function in the national military establishment ⟨the wartime ~ of a Navy is to gain and maintain control of the seas —R.A.Ofstie⟩ **b :** a definite military or naval task assigned to an individual or unit usu. for performance in a combat area or enemy territory ⟨the patrol successfully carried out its ~ of bringing back two enemy prisoners⟩ ⟨~ accomplished⟩ **c :** a flight operation of a single airplane or a group of airplanes charged with the performance of a specific task ⟨flew nineteen ~*s* during the war⟩ ⟨a weather ~⟩
²**mission** \"\ *vb* **missioned; missioned; missioning** \-sh(ə)niŋ\ **missions** *vt* **1 :** to send on or entrust with a mission ⟨~*ed* her . . . servants to enrich the fretted splendor of each nook and niche —John Keats⟩ ⟨for the last several years, she had been ~*ed* at St. Mary's Convent —*Springfield (Mass.) Union*⟩ **2 :** to carry on a religious mission among or in ⟨~*ed* a territory larger than the state of Texas⟩ ~ *vi* **:** to carry on a mission **:** to act as a missionary ⟨now ~*ing* in Argentina for the Midland Bank —*Time*⟩
**mission architecture** *n* **:** a Spanish colonial architectural style used for the early Spanish mission buildings of the southwestern U.S.
¹**mis·sion·ary** \ˈmishəˌnerē, -ri\ *adj* [NL *missionarius*, fr. *mission-, missio* mission + L *-arius* -ary — more at MISSION] **1 a :** of or relating to missions ⟨a ~ undertaking⟩ ⟨the ~ hospital⟩ **b :** engaged in or devoted to mission work ⟨a ~ religion⟩ ⟨~ priests⟩ **2 :** suitable to or characteristic of a person sent on or undertaking a mission ⟨a generous composer with ~ instincts . . . who will attempt to lead other composers —Robert Evett⟩ ⟨threw himself into the campaign with ~ zeal⟩ **3** *Roman Catholicism* **:** not having a canonically established hierarchy and subject immediately to Rome as a mission or prefecture or vicariate apostolic ⟨a ~ territory⟩
²**missionary** \"\ *n* -ES **1 a :** one sent to propagate the faith, doctrine, and principles of a religion or a religious group among nonbelievers ⟨sent *missionaries* into those regions in the early part of the 19th century —*Amer. Guide Series: Pa.*⟩ **b :** one who undertakes a special religious or humanitarian mission among those of his own faith or country ⟨the ~ can . . . put the fear of the Lord into complacent souls that is necessary for their return to grace and salvation —D.J.Corrigan⟩ ⟨became a city ~ devoting his life to helping the down-and-out⟩ **c :** one who attempts to convert others to a specific way of life, set of ideas, or course of action ⟨these early *missionaries* of a new and boundless materialism —M.D. Geismar⟩ ⟨the pressures brought directly or indirectly by the *missionaries* of home ownership —J.P.Dean⟩ ⟨has become an enthusiastic ~ for vitamin E —Eric Hutton⟩ **2 :** one who undertakes a political or diplomatic mission **:** AGENT, EMISSARY ⟨the administration's most-traveled diplomatic ~ —*Newsweek*⟩ **3 :** one who acts to undermine the morale of workers on strike
³**missionary** \"\ *vi* -ED/-ING/-ES [²*missionary*] **:** to work as a missionary ⟨in her wildest dreams of ~*ing* . . . had never looked forward to anything quite like her new home —R.L. Taylor⟩
**missionary apostolic** *n, pl* **missionaries apostolic :** a Roman Catholic missionary sent by commission from the pope
**missionary bishop** *n* **:** a Protestant Episcopal bishop serving in a state, territory, or foreign field not organized into dioceses
**missionary district** *n* **:** an area presided over by a missionary bishop
**missionary rector** *n* **:** a Roman Catholic priest in charge of an important mission or quasi parish
**missionary salesman** *n* **:** a manufacturer's sales representative sent into a territory to stimulate sales of a product (as through special promotions, public-relations work)
**missionary society** *n* **:** a local, denominational, or interdenominational religious organization dedicated to the support of Christian missionary work
**mis·sion·ate** \ˈmishəˌnāt\ *vb* -ED/-ING/-S [¹*mission* + *-ate*] **:** MISSIONIZE
**mission bells** *n pl but sing or pl in constr* **:** either of two herbs (*Fritillaria lanceolata* or *F. mutica*) with purple yellowish mottled flowers
**mission church** *n* **:** a church that is not locally self-supporting but that depends at least partially upon the support of mission funds from the larger religious organization that established it
**mis·sion·er** \ˈmish(ə)nə(r)\ *n* -S [¹*mission* + *-er*] **:** MISSIONARY
**mission furniture** *n* [so called fr. the occurrence of this style in the Spanish missions of the U. S. Southwest] **:** a plain, dark, heavy furniture of a style characterized by straight lines and square sections
**mission home** *n* **:** a benevolent institution (as for the care of the indigent or the aged) maintained by a religious organization
**mission indians** *n pl, usu cap M&I* **:** members of Indian tribes Christianized by Spanish Franciscan missionaries in California
**mis·sion·ization** \ˌmishənəˈzāshən, -ˌnīˈz-\ *n* -S **:** the act or process of conducting a mission
**mis·sion·ize** \ˈmishəˌnīz\ *vb* -ED/-ING/-S [¹*mission* + *-ize*] *vi* **:** to carry on missionary work ⟨was *missionizing* in distant China —*Times Lit. Supp.*⟩ ~ *vt* **:** to conduct a mission or do missionary work among ⟨enable Christians to take heathens from barbaric conditions in order to civilize and ~ them —J. C.Brauer⟩ ⟨were visited, *missionized*, colonized, and civilized from India —A.L.Kroeber⟩ — **mis·sion·iz·er** \-zə(r)\ *n* -S
**missions** *pl of* MISSION
**mission station** *n* **:** a place of missionary residence in or from which missionary activity in a given area is carried on

**missis** *var of* MISSUS

**miss·ish** \'misish\ *adj* [³*miss* + *-ish*] **:** appropriate to or characteristic of a young girl **:** PRIM, AFFECTED ⟨a maudlin, ~, namby-pamby sentimentality —Anthony Trollope⟩ — **miss·ish·ness** *n* -ES

**¹mis·sis·sip·pi** \ˌmisəˈsipē, (ˈ)misˈsi-, -pi *sometimes* ˌmizəˈsi- *or* (ˈ)mizˈsi-\ *adj, usu cap* [*Mississippi* river, central U. S., of Algonquian origin; akin to Ojibwa *Misisipi* Mississippi river, fr. *misi* big + *sipi* river] **1 :** of or relating to the Mississippi river **2** [*Mississippi*, state in the southern U. S., fr. the *Mississippi* river] **:** of or from the state of Mississippi **:** of the kind or style prevalent in Mississippi **3 :** of, relating to, or constituting a culture pattern in the region of the Mississippi drainage system dating A.D.1300–1700 and characterized by the village-state composed of scattered hamlets dominated by a village that is the ceremonial center and has large pyramidal structures around a plaza

**²mississippi** \"\ *n* -s *usu cap* **:** a game resembling bagatelle in which the balls are played against the side cushions and through numbered arches at the end of the table

**¹mis·sis·sip·pi·an** \-pēən\ *adj, usu cap* [*Mississippi* state & river + E *-an*] **1 :** of, relating to, or characteristic of the state of Mississippi or the Mississippi river **2 :** of, relating to, or characteristic of the people of Mississippi or of the Mississippi river region **3 :** of, relating to, or constituting the division of the Paleozoic era or system in No. America following the Devonian and preceding the Pennsylvanian — see GEOLOGIC TIME table

**²mississippian** \"\ *n* -s **1** *cap* **:** a native or resident of Mississippi or of the Mississippi river region **2** *usu cap* **:** the Mississippian period or system of rocks

**mississippi catfish** *also* **mississippi cat** *n, usu cap M* **1 :** BLUE CAT **2 :** FLATHEAD CATFISH

**mississippi kite** *n, usu cap M* **:** a small kite (*Ictinia mississippiensis*) that has chiefly lead-colored plumage with a blackish tail and that is found from southern Illinois to Central America

**¹mis·sive** \'misiv, -sēv *also* -səv\ *adj* [ME, fr. MF or ML; MF *missif*, fr. ML *missivus*, fr. L *missus* (past part. of *mittere* to send) + *-ivus* -ive — more at SMITE] **1 :** specially sent or prepared to be sent — see LETTER MISSIVE **2 :** MISSILE

**²missive** \"\ *n* -s [MF (*lettre*) *missive*, fr. *lettre* letter + *missive*, fem. of *missif*] **1 :** a written communication **:** LETTER ⟨many of their ~s were illiterate, and the more violent of them were unsigned —R.B.Merriman⟩; *often* **:** a formal or official letter ⟨the driver delivered the ~ at the embassy door —Upton Sinclair⟩ **2** *Scots law* **:** a formal authenticated document in the style of a letter by which a party to a contract submits to the other contracting party his own offer or acceptance **3** *obs* **:** MESSENGER ⟨came ~s from the king, who all-hail'd me thane of Cawdor —Shak.⟩ **4 :** something that is thrown or used as a weapon **:** MISSILE ⟨making use of any ~, even a proverb, that came ready to hand —Aldous Huxley⟩

**miss nan·cy** \-'nan(t)sē, -aan-,-ain-, -si\ *n, pl* **miss nancys** *usu cap M&N* [fr. the name *Miss Nancy*] **:** an effeminate boy or man **:** SISSY ⟨"ain't he brave?" he says in a *Miss Nancy* voice, and the rest of them laughed —Helen Eustis⟩ ⟨often mocked as *Miss Nancys* by the more emancipated —Dixon Wecter⟩ — **miss-nancy·ish** \ˌ⸗ˈ⸗(t)sēish\ *adj*

**miss-nancy·ism** \⸗ˈ⸗⸗ˌizəm\ *n* -s **:** EFFEMINACY

**¹mis·sort** \(ˈ)mi(s)+\ *vt* [¹*mis-* + *sort*] **:** to sort badly or incorrectly

**²missort** \"\ *n* -s **:** an item (as a letter or check) that is incorrectly sorted

**¹mis·sou·ri** \məˈzůrə, -zůr-, -rē, -ri\ *adj, usu cap* [*Missouri*, state in the central U. S., fr. the *Missouri* river, fr. F, fr. *Missouri* (people)] **:** of or from the state of Missouri ⟨a *Missouri* mule⟩ **:** of the kind or style prevalent in Missouri **:** MISSOURIAN — **from missouri** *usu cap M* [*Missouri* (state)] **:** not easily fooled **:** hard to convince **:** SKEPTICAL ⟨in social dealings with foreigners, the Englishman is *from Missouri;* he has got to be shown —D.W.Brogan⟩

**²missouri** \"\ *n, pl* **missouri** *or* **missouris** *usu cap* [F, fr. Illinois, lit., owners of big canoes] **1 a :** a Siouan people of the Missouri river valley, Missouri **b :** a member of such people **2 :** a dialect of Chiwere

**¹mis·sou·ri·an** \-rēən\ *adj, usu cap* [*Missouri* (state & people) + E *-an*] **1 :** of, relating to, or characteristic of the state of Missouri **2 :** of, relating to, or characteristic of Missourians **3 :** of or relating to the subdivision of the Pennsylvanian geologic period between the Desmoinesian and the Virgilian — see GEOLOGIC TIME table

**²missourian** \"\ *n* -s *cap* **:** a native or resident of Missouri

**missouri currant** *n, usu cap M* **:** BUFFALO CURRANT 1

**missouri gooseberry** *n, usu cap M* **1 :** a slender spiny shrub (*Ribes missouriense*) of the central U. S. that has greenish white flowers **2 :** the large edible brown or purplish berry of the Missouri gooseberry

**missouri gourd** *n, usu cap M* **:** PRAIRIE GOURD

**missouri grape** *n, usu cap M* **1 :** a woody vine (*Vitis palmata*) of the central and southern U. S. **2 :** the fruit of the Missouri grape

**missouri skylark** *n, usu cap M* **:** SPRAGUE'S PIPIT

**miss-out** \(ˈ)mis+\ *n* -s [fr. *miss out*, v.] **1 :** a loss by the caster of the dice in craps usu. by the throwing of a point and then a seven **2 :** the casting of a 2, 3, or 12 on the first throw — compare ⁵CRAP 2

**mis·speak** \(ˈ)mi(s)+\ *vt* [¹*mis-* + *speak*] **1 :** to speak incorrectly ⟨he uses long words, but he ~s them⟩ **2 :** to express (oneself) badly or imperfectly ⟨*misspoke* himself because he didn't take time to think⟩

**mis·spell** \"+\ *vt* [¹*mis-* + *spell*] **:** to spell incorrectly ⟨~s many words through carelessness⟩

**mis·spelling** \"+\ *n* [¹*mis-* + *spelling*] **:** an incorrect spelling ⟨the occasional ~s and faulty grammar of one more at home in Chinese than in his mother tongue —Vincent Cronin⟩

**mis·spend** \"+\ *vt* [ME *misspenden*, fr. ¹*mis-* + *spenden* to spend — more at SPEND] **:** to spend wrongly **:** SQUANDER, WASTE ⟨a vacation without books would be grievously *misspent* —Orville Prescott⟩ ⟨*misspent* a fortune on fake old masters⟩ — **mis·spender** \"+\ *n*

**mis·state** \"+\ *vt* [¹*mis-* + *state* (v.)] **:** to state wrongly **:** give a false account of ⟨~s the facts to make it appear that he was the injured party⟩ — **mis·stater** \"+\ *n*

**mis·statement** \"+\ *n* [¹*mis-* + *statement*] **:** a false or incorrect statement

**mis·step** \"+\ *n* [¹*mis-* + *step* (n.)] **1 :** a wrong step ⟨made a ~ and fell down the stairs⟩ **2 a :** a mistake in judgment or action **:** BLUNDER ⟨a ~ that could lead to disaster⟩ **b :** a lapse in sexual behavior by a girl or woman; *esp* **:** the bearing of an illegitimate child ⟨a ~ of her youth that she tried to keep a secret⟩

**mis·strike** \"+\ *n* [¹*mis-* + *strike* (n.)] **:** a coin whose design is off center

**mis·sus** *or* **mis·sis** \'misəz, -isəs,-izəz, -izəs\ *n* -ES [alter. of *mistress*] **1 :** WIFE — not in formal use ⟨be sure to bring the ~⟩ **2** *dial* **:** MISTRESS 2

**¹missy** \'misē, -si\ *n* -ES [³*miss* + *-y* (n. suffix)] **:** a young girl **:** MISS ⟨the pious little ~, stiff as a board —Irving Howe⟩

**²missy** \"\ *adj* [³*miss* + *-y* (adj. suffix)] **:** relating to, resembling, or characteristic of a young girl ⟨despite her attempt to seem grown-up, she has a ~ primness of manner⟩

**missy** *abbr* missionary

**¹mist** \'mist\ *n* -s [ME, fr. OE; akin to MD *mist, mest* mist, fog, Icel *mistur* mist, haze, Gk *omichlē* mist, fog, Arm *mēg*, Lith *migla*, Skt *mih* mist, *megha* cloud] **1 :** water in the form of particles suspended in the atmosphere at or near the surface of the earth **:** small water droplets floating or falling, approaching the form of rain, and sometimes distinguished from fog as being more transparent or as having particles perceptibly moving downward ⟨heavy ~s hung in the valley and obscured the mountains —Willa Cather⟩ ⟨still summerlike except for the ~ on the lawn as dusk fell —Kathleen Freeman⟩ **2 :** something that hides or blurs objects or concepts **:** something that dims or obscures one's perceptions or understanding ⟨its origins are lost in the ~s of antiquity —G.G.Coulton⟩ ⟨a revelation of the world of nature that had lain so long under the ~ of erroneous medieval geography —*Saturday Rev.*⟩ ⟨heard through the ~ of sleep the voice . . . praying in her room —Louis Bromfield⟩ **3 :** a dimness of vision **:** a haze or film before the eyes ⟨a ~ seemed to come before her eyes —Gilbert Parker⟩ **4 a :** a cloud of small particles or objects resembling or suggestive of a mist ⟨the thick ~ of smoke and unescaped vapors which filled the room —Liam O'Flaherty⟩ ⟨saw it all in a wondrous light, in the ~ of leaves, in the flash of the river —Van Wyck Brooks⟩ **b :** a suspension of a finely divided liquid in a gas **:** FOG 2c — compare FUME 1b **c :** a fine spray **:** FOG 3b ⟨spraying with insecticidal ~s —*Atlantic*⟩ **5** *or* **mist gray :** a reddish gray that is bluer and paler than evenglow and bluer, lighter, and stronger than opal gray

**²mist** \"\ *vb* -ED/-ING/-s [ME *misten*, fr. OE *mistian*, fr. *mist*, n.] *vi* **1 :** to be or become misty **:** form a mist ⟨it's ~*ing* from the marshes or fogging from the sea —T.H.Fielding⟩ ⟨it was still only ~*ing* when they took their seats —*Pasadena (Calif.) Independent*⟩ **2 :** to become dim or blurred ⟨old eyes ~*ed* as he recalled the most important and tragic day of his life —Barnaby Conrad⟩ ~ *vt* **:** to cover with or as if with mist **:** CLOUD, DIM ⟨damp ~s her glasses —R.P.Warren⟩

**mist** *abbr* [L *mistura*] mixture

**mis·tak·able** \məˈstākəbəl\ *adj* **:** capable of being misunderstood or mistaken ⟨the twins are easily ~ for each other⟩ — **mis·tak·ably** \-blē, -li\ *adv*

**¹mis·take** \məˈstāk\ *vb* **mis·took** \məˈstu̇k, (ˈ)misˈs-\ **mis·tak·en** \məˈstākən\ **mistaking; mistakes** [ME *mistaken*, fr. ON *mistaka* to take by mistake, make a slip, fr. *mis-* ¹mis- + *taka* to take — more at TAKE] *vt* **1 :** to choose wrongly **:** blunder in the choice of ⟨ambition quite ~s her road —Edward Young⟩ ⟨*mistook* the track across the moors, and led the army into boggy ground —T.B.Macaulay⟩ **2 a :** to take in a wrong sense **:** misunderstand the meaning or intention of ⟨don't ~ me; I will do exactly as I say⟩ ⟨had *mistaken* the meaning of her question —Carson McCullers⟩ **b :** to be wrong in the estimation or understanding of **:** MISINTERPRET ⟨*mistook* the class structure and ownership distribution of developed capitalism —Peter Wiles⟩ **c :** to make a wrong judgment of the character or ability of **:** UNDERESTIMATE ⟨they ~ their man if they think they can frighten me⟩ **3 a :** to fail to recognize or to identify wrongly ⟨there's no *mistaking* him⟩ ⟨there's no *mistaking* that house⟩ **b :** to substitute incorrectly in thought or perception **:** take wrongly for someone or something else ⟨~ gush for vigor and substitute rhetoric for imagination —C.D.Lewis⟩ ⟨could be and often was *mistaken* for a farmer —H.S.Canby⟩ **4 :** to be wrong in regard to (time) ⟨somehow *mistook* the hour . . . I had told her nine o'clock, and she came at ten —Mary R. Rinehart⟩ ~ *vi* **:** to be wrong **:** be under a misapprehension ⟨you *mistook* when you thought I laughed at you —Thomas Hardy⟩ ⟨if I ~ not . . . the entire import of the illustration changes —John Dewey⟩ — **mis·tak·er** \-kə(r)\ *n*

**²mistake** \"\ *n* **1 :** a misunderstanding of the meaning or implication of something ⟨it is a ~ to think that the supreme or legislative power of a commonwealth can do what it will —John Locke⟩ ⟨it is a great ~ to think that the bare scientific idea is the required invention —A.N.Whitehead⟩ **2 :** a wrong action or statement proceeding from faulty judgment, inadequate knowledge, or inattention **:** an unintentional error ⟨it would be a ~, however, to drain all bogs —*Boy Scout Handbook*⟩ ⟨gave him a ten-dollar bill in ~ for a one⟩ **3** *law* **:** an erroneous belief **:** a state of mind not in accordance with the facts **syn** see ERROR — **and no mistake :** SURELY, UNDOUBTEDLY ⟨he's the one I saw, *and no mistake*⟩

**mistaken** *adj* [fr. past part. of ¹*mistake*] **1 :** MISUNDERSTOOD, MISCONCEIVED ⟨a case of ~ identity⟩ **2 :** having a wrong opinion or incorrect information ⟨is ~ in his ideas about education⟩ ⟨it is both unfair and immoral to charge perjury against a man who is only ~ —L.P.Stryker⟩ **3 :** wrong in action or thought **:** ERRONEOUS, MISGUIDED ⟨the psychologist is as much interested in ~ behavior as in correct behavior —G.A.Miller⟩ ⟨his ~ venture into poetic drama —H.V. Gregory⟩ ⟨correct some of the ~ ideas about farming —C.R. Hope⟩ — **mis·tak·en·ly** *adv* — **mis·tak·en·ness** \-kən(n)əs\ *n* -ES

**mistake of fact** *law* **:** a mistake other than a mistake of law

**mistake of law :** a mistake as to the legal consequences or significance of an act, transaction, or state of affairs

**mis·tak·ing·ly** *adv* **:** in a mistaking manner

**mis·tal** \'mistᵊl\ *n* -s [prob. of Scand origin; akin to Norw *melkestøl* milking shed in a saeter, fr. *melk* milk (fr. ON *mjolk*) + *stǫl* milking shed, fr. ON *stǫthull* — more at MILK, STADDLE] *dial Eng* **:** a shed for cows

**mis·tas·si·ni** \ˌmistəˈsēnē\ *n* -s [fr. Lake *Mistassini*, Quebec, Canada] **:** a dwarf primrose (*Primula mistassinica*) of northern and alpine America

**mist blower** *n* **:** a machine for the application of insecticides or fungicides in the form of a mist — compare HYDRAULIC SPRAYER

**mist blue** *n* **1 :** DUSTY BLUE **2 :** CAMEO GREEN

**mist board** *n* **:** a paperboard with an outside liner of two fibers of different color typically black and white

**mistbow** \'⸗ˌ⸗\ *n* **:** FOGBOW

**mist brown** *n* **:** BEIGE BROWN

**mist concentrate sprayer** *n* **:** CONCENTRATE SPRAYER

**mis·teach** \(ˈ)misˈtēch\ *vt* [ME *mistechen*, fr. OE *mistǣcan*, fr. ¹*mis-* + *tǣcan* to teach — more at TEACH] **:** to teach wrongly or badly — **mis·teach·er** \-chə(r)\ *n*

**mist·ed** \'mistəd\ *adj* [¹*mist* + *-ed*] **:** covered with or enveloped by or as if by mist ⟨a ~ pitcher of lemonade on the table —John & Ward Hawkins⟩ **:** FOGGED ⟨a mind that was ~ through fatigue⟩

**mis·telle** \məˈstel\ *n* -s [F, fr. Sp *mistela*, fr. *misto*, *mixto* mixed (fr. L *mixtus*, past part. of *miscēre* to mix) + *-ela* (dim. suffix) — more at MIX] **:** grape juice or slightly fermented white wine to which brandy has been added that is used in the production of other wines (as some vermouths and Malaga)

**mis·tempered** \(ˈ)misˈstempə(r)d\ *adj* [¹*mis-* + *tempered*] **1** *archaic* **:** DERANGED **2** *obs* **:** tempered for a bad purpose ⟨throw your ~ weapons to the ground —Shak.⟩

**¹mis·ter** \'mistə(r)\ *n* -s [ME, occupation, kind, need, fr. OF *mestier* — more at MÉTIER] **1** *archaic* **:** CLASS, KIND, SORT ⟨what ~ word is that —Francis Quarles⟩ **2** *chiefly Scot* **:** a case or condition of need

**²mister** \"\ *n* -s [alter. of ¹*master*] **1** — used sometimes in writing instead of the usual *Mr.* **2 :** SIR — used in direct address and not followed by the given name or surname of the man addressed and typically expressing abject deference (as of a beggar) ⟨can you let me have a dime, ~⟩ or stiff formality tinged with displeasure or with anger ⟨try that again, ~, and you'll be sorry⟩ or used simply as a generalized term of direct address of a man that is a stranger esp. by younger persons ⟨hey, ~, do you want to buy a paper⟩ **3 :** a man not entitled to a title of rank or an honorific or professional title ⟨though he was only a ~, he was a greater scholar in his field than any Ph.D.⟩ **4 :** HUSBAND ⟨maybe your *Mister* likes herbs, but then again, he mayn't —Alice Ross⟩

**³mister** \"\ *vt* **mistered; mistered; mistering** \-t(ə)riŋ\ **misters :** to address or refer to as *mister* or *Mr.* ⟨I ~*ed* him and sirred him no longer —*Century Mag.*⟩

**mi·ste·ri·o·so** \məˌstirēˈō(ˌ)sō, (ˌ)miˌs-, -)zō\ *adv* (*or adj*) [It, mysterious, fr. *mistèrio*, *mistèro* mystery (fr. L *mysterium*) + *-oso* -ose (fr. L *-osus*) — more at MYSTERY] **:** in a mysterious manner — used as a direction in music

**mis·term** \(ˈ)misˈtərm\ *vt* [¹*mis-* + *term*] **:** to apply a wrong name or designation to **:** term incorrectly ⟨fly-by-night schools that ~ themselves colleges⟩

**mistery** *var of* MYSTERY

**mis·tetch** \(ˈ)misˈtech\ *vt* -ED/-ING/-ES [alter. of *misteach*] *dial Eng* **:** to teach bad habits to

**mistflower** \'⸗ˌ⸗\ *n* **:** an American herb (*Eupatorium coelestinum*) with violet heads — called also *blue boneset*

**mist·ful** \'mistfəl\ *adj* [¹*mist* + *-ful*] **:** MISTY

**mist gray** *n* **:** MIST 5

**mist green** *n* **:** a variable color averaging a light yellowish green that is lighter and much less strong than apple green (sense 1), greener and paler than pistachio, and greener and duller than ocean green

**mis·think** \(ˈ)mis+\ *vb* [¹*mis-* + *think*] *vi, archaic* **:** to think wrongly, mistakenly, or unfavorably ~ *vt, archaic* **:** to think badly or unfavorably of

**misti** *pl of* MISTUS

**mis·ti·blu** \ˈmistēˌblü\ *n* -s [alter. of *misty blue*] **:** a grayish blue that is redder and paler than electric, greener and paler than copenhagen or old china, and redder and lighter than Gobelin

**mis·tic** \'mistik\ *also* **mis·ti·co** \-təˌkō\ *n* -s [Sp *místico*, perh. fr. Ar *musaṭṭaḥ*, an armed ship] **:** a small lateen-rigged sailing ship used in the Mediterranean

**mistier** *comparative of* MISTY

**mistiest** *superlative of* MISTY

**mis·ti·gris** \'mistēˌgris\ *n* -ES [F *mistigri* pussycat, jack of clubs, card game played with the jack of clubs wild, prob. irreg. fr. *miste, mite* pussycat (prob. of imit. origin) + *gris* gray — more at GRIZZLE] **1 :** a joker or blank card that the holder can play as any card **2 :** poker as played with a mistigris

**mist·i·ly** \'mistəlē, -li\ *adv* [ME, fr. *misty* + *-ly*] **:** in a misty manner **:** OBSCURELY, VAGUELY ⟨the summits of the most distant mountains . . . were dark and ~ purple —Robert Hichens⟩ ⟨explains it somewhat ~ —*Newsweek*⟩

**mis·time** \(ˈ)misˈtīm\ *vt* [ME *mistimen*, fr. ¹*mis-* + *timen* to time — more at TIME] **1 :** to time wrongly or improperly ⟨*mistimed* his arrival⟩ ⟨*mistimed* his swing and struck out⟩ **2 :** to reckon or state the time of incorrectly ⟨~s the accession of Queen Victoria by five years⟩

**mis·timed** \-md\ *adj, chiefly dial Eng* **:** disturbed in regular routine or habits esp. of eating and sleeping

**mist·i·ness** \'mistēnəs, -tin-\ *n* -ES [ME, *mistines*, fr. *misty* + *-nes* -ness] **:** the quality or state of being misty ⟨the vagueness and ~ . . . in his early poems —*H.W.Garrod*⟩

**misting** *pres part of* MIST

**mis·tis** \'mistəs\ *n* -ES [by alter.] *South* **:** MISTRESS

**mist·less** \'mistləs\ *adj* [¹*mist* + *-less*] **:** not misty

**mis·tle thrush** *also* **mis·sel thrush** \'misəl-\ *n* [obs. E *mistle, missel* mistletoe, fr. ME *mistel*, fr. OE — more at MISTLETOE] **:** a large European thrush (*Turdus viscivorus*) that has closely spotted underparts and feeds on mistletoe berries — called also *mistletoe thrush*

**mis·tle·toe** \'misəlˌtō, *chiefly Brit also* 'mizə-\ *n* -s [ME *mistilto* (attested only in the meaning "basil"), fr. OE *misteltān*, fr. *mistel* mistletoe, basil + *tān* twig; OE *mistel* akin to OHG & OS *mistil* mistletoe, ON *mistilteinn* mistletoe and perh. to OHG *mist* dung; OE *tān* akin to OHG *zein* twig, ON *teinn*, Goth *tains;* fr. the seeds being planted in the droppings of birds that have eaten the berries — more at MIXEN] **1 :** a Eurasian hemiparasitic shrub (*Viscum album*) that has dichotomously branching greenish stems, thick persistent leathery leaves, small yellowish flowers, and waxy-white glutinous berries and that grows pendent from various usu. deciduous trees (as the apple) **2 :** any of numerous plants of the family Loranthaceae that are felt to resemble the typical Old World mistletoe: as **a :** any of various American plants of the genus *Phoradendron* that grow on deciduous trees **b :** any of various Old World plants of the genus *Viscum* **c** *Austral* (1) **:** FLAME TREE a(2) (2) **:** a plant of the genus *Loranthus* (3) **:** a plant (*Notothixos incana*) that is parasitic on other mistletoes **d :** AMERICAN MISTLETOE 1 **3** *Austral* **:** DODDER LAUREL

**mistletoe bird** *n* **:** an Australian flower-pecker (*Dicaeum hirundinaceum*)

**mistletoe cactus** *n* **:** a plant of the genus *Rhipsalis*

**mistletoe family** *n* **:** LORANTHACEAE

**mistletoe fig** *n* **:** a shrub or small tree (*Ficus diversifolia*) sometimes grown as a pot plant that has foliage resembling that of the mistletoe and globose to pyriform fruit

**mistletoe gray** *n* **:** a variable color averaging a grayish yellow green that is yellower and paler than average sage green or palmetto and greener and duller than mermaid

**mistletoe green** *n* **:** a variable color averaging a grayish yellow green that is yellower, less strong, and slightly lighter than average sage green and yellower, lighter, and stronger than palmetto

**mistletoe thrush** *n* **:** MISTLE THRUSH

**mist maiden** *n* **:** either of two alpine or arctic perennial herbs (*Romanzoffia sitchensis* or *R. unalaschkensis*) of the family Hydrophyllaceae of western No. America with rounded crenate basal leaves and white funnelform flowers in a loose raceme

**mis·to·nusk** \'mistəˌnəsk\ *n* -s [Cree *mīstanask*, lit., broad, fr. *mist* much + *anāsk* spread out] **:** AMERICAN BADGER

**mistook** *past of* MISTAKE

**mis·train** \(ˈ)misˈtrān\ *vt* [¹*mis-* + *train*] **:** to train badly or incorrectly

**mis·tral** \'mistrəl, məˈsträl\ *n* -s [F, fr. Prov *mistral, mistrau*, fr. *mistral, mistrau* masterful, fr. OProv *maystral*, fr. L *magistralis* — more at MAGISTRAL] **:** a violent cold dry northerly wind of the Mediterranean provinces of France ⟨the ~ blew viciously —Horace Sutton⟩

**mis·transcription** \ˌmis+\ *n* [¹*mis-* + *transcription*] **:** a mistake in transcription **:** an incorrect copy ⟨some errors, ~s and mistranslations impair confidence —*Listener*⟩

**mis·translate** \"+\ *vt* [¹*mis-* + *translate*] **:** to translate incorrectly — **mis·translation** \"+\ *n*

**mis·treat** \(ˈ)misˈtrēt\ *vt* [ME *mistreten*, prob. fr. MF *mestreitier, mestraitier*, fr. OF, fr. *mes-* ¹mis- + *treitier, traitier* to treat — more at TREAT] **:** to treat badly **:** ABUSE ⟨administered a public thrashing to the landlord who had ~*ed* his brother —C.V.Woodward⟩ — **mis·treatment** \"+\ *n*

**¹mis·tress** \'mistrəs; *preceding a name as a title, pronounced like* MRS.\ *n* -ES [ME *maistresse*, fr. MF, fr. OF, fem. of *maistre* master — more at MASTER] **1** *obs* **:** a woman or something personified or venerated as a woman regarded as a guide or protector ⟨conjuring the moon to stand auspicious ~ —Shak.⟩ **2 :** a woman who has power, authority, or ownership: as **a :** the female head of a family or household ⟨having her here as ~ of this house — as your father's wife —Kathleen Freeman⟩ ⟨presided as ~ of the White House during the closing scenes of the administration —T.P.Abernethy⟩ **b :** a woman who employs or supervises servants ⟨the . . . kitchen maid, whose pleasure during the week is in the thought of vying with her ~ on Sunday —Herbert Spencer⟩ **c :** a woman who possesses, owns, or controls something ⟨though she was angry, she was still ~ of her temper⟩ ⟨~ of a large fortune⟩ ⟨a dog whose ~ devoted hours a day to its care⟩ ⟨determined to get a job and become her own ~⟩ **d :** a woman who is in charge of a school or other establishment or group ⟨this guidance is given by a ~ of postulants and the ~ of novices —Mary Augustine⟩ **e :** a woman of the Scottish nobility who holds in her own right a status comparable to that of a master; *specif* **:** the eldest daughter and heiress presumptive of a Scottish peer **3 a** *chiefly Brit* **:** a female teacher or tutor ⟨while classics *mistress* in an East Anglian college —*Irish Digest*⟩ ⟨when I pointed this out to the drawing ~ she rebuked me and told me that the "feeling" was wonderful —Ralph Vaughan Williams⟩ **b :** a woman who is skilled in something or who has achieved mastery in some field ⟨shows herself ~ of almost every conceivable type of fairy lore —Polly Goodwin⟩ ⟨~ of the art of portraiture⟩ ⟨~ of the science of medicine⟩ **4 :** a country or state regarded as having supremacy or control over others ⟨when Rome was ~ of the world⟩ ⟨became undisputed ~ of the continent⟩ **5 :** something personified as female that rules or directs ⟨Mother and *Mistress* of all the churches —William Leonard & Bernard Orchard⟩ ⟨the sea is a stern ~ and an unyielding disciplinarian —Bill Redgrave⟩ **6 a :** a woman with whom a man habitually fornicates ⟨leaving his wife, an actress, behind, he travels with his ~ —Bernice Matlowsky⟩ **b** *archaic* **:** a beloved woman **:** SWEETHEART **7 a** *archaic* **:** MADAM 1 **b** — used archaically as a conventional title of courtesy before the given name or surname or before both names of an unmarried woman **c** *chiefly South & Midland* **:** MRS. 1a **8** *dial chiefly Brit* **:** WIFE

**²mistress** \"\ *vt* -ED/-ING/-ES **1 :** to address as mistress **2 :** to achieve mastery of (an art) — used of a woman **3 :** to rule or control as a mistress **:** DOMINATE — **mistress it :** play the mistress

**mis·tress·ly** *adj* [¹*mistress* + *-ly*] **:** resembling or characteristic of a woman who has a mastery of something ⟨a ~ demonstration of acting⟩

**mistress of ceremonies :** a woman who presides at a public ceremony or who acts as hostess of a stage, radio, or television show

**mistress of the robes** *usu cap M&R* **:** a duchess who is appointed nominally in the British royal household to have charge of the queen's robes and who attends the queen at all state ceremonies

**mistress-ship** \'==,ship\ *n* **:** the condition or position of a mistress ⟨she was looking forward to her *mistress-ship* of the robes —Israel Zangwill⟩ ⟨achieved the *mistress-ship* of the seas⟩ ⟨appointed to the mathematics *mistress-ship*⟩

**mis·trial** \(ˈ)mi¦strīəl\ *n* [¹*mis-* + *trial*] **1 :** a trial that has no legal effect by reason of some error in the proceedings **2 :** a trial not resulting or not likely to result in a lawful decision or verdict because of serious prejudicial misconduct or error

**¹mis·trust** \(ˈ)mi¦strəst\ *n* [ME, fr. ¹*mis-* + *trust*, n.] **:** a lack of confidence **:** DISTRUST, SUSPICION ⟨a certain unbreakable core of ~, suspicion, and disbelief —A.R.Marcus⟩ ⟨realize how weak the love of truth is in the majority and how widespread the ~ of reason —W.R.Inge⟩ **syn** see UNCERTAINTY

**²mistrust** \"\ *vb* [ME *mistrusten*, fr. ¹*mis-* + *trusten* to trust — more at TRUST] *vt* **1 :** to regard with suspicion **:** have no trust or confidence in **:** SUSPECT ⟨~ me and are forever questioning me about my personal life —Isaac Rosenfeld⟩ ⟨she feared an argument; she ~*ed* herself —Arnold Bennett⟩ **2 :** to have doubts about the truth, validity, or effectiveness of ⟨calculated to make the weak-willed reader ~ his own judgment —B.R.Redman⟩ ⟨who ~ the investment of U.S. money, technical and military aid —Adrienne Koch⟩ **3 :** to have a foreboding of the existence or occurrence of **:** feel or believe to be likely **:** SURMISE — often used with noun clause as object ⟨your mind ~*ed* there was something wrong —Robert Frost⟩ **~** *vi* **:** to lack confidence **:** be suspicious ⟨a place so wild that a man less accustomed to these things might have ~*ed* and feared for his life —Willa Cather⟩ — **mis·trust·er** \-tə(r)\ *n*

**mis·trust·ful** \-fəl\ *adj* **1 :** given to mistrust **:** SUSPICIOUS ⟨so ~ of everybody that they never know what to believe —Upton Sinclair⟩ **2 :** full of mistrust **:** marked by mistrust ⟨the ~ atmosphere of dubious peace —J.W.Aldridge⟩ — **mis·trust·ful·ly** *adv* — **mis·trust·ful·ness** *n*

**mis·trust·ing·ly** *adv* **:** in a mistrusting manner

**mis·trust·less** \-ləs\ *adj* **:** having no mistrust **:** UNSUSPECTING

**mis·tryst** \(ˈ)mi¦strīst\ *vb* [¹*mis-* + *tryst*] *vt, chiefly Scot* **:** to break an agreement with; *esp* **:** to fail to keep an engagement with **~** *vi, chiefly Scot* **:** to fail to keep an agreement (as an engagement or an appointed meeting)

**mistrysted** *adj, chiefly Scot* **:** PERPLEXED, FRIGHTENED ⟨they are sore ~ yonder in their parliament house about this robbery —Sir Walter Scott⟩

**mists** *pl of* MIST, *pres 3d sing of* MIST

**mis·tune** \(ˈ)mi¦stün\ *vt* [¹*mis-* + *tune*] **:** to tune incorrectly **:** render discordant ⟨like a pleasant air when performed on a *mistuned* instrument —Sir Walter Scott⟩

**mis·tus** \ˈmistəs\ *n, pl* **mis·ti** \-,stī\ *also* **mistuses** [NL, fr L, past part. of *miscēre* to mix — more at MIX] **:** an intraspecific hybrid plant

**misty** \ˈmistē, -ti\ *adj, usu* -ER/-EST [ME, fr. OE *mistig* misty, fr. *mist* + *-ig* -y — more at MIST] **1 a :** obscured by or covered with mist or something resembling mist ⟨westward the ~ summits of the Coast range —*Amer. Guide Series: Oregon*⟩ ⟨the ~ sheen of the moonlight —O.E.Rölvaag⟩ ⟨was barely heated and ~ with dust —Arthur Miller⟩ **b :** consisting of or marked by mist ⟨the darkness of sky and water was streaked with a long, ~ line of foam —Herman Melville⟩ **c :** unclear in shape or outline **:** INDISTINCT ⟨could perceive the outlines of land, blue and ~ in the distance —C.B.Nordhoff & J.N.Hall⟩ **2 a :** clouded as if by mist **:** DIM, OBSCURE ⟨through the safe and rather ~ glass of ready-made dogmas —Mary Webb⟩ **b :** vague or confused in thought or style ⟨poetry which was essentially vague, ~ and dim —Delmore Schwartz⟩ ⟨a ~ nostalgia for a royalist authoritarianism —Gordon Merrick⟩

**misty blue** *n* **:** DUSTY BLUE

**misty-eyed** \¦==¦=\ *adj* **:** DREAMY, SENTIMENTAL ⟨a *misty-eyed* young lover⟩ ⟨*misty-eyed* recollections⟩

**misty morn** *n* **:** a light grayish brown to reddish brown that is less strong and slightly lighter than sandstone

**mis·understand** \(¦)mis+\ *vt* [ME *misunderstanden*, fr. ¹*mis-* + *understanden* to understand — more at UNDERSTAND] **1 :** to fail to understand **:** miss the true meaning of ⟨~ a poem⟩ ⟨*misunderstood* the idea the lecturer was trying to develop⟩ ⟨*misunderstood* the potentialities of colonization —Albert Hyma⟩ **2 :** to interpret (as something said or done) incorrectly **:** attach a wrong meaning to ⟨the women who blacken your character and ~ your wife's amusements —Rudyard Kipling⟩ — **mis·under·stander** \"+\ *n*

**mis·understanding** \"+\ *n* [ME *misundirstonding*, fr. ¹*mis-* + *undirstonding*, *understanding* understanding] **1 :** a failure to understand **:** MISINTERPRETATION ⟨the ~ which arose from reports of these golden palaces fired the imagination of Columbus —G.F.Hudson⟩ **2 :** DISAGREEMENT, QUARREL ⟨the ~*s* between the two territories have grown during the emergency —Vernon Bartlett⟩

**mis·un·der·stand·ing·ly** *adv* **:** in a misunderstanding manner **:** so as to misunderstand or as a result of misunderstanding

**mis·under·stood** \(¦)mis+\ *adj* [fr. past part. of *misunderstand*] **1 :** wrongly or imperfectly understood ⟨a ~ question⟩ ⟨a ~ criticism⟩ **2 :** not sympathetically appreciated ⟨claimed to be a much ~ husband⟩

**mis·usage** \(ˈ)mi¦shü . . ., (ˈ)mis¦yü . . .— *see* USAGE\ *n* [MF *mesusage*, fr. *mes-* ¹*mis-* + *usage* — more at USAGE] **1 :** bad treatment **:** ABUSE ⟨charged ~ of patients by one of the attendants⟩ **2 :** wrong or improper use (as of words) ⟨an instance of what he regarded as ~ appeared in a conservative publication —Kathryn A. McEuen⟩

**¹mis·use** \(ˈ)mi¦shüz, (ˈ)mis¦yüz\ *vt* [ME *misusen*, partly fr. ¹*mis-* + *usen* to use; partly fr. MF *mesuser* to abuse, use wrongly, fr. OF, fr. *mes-* ¹*mis-* + *user* to use — more at USE] **1 :** to use incorrectly or carelessly **:** MISAPPLY ⟨~*s* words in such number that it is impossible to understand him⟩ **2 :** to use for a wrong or improper purpose ⟨~*s* his talents⟩ ⟨possibility that the members would ~ the organization for inhumane and selfish purposes —Raphael Demos⟩ ⟨regards a battle as a major occasion for *misusing* his social position —William Empson⟩ **3 :** to do harm to **:** ABUSE, MISTREAT ⟨the intent of this regulation is highly commendable, namely to keep the Indians from being *misused* —C.B.Hitchcock⟩

**²mis·use** \(ˈ)mi¦shüs, (ˈ)mis¦yüs\ *n* [ME, partly fr. ¹*mis-* + *use*; partly fr. MF *mesus* abuse, wrong use, fr. *mes-* ¹*mis-* + *us* use — more at USE] **1 :** incorrect or careless use **:** MISAPPLICATION ⟨the first statement involves a ~ of the verb "to create" —Arthur Pap⟩ ⟨the ~ of words which are actually in the language —Barrett Wendell⟩ **2 :** wrong or improper use ⟨intended to keep their secret until adequate controls against its ~ had been devised —Vera M. Dean⟩

**misuse of patents :** an attempt of a patent owner to extend his monopoly beyond the express terms of the patent grant resulting in the denial by the courts of protection to the patent

**¹mis·us·er** \(ˈ)mi¦shüzə(r), (ˈ)mis¦yüz-\ *n* [¹*misuse* + *-er*] **:** one that misuses ⟨these wretched ~*s* of language —S.T. Coleridge⟩

**²misuser** \"\ *n* [AF, fr. OF *mesuser* to misuse] **:** an unlawful use of a right; *esp* **:** an unlawful use of a public office or grant of authority

**mis·value** \(ˈ)mis+\ *vt* [¹*mis-* + *value*] **:** to value wrongly; *esp* **:** UNDERVALUE ⟨neglected and *misvalued* his work for many years⟩

**mis·venture** \"+\ *n* [¹*mis-* + *venture*] **:** an unlucky venture **:** MISADVENTURE

**mis·word** \"+\ *n* [¹*mis-* + *word*] *dial chiefly Brit* **:** a word wrongly spoken **:** a cross word

**mis·write** \"+\ *vt* [ME *miswriten*, fr. OE *miswrītan*, fr. ¹*mis-* + *wrītan* to write — more at WRITE] **:** to write incorrectly **:** make a mistake in writing ⟨*miswrote* the title of the poem he was quoting⟩ ⟨carelessly ~*s* common words⟩

**mis·writing** \"+\ *n* [fr. gerund of *miswrite*] **:** a mistake in writing ⟨the inclusion of many ~*s* mislabeled misspelling helps to invalidate the investigator's conclusions about spelling —Hall Swain⟩

**mit** *var of* MITT

**mit-** *or* **mito-** *comb form* [NL, fr. Gk, fr. *mitos* — more at DIMITY] **1 :** thread ⟨*mito*plast⟩ **2 :** mitosis ⟨*mito*clastic⟩ ⟨*mito*depressive⟩ ⟨*mito*genetic⟩

**mit** *abbr* [L *mitte*, 2nd pers. sing. imper. of *mittere* to send — more at SMITE] send

**MIT** *abbr* milled in transit; milling in transit

**mi·ta** \ˈmēd·ə\ *n* -S [AmerSp, fr. Quechua *mit'a*, lit., turn, time] **:** a forced-labor draft imposed by the Spaniards on the Indians of Peru

**mi·tan·ni** \mə'tanē\ *n, pl* **mitanni** *or* **mitannis** *usu cap* **1 a :** an ancient Subaraean people with an Indo-Iranian ruling class having a kingdom in northern Mesopotamia that was dominant in Mesopotamia and northern Syria from the end of the 15th to the middle of the 14th century B.C. **b :** a member of these people **2 :** the language of the Mitanni people that was of uncertain relationship

**mi·tan·nian** \-nēən, -nyən\ *n* -S *usu cap* [*Mitanni* + E *-an*] **:** MITANNI 1b, 2

**¹mitch** \ˈmich\ *dial Eng var of* MUCH

**²mitch** \", ˈmēch\ *var of* MEECH

**mitch·board** \ˈmich+,=\ *n* [*mitch* (origin unknown) + *board*] **:** an upright timber on the deck of a ship forming a crutch for the mast to rest on when lowered

**mitch·el·la** \mi'chelə\ *n* [NL, fr. John *Mitchell* †1768 Am. botanist born in England] **1** *cap* **:** a genus of creeping evergreen herbs (family Rubiaceae) having shiny evergreen leaves and fragrant white tubular flowers growing in pairs — see PARTRIDGEBERRY **2** -S **:** any plant of the genus *Mitchella* **3** -S **:** the dried plant of the partridgeberry formerly used as a diuretic, tonic, and astringent

**mitch·ell grass** \ˈmichəl-\ *n, usu cap M* [prob. after Thomas L. *Mitchell* †1855 Scot. explorer in Australia] **:** any of several Australian grasses of the genus *Astrebla* with flowering spikes resembling wheat

**mitchell movement** *n, usu cap 1st M* [after John T. *Mitchell* 20th cent. bridge expert, its originator] **:** a method of conducting a game of duplicate bridge or whist so that the North-South pairs play only against the East-West pairs — compare HOWELL SYSTEM

**¹mite** \ˈmīt, *usu* -īd·+V\ *n* -S [ME, fr. OE *mīte* mite (small insect); akin to MD *mite* mite, small copper coin, OHG *mīza* mite (insect), *meizan* to cut, ON *meita* to cut, Goth *maitan* to hew, cut, and to OE *gemād* silly, mad — more at MAD] **1 :** any of numerous small to very minute arachnids of the order Acarina that have a body without a constriction between the cephalothorax and abdomen, mandibles generally chelate or adapted for piercing, usu. four pairs of short legs in the adult and but three in the young larvae, and often breathing organs in the form of tracheae and that include parasites of insects and vertebrates some of which are important disease vectors, parasites of plants in which they frequently cause gall formation, pests of various stored products, and completely innocuous free-living aquatic and terrestrial forms — see BLISTER MITE, CHEESE MITE, CLOVER MITE, ITCH MITE **2** [ME, fr. MF or MD; MF, small Flemish copper coin, fr. OF, fr. MD] **a** (1) **:** LEPTON 2 ⟨a certain poor widow . . . threw in two ~*s* —Mk 12:42 (AV)⟩ (2) **:** half a farthing **b :** a very small theoretical unit of value or coin; *specif* **:** a unit of value in England about 1600 worth usu. 1/24 penny **3 :** an old moneyers' unit of weight equal to 1/20 grain that is no longer used **4 a :** a very little **:** BIT, JOT ⟨only a ~ of what it could have taught was seen and learned —Tom Fitzsimmons⟩ — often used adverbially with *a* ⟨his voice is a ~ less luscious than formerly —R.C.Bagar⟩ **b :** a very small object, creature, or person ⟨a little kindergarten . . . ~ —Marie Imelda⟩

**²mite** \"\ *vt* -ED/-ING/-S [prob. fr. G *meiden* to shun, avoid, fr. OHG *mīdan*; akin to OE *mīthan* to hide, conceal, avoid, shun, MD *miden* to avoid, shun, and to OE *missan* to miss — more at MISS] **:** to impose an Amish mite on ⟨was *mited* by church officials for using an automobile⟩

**³mite** \"\ *n* -S **:** a social and economic boycott applied to a member by an Amish congregation for transgressing church law

**mite box** *n* [¹*mite*] **:** a small box distributed individually to the members of a church or Sunday school for the collection of a special offering ⟨lenten *mite boxes*⟩

**mi·tel·la** \mə'telə\ *n, cap* [NL, fr. L, headband, turban, dim. of *mitra*] **:** a genus of low slender Asiatic and No. American herbs (family Saxifragaceae) having opposite leaves and flowers with trifid or pinnatifid petals and a superior one-celled ovary — see MITERWORT

**¹mi·ter** *also* **mi·tre** \ˈmīd·ə(r), ˈmītə-\ *n* -S [ME *mitre*, fr.

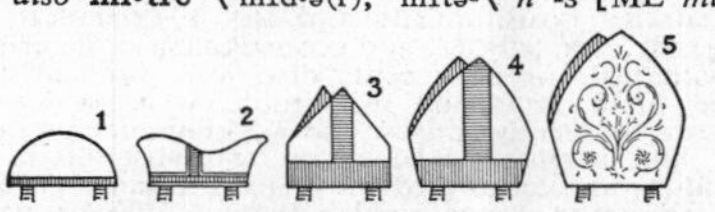

miter 1c: *1* 11th century, *2* 12th century, *3* 15th century, *4* 18th century, *5* 20th century

MF, fr. OF, fr. L *mitra* headband, turban, fr. Gk *mitra*, *mitrē*; akin to Skt *mitra* friend, Av *mithra* friend, treaty, OPer *Mithra* Mithras, god of light and defender of truth] **1 :** any of various turbans, tall caps, or other pieces of headgear: as **a :** a headband worn by women of ancient Greece **b :** the official headdress of the ancient Jewish high priest consisting of a linen turban having attached at the front a gold plate with the inscription "Holy to the Lord" **c :** a liturgical headdress that is worn by bishops and abbots and usu. has high stiff back and front pieces curving to a point and two lappets hanging from the back, is made of white silk or linen or of cloth of gold, and may be plain, orphreyed, or richly ornamented **2** [perh. fr. miter turban] **a** (1) **:** a surface forming the beveled end or edge of a piece where a miter joint is made (2) **:** MITER JOINT (3) **:** MITER SQUARE **b :** a corner or angle joining made by seaming on a diagonal line from the inside angle to the outside point and used esp. in fitting facings or hems and in matching stripes in sewing **3** *or* **miter shell a** *usu* **mitre :** a snail of the genus *Mitra* or family Mitridae **b :** the shell of such a snail **4 :** a piece (as of eaves trough or pipe insulation) made with a right angle bend to fit a corner or elbow ⟨install an inside ~ below the valley⟩

**²miter** *also* **mitre** \"\ *vb* **mitered** *also* **mitred**; **mitered** *also* **mitred**; **mitering** *also* **mitring** \-īd·əriŋ, -ītər-, -ī·tr-\ **miters** *also* **mitres** [ME *mitren*, fr. ML *mitrare*, fr. *mitra* liturgical miter, fr. L] *vt* **1 :** to raise to a rank privileged to wear a miter **:** confer a miter on ⟨~*ed* some of the less radical Protestant leaders —George Willison⟩ **2** [¹*miter* (joint)] **a :** to match together in a miter joint ⟨~ the ends of the boards⟩ **:** bevel the ends of for the purpose of matching together at an angle ⟨~ the side pieces⟩ **:** bring together at an angle without overlapping ⟨~ the cover materials at the inside corner of the book⟩ **b :** to join (lines of a cover decoration) accurately without overrunning at corners or crosslines **c :** to sew together in a miter ⟨stripes are ~*ed* to the waist —*Women's Wear Daily*⟩ **d :** to square off (a bottom corner of a bed sheet) by making a triangular fold and tucking it under **~** *vi* **:** to form a miter joint **:** meet in a miter joint

**miter box** *n* **:** a device for guiding a handsaw at the proper angle in making a miter joint and often in the form of a wooden or metal trough with fixed or adjustable vertical slots in its upright sides

miter box (with saw)

**miter brad** *n* **:** CORRUGATED FASTENER

**miter cap** *n* **:** a molded cushion of a newel post into which the handrail is mitered

**miter clamp** *or* **miter cramp** *n* **:** a clamp for holding together a glued miter joint while the glue sets

**mi·tered** \ˈmīd·ə(r)d, ˈmītə-\ *adj* [ME *mitred*, fr. *mitre* + *-ed*; trans. of ML *mitratus*, fr. L, wearing a turban — more at MITRATE] **1 :** wearing a miter ⟨stood robed and ~ before the altar⟩ **2 :** having an upper part shaped like a miter ⟨the ~ headgear of the knight's lady⟩

**mitered abbey** *n* **:** an abbey under a mitered abbot

**mitered abbot** *n* **:** an abbot papally privileged to wear a miter and in pre-Reformation England entitled to sit and vote in the House of Lords

**mi·ter·er** \ˈmīd·ərə(r), ˈmītə-\ *n* -S **:** one that miters; *esp* **:** a tool or machine for forming miters or bevels

**miter gage** *n* **:** a tool with graduations used to set a saw at any desired angle for a miter joint

**miter gate** *n* **:** one of a pair of canal lock gates that swing out from the side walls and meet at an angle pointing toward the upper level

**miter gear** *n* **:** one of a pair of interchangeable bevel gears with axes at right angles

**miter joint** *n* **:** a joint made by fastening together usu. perpendicularly parts with the ends cut at an angle **:** a butt joint with beveled ends

miter joints: *1* plain, *2* milled, *3* rabbeted

**miter mushroom** *n* [so called fr. the shape of the pileus] **:** a mushroom of the genus *Helvella* (esp. *H. crispa*)

**miter plane** *n* **:** a plane for general use in making angle and butt joints

**miter post** *n* **:** the vertical member at the free edge of a miter gate

**miter rod** *n* **:** a smooth flat plate of steel with one end cut back at a 45 degree angle and used by a plasterer in finishing a reentrant corner

**miter saw** *or* **miter box saw** *n* **:** a saw similar to a backsaw but usu. with a longer blade for cutting miter joints in a miter box

**miter shell** *n* **:** MITER 3

**miter sill** *n* **:** a raised step against which a canal lock gate shuts

**miter square** *n* **1 :** a bevel with an immovable arm at an angle of 45 degrees for striking miter lines **2 a :** a square with an arm adjustable to any angle **b :** a rigid square with a 45 degree bevel on the end of the stock

**miter valve** *n* **:** a valve consisting of a disk fitting in a conical seat faced at 45 degrees to the valve axis

**miterwort** *also* **mitrewort** \'==,=\ *n* -S **1 :** any of various rhizomatous perennial herbs that constitute the genus *Mitella* and have a capsule resembling a bishop's miter — called also *bishop's cap*; see FAIRY CAP **2 :** any of various white-flowered annual herbs constituting a genus (*Cynoctonum*) of the family Loganiaceae; *esp* **:** a plant (*C. mitreola*) of the southeastern U.S.

**mites** *pl of* MITE, *pres 3d sing of* MITE

**mith** \ˈmith\ *chiefly Scot var of* ¹MIGHT

**mith·an** *also* **mith·un** \ˈmithən\ *n, pl* **mithan** *also* **mithun** [native name in Assam and Chittagong] **:** an Indian bison or wild ox related to the gaur

**¹mith·er** \ˈmithər\ *Scot var of* MOTHER

**²mi·ther** \ˈmīthə(r)\ *dial Eng var of* MOIDER

**mithkal** *var of* MISKAL

**mith·rae·um** \mi'thrēəm\ *n, pl* **mith·raea** \-ēə\ *also* **mithraeums** *usu cap* [NL, fr. Gk *Mithraion* shrine of Mithras, fr. *Mithras*, Persian god of light and defender of truth, fr. OPer *Mithra* — more at MITER] **:** an underground room simulating a cave used for mithraic rites (as initiations)

**mith·ra·ic** \mi'thrāik\ *adj, usu cap* [LGk *mithraikos* of Mithras, fr. Gk *Mithras* + *-ikos* -ic] **:** of or relating to Mithraism or its god ⟨acolyte of the *Mithraic* cult —Stuart Cloete⟩

**mith·ra·ism** \ˈmithrə,izəm\ *n* -S *usu cap* [*Mithras*, Persian god of light (fr. L, fr. Gk) + E *-ism*] **:** an oriental mystery cult incorporating elements from Zoroastrianism, the primitive religions of Asia Minor, and Hellenism, having as its deity Mithras, the savior hero of Persian myth, admitting only men to its seven degrees of initiation, and constituting a serious rival of Christianity in the Roman Empire between the second and fourth centuries A.D.

**mith·ra·ist** \-,əst\ *n* -S *usu cap* **:** an adherent of Mithraism — **mith·ra·is·tic** \¦==¦istik\ *adj, usu cap*

**mith·ri·date** \ˈmithrə,dāt\ *also* **mith·ri·da·tum** \,==ˈdād·əm\ *n* -S [ML *mithridatum*, fr. LL *mithridatium* antidote, fr. L, dogtooth violet (used as an antidote) fr. Gk *mithridation*, fr. *Mithridatēs* Mithridates] **:** an antidote against poison **:** ALEXIPHARMIC; *specif* **:** an electuary supposed to be a remedy or a protection against poison

**mithridate mustard** *n* **:** PENNYCRESS

**mith·ri·dat·ic** *or* **mith·ra·dat·ic** \¦mithrə¦dad·ik\ *adj* [*mithridatic* fr. L *Mithridaticus*, fr. *Mithridates* + *-icus* -ic; *mithradatic*, alter. (influenced by Gk *Mithradatēs* Mithridates) of *mithridatic*] **1** *usu cap* **:** of or relating to Mithridates VI of ancient Pontus **2 :** of or relating to mithridatism

**mith·ri·da·tism** \,==ˈdād·,izəm\ *n* -S [*Mithridates* VI †63 B.C. king of ancient Pontus (fr. L *Mithridates*, fr. Gk *Mithridatēs*, *Mithradatēs*) + E *-ism*; fr. the fact that he reputedly produced this condition in himself] **:** tolerance to a poison acquired by taking gradually increased doses of it

**mith·ri·da·tize** \-ād·,īz\ *vt* -ED/-ING/-S **:** to produce mithridatism in

**mit·i·ci·dal** \¦mīd·ə¦sīdᵊl\ *adj* [¹*mite* + *-icidal* (as in *insecticidal*)] **:** ACARICIDAL

**mit·i·cide** \'==,sīd\ *n* -S [¹*mite* + *-icide* (as in *insecticide*)] **:** ACARICIDE

**mitier** *comparative of* MITY

**mitiest** *superlative of* MITY

**mit·i·ga·ble** \ˈmid·əgəbəl, -itə-\ *adj* **:** that can be mitigated

**mit·i·gant** \-gənt\ *n* -S [obs. *mitigant*, adj., mitigative, fr. L *mitigant-*, *mitigans*, pres. part. of *mitigare* to mitigate] **:** something mitigating

**mit·i·gate** \ˈmid·ə,gāt, -itə-, *usu* -ād·+V\ *vt* -ED/-ING/-S [ME *mitigaten*, fr. L *mitigatus*, past part. of *mitigare* to soften, mitigate, fr. *mitis* soft, mild + *agere* to drive; akin to OIr *mōith* soft, *min* smooth, gentle, Skt *mayas* enjoyment, pleasure, Lith *mielas*, *mylas* dear — more at AGENT] **1 :** to cause (as a person) to become more gentle or less hostile **:** MOLLIFY **2 :** to make less severe, violent, cruel, intense, painful **:** SOFTEN, ALLEVIATE ⟨used opium to ~ the horrors to which condemned criminals were subjected —*Science*⟩ ⟨disasters can be, if not prevented, at least *mitigated* —K.S.Davis⟩ **:** TEMPER ⟨in the summer the altitude tempers the heat, and in the winter the latitude ~*s* the cold —C.W.DeKiewiet⟩ **:** LESSEN ⟨a sentence of 20 days solitary confinement may be *mitigated* to 10 days —*Naval Orientation*⟩ ⟨tends to increase rather than to ~ these differences in students —*General Education in a Free Society*⟩ ⟨~ the sincerity of what I said —Mary Austin⟩ **syn** see RELIEVE

**mit·i·gat·ed·ly** *adv* [*mitigated*, past part. of *mitigate* + *-ly*] **:** in a mitigated degree

**mit·i·ga·tion** \,=='gāshən\ *n* -S [ME *mitigacioun*, fr. AF & L; AF *mitigation*, fr. L *mitigation-*, *mitigatio*, fr. *mitigatus* (past part.) + *-ion-*, *-io* -ion] **1 :** the act of mitigating or state of being mitigated: **a :** abatement or diminution of something painful, harsh, severe, afflictive, or calamitous **:** ALLEVIATION, MODERATION, PALLIATION ⟨the cure, prevention, or ~ of disease —*Encyc. Americana*⟩ ⟨prison in ~ of the death sentence —Melitta Schmideberg⟩ **b** *obs* **:** QUALIFICATION, LIMITATION **2 :** a mitigating thing or fact ⟨a large number of drugs and ~*s* . . . at the clinic —*Jour. Amer. Med. Assoc.*⟩

**mit·i·ga·tive** \'==,gād·iv\ *adj* [ME *mitigatif*, fr. MF, fr. LL *mitigativus*, fr. L *mitigatus* (past part.) + *-ivus* -ive] **:** tending to mitigate **:** ALLEVIATING, LENITIVE ⟨an air of being a trifle apologetic; and this ~, tentative quality shows . . . in their stance —*Time*⟩

**mit·i·ga·tor** \-,gād·ə(r)\ *n* -S **:** one that mitigates

**mit·i·ga·to·ry** \ˈmid·əgə,tōrē, -itə-\ *adj* [L *mitigatorius*, fr. *mitigatus* (past part. of *mitigare* to mitigate) + *-orius* -ory] **:** MITIGATIVE

**mit·i·mae** \,mid·ə'mä,ā\ *n* -S [AmerSp (Peru), fr. Quechua *mitma*, lit., foreigner, stranger] **1 :** a member of a part of a conquered Indian people forced by the Incas to settle in a distant area **2 :** compulsory transplantation and colonization of conquered peoples under the Incas

**miting** *pres part of* MITE

**mi·tis** \ˈmīd·əs\ *adj* [L, mild — more at MITIGATE] **:** tending to be less than averagely virulent — used esp. of strains of diphtheria bacilli; compare GRAVIS, INTERMEDIUS

**mi·tis green** \ˈmēd·əs-\ *n* [part trans. of G *mitisgrün*, fr. Ignatz *Mitis* †1842 Ger. manufacturer + G *grün* green] **1** *usu cap M* **:** Paris green used as a pigment **2** *often cap M* **:** EMERALD 2a

**mit·nag·ged** \,mitnä'ged, mi'snägəd\ *or* **mis·na·gid** \mi'snägəd\ *n, pl* **mit·nag·ge·dim** *or* **mit·nag·dim** \,mitnä(g)ə'dēm, mi'snägdəm\ *or* **mis·nag·dim** \mi'snägdəm\ *often cap*

[NHeb *mithnāggēd* & Yiddish *misnaged*, fr. Heb *mithnāggēd* opposing, opponent] **1 :** an orthodox Jew esp. in eastern Europe opposed to the teachings of the Hasidim **2 :** a non-Hasid

**mito-** — see MIT-

**mito·chon·dri·al** \ˌmīd·əˈkändrēəl, ˌmid·ə-\ *adj* [NL *mitochondrion* + E *-al*] **:** of, relating to, or being mitochondria

**mito·chondriome** \ˌ==+\ *n* [NL *mitochondrion* + E *-ome*] **:** CHONDRIOME

**mito·chon·dri·on** \ˌ=='=drēən\ *n, pl* **mitochon·dria** \-ēə\ [NL, fr. *mit-* + Gk *chondrion* small grain — more at CHONDRI-] **:** CHONDRIOSOME; *esp* **:** a granular or globular chondriosome — compare CHONDRIOCONT, CHONDRIOMITE

**mito·cla·sic** \ˌ==ˈklāsik\ *or* **mito·clas·tic** \-ˈklastik\ *adj* [*mitoclasic* fr. F *mitoclasique*, fr. *mito-* mit- + *-clasique* (fr. Gk *klasis* act of breaking + F *-ique* -ic); *mitoclastic*, prob. modif. (influenced by E *-clastic*) of F *mitoclasique* — more at -CLASIA] **:** interrupting the normal course of mitosis ⟨~ chemicals⟩

**mito·ge·net·ic** \ˌmīd·ō, ˌmid·ō+\ *adj* [*mit-* + *-genetic*] **:** producing mitosis ⟨the ~ effect⟩ ⟨~ radiation⟩

**mitogenetic ray** *n* **:** an ultraviolet ray said to be given off by physiologically active cells and to stimulate mitotic activity of adjacent cells — usu. used in pl.

**mito·inhibitory** \ˌ==+\ *adj* [*mit-* + *inhibitory*] **:** retarding or inhibiting mitosis

**mi·tome** \ˈmīd·ˌōm\ *n* -S [G *mitom*, fr. *mit-* + *-om* -ome] **:** the supposed fibrillar reticulum of protoplasm — compare PARAMITOME

**mito·plast** \ˌmīd·əˌplast, ˌmid·-\ *n* -S [ISV *mit-* + *-plast;* prob. orig. formed as F *mitoplaste*] **:** a filamentous plastid

**mi·to·sis** \mīˈtōsəs\ *n, pl* **mito·ses** \-ˌsēz\ [NL, fr. *mit-* + *-osis*] **1 :** cell division in which complex nuclear division usu. involving differentiation and halving of chromosomes precedes cytoplasmic fission and which involves typically a series consisting of the prophase, metaphase, anaphase, and telophase **:** indirect cell division — called also *karyokinesis;* opposed to *amitosis;* compare MEIOSIS 2 **2 :** KARYOKINESIS 1

**mito·some** \ˈmīd·əˌsōm, ˈmid·-\ *n* -S [ISV *mit-* + *-some* (body)] **:** a threadlike cytoplasmic inclusion; *esp* **:** one assumed to be derived from the preceding mitotic spindle that is said to give rise to the middle piece and other parts of a sperm cell

**mi·to·te** \məˈtōd·ē\ *n* -S [Sp, fr. Nahuatl *mitotiqui* dancer] **:** an ancient and modern secular round dance of the Aztecs and other tribes in the Sierra Madre Occidental

**mi·tot·ic** \(ˈ)mīˈtäd·ik, -ätik, -ēk\ *adj* [fr. NL *mitosis*, after such pairs as NL *hypnosis:* E *hypnotic*] **:** of or relating to mitosis **:** KARYOKINETIC — **mi·tot·i·cal·ly** \-ək(ə)lē, -ēk-, -li\ *adv*

**mitotic figure** *n* **:** the spindle-shaped figure presented (as by the chromosomes, asters) during mitosis

**mitotic index** *n* **:** the number of cells per thousand cells actively dividing at a particular time

**mi·tra** \ˈmī·trə\ *n* [NL, fr. L, headband, turban; fr. the shape of the shell — more at MITER] **1** *cap* **:** a genus (the type of the family Mitridae) of chiefly East Indian marine snails having a slender acutely pointed often brightly colored shell **2** -S [NL, fr. L] **a :** GALEA **b :** the thick rounded pileus of various mushroom fungi

**mi·traille** \mē·ˈtrī\ *n* -S [F, fr. MF, old iron, pieces of metal, small coins, change, alter. of OF *mitaille*, fr. *mite* small copper coin — more at MITE (coin)] **1 :** small missiles (as bits of iron grape) for loading cannon **2 :** SMOKED PEARL

**mi·trail·leuse** \ˌmē·trəˈyə(r)z, -ˈyəz\ *n* -S [F, fr. *mitrailler* to fire mitraille, fr. *mitraille*] **1 :** a breech-loading machine gun using small projectiles and consisting of a number of barrels fitted together and so arranged that the barrels can be fired simultaneously or successively and rapidly and first used by the French army in the war of 1870 with Germany **2 :** MACHINE GUN

**mi·tral** \ˈmī·trəl\ *adj* [[1]*miter* + *-al*] **1 :** resembling a miter **2 :** of, relating to, indicating, or adjoining a mitral valve or the mitral orifice

**mitral cell** *n* **:** any of the pyramidal cells of the olfactory bulb about which terminate numerous fibers from the olfactory cells of the nasal mucosa

**mitral commissure** *n* **:** the line of attachment of the mitral valve to the heart wall together with the structures (as muscles and fibers) by which it is secured

**mitral insufficiency** *also* **mitral incompetence** *n* **:** inability of the mitral valve to close perfectly permitting blood to flow back into the auricle and leading to varying degrees of heart failure

**mitral orifice** *n* **:** the left auriculoventricular orifice

**mitral stenosis** *n* **:** a condition usu. the result of disease in which the mitral valve is abnormally narrow

**mitral valve** *n* [trans. of NL *mitralis valvula*] **:** a valve in the heart that guards the opening between the left atrium and the left ventricle, prevents the blood in the ventricle from returning to the atrium, and consists of two triangular flaps attached at their bases to the fibrous ring which surrounds the opening and connected at their margins with the ventricular walls by the chordae tendineae and papillary muscles

**mi·trate** \ˈmī·ˌtrāt\ *adj* [L *mitratus* wearing a turban, turbaned, fr. *mitra* turban + *-atus* -ate — more at MITER] **:** suggestive of a miter or bonnet in shape

**mitre** *var of* MITER

**mit·ri·dae** \ˈmi·trəˌdē\ *n pl, cap* [NL, fr. *Mitra*, type genus + *-idae*] **:** a family of marine snails (suborder Stenoglossa) comprising the miters — see MITRA

**mi·tri·form** \ˈmī·trəˌfȯrm\ *adj* [NL *mitriformis*, fr. L *mitra* turban + *-iformis* -iform] **:** shaped like a bishop's miter

**mits** *pl of* MIT

**mitsch·er·lich·ite** \ˈmichə(r)ləˌkīt\ *n* -S [Eilhardt *Mitscherlich* †1863 Ger. chemist, who first produced it + E *-ite*] **:** a mineral $K_2CuCl_4 . 2H_2O$ consisting of hydrous chloride of copper and potassium

**mitsch·er·lich's law** \ˈmichə(r)(ˌ)liks-\ *n, usu cap M* [after E. *Mitscherlich*] **:** a statement in crystallography and chemistry: isomorphous substances have similar chemical compositions and analogous formulas

**mit·su·ku·ri·na** \ˌmitsəkəˈrīnə, -rēnə\ [NL, fr. Kakichi *Mitsukuri* †1909 Jap. zoologist + NL *-ina*] *syn of* SCAPANORHYNCHUS

**mit·su·ma·ta** \ˌmitsəˈmäd·ə\ *n* -S [Jap, lit., three-pronged fork, fr. *mitsu* three + *mata* forked] **:** a low shrub (*Edgeworthia papyrifera*) of the family Thymelaeaceae of temperate Asia that is cultivated in Japan for its bark used in papermaking

**mitt** *also* **mit** \ˈmit, *usu* -id·+V\ *n* -S [short for *mitten*] **1 a :** a woman's dress glove leaving the fingers uncovered, often extending to or above the elbow, and made of a dressy material (as lace, net, silk) **b :** MITTEN 1 ⟨wearing thick Arctic ~*s*⟩ **c** (1) **:** a baseball catcher's glove with heavy padding and a separate section only for the thumb (2) **:** a first baseman's glove with a padded palm, thumb, and one or two finger sections (3) **:** a protective mitten used in punching bag practice **d :** a device of cloth or similar material shaped (as for household dusting or car washing) to wear over the hand ⟨dust ~⟩ ⟨wash ~⟩ ⟨oven ~⟩ **2** *slang* **:** HAND ⟨dinner pail in his hardened ~ —Sinclair Lewis⟩

mitt 1a

**mit·tel·hand** \ˈmid·ᵊlˌhänt\ *n* [G, lit., middle hand, fr. *mittel* middle + *hand*] **:** MIDDLEHAND

**mit·tel·schmerz** \-ˌshmerts\ *n* -ES *sometimes cap* [G, lit., middle pain, fr. *mittel* middle + *schmerz* pain] **:** pain occurring between the menstrual periods and usu. considered to be associated with ovulation

**mit·ten** \ˈmitᵊn\ *n* -S [ME *mitain*, *mitein*, fr. MF *mitaine*, fr. OF, fr. *mite*] **1 :** a covering for the hand and wrist having a separate section for the thumb only and made in various designs and materials for warmth and protection — distinguished from *glove* **2** *chiefly Scot* **:** a thick worsted glove **3 :** MITT 1a **4** *slang* **:** REFUSAL, REJECTION, DISMISSAL; *esp* **:** the jilting of a suitor — usu. used in the phrases *get the mitten, give* (*someone*) *the mitten, send* (*someone*) *the mitten* **5** *slang* **:** BOXING GLOVE — usu. used in pl.

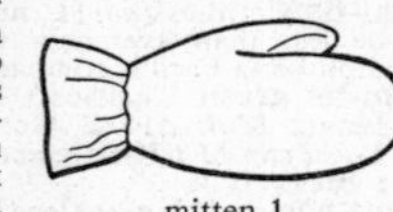

mitten 1

**mit·ti·mus** \ˈmid·əməs\ *n* -ES [L, we send, 1st pers. pl. pres. indic. of *mittere* to send — more at SMITE] **1 a :** a writ formerly used in England for directing the trial of a cause in a county palatine **b :** a warrant of commitment to prison **c :** a writ for removing records from one court to another **2** *Brit* **:** DISCHARGE, DISMISSAL **3** *Brit* **:** MAGISTRATE

**mit·tle** \ˈmitᵊl\ *vt* -ED/-ING/-S [perh. fr. F *mutiler*, fr. MF, fr. L *mutilare* — more at MUTILATE] *Scot* **:** MUTILATE, HURT

**mit·tler's green** \ˈmitlə(r)z-\ *n* [prob. part trans. of G *mittlers grün*, fr. *mittlers* (prob. fr. the name *Mittler*) + *grün* green] **1** *usu cap M* **:** Guignet's green often mixed with barium sulfate **2** *often cap M* **:** GUIGNET'S GREEN 2

**mi·tu** \ˈmēd·(ˌ)ü\ *n* [AmerSp (Argentina) *mitú*, fr. Guarani] **1** -S *archaic* **:** an unidentifiable but prob. gallinaceous Brazilian bird **2** [NL, fr. AmerSp *mitú*] **a** *cap* **:** a genus of curassows **b** -S **:** any curassow of the genus *Mitu*

**mi·tua** \ˈmichəwə\ [NL, fr. *Mitu*] *syn of* MITU

**mity** \ˈmīd·ē, -ītē\ *adj* -ER/-EST [[1]*mite* + *-y*] **:** infested with mites

**mitz·vah** *also* **mits·vah** \ˈmitsvə, -(ˌ)vä\ *n, pl* **mitz·voth** *or* **mitz·vot** \-ˌvōt(h), -ōs\ *or* **mitz·vahs** \-ˌvəz, -(ˌ)väz\ *also* **mits·voth** *or* **mits·vot** \-ˌvōt(h), -ōs\ *or* **mits·vahs** [Heb *miṣwāh* commandment] **1** *Jewish relig* **:** a biblical or rabbinic commandment **2** *Jewish relig* **:** a meritorious performance (as of a religious or civic duty or a humanitarian or charitable act) **:** a good deed **3 :** a privilege of assisting in the ritual in a synagogue

**mi·u·rus** \mīˈyu̇rəs\ *n* -ES [LL, adj., being a miurus, fr. Gk *meiouros*, lit., tapering, prob. alter. of *myouros*, fr. *my-* + *-ouros* -urous] **:** a dactylic hexameter having its last foot an iamb or pyrrhic instead of a spondee or trochee — compare DOLICHURUS

**mi·wok** \ˈmēˌwäk\ *n, pl* **miwok** *or* **miwoks** *usu cap* [Miwok, people] **1 a :** an Indian people of central California **b :** a member of such people **2 :** a Moquelumnan language of the Miwok people **3 :** MOQUELUMNAN

[1]**mix** \ˈmiks\ *vb* **mixed** *also* **mixt** \ˈmikst\ **mixed** *also* **mixt; mixing; mixes** [ME *mixen*, fr. *mixte*, adj., mixed, fr. MF, fr. L *mixtus*, past part. of *miscēre* to mix; akin to Gk *misgein*, *mignynai*, *meignynai* to mix, Skt *miśra* mixed, OIr *mescaim* I mix] *vt* **1 a :** to stir, shake, or otherwise bring together (different substances) with a loss of separateness or identity **:** cause to be scattered or diffused throughout **:** combine (as the ingredients of smokeless powder) in one mass **:** intermingle thoroughly ⟨~ the flour with a little water⟩ ⟨~ the ingredients to a thick paste⟩ ⟨~ sand, clay, and humus⟩ ⟨~ colors to get the right shade⟩ **:** put as an ingredient ⟨~ an egg into the batter⟩ **:** combine with or introduce into a mass already formed **:** put in disorder **:** JUMBLE ⟨~ the slips well in the hat and draw one⟩ **b :** to bring together (as different kinds of people or things) in close association ⟨a party that ~*ed* people of all ages and interests⟩ ⟨~ business with pleasure⟩ ⟨charter granting was ~*ed* with politics —J.D.Magee⟩ ⟨told in a style that ~*es* erudition and bawdiness —*Saturday Rev.*⟩ **2 :** to prepare or form by mixing different components ⟨~ a drink at the bar⟩ ⟨the principals of integrated schools have been making conscious efforts . . . to ~ their classes —Walter Goodman⟩ **3 :** CONFUSE ⟨~*ed* his dates and arrived a week late⟩ ~ *vi* **1 a :** to become mixed **:** enter into combination **:** be capable of mixing ⟨a medicine which will ~ with water⟩ ⟨manual and intellectual labor seldom ~ well —H.S.Canby⟩ **b :** to be compatible — usu. used in negative constructions ⟨insecticides and geese won't ~ —*Springfield* (*Mass.*) *Daily News*⟩ **2 :** to enter into relations **:** ASSOCIATE ⟨on the streets three classes mingle but do not ~ —*Amer. Guide Series: Texas*⟩ ⟨learned to ~ with sons of lawyers, doctors, manufacturers —D.W.Brogan⟩ **3 :** CROSSBREED **4 a :** to enter as a participant ⟨a high-priced lawyer . . . ~*ing* into a case like this —Erle Stanley Gardner⟩ sometimes in an interfering manner ⟨the political crowd ~*ed* in and took over —*Springfield* (*Mass.*) *Union*⟩ **:** become involved **:** take part ⟨not in keeping with his position as a judge to ~ in politics —*Amer. Guide Series: Nev.*⟩ **b :** to become involved in a struggle or fight **:** TANGLE ⟨hesitated to ~ with someone bigger than he was⟩

**syn** MINGLE, COMMINGLE, BLEND, MERGE, COALESCE, AMALGAMATE, FUSE: MIX, MINGLE, and COMMINGLE usu. describe activities with little or no specific direction, often arising from chance or spontaneous inclination, whereas MERGE and COALESCE frequently suggest the working of time or natural force, and BLEND, AMALGAMATE, and FUSE often imply a conscious endeavor toward unity. MIX is the most general term; it usu. applies to elements which, though different, are capable of forming a stable and homogeneous product; sometimes MIX implies a loss of identity in the elements ⟨to *mix* colors in painting⟩, but more often the elements are distinguishable in the combination ⟨to *mix* pepper and salt⟩ ⟨to *mix* a drink⟩ ⟨a building of *mixed* architectural styles⟩ MINGLE implies that the elements are distinguishable both before and after combining; the combination is looser and the interpenetration less thorough than with MIX ⟨a *mixed* marriage⟩ ⟨*mixed* company⟩ but ⟨*mingled* sensations⟩ ⟨*mingled* emotions⟩ ⟨a street displaying *mingled* architectural styles⟩ COMMINGLE is almost interchangeable with MINGLE, but somewhat more intensive ⟨he has brains, wit, humanity, and a delicate acerbity *commingled* with a robust and refreshing ribaldry —*Times Lit. Supp.*⟩ BLEND implies a mixing of like or harmonious things in an intimate union which partakes of the qualities of each of its components, while absorbing their individualities ⟨various kinds of coffee may be *blended*, but coffee is *mixed* with chicory⟩ ⟨kinship with the land . . . she knew that this transfigured instinct was *blended* of pity, memory, and passion —Ellen Glasgow⟩ MERGE emphasizes still more the loss of the constituents in the whole, or the complete absorption of one element into another ⟨still had doubts as to the morality of his procedure, but . . . these doubts would soon be *merged* in . . . admiration of the tactical advantages of his approach —Louis Auchincloss⟩ COALESCE suggests a natural and gradual growing of kindred things into an organic whole ⟨the lips of a wound *coalesce*⟩ ⟨the small white clouds of early morning had swollen and *coalesced* —Osbert Lancaster⟩ ⟨touch and smell and sight and hearing come together and *coalesce* in the commonsense notion of an object —Bertrand Russell⟩ AMALGAMATE implies a union by assimilation, adaptation, or integration without complete loss of individual identity ⟨immigrants of various nationalities are constantly being *amalgamated* with the native American population⟩ ⟨thesis and plot are carefully *amalgamated* —F.B. Millet⟩ FUSE, more than any of the foregoing, stresses the oneness and indissolubility of the resulting product; yet each component plays a necessary and observable part in the whole ⟨one is conscious of the intellectuality and compacted thought which he *fuses* in emotional expression —H.O.Taylor⟩ ⟨in our daily lives we *fuse* our identities as Jew, as American, and as Israeli —Carl Alpert⟩ ⟨what I have done is to *fuse* together in this book all my ideas past and present on freedom of speech —Zechariah Chafee⟩

— **mix it** *or* **mix it up** *slang* **:** to engage in a fight **:** exchange blows aggressively ⟨the two boxers stopped stalling and *mixed it up*⟩ ⟨battle groups were *mixing it* with German tanks — Russell Hill⟩ ⟨hate to see the day when men were afraid to *mix it up* for pretty girls —J.A.Michener⟩

[2]**mix** \"\ *n* -ES **1 :** an act or process of mixing ⟨arming themselves for a big ~⟩ **2 :** a product of mixing **:** MIXTURE: as **a :** a commercially prepared mixture of dry ingredients for a food usu. requiring the addition of only water or sometimes eggs and cooking or baking ⟨roll ~⟩ ⟨soup ~⟩ ⟨cake made from a packaged ~⟩ ⟨an instant pudding ~ that needs only milk and mixing⟩ **b :** a mixture of materials to form a concrete, mortar, or asphaltic batch **c :** MIXTURE 2d **3 :** a state of confusion ⟨so tired he was in a ~⟩ **4 :** the ratio of different constituents going into a product; *specif* **:** an often empirical formula giving the proportions and constituents of a mixture (as of scrap, charcoal, ferroalloy) for making steel **5 :** DISSOLVE

**mix·a·bil·i·ty** \ˌmiksəˈbiləd·ē, -ətē, -i\ *n* **:** the quality or state of being mixable

**mix·able** *also* **mix·ible** \ˈmiksəbəl\ *adj* [[1]*mix* + *-able* or *-ible*] **:** capable of being mixed **:** MISCIBLE — **mix·able·ness** *n* -ES

**mixblood** \ˈ=ˌ=\ *n* [by alter.] **:** MIXED-BLOOD

**mix-crystal** \ˈ=ˌ==\ *or* **mixed crystal** *n* [*mix-crystal*, alter. of *mixed crystal*, trans. of G *mischkristall*, fr. *mischen* to mix + *kristall* crystal] **:** SOLID SOLUTION

**mi·xe** \ˈmēˌhā\ *n, pl* **mixe** *or* **mixes** *usu cap* [AmerSp, fr. Mixe, lit., people of the clouds] **1 a :** a Zoquean people of Oaxaca, Veracruz, and Chiapas, Mexico **b :** a member of such people **2 :** the language of the Mixe people

**mixed** \ˈmikst\ *adj* [alter. (influenced by *mixed*, past part. of [1]*mix*) of ME *mixte* — more at MIX] **1 :** combining the characteristics of more than one kind or class **:** not conforming to a single type ⟨~ grain in lumber⟩ ⟨a horse with a ~ gait⟩: as **a :** having the legal attributes of two or more classes ⟨a personal, real, or ~ action⟩ **b :** uniting features of two or more of the recognized systems of government (as aristocracy, democracy, monarchy) ⟨gave to ~ government the form of a system of checks and balances —G.H.Sabine⟩ ⟨a ~ state⟩ ⟨a ~ constitution, in which King, Lords, and Commons all played their historical part —Ernest Barker⟩ **c :** combining features or exhibiting symptoms of more than one condition or disease ⟨a ~ tumor⟩ **d** *of a hand* **:** having the fingers and palm of more than one type and usu. held by palmists to indicate versatility and ease of comprehension and creativity often combined with erratic behavior and a lack of concentration — compare CONIC, PHILOSOPHIC, PSYCHIC, SPATULATE, SQUARE **e** *of an inflorescence* **:** combining racemose and cymose formations ⟨the ~ thyrsus of the lilac⟩ **f :** involving joint ownership by both government and private individuals or business organizations ⟨a ~ corporation⟩ **g :** of or constituting a life-insurance company having a paid-up capital in addition to its accumulated assets and awarding a small portion of its profits to the proprietors or shareholders and the remainder to the assured (as in the mutual plan) ⟨the ~ plan⟩ ⟨a ~ company⟩ **h** *of a chemical compound* **:** characterized by different groups, radicals, or ions of similar type ⟨~ glycerides⟩ — opposed to *simple* **2 :** made up of or involving individuals or items of more than one kind ⟨a ~ carload⟩ ⟨a highway open to ~ traffic⟩ ⟨a ~ repertory of music old and new —Virgil Thomson⟩ ⟨go to town in fatigues, ~ uniforms and practically anything we want —Glen Carlsen⟩: as **a** (1) **:** made up of or involving persons differing in race, national origin, religion, or class ⟨a ~ trade union with Negroes and whites in the same local⟩ ⟨the ~ group of Alsatians, French, Swiss, Germans . . . who founded and developed the community —*Amer. Guide Series: Texas*⟩ ⟨the religion of children in ~ households⟩ (2) **:** including persons of dubious social status or moral character **:** not select ⟨admit that the early Christians were a very ~ lot —G.B.Shaw⟩ (3) **:** made up of representatives of both sides (as of a matter in dispute) and often one or more neutral members ⟨settle their frontier disputes by means of ~ frontier commissions —*UN Dept. of Public Information*⟩ — compare JOINT (4) **:** constituted by native and foreign judges for the administration of justice between persons of different nationalities ⟨the jurisdiction of the ~ courts extends over all civil cases between Europeans and Egyptians —Evelyn Baring⟩ ⟨set up a ~ tribunal for the suppression of the slave trade —R.E.Crist⟩ **b** (1) **:** made up of or involving individuals of both sexes ⟨a story considered unfit for ~ company⟩ ⟨~ socials⟩ ⟨the couple who sang soprano and bass in the ~ quartet⟩ ⟨a contract bridge contest for ~ pairs⟩ (2) **:** of both men and women performing in combination ⟨a work for ~ voices sung by the men's and women's glee clubs⟩ ⟨a ~ chorus⟩ **c** *of a stable natural community* **:** containing two or more kinds of organism in abundance ⟨a ~ prairie including both short grasses and midgrasses⟩ **d** *of a canasta* **:** containing one or more wild cards **3 a :** including or accompanied by inconsistent or incompatible elements ⟨considered technical advance a ~ blessing⟩ ⟨got a ~ reaction from the family⟩ — often used with plural nouns ⟨acted from ~ motives when money was involved⟩ ⟨~ feelings toward a writer close to him in expression but alien in temperament —Irving Howe⟩ ⟨~ reviews, ranging from "a sound musical drama" to "a very tasteless and pointless production" —*Current Biog.*⟩ **b** *of a market* **:** characterized by price movements in both directions **:** IRREGULAR ⟨the bond market was ~⟩ **4 :** that derives from two or more recognized races or breeds ⟨a person of ~ blood⟩ ⟨a dog of ~ breed⟩

**mixed account** *n* **:** an account that combines the features of a real account and a nominal account (as in showing a trial balance representing both supplies used and supplies on hand)

**mixed acid** *n* **:** a mixture of acids; *esp* **:** a mixture of nitric acid and sulfuric acid used in nitration

**mixed alphabet** *n* **:** an alphabet that has been rearranged or disordered either systematically or at random

**mixed arch** *n* **:** an architectural arch that is struck from several centers

**mixed bag** *n* **:** a miscellaneous collection **:** ASSORTMENT ⟨a *mixed bag* of stocks and bonds⟩ ⟨a prissy individual . . . and a *mixed bag* of other characters —John McCarten⟩

**mixed-blood** \ˈ=ˌ=\ *n* **:** a person whose ancestors belonged to two or more races — compare PUREBLOOD

**mixed bud** *n* **:** a bud (as of an apple, pear, or blackberry) that produces a branch and leaves as well as flowers — compare FLOWER BUD, LEAF BUD, SIMPLE BUD

**mixed chalice** *n* **:** the practice traditional in nearly all ancient Christian rites of adding a few drops of water to the wine in the eucharistic chalice — compare KRASIS

**mixed cropping** *n* **:** the growing of two crops (as corn and soybeans) intermingled together in the same field

**mixed decimal** *n* **:** a mixed number whose fractional part is a decimal fraction (as in 7.238)

**mixed doubles** *n pl* **:** a doubles contest (as in tennis) in which each team is composed of a male and a female player

**mixed drink** *n* **:** an alcoholic beverage prepared from a recipe calling for two or more ingredients stirred or shaken before serving

**mixed economy** *n* **:** an economy in which both publicly and privately owned enterprises operate simultaneously

**mixed ether** *n* **:** an ether (as methyl ethyl ether $CH_3OC_2H_5$) in which the radicals united to oxygen are different

**mixed farming** *n* **:** the growing of food or cash crops, feed crops, and livestock on the same farm ⟨planned to do *mixed farming*, keep a cow, enjoy the black duck —E.A.Weeks⟩ — compare SUBSISTENCE FARMING

**mixed feed** *n* **:** a feed for livestock that consists of a mixture of wheat particles, bran, middlings, shorts, and other material in various proportions and is a by-product of flour milling

**mixed-flow** \(ˈ)=ˈ=\ *adj* [[1]*mixed* + *flow* (n.)] **:** combining or utilizing in succession two or more different types of flow (as axial and radial) — used esp. of turbines and pumps

**mixed forest** *n* **:** a forest with two or more predominant kinds of trees and with at least 20 percent of the stand consisting of other than the most common tree

**mixed foursome** *n* **:** a foursome in which each side consists of a man and a woman

**mixed franking** *n* **:** a franking on a postal cover including stamps of more than one country

**mixed gland** *n* **:** a gland producing more than one kind of secretion; *esp* **:** a mucoserous gland

**mixed grill** *n* **:** several broiled meats and vegetables (as a lamb chop, kidney, bacon, mushroom, and tomato) served on one plate

**mixed larceny** *n* **1 :** a larceny that includes the aggravation of a taking from another's house or person with or without violence and putting that other in fear — compare ROBBERY **2 :** a larceny deemed to be aggravated under circumstances set out in a statute

**mixed·ly** \ˈmiksədlē, -kstlē, -li\ *adv* **:** in a mixed manner ⟨annuals and perennials growing ~ in the bed⟩ ⟨reacted ~ to his going⟩

**mixed marriage** *n* **:** a marriage between persons of different races or religions

**mixed melting point** *n* [[1]*mixed* + *melting point*] **:** the fusion temperature of a mixture of two components that in the case of two different substances is usu. lower than that of either component or that in the case of a mixture of two samples of the same substance prepared by different methods as a check on their identity is not lower than that of either sample

**mixed metaphor** *n* **:** a figure of speech combining two or more inconsistent or incongruous metaphors (as in Shakespeare's "to take arms against a sea of troubles")

**mixed mode** *n* **1 :** an ecclesiastical mode whose ambitus extends through the combined range of an authentic and its related plagal mode **2** *Lockeanism* **:** a mode (as beauty) resulting from the combination of simple ideas of different kinds — contrasted with *simple mode*
**mixed nerve** *n* **:** a nerve containing both sensory and motor fibers
**mixed·ness** \'miksədnəs, -ks(t)n-\ *n* -ES **:** the quality or state of being mixed
**mixed nuisance** *n* **:** a public nuisance that also causes harm or annoyance to a person in the exercise of his private rights as distinct from those common to the public generally
**mixed number** *n* **:** a number that is composed of an integer and a proper fraction and is their sum ⟨5⅔ is a *mixed number*⟩
**mixed planting** *n* **:** a combination of woody and herbaceous plants
**mixed proportion** *n* **:** proportion by addition and subtraction
**mixed salt** *n* **:** a salt (as a double salt) derived from more than one base or more than one acid
**mixed tithe** *n* **:** a tithe arising from animals nourished by the immediate products of the soil (as wool, milk or cheese, or honey and wax) — compare PERSONAL TITHE, PRAEDIAL TITHE
**mixed train** *n* **:** a train made up of both passenger cars and freight cars and used mainly on branch lines
**mixed–up** \(')=¦=\ *adj* [fr. *mixed up*, past part. of *mix up*] **:** marked by bewilderment, perplexity, or disorder **:** CONFUSED ⟨a *mixed-up* character ripe for the analyst —Lucy Crockett⟩ ⟨is only one reflective part of a *mixed-up* age —Norman Cousins⟩
**mix·en** \'miksən\ *n* -S [ME, fr. OE, dung, dunghill; akin to OE *meox* dung, filth, *mīgan* to urinate, MD *mist, mest* dung, OS & OHG *mist* dung, ON *mīga* to urinate, Goth *maihstus* dung, L *mingere, meiere* to urinate, Gk *omichein, omeichein* to urinate, Skt *mehati* he urinates] *dial chiefly Eng* **:** a pile of dung or refuse **:** a manure heap
**mix·er** \'miksə(r)\ *n* -S [¹*mix* + *-er*] **1 :** one that mixes: **a** (1) **:** one whose work is weighing or measuring and mixing the ingredients of a product (as paint, a drug, bread, pottery, cement, glass, fertilizer) (2) **:** one who balances and controls the dialogue, music, and sound effects to be recorded for or with a motion picture or television **b :** a container, device, or machine for mixing: as (1) **:** a valve or burner in which fuel is mixed with air for combustion (2) **:** a storage tank from which molten pig iron drawn from blast furnaces can be transferred to an open-hearth or electric furnace or a converter (3) **:** any of various types of stationary or portable equipment (as an agitator, emulsifier, homogenizer, or pug mill) used for mixing gases, liquids, or solids in industry or in the laboratory (4) **:** an electrical circuit in a sound-recording or broadcasting system for combining the signals from several sources (as microphones, turntables, or wire lines) in any desired proportion (5) **:** MIXING FAUCET (6) **:** MIXING VALVE (7) **:** a stationary or portable kitchen utensil equipped with one or more beaters for mixing, beating, creaming, or whipping a variety of foods (as batters, cream, whites of eggs, boiled potatoes) ⟨electric ~⟩ (8) **:** a revolving drum with paddles attached for mixing concrete and mortar or a hopper with revolving paddles for mixing asphaltic concretes (9) **:** a composing or photocomposing machine in which matrices from more than one magazine can be automatically keyboarded into a single line **c :** a game, stunt, or dance used at a get-together to give members of the group an opportunity to meet one another in a friendly, informal atmosphere — called also *icebreaker* **2 :** one that mixes with others or in combinations: as **a** (1) **:** a person considered as to his casual sociability ⟨was shy and a poor ~⟩ (2) **:** a person marked by easy sociability ⟨the genial extroversion of the salesman, the . . . good ~ —Aldous Huxley⟩ **b :** a nonalcoholic beverage (as ginger ale) used to thin a mixed drink

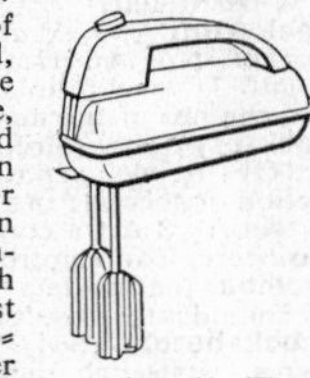
mixer 1b (7)

**mixer tube** *n* **:** an electron tube used for heterodyne operation
**mixes** *pres 3d sing of* MIX, *pl of* MIX
**mix–hellene** \'=¦=,=\ *n, usu cap H* [Gk *mixellēn*, fr. *mix-* mixed (fr. *mixis* act of mixing) + *Hellēn* Hellene] **:** a person of mixed Hellenic and barbarian descent
**mix·hill** \'miks+,-\ *n* [ME *mix* dung, filth (fr. OE *meox*) + E *hill* — more at MIXEN] *dial Eng* **:** MIXEN
**mixible** *var of* MIXABLE
**mixing** *n* -S [fr. gerund of ¹*mix*] **:** the process of operating a mixer in sound recording or broadcasting
**mixing faucet** *n* **:** a faucet that mixes hot and cold water as they pass through the spout in proportions controlled by separate handles
**mixing valve** *n* **:** a device composed of a chamber with a sliding valve controlled often thermostatically by a handle and used to regulate water temperature in a shower or tub
**mix·is** \'miksəs\ *n* -ES [Gk, act of mixing, fr. *mignynai* to mix — more at MIX] **:** the state characteristic of those organisms in which fertilization and related processes result in the existence of well-marked, alternating, diploid and haploid phases — compare APOMIXIS
**-mix·is** \'miksəs\ *n comb form, pl* **-mixes** [NL *-mixis*, fr. Gk, act of mingling, act of mixing, fr. *mixis*] **:** an intermingling in reproduction ⟨apo*mixis*⟩ ⟨endo*mixis*⟩ ⟨pseudo*mixis*⟩ ⟨parthenomixis⟩ — compare -GAMY
**mix·ite** \'mik,sīt\ *n* -S [G *mixit*, fr. A. *Mixa*, 19th cent. Czech mine inspector + G *-it* -ite] **:** a mineral $Cu_{11}Bi(AsO_4)_5(OH)_{10}.6H_2O$ consisting of green to whitish hydrous basic copper bismuth arsenate
**mixo-** *comb form* [Gk, fr. *mixis* act of mingling or mixing] **1 :** mixed ⟨*mixo*trophic⟩ ⟨*mixo*chimaera⟩ **2 :** mixture of isomers of (a specified compound) ⟨*mixo*octane⟩ — compare ISO-
**mixo·biosis** \,miksō+\ *n, pl* **mixobioses** [NL, fr. *mixo-* + *-biosis*] **:** a form of mutualism in which organisms (as ants) of different species live together in composite colonies
**mixo·biotic** \¦==+\ *adj* [fr. NL *mixobiosis*, after such pairs as NL *hypnosis*: E *hypnotic*] **:** of, relating to, or living in mixobiosis
**mixo·chromosome** \¦==+\ *n* [*mixo-* + *chromosome*] **:** a chromosome supposed to be formed by the fusion of all or part of two or more chromosomes
**mixo·dec·tes** \,==ˈdek,tēz\ *n, cap* [NL, fr. *mixo-* + *-dectes*] **:** a genus (the type of the family Mixodectidae) of extinct insectivores having very large incisors from the lower Eocene of the U.S.
**mixo·gram** \'miksə,gram\ *n* [*mixo-* + *-gram*] **:** a graphic record of flour mixes from various wheats as related to the qualities of resultant dough mixes
**mixo·graph** \-,graf\ *n* [*mixo-* + *-graph*] **:** a graphic chart that provides supplementary baking data on dough mixes from various wheats
**mix·ol·o·gist** \mik'säləjəst\ *n* -S [¹*mix* + *-ologist* (as in *psychologist*)] **:** a bartender skilled in preparing mixed drinks
**mix·ol·o·gy** \-jē, -ji\ *n* -ES [*mixologist* + *-y*] **:** the art or skill of preparing mixed drinks
**mixo·lyd·i·an mode** \¦miksə¦lidēən-\ *n* [*mixolydian* fr. Gk *mixolydios* mixolydian (fr. *mixo-* + *lydios* Lydian) + E *-an*; *mixolydian mode* trans. of Gk *mixolydios harmonia*] **1 :** a Greek mode consisting of two disjunct tetrachords represented on the white keys of the piano by a descending diatonic scale from B to B — see GREEK MODE illustration **2 :** an authentic ecclesiastical mode consisting of a pentachord and an upper conjunct tetrachord represented on the white keys of the piano by an ascending diatonic scale from G to G — see MODE illustration
**mixo·ploid** \'miksə,plȯid\ *n* -S [ISV *mixo-* + *-ploid*; prob. orig. formed in G] **:** an organism having different numbers of genomes in different cells **:** CHIMERA — **mixo·ploi·dy** \-,plȯidē\ *n* -ES
**mixo·sau·rus** \,miksə'sȯrəs\ *n, cap* [NL, fr. *mixo-* + *-saurus*] **:** a genus of reptiles of Triassic age similar to *Ichthyosaurus* but with less fully developed paddles
**mixo·troph·ic** \¦miksə¦träfik, -trōf-\ *adj* [*mixo-* + *-trophic*] **:** deriving nourishment from both autotrophic and heterotrophic mechanisms — used esp. of symbionts and partial parasites

**mixt** \'mikst\ *n* -S [ML *mixtum* motley, mixed material, fr. L, neut. of *mixtus*, past part. of *miscēre* to mix — more at MIX] *archaic* **:** COMPOUND 2a
**mix·tec** \'mē,stek\ *or* **mix·te·co** \mē'stā(,)kō, -te(-\ *also* **mix·te·ca** \-,kə\ *n, pl* **mixtec** *or* **mixtecs** *or* **mixteco** *or* **mixtecos** *usu cap* [AmerSp *mixteca, mixteco*, of AmerInd origin] **1 a :** a people of the states of Oaxaca, Guerrero, and Puebla, Mexico, speaking languages of the Mixtecan family **b :** a member of such people **2 :** the language of the Mixtec people
**mix·te·can** \(')mē¦stākən, -tek-\ *n* -S *usu cap* **:** a language family of the states of Oaxaca, Guerrero, and Puebla, Mexico, including Amusgo, Cuicatec, and Mixtec
¹**mix·tie–max·tie** *or* **mix·ty–max·ty** \¦mikstē¦makstē, -ti\ *adj* [alter. & redupl. of *mixt*, obs. var. of ¹*mixed*] *chiefly Scot* **:** jumbled together **:** CONFUSED
²**mixtie–maxtie** *or* **mixty–maxty** \"\ *also* **mix·ter–max·ter** \'mikstər¦makstər\ *n* [*mixter-maxter*, alter. of *mixtie-maxtie*] *chiefly Scot* **:** a heterogeneous mixture
**mixtion** *n* -S [ME *mixcioun*, fr. MF or L; MF *mixtion*, fr. OF *mistion*, fr. L *mixtion-, mixtio, mistion-, mistio* act or process of mixing, fr. *mixtus, mistus* (past part.) + *-ion-, -io* -ion] **1** *obs* **:** the state of being mixed **2** *obs* **:** the process of mixing **3** *obs* **:** a product of mixing
**mix·ture** \'miksche(r)\ *n* -S [MF, fr. OF *misture*, fr. L *mixtura, mistura*, fr. *mixtus, mistus* (past part. of *miscēre* to mix) + *-ura* -ure — more at MIX] **1 a :** an act, process, or instance of mixing ⟨a gradual ~ of languages⟩ ⟨a paste made by the ~ of flour and water⟩ ⟨one of those slight ~*s* in the stock which . . . provides a variant —Lucien Price⟩ **b** (1) **:** the state of being mixed (2) **:** the relative proportions of constituents **:** PROPORTION, RATIO ⟨youngsters do go through phases but with varied timing and in varied ~*s* —Dorothy Barclay⟩; *specif* **:** the fuel-to-air proportions of the charge produced in the carburetor for combustion in an engine or turbine **2** [ME, fr. L *mixtura, mistura* (also, act of mixing)] **:** a product of mixing **:** COMBINATION ⟨beat milk into the dry ingredients until the ~ thickens⟩ ⟨the interior . . . is a ~ of forest and grassland —P.E.James⟩ ⟨a unique ~ of sentimentality and toughness —J.A.Morris b.1904⟩: as **a :** a portion of matter consisting of two or more components that do not bear a fixed proportion to one another and that however thoroughly commingled are regarded as retaining a separate existence — usu. distinguished from *complex* and *compound*; compare ALLOY, MECHANICAL MIXTURE, SOLID SOLUTION, SYSTEM 8 **b :** an aqueous liquid medicine **:** POTION; *specif* **:** a preparation in which insoluble substances are suspended in watery fluids by the addition of a viscid material (as gum, sugar, glycerol) **c :** a combination of several different kinds of some article of consumption (as tea or tobacco) ⟨a smoking ~⟩ **d** (1) **:** a yarn spun from two or more fibers or from a fiber dyed two or more colors (2) **:** a fabric made from such yarn or woven with different yarns in the warp and the weft **e :** a batch or packet of postage stamps sold by weight and usu. comprising stamps gathered by a nonphilatelic agency (as a bank, a government bureau, or a missionary society) — compare KILOWARE
**mixture stop** *also* **mixture** \"\ *n* -S **:** a pipe-organ stop having more than one pipe for each digital — compare PARTIAL STOP
**mix up** *vt* **:** CONFUSE ⟨an explanation that *mixed* me *up* even more⟩ ⟨*mixed up* two similar words⟩
**mix–up** \'=,=\ *n* -S [*mix up*] **1 :** a state or instance of confusion ⟨further the *mix-up* in terminology we have been attempting to correct —Thomas Munro⟩ ⟨sent to the wrong base through a *mix-up* in orders⟩ **2 :** MIXTURE ⟨such a general *mix-up* that our most distinctive . . . endowments disappear —Norman Goodall⟩ ⟨the man is a *mix-up* of cheerful schoolboy and devout elder —Paul Holt⟩ **3 :** MELEE
**mi·ya·ga·wa·nel·la** \,mēyə,gäwə'nelə\ *n, cap* [NL, fr. Yoneji *Miyagawa* b1885 Jap. bacteriologist + connective *-n-* + NL *-ella*] **:** a genus of coccoid to spherical microorganisms (family Chlamydiaceae) usu. placed among the rickettsias and including a number of important parasites (as *M. lymphogranulomatis*, the cause of venereal lymphogranuloma, and *M. psittaci*, the cause of psittacosis)
**miz·maze** \'miz,māz\ *n* [redupl. and alter. of ¹*maze*] **1 :** MAZE ⟨the way lies through . . . an intricate ~ of tracks —S.P.B. Mais⟩ **2** *dial Eng* **:** a state of confusion or bewilderment **:** WHIRL ⟨so surprised he was all of a ~⟩
**miz·pah** \'mizpə\ *adj* [*Mizpah*, place in ancient Palestine where Jacob and Laban erected a heap of stones as a sign of covenant between them (Gen 31:44–49), fr. Heb *Miṣpah*] **:** worn (as by lovers) to signify remembrance ⟨a ~ ring⟩ ⟨~ half coins⟩
**miz·rach** *also* **miz·rah** \'miz,räk\ *n* -S [NHeb *mizrāḥ*, fr. Heb, east, place of sunrise, fr. *zāraḥ* to rise, come forth] **1 :** an ornamental or sacred picture hung on the east wall of a house or synagogue in the direction of Jerusalem toward which Jews face when in prayer **2 :** the eastern wall of a synagogue
**miz·ra·chi** *also* **miz·ra·hi** \miz'räkē\ *adj, usu cap* [*Mizrachi*, movement in Zionism founded in 1902, fr. Heb *Mizrāḥī*, lit., of the east, fr. *mizrāḥ* east] **:** of or relating to a movement in Zionism supported by strictly orthodox Jews
¹**miz·zen** *or* **miz·en** \'miz°n\ *n* -S [ME *mesein, meson*, prob. fr. MF *misaine*, alter. (influenced by OIt *mezzana*) of *migenne*, fr. OCatal *mitjana*; OIt *mezzana* & OCatal *mitjana*, fr. Ar *mazzān* mast] **1 :** a fore-and-aft sail set on the mizzenmast — see SAIL illustration **2 :** MIZZENMAST **3 :** the aftermast and sail of a yawl
²**mizzen** *or* **mizen** \"\ *adj* [ME *meson*, fr. *meson*, n.] **:** of or relating to the mizzenmast ⟨~ shrouds⟩ ⟨the ~ peak halyards⟩
**miz·zen·mast** \-,mast, -,maa(ə)st, -,maist,-,måst, -,məst\ *n* [ME *meson mast*, fr. *meson* (n.) + *mast*] **:** the mast aft or next aft of the mainmast in a ship — see SHIP illustration
¹**miz·zle** \'mizəl\ *vi* **mizzled; mizzled; mizzling** \-z(ə)liŋ\ **mizzles** [ME *misellen*; akin to D dial. *miezelen* to drizzle, MD *misel* mist, dew, drizzle, Flem *mijzelen, mizzelen* to drizzle, LG *mis* foggy weather, MD *mist, mest* mist, fog — more at MIST] *chiefly dial* **:** to rain in very fine drops
²**mizzle** \"\ *n* -S [fr. earlier *mysell, misle*, prob. fr. MD *misel*] *chiefly dial* **:** a fine rain **:** DRIZZLE
³**mizzle** \"\ *vt* -ED/-ING/-S [origin unknown] *chiefly dial* **:** CONFUSE, MUDDLE, MISINFORM
⁴**mizzle** \"\ *vi* -ED/-ING/-S [origin unknown] *slang chiefly Brit* **:** to take oneself off **:** disappear suddenly **:** slink away **:** DECAMP ⟨gone an' *mizzled* to the war —C.J.Dennis⟩
⁵**mizzle** \"\ *vt* -ED/-ING/-S [perh. alter. of obs. E *measle* to cover with or as if with measles, fr. *measle*, sing. of *measles*] *Scot* **:** to make spotted **:** SPECKLE
**miz·zly** \'miz(ə)lē, -li\ *adj* [¹*mizzle* + *-y*] *chiefly dial* **:** characterized by or consisting of mizzle
**miz·zo·nite** \'miz°n,īt\ *n* -S [G *mizzonit*, fr. Gk *meizōn* greater + G *-it* -ite] **:** a mineral of the scapolite group intermediate between meionite and marialite and containing 54 to 57 percent of silica; *specif* **:** a volcanic mizzonite occurring in clear crystals
**mk** *abbr* **1** mark **2** markka
**mkd** *abbr* marked
**mkm** *abbr* marksman
**MKS** *abbr, usu not cap* meter-kilogram-second
**mkt** *abbr* market
**ml** *abbr* **1** mail **2** milliliter
**mL** *abbr* millilambert
**ML** \(')e¦mel\ *abbr or n* -S [L *magister legum*] **:** a master of laws
**ML** *abbr* **1** mean level **2** mine layer **3** mixed lengths **4** mold line **5** motor launch **6** muzzle-loading
**mlanje cedar** *often cap M, var of* MILANJI CEDAR
**mld** *abbr* **1** mild **2** mold; molded; molding
**MLD** *abbr, often not cap* mininum lethal dose
**mldg** *abbr* molding
**mldr** *abbr* molder
**mlech·chha** \mə'lechə\ *n* -S [Skt *mleccha*] *chiefly India* **:** one who does not practice Hinduism; *specif* **:** FOREIGNER
**m level** *n, usu cap M* **:** the energy level of an electron in an M-shell
**mlle** *abbr, often cap* [F] mademoiselle
**mlnr** *abbr* milliner
**MLR** *abbr* **1** main line of resistance **2** muzzle-loading rifle
**MLS** *abbr* microwave landing system

**MLT** *abbr* mean low tide
**MLW** *abbr* mean low water
**MLWN** *abbr* mean low water neaps
**MLWS** *abbr* mean low water springs
**mm** *abbr* millimeter
**mM** *abbr* millimole
**MM** *abbr* **1** machinist's mate **2** made merchantable **3** Maelzel's metronome **4** [L *magistri*] masters **5** Majesties **6** [L, *martyres*] martyrs **7** master mechanic **8** mercantile marine; merchant marine **9** [F] messieurs **10** methyl methacrylate **11** middle marker **12** *often not cap* [L] mutatis mutandis
**mme** *abbr, often cap* [F] madame
**mmf** *abbr* micromicrofarad
**MMF** *abbr, often not cap* magnetomotive force
**mmfd** *abbr* micromicrofarad
**mmm** *abbr* micromillimeter
**MN** *abbr* **1** magnetic north **2** merchant navy
**Mn** *symbol* manganese
**mnem-** *or* **mnemo-** *comb form* [*mnem-*, NL, fr. Gk *mnēm-*, fr. *mnēmē*; *mnemo-* prob. fr. F *mnémo-*, fr. Gk *mnēmo-*, fr. Gk *mnēmē*] **:** memory ⟨*mnemo*genic⟩ ⟨*mnemo*technical⟩
**mne·me** \'nē(,)mē\ *n* -S [NL, fr Gk *mnēmē* memory; akin to Gk *mnasthai* to remember — more at MIND] **:** the persistent or recurrent effect of past experience of the individual or of the race — **mne·mic** \-,mik\ *adj*
¹**mne·mon·ic** \nē'mänik, nə'-, ne'-\ *also* **mne·mon·i·cal** \-änəkəl\ *adj* [Gk *mnēmonikos*, fr. *mnēmon-, mnēmōn* mindful + *-ikos* -ic, -ical; akin to Gk *mnasthai* to remember] **1 :** assisting or intended to assist memory ⟨some ~ device like a string tied around the finger⟩ **:** of or relating to mnemonics **2 :** of or relating to memory ⟨~ skill⟩ — **mne·mon·i·cal·ly** \-änək(ə)lē\ *adv*
²**mnemonic** \"\ *n* -S **1 :** a mnemonic device ⟨made up a word from the initials of the successive steps for a ~⟩ **2 :** MNEMONICS
**mne·mon·ics** \-äniks\ *also* **mne·mon·ic** \-k\ *n pl but usu sing in constr* [*mnemonics* modif. (influenced by E *-ics*) of NL *mnemonica*, fr. Gk *mnēmonika*, fr. neut. pl. of *mnēmonikos* mnemonic; *mnemonic* sing. of *mnemonics*] **:** a technique of improving the efficiency of the memory
**mne·mo·technical** \¦nēmō+-\ *or* **mne·mo·technic** \"+-\ *adj* [*mnemotechnic* fr. *mnemotechnic* (prob. fr. F *mnémotechnique*, fr. *mnémotechnie* mnemonics — fr. *mnémo-* mnem- + *-technie* -techny — + *-ique* -ic) + *-al*] **:** MNEMONIC — **mne·mo·technically** \"+-\ *adv*
**-mne·sia** \(m)'nēzh(ē)ə\ *n comb form* -S [NL, fr. *amnesia*] **:** a (specified) type or condition of memory ⟨crypto*mnesia*⟩ ⟨pan*mnesia*⟩
**mnes·tic** \'nestik\ *adj* [ISV *mnest-* (fr. Gk *mnēstis* memory) + *-ic*; prob. formed as G *mnestisch*; akin to Gk *mnasthai* to remember] **:** of or relating to memory or mneme
**mng** *abbr* managing
**mngr** *abbr* **1** manager **2** monseigneur **3** monsignor
**mni·a·ce·ae** \nī'āsē,ē\ *n pl, cap* [NL, fr. *Mnium*, type genus + *-aceae*] **:** a family of erect mosses (order Eubryales) that is sometimes treated as a subfamily of the Bryaceae but distinguished by the club-shaped paraphyses and the hexagonal cells of the upper leaf surfaces
**mni·oid** \'nī,ȯid\ *adj* [NL *Mnium* + E *-oid*] **:** resembling a moss of the genus *Mnium*
**mnio·til·ti·dae** \,nīə'tiltə,dē\ [NL, fr. *Mniotilta*, genus of warblers (fr. Gk *mnion* moss, seaweed + *tiltos* plucked, verbal of *tillein* to pluck) + *-idae*] *syn of* PARULIDAE
**mni·um** \'nīəm\ *n, cap* [NL, fr. Gk *mnion* moss, seaweed; akin to Gk *mnoos, mnous* soft down, *mateisai*, fem. pl., walking, stepping, MIr *men* meal, W *mathru* to trample, Skt *carnamna* tanner, Lith *miniava* close turf, *minti* to step] **:** a genus of mosses (family Mniaceae) resembling *Bryum* but larger and with usu. horizontal capsules
**MNT** *abbr* mononitrotoluene
**mntn** *abbr* maintenance
¹**mo** \'mō\ *adj or adv or n* [ME — more at MORE] *chiefly dial* **:** MORE
²**mo** \"\ *n* -S [by shortening] *slang* **:** MOMENT
**-mo** \,mō\ *n suffix* -S [duodecimo] — after numerals or their names to indicate the number of leaves made by folding a sheet of paper ⟨sixteen*mo*⟩ ⟨16*mo*⟩ ⟨eighteen*mo*⟩ ⟨18*mo*⟩
**mo** *abbr* month; monthly
**MO** *abbr* **1** mail order **2** manually operated **3** mass observation **4** medical officer **5** [NL] modus operandi **6** money order **7** mustered out
**Mo** *symbol* molybdenum
**moa** \'mōə\ *n* -S [Maori] **:** any of various extinct flightless ratite birds of New Zealand constituting the family Dinornithidae and including numerous forms that range in size from one (*Dinornis giganteus*) which is about 12 feet in height to one (*Anomolopteryx oweni*) which is about the size of a turkey

moa (reconstructed)

¹**mo·ab·ite** \'mōə,bīt\ *n* -S *usu cap* [ME, fr LL *Moabita, Moabites*, fr. Gk *Mōabitēs*, fr. *Mōab* Moab, ancient kingdom in Syria + *-itēs* -ite] **1 :** a member of a people living in Old Testament times east of the Dead sea, north of the Edomites, and at one period south of the Ammonites **2 :** the Semitic language of ancient Moab only dialectally different from Hebrew
²**moabite** \"\ *adj, usu cap* **:** of or relating to Moab or the Moabites or their language
**mo·a·bit·ic** \¦==¦bid·ik\ *also* **mo·a·bit·ish** \'==,bīd·ish\ *adj, usu cap* **:** of or relating to or like the Moabites or their language
**mo·a·bit·ish** \'==,bīd·ish\ *n* -ES *usu cap* [fr. *Moabitish*, adj.] **:** MOABITE 2
¹**moan** \'mōn\ *n* -S [ME *mone, man, mane, moon*, fr. (assumed) OE *mān* lamentation, moan; perh. akin to OE *mǣnan* to have in mind, purpose — more at MEAN] **1 :** LAMENTATION, COMPLAINT ⟨made a great ~ if he had to work —D.H.Lawrence⟩ **2 a :** a low prolonged sound indicative of pain or of grief **b :** any similar low mournful or murmuring sound **3** *obs* **:** a state of lamentation **:** SORROW, GRIEF
²**moan** \"\ *vb* -ED/-ING/-S *vt* **1 :** to bewail audibly **:** LAMENT, BEMOAN ⟨~*ed* that their absence accounted for the low state of learning —Joseph Dorfman⟩ **2 :** to utter wailingly or with lamentation ⟨~ and warble the latest cowboy songs —D.B. Davis⟩ ~ *vi* **1 :** LAMENT, COMPLAIN ⟨~*ing* over the inadequate proofs of the existence of God —W.L.Sullivan⟩ **2 a :** to make a low prolonged sound of grief or pain **:** groan softly **b :** to emit a sound like a moan ⟨the wind ~*ed* in the trees⟩
**moan·ful** \-fəl\ *adj* [¹*moan* + *-ful*] **:** full of moaning **:** expressing sorrow or grief **:** PLAINTIVE, SAD ⟨a ~ song⟩ — **moan·ful·ly** \-fəlē\ *adv*
**moan·ing·ly** *adv* [fr. *moaning*, pres. part. of ²*moan* + *-ly*] **:** in a moaning manner **:** with a moan
**mo·a·no** \mō'ä(,)nō\ *or* **mo·a·na** \-,nə\ *n* -S [Hawaiian, Tahitian, Maori, & Samoan] **:** either of two important Hawaiian food fishes: **a :** a Pacific goatfish (*Pseudupeneus multifasciatus*) banded in light and dark red **b :** a closely related fish (*P. bifasciatus*)
**mo·ar·i·an** \(')mō¦a(a)rēən\ *adj, usu cap* [NL *Moaria*, a hypothetical continental area (fr. E *moa* + L *-aria*, fem. of *-arius* -ary) + E *-an*] **:** of, relating to, or constituting a hypothetical continental area now represented only by New Zealand and adjacent parts of Polynesia
¹**moat** \'mōt, *usu* -ōd·+V\ *n* -S [ME *mot, mote*, prob. fr. MF *motte* hill, bank, mound, fr. OF *mote*] **1 :** a deep and wide trench around the rampart of a castle or other fortified place that is usu. filled with water — see CASTLE illustration **2 a :** an artificial channel resembling a moat (as for confinement of animals in a zoo or for landscaping) **b :** a natural feature resembling a moat (as at the margin of a receding glacier, around the inner cone of a volcano, or on the sea floor at the base of a seamount or beside a coral reef)
²**moat** \"\ *vt* -ED/-ING/-S [ME *moten*, fr. *mote*, n.] **:** to surround with or as if with a moat
**mo·a·za·gotl cloud** \mō'ätsə,gäd·°l\ *n, usu cap M* [*moazagotl*

fr. G dial. (Switzerland)] **:** one or more cloud banks formed on the lee side of a mountain under foehn conditions

**¹mob** \'mäb\ *n* -s **1** [origin unknown] *obs* **:** UNDRESS, DISHABILLE **2** [perh. modif. of obs. D *mop* woman's cap] **:** MOBCAP

**²mob** \"\ *vb* **mobbed; mobbed; mobbing; mobs** *vt* **1** [perh. back-formation fr. *moble*] *archaic* **:** to muffle the head of (as in a hood) **2** [¹*mob*] *archaic* **:** to dress (oneself) negligently ~ *vi, archaic* **:** to go to an unfashionable place disguised or so dressed as to avoid recognition

**³mob** \"\ *n* -s *often attrib* [short for ³*mobile*] **1 :** the lower classes of a community **:** the populace or the lower part of it **:** MASSES ⟨the use of superstition for the purpose of policing the ~ —Benjamin Farrington⟩ ⟨political spellbinding to appeal to the ~ mind⟩ **2 a :** a large and disorderly collection of people tending to acts of violence ⟨windows smashed and police beaten by the angry ~⟩ ⟨a fear of ~ rule⟩ **b** *obs* **:** people in a large disorderly group — used without an article ⟨the lane was full of ~ and the house so full we could not get in —Horace Walpole⟩ **3** *chiefly Austral* **:** a flock, drove, or herd of animals **4 a :** a criminal set or organization (as of pickpockets or gangsters) **:** GANG **b :** CLIQUE, SET **syn** see CROWD

**⁴mob** \"\ *vb* **mobbed; mobbed; mobbing; mobs** *vt* **1 a :** to crowd about and attack or annoy ⟨*mobbed* by autograph hunters before he could enter the theater⟩ **:** attack in a mob ⟨a crowd tried to ~ him and he ran for safety into the superintendent's office —H.S.Warner⟩ **b :** to crowd into or around ⟨bargain hunters that ~ the stores on sale days⟩ **2** *dial Eng* **:** to rail at **:** SCOLD, ABUSE **3 :** to hunt (as a fox) in such a way as to allow the quarry no chance to escape (as by surrounding it) ~ *vi* **:** to form a disorderly mob **:** crowd or riot in a mob ⟨the waiting newsmen *mobbed* forward —*Newsweek*⟩

**mob** *abbr* **1** mobile **2** mobilization; mobilized

**MOB** *abbr* money-order business

**mob·ber** \'mäbə(r)\ *n* -s [⁴*mob* + *-er*] **:** one that mobs

**mob·bish** \-bish\ *adj* [³*mob* + *-ish*] **:** characteristic of a mob **:** LAWLESS ⟨fanned mounting tension into ~ terrorizing —*Time*⟩ — **mob·bish·ly** *adv* — **mob·bish·ness** *n* -ES

**mob·bism** \-,bizəm\ *n* -s **:** mobbish conduct

**mob·bist** \-bəst\ *n* -s **:** one who advocates mobbism **:** MOBBER

**mobcap** \'=,=\ *n* [¹*mob* + *cap*; perh. intended as rendering of obs. D *mopmuts*, fr. *mop* woman's cap, mobcap + *muts* cap] **:** a woman's indoor cap; *esp* **:** a fancy cap made of sheer material with a high full crown and often tied under the chin

**mo·bed** *also* **mo·bad** \'mōbəd\ *n* -s [Per *maubad, mūbad, mūbid*] **:** a Parsi priest of the second rank

**¹mo·bile** \'mōbəl, -,bēl *also* -,bīl *or* -(,)bil *sometimes* mō-'bē(ə)l\ *adj* [MF, fr. L *mobilis*, fr. (assumed) L *movibilis*, fr. L *movēre* to move + *-ibilis* -ible — more at MOVE] **1 :** capable of moving or being moved from one place to another **:** MOVABLE: as **a :** capable of moving or being moved about readily ⟨globular proteins that are ~ and rod-shaped proteins that form solid structures⟩ ⟨the tongue . . . is clearly the most ~ articulator —G.A.Miller⟩; *specif* **:** characterized by an extreme degree of fluidity ⟨ether and mercury are ~ liquids⟩ — compare VISCOUS **b :** organized and equipped for ready movement (as by truck or air transport) ⟨~ fighting forces⟩ ⟨~ television units for on-the-spot reporting⟩ **c :** free for use or service anywhere **:** not restricted or committed ⟨~ dollars to be used where they can best advance the welfare of the whole institution —*Saturday Rev.*⟩ ⟨~ labor . . . could be sent anywhere in England —Henry Green⟩ **d :** designed as a vehicle or mounted on a vehicle or easily placed on or in a vehicle (as a trailer or truck) ⟨~ loudspeakers carrying the campaign speeches into the streets⟩ ⟨a ~ missile launcher⟩ ⟨~ homes⟩ **2 :** capable of or tending to change **:** CHANGEABLE: as **a :** changing readily in appearance and expression under the influence of mind or feeling ⟨his ~ face mirrors every feeling from bitter sadness to ecstasy —Eleanor Harris⟩ **b :** easily swayed in feeling, purpose, or direction ⟨a mind adventurously flexible but not frivolously ~ —Cecil Sprigge⟩ **c :** marked by ready adaptability ⟨industrial resources so ~ that they could be quickly switched from producing for export to producing for home demand⟩ **:** alert and flexible in the use of resources ⟨a ~ imagination⟩ ⟨an organization ~ enough to cope with any emergency⟩ **3 :** characterized by frequent or continuous movement ⟨the wind in ~ grasses⟩; *specif* **:** tending to travel or migrate from place to place ⟨we began as explorers, empire builders, pilgrims, and refugees, . . . and we are still today the most ~ people on the face of the earth —G.W.Pierson⟩ ⟨the Indians of the Great Plains were ~ bison hunters —Clark Wissler⟩ **4 a :** characterized by the mixing of social groups ⟨the general confusion in moral standards which characterizes ~ societies —E.R.Mowrer⟩ **:** affording opportunity for a shift in social status ⟨American society, though highly ~ . . . is not classless —*Times Lit. Supp.*⟩ **b :** having the opportunity for or undergoing a shift in status within the hierarchical social levels of a society ⟨a society in which women are more ~ than men⟩ ⟨born of upward ~ middle-class . . . parents —*Newsweek*⟩ **5 :** marked by the use of vehicles for transportation ⟨~ defense⟩ ⟨~ warfare⟩ ⟨took to their cars for a ~ holiday⟩ **6 :** of, relating to, or having the characteristics of a mobile

**²mo·bile** \'mō,bēl *sometimes* -,bīl *or* -,bil *or* mō'bē(ə)l; *in sense 3* mō'bē(ə)l *or* 'mō,bēl\ *n* -s [MF (*premier*) *mobile* primum mobile, part trans. of ML (*primum*) *mobile*, fr. neut. of L *mobilis*, adj.] **1 :** something that occasions movement or action — see PRIMUM MOBILE **2 a :** a movable or moving body or part **:** one that is mobile **b** (1) **:** a delicately balanced construction or sculpture frequently made of wire and sheet metal shapes and having movable parts that can be set in motion by air currents or mechanical propulsion — compare STABILE (2) **:** a set of lightweight figures (as of animals or story characters) that are suspended on fine wire or string so that they hang in perfect balance and may be moved by a current of air **3** [by shortening] **:** AUTOMOBILE

**³mob·i·le** \'mäbə(,)lē\ *n* -s [L *mobile* (*vulgus*) changeable crowd, the movable common people, neut. of *mobilis*, adj.] **:** ³MOB 1

**⁴mo·bile** \(')mō¦bē(ə)l\ *adj, usu cap* [fr. *Mobile*, Ala.] **:** of or from the city of Mobile, Ala. ⟨*Mobile* gardens⟩ **:** of the kind or style prevalent in Mobile

**-mo·bile** \mō,bēl, mə,- *sometimes* -,bil\ *n comb form* -s [*automobile*] **:** vehicle ⟨club*mobile*⟩ ⟨book*mobile*⟩ ⟨blood*mobile*⟩

**mobile gate** *n* **:** a starting gate affixed to the rear of an automobile and consisting of two metal arms that extend one to each side and fold and swing forward to facilitate a fair start of a harness race

**mobile library** *n* **:** BOOKMOBILE

**mobile station** *n* **:** a radio transmitting station on a ship, airplane, or other vehicle

**mobile terrapin** *n, usu cap M* [⁴*mobile*; fr. its locality] **:** an edible terrapin (*Pseudemys concinna mobilensis*) of the southern U.S. distinguished by a broad scarlet band on each side of the head

**mobile unit** *n* **:** an establishment on wheels (as an automobile or trailer) equipped for some special service (as a traveling library, an ambulance, an X-ray clinic, or television pickup)

**mo·bil·ian** \mō'bēlēən, -lyən\ *n* -s *cap* **1** [*Mobile*, Ala. + E *-ian*] **:** a native or resident of Mobile, Alabama **2 :** a pidgin language based on Choctaw and formerly a lingua franca in the southeastern U.S.

**mo·bil·iary** \mō'bilē,erē, -lyərē\ *adj* [F *mobiliaire*, fr. MF, fr. *mobile* movable property (fr. ML, fr. L *mobilia*, pl., fr. neut. pl. of *mobilis* movable, mobile) + MF *-aire* -ary] **1 :** of or relating to movable property **2 :** of or relating to household furniture

**mo·bil·i·ty** \mō'bilәd·ē, -ətē, -i\ *n* -ES [MF *mobilité*, fr. OF, fr. L *mobilitat-, mobilitas*, fr. *mobilis* mobile + *-itat-, -itas* -ity — more at MOBILE] **1 :** the quality or state of being mobile **:** the capacity or facility of movement **:** MOVABILITY ⟨the ~ of a liquid⟩ ⟨factors of birth, income, and education affecting social ~⟩ ⟨the high ~ of modern labor⟩ **2 :** the measure of the rate at which a solid is deformed under stress after the yield point has been exceeded **3 a :** the average speed at which either gaseous or electrolytic ions move under the influence of a unit potential gradient **b :** the average speed with which molecules in solution diffuse under the influence of a unit osmotic pressure gradient

**mo·bi·liz·able** \¦mōbə¦līzəbəl\ *adj* **:** capable of being mobilized

**mo·bi·li·za·tion** \,mōbələ'zāshən, -,lī'z-\ *n* -s [partly fr. ¹*mobile* + *-ization* and partly fr. F *mobilisation*, fr. *mobiliser* (v.) + *-ation*] **:** the act or process of mobilizing ⟨~ of wealth⟩ ⟨~ of glycogen⟩ ⟨prompt ~ of all national resources⟩

**mo·bi·lize** \'==,līz\ *vb* -ED/-ING/-S *see -ize in Explan Notes* [F *mobiliser*, fr. *mobile* (adj.) + *-iser* -ize] *vt* **1 :** to put into movement or circulation **:** make mobile ⟨mortgages may be *mobilized* like every other instrument of credit and . . . invade the bond market —J.A.Schumpeter⟩; *specif* **:** to release (something stored in the body) for body use ⟨the body ~*s* its antibodies⟩ **2 a :** to assemble (as an army corps or a fleet) and put in a state of readiness for active service in war ⟨~ all reserve forces for overseas duty⟩ ⟨~ industry for the defense effort⟩ **b :** to assemble (as resources) and make ready for use or action **:** ORGANIZE, MARSHAL, RALLY ⟨~ support for the proposal⟩ ⟨the sympathetic nervous system . . . ~*s* the bodily resources as a means of preparing for fight or flight —H.G. Armstrong⟩ **3 :** to separate (an organ or part) from associated structures so as to make more accessible for operative procedures ⟨~ the sigmoid colon⟩ **4 :** to develop to a state of acute activity ⟨ego feeling and ego attitude . . . ~ hostile feelings toward others —Abram Kardiner⟩ ~ *vi* **:** to undergo mobilization **:** assemble and organize for action ⟨in disasters . . . scouts have *mobilized* to give aid —*Boy Scout Handbook*⟩

**mo·bi·liz·er** \-zə(r)\ *n* -s **:** one that mobilizes persons or things

**mo·bil·om·e·ter** \,mōbə'lämәd·ə(r)\ *n* [*mobility* + *-o-* + *-meter*] **:** an apparatus for determining the consistency of plastic materials

**mö·bi·us band** \'mər|bēəs-, 'mə|, 'mā|, 'mē|\ *or* **möbius strip** *n, usu cap M* [after August F. *Möbius* †1868 Ger. mathematician] **:** a one-sided surface formed by holding one end of a rectangle fixed, rotating the opposite end through 180 degrees, and then applying it to the first end

Möbius band

**mo·ble** \'mäbəl\ *vt* -ED/-ING/-S [prob. alter. of ¹*muffle*] *archaic* **:** to wrap or muffle the head of (as in a hood)

**mob·oc·ra·cy** \mä'bäkrəsē\ *n* -ES [³*mob* + *-o-* + *-cracy*] **1 :** the rule of the mob **2 :** the mob as a ruling class **:** a ruling or governing mob **3 :** rule by mobsters or gangsters

**mob·o·crat** \'mäbə,krat\ *n* -s [fr. *mobocracy*, after such pairs as E *democracy: democrat*] **1 :** one who favors mobocracy **2 :** mob leader — **mob·o·crat·ic** \¦==¦krad·ik\ *adj*

**mobs** *pl of* MOB, *pres 3d sing of* MOB

**mobs·man** \'mäbzmən\ *n, pl* **mobsmen** [*mobs* (gen. of ³*mob*) + *man*] **1 :** a member of a mob **2** *Brit* **:** SWELL-MOBSMAN

**mob·ster** \'mäbztə(r), -bst-\ *n* -s [³*mob* + *-ster*] **:** a member of a criminal gang

**mob·u·la** \'mäbyələ\ *n, cap* [NL] **:** a genus of large rays that contains imperfectly known fishes of warm seas and is the type of the family Mobulidae

**mo·bu·li·dae** \mə'byülə,dē\ *n pl, cap* [NL, fr. *Mobula*, type genus + *-idae*] **:** a family of rays that includes the genera *Mobula* and *Manta* — see DEVILFISH

**moc** \'mäk\ *n* -s [by shortening] **:** MOCCASIN 1

**moc·ca·sin** *also* **moc·as·sin** \'mäkəsən\ *n* -s [of Algonquian origin; akin to Natick *mokkussin* shoe, Narraganset *mocussin*, Ojibwa *makisin*] **1 a :** a heelless shoe or boot of soft leather that is the distinctive footwear of American Indians, is widely worn by aborigines of cold climates, and has the sole brought up the sides of the foot and over the toes where it is joined with a puckered seam to a U-shaped piece lying on top of the foot **b :** a regular shoe having a lap seam or saddle seam on the forepart of the vamp imitating the seam of a true moccasin **2 a :** a pit viper of the genus *Agkistrodon*; *esp* **:** WATER MOCCASIN **b :** any snake resembling or thought to resemble a moccasin (as a water snake of the genus *Natrix*) **3 :** ARGUS BROWN

moccasin 1b

**moccasin flower** *n* **:** any of several lady's slippers of the genus *Cypripedium*; *esp* **:** a once common woodland orchid (*C. acaule*) of eastern No. America that has usu. solitary pink or white moccasin-shaped flowers — called also *nerveroot*

**moccasin telegraph** *n* **:** GRAPEVINE 2b

**moch** \'mäk, 'mōk\ *n* -s [alter. of ¹*moth*] *Scot* **:** MOTH

**mo·cha** \'mōkə\ *n* -s [fr. *Mocha*, Arabia, seaport near which the coffee was orig. grown and from which it was orig. exported] **1 a** *or* **mocha coffee** (1) **:** arabica coffee that is grown in Arabia, is characterized by small irregular green or yellowish beans, and produces a superior beverage (2) **:** a coffee of superior quality **b :** a flavoring made of a strong coffee infusion or of a mixture of cocoa or chocolate with coffee **2 :** a soft pliable glove leather made by frizzing off the grain and then suede finishing the grain side of sheepskins from Africa **3** *often cap* **:** ³BARK 3

**mocha bisque** *n* **:** a light to moderate brown that is slightly redder than suede and very slightly yellower than tanbark

**mocha stone** *n, usu cap M* [prob. fr. *Mocha*, Arabia] **:** MOSS AGATE

**mocha ware** *also* **mocha** *n, usu cap M* **:** a coarse English earthenware with soft buff body decorated with colored bands and brush patterns (as of seaweed, earthworms, and tree silhouettes) and made esp. in Staffordshire from the late 18th to the early 20th century

**mo·chi·ca** \mō'chēkə\ *adj, usu cap* [after *Mochica*, a pre-Inca people of high cultural achievement living on the northern coast of Peru (of AmerInd origin)] **:** of or relating to a culture period in the valleys of the northern Peruvian coast A.D. 600–700 characterized by fine red and white modeled pottery for grave offerings and ceremonial use predominantly in the form of a container with a stirrup spout

**mo·chi·la** \mō'chēlə\ *also* **mo·chil·la** \-chilə\ *n* -s [Sp *mochila*, prob. fr. *mochil* errand boy, fr. Basque *mutil, motil* youth, servant, fr. L *mutilus* maimed, mutilated — more at MUTILATE] **1 :** KNAPSACK, HAVERSACK; *specif* **:** a saddle pouch **2 :** a square leather saddle covering having openings for the horn and cantle and sometimes equipped with saddlebags ⟨many riders and even more ponies carried the mail, but only the ~ made the entire trip —J.T.Adams⟩

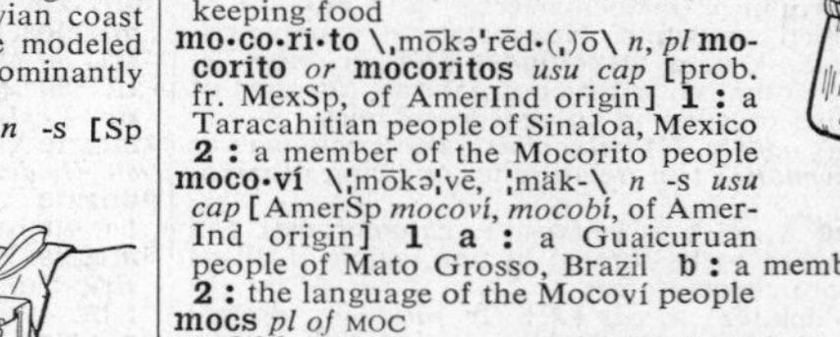

mochila 2

**mochy** \'mäkē, 'mōkē, -ki\ *adj* -ER/-EST [fr. obs. E (Sc) *moch* moist, damp (perh. of Scand origin; akin to ON *mugga* drizzle) + E *-y* — more at ⁴MUG] *Scot* **:** moist and warm; *esp* **:** misty and muggy

**¹mock** \'mäk, 'mȯk\ *vb* -ED/-ING/-S [ME *mocken, mokken*, fr. MF *mocquer*, fr. OF *moquier*] *vt* **1 :** to treat with scorn or contempt or ridicule **:** DERIDE ⟨~*ed* him for showing fear⟩ ⟨insolently ~*ing* the poor⟩ **2 :** to disappoint the hopes of **:** DECEIVE, DELUDE ⟨for any government to ~ men's hopes with mere words and promises and gestures —D.D.Eisenhower⟩ **3 :** DEFY, DISREGARD ⟨it's ~*ing* Heaven to run away and want to earn your own living —Israel Zangwill⟩ **4 :** IMITATE, MIMIC ⟨a mockingbird was ~*ing* a cardinal —Nelson Hayes⟩ **b :** to mimic in sport or derision **:** ridicule by mimicry ⟨followed the old man along the street ~*ing* his gait⟩ **5** *obs* **:** PRETEND, FEIGN, SIMULATE ⟨~*ing* marriage with a dame of France —Shak.⟩ **6 :** to make a sham of ⟨the presence of the Red Army ~*ed* the concessions and vitiated the propaganda —*New Republic*⟩ ~ *vi* **:** to treat a person or thing with scorn, contempt, or ridicule — often used with *at* ⟨was ~*ed* at by the others⟩ **syn** see COPY, RIDICULE

**²mock** \"\ *n* -s [ME *mokk*, fr. *mokken*, v.] **1 :** an act of ridicule or derision **:** SNEER, GIBE ⟨make a ~ of him⟩ **2 :** one that is an object of or is deserving of ridicule, derision, or scorn **3 :** MOCKERY, RIDICULE ⟨take to heart what was said in ~⟩ **4 a :** an act of imitation **b :** something made as an imitation

**³mock** \"\ *adj* **:** of the character of an imitation, parody, or semblance **:** SIMULATED ⟨houses in a variety of styles from ~ Moorish to ~ Tudor —Peter Ustinov⟩ ⟨~ seam⟩ ⟨~ marriage⟩ ⟨~ oyster⟩ ⟨~ epic⟩ **:** SHAM ⟨a custom of appointing a . . . ~ king to represent the real king for a time —J.G.Frazer⟩ **:** FALSE, PSEUDO, QUASI ⟨the curious ~ daylight which even a light fall of snow gives to a morning —Mary Webb⟩ **:** FEIGNED **:** MIMICKED ⟨the ~ solemnity of the parody⟩

**⁴mock** \"\ *adv* **:** in an insincere or counterfeit manner — usu. used in combination ⟨a gabbing, ambitious, *mock*-tough, pretentious young man —Dylan Thomas⟩ ⟨a fawn trench coat *mock*-modestly covering a neat green uniform —Sean O'Casey⟩

**⁵mock** \"\ *n* -s [origin unknown] **1** *dial Eng* **:** the stump and root of a tree **2** *dial Eng* **:** a large block or stick; *specif* **:** a piece of wood usu. burned at Christmas

**mock·able** \-kəbəl\ *adj* **:** that can be mocked

**mock·a·do** \mə'kä(,)dō\ *n* -ES [modif. of obs. It *mocaiardo, mocaiarro* fabric of camel's or goat's hair, mohair — more at MOHAIR] **1 :** a fabric made chiefly in the 16th and 17th centuries usu. of wool and in imitation of velvet **2** *obs* **:** inferior stuff **:** TRUMPERY

**mock·age** \'mäkij, 'mȯk-, -kēj\ *n* -s [ME, fr. *mocken* (v.) + *-age*] **:** MOCKERY

**mock apple** *n* **:** WILD CUCUMBER c

**mockbird** \'=,=\ *n* **1** *dial* **:** a bird that mocks; *esp* **:** MOCKINGBIRD **2 a :** SEDGE WARBLER **b :** BLACKCAP

**mock bishop's-weed** *or* **mock bishop-weed** *n* **:** a plant of the genus *Ptilimnium*; *esp* **:** a slender American marsh herb (*P. capillaceum*)

**mock brawn** *n* **:** HEADCHEESE

**mock chicken** *n* **:** meat other than chicken (as veal) cooked or shaped to resemble chicken

**mock cucumber** *n* **:** WILD CUCUMBER c

**mock cypress** *n* **:** SUMMER CYPRESS

**mock-dominance** \(')=¦===\ *n* **:** PSEUDODOMINANCE

**mock duck** *n* **:** a shoulder of lamb shaped to resemble a duck with the boned foreshank forming the head and neck and the remainder after removal of the blade bones forming the body

**mocked** *past of* MOCK

**mock·er** \'mäkə(r), 'mȯk-\ *n* -s **:** one that mocks; *specif* **:** MOCKINGBIRD

**mockernut** \'=,=\ *also* **mockernut hickory** *n* **:** a smooth-barked No. American hickory (*Carya tomentosa*) with fragrant 7- to 9-foliolate leaves — called also *black hickory* **2 :** the nut of the mockernut tree

**mock·ery** \'mäk(ə)rē, 'mȯk-, -ri\ *n* -ES [ME *moquerie*, fr. MF, fr. OF, fr. *moquier* to mock] **1 :** insulting or contemptuous action or speech **:** DERISION **2 :** a subject of laughter, derision, or sport **3 a :** a counterfeit appearance **:** IMITATION **b :** an insincere, contemptible, or impertinent imitation ⟨arbitrary methods that made a ~ of justice⟩ **4 :** something ridiculously or impudently unavailing

**¹mock-heroic** \¦==¦=\ *adj* **1 :** ridiculing or burlesquing the heroic style, character, or action ⟨a *mock-heroic* poem⟩ **2 :** extravagantly imitating the grand or heroic manner — **mock-heroically** \¦==¦=(=)=\ *adv*

**²mock-heroic** *n* [*mock-heroic*] **:** a mock-heroic composition

**mocking** *pres part of* MOCK

**mockingbird** \'==,=\ *n* **:** a common bird (*Mimus polyglottos*) of the southern U.S. that is remarkable for its exact imitations of the notes of other birds, has the back gray, the underparts grayish white, and the tail and wings blackish marked with white, and is represented by subspecies in Mexico, Central America, and the West Indies

**mock·ing·ly** *adv* **:** in a mocking manner ⟨smiled ~ at his unaccustomed helplessness⟩

**mocking thrush** *n* **:** a bird of the family Mimidae; *esp* **:** THRASHER

**mocking wren** *n* **:** an American wren of the genus *Thryothorus* or of *Thryomanes* — compare CAROLINA WREN

**mock knee** *n* **:** a large pedunculate fibrous tumor in front of the knee esp. in cattle

**mock locust** *n* **:** a fetid false indigo (*Amorpha californica*) with dark purple racemose flowers

**mock moon** *n* **:** PARASELENE

**mock olive** *n* **:** AXBREAKER 1

**mock orange** *n* **1 :** a shrub of the genus *Philadelphus* — called also *syringa* **2 :** any of several American shrubs or trees: as **a :** CHERRY LAUREL **b :** OSAGE ORANGE **c :** SOUTHERN BUCKTHORN **3 :** a gourd resembling an orange **4 :** WILD CUCUMBER c **5** *Austral* **:** NATIVE LAUREL 1

**mock ore** *n* **:** SPHALERITE

**mock pennyroyal** *n* **:** HEDEOMA 2

**mock regent bird** *n* [³*mock* + *regent bird*] **:** FLYING COACHMAN

**mocks** *pres 3d sing of* MOCK, *pl of* MOCK

**mock-strawberry** \'=¦=. . .\ *n* **:** a plant of the genus *Duchesnea*; *esp* **:** INDIAN STRAWBERRY

**mock sun** *n* **:** PARHELION

**mock thrush** *n* **:** MOCKING THRUSH

**mock turtle soup** *n* **:** a soup made of calf's head, veal, or other meat and condiments in imitation of green turtle soup

**mock-up** \'=,=\ *n* -s [¹*mock* (imitate) + *up*] **:** a structural model built accurately to scale (as out of plywood, cardboard, canvas, clay) chiefly for study, testing, or display ⟨a *mock-up* of an airplane⟩

**mock up** *vt* [*mock-up*] **:** to make a mock-up of

**mock willow** *n* **:** MEADOWSWEET 1

**mocky** *also* **mock·ie** \'mäkē, -ki\ *n, pl* **mockies** [prob. fr. Yiddish *makeh* sore, pest, plague, fr. Heb *makāh* blow, wound, plague] **:** JEW — usu. used disparagingly

**mo·co** \mə'kō\ *n* -s [Pg *mocó*, fr. Tupi] **:** a large semiamphibious So. American histricomorph rodent (*Kerodon rupestris*) closely related to the cavies

**mo·coa** \mə'kōə\ *n* -s *usu cap* [Sp, of AmerInd origin] **:** COCHE

**mo·cock** \mə'käk\ *also* **mo·cuck** \-'kək\ *n* -s [of Algonquian origin; akin to Ojibwa *makak* box] **:** a box or basket (as of birch bark) for keeping food

mocock

**mo·co·ri·to** \,mōkə'rēd·(,)ō\ *n, pl* **mocorito** *or* **mocoritos** *usu cap* [prob. fr. MexSp, of AmerInd origin] **1 :** a Taracahitian people of Sinaloa, Mexico **2 :** a member of the Mocorito people

**moco·ví** \¦mōkə¦vē, ¦mäk-\ *n* -s *usu cap* [AmerSp *mocoví, mocobí*, of AmerInd origin] **1 a :** a Guaicuruan people of Mato Grosso, Brazil **b :** a member of such people **2 :** the language of the Mocoví people

**mocs** *pl of* MOC

**mod** \'mōd\ *n* -s *usu cap* [ScGael *mōd*, fr. ON *mōt* meeting; akin to OE *mōt* meeting, assembly — more at MEET] **:** a meeting or gathering for the study and performance of Gaelic arts — compare EISTEDDFOD, FEIS

**mod** *abbr* **1** model **2** moderate **3** moderato **4** moderator **5** modern **6** modification; modified; modify **7** modulator

**MOD** *abbr* **1** mail-order department **2** money-order department

**mod·acrylic fiber** \¦mäd+. . .-\ *n* [*modified acrylic* (n.)] **:** any of various synthetic textile fibers that are long-chain polymers composed of 35 to 85 percent by weight of acrylonitrile units

**¹mod·al** \'mōdᵊl\ *adj* [ML *modalis*, fr. L *modus* measure, manner + *-alis* -al — more at METE] **1 :** of or relating to mode or modality in logic **2 :** containing provisions as to the mode of procedure or the manner of taking effect — used of a contract or legacy **3 :** of or relating to a musical mode; *specif* **:** written in one of the ecclesiastical modes ⟨uses diatonic harmonies with a ~ flavor —Humphrey Searle⟩ **4 :** of or relating to form as opposed to substance **:** having form without reality **5 a :** of, relating to, or constituting a grammatical form or category characteristically indicating predication of an action or state in some manner other than as a simple fact **b :** of, relating to, or constituting a grammatical case that denotes manner **6 :** of or relating to a statistical mode **:** most common **:** TYPICAL ⟨the anthropologist's ~ concept of culture pattern which is based upon observations of what most people seem to be doing —Jacob Fried⟩ ⟨has produced his first novel at the age of sixty . . . approximately thirty years after the American novelist reaches his peak —J.K.Galbraith⟩ **7 :** of or relating to modalism — **mod·al·ly** \-ᵊlē, -li\ *adv*

**²modal** \"\ *n* -s **1 :** a modal proposition or statement in logic **2 :** a grammatical form belonging to a class of words or inflectional affixes with a modal function; *specif* **:** a modal auxiliary in English grammar

**modal auxiliary** *n* **:** a verb or a grammatical form resembling a verb that is characteristically used with a verb of predication and expresses a modal modification (as *can, shall, will, must, might, ought, could, should, would, may, need, dare*) and that in English differs formally from other verbs in lacking *-s, -ing,* and past-tense forms and shares with other auxiliaries the affixing of negative *-n't*

**mod·al·ism** \\-ᵊl,izəm\\ *n* -s [¹*modal* + *-ism*] **:** the theological doctrine that the members of the Trinity are not three distinct persons but rather three modes or forms of activity (the Father, Son, and Holy Spirit) under which God manifests himself

**mod·al·ist** \\-ᵊləst\\ *n* -s [¹*modal* + *-ist*] **:** an adherent of modalism — **mod·al·is·tic** \\¦mōdᵊl¦istik\\ *adj*

**modalistic monarchian** *n, usu cap both Ms* **:** an adherent of Modalistic Monarchianism

**modalistic monarchianism** *n, usu cap both Ms* **:** Monarchianism holding that Jesus Christ was not a distinct person of the Trinity but was rather one of three successive modes or manifestations of God

**mo·dal·i·ty** \\mō'daləd·ē, -ətē, -i\\ *n* -ES [F *modalité,* fr. MF, fr. *modal* (fr. ML *modalis*) + *-ité* -ity] **1 a :** the quality or state of being modal ⟨the ~ of his music⟩ ⟨~ of a circle⟩ **b :** a modal quality, attribute, or circumstance **:** FORM, PATTERN ⟨as the varying subject matter requires, the narrative and style take on the *modalities* of comedy, romance, tragedy, or tragicomedy —J.W.Beach⟩ **2 :** that qualification of logical propositions according to which they are distinguished as asserting or denying the possibility, impossibility, contingency, or necessity of their content — see CATEGORY 1b **3 :** one of the main avenues of sensation (as vision or audition) **4 a :** any of several agencies used in physical therapy (as diathermy, high-frequency currents, or massage) **b :** an apparatus for applying such agencies **5 :** a tendency to conform to a pattern or type ⟨the greater ~ of the male in this regard is indicated by a smaller representation of males than females in the category "Miscellaneous" —Eleanor Smith & J.H. Greenberg Monane⟩

**modal value** *n* **:** MODE 8

**¹mode** \\'mōd\\ *n* -s [ME *moede,* fr. L *modus* measure, manner,

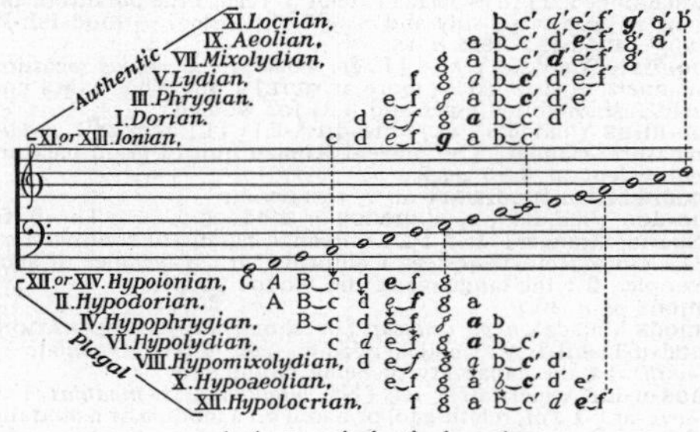

mode 1a : ecclesiastical modes

musical mode — more at METE] **1 a :** a musical arrangement of the eight diatonic notes or tones of an octave according to one of various fixed schemes of their intervals — see ECCLESIASTICAL MODE, GREEK MODE **b :** a rhythmical scheme; *specif* **:** one of the six metrical patterns in 13th and 14th century music corresponding to the feet (as trochee or dactyl) in classical poetry and expressed in triple time **2 :** ²MOOD 2b ⟨the indicative ~ of flat assertion alone —Weston La Barre⟩ **3** [LL *modus,* fr. L, measure, manner] **a :** ²MOOD 1a **b :** the manner in which a logical proposition is asserted or denied esp. as being possible, impossible, necessary, or contingent **4 a :** a particular form or variety of something ⟨a large and overpowering set of brothers and sisters, who were ~*s* or replicas of the same type —Henry Adams⟩ ⟨her anguish of the night before was in another ~ —Josephine Pinckney⟩ ⟨separating movement on foot from other ~*s* of traffic —Lewis Mumford⟩ **b :** a form, pattern, or manner of expression **:** STYLE ⟨the only English poet who has adapted it to his needs as a regular poetic ~ —W.H.Gardner⟩ ⟨his romanticism (his first literary ~) —Austin Warren⟩ ⟨perhaps the major expressive ~ of his day, the ~ of the liberal Emersonian sermon —R.P.Blackmur⟩ **5 :** a manner of doing something or of performing a particular function or activity ⟨as the one or the other ~ of ratification may be proposed by the Congress —*U.S. Constitution*⟩ ⟨new ~*s* of experimentation had to be developed —J.B.Conant⟩ ⟨the Renaissance ~ of thinking in symbols —Michael Kitson⟩ **6 :** a condition or state of being **:** a manifestation, form, or manner of arrangement; *specif* **:** a particular form or manifestation of some underlying substance, or of some permanent aspect or attribute of such a substance — compare MIXED MODE, SIMPLE MODE **7 :** a state or manner of living **:** CUSTOM ⟨a homogeneous population that departs reluctantly from long-accepted institutions and ~*s* —*Amer. Guide Series: Pa.*⟩ ⟨bound up with regional ~*s* of feeling and local traditions —Van Wyck Brooks⟩ ⟨a sedentary agricultural-hunting ~ of life —R.W. Murray⟩ **8 :** the value of the variable in a statistical distribution for which the frequency is a maximum **:** the value that occurs most frequently **:** the most common value ⟨whenever the talk is of Americans the image is always one of the ~ or average person —*Saturday Rev.*⟩ **9 :** any of various stationary-vibration patterns of which an elastic body or an oscillatory system is capable ⟨the vibration ~*s* and frequencies of the airplane were computed —Wilhemina Kroll⟩; *specif* **:** the vibration pattern of electromagnetic waves (as in lines or wave guides) ⟨in the field of radar theory the various ~*s* in which waves are propagated are designated by different symbols —*Television & Radar Encyc.*⟩ **10 :** the actual mineral composition of a rock as distinguished from the norm **11** *crystallog* **:** the type of lattice (as primitive or body-centered) ⟨lattice-*mode*⟩ **syn** see METHOD, STATE

**²mode** \\"\\ *n* -s [F, fr. L *modus* measure, manner — more at METE] **1 :** a prevailing fashion or style of dress or behavior ⟨harbored the cultural backwash of Europe and looked to its stale romanticism as the ~ —H.F.Mooney⟩ ⟨sleeping on top of television sets is the ~ of the day for cats —*New Yorker*⟩ ⟨the contemporary ~⟩ ⟨the newest ~ in dresses⟩ ⟨all the ~⟩ **2 :** ALAMODE **syn** see FASHION

**mode beige** *n* [²*mode*] **:** DRAB 2a

**mo·dec·ca flower** \\mō'dekə-\\ *n* [*modecca* fr. NL *Modecca* (syn. of *Adenia,* genus name of the killer plant *Adenia sinensis*)] **:** KILLER PLANT

**¹mod·el** \\'mädᵊl\\ *n* -s [MF *modelle,* fr. OIt *modello,* fr. (assumed) VL *modellus,* fr. L *modulus* small measure, fr. *modus* measure, manner + *-ulus*] **1** *obs* **:** a set of plans for a building to be erected or of drawings to scale for a structure already built; *also* **:** a ground plan esp. of a garden ⟨we first survey the plot, then draw the ~ —Shak.⟩ **2** *dial Brit* **:** a person or thing that exactly resembles another **:** COPY, IMAGE ⟨had my father's signet in my purse, which was the ~ of that Danish seal —Shak.⟩ **3** *obs* **:** something that encases or wraps around **:** MOLD ⟨~ to thy inward greatness, like little body with a mighty heart —Shak.⟩ **4 :** structural design **:** PATTERN ⟨built his home on the ~ of an old farmhouse⟩ ⟨began his teaching by organizing a seminar on the German ~ —J.S. Bassett⟩ ⟨providing for the founding of New Jersey towns on the New England ~ —*Amer. Guide Series: N.J.*⟩ **5** *archaic* **:** an abstract or summary of a written work **:** EPITOME **6 a :** a usu. miniature three-dimensional representation of something existing in nature or constructed or to be constructed ⟨a mile-long concrete ~ of the Mississippi valley —*Time*⟩ ⟨a 15-foot ~ of a full-rigged ship —*Amer. Guide Series: Md.*⟩ ⟨miniature, like some exquisite ~ seen through a glass case —Osbert Sitwell⟩ **b :** a representation in relief or three dimensions in plaster, papier-mâché, wood, plastic, or other material of a surface or solid **7 :** something made in a usu. pliable material (as clay or wax) and intended to serve as a pattern of an object or figure to be made in a more permanent material ⟨made many ~*s* of the coin before he was satisfied with one⟩ **8 :** a person or thing regarded as worthy of imitation **:** something perfect of its kind ⟨brevity that renders both writers such valuable ~*s* to an age whose worst literary fault is diffuseness —Richard Garnett †1906⟩ ⟨still remains a ~ of scientific argument —B.W.Bacon⟩ ⟨his written addresses are ~*s* of clearness, logical order, and style —A.B. Noble⟩ **9 :** a person or thing that serves as a pattern or source of inspiration for an artist or writer ⟨his father was the ~ for one of the most famous characters in literature⟩; *esp* **:** one who poses for an artist ⟨his wife served as the ~ for many of his early paintings⟩ **10 :** ARCHETYPE **11 :** an organism whose appearance a mimic imitates — compare MIMICRY **12 :** one who is employed to display clothes or to appear in displays of other merchandise (as in a fashion show, in a photograph, or on television) ⟨left school to go to work as a dress ~ in the garment district —*Current Biog.*⟩ ⟨he has appeared as a ~ in advertisements for cigars⟩ **13 a** (1) **:** a specific type or design of clothing ⟨favors the Alaskan-trapper ~ with a high guard at the toe —R.L.Neuberger⟩ (2) **:** an article of clothing (as a dress with a distinctive design) ⟨girls, self-conscious in their Paris ~*s* —Paul Bowles⟩ **b :** a specific type or design of car ⟨offers eight new ~*s* for next year, including a completely restyled convertible⟩ **c :** a modification or variation of a general type or mark of military equipment **14 a :** a description, a collection of statistical data, or an analogy used to help visualize often in a simplified way something that cannot be directly observed (as an atom) **b :** a theoretical projection in detail of a possible system of human relationships (as in economics, politics, or psychology) **:** BLUEPRINT ⟨his ~ of an election procedure based on permanent personal registration reveals some of the problems to be solved⟩ ⟨constructed the first of the world ~*s* of the present century —S.F.Mason⟩

**syn** EXAMPLE, PATTERN, EXEMPLAR, PARADIGM, IDEAL, BEAU IDEAL, STANDARD, MIRROR: MODEL applies to something set up or held out as worthy of imitation, sometimes preeminently so ⟨a workmen's compensation law which is still considered a *model* piece of legislation —*Current Biog.*⟩ ⟨*models* for the development of his own habitual responses to various situations —Ralph Linton⟩ ⟨the very *model* of a modern major general —W.S.Gilbert⟩ EXAMPLE applies chiefly to a person to be imitated or, in some contexts, emphatically not to be imitated since his case serves not as an inducement but as a warning ⟨one of the immortal *examples* of a true man in a world of bounders, cowards, and squeaking specters —W.L. Sullivan⟩ ⟨presents an *example* in modern department store designing —*Retailing Daily*⟩ ⟨making the mutineers *examples* for the rest of the crew⟩ PATTERN may suggest a clear or detailed archetype or prototype ⟨many hymns that set the *pattern* for the stately hymnology of the American Protestant Church —*Amer. Guide Series: N.J.*⟩ ⟨the ancient *pattern* of life had been woven continuously for so many centuries that even illiterate farmers knew how to be courtly and dignified at family celebrations or at the great yearly festivals —John Blofeld⟩ EXEMPLAR indicates either a faultless example to be emulated or a perfect typification ⟨Christianity was primarily an ethical system; Christ was its great teacher and *exemplar;* and to be a Christian meant to conduct one's life in accordance with the principles which governed Him —A.C. McGiffert⟩ ⟨the living *exemplar* of tragedy as the human lot —V.S.Pritchett⟩ PARADIGM, now rare in this sense, may suggest an exemplar of a perfection impossible or unusual in reality ⟨a love worthy of being a *paradigm* of the cosmic relation of universal matter and universal form, this all-comprising power, cannot be a vague feeling —F.P.Bargebuhr⟩ IDEAL indicates the best possible exemplification either in reality or in a mental conception ⟨he had the courage and rebelliousness of his . . . cousins too much on his mind; they were his *ideal* —Glenway Wescott⟩ ⟨a multitude of stories and traditions grew up around his name, to be interpreted according to the hearers' own *ideals* of personality and education —D.E.Smith⟩ BEAU IDEAL sometimes is taken to mean "beautiful ideal" ⟨the very *beau ideal* of a perfect government is the government of a majority, acting through a representative body —J.C.Calhoun⟩ STANDARD may indicate that which embodies criteria for excellence and sets a high example for emulation ⟨the ideal of general cultivation has been one of the *standards* in education —C.W.Eliot⟩ ⟨human life on earth cannot continue unless we ordinary men and women can manage to practice these virtues up to a far higher *standard* —A.J.Toynbee⟩ MIRROR was once often used to mean a model of perfection ⟨bounteous Buckingham, the *mirror* of all courtesy —Shak.⟩

**²model** \\"\\ *vb* **modeled** *or* **modelled; modeled** *or* **modelled; modeling** *or* **modelling** \\-d(ᵊ)liŋ\\ **models** *vt* **1 :** to plan or form after a pattern **:** FRAME, SHAPE ⟨~*ed* a double-decked steamboat —Waldemar Kaempffert⟩ **2** *archaic* **:** to make into an organization (as an army, government, or parish) **3 a :** to shape or fashion in a pliable material (as clay, wax, or dampened leather) ⟨a file of plasticene animals ~*ed* by the little girls —Elizabeth Bowen⟩ **b :** to give a three-dimensional appearance to in painting or drawing esp. by means of chiaroscuro ⟨~*s* the head so that it seems to stand out from the canvas⟩ **c :** to emphasize the three-dimensional qualities of (a photographic subject) by means of highlights and shadows ⟨a ~*ing* light for portraiture⟩ ⟨use shadows to lend interest to the scene, to ~ it, give it emphasis —Aaron Sussman⟩ **4 :** to construct or fashion in imitation of a particular model ⟨~*ed* its constitution on that of the U.S.⟩ ⟨as for the speeches to Congress, they were palpably ~*ed* upon the speeches from the throne of the English kings —H.L.Mencken⟩ **5 :** to display by wearing, using, or posing with ⟨~*ed* her inaugural gowns at a fashion show —*N.Y.Times*⟩ ⟨famous for ~*ing* refrigerators and other appliances⟩ ~ *vi* **1 :** to design or imitate forms **:** make a pattern ⟨she enjoys ~*ing* in clay⟩ **2 :** to work or act as a model ⟨asked each contestant . . . to ~ before the judges' enclosure —Lillian Ross⟩

**³model** \\"\\ *adj* **:** serving as or capable of serving as a model ⟨a ~ house⟩ ⟨a ~ husband⟩ ⟨a ~ farm⟩

**model basin** *or* **model tank** *n* **:** a tank in which ship models are tested (as for inertia) by being towed at various speeds

**mod·el·er** *or* **mod·el·ler** \\'mäd(ᵊ)lə(r)\\ *n* -s **:** one that models: as **a :** a carver of leather shoe vamps and uppers **b :** one who molds in a plastic material designs to be copied for decorative tile or statuary

**mod·el·ist** \\-dᵊləst\\ *n* -s **:** a maker of models

**mod·el·ize** \\-dᵊl,īz\\ *vt, archaic* **:** to give a particular form to **:** SHAPE

**model school** *n* **:** a graded school usu. connected with a normal school or teachers' training college and used as a model in organization and methods of teaching

**model t** *adj, usu cap M&T* [fr. *Model T,* early type of motor car having only two speeds forward and a hand gasoline feed that was manufactured by the Ford Motor Co. between 1909 and 1927] **1 :** belonging to an initial or rudimentary phase of development ⟨when nuclear weapons were in the *Model T* stage of development —*N.Y.Times*⟩ **2 :** OLD-FASHIONED, OUTMODED ⟨a *Model T* school plant⟩

**¹mo·de·na** \\'mōdᵊnə, -ᵊn,ä\\ *adj, usu cap* [fr. *Modena,* city in northern Italy, capital of the province of Modena] **:** of or from the city of Modena, Italy **:** of the kind or style prevalent in Modena

**²modena** \\"\\ *n* [fr. *Modena,* province or its capital city in northern Italy] **1** *usu cap* **:** an Italian breed of small hen pigeons that have an erect carriage and varicolored plumage with the head and wings often of a color different from that of the body **2** -s *often cap* **:** any pigeon of the Modena breed

**mod·e·nese** \\¦mōdᵊn¦ēz, -ēs\\ *n, pl* **modenese** \\"\\ *cap* [It *modenese,* fr. *Modena,* Italy + It *-ese*] **:** a native or resident of Modena

**mod·er·ant** \\'mädərənt\\ *n* -s [²*moderate* + *-ant,* n. suffix] **:** something that moderates

**mod·er·ant·ism** \\-n,tizəm\\ *n* -s [F *modérantisme,* fr. *modérant* (pres. part. of *modérer* to moderate, fr. L *moderare*) + *-isme* -ism] **:** a policy of moderation esp. in politics

**mod·er·ant·ist** \\-,təst\\ *n* -s [F *modérantiste,* fr. *modérant* + *-iste* -ist] **:** an adherent of moderantism

**¹mod·er·ate** \\'mäd(ə)rət, *usu* -ād·+V\\ *adj* [ME, fr. L *moderatus,* past part. of *moderare, moderari* to moderate, fr. *modus* measure, manner — more at METE] **1 a :** characterized by an avoidance of extremes of behavior **:** observing reasonable limits **:** showing discretion and self-control ⟨a ~ drinker⟩ ⟨a ~ eater⟩ ⟨a person of ~ habits⟩ **b :** free from passion or excitement **:** CALM, REASONABLE ⟨though very much in favor of the measure, he expressed himself in ~ language⟩ ⟨his demands were very ~⟩ **2 a :** tending toward the mean or average: as (1) **:** neither small nor large ⟨a family of ~ income⟩ ⟨a room of ~ size⟩ ⟨a ~ crop⟩ (2) **:** neither short nor long ⟨a book of ~ length⟩ ⟨a ~ distance⟩ **b :** having an average or less than average quality **:** MEDIOCRE ⟨cheesecakes very ~ indeed —H.E. Bates⟩ ⟨wrote ~ poetry to the end of his life —Carl Van Doren⟩ **3 :** not violent or rigorous **:** TEMPERATE ⟨a ~ winter⟩ ⟨a ~ wind⟩ ⟨a ~ climate⟩ **4 :** of or relating to a political or social philosophy or program that avoids extreme measures and violent or partisan tactics ⟨has no interest in leading a party that goes off to extremes, that the party direction must be ~ and yet progressive and dynamic —*N.Y. Times*⟩ ⟨all left-wing and some ~ and right-wing groups had boycotted the election —*Collier's Yr. Bk.*⟩ **5 a :** limited in scope or effect ⟨made a ~ change in the bill which failed to satisfy its critics⟩ ⟨his new wealth had only a ~ effect on his way of life⟩ **b :** not severe in effect **:** not seriously or permanently disabling or incapacitating ⟨a few days of ~ illness accompanied by chilly sensations and loss of appetite —Morris Fishbein⟩ ⟨of the 18 cases in which whooping cough developed . . . 13.3 percent were very mild, 4.8 percent were mild and 3.7 percent were ~ —*Jour. Amer. Med. Assoc.*⟩ **6 :** not expensive **:** reasonable or low in price ⟨how to be well dressed at a ~ cost —*Current Biog.*⟩ ⟨a ~ price for a new house⟩ **7** *of a color* **:** of medium lightness and medium chroma

**²mod·er·ate** \\'mädə,rāt, *usu* -ād·+V\\ *vb* -ED/-ING/-S [ME *moderaten,* fr. L *moderatus,* past part. of *moderare, moderari* to moderate] *vt* **1 a :** to lessen the intensity or extremeness of **:** make less violent or excessive **:** keep within bounds **:** make moderate or temperate ⟨considerations of logic and analogy and history and tradition which ~ and temper the promptings of policy and justice —B.N.Cardozo⟩ ⟨*moderated* the harshness of their initial demands⟩ ⟨a quick and efficient job of snow removal *moderated* the effect of the storm⟩ **b :** to lower or soften the tone of (a voice) ⟨*moderated* his voice as they approached the sickroom⟩ ⟨~ your voice if you expect to be listened to⟩ **2** *archaic* **:** to exercise control over **:** REGULATE, RULE **3 :** to preside over or act as chairman at ⟨*moderated* the debate with perfect fairness⟩ ⟨*moderated* a small local variety show —Gladwin Hill⟩ **4 :** to reduce the speed or energy of (neutrons) ~ *vi* **1 :** to act as a moderator ⟨became famous when he *moderated* on a weekly panel show⟩ **2** *archaic* **:** to act as a mediator **3 :** to become less violent, severe, rigorous, or intense ⟨the wind has *moderated*⟩ ⟨loitering a little because the night had *moderated* —Kay Boyle⟩

**syn** QUALIFY, TEMPER, ATTEMPER: MODERATE indicates abating extremes or excesses in keeping within reasonable or due limits ⟨*moderating* his big voice to the dimensions of the room —Clifton Daniel⟩ ⟨if the new poets can bring themselves to *moderate* their attitude of somewhat sensitive resentment towards those who call their art in question —J.L.Lowes⟩ QUALIFY may indicate addition of restriction or precise definition to make a comment less sweeping, inclusive, or open to objection; it may be a close synonym for MODERATE ⟨the neat craftsman has means of *qualifying* or abating his own perilous air of arrant omniscience —C.E.Montague⟩ ⟨but this simple and bare outline of the procedure must be supplemented and *qualified* —Samuel Alexander⟩ ⟨*qualified* his reports in the *Boston News-Letter* according to the demands of the royal governor —F.L.Mott⟩ TEMPER may suggest an alleviating or mitigating of the severe or a modifying to accommodate to a situation ⟨always a cool breeze *tempered* the sunshine —A.B. Osborne⟩ ⟨close to being a major work in war fiction, and only my caution *tempers* my admiration —M.D.Geismar⟩ ⟨the catalogue of one Virginia seminary was promising to *temper* the severities of arithmetic to the delicacy of the female mind —*Amer. Guide Series: Va.*⟩ ATTEMPER is a close but now rarely used synonym for TEMPER in the sense of lessening ⟨the shadow . . . *attempered* the cheery western sunshine —Nathaniel Hawthorne⟩

**³mod·er·ate** \\'mäd(ə)rət, *usu* -əd·+V\\ *n* -s [¹*moderate;* intended as trans. of F *modéré*] **1 :** one who holds moderate views esp. in politics or religion ⟨the middle-of-the-road ~*s* in the world . . . who wanted both stability and liberalism —W.G. Carleton⟩ ⟨always a ~, he deprecated extremists of both sections —H.K.Beale⟩ **2** *often cap* **:** a member or adherent of a political party or group favoring a moderate program ⟨second term as the candidate of the *Moderates* —*Rev. of Reviews*⟩

**moderate breeze** *n* **:** wind having a speed of 13 to 18 miles per hour — see BEAUFORT SCALE table

**moderate gale** *n* **:** wind having a speed of 32 to 38 miles per hour — see BEAUFORT SCALE table

**mod·er·ate·ly** \\'mädər(ə)tlē, -drət-, -li\\ *adv* [ME *moderatly,* fr. *moderat, moderate* moderate + *-ly*] **:** in a moderate manner or to a moderate extent **:** FAIRLY, TEMPERATELY ⟨lived ~⟩ ⟨a ~ hot day⟩

**mod·er·ate·ness** *n* -ES **:** the quality or state of being moderate

**moderate oven** *n* **:** an oven heated to a temperature between 325° and 400° F

**mod·er·a·tion** \\,mädə'rāshən\\ *n* -s [ME *moderacion,* fr. L *moderation-, moderatio,* fr. *moderatus* (past part. of *moderare, moderari* to moderate) + *-ion-, -io* -ion] **1 :** the quality or state of being moderate **:** an avoidance of extremes **:** TEMPERATENESS ⟨a man who knew no ~ in his requests and impulses —Thomas Hardy⟩ ⟨a ~ of speech and of outward attitude which gave conservative constituents a sense of security and radical constituents a gleam of hope —Jeannette P. Nichols⟩ **2 :** the action of moderating; *specif* **:** a lessening of severity or intensity ⟨international policy with respect to the control or ~ of depressions —A.H.Hansen⟩ **3 moderations** *pl* **:** the first public examination for the B.A. in classics or mathematics at Oxford university following responsions — called also *mods* — **in moderation** *adv* **:** without excess **:** TEMPERATELY

**mod·er·a·tion·ist** \\-nəst\\ *n* -s **:** an advocate of moderation

**mod·er·at·ism** \\'mäd(ə)rəd·,izəm, -ə,tiz-\\ *n* -s **:** moderation in doctrines or opinions; *specif* **:** the opinions or policy of a moderate party or group in politics or religion

**mod·er·at·ist** \\-əd·əst, -ətəst\\ *n* -s **:** an adherent of moderatism

**mod·er·a·to** \\¦mädə¦räd·(,)ō\\ *adj (or adv)* [It (past part. of *moderare* to moderate), fr. L *moderatus,* past part. of *moderare, moderari* to moderate — more at MODERATE] **:** MODERATE — used as a direction in music to indicate tempo

**mod·er·a·tor** \\'mädə,rād·ə(r), -rātə-\\ *n* -s [ME *moderatour,* fr. L *moderator,* fr. *moderatus* (past part. of *moderare, moderari* to moderate) + *-or*] **1 :** one that rules or directs **:** GOVERNOR ⟨act in his name as ~ of the Western realm —E.A.Freeman⟩ **2 :** one who arbitrates **:** MEDIATOR ⟨the governor persuaded both sides to continue their talks with the ~ —*Springfield (Mass.) Union*⟩ **3 :** one who presides over an assembly, meeting, or discussion: as **a :** a presiding officer of any of various church meetings or assemblies within Protestant Christianity; *esp* **:** the presiding officer elected within a Presbyterian polity to preside over a general assembly or over a smaller regional meeting **b :** an official presiding over the exercises formerly prescribed for candidates for an academic degree — now used of an examiner for moderations at Oxford as well as of one of the two officers presiding over the mathematical tripos at Cambridge **c :** the nonpartisan presiding officer of a town meeting **d :** a person who acts as chairman of a discussion group (as on radio or television) **4** *archaic* **:** a person or thing that moderates or calms ⟨angling was . . . a ~ of passions —Izaak Walton⟩ **5 a :** a member of a group opposed to the violent methods of the regulators in No. Carolina about 1770 **b :** a member of one of numerous illegal bands active esp. in Texas about the middle of the 19th century **6 :** a candidate for the B.A. at Dublin taking first or second honors **7 :** a substance (as graphite, deuterium in heavy water, or beryllium) used for slowing down neutrons in a nuclear reactor

**mod·er·a·to·ri·al** \\¦mädərə¦tōrēəl, -tȯr-\\ *adj* **:** of, relating to, or characteristic of a moderator

**moderator lamp** *n* **:** a 19th century oil lamp burning colza oil and having a special regulator for the oil supply to the wick

**mod·er·a·tor·ship** \\'mädə,rād·ə(r),ship, -rātə(-\\ *n* **:** the position or duties of a moderator

**¹mod·ern** \R ˈmädərn, — R -dən or -dᵊn; R & — R also ÷ -d(ə)rən\ adj, often -ER/-EST [LL modernus, fr. L modo, adv., just now, fr. abl. of modus measure, manner — more at METE] **1 a :** of, relating to, or characteristic of a period extending from the more or less remote past to the present time ⟨totem poles, therefore, are ~ rather than prehistoric —R.W.Murray⟩ ⟨the difference between the classic and the ~ notion of experience —John Dewey⟩ ⟨links ancient and ~ in many ways —W.H. Ingrams⟩ ⟨~ thought . . . is a very recent affair, dating back only to the seventeenth century —Josiah Royce⟩; specif : of or relating to the historical period extending from about A.D. 1500 to the present day — compare ANCIENT, MEDIEVAL **b :** of, relating to, or characteristic of the present time or the immediate past : CONTEMPORARY, PRESENT-DAY ⟨bipartisanship in foreign policy is a ~ development in American politics —Arthur Krock⟩ ⟨instruments available to ~ government for the wider extension of wealth and well-being —Barbara Ward⟩ **c :** suitable to or expressive of the present time ⟨a ~ look⟩ ⟨~ furnishings⟩ ⟨the second house is even more ~ in appearance —Springfield (Mass.) Daily News⟩ **2 :** produced by or embodying the most recent techniques, methods, or ideas : UP-TO-DATE ⟨going to include in this addition and in this renovation ~ electric wiring and ~ plumbing and ~ means of keeping the offices cool —F.D.Roosevelt⟩ ⟨a very ~ and well-graded surface —L.D. Stamp⟩ **3** obs : COMMONPLACE, ORDINARY, TRITE ⟨full of wise saws and ~ instances —Shak.⟩ **4** usu cap, of a language : of, relating to, or having the characteristics of the present or most recent period of development as contrasted with earlier periods — compare MIDDLE, OLD **5 :** of, relating to, or having the characteristics of a movement or style in the arts marked by a break with traditional esp. academic forms and techniques of expression, an emphasis upon experimentation, boldness, and creative originality, and an attempt to deal with modern themes — compare ABSTRACT, ACADEMIC **syn** see NEW

**²modern** \"\ n -s **1 a :** a person of modern times ⟨the first ~ to state in human terms the principles of democracy —John Dewey⟩ **b :** a person alive at present ⟨the hurried ~ learns to speed quickly down a page, taking in a sentence or paragraph at a glance —Thomas Munro⟩ ⟨the threat of atomic warfare has prompted a mood of hysteria among many ~s —Reinhold Niebuhr⟩ **2 :** a person with modern ideas, tastes, or attitudes ⟨a complete ~, university educated, and trained as an administrator along European lines —Colin Wills⟩ ⟨furniture designed for young ~s⟩ **3 :** a practitioner of modern art ⟨was making a name for himself as one of the ~s —Shirley A. Grau⟩ ⟨turned from his Provençal models except as he continued at times to translate them; he became a ~ —Yvor Winters⟩ **4 :** a style of printing type based on an 18th century design of Giambattista Bodoni and distinguished esp. as contrasted with old style by regularity of shape, precise curves, straight hairline serifs, and heavy downstrokes ⟨this is an example of ~⟩

**mo·derne** \məˈde(ə)rn\ adj [F, modern, fr. LL modernus] : tastelessly or pretentiously modern ⟨a ~ front attached to an old late eighteenth century house —Anthony West⟩

**modern figure** n : LINING FIGURE

**modern game** n, usu cap M&G : the class or breed of game fowls that is characterized by sparse feathering, tall upright carriage, and long neck — see EXHIBITION GAME FOWL, PIT GAME FOWL; compare OLD ENGLISH GAME

**modern greats** n pl, usu cap M&G : an honor school of philosophy, politics, and economics at Oxford University

**modern hebrew** n, usu cap M&H : Hebrew as used in present-day Israel

**mod·ern·ish** \pronunc at MODERN + ish\ adj : suggestive of modern style : somewhat modern

**mod·ern·ism** \pronunc at MODERN + ˌizəm\ n -s [¹modern + -ism] **1 a :** a practice, usage, or expression peculiar to or characteristic of modern times ⟨there is not a house in Warsaw that is not lousy — to use a ~ — with secret passages —Gerald Kelly⟩ **b :** a way of living or thinking characteristic of modern times ⟨opposed to electricity in homes as a concession to ~ —G.P.Musselman⟩ **2 a** often cap : a movement in Protestant Christianity originating in the latter half of the 19th century and continuing to the present that seeks to establish the meaning and validity of the Christian faith in relation to present human experience and to reconcile and unify traditional theological concepts with the requirements of modern knowledge — compare LIBERALISM 2a **b** usu cap, Anglicanism : the position that all knowledge by which religion can be affected necessarily reaffirms the fundamental truths of Christianity but necessitates their official restatement by the Church in the language relevant to the intellectual conditions of the age **c** often cap, Roman Catholicism : a system of interpretation of Christian doctrine developed at the end of the 19th century and condemned by Pope Pius X in 1907 that denied the objective truth of revelation and the whole supernatural world and maintained that the only vital element in any religion and Catholicism in particular was its power to preserve and communicate to others the best religious experiences of the race **3 :** the philosophy and practices of modern art; esp : a self-conscious and deliberate break with the past and a search for new forms of expression in any of the arts ⟨an outraged press and public pounced on it as the very model of loathsome ~ —A.L.Chanin⟩

**¹mod·ern·ist** \-nəst\ n -s [¹modern + -ist] **1 :** an admirer of modern ways or things : one who asserts the superiority of modern times ⟨its subject is the perennial conflict between conservative and ~ —Moses Hadas⟩ **2 :** an adherent of modernism in religion **3 :** one who practices, advocates, or admires modernism in the arts

**²modernist** \"\ adj : of, relating to, or characteristic of modernism or modernists

**mod·ern·is·tic** \ˌ≈≈ˈnistik, -tēk\ adj [¹modernist + -ic] **1 :** MODERNIST ⟨his stimulating, ~ conception of what should be the aims and methods of education —N.Y. Times⟩ ⟨lays bare the emptiness of the ~ substitutes for the ancient certitudes —Va. Quarterly Rev.⟩ **2 :** having the superficial mannerisms or surface characteristics of modern style : falsely modern ⟨his tight suit and stiff hat all angles, like a ~ lampstand —William Faulkner⟩ **syn** see NEW

**mo·der·ni·ty** \mäˈdərnəd·ē, mə'-, -dən-, -dəin-, -nətē, -i\ n -ES [ML modernitat-, modernitas, fr. LL modernus modern + -itat-, -itas -ity] : the quality or state of being modern : MODERNISM ⟨this sleepy little city . . . is waiting for a motor speedway to breathe new life and a spirit of ~ into it —Arnaldo Cortesi⟩

**mod·ern·iza·tion** \R ˌmädərnəˈzāshən, — R -dən- or -dᵊn-; R & — R also ÷ -d(ə)rən-; -ˌnīˈz-\ n -s **1 :** the act of modernizing or the state of being modernized ⟨careful consideration to the ~ of the federal tax structure —H.S.Truman⟩ ⟨only as ~ takes place can countries make their full contribution to the world's wealth —Eugene Mayer⟩ **2 :** a modernized version (as of a play) ⟨produced ~s of a number of Shakespeare's plays⟩

**mod·ern·ize** \pronunc at MODERN + ˌīz\ vb -ED/-ING/-S vt : to make modern : adapt to modern needs, taste, or usage ⟨a determination to ~ poetry, and bring it closer to life —F.R.Leavis⟩ ⟨the method of lumbering has been modernized —Amer. Guide Series: Maine⟩: as **a :** REMODEL, REPAIR ⟨~ the theater⟩ ⟨the curse of many downtown districts . . . is the owner who refuses to ~ his building —Hal Burton⟩ **b :** to change (a text) to make conform to modern usage in spelling and language ⟨has modernized it quite considerably, printing proper names in their modern form, correcting grammatical lapses, and inserting the equivalent of obsolete words in brackets —G.R.Crone⟩ ~ vi : to adopt modern ways : act, write, or speak in a modern manner ⟨it is natural . . . for scribes to ~ and for poets to archaize —C.A.Lynch⟩ — **mod·ern·iz·er** \-zə(r)\ n -s

**modern languages** n pl but sing or pl in constr : the living literary languages esp. of Europe considered as a department of study or teaching

**mod·ern·ly** adv **1 :** in modern times : NOW ⟨society as ~ organized cannot tolerate so broad an area of official irresponsibility —R.H.Jackson⟩ **2 :** in a modern manner ⟨a ~ designed house⟩ ⟨a ~ run office⟩

**mod·ern·ness** \-(n)nəs\ n -ES : MODERNITY ⟨the ~ or antiquity of an action . . . has nothing to do with its fitness for poetical representation —Matthew Arnold⟩

**modern pentathlon** n : a 5-event athletic contest; specif : a composite contest that consists of the 300-meter freestyle swim, the 4000-meter cross-country run, the 5000-meter 30-jump steeplechase, fencing with the épée, and target shooting at 25 meters

**modern school** n : SECONDARY MODERN SCHOOL

**mod·est** \ˈmädəst\ adj, sometimes -ER/-EST [L modestus moderate, modest — more at METE] **1 a :** having a limited and not exaggerated estimate of one's abilities or worth : lacking in vanity or conceit : not bold or self-assertive ⟨the well-bred man . . . is ~ without being bashful, and steady without being impudent —Earl of Chesterfield⟩ ⟨was entirely natural, ~, and unaffected in manner —Eliot Clark⟩ ⟨was so certain he was right he could be rather charmingly simple and ~ —T.R.Ybarra⟩ **b :** diffident and retiring in manner : SHY ⟨the most ~, silent, sheepfaced and meek of little men —W.M. Thackeray⟩ **2 :** arising from or showing a self-effacing and unassertive attitude : free from exaggeration or overstatement : REASONABLE, MODERATE ⟨the reply seems calm, ~ and highly persuasive —R.K.Carr⟩ ⟨what nearly all newsmen were actually doing was a ~ job of explaining the bald facts —F.L.Mott⟩ ⟨his emotions he records in the plain and ~ language of the eighteenth century —Theodore Baird⟩ **3 :** observing conventional standards of proper dress and behavior : free from coarseness or indecency : chaste in thought and conduct ⟨all the females of our family have been perfectly ~ and delicate —Margaret Deland⟩ ⟨the pure bashful maiden was too ~, too tender, too trustful —W.M.Thackeray⟩ **4 a :** limited in size or amount : not excessive ⟨a quietly prosperous rural society, in which landownership, opportunity and ~ wealth were widely distributed —G.M.Trevelyan⟩ ⟨while their means were always ~ there was no trace of dire poverty —J.T.Ellis⟩ ⟨the galaxy of which our sun is a ~ member —B.J.Bok⟩ **b :** limited in extent or aim : not showy or ostentatious : UNPRETENTIOUS ⟨the day-to-day work of the scientist depends on ~ working hypotheses rather than on broad sweeping theories —Eric Ashby⟩ ⟨press agent for a ~ nightclub —Newsweek⟩ ⟨quite famous in a ~ sort of way —Robertson Davies⟩ **syn** see CHASTE, HUMBLE, SHY

**mod·est·ly** adv : in a modest manner or to a modest extent ⟨a book, whose authorship he ~ professed —Sidney Lovett⟩

**mod·es·ty** \ˈmädəstē, -ti\ n -ES [L modestia, fr. modestus moderate, modest + -ia -y] **1 a** archaic : freedom from excess or exaggeration : MODERATION ⟨an excellent play . . . set down with as much ~ as cunning —Shak.⟩ **b :** freedom from conceit or vanity : an awareness of one's limitations ⟨has great natural ~, with a stronger dependence on my judgment than on his own —Jane Austen⟩ ⟨~ . . . is essential to anyone who deals successfully with nature, since the ego must be capable of awe —L.J.Halle⟩ **c :** freedom from coarseness, indelicacy, or indecency : a regard for propriety in dress, speech, or conduct ⟨while retaining all her ~, had lost all her shyness —Arnold Bennett⟩ ⟨that affectation of extreme shyness, silence, and reserve, which misses in their teens are apt to take for an amiable ~ —Sir Walter Scott⟩ **2 :** a plain or decorative fill-in for a low neckline esp. of a dress **3 :** limitation in size, amount, or extent ⟨operates on a budget appropriate to the ~ of its quarters —Report: (Canadian) Royal Commission on Nat'l Development⟩ **4 a :** HARE'S-EAR 1 **b :** FLOWER-OF-AN-HOUR

**modi** pl of MODUS

**mo·dic·i·ty** \mōˈdisəd·ē, -ətē, -i\ n -ES [F modicité, fr. LL modicitat-, modicitas, fr. L modicus moderate + -itat-, -itas -ity] archaic : MODERATENESS ⟨found compensation for the darkness of her frontage in the ~ of her rent —Henry James †1916⟩

**mod·i·cum** \ˈmädəkəm, ˈmōd-\ n -s [ME, fr. L, neut. of modicus moderate, small, fr. modus measure, manner + -icus -ic — more at METE] : a small portion : a limited quantity or amount ⟨a falsehood without even a ~ of truth in it⟩

**mod·i·fi·a·bil·i·ty** \ˌmädəˌfīəˈbiləd·ē, -lətē, -i\ n : the capability of being modified ⟨this ~ is one of the intrinsic qualities of living protoplasm —J.S.Shrike⟩

**mod·i·fi·able** \ˌmädəˈfīəbəl\ adj : capable of being modified ⟨the rhythm of physiological time is not ~ except by interference with certain fundamental processes —Alexis Carrel⟩ — **mod·i·fi·able·ness** n -ES

**mod·i·fi·cand** \ˌ≈≈fəˈkand\ n -s [L modificandum something to be moderated, neut. of modificandus, gerundive of modificare, modificari] : a term having a grammatical qualifier

**mod·i·fi·ca·tion** \ˌ≈≈fəˈkāshən\ n -s [MF, fr. ML modification-, modificatio, fr. L, measure, measuring, fr. modificatus (past part. of modificare, modificari to measure, moderate) + -ion-, -io -ion] **1 :** the act of limiting the meaning or application of a concept or statement : QUALIFICATION, RESTRICTION ⟨with some ~s this statement is true today —J.B.Conant⟩ **2 :** ¹MODE 6 **3 a (1) :** the act or action of changing something without fundamentally altering it ⟨making the exactly minimum degree of ~ to her institutions necessary to fit them to new conditions —John Strachey⟩ **(2) :** the state of being so changed **b :** a result of such partial change : a modified form ⟨a ~ of last year's hardtop⟩ ⟨a ~ of a European breed⟩ ⟨a ~ of his batting style⟩ **c :** a noninheritable change in an organism caused by the influence of its environment **4 a :** a limitation or qualification of the meaning of a word by another word, by an affix, or by internal change **b :** INFLECTION 4a **c :** a change that a linguistic form undergoes when borrowed from one language into another **5 a :** an alteration by environmental influence of the articulatory components of a word or other speech item ⟨the alteration of has to \z\ in \hēz stäpt\ (he's stopped) is a phonetic ~⟩ **b :** UMLAUT 1 **6** Scots law : the action of awarding or decreeing something done or paid in settlement (as the award of a minister's stipend against his parish)

**¹mod·i·fi·ca·tive** \ˈ≈≈≈ˌkād·iv\ n -s [L modificatus + E -ive, n. suffix] : something that modifies

**²modificative** \"\ adj [L modificatus + E -ive, adj. suffix] : serving to modify

**mod·i·fi·ca·tor** \-ˌkād·ə(r)\ n -s [L modificatus + E -or] : MODIFIER

**mod·i·fi·ca·to·ry** \ˈmädəfəkəˌtōrē, ˌmädəˈfik-, mäˈdifək- chiefly Brit ˌmädəfəˈkātəri or -ā·tri\ adj [L modificatus + E -ory] : serving to modify

**modified basket maker** n, usu cap M&B&M : an ancient culture of the plateau area of southwestern U.S. characterized by fired pottery, permanent pithouses, grooved hammers, notched axes, bows and arrows, the cultivation of beans and corn, and the domesticated turkey

**modified life policy** n : a life insurance policy providing for low premiums during an initial period of three or five years

**modified milk** n : milk altered in composition (as by the addition of lactose) esp. for use in infant feeding

**modified soda** n : a mixture of soda ash and sodium bicarbonate in various proportions for use esp. in laundering

**mod·i·fi·er** \ˈmädəˌfī(ə)r, -īə\ n -s **1 :** one that modifies **2 a :** a grammatical qualifier : a subordinate constituent of a grammatical construction **b :** a phonetic symbol of defined meaning that alters the value or provides a more exact description of the symbol to which it is attached (as \ⁿ\ in \aⁿ\ representing a nasalized \a\) : DIACRITIC **3 a :** a gene known only by its effect on the expression of another gene occupying a different locus **b :** a gene that modifies the effect of another **4 :** a substance added during a process or operation to bring about a desired effect or impart desired qualities (as in polymerization processes for controlling cross-linking or in ore flotation for decreasing the tendency of flotation of the undesired particles of gangue)

**mod·i·fy** \-ˌfī\ vb -ED/-ING/-ES [ME modifien, fr. MF modifier, fr. L modificare, modificari to measure, moderate, fr. modus measure, manner + -ficare, -ficari -fy — more at METE] vt **1 :** to make more temperate and less extreme : lessen the severity of : MODERATE ⟨the proximity of the ocean modifies the temperature —Amer. Guide Series: R.I.⟩ ⟨traffic rules were modified to let him pass —Van Wyck Brooks⟩ **2** Scots law : to award or decree as something to be done or paid (as a minister's stipend against his parish) **3 a :** to limit or restrict the meaning of : to be subordinate to in a grammatical construction : QUALIFY **b :** to change (a vowel) by umlaut **4 a :** to make minor changes in the form or structure of : alter without transforming ⟨the aeroplane — as it was called for many years before the word was modified to airplane —A.F.Harlow⟩ ⟨represents a type already partly modified by domestication —P.C.Mangelsdorf⟩ **b :** to make a basic or important change in : ALTER ⟨the older view that laws ~ conduct and that punishment effectively limits crime —Alex Comfort⟩ ⟨the weakening of the geographical factor in social organization must . . . profoundly ~ our attitude toward the meaning of personal relations —Edward Sapir⟩ ⟨have modified my views of conduct to conform with what seem to me the implications of my beliefs —T.S.Eliot⟩ **5 :** to change the form or properties of for a definite purpose ⟨the equipment was modified to produce locomotives —Amer. Guide Series: Va.⟩ ⟨a Navy trainer . . . was modified . . . for flight study of the system of boundary-layer control by blowing —Report: Nat'l Advisory Committee for Aeronautics⟩ ⟨starch is modified by heating to produce British gum⟩ ~ vi : to undergo change **syn** see CHANGE

**mo·dil·lion** \mōˈdilyən\ n -s [It modiglione, fr. (assumed) VL mutilion-, mutilio, fr. L mutulus modillion, mutule] : an enriched block or horizontal bracket generally found under the corona of the cornice of the Corinthian and Composite entablature and sometimes in a plainer form in other orders

modillion

**mo·di·nha** \mōˈdēnyə\ n -s [Pg, dim. of moda mode, fr. F mode] : a Portuguese art song typically romantic and sentimental

**mo·di·o·lar** \məˈdīələ(r)\ adj [prob. fr. (assumed) NL modiolaris, fr. NL ²modiolus + L -aris -ar] : of or relating to the modiolus of the ear

**¹mo·di·o·lus** \-ləs\ n, cap [NL, fr. L, nave of a wheel, cylinder of a pump, dim. of modius] : a genus of sea mussels (family Mytilidae) including the horse mussels

**²modiolus** \"\ n, pl **modio·li** \-ˌlī\ [NL, fr. L] : a central bony column in the cochlea of the ear

**mod·ish** \ˈmōdish, -dēsh\ adj : being in the mode : FASHIONABLE ⟨a ~ hat⟩ ⟨a ~ writer⟩ ⟨tend to regard the pursuit of the new as necessarily silly and ~ —E.R.Bentley⟩ — **mod·ish·ly** adv — **mod·ish·ness** n -ES

**mo·diste** \mōˈdēst\ n -s [F, fr. mode (fr. L modus measure, manner) + -iste -ist — more at METE] : one who makes and sells fashionable dresses and hats for women

**mo·di·us** \ˈmōdēəs\ n, pl **mo·dii** \-ēˌī\ [L; akin to L modus measure, manner] : an ancient Roman unit of grain measure equivalent to 0.96 peck

**modiwarp** or **modiwart** var of MOLDWARP

**mo·doc** \ˈmōˌdäk\ n, pl **modoc** or **modocs** usu cap [prob. fr. Shasta, stranger] **1 a :** a Lutuamian people of southwestern Oregon and northwestern California **b :** a member of such people **2 :** the language of the Modoc people

**¹mods** pl of MOD

**²mods** \ˈmädz\ n pl, usu cap [by shortening] : MODERATIONS

**mod·u·la·bil·i·ty** \ˌmäjələˈbiləd·ē, -ətē, -i\ n [modulate + -ability] : the capability of being modulated

**mod·u·lar** \ˈmäjələ(r)\ adj [NL modularis, fr. modulus + L -aris -ar] **1 :** of, relating to, or based on a module or a modulus **2** [module + -ar] : planned or constructed on the basis of a standard pattern or standard dimensions : capable of being easily joined to or arranged with other parts or units ⟨~ furniture⟩ ⟨a ~ wall unit⟩

**mod·u·late** \-ˌlāt, usu -ād·+V\ vb -ED/-ING/-S [L modulatus, past part. of modulari to measure, modulate, fr. modulus small measure, meter, melody, module, fr. modus measure + -ulus — more at METE] vt **1 :** INTONE, SING ⟨~ a prayer⟩ ⟨~ a song⟩ **2 a :** to tune to a key or pitch : vary in tone : make tuneful or pleasing in sound ⟨the radio engineers do not try to ~ his voice —Current Biog.⟩ ⟨did not scream or roar . . . she was old enough to ~ her voice and conserve her energies —John Mason Brown⟩ **b :** to adjust to or keep in proper measure or proportion : soften or tone down : TEMPER ⟨modulated his thunders according to the tree, shrub, or weed to be blasted —T.S.Eliot⟩ ⟨the humor is either modulated or relegated to the background —Marc Slonim⟩ **3 :** to vary a characteristic (as amplitude, frequency, phase) of (a carrier wave or signal) in a periodic or intermittent manner for the transmission of intelligence ~ vi **1 :** to play or sing with modulation **2 a :** to pass by regular chord progression from one musical key or tonality into another or from one mode to another **b :** to pass by regular melodic progression from one key to another **3 :** to pass gradually from one state to another ⟨had a fierce quality that had modulated, but not softened, to authority —Lionel Trilling⟩

**modulated continuous waves** n pl : CONTINUOUS WAVES 2

**mod·u·la·tion** \ˌ≈≈ˈlāshən\ n -s [ME modulacion, fr. L modulation-, modulatio, fr. modulatus (past part. of modulari to modulate) + -ion-, -io -ion] **1** archaic : a singing or making of music : musical sound : MELODY **2 :** a fitting or regulating according to a certain measure or proportion : a tempering or toning down ⟨appetites so vigorous and senses so vivid do not lend themselves to temperance, to tolerance, to ~ —Francis Hackett⟩ **3 a :** an inflection or varying of the tone or pitch of the voice ⟨that singularly individual voice . . . mature, confident, seldom varying in pitch, but full of slight, very moving ~s —Willa Cather⟩ **b :** a particular intonation or inflection of the voice ⟨told us, in rich nasal ~ —E.V.Lucas⟩ ⟨the soft ~ of her voice soothed the infant⟩ **c (1) :** the use of stress or pitch to convey meaning **(2) :** an instance of such modulation **4 :** the determination of proportions in a classic architectural order by means of the module or unit of length **5 a :** one of four tones (final, dominant, mediant, participant) of an ecclesiastical mode on which a phrase may begin or end **b :** the act or process of changing from one tonality to another without a break in the melody or the chord succession **6 :** a melodious use of language esp. by variations of rhythm and tone : verbal harmony ⟨we read it as much for its pleasing rendition of a state of mind . . . as for the ~ of its prose rhythms —David Daiches⟩ ⟨the metrical mastery which catches so naturally, yet with so true a ~, the faltering accents of the supplicant —Edmund Wilson⟩ **7 :** the variation of a characteristic (as amplitude, frequency, or phase) of a carrier or signal in a periodic or intermittent manner for the transmission of intelligence (as in telegraphy, telephony, radio, television) **8 :** a reversible change in histological structure due to physiological factors

**modulation index** n : a measure of the degree of frequency modulation expressed numerically for a pure tone modulation as the ratio of the frequency deviation to the frequency of the modulating signal

**mod·u·la·tor** \ˈmäjəˌlād·ə(r), -ātə-\ n -s [L, fr. modulatus (past part. of modulari to modulate) + -or] **1 :** one that modulates: as **a :** a device (as an electron tube) for modulating a carrier wave or signal for the transmission of intelligence (as in telegraphy, telephony, radio, television) **b :** LIGHT VALVE — called also light modulator **2 :** any of the nerve fibers that carry impulses from single retinal cones and are believed to be responsible for the transmission of discrete sensations of color

**mod·u·la·to·ry** \-ləˌtōrē, -tȯr-, -ri\ adj : of or relating to modulation (as in music) : serving to modulate ⟨a ~ passage⟩

**mod·ule** \ˈmä(ˌ)jül\ n -s [L modulus small measure, meter, module in architecture, fr. modus measure + -ulus — more at METE] **1 a** archaic : something that serves as a model or pattern : EXEMPLAR ⟨the text ~ is a sentence from . . . Thoreau —William Beebe⟩ **b** obs : a counterfeit image ⟨but a clod and ~ of confounded royalty —Shak.⟩ **2 :** a standard or unit of measurement **3 a** [F, fr. L modulus] : the size of some one part (as the diameter or semidiameter of the base of a shaft) taken as a unit of measure by which the proportions of the other parts of a classical or nonclassical architectural composition are regulated **b :** a unit of size used as a basis for standardizing the design and construction of building parts and materials or articles of furniture ⟨use of dimensional coordination on the four-inch ~ —R.T.Liddicoat⟩ ⟨fabricated for assembly on a 2-foot ~ —S.D.Sturgis⟩ **4 a :** a device used for measuring the flow of water or for delivering a fixed volume of water (as in irrigation systems) **b :** the volume discharged by such a device

**5 :** the diameter of a coin, token, or medal **6 :** the pitch diameter of a gear wheel (as measured in millimeters or inches) divided by the number of teeth

**mod·u·lo** \ˈmäjə,lō\ *prep* [NL, abl. of *modulus*] : with respect to a modulus of

**mod·u·lus** \-ləs\ *n, pl* **moduli** \-,lī\ [NL, fr. L, small measure] **1 :** a constant or coefficient that expresses numerically the degree in which a property is possessed by a substance or body **2 a :** the absolute value of a complex number **b :** an integer (as *x*) whose relationship to two other integers (as *y* and *z*) is such that *y* minus *z* divided by *x* is a whole number **3** *cap* **:** a genus (the type of the family Modulidae) of thin-shelled, bulbous, operculate marine snails of tropical seas

**modulus of a logarithm :** the factor by which the logarithm to a given base of any number must be multiplied to obtain the logarithm of the same number

**modulus of elasticity :** the ratio of the stress in a body to the corresponding strain (as in bulk modulus, shear modulus, and Young's modulus) — called also *coefficient of elasticity, elastic modulus*

**modulus of rigidity :** SHEAR MODULUS

**modulus of rupture :** an ultimate strength pertaining to the failure of beams by flexure equal to the bending moment at rupture divided by the section modulus of the beam

**mo·dus** \ˈmōdəs\ *n, pl* **mo·di** *see sense 2* \-,dī\ [L, measure, manner — more at METE] **1 :** the immediate manner in which property may be acquired (as by occupation or prescription) or the particular tenure by which it is held **2** *pl* **moduses :** a customary mode of tithing by composition instead of by payment in kind ⟨still took his tithe pig or his ~ —George Eliot⟩ **3 :** a mode of procedure **:** a way of doing something ⟨no ~ of accomplishing this desired result —Ezra Pound⟩ **4 :** MODE

**modus ope·ran·di** \-,äpəˈrandē, -,dī\ *n, pl* **modi operandi** [NL] **1 :** a manner of operating or working ⟨their *modus operandi* is the old Indian art of tracking —Frank Cameron⟩ ⟨the *modus operandi* of a particularly nasty type of middle-class woman —John Nerber⟩ **2 :** a distinct pattern or method of procedure thought to be characteristic of an individual criminal and habitually followed by him ⟨got her picture identified, discovered her *modus operandi*, and put a stakeout on her neighborhood —*Time*⟩ — abbr. *M.O.*

**modus po·nens** \-ˈpō,nenz\ *n, pl* **modi ponen·tes** \-,pōˈnen,tēz\ [NL, proposing mode] : a mode of reasoning from a hypothetical proposition according to which if the antecedent be affirmed the consequent is affirmed (as, if A is true, B is true; but A is true; therefore, B is true)

**modus tol·lens** \-ˈtä,lenz\ *n, pl* **modi tol·len·tes** \-(,)täˈlen,tēz\ [NL, removing mode] : a mode of reasoning from a hypothetical proposition according to which if the consequent be denied the antecedent is denied (as, if A is true, B is true; but B is false; therefore A is false)

**modus vi·ven·di** \-vəˈvendē, -,dī\ *n, pl* **modi vivendi** [NL, manner of living] **1 :** an arrangement between two nations or groups that effects a workable compromise on issues in dispute without permanently settling them ⟨essential that a *modus vivendi* be set up if conflict is to be avoided —Donald Davidson⟩ ⟨a *modus vivendi* which both worlds could accept and which would provide to each physical security against military attack —*Newsweek*⟩ **2 :** a manner of living **:** a way of life ⟨after many spiritual fits and starts, he found himself and worked out a satisfactory *modus vivendi* —*New Yorker*⟩ ⟨cocktail parties were a *modus vivendi* in themselves —Jean Stafford⟩

**mody** \ˈmōdē\ *adj* [²*mode* + *-y*] *archaic* **:** MODISH

**moe** \ˈmō\ *adj or adv or n* [ME *mo* — more at MORE] *chiefly dial* **:** MORE

**moeh·rin·gia** \mōˈrinjēə\ *n, cap* [NL, fr. P. H. G. *Moehring* †1792 Ger. naturalist + NL *-ia*] : a genus of low herbs (family Caryophyllaceae) growing in the north temperate regions and having opposite entire leaves, small white flowers, and few-seeded capsules — see SANDWORT

**moel·lon** \(ˈ)mweˈlōⁿ\ *or* **moellon de·gras** \,==dāˈgrä\ *n, pl* **moellons** \-ōⁿ(z)\ *or* **moellons degras** [*moellon* fr. F, prob. fr. *moelle* marrow, fr. OF *moele*, alter. of *meole*, fr. L *medulla* marrow, pith; *moellon degras* fr. *moellon* + *degras* — more at MEDULLA] : DEGRAS 1a

**moeri·there** \ˈmirə,thi(ə)r, ˈmer-\ *n* -S [NL *Moeritherium*] : an animal or fossil of the genus *Moeritherium*

**moeri·the·ri·um** \,==ˈthirēəm\ *n, cap* [NL, fr. Lake *Moeris*, ancient lake in Faiyûm province, northern Upper Egypt where remains of the genus were found + NL *-therium*] : a genus of Upper Eocene and Oligocene northern African mammals (order Proboscidea) that are about as large as tapirs and have a short proboscis and mastodont teeth including enlarged second incisors which are considered precursors of the tusks of later related forms (as mastodons and elephants)

**moe·so·goth** \ˈmēsə, -ēzə+,-\ *n, usu cap* [NL *Moeso-Gothi* (pl.), fr. L *Moesi* inhabitants of Moesia, ancient country south of the Danube river and extending from the Drina river to the Black sea + LL *Gothi* Goths — more at GOTH] : a Goth of the ancient Roman province of the middle Danube or Moesia

**¹moe·so·gothic** \;==+\ *adj, usu cap* [NL *Moeso-Gothicus*, fr. *Moeso-Gothi* + L *-icus -ic*] : of or relating to the Moesogoths or their language

**²moesogothic** \"\ *n, usu cap* **:** the form of Gothic spoken by the Moesogoths

**mo·fette** *also* **mof·fette** \mōˈfet\ *n* -S [F *mofette* gaseous exhalation, mofette, fr. It *mofeta*, of Gmc origin; akin to MHG *müffeln* to smell moldy] : a vent from which carbon dioxide and some nitrogen and oxygen issue from the earth in a last stage of volcanic activity

**mof·fle** \ˈmäfəl\ *var of* MAFFLE

**mo·fus·sil** \mōˈfəsəl\ *n* -S [Hindi *mufassal, mufaṣṣil*, fr. Ar *mufaṣṣal* separated] : the provincial or rural districts of India **:** COUNTRYSIDE ⟨an urgent need for more teachers who can get out to the farming areas in the ~ —*India Internat'l*⟩

**mo·fus·sil·ite** \-,līt\ *n* -S : one who lives in the mofussil

**mog** \ˈmäg, ˈmȯg\ *vb* **mogged; mogged; mogging; mogs** [origin unknown] *vi* **1** *dial* **:** to move away **:** DEPART — usu. used with *off* or *on* **2** *chiefly dial* **:** to walk slowly and steadily **:** JOG ⟨all the men go *mogging* gloomily along —Ralph Knight⟩ ⟨exhausted federal mediators who dutifully *mogged* back & forth —*Time*⟩ ~ *vt, dial Eng* **:** to move or cause to move from one place to another

**mog·a·di·shu** \-di(,)shü\ *or* **mog·a·di·scio** \;mägəˈdi(,)shō, -dē(-, -dishē,ō\ *adj, usu cap* [fr. *Mogadishu* or *Mogadiscio*, Somalia] : of or from Mogadisshu, the capital of Somalia **:** of the kind or style prevalent in Mogadisshu

**mog·a·dor** *also* **mog·a·dore** \;mägəˈdō(ə)r, -dȯ(ə)r\ *n* -S [*Mogador*, seaport city in southwestern Morocco] : a silk or rayon fabric that is similar to fine faille and is usu. made in colorful stripes for neckties and sportswear

**mogador gum** *or* **mogadore gum** *n* **:** MOROCCO GUM

**mog·dad coffee** \(ˈ)mägˈdad-\ *n, often cap M* [*mogdad* fr. native name in Senegal, western Africa] : COFFEE SENNA

**mogen david** *usu cap M&D, var of* MAGEN DAVID

**mog·gan** \ˈmägən\ *n* -S [origin unknown] *Scot* **:** STOCKING; *esp* **:** a long stocking without a foot

**mog·gy** \ˈmägē, -gi\ *n* -ES [prob. fr. *Moggy*, fr. *Mog* (nickname fr. the name *Margaret*) + *-y*] **1** *dial Brit* **a :** COW, CALF — used as a pet name **b :** HOUSE CAT **2** *dial Eng* **:** SLATTERN

**moghul** *cap, var of* MOGUL

**mogi-** *comb form* [NL, fr. Gk, fr. *mogis* barely, with effort; akin to Gk *mogos* exertion, labor, Latvian *smags* burdensome] : with difficulty ⟨*mogiphonia*⟩

**mo·go** \ˈmō,gō\ *n* -S [native name in New South Wales, Australia] : an Australian stone-hatchet

**¹mo·gol·lon** \;mōgəˈyōn, ;mägēˈōn\ *n, pl* **mogollon** *or* **mogollons** *usu cap* [*Mogollon* Mesa, tableland in central Arizona, and *Mogollon* mountains, range in western New Mexico] **1 :** an American Indian people constituting a subdivision of the Gileños **2 :** a member of the Mogollon people

**²mogollon** \"\ *adj, usu cap* **:** of or relating to an ancient culture of west central New Mexico and adjacent Arizona characterized in its earlier stages by polished brown or red ceramic ware, the equal importance of hunting and agriculture, deep pit houses, notched bone awls, and heavy corner-notched projectile points

**mo·go·te** \məˈgōdˌē\ *n* -S [AmerSp, fr. Sp, conical pile of fagots, knoll, budding antler, prob. fr. Basque *moko* point] *Southwest* **:** a patch of brush or thickly grown shrubbery

**¹mo·gul** \ˈmōgəl, (ˈ)mōˈgəl\ *n* -S [Per *Mughul*, fr. Mongolian *Mongol*] **1** *also* **mo·ghul** \"\ *or* **mu·ghal** *or* **mu·ghul** \ˈmügəl\ *cap* **:** an Indian Muslim of or descended from one of several conquering groups of Mongol, Turkish, and Persian origin; *esp* **:** GREAT MOGUL **2 :** a dominant person in a particular business or field ⟨the supposedly omnipotent ~*s* of the dress trade and the advertising trade —F.L.Allen⟩ ⟨found the party ~*s* still canvassing the poor pick of availables —S.H. Adams⟩ ⟨movie ~*s*⟩ ⟨literary ~*s*⟩

**²mogul** \"\ *adj, usu cap* **:** of or relating to the Moguls or their empire

**mogul base** *n* **:** an electric lamp base of larger than standard residential size

**MOH** *abbr* **1** master of otterhounds **2** medical officer of health

**mo·hair** \ˈmō,ha(ə)r|(ə)r, -,he|, |ə\ *n* -S [by folk etymology (influence of ¹*hair*) fr. earlier *mocayare*, fr. obs. It *mocaiarro*, fr. Ar *mukhayyar*, lit., choice, select] **1 :** any of various fabrics or yarns made wholly or in part of the hair of the Angora goat: as **a :** a camlet of mohair **b :** a wiry lustrous clothing fabric of mohair and cotton made in plain or twill weaves **c :** a cut-pile upholstery fabric with a mohair pile and a cotton or wool back **2 :** the long silky hair of the Angora goat

**mohammedan** *usu cap, var of* MUHAMMADAN

**mohammedan blue** *n, often cap M* **:** a dark violet cobalt blue used as an underglaze color on certain Chinese porcelains of the Ming dynasty

**mo·har** \ˈmōhə(r)\ *n* -S [Nepali *mohar, mohor*, fr. Hindi *muhur, muhr* mohur — more at MOHUR] **1 :** a silver coin of Nepal; *also* **:** a corresponding unit of value ⟨½-*mohar* coins⟩

**moharra** *var of* MOJARRA

**moharram** *usu cap, var of* MUHARRAM

**mo·ha·ve** *also* **mo·ja·ve** \mōˈhävē, ,=ˈhäv-, -vi\ *n, pl* **mohave** *or* **mohaves** *also* **mojave** *or* **mojaves** *usu cap* [Mohave *hamakhava* three mountains; fr. the peaks near Needles, California, regarded by the Mohave as the center of their territory] **1 a :** an Indian people of the Colorado river valley in Arizona, California, and Nevada **b :** a member of such people **2 :** a Yuman language of the Mohave people

**mo·hawk** \ˈmō,hȯk\ *n, pl* **mohawk** *or* **mohawks** [of Algonquian origin; akin to Narraganset *Mohowauuck* Mohawk, lit., they eat animate things] **1** *usu cap* **a :** an Iroquoian people of the Mohawk river valley, New York **b :** a member of such people **2** *usu cap* **:** the language of the Mohawk people **3** *often cap* **:** TUSCAN BROWN **4** *sometimes cap, in fancy skating* **:** a stroke forward on either edge of either skate followed by a stroke backward on the corresponding edge of the other skate

**mohawk weed** *n* **:** a bellwort (*Uvularia perfoliata*) of eastern No. America — called also *mealy bellwort*

**mo·he·gan** \mōˈhēgən\ *or* **mo·hi·can** \-ēkən\ *n, pl* **mohegan** *or* **mohegans** *or* **mohican** *or* **mohicans** *usu cap* **1 :** an Indian people of southeastern Connecticut **2 :** a member of the Mohegan people

**mo·hel** \ˈmō(h)el\ *n* -S [Heb *mōhēl*] : a person who circumcises male infants in accordance with Jewish ritual

**mohican** *usu cap, var of* MAHICAN

**moh·ism** \ˈmō,izəm\ *n* -S *usu cap* [*Mo Ti fl* 400 B.C. Chin. philosopher + connective *-h-* + E *-ism*] : the teachings of Mo Ti characterized by an emphasis on equalitarian universal love and opposition to traditionalism and Confucianism

**¹moh·ist** \ˈmōəst\ *n* -S *usu cap* [*Mo Ti* + connective *-h-* + E *-ist*] : an adherent of Mohism

**²mohist** \"\ *adj, usu cap* **:** of or relating to Mo Ti or his teachings or followers

**moh·mand** \ˈmōmənd\ *n, pl* **mohmand** *or* **mohmands** *usu cap* **1 :** a people of eastern Afghanistan related to the Persians and Afghans **2 :** a member of the Mohmand people

**mohn·seed** \ˈmōn,sēd\ *n* [part trans. of G *mohnsame*, fr. *mohn* poppy (fr. MHG *mān, māhen*, fr. OHG *māho*) + *same* seed; akin to OHG *mago* poppy — more at MAW] : POPPY SEED

**¹mo·ho** \ˈmō(,)hō\ *n* [Hawaiian] **1 a** -S **:** any of several Hawaiian honey eaters that have pectoral tufts of yellow feathers **b** *cap* [NL, fr. Hawaiian] **:** a genus comprising such birds **2** -S **:** a small flightless extinct Hawaiian rail (*Pennula millsi*)

**²mo·ho** \"\ *or* **mo·ho·ro·vi·cic discontinuity** \,mōhōˈrōvəˌchich-\ *n* -S *usu cap M* [*moho* short for *mohorovicic discontinuity*, after Andrija *Mohorovičić fl* 1908 Yugoslav geologist] : a point at depths ranging from about three miles beneath the ocean basin floor to about 25 miles beneath the continental surface at which seismological and other studies indicate a change in earth materials from those of the earth's crust to those of the subjacent mantle

**mo·hock** \ˈmō,häk\ *n* -S *usu cap* [alter. of *mohawk*] : one of a gang of aristocratic ruffians who assaulted and otherwise maltreated people in London streets in the early 18th century

**mo·hock·ism** \-,kizəm\ *n* -S *usu cap* **:** the practices of the Mohocks or behavior resembling that of the Mohocks

**mo·ho·li lemur** \məˈhōlē-\ *n* [*moholi* fr. Tswana *mogwêlê*] : a common active gregarious arboreal lemur (*Galago senegalensis*) of tropical Africa

**mohr** *also* **mhorr** \ˈmō(ə)r, ˈmȯ(ə)r\ *n* -S [Ar *muhr, mohr* colt] : a gazelle of northern Africa (*Gazella dama mhorr*) having horns on which are 11 or 12 prominent rings — compare ADDRA

**mohr balance** \ˈmō(ə)r-\ *n, usu cap M* [after Karl F. *Mohr* †1879 Ger. pharmacist] : WESTPHAL BALANCE

**mohr pinchcock** *n, usu cap M* **:** a pinchcock consisting of a wire spring

Mohr pinchcock

**mohr's salt** *n, usu cap M* **:** a light green crystalline salt $FeSO_4.(NH_4)_2SO_4.6H_2O$ used chiefly in iron plating, in photography, and in chemical analysis; ferrous ammonium sulfate

**mohs' scale** \ˈmōz-, -ōs(əz)-\ *n, usu cap M* [After Friedrich *Mohs* †1839 Ger. mineralogist] **1 :** a scale of hardness for minerals ranging from 1 for the softest to 10 for the hardest in which 1 represents the hardness of talc; 2, gypsum; 3, calcite; 4, fluorite; 5, apatite; 6, orthoclase; 7, quartz; 8, topaz; 9, corundum; and 10, diamond **2 :** a revised and expanded version of the original Mohs' scale in which 1 represents the hardness of talc; 2, gypsum; 3, calcite; 4, fluorite; 5, apatite; 6, orthoclase; 7, vitreous pure silica; 8, quartz; 9, topaz; 10, garnet; 11, fused zirconia; 12, fused alumina; 13, silicon carbide; 14, boron carbide; and 15, diamond

**mo·hur** \ˈmōhə(r)\ *n* -S [Hindi *muhur, muhr* gold coin, seal, fr. Per *muhr*; akin to Skt *mudrā* seal, sign, token] **1 :** an old gold coin of the Moguls that circulated in India from the 16th century **2 :** a gold coin of British India equivalent to 15 rupees last issued in 1918 **3 :** any one of several gold coins formerly issued by Indian states (as Bikaner, Gwalior, Hyderabad) and by Nepal and Tibet **4 :** a unit of value equivalent to one mohur coin

**mohurrum** *usu cap, var of* MUHARRAM

**mohwa** *var of* MAHUA

**¹moi** \ˈmȯē\ *n, pl* **moi** *or* **mois** *usu cap* [Annamese] **1 :** a group of Veddoid or Indo-Australoid peoples living in the mountain uplands of Annam **2 :** a member of a Moi people

**²moi** \ˈmōˈē\ *n* -S [Hawaiian *mō'ī*] : a Hawaiian ruling chief or sovereign

**moi·der** \ˈmȯidə(r)\ *or* **moi·ther** \-ōithə-\ *vb* -ED/-ING/-S [origin unknown] *vt* **1** *dial Brit* **:** to throw into disorder or an unsettled state **:** PERPLEX, BEWILDER ⟨had me so ~*ed*, with his talk about securities —*Irish Digest*⟩ **2** *dial Brit* **:** DISTRACT, BOTHER ⟨~ one so with their chatter —Gerald O'Donovan⟩ ~ *vi* **1** *dial Brit* **:** to talk incoherently **:** be delirious **2** *dial Brit* **:** to wander about aimlessly or in a confused manner

**moi·dore** \ˈmȯi,dō(ə)r, =ˈ=\ *n* -S [modif. of Pg *moeda de ouro*, lit., coin of gold] **1 a :** a gold coin of Portugal and Brazil from about 1640 to 1732 containing 4.93 grams of fine gold **b :** a corresponding unit of value **2 :** a gold 2-moidore piece or double moidore

**moi·e·ty** \ˈmȯiəd·ē, -ətē, -i\ *n* -ES [ME *moite*, fr. MF *moitié*, fr. LL *medietat-, medietas*, fr. *medie-* (fr. L *medius* middle) + *-tat-, -tas* -ty — more at MID] **1 a :** one of two equal portions **:** HALF ⟨the site was conveyed by lease in two distinct *moieties* —E.K.Chambers⟩ **b :** one of two approximately equal portions ⟨war, pestilence, and famine had consumed . . . the ~ of the human species —Edward Gibbon⟩ **2 a :** one of the portions into which something is divided **:** COMPONENT, PART ⟨the psychopathic ~ of the personality —*Brit. Jour. of Delinquency*⟩ ⟨the hemoglobin molecule contains four heme *moieties* —Lionel Whitby⟩; *specif* **:** a share paid by the government to an informer out of duties and penalties collected because of his help ⟨the ~ paid to an informer must be 25 percent of the value of the amount recovered —*Chicago Tribune*⟩ **b** *obs* **:** a small portion **:** FRACTION ⟨thine being but a ~ of my grief —Shak.⟩ **3 :** one of two basic complementary tribal subdivisions; *esp* **:** one (as a phratry) of two unilateral usu. exogamous groups

**¹moil** \ˈmȯil, *esp before pause or consonant* ˈmȯiəl\ *vb* -ED/-ING/-S [ME *moillen*, fr. MF *moillier*, fr. (assumed) VL *molliare*, fr. L *mollis* soft — more at MELT] *vt* **1** *chiefly dial* **:** to make wet or dirty **:** DAMPEN, SMEAR ⟨letters ~*ed* with my kisses —Elizabeth B. Browning⟩ **2** *chiefly dial* **:** to make distraught **:** TORMENT, WORRY ~ *vi* **1 :** to work with grueling persistence **:** DRUDGE, GRUB ⟨piles of earth . . . are evidence that here a scant hundred years ago thousands ~*ed* for gold —F.W. Taber⟩ **2** *dial Eng* **:** to be fidgety or restless **:** WORRY **3 a :** to be in continuous agitation **:** CHURN, SWIRL ⟨a crowd of men and women ~*ed* like nightmare figures in the smoke-green haze —Ralph Ellison⟩ ⟨caused all the wrongs of his past life to ~ up inside of him and sear his brain —*True Police Cases*⟩ **b :** to become involved in discussion **:** CHAFFER, WRANGLE ⟨last week's diplomatic ~*ing* in Europe —*Life*⟩

**²moil** \"\ *n* -S **1 :** hard work **:** DRUDGERY, LABOR ⟨escape from the ~ . . . and money-grubbing of ordinary life —*Times Lit. Supp.*⟩ ⟨the drab . . . toil and ~ of a collier's existence —Harry Lauder⟩ **2 a** *dial Eng* **:** MUD, MIRE **b :** BLEMISH, TAINT ⟨undefiled . . . by ~ of printed word —F.L.Gwynn⟩ **3 a :** a jumble of sound or motion **:** UPROAR, TURBULENCE ⟨lost in a vast ~ of noise —Norman Mailer⟩ ⟨the ~ and brine of the sea —D.C.Peattie⟩ **b :** a state of confusion **:** TURMOIL ⟨the ~ of events is . . . unintelligible —H.B.Alexander⟩

**³moil** \"\ *n* -S [IrGael *maol* bald & W *moel* — more at MULEY] *dial Brit* **:** a hornless ox or cow

**⁴moil** \"\ *n* -S [perh. fr. F *meule*, lit., haystack, fr. L *metula* small cone or pyramid — more at METULA] **1 :** excess glass left at the end of an article in contact with the blowing mechanism during the manufacture of blown glass and usu. removed in finishing the article **2 :** a coating of glass on the gathering iron to prevent it from scaling off into the molten glass

**⁵moil** \"\ *n* -S [origin unknown] : a steel bar sharpened to a point or a chisel end for hand use (as in mining) — compare ¹GAD 1c

**moil·er** \-lə(r)\ *n* -S [¹*moil* + *-er*] : one that moils **:** DRUDGE

**moil·ey** \ˈmȯili\ *Irish & Scot var of* MULEY

**moiling** *adj* [fr. pres. part. of ¹*moil*] **1 a :** requiring hard work **:** TOILSOME ⟨~ job⟩ **b :** HARDWORKING, INDUSTRIOUS ⟨~ worker⟩ **2 :** violently agitated **:** NOISY, TURBULENT ⟨the earth a roaring, ~ mass of tanks —*Fortune*⟩ ⟨~ life beyond the quiet close —O.S.J.Gogarty⟩ — **moil·ing·ly** *adv*

**moine** \ˈmȯin\ *adj, usu cap* [prob. fr. *Moin*, moorland in Sutherland, northern Scotland] **:** of or relating to an epoch of the Precambrian era — see GEOLOGIC TIME table

**moi·ra** \ˈmȯirə\ *n, pl* **moi·rai** \-ȯi,rī\ *often cap* [Gk; akin to Gk *meros* part — more at MERIT] **:** individual destiny **:** the will of the gods **:** FATE

**¹moire** *in sense 2 like* MOIRÉ *or sometimes* ˈmȯ(ə)r *or* ˈmwär *or* ˈmȯ(ə)r *or* ˈmwȧ(r; *in sense 1 prob one-syllabled*\ *n* -S [F, fr. E *mohair*] **1** *archaic* **:** a watered mohair **2 :** ²MOIRÉ 2

**²moi·ré** \(ˈ)mȯ;rā, (ˈ)mwä;-\ *or* **moire** *see* ¹MOIRE\ *n* -S [F *moiré*, fr. *moiré*, adj.] **1 a :** an irregular wavy finish usu. produced on a fabric by pressing between engraved rollers **b :** a wavy pattern in fur (as Persian lamb) **c :** a ripple pattern on the face or back of a stamp as a protection against forgery — compare BURELAGE **d :** a dot formation in a halftone print that consists often of geometric figures or wavy lines, is usu. considered an imperfection, and occurs typically in work done from a cut made by rescreening a halftone print or in superimposed impressions in bad register from two or more cuts **2** [alter. (influenced by ³*moiré*) of ¹*moire*] **:** a fabric (as a corded silk or rayon) having a wavy watered appearance ⟨a satchel lined with navy blue ~ —*New Yorker*⟩

**³moiré** *or* **moire** \"\ *adj* [F *moiré*, fr. *moire* + *-é* (fr. L *-atus* -ate)] **:** having a wavy or watery appearance

**⁴moiré** *or* **moire** \"\ *vt* **moiréd** *or* **moired; moiréing** *or* **moireing; moirés** *or* **moires :** to produce a watered pattern on (a fabric)

**mois** *pl of* MOI

**mois·san·ite** \ˈmȯisᵊn,īt\ *n* -S [Henri *Moissan* †1907 Fr. chemist + E *-ite*] **:** a silicon carbide SiC found in the Diablo Canyon meteoric iron — compare CARBORUNDUM

**¹moist** \ˈmȯist\ *adj* -ER/-EST [ME *moiste*, fr. MF, fr. (assumed) VL *muscidus*, alter. (prob. influenced by L *musteus* resembling new wine, fr. *mustum* new wine) of L *mucidus* slimy — more at MUST, MUCID] **1 a** *obs* **:** consisting of water **:** LIQUID ⟨tears, the ~ impediments unto my speech —Shak.⟩ **b** *obs* **:** characterized by succulence **:** LUSH, JUICY ⟨these ~ trees —Shak.⟩ ⟨eat ~ grapes —Num 6: 3 (AV)⟩ **c :** naturally or constitutionally wet — used in ancient and medieval sciences to describe one of the qualities of the four elements; opposed to *dry* **d** *of a sign of the zodiac* **:** having a moist complexion **e** *obs* **:** containing or bringing moisture ⟨the vapors of a ~ pot . . . soar up into the open air —*Return from Parnassus: Part II*⟩ ⟨the ~ daughters of huge Atlas —Edmund Spenser⟩ **2 a :** full of tears **:** WATERY ⟨the eyes of both of us . . . were ~ with the joy of success —Jack London⟩ **b (1) :** slightly or moderately wet **:** DAMP ⟨the gravel paths were ~ . . . with dew —Ernest Hemingway⟩ **(2) :** saturated with moisture **:** HUMID, SOGGY ⟨air which was still warmer and more ~ moved in —G.R. Stewart⟩ ⟨the lush, ~, rice and cotton lands —*Amer Guide Series: Texas*⟩ **c :** characterized by humidity and frequent precipitation ⟨jungles thrive in warm ~ regions⟩ **3 :** employing or accompanied by moisture: as **a (1) :** accompanied by tears **:** TEARFUL ⟨the urgent ~ look in his eyes —Ethel Wilson⟩ **(2) :** emotionally sentimental **:** MAUDLIN ⟨emotionally very ~ about nationalism —A.F.Rolle⟩ **b :** utilizing a washing process ⟨copper, zinc, and silver . . . extracted in the ~ way —William Crookes⟩ **c (1) :** marked by a discharge or exudation of liquid ⟨~ eczema⟩ **(2) :** suggestive of the presence of liquid — used of sounds heard in auscultation ⟨~ rales⟩ **syn** see WET

**²moist** *n* -S [ME *moiste*, fr. *moiste*, adj.] *obs* **:** MOISTURE ⟨myrtles and bays for want of ~ grew wan —Josuah Sylvester⟩

**³moist** *vt* -ED/-ING/-S [ME *moisten*, fr. *moiste*, adj.] *obs* **:** MOISTEN ⟨no more the juice of Egypt's grape shall ~ this lip —Shak.⟩

**moist color** *n* **:** a watercolor pigment in the form of paste

**moist·en** \ˈmȯisᵊn\ *vb* **moistened; moistened; moistening** \-s(ᵊ)niŋ\ **moistens** [¹*moist* + *-en*] *vt* **:** to make moist **:** DAMPEN, SATURATE ⟨~*ed* her lips in anticipation —Beverley Nichols⟩ ⟨broad alluvial plain . . . plentifully ~*ed* by rain-bearing winds —R.S.Billington⟩; *specif* **:** to make moist by immersing in a liquid ⟨passed the cup to his wounded neighbor, without stopping even to ~ his own lips —Andrew Combe⟩ ~ *vi* **:** to become moist ⟨heard a catch in his voice and saw his eyes ~⟩

**moist·en·er** \-s(ᵊ)nə(r)\ *n* -S **:** one that moistens; *specif* **:** a device for moistening gummed surfaces (as stamps, envelopes, labels)

**moist·ful** \ˈmȯistfəl\ *adj* [²*moist* + *-ful*] *archaic* **:** MOIST

**moist gangrene** *n* **:** gangrene that develops in the presence of combined arterial and venous obstruction, is usu. accompanied by a superimposed infection, and is characterized by a watery discharge usu. of foul odor

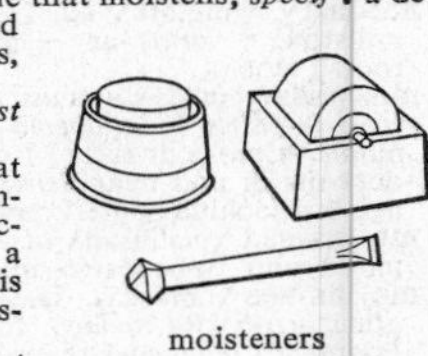

moisteners

**moist·i·fy** \ˈmȯistə,fī\ *vt* -ED/-ING/-ES [¹*moist* + *-ify*] *archaic* **:** MOISTEN

**moist·ish** \-tish\ *adj* **:** somewhat moist

**moist·less** \-tləs\ *adj, archaic* **:** lacking moisture **:** DRY

**moist·ly** *adv* **:** in a moist manner

**moist·ness** *n* -ES [ME *moistnes*, fr. *moiste* moist + *-nes* -ness — more at MOIST] **:** the quality or state of being moist

**mois·ture** \ˈmȯis(h)chə(r)\ *n* -S [ME, modif. (influenced by *-ure*) of MF *moistour*, fr. *moiste* moist — more at MOIST]

1 a : liquid (as water) diffused or condensed in relatively small quantity and dispersed through a gas as invisible vapor or as fog or in or on a solid body in insensible form or as sensible dampness or condensed on a cool surface as visible dew; *specif* : atmospheric water vapor **b** *obs* : the watery component of an object or an individual ⟨all my body's ~ scarce serves to quench my furnace-burning heart —Shak.⟩ **c** : TEARFULNESS ⟨a ~ of the eye —H.S.Scott⟩ **2** : a liquid substance (as water) ⟨rubbing the ~ out of the coat of a . . . fox terrier —Arnold Bennett⟩; *specif* : PRECIPITATION ⟨69 percent of the annual ~ occurred during the growing season —R.H.Brown⟩

**moisture equivalent** *n* : the water content expressed as a percentage of the dry weight that a soil can retain against a centrifugal force one thousand times the force of gravity and used as a convenient laboratory measure of soil moisture conditions

**mois·ture·less** \-(r)ləs\ *adj* : lacking moisture

**moisture meter** *n* : an instrument for determining the percentage of moisture in a material (as timber, flour, soil, or tobacco) commonly by measuring its electrical resistivity

[1]**moistureproof** \ˈ=ˌ=ˌ=\ *adj* [*moisture* + *proof*] : impervious to water vapor — compare WATERPROOF

[2]**moistureproof** \"\ *vt* -ED/-ING/-S : to make impervious to water vapor

**moisty** \ˈmȯistē\ *adj* -ER/-EST [ME *moisty*, fr. *moiste* moist + -*y*] : DAMP, WET ⟨a misty ~ morning⟩

[1]**moit** \ˈmȯit\ *n* -S [alter. of [2]*mote*] : a fragment of stick or other foreign matter found in wool

[2]**moit** \"\ *vb* -ED/-ING/-S : [3]MOTE

**moither** *var of* MOIDER

**moity** \ˈmȯid·ē\ *adj* -ER/-EST : full of moits

**mo·jar·ra** *also* **mo·har·ra** \mōˈhärə\ *n* -S [AmerSp, fr. Sp, lance head, a small flat fish found off the coast of Spain, prob. fr. Ar *muharrab* pointed, fr. *harrab* to sharpen, point] **1** : a fish of the family Gerridae **2** : any of various fishes somewhat similar to the mojarras; *esp* : any of numerous small So. American fishes of the family Cichlidae

**mojave** *usu cap, var of* MOHAVE

**mo·ji** \ˈmōjē\ *adj, usu cap* [fr. *Moji*, Japan] : of or from the city of Moji, Japan : of the kind or style prevalent in Moji

[1]**mo·jo** \ˈmō,hō\ *n, pl* **mojo** *or* **mojos** *usu cap* [Sp, of AmerInd origin] **1 a** : an Arawakan people of northern Bolivia **b** : a member of such people **2** : the language of the Mojo people

[2]**mo·jo** \ˈmō(,)jō\ *n, pl* **mojos** *or* **mojoes** [prob. of African origin; akin to Gullah *moco* witchcraft, magic, Fula *moco'o* medicine man] *chiefly South* : a voodoo spell or amulet

**mo·jon·nier method** *or* **mojonnier test** \mə'jänyə(r)-\ *n, usu cap 1st M* [after *Mojonnier* Bros., Am. food processing equipment firm] : a gravimetric method for determining precisely the fat and total solids content of milk or its derivatives

**mo·ka** *Brit var of* MOCHA

**moke** \ˈmōk\ *n* -S [origin unknown] **1 a** *slang Brit* : DONKEY, ASS **b** *slang Austral* : a horse esp. of poor appearance **2** *slang* : NEGRO — usu. used disparagingly

[1]**mo·ki** *also* **mo·qui** \ˈmōkē\ *n, pl* **moki** *or* **mokis** *usu cap* : HOPI

[2]**moki** \"\ *or* **mo·ki·hi** \-ē,hē\ *n, pl* **moki** *or* **mokis** *or* **mokihi** *or* **mokihis** [Maori] **1** *NewZeal* : a trumpeter fish (*Latridopsis ciliaris*) **2** : a Maori raft made of bundles of flags, rushes, or dry flower stalks of flax

**mo·ki·ha·na** \,mōkēˈhänə\ *n* -S [Hawaiian] : a Hawaiian tree (*Pelea anisata*) of the family Rutaceae growing only on the Island of Kauai and having fragrant fruits that are strung in leis and represent Kauai in the leis of the Islands

**mo·ko** \ˈmō(,)kō\ *n* -S [Maori] **1** : the Maori system of tattooing **2** : a Maori tattoo consisting of pigment rubbed into spiral grooves made in the skin with a small implement resembling an adz

**moko-moko** \ˈmō(,)kōˈmō(,)kō\ *n* -S [Maori] : a common small lizard (*Lygosoma moco*) of New Zealand

**mok·po** \ˈmäk(,)pō\ *adj, usu cap* [fr. *Mokpo* (*Moppo*), Korea] : of or from the city of Mokpo, Korea : of the kind or style prevalent in Mokpo

**mo·ksha** *also* **mo·ksa** \ˈmōkshə\ *n* -S [Skt *mokṣa*; akin to Skt *muñcati* he releases — more at MUCUS] *Hinduism & Jainism* : release from samsara and liberation from karma together with the attainment of Nirvana for the Hindu or kaivalya for the Jain : salvation from the bondage of finite existence — compare DHARMA, KAMA

**mo·kum** *or* **mo·kume** \ˈmōkəm\ *n* -S [Jap *mokume*, lit., wood grain] : a Japanese alloy used in decorative work on gold and silver

**mol** *var of* [7]MOLE

**mol** *abbr* molecular; molecule

**mo·la** \ˈmōlə\ *n* [NL, fr. L, millstone; fr. its shape and rough skin — more at MILL] **1** *cap* : the type genus of the family Molidae including solely a large widely distributed ocean sunfish (*M. mola*) **2** *pl* **mola** *or* **molas** : any fish of the genus *Mola; broadly* : OCEAN SUNFISH

**mo·lal** \ˈmōləl\ *adj* [[7]*mole* + -*al*] *chem* : of, relating to, or containing a mole ⟨the ~ volume of a gas is 22.4 liters at standard conditions⟩; *esp* : containing one mole of solute per 1000 grams of solvent ⟨a ~ solution⟩ — compare MOLAR

**mo·la·la** \mōˈlälə\ *n, pl* **molala** *or* **molalas** **1 a** : a Waiilatpuan people of the Molala and Santiam river valleys in northwestern Oregon **b** : a member of such people **2** : the language of the Molala people

**mo·lal·i·ty** \mōˈlaləd·ē\ *n* -ES : molal concentration

[1]**mo·lar** \ˈmōlə(r)\ *n* -S [L *molaris*, fr. *molaris* of a mill, grinding, fr. *mola* mill, millstone + -*aris* -ar — more at MILL] **1** *also* **molar tooth** : a tooth adapted for grinding by having a broad rounded or flattened though often ridged or tuberculated surface; *specif* : one of the cheek teeth in mammals behind the incisors and canines sometimes including the premolars but more exactly restricted to the three posterior pairs in each jaw on each side in adult man which are not preceded by deciduous teeth — see DENTAL FORMULA, DENTITION illustration **2** : a process with a grinding surface on the inner aspect of the mandible of an insect or crustacean

[2]**molar** \"\ *adj* [L *molaris* of a mill, grinding] **1 a** : pulverizing by friction : GRINDING ⟨~ teeth⟩ ⟨waves, wind, and sand are ~ agents⟩ **b** : of, relating to, or located near the molar teeth ⟨~ gland⟩ **2** [[6]*mole* + -*ar*] : of, relating to, possessing the qualities of, or characterized by a uterine mole ⟨~ pregnancy⟩

[3]**molar** \"\ *adj* [L *moles* mass + E -*ar* — more at MOLE (mound)] **1** : of or relating to a mass of matter as distinguished from the properties or motions of molecules or atoms **2** [[7]*mole* + -*ar*] : of, relating to or containing a mole or molecules : MOLECULAR; *esp* : containing one mole of solute in 1000 milliliters of solution — compare MOLAL **3** : of or relating to larger units of behavior esp. as relatable to a prior deprivation or motivational pattern of the organism ⟨interest in such ~ problems of personality as the ego functions —R.R. Holt⟩ — opposed to *molecular*

**mo·lar·i·form** \mōˈlarə,fȯrm\ *adj* [[1]*molar* + -*iform*] : resembling a molar tooth esp. in shape

**mo·lar·i·ty** \-rəd·ē\ *n* -ES [[3]*molar* + -*ity*] : molar concentration

**mo·lar·iza·tion** \,mōlərəˈzāshən\ *n* -S [[1]*molar* + -*ization*] : the evolution of less specialized teeth into molars

**mo·la·ry** \ˈmōlərē\ *adj* [L *molarius* of a mill, fr. *mola* mill, millstone + -*arius* -ary — more at MILL] : adapted for grinding food : MOLAR

**mo·lasse** \məˈläs\ *n* -S *usu cap* [F, perh. alter. of *mollasse* soft, fr. *mou* (after It *mollaccio* soft: *molle* soft, fr. L *mollis*), fr. L *mollis* — more at MELT] : a series of fossiliferous sedimentary deposits in and near Switzerland that are chiefly of Miocene age but include some Upper Oligocene beds

**mo·las·sed** \məˈlasəd\ *also* **mo·las·sied** \-sēd\ *adj* : impregnated with molasses ⟨~ silage⟩

**mo·las·ses** \məˈlasəz, -laas-,-ˈlais *sometimes* -ləs-, *dial* ˈl-\ *n* -ES *often attrib* [Pg *melaço*, fr. LL *mellaceum* must, fr. neut. of (assumed) *mellaceus* resembling honey, fr. L *mell-, mel* honey + -*aceus* -aceous — more at MELLIFLUOUS] **1** : the thick dark to light brown viscid syrup that is separated from raw sugar in the successive processes of sugar manufacture and graded according to its quality — compare BLACKSTRAP 3, TREACLE **2** : a syrup made by boiling down sweet vegetable or fruit juice or sap ⟨citrus ~⟩ ⟨wood ~⟩

**molasses grass** *n* : a valuable perennial forage grass (*Melinis minutiflora*) native to tropical Africa but widely cultivated and covered with hairs which secrete a sweet substance having the odor of molasses — called also *candy grass*

**mo·la·ve** \mōˈlä(,)vā\ *n* -S [Sp, fr. Tag *mulavin*] **1** : a large Philippine timber tree (*Vitex littoralis*) **2** : the valuable durable heavy hard yellow wood of the molave tree

[1]**mold** *or* **mould** \ˈmōld\ *n* -S [ME *mold, molde*, fr. OE *molde* sand, dust, soil; akin to OHG *molta* dust, soil, ON *mold*, Goth *mulde* dust, soil, OHG *malan* to grind — more at MEAL] **1** : crumbling soft friable earth suited to plant growth : SOIL; *esp* : soil rich in humus — see LEAF MOLD **2** *dial Brit* **a** : the surface of the earth : GROUND ⟨the fairest knight on Scottish ~ —Sir Walter Scott⟩ **b** : the earth of the burying ground ⟨calling his ghost to the ~ —Padraic Gregory⟩ — often used in pl. ⟨were baith in the ~*s* —Sir Walter Scott⟩ **3** *archaic* : earth that is the substance of the human body ⟨leprous sin will melt from human ~ —John Milton⟩ ⟨be merciful great Duke to men of ~ —Shak.⟩

[2]**mold** *also* **mould** \"\ *vb* -ED/-ING/-S *vi* : MOLDER ⟨it was closed for ages, ~*ing* away —Angus Mowat⟩ ~ *vt* : to cover with soil or mold : hill up ⟨potatoes . . . should be kept weed-free and ~*ed* —*New Zealand Jour. of Agric.*⟩

[3]**mold** *or* **mould** \"\ *n* -S *often attrib* [ME *molde, mold*, fr. OF *modle, molle, moule*, fr. L *modulus*, dim. of *modus* measure — more at MODE] **1** : distinctive nature or character : TYPE, STAMP ⟨a philosopher of the grand ~ —D.C.Williams⟩ **2 a** : a pattern or template that serves as a guide for construction; *specif* : a thin wood or paper pattern for part of a ship made in a mold loft **b** (1) : the frame on or around which an object is constructed ⟨laid the dome on a ~ of packed earth —Green Peyton⟩ (2) : a wire-covered frame for forming sheets of paper; *esp* : one of the cylinders covered with wire cloth that forms the sheet on a cylinder machine **3 a** : a cavity in which a fluid or malleable substance is given form: as (1) : a container (as of gypsum, rubber, metal, or wood) in which a piece of ceramic ware is formed (2) : a form for making bricks (3) : a metal form for casting cement, mortar, or concrete test specimens (4) : a matrix in which an article (as of metal, glass, or plastic) is shaped by casting or pressure molding; *specif* : a recessed matrix from which a relief printing surface (as type or a stereotype or electrotype) is cast (5) : a cooking utensil in which a dish (as a pudding or jelly) is given a decorative shape (6) : a carved wooden block by means of which a design is pressed into a soft food (as cookie dough or butter) **b** : a molded object ⟨plaster ~⟩ ⟨fill the center of the ring ~ with cottage cheese⟩ **4 a** : MOLDING **b** : a group of moldings **5 a** *obs* : an example to be followed ⟨the glass of fashion and the ~ of form —Shak.⟩ **b** : a prototype from which an idea or individual is derived ⟨thou all-shaking thunder . . . crack nature's ~*s* —Shak.⟩ ⟨an integral part of the team and cut from the same heroic ~ —A.J.Daley⟩ **c** : a fixed pattern or contour : DESIGN, CAST ⟨compresses all these characters into the relentless ~ of the story —E.B.Garside⟩ ⟨settling in the ~ of a dignified, permanent community —Mabel R. Gillis⟩ **d** *obs* : a fashionable style : MODE ⟨houses of the new ~ in London —Peter Heylin⟩ **6** : a package of goldbeater's skin usu. consisting of about 900 pieces **7 a** : an impression made in earth or rock by the outside of a fossil shell or other organic form **b** : a cast of the inner surface of such a fossil — compare [2]CAST 7a(2) **8** : a grained copper photoengraving plate with the gelatin image on it ready for etching

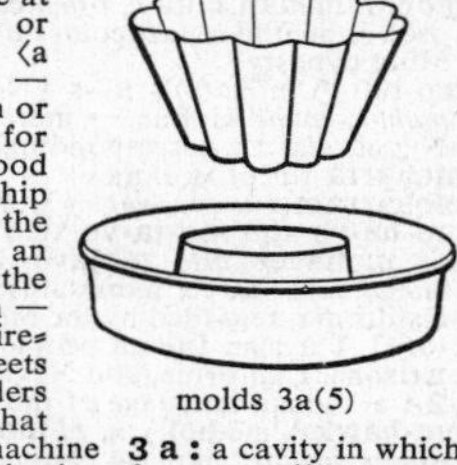

molds 3a(5)

[4]**mold** *or* **mould** \"\ *vb* -ED/-ING/-S [ME *molden*, fr. *molde, mold*, n.] *vt* **1 a** *archaic* : to knead (dough) into a desired consistency or shape **b** : to give shape to (as a fluid or malleable substance) ⟨the wind ~*s* the waves⟩ ⟨his long hands ~*ing* the air —*Time*⟩ ⟨chemical processes that . . . are now ~*ing* the earth's crust —W.H.Bucher⟩ **c** *obs* : to be a component of : help to build ⟨all princely graces that ~ up such a mighty piece as this —Shak.⟩ **2 a** (1) : to form by pouring or pressing into a mold ⟨~ a glass bottle⟩ ⟨to attain a flare in design it is necessary to ~ the plywood into shape —R.J.Whittier⟩ ⟨~ a stereotype⟩ (2) : to make a mold from ⟨~ a type form⟩ **b** : to form a foundry mold of (as in sand) **c** : to exert influence on : determine the ultimate quality or nature of ⟨~ public opinion⟩ ⟨environmental factors which ~ the minds and emotions of youngsters —R.H.Wittcoff⟩ ⟨the culture of the Western world has been ~*ed* by the Bible —I.M.Price⟩ ⟨a great scholar who has ~*ed* his taste and judgment through reflective reading —E.S.McCastney⟩ **3** : to fit the contours of : HUG ⟨~*ed* hipline⟩ ⟨silhouettes that ~ the body —*New Yorker*⟩ **4** : to ornament by molding or carving the material of ⟨ceilings . . . with ~*ed* or precast ornamental patterns —H.S.Morrison⟩ ~ *vi* **1** : to become formed : take shape ⟨the Norman man-at-arms had begun to ~ into the English country gentleman —*Ecclesiologist*⟩ **2** : to become fitted to a contour : ADAPT ⟨cloche . . . so flexible it ~*s* to any head size —*N.Y.Times*⟩ ⟨the river ran, leaped, ~*ed* to rocks and leaped again —Philip Murray b.1924⟩ **3** : to make or use a mold ⟨the outstanding development in ~*ing* —*Technical News Bull.*⟩

[5]**mold** *also* **mould** \"\ *n* -S [ME *mowlde*, perh. alter. (influenced by *molde* soil) of *mowle*, fr. *moulen* to grow moldy — more at MOOL, [1]MOLD] **1** : a superficial often woolly growth produced on various forms of organic matter esp. when damp or decaying and on living organisms **2** : a fungus esp. of the order Mucorales that produces mold — compare BLACK MOLD, BLUE MOLD, MILDEW

[6]**mold** *or* **mould** \"\ *vb* -ED/-ING/-S [ME *mouleden*, fr. *mowlde*, n.] *vt, obs* : to allow to become moldy ⟨hoarding housewives that do ~ their food —William Browne⟩ ~ *vi* **1** : to become moldy ⟨bread tends to ~ in damp weather⟩ **2** *obs* : to deteriorate for lack of use ⟨the man that ~*s* in idle cell —Edmund Spenser⟩

**mold·abil·i·ty** *or* **mould·abil·i·ty** \,mōldəˈbiləd·ē\ *n* : the property of being moldable

**mold·able** *or* **mould·able** \ˈmōldəbəl\ *adj* [[4]*mold, mould* + -*able*] : capable of being molded ⟨clays are plastic and ~ when sufficiently finely pulverized and wet, rigid when dry —R.N.Shreve⟩

[1]**mol·da·vi·an** \mälˈdāvēən, -vyən\ *n* -S *cap* [*Moldavia*, province of Romania + E -*an*] **1** : a native or inhabitant of Moldavia **2** : Romanian as spoken in Moldavia

[2]**moldavian** \(ˈ)=ˈ=(=)=\ *adj, usu cap* : of or relating to the province of Moldavia or to its people

**moldboard** *or* **mouldboard** \ˈ=ˌ=\ *n* [[1]*mold, mould* + *board*] **1 a** : a curved iron plate attached above a plowshare that lifts and turns the soil — called also *breast board* **b** : the flat or curved blade (as of a snowplow or bulldozer) that pushes material to one side as the machine advances **2** [[3]*mold, mould* + *board*] : one of the boards forming a mold for concrete

**moldboard plow** *n* : a plow equipped with a moldboard; *esp* : a general-purpose plow having a moldboard of intermediate length and curvature — called also *turnplow;* compare [1]BREAKER 2b, LISTER, SWIVEL PLOW; see PLOW illustration

**molded** *or* **moulded** *adj* [fr. past part. of [4]*mold, mould*] **1** : decorated or finished with a molding ⟨~ panel⟩ **2 a** : formed in or on a mold ⟨~ pottery⟩ ⟨~ plywood⟩; *specif* : blown in a mold ⟨~ glass is usually called blown-molded by most collectors —G.S. & Helen McKearin⟩ — compare BLOWING 4, PRESSED GLASS **b** : determined by or cut to specifications prepared in a mold loft — used of the parts of a ship ⟨~ line⟩ ⟨~ keel⟩ **3** : CLOSE-FITTING ⟨~ bodice⟩

**molded breadth** *n* : the greatest breadth of a ship's hull exclusive of the outside plating

**molded brick** *n* **1** : brick made in a mold as distinguished from wire-cut brick **2** : brick molded into special shapes for use in ornamental brickwork

**molded depth** *n* : the vertical distance from the top of the keel to the top of the upper deck beams amidships at the gunwale

**molded pulp** *n* : wood pulp formed into protective packaging (as containers for eggs or sleeves for liquor bottles)

[1]**mold·er** *or* **mould·er** \ˈmōldə(r)\ *n* -S [ME *molder*, fr. *molden* to mold + -*er* (n. suffix) — more at MOLD (knead)] **1** : a kneader of bread dough **2 a** : a worker that makes molds or produces molded articles: as (1) : a maker of foundry molds (2) : BRICKMAKER **2** (3) : an operator of a machine with abrasive wheels for cutting decorative designs on stone and concrete products **b** : MOLDING MACHINE **c** (1) : [3]MOLD 3a (2) *or* **molder plate** : CASTER 1b **d** : a firm that makes a business of molding ⟨the sale of . . . plastic material to commercial ~*s* —Milo Perkins⟩ **3** : one that exerts a determining influence on an attitude or course of development ⟨~ of public opinion⟩ ⟨~ of talent⟩ ⟨~*s* of western monasticism —Helen Sullivan⟩

[2]**molder** *or* **moulder** \"\ *vb* **moldered** *or* **mouldered; moldered** *or* **mouldered; moldering** *or* **mouldering** \-d(ə)riŋ\ **molders** *or* **moulders** [freq. of [6]*mold, mould*] *vi* **1 a** : to crumble away : DISINTEGRATE, DECAY ⟨the leaves . . . ~*ed* and went back to the earth —Margaret Kennedy⟩ ⟨body lies a-~*ing* in the grave —*John Brown's Body*⟩ ⟨left the final habitations to ~ into dust —W.E.Swinton⟩ **b** : to deteriorate for lack of exercise ⟨long periods of solitary confinement caused his mental faculties to ~⟩ ⟨air crews ~*ed* in the barracks⟩ **2** *archaic* : to decrease in size : DWINDLE ⟨the Christian army . . . was ~*ing* away with disease —John Lingard⟩ ~ *vt* **1** : to cause to disintegrate ⟨time's . . . gradual touch has ~*ed* into beauty many a tower —William Mason⟩ **2** : to fritter away : WASTE ⟨they have ~*ed* away their time in inactivity —M.G.J. de Crèvecoeur⟩

**mold·i·ness** *or* **mould·i·ness** \ˈmōldēnəs\ *n* -ES : the quality or state of being moldy

**mold·ing** *or* **mould·ing** \ˈmōldiŋ, -dēŋ\ *n* -S [ME *molding*, fr. gerund of *molden* to mold, shape] **1 a** : an act or process of molding ⟨dry sand ~⟩ ⟨opinion ~⟩; *specif* : the shaping of the fetal head to allow it to pass through the birth canal during parturition **b** : an object produced by molding ⟨bronze ~*s* cast in antique forms⟩ **c** : the art or occupation of a molder **2** : the dimensions of a ship's timber measured from inside the plating to the center line — opposed to *siding;* compare MOLDED BREADTH, MOLDED DEPTH **3 a** : a continuous narrow contoured surface either recessed or projecting used singly or in groups for the decorative effect created by the play of light and shadow over it ⟨the piers were short and crowned with square blocks of stone, the ~*s* being ax-hewn —E.H.Short⟩ **b** : a decorative plane or curved strip (as of wood or metal) used for ornamentation or finishing ⟨carved ~*s* applied on doors . . . to form panels —J.E.Gloag⟩ ⟨baseboard ~⟩ ⟨edge ~*s* are designed to meet typical building conditions —*Sweet's Catalog Service*⟩

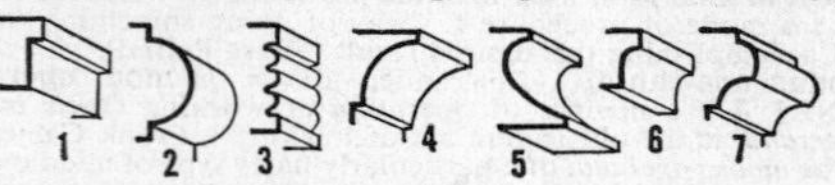


moldings 3a: *1* fillet and fascia, *2* torus, *3* reeding, *4* cavetto, *5* scotia, *6* congé, *7* beak

**molding book** *n* : a book prepared in the mold loft giving the dimensions of the structural members of a ship

**molding machine** *n* **1** : a planing machine for cutting moldings **2** : a foundry machine to assist in making molds; *esp* : a machine to pack the sand

**molding plaster** *n* : a finely ground retarded gypsum plaster for use in molds and for cast ornaments (as rosettes, medallions, friezes)

**molding sand** *n* : a mixture of sand and clay suitable for making foundry molds

**mold loft** *n* [[3]*mold*] : a large building or floor in a building where the lines of a ship or plane are laid down full size and molds and templates made from them for structural units

**mold loftsman** *n* : a worker in a mold loft

**moldmade paper** \ˈ=ˌ=-\ *n* : a machine-made deckle-edged imitation of handmade paper

**mold·man** \ˈ=,man\ *n, pl* **moldmen** **1** : a worker who cleans and readies ingot molds to receive molten metal **2** : an operator of a molding machine

**moldo-** *comb form, usu cap* [[2]*moldavian*] : Moldavian and ⟨*Moldo*-Wallachian⟩

**moldproof** \ˈ=ˌ=\ *adj* [[5]*mold*] : impervious to mildew

**molds** *pl of* MOLD, *pres 3d sing of* MOLD

**mold·warp** \ˈmōl,dwȯrp\ *or* **mold·i·warp** \-ldi,w-\ *n* -S [ME *moldewerp, moldewarp, moldywarp, molwarp;* akin to OS *moldwerp* mole, MD *moldewerp*, MHG *multwerf, moltwerf;* all fr. a prehistoric WGmc compound whose 1st constituent is represented by E [1]*mold* and whose 2d constituent is akin to OE *weorpan* to throw — more at WARP] **1** *dial Brit* : a European mole (*Talpa europaea*) **2** *dial* : a stupid or shiftless person ⟨the old man . . . a shambling ~ —Maristan Chapman⟩

**moldy** *or* **mouldy** \ˈmōldē, -di\ *adj* -ER/-EST [[5]*mold, mould* + -*y*] **1 a** : old and moldering : ANCIENT, CRUMBLING ⟨a dark ~ courtyard on a side street —P.E.Deutschman⟩ **b** : old and outmoded : ANTIQUATED, FUSTY ⟨~ tradition⟩ ⟨helping ~ professors to teach grubby students —Oliver La Farge⟩ **c** *slang* : DISREPUTABLE, MISERABLE ⟨wearing a ~ sport shirt —J.W.Ellison b.1929⟩ **2** : of, resembling, or covered with a mold-producing fungus ⟨~ moss⟩ ⟨~ feed⟩ ⟨~ bread⟩

**moldy corn poisoning** *n* : CORNSTALK DISEASE 2

**moldy nose** *n* : WHITE ROT 2c

**moldy rot** *n* : a disease of the tapping panels of the Para rubber tree caused by a fungus (*Ceratostomella fribriata*)

[1]**mole** \ˈmōl\ *n* -S [ME *mool, mole*, fr. OE *māl* spot, blemish; akin to OHG *meil* spot, Goth *mail* wrinkle, and perh. to Gk *miainein* to pollute, defile, Lith *maiva* swamp] **1** *archaic* : a discolored spot in cloth : STAIN **2 a** : a congenital spot, mark, or small permanent protuberance on the human body; *esp* : a pigmented nevus **b** *obs* : an identifying mark or blemish ⟨a ~ in the fair face of church government —Nathaniel Bacon⟩

[2]**mole** \"\ *vt* -ED/-ING/-S [ME *molen*, fr. *mool, mole*, n.] *archaic* : STAIN, DISCOLOR

[3]**mole** \"\ *n* -S *often attrib* [ME; akin to MD *mol* mole, MLG *mul, mol* mole, and prob. to OE *molde* soil — more at MOLD] **1 a** : any of numerous burrowing mammals chiefly of the family Talpidae living mainly in temperate parts of Europe, Asia, and No. America and having minute eyes often covered with skin, small concealed ears, very soft and often iridescent fur, and strong fossorial feet **b** : MOLE CRICKET **c** : MOLE RAT **d** : the short dense velvety pelt of the mole used as a fur — called also *moleskin* **2** *archaic* : a blind man or one who works in a dark place ⟨well said, old ~! canst work in the earth so fast —Shak.⟩ **3 a** : the borer of a mole plow **b** : MOLE PLOW **4** *or* **mole gray a** : a nearly neutral, slightly bluish, dark gray that is lighter and slightly greener than pewter — called also *moleskin* **b** : TAUPE 1

[4]**mole** \"\ *vi* **moled; moled; moling; moles** : to make or traverse an underground passage : BURROW, TUNNEL ⟨enemy remnants . . . had *moled* in under the wreckage —*Infantry Jour.*⟩ ⟨the diversion tunnel *moled* 1161 feet through an almost solid rock canyon wall —*Civil Engineering*⟩; *specif* : to make a mole drain

[5]**mole** \"\ *n* -S [MF, fr. OIt *molo*, fr. LGk *mōlos*, fr. L *moles*, lit., mass, exertion; akin to OE *mēthe* weary, OHG *muodi*, ON *mōthr* weary, Goth *afmauiths* exhausted, Gk *mōlos* exertion, Russ *mayat'* to fatigue, torment, annoy] **1 a** : a mound or massive work formed of masonry and large stones or earth laid in the sea as a pier or breakwater **b** : the harbor formed by such a work **2** [L *moles*] *obs* : a large piece : MASS, BULK **3** [L *moles*, lit., mass, exertion] : an ancient Roman tomb or mausoleum

[6]**mole** \"\ *n* -S [F *môle*, fr. L *mola* mooncalf, mole (lit., mill, millstone); trans. of Gk *mylē* (lit., millstone) — more at MILL] : an abnormal mass in the uterus: **a** : a blood clot containing a degenerated fetus and its membranes **b** : HYDATIDIFORM MOLE

[7]**mole** *also* **mol** \"\ *n* -S [G *mol*, short for *molekulargewicht* molecular weight, fr. *molekular* molecular + *gewicht* weight] : the quantity of a chemical substance that has a weight in mass units (as grams or pounds) numerically equal to the molecular weight or that in the case of a gas has a volume occupied by such a weight under specified conditions (as 22.4 liters at 0°C and a pressure of 760 millimeters of mercury);

esp : GRAM MOLECULE ⟨a ~ of any substance contains the same number of molecules —Farrington Daniels & R.A.Alberty⟩

⁸**mo·le** \'mō(,)lā\ *n, usu cap* : MOSSI

⁹**mo·le** \'mōlē\ *n* -s [MexSp, fr. Nahuatl *mulli, molli* sauce, stew] : a highly spiced sauce made principally of chile and chocolate but containing numerous other ingredients and served with meat (as beef or turkey)

**molecast** \'=,=\ *n* [³*mole* + *cast*] : MOLEHILL

**mole catcher** *n* : one that catches moles; *specif* : BROWN KING SNAKE

**mole crab** *n* : BAIT BUG

**mole cricket** *n* : an insect of the widespread family Gryllotalpidae (order Orthoptera) having large fossorial front legs adapted for digging in moist soil and feeding largely on the roots of plants

**mo·lec·u·la** \mə'lekyələ\ *n, pl* **molecu·lae** \-yə,lē\ [NL — more at MOLECULE] *archaic* : MOLECULE

**mo·lec·u·lar** \mə'lekyələ(r)\ *adj* [ISV *molecule* + *-ar*] **1** : relating to, connected with, produced by, or consisting of molecules : MOLAR, MOLAL ⟨~ structure⟩ ⟨~ rearrangement⟩ ⟨~ oxygen⟩ **2** : consisting of two or more atomic statements related by logical connectives ⟨~ proposition⟩ — see ¹ATOMIC 4 **3** : relating to or emphasizing individual responses or structures of behavior ⟨proceed by more and more detailed analysis to the ~ facts of perception —G.A.Miller⟩ — opposed to *molar* — **mo·lec·u·lar·ly** *adv*

**molecular beam** *n* : a stream of molecules that escape at thermal speeds from a heated enclosure, that are controlled by slits so as to move in nearly parallel paths, and that are used in determining the electric and magnetic properties of atoms, atomic nuclei, and molecules

**molecular biology** *n* : a branch of biology dealing with the ultimate physicochemical organization of living matter

**molecular compound** *n* : a compound regarded as a union of molecules retaining their identities (as in boron trifluoride-ethyl ether $BF_3.(C_2H_5)_2O$) — called also *addition compound;* compare DOUBLE SALT 2

**molecular distillation** *n* : distillation that is carried out under a high vacuum in an apparatus so designed as to permit molecules escaping from the warm liquid to reach the cooled surface of the condenser before colliding with other molecules and consequently returning to the liquid and that is used in the purification of substances of low volatility (as in the separation of vitamin A and vitamin E from fish-liver oils)

**molecular film** *n* : a monomolecular film or layer : MONOLAYER

**molecular formula** *n* : a chemical formula based on both analysis and molecular weight ⟨$C_2H_4O_2$ and $C_6H_{12}O_6$ are the *molecular formulas* of acetic acid and glucose respectively or twice and six times the empirical formulas respectively⟩ — compare STRUCTURAL FORMULA

**molecular heat** *n* : the heat capacity per gram molecule of any pure substance : the specific heat in calories per degree per gram multiplied by the molecular weight — compare ATOMIC HEAT

**mo·le·cu·lar·i·ty** \mə,lekyə'larəd·ē *also* -'ler-\ *n* -ES : the quality, state, or degree of being molecular; *esp* : the number of molecules or atoms involved in a chemical reaction ⟨there is no necessary correlation between the ~ and the order —Farrington Daniels & R.A.Alberty⟩

**molecular layer** *n* **1** : the outer layer of the cortex of the cerebellum and cerebrum consisting of a mass of unmedullated fibers rich in synapses **2** : either of the two plexiform layers of the retina

**molecular model** *n* : a scale model showing the arrangement of atoms in a molecule (as of an organic compound)

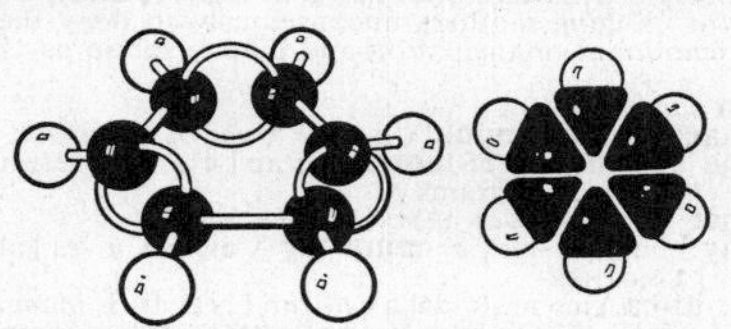

two molecular models of benzene, in which carbon atoms are represented by dark balls and quasi tetrahedrons, and hydrogen atoms by light balls and half spheres

**molecular pump** *n* : a vacuum pump that depends for its action on the adhesion of the gas or vapor molecules to a rapidly moving metal disk or cylinder by which they are carried away

**molecular rotation** *n* : a value obtained by multiplying the specific rotation by the molecular weight

**molecular sieve** *n* : a crystalline substance (as a zeolite) that is characterized by pores of molecular dimensions and uniform size formed by heating to drive off the water of hydration and that by its ability to adsorb small molecules but not large ones can be used esp. in separations (as of gases or liquids) based on differences in sizes of molecules or as a carrier (as of accelerators in rubber vulcanization)

**molecular silver** *n* : a gray powdery active form of silver obtained by reducing silver chloride with zinc

**molecular spectrum** *n* : a spectrum of radiation due to electron transitions and other quantum energy changes within molecules and consisting of series of characteristic spectrum bands which are found upon high dispersion to be made up of very fine lines

**molecular still** *n* : an apparatus for carrying out a molecular distillation

**molecular volume** *n* : the quotient obtained by dividing the molecular weight by the specific gravity — compare ATOMIC VOLUME

**molecular weight** *n* : the weight of a molecule that may be calculated as the sum of the atomic weights of its constituent atoms

**mol·e·cule** \'mälə,kyül, -lē,-\ *n* -s [F *molécule*, fr. NL *molecula*, dim. of L *moles* mass — more at MOLE (structure)] **1 a** : a unit of matter that is the smallest particle of an element or chemical combination of atoms (as a compound) capable of retaining chemical identity with the substance in mass (a few elements (as helium and neon) have monatomic ~s⟩ ⟨the viruses are one kind of giant ~s —Linus Pauling⟩ — see AVOGADRO'S LAW; compare ION, RADICAL **5 b** : a quantity proportional to the molecular weight; *esp* : ⁷MOLE **2** : a tiny bit : FRACTION, FRAGMENT ⟨every tone . . . is a ~ of music —Henry Miller⟩ ⟨a ~ of political honesty —*Time*⟩

**moled** *past of* MOLE

**mole drain** *n* [³*mole*] : an underground channel made by a mole plow and used esp. for draining heavy farm soils of more or less uniform slope

**mole drainage** *or* **mole draining** *n* : an act, instance, or system of drawing off water from farmland by mole drains

**mole fraction** *n* [⁷*mole*] : the ratio of the number of moles of one component of a solution or other mixture to the total number of moles representing all of the components

**mole gray** *n* : ³MOLE 4

**molehill** \'=,=\ *n* [ME, fr. *mole* + *hill*] **1** : a little ridge of earth thrown up by a mole working close to the surface — called also *molecast* **2** : an insignificant obstacle or difficulty : TRIFLE ⟨make a mountain out of a ~⟩

**mole mouse** *n* : SOKHOR

**mole plant** *also* **mole tree** *n* : CAPER SPURGE

**mole plow** *or* **mole drainer** *n* [³*mole*] : a subsoil plow having a vertical knife behind the tooth of which is drawn a round or tapered metal ball that opens an underground channel

**mole rat** *n* : any of various rodents resembling true moles in habit or appearance: as **a** : SOKHOR **b** : a member of the family Spalacidae of the eastern Mediterranean region **c** : a member of the family Bathyergidae and esp. of the African genus *Bathyergus* **d** : a member of the East Indian murid genus *Nesokia*

**moles** *pl of* MOLE, *pres 3d sing of* MOLE

**mole salamander** *n* : a brownish black burrowing salamander (*Ambystoma talpoideum*) of the southeastern U.S.

**mole shrew** *n* **1 a** : an American short-tailed shrew of the genus *Blarina* **b** : any of several shrews of the genus *Anourosorex* that resemble moles, have the ears and eyes greatly reduced, have slate-colored glossy fur, and live in the high mountains of Burma, China, and Siam **2** : SHREW MOLE

**moleskin** \'=,=\ *n* **1** : ³MOLE 1d **2 a** : a heavy durable cotton fabric made in satin weave for industrial, medical, and clothing uses and usu. with a smooth twilled surface on one side and a short thick velvety nap on the other **b** : a garment (as trousers) made of moleskin — usu. used in pl. ⟨got on their boots and ~s —Mary S. Broome⟩ **3** : ³MOLE 4a

**mole snake** *n* **1** : a valuable colubrid snake (*Pseudaspis cana*) that is common in South and East Africa and feeds on rats and mice **2** : BROWN KING SNAKE

¹**mo·lest** \mə'lest\ *vt* -ED/-ING/-S [ME *molesten*, fr. MF *molester*, fr. L *molestare*, fr. *molestus* burdensome, annoying, irreg. fr. *moles* mass — more at MOLE (structure)] **1** *obs* **a** : INCONVENIENCE, HARASS, PLAGUE ⟨the heats of summer are . . . incapable of ~*ing* you —Joseph Addison⟩ **b** : to affect injuriously : AFFLICT ⟨they were generally ~*ed* with . . . sciatica —Sir Thomas Browne⟩ **2 a** : ANNOY, PERSECUTE, DISTURB, TORMENT ⟨painted in a loft, drawing up the ladder after him that he might not be ~*ed* by his family —Laurence Binyon⟩ ⟨leaders . . . should not be ~*ed* in any way nor should their party be outlawed —Sidney Hook⟩; *specif* : RAID ⟨traders turn to ~*ing* the Spanish borderlands —R.A.Billington⟩ **b** : to meddle or interfere with unjustifiably often as a result of abnormal sexual motivation ⟨charges of being drunk and ~*ing* a woman —Frank Yerby⟩ ⟨~*ing* small boys in the washroom of a moving picture house —Wenzell Brown⟩

²**molest** \"\ *n* -s [ME, fr. MF *moleste*, irreg. fr. L *molestia* trouble, fr. *molestus* + *-ia* -y] : MOLESTATION ⟨within his walls, secure from all ~ —W.J.Linton⟩

**mo·les·ta·tion** \,mō,le'stāshən, ,mə'l-\ *n* -s [ME *molestacioun*, fr. MF *molestation*, fr. LL *molestation-, molestatio*, fr. L *molestatus* (past part. of *molestare*) + *-ion-, -io* -ion] **1 a** *archaic* : a cause or state of harassment : VEXATION ⟨all the ~s of marriage are abundantly recompensed with other comforts —Thomas Fuller⟩ **b** : an act or instance of molesting : ANNOYANCE, OBSTRUCTION ⟨liberty to . . . worship without ~ —William Sewel⟩ ⟨seas upon which our ships and planes can travel without ~ —*U.S.Code*⟩ **2 a** *Scots law* : interference with or troubling another in his possession of land **b** : willful injury inflicted upon another by interference with his user of rights as to person, character, social position, or property

**mo·lest·er** \mə'lestə(r)\ *n* -s : one that molests

**mo·lest·ful** \-tfəl\ *adj, archaic* : TROUBLESOME, ANNOYING ⟨~ battle with carnal vices —Thomas Wright⟩

**molet** *var of* MULLET

**mo·le·ta** \mə'lād·ə\ *n* -s [Pg *moleta, muleta*, fr. *muleta* crutch, fr. Sp — more at MULETA] : a short-masted Portuguese fishing boat having a large lateen sail, two outriggers and a bowsprit that carry up to six sails, and an outrigger at the stern with two triangular sails

moleta

**mole-warp** \'mōl,wȯrp\ *var of* MOLDWARP

**mol·ge** \'mōljē\ [NL, fr. G *molch* salamander, fr. OHG *mol, molm, molt;* akin to OS & MLG *mol* salamander, and perh. to Arm *molēz* lizard] *syn of* TRITURUS

**mol·gu·la** \'mälgyələ\ *n, cap* [NL, fr. Gk *molgos* hide, skin + NL *-ula;* perh. akin to OHG *malaha* leather bag, ON *malr* bag] : a cosmopolitan genus (the type of the family Molgulidae) of almost spherical ascidians with long siphons and a thin somewhat transparent tunic — **mol·gu·lid** \-ləd\ *adj or n*

¹**mo·lid** \'mōləd\ *adj* [NL *Molidae*] : of or relating to the Molidae

²**molid** \"\ *n* -s : a fish of the family Molidae

**mol·i·dae** \'mälə,dē\ *n pl, cap* [NL, fr. *Mola*, type genus + *-idae*] : a family of large pelagic marine fishes (order Plectognathi) that have very large heads, short compact bodies, and teeth fused to form a beak and that lack a dorsal fin — see MOLA

**mo·li·men** \mə'līmən\ *n, pl* **mo·lim·i·na** \-limənə\ [NL, fr. L, exertion, fr. *moliri* to struggle, fr. *moles* mass, burden — more at MOLE (structure)] : discomfort or sensations of tension preceding or accompanying menstruation

**moliminous** *adj* [L *molimin-, molimen* + E *-ous*] *obs* : CUMBERSOME, WEIGHTY

**mol·i·nary** \'mälə,nerē, 'mōl-\ *adj* [LL *molina* mill + E *-ary* — more at MILL] : of or relating to a mill or the process of grinding

**mo·line** \'mōlən, mō'līn\ *adj* [fr. (assumed) AF *moliné*, fr. OF *molin* mill, fr. LL *molinum* — more at MILL] *of a cross* : having the end of each arm forked and recurved — compare ANCRÉE, CROSS MOLINE, FOURCHÉE, PATY, RECERCELÉE; see CROSS illustration

**molinet** *n* -s [F *moulinet*, fr. MF *molinet*, dim. of *molin* mill] **1** *obs* : a stick for whipping chocolate **2** *obs* : a small grinding mill

**moling** *pres part of* MOLE

**mo·lin·ia** \mə'linēə\ *n, cap* [NL, fr. Juan Ignacio *Molina* †1829, Chilean naturalist + NL *-ia*] : a small genus of Eurasian grasses having narrow flat leaves, slender panicles, and awnless glumes — see MOOR GRASS 2

¹**mo·li·nism** \'mōlə,nizəm, 'mäl-\ *n* -s *usu cap* [Sp *molinismo*, fr. Luis *Molina* †1600 Span. Jesuit and theologian + Sp *-ismo* -ism] : a doctrine that it is man's free cooperation which makes it possible for him to perform a good act with God's helping grace — compare CONGRUISM, THOMISM

²**molinism** \"\ *n* -s *usu cap* [Sp *molinismo*, fr. Miguel de *Molinos* †*ab*1697 Span. priest and mystic + Sp *-ismo* -ism] : QUIETISM

¹**mo·li·nist** \-nəst\ *n* -s *usu cap* [Sp *molinista*, fr. Luis *Molina* †1600 + Sp *-ista* -ist] : an advocate or follower of the doctrine of Luis Molina

²**molinist** \"\ *n* -s *usu cap* [Sp *molinista*, fr. Miguel de *Molinos* + Sp *-ista* -ist] : an advocate or follower of the quietism of Miguel de Molinos

**mo·lisch reaction** \'mōlish-\ *or* **molisch test** *n, usu cap M* [after Hans *Molisch* †1937 Ger. botanist] : a test for carbohydrate in which a reddish violet color is formed by reaction with alpha-naphthol in the presence of concentrated sulfuric acid

¹**moll** \'mōl\ *adj* [G, fr. ML (*b*) *molle* b flat; fr. *b* + L *molle*, neut. of *mollis* soft, weak — more at MELT] : composed in the minor mode : MINOR ⟨G ~⟩

²**moll** \'mäl, 'mōl\ *n* -s [prob. fr. *Moll*, nickname for *Mary*] **1** : PROSTITUTE **2 a** : DOLL 2 ⟨a sailor and his ~⟩ **b** : a gangster's girl friend — called also *gun moll* ⟨frequently by gangsters and their ~s —W.S.Maugham⟩

**mollah** *var of* MULLAH

**moll-buzzer** \'=,==\ *n* [²*moll*] *slang* : a pickpocket whose victims are women

**mol·le** \'mō(,)yā\ *n* -s [AmerSp, fr. Quechua *mulli*] : PEPPER TREE 1

**mollemock** *var of* MALLEMUCK

**mol·li·crush** \'mäli,krəsh, -rəsh\ *vt* [perh. fr. E dial. *mully* powdery (fr. E ¹*mull* + *-y*) + E *crush*] *dial Eng* : to beat to jelly : CRUSH, PULVERIZE

¹**mollie** *also* **molly** *var of* MOLLY

²**mol·lie** *also* **mol·ly** \'mälē\ *n, pl* **mollies** [by shortening] : MOLLIENISIA 2

**mol·li·e·nis·ia** \,mälēə'nisēə\ *n* [NL, irreg. fr. Comte François N. *Mollien* †1850 Fr. statesman] **1** *cap* : a genus of brightly colored topminnows of the family Poeciliidae highly valued as aquarium fishes — see SAILFIN **2** -s : any fish of the genus *Mollienisia*

**mol·lier diagram** \'mōl(,)yā-\ *or* **mollier chart** *n, usu cap M* [after Richard *Mollier* †1935 Ger. mechanical engineer] : a diagram showing thermodynamic properties of a substance with various quantities (as temperature and pressure) constant esp. in terms of entropy and enthalpy as coordinates

**mollies** *pl of* MOLLY

**mol·li·fi·able** \'mälə,fīəbəl, ,==ˈ===\ *adj* : capable of being mollified

**mol·li·fi·ca·tion** \,mäləfə'kāshən\ *n* -s [ME *mollificacioun*, fr. MF *mollification*, fr. ML *mollification-, mollificatio*, fr. LL *mollificatus* (past part. of *mollificare* to soften) + *-ion-, -io* -ion — more at MOLLIFY] **1** : an act or instance of tempering : AMELIORATION, APPEASEMENT **2** : the quality or state of being mollified

**mollifier** *n* -s : one that mollifies ⟨vinegar . . . is itself a prime corrector and ~ —Thomas Fuller⟩

**mol·li·fy** \'mälə,fī\ *vb* -ED/-ING/-ES [ME *mollefien, mollifien;* fr. MF *mollifier*, fr. LL *mollificare*, fr. L *mollis* soft + *-ficare* -fy — more at MELT] *vt* **1** : to soothe in temper or disposition : CONCILIATE, PACIFY ⟨*mollified* by her flattery⟩ ⟨should have *mollified* their artistic critics —Hunter Mead⟩ ⟨eager to ~ his own . . . nationalists —Claire Sterling⟩ **2** : to reduce the stiffness or rigidity of : SOFTEN ⟨shaving cream *mollifies* the beard⟩ ⟨they have riddled and *mollified* the rocks —D.C. Peattie⟩ ⟨plump cushions with bright covers ~ the lounges —Blanche E. Baughan⟩ **3 a** : to reduce in intensity or violence : ASSUAGE, AMELIORATE ⟨their solicitude *mollifies* his pique⟩ ⟨the behavior was not only *mollified* but improvement continued to recovery —*Diseases of the Nervous System*⟩ **b** : to make more agreeable : TEMPER ⟨prevailed on him to ~ his demands⟩ ⟨nor can the social necessity for the product ~ the process —Lewis Mumford⟩ ~ *vi, archaic* : to become less angry or obstinate : SOFTEN, RELENT ⟨the father *mollifies* and is reconciled to the marriage —*Examiner*⟩ **syn** see PACIFY

**mol·li·fy·ing·ly** *adv* : in a mollifying manner

**mol·li·grant** \'mäli,grant\ *n* -s [origin unknown] *Scot* : a wailing lamentation : COMPLAINT

**mol·lis·i·a·ce·ae** \mə,lisē'āsē,ē\ *n pl* [NL, fr. *Mollisia*, type genus (irreg. fr. L *mollis* soft + NL *-ia*) + *-aceae*] : a family of fungi (order Helotiales having the hymenium of the apothecium surrounded by a pseudoparenchymatous rim of dark mostly thick-walled cells

**mol·lis·i·ose** \mə'lisē,ōs\ *n* -s [NL *Mollisia* + E *-ose*] : LEAF SCORCH b

**mol·li·sol** \'mälə,säl\ *n* -s [L *mollis* soft + *solum* ground — more at MELT, SOIL] : the surface layer of permanently frozen ground in which the ice melts during the summer

**mol·lu·go** \mə'lü(,)gō\ *n, cap* [NL, fr. L, stickseed, fr. *mollis* soft] : a genus of low chiefly tropical American herbs (family Aizoaceae) having whorled leaves and pedicellate flowers — see CARPETWEED

**mol·lus·ca** \mə'ləskə\ *n pl, cap* [NL, fr. L, neut. pl. of *molluscus* soft, fr. *mollis* — more at MELT] : a large phylum of invertebrate animals that include the chitons, tooth shells, snails, mussels and other bivalves, octopuses, and related forms and that have a soft unsegmented body lacking segmented appendages and commonly protected by a calcareous shell secreted by a mantle which extends from the body wall usu. as an enveloping fold; a muscular foot which is formed from part of the ventral surface of the body and is variously modified for creeping, digging, or swimming; a well-developed heart and vascular system and usu. one or more pairs of gills; a complex nervous system with several pairs of ganglia and longitudinal and transverse commissures; and frequently more or less complex eyes and otocysts — compare AMPHINEURA, CEPHALOPODA, GASTROPODA, LAMELLIBRANCHIA, SCAPHOPODA

**mol·lus·can** *also* **mol·lus·kan** \-kən\ *adj* [NL *Mollusca* + E *-an*] : of or relating to the Mollusca

**mol·lus·ci·ci·dal** \mə,ləs(k)ə'sīdᵊl\ *also* **mol·lus·ca·ci·dal** \-skə;-\ *adj* : of, relating to, or being a molluscicide ⟨~ action⟩

**mol·lus·ci·cide** \mə'ləs(k)ə,sīd\ *or* **mol·lus·ca·cide** \-skə,-\ *n* -s [*molluscicide* fr. NL *Mollusca* + E *-i-* + *-cide; molluscacide* fr. NL *Mollusca* + E *-cide*] : an agent for destroying mollusks (as snails)

**mol·lus·civ·o·rous** \,mälə's(k)iv(ə)rəs\ *adj* [NL *Mollusca* + E *-i-* + *-vorous*] : feeding upon mollusks

¹**mol·lus·coid** \mə'lə,skȯid\ *also* **mol·lus·coi·dal** \,mälə-'skȯidᵊl\ *adj* [NL *Molluscoid* fr. NL *Molluscoidea; molluscoidal* fr. NL *Molluscoidea* + E *-al*] : of, like, or relating to the Molluscoidea

²**molluscoid** \"\ *n* -s : one of the Molluscoidea

**mol·lus·coi·da** \,mälə'skȯidə\ [NL, fr. *Mollusca* + *-oida*] *syn of* MOLLUSCOIDEA

**mol·lus·coi·dea** \-dēə\ *n pl, cap* [NL, fr. *Mollusca* + *-oidea*] *in some classifications* : a phylum of invertebrate animals distinguished by possession of a lophophore and typically including the present groups Brachiopoda, Bryozoa, Entoprocta, and Phoronidea — **mol·lus·coi·de·an** \'==ˈskȯidēən\ *adj or n*

¹**mol·lus·cous** \mə'ləskəs\ *adj* [NL *Mollusca* + E *-ous*] : MOLLUSCAN

²**molluscous** \"\ *adj* [NL *molluscum* + E *-ous*] : of, relating to, or having the properties of a molluscum

**mol·lus·cum** \mə'ləskəm\ *n, pl* **mollus·ca** \-kə\ [NL, fr. L *molluscum*, a fungus, fr. neut. of *molluscus* soft — more at MOLLUSCA] : any of several skin diseases marked by soft pulpy nodules — see MOLLUSCUM CONTAGIOSUM

**molluscum con·ta·gi·o·sum** \-kən,tājē'ōsəm\ *n, pl* **mollusca contagio·sa** \-sə\ [NL, lit., contagious molluscum] : a mild chronic viral disease of the skin characterized by the formation of small nodules with a central opening and contents resembling curd

**mol·lusk** *or* **mol·lusc** \'mäləsk\ *n* -s [F *mollusque*, fr. NL *Mollusca*] : one of the Mollusca : SHELLFISH

**mol·wei·de projection** \'mōl,vīdə-\ *n, usu cap M* [after Karl B. *Mollweide* †1825 Ger. mathematician and astronomer] : an equal-area map projection capable of showing the entire surface of the earth in the form of an ellipse with all parallels as straight lines more widely spaced at the equator than at the poles, with the central meridian as one half the length of the equator, and with all other meridians ellipses equally spaced

¹**mol·ly** *or* **mol·lie** \'mälē, -li\ *n, pl* **mollies** [fr. *Molly, Mollie*, nickname for *Mary*] **1** *slang* : ²MOLL **2** *slang* : MOLLYCODDLE

²**molly** *or* **mollie** \"\ *n, pl* **mollies** [by shortening and alter.] : MALLEMUCK

³**molly** *var of* MALI

⁴**molly** *var of* MOLLIE

¹**mollycoddle** \'==,==\ *n* [¹*molly* + *coddle*] **1** : a pampered darling : a spineless weakling ⟨his mother might turn him into a ~ —Aldous Huxley⟩ ⟨catch those ~s getting away from the steam heaters —*Everybody's Mag.*⟩; *specif* : an effeminate man ⟨the men . . . were ~s, and the women were sexually unemployed —Francis Hackett⟩ **2** : GOODY-GOODY ⟨these are the words not of a ~ or a sentimentalist, but of a veteran soldier —*Nation*⟩

²**mollycoddle** \"\ *vt* : to treat with fond indulgence : protect and cater to : PAMPER, SPOIL ⟨believes we have *mollycoddled* women too much —*N. Y. Times*⟩ ⟨judges ~ these young hoods —James McGlincy⟩ **syn** see INDULGE

**mol·ly·cod·dler** \'==,käd(ᵊ)lə(r)\ *n* : one that mollycoddles

**mol·ly·cot** \'mäli,kät\ *n* [¹*molly* + obs. *cot* man who does women's work, short for *cotquean*] *dial Eng* : one unduly concerned with housekeeping; *esp* : a man who takes an interest in or does housework usu. performed by women

**mol·ly·grubs** \'mäli,grəbz\ *var of* MULLIGRUBS

**mol·ly·hawk** \'mälē,hȯk\ *n* -s [by folk etymology fr. *mallemuck*] : MALLEMUCK

**mollymawk** *var of* MALLEMUCK

**mol·man** \'mōlmən\ *n, pl* **molmen** [ME, fr. *mol-* (fr. OE *māl* terms, agreement, pay) + *man* — more at MAIL] : one of a class of tenants in feudal England released from most of their service on condition of paying certain rents for their land

**mo·loch** \'mō,läk, 'mō,lək\ *n* [LL, an ancient Semitic deity, fr. Gk, fr. Heb *Mōlekh*] **1** -s *usu cap* : a tyrannical power to be propitiated by human subservience or sacrifice ⟨duty has become the *Moloch* of modern life —Norman Douglas⟩ ⟨began . . . to suspend members of his staff as a human sacrifice to propitiate the *Moloch* of fear and hysteria —*New Republic*⟩ **2** [NL, fr. LL] **a** *cap* : a genus of small spiny Australian desert lizards **b** -s : any lizard of the genus *Moloch*

moloch 2b

1**mo·loid** \'mō,lȯid\ *adj* [NL *Mola* + E *-oid*] **:** of, relating to, or resembling a mola or the Molidae

2**moloid** \"\ *n* -s **:** an ocean sunfish **:** MOLA

**mol·o·kan** \,mälə'kän\ *n, pl* **molokans** \-nz\ *also* **moloka·ni** \-nē\ *usu cap* [Russ, fr. *moloko* milk; prob. fr. the dietary laws of the sect that permit milk drinking during Lent] **:** a member of a religious sect originating in Russia as an offshoot of the Doukhobors, becoming an antiritualistic group stressing the authority of the Bible, and calling themselves Spiritual Christians

1**mo·los·si·an** \mə'läsh(ē)ən, -äsēən, -äsyən\ *n* -s *usu cap* [*Molossis*, district in northwestern Greece + E *-an*] **1 :** a native or inhabitant of Molossis, a district of ancient Epirus famous for its dogs **2 :** a large dog of ancient times resembling a mastiff

2**molossian** \"\ *adj, usu cap* **:** of, relating to, or characteristic of Molossia or Molossians

1**mo·los·sic** \mə'läsik\ *adj* [*molossus* + *-ic*] **:** of or relating to a molossus

2**molossic** \"\ *n* -s **1 :** MOLOSSUS 1 **2 :** a word whose syllables form a molossus

**mo·los·sid** \mə'läsəd\ *adj* [NL *Molossidae*] **:** of or relating to the Molossidae or to mastiff bats

**mo·los·si·dae** \-sə,dē\ *n pl, cap* [NL, fr. *Molossus*, type genus + *-idae*] **:** a family of Microchiroptera comprising the typical mastiff bats

**mo·los·sus** \mə'läsəs\ *n* [L, fr. Gk *molossos*, fr. *Molossos* Molossian] **1** *pl* **molos·si** \-ä,sī\ *classical prosody* **:** a foot of three long syllables **2** *cap* [NL, fr. L, Molossian, fr. Gk (*kyōn*) *Molossos*, lit., Molossian dog] **:** a genus of mastiff bats that is the type of the family Molossidae

**mol·o·thrus** \'mäləthrəs\ *n, cap* [NL, prob. modif. of Gk *molobros* greedy fellow] **:** a genus of Icteridae consisting of the cowbirds

**mo·lo·tov** \'mälə,tȯf, 'mȯl-, 'mōl-\ *adj, usu cap* [*Molotov*, former name (1940–58) of Perm, city near the Ural mountains U.S.S.R.] **:** PERM

**molotov cocktail** *n, usu cap M* [after Vyacheslav M. *Molotov* *b*1890 Russ. statesman] **:** a crude hand grenade made of a bottle filled with a flammable liquid (as gasoline) and fitted with a wick or saturated rag taped to the bottom and ignited at the moment of hurling

**mol·pa·dia** \mäl'pādēə\ *n, cap* [NL, prob. after *Molpadia*, a minor goddess of Greek mythology, fr. Gk] **:** a widely distributed genus (the type of the family Molpadiidae) comprising smooth-bodied burrowing sea cucumbers having a well-developed respiratory tree and a distinct caudal prolongation of a body — **mol·pa·did** \'mälpədəd\ *n or adj*

1**molt** *or* **moult** \'mōlt\ *vb* -ED/-ING/-S [alter. of ME *mouten*, fr. (assumed) OE *mūtian* to change (as in *bimūtian* to exchange), fr. L *mutare* — more at MUTABLE] *vi* **:** to shed or cast off hair, feathers, shell, horns, or an outer layer of skin in a process of growth or periodic renewal with the cast-off parts being replaced by new growth ⟨birds ~ once or twice a year⟩ ⟨a mature lobster ~*s* . . . in the spring or early summer —Joe McCarthy⟩ ~ *vt* **1 :** to cast off (an outer covering) in a periodic process of growth or renewal ⟨~*ed* its wing feathers —*Nat'l Geographic*⟩ ⟨the crab ~*s* its shell⟩; *specif* **:** to throw off (the old cuticle) — used of an arthropod ⟨a spider, like a lobster, ~*s* its covering as it grows —Eugene Kinkead⟩ **2 :** to free oneself from **:** CHANGE ⟨~ his old notions in a transition period⟩ **syn** see DISCARD

2**molt** *or* **moult** \"\ *n* -s **1 :** the act or process of molting ⟨helps hens to lay right through the ~ —*Poultry Tribune*⟩; *specif* **:** ECDYSIS **2 :** a cast-off covering ⟨bare ground . . . heavily besprinkled with the whitish aphid skins or ~*s* —*Jour. of Agric. Research*⟩ — compare EXUVIAE

**mol·ten** \'mōlt^ən *also* -ltən\ *adj* [ME, fr. past part. of *melten* to melt — more at MELT] **1 a** *obs* **:** formed in a mold **:** CAST **b :** fused or liquefied by heat **:** MELTED ⟨~ lead was poured drop by drop from the top of the tower and . . . solidified as lead shot —*Linguaphone Mag.*⟩ ⟨volcanoes pour forth . . . ~ basalt —R.W.Murray⟩ ⟨~ Parmesan cheese —C.S.Forester⟩ **2 :** having warmth or brilliance **:** HEATED, GLOWING ⟨seething . . . he set himself to compose a ~ political pamphlet —Edgar Johnson⟩ ⟨the ~ sunlight of warm skies —T.B.Costain⟩ — **mol·ten·ly** *adv*

**mol·te·no disease** \mōl'tē(,)nō-\ *n, usu cap M* [after *Molteno* Farmers' Assoc., Union of So. Africa, that first investigated it] **:** a frequently fatal intoxication of southern African cattle marked by liver injury and extreme emaciation due to feeding on a groundsel (*Senecio burchellii*) — compare WINTON DISEASE

**molt·er** *or* **moult·er** \'mōltə(r)\ *n* -s [ME *mowtare*, fr. *mowtan, mouten* to molt + *-are, -er* -er] **:** one that molts or is molting

**mol·to** \'mōl(,)tō\ *adv* [It, fr. L *multum*, fr. neut. of *multus* much — more at MELIORATE] **:** MUCH, VERY — used in musical directions ⟨~ adagio⟩ ⟨~ sostenuto⟩

**mo·luc·ca** \mə'ləkə\ *also* **mo·luc·can** \-kən\ *adj, usu cap* [*Molucca* islands, Indonesia; *Moluccan* fr. *Molucca* islands + E *-an*] **:** of or relating to the Moluccas or Spice islands of the Malay archipelago

**molucca balm** *n, usu cap M* **:** an annual herb (*Moluccella laevis*) with a greenish calyx resembling a bell surrounding the shorter whitish corolla — called also *bells of Ireland, shellflower*

**molucca bean** *n, usu cap M* **:** NICKER NUT

**molucca grains** *n pl, usu cap M* **:** seeds of a tree (*Croton tiglium*) that yield croton oil

**mol·uc·cel·la** \,mäləkˈselə\ *n, cap* [NL, fr. *Molucca* islands, + NL *-ella*] **:** a small genus of mints found in the Mediterranean region, cultivated widely, and usu. having small white pink-tipped flowers in whorls

1**mo·ly** \'mōlē\ *n* -ES [L, fr. Gk *mōly*; akin to Skt *mūla* root] **1 :** a mythical herb described by Homer as having a black root and milk-white blossoms, being possessed of magical powers, and being given by Hermes to Odysseus to counteract the spells of Circe **2 :** a European wild garlic (*Allium moly*) cultivated for its bright yellow flowers

2**moly** \'mälē\ *n* -ES [by shortening] **:** MOLYBDENUM

**molybd-** *or* **molybdo-** *comb form* [L *molybd-*, fr. Gk *molybd-, molybdo-*, fr. *molybdos* — more at PLUMB] **1 :** lead ⟨*molybdo*phyllite⟩ **2** [NL *molybdena* & *molybdenum*] **:** molybdenum **:** molybdous ⟨*molybdo*phosphate⟩ ⟨*molybdo*cyanide⟩

**mo·lyb·date** \mə'lib,dāt\ *n* -s [*molybd-* + *-ate*] **:** a salt of a molybdic acid; *esp* **:** a normal salt derived from the acid $H_2MoO_4$

**molybdate orange** *also* **molybdated orange** *n* **:** a strong brilliant orange pigment made by coprecipitation of lead chromate and lead molybdate often in the presence of lead sulfate and used in protective coatings and printing inks — called also *molybdenum orange*

**mo·lyb·de·na** \mə'libdənə\ *n* -s [NL, fr. L *molybdaena* galena, fr. Gk *molybdaina*, fr. *molybdos* lead] **1** *obs* **a :** MOLYBDENITE **b :** MOLYBDENUM **2 :** an oxide of molybdenum of uncertain structure that is used in catalysis frequently supported on alumina

**mo·lyb·de·nite** \-də,nīt\ *n* -s [NL *molybdena* + E *-ite*] **:** a mineral $MoS_2$ consisting of molybdenum disulfide that is valued as a source of molybdenum and its compounds and occurs in foliated masses or scales resembling graphite but differing from the latter in its bluer color, in giving a greenish streak on porcelain, and in yielding a sulfurous odor before the blowpipe (hardness 1–1.5, sp. gr. 4.7–4.8)

**mo·lyb·de·num** \-dənəm\ *n* -s [NL, fr. *molybdena*] **:** a difficultly fusible polyvalent metallic element that resembles chromium and tungsten in many of its properties, that is obtained as a dark gray powder or hard silver-white metal usu. from its principal ore molybdenite by roasting to molybdenum trioxide and reducing, that is used chiefly in strengthening and hardening steel, and that is a trace element in plant and animal metabolism — symbol *Mo;* see FERROMOLYBDENUM; ELEMENT table

**molybdenum blue** *n* **:** a blue complex substance that is obtained usu. in colloidal form by mild reduction of a molybdate in acid solution and that serves as the basis of some methods of colorimetric analysis

**molybdenum orange** *n* **:** MOLYBDATE ORANGE

**molybdenum steel** *n* **:** steel containing molybdenum whose presence in a percentage of 10 to 15 percent produces a steel similar to tungsten steel

**molybdenum trioxide** *n* **:** a crystalline compound $MoO_3$ made usu. by roasting molybdenite or by heating ammonium molybdate and used chiefly in making other molybdenum compounds and metallic molybdenum and as a catalyst — called also *molybdic oxide*

**mo·lyb·dic** \mə'libdik\ *adj* [*molybd-* + *-ic*] **:** of, relating to, or containing molybdenum — used esp. of compounds in which this element has one of its higher valences (as six)

**molybdic acid** *n* **1 :** any of various acids derived from molybdenum trioxide; *esp* **:** the simplest acid $H_2MoO_4$ obtained as white crystals or as the yellow crystalline monohydrate $H_2MoO_4.H_2O$ but known chiefly in the form of salts many of which are unstable and readily form polymolybdates — compare HETEROPOLY ACID, PHOSPHOMOLYBDIC ACID **2 a :** MOLYBDENUM TRIOXIDE — not used systematically **b :** ammonium molybdate containing added molybdenum trioxide — called also *molybdic acid 85 percent;* not used systematically

**molybdic ocher** *n* **:** FERRIMOLYBDITE

**molybdic oxide** *n* **:** MOLYBDENUM TRIOXIDE

**mo·lyb·dite** \mə'lib,dīt\ *n* -s [G *molybdit*, modif. (influenced by *-it* -ite) of E *molybdine*, fr. *molybd-* + *-ine*] **:** FERRIMOLYBDITE — called also *molybdic ocher*

**mo·lyb·do·me·nite** \mə,libdō'mē,nīt\ *n* -s [F, fr. *molybd-* + Gk *mēnē* moon + F *-ite* — more at MOON] **:** a mineral $PbSeO_3$ consisting of native lead selenite

**mo·lyb·do·phosphate** \mə¦lib(,)dō+\ *n* [*molybd-* + *phosphate*] **:** PHOSPHOMOLYBDATE — used in the system of nomenclature adopted by the International Union or Pure and Applied Chemistry

**mo·lyb·do·phosphoric acid** \"+ . . . -\ *n* [ISV *molybd-* + *phosphoric*] **:** PHOSPHOMOLYBDIC ACID

**mo·lyb·do·phyl·lite** \mə,libdō'fi,līt\ *n* -s [ISV *molybd-* + *phyll-* + *-ite;* fr. its occurrence in foliated masses] **:** a mineral $(Pb,Mg)_2SiO_4.H_2O$(?) consisting of a hydrous lead magnesium silicate

**mo·lyb·dous** \mə'libdəs\ *adj* [*molybd-* + *-ous*] **:** of, relating to, or containing molybdenum — used esp. of compounds in which this element has a lower valence than in molybdic compounds

**mol·y·site** \'mälə,sīt\ *n* -s [It *molisite*, fr. Gk *mōlysis* action of parboiling, simmering (fr. *mōlyein* to parboil + *-sis*) + It *-ite*] **:** a mineral $FeCl_3$ consisting of native ferric chloride found in Vesuvian lava

**mom** \'mäm, 'məm\ *n* -s [short for *momma*] **:** MOTHER ⟨approximately 6000 youngsters, ~*s* and pops watched the two shows —*Springfield (Mass.) Union*⟩

**MOM** *abbr* middle of month

**mom·bin** \mōm'bēn\ *n* -s [AmerSp *mombin*, fr. Carib] **1 :** a common tropical American shrub or small tree (*Spondias purpurea*) with compound leaves and purple paniculate flowers — called also *jocote;* compare HOG PLUM **2 :** the edible purplish fruit of the mombin

1**mom·ble** \'mäm(b)əl\ *vt* -ED/-ING/-S [alter. of 1*mumble*] **1** *dial Eng* **:** to treat roughly **:** ABUSE, BUNGLE **2** *dial Eng* **:** to wrap or conceal in a disordered condition **3** *dial Eng* **:** CONFUSE, BEWILDER ⟨he was so *mombled* he couldn't speak⟩

2**momble** \"\ *n* -s *dial Eng* **:** a state of confusion or untidiness **:** a bungling job

**mombuttoo** *var of* MANGBETU

1**mome** \'mōm\ *n* -s [origin unknown] *archaic* **:** a dull doltish person **:** BLOCKHEAD, FOOL

2**mome** *n* -s [prob. fr. NL *momus*] *obs* **:** a caviling critic

**mo·ment** \'mōmənt\ *n* -s [ME, fr. MF, fr. L *momentum* movement, motion, moment, influence, fr. earlier (assumed) *movimentum*, fr. *movēre* to move + *-mentum* -ment — more at MOVE] **1 a :** a minute portion of time ⟨the ~ stretched out to a minute, the minute to an hour —Hesketh Pearson⟩ ⟨a ~ of dreadful suspense —Graham Greene⟩ **b :** a point of time **:** INSTANT ⟨to us . . . the ~ 8:17 a.m. means something —Aldous Huxley⟩ ⟨at this very ~ of his life's lowest ebb —Osbert Sitwell⟩ ⟨if the great famine had not come along at that particular ~ —Paul Blanshard⟩ **c :** a comparatively brief period of time ⟨this whole ~ of thought hardly lasted five minutes —Carl Jonas⟩ ⟨in ~*s* of solitude when I was milking the cows —David Fairchild⟩ ⟨a presidential candidate . . . must symbolize the forces seeking expression during his ~ in history —V.L.Albjerg⟩ **d :** the present time — usu. used with *the* ⟨at the ~ she is at work on her fourth novel —*Holiday*⟩ ⟨the . . . flavor so much in fashion at the ~ —Kenneth Hince⟩ ⟨a catchword of the ~ —J.A.R.Pimlott⟩ **e :** a particular period (as of importance, significance, or pleasure) ⟨all had their ~*s* when their subject . . . made them greater than their normal selves —R.E.Priestley⟩ ⟨sailors have their ~*s* as in any seaboard town —*Amer. Guide Series: N.H.*⟩ **2** *obs* **:** a minute portion or part **:** PARTICLE ⟨every little ~ of the earth —Thomas Blundeville⟩ **3 :** importance in influence or effect **:** CONSEQUENCE, CONSIDERATION, WEIGHT ⟨decisions of ~ must be made by our government —L.H.Evans⟩ ⟨meanings which are . . . of no ~ to the student —Edward Sapir⟩ ⟨taught men to reckon virtue of more ~ than security —W.F.Hambly⟩ ⟨the political issues of their day seemed . . . of enormous ~ —Christopher Hollis⟩ **4** *obs* **:** a cause or motive of action **:** an influential point or consideration **:** a deciding factor ⟨I have seen her die twenty times upon far poorer ~ —Shak.⟩ **5 :** a definite period or point in a course of events: as **a :** a stage in historical development (as of an institution) ⟨a document of one ~ in the history of thought and sensibility in the nineteenth century —T.S.Eliot⟩ **b :** a stage in logical development, in cognition, or in the growing adequacy of thought **c :** a phase, aspect, or partial apprehension of a subject or thing **d** *in existentialist theology* **:** a timeless point of decision within the inner subjectivity of a person when he freely enacts his relationship to eternity **6 a :** tendency or measure of tendency to produce motion esp. about a point or axis **b :** the product of quantity (as a force) and the distance to a particular axis or point — see MOMENT OF A COUPLE, MOMENT OF A FORCE, MOMENT OF INERTIA **7 :** an essential or constituent element (as of a complex conceptual entity) ⟨the understanding is a necessary ~ in the reason —Bernard Bosanquet⟩ **8 :** the average or sum of the deviations or some power of the deviations of the elements of a frequency distribution from a specified norm **syn** see IMPORTANCE

**momenta** *pl of* MOMENTUM

**mo·men·tal** \mō'ment^əl\ *adj* [prob. fr. F, fr. ML *momentalis* momentary, fr. (assumed) LL (attested as *momentaliter*, adv., in a moment), fr. L *momentum* moment + *-alis* -al] **1** *obs* **:** MOMENTARY 1a ⟨not one ~ minute doth she swerve —Nicholas Breton⟩ **2 :** of or relating to moment or momentum

**mo·men·ta·ne·ous** \¦mōmən¦tānēəs\ *adj* [LL *momentaneus*, fr. L *momentum* moment + *-aneus* (as in *subterraneus* subterranean)] **1 :** MOMENTARY 1a ⟨the rapid ~ association of things which meet and pass —D.H.Lawrence⟩ **2** *archaic* **:** INSTANTANEOUS ⟨in which ~ explosion of the whole quantity all the force consists —William Clarke⟩ **3** *of an aspect or form of a verb* **:** of, relating to, or characterizing action begun and terminated in an instant — **mo·men·ta·ne·ous·ly** *adv* — **mo·men·ta·ne·ous·ness** *n* -ES

**momentany** *adj* [MF *momentané*, fr. LL *momentaneus*] *obs* **:** MOMENTARY 1a ⟨~ as a sound —Shak.⟩

**mo·men·tar·i·ly** \¦mōmən¦terəlē, -li\ *adv* **1 :** for a moment ⟨television serials that ~ distract suburban housewives from their ironing —Wolcott Gibbs⟩ ⟨only ~ troubled by such reports —*Publishers' Weekly*⟩ **2 :** INSTANTLY ⟨the friar groaned, but almost ~ recovered his emotion —Elizabeth Helme⟩ **3 :** at any moment **:** from moment to moment ⟨~ expected his coming —Charlotte Brontë⟩ ⟨when some draperies ~ expected . . . are hung —R.H.Rovere⟩ **4 :** in a few minutes ⟨I'll be there ~⟩

**mo·men·tar·i·ness** \'mōmən,terēnəs\ *n* -ES **:** the quality or state of being momentary ⟨the freshness and ~ of intense life —C.E.Montague⟩

**mo·men·tary** \-rē, -ri\ *adj* [L *momentarius*, fr. *momentum* moment + *-arius* -ary — more at MOMENT] **1 a :** continuing only a moment **:** lasting a very short time **:** TRANSITORY ⟨makes all human trouble appear but a ~ annoyance —Nathaniel Hawthorne⟩ ⟨law and order have reigned with only one ~ breakdown —J.H.Huizinga⟩ **b :** having a very brief life **:** EPHEMERAL — used of a living being ⟨truth more complete than the parcel of truth any ~ individual can seize —Matthew Arnold⟩ **2 :** operative or recurring at every moment ⟨in ~ terror of being hurled headlong down a precipice —T.L. Peacock⟩ **3 :** MOMENTANEOUS 3 **syn** see TRANSIENT

**mo·ment·ly** *adv* **1 :** from moment to moment **:** every moment ⟨amid the ~ increasing confusion —E.A.Poe⟩ ⟨the bill . . . grew ~ larger and larger —Aldous Huxley⟩ **2 :** at any moment ⟨~ expecting death from heart disease —*Time*⟩ **3 :** for a moment ⟨a bedlamite speeds to thy parapets, tilting there ~ —Hart Crane⟩

**momento** *var of* MEMENTO

**moment of a couple :** the product of either of the forces of a couple by the perpendicular distance between them

**moment of a force 1** *of a point* **:** the product of the distance from the point to the point of application of the force and the component of the force perpendicular to the line of the distance **2** *of a line* **:** the product of the perpendicular distance from the axis to the point of application of the force and the component of the force perpendicular to the line of the distance and in a plane perpendicular to the axis

**moment of inertia 1** *of a mass* **:** the ratio of the torque applied to a rigid body free to rotate about a given axis to the angular acceleration thus produced about that axis and equal to the sum of the products of each element of mass by the square of its distance from the axis — called also *rotational inertia* **2** *of an area* **:** the sum of the products of each element of a plane area by the square of its distance from a given axis in the plane of the area

**moment of momentum :** ANGULAR MOMENTUM

**mo·men·tous** \mō'mentəs *also* mə'-\ *adj* [*moment* + *-ous*] **1 :** having moment **:** of moment or consequence **:** very important **:** WEIGHTY ⟨on the eve of another ~ election —*N.Y. Times*⟩ ⟨the ~ character of the choice —M.R.Cohen⟩ ⟨brought about the ~ changes that affect us all —W.S.Maugham⟩ **2 :** having importance or influence — used of a person ⟨made a ~ captive, an Indian . . . prisoner —Bernard DeVoto⟩ — **mo·men·tous·ly** *adv*

**mo·men·tous·ness** *n* -ES **:** the quality or state of being momentous ⟨impress his visitors with the ~ . . . of all he had to say —H.V.Gregory⟩

**mo·men·tum** \mō'mentəm *also* mə'-\ *n, pl* **momen·ta** \-tə\ *also* **momentums** [L, motion — more at MOMENT] **1 :** a property of a moving body that determines the length of time required to bring it to rest when under the action of a constant force or moment — see ANGULAR MOMENTUM, LINEAR MOMENTUM **2 :** MOMENT 7 ⟨a ~ in the spiritual relations of him and God —A.B.Davidson⟩ **3 a :** the force of motion acquired by a moving body as a result of the continuance of its motion **:** IMPETUS — not used technically ⟨steps took him to the door . . . so neatly that he was able to seize the handle and enter without losing ~ —Robertson Davies⟩ ⟨still he galloped, and with a velocity and ~ continually increasing —William Cowper⟩ **b :** something held to resemble such force of motion of a moving body ⟨the . . . music not only lacks passion; it even lacks ~ of any sort —Winthrop Sargeant⟩ ⟨the conspiracy gained ~ and direction —R.C.Doty⟩ ⟨moved along by the ~ of events —Norman Cousins⟩

**momes** *pl of* MOME

**momie cloth** \'mōmē-, 'māmē-\ *n* [prob. alter. (influenced by F *momie* mummy) of *mummy cloth*] **:** a pebble-surfaced crepe with a cotton, rayon, or silk warp and a wool filling that is used for dresses, curtains, and upholstery

**mom·ism** \'mä,mizəm\ *n* -s [*mom* + *-ism*] **:** an excessive popular adoration and oversentimentalizing of mothers that is held to be oedipal in nature and that is thought to allow overprotective or clinging mothers unconsciously to deny their offspring emotional emancipation and thus to set up psychoneuroses

**momma** *var of* MAMMA

**mom·mack** *or* **mom·mick** \'mämək\ *var of* MAMMOCK

**mom·me** \'mämē\ *n, pl* **momme** [Jap] **:** a Japanese unit of weight equal to 3.75 grams

**mom·met** \'mämət\ *var of* MAUMET

**mom·my** \'mämē, -mi\ *or* **mum·my** \'məm-\ *n* -ES [alter. of *mammy*] **:** MOTHER

**mo·mor·di·ca** \mə'mȯ(r)dəkə\ *n, cap* [NL, fr. L *momordisse*, perf. inf. of *mordēre* to bite; fr. the fact that the seeds appear to have been bitten — more at SMART] **:** a genus of tropical Old World herbaceous vines (family Cucurbitaceae) having a campanulate corolla and a warty fruit — see BALSAM APPLE

**momot** *var of* MOTMOT

**mo·mot·i·dae** \mə'mäd·ə,dē\ *n pl, cap* [NL, fr. *Momotus*, type genus + *-idae*] **:** a family of tropical American birds (order Coraciiformes) related to the rollers and kingfishers and consisting of the motmots and in some classifications also the todies

**mo·mo·tus** \mə'mōd·əs\ *n, cap* [NL, fr. *momot*] **:** the type genus of Momotidae

**momser** *or* **momzer** *var of* MAMZER

**mo·mus** \'mōməs\ *n, pl* **momuses** \-səz\ *or* **mo·mi** \-ō,mī\ [NL, fr. *Momus*, god of ridicule in Greek mythology, fr. Gk *Mōmos*, lit., blame, ridicule; perh. akin to Gk *mōkos* mocker] **:** a carping critic **:** FAULTFINDER

1**mon** \'män\ *chiefly dial Brit var of* MAN

2**mon** \"\ *n* -s [Jap] **:** the usu. circular badge of a Japanese family esp. of the ancient feudal nobility consisting typically of conventionalized forms from nature (as flowers, birds, insects, lightning, waves of the sea) or geometric symbolic figures and used on lacquer, pottery, and fabrics — compare CHRYSANTHEMUM 3

mon of the Tokugawa family

3**mon** \'mōn\ *n, pl* **mon** *or* **mons** *usu cap* **1 a :** the dominant native people of Pegu in Burma **b :** a member of such people **2 :** the Mon-Khmer language of the Mon people

4**mon** \'män\ *n, pl* **mon** [native name in the Solomon islands] **:** a usu. large plank boat resembling a canoe and common in Melanesia

**mon-** *or* **mono-** *comb form* [ME, fr. MF & L; MF, fr. OF, fr. L, fr. Gk, fr. *monos* alone, single — more at MONK] **1 a :** consisting of or having only one **:** single ⟨*mon*arch⟩ ⟨*mono*plane⟩ **b :** by or from one only ⟨*mono*genic⟩ ⟨*mono*drama⟩ **c :** restricted to only one ⟨*mono*gamy⟩ ⟨*mono*logue⟩ **d :** only one at a time ⟨*mono*tocous⟩ **e :** alone ⟨*mono*phobia⟩ **2 a :** containing one atom, radical, or group (of a specified kind) ⟨*mon*oxide⟩ ⟨*mono*ether⟩ ⟨*mono*bromide⟩ — usu. omitted in names of specific compounds as being understood ⟨*mono*bromoacetone or bromoacetone⟩ **b :** monomolecular ⟨*mono*film⟩ ⟨*mono*layer⟩ **3 a :** affecting a single part ⟨*mono*plegia⟩ **b :** due to a single cause ⟨*mono*bacillary⟩ **c :** monomeric ⟨*mono*styrene⟩

**mon** *abbr* **1** monastery **2** monetary **3** monitor **4** monsieur **5** monsignor **6** monument

**mo·na** \'mōnə\ *n* -s [NL, prob. fr. Sp or It, monkey, ape — more at MONKEY] **:** a small West African guenon monkey (*Cercopithecus mona*)

1**mona·can** \'mänəkən, mə'näk-, 'mänēk-, mə'nák- *sometimes* 'mōn- *or* mə'nak-\ *adj, usu cap* [*Monaco*, principality of southern Europe + E *-an*] **:** MONEGASQUE

2**monacan** \"\ *n, cap* **:** MONEGASQUE

3**mo·na·can** \'mänəkən\ *n, pl* **monacan** *or* **monacans** *usu cap* **1 :** an extinct Siouan people in the upper James river valley of Virginia **2 :** a member of the Monacan people

1**mon·a·can·thid** \¦mänə¦kan(t)thəd\ *also* **mon·a·can·thine** \-thən, -,thīn\ *adj* [*monacanthid* fr. NL *Monacanthidae*; *monacanthine* fr. NL *Monacanthus*, genus of fishes + E *-ine*] **:** of or relating to the Monacanthidae

2**monacanthid** \"\ *also* **monacanthine** \"\ *n* -s **:** a monacanthid fish

**mon·a·can·thi·dae** \,==ˈkan(t)thə,dē\ *n pl, cap* [NL, fr. *Monacanthus*, type genus (fr. *mon-* + *-acanthus*) + *-idae*] **:** a family of bony fishes (order Plectognathi) including the filefishes

**monacetin** *var of* MONOACETIN

**mon·a·cha** \ˈmänəkə\ [NL, fr. LL, nun, fr. Gk *monachē*, fem. of *monachos*, adj., single — more at MONK] *syn of* MONASA

**mon·a·chal** *or* **mon·a·cal** \ˈmänəkəl\ *adj* [*monachal* fr. MF or LL; MF, fr. LL *monachalis*, fr. *monachus* monk + L *-alis* -al; *monacal* prob. fr. F, fr. MF *monachal* — more at MONK] **:** of, relating to, or having the characteristics of monks or monastic life **:** MONASTIC

**mon·a·chism** \-nə,kizəm\ *n* -s [prob. fr. MF *monachisme*, fr. ML *monachismus*, fr. LGk *monachismos*, fr. Gk *monachos* monk + Gk *-ismos* -ism — more at MONK] **:** MONASTICISM ⟨set itself . . . to reform European ~ —G.G.Coulton⟩

**mon·a·chist** \-kəst\ *adj* **:** MONKISH ⟨lived a life that was essentially ~ in tone —*Times Lit. Supp.*⟩

**monacid** *var of* MONOACID

**mona·co** \ˈmänə,kō, mə'nä(,)kō, 'mänē,-, mə'nä(- *sometimes* 'mōn- *or* mə'na(-\ *adj, usu cap* [fr. *Monaco*, principality in southern Europe] **:** of or from the principality of Monaco **:** of the kind or style prevalent in Monaco **:** MONACAN, MONEGASQUE

**mon·act** \mä'nakt\ *n* -s [*mon-* + *-act* (fr. Gk *aktis* ray) — more at ACTIN-] **:** a monactine sponge spicule

**¹mon·ac·tine** \mä'naktən, -k,tīn\ *also* **mon·ac·ti·nal** \-tənᵊl, ¦mä,nak¦tīnᵊl\ *adj* [*mon-* + *-actine* or *-actinal*] **:** having a single ray — used of a sponge spicule

**²monactine** \"\ *n* -s **:** MONACT

**¹mon·ac·ti·nel·lid** \mä¦naktə¦neləd\ *or* **mon·ac·ti·nel·li·dan** \-lədən\ *adj* [*monactinellid* fr. NL *Monactinellida*; *monactinellidan* fr. NL *Monactinellida* + E *-an*] **:** MONAXONID

**²monactinellid** \"\ *n* -s **:** MONAXONID

**mon·ac·ti·nel·li·da** \ˌ≠ˌ≠ˈneləda\ [NL, fr. *mon-* + *actin-* + *-ella* + *-ida*] *syn of* MONAXONIDA

**¹mo·nad** \ˈmō,nad *sometimes* ˈmä,-\ *n* -s [LL *monad-*, *monas* unit, monad, fr. Gk, fr. *monos* sole, lone, single + *-ad-*, *-as* -ad — more at MONK] **1 a :** a unit in Greek philosophy constituting the number one or an individual; *specif* **:** a metaphysical entity (as the One or an atom) **b :** a metaphysical entity in the philosophy of Giordano Bruno that differs from the Democritean atom in being spatially extended and psychically sensitive **c :** a spiritual being, substance, or soul in Leibnizian philosophy that is unextended, indivisible, unchanging, indestructible, and impenetrable and a center of force from which property all the physical properties of matter are derived — see MONADISM **d :** a similar hypothetical indivisible unit possessing both physical and mental characteristics of various kinds **2 :** a minute simple organism or organic unit: as **a :** ZOOSPORE **b :** a flagellate protozoan; *esp* **:** a member of *Monas* or a related genus **3 :** a univalent element, atom, or radical

**²monad** \"\ *adj* **:** of the nature of a monad

**mo·nad·al** \(ˈ)mō¦nadᵊl, (ˈ)mä¦-\ *adj* [¹*monad* + *-al*] **:** MONADIC 1b

**monadelph** *var of* MONODELPH

**mon·a·del·phous** \¦mänə¦delfəs\ *adj* [*mon-* + *-adelphous*] *of stamens* **:** united by the filaments into one group usu. forming a tube around the gynoecium — compare DIADELPHOUS, POLYADELPHOUS

**monades** *pl of* MONAS

**monadi-** *comb form* [¹*monad*] **:** monad ⟨*monadi*form⟩ ⟨*monadi*gerous⟩

**mo·nad·ic** \(ˈ)mō¦nadik, (ˈ)mä¦-\ *adj* [Gk *monadikos*, fr. *monad-*, *monas* monad + *-ikos* -ic] **1 a :** consisting of monads **b :** of, relating to, or like monads **:** ATOMISTIC, INDIVIDUAL, UNITARY **c :** of or relating to monadism **2 :** having only a single argument — used of a predicate or propositional function ⟨*x* is red is ~, while *x* loves *y* is not⟩

**mo·nad·i·cal** \-dəkəl\ *adj* [Gk *monadikos* monadic + E *-al*] *archaic* **:** MONADIC 1b

**mo·nad·i·dae** \mə'nadə,dē\ *n pl, cap* [NL, fr. *Monad-*, *Monas*, type genus + *-idae*] **:** a family of free-living flagellates (order Protomonadina) that may be active or attached and that often form colonies

**mon·a·di·na** \,mänə'dīnə\ *n pl, cap* [NL, fr. LL *monad-*, *monas* unit, monad + NL *-ina* — more at MONAD] *in some esp former classifications* **:** a group nearly equivalent to Mastigophora

**mo·nad·ism** \ˈmō,na,dizəm, ˈmä,n-, -,nə,d-\ *n* -s [prob. fr. F *monadisme*, fr. *monade* monad + *-isme* -ism] **:** a theory based upon a conception of monads; *specif* **:** the Leibnizian theory that the universe is composed of a hierarchy of monads each of which is a microcosm reflecting the world with differing degrees of clarity from its particular point of view without external stimulation in a system of harmony preestablished by God

**mo·nad·is·tic** \¦≠ˌ≠¦distik, -ˌnə¦-\ *adj* [¹*monad* + *-istic*] **:** of or relating to monadism ⟨~ idealism⟩

**mo·nad·nock** \mə'nad,näk\ *n* -s [fr. Mt. *Monadnock*, N.H.] **:** a hill or mountain of resistant rock surmounting a peneplain

**mo·nad·o·log·i·cal** \¦mō,nadə¦läjəkəl, ¦mä,-, -,nəd-\ *adj* [*monadology* + *-ical*; trans. of G *monadologisch*] **:** of, relating to, or based on monadology **:** MONADIC 1b ⟨culminated in the ~ pluralism —W.A.Kaufmann⟩

**mo·nad·ol·o·gy** \,mō,nə'däləjē, ,mä,-, -,nə'-\ *n* -ES [F *monadologie*, fr. *monade* monad (fr. LL *monad-*, *monas*) + *-o-* + *-logie* -logy] **:** a philosophical theory about monads; *specif* **:** Leibnizian monadism

**mon·a·ghan** \ˈmänəgən, -nəhən, -nəkən\ *adj, usu cap* [fr. *Monaghan*, county in Ireland] **:** of or from County Monaghan, Ireland **:** of the kind or style prevalent in County Monaghan

**mon·a·ker** *var of* MONIKER

**mo·nal** *also* **mo·naul** *or* **moo·nal** *or* **moo·naul** *or* **mi·naul** \mə'nȯl, -näl\ *n* -s [Nepali *munāl*, *monāl*] **:** any of various large pheasants of India; *esp* **:** any of several large showy pheasants of the genus *Lophophorus* found at high altitudes in northern India — see IMPEYAN PHEASANT

**monamide** *var of* MONOAMIDE

**monamine** *var of* MONOAMINE

**mon·an·day** \ˈmənən,de\ *usu cap, Scot var of* MONDAY

**mo·nan·der** \mə'nandə(r)\ *n* -s [*mon-* + *-ander*] **:** a monandrous plant

**mo·nan·dria** \-drēə\ *n pl, cap* [NL, fr. *mon-* + *-andria*] *in former classifications* **:** a class of flowering plants comprising those with flowers that have a single stamen

**mo·nan·dri·an** \-ēən\ *adj* [NL *Monandria* + E *-an*] **:** of or relating to the Monandria

**mo·nan·drous** \-rəs\ *adj* **1** [*mon-* + *-androus*] **a** *of a plant* **:** having flowers with a single stamen ⟨many orchids are ~⟩ **b** *of a flower* **:** having a single stamen **2** [Gk *monandros*, fr. *mon-* + *-andros* having (such or so many) men — more at -ANDROUS] **:** of, relating to, or characterized by monandry ⟨a ~ family system⟩

**mo·nan·dry** \-rē\ *n* -ES [*monandrous* + *-y*] **1 :** a marriage form or custom in which a woman has only one husband at a time — compare POLYANDRY **2 :** a monandrous condition of a plant or flower

**mo·nan·tha vetch** \mə'nan(t)thə-\ *n* [NL *monantha* (specific epithet of *Vicia monantha*), fr. *mon-* + *-antha* (fem. of *-anthus* -anthous)] **:** a weak-stemmed viny vetch (*Vicia articulata*) of southern Europe used for forage and hay in parts of the U.S. having mild winters

**mon·ap·sal** \(ˈ)mä¦napsəl, (ˈ)mō¦-\ *adj* [mon- + *-apsal* (as in *triapsal*)] **:** having only one apse ⟨a ~ church⟩

**¹mon·arch** \ˈmänə(r)k, -ä,närk, -,näk\ *n* -s [LL *monarcha*, fr. Gk *monarchēs*, *monarchos*, fr. *mon-* + *-archēs*, *-archos* -arch (n. comb. form)] **1 :** a person who reigns over a major territorial unit (as a kingdom or empire) usu. for life and by hereditary succession: as **a :** one invested with sovereign power and exercising direct and effective control over the functions of government ⟨an absolute ~⟩ **b :** one acting primarily as chief of state and carrying out political functions limited in nature and extent (as by custom or a written constitution) ⟨a constitutional ~⟩ — compare CZAR, EMPEROR, KAISER, KING, QUEEN **2 :** one held to resemble a monarch in sovereign power or preeminent position ⟨the live oak is the ~ of the Texas low forests —*Amer. Guide Series: Texas*⟩ ⟨of as much interest to them as the business of any money ~ is to him —H.R.Penniman⟩ ⟨cotton, ~ of the textile world —*Wall Street Jour.*⟩ **3** *also* **monarch butterfly :** a large American butterfly (*Danaus plexippus*) having orange-brown wings with black veins and borders and characterized by larvae that feed on milkweed and by an annual two-way migration — compare VICEROY 2

**²monarch** \"\ *vi* -ED/-ING/-S **:** to play the monarch — often used with *it* ⟨~s it in his own closet —*Common Sense*⟩

**³monarch** \"\ *adj* [*mon-* + *-arch* (adj. comb. form)] **:** having only one xylem strand or group — used esp. of roots

**mo·nar·chal** \mə'närkəl, -näk-\ *adj* [¹*monarch* + *-al*] **1** *archaic* **:** MONARCHICAL 2 ⟨~ government⟩ **2** *archaic* **:** having the status or exercising the functions of a monarch **3 :** of, having the characteristics of, or befitting a monarch ⟨the golden age of ~ splendor —Joseph Wechsberg⟩ ⟨an impression of trees, very dark and ~ —H.E.Bates⟩

**mon·arch·ess** \ˈmänə(r)kəs, -ä,närk-\ *n* -ES [¹*monarch* + *-ess*] **:** a female monarch

**mo·nar·chi·al** \mə'närkēəl, -nák-\ *adj* [*monarchy* + *-al*] **:** MONARCHICAL ⟨the ~ institution⟩ ⟨man's subjection to a ~ God—N.A.Ford⟩ ⟨a country that was ~ in tradition —Beverley Baxter⟩

**¹mo·nar·chi·an** \-ēən\ *n* -s *usu cap* [LL *monarchianus*, fr. *monarchia* monarchy, individual rule + L *-anus* -an — more at MONARCHY] **:** an adherent of Monarchianism

**²monarchian** \"\ *adj, usu cap* **:** of or relating to Monarchianism

**mo·nar·chi·an·ism** \-ēə,nizəm\ *n* -s *usu cap* **:** an anti-Trinitarian doctrine or theory current in the Christian church of the 2d and 3d centuries A.D. in several forms and having as a common principle a belief that God is a single person as well as a single being — see DYNAMIC MONARCHIANISM, MODALISTIC MONARCHIANISM; compare PATRIPASSIANISM

**mo·nar·chi·cal** \-kəkəl, -kēk-\ *or* **mo·nar·chic** \-(r)kik, -kēk\ *adj* [MF *monarchique*, fr. Gk *monarchikos*, fr. *monarchos* monarch + *-ikos* -ical, -ic — more at MONARCH] **1 :** MONARCHAL 3 ⟨reconciled to ~ rule —C.G.Bowers⟩ ⟨~ gestures⟩ **2 :** of, possessing, or having the form of a monarchy ⟨~ systems⟩ ⟨a ~ government⟩ **3 :** having the power and functions of a monarch and esp. of one having absolute power ⟨from being primus inter pares he came to be a ~ bishop —C.T. Craig⟩ **4 :** of, relating to, or favoring monarchism ⟨win him over to the ~ side —*Times Lit. Supp.*⟩ ⟨~ candidates⟩

**mo·nar·chi·cal·ly** \-(r)kək(ə)lē, -kēk-, -li\ *adv* **:** in a monarchical form or manner ⟨nor are those provinces . . . aristocratically governed but ~ —Thomas Hobbes⟩

**mon·ar·chism** \ˈmänə(r),kizəm\ *n* -s [F *monarchisme*, fr. *monarchie* monarchy + *-isme* -ism] **1 :** the principles of monarchical government **2 :** belief in or advocacy of the principles of monarchical government

**¹mon·ar·chist** \-kəst\ *n* -s [*monarchy* + *-ist*] **:** one that advocates or believes in monarchy as a form of government

**²monarchist** \"\ *adj* **:** of, relating to, or favoring monarchism

**mon·arch·ize** \-(r),kīz\ *vb* -ED/-ING/-S [¹*monarch* + *-ize*] *vi, archaic* **:** to act or rule as a monarch ⟨vice . . . in every land doth ~ —Thomas Dekker⟩ ~ *vt* **1** *obs* **:** to rule over as a monarch **2** *archaic* **:** to make a monarchy of ⟨efforts to ~ a government⟩

**mo·nar·cho·mach** \mə'närkə,mak\ *n* -s [NL *monarchomachus*, fr. *monarcho-* (fr. LL *monarcha* monarch) + L *-machus* one who fights (fr. Gk *-machos*); akin to Gk *machesthai* to fight — more at MONARCH] **:** one of a group of 16th century political theorists advocating resistance or rebellion against a monarch guilty of acts held to be unlawful

**mo·nar·cho·mach·ic** \¦≠¦≠≠'makik\ *adj* **:** of, relating to, or favoring the doctrines of the monarchomachs ⟨the right of revolution implicitly set forth in . . . ~ pronouncements —H.E.Barnes & H.P.Becker⟩

**mon·ar·chy** \ˈmänə(r)kē, -ki *sometimes* -ä,närk- *or* -,näk-\ *n* -ES [ME *monarchie*, fr. MF, fr. LL *monarchia*, fr. Gk, fr. *monarchēs*, *monarchos* monarch + *-ia* -y — more at MONARCH] **1 :** undivided rule or absolute sovereignty by a single person ⟨if one man be the sole landlord of a territory . . . his empire is absolute ~ —James Harrington⟩ **2 a :** a territorial unit (as a nation or state) having a monarch as chief of state ⟨Morocco is a sovereign independent ~ —*Statesman's Yr. Bk.*⟩ **b :** such a territorial unit having a monarchical government without a monarch as chief of state ⟨officially Spain has been a ~ without a king —*Springfield (Mass.) Union*⟩ **3 a :** a form of government having a single usu. hereditary chief of state with life tenure who may exercise governmental powers varying from nominal to absolute ⟨the constitution of Libya provided for a hereditary ~ —*Statesman's Yr. Bk.*⟩ — compare ¹ABSOLUTE 3, ¹CONSTITUTIONAL 4, LIMITED 2, MIXED 1b **b :** a specific government or governmental institution headed by a monarch ⟨the Russian ~ was never so popular —Malcolm Muggeridge⟩

**mo·nar·da** \mə'närdə\ *n* [NL, after N. *Monardes* †1588 Span. physician and botanist] **1** *cap* **:** a genus of coarse No. American mints having a tubular many-nerved calyx and whorls of variously colored flowers — see HORSEMINT 2, OSWEGO TEA, WILD BERGAMOT **2** -s **:** any plant of the genus *Monarda*

**mo·nar·del·la** \,mänə(r)'delə\ *n, cap* [NL, fr. N. *Monardes* + NL *-ella*] **:** a genus of fragrant herbs (family Labiatae) of the western U.S. having flowers in terminal heads and a 10- to 13-nerved calyx — see MUSTANG MINT

**mon·articular** \¦män, ¦mōn+\ *adj* [*mon-* + *articular*] **:** affecting one body joint only ⟨tuberculous arthritis is usually ~ —*Jour. Amer. Med. Assoc.*⟩

**mo·nas** \ˈmō,nas, ˈmä,-\ *n* [LL & Gk; LL, fr. Gk — more at MONAD] **1** *pl* **mon·a·des** \ˈmänə,dēz\ **:** MONAD **2** *cap* [NL, fr. LL, unit, monad] **:** a genus of small aquatic flagellates that is the type of the family Monadidae

**-mo·nas** \mənəs\ *n comb form* [NL, fr. LL *monas*] **:** unit **:** simple organism of a (specified) kind — in generic names ⟨Chlamydo*monas*⟩ ⟨Cellulo*monas*⟩ ⟨Lepto*monas*⟩

**mon·a·sa** \ˈmänəsə\ *n, cap* [NL] **:** a genus of So. American puffbirds — see NUN BIRD

**¹mon·as·cid·i·an** \¦mänə¦sidēən\ *adj* [NL *Monascidiae* suborder of tunicates (fr. *Mon-* + *Ascidiae*) + E *-an*] **:** of or relating to the simple ascidians

**²monascidian** \"\ *n* -s **:** a simple ascidian

**mon·ase** \ˈmänəs\ *n* -s [NL *Monasa*] **:** NUN BIRD

**mon·aster** \(ˈ)män, (ˈ)mōn+\ *n* [NL, fr. *mon-* + *-aster*] **:** a single aster formed in an aberrant type of mitosis

**mon·as·te·ri·al** \¦mänə¦stirēəl\ *adj* [ME, fr. LL *monasterialis*, fr. *monasterium* monastery + L *-alis* -al] **:** of, relating to, or having the characteristics of a monastery or monastic life

**mon·as·tery** \ˈmänə,sterē, -ri\ *n* -ES [ME *monasterie*, fr. LL *monasterium*, fr. LGk *monastērion*, fr. Gk, hermit's cell, fr. *monazein* to live alone, fr. *monos* lone, sole, single — more at MONK] **:** a house of religious retirement or of seclusion from the world for persons under religious vows **:** CONVENT 3

**¹mo·nas·tic** \mə'nastik, mō'-, -naas-, -tēk\ *adj* [F & LL; F *monastique*, fr. MF, fr. LL *monasticus*, fr. LGk *monastikos*, fr. (assumed) Gk *monastos* (verbal of *monazein* to live alone) + *-ikos* -ic] **1 a :** of, relating to, or connected with a monastery ⟨bishop of a ~ cathedral —F.M.Stenton⟩ ⟨great ~ establishments —G.E.Fussell⟩ ⟨wholesale pillage of ~ assets —M.W.Baldwin⟩ **b :** of, relating to, or having the characteristics of occupants of monasteries ⟨a ~ congregation⟩ ⟨~ vows⟩ **2 :** having or held to have characteristics of life in a monastery ⟨the colleges . . . were still ~ in regimen and spirit —George Willison⟩; *specif* **:** secluded from temporal concerns and devoted to religion ⟨devout Christians . . . not fully embracing the ~ life —Norman Goodall⟩

**²monastic** \"\ *n* -s **:** a member of a monastic order; *specif* **:** MONK

**mo·nas·ti·cal** \-təkəl, -tēk-\ *adj* [ME, fr. LL *monasticus* monastic + ME *-al*] *archaic* **:** MONASTIC ⟨one of the first founders of the ~ orders —William Aglionby⟩

**mo·nas·ti·cal·ly** \-tək(ə)lē, -tēk-, -li\ *adv* **:** in a monastic style or manner ⟨the chairs and table were ~ plain —T.B. Costain⟩

**mo·nas·ti·cism** \-tə,sizəm\ *n* -s **:** the monastic life, system, or condition; *specif* **:** organized asceticism as practiced in a monastery

**mon·atomic** \¦män, ¦mōn+\ *adj* [*mon-* + *atomic*] **1 a :** consisting of one atom **:** having one atom in the molecule **:** ATOMIC 5 ⟨helium is a ~ gas⟩ ⟨~ metals⟩ **b :** having a thickness equal to the diameter of a constituent atom ⟨a ~ layer of cesium⟩ **2 :** UNIVALENT **3 :** having one replaceable atom or radical ⟨~ alcohols⟩

**monaul** *var of* MONAL

**mon·au·lic** \(ˈ)mä¦nȯlik\ *adj* [*mon-* + Gk *aulos* pipe, tube, reed instrument like an oboe + E *-ic* — more at ALVEOLUS] **:** having a single common genital opening — used of an hermaphroditic animal

**mon·aural** \(ˈ)män, (ˈ)mōn+\ *adj* [*mon-* + *aural*] **1 :** of, relating to, affecting, or designed for use with one ear ⟨~ deafness⟩ **2 :** MONOPHONIC 3 — **mon·aurally** \"+\ *adv*

**mon·axial** \(ˈ)män, (ˈ)mōn+\ *adj* [*mon-* + *axial*] **:** having or based on a single axis **:** UNIAXIAL ⟨~ symmetry⟩ — compare PLURIAXIAL

**¹mon·ax·on** \(ˈ)mä¦nak,sän, (ˈ)mō¦-\ *adj* [*mon-* + Gk *axōn* axis — more at AXIS] **1 :** developed by growth along a single axis — used esp. of a sponge spicule **2 :** having monaxon spicules — used of a sponge

**²monaxon** \"\ *n* -s **:** something distinguished by a single axis or axial process (as a nerve cell); *specif* **:** a monaxon sponge spicule

**mon·ax·o·nia** \,mä,nak'sōnēə\ [NL, fr. *mon-* + Gk *axōn* axis + NL *-ia*] *syn of* MONAXONIDA

**mon·ax·on·ic** \¦mä,nak¦sänik, ¦mō,-\ *adj* [*mon-* + Gk *axōn* axis + E *-ic*] **:** having but one axis

**¹mon·ax·on·id** \¦mä,nak¦sänəd\ *adj* [NL *Monaxonida*] **:** of or relating to the Monaxonida

**²monaxonid** \"\ *n* -s **:** a monaxonid sponge

**mon·ax·on·i·da** \ˌ≠ˌ≠'sänədə\ *n pl, cap* [NL, fr. *mon-* + Gk *axōn* axis + NL *-ida*] *in some classifications* **:** a subclass or order of Demospongiae that comprises sponges with siliceous monaxonic megascleres and with or without spongin

**mon·a·zite** \ˈmänə,zīt\ *n* -s [G *monazit*, fr. Gk *monazein* to be alone, live alone + G *-it* -ite; fr. its rarity — more at MONASTERY] **:** a mineral $(Ce,La,Md,Pr,Th)PO_4$ consisting of a yellow, red, or brown phosphate of the cerium metals and thorium and occurring often in sand and gravel deposits (as in the Carolinas and Brazil)

**mond** *var of* MOUND

**¹mon·daine** \mōn'dān\ *n* -s [F, fr. fem. of *mondain*, adj.] **:** a woman belonging to fashionable society **:** woman of the world **:** SOPHISTICATE ⟨all the barbershop roués and millinery-parlor ~s —Sinclair Lewis⟩

**²mondaine** *or* **mon·dain** \"\ *adj* [F *mondaine*, fem., & *mondain*, masc., fr. L *mundanus* of the world — more at MUNDANE] **:** WORLDLY, SOPHISTICATED, FASHIONABLE ⟨a comedy, very corrupt and ~, with a continental background —Margaret Kennedy⟩ ⟨the perfectly coiffed, ~ woman —May Sarton⟩

**mon·day** \ˈməndē, -di *also* -n(,)dā\ *n* -s *usu cap* [ME, fr. OE *mōnandæg*, *mōndæg*; akin to OFris *monendei* Monday, MD *maendach*, *manendach*, MLG *māndach*, *mānendach*, OHG *mānatag*; all fr. a prehistoric WGmc compound formed from components represented by OE *mōna* moon and *dæg* day; trans. of L *dies Lunae*, trans. of Gk *hēmera Selēnēs* — more at MOON, DAY] **:** the second day of the week **:** the day following Sunday

**monday disease** *or* **monday-morning disease** *n, usu cap Monday* **:** azoturia of horses

**monday fever** *n, usu cap M* **:** BYSSINOSIS

**mon·day·ish** \ˈməndēish, -di-ish *also* -n,dāish\ *adj, usu cap* **:** characteristic of Monday; *specif* **:** fagged out after Sunday — **mon·day·ish·ness** *n* -ES *usu cap*

**monday morning quarterback** *also* **monday quarterback** *n, usu cap Monday* [so called fr. the fact that most American football games are played on weekends] **:** a person who using hindsight criticizes what others have done ⟨easy to be a *Monday morning quarterback* . . . and to be omniscient after the event, to expect superhuman deeds from human beings —H.W.Baldwin⟩

**mon·days** \ˈməndēz, -diz *also* -n,dāz\ *adv, usu cap* **:** on Monday repeatedly **:** on any Monday

**mond gas** \ˈmänd-, ˈmōnt-\ *n, usu cap M* [after Ludwig *Mond* †1909 Ger. chemist] **:** a producer gas made by using a large proportion of steam to air at a relatively low temperature so that large amounts of ammonia can be recovered as a by-product

**mon·di·al** \ˈmändēəl\ *adj* [F, fr. LL *mundialis*, fr. L *mundus* world + *-ialis* -ial — more at MUNDANE] **:** of or involving a large part of the world **:** WORLD ⟨in this day, so distraught with ~ events and characters —J.T.Adams⟩

**mon·do** \män'dō\ *n* -s [Jap *mondō*] **:** a rapid question and answer technique employed in Zen Buddhism by a master seeking to lead a pupil into transcending the limitations of conceptual thought

**m-1** \ˈem'wən\ *or* **m-1 rifle** *n, pl* **m-1's** *or* **m-1 rifles** *usu cap M* **:** a gas-operated semiautomatic .30 caliber rifle fed from a magazine containing a clip of eight rounds, mechanically capable of firing 16 to 32 rounds a minute, having an effective range of 500 yards, and weighing 9½ pounds — called also *Garand rifle*

**monecious** *var of* MONOECIOUS

**¹mon·e·gasque** \¦mänə¦gask\ *adj, usu cap* [F *monégasque*, adj. & n., fr. Prov *mounegasc*, fr. *Mounegue* Monaco] **:** of or relating to the principality of Monaco **:** MONACAN

**²monegasque** \"\ *n* -s *cap* [F *Monégasque*] **:** a native or inhabitant of Monaco

**Monel Metal** \mō,nel-\ *trademark* — used for an alloy of approximately 67 percent nickel, 28 percent copper, and 5 percent other elements that is made by direct reduction from ore in which the constituent metals occur in these proportions

**mon·embryonic** \(ˈ)män+\ *also* **mono·embryonic** \¦mänō+\ *adj* **:** characterized by monembryony

**mon·em·bry·o·ny** \mə'nembrēənē, ,mänem'brīə-\ *also* **mono·em·bry·ony** \,mänō'embrēənē, ,mänōem'brīə-\ *n* [*mon-* + *embryony*] **1 :** the condition of having but a single embryo **2 :** production of a single embryo from a single egg

**mon·ep·ic** \(ˈ)mä¦nepik, (ˈ)mō¦-\ *adj* [*mon-* + Gk *epos* word + E *-ic* — more at VOICE] **:** consisting of one word or of sentences of one word

**mon·episcopacy** \,män+\ *n* [*mon-* + *episcopacy*] **:** church government by monarchical bishops **:** monarchical episcopacy — **mon·episcopal** \¦män+\ *adj*

**mon·e·pis·co·pus** \,mänə'piskəpəs\ *n* -ES [NL, fr. *mon-* + LL *episkopus* bishop — more at BISHOP] **:** a monarchical bishop

**monera** *pl of* MONERON

**²mo·ne·ra** \mə'nirə\ *n pl, cap* [NL, fr. pl. of *moneron*] *in some classifications* **a :** a taxon of variable rank comprising the monera **b :** a kingdom or other major division of living beings comprising those (as bacteria and blue-green algae) that lack organized condensed nuclei

**mo·ne·ral** \mə'nirəl\ *or* **mo·ne·ric** \-rik, -ner-\ *adj* [NL *moneron* & ²*Monera* + E *-al* or *-ic*] **:** of, or relating to the monera

**¹mo·ne·ran** \-irən\ *adj* [NL ²*Monera* + E *-an*] **:** of or relating to the Monera

**²moneran** \"\ *or* **mo·ner** \ˈmōnə(r)\ *n* -s **:** a moneran organism

**monergic** *var of* MONOERGIC

**mon·er·gism** \ˈmänə(r),jizəm\ *n* -s [*mon-* + *erg-* + *-ism*] **:** the theological doctrine that regeneration is exclusively the work of the Holy Spirit — compare SYNERGISM

**mon·er·gist** \-jəst\ *n* -s [*mon-* + *erg-* + *-ist*] **:** one who accepts or supports the doctrine of monergism

**mon·er·gis·tic** \¦≠≠¦jistik\ *adj* **:** of or relating to monergism

**mo·ne·ron** \mə'ni,rän\ *n, pl* **mone·ra** \-irə\ [NL, modif. of Gk *monērēs* solitary, singular, fr. *monos* single, alone — more at MONK] **:** a postulated primitive ancestral mass of protoplasm lacking a nucleus

**mo·ne·ro·zoa** \mə,nirə'zōə\ [NL, fr. *moneron* + *-zoa*] *syn of* MONERA

**mo·ne·sia** \mə'nēzhə\ *n* -s [AmerSp] **:** an astringent vegetable extract derived from the bark of a So. American tree (*Pradosia lactescens*) of the family Sapotaceae

**mon·estrous** *also* **mon·oestrous** \(ˈ)män+\ *adj* [*mon-* + *estrous*, *oestrous*] **:** experiencing estrus once each year **:** having a single annual breeding period ⟨most wild carnivorous mammals are ~⟩

**mon·e·tar·i·ly** \¦mänə¦terəlē, -li *sometimes* ¦mən-\ *adv* **:** with respect to money **:** from a monetary standpoint ⟨was incorruptible, both ethically and ~ —R.H.Ferrell⟩

**mon·e·tary** \ˈ≠≠,terē, -ri\ *adj* [LL *monetarius* of a mint, of money, fr. L *moneta* mint, coin, money, + *-arius* -ary — more at MINT] **:** of or relating to money or to the instrumentalities and organizations by which money is supplied to the economy **:** PECUNIARY ⟨~ stocks of gold and silver⟩ ⟨~ reserves⟩ ⟨a ~ system⟩ ⟨~ inflation⟩ ⟨the ~ authorities⟩

**monetary policy** *or* **monetary management** *n* **:** measures taken by the central bank and treasury to strengthen the economy and minimize cyclical fluctuations through the availability and cost of credit, budgetary and tax policies, and other financial factors and comprising credit control and fiscal policy

**monetary unit** *n* **1 :** the standard unit of value of a national currency (as dollar, pound, franc) — called also *currency unit* **2 :** any unit of monetary value ⟨bundles of twenty cotton threads were the *monetary unit* for inexpensive articles — Phares Sigler⟩

**mon·e·tite** \'mänə,tīt\ *n* -s [*Moneta* island, near Puerto Rico + E *-ite*] **:** a mineral $CaHPO_4$ consisting of an acid calcium hydrogen phosphate and occurring in yellowish white crystals

ʹ**mon·e·ti·za·tion** \,mänəd·ə'zāshən *sometimes* ,mən-\ *n* -s **:** the act or process of monetizing (as silver) ⟨~ of credit⟩

**mon·e·tize** \'mänə,tīz *sometimes* 'mən-\ *vt* -ED/-ING/-S [L *moneta* mint, coin, money + E *-ize* — more at MINT] **1 a :** to establish as the standard of a national currency ⟨demonetize gold and ~ silver⟩ **b :** to establish as legal tender **:** authorize for use as national currency with a fixed value in relation to the standard monetary unit **2 a :** to coin into money ⟨the Treasury merely ~*s* the gold that comes in —A.H.Hansen⟩ **b :** to create demand deposits in the banking system based upon assets or against debt instruments ⟨~ the national debt⟩

¹**mon·ey** \'mənē, -ni\ *n, pl* **moneys** *or* **monies** *often attrib* [ME *moneye*, fr. MF *moneie*, fr. L *moneta* mint, coin, money — more at MINT] **1 :** something generally accepted as a medium of exchange, a measure of value, or a means of payment ⟨have used gold, copper, wampum, or cattle for ~⟩: as **a :** officially coined or stamped metal currency **b :** MONEY OF ACCOUNT ⟨a coin worth less than a penny in our ~⟩ **c :** coinage or negotiable paper issued as legal tender by a recognized authority (as a government) ⟨took some ~ from her purse to pay him⟩ ⟨storekeepers who would accept foreign ~⟩ **2 a** (1) **:** assets or compensation in the form of or readily convertible to cash **:** monetary possessions ⟨can lose or make a lot of ~ in that business⟩ ⟨allowed to accept ~ for their services⟩ **:** pecuniary gain ⟨do the job for love or ~⟩ **:** PAY ⟨gets good ~ in that job⟩ (2) **:** property valued in terms of money ⟨died and left all his ~ to charity⟩ **b :** an amount of money ⟨raised the ~ for the new dormitory⟩ ⟨returned the ~ you lent him⟩ ⟨spent all the food ~ before payday⟩ **:** price paid ⟨got his ~'*s* worth⟩ **c :** capital dealt in as a commodity to be loaned or invested ⟨this year . . . mortgage ~ is much more plentiful⟩ ⟨the ~ supply in the country today⟩ ⟨~'*s* cheap these days, particularly on the security we'd be able to offer —John Morrison⟩ **d** *monies or moneys pl* **:** sums of money **:** FUNDS ⟨the collection of tax *monies*⟩ ⟨the servants brawled and stole the royal ~*s* —*Life*⟩ ⟨taking interest for ~*s* lent —G.G.Coulton⟩ **3 a :** a particular form or denomination of coin or paper money — usu. used in pl. ⟨copying the patterns of the ~*s* . . . current at the time of the Roman evacuation —John Craig⟩ **b :** a monetary value (as the silver dollar, pound sterling) taken as the basis of a system of monetary units **4 a :** the group receiving prize money in a contest; *specif* **:** the group finishing first, second, or third in a horse or dog race — used esp. in the phrase *in the money* or *out of the money* **b :** PRIZE MONEY — usu. used with *first, second,* or *third* ⟨his horse took third ~⟩ **5 :** persons or interests possessing or controlling great wealth regarded as a group or class **:** moneyed people ⟨there's a lot of ~ in that town⟩ ⟨politicians at the beck and call of ~⟩ — **for money** *adv* **:** for cash — used on the London stock exchange — **for one's money :** according to one's preference or opinion ⟨*for my money*, the play . . . is extraordinarily good fun —C.J. Rolo⟩ — **in the money** *adv (or adj)* **:** in an affluent state **:** with an ample supply of funds ⟨*in the money* and not worried about costs —Alva Johnston⟩ — **money for jam** *Brit* **:** something of advantage or profit gained with little or no investment or effort **:** EASY MONEY ⟨production grants . . . are *money for jam*, for they mostly benefit farmers who would in any event do the jobs —Clyde Higgs⟩

²**money** \"\ *vt* **moneyed; moneyed; moneying; moneys** **1 :** COIN **2 :** to convert into money by sale **3 :** to supply with money

**moneybags** \'==,=\ *n pl but sing or pl in constr* **1 :** WEALTH ⟨are fighting for the rich and their ~ —Bruce Marshall⟩ **2 :** a person having or believed to have considerable wealth ⟨that fleeting and uneasy dictatorship of the ~ —A.L.Guérard⟩

**money belt** *n* **:** a belt with pockets for carrying money that is usu. worn concealed

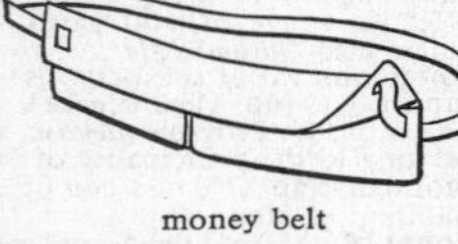

money belt

**money bill** *n* **:** a bill for raising revenue for general public purposes (as for imposing a tax on the people or transferring money or property from the people to the state) as distinguished from one providing a specific service for a fee or charge

**money broker** *n* **:** an intermediary who arranges short-term loans usu. in large amounts for borrowers and who in the U.S. also arranges the sale of excess bank reserve balances to banks short of reserves

**money changer** \'==,==\ *n* [ME *moneye chaunger*] **1 :** one whose occupation is the exchanging of kinds or denominations of currency **2 :** a device for holding and dispensing sorted change

money changer 2

**money changing** *n* **:** the act or occupation of exchanging kinds or denominations of currency

**money chest** *n* **:** a metal container for valuables (as cash, gems) designed to resist burglary

**money cowrie** *n* **:** a cowrie used as money; *specif* **:** a yellow-shelled or white-shelled cowrie (*Cypraea moneta*) of the western Pacific and Indian oceans — see COWRIE illustration

**money crop** *n* **:** CASH CROP

**money economy** *n* **:** a system or stage of economic life in which money replaces barter in the exchange of goods

**mon·eyed** *also* **mon·ied** \'mənēd, -nid\ *adj* [ME *moneyed*, fr. *moneye* + *-ed*] **1 :** supplied with money **:** having money **:** WEALTHY ⟨the ~ tourist from abroad⟩ **2 :** consisting in or composed of money **:** derived from or due to money ⟨the ~ power of the landed gentry —J.W.Beach⟩

**moneyed capital** *n* **:** capital that consists in money or represents money that is used or invested and reinvested from time to time for the sake of making a profit on it as money (as by a bank or investment company)

**moneyed corporation** *n* **:** a corporation authorized to engage in the investment of moneyed capital

**mon·ey·er** \'mənēə(r)\ *n* -s [ME *moneyer, moneyour*, fr. OF *monier*, fr. LL *monetarius* master of a mint, coiner, fr. L *moneta* mint, coin, money + *-arius* -ary — more at MINT] **:** an authorized coiner of money **:** MINTER; *specif* **:** a craftsman formerly employed in England to cut and size blanks and strike coins

**money grass** *n* **:** RATTLE 3a

**moneygrubber** \'==,==\ *n* **:** a person bent on accumulating money

**money illusion** *n* **:** the illusion that the face value of money is representative of its purchasing power **:** preoccupation (as of a wage earner) with wages rather than with real income or prices

**moneylender** \'==,==\ *n* **:** one whose business is lending money; *specif* **:** PAWNBROKER

**moneylending** \'==,==\ *n* **:** the act or occupation of lending money at interest

**mon·ey·less** \'mənēləs\ *adj* **:** having no money ⟨virtually ~ rural regions —*Atlantic*⟩

**money-maker** \'==,==\ *n* [ME *moneyemaker*, fr. *moneye* + *maker*] **1** *obs* **:** one who coins or prints money **:** MINTER; *also* **:** a counterfeiter of money **2 :** one who accumulates money or

MONEY

| NAME | SYMBOL | SUBDIVISIONS | COUNTRY | PAR VALUE |
|---|---|---|---|---|
| afghani | Af | 100 puls | Afghanistan[1] | initial par value established with IMF March 22, 1963=0.0197482 gram fine gold |
| baht *or* tical | Bht *or* B *or* Tc | 100 satang | Thailand[1] | initial par value established with IMF Oct. 20, 1963=0.0427245 gram fine gold |
| balboa | B/ | 100 centesimos | Panama[1] | = U.S. dollar |
| bolivar | B | 100 centimos | Venezuela[1] | as of April 18, 1947=0.265275 gram fine gold |
| cedi | ¢ | 100 pesewas | Ghana[1] | as of July 7, 1967=0.870897 gram fine gold |
| colon | ¢ *or* C | 100 centimos | Costa Rica[1] | as of Sept. 3, 1961=0.134139 gram fine gold |
| colon | ¢ *or* C | 100 centavos | El Salvador[1] | as of Dec. 18, 1946=0.355468 gram fine gold |
| cordoba | C$ | 100 centavos | Nicaragua[1] | as of July 1, 1955=0.126953 |
| cruzeiro | Cr$ | 100 centavos | Brazil[1] | established 1942 in place of the milreis; as agreed with IMF July 14, 1948=0.048036 gram fine gold; "new cruzeiro" with ratio to cruzeiro of 1 to 1000 established Feb. 13, 1967 |
| deutsche mark | DM | 100 pfennigs | West Germany[1] | established 1948 in place of the reichsmark; as of Oct. 24, 1969=0.242806 gram fine gold |
| dinar | DA | 100 centimes | Algeria[1] | no par value agreed with IMF |
| dinar | D | 1000 fils | Bahrain | |
| dinar | ID | 5 riyals<br>20 dirhams<br>1000 fils | Iraq[1] | according to law of April 19, 1931=pound sterling |
| dinar | JD | 1000 fils | Jordan[1] | =pound sterling |
| dinar | KD | 1000 fils | Kuwait[1] | =pound sterling |
| dinar | £sy | 1000 fils | Southern Yemen[1] | no par value established with IMF |
| dinar | D | 1000 millimes | Tunisia[1] | initial par value established with IMF Sept. 28, 1964=1.69271 grams fine gold |
| dinar | Din | 100 paras | Yugoslavia[1] | as of Jan. 1, 1966=0.0710937 gram fine gold |
| dirham | Dh | 100 francs | Morocco[1] | initial par value established with IMF Oct. 16, 1959=0.175610 gram fine gold |
| dollar | $ | 100 cents | United States[1] | according to law of 1934=15.238 grains or 0.888671 gram fine gold |
| dollar | $ | 100 cents | Australia[1] | established Feb. 14, 1966, in place of the pound; par value agreed with IMF Feb. 11, 1966=0.995310 gram fine gold |
| dollar | $ | 100 cents | Bahamas | =1s 2d sterling |
| dollar | $ | 100 cents | Barbados | =4s 2d sterling |
| dollar | $ | 100 cents | Bermuda | =pound sterling |
| dollar | $ | 100 cents | Canada[1] | as first established with IMF Dec. 18, 1946=0.888671 gram fine gold; on May 2, 1962, par value set at 0.822021 gram fine gold |
| dollar | Eth$ *or* E$ | 100 cents | Ethiopia[1] | as of Dec. 13, 1963=0.355468 gram fine gold |
| dollar | G$ | 100 cents | Guyana[1] | as of Nov. 20, 1967=0.444335 gram fine gold |
| dollar | HK$ | 100 cents | Hong Kong | =1s 4½d sterling |
| dollar | $ | 100 cents | Jamaica[1] | as of Sept. 8, 1969=1.06641 grams fine gold |
| dollar | $ | 100 cents | Liberia[1] | =U.S. dollar |
| dollar | M$ *or* Mal$ | 100 cents | Malaysia[1] | as of July 20, 1962=0.290299 gram fine gold |
| dollar | NZ$ | 100 cents | New Zealand[1] | as of Nov. 20, 1967=0.995310 gram fine gold |
| dollar | S$ | 100 cents | Singapore[1] | as of June 9, 1967=0.290299 gram fine gold |
| dollar | TT$ | 100 cents | Trinidad and Tobago[1] | as of Nov. 22, 1967=0.444335 gram fine gold |
| drachma | Dr | 100 lepta | Greece[1] | established March 29, 1961=0.0296224 gram fine gold |
| escudo | E *or* E° | 100 centesimos | Chile [1] | established Jan. 1, 1960 |
| escudo | $ *or* Esc | 100 centavos | Portugal[1] | as of June 1, 1962=0.0309103 gram fine gold |
| florin see GULDEN, below | | | | |
| forint | F *or* Ft | 100 fillers | Hungary | no par value agreed with IMF |
| franc | Fr *or* F | 100 centimes | France[1] | as of Aug. 10, 1969=0.160000 gram fine gold |
| franc | Fr *or* F | 100 centimes | Belgium[1] | first established with IMF Dec. 18, 1946=0.0202765 gram fine gold; as of Sept. 22, 1949=0.0177734 gram |
| franc | Fr *or* F | 100 centimes | Burundi[1] | initial par value established with IMF Jan. 26, 1965=0.0101562 gram fine gold |
| franc | Fr *or* F | 100 centimes | Cameroon[1] | no par value agreed with IMF |
| franc | Fr *or* F | 100 centimes | Central African Republic[1] | no par value agreed with IMF |
| franc | Fr *or* F | 100 centimes | Chad[1] | no par value agreed with IMF |
| franc | Fr *or* F | 100 centimes | Congo (Brazzaville)[1] | no par value agreed with IMF |
| franc | Fr *or* F | 100 centimes | Dahomey[1] | no par value agreed with IMF |
| franc | Fr *or* F | 100 centimes | Gabon[1] | no par value agreed with IMF |
| franc | Fr *or* F | 100 centimes | Guinea[1] | no par value agreed with IMF |
| franc | Fr *or* F | 100 centimes | Ivory Coast[1] | no par value agreed with IMF |
| franc | Fr *or* F | 100 centimes | Luxembourg[1] | =Belgian franc |
| franc | Fr *or* F | 100 centimes | Malagasy Republic[1] | no par value agreed with IMF |
| franc | Fr *or* F | 100 centimes | Mali[1] | no par value agreed with IMF |
| franc | Fr *or* F | 100 centimes | Mauritania[1] | no par value agreed with IMF |
| franc | Fr *or* F | 100 centimes | Niger[1] | no par value agreed with IMF |
| franc | Fr *or* F | 100 centimes | Rwanda[1] | initial par value established with IMF April 6, 1966=0.00888671 gram fine gold |
| franc | Fr *or* F | 100 centimes | Senegal[1] | no par value agreed with IMF |
| franc | Fr *or* F | 100 centimes *or* rappen | Switzerland | according to law of Dec. 17, 1952=0.20322 gram fine gold |
| franc | Fr *or* F | 100 centimes | Togo[1] | no par value agreed with IMF |
| franc | Fr *or* F | 100 centimes | Upper Volta[1] | no par value agreed with IMF |
| gourde | G̸ *or* G *or* Gde | 100 centimes | Haiti[1] | established Sept. 1915=⅕ U.S. dollar |
| guarani | G̸ *or* G | 100 centimos | Paraguay[1] | as of March 1, 1956=0.0148112 gram fine gold |
| gulden *or* guilder *or* florin | G *or* F *or* Fl | 100 cents | Netherlands[1] | as first established with IMF Dec. 18, 1946=0.334987 gram fine gold; as of March 7, 1961=0.245489 gram |
| kip | K | 100 at | Laos[1] | no par value agreed with IMF |
| koruna | Kč | 100 halers | Czechoslovakia[2] | as of June 1, 1953=0.123426 gram fine gold=1/1.80 ruble |
| krona | Kr | 100 aurar | Iceland[1] | as first established with IMF Dec. 18, 1946=0.136954 gram fine gold; as of Nov. 12, 1968=0.0100985 gram |
| krona | Kr | 100 öre | Sweden[1] | as first established with IMF Nov. 5, 1951=0.171783 gram fine gold |
| krone | Kr | 100 öre | Denmark[1] | as first established with IMF Dec. 18, 1946=0.185178 gram fine gold; as of Nov. 1, 1967=0.118469 gram |
| krone | Kr | 100 öre | Norway[1] | as first established with IMF Dec. 18, 1946=0.179067 gram fine gold; as of Sept. 18, 1949=0.124414 gram |

| NAME | SYMBOL | SUBDIVISIONS | COUNTRY | PAR VALUE |
|---|---|---|---|---|
| kwacha | K | 100 ngwee | Zambia[1] | as established with IMF Jan. 16, 1968=1.24414 grams fine gold |
| kyat | K | 100 pyas | Burma[1] | established July 1, 1952 in place of Indian rupee; initial par value agreed with IMF Aug. 7, 1953=0.186621 gram fine gold |
| lek | L | 100 qintars | Albania | established July 1947 |
| lempira | L | 100 centavos | Honduras[1] | established April 3, 1926=½ U.S. dollar; agreed to by IMF Dec. 18, 1946 |
| leone | Le | 100 cents | Sierra Leone[1] | as of Nov. 22, 1967=1.06641 grams |
| leu | L | 100 bani | Romania | from Jan. 27, 1952=0.079346 gram fine gold fixed at 1/.80 ruble; as of Feb. 1, 1954=0.148112 gram fine gold fixed at 1/.50 ruble |
| lev | Lv | 100 stotinki | Bulgaria | as of Jan. 1, 1962=1/.30 ruble |
| lira | L | 100 centesimi | Italy[1] | from March 30, 1960 = 0.00142187 gram fine gold |
| lira see POUND, below | | | | |
| markka | M or Mk | 100 pennia | Finland[1] | as of Dec. 5, 1962=0.27771 gram fine gold |
| pa'anga | T$ | 100 seniti | Tonga | =9s 4d sterling |
| peseta | Pta or P (pl. Pts) | 100 centimes | Equatorial Guinea[1] | no par value agreed with IMF |
| peseta | Pta or P (pl. Pts) | 100 centimos | Spain[1] | initial par value established with IMF July 17, 1959=0.0148112 gram fine gold; as of Nov. 20, 1967=0.0126953 gram |
| peso | $ | 100 centavos | Argentina[1] | initial par value established with IMF Jan. 9, 1957=0.0493706 gram fine gold |
| peso | $B | 100 centavos | Bolivia[1] | computations by IMF made at rate of 11.875 pesos per U.S. dollar |
| peso | $ | 100 centavos | Colombia[1] | as first established with IMF Dec. 18, 1946=0.507816 gram fine gold; as of Dec. 17, 1948=0.455733 gram |
| peso | $ | 100 centavos | Cuba[1] | as established by law of Nov. 7, 1914=0.888671 gram fine gold |
| peso | RD$ | 100 centavos | Dominican Republic[1] | as agreed with IMF April 23, 1948=0.888671 gram fine gold |
| peso | $ | 100 centavos | Mexico[1] | as first established with IMF Dec. 18, 1946=0.183042 gram fine gold; changed June 17, 1949=0.102737 gram fine gold; as of April 19, 1954=0.0710937 gram |
| peso | ₱ or P | 100 centavos | Philippines[1] | as agreed with IMF Nov. 8, 1965=0.227864 gram fine gold |
| peso | $ | 100 centesimos | Uruguay[1] | initial par value established with IMF Oct. 7, 1960=0.120091 gram fine gold |
| piaster | VN$ or Pr | 100 cents | So. Vietnam[1] | no par value agreed with IMF |
| pound | £ | 20 shillings 240 pence | United Kingdom[1] | as first established with IMF Dec. 18, 1946=3.58134 grams fine gold; as reestablished Sept. 18, 1949=2.48828 grams, and Nov. 18, 1967=2.13281 grams |
| pound | £ | 1000 mils | Cyprus[1] | =pound sterling |
| pound | £ | 20 shillings 240 pence | Gambia[1] | =pound sterling |
| pound | £ | 20 shillings 240 pence | Ireland[1] | =pound sterling |
| pound or lira | I£ | 100 agorot 1000 prutoth | Israel[1] | as first established with IMF March 13, 1957 = 0.493706 gram fine gold; as of Nov. 19, 1967=0.253906 gram |
| pound | £L | 100 piasters | Lebanon[1] | as first established with IMF July 16, 1947 = 0.405512 gram fine gold |
| pound | £ | 100 piasters 1000 milliemes | Libya[1] | as of Aug. 12, 1959=2.48828 grams fine gold |
| pound | £ | 20 shillings 240 pence | Malawi[1] | as of Nov. 20, 1967=2.13281 grams fine gold |
| pound | £ | 20 shillings 240 pence | Malta[1] | as agreed with IMF June 27, 1969=2.13281 grams fine gold |
| pound | £N | 20 shillings 240 pence | Nigeria[1] | = pound sterling |
| pound | £S or LSd | 10 rials 100 piasters 1000 milliemes | Sudan[1] | as of July 23, 1958 = 2.55187 grams fine gold |
| pound or lira | £S or LS | 100 piasters | Syria[1] | as of July 29, 1947 = 0.405512 gram fine gold |
| pound or lira | £T or LT or TL | 100 kurus or piasters | Turkey[1] | as of Aug. 20, 1960 = 0.0987412 gram fine gold |
| pound | £E | 100 piasters 1000 milliemes | United Arab Republic | as of Sept. 18, 1949=2.55187 grams fine gold |
| quetzal | Q | 100 centavos | Guatemala[1] | as established with IMF Dec. 18, 1946=0.888671 gram fine gold |
| rand | R | 100 cents | So. Africa[1] | as of Feb. 14, 1961 = 1.24414 grams fine gold |
| rand | R | 100 cents | Botswana[1] | =So. African rand |
| rand | R | 100 cents | Lesotho[1] | =So. African rand |
| rand | R | 100 cents | Swaziland[1] | =So. African rand |
| rial | R or Rl | 100 dinars | Iran[1] | first established with IMF Dec. 18, 1946 = 0.027555 gram fine gold; as of May 22, 1957 = 0.0117316 gram |
| riyal or rial | R | 20 qurshes 100 halala | Saudi Arabia[1] | established with IMF fund Jan. 8, 1960 = 0.197482 gram fine gold |
| riel | ₹ or CR | 100 sen | Cambodia[1] | no par value agreed with IMF |
| ruble | R or Rub | 100 kopecks | U.S.S.R. | as of Jan. 1, 1961 = 0.987412 gram fine gold |
| rupee | Re (pl. Rs) | 100 cents | Ceylon[1] | as of Nov. 21, 1967=0.149297 gram fine gold |
| rupee | Re (pl. Rs) | 100 paise | India[1] | first established with IMF Dec. 18, 1946 = 0.268601 gram fine gold; as of June 5, 1966=0.118489 gram |
| rupee | Re (pl. Rs) | 100 cents | Mauritius[1] | no par value established with IMF |
| rupee | Re (pl. Rs) | 100 paise | Nepal[1] | initial par value established with IMF Dec. 11, 1967=0.087770 gram fine gold |
| rupee | Re (pl. Rs)! | 100 paise | Pakistan[1] | first established with IMF March 19, 1951 = 0.268601 gram fine gold; as of July 30, 1955 = 0.186621 gram |
| rupiah | Rp | 100 sen | Indonesia[1] | no par value agreed with IMF |
| schilling | S or Sch | 100 groschen | Austria[1] | established by law of Dec. 20, 1924; initial par value agreed with IMF April 29, 1953 = 0.034179 gram fine gold |
| shilling | Sh | 100 cents | Kenya[1] | as of Sept. 9, 1966=0.124414 gram fine gold |
| shilling | Sh | 100 cents | Tanzania[1] | as of Aug. 3, 1966=0.124414 gram fine gold |
| shilling | Sh | 100 cents | Uganda[1] | as of Aug. 15, 1966=0.124414 gram fine gold |

*continued*

wealth **3 :** something (as a plan, device, product) that produces money or profit

[1]**moneymaking** \'⸗⸗,⸗⸗\ *adj* **1 :** affording profitable returns ⟨~ investments⟩ **2 :** engaged or successful in gaining money ⟨the ~ members of the family⟩

[2]**moneymaking** \"\ *n* **:** the act or process of making money **:** the acquisition and accumulation of wealth

**moneyman** \'⸗⸗,⸗\ *n, pl* **moneymen :** FINANCIER

**money market** *n* **1 :** the lenders and borrowers of short-term funds and the intermediaries who bring them together **2 :** a financial center where institutions comprising the money market are well developed

**mon·ey·ness** *n* -ES **:** the quality or state of being readily convertible to cash **:** LIQUIDITY

**money of account :** a denominator of value or basis of exchange which is used in keeping accounts and for which there may or may not be an equivalent coin or denomination of paper money

**money of necessity :** NECESSITY MONEY

**money order** *n* **:** an order for the payment of money; *specif* **:** an order issued at a post office upon application by a person making a remittance and payable at another post office

**money plant** *n* **1 :** HONESTY 3 **2 :** MONEYWORT

**money player** *n* **:** a participant in competition (as a sports match) who performs best under pressure

**money-purchase** \'⸗⸗,⸗⸗\ *adj* **:** of, relating to, or being a plan for retirement income in which contributions are at a fixed rate and benefits are determined by what the money thus set aside will buy

**moneys** *pl of* MONEY, *pres 3d sing of* MONEY

**money scrivener** *n* **:** a person engaged in the business of arranging for the loan of money to others

**money spider** *n* **:** a spider popularly supposed to indicate that the person upon whom it crawls will gain money

**money spinner** *n, chiefly Brit* **:** a moneymaking person, product, or activity **:** MONEY-MAKER ⟨in the western province the *money spinner* is cocoa —Wynford Vaughan-Thomas⟩

**money supply** *n* **:** the stock of money consisting of coin, currency, and bank demand deposits that is available for carrying on the business of a country

**money weight** *n* **:** COIN WEIGHT

**moneywort** \'⸗⸗,⸗\ *n* **:** a trailing European herb (*Lysimachia nummularia*) introduced into No. America and having rounded opposite leaves and solitary yellow flowers in their axils

[1]**mong** \'məŋ\ *n* [ME *mong* mixture, short for *ymong*, fr. OE *gemong, gemang* mingling, crowd — more at AMONG] *dial Eng* **:** a mixture of meal for domestic animals

[2]**mong** \"\ *n* -s [short for *mongrel*] *Austral* **:** a mongrel dog

[1]**monger** \'məŋgə(r), 'mäŋ- *sometimes* -ŋə-\ *n* -s [ME *mongere*, fr. OE *mangere*, fr. L *mangon-, mango* dealer in furbished wares, slave dealer, horse trader (of Gk origin; akin to Gk *manganon* charm, ballista) + OE *-ere* -er — more at MANGONEL] **1 :** one engaged in the sale of a commodity **:** DEALER — usu. used in combination ⟨ale*monger*⟩ ⟨cheese*monger*⟩ ⟨pear*monger*⟩ **2 :** a person engaged in petty or discreditable dealings ⟨a ~ of . . . clichés —L.A.Fiedler⟩ ⟨~*s* of class warfare —M.H.Stans⟩ — usu. used in combination ⟨victims of the local slander*mongers* —*New Yorker*⟩ ⟨a patronage-*monger*⟩

[2]**monger** \"\ *vt* **mongered; mongered; mongering** \-ŋ(g)(e)riŋ\ **mongers :** to act as a monger in purveying **:** PEDDLE, SPREAD ⟨no use ~*ing* words unless we know what stands behind them —L.Baralt⟩

**monger·er** \-ŋ(g)ərə(r)\ *n* -s [[2]*monger* + *-er*] **:** MONGER

**mongering** *n* -s [[1]*monger* + *-ing*] **:** the activity of a monger **:** SELLING, TRAFFICKING — usu. used in combination ⟨sensation-*mongering*⟩ ⟨hate*mongering*⟩ ⟨peace*mongering*⟩

**mon·gler** \'məŋglə(r), 'mäŋ-\ *n* -s [alter. of [1]*mongrel*] *dial* **:** STILT SANDPIPER

**mongo** *or* **mongoe** *var of* MUNGO

[1]**mon·gol** \'mäŋgəl, -äŋ,gōl, -än,gōl\ *n* -s [Mongolian *Mongol*] **1** *cap* **:** a member of one of the chiefly pastoral peoples of Mongolia that physically typify the Mongoloid race, conquered much of Asia and eastern Europe in the 12th and 13th centuries, are prevailingly Lamaistic in religion, and include as important tribal groups the Kalmucks to the west, the Khalkhas of the Mongolian People's Republic, the Buryats to the north, and the true Mongols to the east **2** *usu cap* **:** MONGOLIAN 2 **3** *usu cap* **:** MONGOLOID 1 **4** *sometimes cap* **:** MONGOLIAN 3

[2]**mongol** \"\ *adj, usu cap* **:** MONGOLIAN

**mongolfier** *var of* MONTGOLFIER

**mongol-galchic alphabet** *n, usu cap M&G* **:** an alphabet consisting of the Uighur alphabet supplemented by five letters from the Tibetan added to adapt it to the Mongolic speech

**mon·go·lia** \(')mäŋ'gōlēə, -äṇ-, -lyə\ *adj, usu cap* [fr. *Mongolia*, vast territory with indefinite boundaries in east-central Asia] **:** of or from Mongolia **:** of the kind or style prevalent in Mongolia **:** MONGOLIAN

[1]**mon·go·li·an** \-ən\ *adj* [*Mongolia*, territory in Asia + E *-an*] **1** *usu cap* **:** of or relating to Mongolia or the Mongolian People's Republic or to the Mongols or their language ⟨a *Mongolian* pony⟩ ⟨the *Mongolian* embassy⟩ **2** *usu cap* **:** MONGOLOID 1 **3** *sometimes cap* **:** of, relating to, or afflicted with mongolism

[2]**mongolian** \"\ *n* -s **1** *cap* **a :** MONGOL 1 **b :** MONGOLOID 1 **c :** a native or inhabitant of the Mongolian People's Republic **2** *usu cap* **:** the Mongolic language of the Mongol people **3** *sometimes cap* **:** one affected with mongolism

**mongolian bluebeard** *n, usu cap M* **:** a bluebeard (*Caryopteris mongholica*) of China and Mongolia having linear nearly entire leaves and blue flowers in few-flowered clusters

**mongolian fold** *or* **mongoloid fold** *or* **mongolic fold** *n, usu cap M* **:** EPICANTHIC FOLD

**mongolian pheasant** *n, usu cap M* **1 :** a large pheasant (*Phasianus colchicus mongolicus*) native to the colder part of China and similar to the ring-necked pheasant but with the wing coverts almost entirely white **2 :** RING-NECKED PHEASANT

**mongolian release** *n, usu cap M* **:** an arrow release in which the bowstring is drawn by the bent thumb with overlocked forefinger and the arrow held in the hollow at the base of finger and thumb

**mongolian spot** *or* **mongol spot** *n, often cap M* **:** BLUE SPOT

[1]**mon·gol·ic** \(')mäŋ'gälik, -äṇ-\ *adj, usu cap* [[1]*Mongol* + *-ic*] **:** MONGOLOID 1

[2]**mongolic** \"\ *n* -s *usu cap* **:** a group of Altaic languages including Mongolian, Buryat, and Kalmuck

**mon·gol·ism** \'mäŋgə,lizəm\ *or* **mon·go·li·an·ism** \mäŋ'gōlēə,nizəm, män'-, -lyə,-\ *n* -s *sometimes cap* [[2]*Mongol* or [1]*Mongolian* + *-ism*] **:** a congenital idiocy in which a child is born with slanting eyes, a broad short skull, and broad hands with short fingers and which is associated with translocation involving the twenty-first chromosome — called also *Down's syndrome*

**mon·gol·iza·tion** \,mäŋgələ'zāshən\ *n* -s *usu cap* **:** the act or process of mongolizing

**mon·gol·ize** \'mäŋgə,līz\ *vt* -ED/-ING/-S *often cap* [[2]*Mongol* + *-ize*] **1 :** to make Mongolian in racial relationship or characteristics by an admixture of Mongolian blood ⟨*mongolized* Tartars⟩ **2 :** to furnish (a country) with or allow a significant increase in population belonging to the Mongolian race

**mongolo-** *comb form, usu cap* [[2]*Mongol*] **:** Mongolian and ⟨*Mongolo*-Manchurian⟩ ⟨*Mongolo*-Tatar⟩ ⟨*Mongolo*-Turkic⟩

**mon·golo-dravidian** \'mäŋgə,lō+\ *adj, usu cap M&D* [*Mongolo-* + *Dravidian*] **:** of, relating to, or constituting a mixed ethnological type of Bengal and Orissa, India, marked by a broad head, dark complexion, medium stature, somewhat broad nose, and plentiful beard

[1]**mon·gol·oid** \'mäŋgə,lȯid\ *adj* [[1]*Mongol* + *-oid*] **1** *usu cap* **:** of, constituting, or characteristic of a racial stock that is native to Asia, that is commonly distinguished as one of the major racial divisions of mankind and considered to comprise peoples prevalent in northern and eastern Asia, Malaysians, Eskimos, and often American Indians, and that has as typical features a yellowish complexion, coarse straight black hair and scant beard, short stature, a round head, and a broad flat face with small nose and prominent cheekbones and with eyes having an epicanthic fold **2** *sometimes cap* **:** MONGOLIAN 3

[2]**mongoloid** \"\ *n* -s **1** *cap* **:** a person of Mongoloid racial stock **2** *sometimes cap* **:** MONGOLIAN 3

MONEY—*concluded*

| NAME | SYMBOL | SUBDIVISIONS | COUNTRY | PAR VALUE |
|---|---|---|---|---|
| sol | S/ *or* $ | 100 centavos | Peru[1] | no par value agreed upon since new exchange system of Nov. 1949 |
| Somali shilling *also* somalo | SomSh | 100 cents | Somalia[1] | established June 14, 1963 = 0.124414 gram fine gold |
| sucre | S/ | 100 centavos | Ecuador[1] | as first established with IMF Dec. 18, 1946 = 0.0658275 gram fine gold; as of July 19, 1961 = 0.0493706 gram |
| tical see BAHT, above | | | | |
| won | W | 100 chon | So. Korea[1] | established June 10, 1962, in place of the hwan; no par value agreed with IMF |
| yen | ¥ *or* Y | 100 sen | Japan[1] | initial par value agreed with IMF May 11, 1953 = 0.002468 gram fine gold |
| yuan | $ | 10 chiao | China[3] | no par value agreed with IMF |
| zaire | Z | 100 makuta (sing. likuta) 10,000 sengi | Congo (Kinshasa) | no par value agreed with IMF |
| zloty | Zl *or* Z | 100 groszy | Poland | as of Dec. 31, 1961=.225 ruble |

[1]Member of the International Monetary Fund (abbr. IMF), a reserve fund established under terms of an agreement adopted at the Bretton Woods conference July 1944 and made effective by the signing of the articles of agreement Dec. 27, 1945 to promote international monetary cooperation and exchange stability, to aid the contributing nations with loans of foreign exchange during periods of disequilibrium, to prevent unilateral discriminatory currency practices, and to raise the level of world trade.
[2]Czechoslovakia joined the IMF in 1946; the initial par value of the koruna as agreed on Dec. 18, 1946 was 0.017773 grams fine gold; on June 1, 1953 a new rate of exchange was established for the koruna but it was never agreed upon by the IMF and on Dec. 31, 1954 Czechoslovakia's membership in the Fund was terminated.
[3]Nationalist China is a member of the International Monetary Fund.

**mongoloid idiocy** *n, sometimes cap M* **:** MONGOLISM
**mongols** *pl of* MONGOL
**mon·goose** \'mäŋ,güs, |n,- *sometimes* 'mə|\ *n, pl* **mongooses**

mongoose 1a

[Hindi *mūgūs, māgūs*, fr. Prakrit *maṅguso*, perh. of Dravidian origin; akin to Tamil *mūṅkā* mongoose] **1 a :** an agile keen-sighted grizzled brown and black viverrine mammal (*Herpestes nyula*) of India that is about the size of a ferret, has a sharp snout and a long heavy tail, captures and feeds on snakes including the most venomous and on rodents, and is often domesticated **b :** any other member of the genus *Herpestes* or of various related genera native to Asia and Africa — compare ICHNEUMON 1 **2** *or* **mongoose lemur :** a Madagascan lemur (*Lemur mongoz*)
**mongos** *pl of* MONGO
**¹mon·grel** \'məŋgrəl, 'mäŋ-\ *n* -s [prob. fr. ¹*mong*] **1 :** an animal or plant resulting from the interbreeding of two or more breeds or strains; *esp* **:** an individual of unknown ancestry but not necessarily of inferior quality — contrasted with *crossbred* and *grade;* distinguished from *scrub* **2 a :** a person of mixed birth or tendencies or of undefined status **b :** a cross between types of persons or things **3** *dial* **:** STILT SANDPIPER
**²mongrel** \"\ *adj* **1 :** of mixed breeding **:** being a mongrel ⟨a ~ dog⟩ **2 :** of or being a mixed race or nationality **:** of mixed ancestry — sometimes used disparagingly **3 :** of mixed origin, character, or kinds **:** assignable to no definite class, kind, or type ⟨a ~ mixture, including some grass, more weeds, patches of moss —R.M.Yoder⟩
**mongrel buffalo** *n* **:** BLACK BUFFALO
**mon·grel·ism** \-rə,lizəm\ *n* -s **:** the quality or state of being mongrel
**mon·grel·iza·tion** \,məŋgrələ'zāshən, ,mäŋ-, -lī'-\ *n* -s **1 :** the process of mongrelizing ⟨pledged to fight . . . the ~ of the white race —Cabell Phillips⟩ **2 :** the quality or state of being mongrelized ⟨the use of crossbreds . . . will not mean the reversion to ~ of the fowl —L.M.Winters⟩
**mon·grel·ize** \'məŋgrə,līz, 'mäŋ-\ *vt* -ED/-ING/-S [¹*mongrel* + *-ize*] **:** to cause to become mongrel — **mon·grel·iz·er** \-zə(r)\ *n* -s
**mon·grel·ly** \-rəlē\ *adj* **:** having the character of a mongrel ⟨a ~ cur⟩
**mon·grel·ness** *n* -ES **:** the quality or state of being mongrel
**mongrel skate** *n, dial* **:** a monkfish (*Squatina squatina*)
**mongs** *pl of* MONG
**mon·guor** \'män,gwȯ(ə)r, -äŋ,-\ *n, pl* **monguor** *or* **monguors** *usu cap* **1 :** a sinicized group of Mongol peoples inhabiting the Kansu-Chinghai provincial borders in the northeast Tibetan highlands **2 :** a member of any of the Monguor peoples
**mon·hys·ter·i·na** \män,histə'rīnə\ [NL, fr. *mon-* + *hyster-* + *-ina*] *syn of* CHROMADORIDA
**mo·ni·al** \'mōnēəl\ *n* -s [ME *moynel, moniel*, fr. MF *moinel*, perh. fr. *moyen* middle, fr. L *medianus* — more at MEDIAN] **:** MULLION 1
**mo·ni·as** \'mōnēəs\ *n, cap* [NL, fr. Gk, solitary, fr. *monos* alone, single — more at MONK] **:** a monotypic genus of Madagascan birds (family Mesitornithidae) having a longer bill and tail than members of the closely related genus *Mesitornis*
**mon·ie** \'məni\ *chiefly Scot var of* MANY
**monied** *var of* MONEYED
**monies** *pl of* MONEY
**mo·nie·zia** \mə'nezh(ē)ə\ *n* [NL, fr. Romain-Louis *Moniez* †1936 Fr. physician + NL *-ia*] **1** *cap* **:** a genus of cyclophyllidean tapeworms (family Anoplocephalidae) parasitizing the intestine of various ruminants and having a cysticercoid larva in oribatid mites **2** -s **:** any worm of the genus *Moniezia*
**mon·i·ker** *or* **mon·ick·er** \'mänəkə(r), -nēk-\ *n* -s [origin unknown] *slang* **:** NAME, NICKNAME ⟨might have preferred a substantial ~ like Patrick —*Brentano's Bk. Chat*⟩ ⟨when it came to naming their raceway, the hot rodders . . . borrowed the more elegant ~ of Westhampton —J.M.Flagler⟩ ⟨earned him the ~ "Iron-jawed George" —*Pittsfield (Mass.) News*⟩
**mo·nil·e·thrix** *or* **mo·nil·i·thrix** \mə'nilə,thriks\ *n, pl* **mon·i·let·ri·ches** \,mänə'le·trə,kēz\ *or* **mon·i·lit·ri·ches** \-li-\ [NL, fr. L *monili-, monile* necklace + NL *-thrix* — more at MANE] **:** a disease of the hair in which each hair appears as if strung with small beads or nodes
**mo·nil·ia** \mə'nilēə\ *n* [NL, fr. L *monile* necklace; fr. the chain of spores] **1** *cap* **:** the type genus of Moniliaceae comprising imperfect fungi with hyaline or colored oval to short cylindric conidia borne in branched chains that resemble the vegetative hyphae and including in some classifications various fungi that are now usu. placed in other genera (as *Candida*) **2** *pl* **monilias** *or* **monilia :** any fungus of the genus *Monilia* **3** *or* **monilia disease** -s **:** BROWN ROT 1a
**mo·nil·i·a·ce·ae** \mə,nilē'āsē,ē\ *n pl, cap* [NL, fr. *Monilia*, type genus + *-aceae*] **:** a family of imperfect fungi (order Moniliales) having white or brightly colored hyphae and similarly colored spores that are produced directly on the mycelium and not aggregated in fruiting bodies
**mo·nil·i·al** \mə'nilēəl\ *adj* [NL *Monilia* + E *-al*] **:** of, relating to, or caused by a fungus of the genus *Candida* ⟨reports of ~ infection⟩
**mo·nil·i·a·les** \mə,nilē'ā(,)lēz\ *n pl, cap* [NL, fr. *Monilia* + *-ales*] **:** an order of imperfect fungi lacking conidiophores or having conidiophores that are superficial and free or gathered in tufts or pulvinate masses but never enclosed in an acervulus or pycnidium
**mon·i·li·a·sis** \,mänə'līəsəs\ *n, pl* **monilia·ses** \-īə,sēz\ [NL, fr. *Monilia* + *-iasis*] **:** infection with or disease caused by yeastlike fungi of the family Moniliaceae; *specif* **:** THRUSH
**mo·nil·i·form** \mə'nilə,fȯrm\ *adj* [L *monili-, monile* necklace + E *-form* — more at MANE] **:** jointed or constricted at regular intervals so as to resemble a string of beads ⟨a ~ root⟩ ⟨an insect with ~ antennae⟩ — see ANTENNA illustration, ROOT illustration — **mo·nil·i·form·ly** *adv*
**mo·nil·i·for·mis** \mə,nilə'fȯrməs\ *n, cap* [NL, fr. L *monili-, monile* necklace + L *-formis* -form] **:** a genus of acanthocephalan worms usu. parasitic in rodents but occas. found in dogs, cats, or rarely man
**mo·nil·iid** \mə'nilēəd\ *n* -s [NL *Monilia* + E *-id*] **:** a secondary commonly generalized dermatitis resulting from hypersensitivity developed in response to a primary focus of infection with a fungus of the genus *Candida*
**mo·nil·i·oid** \mə'nilē,ȯid\ *adj* [L *monili-, monile* necklace + E *-oid*] **:** MONILIFORM
**mon·i·ment** \'mänimənt\ *n* -s [alter. of *monument*] *Scot* **:** a person whose behavior and actions provoke ridicule
**mo·nim·ia** \mə'nimēə\ *n, cap* [NL, fr. L *Monima* (fr. L, fr. Gk *Monimē*), the wife of Mithridates VI †63B.C. king of ancient Pontus after whom a related genus (*Mithridatea*) had been named + NL *-ia*] **:** a genus (the type of the family Monimiaceae) of shrubs native to the Mascarene islands having opposite leaves and small diclinous flowers
**mo·nim·i·a·ce·ae** \mə,nimē'āsē,ē\ *n pl, cap* [NL, fr. *Monimia*, type genus + *-aceae*] **:** a family of chiefly tropical American trees and shrubs (order Ranales) having evergreen usu. opposite leaves and insignificant generally unisexual flowers
**mo·nim·o·lite** \mə'nimə,līt\ *n* -s [Sw *monimolit*, fr. Gk *monimos* stable, steady (fr. *menein* to remain) + Sw *-lit* -lite — more at MANSION] **:** a yellowish or brownish green mineral $(Pb,Ca)_3Sb_2O_8$(?) consisting of an oxide of lead, calcium, and antimony
**mon·i·mo·sty·lic** \¦mänəmō¦stīlik\ *adj* [Gk *monimos* + E *-stylic*] *of a reptile* **:** having the quadrate bone united to the skull by a suture
**mo·ni·plies** \'mäni,plīz\ *Scot var of* MANYPLIES
**mon·ish** \'mänish\ *vt* -ED/-ING/-ES [ME *monesen, monisshen* alter. (*monest-* being taken as past & past part.) of *monesten*, fr. OF *monester*, fr. (assumed) VL *monestare*, fr. L *monēre* to warn — more at MIND] **:** ADMONISH
**mon·ism** \'mä,nizəm, 'mō,-\ *n* -s [G *monismus*, fr. *mon-* + *-ismus* -ism] **1 a** (1) **:** the metaphysical view that there is only one kind of substance or ultimate reality — compare DUALISM, PLURALISM (2) **:** the metaphysical view that reality is one unitary organic whole with no independent parts — contrasted with *pluralism* **b :** an epistemological theory that proclaims the identity of the object and datum of knowledge — contrasted with *dualism* **2 :** MONOGENESIS **3 :** a viewpoint, theory, or methodology that reduces either all phenomena or those within its particular domain to one fundamental principle ⟨tendency toward ~ . . . toward the reduction of norms to facts —K.R.Popper⟩ **4 :** a sociological doctrine that the laws of man and nature are united in one single harmonious force
**mon·ist** \-nəst\ *n* -s [G, fr. *mon-* + *-ist*] **:** an advocate of monism
**mo·nis·tic** \mə'nistik, mō'-, -tēk\ *also* **mo·nis·ti·cal** \-təkəl, -tēk-\ *adj* **1 :** of, relating to, or involving monism **:** relying on one factor or method in explanation ⟨the ~ school would regard national law and international law as an integrated whole —J.S.Roucek⟩ — distinguished from *dualistic* and *pluralistic* **2 :** of one type or character ⟨that American culture is a ~, unified, homogeneous culture —David Golovensky⟩
**monistic idealism** *n* **:** a system of philosophical idealism emphasizing the primacy of the One (as the Absolute or Nature) rather than of the many — contrasted with *pluralistic idealism;* compare HEGELIANISM, SPINOZISM
**mo·ni·tion** \mə'nishən\ *n* -s [ME *monicioun*, fr. MF *monition*, fr. L *monition-, monitio*, fr. *monitus* (past part. of *monēre* to remind, warn) + *-ion-, -io* -ion — more at MIND] **1 :** instruction or advice given by way of caution **:** ADMONITION, WARNING, CAUTION **2 :** an intimation, indication, or notice of something esp. of a dangerous kind present or impending **3 a :** a legal process in the nature of a summons or citation to appear and answer (as in default of performing some certain act) **b :** an order from a bishop or ecclesiastical court to desist from a specified offense
**¹mon·i·tor** \'mänəd·ə(r), -ətə(r) *sometimes* -ə,tȯ(ə)r *or* -ȯ(ə)\ *n* -s [L, one that reminds or warns, overseer, fr. *monitus* + *-or*] **1 a :** a student appointed to assist a teacher (as by keeping order, performing routine duties, or in some educational systems teaching younger students) **b :** a person or thing that gives advice (as of caution) or instruction regarding conduct **:** one that reproves, reminds, or instructs **:** ADMONISHER, ADVISER ⟨enough practical experience on the fighting line to serve as ~s and instructors for troops green in the game of war —*N. Y. Times*⟩ **:** REMINDER ⟨observed the customary stack of documents on this busy man's reading table, and . . . took it as a silent ~ —Upton Sinclair⟩ **c** (1) **:** one that monitors something ⟨learned from a broadcast heard by a U. S. ~⟩ ⟨an electronic ~⟩ (2) **:** an observer responsible for reporting misdeeds ⟨the correspondents put fresh vigor into their classic role as people's ~ over the Government —*Time*⟩ (3) **:** an instrument that measures (as vital signs during surgery) or gives warning (as of excessive radiation) (4) **:** a screen or receiver used by television personnel to view the picture being picked up by a camera or being broadcast **2** *archaic* **:** a board worn or fastened across the back to give erectness to the figure **3** *also* **monitor lizard** [so called fr. the belief that such lizards give warning of the presence of crocodiles] **:** any of various large tropical Old World pleurodont lizards closely related to the iguanas and constituting the genus *Varanus* and the family Varanidae and including an African lizard (*V. niloticus*) that destroys crocodile eggs — compare KOMODO DRAGON **4** [fr. the *Monitor*, the first ship of this type, designed in 1862 for the U. S. Navy by John Ericsson †1889 Am. engineer and inventor born in Sweden] **a :** a heavily armored warship formerly used in coastal operations, having a very low freeboard and one or more revolving turrets with heavy guns, and sacrificing speed and coal capacity to steadiness as gun platforms and to thickness of armor **b :** a small modern warship with shallow draft and two 15-inch guns for coastal bombardment ⟨the new British ~s . . . which have supported the Allied ground forces in Sicily —*Newsweek*⟩ **5** *also* **monitor top :** a raised central portion of a roof (as along the ridge of a gable roof) having low windows or louvers along its sides and used (as in industrial buildings) to provide light and air **6** *or* **monitor nozzle :** a nozzle capable of turning completely round in a horizontal plane with a limited play in a vertical plane and used in hydraulic mining and fire fighting **7 :** a tool-holding turret on a machine
**²monitor** \"\ *vb* **monitored; monitored; monitoring** \-d·əriŋ, -tər-, -ȯr-, -nə·triŋ\ **monitors** *vt* **1 a :** to check and sometimes to adjust (as a radio or television signal, channel, or program) for quality or fidelity to a band by means of a receiver during or sometimes before transmission ⟨the frequency must be exact, constant, and carefully ~ed —M.H. Aronson⟩ ⟨gradually introducing automatic ~ing of the aural quality of its programs —*Times Rev. of Industry*⟩ **b :** to check (as a radio or television broadcast or a telephone conversation) for military, political, or criminal significance by means of a receiver ⟨~ radiotelephone messages out of Hawaii —*New Republic*⟩ **2 :** to test (as air, a surface, a beam of radiation, clothing, personnel) for intensity of radiation (as from radioactivity) to determine whether the intensity comes within specified limits ⟨~ the upper air to collect telltale evidence of atomic explosions —*Time*⟩ **3 :** to watch, observe, or check esp. for a special purpose ⟨had to ~ every word and thought —Polly Adler⟩ ⟨crew chiefs ~ed engines and the array of dials, switches and lights that told them how each item of equipment was functioning —Gordon Williams⟩ ⟨~ political gossip⟩ **4 :** to keep track of, regulate, or control (as a process or the operation of a machine) ⟨personnel . . . involved in ~ing the work of this contract —A.A.Campbell⟩ — used esp. of an automatic electronic device ⟨the line is ~ed by a new instrument called the quality control indicator —*Science News Letter*⟩; *specif* **:** to keep track of (aircraft in flight) by means of radar ⟨radar stations ~ing all our heavy bombers —W.R. Frye⟩ **5 :** to check or regulate the volume or quality of (sound) in preparation for recording or during recording ⟨sound is ~ed and the correct effect is introduced; it would obviously be ludicrous to have close-up sound in a long shot —O.B.Hanson⟩ ⟨the first soprano . . . either inclines to shred off into shrillness at the top or has been badly ~ed in the recording —Herbert Weinstock⟩ ~ *vi* **:** to act as a monitor
**monitor bug** *n* **:** CONENOSE
**mon·i·to·ri·al** \¦mänə¦tōrēəl, -tȯr-\ *adj* [L *monitorius* monitory + E *-al* — more at MONITORY] **1 :** MONITORY ⟨always teaching the public something, an editorial, ~ urge crowding his brain —H.R.Warfel⟩ **2 :** of, relating to, done by, or in charge of a monitor ⟨~ instruction⟩ — **mon·i·to·ri·al·ly** \-ēəlē, -li\ *adv*
**monitorial system** *n* **:** an educational system formerly in use by many charity schools that consisted in employing older pupils to teach the younger ones — see LANCASTERIAN
**monitor lizard** *n* **:** MONITOR 3
**mon·i·tor·ship** \'mänəd·ə(r),ship\ *n* **:** the position or function of a monitor **:** SUPERVISION ⟨maintain an effective ~ over the various projects in the program⟩
**¹mon·i·to·ry** \'mänə,tōrē, -tȯr-, -ri\ *adj* [L *monitorius*, fr. *monitus* (past part. of *monēre* to warn) + *-orius* -ory — more at MIND] **:** giving admonition **:** WARNING ⟨a ~ proverb⟩ ⟨shook a ~ finger at him⟩
**²monitory** \"\ *n* -ES **:** a monitory letter ⟨exhortations, decrees, and *monitories* of the popes —D.H.Wiest⟩
**mon·i·tress** \'mänə·trəs\ *n* -ES [¹*monitor* + *-ess*] **1 :** a woman that admonishes **2 :** a girl that has monitorial duties in a school
**¹monk** \'məŋk\ *n* -s [ME *munk, monk*, fr. OE *munuc*, fr. LL *monachus*, fr. LGk *monachos*, fr. Gk, adj., single, fr. *monos* single, alone; akin to OHG *mangolōn, mengen* to lack, be without, OIr *mēn* smooth, soft, *menb* small, Toch B *menki* less, Gk *manos* sparse, Skt *manāk* a little; basic meaning: small] **1 :** a man who is a member of a monastic order; *also* **:** a man who has retired from the world to devote himself to asceticism as a solitary or cenobite ⟨many non-Christian as well as early Christian ~s are noted for practicing the solitary life⟩ — compare HERMIT **2 a :** a So. American saki (*Pithecia monachus*) **b** *dial Brit* **:** the European bullfinch **c :** ANGLER 2 **3** *archaic* **:** a blotch or dark spot on a printed sheet caused by excessive deposition of ink — compare FRIAR **4 :** MONK SHOE
**²monk** \"\ *n* -s [by shortening] **:** MONKEY
**monk bat** *n* **:** any of several bats in which the males live in communities; *esp* **:** a bat (*Molossus tropidorhynchus*) of the West Indies
**monkbird** \'=,=\ *n* **:** FRIARBIRD
**monk·ery** \'məŋkərē, -ri\ *n* -ES **1 :** the state, life, or profession of monks **:** monastic life **:** MONASTICISM **2 :** a body or community of monks **:** MONASTERY **3 :** monastic usage, custom, or practice **4** *Brit* **a :** the country as distinguished from the city **b :** the world of tramps **:** TRAMPS **c :** tramping as a practice
**¹mon·key** \'məŋkē, -ki\ *n* -s [prob. of LG, D, or Flem origin; akin to MFlem *Monnekin*, nickname for a monkey, MLG *Moneke*, name of an ape in the epic *Reynard the Fox;* both prob. diminutives of a word of Romance origin; akin to OSp *mona* monkey, prob. short for *maimón, maimona*, prob. fr. Ar *maymūn*, lit., happy] **1 a :** a member of the order Primates excepting man and usu. also the lemurs and tarsiers **b :** any of the smaller longer-tailed primates (as members of the New World family Cebidae) as contrasted with the larger nearly or quite tailless apes — see CAPUCHIN, GUEREZA, LANGUR, SPIDER MONKEY **2 a :** a person resembling a monkey in appearance or behavior (as a mimic or a performer of antics) **b :** a ludicrous figure **:** DUPE ⟨made a ~ of him⟩ **3 :** an unusually active and mischievous child **4 a :** a heavy weight or tup slung from the roof of an ironworks and used in upsetting the end of a piece too long to be treated by the forging hammer **b :** a falling weight used for driving something by percussion (as the falling weight of a pile driver or of a drop hammer) **5 a :** a small pot or crucible used for melting small quantities of glass **b :** MONKEY POT **6** *slang* **:** the sum of 500 pounds or 500 dollars **7** *Brit* **:** TEMPER, ANGER, DANDER ⟨got his ~ up⟩ **8** *Brit* **:** a mortgage on a building **9 :** CINDER NOTCH **10 :** an airway in an anthracite mine **11 :** a desperate irresistible desire for or addiction to drugs regarded as an intolerable burden — often used in the phrase *monkey on one's back* ⟨supporting his yen runs from $35 a week up, though if one "has a ~ on his back", . . . he will be soaked from $50 to $100 a week —Jack Lait & Lee Mortimer⟩
**²monkey** \"\ *adj* **1 :** of, relating to, or having the characteristics of a monkey **:** resembling that of a monkey **2 :** being of small size ⟨a ~ chute in a mine⟩ **3 :** being something on a ship that is small or peculiar in location, arrangement, or use ⟨~ poop⟩ ⟨~ rudder⟩
**³monkey** \"\ *vb* **monkeyed; monkeyed; monkeying; monkeys** [¹*monkey*] *vi* **1 :** to act in a grotesque, mischievous, or meddlesome manner **2 a :** FOOL, TRIFLE — often used with *around* **b :** TAMPER — usu. used with *with* ⟨warned not to ~ with the controls⟩ ~ *vt* **:** to treat as a monkey does **:** MIMIC
**monkey apple** *n* **1 :** POND APPLE **2 :** WILD FIG 3 **3 :** a tropical Old World tree (*Anisophyllea laurina*) of the family Rhizophoraceae having an edible fruit resembling a plum
**monkey bass** *n* **:** PIASSAVA 2
**monkey bear** *n* **:** KOALA
**monkey block** *n* **:** a small single block that is strapped with a swivel
**monkeyboard** \'==,=\ *n, Brit* **:** a footboard at the back of a vehicle (as for a footman or on an omnibus for the conductor)
**monkey boat** *n, Brit* **:** a small usu. half-decked boat used in docks and on the Thames river
**monkey bread** *n* **1 :** the fruit of the baobab **2** *also* **monkey-bread tree :** BAOBAB
**monkey bridge** *n* **:** a high narrow platform above a deck or in an engine room or boiler room
**monkey business** *n* **:** mischievous or questionable activity **:** FOOLING ⟨told the boys to quit their *monkey business*⟩ ⟨suspected *monkey business* at the polls⟩

**monkey cap** *n* **:** a small pillbox equipped with a chin strap
**monkey-faced owl** \'==,=-\ *n* **:** BARN OWL
**monkey fist** *or* **monkey's fist** *n* **:** a large heavy knot resembling a Turk's head used to weight the end of a messenger or heaving line
**monkey flower** *n* **1 :** a plant of the genus *Mimulus* **2 :** TOADFLAX
**monkey flush** *n* **:** three cards of the same suit in poker
**monkey foresail** *n* **:** a square foresail on a sloop or schooner
**mon·key·fy** \'məŋkē,fī\ *vt* -ED/-ING/-ES [*monkey* + *-fy*] **:** to make like or suggestive of a monkey **:** cause to be ridiculous in appearance

monkey cap

**monkey gaff** *n* **:** a light gaff on a mizzenmast above the spanker gaff for the better display of signals
**monkey grass** *n* **:** piassava fiber
**monkey hammer** *or* **monkey press** *n* **:** DROP HAMMER
**mon·key·hood** \'məŋkē,hu̇d\ *n* **:** the state of being a monkey
**mon·key·ish** \-ˌish\ *adj* **:** having the characteristics of a monkey — **mon·key·ish·ly** *adv* — **mon·key·ish·ness** *n* -ES
**monkey island** *n* **:** the top of the pilothouse on a ship

monkey fist

**monkey jack** *n* **:** a jack for pushing over tree trunks and stumps after the lateral roots have been cut
**monkey jacket** *n* **:** MESS JACKET
**monkey ladder** *n* **:** a light ship's ladder (as to the monkey bridge)
**monkey line** *n* **:** a line used in lowering a boat
**monkey-nut** \'==,=\ *n* **1 :** PEANUT **2 :** the fruit of a European basswood (*Tilia glabra*)
**monkey orange** *n* **1 :** either of two deciduous African shrubs or small trees (*Strychnos inocua* and *Strychnos spinosa*) having a hard globose fruit with edible pulp **2 :** the fruit of a monkey orange
**monkeypod** \'==,=\ *n* **:** RAIN TREE
**monkey pot** *n* **1 a :** a large woody urn-shaped operculate fruit characteristic of the sapucaias and various closely related trees (as the manbarklaks) **b :** SAPUCAIA; *also* **:** MANBARKLAK **2 :** a pot used in glassmaking; *specif* **:** any of several round-topped oval cylinders enclosed in firebrick arches at the base of a chimney and used as melting pots in the making of flint glass
**monkey puzzle** *also* **monkey puzzler** *n* **:** a tall Chilean evergreen tree (*Araucaria araucana*) having intertwined branches and stiff sharp-pointed leaves and bearing large edible nuts — called also *Chile pine*
**monkey rail** *n* **:** a second and lighter rail raised a little above the quarter rail of a ship
**monkey-rope** \'==,=\ *n* **1 :** LIANA **2 :** a safety rope secured to a sailor's waist (as when he is working over the ship's side)
**monkey rum** *n, South & Midland* **:** the distilled syrup of sugarcane or sorghum cane
**monkeys** *pl of* MONKEY, *pres 3d sing of* MONKEY
**monkeyshine** \'==,=\ *n* **:** a mischievous or questionable trick or prank **:** a piece of monkey business — usu. used in pl. ⟨the ~s of some political candidates⟩
**monkey skin** *n* **:** a light reddish brown that is redder, lighter, and slightly stronger than copper tan, redder and duller than peach tan, and lighter than peach bisque
**monkey spar** *n* **:** a mast or yard of reduced size (as on a ship on which boys are trained as seamen)
**monkey suit** *n* **1 :** any of various uniforms ⟨difference between the . . . uniforms of other navies and the makeshift *monkey suits* our sailors wear —*Amer. Mercury*⟩ **2 :** TUXEDO
**monkeytail** \'==,=\ *n* **1 :** a piece of rope attached to the bend of a hook to aid in handling it without risk of jamming the hand **2 :** a vertical scroll terminating a handrail
**monkey vine** *n* **:** a tropical Old World morning glory (*Ipomoea nil*) that has large showy often fringed or double flowers and is the source of many cultivated forms
**monkey way** *n* **:** MONKEY 10
**monkeywood** \'==,=\ *n* **:** QUIRA 2
**monkey wrench** *n* **1 :** a wrench with one fixed and one adjustable jaw at right angles to a straight handle **2 :** something disrupting ⟨a speech on foreign policy . . . threw a *monkey wrench* into our foreign relations at a critical time —*Kiplinger Washington Letter*⟩

monkey wrench 1

**monkfish** \'=,=\ *n* **1 :** any of several small bottom-dwelling squaloid sharks (genus *Squatina*) having the pectoral and ventral fins large and lateral in position so that the outline when viewed from above resembles that of a skate or ray rather than a typical shark **2 :** ANGLER 2
**mon-khmer** \'=,=\ *n, usu cap M&K* [³*Mon* + *Khmer*] **1 :** a language family containing Mon, Khmer, Palaung, Wa, Jakun, Sakai, Khasi **2 :** a branch of the Mon-Khmer family containing Mon, Khmer, and a few other closely related languages of southeast Asia
**monk·hood** \'məŋk,hu̇d, -ŋ,ku̇d\ *n* [¹*monk* + *-hood*] **1 :** the character, condition, or profession of a monk **:** MONASTICISM **2 :** monks as a body or a class
**monk·ish** \'məŋkish, -kēsh\ *adj* **1 :** of or relating to monks **:** MONASTIC ⟨the ~ church . . . often included three bays of the nave —E.H.Short⟩ **2 :** characteristic of or befitting monks ⟨the poem is thoroughly medieval and ~ in conception —A. E.Bailey⟩ ⟨brooding and moiling in ~ seclusion —A.M. Schlesinger b.1888⟩ **3 a :** being or resembling a monk ⟨working with much of the patient thoroughness of his ~ predecessors —G.W.Eve⟩ **:** ASCETIC ⟨I esteem even more a man who puts poverty and a shelf of books above profiteering and evenings of jazz; I am naturally ~ —H.L.Mencken⟩ **b :** resembling that of or attributed to a monk or having features attributed to monasticism ⟨a ~ robe⟩ ⟨it is ~, parsimonious, and timid to despise the lavish and complex beauty of life —D.C.Peattie⟩ **4 :** made or used by monks ⟨flesh begins to appear on the bones of these ~ annals —B.R.Redman⟩ ⟨~ Latin⟩ — **monk·ish·ly** *adv* — **monk·ish·ness** *n* -ES
**monk·ism** \-ŋ,kizəm\ *n* -S **:** MONASTICISM
**monk·ist** \-kəst\ *adj* **:** MONASTIC ⟨the ~ vows included chastity —J.H.Robinson †1936⟩
**monk·ly** *adj* **:** of or relating to a monk **:** MONASTIC ⟨many illuminations made by patient ~ hands —T.B.Costain⟩
**monk parrot** *or* **monk parrakeet** *n* **:** a common So. American green and gray parrot (*Myiopsitta monachus*)
**monk saki** *n* **:** a saki (*Pithecia monachus*) of which the ruff suggests a monastic tonsure
**monk's cloth** *n* **:** a coarse heavy fabric in basket weave made orig. of worsted and used for monk's habits but now chiefly of cotton or linen and used for draperies
**monk seal** *n* **:** any of several hair seals (genus *Monachus*) known from the Mediterranean, the Caribbean, and Hawaii but once so extensively hunted for hides and oil that they are now rare in much of their former range
**monk·ship** \'məŋk,ship\ *n* **:** MONKHOOD
**monk shoe** *n* **:** a low shoe having two quarters and a vamp and held to the foot by a strap passing over the instep and usu. buckled at the side — compare MONK STRAP
**monks·hood** \'məŋks,hu̇d\ *n* [*monk's* (gen. of ¹*monk*) + *hood*] **:** ACONITE 1; *esp* **:** a widely distributed Eurasian herb (*Aconitum napellus*) with a thickened or tuberous rootstock and finely palmate leaves that is often cultivated for its showy terminal racemes of cucullate white or purplish flowers and that is extremely poisonous in all its parts — see ACONITE 2; compare WOLFSBANE 1

monk shoe

**monkshood-vine** \'=,=\ *n* **:** a slender Chinese tendril climber (*Ampelopsis aconitifolia*) used as an ornamental vine and having digitately

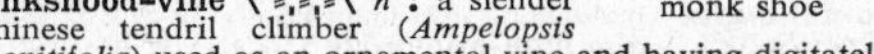

3- to 5-parted leaves, inconspicuous flowers, and orange-colored berries
**monk's pepper tree** *n* **:** AGNUS CASTUS
**monk's seam** *or* **monk seam** *n* **:** an extra middle seam made at the junction of two breadths of canvas ordinarily joined by only two rows of stitches
**monk's tale stanza** *n, usu cap M&T* [fr. the *Monk's Tale* in *The Canterbury Tales* (1386–1400) by Geoffrey Chaucer †1400 Eng. poet, where such stanzas are used] **:** a stanza of eight five-stress lines with the rhyme scheme *ababbcbc*
**monk strap** *n* **1 :** a strap passing over the instep of a monk shoe and holding the shoe to the foot **2 :** MONK SHOE
**monmouth cap** *n, usu cap M* [fr. *Monmouth*, England] **:** a flat round cap formerly worn by soldiers and sailors ⟨did good service . . . wearing leeks in their *Monmouth caps* which your Majesty know to this hour is an honourable badge of the service —Shak.⟩
**mon·mouth·shire** \'mənməth,shi(ə)r, 'män-, -,shiə, -,shə(r)\ *or* **mon·mouth** *adj, usu cap* [fr. *Monmouthshire* or *Monmouth* county, England] **:** of or from the county of Monmouth, England **:** of the kind or style prevalent in Monmouth
¹**mo·no** \'mō(,)nō\ *n, pl* **mono** *or* **monos** *usu cap* [Sp, of AmerInd origin] **1 a :** a Shoshonean people of southeastern California **b :** a member of such people **2 :** the language of the Mono people
²**mono** \'mä(,)nō, 'mō(,)-\ *adj* [*mon-*] **:** containing one atom, radical, or group of a particular kind in the molecule
³**mo·no** \'mō(,)nō\ *n* -S [Sp, monkey, prob. alter. of *mona* — more at MONKEY] **:** a black howler monkey (*Alouatta villosa*) of Central America
⁴**mono** \"\ *n* -S [by shortening] **:** MONOSABIO
⁵**mono** \'mä(,)nō, 'mō(,)-\ *n* -S [by shortening fr. *Monotype*] **:** a typesetting machine
**mono-** —*in pronunciations below*, ¦== = ¦mä(,)nō *also* ¦mō(,)nō *or* -nə\ — see MON-
**mono·acetate** \¦== *at* MONO-+\ *n* [ISV *mon-* + *acetate*] **:** a salt, ester, or acylal containing only one acetate group
**mono·acetin** \"+\ *also* **mon·acetin** \(')män, (')mōn+\ *n* [ISV *mon-* + *acetin*] **:** ACETIN a
¹**mono·acid** \¦== *at* MONO-+\ *or* **mono·acidic** \"+\ *also* **mon·acid** \(')män, (')mōn+\ *adj* [*mon-* + *acid* or *acidic*] **1 :** able to react with only one molecule of a monobasic acid to form a salt or ester **:** characterized by one hydroxyl group — used of bases and sometimes of alcohols **2 :** containing only one hydrogen atom replaceable by a basic atom or radical — used esp. of acid salts
²**monoacid** \"\ *also* **monacid** \"\ *n* **:** an acid (as hydrochloric acid) having only one acid hydrogen atom
**mono·alphabetic substitution** \¦== *at* MONO-+-\ *n* [*mon-* + *alphabetic*] **:** substitution in cryptography that uses a single substitution alphabet so that each plaintext letter always has the same cipher equivalent — compare POLYALPHABETIC
**mono·amide** \"+\ *also* **mon·amide** \(¦)män, (¦)mōn+\ *n* [ISV *mon-* + *amide*] **:** an amide containing only one amido group
**mono·amine** \¦== *at* MONO-+\ *also* **mon·amine** \(¦)män, (¦)mōn+\ *n* [ISV *mon-* + *amine*] **:** an amine containing only one amino group — **mono·amino** \¦== *at* MONO-+\ *adj*
**mono·ammonium phosphate** \¦== *at* MONO-+-\ *n* [*mon-* + *ammonium*] **:** AMMONIUM PHOSPHATE
**mono·azo** \"+\ *adj* [ISV *monaz-, monazo-*, fr. *mon-* + *az-*] **:** containing one azo group in the molecule ⟨~ dyes⟩
**mono·basic** \"+\ *adj* [ISV *mon-* + *basic*] **1 a :** having only one hydrogen atom replaceable by a basic atom or radical — used of acids (as hydrochloric acid) **b :** containing only one atom of a univalent metal or its equivalent ⟨~ sodium phosphate $NaH_2PO_4$⟩ **c :** having only one basic hydroxyl group **:** able to react with only one molecule of a monobasic acid — used of bases and basic salts **2 :** based orig. upon a single species — used of taxonomic genera; compare MONOTYPIC — **mono·basicity** \"+\ *n*
**mono·bath** \'==+,-\ *n* [*mon-* + *bath*] **:** a single solution including ingredients for more than one photographic process (as for developing and fixing)
**mono·blast** \-,blast\ *n* [ISV *mon-* + *-blast*] **:** a motile cell of the spleen and bone marrow that gives rise to the monocyte of the circulating blood
**mono·blastic** \¦==+\ *adj* [*mon-* + *blastic*] **:** having or derived from a single germ layer
**mono·bleph·a·ri·da·les** \,==+,blefərə'dā(,)lēz\ *n pl, cap* [NL, fr. *Monoblepharid-, Monoblepharis* genus of fungi (fr. *mon-* + Gk *blepharid-, blepharis* eyelash) + *-ales*] **:** an order of fungi (subclass Oomycetes) that are distinguished from related forms by possession of a large nonmotile egg which is fertilized by a small uniflagellate motile sperm
**mono·bloc** \'==,=\ *adj* [fr. *mon-* + *bloc*, alter. of *block*] **:** made in one block or casting ⟨a ~ cylinder casting⟩
**mono·branchiate** \¦== *at* MONO-+\ *adj* [*mon-* + *branchiate*] **:** having one gill or set of gills
**monobrom-** *or* **monobromo-** *comb form* [ISV *mon-* + *brom-*] **:** containing one atom of bromine — in names of chemical compounds ⟨*monobromo*naphthalene⟩; compare BROM-
**mono·bromate** \¦== *at* MONO-+\ *vt* [*mon-* + *bromate*] **:** MONOBROMINATE ⟨*monobromated* camphor⟩
**mono·brominate** \"+\ *vt* [*mon-* + *brominate*] **:** to introduce one bromine atom into (as an organic compound) ⟨~ benzene⟩ — **mono·bromination** \"+\ *n*
**Mono·caine** \'==,kān\ *trademark* — used for a crystalline local anesthetic that is an ester of the *para*-aminobenzoic acid
**mono·calcium** \¦== *at* MONO-+\ *adj* [*mon-* + *calcium*] **:** containing one atom or equivalent of calcium in the molecule
**monocalcium phosphate** *n* **:** CALCIUM PHOSPHATE 1a(1)
**mon·o·can·thi·dae** \,mänə'kan(t)thə,dē\ *syn of* MONACANTHIDAE
**mono·carboxylic** \¦== *at* MONO-+\ *adj* [*mon-* + *carboxylic*] **:** containing one carboxyl group
¹**mono·car·di·an** \"+¦kärdēən\ *adj* [*mon-* + Gk *kardia* heart + E *-an* — more at HEART] **:** having a single auricle and ventricle to the heart
²**monocardian** \"\ *n* -S **:** an animal having a monocardian heart
**mono·carp** \'==,kärp\ *n* -S [F *monocarpe*, fr. *mon-* + Gk *karpos* fruit — more at HARVEST] **:** a monocarpic plant — **mono·car·pal** \¦==¦kärpəl\ *adj*
**mono·carpellary** \¦==+\ *adj* [*mon-* + *carpellary*] **:** consisting of a single carpel — compare POLYCARPELLARY
**mono·car·pi·an** \¦kärpēən\ *adj* **:** MONOCARPIC
**mono·car·pic** \-pik\ *adj* [prob. fr. (assumed) NL *monocarpicus*, fr. NL *mon-* + *-carpicus* -carpic] **:** bearing fruit but once and dying — used esp. of annual and biennial flowering plants; compare CENTURY PLANT
**mono·car·pous** \-pəs\ *adj* [NL *monocarpus*, fr. *mon-* + *-carpus* -carpous] **:** having a single ovary ⟨a ~ gynoecium⟩; *esp* **:** MONOCARPELLARY
**mono·cau·lus** \,=='kōləs\ *n, cap* [NL, fr. *mon-* + Gk *kaulos* stalk, stem — more at HOLE] **:** a genus of giant hydroids that may attain a length of eight feet
**mono·cellular** \¦== *at* MONO-+\ *adj* [*mon-* + *cellular*] **:** having or involving a single kind of cell
**mono·centric** \"+\ *adj* [*mon-* + *-centric*] **:** having a single center — compare POLYCENTRIC
**mono·ceph·a·lous** \¦sefələs\ *adj* [*mon-* + *-cephalous*] **:** having a solitary head or capitulum ⟨a ~ aster⟩
**mo·noc·er·os** \mə'näsərəs\ *n* -ES [ME, fr. MF, fr. L, fr. Gk *monokeros*, fr. *mon-* + *-keros* (fr. *keras* horn) — more at HORN] **1** *obs* **:** UNICORN 1a(1) **2 :** a fish (as the swordfish or sawfish) with one hornlike process
**mono·cha·sium** \¦== *at* MONO-+'kāzh(ē)əm\ *n, pl* **monochasia** \-zh(ē)ə\ [NL, fr. *mon-* + *-chasium* (as in *dichasium*)] **:** a cymose inflorescence that produces only one main axis — compare DICHASIUM, POLYCHASIUM
**mono·chla·myd·e·ae** \-klə'midē,ē\ *n pl cap* [NL, fr. *mon-* + *-chlamydeae* (fr. Gk *chlamyd-, chlamys* cloak, mantle)] *in some classifications* **:** a group of Archichlamydeae nearly coextensive with Apetalae and comprising plants with flowers that lack petals or sepals but not both
**mono·chla·myd·e·ous** \¦==+\ *adj* **:** of or relating to the Monochlamydeae
**monochlor-** *or* **monochloro-** *comb form* [ISV *mon-* + *chlor-*] **:** containing one atom of chlorine — in names of chemical compounds ⟨*monochloro*benzene⟩
**mono·chloramine** \¦== *at* MONO- +\ *n* [ISV *monochlor-* + *amine*] **:** the chloramine $NH_2Cl$
**mono·chloride** \"+\ *n* [*monochlor-* + *-ide*] **:** a compound containing one atom of chlorine combined with an element or radical
**mono·chlorinate** \"+\ *vt* [*mon-* + *chlorinate*] **:** to combine with one atom of chlorine either by substitution or addition
**mono·chloro** \"+\ *adj* [*monochlor-*] **:** containing one atom of chlorine in the molecule
**mono·chloroacetic acid** \"+-\ *n* [*monochlor-* + *acetic*] **:** CHLOROACETIC ACID
**mono·chlorobenzene** \"+\ *n* [*monochlor-* + *benzene*] **:** CHLOROBENZENE
**mono·chlorosilane** \"+\ *n* [*monochlor-* + *silane*] **:** CHLOROSILANE 1
**mono·chord** \'mänə,kȯrd, -ō(ə)d\ *n* [ME *monocorde*, fr. MF, fr. ML *monochordum*, fr. Gk *monochordon*, fr. *mon-* + *-chordon* -chord] **1 :** an instrument of ancient origin for measuring and demonstrating the mathematical relations of musical tones that consists of a single string stretched over a sounding board and a movable bridge set on a graduated scale — called also *sonometer* **2 :** an instrument of the late middle ages similar to the single-string monochord but having added strings for sounding chords **3 :** TRUMPET MARINE
**mono·chorial** \¦== *at* MONO- +\ *also* **mono·chorionic** \"+\ *adj* [*mon-* + *chorial* or *chorionic*] *of twins* **:** sharing or developed with a common chorion
**mono·chro·ic** \"+¦krōik\ *adj* [*mon-* + *-chroic*] **:** MONOCHROMATIC
**mono·chro·mat** \¦==¦krō,mat, '==,krō,mat\ *n* -S [L *monochromatos* consisting of one color, fr. Gk *monochrōmatos*, fr. *mon-* + *chrōmat-, chrōma* color — more at CHROMATIC] **1 :** one unable to perceive colors **:** one who responds only to brilliance and sees all colors as tones of gray **:** a completely color-blind individual — compare DICHROMAT, TRICHROMAT **2 :** an optical part (as a microscope objective) that is used only in a limited wavelength range **3 :** a monochromatic filter
**mono·chromatic** \"+\ *adj* [L *monochromatos* + E *-ic*] **1 :** having or consisting of one color or hue **2 :** consisting of radiation of a single wavelength or of a very small range of wave lengths **3 a :** of, relating to, or exhibiting monochromatism **b :** having the characteristics of a monochromat — **mono·chromatically** \"+\ *adv* — **mono·chromaticity** \"+\ *n* -ES
**monochromatic illuminator** *n* **:** MONOCHROMATOR
**mono·chromatism** \"+\ *also* **mono·chro·ma·sy** \,==+'krōməsē\ *n, pl* **monochromatisms** *also* **monochromasies** **:** complete color blindness in which all colors appear as shades of gray — compare TRICHROMATISM
**mono·chromatize** \¦== *at* MONO- +\ *vt* [*monochromatic* + *ize*] **:** to make monochromatic
**mono·chro·ma·tor** \¦==+¦krō,mād·ə(r)\ *n* -S [*monochromatic illuminator*] **:** a spectroscope modified by replacing the eyepiece with a narrow slit parallel to the original slit of the instrument in order to isolate for use a narrow portion of the spectrum
¹**mono·chrome** \'==,krōm\ *n* [ML *monochroma*, fr. L, fem. of *monochromos* of one color, fr. Gk *monochrōmos*, fr. *mon-* + *-chrōmos* -chrome] **1 :** a painting or drawing in a single hue **2 :** a photograph made with a single hue **3 :** MONOCHROMY
²**monochrome** \"\ *adj* **1 :** of, relating to, or made with a single color or hue **2** *of pottery* **:** painted a usu. dark color that contrasts with the usu. light color of the body clay — compare POLYCHROME **3 :** METACHROME 2
**mono·chro·mic** \¦==¦krōmik\ *also* **mono·chro·mi·cal** \-məkəl\ *adj* [¹*monochrome* + *-ic, -ical*] **:** MONOCHROME 1 — **mono·chro·mi·cal·ly** \-mək(ə)lē\ *adv*
**mono·chrom·ist** \'==,krōməst\ *n* -S **:** an artist in monochrome; *also* **:** an advocate of its use
**mono·chro·mous** \==¦krōməs\ *adj* [L *monochromos* consisting of one color — more at MONOCHROME] **:** MONOCHROME 1
**mono·chro·my** \'==,krōmē\ *n* -ES [¹*monochrome* + *-y*] **:** the art or process of producing monochromes
**mo·noch·ro·nous** \mə'näkrənəs\ *adj* [LL *monochronos*, fr. Gk, fr. *mon-* + *-chronos* -chronous] **:** MONOSEMIC
**mono·ciliated** \¦== *at* MONO- +\ *adj* [*mon-* + *ciliated*] **:** UNIFLAGELLATE
**mon·o·cle** \'mänəkəl, -nēk-\ *n* -S [F, fr. LL *monoculus* having one eye, fr. *mon-* + *oculus* eye — more at EYE] **:** an eyeglass for one eye
**mon·o·cled** \-kəld\ *adj* **:** wearing a monocle
**mon·o·cleid** *also* **mono·cleide** \'mänə,klīd, 'mōn-\ *n* -S [*mon-* + Gk *kleid-, kleis* key — more at CLOSE] **:** a cabinet or desk in which all the drawers are locked simultaneously by one key

monocle

¹**mono·cli·nal** \¦== *at* MONO- +¦klīnᵊl\ *adj* [*mon-* + *-clinal*] **:** of or relating to a monocline **:** having a single oblique inclination ⟨~ fold⟩ ⟨~ flexure⟩
²**monoclinal** \"\ *n* -S **:** a monoclinal fold
**mono·cli·nal·ly** \-nᵊlē, -li\ *adv* **:** in a monoclinal manner **:** so as to be monoclinal
**mono·cline** \'==,klīn\ *n* -S [*mon-* + *-cline*] **:** a geologic structure in which the strata are all inclined in the same direction at a uniform angle of dip — compare HOMOCLINE
**mono·clin·ic** \¦==¦klinik\ *adj* [ISV *mon-* + *-clinic*] *crystallog* **:** having one oblique intersection of the axes
**monoclinic system** *n* **:** a crystal system characterized by three unequal axes with one oblique intersection — see CRYSTAL SYSTEM illustration
**mono·clin·ism** \'==,klī,nizəm\ *n* -S [ISV *mon-* + *-clinism*] **:** the condition of being monoclinous
**mono·cli·no·met·ric** \¦==¦klīnō¦me·trik\ *adj* [*monocline* + *-o-* + *-metric*] **:** MONOCLINIC
**mono·cli·nous** \¦==¦klīnəs\ *adj* [NL *monoclinus*, fr. *mon-* + *-clinus* -clinous] **:** having the stamens and pistils in the same flower — compare DICLINOUS
**mono·clo·ni·us** \,==¦klōnēəs\ *n, cap* [NL, fr. *mon-* + *-clonius* (fr. Gk *klōnion*, dim. of *klōn* twig); akin to Gk *klan* to break — more at HALT] **:** a genus of ceratopsian dinosaurs with a large nasal horn found in the Upper Cretaceous of No. America
**mono·coque** \'==,kōk, -,käk\ *n* -S *often attrib* [F *monocoque*, fr. *mon-* + *coque* shell, fr. L *coccum* excrescence on a tree — more at COAK] **1 :** an aircraft structure in which the stressed outer skin (as of metal or plywood) carries all or a major portion of the torsional and bending stresses ⟨~ fuselage⟩ **2 :** the structure of a vehicle (as a motor truck, trailer, or railroad car) in which the body is integral with and shares the stresses with the chassis ⟨~ construction⟩
**mono·cot** \'==,kät\ *or* **mono·cot·yl** \¦==+\ *n* -S [by shortening] **:** MONOCOTYLEDON
**mon·o·cot·y·le·don** \¦==+\ *n* [NL *Monocotyledoneae*] **:** a plant of the subclass Monocotyledoneae — compare DICOTYLEDON
**mono·cot·y·le·do·ne·ae** \,==,käd·ᵊlə'dōnē,ē\ *n pl, cap* [NL, alter. of *Monocotyledones*, fr. *mon-* + *cotyledones*, pl. of *cotyledon*] **:** a subclass of Angiospermae comprising seed plants (as grasses and lilies) that produce an embryo with a single cotyledon and have usu. parallel-veined leaves, stems without central pith or annual rings and with the vascular strands scattered throughout the ground tissue, and floral organs usu. arranged in cycles of three or six, including some chiefly tropical arborescent plants (as the palms), but being chiefly herbaceous in habit — compare DICOTYLEDONEAE
**mono·cot·y·le·do·nes** \-,käd·ᵊl'ēdᵊn,ēz\ *syn of* MONOCOTYLEDONEAE
**mono·cotyledonous** \¦==+\ *adj* [NL *Monocotyledoneae* + E *-ous*] **:** of, relating to, or characteristic of the Monocotyledoneae; *often* **:** having a single cotyledon — contrasted with *dicotyledonous*; compare POLYCOTYLEDONOUS
**mo·noc·ra·cy** \mə'näkrəsē, -si\ *n* -ES [*mon-* + *-cracy*] **:** government by a single person **:** undivided rule **:** AUTOCRACY
**mono·crat** \'== *at* MONO- + ,krat\ *n* -S [*mon-* + *-crat*] **1 :** one who governs alone **:** AUTOCRAT **2 :** one who favors monocracy — **mono·crat·ic** \¦==¦krad·ik\ *adj*

**mono·crotaline** \¦==+\ *n* -s [*mon-* + NL *Crotalaria* + E *-ine*] **:** a poisonous crystalline alkaloid $C_{16}H_{23}NO_6$ found in some plants of the genus *Crotalaria* (as *C. spectabilis*)

**mono·crot·ic** \¦==¦kräd·ik\ *adj* [*mon-* + *-crotic*] *of the pulse* **:** having a simple beat and forming a smooth single-crested curve on a sphygmogram — compare DICROTIC, POLYCROTIC

**¹mo·noc·u·lar** \mə'näkyələ(r)\ *adj* [LL *monoculus* having one eye + E *-ar* — more at MONOCLE] **1 :** of, involving, or affecting a single eye ⟨a ~ cataract⟩ **2 :** relating or adapted to the use of only one eye ⟨~ vision⟩ ⟨a ~ microscope⟩ — **mo·noc·u·lar·ly** *adv*

**²monocular** \"\ *n* **:** a monocular device (as a microscope or a field glass)

**mo·noc·u·lous** \-ləs\ *adj* [LL *monoculus* having one eye] **:** MONOCULAR

**mono·cultural** \¦== *at* MONO-+\ *adj* **:** of or relating to monoculture

**mono·culture** \"+\ *n* [*mon-* + *culture*] **:** the cultivation of a single product (as wheat or wool) to the exclusion of other possible uses of the land

**mono·cycle** \'==+,sīkəl\ *n* [*mon-* + *-cycle* (as in *bicycle*)] **:** a one-wheeled vehicle propelled by its rider — compare UNICYCLE

monocular

**mono·cyclic** \¦==+\ *adj* [ISV *mon-* + *cyclic*] **1 :** arranged in or consisting of one whorl or circle ⟨the floral organs of many plants are ~⟩ **2 :** containing one ring in the molecular structure ⟨a ~ terpene⟩ **3 :** having a single annual maximum of population — used chiefly of planktonic organisms — **mono·cy·cly** \'==,sīklē\ *n* -ES

**mono·cyc·li·ca** \¦==+'siklәkə\ *n pl, cap* [NL, fr. *mon-* + L *cyclica*, neut. pl. of *cyclicus* cyclic — more at CYCLIC] *in some classifications* **:** a division of Crinoidea comprising forms in which the cup of the calyx has a single basal series of ossicles

**mono·cystic** \¦== *at* MONO-+\ *adj* [*mon-* + *cystic*] **1 :** consisting of or having a single cyst **2 :** of or relating to the genus *Monocystis*

**mono·cys·tid** \,=='sistəd\ *adj* [NL *Monocystid-*, *Monocystis* & *Monocystidae*] **:** of or relating to the genus *Monocystis* or the family Monocystidae

**mono·cys·tid·ea** \-(,)si'stidēə\ [NL, fr. *Monocystid-*, *Monocystis*] *syn of* ACEPHALINA

**mono·cys·tis** \-'sistəs\ *n, cap* [NL, fr. *mon-* + *-cystis*] **:** a genus (the type of the family Monocystidae) of acephaline gregarines not having the protoplasm divided into segments by septa and including internal parasites of invertebrates (as *M. agilis* of the reproductive system of earthworms)

**mono·cyte** \'==,sīt\ *n* -s [ISV *mon-* + *-cyte*] **:** a large sluggish phagocytic leukocyte with an oval or horseshoe-shaped nucleus having a chromatin network and with basophilic cytoplasm containing faint eosinophile granulations — **mono·cyt·ic** \¦==¦sid·ik\ *adj* — **mono·cy·toid** \-¦sī,tȯid\ *adj*

**monocytic leukemia** *n* **:** leukemia characterized by the presence of large numbers of monocytes in the circulating blood

**mono·cy·to·pe·nia** \,==,sīd·ə'pēnēə\ *n* -s [NL, fr. ISV *monocyte* + NL *-o-* + *-penia*] **:** a deficiency in circulating monocytes

**mono·cy·to·poi·e·sis** \-,pȯi'ēsəs\ *n* [NL, fr. ISV *monocyte* + NL *-o-* + *-poiesis*] **:** formation of monocytes

**mono·cy·to·poi·et·ic** \¦==¦==+¦ed·ik\ *adj* [*monocyte* + *-o-* + *-poietic*] **:** of or relating to monocytopoiesis

**mono·cy·to·sis** \,==sī'tōsəs\ *n, pl* **monocyto·ses** \-,sēz\ [NL, fr. ISV *monocyte* + NL *-osis*] **:** an abnormal increase in the number of monocytes in the circulating blood; *specif* **:** BLUE COMB — compare GRANULOCYTOSIS, LYMPHOCYTOSIS

**mono·dac·tyle** \¦==¦daktəl\ *adj* [F, fr. Gk *monodaktylos* having one toe] **:** MONODACTYLOUS

**mono·dac·tyl·ism** \,=='daktə,lizəm\ *or* **mono·dac·ty·ly** \-lē\ *n, pl* **monodactylisms** *or* **monodactylies :** the condition of being monodactylous

**mono·dac·ty·lous** \¦==¦daktələs\ *adj* [Gk *monodaktylos* having one toe, fr. *mon-* + *daktylos* finger, toe] **1 :** having one digit or claw **2 :** SUBCHELATE 2

**mono·delph** *or* **mona·delph** \'==,delf\ *n* -s [*monodelph* fr. NL *Monodelphia*; *monadelph* alter. of *monodelph*] **:** EUTHERIAN

**mono·del·phia** \,=='delfēə\ *or* **mono·del·phes** \-,fēz\ [NL, fr. *mon-* + *-delphia* or *-delphes* (fr. Gk *delphys* womb) — more at DOLPHIN] *syn of* EUTHERIA

**mono·del·phi·an** *or* **mona·del·phi·an** \¦==¦delfēən\ *adj or n* [*monodelphian* fr. NL *Monodelphia* + E *-an*; *monadelphian* alter. of *monodelphian*] **:** EUTHERIAN

**mono·del·phic** \-fik\ *also* **monodel·phous** \-fəs\ *adj* [*mon-* + Gk *delphys* womb + E *-ic* or *-ous*] **1 :** having a single female genital tract **2** [NL *Monodelphia* + E *-ic* or *-ous*] **:** EUTHERIAN

**mono·dermic** \¦== *at* MONO- + \ *adj* [*mon-* + *dermic*] **:** of or relating to a single layer of cells

**mo·nod·ic** \mə'nädik, -dēk\ *also* **mo·nod·i·cal** \-dəkəl, -dēk-\ *adj* [Gk or LGk *monōidikos*, fr. Gk *monōidia* monody + *-ikos* -ic, -ical — more at MONODY] **:** of, relating to, or of the nature of monody ⟨the beautiful Hindu melodies, built upon various scales . . . are of course all ~ —Harold Brown⟩ — **mo·nod·i·cal·ly** \-d·ək(ə)lē, -dēk-, -li\ *adv*

**mono·dimetric** \¦== *at* MONO-+\ *adj* [ISV *mon-* + *dimetric*] **:** TETRAGONAL

**mono·disk** *or* **mono·disc** \¦==+\ *adj* [*mon-* + *disk, disc*] *of a scyphistoma* **:** producing but one ephyra at a time — compare POLYDISK

**mono·disperse** \"+\ *also* **mono·dispersed** \"+\ *adj* [*mon-* + *disperse* (adj.) or *dispersed*, past part. of *disperse*, v.] **:** characterized by particles of uniform size in a dispersed phase ⟨~ aerosols⟩

**mon·o·dist** \'mänədəst\ *n* -s [*monody* + *-ist*] **:** a writer, singer, or composer of monody

**mo·nod·o·mous** \mə'nädəməs\ *adj* [*mon-* + Gk *domos* house — more at TIMBER] **:** inhabiting a single nest — used of ant colonies; compare POLYDOMOUS

**mon·odon** \'mänə,dän, 'mōn-\ *n, cap* [NL, fr. *mon-* + *-odon*] **:** a genus (the type of the family Monodontidae) of arctic cetaceans comprising the narwhal

**mon·odont** \'==,dänt\ *adj* [Gk *monodont-*, *monodous*, fr. *mon-* single + *odont-*, *odous* tooth — more at TOOTH] **1** *or* **mon·odon·tal** \¦==¦däntəl\ [*monodontal* fr. Gk *monodontos* + E *-al*] **:** having only one tooth **2** *or* **monodontid** [NL *Monodont-*, *Monodon* & *Monodontidae*] **:** of or relating to the genus *Monodon* or the family Monodontidae

**mono·drama** \¦== *at* MONO- +\ *n* [*mon-* + *drama*] **1 :** a drama acted or designed as if to be acted by a single person **2 :** a dramatic representation of what passes in an individual mind **3 :** a musical drama for a solo performer — **mono·dramatic** \"+\ *adj*

**mono·dramatist** \"+\ *n* [*monodrama* + *-tist* (as in *dramatist*)] **:** a writer or composer of a monodrama

**mon·o·dy** \'mänədē, -di\ *n* -ES [ML *monodia*, fr. Gk *monōidia*, fr. *monōidos* singing alone (fr. *mon-* alone + *ōidē* song) + *-ia* *-y* — more at ODE] **1 a :** an ode sung by one voice (as by one of the actors in a Greek tragedy) **b :** a funeral song or oration **2 :** an elegy or a dirge in which a single mourner laments **3 :** an unaccompanied chant sung in unison **4 a :** the style of musical composition in which but one voice part carries a melody; *specif* **:** the solo style of the earliest operas and oratorios **b :** a melody or monodic composition; *specif* **:** a composition with but a single voice part

**mono·dynamism** \¦== *at* MONO- +\ *n* [*mon-* + *dynamism*] **:** the theory that a single force causes the various forms of activity in nature

**mo·noe·cia** \mə'nēs(h)ēə\ *n pl, cap* [NL, fr. *mon-* + *-oecia*] *in former classifications* **:** a class of plants comprising all monoecious flowering plants — **mo·noe·cian** \-s(h)ēən, -shən\ *adj*

**¹mo·noe·cious** *or* **mo·ne·cious** \-shəs\ *adj* [NL *Monoecia* + E *-ous*] **1 :** having male and female sex organs in the same individual **:** HERMAPHRODITIC **2 :** having pistillate and staminate flowers on the same plant — **mo·noe·cious·ly** \-lē\ *adv*

**²monoecious** *var of* MONOICOUS

**mo·noe·cism** \mə'nē,sizəm\ *or* **monoe·cy** \'mä,nēsē, 'mō,-\ *n, pl* **monoecisms** *or* **monoecies** [NL *Monoecia* + E *-ism* or *-y*] **:** the condition of being monoecious

**mono·embryony** \¦== *at* MONO- +\ *var of* MONEMBRYONY

**mono·energetic** \"+\ *adj* [*mon-* + *energetic*] **1 :** having equal energy — used of particles or radiation quanta **2 :** composed of monoenergetic particles or radiation quanta

**mono·er·gic** \"+¦ərjik\ *also* **mon·er·gic** \(')män, (')mōn+\ *adj* [*mon-* + *-ergic* (fr. *-ergy* + *-ic*)] **:** MONOENERGETIC

**mono·ester** \¦== *at* MONO- +\ *n* [*mon-* + *ester*] **:** an ester (as of a dibasic acid) containing only one ester group ⟨salts of ~s of sulfuric acid⟩

**monoestrous** *var of* MONESTROUS

**mono·ethanolamine** \¦== *at* MONO- +\ *n* [*mon-* + *ethanolamine*] **:** ETHANOLAMINE 1

**mono·ethyl** \"+\ *adj* [*mon-* + *ethyl*] **:** containing one ethyl group esp. in place of hydrogen

**mono·ethylamine** \"+\ *n* [*mon-* + *ethylamine*] **:** ETHYLAMINE 1

**mono·factorial** \"+\ *adj* [*mon-* + *factorial*] **:** MONOGENIC 1b(2)

**mono·fil** \'==+,fil\ *n* -s [by shortening] **:** MONOFILAMENT

**mono·filament** \¦== *at* MONO- +\ *n* [*mon-* + *filament*] **:** a single untwisted synthetic filament (as of nylon) made in varying diameters for use in textiles, hosiery, and screens or as bristles, fishing lines, and sutures — compare MULTIFILAMENT

**mono·flagellate** \"+\ *adj* [*mon-* + *flagellate*] **:** UNIFLAGELLATE

**mono·fuel** \"+\ *n* [*mon-* + *fuel*] **:** a substance (as nitromethane) that contains an oxidizer (as the nitro group) capable of burning the remainder of the substance without recourse to an external oxidizer **:** MONOPROPELLANT

**mono·gamic** \"+¦gamik\ *adj* [*monogamy* + *-ic*] **:** MONOGAMOUS

**mo·nog·a·mist** \mə'nägəməst\ *n* -s [*monogamy* + *-ist*] **:** one who practices or upholds monogamy

**mo·nog·a·mis·tic** \¦==¦mistik\ *adj* **:** of or relating to monogamists or monogamy **:** upholding monogamy

**mo·nog·a·mous** \mə'nägəməs\ *adj* [LL *monogamus* marrying once, fr. Gk *monogamos*, fr. *mon-* + *gamos* marriage — more at BIGAMY] **:** of or relating to monogamy **:** upholding or practicing monogamy ⟨a ~ community⟩ ⟨~ doctrines⟩ — **mo·nog·a·mous·ly** *adv* — **mo·nog·a·mous·ness** *n* -ES

**mo·nog·a·my** \-mē, -mi\ *n* -ES [F *monogamie*, fr. LL *monogamia*, fr. Gk, fr. *monogamos* + *-ia* -y] **1 :** single marriage: **a :** one marriage only during life — compare DIGAMY **b :** marriage with but one person at a time — compare BIGAMY, POLYGAMY **2 :** the condition of having a single mate at any one time

**mono·ganglionic** \¦== *at* MONO- +\ *adj* [*mon-* + *ganglionic*] **:** having one ganglion

**mono·gastric** \"+\ *adj* [F *monogastrique*, fr. *mon-* + *gastrique* gastric, fr. E *gastric*] **1 :** having one digestive cavity **2** *of a muscle* **:** having but one venter

**mo·nog·e·na** \mə'näjənə\ *syn of* MONOGENEA

**mono·gene** \¦== *at* MONO- + ¦jēn\ *adj* [ISV *mon-* + Gk *-genēs* born; prob. orig. formed as G *monogen* — more at -GEN] *geol* **:** built up by a single eruption or by an uninterrupted succession of eruptions

**mono·ge·nea** \,==¦jēnēə\ *n pl, cap* [NL, fr. *mon-* + Gk *genea* race, descent — more at KIN] **:** a subclass of Trematoda comprising worms having a direct life cycle and ordinarily living as ectoparasites on a single fish host throughout the entire cycle — compare ASPIDOGASTREA, DIGENEA — **mono·ge·nean** \¦==¦nēən, -nyən\ *adj*

**mono·ge·ne·i·ty** \,==jə'nēəd·ē, -ətē, -i\ *n* -ES [*monogeneous* + *-ity*] **:** the quality or state of being monogeneous

**mono·ge·neous** \¦== *at* MONO- + ¦jēnēəs, -nyəs\ *adj* [*mon-* + Gk *genea* + E *-ous*] **1 :** developing without cyclic change of form — used esp. of the Monogenea **2 :** MONOGENOUS

**mono·genesis** \"+\ *n* [NL, fr. *mon-* + *genesis*] **:** unity of origin; *specif* **:** the presumed origin of all life from one original entity or cell

**mono·gen·e·sy** \,==¦jenəsē\ *n* -ES [NL *monogenesia*, fr. *mon-* + *-genesia*] **:** MONOGENISM

**mono·genetic** \¦== *at* MONO- +\ *adj* [*mon-* + *-genetic*] **1 :** relating to or involving monogenesis **2 :** resulting from one process of formation — used of a mountain range **3 :** of or relating to the Monogenea **:** MONOGENEAN **4** *of a dye* **:** yielding only one color or shade under any conditions of application

**mono·ge·net·i·ca** \,==jə'ned·əkə\ [NL, fr. ISV *monogenetic*] *syn of* MONOGENEA

**mono·gen·ic** \¦==¦jenik\ *adj* [ISV *mon-* + *-genic*] **1 :** having a single or a common origin: as **a :** relating to an igneous rock composed of but a single mineral species — compare MONOMICT **b** (1) **:** of or relating to monogenesis **:** MONOGENETIC (2) **:** of, relating to, or controlled by a single gene or by either of an allelic pair of genes **:** of or relating to a unit character **c :** descended from one pair **:** characterized by monogenism — compare POLYGENIC **2 :** producing offspring of one sex only — **mono·gen·i·cal·ly** \-nək(ə)lē\ *adv*

**mo·nog·e·nism** \mə'näjə,nizəm\ *n* -s [ISV *mon-* + *-gen* + *-ism*] **:** the doctrine or belief that all human races have descended from a single created pair or from a common ancestral type — compare POLYGENISM

**mo·nog·e·nist** \-,nəst\ *n* -s [ISV *mon-* + *-gen* + *-ist*] **:** one who accepts the doctrine of monogenism

**mo·nog·e·nis·tic** \¦==¦nistik\ *adj* **:** of or relating to monogenism or monogenists

**mo·nog·e·nous** \mə'näjənəs\ *adj* [ISV *mon-* + *-genous*] **:** of or relating to monogenesis

**mo·nog·e·ny** \-nē, -ni\ *n* -ES [ISV *mon-* + *-geny*] **1 a :** the descent of man from a single created pair — compare POLYGENY **b :** MONOGENISM **2** [G *monogenie*, fr. *mono-* mon- + *-genie* -geny] **:** MONOGONY

**¹mono·glot** \'mänə,glät, *usu* -läd·+V\ *adj* [*mon-* + *-glot*] **:** familiar with, making use of, or written in a single language — compare POLYGLOT

**²monoglot** \"\ *n* -s **:** a person familiar with only one language **:** MONOLINGUAL

**mono·glyceride** \¦== *at* MONO- +\ *n* [*mon-* + *-glyceride*] **:** an ester of glycerol in which only one of the three hydroxyl groups is esterified either in the alpha- or 1-position or in the beta- or 2-position

**mono·go·nad·ic** \¦==gō¦nadik\ *adj* [*mon-* + *gonad* + *-ic*] *of a tapeworm* **:** having a single set of reproductive organs in each segment

**mono·go·neu·tic** \¦==gō'n(y)üd·ik\ *adj* [*mon-* + (assumed) Gk *goneutos* (verbal of *goneuein* to produce, beget, fr. *goneus* one that begets, progenitor, father, fr. *gonos* offspring) + E *-ic* — more at GON-] **:** having only one brood in a year

**mono·go·non·ta** \,==gō'näntə\ *n pl, cap* [NL, fr. *mon-* + *gon-* + Gk *-onta* (neut. pl. part. ending)] **:** a large order of Rotifera comprising forms with a single ovary and lateral antennae

**mono·gono·por·ic** \¦==¦gänə¦pȯrik\ *or* **mono·go·nop·o·rous** \-,gə'näpərəs\ *adj* [*mon-* + *gon-* + Gk *poros* passage + E *-ic* or *-ous*] **:** having a single genital opening for both male and female organs

**mo·nog·o·ny** \mə'nägənē, -ni\ *n* -ES [*mon-* + *-gony*] **:** asexual reproduction

**¹mono·gram** \'mänə,gram, -aa(ə)m\ *n* [LL *monogrammus*, fr. L, adj., consisting of lines only, sketched, fr. *mon-* + *-grammus* (fr. Gk *grammē* line, fr. *graphein* to write) — more at CARVE] *archaic* **:** a picture in lines only **:** OUTLINE, SKETCH

**²monogram** \"\ *n* [LL *monogramma*, fr. Gk *mon-* + Gk *gramma* letter — more at GRAM] **:** a character or cipher composed of two or more letters interwoven or combined usu. representing a name or a part of it and often used (as on seals, ornamental pins and rings, linens) to show personal ownership — compare CALLIGRAM

monograms

**³monogram** \"\ *vt* **monogrammed; monogrammed; monogramming; monograms :** to mark with a monogram ⟨always *monogrammed* her handkerchiefs⟩

**mono·gram·mat·ic** \¦==grə¦mad·ik\ *also* **mono·gram·mat·i·cal** \-d·əkəl\ *adj* [LL *monogrammat-*, *monogramma* + E *-ic*] **:** of, relating to, or resembling a monogram

**mono·gram·mic** \¦==¦gramik\ *adj* [²*monogram* + *-ic*] **:** MONOGRAMMATIC

**¹mono·graph** \'==,graf, -aa(ə)f, -aif, -äf\ *n* [*mon-* + *-graph*] **1 a :** a special treatise on a particular subject in natural history **b :** a learned detailed thoroughly documented treatise covering exhaustively a small area of a field of learning ⟨this ~ covers the development of intravenous anesthesia from 1872 —*Jour. Amer. Med. Assoc.*⟩ ⟨his ~ comprises an essay analyzing Irish bookbinding —*Times Lit. Supp.*⟩ **2 :** a written account of a single thing: as **a :** a biographical study ⟨in every language of Europe there are ~s . . . of the man who so affected Christendom and remade it —Hilaire Belloc⟩ **b :** a collection of plates (as reproductions of paintings) showing the work of a single artist and usu. accompanied by biographical or critical text **syn** see DISCOURSE

**²monograph** \"\ *vt* **:** to make a monograph on **:** discuss in a monograph

**mo·nog·ra·pher** \mə'nägrəfə(r)\ *n* -s [NL *monographus* monographer (fr. *mon-* + *-graphus*, fr. Gk *graphein* to write) + E *-er*] **:** one who prepares a monograph

**mono·graph·ic** \¦mänə¦grafik\ *also* **mono·graph·i·cal** \-fəkəl\ *adj* [*monograph* + *-ic*, *-ical*] **1 :** of, relating to, or characteristic of a monograph ⟨the eruditely written ~ volume —M.M.Willey⟩ ⟨~ studies of narrowly specialized topics —A.T.Cutler⟩ **2** [*mon-* + *-graphic*] *in cryptography* **:** involving one letter at a time ⟨~ substitution⟩ — **mono·graph·i·cal·ly** \-fək(ə)lē\ *adv*

**mo·nog·ra·phist** \mə'nägrəfəst\ *n* -s [*monograph* & *monography* + *-ist*] **:** MONOGRAPHER ⟨the historical ~ —F.T.Marsh⟩

**mo·nog·ra·phy** \-fē\ *n* -ES [NL *monographia*, fr. *mon-* + *-graphia* -graphy] **:** MONOGRAPH ⟨*monographies* on the great educators —*Amer. Council of Learned Soc. Newsletter*⟩

**¹mono·grap·tid** \¦== *at* MONO- + ¦graptəd\ *adj* [NL *Monograptus* + E *-id*] **:** of or relating to the genus *Monograptus* or the family Monograptidae

**²monograptid** \"\ *n* -s **:** a graptolite of the genus *Monograptus* or the family Monograptidae

**mono·grap·tus** \,=='taptəs\ *n, cap* [NL, fr. *mon-* + Gk *graptos* engraved, written, fr. *graphein* to write — more at CARVE] **:** a genus (the type of the family Monograptidae) of graptolites with a single row of overlapping thecae

**mono·gyn·ic** \¦==¦jinik\ *also* **mono·gyn·i·ous** \-nēəs\ *adj* [*monogyny* + *-ic* or *-ous*] **:** MONOGYNOUS

**mo·nog·y·nist** \mə'näjənəst\ *n* -s [*monogyny* + *-ist*] **:** one who believes in or practices monogyny

**mono·gy·noe·cial** \¦== *at* MONO- + jə¦nēshəl, gə¦-\ *adj* [*mon-* + NL *gynoecium* + E *-al*] **:** formed from a single pistil

**mo·nog·y·nous** \mə'näjənəs\ *adj* [*mon-* + *-gynous*] **1 :** having one pistil **2 a :** of, relating to, or living in monogyny **:** having but one wife **b :** having only one female mate **3 :** having a single functional female in the colony — used of social insects ⟨the honeybee is a typical ~ insect⟩

**mo·nog·y·ny** \-nē, -ni\ *n* -ES [ISV *mon-* + *-gyny*] **1 :** the quality or state of being monogynous; *specif* **:** the state or custom of having only one wife at a time — compare POLYGYNY **2 :** the state or custom of having one chief, head, or jural wife together with other consorts

**mono·haploid** \¦== *at* MONO- +\ *adj* [*mon-* + *haploid*] **:** having a haploid chromosome number containing a single genome — used of a diploid; compare POLYHAPLOID

**mono·hybrid** \"+\ *n* [*mon-* + *hybrid*] **:** an individual or strain heterozygous for one specified factor or gene

**mono·hydrate** \"+\ *n* [ISV *mon-* + *hydrate*] **:** a hydrate containing one molecule of water — **mono·hydrated** \"+\ *adj*

**mono·hy·dric** \"+¦hīdrik\ *adj* [*mon-* + *-hydric*] **1** *archaic* **:** containing one atom of acid hydrogen **2 :** MONOHYDROXY — used esp. of alcohols and phenols

**mono·hydroxy** \"+\ *adj* [ISV *monohydroxy-*, fr. *mon-* + *hydroxy-*] **:** containing one hydroxyl group in the molecule

**mo·noi·cous** \mə'nȯikəs\ *also* **mo·noe·cious** \-nēshəs\ *adj* [*mon-* + *-oicous* (fr. Gk *oikos* house + E *-ous*) — more at VICINITY] **:** having archegonia and antheridia on different branches of the same plant — compare AUTOICOUS, DIOICOUS, HETEROICOUS, PAROICOUS, POLYOICOUS, SYNOICOUS

**mono·ide·ism** \,== *at* MONO- + 'īdē,izəm\ *n* -s [ISV *mon-* + *idea* + *-ism*] **:** a state of prolonged absorption in a single idea (as in mental depression, trance, hypnosis) — opposed to *polyideism*

**mono·ide·is·tic** \¦==¦==¦istik\ *adj* [ISV *mon-* + *idea* + *-istic*] **:** of, relating to, or characterized by monoideism

**mono·ion** \¦== *at* MONO- +\ *n* [*mon-* + *ion*] **:** an ion having only one charge

**mono·isotopic** \"+\ *adj* [*mon-* + *isotopic*] **:** consisting of a single isotope — used of an element

**mono·ketone** \"+\ *n* [*mon-* + *ketone*] **:** a chemical compound containing one ketonic carbonyl group

**mo·nol·a·ter** \mə'näləd·ə(r)\ *also* **mo·nol·a·trist** \-lətrəst\ *n* -s [*monolatry* + *-er* or *-ist*] **:** one whose religious practices are typified by monolatry

**mo·nol·a·trous** \-ətrəs\ *adj* [*monolatry* + *-ous*] **:** of or relating to monolatry

**mo·nol·a·try** \-ətrē\ *n* -s [*mon-* + *-latry*] **:** HENOTHEISM

**mono·layer** \¦== *at* MONO- +\ *n* [*mon-* + *layer*] **:** a surface layer that is one molecule in thickness **:** a monomolecular layer or film ⟨a ~ of stearic acid⟩

**¹mono·line** \"+\ *adj* [*mon-* + *line* (n.)] **:** having or relating to a single line: as **a :** writing only one main branch of insurance — compare MULTIPLE-LINE **b :** MONORAIL

**²monoline** \"\ *n* [*mon-* + *line*] **:** MONORAIL

**¹mono·lingual** \¦== *at* MONO- +\ *adj* [*mon-* + *lingual*] **:** expressed in or knowing or using only one language

**²monolingual** \"\ *n* -s **:** a person who understands and speaks only one language

**mono·literal** \"+\ *adj* [*mon-* + *literal*] **1 :** consisting of one letter **2 a :** using single letters as cipher equivalents **b :** MONOGRAPHIC — **mono·literally** \"+\ *adv*

**¹mono·lith** \'mänᵊl,ith, 'mōn-\ *n* -s [F *monolithe*, fr. *monolithe*, adj., monolithic, fr. L *monolithus*, fr. Gk *monolithos*, fr. *mon-* + *lithos* stone] **1 a** (1) **:** a single great stone often in the form of an obelisk or column ⟨the 120-ton ~s on three sides of the choir altar —*Amer. Guide Series: Maine*⟩ — compare MEGALITH (2) **:** something resembling a monolith and usu. having tremendous size or strength **:** COLOSSUS ⟨weld together even more tightly the parallel ~s of party and state —*Time*⟩ ⟨his friends see him as a pillar of determination; his enemies consider him a thick-skinned ~ —*Newsweek*⟩ **b** (1) **:** a single large block of concrete serving a specific purpose (2) **:** one of many large blocks cast in place to form gravity-type concrete dams **2 :** a mountain or large hill apparently composed of one kind of rock usu. of a coarse-grained igneous rock **3 :** a column of soil several feet deep removed as a unit

**²monolith** \"\ *adj* [F *monolithe*] **:** MONOLITHIC

**mono·lith·ic** \¦==¦ithik, -thēk\ *adj* [F *monolithe* or L *monolithus* monolithic + E *-ic*] **1 a :** formed or carved from a single block of stone **b :** made up of monoliths ⟨Stonehenge is a ~ monument⟩ **2 a :** consisting of one stone — used of the shaft of a column not built up of drums **b :** having a type of architecture or construction depending upon rock cutting or excavation from the solid rock **3 a** *of a concrete structure* **:** cast as a single piece **b** *of a concrete floor or pavement* **:** having a special quality surface layer which is applied while the bottom layer is still green so that both layers harden to form an integral unit **4 :** constituting one massive undifferentiated whole exhibiting solid uniformity often without diversity or variability ⟨have rejected the idea of the domination of the single ~ party —John Dewey⟩ ⟨a ~ commercial enterprise —*Atlantic*⟩

**mono·lith·ism** \'==,i,thizəm\ *n* -s [F *monolithisme*, fr. *monolithe* + *-isme* -ism] **:** the quality or state of being monolithic ⟨where political ~ inevitably leads —*Saturday Rev.*⟩

**mono·lithologic** \¦== *at* MONO- +\ *adj* [*mon-* + *lithologic*] **:** composed of but one kind of rock

**mono·lobular** \"+\ *adj* [*mon-* + *lobular*] **:** having one lobe

**mono·locular** \"+\ *adj* [ISV *mon-* + *locular*] **:** UNILOCULAR

**mono·log·ic** \¦mänᵊl¦äjik\ *or* **mono·log·i·cal** \-jəkəl\ *adj* [*monology* + *-ic*, *-ical*] **:** of, relating to, or characteristic of a monologue ⟨voice . . . mounted from a ~ mutter to a high-tensioned harangue —L.C.Douglas⟩

**mo·nol·o·gist** \mə'näləjəst, *in sense 3* " *also* 'mänᵊl,ȯgə- *or* -ᵊl,äg- *sometimes* 'mōnᵊl,-\ *n* -s **1 :** one who soliloquizes **2 :** one who monopolizes conversation **3 :** a performer of monologues ⟨greatest ~s in modern minstrelsy —C.F.Witthe⟩

**mo·nol·o·gize** \mə'nälə,jīz *also* 'mänᵊl,ä,gīz *or* -ᵊl,ȯ- *sometimes* 'mōnᵊl,-\ *also* **mon·o·logu·ize** \'==,=,=\ *vi* -ED/-ING/-S [*monology* + *-ize*] **:** to utter a monologue **:** SOLILOQUIZE

**¹mon·o·logue** *also* **mon·o·log** \ˈmänᵊlˌȯg *also* -ᵊlˌäg *sometimes* ˈmōnᵊl-\ *n* -s [F *monologue*, fr. *mon-* + *-logue* (as in *dialogue*) — more at DIALOGUE] **1 a :** a dramatic scene in which one person soliloquizes ⟨such passages as the ~ at the beginning of the second scene —*Manchester Guardian Weekly*⟩ **b :** a dramatic sketch performed by one actor **2 :** a literary composition written in the form of a soliloquy ⟨early poems are the ~s of a young man very isolated . . . in his genius —Stephen Spender⟩ **3 :** a long speech uttered by one person while in company with others ⟨habit of lecturing his friends in ~ —H.S.Canby⟩

**²monologue** \ˈ"\ *vi* -ED/-ING/-S **:** MONOLOGIZE ⟨at once took charge of the meeting and began to ~ —W.A.White⟩

**mon·o·logu·ist** \-gəst\ *n* -s [¹*monologue* + *-ist*] **:** MONOLOGIST

**mon·o·logu·ize** \-ˌgīz\ *vi* -ED/-ING/-S [¹*monologue* + *-ize*] **:** MONOLOGIZE

**mo·nol·o·gy** \məˈnäləjē\ *n* -ES [*mon-* + *-logy*] **1** *obs* **:** MONOLOGUE **2 :** the habit of soliloquizing

**mo·nom·a·chy** \məˈnäməkē\ *n* -ES [MF *monomachie*, fr. L *monomachia*, fr. Gk, fr. *mon-* + *-machia* -machy] **:** a combat between two persons **:** DUEL

**mono·mania** \¦==+\ *at* MONO- +\ *n* [NL, fr. *mon-* + *mania*] **1 :** mental derangement restricted to one idea or group of ideas **:** true paranoia **2 :** such concentration on a single object or idea as to suggest mental derangement

**¹mono·maniac** \ˈ"+\ *n* [*mon-* + *maniac* (n.)] **1 :** a person affected by monomania **2 :** one who has a craze ⟨a complete ~ about his beloved rockets —*Times Lit. Supp.*⟩

**²monomaniac** \ˈ"\ *or* **mono·maniacal** \ˈ"+\ *adj* [*mon-* + *maniac*, *maniacal* (adj.)] **:** relating to, characterized by, or affected with monomania

**Mono·mark** \ˈmänōˌmärk, -mȧk\ *trademark* — used for a system employed chiefly in England by which an individual or a firm may register a combination of letters or figures as an identification mark

**mono·mastigote** \¦== *at* MONO- +\ *adj* [alter. of earlier *monomastigate*, fr. *mon-* + *mastig-* + *-ate*] **:** UNIFLAGELLATE

**mono·me·nis·cous** \ˈ"+məˈniskəs\ *adj* [*mon-* + NL *meniscus* + E *-ous*] **:** having but one lens — used of a simple eye

**mono·mer** \ˈmänəmə(r), ˈmōn-\ *n* -s [ISV *mon-* + *-mer*] **:** the simple unpolymerized form of a chemical compound having relatively low molecular weight ⟨styrene, methyl methacrylate, and other ~s are polymerized in this manner —H.F.Mark⟩ — compare DIMER, POLYMER

**mono·mer·ic** \¦==ˈmerik\ *adj* **:** of, relating to, or consisting of a monomer ⟨a ~ unit . . . contains the same kinds and number of atoms as the real or hypothetical monomer —*Rubber & Rubber-Like Materials*⟩

**mo·nom·er·ous** \məˈnämərəs\ *adj* [Gk *monomerēs* of one part, fr. *mon-* + *meros* part — more at MERIT] **1 a** *of a flower* **:** having a single member in each whorl **b :** MONOCARPELLARY **2 :** having or characterized by one-jointed tarsi

**mono·metallic** \¦== *at* MONO- +\ *adj* [*mon-* + *metallic*] **1 :** consisting of or employing one metal **:** of or relating to monometallism **2 :** containing one atom of metal in the molecule ⟨~ carbonyls⟩

**monometallic balance** *n* **:** a watch or chronometer balance of nickel, steel, or alloy with an uncut rim — compare COMPENSATION BALANCE

**mono·met·al·lism** \¦== *at* MONO- + ¦med·ᵊlˌizəm, -etᵊl-\ *n* -s [ISV *mon-* + *-metallism* (as in *bimetallism*)] **1 :** the legalized use of one metal only (as gold or silver) in the standard currency of a country or as the standard of money values **2 :** the theory, belief, or practice favoring or employing a single metallic standard — compare BIMETALLISM

**mono·met·al·list** \-ᵊləst\ *n* -s [ISV *mon-* + *-metallist* (as in *bimetallist*)] **:** an advocate of monometallism

**mo·nom·e·ter** \məˈnäməd·ə(r)\ *n* [LL, fr. Gk *monometros*, fr. *mon-* + *metron* measure — more at MEASURE] **:** a verse consisting of a single metrical unit (as a foot or dipody)

**mono·methine** \¦== *at* MONO- +\ *n* [*mon-* + *methine*] **:** CYANINE 2

**mono·methyl** \ˈ"+\ *adj* [*mon-* + *methyl*] **:** containing one methyl group esp. in place of hydrogen

**mono·methylamine** \ˈ"+\ *n* [*monomethyl* + *amine*] **:** METHYLAMINE 1

**mono·methylolurea** \ˈ"+\ *n* [NL, fr. *mon-* + ISV *methylol* + NL *-urea*] **:** METHYLOLUREA a

**mono·metric** \ˈ"+\ *adj* [*mon-* + Gk *metron* measure + E *-ic* — more at MEASURE] **:** EQUIGRANULAR

**mono·metrical** \ˈ"+\ *or* **mono·metric** \ˈ"+\ *adj* [*mon-* + *metrical*, *metric*] **:** relating to or consisting of a monometer

**¹mo·no·mi·al** \məˈnōmēəl\ *n* -s [*mon-* + *-omial* (as in *binomial*)] **:** a mathematical expression consisting of a single term

**²monomial** \ˈ"\ *adj* **1 :** of or relating to monomials **2 :** consisting of a single word or term — used of the technical name of a plant or animal

**mono·mict** \ˈ== *at* MONO- + ˌmikt\ *adj* [Ger *monomikt*, fr. *mon-* + Gk *miktos* mixed, blended, fr. *misgein* to mix — more at MIX] **:** relating to a sedimentary rock composed of but a single mineral species — compare MONOGENIC 1a

**mono·mineral** \ˈ"+\ *or* **mono·min·er·al·ic** \ˈ"+¦minəˈralik\ *adj* [ISV *mon-* + *mineral*, *mineralic* (fr. ¹*mineral* + *-ic*); orig. formed as Ger *monomineralisch*] **:** composed wholly or almost wholly of a single mineral species

**mono·molecular** \¦== *at* MONO- +\ *adj* [*mon-* + *molecular*] **:** relating to or consisting of a single or simple molecule ⟨a ~ compound⟩ **:** being only one molecule thick ⟨a ~ film⟩ ⟨a ~ layer⟩ **:** UNIMOLECULAR — **mono·molecularly** \ˈ"+\ *adv*

**mono·mo·ri·um** \ˌ==ˈmōrēəm\ *n*, *cap* [NL, fr. *mon-* + Gk *morion* part, portion, dim. of *moros* lot, fate — more at MERIT] **:** a large widely distributed genus of ants including important household pests — see LITTLE BLACK ANT, PHARAOH ANT

**mono·morphemic** \¦== *at* MONO- +\ *adj* [*mon-* + *morphemic*] **:** consisting of only one morpheme ⟨*raise* is ~ but *rays* is not⟩

**mono·mor·phic** \¦==ˈmȯrfik\ *or* **mono·mor·phous** \-fəs\ *adj* [*mon-* + *-morphic*, *-morphous*] **1 :** having but a single form **:** exhibiting the same or essentially similar structure in all members — used esp. of a taxonomic group **2 a :** retaining the same form throughout various stages of development — used of an ametabolic insect **b :** having but one structural pattern — used of a primitive worker ant; compare POLYMORPHIC **3 :** producing spores of one form or kind — used of a plant

**mono·mor·phism** \ˌ==ˈ=ˌfizəm\ *n* -s **:** the quality or state of being monomorphic

**mono·my·ar·ia** \ˌ==ˌmīˈa(a)rēə\ *or* **mono·mya** \ˌ==ˈmīə\ *n pl*, *cap* [*Monomyaria*, NL, fr. *mon-* + *my-* + *-aria*; *Monomya*, NL, fr. *mon-* + *-mya*] *in some classifications* **:** a division of Lamellibranchia comprising bivalve mollusks (as the oysters, pearl oysters, and scallops) having but one adductor muscle — compare DIMYARIA — **mono·my·ar·i·an** \¦==ˌ=ˈa(a)rēən\ *adj or n*

**mon·onch** \ˈmäˌnäŋk, ˈmō,-\ *n* -s [NL *Mononchus*] **:** a worm of the genus *Mononchus*

**mo·non·chus** \məˈnäŋkəs\ *n*, *cap* [NL, fr. *mon-* + *-onchus* (modif. of Gk *onkos* barbed hook) — more at ANGLE] **:** a genus of predatory nematodes (order Chromadorida) usu. having a single pharyngeal tooth and living in fresh water and in soil where they have been estimated to number up to 300,000,000 to the acre

**mono·neural** \¦== *at* MONO- +\ *adj* [*mon-* + *neural*] *of a muscle* **:** receiving branches from but one nerve

**mo·non·ga·he·la** \məˌnäŋgəˈhēlə, -äŋg-, -hālə\ *n* -s *usu cap* [fr. *Monongahela* river valley in southwestern Pennsylvania and northern West Virginia where it was first produced] **:** American whiskey; *specif* **:** rye whiskey made in western Pennsylvania

**mono·nitrate** \¦== *at* MONO- +\ *n* [*mon-* + *nitrate*] **:** a compound containing a single nitrate group ⟨glycol ~ $HOCH_2CH_2ONO_2$⟩

**mono·nitrated** \ˈ"+\ *adj* [*mon-* + *nitrated*, past part. of *nitrate*, v.] **:** modified by the introduction of one nitro group or one nitrate group

**mono·nitration** \ˈ"+\ *n* [*mon-* + *nitration*] **:** the act or process of modifying by the introduction of one nitro group or one nitrate group

**mono·nitro** \ˈ"+\ *adj* [ISV *mononitro-*, fr. *mon-* + *nitr-*] **:** containing one nitro group in the molecule

**mon·ont** \ˈmäˌnänt, ˈmō,-\ *n* -s [*mon-* + *-ont*] **:** SCHIZONT

**¹mono·nuclear** \¦== *at* MONO- +\ *adj* [ISV *mon-* + *nuclear*] **1 :** having only one nucleus **2 :** MONOCYCLIC 2 ⟨~ aromatic compounds⟩

**²mononuclear** \ˈ"\ *n* -s [ISV, fr. ¹*mononuclear*] **:** a mononuclear cell; *esp* **:** MONOCYTE

**mono·nucleated** \ˈ"+\ *adj* [*mon-* + *nucleated*] **:** MONONUCLEAR

**mono·nu·cle·o·sis** \ˌ==ˌn(y)üklēˈōsəs\ *n*, *pl* **mononucleo·ses** \-ˌsēz\ [NL, fr. ISV ²*mononuclear* + NL *-osis*] **1 :** an abnormal increase in the number of agranulocytes in the circulating blood; *specif* **:** INFECTIOUS MONONUCLEOSIS **2 :** MONOCYTOSIS

**mono·nucleotide** \¦== *at* MONO- +\ *n* [*mon-* + *nucleotide*] **:** a nucleotide derived from one molecule each of a nitrogen base, a sugar, and phosphoric acid

**mon·on·y·chous** \məˈnänəkəs, (ˈ)mäˈnä-, (ˈ)mōˈnä-; ¦mänəˈnikəs, ¦mōn-\ *adj* [*mon-* + *onych-* + *-ous*] **:** having an uncleft claw — used of an insect

**mono·olefin** \¦== *at* MONO- +\ *n* [*mon-* + *olefin*] **:** ALKENE — **mono·olefinic** \ˈ"+\ *adj*

**mono·ou·sian** \¦== *at* MONO- +¦üzēən, -üsēən, -üzh(ē)ən, -üsh(ē)ən\ *or* **mono·ou·sious** \-əs\ *adj* [*monoousian* fr. LGk *monoousios* monoousian (fr. Gk *mon-* + *ousia* substance, essence) + E *-an*; *monoousious* fr. LGk *monoousios* — more at OUSIA] *relig* **:** of one substance or essence

**mono·pack** \ˈ==+ˌ-\ *n* [*mon-* + *pack*] **:** INTEGRAL TRIPACK

**mono·parental** \¦==+\ *adj* [*mon-* + *parental*] **:** having or derived from a single parent

**mono·pectinate** \ˈ"+\ *adj* [*mon-* + *pectinate*] **:** pectinate along one side

**mono·persulfuric acid** \ˈ"+-\ *n* [*mon-* + *persulfuric*] **:** PERMONOSULFURIC ACID

**mono·petalous** \ˈ"+\ *adj* [NL *monopetalus*, fr. *mon-* + *-petalus* -petalous] **1 :** GAMOPETALOUS 1 **2 :** having a solitary petal

**mo·noph·a·gous** \məˈnäfəgəs\ *adj* [*mon-* + *-phagous*] **1 :** feeding on or utilizing a single kind of food **:** feeding on a single kind of plant or animal — used esp. of an insect; compare OLIGOPHAGOUS **2 :** entering only a single host cell — used esp. of the thallus of parasitic fungi; compare POLYPHAGOUS

**mo·noph·a·gy** \-jē\ *n* -ES [*mon-* + *-phagy*] **:** a monophagous character or condition

**mono·phase** \¦== *at* MONO- +\ *adj* [*mon-* + *phase*] **:** SINGLE-PHASE

**mono·pha·sia** \ˌ==ˈfāzh(ē)ə\ *n* -s [NL, fr. *mon-* + *-phasia*] **:** aphasia marked by repeated utterance of one word or phrase

**mono·pha·sic** \¦==¦fāzik\ *adj* [*mon-* + *phasic*] **1 :** SINGLE-PHASE ⟨a ~ electric current⟩ **2** *of an animal* **:** having a single period of activity followed by a period of rest in each 24 hours ⟨man may be considered a naturally ~ being⟩ — compare POLYPHASIC

**mono·pho·bia** \ˌ==ˈfōbēə\ *n* [NL, fr. *mon-* + *-phobia*] **:** a morbid dread of being alone

**mono·phonemic** \¦==+\ *adj* [*mon-* + *phonemic*] **:** constituting, consisting of, or standing for a single phoneme

**mono·phon·ic** \ˈ"+¦fänik\ *also* **mo·noph·o·nous** \məˈnäfənəs\ *adj* [*mon-* + *-phonic*, *-phonous*] **1 :** consisting of a solo voice with accompaniment **2 :** having a single melodic line with little or no accompaniment — compare HOMOPHONIC 3, POLYPHONIC **3 :** of or relating to sound transmission, recording, or reproduction by techniques that provide a single transmission path — compare BINAURAL, STEREOPHONIC

**mo·noph·o·ny** \məˈnäfənē\ *n* -ES [*mon-* + *-phony*] **:** melody for one voice esp. if unaccompanied

**mon·oph·thal·mic** \ˌmäˌnäfˈthalmik, ¦mōˌn-, ÷ -näpˈth-\ *adj* [Gk *monophthalmos* one-eyed (fr. *mon-* + *ophthalmos* eye) + E *-ic* — more at OPHTHALMIA] **:** having one eye

**mon·oph·thong** \ˈmänəfˌthȯŋ, -nəˌth- *also* -thäŋ\ *n* -s [LGk *monophthongos* single vowel, fr. Gk *mon-* + *phthongos* sound] **:** a vowel sound that throughout its duration has a single constant articulatory position and acoustic structure and whose boundary on either side is a consonant or a syllable boundary — compare DIPHTHONG, TRIPHTHONG — **mon·oph·thon·gal** \¦==¦=(g)əl\ *adj*

**mon·oph·thong·ization** \ˌ==ˌ=(g)əˈzāshən, -ˌ(g)īˈz-\ *n* -s **:** the process of monophthongizing

**mon·oph·thong·ize** \ˈ==ˌ=ˌ(g)īz\ *vt* -ED/-ING/-S **:** to change into a monophthong **:** reduce (a diphthong or triphthong) to a simple vowel sound

**mono·phyletic** \¦== *at* MONO- +\ *adj* [ISV *mon-* + *phyletic*] **:** of or relating to a single stock **:** developed from a single common parent form — opposed to *polyphyletic*

**monophyletic theory** *n* **:** a theory in physiology: all the cellular elements of the blood derive from a common stem cell — compare POLYPHYLETIC THEORY

**mono·phyle·tism** \ˌ==ˈfīləˌtizəm, -ˈfil-\ *or* **mono·phyle·ty** \-ləd·ē\ *n*, *pl* **monophyletisms** *or* **monophyleties** [*monophyletism* ISV *monophyletic* + *-ism*; *monophylety* fr. *monophyletic* + *-y*] **:** the quality or state of being monophyletic **:** shared descent from a single common stemform

**mono·phy·odont** \¦==ˈfīəˌdänt\ *adj* [Gk *monophyēs* single (fr. *mon-* + *-phyēs*, fr. *phyein* to bring forth) + *odont-*, *odous* tooth — more at BE, TOOTH] **:** having but one set of teeth of which none are replaced at a later stage of growth — opposed to *diphyodont*; distinguished from *polyphyodont*

**mo·noph·y·sism** \məˈnäfəˌsizəm, mäˈ-, mōˈ-\ *n* -s *usu cap* [F *monophysisme*, fr. *monophysite* (fr. ML *Monophysita*) + *-isme* -ism] **:** MONOPHYSITISM

**¹mo·noph·y·site** \-ˌsīt\ *n* -s *usu cap* [ML *Monophysita*, fr. MGk *Monophysitēs*, fr. Gk *mon-* + *physis* nature + *-itēs* -ite — more at PHYSICS] **:** one who maintains the anti-Chalcedonian doctrine that the human and divine in the person of Jesus Christ constitute only one nature which is regarded either as thoroughly unified or as composite — compare ARMENIAN, DYOPHYSITE

**²monophysite** \ˈ"\ *adj*, *usu cap* **:** MONOPHYSITIC

**mo·noph·y·sit·ic** \=¦=ˈsid·ik\ *adj*, *usu cap* [¹*Monophysite* + *-ic*] **:** of or relating to the Monophysites or Monophysitism **:** supporting Monophysitism

**mo·noph·y·sit·ism** \=ˈ==ˌsīd·ˌizəm\ *n* -s *usu cap* [¹*Monophysite* + *-ism*] **:** the doctrines of the Monophysites

**mono·placula** \¦== *at* MONO- +\ *n* [NL, fr. *mon-* + *placula*] **:** a placula consisting of a single layer of cells — **mono·placular** \ˈ"+\ *adj* — **mono·placulate** \ˈ"+\ *adj*

**mono·plane** \ˈmänəˌplān\ *n* [*mon-* + *plane*] **:** an airplane with only one main supporting surface

**mono·pla·net·ic** \¦== *at* MONO- + pləˈned·ik\ *adj* [*mon-* + Gk *planētikos* migratory — more at DIPLANETIC] *of a fungus* **:** having but a single swarming period — compare DIPLANETIC

**mono·plan·et·ism** \ˌ==ˈplanəd·ˌizəm\ *n* -s [*monoplanetic* + *-ism*] **:** the quality or state of being monoplanetic

**mono·plasmatic** \¦== *at* MONO- +\ *adj* [*mon-* + *plasmatic*] **:** composed of but one substance

**mono·plast** \ˈ==ˌplast\ *n* -s [*mon-* + *-plast*] **:** a single-celled organism or a simple structural element

**mono·plas·tic** \¦==¦plastik\ *adj* [*mon-* + *-plastic*] **:** retaining a primary form **:** UNDIFFERENTIATED, UNIFORM

**mono·ple·gia** \ˌ==ˈplēj(ē)ə\ *n* -s [NL, fr. *mon-* + *-plegia*] **:** paralysis affecting a single limb, body part, or group of muscles — **mono·ple·gic** \¦==¦jik\ *adj*

**¹mono·ploid** \ˈ==ˌplȯid\ *adj* [ISV *mon-* + *-ploid*] **:** having or being a chromosome set comprising a single genome — compare HAPLOID

**²monoploid** \ˈ"\ *n* -s **:** a monoploid individual

**mono·pneu·mo·na** \ˌ==ˈn(y)ümənə, ˌ=ˈnäpˈn-\ *also* **mono·pneu·mo·nes** \-ˌnēz\ *n pl*, *cap* [NL, fr. *mon-* + *-pneumona* (fr. Gk *pneumōn*, *pneumōn* lungs) — more at PNEUMONIA] *in some classifications* **:** an order including the genus *Ceratodus* — **mono·pneu·mo·ni·an** \¦==¦=ˈmōnēən\ *adj or n* — **mono·pneu·mo·nous** \¦==ˈn(y)ümənəs\ *adj*

**mo·nop·o·dal** \məˈnäpəd·ᵊl\ *adj* [*mon-* + *-pod* + *-al*] **:** forming a single pseudopodium at any one time

**¹mono·pode** \ˈ== *at* MONO- + ˌpōd\ *n* [LL *monopodius*] **1 :** a one-footed creature; *specif* **:** a fabulous one-footed Ethiopian that uses his foot as a sunshade **2** [NL *monopodium*] **:** MONOPODIUM

**²monopode** \ˈ"\ *adj* [LL *monopodius*, fr. Gk *monopod-*, *monopous*, fr. *mon-* + *pod-*, *pous* foot — more at FOOT] **:** having only one foot

**mono·po·di·al** \¦==¦pōdēəl\ *adj* [NL *monopodium* + E *-al*] **1 :** of or relating to a monopodium **:** having or involving the formation of offshoots from a main axis ⟨~ theories of evolution⟩ **2 :** RACEMOSE — **mono·po·di·al·ly** \-əlē\ *adv*

**mono·pod·ic** \¦==¦pädik\ *adj* [*monopody* + *-ic*] **:** consisting of or relating to a single metrical foot

**mono·po·di·um** \ˌ==ˈpōdēəm\ *n*, *pl* **monopo·dia** \-ēə\ [NL, fr. *mon-* + *-podium*] **:** a main or primary axis that continues its original line of growth giving off successive axes or lateral branches (as in the excurrent trunk of some coniferous tree) — compare SYMPODIUM

**mo·nop·o·dy** \məˈnäpədē\ *n* -ES [Gk or LGk *monopodia* measurement by single feet, fr. Gk *mon-* + *pod-*, *pous* foot + *-ia* -y — more at FOOT] **:** a measure of a single metrical foot

**mono·polar** \¦== *at* MONO- +\ *adj* [*mon-* + *polar*] **:** UNIPOLAR — **mono·polarity** \ˈ"+\ *n*

**monopole** *n* -s [MF, fr. L *monopolium* — more at MONOPOLY] *obs* **:** MONOPOLY

**monopoler** *n* -s [MF *monopolier*, fr. *monopole* + *-ier* -er] *obs* **:** MONOPOLIST

**mo·nop·o·lism** \məˈnäpəˌlizəm\ *n* -s [*monopoly* + *-ism*] **:** the system, policy, or practices of monopolies or monopolists

**mo·nop·o·list** \-ləst\ *n* -s [*monopoly* + *-ist*] **:** one who monopolizes **:** one who has a monopoly or favors monopoly ⟨a ~ controlling a limited supply of goods —R.W.Firth⟩

**mo·nop·o·lis·tic** \=¦==¦listik, -tēk\ *adj* **:** of, relating to, or characteristic of a monopoly or a monopolist ⟨a ~ conspiracy to determine freight rates —*New Republic*⟩ — **mo·nop·o·lis·ti·cal·ly** \-tək(ə)lē, -tēk-, -lī\ *adv*

**monopolistic competition** *n* **:** competition that is used among sellers whose products are similar but not identical and that takes the form of product differentiation and advertising with less emphasis upon price — compare IMPERFECT COMPETITION

**mo·nop·o·li·za·tion** \məˌnäpələˈzāshən, -ˌlīˈz-\ *n* -s **:** the quality or state of being monopolized; *also* **:** the process of being monopolized

**mo·nop·o·lize** \məˈnäpəˌlīz\ *vt* -ED/-ING/-S *see -ize in Explan Notes* [*monopoly* + *-ize*] **:** to acquire a monopoly of **:** have or get the exclusive privilege of the means of dealing in or the exclusive possession of **:** engross the whole of

**syn** ENGROSS, ABSORB, CONSUME: MONOPOLIZE implies the exclusive, often overbearingly exclusive, possession or control of something which more generally would be distributed, publicly available, or more publicly controlled ⟨*monopolize* the auto market in the area⟩ ⟨*monopolize* the attention of a guest⟩ ⟨*monopolize* a family car⟩ ENGROSS applies usu. to an unprotested monopolizing of attention, interest, or time, as of one charmed or held irresistibly ⟨a group of boys sprawl, teen-age fashion, on couches and chairs, *engrossed* in a drama that blares from a television set —*Lamp*⟩ ⟨they were so *engrossed* in each other that she didn't see me until I was five feet away —Scott Fitzgerald⟩ ⟨an *engrossing* novel⟩ ABSORB is often interchangeable with ENGROSS but usu. has a nonpersonal subject and suggests a monopolizing more often against the will of the one acted upon than does ENGROSS ⟨crammed with ideas, projects, hobbies — enough to keep you *absorbed* and fascinated for the next five hundred years —Glynne Hiller⟩ ⟨petty cares and vexations that *absorb* life's energies —M.R.Cohen⟩ CONSUME, in the somewhat extended sense pertinent here, stresses the monopolizing of the total attention, interest, or time which is its usual object ⟨a *consuming* interest⟩ ⟨a *consuming* curiosity⟩ ⟨the guilt which *consumed* Lawrence during those treacherous moments —H.M.Sachar⟩

**mo·nop·o·liz·er** \-zə(r)\ *n* -s **:** one that monopolizes

**mo·nop·o·loid** \-ˌlȯid\ *adj* [*monopoly* + *-oid*] **:** of, relating to, or resembling a monopoly ⟨~ corporate and financial gigantism —*New Republic*⟩

**mo·nop·o·ly** \məˈnäp(ə)lē, -li\ *n* -ES *see sense 6* [L *monopolium*, fr. Gk *monopōlion*, *monopōlia*, fr. *mon-* + *-pōlion*, *-pōlia* (fr. *pōlein* to sell); prob. akin to MLG *vēle* for sale, MD *veile*, *veil*, OHG *fāli*, *feili*, ON *falr* for sale, Sk *paṇate* he barters, trades] **1 :** ownership or control that permits domination of the means of production or the market in a business or occupation usu. for controlling prices and that is achieved through an exclusive legal privilege (as a governmental grant, charter, patent, or copyright) or by control of the source of supply (as ownership of a mine) or by engrossing a particular article or commodity (as in cornering the market) or by combination or concert of action — compare DUOPOLY, OLIGOPOLY **2 :** exclusive possession ⟨no country has a ~ on morality or truth —Helen M. Lynd⟩ **3 :** the exclusive legal privilege of a monopoly **4 :** the commodity to which the monopoly relates **5 :** a company or combination having a monopoly

**Monopoly** \ˈ"\ *trademark* — used for a board game in which players pretend to buy, rent, and sell real estate

**mono·poly·logue** \ˌ== *at* MONO- + ˈpäləˌlȯg *also* -läg\ *n* -s [*mon-* + *poly-* + *-logue*] **:** an entertainment in which one actor plays many characters

**mono·potassium** \¦==+\ *adj* [*mon-* + *potassium*] **:** containing one atom of potassium in the molecule

**mono·print** \ˈ==+ˌ-\ *n* [*mon-* + *print*] **1 :** an impression made on paper from glass or some equally smooth material (as celluloid or oilcloth) to which oil paint has been applied **2 :** the art or process of making monoprints

**mono·pri·on** \¦==¦prīən\ *or* **mono·pri·o·nid** \-ənəd\ *or* **mono·pri·o·nid·i·an** \-¦nidēən\ *adj* [*monoprion* fr. *mon-* + Gk *priōn* saw; *monoprionid* fr. *mon-* + Gk *priōn* + E *-id*; *monoprionidian* fr. *mon-* + Gk *priōn* + E *-id* + *-ian* — more at PRIOR] **:** of, relating to, or being graptolites that have cells on one side of the stem only

**¹mono·propellant** \¦==+\ *n* [*mon-* + *propellant*] **:** a rocket propellant in which both the fuel and the oxidizer are contained in a single substance — compare BIPROPELLANT

**²monopropellant** \ˈ"\ *adj* **:** of, relating to, or employing a monopropellant

**mo·nop·so·nist** \məˈnäpsənəst\ *n* -s [*monopsony* + *-ist*] **:** one who is a single buyer for a product or service of many sellers — **mo·nop·so·nis·tic** \=¦=¦nistik\ *adj* **:** of, relating to, or characteristic of monopsony

**mo·nop·so·ny** \=ˈ==nē\ *n* -ES [*mon-* + Gk *opsōnia* purchase of victuals, catering — more at DUOPSONY] **:** a market situation in which there is a single buyer for a given product or service from a large number of sellers — compare DUOPSONY, OLIGOPSONY

**mono·psychism** \¦== *at* MONO- +\ *n* [*mon-* + Gk *psychē* soul + E *-ism* — more at PSYCHIC] **:** a doctrine that there is but one immortal soul of which individual souls are manifestations

**mo·nop·ter·al** \(ˈ)mäˈnäptərəl, (ˈ)mō-\ *adj* [L *monopteros* having a single row of columns (fr. Gk, fr. *mon-* + *pteron* wing) + E *-al* — more at FEATHER] *in circular buildings* **:** marked by columniation consisting of a single ring of supporting columns without a cella — see COLUMNIATION illustration

**mo·nop·te·ron** \-ˌrän\ *also* **mo·nop·te·ros** \-ˌräs\ *n*, *pl* **mo·nop·tera** \-rə\ [NL, fr. Gk *monopteron* (neut. of *monopteros*) & *monopteros*, adj.] **:** a monopteral structure

**mon·optic** \(ˈ)män, (ˈ)mōn+\ *also* **mon·optical** \ˈ"+\ *adj* [*mon-* + *optic*, *optical*] **:** having one eye

**mono·py·laea** \ˌ== *at* MONO- + pīˈlēə\ *or* **mono·py·lar·ia** -ˈla(a)rēə\ [NL, fr. *mon-* + *-pylaea* (fr. Gk *pylē* gate) or *-pylaria* (fr. *pyl-* + *-aria*) — more at PYLON] *syn of* MONOPYLEA

**mono·py·lea** \-pīˈlēə\ *n pl*, *cap* [NL, fr. *mon-* + *-pylea* (fr. Gk *pylē* gate)] **:** a suborder of Radiolaria comprising protozoans with or without spiculate skeletons and with the central capsule interrupted by a single perforated plate — **mono·py·le·an** \¦==¦lēən\ *adj or n*

**¹mono·rail** \ˈ== *at* MONO- + ˌ-\ *n* [*mon-* + *rail*] **1 :** a single rail serving as a track for a wheeled conveyance **2 :** a single rail mounted on trestles constituting the track for railway cars that usu. sit astraddle over it or hang suspended from it

**²monorail** \¦==¦=\ *adj* **:** operated by or involving a monorail

**¹mon·or·chid** \(ˈ)mäˈnȯrkəd\ *adj* [irreg. fr. Gk *monorchis*, fr. *mon-* + *orchis* testicle — more at ORCHIS] **:** having but one testis or but one descended into the scrotum — compare CRYPTORCHID

**²monorchid** \ˈ"\ *n* -s **:** a monorchid individual

**mon·or·chid·ism** \-kəˌdizəm\ *also* **mon·or·chism** \-ˌkizəm\ *n* -s **:** the quality or state of being monorchid

**mon·or·chis** \məˈnȯrkəs\ *n*, *pl* **monorchi·des** \-kəˌdēz\ [NL, fr. Gk *monorchis*, adj.] **:** MONORCHID

**mon·organic** \¦män, ¦mōn+\ *adj* [*mon-* + *organic*] **:** of, relating to, or affecting a single organ or set of organs

**mono·rhi·na** *or* **mon·or·rhi·na** \ˌmänəˈrīnə, ˌmōn-, -rēnə\

[NL, fr. mon- + -rhina, -rrhina (fr. Gk rhin-, rhis nose); akin to Gk rhein to flow — more at STREAM] *syn of* CYCLOSTOMI

**mono·rhi·nal** \ˌ==ˈrīnəl\ *or* **mono·rhine** \-ˌrīn\ *adj* [mon- + -rhinal (fr. rhin- + -al) or -rhine] **:** having a single nostril ⟨a ~ cyclostome⟩

**mono·rhin·ic** \ˌ==ˈrinik\ *adj* [mono- + rhin- + -ic] **:** affecting only one nostril ⟨~ stimulation shows that many individuals have keener smell on one side than the other —R.S.Woodworth⟩

**mono·rhyme** *also* **mono·rime** \ˈ==+ˌ-\ *n* [F monorime, fr. mon- + rime rhyme — more at RHYME] **1 :** a strophe or poem in which all the lines have the same end rhyme **2 mono·rhymes** *pl* **:** the lines of a monorhyme — **mono·rhymed** \ˈ==+\ *adj*

**monos** *pl of* MONO

**mo·no·sa·bio** \ˌmänəˈsäbēˌō, ˌmōn-\ *n* -s [Sp, fr. mono monkey + sabio wise, fr. LL sapidus, fr. L savory — more at SAPID] **:** a bullring attendant

**mono·saccharide** \ˌ== *at* MONO- +\ *n* [ISV mon- + sacchar- + -ide; prob. orig. formed as G monosaccharid] **:** any of the class of simple sugars that contain in each molecule one or more alcoholic hydroxyl groups and one carbonyl group of aldehyde or ketone character or its equivalent as a cyclic hemiacetal and that are classed as aldoses or ketoses and further according to the number of carbon atoms present with pentoses and hexoses the most common **:** GLYCOSE 2

**mono·saccharose** \"+\ *n* [mon- + saccharose] **:** MONOSACCHARIDE

**mono·scope** \ˈ==+ˌskōp\ *n* [mon- + -scope] **:** a cathode-ray tube designed to produce for test purposes a video signal of a stationary pattern which has been printed in black foil ink on the aluminum-coated signal plate and sealed in the tube

**mon·ose** \ˈmäˌnōs, ˈmō,-, -ōz\ *n* -s [mon- + -ose] **:** MONOSACCHARIDE

**mono·se·mic** \ˌ== *at* MONO- + ˈsēmik\ *adj* [mon- + -semic] **:** consisting of or equal in duration to one mora ⟨a ~ syllable⟩

**mono·sep·al·ous** \"+ˈsepələs\ *adj* [mon- + -sepalous] **1 :** GAMOSEPALOUS **2 :** having a single sepal

**mono·silane** \"+\ *n* [mon- + silane] **:** a colorless gas $SiH_4$ that is spontaneously flammable in air, is liquefiable only at a low temperature, and is formed by the action of hydrochloric acid on magnesium silicide

**mono·siphonic** \"+\ *or* **mono·siphonous** \"+\ *adj* [mon- + siphon- + -ic or -ous] **:** consisting of a single tube or row of cells (as the thallus of various red algae or the hydrocaulus of some hydrozoans) — compare POLYSIPHONIC

**mono·ski** \ˈ==+\ *n* [mon- + ski] **1 :** a single ski on which a person can stand with both feet and which is equipped with a handle bar that also serves as a brake **2 :** a sled with a single runner in the center

**mon·osmatic** \(ˈ)män, (ˈ)mōn+\ *adj* [mon- + osmatic] **:** lacking a Jacobson's organ — used of a vertebrate in which this typical reptilian structure is absent

**mono·sodium** \ˌ== *at* MONO- +\ *adj* [mon- + sodium] **:** containing one atom of sodium in the molecule

**mon·o·so·di·um glu·ta·mate** *n* **:** a crystalline salt $NaOOCCH_2CH_2CH(NH_2)COOH$ used for enhancing the flavor of foods (as meat or soup)

**monosodium phosphate** *n* **:** SODIUM PHOSPHATE 1a

**mono·some** \ˈ==ˌsōm\ *n* -s [mon- + -some] **1 :** an unpaired X chromosome **2 :** a chromosome lacking a synaptic mate **3 :** an individual or cell lacking one or more chromosomes

**¹mono·so·mic** \ˌ==ˈsōmik\ *adj* [mono- + -somic] **:** having one less than the diploid number of chromosomes

**²monosomic** \"\ *n* -s **:** a monosomic individual

**mono·sperm** \ˈ==+ˌ-\ *n* [mon- + sperm] **:** a monospermous plant

**mono·sper·mic** \ˌ==ˈspərmik\ *adj* [NL monospermicus, fr. mon- + -spermicus -spermic] **:** involving or resulting from a single sperm cell ⟨~ fertilization⟩

**mono·sper·mous** \-məs\ *adj* [NL monospermus, fr. monomon- + -spermus -spermous] **:** having or producing a single seed

**mono·sper·my** \ˈ==ˌspərmē\ *n* -ES [ISV mon- + -spermy] **:** the entry of a single fertilizing sperm into an egg — compare DISPERMY, POLYSPERMY

**mono·spherical** \ˌ==+\ *adj* [mon- + spherical] **:** having or consisting of one sphere only

**mono·spondylic** \"+\ *adj* [mon- + spondylic] **:** having no well-developed intercentra alternating with the true centra of the vertebrae

**mono·spo·ran·gi·um** \ˌ==+spəˈranjēəm\ *n* [NL, fr. ISV monospore + NL -angium] **:** a sporangium which bears monospores

**mono·spore** \ˈ==+ˌ-\ *n* [ISV mon- + spore] **:** a simple nonmotile asexual spore in some algae exhibiting alternation of generations that is produced by a plant of the diploid generation and germinates to form another diploid plant — called also *neutral spore;* contrasted with *tetraspore*

**mono·spored** \ˌ==ˈspō(ə)rd\ *adj* [mon- + spore + -ed] **:** MONOSPOROUS

**mono·sporidial** \"+\ *adj* [mon- + sporidial] **:** of, from, or relating to a single sporidium

**mono·spor·ous** \ˌ==ˈspōrəs, məˈnäspərəs\ *adj* [mon- + -sporous] **1 :** having a single spore **2** *or* **monosporiferous** \ˌ== *at* MONO- +\ **:** reproducing by means of monospores

**mono·stele** \ˈ==ˌstēl *also* ˌ==ˈstēlē\ *n* [mon- + stele] **:** PROTOSTELE — **mono·ste·ly** \ˈ==ˌstēlē\ *n* -ES

**¹mono·stich** \ˈ==ˌstik\ *n* [LL monostichum, fr. Gk monostichon, fr. neut. of monostichos consisting of one verse, fr. mon- + stichos line, verse — more at STICH] **:** a single verse; *also* **:** a poem of one verse

**²monostich** \"\ *adj* [Gk monostichos] **:** consisting of a single verse

**mono·stich·ic** \ˌ==ˈstikik\ *adj* [¹monostich + -ic] **:** of or relating to a single verse or monostich

**mo·nos·ti·chous** \məˈnästəkəs\ *adj* [mon- + -stichous] **1 :** arranged in a single row on one side of an axis **2 :** consisting of a single layer or series

**mono·sto·ma·ta** \ˌ== *at* MONO- + ˈstōmədə\ *n pl, cap* [NL, fr. mon- + -stomata] *in some classifications* **:** a suborder of Digenea comprising trematode worms lacking a ventral sucker — **mono·sto·mate** \ˌ==+\ *adj*

**¹mono·stome** \ˈ==ˌstōm\ *adj* [Gk monostomos, fr. mon- + -stomos -stomous] **1 :** having one mouth or sucker **2** [NL Monostomata] **:** of or relating to the Monostomata

**²monostome** \"\ *n* -s **:** a trematode worm of the suborder Monostomata

**mo·nos·to·mous** \məˈnästəməs\ *adj* [Gk monostomos] **:** MONOSTOME 1

**mono·stot·ic** \ˌ== *at* MONO- + ˈstäd·ik\ *adj* [mon- + Gk osteon bone + E -otic] **:** relating to or affecting a single bone

**mono·stro·mat·ic** \"+strōˈmad·ik\ *adj* [mon- + Gk strōmat-, strōma couch, bed + E -ic — more at STROMA] **:** having the cells in a single layer — used of the leaf of mosses and the thallus of algae

**mono·strophe** \ˈmänəˌstrōf(ē)\ *n* [Gk monostrophos consisting of a single strophe, fr. mon- + strophē strophe — more at STROPHE] **1 :** a poem of one stanza **2 :** a poem in which all the stanzas are of the same metric form

**mono·strophic** \ˌ==ˈsträfik, -rōf-\ *adj* [Gk monostrophikos, fr. mon- + strophikos strophic — more at STROPHIC] **:** consisting of monostrophes

**mono·stroph·ics** \-ks\ *n pl* **:** monostrophic verses

**mono·sty·lous** \"+ˈstīləs\ *adj* [mon- + -stylous] **:** having a single style

**mono·substituted** \"+\ *adj* [mon- + substituted] **:** having one substituent atom or group in the molecule ⟨~ acetylenes⟩ — **mono·substitution** \" + \ *n*

**mono·sulfide** \"+\ *n* [mon- + sulfide] **:** a sulfide containing one atom of sulfur in the molecule

**mono·sulfonic acid** \"+-\ *n* [mon- + sulfonic] **:** a compound containing one sulfonic acid group

**mono·syllabic** \"+\ *adj* [prob. fr. F monosyllabique, fr. monosyllabe + -ique -ic] **1 :** having only one syllable **:** composed of monosyllables **2 a :** using or speaking only monosyllables **b :** conspicuously brief in answering or commenting **:** pointedly terse ⟨merry where he was grave, talkative where he was ~ —Dorothy Sayers⟩ — **mono·syllabically** \"+\ *adv* — **mono·syllabicity** \"+\ *n* -ES

**monosyllabic language** *n* **:** a language all or nearly all of whose words are monosyllables

**mono·syllable** \ˌ== *at* MONO- +\ *n* [modif. (influenced by syllable) of MF or LL; MF monosyllabe, fr. LL monosyllabon, fr. Gk, fr. neut. of monosyllabos having one syllable, fr. mon- + syllabē syllable — more at SYLLABLE] **:** a word or other grammatical unit of one syllable

**monosyllabon** *n, pl* **monosyllaba** [L, fr. Gk, neut. of monosyllabos monosyllabic, fr. mon- + syllabē syllable — more at SYLLABLE] *obs* **:** MONOSYLLABLE

**mono·symmetric** \ˌ== *at* MONO- +\ *or* **mono·symmetrical** \"+\ *adj* [mon- + symmetric, symmetrical] **1 :** MONOCLINIC **2 :** symmetrical bilaterally with reference to a single plane **:** ZYGOMORPHIC — **mono·symmetrically** \"+\ *adv* — **mono·symmetry** \"+\ *n*

**mono·symptomatic** \"+\ *adj* [mon- + symptomatic] **:** exhibiting or manifested by a single principal symptom

**mono·synaptic** \"+\ *adj* [mon- + synaptic] **:** having or involving a single neural synapse

**mono·terpene** \"+\ *n* [mon- + terpene] **:** any of a class of terpenes $C_{10}H_{16}$ (as myrcene or limonene) containing two isoprene units in the molecule; *also* **:** a derivative of such a terpene

**mono·thal·a·mous** \"+ˈthaləməs\ *also* **mono·thalamic** \"+\ *adj* [mon- + thalam- + -ous or -ic] **:** having one chamber **:** UNILOCULAR

**mono·the·cal** \-ˈthēkəl\ *adj* [mon- + Gk thēkē box, case + E -al — more at TICK] **:** UNILOCULAR

**mono·the·ism** \ˈ==(ˌ)thēˌizəm *sometimes* məˈnäthē-\ *n* [mon- + -theism] **:** the doctrine or belief that there is but one God ⟨Christianity and the other ~s —S.E.Hyman⟩

**mono·the·ist** \ˈ==ˌthēəst *sometimes* ·məˈnäthē-\ *n* [mon- + -theist] **:** one who believes in monotheism

**mono·the·is·tic** \ˌ==(ˌ)thēˈistik *sometimes* məˌnäthē-, -tēk\ *also* **mono·the·is·ti·cal** \-təkəl, -tēk\ *adj* **:** of, relating to, or characterized by monotheism — **mono·the·is·ti·cal·ly** \-tək(ə)lē, -tēk-, -li\ *adv*

**mo·noth·e·lism** \məˈnäthəˌlizəm\ *n* -s *usu cap* [Monothelite + -ism] **:** MONOTHELITISM

**mo·noth·e·lite** \-ˌlīt\ *also* **mo·noth·e·lete** \-ˌlēt\ *n* -s *usu cap* [Monothelite fr. ML Monothelita, modif. (influenced by L -ita -ite) of MGk Monotheletēs, fr. Gk mon- + thelētēs one that wills, fr. thelein, ethelein to will, wish; Monothelete fr. MGk Monotheletēs — more at GILDER] **:** an adherent of Monothelitism

**mo·noth·e·lit·ic** \ˌ==ˈlid·ik\ *also* **mo·noth·e·let·ic** \-ˈled-·ik\ *adj, usu cap* **:** of or relating to the Monothelites or Monothelitism

**mo·noth·e·lit·ism** \ˈ==ˌlīd·ˌizəm\ *also* **mo·noth·e·let·ism** \-ˌlēd·ˌ-\ *n* -s *usu cap* **:** the theological doctrine that in Christ there is but one will though two natures — opposed to *Dyothelitism*

**mono·thematic** \ˌ== *at* MONO- +\ *adj* [mon- + thematic] **:** having a single dominating theme; *esp* **:** having a theme continuing through more than one movement of a musical composition

**mono·thet·ic** \"+ˈthed·ik\ *adj* [mon- + Gk thetikos fit for placing, fr. thetos placed, set (fr. tithenai to place, set) + -ikos -ic — more at DO] **:** positing but one essential element

**mono·tint** \ˈ== *at* MONO- + ˌ-\ *n* [mon- + tint] **1 :** a single tint or color **2 :** a picture wholly or chiefly of a single color **:** MONOCHROME

**mo·noto·car·dia** \məˌnäd·əˈkärdēə\ [NL, fr. mon- + Gk ōtoear, auricle (fr. ōt-, ous) + NL -cardia — more at EAR] *syn of* PECTINIBRANCHIA

**mo·noto·car·di·ac** \ˌ==ˈ==ˌak\ *adj* [NL Monotocardia + E -ac (as in cardiac)] **:** of or relating to the Pectinibranchia

**¹mo·noto·car·di·an** \-ēən\ *adj* [NL Monotocardia + E -an] **:** of or relating to the Pectinibranchia

**²monotocardian** \"\ *n* -s **:** a mollusk of the order Pectinibranchia

**mo·not·o·cous** \məˈnäd·əkəs\ *adj* [mon- + Gk tokos birth, offspring — more at TOCO-] **:** producing a single egg or young at one time — compare POLYTOCOUS

**monotomous** *adj* [mon- + -tomous] *obs* **:** having a distinct cleavage in one direction only — used of a mineral

**¹mono·tone** \ˈmänə+ˌ-\ *n* [mon- + tone] **1 a :** a succession of syllables, words, or sentences in one unvaried key or pitch ⟨speaking in an old man's ~, just too loud for ordinary conversation —G.R.Clay⟩ — compare POLYTONE **b :** a sound resembling a monotone ⟨the brook's ~⟩ ⟨a ~ of street noises filtered through⟩ **2 a :** a single unvaried musical tone **b :** recitation esp. of liturgy in such a tone **:** INTONING **c :** a person not able to properly produce or distinguish between musical intervals **3 :** a monotonous reiteration or recurrence **:** tedious repetition ⟨a ~ of flat fields watered by numerous creeks —*Amer. Guide Series: Pa.*⟩ **4 :** uniformity of style usu. characterized by a lack of brilliance esp. in writing ⟨an odd, unconvincing, and regrettably sketchy story, told in a ~ —Brendan Gill⟩ **5 :** uniformity of color ⟨the land itself is often a gray ~ —G.R.Stewart⟩

**²monotone** \"\ *adj* [prob. fr. F, fr. Gk monotonos — more at MONOTONOUS] **1 :** MONOTONOUS ⟨the ~ sound of the sea⟩ **2 :** having a uniform color ⟨her ~ suit⟩ **3 :** MONOTONIC 3

**³monotone** \"\ *vb* [¹monotone] *vt* **:** to talk, recite, or chant in an unvaried tone **:** INTONE ⟨ponderous professors had monotoned us through modern literature —Ellen Hanford⟩ **~** *vi* **:** to recite or chant something in an unvaried tone ⟨listened to the choir *monotoning*⟩

**mono·ton·ic** \ˌ==ˈtänik\ *adj* [¹monotone + -ic] **1 :** of, relating to, or uttered in a monotone ⟨the ~ buzzing of the voices carried —James Jones⟩ **2 :** producing only one musical tone **3 :** being a mathematical function that either never decreases or never increases as the independent variable increases — **mono·ton·i·cal·ly** \-nək(ə)lē\ *adv*

**mo·not·o·nist** \məˈnätᵊnəst *also* -tn-\ *n* -s [monotony + -ist] **:** one who speaks in a monotonous manner **:** one addicted to or preferring monotony

**mo·not·o·nize** \-tᵊnˌīz *also* -tˌnīz\ *vt* -ED/-ING/-S [monotony + -ize] **:** to make monotonic or monotonous

**mo·not·o·nous** \-tᵊnəs *also* -tn-\ *adj* [Gk monotonos, fr. mon- + tonos tone — more at TONE] **1 :** uttered or sounded in one unvarying tone **:** marked by a sameness of pitch and intensity ⟨an owl kept up a faint ~ hooting —Louis Bromfield⟩ ⟨tried to keep his voice calm and ~ as he spoke —Elinor Wylie⟩ **2 :** having no change or variety **:** wearisomely uniform **:** REPETITIOUS ⟨the trim ~ cottages —W.F.Jenkins⟩ ⟨this waste of mud, water and ~ vegetation —Wilfred Thesiger⟩

**mo·not·o·nous·ly** *adv* **:** in a monotonous manner ⟨all men here looked ~ alike —Oscar Handlin⟩ ⟨the theme of rags to riches, exploited ~ but with singular success . . . runs like a bright thread through American folklore —R.B.Morris⟩

**mo·not·o·nous·ness** *n* -ES **:** the quality or state of being monotonous ⟨there is a profound ~ about its facts —Mark Twain⟩

**mo·not·o·ny** \-tᵊnē *also* -tn-, -ī\ *n* -ES [Gk monotonia, fr. monotonos + -ia -y] **1 :** sameness that produces boredom **:** lack of the variety that provides interest and stimulation **:** the same thing over and over **:** depressing uniformity ⟨the desire for change, for novelty, for a relief from the ~ of every day —Aldous Huxley⟩ ⟨the little shows and sports and well-meant activities that relieve the ~ of toil —G.B.Shaw⟩ ⟨the ~ of the brush plains to the eastward —Kenneth Roberts⟩ **2 :** sameness or uniformity of tone or sound or the utterance or use of one unvarying tone or sound ⟨a dominant rhythm persists above loose phrasing and verbal ~ —H.V.Gregory⟩

**mono·top·ic** \ˌ== *at* MONO- + ˈtäpik\ *adj* [mon- + top- + -ic] **:** of, relating to, or characterized by monotopism

**monoto·pism** \ˈmōnəˌtōˌpizəm, ˈmōnə-, məˈnäd·əˌp-\ *n* -s [mon- + top- + -ism] **:** origin of a systematic group only once (as by mutation) or at a single location — compare POLYTOPISM

**mono·tre·mal** \ˌ== *at* MONO- + ·ˈtrēməl\ *or* **mono·tre·mous** \-məs\ *adj* [monotreme + -al or -ous] **:** MONOTREMATOUS

**mono·trema·ta** \ˌ==·ˈtremədə, -rēm-\ *n pl, cap* [NL, fr. mon- + -tremata] **:** the lowest order of Mammalia consisting of the only surviving representatives of the subclass Prototheria — see ECHIDNA, PLATYPUS

**mono·trema·tous** \ˌ==·ˈtremədəs, -rēm-\ *or* **mono·tremate** \-māt, -ˌmāt\ *adj* [monotrematous fr. NL Monotremata + E -ous; monotremate fr. NL Monotremata] **:** of or relating to the order Monotremata

**mono·treme** \ˈ==ˌtrēm\ *n* -s [NL Monotremata] **:** one of the Monotremata

**mo·not·ri·chous** \məˈnä·trəkəs\ *also* **mono·trich·ic** \ˌ== *at* MONO- + ·ˈtrikik\ *or* **mo·not·ri·chate** \məˈnä·trəkət\ *adj* [mon- + -trichous or -trichate (fr. trich- + -ate) or -trichic (fr. trich- + -ic)] **:** having a single flagellum at one pole — used of bacteria

**mono·triglyph** \ˌ== *at* MONO- +\ *n* [L monotriglyphus monotriglyphic, fr. Gk monotriglyphos, fr. mon- + triglyphos triglyph — more at TRIGLYPH] **:** monotriglyphic intercolumniation

**mono·triglyphic** \"+\ *adj* **:** having only one triglyph over the space between two columns

**mono·troch** \ˈmänəˌträk, ˈmōn-\ *or* **mono·troche** \-rōk\ *n* -s [Gk monotrochos wheelbarrow, fr. mon- + trochos wheel — more at TROCHE] *archaic* **:** a one-wheeled vehicle

**mo·not·ro·cha** \məˈnä·trəkə\ *n* -s [NL, fr. mon- + -trocha] **:** a monotrochal larva

**mo·not·ro·chal** \-kəl\ *adj* [NL monotrocha + E -al] **:** having a prototroch only — used of annelid larvae

**mono·tron hardness test** \ˈmälnəˌträn-, ˈmō\ *n* [fr. Monotron, a trademark] **:** an indentation test that measures the load required to produce a definite penetration of steel by a standard spherical penetrator

**mo·not·ro·pa** \məˈnä·trəpə\ *n, cap* [NL, fr. Gk monotropē, fem. of monotropos living alone, fr. mon- + tropos turn, way, fr. trepein to turn — more at TROPE] **:** a genus of leafless fleshy saprophytic herbs (family Pyrolaceae) with solitary polypetalous flowers or with trimerous to pentamerous flowers in racemes — see HYPOPITYS, MONOTROPACEAE; INDIAN PIPE, PINESAP

**mo·not·ro·pa·ce·ae** \məˌnä·trəˈpāsēˌē\ *n pl, cap* [NL, fr. Monotropa, type genus + -aceae] *in some classifications* **:** a family of saprophytic herbs of which *Monotropa* is the type genus

**mono·troph·ic** \ˌ== *at* MONO- + ·ˈträfik, -rōf-\ *adj* [mon- + -trophic] **:** feeding only on one kind of food

**mono·trop·ic** \-·ˈträpik\ *adj* [mon- + -tropic] **1 :** relating to or exhibiting monotropy **2 :** visiting only a single kind of flower for nectar — used of an insect; compare OLIGOTROPIC, POLYTROPIC — **mono·trop·i·cal·ly** \-pək(ə)lē\ *adv*

**mono·trop·sis** \ˌ==·ˈträpsəs\ *n, cap* [NL, blend of *Monotropa* and *-opsis;* fr. its resemblance to Monotropa] **:** a genus of herbs (family Pyrolaceae) that is native to the southeastern U.S. — see CAROLINA BEECHDROPS

**mo·not·ro·py** \məˈnä·trəpē\ *n* -ES [ISV mon- + -tropy; prob. orig. formed as Ger monotropie] **:** the relation of two different forms of the same substance (as white and red phosphorus) that have no definite transition point since only one form (as red phosphorus) is stable and the change from the unstable form to the stable form is irreversible

**mono·typ·al** \ˌ== *at* MONO- + ˈtīpəl\ *adj* [monotype + -al] **:** MONOTYPIC

**mono·type** \ˈ==+ˌ-\ *n* [mon- + type] **1 a :** the only representative of its group (as a single species constituting a genus) **b :** a holotype when there are no paratypes **c :** the type species of a monobasic genus **2 :** an impression on paper of a design that has been painted usu. with the finger or a brush on a metal, glass, or similar surface

**Mono·type** \"\ *trademark* **1** — used for a typesetting apparatus consisting of a keyboard whose operation produces perforations on a roll of paper and a caster which casts and assembles individual pieces of type in justified lines in the order determined by the perforations **2 :** matter produced by a Monotype machine or printing done from such matter

**monotype paper** *n* **:** KEYBOARD PAPER

**mono·typ·ic** \ˌ== *at* MONO- + ˈtipik\ *adj* [mon- + -typic] **1 :** including a single representative — used esp. of a genus with only one species — opposed to *polytypic* **2 :** of or relating to a Monotype machine

**¹mono·valent** \"+\ *adj* [ISV mon- + valent] **1 :** UNIVALENT **2 :** containing antibodies specific for or antigens of a single strain of an organism

**²monovalent** \"\ *n* -s **:** a univalent chromosome or individual

**monovalent antibody** *n* **:** BLOCKING ANTIBODY

**mono·variant** \"+\ *adj* [mon- + variant] **:** UNIVARIANT

**mono·verticillate** \"+\ *adj* [mon- + verticillate] **:** having a single whorl ⟨a ~ shell⟩

**mon·ovular** \(ˈ)män, (ˈ)mōn+\ *adj* [mon- + ovular] **:** derived from a single ovum — used of identical twins or their characteristic state; compare BIOVULAR

**mon·ox·e·nous** \məˈnäksənəs\ *adj* [mon- + -xenous] *of a parasite* **:** living on only one kind of host

**mon·oxide** \məˈn, mäˈn+ˌ-\ *n* [ISV mon- + oxide] **:** an oxide containing one atom of oxygen in the molecule

**mon·oxime** \"+ˌ-\ *n* [mon- + oxime] **:** a compound containing one oxime grouping

**mon·o·zoa** \ˌmänəˈzōə, ˌmōn-\ [NL, fr. mon- + -zoa] *syn of* CESTODARIA

**mon·o·zo·an** \ˌ==ˈzōən\ *adj* [NL Monozoa + E -an] **:** of or relating to the Cestodaria

**mono·zo·ic** \ˌ== *at* MONO- + ˈzōik\ *adj* [mon- + -zoic] **1 :** MONOZOOTIC **2** *of a spore* **:** producing one sporozoite

**mono·zootic** \"+\ *adj* [mon- + zo- + -otic] **:** consisting of a single zooid or individual; *specif* **:** consisting of a single differentiated unit — used of cestodarians; distinguished from *polyzootic* — **mono·zo·o·ty** \ˌ==ˈəd·ē\ *n* -ES

**mono·zygotic** \ˌ==+\ *adj* [mon- + zygotic] *of twins* **:** produced from a single zygote **:** MONOVULAR

**monozy·gous** \"+ˈzīgəs, (ˈ)mäˈnäzəgəs\ *adj* [mon- + -zygous] **:** MONOZYGOTIC

**mon·roe doctrine** \mənˈrō, ˈmanˌrō-\ *n, usu cap M&D* [fr. the *Monroe Doctrine,* a statement proclaimed Dec. 2, 1823 by James *Monroe* †1831, 5th U. S. president, to the effect that the U. S. would not brook any interference in the western hemisphere by European powers] **:** a foreign policy opposed to the extension of outside political, economic, and ideological systems into a nation's existing sphere of influence ⟨the Australians had already proclaimed, in their own hearts, a *Monroe Doctrine* for the South Pacific —W.K.Hancock⟩

**mon·ro·lite** \mənˈrōˌlīt\ *n* -s [Monroe, town in Orange county, N. Y. + E -lite] **:** SILLIMANITE

**mon·ro·via** \mənˈrōvēə\ *adj, usu cap* [fr. Monrovia, Liberia] **:** of or from Monrovia, the capital of Liberia **:** of the kind or style prevalent in Monrovia

**¹mons** \ˈmänz\ *n, pl* **mon·tes** \-nˌtēz\ [NL, fr. L, mountain — more at MOUNT] **:** a body part or area raised above or demarcated from surrounding structures (as the papilla of mucosa through which the ureter enters the bladder)

**²mons** *pl of* MON

**³mons** *abbr, often cap* monsieur

**mon·sei·gneur** \ˌmänˌsānˈyər(·), *n, pl* **mes·sei·gneurs** \ˌmāˌsānˈyər(·), -rz\ [F, fr. OF, lit., my lord] **:** a French dignitary (as a prince or prelate) — used as a title of honor preceding a title of office or rank ⟨*Monseigneur* the Archbishop⟩ ⟨*Monseigneur* the Dauphin⟩; abbr. *Msgr.*

**mon·sieur** \məs(h)ˈyə, -yər(·), -yə; məˈsi(ə)r, -iə; məs(h)ˈyü(ə)r, -üə, məˈshü-; *as a title both syllables may be mi without stress or the first two sounds may be mi with secondary stress and there may or may not be secondary stress on the second syllable*\ *n, pl* **mes·sieurs** \" *or with* mā *or* me *as the first two sounds or with* z *at end*\ [MF, lit., my lord] **1 a :** a Frenchman of high rank or station ⟨would pray our ~s to think an English courtier may be wise —Shak.⟩ **b :** the next collateral heir to the French throne; *specif* **:** the second son or the oldest brother of the king of France **2 :** MISTER — used as a title of courtesy prefixed to the name of a Frenchman; abbr. *M.*

**mon·si·gnor** \(ˈ)mänˈsēnyə(r), *also* mənˈsē- *sometimes* -ēn-ˌyō(ə)r *or* -ēnˌyō(ə)r *or* ˌmänˌsēnˈyō- *or in rapid speech prob by* n *dissimilation* məˈsē-\ *n, pl* **monsigno·ri** \ˌmänˌsēnˈyōrē\ *or* **monsignors** [It monsignore, monsignor (when used as a title) fr. F monseigneur] **1 :** a prelate of the Roman Catholic Church — used as a title of honor; abbr. *Msgr.* **2 :** a strong purple that is redder and deeper than mauve — **mon·si·gno·ri·al** \ˌmänˌsēnˈyōrēəl\ *adj*

**mon·so·ni** \mänˈsōnē\ *n, pl* **monsoni** *or* **monsonis** *usu cap* **1 :** a Cree people of the Moose river region, northeastern Ontario, Canada **2 :** a member of the Monsoni people

**mon·soon** \(ˈ)mänˈsün\ *n* -s [obs. D monssoen, fr. Pg monção, alter. of moução, fr. Ar mawsim time, season] **1 :** a wind blowing part of the year from one direction alternating with a wind from the opposite direction **2 a :** a periodic wind in various latitudes in the Indian ocean and southern Asia generally which blows from the southwest from the latter part of April to the middle of October and from the northeast from about the middle of October to April **b :** the season of the southwest monsoon in India and adjacent countries which is a season of heavy rainfall : rainy season — **mon·soon·al** \-nᵊl\ *adj*

**monsoon forest** *n* **:** open deciduous or partially deciduous forest of tropical regions that develops in areas with alternating seasons of heavy rainfall and prolonged drought

**¹mon·ster** \'mänztə(r), -n(t)st-\ *n* -s [ME *monstre*, fr. MF, fr. L *monstrum* evil omen, monster, monstrosity, prob. fr. *monēre* to remind, warn — more at MIND] **1** *obs* **:** something unnaturally marvelous **:** PRODIGY **2 a :** an animal or plant departing greatly in form or structure from the usual type of its species — compare TERATOLOGY 2 **b :** one who shows a deviation from the normal in behavior or character ⟨at the heart of the legends the researcher too often discovers a stuffed shirt, a faker, or a moral ~ —DeLancey Ferguson⟩ **3 a :** a legendary animal usu. of great size and ferocity that has a form either partly brute and partly human or compounded of elements from several brute forms **b :** a threatening force **:** an engulfing power ⟨the same ~ —Destiny . . . that rolls every civilization to doom —W.L.Sullivan⟩ ⟨that ~ of a forest fire threatening the town⟩ ⟨the swollen rivers . . . are ~s —Gordon Cuyler⟩ **4 a :** an animal of strange and often terrifying shape ⟨visualize this scaleless ~, eight or nine feet long, sprawling in the shade by the side of the mud pools —W.E.Swinton⟩ **b :** a living thing unusually large for its kind ⟨a ~ of nine pounds . . . was said to be the largest weakfish —Hamilton Basso⟩ **c :** something huge and often of unmanageable proportions ⟨better a variety of different sandwiches than one ~ which may prove unwieldy —Al Hine⟩ ⟨a great ~ of a book —*New Yorker*⟩ **5 :** something monstrous; *esp* **:** a person of unnatural or excessive ugliness, deformity, wickedness, or cruelty ⟨the woman is a ~ of egoism —Sylvia T.Warner⟩

**²monster** \"\ *vt* -ED/-ING/-S **1** *obs* **:** to make a monster of ⟨sure her offense must be of such unnatural degree that ~s it —Shak.⟩ **2 :** to exhibit as unusual or wonderful

**³monster** \"\ *adj* **:** enormous in size, extent, or numbers ⟨the shiny black back of a ~ sperm whale —H.A.Chippendale⟩ ⟨new ~ construction is announced —Flora Lewis⟩ ⟨~ entertainment proves a colossal bore —*Saturday Rev.*⟩ ⟨drew up a ~ petition —James Leasor⟩

**mon·stera** \'mänztərə, -n(t)st-\ *n* [NL, perh. irreg. fr. L *monstrum* monster — more at MONSTER] **1** *cap* **:** a genus of tropical American climbing plants (family Araceae) having deeply incised and perforated leaves and a spadix enclosed in a yellow concave spathe — see CERIMAN **2** -s **:** any plant of the genus *Monstera*

**monsterlike** \'==,=\ *adj* **:** having the appearance or qualities of a monster ⟨most ~ be shown —Shak.⟩

**mon·strance** \'mänztrən(t)s, -n(t)st-\ *n* -s [MF, fr. ML *monstrantia*, fr. L *monstrant-, monstrans* (pres. part. of *monstrare* to show, instruct) + *-ia* -y — more at MUSTER] **1 :** a vessel in which the consecrated Host is exposed to receive the adoration of the faithful **2 :** a receptacle holding sacred relics when exposed to view

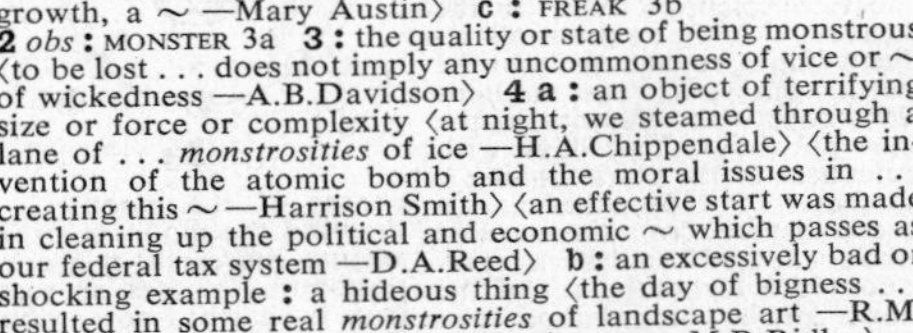
monstrance 1

**mon·stros·i·ty** \mänz'träsəd·ē, -n(t)'st-, -ətē, -i\ *n* -ES [LL *monstrositas*, fr. L *monstrosus*, *monstruosus* monstrous (fr. *monstrum* monster + *-osus* -ous) + *-itas* -ity — more at MONSTER] **1 a :** a malformation of a plant or animal **b :** something showing deviation from the normal ⟨whatever a woman has of intelligence and worth . . . is to be excised as a superfluous growth, a ~ —Mary Austin⟩ **c :** FREAK 3b **2** *obs* **:** MONSTER 3a **3 :** the quality or state of being monstrous ⟨to be lost . . . does not imply any uncommonness of vice or ~ of wickedness —A.B.Davidson⟩ **4 a :** an object of terrifying size or force or complexity ⟨at night, we steamed through a lane of . . . *monstrosities* of ice —H.A.Chippendale⟩ ⟨the invention of the atomic bomb and the moral issues in . . . creating this ~ —Harrison Smith⟩ ⟨an effective start was made in cleaning up the political and economic ~ which passes as our federal tax system —D.A.Reed⟩ **b :** an excessively bad or shocking example **:** a hideous thing ⟨the day of bigness . . . resulted in some real *monstrosities* of landscape art —R.M. Coates⟩ ⟨a ~ of a Victorian chaise longue —M.R.Ridley⟩

**¹mon·strous** \'mänztrəs, -n(t)st-\ *adj* [ME *monstrows*, fr. MF *monstrueux*, fr. L *monstruosus*, fr. *monstrum* monster + *-osus* -ous — more at MONSTER] **1** *obs* **:** STRANGE, UNNATURAL ⟨this ingrateful seat of ~ friends —Shak.⟩ **2 :** having extraordinary often overwhelming size **:** unusually and often unpleasantly big **:** HUGE, GIGANTIC, MAMMOTH ⟨the moon like a ~ crystal —G.K.Chesterton⟩ ⟨a ~ precipice —Thomas Gray⟩ ⟨clad in ~ coat and huge shoes —C.F.Wittke⟩ ⟨the task may well appear ~ —C.W.Shumaker⟩ ⟨he seemed of ~ bulk and significance —G.D.Brown⟩ **3 a :** having the qualities or appearance of a monster ⟨the subtle, ~ horror that broke forth last night and went prowling about the old hallways —W.H.Wright⟩ ⟨hate, a ~ sin that dissolves the bones in the body —Edith Sitwell⟩ **b** *obs* **:** teeming with monsters ⟨under the whelming tide visit'st the bottom of the ~ world —John Milton⟩ **4 a :** extraordinary because of ugliness or viciousness **:** ATROCIOUS, HORRIBLE ⟨the ~ gang who were bringing his country to ruins —Harrison Smith⟩ ⟨a ~ joke, a deception of matchless cruelty —B.R.Redman⟩ **b :** shockingly wrong or ridiculous ⟨the legend assumed ~ proportions —Louis Untermeyer⟩ ⟨the search for truth was largely diverted . . . into a ~ and deadening discussion —P.E.More⟩ **5 :** deviating greatly from the natural form or character **:** ABNORMAL, MALFORMED ⟨a ~ fetus⟩ ⟨a ~ melon⟩ **6 :** very great — used as an intensive ⟨the ~ agnostic —Alistair Cooke⟩ ⟨awakened . . . by a ~ hammering on his door —G.D.Brown⟩

**syn** PRODIGIOUS, TREMENDOUS, STUPENDOUS, MONUMENTAL: MONSTROUS applies to what is like a monster usu. in being abnormally large or often in being deformed or fabulously formed ⟨a procession of some of the most obese and *monstrous* types of humanity. Almost naked, they wandered around the arena, mountains of flesh glistening in the electric light —Hugh Walpole⟩ ⟨*monstrous*, like a doll that is alive and bigger than the child who tries to hold it —Babette Deutsch⟩ ⟨a *monstrous* kind of a creature who had but one leg, and that in the middle of his body —R.L.Stevenson⟩ PRODIGIOUS describes what is extraordinarily vast or immense often unexpectedly or disproportionately ⟨notice his *prodigious* strength. His hand actually seemed like a steel vice that could have crushed mine —Bram Stoker⟩ ⟨the demand was *prodigious*. Almost unimaginably huge quantities of cotton were consumed in its manufacture and virtual armies of men were engaged in making it —A.C.Morrison⟩ TREMENDOUS may apply to the huge or gigantic that arouses dread or awe ⟨the forces that tie an atom together are *tremendous* —Waldemar Kaempffert⟩ ⟨the younger rock slips from time to time, as some earth movement takes place, and the resultant *tremendous* jar is felt throughout the region —*Amer. Guide Series: Wash.*⟩ STUPENDOUS describes what stuns or amazes, usu. because of great size or number, vast complexity, or awesome force ⟨mountain ranges, the most *stupendous* in the world —Faubion Bowers⟩ ⟨a ray of light tells us of a *stupendous* catastrophe that occurred in the constellation —Waldemar Kaempffert⟩ MONUMENTAL refers to that which is impressive or massive enough to serve as a monument — often used figuratively ⟨statues are most successful when they are massive, *monumental*, and have something approaching an architectural context —John Dewey⟩ ⟨the *monumental* character demanded by Americans in their public buildings is achieved by the huge 32-story tower —*Amer. Guide Series: N.Y.*⟩ **syn** see in addition OUTRAGEOUS

**²monstrous** \"\ *adv, chiefly dial* **:** EXCEEDINGLY, VERY ⟨~ pretty girl she was too —Archibald Marshall⟩ ⟨she thought it ~ vulgar —Harrietta Wilson⟩

**mon·strous·ly** *adv* **:** in a monstrous manner ⟨so ~ inept a job of reasoning —Irving Brant⟩ ⟨whales . . . seem quite ~ and impossibly large —Alan Moorehead⟩

**mon·strous·ness** *n* -ES **:** the quality or state of being monstrous ⟨the ~ of the man he plays is kept in bounds — he is scary, but not too scary —*Saturday Rev.*⟩

**mon·stru·os·i·ty** \,mänztrə'wäsəd·ē, -n(t)st-, -ətē, -i\ *n* -ES [ME *monstruosite*, modif. of LL *monstrositas* — more at MONSTROSITY] *archaic* **:** MONSTROSITY

**mon·stru·ous** \'mänztrəwəs, -n(t)st-\ *adj* [ME, fr. L *monstruosus* — more at MONSTROUS] *archaic* **:** MONSTROUS

**mons ve·ne·ris** \-'venərəs\ *n, pl* **montes veneris** [NL, lit., eminence of Venus or of venery] **:** a rounded eminence of fatty tissue upon the pubic symphysis of the human female

**mon·ta·dale** \'mäntə,dāl\ *n* [*Montana* state + *dale* (valley)] **1** *usu cap* **:** an American breed of white-faced hornless sheep developed by crossing Cheviot and Columbia sheep and noted for its efficient production of a heavy fleece on a body of good meat conformation **2** -s *often cap* **:** a sheep of the Montadale breed

**¹mon·tage** \(')män-¦täzh, -tȧzh\ *n* -s [F *montage*, fr. *monter* to mount + *-age* — more at MOUNT] **1 a :** the act or photographic process of combining several distinct pictures so that they often blend with or into each other to produce a composite picture which may or may not appear to be made up of separate pictures **b :** a picture made by montage **2 :** an artistic composition made by combining heterogeneous elements **3 a :** a style of film editing in which contrasting shots or sequences are juxtaposed for the purpose of suggesting a total idea or impression **b :** an impressionistic sequence of images linked usu. by dissolves or superimpositions and introduced into a film or television program to develop a single theme, suggest a state of mind, or bridge a time lapse **4 :** a musical composite of heterogeneous themes or fragments usu. played in quick succession and used to represent or bridge a gap in the sequence of time **5 :** a quick succession of snatches of dialogue, music, and sound effects used as a technique in radio writing **6 a :** a literary technique in which heterogeneous images, themes, or fragments of ideas are juxtaposed to produce a single total effect **b :** a literary composite made by means of such technique **7 :** something felt to resemble a montage ⟨for a few seconds his mind held in ~ all the wrecked towns —Norman Mailer⟩ ⟨recalls this phase of his childhood as a dizzy ~ of whistles, intermeshing gears, ladles spilling ore —R.L.Taylor⟩

**²montage** \"\ *vt* -ED/-ING/-S **:** to combine into or depict in a montage

**mon·ta·gnais** \¦mäntən¦yā\ *n, pl* **montagnais** \-ā(z)\ *also* **monta·gnaises** \-āz\ *usu cap* [F, fr. *montagne* mountain, fr. OF *montaigne* — more at MOUNTAIN] **1 :** CHIPEWYAN **2 a :** an Indian people of northern Quebec, Canada **b :** a member of such people **3 :** a dialect of Cree

**mon·ta·gnard** \-¦yär(d)\ *n, pl* **montagnard** \"\ *or* **montagnards** \", -r(d)z\ *usu cap* [F, lit., mountaineer, fr. *montagne* + *-ard*] **1 :** one of several Athapaskan peoples (as the Sekani and Kaska) in the Rocky mountains of Canada **2 :** a member of the Montagnard people **3 :** SEKANI 2

**mon·taign·esque** \¦män¦tā¦nesk\ *adj, usu cap* [F, fr. Michel Eyquem de *Montaigne* †1592 Fr. essayist + F *-esque*] **:** of, relating to, or having the characteristics of the essayist Montaigne, his literary style, or his thought

**¹mon·tana** \(')män-¦tanə\ *adj, usu cap* [*Montana*, state in the northwestern U. S., fr. L *montana* mountainous regions, fr. neut. pl. of *montanus* of a mountain, mountainous — more at MOUNTAIN] **1 :** of or from the state of Montana ⟨a *Montana* dude ranch⟩ **:** of the kind or style prevalent in Montana **:** MONTANAN **2 :** of or relating to the subdivision of the No. American Cretaceous between the Colorado and the Laramie — see GEOLOGIC TIME table

**²montana** \"\ *n* **1** -s *often cap* **:** a sheep bred or raised in Montana **2 a** *or* **montana number one** *usu cap M&N&O* **:** a breed of productive meat-type hogs developed by crossing Hampshires with Danish Landrace — called also *Hamprace* **b** -s *often cap* **:** an animal of this breed

**³mon·ta·ña** \män-'tanyə\ *n* -s [AmerSp, fr. Sp, mountain, fr. (assumed) VL *montanea* — more at MOUNTAIN] **:** a forested region of the eastern slopes of the Andes

**montana grayling** *n, usu cap M* **:** a fish of a variety (*Thymallus signifer montanus*) of the Arctic grayling that is restricted to various tributaries of the Missouri river

**¹mon·tan·an** \(')män-¦tanən\ *or* **mon·tan·ian** \-anēən, -anyən\ *adj, usu cap* [*Montana* state + E *-an, -ian*] **:** of, relating to, or characteristic of Montana or Montanans

**²montanan** \"\ *or* **montanian** \"\ *n* -s *cap* **:** a native or resident of the state of Montana

**mon·tane** \(')män¦tān\ *adj* [L *montanus* of a mountain, mountainous — more at MOUNTAIN] **1 a :** of, relating to, or being the biogeographic zone made up of relatively moist cool upland slopes below timberline and characterized by the presence of large evergreen trees as a dominant life form — compare ALPINE, SUBALPINE **b :** growing in this zone ⟨~ evergreens⟩ **2 :** of, relating to, or made up of montane plants or animals ⟨a ~ flora⟩

**mon·tan·ic acid** \(')män-¦tanik-\ *n* [*montan* (*wax*) + *-ic*] **:** a crystalline fatty acid $C_{27}H_{55}COOH$ or $C_{28}H_{57}COOH$ found free or in the form of esters in montan wax, beeswax, and other natural waxes

**mon·ta·nism** \'mäntə,nizəm\ *n* -s *usu cap* [*Montanus* + E *-ism*] **:** the doctrines of Montanists

**¹mon·ta·nist** \-nəst\ *n* -s *usu cap* [*Montanus*, 2d cent. A.D. Christian schismatic of Phrygia in Asia Minor + E *-ist*] **:** a follower of Montanus who claimed that the Holy Spirit dwelt in him

**²montanist** \"\ *or* **mon·ta·nis·tic** \¦==¦nistik\ *adj, usu cap* **:** of or relating to Montanists or their doctrines **:** embracing Montanism

**mon·tan·ite** \män-'ta,nīt\ *n* -s [*Montana* state + E *-ite*] **:** a mineral $Bi_2(OH)_4TeO_6$ consisting of a basic bismuth tellurate

**mon·ta·nize** \'mäntə,nīz\ *vi* -ED/-ING/-S *usu cap* [*Montanus* + E *-ize*] **:** to adhere to Montanism

**mon·tan wax** \'män-,tan-\ *n* [L *montanus* of a mountain — more at MOUNTAIN] **:** a hard brittle high-melting mineral wax that is brown when crude but yellow to white after refining, that is obtained usu. from lignites by extraction with solvents, and that is used chiefly in polishes, carbon paper, and insulating compositions

**mont blanc ruby** \(')mōⁿ¦bläⁿ-\ *n, usu cap M&B* [fr. *Mont Blanc*, mountain in southeastern France] **:** RUBASSE

**mont·bray·ite** \mänt'brā,īt, mōⁿ'-\ *n* -s [*Montbray*, Quebec province, Canada, its locality + E *-ite*] **:** a mineral $Au_2Te_3$ consisting of telluride of gold

**¹mont·bre·tia** \mänt'brēsh(ē)ə\ *n* -s [NL, fr. A. F. E. Coquebert de *Montbret* †1801 French naturalist + NL *-ia*] **:** a plant of *Tritonia* or the closely related genus *Crocosmia*; *esp* **:** a hybrid cormose plant (*Crocosmia* × *crocosmiiflora*) that is widely cultivated for its spikes of showy yellow or orange flowers

**²montbretia** \"\ [NL, fr. A. F. E. C. de *Montbret* + NL *-ia*] *syn of* TRITONIA

**mont-de-pié·té** \mōⁿd(ə)pyātā\ *n, pl* **monts-de-piété** \"\ [F, fr. It *monte di pietà*, lit., bank of pity] **:** a public pawnbroker's office for lending money at reasonable rates

**mon·te** \'mäntē\ *n* -s [Sp, lit., bank, fr. It, mountain, heap, bank, fr. L *mont-, mons* mountain — more at MOUNT] **1 a** *or* **monte bank :** a card game in which players select any two of four cards faced in a layout and bet that one of them will be matched before the other as cards are dealt one at a time from the pack **b :** THREE-CARD MONTE **2** [MexSp, fr. Sp] *Southwest* **:** an uncultivated area covered usu. densely with spiny shrubs or small trees (as mesquite) **:** CHAPARRAL — compare PAMPA

**mon·te·bra·site** \,mäntē'brä,zīt\ *n* -s [F, fr. *Montebras*, France, its locality + F *-ite*] **:** a mineral $LiAlPO_4(OH)$ consisting of a basic phosphate of aluminum and lithium isomorphous with amblygonite and natromontebrasite

**mon·teith** \(')män-¦tēth, mən-'-\ *also* **mon·teth** \", -teth\ *n* -s [after *Monteith* (*Monteigh*), 17th cent. Scotchman who wore a cloak scalloped at the bottom] **:** a large usu. silver punch bowl that has a scalloped rim

monteith

**monte-jus** \(')mänt¦jüs, (')mōⁿ¦zhü\ *n* [F, fr. *monter* to mount, raise + *jus* juice — more at MOUNT, JUICE] **:** an apparatus for raising a liquid by pressure of air or steam in a reservoir containing the liquid — compare ACID EGG

**¹mon·te·ne·grin** \¦mäntə¦nēgrən\ *adj, usu cap* [*Montenegro*, region in southwestern Yugoslavia + E *-in*] **1 :** of, relating to, or characteristic of Montenegro **2 :** of, relating to, or characteristic of the people of Montenegro

**²montenegrin** \"\ *also* **mon·te·ne·grine** \"\ *n* -s *cap* **:** a native or inhabitant of Montenegro

**mon·te·ra** \män-'terə\ *n* -s [Sp, fr. *montero* hunter, fr. *monte* mountain, forested region + *-ero* (fr. L *-arius* -ary) — more at MONTE] **:** a cloth cap or hat; *specif* **:** the soft black bicorne hat worn by bullfighters

**mon·te·rey cheese** \¦mäntə¦rā-\ *also* **monterey** *or* **monterey jack** *n, usu cap M&J* [fr. *Monterey* county, Calif.] **:** jack cheese of low moisture content

**monterey cypress** *n, usu cap M* [fr. *Monterey* Bay, Calif.] **:** a tall California cypress (*Cupressus macrocarpa*) endemic on Monterey Bay and now widely used for ornament, reforestation, and shelterbelt planting

**monterey halibut** *n, usu cap M* [fr. *Monterey* Bay, Calif.] **:** CALIFORNIA HALIBUT

**monterey pine** *n, usu cap M* [fr. *Monterey* county Calif.] **:** a southern California pine (*Pinus radiata*) that is often 90 feet high and has leaves in fascicles of two or three, cones lopsided, and cone scales with minute prickles

**monterey spanish mackerel** *n, usu cap M&S* [fr. *Monterey* Bay, Calif.] **:** an unspotted mackerel (*Scomberomorus concolor*) that is found off the California coast and is related to the Spanish mackerel

**mon·te·ro** \män-'te(,)rō\ *n* -s [Sp — more at MONTERA] **1 :** HUNTSMAN **2 :** a round cap with a flap worn by huntsmen **3 :** a forester or ranger in the Philippines

**mon·ter·rey** \¦mäntə¦rā\ *adj, usu cap* [fr. *Monterrey*, Mexico] **:** of or from the city of Monterrey, Mexico **:** of the kind or style prevalent in Monterrey

**montes** *pl of* MONS

**mon·tes·so·ri·an** \¦mäntə¦sōrēən\ *adj, usu cap M* [Maria *Montessori* †1952 Ital. physician & educator + E *-an*] **:** of, following, or relating to a system for training young children emphasizing free physical activity, informal and individual instruction, early development of writing and reading, and extended sensory motor training

**mon·te·video** \¦mäntəvə¦dā,ō *also* -¦vidē,ō\ *adj, usu cap* [fr. *Montevideo*, Uruguay] **:** of or from Montevideo, the capital of Uruguay **:** of the kind or style prevalent in Montevideo

**mon·te·zu·ma cypress** \¦mäntə¦zümə-\ *n, usu cap M* [prob. after *Montezuma* II †1520 Aztec ruler at the time of the Spanish conquest of Mexico] **:** AHUEHUETE

**mont·gol·fi·er** *or* **mon·gol·fi·er** \män(t)'gälfēə(r), mōⁿ-'gälfē,ā\ *n* -s [after Joseph M. *Montgolfier* †1810 and Jacques E. *Montgolfier* †1799 French inventors who built the first practical fire balloon] **:** FIRE BALLOON 1

**¹mont·gom·ery** \,mən(t)'gəmrē, (')män(t)¦gəm-, -ri *also* (')män(t)¦gäm- *sometimes* ¦mən(t)¦gəm- *or* -mər-\ *adj, usu cap* [fr. *Montgomery*, Alabama] **:** of or from Montgomery, the capital of Alabama **:** of the kind or style prevalent in Montgomery

**²montgomery** \"\ *n, usu cap* [fr. *Montgomery*, district in Pakistan where the breed originated] **:** SAHIWAL

**mont·gom·ery·ite** \-¦,īt\ *n* -s [Arthur *Montgomery* *b*1909 Am. geologist + E *-ite*] **:** a mineral $Ca_4Al_5(PO_4)_6(OH)_5.11H_2O$ consisting of a hydrous basic phosphate of calcium and aluminum

**mont·gom·ery·shire** \,mən(t)'=(=)=,shi(ə)r, -,shər, män(t)- *sometimes* ,mən(t)-'\ *adj, usu cap* [fr. *Montgomeryshire* or *Montgomery*, county in Wales] **:** of or from the county of Montgomery, Wales **:** of the kind or style prevalent in Montgomery

**month** \'mən(t)th\ *n, pl* **months** \'mən(t)s, -n(t)ths\ [ME

MONTHS OF THE PRINCIPAL CALENDARS

| GREGORIAN[1] name | number of days | JEWISH name | number of days | MUHAMMADAN name | number of days | HINDU[5] name |
|---|---|---|---|---|---|---|
| January begins 10 days after winter solstice | 31 | Tishri begins with new moon nearest autumnal equinox | 30 | Muharram[4] in A.H. 1378 began July 18, 1948 | 30 | Chait[6] (March-April) |
| February in leap years | 28 / 29 | Heshvan | 29 or 30 | Safar | 29 | Baisakh (April-May) |
| March | 31 | Kislev | 29 or 30 | Rabi I | 30 | Jeth (May-June) |
| April | 30 | Tebet | 29 | Rabi II | 29 | Asarh (June-July) |
| May | 31 | Shebat | 30 | Jumada I | 30 | Sawan (July-August) |
| June | 30 | Adar[2] | 29 or 30 | Jumada II | 29 | Bhadon (August-September) |
| July | 31 | Nisan[3] | 30 | Rajab | 30 | Asin (September-October) |
| August | 31 | Iyar | 29 | Sha'ban | 29 | Kartik (October-November) |
| September | 30 | Sivan | 30 | Ramadan | 30 | Aghan (November-December) |
| October | 31 | Tammuz | 29 | Shawwal | 29 | Pus (December-January) |
| November | 30 | Ab | 30 | Dhu'l-Qa'dah | 30 | Magh (January-February) |
| December | 31 | Elul | 29 | Dhu'l-Hijja in leap years | 29 / 30 | Phagun (February-March) |

[1]The equinoxes occur on March 21 and September 23, the solstices on June 22 and December 22.

[2]In leap years Adar is followed by Veadar or Adar Sheni, an intercalary month of 29 days.

[3]Anciently called Abib; the first month of the postexilic calendar; sometimes called the first month of the ecclesiastical year.

[4]Retrogresses through the seasons; the Muhammadan year is lunar and each month begins at the approximate new moon; the year 1 A.H. began on Friday, July 16, A.D. 622.

[5]An extra month is inserted after every month in which two new moons occur (once in three years). The intercalary month has the name of the one that precedes it.

[6]Baisakh is sometimes considered the first month of the Hindu year.

*moneth, month,* fr. OE *mōnath;* akin to OHG *mānōd* month, ON *mānathr,* Goth *menoths* month, *mena* moon — more at MOON] **1 :** a measure of time corresponding or nearly corresponding to the period of the moon's revolution: as **a :** a period of approximately four weeks, 30 days, or 1/12 of a year based primarily on the period of the moon's revolution and cycle of phase changes — see ANOMALISTIC MONTH, NODICAL MONTH, SIDEREAL MONTH, SYNODIC MONTH, TROPICAL MONTH **b :** one of the twelve portions into which the year is divided in the Gregorian calendar; *also* **:** a similar portion of a year in any calendar **c :** a period of time about the length of a lunar month but not necessarily coinciding with a calendar month **d :** *months, pl* **:** an indefinite usu. extended period of time ⟨been asking you to come forward for ~ —Graham Greene⟩ **2 a** *archaic* **:** a lunar month in common law **b :** a period of time presumed by statute in the U. S. and Great Britain to mean a calendar month **3 :** one ninth of the typical duration of human pregnancy ⟨she was in her eighth ~⟩ — **month of sundays** *usu cap S* **:** an indefinitely long time ⟨hadn't been anywhere for a *month of Sundays*⟩

**¹month·ly** \ˈmən(t)thlē, -li\ *adv* [*month* + *-ly* (adv. suffix)] **:** once a month **:** by the month ⟨the annuity is payable semiannually, quarterly, or ~ —J.B.Maclean⟩

**²monthly** \"\ *adj* [*month* + *-ly* (adj. suffix)] **1 :** of or relating to a month: as **a :** payable every month ⟨~ allowances to parents for the maintenance . . . of the child —*Current Biog.*⟩ **b :** reckoned by the month ⟨an average ~ wage⟩ **c :** based on a month ⟨a ~ rate⟩ ⟨~ statistics⟩ **2 :** having a duration of one month **:** completed in a month ⟨the ~ revolution of the moon⟩ **3 :** occurring, appearing, or being made, done, or acted upon every month or once a month ⟨produces a ~ television show⟩ ⟨a ~ magazine⟩

**³monthly** \"\ *n* -ES **1 :** a periodical that is published regularly once a month **2 monthlies** *pl* **:** a menstrual period

**monthly concert** *n* **:** a monthly meeting formerly held in some Protestant Christian churches for the purpose of offering concerted prayer for missions

**monthly epact** *n* **:** EPACT 1b

**monthly meeting** *n, usu cap both Ms* **1 :** an organizational unit of the Society of Friends made up of one or several local congregations — see QUARTERLY MEETING **2 :** a session of a Monthly Meeting

**month's mind** *n* [ME *moneth mynde,* fr. *moneth* month + *mynde* mind] **1** *Roman Catholicism* **:** a requiem mass for a person a month after his death **2** *Brit* **:** strong desire **:** INCLINATION ⟨I see you have a *month's mind* to them —Shak.⟩

**mon·tia** \ˈmäntēə\ *n, cap* [NL, fr. Giuseppe *Monti* †1760 Ital. botanist & NL *-ia*] **:** a small genus of densely tufted annual herbs (family Portulacaceae) having opposite fleshy leaves, flowers with two sepals and three white petals, and a three-seeded capsule — see BLINKS, TOAD LILY, WATER CHICKWEED

**mon·ti·cel·lite** \ˌmäntəˈseˌlīt, -ˈche-\ *n* -S [Teodoro *Monticelli* †1845 Ital. naturalist + E *-ite*] **:** a mineral $CaMgSiO_4$ consisting of a colorless or gray calcium magnesium silicate related to olivine

**mon·ti·cle** \ˈmäntəkəl\ *n* -S [F *monticule* — more at MONTICULE] **:** a little hill

**mon·tic·u·late** \mänˈtikyələt\ *adj* [*monticule* + *-ate*] **:** having monticules

**mon·ti·cule** \ˈmäntəˌkyül\ *n* -S [F, fr. LL *monticulus,* dim. of L *mont-, mons* mountain — more at MOUNT] **1 :** a little mount **:** HILLOCK **:** a small elevation or prominence **2 :** a subordinate cone of a volcano

**mon·ti·cu·lip·ora** \ˌmäntəkyəˈlipərə\ *n, cap* [NL, fr. LL *monticulus* + NL *-pora*] **:** a genus of fossil bryozoans forming massive zoaria similar to coral and composed of polygonal mostly thin-walled zooecia and represented by numerous species in the Ordovician and extending into the Silurian — **mon·ti·cu·lip·o·rid·e·an** \ˌ==ˌ=ˈridēən\ *adj or n* — **mon·ti·cu·lip·o·roid** \ˌ==ˌ=ˌrȯid\ *adj or n*

**mon·tic·u·lose** \mänˈtikyəˌlōs\ *adj* [LL *monticulus* + E *-ose*] **:** covered with small eminences

**mon·tic·u·lous** \-ləs\ *adj* [ML *monticulosus,* fr. LL *monticulus* + L *-osus* -ous] **:** MONTICULATE

**mon·tic·u·lus** \-ləs\ *n* -ES [LL — more at MONTICULE] **1 :** MONTICULE **2** [NL, fr. LL] **:** the median dorsal projection of the cerebellum

**mon·til·la** \mänˈtilə\ *n* -S [Sp, fr. *Montilla,* town in Spain] **:** a very pale dry sherry

**mont·mar·trite** \mäntˈmärˌtrīt\ *n* -S [F, fr. *Montmartre,* section of Paris, France, its locality + F *-ite*] **:** gypsum from Montmartre

**mont·mo·ril·lon·ite** \ˌmäntməˈriləˌnīt\ *n* -S [F, fr. *Montmorillon,* Dept. Vienne, France + F *-ite*] **:** a soft clay mineral $RMgAl_5Si_{12}O_{30}(OH)_6{\cdot}nH_2O$ with R representing exchangeable bases that is usu. white, grayish, pale red, or blue and that consists of a hydrous aluminum silicate with considerable capacity for exchanging part of the aluminum for magnesium, alkalies, and other bases — compare HECTORITE

**mont·mo·ril·lon·it·ic** \ˌ==ˌ==ˈnid·ik\ *adj* **:** of or containing montmorillonite

**mont·pe·lier** \(ˈ)māntˈpēlyə(r)\ *adj, usu cap* [fr. *Montpelier,* Vt.] **:** of or from Montpelier, the capital of Vermont ⟨*Montpelier* granite⟩ **:** of the kind or style prevalent in Montpelier

**mont·pel·lier green** \ˌmōⁿpelˈyā-\ *n, often cap M* [prob. fr. *Montpellier,* city in southern France] **:** VERDIGRIS 4

**montpellier yellow** *n* **1** *usu cap M* **:** CASSEL YELLOW 1 **2** *often cap M* **:** ORPIMENT 2

**mon·tra·chet** \ˌmōⁿtrăˈshā\ *n* -S *usu cap* [F, fr. *Montrachet,* vineyard in Dept. Côte-d'Or, France] **:** a white Burgundy wine

**mon·tre** \ˈmōⁿtrə\ *n* -S [F, lit., show, display, fr. MF, fr. *montrer* to show, fr. L *monstrare* — more at MUSTER] **1 :** an open diapason or other pipe-organ stop having its pipes displayed as a part of the organ case **2 :** PYROMETRIC CONE

**mon·tre·al** \ˌmän·trēˈȯl, ˌmən-\ *adj, usu cap* [fr. *Montreal,* Canada] **:** of or from the city of Montreal, Quebec **:** of the kind or style prevalent in Montreal

**mon·tre·al·er** \-lə(r)\ *n* -S *cap* [*Montreal,* Canada + E *-er*] **:** a native or inhabitant of Montreal

**mon·troy·dite** \mänˈtrȯiˌdīt\ *n* -S [*Montroyd* Sharpe, 20th cent. Am. mine owner + E *-ite*] **:** a mineral HgO consisting of mercuric oxide

**monts-de-piété** *pl of* MONT-DE-PIÉTÉ

**mon·ture** \ˈmänchə(r)\ *n* -S [F, fr. MF, fr. *monter* to mount + *-ure* — more at MOUNT] **1 :** a frame or setting esp. for a jewel **2 :** a manner of mounting or setting (as a jewel)

**mon·tu·vio** \mänˈtüvēˌō\ *also* **mon·tu·bio** \-bēˌō\ *n* -S [AmerSp, fr. Sp *monte* mountain, forested region — more at MONTE] **:** an Ecuadorian of mixed white, Indian, and Negro descent

**¹mon·u·ment** \ˈmänyəmənt\ *n* -S [ME, fr. L *monumentum, monimentum,* fr. *monēre* to remind + *-mentum* -ment — more at MIND] **1** *obs* **:** a burial vault **:** SEPULCHER ⟨her body sleeps in Capel's ~, and her immortal part with angels lives —Shak.⟩ **2** *archaic* **:** a written legal document or record **:** TREATISE ⟨the critical study of the ~s of Roman and feudal law —Mark Pattison⟩ **3 a :** something that by surviving represents or testifies to the greatness or achievement esp. of an individual or an age ⟨visible ~s to the early struggles of the pioneers . . . are the old forts —*Amer. Guide Series: Maine*⟩ ⟨the circular world map drawn on a single skein of vellum . . . is one of the great cartographic ~s —*Brit. Book News*⟩ ⟨whose life work was a ~ to pure science —H.J.Muller⟩ **b** (1) **:** a conspicuous instance **:** a notable example ⟨the great Connecticut dictionary stood as a ~ of New England learning —Van Wyck Brooks⟩ ⟨that speech . . . was a model, or rather a ~, of beautiful English utterance —George Sampson⟩ ⟨that ~ of dignity would never connive at anything —Margery Allingham⟩ (2) **:** one of unusual prominence **:** a distinguished figure ⟨the answer must be sought in the period before the man became a ~ —G.W.Johnson⟩ ⟨made himself into a ~ within his own lifetime —Walter Millis⟩ **4 :** a structure (as a pillar, stone, or building) erected or maintained in memory of the dead or to preserve the remembrance of a person, event, or action ⟨the Lincoln Memorial is a national ~⟩ ⟨~s celebrating the victories of war —R.B.Fosdick⟩ ⟨run the home as a historic site, reopen the musty old lab as a . . . ~ —*Time*⟩ **5** *archaic* **:** an identifying mark **:** EVIDENCE; *also* **:** PORTENT, SIGN ⟨gaze . . . as if they saw some wondrous ~, some comet or unusual prodigy —Shak.⟩ **6** *obs* **:** a carved statue **:** EFFIGY ⟨if the quick fire of youth light not your mind, you are no maiden but a ~ —Shak.⟩ **7 :** a natural or artificial but permanent object serving to indicate a limit or to mark a boundary (as a lake, stream, blazed tree, iron pin) **8 :** a natural feature (as a mountain or canyon) or an area of special historic or scientific interest (as a battle site or fossil remains) that is set aside by a local or national government as public property **9 :** a rock pinnacle or column resulting from erosion and resembling a man-made monument — compare HOODOO **10 :** a written tribute **:** TESTIMONIAL ⟨a model of appreciative biography, a charming ~ to a great man —T.F.Hamlin⟩

**²mon·u·ment** \-ˌment, -ˌmənt — see ²-MENT\ *vt* -ED/-ING/-S **1 :** to erect a monument to **:** to signalize the memory of **:** COMMEMORATE **2 :** to place or set up monuments on ⟨erected chapels and altars there, and ~*ed* the places of sacred scenes and associations —Hezekiah Butterworth⟩ **3 :** to mark with monuments in surveying ⟨in locating, ~*ing,* and mapping the boundary, extensive use has been made of the geodetic maps of North America —*U.S.Daily*⟩

**mon·u·men·tal** \ˌmänyəˈmentᵊl\ *adj* [LL *monumentalis,* fr. L *monumentum* monument + *-alis* -al] **1 a** *obs* **:** of or relating to a sepulcher ⟨that whiter skin of hers than snow, and smooth as ~ alabaster —Shak.⟩ **b :** serving as a monument ⟨~ chapels of this style —Thomas Rickman⟩ **2 :** resembling a monument: as **a :** having impressive bulk or size **:** IMMENSE, MASSIVE ⟨the entrance on this side is vigorously indicated . . . by a great ~ carriageway —*Amer. Guide Series: N.Y.City*⟩ ⟨the steps are flanked by ~ sculptures —*Amer. Guide Series: La.*⟩ ⟨he could paint superbly on a ~ scale —Herbert Read⟩ **b :** marked by outstanding quality **:** highly significant **:** INESTIMABLE ⟨in this ~ work the entire storehouse of the world's art is surveyed —*advt*⟩ ⟨he was too modest, and had too varied tastes . . . to care to be the ~ critic —T.S.Eliot⟩ **3 :** of, relating to, or belonging to a monument **:** occurring on a monument ⟨failed to carry the use of the arch into ~ architecture —A.L.Kroeber⟩ ⟨a ~ script —Maurice Vieyra⟩ **4 :** very great — used as an intensive ⟨notable for their ~ respectability —John Kobler⟩ ⟨~ failures of the past —W.E.Swinton⟩ ⟨their inertia is as ~ as their grief —John Mason Brown⟩
**syn** MASSIVE, MONSTROUS

**mon·u·men·tal·ism** \ˌ==ˈmentᵊlˌizəm\ *n* -S **:** a monumental style

**mon·u·men·tal·i·ty** \ˌ==mənˈtalədˌē, -ˌmen-, -lətē, -i\ *n* -ES **:** the quality or state of being monumental ⟨differentiates modern design from the immobile and ponderous ~ of the past —Lewis Mumford⟩

**mon·u·men·tal·ize** \ˌ==ˈmentᵊlˌīz\ *vt* -ED/-ING/-S **:** to record or memorialize lastingly by or as if by a monument **:** to make monumental

**mon·u·men·tal·ly** \ˌmänyəˈmentᵊlī\ *adv* **:** in a monumental manner ⟨~ shy —Robert Henderson⟩ ⟨built mostly of sandstone . . . it rises ~ —Christopher Rand⟩

**mon·u·ment·less** *adj* **:** having no monuments

**monument plant** *n* **:** AMERICAN COLUMBO

**mony** \ˈmänē, -ni\ *chiefly Scot var of* MANY

**mon·zo·nite** \ˈmänzəˌnīt, ˈmōn-\ *n* -S [F, fr. Mt. *Monzoni,* northeast Italy + F *-ite*] **1 :** a granular igneous rock composed of plagioclase and orthoclase in about equal quantities together with augite and a little biotite **2 :** any of a large group of rocks intermediate between the syenite group and the diorite-gabbro group — **mon·zo·nit·ic** \ˌ==ˈnid·ik\ *adj*

**¹moo** \ˈmü\ *vb* -ED/-ING/-S [imit.] *vi* **:** to make the natural throat noise of a cow **:** LOW ~ *vt* **:** to utter with a sound resembling the lowing of a cow ⟨meltingly ~ a religious ballad —*Punch*⟩

**²moo** \"\ *n* -S **1 :** the lowing of a cow **2 :** a sound that resembles a moo

**moo·cah** \ˈmükə\ *n* -S [prob. by alter.] **:** MARIHUANA

**¹mooch** \ˈmüch\ *vb* -ED/-ING/-ES [prob. fr. F dial. *muchier* to hide, lurk] *vi* **1** *dial chiefly Brit* **:** to absent oneself **:** play truant **2 :** to move slowly or apathetically **:** wander aimlessly **:** AMBLE, SAUNTER ⟨the crowd ~*ed* away in sullen disinterest —Bruce Marshall⟩ ⟨hateful to be without a garden; there is nowhere to sit or ~ —Gladys B. Stern⟩ ⟨~*ed* forward on to the grass where he sat down . . . and emitted two short, gruff barks —Mervyn Wall⟩ ⟨the destroyer ~*ed* around all over the channel for two weeks —Irwin Shaw⟩; *specif* **:** SLINK ⟨heard I had been ~*ing* round his house and spying —John Buchan⟩ **3 :** to take without giving **:** impose on another's hospitality or generosity **:** SPONGE, CADGE ⟨~*ed* on relatives for a living so he could devote full time to his art⟩ ⟨a rich young man addicted to ~*ing* from his friends —*Newsweek*⟩ **4** *West* **:** to troll (as for salmon) with a spinner or spoon ⟨the angler may spin or ~ on the same trip, as fancy dictates —*Fisherman's Encyc.*⟩ ~ *vt* **1 :** to take surreptitiously **:** make off with **:** SNEAK, STEAL ⟨~ an apple when the huckster isn't looking⟩ **2 :** to get by coaxing or wheedling **:** CADGE, BEG ⟨a dark-eyed urchin came up and tried to ~ a cigarette —*Newsweek*⟩ ⟨forest ponies . . . line the roads on Sundays to ~ tea buns from picnickers —A.J. Liebling⟩

**²mooch** \"\ *n* -ES **1** *slang* **:** an act or instance of mooching **:** PROWL, SLOUCH; *specif* **:** a jazz dance of the 1920s characterized by sensuous hip jerking and knee shivering **2** *slang* **a :** MOOCHER **b :** a customer looking for bargains; *specif* **:** an inexperienced stock speculator ⟨suckers or ~*es* . . . who have in the past bought blue-sky stocks —*Industrial Digest*⟩

**moo·cha** \ˈmüchə\ *n* -S [Zulu *umutsha*] **:** a loincloth of animals' tails or strips of animal skin worn by native peoples of So. Africa

**mooch·er** \ˈmüchə(r)\ *n* -S **1 a** *slang* **:** one that loiters or snoops **b :** an inspector of rivets and welded joints and seams of steel structures **2** *slang* **:** one that begs or takes surreptitiously **:** CADGER, GRAFTER **3** *West* **:** one that trolls for salmon with a spinner or spoon

**¹mood** \ˈmüd\ *n* -S [ME *mod, mood,* fr. OE *mōd;* akin to OHG *muot* emotion, mood, mind, purpose, ON *mōthr* wrath, moodiness, Goth *mōths* courage, anger, L *mos* custom, Gk *maiesthai* to strive, and perh. to Lith *matyti* to see, OSlav *motriti* to look] **1 a :** a conscious subjective state of mind **:** predominant emotion **:** FEELING, TEMPER ⟨it had taken possession of him again — that indomitable, conquering ~ which seemed to give him the right of way wherever he went —O.E.Rölvaag⟩ ⟨sometimes the ~ of one player may cause him to change some detail of interpretation —S.E.Wier⟩ ⟨the ox was his companion . . . and he had walked behind and praised it and cursed it as his ~ was —Pearl Buck⟩ **b :** a particular state of mind predisposing to action **:** receptive spirit ⟨in the ~ to listen to her —Mary Webb⟩ ⟨the House was, at that time, in no giving ~ —T.B.Macaulay⟩ **2** *archaic* **:** a fit of anger **:** RAGE ⟨who, in my ~, I stabbed unto the heart —Shak.⟩ **3 a :** a prevailing attitude **:** general spirit **:** DISPOSITION ⟨our national ~ has changed with our fortunes in battle —J.K. Little⟩ ⟨the Indians betrayed their ~ by accepting only rifles . . . and hatchets in payment for their furs —John Mason Brown⟩ **b :** a distinctive atmosphere or emotional context **:** tonal quality **:** AURA ⟨a large open room that had the ~ of a French commercial outpost somewhere in the tropics —D.W. Dresden⟩ ⟨the emotional ~ of the play —H.F.Helvenston⟩ ⟨the ~ of the landscape, achieved by the beauty of the evening light —Kenneth Clark⟩ ⟨in this book his ~ is doggedly elegiac —Anthony Quinton⟩ **c :** a degree of activity or gradation of illumination **:** ASPECT ⟨the sea in all its ~s —W.H.Taylor⟩ ⟨watching land and water, rocks and trees, and their ever-changing hues and ~s —Richard Semon⟩
**syn** HUMOR, TEMPER, VEIN: MOOD is the comprehensive term for any state of mind in which one emotion or desire or set of them is ascendant, stressing possibly more than the other terms a pervasiveness and compelling quality ⟨the tense limbs of a body possessed by a single *mood* of rapt exaltation —Laurence Binyon⟩ ⟨everything was going along smoothly and the men were in a happy *mood* —H.A.Chippendale⟩ ⟨the disgustingly bilious *mood* which a nasty night at sea never fails to produce —David Fairchild⟩ ⟨practicality was the prevailing *mood* after the war —Dixon Wecter⟩ ⟨the normally sedate neighborhood relaxes in holiday *mood* —*Amer. Guide Series: Md.*⟩ HUMOR in this context applies chiefly to a mood resulting from one's special temperament or physical or mental condition at the moment, suggesting a capriciousness or whimsicality ⟨in no *humor* to be trifled with⟩ ⟨a man of violent *humors* and yet touching affection⟩ ⟨I would not only consult the interest of the people, but I would cheerfully gratify their *humors* —Edmund Burke⟩ TEMPER can apply to a mood dominated by a single strong emotion, usu. anger when the term is unmodified; when modified by an adjective indicating the controlling emotion, the term indicates any humor manifest in a display of feeling ⟨found his friend in quite a *temper*⟩ ⟨wake up in a foul *temper*⟩ ⟨find his boss in a pleasant *temper*⟩ VEIN is often used in the sense of MOOD, usu. suggesting greater transitoriness, or in the sense of HUMOR but almost devoid of any implication of physical or temperamental cause ⟨the whole is written in a *vein* of ironic seriousness — H.J.Laski⟩ ⟨be in a jubilant *vein* after a small triumph⟩ ⟨make a request of a man while he is in an affable and generous *vein*⟩

**²mood** \"\ *n* -S [alter. (influenced by ¹*mood*) of ¹*mode*] **1 a :** the form of a syllogism classified according to the quantity and quality of the constituent propositions and traditionally shown by a sequence formed from the letters A, E, I, O such that the first letter indicates the major premise, the second the minor, and the third the conclusion — compare FIGURE 10, OPPOSITION 2a(2) **b :** MODE 3b **2 a :** distinction of form in a verb to express whether the action or state it denotes is conceived as fact or in some other manner (as command, possibility, or wish) ⟨the Latin verb has person, tense, number, ~, and voice⟩ **b :** a set of inflectional forms of a verb that express whether the action or state it denotes is conceived as fact or in some other manner ⟨the indicative ~⟩ ⟨the imperative ~⟩ ⟨the subjunctive ~⟩ ⟨the optative ~⟩ **c :** the part of the meaning of a verb form that consists of the expression of whether the action or state it denotes is conceived as fact or in some other manner **3 :** MODE 1b

**mood·i·ly** \ˈmüdᵊlˌē, -dəl|, |i\ *adv* **:** in a moody manner **:** DISMALLY, GLOOMILY

**mood·i·ness** \-dēnəs, -din-\ *n* -ES **:** the quality or state of being moody **:** MELANCHOLY, GLOOM

**mood swing** *n* [¹*mood*] **:** a marked change in mood esp. to elation or depression (as in cyclothymia) ⟨certain personality characteristics . . . such as *mood swings,* paranoid features and self-punishment drives —E.F.Kerman⟩

**¹moody** \ˈmüdē, -di\ *adj* -ER/-EST [ME *mody,* fr. OE *mōdig,* fr. *mōd* mood, courage + *-ig* -y — more at MOOD] **1** *obs* **:** full of wrath **:** ANGRY **2 a :** subject to or characterized by depression or discontent **:** SULLEN, GLOOMY ⟨mental depression made him . . . morose, ~, and at times childish —C.N.Boyd⟩ ⟨grew ~ and petulant and would not eat —Pearl Buck⟩ **b :** subject to moods **:** TEMPERAMENTAL ⟨~ artist⟩ ⟨outscheming the ~ winds —K.D.Curtis⟩ **:** expressive of a mood ⟨the meanings come through as a result of some fine ~ direction —Hollis Alpert⟩

**²moody** \ˈmüdi\ *var of* MOUDIE

**mooed** *past of* MOO

**mooing** *n* -S [fr. gerund of ¹*moo*] **:** ²MOO

**mool** \ˈmül\ *n* -S [by alter.] **1** *dial Brit* **:** ¹MOLD 1 **2** *dial Brit* **:** ¹MOLD 2b

**moo·la** *or* **moo·lah** \ˈmülə\ *n* -S [origin unknown] *slang* **:** MONEY ⟨ninety grand is a lot of ~ —Harold Robbins⟩

**mool·ey** \ˈmüli\ *chiefly dial var of* MULEY

**mool·ings** \ˈmülənz, -liŋz\ *n pl* [pl. of *mooling,* gerund of Sc *mool* to crumble, fr. *mool,* n.] *Scot* **:** CRUMB

**moolvee** *var of* MAULVI

**¹moon** \ˈmün\ *n* -S *often attrib* [ME *mone, moone,* fr. OE *mōna;* akin to OHG *māno* moon, ON *māni,* Goth *mena* moon, L *mensis* month, Gk *mēn* month, *mēnē* moon, Skt *mās, māsa* moon, month, and perh. to Skt *māti* he measures — more at MEASURE] **1 a :** the earth's only known natural satellite and next to the sun the most conspicuous object in the heavens shining by the sun's reflected light, revolving about the earth from west to east in about 29½ days with reference to the sun or about 27⅓ days with reference to the stars, having a diameter of 2160 miles and a mean distance from the earth of about 238,857 miles, a mass about one eightieth that of the earth and a volume about one forty-ninth, and rotating as it revolves so that it always presents nearly the same face to the earth **b :** one complete moon cycle consisting of four phases ⟨the old ~ in the arms of the new⟩ — see FULL MOON, NEW MOON; compare ECLIPSE, GIBBOUS, LIBRATION, TIDE **c :** any satellite in the sky ⟨observing the ~s of Jupiter or Saturn⟩ ⟨launching of a man-made ~ —L.V.Berkner⟩ **2 :** the time of a synodic month ⟨labored for many ~s to complete this unusual work of primitive art —*Amer. Guide Series: Conn.*⟩ **3 :** MOONLIGHT ⟨keep out of the ~ or it may turn your head —H.R. Haggard⟩ **4 :** something that resembles a moon: as **a :** a disk on the face of a clock showing the phases of the moon ⟨the plate that carries the ~ —James Ferguson⟩ **b :** a globe surrounding a light ⟨a green ~ of porcelain over a naked electric bulb —Frances Towers⟩ **c :** a slice bar with a nearly circular blade perforated in the middle and used in tending a brickkiln fire **d :** a highly translucent spot in old porcelain **e :** LUNULE **a f :** MOON KNIFE **5 :** something impossible or inaccessible ⟨reach for the ~⟩ **6** *slang* **:** ¹MOONSHINE 3 ⟨five or six good stiff drinks of ~ —Sherwood Anderson⟩ **7 :** PLATY

phases of the moon: *1–8* showing the moon in orbit around the earth; *a–h* corresponding phases as seen from the earth; *1* new moon, *3* first quarter, *5* full moon, *7* last quarter; *a* new moon, *b* waxing crescent, *c* half-moon, *d* gibbous, *e* full moon, *f* gibbous, *g* half-moon, *h* waning crescent

**²moon** \"\ *vb* -ED/-ING/-S *vt* **1** *archaic* **:** to expose to moonlight ⟨the huge man . . . not sunning, but ~*ing* himself —Thomas De Quincey⟩ **2 :** to spend in idle reverie **:** DREAM — used with *away* ⟨~ the afternoon away⟩ **3 :** to locate by sighting against the moon ⟨~ a possum⟩ ⟨darted along . . . till I could ~ the house with the old stack —Joseph Furphy⟩ **4 :** to scrape (a skin or hide) with a moon knife ~ *vi* **:** to behave in an abstracted way **:** move or gaze dreamily or abstractedly **:** DAWDLE, GAPE ⟨~*ed* around the house all day in a dream —Patrick Campbell⟩ ⟨got to ~*ing* over her dead father —Grace Metalious⟩ ⟨~*ing* up into his eyes —Jack Slater⟩ ⟨~s over tape-recorded music —Gilbert Millstein⟩ ⟨~*ing* over a silken phrase and relaxing the flow of melody to a point where the tempo becomes obscured —Roland Gelatt⟩

**moonal** *or* **moonaul** *var of* MONAL

**moonbeam** \ˈ=ˌ=\ *n* **1 :** a ray of light from the moon **2 :** PEARL 6b

**moonbill** \ˈ=ˌ=\ *n, South* **:** RING-NECKED DUCK

**¹moon-blind** \ˈ=ˌ=\ *adj* [¹*moon* + *blind*] **:** afflicted with moon blindness

**²moon-blind** \ˈ=ˌ=\ *n* **:** MOON BLINDNESS

**moon blindness** *n* **:** a periodic ophthalmia or recurrent inflammation of the eye of the horse resulting ultimately in corneal opacity and blindness that has been attributed to genetic factors and to infection but is now usu. considered to be due to a deficiency of riboflavin in the diet

**moon·bow** \ˈ=ˌbō\ *n* [¹*moon* + *rainbow*] **:** a rainbow formed by light from the moon

**moon cake** *n* **:** a small pastry filled with a mixture of meat and other ingredients traditionally associated with the Chinese harvest festival

**mooncalf** \ˈ=ˌ=\ *n* **1 a** *obs* **:** uterine mole **b :** MONSTER 2a **2 :** a foolish or absentminded person **:** DOLT, SIMPLETON

**moon daisy** *n, Brit* **:** DAISY 1b

**moondial** \ˈ=ˌ==\ *n* **:** NIGHT DIAL 1

**moon dog** *n* **:** PARASELENE

**moondown** \ˈ=ˌ=\ *n* [*moon* + *-down* (as in *sundown*)] **:** MOONSET

**¹mooned** *past of* MOON

**²mooned** \ˈmün(ə)d\ *adj, archaic* [¹*moon* + *-ed*] **:** ornamented with or shaped like the moon esp. in the shape of a crescent ⟨with his ~ train the strutting peacock . . . flutters into the Ark —Michael Drayton⟩ ⟨the angelic squadron . . . sharpening in ~ horns their phalanx —John Milton⟩

**moon·er** \ˈmünə(r)\ *n* -S [²*moon* + *-er*] **:** one that moons; *specif* **:** one that moons skins or hides

**mooney** *var of* MOONY

**mooneye** \'⸗,⸗\ *n* **1 a :** an eye affected with moon blindness **b :** MOON BLINDNESS **2 a :** any of three American freshwater fishes constituting the genus *Hiodon* that are closely related to the goldeye, resemble the shad, but are inferior as food; *esp* **:** a fish (*H. tergisus*) of the Great Lakes and Mississippi valley **b :** ³BLOATER 2

**mooneye cisco** *n* **:** ³BLOATER 2

**moon–eyed** \'⸗,⸗\ *adj* **1 :** MOON-BLIND **2 a :** SQUINT-EYED **b :** ROUND-EYED **3** *archaic* **:** able to see well at night

**moonfaced** \'⸗,⸗\ *adj* **:** having a face as round as a full moon

**moon fern** *n* **:** MOONWORT 1

**moonfish** \'⸗,⸗\ *n, pl* **moonfish** *or* **moonfishes :** any of a number of compressed often short deep-bodied silvery or yellowish marine fishes: as **a :** LOOKDOWN FISH; *also* **:** any of several closely related fishes (genus *Vomer*) widely distributed in warm parts of the Atlantic **b :** OPAH **c :** a spadefish (*Chaetodipterus faber*) **d :** an ocean sunfish (*Mola mola*) **e :** PLATY

**moonflower** \'⸗,⸗\ *n* **1** *Brit* **:** DAISY 1b **2 a :** a tropical American night-blooming morning glory (*Calonyction aculeatum*) with fragrant white or purple flowers **b :** any of several plants of the related genera *Ipomoea* and *Quamoclit* **3** *dial Eng* **:** a European wood anemone (*Anemone nemorosa*) **4** *Africa* **:** ANGEL'S-TRUMPET

**moon gate** *n* **:** a circular opening used in Chinese architecture to afford passage through a wall

**moonglow** \'⸗,⸗\ *n* **:** MOONLIGHT

**moon·ie** *or* **moony** \'münē\ *n, pl* **moonies** [*moon* + *-ie, -y*] **:** a little ball cut from translucent stone and used in playing marbles

**moonier** *comparative of* MOONY

**mooniest** *superlative of* MOONY

moon gate

**moon·i·ly** \'münᵊlē, -nəlē\ *adv* **:** in a moony manner **:** ABSTRACTEDLY, DREAMILY

**moon·i·ness** \-nēnəs\ *n* -ES **:** the quality or state of being moony **:** DREAMINESS, INATTENTION

**mooning** *n* -S [fr. gerund of ²*moon*] **1 :** aimless reverie or vacuous contemplation **2** [¹*moon* + *-ing*] **:** an occurrence of small translucent spots in the paste of porcelains (as in Chelsea china of about 1758)

**moon·ish** \'münish\ *adj* **:** DOLTISH, CAPRICIOUS — **moon·ish·ly** *adv*

**moon jelly** *n* **:** a flat white or bluish jellyfish (*Aurelia aurita*) common along both coasts of No. America

**moon knife** *n* **:** a crescent-shaped knife with a handle across the center used in leather finishing

**moon·less** \'münləs\ *adj* **1 :** having no satellite ⟨~ planet⟩ **2 :** lacking the light of or as if of the moon ⟨~ night⟩ ⟨lone is the empty dark, and the ~ heart —Walter de la Mare⟩

**moon·let** \'münlət\ *n* -S **:** a small natural or artificial satellite of the earth or other celestial body ⟨the particles that compose the rings of Saturn are ~s⟩

**moon letter** *n* [trans. of Ar *alḥurūf, alqamarīyah;* fr. the fact that the *l* of the Ar definite article *al* is not assimilated to the initial *q* of *qamar* moon, used as a type word] **:** an Arabic consonant to which the *l* of a preceding definite article *al* is not assimilated in pronunciation — called also *lunar letter;* opposed to *sun letter*

**¹moonlight** \'⸗,⸗\ *n, often attrib* [ME *monelight,* fr. *mone* moon + *light* — more at MOON, LIGHT] **1 :** the light of the moon **:** sunlight reflected by the moon **2 :** FLESH 6

**²moonlight** \"\ *vi* -ED/-ING/-S **:** to engage in moonlighting **:** carry on the activities of a moonlighter

**moonlight blue** *n* **:** a grayish blue that is greener and paler than electric or copenhagen and lighter and slightly greener than Gobelin — called also *infantry*

**moonlighted** \'⸗,⸗⸗\ *adj* **:** MOONLIT

**moon·light·er** \'mün,līd·ə(r), -ītə-\ *n* **:** one that engages in activity by or as if by the light of the moon: as **a :** a participant in a night raid **b :** MOONSHINER **c :** a person holding two jobs at the same time

**moonlight flit** *or* **moonlight flitting** *n, slang Brit* **:** a departure by night with one's possessions to avoid paying rent

**moon·light·ing** \-īd·iŋ, -ītiŋ, |ēŋ\ *n* **:** carrying on activity by or as if by the light of the moon: as **a :** night raiding **b :** holding two jobs at once

**moonlight school** *n* **:** an evening session for adult illiterates esp. in country school districts of the South

**moon·lit** \'mün,lit\ *adj* [*moon* + *lit*] **:** lighted by or as if by the moon ⟨~ path⟩ ⟨his face . . . remained ~ in its pallor —John Mason Brown⟩

**moonmist** \'⸗,⸗\ *n* **:** a yellowish gray that is redder and slightly paler than sand and redder and duller than natural

**moon month** *n* **:** a month determined only and directly by observation of the moon's phase (as in the Hebrew calendar)

**moonpath** \'⸗,⸗\ *n* **:** a lengthened reflection of the moon from slightly agitated water

**moonpenny** \'⸗,⸗⸗\ *n* **:** DAISY 1b

**moon pillar** *n* **:** a light pillar extending vertically above and below the moon

**moon plant** *n* **:** an East Indian vine (*Sarcostemma brevistigma*) of the family Asclepiadaceae whose milky juice yields an intoxicating beverage

**moonproof** \'⸗,⸗\ *adj, archaic* **:** proof against the light or influence of the moon

**moonquake** \'⸗,⸗\ *n* **:** an agitation of the moon's surface that is analogous to a terrestrial earthquake

**moonraker** \'⸗,⸗⸗\ *n* **1** *chiefly Brit* **:** a stupid fellow **:** SIMPLETON **2 :** MOONSAIL

**moonraking** \'⸗,⸗⸗\ *n, archaic* **:** WOOLGATHERING

**moonrat** \'⸗,⸗\ *n* **:** a whitish insectivore (*Echin-osorex gymnurus*) of southeastern Asia having a long snout and a long naked tail

**moonrise** \'⸗,⸗\ *n* **1 :** the rising of the moon above the horizon **2 :** the time of the moon's rising

**moons** *pl of* MOON, *pres 3d sing of* MOON

**moon·sail** \'münsəl (usual nautical pronunciation), -n,sāl\ *n* **:** a light square sail set above a skysail and carried by some clipper ships in light winds

**moon·scape** \'mün,skāp\ *n* [¹*moon* + *-scape*] **:** the surface of the moon either as seen in photographs or through the telescope or as delineated usu. on the basis of photographic or telescopic evidence

**moonseed** \'⸗,⸗\ *n* **:** a plant of the genus *Menispermum* having crescent-shaped seeds and bluish black fruits — see CAROLINA MOONSEED

**moonseed family** *n* **:** MENISPERMACEAE

**moonset** \'⸗,⸗\ *n* **1 :** the descent of the moon below the horizon **2 :** the time of the moon's setting

**moonshee** *var of* MUNSHI

**moon shell** *n* **:** a globose smooth-shelled carnivorous marine snail of the family Naticidae

**¹moon·shine** \'mün,shīn\ *n, often attrib* [¹*moon* + *shine*] **1 :** MOONLIGHT ⟨the world looked very beautiful in the ~ —Fanny K. Wister⟩ **2 :** airy fabrication or empty talk **:** ridiculous chatter **:** NONSENSE ⟨nothing ensues but ~ and mere sentimentality —George Santayana⟩ **3 :** intoxicating liquor; *esp* **:** illegally distilled corn whiskey ⟨charged with possession of ~ —*Tallahassee (Fla.) Democrat*⟩ **4 a :** PEARLY EVERLASTING **b :** a balsamweed (*Gnaphalium obtusifolium*)

**²moonshine** \"\ *vb* -ED/-ING/-S *vi* **:** to operate an illicit still ⟨the Treasury reports an alarming increase in *moonshining* and bootlegging —Howard Brubaker⟩ ~ *vt* **:** to distill illegally ⟨the best of it . . . was *moonshined* during prohibition —J.C. Furnas⟩

**moon·shin·er** \-nə(r)\ *n* **:** one that makes or sells illicit whiskey ⟨married to a convicted ~ —Jacob Hay⟩

**moon·shiny** \-nē\ *adj* **1 :** MOONLIT **2 :** insubstantial or unreal **:** VISIONARY, NONSENSICAL

**moon sight** *n* **:** an observation of the altitude of the moon made for navigational purposes

**moon's man** *n* **:** HOMO SIGNORUM

**moon snail** *n* **:** MOON SHELL

**moon snake** *n* **:** QUEEN SNAKE

**moonstone** \'⸗,⸗\ *n* **:** a transparent or translucent gemstone of pearly or opaline luster that is a feldspar classed according to specimens under orthoclase or under plagioclase

**moonstone blue** *n* **:** a pale purplish blue that is redder and paler than hydrangea blue and redder than starlight blue

**moonstruck** \'⸗,⸗\ *adj* **1 :** affected by or as if by the moon: as **a :** marked by or as if by mental unbalance ⟨to hand over those rights to be interpreted away by lawyers, seemed to him ~ madness —V.L.Parrington⟩ **b :** romantically sentimental ⟨the proper witchery of ~ love —Sinclair Lewis⟩ **2 :** MOONLIT

**moon tide** *n* **:** LUNAR TIDE

**moon type** *n, usu cap M* [after William *Moon* †1894 Eng. inventor] **:** a system of large embossed letters used in printing for the blind and esp. for those blinded late in life that requires less finger sensitivity than braille, consists of nine characters derived from Roman capital letters and used in varying positions to denote the whole alphabet, and is used with full orthography, the lines being printed alternately from left to right and right to left

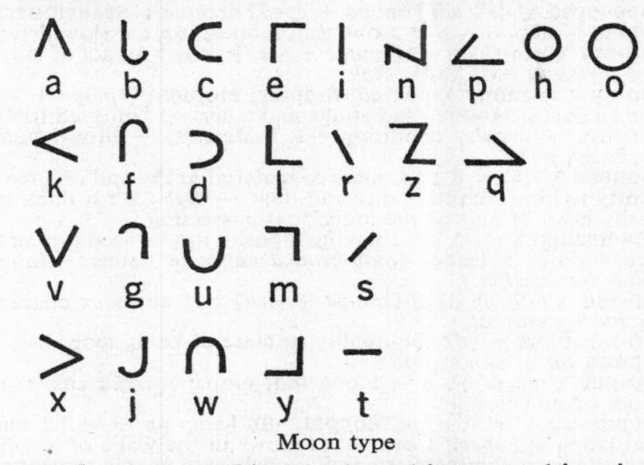

Moon type

**moonvine** \'⸗,⸗\ *n* **:** MOONFLOWER

**moon·ward** \'münwə(r)d\ *or* **moon·wards** \-dz\ *adv* [*moon* + *-ward, -wards*] **:** toward the moon ⟨hurl a rocket ~⟩

**moonwatcher** \'⸗,⸗⸗\ *n* **:** one that tracks the course of a man-made satellite

**moonwort** \'⸗,⸗\ *n* **1 :** a fern of the genus *Botrychium* (esp. *B. lunarium*) **2 :** HONESTY 3

**¹moony** *also* **moon·ey** \'münē, -ni\ *adj* **moonier; mooniest** [¹*moon* + *-y*] **1 :** of or relating to the moon **2 :** shaped like the moon: **a :** resembling or ornamented with the crescent moon ⟨snakes . . . put a trailing, ~ division between weed and weed —Eudora Welty⟩ ⟨the ~ standards of proud Ottoman —Josuah Sylvester⟩ **b :** resembling the full moon **:** ROUND **3 :** MOONLIT ⟨~ night⟩ **4 :** ABSTRACTED, DREAMY ⟨a rather ~ . . . brat, interested mostly in mathematics —F.M.Ford⟩ ⟨conductors are likely to keep these movements low in dynamics and to get ~ over them —Virgil Thomson⟩; *esp* **:** MOONSTRUCK ⟨I always was ~ over you —Zane Grey⟩

**²moony** *var of* MOONIE

**moop** \'müp\ *vi* -ED/-ING/-S [origin unknown] *Scot* **:** to keep company **:** associate closely

**¹moor** \'mu̇(ə)r, -u̇ə *sometimes* 'mō(ə)r *or* 'mȯ(ə)r *or* 'mōə *or* 'mȯ(ə)\ *n* -S *often attrib* [ME *mor,* fr. OE *mōr;* akin to MD *moer* mire, swamp, OHG *muor* swamp, sea, ON *mœrr* land, *marr* sea — more at MARINE] **1 a** *chiefly Brit* **:** an extensive area of open rolling infertile land consisting of sand, rock, or peat usu. covered with heather, bracken, coarse grass, and sphagnum moss **:** HIGH MOOR ⟨an empty desolation of ~s, hill and mountain stretching to the Scottish border —G.E. Fussell⟩ — compare HEATH 2 **b :** a boggy area of wasteland usu. dominated by grasses and sedges growing in a thick layer of peat **:** FEN ⟨boggy ~s are favorite sites for gull colonies —*Brit. Birds in Colour*⟩ ⟨bicycle across the Nantucket ~s — a broad, flat expanse of cranberry bogs . . . and Scotch heather —*Look at America: New England*⟩ — compare LOW MOOR, MUSKEG **2** *Brit* **a :** moorland soil **:** PEAT **b :** moorland vegetation (as heather) ⟨the natural vegetation is largely ~s . . . with a great amount of heather —Samuel Van Valkenburg & Ellsworth Huntington⟩ **c :** a game preserve consisting of moorland

**²moor** \"\ *n* -S *usu cap* [ME *More,* fr. MF, fr. L *Maurus,* prob. of Berber origin] **1 a :** a member of a dark-skinned people of mixed Arab and Berber ancestry inhabiting ancient Mauretania in No. Africa and conquering Spain in the 8th century A.D. **:** MOROCCAN **b :** BERBER **2 :** MUSLIM; *esp* **:** ¹MOORMAN — compare MORO **3 a** *archaic* **:** BLACKAMOOR **b :** one of a group of people of mixed Indian, white, and Negro ancestry in central Delaware — compare NANTICOKE **4 :** a goldfish similar to the fringetail but velvety black

**³moor** \"\ *vb* -ED/-ING/-S [ME *moren;* akin to OE *mǣrels-rāp* ship's rope, MD *maren, meren* to tie, moor, OFris *mere* thong, strap, OHG *marawen* to tie together, connect, LG *vermoren* to moor, and perh. to Gk *mēryesthai* to roll up, *mermis* cord, thread — more at MERMIS] *vt* **1 :** to make fast with cables and lines or with more than one anchor ⟨a motorboat, ~*ed* after dark to a buoy in the harbor —H.M.Parshley⟩ ⟨down went the second anchor, and there we were doubly ~*ed* —Jack London⟩ ⟨~ a dirigible to a mast⟩ ⟨~ an airplane to the ground⟩ **2 :** to attach firmly **:** tie on ⟨suitcases . . . having handles can be more firmly ~*ed* to a bucking vehicle than some other kinds of luggage —E.J.Kahn⟩ ~ *vi* **1 :** to secure a boat by mooring **:** ANCHOR ⟨brought her in through Long Island Sound and ~*ed* off Throgs Neck —James Dugan⟩ **2 :** to be made fast ⟨enables small vessels to ~ close to land —J.H. Bennet⟩

**⁴moor** \"\ *n* -S **:** the act or process of mooring

**moor·age** \'mu̇rij, -rēj *sometimes* 'mōr- *or* 'mȯr-\ *n* -S [*moor* + *-age*] **1 :** an act of mooring **2 :** a charge for mooring

**moorball** \'⸗,⸗\ *n* [¹*moor* + *ball*] **:** a globular mass of filaments of a green alga (*Cladophora holsatica*) often found in lakes and ponds

**moor besom** *n* **:** a heather (*Calluna vulgaris*)

**moorbird** \'⸗,⸗\ *n* **:** RED GROUSE

**moor blackbird** *n, dial Brit* **:** RING OUZEL

**moor·burn** \'mu̇(ə)r,bərn\ *n* [ME(Sc) *murburn,* fr. *mur, mor* moor + *burn*] **1** *Scot* **:** the burning over of a moor to improve the pasturage **2** *Scot* **:** an outburst of temper

**moor buzzard** *n, dial Brit* **:** MARSH HARRIER

**moorcock** \'⸗,⸗\ *n* **1 :** the male of the red grouse **2 :** BLACKCOCK

**moor coot** *n* **:** MOORHEN 2

**moore·ite** \'mu̇,rīt, 'mō,, 'mȯ,-\ *n* -S [Gideon E. *Moore* †1895 Am. chemist + E *-ite*] **:** a mineral $(Mg,Zn,Mn)_8(SO_4)(OH)_{14}·4H_2O$ consisting of a hydrous basic sulfate of magnesium, zinc, and manganese

**moor evil** *n* [¹*moor*] *dial Eng* **:** dysentery in sheep and cattle

**moorfowl** \'⸗,⸗\ *n* **:** RED GROUSE

**moor game** *n* **:** RED GROUSE

**moor grass** *n* **1 :** HEATH GRASS **2 :** a coarse perennial mountain grass (*Molinia coerulea*) of Europe that is considered a good forage grass — called also *flying bent* **3 :** a common cotton grass (*Eriophorum angustifolium*) of the north temperate zone **4 :** a grass growing on a moor

**moor hag** *n* **:** rough moorland

**moor harrier** *n* **:** MARSH HARRIER

**moor hawk** *n, dial Brit* **:** MARSH HARRIER

**moorhen** \'⸗,⸗\ *n* [ME *morhen,* fr. *mor* moor + *hen*] **1 :** the female of the red grouse **2 :** GALLINULE; *esp* **:** the common European gallinule (*Gallinula chloropus*) **3 :** an Australian rail (*Tribonyx ventralis*)

**moorier** *comparative of* MOORY

**mooriest** *superlative of* MOORY

**moor ill** *n, dial Brit* **:** dysentery in cattle

**moor·ing** \'mu̇riŋ, -rēŋ *sometimes* 'mōr- *or* 'mȯr-\ *n* -S [ME *moring,* fr. gerund of *moren* to moor — more at MOOR] **1 :** an act of making fast a boat or aircraft by means of chains, lines, anchors, or other devices **2 a :** a place where or an object to which a craft can be made fast ⟨the lake provides ~ for 166 planes —Elsie M. B. Grosvenor⟩ ⟨yacht clubs . . . of the sort that maintains neither docks nor ~s —M.M.Hunt⟩ **b :** a chain, line, or other device by which an object (as a boat) is secured in place ⟨one of the best tests of a seaman is to let him pick up a ~ under varying conditions of wind, sea and tide —W.P. Moore⟩ **3 :** an established practice or stabilizing influence **:** ANCHORAGE 6 — usu. used in pl. ⟨modern man has been torn from his spiritual ~s —F.L.Baumer⟩ ⟨this shift from normal political ~s —Arthur Krock⟩

**mooring anchor** *n* **:** a mushroom anchor or an anchor with only one fluke used for holding a mooring buoy or channel marker in place

**mooring bitt** *n* **:** BITT

**mooring board** *n* **:** MANEUVERING BOARD

**mooring buoy** *n* **:** an anchored buoy fitted to receive a ship's mooring chain or hawser

**mooring dog** *n* **:** a heavy iron bar on the side of a boat near the waterline to which a mooring line can be secured — called also *mooring staple*

mooring anchor

**mooring mast** *or* **mooring tower** *n* **:** a mast on shore or on a ship with a fitting at the top to receive the mooring device of a rigid dirigible airship

**mooring pipe** *n* **:** an oval or round casting fitted in the bulwark through which mooring lines are passed

**mooring shackle** *n* **:** MOORING SWIVEL

**mooring staple** *n* **:** MOORING DOG

**mooring swivel** *n* **:** a swivel joining the two chain cables of a moored ship near the bow in such a way as to keep them from becoming twisted or entangled — called also *mooring shackle*

**¹moor·ish** \'mu̇rish, -rēsh *sometimes* 'mōr- *or* 'mȯr-\ *adj, usu cap* [ME *morys,* fr. *More* Moor + *-ys, -ish* -ish — more at MOOR] **1 :** of, relating to, or in a style characteristic of the Moors **2** *archaic* **a :** of or relating to the Moormen of India **:** MUHAMMADAN **b :** HINDUSTANI, URDU

**²moorish** \"\ *adj* [ME *morish,* fr. *mor* moor + *-ish*] **1** *obs* **:** MARSHY, SWAMPY — used of soil ⟨it was upon low ~ ground near the sea and I believed it would not be wholesome —Daniel Defoe⟩ **2** *archaic* **a :** abounding in moors ⟨the land is mountainous and ~ —R.G.Preston⟩ **b :** of, relating to, or characteristic of a moor ⟨a . . . ~ place, on the banks of the Poole —Robert Burns⟩

**moorish arch** *n, usu cap M* **:** a horseshoe arch

**moorish architecture** *n, usu cap M* **:** the style developed by the Moors in the later middle ages esp. in No. Africa and Spain — compare ALHAMBRESQUE, HISPANO-MORESQUE, SARACENIC ARCHITECTURE

**moorish idol** *n, usu cap M* **:** a brightly colored fish (*Zanclus cornutus*) or a related form (*Z. canescens*) both widely distributed in the tropical Indo-Pacific from the east coast of Africa to Japan and the west coast of Mexico

**moorish red** *n* **:** a strong orange that is yellower and lighter than pumpkin, yellower and less strong than cadmium orange, and yellower and lighter than mandarin orange

**moor·land** \'⸗,lənd, -,land, -aa(ə)nd\ *n, often attrib* **:** land consisting of moors **:** a stretch of moor ⟨wild ~, bleak and treeless except in the valleys —A.E.Trueman⟩

**moor macaque** *or* **moor monkey** *n* [²*Moor*] **:** a large gray-legged black macaque (*Macaca maura*) of Celebes

**¹moor·man** \'⸗,man, -aa(ə)n, -mən\ *n, pl* **moormen** *usu cap* [²*Moor* + *man*] *India & Ceylon* **:** MUHAMMADAN; *esp* **:** a Muhammadan of mixed Arab and Indian ancestry

**²moorman** \"\ *n, pl* **moormen** [¹*moor* + *man*] **:** an inhabitant of a moor ⟨on Dartmoor . . . there was an old ~'s granite cottage —G.E.Fussell⟩

**moor·mi bhotiah** \'mu̇(ə)rmē'bōd·ē·ə\ *n, pl* **moormi bhotiah** *or* **moormi bhotiahs** *usu cap M&B* **1 :** a non-Tibetan people of Nepal adhering to Lamaism **2 :** a member of the Moormi Bhotiah people

**moor pout** *or* **moor poot** *n* [¹*moor*] *chiefly Scot* **:** a young grouse

**moor·pun·ky** \mȯ(r)'pəŋkē\ *n* -ES [Hindi *morpākhī,* fr. *morpākhī* of a peacock wing, feather (fr. *mor* peacock (fr. Skt *mayūra*) + *pākh* wing, feather (fr. Skt *pakṣa*); fr. its peacock-shaped sternpiece] **:** a large long ornamental pleasure craft propelled by paddles and formerly used as a state barge in India

**moors** *pl of* MOOR, *pres 3d sing of* MOOR

**moor's head** *n, pl* **moor's heads** *or* **moors' heads** *usu cap M* [²*Moor*] **1 a :** a representation of a human head with features characteristic or formerly supposed to be characteristic of a Moor **b :** a heraldic representation of a head usu. with the features and color of a Negro depicted in profile with a band about the forehead unless a different position or a different headdress is specified **2 :** something likened to the head of a Moor: as **a** *obs* **:** a dark or black head usu. occurring on a roan horse **b** *archaic* **:** a globular copper or glass condenser for the top of a still

**moors·man** \'mu̇rzmən\ *n, pl* **moorsmen 1 :** one who lives on a moor **:** MOORMAN **2 :** one who frequents moors

**moor·stone** \'mu̇(ə)r,stōn\ *n* [¹*moor* + *stone*] *dial Eng* **:** granite found esp. in Cornwall

**moor·tet·ter** \'⸗,ted·ə(r)\ *n* -S **:** MOOR TIT

**moor tit** *or* **moor titling** *n* **1 :** a European stonechat (*Saxicola torquata*) **2 :** MEADOW PIPIT

**moo·rup** *or* **mu·rup** \'mü'rüp\ *also* **moo·ruk** \-ük\ *n, pl* **moorup** *or* **murup** *also* **mooruk** [imit.] **:** a cassowary (*Casuarius bennetti*) with rather small stout legs found on the island of New Britain

**moorva** *var of* MURVA

**moorwort** \'⸗,⸗\ *n* [¹*moor* + *wort*] **:** BOG ROSEMARY

**moory** \'mu̇rē *sometimes* 'mōrē *or* 'mȯrē\ *adj* -ER/-EST [¹*moor* + *-y*] **:** of, relating to, or of the nature of a moor **:** MARSHY

**moos** *pres 3d sing of* MOO, *pl of* MOO

**moose** \'müs\ *n, pl* **moose** *often attrib* [of Algonquian origin; akin to Natick *moos* moose, fr. *moos-u* he trims, shaves; fr. the animal's habit of stripping bark and lower branches off trees] **1 a :** a large ruminant mammal (*Alces americana*) of the family Cervidae that inhabits forested parts of Canada and the northern U. S., is closely related to the European elk but slightly larger standing about seven feet high at the humped shoulders and often weighing over 1000 pounds, and has an ungainly form with the legs long, the tail short, and the head large with a thick overhanging snout and broadly palmated antlers with many points **b :** ELK 1a **2** *cap* **:** a member of one of the major benevolent and fraternal orders **3** *sometimes cap* **:** BULL MOOSE

moose 1a

**moose·berry** \'müs- — *see* BERRY\ *n* **1 a :** HOBBLEBUSH **b :** the fruit of the hobblebush **2 :** CRANBERRY BUSH 2

**moosebird** \'⸗,⸗\ *n* **:** CANADA JAY

**moosebush** \'⸗,⸗\ *n* **:** HOBBLEBUSH

**moosecall** \'⸗,⸗\ *n* **:** an instrument (as a piece of birch bark rolled like a horn) used by hunters in calling moose

**moose elm** *n* **:** SLIPPERY ELM

**mooseflower** \'⸗,⸗⸗\ *n* **:** TRILLIUM

**moose fly** *n* **:** a tabanid fly **:** HORSEFLY

**moose maple** *n* **:** MOUNTAIN MAPLE a

**moose·mise** \'mü,smīs\ *or* **moose–misse** \-mis\ *n* -S [of Algonquian origin; akin to Chippewa & Nipissing *monsomish* hobblebush] **:** MOUNTAIN ASH 1b

**moose tick** *n* **:** WINTER TICK
**moosetongue** \ˈ=,=\ *n* **:** WILLOW HERB
**moosewood** \ˈ=,=\ *n* **1 :** STRIPED MAPLE **2 :** LEATHERWOOD 1a **3 :** HOBBLEBUSH

**1moot** \ˈmüt, *usu* -üd.+V\ *n* -s [ME *mot, moot,* fr. OE *mōt* assembly, meeting, encounter; akin to OFris *mōtlik* legal, OS *mōt* meeting, encounter, MHG *muoze* encounter, ON *mōt* meeting, assembly, OE *mētan* to meet — more at MEET] **1 a :** a meeting for discussion and deliberation; *esp* **:** a meeting of freemen (as of a town, city, or shire in early England) or their representatives to administer justice or for administrative purposes — compare FOLKMOOT, GEMOT, HUNDRED, WITENAGEMOT **b :** a place for holding such a meeting **2** *obs* **:** ARGUMENT, DISCOURSE, DISCUSSION ⟨but to end this ~ —John Milton⟩ **3 :** a hypothetical case argued or practice hearing held by law students ⟨elected by his classmates as prosecutor for the weekly ~⟩

**2moot** \ˈ"\ *vb* -ED/-ING/-S [ME *moten,* fr. OE *mōtian,* fr. *mōt,* n.] *vi, obs* **:** to argue a case at law (as a hypothetical case) as a student in a law school ⟨~*ed* seven years in the Inns of Court —John Earle⟩ ~ *vt* **1** *archaic* **:** to discuss from a legal standpoint **:** ARGUE ⟨to ~ cases on the . . . ruin of the constitution —Edmund Burke⟩ **2 a :** to bring up for discussion **:** 2BROACH 6, SUGGEST ⟨condemned such a step when it was first ~*ed* a year before —Ethel Drus⟩ ⟨plans have been ~*ed* for altering the general system of criminal procedure —Ernest Barker⟩ **b :** DISCUSS, DEBATE ⟨the question, so often ~*ed* and never solved, of church unity —*Commonweal*⟩ ⟨the diction of poetry is now, as it has always been, a vigorously ~*ed* point —J.L.Lowes⟩ **3 :** to deprive of practical significance **:** make academic ⟨the case was ~*ed* by unwillingness of the complainant to prosecute⟩

**3moot** \ˈ"\ *adj* [1*moot*] **1 a :** open to question **:** subject to discussion **:** DEBATABLE, UNSETTLED ⟨it is a ~ question what might have happened —O.D.Tolischus⟩ ⟨words of ~ etymology —A.H.Marckwardt⟩ ⟨fill in gaps . . . and to check ~ points —Leslie Spier⟩ **b :** subjected to discussion **:** CONTROVERSIAL, DISPUTED ⟨with a ~ point of law cleared up —John LaFarge⟩ ⟨extract . . . his views on the then ~ subject of a second front —Henry Cassidy⟩ **2 :** deprived of practical significance **:** made abstract or purely academic ⟨thought that the Supreme Court would drop the case as a ~ question, if the bill should become law —*Time*⟩ ⟨appeal does not become ~ when the alien leaves the country, since the possibility of a criminal prosecution for attempted re-entry . . . remains —*Harvard Law Rev.*⟩ **3 :** concerned with a hypothetical situation ⟨~ court⟩ ⟨student participation in a ~ . . . case —*Bulletin of Information: Academy of Advanced Traffic*⟩

**4moot** \ˈmüt\ *vt* -ED/-ING/-S [ME *moten*] *dial Eng* **:** to grub out (as a tree root) or unearth (as an otter)
**moot·able** \ˈmüd·əbəl\ *adj* [2*moot* + *-able*] **:** DEBATABLE
**moot court** *n* **:** a mock court in which students of law argue hypothetical cases for practice
**mooth** \ˈmüth\ *dial Brit var of* MOUTH
**moot hall** *n* [ME *mothalle, moothalle,* fr. *mot, moot* moot + *halle* hall — more at MOOT, HALL] **:** a room or building in which a moot is held; *specif* **:** TOWN HALL
**moot hill** *n* **:** a hill used as the meeting place of a moot in early England ⟨each little village-commonwealth . . . had its *moot hill* or sacred tree as a center —J.R.Green⟩
**mooting** *n* -s [fr. gerund of 2*moot*] **:** DISCUSSION, DEBATE; *specif* **:** participation in a moot court
**moot·man** \ˈmütmən\ *n, pl* **mootmen** *Brit* **:** a student arguing a moot case in the Inns of Court
**moot·ness** *n* -ES **:** the quality or state of being moot — used of an issue, question, or case before a court
**moot-stow** \ˈ=,stō\ *n* [OE *mōtstōw,* fr. *mōt* assembly, meeting + *stōw* place — more at MOOT, STOW] **:** a town or borough serving as the seat of a moot
**mootworthy** \ˈ=,==\ *adj* [1*moot* + *worthy*] *Anglo-Saxon law* **:** qualified to attend a moot as a member **:** FREE

**1mop** \ˈmäp\ *n* -s *often attrib* [ME *mappe,* short for *mappel,* prob. fr. ML *mappula* handkerchief, towel, fr. LL, dim. of L *mappa* napkin — more at MAP] **1 a :** a household implement consisting of a mass of absorbent material (as coarse yarn, cellulose, or rags) fastened to a long handle and used typically for cleaning floors — compare DISHMOP, DRY MOP **b :** a cloth or wad of material for absorbing moisture **:** SWAB ⟨a surgical ~ of absorbent cotton⟩ **2** *dial Eng* **:** STATUTE FAIR **3 :** something that resembles a mop: as **a :** a thick often unruly mass of hair ⟨his hair was a disorderly yellow ~ —T.B.Costain⟩ ⟨grizzled ~*s* of the elderly Fiji chieftains —Mollie Panter-Downes⟩ ⟨perambulating ~*s* known as Yorkshire terriers —*Time*⟩; *specif* **:** the matted forelock of a buffalo ⟨gathered the ~*s* from the heads that were left unskinned on the prairie —Mari Sandoz⟩ **b :** a dauber for applying a liquid ⟨dip this ~ into the barbecue sauce and slap the roasting meat with it —Sheila Hibben⟩ ⟨poisoned syrup was applied to the tops of plants with a ~ —*Amer. Guide Series: Fla.*⟩ **c :** STAR-MOP

mops 1a

**2mop** \ˈ"\ *vb* **mopped; mopped; mopping; mops** *vt* **1 :** to use a mop on: as **a :** to clean by mopping ⟨~ a floor⟩ — often used with *up* ⟨strained to ~ up the debris left by the . . . flood —*N. Y. Times*⟩ **b :** to wipe or polish with a mop ⟨a pitcher . . . should be well *mopped* out, taking care to scrub the whole interior surface —Emily Holt⟩ ⟨*mopped* his brow with a silk handkerchief —Waldo Frank⟩ ⟨*mopped* an imaginary tear from her eye —David Garnett⟩ ⟨*mopping* his plate with a limp piece of new bread —Kenneth Roberts⟩ — often used with *up* ⟨~*s* up his plate with a tortilla folded twice —M.M. Liberman⟩ **c :** to apply (a liquid) with a mop ⟨*mopping* . . . astringents over that area will shorten the period of discomfort —H.G.Armstrong⟩ ⟨built-up roof coverings shall consist of two or more layers of saturated felt sheets . . . thoroughly *mopped* with a hot bituminous cement —*Code for Dwelling Construction*⟩ **2** *slang Brit* **:** to consume eagerly **:** GOBBLE, GUZZLE — usu. used with *up* ⟨swam round with great vigor and *mopped* up his worms greedily —*Irish Digest*⟩ ⟨*mopping* up gin and looking a bit glazed —Anton Vogt⟩ **3 :** to overcome decisively **:** polish off **:** TROUNCE ⟨sent its superb team of oarsmen . . . to ~ the field in the Henley Royal Regatta —David Dodge⟩ — used esp. in the slang phrase *mop the floor with* ⟨the king of Spain *mopped* his floor with him —*London Daily News*⟩; often used with *up* ⟨just let me at him — I'll ~ him up⟩ ⟨a raiding battleship could ~ up any and every convoy . . . guarded only by cruisers —*U. S. Naval Inst. Proceedings*⟩ ~ *vi* **:** to clean a surface (as a floor) with a mop ⟨first she dusted, then she *mopped*⟩ — often used with *up* ⟨residents and workers *mopped* up after a Sunday night flood —*Springfield (Mass.) Daily News*⟩

**3mop** \ˈ"\ *vi* **mopped; mopped; mopping; mops** [perh. fr. obs. *mop* fool — more at MOPPET] **:** to make a face ⟨a shaggy creature . . . came and danced along with her, *mopping* and mowing —Mary Webb⟩
**4mop** \ˈ"\ *n* -s *archaic* **:** GRIMACE, FACE ⟨the ~*s* and mows of the old witch —R.L.Stevenson⟩
**MOP** *abbr* **1** manuscript on paper **2** *often not cap* mother-of-pearl **3** mustering-out pay
**mo·pan** \mōˈpän\ *n, pl* **mopan** *or* **mopans** *usu cap* [Sp *mopán* of AmerInd origin] **1 a :** an American people of northeastern Guatemala **b :** a member of such people **2 :** a Mayan language of the Mopan people closely related to or a dialect of Yucatec
**mo·pa·ni** \mōˈpänē\ *or* **mo·pa·ne** \-nə\ *n, pl* **mopanies** *or* **mopanes** [Sechuana] **:** a tropical African ironwood (*Copaifera mopane*) yielding hard durable timber
**mopboard** \ˈ=,=\ *n* [1*mop* + *board*] **:** BASEBOARD

**1mope** \ˈmōp\ *vb* -ED/-ING/-S [prob. fr. obs. *mope* fool, alter. of *mop* — more at MOPPET] *vi* **1** *chiefly dial Brit* **:** to act in a distracted, bewildered, or stupid manner ⟨a wretched and peevish fellow . . . to ~ with his fat-brained followers so far out of his knowledge —Shak.⟩ **2 :** to give oneself up to brooding **:** become dull, dejected, or listless ⟨doesn't pretend he is glad to be retired but he is not *moping* about it —Katharine Hamill⟩ ⟨the *moping* owl does to the moon complain —Thomas Gray⟩ **3 :** to move slowly or aimlessly **:** DAWDLE ⟨even when the little woman does ~ along in traffic —Paul Jones⟩ ⟨sadly turned his back on us, *moped* into the sea, and took to swimming —*Harper's*⟩ ~ *vt* **1 :** to make dull, dejected, or listless **:** cause to brood ⟨you must come about with me and not ~ yourself —Thomas Hughes⟩ **2 :** to pass (as a period of time) in a dull, dejected, or listless state ⟨directs him not to shut himself up in a cloister alone, there to ~ . . . away his life —George Horne †1792⟩

**2mope** \ˈ"\ *n* -s **1 :** one that mopes **:** a dull or gloomy person ⟨meager, muse-rid ~, adust and thin —Alexander Pope⟩ **2 mopes** *pl* **:** a fit of depression **:** 2BLUES ⟨he's got the ~*s* because she's mad at him⟩
**mope-eyed** \ˈ=;=\ *adj* [1*mope* + *eyed*] *archaic* **:** NEARSIGHTED
**mop·er** \ˈmōpə(r)\ *n* -s **:** one that mopes; *esp* **:** a slow driver
**mop·ery** \-p(ə)rē\ *n* -ES [1*mope* + *-ery*] *slang* **:** an act of moping **:** DAWDLING, VAGRANCY
**mop·ey** *also* **mopy** \-pē\ *adj* **mopier; mopiest** [1*mope* + *-y*] **:** DEPRESSED, DROOPY ⟨sad songs make her ~⟩ ⟨infested fowls are in a ~ drowsy condition —R.L.Metcalf⟩ — **mop·i·ness** \-pēnəs\ *n* -ES
**mophead** \ˈ=,=\ *n* **1 :** the mass of material at the end of a mop ⟨fluffy nylon ~ collects dirt and dust —*advt*⟩ **2 :** a thick or bushy head of hair or the individual possessing it
**mop-headed** \ˈ=;==\ *adj* **:** having a bushy top — used esp. of a tree without a leader ⟨*mop-headed* cabbage palms —*Amer. Guide Series: Fla.*⟩
**mop·ish** \ˈmōpish\ *adj* [1*mope* + *-ish*] **:** given to or characterized by moping
**mop·ish·ness** *n* -ES **:** the quality or state of being mopish
**mopoke** *var of* MOREPORK
**mop·per** \ˈmäpə(r)\ *n* -s **:** one that mops; *specif* **:** one that wipes or polishes
**mopper-up** \ˈ==ˈ=\ *n, pl* **moppers-up** [*mop up* + *-er*] **:** one that mops up; *specif* **:** one that follows in the wake of a military attack to eliminate remaining pockets of enemy resistance and dispose of debris
**mop·pet** \ˈmäpət, *usu* -əd.+V\ *n* -s [obs. E *mop* fool, child (fr. ME) + *-et;* prob. akin to LG *mops* simpleton, pugnosed dog, D *mop, mops* pugnosed dog, obs. D *moppen* to pout, grumble] **1 :** CHILD, YOUNGSTER ⟨a production that will wow the ~*s* and their parents —*Billboard*⟩ ⟨a jury of ~*s* aged from about four through twelve render opinions on the problems of other children —*Pasadena (Calif.) Independent*⟩ **2** *archaic* **a :** a young woman **:** DAMSEL ⟨lustily calling to the landlubbers and to the fair ~*s* about her —*Pall Mall Mag.*⟩; *esp* **:** one given to frivolity **b :** an effeminate man **:** FOP ⟨several times dismissed such manikins as ~*s* —I.J.C.Brown⟩
**mopping** *n* -s [fr. gerund of 2*mop*] **:** a liquid coating applied with a mop ⟨embed each board firmly in the bituminous ~ —P.D.Close⟩
**mop·py** \ˈmäpē\ *adj, usu* -ER/-EST [1*mop* + *-y*] **:** resembling a mop **:** BUSHY ⟨shaking their ~ heads —Christopher Rand⟩ ⟨his ~ black hair —George Moore⟩
**mops** *pl of* MOP, *pres 3d sing of* MOP
**mopstick** \ˈ=,=\ *n* **1 :** the long thin handle of a mop **2** *or* **mopstick rail :** a handrail of nearly round section
**mop·sy** *or* **mop·sey** \ˈmäpsē\ *n, pl* **mopsies** *or* **mopseys** [obs. E *mop* child, fool + *-sy* — more at MOPPET] **1** *obs* **:** a pretty child **:** DARLING, SWEETHEART — used as a term of endearment or deprecation **2** [influenced in meaning by 1*mop*] *archaic* **:** a slovenly woman **:** SLATTERN
**mop up** *vt* **1 :** to dispose of **:** clean up ⟨have heard much less of Brighton's race gangs since the war, so let us hope that they have been *mopped up* —S.P.B.Mais⟩; *specif* **:** to follow in the wake of an attacking military force and clear (an area) of remaining pockets of resistance ⟨the bulk of the troops were still needed to guard and *mop up* the captured territory —*Infantry Jour.*⟩ ⟨it was left to Australians to *mop up* the bypassed Japanese —D.L.Oliver⟩ **2 :** to take up or assimilate **:** GARNER, ABSORB ⟨urchins are abundant in nearby waters and are . . . *mopped up* by the tubful —W.C.Allee⟩ ⟨grabbed seventeen swimming and diving gold medals to the 56 they had *mopped up* in other events —*Newsweek*⟩ ⟨contributes to anti-inflation . . . in that it *mops up* funds that might otherwise be paid out in higher wages and dividends —W.H.Anderson⟩ ⟨sales of assets will serve to *mop up* surplus credit —W.M. Dacey⟩ ~ *vi* **:** to complete a project or transaction **:** clean up ⟨most of the East Cambridge apparatus was *mopping up* at the two engine house fires —*Springfield (Mass.) Union*⟩ ⟨quick-freezers, whose products were not rationed, *mopped up* on the home front —*Harper's*⟩; *specif* **:** to carry out a military cleanup ⟨behind it would come truck-borne infantry and mobile guns to *mop up* and to widen the breach —Tom Wintringham⟩
**mop-up** \ˈ=,=\ *n* -s [*mop up*] **:** an act of concluding or final disposal **:** CLEANUP: as **a :** the clearance of enemy stragglers from a captured area by troops assigned to the task ⟨after the decisive battles come the *mop-ups* —*Time*⟩ **b :** the carrying out of safety measures after a forest fire is brought under control ⟨there was still an endless amount of *mop-up* . . . and some crews would have to be kept on the fire for a week or two —G.R.Stewart⟩
**mo·pus** \ˈmōpəs\ *n, pl* **mopuses** *or* **mopusses** [origin unknown] *slang* **:** MONEY, CASH; *esp* **:** ready money — usu. used in pl.
**mo·que·lum·nan** \,mōkəˈləmnən\ *n* -s *usu cap* **:** a language family of Penutian stock in California comprising three languages all known as Miwok — called also *Miwok*
**mo·quette** \mōˈket\ *n* -s [F, alter. of *moucade*] **1 :** a usu. machine-made pile carpet resembling Axminster but less expensive **2 :** an upholstery fabric similar to the moquette carpeting made with a cut or uncut pile of mohair or wool and a cotton foundation usu. in solid colors or small jacquard patterns
**mo·qui** \ˈmōkē\ *usu cap, var of* MOKI
**mor** \ˈmō(ə)r\ *n* -s [Dan, lit., humus] **:** forest humus that consists characteristically of a layer of largely organic matter abruptly distinct from the mineral soil beneath — compare DUFF, 8MULL
**mor** *abbr* **1** morendo **2** morocco **3** mortar
**1mo·ra** \ˈmōrə, ˈmȯ\ *n, pl* **mo·rae** \-,rē\ *or* **moras** [L, lit., delay — more at MORATORY] **1** *Roman & civil law* **:** delay in the performance of an obligation; *esp* **:** culpable delay **2 a :** the minimal unit of quantitative measure in temporal prosodic systems equivalent in the time value to an average short syllable **b :** such a unit used in linguistic analysis esp. with reference to vowel quantity
**2mo·ra** *or* **mor·ra** \ˈmȯrə\ *n* -s [It] **:** an Italian game in which a player extends a number of fingers of his hand in an attempt to match the number of fingers simultaneously extended by his opponent ⟨the little singing girls playing ~ —Joseph Hergesheimer⟩
**3mo·ra** \mōˈrä\ *n* -s [Hindi *morhā*] *India* **:** a low wicker stool or footstool
**4mo·ra** \ˈmōrə, ˈmȯrə\ *n* [NL, perh. modif. of Tupi *moiratinga,* fr. *moira* tree + *tinga* white] **1 a** *cap* **:** a small genus of tall half-evergreen forest trees (family Leguminosae) of northern So. America that are often included in a closely related genus (*Dimorphandra*) **b -s :** any tree of the genus *Mora;* *esp* **:** a tall buttressed tree (*Mora excelsa* or *Dimorphandra mora*) that often grows in nearly pure stands on alluvial lands chiefly of British Guiana and Trinidad and that yields a strong heavy wood which is highly resistant to dry rot and to termite injury and is used extensively for railway ties, heavy construction, and in shipbuilding **c -s :** the wood of the British Guiana mora **2 -s :** FUSTIC 1
**mor·a·buk·ea** *also* **mor·a·buc·quea** \,mȯrəˈbəkēə\ *n* -s [native name in British Guiana] **:** a leguminous tree (*Mora gonggrijpii* or *Dimorphandra gonggrijpii*) of British Guiana and Surinam that is closely related to the mora, that often grows in dense pure stands, and that yields hard heavy strong often streaked reddish brown wood very resistant to decay
**mo·ra·ce·ae** \məˈrāsē,ē\ *n pl, cap* [NL, fr. *Morus,* type genus + *-aceae*] **:** a family of trees or shrubs (order Urticales) that have a milky juice and small diclinous flowers with a one-celled ovary — see ARTOCARPUS, FICUS, MORUS — **mo·ra·ceous** \-āshəs\ *adj*
**mo·ra·da** \məˈrädə\ *n* -s [AmerSp, fr. Sp, house, dwelling, fr. *morar* to live, dwell, fr. L *morari* to delay, remain — more at MORATORY] **:** a meetinghouse or chapel of the Penitentes ⟨knees growing numb on the stone floor of the ~ —R.V.Hunter⟩
**mo·rad·a·bad** \məˈrädə̇,bäd, -radə̇ˈbad\ *adj, usu cap* [fr. *Moradabad,* city in northern India] **:** of or from the city of Moradabad, India **:** of the kind or style prevalent in Moradabad
**mo·raea** \məˈrēə\ *n* [NL, irreg. fr. Robert *More* †1780 Eng. collector of exotic plants] **1** *cap* **:** a genus of southern African or Australian bulbous or tuberous plants (family Iridaceae) with a divided perianth and petaloid style branches **2 -s :** any plant of the genus *Moraea*
**mora hair** *n* [perh. fr. 4*mora*] **:** SPANISH MOSS
**mo·rain·al** \məˈrānᵊl, mōˈ-, mȯˈ-\ *adj* **:** of or relating to a moraine
**mo·raine** \-ān\ *n* -s [F, fr. F dial. (Savoy) *morêna*] **:** an accumulation of earth and stones carried and finally deposited by a glacier — see END MORAINE, GROUND MORAINE, LATERAL MORAINE, MEDIAL MORAINE, PUSH MORAINE, RECESSIONAL MORAINE, TERMINAL MORAINE; compare ABLATION
**mo·rain·ic** \-nik, -nēk\ *adj* [ISV *moraine* + *-ic*] **:** of or relating to a moraine

**1mor·al** \ˈmȯrəl, ˈmärəl\ *adj* [ME, fr. MF, fr. L *moralis,* fr. *mor-, mos* custom + *-alis* -al — more at MOOD] **1 a :** of or relating to principles or considerations of right and wrong action or good and bad character **:** ETHICAL ⟨~ values⟩ ⟨~ distinctions⟩ ⟨~ conduct⟩ ⟨~ convictions⟩ ⟨a ~ monster⟩ **b :** of or relating to the study of such principles or considerations **2 :** expressing or teaching a conception of right behavior **:** DIDACTIC, MORALIZING ⟨a ~ lesson⟩ ⟨a ~ poem⟩ ⟨a ~ story⟩ **3 a :** capable of being judged as good or evil or in terms of principles of right and wrong action **:** resulting from or belonging to human character, conduct, or intentions ⟨the use of science is a ~ question, that is to say, a human question —Irwin Edman⟩ ⟨a ~ act, the result of a choice —Norman Podhoretz⟩ **b :** capable of right and wrong action or of being governed by a sense of right ⟨a ~ agent⟩ **4 :** of, relating to, or acting upon the mind, character, or will **:** PSYCHOLOGICAL ⟨a whole series of political, organizational, military and . . . ~ triumphs —Joseph Alsop⟩ ⟨gone to the dinner party determined to make a success . . . understanding the ~ importance to herself of this initial contact with society —I.V. Morris⟩ **5 a :** conforming to or proceeding from a standard of what is good and right **:** PRINCIPLED ⟨not exactly a religious man, though a highly ~ one —Katharine F. Gerould⟩ ⟨a ~ life⟩ ⟨took a ~ position on the issue though it cost him the nomination⟩ ⟨show ~ courage⟩ **b** *Hegelianism* **:** relating to virtuous conduct or natural excellence as distinguished from civic or legal righteousness **6 a :** based upon inner conviction ⟨have a ~ certainty that my will is free⟩ **b :** virtual rather than actual, immediate, or completely demonstrable ⟨have a ~ certainty that the prisoner is guilty⟩ **7 :** sanctioned by or operating upon one's conscience or ethical judgment ⟨the ranch was legally all Mother's, except that Grampa . . . had a ~ claim upon it —Mary Austin⟩ ⟨felt under a sort of ~ obligation not to be indifferent —Joseph Conrad⟩ **8 a :** of or relating to the accepted customs or patterns of social or personal relations ⟨a reflection of the ~ imperatives of the community —Kingsley Davis⟩ ⟨the enormous importance of ~ conformity to the stability of society —Talcott Parsons⟩ **b :** sexually virtuous **:** not adulterous or promiscuous ⟨middle-aged and cautious and monogamic and ~ —Sinclair Lewis⟩ **c :** conforming to generally accepted standards of correct behavior ⟨appeared ~, self-controlled, well-bathed, and literate —Jean Stafford⟩ ⟨the teacher had to be more ~ — which usually meant more conventional —J.M.Barzun⟩ **d :** expecting or exacting a strict adherence to conventional standards of speech or conduct **:** PROPER ⟨a highly ~ man who was outraged by the rowdy language of his fellow soldiers⟩

**syn** ETHICAL, VIRTUOUS, RIGHTEOUS, NOBLE: in describing persons and their actions and conduct, MORAL, opposed to *immoral,* may designate conformity to established sanctioned codes or accepted notions of right and wrong, now particularly in sexual conduct ⟨living a *moral* life⟩ ⟨the right thinker, the great *moral* statesman, the perfect model of the Christian cad —H.L.Mencken⟩ ⟨there were black marketeers, but they were not seen as products of the *moral* deficiencies of the ruling class —Edward Shils⟩ ETHICAL may suggest conformity to a code or to the conclusions of other considerations of right, fair, equitable conduct ⟨an *ethical* decision⟩ ⟨an *ethical* solution to the problem —Edward Shils⟩ VIRTUOUS may still indicate blended rectitude and integrity; often it implies abstinence from illicit sex ⟨pacifists assume that other people are as reasonable and *virtuous* as they are themselves —Harold Nicolson⟩ ⟨a man might grind the faces of the poor; but so long as he refrained from caressing his neighbors' wives and daughters, he was regarded as *virtuous* —Aldous Huxley⟩ ⟨all *virtuous* persons . . . whose lives are chaste and placid —Elinor Wylie⟩ RIGHTEOUS suggests freedom from guilt, culpability, or questionability; it may suggest religious or sectarian sanction or sanctimoniousness ⟨persecution seemed justified in reason; it was very logical; broad reasons of Christian statecraft seemed to make for it; and often a *righteous* zeal wielded the weapon —H.O.Taylor⟩ ⟨our wits are much more alert when engaged in wrongdoing (in which one mustn't be found out) than in a *righteous* occupation —Joseph Conrad⟩ ⟨a republic admirable in justice and *righteous* in all its ways —V.L. Parrington⟩ NOBLE may indicate moral eminence with lack of any taint of the petty or dubious ⟨a *noble* ideal, worthy of a Christian —V.L.Parrington⟩ ⟨behavior . . . when the crisis actually came was simple, dignified, and even *noble* —P.E. More⟩ ⟨the true task of man is to create for himself a *noble* memory, a mind filled with grandeur, forgiveness, restless ideals, and the dynamic ethical ferment preached by all religions at their best —J.L.Liebman⟩

**2moral** \ˈ", *in sense 7 like* MORALE\ *n* -s **1 a :** the moral significance or practical lesson taught by or capable of being derived from a story, event, experience, or object ⟨love makes gentlemen even of boors . . . is the constant ~ of medieval story —Henry Adams⟩ ⟨the ~ of his life⟩ ⟨the ~ of recent history⟩ **b :** a passage pointing out usu. in conclusion the lesson to be drawn from a story **:** MAXIM ⟨the view . . . that highly serious art is didactic, ending with a ~ —G.K.Chalmers⟩ **2 :** MORALITY PLAY **3 morals** *pl* **a :** the moral practices of an individual or culture **:** habits of life or modes of conduct ⟨as principal, he maintained a high standard of ~*s* and manners in the school —L.M.Crosbie⟩ ⟨losing touch with the ordinary patterns and ~*s* of life —Alan Moorehead⟩ **b :** sexual conduct ⟨provoked a long and thoughtful discussion of the mores and ~*s* of American womanhood —T.O.Heggen⟩ ⟨a person of loose ~*s*⟩ **4 morals** *pl* **:** the study dealing with the principles of conduct **:** ETHICS ⟨the science of ~*s* endeavors to divide men into the good and the bad —J.W.Krutch⟩ **5 morals** *pl* **:** moral teachings **:** the moral principles of an individual or culture ⟨the Greek dramatists moralize only because ~*s* are woven through and through the texture of their tragic idea —T.S.Eliot⟩ ⟨an authoritative code of ~*s* has force and effect when it expresses the settled customs of a stable society —Walter Lippmann⟩ **6** *archaic* **:** COUNTERPART, IMAGE ⟨the long chin . . . is the very ~ of the governor's —Tobias Smollett⟩ **7** [F, morale, moral nature, fr. *moral,* adj.] **:** MORALE ⟨the ~ of the nation is therefore likely to be as important a factor in war as the ~ of armies has always been —*Atlantic*⟩
**3moral** *like* 1MORAL\ *vb, archaic* **:** MORALIZE
**mo·rale** \məˈral, mōˈ-, mȯˈ-\ *n* -s [in sense 1, fr. F, fr. fem. of *moral,* adj.; in other senses, modif. (influenced by E *morale,* sense 1) of F *moral* morale, moral nature, fr. *moral,* adj. — more at MORAL] **1 :** moral principles, teachings, or conduct **:** MORALITY ⟨conversations which American law and ~ consider privileged —A.F.Westin⟩ ⟨a ~ of fair-mindedness, intellectual integrity —John Dewey⟩ **2 a :** a confident, resolute, willing, often self-sacrificing and courageous attitude of an individual to the function or tasks demanded or expected of him by a group of which he is a part that is based upon such factors as pride in the achievements and aims of the group, faith in its leadership and ultimate success, a sense of fruitful personal participation in its work, and a devotion and loyalty to the other members of the group ⟨high ~ and personal pride are at least barely possible in large firms —Peter Wiles⟩ ⟨whatever happened, ~ meant to them resistance, and capitulation was a proof that they had lost their nerve —Ruth Benedict⟩

**b :** a sense of common purpose or a degree of dedication to a common task regarded as characteristic of or dominant in a particular group or organization **:** ESPRIT DE CORPS ⟨the ~ of the ship improved after two days of shore leave⟩ ⟨the ~ of the faculty was high⟩ ⟨the ~ of the reform group suffered a severe blow when their candidate was defeated⟩ **3 :** a state of individual psychological well-being and buoyancy based upon such factors as physical or mental health, a sense of purpose and usefulness, and confidence in the future ⟨a long period of unemployment had weakened his ~⟩ ⟨the failure of his play did not affect his ~⟩

**moraler** *n* -s [[3]*moral* + *-er*] *obs* **:** MORALIZER ⟨you are too severe a ~ —Shak.⟩

**moral hazard** *n* **:** the possibility of loss to an insurance company arising from the character, habits, or circumstances of the insured

**moral insanity** *also* **moral imbecility** *n* **:** PSYCHOPATHIC PERSONALITY

**mor·al·ism** \\'mȯrə,lizəm, 'mär-\\ *n* -s **1 a :** the habit or practice of moralizing ⟨before he had slipped into transcendentalism and ~ and complacency in mediocrity —George Santayana⟩ **b :** an instance of moralizing **:** a conventional moral attitude or saying ⟨the traditional ~ of melodrama — the idea of Virtue Triumphant —E.R.Bentley⟩ ⟨his brain was clogged with ~*s*, inchoate poetry, and unclear ambitions —H.S.Canby⟩ **2 :** the practice of morality as distinct from religion **:** the doctrine or practice of religion reduced to morality ⟨make out a case for activism and ~ as the fundamental American heresy —*Rev. of Religion*⟩

**mor·al·ist** \\-ləst\\ *n* -s **1 :** one who leads a moral life ⟨a ~ who practices what he preaches⟩ **2 :** a teacher or student of morals **:** a thinker or writer concerned with moral principles and problems ⟨was attracted particularly by the great classical ~*s*, and found in their ethical teaching inspiration and instruction —A.C.McGiffert⟩ ⟨nowadays it is . . . far harder to be a ~ of any true simplicity of spirit —Lionel Trilling⟩ ⟨like all good writers, a ~ at bottom —Bernard Kalb⟩ **3 :** one who is concerned to regulate the morals of others ⟨~*s* looked upon it as a lewd distraction that would take the mind off work —Lewis Mumford⟩ ⟨once the ~ . . . becomes the censor of art, with power to enforce his judgments, art is seriously jeopardized —Hunter Mead⟩

**mor·al·is·tic** \\ˌ==ˈlistik, -tēk\\ *adj* **1 :** characterized by or expressive of a concern with morality ⟨when man developed, when he became more scientific and more ~ —Havelock Ellis⟩ ⟨~ wit, or the joke that teaches a lesson —Ernst Simon⟩ **2 :** characterized by or expressive of a narrow and conventional moral attitude ⟨the conventional and ~ prettifications of life then in vogue —R.M.Coates⟩ ⟨the ponderous and ~ style of the early nineteenth century —*Amer. Guide Series: Tenn.*⟩ — **mor·al·is·ti·cal·ly** \\-tək(ə)lē, -tēk-, -li\\ *adv*

**mo·ral·i·ty** \\mə'ralәd·ē, mȯ'-, mō'-, -ətē, -i\\ *n* -ES [ME *moralitee*, fr. MF *moralité*, fr. LL *moralitat-, moralitas*, fr. L *moralis* moral + *-tat-, -tas* -ty — more at MORAL] **1 moralities** *pl, archaic* **:** moral traits ⟨a saint . . . in her *moralities* —Lord Byron⟩ **2 a :** a moral discourse, statement, or lesson **:** a piece of moralizing ⟨a poem full of commonplace *moralities*⟩ ⟨ended his lecture with a trite ~⟩ **b :** a literary or other imaginative work conceived as a moral allegory and teaching a moral lesson ⟨the book's undeniable power as a ~ is diminished by . . . a style of bright impersonal smartness —*Times Lit. Supp.*⟩ ⟨has managed to turn out a ~ in which he spares his readers any moralizing —*Time*⟩ **c :** MORALITY PLAY ⟨increased use of the comic element marked the development of the *moralities* as popular plays —F.H.O'Hara & Marquerite Bro⟩ **3 a :** a doctrine or system of ideas concerned with conduct ⟨the basic law which an adequate ~ ought to state —Marjorie Grene⟩ ⟨the object of systems of ~ is to take possession of human life —Matthew Arnold⟩ **b moralities** *pl* **:** particular moral principles or rules of conduct ⟨we were all brought up on one of these *moralities* —*Psychiatry*⟩ ⟨instruction in the fundamental *moralities* of life . . . and its decent amenities —W.A. White⟩ **4 :** the quality or fact of conforming to or deriving from right ideals of human conduct ⟨admitted the expediency of the law but questioned its ~⟩ **5 a :** moral conduct **:** goodness and uprightness of behavior **:** VIRTUE ⟨~ consists in the aims at the ideal —A.N.Whitehead⟩ ⟨a new low in public ~ —*Current History*⟩ ⟨a person of strict ~⟩ ⟨today involves a responsible relationship toward the laws of the natural world —P.B.Sears⟩ **b :** conduct conforming to the customs or accepted standards of a particular culture or group ⟨in Christian love and forgiveness lay some reversal of Saxon ~ —H.O. Taylor⟩ ⟨the ~ of a world plunging itself into chaos —G.P. Musselman⟩ ⟨an abyss separated the domestic and business ~ of the Victorian world —F.B.Millett⟩ ⟨customs, *moralities*, scenes, and quaint observances of the time —Joseph Hudnut⟩

**morality play** *n* **:** an allegorical play popular esp. in the 15th and 16th centuries in which the characters personify moral qualities (as charity or vice) or abstractions (as death or youth) and in which moral lessons are taught

**mor·al·iza·tion** \\ˌmȯrələ'zāshən, ˌmär-, -lī'-\\ *n* -s [ME *moralizacion*, fr. ML *moralization-, moralizatio*, fr. *moralizatus* (past part. of *moralizare* to moralize) + L *-ion-, -io* -ion] **1 a :** the giving of a moral interpretation to something **:** an explanation in moral terms ⟨his criticism of the play is simply a ~ of it⟩ **b :** the act of moralizing **:** a moral reflection or discourse ⟨~*s* . . . were the beginnings of thought, feelings, perceptions, which led him to write the novels —J.T.Farrell⟩ **2 a :** the act of making moral ⟨the best government it had ever known, with ~ of public offices —Hubert Herring⟩ **b :** the process of becoming moral ⟨progressive ~ of the idea of holiness in the Old Testament —R.C.Dentan⟩

**mor·al·ize** \\'mȯrə,līz, 'mär-\\ *vb* -ED/-ING/-S *see -ize in Explan Notes* [ME *moralysen*, fr. MF *moraliser*, prob. fr. ML *moralizare*, fr. L *moralis* moral + LL *-izare* -ize] *vt* **1 :** to explain or interpret morally **:** draw a moral from or furnish with a moral meaning ⟨always posed an insoluble problem for those who would ~ the play —D.P.Harding⟩ **2 a :** to give a moral quality or direction to **:** make aware of or subject to the influence of moral values ⟨the sentiments and force of will are neutral . . . and may become antisocial unless they are *moralized* —*General Education in a Free Society*⟩ ⟨has always felt strongly the compulsion to ~ his fellowmen —Asher Moore⟩ **b :** to make more moral **:** improve the morals or moral conduct of ⟨modern efforts to ~ business and to subordinate profit seeking to humane ends —Walter Lippmann⟩ **3** *archaic* **:** to make more tolerable **:** bring into a better state of mind by moral speech or reflection ~ *vi* **:** to make moral reflections **:** talk, write, or think in moral terms ⟨the tendency to ~ upon the relations of beauty to conduct —Bliss Perry⟩ ⟨never descends to the sermonizing and *moralizing* that filled so many pages in Victorian histories —*Saturday Rev.*⟩

**mor·al·iz·er** \\-zə(r)\\ *n* -s **:** one that moralizes

**moralizing** *adj* **:** that moralizes **:** painting a moral ⟨this trite ~ way of regarding natural phenomena —L.P.Smith⟩ — **mor·al·iz·ing·ly** *adv*

**moral law** *n* **:** a general rule of right living; *esp* **:** such a rule or group of rules conceived as universal and unchanging and as having the sanction of God's will, of conscience, of man's moral nature, or of natural justice as revealed to human reason ⟨the basic protection of rights is the *moral law* based on man's dignity —*Time*⟩

**moraller** *var of* MORALER

**mor·al·less** \\'mȯrəlləs, 'mär-\\ *adj* **:** having no moral significance ⟨a ~ story⟩ ⟨regards art as a ~ activity⟩

**mor·al·ly** \\-rəlē, -li\\ *adv* [ME, fr. [1]*moral* + *-ly*] **1 :** from the point of view of moral rules or principles **:** in terms of accepted moral standards ⟨if public administration is ~ bad but legally sound —*Sydney* (*Australia*) *Bull.*⟩ **2 :** according to reason or probability **:** VIRTUALLY ⟨there is precise record of so many East Asiatic junks reaching the Pacific coast . . . during the past hundred years that its having happened again and again in preceding centuries is ~ certain —A.L.Kroeber⟩ **3 :** with respect to the mental and psychological as distinguished from the physical ⟨helped her, ~ rather than physically, to rise —Arnold Bennett⟩ ⟨~ and physically exhausted⟩

**moral philosophy** *or* **moral science** *n* **:** a study of the motivations and principles of human conduct; *esp* **:** such study formerly prominent as a distinct subject in institutions of higher education and including subjects (as psychology) now separately studied — compare MENTAL PHILOSOPHY, NATURAL PHILOSOPHY

**moral re-armament** *n, often cap M&R&A* **:** a movement developing out of the Oxford Group movement and applying its doctrine and techniques esp. to the problems of international relations

**morals** *pl of* MORAL

**moral sense** *n* **:** a feeling of the rightness or wrongness of an action or the ability to have such feelings

**moral theology** *n* **:** a branch of theology that treats of morals; *also* **:** theology or theological doctrines developed as inferences from moral grounds or reasons

**moral theory** *or* **moral influence theory** *n* **:** a theory of the atonement introduced by Peter Abelard in the 12th century and common in modern liberal theology holding that the life and death of Jesus Christ reconcile man to God by so revealing the holiness and love of God as to win man to repentence and faith — called also *subjective theory;* compare SATISFACTION THEORY

**moral turpitude** *n* **1 :** an act or behavior that gravely violates the moral sentiment or accepted moral standards of the community; *esp* **:** sexual immorality ⟨was considered unfit to hold office because of *moral turpitude*⟩ **2 :** the morally culpable quality held to be present in some criminal offenses as distinguished from others ⟨permits may be denied for bad moral character . . . or conviction for an offense involving *moral turpitude* —David Fellman⟩ — compare MALUM PROHIBITUM

**moral victory** *n* **:** an actual defeat regarded as a virtual victory because of the narrowness of the margin or because of some circumstance that gives satisfaction or hope

**moral virtue** *n, Aristotelianism* **:** a virtue concerned with the practical life (as liberality or gentleness) or with the vegetative and appetitive (as temperance or self-control) — contrasted with *intellectual virtue*

**morant hutch** \\mə'rant-\\ *n* [after Major G. F. *Morant*, 19th cent. Eng. agriculturist, its designer] **:** a rabbit hutch with a wire mesh floor used on grassland

**moras** *pl of* MORA

**mo·rass** \\mə'ras, mȯ'-, mō'-, -raa(ə)s-, -rais\\ *n* -ES [D *moeras*, alter. (influenced by obs. D *moer* mire, swamp, fr. MD) of MD *maras, marasch*, fr. OF *mareis, maresc*, of Gmc origin; akin to OE *mersc, merisc* marsh — more at MARSH, MOOR] **1 :** a tract of soft, swampy, or boggy ground **:** MARSH, SWAMP **2 :** something that traps, confuses, or impedes **:** a state of confusion or entanglement ⟨a ~ of clumsy exposition and preposterous dialogue —Bruce Bliven b.1916⟩ ⟨guides her out of her ~ of insecurity —*Newsweek*⟩ — **mo·rassy** \\-sē\\ *adj*

**morass ore** *n* [trans. of G *morasterz*] **:** BOG IRON ORE

**mo·rat** \\'mō,rat\\ *n* -s [ML *moratum*, fr. L *morum* mulberry — more at MULBERRY] **:** a medieval drink of wine flavored with mulberries

**mor·a·to·ri·um** \\ˌmȯrə'tōrēəm, ˌmär-, -tȯr-\\ *n, pl* **morato·riums** \\-mz\\ *or* **moratoria** \\-ēə\\ [NL, fr. LL, neut. of *moratorius* dilatory, retarding] **1 a :** a legally authorized period of delay in the performance of a legal obligation or the payment of a debt ⟨asked the legislature for a ~ of one year on farm mortgage payments⟩ **b :** waiting period set by some authority **:** a delay officially required or granted ⟨usually there was at least one day's ~ on news coming out of such background briefings —Douglass Cater⟩ — compare INDULGENCE 3c **2 :** a suspension of activity **:** a temporary ban on the use or production of something ⟨so thorough was the ~ on brains that nobody in power dared do any primary thinking —J.R. Chamberlain⟩ ⟨a ~ on new systems —C.W.Thornthwaite⟩

**mor·a·tory** \\'==,tōrē, -tȯr-, -ri\\ *adj* [F *moratoire*, fr. LL *moratorius* dilatory, retarding, fr. L *moratus* (past part. of *morari* to delay, remain, fr. *mora* delay) + *-orius* -ory — more at MEMORY] **:** of, relating to, or authorizing delay in payment of an obligation ⟨~ interest⟩ ⟨a ~ law⟩

[1]**mo·ra·vi·an** \\mə'rāvēən, mȯ'-, mō'-, -vyən\\ *n* -s *cap* [ML *Moravia* Moray, region in northern Scotland including the present county of Moray + E *-an*, n. suffix] **:** a native or inhabitant of Moray, Scotland

[2]**moravian** \\"\\ *adj, usu cap* [ML *Moravia* Moray + E *-an*, adj. suffix] **1 :** of, relating to, or characteristic of Moray, Scotland **2 :** of, relating to, or characteristic of the people of Moray

[3]**moravian** \\"\\ *adj, usu cap* [*Moravia*, former province in central Czechoslovakia + E *-an*, adj. suffix] **1 a :** of, relating to, or characteristic of Moravia **b :** of, relating to, or characteristic of the people of Moravia **2 :** of, relating to, or characteristic of the Moravian Church

[4]**moravian** \\"\\ *n* -s **1** *usu cap* **:** a member of a Christian denomination that traces its history back through the evangelical movement in Moravia and Bohemia stemming from the efforts of the reformer John Hus and that accepts the Bible as the sole rule of faith and practice — called also *Herrnhuter* **2** *cap* **a :** a native or inhabitant of Moravia; *esp* **:** a descendant of the Slavic people who ruled Moravia in medieval times **b :** the group of dialects spoken by the Moravian people and transitional between Slovak and Czech

**moravian brethren** *n pl, usu cap M&B* **:** members of the Moravian Church

**mo·ra·vi·an·ism** \\-ēə,nizəm\\ *n* -s *usu cap* **:** the doctrines and practices of Moravians

**mo·ra·vite** \\mə'rā,vīt, 'mōrə,-\\ *n* -s [*Moravia*, former province in central Czechoslovakia + E *-ite*] **:** a mineral $Fe_2(Fe)_4Si_7O_{20}(OH)_4$ consisting of a fine scaly black basic silicate of iron and aluminum of the chlorite group

**mo·rav·ska os·tra·va** \\'mȯrəfskə'ȯstrəvə\\ *adj, usu cap M&O* [fr. *Moravska Ostrava*, city in central Czechoslovakia] **:** of or from the city of Moravska Ostrava, Czechoslovakia **:** of the kind or style prevalent in Moravska Ostrava

[1]**mo·ray** \\mə'rā, 'mȯ(ˌ)rā\\ *or* **moray eel** *n* -s [*moray* fr. Pg *moréia*, fr. L *murena, muraena*, fr. Gk *myraina*; perh. akin to Gk *smyrid-, smyris* powdered emery — more at SMEAR] **:** any of numerous often brightly colored savage voracious eels constituting the family Muraenidae, having small round gill openings, no pectoral or pelvic fins, and usu. narrow jaws with strong knifelike teeth and no tongue, occurring in all warm seas esp. in crevices about coral reefs, and including a Mediterranean eel (*Muraena helena*) valued as a food fish

[2]**mor·ay** \\'mər·ē, 'mə·r|, |i\\ *or* **mor·ay·shire** \\'==,shi(ə)r, -,shiə, -,shə(r)\\ *adj, usu cap* [fr. *Moray, Morayshire*, county in northeast Scotland] **:** of or from the county of Moray, Scotland **:** of the kind or style prevalent in Moray

**mor·bid** \\'mȯrbəd, 'mȯ(ə)b-\\ *adj* [L *morbidus* diseased, unwholesome, fr. *morbus* disease; akin to Gk *marainein* to waste away — more at SMART] **1 a :** of, relating to, or characteristic of disease ⟨~ anatomy⟩ **b :** affected with or induced by disease **:** not sound and healthful ⟨only the sick in mind crave cleverness, as a ~ body turns to drink —H.M.Tomlinson⟩ ⟨a ~ state⟩ ⟨~ alteration of tissues⟩ **c :** productive of disease ⟨introduction into the blood of ~ substances from without —Robert Chawner⟩ **2 :** abnormally susceptible to or characterized by gloomy or unwholesome feelings ⟨a ~, frustrated, sensitive and prophetic man —William Phillips b.1878⟩ ⟨a career of ~ introspection and self-pity —*Times Lit. Supp.*⟩ ⟨an almost ~ sense of guilt about the uses to which their discoveries have been put —Reinhold Niebuhr⟩ **3 :** GRISLY, GRUESOME ⟨a day for ~ joys and gruesome delights —Gertrude Diamant⟩ ⟨war has a ~ fascination for many men and women —D.L.Cohn⟩ **syn** see UNWHOLESOME

**mor·bi·dez·za** \\ˌmȯ(r)bə'detsə\\ *n* -s [It, fr. *morbido* tender, delicate, fr. L *morbidus* diseased, unwholesome] **1 :** an extreme delicacy and softness ⟨marveled at the ~ of the Italian women —Francis Hackett⟩ ⟨had too heroic a style for the ~ of the music he played⟩ **2 :** a sensual delicacy of flesh-coloring in painting ⟨~ in his treatment of flesh —Edward McCurdy⟩

**mor·bid·i·ty** \\mȯ(r)'bidəd·ē, -ətē, -i\\ *n* -ES **1 :** an abnormal or unhealthy state of mind; *esp* **:** one marked by excessive gloom ⟨his very ~ of mind . . . drove him into company as the only refuge from his haunting fears —Robert Lynd⟩ ⟨their passion for privacy verges on ~ —Green Peyton⟩ **2 :** a diseased state or symptom **:** fever up to 100.4°F ⟨lumbar puncture, if improperly performed, may be followed by a significant ~ —*Jour. Amer. Med. Assoc.*⟩ ⟨puerperal ~⟩ **3 :** the incidence of disease **:** the rate of sickness (as in a specified community or group) ⟨while TB mortality has declined fairly steadily, ~ has been rising —*Time*⟩ ⟨the collection of statistics on mental illness ~ —G.N.Raines⟩

**mor·bid·ly** *adv* **:** in a morbid manner or to a morbid extent ⟨~ sensitive⟩ ⟨~ fearful⟩ ⟨~ shy⟩

**mor·bid·ness** *n* -ES **:** the quality or state of being morbid

**mor·bif·ic** \\(')mȯ(r)ˈbifik\\ *adj* [prob. fr. (assumed) NL *morbificus*, fr. L *morbus* disease + *-ficus* -fic] **1 :** causing disease **:** generating a sickly state **2** *archaic* **:** DISEASED

**mor·bil·li** \\mȯ(r)'bi,lī\\ *n pl* [ML, pl. of *morbillus* spot on skin, pustule, dim. of L *morbus* disease] **:** MEASLES 1

**mor·bil·li·form** \\(')mȯrˈbilə,fȯrm\\ *adj* [ISV *morbilli-* (fr. ML *morbilli*) + *-form*] **:** resembling the eruption of measles

**mor·bose** \\(')mȯrˈbōs\\ *adj* [L *morbosus*, fr. *morbus* disease + *-osus* -OSE] **:** DISEASED, MORBID

**mor·bus** \\'mȯrbəs\\ *n, pl* **mor·bi** \\-r,bī\\ [L] **:** DISEASE

**morbus gal·li·cus** \\-'galəkəs\\ *n, usu cap G* [NL, lit., Gallic disease] *archaic* **:** SYPHILIS

**mor·ceau** \\mȯr'sō\\ *n, pl* **mor·ceaux** \\-ō(z)\\ *also* **morceaus** \\-ōz\\ [F, fr. OF *morsel* — more at MORSEL] **:** a short literary or musical piece

**mor·cel·la·tion** \\ˌmȯ(r)sə'lāshən\\ *n* -s [F *morceler* to divide into small pieces (fr. *morceau* morsel) + E *-ation*] **:** division and removal in small pieces (as of a tumor)

**mor·celle·ment** \\ˌmȯ(r)selˈmä^n\\ *n* -s [F, fr. *morceler* to divide into small pieces + *-ment*] **1 :** division into small pieces **2 :** MORCELLATION

**mor·chel·la** \\mȯ(r)'kelə\\ *n, cap* [NL, fr. G *morchel* morel, fr. OHG *morhila* — more at MOREL] **:** a genus of edible fungi (family Helvellaceae) having an irregularly folded and pitted apothecium grown around the upper part of the stalk — see MOREL — **mor·chel·loid** \\-e,lȯid\\ *adj*

**mor·da·cious** \\(')mȯ(r)ˈdāshəs\\ *adj* [L *mordac-, mordax* biting, given to biting (fr. *mordēre* to bite) + E *-ious* — more at SMART] **1 :** biting or given to biting ⟨bitten in as with ~ acid —*Times Lit. Supp.*⟩ **2 :** biting or sharp in manner or style **:** CAUSTIC ⟨the lady's ~ look showed plainly that she hated us all —Pauline R. Fadiman⟩ — **mor·da·cious·ly** *adv*

**mor·dac·i·ty** \\mȯ(r)'dasəd·ē, -aas-, -ətē, -i\\ *n* -ES [L *mordacitat-, mordacitas*, fr. *mordac-, mordax* + *-itat-, -itas* -ity] **1** *archaic* **:** a readiness to bite **2 :** a biting quality of speech

**mor·dan·cy** \\'mȯ(r)dᵊnsē, -si\\ *n* -ES [[1]*mordant* + *-cy*] **1 :** a biting and caustic quality of style **:** INCISIVENESS ⟨the ~ of his comments made his opponent wince⟩ **2 :** a sharply critical or bitter quality of thought or feeling **:** HARSHNESS ⟨marked by a deepening note of grimness and ~ —J.E.M.White⟩ ⟨forceful criticisms of the maladjustments of life, bitterness, ~, and despair —Leslie Rees⟩

[1]**mor·dant** \\-ᵊnt\\ *adj* [MF, pres. part. of *mordre* to bite, fr. L *mordēre*] **1 :** biting and caustic in thought, manner, or style **:** INCISIVE, KEEN ⟨run ranging from slapstick clowning to . . . savage ~ wit —Robert Bendiner⟩ ⟨the ~ things you try to say to listeners, cruelties invariably regarded as merely gently whimsical —Irwin Edman⟩ ⟨a ~ analyst and remorseless judge of snobbery —*Time*⟩ **2 a :** acting as a mordant (as in dyeing) **b :** of, relating to, or subject to application by means of a mordant **3 :** BURNING, PUNGENT ⟨~ pain⟩ **4 :** prone to biting ⟨a ~ dog⟩ — **mor·dant·ly** *adv*

[2]**mordant** \\"\\ *n* -s [F, fr. MF *mordant*, pres. part. of *mordre* to bite] **1 :** a chemical (as a salt or hydroxide of chromium or aluminum or tin) that serves to fix a dye in or on a substance (as a textile fiber, fur, or microscopic preparation of cells or tissues) by combining with the dye to form an insoluble compound **2 :** any sticky matter used to cause leaf metal to adhere **3 :** a corroding substance (as an acid solution) used in etching

[3]**mordant** \\"\\ *vt* -ED/-ING/-S **1 :** to subject (as a textile fabric) to the action of or treat with a mordant or similar chemical ⟨with the old dyewoods, cotton . . . was first ~*ed* with a metallic salt —C.M.Whittaker & C.C.Wilcock⟩ **2 :** to treat (an emulsion or other photographic material) with a chemical that confers the ability to combine with dyes

[4]**mordant** *var of* MORDENT

**mordant acid dye** *n* **:** a mordant dye (as a chrome dye) that dyes in an acid bath — see DYE table I

**mordant dye** *n* **:** a dye (as most natural dyes and many anthraquinone dyes) that becomes fixed on a fiber by forming an insoluble compound with a mordant — see DYE table I

**mordant rouge** *n* **:** RED LIQUOR 2

**mor·del·la** \\mȯ(r)'delə\\ *n, cap* [NL, fr. L *mordēre* to bite + NL *-ella*] **:** the type genus of the family Mordellidae

[1]**mor·del·lid** \\(')mȯ(r)ˈdeləd\\ *adj* [NL *Mordellidae*] **:** of or relating to the Mordellidae

[2]**mordellid** \\"\\ *n* -s [NL *Mordellidae*] **:** a beetle of the family Mordellidae

**mor·del·li·dae** \\mȯ(r)'delə,dē\\ *n pl, cap* [NL, fr. *Mordella*, type genus + *-idae*] **:** a widespread family of small pubescent beetles that have the body strongly arched and tapered to a sharp tip and that are usu. found on flowers

**mor·den·ite** \\'mȯ(r)dᵊn,īt\\ *n* -s [*Morden*, Nova Scotia + E *-ite*] **:** a zeolite approximately $(Ca_1Na_2,K_2)_4Al_8Si_{40}O_{96}$·$28H_2O$ found in minute crystals or fibrous concretions

**mor·dent** *also* **mor·dant** \\'mȯrdᵊnt, 'mȯ(ə)d-\\ *n* -s [It *mordente*, fr. L *mordent-, mordens*, pres. part. of *mordēre* to bite] **1 :** a melodic musical grace made by a quick alternation of a principal tone with an auxiliary tone usu. a half step lower **2 :** ACCIACCATURA

mordents 1: *1* as written, *2* as performed

**mor·di·sheen** \\ˌmȯ(r)də'shēn\\ *n* -s [Pg *mordexim*, fr. Marathi *modśi*, fr. *modṇē* to break, fail, lose health] *India* **:** ASIATIC CHOLERA

**mor·do·ré** \\ˌmȯ(r)də'rā\\ *n* -s [F, fr. *More, Maure* Moor (fr. L *Maurus*) + *doré* gilded, past part. of *dorer* to gild, fr. LL *deaurare* — more at MOOR, DORADO] **:** PENCILWOOD

**mor·do·vi·an** \\mȯ(r)'dōvēən\\ *n* -s *cap* **:** MORDVIN

**mord·va** \\(')mȯrdˈvä\\ *n pl, cap* **:** MORDVINS

**mord·vin** \\-vin\\ *or* **mord·vin·i·an** \\mȯrd'vinēən\\ *n, pl* **mordvin** *or* **mordvins** *or* **mordvinian** *or* **mordvinians** *cap* **1 a :** an agricultural people of the middle Volga provinces of European Russia **b :** a member of such people **2 :** a Finno-Ugric language of the Mordvin people — see URALIC LANGUAGES table

**mord·wil·ko·ja** \\ˌmȯ(r)dwəl'kōjə, mȯ(r)d'wilkəjə\\ *n, cap* [NL, fr. Aleksandr K. *Mordvilko* †1938 Russ. entomologist] **:** a genus of aphids that cause disfiguring galls on cottonwood in western No. America

[1]**more** \\'mō(ə)r, 'mȯ(ə)r, -ōə, -ȯ(ə)\\ *adj* [ME *more, moore, mo*, fr. OE *māra* (adj.), *mā* (adj. & adv. & n.); OE *māra* akin to OHG *mēro* larger, ON *meiri* larger, more, Goth *maiza* greater, elder; OE *mā* akin to OHG *mēr* more, ON *meirr*, Goth *mais;* both OE *māra* and OE *mā* akin to OIr *mór*, *mār* large, Gk *enchesimōros* fighting with a spear, OPruss *muisieson* more] **1 a** *archaic* **:** superior in kind or degree ⟨proceed in their coaches through the city for the ~ solemnity of it —John Evelyn⟩ **b :** superior in quality or intensity ⟨the ~ fool you⟩ ⟨made for something ~ than a guerilla chieftain —H.E. Scudder⟩ **c :** superior in age **:** OLDER ⟨never seemed ~ in years than one of her own . . . brood —Della Lutes⟩ **2 :** ADDITIONAL, FURTHER ⟨offered him ~ coffee⟩ ⟨are going to stake ~ billions on the future —C.F.Craig⟩ ⟨one ~ word and you'll go straight to your room⟩ **3 :** of a larger size or extent ⟨for the ~ part . . . did not talk of ephemerae —Lucien Price⟩ **4 a :** of a larger quantity or amount ⟨the average high school senior does a lot ~ and a lot deeper thinking than his temperamental ways . . . suggest —Milton Lomask⟩ ⟨better democracy is more important than ~ democracy —Francis Biddle⟩ **b :** of a larger number ⟨there are ~ ways than one to skin a cat⟩ ⟨the ~ students who need instruction . . . the greater the demand for my services —H.A.Burton⟩

[2]**more** \\"\\ *adv* [ME *more, moore, mo*, fr. OE *māre* (fr. neut. of *māra*, adj.), *mā* (adj. & adv. & n.)] **1 a :** beyond a previously indicated number, amount, or length of time **:** in addition ⟨went to England a couple of times ~ —Maddy Vegtel⟩ ⟨what ~ could a speaker ask —B.F.Fairless⟩ ⟨the poor man's tired and old . . . and he hasn't much ~ to go —Lenard Kaufman⟩ **b :** in addition to points already enumerated **:** BESIDES, MOREOVER ⟨~, Jefferson failed to anticipate the gigantic changes —J.P.Boyd⟩ **2 a :** to a greater extent or degree ⟨~ as a measure of desperation than as one calculated to achieve victory

—C.E.Black & E.C.Helmreich⟩ — often used with adjectives and adverbs to form the comparative ⟨some of her ~ remarkable sons and visitors —J.P.Marquand⟩ ⟨the ~ learned the writer . . . the harder it is —W.T.Jones⟩ ⟨ostensibly to guard the trains but ~ probably to relieve the fears of Washington —Eben Swift⟩ **b :** to a closer degree : NEARER ⟨the plover has ~ a lark's habits —Alwyn Lee⟩ ⟨the real rates are . . . ~ like 18 per thousand —B.K.Sandwell⟩

**³more** \"\ *n* -s [ME *more, moore, mo,* fr. OE *māre* (fr. neut. of *māra*, adj.), *mā* (adj. & adv. & n.)] **1 :** a larger portion or number ⟨the ~ the merrier⟩ ⟨climb the ~ than four hundred steps —Budd Schulberg⟩ — often used with singular verb ⟨~ than one charge of discrimination was involved —*N.Y.Times*⟩ **2 a :** an additional number, amount, or length of time ⟨it costs a little ~ but it's worth it⟩ **b :** something in addition to what has already been mentioned ⟨what is ~ the gadget can be made to do lovely embossed patterns —Bertram Mycock⟩ **c :** further discussion ⟨~ on this topic later —G.A.Miller⟩ **3** *obs* **:** one that is of superior rank ⟨both ~ and less have given him the revolt —Shak.⟩ **4 :** something different or additional ⟨water is no ~ than ice thawed by heat —Tobias Smollett⟩

**⁴more** \"\ *pron* [¹*more*] **1 a :** something superior or above average ⟨~ is expected of you⟩ **b :** something of greater importance or significance ⟨his book is ~ than a guide —*Geog. Jour.*⟩ ⟨there is ~ to prophecy than the knack of accurate forecasting —D.R.Weimer⟩ **2** *pl in constr* **:** additional persons or things ⟨~ were found as the search continued⟩

**⁵more** \ˈmä(r)\ *n* -s [ME, fr. OE *more, moru* carrot, parsnip; akin to OHG *moraha* carrot, Gk *brakana* wild vegetables, Russ *morkov'* carrot] *dial Eng* **:** ROOT, STUMP

**⁶more** \ˈmō(ə)r\ *archaic var of* MOOR

**⁷mo·ré** \məˈrā\ *n* -s *usu cap* **:** MOSSI

**more and more** *adv* [ME] **:** to a progressively increasing extent ⟨his interest turned *more and more* to meteorology —W.J. Humphreys⟩ ⟨the scientist's theory *more and more* . . . parallels reality —Weston La Barre⟩

**mo·reen** \məˈrēn\ *n* -s [prob. irreg. fr. ¹*moire* + *-een*] **1 :** a strong cross-ribbed upholstery fabric of wool or wool and cotton with a plain glossy or moiré finish **2 :** a cotton imitation of moreen with vertical ribs that is used for clothing

**more·ish** \ˈmōrish, ˈmȯr-\ *adj* [¹*more* + *-ish*] **:** causing a desire for more : PALATABLE

**¹mo·rel** *also* **mo·relle** \məˈrel\ *n* -s [ME, fr. OF *morele,* fr. (assumed) VL *maurella*, fr. L *Maurus* Moor + *-ella* — more at MOOR] **:** any of various nightshades; *esp* **:** BLACK NIGHTSHADE

**²morel** \", ˈmȯrəl, ˈmär\ *n* -s [F *morille,* of Gmc origin; akin to OHG *morhila* morel, dim. of *moraha* carrot] **1 :** an edible fungus of the genus *Morchella* (esp. *M. esculenta*) **2 :** a fungus of any of several genera closely related to *Morchella*

**mo·relles** \məˈrelz\ *n pl* [F *morelles, marelles, mérelles* (pl.), fr. MF *merelles,* fr. pl. of *merelle* counter, disk used in playing a board game, fr. OF *merele, marele* — more at MERELS] **:** ²MORRIS

**mo·rel·lo** \məˈre(ˌ)lō\ *n* -s [prob. modif. of Flem *marelle,* short for *amarelle,* fr. ML *amarellum* sour cultivated cherry — more at AMARELLE] **1** *or* **morello cherry** *also* **morel** \məˈrel\ **:** any of several cultivated cherries derived from the sour cherry and distinguished from the amarelles by their dark-colored skin and juice **2 :** MULBERRY 2b

**mo·re·los orange worm** \məˈrā lōs-\ *n, usu cap M* [*Morelos,* state in south central Mexico] **:** the maggot of the Mexican fruit fly

**mo·ren·cite** \məˈren(t)ˌsīt\ *n* -s [*Morenci,* Arizona + E *-ite*] **:** a hydrated ferric silicate clay mineral in yellow fibrous forms related to chloropal

**mo·ren·do** \məˈren(ˌ)dō\ *adj* (*or adv*) [It, fr. L *moriendum,* gerund of *mori* to die — more at MURDER] **:** dying away : with a gradual softening of tone and slowing of movement — used as a direction in music

**more·ness** *n* -ES **:** the quality or state of being more

**mo·ren·o·site** \məˈrenəˌsīt\ *n* -s [Sp *morenosita,* fr. *Moreno,* 19th cent. Spaniard + connective *-s-* + Sp *-ita* -ite] **:** a mineral $NiSO_4.7H_2O$ consisting of nickel sulfate and occurring in light green crystals or fibrous crusts

**more or less** *adv* [ME *moore or lesse*] **1 :** to a varying or undetermined extent or degree : SOMEWHAT, RATHER ⟨men who are all *more or less* expert in their knowledge —L.M.Judd⟩ ⟨stabilizing the . . . *more or less* arbitrary exchange rates —Jacob Viner⟩ ⟨*more or less* economical⟩ ⟨a copious supply of remedies, *more or less* drastic —W.G.Constable⟩ **2 :** with small variations : APPROXIMATELY, SUBSTANTIALLY ⟨birds . . . looking *more or less* in one direction —James Stevenson-Hamilton⟩ ⟨*more or less* what this article will examine —N.A. Luyten⟩ — used in legal documents to cover trivial differences usu. overlooked when bargaining in good faith ⟨comprising an area of 6600 square feet *more or less*⟩

**more·over** \mōrˈōvə(r), mȯˈrō, ˈ=ˌ==, *sometimes* məˈrō-\ *adv* [ME, fr. ²*more* + *over,* adv.] **:** in addition to what has been said : BESIDES, FURTHER ⟨~, the method has obvious limitations —T.H.Savory⟩ ⟨has therefore an extensive range, and is ~ found in large numbers throughout a considerable portion of it —James Stevenson-Hamilton⟩

**more·pork** \ˈmōrˌpōrk, ˈmȯrˌpȯrk\ *also* **mo·poke** \ˈmōˌpōk\ *or* **more·poke** \ˈmōrˌpōk, ˈmȯr-\ *n* [imit.] **1 :** any of several Australian frogmouths (esp. *Podargus strigoides*) **2 :** BOOBOOK OWL **3** *Austral* **:** a dull-witted person

**mo·res** \ˈmō(ˌ)rāz, ˈmō(ˌ)r, |ēz *sometimes* |ās\ *n pl* [L, pl. of *mor-, mos* custom — more at MOOD] **1 :** the fixed customs or folkways of a particular group that are morally binding upon all members of the group and necessary to its welfare and preservation ⟨the relationship between law and ~, between the decrees of courts and legislatures and the vast body of community beliefs which shape private action —J.P.Roche & M.M. Gordon⟩ ⟨academic ~ have frowned upon the invasion of another man's craft —J.R.Butler⟩ ⟨have tended to withdraw and develop a self-sufficient society of their own, with distinct and rigid ~ —James Stirling⟩ **2 :** moral attitudes ⟨conformity to the evershifting ~ of the moment —Havelock Ellis⟩ ⟨some knowledge of the environment and the dominant ~ of the author —G.W.Sherburn⟩ **3 :** HABITS, MANNERS ⟨her uncanny familiarity with the ~ of feline life —*New Yorker*⟩ ⟨in rural New England, organized dancing developed a whole set of ~ and practices of its own —R.L.Taylor⟩

**¹mo·res·co** \məˈres(ˌ)kō\ *adj, usu cap* [It, fr. *Moro* Moor (fr. L *Maurus*) + *-esco* -esque — more at MOOR] *archaic* **:** of or relating to the Moors : MOORISH

**²moresco** \"\ *n* -ES *usu cap, archaic* **:** MOOR; *esp* **:** a Moorish resident of Spain

**¹mo·resque** *also* **mau·resque** \məˈresk\ *adj, often cap* [F, fr. Sp *morisco,* fr. *Moro* Moor, fr. L *Maurus*] **:** having the characteristics of Moorish art, architecture, or decoration

**²moresque** *also* **mauresque** \"\ *n* -s *often cap* **:** an ornament or decorative motif in Moorish style

**more·ton bay ash** \ˈmōrtᵊn-\ *n, usu cap M&B* [*Moreton Bay,* Queensland, Australia] **:** an Australian tree (*Eucalyptus tessellaris*) with tough durable wood and gum rich in tannin

**moreton bay chestnut** *n, usu cap M&B* **:** BEAN TREE a

**moreton bay fig** *n, usu cap M&B* **:** an Australian fig tree (*Ficus macrophylla*) often planted for shade

**moreton bay pine** *n, usu cap M&B* **:** HOOP PINE

**mor·frey** \ˈmȯrfrī\ *n* -s [alter. of ¹*hermaphrodite*] *dial Eng* **:** a farmer's 2-wheeled cart that can be converted to a 4-wheeled wagon

**morgagni's crypt** *n, usu cap M* **:** CRYPT OF MORGAGNI

**¹mor·gan** \ˈmȯgən\ *n* -s [perh. alter. of E dial. *marg,* perh. short for obs. E *margaret* daisy, fr. ME *margarette,* fr. MF *margarite* daisy, pearl — more at MARGARITE] *dial Eng* **:** any of various plants of the genus *Anthemis*

**²morgan** \ˈmȯrgən, ˈmȯ(ə)g-\ *n* [after Justin *Morgan* †1798 Am. teacher who owned the stallion that became the progenitor of the breed] **1** *usu cap* **:** an American breed of light horses originated in Vermont from the progeny of one thoroughbred stallion with a variety of native mares **2** -s *often cap* **:** a horse of the Morgan breed

**mor·ga·nat·ic** \ˌmȯ(r)gəˈnad·ik\ *adj* [NL *morganatica* morning gift (in the term *matrimonium ad morganaticam* morganatic marriage), prob. alter. of ML *morganaticum,* fr. MHG *morgen* morning (fr. OHG *morgan*) + L *-aticum* -age — more at MORN] **:** of or relating to a form of valid marriage contracted by a member of a European royal or noble family with a person of inferior rank on the understanding that the rank of the inferior partner remains unchanged and that the children of the marriage though legitimate do not succeed to the titles, fiefs, or entailed property of the parent of higher rank — compare LEFT-HANDED 5 — **mor·ga·nat·i·cal·ly** \-d·ək(ə)lē\ *adv*

**mor·gan·ite** \ˈmȯ(r)gəˌnīt\ *n* -s [J. P. *Morgan* †1913 Am. financier + E *-ite*] **:** a rose-colored gem variety of beryl

**mor·gan·ize** \ˈmȯ(r)gəˌnīz\ *vt* -ED/-ING/-S [William *Morgan* †1826? Am. Freemason allegedly murdered by Freemasons for threatening to publish the secrets of Freemasonry + E *-ize*] **:** to assassinate or do away with secretly in order to prevent or punish disclosure of secrets

**mor·gen** \ˈmȯrgən\ *n, pl* **morgen** [D, fr. MD, fr. *morgen* morning; akin to OHG *morgan* morning] **:** an old Dutch unit of land area equal to 2.116 acres that is now used in southern Africa

**mor·gen·age** \-nij\ *n* -s **:** area in morgen

**¹morgue** \ˈmȯrg, ˈmȯ(ə)g\ *n* -s [F] **:** an air of pride and superiority : HAUGHTINESS ⟨had gathered his dignity around him and put on the most terrific ~ as he always did when he had to get into a public vehicle in uniform —Ion Braby⟩ ⟨rigid with caste, insolent with ineffable ~ —*Times Lit. Supp.*⟩

**²morgue** \"\ *n* -s [F, perh. fr. *morgue* haughtiness] **1 :** a place where the bodies of unidentified persons or those who have died of violence or unknown causes are kept until released for burial **2 a :** a collection of reference works and files of reference material (as newspaper clippings and photographs) in the editorial offices of a newspaper or news periodical : a newspaper library **b :** a filing cabinet or storage place (as in a library or office) where material only occas. in use is kept

**¹mor·i·bund** \ˈmȯrəˌbənd, ˈmär-\ *adj* [L *moribundus,* fr. *mori* to die — more at MURDER] **1 :** being in a dying state : approaching death ⟨in the ~ patient deepening stupor and coma are the usual preludes to death —Norman Cameron⟩ ⟨convinced that their textile mills are ~, many weavers are quitting their looms —*Time*⟩ **2 :** being in a state of suspended activity or arrested growth : DORMANT ⟨after being more or less ~ for years, interest in electrolytic diffusion suddenly revived —A.R.Gordon⟩ ⟨a dull ~ form of the faith dozes on in the monasteries and monastic shrines of these secluded highlands —Ellen Semple⟩ — **mor·i·bun·di·ty** \ˌ==ˈbəndəd-ē, -dətē, -i\ *n* -ES

**²moribund** \"\ *n* -s **:** a dying person ⟨the poor ~ was delirious and knew not what he said —Rafael Sabatini⟩

**mo·ri·che** \məˈrēchā\ *or* **moriche palm** *n* -s [Sp *moriche,* fr. Tupi *muriti*] **:** MIRITI PALM

**mo·rig·er·ate** \məˈrijəˌrāt\ *adj* [L *morigeratus,* past part. of *morigerari* to comply with, gratify, fr. *morigerus*] *archaic* **:** MORIGEROUS

**mo·rig·er·a·tion** \ˌ=ˌ==ˈrāshən\ *n* -s [L *morigeration-, morigeratio,* fr. *morigeratus* + *-ion-, -io* -ion] **:** servile obedience : OBSEQUIOUSNESS ⟨a much more contemptible form of ~ than that of courtiers to princes —*Fortnightly Rev.*⟩

**mo·rig·er·ous** \məˈrijərəs\ *adj* [L *morigerus,* fr. *mor-, mos* custom + *-i-* + *-gerus* (fr. *gerere* to bear) — more at MOOD, CAST] *archaic* **:** OBEDIENT, SUBMISSIVE

**mo·ril·lon** \məˈrilən\ *n* -s [F, duck with dark plumage, dark-colored grape fr. OF *morillon, moreillon,* fr. *morel* dark brown, fr. (assumed) VL *maurellus,* fr. L *Maurus* Moor — more at MOOR] **1 :** any of several European ducks; *esp* **:** a female or immature male goldeneye **2 :** a light olive that is greener, stronger, and slightly darker than citrine, greener and deeper than grape green, and greener than old moss green

**mo·rin** \ˈmōrən, ˈmȯr-\ *n* -s [F *morine,* fr. NL *Morus* + F *-ine;* fr. the former belief that the fustic tree belonged to the genus *Morus* — more at MORUS] **:** a pale yellow crystalline flavono pigment $C_{15}H_{10}O_7$ found in old fustic and osage orange

**mo·rin·da** \məˈrində\ *n, cap* [NL, fr. *mor-* (fr. L *morus* mulberry tree) + L *inda,* fem. of *indus* of or connected with India, fr. Gk *indos* — more at MULBERRY, IND-] **:** a large genus of chiefly East Indian tropical trees and shrubs (family Rubiaceae) having small heads of confluent flowers that form an aggregate pulpy fruit and including several that yield yellow dyes

**mo·rin·din** \-dən\ *n* -s [NL *Morinda* + E *-in*] **:** a yellow crystalline glycoside $C_{26}H_{28}O_{14}$ extracted from the root bark of various trees of the genus *Morinda*

**mo·rin·done** \-inˌdōn\ *n* -s [NL *Morinda* + E *-one*] **:** an orange-red crystalline dye $CH_3C_{14}H_4O_2(OH)_3$ derived from anthraquinone and obtained from morindin by hydrolysis

**mor·i·nel** \ˈmȯrəˌnel, ˈmär-\ *n* -s [NL *morinellus,* partly fr. L *Morini,* people inhabiting the part of Gaul nearest to Britain, partly fr. Gk *mōros* stupid; fr. its commonness in northern France and fr. its stupidity — more at MORON] **:** DOTTEREL

**mo·rin·ga** \məˈriŋgə\ *n, cap* [NL, prob. fr. Malayalam *muriṅṅa*] **:** a genus of East Indian and African trees constituting the family Moringaceae and having pinnate leaves and irregular flowers with 10 stamens and a 3-valved capsular fruit — see HORSERADISH TREE

**mo·rin·ga·ce·ae** \ˌmōriŋˈgāsēˌē, ˌmȯr-\ *n pl, cap* [NL, fr. *Moringa,* type genus + *-aceae*] **:** a family of trees (order Rhoeadales) coextensive with the genus *Moringa* — **mo·rin·ga·ceous** \ˌ=ˌ==ˈgāshəs\ *adj*

**mo·rin·gad** \məˈriŋˌgad\ *n* -s [NL *Moringa* + E *-ad*] **:** a tree of the family Moringaceae

**mo·rin·gu·i·dae** \ˌmōriŋˈg(y)üəˌdē, ˌmȯr-\ *n pl, cap* [NL, fr. *Moringua,* type genus (perh. fr. Tamil *malaṅku* eel) + *-idae*] **:** a family of eels comprising the very slender wormlike whip eels

**mo·rin·ite** \ˈmōrəˌnīt, ˈmȯr-\ *n* -s [F, fr. *Morineau,* 19th cent. Fr. mine director + F *-ite*] **:** a mineral $Na_2Ca_3Al_3H(PO_4)_4F_6.8H_2O$ consisting of hydrous acid fluoride and phosphate of sodium, calcium, and aluminum

**mo·ri·o·ka** \məˈrēəkə, ˌmōrēˈōkə\ *adj, usu cap* [fr. *Morioka,* city in northern Honshu, Japan] **:** of or from the city of Morioka, Japan **:** of the kind or style prevalent in Morioka

**¹mo·ri·on** \ˈmōrēən, ˈmȯr-\ *n* -s [MF] **:** a visorless high-crested helmet of Spanish origin worn by foot soldiers in the 16th and 17th centuries ⟨a battered ~ on his brow —Sir Walter Scott⟩

morion

**²morion** \"\ *n* -s [misreading in early editions of Pliny for L *mormorion*] **:** a nearly black variety of smoky quartz or cairngorm

**mo·ri·o·ri** \ˌmōrēˈōrē, ˌmȯrēˈōrē\ *n, pl* **moriori** *or* **morioris** *usu cap* **1 a :** an extinct people surviving until very recent times in the Chatham islands, east of New Zealand **b :** a member of such people **2 :** the Austronesian language of the Moriori

**mo·ris·ca** \məˈriskə\ *or* **mo·ris·co** \-i(ˌ)skō\ *n* -s [modif. (prob. influenced by ¹*morisco*) of It *moresca,* fr. fem. of *moresco* moorish — more at MORESCO] **:** a battle dance symbolizing the victory of the Christians over the Moors that developed during the Crusades, varied in different periods and countries, and is still popular at fiestas of the Iberian peninsula and Latin America

**¹mo·ris·co** \məˈri(ˌ)skō\ *adj, usu cap* [Sp, fr. *Moro* Moor, fr. L *Maurus* — more at MOOR] **:** MOORISH

**²morisco** \"\ *n, pl* **moriscos** *or* **moriscoes** *usu cap* [Sp, fr. *morisco,* adj.] **:** MOOR; *esp* **:** one of the Moorish people in Spain

**mor·lop** \ˈmȯrˌläp\ *n* -s [origin unknown] **:** a variety of jasper found in Australia

**mor·ma·er** *or* **mor·ma·or** \märˈmāər\ *n* -s [ScGael *mòrmhaor,* fr. *mòr* great (fr. OIr *mōr, mār* large, great) + *maor* steward, fr. L *major* larger, greater — more at MORE, MAJOR] **:** the ruler of one of the seven provinces into which medieval Scotland was divided — **mor·ma·er·ship** *or* **mor·ma·or·ship** \-ərˌship\ *n*

**mor·mal** \ˈmȯrməl\ *n* -s [ME, fr. MF *mormal, mortmal,* fr. *mort* dead (fr. L *mortuus,* past part. of *mori* to die) + *mal* disease — more at MURDER, MAL] *archaic* **:** a bad sore or ulcer

**¹mor·mon** \ˈmȯrmən, ˈmȯ(ə)m-\ *n* -s *usu cap* [after *The Book of Mormon* (first published 1830), sacred scriptures of the Latter-day Saints] **:** LATTER-DAY SAINT; *esp* **:** a member of the Church of Jesus Christ of Latter-day Saints

**²mormon** \"\ *adj, usu cap* **:** of or relating to the Mormons

**³mormon** \"\ *n* -s [NL (specific epithet of the mandrill *Mandrillus mormon*), fr. Gk *mormōn, mormō* she-monster, bugbear — more at FORMIDABLE] **:** MANDRILL

**mormon cricket** *n, usu cap M* **:** a large dark wingless katydid (*Anabrus simplex*) that resembles a cricket and is found in the arid parts of western U.S. where it occas. occurs in great numbers and damages crop plants

**mor·mon·dom** \-ndəm\ *n* -s *usu cap* **:** the community of the Mormons or the region inhabited by them

**mor·mon·ess** \-nəs\ *n* -ES *usu cap* **:** a female Mormon

**mor·mon·ism** \-məˌnizəm\ *n* -s *cap* **:** the doctrines and practices of Mormons

**mor·mon·ist** \-ˌnəst\ *n* -s *usu cap* **:** MORMON

**mor·mon·ite** \-məˌnīt\ *n* -s *usu cap* **:** MORMON

**mormon tea** *n, usu cap M* [so called fr. its use in the treatment of gonorrhea, with allusion to Mormon polygamy] **1 :** a plant of the genus *Ephedra* **2 :** a drink made from a plant of the genus *Ephedra*

**mor·mon·weed** \ˈ==ˌ=\ *n, usu cap* **:** INDIAN MALLOW 1

**mor·mo·ops** \mȯ(r)ˈmōˌäps\ *n, cap* [NL, fr. Gk *mormō* she-monster, bugbear + NL *-ops*] **:** a genus of bats (family Phyllostomatidae) comprising the tropical American cinnamon bats

**mor·mo·ran·do** \ˌmȯ(r)məˈrän(ˌ)dō\ *adj* (*or adv*) [It, murmuring, fr. L *murmurandum,* gerund of *murmurare* to murmur — more at MURMUR] **:** in a murmuring manner : MURMURING — used as a direction in music

**¹mor·my·rid** \(ˈ)mȯ(r)ˈmīrəd\ *adj* [NL *Mormyridae*] **:** of or relating to the Mormyridae

**²mormyrid** \"\ *also* **mor·myr** \ˈmȯrmər\ *n* -s [*mormyrid* fr. NL *Mormyridae; mormyr* fr. NL *Mormyrus*] **:** a fish of the family Mormyridae

**mor·myr·i·dae** \mȯ(r)ˈmirəˌdē\ *n pl, cap* [NL, fr. *Mormyrus,* type genus + *-idae*] **:** a family of African freshwater fishes (order Isospondyli) that have the gill openings reduced to small slits, small eyes usu. covered with skin, and the mouth small and often situated at the end of a tubular projection — see MORMYRUS

**mor·my·rus** \mȯ(r)ˈmīrəs\ *n, cap* [NL, fr. Gk *mormyros,* a sea fish] **:** the type genus of the family Mormyridae comprising oily fleshed edible fishes and including the sacred fishes of ancient Egypt

**¹morn** \ˈmȯ(ə)rn, ˈmȯ(ə)n\ *n* -s [ME *morn, morwen* dawn, morning, fr. OE *morgen;* akin to OHG *morgan* morning, ON *morginn,* Goth *maurgins* morning, L *merus* pure, unmixed, Gk *marmairein* to flash, sparkle, Skt *marīci* ray of light] **1 a :** the beginning of the day : DAWN, SUNRISE ⟨it was the lark, the herald of the ~ —Shak.⟩ ⟨a certain ~ broke beautiful and blue —Robert Browning⟩ **b :** the first or early part of the day : MORNING ⟨been on the go since ~ —G.W.Brace⟩ ⟨working from ~ to night, he had no time for frills —John Buchan⟩ **2** *chiefly dial Brit* **:** TOMORROW — used with *the* ⟨the ~'s the Sabbath —J.M.Barrie⟩ **3 :** EAST ⟨the bugle that blows in lands of ~ —A.E.Housman⟩

**²morn** \"\ *adj* **:** MORNING

**mor·nay** \(ˈ)mȯrˈnā\ *also* **mornay sauce** *n* -s *usu cap M* [perh. after Philippe de *Mornay* †1623 Fr. Huguenot leader] **:** a cheese-flavored cream sauce

**¹morne** \ˈmȯ(ə)rn\ *n* -s [ME *moorne,* fr. MF *morne* cap to cover the head of a tilting lance, fr. *morner* to blunt, fr. OF, of Gmc origin; akin to OHG *mornēn* to grieve, mourn — more at MOURN] **:** the head of a lance blunted for tilting

**²mor·né** \(ˈ)mȯrˈnā\ *adj* [F, fr. past part. of *morner* to blunt] **:** of or relating to a heraldic representation of a lion without teeth, tongue, or claws

**³morne** \ˈmȯ(ə)rn\ *adj* [F, fr. OF, fr. *morner* to blunt] **:** having a dismal quality or effect : GLOOMY ⟨the ~ cliffs, the dead cities, the desolate shores of a leaden sea —Boris von Anrep⟩

**¹morn·ing** \ˈmȯrniŋ, ˈmȯ(ə)n-, -nēŋ\ *n* -s [ME *morning, morwening,* fr. *morn, morwen* + *-ing* (as in ME *evening*)] **1 a :** the break of day : DAWN ⟨upon their path the ~ broke —P.B.Shelley⟩ ⟨the red ~ touched him with its light —R.W. Emerson⟩ ⟨tossed and turned all night until ~ finally came⟩ **b :** the early hours of light : the time from rising to noon ⟨uses the ~s for calling on his customers⟩ ⟨does his best work in the ~⟩ **c :** the time from midnight to noon ⟨there was a full moon, and about two o'clock in the ~ a great concourse assembled —John Buchan⟩ ⟨it was then eleven o'clock in the ~ —Nevil Shute⟩ **2 :** the beginning of something : a period of first development or of freshness and vigor ⟨a steamship five times the size of the biggest vessel afloat then, in the ~ of steamers —James Dugan⟩ ⟨the ~ of the world, when life seemed simpler if no less cruel —Herbert Agar⟩ ⟨the ~ of life⟩ **3** *chiefly Scot* **a :** an alcoholic drink taken before breakfast **b :** a light meal eaten before breakfast

**²morning** \"\ *adj* **:** of, belonging to, or intended primarily for use in the morning ⟨~ coffee⟩ ⟨~ freshness⟩ ⟨~ tabloids have a heavy sale among homeward bound theatergoers —Bruce Westley⟩ ⟨once more I was my ~ self, tough, lean, and invulnerable —Nancy Hale⟩

**morning after** *n, pl* **mornings after 1 :** HANGOVER 2a ⟨illusions, headaches, *mornings after* —Carl Sandburg⟩ **2 :** a time when the effects of overindulgence are felt

**morning campion** *n* **:** RED CAMPION

**morning coat** *n* **:** CUTAWAY ⟨in *morning coat,* striped trousers, and, very likely, with a carnation in his buttonhole —Frances Towers⟩

**morning dress** *n* **1 :** a woman's dress suitable for wear around the home; *esp* **:** an informal dress for housework **2 :** the conventional attire for men for highly formal daytime wear including a cutaway coat, striped trousers, and a silk hat all in shades of gray and black — compare EVENING DRESS

**morning gift** *n* **:** a gift made by a husband to his wife on the morning after the consummation of marriage

**morning glory** *n* **1 a :** a plant of the genus *Ipomoea* (esp. *I. pururea*) — see JAPANESE MORNING GLORY **b :** a plant of a related genus (as *Convolvulus*) — compare FIELD BINDWEED, HEDGE BINDWEED **2 :** HOODED MERGANSER **3 a :** someone or something that starts out impressively but fades quickly ⟨was a brilliant student as a freshman, but turned out to be only a *morning glory*⟩ **b** *slang* **:** a racehorse that performs well in morning workouts but runs poorly in races

morning glory 1a

**morning-glory family** *n* **:** CONVOLVULACEAE

**morning gown** *n* **:** an informal dress for wear at home; *esp* **:** an elaborate dressing gown ⟨caught by unexpected guests one day when still in her *morning gown* —Elizabeth Coatsworth⟩

**morning gun** *n* **:** the firing of a gun at the first note of reveille or of a preceding march at military installations

**morning hour** *n* **:** a period of the day devoted by the U.S. Senate and the House of Representatives to routine business (as the introduction of bills)

**morning line** *n* **:** a bookmaker's published list of entries and the probable odds on each for a race meet to be held later in the day

**morning loan** *n* **:** DAY LOAN

**morning prayer** *n, usu cap M&P* **:** a morning service of liturgical prayer in Anglican churches — called also *matins*

**morning report** *n* **:** a daily military report for permanent record made by each company, troop, battery, or higher headquarters and giving its daily history (as strength, movements, or changes in status of individuals)

**morning room** *n* **:** a sitting room for general family use esp. during the day — compare DRAWING ROOM

**morn·ings** \ˈmȯrniŋz, ˈmȯ(ə)n-, -nēŋz\ *adv* **:** in the morning repeatedly : on any morning ⟨goes to the office ~⟩

**morning sickness** *n* **:** nausea and vomiting on rising in the morning occurring esp. during the earlier months of pregnancy

**morning star** *n* **1 a :** a bright planet (as Venus) seen in the eastern sky before sunrise **b :** any of the five planets that may be seen with the naked eye if in the sky at sunrise ⟨Venus, Jupiter, Mars, Mercury, and Saturn may be *morning stars*⟩ **c :** a planet that sets after midnight **2** [trans. of G *morgenstern*] **:** a weapon consisting of a heavy ball set with spikes and either attached to a staff or suspended from one by a chain — called also *holy-water sprinkler* **3 :** an annual California herb (*Mentzelia aurea*) with showy yellow flowers

**morningtide** \ˈ=,=\ *n, archaic* **:** morning time **:** MORNING

**morning watch** *n* **:** the watch on a ship from 4 a.m. to 8 a.m.

**morns** *pl of* MORN

**mo·ro** \ˈmō(,)rō, ˈmȯ(,)-\ *n, pl* **moro** *or* **moros** *usu cap* [Sp, lit., Moor, fr. L *Maurus* — more at MOOR] **1 a :** any of several Muslim peoples of the southern Philippines chiefly of the Sulu archipelago and parts of Mindanao — see MAGINDANAO, MARANAO, SAMAL, TAW-SUG **b :** a member of any of these peoples **2 :** any of the Austronesian languages of the Moro peoples

**mor·oc** \ˈmä,räk\ *n* -s [prob. fr. Tigré *marāḥ* guide] **:** HONEY GUIDE

**mor·o·cain** \ˌmȯrəˌkān\ *n* -s [prob. modif. of F *marocain* Moroccan, fr. *Maroc* Morocco] **:** MOROCCO RED

**¹mo·roc·can** \məˈräkən\ *adj, usu cap* [*Morocco*, sultanate in northwest Africa + E *-an*] **1 :** of, relating to, or characteristic of Morocco **2 :** of, relating to, or characteristic of the people of Morocco

**²moroccan** \ˈ"\ *n* -s **1** *cap* **:** a native or inhabitant of Morocco **2** *often cap* **:** a dark red to reddish orange that is slightly bluer and less strong than autumn glory

**¹mo·roc·co** \-ä(,)kō\ *n* -s [fr. *Morocco*, sultanate in northwest Africa] **1** *or* **morocco leather a :** a fine very firm flexible leather prepared from goatskin tanned with sumac and having a distinctive pebbly grain brought out by graining or boarding **b :** an imitation made from sheepskin or lambskin **2** *often cap* **:** MOROCCO RED

**²morocco** \ˈ"\ *adj, usu cap* [fr. *Morocco*, sultanate in northwest Africa] **:** of or from Morocco **:** of the kind or style prevalent in Morocco **:** MOROCCAN

**morocco gum** *n, usu cap M* **:** gum arabic exported from Morocco and believed to be obtained from any of several acacias (as *Acacia gummifera*) other than those that are usual sources of gum arabic

**morocco–head** \=ˈ=(,)=,=\ *n, usu cap, dial* **:** AMERICAN MERGANSER

**morocco–jaw** \=ˈ=(,)=,=\ *n, usu cap, dial* **:** SURF SCOTER

**morocco millet** *n, usu cap 1st M* **:** JOHNSON GRASS

**morocco red** *n, often cap M* **:** a strong reddish brown that is redder, less strong, and slightly lighter than Sierra — called also *caldron, marocain, morocain, Morocco*

**moro crab** *n* [part trans. of Sp *cangrejo moro*, fr. *cangrejo* crab + *moro* Moorish, fr. *Moro* Moor, fr. L *Maurus* — more at MOOR] **:** STONE CRAB 1

**mo·ron** \ˈmō,rän, ˈmȯ,-\ *n* -s [irreg. fr. Gk *mōros* sluggish, dull, stupid; akin to Skt *mūra* dull, stupid] **1 :** a feebleminded person or mental defective with a potential mental age of between eight and twelve years who is capable of doing routine work under supervision **2 :** a stupid or boorish individual ⟨if it is well-adjusted ~*s* that we must have, then by all means let us encourage dating and going steady —G.A.Panichas⟩ ⟨these ~*s* . . . laugh loudly when a player on the screen is dying, they titter at love scenes —*Auckland (New Zealand) Star*⟩ **3 :** SEXUAL PERVERT ⟨turned and gaped at her with a ~'*s* excited eyes —J.T.Farrell⟩ **syn** see FOOL

**mo·ro·ne** \məˈrōnē\ *n, cap* [NL] **:** a genus of carnivorous fresh and salt water percoid fishes (family Serranidae) including several sport and food fishes — see MORONIDAE, WHITE PERCH, YELLOW BASS

**mo·ron·ic** \məˈränik, (ˈ)mō¦r-, (ˈ)mȯ¦r-, -nēk\ *adj* **1 :** consisting of or having the characteristics of morons ⟨have no difficulty making the ~ millions laugh at ancient jokes —John Dolman⟩ ⟨the sinking of the academic mind to the level of the ~ mob —*Christian Century*⟩ **2 :** like a moron **:** mentally retarded **:** DULL ⟨this ~ but devastating nitwit —*Variety*⟩ **3 :** characteristic of or suitable for morons **:** BRUTISH, STUPID ⟨all the ~ delight of a gangster trying out his first machine gun —Raymond Chandler⟩ ⟨intelligent enough not to fall for such a ~ form of pastime —*Springfield (Mass.) Union*⟩ ⟨an orgy of ~ vulgarity —*No. Amer. Rev.*⟩ — **mo·ron·i·cal·ly** \-nək(ə)lē, -nēk-, -li\ *adv*

**mo·ron·i·dae** \məˈränə,dē\ *n pl, cap* [NL, fr. *Morone*, type genus + *-idae*] *in some classifications* **:** an important family of carnivorous spiny-finned fishes of northeastern No. America, Russia, and Siberia that comprises numerous food and sport fishes and is now usu. included in the family Serranidae

**mo·ron·ism** \ˈmō,rä,nizəm, ˈmȯ,r-\ *n* -s **:** MORONITY

**mo·ron·i·ty** \məˈränəd-ē\ *n* -ES **1 :** a mild degree of feeblemindedness or mental deficiency **2 :** STUPIDITY

**mor·o·pus** \ˈmȯrəpəs, ˈmär-\ *n, cap* [NL, fr. Gk *mōros* sluggish, dull + NL *-pus*; fr. its suggested affinities to the sloth] **:** a genus of American Miocene clawed perissodactyls (family Chalicotheriidae) attaining the size of modern horses

**moror** *var of* MAROR

**moros** *pl of* MORO

**mo·rose** \məˈrōs, (ˈ)mō¦r-, (ˈ)mȯ¦r-\ *adj* [L *morosus*, fr. *mor-, mos* custom, habit + *-osus* -ose — more at MOOD] **1 :** having a sullen and gloomy disposition **:** not friendly or sociable ⟨always found her silent even to the pitch of appearing ~ —Compton Mackenzie⟩ ⟨when deprived of spirits, he became gloomy, ~, and irritable —C.B.Nordhoff & J.N.Hall⟩ **2 :** marked by or expressive of gloom ⟨a ~ little essay on the low state of the short story —James Kelly⟩ ⟨a long, ~ dressing gown grotesquely capped with a derby —Brooks Atkinson⟩ **syn** see SULLEN

**mo·rose·ly** *adv* **:** in a morose manner **:** SULLENLY ⟨ate stoically, ~, saying hardly a word —Harold Sinclair⟩

**mo·rose·ness** *n* -ES **:** the quality or state of being morose ⟨the ~ of age and infirmity never touched him, and he never quarreled with a friend or lost one —Matthew Arnold⟩

**mo·ros·i·ty** \məˈräsəd-ē\ *n* -ES [L *morositat-, morositas*, fr. *morosus* + *-itat-, -itas* -ity] **:** MOROSENESS

**mo·ro·soph** \ˈmȯrə,säf, ˈmȯr-\ *or* **mo·ros·o·phist** \məˈräsəfəst\ *n* -s [*morosoph* fr. obs. F *morosophe*, fr. Gk *mōrosophos*, fr. *mōros* dull, stupid + *sophos* wise; *morosophist* fr. obs. F *morosophe* + E *-ist*] **:** a learned fool

**mo·ro·to·co** \ˌmōrōˈtō(,)kō\ *n, usu cap* **:** a dialect of the Zamuco people

**mo·rox·ite** \məˈräk,sīt\ *n* -s [G *moroxit*, fr. Gk *moroxos* pipe clay, fuller's earth + G *-it* -ite] **:** a greenish blue or bluish variety of apatite

**morph** \ˈmȯ(ə)rf, ˈmȯ(ə)f\ *n* -s [back-formation fr. *morpheme*] **1 :** ²ALLOMORPH **2 :** a phoneme or sequence of phonemes that is presumably an allomorph but that is not considered as assigned to any particular morpheme ⟨the *slep-* \slep\ of *slept* is considered a ~ by a linguist analyzing English who has not yet encountered the *sleep* \slēp\ of *sleep well*⟩ — compare ²ALLOMORPH, MORPHEME 2

**morph-** *or* **morpho-** *comb form* [G *morpho-* form, fr. Gk *morph-, morpho-*, fr. *morphē* — more at FORM] **:** form **:** shape **:** structure **:** type ⟨*morphic*⟩ ⟨*morpho*differentiation⟩

**-morph** \ˌmȯrf, ˌmȯ(ə)f\ *n comb form* -s [ISV, fr. *-morphous*] **:** one having (such) a form ⟨*isomorph*⟩

**morph** *abbr* morphological; morphology

**-mor·pha** \ˈmȯrfə, ˈmȯ(ə)fə\ *n comb form, pl* **-morpha** [NL, fr. fem. sing. & neut. pl. of *-morphus* -morphous, fr. Gk *-morphos* — more at -MORPHOUS] **:** one or ones having (such) a form ⟨Entero*morpha*⟩ — esp. in names of zoological taxa larger than a genus ⟨Cyno*morpha*⟩ ⟨Hystrico*morpha*⟩

**mor·pha·dite** *also* **mor·phi·dite** *or* **mor·pho·dite** \ˈmȯ(r)fə,dīt\ *n* -s [by shortening & alter.] **:** HERMAPHRODITE

**-mor·phae** \ˈmȯr,fē, ˈmȯ(ə),-\ *n pl comb form* [NL, fr. fem. pl. of *-morphus* -morphous] **:** ones having (such) a form — in names of zoological taxa, esp. of birds, larger than a genus ⟨Psittaco*morphae*⟩

**mor·phal·lax·is** \ˌmȯ(r)fəˈlaksəs\ *n, pl* **morphallax·es** \-k,sēz\ [NL, fr. *morph-* + Gk *allaxis* exchange, fr. *allassein, allattein* to change, exchange, fr. *allos* other — more at ELSE] **:** regeneration on a reduced scale of a part or organism from a fragment by reorganization without cell proliferation — compare EPIMORPHOSIS

**mor·phea** *also* **mor·phoea** \mȯ(r)ˈfēə\ *n, pl* **morphe·ae** *or* **morphoe·ae** \-ē,ē\ [ML *morphea*] **:** localized scleroderma

**mor·phe·an** \ˈmȯ(r)fēən\ *adj, usu cap* [*Morpheus* + E *-an*] *archaic* **:** of, relating to, or producing sleep ⟨some drowsy *Morphean* amulet —John Keats⟩

**mor·pheme** \ˈmȯr,fēm, ˈmȯ(ə),-\ *n* -s [F *morphème*, fr. *morph-* + *-ème* -eme] **1 :** a feature of language showing the relations between nouns, verbs, adjectives, and concrete adverbs (as an affix, reduplication, preposition, conjunction, auxiliary verb, copulative verb, intonation, accentuation, ablaut variation, or order of words) — now little used by linguists; distinguished from *semanteme* **2 :** a meaningful linguistic unit whether a free form (as *pin, child, load, pray*) or a bound form (as the *-s* of *pins*, the *-hood* of *childhood*, the *un-* and *-er* of *unloader*, and the *-ed* of *prayed*) that contains no smaller meaningful parts — compare ²ALLOMORPH, MORPH — **mor·phe·mic** \(ˈ)mȯ(r)¦fēmik, -mēk\ *adj* — **mor·phe·mi·cal·ly** \-mək(ə)lē, -mēk-, -li\ *adv*

**morpheme alternant** *or* **morphemic alternant** *n* **:** ²ALLOMORPH

**mor·phe·mics** \mȯ(r)ˈfēmiks, -mēks\ *n pl but sing in constr* **1 :** a branch of linguistic analysis that consists of the study of morphemes (sense 2) **2** *of a language* **:** the structure in terms of morphemes (sense 2) **:** a statement of the structure in terms of morphemes

**mor·pheus** \ˈmȯrfēəs, -,fyüs\ *n, usu cap* [after *Morpheus*, deity represented by Ovid as causing dreams in which a human being appears] **:** something that induces or prolongs sleep ⟨awoke from a deep sleep, jerked from the grip of *Morpheus* —H.A.Smith⟩ ⟨overcome by *Morpheus*⟩

**mor·phew** \ˈmȯr,fyü\ *n* -s [ME *morphue, morphe*, fr. ML *morphea*] *archaic* **:** MORPHEA

**mor·phewed** \-üd\ *adj, archaic* **:** covered with or as if with a morphea ⟨the windows blank and sightless, the walls ~ with scaling —John Masefield⟩

**-mor·phi** \ˈmȯr,fī, ˈmȯ(ə),-\ *n pl comb form* [NL, fr. pl. of *-morphus* -morphous] **:** ones having (such) a form — in names of fish taxa larger than a genus ⟨Halecomorphi⟩

**mor·phia** \ˈmȯ(r)fēə\ *n* -s [NL, fr. *Morpheus*] **:** MORPHINE

**mor·phic** \ˈmȯrfik\ *adj* [*morph-* + *-ic*] **:** of or relating to form **:** MORPHOLOGICAL — **mor·phi·cal·ly** \-fək(ə)lē\ *adv*

**-mor·phic** \ˈmȯrfik, ¦mȯ(ə)f-, -fēk\ *adj comb form* [prob. fr. F *-morphique*, fr. Gk *morphē* form + F *-ique* -ic — more at FORM] **:** having (such) a form ⟨dolicho*morphic*⟩

**morphic effect** *n* **:** a type of effect on the physical properties of a crystal due to the change of symmetry that occurs when a crystal is strained

**-morphies** *pl of* -MORPHY

**mor·phine** \ˈmȯr,fēn, ˈmȯ(ə),- *sometimes* =ˈ=\ *n* -s [F, fr. *Morpheus* + F *-ine*] **:** a bitter crystalline narcotic habit-forming base $C_{17}H_{19}NO_3$ that is the principal alkaloid of opium occurring in amounts up to 15 percent, that is chemically is a complex derivative of phenanthrene, that produces powerful complex physiological and psychic effects similar in some respects to those of opium, and that is used in the form of a soluble salt (as the hydrochloride or sulfate) chiefly as an analgesic and sedative — **mor·phin·ic** \(ˈ)mȯ(r)¦finik\ *adj*

**morphine meconate** *n* **:** the morphine salt of meconic acid that occurs naturally in opium

**mor·phin·ism** \ˈmȯ(r)fə,nizəm\ *n* -s [ISV *morphine* + *-ism*] **:** a condition produced by the habitual use of morphine **:** the morphine habit

**mor·phin·ist** \-ˌnəst\ *n* -s [ISV *morphine* + *-ist*] **:** one addicted to the use of morphine

**mor·phin·ize** \-fə,nīz\ *vt* -ED/-ING/-S **:** to treat with or subject to the influence of morphine

**mor·phi·no·ma·nia** \ˌmȯ(r)fənōˈmānēə\ *also* **mor·phi·o·ma·nia** \-fēō'-\ *n* [*morphinomania* fr. NL, fr. *morphino-* (fr. ISV *morphine*) + LL *mania*; *morphiomania* fr. NL, fr. *morphio-* (fr. *morphia*) + LL *mania*] **:** an habitual and uncontrollable craving for morphine

**mor·phi·no·ma·ni·ac** \-fənōˈmānē,ak\ *also* **mor·phi·o·ma·ni·ac** \-fēō'-\ *n* [fr. NL *morphinomania, morphiomania*, after E *mania: maniac*] **:** one who is afflicted with morphinomania

**-mor·phism** \ˌmȯ(r),fizəm\ *n comb form* -s [LL *-morphus* -morphous (fr. Gk *-morphos*) + E *-ism* — more at -MORPHOUS] **1 :** quality or state of having (such) a form ⟨hetero*morphism*⟩ ⟨iso*morphism*⟩ **2 :** conceptualization in (such) a form ⟨physico*morphism*⟩

**mor·pho** \ˈmȯr(,)fō\ *n* [NL, fr. Gk *Morphō* (epithet of Aphrodite in Sparta)] **1** *cap* **:** a genus (the type of the family Morphoidae) of large showy tropical American butterflies noted for the very brilliant bright blue metallic luster of the upper surface of the wings of some forms **2** -s **:** any butterfly of the genus *Morpho*

**morpho-** — see MORPH-

**mor·pho·differentiation** \¦mȯ(r)(,)fō+\ *n* [*morph-* + *differentiation*] **:** structure or organ differentiation (as in tooth development)

**morphodite** *var of* MORPHADITE

**morphoea** *var of* MORPHEA

**mor·pho·gen·e·sis** \ˌmȯ(r)fəˈjenəsəs\ *n* [NL, fr. *morph-* + L *genesis*] **1 :** BIOGENESIS 2 **2 :** the formation and differentiation of tissues and organs **:** ORGANOGENESIS

**mor·pho·ge·net·ic** \¦mȯ(r)fōjə¦ned·ik\ *adj* [*morph-* + *-genetic*] **:** concerned with or tending to the development of normal organic form ⟨~ movements of early embryonic cells⟩

**mor·pho·gen·ic** \¦mȯ(r)fə¦jenik\ *adj* [*morph-* + *-genic*] **:** MORPHOGENETIC

**mor·phog·e·ny** \mȯ(r)ˈfäjənē\ *n* -ES [ISV *morph-* + *-geny*] **:** MORPHOGENESIS

**mor·pho·graph·ic** \¦mȯ(r)fə¦grafik\ *adj* [NL *morphographicus*, fr. *morphographia* morphography + L *-icus* -ic] **:** of or relating to morphography

**mor·phog·ra·phy** \mȯ(r)ˈfägrəfē\ *n* -ES [NL *morphographia*, fr. *morph-* + *-graphia* -graphy] **1 :** descriptive morphology **2 :** the phenomena or aspect (as of a region) described by morphography

**mor·pho·lide** \ˈmȯ(r)fə,līd\ *n* -s [*morpholine* + *-ide*] **:** an amide derived from morpholine as the amine

**mor·pho·line** \-,lēn, -,lən\ *n* -s [ISV *morphol-* (ISV *morphine* + *-ol*) + *-ine*; fr. a former belief that its molecular structure was similar to that of morphine] **:** an oily cyclic secondary amine $O(CH_2CH_2)_2NH$ made from ethylene oxide and ammonia and used chiefly as a solvent and emulsifying agent; tetrahydro-1,4-oxazine

**mor·pho·log·i·cal** \¦mȯ(r)fə¦läjəkəl, -jēk-\ *also* **mor·pho·log·ic** \-jik, -jēk\ *adj* [*morphological* fr. *morphology* + *-ical*; *morphologic* fr. F *morphologique*, fr. *morphologie* morphology + *-ique* -ic] **1 :** of, relating to, or concerned with form or structure ⟨pre-Darwinian classifications of living things were ~ rather than genetic, the attempt being made to classify according to similarities of fundamental characteristics —W.P. Kent⟩ **2 :** of or relating to points for taking measurements that are present on the skeleton as well as on the living person or the cadaver — compare PHYSIOGNOMIC — **mor·pho·log·i·cal·ly** \-jək(ə)lē, -jēk-, -li\ *adv*

**morphological construction** *or* **morphologic construction** *n* **:** a sequence of morphemes forming a complex or compound word (as *unlike, baseball*) — compare SYNTACTIC CONSTRUCTION

**morphological index** *n* **:** the ratio of the volume of the human trunk to the sum of the lengths of one arm and one leg multiplied by 100

**mor·phol·o·gist** \mȯ(r)ˈfäləjəst\ *n* -s [*morphology* + *-ist*] **:** one who concerns himself with morphology or carries on morphological studies

**mor·phol·o·gy** \-jē, -ji\ *n* -ES [G *morphologie*, fr. Gk *morph-* (fr. *morphē* form) + G *-logie* -logy — more at FORM] **1 a :** a branch of biology that deals with the form and structure of animals and plants **:** a study of the forms, relations, metamorphoses, and phylogenetic development of organs apart from their functions — see ANATOMY; compare PHYSIOLOGY **b :** the features comprised in the form and structure of an organism or any of its parts **2 a :** a study and description of word-formation in a language including inflection, derivation, and compounding — distinguished from *syntax* **b :** the system of word-forming elements and processes in a language **3 a :** a study of the structure or form of something ⟨no one had attempted to sketch out a ~ of the political party as such —*Times Lit. Supp.*⟩ ⟨social ~⟩ **b :** the structure or form of something **:** MAKEUP ⟨the evidence speaks in favor of a number of common genetic factors in the ~ of gamblers —R.M. Lindner⟩ ⟨in general ~ the later Dutch settlements bore a strong resemblance to those of New England —G.T.Trewartha⟩ ⟨the unique ~ of the city —H.J.Nelson⟩ **4 :** the external structure of rocks in relation to the development of erosional forms or topographic features **:** GEOMORPHOLOGY **5 a :** the study of the development of the forms of crystals **b :** the assemblage of forms on a crystal

**mor·pho·ma·ni·ac** \ˌmȯ(r)fəˈmānē,ak\ *n* [by alter.] **:** MORPHINOMANIAC

**mor·phome** \ˈmȯr,fōm\ *n* -s [alter. (influenced by Gk *morphōma* form, fr. *morphē*) of *morpheme*] **:** MORPHEME 2

**mor·pho·met·ric** \¦mȯ(r)fə¦me·trik\ *also* **mor·pho·met·ri·cal** \-rəkəl\ *adj* **:** of, relating to, or involving morphometry ⟨~ studies of the Pacific salmons⟩ — **mor·pho·met·ri·cal·ly** \-rək(ə)lē\ *adv*

**mor·phom·e·try** \mȯ(r)ˈfämə·trē\ *n* -ES [*morph-* + *-metry*] **:** measurement of external form; *esp* **:** a branch of limnology that deals with morphologic measurements of a lake and its basin

**mor·pho·phoneme** \¦mȯ(r)fō+\ *n* [*morpho-* (fr. *morpheme*) + *phoneme*] **:** a class of phonemes that belong to the same morpheme (as the \-s, -z, -əz\ plural suffix of *kits, kids, kisses*; \f, v\ in *knife, knives*); *also* **:** an arbitrarily selected member of such a class as its representative in grammatical description (as the plural suffix -s, or the F in \nīf\) ⟨group together into one ~ the phonemes which replace each other in corresponding parts of the various members of a morpheme —Z.S. Harris⟩

**mor·pho·phonemic** \¦mȯ(r)(,)fō+\ *adj* [*morpho-* (fr. *morpheme*) + *phonemic*] **:** of or relating to a class of phonemes that belong to the same morpheme or to the relations among them and the conditions that determine their occurrences ⟨a ~ alteration of long vowel in open syllable and short vowel in closed syllable —J.H.Greenberg⟩ — **mor·pho·phonemically** \"+\ *adv*

**mor·pho·phonemics** \"+\ *n pl but sing in constr* [*morpho-* (fr. *morpheme*) + *phonemics*] **1 :** a study of the phonemic differences between allomorphs of the same morpheme (as the ē, e difference in slēp, slep ⟨~ thus concerns the phonemic shape of morphemes —J.B.Carroll⟩ **2 :** the distribution in one morpheme of alternants (as the *ed* of *played*, the *o* in *wrote* as distinguished from *write*, the *t* in *built* as distinguished from *build*) and of zero features (as the zero suffix of *let*, past) regardless of whether the assigned members have any phonemes in common **3 :** the structure of a language in terms of morphophonemics or a statement of this ⟨the total class of these differences so described, classified, and compared is called the ~ of the language in question —R.S.Wells⟩

**mor·pho·plasm** \ˈmȯ(r)fə,plazəm\ *n* -s [ISV *morph-* + *-plasm*] **1 :** KINOPLASM **2 :** TROPHOPLASM — **mor·pho·plasmic** \¦=¦plazmik\ *adj*

**mor·pho·sis** \mȯ(r)ˈfōsəs\ *n, pl* **morpho·ses** \-ō,sēz\ [NL, fr. Gk *morphōsis* action or process of forming, fr. *morphoun* to form, fr. *morphē* form] **1 :** the mode of development of an organism or one of its parts **2 :** a nonadaptive structural modification

**-mor·pho·sis** \ˈmȯ(r)fəsəs *sometimes* ˌmȯ(r)ˈfōsəs\ *n comb form, pl* **-morpho·ses** \ˈ=fə,sēz, ˌ=ˈfō,sēz\ [L, fr. Gk *-morphōsis*, fr. *morphōsis*] **1 :** development or change of form of a (specified) thing ⟨cyto*morphosis*⟩ **2 :** development or change of form in a (specified) manner ⟨hetero*morphosis*⟩

**mor·pho·species** \¦mȯ(r)(,)fō+\ *n* [*morph-* + *species*] **:** a taxonomic species based wholly on morphological differences from related species

**mor·pho·tic** \mȯ(r)ˈfäd·ik\ *adj* [fr. *morphosis*, after such pairs as E *narcosis: narcotic*] **:** of or relating to morphosis

**mor·phot·o·my** \mȯ(r)ˈfäd·əmē\ *n* -ES [ISV *morph-* + *-tomy*] **:** ANATOMY 3

**-mor·phous** \ˌmȯrfəs, ¦mȯ(ə)f-\ *adj comb form* [Gk *-morphos*, fr. *morphē* form — more at FORM] **:** having (such) a form ⟨iso*morphous*⟩

**mor·phrey** \ˈmȯrfri\ *var of* MORFREY

**morphs** *pl of* MORPH

**-morphs** *pl of* -MORPH

**-mor·phy** \ˌmȯrfē, ˌmȯ(ə)fē, -fi\ *n comb form* -ES [ISV *-morph* + *-y*] **:** quality or state of having (such) a form ⟨hetero*morphy*⟩ ⟨iso*morphy*⟩

**mor·phy caliper** \ˈmȯrfē-\ *n* [by shortening & alter.] **:** HERMAPHRODITE CALIPER

**mor·pi·on** \ˈmȯ(r)pēən\ *n* -s [MF, fr. *mordre* to bite (fr. L *mordēre*) + *pion*, peon foot soldier, fr. ML *pedon-, pedo* — more at SMART, PAWN] **:** CRAB LOUSE

**morra** *var of* MORA

**mor·ral** \məˈral, -ˈräl\ *n, pl* **morrals** \-lz\ *or* **morra·les** \-ˈä,lās\ [Sp, fr. *morro* protruding lips] *West* **:** a fiber bag usu. used as a food bag for horses **:** NOSE BAG ⟨the provisions were in a ~ hung on a tree —J.F.Dobie⟩

**mor·rhua** \ˈmȯrəwə, ˈmär-\ [NL, fr. ML *morua* cod] *syn of* GADUS

**mor·rhu·ate** \-rə,wāt\ *n* -s [*morrhuic* (in *morrhuic acid*) + *-ate*] **:** a salt or ester of morrhuic acid

**mor·rhu·ic acid** \-rəwik-\ *n* [*morrhuic* fr. NL *Morrhua* + E *-ic*] **:** a mixture of fatty acids obtained from cod-liver oil

**mor·rice** *or* **mor·ris** \ˈmȯrəs, ˈmär-\ *vi* **morriced** *or* **morrised; morriced** *or* **morrised; morricing** *or* **morrising; morrices** *or* **morrises** [ˈmȯris] *archaic* **:** to move off quickly **:** DECAMP

**¹mor·ris** *or* **mor·rice** \ˈmȯrəs, ˈmär-\ *n* -ES *also* **morris dance** *n, pl* **morrises** *or* **morrices** [ME *moreys daunce*, fr. *moreys, morys* Moorish + *daunce* dance — more at MOORISH] **1 :** a vigorous dance done by men wearing costumes and bells and carrying sticks or handkerchiefs and performed as a traditional part of English pageants, processions, and May Day games, often by a group of six men plus solo dancers who represent traditional characters **2 :** a lively and rhythmic movement suggestive of a morris

**²morris** \ˈ"\ *n* -ES [alter. of *merels*] **:** an ancient game for two in which each player has from 3 to 12 counters placed at the angles of a figure consisting of three concentric squares and tries to be first to secure a row of 3 on any line — called also *merels, mill, morelles*

**morris chair** *n* [after William *Morris* †1896 Eng. poet and artist] **:** an easy chair of simple design with adjustable back and removable cushions in the seat and back

morris chair

**mor·ris·ite** \ˈmȯrə,sīt, ˈmär-\ *n* -s *usu cap* [Joseph *Morris* *fl*1860 Am. leader of a dissenting group of Mormons + E *-ite*] **:** one of a schismatic group that broke off from the Mormon Church in 1861

**morris–pike** \ˈ=,=\ *n* [ME *mares-pike*, fr. *mares, morys* Moorish + *pike*] **:** a large pike used by foot soldiers esp. in the 15th and early 16th centuries

**morris style** *n, usu cap M* [after William *Morris* †1896] **:** a simple style of furniture developed in the late 19th century as a protest against overdecoration

**¹mor·row** \ˈmä(,)rō, -rə *also* ˈmȯ(,)-; *often* -,rəw+V\ *n* -s [ME *morwe, morwen* — more at MORN] **1** *archaic* **:** MORNING ⟨I shall say good night till it be ~ —Shak.⟩ **2 :** the next following day **:** the day after any day specified or understood ⟨had expected to go back on the following morning, but instead it looked as if they were going to spend the ~ and a few other morrows in the trenches —Patrick McGill⟩ ⟨told us that the task force would sortie on the ~ —F.J.Bell⟩ **3 :** the time immediately after a specified event ⟨on the ~ of their triumph, jealousy stepped in —*Encyc. Americana*⟩ ⟨has made haste on the ~ of his subject's death to bring out this supplement —*New Yorker*⟩

**²morrow** \ˈ"\ *adj, archaic* **:** of or relating to the next day ⟨a sadder and a wiser man he rose the ~ morn —S.T.Coleridge⟩

**mor·row·an** \ˈmärəwən *also* ˈmȯr-\ *adj, usu cap* [*Morrow* county, Ohio + E *-an*] **:** of, relating to, or constituting a subdivision of the Pennsylvanian — see GEOLOGIC TIME table

**mor·row·ing** \ˈmärəwiŋ\ *n* -s [prob. alter. of *marrowing*, gerund of ³*marrow* in its dial. sense (Northern Ireland) of "to exchange aid with a neighbor"] *Irish* **:** an exchange of aid among farmers

**morrowmass** *n* [ME *morwemasse*, fr. *morwe* morning + *masse* mass] *obs* **:** a mass said early in the morning **:** daily mass
**mors** *pl of* MOR
**mor·sal** \ˈmȯrsəl\ *adj* [L *mors*us bite + E *-al*] **:** OCCLUSAL
[1]**morse** \ˈmȯ(ə)rs, ˈmȯ(ə)s\ *n* -S [ME *mors*, fr. MF, morse, bite, fr. OF, bite] **:** a clasp or brooch used to fasten a cope
[2]**morse** \"\ *n* -S [Lapp *morša*] **:** WALRUS
[3]**morse** \"\ *n* -S *often cap* [after Samuel F. B. *Morse* †1872] **:** MORSE CODE
[4]**morse** \"\ *vb* -ED/-ING/-S *vi* **:** to send Morse code **:** communicate by means of Morse code ~ *vt* **:** to signal to by means of Morse code **:** TELEGRAPH
**morse code** *n*, *usu cap M* [after Samuel F. B. *Morse* †1872 Am. artist and inventor] **:** either of two codes in which letters of the alphabet, numbers, and other symbols are represented by

MORSE CODE

AMERICAN MORSE CODE[1]

| | | | | | | | |
|---|---|---|---|---|---|---|---|
| A | •– | K | –•– | U | ••– | 5 | ––– |
| B | –••• | L | ▬ | V | •••– | 6 | •••••• |
| C | •• • | M | –– | W | •–– | 7 | ––•• |
| D | –•• | N | –• | X | •–•• | 8 | –•••• |
| E | • | O | • • | Y | •• •• | 9 | –••– |
| F | •–• | P | ••••• | Z | ••• • | 0 | ▬ |
| G | ––• | Q | ••–• | 1 | •––• | , (comma) | •–•– |
| H | •••• | R | • •• | 2 | ••–•• | . | ••––•• |
| I | •• | S | ••• | 3 | •••–• | & | • ••• |
| J | –•–• | T | – | 4 | ••••– | | |

INTERNATIONAL CODE[2]

| | | | | | | | |
|---|---|---|---|---|---|---|---|
| A | •– | N | –• | Á | •––•– | 8 | –––•• |
| B | –••• | O | ––– | Ä | •–•– | 9 | ––––• |
| C | –•–• | P | •––• | É | ••–•• | 0 | ––––– |
| D | –•• | Q | ––•– | Ñ | ––•–– | , (comma) | ––••–– |
| E | • | R | •–• | Ö | –––• | . | •–•–•– |
| F | ••–• | S | ••• | Ü | ••–– | ? | ••––•• |
| G | ––• | T | – | 1 | •–––– | ; | –•–•–• |
| H | •••• | U | ••– | 2 | ••––– | : | –––••• |
| I | •• | V | •••– | 3 | •••–– | ' (apostrophe) | •––––• |
| J | •––– | W | •–– | 4 | ••••– | - (hyphen) | –••••– |
| K | –•– | X | –••– | 5 | ••••• | / | –••–• |
| L | •–•• | Y | –•–– | 6 | –•••• | parenthesis | –•––•– |
| M | –– | Z | ––•• | 7 | ––••• | underline | ••––•– |

[1]Formerly used on landlines in the U.S. and Canada; now largely out of use.
[2]Often called the continental code; a modification of this code, with dots only, is used on ocean cables.

dots and dashes or long and short sounds and used for transmitting messages by audible or visual signals (as by telegraphy, wigwag, or light flashes)
[1]**mor·sel** \ˈmȯrsəl, ˈmȯ(ə)s-\ *n* -S [ME, fr. OF, fr. *mors* bite (fr. L *morsus*, fr. *morsus*, past part. of *mordēre* to bite) + *-el* — more at SMART] **1 a :** a small piece or quantity of food **:** BITE ⟨the multitude was kept quiet by the ~*s* of meat which were flung to it —J.A.Froude⟩ ⟨deftly ladled a spoonful of this and a ~ of that into the . . . skillet —Elinor Wylie⟩ ⟨a bitter ~ to swallow⟩ **b :** a small meal **:** SNACK ⟨came home, ate his ~ quickly, and left⟩ **2 :** a small quantity of something **:** a little piece or portion **:** FRAGMENT ⟨that ~ of information lay dormant for over a hundred years —C.C.Furnas⟩ ⟨his last remaining ~ of self-respect⟩ ⟨a tiny ~ of land lost in the ocean⟩ **3 a :** a tasty dish **:** TIDBIT ⟨such exotic ~*s* as Japanese frog legs, Alaskan king crabs, Indian pompano —*Time*⟩ ⟨sitting apart munching his own delectable ~*s* —C.S.Kilby⟩ **b :** something delectable and pleasing ⟨the girl . . . is young and very pretty . . . a ~ worth a little lordly condescension —Eric Blom⟩ ⟨his shorter piano pieces include some choice ~*s*⟩ **4 :** a small or negligible person ⟨this ancient ~ —Shak.⟩
[2]**morsel** \"\ *vt* **morseled** *or* **morselled**; **morseled** *or* **morselled**; **morseling** *or* **morselling**; **morsels :** to divide into or apportion in small pieces
**morse lamp** *n*, *usu cap M* **:** a lamp used for signaling by flashes corresponding to the dashes and dots of the Morse code
**mor·sing** \ˈmȯrsiŋ\ *n* -S [fr. gerund of obs. Sc *mors* to grease, prime (a firearm), modif. of MF *amorcer*, *amorsser* to prime (a firearm), bait, fr. *amorce*, *amorse* bait, fr. OF, fr. *amorse*, fem. of *amors*, past part. of *amordre* to bite, fr. L *admordēre*, fr. *ad-* + *mordēre* to bite] *archaic Scot* **:** PRIMING
**mor·sure** \ˈmȯr͵shu̇r\ *n* -S [ME, fr. MF, fr. LL *morsura*, fr. L *morsus*, past part. of *mordēre* to bite] *archaic* **:** BITE
[1]**mort** \ˈmȯ(ə)rt, ˈmȯ(ə)t, *usu* -d·+V\ *n* -S [prob. alter. (influenced by MF *mort* death, fr. L *mort-*, *mors*) of ME *mot* note of a horn, fr. MF, note of a horn, word, saying — more at MOT] **1 :** a note sounded on a hunting horn when a deer is killed ⟨the hunters, with their horns and voices, whooping and blowing a ~ —Sir Walter Scott⟩ **2 :** the act of putting to death **:** KILLING ⟨~ of the English stag —Glenway Wescott⟩
[2]**mort** \"\ *n* -S [origin unknown] **1** *archaic* **:** GIRL, WOMAN ⟨male gypsies all, not a ~ among them —Ben Jonson⟩ **2** *archaic* **:** MISTRESS, SWEETHEART
[3]**mort** \ˈmȯrt\ *n* -S [prob. alter. of obs. E *morkin* animal that has died a natural death, fr. ME *mortkyn*, prob. modif. (influenced by ME *-kyn*, *-kin* -kin) of MF *morticine* carrion, fr. LL *morticina*, fr. L, fem. of *morticinus* dead of natural causes, fr. *mort-*, *mors* death] *chiefly Scot* **:** the skin or fleece of a sheep that has died a natural death
[4]**mort** \"\ *n* -S [origin unknown] *dial Eng* **:** the fat of a hog from which lard is made **:** LARD
[5]**mort** \ˈmȯ(ə)rt, ˈmȯ(ə)t, *usu* -d·+V\ *n* -S [F or L; F, fr. *mort*, adj., dead, fr. L *mortuus*, past part. of *mori* to die] **:** a dead body **:** CORPSE ⟨unburied ~ —Henry James †1916⟩
[6]**mort** \"\ *n* -S [prob. back-formation fr. [1]*mortal*] **:** a great quantity or number **:** a great deal **:** ABUNDANCE ⟨had a ~ of things to be thankful for —Ellen Glasgow⟩ ⟨after the ~ of trouble I took —James Still⟩
**mor·ta·cious** \mȯrˈtāshəs\ *adv* [prob. fr. [6]*mort* + *-acious* (as in *audacious*)] *dial Eng* **:** EXTREMELY, TERRIBLY
**mor·ta·del·la** \͵mȯ(r)d·əˈdelə\ *n* -S [It, irreg. fr. L *murtatum* sausage seasoned with myrtle berries, fr. *murtus* myrtle + *-atum* -ate — more at MYRTLE] **:** a sausage made of chopped beef, pork, and pork fat, seasoned with pepper and garlic, stuffed into large casings, cooked, and smoked
[1]**mor·tal** \ˈmȯr|d·ᵊl, ˈmȯ(ə)|, |tᵊl\ *adj* [ME, mortal, deadly, subject to death, fr. MF *mortal*, *mortel*, fr. L *mortalis* subject to death, mortal, fr. *mort-*, *mors* death + *-alis* -al; akin to L *mori* to die — more at MURDER] **1 :** destructive to life **:** causing or capable of causing death **:** FATAL ⟨a ~ disease⟩ ⟨a ~ blow⟩ ⟨a ~ wound⟩ ⟨~ danger⟩ ⟨a new fact that was ~ to his theory⟩ **2 :** subject to death **:** destined to die ⟨all men are ~⟩ ⟨attended all that was ~ of their benefactor to the funeral pyre —J.G. Frazer⟩ ⟨these pictures have a very ~ look, but the poems refuse to fade —*N. Y. Herald Tribune Bk. Rev.*⟩ **3 a :** aiming at extermination **:** fought to the death ⟨living in one of those periods of history when wars are frequent and ~ —John Strachey⟩ ⟨won a ~ contest against a totalitarian system which denied all the values of freedom —Alan Barth⟩ **b :** having or marked by an unrelenting hostility **:** IMPLACABLE ⟨a ~ enemy⟩ ⟨a ~ aversion⟩ ⟨a ~ hatred⟩ **4 a :** existing in the greatest degree **:** marked by great intensity or severity **:** EXTREME, OVERPOWERING ⟨was no longer in ~ dread of her job collapsing under her —J.W.Vandercook⟩ ⟨the underworld that was in ~ terror of him —Richard Watts⟩ **b :** very great **:** AWFUL ⟨it's a ~ shame —Ellen Glasgow⟩ ⟨made a ~ mess of things⟩ **5 :** of or relating to man or mankind **:** HUMAN ⟨attempting to thwart me with ~ morals —Sidney Howard⟩ ⟨a nobody with an all too ~ longing to be a somebody —*Time*⟩ ⟨the most marvelous work of ~ genius —W.L.Sullivan⟩ **6 :** not able to be forgiven or condoned **:** deserving or entailing death ⟨a weakening in our purpose, and therefore in our unity . . . is the ~ crime —Sir Winston Churchill⟩ — see MORTAL SIN **7 :** of, relating to, or connected with death ⟨the ~ moment when the bombers, committed to their target, are locked defenseless in their courses —*Time*⟩ ⟨fell with a scream of ~ agony —F.V.W.Mason⟩ **8 :** humanly conceivable or possible **:** EARTHLY ⟨every ~ thing the heart could wish for —A.E. Coppard⟩ ⟨done all you asked — every ~ thing —Michael McLaverty⟩ **9** *archaic* **:** marked by many deaths ⟨a very sickly and ~ autumn —John Evelyn⟩ **10 :** long and wearisome **:** TEDIOUS ⟨here they lay for four ~ hours, their faces close to the muddy water —E.T.Brown⟩ ⟨three ~ hours — a hundred and eighty minutes — ticked off with jerky precision —Ida Treat⟩ **11** *chiefly Scot* **:** DEAD-DRUNK **syn** see DEADLY
[2]**mortal** \"\ *adv* [ME, fr. *mortal*, adj.] *chiefly dial* **:** MORTALLY
[3]**mortal** \"\ *n* -S [[1]*mortal*] **1** *obs* **:** something that is mortal **:** a mortal substance ⟨this corruptible must put on incorruption, and this ~ must put on immortality —1 Cor 15:53 (AV)⟩ **2 :** one who is mortal **:** a human being ⟨what fools these ~*s* be —Shak.⟩ ⟨parallels are risky matters between ~*s* —Claudia Cassidy⟩ **3 :** INDIVIDUAL, PERSON ⟨just the same careless ~ as to small properties that he used to be —Rachel Henning⟩
**mor·tal·ism** \-ᵊl͵izəm\ *n* -S *usu cap* **:** the doctrine that the soul is mortal
**mor·tal·ist** \-ᵊləst\ *n* -S *usu cap* **:** one who holds the soul to be mortal; *specif* **:** a member of a 17th century English sect believing that the soul and body perished together at death and would be resurrected together
**mor·tal·i·ty** \mȯ(r)ˈtaləd·ē, -ətē, -i\ *n* -ES [ME *mortalitee*, fr. MF *mortalité*, fr. L *mortalitat-*, *mortalitas*, fr. *mortalis* mortal + *-tat-*, *-tas* -ty] **1 :** the quality or state of being mortal ⟨salvation is the rescue of men from the ~ which sin has brought upon them —K.S.Latourette⟩ **2 :** the death of large numbers **:** a heavy loss of life (as by war or disease) ⟨the Black Death of 1348 caused a terrible ~ throughout Europe⟩ ⟨those rabbits, frogs, hedgehogs and caterpillars which suffer such ~ on our country roads —*Punch*⟩ **3** *archaic* **:** DEATH ⟨here on my knee I beg ~ —Shak.⟩ **4 :** the human race **:** MANKIND ⟨take these tears, ~'*s* relief —Alexander Pope⟩ **5 a :** the whole sum or number of deaths in a given time or a given community ⟨many died and the ~ among the children mounted daily —*Amer. Guide Series: Minn.*⟩ **b :** the proportion of deaths to population or to a specific number of the population **:** DEATH RATE ⟨for years has had the lowest general ~ and infant death rates —V.G.Heiser⟩ — opposed to *fertility* **c :** the number lost or the rate of loss or failure in a field of human endeavor (as business or education) ⟨the ~ among college students⟩ ⟨the ~ rate of small businesses⟩
**mortality table** *n* **:** an actuarial table based upon statistical records of mortality over a number of years (as a decade) giving the rate of death per 1000 in each age group — called also *life table;* see COMBINED EXPERIENCE TABLE, COMMISSIONERS STANDARD ORDINARY TABLE
**mor·tal·ize** \ˈmȯ(r)d·ᵊl͵īz\ *vt* -ED/-ING/-S **:** to make mortal **:** treat as mortal ⟨contemporary art ~*s* the immortals, stripping them of everything divine and noble —P.A.Sorokin⟩
**mor·tal·ly** \ˈmȯ(r)d·ᵊlē, -(r)tᵊl-, -ᵊli\ *adv* [ME, fr. [1]*mortal* + *-ly*] **1 :** in a deadly or fatal manner **:** to the point of death ⟨his colonel and lieutenant colonel were both ~ wounded —J.D.Hicks⟩ **2 :** to an extreme degree **:** GRIEVOUSLY, INTENSELY ⟨millions have come out of the war lost souls . . . still ~ afraid —F.S.Kinney⟩ ⟨~ hates and fears a fall in farm income —*Time*⟩ **3 :** by way of mortal sin ⟨the souls of those who have sinned ~ —R.M.French⟩ **4 :** AWFULLY, EXTREMELY ⟨all novelists and dramatists without genius . . . are usually being ~ serious about middle-class people entangled by Fate —F.A.Swinnerton⟩
**mortal mind** *n*, *Christian Science* **:** a belief that life, substance, and intelligence are in and of matter **:** ILLUSION — opposed to *Spirit*
**mortal sin** *n* [ME *mortal synne*] *Roman Catholicism* **:** a serious sin or a lesser sin aggravated by circumstances committed willfully and viewed as involving spiritual death and loss of divine grace — contrasted with *venial sin*
[1]**mor·tar** \ˈmȯr|d·ər, ˈmȯ(ə)|d·ə(r, |tə-\ *n* -S [ME *morter*, fr. OE *mortere* & MF *mortier*, fr. L *mortarium* mortar, vessel in which substances are pounded or rubbed, plastic building material that hardens and is used in masonry, trough in which mortar is mixed; akin to Gk *marainein* to waste away — more at SMART] **1 a :** a small usu. bowl-shaped vessel made of a hard material (as porcelain or brass) in which substances are pounded or rubbed with a pestle **b :** a large cast-iron receptacle in which ore is crushed in a stamp mill **2** *archaic* **a :** a bowl of oil with a floating wick **b :** a thick candle **3** [MF *mortier* muzzle-loading cannon having a tube short in relation to its caliber, vessel in which substances are pounded or rubbed] **a :** a muzzle-loading cannon having either a rifled or smooth bore and a tube short in relation to its caliber that is used to throw projectiles with low muzzle velocities at high angles **b :** any of several similar firing devices used for various purposes (as to throw a lifeline or to fire pyrotechnic bombs or shells)

mortars with pestles: *1* glass, *2* porcelain

[2]**mortar** \"\ *vb* -ED/-ING/-S *vt* **:** to direct mortar fire upon or to hit with mortar shells ⟨the enemy . . . was ~*ing* a crossroads behind our lines and interfering with our movements —C.C.Wertenbaker⟩ ⟨the leading tank . . . radioed it had been ~*ed* —*Life*⟩ ~ *vi* **:** to fire mortars ⟨can expect the ~*ing* to begin any minute —Ned Calmer⟩
[3]**mortar** \"\ *n* -S [ME *morter*, fr. OF *mortier*, fr. L *mortarium*] **1 :** a plastic building material that hardens and is used in masonry or plastering; *esp* **:** a mixture of cement, lime, or gypsum plaster with sand and water that is used in either the plastic or hardened state ⟨the masons are calling for ~ —Walt Whitman⟩ **2 :** something that binds or holds together ⟨our dreams are built solidly with the ~ of our toil and blood —Stuart Cloete⟩ ⟨moral and spiritual values . . . the ~ which holds together the other educational ingredients —*Educational and Psychological Measurement*⟩
[4]**mor·tar** \ˈmȯrtər\ *vb* -ED/-ING/-S [ME *morteren*, fr. *morter*, n.] *vt* **:** to plaster or make fast with mortar ~ *vi*, *dial Eng* **:** to tramp about esp. with mud or dirt on one's feet ⟨keep ~*in'* in and out, in and out, for everlastin' trampin' through —H.E. Bates⟩
**mortar bed** *n* **1 :** a shallow box or receptacle in which mortar is mixed **2 :** a layer of sand or gravel cemented by calcium carbonate and resembling hardened mortar
**mortarboard** \ˈ==͵=\ *n* **1 a :** HAWK 3 **b :** a board or platform about 3 feet square for holding mortar **2 :** an academic cap consisting of a closely fitting headpiece surmounted by a broad flat projecting square top ⟨the shape of the hat as stiff and uncoquettish as a ~ —Frances G. Patton⟩ ⟨the candidates for honorary degrees, now sitting fussing nervously with their gowns and ~ hats —*Harper's*⟩

mortarboard 2

**mortar boat** *n* **:** a boat adapted to carrying a mortar or mortars for bombarding
**mor·tar·less** \ˈmȯ(r)d·ə(r)ləs\ *adj* **:** having or using no mortar ⟨a ~ stone foundation⟩
**mor·tar·man** \ˈ==mən\ *n*, *pl* **mortarmen :** a member of a crew that fires a mortar
**mortarware** \ˈ==͵=\ *n* [[1]*mortar* + *ware*] **:** a hard stoneware first made by Wedgwood and used in the manufacture of mortars
**mor·tary** \ˈmȯ(r)d·ərē\ *adj* [[3]*mortar* + *-y*] **:** consisting of, containing, or resembling mortar
**mort·cloth** \ˈmȯrt͵klȯth\ *n* [obs. E *mort* death (fr. MF, fr. L *mort-*, *mors*) + E cloth — more at MORTAL] **1** *chiefly Scot* **:** a funeral pall ⟨let the bedclothes, for a ~, drop into great laps and folds of sculptor's work —Robert Browning⟩ **2** *Scot* **:** money paid for the use of a pall
**mort d'an·ces·tor** \mär'dan͵sestər\ *n* [AF, death of the ancestor] **:** an obsolete writ or brieve in English and Scots law for the recovery by an heir from an abator of a tenement which his deceased ancestor held in seisin at his death
**mor·ter·sheen** \ˈmȯ(r)tə(r)͵shēn\ *n* -S [prob. modif. of (assumed) obs. F *mort d'échine*, lit., death of the spine, fr. MF *mort de eschine*] *Scot* **:** GLANDERS
[1]**mort·gage** \ˈmȯrgij, ˈmȯ(ə)g-, -gēj\ *n* -S [ME *morgage*, fr. MF, fr. OF, fr. *mort* dead (fr. L *mortuus*, past part. of *mori* to die) + *gage* security, gage — more at MURDER, GAGE] **1 a :** a conveyance of property upon condition (as security for the payment of a debt or the performance of a duty) that operates as a lien or charge securing the payment of the money or the performance of an obligation so that the mortgagee may under certain conditions take possession and may foreclose the property upon default, that becomes void upon payment or performance according to stipulated terms, and that leaves possession with the mortgagor and subjects the mortgagee's defeasible estate in the land to the equity of redemption and foreclosure rules of the equity courts — see CHATTEL MORTGAGE, EQUITABLE MORTGAGE, FIRST MORTGAGE, INSTALLMENT MORTGAGE, JUNIOR MORTGAGE, LEASEHOLD MORTGAGE, PARTICIPATING MORTGAGE, PURCHASE-MONEY MORTGAGE, SECOND MORTGAGE, TRUST MORTGAGE; compare ANTICHRESIS, EQUITY OF REDEMPTION, GAGE, HYPOTHEC, LIVING PLEDGE, PLEDGE **b :** the instrument by which a mortgage conveyance is made, the state of the property so conveyed, or the interest of the mortgagee in it **2 :** a binding obligation ⟨however stridently the American writer may protest his Americanism . . . he can never pay off his ~ to the past —*Times Lit. Supp.*⟩ ⟨the first president . . . to feel unencumbered by any ~ to Congress —W.E. Binkley⟩
[2]**mortgage** \", *esp in pres part* -gəj\ *vt* -ED/-ING/-S **1 :** to grant or convey by a mortgage **:** make a mortgage conveyance of **2 :** to subject to a claim or obligation **:** PLEDGE ⟨found myself *mortgaged* to my father for about one hundred and fifty dollars —Roger Eddy⟩ ⟨a view of life . . . in which the individual is *mortgaged* to society —David Riesman⟩
**mortgage bond** *n* **:** a bond secured by a mortgage on property — distinguished from *debenture bond*
**mortgage clause** *or* **mortgagee clause** *n* **:** a clause endorsed on a mortgagor's insurance policy whereby the insurance company agrees to protect the mortgagee's interest regardless of any violation of the policy terms by the mortgagor
**mortgage deed** *n* **:** a deed embodying a mortgage
**mort·ga·gee** \¦mȯ(r)gə¦jē\ *n* -S [[2]*mortgage* + *-ee*] **:** a person who takes a mortgage on another's property as security for a debt or obligation
**mortgage guarantee bond** *n* **:** insurance against loss due to default in payments of interest or principal by a mortgagor
**mortgage insurance** *n* **:** insurance that protects a mortgagee against loss because of default in payments by a mortgagor
**mortgage loan** *n* **:** a loan secured by a mortgage on real property
**mortgage redemption insurance** *n* **:** insurance upon the life of a mortgagor providing for payment of any unpaid balance of the mortgage loan at the insured's death
**mort·ga·gor** \¦mȯrgi¦jȯ(ə)r, ¦mȯgi¦jȯ(ə), ˈ==͵jə(r)\ *also* **mort·gag·er** \ˈ==͵jə(r)\ *n* -S [[2]*mortgage* + *-or* or *-er*] **:** a person who gives a mortgage on his property as security for a loan he receives or other obligation
**mor·tial** \ˈmȯrshəl\ *dial var of* MORTAL
**mortice** *var of* MORTISE
**mor·ti·cian** \mȯ(r)ˈtishən\ *n* -S [L *mort-*, *mors* death + E *-ician* — more at MORTAL] **:** FUNERAL DIRECTOR ⟨saw the old Victorian houses taken over by ~*s* and auto showrooms —*Time*⟩ ⟨on the scene appears a solemn ~ —Robert Frost⟩
**mor·tier** \mȯr·ˈtyā\ *n* -S [F, mortier, vessel in which substances are pounded or rubbed — more at MORTAR] **:** a headdress formerly worn by certain high functionaries of the law in France
**mor·tif·er·ous** \(ˈ)mȯ(r)¦tif(ə)rəs\ *adj* [L *mortifer*, *mortiferus*, fr. *morti-* (fr. *mort-*, *mors* death) + *-fer*, *-ferus* -fer, -ferous] **:** DEADLY, FATAL — **mor·tif·er·ous·ly** *adv* — **mor·tif·er·ous·ness** *n* -ES
**mor·tif·ic** \(ˈ)mȯ(r)¦tifik\ *adj* [LL *mortificus*, fr. L *morti-* (fr. *mort-*, *mors* death) + *-ficus* -fic] *archaic* **:** producing death
**mor·ti·fi·ca·tion** \͵mȯ(r)d·əfəˈkāshən, -(r)təf-\ *n* -S [ME *mortificacion*, fr. MF *mortification*, fr. LL *mortification-*, *mortificatio* mortification, killing, fr. *mortificatus* (past part. of *mortificare* to mortify, kill) + L *-ion-*, *-io* -ion] **1 a :** the subjection and denial of bodily passions and appetites by abstinence or self-inflicted pain or discomfort ⟨fasted for the day as a ~⟩ **b :** something that mortifies **:** a cause of humiliation or chagrin **2** *Scots law* **:** a gift for religious, charitable, or public uses corresponding to mortmain **3** *archaic* **:** a numbing of the vital faculties **:** a loss of consciousness at the approach of death **:** INSENSIBILITY **4 :** local death of tissue in the animal body **:** GANGRENE **5 :** a sense of humiliation and shame caused by something that wounds one's pride or self-respect (as a slight, a deep disappointment, or a personal failure) **:** CHAGRIN ⟨the ~ of being jilted by a little boarding-school girl —Washington Irving⟩ ⟨felt deep ~ at the plight of his invincible fleet —J.L.Motley⟩ ⟨in real life she suffered such bitter ~ in the company of her fellow creatures —Robert Cantwell⟩
**mortification root** *n* **:** MARSHMALLOW 1a
**mortified** *adj* [fr. past part. of *mortify*] **1 :** insensible to worldly or sensual pleasures **:** having the appetites in subjection **:** ASCETIC, AUSTERE ⟨the fame of his ~ life and supernatural gift of counsel —C.M.Rooney⟩ ⟨could be no gainsaying his brilliant intellectual gifts or his ~ daily life —*Times Lit. Supp.*⟩ **2 :** affected by gangrene **:** GANGRENOUS **3** *obs* **:** being without feeling **:** DEADENED ⟨strike in their numbed and ~ bare arms pins, wooden pricks, nails —Shak.⟩ **4** *archaic* **:** DECAYED, ROTTEN ⟨in such a ~ condition, that no other people . . . would feed upon it —Tobias Smollett⟩ **5 :** deeply embarrassed or humiliated ⟨terribly ~ to find that his host had forgotten about him⟩ **syn** see ASHAMED
**mor·ti·fied·ly** *adv* **:** in a mortified manner
**mor·ti·fi·er** \ˈmȯrd·ə͵fī(ə)r\ *n* -S **:** one that mortifies
**mor·ti·fy** \ˈmȯ(r)d·ə͵fī, -(r)tə-\ *vb* -ED/-ING/-ES [ME *mortifien*, fr. MF *mortifier*, fr. LL *mortificare* to mortify, kill, fr. L *morti-* (fr. *mort-*, *mors* death) + *-ficare* -fy] *vt* **1** *obs* **a :** to put to death **:** DESTROY ⟨if ye through the spirit do ~ the deeds of the body, ye shall live —Rom 8:13 (AV)⟩ **b :** to destroy the strength, vitality, or functioning of **:** deaden the effect of ⟨the tendons were *mortified* and . . . he could never have the use of his leg —Daniel Defoe⟩ ⟨the knowledge of future evils *mortifies* present felicities —Sir Thomas Browne⟩ **2 :** to subdue or deaden (as the body or bodily appetites) by abstinence, self-discipline, or self-inflicted pain or discomfort ⟨the flesh tended to corruption, and to achieve the pious ends of life one must ~ it . . . lessening its appetites by fasting and abstention —Lewis Mumford⟩ ⟨one is taught in the noviceship to ~ one's palate at least once during every meal —Monica Baldwin⟩ **3** *Scots law* **:** to grant in mortmain for religious, charitable, or public uses ⟨to administer and manage the whole revenue and property of the University including funds *mortified* for bursaries and other purposes —*Edinburgh Univ. Cal.*⟩ **4** *obs* **:** to make (meat) tender by aging **5 :** to subject to or cause to feel embarrassment, chagrin, or vexation **:** HUMILIATE ⟨it would ~ me that you shouldn't be perfectly dressed —W.S. Maugham⟩ ⟨was no longer *mortified* by comparisons between her sisters' beauty and her own —Jane Austen⟩ ~ *vi* **1 :** to practice mortification **:** lead an ascetic life ⟨a sort of mammoth lay monastery relieved of the obligation to ~ —James Binder⟩ **2 :** to lose organic structure **:** become gangrenous **:** DECAY
**mor·ti·fy·ing·ly** *adv* **:** in a mortifying manner
**mor·tis cau·sa** \ˈmȯrd·əˈskau̇|sə, -kȯ|, |zə\ *adj* [L, because of death] **:** made by reason of or in contemplation of impending death ⟨her last will and testament, or rather her *mortis causa* settlement —Sir Walter Scott⟩
[1]**mor·tise** *also* **mor·tice** \ˈmȯr|d·əs, ˈmȯ(ə)|, |təs\ *n* -S [ME *mortays*, *morteys*, fr. MF *mortaise*] **1 :** a hole, groove, or slot into or through which some other part of any arrangement of parts fits or passes; *specif* **:** a usu. rectangular cavity cut into a piece of timber or other material to receive a tenon **2 :** a hole in a printing plate or cut into which matter (as type) can be inserted
[2]**mortise** *also* **mortice** \"\ *vt* -ED/-ING/-S [ME *morteysen*, fr. *mortays*, *morteys*, n.] **1 :** to join or fasten securely; *specif* **:** to join or fasten by a tenon and mortise ⟨a thin strip of beech is nailed across each corner instead of being *mortised* —Joseph Downs⟩ ⟨this loyalty and this courage, like all virtues not *mortised* in philosophy, are limited —Clifton Fadiman⟩ ⟨a

tightly *mortised*, exciting plot —E.J.Fitzgerald⟩ **2 a :** to cut or make a mortise in **b :** to cut away part of the body of (a printing character) to obtain a closer fit

**mortise gage** *n* **:** a carpenter's tool for scribing parallel lines for mortises

**mortise joint** *n* **:** a joint made by a mortise and tenon

**mortise lock** *n* **:** a door lock inserted in a mortise

**mortise pin** *n* **:** a tapered wooden pin driven either through both members of a mortised joint or through the extended tenon in order to lock and tighten the joint

mortise joint

**mor·tis·er** \-sə(r)\ *n* -s **1 :** one that mortises by hand or by machine **2 :** a woodworking machine for cutting mortises

**mortise wheel** *n* **:** a cast-iron wheel with wooden teeth inserted in mortises

**mort·lake** \'mȯt,lāk\ *n* [prob. fr. *Mortlake*, parish in Barnes municipal borough, southwestern suburb of London, England] *Brit* **:** OXBOW LAKE

**mort·ling** \'mȯrtliŋ\ *n* -s [ME *morlyng*, prob. modif. (influenced by ME *-lyng, -ling* -ling) of MF *morticine* carrion — more at MORT] **:** wool taken from a dead sheep

**mort·main** \'mȯrt,mān, 'mȯ(ə)t-\ *n* -s [ME *morte-mayne*, fr. MF *mortemain*, fr. OF (trans. of ML *mortua manus*), fr. *morte* (fem. of *mort* dead, fr. L *mortuus*, past part. of *mori* to die) + *main* hand, fr. L *manus* — more at MURDER, MANUAL] **1 a :** an inalienable possession or tenure of lands or buildings by an ecclesiastical or other corporation — see STATUTES OF MORTMAIN **b :** the condition of property or other gifts left to a corporation in perpetuity esp. for religious, charitable, or public purposes **2 :** the influence of the past regarded as controlling or restricting the present ⟨the tradition . . . has become a deadweight, a ~ hanging evilly over the school —John Raymond⟩ ⟨in the grip of ~, under thrall of a fascinating past —*Saturday Rev.*⟩

**mor·ton mains disease** \'mȯrtᵊn'mānz-\ *n, usu cap both Ms* [perh. fr. a name *Morton Mains*] **:** cobalt deficiency disease of sheep and cattle in New Zealand — compare ¹PINE 3

**mor·ton's toe** *also* **morton's disease** \'mȯrtᵊnz-\ *n, usu cap M* [after Thomas G. *Morton* †1903 Am. surgeon] **:** METATARSALGIA

**morts** *pl of* MORT

¹**mor·tu·ary** \'mȯ(r)chə,werē, -ri\ *n* -ES [ME *mortuarie*, fr. ML *mortuarium*, fr. L, neut. of *mortuarius*, adj.] **1 :** CORSEPRESENT **2 :** a place in which dead bodies are kept until burial; *esp* **:** FUNERAL HOME

²**mortuary** \"\ *adj* [L *mortuarius* of the dead, fr. *mortuus* dead (past part. of *mori* to die) + *-arius* -ary] **1 :** of or relating to the burial of the dead ⟨ropes, palls, velvet, ostrich feathers, and other ~ properties —W.M.Thackeray⟩ ⟨~ arrangements⟩ **2 :** of, relating to, or characteristic of death ⟨it continues to receive a kind of ~ tribute in the schoolroom —Clifton Fadiman⟩ ⟨an embalmed darkness, a darkness at once soothing and ~ —R.M.Adams⟩

**mor·tu·um va·di·um** \'mȯrchəwəm'vādēəm\ *n* [ML, lit., dead pledge] **:** a mortgage agreement in early English law that gave possession of the mortgaged land and the use of its rents and profits to the mortgagee until such time as the mortgage was paid — compare VIVUM VADIUM

**mort·warp** *or* **mort·worp** \'mȯr,twȯrp\ *var of* MOLDWARP

**mo·ru** \'mō(,)rü, 'mȯ(,)-\ *n, pl* **moru** *or* **morus** *usu cap* **1 a :** a people of the Sudan **b :** a member of such people **2 :** a Central Sudanic language of the Moru people

**mor·u·la** \'mȯrələ, 'mär-\ *n, pl* **moru·lae** \-rə,lē\ [NL, fr. L *morum* mulberry + *-ula*] **1 :** a globular mass of blastomeres formed by cleavage of the egg of many animals in its early development and distinguished from a typical blastula which may arise from it by the absence of any trace of a central cavity — compare GASTRULA **2 :** a cluster of developing male germ cells esp. in certain annelids in which final development of spermatozoa occurs outside the testis — **mor·u·lar** \-lə(r)\ *adj*

**mor·u·la·tion** \,=='lāshən\ *n* -s [NL *morula* + E *-ation*] **:** formation of a morula

**mo·rus** \'mōrəs, 'mȯr-\ *n, cap* [NL, fr. L, mulberry tree, fr. *morum* mulberry — more at MULBERRY] **:** a widely distributed genus of trees that is the type of the family Moraceae and that comprises the mulberries which have usu. dentate or lobed leaves, spicate flowers, and edible multiple fruits consisting of aggregates of juicy one-seeded drupes

**mor·wong** \'mȯr,wäŋ\ *n* -s [native name in New South Wales, Australia] **:** any of several important Australian food fishes of the family Cheilodactylidae — called also *sea carp*

**mos** *pl of* MO

**-mos** *pl of* -MO

**MOS** *abbr or n* -s military occupational specialty ⟨had an ~ of clerk typist⟩

¹**mo·sa·ic** \mō'zāik, -āēk, mə'-\ *n* -s [ME *musycke*, fr. MF *mosaique*, fr. OIt *mosaico*, fr. ML *musaicum*, alter. of LL *musivum*, fr. neut. of *musivus* of a muse, artistic, fr. L *musa* muse + *-ivus* -ive] **1 a :** a surface decoration made by inlaying small pieces of variously colored material (as tile, marble, or glass) to form patterns or pictures **b :** the process of making such a decoration **2 a :** a picture or design made in mosaic **b :** an article decorated in mosaic **3 :** something resembling a mosaic ⟨passages that are ~s of quotations —Malcolm Cowley⟩ ⟨a ~ of colorful bits from history —*College English*⟩ ⟨great cities turn out . . . to be a ~ of segregated peoples —R.E.Park⟩ **4 :** a mosaic individual **:** CHIMERA **5 a :** LEAF MOSAIC 1 **b** *also* **mosaic disease :** any of several virus diseases of plants characterized esp. by more or less diffuse light and dark green or yellow and green mottling or spotting of the foliage and sometimes by pronounced curling, dwarfing, and narrowing of the leaves **6 :** a composite photographic map formed by matching a series of overlapping photographs of adjoining areas of the earth's surface taken vertically from the air at a constant height **7 :** the photosensitive element in a television camera tube consisting of a layer of many minute photoelectric particles that convert light to an electric charge

²**mosaic** \"\ *adj* **1 a** *also* **mosaical** \-āəkəl\ **:** of, relating to, or produced by mosaic ⟨a ~ floor⟩ ⟨bright ~ tile⟩ **b :** resembling mosaic esp. in pattern, variegation, or composition ⟨a ~ compilation⟩ **2 :** exhibiting mosaicism: **a :** CHIMERAL **b :** of, relating to, or constituting a mosaic hybrid or mosaic inheritance **3** *of a plant* **:** affected with mosaic **4 :** GRANOBLASTIC **5 :** DETERMINATE 6 **6 :** of or relating to the mosaic of a television camera tube — **mo·sa·i·cal·ly** \-āək(ə)lē\ *adv*

³**mosaic** \"\ *vt* **mosaicked** *also* **mosaiced** \-ikt,-ēkt\ **mosaicked** *also* **mosaiced; mosaicking** *also* **mosaicing** \-āəkiŋ\ **mosaics** [¹*mosaic*] **1 :** to decorate with or as if with mosaics ⟨doors and roofs were carved and sculptured and painted and *mosaicked* —Rose Macaulay⟩ **2 :** to form into or as if into a mosaic ⟨an artificial patchwork . . . *mosaicked* out of bought, stolen, and plundered provinces —J.L.Motley⟩

⁴**mosaic** \"\ *also* **mo·sa·i·cal** \-āəkəl\ *adj, usu cap* [*Mosaic* fr. NL *Mosaicus*, fr. *Moses* Biblical prophet and lawgiver + L *-icus* -ic; *Mosaical* fr. NL *Mosaicus* + E *-al* — more at MOSES] **:** of or relating to Moses or the institutions or writings attributed to him ⟨the *Mosaic* code⟩

**mosaic binding** *n* **:** a full-leather bookbinding with inlaid colored designs — called also *inlaid binding*

**mosaic dwarf** *n* **:** CURLY DWARF

**mosaic glass** *n* **:** MILLEFIORI

**mosaic gold** *n* **1 :** a yellow scaly crystalline pigment consisting essentially of stannic sulfide **2 :** ORMOLU 2

**mosaic hybrid** *n* **1 :** CHIMERA **2 :** an individual exhibiting mosaic inheritance

**mosaic image** *n* **:** the image formed by a compound eye (as of an insect) in which each visual facet receives independently a small portion of the image and the total visual impression is a composite of the various unit images

**mosaic inheritance** *n* **1 :** supposed inheritance of both of a pair of contrasted parental characters one or the other of which is manifested in pure form at any given point (as in variegated flowers) — compare MOSAICISM **2 :** typical Mendelian inheritance of alternate parental characters

**mo·sa·i·cism** \mō'zāə,sizəm\ *n* -s **:** a condition in which patches of tissue of unlike genetic constitution are mingled in an organism owing esp. to abnormalities of chromosome separation during mitosis

**mo·sa·i·cist** \-səst\ *n* -s **1 a :** a designer of mosaics **b :** a workman who makes mosaics **2 :** a dealer in mosaics

**mosaic law** *n, usu cap M* [⁴*Mosaic*] **:** the ancient Hebrew moral and ceremonial law attributed to Moses

**mosaic rhyme** *n* **:** BROKEN RHYME

**mosaics** *pl of* MOSAIC, *pres 3d sing of* MOSAIC

**mosaic screen** *n* **:** a flat transparent light filter composed of minute colored elements through which the exposure is made on a panchromatic emulsion layer and through which the image is viewed in the screen process of additive color photography

**mosaic structure** *n* **:** irregularity of orientation of small blocks of varying sizes in a crystal

**mosaic-tailed rat** \=¦==¦=-\ *n* **:** any of various large rats (genus *Uromys*) of northern Australia and adjacent islands distinguished by tail scales that do not overlap but meet in a mosaic pattern

**mosaic theory** *n* **:** a theory in embryology: each part of the protoplasm of an egg has its function in forming a special part of the embryo

**mo·sa·ism** \'mōzā,izəm\ *n* -s *usu cap* [⁴*Mosaic* + *-ism*] **1 :** the ancient Hebrew religious and legal system attributed to Moses **2 :** attachment to the Mosaic system or doctrines

**mo·sa·ist** \'mō(,)zāəst, mō'z-\ *n* -s [¹*mosaic* + *-ist*] **:** MOSAICIST

**mo·san** \'mōsᵊn\ *n* -s *usu cap* [*mos-* (fr. *mōs, bōs* "four" in various Chemakuan, Wakashan & Salishan languages) + E *-an*] **:** a language phylum of British Columbia and Washington comprising the Salishan, Wakashan, and Chemakuan stocks

**mo·san·drite** \mō'san,drīt\ *n* -s [G *mosandrit*, fr. Carl G. *Mosander* †1858 Swed. chemist + G *-it* -ite] **:** a mineral approximately $NaCa_6Ce_2(Ti,Zr)_2Si_7O_{24}(OH,F)_7$ consisting of a silicate of sodium, calcium, titanium, zirconium, and the cerium metals

**mo·sa·saur** \'mōsə,sȯ(ə)r\ *n* -s [NL *Mosasaurus*] **:** a reptile of the genus *Mosasaurus* or the family Mosasauridae

**mo·sa·sau·ria** \,==='sȯrēə\ *or* **mo·sa·sau·ri** \-ȯ,rī\ [NL, fr. *Mosasaurus* + *-ia*] *syn of* PYTHONOMORPHA

¹**mo·sa·sau·ri·an** \,==¦==sȯrēən\ *adj* [NL *Mosasaurus* + E *-ian*] **:** of or relating to the genus *Mosasaurus* or the family Mosasauridae

²**mosasaurian** \"\ *n* -s **:** MOSASAUR

**mo·sa·sau·rus** \,=='sȯrəs\ *n, cap* [NL, fr. L *Mosa* the river Meuse (near which the first known species was discovered) + NL *-saurus*] **:** a genus (the type of the family Mosasauridae) of large extinct aquatic Cretaceous fish-eating lizards related to the recent monitors but having the limbs modified into swimming paddles

**mos·cha·tel** \,mäskə¦tel\ *n* -s [modif. (influenced by NL *moschatellina* — specific epithet of *Adoxa moschatellina* — fr. F *moscatelle* or It *moscatella* + NL *-ina*) of F *moscatelle*, fr. It *moscatella*, fr. *moscato* musk (fr. LL *muscus* musk + It *-ato*, fr. L *-atus* -ate) + *-ella* (dim. suffix) — more at MUSK] **:** a small herb (*Adoxa moschatellina*) of the north temperate zone with greenish white musk-scented flowers

**mo·schel·lands·berg·ite** \,mōshə'lan(d)zbə(r),gīt\ *n* -s [*Moschellandsberg*, town in Bavaria, Germany + E *-ite*] **:** a mineral $Ag_2Hg_3$ consisting of a natural alloy or amalgam of silver and mercury

**mos·chi** \'mä,skī\ *n pl, usu cap* [L, fr. Gk *Moschoi*] **:** one of numerous ancient peoples in Armenia associated with ironworking

**mos·chus** \'mäskəs\ *n, cap* [NL, fr. ML, musk — more at MUSK] **:** a genus comprising the Asiatic musk deer usu. segregated in a subfamily of Cervidae but formerly placed in a separate family

**moscovite** *var of* MUSCOVITE

**mos·cow** \'mä,skaü, -ä(,)skō\ *adj, usu cap* [fr. *Moscow*, U.S.S.R.] **:** of or from Moscow, capital of the U.S.S.R. **:** of the kind or style prevalent in Moscow

**mo·selle** \mō'zel\ *n* -s *usu cap* [G *moselwein*, fr. *Mosel* (Moselle) river in southwestern Germany + G *wein* wine] **1 :** a white usu. still but sometimes sparkling table wine made from grapes grown in the valley of the Moselle from Trier to Coblenz and in the valleys of its tributaries, the Saar and the Ruwer **2 :** a wine resembling Moselle ⟨California *Moselle*⟩

**moses** \'mōzəz, -zəs\ *n* -ES [after *Moses*, Biblical prophet and lawgiver who led the Israelites from Egypt to Canaan *ab* 1200 B.C. (Exod 12 ff.), fr. LL *Moses, Moyses*, fr. Gk *Mōsēs, Mōysēs*, fr. Heb *Mōsheh*] **1** *usu cap* **:** LEADER ⟨theatregoers may have found a *Moses* who will lead them out of their wilderness —*Theatre Arts*⟩ **2** *or* **moses boat :** a broad flat-bottomed ship's boat formerly used in the West Indies esp. for lightering hogsheads of sugar

**mo·ses·ite** \'mōzə,zīt, -,sīt\ *n* -s [Alfred J. *Moses* †1920 Am. mineralogist + E *-ite*] **:** a mineral $Hg_2N(X).H_2O$ consisting of a hydrous nitride of mercury with other anions and water exchangeable within wide limits

**moses-on-a-raft** \'====,=\ *also* **moses-in-the-bulrushes** \'====,==,=\ *n, usu cap* [so called fr. the infant Moses' having been placed by his mother in an ark made of bulrushes on the edge of a river to escape death by the Egyptians (Exod 2:3)] **:** OYSTER PLANT 3

**mo·se·te·ne** \,mōsə'tā(,)nā\ *or* **mo·se·te·no** \-nō\ *n, pl* **mosetene** \-nā\ *or* **mosete·nes** \-nās\ *or* **moseteno** \-nō\ *or* **mosete·nos** \-nōs\ *usu cap* **a :** an Amerind people of eastern Bolivia **b :** a member of such people **2 :** the language of the Mosetene people

¹**mo·sey** \'mōzi\ *adj* [ME *mosy*, fr. *mos* moss + *-y* — more at MOSS] **1** *dial Brit* **:** HAIRY; *esp* **:** having soft downy hair **2** *dial Brit* **:** MOLDY, ROTTEN — used esp. of overripe fruit

²**mo·sey** \'mōzē, -zi\ *vi* **moseyed; moseyed; moseying; moseys** [origin unknown] **1 :** to hurry away **:** DECAMP, SCRAM ⟨vamoose, skedaddle, ~ —S.V.Benét⟩ **2 a :** to move in a leisurely, shuffling, or aimless manner **:** SAUNTER, AMBLE ⟨just ~*ed* along, mostly traveling by shanks' mare —Helen Eustis⟩ ⟨~*ed* into position to sneak a look at the owner of the rough voice —Joel Sayre⟩ ⟨a mild river that ~*ed* at will through parks and plowland —W.H.Auden⟩ **b :** to move slowly while observing or inspecting ⟨spend three or four weeks . . . just ~*ing* about, discovering lesser-known museums, galleries, and places of historic interest —Richard Joseph⟩ ⟨~*ed* around the general store, testing the cheese straight off the round —Eric Sevareid⟩

**mosgu** *usu cap, var of* MUSGU

**mo·shav** \mō'shäv\ *n, pl* **mo·sha·vim** \,mōshə'vēm\ [NHeb *mōshābh*, fr. Heb, dwelling] **:** a cooperative small holders' settlement of individual farms in Israel

**mo·sha·va** \,mōshə'vä\ *n, pl* **mosha·voth** *or* **mosha·vot** \-vōt(h)\ [NHeb *mōshābhāh*, fem. of *mōshābh*] **:** a settlement or colony of independent farmers in Israel who own and work their own land

**moshav ov·dim** \-ōv'dēm\ *n, pl* **mosh·vei ovdim** \mōsh'vā-\ [NHeb *mōshābh 'obhēdhīm*, lit., settlement of workers] **:** a workers' settlement of small holders in Israel with independent but cooperatively worked farm units

**moshav shi·tu·fi** \-,shi,tü'fē\ *n, pl* **moshavim shitu·fim** \-'fēm\ [NHeb *mōshābh shittūphī*, lit., partnership settlement] **:** a collective small holders' settlement in Israel

**mos·ke·neer** \,mäskə'niə\ *vt* -ED/-ING/-S [Yiddish *mashken* pledge, pawn (fr. Heb *mashkōn*) + E *-eer* (as in *profiteer*, v.)] *Brit* **:** to pawn for more than the value of the article

¹**mosk·er** \'mäskə(r)\ *vi* -ED/-ING/-S [origin unknown] *dial chiefly Eng* **:** DECAY, MOLDER

²**mosk·er** \'mäskə(r)\ *n* -s [*moskeneer* + *-er*] *Brit* **:** one that moskeneers

**moslem** *usu cap, var of* MUSLIM

**mos·lem·ize** \'mäzlə,mīz, 'mäs-\ *vt* -ED/-ING/-S *often cap* **:** to make Muslim in religion or culture ⟨~ a region⟩ ⟨*moslemized* Christians⟩

**mo·so** \'mō(,)sō\ *also* **mos·so** \'mȯ(-\ *n, pl* **moso** *or* **mosos** *also* **mosso** *or* **mossos** *usu cap* **:** NA-KHI

**mo·so·sau·rus** \,mōsə'sȯrəs\ [NL, alter. of *Mosasaurus*] *syn of* MOSASAURUS

**mosque** \'mäsk\ *n* -s [fr. earlier *moschee, muskie*, fr. MF *musquee, mosquee*, fr. OIt *moschea*, alter. of *mosqueta, meschita*, fr. OSp *mezquita*, fr. Ar *masjid* temple, fr. *sajada* to prostrate oneself] **:** an Islamic place of public religious worship — called also MASJID

**mosque swallow** *n* **:** any of numerous Asian and northern African swallows that commonly nest about buildings

¹**mos·qui·to** \mə'skēd·(,)ō, -ē(,)tō, -ēd·ə, -ētə\ *n, pl* **mosquitoes** *also* **mosquitos** *often attrib* [Sp, fr. *mosca* fly, fr. L *musca* — more at MIDGE] **:** any of numerous two-winged flies of the family Culicidae that have a rather narrow abdomen, usu. a long slender rigid proboscis, and narrow wings with a fringe of scales on the margin and usu. on each side of the wing veins, that have in the male broad feathery antennae and mouthparts not fitted for piercing and in the female slender antennae and a set of needlelike organs in the proboscis with which they puncture the skin of animals to suck the blood, that have the eggs laid on the surface of stagnant water, that in many species pass through several generations in the course of a year and hibernate as adults and in others winter in the egg state, and that in some species are the only vectors of certain diseases — see AEDES, ANOPHELES, CULEX; compare GNAT

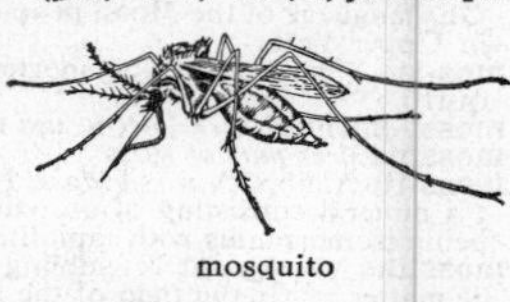
mosquito

²**mosquito** \"\ *n, pl* **mosquito** *or* **mosquitos** *usu cap* [by alter.] **:** MISKITO

**mosquito bar** *n* **:** MOSQUITO NET ⟨slept in hammocks slung between coconut palms and protected by *mosquito bars* —Ralph Watson⟩

**mosquito bee** *n* **:** STINGLESS BEE

**mosquitobill** \=ˈ=(,)=,=\ *n* **:** a California shooting star (*Dodecatheon hendersonii*)

**mosquito blight** *n* **1 :** TEA MOSQUITO **2 :** the disease of tea produced by the punctures of the tea mosquito

**mosquito boat** *n* **:** MOTOR TORPEDO BOAT

**mosquito boot** *n* **:** a high shoe or low boot worn in the tropics ⟨don trousers and, very often, *mosquito boots* in the evening —K.L.Little⟩

**mos·qui·to·ey** \mə'skēd·ōē, -ēt|, |əwē, -i\ *adj* [*mosquito* + *-y*] **:** full of mosquitoes ⟨the screened porch where one might sit in peace during the ~ seasons —Thomas Barbour⟩

**mosquito fern** *n* **:** a water fern of the genus *Azolla*

**mosquito fish** *n* **:** any of numerous small fishes (as gambusia) used to exterminate mosquito larvae

**mosquito fleet** *n* **:** a fleet of comparatively small ships ⟨fast-moving light tanks, agile weaving fighter planes, and high-powered boats of the *mosquito fleet* all operate on the same principles —J.R.Newman⟩

**mosquito hawk** *n* **1 :** NIGHTHAWK **2** *South & Midland* **:** DRAGONFLY

**mosquito net** *n* **:** a net or screen for keeping out mosquitoes; *specif* **:** one suspended from a frame so as to surround a bed

**mosquito netting** *n* **:** netting used for mosquito nets

**mosquito plant** *n* **1** *or* **mosquito trap :** an Asian vine (*Cynanchum acuminatifolium*) whose flowers sometimes entrap small insects **2 :** a plant (as basil mint or pennyroyal) believed to be efficacious in driving away mosquitoes **3 :** MOSQUITO FERN

¹**moss** \'mȯs *also* 'mäs\ *n* -ES *often attrib* [ME *mos, moss*, fr. OE *mōs*; akin to OE *mēos* moss, OHG *mos* moss, swamp, *mios* moss, ON *mosi* moss, swamp, L *mundus* clean, neat, *muscus* moss, Gk *myzein* to suck, *mydan* to be damp, Skt *mūtra* urine, *mudira* cloud; basic meaning: wet] **1 a** *dial chiefly Brit* **:** BOG, MORASS, SWAMP; *esp* **:** PEAT BOG — often used in pl. with *the* ⟨the ~*es* of the English-Scottish border⟩ **b :** spongy soil ⟨the ~ came nearly to the knee —R.L.Stevenson⟩ **2 a :** a plant of the class Musci **b :** a mat, clump, or sward made up of moss plants **3 :** any of various plants more or less like moss in appearance or habit of growth — often used in combination **4 :** a mossy outgrowth or covering (as on the moss rose) **5 :** a fracture or other imperfection (as in a gemstone) having the appearance of moss; *specif* **:** such a fracture in an emerald **6 :** OLD MOSS

²**moss** \"\ *vb* -ED/-ING/-ES [ME *mosen, mossen*, fr. *mos, moss*, n.] *vt* **:** to cover, overgrow, or fill in with moss ⟨an oak whose boughs were ~*ed* with age —Shak.⟩ ⟨frames were ~*ed* in the baggage cars en route —*Florists Exchange*⟩; *specif* **:** to cover (the stems of a cinchona tree) with a layer of moss to increase the yield of alkaloids **~** *vi* **:** to gather moss

**moss agate** *n* **:** a mineral consisting of agate containing brown, black, or green mosslike or dendritic markings due in part to oxide of manganese — called also *Mocha stone*

**moss animal** *or* **moss animalcule** *n* **:** BRYOZOAN

**mossback** \'=,=\ *also* **mossyback** \'===,=\ *n* **1 a :** an old turtle with a mosslike growth on its back ⟨a little clearing where a ~ lived —*McClure's*⟩ **b :** a large sluggish fish (as a muskellunge) ⟨the old ~s . . . big 30 and 40 pound muskies —F.R. Steel⟩; *esp* **:** LARGEMOUTH BLACK BASS **c :** a wild range steer or cow that has evaded many roundups ⟨the old ~ would let us get no closer —*Hunting & Fishing*⟩ **2 a :** a person who lives in the backwoods **:** RUSTIC ⟨an old ~ . . . preaching about some herd of horses —H.L.Davis⟩ **b :** one who is far behind the times **:** an extremely conservative person **:** FOGY ⟨turn-of-the-century ~s —*New Republic*⟩

**moss-backed** \'=¦=\ *also* **mossy-backed** \¦==¦=\ *adj* **1 :** having a mosslike growth on the back **:** overgrown with moss **2 :** marked by sluggishness of thought or life **:** behind the times ⟨*moss-backed* architectural traditions —*Newsweek*⟩ ⟨a *moss-backed* judge —*Nation*⟩

**moss·berry** \'=- — *see* BERRY\ *n* **:** EUROPEAN CRANBERRY

**moss-bound** \'=,=\ *adj* **:** BOGGY

**mossbunker** *also* **mossbanker** *or* **marshbanker** \'=,==\ *n* **:** MENHADEN

**moss bush** *n* **:** MOSS PLANT 2

**moss campion** *n* **:** a low growing perennial herb (*Silene acaulis*) that has small linear leaves and solitary terminal purplish flowers and forms dense mosslike tussocks on barren cliffs and mountains of the northern hemisphere — called also *carpet pink, cushion pink*

**moss cheeper** *n* **1 :** MEADOW PIPIT **2** *dial Brit* **:** REED BUNTING

**moss coral** *n* **:** BRYOZOAN

**moss crab** *n* **:** a large sluggish hairy shallow-water crab (*Loxorhynchus crispatus*) of the California coast

**moss crop** *n, dial Brit* **:** COTTON GRASS

**moss duck** *n, dial Brit* **:** MALLARD

**mossed** \'mȯst *also* 'mäst\ *adj* **:** overgrown with moss

**mossed bark** *n* **:** the bark and bare trunk of a cinchona that remain after alternate strips of bark have been removed and that are covered with moss until the new bark appears — compare NATURAL BARK, RENEWED BARK

**moss·er** \-sə(r)\ *n* -s [²*moss* + *-er*] **:** one that gathers or works with moss

**moss·ery** \-s(ə)rē\ *n* -ES [¹*moss* + *-ery*] **:** a place where mosses are grown

**mosses** *pl of* MOSS, *pres 3d sing of* MOSS

**moss fern** *n* **:** POLYPODY

**moss fiber** *n* **:** one of the complexly ramifying nerve fibers that surround some nerve cells of the cerebellar cortex

**moss forest** *n* **:** wet tropical upland forest characterized by the presence of abundant epiphytic mosses and ferns

**moss fringe** *n* **:** a heavy pile trim used as a decorative cording in upholstery

**moss fruit** *n* **:** SPOROGONIUM

**moss gold** *n* **:** gold in dendritic forms

**moss gray** *n* **:** a grayish green that is bluer and duller than average bayberry, bluer and paler than slate green, and yellower and duller than average blue spruce

**moss green** *n* **:** a variable color averaging a moderate yellow green that is yellower and duller than average pea green or spring green, yellower, lighter, and slightly less strong than spinach green, and less strong and slightly greener and lighter than mosstone — called also *mousse*

**moss-grown** \'=,=\ *adj* **1 :** overgrown with moss ⟨steeples and *moss-grown* towers —Shak.⟩ **2 :** ANTIQUATED ⟨the family

was noble without being . . . *moss-grown* —Francis Hackett⟩ ⟨*moss-grown* regimental traditions —Ralph Thompson⟩
**moss hag** *n, chiefly Scot* **:** a pit or slough in a marshy place; *esp* **:** a place where peat has been cut
**moss hammer** *n* **:** the European bittern
**mosshead** \'ˌ=\ *n* **:** HOODED MERGANSER
**mosshorn** \'ˌ=\ *or* **mossyhorn** \'=ˌ=\ *n, chiefly West* **:** a longhorn steer so old that its horns have become scaly
**mos·si** \'mäsē\ *n, pl* **mossi** *or* **mossis** *usu cap* **1 a :** a people of the west central Sudan **b :** a member of such people **2 :** a Gur language of the Mossi people and of several other peoples in Upper Volta
**mos·sie** \'mäsē\ *n* -S [by shortening & alter.] *Austral* **:** MOSQUITO
**mossi–gurunsi** \ˌ=ˌ=ˌ=\ *n, usu cap M&G* **:** GUR
**mossing** *pres part of* MOSS
**moss·ite** \'mȯ,sīt\ *n* -S [*Moss*, Norway, its locality + E *-ite*] **:** a mineral consisting of an oxide of iron and tantalum and being isomorphous with tapiolite
**mosslike** \'ˌ=\ *adj* **:** resembling moss ⟨~ plants⟩ ⟨patches of ~ matter . . . in the field of the microscope —John Tyndall⟩
**moss locust** *or* **mossy locust** *n* **:** BRISTLY LOCUST
**moss·man fever** \'mȯsmən-\ *n, usu cap M* [fr. *Mossman* district, northern Queensland, Australia] *Austral* **:** TSUTSUGAMUSHI DISEASE
[1]**mos·so** \'mō(,)sō\ *adj (or adv)* [It, fr. past part. of *muovere* to move, fr. L *movēre* — more at MOVE] **:** ANIMATED, RAPID — used as a direction in music
[2]**mosso** *usu cap, var of* MOSO
**moss owl** *n, chiefly Scot* **:** SHORT-EARED OWL
**moss phlox** *n* **:** MOSS PINK
**moss pink** *n* **:** a low tufted perennial phlox (*Phlox subulata*) with needlelike evergreen leaves that is native to the eastern U. S. and is widely cultivated as a ground cover and for its abundant usu. pink or white flowers — called also *dwarf phlox*
**moss plant** *n* **1 :** MOSS; *esp* **:** the leafy gametophyte of the moss **2 :** a small mosslike arctic heath (*Cassiope hypnoides*) of the family Ericaceae having delicate bell-shaped white flowers
**moss polyp** *n* **:** BRYOZOAN
**moss rose** *n* **1 a :** a rose that forms a variety of the cabbage rose and is distinguished by a glandular mossy calyx and flower stalk **b :** a false mallow (*Malvastrum coccineum*) of the western U. S. with racemose red flowers **c :** ROSE MOSS **2 :** a deep to dark pink
**moss silver** *n* **:** silver in dendritic or filiform shapes
**moss stitch** *n* **:** a knitting stitch that is made by alternating knit and purl stitches and that produces a small check pattern
**mosstone** \'ˌ=\ *n* **:** a moderate yellow green that is yellower and deeper than average moss green, yellower and darker than average pea green, yellower and duller than apple green (sense 1), and yellower, lighter, and slightly stronger than spinach green

moss rose 1a

**moss–trooper** \'ˌ=ˌ=\ *n* **1 :** one of a class of 17th century raiders in the marshy border country between England and Scotland **2 :** FREEBOOTER
**moss–trooping** \'ˌ=ˌ=\ *adj* **:** having the characteristics of or suggesting the practices of moss-troopers
**mossy** \'mȯsē, -si *also* 'mäs-\ *adj* -ER/-EST [[1]*moss* + *-y*] **1** *dial Brit* **:** BOGGY **2 :** overgrown with or covered with moss or something like moss **:** DOWNY ⟨some ~ gravestone —Nathaniel Hawthorne⟩ ⟨exposing his round throat, ~ chest —Herman Melville⟩ **3 :** resembling moss ⟨~ green⟩ ⟨~ carpets —Earle Birney⟩ **4 :** ANTIQUATED, MOSS-BACKED ⟨~ ideas that had hung on —*Women's Wear Daily*⟩ ⟨~ old parson —M.L.Bach⟩
**mossyback** *var of* MOSSBACK
**mossy cell** *n* **:** one of the typical astrocytes of the gray matter distinguished by much-branched cytoplasmic processes — see SPIDER CELL
**mossy–cup oak** *n* **:** BUR OAK
**mossyhorn** *var of* MOSSHORN
**mossy saxifrage** *n* **:** a low tufted perennial herb (*Saxifrage hypnoides*) of the mountains of Europe often cultivated for its white flowers
**mossy stonecrop** *n* **:** a stonecrop (*Sedum acre*)
**mossy zinc** *n* **:** a granulated modification of zinc made by pouring melting zinc into water
[1]**most** \'mōst\ *adj* [ME *mest, mast, most*, fr. OE *mǣst, māst;* akin to OHG *meist* most, ON *mestr*, Goth *maists;* superlative fr. the root of OE *mā* more — more at MORE] **1 :** the greatest number of **:** the majority of ⟨~ men⟩ ⟨~ problems⟩ ⟨~ eligible voters went to the polls⟩ — used with the noun in the pl. **2 a :** greatest in quantity, extent, or degree ⟨owning the ~ land⟩ ⟨the car with the ~ speed⟩ ⟨he has the ~ ability⟩ ⟨she has the ~ need of it⟩ — used with the noun in the sing. **b** *obs* **:** in the highest degree **:** GREATEST ⟨these politicians . . . are our ~ fools —George Chapman⟩ **3** *chiefly dial* **:** CHIEF, MAIN ⟨the ~ place where you will be safe —Augusta Gregory⟩ — **for the most part :** in most cases **:** MAINLY
[2]**most** \"\ *adv* [ME *mest, mast, most*, fr. OE *mǣst, māst;* akin to OHG *meist* most, ON *mest*, Goth *maist*, adv., *maists*, adj. — more at [1]MOST] **1 a :** to the greatest or highest degree **:** to the greatest extent ⟨the book that pleased him ~⟩ — often used with adjectives or adverbs to form the superlative ⟨the ~ beautiful woman there⟩ ⟨writes ~ beautifully of all⟩ **b :** to a very great degree ⟨the argument was ~ persuasive⟩ ⟨a ~ careful workman⟩ **2** *obs* **:** for the most part **:** MOSTLY ⟨states are ~ collected into monarchies —Francis Bacon⟩ — **most an end** *adv, dial Eng* **:** GENERALLY, CONTINUALLY
[3]**most** \"\ *n* -S [ME *mest, mast, most*, fr. OE *mǣst, māst*, fr. *mǣst, māst*, adj. — more at [1]MOST] **:** the greatest amount or quantity ⟨the ~ I can give you⟩ ⟨the ~ we can say for him⟩ — **at most** *or* **at the most** *adv* **:** at the furthest point ⟨take a little "recess" every two hours *at most* —Arnold Bennett⟩
[4]**most** \"\ *pron, sing or pl in constr* [[1]*most*] **:** the greatest number or part **:** MAJORITY ⟨some of the people stayed behind but ~ went⟩ ⟨~ who were present⟩ ⟨~ is out of sight⟩
[5]**most** \"\ *adv* [by shortening] **:** ALMOST ⟨~ anywhere in Europe —*N. Y. Herald Tribune*⟩ ⟨you feel the way ~ everybody else has felt —Gwethalyn Graham⟩
**-most** \ˌmōst *also chiefly Brit* məst\ *adj suffix* [ME *-mest, -most*, alter. (influenced by *mast, most* most) of *-mest* (as in *formest* foremost)] **:** most ⟨inner*most*⟩ **:** most toward ⟨head*most*⟩
**moste** [ME, fr. OE *mōste* — more at MUST] *past of* MOTE
**most–favored–nation** \'ˌ=ˌ=ˌ=\ *adj* **:** of or relating to a nation that is the beneficiary of a most-favored-nation clause ⟨*most-favored-nation* treatment⟩ — abbr. *MFN*
**most–favored–nation clause** *n* **:** a clause often inserted in treaties by which a nation binds itself to grant to another nation in certain stipulated matters the same terms as are then or may be thereafter granted to any other nation
**most high** *n, cap M&H* **:** GOD — usu. used with *the* ⟨the *Most High* rules the kingdom of men —Dan 4: 17 (RSV)⟩
**most honorable** — used as a courtesy title for marquesses and also applied to certain distinguished bodies (as the Order of the Bath and the Privy Council)
**mostlike** \'ˌ=\ *adv, dial* **:** very likely
**most·lings** \'mōstlənz, -liŋz\ *adv* [[1]*most* + *-lings*] *dial Brit* **:** for the most part
**most·ly** *adv* [[1]*most* + *-ly*] **1 a :** for the most part ⟨the sky was ~ overcast —Elyne Mitchell⟩ **b :** USUALLY, GENERALLY ⟨it is then that decay ~ sets in —*Punch*⟩ **2 :** MOST ⟨the person whose society she ~ prized —Jane Austen⟩ **3** *dial chiefly Scot* **:** ALMOST ⟨~ blinded both his eyes —D.M.Moir⟩
**most reverend** — used as a courtesy title for various high ecclesiastical officials (as Anglican archbishops, Roman Catholic archbishops and bishops, the presiding bishop of the Protestant Episcopal Church)
[1]**mo·sul** \mō'sül, 'mōsəl\ *adj, usu cap* [fr. *Mosul*, Iraq] **:** of or from the city of Mosul, Iraq **:** of the kind or style prevalent in Mosul
[2]**mosul** \"\ *n, often cap* **:** a light brown to moderate yellowish brown that is very slightly yellower than dogwood
[1]**mot** *n* -S [MF, word, saying, fr. L *muttum* grunt — more at MOTTO] **1** *obs* **:** MOTTO, DEVICE ⟨eye may read the ~ afar —Shak.⟩ **2** \'mō, *pl* -ō(z)\ [F, fr. MF] **:** a pithy or witty saying ⟨the poet . . . delivers three ~s in rapid succession —Peter De Vries⟩
[2]**mot** \'mät\ *n* -S [F *motte* mound, hillock — more at MOTTE] **1** *dial Brit* **:** MARK, TARGET; *esp* **:** the mark in a game of quoits **2 :** [1]MOTTE
**mot** *abbr* motor; motorized
**mo·ta·cil·la** \ˌmōd·ə'silə\ *n* [NL, fr. L *motacilla* wagtail] **1** *cap* **:** a genus (the type of the family Motacillidae) of oscine birds comprising the wagtails **2** -S **:** any bird of the genus *Motacilla*
[1]**mo·ta·cil·lid** \ˌ=ˌ='siləd\ *adj* [NL *Motacillidae*] **:** of or relating to the Motacillidae
[2]**motacillid** \"\ *n* -S **:** a bird of the family Motacillidae
**mo·ta·cil·li·dae** \ˌ=ˌ='silə,dē\ *n pl, cap* [NL, fr. *Motacilla*, type genus + *-idae*] **:** a family of oscine birds comprising the wagtails and the pipits
[1]**mote** \'mōt\ *verbal auxiliary, past* **moste** \'mōst\ [ME *moten*, fr. OE *mōtan* to be allowed to, be able to, have to — more at MUST] *archaic* **:** MAY, MIGHT
[2]**mote** \'mōt, *usu* -ōd·+V\ *n* -S [ME *mot, moot*, fr. OE *mot;* akin to MD & Fris *mot* earth, sand, Norw *mutt* speck] **1 a :** a small particle (as of floating dust) **:** SPECK ⟨~s danced in the shafts of sunlight —Margaret Kennedy⟩ **b** *archaic* **:** a bit of foreign matter in food or drink **c** *obs* **:** something extremely minute **:** TRIFLE, JOT, TITTLE **2** *dial Brit* **:** STRAW, STALK **3 a :** a small undeveloped seed or fragment that has not been removed in cotton ginning **b :** a black spot in yarn or cloth due to such an impurity — **mote in the eye :** a comparatively slight fault noted in another person by one who fails to see a greater fault in himself ⟨why beholdest thou the ~ that is in thy brother's eye, but considerest not the beam that is in thine own eye —Mt 7: 3 (AV)⟩
[3]**mote** \"\ *vt* -ED/-ING/-S **:** to remove motes from (cotton)
[4]**mote** \"\ *n* -S [ME, fr. OF *mote, motte* mound, hillock, mote — more at MOTTE] **1** *or* **mote hill :** HEIGHT, HILL; *esp* **:** an elevated place used as a fortification **2 :** BARROW, TUMULUS
**mot·ed** \-ōd·əd\ *adj* [[2]*mote* + *-ed*] **:** filled with motes ⟨~ sunbeam —Alfred Tennyson⟩
**mo·tel** \(')mō¦tel\ *n* -S [blend of *motor* and *hotel*] **:** a hotel for automobile tourists; *specif* **:** a group of furnished cabins or attached cottages near a highway that offer accommodation to tourists ⟨an endless row of . . . two-story ~s —Bennett Cerf⟩
**mo·tet** \mō'tet, *usu* -ed·+V\ *n* -S [ME, fr. MF, dim. of *mot* word — more at MOT] **1 a :** a polyphonic choral musical composition of a kind originated in the 13th century, based on a sacred Latin text, designed for church performance, and usu. sung unaccompanied — compare MADRIGAL 2a **b :** the English anthem **2 :** a polyphonic instrumental composition intended for church performance
**mo·te·tus** \mō'tēd·əs\ *n* -ES [ML *motetus, motetum*, fr. MF *motet*] **1 :** the middle voice or the voice above the tenor in medieval motets **2 :** MOTET 1a
**motey** \'mōd·ē\ *adj* [[2]*mote* + *-y*] **:** full of motes
[1]**moth** \'mȯth *also* 'mäth\ *n, pl* **moths** \thz, |ths, |z\ *often attrib* [ME *mothe*, fr. OE *moththe;* akin to MD & MLG *motte, mutte* moth, MHG *motte*, ON *motti*, and perh. to OE *matha* worm, maggot — more at MAGGOT] **1 a** (1) **:** CLOTHES MOTH (2) **:** an insect that feeds on materials (as woolens and furs) — compare CARPET BEETLE, DERMESTES **b** *obs* **:** any obnoxious insect (as a mosquito, roach, or maggot) **c :** any of various insects that constitute a major division (Heterocera) of the order Lepidoptera, are usu. nocturnal or crepuscular, have antennae which are often feathery and rarely clubbed, are typically stouter-bodied, less brilliantly colored, and proportionately smaller winged than the butterflies, and have larvae which are caterpillars and feed often very destructively on vegetation — see GYPSY MOTH, SILK MOTH **2** *archaic* **:** a thing or a person that gradually eats away, wastes, or consumes something **3 :** MOTH GRAY **4 :** a class of racing sailboat of varying design but having an overall length of 11 ft. and 73 sq. ft. of sail area; *also* **:** a boat in this class
[2]**moth** \"\ *vi* -ED/-ING/-S **:** to hunt for moths
[1]**mothball** \'ˌ=\ *n* [[1]*moth* + *ball*] **1 :** a ball of the size of a marble made formerly of camphor but now of naphthalene and used to keep moths from clothing **2 mothballs** *pl* **:** the condition of being put into protective storage or relegated to a reserve, standby, or caretaker status ⟨the warships in ~s at the Puget Sound Naval shipyard —*N.Y.Times*⟩ ⟨a million-dollar aluminum powder plant . . . is being taken out of ~s Monday —*Wall Street Jour.*⟩ ⟨then the war ended and ~s took over —E.L.Beach⟩; *also* **:** a state of having been rejected for further use or dismissed from further consideration ⟨you can put that idea into ~s and forget it⟩
[2]**mothball** \"\ *vt* -ED/-ING/-S **:** to inactivate and preserve (as a ship) chiefly by dehumidification ⟨plastic . . . is sprayed over the gun mount of a ship being ~*ed* —*All Hands*⟩ ⟨our sick bay had been ~*ed* —J.J.Micka⟩ ⟨the packing plant ~*ed* for five years —*Newsweek*⟩
[3]**mothball** \"\ *adj* **:** PRESERVED, INACTIVATED ⟨~ ships⟩
**mothball fleet** *n* **:** an aggregate of inactivated preserved warships that can be commissioned and made ready for war in a few months; *specif* **:** the U. S. Navy Reserve Fleet ⟨the entrance of the battleship . . . into the *mothball fleet* —*All Hands*⟩
**moth bean** *also* **moth** *n* -S [*moth* prob. by folk etymology (influence of [1]*moth*) fr. Marathi *maṭh* moth bean, fr. Skt *makuṣṭa*] **1 :** an East Indian bean (*Phaseolus aconitifolius*) that is used esp. in India as a forage and soil-conditioning crop and has hairy foliage, small yellow flowers, and cylindrical pods **2 :** the small yellowish brown seed of the moth bean used as food in India
**moth borer** *n, chiefly Brit* **:** a moth whose larva is a borer
**moth–eaten** \'ˌ=ˌ=\ *adj* **1 a :** eaten into by moths ⟨*moth-eaten* cloth⟩ **b :** having the appearance of something eaten into by moths ⟨a *moth-eaten* horse ready for the glue factory —C.V. Little⟩ **:** PATCHY, RAGGEDY, UNKEMPT ⟨a little man . . . with *moth-eaten* hair —W.A.White⟩ **2 a :** DILAPIDATED ⟨the town had one *moth-eaten* old museum —C.W.Thayer⟩ ⟨a lot of *moth-eaten* barges —John Buchan⟩ **b :** ANTIQUATED, OUTMODED ⟨the *moth-eaten* motto of some of the . . . aristocracy —W.H.Stevenson⟩ ⟨*moth-eaten* . . . theories about race —Dwight Macdonald⟩
[1]**moth·er** \'məthə(r)\ *n* -S [ME *moder*, fr. OE *mōdor;* akin to OHG *muoter* mother, ON *mōthir*, L *mater*, Gk *mētēr*, Skt *mātṛ*] **1 a :** a woman who has given birth to a child **:** a female parent ⟨a ~ of five⟩ ⟨food for the nursing ~⟩ ⟨in the union of the sexual cells the chromosomes coming from the ~ —S.F. Mason⟩ ⟨in chimpanzees the female's functions as ~ and mate alternate in stretches of time —Weston La Barre⟩ **b :** one related to another in a way paralleling or suggesting the relation of mother to child: as (1) **:** one to whom a filial affection and respect are usu. due **:** adoptive mother **:** STEPMOTHER, MOTHER-IN-LAW (2) **:** a woman having authority or dignity like that of a mother ⟨because these class ~s proved so helpful —Gertrude H. Hildreth⟩ **c :** an elderly woman — often used preceding the surname ⟨*Mother* Hubbard⟩ **2 a :** one that has produced or nurtured something **:** parent stock **:** SOURCE ⟨although nature is our ~, she is not a complete guide to human conduct —Brooks Atkinson⟩ ⟨the fertile ~ of . . . civilizations —Edward Clodd⟩ ⟨Hebrew was considered the ~ of European languages —R.W.Weiman⟩ ⟨the free press is the ~ of all our liberties —A.E.Stevenson b.1900⟩ **b :** PROTOTYPE ⟨huge ~ of ocean liners, she was five times the size of the largest vessel then afloat —C.V.Woodward⟩ **3 a** *obs* **:** WOMB ⟨diseases of the ~ —William Coles⟩ **b** *archaic* **:** HYSTERIA ⟨the particular diseases of this sign are . . . hardness of the spleen, ~, hypochondriac melancholy —Ebenezer Sibly⟩ **4 :** feeling (as tenderness or affection) inherited from or characteristic of a mother ⟨all my ~ came into mine eyes and gave me up to tears —Shak.⟩ ⟨all the ~ in her soul awakes —Alexander Pope⟩ **5 :** MOTHER LIQUOR — usu. used in pl. with *the* **6 :** a device for sheltering chickens after incubation — called also *artificial mother* **7 :** MATRIX 4f
[2]**mother** \"\ *vt* **mothered; mothered; mothering** \-th(ə)riŋ\ **mothers 1 a :** to give birth to ⟨she ~*ed* five sons but no daughters⟩ **b :** to give rise to as if by birth **:** PRODUCE ⟨this . . . unexplored country has ~*ed* many legends —V.W.Von Hagen⟩ **2 :** to care for, cherish, or protect in the manner of a mother ⟨all his life . . . he had to be ~*ed* by somebody —Van Wyck Brooks⟩ **3 a :** to acknowledge that one is the mother or author of **b :** to attribute the maternity or origin of to a particular person **4 :** to act as a protective-fire cover or escort for in a military or naval operation ⟨the low-flying contact machines . . . ~*ing* the infantry —*Airman's Outings*⟩ ⟨~*ing* subs off the Grand Banks —*Atlantic*⟩
[3]**mother** \"\ *adj* **1 a :** of, relating to, or being a mother ⟨~ love⟩ ⟨~ pains⟩ **b :** bearing a relationship to others that is parallel to or suggestive of that of a mother ⟨~ lodge⟩ ⟨~ stream⟩ **2 :** derived from or as if from one's mother ⟨~ dialect⟩ **3 :** acting as or providing parental stock — used without reference to sex ⟨~ plant⟩ ⟨~ tubercle⟩ ⟨pollen ~ cells —*Americana Annual*⟩
[4]**mother** \"\ *n* -S [akin to MD *modder, moeder* mud, swamp, dregs, lees, MLG *moder, modder* putrid body, swampland, *mudde* thick mud — more at MUD] **1** *archaic* **:** LEES, DREGS **2** *or* **mother of vinegar :** a slimy membrane that develops on the surface of alcoholic liquids undergoing acetous fermentation, that is composed of yeast cells and bacteria of the genus *Acetobacter* (esp. *A. acetus* syn. *Mycoderma aceti*) which produce the fermentation, and that is added to wine or cider as a starter to produce vinegar
[5]**mother** \"\ *vi* -ED/-S **:** to become mothery ⟨her wines sour and pickles ~ —Samuel Johnson⟩
**mother aircraft** *n* **1 :** an aircraft electronically equipped to direct the flight of a drone **2 :** a large aircraft modified to carry piloted or unpiloted aircraft that can be launched and recovered in flight
**mother bed** *or* **mother block** *n* **:** an area that is devoted to plants known to be free from diseases and true to type and that is used as a source of stock for propagation
**mother bulb** *n* **:** a bulb (as of a narcissus) that produces several offsets
**mother car·ey's chicken** \-'ka(a)rēz-\ *n, usu cap M&1stC* [origin unknown] **:** any of several small petrels; *esp* **:** STORM PETREL
**mother carey's goose** *n, usu cap M&C* **:** GIANT PETREL
**mother carey's hen** *n, usu cap M&C* **:** a petrel of medium size
**mother cell** *n* **:** a cell from which another usu. of a different sort is formed ⟨a sperm *mother cell*⟩
**mother church** *n* **1** *archaic* **:** a parish church ⟨the *mother churches* . . . and rural chapels in the late Saxon and early Norman periods —*Bull. of Inst. of Historical Research*⟩ **2 :** the principal church of a locality or land; *specif* **:** a cathedral or a metropolitan church ⟨the *mother church* . . . which no visitor to these parts should fail to see —T.I.Ellis⟩ **3 :** the original church from which others have sprung ⟨the *mother church* of Unitarianism in America —Leo Pfeffer⟩ **4 :** the original church or communion in which a person has been nurtured ⟨returning to his *mother church*, he died in obscurity —K.S.Latourette⟩
**mother–city** \'=ˌ=ˌ=\ *n* **:** METROPOLIS ⟨they still kept in touch with the *mother-city* —E.R.Bevan⟩
**mother cloves** *n pl* **:** the dried fruits of the clove tree that resemble the true cloves but are less aromatic
**mother country** *n* **1 :** the country of one's parents or ancestors ⟨a sentimental journey back to the *mother country*⟩ **2 :** the country from which the people of a colony derive their origin ⟨a *mother country* . . . in its relationships with its overseas possessions —C.A.Buss⟩ **3 :** a country that is the origin of something ⟨the *mother country* of social graces —*Newsweek*⟩
**mothercraft** \'=ˌ=ˌ=\ *n* **:** knowledge and skill required for the care of babies and young children ⟨courses in ~ for prospective mothers —*N.Y.Times*⟩
**mother earth** *n* **1 :** the mother of everything animate or inanimate upon the earth **2 :** SOIL, GROUND
**mother goose rhyme** *n, usu cap M&G* [after *Mother Goose*, pretended author of *Mother Goose's Melodies*, a collection of nursery rhymes published in London, England, about 1760] **:** NURSERY RHYME
**moth·er·hood** \'məthə(r),hu̇d\ *n* **:** the quality or state of being a mother **:** MATERNITY ⟨~ and childhood are entitled to special care and assistance —*U. N. Declaration of Human Rights*⟩
**motherhouse** \'=ˌ=ˌ=\ *n* **1 :** the monastery or convent in which the superior general or the provincial of a religious community resides **2 :** the original monastery or convent of a religious community
**mother hubbard** \-'həbə(r)d\ *n, pl* **mother hubbards** *often cap M&H* [prob. after *Mother Hubbard*, character in a nursery rhyme (1805) by Sarah C. Martin †1826 Eng. writer; fr. the garb worn by Mother Hubbard in old illustrations] **:** a woman's loose usu. shapeless dress ⟨she had an old *mother hubbard* wrapped loosely about her —Bill Ballinger⟩
**mother·ing** *n* -S **:** a rural custom in England of visiting one's parents on Mid-Lent Sunday and presenting a gift
**mother–in–law** \'məthə(r)ən,lȯ, -thrən-, -thə(r)n-\ *n, pl* **mothers–in–law** \-thə(r)zən-\ [ME *moder in lawe*] **1 :** the mother of one's spouse **2 :** STEPMOTHER
**mother–in–law plant** *n* **:** DUMB CANE
**motherland** \'=ˌ=ˌ=\ *n* **1 :** the land of origin of something ⟨Germany . . . the ~ of philology —René Wellek⟩ **2 :** the home country of colonies or former colonies ⟨ballads brought into this country from the ~ —*Dial*⟩ **3 :** one's native land or country **:** the country to which one claims native allegiance **:** FATHERLAND ⟨nurture our children in affectionate regard for the ~ —J.L.Childs⟩
**moth·er·less** \'məthə(r)ləs\ *adj* [ME *moderles*, fr. OE *mōdorlēas*, fr. *mōdor* mother + *-lēas* -less — more at MOTHER] **:** having no mother; *esp* **:** having no mother living ⟨a ~ child⟩ — **moth·er·less·ness** *n* -ES
**moth·er·li·ness** \-lēnəs, -lin-\ *n* -ES **:** maternal quality **:** the tenderness, warmth, or affection of or befitting a mother ⟨her ~ made her invaluable in caring for the twins —Elizabeth Goudge⟩
**mother liquor** *also* **mother liquid** *n* **:** a residual liquid resulting from crystallization and remaining after the substances that readily or regularly crystallize have been removed — called also *mother water*
**mother lode** *n* **:** the principal vein or lode of a region (as of gold-bearing quartz along the western foothills of the Sierra Nevada, Calif.)
[1]**moth·er·ly** \-lē, -li\ *adj* [ME *moderly* fr. OE *mōdorlīc*, fr. *mōdor* mother + *-lic* -ly] **1 :** of, befitting, or proper to a mother ⟨her ~ instincts had been aroused —Hervey Allen⟩ ⟨~ tenderness —A. Conan Doyle⟩ ⟨in a ~ tone —Ellen Glasgow⟩ **2 :** resembling a mother in love, protectiveness, or conduct **:** maternally soft, warm, or sympathetic **:** MATERNAL ⟨a handsome and ~ young woman —Floyd Dell⟩
[2]**motherly** \"\ *adv* [ME *moderly*, fr. *moderly*, adj.] *archaic* **:** in a motherly manner
**mother mark** *var of* MOTHER'S MARK
**mother–naked** \ˌ=ˌ='=\ *adj* [ME *moder naked*, fr. *moder* mother + *naked*] **:** naked as at birth **:** stark naked ⟨caught *mother-naked* in the full glare of a searchlight —Campbell Nairne⟩ — **mother–na·ked·ness** *n*
**mother of coal :** MINERAL CHARCOAL
**mother–of–millions** \ˌ=ˌ=ˌ='=\ *n pl but usu sing in constr* **:** KENILWORTH IVY
[1]**mother–of–pearl** \ˌ=ˌ=ˌ='=\ *n* -S **:** the hard pearly iridescent internal layer of various mollusk shells (as of pearl oysters, river mussels, abalones) that is extensively used for making small articles (as buttons) and inlays **:** NACRE; *sometimes* **:** a shell or a shellfish having such a pearly layer
[2]**mother–of–pearl** \"\ *adj* [[1]*mother-of-pearl*] **:** IRIDESCENT — used esp. of the luster of a glaze or enamel
**mother–of–pearl cloud** *n* **:** NACREOUS CLOUD
**mother–of–thousands** \ˌ=ˌ=ˌ='=\ *n pl but usu sing in constr* **1 :** KENILWORTH IVY **2 :** STRAWBERRY GERANIUM **3 :** DAISY 1
**mother–of–thyme** \ˌ=ˌ=ˌ='=\ *n* -S **1 :** WILD THYME **2 :** BASIL BALM 2
**mother of vinegar** [[4]*mother*] **:** [4]MOTHER 2
**mother–of–wheat** \ˌ=ˌ=ˌ='=\ *n* -S **1 :** COWWHEAT **2 :** IVY-LEAVED SPEEDWELL
**mother plane** *or* **mother ship** *n* **:** an airplane that carries, launches, or controls another aircraft
**mother right** *n* [prob. trans. of G *mutterrecht*] **:** the matriarchal principle or custom **:** MATRIARCHY 2
**mothers** *pl of* MOTHER, *pres 3d sing of* MOTHER
**mother's boy** *n* **:** a boy or young man who is excessively attached to his mother; *esp* **:** one who as a result of such an at-

tachment is disinclined to follow masculine pursuits or assume masculine responsibilities ⟨his grandfather . . . fearing that the youth was on his way to becoming a *mother's boy*, taught him to swim at an early age —E.J.Kahn⟩ — compare MAMA'S BOY

**mother's day** *n, usu cap M&D* **:** a day (as the second Sunday in May) appointed for the special honoring of mothers by their children

**mother's–heart** \ˈ==,=\ *n, pl* **mother's–hearts :** SHEPHERD'S-PURSE

**mother ship** *n* **1** *chiefly Brit* **:** a naval vessel escorting or guarding smaller craft (as torpedo boats or submarines) **2 :** a ship serving several smaller craft **:** TENDER

**mother–sib** \ˈ==,=\ *n* **:** sib based on matrilineal descent

**mother's mark** *or* **mother mark** *n* **:** BIRTHMARK

**mother superior** *n, pl* **mother superiors** *also* **mothers superior :** a nun who is the head of a religious house

**mother tongue** *n* **1 :** the language of one's mother **:** the language naturally acquired in infancy and childhood **:** one's first language **2 :** a language from which another language originates

**mother tree** *n* **:** SEED TREE

**moth·er·um·bung** \,məthə'rəm,bəŋ\ *or* **moth·er·um·bah** \-mbə\ *n* -s [native name in Australia] **:** a shrub or small tree (*Acacia cheelii*) of Australia having the flowers in spikes or threes and in spikes and the fruit narrow and flat with a thickened margin

**mother water** *n* **:** MOTHER LIQUOR

**mother wit** *n* **:** natural or native wit or intelligence

**motherwort** \ˈ==,=\ *n* -s [ME *moderwort*, fr. *moder* mother + *wort* — more at MOTHER, WORT] **1 :** a plant of the genus *Leonurus; esp* **:** a bitter Old World mint (*L. cardiaca*) with dentate wedge-shaped leaves and axillary whorls of small purple flowers **2 :** MUGWORT 1 **3 :** FEVERFEW **4 :** MARSH MILKWEED **5 :** MONEYWORT

**moth·ery** \ˈməth(ə)rē\ *adj* [⁴*mother* + *-y*] **:** consisting of, containing, or resembling mother ⟨~ vinegar⟩ ⟨~ mold⟩

**mother yaw** *n* **:** the initial superficial lesion of yaws appearing at the site of inoculation after an incubation period of several weeks

**moth fly** *or* **moth gnat** *or* **moth–midge** \ˈ=,=\ *n* **:** a small two-winged fly of the family Psychodidae having hairy or scaly wings

**moth gray** *n* **:** a grayish yellow that is paler and slightly redder than chamois, redder and paler than old ivory, and redder and lighter than crash — called also *sheepskin*

**moth hawk** *or* **moth hunter** *n* **:** GOATSUCKER

**mothing** *pres part of* MOTH

**moth miller** *n* **:** MILLER 2a

**moth mullein** *n* **:** a European mullein (*Verbascum blattaria*) that is naturalized as a weed in America and that has smooth leaves and large yellow or purplish flowers

**moth orchid** *or* **moth plant** *n* **:** an orchid of the genus *Phalaenopsis* (esp. *P. amabilis*)

¹**mothproof** \ˈ=,=\ *adj* [¹*moth* + *proof*] **:** impervious to penetration by moths ⟨~ wool⟩

²**mothproof** \"\ *vt* -ED/-ING/-S **:** to make mothproof ⟨~*ing* textile fabrics —*Chem. Abstracts*⟩

**moths** *pl of* MOTH, *pres 3d sing of* MOTH

**mothy** \ˈmȯthē\ *adj* -ER/-EST **:** full of moths

**mo·tif** \mōˈtēf\ *n* -s [F, motive, motif — more at MOTIVE] **1 a :** a usu. recurring salient thematic element or feature (as in a work of art); *esp* **:** a dominant idea or central theme ⟨the isles of the blest, the mandrake, the stone monster . . . there is enough material from comparative religion to elucidate these ~*s* —G.L.Anderson⟩ ⟨ran like a ~ through his letters of those years —*Atlantic*⟩ ⟨the ~ of disillusion —G.R.Hamilton⟩ ⟨an excellent ~ for a novel —*Times Lit. Supp.*⟩ **b :** a single or repeated design or color (as in interior decoration or clothes designing) ⟨mulberry and silver form the color ~ of the decorations —*N.Y.Times*⟩ ⟨a brown necktie tastily done out in a skyscraper ~ —Pierce Fredericks⟩ **c :** MOTIVE 5 ⟨flute ~⟩ ⟨the familiar device of development by reiteration of short simple ~*s* with chromatic ornamentation —Henry Cowell⟩ **2 :** an influence or stimulus prompting to action ⟨the proselyting ~ was not forgotten —*Atlantic*⟩ ⟨the profit ~ —*Saturday Rev.*⟩ ⟨the ~ of the new measure is reformation —*Spectator*⟩

¹**mo·tile** \ˈmōd·ᵊl, -ōt'l, -ō,tīl, -ō(,)til\ *adj* [L *motus* (past part. of *movēre* to move) + E *-ile* — more at MOVE] **:** exhibiting or capable of movement ⟨~ cilia⟩ ⟨~ spores⟩

²**motile** \"\ *n* -s **:** one whose prevailing mental imagery is motor rather than visual or auditory and takes the form of inner feelings of action (as incipient pronunciation of words, muscular movements) — compare AUDILE, TACTILE, VISUALIZER

**mo·til·i·ty** \mōˈtiləd·ē, -ətē, -i\ *n* -ES **:** the quality or state of being motile **:** CONTRACTILITY ⟨gastrointestinal ~ —*Science*⟩

**mo·ti·lón** \,mōd·ə'lōn\ *n, pl* **motilón** \"\ *or* **motilo·nes** \-lō,nās\ *usu cap* [Sp, of AmerInd origin] **1 a :** a Cariban people of northern Colombia and Venezuela **b :** a member of such people **2 :** the language of the Motilón people

**moting** *pres part of* MOTE

¹**motion** \ˈmōshən\ *n* -s [ME *mocioun*, fr. MF *motion*, fr. L *motion-, motio* movement, fr. *motus* (past part. of *movēre* to move) + *-ion-, -io* -ion — more at MOVE] **1 a** *obs* **:** PROMPTING, SUGGESTION ⟨give ear to his ~ —Shak.⟩ **b :** a formal proposal made in a deliberative assembly ⟨a ~ of censure⟩ ⟨a ~ to adjourn⟩ ⟨the ~ has been seconded⟩ ⟨the ~*s* to discharge and to table may be filed at the same time —Don Irwin⟩ **c :** an application made to a court or judge orally in open court or in written form to obtain an order, ruling, or direction in favor of the applicant usu. to advance the case toward trial or hearing, obtain some interlocutory advantage, or relieve from some injustice but sometimes to obtain for the applicant a final decree or judgment on some matter of law after a hearing or trial on pleadings or after evidence is taken ⟨on ~ of the defendant's lawyer⟩ ⟨~ to quash the indictment⟩ ⟨the ~ for a new trial was denied —Max & Edna A. Lerner⟩ **2 :** an irregular stirring, shaking, or oscillating movement **:** AGITATION ⟨the ~ of the water⟩ ⟨the swaying ~ of the train⟩ ⟨there was no ~ in the heavy sultry atmosphere —W.H.Hudson †1922⟩ **3 a :** the action or process of a body passing from one place or position to another ⟨the ~ of the planets⟩ ⟨a pendulum in ~⟩ **b :** such action or process conceived in terms of one of its characteristics (as direction, course, velocity) ⟨linear ~⟩ ⟨angular ~⟩ ⟨rotational ~⟩ ⟨the earth, according to the Copernican scheme . . . has three ~*s* —G.C.Sellery⟩ ⟨learned in the valuing of ~ . . . I saw that we were now running thirteen miles an hour —Thomas DeQuincey⟩ **c** *obs* **:** a constant moving from place to place ⟨my perpetual ~*s* . . . between Wotton and London —John Evelyn⟩ **d :** a process of change — used chiefly in philosophy ⟨four kinds of ~: substantial (origin and decay); quantitative (change in the size of a body by addition and subtraction); qualitative (transformation of one thing into another); and local (change of place) —Frank Thilly⟩ **4 :** an impulse or inclination of the mind, will, or desires **:** MOVEMENT 2a(1) ⟨between the acting of a dreadful thing and the first ~ —Shak.⟩ ⟨those obscure ~*s* of the mind —J.C. Powys⟩ ⟨the fundamental ~*s* of humanity to good or evil —T.S.Eliot⟩ ⟨studied navigation of his own ~ —*Times Lit. Supp.*⟩ **5 a :** an act or instance of moving the body or any of its members **:** GESTURE ⟨every ~ in the old dances had meaning —Reginald & Gladys Laubin⟩ ⟨every . . . ~ of her head —H.M.Reichard⟩ ⟨signaled with a ~ of his arm⟩ ⟨a sucking ~⟩ **b :** style of moving **:** CARRIAGE 2b ⟨personal habits, such as vocalization . . . ~, and address —William James⟩ **c** *obs* **:** power of moving ⟨devoid of sense and ~ —John Milton⟩ **d :** a conventionalized bodily movement (as a step, gait, athletic movement) ⟨the standard ~*s* of a show horse⟩ **e** *obs* **:** bodily exercise ⟨when in your ~ you are hot and dry —Shak.⟩ **f** *archaic* **:** ACTIVITY — usu. used in pl. ⟨taking advantage of the night to conceal his ~*s* —George Stanhope⟩ **g :** the change or prospective change (as of attitude or position) suggested by the posture of an artistic figure ⟨the expressive ~ of the statue⟩ **6** *obs* **a :** PUPPET SHOW ⟨a ~ of the Prodigal Son —Shak.⟩ **b :** PUPPET ⟨did you think you had married a ~ —Ben Jonson⟩ **7 a :** an evacuation of the bowels ⟨has no control over . . . urine or ~*s* —*Farmer's Weekly* (*So. Africa*)⟩ **b :** the matter evacuated — often used in the pl. ⟨blood in the ~*s* —*Lancet*⟩ **8 a :** the wheelwork of a watch **:** MOVEMENT 3 **b :** MECHANISM ⟨a straight-line ~⟩ ⟨link ~⟩ ⟨loosen lower ~ . . . and turn —*Civil Engineering*⟩ **9 a :** melodic change of pitch in the successive musical tones of a voice part ⟨note repetitions and scalewise ~ quite foreign to characteristic twelve-tone practice —Arthur Berger⟩ **b :** melodic progression of two or more voice parts relatively considered ⟨transition is by way of a passage in contrary ~ for the woodwinds —A.K. Holland⟩

²**motion** \"\ *vb* **motioned; motioned; motioning** \-sh(ə)niŋ\ **motions** *vt* **1** *archaic* **:** PROPOSE, RECOMMEND ⟨what I ~*ed* was of God —John Milton⟩ **2 :** to direct by a motion (as of the hand or head) ⟨~*ed* them to come quietly —Jean Stafford⟩ ⟨~*ed* me to a seat —L.C.Douglas⟩ ~ *vi* **1** *archaic* **:** to propose or suggest a plan or action ⟨well hast thou ~'*d* —John Milton⟩ **2** *archaic* **:** to move in such a way as to suggest an intended action ⟨this he declined, ~*ing* at the same time to go away —Helena Wells⟩ **3 :** to signal by a movement or gesture (as of the hand) ⟨the pitcher ~*ed* to the catcher⟩ **4 :** to vibrate in angular rotation — used of a watch balance ⟨a mainspring should . . . make the watch ~ properly —*Watchmakers' Handbook*⟩

**mo·tion·al** \-shənᵊl, -shnəl\ *adj* **:** of, relating to, or characterized by motion **:** KINETIC

**motional impedance** *n* **:** the part of the electrical impedance in a telephone receiver or loudspeaker that is due to the motion of the diaphragm

**motion and time study** *n* **:** TIME AND MOTION STUDY

**motioner** *n* -s *obs* **:** one that proposes or instigates

**mo·tion·less** \-shənləs\ *adj* **:** being without motion **:** STILL — **mo·tion·less·ly** *adv* — **mo·tion·less·ness** *n* -ES

**motion picture** *n* **1 :** a series of pictures (as photographs taken with a special camera) presented to the eye in very rapid succession with some or all of the objects in the scene represented in successive positions slightly changed so as to produce because of persistence of vision the optical effect of a continuous picture in which the objects move — see SOUND MOTION PICTURE **2 :** a representation of a story or other subject matter by means of motion pictures

**motion–picture camera** *n* **:** a camera adapted to make rapid exposure of moving objects on a strip of film perforated along the edges to ensure accurate registration

**motion–picture projector** *n* **:** a machine that projects and shows motion pictures on a screen and that is usu. fitted with suitable electrical or mechanical attachments for reproducing sound in synchronism with the picture — compare SOUND PROJECTOR

**motion plate** *n, Brit* **:** a transverse plate usu. of annealed cast steel which is situated between the cylinders and driving axle of an inside-cylinder locomotive and to which the slide bars and intermediate valve-rod guides are attached

**motion sickness** *n* **:** sickness induced by motion (as in travel by air, car, or ship) and characterized by nausea

**motion study** *n* **:** TIME AND MOTION STUDY

**motion work** *n* **:** the wheelwork controlling the relative motions of the hour and minute hands of a timepiece

**mo·ti·ta·tion** \,mōd·əˈtāshən\ *n* -s [L *motitatus* (past part. of *motitare* to move often, move about, freq. of *motare* to keep moving, move about, fr. *motus*, past part. of *movēre* to move) + E *-ion* — more at MOVE] **:** a quivering movement

**mo·ti·vate** \ˈmōd·ə,vāt, -ōtə-, *usu* -ād·+V\ *vt* -ED/-ING/-S [¹*motive* + *-ate*] **1 :** to provide with a motive **:** IMPEL, INCITE ⟨the deep unconscious and subconscious factors that ~ people —Vance Packard⟩ ⟨the novelist has adequately *motivated* his hero⟩ **2 a :** to stimulate the active interest of in a study through appeal to associated interests or by special devices ⟨the ingenious teacher can ferret out a thousand methods of *motivating* the child to learn new words —*Education Digest*⟩ **b :** to make (a study) interesting or otherwise appealing to students ⟨program . . . is thoroughly *motivated* —D.H.Patton⟩

**mo·ti·va·tion** \,==ˈvāshən\ *n* -s [¹*motive* + *-ation*] **1 :** the act or process of motivating ⟨Shakespeare . . . neglected ~ when it was already supplied in his sources —Muriel C. Bradbrook⟩ ⟨in the secondary school ~ involves many types of activities —D.G.Tarbet⟩ **2 :** a motivating force or influence **:** DRIVE, INCENTIVE ⟨sex as the ~ of animal behavior —E.A.Armstrong⟩ ⟨economic ~⟩ ⟨the most intrinsic ~ for learning is the child's spontaneous interests —Bernice Neugarten & Nelle Wright⟩ **3 :** the condition of being motivated ⟨found to have good ~ and high morale —*Jour. Amer. Med. Assoc.*⟩ ⟨~ was at a very high level, and the students did not have to be prodded —Haym Kruglak⟩

**mo·ti·va·tion·al** \;==ˈvāshənᵊl, -shnəl\ *adj* **:** of or relating to motivation ⟨~ research⟩ ⟨~ approach⟩ ⟨~ factors⟩

**mo·ti·va·tive** \-ād·iv\ *adj* **:** of, relating to, or providing motivation ⟨it may well be that ethical language has primarily a ~ function —Arthur Pap⟩

¹**mo·tive** \ˈmōd·|iv, -ōt|, |ēv *also* |əv; *in senses 4 and 5* " *or* mōˈtēv\ *n* -s [ME, fr. MF *motif*, fr. *motif*, adj., moving, causing to move, fr. ML *motivus*, fr. L *motus* (past part. of *movēre* to move) + *-ivus* -ive — more at MOVE] **1 a :** something within a person (as need, idea, organic state, or emotion) that incites him to action ⟨ordinarily his ~ is a wish to . . . avoid unfavorable notice and comment —Thorstein Veblen⟩ **b :** the consideration or object influencing a choice or prompting an action ⟨the principal ~ of American policy —C.E.Black & E.C.Helmreich⟩ ⟨the ~ for the crime⟩ **2** *obs* **a :** a prompting force or incitement working on a person to influence volition or action **:** MOVER, INSTIGATOR, CAUSE ⟨nature, whose ~ in this case should stir me most —Shak.⟩ ⟨am I the ~ of these tears —Shak.⟩ **3** *obs* **:** a part of the body capable of movement ⟨her wanton spirits look out at every joint and ~ of her body —Shak.⟩ **4** [F, fr. MF, motive] **a :** the guiding or controlling idea in an artistic work or in one of its parts **b :** MOTIF 1b **5** [G *motiv*, fr. F *motif*] **:** THEME, SUBJECT; *specif* **:** a leading phrase or figure that is reproduced and varied through the course of a musical composition or movement — compare LEITMOTIV

**syn** MOTIVE, SPRING, IMPULSE, INCENTIVE, INDUCEMENT, SPUR, and GOAD can mean, in common, a stimulus prompting a person to act in a particular way. MOTIVE can apply to any emotion, desire, or appetite operating on the will of a person and moving him to act ⟨the habit so prevalent with us of always seeking the *motive* of everyone's speech or behavior —W.C. Brownell⟩ ⟨shielding her husband's murderer, from whatever *motives* of pity or friendship —Rose Macaulay⟩ ⟨it was the deepest *motive* of her soul, this self mistrust —D.H.Lawrence⟩ SPRING, usu. in the plural, is usu. interchangeable with MOTIVE, possibly more frequently applying to a hidden or not fully recognized stimulus to action ⟨the *springs* and consequences of international policy —David Mitrany⟩ ⟨the mysteriously working emotional *springs* of human action⟩ IMPULSE stresses impetus or driving power rather than an effect; in a general sense, it can apply to any strong incitement to activity, esp. one deriving from personal temperament or constitution ⟨the religious *impulse* and the scientific *impulse* —Havelock Ellis⟩ ⟨one strong *impulse* that bound them together — their common love of fine horses —Sherwood Anderson⟩ ⟨the extraordinary vitality of the critical *impulse* in American letters —C.I.Glicksberg⟩ ⟨the *impulse* that led to the evolution of man —Joshua Whatmough⟩ but in a more special use it applies to a spontaneous, often irrational urge to do something ⟨the first *impulse* of a child in a garden is to pick every attractive flower —Bertrand Russell⟩ ⟨suffered an odd *impulse* to get up and kick his chair over —Mary Austin⟩ INCENTIVE applies chiefly to a cause inciting or encouraging to action, applying commonly to some external reward ⟨his love for the family was a strong *incentive* to continued effort in their behalf⟩ ⟨money is not the only *incentive* to work, nor the strongest —G.B.Shaw⟩ ⟨the only *incentive* to travel . . . was the luxury of the accommodation —O.S.Nock⟩ INDUCEMENT implies an external influence and often a purposeful attempt to entice to action ⟨the chief *inducements* to serve were the pension and the right of citizenship which awaited a soldier on his discharge —John Buchan⟩ ⟨a community that . . . holds young people and offers *inducements* to them to stay and help build a greater home town —J.C.Penney⟩ ⟨free gas was offered to factories as an *inducement* for locating in towns —*Amer. Guide Series: Ind.*⟩ SPUR applies to any impetus which can stir to action or increase energy or ardor in an action already undertaken ⟨fear or despair may be a temporary *spur* to action —*Saturday Rev.*⟩ ⟨under the *spur* of his annoyance —Hamilton Basso⟩ ⟨Russia with its drive for warm water ports, China with its inexorable pressure of population — they, too, have a physical *spur* to expansive policies —Barbara Ward⟩ GOAD can apply to anything that strongly incites to action or keeps one in action against one's will or desire ⟨the threat of . . . aggression was a standing *goad* to the defense effort —*N.Y.Times*⟩ ⟨was . . . a *goad* for an indolent writer —Van Wyck Brooks⟩

²**mo·tive** \ˈmōd·|iv, -ōt|, |ēv *also* |əv\ *adj* [MF or ML; MF *motif*, fr. ML *motivus* — more at ¹MOTIVE] **1 :** moving or tending to move to action ⟨the ~ arguments⟩ **2 :** having or concerned with the function of initiating action ⟨the ~ nerves⟩ **3 :** of or relating to motion or the causing of motion ⟨~ energy⟩

³**motive** \"\ *vt* -ED/-ING/-S [¹*motive*] **:** MOTIVATE 1

**mo·tive·less** \|əvləs\ *adj* **:** lacking a motive ⟨~ malignity —S.T.Coleridge⟩ — **mo·tive·less·ly** *adv* — **mo·tive·less·ness** *n* -ES

**motive power** *n* **1 :** an agency (as water, steam, wind, electricity) used to impart motion to machinery **:** MOTOR, MOVER **2 :** the locomotives of a railroad

**mo·ti·vic** \ˈmōd·əvik\ *also* **mo·ti·val** \-vəl\ *adj* [¹*motive* + *-ic* or *-al*] **:** of or relating to a musical motive ⟨~ variation . . . through which the composer is able to create areas of tension and relaxation —Virgil Thomson⟩

**mo·tiv·i·ty** \mōˈtivəd·ē\ *n* -ES [²*motive* + *-ity*] **:** the power of moving or producing motion **:** available energy

**mot juste** \mōzhüst\ *n, pl* **mots justes** \mōzhüst(s)\ [F] **:** the exactly right word **:** precisely expressive phrasing ⟨pride in having found the *mot juste* —Angela Thirkell⟩

¹**mot·ley** \ˈmätlē, -li\ *adj, sometimes* **motleyer** *or* **motlier;** *sometimes* **motleyest** *or* **motliest** [ME *motteley, motley*, perh. fr. *mot* speck — more at MOTE] **1 :** marked by a mixture of usu. startlingly diverse or haphazardly arranged colors **:** PARTI-COLORED ⟨Swiss guardsmen in the strange ~ garb . . . contrived for them —Nathaniel Hawthorne⟩ ⟨clad in a ~ coat with red-and-yellow scarf —J.P.O'Donnell⟩ **2** *obs* **:** made of motley ⟨a leather bag, a ~ jacket —Richard Brathwaite⟩ **3 a :** DIVERSE, HETEROGENEOUS ⟨how ~ are the qualities that go to make up a human being —W.S.Maugham⟩ ⟨these ~ elements of skepticism and reform —Felix Frankfurter⟩ **b :** composed of a haphazard and incongruous mixture of heterogeneous elements ⟨lived in varied cities and very ~ societies —G.K. Chesterton⟩ ⟨the ~ speakers of late provincial Latin —Yakov Malkiel⟩ ⟨a ~ crowd⟩ ⟨a ~ crew⟩ ⟨a ~ scene⟩ **syn** see VARIEGATED

²**motley** \"\ *n* -s [ME *motteley, motley*, prob. fr. *motteley, motley*, adj.] **1 :** a varicolored woolen fabric woven of mixed threads in 14th to 17th century England and used esp. for clothing and cloth bags **2 a :** a garment of this fabric; *esp* **:** the characteristic dress of the professional fool ⟨~'*s* the only wear —Shak.⟩ **b :** the guise or character of a comedian ⟨no circus clown . . . when he has put aside the makeup and the ~ —Emmett Kelly⟩ ⟨a reign where even tragedy was expected to wear ~ —Frances Winwar⟩ **3 a :** a professional fool **:** JESTER ⟨all the ~*s* with their caps and bells —W.H.Dixon⟩ **b :** a person who by overfamiliarity or clowning cuts a ludicrous figure in company ⟨made myself a ~ to the view —Shak.⟩ ⟨making herself a ~ to the view with all fresh acquaintances —Angela Thirkell⟩ **4 :** a heterogeneous collection or mixture of incongruous elements **:** MEDLEY ⟨a ~ of borrowed or invented raiment —Ellen Glasgow⟩ ⟨a ~ of hand-me-downs, baggy generalities, and shabby prejudices —H.J.Muller⟩ ⟨a ~ of nations . . . thrown together —A.L.Kroeber⟩

³**motley** \"\ *vt* **motleyed; motleyed; motleying; motleys** [ME *motleyen*, fr. *motteley, motley*, adj.] **:** to make motley or variegated

**mot·mot** \ˈmät,mät\ *also* **mo·mot** \ˈmō,=\ *n* -s [NL, fr. AmerSp *mot-mot*, of imit. origin] **:** any of numerous birds of the family Momotidae confined to tropical forests from Mexico to Brazil that resemble jays in form, are colored chiefly green with blue, black, and rufous markings, and have long peculiarly shaped tails

**motmot blue** *n* **:** a moderate to strong greenish blue

**motmot green** *n* **:** a moderate yellowish green to light green

**mo·to** \ˈmōd·(,)ō, ˈmō(,)tō\ *n* -s [It, movement, motion, fr. L *motus*, past part. of *movēre* to move — more at MOVE] **:** movement with regard to musical tempo

**moto-** *comb form* [¹*motion* & ²*motor*] **:** motion **:** motor ⟨*moto*facient⟩ ⟨*moto*neuron⟩

**mo·to·neuron** *also* **mo·to·neurone** \;mōd·ō+\ *n* [*moto-* + *neuron, neurone*] **:** a motor nerve cell with its processes

**moto per·pe·tuo** \-perˈped·ə,wō\ *n* [It] **:** PERPETUUM MOBILE

¹**mo·tor** \ˈmōd·ə(r), -ōtə-\ *n* -s [L, fr. *motus* (past part. of *movēre* to move) + *-or* — more at MOVE] **1 :** one that imparts motion **:** a source of mechanical power ⟨in the medieval world view . . . the heavenly spheres and their angelic ~*s* —S.F. Mason⟩ **2 a :** PRIME MOVER **b :** a small compact engine ⟨can take twelve exposures in 5 seconds on 35 mm film with one winding of the clockwork ~ —*Eastman Kodak Monthly Abstract Bull.*⟩ ⟨~*s* powered by compressed air are used in wagon drill feeds, in hoists, and in many other machines which operate near a supply of compressed air —H.L.Nichols⟩ **c :** a gasoline engine (as for an automotive vehicle or motorboat) ⟨internal-combustion type ~ is universally called an engine in the aircraft industry —W.W.Stout⟩ **d :** INTERNAL-COMBUSTION ENGINE **3 a :** AUTOMOBILE ⟨bought the fastest ~ on the market —Victoria Sackville-West⟩ **b :** MOTOR VEHICLE ⟨a cycle and ~ dealer —Christopher Lynch-Robinson⟩ **4 :** a rotating machine that transforms electrical energy into mechanical energy and that consists mainly of a field-magnet winding or a distributed-stator winding which produces a magnetic field and a rotating armature or rotor in whose conductors flow currents which are acted upon by the magnetic field and cause rotation, some of these machines being capable of use as either motors or generators

²**motor** \"\ *adj* **1 a :** causing or imparting motion ⟨~ power⟩ **b :** of, relating to, or being a nerve or nerve fiber that passes from the central nervous system or a ganglion to a muscle and conducts an impulse that causes movement **:** EFFERENT ⟨the normal spinal ~ nerve cell —*Physical Therapy Rev.*⟩ **c :** of, relating to, or involving muscular movement ⟨~ activity⟩ ⟨~ response⟩ ⟨~ behavior patterns⟩ ⟨violent ~ reactions . . . convulsions and shakings —E.T.Clark⟩ ⟨the mental and ~ skills of effective speaking —*Quarterly Jour. of Speech*⟩ **2 a :** equipped with or driven by a motor ⟨a two-man ~ toboggan —R.M.Grant⟩ **b :** of, in, or relating to an automobile ⟨~ trip⟩ ⟨~ industry⟩ **c :** designed for motor vehicles or motorists ⟨~ road⟩ ⟨~ fuels⟩ ⟨~ hotel⟩

³**motor** \"\ *vb* -ED/-ING/-S *vi* **:** to travel by automobile **:** go by car **:** DRIVE ⟨often ~*ed* down from London —Susan Ertz⟩ ~ *vt* **1 :** to convey or transport by motorcar **:** DRIVE ⟨whose parents ~ them to many places of historic . . . interest —*Brit. Book News*⟩ **2 :** to set or keep in motion (as by a motor) ⟨it was not possible to ~ engines connected to the induction-type dynamometer —M.A.Elliott⟩

**mo·tor·able** \-ərəbəl\ *adj* [²*motor* + *-able*] *chiefly Brit* **:** usable by motor vehicles **:** PASSABLE ⟨~ roads⟩

**motor aphasia** *n* **:** the inability to speak or to organize the muscular movements of speech — compare APHASIA

**motor area** *n* **:** any of various areas of cerebral cortex believed to be associated with the initiation, coordination, and transmission of motor impulses to lower centers; *specif* **:** a region immediately anterior to the central sulcus having an unusually thick zone of cortical gray matter, including the giant pyramidal cells, and communicating with lower centers chiefly through the pyramidal tracts

**motor automatism** *n* **1 :** the performance without intent of actions (as speaking or writing) normally under strictly voluntary control **2 :** a product of motor automatism

**motor barrel** *n* **:** the mainspring unit in watches that have the main wheel detached from the barrel but turning as a unit with the barrel arbor to eliminate strain on the main wheel teeth if the mainspring should break — compare GOING BARREL

**motor bicycle** \ˈ==ˈ=(,)==\ *or* **motorbike** \ˈ==,=\ *n* **1 :** MOTORCYCLE **2 a :** a light motorcycle resembling a bicycle in design and structure **b :** a bicycle to which a motor for propulsion is attached

¹**motorboat** \ˈ==,=\ *n* [¹*motor* + *boat*] **1 :** a boat or small ship propelled by an internal-combustion engine or an electric motor **2 :** any of certain classes of boats according to statute (as a boat not more than 65 feet long propelled by machinery) except steam-propelled tugboats and towboats

**²motorboat** \"\ *vi* **1 :** to ride in or drive a motorboat **2 :** to make sounds resembling the exhaust of a motorboat
**motorboating** \'==,==\ *n* **:** an inherent low frequency instability in electronic circuits characterized when heard on a telephone receiver or loudspeaker by a noise similar to the exhaust of a motorboat
**motor boss** *n* **:** one who directs and records mine haulage operations underground or at the surface — called also *dispatcher*
**motor bus** *n* **:** an automotive omnibus **:** MOTOR COACH
**mo·tor·cade** \'mōd·ə(r),kād, -ōtə-\ *n* -s [¹*motor* + *-cade*] **:** a procession of automobiles ⟨the prime minister's ~ passed —*St. John (New Brunswick) Telegraph-Jour.*⟩ ⟨taken in a twenty-five-car ~ to City Hall —Fendall Yerxa⟩
**motorcar** \'==,=\ *n* **1 :** AUTOMOBILE **2** *usu* **motor car a :** a railroad car containing motors for propulsion ⟨several railroads operate electric *motor cars* in suburban passenger train service —*Stories Behind the Pictures*⟩ **b :** a motor-propelled inspection or work car on a railroad
**motor cargo insurance** *n* **:** insurance against loss resulting from damage to goods in transit by motor truck
**motor carriage** *n* **:** a self-propelled mount for a weapon
**motor carrier** *n* **:** a highway passenger and freight carrier regulated by the federal government
**motor cell** *n* **:** BULLIFORM CELL
**motor center** *n* **:** a nervous center that controls or modifies (as by inhibiting or reinforcing) a motor impulse — compare MOTOR AREA
**motor coach** *n* **:** an automotive omnibus **:** MOTOR BUS ⟨a fleet of *motor coaches* —*Motor (London)*⟩
**motor converter** *n* **:** a machine consisting of an induction motor and a synchronous converter mounted on a common shaft with their rotor windings in series with each other
**motor cortex** *n* **:** the cortex of a motor area; *also* **:** the motor areas as a functional whole
**motor court** *n* **:** MOTEL ⟨*motor courts* with swimming pools and finely furnished bungalows —*N.Y.Times*⟩
**¹motorcycle** \'==,==\ *n* [fr. earlier *motor bicycle*] **:** a 2-wheeled tandem automotive vehicle having 1 or 2 riding saddles and sometimes having a 3d wheel for the support of a sidecar
**²motorcycle** \"\ *vi* **:** to ride a motorcycle or go by motorcycle
**motorcyclist** \'==,==\ *n* **:** one that rides a motorcycle
**motor drive** *n* **:** an electric motor and auxiliaries for driving a machine or group of machines
**mo·tor·drome** \'mōd·ə(r),drōm\ *n* [¹*motor* + *-drome*] **:** a track or course usu. enclosed and furnished with seats for spectators at races or tests of automobiles or motorcycles
**mo·tored** \'mōd·ə(r)d\ *adj* [¹*motor* + *-ed*] **:** equipped with a motor — often used in combination ⟨a four-*motored* airplane⟩
**motor end plate** *n* **:** the terminal arborization of a motor axon on a muscle fiber
**motor fiber** *n* **:** a nerve fiber whose stimulation causes muscular contraction
**motor generator** *or* **motor-generator set** *n* **:** one or more motors mechanically coupled to one or more generators for transforming or converting electric currents
**motor horn** *n* **:** a warning horn used on a motor vehicle
**mo·to·ri·al** \mō'tōrēəl\ *adj* [L *motorius* moving + E *-al* — more at MOTORY] **:** MOTOR 1
**mo·tor·ic** \mō'tȯrik, -tär-\ *adj* [¹*motor* + *-ic*] **:** MOTOR 1c — **mo·tor·i·cal·ly** \-rək(ə)lē\ *adv*
**¹motoring** *n* -s [fr. gerund of ³*motor*] **:** the act or recreation of riding in or driving an automobile
**²motor·ing** *adj, chiefly Brit* **:** of or relating to automobiles, the driving of automobiles, or the people who drive automobiles ⟨the design has been virtually dictated by American ~ opinion —Bertram Wycock⟩ ⟨~ offences⟩
**mo·tor·ism** \'mōd·ə,rizəm\ *n* -s [¹*motor* + *-ism*] **:** addiction to or practice of motoring
**mo·tor·ist** \'mōd·ərəst, -ōtə-\ *n* -s **:** one who makes a practice of driving a car or traveling by car
**mo·to·ri·um** \mō'tōrēəm\ *n, pl* **moto·ria** \-ēə\ [NL, fr. LL, neut. of *motorius* moving — more at MOTORY] **1 :** the part of an organism (as of its nervous system) that is concerned in movement as distinguished from that concerned in sensation **2 :** a differentiated cytoplasmic area in certain protozoans that acts as a coordinating neurocenter analogous to the brain of higher animals
**mo·tor·iza·tion** \,mōd·ərə'zāshən, -ōtər-, -rī'-\ *n* -s **:** the act or process of motorizing
**mo·tor·ize** \'mōd·ə,rīz, -ōtə-\ *vt* -ED/-ING/-s *see -ize in Explan Notes* [¹*motor* + *-ize*] **:** to equip with a motor ⟨a *motorized* wheelchair⟩: as **a :** to equip with motor-driven vehicles in substitution for those otherwise propelled ⟨~ a fire department⟩ ⟨~ a farm⟩ **b :** to equip (as ground-fighting troops) with motor-driven vehicles for transportation — distinguished from *mechanize* **c :** to equip with automobiles ⟨the population is becoming increasingly *motorized* —Harold Callender⟩ ⟨~ the police⟩ **d :** to design or adapt (as a machine or a tool) for direct operation esp. by an electric motor ⟨~ a lathe⟩
**motor launch** *n* **:** a launch propelled by an internal-combustion engine
**mo·tor·less** \-ə(r)ləs\ *adj* **:** having no motor
**motor liner** *n* **:** a motor-driven ocean liner
**motor-lorry** \'==,==\ *n, Brit* **:** MOTORTRUCK
**mo·tor·man** \'mōd·ə(r)mən\ *n, pl* **motormen 1 :** an operator of a motor-driven vehicle; *esp* **:** an operator of a street railway car, subway or elevated train, dinkey, or other haulage engine **2 :** one who operates the sound and camera motors used in the making of motion pictures
**motor-minded** \'==¦==\ *adj* **:** inclined to think of things in terms of the muscular movements they involve — compare EYE-MINDED — **mo·tor-mind·ed·ness** *n* -ES
**motor paralysis** *n* **:** paralysis of the voluntary muscles
**motor pendulum** *n* **:** a pendulum that is used to drive the wheelwork and hands of a turret clock and is maintained in motion by electromagnetic impulses applied at regular intervals
**motor phrase** *n* **:** a precisely timed movement division in dancing
**motor point** *n* **:** a small area on a muscle at which electrical or other stimulation is most effective
**motor pool** *n* **:** a group of motor vehicles controlled by a single governmental agency whether or not assembled in one place and dispatched for use as needed by different organizations or individuals
**motor pumper** *n* **:** a unit of automotive fire apparatus with fire pump driven by the engine — compare FIRE ENGINE b
**motor root** *n* **:** a nerve root containing only motor fibers; *specif* **:** the ventral root of a spinal nerve
**motors** *pl of* MOTOR, *pres 3d sing of* MOTOR
**motor sailer** *n* **:** a motorboat with sailing equipment
**motor scooter** *n* **:** a low 2- or 3-wheeled automotive vehicle resembling a child's scooter, having a seat so that the rider does not straddle the engine, sometimes having a parcel compartment, but having smaller wheels and being less powerful than a motorcycle

motor scooter

**motor scythe** *n* **:** a mower with a short reciprocating knife attached to a garden tractor mechanism
**motor ship** *n* **:** a seagoing ship propelled by a motor; *esp* **:** one propelled by an internal-combustion engine
**motor spirit** *n, chiefly Brit* **:** a volatile liquid used as a fuel in internal-combustion engines; *specif* **:** GASOLINE, PETROL
**motor torpedo boat** *n* **:** a high-speed 60 to 100 ft. motorboat mounting two or four torpedo tubes and antiaircraft and machine guns and equipped with depth charges and smoke-making apparatus — called also *mosquito boat, PT boat*
**motor transport** *n* **:** commercial transport (as trucks) on streets and highways
**motortruck** \'==,=\ *n* **:** an automotive truck for transporting freight
**motor unit** *n* **:** a motor neuron together with the muscle fibers on which it acts
**motor vehicle** *n* **:** an automotive vehicle not operated on rails; *esp* **:** one with rubber tires for use on highways
**motor vessel** *n* **:** an inland waterway boat or ocean ship propelled by one or more diesel engines
**motorway** \'==,=\ *n, Brit* **:** a motor highway; *esp* **:** SUPERHIGHWAY
**mo·to·ry** \'mōd·ərē\ *adj* [LL *motorius* moving, fr. L *motus* (past part. of *movēre* to move) + *-orius* -ory — more at MOVE] **:** MOTOR 1
**mo·to·zin·tlec** \,mōd·əsənt¦lek\ *n, pl* **motozintlec** *or* **motozintlecs** *usu cap* [Sp *motozintleca*, fr. *Motozintla*, town in Chiapas state, Mexico] **1 a :** an Indian people of southeastern Mexico **b :** a member of such people **2 :** a Mayan language of the Motozintlec people
**mots** *pl of* MOT
**¹motte** *or* **mott** \'mät\ *n* -s [MexSp *mata*, fr. Sp, bush, shrub, orchard, prob. fr. LL *matta* mat — more at MAT] *chiefly Southwest* **:** a grove or clump of trees; *esp* **:** a shrubby copse in open prairie country ⟨a thick oak ~⟩
**²motte** \"\ *n* -s [F, fr. OF *mote, motte* mound, hillock, fr. OProv *mota*] **:** MOTE 1; *specif* **:** a palisaded mound common in prehistoric Europe
**mot·tet·to** \mō'ted·(,)ō\ *n, pl* **mottettos** *or* **mottet·ti** \-d·ē\ [It, fr. F *motet* — more at MOTET] **:** MOTET
**¹mot·tle** \'mäd·ᵊl, -ät ᵊl\ *n* -s [prob. back-formation fr. ¹*motley*] **1 :** a colored spot ⟨streaks and ~*s*⟩ **2 a :** an appearance like that of a surface having colored spots, blotchings, or cloudings ⟨his chest and flanks were a ~ of bruises —Arthur Morrison⟩ **b :** the arrangement of such markings on a surface ⟨available in a variety of opaque colors or ~*s* —*Modern Plastics Catalog*⟩ **3 :** MOSAIC 5b
**²mottle** \"\ *adj* **:** MOTTLED
**³mottle** \"\ *vt* **mottled; mottled; mottling** \-d·ᵊliŋ, -t(ᵊ)liŋ\ **mottles :** to mark with spots or blotches of different color or shades of color as if stained **:** SPOT, BLOTCH ⟨drifting clouds *mottled* the sea —J.A.Michener⟩
**mottled** *adj* **:** marked with spots of different colors **:** DAPPLED, SPOTTED ⟨~ wood⟩ ⟨a ~ complexion⟩ ⟨~ linoleum⟩ ⟨hills . . . some mantled in green, some ~ with the hues of red clay and white granite —Mabel R. Gillis⟩ ⟨his face was ~ with embarrassment —Mary Austin⟩
**mottled brant** *or* **mottled goose** *n* **:** WHITE-FRONTED GOOSE
**mottled duck** *n* **:** a Louisiana and Texas variety (*Anas fulvigula maculosa*) of the Florida duck
**mottled enamel** *n* **:** a spotted condition of the enamel of teeth caused by continual use of drinking water containing excessive amounts of fluorides during the time the teeth are calcifying
**mottled iron** *n* **:** cast or pig iron that is intermediate between white and gray iron and shows a mottled surface on fracture
**mottled owl** *n* **:** an American screech owl in the gray phase of plumage
**mottle-leaf** \'==,=\ *also* **mottled leaf** *n* **1 :** a zinc deficiency disease of citrus plants characterized by a partial chlorosis, reduced size of leaves and fruits, and stunting **2 :** a virus disease of cherry characterized by chlorotic mottling, puckering, distortion, and wrinkling of the leaves
**mot·tle·ment** \'mäd·ᵊlmənt\ *n* -s **:** mottled condition or appearance
**mot·tler** \'mäd·ᵊlə(r), -ät(ᵊ)l-\ *n* -s **:** one that mottles (as in dyeing or ceramics); *specif* **:** a brush for producing a mottled surface
**mottling** *n* -s **1 :** MOTTLE 2 ⟨inhabitants of certain districts had a curious ~ of their teeth —*Irish Digest*⟩; *specif* **:** a mingling of other-colored spots with the normal green in foliage (as in many variegated plants and in mosaic diseases) **2 :** the act or process of producing mottle
**mot·to** \'mäd·(,)ō, -ä(,)tō\ *n, pl* **mottoes** *also* **mottos** [It, fr. L *muttum* grunt, mumble, fr. *muttire* to mutter, mumble — more at MUTE] **1 :** a sentence, phrase, or word accompanying a heraldic achievement ⟨two bends with the owner's word, reason, or ~ —W.H.St.John Hope⟩ **2 a :** a sentence, phrase, or word inscribed on something as appropriate to or indicative of its character or use ⟨"Cry Aloud and Spare Not", the belligerent ~ of the paper —*Amer. Guide Series: Tenn.*⟩ **b :** a short suggestive expression of a guiding principle **:** MAXIM ⟨the Boy Scout ~ "Be Prepared"⟩ **c :** a short usu. quoted passage prefixed to a literary work (as a novel, essay, or poem) or to one of its divisions (as a chapter or canto) and intended to suggest the subject matter that follows **d** (1) *or* **motto kiss :** a piece of candy in a paper wrapper inscribed with or enclosing a saying or verse (2) **:** a party novelty consisting of a fancy wrapper containing usu. a paper printed with a sentimental or humorous verse, a paper hat, and a small toy or charm — compare CRACKER 2c, FAVOR 4b **3** *also* **motto theme :** a recurring phrase or musical figure possibly varied and usu. alluding to a specific idea
**mot·toed** \-ōd\ *adj* **:** bearing or having a motto
**mot·tram·ite** \'mä·trə,mīt\ *n* -s [*Mottram* St. Andrew, Cheshire, England + E *-ite*] **:** a mineral $(Cu,Zn)Pb(VO_4)(OH)$ that consists of a basic vanadate of lead, copper, and zinc with more copper than zinc and that is isomorphous with descloizite
**mot·ty** *also* **mot·tie** \'mäti\ *adj* [*mot* (Sc. var. of ²*mote*) + *-y*] *Scot* **:** full of motes **:** DUSTY
**¹mo·tu** \'mō(,)tü\ *n, pl* **motu** *or* **motus** *usu cap* **1 a :** a Melanesian people in Papua **b :** a member of such people **2 :** the language of the Motu people used in trade on the southeast coast of Papua
**²motu** \"\ *n, pl* **motu** *or* **motus** [Maori, Tahitian, Tuamotuan, Marquesan, Samoan, & Tongan] **:** a Polynesian reef islet with vegetation
**mo·tu proprio** \,mō(,)tü'prōprē,ō\ *n* [L, by one's own impulse] **:** a rescript initiated and issued by the pope of his own accord and apart from the advice of others
**¹mou** \'mü\ *Scot var of* MOUTH
**²mou** \'maü, 'mü\ *or* **mow** \'maü\ *also* **mu** \'mü\ *n, pl* **mou** *or* **mow** [Chin (Pek) *mou³, mu³*] **:** any of various Chinese units of land area; *esp* **:** one equal to 0.1518 acre
**mouch** *chiefly Brit var of* MOOCH
**mou·char·a·by** \mü'sharəbē\ *or* **mouch·ra·bi·eh** \,müshrə'bē(y)ə\ *or* **mesh·ra·bi·yeh** \,meshrə'bē(y)ə\ *also* **mush·ra·bi·yeh** \,müshrə'bē(y)ə\ *n, pl* **moucharabies** *or* **mouchrabiehs** *or* **meshrabiyehs** [F & Ar; F *moucharaby, moucharabièh*, fr. Ar *mushrabīyah*] **:** a Moorish projecting oriel window or enclosed balcony of which the enclosure is largely made up of carved wooden latticework
**mou·choir** \(')mü¦shwär\ *n* -s [F, fr. *moucher* to blow the nose, fr. (assumed) VL *muccare*, fr. L *muccus, mucus* mucus — more at MUCUS] **:** HANDKERCHIEF
**mou·die** *or* **mou·dy** \'mōdi, 'müdi\ *n, pl* **moudies** [short for *moudiewarp*] *chiefly Scot* **:** ³MOLE 1a
**mou·die·warp** \-,wȯrp\ *or* **mou·die·wort** \-rt\ *Scot var of* MOLDWARP
**moue** \'mü\ *n* -s [F — more at MOW] **:** a little grimace (as of distaste or playful impudence) **:** POUT, MOW ⟨made a ~, to show that he didn't expect to enjoy the occasion —Upton Sinclair⟩ ⟨his ~ of comic disdain permitted their laughter —L.A.Fiedler⟩
**mouf·lon** *or* **mouf·flon** *also* **muf·lon** *or* **muf·flon** \'müflən\ *n, pl* **mouflon** *or* **mouflons** *or* **moufflon** *or* **moufflons** [F *mouflon*, fr. It dial. (Corsica) *mufrone, muvrone* & Sardinian *muvrone*, fr. LL *mufron-, mufro*] **1 :** a wild sheep (*Ovis musimon*) inhabiting the mountains of Sardinia and Corsica and having large curling horns that in the male have a triangular base, a reddish brown coat with a grayish buff patch on the sides, and white on the legs, belly, and buttocks **2 :** a wild sheep with large horns

mouflon 1

**mought** \'mōt, 'maüt\ [ME *moghte*] *chiefly dial past of* MAY
**mouil·la·tion** \mü'yāshən\ *n* -s [*mouillé* + *-ation*] **:** mouillé pronunciation
**mouil·lé** \(')mü¦yā\ *adj* [F, fr. past part. of *mouiller* to wet, moisten, palatalize, fr. (assumed) VL *molliare* to soften with water, fr. L *mollis* soft — more at MELT] **:** pronounced palatally — used esp. in *l mouillé* and with reference to the sound \lʸ\ in Old French and certain dialects of Modern French or rarely with reference to its counterpart \y\ in standard Modern French
**mouil·lure** \mü'yü(ə)r\ *n* -s [F, fr. *mouiller* + *-ure*] **:** MOUILLATION
**moujik** *var of* MUZHIK
**moul** \'mül\ *archaic var of* MOOL
**mou·lage** \(')mü¦läzh\ *n* -s [F, molding, casting, fr. MF, fr. *mouler* to mold (fr. OF, fr. *modle, molle, moule* mold) + *-age* — more at MOLD] **1 a :** the taking of an impression (as of a tire mark or tooth print) for use as evidence in a criminal investigation **b :** an impression or cast made for use as evidence in a criminal investigation **:** MOLDING **2 :** a mold of a lesion or defect used as a guide in applying medical treatment (as in radiation therapy) or in performing reconstructive surgery esp. on the face
**¹mould** *var of* MOLD
**²mould** \'mōld\ *n* -s [ME *molde*, fr. OE *molda* or *molde* — more at -BLAST] **1** *archaic* **:** the top of the head **2 :** FONTANEL
**mouldboard** *var of* MOLDBOARD
**mould·warp** \'mōld,wȯrp\ *archaic var of* MOLDWARP
**moulder** *var of* MOLDER
**mou·lin** \(')mü¦laⁿ\ *n* -s [F, fr. LL *molinum* — more at MILL] **:** a nearly cylindrical vertical shaft in a glacier scoured out by meltwater and rock debris pouring into it
**moul·mein cedar** \(')mül¦mān-, (')mōl-, -¦mīn-\ *n, usu cap M* [fr. *Moulmein*, Burma] **:** TOON
**moult** *var of* MOLT
**moulten** *adj* [*moult* + *-en*] *obs* **:** MOLTED **:** having lost its plumage ⟨a ~ raven —Shak.⟩
**¹moulter** *var of* MOLTER
**²moul·ter** \'mō(l)tə(r)\ *chiefly dial var of* ²MOLDER
**moulvi** *var of* MAULVI
**¹mound** \'maünd\ *vb* -ED/-ING/-s [origin unknown] *vt* **1** *archaic* **a :** to surround with a barrier **:** FENCE ⟨to ~ over the hill would require double the rails —Jethro Tull⟩ **b :** to enclose or fortify with a ridge of earth ⟨heaped hills that ~ the sea —Alfred Tennyson⟩ **2 a :** to gather into a heap **:** PILE ⟨snow ~*ed* in high white cones above the pillars —Josephine Johnson⟩ **b :** to surround or cover with a raised heap **:** BANK, HILL ⟨roses are ~*ed* for winter protection⟩ ⟨the ~*ed* grave of a British Tommy —T.O.Heggen⟩ ⟨spotted the wreck, which the silt of 22 centuries had ~*ed* up —*Nat'l Geographic*⟩ ~ *vi* **:** to become a mound **:** pile up ⟨thunderheads are ~*ing* in the west⟩
**²mound** \"\ *n* -s *often attrib* [origin unknown] **1 a** *dial chiefly Eng* **:** an encompassing hedge or fence **b** *obs* **:** a line of demarcation **:** BOUNDARY ⟨stars, whose whirling courses . . . mark the true ~*s* of years, and months, and days —Josuah Sylvester⟩ **2 a :** an earthwork used as a fortification **:** RAMPART **b :** a prehistoric earthwork constructed by Indian mound builders of No. America over a burial or sacrificial altar or as a foundation or fortification or for ceremonial purposes **3 a :** an accumulated mass or artificially produced heap **:** PILE ⟨~*s* of oyster shells surround the weathered frame shacks —*Amer. Guide Series: Fla.*⟩ ⟨began to process ~*s* of orders —M.E.Harvey⟩ ⟨fluffy ~*s* of mashed potatoes —Jack Alexander⟩ **b :** the slightly elevated area in which a baseball pitcher's plate is set **c :** a natural elevation **:** HILL, KNOLL ⟨~*s* and dunes of loose sand —Willa Cather⟩ ⟨hurricanes . . . dragging in their centers a ~ of seawater —Marjory S. Douglas⟩; *specif* **:** HUMP ⟨under his left eye was a ~ of bluish flesh —G.B.Shaw⟩
**³mound** \"\ *also* **mond** \'mänd\ *n* -s [MF *monde*, lit., world, fr. L *mundus*] **:** ORB 1c(3)
**mound ant** *n, Austral* **:** MEAT ANT
**mound bird** *n* **:** MEGAPODE
**mound builder** *n* **1** *usu cap M&B* **:** a member of one of the prehistoric Indian peoples of central No. America whose extensive earthworks are found esp. around the Great Lakes and in the Mississippi valley region and many of whom were skilled craftsmen in pottery, stone, or copper — compare EFFIGY MOUND, HOPEWELL, MOUND 2b **2 :** MEGAPODE
**mound burial** *n* **:** the practice of laying a corpse on the surface and covering it with earth or stones or of heaping up a mound of soil and sinking a grave into it — compare ¹BARROW 2
**mound layer** *n* **:** a new shoot of a woody plant (as a currant bush) that has been mounded with earth to induce it to root
**mound layering** *also* **mound layerage** *n* **:** a method of propagation in which various woody-stemmed plants (as currants, gooseberries, quinces) are cut back to the ground in early spring and the new shoots that they develop are covered with soil to a depth of six to eight inches to induce root growth which forms individual plants that can be removed in the fall — called also *stool layering*
**mound lily** *or* **mound lily yucca** *n* **:** SPANISH DAGGER 1
**mound maker** *n* **:** MEGAPODE
**mounds·man** \'maün(d)zmən\ *n, pl* **moundsmen :** ²PITCHER 1a
**mound turkey** *n* **:** any of several of the larger megapodes: as **a :** BRUSH TURKEY **b :** JUNGLE FOWL 2a
**moun·seer** \maün'si(ə)r, -iə\ *n* -s [by alter.] *archaic* **:** MONSIEUR
**¹mount** \'maünt\ *n* -s [ME *munt, mont, mount*, partly fr. OE *munt*, fr. L *mont-, mons*; partly fr. OF *mont*, fr. L *mont-, mons*; akin to ON *mænir* ridgepole, *mæna* to project, L *minari* to project, threaten, W *mynydd* mountain, Av *framanyente* they get a head start, *mati-* promontory; basic meaning: mountain] **1 a :** a lofty promontory **:** MOUNTAIN; *specif* **:** a high usu. more or less conical detached hill rising from a landscape ⟨*Mount* Vesuvius⟩ **b :** a lofty position **:** VANTAGE POINT ⟨mystics . . . returned from the ~ of vision —J.S.Bixler⟩ **c** *heraldry* **:** a hill proper vert in base **2 a** *archaic* **:** a protective earthwork **:** RAMPART **b** *obs* **:** CAVALIER 1 **3 a :** an artificial elevation **:** MOUND ⟨~ in the background is the icehouse —*Nat'l Geographic*⟩ **b** *obs* **:** an elevated area in a garden that affords a view of the surrounding countryside ⟨have a ~ of some pretty height . . . to look abroad into the fields —Francis Bacon⟩ **4** *obs* **:** a lending agency **:** BANK, PAWNBROKER — compare MONT-DE-PIÉTÉ **5** *usu cap* **:** a small protrusion of flesh on the palm of the hand esp. at the base of a finger that is held by palmists to indicate predominant traits and degrees of temperament ⟨the absence of *Mounts* . . . indicates the lack of the virtues represented by that *Mount* —Josef Ranald⟩ — see LOWER MARS, MOUNT OF APOLLO, MOUNT OF JUPITER, MOUNT OF LUNA, MOUNT OF MERCURY, MOUNT OF SATURN, MOUNT OF VENUS, UPPER MARS
**²mount** \"\ *vb* -ED/-ING/-s [ME *mounten*, fr. MF *monter*, fr. (assumed) VL *montare*, fr. L *mont-, mons* mountain] *vi* **1 a :** to become greater in amount or extent **:** INCREASE ⟨weekends when passenger volume ~*s* sharply —W.A.Howe⟩ ⟨costs of operation . . . are continually ~*ing* —C.F.Robinson⟩ ⟨you know how those storage bills ~ up —Berton Roueché⟩ **b :** to reach an ultimate amount or extent **:** TOTAL ⟨the cost of champagne . . . is liable to ~ up to a couple of pounds per head —*English Digest*⟩ **2 a :** to wing upward **:** SOAR ⟨the lark . . . ~*ing* from the lea —William Allingham⟩ ⟨the soul ~*ing* toward the eternal forms —Bernard DeVoto⟩ **b :** to make or appear to make a steep ascent **:** CLIMB ⟨~*ing* ivy⟩ ⟨the narrow road ~*s* to higher levels —*Amer. Guide Series: Fla.*⟩ ⟨astride these promontories are . . . residential sections, and even some of the business areas have ~*ed* partway —*Amer. Guide Series: Minn.*⟩ **c :** to reach upward **:** TOWER ⟨the skyscraper ~*s* through the dusk to a winking red light on top⟩ **d :** to move upward **:** RISE ⟨hid her face on the bounteous breast that ~*ed* to her —George Meredith⟩ **e :** to surge up and suffuse the face ⟨blushes ~ to her cheeks —Upton Sinclair⟩ **f :** to attain greater height or magnitude **:** GROW ⟨a vine, remarkable for its tendency . . . to mass and ~ —Willa Cather⟩ ⟨a ~*ing* economic and political problem —Gordon Walker⟩ **g :** to become aroused or amplified **:** KINDLE, INTENSIFY ⟨~ to high moral indignation —M.R. Cohen⟩ ⟨a sense of ~*ing* excitement —T.B.Costain⟩ **h :** ¹COUPLE 1 ⟨meet and ~ like stray dogs in the street —George Barker⟩ **3 a :** to become promoted **:** ADVANCE ⟨younger brother . . . proposed to ~ over the head of the elder by marrying the late King's widow —Edith Sitwell⟩ **b** *archaic* **:** to reach back through the years ⟨an antiquity which ~*s* up to the eighth century of our era —J.M.Jephson⟩ **4 a :** to seat oneself upon a means of conveyance (as a horse) ⟨puts his foot in the stirrup and ~*s*⟩ ⟨~*ed* and rode off in a cloud of dust⟩ **b :** to become elevated by or secured to a support ⟨~ on French heels when

you go to the ball —*London Magazine*⟩ ⟨the transmission ~*s* crosswise in the vehicle —*Principles of Automotive Vehicles*⟩ **5** *slang* **:** to ascend the witness stand **:** TESTIFY ⟨their price is five shillings for what they call ~*ing* —George Parker⟩ ~ *vt* **1 a :** to climb or appear to climb **:** ASCEND ⟨~*ed* a short flight of steps —W.B.Furlong⟩ ⟨the town ~*s* the hills —Claudia Cassidy⟩; *specif* **:** to take one's place on a raised structure ⟨~ a pulpit⟩ ⟨~ the judicial bench⟩ **b** *obs* **:** to soar into ⟨did He . . . not only ~ the firmament but ascend the heaven of heavens —James Hervey⟩ **c** *archaic* **:** to scale for the purpose of assault ⟨first to ~ the breach —Sir Walter Scott⟩ **2 a :** to lift up **:** ELEVATE ⟨hedgehogs . . . ~ their pricks at my footfall —Shak.⟩ ⟨had the brilliant idea of ~*ing* enormous masts . . . down the center of the roadway —H.V.Morton⟩ ⟨clouds . . . ~*ing* thunderheads in the north —Norman Mailer⟩; *specif* **:** to raise (a shotgun) to the shoulder preparatory to firing **b :** to set on something that elevates ⟨a cluster of outbuildings . . . each ~*ed* on poles —Mary Kingsley⟩ **c** *archaic* **:** to raise in esteem or spirituality **:** EXALT ⟨whom his tenth epic ~*s* to fame —Edward Young⟩ ⟨this ~*s* my soul with more heroic fires —Francis Quarles⟩ **3 a :** to dispose in battle array **:** POSITION ⟨on this rampart he ~*ed* his little train of artillery —W.H. Prescott⟩ **b :** to be equipped with or have in position ⟨a war canoe ~*ing* 40 or more oars⟩ ⟨a wooden stockade ~*ing* cannon —P.M.Angle⟩ ⟨vehicles . . . which can ~ 105 mm. recoilless weapons —*Combat Forces Jour.*⟩ **c** (1) **:** to post for defense or observation ⟨~*ed* some guards⟩ (2) **:** to take up (a post of protective custody) ⟨~ guard over the person of the emperor —A.M.Young⟩ **d** (1) **:** to organize and equip (an attacking force) ⟨the logistical support . . . to ~ and support the operation —H.A.Jordan⟩ (2) **:** to launch and carry out (an assault or campaign) ⟨first ship specially designed for ~*ing* helicopter assaults —A.W.Jessup⟩ ⟨~*ed* 1525 effective sorties during the period —*N. Y. Times*⟩ ⟨is ~*ing* a successful trade offensive —D.L.Cohn⟩ **4 :** ¹COVER 10a ⟨crouching like a domestic hen that wants to be ~*ed* —T.H.White b. 1906⟩ **5 a :** to get on (a means of conveyance) ⟨~ a horse⟩ ⟨went running to ~ the motorcycle —Richard Llewellyn⟩ ⟨clouds ~ the wind —Russell Lord⟩ **b :** to sit or be set upon (a means of conveyance) ⟨rode into the barnyard ~*ed* on a tractor⟩ ⟨a horse would be led out and I would be ~*ed* . . . upon it —O.S.J.Gogarty⟩ **c :** to furnish with a means of conveyance ⟨wanted horses to ~ his dragoons —*Amer. Guide Series: Vt.*⟩ **6 a** (1) **:** to attach to a support or assemble for use ⟨after the final polishing . . . the blade is ready to be ~*ed* —L.D.Bement⟩ ⟨the pulley shaft is ~*ed* on large capacity ball bearings —*Whitin Rev.*⟩; *specif* **:** to attach to a base (as of metal or wood) and make type high (a printing plate or cut) (2) **:** to attach to a backing for reinforcement or display ⟨old Roman filet . . . ~*ed* on a net foundation that would give almost invisible support to its fragile threads —*advt*⟩ ⟨black satin motifs ~*ed* on white felt —*Women's Wear Daily*⟩; *specif* **:** to glue or paste (as a sheet of paper) upon firm material in bookbinding **b :** to prepare for display: as (1) **:** to frame or provide with an appropriate setting ⟨classifying, ~*ing*, and labeling specimens —G.O.Blough⟩ ⟨the jeweler ~*s* a pearl in a ring⟩ ⟨a statue on a pedestal⟩; *specif* **:** to place (an object) on a slide for microscopic examination (2) **:** to stuff or arrange (the skin or skeleton of an animal) for exhibition esp. in a natural position or attitude — compare TAXIDERMY ⟨~*ed* a group of orangutans, and then a habitat group of muskrats —Clyde Fisher⟩ (3) **:** to fasten (a stamp) on the page of an album esp. by use of a hinge or on a sheet of paper or cardboard for display **c** (1) **:** to put on view **:** EXHIBIT ⟨one of the finest shows the museum has ever ~*ed* —*Time*⟩; *specif* **:** to arrange (a slide) under a microscope for examination (2) *archaic* **:** to don esp. for display ⟨~*ed* a fashionable greatcoat —*Sporting Mag.*⟩ **d :** to provide with scenery, costumes, lighting, and properties **:** equip for public presentation ⟨the manner in which a play is composed, ~*ed* and performed —Samuel Selden⟩ ⟨a tastefully ~*ed* television show⟩ ⟨a beautifully ~*ed* circus, meaning it had luster and snap and dazzle —T.W.Duncan⟩; *specif* **:** PRODUCE ⟨the manager's stubborn determination to ~ a Wagner opera although he had only a few leading singers to put into it —Marcia Davenport⟩ **syn** see ASCEND, RISE

³**mount** \"\ *n* -s **1 a :** an act or instance of mounting ⟨the circus rider leaped to the horse's back in a flying ~⟩ ⟨took pride in the spread and ~ of his fame —J.L.Davis⟩; *specif* **:** a gymnastic maneuver consisting of a spring from the floor to a position on the apparatus **b :** COUPLING 1 ⟨the copulatory behavior of macaques . . . consists of a series of ~*s* —C.S. Ford & F.A.Beach⟩ **2 :** FRAME, SUPPORT: as **a :** the strips (as of wood or ivory) constituting the framework of a fan **b :** a mat that serves as a background for a picture ⟨salon ~⟩ **c :** a jewelry setting ⟨flexible platinum ~ set with 68 round diamonds —*Precious-Stone Jewelry*⟩ **d :** a decorative border or detail applied to objects (as furniture, clocks, saddles); *also* **:** protective or functional hardware (as escutcheons or drawer pulls) of furniture — usu. used in pl. ⟨a clock with ormolu ~*s*⟩ **e :** an undercarriage or part that fits a device for use or serves to attach an accessory ⟨engine ~⟩ ⟨weapons on towed or self-propelled ~*s* —*U. S. War Dept. Technical Manual*⟩ ⟨invented a ~ for a telescopic gunsight⟩ ⟨a good lens in focusing ~ —R.C.Holslag⟩; *specif* **:** the base upon which a printing plate or cut is mounted to make it type high **f :** a hinge, card, or acetate envelope for mounting a stamp for display (as in an album) **g** (1) **:** a glass slide with its accessories on which objects are placed for examination with a microscope (2) **:** a specimen mounted on a slide for microscopic examination **h :** a piece of material used for reinforcement or backing ⟨~ for a book cover⟩ **3 a :** a means of conveyance ⟨a cavalry action, with jeeps as ~*s* —Blair Clark⟩; *specif* **:** SADDLE HORSE ⟨too many officers' ~*s* and not enough draft animals —F.V.W.Mason⟩ **b :** a supply of saddle horses ⟨told me the color and the brand on every horse that was in my ~ —Ross Santee⟩ — compare ¹STRING 11c **c** (1) **:** an opportunity to ride ⟨offering an unsuspecting person a ~ on a savage horse —Robert Lynd⟩; *specif* **:** an assignment to ride as a jockey in a race ⟨phone is always ringing, with owners and trainers offering ~*s* —Allen Andrews⟩ (2) **:** a horse entered in a competition

**mount·able** \ˈmau̇ntəbəl\ *adj* **:** capable of being mounted

¹**moun·tain** \ˈmau̇ntᵊn, -tən\ *n* -s [ME *mountaine*, fr. OF *montaigne*, fr. (assumed) VL *montanea*, fr. fem. of *montaneus* of a mountain, alter. of L *montanus*, fr. *mont-*, *mons* mountain + *-anus* -an — more at MOUNT] **1 a :** a steep elevation with a restricted summit area projecting 1000 feet or more above the surrounding land surface ⟨a volcanic ~⟩ **b :** a high landmass culminating in several peaks or forming an elongated ridge **c :** any conspicuous hill in an area of low relief; *esp* **:** one that is rounded at the base and has comparatively steep sides ⟨we were in what a Mississippian would call ~*s* but which New Englanders call hills —William Faulkner⟩ **2 a :** an enormous mass or bulk **:** HEAP, HUNK ⟨beaches crowded with ~*s* of supplies —H.L.Merillat⟩ ⟨a ~ of a man —E.K.Brown⟩ **b :** a vast number or quantity **:** PILE, SLEW ⟨the ~ of personnel records accumulated by the armed forces —Seth King⟩ ⟨found a ~ of work awaiting him when he got back from vacation⟩ ⟨crushed by . . . ~*s* of throbbing, elemental sound —*Christian Science Monitor*⟩ **c :** a major obstacle or difficulty **:** CRISIS ⟨make a ~ out of a molehill⟩ **3 :** a region characterized by mountains — usu. used in pl. ⟨preferred the ~*s* to the seashore⟩ **4 a** *archaic* **:** ¹MOUNT 4 **b :** ¹MOUNT 5 **5** *or* **mountain wine :** a sweet white Malaga wine made from grapes picked when thoroughly ripe

²**mountain** \"\ *adj* **1 :** consisting of mountains ⟨~ range⟩ ⟨~ country⟩ **2 a :** situated on a mountain or in or among mountains ⟨~ stream⟩ ⟨~ cabin⟩ ⟨a ~ republic⟩ **b :** characteristic of mountains or a mountain region ⟨~ music⟩ **c :** MONTANE ⟨~ sheep⟩ **3** *archaic* **:** HUGE, MOUNTAINOUS ⟨thy lakes and ~ hills —S.T.Coleridge⟩ **4** *usu cap* **:** ROCKY MOUNTAIN ⟨the *Mountain* states of the U. S.⟩

**mountain accentor** *n* **:** a Siberian oscine bird (*Prunella montanella*) related to the hedge sparrow

**mountain adder** *n* **:** BERG ADDER

**mountain alder** *n* **1 :** any of several trees of the genus *Alnus*; *esp* **:** a tree (*A. rhombifolia*) that is native to upland regions of the western U. S. **2 :** MOUNTAIN MAPLE

**mountain andromeda** *n* **:** MOUNTAIN FETTERBUSH

**mountain antelope** *n* **:** GOAT ANTELOPE

**mountain apple** *n, Hawaii* **:** MALAY APPLE

**mountain ash** *n* **1 :** any of various trees of the genus *Sorbus*: as **a :** ROWAN TREE 1 **b :** AMERICAN MOUNTAIN ASH **c :** WESTERN MOUNTAIN ASH **2 :** any of several Australian eucalypts (esp. *Eucalyptus sieberiana* and *E. regnans*) with deeply furrowed bark suggesting that of old trees of the genus *Fraxinus* — see AUSTRALIAN OAK **3 :** a low-growing Texas ash (*Fraxinus texensis*) having leaves with mostly five leaflets

**mountain-ash sawfly** *n* **:** a European sawfly (*Pristiphora geniculata*) that defoliates mountain ash in the northeastern U. S.

**mountain asp** *n* **:** AMERICAN ASPEN

**mountain avens** *n* **:** a plant of the genus *Dryas*; *esp* **:** an arctic or alpine plant (*D. octopetala*) having large white flowers

**mountain badger** *n* **:** HOARY MARMOT

**mountain balm** *n* **:** either of two yerba santas (*Eriodyctyon californicum* or *E. angustifolium*)

**mountain balsam** *n* **:** any of several American firs: as **a :** a tree (*Abies fraseri*) of the Alleghenies **b :** either of two trees (*A. amabilis* or *A. lasiocarpa*) in the mountains of western U. S.

**mountain banana** *n* **:** FEI

**mountain barometer** *n* **:** a portable barometer used in measuring the heights of mountains

**mountain battery** *n* **:** a battery of mountain artillery

**mountain beaver** *n* **:** a bulky fossorial nocturnal rodent (*Aplodontia rufa*) of the uplands of the Pacific coast of No. America having small ears and eyes and a rudimentary tail and superficially resembling the ground squirrels to which it is actually but distantly related being the sole recent survivor of a once extensive group (Aplodontoidea of the Sciuromorpha), of primitive rodents that first appeared in the Paleocene

**mountain beech** *n, Austral & NewZeal* **:** a tree of the genus *Nothofagus*

**mountain bindweed** *n* **:** SOLDANELLA 2

**mountain birch** *n* **:** WESTERN PAPER BIRCH

**mountain black snake** *n* **:** PILOT BLACK SNAKE

**mountain blue** *n* **1 :** MINERAL BLUE 1a **2 :** AZURITE BLUE

**mountain bluebird** *n* **:** a bluebird (*Sialia currucoides*) of western No. America having a blue rather than a red breast

**mountain bluet** *n* **:** a European perennial herb (*Centaurea montana*) often cultivated for its blue flowers

**mountain bobcat** *n* **:** LYNX CAT

**mountain boomer** *n* **1 :** COLLARED LIZARD **2** *South & Midland* **:** RED SQUIRREL 1 **3** *chiefly Midland* **:** MOUNTAINEER 1

**mountain box** *n* **:** a common New Zealand shrub (*Veronica buxifolia*) with white flowers and leaves resembling heath

**mountain breeze** *n* **:** MOUNTAIN WIND

**mountain brome** *also* **mountain bromegrass** *n* **:** a western bromegrass (*Bromus carinatus* or *B. marginatus*) with large heavy heads that is used as a range grass

**mountain bunch grass** *n* **:** a forage grass (*Festuca viridula*) of the western U. S.

**mountain cabbage** *n* **:** a cabbage palm (*Roystonea oleracea*)

**mountain caribou** *n* **:** a large dark caribou (*Rangifer montanus*) found from British Columbia to Alaska and being the largest of the American caribous

**mountain cat** *n* **1 a :** COUGAR **b :** BAY LYNX **2 :** CACOMISTLE

**mountain cedar** *n* **1 :** any of various junipers; *esp* **:** ROCK CEDAR **2 :** MOUNTAIN PINE 3b

**mountain cherry** *n* **:** any of various trees or shrubs of the genus *Prunus*; *esp* **:** CHICKASAW PLUM

**mountain chickadee** *n* **:** a chickadee (*Penthestes gambeli*) of western No. America that resembles the black-capped chickadee but has a white line over the eye

**mountain clematis** *n* **:** a trailing or climbing vine (*Clematis verticellata*) of northeastern No. America having flowers with thin blue sepals and the outermost stamens usu. altered into prominently veined staminodia that resemble petals

**mountain cock** *n* **:** CAPERCAILLIE

**mountain cork** *n* **:** an asbestos resembling cork in texture and lightness — called also *rock cork*

**mountain crab** *n* **:** BLACK CRAB

**mountain cranberry** *n* **:** a low evergreen shrub (*Vaccinium vitis-idaea*) of high north temperate regions having thick oval leaves, white nodding bell-shaped flowers, and dark red berries — called also *cowberry, foxberry, lingonberry*

**mountain crystal** *n* **:** ROCK CRYSTAL

**mountain curassow** *n* **:** a curassow (*Oreophasis derbianus*) of the high mountains of Guatemala that is greenish black with white underparts and has a white tail band, red feet, and a red casque on the head

**mountain currant** *n* **:** ALPINE CURRANT

**mountain daisy** *n* **:** MOUNTAIN SANDWORT

**mountain damson** *n* **:** PARADISE TREE 1a

**mountain devil** *n* **:** MOLOCH 2b

**mountain dew** *n* **:** MOONSHINE 3

**mountain duck** *n* **1 :** HARLEQUIN DUCK **2** *Austral* **:** a sheldrake (*Casarca tadornoides*)

**mountain eagle** *n* **:** GOLDEN EAGLE

**mountain ebony** *n* **:** a small East Indian tree (*Bauhinia variegata*) having hard dark wood and bark used in tanning

**moun·tained** \ˈmau̇ntᵊnd, -tənd\ *adj* [¹*mountain* + *-ed*] *archaic* **:** heaped as high as a mountain ⟨the ~ sea —William Falconer⟩

¹**moun·tain·eer** \ˌmau̇ntᵊnˈi(ə)r, -tənˈi-, -iə\ *n* -s [¹*mountain* + *-eer*] **1 a :** a native or inhabitant of a mountainous region ⟨encouraging some of these isolated ~*s* to come down and live in more compact settlements —B.M.Bowie⟩; *specif* **:** HILLBILLY ⟨critical of the rural . . . ~*s* —A.N.Votaw⟩ **b :** MOUNTAIN MAN 2 **2 :** one who climbs mountains for sport

²**mountaineer** \"\ *vi* -ED/-ING/-S **:** to climb mountains for sport

**mountaineering** *n* -s **:** the sport or technique of scaling mountains

**mountain fern** *n* **:** either of two common shield ferns (*Dryopteris oreopteris* or *D. phegopteris*)

**mountain fetterbush** *n* **:** an ornamental evergreen shrub (*Pieris floribunda*) of the southeastern U. S. with small white bell-shaped flowers — called also *mountain andromeda*

**mountain fever** *n* **1 :** any of various febrile diseases occurring in mountainous regions: as **a :** COLORADO TICK FEVER **b :** ROCKY MOUNTAIN SPOTTED FEVER **2 :** INFECTIOUS ANEMIA

**mountain finch** *n* **:** BRAMBLING

**mountain flax** *n* **1 a :** PURGING FLAX **b :** SENEGA ROOT **c :** a centaury (*Centaurium umbellatum*) **d :** QUAKING GRASS 1 **e :** CORN SPURRY **f :** a New Zealand herb (*Phormium cookianum*) **2 :** ASBESTOS 1,2

**mountain flower** *n* **:** a common Eurasian cranesbill (*Geranium sylvaticum*)

**mountain fly honeysuckle** *n* **:** a common erect shrub (*Lonicera villosa*) of the north temperate zone with yellow flowers and bluish black berries

**mountain fringe** *n* **1 :** CLIMBING FUMITORY **2 :** a wormwood (*Artemisia frigida*) of Colorado

**mountain geranium** *n* **:** HERB ROBERT

**mountain glacier** *n* **:** ALPINE GLACIER

**mountain goat** *n* **1 :** a goatlike animal (*Oreamnos montanus*) related to the Old World chamois being widely but sparsely distributed in the mountainous parts of northwestern No. America and having a thickset body, small black polished horns present in both sexes, a tufted chin, short legs, and a thick hairy pure white coat — called also *Rocky Mountain goat* **2 :** GOAT ANTELOPE

mountain goat 1

**mountain gorilla** *n* **:** a dark hairy gorilla of the mountain forests of the eastern Congo distinguished from the coast gorilla by a narrower skull and longer palate and separated as a subspecies (*Gorilla gorilla beringeri*) or sometimes as a full species (*G. beringeri*)

**mountain grape** *n* **1 :** SAND GRAPE **2 :** OREGON GRAPE

**mountain green** *n* **1 a :** MALACHITE **b :** GREEN EARTH **2 c :** CHRYSOCOLLA **d :** Paris green mixed with gypsum or barite **2 :** MALACHITE GREEN 3

**mountain gum** *n* **:** either of two Australian eucalypts (*Eucalyptus goniocalyx* or *E. dalrympleana*)

**mountain gun** *n* **:** a gun used by mountain artillery and capable of being transported on muleback

**mountain hare** *n* **1 a :** the American varying hare (*Lepus americanus*) **b :** the large common hare (*Lepus saxatilis*) of southern Africa **2 :** JUMPING HARE

**mountain heath** *n* **:** a small shrub (*Phyllodoce caerulea*) found in cool regions of the north and having tiny evergreen leaves and pink or purple flowers

**mountain hemlock** *n* **:** a hemlock (*Tsuga mertensiana*) of the western U. S. that attains large size and has wood much harder than that of Canadian hemlock — called also *black hemlock*

**mountain hickory** *n* **:** a large Australian timber tree (*Acacia penninervis*) with hard wood similar to blackwood

**mountain holly** *n* **1 :** a shrub (*Nemopanthus mucronata*) of the family Aquifoliaceae of eastern No. America with smooth obovate leaves and scarlet drupes — called also *Canadian holly* **2 :** an upland holly (*Ilex montana*) of the eastern U. S.

**mountain holly fern** *n* **:** HOLLY FERN a

**mountain indigo** *or* **mountain indigo bush** *n* **:** a glabrous shrub (*Amorpha glabra*) of the southeastern U. S. with broad leaflets and clustered racemes of purple flowers

**mountain ivy** *n, chiefly NewEng* **:** MOUNTAIN LAUREL

**mountain juniper** *n* **:** a depressed or trailing juniper that is a variety (*Juniperus communis saxatilis*) of the common juniper, occurs in exposed places and mountains chiefly in northeastern No. America, and has short broad curved pointed leaves with a broad white stripe

**mountain laurel** *n* **1 :** a No. American evergreen shrub (*Kalmia latifolia*) having glossy mostly alternate leaves and umbels of rose-colored or white flowers — called also *American laurel, calico bush* **2 :** CALIFORNIA LAUREL

**mountain leather** *n* **:** an absorbent asbestos occurring in thin tough flexible sheets **:** PALYGORSKITE

**moun·tain·less** \ˈmau̇ntᵊnləs, -tən-\ *adj* **:** lacking mountains

**mountain lilac** *n* **:** a Californian shrub of the genus *Ceanothus*

**mountain lily** *n* **1 :** a Japanese lily (*Lilium auratum*) with showy crimson-spotted yellow-banded white flowers **2 :** a showy white-flowered buttercup (*Ranunculus lyallii*) of New Zealand **3 :** SAND LILY

**mountain limestone** *n* **:** a carboniferous limestone occurring in the hills and mountains of England and generally equivalent to the Mississippian of the No. American section

**mountain lion** *n* **:** COUGAR

**mountain lover** *n* **1 :** a small trailing evergreen shrub (*Pachistima canbyi*) of the southeastern U. S. **2 :** OREGON BOX

**mountain magnolia** *n* **:** any of several upland American magnolias (esp. *Magnolia acuminata* and *M. fraseri*)

**mountain magpie** *n* **1 :** GREEN WOODPECKER **2** *dial Eng* **:** a European butcher-bird (*Lanius exubitor*)

**mountain mahoe** *n* **:** a West Indian tree (*Hibiscus tiliaceus*) related to the majagua and having flowers that change from pale pink in the morning to deep red in the evening — compare CUBAN BAST

**mountain mahogany** *n* **1 :** any of several shrubs or small shrubby trees of western No. America that constitute the genus *Cercocarpus* of the family Rosaceae and are often important browse or forage plants; *esp* **:** an evergreen tree (*C. ledifolius*) with cherry red to chocolate brown very hard strong heartwood that is sometimes used for turnery and carving — see FEATHER TREE 2, HARDTACK 2 **2 :** SWEET BIRCH **3 :** a yew (*Taxus brevifolia*) of the Pacific coast of the U. S.

**mountain-making** \ˈ==ˌ==\ *adj* **:** causing the upthrust of mountains

**mountain man** *n* **1 :** MOUNTAINEER 1a **2 :** a pioneering frontiersman (as a trapper or trader) at home in wilderness country ⟨trappers, traders, scouts, hunters, guides — whatever they were . . . they were all *mountain men* —Frank Waters⟩ ⟨all the way across the continent there would be an advance screen of long hunters and *mountain men* —Bernard DeVoto⟩

**mountain maple** *n* **:** any of various American shrubby maples found in mountain regions: as **a :** a tall shrub or bushy tree (*Acer spicatum*) of the eastern U. S. with flaky or furrowed bark and slender cylindrical panicles of greenish flowers — called also *moose maple, mountain alder* **b :** DWARF MAPLE **c :** VINE MAPLE

**mountain mint** *n* **1 :** an American mint of the genus *Pycnanthemum*; *esp* **:** BASIL MINT **2 :** CALAMINT **3 :** OSWEGO TEA

**mountain misery** *n* **:** a California undershrub (*Chamaebatia foliolosa*) having dark green fernlike leaves and a fragrant gummy exudate — called also *bear clover, bear mat*

**mountain oak** *n* **:** a chestnut oak (*Quercus montana*)

**mountain of venus** *usu cap V* [trans. of NL *mons Veneris*] **:** MONS VENERIS

**moun·tain·ous** \ˈmau̇nt(ᵊ)nəs, -tən-\ *adj* [¹*mountain* + *-ous*] **1 :** characterized by mountains ⟨turn eastward into the ~ Vermont wilderness —Budd Schulberg⟩ **2 :** resembling a mountain **:** HUGE, GIGANTIC ⟨rescued from the ~ seas —*News from New Zealand*⟩ ⟨seemed slender beside that ~ woman —Ann Bridge⟩ **3** *obs* **:** leading a primitive life in an inaccessible mountain region ⟨this wild ~ people —Samuel Purchas⟩ **4** *archaic* **:** MOUNTAIN 2a ⟨the ash and other ~ trees —Richard Warner⟩ — **moun·tain·ous·ly** *adv*

**moun·tain·ous·ness** *n* -ES **:** the quality or state of being mountainous

**mountain oyster** *n* **:** the testis of a bull calf, sheep, boar, or other animal used as food — called also *Rocky Mountain oyster*

**mountain paca** *n* **:** any of several rodents of the mountains of western So. America that constitute a genus (*Stictomys*) closely related to *Dasyprocta*

**mountain panther** *n* **1 :** SNOW LEOPARD **2 :** COUGAR

**mountain paper** *n* **:** an asbestos resembling mountain leather

**mountain parrot** *n* **:** KEA

**mountain parsley** *n* **1 :** a European herb (*Peucedanum oreoselinum*) having an aromatic seed and root **2 :** PARSLEY FERN b(2)

**mountain partridge** *n* **1 :** PARTRIDGE DOVE **2 :** MOUNTAIN QUAIL

**mountain pheasant** *n, South* **:** RUFFED GROUSE

**mountain phlox** *n* **1 :** a common mountain herb (*Phlox ovata*) of the southeastern U. S. having showy pink or red flowers **2 :** MOSS PINK

**mountain pine** *n* **1 a :** any of several pines of the U. S.; *esp* **:** a tall western timber tree (*Pinus monticola*) resembling the white pine **b** (1) **:** SWISS MOUNTAIN PINE (2) **:** MUGHO PINE **2 :** any of several Australian upland cypress pines (as black cypress pine or white cypress pine) **3 :** either of two New Zealand trees: **a :** a tree of the genus *Dacrydium* having tough wood and foliage that resembles cedar **b :** an evergreen tree (*Libocedrus bidwillii*) resembling the kawaka — called also *kaikawaka*

**mountain pine beetle** *n* **:** a bark beetle (*Dendroctonus ponderosae*) of the western U. S. that is extremely destructive to stands of lodgepole and sugar pines

**mountain pink** *n* **:** MOSS PINK

**mountain plover** *n* **:** a small plover (*Eupoda montana*) of the plains of the western U. S.

**mountain plum** *n* **:** the false sandalwood or its fruit

**mountain pride** *n* **:** a pentstemon (*Pentstemon newberryi*) of the mountains of California having pinkish to lavender open-mouthed flowers

**mountain quail** *n* **:** a partridge (*Oreortyx picta palmeri*) of California slightly larger than the California quail

**mountain railroad** *or* **mountain railway** *n* **:** a railroad employing special devices (as cables, racks and pinions, central rails) to hold the cars on the steep track — compare FUNICULAR

**mountain range** *n* **:** a series of mountains or mountain ridges closely related in position and direction — compare OROGEN

**mountain raspberry** *n* **:** CLOUDBERRY

**mountain rat** *n* **:** a bushy-tailed wood rat (*Neotoma cinerea*) of the western U. S.

**mountain rice** *n* **:** BUNCHGRASS; *esp* **:** a valuable forage grass (*Oryzopsis hymenoides*) that is widely distributed in dry upland areas and plains of western No. America

**mountain rimu** *n* **:** a prostrate or suberect shrub (*Dacrydium laxifolium*) of New Zealand with slender trailing branches

**mountain rose** *n* **1 :** a European alpine rose (*Rosa pendulina*) with crimson flowers **2 :** CORALVINE **3 :** CATAWBA RHODODENDRON

**mountain rosebay** *n* **:** CATAWBA RHODODENDRON

**mountains** *pl of* MOUNTAIN

**mountain sage** *n* **1 :** any of several plants of the genus *Artemisia* **2 :** WOOD SAGE 1

**mountain sandwort** *or* **mountain starwort** *n* **:** a boreal or alpine sandwort (*Arenaria groenlandica*) with subulate or filiform leaf blades and small white flowers — called also *mountain daisy*

**mountain sheep** *n* **:** any of various wild sheep inhabiting high mountains in different parts of the world — compare AOUDAD, ARGALI, BIGHORN, DALL SHEEP

**mountain sickness** *n* **:** altitude sickness experienced by mountain climbers or by those ascending or living above 10,000 feet elevation and caused by insufficient oxygen in the air breathed

**mountainside** \ˈ⸗⸗,⸗\ *n* **:** a part of a mountain between the summit and the foot ⟨from every ~ let freedom ring —S.F. Smith⟩

**mountain snow** *n* **:** SNOW-ON-THE-MOUNTAIN

**mountain soap** *n* **:** SAPONITE

**mountain sorrel** *n* **:** a low perennial herb (*Oxyria digyna*) found in northern latitudes in both hemispheres and having kidney-shaped leaves and greenish flowers

**mountain sparrow** *n* **:** TREE SPARROW 1

**mountain specter** *n* **:** BROCKEN SPECTER

**mountain spinach** *n* **:** GARDEN ORACHE

**mountain spleenwort** *n* **:** a spleenwort (*Asplenium montanum*) of eastern No. America

**mountain spruce** *n* **:** ENGELMANN SPRUCE

**mountain sucker** *n* **:** any of several small suckers of the genus *Pantosteus* widely distributed in upland areas of the western U. S.

**mountain sumac** *n* **1 :** DWARF SUMAC **2 :** AMERICAN MOUNTAIN ASH

**mountain tea** *n* **1 :** WINTERGREEN 2a **2 :** an infusion of wintergreen leaves

**mountain tent** *n* **:** a lightweight usu. wedge-shaped tent having a floor and zippered doorway

**mountain thrush** *n* **1** *dial Eng* **:** RING OUZEL **2 :** an Australian thrush (*Zoothera dauma lunulata*)

**mountain time** *or* **mountain standard time** *n, often cap M* **:** the time of the seventh time zone west of Greenwich based on the 105th meridian and used in west central Canada and the U. S. — abbr. *MT* or *MST*

**mountain timothy** *n* **:** a north temperate perennial grass (*Phleum alpinum*) with ovoid or short cylindrical panicles

**mountaintop** \ˈ⸗⸗,⸗\ *n* **:** the summit of a mountain

**mountain trout** *n* **1 :** BROOK TROUT **2 :** an Australian upland minnow (*Galaxias coxi*)

**mountain vizcacha** *n* **:** any of several vizcachas constituting the genus *Lagidium* and living in mountainous parts of western So. America

**mountain wall** *n* **:** a steep mountainside

**moun·tain·ward** \ˈmau̇ntᵊnwə(r)d, -tən-\ *or* **moun·tain·wards** \-dz\ *adv* **:** toward the mountains

**mountain watercress** *n* **:** a bitter cress (*Cardamine rotundifolia*) of streams and damp places of the mountains of eastern No. America having diffuse reclining or trailing stems and simple rounded leaves

**mountain white** *n* **:** a white person inhabiting a mountain region esp. in the southeastern U. S. ⟨the poor *mountain whites*, primitive, rugged, proud —*Amer. Guide Series: Va.*⟩

**mountain willow** *n* **1 :** a much-branched shrubby willow (*Salix planifolia*) of Europe and northeastern No. America **2 :** a tree willow (*Salix scouleriana*) of uplands in the western U. S.

**mountain wind** *n* **:** a breeze of diurnal period depending on the unevenness of land surfaces and blowing down the slope by night — called also *mountain breeze;* compare VALLEY WIND

**mountain winterberry** *n* **:** MOUNTAIN HOLLY 2

**mountain witch** *n* **:** a quail dove (*Geotrygon versicolor*) of the West Indies

**mountain wood** *n* **:** compact fibrous asbestos resembling dry wood in appearance

**moun·tainy** \ˈmau̇nt(ᵊ)nē, -tənē, -ni\ *adj* **1 a :** full of mountains **:** MOUNTAINOUS ⟨~ mass —Rose Macaulay⟩ **b :** of, relating to, or characteristic of mountainous regions **:** MOUNTAIN ⟨worked on a ~ farm —F.M.Ford⟩ ⟨passed from ~ foothills, through green slopes, lush flatlands, and desert —A.J. Liebling⟩ **2 :** living in or associated with the mountains ⟨an old ~ man that had a shirt and trousers of unbleached flannel —W.B.Yeats⟩ ⟨a ~ man and not used to horses —B.T. Cleeve⟩

**mountain zebra** *n* **:** a narrow-striped now nearly extinct zebra (*Equus zebra zebra*) of southern Africa

**moun·tant** \ˈmau̇ntᵊnt\ *n* -s [²*mount* + *-ant*] **1 :** an adhesive used for fastening a print or drawing to a mount **2 :** any substance in which a specimen is suspended between a slide and a cover glass for microscopic examination

¹**moun·te·bank** \ˈmau̇ntə,baŋk, -aiŋk\ *n* -s [It *montambanco, montimbanco*, fr. *montare* to mount, climb (fr. — assumed — VL) + *in* in, on (fr. L) + *banco, banca* bench — more at MOUNT, IN, BANK] **1 a :** an itinerant hawker of pills and patent medicines **:** PITCHMAN, QUACK ⟨bought an unction of a ~ —Shak.⟩ **b :** an entertainer (as a juggler or magician) employed by a quack to attract a crowd ⟨three or four ~*s* . . . manipulated their blue and yellow lion —Nora Waln⟩ **2 :** an unscrupulous cheat or impostor **:** CHARLATAN, SWINDLER ⟨almost all politicians were frauds and ~*s* —J.T.Farrell⟩

²**mountebank** *vt, obs* **:** to beguile or transform by trickery ⟨I'll ~ their loves —Shak.⟩ ⟨amazed to see their money ~*ed* to mercury —Daniel Defoe⟩ ~ *vi* **:** to play the mountebank ⟨you'd better stop ~*ing* round this town —J.B.Priestley⟩

**moun·te·bank·ery** \-ŋkərē\ *n* -ES **1 :** CHARLATANRY, HOCUS-POCUS **2 :** an action characteristic of a mountebank ⟨this is wonderful ~ . . . at once pathetic and uproarious —*N.Y. Times*⟩

**mounted** *adj* [fr. past part. of ²*mount*] **1** *archaic* **:** piled high **:** heaped up ⟨the farthest bourn of ~ eastern cloud —George Meredith⟩ **2 a :** seated or riding on a horse **:** serving on horseback ⟨~ police⟩ **b :** provided with a means of transportation ⟨a ~ messenger shall record the actual number of times he stops his vehicle to make a delivery —*U. S. Post Office Manual*⟩ **c :** performed with the aid of a means of transportation ⟨~ patrol⟩ ⟨no ~ collection is needed in strictly residential territory —*U. S. Post Office Manual*⟩ **3 :** being in working order or placed in position for firing ⟨a completely ~ rifle⟩ ⟨the quarter-deck guns all adrift, and not even ~ —Frederick Marryat⟩ **4 a :** assembled or equipped for use esp. by being attached to a support ⟨tractors with ~ implements —Roy Lewis & Angus Maude⟩ **b :** prepared for display esp. by being furnished with an appropriate frame or setting ⟨~ engraving⟩ ⟨thousands of ~ specimens of tiger beetles —R.K.Plumb⟩; *specif* **:** decorated with applied ornamentation ⟨spied the trim, brass ~ carbine of the ranger —F.V.W. Mason⟩ **c** *of a gemstone* **:** backed with enamel, foil, or dye in order to improve the color **d :** having the pipes displayed as part of the organ case or otherwise specially set up — used of a pipe-organ stop **5 :** equipped with scenery, lighting, costumes, and properties ⟨learn what she is thinking through an impressionistically ~ sound flashback —Lewis Jacobs⟩ ⟨the stage production was cleverly ~ and well performed

**mounted delivery** *n* **:** mail delivery by uniformed carriers using mail trucks in a suburban area too heavily populated for rural free delivery

**mounted route** *n* **:** a postal route served by mounted delivery

**mounted work** *n* **:** silverware with ornaments soldered on

**mount·er** \ˈmau̇ntə(r)\ *n* -s **:** one that mounts: as **a :** a jewelry worker who fashions settings **b :** a worker who mounts optical lenses in frames **c :** a setter of watch jewels **d :** an assembler of radios or radio tubes **e :** a craftsman who attaches carvings and other decorations to furniture **f :** a machine for attaching or inserting small pieces of paper or film in or to a punched card

**mount·ie** *also* **mounty** \ˈmau̇ntē, -ti\ *n, pl* **mounties** *usu cap* [*mount*ed policeman + *-ie, y*] **:** a member of the Royal Canadian Mounted Police ⟨a *Mountie* always gets his man⟩

¹**mount·ing** \ˈmau̇ntiŋ, -tēŋ\ *n* -s [ME, fr. gerund of *mounten* to mount — more at MOUNT] **1 :** an act or instance of mounting; *specif* **:** getting on a horse ⟨one method of ~ is to place the left foot in the stirrup and swing the right leg over the saddle⟩ **2 :** FRAME, SUPPORT, EMBELLISHMENT: as **a :** a jewelry setting ⟨bought a ~ for the pearl —Lynn Groh⟩ **b :** a handle, mount, or coupling for a mechanical device ⟨the ~ of the sword was encrusted with jewels⟩ ⟨guns . . . on portable carriages or stationary ~*s* —*Notes & Queries on Anthropology*⟩ ⟨engines . . . attached to the frame at two, three, or four points according to the type of ~ —Joseph Heitner⟩ **c :** MOUNT 2b ⟨an interesting picture enhanced by an artistic ~⟩ **d :** the harness of a loom **e :** the nonoptical parts of a telescope (as the pier, axes, circles, and tubes); *specif* **:** the standard or support of a telescope ⟨an equatorial ~⟩ **3 :** the decor and lighting of a theatrical production as distinguished from its performance **:** STAGING ⟨technicolor gives the picture a fairly handsome ~ —*Time*⟩

²**moun·ting** \"\ *dial var of* MOUNTAIN

**mounting medium** *n* **:** a medium in which a biological specimen is mounted for preservation or display

**mount of apollo** *usu cap M&A* [after *Apollo*, Greco-Roman god associated with the sun] **:** a mount located at the base of the third finger that when well developed is usu. held by palmists to indicate a love for all things beautiful and artistic — called also *Mount of Brilliancy, Mount of the Sun;* see PALMISTRY illustration

**mount of brilliancy** *usu cap M&B* **:** MOUNT OF APOLLO

**mount of jupiter** *usu cap M&J* [after *Jupiter*, Roman god of the sky, fr. L *Juppiter* — more at DEITY] **:** a mount located at the base of the first finger that when well developed is usu. held by palmists to indicate ambition, pride, enthusiasm, and desire for power — see PALMISTRY illustration

**mount of luna** *usu cap M&L* [*luna* fr. L, moon — more at LUNAR] **:** a mount located on the side of the hand below lower Mars and across the palm from the Mount of Venus that when well developed is usu. held by palmists to indicate refinement, imagination, idealism, and a taste for things romantic and beautiful — called also *Mount of the Moon;* see PALMISTRY illustration

**mount of mars** *usu cap both Ms* [after *Mars*, Roman god of war and agriculture, fr. L *Mart-, Mars*] **1 :** UPPER MARS **2 :** LOWER MARS

**mount of melody** *usu cap both Ms* **:** MOUNT OF VENUS

**mount of mercury** *usu cap both Ms* [after *Mercury*, Roman god of commerce, fr. L *Mercurius*] **:** a mount located at the base of the little finger that when well developed is usu. held by palmists to indicate a predominance of practical qualities (as shrewdness, diplomacy, and adaptability) that often lead to success in business and politics — see PALMISTRY illustration

**mount of saturn** *usu cap M&S* [after *Saturn*, Roman god connected with the sowing of seed, fr. L *Saturnus*] **:** a mount located at the base of the second finger that when well developed is usu. held by palmists to indicate seriousness, prudence, and often a love of quiet and solitude — see PALMISTRY illustration

**mount of the moon** *usu cap both Ms* **:** MOUNT OF LUNA

**mount of the sun** *usu cap M&S* **:** MOUNT OF APOLLO

**mount of venus** *usu cap M&V* [after *Venus*, Roman goddess of love — more at VENUS] **:** a mount constituted by the large development of the hand at the base of the thumb that when well developed is held by palmists to indicate affection, sympathy, sexual attraction, and love of beauty, color, and melody — called also *Mount of Melody;* see PALMISTRY illustration

**mounts** *pl of* MOUNT, *pres 3d sing of* MOUNT

**mounture** *n* -s [²*mount* + *-ure*] *obs* **:** the angle of a gun when raised for firing

**mounty** *usu cap, var of* MOUNTIE

**mourn** \ˈmō(ə)rn, ˈmȯ(ə)rn, ˈmōən, ˈmȯ(ə)n\ *vb* -ED/-ING/-S [ME *mournen, mornen*, fr. OE *murnan;* akin to OHG *mornēn* to mourn, sorrow, ON *morna*, Goth *maurnan* to mourn, sorrow, Gk *mermeros* anxious — more at MEMORY] *vi* **1 a :** to be sorry **:** feel or express deep regret ⟨announced his resignation and everybody ~*ed*⟩ **b** *archaic* **:** to look or act unhappy **:** DROOP, PINE ⟨flowers . . . rejoice at the presence of the sun; and ~ at the absence thereof —Francis Bacon⟩ ⟨cattle ~*ed* for want of milkers —Samuel Purchas⟩ **2 a :** to be sorrowful over a death **:** GRIEVE ⟨time is the great solace of those who ~⟩ ⟨a service which seems spoken by the dead man himself to those who ~ —Walter Besant & James Rice⟩ **b :** to exhibit the conventional signs of mourning; *esp* **:** to wear black ⟨grieve for an hour, perhaps, then ~ a year —Alexander Pope⟩ **3 a :** to murmur mournfully — used esp. of doves **b** *dial* **:** MOAN ~ *vt* **1 :** to be distressed over **:** BEWAIL, PROTEST ⟨led a funeral procession up . . . Fifth Avenue to ~ pogroms —*Time*⟩ ⟨hair-splitting statesmen . . . may ~ the passing of our subjunctive — Weston La Barre⟩ **2 :** to grieve for (someone who has died) ⟨she was ~*ed* by thousands of persons whose lives she had touched —A.J.Kennedy⟩ **3 :** to utter mournfully ⟨let the whirlwind ~ its requiem —W.S.Gilbert⟩ **syn** see GRIEVE

**mourn·er** \-nə(r)\ *n* -s [ME *morener*, fr. *mournen, mornen* to mourn + *-er*] **1 a :** one that mourns ⟨the book business has outlived most of its ~*s* —Aaron Sussman⟩; *esp* **:** one who attends a funeral out of respect or affection for the deceased ⟨when he died, the wayward boys he had befriended were among his chief ~*s*⟩ **b :** one hired to attend a funeral or wail for the dead ⟨~*s* were provided to attend the funeral —Roger L'Estrange⟩ **2 :** one that publicly repents of his sins at a revival meeting ⟨asks for ~*s* to come up and be saved —J.H. Stuart⟩

**mourners' bench** *n* **:** ANXIOUS BENCH 1

**mourn·ful** \-nfəl\ *adj, sometimes* **mournfuller;** *sometimes* **mournfullest 1 a :** full of sorrow **:** SAD ⟨stared with ~ eyes at a daydream of her lost husband —Eric Linklater⟩ **b :** causing sorrow **:** SADDENING ⟨~ news⟩ **2 a :** of a melancholy nature **:** DOLEFUL, DISPIRITED ⟨took a ~ view of human affairs — Ellen Glasgow⟩ ⟨in a ~ rehearsal in Philadelphia I read to my dancers . . . and they took heart —Agnes de Mille⟩ **b :** having a gloomy sound or aspect **:** DISMAL, SOMBER ⟨a long, ~ howl — Lyle Saxon⟩ ⟨the ~ tolling of a bell —Jack London⟩ ⟨a country of ~ cedar thickets —*Amer. Guide Series: Tenn.*⟩ **3 :** causing disappointment **:** REGRETTABLE ⟨a ~ obtuseness of moral feeling in regard to the crimes of military and political life —W.E. Channing⟩ — **mourn·ful·ly** \-fəlē, -li\ *adv*

**mourn·ful·ness** \-lnəs\ *n* -ES **:** the quality or state of being mournful

**mourn·ing** \ˈmō(ə)rniŋ, ˈmȯ(ə)rn-, ˈmōən-, ˈmȯ(ə)n-, -nēŋ\ *n* -s [ME *mourning, morning*, fr. gerund of *mournen, mornen*, to mourn — more at MOURN] **1 :** an act or instance of feeling or expressing sorrow ⟨general ~ over loss of the championship⟩; *specif* **:** grief caused by bereavement ⟨a sound of ~ came from the dead man's room⟩ **2 a :** the ritual observances accompanying a death ⟨~ is repeated for all those who have died during the last few years —*Drums and Shadows*⟩; *specif* **:** the wearing of black ⟨~ is traditional for pallbearers⟩ **b :** the black clothing, draperies, or emblems symbolic of grief esp. among western nations ⟨didn't believe in old-fashioned ~ . . . nobody wore it any longer —Margaret A. Barnes⟩ ⟨lots of people there, and only one man in full ~ —Arnold Bennett⟩ ⟨the room had been cleaned and the ~ pinned up again in newspapers —Ellen Glasgow⟩ — compare CRAPE 3a, ³WEED 2 **c :** the period during which black is worn by a mourner ⟨after a long ~, resume their ordinary dresses —Henry Reed †1854⟩

**mourning bride** *n* **:** a plant of the genus *Scabiosa; esp* **:** a half-hardy annual (*S. atropurpurea*)

**mourning cloak** *or* **mourning cloak butterfly** *n* **:** a blackish brown butterfly (*Nymphalis antiopa*) with a broad yellow border on the wings found in Europe and No. America and having dark spiny larvae that live in clusters esp. on elm, willow, and hackberry — called also *camberwell beauty*

**mourning dove** *n* **:** a wild dove (*Zenaidura macroura carolinensis*) of the U.S. resembling the passenger pigeon in form and plumage though much smaller, having a plaintive note and being represented by distinct subspecies in Cuba and western No. America

**mourn·ing·ly** *adv* **:** MOURNFULLY

**mourning of the chine** [by folk etymology fr. MF *mort de eschine*, lit., death of the spine] *obs* **:** GLANDERS

**mourning warbler** *n* **:** a warbler (*Oporornis philadelphia*) of eastern No. America, the male having the head, neck, and chest deep ash gray mixed with black on the throat and chest with the lower parts pure yellow

**mour·ni·val** \ˈmōrnəvəl\ *n* -s [MF *mornifle*] **1** *archaic* **:** a set of four aces, kings, queens, or knaves in one hand in the game of gleek **2** *obs* **:** a group of four ⟨a ~ of protests; or a gleek at least —Ben Jonson⟩

**mourns** *pres 3d sing of* MOURN

**mous** *pl of* MOU

¹**mouse** \ˈmau̇s\ *n, pl* **mice** \ˈmīs\ *often attrib* [ME *mous*, fr. OE *mūs;* akin to OHG & ON *mūs* mouse, L *mus*, Gk *mys*, Skt *mūṣ* mouse, and perh. to L *movēre* to move — more at MOVE] **1 a :** any of numerous small rodents typically resembling diminutive rats with pointed snout, rather small ears, elongated body, and slender hairless or sparsely haired tail, including all the smaller members of the genus *Mus* and many members of other rodent genera and families having little more in common than their relatively small size — see HARVEST MOUSE, HOUSE MOUSE, JUMPING MOUSE, POCKET MOUSE, WHITE-FOOTED MOUSE **b :** a young muskrat **2 a** *slang* **:** WOMAN, GIRL FRIEND ⟨in the role of . . . the rich Chicago ~ —*Playbill*⟩ ⟨the ~ he was shackin' up with —Earle Birney⟩ **b :** a timid or diffident person ⟨he might be a lion, but in . . . public affairs he must remain a ~ —W.H.Hale⟩ **c :** something trivial or insignificant ⟨labors over a mountain of the chaff of experience to bring forth a poor ~ of reflection —Edward Sapir⟩ **3 :** something that resembles a mouse: as **a** *archaic* **:** a small lump of muscle meat **b** (1) *archaic* **:** a knot on a ship's stays to prevent a rope from slipping (2) **:** MOUSING **c :** a dark-colored swelling caused by a blow ⟨a heavy right to the cheekbone . . . raised a ~ —*New South Wales Bull.*⟩; *specif* **:** BLACK EYE 1a ⟨began the voyage by hanging a ~ on the steward's eye —*Time*⟩ **d :** RAT 3 **e** (1) **:** a small lead weight fastened to a string and used to pull window sash cords into place over pulleys in the jambs of the frame (2) **:** a similar weight used by plumbers to clear a stoppage in a pipe (3) **:** a loose-fitting plug that is forced through a conduit by compressed air and carries with it wires to be drawn into place **4 a :** an olive gray — called also *beige gray* **b :** MOUSE GRAY

mouse 1a

²**mouse** \ˈmau̇z, ˈmau̇s\ *vb* -ED/-ING/-S [ME *mousen*, fr. *mous*, n.] *vi* **1 :** to hunt for or catch mice ⟨the large white owl . . . *moused* in the long grass —Charlotte Yonge⟩ **2 a :** to poke around or make a curious inspection **:** EXPLORE, SNOOP ⟨go *mousing* around libraries . . . looking for dead facts — Garrett Mattingly⟩ ⟨*mousing* politicians —Telford Taylor⟩ **b :** to move stealthily or slowly **:** CREEP, SAUNTER ⟨walked eastward, *mousing* doggedly along on the shady side —John Galsworthy⟩ ⟨just ~ along, putting one saddle shoe in front of the other —Peg Bracken⟩ ~ *vt* **1** *obs* **a :** NIBBLE, GNAW ⟨death . . . feasts, *mousing* the flesh of men —Shak.⟩ **b :** to harass playfully **:** toy with — used chiefly in the phrase *touse and mouse* ⟨none but naughty women sat there, whom they toused and *moused* —William Wycherley⟩ **2 :** to apply a mousing to (a hook) **3 :** to discover by painstaking search — usu. used with *out* ⟨~ out a neighborhood scandal⟩

**mousebane** \ˈ⸗,⸗\ *n* **:** a common European monkshood (*Aconitum napellus*) with poisonous foliage

**mouse barley** *n* **:** WALL BARLEY

**mousebird** \ˈ⸗,⸗\ *n* **1 :** COLY **2 :** WHITE-RUMPED SHRIKE

**mouse bloodwort** *n* **:** MOUSE-EAR 1a

**mouse bur** *n* **:** UNICORN PLANT

**mouse-colored** \ˈ⸗ˈ⸗⸗\ *adj* **:** of the color mouse-gray

**mouse deer** *n* **:** CHEVROTAIN

**mouse-ear** \ˈ⸗,⸗\ *n* [ME *mousere*, fr. *mous* mouse + *ere* ear — more at EAR] **1 a** *or* **mouse-ear hawkweed :** a European hawkweed (*Hieracium pilosella*) having soft hairy leaves — called also *felon herb, mouse bloodwort* **b** *or* **mouse-ear everlasting** *or* **mouse-ear plantain :** an everlasting (*Antennaria plantaginifolia*) with soft gray leaves — called also *cat's-foot* **c :** MARSH CUDWEED **2 :** FORGET-ME-NOT 1a

**mouse-ear chickweed** *or* **mouse-eared chickweed** *also* **mouse-ear** *n* **:** any of several hairy chickweeds of the genus *Cerastium* (esp. *C. vulgatum* and *C. viscosum*) — called also *clammy chickweed*

**mouse-ear cress** *also* **mouse-ear** *n* **:** a Eurasian herb (*Arabidopsis thaliana*) naturalized as a weed in the U.S.

**mouse-eared** \ˈ⸗ˈ⸗\ *adj* **:** having an appendage suggestive of the ear of a mouse

**mousefish** \ˈ⸗,⸗\ *n* **:** a common sargassum fish (*Histrio pictus*)

**mouse galago** *n* **:** a West African galago (*Galago demidoffi*)

**mouse gray** *or* **mouse dun** *n* **:** a brownish gray that is lighter, stronger, and slightly yellower than taupe, yellower and lighter than chocolate, and lighter and slightly redder and stronger than castor — called also *boulevard, murinus, Sakkara, sparrow*

**mouse hare** *n* **:** PIKA

**mousehawk** \ˈ⸗,⸗\ *n* **1** *dial* **:** OWL **2** *dial* **:** any of several hawks (as the marsh hawk or the rough-legged hawk)

**mousehole** \ˈ⸗,⸗\ *n* [ME *moushole*, fr. *mous* mouse + *hole*] **1 a :** a mouse's burrow **b :** a small hole (as in a baseboard) gnawed by a mouse **2 a :** a small opening or passageway **b :** a small space used for storage or for living quarters **:** CUBBY

**mousehunt** \ˈ⸗,⸗\ *n, dial chiefly Eng* **:** WEASEL

**mouse·kin** \ˈmau̇skən\ *n* -s [¹*mouse* + *-kin*] **:** a little mouse

**mouse lemur** *n* **:** any of several small lemurs (as a dwarf lemur or a member of the genus *Cheirogaleus*)

**mouse·let** \ˈmau̇slət\ *or* **mouse·ling** \-liŋ, -lēŋ\ *n* -s **:** a small or baby mouse

**mouselike** \ˈ⸗,⸗\ *adj* **1 :** of, relating to, or characteristic of a mouse ⟨~ tail⟩ **2 :** resembling a mouse in nondescript coloring or timidity of behavior ⟨~ clerk⟩ ⟨a nervous, nondescript, ~ little man⟩

**mouse opossum** *n* **1 :** an opossum of the genus *Marmosa* **2 :** DORMOUSE OPOSSUM

**mouse owl** *n* **:** SHORT-EARED OWL

**mousepox** \ˈ⸗,⸗\ *n* **:** a virus disease of mice that is related to smallpox — called also *ectromelia, infectious ectromelia*

**mouseproof** \ˈ⸗ˈ⸗\ *adj* **:** proof against mice ⟨store grain in a ~ shed⟩

**mous·er** \ˈmau̇zə(r), -au̇sə-\ *n* -s [ME *mowsare*, fr. *mowsen, mousen* to mouse + *-are, -er* -er — more at MOUSE] **:** one that catches mice and rats; *esp* **:** a cat or other animal that habitually catches mice

**mous·ery** \ˈmau̇s(ə)rē, -ri\ *n* -ES **1 :** a place inhabited by a colony of mice or voles **2 :** a place where mice are bred and reared in captivity

**mousetail** \ˈ⸗,⸗\ *n* **1 :** a plant of the genus *Myosurus; esp* **:** a plant (*M. minimus*) with a flower whose receptacle looks like a tail **2 :** any of various plants with an inflorescence resembling a tail

**mouse-tailed bat** \ˈ⸗ˈ⸗-\ *n* **:** any of several rather small insectivorous bats (genus *Rhinopoma*) having a long tail, a reduced interfemoral membrane, and two joints to the index finger and being widely distributed in northern Africa and southern Asia

¹**mousetrap** \ˈ⸗,⸗\ *n* [ME *mowse trape*, fr. *mowse, mous* mouse + *trape, trappe* trap — more at TRAP] **1 a :** a trap for mice **b :** a sharp cheese of the type used for baiting a mousetrap ⟨that wonderful uniform cheddar we call . . . ~ —R.W.Howard⟩ **2 :** something that resembles a mousetrap: as **a :** a stratagem that lures one to defeat or destruction; *specif* **:** a football play in which a defensive player is allowed to cross the line of scrimmage and is unexpectedly blocked from the side while the ball carrier advances through the spot he has vacated — called also *trap, trap play* **b :** a small place **:** HOLE-IN-THE-WALL ⟨this pitiable young man shutting himself up in a ~ —Rebecca West⟩ **c :** a fishing tool for removing small objects from a drilled well **d :** a new or improved product that attracts attention in a highly competi-

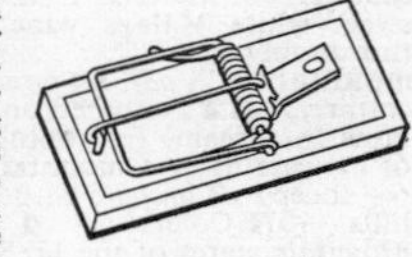
mousetrap 1a

tive market ⟨current experiments amount to attempts at building a better ~ —*Monsanto Mag.*⟩
**²mousetrap** \"\ *vt* **:** to snare in or as if in a mousetrap ⟨two prize motorized armor divisions . . . had been *mousetrapped*, and subsequently destroyed —P.W.Thompson⟩ ⟨~ a politician into a damaging statement⟩; *specif* **:** to block out (a defensive lineman) in a football game by means of the mousetrap play
**mouse-web** \ˈmüˌsweb, ˈmüzˌw-\ *n, chiefly Scot* **:** COBWEB
**mousey** *var of* MOUSY
**mousier** *comparative of* MOUSY
**mousiest** *superlative of* MOUSY
**mous·i·ly** \ˈmau̇sə̇lē, -au̇zə̇-, -li\ *adv* **:** in a mousy manner **:** QUIETLY, TIMIDLY
**mous·i·ness** \-sēnə̇s, -sin-, -zēn-, -zin-\ *n* -ES **:** the quality or state of being mousy **:** DRABNESS, TIMIDITY
**mousing** *n* -s [fr. gerund of ²*mouse*] **1 :** the pursuit or extermination of mice and rats ⟨cats were used for ~ —G.B.Saul⟩ **2 :** a turn or lashing (as of rope yarn) used by seamen esp. across the open end of a hook to prevent the load carried from slipping off
**mousle** *vt* [freq. of ²*mouse*] *obs* **:** MOUSE 1b
**mous·que·taire** \ˌmüskəˈta(a)(ə)r, -te(ə)r, -ta(a)ə, -teə\ *n* -s [F — more at MUSKETEER] **1** *usu cap* **:** a French musketeer; *esp* **:** one of the royal musketeers of the 17th and 18th centuries conspicuous for their daring and their dandified dress **2** *usu* **mousquetaire glove :** a woman's long gauntlet glove often made with a lengthwise buttoned opening at the wrist
**mousse** \ˈmüs\ *n* -s [F, lit., froth, fr. L *mulsa* hydromel, fr. fem. of *mulsus* mixed with honey, sweet as honey — more at MULSE] **1 a :** a frothy dessert; *esp* **:** a dessert of sweetened and flavored whipped cream, or thin cream and gelatin, frozen without stirring **b :** a purée of meat or fish lightened with gelatin or whipped cream or both ⟨chicken ~⟩ **c** *also* **mousse·line** \ˌmüˈslēn, -üsəˈl-\ **:** a food so prepared as to be light, spongy, or creamy in texture and usu. containing gelatin, cream, or whites of eggs ⟨broccoli ~⟩ — compare SOUFFLÉ **2 :** MOSS GREEN
**mousse·line** \(ˈ)müˈslēn, -üsəˈl-\ *n* -s [F, lit., muslin — more at MUSLIN] **1 :** a fine sheer clothing fabric of silk, rayon, wool, or cotton that resembles muslin and has a crisp finish **2 a** *or* **mousseline sauce :** a frothy sauce or purée made so by the addition of whipped cream or beaten egg whites; *specif* **:** hollandaise sauce to which whipped cream or beaten egg whites have been added **b :** MOUSSE 1c ⟨a fluffy ~ of potatoes —*Mag. of Books*⟩
**mousseline de laine** \-dəˈlān\ *n* [F, lit., woolen muslin] **:** DELAINE 1
**mousseline de soie** \-dəˈswä\ *n, pl* **mousselines de soie** [F, lit., silk muslin] **:** a silk muslin resembling chiffon but having a crisp finish and being mainly used for evening dresses and trimmings
**moussena** *var of* MESENNA
**mous·tache** *or* **mus·tache** \ˈməˌstash, ˌməˈs-, -taa(ə)sh, -taish *also* ˌməˈs- *or* -ˈtäsh\ *n* -s [MF *moustache*, fr. OIt *mustaccio, mostaccio, mostacchio*, fr. MGk *moustaki*, fr. Gk (Doric) *mystok-, mystax* upper lip, moustache; akin to Gk (Attic) *mastax* mouth, jaws — more at MOUTH] **1 :** the hair growing on a man's or a woman's upper lip or that on either side of the upper lip ⟨a pair of ~*s*⟩ **2 :** something that resembles a moustache: as **a :** hair or bristles growing around the mouth of an animal **b :** a conspicuous stripe of color on the side of the head beneath the eye of a bird
**moustache cup** *n* **:** a cup having a guard to keep the moustache out of the liquid while one is drinking
**mous·tached** *or* **mus·tached** \(ˈ)məˈstasht, -taa(ə)sht, -taisht *also* -ˈtäsht *or* ˌməˈs-\ *adj* **:** having a moustache
**moustache monkey** *also* **moustache** *n* -s **:** a guenon of western Africa (*Cercopithecus cephus*) having a bluish face with a white stripe on the upper lip
**mous·tach·ial** *pronunc at* MOUSTACHE +ēəl\ *adj* **:** having or being a color marking suggesting a moustache — used of a bird

moustache cup

**moustachio** *var of* MUSTACHIO
**mous·te·ri·an** *or* **mous·tie·ri·an** \(ˈ)müˈsti(ə)rēən\ *adj, usu cap* [F *moustérien, moustiérien*, fr. Le Moustier, cave in Dordogne dept. in southwestern France where archeological finds were made + F *-ien* -ian] **:** of, relating to, or being a late lower Paleolithic period characterized by tools which were primarily flakes with retouched edges but sometimes biface core tools
**mousy** *or* **mousey** \ˈmau̇sē, -au̇zē, -i\ *adj* **mous·i·er; mous·i·est 1 a :** of, relating to, or characteristic of a mouse ⟨~ color⟩ ⟨~ smell⟩ **b :** infested with or smelling of mice ⟨~ cellar⟩ **2 a :** lacking in boldness or definition **:** COLORLESS, TIMID ⟨a ~, respectable novel —*New Yorker*⟩ ⟨the ~, competent little countryman —W.A.White⟩ **b :** making no noise **:** QUIET, STEALTHY ⟨slipped out in the ~ way . . . she so disliked —*Cosmopolitan*⟩ **c :** MOUSE-COLORED ⟨little girls with ~ pigtails —Winifred Bambrick⟩
**¹mout** \ˈmüt\ *dial Brit var of* MOLT
**²mout** \ˈmōt, ˈmau̇t\ *chiefly dial past of* MAY
**mou·tan** \ˈmüˌtan\ *also* **moutan peony** *n* [Chin (Pek) *mou³ tan¹, mu³-tan¹*] **:** TREE PEONY
**¹mouth** \ˈmau̇th\ *n, pl* **mouths** \ˈmau̇thz *also* -au̇z *sometimes* -au̇ths; -au̇ths *esp. in compounds whose meaning is "something having a certain kind of mouth," as "blabbermouth"*\ *often attrib* [ME, fr. OE *mūth*; akin to OHG *mund* mouth, ON *munnr, muthr*, Goth *munths* mouth, L *mandere* to chew, Gk *masasthai* to chew, *mastax* mouth, jaws] **1 a :** the opening through which food passes into the body of an animal; *specif* **:** the orifice in the head of higher vertebrates bounded by the lips or jaws **b :** the cavity bounded externally by the lips or jaws and internally by the pharynx or gullet that encloses in the typical vertebrate the tongue, gums, and teeth **:** the buccal cavity **c :** the structures enclosing or lying within the mouth cavity regarded as a whole ⟨the dog seized the bone in his ~⟩ ⟨my ~ is sore⟩ **2 a :** the lips as a feature of the face ⟨kissed her on the ~⟩ **b :** GRIMACE 1 ⟨make a ~⟩ **c :** response to guiding pressure on the bit — used of a horse ⟨a well-trained horse has a good ~⟩ **d :** an individual requiring food ⟨carnivora . . . keep down the number of useless ~*s* by killing off practically all the weak and aged —James Stevenson-Hamilton⟩ **e** (1) **:** the salivary glands ⟨pastry that makes one's ~ water⟩ (2) **:** the organs of taste **:** PALATE ⟨had my ~ all set for oysters⟩ **f** *obs* **:** a threatening vicinity ⟨we unawares run into danger's ~ —John Milton⟩ **3 a** *archaic* **:** oral communication **:** TONGUE ⟨learned . . . his faith from the ~ of the Roman priest —Mark Pattison⟩ **b** *obs* **:** a means of utterance ⟨the midnight bell did with his . . . brazen ~ sound on —Shak.⟩ **c :** the baying of a dog ⟨the musical ~ of a hound on the scent⟩ **4 a :** one that speaks **:** VOICE ⟨with all the ~*s* of Rome to second you —Joseph Addison⟩ ⟨through the ~ of his chancellor . . . made an unusual demand —R.W.Southern⟩ **b** *archaic* **:** an oral interchange **:** CONVERSATION ⟨the names . . . were in many ~*s* —T.B.Macaulay⟩ **c** (1) **:** a pronouncement attributed to someone ⟨artificial speeches placed in the ~*s* of historical figures —R.A.Hall b.1911⟩ (2) **:** expression in words **:** SPEECH ⟨names came up . . . and she might remember them in her father's ~ —Padraic Fallon⟩ **d** (1) **:** MOUTHPIECE 3a ⟨he is the ~ . . . of the House in its relations with the Crown —T.E. May⟩ (2) *archaic* **:** a gullible person **:** DUPE ⟨the whole gang will be . . . watching an opportunity to make a ~ of you —Charles Cotton⟩ **e** *archaic* (1) **:** a frame of reference **:** VIEW ⟨in a Roman ~, the graceful name of prophet and of poet was the same —William Cowper⟩ (2) **:** a sphere of authority **:** PROVINCE ⟨does it lie in the ~ of members of that government to taunt the . . . party with having no policy —Randolph Churchill⟩ **f** (1) **:** a tendency to excessive talk **:** VOLUBILITY ⟨he is not all ~ . . . he gets results —*Time*⟩ — often modified by *big* ⟨now you've spilled the beans, you and your big ~⟩ (2) **:** saucy or disrespectful language **:** IMPUDENCE, BACK TALK ⟨just don't take any ~ from him —Jackson Burgess⟩ **5 :** something that resembles a mouth: as **a** (1) **:** the place where a tributary enters a larger stream or body of water (2) **:** the entrance to a harbor (3) **:** the place where a valley or gorge begins (4) **:** the place where a side street enters a main thoroughfare **b :** the surface outlet of an underground shaft or passageway ⟨~ of a well⟩ ⟨~ of a mine⟩ ⟨~ of a volcano⟩ ⟨~*s* of all underdrains should be looked to —Adrian Bell⟩ ⟨arriving at the ~ of the burrow he lay down —J.T.McNish⟩ **c :** the opening at the receiving end of a container ⟨~ of a pocket⟩ ⟨~ of a bottle⟩ ⟨~ of a fisherman's trawl⟩; *specif* **:** the curved portion of a hook between the bill and the shank **d** (1) **:** the opening in a metallurgical furnace through which it is charged (2) **:** TAPHOLE (3) **:** any of several furnaces in a pottery kiln each connected by a flue to a central opening in the oven (4) **:** the opening in a covered glass pot **e :** the space between the cutting or gripping edges of a tool (as a vise) **f :** the muzzle of a piece of ordnance ⟨charged right up into the ~*s* of those cannon —F.B.Gipson⟩ ⟨the ~ of the automatic pressed closer against the back in the light overcoat —Kay Boyle⟩ **g :** the space in front of the cutter of a carpenter's plane through which the shavings pass **h** (1) **:** the open end of a wind instrument (as a horn) (2) **:** an opening (as in a flute) across which the player blows (3) **:** the opening between the lips of an organ flue pipe **i :** the summit of the tube of a corolla **j :** the opening of a univalve shell **k** *archit* **:** SCOTIA — **a poor mouth :** a plea of poverty ⟨I've got the millionaire tag because I always pay my bills within seven days and never put on *a poor mouth* —Sam Edgar⟩ ⟨some people put on *a poor mouth* over circumstances less unfortunate than those with more serious problems who accept them in a dignified manner⟩ — **down in the mouth :** sad or sulky in expression **:** DEJECTED, DISGRUNTLED ⟨came home with an empty creel, looking *down in the mouth*⟩ — **from mouth to mouth :** from person to person by word of mouth ⟨the news spread like wildfire *from mouth to mouth*⟩ — **full mouth** *obs* **:** with unrestrained voice **:** LOUDLY ⟨she was coming *full mouth* upon me with her contract —George Farquhar⟩ — **on the wrong side of one's mouth :** RUEFULLY ⟨we shall be laughing *on the wrong side of our mouths* before the day is over —W.E.Norris⟩
**²mouth** \ˈmau̇th\ *vb* -ED/-ING/-S [ME *mouthen*, fr. *mouth*, n.] *vt* **1 a :** to give utterance to **:** SPEAK, PRONOUNCE ⟨taught to ~ the word *cow* —Don Murray⟩ ⟨glibly ~*ed* by so many people —Edna Ferber⟩ ⟨only ~*s* words in talking about the need for faith —R.W.Flint⟩ **b :** to utter sententiously or bombastically ⟨~*ing* big phrases to hide little thought —Bruce Marshall⟩ ⟨~*ing* sonorous Virgil —Robert Keable⟩ **c :** to form soundlessly with the lips ⟨~*ing* the words, "this is what she thinks is tea" —Jean Stafford⟩ **2 a :** to take into the mouth ⟨he keeps them . . . in the corner of his jaw, first ~*ed* to be last swallowed —Shak.⟩; *esp* **:** EAT ⟨~*ed* down a square of cheese —Norman Mailer⟩ **b :** to work over with the mouth or teeth ⟨~*ing* the eggs and young for oxygenation purposes —L.P.Schultz⟩; *specif* **:** MANGLE ⟨a crooked . . . little man who had been ~*ed* by a whale —R.M.Lovett **3 a :** to accustom (a horse) to the bridle and bit ⟨a horse must be carefully ~*ed* before he is taught to jump⟩ **b :** to examine the teeth of (a horse or sheep) esp. as a means of estimating age ⟨sheepmen always ~ . . . sheep they are about to buy, to see if the age is as represented —*Lamb Production*⟩ **4 :** to swage the top of (a metal can) to receive the cover ~ *vi* **1 a :** to express oneself in speech **:** TALK, RECITE ⟨go around annoying people by ~*ing* to yourself —W. R.Benét⟩ ⟨juvenile ~*ing* of the multiplication tables⟩ **b :** to speak bombastically or angrily **:** DECLAIM, RAIL ⟨the bad old tradition of ~*ing* and ranting to bring . . . characters to life —Vernon Jarratt⟩ **c :** to divulge information **:** TELL ⟨wasn't going to have him ~ around the countryside that I had the stove for my own personal comfort —Michael McLaverty⟩ **2** *obs* **:** to caress with the lips **:** KISS ⟨the duke . . . would ~ with a beggar, though she smelt brown bread and garlic —Shak.⟩ **3 a :** to make faces **:** GRIMACE ⟨the children were giggling, bubbling, ~*ing* —Alexander Saxton⟩ **b :** to move the lips silently ⟨the octopus roped down from his hand, suckers still faintly ~*ing* —Norman Lewis⟩ **4 :** to issue into a larger body of water **:** DEBOUCH — used of a tributary ⟨where does this creek ~⟩
**mouth bet** *n* **:** a bet which a player announces but for which he does not put up the stake
**mouth breather** *n* **:** a person who habitually inhales and exhales through the mouth rather than through the nose
**mouthbreeder** \ˈ=,==\ *n* **1 :** any of several small fishes (family Cichlidae) that carry their eggs and young in the mouth; *esp* **:** a No. African fish (*Haplochromes multicolor*) often kept in a tropical aquarium **2 :** any of several marine catfishes that carry the eggs and young in the mouth
**mouthed** \ˈmau̇thd, -au̇tht\ *adj* [¹*mouth* + *-ed*] **1 :** having a mouth ⟨sat me down and took a ~ shell —John Keats⟩ — often used in combination ⟨wide-*mouthed* jar⟩ ⟨large-*mouthed* bass⟩ ⟨many-*mouthed* delta⟩ ⟨gentle-*mouthed* horse⟩ ⟨bull-*mouthed* siren⟩ **2** *obs* **a :** having a mouth of similar shape ⟨beaver . . . ~ like a cony —Thomas Morton⟩ **b :** GAPING, YAWNING ⟨~ graves will give thee memory —Shak.⟩
**mouth·er** \ˈmau̇thə(r)\ *n* -s **:** one that mouths; *esp* **:** a declamatory speaker ⟨a benevolent ~ of platitudes —John Mason Brown⟩
**mouth-filling** \ˈ=ˌ==\ *adj* **:** of notable length or sonority ⟨an impressive, *mouth-filling* sentence —J.N.Hook⟩ ⟨a *mouth-filling* and rather clumsy phrase —Lister Hill⟩
**mouth footed** *adj* **:** having maxillipeds
**mouth·ful** \ˈmau̇thˌfu̇l\ *n, pl* **mouthfuls** \-ˌfu̇lz\ **1 a :** a quantity that fills the mouth ⟨was submerged by a wave and got a ~ of seawater⟩ **b :** the quantity usu. taken into the mouth at one time **:** BITE ⟨assuagement of their hunger by a few more ~*s* —Glenway Wescott⟩ **2 :** a small quantity **:** MORSEL ⟨take a ~ of sweet country air —John Dryden⟩ **3 a :** a mouth-filling word or phrase ⟨the description of his new duties as "administrative coordination of developmental foreign investments" was a ~⟩ **b** *slang* **:** a comment or remark rich in meaning or substance ⟨you said a ~⟩
**mouthier** *comparative of* MOUTHY
**mouthiest** *superlative of* MOUTHY
**mouth·i·ness** \ˈmau̇thēnə̇s, -thin-, -thēn-, -thin-\ *n* -ES **:** the quality or state of being mouthy
**mouthing** *n* -s [fr. pres. part. of ²*mouth*] **1 :** a movement of the lips; *esp* **:** GRIMACE ⟨outward signs of repentance . . . groanings, ~*s*, and eyes upturned —Edith Sitwell⟩ **2 a :** an act or instance of speaking ⟨no matters . . . worth any labor in the ~ —George Barker⟩; *specif* **:** ORATION ⟨listened to the ~*s* of demagogues —*Saturday Rev.*⟩ **b :** a bombastic speech or phrase ⟨let them keep their sanctimonious ~*s* —Farley Mowat⟩ ⟨idealism and spirituality when separated from . . . concrete social situations are vague semantic ~*s* —Agnes Meyer⟩ **3 :** the process of accustoming a horse to a bridle and bit ⟨~ can be begun on the third day when the animal is . . . less inclined to resent gear and fitting —J.A.Miller⟩
**mouthing-bit** \ˈ==,=\ *n* **:** a bit used in mouthing a horse
**mouth·less** \ˈmau̇thlə̇s\ *adj* **:** lacking or appearing to lack a mouth
**mouthless crab** *n* **:** a large hairy-legged land crab (*Cardisoma crassum*) of the western coast of Central and So. America
**mouth-made** *adj, obs* **:** coming from the mouth rather than the heart **:** INSINCERE ⟨those *mouth-made* vows which break themselves in swearing —Shak.⟩
**mouth mirror** *n* **:** a long-handled dental mirror for inspecting the teeth and gums
**mouth organ** *n* **1 a :** PANPIPE **b** *or* **mouth harp :** HARMONICA 3 **2 :** MOUTHPIECE 1
**mouthpart** \ˈ=,=\ *n* **:** a structure or appendage near the mouth (as of an insect) — usu. used in pl.; see TROPHI
**mouthpiece** \ˈ=,=\ *n* **1 :** a structure or appendage that serves as a mouth ⟨~ of a reed organ pipe⟩; *specif* **:** an appendage to an inlet or outlet of a pipe or container that controls the flow of a fluid or other material (as of coal into a coal gas retort)

mouthpiece for tobacco pipe

**2 a :** a part that goes in the mouth ⟨~ of a respirator⟩ ⟨~ of a saxophone⟩ ⟨~ of a briar pipe⟩ ⟨the entire action of the bit should be concentrated in the ~ —W.H.Carter⟩; *specif* **:** a cigar or cigarette holder **b :** a part to which the mouth is applied ⟨~ of a trumpet⟩ ⟨~ of a telephone⟩ **c :** a protective device for the mouth; *specif* **:** a guard worn in the mouth over the upper teeth by a boxer to protect the teeth and reduce the hazard of cut lips **3 a :** one that expresses or interprets another's views ⟨accept her as the conventional ~ for all the discontents the author wishes to discharge —G.J.Becker⟩ ⟨government, as the ~ and executive instrument of the people —A.J.Bruwer⟩; *specif* **:** an official spokesman ⟨his assistants, ~*s*, and messengers . . . carried out his orders —S.G.Morley⟩ ⟨virtually every newspaper was the bought-and-paid-for ~ of a party or clique —W.A.Swanberg⟩ ⟨could create the sense in all who listened to him that he was the ~ of destiny —J.H.Plumb⟩ **b** *slang* **:** CRIMINAL LAWYER
**mouthpipe** \ˈ=,=\ *n* **1 :** an organ flue pipe **2 :** the section of a musical wind instrument into which the mouthpiece is inserted
**mouthroot** \ˈ=,=\ *n* **:** GOLDTHREAD 1
**mouthrot** \ˈ=,=\ *n* **:** a usu. fatal bacterial disease marked by severe necrotic changes of the mouth tissues of snakes esp. in captivity
**mouths** *pl of* MOUTH, *pres 3d sing of* MOUTH
**mouth-to-airway method** \ˌ==ˈ=,=-\ *n* **:** a variation of the mouth-to-mouth method of artificial respiration in which a rescuer blows through an airway inserted in the victim's mouth over the tongue
**mouth-to-mouth method** \ˌ==ˈ=-\ *n* **:** a method of artificial respiration in which a rescuer's mouth is placed tightly over the victim's mouth in order to force air into his lungs by blowing forcefully enough every few seconds to inflate them — called also *rescue breathing*
**mouthwash** \ˈ=,=\ *n* **:** a liquid preparation (as an antiseptic solution) for cleansing the mouth and teeth — called also *collutorium*
**mouth-watering** \ˈ=ˌ===\ *adj* **:** causing a flow of saliva into the mouth **:** APPETIZING ⟨a *mouth-watering* odor came from the kitchen⟩
**mouthy** \ˈmau̇thē, -au̇thē, -i\ *adj* -ER/-EST [¹*mouth* + *-y*] **:** excessively talkative or clamorous **:** GARRULOUS ⟨a ~ character who couldn't stay off the telephone —John & Ward Hawkins⟩; *specif* **:** BOMBASTIC ⟨strides about with many a ~ speech —Washington Irving⟩
**mou·ton** \ˈmüˌtän, =ˈ=\ *n* -s [ME *motoun*, fr. MF *mouton*, lit., ram — more at MUTTON] **1 :** AGNEL **2** [F, lit., sheep, fr. MF, ram] **:** a spy planted in a prison cell to obtain incriminating evidence **3** [F, sheep, sheepskin] **:** processed sheepskin that has been sheared and dyed to resemble beaver or seal and is used esp. for women's coats
**mou·ton·née** \ˌmütᵊnˈā\ *n* -s [by shortening] **:** ROCHE MOUTONNÉE
**MOV** *abbr* manuscript on vellum
**mov·a·bil·i·ty** *or* **move·a·bil·i·ty** \ˌmüvəˈbilə̇d·ē, -lətē, -i\ *n* **:** the quality or state of being movable
**¹mov·able** *or* **move·able** \ˈmüvəbəl\ *adj* [ME *mevable, movable*, fr. *meven, moven* to move + *-able* — more at MOVE] **1** *obs* **a :** FICKLE, INCONSTANT **b :** inclined to move or quick in movement **2 a :** capable of being moved **:** not fixed **:** not stationary ⟨a device with a ~ attachment⟩ **:** not restricted to one position or location ⟨~ hexachord⟩ ⟨~ clef sign⟩ **b** *of property* (1) **:** that can be removed or displaced and that is thus usu. personal rather than real ⟨~ wealth⟩ ⟨~ goods⟩ (2) *Scots law* **:** that does not descend to an heir by inheritance **:** that is not heritable **3 :** that varies chronologically; *specif* **:** that varies in calendar date from one year to the next ⟨a ~ holiday⟩ **4 :** alternating with zero morphophonemically or in etymologies **5** *of a letter or sound* **:** that in some forms or in some verbal environments is sometimes present (as for euphony) and sometimes absent — compare NU MOVABLE, QUIESCENT **6 :** pronounced as distinguished from quiescent ⟨~ consonants and syllables in Hebrew⟩
**²movable** *or* **moveable** \"\ *n* -s [ME *mevable*, fr. *mevable, movable*, adj.] **1 :** a piece of property (as an article of furniture) that can be removed or displaced **:** a movable piece of property **2** *Scots law* **:** a piece of property that is not heritable
**movable-do system** \ˌ===ˈdō-\ *n* **:** a system of solmization in which the sol-fa syllables may be transposed to any key — compare FIXED-DO SYSTEM
**movable exchange** *n* **:** INDIRECT EXCHANGE 2
**movable finger** *n* **:** the dactylopodite of a chela
**movable fixture** *n* **:** FIXTURE 2c(2)
**movable kidney** *n* **:** NEPHROPTOSIS
**mov·able·ness** *n* -ES [ME *mevablenes*, fr. *mevable, movable* + *-nes* -ness] **:** MOVABILITY
**movable type** *n* **:** printing type made up of individual pieces each carrying usu. a single letter or other character so that the pieces can be freely assembled or reassembled for printing any desired combination or line
**mov·ably** \ˈmüvəblē, -li\ *adv* **:** so as to be movable ⟨a rod that is attached ~ to the device⟩
**mov·ant** *also* **mov·ent** \ˈmüvənt\ *n* -s [¹*move* + *-ant* or *-ent*] **:** one that makes an application or petition to a court of law or to a judge with the intention of obtaining a favorable ruling
**¹move** \ˈmüv\ *vb* **moved; moved; moving** *with speakers who "drop the g" of present participles, often* ˈmüb°m, *often satirized by the spelling "moom pictures"*\ **moves** [ME *meven, moven*, fr. MF *movoir, mouvoir*, fr. L *movēre*; prob. akin to Gk *ameusasthai* to surpass, *amynein* to ward off, Skt *mīvati* he pushes, shoves, Lith *mauti* to pull (a garment) on or off; basic meaning: to push] *vi* **1 a** (1) **:** to go continuously from one point or place to another usu. with marked deliberation ⟨*moved* slowly along the road⟩ (2) **:** to go forward **:** get along **:** make progress **:** PROCEED, ADVANCE ⟨wanted to keep *moving*, no matter what the obstacles⟩; *specif* **:** MARCH ⟨a victorious army *moving* through the countryside⟩ (3) **:** to become more fully worked out through the addition or accretion of successive details or greater elaboration or some other form of further development ⟨the plot of the drama ~*s* swiftly⟩ ⟨a novel that hardly seems to ~⟩ (4) **:** to go along from one note or group of notes of music to the next in the course of the development or performance of a musical composition ⟨a melody that ~*s* smoothly⟩ ⟨at this point the tenor part ~*s* upward⟩ **b** (1) **:** to leave one point or place and go on to a new one ⟨remained outside the town for about one day and then *moved* inside and began the campaign⟩ (2) **:** to start away from some point or place **:** be on one's way **:** DEPART ⟨it was getting late and I thought it was time to be *moving*⟩ **c** (1) **:** to become transferred from one position to another in the course of play — used of pieces used in some games (as checkers, chess) ⟨in chess the bishop ~*s* diagonally⟩ (2) **:** to transfer a piece used in some games (as checkers, chess) from one position to another ⟨his turn to ~⟩ **d :** to settle in a new or different place (as of residence, business) usu. abandoning a former one **:** change one's abode or location ⟨did not like small towns and decided to ~ to the city⟩ **e** (1) **:** to become disposed of or to change hands by being sold or rented ⟨had a line of goods that was *moving* very slowly⟩ (2) **:** to become distributed through being borrowed by readers **:** find readers ⟨some books in public libraries hardly ever seem to ~⟩ **2 a** (1) **:** to change position or posture or otherwise exhibit outward activity **:** cause or allow the self or a part of the self to change position or posture **:** STIR ⟨so frightened that she stood rigid and didn't ~⟩ ⟨told him not to ~ or he would shoot⟩ (2) **:** to indicate recognition by some outward act (as inclining the head) ⟨thought she *moved* slightly when we were introduced, but it was impossible to be sure⟩ **b** (1) **:** to produce outwardly noticeable changes in position or in alignment of parts through being subjected to some external force ⟨the boat *moved* slowly from side to side at its mooring as the wind rose⟩ ⟨the trees *moved* gently in the breeze⟩ (2) **:** to become activated into operating or functioning or working in a designed or usual or expected way ⟨pushed and pushed but the door wouldn't ~⟩ ⟨pressed a button and the machine began *moving*⟩ **c :** to show marked activity **:** be very busy **:** snap into or maintain lively activity **:** HUM ⟨for a while there was not much to do, but suddenly things really began to ~⟩ **3 a :** to carry on one's life **:** EXIST ⟨in him we live, and ~, and have our being —Acts 17: 28 (AV)⟩ **b :** to live one's life in a specified environment **:** pass one's life or carry on one's activities in everyday acquaintance or familiarity with something indicated ⟨now ~*s* in only the best of circles⟩ **c :** to comport oneself in a specified way **:** behave in a particular manner ⟨must ~ very carefully so as not to offend her⟩ **4 :** to go ahead and do something **:** take action or begin to take action **:** ACT ⟨the time has come for us to make up our mind and ~⟩ **5 :** to make a formal request or proposal or application or appeal — used with *for* ⟨the delegate *moved for* a reconsideration of the suggestion⟩ ⟨the plaintiff *moved* for a rehearing⟩ **6** *of the bowels* **:** to eject fecal matter **:** EVACUATE, VOID ~ *vt* **1 a** (1) **:** to change the place or position of **:** cause to be shifted

or removed from one place or position to another ⟨*moved* the chair to a different part of the room⟩ (2) **:** to dislodge or displace from a fixed position **:** force loose or out **:** BUDGE ⟨the knife had sunk deeply into the wood and couldn't be *moved*⟩ ⟨was unable to ~ him from his obstinate convictions⟩ **b :** to transfer (a piece used in some games, as checkers or chess) from one position to another **c :** to take off or lift or tip (one's hat, cap) in salutation ⟨*moved* his hat politely when he saw her⟩ **d :** to cause to be disposed of or cause to change hands through sale or rent — usu. used in passive ⟨the new cars were *moved* very quickly⟩ **2 a** (1) **:** to cause to go or cause to keep on going continuously from one point or place to another ⟨*moved* the flag slowly up and down as a signal⟩ (2) **:** to cause to advance or cause to keep on advancing ⟨*moving* the troops farther into enemy territory⟩ **b** (1) **:** to activate into operating or functioning or working in a designed or usual or expected way **:** ACTUATE ⟨this button ~*s* the whole mechanism⟩ (2) **:** to cause (as an implement) to go or act or be driven or agitated in a direction or manner designed to produce a particular result ⟨*moved* the handle first to the left and then to the right and the door finally opened⟩ **c :** to put into activity or cause to continue in activity **:** rouse up from inactivity **:** cause not to remain at rest ⟨the breeze *moved* the branches of the trees⟩ ⟨news that *moved* them from their torpor⟩ **3 :** to cause (the self or a part of the self) to change position or posture or otherwise exhibit outward activity ⟨*moved* his lips but not a sound could be heard⟩ **4 :** to prompt or impel or rouse to the doing of something by reason of being a motive or incentive or similar influence **:** serve as an influence on the mind or will of **:** PERSUADE ⟨the happiness that could be his *moved* him to acting swiftly⟩ ⟨the logic and sanity of the argument *moved* them to reconsider the plan⟩ **5 a** (1) **:** to stir the emotions of **:** affect emotionally **:** rouse the feelings or passions of ⟨was greatly *moved* by such kindness⟩; *esp* **:** to cause to experience emotions of tenderness or compassion or sympathy ⟨her grief deeply *moved* them⟩ (2) **:** to affect in such a way as to lead to an indicated manifestation of emotion or passion ⟨a story that *moved* them to tears⟩ ⟨ingratitude that *moved* him to anger⟩ **b** *archaic* **:** to bring forth or excite or evoke (an indicated reaction) ⟨the exaggerations of both the great parties in the state *moved* his scorn —T.B.Macaulay⟩ **6 a** *obs* **:** to make an appeal to **:** earnestly solicit **:** BEG **b :** to make a formal application to (as a legislative body) — used with *for* ⟨*moved* the assembled delegates for reconsideration of the bill⟩ **7 :** to propose (as a question, resolution) formally in a deliberative assembly for consideration and determination ⟨*moved* that the meeting adjourn⟩ **8 :** to cause (the bowels) to eject fecal matter

**syn** ACTUATE, DRIVE, IMPEL: MOVE indicates simply the fact of altering position or place of setting or keeping going or in motion ⟨*move* furniture about the room⟩ ⟨the car *moves* slowly in low gear⟩ ⟨a plane *moved* across the sky⟩ ⟨retail prices *moved* steadily upward —*Americana Annual*⟩ ACTUATE, generally used in connection with machinery or mechanisms, lays stress upon the communication of the power to work or set in action; in application to persons the activation is usu. a specified motive ⟨as you entered a driveway you could throw out a short electrical impulse which would *actuate* equipment installed in the garage to open the doors mechanically —*Science Yr. Bk.*⟩ ⟨figurines which once performed amusing antics *actuated* by power from a waterwheel —*Amer. Guide Series: Conn.*⟩ ⟨*actuated* by altruistic motives⟩ ⟨*actuated* by jealousy⟩ DRIVE often signifies providing or communicating the power to set and keep in action ⟨a small turbine engine *drives* the wheel⟩ generally stresses the movement imparted, often suggesting the effect of speed or force ⟨the engine *drives* the crane back and forth across the short elevated track⟩ ⟨a propeller-*driven* plane⟩ ⟨a blade *driven* at a terrific speed by a small engine sliced the material into small strips⟩ ⟨*drive* a rod through a wall⟩ IMPEL, usu. used in figurative applications, is to drive with a great impetus ⟨he was *impelled* down the stairs by a pair of powerful arms⟩ ⟨*impelled* by a sense of duty —R.M.Lovett⟩ ⟨the motives which *impelled* him to take up and carry forward so difficult and thankless a work —V.L.Parrington⟩

**syn** MOVE, REMOVE, SHIFT, TRANSFER can mean, in common, to change or cause to change from one place to another. MOVE in itself implies no more than the motion or activity except in the special sense of to move one's habitation ⟨*move* along a street⟩ ⟨*move* a chair back⟩ ⟨*move* into a new house⟩ REMOVE usu. adds to MOVE the implication of a change from a normal, original, or usual location, station, or occupation; it is preferred to MOVE when the idea of eradicating is stressed ⟨*remove* a box from a shelf⟩ ⟨*remove* a wart from a finger⟩ ⟨*remove* faults by effort of will⟩ SHIFT throws emphasis on the change of location or direction, often suggesting unrest or instability ⟨*shift* from job to job⟩ ⟨*shift* from foot to foot⟩ ⟨the wind *shifted* to the east⟩ ⟨help a man *shift* a bureau to one side⟩ TRANSFER commonly implies a change from hand to hand, from one mode of conveyance to another, from one depository to another ⟨*transfer* a heavy package from one hand to the other⟩ ⟨*transfer* from the train to the bus⟩ ⟨*transfer* property from a man to his son⟩ ⟨*transfer* one's affection from person to person easily⟩

²**move** \"\ *n* -S **1 a** (1) **:** the action of moving a piece (as in checkers, chess) (2) **:** the turn of a player to move a piece (as in checkers, chess) **b :** advantage in end play in checkers or chess depending on which player must move in a given position — used with *the* ⟨after the exchange White has the ~ and wins⟩ — compare OPPOSITION 4b **2 a :** a step taken so as to gain some objective **:** a calculated procedure **:** MANEUVER ⟨made a clever ~ that outwitted all his rivals⟩ ⟨what's our next ~⟩ **b** (1) **:** the action of moving from a motionless position **:** the action of becoming active after previously being stationary or otherwise inactive ⟨the silence was appalling and no one dared to make a ~⟩ (2) **:** the action of rising from table ⟨sat there politely, waiting for someone else to make the first ~⟩ (3) **:** an incipient or initial action of moving esp. out of or away from a place ⟨was bored with their company, but no one seemed ready to make a ~⟩ **c :** a change of abode or location ⟨will make their ~ to the city next week⟩ **3 a :** a nominal period of time during which a certain amount of work can on the average be done or produced and which is sometimes used as a basis for paying a worker in proportion to the work actually done or produced **b :** the amount of work theoretically capable of being done or produced in the course of such a period of time — **on the move** *adv* (*or adj*) **1 :** in a state or process of moving about from place to place ⟨is a salesman and is constantly *on the move*⟩ **2 a :** in a state or process of moving ahead or making progress ⟨said that civilization is always *on the move*⟩ **b :** in a state of marked activity or distinct motion ⟨was not content to twiddle his thumbs but wanted to be *on the move*⟩

**moveable** *var of* MOVABLE

**moved** *past of* MOVE

**move·less** \ˈmüvlə̇s\ *adj* **:** that is without movement **:** MOTIONLESS, FIXED, IMMOBILE ⟨banks of ~ cloud hung about the horizon —George Meredith⟩ ⟨a crowd of quite 200 persons, standing ~ —Arnold Bennett⟩ — **move·less·ly** *adv* — **move·less·ness** *n* -ES

**move·man** \-ˌman, -mən\ *n, pl* **movemen :** a worker in an industrial plant who keeps materials or products moving on schedule from one operation or processing job to the next

**move·ment** \-vmənt, *in rapid speech sometimes* -bm-\ *n* -S [ME *movement, mevement,* fr. MF *movement, mouvement,* fr. *movoir, mouvoir* to move + *-ment* — more at MOVE] **1 a** (1) **:** the action or process of moving; *esp* **:** change of place or position or posture ⟨the ~ of pioneers to the West⟩ ⟨studying the ~ of planets⟩ (2) **:** a particular instance or manner of such moving ⟨made an impatient ~⟩ ⟨was entranced with her graceful ~*s*⟩ **b** (1) **:** a tactical or strategic shifting of a military unit (as an army division) **:** MANEUVER (2) **:** the orderly advance or progress of a military unit toward some point or in the course of some maneuver ⟨a steady ~ of troops over the border⟩ **c :** ACTION, ACTIVITY — usu. used in pl. ⟨carefully watched the ~*s* of the crowd⟩ **d :** a change or marked direction in the price of a commodity or stock ⟨an upward ~ in the price of coffee⟩ **2 a** (1) **:** a particular impulse or inclination (as of the will) ⟨had some good ~*s* in him —W.M.Thackeray⟩ ⟨a ~ of the will toward what appears good⟩ (2) **:** TENDENCY, TREND ⟨an age marked by a strong ~ toward materialism⟩ (3) **:** a progression in a particular direction or toward a particular objective ⟨was not sure toward what conclusion the ~ of the argument was leading⟩ **b** (1) **:** a series of actions taken by a body of persons to achieve an objective (2) **:** the body of persons taking part in such a series of actions **3 :** the moving parts of a mechanism that transmit a definite motion or transform motion; *esp* **:** a delicate train of wheelwork (as in a watch) **4 a :** MOTION 9 **b :** the rhythmic character or quality of a musical composition ⟨a dance ~⟩ **c :** TIME 7c **d :** TEMPO **e :** a distinct structural unit or division complete in its own key, rhythmic structure, and themes, and forming part of an extended musical composition ⟨a ~ of a suite⟩ ⟨the largo ~⟩ **5 a** (1) **:** a quality in a fine arts work (as a piece of sculpture, a painting) of representing or suggesting motion (2) **:** a quality in a fine arts work of dynamic rhythm and of harmonious variation and progression and of freedom from incongruity and from monotony **b** (1) **:** the quality in a piece of prose or poetry of being vibrant and alive through having a quickly moving plot or an abundance of interesting incidents or through having a fresh smooth stimulating style or through some other device that engages the constant interest of the reader (2) **:** the particular rhythmic flow of a piece of poetry **:** CADENCE **6 a :** an act of evacuation of the bowels **b :** matter evacuated from the bowels at one passage **:** STOOL

**movent** *var of* MOVANT

**mov·er** \ˈmüvə(r)\ *n* -S [ME *mover, mever,* fr. *moven, meven* to move + *-er* — more at MOVE] **:** one that moves: as **a** (1) **:** one that sets something into motion **:** ACTUATOR ⟨viewing God as the ~ of the universe⟩ (2) **:** one that incites or instigates to action or that promotes an action that has been begun ⟨hotheaded ~*s* of rebellion⟩ (3) **:** one that proposes something in a deliberative assembly ⟨the ~ of a resolution⟩ (4) **:** one whose business or occupation is the moving of household goods from one residence to another **b** (1) **:** one that is in motion or that is capable of motion ⟨a deer is a fast ~⟩ (2) **:** MIGRANT; *specif* **:** one participating in the extensive 19th century migration to the West of the U.S.

**moves** *pres 3d sing of* MOVE, *pl of* MOVE

**mov·ie** \ˈmüvē, -vi\ *n* -S [*moving* picture + *-ie*] **1 a :** MOTION PICTURE ⟨saw her favorite star in a new ~⟩ **b :** material or method suitable for motion pictures ⟨a novel with a plot that is good ~⟩ ⟨a style of direction that was authentic ~⟩ **2 :** a theater designed or used for the presentation of motion pictures ⟨dropped in at a neighborhood ~⟩ **3 movies** *pl* **a** (1) **:** motion pictures considered esp. as a source of entertainment or as an art form — usu. used with *the* ⟨liked nothing better than the ~*s*⟩ (2) **:** the motion-picture industry ⟨worked for years in the ~*s*⟩ **b :** a showing of a motion picture — used with *the* ⟨felt like going to the ~*s*⟩

**mov·ie·dom** \ˈ==dəm\ *n* -S **:** FILMDOM

**moviegoer** \ˈ==ˌ==\ *n* **:** one that goes to see motion pictures esp. frequently

**moviegoing** \ˈ==ˌ==\ *n* **:** the act or habit of going to see motion pictures

**movie house** *n* **:** an indoor theater designed for the public presentation of motion pictures

**movieland** \ˈ==ˌ=\ *n* **:** FILMDOM

**moviemaker** \ˈ==ˌ==\ *n* **:** one engaged in the production of motion pictures **:** a motion-picture magnate

**mo·vi·men·to** \ˌmōvəˈmen(ˌ)tō\ *n* -S [It, lit., movement, fr. *movere* to move (fr. L *movēre*) + *-mento* -ment — more at MOVE] **:** TEMPO

**mov·ing** *see pres part at* ¹MOVE\ *adj* [ME, fr. pres. part. of *moven* to move — more at MOVE] **1 a :** that is marked by or capable of movement **:** that is not fixed or stationary ⟨a device with ~ parts⟩ **b :** that advances or progresses ⟨living in a ~ world⟩ **2 a** (1) **:** that causes or produces or carries on motion or action or change **:** ACTUATING ⟨the ~ force of a machine⟩ (2) **:** that originates or instigates or promotes something ⟨was one of the ~ spirits behind the plan⟩ **b :** that stirs up or arouses or plays upon the emotions **:** that affects one's feelings or influences the mental outlook emotionally **:** that affects the sensibilities ⟨a ~ plea for justice⟩ ⟨a ~ tale of heroism⟩ **c :** that excites interest and discussion and controversy **:** VITAL ⟨one of the ~ questions of the day⟩

**syn** IMPRESSIVE, POIGNANT, AFFECTING, TOUCHING, PATHETIC: MOVING applies to any strong emotional excitation, including thrilling, entrancing, saddening, or calling forth pity and sympathy ⟨a modern version of the hero who for the good of mankind exposed himself to the agonies of the damned. It is always a *moving* subject —W.S.Maugham⟩ ⟨a *moving* revelation of child life in an orphanage —Mary MacColl⟩ IMPRESSIVE may describe that which forcibly commands attention, respect, admiration, awe, wonder, or conviction ⟨he was especially *impressive* before a court or jury and on account of his masterly arguments and effective oratorical powers the courtroom was always filled when it was known that he would speak —Marie B. Owen⟩ ⟨the southern entrance is *impressive*, with great rock walls rising abruptly on each side of the river bed in barren and forbidding grandeur —*Amer. Guide Series: Texas*⟩ POIGNANT refers to whatever keenly or sharply affects one's sensitivities, now esp. to whatever compels pity ⟨the most *poignant* of all perfumes: that which rises from a meadow on a July night —Kenneth Roberts⟩ ⟨that tenderness became sometimes so *poignant* that perhaps neither of us knew whether it was joy or pain —Havelock Ellis⟩ ⟨is anything in the world more *poignant* than youth and love —Virgil Thomson⟩ AFFECTING applies to whatever deeply moves the emotions; it is less specific than others in this list but is commonly used in situations involving pathos ⟨funeral the next day was a more *affecting* spectacle than anything ever seen in his theater —Green Peyton⟩ TOUCHING may describe that which calls forth tenderness or compassion ⟨a clean sober little maid, with a very *touching* upward look of trust —John Galsworthy⟩ ⟨when an aging man begins to cry in front of his colleagues, he presents a *touching* spectacle —Francis Hackett⟩ PATHETIC suggests pity for sorrow and distress, but unlike others in this group and like the word *pitiful* it may connote blended pity and amusement or contempt for weakness, inadequacy, and futility ⟨infant mortality, as the *pathetic* little cemeteries bore witness, was cruelly high —Allan Nevins & H.S.Commager⟩ ⟨her death has all the *pathetic* uselessness of martyrdom —Oscar Wilde⟩ ⟨staged the *pathetic* little rebellion of 1798 against England. It ended in quick disaster —Paul Blanshard⟩ ⟨this southern tradition was *pathetic* because it was but a remnant of an old aristocratic society —Reinhold Niebuhr⟩

**moving average** *n* **:** the average of statistical data (as in a time series) computed over a progressively shifting interval

**moving cluster** *n* **1 :** a cluster of stars that have common motions in space **2 :** an open cluster comparatively near the sun whose individual proper motions may be measured

**moving-coil** \ˈ==ˌ=\ *adj* **1 :** operated by the force exerted upon a movable electric-current-carrying coil suspended in a magnetic field ⟨a *moving-coil* galvanometer⟩ **2 :** operating by means of an electric-current-carrying coil or a single conductor that moves in a magnetic field (as in a dynamic loudspeaker or a dynamic pickup)

**moving-iron meter** \ˈ==ˈ==(=)-\ *n* **:** an instrument in which a vane or plunger of soft iron is moved by the magnetic field set up by a coil carrying the current to be measured — called also *iron-vane meter*

**mov·ing·ly** *adv* **:** in a moving manner **:** in such a way as to touch one's feelings or sensibilities **:** TOUCHINGLY, AFFECTINGLY ⟨spoke ~ of the country's glorious past⟩ ⟨writes ~ of his disappointment —Jay Walz⟩

**moving picture** *see pres part at* ¹MOVE\ *n* **:** MOTION PICTURE

**moving sidewalk** *n* **:** a sidewalk constructed on the principle of an endless belt or a series of such belts side by side and moving at different gradated speeds so that a person stepping on it will be carried along

**moving staircase** *or* **moving stairway** *n* **:** a set of stairs arranged like an endless belt and power driven so that the steps or treads may be made to ascend or descend continuously — called also *escalator*

**mo·vin·gui** *or* **mo·vin·gue** \mōˈviŋgē\ *n* -S [native name in western Africa] **1 :** a West African leguminous tree (*Distemonanthus benthamianus*) having straw-colored wood with evident pores **2 :** the wood of the movingui used esp. for veneers

¹**mow** \ˈmau̇\ *n* -S [ME *mowe, mow, mough,* fr. OE *mūga, mūha, mūwa*; akin to MHG *mūche* disease of a horse's foot, *mocke* lump, ON *mūgi, mūgr* crowd, heap, Gk *mykōn* heap] **1 :** a stack or heap of hay or straw or grain or similar produce esp. when stored in a barn **2 :** the part of a barn where hay, straw, or grain is stored

²**mow** \"\ *vt* -ED/-ING/-S [ME *mowen,* fr. *mowe,* n.] **:** to stack or store in or as if in a haymow — usu. used with *away*

³**mow** \ˈmō\ *vb* **mowed; mowed** *or* **mown; mowing; mows** [ME *mowen,* fr. OE *māwan*; akin to OHG *māen* to mow, MLG *meien, meigen,* MD *maeyen* to mow, L *metere* to reap, mow, W *medi* to reap, Gk *aman* to cut, mow, reap] *vt* **1 a :** to cut down (as standing grass, grain) with a scythe or sickle or machine; *esp* **:** to crop (relatively short standing grass) close to the ground with a lawn mower ⟨agreed to ~ the grass once a week⟩ **b :** to cut the standing grass or grain or similar produce of with a scythe or sickle or machine ⟨~*ed* the field so as to provide the cattle with fodder⟩; *esp* **:** to crop close to the ground the relatively short standing grass of with a lawn mower ⟨~*ed* the lawn regularly⟩ **2 a** (1) **:** to kill or destroy in rapid succession and in great numbers and indiscriminately ⟨~*ed* down with machine-gun fire⟩ (2) **:** to kill or destroy with sudden savage swiftness and without mercy or concern ⟨was ~*ed* down by gunmen after being lured from his home —Len Arthur⟩ (3) **:** to cause to fall from a standing position with sudden impetuous force **:** cause to tumble from an upright position **:** bowl over **:** knock over **:** knock down ⟨burst through the revolving door and ~*ed* down a couple of shoppers⟩ **b :** to meet and overcome swiftly and completely and decisively **:** make short work of **:** utterly crush **:** ROUT, SMASH ⟨~ down the opposition —Ira Wolfert⟩ ~ *vi* **:** to cut down standing grass or grain or similar produce with a scythe or sickle or machine

⁴**mow** *also* **mowe** \ˈmau̇, ˈmō\ *n* -S [ME *mowe,* fr. MF *moue,* of Gmc origin; akin to MD *mouwe* thick or protruding lip] **:** a contortion of the face or lips; *esp* **:** a mocking or derisive grimace ⟨watched the monkeys making ~*s* at us⟩

⁵**mow** \"\ *vi* -ED/-ING/-S [ME *mowen,* fr. *mowe,* n.] **1 :** to contort the face esp. so as to produce a mocking or derisive expression **:** make faces ⟨when the unintelligent brute force that lies at the bottom of society is made to growl and ~ —R.W.Emerson⟩ **2 :** to keep the lips constantly moving and contorting without actually speaking ⟨then he jabbers and ~*s* and trembles —Rudyard Kipling⟩

⁶**mow** *var of* MOU

**mowburnt** \ˈ=ˌ=\ *adj* **:** fermented or moldy through being stored in a mow while still damp ⟨~ hay⟩

**mow·die** \ˈmōdi\ *var of* MOUDIE

**mow·er** \ˈmō(ə)r, -ōə\ *n* -S [³*mow* + *-er*] **1** *also* **mowing machine :** an agricultural implement for cutting standing grass or grain or similar produce consisting of a reciprocating knife or sickle operated through guards or fingers and driven by a connecting rod from a crank and of gearing governing the speed of the crank and of dividers to divide the cut produce from the standing produce **2 :** LAWN MOWER

**mow·ha** \ˈmau̇hə\ *n* -S [Hindi *mahūā* — more at MAHUA] **:** MAHUA

**mowhay** \ˈ=ˌ=\ *n* [¹*mow* + *hay*] *dial Eng* **:** STACKYARD

**mowing** *n* -S [fr. gerund of ³*mow*] **1 :** the amount of produce (as grass or grain) mowed at one time **2 :** HAYFIELD

**mowle** \ˈmōl\ *var of* MOOL

**mown** *past part of* MOW

**mow·ra** *or* **mow·rah** \ˈmau̇rə\ *n* -S [Hindi *mahūā* — more at MAHUA] **:** MAHUA

**mowrah butter** *or* **mowrah oil** *also* **mahua butter** *n* **:** a bitter-tasting white or yellow soft fat obtained from the seeds of various East Indian trees of the genus *Madhuca* (as *M. latifolia* and *M. longifolia*) and used in soap, candles, and foods — compare INDIAN BUTTER

**mowrah meal** *n* **:** a meal produced as a by-product of mowrah butter and used to kill earthworms in lawns and other fine turfs and in greenhouses

**mows** \ˈmōz\ *n pl* [fr. pl. of obs. *mow* jest, fr. ME *mowe* grimace, jest — more at MOW] *chiefly Scot* **:** something that causes laughter **:** a laughing matter ⟨it's not ~ to be out at such a time —J.M.Barrie⟩

**mowt** \ˈmōt, ˈmau̇t\ [ME *moghte*] *chiefly dial past of* MAY

**moxa** \ˈmäksə\ *n* -S [NL, fr. Jap *mogusa*] **1 :** a soft woolly mass prepared from the young leaves of various wormwoods of eastern Asia and used esp. in Japanese popular medicine as a cautery by being ignited on the skin **2 :** any of various substances applied and ignited like moxa as a counterirritant

**mox·ie** \ˈmäksē, -si\ *n* -S [fr. *Moxie,* a trademark for a soft drink] **1** *slang* **:** ENERGY, PEP, LIFE ⟨she shook out of my grip, but there wasn't much ~ in it —P.W. Denzer⟩ **2** *slang* **a** (1) **:** COURAGE, PLUCK ⟨had plenty of ~ and was afraid of nothing⟩ (2) **:** AUDACITY, NERVE ⟨only in the outposts of the British Empire do males have the ~ to regularly wear shorts in mixed company —*Fortnight*⟩ **b :** STAMINA, BACKBONE, GUTS ⟨show that mob in the stadium that you've got the old ~ —*Saturday Rev.*⟩

**mox·ie·ber·ry** \ˈ==- — *see* BERRY\ *also* **mox·ie** \ˈ==\ *or* **mox·ie·plum** \ˈ==ˌ=\ *n* [origin unknown] **:** CREEPING SNOWBERRY

**moy** *abbr* money

**moy·en** \ˈmȯi(y)ən\ *n* -S [ME, fr. MF *meien, moien, moyen* — more at MEAN] **1 a** *chiefly Scot* **:** a means of doing something **b** *obs* **:** MEDIATION, INTERCESSION **2** *chiefly Scot* **:** a course of action

**moyen-âge** \ˌmwäyəˈnäzh\ *adj, often cap M&A* [F *moyen âge* middle ages; trans. of NL *Medium Aevum* — more at MIDDLE-AGE] **:** of, relating to, or suggestive of medieval times **:** MIDDLE-AGE ⟨a *moyen-âge* costume⟩

**mo·zab·ite** \mōˈzaˌbīt, ˈmōzə,-\ *n* -S *cap* [F, fr. *Mzab* (*M'zab*), group of oases in Ghardaïa territory, Algeria + F *-ite*] **:** a Berber of the Ibadite sect holding to a literal interpretation of the Koran

**mo·zam·bi·can** \ˌmōzəmˈbēkən, -ˌzam-\ *adj, usu cap* [*Mozambique,* colony in southeastern Africa + E *-an*] **:** of or relating to Mozambique or its inhabitants

**mo·zam·bique** \ˌmōzəmˈbēk -ˌzam-\ *n* -S [fr. *Mozambique,* colony in southeastern Africa] **:** a lightweight dress fabric in small fancy patterns that is loosely woven with a cotton warp and a mohair weft

**moz·ar·ab** \mōˈzarəb *also* -zer-\ *n, usu cap* [Sp *mozárabe,* fr. Ar *Musta'rib* would-be Arab, fr. *'Arab* Arab] **:** a Spanish Christian in the period of Muslim domination of Spain from about the 9th century to the 15th century

**moz·ar·a·bic** \(ˈ)mōˈzarəbik\ *adj, usu cap* [F *mozarabique,* fr. Sp *mozárabe* + F *-ique* -ic] **:** of, relating to, or used by Mozarabs ⟨*Mozarabic* poetry⟩ ⟨the *Mozarabic* liturgy⟩

**mo·zar·te·an** *also* **mo·zar·ti·an** \(ˈ)mōtˈsärd·ēən\ *adj, usu cap* [Wolfgang A. *Mozart* †1791 Austrian composer + E *-ean, -ian*] **:** of, relating to, or characteristic of Mozart or his music

**mozca** *usu cap, var of* MUISCA

**mo·zo** \ˈmō(ˌ)sō\ *n* -S [Sp, lit., boy, fr. OSp *moço*] **1** *chiefly Southwest* **a :** a male hired to assist with household work or to attend to various small jobs or to do chiefly manual work of a usu. somewhat heavy or menial kind: as (1) **:** a male servant **:** male domestic (2) **:** HANDYMAN (3) **:** a luggage porter (4) **:** LABORER **b :** a waiter in a restaurant or other dining room **2** *chiefly Southwest* **:** a male hired to assist with a train of pack animals

**moz·za·rel·la** \ˌmätsəˈrelə, ˌmōt-\ *n* -S [It, dim. of *mozza,* a kind of cheese, fr. *mozzare* to cut off] **:** a moist white rubbery unsalted cheese that has a somewhat acid flavor

**moz·zet·ta** *also* **mo·zet·ta** \mōtˈsedə, mōˈze-\ *n* -S [It, short for *almozzetta,* irreg. fr. ML *almutia* amice + It *-etta,* dim. suffix] **:** a short cape with a small ornamental hood worn on occasion over the rochet by some ecclesiastics

**moz·zie** \ˈmäzē\ *var of* MOSSIE

**MP** \(ˈ)emˈpē\ *abbr or n* -S **1 :** a member of Parliament **2 :** a group of military police **3 :** a member of a group of military police **:** a military policeman

**mp** *abbr* melting point

**MP** *abbr* **1** mail payment **2** meeting point **3** memorandum of partnership **4** metropolitan police **5** mezzo piano **6** milepost **7** minister plenipotentiary **8** morning prayer **9** motion picture **10** mounted police **11** multipole **12** municipal police

**m paper** *n, usu cap M* **:** paper containing minor imperfections and graded second quality — compare N PAPER, P PAPER

**MPB** *abbr* missing persons bureau

**MPG** *abbr, often not cap* miles per gallon

**MPH** *abbr, often not cap* miles per hour
**MPHPS** *abbr, often not cap* miles per hour per second
**MPI** *abbr, often not cap* mean point of impact
**MPM** *abbr* **1** *often not cap* meters per minute **2** multipurpose meal
**MPO** *abbr* military post office
**mpon·do** \əm'pän(,)dō\ *n, pl* **mpondo** *or* **mpondos** *usu cap* : PONDO
**mpong·we** \əm'päŋ(,)wā\ *n, pl* **mpongwe** *or* **mpongwes** *usu cap* **1 a** : a people of the southern part of French Equatorial Africa just north of the equator and distributed chiefly about the estuary of the Gabon river **b** : a member of such people **2** : a Bantu language of the Mpongwe people
**MPS** *abbr* **1** marbled paper sides **2** *often not cap* meters per second
**m-q developer** *n, usu cap M&Q* [*Metol* (trademark applied to *N*-methyl-*para*-aminophenol) + *quinol*] : a photographic developer containing the developing agents *para*-methylaminophenol sulfate and hydroquinone and usu. a preservative, an activator, and an antifoggant
**mr.** \ˈmistə(r), *in rapid speech sometimes* (ˌ)mist\ *n, pl* **messrs.** \ˈmesə(r)z *sometimes* -eshə- *or* -es(h)yə- *or* -ezə- *or* -ezhə- *or* -ez(h)yə-\ *usu cap* [ME *Mr*, abbr. of *maister* master — more at MASTER] **1 a** — used as a conventional title of courtesy except when usage requires the substitution of a title of rank or the substitution of an honorific or professional title before a man's surname ⟨spoke to *Mr.* Doe⟩ ⟨may I have a word with you, *Mr.* Doe⟩ or sometimes before a man's given name and surname when the two are used together ⟨a *Mr.* John Doe has left a message for you⟩ **b** — used in direct address as a conventional title of respect before a man's title of office now usu. only when the title of office is not followed by the surname ⟨may I ask one more question, *Mr.* President⟩ **c** — used before the name of a place (as a country, city) or of a profession or other line of activity (as a sport) or before some epithet (as *clever*) to form a title applied to a male viewed or recognized as esp. outstanding in or as representative of the thing indicated ⟨was *Mr.* Baseball to many for a number of years⟩ ⟨was elected *Mr.* America⟩ **2** *obs* : MASTER ⟨refused the title of *Mr.* of Arts —Robert Godfrey⟩ **3** : ²MISTER
**mr** *abbr* milliroentgen
**MR** *abbr* **1** map reference **2** master of the rolls **3** mate's receipt **4** mill run **5** mineral rubber **6** mine-run **7** minister resident **8** missionary rector
**MRA** *abbr* moral rearmament
**MRC** *abbr* medical reserve corps
**MRD** *abbr* minimum reacting dose
**mrg** *or* **mrgn** *abbr* margin; marginal
**mrkr** *abbr* marker
**mrng** *abbr* morning
**MRO** *abbr* maintenance, repair, and operation
**m roof** *n, cap M* : a roof formed by the junction of two common gable roofs with a valley between them — compare SAWTOOTH ROOF

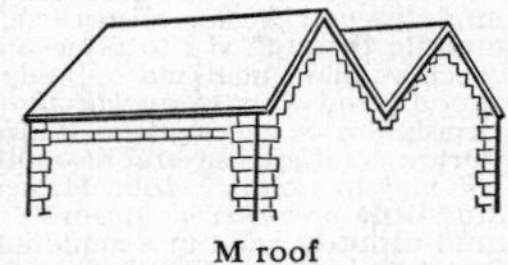
M roof

**mrs.** \ˈmisəz, ˈmisəs, ˈmizəz, ˈmizəs, (ˌ)mis, _məs (*in the southern U S these last two forms occur chiefly before a Christian name*), (ˌ)miz, _məz *sometimes chiefly in substand speech or in the speech of older persons* ˈmisərz *or* ˈmisərs *or* ˈmizərz *or* ˈmizrəs *or* ˈmizrəz; *the forms with z immediately following the first or only vowel occur chiefly in the southern U S*\ *n, pl* **mrs.** *any of the preceding two-syllable pronunciations*\ *or* **mes·dames** \(ˈ)māˈdäm, -dam, -daa(ə)m, -däm\ *usu cap* [fr. abbr. of *mistress*] **1 a** — used as a conventional title of courtesy except when usage requires the substitution of a title of rank or the substitution of an honorific or professional title before a married woman's surname ⟨spoke to *Mrs.* Doe⟩ ⟨may I have a word with you, *Mrs.* Doe⟩ or sometimes before a married woman's surname with the given name of her husband or her own given name intervening ⟨a *Mrs.* John Doe has left a message for you⟩ **b** — used before the name of a place (as a country, city) or of a profession or other line of activity (as a sport) or before some epithet (as *clever*) to form a title applied to a married female viewed or recognized as esp. outstanding in or as representative of the thing indicated ⟨was elected *Mrs.* Homemaker⟩ **2** *obs* : MISTRESS **3** *obs* — used as a conventional title of courtesy before the surname or before the given name and surname of an unmarried woman **4** : WIFE ⟨pick up the *Mrs.* at the five-and-dime —Alan Kapelner⟩
**MRS** *abbr* medical receiving station
**mrs. grun·dy** \-ˈgrəndē, -di\ *n, pl* **mrs. grundys** *also* **mrs. grundies** *usu cap M&G* [fr. *Mrs. Grundy*, character alluded to in the play *Speed the Plough* (1798) by Thomas Morton †1838 Eng. playwright] : a person marked by a narrowly conventional outlook or by prudishness or by stiff intolerance of any breach of propriety
**mrtm** *abbr* maritime
**mru** \məˈrü\ *n, pl* **mru** *or* **mrus** *usu cap* **1 a** : an Indo-Chinese people of the hill districts of Chittagong and Arakan in the western part of Burma **b** : a member of such people **2** : the Tibeto-Burman language of the Mru people
**MS** \(ˈ)eˈmes\ *abbr or n* -s Master of Science
**ms** *abbr* **1** *often cap M&S* manuscript **2** *usu ital* meso- **3** millisecond
**MS** *abbr* **1** machinery survey **2** mail steamer **3** main switch **4** [It *mano sinistra*] left hand **5** margin of safety **6** master sergeant **7** maximum stress **8** mean square **9** medium shot **10** medium steel **11** [L *memoriae sacrum*] sacred to the memory **12** meters per second **13** metric system **14** mild steel **15** minesweeper **16** mint state **17** months after sight; month's sight **18** morphine sulfate **19** motor ship **20** multiple sclerosis
**m's** *or* **ms** *pl of* M
**msa·sa** \əmˈsäsə\ *n* -s [native name in southern Rhodesia] : any of various African trees of the genus *Brachystegia*
**MSc** \ˌe,me(s)ˈsē\ *abbr or n* -s Master of Science
**msc** *abbr* **1** millisecond **2** miscellaneous; miscellany
**MSC** *abbr* **1** mile of standard cable **2** moved, seconded, and carried
**MSCP** *abbr, often not cap* mean spherical candlepower
**msec** *abbr* millisecond
**MSF** *abbr* muscle shock factor
**msg** *abbr* message
**MSG** *abbr* monosodium glutamate
**msgr** *abbr* **1** messenger **2** *often cap* monseigneur **3** *often cap* monsignor
**MSH** *abbr* master of staghounds
**m-shell** \ˈ=,=\ *n, usu cap M* : the third innermost shell of electrons surrounding an atomic nucleus — compare K-SHELL, L-SHELL
**MSL** *abbr, often not cap* mean sea level
**MSM** *abbr* [L *mille* thousand] thousand feet surface measure
**msn** *abbr* mission
**msngr** *abbr* messenger
**mss** *abbr, often cap M & both Ss* manuscripts
**mst** *abbr* measurement
**MST** *abbr* **1** mean solar time **2** mountain standard time
**m star** *n, usu cap M* : a star of spectral type M — see SPECTRAL TYPE table
**MsTh₁** *symbol* mesothorium a
**MsTh₂** *symbol* mesothorium b
**mstr** *abbr* **1** master **2** moisture
**mt** *abbr* **1** empty **2** might **3** most **4** mount; mountain
**MT** *abbr* **1** mail transfer **2** mandated territory **3** mean tide **4** mean time **5** measurement ton **6** mechanical transport **7** metric ton **8** military training **9** motor transport **10** mountain time
**MTB** *abbr or n* -s motor torpedo boat
**MTC** *abbr* **1** mechanical transport corps **2** motor transport corps
**mtd** *abbr* mounted
**MTD** *abbr* mean temperature difference
**MTF** *abbr* mechanical time fuse
**mtg** *abbr* **1** meeting **2** mortgage **3** mounting
**mtgd** *abbr* mortgaged
**mtge** *abbr* mortgage
**mtgee** *abbr* mortgagee
**mtgor** *abbr* mortgagor
**mth** *abbr* month
**MTI** *abbr* moving target indicator
**mtl** *abbr* material
**MTL** *abbr* mean tidal level
**mtn** *abbr* mountain
**mtr** *abbr* motor
**MTR** *abbr* **1** materials testing reactor **2** multiple track radar
**mtrl** *abbr* material
**¹mu** \ˈmyü, ˈmü, *in sense 1 sometimes* ˈmüē\ *n* -s [Gk *my*] **1** : the 12th letter of the Greek alphabet — symbol M or *μ*; see ALPHABET table **2** *or* **mu factor** : the amplification factor in an electron tube ⟨the tube oscillates as a low ~ tube —*Radio Corp. of Amer. Rev.*⟩ **3** : MICRON **4** : a bridging position or group joining two or more central atoms or ions in a polynuclear coordination complex — symbol *μ* ⟨tetraethyl-*μ*-dibromo-di-gold⟩
**²mu** *var of* MOU
**³mu** \ˈmü\ *n* -s [Hawaiian] : MAMAMU
**MU** *abbr* **1** maintenance unit **2** mobile unit **3** motor union
**muazzin** *also* **mu'adhdhin** *var of* MUEZZIN
**muc-** *or* **muci-** *or* **muco-** *comb form* [L *muc-*, fr. *mucus* nasal mucus — more at MUCUS] **1** : mucus : mucous ⟨*mucific*⟩ ⟨*mucocele*⟩ ⟨*mucoid*⟩ **2** : mucous and ⟨*mucopurulent*⟩
**muc** *abbr* mucilage
**mu·ced·i·na·ceous** \(ˌ)myüˌsedᵊnˈāshəs\ *adj* [NL *Mucedinaceae*, family of mold fungi in some classifications (fr. L *mucedin-*, *mucedo* nasal mucus — fr. *mucus* — + NL *-aceae*) + E *-ous*] : MUCEDINOUS
**mu·ce·dine** \ˈmyüsə,dēn, -dən\ *n* -s [NL *Mucedineae*, family of mold fungi in some classifications, fr. L *mucedin-*, *mucedo* + NL *-eae*] : a mold fungus
**mu·ced·i·nous** \(ˌ)myüˈsedᵊnəs\ *or* **mu·ce·din·e·ous** \ˌmyüsəˈdinēəs\ *adj* [NL *mucedinous* fr. L *mucedin-*, *mucedo* + E *-ous*; *mucedineous* prob. fr. NL *Mucedineae* + E *-ous*] : having the nature of or resembling mold or mildew
**¹much** \ˈməch\ *adj* **more** \(ˌ)mō(ə)r, -ō(ə)r, -ōə, -ȯ(ə)\ **most** \(ˌ)mōst\ [ME *muche*, *miche*, fr. *muchel*, *michel* great, large, much, fr. OE *micel*, *mycel*; akin to OHG *mihhil* great, large, ON *mikill*, Goth *mikils*, L *magnus*, Gk *megas*, Skt *mahat*] **1 a** : that exists or is present in a great quantity or amount or to a considerable extent or degree ⟨has ~ money⟩ ⟨spent ~ time⟩ ⟨there is ~ truth in what you say⟩ **b** : that exists or is present in an indicated relative quantity or amount or to an indicated relative extent or degree — used with a qualifying adverb ⟨how ~ money have you got⟩ ⟨has taken too ~ time⟩ ⟨there is as ~ validity in the one theory as in the other⟩ **2** : MANY ⟨~ thanks⟩ ⟨came out against him with ~ people —Num 20:20 (AV)⟩ **3** : very good ⟨wouldn't think I was ~ on literature —C.B.Kelland⟩ ⟨he's not so ~ on looks, but he really is charming —*Atlantic*⟩
**²much** \"\ *adv* **more** \"\ **most** \"\ [ME *muche*, *miche*, fr. *muche*, *miche*, adj.] **1 a** (1) : to a great degree or extent : very considerably or notably : GREATLY ⟨is ~ happier now⟩ (2) : VERY — usu. used with adjectival past participles ⟨~ interested⟩ ⟨~ pleased by the compliment⟩ ⟨~ gratified⟩ and in negative constructions ⟨not ~ good at all⟩ **b** (1) : FREQUENTLY, OFTEN ⟨went ~ to the theater⟩ (2) : for a considerable length of time ⟨was with her ~, but didn't find out anything⟩ : LONG ⟨didn't get there ~ before midnight **2 a** : just about : APPROXIMATELY ⟨the patient was ~ the same as he had been earlier⟩ ⟨comes to ~ the same thing —George Sampson⟩ ⟨the two writers, who are ~ of an age —*Times Lit. Supp.*⟩ **b** : NEARLY ⟨speaks and thinks very ~ as his father used to⟩
**³much** \ˈməch\ *n* -ES [ME *muche*, *miche*, fr. *muche*, *miche*, adj.] **1** : a great quantity or amount or extent or degree : a great deal ⟨learned ~ from this experience⟩ ⟨gave away ~ of what he owned⟩ — often used in negative or interrogative constructions with a following dependent specifying phrase consisting of a generalized category introduced by *of a* and used typically to belittle or query the extent to which something exists in the indicated category ⟨wasn't ~ of a teacher⟩ **2** : something considerable or important or significant or impressive ⟨the evidence didn't amount to ~⟩ ⟨thought it ~ to have made even a little progress⟩ ⟨was not ~ to look at⟩
**⁴much** \"\ *vt* -ED/-ING/-ES *dial* : to make much of: **a** : to show affection for (as by petting or caressing) ⟨~ that dog and see won't he come along —Horace Kephart⟩ **b** : CODDLE ⟨my mother shielded me and ~*ed* me —W.A.White⟩
**mu·cha·cha** \müˈchächə\ *n* -s [Sp, fem. of *muchacho*] **1** *chiefly Southwest* : a young woman : GIRL **2** *chiefly Southwest* : a female servant
**mu·cha·cho** \-(,)chō\ *n* -s [Sp, fr. obs. Sp *mochacho*, fr. Sp *mocho* cropped, shorn] **1** *chiefly Southwest* : a young man : BOY **2** *chiefly Southwest* : a male servant
**much as** *conj* : however much : even though ⟨when a person's afraid — *much as* he might wish to blame his fear on others ... — he's really afraid of himself —W.J.Reilly⟩
**much-hunger** \ˈ=,==\ *n* : a plant of the genus *Trillium*
**much·ly** *adv* : MUCH — now not often in formal use ⟨wore a voluminous navy-blue cotton print wrapper, ~ patched —Willie S. Ethridge⟩
**much·ness** *n* -ES [ME *mochenes*, fr. *moche*, *muche*, *miche* much + *-nes* -ness] *archaic* : the quality or state of being great in quantity or amount or extensive in degree — **much of a muchness** : very much the same : just about the same ⟨when we grow a little older we discover we're all very *much of a muchness* —W.S.Maugham⟩
**mu·cic acid** \ˈmyüsik-\ *n* [*mucic* ISV *muc-* + *-ic*] : an optically inactive crystalline acid $HOOC(CHOH)_4COOH$ obtained from galactose or lactose by oxidation with nitric acid
**mu·cid** \ˈmyüsəd\ *adj* [L *mucidus*, fr. *mucēre* to be moldy or musty — more at MUCUS] *archaic* : MOLDY, MUSTY
**mu·cif·er·ous** \(ˌ)myüˈsif(ə)rəs\ *adj* [*muc-* + *-ferous*] : containing or producing or filled with mucus ⟨~ ducts⟩ ⟨~ glands⟩
**mu·cif·ic** \-fik\ *adj* [*muc-* + *-fic*] : secreting mucus ⟨a ~ gland⟩
**mu·ci·fi·ca·tion** \ˌmyüsəfəˈkāshən\ *n* -s [*mucific* + *-ation*] : acquisition by epithelial cells of the capacity to form and secrete mucus
**mu·ci·fy** \ˈ==sə,fī\ *vi* -ED/-ING/-ES [*muc-* + *-fy*] : to produce or cause the production of mucus
**mu·ci·gen** \-jən, -,jen\ *n* -s [ISV *mucin* + *-gen*] : MUCINOGEN
**mu·ci·lage** \ˈmyüs(ə)lij, -lēj\ *n* -s [ME *muscilage*, fr. LL *mucilago* musty juice, fr. L *mucus* nasal mucus — more at MUCUS] **1** : a gelatinous substance that contains protein and polysaccharides and usu. uronides and that is obtained esp. from the seed coats of various plants (as fucoid seaweeds, marshmallows, flaxes, quinces) and that is similar to plant gums (as gum arabic) but that swells in water without dissolving and forms a slimy mass **2 a** : an aqueous usu. viscid solution of a gum or of some other substance resembling a gum that is used as an adhesive and that is used specif. in pharmacy as an excipient and in medicine as a demulcent — compare PASTE 2 **b** : a similar liquid adhesive of low bonding strength
**mucilage cell** *n* : a plant cell that secretes mucilage (sense 1) usu. by disorganization of its wall
**mu·ci·lag·i·nous** \ˌmyüsəˈlajənəs\ *adj* [LL *mucilaginosus*, fr. *mucilagin-*, *mucilago* mucilage + L *-osus* -ose] **1 a** : relating to mucilage or the secretion of mucilage ⟨~ disorganization in a plant cell⟩ **b** : resembling mucilage: as (1) : viscid and moist (2) : slimily sticky **2** : containing or secreting mucilage ⟨a ~ gland⟩ — **mu·ci·lag·i·nous·ly** *adv*
**mu·cin** \ˈmyüsᵊn\ *n* -s [ISV *muc-* + *-in*] : any of a group of mucoproteins that are found in various secretions and tissues of man and lower animals (as in saliva, lining of the stomach, skin) and that are white or yellowish powders when dry and that are viscid when moist ⟨gastric ~⟩
**mu·cin·o·gen** \myüˈsinəjən, -,jen\ *n* -s [ISV *mucin* + *-o-* + *-gen*] : any of various substances easily converted into mucins (as by the action of alkalies)
**mu·cin·oid** \ˈmyüsᵊn,ȯid\ *adj* [ISV *mucin* + *-oid*] : resembling mucin
**mu·ci·no·lyt·ic** \ˌmyüsᵊnōˈlid·ik\ *adj* [*mucin* + *-o-* + *-lytic*] : able or tending to break down or lower the viscosity of mucin-containing body secretions or components ⟨a ~ enzyme⟩
**mu·ci·nous** \ˈmyüsᵊnəs\ *adj* [*mucin* + *-ous*] : relating to or containing mucin : MUCOID
**¹muck** \ˈmək\ *n* -s [ME *muk*, perh. fr. OE *-moc*; akin to ON *myki* dung — more at MUCUS] **1** : soft moist farmyard manure esp. when mixed with decomposing vegetable material and used as a fertilizer **2** *obs* : MONEY **3 a** (1) : wet clinging slimy dirt or filth ⟨spattered with ~ from the pigpen⟩ (2) : something (as defamatory remarks) that injures or tends to injure the reputation or standing of another ⟨throwing as much ~ as possible at her rivals⟩ **b** (1) *chiefly dial* : RUBBISH, TRASH, JUNK (2) : idle remarks or observations : NONSENSE, GUFF ⟨recall some ~ about chucking someone out —Ernest Hemingway⟩ ⟨the usual ~ of old-timers and loafers —S.E.White⟩ **4 a** : an untidy or messy condition ⟨was all in a ~ of sweat⟩ **b** : a state of confusion, uncertainty, or disorganization : a fouled-up condition ⟨has made such a ~ of things —Agatha Christie⟩ ⟨we're all in a ~, and we're to do the best we can —Richard Llewellyn⟩ **5 a** (1) : a dark usu. black earth that is capable of absorbing much water, that is usu. moist or wet so as to have a consistency like that of moist or wet loam or humus, that is marked by the presence of organic usu. plant matter in an advanced state of decomposition and in a proportion of usu. less than 50 percent, that is rich in nitrogen and relatively low in mineral content (as potash) and that is very fertile (2) : earth resembling such muck in wetness or sogginess : soft wet mud : MIRE ⟨floundering through the wet black ~ —Marjory S. Douglas⟩ **b** : something that is oozy, viscid, or sticky like such muck : GOO, GUNK ⟨was given some kind of ~ to use as a salve⟩ **c** : a heavy soggy, slushy, or slimy deposit or mass of sedimentation or some similar heavy wet mass : SLUDGE ⟨oily ~ on the floor of a garage⟩ ⟨pushed through the ~ of dirty snow and half-thawed ice⟩ ⟨~ at the bottom of the drainpipe⟩ **6** : material removed in the process of excavating or mining: as **a** : the total mass of material (as soft earth, hardpan, gravel, rock) so removed **b** : ore or rock in a loose heap as first broken in the process of mining **c** : the material removed by hydraulic mining
**²muck** \"\ *vb* -ED/-ING/-S [ME *mukken*, fr. *muk*, n.] *vt* **1 a** : to clean up; *esp* : to clear of manure or filth ⟨an old pair of boots with rubber feet and felt tops that were used for ~*ing* out the corrals and the pigpen —W.V.T.Clark⟩ **b** (1) : to clear of material (as soft earth, gravel, rock) in the process of excavating or mining ⟨~*ing* an excavation⟩ (2) : to dig out or otherwise remove (as soft earth, gravel, rock) in the process of excavating or mining ⟨after each blast they ~*ed* out the rock⟩ **2** : to cover with manure or some other fertilizing muck ⟨~*ing* the orchards each year⟩ **3 a** : to dirty with or as if with muck : SOIL ⟨you can't touch pitch and not be ~*ed* —R.L.Stevenson⟩ **b** : to dirty by tracking or littering : make untidy or messy ⟨~*ed* up the floor⟩ **4** *chiefly Brit* **a** : to make a mess of : BOTCH, BUNGLE ⟨was afraid of ~*ing* up the experiment⟩ **b** : to throw into a state of confusion or disorganization : foul up : SNARL, TANGLE ⟨acting ~*s* up childhood —Clemence Dane⟩ ⟨~*ed* up every plan⟩ **5** *chiefly Brit* : to push around : SHOVE ⟨still ~*ing* the salt about —Richard Llewellyn⟩ ⟨~*ed* about by the last war, by inflations and depressions —*Time*⟩ ~ *vi* **1** *dial Eng* : to work energetically or slavishly : TOIL, DRUDGE **2** *chiefly Brit* **a** (1) : to move about aimlessly or idly : WANDER, LOITER ⟨the country was full of people ~*ing* about the fields —A.J.Liebling⟩ (2) : to waste time in trivial or altogether useless activities : DAWDLE, PUTTER ⟨~*ing* about in the affairs of other peoples —A.J. Nock⟩ **b** : to play around : mess around : FOOL, TRIFLE ⟨hadn't ~*ed* around with boys since the time when she was little —Ruth Park⟩ ⟨~*ing* about with some sort of occultism —Ngaio Marsh⟩
**³muck** \"\ *n* -s [alter. of *amuck* (initial vowel taken as indefinite article *a*)] *archaic* : the act of running amok
**¹muck·a·muck** \ˈməkə,mək\ *vb* [Chinook jargon] *Northwest* : EAT
**²muckamuck** \"\ *n* [Chinook jargon] *Northwest* : FOOD
**³muckamuck** \"\ *also* **muck·ety-muck** \ˈməkəd·ē,mək\ *n* [short for *high-muck-a-muck*, *high-muckety-muck*] : an individual of great importance or consequence : BIG SHOT
**muck·en·der** \ˈməkəndə(r), ˈmu̇k-\ *n* -s [alter. of ME *mokadour*, prob. fr. (assumed) OProv *mocador* (whence Prov *moucadou*), fr. OProv *mocar* to blow or wipe the nose, fr. *moc* nasal mucus, fr. L *mucus* — more at MUCUS] *dial Eng* : HANDKERCHIEF
**¹muck·er** \ˈməkə(r)\ *vb* -ED/-ING/-S [freq. of ²*muck*] *vt* : BOTCH, BUNGLE, SNARL, TANGLE ~ *vi* : WANDER, LOITER, DAWDLE, PUTTER, FOOL, TRIFLE
**²mucker** \"\ *n* -s *chiefly Brit* : MUCK 4
**³mucker** \"\ *n* -s [¹*muck* + *-er*] **1** *chiefly Brit* : ³CROPPER **2 a** (1) : a coarse boorish person : OAF, PHILISTINE (2) : CAD (3) : one that lacks the qualities of a good sportsman (4) : BASTARD 7 **b** : a tough sometimes vicious individual : ROUGHNECK — **muck·er·ish** \-k(ə)rish\ *adj*
**⁴muck·er** \ˈməkə(r)\ *n* -s [²*muck* + *-er*] : one that clears away material (as earth, gravel, rock) from a working area: as **a** : a mine worker who scrapes up the chippings left in the channels made by a coal-cutting machine **b** : one that clears bark and debris from a log landing
**muck·er·ism** \ˈməkə,rizəm\ *n* -s : behavior characteristic of a mucker
**muck·et** \ˈməkət, *usu* -əd·+V\ *n* -s [origin unknown] : any of several freshwater mussels; *esp* : the common mussel (*Actinonaias carinata*) with a lustrous nacreous shell that is used in button manufacture
**muck grower** *also* **muck farmer** *n* : one who grows vegetables on a muck soil
**muckhill** \ˈ=,=\ *or* **muckheap** \ˈ=,=\ *n* [*muckhill* fr. ME *mukhill*, fr. *muk* muck + *hill*; *muckheap* fr. ME *mukhepe*, fr. *muk* muck + *hepe* heap] : a pile of manure
**muck in** *vi* **1** *slang* : to share rations **2** *slang* : to share the burden of some work or project
**mucking** *adj* [fr. pres. part. of ²*muck*] : DAMNED 2 ⟨if I ever hit you I'll break your ~ jaw —Ernest Hemingway⟩
**muck·ite** \ˈmə,kīt, ˈmu̇,k-\ *n* -s [G *muckit*, fr. H. *Muck*, 19th cent. Ger. mineralogist, its discoverer + G *-it* -ite] : a yellow resinous hydrocarbon that is a variety of retinite and that is found in a region of central Europe about the upper valley of the Oder river
**muck·land** \ˈmə,kland\ *n* : a land area marked by the occurrence of extensive tracts of fertile muck soil
**muck·le** \ˈməkəl\ *var of* MICKLE
**muck·le·shoot** \ˈməkəl,shüt\ *n, pl* **muckleshoot** *or* **muckleshoots** *usu cap* **1 a** : a Salishan people of the White river valley, Washington **b** : a member of such people **2** : a dialect related to Skagit
**muckluck** *also* **mucluc** *var of* MUKLUK
**muck·ment** \ˈməkmənt, ˈmu̇k-\ *n* -s [²*muck* + *-ment*] *dial Eng* : MUCK
**muckmidden** \ˈ=,==\ *n, chiefly Scot* : MUCKHILL
**¹muck·rake** \ˈmək,rāk\ *vb* [fr. obs. E *muckrake*, n., rake for gathering dung into a heap, fr. ¹*muck* + *rake*] *vi* : to search out and charge with and seek to expose publicly real or apparent misconduct or vice or corruption on the part of prominent individuals (as public officials) ⟨a politician that ~*s* at every opportunity⟩ : dig up scandal ⟨would enjoy himself if he could ~ in his own backyard —Reginald Reynolds⟩ ~ *vt* **1** : to subject to muckraking ⟨*muckraked* his rivals with great relish⟩ **2** : to investigate or go over assiduously with the purpose of digging up scandal or of incriminating ⟨~*s* his subject with pious zeal —*Time*⟩
**²muckrake** \"\ *n* [fr. obs. E *muckrake*, n.] **1 a** : MUCKRAKING — used with *the* ⟨jeered at me and my colleagues of the ~ —Lincoln Steffens⟩ ⟨such a bold defender of the people, if it be necessary, will use the much dreaded ~ —A.M.Grussi⟩ **b** : a book, article, speech, or other medium used as a vehicle for a muckraking disclosure ⟨will publish his newest ~ later this year⟩ **2** : MUCKRAKER ⟨a confirmed holier-than-thou ~⟩
**muck·rak·er** \-kə(r)\ *n* : one marked by or given to muckraking ⟨had no patience with ~*s*⟩
**¹muckraking** *adj* [fr. pres. part. of ¹*muckrake*] : marked by preoccupation with or inclination toward muckraking ⟨had grown famous for its ~ articles —Ben Riker⟩ ⟨the ~ magazines and those novelists with similar reformist zeal —W.V.O'Connor⟩ ⟨~ journalism⟩ ⟨a ~ political campaign⟩
**²muckraking** *n* [fr. gerund of ¹*muckrake*] : the action or prac-

tice of one that muckrakes ⟨~ and other sad substitutes for an intelligent policy⟩
**muck rolls** *n pl* [¹*muck*] : the first pair of a train of rolls for rolling wrought iron
**mucks** *pl of* MUCK, *pres 3d sing of* MUCK
**muck soil** *n* : soil consisting wholly or nearly wholly of muck
**muckstick** \ˈ=,=\ *n* : SHOVEL
**muck·sy** \ˈməksi, ˈmu̇k-\ *adj* [prob. by alter. (influence of *mixen*)] *dial Eng* : MUCKY
**muckworm** \ˈ=,=\ *n* **1 a** : MISER **b** : GUTTERSNIPE **2** : WORM; *specif* : a worm found in mucky soil or manure — not used technically
¹**mucky** \ˈməkē, -ki\ *adj, usu* -ER/-EST [¹*muck* + -*y*] **1 a** : DIRTY, MESSY, FILTHY ⟨a ~ stable⟩ **b** *chiefly Brit* (1) : DISGUSTING, CONTEMPTIBLE ⟨a ~ way of doing things⟩ (2) : UNPLEASANT, DISAGREEABLE ⟨an embarrassing and altogether ~ situation⟩ (3) : MEAN, CHEAP, UNDERHANDED ⟨had played a ~ trick on him —Mary Deasy⟩ (4) : revoltingly fulsome : STICKY ⟨his ~ flattery —Samuel Butler †1902⟩ **c** (1) : MUGGY, HUMID ⟨~ weather⟩ (2) : MURKY, CLOUDED ⟨the slow ~ water of the creek⟩ **2** : consisting of, marked by, or full of muck ⟨the ~ bottom of a pond⟩ : MIRY, MUDDY ⟨a ~ ditch⟩ ⟨a ~ road⟩
²**mucky** \ˈməki, ˈmu̇ki\ *vt* -ED/-ING/-ES *dial Eng* : to make dirty
**muco-** — see MUC-
**mu·co·cele** *also* **mu·co·coele** \ˈmyükə,sēl\ *n* -S [*muc-* + -*cele* or -*coele*] : a swelling like a sac that is due to distention of a hollow organ or cavity with mucus ⟨a ~ of the appendix⟩; *specif* : a dilated lacrimal sac
**mu·co·cutaneous** \ˌmyü(ˌ)kō+\ *adj* [*muc-* + *cutaneous*] : made up of, affecting, or involving both typical skin and mucous membrane ⟨the ~ junction of the mouth⟩ ⟨~ syphilis⟩
**mu·co·flocculent** \ˌ==+\ *adj* [*muc-* + *flocculent*] : consisting of or containing flaky shreds of mucus
¹**mu·coid** \ˈmyü,kȯid\ *also* **mu·coi·dal** \(ˈ)myüˈkȯidᵊl\ *adj* [*mucoid* ISV *muc-* + -*oid*; *mucoidal* fr. *mucoid* + -*al*] **1** : resembling mucus **2** : forming large moist sticky colonies — used of dissociated strains of bacteria; contrasted with *rough* and *smooth*
²**mu·coid** \ˈmyü,kȯid\ *n* -S [ISV *mucin* + -*oid*] **1** : any of a group of complex proteins similar to mucins or mucoproteins but occurring esp. in connective tissue and in cysts : ²COLLOID 2 **2** : MUCOPROTEIN
**mucoid degeneration** *n* [¹*mucoid*] : tissue degeneration marked by conversion of cell substance into a glutinous substance like mucin
**mucoid tissue** *n* : MUCOUS TISSUE
**mu·co·i·tin-sulfuric acid** *also* **mucoitin sulfate** \(ˈ)myü¦kōətᵊn+-\ *n* [*mucoitin* ISV *muc-* + -*itin* (as in *chondroitin*)] : an acidic mucopolysaccharide that is found esp. in the cornea of the eye and in gastric mucosa and that is a derivative of glucosamine and glucuronic acid; an ester of hyaluronic acid and sulfuric acid
**mu·co·lyt·ic** \ˌmyükəˈlid·ik\ *adj* [ISV *muc-* + -*lytic*] : that hydrolyzes mucopolysaccharides : MUCINOLYTIC ⟨a ~ enzyme⟩
**mu·con·ic acid** \(ˈ)myü¦känik-\ *n* [*muconic* ISV *mucic* + *itaconic*] : a crystalline unsaturated acid $(CHCHCOOH)_2$ obtained indirectly from mucic acid and formed by oxidation of benzene in the animal body; 1,3-butadiene-1,4-dicarboxylic acid
**mu·co·periosteal** \ˌmyükō+\ *adj* [NL *mucoperiosteum* + E -*al*] : of or relating to the mucoperiosteum
**mu·co·periosteum** \"+\ *n* [NL, fr. *muc-* + *periosteum*] : a periosteum backed with mucous membrane (as that of the palatine surface of the mouth)
**mu·co·polysaccharide** \"+\ *n* [ISV *muc-* + *polysaccharide*] : any of a class of polysaccharides (as chondroitinsulfuric acid, mucoitinsulfuric acid, or heparin) that are widely distributed in the body, that bind water to form thick gelatinous material serving to cement cells together and to lubricate joints and bursas, that are derived from a hexosamine (as glucosamine), a uronic acid, and often sulfuric acid, and that are constituents of mucoproteins, glycoproteins, and blood-group substances
**mu·co·protein** \"+\ *n* [*muc-* + *protein*] : any of a group of complex compounds (as mucins) containing mucopolysaccharides (as chondroitinsulfuric acid or mucoitinsulfuric acid) combined with amino acid units or polypeptides and occurring in body fluids and tissues — called also *mucoid*; compare GLYCOPROTEIN
**mu·co·purulent** \"+\ *adj* [ISV *muc-* + *purulent*] : containing both mucus and pus
**mu·co·pus** \ˌmyükō+\ *n* [ISV *muc-* + *pus*] : mucus mingled with pus
**mu·cor** \ˈmyükə(r), -ˌkȯ(ə)r\ *n* [NL, fr. L, mold, moldiness, fr. *mucēre* to be moldy or musty — more at MUCUS] **1** *cap* : a genus (the type of the family Mucoraceae) of molds that are distinguished from molds of the genus *Rhizopus* through having round usu. cylindrical or pear-shaped sporangia not clustered and not limited in location to the points where rhizoids develop **2** -S : any mold of the genus *Mucor*
**mu·co·ra·ce·ae** \ˌmyükəˈrāsē,ē\ *n pl, cap* [NL, fr. *Mucor*, type genus + -*aceae*] : a large family of chiefly saprophytic molds (order Mucorales) having a well-developed branching mycelium that lacks septa and including many molds (as members of the genera *Rhizopus* and *Mucor*) that are destructive to food products (as bread, fruits, or vegetables) — **mu·co·ra·ceous** \ˌ==ˈrāshəs\ *adj*
**mu·co·ra·les** \ˌ==ˈrā(ˌ)lēz\ *n pl, cap* [NL, fr. *Mucor* + -*ales*] : an order of mostly saprophytic fungi (subclass Zygomycetes) that reproduce asexually by spores borne within sporangia and sexually by homothallic or heterothallic zygospores and that include many common domestic molds
**mu·cor·my·co·sis** \ˌmyükə(r)+\ *n* [NL, fr. *Mucor* + *mycosis*] : mycosis caused by fungi of the genus *Mucor* usu. primarily involving the lungs and invading other tissues by means of metastatic lesions
**mu·cor·rhea** *or* **mu·cor·rhoea** \ˌmyükəˈrēə\ *n* -S [NL, fr. *muc-* + -*rrhea*, -*rrhoea*] : discharge of mucus esp. when excessive
**mu·co·sa** \myüˈkōsə, -ōzə\ *n, pl* **muco·sae** \-ˌsē, -ˌzē\ *or* **mucosa** *or* **mucosas** [NL, fr. L, fem. of *mucosus* mucous] : MUCOUS MEMBRANE — **mu·co·sal** \(ˈ)=ˈ=səl, -zəl\ *adj*
**mu·co·sanguineous** \ˌmyü(ˌ)kō+\ *adj* [*muc-* + *sanguineous*] : containing mucus and blood ⟨~ feces⟩
**mu·cose** \ˈmyü,kōs\ *adj* [L *mucosus*] : MUCOUS
**mu·co·serous** \ˌmyükō+\ *adj* [*muc-* + *serous*] : containing both mucous and serous matter ⟨a ~ discharge⟩; *esp* : producing both mucus and a serous secretion ⟨a ~ cell⟩ ⟨a ~ gland⟩
**mu·cos·i·ty** \myüˈkäsəd·ē, -ətē, -i\ *n* -ES [F *mucosité*, fr. L *mucosus* mucous + F -*ité* -ity] : the quality or state of being mucous
**mucoso-** *comb form* [L *mucosus* mucous] : mucous and ⟨*mucoso*purulent⟩ ⟨*mucoso*saccharine⟩
**mu·cous** \ˈmyükəs\ *adj* [L *mucosus*, fr. *mucus* nasal mucus + -*osus* -ose] **1** : covered with mucus or similar viscous matter : SLIMY ⟨a ~ surface⟩ **2** : of, relating to, or resembling mucus ⟨a ~ secretion⟩ **3** : secreting or containing mucus ⟨~ glands of the intestine⟩
**mucous colitis** *n* : a functional commonly psychosomatic disorder of the colon characterized by the secretion and passage of large amounts of mucus, constipation alternating with diarrhea, and cramping abdominal pain
**mucous membrane** *n* : a membrane rich in mucous glands; *specif* : the membrane that lines the passages and cavities of the body which communicate directly or indirectly with the exterior (as the alimentary, respiratory, and genitourinary tracts) and that consists of two chief layers of which one is a deep vascular connective-tissue stroma which in many parts of the alimentary canal contains a thin but definite layer of nonstriated muscle and the other is a superficial epithelium varying in kind and thickness but always soft and smooth and kept lubricated by the secretions of the cells and numerous glands embedded in the membrane
**mucous patch** *n* : a broad flat syphilitic condyloma that is often marked by a yellowish discharge and that occurs on moist skin or mucous membranes
**mucous tissue** *n* : a gelatinous connective tissue containing stellate cells with long processes in a soft matrix that occurs in the umbilical cord and in the embryo and in myxomas

**mu·co·vis·ci·do·sis** \ˌmyükō,visəˈdōsəs\ *n, pl* **mucoviscidoses** \-ˌsēz\ [NL, fr. *muc-* + LL *viscidus* viscid + NL -*osis*] : an hereditary disease of infants and young children characterized by the presence of cysts and excessive fibrous tissue in glandular organs (as the pancreas and lungs), by excess mucous secretion which causes a blocking of respiratory passages and pancreatic ducts, and by resulting malnutrition, diarrhea, cough, and wheezing respiration — called also *cystic fibrosis, pancreatic fibrosis*
**mu·cro** \ˈmyü(ˌ)krō\ *n, pl* **mucro·nes** \=ˈ=ˌnēz\ *also* **mucros** [NL, fr. L, point, edge; akin to Gk *amyssein* to scratch, sting and prob. to Lith *mušti* to strike] : an abrupt sharp terminal point or tip or process of an animal part or a plant part: as **a** : the terminal segment of the springing appendage of an arthropod of the order Collembola **b** : the terminal point or tip of some leaves
**mu·cro·nate** \ˈmyükrənət, -ˌnāt, *usu* -d·+V\ *also* **mu·cro·nat·ed** \-ˌnād·əd\ *adj* [*mucronate* fr. L *mucronatus*, fr. *mucron-*, *mucro* point + -*atus* -ate; *mucronated* fr. L *mucronatus* + E -*ed*] : ending in an abrupt sharp terminal point or tip or process : marked by a mucro ⟨a ~ leaf⟩
**mu·cro·na·tion** \ˌ==ˈnāshən\ *n* -S [*mucronate* + -*ion*] **1** : the quality or state of being mucronate **2** : a mucronate point, tip, or process
**mu·cu·lent** \ˈmyükyələnt\ *adj* [LL *muculentus* sniveling, fr. L *mucus* nasal mucus + -*ulentus* -ulent] : MUCOID
**mu·cu·na** \myüˈkyünə\ *n, cap* [NL, fr. Pg *mucunã*, *mucuna* any of several plants of the genus *Mucuna*, fr. Tupi *mucunán*, *mucunã*] : a genus of tropical herbs and woody vines (family Leguminosae) with trifoliolate leaves and showy flowers in axillary stalked clusters — see COWAGE
**mu·cus** \ˈmyükəs\ *n* -ES [L, nasal mucus; akin to ON *myki* dung, *mjūkr* soft, gentle, Goth *muka-* gentle, L *mucēre* to be moldy or musty, Gk *myxa* lamp wick, nasal mucus, Skt *muñcati* he releases, lets loose; basic meaning: slippery] **1** : a viscid slippery secretion rich in mucins that is produced by mucous membranes and that serves to moisten and protect such membranes **2** : a viscid animal secretion (as from the external body surface of snails) that resembles mucus
¹**mud** \ˈməd\ *n* -S *often attrib* [ME *mode*, *mudde*, prob. fr. MLG, thick mud; akin to MHG *mot* mud, morass, Sw *modd* dirty snow, OE *mōs* bog, swamp — more at MOSS] **1** : a slimy sticky fluid-to-plastic mixture of finely divided particles of solid material and water ⟨a drizzling rain . . . turned the dust of the roads into ~ —George Borrow⟩ **2 a** : the worst part of a thing : DREGS ⟨the ~ of the earth . . . remains bespattering his spirit —Havelock Ellis⟩ **b** : the lowest place : DEPTHS ⟨that you should have been dragged down into the ~ —Christopher Isherwood⟩ **3** : abusive and malicious remarks or charges ⟨a sorely bedeviled body of men who have had much ~ thrown at and around them —Roy Lewis & Angus Maude⟩ **4** : a geological deposit having the physical character of mud ⟨sands and ~s . . . have been transformed by the stresses of millions of years into white marble —*Amer. Guide Series: Md.*⟩ **5** : DRILLING FLUID **6** : ²ANATHEMA 2b — used esp. in the phrase *name is mud* ⟨don't know what his right name is . . . but his name's ~ with me —S.V.Benét⟩ **7** *slang* : OPIUM
²**mud** \"\ *vb* **mudded; mudded; mudding; muds** *vt* **1** : to make muddy or turbid ⟨the dog scampered through the brook, *mudding* it⟩ **2** : to spread or plaster with mud ⟨these tanks were *mudded* up for camouflage —*Infantry Jour.*⟩ ⟨choose deliberately the path well-*mudded* —Roland Mathias⟩ ⟨~ the chinks in his cabin⟩ **3** : to introduce mud into; *esp* : to introduce artificial muds containing a heavy constituent (as barite) into (an oil well) to seal against natural gas or water during drilling — often used with *off* ~ *vi* : to burrow or hide in mud ⟨a place where the eels ~⟩
³**mud** *var of* MUID
**mu·dar** *also* **mud·dar** *or* **ma·dar** \məˈdär, -dȧ(r\ *n* -S [Hindi *madār*] : either of two East Indian shrubs (*Calotropis gigantea* and *C. procera*) whose fine bast fiber resembles flax in strength but is too short to be of great commercial value
**mud-baby** \ˈ=,==\ *n* : BURHEAD 2
**mudbank** \ˈ=,=\ *n* : a submerged or partly submerged bank of mud along a shore or in a river ⟨an old dismantled steamer he had seen years ago rotting on a ~ —Joseph Conrad⟩
**mud bass** *n* **1** : a small freshwater sunfish (*Acantharchus pomotis*) of the eastern U.S. **2** : WARMOUTH
**mud bath** *n* : an immersion of the body or a part of it in mud (as for the alleviation of rheumatism or gout)
**mud-blister worm** \ˈ=ˈ==\ *n* : a polychaete worm (*Polydora ciliata*) that lives in a mud-walled tube with which it lines U-shaped borings in chalky formations or in the shells of oysters on which it may be a destructive pest
**mud boat** *n* **1** : a large flatboat used in dredging to carry off the mud and silt to deep water or elsewhere **2** : a low sled with broad runners on which logs are hauled in swamps
¹**mudcap** \ˈ=,=\ *n* [¹*mud* + *cap*] : a blasting method in which explosive is placed on the surface of a rock fragment and covered with mud or clay — called also *adobe*
²**mudcap** \"\ *vt* : to blast by the mudcap process
**mud cat** *also* **mud catfish** *n* [¹*mud*] **1** : FLATHEAD CATFISH **2** : a large freshwater catfish of the Mississippi valley and adjoining regions
**mudcat** \ˈ=,=\ *n, usu cap* : MISSISSIPPIAN — used as a nickname
**mud clerk** *n* : the assistant to the purser of a river steamboat ⟨even her two *mud clerks* . . . wore uniforms —I.S.Cobb⟩
**mud coot** *n* : AMERICAN COOT
**mud crab** *n* **1** : any of numerous marine crabs (family Xanthidae) dwelling on muddy bottoms; *esp* : one of a widely distributed genus (*Panopeus*) found along both coasts of No. and So. America and near western Africa **2** : YELLOW SHORE CRAB
**mud crack** *n* : one of a system of cracks by which drying mud is divided; *specif* : one of the cracks after it has been filled and the mud and filling material changed to rock
**mud dab** *n* **1** : WINTER FLOUNDER **2** : any of several flounders (family Pleuronectidae) of the genus *Limanda*; *esp* : a flounder (*L. limanda*) of northern Europe resembling the winter flounder
**mud dabbler** *n* : a killifish (*Fundulus heteroclitus*) of the U.S.
**mud dauber** *n* : any of various wasps of the families Sphecidae and sometimes Eumenidae that construct mud cells on a solid base (as stone or woodwork of buildings) in which the female places an egg with spiders or insects paralyzed by a sting to serve as food for the larva
**mud·der** \ˈmədə(r)\ *n* -S [¹*mud* + -*er*] **1** : a race horse that runs well on a wet or muddy track **2** : a player or a team (as in football) that performs well on a wet field
**mud devil** *n* : HELLBENDER 1
**muddied** *past of* MUDDY
**muddier** *comparative of* MUDDY
**muddies** *pres 3d sing of* MUDDY
**muddiest** *superlative of* MUDDY
**mud·di·ly** \ˈmədəlē, -li\ *adv* : in a muddy manner
**mud·di·ness** \-dēnəs, -din-\ *n* -ES : the quality or state of being muddy ⟨the language is pure and correct, free from ~ —T.S. Eliot⟩
**mudding** *pres part of* MUD
**mud dipper** *n* : RUDDY DUCK
¹**mud·dle** \ˈmədᵊl\ *vb* **muddled; muddled; muddling** \-d(ᵊ)liŋ\ **muddles** [prob. fr. obs. D *moddelen* to make muddy or turbid, fr. MD, freq. of *modden* to make muddy or turbid, fr. *modde* mud; akin to MLG *mode*, *mudde* thick mud — more at MUD] *vt* **1** : to spoil the clearness of (colors) ⟨the transparent freshness of watercolor drawings when the washes are not *muddled* —E.V.Neale⟩ **2** : to make turbid or muddy ⟨*muddled* the brook with his splashings⟩ **3** : to make (one's brain) cloudy or foggy : make stupid esp. with liquor ⟨the drink *muddled* him and his voice became loud and domineering⟩ **4** : to make indistinct (as speech) : MUMBLE ⟨the unforgivable sin in a pupil is not ungrammatical speech but *muddled* speech —George Sampson⟩ **5** : to waste or squander without purpose — usu. used with *away* ⟨~ away a fortune⟩ ⟨~ away the hours until train time⟩ **6** : to mix confusedly : jumble together without purpose ⟨two worlds of discourse become *muddled* together in the same language and become nonsense —F.S.C.Northrop⟩ **7** : to make a mess of : BUNGLE ⟨*muddled* themselves into the most indefensible positions —A.N.Whitehead⟩ ⟨too much is at stake in government for them to be permitted to ~ policies —V.L.Parrington⟩ **8** *of mixed drinks* : to crush and mix (as mint and sugar) by working a spoon or similar utensil on the bottom of a glass or mixer ~ *vi* **1 a** : to dabble or wallow in mud or dirt ⟨cats and dogs *muddling* round a fire —E.M.Forster⟩ **b** *archaic* : to do hard often dirty work : GRUB **2** : to think, act, or go in a confused aimless way or in a way that tends to make a mess of things ⟨the story . . . is one of *muddling* and halfheartedness —R.C.K. Ensor⟩ ⟨~ around a house for a week —Peggy Durdin⟩ ⟨let her ~ along thinking she is getting ready —Marcia Davenport⟩
²**muddle** \"\ *n* -S **1** : a state of confusion: as **a** : thinking that lacks clarity and precision : intellectual cloudiness : VACUITY ⟨the ~ in the argument —John Holloway⟩ ⟨surrounded by a vast ~ of hearsay —Janet Flanner⟩ **b** : a condition marked by bungling, uncertainty, and lack of clear procedure or aim ⟨dislike of the ~ and the misdirection of our institutions —*Times Lit. Supp.*⟩ ⟨the world's been confused and poor, a thorough ~ —H.G.Wells⟩ ⟨saw what faulty coordination and general ~ can do to an army —G.A.Craig⟩ **c** : an untidy litter of heterogeneous things out of place or order ⟨I'll move these newspapers, excuse the *muddle* —Janet Frame⟩ ⟨a mixture of Gothic and Renaissance, a ~ of gables and projections —S.P.B.Mais⟩ ⟨the shelves in ascending degrees of ~ covered the wall —John Updike⟩ **2 a** : a fish stew **b** : a gathering where muddle is served **syn** see CONFUSION
**muddlebrained** \ˈ=ˈ=ˈ=\ *adj* : MUDDLEHEADED
**mud·dled** \ˈmədᵊld\ *adj* [fr. past part. of ¹*muddle*] : characterized by a confused state: as **a** : dull of mind : slightly stupid; *also* : INTOXICATED ⟨being at the same time slightly ~ with liquor —Charles Dickens⟩ **b** : having little reality : CLOUDY, VAGUE ⟨in a ~ platonic way he feels some affection for the girl —*Sydney (Australia) Bull.*⟩ ⟨the mixed and ~ skepticism of the Renaissance —T.S.Eliot⟩ ⟨~ thinking as ignoble as dirty conduct —H.G.Wells⟩ ⟨her ~ yearnings and dreamings dissolved into storms of furious tears —Ruth Park⟩ **c** : MIXED-UP, JUMBLED ⟨the gigantic growth of government expenditures, the ~ tax situation —E.B.George⟩ ⟨much of the information he gives is ~ —H.P.Stern⟩
**mud·dled·ness** *n* -ES : the quality or state of being muddled ⟨~ in the activities of the world —S.C.Pepper⟩
**mud·dle·dom** \ˈmədᵊldəm\ *n* -S **1** : thinking or acting in an aimless or confused manner ⟨in a constant state of ~⟩ **2** : a realm of unintelligible confusion ⟨a spiritual ~ is set up —E.M. Forster⟩
**muddlehead** \ˈ==,=\ *n* : a stupid person : BLOCKHEAD
**muddleheaded** \ˈ==ˈ==\ *adj* : characterized by a state of confused thought or by bungling and ineptitude ⟨such a confused, puddingheaded, ~ fellow —Laurence Sterne⟩ — **mud·dle·head·ed·ness** *n*
**mud·dle·ment** \ˈmədᵊlmənt\ *n* -S : MUDDLEDNESS ⟨made her feel remote from the usual ~ of her thoughts —Ruth Park⟩
**muddle-minded** \ˈ==ˈ==\ *adj* : MUDDLEHEADED
**mud·dler** \ˈməd(ᵊ)lə(r)\ *n* -S **1** : one that muddles; *specif* : a utensil usu. shaped like a pestle for crushing and mixing (as the flavoring agents of a mixed drink) **2** : MILLER'S-THUMB 1
**muddles** *pres 3d sing of* MUDDLE, *pl of* MUDDLE
**muddle through** *vi* : to achieve a degree of success without a decisive plan ⟨mankind . . . only learns enough from glaciers, floods, and wars to *muddle through* —Henry Hewes⟩ ⟨social legislation *muddled through* in the right direction —W.A. Orton⟩ ⟨suffered several resounding disasters before *muddling through* to victory —John Masters⟩
**muddling** *pres part of* MUDDLE
**mud·dling·ly** *adv* : in a muddling manner
¹**mud·dy** \ˈmədē, -di\ *adj* -ER/-EST [ME *moddy*, fr. *mode*, *mudde* mud + -*y*] **1** : morally impure : BASE ⟨has avoided any off-color ~ humor —*Newsweek*⟩ ⟨graft-ridden and ~ regime —D.M.Friedenberg⟩ **2 a** : having a great deal of mud : covered with mud ⟨clambering on the divan with ~ shoes —Lucius Garvin⟩ ⟨waded through the ~ water —Robert Hichens⟩ ⟨eyes were fixed on the ~ coastline —T.B.Costain⟩ **b** : characteristic of or resembling mud ⟨a ~ flavor in freshwater fish caught in a *muddy*-bottomed lake —Jane Nickerson⟩ ⟨a sky that had a ~ color⟩ **c** : turbid with sediment ⟨quaff ~ ale in the bar —Max Peacock⟩ ⟨the horrible ~ coffee⟩ **3** : cloudy in color : having no brightness or clarity : DULL ⟨eyes a little wild, ~ with anger and lack of sleep —John & Ward Hawkins⟩ ⟨colors . . . are subdued, hinting thus at the ~ monotony of his later paintings —R.M.Coates⟩ **4** : living naturally close to or in mud ⟨the coot is a ~ bird⟩ **5 a** : cloudy in mind : MUDDLED ⟨are you able to reconstruct happenings clearly . . . in your mind, or do they come ~ and distorted —Charles Yerkow⟩ ⟨a ~ thinker, but a superb artist —J.D.Adams⟩ **b** : obscure in meaning : CONFUSED ⟨his style is never ~ —W.J.M.Rankine⟩ **6** : DEJECTED, GLOOMY ⟨the glandular, torpid, ~ stare —George Biddle⟩ **7** *of musical tones* : run together : not clearly defined or articulated : INDISTINCT **syn** see TURBID
²**muddy** \"\ *vb* -ED/-ING/-ES *vt* **1** : to soil or stain with or as if with mud ⟨*muddied* and weary horsemen —S.H.Adams⟩ ⟨~ and cheapen the quality of our actual everyday life —Thomas Wolfe⟩ **2** : to make turbid ⟨what are you doing in my well, ~*ing* it up like that —Erskine Caldwell⟩ **3** : to make cloudy or dull in color ⟨a common admonition of the instructors is . . . "~ your colors" —*Amer. Fabrics*⟩ **4** : to produce confusion in ⟨exhaustion broke him down . . . and *muddied* his mind —Norman Mailer⟩ ⟨emotionalism which has *muddied* discussion —C.J.Rolo⟩ ~ *vi* : to become muddy
**muddybreast** \ˈ==,=\ *n* : GOLDEN PLOVER
**muddyheaded** \ˈ==ˈ==\ *adj* : MUDDLEHEADED
**muddy-mettled** \ˈ==ˈ==\ *adj* : having a dull spirit ⟨a dull and *muddy-mettled* rascal —Shak.⟩
**muddy-minded** \ˈ==ˈ==\ *adj* : MUDDLEHEADED ⟨the expression of a *muddy-minded* humanitarianism —Raymond Moley⟩
**mud eel** *n* : a siren (*Siren lacertina*) that is lead gray in color, attains a length of about two feet, and inhabits the swamps and ditches of the southern U.S.
¹**mu·de·jar** \müˈt͟heˌhär\ *n, pl* **mudeja·res** \-ˌhä(ˌ)rās\ *usu cap* [Sp *mudéjar*, fr. Ar *mudajjan*, lit., allowed to remain] : a Muslim living under a Christian king esp. during the 8th to 11th centuries but retaining his religion, laws, and customs
²**mudejar** \"\ *adj, usu cap* : of, relating to, or characteristic of the Mudejars and esp. of their architecture ⟨cloisters separated from green gardens and fountains by delicate Gothic tracery or *Mudejar* colonnades —S.E.Morison⟩
**mud fever** *n* **1** : a chapped inflamed condition of the skin of the legs and belly of a horse due to irritation from mud or drying resulting from washing off mud-spatters and closely related or identical in nature to grease heel **2** : a severe enteritis of turkeys **3** : a mild leptospirosis that occurs chiefly in European agricultural and other workers in wet soil, is caused by infection with an organism (*Leptospira grippotyphosa*) present in native field mice, and is marked by fever and headache without accompanying jaundice
**mudfish** \ˈ=,=\ *n* : any of several fishes that frequent muddy water or burrow in the mud: as **a** : BOWFIN **b** : MUD MINNOW **c** : a New Zealand fish (*Neochanna apoda*) of the family Galaxiidae that lives in burrows like a crayfish
**mud flap** *n* : a sheet of thin material suspended behind each rear wheel of a motor vehicle to intercept spattered mud and water
**mud flat** *n* : ²FLAT 1a(2)
**mudflow** \ˈ=,=\ *n* **1 a** : a mass of mingled volcanic particles and water which flows like lava from a volcano **b** : a body of rock formed in this manner **2** : an eruption of mud from a mud volcano or mud spring **3** : a moving mass of soil made fluid by rain or melting snow : a mud avalanche — compare EARTHFLOW **4** : a minor structure present in various fine-grained sedimentary rocks and indicative of local flowage while the material was still soft
¹**mudge** \ˈməj\ *vi* -ED/-ING/-S [perh. alter. (influenced by ¹*move*) of ²*budge*] *chiefly Scot* : BUDGE, MOVE
²**mudge** \"\ *n* -S *Scot* : MOVEMENT
**mud goose** *n* : HUTCHINS'S GOOSE
**mudguard** \ˈ=,=\ *n* **1** : FENDER 1d(1) **2** : a strip of material (as of leather or rubber) applied to a shoe upper just above the sole intended as a protection against dampness or as an ornament — see SHOE illustration
**mud gun** *n* : a device for forcibly applying stiff mud or clay (as to the taphole of a blast furnace for closing it)
**mudhead** \ˈ=,=\ *n* : one of a Zuñi ceremonial clown fraternity appearing in tribal rites in mud-daubed masks symbolizing an early stage in the development of man

**mud hen** *n* : MARSH HEN 1
**mudhole** \ˈ=,=\ *n* **1** : a hole or hollow place containing much mud ⟨his swimming pool was nothing but a ~⟩ ⟨a dirt road full of ~*s*⟩ **2** : a very small town ⟨drifted into some rural ~ and set up shop —*Amer. Mercury*⟩
**mudhook** \ˈ=,=\ *n* : the anchor of a ship ⟨dropped his ~ . . . and ran up the American flag —*Nat'l Geographic*⟩
**mudhopper** \ˈ=,==\ *n* : MUDSKIPPER
**mu·dir** \mü'di(ə)r\ *n* -s [Ar *mudīr*] : the governor of a mudiria
**mu·di·ria** *also* **mu·di·ri·eh** \,müdəˈrē(y)ə\ *n* -s [Ar *mudīrīyah*] : a province in Egypt, the Sudan, and the Zanzibar protectorate
**mud jacking** *n* [*jacking* fr. gerund of ²*jack*] : the raising of a pavement or railroad subgrade by means of mud pumped under it through drilled holes
**mud lark** *n* **1** : a person who grubs in mud (as in search of stray bits of coal, iron, rope); *specif* : an urchin who grubs for a living along the tide flats of the English Thames **2 a** *dial Eng* : PIPIT **b** : any of various birds (as the meadowlark or the shoveler) that live in moist places **c** : the Australian magpie lark (*Grallina cyanoleuca*) that makes mud nests
**mudlark** \ˈ=,=\ *vi* [*mud lark*] : to play, dig, or search in mud or on muddy ground ⟨had been out all the morning sailing cork boats and ~*ing* in the marshes —Crosbie Garstin⟩
**mud lava** *n* : MUD 4
**mud·less** \ˈmədləs\ *adj* : having no mud
**mud lump** *n* : a broad low mound of clay or silt on a delta usu. near its outer margin (as on the delta of the Mississippi river)
**mud mark** *n* : MUDFLOW 4
**mudminnow** \ˈ=,=(,)=\ *n* : a small fish of the genus *Umbra* (order Haplomi); *esp* : a common small fish (*U. limi*) of the Mississippi valley
**mudpack** \ˈ=,=\ *n* **1** : a cosmetic paste for the face composed chiefly of fuller's earth, bleaches, and astringents **2** : the powder from which this paste is prepared
**mud peep** *n* : LEAST SANDPIPER
**mud pickerel** *n* : GRASS PICKEREL 1
**mud plantain** *n* **1** : a plant of the genus *Heteranthera; esp* : a No. American marsh or water plant (*H. dubia*) **2** : WATER PLANTAIN
**mud plover** *n* : BLACK-BELLIED PLOVER
**mud puddle** *n* : a small pool of dirty water usu. left by a rain storm ⟨*mud puddles* and ragged weeds by the road —Sinclair Lewis⟩
**mud puppy** *n* : any of various mostly large American salamanders: as **a** : HELLBENDER **b** : AXOLOTL **c** : a member of the genus *Necturus*
**mud purslane** *n* : a plant of the genus *Elatine*
**mud puss·er** \-,pùsə(r)\ *n* -s [¹*mud* + *pusser* (of unknown origin)] : the native mollienisia (*Mollienisia latipinna*) of Florida
**mu·dra** \məˈdrä\ *n* -s [Skt *mudrā* seal, sign, token] : symbolic hand gestures of India's natya dance crystallized by ancient sages from descriptive and expressive movements into an elaborate code
**mud ring** *n* : the ring or frame forming the bottom of a water leg in a steam boiler
**mud–runner** \ˈ=,==\ *n* : MUDDER
**muds** *pl of* MUD, *pres 3d sing of* MUD
**mud saw** *n* : a cutting tool for very hard materials (as gems) consisting of a metal disk that dips into a semifluid abrasive mixture as it revolves and carries it to the point of cutting
**mud shark** *n* : any of several sluggish bottom-dwelling sharks esp. of the family Hexanchidae
**mudsill** \ˈ=,=\ *n* **1** : the lowest sill of a structure (as of a house, bridge, dam) usu. embedded in soil or mud **2** : a person of the lowest stratum of society ⟨a ~ like me trying to push in and help —Mark Twain⟩ ⟨all classes and conditions of society from the millionaire to the ~ —D.D.Martin⟩
**mudskipper** \ˈ=,==\ *n* : any of several small Asiatic and Polynesian gobies (genera *Periophthalmus* and *Boleophthalmus*) that are able to leave the water and skip about actively over wet mud and sand and even to climb the roots of mangroves by means of fleshy modified pectoral fins
**mudslinger** \ˈ=,==\ *n* : one that employs mudslinging
**mudslinging** \ˈ=,==\ *n* : the use of offensive epithets and invective against an individual esp. during a political campaign ⟨acrimonious debate and ~ —*Amer. Guide Series: Ind.*⟩
**mud snail** *n* **1** : BASKET SHELL **2** : a common Old World pond snail (*Lymnaea truncatella*) that is the English intermediate host of the sheep liver fluke
**mud snake** *n* : HOOP SNAKE 2a
**mud snipe** *n* : WOODCOCK 1a(2)
**mudspate** \ˈ=,=\ *n* : MUDFLOW 3
**mudspringer** \ˈ=,==\ *n* : MUDSKIPPER
**mud–star** \ˈ=,=\ *n* : any of various active bottom-dwelling starfishes that constitute the genus *Luidia*
**mudstone** \ˈ=,=\ *n* : an indurated shale produced by the consolidation of mud
**mudsucker** \ˈ=,==\ *n* **1** : any bird that thrusts its bill into mud in search of food (as the woodcock and certain ducks) **2** : a common goby (*Gillichthys mirabilis*) of muddy bays and sloughs of the southern California and Lower California coast that is much used as a baitfish
**mud sunfish** *n* : MUD BASS
**mud swallow** *n* : CLIFF SWALLOW
**mud time** *n*, *NewEng* : the muddy season in spring
**mud turtle** *or* **mud terrapin** *or* **mud tortoise** *n* : any bottom-dwelling freshwater turtle: as **a** : a musk turtle (genus *Kinosternon*) **b** : the Pacific mud turtle (*Clemmys marmorata*) **c** : SOFT SHELLED TURTLE
**mu·du·ga** \məˈdügə\ *n*, *pl* **muduga** *or* **mudugas** *usu cap* **1** : one of several peoples in the Nilgiri hills of southwest India with hereditary ties of friendship with the Toda people of this area **2** : a member of any of the Muduga peoples
**mud volcano** *n* : an orifice in the earth from which gas or vapor issues either through a pool of mud or with the ejection of mud which may accumulate in a conical mound — compare AIR VOLCANO
**mud wagon** *n* : a stagecoach lighter and smaller than the Concord coach with flat sides and simpler joinery
**mud wasp** *n* : a wasp that builds a nest of mud for its young; *esp* : MUD DAUBER
**mudweed** \ˈ=,=\ *n* : MUDWORT
**mud whelk** *n* : HERCULES CLUB
**mudworm** \ˈ=,=\ *n* **1** *NewEng* : EARTHWORM **2** : MUD-BLISTER WORM
**mudwort** \ˈ=,=\ *n* : an herb of the genus *Limosella* (esp. *L. aquatica*)

mud wagon

**mueh·len·beck·ia** \,myülən-ˈbekēə\ *n*, *cap* [NL, fr. H. G. *Mühlenbeck* †1845 Alsatian physician + NL *-ia*] : a genus of somewhat erect or climbing plants (family Polygonaceae) that are native to temperate parts of the southern hemisphere, have small opposite leaves or leaves replaced by cladophylls, and are sometimes grown as ornamentals or ground covers in mild regions
**muelheim** *usu cap*, *var of* MÜLHEIM
**muellerian** *sometimes cap*, *var of* MÜLLERIAN
**muel·le·ri·us** \myüˈlirēəs\ *n*, *cap* [NL, prob. fr. Fritz *Müller* †1897 Ger. zoologist] : a genus of lungworms (family Metastrongylidae) that are nearly cosmopolitan in sheep and goats and have larval stages in various snails and slugs
**muenchen–gladbach** *usu cap M&G*, *var of* MÜNCHEN-GLADBACH
¹**muenster** *usu cap*, *var of* MÜNSTER
²**muen·ster** *or* **muenster cheese** *also* **mun·ster** \ˈm(y)ün-ztə(r), ˈmùn-,ˈmən-,ˈmin-,ˈmæn-, -n(t)st-\ *n*, *usu cap M* [*Münster*, *Munster*, city in Haut-Rhin department, northeastern France] : a semisoft cheese that may be bland or sharp in flavor depending upon the length of cure
**muer·mo** \ˈmwer(,)mō\ *n* -s [AmerSp, fr. Araucan] **1** : a tall Chilean timber tree (*Eucryphia cordifolia*) **2** : the hard wood of the muermo tree
**muet** \mwᵊe\ *or* **muette** \-et\ *adj* [*muet* fr. F, lit., mute, fr. MF; *muette* fr. F, fem. of *muet* — more at MUTE] **1** *of e in French* : silent or sometimes silent and sometimes pronounced **2** *of h in French* : initial in the orthography of a word before which elision and liaison occur — compare ASPIRÉ
**mu·ez·zin** *or* **mu·az·zin** *also* **mu'·adh·dhin** \m(y)üˈezᵊn, -ˈaz-; ˈmüəzən, -,zēn\ *n* -s [Ar *mu'adhdhin*] : a Muslim crier who calls the hour of daily prayers from the minaret of a mosque
**MUF** *abbr*, *often not cap* maximum usable frequency
¹**muff** *n* -s [D *mof* German, fr. G *muff* grumbler, sulky person, of imit. origin] *obs* : GERMAN, SWISS — usu. used disparagingly
²**muff** \ˈməf\ *n* -s [D *mof*, fr. MD *moffe*, *moffel*, *muffel* mitten, thick glove, muff, fr. MF *moufle* mitten, fr. ML *muffula*] **1** : a warm tubular covering with open ends into which the hands may be thrust that is usu. made of cloth or fur, usu. lined and padded, and used by men in the 18th century and now only by women and children **2 a (1)** : a cluster of feathers on the side of the face of domestic fowls of certain breeds **(2)** : feathering on the feet and shanks of some pigeons **b** : a protective pad or covering for the natural spurs of a cock worn during training fights — usu. used in pl. **3** : a blown cylinder of glass which is afterward flattened out to make a sheet **4** : a short hollow cylinder surrounding an object or used to connect two abutting objects (as pipes or shafts)
³**muff** \"\ *n* -s [prob. fr. ²*muff*] **1 a** : a bungling performance : a clumsy failure **b** : a failure to hold a ball in attempting to catch it **2 a** : an awkward person; *esp* : one who is poor in an athletic sport ⟨a complete ~ at cricket —G.M.Trevelyan⟩ **b** : a poor-spirited person : DUFFER
⁴**muff** \"\ *vb* -ED/-ING/-S *vt* **1** : to handle awkwardly : do awkwardly : BUNGLE, FLUFF ⟨gave me another chance to make good on a job I once ~*ed* —Agnes M. Cleaveland⟩ **2** : to fail to hold (a ball) when attempting a catch : FUMBLE ~ *vi* **1** : to act or do something stupidly or clumsily : BUNGLE, FLUFF **2** : to muff a ball — compare FUMBLE
**muffed** \ˈməft\ *adj* [²*muff* + *-ed*] **1** : having or wearing a muff : CRESTED **2** [fr. past part. of ⁴*muff*] : poorly executed ⟨a ~ pass⟩ ⟨a ~ play⟩
**muff·et** \ˈməfət, *usu* -fəd-+V\ *n* -s [prob. fr. ²*muff* + *-et*; fr. the ring of feathers around its neck] *Brit* : WHITETHROAT
**muf·fe·tee** *also* **muf·fa·tee** \,məfəˈtē, ˈmùf-\ *n* -s [irreg. fr. ²*muff*] *dial chiefly Brit* **1** : a scarf or muffler worn around the neck **2** : WRISTLET
**muf·fin** \ˈməfən\ *n* -s [prob. fr. LG *muffen*, pl. of *muffe* cake] **1 a** : a quick bread made of batter containing egg and baked in a small cup-shaped pan **b** : a similarly shaped biscuit made from yeast dough — see ENGLISH MUFFIN **2** : a small-sized plate (as of clay or glass) **3** : HAZEL 4
**muf·fin·eer** \,məfəˈni(ə)r, -niə\ *n* -s : a shaker for sifting sugar on muffins
**muffin pan** *n* : a baking pan formed of a group of connecting cups usu. used for muffins or cupcakes
**muffin ring** *n* : a metal ring in which English muffins are baked
**muffin stand** *n* : a small three-tiered table for holding food (as sandwiches or cakes)

muffin pan

¹**muf·fle** \ˈməfəl\ *vt* **muffled; muffled; muffling** \-f(ə)liŋ\ **muffles** [ME *muflen*, perh. fr. (assumed) MF *moufler* to envelop in mittens, fr. MF *moufle* mitten] **1** : to wrap up so as to conceal or protect : cover over : ENVELOP ⟨*muffling* his neck with a knitted scarf —Agatha Christie⟩ ⟨the cloud . . . *muffled* the plane —Ira Wolfert⟩ ⟨the grey fog which *muffled* the sky —Ellen Glasgow⟩ ⟨still drowsy, he *muffled* his face and went to sleep —C.G.D.Roberts⟩ **2 a** *obs* : to prevent from seeing : BLINDFOLD ⟨love, whose view is *muffled* still, should without eyes see pathways to his will —Shak.⟩ **b** : to prevent from speaking : SILENCE ⟨let's ~ all the gossip —Louis Bromfield⟩ **3 a** : to wrap or pad with something to dull the sound of ⟨the rowlocks were *muffled* in chamois —A.B.Mayse⟩ **b** : to deaden the sound of ⟨~ the noises of the street —Virginia Woolf⟩ ⟨the sands . . . have *muffled* the tread of countless armies —Rex Keating⟩ **4** : to keep down : SUPPRESS ⟨the abrupt, bony, closemouthed prose . . . ~*s* his social comment —John Woodburn⟩ ⟨made an admirable effort to ~ his feelings —*Time*⟩
²**muffle** \"\ *n* -s **1 a** *archaic* : something that covers the neck or face : MUFFLER **b** : something resembling a muffle ⟨it had a soothing . . . influence, that ~ of snow —*Harper's*⟩ **2** [F *moufle*, lit., mitten, fr. MF] : a compartment or oven used in a furnace in firing wares (as those decorated over the glaze) that must be protected from flame — see MUFFLE FURNACE **3** : something that deadens sound; *also* : the sound deadened ⟨the ~ of distant thunder⟩ ⟨~ of marching feet⟩ **4** [F *moufle* mitten, fr. MF] *archaic* : BOXING GLOVE ⟨sometimes we must box without a ~ —Lord Byron⟩ **5** [F, lit., mitten, fr. MF] : a pulley block with several sheaves
³**muffle** \"\ *n* -s [F *mufle*, fr. MF, alter. (prob. influenced by MF *museau* muzzle, fr. OF *musel*) of *moufle* fat coarse face, fr. G *muffel* short snout, sulky person, of imit. origin — more at MUZZLE] : the rhinarium of mammals in which it is heavy and flabby
**muf·fled** \ˈməfəld\ *adj* **1** : wrapped up closely : COVERED ⟨the house itself ~ in ramblers and ivy —Edmund Wilson⟩ ⟨they were ~ figures deep in thick coats —John Steinbeck⟩ **2 a** : sounding as if from a distance : deadened in intensity : FAINT ⟨with the ~ roar of London around them —George Meredith⟩ ⟨the ~ footsteps of innumerable pilgrims —L.P. Smith⟩ **b** : said under the breath : MUTTERED ⟨made a ~ sound of disgust —Kenneth Roberts⟩ **3** : decorated or painted and treated in a muffle furnace to fix the color **4** : SUPPRESSED ⟨~ fighting —*Atlantic*⟩ — **muf·fled·ly** *adv*
**muffle furnace** *n* : a furnace having its charge inside a muffle and the source of heat outside so that the charge has no contact with the flame
**muffle–jaw** \ˈ=,=\ *n* [³*muffle*] : MILLER'S-THUMB 1
¹**muf·fler** \ˈməflə(r)\ *n* -s **1 a** : a covering (as a veil or scarf) worn as a protection or disguise ⟨some awkwardness in her management of the ~ . . . a principal accomplishment of the coquettes of the time —Sir Walter Scott⟩ **b** *obs* : a bandage placed over the eyes ⟨fortune is painted . . . with a ~ afore her eyes —Shak.⟩ **c** : a scarf worn around the neck ⟨the outlandish sports coats and garish ~*s* —Bennett Cerf⟩ **d** : something that hides or disguises ⟨the mask and ~ of allegoric rhapsody —A.C.Swinburne⟩ **2** : a cushion for terminating or softening the tones made by a musical instrument (as the piano or drum) **3 a** : any of various devices to deaden the noise of escaping gases or vapors; *specif* : a tube filled with baffles through which the exhaust gases of an internal-combustion engine are passed **b** : something that silences ⟨nobody had ever put a ~ on him yet —S.H.Adams⟩
²**muffler** \"\ *adj* : relating to a device or a stage of amplification used with a radiating receiving set to suppress the radiation
**muf·flin** \-lən\ *n* -s [perh. irreg. fr. ¹*muffle*] *Brit* : LONG-TAILED TIT
**mufflon** *or* **muflon** *var of* MOUFLON
**muffs** *pl of* MUFF, *pres 3d sing of* MUFF
**muffy** \ˈməfē\ *adj* [²*muff* + *-y*] : of, relating to, or resembling a muff
¹**muf·ti** \ˈməftē, ˈmùf-, -ti\ *n* -s [Ar *muftī*] **1** : a professional jurist who interprets Muslim religious law **2** : the chief mufti of a district — called also *grand mufti*
²**muf·ti** \ˈməftē, -ti\ *n* -s [prob. fr. ¹*mufti*] : ordinary dress as distinguished from that denoting a calling or station; *esp* : civilian dress when worn by one in military service
¹**mug** \ˈməg\ *n* -s [origin unknown] **1 a** : a drinking cup usu. of metal or earthenware and usu. cylindrical with no lip but with a handle **b** : the quantity that a mug will hold : MUGFUL **2 a (1)** : the face or mouth of a person ⟨the sagebrush hero with the vacant ~ —Walker Gibson⟩ ⟨that lovable, ugly ~ of his —D.G.Peattie⟩ **(2)** *slang* : MUG SHOT **b** : a grotesque facial gesture : GRIMACE ⟨started making faces, pulling wide, ill-mannered ~*s* —*Picture Post*⟩ **3 a (1)** : an extremely stupid person : BLOCKHEAD, FOOL ⟨he knew he might look a ~ standing there just looking —Richard Llewellyn⟩ **(2)** *Brit* : a gullible person; *specif* : the victim of a swindle or fraud **b** : one of a criminal element : PUNK, THUG ⟨that hooey about what good guys the ~*s* are at heart —John Byron⟩ **syn** see FACE

mug 1a

²**mug** \"\ *vb* **mugged; mugged; mugging; mugs** *vi* : to make faces; *esp* : to call attention to oneself by grimacing or exaggerated gestures usu. on the stage or before a camera frequently for comic effect ⟨the technique of the ham actor *mugging* to the audience —Edward Montgomery⟩ ⟨students were on hand to ~ for TV cameras —*Newsweek*⟩ ~ *vt* **1** : to display by grimacing ⟨*mugged* displeasure at the offer —James Dugan⟩ **2** : PHOTOGRAPH ⟨he ~*s* criminals⟩
³**mug** \"\ *n* -s [origin unknown] *archaic Scot* : a breed of sheep with wool over the face
⁴**mug** \", ˈmùg\ *n* -s [prob. of Scand origin; akin to ON *mugga* drizzle; akin to ON *mjūkr* soft — more at MUCUS] *dial Eng* : DRIZZLE
⁵**mug** \ˈməg\ *vb* **mugged; mugged; mugging; mugs** [origin unknown] *vi*, *Brit* : to study (as for an examination) often with little understanding or spontaneous interest : CRAM — often used with *up* ⟨~ up on this assault engineering —*Springfield (Mass.) Republican*⟩ ~ *vt*, *Brit* : STUDY — often used with *up* ⟨been *mugging* up Greek —Thomas Wood †1950⟩ ⟨~ up other people's judgments and repeat them mechanically —Aldous Huxley⟩
⁶**mug** \"\ *vb* **mugged; mugged; mugging; mugs** [back-formation fr. ³*mugger*] *vi* : to assault someone esp. by garroting usu. with intent to rob ⟨supported themselves by *mugging* —*Sat. Eve. Post*⟩ ~ *vt* : to assault esp. by garroting usu. with intent to rob —was *mugged* from behind and forced into a hallway —*N.Y. Times*⟩
**mu·ga** \ˈmügə\ *n* -s [Bengali *mūgā*] **1** : a silk from the cocoon of an Indian moth (*Antheraea assamensis*) **2** : the caterpillar producing muga
**mug·ful** \ˈməg,fùl\ *n*, *pl* **mugfuls** *also* **mugs·ful** \-g,fùlz, -gz,fùl\ [¹*mug* + *-ful*] : the amount that a mug will hold ⟨making slow progress with my ~ —Adrian Bell⟩
**mug·ga** \ˈməgə\ *n* -s [native name in New South Wales, Australia] : RED IRONBARK
¹**mug·ger** \ˈmùgər, ˈməg-\ *n* -s [¹*mug* + *-er*] *chiefly Scot* : a peddler of earthenware : TINKER
²**mug·ger** \ˈməgə(r)\ *n* -s [Hindi *magar*, fr. Skt *makara* water monster] : the common freshwater crocodile (*Crocodylus palustris*) of southeastern Asia that is usu. harmless to man although it may attain a length of 16 feet
³**mugger** \"\ *n* -s [prob. fr. obs. E *mug* to punch in the face (fr. E ¹*mug*) + E *-er*] : one that attacks usu. from behind with intent to rob
⁴**mugger** \"\ *n* -s [²*mug* + *-er*] : one that mugs; *esp* : an actor who depends on grimaces and exaggerated gestures for audience response
**mug·get** \ˈməgət\ *n* -s [origin unknown] *dial Eng* : entrails of a sheep or calf esp. when used as food
**mug·gi·ly** \ˈməgəlē\ *adv* : in a muggy manner
**mug·gi·ness** \-gēnəs, -gin-\ *n* -ES : the quality or state of being muggy
**mugging** *n* -s [in sense 1, fr. gerund of ²*mug*; in sense 2, fr. gerund of ⁶*mug*] **1** : the exaggerated action of an actor used to get audience response **2** : the act of strong-arming a robbery victim from behind; *also* : a street assault or beating esp. when robbery is involved
**mug·gins** \ˈməgənz\ *n*, *pl* **muggins** *often cap* [prob. fr. the name *Muggins*] **1 a** : a provision in many games played in England that if a player fails to record an earned score promptly his opponent may say *muggins* and claim that score — used esp. in cribbage and dominoes **b** : a dominoes game identical with sniff except that the muggins provision is included **c** : any of various card games in which a score overlooked may be claimed by saying *muggins* or in which the player with the worst score is called *muggins* — used esp. in children's games **2** : SIMPLETON ⟨had seen too many ~ come bowing and smiling —Enid Bagnold⟩
**mug·gles** \ˈməgəlz\ *n*, *pl* **muggles** [origin unknown] *slang* : ²REEFER
**mug·gle·to·nian** \,məgəlˈtōnēən, -nyən\ *n* -s *usu cap* [Lodowicke *Muggleton* †1698 Eng. Puritan tailor, one of the founders + E *-an*] : one of a British sect identifying its two founders with the witnesses of Revelation 11:3–6, rejecting the doctrine of the Trinity, condemning preaching and prayer, and believing matter to be eternal and reason the creation of the devil
¹**mug·gy** \ˈməgē, -gi\ *adj* -ER/-EST [⁴*mug* + *-y*] : marked by warm dampness : HUMID ⟨horribly ~ weather⟩
²**mug·gy** \ˈmügi, ˈməgi\ *n* -ES [perh. alter. of *Maggie*, feminine name, dim. of *Mag*, nickname for *Margaret*] *dial Eng* : WHITETHROAT
**mughal** *or* **mughul** *cap*, *var of* MOGUL
**mu·gho pine** *or* **mu·go pine** \ˈm(y)ü(,)gō-\ *n* [*mugho* prob. fr. F, mugho pine, fr. It *mugo*] : a shrubby spreading pine (*Pinus mugo mughus*) that is a variety of the Swiss mountain pine and is widely cultivated as an ornamental
**mughouse** \ˈ=,=\ *n* : ALEHOUSE ⟨shrouded in the fumes of taverns and ~*s* —*Time*⟩
**mu·gi·ent** \ˈmyüjēənt\ *adj* [L *mugient-*, *mugiens*, pres. part. of *mugire* to bellow, moo; akin to Gk *myzein* to moan, Skt *muñjati*, *mojati* he emits a sound, L *mutus* mute — more at MUTE] : making a lowing sound : BELLOWING ⟨the ~ herds are turned out to pasture —Richard Amper⟩
**mu·gil·i·dae** \myüˈjilə,dē\ *n pl*, *cap* [NL, fr. *Mugil*, type genus (fr. L *mugil* mullet) + *-idae*; akin to L *mucus* nasal mucus — more at MUCUS] : a family of fishes (suborder Mugiloidea) consisting of the gray mullets
¹**mu·gi·loid** \ˈmyüjə,lòid\ *adj* [NL *Mugiloidea*] **1** : of or relating to the Mugiloidea **2** : resembling a gray mullet
²**mugiloid** \"\ *n* -s [NL *Mugiloidea*] : a fish of the suborder Mugiloidea
**mu·gi·loi·dea** \,==ˈlòidēə\ *n pl*, *cap* [NL, fr. *Mugil* + *-oidea*] : a suborder of the order Percomorphi that is distinguished by abdominal pelvic fins and that includes the families Mugilidae, Atherinidae, and Sphyraenidae
**mu·gon·go** \müˈgäŋ(,)gō, -ˈgȯŋ-\ *n* -s [origin unknown] **1** : either of two African trees (*Ricinodendron rautanenii* and *R. africanum*) of the family Euphorbiaceae having extremely light wood **2** : the wood of the mugongo tree
**mugs** *pl of* MUG, *pres 3d sing of* MUG
**mugsful** *pl of* MUGFUL
**mug shot** *n* : a photograph of a person's face — usu. used of official police photographs
**mu·guet** \mœˈgā\ *n* -s [F, lily-of-the-valley, woodruff, fr. OF, fr. *muguete*, *muguede* (in *nois muguete*, *nois muguede* nutmeg); fr. the odor — more at NUTMEG] : LILY OF THE VALLEY 1
**mug–up** \ˈ=,=\ *n* -s [fr. E dial. *mug up*, v., to have a snack, prob. fr. E ¹*mug* + *up*] : a cup of coffee or tea and sometimes a snack between meals
**mugweed** \ˈ=,=\ *n* [ME *mugwed*, fr. *mug-* (in *mugwort*) + *wed*, *weed* weed] : MUGWORT 1
**mug·wet** \ˈmə,gwet\ *n* [by folk etymology fr. earlier *muguet*, fr. MF, fr. OF] **1** : SWEET WOODRUFF **2** : GUELDER ROSE
**mug·wort** \ˈməg+,-\ *n* [ME, fr. OE *mucgwyrt*, fr. *mucg-* (perh. akin to OE *mycg* midge) + *wyrt* wort — more at MIDGE, WORT] **1** : any of several wormwoods; *esp* : a Eurasian perennial herb (*Artemisia vulgaris*) **2** : BASTARD FEVERFEW **3** : CROSSWORT c
¹**mug·wump** \ˈmə,gwəmp\ *n* -s [Natick *mugquomp*, *mugwomp* captain, prob. fr. *mogki* great + *-omp* man] **1** : a person of importance : CHIEF 2a — often a generalized expression of disapproval **2 a** *often cap* : a bolter from the Republican party in the presidential election of 1884 **b** : one that withdraws his support from a political group or organization : a regular member who bolts a party and adopts an independent position **3** : one who is undecided or neutral (as in politics) often as a result of an inability to make up his mind : FENCE-SITTER ⟨too much of a ~ to be a politician —Bernard Kalb⟩ ⟨was at twenty still a restless mental ~ —D.C.Peattie⟩ ⟨a party question with the partisans lined up pro and contra and the ~*s* sorely perplexed —*Century Mag.*⟩
²**mugwump** \"\ *vi* -ED/-ING/-S : to act as or adopt the position of a mugwump
**mug·wump·ery** \ˈ=,gwəmp(ə)rē\ *n* -ES : the views and practices of mugwumps ⟨endeavoring to put a respectable front on his ~ —George Barker⟩

**mug·wump·i·an** \(ˈ)=ˈgwəmpēən\ *adj* **:** of, suggesting, or being a mugwump ⟨tainted with a certain New England ~ independence —W.A.White⟩ ⟨a ~ Democrat —*Boston Jour.*⟩

**mug·wump·ish** \-pish\ *adj* **:** suggesting or having the characteristics of mugwumpery ⟨a ~ policy⟩

**mug·wump·ism** \-,pizəm\ *n* -s **:** independent action in politics; *esp* **:** MUGWUMPERY ⟨an inveterate organization Republican intolerant of ~ —Robert White⟩

**mu·ha·ji·run** \(,)mü,häjəˈrün, ='==,=\ *n pl, often cap* [Ar *muhājirūna*] **:** fellow emigrants who fled with Muhammad during the Hegira

**¹mu·ham·mad·an** *or* **mo·ham·med·an** \mōˈhaməd°n, -hām-, -həm-, -dən *sometimes* mə- *or* mü'-\ *adj, usu cap* [*Muhammad, Mohammed* †A.D.632 Arabian prophet and founder of Islam + E *-an*, adj. suffix] **:** of or relating to Muhammad or the religion and institutions founded by Muhammad

**²muhammadan** \"\ *or* **mohammedan** \"\ *n* -s *usu cap* [*Muhammad, Mohammed* †A.D.632 + E *-an*, n. suffix] **:** MUSLIM — used predominantly by those outside the faith of Islam and usu. taken to be offensive by the Islamic believer

**muhammadan era** *n, usu cap M* **:** the era in use in Muhammadan countries for numbering Muhammadan calendar years since the hegira

**mu·ham·mad·an·ism** *or* **mo·ham·med·an·ism** \-d°n,izəm, -də,ni-\ *n* -s *usu cap* **:** ISLAM

**mu·har·ram** \müˈharəm\ *or* **mo·har·ram** \mō'-\ *or* **mo·hur·rum** \-ˈhərəm\ *n* -s *usu cap* [Ar *muḥarram*, lit., sacred, forbidden] **1 :** the first month of the Muhammadan year — see MONTH table **2 :** a Muslim festival held during the first ten days of the month of Muharram

**muh·len·ber·gia** \,myülənˈbərjēə\ *n, cap* [NL, fr. Gotthilf H. E. *Mühlenberg* †1815 Am. clergyman and botanist + NL *-ia*] **:** a genus of slender often wiry perennial American and Asiatic grasses with small spikelets and capillary awns of some importance in the western U. S. as forage

**muh·len·berg's turtle** \ˈmyülən,bərgs-\ *n, usu cap M* [prob. after Gotthilf H. E. *Mühlenberg* †1815] **:** a small American freshwater turtle (*Clemmys muhlenbergii*)

**muhly** \ˈmyülē\ *also* **muhly grass** *n* -s [*muhly* fr. *muhl-* (fr. NL *Muhlenbergia*) + *-y*] **:** a grass of the genus *Muhlenbergia*

**mu·hu·hu** \məˈhü(,)hü\ *also* **mu·hu·gu** \-)gü\ *or* **mu·hu·ga** \-,gə\ *n* -s [native name in East Africa] **1 :** an East African tree (*Brachylaena hutchinsii*) of the family Compositae with strongly aromatic hard heavy durable wood similar to sandalwood **2 :** the wood of the muhuhu tree

**muid** *or* **mud** \ˈmə(r)d, ˈməd\ *n* -s [Afrik *mud*, fr. D, fr. MD *mudde*; akin to OE *mydd* bushel, OHG *mutti*; all fr. a prehistoric WGmc word borrowed fr. L *modius* — more at MODIUS] **:** a Dutch unit of capacity used in southern Africa equal to about three bushels

**mu·il·la** \myüˈilə\ *n, cap* [NL, backward spelling of *Allium* — more at ALLIUM] **:** a genus of bulbous California herbs (family Liliaceae) with greenish white flowers and foliage that resembles that of an onion but is odorless

**muir** \ˈmyü(ə)r\ *n* -s [ME (Sc) *mur*, alter. of ME *mor* — more at MOOR] *chiefly Scot* **:** ¹MOOR

**mu·i·ra·pi·ran·ga** \,müə,räpəˈraŋgə\ *n* -s [Pg, prob. fr. Tupi, fr. *muirá* wood, stick + *piranga* red] **:** SATINÉ

**muir·burn** \ˈmyü(ə)r,bərn\ *n* [ME (Sc) *murbyrn*, fr. *mur* moor + *-byrn* (fr. ME *birnen* to burn) — more at BURN] *Scot* **:** the burning of the heath and stubble on a moor

**muircock** \ˈ=,=\ *n* [ME (Sc) *mur cok*, fr. *mur* + ME *cok* cock] *Scot* **:** MOORCOCK

**muirfowl** \ˈ=,=\ *n* [*muir* + *fowl*] *Scot* **:** RED GROUSE

**muis·ca** \ˈmwēskə\ *or* **moz·ca** \ˈmōskə\ *n, pl* **muisca** *or* **muiscas** *or* **mozca** *or* **mozcas** *usu cap* **:** CHIBCHA

**muis·hond** \ˈmīs,hänt, ˈmās-\ *n* -s [Afrik, fr. D, cat, weasel, fr. MD *muushont*, fr. *muus* mouse + *hont* dog; akin to OE *mūs* mouse and to OE *hund* dog — more at MOUSE, HOUND] **:** either of two southern African weasels that are black with white stripes and that emit a fetid odor when disturbed — see SNAKE MUISHOND, STRIPED MUISHOND

**mui–tsai** \ˈmüēˈjī\ *n, pl* **mui–tsai** [Chin (Cant) *moot-tsai*, fr. *moot* younger sister + *tsai* little; akin to Chin (Pek) *mei⁴-tsai³* little younger sister, fr. *mei⁴* younger sister + *tsai³* child] **1 :** a young slave girl in South China **2 :** a system of girl slavery in South China

**mujik** *var of* MUZHIK

**muj·ta·hid** \müjˈtä,hid\ *n* -s [Ar, one who exerts himself] **:** an authoritative interpreter of the religious law of Islam; *esp* **:** a living religious teacher that is recognized by the Shi'a as competent to exercise private judgment in formulating authoritative answers to legal questions

**muk·den** \ˈmükdən, ˈmək-; (ˈ)mük,den, (ˈ)mük-\ *adj, usu cap* [fr. *Mukden*, city in southern Manchuria, northeast China] **:** of or from Mukden, Manchuria **:** of the kind or style prevalent in Mukden

**mukh·tar** \(ˈ)mükˈtär\ *n* -s [Ar *mukhtār*, lit., chosen] **:** the head of the local government of a town

**muk·luk** *also* **muck·luck** *or* **muc·luc** \ˈmə,klək\ *n* -s [Esk *muklok* large seal] **1 :** a sealskin or reindeer-skin boot worn by Eskimos **2 :** a boot similar in style to the Eskimo mukluk often made of duck with a soft leather sole and worn over several pairs of socks

**muk·ri** \ˈmükrē\ *n, pl* **mukri** *or* **mukris** *usu cap* **1 a :** an ancient Kurdish people of Persia **b :** a member of such people **2 :** the Kurdish dialect of the Mukri people

**muk·ti** \ˈmüktē, -ti\ *n* -s [Skt, fr. *muñcati* he releases — more at MUCUS] **:** MOKSHA

**muk·tuk** \ˈmək,tək\ *n* -s [Esk] **:** whale skin used for food

**mu·la·da** \müˈlädə\ *n* -s [Sp, fr. *mulo* mule] *Southwest* **:** a drove of mules

**mu·la·dí** \,müləˈthē\ *n, pl* **muladí·es** \-(,)ās\ [Sp, fr. Ar *muwalladīn* adopted ones] **:** a Spaniard who adopted the Muslim religion during the Moorish occupation — compare MOZARAB

**mu·lat·ta** \məˈladə, myə'-, myü'-, -atə\ *n* -s [Sp *mulata*, fem. of *mulato*] **:** MULATTRESS

**¹mu·lat·to** \-ad·(,)ō, -adə, -a(,)tō, -atə\ *n, pl* **mulattoes** *also* **mulattos** [Sp *mulato*, fr. *mulo* mule, fr. L *mulus* — more at MULE] **1 :** the first-generation offspring of a Negro and a white **2 :** a person of mixed Caucasian and Negro ancestry

**²mulatto** \"\ *adj* **1 :** of or relating to a mulatto; *esp* **:** having the color of a mulatto **2** *South* **:** composed of or characterized by brown clay ⟨~ soil⟩ ⟨~ land⟩

**mulatto land crab** *n* [so called fr. its grayish color] **:** GREAT LAND CRAB

**mulatto–wood** \=ˈ=(,)=,=\ *n* **:** the wood of any of several Mexican timber trees (as of the genera *Celtis, Bursera*, and *Zanthoxylum*)

**mu·lat·tress** \=ˈla·trəs\ *n* -ES [F *mulâtresse*, fr. *mulâtre* mulatto (modif. of Sp *mulato*) + *-esse* -ess] **:** a female mulatto

**mulay saw** *var of* MULEY SAW

**mul·ber·ry** \ˈməl,berē, -b(ə)rē, -ri — *see* BERRY\ *n* [ME *mulberie, murberie*, fr. OF *moure, meure* mulberry (fruit), (fr. — assumed — VL *mora*, fr. L, pl. of *morum* mulberry — fruit —, fr. Gk *moron* mulberry — fruit —, blackberry) + ME *berie, berye* berry; prob. akin to Arm *mor* blackberry] **1 a :** a tree of the genus *Morus* — compare PAPER MULBERRY **b :** the edible pleasantly acid berrylike usu. dark purple fruit of the mulberry tree **c :** THIMBLEBERRY **d :** any of several blackberries **e :** any of several other plants (as dodder and whitebeam) **2 a :** a dark purple that is bluer, lighter, and stronger than average prune or plum (sense 6b) and redder and paler than mulberry purple **b :** a purplish black that is bluer and stronger than black plum — called also *morello, murrey*

mulberry

**mulberry bird** *n* **:** ROSE-COLORED STARLING

**mulberry family** *n* **:** MORACEAE

**mulberry fig** *n* **:** SYCAMORE 1

**mulberry fruit** *n* **:** a very dark red that is slightly redder than port

**mulberry purple** *n* **:** a dark purple that is bluer, lighter, and stronger than average prune, bluer and deeper than mulberry (sense 2a), and bluer and stronger than plum (sense 6b)

**mulberry whelk** *n* **:** a boring mollusk (*Morula uva*) having a bluish white shell with black tubercles and a violet aperture and being sometimes a serious pest of Australian oyster beds

**¹mulch** \ˈməlch\ *n* -ES [perh. irreg. fr. *melch*] **1 :** rotting straw strewn over the ground and often mixed with mud or manure ⟨maids walking in pattens . . . to keep their shoes above the ~ —Thomas Hardy⟩ **2 :** a protective covering (as of sawdust, moss, compost, gravel, or paper) spread or left upon the ground to reduce evaporation, maintain even soil temperature, prevent erosion, control weeds, or enrich the soil **:** LITTER, TOPDRESSING — compare STUBBLE MULCH **3 :** DUST MULCH

**²mulch** \"\ *vt* -ED/-ING/-ES **1 :** to cover or dress with mulch ⟨~ an orchard⟩ **2 :** to make a layer of dry mulch on ⟨plow under green manure and ~ the ground afterward —*Farmer's Irrigation Guide*⟩

**mulch·er** \-chə(r)\ *n* -s **:** a device for applying mulch

**¹mulct** \ˈməlkt\ *n* -s [L *multa, mulcta*] **1 :** FINE, PENALTY, AMERCEMENT **2 :** an arbitrary exaction esp. of money ⟨a bill requiring bookmakers to buy a fifty-dollar tax stamp and then pay a ~ of 10 percent on their gross business —A.J.Liebling⟩

**²mulct** \"\ *vt* **mulcted; mulcted** *or* **mulct; mulcting; mulcts** [L *multare, mulctare*, fr. *multa, mulcta*, n.] **1 :** to punish or penalize by imposing a usu. pecuniary fine or forfeiture **:** exact a mulct from **:** FINE ⟨be ~*ed* or expelled by the stock exchange committee —G.B.Shaw⟩ **2 a :** to defraud esp. of money (as by extortion) **:** BLEED, MILK, SWINDLE ⟨aid the claimants in ~*ing* the insurance company —B.C.Dawkins⟩ ⟨~*ed* of their meager savings by thieves and swindlers —*Amer. Guide Series: N.Y.*⟩ **b :** to obtain (as money) from someone in an excessive amount or by fraud, duress, or theft ⟨mail fraud in ~*ing* $60,000 from clients —*Time*⟩ ⟨had ~*ed* an object of no value —S.J.Perelman⟩

**mul·der** \ˈmüldə(r), ˈməl-\ *dial Brit var of* MOLDER

**¹mule** \ˈmyül\ *n* -s [ME, fr. OF *mul*, fr. L *mulus*, prob. of non-IE origin; akin to the source of LGk dial. (Phocian) *mychlos* male ass] **1 :** a hybrid between the horse and the ass: as **a :** the usu. sterile offspring of a male ass and a mare having the large head, long ears, and small hoofs of the ass and the form and size of the horse and being valued as a draft and pack animal because of its endurance and surefootedness **b :** HINNY **2 :** a very stubborn person **3 :** a plant that is self-sterile because of either infertile pollen or rudimentary pistils; *usu* **:** a hybrid that is self-sterile and cross-sterile **4 :** HYBRID; *esp* **:** one that is sterile — used esp. of hybrids between the canary and related birds **5** [prob. so called fr. its being regarded as combining the principles of two earlier machines] **:** a machine having a moving carriage for simultaneously drawing and twisting a sliver into yarn or thread and winding it into cops and used orig. for cotton but now limited largely to wool — called also *mule-jenny* **6 :** a sharp-sterned coble used on the northeast coast of England **7 :** a coin or token struck from dies belonging to two different issues (as the obverse die of a cent and the reverse die of a halfpenny) **8 a :** a small usu. electric locomotive (as for towing ships through a lock or pulling mine cars) **b :** a light tractor (as for hauling trucks on a dock or dollies in a warehouse) **9 :** a device that can be lowered vertically from across the bow of a boat so as to catch the current in the water and draw the boat along **10 :** a large wooden board pulled by a windlass and used to unload grain from a railroad car

**²mule** \"\ *adj* **:** HYBRID ⟨~ cabbage⟩ ⟨~ lamb⟩ ⟨a ~ plant⟩

**³mule** \"\ *vt* -ED/-ING/-S **1 :** to combine (dies that do not match) to make a mule ⟨~ the obverse of one token with the reverse of another⟩ **2 :** to strike (a coin or token) with non-matching dies making a mule

**⁴mule** *n* -s [ME, fr. MF, chilblain, slipper] *obs* **:** CHILBLAIN

**⁵mule** \ˈmyül\ *n* -s [MF, chilblain, slipper, fr. L *mulleus* red shoe worn by dignitaries; prob. akin to Gk *melas* black — more at MULLET] **:** a shoe or house slipper without quarter and usu. without counter and often with a low heel

mule

**mule armadillo** *n* [¹*mule*] **:** a So. American armadillo (*Dasypus septemcinctus*)

**¹muleback** \ˈ=,=\ *n* **:** the back of a mule

**²muleback** \"\ *adv* **:** on the back of a mule

**mule chest** *n* [¹*mule*] **:** BLANKET CHEST

**mule deer** *n* **:** a long-eared deer of western No. America (*Odocoileus hemionus* syn. *Cariacus macrotis*) that is larger and more heavily built than the Virginia deer — called also *black-tailed deer*

**mule–ears** \ˈ=,=\ *n pl but sing in constr* **:** a plant of the genus *Wyethia*

**mule fat** *n* **:** a California composite shrub (*Baccharis viminea*) with slender leafy branching shoots that are an important browse for mule deer

**¹mule–foot** \ˈ=,=\ *or* **mule–footed** \ˈ=;==\ *adj* [¹*mule* + *foot* or *footed*] **1** *of a cloven-hoofed animal* **:** having a solid rather than a cleft hoof ⟨a *mule-foot* hog⟩ ⟨a *mule-foot* calf⟩ **2** *of a horse* **:** having a foot with small frog, upright hoof wall, and high heel like that of a mule

**²mule–foot** \ˈ=,=\ *n* **1** *pl* **mule–feet :** a mule-foot hoof **2** *pl* **mule–foots :** a mule-foot animal

**mule foot** *n, pl* **mule foots** [¹*mule* + *foot*; fr. the shape of the shell] *South* **:** BOX TORTOISE

**muleheaded** \ˈ=;==\ *adj* **:** STUBBORN, PIGHEADED — **mule·head·ed·ly** \ˈ=;===\ *adv*

**mule–jenny** \ˈ=;==\ *n* **:** MULE 5

**mule killer** *n, chiefly South* **:** any of several arthropods: as **a :** WHIP SCORPION **b :** STICK INSECT **c :** MANTIS **d :** WHEEL BUG **e :** a mutillid wasp

**mule·man** \ˈ=mən\ *n, pl* **mulemen :** one who tends mules

**mule mark** *n* **:** a dark dorsal stripe (as on a mule)

**mule pulley** *n* **:** an adjustable idler pulley for a belt; *esp* **:** one making an angle turn

**mules** \ˈmyülz\ *vt* -ED/-ING/-ES [after J. H. W. *Mules*] **:** to perform the Mules operation

**mule skinner** *n* **:** MULETEER

**mules operation** *n, usu cap M* [after J. H. W. *Mules*, 20th cent. Australian grazier who first suggested it] **:** removal of excess loose skin from either side of the crutch of a sheep to reduce the incidence of blowfly strike

**mu·le·ta** \müˈlād·ə, -ledə\ *n* -s [Sp, muleta, crutch, dim. of *mula* she-mule, fr. L, fem. of *mulus* mule — more at MULE] **:** a small cloth attached to a short tapered stick and used by a matador during the faena in place of the large fighting cape

**mu·le·teer** \,myüləˈti(ə)r, -iə\ *n* -s [MF *muletier*, fr. *mulet* mule (fr. OF, fr. *mul* mule + *-et*) + *-ier* -eer — more at MULE] **:** a driver of mules or team of mules

**mu·let·ta** \m(y)üˈled·ə\ *n* -s [Pg *muleta*, prob. dim. of *mula* she-mule, fr. L] **:** a Portuguese coasting ship that is similar to a tartan, has a large lateen sail, uses a jumble of sails when fishing, and has a pointed bow painted with a human eye

**¹mu·ley** *also* **mul·ley** \ˈmyülē, ˈmül-, ˈmül-, -li\ *n* -s [IrGael & ScGael *maol* bald, hornless & W *moel* bald, hornless + E *-y*, n. suffix; IrGael & ScGael *maol* & W *moel* akin to each other and prob. to ON *meitha* to hurt, mutilate — more at MAD] **1 :** a polled or hornless animal; *esp* **:** a muley cow **2 :** cow — used as a pet name

**²muley** *also* **mulley** \"\ *adj* **:** POLLED, HORNLESS, DEHORNED; *esp* **:** naturally hornless ⟨occasionally a male deer will be ~ —Lyle St. Amant & Carrol Perkins⟩ — used esp. of cattle ⟨a ~ ⟨a big brindle, ~ ox —Andy Adams⟩

**³muley** \ˈmyülē, -li\ *adj* [¹*mule* + *-y*, adj. suffix] **:** MULISH

**muley axle** *n* [²*muley*] **:** a railroad car axle without collars at the outer ends of the journals

**muley saw** *also* **mu·lay saw** *pronunc at* ¹MULEY +\ *n* [²*muley*] **:** a stiff saw with vertical reciprocating motion used in sawmills

**mul·ga** \ˈməlgə\ *n, pl* **mulgas** *or* **mulga** [native name in Australia] **1 a :** a widely distributed irregular and often shrubby Australian acacia (*Acacia aneura*) that has usu. linear grayish green phyllodes, yields a very hard tough heavy wood, and is an important forage plant in much of the drier part of Australia **b :** any of several other Australian acacias that resemble mulga; *broadly* **:** any Australian tree of scrubby growth and notably hard wood **2 :** the wood of a mulga **3** *or* **mulga scrub** *or* **mulga country :** arid land of Australia on which the mulga (*Acacia aneura*) is the dominant form of vegetation

**mül·heim** *or* **mul·heim** *or* **muel·heim** \ˈm(y)ül,hīm, ˈmēl-\ *adj, usu cap* [fr. *Mülheim* an der Ruhr, city in western Germany] **:** of or from the city of Mülheim an der Ruhr, Germany **:** of the kind or style prevalent in Mülheim an der Ruhr

**mul·house** \məˈlüz, mē'-\ *adj, usu cap* [fr. *Mulhouse*, city in northeast France] **:** of or from the city of Mulhouse, France **:** of the kind or style prevalent in Mulhouse

**mu·li·ebral** \ˈmyülēˌebrəl, -lēˌēb-\ *adj* [L *muliebris* + E *-al*] **:** of, relating to, or characteristic of women **:** FEMININE ⟨the sheer ~ warmth of her —Richard Llewellyn⟩

**mu·li·ebria** \,=ˈebrēə, -ˈēb-\ *n pl* [L, fr. neut. pl. of *muliebris*] **:** the female genitalia

**mu·li·eb·ri·ty** \,==ˈebrəd·ē\ *n* -ES [LL *muliebritat-, muliebritas*, fr. L *muliebris* of a woman (fr. *mulier* woman) + *-itat-, -itas* -ity; prob. akin to L *mollis* soft — more at MELT] **1 :** the state of being a woman or of possessing full womanly powers **:** WOMANHOOD — compare VIRILITY **2 a :** WOMANLINESS, FEMININITY **b :** EFFEMINACY

**mu·li·er puis·ne** \;myülēə(r)ˈpyünē\ *or* **mulier younger** *n, pl* **muliers puisne** *or* **muliers younger** [*mulier puisne* fr. (assumed) AF *mulieré puisné*, fr. AF *mulieré* legitimate son (fr. *mulier* wife, fr. L, woman, wife) + MF *puisné* younger; *mulier younger* part trans. of (assumed) AF *mulieré puisné* — more at PUNY] **:** a younger legitimate son of a married woman who prior to her marriage has had an older illegitimate son by the father of her legitimate child — compare BASTARD EIGNE

**muling** *n* -s [fr. gerund of ³*mule*] **:** ¹MULE 7

**mul·ish** \ˈmyülish, -lēsh\ *adj* [¹*mule* + *-ish*] **:** STUBBORN, INFLEXIBLE, UNCOMPROMISING, UNYIELDING ⟨that expression of ~ obstinacy which no one can better assume at will than the French peasant —Dorothy Sayers⟩ **syn** see OBSTINATE

**mul·ish·ly** \-lāshlē, -lēsh-, -shli\ *adv* **:** in a mulish manner **:** STUBBORNLY, OBSTINATELY

**mul·ish·ness** \-lishnəs, -lēsh-\ *n* -ES **:** STUBBORNNESS, OBSTINACY

**mu·li·ta** \müˈlēd·ə\ *n* -s [AmerSp, dim. of Sp *mula* she-mule — more at MULETA] **:** MULE ARMADILLO

**¹mull** \ˈməl, *dial Brit* " *or* ˈmül\ *n* -s [ME *mul, mol*, prob. fr. MD; akin to OE *myl* dust, *melu* meal — more at MEAL] **1 a** *chiefly dial Brit* **:** DUST **:** dry mold **b** *chiefly dial Brit* **:** PEAT **2** [prob. fr. ²*mull*] **:** MIXTURE, MESS, MUDDLE ⟨~ of subtly flavored shrimps-of-the-sea heaped on a snowy hillock of rice —Jean Austen⟩ ⟨made a ~ of things up to now —Marguerite Steen⟩

**²mull** \ˈməl\ *vb* -ED/-ING/-S [ME *mullen*, fr. *mul, mol*, n.] *vt* **1 :** to grind or mix thoroughly (as in a mortar) **:** PULVERIZE, CRUMBLE, STIR ⟨~ a portion of the pigment with the oil —H.J. Wolfe⟩ ⟨the alloy, after removal from the amalgamator, was ~*ed* in the palm of the hand —*Jour. of Amer. Dental Assoc.*⟩ ⟨~ tobacco in making snuff⟩ **2 a** *Brit* **:** to make a mess of **:** BOTCH, FUMBLE, MUFF ⟨~ a catch in cricket⟩ **b** (1) **:** BLUNT, DULL, DEADEN ⟨walls were red brick, not a bright, brawling color, but sufficient to ~ the edge of a bitter day —Audrey Barker⟩ (2) **:** BEFUDDLE, BEMUSE ⟨pleasantly ~*ed* by the martinis —C.O.Gorham⟩ ⟨nerves dulled and ~*ed* by copious wine —Francis Hackett⟩ **3 :** to consider or talk over the aspects of (as a problem) at length or at leisure **:** go over in one's mind **:** PONDER ⟨tax experts, ~*ing* how to keep on a pay-as-you-go basis —*Time*⟩ ⟨aides ~ a batch of overseas disposal plans —*Wall Street Jour.*⟩ — often used with *over* ⟨the idea he was ~*ing* over that spring —Virginia D. Dawson & Betty D. Wilson⟩ ⟨sat ~*ing* over what she had said —Cortland Fitzsimmons⟩ ⟨~*ing* over a new quilt pattern —Julian Dana⟩ ⟨~*ed* the book over in his mind —Henry Giniger⟩ **4 :** TEMPER 3e ~ *vi* **1 :** MEDITATE, PONDER, THINK ⟨~ about for words that will convey suspicions as well as impressions —*Everybody's Mag.*⟩ ⟨all his talk of ~*ing* and weighing and balancing was vacillation —J.P.Marquand⟩ **2 :** MESS, MUDDLE, DAWDLE ⟨don't ~ over your breakfast —Lionel Shapiro⟩ ⟨spend two hours after dinner ~*ing* around with your agent —Niven Busch⟩

**³mull** \"\ *n* -s [ME (Sc) *mole*, prob. fr. ON *mūli* projecting crag, snout, muzzle; akin to OHG *mūla, mūl* mouth (of an animal), Goth *faurmūljan* to muzzle, Gk *myllon* lip, L *mutus* mute — more at MUTE] *Scot* **:** HEADLAND, PENINSULA ⟨the *Mull* of Galloway⟩ ⟨the *Mull* of Kintyre⟩

**⁴mull** \"\ *vt* -ED/-ING/-S [origin unknown] **:** to heat, sweeten, and flavor (as wine or cider) with spices

**⁵mull** \"\ *n* -s **:** a mulled beverage (as wine)

**⁶mull** \"\ *chiefly Scot var of* MILL

**⁷mull** \"\ *n* -s [by shortening & alter. fr. *mulmul*] **1 :** a soft fine sheer fabric in plain weave made of cotton, silk, or rayon singly or in combination and used with or without special finishes for clothing and in bookbinding **2 :** an ointment of high melting point intended to be spread on muslin or mull and used like a plaster ⟨zinc ~⟩

**⁸mull** \"\ *n* -s [G, fr. Dan *muld*, fr. ON *mold* dust, soil — more at MOLD] **:** granular forest humus consisting characteristically of a layer of mixed organic matter and mineral soil merging gradually into the mineral soil beneath — compare DUFF, MULCH

**⁹mull** \"\ *n* -s [by shortening] **:** MULLION

**mull** *abbr* mullion

**mullagatawny** *var of* MULLIGATAWNY

**mul·lah** *or* **mul·la** \ˈmələ, ˈmülə, ˈmúlə\ *or* **mol·lah** \ˈmōlə\ *n* -s [Turk *molla* & Per & Hindi *mulla*, fr. Ar *mawlā*] **:** a learned teacher or expounder of the religious law and doctrines of Islam

**mul·lar** \ˈmələ(r)\ *n* -s [perh. alter. of ¹*muller*] **:** a die cut in intaglio for stamping an ornament in relief (as upon metal)

**mul·lein** *also* **mul·len** \ˈmələn\ *n* -s [ME *moleyne*, fr. AF *moleine*, prob. fr. OF *mol* soft, fr. L *mollis* — more at MELT] **:** an herb of the genus *Verbascum* (esp. *V. thapsus*) **:** GREAT MULLEIN — see MOTH MULLEIN

**mullein foxglove** *n* **:** an American herb (*Seymeria macrophylla*) with coarse leaves and yellow tubular flowers

**mullein pink** *n* **:** a European herb (*Lychnis coronaria*) often cultivated for its attractive white woolly herbage and showy crimson flowers — called also *gardener's-delight, rose campion*

**Mul·len Tester** \ˈmələn-\ *trademark* — used for a machine for testing the bursting strength of paper

**¹mull·er** \ˈmələ(r)\ *n* -s [alter. (influenced by *-er*) of ME *molour*, prob. fr. *mullen* to pulverize, grind as in a mortar + *-our, -or* -or — more at MULL] **1 :** a stone or piece of wood, metal, or glass having a usu. flat base and often a handle and held in the hand to pound, grind, or mix a material (as grain, pigments, or drugs) or to polish a surface (as of glass) **:** MANO, PESTLE **2 :** any of several rotating shoes bearing against the bottom of a cylindrical pan used for agitating, mixing, and grinding molding sand; *also* **:** the whole of such apparatus **3 :** a heavy wheel rolling in the flat-bottomed cylindrical pan of a grinding wheel; *also* **:** the mill employing such a wheel **4 :** BUCKING HAMMER

**²muller** \"\ *n* -s [⁴*mull* + *-er*] **:** a vessel in which a beverage (as wine) is mulled over a fire

**³muller** \"\ *n* -s [²*mull* + *-er*] **1 :** a worker who moistens hat bodies for blocking **2 :** DAMPENER b(1)

**mül·le·ri·an** *also* **muel·le·ri·an** \myüˈlirēən, mi'-, mú'-, ,mə'-, mɛ'-\ *adj, sometimes cap* [Johannes Peter *Müller* †1858 Ger. physiologist and comparative anatomist, Heinrich M. *Müller* †1864 Ger. anatomist, & Fritz *Müller* †1897 Ger. zoologist + E *-an*] **1 :** discovered by or named after the German physiologist Johannes Peter Müller **2 :** discovered by or named after the German anatomist Heinrich M. Müller **3 :** discovered by or named after the German zoologist Fritz Müller

**müllerian body** *n, sometimes cap M* [*müllerian* prob. fr. the name *Müller* + E *-an*] **:** one of the minute nitrogenous and oily glands on the leaves of a myrmecophyte (*Cecropia adenopus*) serving as food for the symbiotic ants that inhabit the plant

**müllerian duct** *n, sometimes cap M* [*müllerian* fr. Johannes Peter *Müller* + E *-an*] **:** either of a pair of ducts parallel to the wolffian ducts in vertebrate animals and giving rise in the female to the oviducts

**müllerian fiber** *n, usu cap M* **:** FIBER OF MÜLLER

**müllerian mimicry** *n, sometimes cap 1st M* [*müllerian* fr.

Fritz *Müller* + E *-an*] **:** mimicry between two distasteful or dangerous species (as of butterflies)

**mül·ler's larva** \'myülə(r)z-, 'mil-, 'mul-, 'məl-, 'mœl-\ *n, usu cap M* [after Johannes Peter *Müller*] **:** a ciliated larva that resembles a modified ctenophore and is characteristic of various polyclad turbellarians

**müller's muscle** *n, usu cap 1st M* [after Heinrich M. *Müller*] **:** the circular fibers of the ciliary muscle of the eye

**¹mul·let** \'mələt\ *or* **mol·et** \'mäl-\ *n* -s [ME *molet*, fr. MF *molette* mullet, rowel of a spur] *heraldry* **:** a figure of a usu. 5-pointed star — compare ESTOILE

**²mul·let** \'mələt, *usu* -əd.+V\ *n, pl* **mullet** *or* **mullets** [ME *molet*, fr. MF *mulet*, fr. L *mullus* red mullet, fr. Gk *myllos*; akin to Gk *melas* black, Skt *malina* dirty, black] **1 :** a fish of the family Mugilidae occurring in streams and most seas, living chiefly near the shore, reaching a length of from one to two feet, and being valued as food — called also *gray mullet*; see STRIPED MULLET, WHITE MULLET **2 :** any of various fishes that constitute the family Mullidae, are of moderate size with a small mouth, large scales, and two long barbels on the chin and of brilliant usu. red or golden color, and include many excellent food fishes as well as several reputed to have a powerful neurotoxin in the brain — called also *goatfish, red mullet, surmullet* **3 :** any of various other fishes; *esp* **:** any of several American suckers (family Catostomidae)

**³mullet** \"\ *n* -s [origin unknown] *Brit* **:** PUFFIN

**mullet hawk** *n* [²*mullet*] *dial Eng* **:** OSPREY

**mulley** *var of* MULEY

**mul·lid** \'mələd\ *n* -s [NL *Mullidae*] **:** a fish of the family Mullidae

**mul·li·dae** \-lə,dē\ *n pl, cap* [NL, fr. *Mullus*, type genus + *-idae*] **:** a family of percoid fishes consisting of the red mullets

**¹mul·li·gan** \'məlǝgən, -lēg-\ *also* **mulligan stew** *n* -s [prob. fr. the name *Mulligan*] **:** a stew of vegetables, meat or fish, and other available foodstuffs

**²mulligan** \"\ *n* -s [prob. fr. the name *Mulligan*] **:** a free shot sometimes awarded a golfer in nontournament play when the preceding shot has been poorly played

**mul·li·ga·taw·ny** *also* **mul·la·ga·taw·ny** \¦məlǝgə¦tȯnē, -ni\ *n* -ES [Tamil *milakutaṇṇi*, fr. *milaku* pepper + Tamil (colloquial) *taṇṇi* water, fr. Tamil *taṇṇīr*, fr. *taṇ* cold + *nīr* water] **:** a soup usu. of chicken stock strongly seasoned with curry

**mul·li·grubs** *or* **mul·ly·grubs** \'mәlē,grəbz\ *also* **mol·ly·grubs** \'mäl-\ *n pl* [alter. (prob. influenced by *grub*) of earlier *mulliegrums*, perh. alter. (perh. influenced by obs. E *mully* dusty, moldy, fr. E ¹*mull* + *-y*) of *megrims*, pl. of ¹*megrim*] **1 :** a despondent, sullen, or ill-tempered mood **:** SULKS, BLUES **2 :** a griping of the intestines **:** COLIC

**mulling** *pres part of* MULL

**¹mul·lion** \'məlyən\ *n* -s [prob. alter. of *monial*] **1 :** a slender vertical usu. nonstructural bar or pier forming a division between lights of windows, doors, or screens — distinguished from *transom*; compare MUNTIN; see DOOR illustration **2 :** an upright member of a framing (as of panels in wainscoting) — compare STILE **3 :** a pattern or structure found on some faulted rock surfaces consisting of rounded grooves or small stepped irregularities — compare SLICKENSIDE

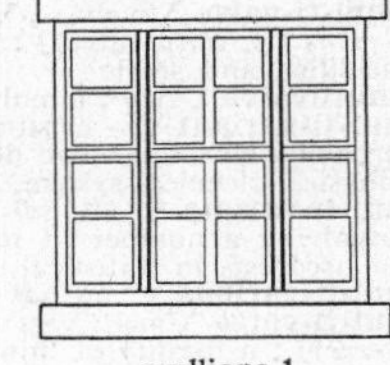

mullions 1

**²mullion** \"\ *vt* -ED/-ING/-S **:** to furnish with mullions **:** divide by mullions

**mull·ite** \'mə,līt\ *n* -s [*Mull*, island off the west coast of Scotland + E *-ite*] **:** a mineral $Al_6Si_2O_{13}$ or $3Al_2O_3.2SiO_2$ consisting of a silicate of aluminum that is orthorhombic in form and resistant to corrosion and heat and is found naturally and also made synthetically for use as a refractory

**mull·i·ti·za·tion** \,mə,līd·ə'zāshən\ *n* -s **:** the formation of mullite in a fireclay body or from minerals of the sillimanite group by heating

**¹mul·lock** \'mələk, 'mul-\ *n* -s [ME *mullok*, fr. *mul, mol* dust, dry mold — more at MULL] **1** *chiefly dial Brit* **:** RUBBISH, REFUSE, DIRT **2** *dial* **:** a state of confusion **:** MUDDLE, MESS **3** *Austral* **a :** refuse earth or rock from a mine **b :** earth or rock bearing no gold

**²mullock** \"\ *vb* -ED/-ING/-s *vi, dial Brit* **:** to work in a slipshod way ~ *vt, dial Brit* **:** MESS, WASTE, SPOIL

**mul·lock·er** \-kə(r)\ *n* -s **:** one that mullocks; *esp* **:** a mucker who shovels waste material for removal from a mine

**mul·locky** \-kē\ *adj* [¹*mullock* + *-y*] **:** consisting or having the quality of mullock

**mul·lo·way** \'mələ,wā\ *n* -s [origin unknown] **:** a large Australian marine sciaenid fish (*Sciaena antarctica*) that is scarcely distinguishable from the European maigre and is a leading food fish of southern and eastern Australia — called also *jewfish*

**mulls** *pl of* MULL, *pres 3d sing of* MULL

**mul·lus** \'mələs\ *n, cap* [NL, fr. L, red mullet — more at MULLET] **:** a genus of percoid fishes that is the type of the family Mullidae

**mulm** \'məlm\ *n* -s [origin unknown] **:** organic sediment that accumulates in an aquarium

**mul·mul** \'məl,məl\ *n* -s [Hindi *malmal*, fr. Per] *India* **:** MUSLIN

**mulse** *n* -s [L *mulsum*, fr. neut. of *mulsus* mixed with honey, sweet as honey; akin to L *mel* honey — more at MELLIFLUOUS] *obs* **:** a beverage of honey mixed with wine or water

**mult** *abbr* multiple

**mul·tan** \(')mul,'tän\ *adj, usu cap* [fr. *Multan*, Pakistan] **:** of or from the city of Multan, Pakistan **:** of the kind or style prevalent in Multan ⟨a *Multan* rug⟩

**mult·angular** \¦məl¦t+\ *adj* [NL *multangularis*, fr. *multangulum* polygon (fr. L, neut. of *multangulus* having many angles, fr. *multus* much, many + *angulus* angle) + L *-aris* -ar — more at ANGLE] **:** having many angles ⟨overlooking a ~ pool — Christopher Hussey⟩

**mult·an·gu·lum** \,məl'taŋgyələm, -taiŋ-\ *n, pl* **multangu·la** \-lə\ [NL, multangulum, polygon] **:** either the greater wrist bone articulating with the first metacarpal or the lesser wrist bone articulating with the second metacarpal

**mul·ta·ni** \mul'tänē\ *n* -s *cap* **:** the Lahnda dialect of Multan and vicinity

**mul·te·i·ty** \,məl'tēəd·ē, -ətē, -i\ *n* -ES [L *multus* much, many + E *-eity* (as in *spontaneity*)] **:** MULTIPLICITY

**mul·ti-** *in pronunciations below*, ¦==¦məltə *or* -tē *or* -l,tī\ *comb form* [ME, fr. MF or L; MF, fr. L, fr. *multus* much, many — more at MELIORATE] **1 a :** many **:** multiple **:** much ⟨*multi*coupler⟩ ⟨*multi*dimensional⟩ ⟨*multi*perforated⟩ **b :** consisting of, containing, or having more than two ⟨*multi*cuspid⟩ ⟨*multi*level⟩ **c :** consisting of, containing, or having more than one ⟨*multi*family⟩ **2 :** many times over ⟨*multi*millionaire⟩ **:** in many respects ⟨*multi*specialist⟩ **3 :** affecting many parts ⟨*multi*glandular⟩

**mul·ti·angular** \¦== *at* MULTI- +\ *adj* [by alter. (influenced by *multi-*)] **:** MULTANGULAR

**mul·ti·break** \'məltə,brāk\ *adj* [*multi-* + *break*, n.] **:** being an electrical switch that breaks the circuit at two or more points at the same time

**mul·ti·brood·ed** \¦== *at* MULTI- +¦brüdəd\ *adj* [*multi-* + *brood*, n. + *-ed*] **:** having several batches of young in a season — used chiefly of parasitic insects

**mul·ti·cellular** \"+\ *adj* [ISV *multi-* + *cellular*] **:** having or consisting of many cells

**mul·ti·ceps** \'məltə,seps\ *n* [NL, fr. L *multi-* + *-ceps* (as in *biceps* two-headed) — more at BICEPS] **1** *cap* **:** a genus of cyclophyllidean tapeworms (family Taeniidae) having a coenurus larva that is parasitic in ruminants, rodents, and rarely man including the parasite of gid (*M. multiceps*) and other worms that are typically parasites of carnivores **2** -ES **:** COENURUS

**mul·ti·channel** \¦== *at* MULTI- +\ *adj* **:** using two or more channels

**¹mul·ti·color** \'məltə, -tē+,-\ *adj* [L, fr. *multi-* + *color*, n.] **1 :** MULTICOLORED **2 :** that prints in several colors at one operation ⟨~ press⟩

**²multicolor** \"\ *n* **:** a combination of several colors **:** a color scheme using more than two colors ⟨a postage stamp in ~⟩

**mul·ti·colored** \"+,-\ *adj* [*multi-* + *colored*] **:** having more than two colors **:** of various colors **:** PARTI-COLORED

**mul·ti·component** \¦== *at* MULTI- +\ *adj* [*multi-* + *component*, n.] **:** having or consisting of two or more components ⟨vapor-liquid equilibria of ~ systems⟩

**mul·ti·coupler** \'məltə+,-\ *n* [*multi-* + *coupler*] **:** a device to permit a number of radio or television receivers to operate efficiently from a single antenna

**mul·ti·cylinder** \¦== *at* MULTI- +\ *adj* [*multi-* + *cylinder*] **:** marked by several or many cylinders

**mul·ti·dimensional** \"+\ *adj* [*multi-* + *dimensional*] **:** of, relating to, or marked by several dimensions

**mul·ti·disciplinary** \"+\ *adj* [*multi-* + *disciplinary*] **:** combining several specialized disciplines (as those in the field of applied social science) for a common purpose ⟨use of a ~ approach by a child guidance clinic⟩

**mul·ti·engine** \"+\ *adj* [*multi-* + *engine*, n.] **:** having several engines

**mul·ti·factorial** \"+\ *adj* [*multi-* + *factorial*] **:** having characters or a mode of inheritance dependent on the interaction of a number of genes at different loci — compare MULTIPLE FACTOR

**mul·ti·far·i·ous** \¦məltə¦fa(a)rēəs, -fer-, -får-\ *adj* [L *multifarius*, fr. *multifariam* on many sides, in many places, fr. *multi-* + *-fariam* (as in *bifariam* in two ways) — more at BIFARIOUS] **1 :** having multiplicity **:** having great diversity or variety **:** of various kinds ⟨the ~ activities of a farm —Kenneth Roberts⟩ ⟨the ~ problems of our troubled times —C.L.R.James⟩ ⟨~ noise of a great city —A.L.Kroeber⟩ **2** *of a pleading in law* **:** improperly uniting distinct and independent matters and thereby confounding them whether against one or several defendants — **mul·ti·far·i·ous·ly** *adv* — **mul·ti·far·ious·ness** *n* -ES

**mul·ti·fid** \'məltə,fid\ *adj* [L *multifidus*, fr. *multi-* + *-fidus* -fid] **:** cleft into several or many parts ⟨a ~ leaf⟩ — **mul·ti·fid·ly** *adv*

**mul·tif·i·dus** \,məl'tifədəs\ *n, pl* **multifi·di** \-fə,dī\ [NL, fr. L, multifid] **:** a muscle of the fifth and deepest layer of the back filling up the groove on each side of the spinous processes of the vertebrae from the sacrum to the skull and consisting of many fasciculi that pass upward and inward to the spinous processes and help to erect and rotate the spine

**mul·ti·fil** \'məltə,fil\ *n* -s [by shortening] **:** MULTIFILAMENT

**mul·ti·filament** \¦== *at* MULTI- +\ *n* [*multi-* + *filament*] **:** yarn composed of many individual filaments — compare MONOFILAMENT

**mul·ti·flash** \'məltə+,-\ *adj* [*multi-* + *flash*, n.] **:** employing or made with two or more photoflash lamps in synchronization with the shutter ⟨a ~ photograph⟩

**mul·ti·flo·ra bean** \¦məltə¦flōrə-\ *n* [NL *multiflora* (specific epithet of *Lipusa multiflora*, syn. of *Phaseolus coccineus*, species name of the scarlet runner), fr. ML, fem. of *multiflorus* having many flowers, fr. L *multi-* + LL *-florus* -florous] **:** SCARLET RUNNER

**multiflora rose** *or* **multiflora** *n* -s [NL *multiflora* (specific epithet of *Rosa multiflora*), fr. ML, fem. of *multiflorus* having many flowers] **:** a rose (*Rosa multiflora*) characterized by clusters of numerous small flowers and used because of its vigorous growth as a grafting stock and for wildlife shelter and hedges — called also *Japanese rose*

**¹mul·ti·foil** \'məltə+,-\ *n* [*multi-* + *foil*] **:** a foil of more than five divisions — used esp. of a window foil

**²multifoil** \"\ *adj* **:** composed of or ornamented with many foils **:** SCALLOPED ⟨a coin having a ~ border⟩; *specif* **:** having an intrados composed of more than five foils ⟨a ~ arch⟩

**mul·ti·fold** \'məltə,fōld\ *adj* [*multi-* + *-fold*] **:** many times doubled **:** MANIFOLD, NUMEROUS ⟨regulate ~ and complex economic and social relationships —F.A.Ogg & P.O.Ray⟩

**¹mul·ti·form** \'məltə,fȯrm, -ō(ə)m\ *adj* [F *multiforme*, fr. L *multiformis*, fr. *multi-* + *-formis* -form] **:** having many forms, shapes, or appearances ⟨the ~ universe of nature and man —John Dewey⟩ ⟨a protean and ~ ego —J.L.Lowes⟩

**²multiform** \"\ *n* **:** something that is multiform ⟨the ~s of Christianity —F.S.Kinney⟩

**mul·ti·formed** \-md\ *adj* [*multi-* + *formed*] **:** MULTIFORM ⟨the ~ paraphernalia of modern battle —*Newsweek*⟩

**mul·ti·form·i·ty** \,məltə'fȯ(r)məd·ē\ *n* -ES [LL *multiformitat-, multiformitas*, fr. L *multiformis* multiform + *-tat-, -tas* -ty] **:** the state of being multiform **:** DIVERSITY ⟨the ~ and at the same time the regularity of the shapes in the structure of plants and animals —M.M.Novikoff⟩ ⟨our institutions, with all their historic ~ —Charles Madge⟩

**mul·ti·gen·ic** \¦məltə¦jenik\ *adj* [*multi-* + *genic*] **:** MULTIFACTORIAL ⟨~ chromosomal blocks —*Advances in Genetics*⟩

**mul·ti·graph** \'məltə,graf, -räf\ *vt* **:** to print on a Multigraph machine

**Mul·ti·graph** \"\ *trademark* — used for a machine consisting essentially of a cylinder with grooves into which type or electrotypes are inserted

**mul·ti·grav·i·da** \,məltə'gravədə\ *n* [NL, fr. *multi-* + L *gravida*] **:** a woman who has been pregnant more than once — compare MULTIPARA

**mul·ti·hued** \¦== *at* MULTI- +\ *adj* [*multi-* + *hued*] **:** MULTICOLORED

**mul·ti·lacunar** \"+\ *adj* [*multi-* + *lacunar*] **:** having more than three leaf gaps — compare UNILACUNAR

**mul·ti·lane** \'məltə,lān\ *adj* [*multi-* + *lane*, n.] **:** having two or more lanes for traffic in one direction or four or more lanes for traffic in two directions ⟨a ~ divided highway⟩

**mul·ti·lateral** \¦== *at* MULTI- +\ *adj* [*multi-* + *lateral*] **1 :** having many sides **:** MANY-SIDED **2 a :** participated in by or involving more than two states ⟨~ treaty⟩ ⟨~ guarantees⟩ ⟨~ trade⟩ ⟨~ payments⟩ **b** *of a contract* **:** having three or more parties **3** *of a secondary school* **:** offering several distinct curricula — compare COMPREHENSIVE 3b — **mul·ti·laterally** \"+\ *adv*

**mul·ti·lat·er·al·ism** \,məltə'lad·ərə,lizəm\ *n* -s **:** freedom of international trade and currency transfers so as to achieve for each country a trading balance with the total trading area but not necessarily with any one particular country — contrasted with *bilateralism*

**¹mul·ti·layer** \¦== *at* MULTI- +\ *adj* [*multi-* + *layer*, n.] **:** having or relating to two or more layers of sensitive emulsion of differing color characteristics coated in superposition on a single support — used of a photographic material or process

**²mul·ti·layer** \'==+,-\ *n* [*multi-* + *layer*, n.] **:** a layer built up from two or more monolayers **:** a polymolecular layer

**¹mul·ti·lingual** \¦== *at* MULTI- +\ *adj* [*multi-* + *lingual*] **1 :** containing or expressed in several languages ⟨a ~ signboard⟩ **2 :** versed in or using several languages ⟨a ~ stewardess⟩

**²multilingual** *n* -s **:** one who speaks and understands several languages

**mul·ti·linguist** \"+\ *n* [*multi-* + *linguist*] **:** MULTILINGUAL

**mul·ti·lith** \'məltə,lith\ *vt* -ED/-ING/-S **:** to print on a Multilith machine

**Mul·ti·lith** \"\ *trademark* — used for a small offset press used typically for duplicating office forms

**mul·ti·lobed** \¦məltə¦lōbd\ *adj* **:** having two or more lobes

**mul·ti·locular** \¦== *at* MULTI- +\ *adj* [ISV *multi-* + *locular*] **:** having or divided into many small chambers or vesicles ⟨a ~ cyst⟩

**mul·ti·loculate** \"+\ *adj* [*multi-* + *loculate*] **:** MULTILOCULAR

**mul·til·o·quence** \,məl'tiləkwən(t)s\ *n* -s [LL *multiloquentia*, fr. L *multi-* + *-loquentia* (as in *eloquentia* eloquence)] **:** GARRULOUSNESS, TALKATIVENESS

**mul·til·o·quent** \-nt\ *adj* [*multi-* + *loquent*] **:** GARRULOUS, TALKATIVE — **mul·til·o·quent·ly** *adv*

**mul·ti·lo·qui·ous** \¦məltə¦lōkwēəs\ *adj* [obs. E *multiloquy* garrulousness (fr. L *multiloquium*, fr. *multi-* + *-loquium* — as in *colloquium* colloquy) + E *-ous*] **:** MULTILOQUENT

**mul·ti·mammate mouse** *or* **mul·ti·mammate rat** \¦== *at* MULTI- + . . .-\ *n* [*multimammate* fr. *multi-* + *mammate*] **:** any of several common African rodents (genus *Rattus*) having 12 rather than the usual 5 or 6 mammae on each side

**mul·ti·member district** \'məltə+,- . . . -\ *n* [*multimember* fr. *multi-* + *member*, n.] **:** an electoral district from which two or more members are sent to the legislature

**Mul·tim·e·ter** \,məl'timəd·ə(r)\ *trademark* — used for an electric meter

**mul·ti·million** \¦== *at* MULTI- +\ *n* [back-formation fr. *multimillionaire*] **:** many millions (as of dollars) — usu. used in pl. ⟨~s in almost pure silver and lead —J.A.Michener⟩

**mul·ti·millionaire** \"+\ *n* [*multi-* + *millionaire*] **:** one worth many millions (as of dollars, pounds, francs) ⟨an oil ~⟩ ⟨a resort frequented by ~s⟩

**mul·ti·modal** \"+\ *adj* [*multi-* + *modal*] **:** having several modes: as **a :** having several regions of maximum frequency ⟨~ distribution⟩ **b :** composed of several distinct types of activity ⟨a ~ conception of intelligence⟩ — **mul·ti·modality** \"+\ *n*

**mul·ti·no·mi·al** \¦məltə¦nōmēəl\ *adj or n* [*multi-* + *-nomial* (as in *binomial*)] **:** POLYNOMIAL

**mul·ti·nucleate** *or* **mul·ti·nuclear** \¦== *at* MULTI- +\ *adj* [ISV *multi-* + *nucleate* or *nuclear*] **:** having more than two nuclei — compare BINUCLEATE, UNINUCLEATE

**mul·tip·a·ra** \,məl'tipərə\ *n* [NL, fr. *multi-* + *-para*] **:** a woman who has borne more than one child — compare MULTIGRAVIDA

**mul·ti·par·i·ty** \,məltə'parəd·ē\ *n* [prob. fr. (assumed) NL *multiparitat-, multiparitas*, fr. NL *multiparus* multiparous + L *-itat-, -itas* -ity] **1 :** the production of two or more young at a birth **2 :** the condition of having borne a number of children

**mul·tip·a·rous** \,məl'tipərəs\ *adj* [NL *multiparus*, fr. *multi-* + L *-parus* -parous] **1 :** producing many or more than one at a birth **:** of or relating to multiparity **2 a :** of or relating to a multipara **b :** having experienced one or more previous parturitions ⟨a ~ heifer⟩ — compare PRIMIPAROUS **3 :** producing several lateral axes ⟨a ~ cyme⟩

**mul·ti·par·tite** \,məltə'pär,tīt\ *adj* [L *multipartitus*, fr. *multi-* + *partitus*, past part. of *partire* to divide, fr. *part-, pars* part — more at PART] **:** divided into several or many parts **:** having numerous members or signatories ⟨~ curve⟩ ⟨~ treaty⟩

**mul·ti·path** \'məltə+,-\ *adj* [*multi-* + *path*, n.] **:** of, relating to, or resulting from the propagation of electric waves over a number of different paths ⟨~ transmission⟩ ⟨~ phenomena⟩

**¹mul·ti·ped** \'məltə,ped\ *n* -s [L *multipeda* & LL *multiped-, multipes*; L *multipeda* fr. *multi-* + *-peda* (fr. *ped-, pes* foot); LL *multiped-, multipes* fr. L *multiped-, multipes*, adj. — more at FOOT] **:** a multiped animal ⟨bipeds, quadrupeds, and all the small ~s⟩

**²multiped** \"\ *adj* [L *multiped-, multipes*, fr. *multi-* + *ped-, pes* foot] **:** having many feet; *sometimes* **:** having more than four feet

**mul·ti·phase** \'məltə+,-\ *adj* [*multi-* + *phase*, n.] **:** having many phases; *specif* **:** POLYPHASE ⟨a ~ electrical system⟩

**mul·ti·phasic** \¦== *at* MULTI- +\ *adj* [*multi-* + *phasic*] **:** having many phases or aspects ⟨the ~ nature of speech —O.W. Nelson⟩ ⟨~ mass screening technique —E.R.Weinerman⟩

**mul·ti·phyletic** \"+\ *adj* [*multi-* + *phyletic*] **:** of multiple or complex origin ⟨the complexity and ~ nature of Southwestern cultures —W.W.Taylor⟩

**mul·ti·plane** \'məltə+,-\ *n* [ISV *multi-* + *plane*] **:** an airplane with two or more main supporting surfaces placed one above another

**¹mul·ti·ple** \'məltəpəl\ *adj* [F, fr. L *multiplex*, fr. *multi-* + *-plex* -fold — more at SIMPLE] **1 :** consisting of, including, or involving more than one ⟨~ birth⟩ ⟨~ burial of plague victims⟩ ⟨~ cable⟩ ⟨~ corolla⟩ ⟨~ drill⟩ ⟨~ rate⟩ ⟨~ skin eruption⟩ **2 :** MANY, MANIFOLD, SEVERAL ⟨~ achievements in politics and public life —B.H.Wall⟩ ⟨~ minds functioning together —*Amer. Scholar*⟩ ⟨plants were on a *multiple*-shift basis —*Annual Report General Motors Corp.*⟩ ⟨~ copies of a speech⟩ ⟨*multiple*-restaurant chain⟩ ⟨*multiple*-party system⟩ **3 :** occurring more than once or in higher degree than the first **:** REPEATED ⟨~ roots⟩ **4 :** belonging to or divided among several or many ⟨~ ownership⟩ ⟨~ responsibility⟩ **5 :** having numerous aspects or functions **:** VARIOUS, COMPLEX ⟨life is very ~, full of movements, facts, and news —John Galsworthy⟩ ⟨she is ~ and ghostly on stage —Leo Lerman⟩ ⟨the ~ executive has been widely used in business and in government —Harold Koontz & Cyril O'Donnell⟩ **6 a :** being a circuit with a number of conductors in parallel **b :** being a group of terminals which make a circuit available at a number of points **7 :** developed by coalescence of the ripening ovaries of several distinct flowers (as in the mulberry and the pineapple) **:** COLLECTIVE — distinguished from *aggregate*; see FRUIT illustration **8 :** having a value equal to some multiple of a single unit ⟨~ dollars from 2- to 20-dollar pieces⟩ ⟨~ thaler⟩

**²multiple** \"\ *n* -s **1 a :** the product of a quantity by an integer ⟨35 is a ~ of 7⟩ ⟨gases . . . are adsorbed in ~s of the molecular weight —F.H.Getman⟩ **b :** an assemblage with respect to any of its divisions or parts ⟨lay mines in ~⟩ ⟨four road switchers running in ~ —*Trains*⟩ **2 :** PARALLEL 4b ⟨connected in ~⟩ **3 :** a multiple coin

**multiple allele** *or* **multiple allelomorph** *n* **:** any of more than two allelic factors located at one chromosome locus

**multiple allelism** *n* **:** the state of having more than two alternative contrasting characters controlled from a single gene locus

**multiple–alphabet cipher** *n* **:** polyalphabetic substitution in which the choice of alphabets is limited (as by a key word) — compare PROGRESSIVE-ALPHABET CIPHER

**multiple–choice** *adj* **:** having several answers given from which the correct or most commonly selected is to be chosen ⟨a *multiple-choice* question⟩ ⟨*multiple-choice* tests⟩

**multiple correlation** *n* **:** correlation involving two or more independent mathematical variables

**multiple cropping** *n* -s **:** the taking of two or more crops from the same field in one year

**multiple–die press** *n* **:** a punch press that operates two or more identical dies at a single stroke — called also *gang press*

**multiple dwelling** *n* **:** a residential structure to house three or more families

**multiple–effect** \'====,-\ *adj* **:** relating to or consisting of a series of evaporators in which the pressure decreases progressively from one to the next so that the vapor from each unit except the last heats the liquid in the next unit

**multiple factor** *n* **1 :** MULTIPLE ALLELE **2 :** one of a group of nonallelic genes that according to the multiple-factor hypothesis control various quantitative hereditary characters (as size and skin color) — compare POLYGENE, QUANTITATIVE INHERITANCE

**multiple fission** *n* **:** division of a cell into more than two parts — compare BINARY FISSION

**multiple–line** \'===,-\ *adj* **:** writing all or many kinds of insurance ⟨a *multiple-line* insurance company⟩ — compare MONOLINE

**multiple listing** *n* **:** a system of listing all properties for sale or rent by each real estate broker with a central bureau or on a list available to all brokers participating who may then sell or rent the properties with the commissions being split in agreed proportions between the brokers listing the properties and the brokers selling them — compare OPEN LISTING

**multiple management** *n* **:** a plan of management that permits employee participation in the formulation of policy

**multiple myeloma** *n* **:** a disease of bone marrow characterized by the presence of numerous myelomas in various bones of the body

**multiple–party** \'===,==\ *adj* **:** consisting of three or more political parties with no single party having a majority ⟨the *multiple-party* system prevailing in some continental European countries⟩

**multiple personality** *n* **:** a disorder of consciousness in which a person esp. of suggestible temperament appears to have two or more distinct personalities each of which may be alternatively unaware of the others and which may be present either concurrently or successively — see ALTERNATING PERSONALITY

**multiplepoinding** \'===¦==\ *n* [¹*multiple* + *poinding*] *Scots law* **:** a proceeding brought by one having in his possession money or goods belonging to another to which two or more persons make claim **:** INTERPLEADER

**multiple point** *n* **1 :** a point on a curve through which two or more branches of the curve pass **:** a point on a surface through which three or more nappes of the surface pass **2 :** a point representing a set of conditions under which two or more phases can exist together

**multiple press** *n* **:** MULTIPLE-DIE PRESS

**multiples** *pl of* MULTIPLE

**multiple sclerosis** *n* **:** a chronic progressive disease of the central nervous system marked by patchy demyelination and hardening of nerve tissue and associated with varied motor and psychic changes depending upon the location of the lesions

**multiple shop** *or* **multiple store** *n, Brit* **:** CHAIN STORE

**multiple-speed transmission** *n* **:** transmission that provides a choice of gear ratios between the motor and the shaft or axle finally driven

**multiple standard** *n* **:** TABULAR STANDARD

**multiple star** *n* **:** several stars in close proximity that appear to form a single system

**multiple switchboard** *n* **:** a manual telephone switchboard in the jack field of which some or all subscriber lines appear more than once so as to be within reach of all operators

**multiple synchronous telegraph** *n* **:** a multiplex telegraph in which at the receiving station apparatus is maintained in exact synchronism with corresponding apparatus at the sending station

**mul·ti·plet** \'məltəplət\ *n* -S [ISV 1*multiple* + *-et*] **:** a spectrum line having several components

**multiple thread** *n* **:** a screw thread composed of two or more distinct parallel intertwined threads or helices

**multiple-tuned** \¦⸗⸗⸗¦⸗\ *adj* **:** tuned to more than one frequency or by more than one circuit or element — usu. used of antennas or electrical networks

**multiple-unit** \'⸗⸗⸗,⸗⸗\ *adj* **:** of or relating to a system of electric traction in which two or more cars controlled from a single car are used to propel a train (as in commuter service)

**multiple voting** *n* **1 :** voting by the same individual at the same election in various places in each of which he possesses the legal qualifications **2 :** unauthorized and illegal voting by one person in two or more constituencies (as voting by floaters)

**multiple watermark** *n* **:** a watermark on a stamp that consists of more than one or portions of more than one unit of design

1**mul·ti·plex** \'məltə,pleks\ *adj* [L *multiplex* — more at MULTIPLE] **1 :** having numerous parts or elements **:** MANIFOLD, MULTIPLE ⟨the ~ moods of our human nature —Herbert Read⟩ ⟨the sprawling metropolis so ~ in its aspects —Brander Matthews⟩ ⟨giants and the genii, ~ of wing and eye —G.K. Chesterton⟩ **2 :** being or relating to a system of transmitting several messages or signals simultaneously on the same circuit (as in telephony or telegraphy) or on the same channel (as in radio or television) ⟨favored the development and use of ~ sound and facsimile broadcasting —*Proceedings of the Institute of Radio Engineers*⟩

2**multiplex** \"\ *vb* -ED/-ING/-ES *vt* **:** to send (several messages or signals) by a multiplex system **~** *vi* **:** to multiplex messages or signals ⟨granted permission for FM stations to test stereo *~ing*, a system that sends the two separate signals over a single radio frequency —*Time*⟩

3**multiplex** \"\ *n* -ES **1 :** a multiplex system **2 :** a stereoscopic instrument used in preparing topographic maps by projecting aerial photographs onto a surface so that the projected images when viewed with anaglyphic spectacles give a three-dimensional effect

**mul·ti·plex·er** \-sə(r)\ *n* -S [2*multiplex* + *-er*] **:** a device for multiplex transmission of signals

**mul·ti·pli·able** \'məltə,plīəbəl, ,⸗⸗'⸗⸗⸗\ *adj* [F, fr. OF, fr. *multiplier* to multiply + *-able* — more at MULTIPLY] **:** capable of being multiplied

**mul·ti·plic·a·ble** \¦məltə¦plikəbəl\ *adj* [ME, fr. ML *multiplicabilis*, fr. L *multiplicare* to multiply + *-abilis* -able] **:** MULTIPLIABLE

**mul·ti·pli·cand** \,məltəplə'kand, -aa(ə)nd\ *n* -S [L *multiplicandum* something to be multiplied, neut. of *multiplicandus*, gerundive of *multiplicare* to multiply] **:** the number that is to be multiplied by another number — compare MULTIPLIER

1**mul·ti·pli·cate** \'məltəplə,kāt\ *adj* [ME, fr. L *multiplicatus*, past part. of *multiplicare* to multiply] **1 :** consisting of many or of more than one **:** MULTIPLE, MULTIFOLD ⟨~ forms⟩ **2 :** having many folds ⟨~ shells⟩

2**multiplicate** \"\ *n* -S **:** the form or condition of being exactly reproduced in many copies ⟨have copies made in ~⟩

**mul·ti·pli·ca·tion** \,məltəplə'kāshən\ *n* -S [ME *multiplicacioun*, fr. MF *multiplication*, fr. L *multiplication-*, *multiplicatio*, fr. *multiplicatus* (past part. of *multiplicare* to multiply) + *-ion-*, *-io* -ion — more at MULTIPLY] **1 a :** the act or process of multiplying ⟨combat the weevil and prevent its ~ —*Encyc. Americana*⟩ ⟨the ~ and distribution of a printed and bound message —B.L.Stratton⟩ **b :** the state of being multiplied ⟨this ~ of security investigations is institutionalized —H.J.Morgenthau⟩ ⟨when the converter is developing its greatest torque ~ —Joseph Heitner⟩ **2 a :** a mathematical operation commonly indicated by $ab$, $a{\cdot}b$, or $a \times b$ and having various significances according to the type of numbers involved, the simplest being in the case of positive integers where the process is that of repeating $b$ as many times as there are units in $a$ or vice versa **b :** the mathematical process involving an operand and an operator each of which may consist of various kinds of numbers, symbols, expressions, assemblages, or magnitudes and in which the operand is affected by the operator in a manner governed by defined laws some of which are usu. the same as those that apply to the multiplication of numbers even when numbers are not involved ⟨the ~ of derivatives to yield derivatives of derivatives⟩ **3 :** the logical operation of forming a conjunction or product — rarely used outside the algebra of classes

**multiplication dance** *n* **:** a mixer in American social dances starting with one couple and multiplying by continual choice of new partners

**multiplication factor** *n* **:** the ratio of the number of neutrons produced in a nuclear pile to the number disappearing that must equal or exceed unity for a chain reaction to take place — called also *reproduction constant*, *reproduction factor*

**multiplication table** *n* **:** a table of the products of a set of

MULTIPLICATION TABLE

| | | | | | | | | | | | |
|---|---|---|---|---|---|---|---|---|---|---|---|
| 1 | 2 | 3 | 4 | 5 | 6 | 7 | 8 | 9 | 10 | 11 | 12 |
| 2 | 4 | 6 | 8 | 10 | 12 | 14 | 16 | 18 | 20 | 22 | 24 |
| 3 | 6 | 9 | 12 | 15 | 18 | 21 | 24 | 27 | 30 | 33 | 36 |
| 4 | 8 | 12 | 16 | 20 | 24 | 28 | 32 | 36 | 40 | 44 | 48 |
| 5 | 10 | 15 | 20 | 25 | 30 | 35 | 40 | 45 | 50 | 55 | 60 |
| 6 | 12 | 18 | 24 | 30 | 36 | 42 | 48 | 54 | 60 | 66 | 72 |
| 7 | 14 | 21 | 28 | 35 | 42 | 49 | 56 | 63 | 70 | 77 | 84 |
| 8 | 16 | 24 | 32 | 40 | 48 | 56 | 64 | 72 | 80 | 88 | 96 |
| 9 | 18 | 27 | 36 | 45 | 54 | 63 | 72 | 81 | 90 | 99 | 108 |
| 10 | 20 | 30 | 40 | 50 | 60 | 70 | 80 | 90 | 100 | 110 | 120 |
| 11 | 22 | 33 | 44 | 55 | 66 | 77 | 88 | 99 | 110 | 121 | 132 |
| 12 | 24 | 36 | 48 | 60 | 72 | 84 | 96 | 108 | 120 | 132 | 144 |

numbers multiplied in some regular order; *usu* **:** a table of the products of the first 10 or 12 integers multiplied successively by 1, 2, 3, etc., up to 10 or 12

1**mul·ti·pli·ca·tive** \¦məltəplə¦kād·|iv, -āt|, |ēv *also* |əv\ *adj* [LL *multiplicativus*, fr. L *multiplicatus* (past part. of *multiplicare* to multiply) + *-ivus* -ive] **:** tending or having the power to multiply numbers ⟨the ~ tendency of proportional representation —Barbara & Robert North⟩ ⟨a ~ scale of monetary weight units —A.L.Kroeber⟩ — **mul·ti·pli·ca·tive·ly** \|əvlē, -li\ *adv*

2**multiplicative** *n* -S **:** a numeral adjective (as *single*, *treble*, *twofold*) denoting how many times something is taken

**mul·ti·pli·ca·tor** \'məltəplə,kād·ə(r)\ *n* -S [LL, fr. L *multiplicatus* (past part. of *multiplicare* to multiply) + *-or*] **:** MULTIPLIER ⟨provides the necessary circulation in a ~ circuit —Anna Akeley⟩

**multiplicious** *adj* [L *multiplic-*, *multiplex* multiple + E *-ious*] *obs* **:** MULTIPLEX, MANIFOLD

**mul·ti·plic·i·ty** \,məltə'plisəd·ē, -ətē, -i\ *n* -ES [MF *multiplicité*, fr. LL *multiplicitat-*, *multiplicitas*, fr. L *multiplic-*, *multiplex* multiple + *-itat-*, *-itas* -ity] **1 :** the quality or state of being multiple, manifold, or various **:** multiple or multiform character **:** MULTIFARIOUSNESS ⟨try to reduce the incomprehensible ~ of the universe to a comprehensible simplicity —F.L.Mott⟩ ⟨the ~ and heterogeneity of our environment —Hunter Mead⟩ ⟨there is a vast ~ of duty for the squadron commander —H.H.Arnold & I.C.Eaker⟩ **2 :** a great number ⟨a ~ of interesting paths crossed the featureless land —E.E. Shipton⟩ ⟨booklet is unfortunately marred by a ~ of minor errors —R.S.Churchill⟩ **3 a :** the number of components or sublevels in a given electronic multiple-energy state **b :** the number of components of a multiplet

**mul·ti·pli·er** \'məltə,plī(ə)r, -īə\ *n* -S [ME, fr. *multiplien* to multiply + *-er*] **:** one that multiplies: as **a :** a number by which another number is multiplied — compare MULTIPLICAND **b** (1) **:** an instrument or device for multiplying or intensifying some effect ⟨~ phototube⟩ — compare VOLTAGE MULTIPLIER (2) **:** MULTIPLYING COIL **c** (1) **:** a set of gears causing the spool of a fishing reel to revolve faster than the crank thereby accelerating the speed at which the fishing line is reeled in (2) *or* **multiplier reel** *or* **multiplying reel :** a reel so equipped **d :** a key-operated machine or a key-operated mechanism or circuit on a machine (as on a calculating machine) that multiplies figures and records the products **e** (1) **:** one of the underground bulbils or offsets by which a multiplier onion increases — compare TOP ONION (2) *chiefly NewEng* **:** WINTER ONION; *esp* **:** MULTIPLIER ONION **f :** a factor in the game of skat that is derived by adding 1 for each matador held by the bidder or his opponents, 1 for fulfilling or failing to fulfill the contract, and 1 each for schneider or schwarz and predation thereof and that is used by multiplying by the base value of a game to determine the total score **g :** the ratio of the income held to result from an addition to investment to the amount of such addition ⟨the ~, which began as an analysis of the effects of public spending, has thus broadened into a general concept of income formation⟩ — compare ACCELERATOR

**multiplier onion** *n* **:** any of several perennial garden onions that constitute a variety (*Allium cepa* var. *aggregatum*) of the common onion and are grown chiefly for salad onions

1**mul·ti·ply** \'məltə,plī\ *vb* -ED/-ING/-ES [ME *multiplien*, fr. OF *multiplier*, fr. L *multiplicare*, fr. *multiplic-*, *multiplex* multiple — more at MULTIPLE] *vt* **1 :** to increase in number esp. greatly or in multiples **:** make more numerous **:** add quantity to **:** AMPLIFY, AUGMENT ⟨the spread of such a prejudice may ~ readers —R.P.Blackmur⟩ ⟨no organized attempt to ~ good writings —G.G.Coulton⟩ ⟨when an original manuscript could only be *multiplied* by handwritten copies —G.F.Hudson⟩ ⟨inspiring other property owners to ~ their prices —Louise Levitas⟩ ⟨ask you not to ~ those errors into misfortunes for all of us —Irving Stone⟩ ⟨commerce *multiplied* wealth and comfort —Stringfellow Barr⟩ **2 a :** to find the product of **:** perform multiplication on **b :** to combine with (another number) by multiplication **3** *obs* **:** MAGNIFY **~** *vi* **1 a :** to become greater in number **:** increase in extent **:** SPREAD ⟨as time passed, the forges and the furnaces *multiplied* —Desmond Sprague⟩ ⟨the natural secrecy in which errors breed and ~ —Norman Cousins⟩ **b :** BREED, PROPAGATE ⟨every species of animals naturally *multiplies* in proportion to the means of their subsistence, and no species can ever ~ beyond it —Adam Smith⟩ ⟨allows virus to ~ more than a millionfold —*Monsanto Mag.*⟩ **2 :** to perform the mathematical operation of multiplication **syn** see INCREASE — **multiply the earth :** to add to the world's population ⟨front soldiers who have just returned from killing and destruction now begin calmly to *multiply the earth* as though nothing had happened —Lawrence Thompson⟩ — **multiply words :** to be verbose or garrulous ⟨a fool *multiplies words* —Eccles. 10: 14 (RSV)⟩

2**mul·ti·ply** \'məltəplē, -li\ *adv* [1*multiple* + *-ly*] **:** in a multiple manner **:** in several or many ways **:** in multiple ⟨the use of ~ applicable names —A.I.Melden⟩ ⟨that physical objects are ~ accessible to different people —J.W.Yolton⟩ ⟨~ connected electrical devices⟩ ⟨a ~ connected surface⟩

**mul·ti-ply** \'məltə,plī\ *adj* [*multi-* + *ply*, n.] **:** composed of several or many plies ⟨*multi-ply* nylon⟩ ⟨*multi-ply* glass⟩

**mul·ti·ply·ing** \'məltə,plīiŋ\ *adj* [ME *multepliynge*, fr. pres. part. of *multeplien*, *multiplien* to multiply] **:** that multiplies ⟨the ~ train in a timepiece⟩ ⟨~ camera⟩

**multiplying coil** *n* **:** a resistor connected in parallel with an ammeter or in series with a voltmeter and so adjusted that the readings of the instrument must be multiplied in a fixed ratio (as 10: 1) to give the correct value — called also *multiplier*

**multiplying reel** *n* **:** MULTIPLIER c(2)

**mul·ti·polar** \¦⸗⸗ *at* MULTI- +\ *adj* [ISV *multi-* + *polar*] **:** having several poles: as **a :** having several dendrites ⟨~ nerve cells⟩ **b :** having a number of pairs of magnetic poles of alternate north and south polarity ⟨a ~ electric machine⟩

1**mul·ti·pole** \'məltə,pōl\ *adj* [*multi-* + *pole*, n.] **:** MULTIPOLAR ⟨~ radiation field⟩

2**multipole** \"\ *n* [ISV *multi-* + *pole*] **:** a system (as a molecule) involving two or more pairs of electric or magnetic dipoles and having an electric or a magnetic moment

**mul·tip·o·tent** \,məl'tipəd·ənt\ *adj* [L *multipotent-*, *multipotens*, fr. *multi-* + *potent-*, *potens* potent — more at POTENT] **:** having power to do many things ⟨~ goblins gyrated in a danse macabre —Saul Carson⟩ ⟨the synthesis of new ~ derivatives —*Jour. Amer. Med. Assoc.*⟩

**mul·ti·purpose** \¦məltə+,-\ *adj* [*multi-* + *purpose*, n.] **:** having several purposes ⟨~ dam⟩ ⟨~ furniture⟩

**mul·ti·racial** \¦⸗⸗ *at* MULTI- +\ *adj* [*multi-* + *racial*] **:** of, relating to, or representing various races ⟨~ government⟩

**mul·ti·seriate** \"+\ *adj* [prob. fr. (assumed) NL *multiseriatus*, fr. NL *multi-* + (assumed) NL *seriatus* seriate] **:** consisting of or arranged in several or many series

**mul·ti·spiral** \"+\ *adj* **:** having several whorls

**mul·ti·stage** \'məltə,stāj\ *adj* [*multi-* + *stage*, n.] **1 :** having successive operating stages ⟨~ compressor⟩ ⟨~ pump⟩ ⟨~ turbine⟩; *specif* **:** having two or more propulsion units that operate in turn ⟨~ rocket⟩ **2 :** conducted by stages ⟨~ amplification⟩ ⟨~ milling⟩ ⟨a ~ investigation⟩ ⟨~ sampling⟩

**mul·ti·story** \'məltə+,-\ *adj* [*multi-* + *story*, n.] **:** having a number of stories ⟨a ~ parking garage⟩; *esp* **:** having a floor plan that is repeated on levels above the ground floor ⟨a ~ hotel⟩

**mul·ti·syllabic** \¦⸗⸗ *at* MULTI- +\ *adj* [*multi-* + *-syllabic*] **:** POLYSYLLABIC

**mul·ti·syllability** \,məltə,silə'biləd·ē\ *n* [*multisyllable* + *-ity*] **:** the quality or state of being multisyllabic

**mul·ti·syllable** \'məltə+,-\ *n* [*multi-* + *syllable*] **:** a word of many syllables

**mul·ti·tubercular** \¦⸗⸗ *at* MULTI- +\ *adj* [*multi-* + *tubercular*] **:** MULTITUBERCULATE

**mul·ti·tu·ber·cu·la·ta** \,məltətə,bərkyə'läd·ə, -lād·ə\ *n pl, cap* [NL, fr. neut. pl. of *multituberculatus* multituberculate] **:** an order of relatively small Mesozoic and Eocene mammals coextensive with the subclass Allotheria and resembling the rodents although not considered ancestral to any recent mammals

**mul·ti·tuberculate** \¦⸗⸗ *at* MULTI- +\ *adj* [NL *multituberculatus*, fr. *multi-* + *tuberculatus* tuberculate] **1** *of teeth* **:** having many simple conical cusps ⟨primitive ~ mammals⟩ **2 :** of or relating to the Multituberculata **3 :** of or relating to multituberculy

**mul·ti·tu·ber·cu·lism** \,məltətə'bərkyə,lizəm\ *n* -S [*multituberculate* + *-ism*] **:** MULTITUBERCULY

**mul·ti·tu·ber·cu·ly** \-,lē\ *n* -ES [*multituberculate* + *-y*] **:** the state of having many tubercles — used esp. in ref. to a theory of the origin of mammalian teeth; compare TRITUBERCULY

**mul·ti·tude** \'məltə,tüd, -tə·,tyüd\ *n* -S [ME, fr. MF or L; MF, fr. L *multitudo*, fr. *multi-* + *-tudo* -tude] **1 :** the state of being many **:** NUMEROUSNESS ⟨whereas you were as the stars of heaven for ~ —Deut. 28:62 (RSV)⟩ ⟨the mind falters, confused by the ~ and yet the harmony of the detail —Theodore Dreiser⟩ ⟨of large numbers, note whether they are used precisely, or merely to express ~ —*Notes & Queries on Anthropology*⟩ **2 :** a great number **:** HOST ⟨*~s* in the valley of decision —Joel 3:14 (RSV)⟩ ⟨love covers a ~ of sins —1 Pet 4:8 (RSV)⟩ ⟨a language in which the same sound has to stand for a ~ of ideas —Edward Clodd⟩ ⟨a ~ of stories and traditions grew up around his name —D.E.Smith⟩ **3 :** a great number of persons collected together **:** CROWD, THRONG ⟨all the ~ was astonished —Mk 11:18 (RSV)⟩ ⟨the tourist buses disgorged their *~s* —Mollie Panter-Downes⟩ **4 :** POPULACE, PUBLIC ⟨both scorns and seeks the understanding and approbation of the ~ —Arthur Knight⟩ ⟨does not like his defeat in a matter of the heart to be known, and needs must dissemble to the ~ —Rex Ingamells⟩

**mul·ti·tu·di·nal** \¦məltə¦tüdᵊnəl, -tə·¦tyü-\ *adj* [L *multitudin-*, *multitudo* multitude + E *-al*] **:** MULTITUDINOUS

**mul·ti·tu·di·nism** \,⸗⸗'tüdᵊn,izəm, --'tyü-\ *n* -S [L *multitudin-*, *multitudo* multitude + E *-ism*] **:** a doctrine or policy giving primary importance to the interests of the multitude as opposed to the individual

**mul·ti·tu·di·nous** \¦məltə¦tüdᵊnəs, -tə·¦tyü-\ *adj* [L *multitudin-*, *multitudo* multitude + E *-ous*] **1 :** including a multitude of individuals **:** POPULOUS ⟨the invasion of nature by ~ man —H.S.Canby⟩ ⟨in the ~ city —W.S.Maugham⟩ **2 :** existing in a great multitude **:** MYRIAD ⟨the mosquitoes were ~ and fierce —Claud Cockburn⟩ ⟨evaluates the ~ happenings of the day —F.L.Mott⟩ ⟨lunch of ~ hors d'oeuvres —Jean Stafford⟩ ⟨the ~ arrangements necessitated by a great military undertaking —A.T.Mahan⟩ **3 :** existing in or consisting of innumerable forms, particles, elements, or aspects ⟨filling the air with a ~ musical clamor —John Burroughs⟩ ⟨urgent demand upon my attention made by the ~ world around me —Richard Church⟩ ⟨the long ~ rain —Carl Sandburg⟩

**mul·ti·tu·di·nous·ly** *adv* **:** in a multitudinous manner

**mul·ti·tu·di·nous·ness** *n* -ES **:** the state or quality of being multitudinous ⟨the ~ of their wants —Douglas Rimmer⟩

**mul·ti-unit tube** \'məltə+,- . . . -\ *n* [*multi-unit* fr. *multi-* + *unit*, n.] **:** a single electron tube that contains in one envelope elements enabling it to perform the functions of two or more separate tubes

**mul·ti·va·lence** \,məltə'vālən(t)s\ *n* -S [fr. 1*multivalent*, after such pairs as E *absent: absence*] **1** *or* **mul·ti·va·len·cy** \-nsē\ **:** POLYVALENCE **2 :** the quality or state of having many values, meanings, or appeals ⟨while ~ in the sense of appeal to different periods can not be demonstrated —*Western Rev.*⟩ ⟨the admission of relativity and ~ does not make value illusory or judgment futile —H.J.Muller⟩ ⟨the ~ of his imagery —James Burnham⟩

1**mul·ti·va·lent** \¦⸗⸗ *at* MULTI- +\ *adj* [ISV *multi-* + *valent*] **1 :** POLYVALENT **2 :** MULTIPLE — used of homologous chromosomes when more than two are present and associate in synapsis **3 :** having many values, meanings, or appeals ⟨even in the field of the terminal values of form, a work of art is ~ —George Boas⟩ ⟨as great and ~ a poet —Ramon Guthrie⟩

2**multivalent** \"\ *n* -S **:** one that is multivalent; *esp* **:** a multivalent chromosome group

**mul·ti·valued** \"+\ *adj* [*multi-* + *valued*] **:** having several or many values

1**mul·ti·valve** \'məltə+,-\ *adj* [NL *multivalvis*, fr. *multi-* + *-valvis* (fr. *valva* valve)] **:** having many valves — used esp. of shellfish and shells

2**multivalve** \"\ *n* **:** a multivalve shellfish or shell

**mul·ti·variant** \¦⸗⸗ *at* MULTI- +\ *adj* [*multi-* + *variant*, adj.] **:** having more than two degrees of freedom — used esp. of a physical-chemical system; compare PHASE RULE

**mul·ti·variate** \"+\ *adj* [*multi-* + *variate*, n.] **:** having or involving a number of independent mathematical variables — used esp. in statistical analysis

**mul·ti·various** \"+\ *adj* [*multi-* + *various*] **:** widely diverse

**mul·ti·verse** \'məltə,vərs\ *n* -S [*multi-* + *-verse* (as in *universe*)] **:** a totality of things and forces that are disparate or lacking in ultimate unity ⟨neither a universe pure and simple nor a ~ pure and simple —William James⟩ ⟨the part that mind plays in changing individuals and their ~ —Maynard Whitlow⟩ — compare PLURIVERSE

**mul·ti·vibrator** \,məltə+\ *n* [ISV *multi-* + *vibrator*] **:** a radio-frequency oscillator that produces a controlled fundamental frequency but distributes its energy chiefly among several harmonic or subharmonic frequencies

**mul·ti·vin·cu·lar** \¦məltə¦viŋkyələ(r)\ *adj* [*multi-* + *vinculum* + *-ar*] **:** having several small separate ligaments — used of the hinge of various bivalves

**mul·tiv·i·ous** \,məl'tivēəs\ *adj* [L *multivius*, fr. *multi-* + *-vius* (fr. *via* way, road) — more at VIA] **:** having many ways or roads

1**mul·ti·vitamin** \¦⸗⸗ *at* MULTI- +\ *adj* [*multi-* + *vitamin*, n.] **:** containing or employing several vitamins

2**multivitamin** \"\ *n* **:** a multivitamin preparation

**mul·tiv·o·cal** \,məl'tivəkəl\ *adj* [*multi-* + *-vocal* (as in *equivocal*)] **1 :** signifying many things **:** of manifold meanings **:** EQUIVOCAL ⟨meet with an ambiguous or ~ word —S.T. Coleridge⟩ **2** [*multi-* + *vocal*] **:** VOCIFEROUS ⟨so bustling and ~ in pacifism —F.L.Paxson⟩ ⟨scandals and horrors of the moment in ~, multigraphic clamor —S.H.Adams⟩

**mul·ti·vol·tine** \¦məltə¦vōl,tēn, -,tᵊn\ *adj* [*multi-* + *-voltine* (as in *bivoltine*)] **:** having several broods in a season — used esp. of an insect

**mul·ti·volume** \¦⸗⸗ *at* MULTI- +\ *or* **mul·ti·volumed** *adj* [*multi-* + *volume* (n.) or *volumed*] **:** comprising several volumes ⟨a ~ atlas⟩

1**mul·ti·wall** \'məltə,wȯl\ *adj* [*multi-* + *wall*, n.] **:** constructed of three or more plies of kraft or special papers usu. with glued body seams and sewn or glued top and bottom ⟨~ cement bag⟩ ⟨~ sack⟩

2**multiwall** \"\ *n* **:** a multiwall bag

**mul·ture** \'myütə(r)\ *n* -S [ME *multyr*, *multer*, fr. OF *molture*, lit., grinding, fr. (assumed) VL *molitura*, fr. L *molitus* (past part. of *molere* to grind) + *-ura* -ure — more at MEAL] *chiefly Scot* **:** a fee in the form of money, grain, or meal paid to a land proprietor or a tenant miller for the grinding of grain

**mul·tur·er** \-tərə(r)\ *n* -S **1** *chiefly Scot* **:** one who has grain ground at a mill **2** *chiefly Scot* **:** a miller to whom multure is paid

1**mum** \'məm\ *adj* [prob. imit. of a sound made with closed lips] **:** having no speech **:** SILENT ⟨to all of which I listened, ~ as an oyster —Carleton Beals⟩ ⟨officially he is still ~ on the subject —*Newsweek*⟩ — often used interjectionally to express a desire or need for silence

2**mum** \"\ *n* -S **:** abstention from speaking **:** SILENCE — often used in the expression *mum's the word*

3**mum** \"\ *vb* **mummed; mummed; mumming; mums** [ME *mommen*, fr. MF *momer* to go masked] *vi* **1 :** to act or play (as in a pantomime) usu. in mask or disguise ⟨miserable *mumming* on the stage —Donn Byrne⟩ **2 :** to go about merrymaking in disguise esp. during festivals ⟨the crowds *mumming* in the streets at Mardi Gras⟩ **~** *vt* **:** to make (one's way) esp. in disguise during festivals ⟨with soot-blackened faces and grotesque attire, *mumming* their way . . . singing for sixpences —A.J.Cronin⟩

4**mum** \"\ *n* -S [G *mumme*] **:** a strong ale or beer orig. made in Brunswick, Germany

5**mum** \"\ *chiefly Brit var of* MOM

6**mum** \", ,məm, -əm\ *n* -S [alter. of *ma'am*] **:** MADAM

7**mum** \'məm\ *n* -S [by shortening] **:** CHRYSANTHEMUM

1**mum·ble** \'məmbəl\ *vb* **mumbled; mumbled; mumbling** \-b(ə)liŋ\ **mumbles** [ME *momelen*, of imit. origin] *vi* **1** *archaic* **:** to chew something gently with closed lips or with little use of the teeth **2 :** to make speech sounds that are hard to understand because of minimal displacement of the speech organs from their rest position **:** utter words in a low confused indistinct manner **:** MUTTER ⟨he lay . . . gray and limp, with a parson *mumbling* over him —Francis Yeats-Brown⟩ **~** *vt* **1 :** to utter with a low inarticulate voice ⟨*mumbled* something about not having a license —George Meredith⟩ **2 :** to chew or bite with or as if with toothless gums ⟨the old women *mumbling* soft sandwiches —A.P.Gaskell⟩ **3 :** to press or caress with the lips ⟨she *mumbled* his cheek and called him "lovey" —Robertson Davies⟩ **4** *chiefly dial Eng* **:** MOMBLE

2**mumble** \"\ *n* -S **:** a low confused indistinct utterance **:** MUTTERING ⟨the ~ of his voice vanished —Gwyn Thomas⟩

**mumblebee** \'⸗⸗,⸗\ *n* -S [origin unknown] **:** a sloop-rigged Devonshire fishing boat with a mast stepped far aft, a large foresail, and a jib

**mumblenews** \'⸗⸗,⸗\ *n pl but sing or pl in constr* **:** TALEBEARER

**mum·bler** \'məmb(ə)lə(r)\ *n* -S **1 :** one that mumbles **2** *Brit* **:** GLASSBLOWER

**mum·ble·ty-peg** \'məmbəltē,peg, -pāg\ *or* **mumble-the-peg** \'≈≈≈,≈\ *or* **mumble peg** *also* **mum·ble·de·peg** \'məmbəldē-,peg, -pāg\ *or* **mum·bly-peg** \-blē-\ *n* [fr. the phrase *mumble the peg;* fr. the loser's originally having to pull out with his teeth a peg driven into the ground] **:** a game in which the players try to flip or throw a knife from various positions so that the blade will stick into the ground

**mum·bling·ly** *adv* **:** in a mumbling manner

**mum·bo jum·bo** \'məm(,)bō'jəm(,)bō\ *n, pl* **mumbo jumbos** [perh. fr. Mandingo *mama dyumbo,* fr. *mama* ancestor + *dyumbo* pompon, wearer of a pompon] **1** *usu cap M&J* **a :** an idol or deity held to have been worshiped by various African peoples **b :** an object of superstitious homage and fear **2 a :** a complicated observance that is often ritualistic and accompanied by elaborate trappings ⟨spell woven by the *mumbo jumbo* of a ritual and the glamour of regalia —C.W. Ferguson⟩ ⟨the *mumbo jumbo* of the . . . coronation —Victoria Sackville-West⟩ **b :** complicated and sometimes purposeless activity intended to obscure and confuse ⟨the exchange of notes is not mere diplomatic *mumbo jumbo* —*Time*⟩ ⟨personal combat is not *mumbo jumbo* —J.V.Grombach⟩ **3 :** language that is unnecessarily involved and difficult to understand **:** GIBBERISH ⟨created a *mumbo jumbo* beyond . . . many a lawyer to translate —Stuart Chase⟩ ⟨professional *mumbo jumbo* of much of our scholarly writing —P.G.Hoffman⟩

**¹mumbudget** *n* [prob. fr. ¹*mum* + *budget*] *obs* **:** SILENCE

**²mumbudget** *adj, obs* **:** SILENT

**³mumbudget** \,≈'≈≈\ *vi, obs* **:** to be silent

**¹mum·chance** \'məm,chan(t)s, -cha(a)n-, -chain-, -chän-\ *n* [LG *mummenschanze* throw in a dice game played by masked revelers, fr. MLG, fr. *mummen* dice game played by masked revelers (fr. *mummen* to go masked, perh. fr. MF *momer*) + (assumed) MLG *schanze* throw of dice, fr. MF *chance* throw of dice, chance — more at CHANCE] **1 :** an old dice game in which the caster is not permitted to choose the player with whom he contests the stake — compare HAZARD **2** [influenced in meaning by ¹*mum*] *dial Eng* **:** a silent stupid person

**²mumchance** \"\ *vi* **1 :** MASQUERADE **2** *chiefly dial* **:** to be silent out of caution or stupidity

**³mumchance** \"\ *adj, chiefly dial* **:** SILENT

**⁴mumchance** \"\ *adv* [³*mumchance*] *chiefly Brit* **:** SILENTLY ⟨peering down ~ at its reflection in the river —Richard Llewellyn⟩

**mu·me** \'müme\ *n* -S [Jap] **:** JAPANESE APRICOT

**mu–meson** \'≈;≈,≈\ *n* [¹*mu* + *meson*] **:** a meson having a mass approximately 200 times that of the electron

**mum·mer** \'məmə(r)\ *n* -S [MF *mommeur, momeur* masker, fr. OF *momeor,* fr. *momer* to go masked + *-eor* -or] **1 a :** an actor in a pantomime **b :** a theatrical performer **2 :** one who goes merrymaking in disguise esp. during festivals ⟨this first of May morning when ~s were dancing in the fields —Winifred Bryher⟩

**mum·mery** \'məmərē\ *n* -ES [MF *momerie* masquerade, fr. *momer*] **1 :** a performance given by mummers **2 :** a ridiculous, hypocritical, or pretentious ceremony, observance, or performance ⟨practices . . . commonly regarded as superstitious *mummeries* were revived —T.B.Macaulay⟩ ⟨the ~ and ceremonial of modern life —W.P.Webb⟩

**mummia** *n* -S [ME *momyan,* fr. ML *mumia* — more at MUMMY] *obs* **:** MUMMY 1

**mum·mi·chog** *also* **mum·ma·chog** \'məmə,chäg\ *or* **mum·my·chog** \-mē,-\ *n* -S [Narraganset *moamitteaúg,* lit., they go in great numbers] **:** any of various killifishes; *esp* **:** a common American killifish (*Fundulus heteroclitus*)

**mum·mick** \'məmik\ *var of* MAMMOCK

**mum·mi·fi·ca·tion** \,məməfə'kāshən\ *n* -S [fr. *mummify,* after such pairs as E *amplify: amplification*] **1 a :** the process of mummifying or the state of being mummified **b :** a condition resembling mummification ⟨no time for empty formalities . . . or ~ in bandages of red tape —*Newsweek*⟩ **2 :** the devitalization of a tooth pulp followed by amputation of the coronal portion leaving the remainder of the devitalized tissue in the tooth canal **3 :** DRY GANGRENE

**mum·mi·form** \'məmə,fȯrm\ *adj* [¹*mummy* + *-form*] **:** resembling or suggestive of a mummy in appearance

**mum·mi·fy** \'məmə,fī\ *vb* -ED/-ING/-ES [¹*mummy* + *-fy*] *vt* **1 :** to embalm and dry (as the body of an animal) ⟨cats and other sacred animals of Egypt were *mummified* like kings —Emma Hawkridge⟩ **2 a :** to make into or like a mummy ⟨dead love affairs, *mummified* and bound in a book —C.W. Cunnington⟩ ⟨Arab women . . . bundled up and *mummified,* white shadows scurrying —Vincent Sheean⟩ ⟨*mummified* customs that have long outlasted their usefulness —W.R.Inge⟩ **b :** to cause to dry up and shrivel ⟨brown rot not only causes decay of fruits but *mummifies* many of them —Raymond Bush⟩ **3 :** to wrap (a body) in sheets to restrain movement ~ *vi* **:** to dry up and shrivel like a mummy

**mum·ming** \'məmiŋ\ *n* -S [ME *mommyng,* fr. gerund of *mommen*-to mum — more at MUM] **:** participation in mummery **:** MASKING

**mum·mock** \'məmək\ *dial Eng var of* MAMMOCK

**¹mum·my** \'məmē, -mi\ *n* -ES [ME *mummie,* fr. MF *momie,* fr. ML *mumia,* fr. Ar *mūmiyah* mummy, bitumen, fr. Per *mūm* wax] **1 :** a concoction formerly used as a medicament or drug containing powdered parts of a human or animal body **2 a** *obs* **:** lifeless flesh ⟨should have a mountain of ~ —Shak.⟩ **b** *chiefly dial* **:** a soft pulpy mass **3 a** (1) **:** a body of a human being or other animal embalmed or treated for burial with preservatives after the manner of the ancient Egyptians (2) **:** a body unusually well preserved owing to the manner of its burial or to some special preparation for burial ⟨a Peruvian ~⟩ (3) **:** a carcass fortuitously preserved (as by being sun-dried) **b :** one resembling a mummy; *esp* **:** a person whose energies have withered ⟨sat like a couple of *mummies* ever since we left home —Richard Blaker⟩ **4 :** a brown bituminous artists' pigment of varying properties (as made by grinding the bones of mummies) **5 a :** CONGO 4 **b :** MUMMY BROWN 2b **c :** a moderate yellowish brown that is redder and very slightly darker than Bismarck brown and darker and slightly redder than maple sugar **6 :** a dried-up or shriveled fruit first rotted by a fungus ⟨the brown-rot *mummies* of stone fruits⟩

**²mummy** \"\ *vb* -ED/-ING/-ES **:** MUMMIFY ⟨the *mummied* heath-bells of the past summer —Thomas Hardy⟩

**³mummy** *var of* MOMMY

**mummy apple** *n* [alter. of *mammee*] **:** PAPAYA

**mummy bag** *n* **:** a sleeping bag tapered at the feet and sometimes enclosed at the head with an opening for the face

**mummy berry** *n* **:** a disease of blueberries caused by a fungus (*Sclerotinia vaccinii*) characterized mainly by cream colored or brown shriveled fruit

**mummy brown** *n* **1 :** MUMMY 4 **2 a :** ²BAY 2 **b :** a grayish brown to yellowish brown that is slightly paler than soot brown and slightly paler than gold bronze — called also *chukker brown, snuff, tamarack*

**mummy case** *n* **:** a case fitted closely to a swathed mummy usu. having the face modeled and the body covered with ritualistic emblems

mummy case

**mummychog** *var of* MUMMICHOG

**mummy cloth** *n* **1 :** a fabric used to wrap mummies **2 :** a heavy unbleached linen or cotton fabric in plain weave used as a foundation for embroidery **3 :** MOMIE CLOTH

**mummy pot** *n* **:** a vase used by the ancient Egyptians for keeping the mummies of small animals — compare CANOPIC JAR

**mummy wheat** *n* [so called fr. its having been found in Egyptian mummy cases] **:** POULARD WHEAT

**¹mump** \'məmp, *dial Eng* " *or* 'mu̇mp\ *vb* -ED/-ING/-S [prob. of imit. origin] *vt, chiefly dial* **:** MUMBLE ⟨ladies who ~ their passion —Oliver Goldsmith⟩ ~ *vi* **1** *dial Eng* **:** to grimace with the mouth **:** GRIN **2** *dial Eng* **:** MUMBLE **3** *dial Eng* **:** to be sullen or sulky ⟨make a shift at bearing yourself like a man, not ~*ing,* not moping —J.G.Cozzens⟩

**²mump** \'məmp\ *n* -S **1** *obs* **:** GRIMACE, GRIN **2 mumps** *pl* **:** SULLENNESS **:** silent displeasure

**³mump** \'məmp, *dial Eng* " *or* 'mu̇mp\ *vb* -ED/-ING/-S [obs. D *mompen*] *vt, chiefly dial* **:** CHEAT ⟨some debauched person who will ~ you of your daughter —William Wycherley⟩ ~ *vi* **1** *dial Eng* **:** BEG, SPONGE ⟨one prince came ~*ing* to them annually —T.B.Macaulay⟩ **2** *dial Eng* **:** CHEAT

**¹mump·er** \'məmpə(r), 'mu̇m-\ *n* -S [³*mump* + *-er*] *dial Eng* **:** a begging impostor **:** BEGGAR

**²mumper** \"\ *n* -S [¹*mump* + *-er*] *dial Eng* **:** one that sulks

**mump·ish** \'məmpish\ *adj* [²*mump* + *-ish*] **:** SULLEN, SULKY

**mumps** \'məmps\ *n pl but sing in constr* [fr. pl. of ²*mump*] **:** an acute contagious viral disease marked by fever and by swelling of the parotid gland and sometimes other salivary glands and ovaries or testes **:** PAROTITIS

**mump·si·mus** \'məmpsəməs\ *n* -ES [error for L *sumpsimus* we have taken, 1st pl. perf. ind. of *sumere* to take; fr. a familiar story in which this error was made in the ritual of the mass by an illiterate priest who when corrected replied that he would not change his old *mumpsimus* for his critic's new *sumpsimus* — more at ASSUME] **1 :** a bigoted adherent to exposed but customary error **2 :** a custom or tenet adhered to by a mumpsimus

**mum·ruf·fin** \'müm,rüfin, 'məm,rəf-\ *n* -S [origin unknown] *dial Eng* **:** LONG-TAILED TIT

**mums** *pl of* MUM, *pres 3d sing of* MUM

**mu·mu** \'mü(,)mü\ *n* -S [Samoan, lit., red] **:** BANCROFTIAN FILARIASIS

**¹mun** \'mu̇n, ,mən\ *verbal auxiliary* [ME *mun, mon,* must, shall, fr. ON *mon* shall (1st & 3d sing. pres indic; infin. *munu, monu*); akin to OE *man, mon* he remembers, thinks of (infin. *munan*) Goth *man* he thinks, believes, intends (infin. *munan*), L *ment- mens* mind — more at MIND] **1** *dial Brit* **:** MUST **2** *dial Eng* **:** MAY

**²mun** \'mu̇n, 'mən\ *n* -S [of Scand origin; akin to ON *munnr* mouth — more at MOUTH] *dial Eng* **:** MOUTH

**³mun** \,mən\ *pron* [ME, by shortening & alter. fr. *hemen*] **1** *dial Eng* **:** THEM **2** *dial Eng* **a :** HIM **b :** IT

**⁴mun** \'mən\ *n* -S [origin unknown] **:** one of a class of London street roisterers of the mid-seventeenth century

**⁵mun** \"\ *n* -S [alter. of ¹*man*] *chiefly dial* **:** MAN, FELLOW

**mun** *abbr* **1** municipal; municipality **2** munitions

**mun·ce·ri·an** \,mən'sirēən\ *n* -S *usu cap* [NL *Muncerianus,* fr. Thomas *Muncerus* (Münzer) †1525 Ger. religious leader + L *-ianus* -ian] **:** a follower of Thomas Münzer the Anabaptist

**¹munch** \'mənch\ *vb* -ED/-ING/-ES [ME *monchen,* prob. of imit. origin] *vt* **1 :** to chew with a crunching sound **:** eat with relish ⟨a cow ~*ing* clover in a field —J.P.McGranery⟩ ⟨one of the most toothsome chicken dinners you'll ever ~ —Gelston Hardy⟩ **2 :** to move (the jaws) up and down as if chewing ⟨~*ed* her feeble old toothless jaws —Samuel Butler †1902⟩ ~ *vi* **1 :** to chew food with a crunching sound **:** eat food with relish **2 :** to move the jaws as if chewing

**²munch** \"\ *n* -ES **1 :** the act or sound of munching ⟨the ~ and stamp of work stock —A.B.Guthrie⟩ **2 :** a bite to munch ⟨between ~*es* of the big red apple —*Century Mag.*⟩

**mun·chau·sen** \'mən,chau̇zᵊn, 'mu̇n- *also* 'mən,chȯz- *or* ,mən- *or* mün'-\ *adj, usu cap* [after Baron Karl Friedrich Hieronymus von *Münchhausen* †1797 Ger. huntsman and soldier famous for his tall tales] **:** of, relating to, or resembling the fabulous stories of his exploits told by Baron Munchausen ⟨mystify people by making them swallow as many of his more or less *Munchausen* stories as possible —C.D.Ley⟩

**mun·chau·sen·ism** \-ᵊn,izəm\ *n* -S *usu cap* [Baron von *Münchausen* + E *-ism*] **:** a tall tale ⟨it sounds like a *Munchausenism* but it's the truth —A.F.Collins⟩

**mun·cheel** \,mən'chē(ə)l\ *n* -S [Malayalam *manjīl*] **:** a litter used in India

**mün·chen–glad·bach** *or* **mun·chen–glad·bach** *or* **muen·chen–glad·bach** \'münkən'glät,bäk\ *adj, usu cap M&G* [fr. *München-Gladbach,* Germany] **:** of or from the city of München-Gladbach, Germany **:** of the kind or style prevalent in München-Gladbach

**munch·er** \'mənchə(r)\ *n* -S **:** one that munches

**mun·chi** \'münchē\ *or* **mun·shi** \-nshē\ *n, pl* **munchi** *or* **munchis** *or* **munshi** *or* **munshis** *usu cap* **:** TIV

**mund** \'mənd\ *n* -S [ME, fr. OE, protection, hand — more at MANUAL] **1** *early Eng law* **:** right of protection or guardianship (as over the person and property of a wife, a widow, an orphan, or the members of one's household or dependents) **2 :** GRITH 1b

**mun·da** \'mu̇ndə\ *n* -S *usu cap* **1 :** a member of any of various peoples representing an ancient pre-Aryan stock of India pushed back or nearly absorbed by incoming Caucasians or Mongolians **2 :** a language family restricted to central India including Asuri, Gadaba, Ho, Juang, Kharia, Korwa, Korku, Mundari, Santali, and Savara and included by some in the Austroasiatic family

**mun·dane** \,mən;dān\ *adj* [ME *mondeyne,* fr. MF *mondain,* fr. LL *mundanus,* fr. L *mundus* world + *-anus* -an] **1 a :** of, relating to, or characteristic of the world **:** characterized by human affairs, concerns, and activities that are often practical, immediate, transitory, and ordinary ⟨a reviewer is not expected to mention anything so ~ as the price of books —A.J.P.Taylor⟩ ⟨nothing but ~ businessmen —T.H.Fielding⟩ ⟨the occupations and distractions of ~ life —Harold Nicolson⟩ **b :** belonging to the world and having no concern for the ideal or the heavenly ⟨the trend which marks distinguished art from the more ~ —Carlyle Burrows⟩ ⟨a fairy palace, no: but a ~ wonder of a quite unimagined kind —R.A.W. Hughes⟩ **2 :** of or relating to the cosmos **:** COSMIC **syn** see EARTHLY

**mundane astrology** *n* **:** JUDICIAL ASTROLOGY

**mundane house** *n* **:** one of the twelve equal sectors in which the celestial sphere is divided in judicial astrology by six great circles intersecting at the north and south points of the horizon and which are regarded as fixed with respect to the horizon, the stars and planets passing through them each 24 hours — see HOROSCOPE

**mun·dane·ly** *adv* **:** in a mundane manner ⟨he spoke so ~ of university life⟩

**mun·dane·ness** \-ānnəs\ *n* -ES **:** the quality or state of being mundane

**mun·dan·i·ty** \,mən'danəd·ē\ *n* -ES [MF or ML; MF *mondanité,* fr. ML *mundanitat-, mundanitas,* fr. LL *mundanus* mundane + L *-itat-, -itas* -ity] **1 :** the quality or state of being mundane **:** WORLDLINESS ⟨an ideal opposed to ~⟩ **2 :** worldly inclinations — often used in pl. ⟨charm and graciousness, — her appreciation of fine clothes and houses — these are all *mundanities* —*Harper's Bazaar*⟩

**mun·da·ri** \,mən'därē\ *n* -S *usu cap* **:** a Munda dialect of the Kol people

**mun·da·tory** \'məndə,tōrē\ *n* -ES [LL *mundatorius* of cleaning, fr. L *mundatus* (past part. of *mundare* to clean, fr. *mundus* clean) + *-orius* -ory — more at MOSS] **:** a towel or cloth used to cleanse ecclesiastical vessels used in Holy Communion

**mun·dic** \'məndik\ *n* -S [perh. fr. Corn *mēn tēk,* fr. *mēn* stone + *tēk* pretty; akin to W *teg* pretty, OIr *ētig* ugly, ON *thægr* pleasant, *thiggja* to take, receive — more at MENHIR, THIG] *Cornwall* **:** PYRITE

**mun·di·fy** \'məndə,fī\ *vt* -ED/-ING/-ES [MF or LL; MF *mondifier* to cleanse, fr. LL *mundificare,* fr. L *mundus* clean + *-ificare* -ify — more at MOSS] **:** to wash thoroughly **:** DETERGE

**mun·div·a·gant** \,mən'divəgənt\ *adj* [L *mundus* world + *-i-* + *vagant- vagans* wandering, fr. pres. part. of *vagari* to wander — more at VAGARY] *archaic* **:** wandering over the world

**mun·dle** \'mu̇ndᵊl\ *n* -S [of Scand origin; akin to ON *möndull* handle; akin to (assumed) Oscan *manfur,* a part of a turner's lathe (whence L *mamphur*), Gk *mothos* din of battle, Skt *manthati* it swirls] *dial Eng* **:** a stick that is used for stirring

**mun·du·gu·mor** \,mən'dügə,mō(ə)r\ *n, pl* **mundugumor** *or* **mundugumors** *usu cap* **1 :** a Papuan people in the Sepik district, Territory of New Guinea **2 :** a member of the Mundugumor people

**mun·dun·gus** \,mən'dəŋgəs\ *n* -ES [modif. of Sp *mondongo* tripe] **1** *archaic* **:** REFUSE, TRASH **2 :** tobacco having an offensive smell

**mun·du·ru·cú** \,mündürü'kü\ *n, pl* **mundurucú** *or* **mundurucús** *usu cap* [Pg *mundurucú, mundurucu,* of AmerInd origin] **1 a :** a Tupian people of the upper Tapajoz river valley of Brazil **b :** a member of such people **2 :** the language of the Mundurucú people

**mune** \'mün\ *dial var of* MOON

**mung** *slang Austral var of* MONG

**mun·ga** \'məŋgə\ *n* -S [Kanarese *maṅga,* fr. Skt *marka*] **:** BONNET MONKEY

**mung bean** \'məŋ-\ *also* **mung** *n* -S [short for ³*mungo*] **:** an erect bushy annual bean (*Phaseolus aureus*) that is probably native to India, is widely cultivated in warm regions for its edible usu. green or yellow seeds, for green manure, or for forage, and is the chief source of the bean sprouts used in Chinese cookery — called also *green gram;* see URD

**¹munge** \'mu̇nzh, 'mənzh\ *vb* -ED/-ING/-S [perh. alter. (influenced by ¹*munch*) of obs. *mange* to eat, fr. ME *mangen,* fr. MF *mangier* — more at MANGE] *dial Brit* **:** MUNCH

**²munge** \"\ *vi* -ED/-ING/-S [origin unknown] *dial Brit* **:** GRUMBLE, MOAN

**mungeet** *var of* MUNJEET

**¹mun·go** \'məŋ(,)gō\ *n* -S [prob. after *Mungo,* a Negro slave in the farce *The Padlock* (1768) by Isaac Bickerstaffe †*ab*1812 Ir. playwright] *archaic* **:** NEGRO

**²mungo** \"\ *also* **mon·go** *or* **mon·goe** \'mäŋ-\ *n* -S [origin unknown] **:** wool of poor quality and very short staple recovered from heavily felted wool goods and wastes — see SHODDY 1

**³mun·go** \'məŋ(,)gō\ *also* **mungo bean** *n* -S [Tamil *mūṅgu,* fr. Hindi *mūg,* fr. Skt *mudga*] **1 :** MUNG BEAN **2 :** URD

**mun·goos** *or* **mun·goose** *var of* MONGOOSE

**mun·gu·ba** \,məŋ'gübə\ *n* -S [Pg *munguba, monguba,* fr. Tupi] **:** a Brazilian silk-cotton tree (*Bombax munguba*)

**mu·ni** \'münē\ *n* -S [Skt — more at MANTIS] **:** a Hindu hermit sage

**¹mu·nich** \'myünik, -nēk\ *adj, usu cap* [fr. *Munich,* Germany] **:** of or from the city of Munich, Germany **:** of the kind or style prevalent in Munich

**²munich** \"\ *n* -S *usu cap* [fr. *Munich,* Germany, the site of a 1938 agreement among England, France, and Italy that approved the dismemberment of Czechoslovakia by Hitler] **:** an instance of unresisting compliance with and capitulation to the demands of an aggressor nation ⟨the truce . . . was another *Munich* —R.T.Oliver⟩ ⟨do not think that a modus vivendi to save what can be saved . . . is necessarily a *Munich* —Frank Gorrell⟩

**mu·nich·ism** \-ni,kizəm\ *n* -S *usu cap* [²*munich* + *-ism*] **:** an attitude favoring appeasement ⟨the principal conservative critic of *Munichism* —*New Republic*⟩

**munich lake** *n, often cap M* **:** CARMINE 2

**¹mu·nic·i·pal** \myü'nisəpəl, myə'-, ÷mə'- *or* ÷¦myünə¦sipəl\ *adj* [L *municipalis,* fr. *municip- municeps* inhabitant of a municipium, lit., undertaker of duties (fr. *munus* duty, service, gift + *-cip-, -ceps,* fr. *capere* to take) + *-alis* -al — more at MEAN, HEAVE] **1 :** of or relating to the internal affairs as distinguished from the foreign relations of a nation or other major political unit ⟨international law . . . only authorizes a belligerent to punish a spy under its ~ law —J.L.Kunz⟩ ⟨~ legislation . . . enacted for the fulfillment of the treaties —*U. S. Stat. 750*⟩ — compare INTERNAL LAW, INTERNATIONAL LAW **2 a :** of or relating to a municipality ⟨~ reform acts⟩ ⟨a ~ golf course⟩ ⟨~ university⟩ ⟨~ government⟩ ⟨~ architecture⟩ **b :** appointed, elected, or empowered by a municipality **:** functioning in a municipality ⟨~ council⟩ ⟨~ officer⟩ ⟨~ police⟩ **c :** issued by or under the authority of a municipality ⟨~ bond⟩ ⟨~ regulation⟩ **3 :** of, relating to, or having the characteristics of a municipium **4 :** restricted to one locality **:** having narrow limits ⟨a new very ~ variety of dwarf sweet pea —Osbert Sitwell⟩ ⟨the sacredness of human life is a purely ~ ideal of no validity outside the jurisdiction —O.W.Holmes †1935⟩

**²municipal** \"\ *n* -S **1 :** an inhabitant of a municipium **2 :** a member of the municipal guard of Paris **3 :** a security issued by a state or local government or by an authority set up by such a government — usu. used in pl. ⟨prospects . . . seemed better in low interest rate corporation issues than in ~*s* —*World's Work*⟩

**municipal borough** *n* **:** a borough in England or Wales having powers of self-government limited by its inclusion in an administrative county

**municipal corporation** *n* **:** a political unit (as a town, city, or borough) created and given quasi-independent status by a nation, state, or other major governing authority and usu. endowed with powers of local self-government **:** a public corporation created by law to act as an agency of administration and local self-government

**municipal district** *n* **:** a chiefly rural unit of local government in Canada and in some parts of Australia

**municipal engineer** *n* **:** one whose training or occupation is in municipal engineering

**municipal engineering** *n* **:** a branch of engineering that deals with the operation and problems (as laying out additions and parks, and constructing and maintaining sewer systems, waterworks, and pavements) peculiar to urban life

**mu·nic·i·pal·i·ty** \myü,nisə'paləd·ē, myə,-, -lətē, -i ÷mə,-\ *n* -ES [F *municipalité,* fr. *municipal* (fr. L *municipalis*) + *-ité* -ity — more at MUNICIPAL] **1 a :** a primarily urban political unit (as a town or city) having corporate status and usu. powers of self-government ⟨a ~ . . . has no powers save those conferred upon it by the laws of the state —S.J.Ervin⟩ **b :** the governing body of such a unit **2 :** an administrative area into which Philippine provinces are divided, comprising a number of barrios — compare POBLACIÓN

**mu·nic·i·pal·iza·tion** \myü,nisəpələ'zāshən, myə,-, ÷mə,-\ *n* -S **:** the action or result of municipalizing ⟨the ~ of a gas supply is not . . . a way of cheapening the public service —W.H.Y.Webber⟩

**mu·nic·i·pal·ize** \≈'≈≈pə,līz\ *vt* -ED/-ING/-S **:** to bring under municipal ownership, control, or supervision ⟨water and gas supply in practically all German towns . . . had been *municipalized* —G.M.Harris⟩

**mu·nic·i·pal·ly** \-p(ə)lē\ *adv* **:** by or in terms of a municipality ⟨the club . . . had grown into a ~ sponsored organization —*Amer. Guide Series: Ark.*⟩

**municipal security** *n* **:** a security (as a bond) issued by the government or a governmental agency of a municipality — usu. used in pl.

**mu·ni·cip·i·um** \,myünə'sipēəm\ *n, pl* **municip·ia** \-ēə\ [L, fr. *municip-, municeps* inhabitant of a municipium — more at MUNICIPAL] **:** a Roman municipality; *esp* **:** one giving its citizens the privileges of Roman citizenship and often the right of living according to their own laws and customs

**mu·nif·i·cence** \myü'nifəsən(t)s, myə'-, ÷mə'-\ *n* -S [MF, fr. L *munificentia,* fr. *munificus* generous (fr. *munus* service, gift + *-ficus* -fic) + *-entia* -ence — more at MEAN] **:** the quality or state of being munificent **:** a giving or bestowing with extraordinary liberality **:** lavish generosity ⟨the ~ of princes made possible the painting and sculpture of the Renaissance —Curt Stern⟩

**munificency** *n* -ES [L *munificentia*] *obs* **:** MUNIFICENCE

**mu·nif·i·cent** \-nt\ *adj* [fr. *munificence,* after such pairs as E *magnificence: magnificent*] **1 :** very liberal in giving or bestowing **:** LAVISH ⟨my father gave me ten shillings and my mother five and I thought them ~ —Samuel Butler †1902⟩ **2 :** characterized by great liberality or generosity ⟨a handful of fruit which in her station was a ~ gift —William Beebe⟩ ⟨~ endowment of $22,000,000 —*Amer. Guide Series: Va.*⟩ **syn** see LIBERAL

**mu·nif·i·cent·ly** *adv* **:** in a munificent manner

**mu·nif·i·cent·ness** *n* -ES **:** the quality or state of being munificent

**mu·ni·fy** \'myünə,fī\ *vt* -ED/-ING/-ES [irreg. fr. L *munire* to fortify + E *-fy* — more at MUNITION] **:** to provide defenses for **:** FORTIFY

**mu·ni·ment** \'myünəmənt\ *n* -S [MF, fr. L *munimentum,* fr. *munire* to fortify + *-mentum* -ment] **1 muniments** *pl* **a :** the evidences or writings that enable one to defend the title to an estate or maintain a claim to rights and privileges; *also* **:** title deeds and papers, statutory grants, charters, and judgments **b** *archaic* **:** things provided as furnishings ⟨bedrooms contain little beyond the ~*s* necessary for sitting and lying —G.C. Munday⟩ **2** *archaic* **:** something that supports or defends **:** a means of defense ⟨we cannot spare the coarsest ~ of virtue —R.W.Emerson⟩

**muniment room** *n* **:** a storage room for preservation of family

or sometimes official or parochial records, papers, notebooks ⟨old manuscript treasures accumulated during the centuries in the *muniment rooms* of most of the noble and ancient families of Britain —St. Vincent Troubridge⟩ ⟨cobwebby old *muniment rooms* —R.D.Altick⟩
**munite** *vt* -ED/-ING/-S [ME *munyten*, fr. L *munitus*, past part. of *munire*] *obs* : to strengthen usu. by fortifying
[1]**mu·ni·tion** \myü'nishən, myə'-\ *n* -S [MF, fr. L *munition-, munitio*, fr. *munitus* (past part. of *munire* to fortify, fr. *moenia* walls) + *-ion-, -io* -ion; akin to OE *mǣre, gemǣre* boundary, MD *mere* stake, ON *landamæri* borderland, L *murus* wall, *meta* pyramid, boundary mark, Skt *minoti* he fixes in the earth, builds; basic meaning: stake] **1 a** *obs* : RAMPART, FORTIFICATION, FORTRESS, STRONGHOLD ⟨his place of defense shall be the ~*s* of rocks —Isa. 33:16 (AV)⟩ **b** *archaic* : something that serves as a defense ⟨whose might, the chief ~ is of all our host —William Cowper⟩ **2 a** : material used in war for defense or attack : ammunition and all supplies for direct military action : ARMAMENT 2b **b** : necessary equipment or provision — usu. used in pl. ⟨~*s* for a political campaign⟩
[2]**munition** \"\ *vt* -ED/-ING/-S : to provide with munitions ⟨they were ~*ed* and ready for the campaign⟩
**mu·ni·tion·eer** \myü¦nishə¦ni(ə)r, myə¦-\ *n* -S **1** : MUNITIONER **2** : a profiteer in the sale of munitions
**mu·ni·tion·er** \-'ish(ə)nə(r)\ *n* -S : one who is engaged in the manufacture of munitions
**mu·ni·tion·ment** \-nmənt\ *n* -S : a munition supply ⟨the army faced the problem of ~ for its forces⟩
**mu·ni·ty** \'myünəd·ē\ *n* -ES [ME *munitie*, short for *immunitie* exemption from duty, privilege of exemption — more at IMMUNITY] : a privilege that is granted
**munj** \'münj, 'mənj\ *also* **mun·ja** \-jə\ *n, pl* **munjes** *also* **munjas** [Hindi & Skt; Hindi *mūj*, *mūñj*, fr. Skt *muñja*] : a tough Asiatic grass (*Saccharum munja*) whose tenacious culms are used for ropes, twine, and baskets
**mun·jeet** *or* **mun·geet** \,mən'jēt\ *n* -S [Hindi *majīṭh*, fr. Skt *mañjiṣṭhā*, fem. of *mañjiṣṭha* bright red] : INDIAN MADDER 1
**mun·jis·tin** \,mən'jistən\ *n* -S [NL *munjista* Indian madder (fr. Skt *mañjiṣṭhā*) + E *-in*] : a yellow crystalline compound $C_{15}H_8O_6$ obtained from the Indian madder; purpuroxanthin-carboxylic acid
**mun·nion** *also* **mun·ion** \'mənyən\ *or* **min·ion** \'min-\ *n* -S [alter. of *monial*] : MULLION
**mun·nop·sis** \,mə'näpsəs\ *n, cap* [NL, fr. *Munna*, genus of isopods + *-opsis*] : a genus of eyeless marine isopods that somewhat resemble shrimps and have greatly enlarged antennae
**mun·roe effect** \mən'rō-\ *n, usu cap M* [after Charles E. *Munroe* †1938 Am. chemist and inventor] : the greatly increased penetration of an explosive into a surface (as of metal or concrete) that is caused by shaping a conical or hemispherical hollow in the forward end of an explosive cartridge
**mun·see** \'mən(t)sē\ *n, pl* **munsee** *or* **munsees** *usu cap* [Delaware *Min-asin-ink*, lit., at the place where stones are gathered together] **1** : a Delaware Indian people of northern New Jersey and neighboring parts of New York west of the Hudson **2** : a member of the Munsee people
[1]**mun·shi** *or* **moon·shee** \'münshē\ *n* -S [Hindi *munshī*, fr. Ar *munshi'*] **1** : a Hindu secretary or clerk **2** : a Hindu interpreter or language teacher
[2]**munshi** *usu cap, var of* MUNCHI
**mun·son system** \'mən(t)sən-\ *n, usu cap M* [after T. V. *Munson* †1913 Amer. viticulturist] : a system for training grape vines in which double wires spaced 18 to 24 inches apart with a third single wire between them are attached to posts about 6 feet in height
[1]**mun·ster** \'mənztə(r), -n(t)st-\ *adj, usu cap* [fr. *Munster*, province in southern Ireland] : of or from the province of Munster, Ireland : of the kind or style prevalent in Munster
[2]**mün·ster** *or* **mun·ster** *or* **muen·ster** \'minztə(r), 'mæn-, m(y)ün-, 'mün-, 'mən-, -n(t)st-\ *adj, usu cap* [fr. *Münster*, city in northwest Germany] : of or from the city of Münster, Germany : of the kind or style prevalent in Münster
[3]**munster** *usu cap, var of* MUENSTER
**mun·ti·a·cus** \,mən·'tīəkəs\ *n, cap* [NL, fr. E *muntjac*] : a genus of mammals consisting of the muntjacs
**mun·tin** \'mənt°n\ *or* **mun·ting** \-tiŋ\ *n* -S [alter. of earlier *montant* vertical dividing bar or timber, fr. F, fr. pres. part. of *monter* to rise — more at MOUNT] : a strip member separating panes of glass with a sash — compare MULLION
**munt·jac** *also* **munt·jak** \'mənt,jak\ *or* **mun·jak** \-n,-\ *n* -S [prob. modif. of Jav *mindjangan* deer] **1** : any of various small deer (genus *Muntiacus*) of southeastern Asia and the East Indies having the male distinguished by sharp exposed canine tusks and small upright antlers — called also *barking deer* **2** : a Tibetan deer (*Elaphodus cephalophus*) closely related to the muntjac and with it and various extinct related forms constituting a subfamily of the Cervidae
**muntshi** *var of* MUNCHI
**muntz metal** \'mən(t)s-\ *n, usu cap 1st M* [after George F. *Muntz* †1857 Eng. metal manufacturer] : an alloy of copper and zinc that contains 60 percent of copper, can be rolled hot, and is used esp. for sheathing and bolts
**mu·on** \'myü,än, 'mü-\ *n* -S [by contr.] : MU-MESON
**muong** \'mwäŋ\ *n, pl* **muong** *or* **muongs** *usu cap* **1 a** : an Indo-Chinese people of Tonkin and northern Annam **b** : a member of such people **2** : the language of the Muong people that is related to Vietnamese
[1]**mu·ra** \'mürə\ *n, pl* **mura** *or* **muras** *usu cap* [Pg, of AmerInd origin] **1 a** : an Indian people of northwestern Brazil **b** : a member of such people **2** : the language of the Mura people that constitutes the Muran language family
[2]**mu·ra** \'mürə\ *n* -S [Jap, village, hamlet] : a rural community in Japan
**mura·bit** \'mürə,bit\ *n* -S [Ar *murābiṭ* hermit, ascetic] : MARABOUT
**mu·rae·na** *or* **mu·re·na** \myü'rēnə\ *n* [NL, fr. L *muraena*, *murena* moray — more at MORAY] **1** *cap* : the type genus of Muraenidae **2** -S : MORAY
**mu·rae·ni·dae** \-rēnə,dē, -ren-\ *n pl, cap* [NL, fr. *Muraena*, type genus + *-idae*] : a family of eels comprising the morays
[1]**mu·rae·noid** \-rē,nȯid\ *adj* [ISV *muraen-* (fr. NL *Muraena*) + *-oid*] : of, relating to, or resembling the Muraenidae
[2]**muraenoid** \"\ *n* -S : MORAY
**mu·rage** \'myürij\ *n* -S [ME, fr. MF, fr. *murer* to enclose with a wall + *-age* — more at MURE] *Brit* : a tax paid for building or repairing the walls of a fortified town
[1]**mu·ral** \'myürəl, 'myür-\ *adj* [L *muralis*, fr. *murus* wall + *-alis* -al — more at MUNITION] **1** : of, relating to, or resembling a wall ⟨a margin of lofty unbroken ~ precipices —Samuel Haughton⟩ **2** : applied to and made integral with a wall surface ⟨paused to read the carved ~ tablet⟩ **3** : attached to and limited to a wall or a cavity ⟨~ thrombus⟩ ⟨~ abscess⟩
[2]**mural** \"\ *n* -S : a painting or other work applied to and made integral with a wall surface
**mural arch** *or* **mural arc** *n* : the wall or arch in the plane of the meridian formerly used for the attachment of an astronomical circle
**mural crown** *n* [trans. of L *corona muralis*] **1** : an open crown of gold having the upper rim indented to resemble a battlement bestowed among the ancient Romans on one that first mounted the wall of a besieged place and lodged a standard there **2** *or* **mural coronet** : a representation of an embattled open crown in heraldry

mural crown 2

**mu·ral·ist** \-ləst\ *n* -S : a painter of mural pictures or decorations
**mu·ral·ly** \-rəlē\ *adv* : with a mural crown
**mu·ran** \'mürən\ *adj, usu cap* [[1]*Mura* + *-an*] : relating to or being the language family consisting of the language of the Mura people of Brazil
**mu·ra·no glass** \mü'rä(,)nō-\ *n, usu cap M* [fr. *Murano*, Italy] : glassware made at Murano, Italy
**mu·rar·i·um** \myü'ra(a)rēəm\ *n* -S [L *mur-, mus* mouse + E *-arium* — more at MOUSE] : a place for rearing mice or rats under controlled conditions
**mu·ra·to·ri·an** \¦myürə¦tōrēən\ *adj, usu cap* [Lodovico Antonio *Muratori* †1750 Ital. antiquary and historian + E *-an*] : of or relating to the antiquary Muratori

**mur·cia** \'mərsh(ē)ə\ *adj, usu cap* [fr. *Murcia*, Spain] : of or from the city of Murcia, Spain : of the kind or style prevalent in Murcia
**mur·ci·a·na** \,mərshē'änə\ *n* -S [Sp, fr. fem. of *murciano* of Murcia, fr. *Murcia* + *-ano* -an] : a fandango of Murcia, Spain
[1]**mur·der** \'mərdər, 'mədə(r, 'məidə(r\ *n* -S [partly fr. ME *murther*, fr. OE *morthor*; partly fr. ME *mordre, murdre*, fr. OF *murdre, murtre*, of Gmc origin; akin to OE *morthor*; akin to OE *morth* death, murder, Goth *maurthr* murder, OHG *mord*, ON *morth* murder, L *mort-, mors* death, *mori* to die, Gk *brotos, mortos* mortal, Skt *mṛta* death, *marate, mriyate* he dies] **1** *early Eng law* : the killing of a person secretly or with concealment as opposed to an open killing **2** : the crime of killing a person under circumstances precisely defined by statute: as **a** : first-degree murder that deserves either capital or severe punishment because of being willful and premeditated, being committed with atrocity or cruelty (as by poisoning, starvation, mayhem, or torture), being committed in the course of the commission of a serious felony (as arson, burglary, or kidnapping), or being committed after lying in wait for the purpose of killing the victim **b** : second-degree murder that in most states is all other murder not classified as first-degree murder **3** : the killing of people in war ⟨war is mass ~⟩ **4** : something extraordinarily difficult or dangerous ⟨it'll be ~ on those roads up in the Sierras —G.A.Wagner⟩ ⟨in the more modest cafeteria . . . the crush is ~ —Herbert Kubly⟩ **5** : a parlor game in which after a mock murder has been committed in the dark the lights are turned on and one player as the detective questions the others to try to find out who is the criminal
[2]**murder** \"\ *vb* **murdered; murdered; murdering** \-d(ə)riŋ\ **murders** [partly fr. ME *murthren*, fr. *murther*, n.; partly fr. ME *mordren, murdren*, fr. MF *mordrir, murdrir*, fr. OF, fr. *murdre, murtre*, n.] *vt* **1** : to kill (a human being) unlawfully and with premeditated malice or willfully, deliberately, and unlawfully **2** : to slaughter in a brutal manner esp. in war ⟨bombs ~*ed* people as they stood in the street⟩ **3 a** : to put an end to : DESTROY ⟨if ever he were in power would . . . ~ truth, freedom, and art —*Saturday Rev.*⟩ **b** : to harass or depress grievously : TEASE, TORMENT ⟨~*ed* this poor heart of mine —Shak.⟩ **c** : to mutilate, spoil, or deform by wretched performance : MANGLE ⟨someone's difficult sonata was ~*ed* on the piano —Anne Green⟩ ⟨the average British traveler leads the world in ~*ing* the French tongue —*Times Lit. Supp.*⟩ ~ *vi* : to commit murder **syn** see KILL
**mur·der·ee** \¦mərdə¦rē\ *n* -S [[2]*murder* + *-ee*] : the victim or intended victim of a murderer ⟨played the ~ in the . . . crime picture —Speed Lamkin⟩
**mur·der·er** \'mərdərər, 'mədərə(r, 'məidərə(r\ *n* -S [partly fr. ME *murtherer*, fr. *murthren* + *-er*; partly fr. ME *mordrour*, fr. MF *mordreur, murdreur*, fr. OF, fr. *mordrir, murdrir* + *-eur* -or] **1 a** : one legally guilty of committing murder **b** : one who slays a living creature **2** *obs* : a cannon used esp. for clearing a ship's decks **3** : a metal bar carrying several hooks for cod
**mur·der·ess** \-dərəs\ *n* -ES [*murderer* + *-ess*] : a female murderer
**murdering** *adj* [fr. pres. part. of [2]*murder*] **1** : characterized by murder or the commitment of murder ⟨his ~ guns —John Dryden⟩ **2** : characterized by an intent or ability to injure or harm ⟨a ~ tongue⟩
**murdering piece** *n, obs* : MURDERER 2
**mur·der·ous** \'mərd(ə)rəs, 'məd-, 'məid-\ *adj* **1** : having the purpose or capability of murder : characterized by or causing murder or bloodshed ⟨the charge . . . was covered at a disciplined trot under ~ fire —Al Newman⟩ ⟨the ~ inadequacy of lifeboats and rafts —F.L.Paxson⟩ ⟨some uncontrollable impulse . . . may have driven the defendant to the commission of the ~ act —B.N.Cardozo⟩ ⟨the anger . . . crystallized in his demented brain into a cold, ~ fury —J.C.Powys⟩ **2** : having the ability or power to overwhelm : DEVASTATING ⟨the ~ heat that attended the opening —Wolcott Gibbs⟩ ⟨a hard-hitting and exhilarating book . . . full of quietly ~ thrusts —C.J.Rolo⟩ **3** : characterized by extreme difficulty ⟨the exams . . . are ~ —E.O.Hauser⟩ ⟨those unmanageable verbs, those ~ moods and tenses —*Times Lit. Supp.*⟩
**mur·der·ous·ly** *adv* : in a murderous manner ⟨a . . . schnauzer tore down from the garden barking ~ —Jean Stafford⟩
**mur·der·ous·ness** *n* -ES : the quality or state of being murderous
**mur·drum** \'mərdrəm\ *n* -S [ML, murder, fine for murder, fr. OF *murdre* murder — more at MURDER] *early Eng law* **1** : MURDER; *esp* : a killing in secret **2** : a fine exacted under the Norman kings from the hundred in which a person was slain unless the slayer was produced or proof was given that the slain person was not a Franco-Norman
[1]**mure** \'myü(ə)r\ *vt* -ED/-ING/-S [ME *muren*, fr. MF *murer*, fr. LL *murare*, fr. L *murus* wall — more at MUNITION] **1** : IMMURE **2** : THRUST, SQUEEZE ⟨~ against a wall⟩
[2]**mure** *n* -S [MF *mur*, fr. L *murus*] *obs* : WALL : something resembling a wall
[3]**mure** \'myü(ə)r\ *adj* [ME, fr. MF *meur*, lit., ripe, fr. L *maturus* — more at MATURE] *dial Brit* : HUMBLE, MEEK
[4]**mure** \"\ *dial Eng var of* MOOR
**murena** *syn of* MURAENA
**mu·ren·ger** \'myürənjə(r)\ *n* -S [alter. of earlier *murager*, fr. ME, fr. *murage* + *-er*] : one in charge of the wall of a town and its repairs
**mu·rex** \'myü,reks\ *n* [NL, fr. L, purple shell; akin to Gk *myak-, myax* sea-mussel, and prob. to L *mur-, mus* mouse — more at MOUSE] **1 a** *cap* : a genus (the type of the family Muricidae) of marine gastropods having a rough and often spinose shell and abounding in tropical seas **b** *pl* **mu·ri·ces** \-ürə,sēz\ *or* **murexes** : any mollusk of this genus or of the family Muricidae formerly much valued as the chief source of Tyrian purple dye **2** *pl* **murices** *or* **murexes** : a shell used as a trumpet
**mu·rex·an** \myü'rek,san\ *n* -S [*murexide* + *-an*] : URAMIL
**mu·rex·ide** \-,sīd, -,sə̇d\ *n* -S [G *murexid*, fr. NL *Murex* + G *-id* -ide] : a red crystalline compound $C_8H_8N_6O_6$ having a green luster, forming purple-red solutions with water, and formerly used as a dye; the ammonium salt of purpuric acid
**murexide reaction** *or* **murexide test** *n* : a reaction giving rise to murexide when uric acid or a related compound is heated with nitric acid and the product is treated with ammonia
**mur·geon** \'mərjən\ *n* -S [origin unknown] **1** *Scot* **a** : a wry face : GRIMACE **b** : a body contortion **2** *Scot* : GRUMBLINGS — usu. used in pl.
**mu·ria** \'mürēə\ *n, pl* **muria** *or* **murias** *usu cap* : one of a Gond hill people of India inhabiting the Bastar region of Madhya Pradesh
**mu·ri·ate** \'myürē,āt\ *n* -S [F, back-formation fr. *muriatique* (in *acide muriatique* muriatic acid), fr. L *muriaticus* pickled in brine, fr. *muria* brine; akin to L *muscus* moss — more at MOSS] : CHLORIDE — used chiefly commercially
**mu·ri·at·ed** \-ād·əd\ *adj* [fr. past part. of obs. *muriate* to pickle in brine, fr. L *muria* + E *-ate*, v. suffix] : combined or impregnated with a chloride or chlorides: as **a** : put in brine : PICKLED **b** : containing much salt : BRINY ⟨~ waters⟩
**muriate of potash** : POTASSIUM CHLORIDE — used chiefly of fertilizer grades
**mu·ri·at·ic acid** \¦myürē¦ad·ik-, -at|, |ēk-|\ *n* [F *muriatique*] : HYDROCHLORIC ACID — now used esp. of commercial grades
**mu·ri·cate** \'myürə,kāt, -,kət\ *also* **mu·ri·cat·ed** \-,kād·əd\ *adj* [*muricate* fr. L *muricatus* pointed like a purple fish, fr. *muric-, murex* purple shell + *-atus* -ate; *muricated* fr. L *muricatus* + E *-ed* — more at MUREX] : roughened with sharp hard points — compare ECHINATE
[1]**muricid** \'myürəsəd, myü'ris-\ *adj* [NL *Muricidae*] : of or relating to the Muricidae
[2]**muricid** \"\ *n* -S : a mollusk of the family Muricidae : MUREX 1b
**mu·ric·i·dae** \myü'risə,dē\ *n pl, cap* [NL, fr. *Muric-*, *Murex*, type genus + *-idae*] : a large family of gastropod mollusks (suborder Stenoglossa) marked by elongated sculptured shells often with rows of protuberances or spines, long siphon canal, and sessile eyes — **mu·ric·i·form** \-,fȯrm\ *adj* — **mu·ri·cine** \'myürə,sīn, -,sən\ *adj* — **mu·ri·coid** \-rə,kȯid\ — *adj*
**mu·ric·u·late** \myü'rikyə,lāt, -,lət\ *adj* [L *muriculus*, dim. of *muric-, murex* purple shell + E *-ate*] : minutely muricate
[1]**mu·rid** \mü'rēd\ *n* -S [Ar *murīd*] *Islam* : DISCIPLE; *esp* : a Sufi disciple

[2]**mu·rid** \'myürəd\ *adj* [NL *Muridae*] : of or relating to the Muridae
[3]**murid** \"\ *n* -S : a rodent of the family Muridae
**mu·ri·dae** \'myürə,dē\ *n pl, cap* [NL, fr. *Mur-, Mus*, type genus + *-idae*] : a very large family of relatively small rodents (superfamily Muroidea) that include various orig. Old World rodents (as the house mouse and the common rats) that are now cosmopolitan in distribution and that are distinguished from the related cricetid rodents by complete absence of cheek pouches
[1]**mu·ri·form** \'myürə,fȯrm\ *adj* [L *murus* wall + E *-iform* — more at MUNITION] : resembling courses of bricks in arrangement; *esp* : having both horizontal and vertical septa ⟨~ spores⟩ — **mu·ri·form·ly** *adv*
[2]**muriform** \"\ *adj* [L *mur-, mus* mouse + E *-iform* — more at MOUSE] : resembling a mouse or rat in form or appearance
**mu·ril·lo** \myü'ri(,)lō, mə'rē(,)(y)ō\ *n, often cap* [after Bartolomé E. *Murillo* †1682 Span. painter] : a moderate blue that is greener and duller than average copen, redder and deeper than azurite blue, and greener and darker than Dresden blue
**murillo bark** *n* : SOAPBARK
[1]**mu·rine** \'myü,rīn, -,rən, myü'rēn\ *adj* [L *murinus* of mice, fr. *mur-, mus* mouse + *-inus* -ine — more at MOUSE] **1 a** : of or relating to the genus *Mus* or to the subfamily of Muridae that includes it and contains most of the rats and mice which habitually live in intimate association with man ⟨~ rodents⟩ **b** : of, relating to, or produced by the common house mouse ⟨a ~ odor⟩ **2** : affecting or transmitted by rats or mice ⟨~ rickettsial diseases⟩
[2]**murine** \"\ *n* -S : a murine animal
**murine opossum** *n* : any of several small arboreal opossums (genus *Marmosa*) widely distributed in So. and Central America
**murine typhus** *n* : a mild febrile disease marked by headache and rash, caused by a rickettsia (*Rickettsia mooseri*) widespread in nature in rodents, and transmitted to man by the common rat flea
**mu·ri·nus** \myü'rīnəs\ *n* -ES [L, of mice] : MOUSE GRAY
**mu·ri·ti palm** \¦mürə¦tē-\ *n* [Pg *muriti, buriti* muriti palm, miriti palm, fr. Tupi] : a large Brazilian fan palm (*Mauritia vinifera*) yielding edible nuts and a useful fiber
**mu·ri·um** \'myürēəm\ *n* -S [NL, back-formation fr. ISV *muriatic* (acid) + NL *-ium*] : a hypothetical element having muriatic acid as the oxide
**mur·ji'·ite** \'mərjē,īt\ *or* **murj·ite** \-r,jīt\ *n* -S *usu cap* [Ar *murji'ah* believers in suspension of judgment + E *-ite*] **1** : an early Muslim sect emphasizing a suspension of judgment against erring believers and the unfailing efficacy of faith over works **2** : a member of the Murji'ite sect
[1]**murk** *or* **mirk** \'mərk, 'mək, 'məik\ *adj* -ER/-EST [ME *mirke*, prob. fr. ON *myrkr*; akin to OE *mirce* dark, & prob. to *morgen* morn — more at MORN] **1** *archaic* : having little or no light : dark and gloomy ⟨the heavens are ~ as the midnight —William Morris⟩ **2** *archaic* : obscured by or as if by mist : FOGGY
[2]**murk** *or* **mirk** \"\ *n* -S [ME *mirke*, prob. fr. ON *myrkr*, fr. *myrkr*, adj.] : DARKNESS, GLOOM; *also* : thick heavy air : FOG ⟨~ without, and leaden dusk in the huts —O.E.Rölvaag⟩ ⟨an early gull rose from the water . . . and soared away into the ~ —Nevil Shute⟩ ⟨out in the ~ and rain —H.W.Longfellow⟩
[3]**murk** *or* **mirk** \"\ *vt* -ED/-ING/-S [ME *mirken*, fr. *mirke*, adj.] : to make dark, dim, or gloomy; *also* : SOIL
**murk·i·ly** *or* **mirk·i·ly** \-kəlē\ *adv* : in a murky manner : DARKLY ⟨can imagine that ~ passionate nature —H.J. Laski⟩
**murk·i·ness** *or* **mirk·i·ness** \-kēnəs\ *n* -ES : the quality or state of being murky ⟨her abiding sense of the ~ of human life —Thomas Hardy⟩
**murk·ness** *n* -ES [ME *mirknesse*, fr. *mirke*, adj. + *-nesse* -ness] : MURKINESS
**murk·some** *or* **mirk·some** \-ksəm\ *adj* [[2]*murk, mirk* + *-some*] : quite murky
[1]**murky** *or* **mirky** \'mərkē, 'məkē, 'məikē, -ki\ *adj* -ER/-EST [[2]*murk, mirk* + *-y*] **1 a** : characterized by intense darkness or gloominess ⟨a brown adobe structure with . . . no window to shed light in its ~ depths —Tom Marvel⟩ ⟨the ~ bayous that are the highways of the marsh country —*Lamp*⟩ **b** : difficult to understand : CLOUDY, OBSCURE ⟨however ~ the subject matter may be, the language is always crystal clear —James Yaffe⟩ ⟨the ~ field of politics —P.H.Douglas⟩ ⟨the ~ depths of public opinion —M.W.Childs⟩ **2** : characterized by thickness and heaviness of air : FOGGY, MISTY ⟨rain poured down from ~ skies —*Newsweek*⟩ ⟨the air was ~ with the smoke of brush fires —Christopher Rand⟩ **3** : dark or dull in color ⟨her tweeds are soft and ~ —Lois Long⟩ ⟨nighthawks sheer the gloom, the white bar just visible on the . . . ~ plumage —D.C.Peattie⟩ ⟨a rather wiry and very dark animal, with a ~ brooding eye —J.B.Priestley⟩ **4** : covered with dirt and grime ⟨dimly saw the ~ fanlight over the door —A. Conan Doyle⟩ **syn** see DARK
[2]**murky** \"\ *n* -ES [origin unknown] : a musical composition for keyboard instruments with a bass in broken octaves
**murky bass** *n* : an accompanying bass in broken octaves
**murl** \'mərl\ *vb* -ED/-ING/-S [perh. of Celt origin; akin to IrGael *muirlim* I crumble] *dial Brit* : CRUMBLE, MOLDER
**mur·lin** \'mərlən\ *n* -S [origin unknown] *Irish* : BADDERLOCKS
**murly** \'mərlī\ *adj* [*murl* + *-y*] *dial Eng* : CRUMBLY — used esp. of soil
**mur·mansk** \(')mür¦man(t)sk\ *adj, usu cap* [fr. *Murmansk*, U.S.S.R.] : of or from the city of Murmansk, U.S.S.R. : of the kind or style prevalent in Murmansk
**mur·mi** \'mürmē\ *n, pl* **murmi** *or* **murmis** *usu cap* **1** : a member of a people that live on the border between Nepal and Sikkim, that are a pastoral division of the Bhutanese, and that have Mongolian features **2** : the Tibeto-Burman language of the Murmi people
[1]**mur·mur** \'mərmər, 'məmə(r, 'məimə(r\ *n* -S [ME *murmure*, fr. MF, fr. L *murmur* murmur, grumbling, roar; akin to OHG *murmurōn, murmulōn* to murmur, ON *murra* to murmur, Gk *mormyrein* to roar and boil (of water), Skt *marmara* murmuring, rustling; of imit. origin] **1** : a complaint half suppressed or uttered in a low muttering voice : GRUMBLING ⟨the tax on chimneys . . . raised far louder ~*s* —T.B.Macaulay⟩ ⟨devices . . . which writers use confidently and readers accept without a ~ —Robert Humphrey⟩ ⟨a ~ of impatience in the crowd —G.B.Shaw⟩ **2 a** : a low indistinct but often continuous sound ⟨the ~ of voices in the street —Sherwood Anderson⟩ ⟨the ~ of the waves along the shore⟩ **b** : a soft-spoken word : gentle speech ⟨her ~ was a comforting word⟩ ⟨there was a ~, "Yes, Yes" —Millen Brand⟩ ⟨amid a ~ of salaams we seated ourselves —William Beebe⟩ **3** : RUMOR, WHISPER ⟨was fresh in ~ . . . that he did seek the love of fair Olivia —Shak.⟩ **4** : an abnormal sound of the heart heard through the chest wall indicating a functional abnormality or the site of a structural abnormality **5** *also* **murmur vowel** : the unstressed voiced or voiceless vowel \ə\ when morphemically incidental to the articulation of a consonant
[2]**murmur** \"\ *vb* **murmured; murmured; murmuring** \-m(ə)riŋ\ **murmurs** [ME *murmuren*, fr. MF *murmurer*, fr. L *murmurare*, fr. *murmur*] *vi* **1** : to make a low continuous sound ⟨the brook ~*ed* under the ice —Elliott Merrick⟩ ⟨a breeze ~*ed* in the trees —Wilfrid Campfield⟩ **2** : to utter complaints in a low half-articulated voice : express discontent : GRUMBLE ⟨no one dares ~ in public —*Time*⟩ ⟨the ignorant and ungrateful nation ~*ed* against its deliverers —T.B. Macaulay⟩ ~ *vt* **1 a** *Scot* : to murmur against : ACCUSE **b** : to utter with dissatisfaction : COMPLAIN ⟨critics . . . today that it lacks a forward looking concept —M.W.Straight⟩ **2** : to utter or give forth in low or indistinct sounds or words ⟨the sentences men ~ again and again for years —W.B.Yeats⟩ ⟨she would be ~*ing* into the telephone important secrets —Elizabeth Headley⟩
**mur·mur·a·tion** \,mərmə'rāshən\ *n* -S [ME *murmuracioun*, fr. MF *murmuration*, fr. L *murmuration-, murmuratio*, fr. *murmuratus* (past part. of *murmurare*) + *-ion-, -io* -ion] **1** : the act of murmuring : the utterance of low continuous sounds or complaining noises ⟨the ~ of the crowds —A.E. Richardson⟩ ⟨ceaseless, inarticulate ~ of prayer —Frederic Prokosch⟩ **2** *of starlings* : FLOCK ⟨in the stackyard there was a great ~ of starlings —Mary Webb⟩

**murmur diphthong** *n* **:** a falling diphthong whose ending position is that of \ə\ **:** a centering diphthong
**mur·mur·er** \ˈmərmərər, ˈmə̄mərə(r, ˈməimərə(r\ *n* -s **:** one that murmurs
**mur·mur·ing·ly** *adv* **:** in a murmuring manner
**mur·mur·less** \ˈmərmərlə̇s\ *adj* **:** having no murmur — **mur·mur·less·ly** *adv*
**mur·mur·ous** \ˈmərm(ə)rəs, ˈmə̄m-, ˈməim-\ *adj* **1 :** filled with murmurs **:** characterized by low indistinct but often continuous sound ⟨the empty chimneys became so alive with swallows that the whole place was faintly ~ —Ellen Glasgow⟩ ⟨the garden is ~ with bees —Booth Tarkington⟩ **2 :** spoken softly and gently **:** low and sometimes indistinct ⟨his voice . . . was of a ~ character, soft, attractive —Nathaniel Hawthorne⟩
**mur·mur·ous·ly** *adv* **:** in a murmurous manner ⟨palm trees . . . wave ~ —Sam Boal⟩
**murn·gin** \ˈmərnjə̇n\ *n, pl* **murngin** *or* **murngins** *usu cap* **:** an Australian people of Arnhemland
**¹mu·roid** \ˈmyu̇,rȯid\ *adj* [NL *Muroidea*] **:** of or relating to the Muroidea
**²muroid** \"\ *n* -s **:** a rodent of the superfamily Muroidea
**mu·roi·dea** \myu̇ˈrȯidēə\ *n pl, cap* [NL, fr. *Mur-, Mus* + *-oidea*] **:** a superfamily of rodents approximately equal to Myomorpha with the Dipodidae excluded
**mu·ro·mon·tite** \,myu̇rəˈmän,tīt\ *n* -s [G *muromontit*, fr. *Muromontium* (Mauersberg) in Saxony, Germany, its locality + G *-it* -ite] **:** a mineral $Be_2FeY_2(SiO_4)_3$(?) consisting of a silicate of yttrium, iron, and beryllium that is perhaps identical with gadolinite or is a variant of clinozoisite
**muron** *var of* MYRON
**mur·phy** \ˈmərfē\ *n* -ES [fr. *Murphy*, a common Irish surname; fr. the potato's being regarded as the staple food of Ireland] **:** POTATO
**murphy bed** *n, usu cap M* [after William L. *Murphy*, 20th cent. Amer. inventor] **:** a bed that may be folded or swung into a closet when not in use

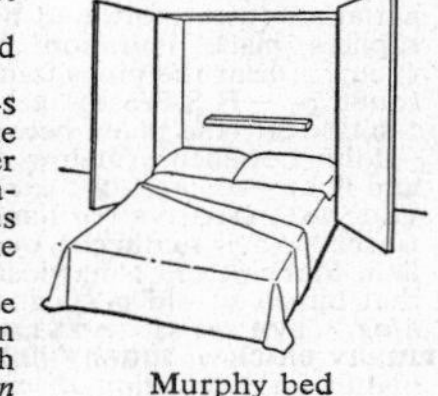
Murphy bed

**murr** *n* -s [ME *murre*] *obs* **:** a cold with hoarseness **:** CATARRH
**mur·ra** *or* **mur·rha** \ˈmərə\ *n* -s [L, prob. of Iranian origin like Gk *morrhia* murra; akin to Per *mori, muri* little glass ball] **:** a material thought to be of semiprecious stone or porcelain used to make costly vessels in ancient Rome
**mur·rah** \ˈmərə\ *n* [native name in India] **1** *usu cap* **:** an Indian breed of dairy type buffaloes with distinctive coiled horns **2** -s *often cap* **:** an animal of the Murrah breed
**mur·rain** \ˈmər·ə̇n, ˈmə·rə̇n\ *n* -s [ME *moreyne, moryne*, fr. MF *morine*, fr. *morir* to die, fr. L *mori* — more at MURDER] **1 a** *obs* **:** a deadly plague **:** PESTILENCE **b :** something resembling a murrain ⟨the beginnings of the Puritan ~ —H.L. Mencken⟩ **2 :** a pestilence or plague affecting domestic animals or plants (as anthrax or Texas fever of cattle or late blight of the potato) **3 :** PLAGUE — used as an imprecation ⟨muttering "a ~ on all your planning" —*Country Life*⟩ **4 :** leather from a diseased or poor-conditioned animal or from an animal that has died naturally
**mur·ral** *or* **mur·rel** \ˈmərəl\ *n* -s [Skt *murala*] **:** a common freshwater snakehead (*Ophiocephalus striatus*) of southeast Asia and the Philippines that is an important food fish
**mur·raya** \məˈrāə\ *n, cap* [NL, after Johan A. *Murray* †1791 Swed. botanist] **:** a genus of tropical Asiatic and Australian trees (family Rutaceae) having pinnate leaves and flowers with imbricated petals — see ORANGE JESSAMINE
**mur·ray cod** \ˈmərē-\ *n, usu cap M* [fr. *Murray* river, southeastern Australia] **:** a large serranid fish (*Oligorus macquariensis*) that is a leading freshwater food fish of Australia
**murray crayfish** *or* **murray lobster** *n, usu cap M* [fr. *Murray* river] **:** a large light-colored Australian crayfish (*Astacopsis serratus*) that is sought as a delicacy
**murray down** *n, usu cap M* [fr. *Murray* river] **:** the floss from the inflorescence of the carbungi
**mur·ray·ian** *or* **mur·ray·an** *also* **mur·ri·an** \ˈmərēən\ *n* -s *usu cap* [*Murray* river + E *-an*] **:** a member of an almost extinct ethnic group of southeastern Australia — compare CARPENTARIAN
**murray pine** *n, usu cap M* [in sense 1 after Andrew *Murray* †1878 Scot. naturalist; in sense 2 fr. *Murray* river] **1 :** LODGEPOLE PINE b **2** *or* **murray river pine :** a spreading Australian cypress pine (*Callitris glauca*) with dark green foliage
**murray red gum** *n, usu cap M* [fr. *Murray* river] **:** a gum tree (*Eucalyptus camaldulensis*) that is native to Australia but is grown elsewhere in warm regions for ornament and shade and that has smooth gray bark, red wood, and umbellate flowers
**murre** \ˈmər(·)\ *n* -s [origin unknown] **1 :** any of several guillemots of the genus *Uria*: as **a :** FOOLISH GUILLEMOT **b :** THICK-BILLED MURRE **2 :** RAZORBILL
**murree** *usu cap, var of* MARI
**murre·let** \ˈmərlə̇t\ *n* -s [*murre* + *-let*] **:** any of several small sea birds (family Alcidae) found chiefly on islands of the north Pacific
**mur·rey** \ˈmərē\ *n* -s [ME *murrey, murreye*, fr. MF *moré, morée*, fr. ML *moratum, morata*, fr. neut. and fem. respectively of *moratus* mulberry-colored, fr. L *morum* mulberry + *-atus* -ate — more at MULBERRY] **1 :** MULBERRY 2b **2** *obs* **:** a fabric colored murrey
**murrha** *var of* MURRA
**¹mur·rhine** *also* **myr·rhine** \ˈmərə̇n, ˈmə,rīn\ *adj* [L *murrinus, murrhinus, myrrhinus*, fr. *murra, murrha* + *-inus* -ine] **:** of, relating to, or made of murra ⟨sent him the poison to drink in a ~ cup —*Time*⟩
**²murrhine** *also* **myrrhine** \"\ *n* -s [L *murrinum, murrhinum, myrrhinum*, fr. neut. of *murrinus, murrhinus*] **:** a murrhine vase
**mur·ri·na** \məˈrīnə\ *n* -s [Sp *morriña*] **:** a disease of Central American horses and mules attributed to a protozoan blood parasite (*Trypanosoma hippicum*), characterized by emaciation, anemia, edema, conjunctivitis, fever, and paralysis of the hind legs, and often considered identical to surra
**murr·nong** \ˈmər,näŋ\ *n* -s [native name in Australia] **:** an Australian herb (*Microseris forsteri*) of the family Compositae having leaves all radical, flower heads solitary, and pappus bristles dilated at the base
**murry** \ˈməri\ *dial Brit var of* MERRY
**mur·shid** \ˈmu̇rshēd\ *n* -s [Ar] **:** a Muslim religious teacher; *also* **:** the head of a religious order
**mur·ther** \ˈmərt͟hər\ *chiefly dial var of* MURDER
**mu·ru·mu·ru** \mə̇ˈrüməˈrü\ *n* -s [Pg *murumurú, murumuru*, fr. Tupi] **:** a palm tree of Brazil (*Astrocaryum murumuru*) with small pear-shaped spiny fruits that turn yellow when ripe
**murumuru fat** *or* **murumuru oil** *n* **:** a fat obtained from the nuts of the murumuru and used chiefly in making soap
**murup** *var of* MOORUP
**mu·rut** \ˈmü,ru̇t\ *n, pl* **murut** *or* **muruts** *usu cap* **1 a :** any of several Dayak peoples in Sarawak and British No. Borneo sometimes considered to be a subdivision of the Klamantan people **b :** a member of any of the Murut peoples **2 :** the Austronesian language of the Murut people
**mur·va** *also* **moor·va** \ˈmu̇rvə\ *n* -s [Skt *mūrvā*] **1 :** an Asiatic bowstring hemp (*Sansevieria roxburghiana*) widely cultivated in India for its soft silky leaf fiber **2 :** the fiber yielded by the murva
**¹mus** *pl of* MU
**²mus** \ˈməs\ *n, cap* [NL, fr. L, mouse — more at MOUSE] **:** a genus (the type of the family Muridae) of rodents including the common house mouse and a few related small forms distinguished by the square-notched tip of the upper incisors as seen in profile
**mus** *abbr* **1** museum **2** music; musical; musician
**mu·sa** \ˈmyüzə\ *n, cap* [NL, fr. Ar *mawzah* banana] **:** a genus of perennial herbs (family Musaceae) that resemble trees, and have huge sheathing leaves, flower clusters subtended by bright-colored bracts, and a fleshy baccate fruit — see ABACA, BANANA, PLANTAIN
**MUSA** *abbr* multiple-unit steerable antenna
**mu·sa·ce·ae** \myüˈzāsē,ē\ *n pl, cap* [NL, fr. *Musa*, type genus + *-aceae*] **:** a family of trees or arborescent herbs (order Musales) that have clustered flowers subtended by spathaceous bracts, a perianth of two petaloid series, five anthers with one staminodium, and a baccate or capsular fruit — **mu·sa·ceous** \-āshəs\ *adj*
**mu·saf** *or* **mu·saph** \ˈmüsəf\ *n* -s [Heb *mūsāph* addition] **:** an additional morning service on the Sabbath and on festivals in the liturgy of the Jews — compare SHAHARITH
**mu·sa·har** \ˌmüsəˈhär\ *n* -s *usu cap* [Bengali] **:** a member of a caste of hinduized jungle people of India who perform tasks such as crop watching and the bearing of palanquins
**mu·sa·les** \myüˈzā(,)lēz\ *n pl, cap* [NL, fr. *Musa* + *-ales*] **:** an order of monocotyledonous tropical plants characterized by the cyclic flowers often with irregular perianth and one or more of the stamens suppressed
**musalman** *var of* MUSSULMAN
**mu·sang** \müˈsäŋ, myüˈsaŋ\ *n* -s [Malay] **:** an East Indian palm civet (*Paradoxurus hermaphroditus*) with long shaggy fur obscurely patterned with spots and stripes
**¹mu·sar** \ˈmyü,zär\ *n* -s [F *musard*, fr. OProv *musart, muzart*, lit., idler, fr. *musar, muzar* to gape, idle, loiter (fr. *mus* mouth of an animal, fr. ML *musus*) + *-art* -ard] **:** a 12th century ballad singer of Provence
**²mu·sar** \ˈmü,sär\ *n* -s [NHeb *mūsār*, fr. Heb, discipline, fr. *yōser* to discipline, punish] **:** a 19th century Jewish religio-ethical movement stressing strict moral discipline and piety
**musc-** *or* **musci-** *also* **musco-** *comb form* [L *musc-*, fr. *muscus* — more at MOSS] **:** moss ⟨*Muscites*⟩ ⟨*muscoid*⟩ ⟨*muscicolous*⟩ ⟨*muscology*⟩
**mus·ca** \ˈməskə\ *n, cap* [NL, fr. L, fly — more at MIDGE] **:** a genus (the type of the family Muscidae) of flies now restricted to the common housefly (*M. domestica*) and closely related flies
**mus·cade** \,məˈskäd\ *n* -s [F, nutmeg, fr. MF (*nois*) *muscade*, fr. OF — more at NUTMEG] **:** a light brown that is stronger and slightly yellower than blush and redder, lighter, and stronger than cork — called also *woodland rose*
**mus·ca·din** \ˈməskədə̇n\ *n* -s [F, lit., musk-scented lozenge — more at *muscardinus*] **:** a young French fop; *esp* **:** one of royalist sympathies during the French Revolution
**mus·ca·dine** \ˈməskədīn, -,dən\ *n* -s [prob. alter. (influenced by F *muscade* nutmeg & E *-ine*) of *muscatel*] **1** *archaic* **:** MUSCATEL **2** *or* **muscadine grape :** a tall-growing grape (*Vitis rotundifolia*) of the southern U.S. having rounded leaves and thick-skinned somewhat musky fruits in small clusters and being the source of several cultivated grapes (as the scuppernong)
**mus·ca·din·ia** \,məskəˈdinēə\ *n, cap* [NL, fr. E *muscadine* + NL *-ia*] *in some esp former classifications* **:** a small genus of woody vines (family Vitaceae) having simple tendrils and a continuous pith
**mus·cae vo·li·tan·tes** \ˈmə,skī,wōləˈtän·,tās\ *n pl* [NL, lit., flying flies] **:** spots before the eyes, usu. in the form of dots, threads, beads, or circles, due to cells and cell fragments in the vitreous humor and lens
**mus·car·dine** \ˈməskə(r)də̇n, -(r),dēn\ *also* **muscardine disease** *n* -s [F *muscardine*] **:** any of various fungus diseases of insects caused by imperfect fungi that proliferate and ramify throughout the body of the host; *esp* **:** CALCINO — see GREEN MUSCARDINE
**mus·car·din·i·dae** \,məskə(r)ˈdinə,dē\ [NL, fr. *Muscardinus*, type genus + *-idae*] *syn of* GLIRIDAE
**mus·car·di·nus** \-dīnəs\ *n, cap* [NL, fr. F *muscardin, muscadin* musk-scented lozenge, hazel mouse, fr. *muscat* musky, fr. Prov — more at MUSCAT] **:** a genus of dormice (family Gliridae) comprising the hazel mouse and related small mice
**mus·ca·ri** \,məˈskä,rī\ *n, cap* [NL, fr. (assumed) obs. NGk *moschari* grape hyacinth, fr. Gk *moschos* musk — more at MUSK] **:** a genus of Old World bulbous herbs (family Liliaceae) having narrow fleshy leaves and racemes or spikes of urn-shaped flowers with the lower portion of the perianth segments united — see GRAPE HYACINTH
**mus·ca·rine** \ˈməskə,rēn, -,rə̇n\ *n* -s [G *muskarin*, fr. NL *muscaria* (specific epithet of *Amanita muscaria*, fr. L, fem. of *muscarius* of a fly, fr. *musca* fly + *-arius* -ary) + G *-in* -ine — more at MIDGE] **:** a quaternary ammonium base $C_8H_{19}NO_3$ that is chemically related to choline, was first found in the fly agaric, stimulates smooth muscle, and when ingested produces profuse salivation and sweating, abdominal colic with evacuation of bowels and bladder, contracted pupils and blurring of vision, excessive bronchial secretion, bradycardia, and respiratory depression
**mus·ca·rin·ic** \ˌ=ˈrinik\ *adj* **:** of, resembling, or characteristic of muscarine ⟨a ~ drug⟩; *esp* **:** producing direct stimulation of smooth muscle ⟨~ physiologic effects⟩
**mus·cat** *also* **mus·kat** \ˈmə,skat, -,skət, usu -d.+V\ *n* -s [F *muscat*, fr. MF, fr. OProv, fr. *muscat* musky, fr. *musc* musk (fr. LL *muscus*) + *-at* -ate (fr. L *-atus*) — more at MUSK] **1 :** any of several cultivated vinifera grapes used esp. in making wine and raisins **2 :** MUSCATEL 1, 2
**mus·cat and oman** \ˈməs,kad·ən(d)ōˈmän, -,kəd-·\ *adj, usu cap* [fr. *Muscat and Oman*, country in southeast Arabia] **:** of or relating to Muscat and Oman **:** of the kind or style prevalent in Muscat and Oman
**mus·ca·tel** \ˌməskəˈtel\ *also* **mus·ca·del** *or* **mus·ca·dell** *or* **mus·ca·delle** \-ˈdel\ *n* -s [ME *muskadelle*, fr. MF *muscadel, muscatel*, fr. OProv *muscadel*, fr. *muscadel* resembling musk, fr *muscat* musky] **1 :** a sweet dessert wine that is golden to dark amber in color with a flavor and aroma peculiar to the muscat grapes from which it is made **2 :** a raisin produced from muscat grapes **3 :** MUSCAT 1
**muscavado** *var of* MUSCOVADO
**mu·schel·kalk** \ˈmu̇shəl,kälk\ *adj, usu cap* [G, shell lime, fr. *muschel* mussel, shell + *kalk* lime] **:** of, relating to, or constituting a subdivision of the European Triassic — see GEOLOGIC TIME table
**mus·ci** \ˈmə,sī\ *n pl, cap* [NL, fr. pl. of L *muscus* moss — more at MOSS] **:** a class of Bryophyta comprising the mosses and being characterized by a well-developed leafy gametophyte that arises by budding from a protonema and bears sex organs among the leaves at its tip and by a sporophyte that develops from the fertilized egg, remains attached to the tip of the gametophyte, and is a naked usu. stalked and operculate capsule in which asexual spores are borne — see ANDREAEALIS, BRYALES, SPHAGNALES; compare EUBRYALES, HEPATICAE
**¹musci-** *comb form* [NL, fr. L *musca* — more at MIDGE] **:** fly ⟨*Muscicapidae*⟩
**²musci-** — see MUSC-
**mus·cic·a·pa** \məˈsikəpə\ *n, cap* [NL, fr. ¹*musci-* + *-capa* (fr. L *capere* to take, seize) — more at HEAVE] **:** a genus of flycatchers including the common European spotted flycatcher (*Muscicapa striata* syn. *M. grisola*) and being the type of the family Muscicapidae — compare SYLVIIDAE
**mus·ci·cap·i·dae** \,məsəˈkapə,dē\ *n pl, cap* [NL, fr. *Muscicapa*, type genus + *-idae*] **:** a very large family of oscine passerine birds consisting of the Old World or true flycatchers and sometimes including also the thrushes, warblers, and babblers
**mus·cic·a·pine** \məˈsikə,pīn, -,pə̇n\ *adj* [NL *Muscicapa* + E *-ine*] **:** of or relating to the Muscicapidae
**mus·cic·o·lous** \məˈsikələs\ *adj* [*musc-* + *-colous*] **:** growing on decaying mosses or hepatics
**¹mus·cid** \ˈməsə̇d\ *adj* [NL *Muscidae*] **:** of or relating to the Muscidae
**²muscid** \"\ *n* -s [NL *Muscidae*] **:** a fly of the family Muscidae
**mus·ci·dae** \ˈməsə,dē\ *n pl, cap* [NL, fr. *Musca*, type genus + *-idae*] **:** a family of two-winged flies (order Diptera) including the housefly (*Musca domestica*)
**¹mus·ci·form** \ˈməsə,fȯrm\ *adj* [*musc-* + *-form*] **:** resembling moss in form or appearance
**²musciform** \"\ *adj* [ISV ¹*musci-* + *-form*] **:** having the form or structure of an insect of the family Muscidae
**mus·ci·ne·ae** \məˈsinē,ē\ [NL, fr. *musc-* + *-ineae*] *syn of* BRYOPHYTA
**mus·ci·tes** \ˈməsə,tēz\ *n, cap* [NL, fr. *musc-* + L *-ites* -ite] **:** a form genus of fossil plants that resemble present-day tree mosses and may belong to the class Musci
**¹muscle** *var of* MUSSEL
**²mus·cle** \ˈməsəl\ *n* -s *often attrib* [MF, fr. L *musculus*, fr. dim. of *mus* mouse — more at MOUSE] **1 a :** a tissue that functions to produce motion and is made up of variously modified elongated cells capable of contracting when stimulated — see CARDIAC MUSCLE, SMOOTH MUSCLE, STRIATED MUSCLE **b :** an organ that contracts to produce, enhance, or check a particular movement and is made up of usu. striated muscle tissue enclosed in a perimysium and firmly attached at either end to a bone or other fixed point — see AGONIST, ANTAGONIST, SYNERGIST **2 a :** something that resembles or is likened to a muscle ⟨electronic circuits . . . are the ~s which carry out its orders —*Boeing Mag.*⟩ ⟨the ~s of England . . . the factories —Richard Joseph⟩ ⟨limbered his mental and moral ~s —Janet Whitney⟩ **b** (1) **:** muscular strength **:** BRAWN ⟨got the nerve for anything, only he hasn't got the ~ —Joseph Conrad⟩ (2) **:** effective strength or authority **:** FORCE, POWER ⟨put military ~ into the mutual defense pact —*N. Y. Herald Tribune*⟩ ⟨chosen less for polish and background, more for economic and executive ~ —*Time*⟩ ⟨a cup of . . . coffee that really has some ~ —R.M.Hodesh⟩ **c :** an essential item or service **:** NECESSITY ⟨economies that would cut out fat rather than ~ —D.W.Mitchell⟩ **3 a :** muscular tissue **b :** lean meat
**³muscle** \"\ *vb* **muscled; muscled; muscling** \-s(ə)liŋ\ **muscles** *vt* **1** *dial* **:** to move by muscular effort ⟨needed men to ~ chairs and tables —Linnell Jones⟩ **2 :** to use strength or influence on **:** achieve by coercion **:** FORCE, SHOVE ⟨was suddenly *muscled* aside as a swarm of his fellows rushed out —*Sydney (Australia) Bull.*⟩ ⟨a plane ~s its way through the . . . sound barrier —*Springfield (Mass.) Daily News*⟩ ⟨dreamers were *muscled* out of patent rights —Scott Fitzgerald⟩ **3 :** to furnish with strength or muscle **:** REINFORCE, CONDITION ⟨even the years of ballet exercises . . . had not *muscled* them into hardness —Winifred Bambrick⟩ ⟨~ up our diplomatic approach —*Newsweek*⟩ ⟨*muscling* their minds to strike —Rose Thurburn⟩ **~** *vi* **1 a :** to make one's way by brute strength ⟨slowly *muscled* up the cliff⟩ **b :** to overcome opposition by force — usu. used with *in* or *into* ⟨*muscled* into the queue —Bruce Marshall⟩ **2 :** to force one's way in (as by trickery or intimidation) against hostility or opposition esp. for fraudulent gain — usu. used with *in* ⟨some competing journalist would ~ in on my exclusive story —*N.Y.Times*⟩ ⟨*muscling* in on his territory —Green Peyton⟩ ⟨would ~ in on the racket⟩
**muscle-bound** \ˈ==,=\ *adj* **1 :** having some of the muscles tense and enlarged and of impaired elasticity sometimes as a result of excessive exercise **2 :** lacking in flexibility **:** RIGID, STIFF ⟨suffers from *muscle-bound* doctrinaire inflexibility —Mollie Panter-Downes⟩ ⟨television is becoming *muscle-bound*, repetitious, unenterprising —*Saturday Rev.*⟩
**muscled** *adj* **:** furnished with muscles — often used in combination ⟨hard-*muscled* arms⟩
**muscle fiber** *n* **:** one of the cells of muscle
**mus·cle·less** \ˈməsəllə̇s\ *adj* **:** lacking muscle
**muscleman** \ˈ==,=\ *n, pl* **musclemen :** a man hired (as by a gangster) to enforce compliance by strong-arm methods **:** GOON 1, ENFORCER ⟨ran the gambling games, acted as . . . *musclemen*, fixers, thugs —G.A.Hamid⟩
**muscle plate** *n* **:** a differentiated part of a primitive segment in a vertebrate embryo that forms voluntary muscle tissue
**muscle reading** *n* **:** a technique practiced by some magicians of detecting slight involuntary movements of a subject's muscles that furnish clues to the solution of problems or the finding of hidden objects
**muscle scar** *also* **muscle mark** *n* **:** one of the differentiated usu. depressed areas on the inner surface of a bivalve shell to which a muscle is fixed
**muscle segment** *n* **:** MYOCOMMA
**muscle sense** *n* **:** sensations arising from proprioceptors in the muscles and including those that are usu. held to give rise to awareness of the position in space of body parts
**muscle spasm** *n* **:** persistent involuntary hypertonicity of one or more muscles usu. of central origin and commonly associated with pain and excessive irritability
**muscle spindle** *n* **:** a proprioceptive sensory end organ in a muscle consisting of small striated muscle fibers richly supplied with nerve endings and enclosed in a connective tissue sheath
**muscle sugar** *n* **:** INOSITOL
**mus·cling** \ˈməs(ə)liŋ\ *n* -s [³*muscle* + *-ing*] **1 :** the distribution and state of development of muscles ⟨a heifer with splendid rump ~⟩ **2 :** MUSCULATURE 3
**mus·cly** \-lē\ *adj* **:** constituted of muscle ⟨the ~ mass from neck to shoulder blade —Robert Browning⟩
**musco-** — see MUSC-
**¹mus·coid** \ˈmə,skȯid\ *adj* [ISV *musc-* + *-oid*] **:** of, relating to, or resembling moss
**²muscoid** \"\ *adj* [NL *Muscoidea*] **:** of or relating to the superfamily Muscoidea; *specif* **:** resembling the muscoid fly maggot esp. in being headless, posteriorly truncate, and cylindrical to spindle-shaped
**mus·coi·dea** \,məˈskȯidēə\ *n pl, cap* [NL, fr. *Musca* + *-oidea*] **:** a superfamily of two-winged flies (suborder Brachycera) including the houseflies and many related flies (as of the families Muscidae, Gasterophilidae, Calliphoridae, Tachinidae) that have the head freely movable and the abdomen usu. oval and bristly
**mus·co·log·ic** \ˌməskəˈläjik\ *or* **mus·co·log·i·cal** \-jə̇kəl\ *adj* **:** of or relating to muscology **:** BRYOLOGICAL
**mus·col·o·gist** \,məˈskäləjə̇st\ *n* -s [ISV *muscology* + *-ist*] **:** a specialist in muscology
**mus·col·o·gy** \-jē\ *n* -ES [NL *muscologia*, fr. *musc-* + *-logia* -logy] **:** BRYOLOGY; *esp* **:** a part of bryology that deals with the mosses — compare HEPATICOLOGY
**mus·cone** *or* **mus·kone** \ˈmə,skōn\ *n* -s [ISV ¹*musk* + *-one*] **:** an oily macrocyclic ketone $C_{16}H_{30}O$ that is the chief odoriferous constituent of musk and is used similarly in perfumes; 3-methyl-cyclo-pentadecan-one
**mus·cose** \ˈmə,skōs\ *adj* [L *muscosus*, fr. *musc-* + *-osus* -ose] **:** MOSSY
**mus·co·va·do** *also* **mus·ca·va·do** \,məskəˈvä(,)dō, -vā(,)-\ *n* -s [Sp or Pg; Sp (*azúcar*) *mascabado*, fr. Pg (*açúcar*) *mascavado*, fr. *açúcar* sugar + *mascavado*, past part. of *mascavar* to adulterate, separate raw sugar (from molasses), fr. (assumed) VL *minuscapare*, fr. L *minus* less + *caput* head — more at MINUS, HEAD] **:** unrefined or raw sugar obtained from the juice of the sugarcane by evaporation and draining off the molasses
**muscovian** *adj, cap* [NL *Moscovia* + E *-an*] *obs* **:** MUSCOVITE
**¹mus·co·vite** \ˈməskə,vīt, *usu* -īd·+V\ *also* **mos·co·vite** \ˈmäskō,-\ *n* -s [ML or NL *Muscovia, Moscovia* Moscow (fr. ORuss *Moskovŭ*) + E *-ite*] **1** *cap* **a :** a native or resident of the ancient principality of Moscow or of the city of Moscow **b :** RUSSIAN **2** [*muscovy (glass)* + E *-ite*] **:** a mineral essentially $KAl_3Si_3O_{10}(OH)_2$ consisting of common or potassium mica that is usu. colorless or pale brown — see MICA **3 :** a dark greenish gray that is bluer and lighter than sagebrush green and bluer and stronger than castor gray
**²muscovite** \"\ *adj, usu cap* **1 :** of, belonging to, or characteristic of the ancient principality of Moscow, the city of Moscow, or Muscovites **2 :** RUSSIAN
**mus·co·vit·iza·tion** \,məskə,vīd·ə̇ˈzāshən\ *n* -s **:** conversion of a rock or mineral into muscovite
**mus·co·vit·ize** \ˈməskə,vīd·,īz\ *vt* -ED/-ING/-S **:** to convert (a rock or mineral) wholly or partially into muscovite
**mus·co·vy duck** \ˈmə,skōvē-, (,)məˈskōvē-\ *also* **muscovy** *n* -ES *usu cap M* [fr. *Muscovy* principality of Moscow, Russia, fr. ML or NL *Muscovia*] **:** a duck (*Cairina moschata*) native from Mexico to southern Brazil but widely kept in domestication that is larger than the mallard and has a small crest and red caruncles about the eyes and forehead — called also *musk duck*
**muscul-** *or* **musculo-** *comb form* [LL *muscul-*, fr. L *musculus* — more at MUSCLE] **1 :** muscle ⟨*muscul*ar⟩ ⟨*muscul*in⟩ ⟨*musculo*spiral⟩ **2** *usu* **musculo- :** muscular and ⟨*musculo*epithelial⟩ ⟨*musculo*fibrous⟩
**mus·cu·lar** \ˈməskyələ(r)\ *adj* [*muscul-* + *-ar*] **1 a :** constituting or consisting of muscle ⟨~ fiber⟩ ⟨~ tissue⟩ **b :** of, relating to, or performed by the muscles ⟨~ energy⟩ ⟨~ activity⟩ **2 :** affecting the muscles ⟨~ fatigue⟩ ⟨~ atrophy⟩ **3 :** characterized by good musculature **:** SINEWY ⟨a ~ young man⟩ ⟨the swordfish is very ~ and a very rapid swimmer

—S.W.Tinker⟩ **4 a** : of or relating to physical strength : having actual or potential power : BRAWNY, MIGHTY ⟨~ rivers of the Rockies —J.H.Bradley⟩ ⟨white yawls, ~ with sail —George Loveridge⟩ **b** : of or relating to strength of expression or character : VIGOROUS, FORCEFUL ⟨capable of writing intensely ~ dramatic prose —Kenneth Tynan⟩ ⟨brings a fine resounding voice to the singing that fits the ~ music of the . . . fisherfolk —Oscar Brand⟩ ⟨for all its . . . ~ decisiveness, it is a calm and reasoned performance —H.S.Commager⟩ **c** : expressed in physical works or healthy activity ⟨~ Christianity⟩ — **mus·cu·lar·ly** *adv*

**muscular dystrophy** *n* : a hereditary disease characterized by progressive wasting of muscles

**mus·cu·la·ris** \ˌməskyəˈla(a)rəs\ *n* -ES [NL, fr. *muscul-* + *-aris* -ar] **1** : the smooth muscular layer of the wall of various more or less contractile organs (as the bladder) — called also *muscularis propria* **2** : the thin layer of smooth muscle that forms part of a mucous membrane — called also *muscularis mucosae*

**mus·cu·lar·i·ty** \ˌməskyəˈlarəd·ē, -ətē, *also* -ler-\ *n* -ES : the quality or state of being muscular : VIGOR, BRAWN

**muscular rheumatism** *n* : FIBROSITIS

**muscular stomach** *n* : GIZZARD 1

**mus·cu·la·tion** \ˌməskyəˈlāshən\ *n* -S [ISV *muscul-* + *-ation*] : MUSCULATURE

**mus·cu·la·ture** \ˈməskyələˌchu̇(ə)r, -ü̇ə, -ˌchə(r) *sometimes* -lə-ˌtyü-\ *n* -S [F, fr. *muscul-* + L *-atus* -ate + F *-ure*] **1** : the muscles of an animal or of any part of it that are related to each other and function together ⟨~ of the leg⟩ ⟨~ of the heart⟩ **2** : the muscular system ⟨tensions are transferred . . . across the footlights and into the ~ of every spectator —John Martin⟩ **3** : a well-developed underlying structure of or as if of muscles ⟨elaborate ~ of the male figures —J.T.Soby⟩ ⟨a sustaining pulse for the whole musical ~ —Virgil Thomson⟩

**mus·cu·lo·cutaneous nerve** \ˌməskyəlō+ . . . -\ *n* [ISV *muscul-* + *cutaneous*] **1** : a mixed nerve giving off motor fibers to muscles and receiving sensory fibers from muscles and skin **2 a** : a large branch of the brachial plexus supplying various parts of the upper arm (as flexor muscles) and forearm (as the skin) **b** : the superficial peroneal nerve

**mus·cu·lo·epithelial** \"+\ *adj* [*muscul-* + *epithelial*] : having both an epithelial and a muscular function — used of ectodermal cells of invertebrates (as hydra) that cover the body surface and contract the body

**mus·cu·lo·membranous** \"+\ *adj* [*muscul-* + *membranous*] : composed of both muscle and membrane

**mus·cu·lo·phrenic** \"+\ *adj* [*muscul-* + *phrenic*] : supplying the muscles of the body wall and the diaphragm ⟨~ nerve⟩ ⟨~ blood vessel⟩

**mus·cu·lo·skeletal** \"+\ *adj* [*muscul-* + *skeletal*] : of, relating to, or involving both musculature and skeleton ⟨~ defects⟩ ⟨the ~ organization of the arm⟩

**mus·cu·lo·spiral** \"+\ *adj* [*muscul-* + *spiral*] : of, relating to, or characterizing muscles having a spiral direction or structures having a spiral arrangement in relation to muscles

**musculospiral groove** *n* : a long shallow oblique groove in the shaft of the humerus that lodges the radial nerve

**mus·cu·lo·trop·ic** \ˌməskyəlōˈträpik\ *adj* [*muscul-* + *-tropic*] : having a direct usu. stimulatory effect on muscle

**musculous** *adj* [MF *musculeux*, fr. L *musculosus*, fr. *muscul-* + *-osus* -ous] *obs* : MUSCULAR

**mus·cu·lus** \ˈməskyələs\ *n*, *pl* **mus·cu·li** \-yəˌlī\ [L — more at MUSCLE] : MUSCLE

[1]**muse** \ˈmyüz\ *vb* -ED/-ING/-S [ME *musen*, fr. MF *muser* to idle, loiter, muse (prob. orig., "to gape, stare"), fr. *muse* mouth of an animal, snout, fr. ML *musus*] *vi* **1 a** : to become absorbed in thought : RUMINATE ⟨~ upon the continuity and the tragic finality of life —Irving Howe⟩ ⟨its suggestions set the imagination *musing* —Irwin Edman⟩ **b** *archaic* : to look reflectively ⟨the mind is left to ~ upon the solemn scene —William Wordsworth⟩ **2** *archaic* : to become astonished : WONDER, MARVEL ⟨do not ~ at me my most worthy friends —Shak.⟩ ~ *vt* **1** *archaic* : to ask oneself : WONDER ⟨~ what this young fox may mean —Matthew Arnold⟩ **2 a** : to ruminate on ⟨*mused* the question considerably once more —*Harper's*⟩ **b** : to say or think reflectively ⟨I could sell the house, she *mused*, but then where would I go⟩ **3** *obs* : to puzzle over (a fact or occurrence) : be surprised that ⟨I ~ my Lord of Gloucester is not come —Shak.⟩ **syn** see PONDER

[2]**muse** \"\ *n* -S [ME, fr. *musen*, v.] : a state of deep thought or dreamy abstraction : BROWN STUDY

[3]**muse** \"\ *n* -S [ME, fr. MF, fr. L *Musa*, fr. Gk *Mousa*; prob. akin to Gk *mnasthai* to remember — more at MIND] **1 a** *usu cap* : any of nine sister goddesses associated with the Graces in Greek mythology and regarded as presiding over learning and the creative arts (as poetry and music) — usu. used in pl. ⟨the *Muses* . . . gave the poet his song and sang it through his lips —T.B.L.Webster⟩ **b** *sometimes cap* : the personification of a guiding genius or principal source of inspiration ⟨an atmosphere in which the ~ of serendipity is most likely to be wooed and won —*Lamp*⟩ **2** *sometimes cap* : the creative spirit of an individual ⟨the situations that tempt his dramatic ~ are strained, acute situations —Leslie Rees⟩ ⟨pay the writing schools hard cash to liberate their ~ —Edward Uhlan⟩ **3 a** : a composer of songs or verse : POET ⟨so may some gentle ~ with lucky words favor my destined urn —John Milton⟩ **b** *archaic* : LIBERAL ARTS; *esp* : the creative arts — usu. used in pl. ⟨his retirement . . . was to the last devoted to the ~*s* —Connop Thirlwall⟩

[4]**muse** \"\ *n* -S [ME, fr. MF, fr. *muser* to muse, play the bagpipe — more at [1]MUSE] **1** : BAGPIPE **2** : the mouthpiece of a bagpipe

[5]**muse** \ˈmyüs, -üz\ *dial Eng var of* MEUSE

**muse·ful** \ˈmyüzfəl\ *adj* [[2]*muse* + *-ful*] *archaic* : BEMUSED, MEDITATIVE — **muse·ful·ly** \-fəlē\ *adv*

**mu·se·ist** \(ˈ)myüˈzēəst, ˈ=ˌ==\ *n* -S [*museum* + *-ist*] : MUSEOLOGIST

**muse·less** \ˈmyüzləs\ *adj* [[3]*muse* + *-less*] *archaic* : ILLITERATE, UNCULTURED

**musenna** *var of* MESENNA

**museo-** *comb form* [*museum*] : museum ⟨*museology*⟩

**mu·se·og·ra·phy** \ˌmyüzēˈägrəfē\ *n* -ES [F *muséographie*, fr. *muséo-* museo- + *-graphie* -graphy] : museum methods of classification and display

**mu·seo·log·i·cal** \ˌmyüzēəˈläjəkəl\ *adj* : of or relating to museology

**mu·se·ol·o·gist** \ˌ==ˈäləjəst\ *n* -S : a specialist in museum work

**mu·se·ol·o·gy** \-jē\ *n* -ES [*museo-* + *-logy*] : the science or profession of museum organization, equipment, and management

**mus·er** \ˈmyüzə(r)\ *n* -S [ME, fr. *musen* to muse + *-er* — more at MUSE] : one that muses

**muset** *n* -S [MF *mussette*, *mucette*, dim. of *musse*, *muce* — more at MEUSE] *obs* : MEUSE

**mu·sette** \myüˈzet\ *n* -S [F, fr. MF, dim. of *muse* bagpipe — more at MUSE] **1 a** : a small bellows-filled bagpipe popular in France esp. in the 18th century and having a soft sweet tone **b** *also* **musette pipe** : a small simple oboe **c** : a reed stop of 4-foot or 8-foot pitch with a bright pleasing tone **2 a** : a quiet pastoral air that often has a drone bass, is adapted to the musette, and often constitutes the middle or trio of a group of three gavottes in which the first and third are the same **b** : a gavotte danced to the tune of a musette **3** *or* **musette bag** : a small canvas or leather knapsack suspended by a strap from the shoulder and used esp. by members of the armed forces for carrying provisions and personal belongings

**mu·se·um** \(ˈ)myüˈzēəm, ÷ ˈ=ˌ=\ *n* -S [L *Museum*, fr. Gk *Mouseion*, fr. neut. of *Mouseios* of the Muses, fr. *Mousa* Muse — more at MUSE] **1** *obs* : a scholar's library : STUDY ⟨admitted to an audience in his ~ —Charles Johnstone⟩ **2 a** : an institution devoted to the procurement, care, and display of objects of lasting interest or value ⟨British *Museum*⟩ ⟨American *Museum* of Natural History⟩ **b** : a room, building, or locale where a collection of objects is put on exhibition ⟨art ~⟩ ⟨science ~⟩ ⟨striking outdoor ~, two hundred acres of it —Bernard De Voto⟩ **c** : EXHIBIT, COLLECTION ⟨the little ~ of . . . lore assembled in the foyer —Claudia Cassidy⟩ **3** : something that resembles a museum ⟨the parlor was a ~ of Victorian bric-a-brac⟩ ⟨codes are maintained as no mere ~*s* of legal rules and principles —F.A.Ogg & Harold Zink⟩

**museum beetle** *n* : any of several beetles (esp. of the genera *Anthrenus* and *Dermestes*) that feed as larvae esp. on dried animal products (as skins or insect specimens)

**mu·se·um·ist** \-məst\ *n* -S : MUSEOLOGIST

**museum jar** *n* : a glass or pottery container capable of being tightly closed or sealed and used esp. for the storage or display of preserved organisms or dissections

**museum piece** *n* **1** : an object of lasting interest or value (as an antique) suitable for or preserved in a museum ⟨early pie plates, now *museum pieces* —*Amer. Guide Series: Conn.*⟩ ⟨a *museum piece* volume —Claudia Cassidy⟩ ⟨some classics, no longer appropriate for daily use, become . . . *museum pieces* periodically dusted off by the critics —Waldo Frank⟩ **2** : something antiquated or obsolete : a thing of the past ⟨tended to regard the old clerk of court as a *museum piece*⟩ ⟨the taxicabs . . . are early-century *museum pieces* —E.O.Hauser⟩ ⟨contains the substance of lectures . . . which now are almost dated *museum pieces* —Irwin Edman⟩

**mus·gu** \ˈməsˌgü\ *also* **mos·gu** \ˈmäs-\ *n*, *pl* **musgu** *or* **musgus** *also* **mosgu** *or* **mosgus** *usu cap* **1 a** : a Negro people of the central Sudan in the Logone valley south of Lake Chad **b** : a member of such people **2** : the language of the Musgu people

[1]**mush** \ˈməsh, *chiefly dial* ˈmu̇sh\ *n* -ES [prob. alter. of *mash*] **1** : cornmeal boiled in water, eaten hot as a cereal or pudding, fried as cakes, or molded until cold and then sliced and fried — compare HASTY PUDDING **2** : something having the consistency of cornmeal mush ⟨perspired so much the cast under his armpits . . . turned to ~ —Earle Birney⟩ **3** : something soft and spongy or shapeless: as **a** : a formless mass **b** : weak sentimentality or mawkish amorousness : DRIVEL ⟨oratorical ~⟩ ⟨the tenderness never becomes ~ —Coulton Waugh⟩ ⟨it isn't youthful romance, it's the ~ of senility —Erle Stanley Gardner⟩ **c** *slang* : MOUTH, FACE ⟨slammed him in the ~ with the ball, and his eyes watered —J.T.Farrell⟩

[2]**mush** \"\ *vb* -ED/-ING/-ES *vt* **1** *chiefly dial* : to reduce to or mix up in a crumbly mass : CRUSH, PULVERIZE — often used with *up* ⟨~ up papier-mâché animals —R.L.Shayon⟩ **2** *slang* : to make amorously sentimental — used with *up* ⟨he would ~ it up and . . . we would sway sweet and slow —R.P.Warren⟩ ~ *vi* **1** : to give way : CRUMBLE, SQUASH ⟨does not ~ down —*advt*⟩ ⟨the top of the pile sank, the lower logs ~*ing* out toward the water —*Mich. Log Marks*⟩ **2** *of an airplane* **a** : to fly in a half-stalled condition with controls ineffective ⟨throttled back and ~*ed* in —Walt Sheldon⟩ **b** : to fail to gain altitude or to lose it when the angle of attack would normally indicate a gain ⟨he was miles high, ~*ing*, nearly slumping, in the rare air —J.G.Cozzens⟩ **3** *slang* : to be effusive : GUSH; *esp* : to make love in public

[3]**mush** \ˈməsh\ *n* -ES [short for *mushroom*] *slang* : UMBRELLA

[4]**mush** \ˈməsh, *chiefly dial* ˈmu̇sh\ *vb* -ED/-ING/-ES [prob. fr. AmerF *moucher* to go fast, fr. F *mouche* fly, fr. L *musca* — more at MIDGE] *vi* : to hike or travel esp. over snow with a dogsled ⟨~ over a wilderness that no sled track has ever crossed before —Klondy Nelson⟩ ⟨huskies bark excitedly as they ~ across the ice and snow —Robert Meyer⟩ — often used in the imperative as a command to a dog team ⟨snapped the long lash of his whip . . . cried ~ —Frederick Palmer⟩ ~ *vt* : to urge (a dog team) forward ⟨the driver ~*ed* the dogs —Nan Dorland⟩ : transport by means of a dog team

[5]**mush** \"\ *n* -ES : a hike esp. across snow with a dog team

**musha** \ˈmu̇shə\ *interj* [IrGael *māiseadh*, fr. *mā* if + *is* is + *eadh* it] *Irish* — used esp. to express surprise or annoyance

**mus·haa** \müsˈhä\ *n* -S [Ar *mushā'* common] *Islam* : undivided common property

**mush·a·roon** *also* **mush·er·oon** \ˌməshəˈrün\ *dial var of* MUSHROOM

**mushball** \ˈ=ˌ=\ *n* [[1]*mush* + *ball*] : SOFTBALL

**mush·er** \ˈməshə(r), *chiefly dial* ˈmu̇sh-\ *n* -S [[4]*mush* + *-er*] : one that mushes; *esp* : the driver of a dog team

**mush·et steel** \ˈməshət-\ *or* **mushet's steel** *n*, *usu cap M* [after Robert F. *Mushet* †1891 Eng. metallurgist] : the first self-hardening steel

**mushier** *comparative of* MUSHY

**mushiest** *superlative of* MUSHY

**mush·i·ly** \ˈməshəlē, -li, *chiefly dial* ˈmu̇sh-\ *adv* : in a mawkish or mushy manner

**mush·i·ness** \-shēnəs, -shin-\ *n* -ES : the quality or state of being mushy or mawkishly sentimental

**mush·mel·on** \ˈməshˌmelən\ *n* [by alter.] *dial var of* MUSKMELON

**mushquash** *var of* MUSQUASH

**mush·rat** \ˈməshˌrat\ *dial var of* MUSKRAT

**mushrebiyeh** *var of* MOUCHARABY

[1]**mush·room** \ˈməˌshrüm, -ru̇m, *chiefly dial* |n\ *n* -S *often attrib* [ME *musseroun*, *muscheron*, fr. MF *mousseron*, fr. OF *meisseron*, fr. LL *mussirion-*, *mussirio*] **1 a (1)** : any of various enlarged complex aerial fleshy fruiting bodies of fungi (as most members of the class Basidiomycetes) that are technically sporophores, arise from an underground mycelium, and consist typically of a stem bearing a flattened pileus with spores developing in the folds or pores of a hymenium on its undersurface **(2)** : such a fruiting body that is edible; *esp* : MEADOW MUSHROOM — compare TOADSTOOL **b** : FUNGUS 1 **2** *archaic* : UPSTART 1 **3** *slang* : UMBRELLA **4** : a woman's low-crowned hat with a convex brim **5 a** : MUSHROOM ANCHOR **b** : the head of a mushroom anchor without the shank **6** : a metal traffic guide about 18 inches in diameter fixed in the pavement surface at an intersection **7** : a bullet with a soft or hollow point that flattens on impact **8** : an obturator for a cannon **9** : a lateral and radial extension of reinforcing rods into the slab at the top of each column in a system of reinforced-concrete construction permitting the weight of the floors to be borne by the columns rather than by external walls **10** : a spreading cloud (as of smoke or debris) ⟨~ of exploding five-inch shells —K.M.Dodson⟩ ⟨radioactive ~ from an atom-bomb explosion⟩ ⟨the stem of the ~ caused by the intense heat sucking up . . . debris —E.P.Boland⟩ **11** : BEAVER 6

mushroom 1a(1)

[2]**mushroom** \"\ *vb* -ED/-ING/-S *vi* **1** : to spring up suddenly or multiply rapidly ⟨towns . . . ~*ed* about factories near water power —R.H.Brown⟩ ⟨accidents ~*ed* so prodigiously . . . that it was evident some basic factor had been overlooked —Stanley Frank⟩ — often used with *up* ⟨stools and benches decorated with her handiwork had ~*ed* up all over the house —Virginia D. Dawson & Betty D. Wilson⟩ **2 a** : to flatten at the end due to impact — used esp. of a bullet ⟨bullets ~*ed* well, so the animal did not go far —W.Z.Bradley⟩ **b** : to puff out or spread ⟨the cloud of radioactive ash . . . ~*s* from the bomb —*Newsweek*⟩ ⟨the homely aroma . . . came ~*ing* over us —William Sansom⟩; *esp* : to well up and spread out laterally from a central source ⟨the fire was ~*ing* under the ceiling when fire fighters . . . arrived —*Springfield (Mass.) Union*⟩ **c** : to become enlarged or extended : EXPAND, GROW ⟨appetites ~ on the trail —Joyce R. Muench⟩ ⟨from a sleepy little rural community . . . it has ~*ed* into a fast-growing center —Martha Alexander⟩ ⟨the vast ~*ing* of air travel —*Fortune*⟩ **d** : EXPLODE ⟨an enemy plane . . . ~*s* in your gunsight —R.L.Scott⟩ **3** : to gather mushrooms ~ *vt* **1** : to cause to spread or flatten out ⟨hammering can . . . ~ the end of the handle —H.D.Burghardt & Aaron Axelrod⟩ **2** : to cause to extend or multiply suddenly or rapidly : EXPAND ⟨a city swollen with a ~*ed* population —Earl Brown⟩ ⟨~*ed* his interests over three quarters of the U.S. —*Time*⟩

**mushroom anchor** *n* : an anchor that has a bowl-shaped head with the shank welded to its center, is capable of grasping the ground however it falls, and is used chiefly for permanent moorings

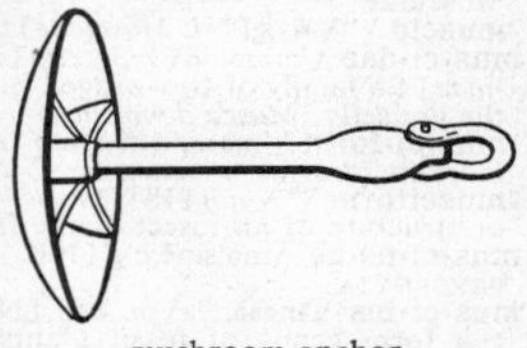

mushroom anchor

**mushroom body** *n* : any of various neural centers in the insect brain that are esp. well developed in social insects and are thought to be possible integration or association centers

**mushroom chair** *n* : a turned chair of the 17th and early 18th centuries having enlarged and usu. flattened balls topping and made in one piece with the front posts

**mushroom coral** *n* : any of various flattened disk-shaped stony corals of *Fungia* or related genera that are usu. solitary and in the adult stage completely free from the substrate

**mushroom jellyfish** *n* : a nearly globular brownish scyphozoan jellyfish (*Stomolophus meleagris*) having a greatly reduced mouth and often occurring in swarms many miles in extent

**mushroomlike** \ˈ=ˌ=ˌ=\ *adj* **1** : resembling a mushroom in appearance **2** : springing up suddenly

**mushroom mite** *n* : an Australian tarsonemid mite (*Tyrophagus putrescentiae*) or a related mite that infests fungi and is sometimes a house pest

**mushroom pin** *n* : SPOOL PIN

**mushroom root rot** *n* : a root rot caused by an agaric, esp. by the oak fungus (*Armillaria mellea*)

**mushrooms** *pl of* MUSHROOM, *pres 3d sing of* MUSHROOM

**mushroom steamer** *n* : TRAMP STEAMER

**mushroom valve** *n* : a LIFT valve resembling a mushroom in shape

**mushroom ventilator** *n* : a ship's ventilator with a curved hood that may be raised or lowered to regulate the air in cabins below deck

**mush·roomy** \ˈməˌshrümē, -ru̇m-\ *adj* : resembling a mushroom

**mushroon** *dial var of* MUSHROOM

**mush rot** *n* [[1]*mush*] : LEAK 3

**mushsquash** *var of* MUSQUASH

**mushy** \ˈməshē, -shi, *chiefly dial* ˈmu̇sh-\ *adj* -ER/-EST [[1]*mush* + *-y*] **1 a** : having the consistency of mush : SOFT, SPONGY ⟨concrete mix should be ~ but not soupy —*Building Estimating & Contracting*⟩ ⟨the ground is covered with a soft, ~ tundra carpet —W.W.Atwood b.1906⟩ **b** : lacking in definition : HAZY, BLURRED ⟨with more and more ~ effects, "artistic" photographers made imitation paintings —T.H.Benton b.1889⟩ ⟨you . . . hear the pings faintly through a voice tube and they sound ~ —H.S.Pease⟩ **c** : lacking precision of performance : SLUGGISH ⟨the plane became ~ and controls lost efficiency —John Lewellen⟩ ⟨at low speeds, aileron movements feel ~ and light —*Flying*⟩ **2** : excessively tender or emotional : SENTIMENTAL, EFFUSIVE ⟨~ handling of crime —*Emporia (Kans.) Gazette*⟩ ⟨a ~ sentiment, unstable and only half-sincere —William McFee⟩; *esp* : mawkishly amorous ⟨find a love story in that bunch of old magazines — a nice ~ one —*Lippincott's Mag.*⟩ **syn** see SENTIMENTAL

**mushy chick** *or* **mushy chick disease** *n* : a nonspecific and highly fatal infection of newly hatched chickens or turkeys marked by a soft swollen abdomen and foul odors and caused by bacteria entering the body through the umbilical opening

[1]**mu·sic** \ˈmyüzik, -zēk\ *n* -S *often attrib* [ME *musik*, fr. OF *musique*, fr. L *musica*, fr. Gk *mousikē*, any art presided over by the Muses, esp. music, fr. fem. of *mousikos* of the Muses, musical, fr. *Mousa* Muse + *-ikos* -ic — more at MUSE] **1 a** : the science or art of incorporating pleasing, expressive, or intelligible combinations of vocal or instrumental tones into a composition having definite structure and continuity ⟨~ as . . . a combination of rhythm, melody, harmony, and counterpoint, has existed less than a thousand years —Deems Taylor⟩ **b** : vocal or instrumental sounds having rhythm, melody, or harmony ⟨~ of a choir⟩ ⟨~ of a hurdy-gurdy⟩ **2 a** : an agreeable sound that is likened to a musical composition : EUPHONY ⟨~ of the nightingale⟩ ⟨the morning on the water has sharpened our appetites, and the sizzling and spluttering below is ~ in our ears —T.C.Roughley⟩; *specif* : the cry of hounds at sight of the game **b** : an unpleasant medley of sound : RACKET, DIN ⟨the stairwell echoed the ~ of clashing swords⟩; *esp* : a reprimand or legal prosecution for a misdeed ⟨urged the hunted man to give himself up and face the ~⟩ **c** : a quality of expression or movement characterized by tonal harmony or rhythmical grace ⟨to him two blending thoughts give a ~ perceptible as two blending notes of a lute —Ezra Pound⟩ ⟨the ~ of lovingly orchestrated words —*Saturday Rev.*⟩ ⟨a purely abstract language of form — a visual ~ —Roger Fry⟩ ⟨women with . . . waists of agile ~ —Dudley Fitts⟩ **d** : spiritual impulse or animation ⟨that sad and universal ~ which stirs when we look back upon our youth —V.S.Pritchett⟩ ⟨the ~ of her own happiness —Helen Howe⟩ ⟨the sweet ~ of free institutions —A.E.Stevenson b.1900⟩ **3 a** *obs* : a piece of music composed or performed ⟨I have assailed her with ~*s* —Shak.⟩ **b** : a musical accompaniment ⟨a play set to ~⟩ **4 a** : a musical ensemble — now used chiefly of a military band ⟨another field ~, equipped with drums, cymbals, horns . . . played with great abandon —G.S.Patton⟩ **b** *chiefly dial* : a musical instrument ⟨fetch your ~ into the house —Vance Randolph & G.P.Wilson⟩ **5 a** : the score of a musical composition set down on paper ⟨leafed through the ~⟩ **b** : a recorded performance of a musical composition ⟨stacked the hi-fi with soft ~⟩

[2]**music** \"\ *vb* **musicked; musicked; musicking; musics** *vi* : to compose or perform music ⟨the man could talk in Latin, ~, mime —J.C.Ransom⟩ ~ *vt* **1** *archaic* : to instruct in music **2** : to express in or set to music ⟨~*s* every jingle and clash and call —John Collier b.1901⟩

**mu·si·ca fal·sa** \ˌmyüzəkəˈfȯl(t)sə\ *n* [ML, lit., false music] : MUSICA FICTA

**musica fic·ta** \-ˈfiktə\ *n* [ML, lit., feigned music] : contrapuntal music in which accidentals or notes foreign to the mode are introduced — called also *false music*

[1]**mu·si·cal** \ˈmyüzəkəl, -zēk-\ *adj* [ME, fr. MF, fr. ML *musicalis*, fr. L *musica* music + *-alis* -al — more at MUSIC] **1 a** : of or relating to music or to its notation or performance ⟨~ form⟩ ⟨~ instrument⟩ **b** : having the pleasing harmonious qualities of music : MELODIOUS ⟨~ voice⟩ ⟨~ name⟩ ⟨the piano sonata is an . . . exquisitely ~ piece —Edward Sackville-West & Desmond Shawe-Taylor⟩ ⟨the little frogs are ~ —John Burroughs⟩ **2 a** : having an interest in or talent for music ⟨comes from a ~ family⟩ **b** : versed in music ⟨a galaxy of ~ artists⟩ **3** : set to or accompanied by music ⟨~ extravaganza⟩ **4** : of or relating to musicians or music lovers ⟨~ organization⟩ — **mu·si·cal·ly** \-zək(ə)lē, -zēk-, -li\ *adv*

[2]**musical** \"\ *n* -S **1** *archaic* : MUSICALE **2** : a film or theatrical production typically of a sentimental or humorous nature and consisting of musical numbers and dialogue based upon a unifying plot — called also *musical comedy*

**musical accent** *n* : PITCH ACCENT 2, INTONATION

**musical box** *n*, *chiefly Brit* : MUSIC BOX

**musical chairs** *n pl but sing in constr* **1** : a game in which players march to music in single file around a row of chairs numbering one less than the players and scramble for seats when the music stops, one player and one chair being eliminated each time until one of the last two marchers claims the only remaining seat — called also *going to Jerusalem* **2** : manipulating resources or maneuvering for advantage ⟨it was the game of *musical chairs* in Washington last month as . . . aviation leaders all moved up a notch —*Aero Digest*⟩ ⟨motorists played *musical chairs* while parking lot owners did a land-office business —*Springfield (Mass.) Union*⟩

**musical clock** *n* : a clock that plays a tune at set intervals or as desired

**musical comedy** *n* : MUSICAL

**mu·si·cale** \ˌmyüzəˈkal, -zē-, *sometimes* -ˈkäl *or* -ˈkȧl\ *n* -S [F (*soirée*) *musicale*, lit., musical evening] : a usu. private concert of music typically comprising a social entertainment

**musical flame** *n* : a flame that produces a musical note by setting in vibration the air in an open tube held over it

**musical glasses** *n pl* **1** : GLASS HARMONICA, HARMONICA b **2** : a set of drinking glasses tuned to the scale and played by rubbing their brims with moistened fingers

**mu·si·cal·i·ty** \ˌmyüzəˈkaləd·ē, -zē-, -lətē, -i\ *n* -ES **1** : the quality or state of being musical : MELODIOUSNESS ⟨the supreme ~ of Verdi's opera —Herbert Kupferberg⟩ ⟨~ of her words —*Saturday Rev.*⟩ **2** : sensitivity to, knowledge of, or talent for producing music ⟨an audience of genuine ~ —*Saturday Rev.*⟩ ⟨enabled his ~ to flower —Virgil Thomson⟩

**mu·si·cal·ization** \ˌmyüzəkələˈzāshən, -zēk-, -ˌlīˈz-\ *n* -S : an act or instance of setting to music ⟨a ~ of the novel⟩

**mu·si·cal·ize** \ˈ==kəˌlīz\ *vt* -ED/-ING/-S [[1]*musical* + *-ize*] : to set to music ⟨refused to let them ~ his play⟩

**mu·si·cal·ness** *n* -ES : MUSICALITY
**musical prawn** *n* : a rather small prawn (*Penaeopsis novae-guineae*) both sexes of which possess stridulating organs on the thorax
**musical sand** *n* : sand that emits a musical note when stirred or trodden on
**musical saw** *n* : a handsaw made to produce melody by bending the blade with varying tension while sounding it with a small hammer or a violin bow
**mu·si·ca men·su·ra·ta** \ˌmyüzəkəˌmenchəˈrädə, -ˌmen(t)səˈ-, -rädˑə\ *n* [NL, lit., measured music] : MENSURAL MUSIC
**music box** *n* **1** : a container enclosing an apparatus capable of mechanically reproducing music esp. activated by clockwork ⟨Swiss *music box*⟩ **2** : JUKEBOX ⟨more nickels were shoved into the mechanical *music box* —Robert Hazel⟩
**music director** *n* : one in charge of musical activities (as in a school)
**music drama** *n* : an opera in which the action is not interrupted by formal song divisions (as recitatives or arias) and the music is determined solely by dramatic appropriateness — compare LEITMOTIV
**music gallery** *n* : MINSTREL GALLERY
**music hall** *n* : a vaudeville theater or variety show ⟨a song-and-dance man famous in London *music halls*⟩
**mu·si·cian** \myüˈzishən\ *n* -S [ME *musicien*, fr. MF, fr. L *musica* + MF *-ien* -ian — more at MUSIC] : one skilled in music; *esp* : a composer, conductor, or professional performer of music
**mu·si·cian·er** \-sh(ə)nə(r)\ *n* -S : MUSICIAN
**mu·si·cian·ly** \-shənlē, -li\ *adj* : having or exhibiting the taste or artistry appropriate to a skilled musician ⟨a ~ interpretation⟩ ⟨the tenor's wife is his ~ accompanist —Roland Gelatt⟩
**mu·si·cian·ship** \-ˌship\ *n* : artistry and insight displayed in the interpretation or rendition of music ⟨the finesse, the virtuosity and the ~ of this performance —Robert Donington⟩
**musicked** *past of* MUSIC
**mu·sick·er** \ˈmyüzəkə(r)\ *n* -S [²*music* + *-er*] *chiefly dial* : MUSICIAN
**musicking** *pres part of* MUSIC
**mu·sic·less** \ˈmyüziklės, -zēk-\ *adj* : lacking in harmony or melodious quality ⟨~ instruments⟩ ⟨this ~ biography of a musician —P.H.Lang⟩
**music lyre** *n* : a lyriform spring clamp on a stem that is used to hold the music book of a player in a marching band and is attachable to the instrument or the player's arm
**mu·si·co** \ˈmyüzəˌkō\ *n* -S [It, fr. L *musicus*, fr. *musicus*, adj., of music, fr. Gk *mousikos* of the Muses, musical — more at MUSIC] : MUSICIAN
**musico-** *comb form* [¹*music*] **1** : music ⟨*musicography*⟩ ⟨*musicotherapy*⟩ **2** : musical and ⟨*musicodramatic*⟩ ⟨*musicoliturgical*⟩
**music of the spheres** : an ethereal harmony supposed by the Pythagoreans to be produced by the vibration of the celestial spheres upon which the stars and planets were thought to move — compare HARMONY OF THE SPHERES
**mu·si·cog·ra·phy** \ˌmyüzəˈkägrəfē, -zē-, -fi\ *n* -ES [*musico-* + *-graphy*] : the art or science of writing music
**mu·si·co·log·i·cal** \ˌmyüzəkəˈläjəkəl\ *adj* : of or relating to musicology
**mu·si·col·o·gist** \ˌ==ˈkäləjəst\ *n* -S : a specialist in musicology

music lyre

**mu·si·col·o·gy** \-jē, -ji\ *n* -ES [It *musicologia*, fr. *musico-* + *-logia* -logy] : a study of music as a branch of knowledge or field of research; *esp* : the historical and theoretical investigation and analysis of specific types of music
**mu·si·co·therapy** \ˌmyüzə(ˌ)kō+\ *n* [*musico-* + *therapy*] : the treatment of disease (as mental disease) by means of music
**music roll** *n* : a roll of paper on which music for a player piano is recorded in perforations that actuate the keys by regulating the flow of air from a bellows
**musics** *pl of* MUSIC, *pres 3d sing of* MUSIC
**music shell** *n* : a marine gastropod shell (esp. *Voluta musica* of the East Indies or a related species) having color markings suggesting printed music
**music supervisor** *n* : one who has general oversight of musical instruction in a school system or in some division of it
**music visualization** *n* **1** : the creation of a modern or ballet dance entirely from designs suggested by musical accompaniment **2** : a dance that constitutes a direct translation of music into motion
**music wire** *n* : steel wire used for the strings of musical instruments or for helical springs; *specif* : PIANO WIRE
**mus·i·mon** \ˈmyüsəˌmän\ *n* -S [L *musimon-, musimo, musmon-, musmo*] : MOUFLON
¹**musine** \ˈmyüˌsīn, ˈməˌs-\ *adj* [irreg. fr. L *mus* mouse + E *-ine* — more at MOUSE] : of or relating to mice : MURINE : resembling a mouse : MOUSY
²**musine** \"\ *n* -S : MURINE
¹**mus·ing** \ˈmyüziŋ, -zēŋ\ *n* -S [ME, fr. gerund of *musen* to muse — more at MUSE] : MEDITATION
²**musing** \"\ *adj* [ME, fr. pres. part. of *musen* to muse] : thoughtfully abstracted : MEDITATIVE — **mus·ing·ly** *adv*
**mu·sique con·crète** \mü̅ēzēkkōⁿkret\ *n* [F, lit., concrete music] : the composition by tape-recording of freely selected and treated sounds and natural noises into an artistically ordered continuum
**mu·sive** \ˈmyüsiv, -uziv\ *adj* [fr. obs. E *musive*, n., mosaic, fr. LL *musivum* — more at MOSAIC] *archaic* : MOSAIC
¹**musk** \ˈməsk\ *n* -S [ME *muske*, fr. MF *musc*, fr. LL *muscus*, fr. Gk *moschos*, fr. Per *mushk* castoreum, musk, fr. Skt *muṣka* testicle, scrotum, vulva, dim. of *mūṣ*, mouse — more at MOUSE] **1 a** : a substance that has a penetrating persistent odor, that is obtained from a sac situated under the skin of the abdomen of the male musk deer, that when fresh in the pods is brown and unctuous and when dried is a grainy powder, that varies in quality according to the season and age of the animal, and that is used chiefly in the form of a tincture as a fixative in perfumes **b** : any of various strong-smelling substances obtained from other animals (as the musk-ox, muskrat, or civet cat) **c** : any of various synthetic compounds (as muscone, civetone, or musk ambrette) having musky odors and used similarly to natural musk **2** : the musk deer or a similar animal **3 a** : MUSK PLANT **b** : MUSK MALLOW **c** : MUSK CLOVER **d** : GRAPE HYACINTH **e** *Austral* : any of several shrubs of the genus *Olearia* **4** : a dark grayish yellowish brown that is stronger, slightly yellower, and lighter than seal brown, slightly redder and lighter than sepia brown, lighter and stronger than otter brown, and very slightly redder and deeper than lama or bison — called also *café noir*, *cattail* **5 a** : the odor of musk **b** : an odor (as an animal scent) that resembles musk ⟨~ of mignonette —Elizabeth S. Hardy⟩ ⟨the ~ where a polecat had passed —Edwin Granberry⟩
²**musk** \"\ *vt* -ED/-ING/-S : to perfume with musk
**muskadel** *var of* MUSCATEL
**musk ambrette** *n* : a white to yellow powdery synthetic musk $C_{12}H_{16}N_2O_5$ made from *meta*-cresol; methyl-*tert*-butyl-dinitro-anisole
**muskat** *var of* MUSCAT
**muskat nut** *n* : any of several nuts yielded by trees of the genus *Myristica* that resemble nutmegs and are used for oil
**musk bag** *n* : an odor-producing gland; *esp* : the preputial odor-bearing gland of the male musk deer — called also *musk gland*
**musk beaver** *n* : MUSKRAT
**musk beetle** *n* : a European longicorn beetle (*Aromia moschata*) having an odor suggesting that of attar of roses
**musk buffalo** *n* : MUSK-OX
**musk cat** *n* **1** : an animal producing musk: as **a** : CIVET CAT **b** : GENET **2** *obs* **a** : COURTESAN **b** : FOP
**musk cattle** *n* : MUSK-OXEN
**musk cavy** *n* : HUTIA
**musk clover** *n* : a low annual European herb (*Erodium moschatum*) resembling alfilaria — called also *muskus grass*
**musk cow** *n* : a female musk-ox
**musk cucumber** *n* : CASSABANANA
**musk deer** *n* **1** : a small heavy-limbed deer (*Moschus moschiferus*) of the central Asiatic uplands valued for the musk bag of the male and unique among the deers in the possession of a gallbladder **2** : CHEVROTAIN
**musk duck** *n* **1** [alter. of *muscovy duck*] : MUSCOVY DUCK **2** [so called fr. its characteristic odor during the breeding season] : an Australian duck (*Biziura lobata*) having a disk-shaped leathery chin lobe and exuding a musky odor during the breeding season
**mus·keg** \ˈməˌskeg\ *also* **mas·keeg** \ˈmaˌskēg\ *n* -S [of Algonquian origin; akin to Ojibwa *mŭskeg* grassy bog, Cree *maskek*, Fox *maskyägi*] **1** : BOG; *esp* : a sphagnum bog of northern No. America often with tussocks — compare ¹MOOR 1b **2** : an often very thick usu. imperfectly consolidated deposit of partially decayed vegetable matter characteristic of wet boreal regions

musk deer 1

**muskeg moss** *n* : any of various mosses (as of the genera *Sphagnum* or *Hypnum*) that thrive on muskeg
**mus·kel·lunge** *or* **mus·kal·lunge** \ˈməskəˌlənj\ *or* **mas·ki·nonge** \ˈmaskəˌnänj\ *also* **mus·kal·longe** \ˈməskəˌlänj\ *or* **mas·ka·longe** \ˈmas-\ *n, pl* **muskellunge** *or* **muskellunges** *or* **muskallunge** *or* **muskallunges** *or* **maskinonge** *or* **maskinonges** [of Algonquian origin; akin to Ojibwa & Cree *maskinonge, mashkinonge* muskellunge, prob. lit., big fish] : a large No. American pike (*Esox masquinongy*) which may exceed six feet in length with a weight of 60 to 80 pounds and is highly prized as a game fish, the typical form occurring in the Great Lakes and being brownish green spotted with black — see CHAUTAUQUA MUSKELLUNGE
¹**mus·ket** \ˈməskət, *usu* -əd·+V\ *n* -S [ME *muskett*, fr. ONF *mousquet*, dim. of *mousque* fly, fr. L *musca* — more at MIDGE] : the male of the sparrow hawk
²**musket** \"\ *n* -S [MF *mousquet, mousquette*, fr. OIt *moschetto, moschetta* arrow for a crossbow, musket, dim. of *mosca* fly, fr. L *musca*] : a large-caliber usu. muzzle-loading and smoothbore military shoulder firearm superseded by the rifle
**musket arrow** *n* : a feathered wooden arrow fired from a musket or other firearm of the 16th century
**mus·ke·teer** \ˌməskəˈti(ə)r, -iə\ *n* -S [modif. (influenced by *-eer*) of MF *mousquetaire*, fr. *mousquet* + *-aire* -ary] **1** : a soldier armed with a musket **2** [so called fr. the loyal friendship of the musketeers who are principal characters in the novel *Les Trois Mousquetaires* (1844) by Alexandre Dumas †1870 Fr. novelist] : a boon companion
**mus·ke·toon** \ˌməskəˈtün\ *n* -S [MF *mousqueton*, fr. OIt *moschettone*, aug. of *moschetto* musket — more at MUSKET] : a short musket with a large bore
**musketproof** \ˈ==ˌ=\ *adj, archaic* : capable of resisting penetration by a musket ball
**mus·ket·ry** \ˈməskətrē\ *n* -ES [F *mousqueterie*, fr. *mousquet* musket + *-erie* -ery — more at MUSKET] **1** : MUSKETS **2** : MUSKETEERS **3 a** : musket or rifle fire ⟨rattle of ~⟩ **b** : the technique of using small arms or of concentrating the collective fire of rifle and automatic rifle-fire units ⟨had not had enough training in . . . ~ —J.H.Michaelis⟩
**muskflower** \ˈ=ˌ==\ *n* : MUSK PLANT
**musk gland** *n* : MUSK BAG
**muskgrass** \ˈ=ˌ=\ *n* : CHARA 2
**musk hog** *n* : PECCARY
**mus·kie** *or* **mus·ky** \ˈməskē\ *n, pl* **muskies** [by shortening & alter.] : MUSKELLUNGE
**muskier** *comparative of* MUSKY
**muskiest** *superlative of* MUSKY
**muskie weed** *n* : an aquatic plant of the genus *Potamogeton*; *esp* : a large-leaved pondweed (*P. praelongus*)
**mus·ki·ness** \ˈməskēnəs\ *n* -ES [¹*musky* + *-ness*] : the quality or state of being musky
**musking** *pres part of* MUSK
**musk·ish** \-kish\ *adj* : somewhat musky
**musk kangaroo** *n* : a small kangaroo (*Hypsiprymnodon moschatus*) of northeastern Australia characterized by a musky odor and closely related to the rat kangaroos — called also *muskrat*
**musk ketone** *n* : a white to yellow crystalline synthetic musk $C_{14}H_{18}N_2O_5$; *tert*-butyl-dinitro-xylyl methyl ketone
**musk lorikeet** *or* **musk parakeet** *n* : a green Australian lorikeet (*Glossopsitta concinna*) with bright red ear coverts and forehead
**musk mallow** *n* **1** : a European mallow (*Malva moschata*) adventive in No. America and having faintly musk-scented foliage — called also *musk rose* **2** : ABELMOSK
**musk·melon** \ˈməsk, *chiefly in dial or substand speech* ˈməsh+ˌ-\ *n* : a usu. sweet musky-odored edible melon that is the fruit of a trailing or climbing Asiatic herbaceous vine (*Cucumis melo*): as **a** : any of various green-fleshed or orange-fleshed melons of small or moderate size with superficially netted skin and often fluted surface that constitute a distinct variety (*C. melo reticulatus*) and include most of the muskmelons cultivated in No. America — distinguished from *cantaloupe* (sense 1) **b** : CANTALOUPE 1 **c** : WINTER MELON
**musk mole** *n* : a grayish brown mole (*Scaptochirus moschatus*) of Siberia and northeastern China
**mus·ko·ge·an** *or* **mus·kho·ge·an** *also* **mus·ko·gi·an** \ˌməˈskōgēən\ *n, usu cap* **1** : a language family of southeastern U.S. that forms with the Natchesan the Natchez-Muskogean stock and includes Alabama, Choctaw, Hitchiti, Koasati, Muskogee, and Apalachee **2** : the peoples speaking Muskogean languages
**mus·ko·gee** \ˌməˈskōgē\ *n, pl* **muskogee** *or* **muskogees** *usu cap* **1 a** : a Muskogean people of Georgia and eastern Alabama constituting the nucleus of the Creek Confederacy **b** : a member of such people **2** : the language of the Muskogee people and of part of the Seminole people
**muskone** *var of* MUSCONE
**musk orchis** *or* **musk orchid** *n* : a European orchid (*Herminium monorchis*) having a musky scent
**musk–ox** \ˈ=ˌ=\ *n, pl* **musk–oxen** : a heavy-set bovid mammal (*Ovibos moschatus*) circumpolar in distribution during the Pleistocene period but now confined to Greenland and the barren northern lands of No. America, being between the sheep and the oxen in size and in many characters but having a thick long shaggy pelage that is dark grayish brown or blackish with a light saddle marking — called also *musk sheep*

musk-ox

**musk parrot** *n* **1** : a large brightly colored Fijian parrot (*Prosopeia tabuensis*) with a pronounced musky odor that is readily domesticated and trained to speak **2** : any of several parrots related to the musk parrot
**musk plant** *n* **1** : a yellow-flowered No. American herb (*Mimulus moschatus*) with hairy foliage formerly of musky odor — called also *muskflower* **2** : MUSK MALLOW
**musk·rat** \ˈməˌskrat, *usu* -ad·+V\ *n, pl* **muskrat** *or* **muskrats** [prob. by folk etymology fr. a word of Algonquian origin — more at MUSQUASH] **1 a** *or* **muskrat beaver** : an abundant aquatic rodent (*Ondatra zibethica* syn. *Fiber zibethica*) found throughout the U.S. and Canada living in holes in the banks of ponds or streams or in dome-shaped houses of rushes and mud, being as large as a small cat with the tail long, scaly, and laterally compressed, the hind feet webbed, the fur dark glossy brown, and having small glands that emit a musky odor — called also *musquash* **b** : the fur or pelt of the muskrat **2** : any of various other musky-smelling or musk-producing animals (as the musk kangaroo, hutia, So. African genet, or musk shrew)

muskrat 1a

**muskrat potato** *n* : WAPATOO
**muskrat weed** *n* : TALL MEADOW RUE
**muskroot** \ˈ=ˌ=\ *n* **1** : any of several plants having strong-scented roots: as **a** : MOSCHATEL **b** : an umbelliferous plant (*Ferula sumbul*) of central Asia whose musky aromatic roots constitute the chief sumbul of commerce **2** : SUMBUL 1
**musk rose** *n* **1** : a rose (*Rosa moschata*) of the Mediterranean region with curved or somewhat climbing branches and flowers having a musky odor **2** : MUSK MALLOW
**musks** *pl of* MUSK, *pres 3d sing of* MUSK
**musk seed** *n* : AMBER SEED
**musk sheep** *n* : MUSK-OX
**musk shrew** *n* **1** : any of various East Indian shrews having a powerful musky odor; *esp* : CROCIDURA 2 **2** : DESMAN
**musk thistle** *n* : a Eurasian thistle (*Carduus nutans*) naturalized in eastern No. America with nodding musky flower heads — called also *nodding thistle*
**musk tree** *n* : any of several Australasian musk-scented trees (as *Olearia argophylla*) — see MUSKWOOD 2
**musk turtle** *also* **musk terrapin** *or* **musk tortoise** *n* : any of several small American freshwater turtles of the genera *Sternotherus* and *Kinosternon*; *esp* : a turtle (*S. odoratus*) having a strong musky odor
**mus·kus grass** \ˈməskəs-\ *n* [D *muskus* musk, fr. L *muscus* — more at MUSK] : MUSK CLOVER
**muskwood** \ˈ=ˌ=\ *n* **1 a** : a usu. small to medium-sized widely distributed tropical American musky-odored tree (*Guarea trichilioides*) **b** : the reddish brown rather light straight-grained wood of this tree used esp. formerly in the West Indies as a substitute for mahogany **2 a** : a musk tree (*Olearia argophylla*) **b** : the hard white wood of the musk tree used for cabinetwork
**musk xylene** *n* : a white to yellow crystalline synthetic musk $C_{12}H_{15}N_3O_6$ used esp. in perfumes for soaps; *tert*-butyl-trinitro-xylene
¹**musky** \ˈməskē\ *adj* -ER/-EST [¹*musk* + *-y*] : having an odor of or resembling musk
²**musky** *var of* MUSKIE
¹**mus·lim** \ˈməzləm, ˈmu̇z-, ˈmu̇s- *sometimes* ˈməsləm\ *or* **mos·lem** \ˈmäzləm *sometimes* ˈmäsl-\ *also* **mus·lem** *like* MUSLIM\ *n, pl* **muslim** *or* **muslims** *or* **moslem** *or* **moslems** *usu cap* [Ar *muslim*, fr. *aslama* to surrender (to God)] : an adherent of or believer in Islam : one who submits to the will of Allah
²**muslim** \"\ *or* **moslem** \"\ *also* **muslem** \"\ *adj, usu cap* : of or relating to the religion, believers, or the institutions of Islam
**mus·lim·ism** \-ləˌmizəm\ *n* -S *cap* : ISLAM
**mus·lin** \ˈməzlən\ *n* -S *often attrib* [F *mousseline*, fr. It *mussolina*, fr. Ar *mawṣilīy* of Mosul, fr. al-*Mawṣil* Mosul, city in northern Iraq where it was formerly made] **1 a** : a plainwoven cotton fabric that is produced in various qualities from sheer to coarse, used bleached or unbleached for sheeting, embroidery, or other purposes, given special finishes for industrial purposes (as in bookbinding), and dyed or printed for clothing — see BOOK MUSLIN, ORGANDY **b** : a garment (as a gown) made of muslin **2 a** : a trial model of a garment or manufactured article (as a handbag) worked out in muslin for preliminary showing or fitting and then used as a pattern **b** : a frame or backing (as for a fur coat) ⟨~s . . . are made in Paris and befurred over here —Lois Long⟩ — **in muslin** : covered with muslin and sold with or without upholstering in decorator fabrics of the buyer's choosing — used of upholstered furniture
**muslin delaine** *n* : DELAINE 1
**mus·lin·et** *or* **mus·lin·ette** \ˌməzləˈnet\ *n* -S [*muslin* + *-et* or *-ette*] *archaic* : a heavy muslin
**muslin house** *n* : CLOTH HOUSE
**muslin kail** *n*, *Scot* : broth of barley and greens
**mus·nud** \ˈməˌsnəd\ *n* -S [Hindi *masnad*, fr. Ar] : a cushioned seat used as a throne by native princes of India
**mu·soph·a·ga** \myüˈsäfəgə\ *n, cap* [NL *muso-* (fr. *Musa*) + *-phaga*] : the type genus of the family Musophagidae comprising various typical touracos
**mu·so·phag·i·dae** \ˌmyüsəˈfajəˌdē\ *n pl, cap* [NL, fr. *Musophaga*, type genus + *-idae*] : a family of African birds (order Cuculiformes) consisting of the touracos
**mu·soph·a·gine** \myüˈsäfəˌjīn, -ˌjən\ *adj* [NL *Musophaginae*, subfamily of African birds, fr. *Musophaga*, type genus + *-inae*] : of or relating to the Musophagidae
**mus·quash** \ˈməˌskwäsh, -wȯsh\ *also* **mush·squash** \ˈməsh-k-\ *n* -ES [of Algonquian origin; akin to Natick *musquash*] **1** : MUSKRAT 1a **2** *chiefly Brit* : MUSKRAT 1b
**musquash root** *n* : SPOTTED COWBANE
**musquashweed** \ˈ=ˌ=ˌ=\ *n* : TALL MEADOW RUE
**mus·quaw** \ˈməˌskwȯ\ *n* -S [of Algonquian origin; akin to Cree *maskwa* black bear, Natick *mosq, masq*, Delaware *machk*, Mohegan *mquoh*] : BLACK BEAR 1
**mus·rol** \ˈməzˌrōl\ *n* -S [MF *muserole*, fr. It *museruola, musarola*, fr. *muso* muzzle, snout, fr. ML *musus*] *archaic* : the noseband of a horse's bridle
¹**muss** \ˈməs\ *n* -ES [origin unknown] **1** *obs* **a** : a game in which players at a given signal scramble for small objects that have been thrown to the ground ⟨when I cried ho, like boys unto a ~, kings would start forth —Shak.⟩ **b** : SCRAMBLE ⟨bauble and cap no sooner are thrown down, but there's a ~ of more than half the town —John Dryden⟩ **2** *slang* : a confused conflict : DISTURBANCE, BRAWL, FIGHT ⟨kick up a ~⟩ **3** : a state of confusion or disorder : MESS ⟨can be quickly installed, without ~ or fuss⟩
²**muss** \"\ *vt* -ED/-ING/-ES : to make untidy : WRINKLE, DISARRANGE, RUMPLE, DISHEVEL ⟨if these fabrics are very ~*ed*, use dry press cloth —Mary B. Picken⟩ ⟨most of the new hats manage to ~ the hairdos —Lois Long⟩ — often used with *up* ⟨a hard apartment to ~ up and easy to straighten out —Dorothy Baker⟩
**mus·saen·da** \məˈsendə\ *n, cap* [NL, fr. Singhalese *mussænda*, a species of this genus] : a large genus of herbs or shrubs (family Rubiaceae) found in the Old World tropics and having an ornamental calyx with one sepal that is much enlarged and showy
**mussaenda coffee** *n* : the seeds of a tree (*Gaertnera vaginata*) of the family Loganiaceae that contain no caffeine but are used as a coffee substitute
**mus·sal** \məˈsäl\ *n* -S [Hindi *masāl, mashāl*, fr. Ar *mash'al*] *India* : a torch usu. of oil-soaked rags
**mus·sal·chee** \-lˌchē\ *n* -S [Hindi *mash'alcī*, fr. Per, fr. Ar *mash'al* torch + Turk *-ci* (suffix denoting an agent)] *India* **1** : one that tends or carries a mussal : TORCHBEARER **2** : a kitchen servant : SCULLION — used by Europeans
**mus·sel** *also* **mus·cle** \ˈməsəl\ *n* -S *often attrib* [ME *muscle*, fr. OE *muscelle, muscle, musle*; akin to OS & OHG *muscula* mussel, MD *mosschele*; all fr. a prehistoric WGmc word borrowed fr. (assumed) VL *muscula*, alter. of L *musculus* small mouse, muscle, mussel — more at MUSCLE] **1** : a marine bivalve mollusk of *Mytilus* or a related genus usu. having an oval or elongated shell with a dark horny periostracum and being attached to the substrate by a byssus of fine threads secreted by the animal **2** : a freshwater bivalve mollusk of *Unio*, *Anodonta*, or related genera that is esp. abundant in rivers of the central U.S. and has a shell with a lustrous nacreous lining much used in making buttons — called also *freshwater clam, freshwater mussel*
**mussel bill** *n* : SURF SCOTER
**mussel crab** *n* **1** : a small American commensal crab (*Pinnotheres maculatus*) sometimes found in the mantle cavity of the mussel and other bivalves **2** : any of various crabs of the family Pinnotheridae — compare OYSTER CRAB
**musselcracker** *or* **musselcrusher** \ˈ==ˌ==\ *n* [so called fr. its large incisors] : BISKOP

**mussel digger** *n* [so called fr. its habit of digging in the mud] : GRAY WHALE

**mussel duck** *n* **1** : SCAUP DUCK **2** : SCOTER

**mussel poisoning** *n* : a toxic reaction following the eating of mussels; *esp* : a severe often fatal intoxication following the consumption of mussels that have fed on gonyaulax or other red tide flagellates and stored up a dangerous alkaloid in their tissues

**mussel scale** *n* : any of numerous scale insects (as of the genus *Lepidosaphes*) shaped like a mussel shell

**mussel-shrimp** \'ˌ=ˌ=\ *n* : OSTRACOD

**mus·si·dae** \'məsəˌdē\ *n pl, cap* [NL, fr. *Mussa*, type genus + *-idae*] : a family of imperforate corals that includes massive reef-building corals with compound polyps — see CACTUS CORAL

**muss·i·ly** \'məsəlē\ *adv* : in a mussy manner

**muss·i·ness** \-sēnəs\ *n* -ES : the quality or state of being mussy

**mussitate** *vi* -ED/-ING/-S [L *mussitatus*, past part. of *mussitare* to mutter, be silent, fr. *mussare*, prob. of imit. origin] *obs* : MUTTER

**mus·si·ta·tion** \ˌməsə'tāshən\ *n* -S [L *mussitation-*, *mussitatio* action of muttering, fr. *mussitatus* + *-ion-*, *-io* -ion] : movement of the lips as if in speech but without accompanying sound

**mus·so** \'mə(ˌ)sō\ *n, pl* **musso** *or* **mussos** *usu cap* : LAHU

**mus·sul·man** *or* **mus·sal·man** *also* **mus·ul·man** *or* **mus·al·man** \'məsəlmən\ *n, pl* **mussulmen** *or* **musulmen** *usu cap* [Turk *müslüman* & Per *musulmān*, modif. of Ar *muslim* (pl. *muslimūn*)] : MUSLIM

**muss up** *vt* **1** : to batter or handle roughly : BEAT, MAUL ⟨wanted to get there in time to *muss* him *up* a bit —J.F. Fishman⟩ **2** : to make chaotic or incoherent : CONFUSE ⟨sold them liquor, and generally *mussed up* the situation —William Kent⟩

**mus·su·ra·na** \ˌmüsə'rānə\ *n* -S [Pg *muçurana* fr. Tupi, lit., cord] : a large harmless colubrid snake (*Cloelia cloelia* syn. *Pseudoboa cloelia*) of the West Indies and tropical America which constricts and swallows poisonous snakes

**mussy** \'məsē, -si\ *adj* -ER/-EST [[1]*muss* + *-y*] : characterized by clutter or muss : MESSY, SLOVENLY

[1]**must** \(ˈ)məs(t)\ *vb, pres & past all persons* **must** [ME *moste* (past ind. & subj. of *moten* to be allowed to, be able to, have to), fr. OE *mōste*, past ind. & subj. of *mōtan* to be allowed to, be able to, have to; akin to OS *mōtan* to have cause for, be obliged to, have to, OHG *muozan* to be allowed to, be able to, have to, Goth *gamotan* to have room, fit; basic meaning: to have allotted to one; derivative fr. the stem of OE *metan* to measure — more at METE] *verbal auxiliary* **1 a** : is commanded or requested to ⟨you ~ stop that noise⟩ ⟨you ~ hear my side of the story⟩ ⟨he ~ be made to obey⟩ ⟨I told him what he ~ do⟩ **b** : is urged to : ought by all means to ⟨you ~ read that book⟩ ⟨you ~ come to visit us soon⟩ **2** : is compelled by physical necessity to ⟨man ~ eat to live⟩ : is required by immediate or future need or purpose to ⟨we ~ hurry if we want to catch the bus⟩ ⟨you take all that luggage along⟩ ⟨if you wished to see it you ~ queue —Leslie Eytle⟩ **3** : is obliged to : is compelled by social considerations to ⟨I ~ say you're looking much better⟩ ⟨I ~ admit your plane's safer⟩ ⟨realized that he ~ say nothing about it⟩ **4** : is required by law, custom, or moral conscience to ⟨we ~ obey the rules⟩ ⟨you ~ respect your father's wishes⟩ ⟨the present government ~ go . . . for it is too gross a scandal —John Buchan⟩ **5 a** : is compelled by resolve : is determined to ⟨if you ~ go at least wait till the storm is over⟩ **b** : is unreasonably or perversely compelled to ⟨I was planning a surprise for you, if you ~ know⟩ ⟨why ~ you be so stubborn⟩ ⟨why ~ it always rain on weekends⟩ **6** : is logically inferred or supposed to ⟨he ~ be out of his mind to say that⟩ ⟨it ~ be nearly dinner time⟩ ⟨he ~ have done it, no one else was there⟩ ⟨it ~ have been the coffee that kept me awake⟩ **7** : is compelled by fate or by natural law to ⟨what ~ be will be⟩ ⟨the innocent ~ suffer with the guilty⟩ ⟨three men who ~ leave their Queen on her death bed —Edith Sitwell⟩ ⟨a woman ~ have children to love —Edith Wharton⟩ **8** : was presumably certain to : would surely or necessarily : was bound to ⟨if he had really been there I ~ have seen him⟩ ⟨buffalo . . . beat out a track where human beings ~ have measurably failed —S.C.Williams⟩ ⟨~ have fallen had the railing not been there⟩ ⟨my rifle was slung on my back . . . else I ~ have lost it —Lea MacNally⟩ **9** *dial* : MAY, SHALL — used chiefly in questions ⟨~ I bring in the soup now⟩ ~ *vi* **1** : is obliged or compelled ⟨when Duty whispers low "thou ~" the youth replies "I can" —R.W.Emerson⟩ ⟨shoot if you ~ this old gray head —J.G. Whittier⟩ **2** *archaic* : ought to go : is obliged to go — used with adverb or adverbial phrase ⟨I ~ to Coventry —Shak.⟩ ⟨I ~ now to breakfast —John Buchan⟩ **syn** see OUGHT

[2]**must** \'məst\ *n* -S *often attrib* **1 a** : an imperative need or duty : OBLIGATION, REQUIREMENT ⟨in highly competitive modern industry, technological progress is a ~ —*Annual Report General Motors Corp.*⟩ ⟨told Republican leadership that the bill was a ~ —*N. Y. Times*⟩ ⟨less plagued . . . by rigid ~s —Walter de la Mare⟩ **b** : an indispensable item : ESSENTIAL, NECESSITY ⟨a raincoat is an absolute ~ —Richard Joseph⟩ ⟨facility, capacity and dependability of project equipment are ~s —*Military Engineer*⟩; *specif* : a priority item marked for inclusion without fail in a particular edition of a newspaper **2** : something that deserves attention because of its outstanding merit ⟨this is a lovely place, a real ~ for visitors —Richard Joseph⟩ ⟨for the thrill of being close to the original . . . the volume is a ~ —Louis Marder⟩

[3]**must** \"\ *n* -S [ME, fr. OE, fr. L *mustum*, fr. neut. of *mustus* young, fresh, new; perh. akin to Gk *mysos* spot, stain, defect, OIr *mossach* dirty, OE *mos* moss — more at MOSS] **1 a** : the juice of grapes or other fruit before and during fermentation **b** : the juice in combination with the pulp and skins of the crushed fruit **2** *dial Eng* : the pomace of apples or pears often used as fodder for livestock

[4]**must** \"\ *n* -S [MF, alter. of *musc* — more at MUSK] **1** : MUSK **2** : MUSTINESS, MOLD ⟨the dust and ~ of a decade —Marcia Davenport⟩

[5]**must** \"\ *vi* : to become musty or moldy ~ *vt, archaic* : to powder (the hair) with musk

[6]**must** *var of* MUSTH

**mustache** *var of* MOUSTACHE

**mus·ta·chio** *or* **mous·ta·chio** \məs'tä|shē,ō, -ta|, |(ˌ)shō\ *n* -S [Sp & It; Sp *mostacho*, fr. It *mustaccio*, *mostaccio* — more at MOUSTACHE] : MOUSTACHE; *esp* : a large moustache

**mus·ta·chioed** *or* **mous·ta·chioed** \-ōd\ *adj* : having mustachios

**mus·ta·fi·na** \ˌməstə'fēnə\ *also* **mus·tee·fi·no** \-tē'fē(ˌ)nō\ *n* -S [perh. fr. *mustee* + Sp *fino* fine — more at FINO] : the offspring of a white person and a mustee

[1]**mus·tang** \'məˌstaŋ\ *n* -S [MexSp *mesteño*, *mestengo*, fr. Sp, animal without an owner, stray, fr. *mesteño*, *mestengo*, adj., ownerless, strayed, fr. *mesta*, annual roundup of cattle formerly held in Spain, annual meeting of the owners of such cattle that disposed of strays, fr. ML (*animalia*) *mixta* mixed animals, fr. L *animalia* animals + *mixta*, neut. pl. of *mixtus*, past part. of *miscēre* to mix — more at MIX] **1 a** : the small hardy naturalized horse of the western plains directly descended from horses brought in by the Spaniards — compare CAYUSE 3, INDIAN PONY **b** : BRONCO **2** *slang* : a commissioned officer (as in the U. S. Navy) who has risen from the ranks **3** : SPHINX 4

[2]**mustang** \"\ *vi* -ED/-ING/-S : to hunt wild horses

**mus·tang·er** \-ŋə(r)\ *n* -S : one who rounds up wild horses on the open range and sells them esp. for horsemeat

**mustang grape** *n* : a woody vine (*Vitis candicans*) of the southwestern U. S. having light-colored berries with a pungent pulp

**mustang mint** *n* : a fragrant California annual herb (*Monardella lanceolata*) with rose-purple flowers in bracted clusters

**mus·tard** \'mastə(r)d\ *n* -S *often attrib* [ME *mostard*, *mustard*, fr. OF *mostarde*, *moustarde* condiment made from mustard seed and must, mustard, fr. *moust* must, fr. L *mustum* — more at MUST] **1 a** : a pungent yellow condiment consisting of the pulverized seeds of the black mustard or sometimes the white mustard either dry or made into a paste (as with water or vinegar) and sometimes adulterated with other substances (as turmeric) or mixed with spices and serving as a stimulant and diuretic or in large doses as an emetic and as a counterirritant when applied to the skin as a poultice **b** *slang* : something that adds strength or piquancy : ENTHUSIASM, ZEST ⟨kick a lot of ~ out of . . . 'em —J.T.Farrell⟩ ⟨a lot of muscle and ~ —*Time*⟩ **2 a** (1) : any of several plants of the genus *Brassica* that have lyrately lobed leaves, yellow flowers, and linear beaked pods and that include some which are cultivated for their pungent seed or for their edible foliage — see BLACK MUSTARD, INDIAN MUSTARD, WHITE MUSTARD (2) : any of various other plants of the family Cruciferae — used chiefly in combination; see HEDGE MUSTARD, WORMSEED MUSTARD **b** : TOOTHBRUSH TREE **3 a** : a dark yellow **b** : a moderate yellow — compare MUSTARD YELLOW **4 a** : MUSTARD GAS **b** : NITROGEN MUSTARD

**mustard beetle** *n* : a small black European leaf beetle (*Phaedon cochleariae*) destructive to mustard and other cruciferous plants

**mustard brown** *n* **1** : a variable color averaging a moderate olive brown that is greener and deeper than old olive **2** : a moderate yellowish brown that is lighter, stronger, and slightly redder than chestnut brown, and yellower, lighter, and stronger than auburn

**mus·tard·er** \-tə(r)dər, -tədə(r\ *n* -S : a maker or seller of mustard

**mustard family** *n* : CRUCIFERAE

**mustard gas** *n* [so called fr. its odor] : a vesicant war gas ($(ClCH_2CH_2)_2S$) that also attacks the eyes and lungs and is a systemic poison, that is a high-boiling oily liquid with a pungent odor only when impure, and that is obtained by treating thiodiglycol with gaseous hydrogen chloride or ethylene with sulfur monochloride; bis-(2-chloroethyl) sulfide — called also *dichloroethyl sulfide, sulfur mustard*

**mustard gold** *n* : a variable color averaging a light olive brown that is much stronger and slightly lighter than drab or sponge

**mustard oil** *n* **1** : an oil from mustard: as **a** *or* **mustard-seed oil** : a greenish yellow bland semidrying fatty oil that is expressed from the seeds usu. of black mustard and is used chiefly in soapmaking and as a salad oil **b** : a colorless to pale yellow pungent irritating essential oil that is obtained by distillation from the seeds usu. of black mustard after expression of the fatty oil and maceration with water, that consists largely of allyl isothiocyanate, and that is used esp. in liniments and medicinal plasters — compare SINIGRIN **2 a** : ALLYL ISOTHIOCYANATE **b** : an isothiocyanate ester ⟨phenyl *mustard oil* $C_6H_5NCS$⟩

**mustard plaster** *n* **1** : a poultice made by spreading a paste of mustard, flour, and cold water on cloth **2** *or* **mustard paper** : a counterirritant and rubefacient plaster prepared by spreading a mixture of powdered black mustard and a rubber solution on fabric

**mustard seed** *n* **1** *or* **mustard-seed shot** : DUST SHOT **2** *also* **mustard-seed coal** : the smallest size of buckwheat coal

**mustard spinach** *n* : INDIAN MUSTARD

**mustard tan** *n* : a variable color averaging a light olive brown that is stronger and slightly greener than drab or sponge and deeper and slightly greener than dust

**mustard yellow** *n* : a moderate yellow that is duller than colonial yellow, greener and paler than brass, and redder and less strong than quince yellow — compare MUSTARD 3

**mus·tee** \ˌmə'stē, 'ˌ=\ *n* -S [modif. & shortening of Sp *mestizo* — more at MESTIZO] **1** : OCTOROON **2** : HALF-BREED

**musteefino** *var of* MUSTAFINA

**mus·te·la** \mə'stēlə\ *n, cap* [NL, fr. L, weasel, prob. fr. *mus* mouse + *-tela* (origin unknown) — more at MOUSE] : a genus of carnivorous mammals (the type of the family Mustelidae) comprising active predators and valuable furbearers

[1]**mus·te·lid** \'məstələd\ *adj* [NL *Mustelidae*] : of or relating to the Mustelidae

[2]**mustelid** \"\ *n* -S : a mammal of the family Mustelidae

**mus·tel·i·dae** \ˌmə'steləˌdē\ *n, pl, cap* [NL, fr. *Mustela*, type genus + *-idae*] : a large widely distributed family (superfamily Arctoidea) of rather small lithe active carnivorous mammals including many important furbearers (as the mink, fisher, and otter) and some destructive predators (as the weasels and polecats) and varying greatly in appearance and habits from the tiniest slender bloodthirsty weasel to the relatively large stocky slow-moving skunk or the burly wolverine

**mus·te·line** \'məstəˌlīn, -lən\ *adj* [NL *Mustela* + E *-ine*] : of or relating to weasels : like or related to weasels

**mus·te·lus** \ˌmə'stēləs\ *n, cap* [NL, fr. L *mustela* weasel, a fish — more at MUSTELA] : a genus of dogfishes of the family Triakidae including the smooth hound

[1]**mus·ter** \'məstə(r)\ *vb* **mustered; mustered; mustering** \-t(ə)riŋ\ **musters** [ME *mostren*, *mustren* to show, muster, fr. OF *mostrer*, *monstrer*, *moustrer*, fr. L *monstrare* to show, point out, fr. *monstrum* evil omen, monster, monstrosity, marvel — more at MONSTER] *vt* **1 a** : ENLIST, ENROLL ⟨had been . . . ~*ed* as surgeon's mate —Tobias Smollett⟩ — used chiefly with *in* or *into* ⟨the army ~*s* in recruits⟩ ⟨a businessman recently ~*ed* into government service —*New Yorker*⟩ **b** (1) : to cause to gather : CONVENE, ASSEMBLE ⟨all hands were ~*ed* aft for watches to be told off —H.A.Chippendale⟩ ⟨~*ed* the ladies together and urged them into another room —Maurice Cranston⟩ ⟨did not ~ much of a crowd —Ben Riker⟩ (2) *Austral* : ROUND UP ⟨went up into the reserve to ~ our stock —F.S.Anthony⟩ **c** : to call the roll of ⟨fell out on deck and the mate ~*ed* the ship's company⟩ **2 a** : to bring together : COLLECT, ACCUMULATE ⟨~ a few pounds to buy some seed corn —Adrian Bell⟩ ⟨~*ed* shirts and socks and neckties from his chest of drawers —Richard Blaker⟩ ⟨could only ~ . . . two hundred votes —E.H.Collis⟩ **b** : to call forth : DEVELOP, INVOKE : work up ⟨couldn't ~ courage to pop the question —Agnes S. Turnbull⟩ ⟨have to ~ the right words as well as the midnight courage —E.B.White⟩ ⟨as soon as sufficient public support can be ~*ed* —Chester Bowles⟩ — often used with *up* ⟨cannot ~ up much sympathy for the . . . privations which he endured —W.E.Channing⟩ **3** : to amount to : COMPRISE, INCLUDE, NUMBER ⟨the book-reading public ~*s* 55 percent of the population —J.D.Adams⟩ ⟨the senior program . . . ~*ed* 123,299 students —*Americana Annual*⟩ ~ *vi* **1 a** : to come together : CONGREGATE, FORGATHER ⟨thirty thousand men . . . were to ~ in the disguise of pilgrims —T.B. Macaulay⟩ **b** *obs* : GATHER ⟨vapors . . . drawn from the sea to ~ in the skies —Richard Blackmore⟩ **2** *Austral* : to conduct a roundup of livestock ⟨~*ed* in March this year on account of the late season and drove the stock down . . . in April —Nevil Shute⟩

[2]**muster** \"\ *n* -S [ME *mustre*, *moustre*, fr. MF *mostre*, *monstre*, *moustre*, fr. *mostrer*, *monstrer*, *moustrer*, v.] **1** : a representative specimen : SAMPLE ⟨~*s* of goods for sale, in reasonable quantities —*Tariffs of Foreign Countries*⟩ **2** *obs* : PRESENTATION, DISPLAY ⟨begin to make some ~ and show of their learning —Richard Mulcaster⟩ **3 a** (1) : an act of assembling for enumeration or inspection ⟨the boys in the squad room sat around between ~*s* —Seymour Ettman⟩ (2) : an act or process of critical examination ⟨slipshod work that would never pass ~⟩; *specif* : formal military inspection ⟨call out the troops to stand ~⟩ **b** : a competitive demonstration ⟨eleven hand tub fire pumpers . . . have entered the Riverside Park Championship Fireman's ~ —*Springfield (Mass.) Daily News*⟩ **c** *Austral* : ROUNDUP — compare CAMP 1d **d** (1) : an assembled group : ACCUMULATION, GATHERING ⟨a ~ of biographical facts —*Time*⟩ ⟨last week's ~ of the heads of . . . governments —R.H.Rovere⟩ (2) *of peacocks* : FLOCK **e** : INVENTORY, ROSTER; *esp* : MUSTER ROLL ⟨were sent . . . to take the ~*s* of this expedition —G.R.Elton⟩

**mus·ter·er** \-tərə(r)\ *n* -S **1** : one that musters **2** *Austral* : a ranch hand who rounds up livestock

**mustering** *n* -S [ME, fr. gerund of *mustren* to muster] **1** : an act or instance of assembling **2** *Austral* : ROUNDUP

**muster-master** \'ˌ=ˌ=\ *n* : an officer or official charged with keeping a muster roll

**muster out** *vt* : to discharge from service (as military) ⟨at the end of the war was *mustered out* as an ensign —E.P.Snow⟩ ⟨tired liberals . . . *mustered* themselves *out* —Bruce Bliven b.1889⟩

**muster-out** \'ˌ=ˌ=\ *n, pl* **musters-out** [*muster out*] : an act or process of mustering out : DISCHARGE ⟨the first great commands to complete their *musters-out* —Dixon Wecter⟩ ⟨ordered the *muster-out* of all troops not needed for occupation duties⟩

**muster roll** *n* : INVENTORY, ROSTER; *specif* : a register of all the officers and men in a military unit or ship's company

**musth** *or* **must** \'məst\ *n* -S [Hindi *mast* intoxicated, ruttish, fr. Per *mast*; akin to Skt *madati* he rejoices, is drunk — more at MEAT] : a periodic state of murderous frenzy of the bull elephant usu. connected with the rutting season and marked by the exudation of a dark brown odorous ichor from tiny holes above the eyes — **on must** *also* **in must** : in a state of belligerent fury — used of the bull elephant

**must·i·ly** \'məstəlē\ *adv* : in a musty manner

**must·i·ness** \-tēnəs\ *n* -ES : the quality or state of being musty

**mustn't** \'məsᵊnt\ [by contr.] : must not

**musts** *pl of* MUST

[1]**musty** \'məstē, -ti\ *adj* -ER/-EST [[4]*must* + *-y*] **1 a** : impaired by damp or mildew : MOLDY ⟨~ relic⟩ **b** : tasting of mold ⟨~ wine⟩ **c** : smelling of damp and decay : FUSTY ⟨a pathetic air of dilapidation . . . and a ~, shut-up smell —George du Maurier⟩ **2 a** : TRITE, DULL, STALE ⟨the proverb is something ~ —Shak.⟩ **b** : ANTIQUATED, SUPERANNUATED ⟨~ statute⟩ ⟨a ~ clerk on a high stool⟩

[2]**musty** *vi* -ED/-ING/-ES *obs* : to become musty

**musulman** *usu cap, var of* MUSSULMAN

**mut** *var of* MUTT

**mut** *abbr* **1** mutilated **2** mutual

[1]**mu·ta** \'mü(ˌ)tä, -üd·ə\ *n* -S [It, fr. *mutare* to change, fr. L] : CHANGE — used as a direction in ensemble music for various instruments (as timpani) to change tuning preparatory to a change in key

[2]**muta** \"\ *n* -S [Ar *mut'ah* enjoyment] : a form of Muslim usufruct marriage for a specified period — compare BEENA MARRIAGE

**mu·ta·bil·ia** \ˌmyüd·ə'bilēə, -lyə\ *n pl, cap* [NL, fr. L, neut. pl. of *mutabilis*] **1** *in former classifications* : a suborder of Caudata comprising all salamanders that normally undergo metamorphosis **2** *in some classifications* : a suborder of Caudata including all true salamanders as opposed to the Proteida and Meantes

**mu·ta·bil·i·ty** \ˌmyüd·ə'biləd·ē, -ütə-, -lətē, -i\ *n* -ES [ME *mutabilite*, fr. MF *mutabilité*, fr. L *mutabilitat-*, *mutabilitas*, fr. *mutabilis* + *-itat-*, *-itas* -ity] **1** : the quality or state of being mutable or capable of mutation **2** : an instance of being mutable

[1]**mu·ta·ble** \'myüd·əbəl, -ütəb-\ *adj* [L *mutabilis*, fr. *mutare* to change + *-abilis* -able — more at MISS] **1** : prone or liable to change : INCONSTANT, FICKLE ⟨a ~ mind⟩ ⟨a ~ foreign policy⟩ **2 a** : capable of change or of being changed in form, quality, or nature ⟨a ~ substance⟩ **b** : subject to or capable of mutation : liable to mutate ⟨~ vowels⟩ — **mu·ta·ble·ness** *n* -ES

[2]**mutable** *n* -S : a mutable sound or grammatical form

**mu·ta·bly** \-blē, -li\ *adv* : in a mutable manner

**mu·ta·fa·cient** \ˌmyüd·ə'fāshənt\ *adj* [*mutation* + *-facient*] : capable of inducing biological mutation — used chiefly of intracellular agents; compare MUTAGENIC

**mu·tage** \'myüd·ij\ *n* -S [F, fr. *muter* to check fermentation (prob. fr. *muet* mute) + *-age* — more at MUTE] : the checking of fermentation (as by adding alcohol) in the must of grapes

**mu·ta·gen** \'myüd·əjən, -ˌjen\ *n* -S [ISV *mutation* + *-gen*] : an agent (as mustard gas, various radiations, or possibly some viruses) that tends to increase the occurrence or extent of mutation

**mu·ta·gen·e·sis** \ˌmyüd·ə'jenəsəs\ *n* [NL, fr. ISV *mutation* + NL *genesis*] : the occurrence or induction of mutation

**mu·ta·gen·ic** \ˌ=ˌ='jenik\ *adj* : capable of inducing mutation — used chiefly of extracellular agents (as chemicals or X ray); compare MUTAFACIENT — **mu·ta·gen·i·cal·ly** \-nək(ə)lē\ *adv*

**mu·ta·kal·li·mun** \ˌmü|tä,kalə'mün\ *n pl* [Ar *mutakallimūna*] : scholastic theologians of Islam — compare KALAM

**mu·tan·kiang** \ˌmü,dän|jē|äŋ\ *adj, usu cap* [fr. *Mutankiang*, Manchuria] : of or from the city of Mutankiang, Manchuria : of the kind or style prevalent in Mutankiang

[1]**mu·tant** \'myütᵊnt\ *adj* [L *mutant-*, *mutans*, pres. part. of *mutare* to change — more at MISS] : of, relating to, or produced by mutation ⟨a ~ gene⟩

[2]**mutant** \"\ *n* -S : a mutant individual

**mu·ta·rotate** \ˌmyüd·ə+\ *vi* [back-formation fr. *mutarotation*] : to undergo mutarotation

**mu·ta·rotation** \"+\ *n* [L *mutare* to change + E *rotation*] : a change in optical rotation shown by various solutions on standing as a result of chemical change (as of alpha-D-glucose into an equilibrium mixture containing both alpha- and beta-D-glucose)

**mutasarrif** *var of* MUTESSARIF

**mu·tase** \'myü,tās, -āz\ *n* -S [ISV *mut* -(fr. L *mutare* to change) + *-ase*] **1** : an enzyme regarded as able to catalyze a dismutation (as of acetaldehyde to alcohol and acetic acid) **2** : any of various enzymes (as phosphoglucomutase) that catalyze molecular rearrangements — compare ISOMERASE

[1]**mu·tate** \'myü,tāt, ='=\ *vb* [L *mutatus*, past part. of *mutare* to change — more at MISS] : to undergo or cause to undergo mutation

[2]**mutate** *n* -S **1** : MUTANT **2** : a word form with mutated vowel

**mu·ta·tion** \myü'tāshən\ *n* -S [ME *mutacioun*, fr. MF *mutation*, fr. L *mutation-*, *mutatio*, fr. *mutatus* + *-ion-*, *-io* -ion] **1** : a major change : a significant and basic alteration ⟨changes are not all gradual; they culminate in sudden ~*s* —John Dewey⟩ **2 a** *in medieval solmization* : the change from one hexachord to another involving a change of syllable for a given musical tone **b** : MUTATION STOP **3 a** (1) : any of several changes undergone by stops in Celtic languages because of their phonetic surroundings (2) : the phonetic changes that some initial consonants in Celtic languages undergo under certain sandhi conditions **b** : UMLAUT **4 a** : a hypothetical sudden fundamental change in heredity believed to result in the production of new individuals that are basically unlike their parents and that can be acted upon by natural selection to fix desirable changes and establish new species — compare DARWINISM, EVOLUTION, MACROEVOLUTION, SALTATION **b** : a relatively permanent change in hereditary material other than one brought about by Mendelian recombination of factors involving either a physical change in chromosome relations (as in polyploidy, nondisjunction, or deficiency) or a fundamental change in genes and occurring either in germ cells or in somatic cells but with only those in germ cells being capable of perpetuation by sexual reproduction — see GENE MUTATION, SOMATIC MUTATION **c** (1) : an individual or strain resulting from mutation — compare FREAK 3b (2) : an animal (as a mink) of a domesticated strain which differs esp. in coat color from typical animals of the wild type and whose difference is maintained by selective breeding; *also* : the coat color of such an animal — compare COLOR PHASE **5** : one of a series of palaeontologic stages that are comparable to subspecies and that occur in the temporal succession of a line of fossils in successive horizons

**mu·ta·tion·al** \(ˈ)myü|tāshənᵊl, -shnəl\ *adj* : of or relating to mutation — **mu·ta·tion·al·ly** \-ᵊlē, -əl|, |i\ *adv*

**mu·ta·tion·ism** \=ˈ=shə,nizəm\ *n* -S : the theory that mutation is a fundamental factor in evolution

**mu·ta·tion·ist** \-.nəst\ *n* -S : a believer in or upholder of mutationism

**mutation plural** *n* : a plural form differing from the singular by a vowel (as in *teeth, mice*)

**mutation pressure** *n* : a hypothetical tendency for biological mutation in one direction to occur disproportionately

**mutation stop** *n* : a pipe-organ stop sounding pitches other than those indicated by the notes or one of their octaves (as a fifth, a twelfth) — compare FOUNDATION STOP

**mu·ta·tis mu·tan·dis** \mü|täd·əsmü'tändəs, myü|tad·əsmyü'tan-\ *adv* [L] **1** : with the necessary changes having been made **2** : with the respective differences having been considered

**mu·ta·tive** \'myüd·əd·iv\ *adj* [L *mutatus* + E *-ive*] **1** : of, relating to, or marked by mutation **2** : expressive of change : passing from one place or state into another : PACTIVE ⟨~ verbs like *fall, rise, melt*⟩

**mu·ta·wal·li** \ˌmüd·ə'wä|lē\ *n* -S [Ar *mutawallī* one entrusted with something] : the trustee of a waqf (as a religious building)

**mu·'ta·zi·la** *also* **mu·'ta·zi·lah** \mü'täzələ\ *n* -s *usu cap* [Ar *mu'tazilah* body of seceders] **:** the Mu'tazilite school
**mu·'ta·zi·lism** *or* **mu·ta·zi·lism** \-,lizəm\ *n* -s *usu cap* **:** the theological doctrines and methods of the Mu'tazilites
**mu·'ta·zi·lite** *or* **mu·ta·zi·lite** \-,līt\ *n* -s *usu cap* [Ar *mu'tazilah* + E *-ite*] **1 :** a Muslim philosophical school founded in the 8th century A.D. emphasizing reason in religious interpretation, free will in opposition to predestination, and the unity and justice of Allah **2 :** a member of the Mu'tazilite school
**mutch** \ˈməch\ *n* -ES [ME (Sc dial.) *much*, fr. MD *mutse* cap, fr. ML *almutia* amice] *chiefly Scot* **:** a close-fitting cap (as of linen or muslin) often worn by old women or babies
**mutch·kin** \-kən\ *n* -s [ME (Sc) *muchekyn*] **:** a Scotch unit of liquid capacity equal to 0.90 pint
**¹mute** \ˈmyüt, *usu* -üd·+V\ *adj* -ER/-EST [alter. (influenced by L *mutus*) of ME *muet, mewet*, fr. MF *muet*, fr. OF *mu*, fr. L *mutus*; akin to OHG *māwen* to cry out, shriek, Norw *mua* to be silent, Gk *mykos, mytis* mute, Skt *mūka*; basic meaning: inarticulate sound] **1 :** characterized by the inability to speak; *specif* **:** unable to utter articulate sounds as a result of never having heard speech sounds **2 :** characterized by absence of speech: as **a :** unable for a limited time to speak (as from astonishment, grief, shock, or other strong emotion) **b :** felt or experienced but not expressed ⟨gave him her hand with ~ thanks —George Meredith⟩ **c** *of a person arraigned by law* **:** making no answer, maintaining silence, or refusing to plead directly or stand trial — usu. used with *stand* **3 :** not giving tongue when hunting **:** SILENT — used of a hound **4 a** *of a coin* **:** devoid of inscription or means of identification other than heraldic or symbolical devices **b** *of a mineral* **:** not giving a ringing sound when struck **5 a** *of a written or printed character* (1) **:** contributing nothing to the pronunciation of a word (as *b* in *plumb* or the second *e* in *every* as it is usu. pronounced) (2) **:** contributing to the pronunciation of a word but not representing the nucleus of a syllable (as the *e* in *mate* which produces \māt\ instead of \mat\) **b** *of the e in French* **:** having no counterpart in the pronunciation in some environments or styles of utterance but pronounced \ə\ in other environments or styles of utterance (as *e* in *cheval* which is sometimes pronounced \shvál\ and sometimes \shəvál\) **syn** see DUMB
**²mute** \"\ *n* -s **1 a :** one that does not speak (as from physical inability or unwillingness) **b** *archaic* **:** a person whose part in a play does not require him to speak **c :** one hired to attend a funeral as a mourner **2 :** STOP 9 — used esp. in the study of Greek and Latin **3 a :** a device on a musical instrument serving to reduce, soften, or muffle its tone: as **a :** a metal, ivory, or wood clamp that can be attached to the bridge of a bowed stringed instrument **b :** a cone or cylinder or pad inserted in the bell of a wind instrument — compare SORDINE **c :** one of the dampers of a piano action

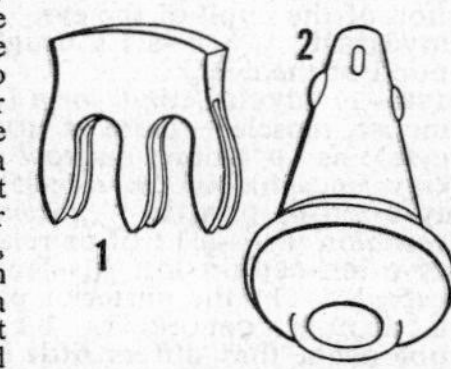

mutes 3: *1* for violin, *2* for trumpet

**³mute** \"\ *vt* -ED/-ING/-S **1 :** to muffle or reduce the sound of (as by a mute) **2 :** to subdue or tone down (a color)
**⁴mute** \"\ *vi* -ED/-ING/-S [ME *muten*, fr. MF *meutir*, short for *esmeutir*, fr. OF *esmeltir*, of Gmc origin; akin to MD *smelten* to melt, defecate (used of birds)] *of a bird* **:** DEFECATE
**⁵mute** \"\ *n* -s **:** the excrement of a bird
**⁶mute** *vi* -ED/-ING/-S [perh. fr. L *muttire* to mutter — more at MUTTER] *obs Scot* **:** COMPLAIN
**mut·ed** \ˈmyüdəd, -ütəd\ *adj* **1 :** being mute **:** SPEECHLESS, SILENT **2 :** provided with, produced by means of, or modified through the presence of a mute
**mut·ed·ly** *adv* **:** in a muted manner
**mute·ly** *adv* [¹*mute* + *-ly*] **:** in a mute manner
**mute·ness** *n* -ES **:** the quality or state of being mute
**mute of malice** *Eng law* **:** the silence assumed by a prisoner able to plead a felony but refusing to do so and thereby formerly exposing himself to the penalty of torture and death
**¹muter** *comparative of* MUTE
**²mu·ter** \mü'ter\ *n, pl* **muter** *or* **muters** *usu cap* **1 :** a nomadic Bedouin people in Arabia **2 :** a member of the Muter people
**mu·tes·sar·if** *also* **mu·ta·sar·rif** \,müd·ə'sarəf\ *n* -s [Turk *mutasarrif*, fr. Ar *mutaṣarrif*] **:** an administrative authority of various sanjaks (as in the Ottoman Empire or in Iraq)
**mutest** *superlative of* MUTE
**mute swan** *n* **:** the common white swan (*Cygnus olor*) of Europe and western Asia that produces no loud notes
**muth** *var of* MATH
**muth·mann·ite** \ˈmüt(h)mə,nīt\ *n* -s [G *muthmannit*, fr. F. W. *Muthmann* †1913 Ger. chemist + G *-it* -ite] **:** a silver gold telluride (Ag, Au)Te
**mu·ti** \ˈmüd·ē, ˈmüd·ē\ *n* -s [Zulu *umuti* tree, shrub, herb, medicine] *Africa* **:** MEDICINE
**mu·tic** \ˈmyüd·ik\ *adj* [L *muticus* curtailed, docked — more at MUTILATE] **1 :** lacking the usu. defensive parts (as teeth or claws) **2 :** MUTICATE
**mu·ti·ca** \ˈmyüd·əkə\ [NL, fr. L, neut. pl. of *muticus* docked] *syn of* CETACEA
**mu·ti·cate** \-d·ə,kāt, -d·əkət\ *also* **mu·ti·cous** \-d·əkəs\ *adj* [*muticate* fr. L *muticus* docked + E *-ate*; *muticous* fr. L *muticus*] **:** growing without an awn or point
**¹mu·ti·late** \ˈmyüd·ᵊl,āt, -üt·ᵊl,-, *usu* -ād·+V\ *adj* [L *mutilatus*, past part.] **1 :** MUTILATED **2 a :** having no hind limbs ⟨a ~ cetacean⟩ **b :** ABBREVIATED — used of the elytra of an insect
**²mutilate** \"\ *vt* -ED/-ING/-S [L *mutilatus*, past part. of *mutilare*, fr. *mutilus* mutilated, maimed; akin to L *muticus* docked, OIr *mut* short] **1 :** to cut off or permanently destroy a limb or essential part of ⟨~ a body⟩ ⟨~ a statue⟩; *sometimes* **:** CASTRATE **2 :** to cut up or alter radically so as to make imperfect ⟨~ a medieval manuscript⟩ **syn** see MAIM
**³mutilate** *n* -s [NL *Mutilata*, a former group of mammals comprising the whales and sirenians, fr. L, neut. pl. of *mutilatus*] *obs* **:** CETACEAN, SIRENIAN
**mu·ti·la·tion** \,myüd·ᵊl'āshən, -üt·ᵊl'-\ *n* -s [LL *mutilation-, mutilatio*, fr. L *mutilatus* + *-ion-, -io* -ion] **1 :** deprivation of a limb or essential part esp. by excision ⟨the ~ of a body⟩ **2 :** an instance of mutilating
**mu·ti·la·tive** \ˈmyüd·ᵊl,ād·iv\ *also* **mu·ti·la·to·ry** \-ᵊlə,tōrē\ *adj* **:** of or relating to mutilation ⟨a ~ deed⟩
**mu·ti·la·tor** \ˈmyüd·ᵊl,ād·ə(r), -üt·ᵊl,-, -ātə-\ *n* -s **:** one that mutilates
**mu·til·la** \myü'tilə\ *n, cap* [NL, irreg. fr. L *mutilus* mutilated — more at MUTILATE] **:** a genus of parasitic wasps having wingless females — compare VELVET ANT
**¹mu·til·lid** \-ləd\ *adj* [NL *Mutillidae*] **:** of or relating to the Mutillidae
**²mutillid** \"\ *n* -s **:** a wasp of the family Mutillidae **:** VELVET ANT
**mu·til·li·dae** \-lə,dē\ *n pl, cap* [NL, fr. *Mutilla*, type genus + *-idae*] **:** a family of wasps of which *Mutilla* is the type genus
**mutilous** *adj* [L *mutilus* — more at MUTILATE] *obs* **:** MUTILATED, DEFECTIVE, IMPERFECT
**¹mutine** *vb* -ED/-ING/-S [MF (*se*) *mutiner* to rebel, *mutiner* to incite to rebellion, fr. *mutin* insubordinate, mutinous, fr. *meute* revolt, fr. (assumed) VL *movita*, fr. fem. of *movitus*, alter. of L *motus*, past part. of *movēre* to move — more at MOVE] *vi, obs* **:** REBEL, MUTINY ~ *vt, obs* **:** to urge to rebel
**²mutine** *n* -s [MF *mutin*, fr. *mutin*, adj.] **1** *obs* **:** MUTINY **2** *obs* **:** MUTINEER
**¹mu·ti·neer** \,myüt·ᵊn'i(ə)r, -iə\ *n* -s [MF *mutinier*, fr. *mutin* mutiny + *-ier* -eer] **:** one that mutinies
**²mutineer** \"\ *vi* -ED/-ING/-S *archaic* **:** MUTINY
**muting** *pres part of* MUTE
**muting switch** *n* **:** a record changer switch which shuts off the phonograph pickup during the record changing cycle
**mu·ti·nize** \ˈmyüt·ᵊn,iz\ *vi* -ED/-ING/-S [²*mutine* + *-ize*] *archaic* **:** MUTINY
**mu·ti·nous** \-ᵊnəs\ *adj* [²*mutine* + *-ous*] **1 a :** disposed to or in a state of mutiny **:** REBELLIOUS ⟨a ~ crew⟩ **b :** TURBULENT, UNRULY ⟨~ passions⟩ **2 :** constituting or characterized by mutiny ⟨~ acts⟩ **:** expressive of an inclination or readiness to mutiny ⟨~ thoughts⟩ **:** inciting mutiny ⟨a ~ speech⟩ **syn** see INSUBORDINATE
**mu·ti·nous·ly** *adv* **:** in a mutinous manner
**mu·ti·nous·ness** *n* -ES **:** the quality or state of being mutinous
**¹mu·ti·ny** \ˈmyüt(ᵊ)nē, -ni\ *n* -ES [¹*mutine* + *-y*] **1** *obs* **:** violent commotion **:** TUMULT, STRIFE **2 :** insurrection against or willful refusal to obey constituted, recognized, or traditional authority **:** forcible or passive resistance to existing authority ⟨a colonial ~⟩; *specif* **:** concerted revolt against the rules of discipline or the lawful commands of a superior officer **syn** see REBELLION
**²mutiny** \"\ *vb* -ED/-ING/-S *vi* **1 a :** to rise against or refuse to obey or observe authority; *specif* **:** to rebel against military authority **b :** to be guilty of mutiny **2 :** to turn against one's group without warning ⟨the extreme left wing *mutinied* just before the election⟩ ~ *vt, archaic* **:** to incite to mutiny
**mu·ti·sia** \myü'tizh(ē)ə\ *n, cap* [NL, fr. José C. *Mutis* †1808 Sp. naturalist + NL *-ia*] **:** a large genus of So. American often climbing shrubs (family Compositae) having large heads of pistillate flowers with plumose pappus
**mut·ism** \ˈmyüd·,izəm\ *n* -s [F *mutisme*, fr. L *mutus* mute, + F *-isme* -ism — more at MUTE] **:** the condition of being mute: **a :** inability to speak whether from physical or functional cause **b :** a condition of persistent failure to speak in the absence of evident direct cause (as in mental disease)
**mu·trie yellow** \ˈmü·trē-\ *n, often cap M* [prob. fr. the name *Mutrie*] **:** CADMIUM LEMON
**muts** *pl of* MUT
**mut·sud·dy** \(ˈ)mət¦sədi\ *n* -ES [Hindi *mutasaddī*, fr. Ar] **:** a native accountant or clerk in British India
**mutt** *also* **mut** \ˈmət, *usu* -əd·+V\ *n* -s [short for *muttonhead*] **1 :** a stupid or commonplace person **2 :** a mongrel dog **:** CUR
**¹mut·ter** \ˈməd·ə(r), -ətə-\ *vb* **muttered; muttered; muttering** \-əd·əriŋ, -ətər-, -ə·tr-\ **mutters** [ME *muteren*; akin to Norw dial. *mutra* to mutter, OHG *mutilōn* to murmer, ON *muthla*, L *muttire* to mutter, *mutus* mute — more at MUTE] *vi* **1 :** to utter indistinctly or with a low voice and lips partly closed ⟨~*s* just before dying⟩ **2 :** to murmur complainingly or angrily **:** GRUMBLE, GROWL ⟨a ~*ing* group of workers⟩ **3 :** to make a low rumbling sound **:** murmur continuously or rumblingly ⟨forest noises ~*ing*⟩ ~ *vt* **1 :** to utter esp. in a low or imperfectly articulated manner ⟨~ an answer⟩ **2 :** to sound reverberatingly ⟨a fog horn ~*ing* danger⟩
**²mutter** \"\ *n* -s **1 :** a subdued scarcely audible utterance ⟨the ~ of an audience⟩ **2 :** a low continuous sound ⟨the ~ of surf⟩
**mut·ter·er** \-ərə(r)\ *n* -s **:** one that mutters
**mut·ter·ing·ly** *adv* **:** in a muttering manner
**mut·ton** \ˈmətᵊn\ *n* -s [ME *motoun*, fr. OF *moton, mouton* ram, wether, agnel, of Celt origin; akin to MIr *molt* wether, MBret *mout*, W *mollt*; prob. akin to L *molere* to grind — more at MEAL] **1 a :** the flesh of a mature ovine animal when killed for food **b :** the dressed carcass of a sheep usu. one year of age or older characterized by the dark red color of the flesh, whiteness of the fat, and hardness of the bone **2 :** AGNEL **3 :** the matter at hand **:** the central issue — usu. used in pl. ⟨now I must get to my ~*s* and write —H.J.Laski⟩
**muttonbird** \ˈ==,=\ *n* **:** any of several Australasian sea birds often used (as by the Maori) for their meat, oil, and feathers: as **a** (1) **:** a short-tailed shearwater (*Puffinus tenuirostris*) of Australia and New Zealand (2) **:** a sooty shearwater (*Puffinus griseus*) of New Zealand **b :** any of several petrels (as *Pterodroma macroptera, P. lessoni*, and *P. neglecta*)
**muttonchops** \ˈ==,=\ *also* **muttonchop whiskers** *n pl* [so called fr. the shape] **:** side-whiskers that are narrow at the temple and broad and round by the lower jaws

muttonchops

**mutton corn** *n, chiefly South* **:** sweet corn that is just ripe enough to be eaten **:** ROASTING EARS
**muttonfish** \ˈ==,=\ *n* [so called fr. its flavor] **1 :** a snapper (*Lutjanus analis*) of the warmer parts of the western Atlantic that is usu. olive green and sometimes nearly white or tinged with rosy red and that is an excellent food and sport fish **2 :** an eelpout (*Zoarces anguillaris*) of the northerly eastern coastal waters of No. America **3** *also* **mutton shell** *Austral* **:** ABALONE
**mutton fist** *n* **1 :** a large brawny fist or hand **2** *archaic* **:** FISTNOTE
**mutton grass** *also* **mutton bluegrass** *n* **:** a bluegrass (*Poa fendleriana*) of drier parts of the western U.S. used as forage
**mutton ham** *n* **1** *chiefly Scot* **:** a leg of mutton cured like a ham **2** *Midland* **:** a large sail on a fishing boat
**muttonhead** \ˈ==,=\ *n* **:** a dull-witted person **:** OAF — **mutton·head·ed** \¦==¦==\ *adj*
**mutton quad** *n* [*mutton* so called fr. its use as a code word to distinguish pronounced *em quad* fr. *en quad*] **:** EM QUAD
**mutton snapper** *n* **:** MUTTONFISH 1
**mut·tony** \ˈmət(ᵊ)nē, -ni\ *adj* **1 :** suggesting mutton ⟨a ~ taste⟩ **2 a** *of a sheep* **:** having conformation suitable for production of meat **b** *of lamb meat* **:** coarse in texture and flavor
**mutua** *pl of* MUTUUM
**mu·tu·al** \ˈmyüch(ə)wəl, -chəl\ *adj* [ME *mutuall*, fr. MF *mutuel*, fr. L *mutuus* lent, borrowed, reciprocal, mutual + MF *-el* -al; akin to L *mutare* to change — more at MISS] **1 a :** entertained, proffered, or exerted by each with respect to the other of two or to each of the others of a group **:** given and received in equal amount ⟨~ love⟩ **b :** having the same feelings one for the other ⟨~ enemies⟩ ⟨~ lovers⟩ **c :** shared in common **:** enjoyed by each **:** COMMON ⟨a ~ friend⟩ ⟨a ~ hobby⟩ **d :** possessed, experienced, or done by two or more persons or things at the same time **:** JOINT ⟨~ effort⟩ ⟨~ advantage⟩ **2 :** characterized by or suggestive of intimacy or familiarity ⟨~ contacts⟩ **3 :** belonging to each of two or more associates **:** RESPECTIVE ⟨~ property⟩ **4 :** of or relating to a plan whereby the members of an organization share in the profits, benefits, expenses, and liabilities; *specif* **:** of, relating to, or taking the form of a method or plan in insurance in which the policyholders constitute the members of the insuring company or association, elect their own managers or directors, and share in the profits and in which assessments may or may not be provided for — compare INSURANCE 2b **syn** see RECIPROCAL
**mutual aid** *n* **:** reciprocal aid and cooperation as among men in social groups
**mutual aid association** *n* **1 :** an organization whose purpose is not primarily to distribute earnings to its members but to assist, benefit, or protect them in some common matters or objectives **:** a beneficial association **2 :** BENEFIT SOCIETY
**mutual benefit society** *n* **:** BENEFIT SOCIETY
**mutual conductance** *n* **:** the quotient of a change in plate current in an electron tube by the change in grid voltage producing it, the plate voltage remaining unchanged
**mutual fund** *n* **:** an open-end investment company that invests money of its shareholders in a usu. diversified group of securities of other corporations
**mutual gable** *or* **mutual wall** *n, Scots law* **:** PARTY WALL
**mutual inductance** *n* **:** the measure of the inductance between two circuits or parts thereof
**mutual induction** *n* **:** the induction produced on each other by two adjacent circuits **:** the induction produced in charged conductors adjacent to each other
**mutual inductor** *n* **:** a device providing mutual inductance and usu. consisting of two inductance coils not connected by conductors
**mutual investment company** *or* **mutual investment trust** *n* **:** an investment company that has a variable number of shares outstanding and that is ready at any time to issue or redeem shares at or near current liquidating value
**mu·tu·al·ism** \ˈmyüch(ə)wə,lizəm, -chə,l-\ *n* -s **1 a :** the doctrine or practice of mutual dependence as the condition of individual and social welfare **b :** a socialistic theory advocating a social organization based on common ownership, effort, and control and regulated by sentiments of mutual help and brotherhood **2 a :** mutually beneficial association between different kinds of organisms (as between various ants and aphids); *esp* **:** interaction between organisms of two kinds whereby a shared way of life becomes obligatory for both if the population of each is to increase — compare PREDATION **b :** the supposed factor or principle of mutual aid and cooperation among the lower animals
**mu·tu·al·ist** \-ləst\ *n* -s **1 :** an advocate of mutualism **2 :** one (as a commensal animal) that exists in a state of mutualism — **mu·tu·al·is·tic** \¦=(=)=¦listik\ *adj*
**mu·tu·al·i·ty** \,myüchə'walәd·ē, -lətē, -i\ *n* -ES **1 :** the quality or state of being mutual **:** quality of reciprocity **:** INTERCHANGE, INTERACTION, INTERDEPENDENCE **2 :** a sharing of sentiments between persons **:** interchange of kind acts or expressions
**mu·tu·al·ization** \,myüch(ə)wələ'zāshən, -chəl-, -,lī'z-\ *n* -s **:** the act or action of making or becoming mutual
**mu·tu·al·ize** \ˈ=(=)=,līz\ *vt* -ED/-ING/-S [*mutual* + *-ize*] **1 :** to make mutual **2 :** to convert (a corporation) into a mutual plan by purchase and retirement of its stocks
**mutual loan association** *n* **:** SAVINGS AND LOAN ASSOCIATION
**mu·tu·al·ly** \ˈmyüchəlē, -ch(ə)wəlē, -li\ *adv* **:** in a mutual manner
**mu·tu·al·ness** *pronunc at* MUTUAL + nəs\ *n* -ES **:** the quality or state of being mutual
**mutual savings bank** *n* **:** a bank organized without stock which receives savings deposits and whose earnings accrue entirely to the benefit of its depositors
**mutual wills** *n pl* **:** wills pursuant to agreement between and made by two or more persons that contain similar or identical testamentary provisions in favor of each other or of the same beneficiary — called also *reciprocal wills*
**mu·tu·ary** \ˈmyüchə,werē\ *n* -ES [L *mutuarius* mutual, in exchange, fr. *mutuus* borrowed, lent + *-arius* -ary — more at MUTUAL] *Roman & civil law* **:** the borrower in a contract of mutuum
**mutuate** *vt* -ED/-ING/-S [L *mutuatus*, past part. of *mutuari* to borrow, fr. *mutuus* borrowed, lent] *obs* **:** BORROW — **mutuation** *n* -s *obs*
**mu·tu·a·ti·tious** \¦myüchəwə¦tishəs\ *adj* [L *mutuaticius*, fr. *mutuatus* + *-icius* -itious — more at MUTUATE] *archaic* **:** BORROWED
**mu·tu·el** \ˈmyüch(ə)wəl, -chəl\ *n* -s *often attrib* [by shortening] **:** PARI-MUTUEL
**mu·tu·lar** \ˈmyüchələ(r)\ *or* **mu·tu·lary** \-,lerē\ *adj* **:** of or relating to the Doric order whose cornices bear mutules rather than dentils
**mu·tule** \-(,)chül\ *n* -s [L *mutulus*] **:** a flat block projecting under the corona of the Doric cornice in the same position as the modillion of other orders — compare GUTTA
**mu·tu·um** \-chəwəm\ *n, pl* **mu·tua** \-wə\ [ME, fr. L, fr. neut. of *mutuus* borrowed, lent — more at MUTUAL] **:** a loan in Roman and civil law of fungible things to be restored in similar property of the same quantity and quality; *also* **:** a contract in which movables are so loaned
**muu·muu** \ˈmü(,)mü\ *n* -s [Hawaiian *mu'u mu'u*, lit., cut-off; fr. the yoke's having formerly been omitted] **:** a loose dress worn chiefly in Hawaii, having gay colors and patterns, and adapted from the dresses orig. distributed by missionaries to the native women
**mu·vu·le** *also* **mu·vu·li** *or* **mvu·le** *or* **mvu·li** \mə'vü(,)lē\ *n* -s [native name in Africa] **:** IROKO
**¹mux** \ˈməks\ *vt* -ED/-ING/-ES [prob. back-formation fr. *mucksy*] *chiefly NewEng* **:** to put in disorder **:** make a mess of
**²mux** \"\ *n* -ES *chiefly NewEng* **:** a state of disorder **:** MESS
**mu·yu·sa** \mü'yüsə\ *n* -s [AmerSp] **:** the white-fleshed edible fruit of a stout cylindrical cactus (*Borzicactus sepium*) of Ecuador
**mu·zhik** *or* **mu·zjik** *or* **mu·jik** *or* **mou·jik** \(ˈ)mü¦zhik, -zhēk\ *n* -s [Russ *muzhik* peasant, dim. of *muzh* man, husband; fr. the fact that under old Russian law peasants were regarded as minors; akin to OSlav *mǫžĭ* man, OE *man* — more at MAN] **:** a Russian peasant
**¹muzz** \ˈməz\ *vt* -ED/-ING/-ES [back-formation fr. *muzzy*] *Brit* **:** to make muzzy
**²muzz** \"\ *n* -ES *Brit* **:** MUDDLE
**muz·zi·ly** \ˈməzəlē, -li\ *adv* **:** in a muzzy manner
**muz·zi·ness** \-zēnəs, -zin-\ *n* -ES **:** the quality or state of being muzzy
**¹muz·zle** \ˈməzəl\ *n* -s [ME *musell, mosel*, fr. MF *musel*, dim. of *muse* snout, muzzle, mouth of an animal, fr. ML *musus*] **1 a :** the projecting jaws and nose of an animal (as a horse or dog) **:** SNOUT — see COW illustration **b :** the human face or mouth **2 a :** a fastening or covering (as a band or cage) for the mouth of an animal used to prevent eating or biting **b :** something that restricts, censors, or otherwise circumscribes natural or normal expression ⟨a dictator's ~ on the popular press⟩ **3 :** the open end of an implement; *esp* **:** the end of a weapon from which the projectile emerges — see CANNON illustration **4** *archaic* **:** the clevis of a plow

muzzle 2a

**²muzzle** \"\ *vb* **muzzled; muzzled; muzzling** \-z(ə)liŋ\ **muzzles** *vi, dial chiefly Eng* **:** to push or root about with the muzzle ~ *vt* **1 :** to bind the muzzle of ⟨~ a dog⟩ **2 :** to restrain from expression (as by speech or action) **:** GAG ⟨~ freedom of speech⟩ **3 :** to press or rub with the muzzle or snout **:** NUZZLE **4 :** to take in (sail)
**muzzlebag** \ˈ==,=\ *n* **:** a cover for the muzzle (as of a naval gun) used to keep out rain and spray and made usu. of canvas
**muzzle blast** *n* **:** an excessively loud report produced by a gun often having a barrel shorter than standard or using a powder charge greater than standard and usu. attributed to powder exploding both within and without the barrel as well as to the impact of gases on the outside atmosphere; *also* **:** the flash or flame at the muzzle accompanying such a report
**muzzle brake** *n* **:** a device attached to the muzzle of a gun tube that utilizes escaping gases to reduce the force of recoil — compare COMPENSATOR
**muzzle device** *n* **:** a device fixed to the muzzle of a shotgun to act as a muzzle brake and usu. to allow a selection of chokes
**muzzle energy** *n* **:** the energy of impact of a bullet at the velocity developed at the muzzle of the piece and calculated according to the formula

$$ME=\frac{V^2}{7000}\div 2g\times w$$

where *ME* represents muzzle energy in foot-pounds, $V^2$ the square of the muzzle velocity in feet per second, *g* the acceleration due to gravity, and *w* the weight of the bullet in grains avoirdupois
**muzzle-loader** \¦==¦==\ *n* **:** a muzzle-loading firearm
**muzzle-loading** \¦==¦==\ *adj, of a firearm* **:** receiving the cartridge or projectile at the muzzle
**muz·zler** \ˈməz(ə)lə(r)\ *n* -s **1 :** one that muzzles **2 :** a head-on wind
**muzzle ring** *n* **:** a ring or ringlike projection near the muzzle of a piece
**muzzle velocity** *n* **:** the speed of a projectile at the moment of leaving the muzzle of a gun
**muzzlewood** \ˈ==,=\ *n* **:** BLACK SALLY
**muz·zy** \ˈməzē, -zi\ *adj* -ER/-EST [perh. blend of *muddled* and *fuzzy*] **1 :** muddled or confused in mind **:** DULL ⟨men ~ with drink⟩ **2 :** DULL, DEPRESSING ⟨a ~ day⟩; *also* **:** BLURRED ⟨a ~ brain⟩
**mv** *abbr* millivolt
**MV** *abbr* **1** main verb **2** market value **3** mean variation **4** medium voltage **5** merchant vessel **6** methyl violet **7** million volts **8** motor vessel **9** muzzle velocity
**Mv** *symbol* mendelevium
**MVC** *abbr* manual volume control
**mvt** *abbr* movement
**mw** *abbr* milliwatt
**MW** *abbr* **1** mixed widths **2** most worshipful **3** most worthy **4** music wire
**Mw** *abbr* megawatt
**mwa·mi** \mə'wämē\ *n* -s [native name in Africa] **:** the native ruler or king of Ruanda-Urundi, Africa
**MWG** *abbr* music-wire gauge
**mwh** *abbr* megawatt-hour
**MWP** *abbr* maximum working pressure
**mx** *abbr* **1** maxwell **2** multiplex
**mxd** *abbr* mixed
**¹my** [ME *my, mi, min*, fr. OE *mīn*, suppletive gen. of *ic* I] *obs possessive of* ²I
**²my** \(ˈ)mī, ˌmə\ *adj* [ME *my, mi, min*, fr. OE *mīn*, fr. *mīn*, suppletive gen. of *ic* I — more at MINE] **1 a :** of or belonging

to me or myself as possessor : due to me : inherent in me : associated or connected with me ⟨bumped ~ head⟩ ⟨defending ~ rights⟩ ⟨all ~ relatives⟩ **b** : of or relating to me or myself as author, doer, giver, or agent : effected by me : experienced by me as subject : that I am capable of ⟨criticized all ~ words and actions⟩ ⟨kept ~ promise⟩ ⟨was angry because of ~ being late⟩ ⟨did ~ very best⟩ **c** : of or relating to me as object of an action : experienced by me as object ⟨expected ~ election as secretary⟩ ⟨~ injuries didn't amount to much⟩ **d** : that I have to do with or am believed to possess or to have knowledge or a share of or some special interest in ⟨I like golf and I know ~ game⟩ **e** : that is esp. significant for me : that brings me good fortune or prominence — used with *day* or sometimes with other words indicating a division of time ⟨today was really ~ day: everything went fine⟩ **2 a** — used with a noun of address to express endearment ⟨tell me, ~ little sister⟩ or jocularity ⟨I see you're stepping out, ~ boy⟩ or familiarity ⟨come along, ~ man⟩ or compassion ⟨~ poor fellow⟩ **b** — used esp. with *lord* or *lady* functioning as a noun of address to express special deference or submission ⟨I'll obey your command, ~ lord⟩ **c** — used interjectionally to express surprise and sometimes reduplicated ⟨~, ~⟩ ⟨~ oh ~⟩; used also interjectionally with names of various parts of the body to express doubt or disapproval ⟨~ foot⟩ ⟨~ eye⟩; used also as an intensive in oaths ⟨oh ~ lord⟩

**my-** *or* **myo-** *comb form* [NL, fr. Gk, fr. *mys* — more at MOUSE] **1** : mouse ⟨*myomorpha*⟩ **2 a** : muscle ⟨*myology*⟩ : muscle and ⟨*myoelastic*⟩ **b** : myoma and — with words ending in *-oma* ⟨*myofibroma*⟩

**my** *abbr* **1** muddy **2** myopia

**MY** *abbr* motor yacht

**mya** \ˈmīə\ *n, cap* [NL, fr. L, mussel, irreg. fr. Gk *myax* — more at MUREX] : a genus (the type of the family Myacidae) of bivalve mollusks including the common soft-shell clam — see MYACEA

**-mya** \ˈmīə\ *n pl comb form* [NL, fr. Gk *mys* mouse, muscle] : creatures having such, so many, or so arranged musculature — in higher taxa of mollusks ⟨*Dimya*⟩ ⟨*Heteromya*⟩

**my·a·cea** \mīˈāshēə\ *n pl, cap* [NL, fr. *Mya* + *-acea*] : a suborder of Eulamellibranchia that comprises bivalve mollusks with well-developed siphons, gaping valves, and a pallial sinus and includes various economically important edible mollusks (as of the genus *Mya*) — see MYACIDAE

**my·ac·i·dae** \mīˈasə,dē\ *n pl, cap* [NL, fr. *Myac-*, *Mya*, type genus + *-idae*] : a family of marine bivalve mollusks (suborder Myacea) comprising the soft-shell clams

**my·al** \ˈmīəl\ *adj* [origin unknown] : of or relating to myalism

**my·al·gia** \mīˈalj(ē)ə\ *n* -s [NL, fr. *my-* + *-algia*] : pain in one or more muscles

**my·al·gic** \-jik\ *adj* [NL *myalgia* + E *-ic*] : characteristic of or affected with myalgia

**my·al·ism** \ˈmīə,lizəm\ *n* -s : a cult among West Indian Negroes akin to obeah and prob. of West African origin

**¹my·all** \ˈmī,ȯl\ *adj* [native name in Australia] *Austral* : WILD, UNCIVILIZED

**²myall** \"\ *n* -s *often attrib* : an Australian aborigine ⟨~ tribes still roaming the wildest backcountry —W.L.Worden⟩

**³myall** \"\ *n* -s [native name in Australia] **1** : any of various Australian acacias with hard fragrant wood: as **a** : WEEPING MYALL **b** : YARRAN **2 c** : BASTARD MYALL **2** *also* **myall wood** : the hard heavy fine-grained wood of a myall that is used esp. for carving and small articles of fine woodworking

**My·an·e·sin** \mīˈanəsən\ *trademark* — used for mephenesin

**my·ar·ia** \mīˈa(a)rēə\ *n pl, cap* [NL, fr. *Mya* + *-aria*] *in some classifications* : a group of marine bivalves nearly equivalent to Myacea

**-my·ar·ia** \,mīˈa(a)rēə, -ˈer-, -ˈār-\ *n pl comb form* [NL, fr. *my-* + *-aria*] : -MYA

**my·as·the·nia** \,mīəsˈthēnēə\ *n* -s [NL, fr. *my-* + *asthenia*] : muscular debility

**myasthenia gravis** *n* [NL, lit., grave myasthenia] : a disease characterized by progressive weakness and exhaustibility of voluntary muscles without atrophy or sensory disturbance

**my·as·then·ic** \ˌ⸗⸗ˈthenik\ *adj* [NL *myasthenia* + E *-ic*] : of, relating to, or characterized by myasthenia

**my·a·to·nia** \,mīəˈtōnēə\ *n* -s [NL, fr. *my-* + LL *atonia* atony — more at ATONY] : lack of muscle tone : muscular flabbiness

**myc-** *or* **myco-** *comb form* [NL, irreg. fr. Gk *mykēs* fungus, mushroom; akin to Gk *myxa* lampwick, nasal mucus — more at MUCUS] : fungus ⟨*mycelium*⟩ ⟨*mycobiota*⟩ ⟨*mycogenetic*⟩ ⟨*mycology*⟩ ⟨*mycosis*⟩; *specif* : mushroom ⟨*mycophile*⟩

**my·ce·li·al** \mīˈsēlēəl\ *adj* [NL *mycelium* + E *-al*] : of, relating to, or characterized by mycelium

**my·ce·lia ste·ri·lia** \mī¦sēlēəstəˈrilēə\ *n pl, cap M&S* [NL, lit., sterile mycelia] : a group that is usu. considered more or less equivalent to an order and that comprises genera of imperfect fungi having no known spore stage and producing sclerotia, rhizomorphs, or simply mycelial masses — see OZONIUM, RHIZOCTONIA, SCLEROTIUM

**my·ce·li·oid** \mīˈsēlē,ȯid\ *adj* [NL *mycelium* + E *-oid*] : resembling mycelium

**my·ce·li·um** \-lēəm\ *n, pl* **myce·lia** \-ēə\ [NL, fr. *myc-* + Gk *hēlos* nail, wart, callus + NL *-ium*; perh akin to Gk *eilyein* to fold — more at VOLUBLE] : the mass of interwoven hyphae that forms esp. the vegetative portion of the thallus of a fungus and that in the larger forms (as the mushrooms) forms cobwebby filaments penetrating the substrate but in many smaller fungi (as most parasitic forms) is invisible to the naked eye but ramifies through the substrate or tissues of the host usu. producing its spore fruits on the surface; *also* : a similar mass of filaments formed by a higher bacterium

**¹my·ce·nae·an** \,mīsəˈnēən\ *also* **my·ce·ni·an** \mīˈsēnēən\ *adj, usu cap* [*Mycenae*, ancient city of Greece (fr. L, fr. Gk *Mykēnai*) + E *-an* or *-ian*] **1 a** : of, relating to, or characteristic of the ancient city of Mycenae **b** : of, relating to, or characteristic of the people of Mycenae **2 a** : AEGEAN **b** (1) : of, relating to, or characteristic of the period of Mycenae's political ascendancy extending from about 1400 to 1100 B.C. (2) : of, relating to, or characteristic of the Bronze Age culture of the eastern Mediterranean area characterized by objects of Mycenaean style

**²mycenaean** \"\ *also* **mycenian** \"\ *n* -s *cap* **1** : a native or inhabitant of ancient Mycenae **2** : the early Greek language of the Mycenaeans known from inscriptions

**-my·ces** \ˈmī,sēz\ *n comb form* [NL, fr. Gk *mykēs*] : fungus ⟨Actino*myces*⟩ ⟨Phyco*myces*⟩

**mycet-** *or* **myceto-** *comb form* [ISV, fr. Gk *mykēt-*, *mykēs* — more at MYC-] : fungus ⟨*mycetocolous*⟩ ⟨*mycetogenetic*⟩ ⟨*mycetoma*⟩ ⟨*Mycetozoa*⟩

**-my·cete** \ˈmī,sēt, ,mīˈsēt, *usu* -ēd.+V\ *n comb form* -s [NL *-mycetes*] : fungus ⟨*micromycete*⟩

**my·ce·tes** \mīˈsēd·ēz\ [NL, fr. Gk *myketēs* one that bellows, fr. *mykasthai* to bellow; akin to MHG *mūhen*, *mūgen*, *mūwen* to roar, bellow, L *mutus* mute — more at MUTE] *syn of* ALOUATTA

**-my·ce·tes** \,mīˈsēd·ēz, -ētēz\ *n pl comb form* [NL, fr. Gk *mykētes*, pl. of *mykēt-*, *mykēs* fungus, mushroom — more at MYC-] : fungi — chiefly in names of classes and subclasses ⟨Asco*mycetes*⟩ ⟨Schizo*mycetes*⟩

**my·ce·tism** \ˈmīsə,tizəm\ *n* -s [*mycet-* + *-ism*] : MYCETISMUS

**my·ce·tis·mus** \,mīsəˈtizməs\ *n, pl* **mycetis·mi** \-z,mī\ [NL, fr. *mycet-* + L *-ismus* -ism] : mushroom poisoning

**my·ce·to·cyte** \mīˈsēd·ə,sīt\ *n* -s [*mycet-* + *-cyte*] : a cell in various insects (as most true bugs) of a type that contains unicellular and prob. symbiotic fungi and is usu. clustered with others of its kind into paired mycetomes

**my·ce·toid** \mīˈsē,tȯid\ *adj* [ISV *mycet-* + *-oid*] : of, relating to, or resembling a fungus : FUNGOID

**my·ce·to·ma** \,mīsəˈtōmə\ *n, pl* **mycetomas** \-məz\ *or* **mycetoma·ta** \-məd·ə\ [NL, fr. *mycet-* + *-oma*] : a condition marked by invasion of the deep subcutaneous tissues with fungi or actinomycetes: **a** : MADUROMYCOSIS **b** : NOCARDIOSIS — **my·ce·tom·a·tous** \ˌ⸗⸗ˈtämədəs, -tōm-\ *adj*

**my·ce·tome** \ˈmīsə,tōm\ *n* -s [*mycet-* + *-ome*] : either of a pair of organs in an insect (as a true bug) that consist of a cellular mass of mycetocytes and are located one in either fat body

**my·ce·tom·ic** \ˌmīsəˈtämik\ *adj* : of, relating to, or occurring in a mycetome ⟨~ yeasts⟩

**my·ce·to·phag·i·dae** \mī,sēd·əˈfajə,dē\ *n pl, cap* [NL, fr. *Mycetophagus*, type genus (fr. *mycet-* + *-phagus*, fr. Gk *phagein* to eat) + *-idae* — more at BAKSHEESH] : a family of small oval usu. hairy beetles having 5-jointed tarsi and generally feeding on fungi

**my·ce·toph·a·gous** \ˌmīsəˈtäfəgəs\ *adj* [*mycet-* + *-phagous*] : feeding on fungi : FUNGIVOROUS ⟨~ insects are themselves fed upon —Orlando Park⟩

**¹my·ce·toph·i·lid** \ˌmīsəˈtäfələd\ *adj* [NL *Mycetophilidae*] : of or relating to the family Mycetophilidae

**²mycetophilid** \"\ *n* -s [NL *Mycetophilidae*] : a fungus gnat of the family Mycetophilidae

**my·ce·to·phil·i·dae** \mī,sēd·əˈfilə,dē\ *n pl, cap* [NL, fr. *Mycetophila*, type genus (fr. *mycet-* + *-phila*) + *-idae*] : a large widely distributed family of small nematocerous two-winged flies that includes the majority of the fungus gnats — compare SCIARIDAE

**my·ce·tous** \mīˈsēd·əs\ *adj* [*mycet-* + *-ous*] : of, relating to, or resembling a fungus

**my·ce·to·zoa** \,mī,sēd·əˈzōə\ *n pl, cap* [NL, fr. *mycet-* + *-zoa*] : the Myxomycetes regarded as an order of rhizopod protozoans

**¹my·ce·to·zo·an** \⸗ˌ⸗⸗ˈzōən\ *adj* [NL *Mycetozoa* + E *-an*] : of or relating to the Mycetozoa

**²mycetozoan** \"\ *n* -s : MYXOMYCETE

**my·ce·to·zo·on** \⸗ˌ⸗⸗ˈzō,än\ *n, pl* **myceto·zoa** \-ōə\ [NL, fr. *mycet-* + *-zoon*] : MYXOMYCETE

**-my·cin** \ˈmīsᵊn\ *n comb form* -s [ISV *myc-* + *-in*] : substance obtained from a fungus ⟨carbo*mycin*⟩ ⟨erythro*mycin*⟩

**myco-** — see MYC-

**my·co·bac·te·ria** \,mīkō,bakˈtirēə\ [NL, fr. *myc-* + *bacteria*] *syn of* ACTINOMYCETALES

**my·co·bac·te·ri·a·ce·ae** \,⸗⸗,⸗,tirēˈāsē,ē\ *n pl, cap* [NL, fr. *Mycobacterium*, type genus + *-aceae*] : a family of rod-shaped bacteria (order Actinomycetales) rarely filamentous and with only occasional slight branching

**my·co·bac·te·ri·al** \ˌ⸗⸗,⸗ˈtirēəl\ *adj* [NL *Mycobacteria* + E *-al*] : of, relating to, or caused by Mycobacteria

**my·co·bacterium** \ˌ⸗⸗,⸗ˈtirēəm\ *n* [NL, fr. *myc-* + *Bacterium*] **1** *cap* : a genus of nonmotile acid-fast aerobic bacteria (family Mycobacteriaceae) that are usu. slender and difficult to stain and that include forms causing tuberculosis and leprosy as well as numerous purely saprophytic forms **2** : any bacterium of *Mycobacterium* or a closely related genus

**my·co·cecidium** \ˌmīkō+\ *n* [NL, fr. *myc-* + *cecidium*] : a gall produced by the attacks of a parasitic fungus

**my·co·cide** \ˈmīkə,sīd\ *n* -s [*myc-* + *-cide*] : a fungicide that destroys molds

**my·co·der·ma** \,mīkəˈdərmə\ *n* [NL, fr. *myc-* + *-derma*] **1** -s **a** : ⁴MOTHER 2 **b** *or* **my·co·derm** \ˈmīkə,dərm\ : a bacterium or yeast that is a constituent of a mother or flor **2** *cap* : a genus of microorganisms recovered from mothers or flors orig. including a varied assortment of yeasts and acetobacters but now usu. restricted to various yeasts of the family Pseudosaccharomycetaceae that do not form ascospores but grow vegetatively in the presence of air producing a scum on the surface of alcoholic solutions (as wine and beer) — **my·co·der·ma·toid** \ˌmīkəˈdərmə,tȯid\ *adj* — **my·co·der·ma·tous** \-məd·əs\ *adj*

**my·co·der·mic** \-mik\ *adj* : of or relating to a mycoderm

**my·co·flora** \ˌmīkō+\ *n* [NL, fr. *myc-* + *flora*] : a flora of fungi — **my·co·floral** \"+\ *adj*

**my·co·gone** \ˈmīkə,gōn\ *n, cap* [NL, fr. *myc-* + Gk *gonē* offspring, race, seed, womb, fr. the stem of *gignesthai* to be born — more at KIN] : a form genus of imperfect fungi (family Moniliaceae) having unequally two-celled conidia on short lateral conidiophores — see BUBBLE DISEASE

**my·col·ic acid** \(ˈ)mīˌkälik-\ *n* [*myc-* + L *oleum* oil + E *-ic* — more at OIL] : any of several hydroxy fatty acids that have very long branched chains and are obtained esp. from the wax of tubercle bacilli

**my·co·log·ic** \ˌmīkəˈläjik\ *or* **my·co·log·i·cal** \-jəkəl\ *adj* : of or relating to mycology — **my·co·log·i·cal·ly** \-jək(ə)lē\ *adv*

**my·col·o·gist** \mīˈkäləjəst\ *n* -s : a specialist in mycology

**my·col·o·gize** \-lə,jīz\ *vi* -ED/-ING/-S : to study fungi

**my·col·o·gy** \-jē, -ji\ *n* -ES [NL *mycologia*, fr. *myc-* + L *-logia* -logy] **1** : a branch of botany dealing with fungi **2** : fungal life (as of a region) ⟨the ~ of a swamp⟩ **3** : the properties and life phenomena exhibited by a fungus, fungus type, or fungus group ⟨the ~ of a mold⟩ **4** : a treatise on fungi

**my·co·my·cete** \,mīkōˈmī,sēt, ¦⸗⸗,⸗ˈ⸗\ *n* -s [NL *Mycomycetes*] : one of the Mycomycetes

**my·co·my·ce·tes** \,mīkō,mīˈsēd·ēz\ *n pl, cap* [NL, fr. *myc-* + *-mycetes*] *in some classifications* : a class of fungi including the Ascomycetes and Basidiomycetes — compare PHYCOMYCETES — **my·co·my·ce·tous** \ˌ⸗⸗⸗ˈsēd·əs\ *adj*

**my·co·mycin** \,mīkəˈmīsᵊn\ *n* -s [ISV *myc-* + *-mycin*] : a highly unsaturated antibiotic acid $C_{13}H_9COOH$ obtained from an actinomycete (*Nocardia acidophilus*)

**my·coph·a·gist** \mīˈkäfəjəst\ *n* -s [*mycophagy* + *-ist*] : one that eats fungi (as mushrooms)

**my·coph·a·gous** \-fəgəs\ *adj* [*myc-* + *-phagous*] : feeding on fungi : eating mushrooms ⟨a ~ coccinellid —*Biol. Abstracts*⟩

**my·coph·a·gy** \-fəjē\ *n* -ES [*myc-* + *-phagy*] : the eating of fungi (as mushrooms)

**my·co·phenolic acid** \ˌmīkō+ . . .-\ *n* [ISV *myc-* + *phenolic*] : a crystalline antibiotic $C_{17}H_{20}O_6$ obtained from fungi of the genus *Penicillium*

**my·coph·tho·rous** \mīˈkäfthərəs\ *adj* [*myc-* + Gk *phthor-* (stem of *phtheirein* to destroy, corrupt) + *-ous* — more at PHTHIRIASIS] *of a fungus* : parasitizing a fungus

**my·co·plasm** \ˈmīkə,plazəm\ *also* **my·co·plas·ma** \ˌ⸗⸗ˈplazmə\ *n* [NL *mycoplasma*, fr. *myc-* + *-plasma*] : a hypothetical hibernating form of various fungi (as rusts) in which the fungus protoplasm is intimately fused with that of dormant structures (as seeds) of the host plant

**my·co·plas·ma** \ˌ⸗⸗ˈplazmə\ *n, cap* [NL *Mycoplasmat-*, *Mycoplasma*, fr. *myc-* + *-plasmat-*, *-plasma* -plasma] : the type and usu. sole genus of the family Mycoplasmataceae

**my·co·plas·ma·ta·ce·ae** \,mīkə,plazməˈtāsē,ē\ *n pl, cap* [NL, fr. *Mycoplasmat-*, *Mycoplasma*, type genus + *-aceae*] : a family (coextensive with the order Mycoplasmatales) of minute pleomorphic gram-negative nonmotile microorganisms that are intermediate in some respects between viruses and bacteria, are reported to have complex life cycles, and are mostly parasitic usu. in mammals — compare PLEUROPNEUMONIA; see BORRELOMYCETACEAE

**my·cor·rhi·za** *also* **my·co·rhi·za** \,mīkəˈrīzə\ *n, pl* **my·corrhi·zae** \-rī,zē\ *or* **mycorrhizas** [NL, fr. *myc-* + *-rhiza*] : the symbiotic association of the mycelium of a fungus (as various basidiomycetes and ascomycetes) with the roots of a seed plant (as various conifers, beeches, heaths, and orchids) in which the hyphae form an interwoven mass investing the root tips or penetrate the parenchyma of the root — compare ECTOTROPHIC, ENDOTROPHIC — **my·cor·rhi·zal** *also* **my·co·rhi·zal** \ˌ⸗⸗ˈrīzəl\ *adj*

**my·co·sis** \mīˈkōsəs\ *n, pl* **myco·ses** \-ō,sēz\ [NL, fr. *myc-* + *-osis*] : infection with or disease caused by a fungus

**mycosis fun·goi·des** \fəŋˈgȯidēz\ *n* [NL, lit., fungoid mycosis] : a chronic progressive disease possibly related to leukemia and marked by the development of reddish tumors esp. upon the scalp, face, and chest and sometimes by cellular infiltration of various visceral organs

**my·co·sphaerella** \ˌmīkō+\ *n, cap* [NL, fr. *myc-* + *Sphaerella*] : a genus (the type of the family Mycosphaerellaceae) of fungi of the order Sphaeriales having 2-celled ascospores borne in perithecia that are immersed in dead portions of the host — see CURRANT LEAF SPOT

**my·co·stat** \ˈmīkə,stat\ *n* -s [*myc-* + *-stat*] : an agent that inhibits the growth of molds

**my·co·stat·ic** \ˌ⸗⸗ˈstad·ik\ *adj* : of or relating to a mycostat ⟨~ vapors⟩

**my·cos·ter·ol** \mīˈkästə,rōl, -rȯl\ *n* [*myc-* + *sterol*] : any of a class of sterols obtained from fungi

**my·co·symbiosis** \ˌmīkō+\ *n* [NL, fr. *myc-* + *symbiosis*] : symbiosis in which a fungus participates

**my·cot·ic** \(ˈ)mīˈkäd·ik\ *adj* [G *mykotisch*, fr. *mykose* mycosis (fr. NL *mycosis*), after such pairs as G *hypnotisch* hypnotic: *hypnose* hypnosis, fr. NL *hypnosis*] : of, relating to, or characterized by mycosis ⟨~ dermatitis⟩

**mycotic pneumonia** *n* : brooder pneumonia of the chicken

**mycotic stomatitis** *n* : thrush of cattle and other ruminants

**my·co·troph·ic** \ˌmīkəˈträfik\ *adj* [ISV *myc-* + *-trophic*] : obtaining food by association with a fungus — **my·cot·ro·phy** \mīˈkä·trəfē\ *n* -ES

**myc·te·ria** \mikˈtirēə\ *n, cap* [NL, fr. Gk *myktēr* nostril, nose + NL *-ia*; akin to Gk *myxa* lampwick, nasal mucus — more at MUCUS] : a genus of storks now consisting only of the American wood ibis (*M. americana*)

**myc·ter·ic** \(ˈ)mikˈterik\ *adj* [Gk *myktēr* + E *-ic*] : of or relating to the nasal cavities

**myc·ter·o·per·ca** \,miktərōˈpərkə\ *n, cap* [NL, fr. Gk *myktēr* + L *perca* perch — more at PERCH] : a widely distributed genus of groupers

**myc·to·de·ra** \,miktəˈdirə\ [NL, fr. *mycto-* (fr. Gk *myktēr* nostril, nose) + L *-dera* (fr. Gk *derē*, *deirē* neck) — more at DER-] *syn of* MUTABILIA

**myc·to·phid** \ˈmiktəfəd\ *n* -s [NL *Myctophidae*] : one of the Myctophidae

**myc·toph·i·dae** \mikˈtäfə,dē\ *n pl, cap* [NL, fr. *Myctophum*, type genus + *-idae*] : a family of marine fishes (order Isospondyli) comprising the true lantern fishes

**myc·to·phum** \mikˈtōfəm\ *n, cap* [NL, fr. Gk *myktēr* nose, nostril + *-ophum* (fr. Gk *ophis* snake) — more at ANGUIS] : a genus (the type of the family Myctophidae) of lantern fishes

**my·da·i·dae** \mīˈdāə,dē\ *n pl, cap* [NL, fr. *Mydas*, type genus (irreg. fr. Gk *midax*, an insect destructive to beans) + *-idae*] : a small family of American and Australian dipterous insects containing the largest known two-winged flies

**my·das fly** *or* **mi·das fly** \ˈmīdəs-\ *n* [NL *Mydas*, genus of dipterous insects] : a fly of the family Mydaidae

**myd·a·us** \ˈmidāəs\ *n, cap* [NL, fr. Gk *mydan* to be damp — more at MOSS] : a genus of mammals (family Viverridae) consisting of the teledu

**my·dri·a·sine** \məˈdrīə,sēn, mīˈ-, -ˌsən\ *n* -s [ISV *mydrias-* (fr. L *mydriasis*) + *-ine*] : a white crystalline compound $C_{17}H_{23}NO_3.CH_3Br$ used like atropine; atropine methobromide

**my·dri·a·sis** \məˈdrīəsəs, mīˈ-\ *n, pl* **mydria·ses** \-ə,sēz\ [L, fr. Gk] : dilatation of the pupil of the eye esp. when prolonged (as from the effect of drugs) or excessive

**¹myd·ri·at·ic** \ˌmidrēˈad·ik\ *adj* [fr. *mydriasis*, after such pairs as E *hypostatic*: *hypostasis*] : causing or involving dilatation of the pupil of the eye

**²mydriatic** \"\ *n* -s : a drug that produces dilatation of the pupil of the eye

**myel-** *or* **myelo-** *comb form* [NL, fr. Gk, fr. *myelos*, fr. *mys* mouse, muscle — more at MOUSE] : marrow ⟨*myelin*⟩ ⟨*myelocyte*⟩: as **a** : bone marrow ⟨*myelogenous*⟩ **b** : spinal cord ⟨*myelencephalon*⟩ ⟨*myelocele*⟩

**my·e·len·ce·phal·ic** \ˌmīəlˌensəˈfalik\ *adj* [NL *myelencephalon* + E *-ic*] : of or relating to the myelencephalon

**my·e·len·ceph·a·lon** \ˌ⸗⸗lənˈsefə,län\ *n* [NL, fr. *myel-* + *encephalon*] : the posterior portion of the rhombencephalon: **a** : MEDULLA OBLONGATA **b** : the posterior part of the medulla oblongata that differs little in structure from the spinal cord with which it is continuous

**-my·e·lia** \,mīˈēlēə\ *n comb form* -s [NL, fr. *myel-* + *-ia*] : (specified) condition of the spinal cord ⟨*hematomyelia*⟩ ⟨*syringomyelia*⟩

**my·el·ic** \(ˈ)mīˈelik\ *adj* [*myel-* + *-ic*] : of or relating to the spinal cord

**my·e·lin** \ˈmīələn\ *also* **my·e·line** \", -ə,lēn\ *n* -s [ISV *myel-* + *-in*, *-ine*; orig. formed as G *myelin*] : a soft white somewhat fatty material that in medullated nerve fibers forms a thick medullary sheath about the axis cylinder and contains lipides (as lecithin and cerebrosides) and proteins usu. combined with lipides — **my·e·lin·ic** \ˌmīəˈlinik\ *adj*

**my·e·li·nat·ed** \ˈmīələ,nād·əd\ *adj, of a nerve* : having a medullary sheath

**my·e·li·na·tion** \ˌ⸗⸗⸗ˈnāshən\ *or* **my·e·lin·iza·tion** \,mīələnəˈzāshən\ *n* -s **1** : the process of acquiring a medullary sheath **2** : the condition of being myelinated

**myelino-** *comb form* [NL, fr. ISV *myelin*] : myelin ⟨*myelinoclasis*⟩ ⟨*myelinoclastic*⟩ ⟨*myelinogenesis*⟩ ⟨*myelinogenetic*⟩

**myelin sheath** *n* : MEDULLARY SHEATH 1

**my·e·lit·ic** \ˌmīəˈlid·ik\ *adj* [*myel-* + *-itic*] : affecting or attracted to the spinal cord ⟨a ~ virus⟩

**my·e·li·tis** \ˌmīəˈlīd·əs\ *n, pl* **myelit·i·des** \-lid·ə,dēz\ [NL, fr. *myel-* + *-itis*] : inflammation of the spinal cord or of the bone marrow

**my·e·lo·blast** \ˈmīəlō,blast\ *n* [ISV *myel-* + *-blast*] **1** : HEMOCYTOBLAST **2** : a cell derived from the hemocytoblast and serving as precursor for the blood granulocytes — **my·e·lo·blas·tic** \ˌ⸗⸗⸗ˈblastik\ *adj*

**my·e·lo·blas·te·mia** \ˌ⸗⸗⸗,blaˈstēmēə\ *n* -s [NL, fr. ISV *myeloblast* + NL *-emia*] : the presence of myeloblasts in the circulating blood (as in myelogenous leukemia)

**myeloblastic leukemia** *n* : MYELOGENOUS LEUKEMIA

**my·e·lo·blas·to·ma** \ˌ⸗⸗⸗,blaˈstōmə\ *n, pl* **myeloblastomas** \-məz\ *or* **myeloblastoma·ta** \-məd·ə\ [NL, fr. ISV *myeloblast* + NL *-oma*] **1** : a myeloma consisting of myeloblasts **2** : MYELOGENOUS LEUKEMIA

**my·e·lo·brachium** \ˌmīəlō+\ *n* [NL, fr. *myel-* + *brachium*] : RESTIFORM BODY

**my·e·lo·cele** *also* **my·e·lo·coele** \ˈmīəlō,sēl\ *n* -s [ISV *myel-* + *-cele*, *-coele*] : the central canal of the spinal cord

**my·e·lo·cerebellar** \ˌmīəlō+\ *adj* [*myel-* + *cerebellar*] : of or relating to the spinal cord and cerebellum

**my·e·lo·cyte** \ˈmīəlō,sīt\ *n* -s [ISV *myel-* + *-cyte*] **1** : a bone-marrow cell; *esp* : a motile cell with cytoplasmic granules that gives rise to the granulocytes of the blood but is not itself present in normal blood **2** : a nerve cell of the gray matter of the central nervous system — **my·e·lo·cyt·ic** \ˌ⸗⸗⸗ˈsid·ik\ *adj*

**my·e·lo·cy·to·ma** \,mīəlō,sīˈtōmə\ *n, pl* **myelocytomas** \-məz\ *or* **myelocytoma·ta** \-məd·ə\ [NL, fr. ISV *myelocyte* + NL *-oma*] : a tumor of which the typical cellular element is a myelocyte or a cell of similar differentiation — **my·e·lo·cy·to·ma·to·sis** \ˌ⸗⸗⸗,⸗,tōməˈtōsəs\ *n, pl* **myelocytomato·ses** \-ˈtō,sēz\

**my·e·lo·cy·to·sis** \,mīəlō,sīˈtōsəs\ *n, pl* **myelocyto·ses** \-ˈtō,sēz\ [NL, fr. ISV *myelocyte* + NL *-osis*] : the presence of excess numbers of myelocytes in blood, bone marrow, or other parts of the body

**my·e·log·e·nous** \ˌmīəˈläjənəs\ *also* **my·e·lo·gen·ic** \ˌmīəlōˈjenik\ *adj* [ISV *myel-* + *-genous*, *-genic*] : of, relating to, originating in, or produced by the bone marrow ⟨~ sarcoma⟩

**myelogenous leukemia** *n* : leukemia characterized by proliferation of myeloid tissue (as of the bone marrow and spleen) and an abnormal increase in the number of granulocytes, myelocytes, and myeloblasts in the circulating blood

**my·e·lo·gram** \ˈmīəlō,gram\ *n* [ISV *myel-* + *-gram*] **1** : a differential study of the cellular elements present in bone marrow usu. made on material obtained by sternal biopsy **2** : a roentgenogram of the spinal cord made by myelography

**my·e·lo·graph·ic** \ˌ⸗⸗⸗ˈgrafik\ *adj* [*myel-* + *-graphic*] : of, relating to, or by means of a myelogram or myelography — **my·e·lo·graph·i·cal·ly** \-fək(ə)lē\ *adv*

**my·e·log·ra·phy** \,mīəˈlägrəfē\ *n* -ES [ISV *myel-* + *-graphy*] : roentgenographic visualization of the spinal subarachnoid space after the injection of a contrast medium

**my·e·loid** \ˈmīə,lȯid\ *adj* [ISV *myel-* + *-oid*] **1** : of or relating to the spinal cord **2** : of, relating to, arising from, or like the bone marrow; *esp* : of or relating to myeloblasts or to cells derived from them ⟨the ~ series consists of myeloblasts, myelocytes, and true granulocytes⟩ — compare ERYTHROID

**myeloid leukemia** *n* : MYELOGENOUS LEUKEMIA

**my·e·lo·ma** \,mīəˈlōmə\ *n, pl* **myelomas** \-məz\ *or* **myeloma·ta** \-məd·ə\ [NL, fr. *myel-* + *-oma*] : a primary tumor of the bone marrow formed of any one of the bone-marrow cells (as myelocytes or plasma cells) and usu. involving several different bones at the same time — see MULTIPLE MYELOMA

**my·e·lo·ma·to·sis** \,mīə,lōməˈtōsəs\ *n, pl* **myelomato·ses** \-tō,sēz\ [NL, fr. *myelomat-*, *myeloma* + *-osis*] : the condition of being affected with multiple myeloma

**my·e·lom·a·tous** \ˌmīəˈlämədəs, -lōm-\ *adj* [NL *myelomat-*, *myeloma* + E *-ous*] : of or relating to a myeloma or to myelomatosis

**my·e·lo·mere** \ˈmīəlōˌmi(ə)r\ *n* -s [ISV *myel-* + *-mere*] **:** any of the segments of the developing central nervous system corresponding with a mesoblastic somite on either side

**my·e·lon·ic** \ˌmīəˈlänik\ *adj* [NL *myelon* spinal cord (fr. Gk *myelos* marrow) + E *-ic* — more at MYEL-] **:** of or relating to the spinal cord

**my·e·lo·path·ic** \ˌmīəlōˈpathik\ *adj* [ISV *myel-* + *-pathic*] **:** of or relating to a myelopathy **:** resulting from abnormality of the spinal cord or the bone marrow ⟨~ anemia⟩

**my·e·lop·a·thy** \ˌmīəˈläpəthē\ *n* -ES [ISV *myel-* + *-pathy*] **:** a disease or disorder of the spinal cord or the bone marrow

**my·e·lo·phthisic anemia** \ˌmīəlō+ . . . -\ *n* [ISV *myel-* + *phthisic*] **:** anemia in which the blood-forming elements of the bone marrow are unable to reproduce normal blood cells and which is commonly caused by specific toxins or by overgrowth of tumor cells

**my·e·lo·phthisis** \"+\ *n* [NL, fr. *myel-* + *phthisis*] **:** MYELOPHTHISIC ANEMIA

**my·el·o·plax** \mīˈeləˌplaks\ *n, pl* **myeloplaxes** \-ksəz\ *or* **my·e·lo·pla·ces** \ˌmīəˈläpləˌsēz\ [NL, fr. *myel-* + Gk *plax* flat object — more at PLEASE] **:** one of the large multinucleate cells in bone marrow **:** MEGAKARYOCYTE, OSTEOCLAST

**my·e·lo·poi·e·sis** \ˌmīəlōˌpoiˈēsəs\ *n, pl* **myelopoie·ses** \-ēˌsēz\ [NL, fr. *myel-* + *-poiesis*] **1 :** production of marrow or marrow cells **2 :** production of blood cells in bone marrow; *esp* **:** formation of blood granulocytes

**my·e·lo·poi·et·ic** \ˌ≈≈≈ˈed·ik\ *adj* [*myel-* + Gk *poiētikos* capable of making — more at POETIC] **:** of or relating to myelopoiesis

**my·e·lo·sclerosis** \ˌmīəlō+\ *n* [NL, fr. *myel-* + *sclerosis*] **:** abnormal hardening of the bone marrow commonly associated with splenic disorder and constitutional symptoms

**my·e·lo·sis** \ˌmīəˈlōsəs\ *n, pl* **myelo·ses** \-ōˌsēz\ [NL, fr. *myel-* + *-osis*] **1 a :** the proliferation of marrow tissue to produce the changes in cell distribution typical of myelogenous leukemia **b :** LEUKEMIA; *esp* **:** MYELOGENOUS LEUKEMIA **2 :** the formation of a tumor of the spinal cord

**my·e·lo·spon·gi·um** \ˌmīəlōˈspänjēəm\ *n, pl* **myelospongia** \-ēə\ [NL, fr. *myel-* + *-spongium*] **:** a network in the embryonic central nervous system derived from the spongioblasts and giving rise to the neuroglia

**my·e·lo·toxic** \ˌmīəlō+\ *adj* [*myel-* + *toxic*] **:** destructive to bone marrow or any of its elements

**my·e·lo·zoa** \ˌmīəlōˈzōə\ [NL, fr. *myel-* + *-zoa*] *syn of* LEPTOCARDII

**my·en·ter·ic** \ˌmīənˈterik\ *adj* [*my-* + *enteric*] **:** of or relating to the muscular coat of the intestinal wall

**myenteric plexus** *n* **:** AUERBACH'S PLEXUS

**my·en·ter·on** \mīˈentəˌrän\ *n* [NL, fr. *my-* + *enteron*] **:** the muscular coat of the intestine

**myg** *abbr* myriagram

**¹myg·a·le** \ˈmigəlē\ *n* -s [L, fr. Gk *mygalē*] **:** SHREWMOUSE

**²mygale** \"\ [NL, fr. L, shrewmouse] *syn of* AVICULARIA

**myg·a·lo·morph** \ˈmigələˌmȯrf\ *n* [NL *Mygalomorphae*] **:** one of the Mygalomorphae

**myg·a·lo·mor·phae** \ˌ≈≈≈ˈmȯrˌfē\ *n pl, cap* [NL, fr. *mygale* + *-morphae*] **:** a suborder of spiders comprising those in which the fangs move vertically and four book lungs are present — see TARANTULA

**myi-** *or* **myio-** *comb form* [NL, fr. Gk, fr. *myia* — more at MIDGE] **:** fly ⟨*Myi*archus⟩

**-my·ia** \ˈmī(y)ə\ *n comb form* -s [NL, fr. Gk *myia*] **:** fly ⟨antho*myia*⟩ ⟨Cephenom*yia*⟩

**my·iar·chus** \mīˈyärkəs\ *n, cap* [NL, fr. *myi-* + Gk *archos* ruler] **:** a genus of large plainly colored tyrant flycatchers widely distributed in America

**my·ia·sis** \ˈmī(y)əsəs\ *n, pl* **myia·ses** \-əˌsēz\ [NL, fr. *myi-* + *-iasis*] **:** infestation with or disease caused by fly maggots

**my·i·dae** \ˈmīəˌdē\ [NL, fr. *Mya* + *-idae*] *syn of* MYACIDAE

**my·if·er·ous** \(ˈ)mīˈif(ə)rəs\ *adj* [*my-* + *-ferous*] **:** MYOPHOROUS

**my·io·sis** \mīˈyōsəs\ *n, pl* **myio·ses** \-ōˌsēz\ [NL, fr. *myi-* + *-osis*] **:** MYIASIS

**myl-** *or* **mylo-** *comb form* [NL, fr. Gk, mill, molar, fr. *mylē* — more at MEAL] **:** molar ⟨*mylo*hyoid⟩

**myl** *abbr* myrialiter

**¹myl·i·ob·a·tid** \ˌmilēˈäbəd·əd\ *adj* [NL *Myliobatidae*] **:** of or relating to the Myliobatidae

**²myliobatid** \"\ *n* -s [NL *Myliobatidae*] **:** one of the Myliobatidae

**myl·i·o·bat·i·dae** \ˌmilēōˈbad·əˌdē\ *n pl, cap* [NL, fr. *Myliobatis*, type genus (fr. Gk *mylias*, *mylios* of a mill — fr. *mylē* mill, molar — + *batis*, a flat fish, prob. a skate or ray) + *-idae*] **:** a family of large flattened chiefly tropical sting rays — see EAGLE RAY

**my·lo·don** \ˈmīləˌdän\ *n* [NL, fr. *myl-* + *-odon*] **1** *cap* **:** a genus (the type of the family Mylodontidae) of large edentates of the Pleistocene of So. America **2** -s **:** a mammal of the genus *Mylodon*

**¹my·lo·dont** \-nt\ *adj* [NL *Mylodont-*, *Mylodon*] **:** of or relating to the genus *Mylodon* or the family Mylodontidae

**²mylodont** \"\ *n* -s [NL *Mylodont-*, *Mylodon*] **:** a mammal of the genus *Mylodon* or the family Mylodontidae

**¹my·lo·hy·oid** \ˌmīlōˈhīˌȯid\ *also* **my·lo·hy·oi·de·an** \ˌ≈≈-ˌhīˌȯidēən\ *adj* [*mylohyoid* fr. NL *mylohyoideus*, fr. *myl-* + *hyoides* hyoid bone; *mylohyoidean* fr. NL *mylohyoideus* + E *-an* — more at HYOID BONE] **:** of, indicating, or adjoining a muscle that extends from the inner surface of the mandible to the hyoid and forms the floor of the mouth

**²mylohyoid** \"\ *or* **my·lo·hy·oi·de·us** \ˌ≈≈ˌ≈ˈȯidēəs\ *n, pl* **mylohyoids** \-dz\ *or* **mylohyoi·dei** \-dēˌī\ [NL *mylohyoideus*, fr. *mylohyoideus*, adj.] **:** a mylohyoid muscle

**my·lo·nite** \ˈmīləˌnīt, ˈmil-\ *n* -s [Gk *mylōn* mill (fr. *mylē* mill) + E *-ite* — more at MEAL] **:** a siliceous schist produced by intense crushing of rocks

**my·lo·nit·ic** \ˌ≈≈ˈnid·ik\ *adj* **:** CATACLASTIC

**my·lo·nit·iza·tion** \ˌ≈≈ˌnid·əˈzāshən\ *also* **my·lo·ni·za·tion** \ˌ≈≈nəˈzāshən\ *n* -s **:** the process of producing mylonite

**my·lo·nit·ize** \ˈ≈≈ˌnīˌtīz\ *also* **my·lo·nize** \ˈ≈≈ˌnīz\ *vt* -ED/-ING/-S *see -ize in Explan Notes* **:** to form by or subject to the process of mylonitization ⟨*mylonitized* dunite —*Jour. of Geol.*⟩

**mym** *abbr* myriameter

**¹my·mar·id** \(ˈ)mīˈmarəd\ *adj* [NL *Mymaridae*] **:** of or relating to the Mymaridae

**²mymarid** \"\ *n* -s [NL *Mymaridae*] **:** a chalcid fly of the family Mymaridae

**my·mar·i·dae** \mīˈmarəˌdē\ *n pl, cap* [NL, fr. *Mymar*, type genus (fr. Gk *mymar*, *mōmar*, *mōmos* blame, blemish) + *-idae*] **:** a family of minute chalcid flies that are parasitic in the larval state living principally in the eggs of other insects

**my·na** *or* **my·nah** \ˈmīnə\ *n* -s [Hindi *mainā*, fr. Skt *madana*, *madanaka*] **:** any of various Asiatic starlings esp. of the genera *Acridotheres*, *Gracula*, and *Sturnus:* as **a :** a dark brown slightly crested bird (*A. tristis*) of southeastern Asia that has white tail tip and wing markings and bright yellow bill and feet, is semigregarious and very aggressive, and has when introduced to other areas often replaced native birds and proved very destructive to crops (as small grains and some fruits) **b :** HILL MYNA

**myn·heer** \mīnˈhe(ə)r, -hi(ə)r\ *n* -s [D *mijnheer* (formerly spelled also *mynheer*), fr. *mijn* my + *heer* sir] **1 a :** MISTER — used as a title prefixed to the name of a male Netherlander or Dutch-speaking man **b :** SIR — used as a form of respectful or polite address to a male Netherlander or Dutch-speaking man **2 a :** GENTLEMAN — used esp. of a Netherlander of good birth **b :** DUTCHMAN ⟨the ~s of New Amsterdam⟩

**myn·pacht** \ˈmīnˌpäkt\ *n* -s [Afrik, fr. *myn* mine + *pacht* lease] **1** *southern Africa* **:** a mining concession; *esp* **:** one by the government to the owner of the surface concerned **2** *southern Africa* **:** a landowner's mining location covering one tenth of the surface leased to the government

**myo-** — see MY-

**my·o·blast** \ˈmīəˌblast\ *n* [ISV *my-* + *-blast*] **:** an undifferentiated cell capable of giving rise to muscle cells

**my·o·car·di·al** \ˌmīəˈkärdēəl\ *adj* [NL *myocardium* + E *-al*] **:** of, relating to, or involving the myocardium

**myocardial infarction** *n* **:** infarction of the myocardium, typically resulting from coronary occlusion

**myo·cardiograph** \ˌmīō+\ *n* [*my-* + *cardiograph*] **:** a recording instrument for making a tracing of the action of the heart

**my·o·car·di·tis** \ˌmīəˌkärˈdīd·əs\ *n* [NL, fr. *myocardium* + *-itis*] **:** inflammation of the myocardium

**my·o·car·di·um** \ˌmīəˈkärdēəm\ *n, pl* **myocar·dia** \-ēə\ [NL, fr. *my-* + *-cardium*] **:** the middle muscular layer of the heart wall

**my·o·cas·tor** \ˈmīəˌkastə(r)\ *n, cap* [NL, fr. *my-* + L *castor* beaver — more at CASTOR] **:** a genus of hystricomorph rodents comprising the coypu

**my·o·clo·nia** \ˌmīəˈklōnēə\ *n* -s [NL, fr. *myoclonus* + *-ia*] **1 :** a disturbance marked by myoclonus **2 :** MYOCLONUS — **my·o·clon·ic** \ˌ≈≈ˈklänik\ *adj*

**my·oc·lo·nus** \mīˈäklənəs\ *n* [NL, fr. *my-* + *clonus*] **:** irregular involuntary contraction of a muscle usu. resulting from functional disorder of controlling motoneurons

**my·o·coel** *also* **my·o·coele** \ˈmīəˌsēl\ *n* -s [*my-* + *-coel*, *-coele*] **:** the cavity of a myotome

**my·o·com·ma** \ˌmīəˈkämə\ *n, pl* **myocomma·ta** \-məd·ə\ *also* **myocommas** [NL, fr. *my-* + *comma*] **1 :** one of the segments into which the muscles of the body or trunk of vertebrates are separated by connective-tissue septa **2 :** MYOSEPTUM

**my·o·cyte** \ˈmīəˌsīt\ *n* -s [*my-* + *-cyte*] **:** a contractile cell; *specif* **:** a muscle cell

**my·o·dar·ia** \ˌmīəˈda(a)rēə\ *n pl, cap* [NL, irreg. fr. Gk *myia* fly + *-ōdēs* -ode + NL *-aria* — more at MIDGE] **:** a very large section of the suborder Brachycera that comprises typical two-winged flies having 3-jointed antennae with an arista on the third segment, a distinctly segmented abdomen, leg bases near together on each segment, and modified wing venation — **my·o·dar·i·an** \ˌ≈≈ˈda(a)rēən\ *adj or n*

**my·o·des** \mīˈōdēz\ [NL, fr. Gk *myōdēs* mouselike, fr. *my-* + *-ōdēs* -ode] *syn of* LEMMUS

**myo·dynamics** \ˌmīō+\ *n pl but often sing in constr* [*my-* + *dynamics*] **:** the physiology of muscular contraction

**myo·elastic** \"+\ *adj* [*my-* + *elastic*] **:** made up of muscular and elastic tissues ⟨a ~ junction⟩

**myo·epicardial layer** \"+ . . . -\ *n* [*my-* + *epicardial*] **:** the layer of mesocardium that enters into the formation of the muscular and epicardial walls of the heart

**myo·epithelial** \"+\ *adj* [*my-* + *epithelial*] **:** of, relating to, or being large stellate cells that are associated with the secretory cells of the salivary glands or the alveolae of some other glands and are believed to play a mechanical role in expressing secretion

**myo·fibril** *also* **myo·fibrilla** \"+\ *n* [NL *myofibrilla*, fr. *my-* + *fibrilla*] **1 :** a bundle of contractile micelles of a muscle cell **2 :** MYONEME

**myo·fibroma** \"+\ *n* [NL, fr. *my-* + *fibroma*] **:** a tumor composed of fibrous and muscular tissue

**my·o·gen** \ˈmīəjən, -ˌjen\ *n* -s [ISV *my-* + *-gen*] **:** a mixture of albumins obtained by extracting muscle with cold water

**my·o·gen·ic** \ˌ≈≈ˈjenik\ *adj* [ISV *my-* + *-genic*] **1 :** originating in muscle ⟨~ pain⟩ **2** *of cardiac muscular contraction* **:** taking place in ordered rhythmic fashion because of inherent properties of cardiac muscle rather than by reason of specific neural stimuli — compare NEUROGENIC 2b — **my·o·ge·nic·i·ty** \ˌ≈≈jəˈnisəd·ē\ *n* -ES

**myo·globin** \ˌmīə+\ *n* [ISV *my-* + *globin*] **:** a red iron-containing protein pigment in muscles that is similar to hemoglobin but differs in the globin portion of its molecule, in the smaller size of its molecule (as in the mammalian heart muscle which has only one fourth the molecular weight of the hemoglobin in the blood of the same animal), in its greater tendency to combine with oxygen, and in its absorption of light at longer wavelengths — called also *myohemoglobin*

**my·o·glo·bi·nu·ria** \ˌmīəˌglōbəˈn(y)u̇rēə\ *n* -s [NL, fr. ISV *myoglobin* + NL *-uria*] **:** the presence of myoglobin in the urine

**my·o·gram** \ˈmīəˌgram\ *n* [*my-* + *-gram*] **:** a graphic representation of the phenomena (as velocity and intensity) of muscular contractions

**my·o·graph** \-raf, -räf\ *n* [*my-* + *-graph*] **:** an apparatus for producing myograms usu. consisting essentially of a series of transmitting levers and a revolving recording surface (as a kymograph) — **my·o·graph·ic** \ˌ≈≈ˈgrafik\ *adj* — **my·o·graph·i·cal·ly** \-fək(ə)lē\ *adv*

**my·og·ra·phy** \mīˈägrəfē\ *n* -ES [ISV *my-* + *-graphy*] **:** use of the myograph

**myo·hematin** \ˌmīō+\ *n* [*my-* + *hematin*] **:** CYTOCHROME

**myo·hemoglobin** \"+\ *n* [ISV *my-* + *hemoglobin*] **:** MYOGLOBIN

**myo·he·mo·glo·bi·nu·ria** \ˌmīōˌhēməˌglōbəˈn(y)u̇rēə\ *n* -s [NL, fr. ISV *myohemoglobin* + NL *-uria*] **:** MYOGLOBINURIA

**my·oid** \ˈmīˌȯid\ *adj* [ISV *my-* + *-oid*] **:** resembling muscle

**myo·i·dea** \mīˈȯidēə\ [NL, fr. *my-* + *-oidea*] *syn of* MUROIDEA

**myo·inositol** \ˌmīō+\ *n* [*my-* + *inositol*] **:** INOSITOL a

**myo·kinase** \"+\ *n* [*my-* + *kinase*] **:** a crystallizable enzyme that promotes the reversible transfer of phosphate groups in adenosine diphosphate with the formation of adenosine triphosphate and adenylic acid and that occurs in muscle and other tissues

**my·o·lemma** \ˌmīəˈlemə\ *n* -s [NL, fr. *my-* + *-lemma*] **:** SARCOLEMMA

**my·o·log·ic** \ˌmīəˈläjik\ *or* **my·o·log·i·cal** \-jəkəl\ *adj* **:** of or relating to myology

**my·ol·o·gy** \mīˈäləjē\ *n* -ES [F or NL; F *myologie*, fr. NL *myologia*, fr. *my-* + L *-logia* -logy] **1 :** a scientific study of muscles **2 :** the muscular makeup of an animal or part

**myom-** *or* **myomo-** *comb form* [NL *myoma*] **:** myoma ⟨*myom*ectomy⟩ ⟨*myomo*hysterectomy⟩ ⟨*myomo*tomy⟩

**my·o·ma** \mīˈōmə\ *n, pl* **myomas** \-məz\ *or* **myoma·ta** \-məd·ə\ [NL, fr. *my-* + *-oma*] **:** a tumor consisting of muscle tissue — **my·om·a·tous** \(ˈ)mīˌämədˑəs, -ˈōm-\ *adj*

**my·o·mec·to·my** \ˌmīəˈmektəmē\ *n* -ES [ISV *myom-* + *-ectomy*] **:** excision of a myoma

**my·o·mere** \ˈmīəˌmi(ə)r\ *n* -s [ISV *my-* + *-mere*] **:** a muscle segment — compare METAMERE, MYOCOMMA — **my·o·mer·ic** \ˌ≈≈ˈmerik\ *adj*

**my·o·me·tri·al** \ˌmīəˈmē·trēəl\ *adj* [NL *myometrium* + E *-al*] **:** of, relating to, or affecting the myometrium

**my·o·me·tri·um** \ˌ≈≈ˈmē·trēəm\ *n* -s [NL, fr. *my-* + *metr-* + *-ium*] **:** the muscular layer of the wall of the uterus

**¹my·o·morph** \ˈmīəˌmȯrf\ *adj* [NL *Myomorpha*] **:** of or relating to the Myomorpha

**²myomorph** \"\ *n* -s [NL *Myomorpha*] **:** a rodent of the suborder Myomorpha

**my·o·mor·pha** \ˌ≈≈ˈmȯrfə\ *n pl, cap* [NL, fr. *my-* + *-morpha*] **:** the largest suborder of Rodentia comprising the true rats, mice, and related rodents — compare HYSTRICOMORPHA, SCIUROMORPHA — **my·o·mor·phic** \ˌ≈≈ˈmȯrfik\ *adj*

**my·o·neme** \ˈmīəˌnēm\ *also* **my·o·ne·ma** \ˌ≈≈ˈnēmə\ *n* -s [NL *myonema*, fr. *my-* + *-nema*] **:** a contractile fibril in the body of a protozoan

**myo·neural** \ˌmīō+\ *adj* [*my-* + *-neural*] **:** of or relating to both muscle and nerve

**myoneural junction** *n* **:** the modified point of contact between muscle and motor nerve usu. considered to consist of specialized receptive matter of muscular origin, specialized transmitting matter of nervous origin, and intervening substance that is neither nerve nor muscle

**my·o·path·ic** \ˌmīəˈpathik\ *adj* [ISV *my-* + *-pathic*] **:** involving abnormality of the muscles ⟨~ syndrome⟩ **:** of or relating to myopathy

**my·op·a·thy** \mīˈäpəthē\ *n* -ES [ISV *my-* + *-pathy*] **:** a disorder of muscle tissue or muscles

**my·ope** \ˈmīˌōp\ *n* -s [F, fr. LL *myops* myopic, fr. Gk *myōps*, fr. *myein* to close (used of the lips and eyes), close the eyes + *ōps* eye, face — more at MYSTERY, EYE] **:** a myopic person

**my·o·phan** \ˈmīəˌfan\ *n* -s [*my-* + Gk *phan-*, stem of *phainein* to show — more at FANCY] **:** MYONEME

**my·o·phore** \ˈmīəˌfō(ə)r, -fȯ(ə)r\ *n* -s [*my-* + *-phore*] **:** a part or process of a shell (as of a clam) adapted for the attachment of a muscle — **my·oph·o·rous** \(ˈ)mīˈäf(ə)rəs\ *adj*

**my·o·phrisk** \ˈmīəˌfrisk\ *n* -s [NL *myophrisca*, prob. irreg. fr. *my-* + *phor-* + *-isca* (fr. Gk *-iskos*, dim. suffix) — more at -ISH] **:** MYONEME

**myo·physics** \ˌmīō+\ *n pl but sing or pl in constr* [*my-* + *physics*] **:** the physics of muscular action

**my·o·pia** \mīˈōpēə\ *n* -s [NL, fr. Gk *myōpia*, fr. *myōp-*, *myōps* myopic + *-ia* -y — more at MYOPE] **1 :** a condition in which the visual images come to a focus in front of the retina of the eye because of defects in the refractive media of the eye or of abnormal length of the eyeball resulting esp. in defective vision of distant objects — called also *nearsightedness, shortsightedness;* compare EMMETROPIA **2 :** deficiency or lack of foresight, discernment, or liberality esp. in a particular field ⟨the ~ of the single mind is corrected through the perspectives of other minds —F.K.Davis⟩ ⟨the ~ of contemporary opinion —J.T.Soby⟩ ⟨a persistent emotional ~ —D.M.Friedenberg⟩ ⟨political ~⟩

**my·o·pic** \(ˈ)mīˈōpik, -ˈäp-\ *adj* [E *myope* & NL *myopia* + E *-ic*] **1 :** affected by myopia **:** of, relating to, or exhibiting myopia **2 :** lacking in foresight, discernment, or liberality ⟨the ~ perspective of the specialist —Erwin Schrödinger⟩ ⟨policies which are dangerously self-centered and ~ —N.D. Palmer⟩ — **my·o·pi·cal·ly** \-pək(ə)lē, -li\ *adv*

**myo·polar** \ˌmīō+\ *adj* [*my-* + *polar*] **:** of or relating to muscular polarity

**my·op·o·ra·ce·ae** \mīˌäpəˈrāsēˌē\ *n pl, cap* [NL, fr. *Myoporum*, type genus + *-aceae*] **:** a family of chiefly Australian shrubs and trees (order Polemoniales) having an irregular or bilabiate corolla, didynamous stamens, and berrylike fruit — **my·op·o·ra·ceous** \≈ˌ≈≈ˈrāshəs\ *adj* — **my·op·o·rad** \≈ˈ≈≈ˌrad\ *n* -s

**my·op·o·rum** \mīˈäpərəm\ *n, cap* [NL, fr. *myo-* (fr. Gk *myein* to close — used of the lips and eyes) + *-porum* (fr. Gk *poros* pore) — more at MYSTERY, PORE] **:** a genus (the type of the family Myoporaceae) of mostly Australasian shrubs or trees that have small axillary white flowers with a 5-parted bell-shaped calyx — see BASTARD SANDALWOOD

**my·o·pus** \ˈmīəpəs\ *n, cap* [NL, fr. *my-* + *-pus*] **:** a genus of rodents comprising the Old World red-backed lemmings

**myo·sarcoma** \ˌmīō+\ *n* [NL, fr. *my-* + *sarcoma*] **:** sarcomatous myoma

**myo·septum** \"+\ *n* [NL, fr. *my-* + *septum*] **:** the septum between adjacent myotomes

**my·o·sin** \ˈmīəsən\ *n* -s [ISV *myos-* (fr. Gk *myos*, gen. of *mys* mouse, muscle) + *-in* — more at MOUSE] **:** either of two proteins that are extracted from muscle by salt solutions and that are thought to constitute the chief components of the contractile mechanism: **a :** ACTOMYOSIN **b :** a fibrous globulin that interreacts with actin and adenosine triphosphate with resulting enzymatic hydrolysis of the triphosphate to adenosine diphosphate and inorganic phosphate

**myosis** *var of* MIOSIS

**my·o·si·tis** \ˌmīəˈsīd·əs\ *n* -ES [NL, fr. Gk *myos* (gen. of *mys* mouse, muscle) + NL *-itis*] **:** muscular discomfort or pain from infection or an unknown cause

**my·os·mine** \mīˈäsˌmēn, ˈäz, ˈmən\ *n* -s [*my-* + *osm-* + *-ine*; fr. the mouselike odor] **:** a heterocyclic liquid base $C_9H_{10}N_2$ formed during smoking of tobacco and obtained by pyrolysis of nicotine; 3-(dihydro-pyrryl)-pyridine

**my·o·sote** \ˈmīəˌsōt\ *n* -s [NL *Myosotis*] **:** MYOSOTIS 2

**my·o·so·tis** \ˌ≈≈ˈsōd·əs\ *n* -s [NL, fr. L, mouse ear, fr. Gk *myosōtis*, fr. *myos* (gen. of *mys* mouse) + *-ōtis* (fr. *ōt-*, *ous* ear) — more at MOUSE, EAR] **1** *cap* **:** a large genus of herbs (family Boraginaceae) with racemose flowers having a salver-form or funnelform corolla, the lobes rounded, and basally attached nutlets — see FORGET-ME-NOT **2** -ES **:** any plant of the genus *Myosotis* — called also *myosote*

**myosotis blue** *n* **:** FORGET-ME-NOT 2b

**my·o·su·rus** \ˌmīəˈs(h)u̇rəs, -īəsˈyü-\ *n, cap* [NL, fr. Gk *myos* (gen. of *mys* mouse) + NL *-urus* — more at MOUSE] **:** a genus of small annual herbs (family Ranunculaceae) found in temperate regions and having tufted linear-spatulate radical leaves and flowers with the receptacle slender and elongated in fruit — see MOUSETAIL

**my·o·tat·ic** \ˌmīəˈtad·ik\ *adj* [ISV *my-* + Gk *tatikos* exerting tension, fr. *tatos* stretchable (fr. *teinein* to stretch) + *-ikos* -ic — more at THIN] *of muscular contraction* **:** resulting from stretching — used chiefly of reflexes (as the knee jerk) in which stretching of the associated tendon is followed by a sharp reflex contraction of a muscle

**myotic** *var of* MIOTIC

**my·o·tis** \mīˈōd·əs\ *n, cap* [NL, fr. *my-* + *-otis* (fr. Gk *ōt-*, *-ous* ear) — more at EAR] **:** a very large cosmopolitan genus of vespertilionid bats comprising the common brown bats and numerous related forms

**my·o·tome** \ˈmīəˌtōm\ *n* -s [ISV *my-* + *-tome*] **1 a :** the portion of an embryonic somite from which skeletal musculature is produced **b :** MYOCOMMA **c :** the muscles of a metamere esp. in a segmented invertebrate **2 :** an instrument for myotomy

**my·ot·o·my** \mīˈäd·əmē\ *n* -ES [ISV *my-* + *-tomy*] **:** incision or division of a muscle

**my·o·to·nia** \ˌmīəˈtōnēə\ *n* -s [NL, fr. *my-* + *-tonia*] **:** tonic spasm of one or more muscles; *also* **:** a condition characterized by such spasms

**my·o·ton·ic** \ˌ≈≈ˈtänik\ *adj* [NL *myotonia* + E *-ic*] **:** of, relating to, or exhibiting myotonia

**my·o·trop·ic** \ˌmīəˈträpik\ *adj* [*my-* + *-tropic*] **:** affecting or tending to invade muscles ⟨a ~ infection⟩

**my·ox·ine** \mīˈäkˌsīn, -ˌsən\ *adj* [LGk *myōxos* dormouse + E *-ine*] **:** of or relating to dormice

**my·ox·us** \mīˈäksəs\ [NL, fr. LGk *myōxos* dormouse] *syn of* GLIS

**myr·a·bal·a·nus** \ˌmirəˈbalənəs\ *n* -ES [NL, alter. of L *myrobalanum* — more at MYROBALAN] **:** MYROBALAN

**myrabolam** *var of* MYROBALAN

**myrabolan** *var of* MYROBALAN

**myrbane oil** *var of* MIRBANE OIL

**myr·cene** \ˈmərˌsēn, -sən\ *n* -s [ISV *myrcia* (*oil*) + *-ene*] **:** a liquid acyclic terpene hydrocarbon $C_{10}H_{16}$ that is isomeric with ocimene, occurs in bay oil, hop oil, and other essential oils, and polymerizes readily

**myr·cia** \ˈmərsh(ē)ə\ *n, cap* [NL, alter. of L *myrtus* myrtle + NL *-ia* — more at MYRTLE] **:** a large genus of tropical American trees and shrubs (family Myrtaceae) distinguished by their few-seeded berries

**myrcia oil** *n* **:** BAY OIL

**myri-** *or* **myrio-** *comb form* [Gk, fr. *myrios* — more at MYRIAD] **:** indefinitely numerous **:** countless ⟨*myrio*phyllous⟩ ⟨*Myrio*phyllum⟩ ⟨*myrio*sporous⟩

**myria-** *comb form* [F, fr. Gk *myrios* — more at MYRIAD] **1 :** ten thousand ⟨*myria*coulomb⟩ — esp. in terms belonging to the metric system ⟨*myria*gram⟩ ⟨*myria*liter⟩ **2 :** MYRI- ⟨*Myria*poda⟩

**myr·i·a·can·thous** \ˌmirēəˈkan(t)thəs\ *adj* [*myri-* + *acanthous*] *biol* **:** having numerous spines or prickles

**¹myr·i·ad** \ˈmirēəd\ *n* -s [Gk *myriad-*, *myrias*, fr. *myrios* countless, *myrioi* (its pl.) ten thousand; perh. akin to MIr *mūr* abundance] **1 :** the number of ten thousand **:** ten thousand persons or things — used esp. in translations from the Greek and Latin **2 :** an immense number **:** an indefinitely large number **:** a great multitude — usu. used with *of* and often used in pl. ⟨beset with a ~ of profound emotional stresses —H.G.Armstrong⟩ ⟨a ~ of mathematical possibilities —John Haverstick⟩ ⟨~s of insects, flying before north winds —R.A. Billington⟩ ⟨~s of freshman texts —W.N.Francis⟩

**²myriad** \"\ *adj* **1 :** consisting of a very great but indefinite number **:** INNUMERABLE, MULTITUDINOUS ⟨the involved and ~ events which fill the world's past —Edward Clodd⟩ ⟨the intricacies of human action are ~ —F.A.Geldard⟩ ⟨the faces ~ yet curiously identical in their lack of individual identity —William Faulkner⟩ **2 :** having innumerable aspects or elements ⟨the ~ activity of the new land —Meridel Le Sueur⟩ ⟨a ~ murmur of insects —Hamilton Basso⟩ ⟨the soft ~ darkness of a May night —William Faulkner⟩

**¹myr·i·ad-fold** \ˈ≈≈≈ˌfōld\ *adj* **1 :** having myriad parts or aspects **2 :** being a myriad times as large, as great, or as many as some understood size, degree, or amount

**²myriadfold** \"\ *adv* **:** to a myriad times as much or as many **:** by a myriad times

**myr·i·ad·ly** *adv* **:** a myriad times **:** to a myriad degree **:** INNUMERABLY

**myriad-minded** \ˈ≈≈≈ˈ≈≈\ *adj* **:** having a mind of extreme versatility and power

**myr·ia·me·ter** \ˈmirēəˌmēd·ə(r)\ *n* [F *myriamètre*, fr. *myria-* + *-mètre* -meter] **:** a metric unit of length equal to 10,000 meters — see METRIC SYSTEM table

**myr·i·an·gi·a·les** \ˌmirēˌanjēˈā(ˌ)lēz\ *n pl, cap* [NL, fr. *Myriangium* + *-ales*] : an order of fungi (subclass Euascomycetes) having a single ascus in each chamber of the well-developed and often gelatinous stroma

**myr·i·an·gi·um** \ˌmirēˈanjēəm\ *n, cap* [NL, fr. *myri-* + *-angium*] : a genus of ascomycetous fungi (order Myriangiales) having asci borne at different levels in the stroma and including several forms that are parasitic on insects (as scales)

**myr·i·an·i·da** \ˌmirēˈanədə\ *n, cap* [NL, fr. Gk *myrios* countless — more at MYRIAD] : a genus of annelid worms related to *Autolytus* and reproducing similarly

**myr·i·a·pod** \ˈmirēəˌpäd\ *adj or n* [NL *Myriapoda*] : MYRIOPOD

**myr·i·ap·o·da** \ˌmirēˈapədə\ [NL, fr. *myria-* + *-poda*] *syn of* MYRIOPODA

**myr·i·arch** \ˈmirēˌärk\ *n* -s [Gk *myriarchēs, myriarchos*, fr. *myrioi* ten thousand + *-archēs, archos* -arch — more at MYRIAD] : a commander of ten thousand men in ancient Greece — **myr·i·archy** \-kē\ *n* -ES

**my·ri·ca** \məˈrīkə\ *n, cap* [NL, fr. L, tamarisk, fr. Gk *myrikē*, prob. of Sem origin; akin to the source of Gk *myrrha* myrrh — more at MYRRH] : a large widely distributed genus (the type of a family Myricaceae) of aromatic shrubs having exstipulate leaves and ovary with 2 to 4 bractlets

**myr·i·ca·ce·ae** \ˌmirəˈkāsēˌē\ *n pl, cap* [NL, fr. *Myrica*, type genus + *-aceae*] : a family of shrubs constituting an order Myricales having simple alternate mostly coriaceous leaves with small diclinous flowers borne in aments in the axils of bracts and infruit forming a small drupe or nut — **myr·i·ca·ceous** \¦==¦kāshəs\ *adj*

**myr·i·ca·les** \ˌ==ˈkā(ˌ)lēz\ *n pl, cap* [NL, fr. *Myrica* + *-ales*] : an order of dicotyledonous plants coextensive with the family Myricaceae

**myrica tallow** *n* : BAYBERRY WAX

**my·ric·e·tin** \məˈrisəd·ən\ *n* -s [ISV *myric-* (fr. NL *Myrica*) + *-et-* + *-in*] : a yellow crystalline flavone dye $C_{15}H_{10}O_8$ obtained from many plants (as from the bark of the box myrtle and the leaves of sumacs)

**my·ric·i·trin** \məˈrisəˌtrən\ *n* -s [ISV *myric-* (fr. NL *Myrica*) + *-itrin* (as in *quercitrin*)] : a crystalline glycoside $C_{21}H_{20}O_{12}$ obtained esp. from the bark of the box myrtle and yielding myricetin and rhamnose on hydrolysis

**my·ri·cyl alcohol** \ˈmirəˌsil-\ *n* [ISV *myric-* (fr. NL *Myrica*) + *-yl*] : a crystalline alcohol $CH_3(CH_2)_{29}OH$ occurring in the form of esters (as the palmitate) in beeswax and other waxes — called also *melissyl alcohol*

**myr·i·en·to·ma·ta** \ˌmirēən·ˈtōməd·ə\ *n pl, cap* [NL, fr. *Myriopoda* + *entom-* + *-ata*] *in some classifications* : a class of Arthropoda comprising the order Protura — used when the order is excluded from Insecta

**myring-** *or* **myringo-** *comb form* [NL, fr. *myringa*] : myringa ⟨*myringo*dermatitis⟩ ⟨*myringo*scope⟩ ⟨*myringo*tomy⟩

**my·rin·ga** \məˈriŋgə\ *n* -s [NL, alter. of ML *miringa* membrane, alter. of LL *mininga, meninga*, fr. Gk *mēninga, mēninx* — more at MEMBER] : TYMPANIC MEMBRANE

**myr·in·gi·tis** \ˌmirənˈjīd·əs\ *n* -ES [NL, fr. *myring-* + *-itis*] : inflammation of the tympanic membrane

**myr·in·got·o·my** \ˌmirənˈgäd·əmē\ *n* -ES [ISV *myring-* + *-tomy*] : incision of the tympanic membrane

**myrio-** — see MYRI-

**myr·i·o·ne·ma** \ˌmirēōˈnēmə\ *n, cap* [NL, fr. *myri-* + *-nema*] : a genus (the type of the family Myrionemataceae) of the order Chordariales of brown algae having a minute thallus consisting of a parenchymatous disk made up of radiating filaments and growing epiphytically on other algae (as the sea lettuces) — **myr·i·o·ne·moid** \¦==¦nēˌmȯid\ *adj*

**myr·i·o·phyl·lum** \ˌmirēōˈfiləm\ *n, cap* [NL, fr. L *myriophyllon* water milfoil, fr. Gk, fr. *myrio-* myri- + *phyllon* leaf — more at BLADE] : a widely distributed genus of submerged aquatic plants (family Haloragaceae) having much-divided whorled or alternate leaves and emersed wind-pollinated flowers — see WATER MILFOIL

**¹myr·i·o·pod** \ˈmirēəˌpäd\ *adj* [NL *Myriopoda*] : of or relating to the Myriopoda

**²myriopod** \"\ *n* -s [NL *Myriopoda*] : an arthropod of the group Myriopoda

**myr·i·op·o·da** \ˌmirēˈäpədə\ *n pl, cap* [NL, fr. *myri-* + *-poda*] *in some classifications* : a diverse group formerly regarded as a class of arthropods that have a more or less elongated segmented body, one pair of antennae, and several to many pairs of segmentally arranged legs and that in current classification make up the classes Diplopoda, Pauropoda, Chilopoda, and Symphyla

**myr·i·o·ra·ma** \ˌmirēəˈramə, -ˈrämə\ *n* -s [*myri-* + *-orama* (as in *panorama*)] : a picture made of several sections combinable in different ways so as to produce a variety of scenes

**my·ris·tate** \məˈriˌstāt\ *n* -s [ISV *myristic* + *-ate*] : a salt or ester of myristic acid

**my·ris·ti·ca** \-stəkə\ *n, cap* [NL, fr. LGk *myristikē*, fem. of *myristikos* fragrant, fr. Gk *myron* unguent, perfume + *-istikos* -istic — more at SMEAR] : a large genus of tropical trees (the type of a family Myristicaceae) with entire leaves and small white or yellow flowers succeeded by fleshy fruits — see NUTMEG

**my·ris·ti·ca·ce·ae** \məˌristəˈkāsēˌē\ *n pl, cap* [NL, fr. *Myristica*, type genus + *-aceae*] : a family of trees (order Ranales) having unisexual flowers, monadelphous stamens, and arillate seeds — see BECUIBA, NUTMEG — **my·ris·ti·ca·ceous** \¦==¦kāshəs\ *adj*

**my·ris·tic acid** \məˈristik-, (ˈ)mīˌristik-\ *n* [ISV *myristic*, fr. NL *Myristica*] : a crystalline fatty acid $CH_3(CH_2)_{12}COOH$ occurring esp. in the form of glycerides in most fats (as in nutmeg butter, sperm oil, coconut oil) — called also *tetradecanoic acid*

**myristica oil** *n* : NUTMEG OIL a

**my·ris·ti·cin** \məˈristəsən\ *n* -s [ISV *myristic* + *-in*] : a crystalline phenolic ether $C_{11}H_{12}O_3$ that has a strong odor and occurs in various essential oils (as nutmeg oil, mace oil, parsley oil)

**my·ris·ti·civ·o·ra** \məˌristəˈsiv(ə)rə\ *n, cap* [NL, fr. *Myristica* + *-vora*] *in some classifications* : a genus consisting of the nutmeg pigeons and now usu. included in the genus *Ducula*

**my·ris·tin** \məˈristən, mīˈ-\ *n* -s [ISV *myristic* + *-in*] : a glycerol ester of myristic acid; *esp* : TRIMYRISTIN

**myrmec-** *or* **myrmeco-** *comb form* [Gk *myrmēk-, myrmēko-*, fr. *myrmēk-, myrmēx* — more at PISMIRE] : ant ⟨*Myrmecia*⟩ ⟨*Myrmeco*phyte⟩ ⟨*myrmeco*logy⟩ ⟨*myrmeco*phobic⟩

**myr·me·cia** \mərˈmēsh(ē)ə, -ēsēə\ *n, cap* [NL, fr. *myrmec-* + *-ia*] : a genus containing the bulldog ant

**myr·me·co·bi·ine** \¦mərməˈkōbēˌīn, -ēən\ *adj* [NL *Myrmecobius* + E *-ine*] : of or relating to the genus *Myrmecobius*

**myr·me·co·bi·us** \ˌ==ˈkōbēəs\ *n, cap* [NL, fr. *myrmec-* + *-bius*] : a genus of insectivorous marsupials including a single species (*M. fasciatus*) that is rufous gray banded with white on the back and has a long extensile tongue and 50 to 56 small teeth — see BANDED ANTEATER

**myr·me·co·cho·rous** \ˌmərməkōˈkōrəs\ *adj* [*myrmec-* + *-chorous*] : dispersed by ants ⟨~ seeds⟩ — **myr·me·co·cho·ry** \¦===ˈkōrē\ *n* -ES

**¹myr·me·coid** \ˈmərməˌkȯid\ *adj* [G or LGk *myrmēkoeidēs*, fr. Gk *myrmēk-* myrmec- + *-oeidēs* -oid] : resembling an ant

**²myrmecoid** \"\ *n* -s : a myrmecoid insect or spider

**myr·me·coidy** \-dē\ *n* -ES [²*myrmecoid* + *-y*] : the mimicking of ants by other insects

**myr·me·co·log·i·cal** \ˌmərməkəˈläjəkəl\ *adj* : of or relating to myrmecology

**myr·me·col·o·gist** \ˌmərməˈkäləjəst\ *n* -s : a specialist in myrmecology

**myr·me·col·o·gy** \-jē\ *n* -ES [ISV *myrmec-* + *-logy*] : a scientific study of ants

**myr·me·coph·a·ga** \ˌmərməˈkäfəgə\ *n, cap* [NL, fr. *myrmec-* + *-phaga*] : a genus (the type of a family Myrmecophagidae) of edentate mammals comprising the So. American ant bear — **myr·me·coph·a·gid** \-fəjəd\ *n or adj* — **myr·me·coph·a·gine** \-fəˌjīn, -jən\ *n or adj* — **myr·me·coph·a·goid** \-fəˌgȯid\ *n or adj*

**myr·me·co·phag·i·dae** \ˌmərməkōˈfajəˌdē\ *n pl, cap* [NL, fr. *Myrmecophaga*, type genus + *-idae*] : a family of edentate mammals including the So. American ant bear, the tamandua, and the silky anteater

**myr·me·coph·a·gous** \¦mərməˈkäfəgəs\ *adj* [*myrmec-* + *-phagous*] : feeding on ants — used esp. of organisms that prey on but do not live with ants

**myr·me·co·phile** \ˈmərməkōˌfīl\ *n* -s [ISV *myrmec-* + *-phile*] : an organism (as an insect) that habitually shares the nest of a species of ant — **myr·me·coph·i·ly** \ˌmərməˈkäfəlē\ *n* -ES

**myr·me·coph·i·lism** \ˌmərməˈkäfəˌlizəm\ *n* -s : the practice or characteristic of habitually sharing the nest of a species of ant

**myr·me·coph·i·lous** \¦==¦käfələs\ *adj* [*myrmec-* + *-philous*] : fond of or benefited by ants — used esp. of an insect

**myr·me·co·pho·bic** \¦mərməkō¦fōbik *also* -fäb-\ *adj* [*myrmec-* + *-phobic*] : having a repulsion for ants — used of a plant that repels ants (as by hairs or glands)

**myr·me·co·phyte** \ˈmərməkōˌfīt\ *n* -s [ISV *myrmec-* + *-phyte*] : a plant that affords shelter or food or both to ants that live in symbiotic relations with it — **myr·me·co·phyt·ic** \¦===¦fid·ik\ *adj*

**myr·me·cox·ene** \ˌmərməˈkäkˌsēn\ *n* -s [*myrmec-* + *-xene*] : SYMPHILE

**myr·me·kite** \ˈmərməˌkīt\ *n* -s [G *myrmekit*, fr. Gk *myrmēkia* anthill, wart (fr. *myrmēk-* myrmec-) + G *-it* -ite] : an intergrowth of vermicular quartz and feldspar (as oligoclase) formed during the later stages in the consolidation of an igneous rock — **myr·me·kit·ic** \¦==¦kid·ik\ *adj*

**myr·me·le·on** \mərˈmēlēən\ *n, cap* [NL, modif. of Gk *myrmekoleōn* ant lion, fr. *myrmēk-* myrmec- + *leōn* lion — more at LION] : a genus (the type of the family Myrmeleontidae) of ant lions

**myr·me·le·on·i·dae** \ˌmərˌmēlēˈänəˌdē\ [NL, fr. *Myrmeleon* + *-idae*] *syn of* MYRMELEONTIDAE

**myr·me·le·ont·i·dae** \-ntə-\ *n pl, cap* [NL, fr. *Myrmeleont-, Myrmeleon*, type genus + *-idae*] : a family of insects (order Neuroptera) comprising the ant lions

**myr·mi·cine** \ˈmərməˌsīn, -sən\ *n* -s [NL *Myrmicinae*, subfamily of ants, fr. NL *Myrmica*, type genus (irreg. fr. Gk *myrmēk-, myrmēx* ant) + *-inae*] : any of a large subfamily of ants having the pedicel of the abdomen in two well-marked segments and including many of the commonly encountered forms (as the little black ant, leaf-cutting ants, and the pavement ant)

**myr·mi·don** \ˈmərməˌdän, -dən\ *n* -s [L *Myrmidon-, Myrmido*, fr. Gk *Myrmidon-, Myrmidōn*] **1** *usu cap* : one of a legendary Thessalian people accompanying Achilles to the Trojan War **2 a** : a loyal retainer or attendant **b** : a follower or subordinate who unquestioningly or pitilessly executes orders : HIRELING

**myr·mo·the·rine** \ˌmərməˈthēˌrīn, -rən\ *adj* [Gk *myrmos* ant + *thēran* to hunt (fr. *thēr* wild animal) + E *-ine* — more at PISMIRE, FIERCE] : MYRMECOPHAGOUS

**my·rob·a·lan** \mīˈräbələn, məˈ-\ *also* **my·rob·a·lam** \-ləm\ *or* **my·rab·o·lam** \-rabələm\ *or* **my·rab·o·lan** \-lən\ *or* **myrob·o·lan** \-räbələn\ *n* -s [MF *mirobolan, mirabolan*, fr. L *myrobalanus, myrobalanum*, fr. Gk *myrobalanos*, fr. *myron* unguent, perfume + *balanos* acorn — more at SMEAR, GLAND] **1 a** : the dried astringent fruit of any of several East Indian trees of the genus *Terminalia* (as *T. chebula* and *T. bellerica*) used chiefly in tanning and in inks **b** : a tree producing myrobalans **2 a** : CHERRY PLUM 1 **b** : EMBLIC

**myrobalan family** *n* : COMBRETACEAE

**myrobalan plum** *n* : CHERRY PLUM

**my·ron** *or* **mu·ron** \ˈmēˌrȯn\ *n* -s [Gk *myron* ointment — more at SMEAR] *Eastern Church* : CHRISM

**myr·o·sin** \ˈmirəsən, ˈmīr-\ *n* -s [alter. of earlier *myrosyne*, fr. F, fr. Gk *myron* unguent + connective *-s-* + *-yne* — more at SMEAR] : an enzyme occurring in various brassicaceous plants (as mustard) that hydrolyzes the glucoside sinigrin

**myr·o·sin·ase** \-səˌnās\ *n* -s [*myrosin* + *-ase*] : MYROSIN

**my·ro·tham·na·ce·ae** \ˌmīrəˌthamˈnāsēˌē\ *n pl, cap* [NL, fr. *Myrothamnus*, type genus + *-aceae*] : a family of plants (order Rosales) coextensive with the genus *Myrothamnus*

**my·ro·tham·nus** \ˌ==ˈthamnəs\ *n, cap* [NL, fr. Gk *myron* unguent, perfume + *thamnos* shrub] : a small genus of xerophytic southern African shrubs constituting a family (Myrothamnaceae) having small dioecious apetalous spicate flowers

**my·rox·y·lon** \mīˈräksəˌlän\ *n, cap* [NL, fr. Gk *myron* + NL *-xylon*] : a genus of tropical American trees (family Leguminosae) having pinnate leaves, white papilionaceous flowers, and one-seeded winged pods

**myrrh** \ˈmər, ˈmə\ *n* -s [ME *myrre, mirre*, fr. OE *myrre, myrra*, fr. L *murra, murrha, myrrha*, fr. Gk *myrrha*, of Sem origin; akin to Heb *mōr* myrrh, *mar* bitter, Ar *murr* myrrh, bitter] **1** : a yellow to reddish brown aromatic bitter gum resin that is obtained from various trees of the genus *Commiphora* esp. of East Africa and Arabia (as *C. myrrha* or *C. abyssinica*), that was used by the ancients as an ingredient of incense and perfumes and as a remedy for local application, and that is used today chiefly in the manufacture of dentifrices and perfumes and as a stimulating tonic — see BISABOL, HERABOL MYRRH; compare BDELLIUM **2** : labdanum or a mixture of myrrh and labdanum ⟨they offered him gifts, gold and frankincense and ~—Mt 2:11(RSV)⟩ **3** : the European sweet cicely

**myrrhed** \ˈmərd\ *adj* [ME *myrred*, fr. *myrre* + *-ed*] : containing myrrh

**myrrh·ic** \ˈmərik, ˈmir-\ *adj* : of or relating to myrrh

**myrrhine** *var of* MURRHINE

**myr·rhis** \ˈmirəs\ *n, cap* [NL, fr. L, sweet cicely, fr. Gk] : a genus of European pubescent perennial herbs (family Umbelliferae) having pinnate leaves, compound umbels of white flowers, and linear oblong beaked fruit — see SWEET CICELY

**myr·rho·phore** \ˈmirəˌfō(ə)r\ *n* -s *usu cap* [modif. (influenced by *myrrh*) of LGk *myrophoros*, fr. Gk, fem. of *myrophoros* bearing unguent, fr. *myron* unguent + *-phoros* -phore — more at SMEAR] : one of the women bearing spices to the sepulcher of Christ

**myr·si·na·ce·ae** \ˌmərsəˈnāsēˌē\ *n pl, cap* [NL, fr. *Myrsine*, type genus (fr. Gk *myrsinē* myrtle, prob. of Sem origin; akin to the source of Gk *myrrha* myrrh) + *-aceae* — more at MYRRH] : a family of tropical trees and shrubs (order Primulales) of which some occur in Florida and which have alternate glandular leaves, white or pink tetramerous flowers, and one-celled indehiscent fruit — see ARDISIA — **myr·si·na·ceous** \¦==¦nāshəs\ *adj*

**myr·si·ne family** \ˈmərsənē-\ *n* [NL *Myrsine*, genus of shrubs] : MYRSINACEAE

**myr·si·phyl·lum** \ˌmərsəˈfiləm\ *n, cap* [NL, fr. Gk *myrsinē* myrtle + NL *-phyllum*] *in some classifications* : a genus of plants comprising the smilax of the florist's trade that is now usu. included in the genus *Asparagus*

**myr·ta·ce·ae** \mərˈtāsēˌē\ *n pl, cap* [NL, fr. *Myrtus*, type genus + *-aceae*] : a family of trees and shrubs (order Myrtales) characterized by numerous stamens, cymose flowers with inferior ovary, and opposite exstipulate leaves that yield a fragrant oil — **myr·ta·ceous** \-āshəs\ *adj*

**myr·ta·les** \mərˈtā(ˌ)lēz\ *n pl, cap* [NL, fr. *Myrtus* + *-ales*] : an order of dicotyledonous herbs, shrubs, or trees including among others the Myrtaceae, Melastomaceae, Lythraceae, Rhizophoraceae, and Onagraceae and having simple leaves, flowers with inferior compound ovary and numerous ovules, and capsular or baccate fruit

**myr·ti·flo·rae** \ˌmərd·əˈflōˌrē\ *n pl* [NL, fr. L *myrtus* myrtle + *-i-* + NL *-florae* (fr. LL, fem. pl. of *-florus* -florous)] *syn of* MYRTALES

**myr·ti·form** \ˈmərd·əˌfȯrm\ *adj* [L *myrtus* myrtle + E *-iform*] : resembling myrtle or myrtle berries

**myr·tle** \ˈmər|d·ᵊl, ˈmə|, |tᵊl\ *n* -s *often attrib* [ME *mirtille*, fr. MF *mirtille, myrtille*, fr. ML *myrtillus*, fr. L *myrtus, murtus*, fr. Gk *myrtos*, prob. of Sem origin; akin to the source of Gk *myrrha* myrrh — more at MYRRH] **1** : any of various plants of the family Myrtaceae; *esp* : a European shrub (*Myrtus communis*) having ovate or lanceolate evergreen leaves and solitary axillary white or rosy flowers followed by black berries **2 a** : PERIWINKLE 1a **b** : CALIFORNIA LAUREL **c** : MONEYWORT **3** *or* **myrtle green a** : a variable color averaging a moderate green that is yellower and deeper than sea green (sense 1a) or laurel green (sense 1) **b** : a dark grayish green to dark bluish green — called also *Baltic*

myrtle

**myrtle beech** *n* : an Australian and Tasmanian evergreen beech (*Nothofagus cunninghamii*)

**myrtle family** *n* : MYRTACEAE

**myrtle oak** *n* : a small shrubby oak (*Quercus myrtifolia*) of the southeastern U.S. that has stiff much-branched stems and small glossy oval to oblong dark green leaves and that often forms nearly impenetrable thickets in sandy coastal areas

**myrtle oil** *n* : a yellow to greenish fragrant essential oil obtained from the leaves and flowers of the European myrtle and formerly used in medicine

**myrtle spurge** *n* : CAPER SPURGE

**myrtle tree** *n* **1** : MYRTLE **2** : a wax myrtle (as *Myrica carolinensis* and *M. cerifera*) **3** : MYRTLE BEECH

**myrtle warbler** *or* **myrtle bird** *n* : a No. American warbler (*Dendroica coronata*) of which the male in full plumage is bluish gray streaked with black above and largely white below with a yellow patch on the crown, rump, and each side of the breast

**myrtle wax** *n* : BAYBERRY WAX

**myr·tus** \ˈmərd·əs\ *n, cap* [NL, fr. L, myrtle — more at MYRTLE] : a genus of chiefly So. American shrubs (the type of the family Myrtaceae) having flowers with numerous ovules — see MYRTLE

**-mys** \ˌmis\ *n comb form* [NL, fr. Gk *mys* — more at MOUSE] : mouse : mouselike creature — in generic names in zoology ⟨Cyno*mys*⟩ ⟨Phascolo*mys*⟩

**my·sel** *or* **my·sell** \məˈsel\ *or* **my·sen** \-en\ *dial var of* MYSELF

**my·self** \mīˈself, məˈ-, -euf\ *pron* [ME, alter. (influenced by *my* & *herself*) of *meself*, fr. OE *mē seljum* & *mē selfne*, dat. & acc. respectively of *ic self* I myself — more at I, ME, SELF] **1** : that identical one that is I : the self that belongs to me : the self that is mine — used (1) reflexively as object of a preposition or direct or indirect object of a verb ⟨I'm doing it solely for ~⟩ ⟨busying ~ only with what concerns me⟩ ⟨I'm going to get ~ a new suit⟩; (2) for emphasis in apposition with *I* or *who* ⟨I ~ will go⟩ ⟨I told him so ~⟩ ⟨I can sympathize with you, I who have ~ had to go through the same thing⟩; (3) for emphasis instead of nonreflexive *me* as object of a preposition or direct or indirect object of a verb ⟨my income supports my wife and ~⟩; (4) for emphasis instead of *I* or instead of *I myself* as predicate nominative ⟨there is only one that wants to do it and that's ~⟩ or in comparisons after *than* or *as* ⟨no one knows more about it than ~⟩ or as part of a compound subject ⟨my brother and ~ will be glad to come⟩ or archaically or dialectally as only subject of a verb ⟨~ when young did eagerly frequent Doctor and Saint —Edward FitzGerald⟩; (5) in absolute constructions ⟨~ without a care in the world, I'll do it whenever I choose⟩ **2** : my normal, healthy, or sane condition ⟨the bewilderment passed quickly and I again came to ~⟩ : my normal, healthy, or sane self ⟨I had been somewhat unwell, but that day I was once more ~⟩

**¹my·si·an** \ˈmishēən\ *adj, usu cap* [*Mysia*, ancient country in northwestern Asia Minor + E *-an*] : of or relating to Mysia or to its inhabitants

**²mysian** \"\ *n* -s *cap* **1** : a native or inhabitant of Mysia **2** : the language of the Mysian people that is prob. related to Phrygian

**¹my·sid** \ˈmīsəd\ *adj* [NL *Mysidae*] **1** : of or relating to the Mysidae **2** : resembling a crustacean of the family Mysidae : of or relating to a mysis

**²mysid** \"\ *n* -s [NL *Mysidae*] **1** : a crustacean of the family Mysidae **2** : MYSIS

**mys·i·da·cea** \ˌmisəˈdāshēə\ *n pl, cap* [NL, fr. *Mysid-, Mysis*, + *-acea*] : an order of Crustacea including the Mysidae and related families and formerly with the Euphausiacea constituting the Schizopoda — see OPOSSUM SHRIMP

**mys·i·dae** \ˈmisəˌdē\ *n pl, cap* [NL, fr. *Mysis*, type genus + *-idae*] : a family of small crustaceans (order Mysidacea) that resemble shrimps, have stalked eyes and 6 pairs of leglike appendages each bearing an exopodite, occur in both fresh and salt water, and form an important food supply of valuable fishes and whales

**my·sis** \ˈmīsəs\ *n* [NL, fr. Gk *mysis* action of closing (used of the lips or eyes), fr. *myein* to close (used of the lips or eyes), close the eyes + *-sis* — more at MYSTERY] **1** *cap* : the type genus of the family Mysidae **2** *or* **mysis stage** -ES : a larva of higher crustaceans (as macrurans and peneids) having all the thoracic appendages biramous

**my·so·phil·ia** \ˌmīsəˈfilēə\ *n* -s [NL, fr. Gk *mysos* uncleanness + NL *-philia*; akin to Gk *mydan* to be damp — more at MOSS] : abnormal attraction to filth

**my·so·pho·bia** *also* **mi·so·pho·bia** \-ˈfōbēə\ *n* [NL, fr. Gk *mysos* uncleanness + NL *-phobia*] : abnormal fear of or distaste for uncleanliness or contamination — **my·so·pho·bic** \¦==¦fōbik *also* -fäb-\ *adj*

**my·sore** \(ˈ)mīˌsō(ə)r, -sȯ(ə)r\ *adj, usu cap* [fr. *Mysore*, India] : of or from the city of Mysore, India : of the kind or style prevalent in Mysore

**mysore thorn** *n, usu cap M* : a spreading thorny leguminous shrub (*Caesalpinia sepiaria*) that bears large erect racemes of red-marked yellow flowers, is native to India where it is used for hedging, and is often cultivated in the greenhouse for its showy flowers

**my·sost** \ˈmīˌsäst\ *n* -s [Norw *myseost, mysost*, fr. *myse* whey + *ost* cheese] : a hard brown cheese of mild flavor made from whey esp. of goat's milk

**myst** \ˈmist\ *n* -s [L *mystes*, fr. Gk *mystēs* — more at MYSTES] : MYSTES

**myst** *abbr* mysteries; mystery

**mys·ta·ci·al** \məˈstāsh(ē)əl\ *also* **mys·ta·cal** \ˈmistəkəl\ *or* **mys·ta·cine** \-təˌsin, -sən\ *or* **mys·ta·ci·nous** \¦mistə¦sīnəs\ *adj* [Gk (Doric) *mystak-, mystax* moustache + E *-ial* or *-al* or *-ine* or *-inous* (fr. L *-inus*) — more at MOUSTACHE] : having a stripe or fringe of hairs suggestive of a moustache

**mys·ta·co·car·i·da** \ˌmistəkōˈkarədə\ *n pl, cap* [NL, fr. Gk (Doric) *mystak-, mystax* upper lip, moustache + NL *Carida*] : an order of obscure microscopic crustaceans living in intertidal sands and considered to be related to the copepods

**mys·ta·co·ce·te** \ˌmistəkōˈsēˌtē\ *or* **mys·ta·co·ce·ti** \-ˌtī\ [NL, by alter.] *syn of* MYSTICETI

**mystae** *or* **mystai** *pl of* MYSTES

**mys·ta·gog·ic** \¦mistə¦gäjik\ *also* **mys·ta·gog·i·cal** \-jəkəl\ *adj* : of or relating to a mystagogue or mystagogy — **mys·ta·gog·i·cal·ly** \-jək(ə)lē\ *adv*

**mys·ta·gogue** \ˈmistəˌgäg *sometimes* -gȯg\ *n* -s [L *mystagogus*, fr. Gk *mystagōgos*, fr. *mystēs* initiate + *agōgos* leader, fr. *agein* to lead — more at MYSTERY, AGENT] : one who initiates into or interprets mysteries (as the Eleusinian mysteries) : a teacher or disseminator of mystical doctrines

**mys·ta·go·gy** \-ˌgōjē\ *n* -ES [Gk *mystagōgia*, fr. *mystagōgein* to initiate (fr. *mystagōgos*) + *-ia* -y] : the doctrines, principles, or practice of a mystagogue : interpretation of mysteries

**mys·tax** \ˈmiˌstaks\ *n* -ES [NL, fr. Gk (Doric) *mystax* upper lip, moustache — more at MOUSTACHE] : a cluster or row of hairs above the mouth of insects (as various two-winged flies)

**mys·te·ri·al** \məˈstirēəl, -tēr-\ *adj* [LL *mysterialis*, fr. L *mysterium* mystery + *-alis* -al — more at MYSTERY] : MYSTIC, MYSTERIOUS

**mys·te·ri·arch** \-rēˌärk\ *n* -s [LL *mysteriarches*, fr. LGk *mystēriarchēs*, fr. Gk *mystērion* mystery + *-archēs* -arch — more at MYSTERY] : one that presides over mysteries

**mys·te·ri·os·o·phy** \məˌstirēˈäsəfē\ *n* -ES [Gk *mystērion* mystery + E *-sophy*] : esoteric doctrine concerning the ancient mysteries

**mys·te·ri·ous** \məˈstirēəs, -tēr-\ *adj* [MF *mysterieux*, fr. *mystere* mystery (fr. L *mysterium*) + *-ieux* -ious] **1** : of or relating to mystery : containing, conveying, intimating, or implying a mystery : difficult or impossible to understand : OBSCURE, ENIGMATICAL ⟨a ~ event⟩ ⟨these ~ changes⟩ **2 a** : proper to or characteristic of a mystery or solemn rite **b** : stirred by or attracted to the inexplicable — **mys·te·ri·ous·ly** *adv* — **mys·te·ri·ous·ness** *n* -ES

**mysterious plant** *n* : MEZEREON 1

**mys·ter·ize** \ˈmistəˌrīz\ *vi* -ED/-ING/-S : to cultivate mystery or a mysterious air

**¹mys·tery** \'mist(ə)rē, -ri\ *n* -ES [ME *misterie, mysterie,* fr. L *mysterium,* fr. Gk *mystērion,* fr. (assumed) *mystos,* verbal of *myein* to initiate into religious rites, fr. *myein* to close (used of the eyes and lips), close the eyes; perh. akin to Norw *mysa* to wink, Latvian *musinât* to whisper, murmur, L *mutus* mute — more at MUTE] **1 a** *obs* **:** a purely spiritual form or interpretation **b :** a religious truth revealed by God that man cannot know by reason alone and that once it has been revealed cannot be completely understood **c** *usu cap* **:** a Christian religious rite or sacrament: as (1) **:** EUCHARIST 1 (2) **mysteries** *pl* **:** HOLY MYSTERIES (3) **:** any of the 15 meditations on the events of the life of Christ forming the major part of the rosary devotion **d** (1) **:** a secret non-Christian religious rite marked by the showing of sacred objects to duly initiated worshipers, the pronouncing of formulas, and the performing of ritual acts (as washing, eating and drinking, sacrificing) with a view to bettering the worshipers in this life and assuring them of life after death through union with the god thus worshiped (2) *or* **mystery cult** *or* **mystery religion** *often cap M* **:** a cult chiefly among ancient Mediterranean peoples characterized by such rites — often used in pl. ⟨the Eleusinian *mysteries* of the Greeks and the Mithras *mysteries* of Persia⟩ **2 :** something that has not been or cannot be explained, that is unknown to all or concealed from some and therefore exciting curiosity or wonder, or that is incomprehensible or uncomprehended ⟨the ~ of his disappearance has never been solved⟩ ⟨it's a ~ to me⟩ ⟨why are they making such a ~ of their troubles⟩: as **a** *obs* **:** a private secret **b** (1) **:** the secret or specialized operations or processes peculiar to an occupation or accomplishment ⟨learned the *mysteries* of his trade as an apprentice⟩ ⟨baffled by the *mysteries* of his wife's toilette⟩ — usu. used in pl. (2) **:** a ritual or the practices or doctrines peculiar to some body of people (as a fraternal order or a primitive community) that are revealed only to members or initiates of that body — usu. used in pl. **c** *archaic* **:** a state or political secret **d :** something that is incomprehensible at a particular period or under particular circumstances but that is not normally so to people in general ⟨the thrilling *mysteries* of childhood, so soon outgrown⟩ **e** *or* **mystery story :** a piece of fiction in which the evidence relating to a crime or occasionally to another mysterious event is so presented that the reader has an opportunity to solve the problem, the author's solution being the final phase of the piece **3** *obs* **:** a mystical or recondite cause or significance **4 a :** profound and inexplicable quality or character **:** INCOMPREHENSIBILITY ⟨the *mysteries* and beauties of nature⟩ **:** the quality or state of defying solution or analysis ⟨puzzled by the ~ of her sly glance⟩ **b :** a tendency to surround things with puzzling circumstances or to make them obscure **:** an affectation of needless or excessive secrecy ⟨despising ~ in their rulers⟩ ⟨wrapped in ~ as in a cloak⟩

**syn** PROBLEM, PUZZLE, ENIGMA, RIDDLE, CONUNDRUM: MYSTERY refers to a matter inexplicable, one that defies attempts at explanation, or to something kept secret but intriguing and compelling speculation ⟨this *mystery* of growth of life —Richard Jefferies⟩ ⟨the veil of *mystery* that shrouds human sleep —Webb Garrison⟩ ⟨the disappearance of the Erebus and Terror in the Arctic was one of the great mid-Victorian *mysteries* —*Times Lit. Supp.*⟩ PROBLEM, more commonplace in its suggestions, refers to any question calling for solution or answer or to any factor causing perplexity and concern ⟨the *problem* of spontaneous generation —J.B. Conant⟩ ⟨with the shipping *problem* resolved by the allocation of ships to France —*Current Biog.*⟩ ⟨the withdrawn child or adolescent is, in the long run, more likely to become a serious psychological *problem* than is the mildly aggressive child —Paul Woodring⟩ PUZZLE applies to any problem notably baffling and challenging one's ingenuity or skill ⟨there are few things in the world so difficult to explain as real change; it appears to me that most scientists are far from realising the complexity of this metaphysical *puzzle* —W.R.Inge⟩ ENIGMA applies to whatever is quite obscure or inscrutable and challenges one's ingenuity for an answer ⟨he became an *enigma.* One side or the other of his nature was perfectly comprehensible; but both sides together were bewildering —Jack London⟩ ⟨just what his objectives are is an *enigma,* for he has been extremely adept in refusing to commit himself too far —Vance Johnson⟩ RIDDLE indicates a question or problem involving paradox or contradictions, often light, and usu. proposed for solution as an indication of wit or intellect ⟨I've got a brand-new *riddle* for you . . . what's the difference between a cat and a comma? . . . a comma's a pause at the end of a clause, and a cat's got claws at the end of its paws —J.W.Ellison b.1929⟩ CONUNDRUM may apply to punning riddles or to unsolvable problems inviting speculation ⟨Octavius — he was not for nothing the scion of banking stock — looked beyond the political *conundrum* to the economic problems of the land —John Buchan⟩

**²mystery** *or* **mis·tery** \"\ *n* -ES [LL *mysterium, misterium,* alter. (influenced by L *mysterium* mystery) of L *ministerium* work, occupation, ministry — more at MINISTRY] **1** *archaic* **:** one's occupation or calling **:** TRADE, CRAFT, HANDICRAFT, ART **2** *archaic* **:** a body of persons engaged in a particular trade, business, or profession **:** GUILD ⟨fie upon him, he will discredit our ~ —*Shak.*⟩ **3** *or* **mystery play** [ML *misterium, mysterium,* fr. LL] **a :** one of a class of medieval religious dramas based on Scriptural incidents and usu. centering in the life, death, and resurrection of Christ **b :** this type of drama — compare MIRACLE PLAY, MORALITY PLAY

**mystery clock** *n* **:** a clock so constructed as to run without gears or a visible source of power

**mystery grass** *n* **:** DEATH CAMAS

**mystery ship** *or* **mystery boat** *n* **:** Q-BOAT — first used of one of a class of ships built in England during World War I

**mystery snail** *n* **:** an apple snail (*Ampullaria cuprina*) often kept as a scavenger in aquariums

**mys·tes** \'mistēz\ *n, pl* **mys·tae** \-,stē\ *or* **mys·tai** \-,stī\ [L, fr. Gk *mystēs,* fr. *myein* to initiate into religious rites — more at MYSTERY] **:** an initiate in a mystery (as in the Eleusinian mysteries)

**¹mys·tic** \'mistik, -tēk\ *adj* [ME *mistik,* fr. L *mysticus,* fr. Gk *mystikos,* fr. (assumed) *mystos* (verbal of *myein* to initiate into religious rites) + *-ikos* -ic — more at MYSTERY] **1 :** MYSTICAL 1 **2 a :** of or relating to ancient mysteries (as the Eleusinian) **b :** constituting or belonging to something occult or esoteric — used of rites, observances, religions, and comparable matters **c** *of a fraternal order* **:** having a ritual known or practiced only by initiates **3 :** of or relating to mysticism, mystics, the mystical experience ⟨~ state⟩ ⟨the ~ way⟩ **4 a :** baffling or incomprehensible to the understanding **:** MYSTERIOUS ⟨the ~ gulf from God to man —R.W.Emerson⟩ **b :** ENIGMATIC, OBSCURE, MYSTIFYING, VAGUE ⟨the ~ words of the stranger⟩ **c :** inducing a feeling of awe, wonder, or similar response ⟨the ~ beauty of the night⟩ **d :** having magical properties or associations ⟨~ numbers⟩ **5** *obs* **:** SECRET, HIDDEN, COVERT, DISGUISED

**²mystic** \"\ *n* -S **1 :** a person subject to mystical experiences **:** a follower or an expounder of a mystical way of life **2 :** an initiate of a mystery **3 :** a holder or advocate of a theory of mysticism

**mys·ti·cal** \-tәkәl, -tēk-\ *adj* [L *mysticus* + E *-al*] **1 :** having a spiritual meaning, existence, reality, or comparable value that is neither apparent to the senses nor obvious to the intelligence **:** relating to such a value **:** SYMBOLICAL, ANAGOGIC ⟨the church is the ~ body of Christ⟩ ⟨the ~ interpretation of Scriptures⟩ ⟨the ~ style of Blake⟩ **2 a :** of, resulting from, or manifesting an individual's direct or intimate knowledge of or communion with God (as through contemplation, vision, an inner light) ⟨~ rapture⟩ ⟨~ experience⟩ **:** concerned with or relating to such experience ⟨a ~ artist⟩ **b :** derived immediately rather than mediately **:** based upon intuition, insight, or similar subjective experience ⟨the ~ character of Neoplatonism⟩ ⟨the ~ religions of the East⟩ **3 a :** beyond ordinary human knowledge or comprehension **:** UNINTELLIGIBLE, CRYPTIC, ENIGMATIC, OBSCURE **b :** FURTIVE, SECRET **4 :** MYSTIC 2

**mys·ti·cal·i·ty** \,mistә'kalәd·ē, -әtē, -i\ *n* -ES **:** mystical quality

**mys·ti·cal·ly** \'mistәk(ә)lē, -tēk-, -li\ *adv* **:** in a mystic or mystical manner **:** so as to produce a mystic or mystical effect

**mys·ti·cal·ness** *n* -ES **:** MYSTICALITY

**mystic cross** *n, sometimes cap M&C* **:** a mark resembling a cross that is sometimes found on the center of the palm between the line of Heart and the line of Head and under the Mount of Saturn and that is usu. held by palmists to indicate a great interest in mysticism and occult subjects

**¹mys·ti·ce·te** \,mistә'sē,tē\ *syn of* MYSTICETI

**²mys·ti·cete** \'mistә,sēt\ *n* -S [NL *Mysticeti*] **:** WHALEBONE WHALE

**mys·ti·ce·ti** \,mistә'sē,tī\ *n pl, cap* [NL, pl. of *mysticetus* Greenland whale, fr. Gk *mystikētos,* a whale (dubious reading in some early editions of Aristotle where some recent editions read *ho mys to ketos* and interpret as "the 'mouse' — that is, the whale so called")] **:** a suborder of Cetacea consisting of the whalebone whales — compare ODONTOCETI — **mys·ti·ce·tous** \¦==¦sēd·әs\ *adj*

**mys·ti·cism** \'mistә,sizәm\ *n* -S [¹*mystic* + *-ism*] **1 :** the experience of mystical union or direct communion with ultimate reality reported by mystics **2 :** a theory of mystical knowledge **:** the doctrine or belief that direct knowledge of God, of spiritual truth, of ultimate reality, or comparable matters is attainable through immediate intuition, insight, or illumination and in a way differing from ordinary sense perception or ratiocination ⟨nature ~⟩ **3 a :** vague speculation **:** VAGARY **:** a belief without foundation **b :** any theory postulating or based on the possibility of direct and intuitive acquisition of ineffable knowledge or power

**mys·tic·i·ty** \mә'stisәd·ē\ *n* -ES [F *mysticité,* fr. L *mysticus* mystic + F *-ité* -ity — more at MYSTIC] **:** mystic quality or state

**mys·ti·cize** \'mistә,sīz\ *vb* -ED/-ING/-S [¹*mystic* + *-ize*] **:** to make mystic or mystical

**mys·tic·ly** *adv* **:** in a mystic manner **:** so as to produce a mystic effect

**mystico-** *comb form* [¹*mystic*] **:** mystical and ⟨*mystico*allegoric⟩

**mystic will** *or* **mystic testament** *n* **:** a will prepared by or at the instance of a testator, sealed up in an envelope, acknowledged on the outside of the envelope, and executed in accordance with required formalities before a notary

**mys·tif·ic** \mә'stifik\ *n* -S [back-formation fr. *mystification*] **:** MYSTIFICATOR

**mys·ti·fi·ca·tion** \,mistәfә'kāshәn\ *n* -S [F, fr. *mystifier* to mystify, after such pairs as F *falsifier* to falsify: *falsification* — more at MYSTIFY] **1 :** an act or instance of mystifying **2 :** the quality or state of being mystified **3 :** something that is designed to or that does mystify

**mys·ti·fi·ca·tor** \-ād·ә(r)\ *n* -S [F *mystificateur,* fr. *mystifier,* after such pairs as F *falsifier: falsificateur* falsifier] **:** one that mystifies

**mys·tif·i·ca·to·ry** \mә'stifәkә,tōrē\ *adj* **:** MYSTIFYING

**mys·ti·fied·ly** *adv* **:** in a mystified manner

**mys·ti·fi·er** \'mistә,fī(ә)r\ *n* -S **:** one that mystifies

**mys·ti·fy** \-,fī\ *vt* -ED/-ING/-ES [F *mystifier,* fr. *mystère* mystery + *-ifier* -ify — more at MYSTERIOUS] **1 :** to intentionally perplex the mind of **:** impose upon the credulity of **:** BEWILDER ⟨caught trying to confuse and ~ his opponent⟩ **2 a :** to involve in mystery **:** make obscure or difficult to understand ⟨~ a passage of Scripture⟩ **b :** to embellish (as fact) mystically or fancifully **syn** see PUZZLE

**mys·ti·fy·ing·ly** *adv* **:** in a mystifying manner **:** so as to cause mystification

**mys·tique** \mi'stēk\ *n* -S [F, fr. *mystique,* adj., mystic, fr. L *mysticus* — more at MYSTIC] **1 a :** a complex of transcendental or semimystical beliefs and attitudes directed toward or developing around an object (as a person, institution, idea, or pursuit) and enhancing the value or significance of the object by enduing it with an esoteric truth or meaning ⟨the ~ of the leader⟩ ⟨a ~ of mountain climbing⟩ **b :** an object of a mystique or of the veneration characteristic of a mystique **:** a mystic symbol **2 :** the special esoteric skill or mysterious faculty essential in a calling or activity ⟨a dozen handicrafts each with its own ~⟩ **3 :** a mystical or metaphysical interpretation of reality or a real situation, usu. expressed in a creed or credo, often served by a cult, and serving or intended to serve as a guide to action (as of a religious or a political group)

**my·ta·cism** \'mīd·ә,sizәm\ *n* -S [Gk *mytakismos,* irreg. fr. *my* mu (the letter) + *-ismos* -ism] **:** excessive or wrong use of the letter *m* or of the sound it represents (as in writing or in defective speech)

**myth** \'mith\ *n* -S [Gk *mythos* tale, speech, myth; perh. akin to Goth *maudjan* to remind, OIr *smuainim* I think, OSlav *myslĭ* thought, Lith *maũsti* to desire ardently] **1 :** a story that is usu. of unknown origin and at least partially traditional, that ostensibly relates historical events usu. of such character as to serve to explain some practice, belief, institution, or natural phenomenon, and that is esp. associated with religious rites and beliefs — compare EUHEMERISM, FABLE, FOLKTALE **2 a :** a story invented as a veiled explanation of a truth **:** PARABLE, ALLEGORY; *esp* **:** one of Plato's philosophical allegories **b :** the theme or plot of a mythical tale occurring in forms differing only in detail **3 :** a person or thing existing only in imagination or whose actuality is not verifiable: as **a :** a belief given uncritical acceptance by the members of a group esp. in support of existing or traditional practices and institutions ⟨a ~ of racial superiority used to justify discrimination⟩ **b :** a belief or concept that embodies a visionary ideal (as of some future utopian state or condition) ⟨the Marxian-fostered ~ of a classless society⟩ **4 :** mythical matter **:** the whole body of myths ⟨features distinguishing modern fiction from ~⟩

**syn** LEGEND, SAGA: MYTH varies considerably in its denotation and connotation depending on the persuasion of the user. Often the word is used to designate a story, usu. fanciful and imaginative, that explains a natural phenomenon or a social practice, institution, or belief ⟨the old *myth,* imported hazily from the East, which represented the cat-moon devouring the gray mice of twilight —Agnes Repplier⟩ It is also used to designate a story, belief, or notion commonly held to be true but utterly without factual basis ⟨the doubts that women have about themselves are man-made, and most women are so enslaved to the *myths* of their own inferiority they are unable to see the truth for the *myth* —M.F.A.Montagu⟩ The word may be used with wide comprehensiveness in general writing or with narrow exclusiveness and specificity in more limited use ⟨*myths* may be subdivided into such classifications as origin *myths,* ritual *myths,* incidents involving the lives of the gods, stories of culture heroes, trickster tales, journeys to the other world, human and animal marriages, adaptations of old world *myths,* and retellings of biblical stories —L.J.Davidson⟩ ⟨*myths* are said to be expressions or objectifications of "collective wishes" which are personified in the "leader" who is endowed by a given society with powers of social magic to fulfill the collective wishes —A.L.Kroeber⟩ LEGEND is likewise used with latitude: it is likely to indicate a story, incident, or notion often fanciful, fabulous, or incredible, attached to a particular person or place ⟨the medieval *legends* of the saints⟩ ⟨the wrecking of the Palatine which, according to *legend,* did not sink but rose flaming into the sky —Fred Zimmer⟩ ⟨the violent deaths of several slaves quartered in them gave rise to a *legend* that this part of the house is haunted —*Amer. Guide Series: Md.*⟩ SAGA may refer to a long, continued, heroic story that is action-packed but not especially romantic, that deals with a person or group, and that is historical or legendary or both ⟨the *Saga* of Burnt Njal⟩ ⟨the building of the railroad in the Northwest was one of the great *sagas* of man's enterprise —Meridel Le Sueur⟩ **syn** see in addition ALLEGORY

**mythi** *pl of* MYTHUS

**myth·i·cal** \'mithәkәl, -thēk-\ *or* **myth·ic** \-thik, -thēk\ *adj* [*mythical* fr. LL *mythicus* (fr. Gk *mythikos,* fr. *mythos* myth + *-ikos* -ic) + E *-al; mythic* fr. LL *mythicus*] **1 a :** based on or described in a myth esp. as contrasted with factual history **:** imaginary, fancied, and existent only in myths ⟨the founder of the sacred grove . . . is clearly the ~ predecessor or archetype of the line of priests who served Diana —J.G.Frazer⟩ **b :** fabricated, invented, or imagined in a consciously arbitrary way ⟨a ~ all-star team⟩ or ignorantly and willfully without facts or in defiance of facts ⟨history . . . shows that the claim to purity of race on the part of any civilized people is entirely ~ —M.R.Cohen⟩ **c :** characterized by qualities suitable to myth esp. by fantastic or bizarre characteristics ⟨a ~ monster⟩ **d :** constituting myth ⟨~ accounts⟩ **2 a :** characterized by or using myths or mythical matter ⟨~ writers⟩ **b :** construing religious or other narratives about supernatural events to have originated as or to be based on myth ⟨the ~ theory of the Gospels⟩ **syn** see FICTITIOUS

**myth·i·cal·ly** \-thәk(ә)lē, -thēk-, -li\ *adv* **:** in a mythical manner **:** so as to constitute or give the effect of myth

**myth·i·cal·ness** *n* -ES **:** the quality or state of being mythical

**myth·i·cist** \'mithәsәst\ *n* -S **1 :** a student or interpreter of myths **2 :** an adherent of the view that apparently supernatural persons or events have their origin in human imagination esp. as revealed in myth

**myth·i·cize** \'mithә,sīz\ *vt* -ED/-ING/-S **1 :** to make mythical **:** envelop or obscure in myths ⟨*mythicizing* the scanty historic remains of the earlier saints⟩ **2 :** to treat or represent as mythical or fabricated as a myth — **myth·i·ciz·er** \-zә(r)\ *n* -S

**mythico-** *comb form* [*mythical*] **:** mythical and ⟨*mythico*historical⟩ ⟨*mythico*romantic⟩

**mythier** *comparative of* MYTHY

**mythiest** *superlative of* MYTHY

**myth·i·fy** \'mithә,fī\ *vt* -ED/-ING/-ES [*myth* + *-ify*] **:** to make myth of **:** give a mythical cast to

**mythmaker** \'=,==\ *n* **:** a creator of myths or of mythical situations or lore

**mythmaking** \'=,==\ *n* **:** the creation of myths or of mythical situations or lore

**myth·o·clast** \'mithә,klast\ *n* -S [*myth* + *-o-* + *-clast*] **:** a decrier of myths — **myth·o·clas·tic** \¦==¦klastik\ *adj*

**mytho·genesis** \,mithә+\ *also* **my·thog·e·ny** \mә'thäjәnē\ *n, pl* **mythogeneses** *also* **mythogenies** [*myth* + *-o-* + *genesis* or *-geny*] **1 :** formation or production of myths **2 :** the tendency to make myths or to give mythical status to something (as a tradition or belief)

**my·thog·ra·pher** \mә'thägrәfә(r)\ *n* -S [Gk *mythographos* mythographer (fr. *mythos* myth + *graphein* to write) + E *-e* — more at MYTH, CARVE] **:** a compiler of or writer about myths

**my·thog·ra·phy** \-fē\ *n* -ES [Gk *mythographia,* fr. *mythos* + *-graphia* -graphy] **1 :** the representation of mythical subjects in art **2 a :** descriptive mythology **b :** a critical compilation of myths

**mytho green** \'mi(,)thō-\ *n* [*mytho* of unknown origin] **:** a grayish to moderate yellow green that is greener and lighter than gage green or pois green

**mytho·heroic** \¦mithō+\ *adj* [*myth* + *-o-* + *heroic*] **:** celebrating the deeds of heroes of myths ⟨~ poetry⟩

**mythoi** *pl of* MYTHOS

**my·thol·o·gem** \mә'thälәjәm\ *n* -S [Gk *mythologēma* mythical narrative, fr. *mythologein* to narrate mythical tales — more at MYTHOLOGY] **:** a basic or recurrent theme of myth ⟨the universal flood and the fire bringer are ~*s* of diverse times and races⟩

**my·thol·o·ger** \mә'thälәjә(r)\ *n* -S [Gk *mythologos* teller of myths or legends + E *-er* — more at MYTHOLOGIST] **:** MYTHOLOGIST

**myth·o·log·i·cal** \¦mithә¦läjәkәl, -jēk-\ *also* **myth·o·log·ic** \-jik, -jēk\ *adj* [LL *mythologicus,* fr. Gk *mythologikos,* fr. *mythologia* legend, story-telling + *-ikos* -ic, -ical] **1 :** of or relating to mythology or myths **:** dealt with in mythology **2 :** lacking factual basis or historical validity **:** MYTHICAL, FABULOUS — **myth·o·log·i·cal·ly** \-jәk(ә)lē, -jēk-, -li\ *adv*

**my·thol·o·gist** \mә'thälәjәst\ *n* -S [Gk *mythologos* teller of myths or legends (fr. *mythos* myth + *-logos,* fr. *logos* word, speech, account) + E *-ist* — more at MYTH, LEGEND] **1 :** a student of mythology or myths **2 :** MYTHMAKER

**my·thol·o·gi·za·tion** \mә,thälәjә'zāshәn\ *n* -S **:** the act or practice of mythologizing **:** the imparting of a mythical quality to something

**my·thol·o·gize** \mә'thälә,jīz\ *vb* -ED/-ING/-S *see -ize in Explan Notes* [F *mythologiser,* fr. *mythologie* mythology (fr. LL *mythologia* interpretation of myths) + *-iser* -ize] *vt* **1** *obs* **:** to explain the mythological references or the symbolical significance of **2 a :** to build a myth round **:** make the subject of mythical treatment **b :** to represent mythologically or as mythological **:** MYTHICIZE ~ *vi* **1 :** to relate, classify, and explain or attempt to explain myths **:** write about myths **2 :** to construct and propagate myths — **my·thol·o·giz·er** \-zә(r)\ *n* -S

**my·thol·o·gy** \mә'thälәjē, -ji\ *n* -ES [F or LL; F *mythologie,* fr. LL *mythologia* interpretation of myths, fr. Gk, legend, myth, storytelling, fr. *mythologein* to narrate mythical tales (fr. *mythos* myth + *-logein,* fr. *logos* word, speech, account) + *-ia* -y — more at MYTH, LEGEND] **1** *obs* **:** the symbolical significance of something (as a name or a fable) **2 a :** an allegorical narrative **:** MYTH, PARABLE **b :** a body of myths: as (1) **:** the myths dealing with the gods, demigods, and legendary heroes of a particular people in stories that involve supernatural elements ⟨the ~ of ancient Greece⟩ (2) **:** a body of myths arising from a situation (as an activity or a historical event) or more or less consciously propagated by an agency (as a group or political party) ⟨the ~ that emerged out of World War II⟩ ⟨the ~ of Fascism⟩ **3 a :** a branch of knowledge that deals with myth **b :** a treatise on myths

**myth·o·ma·nia** \,mithә'mānēә\ *n* [NL, fr. Gk *mythos* myth + NL *-mania*] **:** an abnormal propensity for lying and exaggerating — **myth·o·ma·ni·ac** \¦==¦mānē,ak\ *n or adj*

**myth·o·poe·ia** \,mithә'pēә\ *n* -S [LL, fr. Gk *mythopoiia,* fr. *mythopoiein* to make a myth (fr. *mythos* myth + *poiein* to make) + *-ia* -y — more at POEM] **:** a creating of myth or a giving rise to myths

**myth·o·poe·ic** \¦==¦pēik\ *adj* [Gk *mythopoios* teller of legends or myths (fr. *mythopoiein*) + E *-ic*] **1 a :** creating or tending to create myth or myths ⟨the ~ stage of human culture⟩ **b :** preoccupied with mythological matters ⟨the ~ mind of the savage —David Bidney⟩ **2 :** giving rise to myths ⟨some great ~ event —J.C.Powys⟩

**mytho·poem** \¦mithә+\ *n* [*myth-* + *-o-* + *poem*] **:** a mythological poem

**myth·o·po·e·sis** \,mithәpō'ēsәs\ *n* -ES [NL, fr. Gk *mythopoiēsis,* fr. *mythopoiein* + *-sis*] **:** the making of myths

**mytho·poet** \¦mithә+\ *n* [*myth-* + *-o-* + *poet*] **:** MYTHMAKER

**myth·o·po·et·ic** \¦mithәpō¦ed·ik\ *adj* [*myth* + *-o-* + Gk *poiētikos* able to make, poetic — more at POETIC] **:** MYTHOPOEIC 1a

**myth·o·po·et·i·cal** \-d·әkәl\ *adj* [*myth* + *-o-* + Gk *poiētikos* able to make + E *-al*] **:** MYTHOPOEIC 2

**mytho·poetry** \¦mithә+\ *n* [*myth* + *-o-* + *poetry*] **:** mythological poetry

**my·thos** \'mī,thäs\ *n, pl* **my·thoi** \-thȯi\ [Gk — more at MYTH] **1 a :** MYTH 1 **b :** MYTHOLOGY 2b **2 :** the pattern of meaning and valuation expressive of the basic truths and enduring apprehensions of a people's historic experience characteristically expressed through a medium of high symbolism (as poetry, art, or drama) **3 :** the underlying theme or symbolic meaning of a creative work; *sometimes* **:** PLOT 4

**myths** *pl of* MYTH

**my·thus** \'mīthәs\ *n, pl* **mythi** [NL, fr. Gk *mythos*] **1 :** MYTH 1 **2 :** MYTHOS 2

**mythy** \'mithē\ *adj* -ER/-EST [*myth* + *-y*] **:** resembling, concerned with, or a subject for myth or myths ⟨a ~ mind⟩ ⟨a ~ theme⟩

**myt·i·la·cea** \,mid·ә'lāshēә\ *n pl, cap* [NL, fr. *Mytilus* + *-acea*] **:** a suborder of Filibranchia including the family Mytilidae and sometimes related families (as Pteriidae) — **myt·i·la·cean** \¦==¦lāshәn\ *adj or n* — **myt·i·la·ceous** \-shәs\ *adj*

**¹myt·i·lid** \'mid·ᵊlәd\ *adj* [NL *Mytilidae*] **:** of or relating to the Mytilidae

**²mytilid** \"\ *n* -S [NL *Mytilidae*] **:** a mollusk of the family Mytilidae **:** MUSSEL

**my·til·i·dae** \mī'tilә,dē\ *n pl, cap* [NL, fr. *Mytilus,* type genus + *-idae*] **:** a family of marine bivalve mollusks (order Filibranchia) having the shell elongated and equivalve with a large narrow internal ligament and a byssus for attachment to the substrate — compare MUSSEL

**my·til·i·form** \-,fȯrm\ *adj* [L *mytilus* + E *-iform*] **:** shaped like a mussel shell

**myt·i·lus** \'mid·ᵊlәs\ *n, cap* [NL, fr. L *mytilus, mytulus, mitulus,* a mussel, fr. Gk *mytilos, mitylos*] **:** the type genus of Mytilidae comprising usu. smooth-shelled marine mussels that live attached to solid objects chiefly in the intertidal zone and include the common edible mussel (*M. edulis*)

**myx-** *or* **myxo-** *comb form* [NL, fr. Gk, fr. *myxa* lampwick, nasal slime — more at MUCUS] **1 :** mucus **:** slime ⟨*myx*adenitis⟩ ⟨*myxo*cyte⟩ ⟨*Myxo*mycetes⟩ **2 :** myxoma ⟨*myxo*fibroma⟩ ⟨*myxo*sarcoma⟩

**-myxa** \'miksə\ *n comb form, pl* **-myxa** [NL, fr. Gk *myxa* lampwick, nasal slime] **:** one or ones consisting of or resembling slime — in taxonomic names esp. in protozoology ⟨Chlamydo*myxa*⟩ ⟨Proteo*myxa*⟩

**myx·amoe·ba** \ˌmiks+\ *n* [NL, fr. *myx-* + *amoeba*] **:** a naked amoeboid uninucleate protoplast that lacks both cilia and flagella, is a characteristic stage in the life cycle of slime molds and some other fungi, arises from a haploid derivative of a swarm spore or by fusion of two haploid zoospores, and typically develops into a plasmodium either by repeated nuclear fission or by fusion of individual myxamoebas

**myx·ede·ma** \ˌmiksə'dēmə\ *n* -s [NL, fr. *myx-* + *edema*] **:** severe hypothyroidism characterized by firm inelastic edema, dry skin and hair, and loss of mental and physical vigor — **myx·edem·a·tous** \ˌ≈≈¦deməd·əs, -dēm-\ *adj*

**myx·i·ne** \mik'sīnē\ *n, cap* [NL, fr. Gk *myxinos*, a kind of mullet, fr. *myxa* lampwick, nasal mucus + *-inos* -ine — more at MUCUS] **:** a genus (the type of the family Myxinidae) of cyclostomes containing the typical hagfishes that have on each side only a single external gill opening

**myx·i·noid** \'miksəˌnȯid\ *adj or n* [NL *Myxine* + E *-oid*] **:** HYPEROTRETAN

**myx·i·noi·dei** \ˌ≈≈'nȯidēˌī\ [NL, fr. *Myxine* + *-oidei*] *syn of* HYPEROTRETA

**myx·o·bac·ter** \'miksəˌbaktə(r)\ *n* -s [NL *Myxobacter*, former genus of bacteria, fr. *myx-* + *-bacter*] **:** a bacterium of the order Myxobacterales

**myx·o·bac·ter·a·les** \ˌmiksəˌbaktə'rā(ˌ)lēz\ *n pl, cap* [NL, fr. *Myxobacter* + *-ales*] **:** an order of higher bacteria having long slender nonflagellated vegetative cells that form colonies capable of creeping slowly over a layer of slime secreted by the cells, forming spores usu. in distinct fruiting bodies, and living chiefly as saprophytes on substrates rich in carbohydrates

**myxo·bac·te·ria** \ˌmiksəˌbak'tirēə\ [NL, fr. *myx-* + *bacteria*, pl. of *bacterium*] *syn of* MYXOBACTERALES

[1]**myx·o·bac·te·ri·a·ce·ae** \ˌ≈≈ˌ≈ˌtirē'āsēˌē\ [NL, fr. *Myxobacterium* + *-aceae*] *syn of* MYXOBACTERALES

[2]**myxobacteriaceae** \"\ [NL, fr. *Myxobacterium* + *-aceae*] *syn of* POLYANGIACEAE

**myx·o·bac·te·ri·al** \¦≈≈ˌ≈¦tirēəl\ *adj* [NL *Myxobacteriales*] **1 :** of or relating to the Myxobacterales **2 :** like or like that of a myxobacter

**myx·o·bac·te·ri·a·les** \ˌ≈≈ˌ≈ˌtirē'ā(ˌ)lēz\ [NL, fr. *Myxobacterium* + *-ales*] *syn of* MYXOBACTERALES

**myx·o·bac·te·ri·um** \ˌmiksəˌbak'tirēəm\ *n* [NL, former genus of bacteria, fr. *Myx-* + *bacterium*] **:** a bacterium of the order Myxobacterales

**myx·ob·o·lus** \mik'säbələs\ *n, cap* [NL, fr. *myx-* + Gk *bōlos* lump — more at BOLE] **:** a genus of cnidosporidian protozoans that includes the causative organism of boil disease of fishes

**myx·o·coc·cus** \ˌmiksə'käkəs\ *n* [NL, fr. *Myx-* + *-coccus*] **1** *cap* **:** a genus of myxobacteria in which the rod-shaped vegetative cells are transformed into ovoidal to spherical spores **2** *pl* **myxococ·ci** \-äˌkī, -ä(ˌ)kē, -äkˌsī, -äk(ˌ)sē\ **:** an organism of the genus *Myxococcus*

**myx·o·coel** \'miksəˌsēl\ *n* -s [*myx-* + Gk *koilos* hollow, concave — more at CAVE] **:** a body cavity that is only partly of coelomic origin

**myx·o·cyte** \'miksəˌsīt\ *n* -s [*myx-* + *-cyte*] **:** a stellate cell that is characteristic of mucous tissue

**myx·o·flag·el·late** \ˌmiksə'flajəˌlāt\ *n* [*myx-* + *flagellate*] **:** a flagellated zoospore that follows the myxamoeba in various myxomycetes

**myx·o·gas·ter** \'miksəˌgastə(r), ˌ≈≈'≈≈\ *n* -s [NL, former genus of slime molds, fr. *myx-* + *-gaster*] **:** MYXOMYCETE

**myx·o·gas·te·res** \ˌ≈≈'gastəˌrēz\ [NL, fr. pl. of *Myxogaster*] *syn of* MYXOGASTRES

**myx·o·gas·tra·les** \ˌ≈≈ˌga'strā(ˌ)lēz\ *n pl, cap* [NL, fr. *Myxogastr-*, *Myxogaster* + *-ales*] *in some classifications* **:** an order equivalent to the subclass Myxogastres

**myx·o·gas·tres** \ˌ≈≈'gaˌstrēz\ *n pl, cap* [NL, fr. pl. of *Myxogaster*] **:** a subclass of Myxomycetes comprising those typical slime molds that develop definite fruiting bodies in which are produced spores which on germinating release one, two, or rarely several swarm spores — compare EXOSPOREAE — **myx·o·gas·tric** \¦≈≈¦gastrik\ *or* **myx·o·gas·trous** \-rəs\ *adj*

**myx·oid** \'mikˌsȯid\ *adj* [*myx-* + *-oid*] **:** like mucus

**myx·o·ma** \mik'sōmə\ *n, pl* **myxomas** \-məz\ *or* **myxoma·ta** \-məd·ə\ [NL, fr. *myx-* + *-oma*] **:** a soft tumor made up of gelatinous connective tissue resembling that found in the umbilical cord — **myx·om·a·tous** \(')mik¦säməd·əs, -sōm-\ *adj*

**myx·o·ma·to·sis** \mikˌsōmə'tōsəs\ *n, pl* **myxomato·ses** \-tōˌsēz\ [NL, fr. *myxomat-*, *myxoma* + *-osis*] **1 :** a condition characterized by the presence of myxomas in the body; *specif* **:** a severe virus disease of rabbits that is marked by fever, swelling and inflammation, and myxomatous subcutaneous tumors tending to become necrotic, is transmitted by mosquitoes, and has been used in biological control of rabbits in plague areas **2 :** mucoid degeneration

**myx·o·my·ce·tae** \ˌmiksəˌmī'sē(ˌ)d·ē\ [NL] *syn of* MYXOMYCETES

**myx·o·my·cete** \ˌmiksə'mīˌsēt, ¦≈≈ˌ≈¦≈ *sometimes* mik¦sämə¦sēt\ *n* -s [NL *Myxomycetes*] **:** an organism of the class Myxomycetes

**myx·o·my·ce·tes** \ˌmiksəˌmī'sēd·ēz\ *n pl, cap* [NL, fr. *Myx-* + *-mycetes*] **:** a class of organisms of uncertain systematic position that are sometimes considered to be protozoans but are now usu. regarded as plants and associated with the fungi or placed in a separate division, that exist vegetatively as complex mobile plasmodia, reproduce by means of spores which in almost all cases are borne in characteristic fruiting bodies, and have complex variable life cycles — see EXOSPOREAE, MYXOGASTRES; MYCETOZOA, MYXOPHYTA; SLIME MOLD — **myx·o·my·ce·tous** \¦≈≈ˌ≈¦sēd·əs *sometimes* mik¦sämə¦s-\ *adj*

**myx·o·my·ce·ti·dae** \ˌ≈≈ˌ≈'sēd·əˌdē\ [NL, fr. *Myxomycetes* + *-idae*] *syn of* MYXOGASTRES

**myx·o·my·coph·y·ta** \ˌmiksəˌmī'käfəd·ə\ [NL, fr. *myx-* + *myc-* + *-phyta*] *syn of* MYXOPHYTA

**myx·o·phy·ce·ae** \ˌmiksə'fisēˌē\ *n pl, cap* [NL, fr. *myx-* + *-phyceae*] **:** a class of unicellular or filamentous algae of simple structure that comprise the blue-green algae, have the chlorophyll masked by bluish green pigments, lack a condensed nucleus and chloroplasts, reproduce only by simple fission, and have been sometimes considered related to the bacteria — compare NOSTOC, OSCILLATORIA — **myx·o·phy·ce·an** \¦≈≈¦fisēən\ *adj or n*

**myx·oph·y·ta** \mik'säfəd·ə\ *n pl, cap* [NL, fr. *myx-* + *-phyta*] *in some esp former classifications* **:** a division of plants coextensive with the class Myxomycetes — used when the myxomycetes are considered to constitute a group independent of Fungi

**myx·op·o·da** \mik'säpədə\ [NL, fr. *myx-* + *-poda*] *syn of* RHIZOPODA

**myx·o·po·di·um** \ˌmiksə'pōdēəm\ *n, pl* **myxopo·dia** \-ēə\ [NL, fr. *myx-* + *-podium*] **:** a pseudopodium that tends to branch or anastomose like the foraminiferans, radiolarians, and myxomycetes

**myx·op·o·dous** \mik'säpədəs\ *adj* [NL *myxopodium* + E *-ous*] **:** having myxopodia

**myxo·pterygium** \ˌmiksə+\ *n* [NL, fr. *myx-* + *pterygium*] **:** a clasper of an elasmobranch fish

**myxo·sarcoma** \¦miksō+\ *n* [NL, fr. *myx-* + *sarcoma*] **:** a sarcoma with myxomatous elements — **myxo·sarcomatous** \"+\ *adj*

**myx·o·spon·gia** \ˌmiksə'spänjēə\ *or* **myx·o·spon·gi·ae** \-ēˌē\ [NL, fr. *myx-* + *-spongia*, *-spongiae*] *syn of* MYXOSPONGIDA

**myxo·spongida** \ˌmiksə+\ *n pl, cap* [NL, fr. *myx-* + *Spongida*] **:** an order of Demospongiae comprising sponges without either spicules or horny fibers

**myx·o·spo·rid·ia** \ˌmiksəspə'ridēə\ *n pl, cap* [NL, fr. *myx-* + *-sporidia*] **:** an order of cnidosporidian protozoans that are mostly parasitic in fishes and include various serious pathogens — compare BOIL DISEASE, TWIST DISEASE, WORMY HALIBUT — **myx·o·spo·rid·i·an** \¦≈≈¦ridēən\ *adj or n*

**myx·o·spo·ri·di·ida** \ˌmiksəˌspōrə'dīədə\ [NL, fr. *myx-* + *sporidium* + *-ida*] *syn of* MYXOSPORIDIA

**myx·os·to·ma** \mik'sästəmə\ *n, cap* [NL, fr. *myx-* + *-stoma*] **:** a genus of cnidosporidian protozoans containing the organism causing twist disease

**myxo·thallophyta** \ˌmiksə+\ [NL, fr. *myx-* + *Thallophyta*] *syn of* MYXOPHYTA

**myx·o·the·ca** \ˌmiksə'thēkə\ *n, pl* **myxothe·cae** \-ē(ˌ)sē\ [NL, fr. *myx-* + *-theca*] **:** the horny sheath of the end of a bird's lower mandible

**myxo·xanthin** \ˌmiksə+\ *n* [*myx-* + *xanthin*] **:** a violet crystalline carotenoid ketone $C_{40}H_{54}O$ that occurs in blue-green algae and is a provitamin A

**-my·za** \'mīzə\ *or* **-my·zon** \'mīˌzän\ *n comb form*, [NL, fr. Gk *myzein*, *myzan* to suck; akin to Gk *mydan* to be damp — more at MOSS] **:** one that sucks or feeds by suction — in generic names in zoology ⟨Petro*myzon*⟩ ⟨Agro*myza*⟩

**myzo-** *comb form* [NL, fr. Gk *myzan*, *myzein* to suck] **:** sucking **:** sucker ⟨*myzo*dendron⟩ ⟨*Myzo*rhynchus⟩

**my·zo·den·dron** \ˌmīzə'dendrən\ *n, cap* [NL, fr. *myzo-* + *-dendron*] **:** a genus (coextensive with the family Myzodendraceae) of semiparasitic plants of the order Santalales that usu. have unisexual flowers with the small perianth parts opposite the aduate stamens and 3-angled fruits with a greatly elongated hairy process projecting from each angle

**my·zon·tes** \mī'zänˌtēz\ [NL, fr. Gk, nom. masc. pl. of *myzōn*, pres. part. of *myzein* to suck] *syn of* CYCLOSTOMI

**my·zop·o·da** \mī'zäpədə\ *n, cap* [NL, fr. Gk *myzo-* + *-poda*] **:** a genus of bats including solely the sucker-footed bat

**my·zo·rhyn·chus** \ˌmīzə'riŋkəs\ *n, pl* **myzorhyn·chi** \-ŋˌkī\ [NL, fr. *myzo-* + *-rhynchus*] **:** an apical sucker on the scolex of various tapeworms that is often stalked

**my·zo·sto·mar·ia** \ˌmīzəstə'ma(a)rēə\ *n pl, cap* [NL, fr. *Myzostomum*, type genus (fr. *myzo-* + *-stomum*) + *-aria*] **:** a class or other division of aberrant annelid worms that are probably related to the polychaetes, are parasites of echinoderms, have the form as an adult of an unsegmented disk with ventrally located parapodia, adhesive suckers, distinctive marginal cirri, a coelom obscured by connective tissue, no vascular system, and a single pair of nephridia opening into the posterior intestine, develop indirectly, and have a typical trochophore

**my·zos·tome** \mī'zäˌstōm\ *n* -s [NL *Myzostomum*] **:** a worm of the class Myzostomaria

**my·zus** \'mīzəs\ *n, cap* [NL, fr. Gk *myzei* to suck — more at -MYZA] **:** a large widely distributed genus of aphids that includes several economically important plant pests — see GREEN PEACH APHID

**mza·bite** \em'zäˌbīt\ *n* -s *cap* [*Mzab*, oasis in Algeria + E *-ite*] **:** a member of a Berber people of the Ghardaia oasis in the Algerian Sahara

[1]**n** \'en\ *n, pl* **n's** *or* **ns** \'enz\ *often cap, often attrib* **1 a :** the 14th letter of the English alphabet **b :** an instance of this letter printed, written, or otherwise represented **c :** a speech counterpart of orthographic *n* (as *n* in *nine, snow,* or Spanish *nuevo*) **2 :** a printer's type, a stamp, or some other instrument for reproducing the letter *n* **3 a :** someone or something arbitrarily or conveniently designated *n* esp. as the 13th or when *j* is used for the 10th the 14th in order or class **b :** an indefinite number; *esp* **:** a constant integer denoting degree, order, class, or power (as of an equation, curve, or algebraic expression) ⟨the rules for the permutations of ~ things taken *r* at a time —D.E.Smith⟩ — see NTH **c** (1) **:** the gametic number of chromosomes (2) **:** the basic number of chromosomes (as of a species or species group) — compare X **4 :** something having the shape of the capital letter N **5 :** EN 2 **6 :** an antigen of human blood that shares a common genetic locus with the M antigen

[2]**n** *abbr, often cap* **1** nail **2** name **3** nasal **4** national; nationalist **5** [L *natus*] born **6** naval **7** navigate; navigating; navigation **8** navy **9** Negro **10** nephew **11** net **12** neuter **13** new **14** newspaper **15** newton **16** night **17** night stop **18** [L *nocte*] at night **19** [L] nomen **20** nominative **21** none **22** noon **23** normal **24** *usu ital* normal (sense 10a) — used of solutions ⟨0.1 *N* hydrochloric acid⟩; normal (sense 10e) — with names of aliphatic hydrocarbons, their derivatives, or alkyl radicals ⟨*n*-pentane⟩ ⟨*n*-butyl⟩ **25** north; northern **26** note **27** noun **28** [F *nous*] we; us **29** November **30** [L *novus*] new **31** number

[3]**n** *symbol* **1** *cap* **a** place for the insertion of the given name of a bride or of a female person — compare [3]M 1 **b** place for the insertion of the given name of a person (as in a ceremonial statement) — compare NN **2** *usu ital* neutron **3** *cap* nitrogen **4** *usu ital* index of refraction **5** *cap, ital* Avogadro number **6** *cap* knight

[1]**'n** *or* **'n'** \ən, *usu* ᵊn *after* t, d, s *or* z\ *conj* [by alter.] **:** AND ⟨sugar 'n spice⟩ — not often in formal use

[2]**'n** \"\ *conj* [by shortening] **:** THAN ⟨hotter'n blazes⟩ — not often in formal use

[3]**'n** \"\ *prep* [by shortening] **:** IN ⟨where'n blazes is he⟩ — not often in formal use

**-n** — see -EN

[1]**na** \nə\ *adv* [ME (northern dial.), fr. OE *nā* — more at NO] *chiefly Scot* **:** by no means **:** NO, NOT — often combined with a preceding verb ⟨a wooer like me mau*na* hope to come speed —Robert Burns⟩

[2]**na** \"\ *conj* **1** [ME, fr. OE *nā*, fr. *nā*, adv.] *chiefly Scot* **:** NOR **2** *chiefly Scot* **:** THAN

**na** *abbr* **1** nadir **2** nail

**NA** *abbr* **1** national academician; national academy **2** national association **3** nautical almanac **4** naval academy **5** naval architect **6** naval attaché **7** naval aviator **8** no account **9** no advice **10** nonacceptance **11** numerical aperture **12** nursing auxiliary

**Na** [NL *natrium*] *symbol* sodium

**NAA** *abbr, often not cap* not always afloat

**naam** *or* **nam** \'näm\ *n* -S [ME, fr. OE *nām*, fr. ON, action of taking or seizing (attested only in compounds such as *landnām* act of taking possession of land), learning; akin to OE *nǣm* action of taking, OHG *nāma* robbery; derivative fr. the stem of ON *nema* to take — more at NIMBLE] **1** *early Eng law* **:** distraint of chattels **2** *early Eng law* **:** things distrained

**naart·je** \'närchə\ *or* **naart·jie** \-chē\ *n* -S [Afrik, fr. Tamil *nārattai*, fr. *nāram* lemon] *southern Africa* **:** TANGERINE 2

**na·as·sene** \nā'a,sēn\ *n* -S *usu cap* [LGk *Naassēnos*, fr. *naas* snake, fr. Heb *naḥash*] **:** a member of one of the Ophite group of Gnostic sects noted for its worship of the serpent as the principle of generation

[1]**nab** \'nab\ *n* -S [ME *nabb*, of Scand origin; akin to Norw *nabbe* crag, ON *nabbi* small conical protuberance; akin to ON *nef* beak — more at NEB] **1** *Scot* **:** a projecting part of an eminence (as a peak or promontory) **2 a** *obs slang* **:** HEAD **b** *archaic slang* **:** HAT **3 a :** the shoulder of the bolt of a lock on which the key acts to shoot the bolt **b :** the keeper of a door lock

[2]**nab** \'nab, 'naa(ə)b\ *vt* **nabbed; nabbed; nabbing; nabs** [perh. alter. of [5]*nap*] **1 :** to catch or seize in arrest **:** take into custody **:** APPREHEND **2 :** to seize or catch suddenly **:** lay hold of **:** obtain possession of usu. by some improper or irregular method ⟨*nabbed* the best seats in the house⟩; *esp* **:** STEAL

[3]**nab** \"\ *n* -S **1** *slang* **:** POLICEMAN **2** *slang* **:** ARREST

[4]**nab** \'nab\ *Scot var of* [3]NOB

**NAB** *abbr* **1** national aircraft beacon **2** naval air base

**na·bal** \'nābəl\ *n* -S *usu cap* [fr. *Nabal*, wealthy sheep owner who refused to pay tribute to King David for protecting his flocks (1 Sam 25:2), fr. Heb *Nābhāl*] **:** a churlish or niggardly man **:** MISER

**na·ba·loi** \¦näbə¦lȯi\ *n, pl* **nabaloi** *or* **nabalois** *usu cap* **1 a :** a people inhabiting northern Luzon, Philippines — compare IGOROT 1a **b :** a member of such people **2 :** an Austronesian language of the Nabaloi people

**na·bam** \'nā,bam\ *n* -S [*Na* (symbol) + dithiocar*bam*ate] **:** a crystalline fungicide $(-CH_2NHCSSNa)_2$; disodium ethylene-bis-dithiocarbamate

**nab·a·tae·an** *also* **nab·a·te·an** \,nabə'tēən\ *n* -S *usu cap* [L *Nabataeus, Nabathaeus*, Nabataeau (fr. *Nabataea, Nabathaea*, ancient Arab kingdom to the east and southeast of Palestine, fr. Ar *Nebāṭu*) + E *-an*] **1 :** an Arab of an ancient kingdom of Palestine that lasted from about 312 B.C. to A.D.106 when it was made a Roman province **2 :** a dialect of Aramaic spoken by the Nabataeans as shown in their inscriptions

**nab·ber** \'nabə(r)\ *n* -S [[2]*nab* + *-er*] **:** one that nabs

**nab·by** \'nabē\ *n* -ES [origin unknown] **:** an open sailboat with a lug rig and jib and a raking mast that is used esp. for fishing off the eastern coast of Scotland

nabby

**nabcheat** *n* [[1]*nab* (hat) + *cheat* (thing)] *obs slang* **:** HAT

**nabe** \'nāb\ *n* -S [by shortening & alter. fr. *neighborhood (theater)*] **:** a neighborhood theater

**na·bel** *or* **na·ble** \'nābəl\ *dial var of* NAVEL

**na·be·shi·ma ware** \¦näbə¦shēmə-\ *n, usu cap N* [after the *Nabeshima*, 15th–19th cent. feudal lords of Hizen, Japan] **:** a Hizen porcelain noted for its clean design and brilliant coloring

**na·bes·na** \nə'beznə\ *n, pl* **nabesna** *or* **nabesnas** *usu cap* [fr. the *Nabesna* river, southeastern Alaska] **1 :** an Athapaskan people of southeastern Alaska **2 :** a member of the Nabesna people

**na·bi** \'näbē\ *n* -S *often cap* [F, fr. Heb *nābhī* prophet] **:** a member of a group of French artists that was active about 1890 and followed a synthetic direction — compare SYNTHETISM

[1]**nab·id** \'nabəd, 'nāb-\ *adj* [NL *Nabidae*] **:** of or relating to the Nabidae

[2]**nabid** \"\ *n* -S [NL *Nabidae*] **:** a bug of the family Nabidae

**nab·i·dae** \'nabə,dē\ *n pl, cap* [NL, fr. *Nabis*, type genus (fr. L, giraffe) + *-idae*] **:** a widely distributed family of predaceous bugs that are related to the assassin bugs and typically have a four-segmented rostrum through which they suck the blood of soft-bodied insects

**nab·la** \'nablə\ *n* -S [Gk, of Sem origin; akin to Heb *nēbhel* harp] **1 :** an ancient stringed instrument probably like a Hebrew harp of 10 or 12 strings — called also *nebel* **2** [prob. so called fr. the resemblance of its symbol, the inverted Greek delta, to a harp] **:** DEL

**na·bob** \'nā,bäb\ *n* -S [Hindi *nawwāb, nawāb, nabāb*, fr. Ar *nuwwāb*, pl. of *nā'ib* vice-regent, governor] **1 :** a native deputy or viceroy in India **:** a governor of a province of the Mogul empire **2 a :** one who returns to Europe from the East with great riches **b :** man of great wealth **c :** a man of unusual prominence in a particular field ⟨these scientific ~*s*⟩ — sometimes a generalized expression of disapproval

**na·bob·ess** \-äbəs\ *n* -ES **1 :** a female nabob **2 :** a woman of a nabob's family

**na·boom** \'nä,bōm\ *n* -S [Afrik, fr. Hottentot *ngha* naboom + Afrik *boom* tree, fr. MD — more at BOOM] **:** a small tree (*Euphorbia ingens*) of dry open parts of southern Africa that has erect 4-angled branches which form a broad head suggesting a candelabra

**na·bo·thi·an cyst** *or* **na·bo·thi·an follicle** \nə'bōthēən-\ *n, sometimes cap N* [Martin *Naboth* †1721 Ger. anatomist + E *-ian*] **:** a mucous gland of the uterine cervix esp. when occluded and dilated

[1]**nabs** *pl of* NAB, *pres 3d sing of* NAB

[2]**nabs** \'nabz\ *n pl but sing or pl in constr* [origin unknown] *slang* **:** FELLOW, PERSON, CHAP — used with *my* and chiefly in nonspecific identification or as a mode of address ⟨my ~ of an officer⟩ ⟨well, my ~, shall we get along⟩; compare NIBS

**nac** *abbr* nacelle

**NAC** *abbr* **1** national advisory committee; national advisory council **2** naval aircraftsman **3** non-airline-carrier

**nac·a·rat** \'nakə,rat\ *n* -S [F, fr. MF *nacarade*, fr. OSp *nacarado*, fr. *nácar* nacre (fr. Ar *naqqārah* drum) + *-ado* (fr. L *-atus* -ate)] **:** GERANIUM LAKE 2

**na·celle** \nə'sel\ *n* -S [F, lit., small boat, fr. LL *navicella*, dim. of L *navis* ship — more at NAVE] **:** an enclosed shelter on an aircraft for an engine or sometimes for crew

**nach·i·ku·fu** \¦nachə¦kü(,)fü\ *also* **nach·i·ku·fan** \-küfən\ *adj, usu cap* [*Nachikufu* fr. *Nachikufu*, locality in Nyasaland; *Nachikufan* fr. *Nachikufu*, Nyasaland + E *-an*] **:** of or belonging to a late Stone-Age culture of central Nyasaland characterized by tranchet-type microliths, bored stones, and scrapers

**nach·schlag** \'näk,shläk\ *n, pl* **nachschlä·ge** \-lägə\ *or* **nachschlags** [G, lit., afterstroke, fr. MHG *nāchslac* blow struck from behind, fr. *nāch* after, behind (fr. OHG *nāh*) + *slac* blow (fr. OHG *slag*); akin to OHG *slahan* to beat, strike — more at NIGH, SLAY] **1 :** a musical ornament consisting of one or several short unaccented grace notes attached to and played in the time of the preceding main note or tone **2 :** the auxiliary closing note or notes usu. played at the end of a trill

**nacht·horn** \'näkt,hȯrn\ *n, pl* **nachthör·ner** \-hərnər\ *or* **nachthorns** [G, fr. *nacht* night (fr. OHG *naht*) + *horn* (fr. OHG) — more at NIGHT, HORN] **:** COR-DE-NUIT

**nacht·mu·sik** \'näktmü,zēk\ *n, pl* **nachtmusi·ken** \-kən\ *or* **nachtmusiks** [G, fr. *nacht* night + *musik* music, fr. F *musique* — more at NIGHT, MUSIC] **:** SERENADE

[1]**nack·et** \'nakət\ *n* -S [obs. Sc *nacket* caddie at tennis, fr. MF *naquet* valet, caddie at tennis, prob. fr. *naquer* to bite, gnaw, cheat, of imit. origin] *Scot* **:** a mischievous or brattish boy

[2]**nacket** \"\ *n* -S [perh. contr. of *noon cate*] **1** *Scot* **:** a light lunch **2** *Scot* **:** a small cake resembling a pasty

[1]**nacre** \'nākə(r)\ *n* -S [MF, fr. OIt *naccara, nacchera* nacre, drum, fr. Ar *naqqārah* drum] **1** *archaic* **:** a shellfish that yields mother-of-pearl **2 :** the iridescent inner layer of various mollusk shells consisting chiefly of calcium carbonate deposited in thin overlapping sheets with some organic matter (as conchiolin) **:** MOTHER-OF-PEARL

[2]**na·cré** \nə'krā\ *also* **na·cre** \'nākə(r)\ *adj* [F *nacré*, fr. *nacre*, n.] **:** resembling nacre esp. in pearly iridescent luster: as **a** *of a fabric* **:** having a changeable iridescent luster produced usu. by use of a warp of one color and a filling of another ⟨~ taffeta⟩ **b** *of a plant sieve element* **:** having a thickened hydrated wall that appears pearly in section

**na·cred** \'nākə(r)d\ *adj* **:** lined with or like nacre

**na·cre·ous** \'nākrēəs\ *also* **na·crous** \-krəs\ *adj* **:** consisting of or resembling nacre **:** PEARLY

**nacreous cloud** *n* **:** a luminous iridescent cloud that occurs at altitudes of about 85,000 feet — called also *mother-of-pearl cloud*

**na·crite** \'nā,krīt\ *n* -S [F, fr. *nacre* + *-ite*; fr. its pearly scales] **:** a clay mineral $Al_2Si_2O_5(OH)_4$ consisting of hydrous silicate of aluminum and being polymorphous with kaolinite

**NAD** *abbr* **1** no appreciable disease **2** nothing abnormal discovered

**na·da** \'nädə, 'näthə\ *n* -S [Sp, nothing, fr. L (*res*) *nata* lit., thing born, small, insignificant thing (only attested in sense of "the question on hand"), fr. *res* thing + *nata*, fem. of *natus* born, past part. of *nasci* to be born — more at NATION] **:** a state of or as if of nonexistence **:** NOTHINGNESS ⟨the typical situation is love, with some drinking, against the background of ~ of civilization gone to pot, or war, or death —R.P. Warren⟩

**nad·der** \'nadə(r)\ *n* -S [ME *naddre* — more at ADDER] *dial* **:** ADDER

**na-de·ne** *also* **na-dé·né** \¦nä¦dā¦nā\ *n, pl* **na-dene** *usu cap N & sometimes cap D* [*na-* (fr. an Athapaskan word stem akin to Haida *na* to dwell, house, Tlingit *na* people) + *Déné*] **:** a language phylum comprising the Athapaskan, Eyak, Haida, and Tlingit stocks

[1]**na·dir** \'nādə(r), -ā,di(ə)r, -iə\ *n* -S [ME, fr. MF, fr. Ar *naẓīr* opposite (in the phrase *naẓīr as-samt* opposite the zenith)] **1 :** the point of the celestial sphere that is directly opposite the zenith and vertically downward from the observer **2 :** the lowest point ⟨the novel's ~ of degradation —Robert Hunting⟩ **:** the time of greatest depression

[2]**na·dir** \'nä,di(ə)r\ *n* -S [Malay] **:** a Malayan light-draft fishing boat

**na·dir·al** \'nādərəl\ *adj* [F, fr. *nadir* + *-al*] **:** relating to or constituting a nadir

**nad·or·ite** \'nadə,rīt, 'nād-\ *n* -S [F, fr. Jebel *Nador*, locality in northern Algeria + F *-ite*] **:** a mineral $PbSbO_2Cl$ consisting of a brownish yellow lead chloride and stibnite

**nae** \'nā\ *dial Brit var of* NA

**nae·body** \'nābədē\ *Scot var of* NOBODY

**nae·ge·lia** \nā'gēlēə\ *n* [NL, fr. Karl Wilhelm von *Naegeli* †1891 Ger. botanist + NL *-ia*] **1** *cap* **:** a small tropical American genus of rhizomatous perennial herbs (family Gesneriaceae) that are often cultivated for their showy tubular flowers and their velvety foliage **2** -S **:** any plant of the genus *Naegelia*

**naem·o·rhe·dus** \,nemə'rēdəs\ *n, cap* [NL, irreg. fr. L *nemor-, nemus* grove + *haedus* kid — more at NEMORAL, GOAT] **:** a genus of ruminant mammals comprising the Asiatic gorals

**nae·thing** \'nāthiŋ\ *Scot var of* NOTHING

**naeve** *n* -S [LL *naevus*, fr. L, mole, birthmark — more at NEVUS] *obs* **:** FLAW, SPOT, BLEMISH

**naevus** *var of* NEVUS

[1]**nag** \'nag, 'naa(ə)g, 'naig\ *n* -S [ME *nagge*; akin to D *negge* small horse and prob. to OE *hnǣgan* to neigh — more at NEIGH] **1 a** *archaic* **:** a small light saddle horse **:** a riding pony **b :** an inferior or aged and unsound horse **c** *slang* **:** RACEHORSE **2** *obs* **:** PROSTITUTE

[2]**nag** \"\ *vb* **nagged; nagged; nagging; nags** [prob. of Scand origin; akin to Sw & Norw dial. *nagga* to gnaw, bite, hurt ON *gnaga* to gnaw — more at GNAW] *vi* **1 :** to engage in persistent petty faultfinding, scolding, or urging ⟨a good wife but she does ~ so⟩ **2 :** to cause distress by persistent small assaults (as of pain or words) — usu. used with *at* ⟨this tooth has been *nagging* at me for days⟩ ~ *vt* **1 :** to annoy by persistent petty faultfinding, scolding, or urging ⟨*nagged* her husband at every opportunity⟩ **2 :** to affect with recurrent awareness, uncertainty, need for consideration, or concern **:** make recurrently conscious of something (as a problem, solution, situation) ⟨a possible solution *nagged* the back of my mind⟩ ⟨that tattoo *nagged* my memory⟩ **syn** see WORRY

[3]**nag** \"\ *n* -S **1 :** an act of nagging **:** nagging conduct or speech **2 :** a person who nags habitually

[1]**na·ga** \'nägə\ *n, pl* **naga** *or* **nagas** *usu cap* **1 a :** one of a group of Tibeto-Burman peoples in the Naga hills, Assam and in adjoining parts of Burma east of the Chindwin river and the Hukawng valley **b :** a member of any such group **2 :** any of the Tibeto-Burman languages of the Naga peoples

[2]**naga** \"\ *n* -S [Skt *nāga* serpent] **1 :** a member of a race of spirits recognized in Hinduism and Buddhism that have mingled superhuman and serpent qualities, are genii of waters and rain, and live in a subaqueous kingdom **2 :** a Hindu mendicant of any of various sects **3** *also* **nag** \'näg\ [nag fr. Hindi *nāg*, fr. Skt *nāga*] **:** SNAKE; *esp* **:** COBRA

**na·gaed wood** \'nägəd-\ *n* [*nagaed* prob. fr. Tag & Bisayan *naga* Honduras rosewood + E *-ed*] **:** HONDURAS ROSEWOOD

**na·gai·ka** \nə'gīkə\ *n* -S [Russ, of Turkic origin; akin to Kirghiz *nogai* Kazan Tatar] **:** a thick tightly twisted whip used by Cossacks

**na·ga·mi kumquat** \nə'gämē-\ *or* **nagami** *n* -S [*nagami* of unknown origin] **:** a kumquat (*Fortunella margarita*) having oval fruit and a persistent style base — compare MARUMI KUMQUAT

**na·ga·na** *or* **n'ga·na** \nə'gänə\ *n* -S [Zulu *u-nakane, ulu-nakane*] **1 :** a highly fatal disease of domestic animals in tropical Africa caused by a trypanosome (*Trypanosoma brucei*), marked by fluctuating fever, inappetence, edematous swelling, and sluggishness, and transmitted by tsetse and possibly other biting flies **2 :** an African trypanosomiasis of domestic animals

**na·ga·ri** \'nägərē\ *n* -S *usu cap, often attrib* [Skt *nāgarī*, lit., (writing) of the city, fr. *nagara* city, of Dravidian origin; akin to Tamil *nakar* dwelling, city, Telugu *nagaru* palace] **1 :** DEVANAGARI **2 :** the family of related alphabets of the Indian subcontinent of which Devanagari is a member

**na·ga·sa·ki** \¦nägə¦säkē, ¦nag- ¦nagə¦sakē\ *adj, usu cap* [fr. *Nagasaki*, Japan] **:** of or from the city of Nagasaki, Japan **:** of the kind or style prevalent in Nagasaki

**naga sore** *n, usu cap N* [fr. *Naga* hills, region in Assam and Burma] **:** TROPICAL ULCER 2

**nag·a·tel·ite** \,nagə'te,līt\ *n* -S [*Nagatej*ima, headland on the Noto peninsula, Japan + E *-lite*] **:** a rare mineral $Ca_2(Ce,La)_2Al_4Fe_2(Si,P)_6O_{25}(OH)(?)$ that consists of phosphosilicate of aluminum, the rare earths, calcium, and iron, that is related to clinozoisite, and that occurs in black tabular masses

**na·gel·fluh** \'nägəl,flü\ *n* -S [G, fr. *nagel* nail (fr. OHG *nagal*) + G dial. (Switzerland) *fluh* cliff, mass of rock, fr. OHG *fluoh* cliff — more at NAIL, PLEASE] **:** a massive variegated conglomerate forming a prominent member of the Miocene series in the Alps

**nag·gar** \nə'gär\ *n* -S [Ar *nuqqār*] **:** a cargo boat used on the upper Nile river

**nag·ger** \'nagə(r)\ *n* -S [[2]*nag* + *-er*] **:** one that nags

**naggin** *var of* NOGGIN

**nagging** *adj* [fr. pres. part. of [2]*nag*] **1 :** persistently annoying, irritating, or faultfinding ⟨a ~ husband⟩ **2 :** characterized by nagging ⟨a ~ fear⟩ — **nag·ging·ly** *adv* — **nag·ging·ness** *n* -ES

[1]**nag·gish** \'nagish\ *adj* [[1]*nag* + *-ish*] **:** having the quality of a nag **:** SMALL, INFERIOR

[2]**naggish** \"\ *adj* [[2]*nag* + *-ish*] **:** somewhat nagging

**nag·gle** \'nagəl\ *vi* -ED/-ING/-S [freq. of [2]*nag*] **:** to haggle or dispute pettily

**nag·gly** \'nag(ə)lē\ *adj*, -ER/-EST [*naggle* + *-y*] **:** of a naggling nature **:** petty and contentious ⟨~ arguments⟩

[1]**nag·gy** \'nagē\ *n* -ES [[1]*nag* + *-y* (dim. suffix)] **:** a little nag **:** PONY

[2]**naggy** \"\ *adj* -ER/-EST [[1]*nag* + *-y* (adj. suffix)] **:** [1]NAGGISH

[3]**naggy** \"\ *adj* -ER/-EST [[2]*nag* + *-y* (adj. suffix)] **1 :** given to or characterized by nagging **2** *dial Eng* **:** IRRITABLE, CROSS

**na·gid** \nä'gēd\ *n, pl* **na·gi·dim** \,nägē'dēm\ *also* **ne·gi·dim** \nə'gēdəm\ [Heb *nāgīd*] **:** a Jewish ruler and religious authority presiding over former Jewish communities esp. in medieval Spain and Egypt

**nag·kassar** \näg'kasə(r)\ *also* **nag·kes·ar** \-kes-\ *n* -S [Marathi & Hindi *nāgkesar*, fr. Skt *nāgakesara*, fr. *nāga* snake + *kesara* hair, nagkassar (*Mesua ferrea*); akin to L *caesaries* hair of the head] **:** either of two East Indian trees (*Mesua ferrea* and *Ochrocarpus longifolius*) of the family Guttiferae from whose flower buds a red or orange dye is obtained

**nag·maal** \'näk,mäl\ *n* -S [Afrik, fr. MD *nachtmael*, fr. *nacht* night + *mael* meal; akin to OE *niht* night and to OE *mǣl* appointed time, mealtime, meal — more at NIGHT, MEAL] **1** *Africa* **:** evening meal **2** *Africa* **:** COMMUNION 2

**nag·nag** \'nag,nag\ *vb* [by redupl.] **:** NAG

**na·go** \'nä(,)gō\ *n, pl* **nago** *or* **nagoes** *usu cap* **:** YORUBA

**na·gor** \'nā,gȯ(ə)r\ *n* -S [F, alter. of *nanguer* nanger — more at NANGER] **:** a reddish brown reedbuck (*Redunca redunca*) of western Africa

**na·go·ya** \nə'gōyə\ *adj, usu cap* [fr. *Nagoya*, Japan] **:** of or from the city of Nagoya, Japan **:** of the kind or style prevalent in Nagoya

**nag·pur** \'näg,pu̇(ə)r\ *adj, usu cap* [fr. *Nagpur*, India] **:** of or from the city of Nagpur, India **:** of the kind or style prevalent in Nagpur

**nags** *pl of* NAG, *pres 3d sing of* NAG

**nags·man** \'nagzmən\ *n, pl* **nagsmen** [*nags* (pl. of [1]*nag*) + *man*] **:** a man employed to ride and show horses esp. in a sales ring

**na·gual** \nə'(g)wäl\ *also* **na·hual** \nə'(h)wäl\ *n, pl* **naguals** \-älz\ *or* **nagua·les** \-ä,läs\ *also* **nahuals** [Sp, fr. Nahuatl *nahualli, naualli*, fr. *nahua* to dance with tied hands] **1 a :** a personal guardian spirit or protective alter ego assumed by various Middle American Indians to reside in an animal or less frequently in some other embodiment — compare HUACA **b :** the animal double or guardian itself **2 :** a sorcerer believed by various Middle American Indians to be capable of transforming himself into animal form

**na·gual·ism** \-ä,lizəm\ *n* -S **:** belief in naguals

**nag·ya·gite** \'nagyə,gīt, 'najə,-\ *n* -S [G *nagyagit*, fr. *Nagyág* (*Săcărâmbu*), Romania + G *-it* -ite] **:** a mineral $Pb_5Au(Te,Sb)_4S_{5-8}$ that is a sulfide of lead, gold, tellurium, and antimony

**nah** *substand var of* NO

**na·hal** \nə'häl\ *n, pl* **nahal** *or* **nahals** *usu cap* **1 :** one of a group of peoples of the hill land of central India **2 :** a member of such people

**na·ha·ne** *or* **na·ha·ni** \nə'hänē\ *n, pl* **nahane** *or* **nahanes** *or* **nahani** *or* **nahanis** *usu cap* **:** KASKA

**nah·co·lite** \'näkə,līt\ *n* -S [*NaHCO* (in $NaHCO_3$, formula for sodium bicarbonate) + E *-lite*] **:** a mineral consisting of natural sodium bicarbonate

**na·he·carida** \,näə'karədə\ *n pl, cap* [NL, fr. *Nahecaris*, genus of crustaceans in some classifications (prob. fr. *Nahe*, river in western Germany + NL *-caris*) + *-ida*] **:** a subdivision of Malacostraca comprising extinct crustaceans that are similar in some respects to members of Phyllocarida

**na·hoor** \nə'hu̇(ə)r\ *n* -S [prob. fr. Nepali *nahūr*] **:** BHARAL

**na·hua** \'näwə\ *n, pl* **nahua** *or* **nahuas** *usu cap* [Sp, fr. Nahuatl (n. pl.)] **:** NAHUATL

**na·huan** \-ən\ *adj, usu cap* [*Nahua* + *-an*] **:** NAHUATLAN

**na·hua·tl** \'nä,wäd·ᵊl, -wät³l\ *n, pl* **nahuatl** *or* **nahuatls** *usu cap* [Sp, fr. Nahuatl, sing. of *Nahua*] **1 a :** a group of peoples of southern Mexico and Central America including the Aztec **b :** a member of any such people **2 :** the Uto-Aztecan language of the Nahuatl people

[1]**na·huat·lan** \-wätlən\ *adj, usu cap* [*Nahuatl* + *-an*] **:** of or relating to the Nahuatl or to Nahuatlan

[2]**nahuatlan** \"\ *n, pl* **nahuatlan** *or* **nahuatlans** *usu cap* **1 :** NAHUATL **2 :** a language family of the Uto-Aztecan phylum comprising Nahuatl and Pipil

**na·hys·san** \nə'hisᵊn\ *n, pl* **nahyssan** *usu cap* **1 a :** a Siouan people in the James river valley, Virginia **b :** a member of such people **2 :** the language of the Nahyssan people

**nai** \'nī\ *n* -S *usu cap* [Hindi *nāī*, fr. Skt *nāpita*; akin to Skt *snāti* he bathes — more at NOURISH] **:** a member of a barber caste of Hindus in India that grooms the living and the dead and thus is intimately associated with Hindu ceremonial life including the contraction of marriages

**na·ia** \'nāə\ *syn of* **naja**

**na·iad** \'nā,əd, 'nī,|,ad\ *n, pl* **naiads** \-dz\ *or* **naia·des** \|ə,dēz\ [F or L; F *naïade*, fr. L *naiad-, naias*, fr. Gk, fr. *nan* to flow — more at NOURISH] **1 :** one of the nymphs believed by the ancient Greeks and Romans to live in and give life and perpetuity to lakes, rivers, springs, and fountains **2 :** one of the distinctive aquatic young of mayflies, dragonflies, damselflies, and stone-flies that differ markedly from the corresponding adults **3** [NL *Naiad-, Naias*] **:** a plant of the genus *Naias* or family Naiadaceae **4** [NL *Naiades*] **:** a mollusk of the tribe Naiades **:** a freshwater mussel

**na·ia·da·ce·ae** \,nāə'dāsē,ē, ,nīə-\ *n pl, cap* [NL, fr. *Naiad-, Naias*, type genus + *-aceae*] **:** a monotypic family of aquatic plants (order Naiadales) — see NAIAS — **na·ia·da·ceous** \¦=¦dāshəs\ *adj*

**na·ia·da·les** \,=='dā(,)lēz\ *n pl, cap* [NL, fr. *Naiad-, Naias* + *-ales*] **:** an order of aquatic monocotyledonous herbaceous plants that have flowers either with or without perianth, apocarpous ovaries, and seeds without endosperm — see HYDROCHARITACEAE, JUNCAGINACEAE, NAIADACEAE

**na·ia·des** \'nāə,dēz, 'nīə-\ *n pl, cap* [NL, fr. L, pl. of *naiad-, naias* naiad] *in former classifications* **:** a tribe of mollusks that is practically equivalent to the family Unionidae and includes the freshwater mussels

**na·iant** \'nāənt\ *adj* [modif. of MF *noiant*, pres. part. of *noier* to swim, fr. L *natare* — more at NATANT] *heraldry* **:** represented in a horizontal position as if swimming ⟨a roach ~⟩ ⟨a sea horse ~ in waves⟩

**na·ias** \'nā|əs, 'nī|, |,as\ *n, cap* [NL *Naiad-, Naias*, fr. L *naiad-, naias* naiad] **:** a genus (coextensive with the family Naiadaceae) of submerged aquatic plants that have filiform stems, sheathing leaves, and minute diclinous flowers with a double perianth

**na·ib** *or* **na·ibe** \'nä,ēb\ *n* -s [It *naibi* playing cards, tarot, fr. Sp *naipes*, pl. of *naipe* playing card, perh. fr. Ar *nā'ib* vice-regent, governor] **:** TAROT 1

**na·id** \'nāəd\ *n* -s [L *naid-, nais*, fr. Gk, fr. *nan* to flow + *-id-, -is* -id] **1** *obs* **:** NAIAD **2** [NL *Naid-, Nais* genus of annelids fr. L, naiad] **:** any of numerous small freshwater annelids constituting *Nais* and related genera of the order Oligochaeta

**na·i·dae** \'nāə,dē\ [NL, fr. pl. of *Nais*] *syn of* NAIDIDAE

**naides** *pl of* NAIS

**na·id·i·dae** \nā'idə,dē\ *n pl, cap* [NL, fr. *Naid-, Nais*, type genus + *-idae*] **:** a family of small aquatic oligochaete worms that commonly reproduce by vegetative transverse segmentation and form chains of worms in various stages of development

**na·i·do·mor·pha** \,nāədō'mȯrfə\ *n pl, cap* [NL, fr. *Naid-, Nais* + *-o* + *-morpha*] *in some classifications* **:** a group of aquatic worms nearly coextensive with Archioligochaeta

[1]**na·ïf** *or* **na·if** \nä'ēf\ *adj* [MF *naif*, — more at NAÏVE] **1 :** NAÏVE **2** *or* **na·ife** \"\ **:** having a true luster when uncut — used of precious stones

[2]**naïf** *or* **naif** \"\ *n* -s [F *naïf*, fr. *naïf*, adj.] **:** a naïve person

**naig** \'nāg\ *chiefly Scot var of* NAG 1

**na·ik** \'nä|ik\ *also* **na·ig** \|ig\ *or* **na·igue** \|,ēg\ *or* **na·ique** \|,ēk\ *or* **na·yak** \|yək\ *n* -s [Hindi *nāyak*, fr. Skt *nāyaka*, lit., leader, fr. *nayati* he leads; akin to MIr *nē*, *nīa* warrior, hero, Av *nayeiti* he leads, brings, Hitt *nāi-* to control, lead] **1 :** a leader, chief, or governor in India — used as a title of authority or form of address **2 :** a native subordinate officer in the British India army; *specif* **:** CORPORAL

**na·ik·pod** \'näik,päd\ *n* -s *usu cap* **1 :** one of various peoples that inhabit the jungle of Central India and practice shifting agriculture with the use of a digging stick **2 :** a member of any of such peoples

[1]**nail** \'nāl, *esp before pause or consonant* 'nāəl\ *n* -s *often attrib* [ME, fr. OE *nægl, nægel;* akin to OS & OHG *nagal* nail, fingernail, ON *nagl* fingernail, L *unguis* nail of the finger or toe, claw, Gk *onyx*, Lith *nagas*, Skt *nakha*] **1 a :** the horny plate of thickened and condensed epithelial stratum lucidum that grows out from a vascular matrix of cutis and sheathes the upper surface of the end of each finger and toe of man and most other primates and that is strictly homologous with the hoof or claw of other mammals from which it differs chiefly in shape and size **b :** a corresponding structure (as a claw or talon) terminating a digit **c :** a terminal horny process not associated with a digit: as (1) **:** a plate at the end of the bill of ducks and related birds (2) **:** a horny spur on the end of the tail of a few vertebrates — compare NAIL-TAILED WALLABY **2 a :** a slender and usu. pointed and headed fastener designed for impact insertion — see TREENAIL, WIRE NAIL; compare BRAD, SPIKE, TACK **b :** DATING NAIL **c :** a rod (as of metal) used to fix the parts of a broken bone in normal relation ⟨medullary ~⟩ **3 :** something resembling a nail (as in shape or color) **4 a :** [3]CLOVE **b :** an English unit of length once used esp. for cloth equal to 1/16 yard or 2¼ inches — **nail in one's coffin :** something regarded as likely to shorten one's life — **on the nail** *adv (or adj)* **:** on the spot **:** immediately when due **:** at once ⟨paid his bills *on the nail*⟩ — **to the nail** *adv (or adj)* **:** to the last degree **:** PERFECTLY ⟨finished *to the nail*⟩

[2]**nail** \"\ *vt* -ED/-ING/-S [ME *nailen*, fr. OE *næglian;* akin to OHG *negilen* to nail, ON *negla*, Goth *ganagljan* to nail to, attach; denominative fr. the root of E [1]*nail*] **1 a :** to attach with a nail ⟨~*ed* the proclamation to the church door⟩ **b** *archaic* **:** to pierce with a nail **c :** to put together with nails ⟨~*ed* the timbers into a sturdy frame⟩ **d** *obs* **:** to stud with or as if with nails **e :** to close or make secure with nails — usu. used with adverbs expressive of direction or condition ⟨~*ed* the box up⟩ ⟨~ down the windows⟩ **f** *archaic* **:** [2]SPIKE 2a **g :** to fix in position with a nail ⟨~*ed* the vines to the wall⟩ **h :** to block (fur garments) by dampening and attaching to a pattern board with nails **i :** to unite (parts of a broken bone) with a nail **2 a** *archaic* **:** to make fast as if with nails **b :** to secure or fasten to something ⟨~*ed* to the tree by an Indian's arrow⟩ **c :** to be unalterably fixed to or associated with something (as a profession, a course of action) ⟨the clerk ~*ed* to his counter⟩ **d :** to fix in steady attention ⟨~*ing* his eyes on the crack⟩ **3 a :** CATCH, TRAP; *esp* **:** to detect and expose (as a lie or scandal) so as to stop currency or circulation ⟨~*ed* the source of the story and forced a retraction⟩ **b** *slang* **:** to get hold of **:** SNATCH, STEAL ⟨~ an apple⟩ **c** *slang* **:** CHECK, ARREST **d** *of a bird dog* **:** to point (as a covey) quickly, sharply, and accurately **4 a** *slang* **:** STRIKE, HIT ⟨~*ed* him in the head with a rock⟩ **b :** to put out (a runner) in baseball — **nail one's colors to the mast :** to assume and manifest an inflexible attitude (as of determination not to acknowledge defeat)

**nail·abil·i·ty** \,nālə'biləd·ē\ *n* **:** suitability for being nailed ⟨a sheathing of superior ~⟩

**nail apron** *n* **:** a coarse work apron with pockets for nails or similar small articles

**nail bed** *n* **:** MATRIX 1c

**nail bit** *n* **:** a wood-boring tool used for cutting across the grain

**nail-biting** \'=,==\ *n* **1 a :** habitual biting at the fingernails usu. being symptomatic of emotional tensions and frustrations **b :** an act or instance of this behavior **2 :** a hopelessly or helplessly frustrated condition or activity ⟨their critical work has become largely a kind of ethical *nail-biting* —S.E.Hyman⟩

**nail bone** *n* **1 :** LACRIMAL BONE **2 :** the terminal phalanx of a digit

**nail brush** *n* **:** a small firm-bristled brush for cleaning the fingernails

**nail down** *vt* **:** to settle or establish clearly and unmistakably ⟨*nailed* his argument *down* with a quotation from the Bible⟩ ⟨called its 400 local drivers to a meeting . . . to *nail down* final strategy for the walkout —*Sacramento (Calif.) Bee*⟩

**nailed shoe** *n* **:** a shoe in which the upper is attached to the sole by means of nails

**nail enamel** *n* **:** nail polish in the form of a plastic liquid that forms a usu. colored coating on the nails

**nail·er** \'nālə(r)\ *n* -s [ME, fr. *nailen* to nail + *-er*] **1 :** a nail maker **2 :** one that drives nails or fastens together with nails: as **a :** a maker or lidder of wooden boxes **b :** a machine for automatic nailing **c :** an operator of such a machine **3** *slang* **:** something highly superior of its kind **:** one that is extremely capable at something

**nail·ery** \'nāl(ə)rē\ *n* -ES **:** a place where nails are made

**nail fiddle** *n* **:** NAIL VIOLIN

**nail file** *n* **:** [1]FILE 1b

**nail fold** *n* **:** the fold of the cutis at the margin of a fingernail or toenail

**nail harmonica** *n* **:** NAIL VIOLIN

**nailhead** \'=,=\ *n, often attrib* **1 a :** the usu. flattened boss that forms the end of a nail opposite to the point **b :** an ornament suggesting a nailhead ⟨a belt studded with enamel ~*s*⟩ ⟨~ taffeta⟩ **2 :** NAIL-HEADED MOLDING; *also* **:** one of the pyramids forming such molding

**nail-headed** \'=¦==\ *adj* **:** having a head like that of a nail **:** formed so as to resemble the head of a nail

**nail-headed molding** *or* **nailhead molding** *n* **:** an architectural ornament consisting of a series of low four-sided pyramids suggestive of nailheads

**nailhead rust** *n* **:** LEPROSIS

**nailhead spar** *n* **:** calcite that crystallizes in nail-headed forms

**nailhead spot** *n* **:** a rot of the tomato that is caused by an imperfect fungus (*Alternaria tomato*) and is characterized by small sunken brown to black fruit spots resembling the head of a nail

**nailing strip** *n* **:** a strip of wood made fast (as by bolting) to a surface (as of concrete or metal) unsuitable for nailing in order to provide a means of attaching something (as flooring or lathing) by nailing

**nail·less** \'nā(ə)lləs\ *adj* **1 :** having no nails ⟨~ fingers⟩ **2 :** requiring no nails for fastening ⟨a ~ horseshoe⟩

**naillike** \'=,=\ *adj* **:** resembling a nail: as **a :** CORNEOUS ⟨a hard ~ layer of tissue⟩ **b :** shaped like a fingernail or toenail ⟨a ~ bone⟩ **c :** slender and tapered or pointed ⟨developed a ~ colony in agar⟩

**nail plate** *n* **1 :** NAIL 1a; *also* **:** the homologous hard sheath of a claw **2 :** a sheet of iron from which cut nails are made

**nail polish** *n* **:** a dry or liquid preparation for giving a sheen to fingernails and toenails; *usu* **:** a lacquer or enamel that may be clear or opaque and colored or colorless and that forms a substantial covering over the surface of the nail

**nail puller** *n* **:** a device (as a bar with a notched end) for gripping and drawing a nail

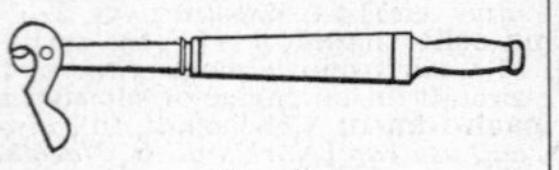

nail puller

**nailrod** \'=,=\ *n* **1 a :** iron in rods or strips for cutting into nails **b :** a rod or strip of such iron **2** *Brit* **:** hard-pressed and usu. very dark tobacco made up in short rods or sticks

**nails** *pl of* NAIL, *pres 3d sing of* NAIL

**nail-scissors** \'=,==\ *n pl* **:** small scissors with slender shaft and brief curved blades that are used chiefly for shaping and trimming the fingernails

**nail·sea glass** \'nā(ə)l,sē-\ *n, usu cap N* [fr. *Nailsea*, England] **:** glassware produced at Nailsea, England during the 18th and 19th centuries and typically ornamented with latticinio striping

**nail set** *n* **:** [3]PUNCH 1a(3)

**nailsick** \'=,=\ *adj* **1 :** weakened by repeated nailing ⟨patched the roof with ~ boards⟩ **2 :** leaking at the nail holes ⟨a ~ boat⟩

**nail-tailed wallaby** *also* **nail-tailed kangaroo** \'=,=-\ *or* **nail-tail** \'=,=\ *n* **:** any of a genus (*Onychogalea*) of small kangaroos with brightly marked silky fur and a horny nail on the tip of the tail

**nail violin** *n* **:** an 18th century musical instrument that consists of a semicircular sounding board with nails or iron pins of graduated size driven along its edge and that is played with a violin bow

**nailwort** \'=,=\ *n* **1 :** either of two whitlow grasses (*Draba verna* and *Saxifraga tridactylites*) **2 :** a plant of the genus *Paronychia*

**naily** \'nālē\ *adj* **:** full of nails ⟨a ~ board⟩

**nain** \'nān\ *adj* [alter. (resulting from incorrect division of *mine ain*) of [2]*ain*] *Scot* **:** OWN

**nain·sel** *or* **nain·sell** \nān'sel\ *pron* [*nain* + *sel, sell*] **1** *Scot* **:** own self **2** *Scot* **:** a Scottish Highlander

**nain·sook** \'nān,su̇k\ *n* -s [Hindi *nainsukh*, fr. *nain* eye (fr. Skt *nayana*, fr. *nayati* he leads) + *sukh* delight, fr. Skt *sukha* — more at NAIK] **:** a soft lightweight cotton fabric in plain weave and various finishes that is used esp. for clothing and curtains

**naio** \'nī(,)ō\ *n* -s [Hawaiian] **:** any of several trees of the genus *Myoporum:* as **a :** NGAIO **b :** BASTARD SANDALWOOD 2a (1) **c :** a tall Hawaiian tree (*M. sandwicense*) that has rough gray bark and pink or white flowers in terminal clusters and that yields a lumber which is sometimes substituted for sandalwood

**nai·pa·li** \nā'p-,nī'p-\ *cap, var of* NEPALI

**naique** *var of* NAIK

[1]**nair** *usu cap, var of* NAYAR

[2]**na·ir** \'nä,i(ə)r\ *n* -s [native name in India] **:** BEGTI

[3]**nair** \"\ *n* -s [native name in India] **:** the common Indian otter (*Lutra nair*)

**nairn·shire** \'naa(ə)rn,shi(ə)r, 'ne(ə)rn-, 'nārn-, -,shər\ *or* **nairn** *adj, usu cap* [fr. *Nairnshire* or *Nairn* county, Scotland] **:** of or from the county of Nairn, Scotland **:** of the kind or style prevalent in Nairn

**nai·ro·bi** \(')nī¦rōbē\ *adj, usu cap* [fr. *Nairobi*, Kenya] **:** of or from Nairobi, the capital of Kenya **:** of the kind or style prevalent in Nairobi

**nairobi disease** *n, usu cap N* **:** a severe and frequently fatal gastroenteritis of sheep or sometimes goats that occurs in parts of Kenya and is considered due to a virus transmitted by the bite of the brown tick

**nairy** *dial var of* NARY

**na·is** \'nāəs\ *n* [L — more at NAID] **1** *pl* **naises** \-səz\ *or* **na·i·des** \'nāə,dēz\ **:** a river nymph **:** NAIAD **2** *cap* [NL, fr. L, naiad] **:** a large genus of small aquatic oligochaete worms that is the type of the family Naididae

**naish** \'nāsh\ *var of* NESH

**nais·sance** \'nās°n(t)s\ *n* -s [F, birth, origin, fr. MF, fr. *nais-* (stem of *naitre* to be born) + *-ance*] **:** an original issue or growth ⟨educational broadcasting, now in its crisis of ~ —R.L.Shayon⟩ — sometimes distinguished from *renaissance*

**nais·sant** \-°nt\ *adj* [MF, pres. part. of *naitre* to be born, fr. L *nascere*, fr. *nasci* — more at NATION] **1** *heraldry* **a :** ISSUANT **b :** rising or issuing from the middle of an ordinary (as a fess) in the instance of an animal with only the upper part visible **2 :** NASCENT

[1]**na·ïve** *also* **na·ive** \(')nä¦ēv, (')nȧ¦-, (')nī¦-\ *adj, sometimes* -ER/-EST [F *naïve*, fem. of *naïf*, fr. OF *naif* inborn, native, natural, fr. L *nativus* native — more at NATIVE] **1 :** marked by simplicity, ingenuousness, artlessness: **a :** showing candor, freshness, and spontaneity unchecked by convention, social diffidence, or guile ⟨when the experienced man speaks simply and wisely to the ~ girl —Gilbert Highet⟩ **b :** showing lack of worldly experience **:** INNOCENT, SIMPLE ⟨their ~ ignorance of life, hers and his, when they were first married —Arnold Bennett⟩ ⟨the same ~ belief in an anthropomorphic Creator —H.L.Mencken⟩ ⟨the *naïvest* person imaginable⟩ **c :** unsuspecting, credulous, and unwary about duplicity or distortion ⟨the work exhibits a ~ acceptance of every kind of miracle —H.O.Taylor⟩ **2 :** marked by lack of instruction, experience, perception, learning **:** exhibiting lack of analysis, subtlety, or depth by ready acceptance without consideration **:** UNPHILOSOPHIC ⟨a little ~ to suppose that when really vital differences emerge, one nation or another is likely to abandon its position on the first interchange of views —J.F.Byrnes⟩ **syn** see NATURAL

[2]**naïve** *also* **naive** \"\ *n* -s **:** a naïve person

**na·ïve·ly** *also* **na·ive·ly** *adv* **:** in a naïve manner **:** with naïveté

**na·ïve·ness** *n* -ES **:** NAÏVETÉ

**naïve realism** *n* **:** the commonsense viewpoint that our perception of the external world is a direct copy of it

**na·ïve·té** *also* **na·ive·té** \(,)nä,ēvə'tā, (,)nȧ,-, (,)nī,-, ='==,=, ¦=,ēv¦tā\ *n* -s [F *naïveté*, fr. OF *naiveté* inborn character, fr. *naif* inborn, native, natural + *-ité* -ity] **1 :** the quality or state of being naïve **:** native simplicity or unaffected naturalness **:** INGENUOUSNESS, ARTLESSNESS **2 :** a naïve act

**na·ïve·ty** \nä'ēvəd·ē, nȧ'-, -v(ə)tē, -i\ *n* -ES [modif. of F *naïveté*] **:** NAÏVETÉ

**na·ja** \'nājə\ *n, cap* [NL, fr. Skt *nāga* serpent] **:** a genus of elapid snakes comprising the true cobras

**na·ja·da·ce·ae** \,nājə'dāsē,ē\ *syn of* NAIADACEAE

**na·ja·da·les** \,nājə'dā(,)lēz\ *syn of* NAIADALES

**naj·di** \'najdē\ *n, pl* **najdi** *or* **najdis** *usu cap* **:** one of a major Arab people in the Kuwait region of Arabia

**nak** \'nak\ *n* -s [perh. fr. Hindi *nāk* nose; akin to Skt *nāsā* nose — more at NOSE] **:** the stigmatic point of the fruit of the mango (*Mangifera indica*)

**nake** \'nāk\ *vt* [ME *naken*, back-formation fr. *naked* (taken as past part.)] *archaic* **:** to make naked **:** lay bare **:** STRIP

[1]**na·ked** \'nākəd, *chiefly in southern US* 'nek-\ *adj, sometimes* -ER/-EST [ME, fr. OE *nacod, nacud, naced;* akin to OHG *nackot, nackut* naked, ON *nökkvithr*, Goth *naqaths*, L *nudus*, Gk *gymnos*, Skt *nagna*] **1 :** lacking covering **:** UNCOVERED: as **a** (1) **:** not wearing, covered by, or protected with clothing **:** NUDE ⟨the man and his wife were both ~, and were not ashamed —Gen 2:25 (RSV)⟩ — used of a person, the body, or one of its parts ⟨~ arms plunged into the dough⟩ ⟨never saw a colder ~*er* man⟩ (2) **:** inadequately or partially clothed esp. so as to be socially unacceptable ⟨that blouse is a disgrace, the girl is simply ~⟩ **b** *of a saddle or draft animal* **:** lacking the usual harness or trappings **c** (1) *of a sword or similar weapon* **:** free from its sheath **:** unsheathed and ready for immediate use ⟨advancing, ~ sword in hand⟩ (2) **:** freed from or not provided with a protective enclosure ⟨a ~ light⟩ **d** *of a plant or one of its parts* (1) **:** lacking pubescence ⟨smooth ~ stems⟩ (2) **:** lacking some enveloping or subtending structure (as leaves, hulls, scales) ⟨a ~ bud⟩ **e** *of an animal or one of its parts* **:** lacking some natural external covering (as of hair, feathers, or shell) ⟨a ~ rhizopod⟩ ⟨the Transylvanian *naked-necked* fowl⟩ **f :** not clothed in substance or flesh — used esp. of personified concepts or unembodied entities ⟨the ~ spirits of the air⟩ **g :** lacking a final covering layer ⟨a ~ wall is one fully lathed but not yet plastered⟩ **2 a :** unprovided with needful or adequate clothing or other necessities of life **:** poverty-stricken **:** DESTITUTE ⟨~ of comfort⟩ **b :** empty and barren **:** seeming bare by reason of the lack of usual covering, adornment, or furnishings ⟨glanced about the drab ~ room⟩: as (1) **:** devoid of ornaments or embellishments ⟨hands ~ of rings⟩ (2) **:** lacking foliage ⟨wintry trees spreading their gray ~ arms⟩ (3) **:** devoid of or sparsely furnished with vegetation ⟨a ~ desert⟩ ⟨the ~ hills towering above⟩ **c :** lacking weapons or means of defense or offense **:** UNARMED, DEFENSELESS ⟨unwilling to slay a ~ man⟩ **3 a :** devoid of anything that strengthens, supports, or confirms **:** lacking evident or proven authority or authoritativeness **:** MERE, SIMPLE ⟨a ~ command⟩ ⟨~ belief⟩ **b :** lacking in some material matter, or having nothing to validate, confirm, or support it ⟨a ~ title⟩ ⟨such ~ contracts are difficult to enforce⟩ **c :** lacking estimable qualities (as of worth, dignity, adequacy) **:** BALD, MEAGER, SCANTY ⟨a ~ account of the conference⟩ **4 :** devoid of concealment or disguise ⟨confront ~ realities at their source —Richard Eberhart⟩: as **a :** outspoken and straightforward **:** presented without reserve or embellishment ⟨a ~ confession⟩ ⟨the ~ truth⟩ **b :** open to view **:** plainly manifest **:** CLEAR, OBVIOUS ⟨the ~ facts of the case⟩ ⟨an act of ~ aggression⟩ **5** *chiefly dial* **a :** of full strength **:** UNDILUTED ⟨~ spirits⟩ **b :** free from contamination or admixture **:** PURE ⟨~ water⟩ **syn** see BARE

[2]**naked** *n* -s **1** *archaic* **:** NUDE ⟨covered the ~ with a garment —Ezek 18:7 (AV)⟩ **2 :** the inadequately clothed ⟨clothes for the ~⟩

**naked bat** *n* **:** a large Indo-Malayan bat (*Cheiromeles torquatus*) hairless except for a thin half collar

**naked bed** *n* [ME] *archaic* **:** a bed in which one sleeps unclothed

**naked boys** *n pl but sing or pl in constr* **:** MEADOW SAFFRON

**naked broom rape** *n* **:** a cancer root (*Orobanche uniflora*) that occurs chiefly in eastern No. America and has broad minutely ciliolate corolla lobes

**naked bulb** *n* **:** a plant bulb consisting of scales as distinguished from a tunicate bulb

**naked catfish** *n* **:** a catfish lacking dermal bony plates — distinguished from *armored catfish*

**naked eye** *n* **:** the eye unaided by any instrument that changes the apparent size or distance of an object or otherwise alters visual powers ⟨just visible to the *naked eye*⟩

**naked fallow** *n* **:** a fallow in which land is kept bare (as by repeated cultivation) rather than fallowed under a green manure or cover crop

**naked floor** *n* **1 :** a floor completely framed but as yet uncovered by flooring **2 :** a floor in which the joists extend unbroken from wall to wall

**naked flower** *n* **:** a flower lacking floral leaves

**naked heeler** *n* **:** a gamecock that is fought with natural spurs only

**na·ked·ize** \'nākə,dīz\ *vi* -ED/-ING/-S [[1]*naked* + *-ize*] **:** to be or go naked

**naked lady** *n* **:** MEADOW SAFFRON

**na·ked·ly** *adv* [ME, fr. *naked* + *-ly*] **:** in a naked manner: as **a :** without covering, disguise, or addition **:** MANIFESTLY, OPENLY, SIMPLY, BARELY **b :** as standing by or considered by itself alone ⟨a question discussed ~⟩ **c :** in an unclothed, exposed, defenseless, or unprotected manner **d :** in a deficient or imperfect manner **:** POORLY, INADEQUATELY

**naked mollusk** *n* **:** a nudibranch mollusk

**naked neck** *n, usu cap both Ns* **:** a breed or strain of the domestic fowl having the neck bright red and wholly free from feathers

**na·ked·ness** *n* -ES [ME *nakednesse*, fr. OE *nacednisse*, fr. *nacod, nacud, naced* naked + *-nisse* -ness — more at NAKED] **1 a :** the quality or state of being naked **b :** one that is naked **2 :** something that should be covered; *esp* **:** PRIVATES

**naked oat** *n* **:** an oat (*Avena nuda*) that has multiple-flowered spikelets and naked mature kernels and that is sometimes cultivated esp. in interior Asia as a cereal grain

**naked power** *n* **:** COLLATERAL POWER **:** a power in gross as distinguished from one coupled with an interest

**naked reverse** *n* **:** a reverse play in football in which the ball is handed off to a player who runs without interference as though covering up a fake until he is outside the end and then goes downfield

**naked smut** *n* **:** a smut fungus (as *Ustilago nuda* or *U. tritici*) that converts the entire inflorescence of the host into a loose powdery mass of spores — compare COVERED SMUT

**naked stopper** *n* **:** any of several tropical American trees and shrubs constituting a genus (*Anamomis*) of the family Myrtaceae

**naked trust** *n* **:** PASSIVE TRUST

**nakedwood** \'==,=\ *n* **1 :** any of several small or medium-sized trees (genus *Colubrina*) of Florida and the West Indies with thin scaly bark and strong hard heavy heartwood — see MABI **2 :** a stopper (*Eugenia dicrana*) of extreme southern Florida and the West Indies with thin scaly bark, aromatic fruits and fragrant seeds, and hard heavy close-grained wood **3 :** WILD CINNAMON 1

**na·ker** \'nākə(r)\ *n* -s [ME, fr. MF *nacaire*, fr. OIt *nacchera* kettledrum, nacre — more at NACRE] **:** KETTLEDRUM

**na-khi** \'nä'kē\ *also* **na·shi** \'näshē\ *n* -s *usu cap N&K* **:** one of a people closely related to the northern Lolo and found mainly in the high plateaus and mountains of the Yunnan-Szechwan borderlands of southwest China

**na·kho·da** \'näkə,dä\ *or* **nuc·que·dah** \'nək-\ *n* -s [Per *nākhudā*, fr. *nāv* boat (fr. OPer) + *khudā* master, fr. MPer *khutāī;* akin to Skt *nau* ship — more at NAVE] **:** a master of a native Indian vessel

**na·kong** \nə'käŋ\ *n* -s [Sechuana] **:** a western African antelope that is a variety (*Strepsiceros spekei gratus*) of the sitatunga

**naks** *pl of* NAK

**nak·sha·tra** \'nəkshə·trə\ *n* -s *usu cap* [Skt *nakṣatra*, lit., dominion over the night, fr. *nakt* night + *kṣatra* dominion — more at NIGHT, KSHATRIYA] **:** one of the asterisms in the moon's path or one of its celestial houses in Hindu astrology

**na·ku·ru·i·tis** \nə,kü,rü'īd·əs\ *n* -ES [NL, prob. fr. *Nakuru*, town in central Kenya + NL *-itis*] *eastern Africa* **:** a cobalt deficiency disease of sheep and cattle **:** PINE

**nal** \'nəl\ *n* -s [Hindi *nal*, fr. [Skt *nala* reed] *India* **:** GIANT REED 1

**nall** \'nȯl\ *dial Eng var of* AWL

**nallah** *or* **nalla** *or* **nala** *var of* NULLAH

**nal·or·phine** \'nalə(r),fēn\ *n* -s [*N-allylnormorphine*] **:** ALLYLNORMORPHINE

**nam** *var of* NAAM

[1]**na·ma** \'nämə\ *n, pl* **nama** *or* **namas** *usu cap* **1** *also* **na·man** \-ən\ **:** one of a Hottentot people of Great Namaqualand in South-West Africa **2 :** a dialect of Hottentot

[2]**na·ma** \'nāmə\ [NL, fr. Gk, stream; akin to Gk *nan* to flow — more at NOURISH] *syn of* HYDROLEA

**namable** *var of* NAMEABLE

**namad** *var of* NUMDAH

**na·ma·ma·hay** \,nämәmə'hī\ *n* -s [Tag] **:** a member of a former Philippine group or caste of serfs who were chiefly employed in agriculture

[1]**na·ma·qua** \nə'mäkwə\ *n* -s [fr. *Namaqua*land, coast region

in southwestern Africa] : a long-tailed African dove (*Oena capensis*)

²**namaqua** \"\ *or* **na·ma·quan** \-wən\ *n* -s *usu cap* : ¹NAMA

**nam·ay·cush** \'namē,kash, -mə,-\ *n* -ES [of Algonquian origin; akin to Cree *namekus* lake trout] : LAKE TROUT

**na·maz** \nə'mäz\ *n, pl* **namaz** [Pers *namāz*; akin to Skt *namas* obeisance — more at NEMORAL] : Islamic worship or prayer

**nam·be** \näm'bā\ *n, pl* **nambe** *or* **nambes** *usu cap* **1** : a Tanoan people occupying a pueblo in New Mexico **2** : a member of the Nambe people

**nam·bi·cua·ra** *or* **nam·bi·kua·ra** \,nambē'kwärə\ *or* **nham·bi·qua·ra** *or* **nham·bi·cu·a·ra** *n* -s *usu cap* [Pg *nambicuara, nhambicuara*, fr. Tupi, lit., long-eared] **1 a** : a people of Mato Grosso, Brazil **b** : a member of such people **2** : the language of the Nambicuara people

**nam·by** \'nambē\ *adj or n* [by shortening] : NAMBY-PAMBY

**nam·by-pam·bi·ness** \,nambē,pambēnəs\ *n* -ES : the quality or state of being namby-pamby

¹**nam·by-pam·by** \,nambē;pambē, ;naam . . . aambē, -bi . . . bi\ *adj* [fr. *Namby Pamby*, nickname given to *Ambrose Philips* †1749 Eng. poet by some satirists of his time to ridicule the style of his verses] **1** : characterized by feeble sentimentality or insipid and artificial prettiness or elegance ⟨*namby-pamby* rhymes⟩ **2 a** *of a person* : lacking in vigor or manliness : weak, trifling, or childish in character or behavior ⟨*namby-pamby* boys afraid to leave their mothers' apron strings⟩ **b** : lacking in real worth, substance, or quality : unduly lax, soft, or conciliatory ⟨the *namby-pamby* handling of juvenile delinquents⟩ ⟨*namby-pamby* educational standards⟩

²**namby-pamby** \"\ *n* -ES : something (as talk, writing, or a person) that is namby-pamby

**nam·by-pam·by·ism** \"+,izəm\ *n* -s : NAMBY-PAMBINESS

¹**name** \'nām\ *n* -s [ME, fr. OE *nama*; akin to OHG & Goth *namo* name, ON *nafn*, L *nomen*, Gk *onyma, onoma*, Skt *nāma*] **1 a** : a word or sound or a combination of words or sounds by which an individual or a class of individuals (as persons or things) is regularly known or designated : a distinctive and specific appellation ⟨the ~ of the boy is Mark⟩ ⟨the ~ of this fruit is apple⟩ ⟨metal is the ~ of a class of substances each of which has an individual ~ (as gold, silver, lead, copper, iron)⟩ — see LEGAL NAME **b** (1) : a word usu. with little or no connotation that can serve as the subject of a sentence; *also* : the symbolic equivalent of such a word (2) : a designating or identifying expression ⟨"the smallest prime" and "the proposition that all men are equal" may be construed as ~*s*⟩ **2** *usu cap* : a symbol of divinity or an actual vehicle of divine attributes ⟨the ascetics testify that this *Name* has in itself the power of the presence of God —Elizabeth Cram⟩ ⟨*Name* — may mean either character, or manifestations of Jehovah, or Jehovah himself —W.A.Shelton⟩ **3 a** : a descriptive or qualifying appellation based on character, attributes, or acts ⟨his ~ shall be called Wonderful —Isa 9:6 (AV)⟩ **b** : an unpleasant, vulgar, or offensive appellation often based on some attribute ⟨it is wrong to call ~*s*⟩ **4 a** : reputed character : good or bad reputation ⟨had the ~ of a miser⟩ **b** : honorable reputation or illustrious fame ⟨had a ~ for learning⟩ ⟨a ~ to conjure with⟩ **5 a** : the designation of an individual regarded as his individuality or character ⟨one of the most detested ~*s* in history⟩ ⟨polio and cancer are among the most dread ~*s* today⟩ **b** : individuals sharing a name : RACE, FAMILY, CLAN **c** : a person or thing that is outstanding in importance, prominence, or interest ⟨tried to get several ~*s* to give glamor to the party⟩ **6** : the appellation of a thing in distinction to the reality : mere seeming ⟨the place was a town in ~ only⟩ ⟨a poet in ~ but scarcely in production⟩ ⟨gradual attrition reduced it to an empty ~⟩ **7** : the mystic essence, character, or spiritual attribute of a person — **by name** *adv* **1** : with specific personal designation : with the according of individual recognition ⟨mentioned each student *by name*⟩ **2 a** : as individuals : INDIVIDUALLY ⟨knew them all *by name*⟩ **b** : by reputation rather than by personal acquaintance or appearance ⟨knew the new supervisor *by name* only⟩ — **to one's name** : as one's property : among one's possessions

²**name** \"\ *vt* -ED/-ING/-s [ME *namen*, fr. OE *namian*, fr. *nama*, n.] **1** : to give a distinctive name or appellation to : ENTITLE, DENOMINATE, STYLE, CALL ⟨*named* the child after her grandmother⟩ **2** : to mention or identify by name : utter or publish the name of ⟨~ one person who would do such a thing⟩ ⟨everyone *named* him with praise⟩: as **a** : to introduce (as oneself) by name ⟨may I ~ these gentlemen⟩ **b** (1) : to mention the name of (a member of a legislative body) in formal reprimand — used of the speaker of the house (2) : to accuse by name ⟨~ the villain if you can⟩ **c** : to identify by naming ⟨~ that tree⟩ : tell over the names of : recognize or recount by name ⟨can ~ the books of the Bible in perfect order⟩ **3** : to appoint specif. or by name : assign to some purpose : NOMINATE ⟨the king *named* his eldest son to succeed him⟩ ⟨let's ~ an early day for the wedding⟩ **4 a** : to speak about : MENTION, STIPULATE, CITE, STATE, QUOTE ⟨will he ~ a price⟩ ⟨refused to ~ the source of the story⟩ **b** : to bring up in conversation : INDICATE, SUGGEST — usu. used with an indefinite *it* as object ⟨if you don't see what you want, ~ it⟩ ⟨I'll ~ it to him the next time we meet⟩ **syn** see DESIGNATE, MENTION

³**name** \"\ *adj* ['name] **1** : bearing or intended for a name or names ⟨leather ~ tag⟩ ⟨ornately painted ~ signs⟩ **2 a** : named in honor or remembrance of another ⟨~ child⟩ **b** : being the person for whom another is named ⟨~ ancestor⟩ **3** : giving its or the name to a collection or composition ⟨the anthology opens with the ~ article⟩ **4** : accorded top rank for preeminence in performance under a distinctive name recognized as a mark of celebrity ⟨a ~ band⟩ ⟨a ~ writer⟩ ⟨a ~ train⟩ **5** : bearing a name (as a trade name) accepted by a widely distributed public as the mark of approved or quality products supplied by a particular enterprise ⟨insisting on ~ brands⟩ ⟨sales of ~ merchandise⟩

**name·abil·i·ty** *also* **nam·abil·i·ty** \,nāmə'biləd·ē\ *n* : the quality or state of being nameable

**name·able** *also* **nam·able** \'nāməbəl\ *adj* **1** : capable of being named : IDENTIFIABLE ⟨pick any ~ item⟩ **2** : worthy of being recalled or mentioned : MEMORABLE, NOTEWORTHY

**nameboard** \'ₛ,ₛ\ *n* : an identifying signboard (as for a station, a shop, or a ship); *also* : an identifying name displayed (as on the side of a ship) other than on a board — see SHIP illustration

**name-caller** \'ₛ,ₛₛ\ *n* : one that habitually engages in name-calling

**name-calling** \'ₛ,ₛₛ\ *n* : the use of opprobrious designations esp. to win an argument or to induce rejection or condemnation (as of a person or project) without due and unimpassioned consideration of relevant facts ⟨the campaign degenerated into mere scurrilous *name-calling*⟩ ⟨not above *name-calling* when it served his purposes⟩

**named** \'nāmd\ *adj* [ME *namyd*, fr. past part. of *namen* to name] **1** : mentioned by name : SPECIFIED ⟨arrived on the ~ date⟩ **2** : having a well-known name : NOTABLE ⟨this highly ~ philosopher⟩ **3** : having or known by a distinctive name ⟨there are hundreds of ~ roses that are no longer planted⟩

**name day** *n* **1** : the day of the saint whose name one bears **2** : the day under London stock exchange rules on which a ticket giving the name of the buyer of securities and the consideration is issued by the purchasing broker to the seller to be passed through the hands of all the parties to the transaction to the original seller so that the middlemen may settle differences and the actual transfer be made between the final holder of the ticket and the issuing broker

**named insured** *n* : a person specif. named in an insurance contract as the insured as distinguished from one protected under a policy whether so named or not

**name-drop** \'ₛ,ₛ\ *vi* [back-formation fr. *name-dropper* & *name-dropping*] : to engage in name-dropping ⟨we *name-drop* in order to establish some contact with a tradition more acceptable than our own —Clifton Fadiman⟩

**name-dropper** \'ₛ,ₛₛ\ *n* ['name + *dropper*] : one who engages in name-dropping

**name-dropping** \'ₛ,ₛₛ\ *n* ['name + *dropping*] : the practice of seeking to impress others by studied but apparently casual mention of prominent or powerful persons as friends or associates ⟨cultivate an air of Broadway knowingness largely by means of *name-dropping* —Henry Hewes⟩

**name·less** \'nāmləs\ *adj* [ME *nameles*, fr. ¹*name* + *-les* -less — more at NAME] **1** : lacking a distinguished name : not noted : OBSCURE ⟨understood the ~ men who fought and swore . . . and won a war —Merle Miller⟩ **2** : not known, specified, or mentioned by name often to avoid giving offense ⟨the hero of this tale must remain ~⟩ **3** : having no legal right to a name (as by reason of illegitimacy) : BASTARD **4** : having no name : not having been given a name ⟨discovered several ~ species of moss⟩ **5** : not marked with any name ⟨a ~ grave⟩ **6 a** : impossible to identify precisely or by name ⟨the ~ ills of old age⟩ : being such as to defy description usu. by reason of indefiniteness ⟨troubled by ~ fears and uncertainties⟩ **b** : too horrible, repulsive, or distressing to be mentioned ⟨this ~ abomination⟩ ⟨their ~ sensualities⟩ — **name·less·ly** *adv* — **name·less·ness** *n* -ES

¹**namely** *adv* [ME, fr. ¹*name* + *-ly* (adv. suffix)] **1** *obs* : SPECIFICALLY, ESPECIALLY, EXPRESSLY **2** : that is to say : to wit ⟨dropping one preconception, ~ the qualitative distinction between the heavens and the earth —S.F.Mason⟩

²**name·ly** \'nāmli\ *adj* [ME, fr. ¹*name* + *-ly* (adj. suffix)] *Scot* : FAMOUS ⟨~ for witches⟩ ⟨to be a ~ piper it was necessary to study for 7 years —Seton Gordon⟩

**name part** *n* : the title role in a play

**nameplate** \'ₛ,ₛ\ *n* **1** : a plate or plaque bearing or designed to bear a name (as of a resident, proprietor, or manufacturer) **2** : the name of a newspaper or periodical as it is regularly displayed usu. on the top of the first page of the newspaper or on the front cover or title page of the periodical

**name prefix** *n* : a patronymic prefix

**nam·er** \'nāmə(r)\ *n* -s : one that bestows a name or calls by name

**names** *pl of* NAME, *pres 3d sing of* NAME

**namesake** \'ₛ,ₛ\ *n* [prob. fr. *name's sake* (i.e., one named for the sake of another's name)] : one that has the same name as another; *esp* : one named after another

**name tape** *n* : firmly woven cotton tape with the name of a person interwoven or printed in linear series to be divided into single name-bearing segments for attachment to items (as garments) likely to require identification; *also* : one name-bearing section of such tape ⟨sewed *name tapes* on all her underwear⟩

**naming** *pres part of* NAME

**nammad** *var of* NUMDAH

**nams** *pl of* NAM

**na·mu·ri·an** \nə'm(y)u̇rēən\ *adj, usu cap* [*Namur*, town and province in Belgium + E *-ian*] : of or relating to a division of the Upper Carboniferous — see GEOLOGIC TIME table

**nan** \'nan, -aa(ə)-\ *usu cap* [fr. *Nan*, nickname fr. the name *Nancy*] — a communications code word for the letter *n*

**NAN** *abbr* [L *nisi aliter notetur*] unless otherwise noted

**nan-** *or* **nano-** *comb form* [F, fr. L *nanus* dwarf, fr. Gk *nanos, nannos*; prob. akin to Gk *nanna, nenna* female relative, aunt — more at NUN] : dwarf ⟨*nanocephaly*⟩ ⟨*nanoid*⟩ ⟨*nanosomia*⟩

¹**na·na** \'nanə, 'nänə, 'nȧnə\ *n* -s [prob. of baby-talk origin] : a child's nurse or nursemaid

²**na·na** \'nänə\ *n* -s [Pg *naná*, fr. Guarani & Tupi] : PINEAPPLE

³**nana** \"\ *n* -s [Ar *na'nā'*] : MINT

⁴**na·na** \'nānə\ *adj* [NL, fr. LL, female dwarf, fem. of L *nanus* dwarf — more at NAN-] : DWARF, DWARFISH — used esp. of genetic variants of economic plants ⟨a ~ strain of corn⟩

**na·nai·mo** \nə'nī(,)mō\ *n, pl* **nanaimo** *usu cap* [Nanaimo *Sananaimux*, lit., people of Nanoose bay] **1 a** : a Salishan people of the east coast of Vancouver Island, British Columbia **b** : a member of such people **2** : a Salishan language of the Nanaimo people

**na·nak·pan·thi** \,nänək'pən(t)thē\ *n* -s *usu cap* [Hindi *nānakpanthī*, fr. Guru *Nanak* †1538 Indian religious leader who founded Sikhism + Skt *panthan, patha* way, path, course — more at FIND] : a member of a major Sikh party distinguished by its primary emphasis on the peaceful tenets of Guru Nanak — compare KHALSA

**na·nan·der** \nə'nandə(r)\ *n* -s [*nan-* + *-ander*] : NANNANDER

**na·na·wood** \'nänə'wu̇d\ *n* [Marathi *nānā* ben-teak (prob. fr. Skt *nandin*, any of various plants) + E *wood*] : BEN-TEAK

¹**nan·ce** \'nän(t)sā\ *also* **nan·che** \-nchā\ *n* -s [AmerSp, fr. Nahuatl *nantzi*] **1** : a tree of the genus *Byrsonima* **2** : the fruit of a nance and esp. of the golden spoon (*Byrsonima crassifolia*)

²**nance** \'nan(t)s\ *n* -s [short for ²*nancy*] *slang* : an effeminate male : HOMOSEXUAL

**nan·chang** \'nän'chäŋ\ *adj, usu cap* [fr. *Nanchang*, China] : of or from the city of Nanchang, China : of the kind or style prevalent in Nanchang

¹**nan·cy** \'nan(t)sē\ *adj, usu cap* [fr. *Nancy*, France] : of or from the city of Nancy, France : of the kind or style prevalent in Nancy

²**nancy** \"\ *n* -ES *sometimes cap* [fr. the female name *Nancy*] : ²NANCE

**nancy-story** \'ₛₛ,ₛₛ\ *also* **nancy** *n* [*nancy* by folk etymology (influence of name *Nancy*) fr. a West African word akin to Twi *a³na¹nse¹* spider, Ewe *a¹na³nse³*] : a folktale of the Negroes of the African Gold Coast or their West Indian descendants

¹**nan·di** \'nan,dē\ *n, pl* **nandi** *usu cap* **1 a** : a pastoral people on the Uganda-Kenya frontier **b** : a member of such people **2** : a Nilotic language of the Nandi people — called also *Kipsigis*

²**nandi** \"\ *n* -s [Skt *nāndī* joy, vigor, freshness] : a benediction or invocation spoken at the beginning of an Indian drama and usu. addressed to Vishnu or Siva but sometimes to Buddha

³**nandi** \"\ *n* -s [Telugu, prob. fr. Skt *nandin*, any of various plants] : BEN-TEAK

**nan·di bear** \'nändē-\ *n, often cap N* [prob. fr. *Nandi*, town in Kenya] : a large carnivorous animal that is said to resemble a bear and has been reported repeatedly from parts of southern and eastern Africa

¹**nan·did** \'nandəd\ *adj* [NL *Nandidae*] : of or relating to the Nandidae

²**nandid** \"\ *n* -s [NL *Nandidae*] : a fish of the family Nandidae

**nan·di·dae** \'nandə,dē\ *n pl, cap* [NL, fr. *Nandus*, type genus (perh. fr. Skt *nāndī* joy) + *-idae*] : a family of small deep-bodied percoid fishes of warm fresh and salt waters of the southern hemisphere — compare LEAF FISH

**nan·di·na** \nan'dīnə, -dēnə\ *n* [NL, fr. Jap *nandin* nandina] **1** *cap* : a monotypic genus of Chinese and Japanese evergreen shrubs (family Berberidaceae) having decompound leaves and small white paniculate flowers with numerous sepals that are followed by bright red or purplish fruits and being grown in warm regions as an ornamental **2** *also* **nan·din** \'nandən\ -s : any shrub of the genus *Nandina* — called also *sacred bamboo*

**nan·dine** \'nandən\ *n* -s [native name in Africa] : either of two spotted ring-tailed African palm civets (*Nandinia binotata* and *N. gerrardi*)

**nan·du** *also* **nan·dow** \'nan(,)dü\ *n* -s [Pg *nandu, nandú, nhandu, nhandú* & Sp *nandú, ñandú*, fr. Guarani & Tupi] : RHEA

**nan·du·bay** \;nyändə;bī\ *n* -s [Sp *ñandubay*, fr. Guarani] : a So. American tree or shrub (*Prosopis nandubay*) with rough hard bark and durable wood that is sometimes used for fence posts

**nan·du·ti** *or* **nan·du·ty** \;nyändə;tē\ *n* -ES [AmerSp *ñandutí*, fr. Guarani, web] : a delicate intricately patterned lace made in Paraguay from cotton or other fine vegetable fibers

¹**nane** \'nān\ *chiefly dial var of* NONE

²**nane** \"\ *var of* NAIN

**nang·ca** *or* **nang·ka** \näŋ'kä, 'näŋkə\ *n* -s [Tag] *Philippines* : the jackfruit tree or its fruit

**nan·ger** \'naŋgə(r)\ *n* -s [F *nanguer*, fr. a native name in Senegal] : ADDRA

**na·ni·go** \'nyänyē,gō\ *n -s sometimes cap* [AmerSp *ñáñigo*] : a men's secret society among Cuban Negroes; *also* : a member of this society

**na·nism** \'nā,nizəm, 'na,-\ *n* -s [F *nanisme*, fr. *nan-* + *-isme* -ism] : the condition of being abnormally or exceptionally small in stature : DWARFISHNESS — opposed to *gigantism* ⟨the ~ of the early generations of nonsexual castes of many social insects results from food shortage in a new or weak colony⟩

**na·nit·ic** \nā'nid·ik, na'-\ *adj* [*nan-* + *-itic*] : exhibiting or affected with nanism : atypically small ⟨~ worker ants⟩

**na·ni·za·tion** \,nānə'zāshən, ,nan-\ *n* -s [F *naniser* to dwarf (fr. *nan-* + *-iser* -ize) + E *-ation*] : artificial dwarfing (as of trees by horticulturists)

**nan·keen** \(')nan;kēn\ *also* **nan·kin** \-kin\ *or* **nan·king** \-kiŋ\ *n* -s [fr. *Nanking*, China, where it was first manufactured] **1 a** : a durable fabric handloomed in China from local cottons that had naturally a yellowish color; *also* : a firm twilled cotton fabric dyed to imitate the Chinese fabric **b** *or* **nankeen cotton** : a tree cotton (*Gossypium religiosum*) used for weaving the original nankeen fabric **2 nankeens** *pl* : trousers made of nankeen **3** *or* **nankeen yellow** *often cap N* : NAPLES YELLOW 2 **4** *usu cap* : NANKEEN PORCELAIN

**nankeen bird** *or* **nankeen night heron** *n* : an Australian night heron (*Nycticorax caledonicus*)

**nankeen hawk** *or* **nankeen kestrel** *n* : a pale yellowish Australian kestrel (*Falco cenchroides* syn. *Cerchneis cenchroides*)

**nankeen lily** *n* : a hybrid garden lily (*Lilium* × *testaceum*) with fragrant yellow flowers

**nankeen porcelain** *n, usu cap N* : chinese porcelain painted in blue on white — used esp. by dealers of all except the roughest sorts both ancient and modern

**nankin** *n* -s : NAPLES YELLOW 2

**nan·king** \(')nan;kiŋ\ *adj, usu cap N* [fr. *Nanking*, China] : of or from the city of Nanking, China : of the kind or style prevalent in Nanking

**nanking cherry** *n, usu cap N* : a large spreading hardy shrub or small compact tree (*Prunus tomentosa*) that has nearly sessile flowers, leaves tomentose on the under surface, and globular light red edible fruit and that is native to Asia but widely cultivated as an ornamental and for its fruit in regions of rigorous climate — called also *Manchu cherry*

**nan·mu** \'nan(,)mü\ *n* -s [Chin (Pek) *nan² mu⁴*] : a durable fragrant close-grained brown lumber obtained in western China from a lauraceous tree (esp. *Machilis namu*) and used by the Chinese esp. for fine framing and architectural adjuncts (as pillars)

**nann-** *or* **nanno-** *comb form* [NL, fr. Gk *nann-*, fr. *nannos, nanos* — more at NAN-] : dwarf ⟨*Nannippus*⟩ ⟨*nannocephaly*⟩

**nan·nan·der** \na'nandə(r)\ *or* **nan·nan·dri·um** \-drēəm\ *n, pl* **nannanders** \-(r)z\ *or* **nannan·dria** \-ēə\ [*nannander* fr. *nann-* + *-ander*; *nannandrium*, NL, fr. *nann-* + *andr-* + *-ium*] : DWARF MALE 1

**nan·nan·drous** \-drəs\ *adj* [*nann-* + *-androus*] : having oogonia borne on normal-sized plants and antheridia borne on greatly reduced plants or filaments — used of green algae of the family Oedogoniaceae; compare MACRANDROUS

**nan·nie** *or* **nan·ny** \'nanē, -ni\ *n, pl* **nannies** [prob. of baby-talk origin] *chiefly Brit* : a child's nurse : NURSEMAID

**nan·ning** \(')nän;niŋ\ *adj, usu cap* [fr. *Nanning*, China] : of or from the city of Nanning, China : of the kind or style prevalent in Nanning

**nan·ni·nose** \'nanə,nōs\ *n* -s [alter. of earlier *maninose, mananosay* — more at MANANOSAY] *dial* : SOFT-SHELL CLAM

**nan·nip·pus** \na'nipəs\ *n, cap* [NL, fr. *nann-* + *-hippus*] : a genus of tiny extinct three-toed American Pliocene horses

**nan·no·plankton** \;nanō+\ *n* [NL, fr. *nann-* + *plankton*] : the smallest plankton comprising those organisms (as various flagellates, algae, bacteria) that pass through nets of number 25 mesh silk bolting cloth — compare NET PLANKTON — **nan·no·planktonic** \"+,ₛ;ₛₛ\ *adj*

**nan·ny** \'nanē, -ni\ *or* **nanny goat** *n* -ES [fr. *Nanny*, nickname for *Anne*] : a female domestic goat : a goat doe

**nan·ny·berry** \'nanē- — see BERRY\ *n* **1** *or* **nannybush** : SHEEPBERRY 1a **2** : SHEEPBERRY 1b

**nan·ny·gai** \'nanē,gī\ *n* -s [native name in New So. Wales, Australia] : a red iridescent Australian food fish (*Trachichthodes affinis*) of the family Berycidae

**nanny plum** *n* : SHEEPBERRY 1

**nanny tea** *n* : a folk remedy for many ailments that consists of a hot infusion of sheep manure in water often with sugar

¹**nano-** — see NAN-

²**nano-** *comb form* [ISV, fr. L *nanus* dwarf — more at NAN-] : one billionth ($10^{-9}$) part of ⟨*nanosecond*⟩

**na·no·gram** \'nanə,gram, 'nan-\ *n* [*nan-* + *gram*] : a unit of mass equal to one billionth of a gram

**na·noid** \'nā,nȯid, 'na,-\ *adj* [*nan-* + *-oid*] : having an abnormally small body : DWARFISH

**na·no·phy·e·tus** \,nānə,fī'ēd·əs, ,nan-\ *or* **na·no·phy·es** \,ₛₛ'fīēz\ [NL, fr. *nan-* + *-phyetus, -phyes* (fr. Gk *phyein* to bring forth) — more at BE] *syn of* TROGLOTREMA

**na·no·plankton** \;nānō, ;nanō+\ *n* [NL, fr. *nan-* + *plankton*] : NANNOPLANKTON

**na·no·so·mia** \,nānə'sōmēə, ,nan-\ *n* -s [NL, fr. *nan-* + *-somia*] : DWARFISM

**na·no·so·mus** \-məs\ *n* -ES [NL, fr. *nan-* + *-somus*] : DWARF

**nan·pie** \'nan,pī\ *n* [*Nan* (nickname fr. *Anne*) + *pie*] *dial Eng* : MAGPIE

**nan·sen bottle** \'nan(t)sən-\ *n, usu cap N* [after Fridtjof *Nansen* †1930 Norw. explorer and statesman] : an apparatus used in oceanographic studies for collecting water samples at predetermined depths

**nansen passport** *n, usu cap N* [after Fridtjof *Nansen*] : a passport issued through the agency of the League of Nations to a person without a home government

**nantes** \'nan(t)s\ *adj, usu cap* [fr. *Nantes*, France] : of or from the city of Nantes, France : of the kind or style prevalent in Nantes

**nan·ti·coke** \'nantə,kōk\ *n, pl* **nanticoke** *or* **nanticokes** *usu cap* [Nanticoke *Naitaquok*, lit., tidewater people] **1 a** : an Indian people of eastern Maryland and southern Delaware **b** : a member of such people **2** : an Algonquian language of the Nanticoke and Conoy peoples **3** : one of a group of people of mixed Indian, white, Negro ancestry in southern Delaware

**nan·to·kite** \'nantə,kīt\ *n* -s [Sp *nantoquita*, fr. *Nantoco*, village north of Copiapó, Chile + Sp *-ita* -ite] : a native cuprous chloride CuCl

**nan·tuck·et·er** \nan-'təkəd·ə(r)\ *n* -s *cap* [*Nantucket* Island, Mass. + E *-er*] : a native or resident of Nantucket Island

**nan·tuck·et pine tip moth** \(')nan-;təkət-\ *n, usu cap N* [fr. *Nantucket* Island] : a small reddish brown silver-marked olethreutid moth (*Rhyacionia frustrana*) of the eastern and central U.S. with yellowish brown larva that feeds in and damages the new growth of various pines

**nantucket sleighride** *n, usu cap N* [fr. *Nantucket* Island] : a run in a whaling boat fast to a harpooned whale

**nan·tung** \(')nän;tu̇ŋ\ *adj, usu cap* [fr. *Nantung*, China] : of or from the city of Nantung, China : of the kind or style prevalent in Nantung

**nan·yu·ki·an** \(')nän;yükēən\ *adj, usu cap* [*Nanyuki*, town in Kenya + E *-an*] : of or belonging to an Upper Pleistocene culture of Kenya, East Africa, typified by a slightly modified Acheulean industry

**nao** \'naů\ *n* -s [Sp, fr. Catal *nau*, fr. L *navis* ship — more at NAVE] : a medium-sized sailing ship of the late middle ages

**na·ol·o·gy** \nā'äləjē\ *n* -ES [Gk *naos* temple + E *-logy*] : a study of sacred edifices

**na·os** \'nā,äs\ *n, pl* **na·oi** \-,ȯi\ [Gk, temple; akin to Gk *nostos* return home — more at NOSTALGIA] **1** : an ancient temple or shrine **2** : CELLA

¹**nap** \'nap\ *vi* **napped; napped; napping; naps** [ME *nappen*, fr. OE *hnappian*; akin to OHG *hnaffezen* to doze, nap, Norw *napp* nap] **1** : to sleep briefly esp. during the day : DOZE, SNOOZE **2** : to be in a careless unguarded state : NOD — often used with *catch* ⟨was caught *napping*⟩ **syn** see SLEEP

²**nap** \"\ *n* -s [ME *nap, nappe*, fr. *nappen*, v.] : a short sleep esp. during the day ⟨take a ~⟩ : DOZE, SIESTA, SNOOZE

³**nap** \"\ *n* -s [ME *noppe*, fr. MD, flock of wool, nap; akin to OE *hnoppian* to pluck, *āhnēopan* to pluck off, MLG *noppe* flock of wool, OSw *niupa* to pinch, Goth *dishniupan* to tear apart, Gk *konis, konia* ashes, dust — more at INCINERATE] **1** : a soft fuzzy fibrous surface (as on yarn and cloth) usu. raised by brushing against a rough surface (as by a cylinder covered with wire) : COVER — compare PILE **2** : a downy, shaggy, or tufted surface (as of fur) resembling the nap of a fabric ⟨hills with a mottled ~ of gray-green sagebrush —*Amer. Guide Series: Wash.*⟩

**⁴nap** \"\ *vt* **napped; napped; napping; naps :** to raise a nap on (fabric or leather)
**⁵nap** \"\ *vt* **napped; napped; napping; naps** [prob. of Scand origin; akin to Sw *nappa* to snatch, pinch, pluck, Dan & Norw *nappe* to snatch, pinch, & prob. to OSw *niupa* to pinch — more at ³NAP] *chiefly dial Eng* **:** GRAB, NAB
**⁶nap** \"\ *var of* KNAP
**⁷nap** \"\ *n* -s [by shortening] **1 :** NAPOLEON 1 **2 :** NAPOLEON 3
**⁸nap** *chiefly dial var of* NAPE
**⁹nap** \'nap\ *n* -s [by shortening & alter.] *Austral* **:** KNAPSACK
**NAP** *abbr* naval aviation pilot
**napa leather** \'napə-\ *or* **napa** *n* -s [fr. *Napa*, Calif.] **1 :** a glove leather made in Napa, Calif., by tawing sheepskins with a soap-and-oil mixture **2 :** a leather resembling the original Napa leather in softness
**¹na·palm** \'nā,pälm, -pȧm, *also* -pälm\ *n* -s [*na*phthenate + *palm*itate] **1 :** a thickener consisting of a mixture of aluminum soaps used in jellying gasoline esp. for incendiary bombs and flamethrowers **2 :** the jellied fuel made by the addition of napalm to gasoline ⟨~ bomb⟩
**²napalm** \"\ *vt* -ED/-ING/-S **:** to attack with napalm bombs or flamethrowers
**napa thistle** *n, often cap N* [fr. *Napa*, Calif.] **:** TOCALOTE
**nap-at-noon** \'=='=\ *n* [so called fr. the fact that its flowers close during the morning] **:** STAR-OF-BETHLEHEM
**nape** \'nāp, 'nap\ *n* -s [ME] **:** the back part of the neck — often used in the phrase *nape of the neck*
**napecrest** \'=,=\ *n* [*nape* + *crest*] **:** an African bird of the genus *Crinifer* related to the plantain eaters
**na·per·er** \'nāpərə(r)\ *n* -s [*napery* + *-er*] **:** an officer in a royal household having charge of the table linen
**naperian** *usu cap, var of* NAPIERIAN
**na·pery** \'nāp(ə)rē\ *n* -ES [ME, fr. MF *naperie, napperie*, fr. *nape, nappe* tablecloth + *-erie* -ery — more at NAPKIN] **:** household linen; *esp* **:** TABLE LINEN
**napf·kuchen** \'näpf+,-\ *n* [G, fr. *napf* bowl, drinking vessel (fr. OHG *hnapf*) + *kuchen* cake — more at HANAP, KUCHEN] **:** GUGELHUPF
**nap hand** *n* [⁸*nap*] **:** a favorable chance that invites the taking of risks
**na·phaz·o·line** \nə'fazə,lēn\ *n* -s [*naph*thalene + imid*azoline*] **:** a base $C_{14}H_{14}N_2$ derived from naphthalene and imidazoline and used locally in the form of its bitter crystalline hydrochloride esp. to relieve nasal congestion
**naph·ta·lite** \'naftə,līt\ *n* -s *usu cap* [*Naphtali*, second son of Jacob and ancestor of the tribe (fr. LL, fr. Heb *Naphtālī*) + E *-ite*] **:** a member of the Hebrew tribe of Naphtali
**naphth-** *or* **naphtho-** *also* **naphtha-** *comb form* [ISV, fr. *naphtha & naphthaline*] **1 :** naphtha ⟨*naphth*ene⟩ ⟨*naphth*yl⟩ **2 a :** related to naphthalene **:** naphthoic acid ⟨*naphtho*quinone⟩ ⟨*naphth*amide⟩ — sometimes in names of compounds in which a benzene nucleus has been replaced by a naphthalene nucleus ⟨*naphtho*resorcinol $C_{10}H_6(OH)_2$⟩ **b :** naphthol ⟨*naphth*oxide⟩ **3 a :** containing a naphthalene nucleus fused on one or two sides to one or two other rings ⟨*naphth*acridine⟩ ⟨*naphtho*pyran⟩ ⟨*naphtha*diazine⟩ **b :** BENZ- 2 — not used systematically ⟨*naphth*anthracene⟩
**naph·tha** \'nafthə, ÷ 'nap-\ *n* -s [L, fr. Gk, of Iranian origin; akin to Av *napta* moist, Pers *neft* naphtha; perh. akin to Gk *nephos* cloud, mist — more at NEBULA] **1 :** petroleum esp. when occurring in any of its more volatile varieties **2** *archaic* **:** any of various volatile strong-smelling flammable liquids (as ether or ethyl acetate) **3 :** any of various volatile often flammable liquid hydrocarbon mixtures used chiefly as solvents and diluents and as raw materials for conversion to gasoline: as **a :** a petroleum distillate containing principally aliphatic hydrocarbons and boiling usu. higher than gasoline and lower than kerosine — called also *petroleum naphtha; see* LIGROIN, STODDARD SOLVENT **b :** SOLVENT NAPHTHA
**naph·tha·cene** \'nafthə,sēn, ÷ 'napth-\ *n* -s [ISV *naphth-* + *-acene*] **:** an orange crystalline tetracyclic hydrocarbon $C_{18}H_{12}$ isomeric with chrysene and benzanthracene and present in small amounts in coal tar
**naph·tha·late** \'nafthə,lāt, ÷ 'napth-\ *n* -s [ISV *naphthalic* + *-ate*] **:** a salt or ester of naphthalic acid
**naph·tha·lat·ed** \'nafthə,lād·əd, ÷ napth-\ *adj* [*naphthalene* + *-ate* + *-ed*] **:** cleaned with naphtha to preserve its strength and resiliency ⟨~ wool⟩
**naph·tha·lene** \'nafthə,lēn, ÷ 'napth-\ *n* -s [alter. (influenced by *-ene*) of earlier *naphthaline*, fr. *naphtha* + connective *-l-* + *-ine*] **:** a crystalline aromatic hydrocarbon $C_{10}H_8$ that has a characteristic odor, that is the most abundant component of coal tar and is usu. obtained by distillation of tar and by recovery from coke-oven gas, that is constituted of two fused benzene rings and yields two varieties of monosubstitution products by substitution in the alpha or 1- and beta or 2-positions, and that is used chiefly as a raw material in organic syntheses (as of phthalic anhydride and many dye intermediates) and as a fumigant (as in moth balls) — see DECAHYDRONAPHTHALENE, TETRAHYDRONAPHTHALENE; compare STRUCTURAL FORMULA

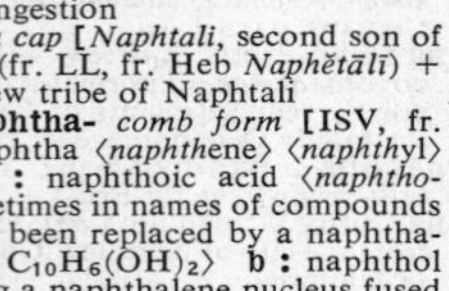

naphthalene

**naph·tha·lene·acetic acid** \'==,=+ . . . -\ *n* [*naphthalene* + *acetic*] **:** either of two crystalline naphthyl derivatives $C_{10}H_7CH_2COOH$ of acetic acid; *esp* **:** the alpha or 1-compound used as a growth regulator for plants (as for preventing drop of apples before normal harvest time)
**naph·tha·lene·disulfonic acid** \"+ . . . -\ *n* [*naphthalene* + *disulfonic*] **:** any of several disulfonic acids $C_{10}H_6(SO_3H)_2$ derived from naphthalene and used esp. in the form of hydroxy and amino derivatives (as chromotropic acid, H acid, G acid, R acid) as dye intermediates
**naphthalene green V** *n, usu cap N&G* **:** an acid dye — see DYE table I (under *Acid Green 16*)
**naph·tha·lene·sulfonic acid** \'==,=+ . . . -\ *n* [ISV *naphthalene* + *sulfonic*] **1 :** either of two crystalline monosulfonic acids $C_{10}H_7SO_3H$ obtained by sulfonation of naphthalene and used in the synthesis of dyes and naphthols **2 :** any of numerous sulfonic acids derived from naphthalene
**naph·tha·lene·trisulfonic acid** \"+ . . . -\ *n* [*naphthalene* + *trisulfonic*] **:** any of several trisulfonic acids $C_{10}H_5(SO_3H)_3$ that are derived from naphthalene and that in some cases are used as dye intermediates
**naph·tha·len·ic** \¦nafthə¦lenik, ÷ ¦napth-\ *adj* [ISV *naphthalene* + *-ic*] **:** of, relating to, or derived from naphthalene
**naph·tha·len·oid** \¦==¦lē,nȯid\ *adj* [*naphthalene* + *-oid*] **:** like naphthalene esp. in structure — sometimes contrasted with *benzenoid*
**naph·thal·ic acid** \(')naf¦thalik-, ÷ (')nap¦\ *n* [*naphthalic* (fr. ISV *naphthaline* + *-ic* + *acid*; prob. orig. formed as F *acide naphtalique*] **1 :** a crystalline acid $C_{10}H_6(COOH)_2$ formed by oxidation of acenaphthene; 1,8-naphthalene-dicarboxylic acid **2** *obs* **:** PHTHALIC ACID
**naph·tha·mine dye** \'naf¦thə,mēn-, ÷ 'nap¦, -mən-\ *n* [ISV *naphth-* + *amine*] **:** any of several direct azo dyes — see DYE table I (under *Direct Yellow 9* and *Direct Black 19*)
**naphthaquinone** *var of* NAPHTHOQUINONE
**naphthas** *pl of* NAPHTHA
**naph·the·nate** \'nafthə,nāt, ÷ 'napth-\ *n* -s [*naphthene* + *-ate*] **:** a salt or ester of a naphthenic acid ⟨~ drier⟩
**naph·thene** \'naf,thēn, ÷ 'nap,-\ *n* -s [ISV *naphth-* + *-ene*] **:** any of a series of saturated cyclic hydrocarbons of the general formula $C_nH_{2n}$ **:** CYCLOPARAFFIN — used esp. of those members (as cyclopentane and cyclohexane and their alkyl derivatives) that occur in various kinds of petroleum, in shale, and in tar oil, and that yield useful aromatic hydrocarbons on dehydrogenation
**naphthene-base** \'=,=¦=\ *adj* **:** containing relatively large amounts of various cyclic hydrocarbons (as naphthenes) — used esp. of crude petroleum; compare ASPHALT-BASE, PARAFFIN-BASE
**naph·the·nic** \-thēnik, -then-\ *adj* [ISV *naphthene* + *-ic*] **:** of, relating to, containing, or being a naphthene ⟨~ hydrocarbons⟩
**naphthenic acid** *n* **:** any of numerous chiefly monocarboxylic acids derived from naphthenes and obtained from naphthene-base and asphalt-base petroleums; *usu* **:** a commercial viscous liquid mixture of such acids used esp. in the form of salts (as copper naphthenate) as paint driers and preservatives for wood and textiles — see METALLIC SOAP
**naph·thi·o·nate** \'nafthēə,nāt, ÷'napth-\ *n* -s [ISV *naphthionic* + *-ate*] **:** a salt of naphthionic acid
**naph·thi·on·ic acid** \¦==¦änik-\ *n* [ISV, fr. *naphthyl*aminesulfonic] **:** a crystalline naphthylaminesulfonic acid made by baking a mixture of alpha-naphthylamine and sulfuric acid and used in the preparation of Congo red and other dyes; 4-amino-1-naphthalenesulfonic acid
**naphtho-** — see NAPHTH-
**naph·tho·ate** \'nafthə,wāt, ÷'napth-\ *n* -s [ISV *naphth-* (in *naphthoic acid*) + *-oate*] **:** a salt or ester of a naphthoic acid
**naph·tho·chrome violet R** \'naf¦thə,krōm-, ÷'nap¦t\ *n, usu cap N&V* [*naphth-* + *-chrome*] **:** a mordant dye — see DYE table I (under *Mordant Violet 1*)
**naph·tho·ic acid** \(')naf¦thōik-, ÷(')nap¦\ *n* [ISV *naphth-* + *-oic*] **:** either of two crystalline monocarboxylic acids $C_{10}H_7COOH$ derived from naphthalene
**naph·thol** \'naf,thōl, ÷'nap,-, -thōl\ *n* -s [ISV *naphth-* + *-ol*] **1 :** either of two crystalline monohydroxy derivatives $C_{10}H_7OH$ of naphthalene found in small amounts in coal tar: **a :** the compound made usu. by hydrolysis of alpha-naphthylamine and used chiefly as a dye intermediate — called also *alpha-naphthol, 1-naphthol* **b :** the compound made usu. by alkali fusion of beta-naphthalenesulfonic acid and used chiefly as an intermediate (as for dyes, pharmaceuticals, and antioxidants for rubber) and esp. formerly in medicine as an antiseptic and parasiticide — called also *beta-naphthol, 2-naphthol;* see DYE table I (under *Developer 5*) **2 :** any of various hydroxy derivatives of naphthalene that resemble the simpler phenols but are in general more reactive **3** *often cap* **:** any of a series of compounds (as Naphthol AS) derived esp. from beta-naphthol and used as coupling components for azoic dyes
**naphthol AS** *n, usu cap N* [G *naphthol AS*, fr. *naphthol* + *AS*, fr. *anilid* anilide + *säure* acid] **1 :** a crystalline phenolic anilide $HOC_{10}H_6CONHC_6H_5$ used as a coupling component for azoic dyes; the anilide of 3-hydroxy-2-naphthoic acid — see DYE table I (under *Azoic Coupler 2*) **2 :** any of a series of arylides of either *ortho*-hydroxy aromatic carboxylic acids (as 3-hydroxy-2-naphthoic acid) or acyl derivatives (as acetoacetic acid) of acetic acid used as coupling components for azoic dyes — see DYE table I (under *Azoic Coupler*)
**naphthol blue black** *n, usu cap N & both Bs* **:** either of two acid dyes — see DYE table I (under *Acid Black 1 & 41*)
**naphthol green B** *n, usu cap N&G* **:** an acid dye — see DYE table I (under *Acid Green 1*)
**naphthol NEL** *n, usu cap 1st N* **:** a coupling agent for azoic dyes — see DYE table I (under *Azoic Coupler 34*)
**naph·thol·sulfonic acid** \¦=,=+ . . . -\ *n* [ISV *naphthol* + *sulfonic*] **:** any of several sulfonic acids derived from the naphthols and used as dye intermediates: as **a :** NEVILE AND WINTHER'S ACID **b :** SCHAEFFER'S ACID **c :** CROCEIN ACID
**naphthol yellow S** *n, usu cap N&Y* **:** an acid dye — see DYE table I (under *Acid Yellow 1*)
**naph·tho·quinone** *also* **naph·tha·quinone** \¦nafthə, ÷¦napthə+\ *n* [ISV *naphth-* + *quinone*] **:** any of three isomeric yellow to red crystalline compounds $C_{10}H_6O_2$ derived from naphthalene; *esp* **:** the alpha or 1, 4-compound that occurs naturally in the form of derivatives (as juglone, lawsone, vitamin K)
**naph·thox·ide** \naf'thäk,sīd, ÷ nap'-, -səd\ *n* [*naphth-* + *oxide*] **:** a derivative of naphthol formed by replacing its phenolic hydrogen by a metal or other cation (as sodium naphthoxide $C_{10}H_7ONa$)
**naphthoxy-** *comb form* [*naphth*yl + *oxy-*] **:** containing the univalent radical $C_{10}H_7O$— composed of naphthyl united with oxygen; naphthyl-oxy- ⟨*β-naphthoxy*acetic acid $C_{10}H_7OCH_2COOH$⟩
**naph·tho·yl** \'nafthə,wil, ÷'napth-\ *n* -s [ISV *naphthoic* + *-yl*] **:** either of the radicals $C_{10}H_7CO$— of the naphthoic acids
**naph·thyl** \'naf,thil, ÷'nap,-\ *n* -s [ISV *naphth-* + *-yl*] **:** either of two univalent hydrocarbon radicals $C_{10}H_7$ derived from naphthalene: **a :** the radical derived by removal of a hydrogen atom in the alpha or 1-position — called also *alpha-naphthyl, 1-naphthyl* **b :** the radical derived by removal of a hydrogen atom in the beta or 2-position — called also *beta-naphthyl, 2-naphthyl*
**naph·thyl·acetic acid** \¦=,=+ . . . -\ *n* [*naphthyl* + *acetic*] **:** NAPHTHALENEACETIC ACID
**naph·thyl·amine** \"+\ *n* [ISV *naphthyl* + *amine*] **:** either of two crystalline bases $C_{10}H_7NH_2$ that are amino derivatives of naphthalene and are used chiefly as dye intermediates: **a :** the alpha or 1-derivative made usu. by reduction of alpha-nitronaphthalene **b :** the carcinogenic beta or 2-derivative made usu. from beta-naphthol, ammonia, and ammonium sulfite
**naphthylamine black** *n, usu cap N&B* **:** either of two acid dyes — see DYE table I (under *Acid Black 1 and 7*)
**naph·thyl·amine·sulfonic acid** \"+ . . . -\ *n* [ISV *naphthylamine* + *sulfonic*] **:** any of several amino sulfonic acids that are derived from the naphthylamines, have the properties of inner salts, and are used as dye intermediates: as **a :** BRÖNNER'S ACID **b :** CLEVE'S ACID **c :** LAURENT'S ACID **d :** NAPHTHIONIC ACID **e :** TOBIAS ACID
**naph·thy·lene** \'nafthə,lēn, ÷'napth-\ *n* -s [ISV *naphthyl* + *-ene*] **:** any of several bivalent radicals $-C_{10}H_6-$ derived from naphthalene
**naph·thyl·ic** \(')naf¦thilik, ÷(')nap¦-\ *adj* [ISV *naphthyl* + *-ic*] **:** of or relating to naphthyl
**naphthyl methyl ketone** *n* **:** ACETONAPHTHONE
**naph·thyl·thiourea** \¦=,=+\ *n* [NL, fr. ISV *naphthyl* + NL *thiourea*] **:** either of two crystalline compounds $C_{10}H_7NHCSNH_2$ derived from thiourea — see ANTU
**na·pi·er grass** \'nāpēə(r)-\ *also* **napier** *or* **napier fodder** *n, often cap N* [fr. *Napier*, town in Cape Province, Union of So. Africa] **:** a tall stout perennial grass (*Pennisetum purpureum*) resembling sugarcane and first cultivated in Rhodesia but now grown in many countries for forage — called also *elephant grass*
**na·pier·i·an** *or* **na·per·i·an** \nə'pirēən\ *adj, usu cap N* [John *Napier*, Laird of Merchiston †1617 Scot. mathematician + E *-ian*] **:** of, relating to, or discovered by Napier
**napierian logarithm** *n, usu cap N* [John *Napier* + E *-ian*] **:** NATURAL LOGARITHM
**na·pi·er's analogies** \'nāpēə(r)z-\ *n pl, usu cap N* [after John *Napier*] **:** four formulas giving the tangent of half the sum or difference of two of the angles or sides of a spherical triangle in terms of the others
**napier's bones** *or* **napier's rods** *n pl, usu cap N* [after John *Napier*] **:** a set of 11 rods (as of wood) invented by Napier for the purpose of making numerical calculations
**napier's circular parts** *n pl, usu cap N* [after John *Napier*] **:** five parts of a right spherical triangle including the two legs and the complements of their opposite angles and of the hypotenuse
**napier's rule** *n, usu cap N* [after John *Napier*] **:** either of two rules in spherical trigonometry: the sine of any part is equal to the product of the tangents of the adjacent parts and the sine of any part is equal to the product of the cosines of the opposite parts
**na·pi·form** \'nāpə,fȯrm\ *adj* [ISV *nap-* (fr. L *napus* turnip, fr. Gk *napy* mustard) + *-iform*; akin to Gk *sinapy* mustard] *of roots* **:** shaped like a turnip **:** large and round above and tapering abruptly below — see ROOT illustration
**¹nap·kin** \'napkən\ *n* -s [ME *napekin, nappekin*, fr. *nappe* tablecloth (fr. MF *nape, nappe*, fr. L *mappa* napkin) + ME *-kin* — more at MAP] **1 :** a usu. square piece of woven fabric or paper of variable size that is used to wipe the lips or the fingers ⟨cocktail ~⟩ ⟨dinner ~⟩ **2 :** a small cloth or towel ⟨the soul is sometimes shown borne upwards by angels in a ~ —Mary D. Anderson⟩; *specif* **a** *dial Brit* **:** HANDKERCHIEF **b** *chiefly Scot* **:** KERCHIEF, NECKERCHIEF **c** *chiefly Brit* **:** DIAPER 2 b **3 :** SANITARY NAPKIN
**²napkin** \"\ *vt* -ED/-ING/-S **1 :** to cover, provide, serve, or wipe with a napkin ⟨after a most meticulous ~*ing* of his mouth —Alan Kapelner⟩ ⟨a ~*ed* tray⟩ **2** *archaic* **:** to conceal as if by hiding under a napkin ⟨a golden talent ~*ed* and hid away —*Saturday Rev.*⟩
**napkin pattern** *n* **:** LINENFOLD
**napkin ring** *n* **:** a usu. ring-shaped device used to enclose a folded table napkin

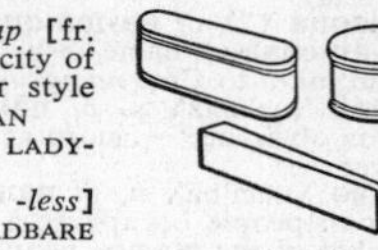

napkin rings

**na·ples** \'nāpəlz\ *adj, usu cap* [fr. *Naples*, Italy] **:** of or from the city of Naples, Italy **:** of the kind or style prevalent in Naples **:** NEAPOLITAN
**naples biscuit** *n, usu cap N* **:** LADYFINGER 2
**nap·less** \'napləs\ *adj* [³*nap* + *-less*] **:** being without nap **:** THREADBARE — **nap·less·ness** *n* -ES
**naples yellow** *n* **1** *usu cap N* **a :** a poisonous pigment consisting essentially of a basic lead antimonate used as an enamel color and in oil painting — called also *antimony yellow* **b :** any of several yellow pigments (as a mixture of chrome yellow and zinc white) substituted for Naples yellow **2** *often cap N* **:** a pale to grayish yellow that is redder and stronger than wine yellow and slightly redder than cream buff — called also *Nankeen, Nankin, Neapolitan Yellow*
**na·po·leon** \nə'pōlyən, -lēən\ *n* -s [after *Napoleon* I (Napoléon Bonaparte or Napoleone Buonaparte) †1821 Fr. emperor] **1** [F *napoléon* (*d'or*), lit., Napoleon of gold, after *Napoléon I*] **:** a French 20-franc gold coin first issued in 1805 by Napoleon I but not in general circulation since World War I **2** *or* **napoleon boot :** a man's high boot worn esp. in the 19th century **3 a :** a card game played with hands of five cards in which the highest bidder having named the number of tricks he will try to take collects from each player the number of chips of the bid if he makes it or pays out that number if he fails; *also* **:** a bid to win all five tricks for a double premium **b :** any of various forms of solitaire **4 :** a rich pastry consisting of several oblong layers of puff paste with a filling of cream, custard, or jelly **5 a :** CRIMSON CLOVER **b :** CYPRESS SPURGE **6** *usu cap* **:** one like Napoleon I (as in ambition, discipline, strategy, or power) ⟨a *Napoleon* in the management of men —Cy Warman⟩ ⟨the little *Napoleon* of an automaking empire —*Time*⟩ ⟨a *Napoleon* of finance⟩
**napoleon blue** *n, often cap N* [after *Napoleon* I] **:** a deep blue that is greener and very slightly deeper than Yale blue and greener, lighter, and stronger than royal (sense 8b) — called also *Helvetia blue*
**na·po·le·on·ic** \nə¦pōlē¦änik, -nēk\ *adj, usu cap* [*Napoleon* I †1821 + E *-ic*] **:** of, relating to, or resembling Napoleon I ⟨*Napoleonic* Wars⟩ ⟨*Napoleonic* in loyalty to his family and early acquaintances —E.S.Bates⟩ ⟨*Napoleonic* ambitions⟩ — **na·po·le·on·i·cal·ly** \-nək(ə)lē, -nēk-, -li\ *adv, often cap*
**na·po·leon·ism** \nə'pōlyə,nizəm, -lēə,-\ *n* -s *usu cap* [*Napoleon* I + E *-ism*] **1 :** the policy of Napoleon I or the Napoleons **2 :** attachment to or advocacy of the Napoleonic dynasty — compare BONAPARTISM
**na·po·leon·ist** \-,nəst\ *n* -s *usu cap* [*Napoleon* I + E *-ist*] **:** a supporter of Napoleon I or the Napoleons **:** an advocate of Napoleonism
**napoleon's-bell** \=¦=(=)=¦=\ *n, pl* **napoleon's-bells** *usu cap N* [after *Napoleon* I; fr. the fact that the genus to which it belongs was named after the Empress Josephine (Joséphine de la Pagerie) †1814 Napoleon's consort] **:** a climbing plant (*Lapageria rosea*) having large leaves similar to smilax and rose-colored flowers
**napoleon's-willow** \=¦=(=)=¦=(,)=\ *n, pl* **napoleon's-willows** *usu cap N* [after *Napoleon* I; fr. the fact that his tomb at Saint Helena is overshadowed by a tree of this species] **:** WEEPING WILLOW
**na·po·li·ta·na** *also* **na·po·le·ta·na** \nə,pōlə'tänə\ *n* -s [It, fr. fem. of *napolitano, napoletano* Neapolitan, fr. L *Neapolitanus* — more at NEAPOLITAN] **:** a simple madrigal originating in 16th century Naples and similar to the villanella in style
**¹na·poo** *or* **na·pooh** \nə'pü\ *interj* [modif. of F *il n'y en a plus* there is no more, it's over] *Brit* — used to indicate that something is finished, incapacitated, dead, all gone, or nonexistent or that the answer is no
**²napoo** *or* **napooh** \"\ *adj, slang Brit* **:** all gone **:** no more **:** FINISHED, INCAPACITATED, NONEXISTENT, DEAD
**³napoo** *or* **napooh** \"\ *vb* -ED/-ING/-S *vt, slang Brit* **:** to put an end to **:** STOP, FINISH, INCAPACITATE, EXHAUST, KILL ⟨the corporal's right arm being ~*ed* —*N. Y. Herald Tribune*⟩ ~ *vi, slang Brit* **:** to come to an end **:** DIE
**nappe** \'nap\ *n* -s [F, tablecloth, cover, sheet — more at NAPKIN] **1** [F *nappe* (*d'eau*), lit., sheet of water] **:** a sheet of water falling from the crest of a weir **2 :** a large mass thrust over other rocks by a recumbent anticlinal fold, by thrust faulting, or by a combination of both **3 a :** SHEET 6 **b :** one of the two sheets that lie on opposite sides of the vertex and together make up a cone
**napped** \'napt\ *adj* [ME *noppyd*, fr. *noppe* nap (of cloth) + *-yd* -ed — more at NAP] **:** having a nap ⟨~ cloth⟩ ⟨~ leather⟩
**¹nap·per** \'napə(r)\ *n* -s [¹*nap* + *-er*] **1 :** one that takes a nap **:** one given to napping **2** *slang Brit* **:** HEAD ⟨had come within an ace of copping me on the ~ —P.G.Wodehouse⟩ ⟨nearly laughed his ~ off —Emlyn Williams⟩ ⟨gone off his ~ at last —William Sansom⟩
**²napper** \"\ *n* -s [⁴*nap* + *-er*] **:** one that naps cloth
**³napper** \"\ *var of* KNAPPER
**nappe structure** *n* **:** a mass of rocks that includes parts of one or more nappes
**¹nap·pi·ness** \'napēnəs\ *n* -ES [¹*nappy* + *-ness*] **:** the quality of having a nap **:** abundance of nap (as on cloth)
**²nappiness** \"\ *n* -ES [¹*nappy* + *-ness*] *of a horse* **:** STUBBORNNESS, BALKINESS
**napping** *n* -s [fr. gerund of ⁴*nap*] **:** the process of raising a nap (as on a textile)
**napping hammer** *var of* KNAPPING HAMMER
**¹nap·py** \'napē, -pi\ *adj* -ER/-EST [ME *noppy*, fr. ME *noppe* nap (of cloth) + *-y* — more at NAP] **1 :** having a nap **:** DOWNY, SHAGGY **2 :** KINKY — used esp. of Negroes' hair ⟨carried on ~ heads —J.P.Bishop⟩ ⟨~ hair —Richard Wright⟩ **3 a** *of liquor* **:** FOAMING, STRONG, HEADY ⟨~ ale⟩ **b** *archaic* **:** somewhat intoxicated **4** *of a horse* **:** given to sudden tricks or starts **:** STUBBORN, BALKY
**²nap·py** \'napi\ *n* -ES *chiefly Scot* **:** LIQUOR; *specif* **:** ALE
**³nap·py** \'napē\ *n* -ES [E dial. *nap* bowl (fr. ME, fr. OE *hnæpp* bowl, drinking vessel) + *-y* — more at HANAP] **:** a shallow open serving dish sometimes having one handle
**⁴nap·py** *or* **nap·pie** \'napi\ *n, pl* **nappies** [¹*napkin* + *-y, -ie*] *chiefly Brit* **:** DIAPER 2b

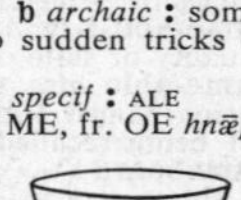

nappies

**nap·ra·path** \'naprə,path\ *n* -s [Czech *naprava* correction + E *-path*] **:** a practitioner of naprapathy
**na·prap·a·thy** \nə'prapəthē\ *n* -ES [Czech *naprava* correction + E *-pathy*] **:** a therapeutic system of drugless treatment by manipulation depending on the theory that disease symptoms result from disorder in the ligaments and connective tissues
**naps** *pres 3d sing of* NAP, *pl of* NAP
**na·pu** \'nä(,)pü\ *n* -s [Malay *napoh*] **:** any of several Indo-Malayan chevrotains resembling but larger than the kanchils and probably all varieties of a single species (*Tragulus javanicus*)
**nar** \'när\ *chiefly dial var of* NEAR
**nar** *abbr* narrow
**na·ra** \'närə\ *adj, usu cap* [fr. *Nara*, city in Honshu, Japan, that was the chief Buddhist center of early Japan] **:** of or relating to the eighth century Buddhistic renaissance in Japan or the art that flourished during that time
**na·ran·ji·lla** \,närən'hēyə\ *n* -s [Sp, dim. of *naranja* orange, fr. Ar *nāranj* — more at ORANGE] **1 :** a shrubby perennial herb (*Solanum quitoense*) cultivated in the uplands of northern So. America for its tomentose edible bright orange fruits that resemble tomatoes or small oranges **2 :** the richly flavored acid fruit of the naranjilla; *also* **:** a beverage made from this fruit
**nar·as** \'narəs\ *n* -ES [Hottentot (Nama dial.) *ǂnarab*] **:** a spiny southern African desert shrub (*Acanthosicyos horrida*) of the family Cucurbitaceae having a fruit resembling a melon and oily edible seeds
**nar·bonne vetch** \(')när¦bän- *or* **nar·bo·nus vetch** \(')när¦bōnəs-\ *n* [*narbonne* fr. *Narbonne*, France; *narbonus* NL, fr. L *Narbon-, Narbo* Narbonne] **:** an annual vetch (*Vicia*

*narbonensis*) that is native to southern Europe but used elsewhere as a forage crop and that has leafy stipules and leaves ¾ inch or more broad

**narc-** or **narco-** *comb form* [ME *nark-*, fr. MF *narc-*, fr. ML, fr. Gk *nark-*, fr. *narkoun* to benumb — more at NARCOTIC] **1 :** numbness : stupor ⟨*narco*hypnia⟩ **2 :** narcosis : narcotic ⟨*narc*oma⟩ ⟨*narco*hypnosis⟩ ⟨*narco*anesthesia⟩ : narcotic and ⟨*narco*stimulant⟩ **3 :** deep sleep ⟨*narco*lepsy⟩ **4 :** electric ray ⟨*Narc*acion⟩ ⟨*Narco*batus⟩

**nar·ca·ci·on·tes** \när,kāshē'än·,tēz\ [NL, fr. pl. of *Narcacion*, genus of electric rays in some classifications, irreg. fr. *narc-* + Gk *akē* point + *-ōn*, pres. part. ending — more at EDGE] *syn of* NARCOBATOIDEA

**nar·ce·ine** \'närsē,ēn, -sēən\ *n* -s [F *narcéine*, fr. Gk *narkē* numbness + F *-ine* — more at SNARE] **:** a bitter crystalline narcotic amphoteric alkaloid $C_{23}H_{27}NO_8$ found in opium and also obtainable from narcotine

**nar·cism** \'när,sizəm\ *n* -s [G *narzissmus* (formerly spelled *narcismus*), fr. *Narziss* Narcissus (fr. L *Narcissus*) + G *-ismus* -ism] **:** NARCISSISM

**nar·cis·san** \(')när¦sis°n\ *adj, often cap* [*Narciss*us, beautiful youth of Greco-Roman mythology who fell in love with his own image, died of unrequited love and was turned into the flower narcissus (fr. L, fr. Gk *Narkissos*) + E *-an*] **1 :** of or relating to the mythological Narcissus **2 :** NARCISSISTIC

**nar·cis·sine** \", -ī,sīn\ *adj, often cap* [L *Narcissus* + E *-ine*] **:** NARCISSAN

**nar·cis·sism** \'närsə,sizəm, 'nȧs-\ *n* -s [G *narzissismus*, fr. *Narziss* Narcissus (fr. L *Narcissus*) + *-ismus* -ism] **1 a :** EGOISM, EGOCENTRISM **b :** overevaluation of one's own attributes or achievements or of those of one's group **2 :** love of or sexual desire for one's own body **3 :** the state or stage of development in which there is a heavy investment of libido in one's own ego and which in abnormal forms persists through fixation or reappears through regression

**nar·cis·sist** \-sȯst\ *n* -s [G *narzissist*, fr. *Narziss* + G *-ist* (fr. L *-ista*)] **:** one showing symptoms of or suffering from narcissism

**nar·cis·sis·tic** \¦närsə¦sistik, ¦nȧs-, -tēk\ *also* **narcissist** *adj* [*narcissistic* fr. G *narzissistisch*, fr. *narzissist* narcissist + *-isch* -ic (fr. OHG *-isc*, *-isk* -ish); *narcissist* fr. *narcissist*, n.] **:** of or relating to narcissism — **nar·cis·sis·ti·cal·ly** \-tək(ə)lē, -tēk-, -li\ *adv*

**nar·cis·sus** \när'sisəs, nȧ'-\ *n* [NL, fr. L, any of various plants of the genus Narcissus, fr. Gk *narkissos*, prob. by folk etymology (influence of *narkē* numbness) fr. a word of non-IE origin; fr. the plant's narcotic properties — more at NARCOTIC] **1** *cap* **:** a genus of Old World bulbous herbs (family Amaryllidaceae) having erect linear leaves and showy yellow or white or bicolor flowers with a large cup-shaped corona — see DAFFODIL 1, JONQUIL 1 **2** *pl* **narcissus** \"\ *or* **narcissuses** \-'sisəsəz\ *or* **narcis·si** \-'si-,sī\ **:** any plant of the genus *Narcissus*; *esp* **:** any of numerous such plants (as from the species *N. poeticus*) of which the flowers have a short corona and are usu. borne separately — compare DAFFODIL, JONQUIL

narcissus 2

**narcissus bulb fly** *n* **1 :** a large yellow and black hairy syrphid fly (*Merodon equestris*) that resembles a small bumblebee, is native to Europe but now widespread in the U. S., and has a yellowish or whitish larva that bores in and destroys the bulbs of various plants (as narcissus, amaryllis, hyacinth) — called also *greater bulb fly* **2 :** LESSER BULB FLY

**nar·cist** \'närsəst\ *n* -s [G *narzisst*, irreg. fr. *Narziss* Narcissus + G *-ist*] **:** NARCISSIST

**nar·cis·tic** \(')när¦sistik\ *adj* [G *narzisstisch*, fr. *narzisst* narcist + *-isch* -ic] **:** NARCISSISTIC

**nar·co·analysis** \¦närkō+\ *n* [NL, fr. *narc-* + *analysis*] **:** psychotherapy under sedation for the recovery of repressed memories together with the emotion accompanying the experience which is designed to facilitate an acceptable integration of the experience in the patient's personality

**nar·co·anesthesia** *also* **nar·co·anaesthesia** \"+\ *n* [NL, fr. *narc-* + *anesthesia, anaesthesia*] **:** anesthesia produced by a narcotic drug (as morphine)

**nar·co·bat·i·dae** \,närkə'bad·ə,dē\ [NL, fr. *Narcobatus*, genus of electric rays in some classifications (fr. *narc-* + Gk *batos*, a skate) + *-idae*] *syn of* TORPEDINIDAE

**nar·co·ba·toi·dea** \,närkōbə'tȯidēə\ *n pl, cap* [NL, fr. *Narcobatus* + *-oidea*] **:** a suborder of Hypotremata coextensive with the family Torpedinidae comprising the electric rays

**nar·co·diagnosis** \¦närkō+\ *n* [NL, fr. *narc-* + *diagnosis*] **:** the use of sedative or hypnotic drugs for diagnostic purposes (as in psychiatry)

**nar·co·hyp·nia** \,närkō'hipnēə\ *n* -s [NL, fr. *narc-* + *hypn-* + *-ia*] **:** numbness felt on awaking from sleep

**nar·co·hypnosis** \¦närkō+,=¦==\ *n* [NL, fr. *narc-* + *hypnosis*] **:** a hypnotic state produced by drugs and sometimes used in psychotherapy — compare NARCOANALYSIS, NARCOSYNTHESIS

**nar·co·lep·sy** \'närkə,lepsē\ *n* -ES [ISV *narc-* + *-lepsy*; orig. formed as F *narcolepsie*] **:** a condition characterized by a transient compulsive tendency to attacks of deep sleep usu. of unknown cause

**¹nar·co·lep·tic** \¦==¦leptik\ *adj* [fr. *narcolepsy*, after such pairs as E *epilepsy: epileptic*] **:** of, relating to, or affected with narcolepsy

**²narcoleptic** \"\ *n* -s **:** a person subject to attacks of narcolepsy

**nar·co·ma** \när'kōmə\ *n, pl* **narcomas** \-məz\ *also* **nar·coma·ta** \-məd·ə\ [NL, fr. Gk *narkoun* to benumb] **:** the stuporous state produced by narcotics

**nar·co·mania** \,närkə+\ *n* [NL, fr. *narc-* + *mania*] **:** uncontrollable desire for narcotics

**nar·co·medusae** \"+\ *n pl, cap* [NL, fr. *narc-* + *medusae*] **:** a suborder of trachyline medusae sometimes regarded as an independent order — **nar·co·medusan** \¦==+\ *adj or n*

**nar·cose** \'när,kōs\ *also* **nar·cous** \-rkəs\ *adj* [ISV *narc-* + *-ose* or *-ous*] **:** marked by a condition of stupor

**nar·co·sis** \när'kōsəs, nȧ'-\ *n, pl* **narco·ses** \-ō,sēz\ [NL, fr. Gk *narkōsis*, action of benumbing, fr. *narkoun* to benumb + *-sis* — more at NARCOTIC] **1 :** a state of stupor, insensibility, or unconsciousness from which recovery is possible produced by the influence of narcotics or other chemicals **2 :** a reversible state of arrested activity of various protoplasmic structures under the influence of various concentrations of some chemicals (as carbon dioxide, alcohols, or magnesium salts)

**nar·co·stimulant** \¦närkō+\ *n* [*narc-* + *stimulant*] **:** a substance possessing both narcotic and stimulant properties

**nar·co·suggestion** \"+\ *n* [*narc-* + *suggestion*] **:** the psychoanalytic use of suggestion in subjects who have received sedative or hypnotic drugs

**nar·co·synthesis** \"+\ *n* [NL, fr. *narc-* + *synthesis*] **:** narcoanalysis which has as its goal a reintegration of the patient's personality

**nar·co·therapy** \"+\ *n* [ISV *narc-* + *therapy*] **:** psychotherapy carried out with the aid of sedating or hypnotic drugs

**¹nar·cot·ic** \när'käd·ik, -kät, ¦ēk\ *n* -s [ME *narkotik*, fr. MF *narcotique*, fr. *narcotique*, adj., fr. ML *narcoticus*, fr. Gk *narkōtikos* benumbing, narcotic, fr. (assumed) *narkōtos* (verbal of *narkoun* to benumb, fr. *narkē* numbness, cramp, electric ray) + *-ikos* -ic — more at SNARE] **1 :** a drug (as of the opium, belladonna, or alcohol groups) that in moderate doses allays sensibility, relieves pain, and produces profound sleep but that in poisonous doses produces stupor, coma, or convulsions — often used in the pl. in attributive position ⟨~s addiction⟩ **2 :** something that soothes, relieves, or lulls ⟨a public comforted by the ~ of military supremacy⟩

**²narcotic** \(')=¦=¦==\ *adj* [F or ML; F *narcotique*, fr. ML *narcoticus*] **1 :** having the properties of or yielding a narcotic; *sometimes* **:** inducing mental lethargy : SOPORIFEROUS ⟨a ~ speech⟩ **2 :** of, induced by, or concerned with narcotics **3 :** of, involving, or for narcotic addicts or their care

**nar·cot·i·cal·ly** \|äk(ə)lē\ *adv* **:** in a narcotic manner

**nar·cot·i·cism** \när'käd·ə,sizəm\ *n* -s [¹*narcotic* + *-ism*] **:** addiction to habit-forming drugs

**nar·cot·ic·ness** *n* -ES **:** the quality or state of being narcotic or a narcotic

**nar·co·tine** \'närkə,tēn, -,tən\ *n* -s [F, fr. *narcotique* narcotic + *-ine*] **:** a crystalline alkaloid $C_{22}H_{23}NO_7$ that is found in opium and possesses antispasmodic but no narcotic properties **:** a methoxy derivative of hydrastine

**nar·co·tism** \'närkə,tizəm\ *n* -ES [F *narcotisme*, fr. *narcotique* narcotic + *-isme* -ism] **:** NARCOSIS : NARCOTICISM

**nar·co·ti·za·tion** \,närkəd·ə'zāshən\ *n* -s **:** the act or process of inducing narcosis

**nar·co·tize** \'närkə,tīz\ *vt* -ED/-ING/-S [ISV *narcot*ic + *-ize*] **1 :** to imbue with or subject to the influence of a narcotic : put into a state of narcosis **2 :** to soothe to unconsciousness or unawareness ⟨*narcotizing* the pains of confusion and soothing the fevers of frustration —D.L.Cohn⟩

**nar·co·tol·ine** \'närkə,tō,lēn, -tō,-, -,lən\ *n* -s [ISV, blend of *narcotine* and *-ol*] **:** a crystalline alkaloid $C_{21}H_{21}NO_7$ found in the seed capsules of the opium poppy

**narcous** *var of* NARCOSE

**¹nard** \'närd, 'nȧd\ *n* -s [ME *narde*, fr. MF or L; MF, fr. L *nardus*, fr. Gk *nardos*, fr. a Sem word (akin to Heb *nērd* nard) prob. derived fr. Skt *nalada* Indian spikenard] **1 a :** SPIKENARD 1b **b :** MATGRASS 1b **2 :** an ointment made partly from nard : SPIKENARD 1a **3 :** the rhizomes of any of several pharmaceutically useful plants of the genus *Valeriana* (as *V. celtica*, *V. tuberosa*) or of the related plant (*Nardostachys jatamansi*)

**²nard** \"\ *vt* -ED/-ING/-S **:** to anoint with nard

**nar·dine** \'närdən, -r,dīn\ *adj* [ME, fr. L *nardinus*, fr. Gk *nardinos*, fr. *nardos* nard + *-inos* -ine] **:** of or relating to nard : having the qualities of nard

**nar·doo** \när'dü\ *or* **nar·do** \-dō\ *n* -s [native name in Australia] **1 :** an Australian clover fern (*Marsilea drummondii*) **2** *India* **:** a plant (*Sesbania aculeata*) whose seeds are ground into meal — compare DAINCHA

**nar·dus** \'närdəs\ *n, cap* [NL, fr. L, nard — more at NARD] **:** a genus of grasses having spikelets forming a one-sided spike with each spikelet having a single flower — see MATGRASS

**nar·gil** \'när,gēl\ *n* -s [Per *nārgīl*] **:** the Indian coconut

**nar·gi·leh** \'närgə,le\ *also* **nar·ghi·le** \'närgəlē\ *n* -s [Per *nārgīla*, fr. *nārgīl* coconut (of which the bowls were orig. made), of Indic origin; akin to Skt *nārikela*, *nādikela* coconut, Hindi *nāriyal*] **:** a pipe used chiefly in the Near East that cools the tobacco smoke by passing it through a reservoir of water and that is provided with long flexible stems resembling tubes — compare HOOKAH

nargileh

**nar·i·al** \'na(a)rēəl\ *also* **nar·ic** \'narik\ *adj* [*naris* nostril + *-al* or *-ic*] **:** of or relating to the nares ⟨the ~ septum⟩

**nar·i·ca** \'narəkə\ *n* -s [NL, fr. L *naris* + *-ica* (fem. of *-icus* -ic)] **:** BROWN COATI

**nar·i·corn** \'na(a)rə,kȯrn\ *n* [NL *naris* nostril + *cornu* horn — more at HORN] **:** the horny segment of the rhinotheca covering the nostrils of albatrosses and some other birds

**nar·in·gen·in** \,narən'jenən, -'ge-, nə'rinjən-\ *n* -s [ISV, blend of *naringin* and *-ene*] **:** a crystalline flavanone $C_{15}H_{12}O_5$ obtainable esp. by hydrolysis of naringin

**na·rin·gin** \nə'rinjən, -iŋgən\ *n* -s [ISV *naring-* (fr. Skt *nāraṅga*, *nāriṅga* orange tree) + *-in*; orig. formed in G] **:** a bitter crystalline glycoside $C_{27}H_{32}O_{14}$ that is found in the blossoms or fruit of the grapefruit and that on hydrolysis yields naringenin and a disaccharide constituted of D-glucose and L-rhamnose

**naris** \'na(a)rəs, 'ne\, 'nā\ *n, pl* **nares** \|(,)rēz\ [L; akin to L *nasus* nose — more at NOSE] **:** the opening of the nose or nasal cavity of a vertebrate; *esp* **:** either of the actual orifices internal or external of the nasal cavity

**¹nark** \'närk\ *n* -s [perh. fr. Romany *nok*, *nak* nose; akin to Skt *nāsā* nose — more at NOSE] *Brit* **:** a spy employed by the police : INFORMER, STOOL PIGEON

**²nark** \"\ *vb* -ED/-ING/-S *vt, Brit* **:** to inform or spy on ~ *vi, Brit* **:** to act as an informer

**³nark** \"\ *vt* -ED/-ING/-S [origin unknown] *Brit* **:** IRRITATE, ANNOY ⟨hope you aren't ~ed with me —Norman Lindsay⟩

**⁴nark** \"\ *n* -s **1** *chiefly Austral* **:** KILLJOY, WET BLANKET **2** *chiefly Austral* **:** an unpleasant irritating person

**⁵nark** \"\ *v imper* [origin unknown] *Brit* — sometimes used with *it* as a command or entreaty to cease ⟨~ it⟩

**narky** \-ki\ *adj* [³*nark* + *-y*] *Brit* **:** marked by ill temper and irritability ⟨a great deal of ~ petulance —*Listener*⟩

**narr** \'när\ *n* -s [ML *narratio*, fr. L, narration — more at NARRATION] *archaic* **:** a declaration in legal pleading

**nar·ra** \'närə\ *n* -s [Tag & Bisayan] **1 :** any of several timber trees of the genus *Pterocarpus* **2** *also* **narrawood** \'==,=\ **:** the hard wood of narra noted for its ability to take a high polish — called also *Philippine mahogany*

**nar·ra·gan·set** \,narə'gan(t)sət, -gaan- *also* ,ner-, *usu* -əd-+V\ *n, pl* **narraganset** *or* **narragansets** *usu cap* [prob. modif. of Narraganset *naiaganset*, lit., people of the small point, fr. *naiagans* small point of land (dim. of *naiag* point) + *-et*, locative suffix] **1 a :** an Indian people of Rhode Island west of Narragansett Bay **b :** a member of such people **2 :** an Algonquian language of the Narraganset people **3 :** NARRAGANSETT

**nar·ra·gan·sett** \"\ *n, usu cap* [fr. *Narragansett*, Rhode Island] **1** *also* **narranganset pacer a** *usu cap N&P* **:** an extinct breed of American pacing saddle horses **b** -s *usu cap N* **:** an animal of this breed **2** -s **:** a domestic turkey of a variety developed in Rhode Island that is characterized by medium size and black plumage marked with white giving a grayish cast to the feathers

**nar·ran·te** \nä'räntā\ *adv (or adj)* [It, narrating, pres. part. of *narrare* to narrate, fr. L — more at NARRATE] **:** in a declamatory style — used as a direction in music

**nar·rat·able** \(')na¦rād·əbəl\ *adj* **:** capable of being narrated

**nar·ra·tage** \'narəd·ij\ *n* -s [*narrate* + *-age*] **:** a technique sometimes used in plays and films and on television whereby the voice of a narrator usu. begins and often supplements the actual story and gives thereby the illusion that the story itself is merely an expansion of his own words

**nar·rate** \'na,rāt, na'r- *also* 'ne,r- *or* ne'r- *sometimes* nə'r-, *usu* -ād-+V\ *vb* -ED/-ING/-S [L *narratus*, past part. of *narrare* to make known, narrate, fr. L *gnarus* knowing, known; akin to L *gnoscere*, *noscere* to know — more at KNOW] *vt* **:** to tell or recite the happenings of (a story) ~ *vi* **:** to act or function as a storyteller **syn** see RELATE

**nar·ra·tion** \na'rāshən *also* ne'- *sometimes* nə'-\ *n* -s [ME *narracioun*, fr. L *narration-*, *narratio*, fr. *narratus* + *-ion-*, *-io* -ion] **1 :** the act or process of telling the particulars of an act, occurrence, or course of events ⟨the ~ of the course of battle⟩ ⟨the ~ of a fairy story⟩ **2 :** something that is narrated : STORY, NARRATIVE **3 :** the recitation of a succession of events usu. in chronological order and usu. with description of the persons involved — **nar·ra·tion·al** \-shən°l, -shnəl\ *adj*

**¹nar·ra·tive** \'narəd·|iv, -at| *also* 'ner-\ *n* -s [MF, fr. fem. of *narratif*, adj.] **1** *Scots law* **:** the part of a document containing the recitals; *specif* **:** the part of a deed immediately following the name and designation of the grantor reciting the inducement for making it **2 :** something that is narrated (as the account of a series of events) : STORY, NARRATION **3 :** the art or study of narrating **4 :** the representation in painting of an event or story or an example of such a representation ⟨the ~ of St. Francis of Assisi⟩

**²narrative** \"\ *adj* [F or LL; F *narratif*, fr. LL *narrativus*, fr. L *narratus* (past part. of *narrare* to make known, narrate) + *-ivus* -ive — more at NARRATE] **1 a :** of or relating to narration ⟨a good ~ technique⟩ **b :** having the form of a story ⟨a ~ treatment of an historical event⟩ **2** *of a painting* **:** showing or having the quality of a narrative

**nar·ra·tive·ly** \|əvlē\ *adv* **1 :** in the style or manner of narration **2 :** in respect to narrative character ⟨a book amusing ~ but shallow⟩

**narrative past** *or* **narrative preterit** *n* **:** PAST TENSE

**nar·ra·tor** \'na,rād·ə(r), na'r- -ātə- *also* 'ne,- *or* ne'r- *sometimes* nə'r- *or* 'narəd-- *or* 'nerəd--\ *n* -s [L, fr. *narratus* + *-or*] **:** one that narrates

**narrawood** *var of* NARRA

**nar·rin·yeri** \,narən'yerē\ *n, pl* **narrinyeri** *or* **narrinyeris** *usu cap* **1 a :** a people native to the Lake Alexandria region of So. Australia **b :** a member of such people **2 :** the language of the Narrinyeri people

**¹nar·row** \'na(,)rō, -,rə *also* 'ne(-, *often* -,rəw+V\ *adj* -ER/-EST [ME *narwe*, *naru*, *narowe*, fr. OE *nearu*; akin to OHG *narwa* scar, narrow mark of a scar, *snuor* cord, ON *snæri* twisted rope, Goth *snorjo* basket, net, Gk *narnax* box, chest, Lith *nerti* to dive, thread; basic meaning: twisting] **1 a :** of little breadth esp. in comparison with length ⟨a ~ bay⟩ ⟨a ~ table⟩ **b :** not possessing usual or expected width ⟨a ~ sidewalk⟩ **c** *of a textile* **:** woven narrow (as in widths less than 18 inches) and suitable for ribbon, tape, webbing, or braid — compare BROAD **2 a :** limited in size or scope : RESTRICTED, CIRCUMSCRIBED ⟨~ resources⟩ ⟨~ nations⟩ ⟨in a ~er sense, history is the record of human events —A.L.Guérard⟩ **b :** close around : CONFINING ⟨~ bounds⟩ **3 a (1) :** possessed of insufficient means : MEAGER ⟨a ~ income⟩ ⟨~circumstances⟩ **(2) :** MEAGER, BIGOTED, SMALL ⟨a ~ individual⟩ ⟨a ~ mind⟩ **b** *chiefly dial* **:** STINGY, NIGGARDLY **4 a :** having only a little margin : having barely sufficient space, time, or number : CLOSE ⟨winner in the election by a ~ margin⟩ **b :** uncomfortably close to failure : barely successful ⟨a ~ escape⟩ **5 a :** concentrating on minute particulars : CLOSE ⟨a ~ inspection⟩ **b :** extremely precise ⟨a machine with ~ tolerances⟩ **6** *of an animal ration* **:** relatively rich in protein as compared with carbohydrate and fat — compare WIDE **7 a :** TENSE 3 **b** *of pronunciation transcription* **:** representing by diacritical symbols many differences in and varieties of sounds including nonphonemic differences — compare BROAD **8 :** of limited activity (as with little or no demand or supply for particular issues) ⟨a ~ market⟩; *also* **:** characterized by very small price changes ⟨a ~ price range⟩

**syn** STRAIT: NARROW is the ordinary term signifying not broad or wide ⟨a *narrow* tape⟩ ⟨a *narrow* street⟩ ⟨a *narrow* entrance⟩ It commonly extends to signify cramped, restricted, or circumscribed ⟨a *narrow* squeeze through a passage⟩ ⟨a *narrow* interpretation of a law⟩ and often suggests the provincial, sectional, or partisan ⟨a *narrow* sectarian opinion on a national problem⟩ ⟨a *narrow* mind⟩ STRAIT, now archaic or dialect except in the phrase *the strait and narrow path*, more strongly than *narrow* implies tightness and closeness, commonly extending in meaning to include the idea of the strictness or rigorousness of great and distressing restraints ⟨*narrow* is the gate and *strait* is the way, which leadeth unto life —Mt 7:14 (DV)⟩ ⟨a *strait* prison⟩ ⟨to reform . . . some *strait* decrees that lie too heavy on the commonwealth —Shak.⟩

**²narrow** \"\ *n* -s [ME *narwe*, fr. *narwe*, adj.] **:** the narrow part of something: as **a :** a narrow passage (as in a mountain pass or street) **b :** a contracted part of a stream, lake, or sea; *specif* **:** a strait connecting two bodies of water ⟨the *Narrows* of New York harbor⟩ — usu. used in pl. but sometimes sing. in constr. **c :** a narrow gallery in a mine

**³narrow** \"\ *vb* -ED/-ING/-S [¹*narrow*] *vt* **1 :** to decrease the breadth or extent of : CONTRACT; *specif* **:** DECREASE 2 **2 :** to contract the reach or sphere of ⟨~ the powers of executive authority⟩ : make less liberal or broad : LIMIT ⟨~ one's views on education⟩ ~ *vi* **:** to become less broad : CONTRACT, LESSEN ⟨the river ~s above the town⟩

**narrow dock** *n* **:** CURLED DOCK

**nar·row·er** \'narōə(r), -rəwə(r) *also* 'ner-\ *n* -s **:** one that narrows

**narrow–fisted** \¦=(,)=¦=\ *adj* **:** CLOSEFISTED

**¹narrow–gage** *also* **narrow–gaged** \¦=(,)=¦=\ *adj* **1 :** using track of less than standard gage ⟨a *narrow-gage* railway⟩; *also* **:** of a gage less than standard ⟨*narrow-gage* track⟩ **2** *usu* **narrow–gauge :** RESTRICTED, PROVINCIAL, PETTY ⟨*narrow-gauge* views⟩ the stereotypes of *narrow-gauge* business standards —Lewis Mumford⟩

**²narrow–gage** \¦=(,)=,=\ *n* [¹*narrow-gage*] **:** a narrow-gage railway, track, locomotive, or car

**narrowhearted** \¦=(,)=¦=\ *adj* **:** MEAN, PARSIMONIOUS, UNGENEROUS — **nar·row·heart·ed·ness** *n* -ES

**narrowing** *n* -s [fr. gerund of ³*narrow*] **1 :** the act or process of becoming or making narrow **2 :** an instance of narrowing; *specif* **:** DECREASE 3

**nar·row·ing·ness** *n* -ES **:** the quality of becoming narrow or a tendency to become narrow

**narrow–leaved plantain** \'=(,)=,=-\ *n* **:** a ribgrass (*Plantago lanceolata*)

**narrow–leaved vetch** *n* **:** an annual or winter annual vetch (*Vicia angustifolia*) with linear upper leaves

**nar·row·ly** *adv* [ME *narowly*, fr. OE *nearulīce*, fr. *nearu* narrow + *-līce* -ly — more at NARROW] **:** in a narrow manner: as **a :** with little width or extent ⟨a ~ constructed causeway⟩ **b :** by a slight margin : BARELY ⟨~ escaped⟩ ⟨the Indian onslaught . . . ~ missed extinguishing the colony —*Amer. Guide Series: Va.*⟩ **c (1) :** with strict adherence to details, rules, or norms ⟨a ~ interpreted constitution⟩ **(2) :** with minute scrutiny : CAREFULLY ⟨search an area ~⟩ **d :** with utmost vigor : INTENSELY ⟨a ~ pursued course of action⟩ **e :** in a particularly petty, illiberal, or narrow-minded way ⟨not ~ moral —F.R.Leavis⟩

**narrow–minded** \¦=(,)=¦==\ *adj* **1 a :** of limited mental or spiritual capabilities : SHALLOW ⟨*narrow-minded* public officials⟩ **b :** PETTY, PROVINCIAL ⟨*narrow-minded* blue laws⟩ **2 :** restricted or hampered by bigotry ⟨a *narrow-minded* interpretation⟩ ⟨brilliant, but *narrow-minded* judges⟩ — **narrow–mind·ed·ly** *adv* — **nar·row–mind·ed·ness** *n* -ES

**narrow–mouthed toad** \'=(,)=,=-\ *n* **:** a toad of the family Brevicipitidae

**nar·row·ness** *n* -ES **:** the quality or state of being narrow ⟨the ~ of a point of view⟩ ⟨the ~ of a road⟩

**narrow pennant** *n* **:** LONG PENNANT

**narrows** *pl of* NARROW, *pres 3d sing of* NARROW

**nar·sar·suk·ite** \,närsə(r)'sə,kīt\ *n* -s [*Narsarssuak*, near Ivigtut, So. Greenland + E *-ite*] **:** a mineral $Na_2(Ti,Fe)Si_4(O,F)$ consisting of a silicate and fluoride of sodium, iron, and titanium

**nar·sin·ga** \nər'siŋgə\ *n* -s [Hindi *narsīgā*, perh. fr. Skt *nala* reed, tube + *śṛṅga* horn — more at HORN] **:** a curved metal trumpet used throughout India

**nar·the·cal** \(')när¦thēkəl\ *adj* [LGk *narthēk-*, *narthēx* + E *-al*] **:** of the nature of or relating to a narthex of a church

**nar·the·ci·um** \när'thē(s)ēəm\ *n, cap* [NL, fr. Gk *narthēkion* asphodel, dim. of *narthēk-*, *narthēx* giant fennel] **:** a genus of bog herbs (family Liliaceae) having linear leaves and greenish yellow flowers in racemes and with conspicuously bearded filaments — see BOG ASPHODEL

**nar·thex** \'när,theks\ *n* -ES [LGk *narthēx*, fr. Gk, giant fennel, prob. of Sem origin like Gk *nardos* nard; fr. the resemblance in shape of the thin porch to a stalk of giant fennel — more at NARD] **1 :** a western porch (as in early Christian churches) used orig. by persons (as women, penitents, or catechumens) not entering the church itself and being usu. one side or member of the atrium or outer court surrounded by ambulatories; *also* **:** a vestibule (as within an early Christian church) used for similar purposes **2 :** a vestibule leading to the nave of a church — see BASILICA illustration

**nartje** *or* **nartjie** *var of* NAARTJE

**nar·whal** *or* **nar·wal** \'när,(h)wäl, -rwəl, -,(h)wōl\ *or* **nar-**

narwhal

**whale** \-,(h)wāl\ *n* -s [*narwhal*, *narwal* modif. (influenced by E *whale*) of Norw & Dan *narhval* & Sw *narval*, prob. modif. of Icel *náhvalur*, fr. ON *náhvalr*, fr. *nār* corpse + *hvalr* whale; *narwhale* part trans. of Dan & Norw *narhval* & Sw *narval*; fr. the resemblance of its color to that of a human corpse; akin to OE *nēo-*, *-nē* corpse, Goth *naus*, ORuss *navĭ* corpse, Goth *nauths* need — more at NEED, WHALE] **:** an arctic cetacean (*Monodon monoceros*) that has no dorsal fin, is marbled gray or white in color, becomes when mature about 20 feet long, and possesses in the male one or infrequently two long twisted pointed tusks projecting like a horn and furnishing ivory of commercial value — **nar·whal·ian** \(')när¦(h)wälēən, -wōl-, -wāl-\ *adj*

**nary** \ˈnarē, ˈner-,ˈnaar-, -ri, *South also* ˈar *or* ˈaə\ *adj* [alter. of *ne'er a*, fr. *ne'er* + ²*a*] *dial*: not one — **nary a** *or* **nary an** : not a single : never a ⟨sold merchandise to a friend, with *nary an* entry on the books —J.K.Lasser⟩

**nas-** *or* **naso-** *also* **nasi-** *comb form* [L *nasus* nose — more at NOSE] **1** : nose : nasal ⟨*nasi*corn⟩ ⟨*nas*itis⟩ ⟨*naso*logy⟩ ⟨*naso*scope⟩ ⟨*naso*sinusitis⟩ **2** : nasal and ⟨*nas*ethmoid⟩ ⟨*naso*palatine⟩ ⟨*naso*labial⟩

**NAS** *abbr* naval air station

¹**na·sal** \ˈnāzəl\ *n* -s [MF *nasal, nasel*, fr. OF, fr. *nes* nose, fr. L *nasus* — more at NOSE] **1** : a part of a helmet serving as a guard for the nose — called also *nosepiece* **2** : a part near or entering into the structure of the nose (as a nasal bone or scale) **3** : a nasal consonant or vowel

²**nasal** \"\ *adj* [F, fr. L *nasus* nose + F *-al* (adj. suffix)] **1 a** : of or relating to the nose ⟨~ inflammation⟩ **b** : of or relating to a plate or scale through or by which the nostril opens (as in various reptiles) **2 a** : uttered with the nose passage open by reason of a lowered velum and with the mouth passage occluded at some point (as at the lips in \m\, the tongue tip in \n\, or the tongue back in \ŋ\ **b** (1) : uttered with the mouth open, with the velum lowered, and with the nose passage producing a phonemically essential resonance — used of a vowel as in French and Portuguese (2) : uttered by some speakers with purely oral resonance (as in English) : uttered with the mouth open, with the velum at least partly open, and with the nose passage producing a phonemically nonessential resonance objectionable to some listeners — used of a vowel or a continuant **c** : containing or using sounds that are nasal or that are made through the nose — used of speech or a speaker **3** *of a musical tone* : having a quality characteristically sharp and penetrating and lacking in resonance; *esp* : having a predominance of upper partials

**nasal bone** *n* : either of two bones of the skull of vertebrates above the fishes lying in front of the frontal bones and being in man oblong in shape forming by their junction the bridge of the nose and partly covering in the nasal cavity

**nasal breadth** *n* **1** *on the skull* : the distance between the two most lateral points on the rim of the nasal opening **2** *on the living* : the distance between the two most lateral points on the wings of the nostrils

**nasal capsule** *n* : the structures enclosing the nasal fossae or olfactory organ of a vertebrate

**nasal cartilage** *n* : any of the cartilages forming the anterior part of the nose

**nasal cavity** *n* : the vaulted chamber that lies between the floor of the cranium and the roof of the mouth of higher vertebrates extending from the external nares to the pharynx, being enclosed by bone or cartilage and usu. incompletely divided into lateral halves by the septum of the nose, and having its walls lined with mucous membrane that is rich in venous plexuses and ciliated in the lower part which forms the beginning of the respiratory passage and warms and filters the inhaled air and that is modified as sensory epithelium in the upper olfactory part — see NOSE 1

**nasal concha** *n* : TURBINATE BONE

**nasal duct** *n* : a nasolacrimal duct

**nasal eminence** *n* : GLABELLA

**nasal fly** *n* : any of several botflies that develop in nasal passages and frontal sinuses of various mammals

**nasal fossa** *n* **1** : either lateral half of the nasal cavity **2** : one of the depressions or grooves on the bill in which the nostrils of most birds are situated

**nasal gamma** *n* : GAMMA NASAL

**nasal height** *n* : the height of the nose from the nasion to the middle of the lower margin of the anterior nares

**nasal index** *n* : the ratio of nasal breadth to nasal height multiplied by 100

**na·sa·lis** \nāˈz|aləs, -ˈs|, |āl-, |äl-\ *n* [NL, fr. L *nasus* nose + *-alis* -al — more at NOSE] **1** -ES : a small muscle on each side of the nose that constricts the nasal aperture by the action of (1) a triangular transverse portion which draws the lateral part of the aperture upward and (2) a quadrangular alar portion which draws it downward **2** *cap* : a genus of monkeys (family Cercopithecidae) that comprises the proboscis monkey

**na·sal·ism** \ˈnāzə,lizəm\ *n* -s : nasality of utterance

**na·sal·i·ty** \nāˈzaləd·ē, -ətē, -i\ *n* -ES [prob. fr. F *nasalité*, fr. *nasal* + *-ité* -ity — more at NASAL] : the quality or an instance of being nasal esp. in utterance

**na·sal·iza·tion** \,nāzələˈzāshən, -,līˈ-\ *n* -s : the act or process of making, being, or becoming nasal

**na·sal·ize** \ˈnāzə,līz\ *vb* -ED/-ING/-S *vt* : to make nasal; *specif* : to change to a sound that is nasal ~ *vi* : to speak in a nasal manner

**na·sal·ly** \-lē, -li\ *adv* **1** : in a nasal manner ⟨~ pronounced⟩ **2** : in the direction of nasalization ⟨a ~ altered consonant⟩

**nasal mite** *n* : any of several mites of the family Rhinonyssidae and order Acarina that are parasitic in the nasal passages of birds

**nasal nerve** *n* : NASOCILIARY NERVE

**nasal notch** *n* : the rough surface on the anterior lower border of the frontal bone between the orbits which articulates with the nasal bones and superior maxillaries

**nasal process** *n* : the upwardly extending part of the maxillary bone that forms part of the sides of the nose

**nasal sac** *n* : OLFACTORY PIT 2

**nasal scale** *n* : NARICORN

**nasal septum** *n* : the bony and cartilaginous partition between the nasal passages

**nasal sill** *n* : the floor of the nasal opening

**nasal spine** *n* : any of three median bony processes adjacent to the nasal passages — see ANTERIOR NASAL SPINE, FRONTAL NASAL SPINE, POSTERIOR NASAL SPINE

**nasal twang** *n* : TWANG 2a

**nasard** *var of* NAZARD

**na·sat** \ˈnä,zät\ *n* -s [G, modif. of F *nazard* — more at NAZARD] : NAZARD

**na·saump** \nəˈsȯmp\ *n* -s [Narraganset] : HOMINY

**nasca** *usu cap, var of* NAZCA

**nas·cence** \ˈnasᵊn(t)s, ˈnās-,ˈnaas-,ˈnais-\ *n* -s [L *nascentia*] : NASCENCY

**nas·cen·cy** \-sᵊnsē, -si\ *n* -ES [L *nascentia*, fr. *nascent-, nascens* (pres. part. of *nasci* to be born) + *-ia* -y — more at NATION] : condition of being nascent : BIRTH, ORIGIN

**nas·cent** \-ᵊnt\ *adj* [L *nascent-, nascens*, pres. part. of *nasci* to be born] **1** : undergoing the process of being born : beginning to exist ⟨~ revolutionary tendencies⟩ **2** : of, relating to, or being an atom or substance at the moment of its formation usu. with the implication of greater reactivity than otherwise ⟨~ hydrogen⟩ ⟨~ state⟩

**nase** *var of* NAZE

**nase·ber·ry** \ˈnāz- — *see* BERRY\ *n* [by folk etymology (influence of E *berry*) fr. Sp *néspera, níespera*, fr. L *mespila* — more at MEDLAR] : SAPODILLA 2

**na·seth·moid** \(ˈ)nā¦zeth,mȯid\ *adj* [*nas-* + *ethmoid*] : of or relating to the nasal and ethmoid bones

**nash** \ˈnash\ *var of* NESH

**nash·gab** \ˈnash,gab\ *also* **nash·gob** \-gäb\ *n* [Sc *nash* impertinence + *gab* or *gob* alter. of *gab*] **1** *archaic Scot* : rude gossip **2** *archaic Scot* : an impertinent oaf

**nashi** *usu cap, var of* NA-KHI

**nash·ville** \ˈnash,vil, ˈnaash-,ˈnaish-, *esp in southern US* -vəl\ *adj, usu cap* [fr. *Nashville*, Tennessee] : of or from Nashville, the capital of Tennessee ⟨an old *Nashville* mansion⟩ : of the kind or style prevalent in Nashville

**nashville warbler** *n, usu cap N* : a common greenish-backed yellow-breasted swamp warbler (*Vermivora ruficapilla*) of eastern No. America — see CALAVERAS WARBLER

**nash·vil·lian** \nashˈvilyən\ *n* -s *cap* [*Nashville*, Tennessee + E *-ian*] : a native or resident of Nashville, Tenn.

¹**nasi** *pl of* NASUS

²**na·si** \ˈnä(,)sē\ *n* -s [Heb *nāsī'* exalted one] **1** *often cap* : the chief presiding officer of the Sanhedrin according to the rabbinical tradition **2** : PATRIARCH

**nasi-** — see NAS-

**na·si·al** \ˈnāzēəl\ *adj* [NL *nasion* + E *-al*] : of or relating to the nasion

¹**na·si·corn** \ˈnāzə,kȯrn\ *adj* [*nas-* + L *cornu* horn] **1** : bearing a horn or horns on the nose **2** [NL *Nasicornia*, division of mammals containing the rhinoceroses in former classifications, fr. *nas-* + *-cornia* (fr. L *cornu* horn + NL *-ia*) — more at HORN] : of or relating to a former taxonomic group consisting of the rhinoceroses

²**nasicorn** \"\ *n* -s [(assumed) NL *nasicornus*] : RHINOCEROS

**na·si·on** \ˈnāzē,än\ *n* -s [NL, fr. *nas-* + Gk *-ion*, dim. suffix] : the middle point of the nasofrontal suture — see CRANIOMETRY illustration

**nas·ka·pi** \ˈnaskəpē\ *n, pl* **naskapi** *or* **naskapis** *usu cap* **1 a** : an Indian people of northern Quebec and interior Labrador, Canada **b** : a member of such people **2** : a dialect of Cree

**naskhi** *usu cap, var of* NESKHI

**nas·myth's membrane** \ˈnā¦z,miths-, ˈna¦, ¦,smiths-\ *n, usu cap N* [after Alexander *Nasmyth* †1848 Scottish anatomist and dentist] : the thin cuticular remains of the enamel organ which surrounds the enamel of a tooth during its fetal development and for a brief period after birth

**naso-** — see NAS-

**na·so·basilar** \¦nāzō+\ *adj* [*nas-* + *basilar*] : of or relating to the nasion and the basion ⟨~ diameter⟩

**na·so·ciliary** \"+\ *adj* [*nas-* + *ciliary*] : nasal and ciliary

**nasociliary nerve** *n* : a branch of the ophthalmic division of the trigeminal nerve distributed in part to the ciliary ganglion and in part to the mucous membrane and skin of the nose

**na·so·labial fold** \"+ . . . -\ *n* [ISV *nas-* + *labial*] : the crease that runs from the ala of the nose to the corner of the mouth of the same side

**na·so·lacrimal** *also* **na·so·lachrymal** \"+\ *adj* [*nas-* + *lacrimal, lachrymal*] : of or relating to the lacrimal apparatus and nose ⟨the ~ duct transmits tears from the lacrimal sac to the inferior meatus of the nose⟩

**na·sol·o·gy** \nāˈzäləjē\ *n* -ES [*nas-* + *-logy*] : a scientific study of noses

**na·son flute** \ˈnāzᵊn-\ *n* [*nason* perh. irreg. fr. L *nasus* nose — more at NOSE] : a 4-foot or 8-foot gedeckt with a prominent second harmonic

**na·son·ite** \ˈnāsᵊn,īt\ *n* -s [Frank L. *Nason* †1928 Am. geologist + E *-ite*] : a mineral $Ca_4Pb_6Si_6O_{21}Cl_2$ consisting of lead calcium silicate with chloride and occurring as granular white masses

**na·so·palatine** *also* **na·so·palatal** \¦nāzō+\ *adj* [*nas-* + *palatine* or *palatal*] : of, relating to, or connecting the nose and the palate

**na·so·pharyngeal** \"+\ *adj* [*nas-* + *pharyngeal*] : of or relating to the nose and pharynx or the nasopharynx

**na·so·phar·yn·gi·tis** \,nāzō,farənˈjīd·əs\ *n* [NL, fr. *nas-* + *pharyngitis*] : inflammation of the nose and pharynx

**na·so·pha·ryn·go·scope** \,nāzōfəˈriŋgə,skōp\ *n* [NL *nasopharyng-, nasopharynx* + E *-o-* + *-scope*] : an instrument equipped with an optical system and used in examining the nasal passages and pharynx — **na·so·pha·ryn·go·scop·ic** \¦≈≈¦≈¦skäpik\ *adj*

**na·so·pharynx** \¦nāzō+\ *n* [NL, fr. *nas-* + *pharynx*] : the upper part of the pharynx continuous with the nasal passages

**na·so·scope** \ˈnāzə,skōp\ *n* [*nas-* + *-scope*] : an instrument for inspecting the nasal passages

**na·so·sinusitis** *also* **na·so·sinuitis** \¦nāzō+\ *n* [NL, fr. *nas-* + *sinusitis, sinuitis*] : inflammation of the nasal sinuses

**na·so·spi·na·le** \,nāzō,spīˈnalē, -nälē, -nälē\ *n* -s [NL, fr. *nas-* + LL *spinale*, neut. of *spinalis* spinal — more at SPINAL] *anthropol* : the point of intersection of a line uniting the lowest points on the margin of each nasal opening with the midsagittal plane

**na·so·turbinal** \¦nāzō+\ *n* [ISV *nas-* + *turbinal*] : the middle turbinate bone

**nas·sa** \ˈnasə\ *n* [NL, fr. L, fish basket — more at NET] *syn of* NASSARIUS

**nas·sa·ri·idae** \,nasəˈrīə,dē\ *n pl, cap* [NL, fr. *Nassarius*, type genus + *-idae*] : a large family of widely distributed marine snails (suborder Stenoglossa) having a long broad foot, long siphon, and a heavy usu. sculptured shell and including numerous basket shells

**nas·sar·i·us** \nəˈsa(a)rēəs\ *n, cap* [NL, fr. *Nassa* + L *-arius* -ary] : the type genus of Nassariidae comprising various typical basket shells

**nas·sau** \ˈna(,)sȯ\ *n* -s *usu cap* [fr. *Nassau*, capital city of the Bahama islands] : a golf match in which winning the first nine holes counts one point, winning the second nine one point, and winning eighteen one point

**nassau grouper** *n, usu cap N* [fr. *Nassau*, Bahama islands] : ²HAMLET

**nas·sel·la** \nəˈselə\ *n, cap* [NL, dim. of L *nassa* fish basket — more at NET] : a small genus of So. American and chiefly Chilean tufted perennial grasses that resemble sedges and have narrow few-branched panicles — see NASSELLA TUSSOCK

**nassella tussock** *n* : an aggressive Chilean grass (*Nassella trichotoma*) that has been introduced accidentally in various regions and is a serious weed in New Zealand rangeland

**nast** \ˈnast\ *n* -s [back-formation fr. ¹*nasty*] *dial Eng* : FILTH, DIRT

**nas·ta·liq** \ˈnastə,lēk\ *n* -s [Per *nasta'līq*, fr. Ar *naskhīy ta'līq*, fr. *naskhīy* neskhi + *ta'līq*, a script — more at NESKHI] : an Arabic script developed about the 15th century, characterized by a tendency to slope downward from right to left, and used mainly for Persian poetical writings and in Urdu and Malay manuscript

**nas·tic** \ˈnastik\ *adj* [Gk *nastos* close-pressed, firm, solid (fr. *nassein* to press, stamp down) + E *-ic*] : of, relating to, or constituting a nastic movement

**nastic movement** *n* : movement of a flat plant part (as a leaf or bud scale) that is oriented in respect to the plant rather than an external source of stimulation, is brought about by disproportionate growth or increase of turgor in the tissues of one surface of the part, and typically involves a curling or bending outward or inward of the whole part in a direction away from the more active surface ⟨the opening and closing of four-o'clocks involves *nastic movements*⟩ — compare TROPISM

**nas·ti·ly** \ˈnastəlē, -aas-, -li\ *adv* : in a nasty manner or condition

**nas·ti·ness** \-tēnəs, -tin-\ *n* -ES **1** : the quality or state of being nasty ⟨the ~ of crooked politics⟩ ⟨the ~ of weather in the north Atlantic⟩ **2** : something that is nasty ⟨the vermin, rags, disease, and other ~*es* of slum areas⟩

**nas·tur·tium** \nəˈstərshəm, naˈ-, naaˈ-, -stəsh-\ *n* [NL, fr. L *nasturtium, nasturcium*, a cress, perh. fr. *nasus* nose + *-turtium, -turcium* (fr. *torquēre* to twist); fr. its strong smell — more at NOSE, TORTURE] **1** *cap* : a genus of aquatic herbs (family Cruciferae) with succulent smooth stems, often pinnate leaves, and flowers with white petals twice as long as the sepals — see WATERCRESS **1** **2** -s : any plant of the genus *Tropaeolum* (as *T. majus* and *T. minus*) **3** -s **a** : NASTURTIUM RED **b** : CADMIUM YELLOW

nasturtium

**nasturtium family** *n* : TROPAEOLACEAE

**nasturtium red** *n* **1** *or* **nasturtium** : a strong reddish orange **2** : a dark reddish orange

**nasturtium yellow** *n* **1** : CADMIUM YELLOW **2** : a strong orange yellow that is redder and paler than average marigold (sense 3b) and slightly stronger and very slightly lighter than Spanish yellow

¹**nasty** \ˈnastē, -aas-, -ais-, -äs-, -ti\ *adj* -ER/-EST [ME] **1 a** : filthy to the point of exciting disgust ⟨~ living conditions⟩ **b** : exciting physical repugnance : VILE ⟨a ~ taste⟩ ⟨~ food⟩ ⟨~ medicine⟩ **2 a** : morally reprehensible : INDECENT, OBSCENE ⟨~ language⟩ **b** : lacking the decencies of good taste : grossly indelicate ⟨~ literature⟩; *specif* : crudely or immaturely preoccupied with matters of sex ⟨a ~ book⟩ **c** : devoid of real value : TAWDRY, CHEAP ⟨using cheap and ~ articles and living a cheap and ~ life —G.B.Shaw⟩ **3 a** : extremely difficult, hazardous, or threatening ⟨~ storms⟩ ⟨a ~ tide rip⟩ ⟨a ~ crossfire⟩ **b** : excessively unpleasant, uncomfortable, or awkward ⟨would not go again in that ~ little clipper ship . . . where the passengers were cooped up —George Santayana⟩ **4 a** : difficult to understand, handle, or solve : VEXATIOUS ⟨a ~ question⟩ **b** : psychologically unsettling : DISTURBING ⟨the ~ realization that money has run out⟩ **5 a** : characterized by a sharp lack of sportsmanship, generosity, or good nature : MEAN ⟨a ~ trick⟩ ⟨a ~ disposition⟩ **b** : prone to display petty maliciousness : SNIDE ⟨~ underpaid clerks⟩ **c** : socially offensive : ILL-BRED, OAFISH ⟨~ little urchins⟩ **syn** see DIRTY

²**nasty** \"\ *vt, chiefly dial* : to get dirty : SOIL ⟨don't ~ your new dress⟩

**-nas·ty** \,nastē, -aas-, -ti\ *n comb form* -ES [G *-nastie*, fr. Gk *nastos* close-pressed, firm + G *-ie* -y] : nastic movement of a plant part in a (specified) direction, of a (specified) kind, or resulting from a (specified) class of stimulus ⟨*epinasty*⟩ ⟨*nyctinasty*⟩ ⟨*thermonasty*⟩

**na·sua** \ˈnashəwə\ *n* [NL, fr. L *nasus* nose] **1** *cap* : a genus of mammals (family Procyonidae) consisting of the coatis **2** -s : COATI

**na·sus** \ˈnāsəs\ *n, pl* **na·si** \-ā,sī\ [NL, fr. L, nose — more at NOSE] : a prolongation on the front of the head of a crane fly or of various termites

¹**na·sute** \(ˈ)nā¦süt\ *adj* [L *nasutus* having a large nose, fr. *nasus* nose] **1** : having a well-developed proboscis ⟨a lean, ~ leprechaun, given to tricks —*Newsweek*⟩ **2** : having a nasus — **na·sute·ness** *n* -ES

²**nasute** \"\ *n* -s : a member of a caste of highly modified soldier termites in which the jaws are reduced and the top of the head is drawn out into a snoutlike process from which a sticky fluid can be ejected

**na·su·ti·form** \(ˈ)nā¦süd·ə,fȯrm\ *adj* [¹*nasute* + *-iform*] : having a nasus projection of the front of the head

**na·su·ti·ter·mes** \nā,süd·əˈtər(,)mēz\ *n, cap* [NL, fr. *nasuti-* (fr. L *nasutus*) + L *termes* woodworm — more at TERMITE] : a large genus of termites of the family Termitidae whose soldiers are mainly nasutes

**na·su·tus** \nāˈsüd·əs\ *n, pl* **na·su·ti** \-ü,tī\ [NL, fr. L, having a large nose] : NASUTE

¹**nat** \ˈnat\ *dial Brit var of* NOT

²**nat** \ˈnät\ *n* -s [Burmese *nāt*, fr. Skt *nātha* protector, lord] : one of a general class of spirits in the folklore and aboriginal religion of Burma ⟨house ~s and river ~s — all of whom have to be propitiated —*N. Y. Times*⟩

**nat** *abbr* **1** national; nationalist **2** native **3** natural; naturalist; naturalized

**na·ta·ka** \ˈnäd·əkə\ *n* -s [Skt *nāṭaka*] : the drama in India; *specif* : the heroic comedy that is the chief of the ten main types of the drama in India

¹**na·tal** \ˈnād·ᵊl, -ātᵊl\ *adj* [ME, fr. L *natalis*, fr. *natus* (past part. of *nasci* to be born) + *-alis* -al — more at NATION] **1** : NATIVE — used of places ⟨princes' children took names from their ~ places —William Camden⟩ ⟨most weeds have ~ countries whence they have sortied —D.C.Peattie⟩ **2 a** : of or relating to birth ⟨on the nation's ~ day —C.G.Bowers⟩ ⟨lowering the ~ death rate —*Jour. Amer. Med. Assoc.*⟩ **b** : connected with or dating from one's birth ⟨~ star⟩ **c** : present at birth ⟨the ~ down of the young ducklings is soon dry —*Canadian Geog. Jour.*⟩ ⟨their ~ and acquired faculties —H.O.Taylor⟩

²**natal** \"\ *adj* [L *natis* buttock + E *-al* — more at NATES] : of or relating to the buttocks : GLUTEAL

**na·tal aloes** \nəˈtal-, -täl-\ *n pl, usu cap N* [fr. *Natal*, province of Union of So. Africa] : a commercial variety of aloes — compare ALOIN

**natal brown** *n, usu cap N* : NEW COCOA

**natal grass** *also* **natal redtop** *n, usu cap N* : a showy grass (*Rhynchelytrum roseum* syn. *Tricholaena rosea* or *T. repens*) of southern Africa grown for forage and hay esp. in Australia

**natal hemp** *n, usu cap N* : SISAL

**na·tal·ian** \nəˈtalēən, -täl-, -lyən\ *n* -s *cap* [*Natal*, province of Union of So. Africa + E *-ian*] : a native or resident of Natal, Union of So. Africa

**natalitial** *adj* [L *natalitius, natalicius* (fr. *natalis* natal) + E *-al* — more at NATAL] *obs* : NATAL

**na·tal·i·ty** \nəˈtaləd·ē, nāˈ-, -ətē, -i\ *n* -ES [F *natalité*, fr. *natal* (fr. L *natalis*) + *-ité* -ity] : BIRTHRATE ⟨looked on the decreasing ~ of France as a source of economic . . . weakness —*Century Mag.*⟩ ⟨the effect of crowding upon the ~ of grain-infesting insects —*Experiment Station Record*⟩

**natal mahogany** *n, usu cap N* [fr. *Natal*, province of Union of So. Africa] : MAFURA

**natal orange** *n, usu cap N* : a spiny shrub (*Strychnos spinosa*) of tropical and southern Africa having greenish yellow edible berries and ovate to orbicular leaves with veins hairy beneath and cultivated as an ornamental

**natal plum** *n, usu cap N* **1** : either of two shrubs of southern Africa (*Carissa bispinosa* and *C. grandiflora*) having forked spines and edible scarlet fruits resembling plums **2** : the fruit of the Natal plum

**na·tant** \ˈnātᵊnt\ *adj* [L *natant-, natans*, pres. part. of *natare* to swim, float; akin to L *nare* to swim, float — more at NOURISH] : swimming or floating in water

**na·tan·tia** \nəˈtanchə\ *n pl, cap* [NL, fr. L, neut. pl. of *natant-, natans*, pres. part. of *natare*] : a suborder of Decapoda comprising crustaceans (as the shrimps, prawns, and related forms) that have the rostrum usu. long, the first antenna with a stylocerite, the second antennal scale larger, and the abdomen well-developed, somewhat compressed laterally, and frequently flexed ventrally — compare REPTANTIA

**na·ta·tion** \nəˈtāshən, nāˈ-\ *n* -s [L *natation-, natatio*, fr. *natatus* (past part. of *natare*) + *-ion-, -io* -ion] : the action or art of swimming ⟨their dexterity at ~ —George Borrow⟩

**na·ta·tor** \ˈnād·əd·ə(r)\ *n* -s [L, fr. *natatus* + *-or*] : SWIMMER ⟨the first woman ~ to negotiate the . . . passage —*Emporia (Kans.) Gazette*⟩

**na·ta·to·ri·al** \¦nād·ə¦tōrēəl, -ātə¦-, -tȯr-\ *adj* [LL *natatorius* + E *-al*] **1** : of or relating to swimming ⟨~ skill⟩ **2** : adapted to or characterized by swimming ⟨~ birds⟩

**na·ta·to·ri·um** \,≈≈ˈtōrēəm, -tȯr-\ *n* -s [LL, fr. L *natatus* + *-orium*] : a place for swimming; esp : an indoor swimming pool

**na·ta·to·ry** \ˈ≈≈,tōrē, -tȯr-, -ri\ *adj* [LL *natatorius*, fr. L *natatus* + *-orius* -ory] **1** : adapted for or used in swimming ⟨~ organs⟩ **2** : of, relating to, or characterized by swimming ⟨~ feats⟩

¹**natch** \ˈnach\ *dial Brit var of* NOTCH

²**natch** \"\ *n* -ES [prob. fr. ¹*natch*] : a knob and a corresponding notch on respective halves of a plaster mold used in ceramics to keep the halves in proper position

³**natch** \"\ *adv* [by shortening and alter.] *slang* : NATURALLY ⟨the witch doctor charged for his services, ~ —Jeff Daniels⟩

**natch·bone** \ˈnach,bōn\ *n* [fr. (assumed) ME *nachebon* — more at AITCHBONE] : AITCHBONE

**natch·e·san** \ˈnachəsən\ *n* -s *usu cap* [*Natchez* (of AmerInd origin) + E *-an*] **1** : a linguistic family of the Natchez-Muskogean stock comprising the Natchez language **2 a** : the peoples speaking Natchesan languages (as the Natchez, Taensa, and Avoyel) **b** : a member of any of the Natchesan peoples

**natch·ez** \ˈnachəz\ *n, pl* **natchez** *usu cap* [F, of AmerInd origin] **1 a** : a Natchesan people of southwestern Mississippi **b** : a member of such people **2** : the language of the Natchez people

**natchez-muskogean** \¦≈≈¦≈≈≈\ *n, usu cap N&M* : a language stock comprising the Natchesan and Muskogean language families

**natch·i·toches** \ˈnakə,tāsh\ *n, pl* **natchitoches** *usu cap* **1 a** : a Caddo confederacy of northwestern Louisiana **b** : a member of any of the peoples of such confederacy **2 a** : an Indian people of the Natchitoches confederacy **b** : a member of such people

**na·tes** \ˈnā,tēz\ *n pl* [NL, fr. L, pl. of *natis* buttock, rump; akin to Gk *nōtos, nōton* back] **1** : something suggesting the buttocks: as **a** : the anterior pair of elevations of the corpora quadrigemina **b** : the umbones of a bivalve shell **2** [L] : BUTTOCKS

**nathe** *n* -s [ME, by alter.] *obs* : ¹NAVE

**nathe·less** \ˈnāthləs\ *or* **nath·less** \ˈnath-\ *adv* [ME *natheles, nathles*, fr. OE *nā thē lǣs*, fr. *nā* not + *thē, thȳ* (instrumental of *sē* the, that) + *lǣs* less — more at NO, THE, LESS] : NEVERTHELESS : NOTWITHSTANDING ⟨somewhat they doubted, ~ forth they passed —William Morris⟩

**nathemore** *adv* [ME *nathemore*, fr. *na* not + *the* (adv.) + *more*

— more at MORE] obs : never the more ⟨but ~ would that courageous swain to her yield passage —Edmund Spenser⟩

**nathless** prep [natheless, nathless, adv.] : in spite of : NOTWITHSTANDING ⟨~ the dread which I had of these creatures —Edmund O'Donovan⟩

**nat·i·ca** \'nad·ək·ə\ n, cap [NL, perh. fr. LL, buttock, fr. L *natis* — more at NATES] : a large genus (the type of the family Naticidae) of active marine snails having a thick nearly smooth shell and a large foot with a fold reflected over the head and characterized by burrowing beneath sand or mud along the seashore and drilling other shells

**na·tic·i·dae** \nə'tisə,dē\ n pl, cap [NL, fr. *Natica*, type genus + *-idae*] : a family of carnivorous marine gastropod mollusks (suborder Taenioglossa) that have strong globose umbilicate shells, a long retractile proboscis, and a firm dark-colored operculum and that deposit their eggs in firm sandy ribbons — see MOON SHELL, NATICA, SAND COLLAR

**na·tick** \'nād·ik\ n -s usu cap : a dialect of Massachuset

[1]**nat·i·coid** \'nad·ə,kȯid\ adj [ISV *natic-* (fr. NL *Natica*) + *-oid*] : resembling or related to the Naticidae

[2]**naticoid** \"\ n -s : a naticoid snail

**na·ti·form** \'nād·ə,fȯrm\ adj [L *natis* buttock + E *-form* — more at NATES] : resembling the buttocks

[1]**na·tion** \'nāshən\ n -s [ME *nacioun*, fr. MF *nation*, fr. L *nation-, natio* birth, race, people, nation, fr. *gnatus, natus* (past part. of *nasci* to be born) + *-ion-, -io* -ion; akin to L *gignere* to beget — more at KIN] **1 a** (1) : NATIONALITY 5a ⟨after the division of Poland . . . the ~ existed without a state —F.A.Magruder⟩ ⟨three Slav peoples . . . forged into a Yugoslavia without really fusing into a Yugoslav ~ —Hans Kohn⟩ (2) : a politically organized nationality; *esp* : one having independent existence in a nation-state **b** : a community of people composed of one or more nationalities and possessing a more or less defined territory and government ⟨India is . . . a member ~ of the British Commonwealth —*N. Y. Times Mag.*⟩ ⟨Canada is a ~ with a written constitution —B.K.Sandwell⟩ — compare STATE **c** : a territorial division containing a body of people of one or more nationalities and usu. characterized by relatively large size and independent status ⟨a Roman province was far above a satrapy though far below a ~ —Goldwin Smith⟩ ⟨a ~ of vast size with a small population —Mary K. Hammond⟩ **2** *archaic* : a particular group or aggregation (as of men or animals) ⟨the scaly ~s of the sea profound —John Dryden⟩ ⟨you are a subtle ~, you physicians —Ben Jonson⟩ **3 a** : a division of the student body forming a relatively independent community within a medieval university and comprising students from a particular locality (as a country or region) **b** : a similar division of students at Glasgow and Aberdeen universities in Scotland for the purpose of electing a rector ⟨the ~s into which the body of matriculated students is divided —*Glasgow Univ. Cal.*⟩ **4 a** : TRIBE : a federation of tribes (as of American Indians); *specif* : one having a measure of political cohesion ⟨that part of the Shawnee ~ inhabiting the upper Savannah river —Geraldine De Courcy⟩ ⟨the five ~s of Iroquois⟩ **b** : the territory occupied by such a tribe or federation of American Indians **syn** see RACE

[2]**nation** \"\ adj [short for *damnation*, fr. *damnation*, n.] *chiefly dial* : GREAT, LARGE ⟨there was a ~ sight of folks there —T.C.Haliburton⟩

[3]**nation** \"\ adv [short for *damnation*, fr. *damnation*, n.] *chiefly dial* : EXTREMELY, VERY ⟨I'm ~ sorry for you —Mark Twain⟩

[4]**nation** \"\ n -s [short for *damnation*] *chiefly dial* : DAMNATION ⟨~ seize such husbands as you seem to get —Thomas Hardy⟩ ⟨what in the ~ are we doing down here —MacKinlay Kantor⟩ ⟨how in the ~ are these fellows going to be ransomed —Mark Twain⟩

[1]**na·tion·al** \'nashənᵊl, -shnəl, -'naash-, 'naish-\ adj [MF, fr. *nation* + *-al*] **1** : of or relating to a nation: as **a** : of, affecting, or involving a nation as a whole esp. as distinguished from subordinate areas ⟨the ~ desire to win a war —E.L.Bernays⟩ ⟨the Republican party is not ~ in scope —Arthur Krock⟩ ⟨~ newspapers⟩ ⟨~ advertising⟩ — compare LOCAL **b** : of, relating to, or affecting one nation as distinguished from several nations or a supranational group ⟨protected only by ~ action in concert with that of another power —O.W.Holmes †1935⟩ ⟨the basis . . . is neither ~ nor continental but planetary —Lewis Mumford⟩ ⟨a ~ king⟩ — compare INTERNATIONAL **c** : identified with or symbolic of a specific nation ⟨regards wine and brandy as ~ beverages —G.G.Weigend⟩ ⟨the ~ poet of the empire —James Bryce⟩ ⟨~ game⟩ ⟨~ flower⟩ ⟨~ costume⟩ **d** : having a size or importance of significance for a nation as a whole ⟨his performances . . . brought him ~ distinction —*Providence (R. I.) Evening Bull.*⟩ ⟨a vice-president . . . is not a ~ figure in the fullest sense —R.H.Rovere⟩ **2** : NATIONALIST ⟨intensely ~⟩ **3** : of, having the characteristics of, or being a nationality ⟨his ~ accent was plainly audible —Elinor Wylie⟩ ⟨the doctrine of ~ self-determination acquired greater prominence —Oscar Handlin⟩ ⟨the various ~ groups that settled in the state —*Amer. Guide Series: Pa.*⟩ **4** : of, maintained, or sponsored by the government of a nation ⟨one mile from a ~ tarred road —*advt*⟩ ⟨one of four ~ cemeteries in Louisiana —*Amer. Guide Series: La.*⟩ ⟨a ~ park⟩ **5** : of, relating to, or being a government formed in a parliamentary system by representatives of most or all major political parties usu. in a period of crisis **6** *usu cap* : of, relating to, or constituting a minor political party composed of the Greenbackers **7** *usu cap* : of, relating to, or being a major political party in New Zealand generally favoring private enterprise and tending to represent agricultural and business as contrasted with labor interests ⟨the anti-Labour forces represented in the *National* party are miscellaneous —Alexander Brady⟩

[2]**national** \"\ n -s **1** : one that owes permanent allegiance to a nation without regard to place of residence or to possession of a more formal status (as that of citizen or subject) ⟨citizens of Guam and ~s but not citizens of the United States —D.L. Oliver⟩ ⟨under that act a person might be a Canadian ~ without being a British subject —T.N.M.Buesst⟩ ⟨American ~s in China⟩ **2** : NATIONAL BLUE **3** : the national or major competition held in various sports — usu. used in pl. ⟨runner-up to the champion in the ~s —*Springfield (Mass.) Union*⟩ **4** : an organization (as a fraternity or labor union) having local units on a nationwide basis **syn** see CITIZEN

**national anthem** *or* **national air** *or* **national hymn** n : a patriotic song or hymn; *esp* : one adopted officially and played or sung on formal occasions as a mark of loyalty to the nation

**national assembly** n : an assembly composed of the representatives of a nation and usu. constituting a legislative body or a constituent assembly

**national bank** n **1** : a bank having association with the finances of a nation ⟨a *national bank* of Libya was established —*Statesman's Yr. Bk.*⟩ **2** : a commercial bank that is organized under the provisions of congressional legislation and that is chartered by and operates under the supervision of the federal government

**national bank note** n : a bank note issued by a national bank on the security of government bonds deposited with the U. S. Treasury and circulating as full legal tender

**national blue** n : a moderate to deep blue — called also *bleu de Lyon, opal blue*

**national chairman** n : the chairman of the national committee of a political party who usu. acts as the head of the party's permanent organization and has general direction of party strategy esp. during election campaigns

**national church** n **1** : an autonomous church organized and administered on a national scale ⟨the churches of Norway and Denmark are both *national churches*⟩ **2** : a church established by law in a particular nation as a national institution

**national committee** n : the chief executive agency of a political party usu. consisting of members chosen by the national convention to represent geographical areas or constituent elements in the party and having general supervisory powers over the organization of national conventions and the planning of campaigns ⟨the *national committee* . . . was brought into being for the purpose of directing the presidential campaign —H.R. Penniman⟩

**national convention** n : a convention of a political party usu. composed of delegates chosen by state primaries or conventions and meeting primarily to nominate candidates for president and vice-president and to adopt a platform ⟨the supreme organ of the national party is still the *national convention* —F. A.Ogg & P.O.Ray⟩

**national day** n : a day having significance for and usu. celebrated throughout a nation ⟨the 26th is a *national day* of mourning and all activities cease —*Stamps*⟩; *specif* : NATIONAL HOLIDAY ⟨each colony tended to celebrate its own foundation day to the exclusion of the *national day* —Ira Raymond⟩

**national debt** n : the total financial obligations of the central government of a nation usu. in the form of interest-bearing government bonds — called also *public debt*

**national democratic** adj, *usu cap N&D* : of, relating to, or being a political party composed of Gold Democrats running a separate ticket in the presidential election of 1896 in opposition to the stand of the regular Democrats in favor of the free coinage of silver

**national economy** n : the economy of a nation; *specif* : the economy of a nation as a whole that is an economic unit and is usu. held to have a unique existence greater than the sum of the individual units within it

**national emergency** n : a state of emergency resulting from a danger or threat of danger to a nation from foreign or domestic sources and usu. declared to be in existence by governmental authority ⟨therefore I . . . do proclaim the existence of a *national emergency* —H.S.Truman⟩

**national ensign** n : ENSIGN 1

**national flag** n : a flag serving as a distinctive emblem of a particular nation; *esp* : one so designated (as by custom, decree, or law) in distinction from other flags of the nation serving other purposes — compare ENSIGN 1, MERCHANT FLAG

**national flag blue** n : a dark purplish blue that is slightly darker than Scotch blue and slightly stronger and very slightly darker than homage blue

**national forest** n : a usu. forested area of considerable extent that is preserved by government decree from private exploitation and harvested only under supervision and that is often used for the practice and demonstration of proper silvicultural methods

**national guard** n, *usu cap N&G* : a militia force that is recruited and partly maintained by each state and equipped and partly maintained by the federal government and that may be employed by the state (as in law enforcement or the suppression of insurrection) or called into federal service as part of the U. S. Army — compare HOME GUARD

**national holiday** n **1** : a holiday celebrated throughout a nation; *esp* : one commemorating the birth or independence of a nation ⟨the Bolivian *national holiday*⟩ **2** : a legal holiday established by the central government of a nation rather than by state or local authorities ⟨there are no annual legal *national holidays* in the United States —*Literary Digest*⟩

**national income** n : the aggregate of all earnings arising from the current production of goods and services in a nation's economy and comprising the compensation of employees, the profits of business after taxes, interest, and rental income ⟨net national product . . . less indirect business taxes equals *national income* —H.H.Maynard & T.N.Beckman⟩ — compare GROSS NATIONAL PRODUCT, NET NATIONAL PRODUCT

**national interest** n : the interest of a nation as a whole held to be an independent entity separate from the interests of subordinate areas or groups and also of other nations or supranational groups ⟨any foreign policy which operates under the standard of the *national interest* —H.J.Morgenthau⟩

**na·tion·al·ism** \'nashənᵊl,izəm, -shnə,li-, 'naash-, 'naish-\ n -s [[1]*national* + *-ism*] : loyalty and devotion to a nation; *esp* : an attitude, feeling, or belief characterized by a sense of national consciousness, an exaltation of one nation above all others, and an emphasis on loyalty to and the promotion of the culture and interests (as political independence) of one nation as opposed to subordinate areas or other nations and supranational groups ⟨~ is a relatively recent phenomenon —F.H.Heller⟩ — compare INTERNATIONALISM, LOCALISM, PARTICULARISM, PATRIOTISM

[1]**na·tion·al·ist** \-shənᵊləst, -shnəl-\ n -s [[1]*national* + *-ist*] **1** : an advocate of or believer in nationalism ⟨a true ~ places his country above everything —C.J.H.Hayes⟩ ⟨has gone through evolution as a cultural ~ and today is a cultural chauvinist —J.T.Farrell⟩ **2** *usu cap* : a member of a political group usu. associated with advocacy of national independence or the creation and development of a strong national government: as **a** : a member of a British political party advocating the independence of Ireland and constituting an important element in the House of Commons until the establishment of Irish independence **b** : a member of a political party in the Union of So. Africa characterized chiefly by strong Afrikaner nationalism **c** : a member of an Australian political party evolving from groups opposed to the Labour party and later becoming part of the Liberal party

[2]**nationalist** \"\ adj **1** : of, relating to, or advocating nationalism ⟨the ~ aspirations of the Korean people —Homer Bigart⟩ ⟨an alleged ~ orthodoxy . . . seeking to control the schools —*Living Church*⟩ **2** *usu cap* : of, relating to, or being a political group advocating or associated with nationalism ⟨the Turkish *Nationalist* forces attack the sultan's troops —*Literary Digest*⟩

**na·tion·al·is·tic** \¦nashənᵊl¦istik, -shnə,li-, ¦naash-, ¦naish-, -tēk\ adj **1** : of, favoring, or having the characteristics of nationalism ⟨the highly ~ tone of the election speeches —*Listener*⟩ ⟨the ~ demand that America rise to meet her destiny —R.A.McConnell⟩ **2** : of, relating to, or favoring a nation : NATIONAL 1 ⟨examined from a world rather than a strictly ~ standpoint —W.A.Noyes b.1898⟩ ⟨minor ~ differences —A.E.Wier⟩ — **na·tion·al·is·ti·cal·ly** \-tək(ə)lē, -tēk-, -li\ adv

**na·tion·al·i·ty** \,nashə'naləd·ē, ,naash-, ,naish-, -ətē, -i\ n -ES [[1]*national* + *-ity*] **1 a** : national quality or character ⟨those peculiar institutions which colored all their ~ —J.T.Graves⟩ **b** : the quality of being distinctively national ⟨the question of the value of ~ in art —Edward Hopper b. 1882⟩ **2** : NATIONALISM ⟨the anglicizing policy . . . robbed Irish ~ of a great deal of its native force —Aidan Mulloy⟩ **3 a** : the fact or state of belonging to a nation : the status of being a national; *specif* : a legal relationship between an individual and a nation involving allegiance on the part of the individual and usu. protection on the part of the state ⟨until . . . recently voluntary resignation of ~ was not generally recognized —Edward Jenks⟩ **b** : the quality or state of being a national of a particular nation ⟨a local citizenship in addition to their British ~ —*News from New Zealand*⟩ ⟨before a national can acquire the ~ of another state —D.V.Sandifer⟩ **4** : the quality or state of being a nation; *specif* : political independence or existence as a separate nation ⟨product of Canada's own evolving ~ —H.W.Baehr⟩ ⟨if the ~ of any of the smaller German states were extinguished —*Examiner*⟩ **5 a** : a usu. large and closely associated aggregation of people having a common and distinguishing origin, tradition, and language and potentially capable of or actually being organized in a nation-state ⟨the diverse *nationalities* of the Austro-Hungarian Empire desired independence⟩ **b** : a group of people having a common and distinguishing racial, linguistic, and cultural background and forming one constituent element of a larger group (as a nation) : an ethnic group ⟨in China . . . some fifty *nationalities* have been noted —John De Francis⟩ ⟨Russia's population consists of some 140 *nationalities* —*Pulaski Foundation Bull.*⟩ **6** : national or ethnic background ⟨immigrants . . . of the same language and ~ seek one another —Edith T. Bremer⟩

**na·tion·al·iza·tion** \,nashənᵊlə'zāshən, -shnələ'-, ,naash-, ,naish-, -ᵊl,ī'-, -nə,lī'-\ n -s : the action or process of nationalizing : the state of being nationalized ⟨the ~ of culture, taste, mind —P.W.Kutz⟩ ⟨a bill proposing the ~ of mines —C.W.A. Veditz⟩ ⟨the Bolsheviks . . . decreed immediate ~ and distribution of all the land —M.W.Straight⟩

**na·tion·al·ize** \'nashənᵊl,īz, -shnə,līz, 'naash-, 'naish-\ vt -ED/-ING/-S *see -ize in Explan Notes* [prob. fr. F *nationaliser*, fr. *national* + *-iser* -ize] **1** : to give a national character to : make distinctively national ⟨factors tending to ~ American politics⟩ **2** : to invest in the central government of a nation the control or ownership of ⟨it . . . *nationalized* ownership of all agricultural estates, factories, . . . and all means of production —A.J.Osgniach⟩ ⟨the movement to ~ industry —P.H. Douglas⟩ — compare COLLECTIVIZE, SOCIALIZE

**na·tion·al·iz·er** \-ze(r)\ n -s : one that advocates nationalization ⟨the English railway ~s proposed that the state should own the lines —*Contemporary Rev.*⟩

**na·tion·al·ly** \-nᵊlē, -nəlē, -i\ adv **1** : by, with regard to, or in terms of a nation as a whole ⟨farm purchasing power has declined ~ —A.G.Mezerik⟩ ⟨the people . . . might be represented as ~ Christianized —Rufus Anderson⟩ **2** : on a national scale : throughout a nation ⟨it costs a lot of money to advertise ~ —Sherwood Anderson⟩ ⟨made available ~ at prices . . . everyone could afford —Gordon Russell⟩

**national meridian** n : a meridian chosen in a particular nation as the zero point in measuring longitude for that nation — compare PRIME MERIDIAN

**national mission** n : HOME MISSION

**national monument** n : a monument reserved by the federal government as public property ⟨permits presidents to make *national monuments* of historically . . . interesting places —C.L.Wirth⟩

**national park** n : an area of special scenic, historical, or scientific importance set aside and maintained by a national government esp. for recreation or study ⟨the fourth of Britain's *national parks* —*Brit. Book News*⟩ ⟨Canada's western *national parks* —L.S.Marceau⟩ ⟨*national parks* in the U.S. are managed by the Department of the Interior⟩

**national product** n **1** : GROSS NATIONAL PRODUCT **2** : NET NATIONAL PRODUCT

**national republican** n, *usu cap N&R* : a member of a political party formed in opposition to the Jacksonian Democrats and after being decisively defeated in the presidential election of 1832 fused with other elements to form the Whig party

**nationals** *pl of* NATIONAL

**national salute** n **1** : a salute of 21 guns in honor of the president of the U.S. or of the head or flag of an independent foreign nation **2** : SALUTE TO THE UNION

**national school** n : a voluntary school in Great Britain established or aided by a national society (as the National Society for Promoting the Education of the Poor in the Principles of the Established Church)

**national school-bus chrome** n : a variable color averaging a vivid orange yellow that is redder, lighter, and stronger than bright marigold

**national service** n, *Brit* : SELECTIVE SERVICE

**national service life insurance** : life insurance made available by the federal government to members of the armed forces during and after World War II

**national silver** adj, *usu cap N&S* : of, relating to, or being a political party composed of dissident Republicans favoring the free coinage of silver and endorsing the Democratic ticket in the election of 1896 — compare GOLD DEMOCRAT, NATIONAL DEMOCRATIC

**national socialism** n [trans. of G *nationalsozialismus*] : NAZISM 1 ⟨the anti-Jewish policy of *national socialism* —G.H. Sabine⟩

**national socialist** adj [trans. of G *nationalsozialistisch*] : of, relating to, or having the characteristics of nazism ⟨theories . . . advanced to explain the *national socialist* movement in Germany —J.H.Hallowell⟩ ⟨the *national socialist* notion of the racial folk —G.H.Sabine⟩

**national state** n : NATION-STATE ⟨in the nineteenth century the *national state* became the basis of all political systems —W.J. Ehrenpreis⟩

**na·tion·hood** \'nāshən,hu̇d\ n : the quality or state of being a nation ⟨colonies emerging into ~ —R.S.Sayers⟩ ⟨claim the full status of ~ for the Dominions —*Nineteenth Century*⟩ ⟨animated by a . . . strong sense of ~ —Isaac Deutscher⟩

**na·tion·less** \-nləs\ adj : belonging to no nation

**nations** *pl of* NATION

**nation-state** \'=,=\ n : a form of international political organization developing in the 16th century from earlier feudal units and characterized chiefly by a relatively homogeneous group of people with a feeling of common nationality living within the defined boundaries of an independent and sovereign state : a state containing one as opposed to several nationalities

**nationwide** \'==¦=\ adj : extended or existing throughout an entire nation ⟨political oratory . . . in this day of the ~ broadcast —Max Eastman⟩ ⟨a ~ coal strike⟩ ⟨attracted ~ attention⟩

[1]**na·tive** \'nād·|iv, -ät|, |ēv *also* |əv\ adj [ME *natif*, fr. MF, fr. L *nativus*, fr. *natus* (past part. of *nasci* to be born) + *-ivus* -ive — more at NATION] **1** : belonging to one by nature : conferred by birth : derived from origin : born with one : not acquired : INHERENT, INBORN ⟨a ~ shrewdness and an ability to make the right decision by instinct —A.J.P.Taylor⟩ ⟨ambition and ~ aptitude —Bertrand Russell⟩ ⟨a certain ~ capacity is needed to meet academic requirements —W.K.Hicks⟩ **2** : belonging to or associated with a particular place (as a region or country) by birth ⟨~ artists left the state and studied . . . abroad —*Amer. Guide Series: Mich.*⟩ ⟨a ~ Englishman⟩ **3** *archaic* : closely related (as by birth or race) ⟨the head is not more ~ to the heart . . . than is the throne of Denmark to thy father —Shak.⟩ **4 a** : of, relating to, or connected with one as a result of birth in a given place or circumstances ⟨hailed in his ~ Sweden as an influential dramatist —William Peden⟩ ⟨returned to his ~ countryside —I.M.Price⟩ ⟨my foot is on my ~ heath —Sir Walter Scott⟩ **b** : belonging to or associated with one by birth into a particular region or people ⟨~ language⟩ ⟨~ costume⟩ **5 a** : according to nature : NATURAL, NORMAL ⟨think France and England . . . the ~ leaders of Europe —Janet Flanner⟩ ⟨if fiction chooses to abandon its ~ approach —Bernard DeVoto⟩ — often used with following *to* ⟨sitting there, as ~ to the stool as a cat —Jean Stafford⟩ **b** : naturally implied or involved (as in a text or term) : not forced in interpretation or construction ⟨the ~ sense of a word⟩ **6 a** : grown, produced, or originating in a particular place (as a region or country) : not foreign or exotic ⟨whose paintings retained a ~ quality despite his close familiarity with the styles of European art —*Amer. Guide Series: Pa.*⟩ ⟨the Edinburgh groat . . . was the first ~ coin of Scotland —*advt*⟩ ⟨the first ~ use of the harp in Ireland —Richard Hayward⟩ **b** : grown, produced, or originating in the vicinity : not transported from a distant region : LOCAL ⟨your requirements are either ~ or nearby —*Delaware*⟩ ⟨a one-story structure of ~ stone —Seth King⟩ **c** : living or growing naturally in a given region : INDIGENOUS ⟨tobacco is ~ to the American continent —C.H.Thienes⟩ ⟨where tropical . . . plants will grow ~ —Marjory S. Douglas⟩ ⟨a ~ species⟩ **d** : of, relating to, or being livestock found typically in a particular region; *often* : inferior and not of a recognized breed **7** : left or remaining in a natural state : being without embellishment or artificial change : SIMPLE, UNADORNED, UNAFFECTED ⟨our feelings still ~ and entire, unsophisticated by pedantry —Edmund Burke⟩ **8** *archaic* : belonging to or associated with one by birth ⟨that man should thus . . . abridge him of his just and ~ rights —William Cowper⟩ **9** *obs* : having a right or title by birth : RIGHTFUL **10** : constituting the original substance or source of something ⟨the way I must return to ~ dust —John Milton⟩ **11 a** : occurring in nature esp. uncombined with other elements ⟨~ gold⟩ ⟨~ sulfur⟩ **b** : as found in nature : not artificially prepared ⟨~ gypsum⟩ ⟨salt in the ~ state⟩ ⟨conversion of a ~ protein to a denatured protein⟩ **12** [[2]*native*] **a** : of, relating to, or composed of a people inhabiting a territorial area at the time of its discovery or its becoming familiar to a foreigner ⟨~ societies⟩ ⟨a ~ worker⟩ **b** : of, relating to, or having the characteristics of such a people having a less complex civilization ⟨the ~ Indian tribes of the American prairie⟩ ⟨~ reserve⟩ **c** *usu cap, Africa* : of, relating to, or being a Negro of unmixed descent ⟨the vast *Native* labor resources of the country —A.J.Bruwer⟩ ⟨the third *Native* woman to qualify as a doctor —*Johannesburg Sunday Express*⟩ **13** *chiefly Austral* : having a usu. superficial resemblance to a specified English plant or animal ⟨~ cat⟩ ⟨~ robin⟩ ⟨~ cherry⟩ **14** : free from branding marks : UNBRANDED — used of cattle and hides

**syn** INDIGENOUS, ENDEMIC, ABORIGINAL, AUTOCHTHONOUS: NATIVE applies to one having birth or origin in a locality indicated; it may imply concord or compatibility with that locality ⟨except for highly technical work, the company employs only *native* whites —*Amer. Guide Series: La.*⟩ ⟨2,479 European and 37,032 *native* teachers —*Americana Annual*⟩ ⟨interest centers on our *native* roots, the American past that here is many strata deep —Bernard DeVoto⟩ INDIGENOUS may apply to that which is not only native but which, insofar as can be known, has never been introduced, transported, or brought from another area into the locality in question ⟨southern Rhodesia at present employs about half a million Africans, of whom half are *indigenous* and half are migrants from neighboring territories —Peter Scott⟩ ⟨the sugarcane, a plant *indigenous* to the island —Herman Melville⟩ ⟨no rich heritage of *indigenous* folk song —C.A. & Mary Beard⟩ ENDEMIC may but does not necessarily add to INDIGENOUS the notion of being peculiar to a specific locality or sphere ⟨the Russia of the czars was backward, poor, threatened by an *endemic* revolutionary crisis, tyrannical and inefficient in practically all aspects of its life —D.W.Brogan⟩ ⟨keen competition among universities in educational affairs and the pursuit of knowledge is necessary as a corrective to that complacency which is an *endemic* disease of academic groups —J.B.Conant⟩ ⟨malaria is *endemic* in 17 states of our own South and Southwest —*Harper's*⟩ ABORIGINAL is likely to apply to the primitive native belonging to the earliest extant race inhabiting an area ⟨a primitive *aboriginal* race in the southeast of Sumatra —J.G. Frazer⟩ ⟨the squatters who staked off so-called government lands pushed the *aboriginal* inhabitants back into the mountains and deserts —*Amer. Guide Series: Calif.*⟩ AUTOCHTHONOUS (along with its variants) applies to that which either definitely or presumably had its eventual origin or emergence at the locality in question ⟨*autochthonous* cases of malaria have never been reported from these islands —*Biol. Abstracts*⟩ ⟨born in the West of Britain, a Welshman, into that tribe of *autochthonous* types who were living in the Island before the Danes, Romans, Angles, Saxons, Vikings, and other aggressors arrived —Henry Williamson⟩

[2]**native** \"\ *n* -S [in sense 1, fr. ME *natif*, fr. ML *nativus*, fr. L *nativus*, adj., belonging by birth, native; in other senses fr. [1]*native*] **1 :** one born in a state of bondage or serfdom **:** a born thrall ⟨these lairds had also their ~*s* and husbandmen for labor in feudal services —James Colville⟩ **2** *archaic* **a :** one born under a particular sign or planet **b :** the subject of a nativity or other horoscope **3 a :** one born in a particular place **:** one connected with a place (as by parental domicile or childhood residence) even though actually born or later resident elsewhere ⟨the total numbers of ~*s* and foreign-born persons —*Population Census Methods*⟩ — often used with following *of* ⟨a ~ of Hoboken, where he was born on March 26 —*Current Biog.*⟩ **b** *Austral* **:** a white person born in the country as distinguished from one born abroad **4** *obs* **:** a fellow countryman **:** COMPATRIOT — used in pl. ⟨the king (distrusting his ~*s*) employed . . . many French foreigners —Thomas Fuller⟩ **5 a :** one of a people inhabiting a territorial area at the time of its discovery or becoming familiar to a foreigner; *esp* **:** one belonging to a people having a less complex civilization ⟨a protest against the attitude of the white population toward the ~*s* —*Irish Digest*⟩ **b :** one held to resemble such a person **:** an inhabitant of a region spoken of as if strange or newly discovered **c** *usu cap, Africa* **:** a Negro of unmixed descent; *specif* **:** BANTU ⟨*Natives* and Coloreds who live along this public road —*Farmer's Weekly So. Africa*⟩ — compare [2]AFRICAN 1, AFRIKANER, [2]ASIATIC 2, CAPE COLORED, [2]EUROPEAN 2b **6** *dial Brit* **:** one's native country or locality ⟨when he came back to his ~ . . . he knew no one —*Cornhill Mag.*⟩ **7 a :** a local resident; *esp* **:** a person who has lived all his life in a place as distinguished from a visitor or a temporary resident ⟨give visitors — and the mere . . . ~ — a new aspect of a city —*Irish Digest*⟩ ⟨~*s* and old-time summer residents —*N.Y.Times*⟩ ⟨the split between ~*s* and refugees —Dolf Sternberger⟩ **b :** such a person inhabiting a small town or village **8 a :** something (as an animal, vegetable, or mineral) indigenous to a particular locality **:** one produced in a given area and not normally produced or found elsewhere ⟨improbable that corn could have been a ~ of the region —P.C.Mangelsdorf⟩ ⟨the Mexican bean beetle, a ~ of Central America —*Amer. Guide Series: N.J.*⟩ **b** *Brit* **:** an oyster grown in local waters ⟨eating ~*s* until the man who opened them grew pale —Charles Dickens⟩ **9 :** a very old and large snapper — called also *rock native*

[1]**native american** *adj, usu cap N&A* [[1]*native*] **:** of, relating to, or characterized by Native Americanism ⟨in 1835 a *Native American* party was formed —D.D.McKean⟩

[2]**native american** *n, usu cap N&A* **:** a member of a minor American political group having a brief existence in the early 19th century before evolving into the Know-Nothing party ⟨the *Native Americans* . . . were pledged not to vote for any foreigner for office —C.H.Haswell⟩

**native american church** *n, usu cap N&A&C* **:** an intertribal American Indian religious organization adapting Christianity to native beliefs and practices and including esp. the sacramental use of peyote

**native americanism** *n, usu cap N&A* **:** the principles and policies of the Native Americans; *esp* **:** hostility toward all but native-born Protestant Americans

**native bear** *n, Austral* **:** KOALA

**native beech** *n* **1 :** either of two Australian trees: **a :** FLINDOSA **b :** a shrubby tree (*Callicoma serratifolia*) of the family Cunoniaceae having wood that contains saponin and being often cultivated for its heads of petalless bright yellow flowers with showy elongated stamens and anthers **2** *or* **native birch** *NewZeal* **:** NEW ZEALAND BEECH

**native-born** \ˌ==ˌ=\ *adj* **:** belonging to or associated with a particular place (as a country) by birth therein ⟨a *native-born* American⟩ ⟨*native-born* stock —*Survey Graphic*⟩ ⟨supply of *native-born* labor in the South is equal to the demand —*Textile World*⟩ — compare NATURAL-BORN

**native box** *n* **:** an Australian prickly shrub or small tree (*Bursaria spinosa*) useful as a browse plant — called also *boxthorn*

**native bread** *n* **:** BLACKFELLOWS' BREAD

**native broom** *n* **:** DOGWOOD 2d(1)

**native cabbage** *n* **:** a succulent Australian shrub (*Scaevola koenigii*)

**native cat** *n* **:** any of several Australian predaceous carnivorous marsupials of the genus *Dasyurus* (esp. *D. viverrinus*)

**native cherry** *n* **1 :** a low shrubby Australian tree (*Exocarpus cupressiformis*) of the family Santalaceae with a fruit that is a drupe and rests on an enlarged succulent bright red edible pedicel **2 :** the fruit or pedicel of the native cherry

**native cod** *n* **:** SHORE COD

**native companion** *n, Austral* **:** BROLGA

**native cranberry** *n* **:** either of two Australian shrubs of the genus *Styphelia* (*S. sapida, S. humifusa*) having thin-fleshed fruits resembling cranberries

**native currant** *n* **:** any of several Australian trees bearing small edible acid berries resembling currants: as **a :** a tree (*Coprosma billardieri*) **b :** any of several shrubs or trees of the genus *Leptomeria* (family Santalaceae) **c :** BLUEBERRY 2a(1) **d :** BLACK NIGHTSHADE

**native daphne** *n* **:** NATIVE LAUREL

**native dog** *n, Austral* **:** DINGO

**native flax** *n* **1 :** an Australian flax (*Linum marginale*) **2 :** NEW ZEALAND FLAX

**native fuchsia** *n* **1** *NewZeal* **:** KONINI **2 :** any of several plants of the genera *Correa* or *Epacris* having showy flowers

**native guava** *n* **1 :** an Australian shrub or small tree (*Rhodomyrtus psidioides*) of the family Myrtaceae resembling the true guava **2 a :** an Australian timber tree (*Eupomatia laurina*) **b :** the edible fruit of the native guava **3 :** IVORYWOOD

**native hen** *n* **:** an Australian rail (*Tribonyx mortierii*)

**native hop** *n, Austral* **:** HOPBUSH

**native juniper** *n* **:** BLUEBERRY 2a(2)

**native laurel** *n* **1 :** a medium-sized Australian tree (*Pittosporum undulatum*) with shining evergreen leaves and fragrant creamy white flowers in terminal clusters **2 :** an Australian timber tree (*Polyscias elegans*) of the family Araliaceae having whitish wood

**native lime** *n* **1 :** either of two Australian citrus trees (*Citrus australis* and *Microcitrus australasica*) having very acid fruit **2 :** the fruit of a native lime tree

**na·tive·ly** \ˈnād·əvlē, -ātə-, -li\ *adv* **:** in a native manner; *specif* **:** by birth, origin, or inherent qualities **:** INNATELY, NATURALLY ⟨a ~ gifted . . . individual —A.L.Kroeber⟩ ⟨they were ~ courteous —Ernie Pyle⟩

**native millet** *n* **:** AUSTRALIAN MILLET

**native mistletoe** *n* **:** an Australian plant of the genus *Loranthus*

**native mulberry** *n* **:** any of several Australian trees that are felt to resemble the mulberry: as **a :** a tree (*Pipturus argenteus*) of the family Urticaceae having edible white berries **b :** a tree (*Hedycarya angustifolia*) of the family Monimiaceae **c :** an evergreen tree (*Litsea dealbata*) of the family Lauraceae **d :** a thorny bush (*Cudrania javanensis*) of the family Moraceae

**native myrtle** *n* **:** any of several Australian shrubs or trees that are felt to resemble the true myrtles: as **a :** BRUSH CHERRY 1 **b :** AUSTRALIAN MYRTLE **c :** BLUEBERRY 2a(2)

**na·tive·ness** *n* -ES **:** the quality or state of being native **:** NATURALNESS

**native olive** *n* **1 a :** an indigenous Australian olive (*Olea paniculata*) **b :** the fruit of this plant **2 :** an Australian ironwood (*Notelaea ligustrina*)

**native orange** *n* **1** *Austral* **:** NATIVE LIME 1 **2** *Austral* **:** NATIVE POMEGRANATE

**native peach** *n* **1** *Austral* **a :** QUANDONG **b :** the fruit of the quandong **2** *Austral* **:** EMU APPLE 1

**native pear** *n* **:** an Australian tree (*Xylomelum pyriforme*) of the family Proteaceae having a pear-shaped fruit with a thick woody epicarp

**native pheasant** *n* **:** LEIPOA

**native plum** *n* **1 :** any of several Australian trees that are felt to resemble the plums: as **a :** BLACK APPLE **b :** a Tasmanian tree (*Cenarrhenes nitida*) of the family Proteaceae **c :** a plant of the genus *Owenia* **2 :** the fruit of a native plum

**native pomegranate** *n* **1 :** any of several Australian plants of the genus *Capparis* **2 :** the edible fruit of a native pomegranate resembling the pomegranate

**native porcupine** *n, Austral* **:** ECHIDNA

**native potato** *n* **1 :** an Australian orchid (*Gastrodia sesamoides*) having tubers resembling potatoes **2 :** an Australian plant of the genus *Marsdenia*

**native quince** *n* **:** a small shrubby Australian tree (*Petalostigma quadriloculare*) that is related to the eucalypts and has a very bitter bark

**native rabbit** *n, Austral* **:** a bandicoot (*Thylacomys lagotis*)

**native rat** *n, NewZeal* **:** KIORE

**natives** *pl of* NATIVE

**native sarsaparilla** *n* **:** an Australian purple-flowered twining plant (*Kennedya monophylla*) of the family Leguminosae having roots sometimes used as a substitute for sarsaparilla

**native sloth** *n* **:** KOALA

**native son** *n* **:** NATIVE 3a

**native sparrow** *n* **:** either of two Australian weaverbirds (*Zonaeginthus oculatus* and *Z. bellus*)

**native state** *n* **:** a former territorial division of India not constituting an integral part of British India but ruled by its own prince with British advice and supervision

**native teak** *n* **:** either of two Australian trees: **a :** a flindersia (*Flindersia bennettiana*) that is native to New So. Wales and has been introduced into southern Africa as a shelter and timber tree **b :** FLINDOSA

**native thrush** *n* **:** an Australian whistler (*Pachycephala olivaceus*)

**native trout** *n* **1 a :** BROOK TROUT **b :** CUTTHROAT TROUT **2 :** a small pale green Australian salmonoid fish (*Galaxias attenuatus*)

**native turkey** *n* **:** PLAIN TURKEY

**native willow** *n* **:** any of several Australian trees having foliage resembling that of a willow: as **a :** BOOBYALLA **b :** COOBA **c :** POISONBERRY TREE **d :** WILGA

**native yam** *n* **:** an Australian yam (*Dioscorea transversa*)

**na·tiv·ism** \ˈnād·əˌvizəm, -ātə-\ *n* -S **1 :** the attitude or policy of favoring the native inhabitants of a country as against immigrants ⟨forces of racism and ~ —D.S.Myer⟩ ⟨a persistent ~ in American politics —D.D.McKean⟩; *specif* **:** such an attitude or policy held by the 19th century Native Americans ⟨the rise of ~ and eventually Know-Nothingism —Wallace Stegner⟩ **2 a :** the doctrine that the mind possesses elements of knowledge not derived from sensation **b :** a theory emphasizing heredity or bodily constitution in determining man's perceptions, attitudes, and behavior — compare EMPIRICISM, GENETICISM **3 :** a nativistic reaction of a usu. primitive people against acculturation

[1]**na·tiv·ist** \-ˌvəst\ *n* -S [[1]*native* + *-ist*] **:** one that believes in or advocates nativism ⟨a bigoted ~ who published feverish anti-immigration and anti-Catholic tracts —Marshall Davidson⟩

[2]**nativist** \"\ *adj* **1 :** of, having the characteristics of, or supporting political nativism ⟨the die-hard Know-Nothings . . . were both ~ and proslavery —M.M.Hunt⟩ ⟨old ~ prejudice against the . . . foreign businessman —*Springfield (Mass.) Republican*⟩ **2 :** of, relating to, or composed of nativists ⟨~ rural audiences in the south —W.G.Carleton⟩

**na·tiv·is·tic** \ˌ==ˈvistik, -tēk\ *adj* **1 :** NATIVIST ⟨the ~ tendencies of the Whig party —*Nation*⟩ **2 :** of, advocating, or having the characteristics of psychological nativism ⟨the traditional controversy between the ~ and empiristic theories of space perception —H.H.Price⟩ **3 :** of, being, or having the characteristics of a movement (as among a primitive people) advocating or advancing the perpetuation or reestablishment of native culture traits and a concomitant restriction or removal of foreign culture elements often accompanied by a strong messianic or ceremonial cult ⟨the ~ faith preaches the old values —C.K.Kluckhohn⟩

**na·tiv·i·ty** \nəˈtivəd·ē, nāˈ-, -ətē, -i\ *n* -ES [ME *nativite*, fr. MF *nativité*, fr. ML *nativitat-, nativitas* birth, birth of Christ, fr. LL, birth, fr. L *nativus* native + *-itat-, -itas* -ity — more at NATIVE] **1** *usu cap* **:** the birth or coming into the world of Christ — usu. used with *the* ⟨his sermons on the *Nativity* —R.H.Bainton⟩ **2** *usu cap* **a :** an annual church festival commemorating the birth of Christ **:** CHRISTMAS 1 **b :** an annual festival held in some churches to commemorate the birth of other religious figures (as the Virgin Mary and St. John the Baptist) **3 :** the process, fact, or circumstances (as time, place, or manner) of being born **:** BIRTH ⟨the country of one's ~⟩ ⟨I have served him from the hour of my ~ —Shak.⟩ **4 :** a horoscope at or of the time of one's birth **5 :** the fact or status of being born a native of a particular place ⟨the Yankee ~ of many Florida editors —*Amer. Guide Series: Fla.*⟩ ⟨percentage distribution of the population by ~ for Connecticut —*Amer. Guide Series: Conn.*⟩ **6** *usu cap* **:** a work of art (as a picture or relief sculpture) representing or symbolizing the earliest infancy of Christ

**nativity play** *n* **:** a play dealing with the nativity of Christ — compare PASSION PLAY

**na·tiv·ize** \ˈnād·əˌvīz\ *vt* -ED/-ING/-S [[1]*native* + *-ize*] **:** to modify in conformity with local customs or usages

**natl** *abbr* national

**natr-** *or* **natro-** *comb form* [G, fr. *natron*, fr. F — more at NATRON] **1 :** natron **2 :** sodium ⟨*natr*ium⟩ ⟨*natro*lite⟩ ⟨*natro*philite⟩

**nat·ri·cine** \ˈnatrəˌsīn, -ˌsən\ *n* -S [NL *Natric-, Natrix* + E *-ine*] **:** any of various predominantly aquatic snakes belonging to *Natrix* and closely related genera

**na·tri·um** \ˈnā·trēəm\ *n* -S [NL, fr. *natr-* + *-ium*] **:** SODIUM — symbol *Na*

**na·trix** \ˈnā·triks\ *n, cap* [NL, fr. L, water snake — more at ADDER] **:** a large widely distributed genus of colubrid aquatic snakes that includes all the true water snakes of No. America

**na·tro·alunite** \ˌnā·trō, ˌna·trō+\ *n* [*natr-* + *alunite*] **:** a mineral $NaAl_3(SO_4)_2(OH)_6$ consisting of a basic sulfate of aluminum and sodium isomorphous with alunite — called also *almerite*

**na·tro·chal·cite** \ˌnā·trōˈkalˌsīt, ˌna·-\ *n* -S [G *natrochalzit*, fr. *natro-* natr- + *chalz-* chalc- + *-it* -ite] **:** a mineral $NaCu_2(SO_4)_2(OH).H_2O$ consisting of a hydrous basic sodium copper sulfate

**na·tro·jarosite** \ˌnā·trō, ˌna·trō+\ *n* [*natr-* + *jarosite*] **:** a mineral $NaFe_3(SO_4)_2(OH)_6$ in which sodium takes the place of potassium in jarosite

**na·tro·lite** \ˈnā·trəˌlīt, ˈna·-\ *n* -S [G *natrolith*, fr. *natro-* natr- + *-lith* -lite] **:** a hydrous sodium aluminum silicate $Na_2Al_2Si_3O_{10}.2H_2O$ belonging to the zeolite family

**na·tro·montebrasite** \ˌnā·trō, ˌna·trō+\ *n* [F, fr. *natr-* + *montebrasite*] **:** a mineral (Na, Li)Al($PO_4$)(OH, F) consisting of a basic phosphate of sodium, lithium, and aluminum isomorphous with amblygonite and montebrasite

**na·tron** \ˈnāˌträn, ˈna-, -ˌtrən\ *n* -S [F, fr. Sp *natrón*, fr. Ar *natrūn*, fr. Gk *nitron* — more at NITER] **:** a hydrous sodium carbonate $Na_2CO_3.10H_2O$ occurring mainly in solution or solid and with other salts

**na·troph·i·lite** \nəˈträfəˌlīt\ *n* -S [*natr-* + *-phil* + *-ite*] **:** a mineral $NaMn(PO_4)$ consisting of phosphate of sodium and manganese almost isostructural with varulite but having sodium and manganese disordered

**nats** *pl of* NAT

**nat·te** \nəˈtā\ *n* -S [F *natté*, fr. past part. of *natter* to plait, braid, fr. *natte* mat, fr. LL *natta*, alter. of *matta* — more at MAT] **:** a basket weave made with contrasting colors in the warp and weft; *also* **:** a fabric with such a weave woven usu. from silk, rayon, and cotton

[1]**nat·ter** \ˈnad·ə(r), -atə-\ *vi* -ED/-ING/-S [alter. of *gnatter*] **1** *dial Eng* **:** to find fault **:** GRIPE **2** *chiefly Brit* **:** to talk a great deal but say little **:** CHATTER ⟨willing to sit for hours and ~ away about nothing —*Vancouver (Canada) Sun*⟩ ⟨~ to the neighbors' women, exchanging gossip —Peter Mayne⟩

[2]**natter** \"\ *n* -S *chiefly Brit* **:** a conversation usu. of a trivial nature **:** CHAT

**nat·ter·jack** \ˈnad·ə(r)ˌjak\ *n* [origin unknown] **:** a common brownish yellow toad (*Bufo calamita*) of western Europe having short hind legs and progressing by running rather than by hopping

**nat·tier blue** \nəˈtyā-\ *n* [after Jean Marc *Nattier* †1766 Fr. portrait painter] **:** a moderate azure

**nat·ti·ly** \ˈnad·ᵊlē\ *adv* **:** in a natty manner **:** SMARTLY ⟨everything seemed to be arranged so carefully and ~ —Hall Caine⟩

**nat·ti·ness** \-d·ēnəs\ *n* -ES **:** the quality or state of being natty **:** SMARTNESS ⟨his familiar ~ of attire —John Buchan⟩

**nat·tle** \ˈnatᵊl\ *vi* -ED/-ING/-S [imit.] *dial Eng* **:** to make a usu. slight rattling or tapping noise

**nat·tock** \ˈnad·ək\ *n* -S [origin unknown] **:** WEASEL LEMUR

**nat·ty** \ˈnad·|ē, -at|, |i\ *adj* -ER/-EST [perh. alter. of earlier *netty*, fr. [3]*net* + *-y*] **:** trimly neat and tidy **:** SMART, SPRUCE ⟨a glamorous air hostess in gray uniform and a ~ cap —*Blackwood's*⟩ ⟨a ~ marine captain —E.L.Beach⟩

[1]**na·tu·fi·an** \nəˈtüfēən\ *adj, usu cap* [Wadi en-*Natuf*, valley in Palestine + E *-ian*] **:** of, relating to, or having the characteristics of a food-gathering, cave-dwelling Mesolithic culture of Palestine characterized by microliths, composite tools of microliths, small bare zoomorphic carvings in bone or stone, and the use of sickles suggesting some agriculture

[2]**natufian** \"\ *n* -S *usu cap* **:** a Mesolithic cave dweller of Mount Carmel and other localities in Palestine

[1]**nat·u·ral** \ˈnach(ə)rəl + V *also* -chərl\ *adj* [ME, fr. MF *natural, naturel*, fr. L *naturalis*, fr. *natura* nature + *-alis* -al — more at NATURE] **1 :** based upon the innate moral feeling or inherent sense of right and wrong held to characterize mankind ⟨principles of equity and ~ justice —J.D.Johnson⟩ — see NATURAL LAW **2 a :** in accordance with or determined by nature **:** based upon the operations of the physical world ⟨~ year⟩ — see NATURAL LOGARITHM, NATURAL NUMBER; compare DAY 1, 2 **b :** having or constituting a classification or other method of arrangement based on features existing in nature **3 a** *chiefly dial* (1) **:** begotten as distinguished from adopted; *esp* **:** begotten in wedlock **:** LEGITIMATE ⟨all the children, whether male or female, ~ or adopted —Thomas Robinson⟩ (2) **:** being a relation by actual consanguinity or kinship by descent as distinguished from adoption ⟨any child . . . found guilty of cursing or striking his ~ parents —*Amer. Guide Series: Conn.*⟩ **b** (1) **:** born out of wedlock; *specif* **:** ILLEGITIMATE — see NATURAL CHILD (2) **:** being a relation by consanguinity as opposed to a legally recognized relationship **4 :** having an essential relationship with someone or something **:** possessing a normal connection with someone or something **:** consonant with the nature or character of someone or something ⟨his guilt is a ~ deduction from the facts⟩ **5 :** implanted or held to be implanted by nature **:** existing or present from birth **:** being part of the constitution of a person **:** not acquired **:** INBORN, INNATE ⟨some ~ inability to observe —Ellen Glasgow⟩ ⟨our ~ abhorrence of war —F.D.Roosevelt⟩ — see NATURAL PARTS 2 **6 :** of, relating to, or concerned with nature as an object of study and research ⟨some ~ observations made —*Philosophical Transactions*⟩ — see NATURAL HISTORY, NATURAL PHILOSOPHY, NATURAL SCIENCE **7 :** having a specified character by nature ⟨~ fool⟩ ⟨~ idiot⟩ ⟨~ pacer⟩ ⟨a ~ leader⟩ **8 :** WHITE 3c ⟨~ magic⟩ **9 a :** occurring in conformity with the ordinary course of nature **:** not supernatural, marvelous, or miraculous ⟨the ~ process of growth —H.W.H.King⟩ ⟨a world where ~ forces overwhelmed him —R.B.West⟩ ⟨the rate of ~ increase of the . . . population was quite high —Kingsley Davis⟩ ⟨~ causes⟩ **b :** having a normal or usual character **:** not exceptional ⟨digressions . . . ~ in a work taken down from oral dictation —G.F.Hudson⟩ **10 :** having a relationship with something by reason of the conditions, events, or circumstances of the case or in line with normal experience ⟨theory and practice are a kind of ~ opposites —C.E.Montague⟩ ⟨the ~ enemies of originality —Clive Bell⟩ **11 :** characterized by qualities (as warm and genuine feelings, affection, or gratitude) held to be part of the nature of man ⟨a wicked old screw . . . why wasn't he ~ in his lifetime —Charles Dickens⟩ **12** *obs* **:** NATURAL-BORN ⟨~ subjects⟩ **13 a :** planted or growing by itself **:** not cultivated or introduced artificially ⟨~ grass⟩ **b :** existing in or produced by nature **:** consisting of objects so existing or produced **:** not artificial (as in form or construction) ⟨agricultural commodities in their raw and ~ state —*U.S. Code*⟩ ⟨these ~ deposits of potassium salts —A.C.Morrison⟩ ⟨the vast ~ wealth of the country —William Tate⟩ **14 a :** being in a state of nature without spiritual enlightenment **:** UNREGENERATE ⟨the ~ man receiveth not the things of the Spirit of God —1 Cor 2:14 (AV)⟩ **b :** living in or as if in a state of nature untouched by the influences of civilization and society ⟨an apotheosis of ~ man, with consequent exaltation of appetite —W.L.Grossman⟩ **15 a :** having a physical or real existence as contrasted with one that is spiritual, intellectual, or psychical ⟨the ~ world⟩ **b :** of, relating to, or operating in the physical as opposed to the spiritual world ⟨~ laws . . . merely describe what actually happens —Maurice Cranston & J.W.N.Watkins⟩ **16** *obs* **:** NATIVE-BORN **17 a :** closely resembling the object imitated **:** true to nature **:** according to life ⟨the Israeli flag . . . illustrated in ~ colors —K.B.Stiles⟩ ⟨doves ~ do not have little crests —F.M. Ford⟩ ⟨drawn to ~ scale⟩ **b :** having the ease or simplicity of nature **:** free from artificiality, affectation, or constraint **:** springing from true sentiment **:** EASY, SIMPLE ⟨successful people are genuine and ~ rather than synthetic and imitative — —Gilbert Seldes⟩ ⟨at ease with us . . . , always spontaneous and ~ —Dorothy Bussy⟩ **c :** having a form or appearance found in nature ⟨~ hair⟩ **18 a :** having neither flats nor sharps — used of a key or scale in music ⟨the ~ scale of C major⟩ **b :** being neither sharped nor flatted — used of a musical note or tone **c :** having the pitch as indicated in musical notation modified by the natural (sense 7a) **d :** produced without aid of stops, valves, slides, or other supplementary devices — used of a harmonic or tone from a wind and stringed instrument **e :** not falsetto — used of a man's singing voice **19 a :** not being the joker or a wild card — used of a playing card **b :** containing no wild card — used of a combination of cards **20 :** of the color natural

**syn** SIMPLE, UNAFFECTED, ARTLESS, UNSOPHISTICATED, INGENUOUS, NAÏVE: NATURAL stresses easy freedom from the artificial, stiff, constrained, or formal ⟨the fact is that a poetic language which appears *natural* to one age will appear unnatural or artificial to another —C.D.Lewis⟩ ⟨the poor man had no *natural*, spontaneous human speech . . . he habitually expressed himself in a book-learned language —Willa Cather⟩ SIMPLE indicates lack of duplicity and artifice in one's character or thought along with suggestion of lack of complexity and artificiality ⟨the straight and *simple*, the homespun, *simple*, valiant English Truth —H.G.Wells⟩ ⟨*simple* and earnest people, however, being accustomed to speak from their genuine impulses, cannot easily, as craftier men do, avoid the subject which they have at heart —Nathaniel Hawthorne⟩ UNAFFECTED stresses lack of affectation and indicates a simple naturalness without connoting much else ⟨his simple manners and *unaffected* friendliness were attractive —A.W.Long⟩ ⟨she's the best-natured and most *unaffected* young creature —W.M. Thackeray⟩ ARTLESS indicates freedom from calculation about the effects of what one says or does and a consequent ease ⟨her simple, *artless* behaviour, and modest kindness of demeanour, won all their unsophisticated hearts —W.M.Thackeray⟩ ⟨almost every turn in the *artless* little maid's prattle touched a new mood in him —George Meredith⟩ UNSOPHISTICATED stresses lack of knowledge of and experience with worldly matters bringing discretion, reserve, adroitness, smoothness ⟨not elegant or artificial, too much the *unsophisticated* child of nature —Rose Macaulay⟩ ⟨a race almost wholly *unsophisticated* by intercourse with strangers —Herman Melville⟩ INGENUOUS indicates lack of any subtlety, dissimulation, calculation; it indicates unrestrained and unmasked frankness ⟨Father had set a dog on him. A less *ingenuous* character would be silent about such passages —H.G.Wells⟩ ⟨"yet I've done very well this year. Oh yes," he went on with *ingenuous* enthusiasm —Thomas Hardy⟩ NAÏVE stresses lack of worldly wisdom and sophistication with resulting freshness, candor, or innocence untutored and unchecked by convention ⟨the future arch master of love proved to be a *naïve* and candid swain at the beginning of his career —P.H.Lang⟩ ⟨that *naïve* patriotism which leads every race to regard itself as evidently superior to every other —J.W.Krutch⟩ **syn** see in addition REGULAR

**²natural** \"\ *n* -s [partly fr. MF *naturel, natural,* fr. *naturel, natural,* adj.; partly fr. E ¹*natural*] **1** *obs* **:** a native inhabitant of a place (as a region or country) **2 naturals** *pl, obs* **:** the gifts, powers, and abilities with which a person is endowed by nature ⟨a person of excellent ~s —Theophilus Gale⟩ **3 :** one born without the usual powers of reason and understanding **:** a half-witted person **:** IDIOT ⟨with the vacant grin of a ~ —Charles Gibbon⟩ **4 naturals** *pl, obs* **:** the objects of the natural world **:** natural as distinguished from unnatural or supernatural things **5** *obs* **:** the natural character or disposition of a person **:** the natural form or condition of an animate object (as a flower) **6 naturals** *pl, obs* **a :** a natural state or condition ⟨in their pure ~s, they were wonderfully abstemious —Thomas Fuller⟩ **b :** a state of nakedness — usu. used in the phrase *in one's pure naturals* **7 a :** the character or sign ♮ placed on any degree of the musical staff to nullify the effect of a preceding sharp or flat **b :** a note or tone affected by the natural sign **8 :** a result or combination that immediately wins the stake in a game: as **a :** a throw of 7 or 11 on the first cast in craps **b :** BLACKJACK 6c **c :** a count of 8 or 9 in the first two cards at baccarat **d :** RANCHE **9 :** something that is natural as distinguished from artificial or supernatural ⟨all culture is thus . . . a negation of the ~ —Leon Livingstone⟩ ⟨this social philosophy, based like contemporary science on the ~ —*New Republic*⟩ ⟨study the supernatural as the philosopher studies the ~ —Frederic Myers⟩ **10 :** a shot in billiards held to be easy because the ball can be pocketed directly or in carom billiards by a simple angle shot **11 :** a variable color averaging a yellowish gray that is lighter and slightly redder than average sand and redder and deeper than ivory tint **12 a :** one having natural skills, talents, or abilities often to an unusual degree and usu. requiring no special training or development for success in a specific line of endeavor ⟨as an actor, he was a ~⟩ **b :** something that by its very nature is or is likely to become an immediate and genuine success ⟨as much a ~ as rubber on the end of a pencil —Irving Kolodin⟩ ⟨fight fans discussed the . . . rematch as a ~ —*Newsweek*⟩ ⟨the idea of this book is a ~ —Carl Bridenbaugh⟩ **c :** one constituting an easy, appropriate, and usu. successful selection for a specific purpose by possession of various natural qualities ⟨the review characterizing some new novel as a ~ for pictures —P.S. Nathan⟩ ⟨the legal process . . . is a ~ for delaying tactics —Titus Lord⟩ ⟨fearless and cool in the face of disaster, he was a ~ for the job —*Newsweek*⟩ **13 :** a close pase in bullfighting done with the muleta in the left hand—compare DERECHAZO **syn** see FOOL

**natural allegiance** *n* **:** the allegiance owed to his country by a native-born subject or citizen — compare ALLEGIANCE 1 b (2), LOCAL ALLEGIANCE

**natural area** *n* **:** a geographical area (as in a city) having a physical and cultural individuality developed through natural growth rather than design or planning

**natural astrology** *n* **:** a branch of astrology formerly concerned with the prediction of events in inanimate nature and being in part legitimate astronomical science

**natural bark** *n* **:** virgin cinchona bark; *specif* **:** the bark first removed from the tree in alternate longitudinal strips — compare MOSSED BARK, RENEWED BARK

**natural-born** \¦=(ˌ)=¦=\ *adj* **:** having a specified status or character by birth ⟨a *natural-born* describer with a memory for details —Ernestine Evans⟩ ⟨she's a *natural-born* nurse —Winston Churchill⟩; *esp* **:** having the legal status of citizen or subject ⟨no person except a *natural-born* citizen . . . shall be eligible to the office of president —*U. S. Constitution*⟩ — compare NATIVE-BORN

**natural bridge** *n* **:** a usu. arch formation created by nature and resembling a bridge

**natural cement** *n* **:** a hydraulic cement made from a naturally occurring limestone containing up to 25 percent argillaceous material — compare PORTLAND CEMENT

**natural child** *n* **1 :** a child born out of lawful wedlock **:** an illegitimate child **:** BASTARD 1 **2 :** a child under Louisiana law that is born out of lawful wedlock but to parents capable of entering into lawful marriage at the time of the birth and that unlike a bastard may be legitimized

**natural childbirth** *n* **:** a system of management of parturition in which prenatal reeducation and psychologic conditioning largely replace the use of anesthesia, sedation, or surgical intervention in the course of normal childbirth

natural bridge

**natural day** *n* **1 :** DAY 1 **2 :** DAY 2

**natural death** *n* **:** death occurring in the course of nature and from natural causes (as age or disease) as opposed to accident or violence ⟨Hindu orthodoxy opposes any cattle slaughter . . . on the grounds sacred beasts should be allowed *natural deaths* —*Associated Press*⟩ ⟨the industry died a *natural death* —Ada Darling⟩ — compare CIVIL DEATH, NATURAL LIFE

**natural dualism** *n* **:** NATURAL REALISM

**natural dye** *n* **:** a dye (as logwood or cochineal) from a plant or animal source — see DYE table I

**na·tu·ra·le** \¦nätü¦rälā\ *adv (or adj)* [It, natural, fr. L *naturalis* — more at NATURAL] **:** in a natural manner — used as a direction in music to cancel a previous direction

**natural english** *n, usu cap E* **:** RUNNING ENGLISH

**nat·u·ral·esque** \¦nach(ə)rə¦lesk *also* -chər¦-\ *adj* **:** faithfully imitating nature **:** conforming closely to natural details (as of objects represented) ⟨~ designs of birds⟩

**natural frequency** *n* **1 :** the frequency or wavelength with which a circuit or part of a circuit is in tune **2 :** the lowest frequency or highest wavelength with which an antenna without added capacity or inductance is in tune — called also NATURAL WAVELENGTH

**natural function** *n* **:** a trigonometric function as distinguished from its logarithm

**natural gas** *n* **:** gas issuing from the earth's crust through natural openings or bored wells; *esp* **:** any of various combustible gaseous mixtures that when in the dry state contain largely methane and in the wet state in association with petroleum contain also higher hydrocarbons (as ethane, propane, butanes, and pentanes) and that are used chiefly as fuels directly or by recovery of gasoline or conversion to other liquid fuels and as raw materials for the manufacture of carbon black and many other products (as nitroparaffins and synthesis gas) — see CASINGHEAD GAS

**natural gasoline** *n* **:** a very volatile gasoline recovered from natural gas and used in blending with gasoline from petroleum and other sources to increase the volatility — called also *casinghead gasoline*

**natural gender** *n* **:** the phenomena in a language that resemble grammatical gender but are not ⟨the use of the pronoun *she* in the sentence *the girl may do as she likes* is an instance of *natural gender,* since the choice of the pronoun *she* is not determined by the noun *girl* but by the actual sex of the person to whom the noun *girl* refers⟩

**natural glass** *n* **:** a silica-rich noncrystalline solid of either volcanic or cosmic origin — compare OBSIDIAN, TEKTITE

**natural guardian** *n* **1 :** a guardian by natural relationship having custody of the person but not the property of a minor and under common law being constituted by the father if fit and upon his death or incapacity the mother and in the absence of lawful parents the grandparents or other close relatives **2 :** the person who is in fact exercising parental authority over a minor as distinguished from a guardian appointed by a court to have custody of the person or property of the minor — called also *guardian by nature;* compare GUARDIAN FOR NURTURE, GUARDIAN IN SOCAGE

**natural harmonic** *n* **1 :** a harmonic produced on an open string of a stringed musical instrument — compare ARTIFICIAL HARMONIC **2 :** one of the overtones produced without the use of a slide or valves on a wind instrument

**natural hexachord** *n* **:** the hexachord beginning on C

**natural historian** *n* **:** a student of or writer on natural history

**natural history** *n* **1 :** a treatise on any aspect of natural history but esp. on ecology ⟨edited a *natural history* of spiders⟩ **2 a :** the natural development of something (as of an organism or disease) over a period of time ⟨increasing knowledge of the *natural histories* of tumors —H.S.N.Greene⟩ **b :** a chronicle of the natural development of something over a period of time usu. presenting an assemblage of principal facts and characteristics ⟨the plays are a shrewd *natural history* of . . . Bohemian New York —Francis Fergusson⟩ **3 a :** a former branch of knowledge embracing the study, description, and classification of natural objects (as animals, plants, and minerals) and thus including the modern sciences of zoology, botany, and mineralogy in so far as they existed at that time **b :** a modern branch of inquiry usu. restricted to a consideration of these subjects from an amateur or popular rather than a technical and professional point of view

**natural horn** *n* **:** the simplest form of the horn consisting of a tapering brass tube with mouthpiece and bell curved upon itself and without keys or valves and producing only those tones appearing in the harmonic series

natural horn

**natural immunity** *n* **:** immunity possessed by a group (as a race, strain, or species) and occurring in an individual as part of its natural biologic makeup — compare ACQUIRED IMMUNITY

**nat·u·ral·ism** \ˈnach(ə)rəˌlizəm *also* -chərˌ-\ *n* -s **1 :** action, inclination, or thought based on natural desires and instincts alone **2 :** a theory that expands conceptions drawn from the natural sciences into a world view and that denies that anything in reality has a supernatural or more than natural significance; *specif* **:** the doctrine that cause-and-effect laws (as of physics and chemistry) are adequate to account for all phenomena and that teleological conceptions of nature are invalid **3 a :** a theory that art or literature should conform exactly to nature or depict every appearance of the subject that comes to the artist's attention; *specif* **:** a theory in literature emphasizing the role of heredity and environment upon human life and character development **b :** the quality, rendering, or expression of art or literature executed according to this theory **:** close adherence to nature — compare REALISM **4 :** a doctrine that religious truth is derived from nature and not from miraculous or supernatural revelation **:** a denial of the miraculous and supernatural in religion **5 :** a view in ethics that distinctions between good and bad and right and wrong can be made on the basis of natural phenomena or that ethical terms and statements can be expressed in terms of or be reduced to nonnormative factual terms and statements

**¹nat·u·ral·ist** \-ˌləst\ *n* -s [MF *naturaliste,* fr. *natural, naturel* natural + *-iste* -ist — more at NATURAL] **1 a :** an adherent of naturalism (as in theology or philosophy) **b :** one that believes in, practices, or teaches naturalism (as in art or literature) **2 a** *archaic* **:** one versed in natural science **:** NATURAL PHILOSOPHER **b :** a student of natural history; *esp* **:** a field biologist in contrast to a laboratory worker

**²naturalist** \"\ *adj* **:** NATURALISTIC ⟨belong to the ~ school, an offshoot of realism —Marjorie Wheeler⟩ ⟨the ~ imprint upon a work of fiction —Philip Rahv⟩

**nat·u·ral·is·tic** \¦nach(ə)rə¦listik, -tēk *also* -chər¦-\ *adj* **:** of, characterized by, or in accordance with naturalism ⟨more ~ behavior⟩ ⟨in ~ colors⟩ ⟨the school of ~ writers⟩ ⟨a ~ interpretation of the deity —Helmut Kuhn⟩

**nat·u·ral·is·ti·cal·ly** \-tək(ə)lē, -tēk-, -li\ *adv* **:** in a naturalistic style or manner ⟨animals shown ~ and humans fantastically —*African Abstracts*⟩ ⟨a ~ constructed novel⟩

**naturalistic fallacy** *n* **:** the process of defining ethical terms (as the good) in nonethical descriptive terms (as happiness, pleasure, and utility)

**nat·u·ral·i·ty** \ˌnachəˈraləd·ē\ *n* -ES [MF *naturalité,* fr. LL *naturalitat-, naturalitas,* fr. L *naturalis* natural + *-itat-, -itas* -ity — more at NATURAL] **1** *obs* **:** natural quality or character **2 :** natural feeling or behavior ⟨to rouse lethargic friends into ~ —Jane W. Carlyle⟩

**nat·u·ral·iza·tion** \ˌnach(ə)rəl|əˈzāshən |,ˌlīˈ- *also* -chər|\ *n* -s [MF *naturalisation,* fr. *naturaliser* to naturalize + *-ation*] **:** the act or process of naturalizing **:** the state of being naturalized ⟨Australian citizenship may also be acquired by . . . ~ —T.N.M.Buesst⟩ ⟨the ~ of . . . these new terms in English —A.E.Bestor⟩

**nat·u·ral·ize** \ˈnach(ə)rəˌlīz *also* -chərˌ-\ *vb* -ED/-ING/-S [MF *naturaliser,* fr. *natural, naturel* natural + *-iser* -ize — more at NATURAL] *vt* **1 a :** to establish in new surroundings **:** introduce into a new area or into common use ⟨he *naturalized* among us the Renaissance manner which he had learned —F.J.Mather⟩ ⟨these tales . . . had become *naturalized,* developed, adapted to American settings —DeLancey Ferguson⟩ **b :** to receive or adopt into the vernacular language ⟨some Latin phrases . . . have become completely *naturalized* —A.H. Weston⟩ **c :** to cause to adapt and grow or multiply as if native ⟨several Old World weeds have become *naturalized* here⟩ ⟨the steelhead and rainbow trout have become *naturalized* . . . in the Lake Superior region —*Amer. Guide Series: Minn.*⟩ **d :** to plant (as a flowering bulb) in sod so as to give an effect of wild growth ⟨*naturalized* daffodils in open shade⟩ **2 :** to make less artificial or conventional **:** to bring into accord or conformity with nature **3 :** to confer the rights and privileges of a native subject or citizen on **:** admit (an alien) to the rights and status of citizenship ⟨all persons born or *naturalized* in the United States . . . are citizens —*U. S. Constitution*⟩ **4** *obs* **:** to render familiar by custom and habit ⟨custom has *naturalized* his labor to him —Robert South⟩ **5 a :** to treat as natural as opposed to supernatural **:** place on a natural basis ⟨willing to contradict the falsity and thus ~ the miracle —Jeremy Bentham⟩ **b :** to express in natural terms esp. in a manner not conflicting with scientific theories ⟨find a way to ~ the idealistic traditions —J.H.Randall⟩ ~ *vi* **1 :** to become naturalized **:** become as if native **2 :** to carry on investigations in natural history

**natural key** *n* **:** a key used to determine the name of a plant or animal and based on genetic relationships esp. as shown by chromosome counts — compare ARTIFICIAL KEY

**natural language** *n* **:** a language that is the native speech of a people (as English, Tamil, Samoan) — compare ARTIFICIAL LANGUAGE

**natural law** *n* **1 :** a body of law derived from nature and binding upon human society in the absence of or in addition to institutional law: as **a :** the principles of justice discernible (as by the Stoics) by right reason **b :** JUS GENTIUM **c :** the part of divine law discernible (as by the Scholastics) to reason but not directly revealed **d :** a set of principles derived from an analysis of human societies and based (as by 18th century rationalists) principally upon certain natural rights having prior validity to institutional law **e :** the body of rules or customs derived from the general development of mankind and essential to the maintenance of human society **2 :** a specific principle belonging to the total body of natural law **3 :** LAW OF NATURE

**natural life** *n* [ME] **:** the period of a person's earthly existence terminated by natural as opposed to civil death

**natural logarithm** *n* **:** a logarithm with *e* as a base

**nat·u·ral·ly** \ˈnach(ə)rəlē, -li *also* -chərl-\ *adv* [ME, fr. *natural* + *-ly*] **1 :** by nature **:** by natural or inherent character **:** by native endowment **:** by innate tendency or feeling ⟨one child . . . was ~ good —Margaret Deland⟩ ⟨poetry or music . . . may be said to be ~ pleasing —Joshua Reynolds⟩ ⟨her face, ~ pale as marble —Charlotte Brontë⟩ **2 a :** according to or by the operation of the laws of nature ⟨the snow loads will begin to slide off the ~ drooping branches —G.R.Stewart⟩ ⟨the changes which are ~ wrought by time —H.F.Tozer⟩ **b :** as a natural result or consequence **:** as might be expected from the circumstances ⟨the doomed retainers . . . ~ bewailed their sad fate —A.M.Young⟩ ⟨its insular situation . . . led ~ to the seafaring activities —Kemp Malone⟩ ⟨money flows ~ to those who can produce something of value —W.J.Reilly⟩ **3 :** in a natural manner ⟨she did not seem to die ~ —Ann Radcliffe⟩ ⟨you will feel your body weight shift ~ to the left leg —Bob Nichols⟩ **4 a :** by natural growth **:** without cultivation **:** without the use of art or effort **:** SPONTANEOUSLY ⟨her hair curls ~⟩ ⟨an older and more ~ wooded area —*Amer. Guide Series: Minn.*⟩ **b :** INDIGENOUSLY ⟨the cypress grows ~ in the southeastern U. S.⟩ **5 :** with truth to nature or life **:** in a lifelike manner **:** REALISTICALLY ⟨the artist who represents objects ~⟩ **6 :** with ease and simplicity **:** without affectation ⟨write ~ and spontaneously, just as you'd thank your friend in person —Barbara Peterson⟩

**natural magnet** *n* **:** MAGNET 1a

**natural minor scale** *n* **:** a minor scale with the diatonic intervals being whole steps except those half-steps between 2–3 and 5–6 and corresponding in pattern to the Aeolian church mode — compare HARMONIC MINOR SCALE, MELODIC MINOR SCALE

**nat·u·ral·ness** *n* -ES **1** *obs* **:** natural feeling, conduct, or sympathy **2 :** the quality or state of being natural ⟨the spontaneous ~ . . . of his manner —Frank Budgen⟩

**natural number** *n* **:** any one of the numbers 1, 2, 3, 4, etc. **:** a positive integer

**natural order** *n* **1 :** the orderly system comprising the physical universe and functioning according to natural as distinguished from human or supernatural laws **2 :** FAMILY 6 a — not now used technically

**natural parts** *n pl* **1** *obs* **:** GENITALIA **2** *archaic* **:** native ability ⟨a rough man, with good *natural parts* —Horace Walpole⟩

**natural period** *n* **:** the period of one complete oscillation of a body or system

**natural person** *n* **:** a human being as distinguished in law from an artificial or juristic person ⟨extended to corporations the rights and immunities guaranteed to *natural persons* —G.W. Johnson⟩ — compare CORPORATION 3

**natural philosopher** *n* **:** one that studies or is skilled in natural philosophy

**natural philosophy** *n* [ME] **:** the study of nature in general; *specif* **:** NATURAL SCIENCE — compare MENTAL PHILOSOPHY, MORAL PHILOSOPHY

**natural porcelain** *n* **:** a porcelain (as Chinese porcelain) made from a single raw material

**natural premium** *n* **:** the amount required to meet the mortality cost of life insurance for each particular year and increasing from year to year for any given unit of protection

**natural price** *n* **:** a price which is determined by the costs of production and about which the market price can oscillate

**natural pruning** *n* **:** a natural falling or dropping off of branches and twigs of trees and shrubs esp. as caused by suppression or death of branches and twigs — compare ABSCISSION 2

**natural rate of interest :** the rate of interest at which the demand for funds and the supply of savings exactly agree

**natural realism** *n* **:** a doctrine (as elaborated by the philosophers of the Scottish school) that perception gives direct and indubitable evidence of the independent existence of both mind and matter — called also *commonsense realism*

**natural religion** *n* **:** a religion validated on the basis of human reason and experience apart from miraculous or supernatural revelation; *specif* **:** a religion that is universally discernible by all men through the use of human reason apart from any special revelation — compare REVEALED RELIGION

**natural resin** *n* **:** an unmodified resin (as a copal or a dammar) from a natural source (as a tree) **:** RESIN 1 a — distinguished from *synthetic resin*

**natural resources** *n pl* **:** capacities (as native wit) or materials (as mineral deposits and waterpower) supplied by nature

**natural right** *n* **:** a right conferred upon man by natural law ⟨a *natural right* . . . would hold in the absence of organized government —Lucius Garvin⟩ — compare LEGAL RIGHT

**natural rubber** *n* **:** rubber or rubber latex from a plant (esp. *Hevea brasiliensis*) **:** RUBBER 2a — distinguished from *synthetic rubber*

**naturals** *pl of* NATURAL

**natural science** *n* **:** branches of science (as physics, chemistry, biology) that deal with matter, energy, and their interrelations and transformations or with objectively measurable phenomena

**natural selection** *n* **:** a natural process tending to cause the survival of those individuals or groups best adjusted to the conditions under which they live, resulting from the interaction of the organism in its entirety with all the factors of the environmental complex although any one factor may appear to be decisive for survival or extinction in particular circumstances, and recognized today as a mechanism equally important for the perpetuation of desirable genetic qualities and for the elimination of undesirable as these are brought forward by recombination or mutation of genes — compare DARWINISM, MACROEVOLUTION, MENDEL'S LAWS, MICROEVOLUTION

**natural slope** *n* **:** the slope assumed by a mass of earth thrown up into a heap

**natural spirits** *n pl, obs* **:** a vaporous principle formerly supposed to arise from the blood and exert control over the functions of nutrition, growth, and reproduction

**natural steel** *n* **:** steel made by the direct refining of cast iron in a refinery or (as wootz) by a direct process from the ore

**natural system** *n* **:** a biological classification based upon morphological and anatomical relationships and affinities considered in the light of phylogeny and embryology; *specif* **:** a system in botany other than the artificial or sexual system established by Linnaeus

**natural theologian** *n* **:** a theologian who uses the methodology of natural theology

**natural theology** *n* **:** theology deriving its knowledge of God from the study of nature independent of special revelation

**natural virtue** *n* **:** one of the four cardinal virtues prudence, justice, temperance, or fortitude distinguished in scholasticism from the three theological virtues

**natural wavelength** *n* **:** NATURAL FREQUENCY

**natural wine** *n* **:** TABLE WINE

**¹na·ture** \ˈnāchə(r)\ *n* -s [ME, fr. MF, fr. L *natura,* fr. *natus,* (past part. of *nasci* to be born) + *-ura* -ure — more at NATION] **1** *dial Eng* **:** normal and characteristic quality, strength, vigor, or resiliency ⟨she cooked the meat till it lost all its ~⟩ **2 a :** the essential character or constitution of something ⟨the ~ of the controversy⟩ ⟨inquire into the ~ of heredity —Theodosius Dobzhansky⟩; *esp* **:** the essence or ultimate form of something **b :** the distinguishing qualities or properties of something ⟨the ~ of mathematics⟩ ⟨the ~ of a literary movement⟩ **3 a :** the fundamental character, disposition, or temperament of a living being usu. innate and unchangeable ⟨it was in his ~ to look after others —F.A.Swinnerton⟩ ⟨devotion that it was not in her ~ to return —Naomi Lewis⟩ **b :** the fundamental character, disposition, or temperament of mankind as a whole **:** HUMAN NATURE b ⟨not interested in any particular man . . . but in the ~ of man —Peter Dunne⟩ **c** (1) **:** a specified kind of individual character, disposition, or temperament ⟨his kindly ~⟩ (2) **:** a being possessing or characterized by such a specified character, disposition, or temperament ⟨who, like so many buoyant ~s, had a talent for worrying —S.H.Adams⟩ **4 :** a creative and controlling agent, force, or principle operating in something and determining wholly or chiefly its constitution, development, and well-being: **a :** such a force or agency in the universe acting as a creative guiding intelligence **:** a set of principles held to be established for the regulation of the universe or observed in its operation **b :** an inner driving or prompting force (as instinct, appetite, desire) or the sum of such forces in an individual **5 :** a life-giving or health-giving force in an animate being **6 :** kind, order, or general character ⟨most of his public acts are of a ceremonial ~ —*London Calling*⟩ ⟨island songs of a Hawaiian ~ —Eve Langley⟩ **7 :** the qualities, characteristics, properties, organs, and functions that together make up the vital being of a human being or other organism: **a :** such organs or functions requiring nourishment **b :** an excretory organ or function — usu. used in the phrase *call of nature* **8 :** normality esp. as prescribed by law for sexual relations — usu. used in the phrase *against nature* ⟨their women did change the natural use into that which is against ~ —Rom. 1:26 (AV)⟩; compare CRIME AGAINST NATURE **9 :** feeling (as kindliness or affection) that is genuine, spontaneous, or unstudied in expression **:** NATURALNESS 2 ⟨that no compunctious visitings of ~ shake my fell purpose —Shak.⟩ **10 a (1) :** the created world in its entirety **(2) :** the totality of physical reality exclusive of things mental **b :** the total system of spatiotemporal phenomena and events that can be explained by other occurrences in the same system **11 :** the state of an unregenerate soul ⟨the difference between a state of ~ and a state of grace —Robert South⟩ ⟨the congenital ~ of men is evil, the goodness in them acquired —E.R.Hughes⟩ **12 a :** a theoretical condition or stage of existence usu. held to reveal man in his original or proper state: as (1) **:** the normal and ideal character both of particular things and of the universe as a whole sometimes equated with reason and the rational ⟨the full meaning of the Stoic injunction that we live according to ~ —Frank Thilly⟩ (2) **:** a simple, undomesticated, uncivilized mode of life among primitive men having few wants and obligations **:** a state of existence preceding the foundation of organized society **b :** a simplified mode of life esp. as lived out of doors apart from communities and other civilizing and restraining influences ⟨escape from civilization and get back to ~⟩ **13 :** substance or essence that is the principle of specific proper acts or operations ⟨the union of two ~s in Christ⟩ ⟨in the Trinity, three persons in one divine ~⟩ **14 :** the genetically controlled qualities of an organism ⟨~ . . . modified by nurture —E.G.Conklin⟩ — compare NURTURE **15 :** a particular order of existence or of existing things that is the subject matter of art: as **a :** one having an unchanged as contrasted with a developed, ordered, perfected, or man-made character **b :** real and objective existence **:** the world of mind and matter external to an observer **:** reality as observed **c :** the aspect of out-of-doors (as a landscape) **:** natural scenery **syn** see TYPE

**²nature** \"\ *vi* -ED/-ING/-S [ML *naturare*, fr. L *natura*] **:** to give to each thing its specific nature

**³nature** \"\, *in sense 2* nə'tü(ə)r\ *adj* [¹*nature*] **1 :** of or relating to nature **2** [F, plain, unadulterated (used of food or drink), fr. *nature*, n.] **:** BRUT

**na·tured** \ˈnāchə(r)d\ *adj* [¹*nature* + *-ed*] **:** having a specified nature, temper, or disposition ⟨others, similarly ~, will not permit him . . . to do this —Herbert Spencer⟩ — usu. used in combination ⟨*good-natured*⟩ ⟨*ill-natured*⟩

**nature faker** *n* **:** one (as a writer) that misrepresents facts about nature usu. attributing to animals traits or habits which they are not known to possess

**nature philosophy** *n* **:** NATURAL PHILOSOPHY; *esp* **:** an ancient Grecian and Renaissance philosophy undertaking to explain phenomena by natural causes and without recourse to mythical beings

**nature print** *n* **:** a print made by nature printing

**nature printing** *n* **:** a process in which an object (as a leaf or piece of lace) is pressed into a plane surface (as of soft metal) to make either a direct printing surface or a matrix

**nature study** *n* **:** a study of the objects and phenomena of nature (as birds, flowers, minerals, and weather) usu. on an amateur or superficial basis ⟨botany is taught in every high school and *nature study* in the grades —*Amer. Botanist*⟩

**na·tur·ism** \ˈnāchə,rizəm\ *n* -s **1 :** NATURALISM **2 :** a form of religious belief and practice characterized by a worship of usu. personified powers of nature — compare ANIMISM **3 :** NUDISM

**na·tur·ist** \-rəst\ *n* -s **:** a follower of nature; *specif* **:** a believer in or adherent of naturism

**na·tur·is·tic** \ˌ==ˈristik\ *adj* **:** of, relating to, or resembling naturism

**na·tur·o·path** \ˈnāchərə,path, ˈnach-\ *n* -s [*nature* + *-o-* + *-path*] **:** a practitioner of naturopathy

**na·tur·o·path·ic** \ˌ===ˈpathik\ *adj* **:** of, relating to, or by means of naturopathy

**na·tur·op·a·thy** *also* **na·ture·op·a·thy** \ˌnāchəˈräpəthē, ˌnach-\ *n* -ES [*nature* + *-o-* + *-pathy*] **:** a system of treatment of disease emphasizing assistance to nature and sometimes including the use of various medicinal substances (as herbs, vitamins, and salts) and certain physical means (as manipulation and electrical treatment)

**na·tya** \ˈnätyə\ *n* -s [Skt *nāṭya*; prob. akin to Skt *nṛtyati* he dances] **:** the theatrical dance art of India originating in the temple and still devoted largely to the enactment of divine epics and embracing an elaborate system of body postures, hand gestures, and foot movements

**¹nau·co·rid** \ˈnökərəd, -ˌrid\ *adj* [NL *Naucoridae*] **:** of or relating to the Naucoridae

**²naucorid** \"\ *n* -s **:** a bug of the family Naucoridae

**nau·cor·i·dae** \nöˈkȯrə,dē, -kär-\ *n pl, cap* [NL, fr. *Naucoris*, type genus + *-idae*] **:** a widely distributed family of aquatic predaceous hemipterous insects comprising the water creepers and having the body broad, oval, and flat and the front femora greatly enlarged

**nau·co·ris** \ˈnökərəs\ *n, cap* [NL, fr. Gk *naus* ship + *koris* bedbug — more at NAVE, COREIDAE] **:** the type genus of the family Naucoridae comprising water creepers of Europe and Asia

**nau·cra·tes** \ˈnökrə,tēz\ *n, cap* [NL, fr. LGk *naukratēs* pilot fish, fr. Gk *naus* ship + *-kratēs* ruler (fr. *kratos* strength, power) — more at HARD] **:** a genus of amberfishes including the pilot fish (*N. ductor*)

**naufrage** *n* -s [MF, fr. L *naufragium*, *navifragium*, fr. *navis* ship + *-fragium* (fr. *frangere* to break) — more at NAVE, BREAK] *obs* **:** SHIPWRECK

**nau·ger** \ˈnögə(r)\ *n* -s [ME — more at AUGER] *chiefly dial* **:** AUGER

**¹naught** *or* **nought** \ˈnȯt, ˈnät, *usu* -d.+V\ *pron* [ME, fr. OE *nāwiht*, *nōwiht* (akin to OHG *neowiht*), fr. *nā*, *nō* no + *wiht* creature, thing — more at NO, WIGHT] **1 a :** NOTHING ⟨can do ~ but give ourselves wholly to it —L.A.White⟩ ⟨has heard ~ but good of me —J.H.Wheelwright⟩ **b :** a state of utter ineffectualness **:** an insignificant result ⟨these promising beginnings . . . were brought to ~ —Stephen Ullmann⟩ ⟨his efforts to purge his own party came to ~ —Norman Thomas⟩ **2** *obs* **:** what is wrong in morals or method **:** EVIL, ERROR

**²naught** *or* **nought** \"\ *n* -s [ME, fr. OE *nāwiht*, *nōwiht*, fr. *nāwiht*, *nōwiht*, pron.] **1 a :** NOTHING **b (1) :** NOTHINGNESS, NONEXISTENCE ⟨a shift of emphasis from existential analysis to ontology . . . from the ~ to what the ~ manifests concerning the real —James Collins⟩ (2) *usu cap, cabalism* **:** the depths of the Godhead ⟨communion with the *Naught*, . . . a much higher rank than communion with the Shekhinah —G.G. Scholem⟩ **2 :** the arithmetical symbol 0 **:** ZERO, CIPHER — see NUMBER table

**³naught** *or* **nought** \"\ *adj* [ME, fr. OE *nāwiht*, fr. *nāwiht*, pron.] **1** *archaic* **:** of no worth **:** BAD, UNFIT ⟨the water is ~ and the ground barren —2 Kings 2:19 (AV)⟩ **2 :** of no existence, importance, or effect **:** INSIGNIFICANT ⟨why give him publicity and importance when our critics are convinced that he is ~ —*United India & Indian States*⟩ **:** NONEXISTENT ⟨a whole city made ~ by the bomb⟩ **:** RUINED

**naugh·ti·ly** \ˈnöd·ᵊlē, |t|, |ᵊli, |əl- *also* ˈnäl\ *adv* **:** in a naughty manner **:** MISCHIEVOUSLY ⟨behaved ~ before guests⟩

**naugh·ti·ness** \|ēnəs, |in-\ *n* -ES **1 :** the quality or state of being naughty **2 :** a naughty act or impulse

**naughts-and-crosses** *var of* NOUGHTS-AND-CROSSES

**naugh·ty** \ˈnöd·|ē, |t|, |i *also* ˈnäl\ *adj* -ER/-EST [²*naught* + *-y*] **1 a** *archaic* **:** of inferior quality **:** POOR ⟨very ~ figs, which could not be eaten —Jer 24:2 (AV)⟩ **b** *chiefly Scot* **:** INSIGNIFICANT, GOOD-FOR-NOTHING **2 a** *archaic* **:** vicious in moral character **:** WICKED ⟨~ persons . . . have practiced dangerously against your state —Shak.⟩ **b :** guilty of disobedience or misbehavior ⟨treated like a grown-up gangster, whereas he ought to be treated as a ~ boy —*Times Lit. Supp.*⟩ **3 :** violating accepted standards of morality, good taste, or polite behavior ⟨books . . . with ~ illustrations —Thomas Wolfe⟩ ⟨will be ~ for the young generation to question anything —Sinclair Lewis⟩ **syn** see BAD

**naughty pack** *n, archaic* **:** a person of bad character; *esp* **:** a loose woman ⟨she was a *naughty pack* —Jonathan Swift⟩

**nau·ja·ite** \ˈnaüyə,īt\ *n* -s [*Nauj*akasik, Greenland + E *-ite*] **:** a nephelite-sodalite-syenite rock having a poikilitic texture

**nau·ja·ka·site** \ˌ==ˈkä,sīt\ *n* -s [*Naujakasik*, Greenland + E *-ite*] **:** a mineral $Na_4FeAl_4Si_8O_{25}.2H_2O$ (?) consisting of a hydrous aluminosilicate of sodium or of sodium and iron

**nau·ma·chia** \nöˈmākēə\ *n, pl* **naumachi·ae** \-kē,ē\ *or* **naumachias** [L, fr. Gk, naval battle, fr. *naus* ship + *-machia* -machy — more at NAVE] **1 :** an ancient Roman spectacle representing a naval battle **2 :** a place for naumachiae; *esp* **:** an artificial body of water surrounded by seats

**nau·mann·ite** \ˈnȯmə,nīt, ˈnaüm-\ *n* -s [G *naumannit*, fr. Karl F. *Naumann* †1873 Ger. mineralogist + G *-it* -ite] **:** a mineral ($Ag_2Se$) consisting of a silver selenide in iron-black cubic crystals or massive (sp. gr. 8)

**¹naum·keag** \ˈnȯm,kēg\ *or* **naumkeag machine** *or* **naumkeag scourer** *n* -s *often cap N* [prob. fr. *Naumkeag*, old name for Salem, Mass., shoe manufacturing city] **:** a machine having a rubber buffing disk for smoothing the surface of shoe soles or heels before finishing

**²naumkeag** \"\ *vb* -ED/-ING/-S *vi* **:** to buff a shoe bottom (as on a naumkeag machine) prior to the finishing process ~ *vt* **:** to buff (a shoe bottom) prior to finishing

**naum·keag·er** \-gə(r)\ *n* -s **:** an operator of a naumkeag machine

**naunt** \ˈnänt, -ā-,-ä-\ *n* -s [alter. (resulting fr. incorrect division of *mine aunt*) of *aunt*] *dial chiefly Eng* **:** AUNT

**nau·pa·ka** \naüˈpäkə\ *n* -s [Hawaiian] **:** a Hawaiian shrub (*Scaevola frutescens*) of the family Goodeniaceae found in mountains and near the coast and conspicuous for their white flowers that look like half flowers

**nau·path·ia** \nȯˈpathēə\ *n* -s [NL, fr. Gk *naus* ship + NL *-pathia* — more at NAVE] **:** SEASICKNESS

**nau·pli·ar** \ˈnȯplēə(r)\ *adj* [NL *nauplius* + E *-ar*] **:** of, relating to, or being a nauplius

**nau·pli·iform** \ˈnȯplē,fȯrm\ *adj* [NL *nauplius* + E *-iform*] **1 :** resembling the nauplius of a crustacean **2** *of a hymenopterous larva* **:** having large sickle-shaped mandibles and a pair of bifurcate caudal processes

**nau·pli·o·so·ma** \ˌ==əˈsōmə\ *n* -s [NL, fr. *nauplius* + *-o-* + *-soma*] **:** a pelagic larva that precedes the phyllosoma of various marine decapod crustaceans (as some spiny lobsters)

**nau·pli·us** \ˈnȯplēəs\ *n, pl* **nau·plii** \-ē,ī\ [NL, fr. L, a shellfish, fr. Gk *nauplios*] **:** a crustacean larva in usu. the first stage after leaving the egg and with three pairs of appendages corresponding to antennules, antennae, and mandibles, a median eye, and little or no segmentation of the body

**na·u·ru** \näˈü(,)rü\ *adj*, [fr. *Nauru*, island in the western Pacific] **:** of or from the island of Nauru **:** of the kind or style prevalent in Nauru

**na·u·ru·an** \näˈürəwən\ *n* -s *usu cap* [*Nauru* + E *-an*] **:** a Micronesian native or inhabitant of Nauru

**nau·ruz** \(ˈ)naüˈrüz\ *n* -ES *usu cap* [Per *naurūz*, *naurōz*, lit., new day, fr. *nau* new + *rūz*, *rōz* day, fr. OPer *raucha-*; akin to Skt *nava* new & to Skt *rocate* he shines — more at NEW, LIGHT] **:** the Persian New Year's Day celebrated at the vernal equinox as a day of great festivity

**nau·sea** \ˈnȯ|shə, |zēə, |sēə, |zhə *sometimes* |zyə, |syə, |shēə, |zhēə\ *n* -s [L, lit., seasickness, fr. Gk *nausia*, *nautia* nausea, seasickness, fr. *naus* ship — more at NAVE] **1 a :** a sensation of discomfort in the region of the stomach usu. associated with an urge to retch or vomit **b :** a feeling of distress associated with loathing of food and sometimes aroused by the sight of food **2 :** extreme disgust **:** LOATHING ⟨the victory of his party . . . is considerably more the product of ~ with the present situation —P.B.Rice⟩ **3 :** a state of revulsion accompanying the frightening awareness of one's inescapable freedom as an individual human self

**¹nau·se·ant** \|shēənt, |zē-, |sē-, |zhē-\ *n* -s [*nausea* + *-ant*, n. suffix] **:** an agent that induces nausea; *esp* **:** an expectorant that liquefies and increases the secretion of mucus

**²nauseant** \"\ *adj* [*nausea* + *-ant*, adj. suffix] **:** inducing nausea **:** NAUSEATING

**nau·se·ate** \-ē,āt, *usu* -ād.+V\ *vb* -ED/-ING/-S [L *nauseatus*, past part. of *nauseare*, fr. *nausea*] *vi* **1 :** to become affected with nausea **2 :** to feel disgust ~ *vt* **1 a** *archaic* **:** to reject with nausea or loathing **:** sicken at **b :** to feel disgust or aversion to **:** ABHOR, LOATHE ⟨the mind ~s the thought of processions of learned dunces —Holbrook Jackson⟩ **2 a :** to cause to sicken **:** affect with nausea ⟨was something in the dinner that *nauseated* him⟩ **b :** to create an aversion in **:** affect with loathing ⟨the antics of Party discipline soon *nauseated* him —Eugene Gressman⟩ **syn** see DISGUST

**nau·se·at·ing·ly** *adv* **:** in a nauseating manner or to a nauseating degree ⟨of America . . . he expressed the view that it was ~ materialist —H.J.Laski⟩

**nau·se·at·ing·ness** *n* -ES **:** the quality or state of being nauseating

**nau·seous** \ˈnȯ|shəs, |zēəs, |sēəs, |zhəs\ *adj* [L *nauseosus* causing nausea, fr. *nausea* + *-osus* -ous] **1 :** affected with or inclined to nausea **:** NAUSEATED ⟨began to feel ~⟩ **2 :** causing or such as might be expected to cause nausea **:** SICKENING, LOATHSOME, DISGUSTING ⟨a ~ odor⟩ ⟨~ hypocrisy⟩ — **nau·seous·ly** *adv* — **nau·seous·ness** *n* -ES

**nau·set** \ˈnȯsət\ *n, pl* **nauset** *also* **nausetts** *usu cap* **1 :** an Indian people of Cape Cod **2 :** a member of the Nauset people

**naut** *abbr* nautical

**nautch** \ˈnȯch\ *n* -ES [Hindi *nāc*, fr. Prakrit *nacca*, fr. Skt *nṛtya*, fr. *nṛtyati* he dances, acts] **1 :** an entertainment in India consisting chiefly of dancing by professional dancing girls **2** *or* **nautch dance :** a suggestive Eastern dance performed by a dancing girl

**nau·ther** \ˈnȯthə(r)\ *conj* [ME — more at NEITHER] *dial chiefly Eng* **:** NEITHER

**nau·ti·cal** \ˈnöd·|əkəl, ˈnä|, |t|, |ēk-\ *adj* [L *nauticus* (fr. Gk *nautikos*, fr. *nautēs* sailor — fr. *naus* ship — + *-ikos* -ic) + E *-al* — more at NAVE] **:** of, relating to, or associated with seamen, navigation, or ships ⟨a glossary of ~ terms⟩

**nautical astronomy** *n* **:** practical astronomy by which the position of a ship or airplane is found by astronomical observations

**nautical distance** *n* **:** the length in nautical miles of the rhumb line joining any two places on the earth's surface

**nau·ti·cal·i·ty** \ˌnöd·əˈkaləd·ē\ *n* -ES **:** the quality of being nautical ⟨a seaman of overpowering ~ —John Lardner⟩

**nau·ti·cal·ly** \ˈnöd·|ək(ə)lē, ˈnä|, |t|, |ēk-, -li\ *adv* **:** in a nautical manner **:** with reference to nautical affairs ⟨a ~ powerful nation⟩

**nautical mile** *n* **:** any of various units of distance used for sea and air navigation based on the length of a minute of arc of a great circle of the earth and differing because the earth is not a perfect sphere: as **a :** a British unit equal to 6080 ft. or 1853.2 meters — called also *Admiralty mile* **b :** a U.S. unit no longer in official use equal to 6080.20 ft. or 1853.248 meters **c :** an international unit equal to 6076.11549 ft. or 1852 meters used officially in the U.S. since July 1, 1959

**nautical planisphere** *n* **:** the projection of the terrestrial globe on a plane for navigators' use

**nautical star** *n* **:** a star selected with special reference to its fitness for navigators' use in ascertaining longitude and latitude

**nautical tables** *n pl* **:** arithmetical tables esp. adapted to facilitate a navigator's work in solving problems particularly in nautical astronomy

**nautical twilight** *n* **:** the period before sunrise or after sunset during which the sun is not more than 12 degrees below the horizon

**nau·ti·la·cea** \ˌnöd·ᵊlˈāshēə\ [NL, fr. *Nautilus* + *-acea*] *syn of* NAUTILOIDEA

**¹nau·ti·la·cean** \ˌ==ˈāshən\ *adj* [NL *Nautilacea* + E *-an*] **:** NAUTILOID

**²nautilacean** \"\ *n* -s **:** NAUTILOID

**nau·til·i·cone** \nöˈtilə,kōn\ *n* [NL *Nautilus* + E *-i-* + *cone*] **:** a nautiloid cephalopod shell coiled in a plane spiral with the outer whorls embracing the inner

**nau·til·i·dae** \-ˌdē\ *n pl, cap* [NL, fr. *Nautilus*, type genus + *-idae*] **:** a family of cephalopod mollusks that comprises nautiloids with closely coiled shells and includes all recent members of the order Nautiloidea — see NAUTILUS 1 b

**nau·til·i·form** \-ˌfȯrm\ *adj* [NL *Nautilus* + E *-iform*] **:** having the form of a nautilus shell

**nau·ti·lite** \ˈnöd·ᵊl,īt\ *n* -s [NL *Nautilus* + E *-ite*] **:** a fossil nautilus

**¹nau·ti·loid** \-ˌȯid\ *adj* [NL *Nautiloidea*] **1** *also* **nau·ti·loi·de·an** \ˌ==ˈȯidēən\ [*nautiloidean* fr. NL *Nautiloidea* + E *-an*] **:** of or relating to the Nautiloidea **2** [*nautilicone* + *-oid*] *of a shell* **:** having the form of a nautilicone

**²nautiloid** \"\ *also* **nautiloidean** \"\ *n* -s **:** a mollusk of the group Nautiloidea

**nau·ti·loi·dea** \ˌ==ˈȯidēə\ *n pl, cap* [NL, fr. *Nautilus* + *-oidea*] **1 :** an order or other subdivision of Tetrabranchia comprising cephalopods having an external chambered shell that is either straight (as in *Orthoceras*) or variously curved or coiled and being important in the Ordovician and esp. the Silurian but now represented only by the genus *Nautilus* **2** *in some classifications* **:** a subclass or other subdivision of Cephalopoda that is coextensive with Tetrabranchia

**nau·ti·lus** \ˈnöd·ᵊləs, ˈnäl, |tᵊl-\ *n* [NL, fr. L, paper nautilus, fr. Gk *nautilos*, lit., sailor, fr. *naus* ship — more at NAVE] **1 a** *pl* **nautilus·es** \-ᵊləsəz\ *or* **nauti·li** \-ᵊl,ī\ **:** any of several cephalopod mollusks of the southern Pacific and Indian oceans that constitute a genus (*Nautilus*), that are contained in the outermost chamber of a spiral chambered shell with an outer porcelaneous layer and an inner pearly layer, and that have numerous small tentacles arranged in groups and without suckers or hooks, no ink sac, four gills, four auricles, four nephridia, and a siphon consisting of two lobes not fused to form a tube — called also *chambered nautilus, pearly nautilus* **b** *cap* **:** the type genus and sole recent representative of the family Nautilidae comprising nautiluses and extinct related forms of which some date back to the Tertiary **2** [L] **:** PAPER NAUTILUS

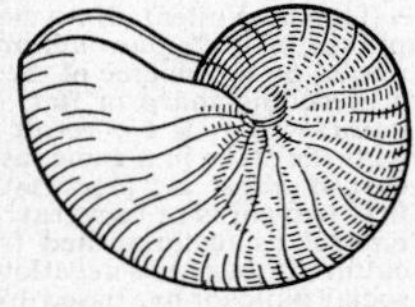

shell of pearly nautilus

**nav** *abbr* **1** naval **2** navigable **3** navigate; navigation; navigator **4** navy

**nava·ho** *or* **nava·jo** \ˈnavə,hō, ˈnäv-\ *n, pl* **navaho** *or* **navahos** *or* **navahoes** *or* **navajo** *or* **navajos** *or* **navajoes** [Sp (*Apache de*) *Navajó*, lit., Apache of Navajó, fr. *Navajó*, a pueblo, fr. Tewa *Navahú*, lit., great planted-fields] **1** *usu cap* **a :** an Athapaskan people of northern New Mexico and Arizona ranging also into Colorado and Utah — called also *Diné* **b :** a member of such people **2** *usu cap* **:** the language of the Navaho people **3** *usu navaho, pl navahos, often cap* **:** a strong to vivid orange that is redder than orpiment orange and slightly redder and darker than Big Four yellow

**navaho blanket** *also* **navaho rug** *n, usu cap N* **:** a blanket woven by the Navaho in geometric designs of symbolic meaning

**navajo stitch** *n, usu cap N* **:** a coiled basketry stitch in which the binding strand encloses the working coil and the previous coil in a figure eight

**¹na·val** \ˈnāvəl\ *adj* [L *navalis*, fr. *navis* ship + *-alis* -al — more at NAVE] **1** *obs* **:** of or relating to ships or shipping **2 a :** of, relating to, or belonging to, connected with, or used in a navy ⟨~ vessels⟩ ⟨U. S. ~ history⟩ ⟨~ personnel⟩ ⟨a ~ academy⟩ ⟨~ supplies⟩ **b :** engaged in by ships of war ⟨a ~ battle⟩ ⟨a ~ bombardment⟩ **c :** consisting of or based on a navy ⟨a ~ force⟩ ⟨~ power⟩

Navajo stitch

**²naval** *or* **naval orange** *var of* NAVEL ORANGE

**naval architect** *n* **:** MARINE ARCHITECT

**naval attaché** *n* **:** a naval officer detailed on duty with the diplomatic representative of his country at a foreign capital

**naval auxiliary** *n* **:** a naval vessel (as a tanker or supply ship) auxiliary to the fighting ships

**naval aviator** *n* **:** an officer or petty officer in the U. S. Navy who has completed the requisite course of training as a pilot of heavier-than-air craft

**naval base** *n* **:** an area command normally including a seaport that includes and integrates the shore activities (as a shipyard, ammunition depot, hospital) which provide local logistic services to the fleet

**naval brass** *also* **naval bronze** *n* **:** brass composed usu. of 60 percent copper, 39 percent zinc, 1 percent tin and used for bolts or other parts usu. under water

**naval brigade** *n* **:** NAVAL MILITIA

**naval cadet** *n* **:** a young man in training for service as a naval officer; *specif* **:** a midshipman in the U. S. Naval Academy between 1882 and 1902

**naval crown** *n* [trans. of L *corona navalis*] **1 :** a golden crown given as a reward for sea service in ancient Rome that consists of galley prows arranged in a circle to form the rim **2** *or* **naval coronet :** a heraldic representation of a crown of gold with ship sterns and square sails arranged alternately on the fillet

naval crown 2

**naval district** *n* **:** a geographical area in which all naval activities except those of the fleet come under the command of its commandant

**naval establishment** *n* **:** all the activities under the secretary of the navy including the operating forces, the navy department, and the shore establishment

**na·val·ism** \ˈnāvə,lizəm\ *n* -s **:** the policy of maintaining naval interests; *also* **:** dominance of the naval class or of naval policies ⟨radio propaganda for ~ —*N. Y. Herald Tribune*⟩

**na·val·ist** \-ləst\ *n* -s **:** an advocate of navalism — **na·val·is·tic** \ˌ==ˈlistik\ *adj* — **na·val·is·ti·cal·ly** \-tək(ə)lē\ *adv*

**na·val·ly** \ˈnāvəlē, -li\ *adv* [*naval* + *-ly*] **1 :** with a naval crown ⟨an eagle . . . and on the sinister a stork proper, each ~ gorged —*Burke's Peerage*⟩ **2 :** in a naval manner or from a naval standpoint ⟨~, the U. S. controls the Pacific —F.H. Cramer⟩

**naval militia** *n* **:** a naval force maintained by some states in a similar manner to the National Guard

**naval officer** *n* **1 :** an officer in a navy **2 :** a customs official of the U. S. who handles manifests and entries, permits, clearances, and other documents

**naval pipe** *n* **:** CHAIN PIPE

**naval reserve** *n* **:** an organization of trained officers and men that can be called upon to strengthen the regular navy in war

**naval shipyard** *n* **:** a naval activity manned by civilian engineers and workers and administered by engineer duty officers that builds, repairs, alters, docks, converts, and fits out all types of warship — called also *navy yard*

**naval station** *n* **:** a command ashore whose mission is to provide local logistic support to units of the operating forces (as in ship repair, personnel administration, pilotage, aerology, flight control, medical care)

**naval stores** *n pl* **1 :** permanent or consumable supplies for warships excluding armament stores **2 :** products (as tar, pitch, turpentine, pine oil, rosin, terpenes) obtained from the oleoresin of pine and other coniferous trees

**nav·ar** \'na,vär, -vå(r\ *n* -s [*navigational and traffic control radar*] : a system of radar navigation in which the position and identity of all planes in the area about an airport are determined by ground radar and retransmitted so that a pilot has a detailed picture of all aerial activity on his radarscope

**na·va·ra·tra** \,nəvə'rä·trə\ *n* -s [Skt *navarātra* period of nine nights, fr. *nava* nine + *rātri* night; perh. akin to Skt *rāma* black — more at NINE] : a nine-day Hindu festival in honor of Durga held in the month Asin

**na·varch** \'nä,värk\ *n* -s [L *navarchus, nauarchus,* fr. Gk *nauarchos,* fr. *naus* ship + *-archos* -arch — more at NAVE] : the commander of a fleet in ancient Greece

**nav·a·rho** \'navə,rō\ *n* -s [*navigation* + *aid* + *rho* (ρ), a symbol for distance in navigation] : a long-range omnidirectional radio navigation system presenting position information in the simplified form of an azimuth reading and a distance reading on two dials in the cockpit

**na·va·rin** \nàvàraⁿ\ *n, pl* **navarins** \"\ [F] : a mutton stew prepared with vegetables

**¹na·var·rese** \'navə'rēz, 'näv-, -rēs\ *adj, usu cap* [*Navarre* ancient kingdom now divided between Spain and France + E *-ese*] : of, relating to, or characteristic of Navarre

**²navarrese** \"\ *n, pl* **navarrese** \"\ *cap* **1** : a native or inhabitant of Navarre **2** : a dialect of Basque spoken on both sides of the French-Spanish border in the western Pyrenees

**¹nave** \'nāv\ *n* -s [ME, fr. OE *nafu;* akin to OHG *naba* nave, ON *nǫf* nave, OE *nafela* navel — more at NAVEL] : a block in the center of a wheel from which the spokes radiate and in which the axle is fixed : HUB

**²nave** \"\ *n* -s [ML *navis,* fr. L, ship; akin to OE *nōwend* skipper, sailor, OHG *nuosc* trough, ON *nōr* ship, Gk *naus,* Skt *nau*] **1** : the main part of the interior of a church: as **a** : the long narrow central hall in a cruciform church that rises higher than the aisles flanking it to form a clerestory and is usu. not considered to include the central part of the transept and choir — see BASILICA illustration **b** : the part of a church between the rear wall and the chancel **2** : a large open central space in a building (as a railway station)

**nave arcade** *n* : an arcade marking the separation between a nave and its side aisles

**na·vel** \'nāvəl\ *n* -s [ME *navel, navele,* fr. OE *nafela;* akin to OHG *nabalo* navel, ON *nafli,* L *umbilicus* navel, *umbo* boss of a shield, Gk *omphalos* navel, Skt *nabhya* nave of a wheel, *nābhi* navel, nave of a wheel] **1** : a mark or depression in the middle of the abdomen, marking the point of attachment of the umbilical cord or yolk stalk : UMBILICUS **2** : the central point or part of something : MIDDLE ⟨the blessed Mediterranean . . . the ~ of the earth —Harold Nicolson⟩ ⟨the hero as the incarnation of God is himself the ~ of the world, the umbilical point through which the energies of eternity break into time —Joseph Campbell⟩ **3** *or* **navel point** : NOMBRIL

**navel ill** *n* : a serious septicemia of newborn animals caused by pus-producing bacteria entering the body through the umbilical cord or opening and typically marked by joint inflammation or arthritis accompanied by generalized pyemia, rapid debilitation, and commonly death — called also *joint evil;* compare MUSHY CHICK

**navel orange** *also* **navel** \"\ *or* **na·val** \"\ *or* **naval orange** *n* -s [*naval* by folk etymology fr. *navel*] : a seedless or nearly seedless orange originated in Brazil and much grown in California with fruit that encloses a small secondary fruit and has a rind showing on the exterior a pit at the apex

**navel orangeworm** *n* : a caterpillar that is the larva of a phycitid moth (*Paramyelois transitella*) and that is a serious pest of almonds and walnuts esp. in California

**navel string** *n* : UMBILICAL CORD

**navelwort** \'==,=\ *n* [ME, fr. *navel* + *wort*] **1** : a European succulent herb (*Cotyledon umbilicus*) having round peltate leaves with a central depression **2** : an herb of the genus *Omphalodes* of the family Boraginaceae **3** : MARSH PENNYWORT

**na·vet** \nàvā\ *or* **na·vette** \nàvet\ *n* -s [MF *navet* turnip, rape (fr. OF *naviet,* dim. of *nef* turnip, rape, fr. L *napus*) & *navette* rape, alter. of *navet*] : RAPE 2

**na·ve·ta** \nə'vād·ə, -ved·ə\ *n* -s [Catal, navicula, naveta, dim. of *nau* ship, fr. L *navis*] : a megalithic long barrow of the Balearic islands resembling an inverted boat

**na·vette** \nàvet\ *n* -s [F, shuttle, navicula, marquise, fr. OF, shuttle, dim. of *nef* ship, fr. L *navis* — more at NAVE] : MARQUISE 3

**nav·i·cel·la** \,navə'selə\ *n* -s [ML, fr. LL, small ship, dim. of L *navis* ship — more at NAVE] : an ornamental object shaped like a ship

**nav·i·cert** \'navə,sərt\ *n* -s [*navigation certificate*] : a certificate issued by authorized British officials (as consular officers) exempting a noncontraband consignment from seizure or search by British blockade patrols

**na·vic·u·la** \nə'vikyələ\ *n* [in sense 1, fr. ML, fr. L, small ship, dim. of L *navis* ship; in sense 2, NL, fr. L] **1** -s : an incense boat **2 a** *cap* : a very large genus (the type of the family Naviculaceae) of diatoms having a lanceolate or boat-shaped usu. free-floating frustule covered with minute striae **b** -s : a plant of the genus *Navicula*

**¹na·vic·u·lar** \-lə(r)\ *adj* [in sense 1, fr. L *navicula* small ship + E *-ar;* in sense 2, fr. NL *Navicula* + E *-ar;* in sense 3, irreg. fr. MF *naviculaire,* fr. L *navicula* + MF *-aire* -ary] **1** : resembling or having the shape of a boat ⟨a ~ bone⟩ : CYMBIFORM, SCAPHOID **2** : resembling a diatom of the genus *Navicula* **3** : of, relating to, or involving a navicular bone ⟨~ fractures⟩

**²navicular** \"\ *also* **na·vic·u·la·re** \=,==la(a)rē, -lärē\ *n* -s [partly fr. ¹*navicular;* partly fr. NL (*os*) *naviculare* navicular bone] : a navicular bone; *esp* : the lateral bone on the radial side of the proximal row of the carpus

**navicular disease** *also* **navicular** *n* -s : inflammation of the navicular bone and forefoot of the horse resulting in a shortened stride and persistent lameness and regarded as due to repeated bruising or strain esp. in individuals exhibiting a hereditary predisposition

**navies** *pl of* NAVY

**nav·i·ga·bil·i·ty** \,navəgə'biləd·ē, -ətē, -i\ *n* : the quality or state of being navigable

**nav·i·ga·ble** \'==gəbəl\ *adj* [MF or L; MF *navigable,* fr. L *navigabilis,* fr. *navigare* to navigate + *-abilis* -able] **1** : capable of being navigated : deep enough and wide enough to afford passage to ships ⟨a ~ river⟩ ⟨canals ~ at a length of about 2,700 miles and floatable at a length of about 26,500 miles —*Statesman's Yr. Bk.*⟩ **2** : capable of being navigated or steered ⟨a ~ balloon⟩ — **nav·i·ga·ble·ness** *n* -ES

**navigable airspace** *n* : airspace above the minimum safe altitudes of flight as legally prescribed

**navigable waters** *n pl, law* : waters which form in their ordinary condition by themselves or by uniting with other waters a continuous highway over which commerce in the waters is or may be conducted by water is or may be carried on with other states or foreign countries, their status as such waters being established by evidence of actual commercial or private use or of the feasibility of removing the obstructions to their use for such interstate or foreign commerce

**nav·i·ga·bly** \-blē, -li\ *adv* : in a navigable manner or to a navigable degree

**nav·i·gate** \'navə,gāt, *usu* -ād·+V\ *vb* -ED/-ING/-S [L *navigatus,* past part. of *navigare,* fr. *navis* ship + *-igare* (fr. *agere* to lead, drive) — more at NAVE, AGENT] *vi* **1 a** : to go from one place to another by water : SAIL **b** : to sail or manage a boat **2** : to direct one's course through any medium; *specif* : to operate an airplane or airship ⟨~ by instrument⟩ **3** : to get about : WALK ⟨well enough to ~ under his own power⟩ : MOVE ⟨as to the state of the roads . . . it might be another week or two before wheels could ~ in any comfort —Esther Forbes⟩ ~ *vt* **1 a** : to sail over, on, or through ⟨the first ships to ~ the Atlantic⟩ ⟨cargo ships that can ~ inland waters⟩ ⟨having successfully *navigated* the pack ice off the . . . coast —Rene Cutforth⟩ **b** : to make one's way on, about, or through ⟨had trouble *navigating* the stairs⟩ ⟨managed to ~ the house on his knees —Alice Lake⟩ ⟨~ the dangerous age range from 50 to 70 —Flanders Dunbar⟩ **2 a** : to steer, direct, or manage in sailing : conduct (a boat) upon the water by the art or skill of seamen **b** : to operate, steer, or control the course of (an aircraft)

**navigating officer** *n* : a navigator of a ship or aircraft

**nav·i·ga·tion** \,navə'gāshən\ *n* -s [MF or L; MF *navigation* fr. L *navigation-, navigatio,* fr. *navigatus* + *-ion-, -io* -ion] **1** : the act or practice of navigating ⟨feats of ~ among migratory animals —W.H.Dowdeswell⟩ **2 a** : the science or art of conducting ships or aircraft from one place to another; *esp* : the method of determining position, course, and distance traveled over the surface of the earth by the principles of geometry and astronomy and by reference to devices (as radar beacons or instruments) designed as aids **b** : skill in this art or science **3** : an instance of navigating : VOYAGE ⟨pigeons and shearwaters can exhibit . . . a successful ~ homeward —R.M.Lockley⟩ **4** : ship traffic or commerce : SHIPPING ⟨open to ~ as soon as the ice is out⟩ **5** : a navigable waterway formed artificially : PASSAGE ⟨the lake itself being some six miles long, tolerable ~ was thus established for a distance of eleven miles —John Burroughs⟩

**nav·i·ga·tion·al** \;==;gāshənᵊl, -shnəl\ *adj* : of, relating to, or used in navigation ⟨~ difficulties⟩ ⟨~ astronomy⟩ ⟨the ~ planets Venus, Mars, Jupiter, and Saturn⟩ — **nav·i·ga·tion·al·ly** \-ᵊlē, -əlī, \i\ *adv*

**navigation light** *n* : one of a set of lights on an airplane indicating its position and direction of motion and consisting of a red light and a green light on the port and starboard wing tips respectively and a white light at the tail

**nav·i·ga·tor** \'navə,gād·ə(r), -gāt-\ *n* -s [L, fr. *navigatus* + *-or*] **1** : one that navigates or is qualified to navigate: as **a** : an officer on a ship or aircraft responsible for its navigation **b** : one who explores by ship **c** : an automatic device that registers or directs the course of an aircraft or missile **2 a** *Brit* : a laborer employed in constructing a canal **b** : NAVVY

**na·vite** \'nä,vīt\ *n* -s [G *navit,* fr. L *Nava* Nahe river, Germany + G *-it* -ite] : a mineral consisting of a coarse-grained olivine-basalt with phenocrysts of altered olivine and a little augite and basic plagioclase in a holocrystalline groundmass of labradorite and augite

**navr** *abbr* navigator

**¹nav·vy** \'navē\ *n* -ES [by shortening & alter. fr. *navigator*] **1** *Brit* : an unskilled laborer; *esp* : one doing excavation or construction **2** *Brit* : a machine for excavating : STEAM SHOVEL

**²navvy** \"\ *vb* -ED/-ING/-ES *Brit, vi* : to work as a navvy ~ *vt* : EXCAVATE

**na·vy** \'nāvē, -vi\ *n, pl* **navies** *see sense 4, often attrib* [ME *navie,* fr. MF, fr. L *navigia,* pl. of *navigium* ship, fr. *navigare* to navigate] **1** : the ships of one nation or owner or gathering : FLEET ⟨the country's merchant ~⟩ **2** : the war vessels belonging to a nation composed formerly chiefly of ships of the line, frigates, and gun vessels and in modern times of warships (as aircraft carriers, battleships, cruisers, command ships, destroyers and submarines), amphibious ships (as attack transports and attack cargo ships), patrol vessels (as escort vessels and gunboats), mine warfare vessels (as minelayers and minesweepers), and logistic support vessels (as tenders, tankers, repair ships and ammunition ships) **3** *often cap* : the complete military organization of a nation for sea warfare including yards, shops, stations, men, ships, offices, and officers : the naval establishment **4** *pl* **navys** : NAVY BLUE **5** *or* **navy plug** : a strong dark plug tobacco

**navy agent** *n* : a British attorney who acts for naval officers in financial matters connected with the service (as distribution of prize money)

**navy bean** *n* : a white-seeded kidney bean that is grown esp. for its nutritious seeds

**navy blue** *n* : a variable color averaging a grayish purplish blue that is duller and slightly bluer than average delft, bluer and duller than Windsor blue or Turkish blue, bluer and darker than regimental, and duller than Wedgwood (sense 2b)

**navy exchange** *n* : SHIP'S SERVICE

**navy green** *n* : LIGHT CHROME GREEN

**navy yard** *n* : NAVAL SHIPYARD

**na·wab** \nə'wäb, -wōb\ *n* -s [Hindi *nawāb* — more at NABOB] **1 a** : a deputy ruler or viceroy under the Mogul government **b** : a Muslim prince inferior only to a Nizam — sometimes used as a courtesy title **2** : NABOB

**¹nay** \'nā\ *adv* [ME *nay, nei,* fr. ON *nei,* fr. *ne* not + *ei* ever — more at NE, AYE] **1** : NO — used formerly as a negative answer to a question asked or a request made and now superseded by *no* except in oral voting **2** : not this merely but also : not only so but — used to mark addition or substitution of a more explicit or emphatic phrase and thus interchangeable with *yea* ⟨each of us is peculiar, ~, in a sense, unique —S.J. Brown⟩

**²nay** \"\ *n* -s **1** : DENIAL, REFUSAL, PROHIBITION **2 a** : a negative reply or vote ⟨the ~s outnumbering the ayes⟩ **b** : one who votes no ⟨voted among the ~s⟩

**³nay** \"\ *n* -s [Ar *nāy,* fr. Per] : a vertical end-blown flute of ancient origin used in Muslim lands

**na·ya·di** \'nīədē\ *n, pl* **nayadi** *or* **nayadis** *usu cap* [Malayalam *nāyāti* hunter, fr. *nay* dog + *āti* one who moves] : a member of one of the lowest of the untouchable Hindu castes of the Malabar coast of India

**nayak** *var of* NAIK

**na·ya pai·sa** \nə,yä,pī'sä\ *n, pl* **na·ye pai·se** \nə,yā,pī'sā\ [Hindi *nayā paisā,* lit., new pice] : a subsidiary unit of value of the Republic of India equal to 1/100 rupee established April 1957 : PAISA

**nayar** *or* **nair** \'nī(ə)r\ *n, pl* **nayar** *or* **nayars** *or* **nair** *or* **nairs** *usu cap* [Malayalam *nāyar,* fr. Skt *nāyaka* — more at NAIK] **1** : a people of the Malabar coast of India that are probably Dravidians with Aryan admixture and are noted for polyandry in which women are free to contract alliances as they please outside their own clan with men of equal or better rank, children belong to the mother's clan, and property descends through the female line **2** : a member of the Nayar people

**na·ya·rit** \,näyə'rēt\ *or* **na·ya·ri·ta** \-rēd·ə\ *n* -s *usu cap* [Sp *nayarita,* of AmerInd origin] : CORA 2

**na·yaur** \nə'yȯr\ *n* -s [perh. modif. of Nepali *nahūr* nahoor] : a Tibetan wild sheep (*Ovis ammon hodgsoni*) that is a variety of the argali

**nay·say** \'nā,sā\ *n* [¹*nay* + *say,* n.; after the phrase *to say one nay*] : REFUSAL, DENIAL

**²naysay** \(')=;=\ *vt* [¹*nay* + *say,* vb.] : DENY, REFUSE, OPPOSE ⟨there might have been . . . for anything he could ~ —W.F. DeMorgan⟩ — **naysayer** \(')=;==\ *n* -s

**nay·word** \'nā,=\ *n* [*nay-* (of unknown origin) + *word*] **1** : a word used as a signal : WATCHWORD 1b **2** *obs* : a proverb of reproach : BYWORD

**na·zard** *or* **na·sard** \nə'zär(d)\ *n* -s [F, *nazard, nasard,* having a nasal sound, fr. L *nasus* nose — more at NOSE] : a mutation organ stop of 2⅔-foot pitch with metal pipes

**naz·a·re·an** \,nazə'rēən\ *n* -s *cap* [LL *Nazaraeus* (fr. Gk *Nazōraios,* fr. *Nazareth, Nazeret* Nazareth) + E *-an*] : NAZARENE 1

**¹naz·a·rene** \;nazə;rēn\ *n* -s [ME *Nazaren,* fr. LL *Nazarenus,* fr. Gk *Nazarēnos,* fr. *Nazareth, Nazeret* Nazareth, town in ancient Palestine] **1** *cap* : a native or resident of Nazareth in Galilee, Palestine ⟨Jesus Christ, the *Nazarene*⟩ **2** *usu cap* **a** : a follower of Jesus of Nazareth : CHRISTIAN **b** : a member of an early sect of Jewish-Christians holding that Christians of Jewish descent should observe the Jewish law **c** : a member of a sect of pietistic, pacifistic Christians in Hungary **d** : a member of the Church of the Nazarene, a Protestant Christian denomination deriving from the merging in 1907–8 of three independent holiness groups and adhering closely to the original teachings of Methodism (as the doctrines of holiness and sanctification) **3** *usu cap* : one of a group of 19th century German painters in Rome seeking to restore Christian art to its medieval purity

**²nazarene** \"\ *adj, usu cap* : of or relating to Nazareth or the Nazarenes

**naz·ca** *also* **nas·ca** \'näskə\ *adj, usu cap* [fr. *Nazca* (*Nasca*), town in southwestern Peru] : of or relating to a culture of the coast of southern Peru dating from about 2000 B.C. and characterized by a thin hard coiled pottery painted in many brilliant colors and conventionalized symbolic design, by expert weaving, and by irrigated agriculture in an area now desert

**naze** *or* **nase** \'nāz\ *n* -s [perh. from the *Naze,* promontory in Essex, England] : PROMONTORY, HEADLAND

**¹na·zi** \'nä|ts|ē, 'na|, 'nà|, |i *sometimes* |z|\ *n* -s [G, by shortening and alter. fr. *nationalsozialist* National Socialist, fr. *national* + *sozialist* socialist] **1** *usu cap* : a member of the former National Socialist German Workers' party founded on fascist principles in 1919 and headed by Adolf Hitler from 1921 **2** *often cap* : an adherent of a party or movement similar to that of the Nazis

**²nazi** \"\ *adj, often cap* **1** : of or relating to Nazism or a Nazi ⟨~ ideology⟩ ⟨~ officials⟩ ⟨the ~ party⟩ **2** : controlled or carried out by Nazis ⟨a ~ government⟩ ⟨~ persecution⟩

**na·zi·dom** \-dəm\ *n* -s *often cap* : NAZISM 2

**na·zi·fi·ca·tion** \,==fə'kāshən\ *n* -s *often cap* [fr. *nazify,* after such pairs as E *amplify: amplification*] : the act or process of nazifying

**na·zi·fy** \'==,fī\ *vt* -ED/-ING/-ES *often cap* [¹*Nazi* + *-fy*] : to subject to Nazi control or imbue with Nazism

**na·zim** \'näzəm\ *n* -s [Hindi *nāzim,* fr. Ar *nāzim* arranger, organizer] : a military governor in India

**na·zi·phile** *pronunc at* NAZI + ,fīl\ *n* -s *often cap* [¹*Nazi* + *-phile*] : a person favorable toward Nazism

**na·zir** \'nä,zi(ə)r\ *n* -s [Hindi *nāzir,* fr. Ar *nāzir*] **1** : a native court official in India who serves processes, acts as treasurer, and performs other similar duties **2** : any of various officials in Muslim countries

**naz·i·rite** *or* **naz·a·rite** \'nazə,rīt, *usu* -īd·+V\ *n* -s *usu cap* [LL *nazaræus* Nazarite (fr. Gk *nazaraios, naziraios,* fr. Heb *nāzīr,* fr. *nāzar* to consecrate) + E *-ite*] : a man of ancient Israel or Judah consecrated to God for a given time by an ascetic vow esp. to avoid drinking wine, cutting the hair, and being defiled by a corpse

**naz·i·rit·ism** \-,rīd·,izəm\ *n* -s *usu cap* : the practice of a Nazirite

**na·zism** \'nät,sizəm *sometimes* 'nä,zizəm *or* 'na- *or* 'nà-\ *or* **na·zi·ism** *pronunc at* NAZI +,izəm\ *n* -s *usu cap* [¹*Nazi* + *-ism*] **1** : the body of political and economic doctrines held and put into effect by the National Socialist German Workers' party in the Third German Reich including the totalitarian principle of government, state control of all industry, predominance of groups assumed to be racially superior, and supremacy of the führer : German fascism **2** : a Nazi movement or regime

**na·zist** \'nä|ts|əst, 'na|, |'nà *sometimes* |z|\ *or* **na·zis·tik** \(')nät¦sistik *sometimes* (')nä¦zi- *or* (')na- *or* (')nà-\ *adj, usu cap* : adhering to or resembling Nazism

**naz·o·re·an** \,nazə'rēən\ *n* -s *cap* [Gk *nazōraios,* fr. *Nazareth* Nazareth] : NAZARENE 1

**NB** *abbr* **1** naval base **2** no ball **3** no bid **4** northbound **5** [L *nota bene*] note well; take notice

**Nb** *symbol* niobium

**n balance** *n, usu cap N* : NITROGEN BALANCE

**NBP** *abbr* normal boiling point

**NC** *abbr* **1** new charter **2** new crop **3** nitrocellulose **4** no change **5** no charge **6** no connection **7** noncollectible **8** nurse corps

**NCA** *abbr* neurocirculatory asthenia

**NCO** \¦en,sē¦ō\ *abbr or n* -s noncommissioned officer

**NCS** *abbr* net control station

**NCUP** *abbr* no commission until paid

**NCV** *abbr, often not cap* no commercial value

**-nd** *symbol* — used after the figure 2 to form the ordinal *second* or an ordinal that ends in *second* ⟨a 32*nd* note⟩ — compare -D

**ND** *abbr* **1** national debt **2** navy department **3** *often not cap* no date; not dated

**Nd** *symbol* neodymium

**NDB** *abbr* nondirectional beacon

**nde·be·le** \,endə'bē(,)lē\ *n, pl* **ndebele** *or* **ndebeles** *usu cap* **1 a** : a Bantu people of the northern Transvaal and Southern Rhodesia — called also *Matabele* **b** : a member of such people **2** : a dialect of Zulu spoken by the Ndebele people

**NDGA** *abbr* nordihydroguaiaretic acid

**ndon·ga** *n, pl* **ndonga** \ən'dȯŋgə\ *or* **ndongas** *usu cap* **1 a** : a people of South-West Africa near the Angola border **b** : a member of such people **2** : a Bantu language spoken by the Ndonga people

**ndo·ro·bo** \,endə'rō(,)bō\ *n, pl* **ndorobo** *or* **ndorobos** *usu cap* **1** : a hunting people of small stature living in the Kikuyu-Masai region and northward in Kenya and possibly related to the Pygmies **2** : a member of the Ndorobo people

**¹ne** \'nē, ,nə\ *adv* [ME, fr. OE *ne, ni* — more at NO] *chiefly dial* : NOT

**²ne** \"\ *conj* [ME, fr. OE *ne, ni,* fr. ¹*ne*] *chiefly dial* : NOR

**³né** \'nā\ *adj* [F, lit., born (past part. of *naître* to be born, fr. L *nascere,* fr. *nasci*), fr. L *natus,* past part. of *nasci* to be born — more at NATION] : originally or formerly called or named — used (1) to indicate and introduce the former name of a man or boy usu. after mention of the name actually being used ⟨John Doe ~ Smith⟩ or (2) sometimes to indicate and introduce the former name of a group ⟨the Milwaukee Braves ~ the Boston Braves⟩ or thing ⟨Kernville ~ Whiskey Flat⟩ usu. after mention of the name actually being used; compare NÉE

**ne-** *or* **neo-** *comb form* [Gk, fr. *neos* new — more at NEW] **1 a** : new : recent ⟨*neo*logism⟩ ⟨*neo*phyte⟩ **b** : a new and different period or form of something (as a faith, school, or language) — often joined to the second element with a hyphen ⟨*Neo*-Chippendale⟩ ⟨*Neo*-Darwinism⟩ ⟨*Neo*-Latin⟩ ⟨*Neo*platonism⟩ **c** : of recent forms — opposed to *pale-* ⟨*neo*botanist⟩ ⟨*neo*botany⟩ ⟨*neo*ntology⟩ **d** : neozoic — opposed to *pale-* ⟨*Neo*crinoidea⟩ ⟨*Neo*lithic⟩ **e** : imitation : pseudo **f** : the New World ⟨*Ne*arctic⟩ ⟨*Neo*tropical⟩ **g** : an immature form ⟨*neo*fetus⟩ **h** : a more recently developed part (as of a plant or animal) ⟨*neo*morph⟩ **i** : an abnormal new formation ⟨*neo*plasm⟩ **2 a** : the one among several isomeric hydrocarbons that has been recently classified and contains at least one carbon atom connected directly with four other carbon atoms ⟨*neo*hexane⟩ — compare IS-, NORMAL 10e **b** : a new chemical compound isomeric with or otherwise related to the one to whose name it is prefixed ⟨*neo*arsphenamine⟩ **3** : the latest subdivision of a division of geologic time ⟨*Neo*paleozoic⟩ — distinguished from *mes-* and *eo-*

**NE** *abbr* **1** national emergency **2** new edition **3** no effects **4** nonessential **5** northeast; northeastern **6** not exceeding; not to exceed

**Ne** *symbol* neon

**neaf** \'nēf\ *chiefly dial var of* ¹NIEVE

**neal** \'nēl, -ēəl\ *vb* [by shortening] *chiefly dial* : ANNEAL

**ne·allotype** \(')nē+\ *n* [*ne-* + *allotype*] : a type specimen of the opposite sex to the holotype and collected and described later than the holotype — compare ALLOTYPE

**¹ne·an·der·thal** *also* **ne·an·der·tal** \nē'andə(r),t(h)ȯl, -'aan-; nā'ändə(r),täl, nā'ändə(r),tål\ *adj, usu cap* [*Neanderthal* (*man*) *or Neandertal* (*man*)] **1** : belonging or relating to or resembling Neanderthal man ⟨*Neanderthal* cave⟩ ⟨*Neanderthal* jaw⟩ **2 a** : suggesting primitive man in appearance or behavior ⟨*Neanderthal* ferocity⟩ **b** : extremely old-fashioned or out-of-date ⟨*Neanderthal* conservatism⟩

**²neanderthal** \"\ *n* -s *usu cap* **1** : a member of the Neanderthal race **2** : a rugged or uncouth person : CAVEMAN

**ne·an·der·thal·er** \-lə(r)\ *n* -s *usu cap* [G, lit., inhabitant of the Neanderthal, fr. *Neanderthal,* valley in western Germany] : NEANDERTHAL

**¹ne·an·der·thal·ian** \=¦=;=¦lēən, -lyən\ *adj, usu cap* [*Neanderthal* (*man*) + *-ian*] : belonging or relating to Neanderthal man

**²neanderthalian** \"\ *n* -s *usu cap* : NEANDERTHAL

**neanderthal man** *also* **neandertal man** *n, usu cap N* [fr. *Neanderthal* (*Neandertal*), valley in western Germany where the remains were first discovered] : a type or race or species of Middle Paleolithic man (*Homo neanderthalensis* or *Palaeoanthropus neanderthalensis*) known from skeletal remains found at many sites in Europe, northern Africa, and western Asia usu. in association with Mousterian artifacts and distinguished by a stocky, heavily muscled build, proportionally short forearm and lower leg, and an extremely dolichocephalic skull with projecting occiput, heavy supraorbital torus, receding forehead, and undeveloped chin

**¹ne·an·der·thal·oid** \=¦=;=,lȯid\ *adj, usu cap* [*Neanderthal* (*man*) + *-oid*] : like or relating to Neanderthal man or to the Neanderthal type of skull

[2]**neanderthaloid** \"\ *n* -s *often cap* **:** a specimen or a fossil type resembling Neanderthal man

**ne·an·ic** \nē'anik\ *adj* [Gk *neanikos* youthful, vigorous, fr. *neanias* young man + *-ikos* -ic; akin to Gk *neos* new — more at NEW] **:** YOUTHFUL; *specif* **:** constituting the pupal stage of insect development

**ne·anthropic** \ˌnē+\ *also* **neo·anthropic** \ˌnēō+\ *adj* [*ne-* + *anthrop-* + *-ic*] **:** of, like, or belonging to man of the surviving species (*Homo sapiens*) as distinguished from primitive hominids (as Neanderthal man or Pithecanthropus) that are known only through fossil remains ⟨~ man⟩

**ne·an·thro·pi·nae** \nēˌan(t)thrə'pīˌnē\ *n pl, usu cap* [NL, fr. *ne-* + *anthrop-* + *-inae*] **:** recent man (*Homo sapiens*) when treated by anthropologists as though distinct from more primitive species of the same genus at the subfamily level

[1]**neap** \'nēp\ *adj* [ME *neep*, fr. OE *nēp* being at the stage of neap tide] **:** of, relating to, or constituting a neap tide

[2]**neap** \"\ *vi* -ED/-ING/-S [[1]*neap*] *of a tide* **:** to tend toward the neap stage

[3]**neap** \"\ *n* -s [prob. fr. E dial. *nape, neap* piece of wood used to hold up the front or the tongue of a wagon, of Scand origin; akin to Norw dial. *neip* forked stick, hayfork, Icel *neip* space between two fingers, ON *hnippa* to prod — more at NIP] *NewEng* **:** the tongue of a cart

**neaped** *adj* [fr. past part. of [2]*neap*] **:** left aground by the high water of a spring tide **:** STRANDED, GROUNDED

[1]**ne·a·pol·i·tan** \ˌnēə'pälət°n *also* -ətən *or* -əd·ən\ *adj, usu cap* [L *neapolitanus*, fr. Gk *neapolitēs* citizen of Naples (fr. *Neapolis* Naples + *-itēs* -ite) + L *-anus* -an] **:** of, relating to, or characteristic of Naples, Italy, or its residents

[2]**neapolitan** \"\ *n* -s **1** *cap* **:** a native or resident of Naples, Italy **2** *usu cap* **:** NEAPOLITAN ICE CREAM

**neapolitan ice cream** *n, usu cap N* **:** a brick of from two to four layers of ice cream of different flavors usu. including lemon ice or orange ice

**neapolitan mandolin** *n, usu cap N* **:** a mandolin having four pairs of strings — compare MILANESE MANDOLIN

**neapolitan ointment** *n, usu cap N* **:** MERCURIAL OINTMENT

**neapolitan sixth** *n, usu cap N* **:** the first inversion of the major triad formed on the lowered second degree of the musical scale

**neapolitan yellow** *n, often cap N* **:** NAPLES YELLOW

**neap rise** *n* **:** the difference in level between low water at spring tide and high water at neap tide

**neap tide** *also* **neap** *n* -s **:** a tide of minimum range occurring at the first and the third quarters of the moon — compare SPRING TIDE

[1]**near** *adv* [ME *ner, nere*, fr. OE *nēar* — more at [2]NEAR] *obs* **:** NEARER

[2]**near** \'ni(ə)r, -iə\ *adv* -ER/-EST [ME *ner, nere*, partly fr. *ner, nere* nearer, fr. OE *nēar*, comparative of *nēah* nigh; partly fr. ON *nær* nearer, near, comp. of *nā-* near — more at NIGH] **1 :** at, within, or to a short distance ⟨don't shoot until they come ~⟩ or a short time ⟨sunset was drawing ~⟩ ⟨getting ~*er* to the true explanation⟩ **2 :** within little **:** ALMOST, NEARLY ⟨~ exhausted by the heat⟩ ⟨dark brown coming ~ to black⟩ ⟨not ~ so many⟩ ⟨came ~ to being the best speller in the class⟩ **3 a :** CLOSELY ⟨copy it as ~ as you can⟩ ⟨*near*-related terms⟩ ⟨*near*-actual mock battle⟩ **b :** INTIMATELY ⟨~ allied unto the duke —Shak.⟩ **4 :** THRIFTILY, STINGILY

[3]**near** \"\ *prep* [ME *ner, nere*, fr. *ner, nere* adv.] **:** not far distant from esp. in place, time, or degree **:** close to ⟨bombs fell ~ the building⟩ ⟨several beaches ~ the city⟩ ⟨came home ~ midnight⟩ ⟨seemed to be ~ death⟩ ⟨was in a state ~ collapse⟩

[4]**near** \"\ *adj* -ER/-EST [ME *ner, nere*, fr. *ner, nere*, adv.] **1 a :** closely akin ⟨~ relative⟩ **b :** closely or intimately related or associated ⟨~ relations⟩ ⟨~ affairs⟩ ⟨his ~*est* and dearest friend⟩ **2 a :** not far distant in time, place, or degree ⟨in the ~ future⟩ ⟨his ~*est* approach to success⟩ **:** ADJACENT, NIGH ⟨saw only his ~*est* neighbors⟩ ⟨hunting rabbits in the ~ fields⟩ **b :** that barely avoids, passes, or misses ⟨~ disaster⟩ ⟨~ miracle⟩ **:** CLOSE, NARROW ⟨he won the match but it was a very ~ thing⟩ **3 a :** being the closer of two ⟨~ side of the mountain⟩ — opposed to *far* **b :** being the left-hand one of a pair ⟨~ horse⟩ ⟨~ hind foot⟩ ⟨~ wheel of a cart⟩ — opposed to *off* **4 :** DIRECT, SHORT — used chiefly in the comparative or superlative ⟨four miles by the ~*est* road⟩ **5 :** CLOSEFISTED, PARSIMONIOUS, STINGY **6 a :** closely resembling or following ⟨a version very ~ the original⟩ **b :** approaching closely in extent or degree ⟨~ equivalent⟩ ⟨the ~*est* thing to perfect happiness⟩ **c :** approximating the genuine ⟨~ silk⟩ — often used in combination ⟨*near*-antique⟩

[5]**near** \"\ *vb* -ED/-ING/-S [[2]*near*] *vi* **:** to come closer in space or time ⟨every year when the baseball season ~s⟩ ~ *vt* **:** to draw near to **:** APPROACH ⟨ship was ~*ing* the dock⟩

[6]**near** *var of* NEER

**nearabout** \'≠ˌ≠\ *also* **nearabouts** \'≠ˌ≠\ *adv* [*nearabout* fr. [2]*near* + *about*; *nearabouts* fr. [2]*near* + *about* + *-s*] *chiefly South & Midland* **:** NEARLY, ALMOST

**near-at-hand** \'≠ˌ≠\ *adj* [fr. *near at hand*, adv. phrase, fr. ME *nere at hand*] **:** NEARBY ⟨lumber from *near-at-hand* sources⟩ **:** IMMEDIATE ⟨concerned mostly with *near-at-hand* problems⟩

**near beer** *n* **:** any of various malt liquors resembling beer but considered nonalcoholic because containing less than ½ percent alcohol

[1]**nearby** \'≠ˌ≠\ *adv* [ME *nerby, nere by*, fr. *ner, nere near* + *by*, adv.] **1 :** near at hand **:** close by ⟨~ flows a river⟩ ⟨plane lands ~⟩ **2** *Scot* **:** NEARLY, THEREABOUTS ⟨sixty miles or ~⟩

[2]**nearby** \"\ *prep* [ME *nerby, nereby*, fr. *nerby, nere by*, adv.] **:** close to **:** hard by **:** NEAR ⟨put up attractive churches ~ a university —W.L.Sperry⟩

[3]**nearby** \"\ *adj* [[1]*nearby*] **:** being or set close at hand **:** ADJACENT, NEIGHBORING ⟨water from a ~ river⟩

[4]**nearby** \'≠ˌ≠\ *n* -s **:** something produced in the neighborhood — usu. used in pl. ⟨steady market on . . . colored eggs . . . but ~s were weaker —*Jour. of Commerce*⟩

**ne·arctic** \(')nē+\ *adj, usu cap* [*ne-* + *arctic*] **:** of, relating to, or being the biogeographic subregion that includes Greenland, arctic America, and the northern and mountainous parts of No. America and that is now usu. considered a subdivision of the Holarctic region

**near eastern** *adj, usu cap N&E* **:** of, relating to, or concerned with the countries of the Near East — used orig. of the Balkan States, later of the region included in the Ottoman Empire, and now often of all the countries of southeastern Europe, No. Africa, and southwestern Asia, sometimes including the entire area extending from Libya or Morocco, Ethiopia, and Somalia to Greece, Turkey, Iran, Afghanistan, and sometimes India; compare FAR EASTERN, MIDDLE EASTERN

**near-fall** \'≠ˌ≠\ *n* **:** a wrestling fall scoring usu. two points and achieved by pinning both shoulders to the mat for more than one but less than two seconds or by holding both shoulders to within two inches of the mat for at least two seconds

[1]**near hand** *adv* [ME *nerhand, nerehand*, fr. *ner, nere* near + *hand*] *chiefly Scot* **1 :** close by **2 :** ALMOST, NEARLY

[2]**near hand** *prep* [ME *nerhand, nerehand*, fr. *nerhand, nerehand*, adv.] *chiefly Scot* **:** close to **:** next to **:** NEAR

[3]**near hand** *adj* [[1]*near hand*] *chiefly Scot* **:** ADJACENT, NEAR

**near·ish** \'ni(ə)rish, -rēsh\ *adj* [[4]*near* + *-ish*] **:** rather near ⟨not really miserly, but just ~⟩ ⟨a ~ escape from serious injury⟩

**near-legged** *U S usu* '≠ˌlegəd, *Brit usu* -gd\ *adj, of a horse* **:** having the two fore or two hind legs set close together; *esp* **:** having them so near that the feet interfere

**near·ly** \'ni(ə)rlē, -iəlē, -li\ *adv, sometimes* -ER/-EST [[4]*near* + *-ly*] **1 :** at close range **:** with careful scrutiny **2 a :** closely as to relationship, personal connection, or interest ⟨~ related⟩ **:** PARTICULARLY ⟨other things that concerned me more ~ to think of —W.H.Hudson †1922⟩ ⟨~ acquainted⟩ **b :** closely as to similarity ⟨~ identical⟩ ⟨two cities . . . grown to a status so ~ equal —*Amer. Guide Series: Minn.*⟩ **c :** with an approach to completeness or exactness **:** APPROXIMATELY ⟨such words are ~ meaningless⟩ ⟨lying ~ at right angles⟩ **d** *archaic* **:** closely as to location ⟨some danger does approach you ~ —Shak.⟩ **3 :** within a little **:** all but **:** ALMOST ⟨~ a year later⟩ ⟨~ a hundred dollars⟩ ⟨~ missed the train⟩

**near-miss** \'≠ˌ≠\ *n* **:** a miss (as with a bomb) close enough to the target to cause damage; *broadly* **:** something that falls just short of complete success

**near-money** \'≠ˌ≠\ *n* **:** demand or short-term obligations easily converted into cash or bank deposits **:** liquid assets

**near·most** \'≠ˌmōst *also chiefly Brit* -ˌməst\ *adj* [[4]*near* + *-most*] **:** NEAREST

**near·ness** *n* -ES [ME *nernes*, fr. *ner* near + *-nes* -ness] **:** the quality or state of being near: as **a :** close relationship or resemblance ⟨confused by the ~ of their names⟩ **b :** INTIMACY ⟨lost the ~ of the first months of their marriage⟩ **c :** proximity in space or time ⟨shyly aware of her ~ to the cowboy —Zane Grey⟩ **d :** FRUGALITY, STINGINESS

**near point** *n* **:** the point nearest the eye at which an object is accurately focused on the retina when the maximum degree of accommodation is employed, having an approximate value of 4 inches in infancy, 10 inches in the normal adult eye, and 13 inches in extreme old age — compare FAR POINT; see RANGE OF ACCOMMODATION

**near-print** \'≠ˌ≠\ *n* **:** a duplicating process (as typewriting and offset) that resembles typographical printing but does not involve the setting of metal type — called also *nomic*

**nears** *pres 3d sing of* NEAR

**near seal** *n* **:** a fur (as rabbit) dressed to simulate true seal

**nearshore** \'≠ˌ≠\ *adj* **:** extending seaward or lakeward an indefinite but generally short distance from a shore ⟨~ deposits⟩ ⟨~ current⟩

**nearside** \'≠ˌ≠\ *adj* [so called fr. the custom of approaching, mounting, or leading horses and cattle from the left side] *chiefly Brit* **:** being on the left-hand side ⟨never quite knows where his ~ wheels are —*New Statesman & Nation*⟩

**nearsighted** \'≠ˌ≠≠\ *adj* **:** seeing distinctly at short distances only **:** affected with myopia **:** SHORTSIGHTED, MYOPIC

**near·sight·ed·ly** *adv* **:** in a nearsighted manner ⟨peered ~ at the visitor —Josephine Pinckney⟩

**near·sight·ed·ness** *n* -ES **1 :** the quality or state of being nearsighted **2 :** MYOPIA

**ne·ar·thro·sis** \ˌnē+\ *n* [NL, fr. *ne-* + *arthrosis*] **:** a false joint **:** PSEUDARTHROSIS

**near wilt** *n* **:** a disease of peas caused by a fungus (*Fusarium oxysporum pisi*) and differing from true wilt in that it is found only on scattered plants, develops more slowly, and causes brick red rather than orange coloration

**ne·as·cus** \nē'askəs\ *n* -ES [NL, fr. *ne-* + Gk *askos* sack, bladder — more at ASCUS] **:** BLACK GRUB

[1]**neat** \'nēt, *usu* -ēd·+V\ *n, pl* **neat** [ME *net, neet*, fr. OE *nēat*; akin to OHG *nōz* head of cattle, ON *naut*; all fr. a prehistoric NGmc-WGmc noun akin to OE *nēotan* to make use of, enjoy, OHG *niozzan*, ON *njōta*, Goth *niutan*] **:** the common domestic bovine (*Bos taurus*); *also* **:** cattle of this or sometimes of other species of the genus *Bos* ⟨~ cattle⟩ ⟨~ stall⟩ ⟨~ leather⟩ ⟨a lion in a herd of ~ —Shak.⟩

[2]**neat** \"\ *adj* -ER/-EST [MF *net*, fr. L *nitidus* bright, lustrous, neat, fr. *nitēre* to shine; akin to MIr *niam* luster, beauty, OIr *nōib* holy, OPer *naiba-* beautiful] **1 :** BRIGHT, SHINING — used chiefly in the phrase *neat as a new pin* **2 a :** free from admixture or adulteration **:** UNDILUTED ⟨~ brandy⟩ ⟨a remark is not to be taken ~, but watered with the ideas of common sense —O.W.Holmes †1894⟩ **b :** made without sand ⟨~ cement⟩ ⟨~ plaster⟩ **c** *of raw silk* **:** free from loops, lumps, breaks, or hairiness **3** *obs* **:** finely or smartly dressed ⟨still to be ~, still to be dressed as if going to a feast —Ben Jonson⟩ **4 a :** free from whatever clutters, blurs, or confuses **:** having sharp outlines on even, smooth surfaces ⟨~ patch⟩ ⟨~ joint⟩ ⟨~ handwriting⟩ **b :** free from complication or irregularity or contradiction **:** simply or symmetrically arranged or constituted ⟨~ set of rules⟩ ⟨hated to have her ~ plans upset⟩ ⟨not all human problems have ~ solutions⟩ **c :** achieved or performed with precision and economy of effort **:** DEFT, ADROIT ⟨~ theft⟩ ⟨a ~ way of carving up a chicken⟩ ⟨mathematics . . . retains the ~ exactness of the surgeon's knife —Bertrand Russell⟩ **d :** CLEVER, INGENIOUS ⟨saw through his ~ little plan⟩ ⟨~ device for shelling peas⟩ **e :** capable of quick and accurate performance ⟨small ~ hands⟩ ⟨a *neat*-fingered worker⟩ **5 :** ORDERLY, TIDY ⟨~ housewife⟩ ⟨the cat is ~ in its habits⟩ **6 a :** CLEAR, NET ⟨~ profit⟩ **b :** GRATIFYING ⟨a ~ little fortune⟩ **7** *slang* **:** WONDERFUL, FINE, ADMIRABLE — used to express general enthusiastic approval ⟨~ bicycle⟩ ⟨we had a ~ time at the circus⟩

**syn** TIDY, TRIM, TRIG, SNUG, SHIPSHAPE, SPICK-AND-SPAN: NEAT may call forth suggestions of blended clearness and order, particularly the latter, freedom from clutter, jumble, disorder, confusion, complication, or adventitious addition ⟨she could be to the last degree slatternly. Or she could be as *neat* as a pin —Arnold Bennett⟩ ⟨as a rule he was *neat* in his person, but now his clothes were in disorder —W.S.Maugham⟩ ⟨*neat* minds, who prefer things in their proper places, ticketed and pigeon-holed —W.M.Dixon⟩ TIDY now commonly suggests a pleasing neatness and order diligently maintained ⟨he's always *tidy* without being smart; his coat is old and his trousers are uncreased, but they're both clean, and nothing's loose or torn —Richard Harrison⟩ ⟨he told me of his childhood in the *tidy* brick house, and of his mother's passionate orderliness —W.S. Maugham⟩ TRIM suggests neat smartness like that given by clean lines, good proportion, and compact, orderly arrangement ⟨a *trim* clipper ship⟩ ⟨spotless and *trim*, with shining spectacles and a white apron —Eden Phillpotts⟩ ⟨the sward was *trim* as any garden lawn —Alfred Tennyson⟩ TRIG may suggest jaunty neatness ⟨so *trig* in fashionable clothes that he made me feel awkward and uncomfortable —Irving Bacheller⟩ SNUG may suggest trim neatness with compact order in stowage and fine firmness of line and construction ⟨a *snug* little ship⟩ ⟨Farmer Matson reached the *snug* little cabin which was his headquarters —F.V.W.Mason⟩ SHIPSHAPE implies a tidiness and order befitting a ship likely to undergo sudden peril or difficulty ⟨in *shipshape* order⟩ ⟨leaving the account in *shipshape* condition⟩ SPICK-AND-SPAN suggests the brightness and freshness of the completely clean ⟨no spots came on his clothes. No slovenly habits crept upon him. He was always *spick-and-span* —W.A.White⟩ ⟨the automobile owner who likes to keep his car *spick-and-span* between washings —*New Yorker*⟩

[3]**neat** *vt* -ED/-ING/-S **1** *obs* **:** to make neat **:** TRIM, GROOM **2** *obs* **:** [4]NET

[4]**neat** \'nēt, *usu* -ēd·+V\ *adv* **:** NEATLY

**neat·en** \'nēt°n\ *vt* **neatened; neatened; neatening** \-t-(°)niŋ\ **neatens** [[2]*neat* + *-en*] **1 :** to set in order **:** make neat ⟨~*ing* the books in a low bookcase —E.B.White⟩ **2 :** to finish (as a piece of sewing) carefully ⟨oversewing edges to ~ them⟩

**neater** *comparative of* NEAT

**neatest** *superlative of* NEAT

**neath** \'nēth, -ēth\ *prep* [by shortening fr. *aneath & beneath*] *dial* **:** BENEATH

**neat-handed** \'≠ˌ≠≠\ *adj* **:** neat and deft in handling things **:** DEXTEROUS — **neat-hand·ed·ly** *adv* — **neat-hand·ed·ness** *n* -ES

**neat·herd** \'nētˌhərd, -hōd, -əid\ *n* [ME *netherde*, fr. *net* head of cattle + *herde* herdsman — more at NEAT, HERD] **:** HERDSMAN, COWHERD

**neath·most** \'≠ˌmōst *also chiefly Brit* -ˌməst\ *adj* [*neath* + *-most*] *Scot* **:** LOWEST

**neat line** *n* [[2]*neat*] **1 :** the line to which the face of a masonry wall is supposed to conform disregarding minor irregularities **2 :** the innermost of a series of lines that frame a map or mechanical drawing

**neat·ly** *adv* [[2]*neat* + *-ly*] **:** in a neat manner ⟨hair ~ combed⟩ **:** TIDILY ⟨~ kept room⟩ **:** DEFTLY, CLEVERLY ⟨~ removed the bones from the fish⟩

**neat·ness** *n* -ES **:** the quality or state of being neat

**neat's-foot oil** \'≠ˌ≠-\ *n* [[1]*neat*] **:** a pale yellow fatty oil made by boiling the feet and shinbones esp. of cattle and used chiefly as a leather dressing and fine lubricant

**neat soap** *n* [[2]*neat*] **:** molten soap formed during manufacture esp. after fitting and settling out of nigre and lye and used for making bars, chips, or powders

**neb** \'neb\ *n* -S [ME *neb, nebb*, fr. OE; akin to ON *nef* beak, nose, MLG *nebbe*, and prob. to OHG *snabul* beak] **1 :** the beak of a bird or tortoise **:** BILL; *also* **:** a person's mouth **2 :** something suggestive of a bill esp. in being jutting or pointed; *specif* **:** NOSE 1 **3 :** the pointed or narrowed end of a thing **:** TIP; *specif* **:** the point of a pen or pencil **4 :** [1]EAR 4h

**ne·ba·lia** \nə'bālēə\ *n, cap* [NL] **:** a genus of small marine crustaceans (order Nebaliacea) having the body enclosed in a bivalved carapace, the thoracic feet leaflike, the abdominal feet biramous, and the abdomen composed of eight segments — **ne·ba·li·an** \-ēən\ *adj or n* — **ne·ba·li·oid** \-ēˌȯid\ *adj or n*

**ne·ba·li·a·cea** \≠ˌ≠≠'āsh(ē)ə\ *n pl, cap* [NL, fr. *Nebalia* + *-acea*] **:** a small order of marine crustaceans (division Phyllocarida) comprising *Nebalia* and a few other genera of recent or extinct forms

**nebbed** \'nebd\ *adj* **:** having a neb

**neb·by** \'nebē, -bi\ *adj* -ER/-EST [*neb* + *-y*] **1** *dial* **:** rudely inquisitive **:** MEDDLESOME **2** *dial Brit* **:** sharp-natured **:** SPITEFUL

**ne·bel** \'nā|bəl, 'nē|\ *or* **ne·vel** \|vəl\ *n* -S [Heb *nēbhel*] **:** NABLA

**ne·ben·kern** \'nābənˌkərn\ *n* -S [G, fr. *neben-* secondary, accessory (fr. *neben* beside, next to) + *kern* kernel, nucleus] **:** an extranuclear organized body of the spermatid possibly derived from the chondriosomes — compare ACROSOME

**neb-neb** \'nebˌneb\ *n* -S [Senegalese] **:** BABUL 2

**ne·bras·ka** \nə'braskə, -raas-\ *adj, usu cap* [*Nebraska*, state in the central U. S., fr. *Nebraska*, former name for the Platte river] **:** of or from the state of Nebraska ⟨*Nebraska* farmers⟩ **:** of the kind or style prevalent in Nebraska **:** NEBRASKAN

[1]**ne·bras·kan** \-kən\ *also* **ne·bras·ki·an** \-kēən\ *adj, usu cap* [*Nebraska* state + E *-an, -ian*] **1 :** of, relating to, or characteristic of Nebraska or Nebraskans **2 :** belonging to the first glacial stage during the glacial epoch in No. America

[2]**nebraskan** \"\ *also* **nebraskian** \"\ *n* -S *cap* **:** a native or resident of the state of Nebraska

**neb·ris** \'nebrəs\ *n* -ES [L, fr. Gk, fr. *nebros* fawn] **:** a fawn skin shown in classic art as worn by Dionysus, Silenus, satyrs, and bacchanals

**neb·u·chad·nez·zar** \ˌneb(y)əkəd'nezə(r)\ *n* -S *usu cap* [after *Nebuchadnezzar* II †562 B.C. king of Babylon] **:** an oversize wine bottle holding about 20 quarts ⟨a ~ of champagne⟩

**neb·u·la** \'nebyələ\ *n, pl* **nebu·las** \-ləz\ *or* **nebu·lae** \-ˌlē, -ˌlī\ [NL, fr. L, mist, cloud; akin to OE *nifol* cloudy, dark, OS *nebal* fog, OHG *nebul* fog, ON *njōl* darkness, night, Gk *nephelē, nephos* cloud, Skt *nabhas* mist] **1 a :** any of many immense bodies of highly rarefied gas or dust in the interstellar space of our own Milky Way and other galaxies that when located in our own Milky Way may by absorption of light from objects farther away be observed as a dark cloud or may by reflection or reemission of light from associated nearby stars be observed as a bright cloud **b :** GALAXY; *specif* **:** a galaxy outside the Milky Way galaxy — see PLANETARY NEBULA, SPIRAL NEBULA **2 a :** a white spot or a slight opacity of the cornea **3 :** a liquid preparation intended for medicinal spraying

**neb·u·lar** \-lə(r)\ *adj* [NL *nebula* + E *-ar*] **:** of or relating to a nebula **:** of the nature of or resembling a nebula **:** CLOUDY

**nebular hypothesis** *n* **:** a hypothesis in astronomy: the solar system has evolved from a hot gaseous nebula

**neb·u·lat·ed** \'nebyəˌlād·əd\ *adj* [LL *nebulatus* (past part. of *nebulare* to cloud, obscure, fr. L *nebula* mist, cloud) + E *-ed*] **:** indistinctly marked **:** CLOUDED, CLOUDY

**neb·u·lé** \ˌnebyə'lā, -'lē\ *also* **neb·u·ly** \'nebyəlē\ *adj* [MF *nebulé*, fr. L *nebula* + F *-é* -ate, adj. suffix (fr. L *-atus* -ate)] **1 :** composed of successive short curves made to resemble a cloud — used of a heraldic line by which an ordinary or subordinary may be bounded **2** *of a molding* **:** consisting of an overhanging band the lower projecting edge of which conforms in shape to a continuous undulating curve

**ne·bu·li·um** \nə'byülēəm, ne'-\ *n* -S [NL, fr. *nebula* + *-ium*] **:** a hypothetical chemical element formerly inferred from certain lines in the spectra of nebulae now believed to arise from transitions in oxygen and nitrogen that are forbidden under ordinary laboratory conditions

**neb·u·li·za·tion** \ˌnebyələ'zāshən, -ˌlī'z-\ *n* -S **:** reduction (as of a medicinal solution) to a mist, spray, or vapor

**neb·u·lize** \'≠≠ˌlīz\ *vt* -ED/-ING/-S [NL *nebula* + E *-ize*] **:** to reduce (as a medicinal solution) to a fine spray **:** AEROSOLIZE — **neb·u·liz·er** \-zə(r)\ *n* -S

**neb·u·lose** \-ˌlōs\ *adj* [L *nebulosus* — more at NEBULOUS] **:** NEBULOUS

**neb·u·los·i·ty** \ˌ≠≠'läsəd·ē, -ətē, -i\ *n* -ES [F or LL; F *nébulosité*, fr. LL *nebulositat-, nebulositas*, fr. L *nebulosus* + *-itat-, -itas* -ity] **1 :** the quality or state of being nebulous **:** CLOUDINESS **2 :** nebulous matter **:** NEBULA ⟨faintly luminous ~ is abundant in the vicinity of Orion —R.H.Baker⟩

**neb·u·lous** \'≠≠ləs\ *adj* [L *nebulosus*, fr. *nebula* mist, cloud + *-osus* -ous, -ose — more at NEBULA] **1** *archaic* **:** full of clouds **:** CLOUDY, FOGGY **2 a :** lacking clarity of feature or sharpness of outline **:** HAZY, INDISTINCT ⟨~ memory⟩ ⟨~ line between confidence and overconfidence —*Wall Street Jour.*⟩ **b :** vaguely defined **:** poorly grasped **:** dimly realized ⟨~ hopes and fears⟩ ⟨~ social values —A.H.MacCormick⟩ **3 :** not transparent **:** TURBID, CLOUDED **4 :** of, relating to, or resembling a nebula **:** NEBULAR — **neb·u·lous·ly** *adv* — **neb·u·lous·ness** *n* -ES

**nebulous cluster** *n* **:** a cluster of stars containing or enveloped in nebulosity

**ne·ca·tor** \nə'kād·ə(r)\ *n* [NL, fr. LL, killer, fr. L *necatus* (past part. of *necare* to kill, fr. *nec-, nex* violent death) + *-or* — more at NOXIOUS] **1** *cap* **:** a common genus of hookworms that have buccal teeth resembling flat plates, that include internal parasites of man and various other mammals, and that are prob. of African origin though first identified in No. America — compare ANCYLOSTOMA **2 -s :** any hookworm of the genus *Necator*

**nec·es·sar** \'nesəsər\ *Scot var of* NECESSARY

**nec·es·sar·i·an** \ˌnesə'serēən -sa(a)r-, -sār-\ *n or adj* [*necessary* + *-an*] **:** NECESSITARIAN

**nec·es·sar·i·an·ism** \ˌ≠≠'≠≠əˌnizəm\ *n* -S [[1]*necessarian* + *-ism*] **:** NECESSITARIANISM

**nec·es·sar·i·ly** \ˌ≠≠'serəlē, -li\ *adv* [ME, fr. *necessary* + *-ly*] **1 :** in such a way that it cannot be otherwise **:** of necessity **:** INEVITABLY, UNAVOIDABLY ⟨the audience was ~ small⟩ ⟨political philosophy ~ implies the attitude of the philosopher toward politics —Hannah Arendt⟩ ⟨occupying precious space with a ~ lengthy chapter —Peter Heaton⟩ **2 a :** as a necessary result or consequence ⟨their whole political outlook was ~ determined by this condition —G.L.Dickinson⟩ ⟨inconsistency, flat contradiction, and irrelevance ~ prevent an armed doctrine from achieving great success —D.W.Brogan⟩

**nec·es·sar·i·ness** \-rēnəs, -rin-\ *n* -ES *archaic* **:** the quality or state of being necessary **:** NECESSITY

[1]**nec·es·sary** \'nesəˌserē, -ri, *in rapid speech* 'nesˌse-\ *n* -ES [ME *necessaries* (pl.), fr. L *necessaria*, fr. neut. pl. of *necessarius* necessary (adj.)] **1 a** (1) **necessaries** *pl* **:** items (as of food, clothing, shelter, medical care, equipment or furnishing) that cannot be done without **:** things that must be had (as for the preservation and reasonable enjoyment of life) **:** ESSENTIALS ⟨was provided with at least the *necessaries* of life⟩ ⟨gave away so much that he could only have kept just enough to keep himself in bare *necessaries* —Flora Thompson⟩ ⟨household *necessaries*⟩; *specif* **:** such items as are essential to the proper maintenance and support of those (as married women) who are legally dependent or those (as infants, children, the mentally ill) who are legally incompetent (2) **:** one such essential item ⟨salt is a ~⟩ **b :** whatever is essential for some purpose ⟨supplies of the ~ were hard to come by —Brian James⟩; *esp* **:** MONEY — used with *the* **2** *chiefly NewEng* **:** PRIVY 2

[2]**necessary** \"\ *adj* [ME *necessarie*, fr. L *necessarius*, fr. *necesse* unavoidable, inevitable, necessary (fr. *ne* not + *-cesse*, fr. *cedere* to withdraw) + *-arius* -ary — more at NO, CEDE] **1 a :** that must be by reason of the inherent nature of things **:** that cannot be otherwise by reason of inherent qualities **:** that is or exists or comes to be by reason of the nature of being and that cannot be or exist or come to be in any other way **:** that is determined and fixed and inevitable ⟨death is a ~ feature of the human condition⟩ ⟨it is ~ that a whole be greater than any of its parts⟩ ⟨patience . . . is a ~ mark of the liberal mind —John Dewey⟩ **b :** of, relating to, or having the character of something that is logically required or logically inevitable or that cannot be denied without involving contradiction ⟨a ~ judgment⟩ ⟨a ~ relation between two things⟩ ⟨a ~ truth⟩ ⟨a ~ conclusion⟩ — opposed to *contingent* **c :** that is inevitably fixed or determined or produced by a previous condition of things ⟨a ~ result⟩ ⟨the ~ outcome of the affair⟩ **d** (1) **:** that is produced in a mechanical way through conditioning (as by previous actions, experiences) so as to be devoid of freedom of the will ⟨a ~ submission to evil⟩ (2) **:** that is driven by

circumstances or other outside forces so as to have little or no independence of volition : not exercising free choice : acting under compulsion ⟨the ~ agent of some crimes⟩ **2 :** that cannot be done without : that must be done or had : absolutely required : ESSENTIAL, INDISPENSABLE ⟨food is ~ for all⟩ ⟨was ~ to her peace of mind⟩ ⟨the ~ secrecy of my trip —F.D. Roosevelt⟩ ⟨the ~ conditions of freedom —F.C.Neff⟩ ⟨a ~ tool⟩ ⟨a ~ law⟩ ⟨took all ~ steps⟩ ⟨a ~ act⟩ **syn** see NEEDFUL

**necessary condition** *n* **:** CONDITION 2a(3)

**necessary deposit** *n* **:** a deposit arising where the owner of property entrusts it to another in a sudden emergency or overwhelming calamity (as in case of fire or earthquake)

**necessary house** *n, chiefly dial* **:** PRIVY

**necessary improvement** *n* **:** an improvement to property that is made to prevent its deterioration

**necessary woman** *n, archaic* **:** a personal maid

**¹ne·ces·si·tar·i·an** \nə̇ˌsesəˈterēən, -ta(a)r-, -tär-\ *n* -s [*necessity* + *-arian*] **:** one that accepts or advocates necessitarianism — contrasted with *libertarian*

**²necessitarian** \"\ *adj* **:** of or relating to a necessitarian or necessitarianism

**ne·ces·si·tar·i·an·ism** \-əˌnizəm\ *n* -s **:** the theory or doctrine that results follow by invariable sequence from causes **:** the doctrine of philosophical necessity **:** DETERMINISM

**¹ne·ces·si·tate** \ə̇ˈ==ˌtāt, *usu* -ād+V\ *vt* -ED/-ING/-S [ML *necessitatus*, past part. of *necessitare* to compel, constrain, fr. L *necessitas* necessity — more at NECESSITY] **1 :** to make necessary: as **a** (1) **:** to make inevitable **:** make unavoidable ⟨difficult circumstances seemed to ~ a certain gloominess on his part⟩ (2) **:** to involve as an essential element or inevitable outcome or unavoidable consequence ⟨goodness ~*s* a sharing of itself⟩ ⟨his private practice grew to large proportions, *necessitating* the employment of assistants —G.M.Lewis b.1899⟩ **b :** to cause to be required as an indispensable preparation, condition, or accompaniment ⟨the complexity of the problem ~*s* careful thought and good judgment⟩ ⟨world changes which *necessitated* a new approach —Bruce Bliven b.1889⟩ **2 :** to put under the obligation of **:** force into **:** CONSTRAIN, COMPEL ⟨was *necessitated* to choose some other route⟩ **3** *archaic* **:** to reduce to a state of necessity **:** cause to be hard up

**²necessitate** *adj* [ML *necessitatus*] *obs* **:** forced by necessity ⟨being ~ to leave London —Anne Halkett⟩

**ne·ces·si·ta·tion** \=ˌ==ˈtāshən\ *n* -s **:** the act of necessitating or condition of being necessitated ⟨the absence of ~ by the past —A.C.Ewing⟩ ⟨is good by free choice, not ~ —Nicholas Rescher⟩

**ne·ces·si·tous** \=ˈsesəd·əs, -ətəs\ *adj* [F *nécessiteux*, fr. *nécessité* necessity (fr. L *necessitat-, necessitas*) + *-eux* -ous] **1 a :** hard up **:** reduced to a state of marked want **:** NEEDY ⟨was a ~ widower with a marriageable daughter —Norman Douglas⟩ ⟨the most ~ members of the community —T.B. Macaulay⟩ **b :** STRAITENED ⟨~ circumstances⟩ **2 :** URGENT, PRESSING ⟨except for the most ~ reasons —Walter Goodman⟩ **3 :** that is essential by reason of circumstances **:** that is unavoidable ⟨will be unable to do its ~ financing —Allan Sproul⟩ **syn** see POOR

**ne·ces·si·tude** \-əˌtüd, -əˌtyüd\ *n* -s [L *necessitudo*, fr. *necesse* necessary + *-i-* + *-tudo* -tude] *archaic* **:** NECESSITY

**¹ne·ces·si·ty** \nə̇ˈsesəd·ē, -ətē, -ˈsestē, -i\ *n* -ES [ME *necessite*, fr. MF *necessité*, fr. L *necessitat-, necessitas*, fr. *necesse* necessary + *-itat-, -itas* -ity — more at NECESSARY] **1 :** the quality or state or fact of being necessary: as **a :** a condition arising out of circumstances that compels to a certain course of action ⟨as if there were some ~ for being together that only the two of them understood —C.B.Flood⟩ **b :** INEVITABLENESS, UNAVOIDABILITY ⟨the ~ of death⟩ **c :** great or absolute need **:** INDISPENSABILITY ⟨the ~ of full and fair news service —F.L. Mott⟩ ⟨the ~ of civil, academic, and scientific liberty —George Soule⟩ **d** (1) **:** absence of physical or moral liberty **:** physical or moral compulsion ⟨did it, not because he wanted to, but by ~⟩ ⟨making a virtue of ~⟩ (2) **:** constraint or compulsion arising out of the natural constitution of things **:** impossibility of a contrary order or condition of things ⟨submitting to the ~ imposed by the physical laws of the universe⟩ ⟨logical ~⟩ ⟨physical ~⟩ **2 :** the quality or state or fact of being in difficulties or in need ⟨came to help them in their ~⟩; *esp* **:** POVERTY ⟨was reduced to the most abject ~⟩ **3 :** something that is necessary **:** REQUIREMENT, REQUISITE ⟨daily *necessities*⟩ ⟨is a ~ for happy living⟩ ⟨the *necessities* of life⟩ — **of necessity** *adv* **:** NECESSARILY ⟨something that *of necessity* must be so⟩

**²necessity** \"\ *adj* [*necessity (money)*] **:** consisting of, used as, or designed for necessity money ⟨a ~ coin⟩

**necessity money** *n* **:** money (as a coin, token, note) issued for a period of emergency (as a war, siege, financial crisis) and typically consisting of substitute materials

**¹neck** \ˈnek\ *n* -s [ME *necke, nekke*, fr. OE *hnecca;* akin to OHG *hnac* nape of the neck, ON *hnakki* nape of the neck, OE *hnutu* nut — more at NUT] **1 a** (1) **:** the usu. constricted part of an animal that connects the head with the body; *specif* **:** the cervical region of a vertebrate (2) **:** the part of a tapeworm immediately behind the scolex from which new proglottides are produced — see ECHINOCOCCUS illustration (3) **:** the siphon of a bivalve mollusk (as a clam) — not used technically **b :** the part of a garment that covers or is next to the neck; *esp* **:** NECKLINE **2 :** a relatively narrow or constricted part joining two other parts or located at an end and suggestive of a neck: as **a** (1) **:** the narrowed part of a bottle running from the body of the bottle to the mouth (2) **:** the slender end of a gourd or of some other fruits **b :** the narrow part of the uterus **:** CERVIX **c** (1) **:** COLLET 3 (2) **:** the tapering distal part of an archegonium (3) **:** the terminal usu. elongated part of a perithecium or pycnidium in some fungi (4) **:** the part of the trunk of a tree or of the stem of a shrub that is at the surface of the soil (5) **:** the restricted part of the leaf cluster just above the bulb of an onion **d** (1) **:** GORGERIN (2) **:** the narrow part of a column or baluster shaft just below the capital **e :** a part reduced in circumference (as the part forming the journal of a shaft) formed by a groove around and usu. near the end of an object **f** (1) **:** the slender part of a cascabel between the knob and the fillet (2) **:** the part of a cannon immediately behind the swell of the muzzle (3) **:** the cylindrical part of a cartridge case that has an inside diameter about equal to the projectile diameter **g :** the part of a stringed musical instrument which extends from the body and to which are attached the fingerboard and the strings **h :** BEARD 4d **i :** a thread shank for a button **3 a :** a narrow stretch of land (as an isthmus, cape, promontory, or mountain pass) **b** (1) **:** a narrow body of water between two larger bodies **:** STRAIT (2) **:** a narrow current flowing seaward through incoming surf **c :** a mass of solidified massive or fragmental lava or igneous rock that fills or formerly filled a conduit leading upward to a volcanic vent or a laccolith **d :** a narrow vertically elongated ore body **4 :** a brick wall that is usu. 60 bricks long, 24 to 30 high, and 3 thick placed on each side of an upright or double battering wall to form a clamp **5 a :** the approximate length of the neck of a horse plus that of the head ⟨won by a ~⟩ **b :** a narrow margin of victory ⟨won the election campaign by a ~⟩ **6 :** WAKE, TRAIL — used with *in, on, upon* ⟨this bad news followed on the ~ of the letter⟩ — **in the neck** *adv* **:** to a severe or painful extent **:** without sparing ⟨really got it *in the neck* for his impudence⟩

**²neck** \"\ *vb* -ED/-ING/-S *vt* **1 a :** to strike sharply (as with the side of the hand) on the neck **b :** BEHEAD **c :** to twist or pull the neck of (as a fowl) so as to kill **2 :** to reduce the diameter of esp. by making a groove around — often used with *down* or *in* ⟨~ down a cylinder⟩ ⟨~*ing* down a cartridge case⟩ **3** *chiefly West* **:** to tie (animals) loosely together by means of something (as a rope, thong) fastened about the neck **4 :** to hold tightly and fondle and kiss amorously ⟨~*ing* the co-eds on the steps of the lecture hall —*Time*⟩ ~ *vi* **1 :** to engage in fondling and kissing ⟨a young couple ~*ing* on the park bench⟩ **2 :** to undergo a constriction or reduction of cross section — used esp. of a solid rod subjected to tension beyond the yield value

**³neck** \"\ *n* -s [origin unknown] *dial Eng* **:** the last sheaf of grain cut often with traditional ceremonies at harvest time and sometimes decorated and preserved

**neck ail** *n, chiefly NewEng* **:** a cobalt deficiency disease of sheep and cattle

**neck and crop** *adv* **:** with brisk dispatch and completeness **:** SUMMARILY ⟨turned her out into the street *neck and crop* —W.S.Maugham⟩

**neck and heels** *adv* **1 :** neck and crop **2 :** SECURELY ⟨tied him up *neck and heels*⟩

**neck and neck** *adj (or adv)* **:** very close together (as in a race, contest, campaign, game) so that the winner is not yet certain ⟨were *neck and neck* in the polls through most of the election campaign⟩

**neckatee** *n* -s [¹*neck* + *-atee* (origin unknown)] *obs* **:** NECKERCHIEF

**neckband** \ˈ=ˌ=\ *n* [ME *nekbande*, fr. *nek, nekke* neck + *bande* strip — more at BAND] **1 :** a usu. ornamental band worn about the neck **2 a :** the part of a garment that encircles the neck and finishes the neckline ⟨the ~ of a sweater⟩ **b :** the band of a shirt to which a collar is sewed or buttoned

**neckbreaking** \ˈ=ˌ==\ *adj* **:** BREAKNECK

**neck canal cell** *n* [trans. of G *halskanalzelle*] **:** one of the cells in the neck of an archegonium

**neck cell** *n* **:** one of the sterile cells constituting the jacket that surrounds the canal cells in an archegonium

**neckcloth** \ˈ=ˌ=\ *n* **1 a :** a large folded ornamental cloth formerly worn loosely about the neck by men **b :** NECKERCHIEF **2** *archaic* **:** NECKTIE

**neck-deep** \ˈ=ˈ=\ *adj (or adv)* **:** sunk or absorbed or involved in something almost to the point of total submersion ⟨was *neck-deep* in trouble —*Time*⟩ **:** up to the limit of involvement ⟨fell *neck-deep* into difficulties⟩

**necked** \ˈnekt\ *adj* [¹*neck* + *-ed*] **1 :** having a neck or necks of a specified kind or number ⟨red-*necked*⟩ ⟨short-*necked*⟩ ⟨two-*necked*⟩ **2 :** having a neck ⟨~ barnacles⟩

**neck·er** \ˈnekə(r)\ *n* -s [¹*neck* + *-er*] **:** one that stitches around the neckline of neckties

**neck·er·cher** \ˈnekə(r)chə(r)\ *n* -s [¹*neck* + *kercher*] *chiefly dial* **:** NECKERCHIEF

**neck·er·chief** \-chəf, -(ˌ)chif, -ˌchēf\ *n, pl* **neckerchiefs** *also* **neckerchieves** \-fs, -vz; *see pl at* HANDKERCHIEF\ [ME *nekkerchef*, fr. *nekke* neck + *kerchef* kerchief — more at NECK, KERCHIEF] **:** a folded ornamental square of cloth worn about the neck like a scarf or worn esp. by sailors as part of a uniform

**neck handkerchief** *n, archaic* **:** NECKCLOTH

**neckhole** \ˈ=ˌ=\ *n* **:** an opening in a garment for the head and neck to pass through

**neck·ing** \ˈnekiŋ, -ēŋ\ *n* -s [¹*neck* + *-ing*] **1 :** a small molding near the top of a column or pilaster **2 :** GORGERIN

**¹neck·lace** \ˈnekləs\ *n* [¹*neck* + *lace*] **1 a** (1) **:** a string of beads or of other small objects (as precious stones) that is worn about the neck as an ornament (2) **:** a chain or band usu. of metal often specially decorated (as with enamel work, precious stones) and worn about the neck as an ornament **b** (1) **:** a trimming or decoration that resembles or is suggestive of a necklace (2) **:** a stripe of different color about the neck of an animal **c :** a series of identical or similar things arranged or lying in a circular or semicircular pattern or otherwise linked together like a necklace ⟨with a ~ of barbed wire gun pits ringing it about —T.H.White b.1915⟩ ⟨a ~ of islands⟩ **2 :** a rope or chain fitted around a mast near the top to hold hanging blocks

**²necklace** \"\ *vt* **:** to provide with or as if with a necklace ⟨*necklaced* the statue with a wreath of flowers⟩ ~ *vi* **:** to become formed into or as if into a necklace ⟨boats *necklacing* about the pier⟩

**necklace poplar** *n* [so called fr. the arrangement of its pods] **:** BALSAM POPLAR

**necklace tree** *n* [so called fr. the use of its seeds as beads] **:** a tree of the genus *Ormosia*; *esp* **:** JUMBY BEAN 1a

**necklaceweed** \ˈ==ˌ=\ *n* [so called fr. its pearly white berries] **1 :** WHITE BANEBERRY **2 :** FALSE GROMWELL

**neck·less** \ˈnekləs\ *adj* **:** having no neck

**neck·let** \-lət\ *n* -s [¹*neck* + *-let*] **1 :** an ornamental piece (as of fur) worn about the neck **2 :** a close-fitting necklace

**necklike** \ˈ=ˌ=\ *adj* **:** resembling a neck

**neckline** \ˈ=ˌ=\ *n* **1 :** the line formed by the neck opening of a garment ⟨the little pleated frill that finished the ~ of her gown —Edna Ferber⟩ **2 :** the line formed by the edge of the hair across the back of the neck

**neckmold** \ˈ=ˌ=\ *or* **neck molding** *n* **:** NECKING

**neck of the woods 1 :** a settlement in a wooded country **2 :** NEIGHBORHOOD, REGION ⟨haven't been in that *neck of the woods* for a long time⟩

**neck or nothing** *also* **neck or nought** *adv* **:** with complete abandon and recklessness ⟨launched my scheme *neck or nought* —W.C.Hazlitt⟩

**neckpiece** \ˈ=ˌ=\ *n* **1 :** an article of apparel (as a fur) worn about the neck **2 :** MIDDLE PIECE

**neck-rein** \ˈ=ˌ=\ *vi, of a saddle horse* **:** to respond to the pressure of a rein on one side of the neck by turning in the opposite direction ~ *vt* **:** to guide or direct (a horse) by pressures of the rein on the neck

**neck rot** *n* **:** a disease of onions caused by a fungus of the genus *Botrytis* and marked by rotting of the leaf cluster just above the bulb

**necks** *pl of* NECK, *pres 3d sing of* NECK

**necktie** \ˈ=ˌ=\ *n* **:** a rather long narrow length of soft material (as silk or wool) worn about the neck usu. under a collar with a knot, loop, or bow tied in front and with the two ends usu. falling free vertically; *esp* **:** FOUR-IN-HAND — compare BOW TIE

**necktie party** *n, slang* **:** LYNCHING, HANGING ⟨were threatened with mob violence, with tar and feathering and a *necktie party* —Mari Sandoz⟩

**neck-verse** \ˈ=ˌ=\ *n* [ME *neke verse;* fr. the possibility of its saving the accused person's neck] **:** a verse usu. consisting of the first lines of a Latin version of the 51st psalm formerly set before an accused person claiming benefit of clergy so that the person might vindicate his claim by an intelligent reading aloud of the verse before examiners

**neckwear** \ˈ=ˌ=\ *n* **:** articles of clothing worn about the neck (as ties, collars, scarfs)

**neckweed** \ˈ=ˌ=\ *n* [so called fr. its use for treating scrofula] **:** an American speedwell (*Veronica peregrina*)

**necr-** *or* **necro-** *comb form* [LL, fr. Gk *nekr-, nekro-*, fr. *nekros* dead body, dead person — more at NOXIOUS] **1 a :** those that are dead **:** the dead **:** corpses ⟨*necro*philism⟩ **b :** one that is dead **:** corpse ⟨*necro*psy⟩ **2 :** death ⟨*necro*biosis⟩ **:** conversion to dead tissue **:** atrophy ⟨*necr*osis⟩ **3 :** extinct **:** fossil ⟨*necro*type⟩

**ne·cro** \ˈne(ˌ)krō\ *n* -s [by shortening] **:** NECROTIC ENTERITIS

**ne·cro·bacillary** \ˌnekrō+\ *adj* [NL *necrobacillosis* + E *-ary*] **:** of, relating to, or marked by necrobacillosis

**ne·cro·bacillosis** \"+\ *n* [NL *necrophorus* & *necrophorum* (specific epithets of *Sphaerophorus necrophorus* & *Necrobacterium necrophorum* respectively; fr. *necr-* + *-phorus* or *-phorum*, neut. of *-phorus*) + *bacillosis*] **:** infection with or disease caused by a bacterium (*Sphaerophorus necrophorus* or *Necrobacterium necrophorum*) that is either localized (as in foot rot) or disseminated through the body of an affected mammal and that is characterized by inflammation and ulcerative or necrotic lesions — compare BULLNOSE, CALF DIPHTHERIA, QUITTOR

**ne·cro·bia** \nəˈkrōbēə, neˈ-\ *n, cap* [NL, fr. *necr-* + *-bia*] **:** a genus of widely distributed beetles that include the copra beetle, are related to the family Cleridae, and feed on animal and cereal products

**ne·cro·bi·o·sis** \ˌnekrō,bīˈōsə̇s\ *n, pl* **necrobioses** \-ˌsēz\ [NL, fr. *necr-* + *-biosis*] **:** death of a cell or group of cells within a tissue whether normal (as in various epithelial tissues) or part of a pathologic process — compare NECROSIS

**ne·cro·biotic** \"+\ *adj* [fr. NL *necrobiosis*, after such pairs as NL *neurosis:* E *neurotic*] **:** of, relating to, or being in a state of necrobiosis

**ne·cro·gen·ic** \ˌ==ˈjenik\ *or* **ne·crog·e·nous** \nəˈkräjənəs, neˈ-\ *adj* [*necr-* + *-genic, -genous*] **:** relating to, living in, or coming from carrion

**ne·crog·ra·pher** \nəˈkrägrəfə(r), neˈ-\ *n* -s [*necr-* + *-grapher*] **:** NECROLOGIST

**ne·crol·a·try** \=ˈkrälə·trē, -ri\ *n* -ES [LGk *nekrolatreia*, fr. Gk *nekr-* necr- + *-latreia* -latry] **:** superstitious worship or veneration of the dead

**ne·ro·log·i·cal** \ˌnekrəˈläjəkəl\ *also* **nec·ro·log·ic** \-jik\ *adj* **:** of, relating to, or having the nature of a necrology ⟨a ~ notice in a newspaper⟩ — **nec·ro·log·i·cal·ly** \-jək(ə)lē\ *adv*

**ne·crol·o·gist** \nəˈkrälə̇jə̇st, neˈ-\ *n* -s **:** one that writes or compiles a necrology

**nec·ro·logue** \ˈnekrəˌlȯg *also* -läg\ *n* -s [alter. (influenced by *catalogue*) of *necrology*] **:** NECROLOGY

**ne·crol·o·gy** \nəˈkräləjē, neˈ-, -ji\ *n* -ES [NL *necrologium*, fr. *necr-* + *-logium* (as in *eulogium* eulogy, epitaph) — more at EULOGY] **1 a :** an ecclesiastical or monastic register in which are recorded the dates of death of persons (as benefactors) closely associated with the church or monastery where the register is kept **b :** a list of persons that have died at or within a certain time ⟨the publication carried a ~ of contributors who had died during the year⟩ **2** [F *nécrologie*, fr. NL *necrologium*] **:** a death notice **:** OBITUARY

**nec·ro·man·cer** \ˈnekrəˌman(t)sə(r)\ *n* -s [alter. (influenced by LL *necromantia* necromancy) of *nigromancer*, fr. ME, fr. MF, fr. *nigromance* necromancy + *-er*] **:** one that practices necromancy

**¹nec·ro·manc·ing** \-ˌman(t)siŋ, -sēŋ\ *adj* [*necromancer* + *-ing*] **:** practicing necromancy

**²necromancing** \"\ *n* -s **:** the practice of necromancy

**nec·ro·man·cy** \-n(t)sē, -si\ *n* -ES [alter. (influenced by LL *necromantia*) of ME *nigromancie*, fr. MF *nigromance, nigromancie*, fr. ML *nigromantia*, by folk etymology (influence of L *nigr-, niger* black) fr. LL *necromantia*, fr. LGk *nekromanteia*, fr. Gk *nekr-* necr- + *-manteia* -mancy — more at NEGRO] **1 a** (1) **:** the art or practice of magically revealing the future, of magically influencing the course of natural events, or of magically attaining other purposes esp. through communication with and the intervention of the dead (2) **:** the art or practice of magically conjuring up the souls of the dead **b :** magic in general esp. when directed toward the attainment of evil purposes **:** WITCHCRAFT, SORCERY **2 :** an instance of the practice of necromancy

**nec·ro·mant** \-ˌmant\ *n* -s [Gk *nekromantis*, fr. *nekr-* necr- + *mantis* seer, prophet — more at MANTIS] **:** NECROMANCER

**nec·ro·man·tic** \ˌ==ˈmantik\ *adj* [LL *necromanticus*, fr. *necromantia* + L *-icus* -ic] **1 :** given to the practice of necromancy ⟨a ~ sorcerer⟩ **2 a :** of, relating to, or associated with necromancy ⟨mysterious ~ rites⟩ **b :** accomplished or produced by necromancy ⟨~ delusions⟩ **3 :** used in necromancy ⟨strange ~ powders and other weird objects⟩ — **nec·ro·man·ti·cal·ly** \-tə̇k(ə)lē\ *adv*

**nec·ro·man·ti·cal** *obs var of* NECROMANTIC

**ne·croph·a·ga** \nəˈkräfəgə, neˈ-\ *n pl, cap* [NL, fr. *necr-* + *-phaga*] **:** a group composed of the burying beetles

**nec·ro·pha·gia** \ˌnekrəˈfājēə\ *n* -s [NL, fr *necr-* + *-phagia*] **:** the act or practice of eating corpses or carrion

**ne·croph·a·gous** \nəˈkräfəgəs, neˈ-\ *adj* [Gk *nekrophagos*, fr. *nekr-* necr- + *-phagos* -phagous] **:** feeding on corpses or carrion ⟨~ savages⟩ ⟨~ insects⟩

**ne·croph·a·gy** \-jē\ *n* -ES [*necr-* + *-phagy*] **:** NECROPHAGIA

**nec·ro·phile** \ˈnekrəˌfīl\ *also* **nec·ro·phil** \-ˌfil\ *n* -s [*necr-* + *-phile, -phil*] **:** one that is affected with necrophilia

**nec·ro·phil·ia** \ˌ==ˈfilēə\ *n* -s [NL, fr. *necr-* + *-philia*] **:** fascination with the dead; *specif* **:** obsession with and usu. erotic attraction toward and stimulation by corpses typically evidenced by overt acts (as copulation with a corpse)

**¹nec·ro·phil·i·ac** \ˌ==ˈfilēˌak\ *adj* [NL *necrophilia* + E *-ac* (fr. Gk *-akos*, adj. suffix)] **:** NECROPHILIC

**²necrophiliac** \"\ *n* -s **:** NECROPHILE

**¹nec·ro·phil·ic** \-lik\ *adj* [*necr-* + *-philic*] **:** of, relating to, or marked by necrophilia

**²necrophilic** \"\ *n* -s **:** NECROPHILE

**ne·croph·i·lism** \nəˈkräfəˌlizəm, neˈ-\ *n* -s **1 :** NECROPHILIA **2 :** an act prompted by necrophilia

**ne·croph·i·list** \-lə̇st\ *n* -s **:** NECROPHILE

**ne·croph·i·lous** \-ləs\ *adj* [*necr-* + *-philous*] **1 :** NECROPHAGOUS **2 :** NECROPHILIC

**ne·croph·i·ly** \-lē\ *n* -ES [*necr-* + *-phily*] **:** NECROPHILIA

**nec·ro·phobe** \ˈnekrəˌfōb\ *n* -s [*necr-* + *-phobe*] **:** one that exhibits necrophobia

**nec·ro·pho·bia** \ˌ==ˈfōbēə\ *n* [NL, fr. *necr-* + *-phobia*] **:** an exaggerated fear of death or horror of dead bodies — **nec·ro·pho·bic** \ˌ==ˈfōbik *also* -ˈfäb-\ *adj*

**ne·croph·o·rus** \nəˈkräf(ə)rəs, (ˈ)neˈk-\ *n, cap* [NL, fr. Gk *nekrophoros* burying the dead, fr. *nekr-* necr- + *-phoros* bearing, burying (fr. *pherein* to bear, carry to burial) — more at BEAR] **:** a genus of large burying beetles

**nec·ro·pole** \ˈnekrəˌpōl\ *n* -s [back-formation fr. NL *necropoles*, pl. of *necropolis*] **:** NECROPOLIS

**ne·crop·o·lis** \nəˈkräpələs, neˈ-\ *n, pl* **necropolis·es** \-lə̇səz\ *or* **necropo·les** \-ˌlēz\ *also* **necropo·leis** \-ˌlīs\ *or* **necropo·li** \-ˌlī\ [LL, city of the dead, fr. Gk *nekropolis*, fr. *nekr-* necr- + *-polis*] **1 a :** CEMETERY; *esp* **:** a large elaborate cemetery of an ancient city **b :** an ancient or prehistoric burying place **2 :** a place (as an abandoned city or town) devoid of life and inhabited by or as if by only the dead

**¹ne·crop·sy** \ˈneˌkräpsē, -nəˈk-, neˈk-\ *n* -ES [*necr-* + *-opsy*] **:** POSTMORTEM EXAMINATION

**²necropsy** \"\ *vt* -ED/-ING/-ES **:** to perform a postmortem examination upon

**necrose** \nəˈkrōs, neˈ-, -ōz, ˈneˌk-\ *vb* -ED/-ING/-S [back-formation fr. *necrosis*] *vi* **:** to undergo necrosis ⟨tissues subjected to prolonged pressure may ~ to form bedsores⟩ ~ *vt* **:** to affect with or cause to undergo necrosis ⟨infarction commonly ~*s* tissues deprived of blood⟩

**ne·cro·sin** \ˈnekrəsə̇n\ *n* -s [ISV *necros-* (fr. *necrosis*) + *-in*] **:** a toxic substance associated with euglobulin in injured tissue and inflammatory exudates that induces leukopenia and hastens blood coagulation and is regarded by some as a proteolytic enzyme

**ne·cro·sis** \nəˈkrōsə̇s, neˈ-\ *n, pl* **necro·ses** \-ˌsēz\ [LL, fr. Gk *nekrōsis*, fr. *nekroun* to make dead, mortify, fr. *nekros* dead body — more at NOXIOUS] **1 :** death of living tissue: as **a :** death of a portion of animal tissue differentially affected by loss of blood supply, corrosion, burning, the local lesion of a disease (as tuberculosis), or other local injury — compare NECROBIOSIS **b :** localized or general death of plant tissue caused by low temperatures, fungi, or other factors and often characterized by a brownish or black discoloration **2 :** DEADARM

**nec·ro·sper·mia** \ˌnekrəˈspərmēə\ *n* -s [NL, fr. *necr-* + *-spermia*] **:** a condition in which the spermatozoa in seminal fluid are dead or motionless

**ne·crot·ic** \nəˈkräd·ik, neˈ-, -ätik\ *adj* [Gk *nekrōtikos*, fr. (assumed) *nekrōtos* (verbal of *nekroun*) + *-ikos* -ic] **:** affected with, characterized by, or producing necrosis

**necrotic enteritis** *n* **:** a serious infectious disease of young swine caused by a bacterium (*Salmonella suipestifer* or *S. choleraesuis*) and marked by fever and by necrotic and ulcerative inflammation of the intestinal wall — called also *necro, swine typhoid, paratyphoid;* see HOG CHOLERA

**necrotic ring spot** *n* **:** a virus leaf spot of cherries characterized by small dark water-soaked sometimes incomplete rings which may alternate with the normal green tissue and later often drop out and give the leaf a shredded or tattered appearance

**necrotic stomatitis** *n* **:** CALF DIPHTHERIA

**nec·ro·tize** \ˈnekrəˌtīz\ *vb* -ED/-ING/-S *see -ize in Explan Notes* [*necrotic* + *-ize*] *vi* **:** to undergo necrosis ⟨a *necrotizing* lesion⟩ ~ *vt* **:** to cause or affect with necrosis

**ne·crot·o·my** \nəˈkräd·əmē, neˈ-, -mi\ *n* -ES [*necr-* + *-tomy*] **1 :** dissection of dead bodies **2 :** surgical removal of necrosed bone

**nec·ro·type** \ˈnekrəˌtīp\ *n* [*necr-* + *type*] **:** an extinct organism or group of organisms

**nect-** *or* **necto-** *comb form* [NL, fr. Gk *nēktos*, fr. *nēchein* to swim — more at NESO-] **:** swimming **:** for swimming ⟨*necto*calyx⟩

**-nec·tae** \ˈnek(ˌ)tē\ *n pl comb form* [NL, fr. Gk *nēktai*, pl. of *nēktēs* swimmer, fr. *nēchein* to swim] **:** ones that swim in a (specified) way — in taxonomic names in zoology ⟨Cysto*nectae*⟩

**nec·tan·dra** \nekˈtandrə\ *n, cap* [NL, fr. L *nectar* + NL *-andra;* fr. the nectar glands of the anthers] **:** a large genus of tropical American trees of the family Lauraceae having pinnately veined leaves and small paniculate flowers — see BEBEERU, GREENHEART

**¹nec·tar** \ˈnektə(r)\ *n* -s [L, fr. Gk *nektar*, prob. lit., overcoming death, fr. *nek-* (prob. akin to L *nec-, nex* death) + *-tar* (prob. akin to Skt *tarati* he crosses over, overcomes) — more at NOXIOUS, TERM] **1 a :** the drink of the Greek and Roman gods b : any delicious drink; *often* : one of blended fruit juices **c** : a sweet liquid that is secreted by the nectaries of a plant and that is the chief material used by bees in the production of honey **2** : a grayish red that is yellower and paler than apple-blossom, bluer and paler than bois de rose, and bluer, less strong, and slightly lighter than Pompeian red

**²nectar** \"\ *usu cap* — a communications code word for the letter *n*

**nectar bird** *n* **1** : HONEY EATER **2** : SUNBIRD

**nec·tar·e·al** \(ˈ)nekˈta(a)rēəl\ *adj* [L *nectareus* of or like nectar (fr. Gk *nektareos*, fr. *nektar*) + E *-al*] *archaic* : NECTAROUS

**nec·tar·e·an** \-ēən\ *adj* [L *nectareus* + E *-an*] *archaic* : NECTAROUS

**nec·tared** \ˈnektə(r)d\ *adj* [*nectar* + *-ed*] **1** *archaic* : filled or imbued or mingled with nectar ⟨each to his lips applied the ~ urn —Alexander Pope⟩ **2** *archaic* : deliciously sweet or fragrant : NECTAROUS ⟨the blue ~ air —Julian Hawthorne⟩

**nec·tar·e·ous** \(ˈ)nekˈta(a)rēəs\ *adj* [L *nectareus*] : NECTAROUS

**nec·tar·i·al** \-rēəl\ *adj* [*nectary* + *-al*] : relating to or consisting of a nectary

**nec·tar·i·an** \-ən\ *adj* [alter. of *nectarean*] *archaic* : NECTAROUS

**nec·ta·ried** \ˈnektərēd\ *adj* [*nectary* + *-ed*] : having nectaries

**nec·tar·if·er·ous** \ˌnektəˈrif(ə)rəs\ *adj* [*nectar* + *-i-* + *-ferous*] : producing nectar ⟨the ~ organs of flowers⟩

**¹nec·tar·ine** \ˈnektərən\ *adj* [*nectar* + *-ine*] *archaic* : NECTAROUS

**²nec·tar·ine** \ˌ==ˈrēn\ *n* -s [¹*nectarine*] **1** : a peach (*Prunus persica nectarina*) that has a smooth-skinned fruit and is a frequent somatic mutation of the normal peach; *also* : its fruit **2** : a light to moderate yellowish pink that is redder and stronger than seashell pink

**nec·ta·rin·ia** \ˌ==ˈrinēə\ *n, cap* [NL, fr. L *nectar* + *-inus* -ine + NL *-ia*] : a genus (the type of the family Nectariniidae) of Old World oscine birds

**nec·ta·ri·ni·idae** \=ˌ=rəˈnīəˌdē\ *n pl, cap* [NL, fr. *Nectarinia*, type genus + *-idae*] : a family of Old World oscine birds consisting of the sunbirds

**nec·tar·i·ous** \(ˈ)nekˈta(a)rēəs\ *adj* [alter. of *nectareous*] *archaic* : NECTAROUS

**nec·tar·i·um** \=ˈta(a)rēəm, -terē-, -tär-\ *n, pl* **nectar·ia** \-rēə\ *or* **nectariums** [NL, irreg. fr. L *nectar* + *-arium*] : NECTARY

**nec·tar·iv·o·rous** \ˌnektəˈriv(ə)rəs\ *adj* [*nectar* + *-i-* + *-vorous*] : feeding on nectar ⟨~ insects⟩

**nec·tar·ous** \ˈnektərəs\ *adj* [*nectar* + *-ous*] : having the nature of or consisting of nectar : resembling nectar (as in deliciousness, sweetness, fragrance) ⟨~ drinks —Andrew Young⟩

**nec·ta·ry** \-rē\ *n* -ES [NL *nectarium*] **1** : a plant gland that secretes nectar and that in flowers is usu. at the base of the corolla or petals or (as in the larkspur or violet) in the spur **2** : an organ or part that contains a nectary

**-nec·tes** \ˈnekˌtēz\ *n comb form* [NL, fr. Gk *nēktēs* swimmer, fr. *nēchein* to swim — more at NESO-] : one that swims in a (specified) way — in generic names in zoology ⟨*Chironectes*⟩

**necto-** — see NECT-

**nec·to·calycine** \ˌnektō+\ *adj* [NL *nectocalyc-*, *nectocalyx* + E *-ine*] : of, relating to, or resembling a nectocalyx

**nec·to·calyx** \"+\ *n* [NL, fr. *nect-* + *calyx*] : a swimming bell of a siphonophore

**necton** *var of* NEKTON

**nec·to·nematoidea** *n pl, cap* \ˌnektō+\ [NL, fr. *Nectonemat-*, *Nectonema* (fr. *nect-* + *-nema*) + *-oidea*] : a cosmopolitan order (coextensive with a family Nectonematidae and genus *Nectonema*) of Nematomorpha comprising marine hairworms with a parasitic stage in various crustaceans, a double row of natatory bristles, and an expansive pseudocoel — compare GORDIOIDEA

**nec·to·phore** \ˈnektəˌfō(ə)r\ *n* -s [*nect-* + *-phore*] : NECTOCALYX

**nec·to·pod** \-ˌpäd\ *n* -s [*nect-* + *-pod*] : a limb (as of a mollusk) adapted for swimming

**nec·to·some** \-ˌsōm\ *n* -s [*nect-* + *-some*] : the part of the colony of some complex siphonophores that bears swimming bells

**nec·tria** \ˈnektrēə\ *n* [NL, irreg. fr. Gk *nēktris* female swimmer, fr. *nēchein* to swim — more at NESO-] **1** *cap* : a genus (the type of the family Nectriaceae) of ascomycetous fungi that have bright-colored superficial perithecia — see CORAL SPOT, EUROPEAN CANKER **2** -s : any fungus of the genus *Nectria*

**nec·tri·a·ce·ae** \ˌ==ˈāsēˌē\ *n pl, cap* [NL, fr. *Nectria*, type genus + *-aceae*] : a family of ascomycetous fungi (order Hypocreales) that have superficial perithecia with or without a stroma

**nec·tri·a·ceous** \ˌ==ˈāshəs\ *adj* [NL *Nectriaceae* + E *-ous*] : of or relating to the Nectriaceae

**nec·trid·ia** \nekˈtridēə\ *n pl, cap* [NL, fr. Gk *nēktrid-*, *nēktris* female swimmer + NL *-ia*] : an order of Lepospondyli comprising extinct amphibians of the Pennsylvanian and Lower Permian characterized by markedly aquatic forms with the limbs weak or reduced and the body elongated like that of an eel or broadly flattened like that of a skate — **nec·trid·i·an** \(ˈ)=ˈtridēən\ *adj or n*

**nec·tri·oid·a·ce·ae** \ˌnektrēˌōiˈdāsēˌē\ [NL, fr. *Nectria* + L *-oides* -oid + NL *-aceae*] *syn of* ZYTHIACEAE

**nec·tu·rus** \nekˈtyu̇rəs\ *n* [NL, fr. *nect-* + *-urus*] **1** *cap* : a genus of large No. American gilled aquatic salamanders of the family Proteidae — see MUD PUPPY **2** *pl* **nectu·ri** \-ˌrī\ *or* **necturuses** : a salamander of the genus *Necturus*

**ned·der** \ˈnedə(r)\ *n* -s [ME *neddre*, *naddre* — more at ADDER] *dial chiefly Brit* : ADDER

**ned·dy** \ˈnedē, -di\ *n* -ES [fr. *Neddy*, nickname for *Edward*] **1** *dial chiefly Brit* : DONKEY **2** *dial chiefly Brit* : HORSE

**ne·der·lands** \ˈnādə(r)ˌlän(t)s\ *n* -ES *cap* [D, fr. *Nederland* Netherlands] : DUTCH 1b

**née** *or* **nee** \ˈnā *sometimes* ˈnē\ *adj* [F *née*, fem. of *né*] **1** : born into a family surnamed ⟨Rebecca Crawley, ~ Sharp —W.M. Thackeray⟩ ⟨Mrs. Jane Doe ~ Roe⟩ ⟨Mrs. John Doe ~ Roe⟩ ⟨Aunt Margaret, ~ Sheridan —Mary McCarthy⟩ — used to identify a woman by her maiden family name usu. after mention of her name by marriage; sometimes used of a male ⟨Don Lockwood ~ Kosinski —J.S.Redding⟩ **2** : originally or formerly called or named — used to identify (1) a girl or woman usu. after mention of an assumed or acquired name ⟨John Doe, whose widow ~ Jane Roe⟩ ⟨with his charming bride, ~ Miss Carol Milford —Sinclair Lewis⟩ ⟨the actress Madam X ~ Jane Roe⟩ ⟨requiem high mass for Sister AB ~ Jane Roe⟩; (2) sometimes a man or boy usu. after mention of another name being used ⟨Lord Byron, ~ George Pappas — Joseph Auslander & Audrey Wurdemann⟩; and (3) sometimes similarly a group ⟨the Milwaukee Braves ~ the Boston Braves⟩, place ⟨Kernville, ~ Whiskey Flat —Roy Millholland⟩, or thing ⟨sonata for flute, oboe, and basso continuo ~ sonata for violin and harpsichord —P.H.Lang⟩; compare NÉ

**¹need** \ˈnēd\ *n* -s [ME *ned*, *nede*, fr. OE *nēd*, *nīed*, *nēad*, *nēod* distress, force, necessity, need; akin to OHG *nōt* distress, force, necessity, need, ON *nauth*, Goth *nauths*, and prob. to OE *nēo* corpse, ON *nār*, Goth *naus*; basic meaning: to be exhausted] **1** : necessary duty : OBLIGATION ⟨if ~ be⟩ ⟨no ~ to apologize —B.K.Thorne⟩ ⟨the ~ to pay taxes —Peter Scott⟩ ⟨the ~ to evade in order to survive —S.D.Cutter⟩ **2 a** : a want of something requisite, desirable, or useful ⟨our daily ~s⟩ ⟨meet every ~⟩ ⟨a building adequate for the company's ~s⟩ ⟨eliminates all ~ for stitches and glue —*Book Production*⟩ ⟨the urgent ~ for discussion —*Manchester Guardian Weekly*⟩ ⟨order and discipline were the crying ~s —Kemp Malone⟩ ⟨the classless society in which each would receive according to his ~s —C.I.Glicksberg⟩ **b** : a physiological or psychological requirement for the maintenance of the homeostasis of an organism ⟨tissue ~s⟩ ⟨the ~ of a better education⟩ ⟨fundamental ~s (besides sex and organic satisfaction) are for prestige, security, and some form of generalized activity — Frederick Creedy⟩ ⟨she experienced the ~ of being petted and made much of by a man —Robert Grant †1940⟩ ⟨an equilibrium in which society's ~s and the ~s of the individual are one —W.H.Whyte⟩ **3** : a condition requiring supply or relief : EXIGENCY ⟨in his ~⟩ ⟨at a time of ~⟩ ⟨whenever the ~ arises⟩ ⟨a friend in ~ is a friend indeed⟩ **4** : want of the means of subsistence : DESTITUTION, POVERTY ⟨the community provides for those in ~⟩ — **at need** *adv* : in time of need ⟨a supply to draw on *at need*⟩

**²need** *adv* [ME *nede*, fr. OE *nēde*, *nīede*, *nēade*, *nēode*, instrumental of *nēd*, *nīed*, *nēad*, *nēod* necessity] *obs* : NEEDS

**³need** \ˈnēd\ *vb* **needed; needed; needing; needs** *or* **need** [ME *neeeden*, *neden*, fr. OE *nēodian* to be necessary, fr. *nēod* necessity] *vi* **1** : to be in want ⟨give to them who ~⟩ **2** : to be needful : be necessary ⟨playing as quietly as ~ed —Warwick Braithwaite⟩ ⟨is less effective than ~s be —Leo Wiener⟩ ~ *vt* : to be in need of : have cause or occasion for : REQUIRE ⟨children ~ milk⟩ ⟨he ~s advice⟩ ⟨great art does not ~ a theory —Herbert Read⟩ ⟨he does not ~ to be told when he is failing⟩ ⟨we ~ to guard against the private seizure of power —T.W.Arnold⟩ ⟨really ~ to ask ourselves —Frank Fremont-Smith⟩ ⟨something urgently ~s doing —Joaquin Noval⟩ ⟨it ~s little more than wise words —Barbara Ward⟩ — sometimes used before an infinitive without *to* ⟨I did not ~ appear —Herbert Hoover⟩ ⟨one ~s point out —J.B.Cabell⟩ ~ *verbal auxiliary* : be under necessity or obligation to ⟨the last group . . . we ~ deal with —W.E.Swinton⟩ ⟨one ~ only look at the management . . . to realize —Wayne Morse⟩ ⟨no necessitarian ~ ever abandon his hypothesis —L.S.Feuer⟩ ⟨talks more than he ~⟩ ⟨he ~ not answer⟩ ⟨~ she explain⟩ ⟨all the poet ~ do is to remind the reader —Joseph Jones⟩ **syn** see LACK

**need-be** \ˈ=,=\ *n* -s [fr. the phrase *need be*, fr. ³*need* + *be*, vb.] *archaic* : a necessary reason : NECESSITY

**need·ces·si·ty** \nēdˈsesədē\ *n* -ES [alter. (influenced by *need*) of *necessity*] *dial* : NECESSITY

**needfire** \ˈ=,=\ *n* [¹*need* + *fire*] : a purificatory fire traditionally kindled usu. by friction of dry wood in time of distress (as during a cattle plague) in the belief that it would ward off evil spirits; *specif* : the fire lighted on the night of St. John the Baptist's Day (June 24) to ward off sickness and ill luck — compare SAINT JOHN'S FIRE

**¹need·ful** \ˈnēdfəl\ *adj* [ME *nedefull*, *nedfull*, fr. *nede*, *ned* need + *-full* -ful] : necessary for supply or relief : REQUISITE, INDISPENSABLE ⟨the one thing ~⟩ ⟨provided with everything ~ and remain aboard —Herman Melville⟩ ⟨power to . . . make all ~ rules and regulations —*U. S. Constitution*⟩ ⟨buying only what was strictly ~ —W.S.Maugham⟩

**syn** NEEDFUL, NECESSARY, REQUISITE, INDISPENSABLE, and ESSENTIAL can mean, in common, required, usu. urgently. NEEDFUL is the weakest, applying to anything required to fill a want or need ⟨the town fathers found it *needful* to seek a new place to the west for grazing —*Amer. Guide Series: Mass.*⟩ ⟨pots and pans, kettles and cranes, axes and nails, and other *needful* things which could not be made by men hewing homes from a wilderness —Harriot B. Barbour⟩ NECESSARY implies more pressing need ⟨until we know how much of this damage can be repaired and how quickly the *necessary* repairs can be made —F.D.Roosevelt⟩ ⟨we are making them independent of the knowledge *necessary* to make their work satisfactory —M. R.Cohen⟩ ⟨amino acids *necessary* for protein synthesis —*Americana Annual*⟩ REQUISITE suggests an imposed requirement, applying usu. to what is necessary by the nature of the end or the larger purpose to be served ⟨attack their other studies with the vigor *requisite* to success —C.H.Grandgent⟩ ⟨the skill *requisite* to direct these immense machines is proportionate to their magnitude and complicated mechanism —T.L.Peacock⟩ INDISPENSABLE applies to something that cannot be done without if the end is to be attained ⟨eliminate irrelevancies and retain what is *indispensable* —John Dewey⟩ ⟨reading quite *indispensable* to a wise man —R.W.Emerson⟩ ⟨stability of cost is *indispensable* to sound business planning —H.S.Truman⟩ ESSENTIAL is often interchangeable with *indispensable* though less dramatic in implication, implying simply inherent necessity ⟨food is *essential* to life⟩ ⟨the award of fellowships and research grants is *essential* to the accomplishment of this high purpose —Dexter Perkins⟩ ⟨unrestrained competition, which is generally regarded as *essential* to modern capitalism —M.R.Cohen⟩

**²needful** \"\ *n* -s : something needed or requisite: **a** : the thing that must be done — used with *the* ⟨do the ~⟩ **b** : a personal necessary (as a piece of apparel or a toilet article) ⟨summer ~s⟩ ⟨small ~s⟩ **c** : MONEY — used with *the* ⟨had the ~ to buy what he wanted⟩

**need·ful·ly** \ˈnēdfəlē\ *adv* [ME *nedfully*, fr. *nedfull* + *-ly*] *archaic* : NECESSARILY

**need·ful·ness** *n* -ES [ME *nedefulnes*, fr. *nedefull* + *-nes* -ness] : the quality or state of being needful

**needier** *comparative of* NEEDY

**neediest** *superlative of* NEEDY

**need·i·ness** \ˈnēdēnəs\ *n* -ES [ME *nedynes*, fr. *nedy* needy + *-nes* -ness] : the quality or state of being needy

**¹nee·dle** \ˈnēdᵊl\ *n* -s *often attrib* [ME *nedle*, fr. OE *nǣdl*; akin to OHG *nādala* needle, ON *nāl*, Goth *nethla*; all fr. a prehistoric Gmc noun akin to OHG *nājan* to sew, L *nēre* to spin, Gk *nēn* to spin, *nēma* thread, Skt *snāyu* sinew] **1 a** (1) : a small slender rodlike instrument for hand sewing that has a round or elongated eye for thread at one end and a blunt or sharp point at the other and that is made usu. of steel or bone in straight or curved form (2) : a similar steel instrument for machine sewing that has an eye in the pointed end and is shaped at the other end for attachment to the machine **b** : any of various devices for carrying thread and making stitches in crocheting, knitting, netting, or hooking — see KNITTING NEEDLE **c** (1) : a pointed slender instrument used for sewing or puncturing tissues : SURGICAL NEEDLE (2) : a slender hollow instrument that has one end pointed and beveled and the other enlarged and modified for attachment to various devices and that is used chiefly for introducing material into or removing material from the body parenterally ⟨intravenous ~⟩ ⟨hypodermic ~⟩ (3) : a hollow device designed to contain radioactive material (4) : ELECTRIC KNIFE **2** : a slender usu. sharp-pointed indicator on a dial instrument (as a magnetic compass or an ammeter); *specif* : MAGNETIC NEEDLE **3 a** : a slender pointed object resembling a needle: as (1) : a pointed crystal (2) : a sharp rock (3) : OBELISK ⟨Cleopatra's ~⟩ **b** : a needle-shaped leaf (as of the pine, spruce, larch) **4** : a short stout timber, steel, or iron beam passing through a hole in a wall esp. to support the end of a shore **5 a** : ETCHING NEEDLE **b** : a slender piece of a jewel or of steel, wood, or fiber with a rounded tip used in a phonograph to transmit vibrations from the record — called also *stylus* **6** [by shortening] *archaic* : NEEDLEWOMAN **7 a** : one of a set of parallel wires found in knitting machines and jacquard looms **b** : a usu. platinum wire used for transferring microorganisms into culture mediums **8 a** : part of the knotting mechanism of a grain binder **b** : a slender tapering rod set in a bore during charging and then withdrawn leaving an opening for the priming, fuse, or squib — called also *pricker* **c** : a slender pointed rod controlling a fine inlet or outlet (as in a valve) **d** : a slender pointed rod mounted on a handle and used to sort or to arrange hand-sorted punched cards — **needle in a haystack** : an object hard to find or attain

1 2 3 4

needles 1 a (1) and 1b: *1* dressmaker's needle, *2* crochet needle, *3* knitting needle, *4* netting needle

**²needle** \"\ *vb* **needled; needled; needling** \-d(ᵊ)liŋ\ **needles** *vt* **1** : to sew with a needle ⟨fabrics which are woven, *needled* and printed —W.C.Smith⟩ **2 a** : to pierce or treat with or as if with a needle ⟨*needling* a blister until it bursts —James Baldwin⟩ ⟨the pangs of terror now *needled* his soul —James Hogg⟩ **b** : to puncture, operate on, or inject (as a person) with a needle ⟨*needling* a cataract⟩ ⟨~s the population against polio⟩ **3 a** : to push (something) through like a needle ⟨words . . . *needled* into one's self —Christopher Morley⟩ ⟨have to talk fast to ~ it in between . . . speeches —*Nat'l Home Monthly*⟩ ⟨*needling* their way through a crowd⟩ **b** : to put a needle beam under a wall for support **4** : to vex by repeated sharp prods or gibes : goad or incite often to a specified action ⟨thoroughly enjoys *needling* his stuffy relatives —James Gray⟩ ⟨*needled* him into it —James Jones⟩ **5** : to increase the interest and attractiveness of : add strength or pungency to ⟨~ a speech with humor⟩ ⟨*needled* with irony⟩; *specif* : to strengthen (a beverage) by adding raw alcohol ⟨~ beer⟩ ~ *vi* : to sew or embroider with a needle ⟨groups of women . . . *needling* away —W.M.Thackeray⟩

**³needle** \"\ *adj* [¹*needle*] *chiefly Brit, of a game or athletic contest* : highly important : CRUCIAL ⟨the most heated moments of a ~ match —*Rugger*⟩

**needle and thread** *n* : a needlegrass (*Stipa comata*)

**needlebar** \ˈ==,=\ *n* : a bar on a sewing or knitting machine for holding the needle or needles

**needle bath** *n* : a bath in which water is forcibly projected on the body in fine jets

**needle beam** *n* **1** : NEEDLE 4 **2** : a transverse floor beam in a bridge

**needle bearing** *n* : a roller bearing with very slender rollers varying typically from 0.08 to 0.16 inch in diameter

**needle beer** *n* [²*needle*] : beer made with ether alcohol often illicitly and under makeshift conditions ⟨for a big depression buck, you could get ten glasses of *needle beer* —*Crime Detective*⟩

**needlebill** \ˈ==,=\ *also* **needle-billed snipe** \ˈ==,=-\ *n* : WILSON'S PHALAROPE

**needle biopsy** *n* : a biopsy esp. of deep tissues done with a hollow needle

**needle blight** *or* **needle cast** *n* : LEAF CAST

**needle board** *n* **1** : a board covered with very short fine wires that is used for pressing pile fabrics **2 a** : the perforated board in a jacquard mechanism through which the ends of the actuating needles project **b** : a board carrying the needles in a punch loom or needle loom

**needle bug** *n* [so called fr. its long slender body] : a bug of the genus *Ranatra*

**needlebush** \ˈ==,=\ *n* **1** : any of several Australian shrubs or trees with rigid needle-shaped leaves; *esp* : a plant of the genus *Hakea* **2** : CHAPARRAL PEA

**needle chatter** *n* : NEEDLETALK

**needlecraft** \ˈ==,=\ *n* [ME *nedle craft*, fr. *nedle* needle + *craft*] : NEEDLEWORK

**needled** *adj* [fr. past part. of ²*needle*] **1** : done with a needle ⟨~ embroidery⟩ **2** [¹*needle* + *-ed*] : resembling a needle ⟨~ crystals⟩

**needle dam** *n* : a barrier consisting of horizontal bars dropped into grooves in the abutments of a pass through a dam or of planks set on end and removable in case of flood

**needle file** *n* : a very small file having any of the usual shapes of cross section and having the tang end extended to a long rodlike handle

**needle fir** *n* : a Chinese evergreen tree (*Abies holophylla*) with pectinate leaves and erect cones

**needlefish** \ˈ==,=\ *n, pl* **needlefish** *or* **needlefishes** **1** : any of numerous voracious elongate teleost fishes of *Belone* and related genera that resemble superficially but are not related to the freshwater ganoids, that are green and silvery in color with even the bones often bright green, and that include a common European fish (*Belone belone*) and well-known American forms belonging to the genus *Tylosurus* — called also *billfish*, *gar* **2** : any of various other slender elongated fishes (as a halfbeak or a pipefish) with projecting jaws

**needle furze** *n* : a prickly shrub (*Genista anglica*) of western Europe having bluish green foliage and racemose yellow flowers

**needle grama** *n* : an annual grama (*Boutelona aristidoides*) with three awns longer than the spikelet

**needlegrass** \ˈ==,=\ *n* **1** : any of several grasses of the genus *Stipa* (esp. *S. comata*) of the western U. S. with filiform leaves and slender awns on the spikelet **2** : any of several grasses of the genus *Aristida* (esp. *A. longiseta*) of the western U. S. furnishing poor forage — called also *triple-awned grass*

**needle gun** *n* : a rifle of the later 19th century having a needle-shaped firing pin which upon penetrating a paper, oiled linen, or oiled silk cartridge passes through the powder charge to detonate the cap loaded at the base of the bullet

**needle ice** *n* : FRAZIL

**needle ironstone** *or* **needle iron ore** *n* : goethite in acicular crystals

**needle juniper** *n* : an Asiatic evergreen shrubby tree (*Juniperus rigida*) with needle-shaped rigid leaves that is sometimes used as an ornamental

**needle lace** *n* : NEEDLEPOINT 1

**needlelike** \ˈ==,=\ *adj* : resembling a needle in slenderness, pointedness, or sharpness ⟨~ crystals⟩ ⟨~ leaves⟩ ⟨~ pick⟩ ⟨~ spire⟩

**needle loom** *n* **1** : a loom in which the filling is carried through the shed by a long eye-pointed needle **2** : PUNCH LOOM

**nee·dle·man** \ˈnēdᵊlmən\ *n, pl* **needlemen** *archaic* : TAILOR

**needle-miner** \ˈ==,==\ *n* : an insect larva that forms minute mines within the needles of various coniferous trees; *esp* : a lepidopterous larva of such habits

**needle ore** *n* : AIKINITE

**needle palm** *n* : BLUE PALMETTO

**¹needlepoint** \ˈ==,=\ *n* **1** : lace worked entirely with a needle over a paper pattern in buttonhole stitch — compare BOBBIN LACE **2** : embroidery worked over or on canvas usu. in simple even stitches across counted threads; *esp* : GROS POINT

**²needlepoint** \"\ *adj* **1** : of, relating to, or resembling needlepoint ⟨~ lace⟩ ⟨~ embroidery⟩ ⟨~ silk⟩ ⟨~ holder⟩ **2** : of or relating to a fabric with a fine pebbled or nubby surface formed by uneven yarns or fancy weaves

**³needlepoint** \"\ *n* : something resembling the point of a needle (as in sharpness or minuteness) ⟨admits the ~ of that argument —*Times Lit. Supp.*⟩ ⟨the towerman has to balance on a thin beam . . . virtually on a ~ —Beatrice Schapper⟩

**needle-pointed** \ˌ==ˈ==\ *adj* : resembling a needle in sharpness of point ⟨*needle-pointed* cleaners used to clear clogged burner holes —K.A.Henderson⟩

**nee·dler** \ˈnēd(ᵊ)lə(r)\ *n* -s [in sense 1, fr. ¹*needle* + *-er*; in other senses fr. ²*needle* + *-er*] **1** : one that makes, uses, or deals in needles **2** *Brit* : one that sews up packages **3** : one that goads or prods; *esp* : one that indulges in sharp and often captious criticism of others ⟨provided the moderator was an able discussion leader rather than just a plain ~ —John Withall⟩

**needlerun** \ˈ==,=\ *adj* [¹*needle* + *run*, past part. of *run* to sew] : ornamented or joined by needlework — used esp. of pillow lace or machine-made net with hand-sewn designs

**needlerush** \ˈ==,=\ *n* **1** : a rush (*Juncus roemerianus*) chiefly of the southeastern U. S. with terete rigid leaves and sharp-pointed sepals **2** : NEEDLE SPIKE RUSH

**needles** *pl of* NEEDLE, *pres 3d sing of* NEEDLE

**needle scale** *n* : a homopterous insect of the family Coccidae that feeds on conifers

**needle scratch** *n* : SURFACE NOISE

**needle spike rush** *n* : a common perennial sedge (*Eleocharis acicularis*) with needlelike leaves — called also *needlerush*

**need·less** \ˈnēdləs\ *adj* [ME *nedeles*, fr. *nede* need + *-les* -less] : not needed : UNNECESSARY, GRATUITOUS ⟨~ movement⟩ ⟨~ controversy⟩ ⟨~ to say⟩ ⟨utterly ~ —~ wickedness —F.L.Paxson⟩ — **need·less·ly** *adv* — **need·less·ness** *n* -ES

**needletalk** \ˈ==,=\ *n* : noise radiated directly by the needle of a phonograph pickup or by a record as distinguished from the sound produced by the complete phonograph — called also *needle chatter*

**needle telegraph** *n* : a telegraph signaling by the deflections of a magnetic needle (as when the receiver is a galvanometer with vertical needle)

**needle tooth** *n* : a small dark sharp tooth of a newborn pig — called also *black tooth*

**needle trade** *n* : any of the various businesses involved in the manufacture of clothing — usu. used in pl. with *the* ⟨immigrants worked as peddlers or entered the expanding *needle trades* —*Amer. Guide Series: N.Y. City*⟩

**needle valve** *n* : a valve consisting essentially of a slender pointed rod or needle fitting into a conoidal seat and capable of fine adjustment

**needle whin** *n* : NEEDLE FURZE

**needlewoman** \ˈ==,==\ *n, pl* **needlewomen** : a woman who does needlework

**needle wood** *n* **1** *usu* **needlewood** \ˈ==,=\ : a needlebush of the genus *Hakea*; *esp* : a white-flowered shrub or small shrubby tree (*H. leucoptera*) with a hard tough heavy reddish brown wood that is used locally for small cabinetwork **2 :** an Indian-Burmese tree (*Schima wallichii*) of the family Theaceae with light red or reddish brown wood **3 :** the wood of a needle wood

**needlework** \'==,=\ *n* [ME *nedle werk*, fr. *nedle* needle + *werk* work] **1 :** work done with a needle; *specif* **:** work (as embroidery, knitting, needlepoint) other than plain sewing **2 :** the occupation of one who does needlework

**needleworker** \'==,==\ *n* **:** one that does needlework

**needle zeolite** *n* [so called fr. the shape of its crystals] **:** NATROLITE

**needling** *n* -s [fr. gerund of ²*needle*] **1 :** the action or process of using a needle ⟨from their authentic styling to their fine ~ —*N.Y. Times*⟩; *specif* **:** the action or process of using an etching needle **2 :** a temporary support of needle beams **3 :** irritatingly persistent goading or prodding ⟨the give-and-take, the ~ . . . and sometimes the downright abuse involved in dealing with newsmen —F.L.Mott⟩

**nee·dly** \'nēd(ᵊ)lē\ *adj* -ER/-EST [¹*needle* + -*y*] **:** resembling a needle ⟨ragged and ~ ice —Rudyard Kipling⟩

**need·ment** \'nēdmənt\ *n* -s **:** a thing needed or wanted; *esp* **:** a necessary item of personal luggage — usu. used in pl. ⟨the old canvas bag in which all his poor ~s for a long journey were packed —Jack Kerouac⟩

**need-not** \'=,=\ *n* -s [fr. the phrase *need not*, fr. ³*need* + *not*] **:** something not needed **:** SUPERFLUITY ⟨purchasing *need-nots*⟩

**needs** \'nēdz\ *adv* [ME *nedes*, fr. OE *nēdes*, fr. gen. of *nēde* necessity — more at NEED] **:** of necessity **:** NECESSARILY, INDISPENSABLY ⟨would ~ be left open —*U. S. Daily*⟩ — usu. used with *must* ⟨must ~ be objective —W.B.Yeats⟩ ⟨must ~ examine her bracelet —Henry Lapham⟩

¹**needy** \'nēdē, -di\ *adj* -ER/-EST [ME *nedy*, fr. *ned* need + -*y*] **:** marked by want of the means of living **:** POVERTY-STRICKEN ⟨~ families⟩ ⟨the ~ blind⟩ ⟨the *neediest* cases⟩ **syn** see POOR

²**needy** \"\ *n, sing or pl in constr* **:** one that is unable to maintain economic self-sufficiency or that must receive public or private assistance of some kind ⟨take care of the ~⟩

**neeld** \'nēld\ *dial chiefly Eng var of* NEEDLE

**neem** \'nēm\ *or* **neem tree** *also* **neemba** \'nēmbə\ *n* -s [Hindi & Skt; Hindi *nīm*, fr. Skt *nimba*] **:** MARGOSA

**neem-oil** \'=,=\ *n, sometimes cap* **:** a medicinal aromatic oil yielded by the fruit and seeds of the neem tree

**ne·encephalon** \¦nē+\ *n* [NL, fr. *ne-* + *encephalon*] **:** the part of the brain having the most recent phylogenetic origin; *specif* **:** the cerebral cortex and parts developed in relation to it — compare PALEENCEPHALON

**neep** \'nēp\ *n* -s [ME *nepe*, fr. OE *nǣp*, fr. L *napus*] *chiefly Scot* **:** TURNIP

**neep·er** \'nēpə(r)\ *Scot var of* NEIGHBOR

**neer** \'nēr\ *n* -s [ME *nere* — more at NEPHRITIS] *chiefly Scot* **:** KIDNEY

**ne'er** \(')ne|(ə)r, (')na(a)|, |ə\ *adv* [ME *ner*, *nere*, contr. of *never*, *nevere*] **:** NEVER

**ne'er-do-weel** \'ner(,)dü,wēl\ *chiefly Scot var of* NE'ER-DO-WELL

¹**ne'er-do-well** \'ner(,)dü,wel, 'neə(-\ *n* -s [fr. the phrase *ne'er do well*] **:** a person who never does well **:** GOOD-FOR-NOTHING ⟨the backwash of society . . . tramps, prostitutes and *ne'er-do-wells* —F.J.Jirka⟩ ⟨charming, desirable, yet essentially a *ne'er-do-well* —John Nerber⟩

²**ne'er-do-well** \"\ *adj* **:** never doing well **:** SHIFTLESS, INCOMPETENT ⟨a *ne'er-do-well* couple that has neglected farm, home, and church —H.H.Reichard⟩

**neet** \'nēt\ *dial Eng var of* NIGHT

**ne ex·e·at** \nē'eksē,at\ *n* [L, let him not leave] **1 :** a high prerogative writ formerly used in England in matters of state to restrain a person from leaving the country **2 :** a writ issued out of chancery or equity to restrain a person from leaving the jurisdiction of the court pending an action

**ne exeat re·pub·li·ca** \-rē'pəblәkə\ *n* [L, let him not leave the state] **:** a writ issued to restrain a person from leaving the jurisdiction of the court pending an action — compare NE EXEAT

¹**neeze** *also* **neese** \'nēz\ *vi* -ED/-ING/-S [ME *nesen*, of Scand origin; akin to ON *hnjōsa* to sneeze; akin to OHG *niosan* to sneeze] *chiefly Scot* **:** SNEEZE

²**neeze** *also* **neese** \"\ *n* -s *chiefly Scot* **:** SNEEZE

**nef** \'nef\ *n* -s [F, nave, boat-shaped vessel, fr. ML *navis* — more at NAVE] **1** *obs* **:** NAVE **2 :** a 16th century clock in the form of a ship having mechanical devices to illustrate astronomical movements **3 :** an ornamental table utensil (as for holding a napkin, knife, and spoon) shaped like a ship

**ne·fan·dous** \nə'fandəs\ *adj* [L *nefandus*, fr. *ne-* not + *fandus*, gerundive of *fari* to speak — more at NO, BAN] **:** unfit to be spoken of **:** IMPIOUS, EXECRABLE ⟨~ wickedness —Increase Mather⟩

**ne·far·i·ous** \nə'fa(a)rēəs, nē'-, -fer-, -fār-\ *adj* [L *nefarius*, fr. *nefas* crime, wrong, fr. *ne-* not + *fas* right, divine law; akin to L *fari* to speak] **:** heinously or impiously wicked **:** DETESTABLE, INIQUITOUS ⟨~ schemes⟩ ⟨~ practice⟩ ⟨race prejudice is most ~ on its politer levels —H.E.Clurman⟩ **syn** see VICIOUS

**ne·far·i·ous·ly** *adv* **:** in a nefarious manner ⟨~ involved in a conspiracy⟩

**ne·far·i·ous·ness** *n* -ES **:** the quality or state of being nefarious ⟨the ~ of the deed⟩

**ne·fast** \nə'fast\ *adj* [L *nefastus*, fr. *nefas* crime, wrong] **:** WICKED

**nef·fy** \'nefē\ *dial var of* NEPHEW

**neft·gil** \'neft,gil\ *n* -s [G, fr. Per *naftdagil* naphtha clay] **:** OZOKERITE

**neg** *abbr* **1** negative **2** negotiable

**ne·ga·ra** \nə'gärə\ *n* -s [Indonesian, fr. Skt *nagara* city] **:** an autonomous or federative state in the republic of Indonesia

¹**ne·gate** \nə'gāt, nē'-, *usu* -ād.+V *sometimes* 'ne,g *or* 'nē,g-\ *vb* -ED/-ING/-S [L *negatus*, past part. of *negare*] *vt* **1 :** to deny the existence or truth or fact of **:** refuse to admit ⟨*negated* and denied her own honest reactions —Sara H. Hay⟩ **2 :** to cause to be ineffective or invalid **:** NEGATIVE ⟨the conception of limitless growth is even more obviously *negated* by the death of the individual —Reinhold Niebuhr⟩ ~ *vi* **:** to deny something **:** negative something ⟨the . . . dictator is the force that always ~s —F.H.Cramer⟩ **syn** see NULLIFY

²**negate** \"\ *n* -s [L *negatus*, past part. of *negare*] **:** the contradictory of something ⟨either this statement or its ~ is verifiable —R.J.Richman⟩

**ne·ga·tion** \nə'gāshən, nē'-, ne'-\ *n* -s [MF or L; MF *negation*, fr. L *negation-*, *negatio*, fr. *negatus* (past part. of *negare* to say no, deny, fr. *neg-* no, not, akin to *ne-* not) + -*ion-*, -*io* -ion — more at NO] **1 a :** the action of negating **:** DENIAL, CONTRADICTION ⟨conformity is the very ~ of the liberties enjoyed by a free society —*New Republic*⟩; *specif* **:** the operation of forming a negation **b :** an instance of negating **:** a negative doctrine or statement or proposition or judgment; *specif* **:** a statement that is true provided the unqualified original statement is false **c :** a negating particle (as *not*) **:** NEGATIVE **2 a :** something that is merely the absence of something actual **:** something without real existence of its own **:** NONENTITY ⟨anarchy is not law but its ~ —B.N.Cardozo⟩ **b :** something that is the negative opposite of something positive ⟨black is the ~ of all color⟩ — **ne·ga·tion·al** \-shənᵊl, -shnəl\ *adj*

**ne·ga·tion·ist** \-sh(ə)nəst\ *also* **ne·ga·tion·al·ist** \-shənᵊl-əst, -shnel-\ *n* -s **:** an adherent of a doctrine or theory of mere negation

**neg·a·tiv·ate** \'negəd·ə,vāt\ *vt* -ED/-ING/-S [¹*negative* + -*ate*] **:** NEGATE ⟨is directly *negativated* by plain facts —A.N.Whitehead⟩

¹**neg·a·tive** \'negəd·iv, -ətiv\ *adj* [MF or L; MF *negatif*, fr. L *negativus*, fr. *negatus* + -*ivus* -ive] **1 a :** that expresses or implies or contains negation **:** that denies or contradicts or prohibits or refuses ⟨a ~ answer⟩ ⟨a ~ opinion⟩ **b (1) :** denying a predicate of a subject or of a part of a subject or asserting the falsity of something (“no A is B”, “some A is not B”, and “it is false that A is B” are ~ propositions)— contrasted with *affirmative* **(2) :** denoting the absence of something or the contradictory of something ⟨*not-white* is a ~ term⟩ **2 a :** that is marked by the absence of positive features ⟨a colorless ~ personality⟩ **b :** that is marked by features (as hostility, perversity, withdrawal) that oppose constructive treatment or development ⟨delinquents retarded by their ~ outlook on life⟩ **3 a :** less than zero and of such nature that when added to a like number of positive sign zero is produced ⟨the ~ number −2 added to +2 yields zero⟩ **b :** that is opposite in direction or position to an arbitrarily chosen regular direction or position **4 a :** relating to, charged with, or composed of negative electricity **b :** gaining electrons **:** ELECTRONEGATIVE 2a, ACID 2a **5 a :** not affirming the presence of the organism or condition in question ⟨a ~ diagnosis⟩ ⟨a ~ reaction⟩ **b :** directed or moving away from a source of stimulation ⟨a ~ tropism⟩ **c :** less than the pressure of the atmosphere ⟨the role of intrathoracic ~ pressure in respiration⟩ **6 a :** being or exhibiting rotation to the left **:** LEVOROTATORY **b :** having or characterized by a smaller index of refraction for the extraordinary ray than for the ordinary ray — used of doubly refracting crystals **7 :** having or reproducing the bright parts of the original subject as dark areas and the dark parts as light areas — used of a photographic image or of the material on which it is reproduced **8** *geol* **a :** frequently submerged **b :** subjected to downward movement or extensive erosion **c :** displaying less than normal gravitational or magnetic properties **9 a :** that is a no-trump response made on a weak hand in bridge for the purpose of keeping the bidding open **b** *of a double in bridge* **:** INFORMATORY

²**negative** \"\ *n* -s **1 a :** a proposition by which something is denied or contradicted **:** an opposite or contradictory term or conception or sense; *specif* **:** a statement or judgment expressing or implying or containing denial or contradiction **b (1) :** a reply by which is indicated the withholding of assent about something **:** REFUSAL **(2)** *archaic* **:** a right of veto **(3)** *obs* **:** a vote expressing opposition **:** adverse vote **2 :** something that is the opposite or negation of something else **3 a :** a word or particle or term or phrase (as *not*, *no*) that expresses negation or denial — often used adverbially esp. in radiotelephone communication ⟨is he there? —~⟩ **b :** a mathematical quantity or symbol that has a minus value **4 a :** the side that upholds the contradictory proposition in a debate — opposed to *affirmative* **b :** a speaker on the contradictory side in a debate **5 :** the plate of a voltaic or electrolytic cell that is at the lower potential **6 a :** a photographic image that reproduces the bright parts of the photographed subject as dark areas and the dark parts as light areas, that is usu. on transparent material, and that is used for printing positive pictures **b :** the material on which this image is reproduced **7 :** a reverse impression or mold taken from a piece of sculpture or ceramics — **in the negative** *adv (or adj)* **1 :** in favor of or with the effect of rejection or refusal ⟨the vote was wholly *in the negative*⟩ **2 :** with a negative answer ⟨invited her to go but she answered *in the negative*⟩

³**negative** \"\ *vb* -ED/-ING/-S *vt* **1 a :** to refuse assent to (as a candidate, proposal, program) **:** refuse to accept **b (1) :** to reject by or as if by a vote **(2) :** VETO **2 :** to demonstrate the falsity of **:** DISPROVE **3 :** CONTRADICT **4 :** COUNTERACT ~ *vi* **:** to deny or reject or refuse something **syn** see DENY, NEUTRALIZE

**negative acceleration** *n* **1 :** RETARDATION **2 :** acceleration in a negative direction

**negative afterimage** *n* **1 :** COMPLEMENTARY AFTERIMAGE **2 :** a visual afterimage in which light portions of the original sensation are replaced by dark portions and dark portions are replaced by light portions — opposed to *positive afterimage*

**negative angle** *n* **:** an angle generated in a direction opposite to an arbitrarily chosen usu. clockwise direction

**negative catalysis** *n* **:** catalysis in which the catalyst has an inhibiting effect on the reaction (as the retardation of the aging of rubber and oils by antioxidants)

**negative catalyst** *n* **:** a substance that brings about negative catalysis

**negative crystal** *n* **1 :** a cavity that has the form of a crystal and occurs in a mineral mass **2 :** a crystal showing negative double refraction

**negative curvature** *n* **:** curvature of a graph in such a way that it is concave downward

**negative easement** *or* **negative servitude** *n* **:** an easement enabling its holder to prevent the possessor of the land subject to the easement from doing certain acts or exercising certain rights of ownership he would otherwise have a legal right to ⟨a *negative easement* to receive air and light without interference by an adjoining owner⟩

**negative electricity** *n* **:** electricity of which the elementary unit is the electron

**negative electron** *n* **:** ELECTRON

**negative eugenics** *n pl but usu sing in constr* **:** improvement of the genetic makeup of a population by preventing the reproduction of the obviously unfit

**negative feedback** *n* **:** the returning of a fraction of the output of an electric oscillator to the input in such a way as to decrease the oscillation amplitude **:** DEGENERATION — called also *inverse feedback*

**negative form** *n* **:** one of a pair of congruent crystal forms that together correspond to a single form in a crystal class of higher symmetry

**negative glow** *n* **:** a narrow luminous region that occurs in an electrical discharge in a gas at low pressure (as in a Crookes tube) and that is often the second such region from the cathode

**negative lens** *n* **:** DIVERGING LENS

**negative logarithm** *n* **:** COLOGARITHM

**neg·a·tive·ly** \'negəd·əvlē, -ətə-, -li\ *adv* **:** in a negative manner: as **a (1) :** by way of denial or contradiction **:** in the negative **:** on the negative side ⟨answered ~⟩ ⟨with a sphere of action defined more ~ than positively —*Times Lit. Supp.*⟩ **(2) :** in a negative direction ⟨a disk rotating ~⟩ **(3) :** in such a way as to indicate refusal or lack of agreement or of sympathy ⟨viewed all their efforts ~⟩ **b :** with negative electricity ⟨~ charged⟩

**negative misprision** *n* **:** concealment of something known by one that has the duty of revealing it to proper authority — distinguished from *positive misprision*

**negative modulation** *or* **negative transmission** *n* **:** amplitude-modulated signals in television in which the maximum carrier corresponds to the dark part of the picture

**neg·a·tive·ness** *n* -ES [¹*negative* + -*ness*] **:** NEGATIVITY

**negative-painted** \¦===¦==\ *adj* **:** painted by negative painting

**negative painting** *n* **:** an ancient process of decorative painting (as of Peruvian Indian pottery) marked by application of wax or gum to parts of a surface and by application of color to the entire surface and by subsequent removal of the wax or gum so as to leave a pattern created by the parts of the surface thus left unpainted

**negative phase** *n* **:** a phase of lowered resistance that may follow the injection of foreign antigen in active immunization

**negative plate** *n* **:** the electrode of a voltaic cell or storage cell that is at the lower potential when the circuit is open

**negative pole** *n* **:** the terminal of a voltaic cell or storage cell that is connected to the negative plate

**negative potential** *n* **:** an electric potential lower than that of the earth or other conductor taken as an arbitrary zero of potential

**negative pregnant** *n, pl* **negatives pregnant** [²*negative* + *pregnant*, adj.] **:** a legal denial that admits or involves an affirmative implication which is favorable to the pleader's adversary

**negative pressure** *n* [¹*negative*] **:** pressure that is less than existing atmospheric pressure taken as a zero of reference

**negative proton** *n* **:** ANTIPROTON

**negative resistance** *n* **:** a resistance phenomenon (as exhibited by an electric arc or vacuum tube) in which the voltage drop across the circuit decreases as the current increases

**negative sign** *n* **:** MINUS SIGN 1

**negative skewness** *n* **:** skewness in which the mean is less than the mode

**negative staining** *n* **:** a method of demonstrating the form of small objects (as bacteria) by surrounding them with a stain that they do not take up so that they appear as sharply outlined unstained bright bodies on a colored ground

**negative theology** *n* **:** theology that conceives of ultimate reality as so transcending human thought that it can be described only negatively — distinguished from *positive theology*

**negative valence** *n* **1 :** the valence of a negatively charged ion **2 :** the number of electrons an atom can take up ⟨oxygen has a *negative valence* of 2⟩

**neg·a·tiv·ism** \'negəd·ə,vizəm, -gətə,-\ *n* -s [¹*negative* + -*ism*] **1 :** an attitude of mind marked by regular denial of or skepticism about nearly everything affirmed by others **:** habitual skepticism **2 :** a tendency to refuse to do what is asked, to do the opposite of what is asked, or to do something capriciously at variance with what is asked

**neg·a·tiv·ist** \-,vəst\ *n* -s **:** one who adheres to or practices negativism

**neg·a·tiv·is·tic** \¦===¦vistik, -tēk\ *also* **negativist** *adj* **:** of, relating to, or marked by negativism

**neg·a·tiv·i·ty** \,negə'tivəd·ē\ *n* -ES **:** the quality or state of being negative **:** NEGATIVISM

**ne·ga·tor** *or* **ne·gat·er** \nə'gād·ə(r)\ *n* -s [*negator* fr. LL, fr. L *negatus*, past part. of *negare* to deny + -*or* -or; *negater* fr. ¹*negate* + -*er* — more at NEGATION] **:** one that negates

**neg·a·to·ry** \'negə,tōrē\ *adj* [MF and LL; MF *negatoire*, fr. LL *negatorius*, fr. L *negatus* + -*orius* -ory] **:** marked by or having the nature of negation **:** NEGATIVE ⟨~ criticism⟩

**neg·a·tron** \'negə,trän\ *also* **neg·a·ton** \-gə,tän\ *n* -s [*negatron* fr. ¹*negative* + *electron*; *negaton* fr. ¹*negative* + -*on*] **:** ELECTRON

**ne·ger** \'nēgə(r)\ *n* -s [MF *negre*, fr. Sp or Pg *negro*, black, Negro] *dial chiefly Eng* **:** NEGRO

**negidim** *pl of* NAGID

¹**ne·glect** \nə'glekt, nē'-\ *vt* -ED/-ING/-S [L *neglectus*, past part. of *neglegere*, *negligere*, *neclegere*, fr. *nec-* not (akin to *ne-* not) + *legere* to choose, gather — more at NO, LEGEND] **1 a :** to give little or no attention or respect to **:** consider or deal with as if of little or no importance **:** DISREGARD, SLIGHT ⟨some of the most significant issues have been ~*ed* —Bruce Payne⟩ ⟨~*ed* the real needs of the students⟩ **b :** to fail to attend to sufficiently or properly **:** not give proper attention or care to ⟨a great deal of its important work must either be ~*ed* or only inadequately done —J.E.Smith⟩ ⟨~*ed* her clothes and hair⟩ ⟨~*ed* his correspondence⟩ **2 :** to carelessly omit doing (something that should be done) either altogether or almost altogether **:** leave undone or unattended to through carelessness or by intention **:** pass lightly over ⟨~*ing* their obvious duty⟩ ⟨~*ed* to mention that he was a convict —Bernard Smith⟩ **3** *obs* **:** to cause to be neglected ⟨my absence doth ~ no great design —Shak.⟩

**syn** NEGLECT, OMIT, DISREGARD, IGNORE, OVERLOOK, SLIGHT, and FORGET can mean in common to pass over something without giving it due or sufficient attention. NEGLECT implies failure to give full or proper attention to someone or something that has a claim on one's attention ⟨*neglect* the duties of a citizen⟩ ⟨*neglect* one's friends⟩ OMIT implies to neglect entirely, as by oversight or inattention, an important detail or aspect of a whole or of a series of related things ⟨wished his parents had *omitted* to have him baptized —Bruce Marshall⟩ ⟨small possessions of her own which she had *omitted* to remove from the . . . room —Arnold Bennett⟩ DISREGARD usu. implies a voluntary inattention ⟨efface and injure something in ourselves, when we hurry by and *disregard* what does not seem to profit our own existence —Laurence Binyon⟩ ⟨wished to affirm her right to *disregard* the feelings of all the world —Joseph Conrad⟩ IGNORE implies an intention to disregard or a failure to regard something more or less obvious ⟨he who *ignores* outsiders is naturally ignored himself —G.G.Coulton⟩ ⟨get a reputation for clarity by avoiding or *ignoring* all the tangled jungles, by detouring round the blind alleys and dead ends of thought —Irwin Edman⟩ ⟨*ignore* trivial irritations⟩ OVERLOOK implies a disregarding typically through haste or lack of care ⟨some of the most significant issues have been neglected, and many revealing lessons of past experience have been *overlooked* —Bruce Payne⟩ ⟨promised to give him some background work, a promise he later *overlooked* —*Amer. Guide Series: La.*⟩ SLIGHT usu. implies cursory treatment, often contemptuous, or a disdainful disregarding ⟨nothing in the service was *slighted*, every phrase and gesture had its full value —Willa Cather⟩ ⟨these systems sometimes do not receive their full share of attention and may be *slighted* in the design —H.J. Petersen⟩ ⟨felt as if he had been *slighted* by a close friend⟩ FORGET in this comparison can imply a willful ignoring but more often suggests an absentminded neglecting ⟨the matter seemed important but I was told by my superiors, who were afraid of trouble, to *forget it*⟩ ⟨*forgot* to turn off the gas before leaving the house⟩

²**neglect** \"\ *n* -s [L *neglectus*, fr. *neglectus*, past part. of *neglegere*] **1 a :** the action of neglecting something ⟨could not understand his ~ of her⟩ ⟨one other element which may have contributed to the ~ of this problem —H.G.Armstrong⟩ **b :** the condition of being neglected ⟨would sink back into relative ~ and stagnation —Harold Griffin⟩ **2 a :** the fact of neglecting or of being neglected ⟨cannot deny the total ~ of the house⟩ **b** *archaic* **:** an instance of neglecting or of being neglected ⟨recovering from . . . ravages and ~s —J.H.Stocqueler⟩ **syn** see FAILURE

**ne·glect·able** \-təbəl\ *adj* [¹*neglect* + -*able*] *archaic* **:** NEGLIGIBLE

**neglected** *adj* [fr. past part. of ¹*neglect*] **1 :** not properly or sufficiently attended to or cared for ⟨a very ~ child⟩ **2 :** that evidences improper or insufficient attention or care ⟨had a ~ appearance⟩ — **ne·glect·ed·ly** *adv* — **ne·glect·ed·ness** *n* -ES

**ne·glect·er** *also* **ne·glec·tor** \-tə(r)\ *n* -s [*neglecter* fr. ¹*neglect* + -*er*; *neglector* fr. LL, fr. L *neglectus* (past part. of *neglegere*) + -*or* -or] **:** one that neglects

**ne·glect·ful** \-tfəl\ *adj* [²*neglect* + -*ful*] **1 :** that neglects or is given to neglecting **:** CARELESS, HEEDLESS ⟨~ of what people might think⟩ ⟨telling the nurse was as ~ as the rest of us —W.H.Wright⟩ **2 :** NEGLECTED 2 ⟨the ~ condition of the cemetery⟩ **syn** see NEGLIGENT

**ne·glect·ful·ly** \-fəlē, -li\ *adv* **:** in a neglectful manner

**ne·glect·ful·ness** *n* -ES **:** the quality or state of being neglectful

**ne·glec·tion** \nə'glekshən\ *n* -s [L *neglection-*, *neglectio* neglect, fr. *neglectus* (past part. of *neglegere* to neglect) + -*ion-*, -*io* -ion — more at NEGLECT] *chiefly dial* **:** NEGLECT

**ne·glec·tive** \-ktiv\ *adj* [¹*neglect* + -*ive*] *archaic* **:** NEGLECTFUL

**neg·li·gee** *or* **neg·li·gée** *or* **né·gli·gé** *or* **ne·gli·gé** *also* **neg·li·ge** \,neglə'zhā, '===\ *n* -s [F *négligé*, fr. past part. of *négliger* to neglect, fr. L *negligere*, *neglegere*] **1 a :** a loose gown worn by women in the 18th century **b :** a woman's long flowing dressing gown usu. dressy in style and trimmed (as with lace, ruffles, fur) **2 :** carelessly informal or incomplete attire ⟨was lounging about at home in ~⟩

**neg·li·gence** \'negləjən(t)s\ *n* -s [ME *negligence*, *necgligence*, fr. MF & L; MF *negligence*, fr. L *negligentia*, *neclegentia*, fr. *neglegent-*, *neglegens* + -*ia* -y] **1 a :** the quality or state of being negligent **b :** a failure to exercise the care that a prudent person usu. exercises — opposed to *diligence*; see GROSS NEGLIGENCE, ORDINARY NEGLIGENCE, SLIGHT NEGLIGENCE **2 :** an instance of negligence ⟨remembered his past ~s⟩

**neg·li·gen·cy** \-nsē\ *n* -ES [L *neglegentia*] *archaic* **:** NEGLIGENCE

¹**neg·li·gent** \-nt\ *adj* [ME *negligent*, *necgligent*, fr. MF & L; MF *negligent*, fr. L *neglegent-*, *neglegens*, pres. part. of *neglegere* to neglect — more at NEGLECT] **1 :** that is marked by or given to neglect **:** that is neglectful esp. habitually or culpably ⟨was a careless workman, ~ of detail —Edith Hamilton⟩ ⟨~ in his correspondence⟩; *specif* **:** not exercising the care usu. exercised by a prudent person ⟨~ about traffic regulations⟩ **2 :** that is marked by or given to a carelessly easy manner in such a way as to produce a usu. agreeable effect ⟨~ speech⟩ ⟨~ action⟩ **:** marked by a nonchalant indifference **:** free from stiffness or restraint **:** not labored or artificial **:** UNSTUDIED, OFFHAND ⟨converse with ~ ease upon indifferent topics —Arnold Bennett⟩ ⟨wore clothes with a ~ grace⟩

**syn** NEGLECTFUL, LAX, SLACK, REMISS: NEGLIGENT suggests culpable inattentiveness resulting in imperfection, incompleteness, slovenliness, or danger or damage to others ⟨so *negligent* in his poetical style . . . so slovenly, slipshod, and infelicitous —Matthew Arnold⟩ ⟨would come from the kitchen and pass slowly about the table, vaguely *negligent* unless she was directed by . . . brief orders —Elizabeth M. Roberts⟩ ⟨*negligent* about not maintaining a steady watch on the fire⟩ NEGLECTFUL may be more censorious in centering attention without palliation on the fact of neglect ⟨was not *neglectful* and would write as soon as he found anything good —Upton Sinclair⟩ ⟨peoples who when they dress themselves are utterly *neglectful* of what we consider the first requirements of decency —Edward Westermarck) LAX implies a want of strictness, stringency, precision, severity, or careful attention, usu. a blameworthy want ⟨scandalously *lax* in restraining drunkards from annoying the sober —G.M.Trevelyan⟩ ⟨their rather *lax* mental processes allow sweeping generalizations about the riddle of the universe and the mystery that is man —W.L.Sperry⟩ SLACK suggests want of necessary due care, diligence, attention, or application ⟨if they were *slack* in performing these arduous duties —G.M.Trevelyan⟩ ⟨one of the oars slipped from her *slack* grasp and floated beside the drifting skiff —B.A.Williams⟩ REMISS strongly implies the fact of blameworthiness or culpability without implication about the degree ⟨so *remiss* did they become in their attentions that we could no longer rely upon their bringing us the daily supply of food —Herman Melville⟩ ⟨shamefully *remiss* about paying them —H.E.Scudder⟩

**²negligent** \"\ *n* -s *archaic* : a negligent person

**negligent escape** *n* : the escape of a prisoner without prison breach and without the custodian's consent and arising through the custodian's negligence — contrasted with *voluntary escape*

**neg·li·gent·ly** *adv* [ME, fr. ¹*negligent* + *-ly*] : in a negligent manner ⟨did their work ~⟩ ⟨was strolling ~ toward them, smoking a cigarette —Dorothy Sayers⟩

**neg·li·gi·bil·i·ty** \ˌneglәjә'bilәd·ē, -lēj-, -әtē, -i\ *n* -ES : the quality or state of being negligible ⟨differences between the two positions dwindle to ~ —Lucius Garvin⟩

**neg·li·gi·ble** *also* **neg·lige·able** \'neglәjәbәl, -lēj-\ *adj* [*negligible* fr. *neglig-* (fr. L *negligere*) + *-ible*; *negligeable* fr. F *négligeable*, fr. *négliger* to neglect (fr. L *negligere*) + *-able*] : that can or should easily be disregarded: **a** : that is so tiny or unimportant or otherwise of so little consequence as to require or deserve little or no attention : TRIFLING ⟨the error involved is ~ —W.H.Dowdeswell⟩ **b** : that is of so little substance or extent or worth as to be practically nonexistent and so requiring or deserving little or no attention or respect ⟨trade or industry is practically ~ —S.J.Roche⟩ ⟨made ~ progress⟩ ⟨poisonous plants in Arizona are so rare as to be ~ —*Amer. Guide Series: Ariz.*⟩ ⟨a pious and good man, but an utterly ~ personality —Compton Mackenzie⟩

**neg·li·gi·bly** \-blē\ *adv* [*negligible* + *-ly*] : to a negligible extent ⟨are small, but not ~ small —Fred Hoyle⟩

**negociate** *archaic var of* NEGOTIATE

**ne·go·tia·bil·i·ty** \nә͵gōsh(ē)ә'bilәd·ē, nē͵-, -әtē, -i\ *n* : the quality or state of being negotiable

**ne·go·tia·ble** \nә'gōsh(ē)әbәl, nē'-\ *adj* [*negotiate* + *-able*] : that can be negotiated: as **a** : that can be transferred or assigned from one person to another in return for equivalent value by being delivered either with endorsement (as of an instrument payable to order) or without endorsement (as of an instrument payable to bearer) so that the title passes to the transferee who is not prejudiced in his rights by any defect or flaw in the title of prior parties nor by personal defenses available to prior parties among themselves provided in both cases that the transferee is a bona fide holder without notice ⟨bills of exchange, promissory notes, and checks that are payable to bearer or order are ~ instruments, as are also, in some jurisdictions, some other instruments (as bonds, some forms of stock)⟩ ⟨~ paper⟩ ⟨~ securities⟩ **b** (1) : that can be successfully traversed ⟨the road, normally ~ by jeep —Herbert Passin⟩ ⟨a difficult but ~ path through the forest⟩ or gone up or down ⟨a ~ hill⟩ or otherwise successfully managed ⟨a sharp curve in the road that is ~ if one goes slowly⟩ (2) : that can be met and successfully dealt with : that does not pose insurmountable problems ⟨familiar and ~ situations —Anthony West⟩ (3) : that can be arrived at : that can be done or accomplished or realized : ATTAINABLE ⟨thought that some kind of treaty was ~⟩ ⟨not readily ~ by empirical method —V.C. Aldrich⟩ (4) : that can be readily understood ⟨disclose its fundamental motives in widely ~ language —H.E.Clurman⟩ **c** (1) : that is utilizable in a practical way ⟨the old rhetoric . . . is no longer ~ —E.R.Bentley⟩ (2) : that has characteristics favoring wide acceptance ⟨have found a home where their ideas are ~ —R.M.Weaver⟩ ⟨is ~ to the widest possible public —W.L.Miller⟩ : that has high commercial value ⟨seems to be highly ~ at the box office —Barbara B. Jamison⟩ **d** : that is open to discussion or question or dispute ⟨criticism, which is public and ~ —J.C.Ransom⟩ ⟨he declared that their claim . . . is not ~ —*New Republic*⟩

**ne·go·ti·ant** \-sh(ē)ənt\ *n* -s [L *negotiant-, negotians* trader, fr. pres. part. of *negotiari*] : NEGOTIATOR

**ne·go·ti·ate** \-s(h)ē͵āt, *usu* -ād·+V\ *vb* -ED/-ING/-S [L *negotiatus*, past part. of *negotiari* to carry on business, fr. *negotium* business, fr. *neg-* not (akin to *ne-* not) + *otium* leisure — more at NO] *vi* **1** : to communicate or confer with another so as to arrive at the settlement of some matter : meet with another so as to arrive through discussion at some kind of agreement or compromise about something : come to terms esp. in state matters by meetings and discussions ⟨*negotiated* with him on the political and economic program to be carried out —*Current Biog.*⟩ ⟨wanted to ~ before naming a final price⟩ ⟨*negotiating* with the foreign ministers⟩ **2** *obs* : to carry on business or trade : TRAFFIC ~ *vt* **1 a** : to deal with (some matter or affair that requires ability for its successful handling) : MANAGE, HANDLE, CONDUCT ⟨*negotiated* his business deals with remarkable skill⟩ **b** (1) : to arrange for or bring about through conference and discussion : work out or arrive at or settle upon by meetings and agreements or compromises ⟨*negotiating* a peace treaty⟩ ⟨one of his first actions was to ~ a monetary understanding with the British government —*Current Biog.*⟩ (2) : to influence successfully in a desired way by discussions and agreements or compromises ⟨*negotiated* them into doing exactly what he wanted⟩ **2 a** : to transfer or assign (as a check, bill of exchange, promissory note) to another by delivery or endorsement or both in return for equivalent value **b** : to convert (as a check) into cash or the equivalent value ⟨*negotiating* securities⟩ **c** : to give equivalent value for (as a check) ⟨offered to ~ any checks properly drawn up⟩ **3 a** : to successfully get over or across (as a road) or up or down (as a hill) or through (as an obstacle) ⟨carefully *negotiated* the winding road⟩ ⟨took me almost an hour to ~ the almost perpendicular trail —V.W. Von Hagen⟩ **b** : to encounter and dispose of (as a problem, challenge) with completeness and satisfaction : tackle successfully ⟨*negotiated* the difficult arpeggios of the song cleanly and confidently —*Current Biog.*⟩ **c** : COMPLETE, ACCOMPLISH ⟨~*s* the trip in 4 hours⟩

**ne·go·ti·a·tion** \≈͵≈≈'āshən\ *n* -s [L *negotiation-, negotiatio*, fr. *negotiatus* + *-ion-, -io* -ion] **1** *obs* **a** : a business transaction **b** : TRADING, TRAFFICKING **2** : the action or process of negotiating or of being negotiated ⟨the dispute is now under ~⟩ — often used in pl. ⟨proposed resumption of ~*s* on the long treaty draft —*Americana Annual*⟩

**ne·go·ti·a·tor** \≈'≈≈͵ād·ə(r), -ātə-\ *n* -s [L, trader, fr. *negotiatus* + *-or* -or] : one that negotiates

**ne·go·ti·a·to·ry** \nə'gōshēə͵tōrē\ *adj* [*negotiate* + *-ory*] : of or relating to negotiation ⟨a ~ association that was formed for carrying on discussions with trade unions⟩ ⟨have been restricted to ~ functions —Dale Yoder⟩

**ne·go·ti·a·tress** \nə'gōshēə·trəs\ *n* -ES [*negotiator* + *-ess*] : a female negotiator

**ne·go·ti·a·trix** \-riks\ *n* -ES [NL, fem. of *negotiator*] : NEGOTIATRESS

**ne·go·ti·o·rum ges·tio** \nə͵gōd·ē'ō͵rüm'gestē͵ō\ *n* [LL, fr. L, management of business] : GESTION 2

**ne·gre** \'negrā\ *n* -s [origin unknown] : RED GROUPER

**ne·gress** \'nēgrəs\ *n* -ES *usu cap* [F *négresse*, fr. *nègre* Negro (fr. Sp or Pg *negro*, black, Negro) + *-esse* -ess] : a female Negro — usu. taken to be offensive

**ne·gri body** \'nāgrē-\ *n*, *usu cap N* [after Adelchi *Negri* †1912 Ital. physician] : an inclusion body found in the nerve cells in rabies

**ne·grid** \'nēgrəd\ *n* -s *often cap* [ISV *negr-* Negro (fr. ¹*negro*) + *-id*] **1** : NEGRITO **2** : NEGRILLO

**ne·gril·lo** \nə'gri(͵)lō\ *n*, *pl* **negrillos** *or* **negrilloes** *usu cap* [Sp, dim. of *negro* black, Negro] : a member of a people (as Bushmen, Pygmies) belonging to a group of negroid peoples of small stature found in Africa — usu. distinguished from *Negrito*

**ne·grit·ic** \nə'grid·ik\ *adj*, *often cap* [partly fr. *negro* + *-itic*; partly fr. *negrito* + *-ic*] : of, relating to, or resembling Negroes or Negritos

**ne·gri·to** \nə'grē(͵)tō\ *n*, *pl* **negritos** *or* **negritoes** [Sp, dim. of *negro*] **1** *usu cap* : a member of a people (as the Andamanese) belonging to a group of negroid peoples of small stature found in Oceania and the southeastern part of Asia — usu. distinguished from *Negrillo* **2** : PARADISE TREE 1a

**ne·grit·oid** \-ri͵tȯid\ *adj*, *often cap* [*negrito* + *-oid*] : of, relating to, or having the characteristics of Negritos

**¹ne·gro** \'nē(͵)grō, *esp South* 'ni(͵)- *or* -͵grə\ *n* -ES [Sp or Pg, black, Negro, fr. L *nigr-, niger* black] **1** *usu cap* **a** : a member of the black race of mankind as opposed by classification according to physical features (as skin color, hair form, or body or skeletal characteristics) but without regard to language or culture to members of the Caucasian, Mongoloid, or other races of mankind; *esp* : a member of a people belonging to the African branch of the black race and marked typically by dark pigmentation and woolly hair and everted lips and broad flat noses and prognathism **b** : a person of Negro ancestry; *esp* : a person whose pigmentation is dark like that of typical African Negroes and who often (as with mulattoes) has other physical characteristics of typical African Negroes **2** : a black to dark grayish yellowish brown — called also *Saint Benoit*; see MINERAL BROWN

**²negro** \"\ *adj*, *usu cap* : of, relating to, or having the characteristics of Negroes

**negro-african** \≈(͵)≈¦≈≈≈\ *n*, *cap N&A* **1** *in former classifications* : a family of African languages **2** : the indigenous languages of Africa south of the Sahara

**negro ant** *n* : a common widely distributed black ant (*Formica fusca*)

**negro bug** *n*, *sometimes cap N* : any of numerous minute convex black bugs that constitute the genus *Corimelaena* and that feed on plant juices and impart a foul taste to fruits (as raspberries) over which they crawl; *esp* : a common pest (*C. pulicaria*) of the U.S. east of the Rocky mountains that is sometimes very destructive to celery, corn, and wheat

**negro cloth** *or* **negro cotton** *n*, *often cap N* : a strong coarse cloth formerly used in making clothes for Negro slaves

**negro coffee** *n*, *often cap N* : COFFEE SENNA

**negrohead** \≈(͵)≈͵≈\ *n* [fr. its color] **1** : a dark lump or mass of tobacco or inferior rubber **2** : NIGGERHEAD 3

**negrohead beech** *n* : an Australian timber tree (*Nothofagus moorei*) having dark green foliage

**¹ne·groid** \'nē͵grȯid\ *adj*, *often cap* [ISV *negr-* Negro (fr. ¹*negro*) + *-oid*] : of, resembling, or related to the Negro race

**²negroid** \"\ *n* -s *usu cap* : a negroid individual

**ne·gro·ism** \'nēgrō͵izəm\ *n* -s *often cap* **1** : advancement of Negro interests; *specif* : advocacy of the cause of equal rights for Negroes **2** : a quality or trait distinctive or taken to be distinctive of Negroes; *esp* : a word, phrase, or manner of expression distinctive or taken to be distinctive of the speech of Negroes

**ne·gro·ize** \-͵īz\ *vt* -ED/-ING/-S *sometimes cap* **1** : to cause to be Negro (as in qualities, personnel) ⟨*negroized* speech⟩ ⟨a new *negroized* stage production⟩ ⟨a *negroized* unit⟩ **2** : to imbue with negroism ⟨a *negroized* philanthropic group⟩

**negro monkey** *n* **1** : MOOR MACAQUE **2** : a black langur (*Presbytis maurus*) **3** *or* **negro tamarin** : a black Brazilian tamarin (*Leontocebus ursulus*)

**negro peach** *n* **1** : a stout spreading or semiclimbing shrub (*Sarcocephalus esculentus*) of tropical Africa and Ceylon with round brownish warty fruit having a reddish watery pulp **2** : the fruit of the negro peach

**¹ne·gro·phile** \'nēgrō͵fīl\ *also* **ne·gro·phil** \-fil\ *n* -s *often cap* [¹*negro* + *-phile*] : one that is esp. friendly to Negroes and their interests; *esp* : one that favors negroism

**²negrophile** \"\ *adj*, *often cap* : having the qualities of a negrophile

**ne·groph·i·lism** \nə'gräfə͵lizəm\ *n* -s *often cap* : NEGROISM

**ne·groph·i·list** \nə'gräfələst\ *n* -s *often cap* : NEGROPHILE

**¹ne·gro·phobe** \'nēgrō͵fōb\ *n* -s *often cap* : one that strongly dislikes or fears Negroes

**²negrophobe** \"\ *adj*, *often cap* : having the qualities of a negrophobe

**ne·gro·pho·bia** \͵≈≈'fōbēə\ *n*, *often cap* [NL, fr. E *negro* + NL *-phobia*] : strong dislike or fear of Negroes — **ne·gro·pho·bic** \¦≈≈¦fōbik, -bēk *also* -fäb-\ *adj*, *often cap*

**negro vine** *n* : an herbaceous vine (*Vincetoxicum hirsutum*) with hairy foliage and dark purple flowers

**ne·gun·do** \nə'gən(͵)dō\ *n* [NL, fr. a native name in India for plants of the genus *Vitex*, fr. Skt *nirguṇḍī*] **1** *cap, in some classifications* : a genus of trees set off from *Acer* on the basis of the pinnate leaves **2** -s : BOX ELDER

**¹ne·gus** \'nēgəs\ *n* -ES [Amharic *negūs*, fr. Eth *nĕgūša*, *nagašt* king of kings] : KING — used as a title of the sovereign of Ethiopia

**²negus** \"\ *n* -ES [after Francis *Negus* †1732 Eng. colonel, its originator] : a beverage of claret, port, or other wine heated with hot water, sweetened, and often flavored with lemon juice and nutmeg

**ne·hu** \'ne(͵)hü\ *n*, *pl* **nehu** *or* **nehus** [Hawaiian] : a small Hawaiian anchovy (*Anchoviella purpureus*) much used for bait

**NEI** *abbr*, *often not cap* **1** [L *non est inventus*] he was not found **2** not elsewhere included; not elsewhere indicated

**nei·bour** \'nēbə(r)\ *Scot var of* NEIGHBOR

**neid** \'nēd\ *Scot var of* NEED

**ne·id·i·dae** \nē'idə͵dē\ *n pl*, *cap* [NL, fr. *Neides*, type genus, + *-idae*] : a family of long-legged slender-bodied bugs with elbowed antennae of which the first joint is long and clubbed and the last is spindle-shaped — see STILT BUG

**¹neif** \'nēf\ *n* -s [fr. (assumed) AF *neif, naif*, fr. OF *naif* native, fr. L *nativus* — more at NATIVE] : one born a serf

**²neif** \'nēf\ *chiefly dial var of* ¹NIEVE

**¹neigh** \'nā\ *vb* -ED/-ING/-S [ME *neyen*, fr. OE *hnǣgan*; akin to MHG *nēgen* to neigh, ON *gneggja*; all fr. a prehistoric Gmc vb. of imit. origin] *vi* : to make the loud prolonged calling cry typical of a horse ~ *vt* : to utter by or as if by neighing

**²neigh** \"\ *n* -s : the loud prolonged calling cry typical of a horse

**¹neigh·bor** \'nābə(r)\ *n* -s *see -or in Explan Notes* [ME *neighbor, neighebor*, fr. OE *nēahgebūr*; akin to MD *nāgebuur*, OHG *nāhgibūr*; all fr. a prehistoric WGmc compound whose first element is represented by OE *nēah* near and whose second element is represented by OE *gebūr* dweller — more at NIGH, BOOR] **1 a** : one whose house or other place of residence immediately adjoins or is relatively near that of another : one that lives next to or near another **b** : one whose town or district or country immediately adjoins or is relatively near that of another **c** (1) : one whose position (as in sitting, standing) immediately adjoins or is relatively near that of another ⟨each of the students in the classroom passed his paper to his ~⟩ (2) : CORNER 7 **d** : something located in a position immediately adjoining or relatively near that of another ⟨Canada is the northern ~ of the U.S.⟩ ⟨Venus is one of Earth's nearest ~*s*⟩ **2 a** : a fellow creature; *esp* : a fellow human being ⟨thou shalt love thy ~ as thyself —Mt 19:19 (AV)⟩ ⟨closing their eyes and their hearts to the misfortune of a ~ who is unknown and far away —Pius XII⟩ **b** : one that evidences true kindness and charity toward his fellowman ⟨proved ~ to the man who fell among the robbers —Lk 10:36 (RSV)⟩ **3** — used as a term of familiar direct address esp. to one whose name is not known ⟨say, ~, give me a hand⟩ and often with an implication of stiff reserve or condescension or mild hostility ⟨better not say things you oughtn't, ~⟩ **4** *chiefly Scot* : one of a pair

**²neighbor** \"\ *adj* : that immediately adjoins or is relatively near another : that is a neighbor : NEIGHBORING ⟨promised our ~ American republics —Blair Bolles⟩

**³neighbor** \"\ *vb* **neighbored; neighbored; neighboring** \-b(ə)riŋ\ **neighbors** *vt* **1 a** : to adjoin immediately or lie relatively near to : border upon ⟨the U.S. ~*s* the northern border of Mexico⟩ **b** *archaic* : to come close to : APPROACH ⟨can pretty nigh ~ it with a guess —George Meredith⟩ **2** : to put into the position or relationship of having (something indicated) immediately adjoining or closely situated ⟨a building of admirable proportions is this, ~*ed* by other public structures of vast size —Aubrey Drury⟩ ~ *vi* **1 a** : to have one's house or other place of residence immediately adjoining or relatively near that of another ⟨she ~*ed* close upon the street where her former friend lived⟩ **b** : to have an immediately adjoining or relatively near position or location ⟨the earth ~*s* near to the sun⟩ **2** : to associate in a friendly way (as by exchanging visits, having informal chats, offering ordinary help and advice) with another that is a neighbor : make the agreeable easy social contacts usual among congenial neighbors ⟨it was a quiet farmplace, standing among fields . . . yet it was near enough the town for ~*ing* —Maristan Chapman⟩ ⟨had no mind to ~ with them —V.L.Parrington⟩

**neigh·bor·hood** \-(r)͵hu̇d\ *n* [ME *neighborhode*, fr. ¹*neighbor* + *-hode*, -hood] **1** : friendly association with another that is a neighbor : the agreeable easy relationship usual among congenial neighbors ⟨if there are remoter nations that wish us not good but ill, they know that we are strong; they know that we can and will defend our ~ —F.D.Roosevelt⟩ **2** : the quality or state of being immediately adjacent or relatively near to something : PROXIMITY ⟨the ~ of the earth to the sun⟩ ⟨refugees from the country, driven by fear or the ~ of armies —F.L.Paxson⟩ **3 a** : the approximate area or point of the location or position of something ⟨traveled to a region somewhere in the ~ of that city⟩ **b** : the approximate amount or extent or degree — usu. used with *in* and a qualifying phrase ⟨has in the ~ of $10,000,000⟩ ⟨a highway in the ~ of 100 miles long⟩ **4 a** : a number of people forming a loosely cohesive community within a larger unit (as a city, town) and living close or fairly close together in more or less familiar association with each other within a relatively small section or district of usu. somewhat indefinite boundaries and usu. having some common or fairly common identifying feature (as approximate equality of economic condition, similar social status, similar national origins or religion, similar interests) and usu. some degree of self-sufficiency as a group (as through local schools, churches, libraries, business establishments, cultural and recreational facilities) ⟨thought the whole ~ would hear about it⟩ **b** : the particular section or district that is lived in by these people and that is marked by individual features (as type of homes and public establishments) that together establish a distinctive appearance and atmosphere ⟨now lives in a beautiful ~⟩ **c** : an area or region of usu. vague limits that is usu. marked by some fairly distinctive feature of the inhabitants or terrain ⟨would never want to live in that ~ of the country⟩ **5** : the assemblage of all points whose distances from a given point are not greater than a given positive number

**neighborhood house** *n* : SETTLEMENT 6g

**neighboring** *adj* [fr. pres. part. of ³*neighbor*] **1** : that is immediately adjacent or relatively near ⟨where the men from the ~ towns gathered —Phyllis Duganne⟩ ⟨~ countries⟩ ⟨~ planets⟩ **2** *of atoms or groups in a molecule* : attached to atoms united to each other; *esp* : attached to carbon atoms united to each other in aliphatic or alicyclic compounds — compare VICINAL 3

**neighboring tone** *n* : AUXILIARY TONE

**neigh·bor·less** \'nābə(r)ləs\ *adj* : having no neighbor

**neighborlike** \'≈≈͵≈\ *adj* : NEIGHBORLY

**neigh·bor·li·ness** \'nābə(r)lēnəs, -lin-\ *n* -ES : the quality or state of being neighborly

**¹neigh·bor·ly** \-lē, -li\ *adv* [*neighbor* + *-ly*, adv. suffix] *archaic* : in a neighborly manner ⟨you called in here ~ —John Drinkwater⟩

**²neighborly** \"\ *adj* [*neighbor* + *-ly*, adj. suffix] **1** : of, relating to, or typical of neighbors, esp. congenial neighbors : suited to neighbors ⟨a ~ conversation⟩ ⟨has ~ chores —Mary Welsh⟩ ⟨~ helpfulness⟩ **2** : that readily associates in a friendly way (as by exchanging visits, having informal chats, offering ordinary help and advice) with a neighbor : that has the agreeable easy sociability typical of a congenial neighbor ⟨a pleasant ~ person⟩ **syn** see AMICABLE

**neigh·bor·ship** \-(r)͵ship\ *n* [ME *nychtbourschip*, fr. *nychtbour, neighbor* neighbor + *-schip*, *-ship* -ship] **1** *archaic* : PROXIMITY **2** *archaic* : the relationship and activity of a neighbor ⟨its true interest is a good ~ —Jedediah Morse⟩

**neigh·er** \'nikə(r)\ *vi* -ED/-ING/-S [imit.] *Scot* : ⁴NICKER

**ne·i·lah** \͵neē'lä, ne'ēlə\ *n* -s [Heb *nĕʽīlāh* closing of gates; fr. the closing of the gates of the Temple at Jerusalem at the end of the service] : the concluding portion of the liturgy on Yom Kippur

**nei·per** \'nēpə(r)\ *Scot var of* NEIGHBOR

**neis·se·ria** \nī'sirēə\ *n*, *cap* [NL, fr. Albert L. S. *Neisser* †1916 Ger. physician + NL *-ia*] : a genus of parasitic bacteria (the type of the family Neisseriaceae) growing in pairs and occas. tetrads and thriving best at 98.6°F in the animal body or serum media — see GONOCOCCUS, MENINGOCOCCUS

**neis·ser·i·a·ce·ae** \nī͵sirē'āsē͵ē\ *n pl*, *cap* [NL, fr. *Neisseria*, type genus + *-aceae*] : a small family of spherical nonmotile gram-negative bacteria (order Eubacteriales) that are obligate parasites of warm-blooded vertebrates — see NEISSERIA

**neis·se·ri·an** \(')nī¦sirēən\ *adj* [NL *Neisseria* + E *-an*] : of, relating to, or caused by the gonococcus

**neist** \'nēst\ *chiefly Scot var of* NEXT

**¹nei·ther** \'nēthə(r), 'nīth-; *see* EITHER\ *pron* [ME *neither, naither* not either of two, pron., conj. & adj., alter. (influenced by *either, aither* either) of *nauther*, pron. & conj., *nouther, nowther*, pron., conj. & adj., *nother*, pron. & adj., fr. OE *nāhwæther, nāwther*, pron. & conj., *nōhwæther, nowther*, pron., *nōther*, pron., fr. *nā, nō* not + *hwæther* which of two, whether — more at NO, WHETHER] : not one of two or more : not either: **a** : not the one and not the other of two ⟨made two suggestions and ~ was accepted⟩ **b** : not any one of more than two ⟨~ of the three men stood up —Luke Short⟩ — usu. sing. in constr. except when a periphrastic genitive intervenes between *neither* and the verb form in which circumstance the verb is often plural in form ⟨~ of them were in —John Galsworthy⟩; often qualified by a periphrastic genitive and used in apposition with a plural pronominal subject to emphasize the exclusion of each of the individuals included in the subject from the thing predicated ⟨we ~ of us moved —Wendy Wood⟩ ⟨two English painters who are ~ of them abstract or surrealist —Geoffrey Grigson⟩

**²neither** \"\ *conj* [ME *neither, naither*] **1** — used as a function word before two or more coordinate words, phrases, or clauses now joined usu. by *nor* or sometimes by *or* or archaically by *neither* to indicate that what immediately follows is the first of two or more alternatives both or all of which are rejected ⟨~ my father nor I were by nature inclined to faith in the unintelligible —George Santayana⟩ **2** : nor yet : also not : no more ⟨just as the serf was not permitted to leave the land, so ~ was his offspring —G.G.Coulton⟩ ⟨an illiterate author cannot get very far, and ~ can a musical composer who has not learned musical notation —Thomas Munro⟩ ⟨justice is ~ new nor old —Mark Van Doren⟩ ⟨sat at bare tables and ~ ate, drank, nor smoked —Mary Cable⟩ ⟨~ by day nor by night⟩ ⟨we believe ~ in prescribing or proscribing books —*Publisher's Weekly*⟩ ⟨this court ~ approves or condemns any legislative policy —O.J.Roberts⟩

**³neither** \"\ *adj* [ME *neither, naither*] : not either ⟨on ~ side of the street are there any trees⟩

**⁴neither** \"\ *adv*, *chiefly dial* : EITHER — used esp. to emphasize a negative in a foregoing clause ⟨others speak so fast and sputter that they are not to be understood ~ —Earl of Chesterfield⟩

**neive** \'nēv\ *chiefly dial var of* ¹NIEVE

**nejd** \'nejd\ *also* **nej·di** \-dē\ *adj*, *usu cap* [*nejd* fr. *Nejd*, state of Saudi Arabia; *nejdi* fr. Ar *najdīy*, fr. *Najd* Nejd] : of or relating to the inland state of Nejd in Saudi Arabia

**nejdi** *n* -s *cap* [Ar *najdīy*] : a native or inhabitant of Nejd

**nek·ton** *also* **nec·ton** \'nektən\ *n* -s [G *nekton*, fr. Gk *nēkton*, neut. of *nēktos* swimming — more at NECT-] : free swimming aquatic animals essentially independent of wave and current action — compare PLANKTON — **nek·ton·ic** \(')nek¦tänik\ *adj*

**nell** \'nel\ *n* -s [by shortening & alter.] : MENEL

**nel·lore** \nə'lō(ə)r\ *n*, *usu cap* [fr. *Nellore*, town in southeast Indian Union] : an Indian breed of large steel-gray to almost white cattle used chiefly for heavy draft and introduced in many warm regions for crossbreeding with European cattle

**nel·ly** \'nelē\ *n* -ES [perh. fr. *Nelly*, nickname for *Helen*] **1** : GIANT PETREL **2** : SOOTY ALBATROSS

**nel·ma** \'nelmə\ *n* -s [Russ *nel'ma*] : INCONNU

**¹nel·son** \'nelsən\ *adj*, *usu cap* [fr. *Nelson*, provincial district of New Zealand] : of or from the provincial district of Nelson, New Zealand : of the kind or style prevalent in the Nelson provincial district

[2]**nelson** \"\ *n* -s [prob. fr. the name *Nelson*] **:** a wrestling hold marked by a distinctive application of leverage against an opponent's arm and neck and head — see FULL NELSON, HALF NELSON, QUARTER NELSON, THREE-QUARTER NELSON

**nelson bighorn sheep** *n, usu cap N* [prob. fr. the name *Nelson*] **:** a large dark-coated wild sheep that is a variety (*Ovis Canadensis nelsoni*) of the bighorn distinguished by its very large horns and now rare over much of its range in the mountainous regions of western No. America

**nelson's oriole** *n, usu cap N* [after Edward W. *Nelson* †1934 Am. naturalist] **:** HOODED ORIOLE

**ne·lum·bi·um** \nə̇'ləmbēəm\ [NL, fr. Sinhalese *neḷumbu* + NL *-ium*] *syn of* NELUMBO

**ne·lum·bo** \-ləm(,)bō\ *n* [NL, fr. Sinhalese *neḷumbu*, Indian lotus] **1** *cap* **:** a genus that includes large water lilies having flowers with 4 to 5 sepals, numerous petals, and the discrete carpels embedded in a fleshy receptacle and that is usu. considered to constitute a subfamily of Nymphaeaceae but is sometimes isolated in a separate family **2** *or* **nelumbium** -s **:** any plant of the genus *Nelumbo* — compare LOTUS 3

**nem-** *or* **nema-** *or* **nemo-** *comb form* [Gk & NL; NL *nem-*, *nemo-*, fr. Gk *nēma*] **1 :** thread ⟨*nema*thecium⟩ ⟨*Nem*ichthys⟩ ⟨*Nemo*cera⟩ **2 :** nematode ⟨*nema*cide⟩ ⟨*nem*ic⟩

**NEM** *abbr, often not cap* not elsewhere mentioned

**ne·ma** \'nēmə\ *n* -s [NL, fr. Gk *nēma* thread — more at NEEDLE] **1 :** a tubular filament that connects the disk of attachment of a graptolite with the primary theca **2 :** NEMATODE, ROUNDWORM, EELWORM

**-ne·ma** \'nēmə\ *n comb form, pl* **-nema·ta** \'nēməd·ə, 'nem-, -mətə\ *or* **-nemas** [NL, fr. Gk *nēma* thread] **:** one having, being, or resembling (such) a thread ⟨chromo*nema*⟩ — esp. in generic names in botany and zoology ⟨Hyalo*nema*⟩ ⟨Scyto*nema*⟩

**nemacide** *var of* NEMATOCIDE

**nem·a·line** \'nemə,līn, -,lə̇n\ *adj* [*nem-* + connective *-l-* + *-ine*] *of a mineral* **:** having the form of threads **:** FIBROUS

**ne·ma·li·on** \nə̇'mālēən\ *n, cap* [NL, irreg. fr. Gk *nēma* thread] **:** a genus of reddish brown gelatinous wormlike branching algae (family Helminthocladiaceae) found clinging to rocks in the intertidal zone in the north Atlantic

**ne·ma·li·o·na·ce·ae** \nə̇,mālēə'nāsē,ē\ [NL, fr. *Nemalion* + *-aceae*] *syn of* HELMINTHOCLADIACEAE

**ne·ma·li·o·na·les** \-'nā(,)lēz\ *n pl, cap* [NL, fr. *Nemalion* + *-ales*] **:** an order of red algae (class Rhodophyceae) that have only a gametophytic generation and carpospores which develop from end cells of short filaments sprouting from a carpogonium

**nem·a·lite** \'nemə,līt\ *n* -s [Gk *nēma* thread + E *-lite*] **:** a fibrous brucite

**nem·a·sto·ma·ce·ae** \,neməstō'māsē,ē, nə̇,mas-\ *n pl, cap* [NL, fr. *Nemastoma*, type genus (fr. *nem-* + *stoma*) + *-aceae*] **:** a family of red algae (order Cryptonemiales) with cylindrical, flat, or leaflike thalli and sunken cystocarps

**nema·sty·lis** \,nemə'stīlə̇s\ *n, cap* [NL, fr. *nem-* + Gk *stylis* small pillar, dim. of *stylos* pillar — more at STOW] **:** a genus of bulbous perennial herbs (family Iridaceae) that are characterized by terete stems, few plicate leaves, few-flowered spathes, and threadlike style branches

**nemat-** *or* **nemato-** *comb form* [NL, fr. Gk *nēmat-*, fr. *nēmat-*, *nēma* thread] **1 :** thread ⟨*nemat*ic⟩ ⟨*Nemato*spora⟩ **2 :** nematode ⟨*nemato*cide⟩

**nem·a·tel·mia** \,nemə'telmēə\ *or* **nem·a·tel·min·thes** \-,tel'min(t)(,)thēz\ [*Nematelmia* fr. NL, fr. *nemat-* + *-elmia* (fr. Gk *helminth-*, *helmis* intestinal worm, parasitic worm); *Nematelminthes* fr. NL, fr. *nemat-* + *-elminthes* (fr. Gk *helminth-*, *helmis*) — more at HELMINTH-] *syn of* NEMATHELMINTHES

**nem·a·the·cial** \¦nemə¦thēsh(ē)əl, -thēsēəl\ *adj* [*nemathecium* + *-al*] **:** of or relating to a nemathecium

**nem·a·the·ci·um** \,nemə'thēs(h)ēəm\ *n, pl* **nemathe·cia** \-)ēə\ [NL, fr. *nem-* + *-thecium*] **:** a wartlike prominence on the thallus of a red alga containing tetraspores, antheridia, or cystocarps

**nem·a·thel·mia** \,nemə'thelmēə\ [NL, fr. *nemat-* + *-helmia* (fr. Gk *helminth-*, *helmis*)] *syn of* NEMATHELMINTHES

**nem·a·thel·minth** \-l,min(t)th\ *n* -s [NL *Nemathelminthes*] **:** a worm of the phylum Nemathelminthes

**nem·a·thel·min·thes** \-,thel'min(t)(,)thēz\ *n pl, cap* [NL, fr. *nemat-* + *Helminthes*] *in some classifications* **:** a phylum including the Nematoda and Nematomorpha and sometimes the Acanthocephala, the Rotifera, the Gastrotricha, and the Kinorhyncha, all being more or less wormlike animals with a cylindrical unsegmented body covered by an unciliated ectoderm that secretes an external cuticle

**ne·mat·ic** \nə̇'mad·ik\ *adj* [ISV *nemat-* + *-ic*] **:** relating to, existing in, or being a mesomorphic state which is the first state formed on cooling from a liquid melt and in which the orientation of the molecules or atoms is in parallel lines but not in layers — compare SMECTIC

**nem·a·to·blas·tic** \¦neməd·ə¦blastik, nə̇¦mad·-\ *adj* [ISV *nemat-* + *blastic*] *of metamorphic rock* **:** having a texture corresponding to the fibrous texture in igneous rock

**nem·a·toc·era** \,nemə'täsərə\ *n pl, cap* [NL, fr. *nemat-* + *-cera*] **:** a suborder of Diptera including the mosquitoes, fungus gnats, and crane flies — **nem·a·toc·er·an** \¦≈≈¦≈≈rən\ *adj or n* — **nem·a·toc·er·ous** \-rəs\ *adj*

**nem·a·to·ci·dal** *also* **nem·a·ti·ci·dal** \¦neməd·ə¦sīdᵊl, nə̇¦mad·-\ *or* **nema·ci·dal** \¦nemə¦s-\ *adj* [*nematocide*, *nematicide*, *nemacide* + *-al*] **:** capable of destroying nematodes

**nem·a·to·cide** *also* **nem·a·ti·cide** \'neməd·ə,sīd, nə̇'mad·-\ *or* **nem·a·cide** \'nemə,s-\ *n* -s [*nematocide* fr. *nemat-* + *-cide*; *nematicide* fr. *nemat-* + *-i-* + *-cide*; *nemacide* fr. *nem-* + *-cide*] **:** a substance or preparation used to destroy nematodes, esp. those that attack crop plants — compare ANTHELMINTIC

**nem·a·to·cyst** \'neməd·ə,sist, nə̇'mad·-\ *n* [ISV *nemat-* + *cyst*] **:** one of the minute stinging organs of hydrozoans, scyphozoans, and actinozoans — compare TRICHOCYST — **nem·a·to·cys·tic** \¦≈≈≈¦sistik, ≈¦≈≈-\ *adj*

**nem·a·to·cyte** \'≈≈≈,sīt, ≈'≈≈-\ *n* -s [*nemat-* + *-cyte*] **:** CNIDOBLAST

**nem·a·to·da** \,nemə'tōdə\ *n pl, cap* [NL, fr. *nemat-* + *-oda* (irreg. fr. *-oidea*)] **:** a class of Aschelminthes or a separate phylum comprising elongated cylindrical worms without an epithelial coelomic lining, with dorsal and ventral nerve cords, and with lateral excretory ducts, that are parasites of man, animals, or plants or free-living dwellers in soil or water and are known as roundworms, eelworms, or nematodes

[1]**nem·a·tode** \'nemə,tōd\ *adj* [NL *Nematoda*] **:** of or relating to the Nematoda

[2]**nematode** \"\ *n* -s [NL *Nematoda*] **:** a worm of the class or phylum Nematoda

**nem·a·to·di·a·sis** \,nemə(,)tō'dīəsə̇s\ *n, pl* **nematodia·ses** \-ə,sēz\ [NL, fr. *Nematoda* + *-iasis*] **:** infestation with or disease caused by nematode worms

**nem·a·to·di·rus** \,neməd·ə'dīrəs, nə̇,mad·-\ *n, cap* [NL, fr. *nemat-* + *-dirus* (prob. fr. Gk *deirē* neck, throat) — more at DER-] **:** a genus of reddish nematode worms (family Strongylidae) having slender elongated necks and being parasitic in the small intestine of ruminants and sometimes other mammals

**ne·mat·o·gen** \nə̇'mad·əjə̇n, 'neməd·-, -,jen\ *also* **ne·mat·o·gene** \-,jēn\ *n* -s [*nemat-* + *-gen*] **:** the form of a mesozoan of the order Dicyemida that occurs in the immature host and that consists of an outer layer of cells enclosing one or more large elongated axial cells which give rise to other nematogens by means of agametes — compare RHOMBOGEN

**nem·a·tog·nath** \,nemə'täg,nath\ *n* -s [NL *Nematognathi*] **:** a siluroid fish **:** CATFISH

**nem·a·tog·na·thi** \,nemə'tägnə,thī\ *n pl, cap* [NL, fr. *nemat-* + *-gnathi* (fr. *-gnathi*, pl. of *-gnathus* -gnathous)] *in some classifications* **:** an order of scaleless fishes that comprises the catfishes and is equivalent to the suborder Siluroidea of the order Ostariophysi — **nem·a·tog·na·thous** \¦≈≈¦≈≈,thəs\ *adj*

**ne·mat·o·gone** \nə̇'mad·ə,gōn, 'neməd·-\ *n* -s [ISV *nemat-* + *-gone* (fr. Gk *gonē* seed, offspring) — more at GONE] **:** one of the thin-walled propagative cells in the gemmae of various mosses

**nem·a·tog·o·nous** \¦nemə¦tägənəs\ *adj* **:** of or relating to a nematogone

[1]**nem·a·toid** \'nemə,tȯid\ *or* **nem·a·toi·de·an** \¦≈≈¦tȯidēən\ *adj* [*nematoid* fr. NL *Nematoidea*; *nematoidean* fr. NL *Nematoidea* + E *-an*, adj. suffix] **1 :** resembling or related to the Nematoda **2 :** NEMATODE

[2]**nematoid** \"\ *or* **nematoidean** \"\ *n* -s [*nematoid* fr. NL *Nematoidea*; *nematoidean* fr. NL *Nematoidea* + E *-an*, n. suffix] **1 :** a nematoid worm **:** NEMATHELMINTH **2 :** NEMATODE

**nem·a·toi·dea** \,≈≈'tȯidēə\ [NL, fr. *nemat-* + *-oidea*] *syn of* NEMATODA

**nem·a·to·log·i·cal** \¦neməd·ə¦läjə̇kəl, nə̇¦mad·-\ *adj* **:** of or relating to nematology

**nem·a·tol·o·gist** \,nemə'täləjə̇st\ *n* -s **:** a specialist in nematology

**nem·a·tol·o·gy** \-jē\ *n* -ES [*nemat-* + *-logy*] **:** a branch of zoology that deals with nematodes

**nem·a·to·mor·pha** \,neməd·ə'mȯrfə, nə̇,mad·-\ *n pl, cap* [NL, fr. *nemat-* + *-morpha*] **:** a class of Aschelminthes or a separate phylum comprising the horsehair worms formerly often grouped with the nematodes but distinguished from these by possession of a true body cavity, gonads discontinuous with their ducts, and an atrophied digestive tract in the adult — see GORDIOIDEA, NECTONEMATOIDEA — **nem·a·to·mor·phan** \¦≈≈≈¦mȯrfən, ≈¦≈≈-\ *adj or n*

**nem·a·toph·o·ra** \,nemə'täfərə\ *n pl, cap* [NL, fr. *nemat-* + *-phora*] *in former classifications* **:** a phylum or other division of invertebrates comprising the true nematocyst-bearing coelenterates as distinguished from the Ctenophores

**nem·a·toph·y·ton** \,nemə'täfə,tän\ *n* -s [NL, fr. *nemat-* + Gk *phyton* plant — more at PHYT-] **:** a large branching fossil plant found in Devonian rocks, believed to be a thallophyte, and often considered to offer evidence of a relationship between brown algae and vascular plants

**nem·a·tos·po·ra** \,nemə'täspərə; ,neməd·ə'spōrə, nə̇,mad·-\ *n, cap* [NL, fr. *nemat-* + *-spora*] **:** a genus of yeasts (family Saccharomycetaceae) having ascospores with needle-shaped, fusiform, or threadlike nonvibratile extensions

**nem·a·to·zooid** \¦neməd·ə, nə̇¦mad·ə+\ *n* [*nemat-* + *zooid*] **:** a defensive zooid in a hydroid or siphonophore

**Nem·bu·tal** \'nembyə,tȯl *sometimes* -tal\ *trademark* — used for the sodium salt of pentobarbital

**nem·bu·tsu** \nem'bu̇t(,)sü\ *n* -s *often cap* [Jap, contr. of *namu Amida Butsu* reverence to the Buddha Amitabha] **:** repetition of an Amidist devotional formula as a means of salvation

**nem con** *abbr* [NL *nemine contradicente*] no one contradicting

**nem diss** *abbr* [NL *nemine dissentiente*] no one dissenting

**-neme** \,nēm\ *n comb form* -s [NL *-nema*] **:** thread ⟨axo*neme*⟩ ⟨desmo*neme*⟩

**ne·me·an** \'nēmēən, nə̇'m-\ *adj, usu cap* [L *neme*us Nemean (fr. Gk *nemeos*, *nemeois*, fr. *Nemea*, valley in northern Argolis in ancient Greece) + E *-an*] **:** of, relating to, or held in Nemea in ancient Greece

**ne·mer·tea** \nə̇'mərd·ēə\ *n pl, cap* [NL, fr. *Nemertes*, included genus (fr. Gk *Nēmertēs* Nemertes, one of the Nereids) + *-ea* (fr. L, neut. pl. of *-eus* -eous)] **:** a class or other category of Platyhelminthes comprising soft-bodied often brightly colored unsegmented acoelomate worms that have an anterior mouth and posterior anus, a long eversible proboscis, and a definite circulatory system, are typically elongate and contractile, and are usu. marine and littoral and burrow in sand or mud though a few live in fresh water or on land — see ANOPLA, ENOPLA — **ne·mer·te·an** \-ēən\ *adj or n*

[1]**nem·er·tine** \'nemə(r),tin, -tēn\ *or* **nem·er·tin·e·an** \¦≈≈¦tinēən\ *adj* [*nemertinean* fr. NL *Nemertinea* + E *-an*, adj. suffix; *nemertine* fr. NL *Nemertinea*, *Nemertina*, *Nemertini*] **:** of or relating to the Nemertea

[2]**nemertine** \"\ *or* **nemertinean** \"\ *n* -s [*nemertinean* fr. NL *Nemertinea* + E *-an*, n. suffix; *nemertine* fr. NL *Nemertinea*, *Nemertina*, *Nemertini*] **:** a worm of the group Nemertea

**nem·er·tin·ea** \,nemər'tinēə\ *also* **nem·er·ti·na** \-tīnə,-tēnə\ *or* **nem·er·ti·ni** \-tī,nī, -tē(,)nē\ [*Nemertinea* fr. NL, fr. *Nemertes* + *-inea* (fr. L, neut. pl. of *-ineus* — as in *gramineus* gramineous); *Nemertina*, *Nemertini* fr. NL, fr. *Nemertes* + *-ina* or *-ini*] *syn of* NEMERTEA

[1]**nem·er·toid** \'nemər,tȯid, nə̇'mər-\ *adj* [NL *Nemertea* + E *-oid*] **:** resembling or related to the Nemertea **:** NEMERTEAN

[2]**nemertoid** \"\ *n* -s **:** one of the Nemertea **:** a nemertoid worm

**ne·me·sia** \nə̇'mēzh(ē)ə\ *n* [NL, fr. Gk, pl. of *nemesion* catchfly] **1** *cap* **:** a genus of African herbs or subshrubs (family Scrophulariaceae) having variously colored, irregular, slightly spurred, mostly racemose flowers **2** -s **:** a plant of the genus *Nemesia*

**nem·e·sis** \'neməsə̇s\ *n, pl* **neme·ses** \-ə,sēz\ *or* **neme·sis·es** [L *Nemesis*, goddess of divine retribution, fr. Gk, fr. *nemesis* retribution, righteous anger, fr. *nemein* to distribute — more at NIMBLE] **1 a :** one that inflicts retribution ⟨many a pursued man fell before his ~ in the streets —Agnes M. Cleaveland⟩ **b :** one that avenges relentlessly or destroys inevitably **c :** a formidable and usu. victorious rival or opponent ⟨the baseball team was defeated by the first-rate pitching of its old ~⟩ **2 a :** an act or effect of retributive justice ⟨whether in the individual or in the community, overweening self-assertion . . . was regarded as justly provoking ~ —Walter Moberly⟩ ⟨if they jumped their duty, not one survivor would there be to pursue them with the ~ of outraged humanity —D.C. Peattie⟩ **b :** an inevitable result ⟨this propensity to self-destruction is the ~ of irrationality —Lewis Mumford⟩

[1]**nem·e·stri·nid** \¦nemə¦strīnə̇d\ *adj* [NL *Nemestrinidae*] **:** of or relating to the Nemestrinidae

[2]**nemestrinid** \"\ *n* -s [NL *Nemestrinidae*] **:** an insect of the family Nemestrinidae

**nem·e·strin·i·dae** \-rinə,dē\ *n pl, cap* [NL, fr. *Nemestrinus*, type genus (perh. fr. LL *Nemestrinus*, god of groves) + *-idae*] **:** a family of dipterous insects occurring mostly in hot and arid regions and having larvae that are parasitic on other insects

**nem·ic** \'nemik\ *adj* [*nem-* + *-ic*] **:** of or relating to nematodes

**nem·ich·thy·i·dae** \,nemik'thīə,dē\ *n pl, cap* [NL, fr. *Nemichthys*, type genus + *-idae*] **:** a family of eels (order Apoda) comprising the snipe eels and related deep-sea forms — see NEMICHTHYS

**nem·ich·thys** \nə̇'mikthə̇s\ *n, cap* [NL, fr. *nem-* + *-ichthys*] **:** a genus (the type of the family Nemichthyidae) of fragile slender-bodied deep-sea eels

**ne·mi·ne con·tra·di·cen·te** \¦nemənē,kän·trədə̇'sentē\ *adv* (*or adj*) [NL, lit., no one contradicting] **:** without a dissenting vote ⟨the votes of thanks were endorsed by . . . all parties and were passed *nemine contradicente* —*Times Hist. of the War*⟩

**ne·mi·ne dis·sen·ti·en·te** \-,də̇,sentē'entē\ *adv* (*or adj*) [NL, lit., no one dissenting] **:** without dissent ⟨resolutions are sometimes . . . agreed to *nemine dissentiente* in the House of Lords —T.E.May⟩

**ne·mo** \'nē(,)mō\ *n* -s [perh. alter. of *remote*] **:** a radio or television broadcast that originates outside the studio (as at a football game or a banquet)

**nemo-** — see NEM-

**ne·mo·bi·us** \nə̇'mōbēəs\ *n, cap* [NL, fr. Gk *nemos* wooded pasture, glade + NL *-bius*] **:** a widely distributed genus of crickets most of which inhabit open fields

**ne·moc·era** \nə̇'mäsərə\ [NL, fr. *nem-* + *-cera*] *syn of* NEMATOCERA

**ne·moph·i·la** \nə̇'mäfələ\ *n* [NL, fr. Gk *nemos* wooded pasture, glade + NL *-phila*] **1** *cap* **:** a genus of ornamental chiefly Californian annual herbs (family Hydrophyllaceae) having flowers with a reflexed or spreading appendage in each sinus of the calyx — see BABY BLUE-EYES **2** -s **:** a plant of the genus *Nemophila*

[1]**ne·mop·ter·id** \nə̇'mäptərə̇d\ *adj* [NL *Nemopteridae*] **:** of or relating to the Nemopteridae

[2]**nemopterid** \"\ *n* -s [NL *Nemopteridae*] **:** an insect of the family Nemopteridae

**nemop·ter·i·dae** \,nē,mäp'terə,dē, ,ne,-\ *n pl, cap* [NL, fr. *Nemoptera*, type genus (fr. *nem-* + *-ptera*) + *-idae*] **:** a family of neuropterous insects whose hind wings are elongate and ribbonlike and whose larvae inhabit dusty or sandy regions and prey on small insects

**nem·o·ral** \'nem(ə)rəl\ *adj* [L *nemoralis*, fr. *nemor-*, *nemus* wood, grove + *-alis* -al; akin to Gk *nemos* wooded pasture, glade, Skt *namas* obeisance, *namati* he bends, bows] **:** of, relating to, or inhabiting a wood or grove

**nemorhaedus** *syn of* NAEMORHEDUS

**ne·mori·cole** \nə̇'mȯrə,kōl, 'nemər-\ *or* **nem·o·ric·o·line** \¦nemə¦rikə,līn, -,lə̇n\ *or* **nem·o·ric·o·lous** \-,ləs\ *adj* [L *nemor-*, *nemus* grove + E *-i-* + *-cole* or *-coline* or *-colous*] **:** inhabiting groves

[1]**ne·mou·rid** \nə̇'mu̇rə̇d\ *adj* [NL *Nemouridae*] **:** of or relating to the Nemouridae

[2]**nemourid** \"\ *n* -s [NL *Nemouridae*] **:** a stone fly of the family Nemouridae

**ne·mou·ri·dae** \-rə,dē\ *n pl, cap* [NL, fr. *Nemoura*, type genus (fr. *nem-* + Gk *oura* tail) + *-idae* — more at -URA] **:** a widely distributed family of stone flies (order Plecoptera) having small or vestigial cerci

**ne·ne** \'nā(,)nā\ *n, pl* **nene** [Hawaiian *nēnē*] **:** a nearly extinct goose (*Nesochen sandvicensis*) of the Hawaiian islands that inhabits waterless uplands and feeds on berries and vegetation

**nen·tsi** *or* **nen·tsy** \'nentsē\ *or* **nien·tsi** \nē'e-\ *n, pl* **nentsi** *or* **nentsy** *or* **nientsi** *cap* [Russ *Nentsy*, pl. of *Nenets*, fr. Yurak *ńeneś* man] **:** SAMOYED

**nenu·phar** \'nenyə,fär, nə̇'n(y)üfər\ *n* -s [ML *nenufar*, fr. Ar *naynūfar*, *naylūfar*, fr. Per *nīlūfar*, fr. Skt *nīlotpala*, fr. *nīla* dark blue + *utpala* nenuphar blossom] **:** WATER LILY; *esp* **:** EGYPTIAN LOTUS 1

**neo-** — see NE-

**neo·abietic acid** \¦nē(,)ō+. . .\ *n* [*neoabietic* fr. *ne-* + *abietic* (in *abietic acid*)] **:** a crystalline resin acid $C_{19}H_{29}COOH$ that is isomeric with abietic acid and is found esp. in oleoresins from pine trees

**Neo–Ant·er·gan** \¦nē(,)ō,ant·'ərgən\ *trademark* — used for pyrilamine

**neo·anthropic** \¦nē(,)ō+\ *adj* [*ne-* + *anthrop-* + *-ic*] **:** belonging to the same species (*Homo sapiens*) as recent man **:** modern in anatomy or type — used of fossil hominids; compare PALAEOANTHROPIC

**neo·an·thro·pi·nae** \¦nē(,)ō,anthrə'pī(,)nē\ *n pl, cap* [NL, fr. *ne-* + *anthrop-* + *-inae*] **:** an anthropological subdivision of Hominidae coextensive with a species (*Homo sapiens*) but regarded as comparable to a subfamily — compare ARCHANTHROPINAE, PALEOANTHROPINAE — **neo·an·thro·pine** \¦nē(,)ō¦anthrə,pīn\ *adj or n*

**neo·aplec·ta·na** \¦nē(,)ō(,)ā'plektənə\ *n, cap* [NL, fr. *ne-* + *Aplectana*, genus of nematode worms, fr. *a-* + *-plectana* (fr. Gk *plektanē* coil, fr. *plekein* to plait, twine) — more at PLY] **:** a genus of nematode worms (order Rhabditida) that are parasitic in insects and that include one form (*N. glaseri*) which has been used in attempts to establish biological control of the Japanese beetle

**neo·arsphenamine** \¦nē(,)ō+\ *n* [*ne-* + *arsphenamine*] **:** a yellow powder $C_{12}H_{11}As_2N_2O_2CH_2SO_2Na$ similar to arsphenamine in structure and uses

**neo–assyrian** \"+\ *n, often cap N & usu cap A* [*ne-* + *assyrian*] **:** a dialect of Akkadian used in Assyria after 1000 B.C.

[1]**neo–babylonian** \"+\ *adj, often cap N & usu cap B* [*ne-* + *babylonian*] **:** of or relating to the later Babylonian empire

[2]**neo–babylonian** \"\ *n, often cap N & usu cap B* **:** CHALDEAN 1 b

**neo·balaena** \¦nē(,)ō+\ *n, cap* [NL, fr. *ne-* + *Balaena*] **:** a genus of relatively small whalebone whales of the waters about Australia and New Zealand

**neo·baroque** \"+\ *adj* [*ne-* + *baroque*] **:** of, relating to, or having the characteristics of art or architecture based on study of 17th century baroque

**ne·o·blast** \'nēə,blast\ *n* [ISV *ne-* + *-blast*] **:** any of various large undifferentiated cells of annelid worms that participate in regeneration of lost parts

**ne·o·blas·tic** \¦nēə¦blastik\ *adj* [*ne-* + *-blastic*] **:** relating to or constituting new growth

**neo·calamites** \¦nē(,)ō+\ *n, cap* [NL, fr. *ne-* + *Calamites*] **:** a genus of Mesozoic fossil plants (order Equisetales) having large strap-shaped leaves

[1]**ne·o·cene** \'nēə,sēn\ *adj, usu cap* [*ne-* + *-cene*] **:** relating to or being the later portion of the Tertiary including both the Miocene and Pliocene

[2]**neocene** \"\ *n* -s *usu cap* **:** the Neocene period or system

**neo·ceratodus** \¦nē(,)ō+\ *n, cap* [NL, fr. *ne-* + *Ceratodus*] **:** a genus of dipnoan fishes comprising the recent lungfishes of Australia — see BARRAMUNDA; compare CERATODUS

**neo·cerebellar** \"+\ *adj* [*neocerebellum* + *-ar*] **:** of or relating to the neocerebellum

**neo·cerebellum** \"+\ *n* [NL, fr. *ne-* + ML *cerebellum*] **:** the phylogenetically youngest part of the cerebellum associated with the cerebral cortex in the integration of voluntary limb movements and comprising most of the cerebellar hemispheres and the superior vermis — compare ARCHICEREBELLUM, PALEOCEREBELLUM

**neo–christianity** \"+\ *n, often cap N & usu cap C* [*ne-* + *christianity*] **:** a reinterpretation of Christianity in terms of a current philosophy (as rationalism in the 19th century)

**neo·classic** *or* **neo·classical** \"+\ *adj* [*ne-* + *classic* or *classical*] **1 :** of, relating to, or having the characteristics of a style of artistic expression that is based on or felt to be based on the classical style: as **a :** of or relating to a revival or contemporary adaptation of classical taste or style in art or architecture ⟨not all buildings erected in Rome during the Fascist era were in the severe *neoclassical* style —*Architectural Rev.*⟩ ⟨in France meanwhile the classic grandeur of Versailles had given way to the *neoclassical* delicacy of the Place de la Concorde and the Petit Trianon —Nikolaus Pevsner⟩ **b :** of or relating to a revival or adaptation of classical style in literature; *esp* **:** of, relating to, or being the dominant style of English literature of the 18th century ⟨*neoclassical* poetry, for example, is characterized by the simile, periphrasis, the ornamental epithet, epigram, balance, antithesis —René Wellek & Austin Warren⟩ ⟨the most accomplished poet of the ~ school itself, however, was Alexander Pope; other members of the school included Addison, Swift, and Dr. Samuel Johnson —D.S.Norton & Peters Rushton⟩ — compare ROMANTIC **c :** of or relating to a style of musical composition of the 20th century characterized by the incorporation of the impersonal features and formal restrictions of the classic and earlier periods into a contemporary style **2 :** of, relating to, or being the theories or teachings of the postclassical economists esp. Alfred Marshall and his followers whose most distinguishing feature is their substitution of marginal utility for the labor theory of value of the classical school

**neoclassical arabic** *n, cap A* **:** literary Arabic that follows the grammatical conventions of classical Arabic, has a modernized vocabulary, and is commonly the written language of Arab countries

**neo·classicism** \"+\ *n* [*ne-* + *classicism*] **1 :** the principles or the style of neoclassical literature, art, architecture, music, or economics ⟨in drama, ~ was marked by devotion to the "Rules": the three unities, the use of a chorus, the avoidance of violence on the stage, the use of only royal or noble characters in tragedy —Cleanth Brooks & R.B.Heilman⟩ **2 :** CLASSICISM 3

**neo·classicist** \"+\ *n* [*ne-* + *classicist*] **:** an advocate or follower of neoclassical style, models, or theory — compare ROMANTICIST

**ne·o·co·mi·an** \¦nēə¦kōmēən\ *adj, usu cap* [F *néocomien*, fr. *Neocomium* (latinized form of *Neuchâtel*, canton in western Switzerland) + F *-en* -an (fr. L *-anus*)] **:** of or relating to a division of the European Cretaceous — see GEOLOGIC TIME table

**neo–confucian** *or* **neo–confucianist** \¦nē(,)ō+\ *adj, often cap N & usu cap C* [*ne-* + *confucian* or *confucianist*] **:** of or relating to neo-Confucianism or the neo-Confucianists

**neo–confucianism** \"+\ *n, often cap N & usu cap C* [*ne-* + *confucianism*] **:** a rationalistic revival of Confucian philosophy in the 11th century A.D. that exercised a pronounced influence on Chinese thought for over 800 years

**neo–confucianist** \"+\ *n* -s *often cap N & usu cap C* [*ne-* + *confucian* + *-ist*] **:** an adherent or advocate of neo-Confucianism

**neo·cortex** \"+\ *n* [NL, fr. *ne-* + L *cortex* bark — more at CORTEX] **:** the cortical part of the neencephalon

**neo·cosmic** \"+\ *adj* [*ne-* + *cosmic*] **:** of or relating to the universe in its present state or to races of men known to history

**neo·crinoidea** \"+\ *n pl, cap* [NL, fr. *ne-* + *Crinoidea*] *in some classifications* : an order of crinoids comprising forms in which the actinal surface is not closed — compare PALAEOCRINOIDEA

**neo·criticism** \"+\ *n* [ISV *ne-* + *criticism*] : a form of neo-Kantianism developed principally by C. B. Renouvier and his followers rejecting the noumena of Kant and restricting knowledge to phenomena as constituted by a priori categories

**neo·cyanine** \"+\ *n* [*ne-* + *cyanine*] : a cyanine dye derived from lepidine and used for sensitizing photographic emulsions to infrared rays

**neo–darwinian** \"+\ *adj, often cap N & usu cap D* [*ne-* + *darwinian*] : of or relating to neo-Darwinism

**neo–darwinism** \"+\ *n, often cap N & usu cap D* [*ne-* + *darwinism*] : a theory that holds natural selection to be the chief factor in the evolution of plants and animals and specif. denies the possibility of inheriting acquired characters — compare NATURAL SELECTION, NEO-LAMARCKISM, WEISMANNISM

**neo–darwinist** \"+\ *n, often cap N & usu cap D* [*ne-* + *darwinist*] : an advocate or follower of neo-Darwinism

**neo·di·pri·on** \¦nē(,)ō,dī'prī,än\ *n, cap* [NL, fr. *ne-* + *Diprion*, genus of sawflies, fr. *di-* + *-prion*] : a genus of sawflies including forms that in the larval stage feed on and often cause serious defoliation of pines and other conifers

**neo·dym·i·um** \,nēō'dimēəm\ *n* -s [NL, fr. *ne-* + *-dymium* (fr. *didymium*)] : a faintly yellow trivalent metallic element of the rare earth group that occurs in monazite sand associated esp. with cerium, lanthanum, and praseodymium, that forms pink salts, and that is used chiefly in the form of the oxide to impart a violet color to glass and porcelain — symbol *Nd;* see DIDYMIUM, ELEMENT table

**neo–egyptian** \¦nē(,)ō+\ *n, often cap N & cap E* [*ne-* + *egyptian*] : NEW EGYPTIAN

**neo·fabraea** \"+\ *n, cap* [NL, fr. *ne-* + *Fabraea*] : a genus of plant-parasitic fungi (family Mollisiaceae) that form brightly colored apothecia in conidial stromata — see APPLE ANTHRACNOSE

**neo·fascism** \"+\ *n* [ISV *ne-* + *fascism*] : a political movement arising in Europe after World War II and characterized by policies designed to incorporate the basic principles of fascism (as nationalism and opposition to democracy) into existing political systems

[1]**neo·fascist** \"+\ *n* [ISV *ne-* + *fascist*] : one who advocates or supports neofascism

[2]**neofascist** \"\ *adj* : of, relating to, or favoring neofascism ⟨a ~ party⟩

**neo·fetus** \¦nē(,)ō+\ *n* [NL, fr. *ne-* + L *fetus*] : the embryo during the eighth and ninth weeks of gestation

**neo·fiber** \"+\ *n, cap* [NL, fr. *ne-* + *Fiber*] : a genus of rodents (family Cricetidae) comprising solely the round-tailed muskrat

**neo·formation** \"+\ *n* [ISV *ne-* + *formation*] : a new growth: as **a** : TUMOR **b** : an anatomical anomaly peculiar to a small racial group and regarded as recent in appearance — **neo·formative** \"+\ *adj*

**neo–freudian** \"+\ *n, often cap N & usu cap F* [*ne-* + *freudian*] : any of a group of psychoanalysts who differ from orthodox Freudians in emphasizing the importance of socio-cultural factors in the development of an individual's personality

**neo·gae·an** *or* **neo·ge·an** \¦nēə¦jēən\ *adj, usu cap* [NL *Neogaea, Neogea*, biogeographic region that is coextensive with the neotropical biogeographic region and is regarded as one of three primary biogeographic realms (fr. *ne-* + *-gaea*) + E *-an*] : NEOTROPICAL

**ne·og·a·mous** \(')nē¦ägəməs\ *adj* [*ne-* + *-gamous*] : of or relating to neogamy

**ne·og·a·my** \nē'ägəmē\ *n* -ES [*ne-* + *-gamy*] : association in gregarines occurring prior to the adult stage of the life cycle

**ne·o·gene** \'nēə,jēn\ *adj or n, usu cap* [ISV *ne-* + *-gene* (fr. Gk *-genēs* born) — more at -GEN] : NEOCENE

**neo·genesis** \¦nēō+\ *n* [NL, fr. *ne-* + L *genesis*] : new formation : REGENERATION ⟨~ of tissue⟩

**neo·ge·net·ic** \-¦jə¦ned·ik\ *or* **neo·gen·ic** \-¦jenik\ *adj* [*neogenetic* ISV, fr. *neogenesis*, after such pairs as E *antithesis: antithetic; neogenic* alter. (influenced by *-genic*) of *neogenetic*] : of, relating to, or characterized by neogenesis

**ne·og·na·thae** \nē'ägnə,thē\ *n pl, cap* [NL, fr. *ne-* + *-gnathae*] : a superorder of Neornithes that includes most existing birds and that is characterized by reduction of the median bones of the palate — see PALAEOGNATHAE — **ne·og·nath·ic** \¦nē,äg¦nathik\ *adj* — **ne·og·na·thous** \(')nē¦ägnəthəs\ *adj*

**neo–gothic** \¦nē(,)ō+\ *adj, often cap N & usu cap G* [*ne-* + *gothic*] : of, relating to, or having the characteristics of art or architecture based on study of medieval Gothic models (as in the Gothic revival of 1840 in England and similar movements in Germany, France, and the U.S.) ⟨the *neo-Gothic* treatment of railway signal towers —R.D.Altick⟩ ⟨a *neo-Gothic* library building⟩

**neo·grammarian** \"+\ *n* [*ne-* + *grammarian;* trans. of G *junggrammatiker*] : one of a school of philologists arising in Germany about 1875, advocating the more exact formulation of phonetic law and its more rigid application to linguistic phenomena, maintaining that phonetic laws admit no real exceptions, and recognizing analogy as a normal factor in linguistic change

**neo–greek** \"+\ *n, often cap N & cap G* [ISV *ne-* + *greek*] : the modern Greek language

**neo–hawaiian** \"+\ *n, often cap N & cap H* [*ne-* + *hawaiian*] : an individual born in Hawaii of Hawaiian and other (usu. Caucasian, Chinese, or Japanese) ancestry

**neo–hebraic** \"+\ *n, often cap N & cap H* [*ne-* + *hebraic*] : NEO-HEBREW

**neo–hebrew** \"+\ *n, often cap N & cap H* [*ne-* + *hebrew*] : Hebrew as used by learned Jews of the Christian era

[1]**neo–hegelian** \"+\ *n, often cap N & usu cap H* [*ne-* + *hegelian*] : an advocate of neo-Hegelianism

[2]**neo–hegelian** \"\ *adj, often cap N & usu cap H* : of or relating to neo-Hegelianism

**neo–hegelianism** \"+\ *n, often cap N & usu cap H* [*ne-* + *hegelianism*] **1** : the philosophy of a school of chiefly British and American idealists following Hegel in his logical method and emphasizing organismic rather than atomistic conceptions **2** : one of a group of philosophical theories based on Hegelian principles advanced esp. by German and Italian philosophers

**neo–hellenism** \"+\ *n, often cap N & usu cap H* [*ne-* + *hellenism*] : Hellenism as surviving or revived in modern times : the practice of ancient Greek ideals in modern life or art

**neo·hexane** \¦nē(,)ō+\ *n* [*ne-* + *hexane*] : a volatile flammable liquid hydrocarbon $(CH_3)_3CC_2H_5$ that is usu. made from isobutane and ethylene and is used in aviation fuel and other special fuels for increasing power; 2,2-dimethyl-butane

**neo·hipparion** \"+\ *n, cap* [NL, fr. *ne-* + *Hipparion*] : a genus of extinct American Pliocene horses with one large and two small toes on each foot

**neo–humanism** \"+\ *n* [*ne-* + *humanism*] : NEW HUMANISM

**neo–humanist** \"+\ *n* [*ne-* + *humanist*] : NEW HUMANIST

**neo–impressionism** \"+\ *n, often cap N&I* [F *néo-impressionisme*, fr. *né-* ne- + *impressionisme* impressionism] : art whose exponents are critical of impressionism and seek a carefully integrated pictorial structure involving simplified and solidified forms and a pointillist rendering of light; *specif* : a French art theory and practice of the last decade of the 19th century characterized by an attempt to make impressionism more precise in form and the use of a pointillist painting technique — compare DIVISIONISM

[1]**neo–impressionist** \"+\ *n, often cap N&I* [F *néo-impressioniste*, fr. *né-* ne- + *impressioniste* impressionist] : a practitioner or advocate of neo-impressionism

[2]**neo–impressionist** \"\ *adj, often cap N&I* : of, relating to, or having the characteristics of neo-impressionism or the neo-impressionists

[1]**neo–kantian** \¦nē(,)ō+\ *n, often cap N & usu cap K* [*ne-* + *kantian;* prob. trans. of G *neukantianer*] : an adherent of neo-Kantianism

[2]**neo–kantian** \"\ *adj, often cap N & usu cap K* : derived from Kant or based on his theories or his philosophy ⟨a *neo-Kantian* movement⟩ ⟨a *neo-Kantian* hypothesis⟩

**neo–kantianism** \¦nē(,)ō+\ *n, often cap N & usu cap K* [*ne-* + *kantianism;* prob. trans. of G *neukantianismus*] : a philosophical movement opposing mid-19th century materialism and idealism, developing from Kant's epistemology, considering the thing-in-itself as a borderline concept and emphasizing normative considerations in ethics and jurisprudence

**neol** *abbr* neologism

**ne·o·la·lia** \,nēō'lālēə\ *n* -s [NL, fr. *ne-* + *-lalia*] : speech esp. of a psychotic that includes words that are new and meaningless to the hearer

[1]**neo–lamarckian** \¦nē(,)ō+\ *adj, often cap N & usu cap L* [*ne-* + *lamarckian*] : of or relating to neo-Lamarckism

[2]**neo–lamarckian** \"+\ *n, often cap N & usu cap L* : an advocate or follower of neo-Lamarckism

**neo–lamarckism** \¦nē(,)ō+\ *n, often cap N & usu cap L* [*ne-* + *lamarckism*] : a modern theory of evolution based on Lamarckism and retaining the fundamental concept that acquired characters are inherited: as **a** : the theory that evolution results from the action of natural selection upon acquired characters **b** : the theory that evolutionary change is the direct product of the interaction of organism and environment — compare NEO-DARWINISM

**neo·la·si·op·tera** \¦nē(,)ō,lāzē¦äptərə, -āsē-\ *n, cap* [NL, fr. *ne-* + *Lasioptera*, genus of Diptera, fr. *lasio-* (fr. Gk *lasios* shaggy) + *-ptera;* akin to Gk *lēnos* wool — more at WOOL] : a genus of gall midges (family Cecidomyiidae) whose larvae cause the formation of galls chiefly on the stems of asters, viburnums, dogwoods, and various other plants

**neo–latin** \¦nē(,)ō+\ *n, often cap N & cap L* [ISV *ne-* + *latin*] : NEW LATIN : ROMANCE

**neo·liberal** \"+\ *n* [ISV *ne-* + *liberal*] : an advocate or adherent of neoliberalism

**neo·liberalism** \"+\ *n* [ISV *ne-* + *liberalism*] **1** : a movement or doctrine that attempts to modify the principles of classical liberalism in the light of 20th century conditions **2** : a modern movement in Protestant Christian theology that is critical of earlier 20th century liberalism while affirming many of its fundamental assumptions and that is held to have arisen as a reaction against the new supernaturalism and the conservative doctrines of neoorthodoxy

**ne·oligochaeta** \(¦)nē+\ *n pl, cap* [NL, fr. *ne-* + *Oligochaeta*] *in some classifications* : a division of Oligochaeta comprising relatively large complex chiefly terrestrial worms that ordinarily reproduce only by sexual means (as those of the genera *Lumbricus, Allolobophora,* and *Megascolex*) — compare EARTHWORM, MEGADRILI, TERRICOLAE — **ne·oligochaete** \"+\ *adj or n*

**neo·linguist** \¦nē(,)ō+\ *n* [*ne-* + *linguist;* trans. of It *neolinguista*] : an adherent of areal linguistics

**neo·linguistic** \"+\ *adj* [*ne-* + *linguistic;* trans. of It *neolinguistico*] : of or relating to areal linguistics

**neo·linguistics** \"+\ *n pl but usu sing in constr* [*ne-* + *linguistics;* trans. of It *neolinguistica*] : AREAL LINGUISTICS

**ne·o·lith** \'nēə,lith\ *n* -s [back-formation fr. *neolithic*] : a neolithic stone implement

**ne·o·lith·ic** \¦nēə¦lithik\ *adj* [*ne-* + *-lithic*] **1** *usu cap* : of, being, or relating to the latest period of the Stone Age following the Mesolithic and Aeneolithic and characterized by the use of polished stone implements, the art of grinding stone, horn, bone, and ivory tools with sandstone, pottery making, the use of bow and arrow, domestication of animals, the cultivation of grain and fruit trees, the invention of the wheel, linen weaving, and the beginning of settled village life **2** : belonging to an earlier age and now outmoded ⟨defense of the ~ liberals who once inhabited these lands —W.A.White⟩

**neo·local** \¦nēō+\ *adj* [*ne-* + *local*] : having a new location; *specif* : located apart from the families of either spouse ⟨a ~ residence⟩ — compare AVUNCULOCAL, MATRILOCAL, PATRILOCAL — **neo·locality** \¦nē(,)ō+\ *n*

**ne·o·lo·gian** \,nēə'lōj(ē)ən\ *n* -s [*neology* + *-an*] : NEOLOGIST

**ne·o·log·i·cal** \¦nēə¦läjəkəl\ *also* **ne·o·log·ic** \-jik\ *adj* [*neological* fr. F *néologique* neological (fr. *né-* ne- + *-logique*, fr. *-logie* -logy + *-ique* -ic) + E *-al; neologic* fr. F *néologique*] : of, relating to, or characterized by neology

**ne·ol·o·gism** \nē'äla,jizəm *sometimes* 'nēəl-\ *n* -s [F *néologisme*, fr. *né-* ne- + *log-* + *-isme* -ism] **1 a** : a new word, usage, or expression ⟨all ~s begin as slang, except in those branches of terminology where . . . there is an established tradition of word coinage or redefinition —R.A.Hall b.1911⟩ **b** : a usu. compound word coined by a psychotic and meaningless to the hearer **2** : NEOLOGY 2

**ne·ol·o·gist** \nē'äləjəst\ *n* -s [prob. fr. F *néologiste*, fr. *neologisme*, after such pairs as F *purisme* purism: *puriste* purist] : a proponent of a new doctrine : an advocate of neology

**ne·ol·o·gis·tic** \(¦)nē¦älə¦jistik, ¦nēəl-\ *adj* [*neologist* + *-ic*] : of or relating to neology

**ne·ol·o·gize** \nē'älə,jīz *sometimes* 'nēəl-\ *vi* -ED/-ING/-S [*neology* + *-ize*] : to practice neology

**ne·ol·o·gy** \nē'äləjē\ *n* -ES [F *néologie*, fr. *né-* ne- + *-logie* -logy] **1 a** : the use of a new word or expression or of an established word in a new or different sense : the use of new expressions that are not sanctioned by conventional standard usage : the introduction of such expressions into a language **b** : NEOLOGISM 1a **2** : a new doctrine; *esp* : a new method of theological interpretation

**neo–malthusian** \¦nē(,)ō+\ *adj, often cap N & usu cap M* [*ne-* + *malthusian*] : being or relating to the doctrine that only through the limitation of births by the use of artificial contraceptives can the numbers of the population be sufficiently controlled to make possible the elimination of vice and misery and a general elevation of the standard of living

**neo–malthusianism** \¦nē(,)ō+\ *n, often cap N & usu cap M* : neo-Malthusian views or beliefs

**neo–melanesian** \¦nē(,)ō+\ *n, often cap N & cap M* [*ne-* + *melanesian*] : an English-based pidgin language used in New Guinea and the Solomon islands

**neo–mendelian** \"+\ *adj, often cap N & usu cap M* [*ne-* + *mendelian*] : of or relating to neo-Mendelism

**neo–mendelism** \"+\ *n, often cap N & usu cap M* [*ne-* + *mendelism*] : Mendelism as modified and extended by recent biologists; *esp* : such principles including the concepts of linkage and multiple factors

**ne·o·me·nia** \,nēə'mēnēə\ *n* -s [ME, fr. LL, fr. Gk *neomēnia*, fr. *ne-* + *-mēnia* (fr. *mēnē* moon) — more at MOON] : the time of the new moon; *also* : the festival of the new moon

**neo–mercantilism** \¦nē(,)ō+\ *n* [*ne-* + *mercantilism*] : a revived theory of mercantilism emphasizing trade restrictions and commercial policies as means of increasing domestic income and employment

**neo·modal** \¦nēə+\ *adj* [*ne-* + *modal*] : characterized by the modification of major-minor tonality by the use of ecclesiastical modes or of new modes (as whole-tone scale, pentatonic scale)

**neo·morph** \'nēə,mȯrf\ *n* [*ne-* + *-morph*] **1** : a structure that is not derived from a similar structure in an ancestor **2** : a mutant gene having a function distinct from that of any nonmutant gene of the same locus — **neo·mor·phic** \¦nēə¦mȯrfik\ *adj* — **neo·mor·phism** \'nēə,mȯr,fizəm\ *n* -s

**neo·mor·pha** \,nēə'mȯrfə\ *n, cap* [NL, fr. *ne-* + *-morpha*] : a genus of New Zealand passerine birds including solely the huia

**neo·mor·pho·sis** \,nēə'mȯrfəsəs, -,mȯr'fōs-\ *n* [NL, fr. *ne-* + *-morphosis*] : regeneration in which one part is replaced by an unlike part (as production of a leg in place of an antenna)

**ne·o·my·cin** \¦nēə¦mīsᵊn\ *n* -s [*ne-* + *-mycin*] : an antibiotic or mixture of antibiotics that is produced by a soil actinomycete (*Streptomyces fradiae*) and that is active against a wide variety of bacteria — compare FRADICIN

[1]**ne·on** \'nē,än *sometimes* 'nēən\ *n* -s [Gk, neut. of *neos* new — more at NEW] **1** : a colorless odorless inert gaseous element that occurs in air to the extent of about two thousandths of a percent by volume, is obtained by separating from liquid air, gives a reddish glow in a vacuum tube, and is used in electric lamps — symbol *Ne;* see ELEMENT table **2 a** : NEON LAMP **b** : a sign composed of neon lamps; *esp* : one used for advertising **c** : the illumination provided by such lamps or signs ⟨a street of narrow shops and faulty ~ —Martin Dibner⟩

[2]**neon** \"\ *adj* **1** : of, relating to, or resembling the light of neon lamps **2** : lighted by or composed of neon lamps ⟨a ~ roadside stand⟩ ⟨a ~ sign⟩

**neo·natal** \¦nēə+\ *adj* [*ne-* + *natal*] : of, relating to, or affecting the newborn and esp. the human infant during the first month after birth ⟨~ period⟩ ⟨~ death⟩ ⟨~ serum⟩ — compare ANTENATAL, INTRANATAL, POSTNATAL — **neo·natally** \"+\ *adv*

**ne·o·nate** \'nēə,nāt\ *n* -s [NL *neonatus*, fr. *ne-* + L *natus*, past part. of *nasci* to be born — more at NATIVE] : a newborn child; *specif* : a child less than one month old

**neo·naturalism** \¦nē(,)ō+\ *n* [*ne-* + *naturalism*] : a Protestant theology that seeks to reinterpret the Christian faith with new relevance on the basis of the biblical gospel and within the philosophical framework of process philosophy

**neo·naturalist** \"+\ *adj* [*ne-* + *naturalist*] : of, relating to, or adhering to neonaturalism

**ne·oned** \'nē,änd *sometimes* 'nēənd\ *adj* [[1]*neon* + *-ed*] : of, equipped with, or lighted by neon lamps

**neon lamp** *also* **neon light** *or* **neon tube** *n* : a gas-discharge lamp in which the electrical discharge takes place through a mixture of gases containing a large proportion of neon

**ne·o·no·mi·an** \,nēə'nōmēən\ *n* -s [*ne-* + *-nomian* (as in *antinomian*)] : one who advocates or adheres to new laws; *esp* : one who holds that the Christian gospel is a new law supplanting the Mosaic

**ne·o·no·mi·an·ism** \-mēə,nizəm\ *n* -s : the doctrine of the neonomians

**neon tetra** *n* : a brightly colored So. American characin fish (*Hyphessobrycon innesi*) often kept in a tropical aquarium

**ne·on·to·log·ic** \(¦)nē¦äntə¦läjik\ *or* **ne·on·to·log·i·cal** \-jəkəl\ *adj* [*neontology* + *-ic* or *-ical*] : of or relating to neontology

**ne·on·tol·o·gist** \,nē,än'täləjəst, ,nēən-\ *n* -s [*neontology* + *-ist*] : a specialist in neontology

**ne·on·tol·o·gy** \-jē\ *n* -ES [*ne-* + *ont-* + *-logy*] : the study of recent organisms — distinguished from *paleontology*

**neo·nych·i·um** \,nēə'nikēəm\ *n, pl* **neonych·ia** \-kēə\ *or* **neonychi·ums** [NL, fr. *ne-* + *-onychium*] : a protective pad enclosing a fetal claw

**neo·orthodox** \¦nē(,)ō+\ *adj* [*ne-* + *orthodox*] : of, relating to, or adhering to neoorthodoxy

**neo·orthodoxy** \"+\ *n* [*ne-* + *orthodoxy*] : a 20th century movement in Protestant theology characterized by a reaction against liberalism, reemphasis on some orthodox Reformation doctrines (as God's transcendence, the fallen state of man, the inevitability of man's sin and his responsibility for it, discontinuity between time and eternity), and renewed stress on classic Protestant formularies interpreted through biblical language and symbolism — compare CRISIS THEOLOGY, DIALECTICAL THEOLOGY

**neo·pagan** \"+\ *adj* [*ne-* + *pagan*] : of, relating to, or characterized by neopaganism

**neo·paganism** \"+\ *n* [*ne-* + *paganism*] : revived or new paganism

[1]**neo·paleozoic** \"+\ *adj, usu cap* [*ne-* + *paleozoic*] : late Paleozoic — used of the entire period including the Devonian and the Permian

[2]**neopaleozoic** \"\ *n, usu cap* : the Neopaleozoic period

**neo·pal·li·al** \¦nēō¦palēəl\ *adj* [*neopallium* + *-al*] : of, relating to, or mediated by the neopallium

**neo·pal·li·um** \-lēəm\ *n* [NL, fr. *ne-* + *pallium*] : the phylogenetically new part of the cerebral cortex that develops from the area between the pyriform lobe and the hippocampus, comprises the nonolfactory region of the cortex, and attains its maximum development in man where it makes up the greater part of the cerebral hemisphere on each side — compare ARCHIPALLIUM

**neo·pentane** \¦nē(,)ō+\ *n* [*ne-* + *pentane*] : a gaseous or very volatile liquid hydrocarbon $(CH_3)_4C$ found in small amounts in petroleum and natural gas; dimethyl-propane or tetramethyl-methane

**neo·pentyl** \"+\ *n* -s [*neopentane* + *-yl*] : the pentyl radical $(CH_3)_3CCH_2$— derived from neopentane; 2,2-dimethyl-propyl

**neo·phobia** \,nēə+\ *n* [NL, fr. *ne-* + *-phobia*] : dread of or aversion to novelty — **neophobic** *adj*

**ne·o·phron** \'nēə,frän\ *n, cap* [NL, fr. Gk *Neophrōn*, man transformed into a vulture in the *Metamorphoses* of Antoninus Liberalis, 2d cent. A.D. Greek writer of narrative prose] : a genus of Old World vultures characterized by horizontal nostrils and containing the Egyptian vulture

**neo·phy·o·sis** \,neə,fī'ōsəs\ *n* -ES [NL, fr. *ne-* + Gk *phyein* to grow + *-osis* -osis] : rejuvenation of a citrus strain long vegetatively reproduced by seedlings developing from nucellar buds and reproducing the original characters of the strain

**ne·o·phyte** \'nēə,fīt, *usu* -īd·+V\ *n* -s [LL *neophytus* recently converted, recently planted, fr. Gk *neophytos*, fr. *ne-* + *phytos*, verbal of *phyein* to grow, bring forth — more at BE] **1** : a new convert : PROSELYTE; *esp* : a convert to the Christian faith in the early church **2** *Roman Catholicism* **a** : a newly ordained priest **b** : a novice in a convent **3** : a young or inexperienced practitioner or student : TYRO, BEGINNER ⟨to the ~, the desert may be only a barren waste —Gladwin Hill⟩ ⟨psychic code-deciphering that makes Freud look like a ~ and Jung like an amateur —Joseph Frank⟩ **syn** see NOVICE

**ne·o·phyt·ic** \¦nēə¦fid·|ik, -it|, |ēk\ *adj* : of or relating to a neophyte

**ne·o·phyt·ism** \'nēə,fīd·,izəm, -ī,ti-\ *n* -s : the state of being a neophyte

**neo·pilina** \¦nē(,)ō+\ *n, cap* [NL, fr. *ne-* + *Pilina*, genus of mollusks] : a genus of primitive segmented mollusks that have conical shells, are believed to have existed from the Cambrian on, and are of uncertain systematic position often being isolated in a distinct class

**ne·o·pine** \'nēə,pēn, -,pən\ *n* -s [ISV *ne-* + *-opine* (as in *atropine*)] : an opium alkaloid $C_{18}H_{21}NO_3$ isomeric with codeine

**ne·o·pla·sia** \,nēə'plāzh(ē)ə\ *n* -s [NL, fr. *ne-* + *-plasia*] **1** : the abnormal state characterized by the growth and development of tumors **2** : the bodily alterations involved in the formation of tumors and esp. of malignant tumors

**ne·o·plasm** \'nēə,plazəm\ *n* [ISV *ne-* + *-plasm*] : a new growth of animal or plant tissue resembling more or less the tissue from which it arises but serving no physiologic function and being benign, potentially malignant, or malignant in character — compare CARCINOMA, NEOPLASIA, SARCOMA

**ne·o·plas·tic** \¦nēə¦plastik\ *adj* [ISV *ne-* + *-plastic*] **1** : of, relating to, or having the characteristics of a neoplasm or neoplasia **2** : of or relating to neoplasticism

**neo·plasticism** \¦nē(,)ō+\ *n* [*ne-* + *plasticism;* intended as trans. of D *nieuwe beelding* new form-construction] : the de Stijl art principle of reducing form to horizontal and vertical lines and planes and excluding all colors except white, black, and the primaries

**neo·plas·ti·cist** \-,səst\ *n* -s [*neoplasticism* + *-ist*] : an advocate or a practitioner of neoplasticism

**neo·platonic** \¦nē(,)ō+\ *adj, usu cap* [*ne-* + *platonic*] : of, relating to, or resembling Neoplatonism or Neoplatonists

**neo·platonism** \"+\ *n, usu cap* [ISV *ne-* + *platonism*] **1** : a philosophical school originating in Alexandria about A.D. 200, modifying the teachings of Plato to accord with Aristotelian, post-Aristotelian, and oriental conceptions and conceiving of the world as an emanation from the One with whom the soul is capable of being reunited in trance or ecstasy — compare EMANATION, NOUS **2** : teachings and doctrines similar to those of the ancient Neoplatonists (as those promulgated in medieval times by mystics and in the Renaissance by Italian humanists) — compare CAMBRIDGE PLATONISTS

**neo·platonist** \"+\ *n, usu cap* [*ne-* + *platonist*] : an advocate of Neoplatonism

**neo·positivism** \"+\ *n* [ISV *ne-* + *positivism*] : LOGICAL POSITIVISM

**neo·positivist** \"+\ *n* : an advocate or adherent of neopositivism — **neo·positivistic** \"+\ *adj*

**ne·o·prene** \'nēə,prēn\ *n* -s [*ne-* + *-prene* (as in *chloroprene*)] : a synthetic rubber made by the polymerization of chloroprene and characterized by superior resistance to oils, gasoline, sunlight, ozone, and heat and by lower permeability to gases than rubber — compare POLYCHLOROPRENE

**ne·op·tera** \nē'äptərə\ *n pl, cap* [NL, fr. *ne-* + *-ptera*] : a major division of the subclass Pterygota comprising winged insects that are able to flex the wings over the abdomen when not in use and including all orders of winged insects except Odonata and Plectoptera — **ne·op·ter·ous** \(')nē¦äptərəs\ *adj*

[1]**ne·opte·ryg·ian** \(¦)nē,äptə¦rij(ē)ən, ¦nē(,)ōtə-\ *adj* [NL *Neopterygii* + E *-an*] : of or relating to the Neopterygii

[2]**neopterygian** \"\ *n* -s : a fish of the subclass Neopterygii

**ne·opte·ryg·ii** \(,)nē,äptə'rijē,ī, ,nē(,)ōtə-\ *n pl, cap* [NL, fr. *ne-* + *-pterygii*] *in some classifications* : a subclass of Osteichthyes including all the higher bony fishes — compare PALAEOPTERYGII

**neo·pterygota** \ˌnē(ˌ)ō+\ [NL, fr. *ne-* + *Pterygota*] *syn of* NEOPTERA

**neo–punic** \"+\ *n, often cap N & cap P* [*ne-* + *punic*] : the later Punic language

**neo–pythagorean** \"+\ *n, often cap N & usu cap P* [*ne-* + *pythagorean*] : an advocate of neo-Pythagoreanism

**neo–pythagoreanism** \"+\ *n, often cap N & usu cap P* [*ne-* + *pythagoreanism*] : the doctrines of a school of philosophy originating in Alexandria about the beginning of the first century A.D. and reviving with mystical interpretations many Pythagorean ideas

**neo·realism** \"+\ *n* [*ne-* + *realism*] **1** : NEW REALISM **2** : a revived realism ⟨like the postwar Italian movies of consequence, the novels have turned to ~, with truth taking the place of a happier ending —*New Yorker*⟩

**neo·realist** \"+\ *n* [*ne-* + *realist*] : an advocate or follower of neorealism — **neo·realistic** \"+\ *adj*

**ne·or·ni·thes** \nēˈȯrnəˌthēz, ˌnēˌȯrˈnī(ˌ)thēz\ *n pl, cap* [NL, fr. *ne-* + *-ornithes*] : a subclass of birds comprising all recent and fossil birds except the Archaeornithes — **ne·or·nith·ic** \ˌnēˌȯrˈnithik\ *adj*

**¹neo·romantic** \ˌnē(ˌ)ō+\ *adj* [*ne-* + *romantic*] : of or relating to a new or revived romanticism esp. in art or literature ⟨~ is a term that may most accurately be applied to those writers of recent years who have shown marked allegiance to the principles of Wordsworth, Coleridge, and Shelley or who have in a distinctive way exemplified romantic modes of mind and practice —C.D.Thorpe & N.E.Nelson⟩ ⟨the unhampered imaginative and emotional conception of the art of painting that distinguishes what is best in British art at this moment and may be qualified, for reasons of convenience, as ~ —Robin Ironside⟩

**²neoromantic** \"\ *n* : an advocate or follower of neoromanticism

**neo·romanticism** \ˌnē(ˌ)ō+\ *n* [*ne-* + *romanticism*] : neoromantic principles or characteristics

**Neo·sal·var·san** \ˌnē(ˌ)ōˈsalvə(r)ˌsan\ *trademark* — used for neoarsphenamine

**neo–sanskrit** \ˌnē(ˌ)ō+\ *n, often cap N & cap S* [*ne-* + *sanskrit*] : the modern Indic languages — **neo–sanskritic** \"+\ *adj, often cap N & usu cap S*

**neo–scholastic** \"+\ *adj, sometimes cap S* [ISV *ne-* + *scholastic*] : of or relating to neo-scholasticism

**neo–scholasticism** \"+\ *n, sometimes cap S* [*ne-* + *scholasticism*] **1** : a movement begun in the middle of the 19th century among Catholic scholars and having for its aims the restatement and exposition of the methods and teachings of the medieval Schoolmen in a manner suited to the intellectual needs of the present and further speculation that makes use of the findings of modern research and is grounded on principles derived from the Greeks and the Schoolmen **2** : SCHOLASTICISM 2

**neo·schon·gas·tia** \ˌnē(ˌ)ōˌshänˈgastēə\ *n, cap* [NL, fr. *ne-* + *Schongastia*, genus of Arachnida, prob. fr. the name *Schöngast* + NL *-ia*] : a genus of trombiculid mites parasitic in their larval stage on poultry

**neo·sisten** \ˌnē(ˌ)ō+\ *or* **neosistens** *n, pl* **neosistens** *or* **neosistentes** [NL *neosistens*, fr. *ne-* + *sistens* sisten] : a first-stage nymph of an adelgid bug that hibernates, reaches maturity in the spring, and lays eggs which develop parthenogenetically

**neo–sogdian** \"+\ *n, often cap N & usu cap S* [*ne-* + *sogdian*] : UIGHUR 2b

**neo·spo·rid·ia** \ˌnē(ˌ)ōspəˈridēə\ *n pl, cap* [NL, fr. *ne-* + *-sporidia*] *in some classifications* : a division of Sporozoa including Cnidosporidia and Acnidosporidia — **neo·spo·rid·i·an** \-ēən\ *adj or n*

**ne·os·sol·o·gy** \ˌnēˌäˈsäləjē, ˌnēəˈs-\ *n* -ES [Gk *neossos* young bird (fr. *neos* young, new) + E *-logy*] : the study of young birds

**ne·os·sop·tile** \ˌnēəˈsäptəl, -ˌtīl\ *n* -S [Gk *neossos* young bird + E *-ptile*] : one of the downy feathers of a newly hatched bird

**neo·stig·mine** \ˌnē(ˌ)ōˈstigˌmēn, -mən\ *n* -S [*ne-* + *-stigmine* (as in *physostigmine*)] : a cholinergic drug used in the form of the bromide $[(CH_3)_2NCOOC_6H_4N(CH_3)_3]Br$ or the methyl sulfate derivative in the diagnosis and treatment of myasthenia gravis and the relief of postoperative atony of the intestines and urinary bladder

**neo·striatum** \ˌnē(ˌ)ō+\ *n, pl* **neostriatums** *or* **neostriata** [NL, fr. *ne-* + *striatum*] : the phylogenetically new part of the corpus striatum consisting of the caudate nucleus and putamen

**neo–sumerian** \"+\ *n, often cap N & cap S* [*ne-* + *sumerian*] : the later form of the Sumerian language

**neo·supernaturalism** \"+\ *n* [*ne-* + *supernaturalism*] : a revival of supernaturalism esp. in religious thought; *specif* : NEOORTHODOXY

**Neo–Sy·neph·rine** \ˌnē(ˌ)ōsəˈnefrən, -ˌrēn\ *trademark* — used for phenylephrine

**neo–syriac** \ˌnē(ˌ)ō+\ *n, often cap N & cap S* [*ne-* + *syriac*] : a modern form of Syriac that is spoken by Aramaean Christians and that is akin to the ancient literary Syriac though not directly from it

**neo·technic** \ˌnēō+\ *adj* [*ne-* + *technic*] : of, relating to, or constituting the most recent period of industrial development marked by the use of electricity and alloys — compare PALEOTECHNIC

**ne·o·tenic** \ˌnēəˈtēnik, -ten-\ *also* **ne·o·te·nous** \-tēnəs\ *or* **ne·o·tei·nic** \-tēnik, -tīn-, -tān-\ *adj* [*neotenic, neoteinic* ISV *neoten-, neotein-* (fr. NL *neotenia, neoteinia* neoteny) + *-ic*; *neotenous* fr. *neoteny* + *-ous*] **1** : of, relating to, or exhibiting neoteny **2** *usu neoteinic* : being a newly developed king or queen of a termite colony following the loss of the previous royalties

**ne·o·te·ny** \nēˈätənē\ *also* **ne·o·tei·nia** \ˌnēəˈtēnēə, -tīn-, -tān-\ *n, pl* **neotenies** *also* **neoteinias** [NL *neotenia, neoteinia*, fr. *ne-* + *-tenia, -teinia* (fr. Gk *teinein* to stretch) — more at THIN] **1** : the attainment of sexual maturity during the larval stage (as in the axolotl) **2** : the retention of some larval or immature characters in adulthood (as in complemental reproductives of termites) — compare FETALIZATION

**¹ne·o·ter·ic** \ˌnēəˈterik\ *adj* [LL *neotericus*, fr. LGk *neōterikos*, fr. Gk, youthful, fr. *neōteros* more recent, newer (compar. of *neos* young, new) + *-ikos* -ic — more at NEW] : recent in origin : MODERN **syn** see NEW

**²neoteric** \"\ *n* -S : MODERN 1; *esp* : a modern writer

**ne·o·ter·i·cal·ly** \-rək(ə)lē\ *adv* : in a neoteric manner

**ne·ot·er·ism** \nēˈädəˌrizəm\ *n* -S [Gk *neōterismos* innovation, fr. *neōteros* + *-ismos* -ism] : a newly invented word or phrase : the introduction of new expressions — compare NEOLOGISM

**neo·thalamus** \ˌnē(ˌ)ō+\ *n* [NL, fr. *ne-* + *thalamus*] : the phylogenetically more recent part of the thalamus including the lateral nucleus and the pulvinar together with the geniculate bodies

**neo–thomism** \ˌnē(ˌ)ō+\ *n, often cap N & usu cap T* [ISV *ne-* + *thomism*] : neo-scholastic philosophy or theory concerned with the teachings of Thomas Aquinas

**¹neo–thomist** \"+\ *n, often cap N & usu cap T* [ISV *ne-* + *Thomist*] : an adherent of neo-Thomism

**²neo–thomist** \"\ *or* **neo–thomistic** *adj, often cap N & usu cap T* : of or relating to neo-Thomism or neo-Thomists

**neo·thunnus** \ˌnē(ˌ)ō+\ *n, cap* [NL, fr. *ne-* + *Thunnus*] : a genus of fishes (family Scombridae) containing the yellowfin tuna

**ne·ot·o·cite** \nēˈädəˌsīt\ *n* -S [Sw *neotokit*, fr. Gk *neotokos* newborn (fr. *ne-* + *tokos* childbirth, offspring, fr. *tiktein* to give birth to, beget) + Sw *-it* -ite — more at THANE] : a mineral consisting of a hydrous silicate of manganese and iron but having an uncertain formula

**ne·ot·o·ma** \nēˈädəmə\ *n, cap* [NL, fr. *ne-* + *-toma* (fr. Gk *temnein* to cut) — more at TOME] : a genus of rodents (family Cricetidae) comprising the wood rats or pack rats of western No. America

**ne·ot·ra·gus** \nēˈä·trəgəs\ *n, cap* [NL, fr. *ne-* + Gk *tragos* he-goat — more at TRAGEDY] : a genus of western African antelopes including only the royal antelope

**ne·o·trema·ta** \ˌnēəˈtremədə, -rēm-\ *n pl, cap* [NL, fr. *ne-* + *-tremata*] : an order of inarticulate brachiopods that have the peduncle restricted throughout life to the ventral valve or atrophied in the adults and are known from the Cambrian to the present — **ne·o·tremate** \ˌ==ˈ=ˌmāt\ *n* -S — **ne·o·trema·tous** \ˌ==ˈ=mədəs\ *adj*

**ne·o·treme** \ˈnēəˌtrēm\ *adj* [NL *Neotremata*] : of or relating to the Neotremata

**neo·tropical** *also* **neo·tropic** \ˌnē(ˌ)ō+\ *adj, usu cap* [ISV *ne-* + *tropical* or *tropic*] : of, relating to, or constituting the biogeographic region that includes So. America, the West Indies, and tropical No. America

**neo·tropics** \"+\ *n pl* [*ne-* + *tropics*] : the Neotropical region

**neo·type** \ˈnēəˌtīp\ *n* [*ne-* + *type*] : a type specimen selected subsequent to the description of a species to replace a preexisting type that has been lost or destroyed

**neo·vitalism** \ˌnē(ˌ)ō+\ *n* [ISV *ne-* + *vitalism*] : modern vitalism

**neo·vitalist** \"+\ *n* [*ne-* + *vitalist*] : an advocate of neovitalism

**neo·washingtonia** \ˌnē(ˌ)ō+\ [NL, fr. *ne-* + *Washingtonia*] *syn of* WASHINGTONIA

**ne·o·za pine** \nēˈōzə-\ *n* [Bhutanese *neoza*] : a tall Himalayan pine (*Pinus gerardiana*) with silvery bark and edible nuts

**neo·zo·ic** \ˌnēəˈzōik\ *adj, usu cap* [ISV *ne-* + *-zoic*] : of, relating to, or constituting the entire period from the end of the Mesozoic to the present time

**¹nep** \ˈnep\ *n* -S [ME *nep, nepte*, fr. OE *nepte*, fr. L *nepeta*] *dial chiefly Brit* : CATNIP

**²nep** \"\ *vt* **nepped; nepped; nepping; neps** [origin unknown] : to form neps in (cotton) during processing

**³nep** \"\ *n* -S **1** : any of the little knots formed by irregular growth of cotton fibers or by the rubbing together of the fibers esp. in ginning **2** : a cluster of fibers occurring in wool staple

**NEP** *abbr* new economic policy

**ne·pa** \ˈnēpə\ *n, cap* [NL, fr. L, scorpion] : the type genus of the family Nepidae containing various typical elongate-oval water scorpions — compare RANATRA

**NEPA** *abbr* nuclear energy for propulsion of aircraft

**ne·pal** \nəˈpȯl, -päl,-pal,-pål\ *adj, usu cap* [fr. *Nepal*, country on northeast frontier of India] : of or from Nepal : of the kind or style prevalent in Nepal : NEPALESE

**¹nep·a·lese** \ˌnepəˈlēz, -ēs\ *adj, usu cap* [*Nepal* + E *-ese*] **1** : of, relating to, or characteristic of Nepal **2** : of, relating to, or characteristic of the people of Nepal

**²nepalese** \"\ *n, pl* **nepalese** *cap* : NEPALI

**¹ne·pali** \nəˈpȯlē, -pä-,-pa-,-på-\ *adj, usu cap* [Hindi *naipālī*, fr. Skt *naipālīya*, fr. *Nepāla* Nepal] **1 a** : of, relating to, or characteristic of Nepal **b** : of, relating to, or characteristic of the people of Nepal **2** : of, relating to, or characteristic of the Nepali language

**²nepali** \"\ *n, pl* **nepali** *also* **nepalis** *cap* **1** : the Indic language of Nepal **2** : a native or inhabitant of Nepal

**nepen·tha·ce·ae** \ˌnepənˈthāsēˌē, ˌnēˌpen-\ *n pl, cap* [NL, fr. *Nepenthes*, type genus + *-aceae*] : a family of plants coextensive with the genus *Nepenthes*

**ne·pen·the** \nəˈpen(t)thē\ *n* -S [L *nepenthes*, fr. Gk *nēpenthes*, neut. of *nēpenthēs* banishing pain and sorrow, fr. *nē-* not + *penthos* grief, sorrow — more at NO, PATHOS] **1 a** : a potion or drug used by the ancients to give forgetfulness of pain and sorrow and held by some to have been opium or hashish **b** : something capable of causing oblivion of grief or suffering ⟨only in occasional visits to the movies and lending libraries, in idle chatter and consoling gossip and scandal, and in the more unendurable cases in drink, can they find ~ —G.J. Nathan⟩ **2** : a plant yielding nepenthe — **ne·pen·the·an** \-ēən\ *adj*

**ne·pen·thes** \-n(t)(ˌ)thēz\ *n* [L] **1** *pl* **nepenthes** : NEPENTHE **2** *cap* [NL, fr. L, nepenthe] : a genus of Malaysian climbing insectivorous plants constituting a distinct family of the order Sarraceniales and having leaves with the midrib prolonged to a tendril and the apex expanded to a pitcher-shaped appendage — see PITCHER PLANT

**ne·per** \ˈnēpə(r), ˈnāp-\ *n* -S [after John *Neper* (Napier) †1617 Scot. mathematician who invented logarithms] : a unit on a natural logarithmic scale for expressing the relationship between two amounts of power (as electric power or acoustic power) equal to one half the natural logarithm of the ratio of the two powers compared : 8.686 decibels

**nep·e·ta** \ˈnepədə\ *n, cap* [NL, fr. L, catnip] : a large genus of Eurasian mints having dentate leaves and verticillate clusters of white or blue flowers with a tubular 15-nerved calyx and a 2-lipped corolla — see CATNIP, GROUND IVY

**neph·a·lism** \ˈnefəˌlizəm\ *n* -S [MGk *nēphalismos* soberness, fr. Gk *nēphalios* sober (fr. *nēphein* to be sober, drink no wine) + *-ismos* -ism; akin to Arm *nautʻi* sober] : total abstinence from alcoholic beverages

**neph·a·list** \-ləst\ *n* -S : an advocate or practitioner of nephalism — **neph·a·lis·tic** \ˌnefəˈlistik\ *adj*

**nephel-** *or* **nephelo-** *comb form* [F *néphél-*, fr. Gk *nephel-, nephelo-*, fr. *nephelē* — more at NEBULA] **1** : cloud ⟨*nephelognosy*⟩ **2** : cloudiness ⟨*nephelometer*⟩

**neph·e·line** \ˈnefəˌlēn, -lən\ *or* **neph·e·lite** \-ˌlīt\ *n* -S [*nepheline* fr. F *néphéline*, fr. Gk *nephelē* cloud + F *-ine*; *nephelite* fr. *nepheline* + *-ite*] : a hexagonal mineral $KNa_3Al_4Si_4O_{16}$ consisting of a silicate of sodium, potassium, and aluminum, occurring as glassy crystals or grains or as coarse crystals or masses of greasy luster without cleavage in various igneous rocks, and constituting an essential constituent of some rocks — **neph·e·lin·ic** \ˌnefəˈlinik\ *adj*

**neph·e·lin·ite** \ˈnefələˌnīt\ *n* -S [ISV *nepheline* + *-ite*; prob. orig. formed as G *nephelinit*] : a silica-deficient igneous rock having nepheline as the predominant mineral

**neph·e·lin·iza·tion** \ˌnefələnəˈzāshən, -ˌlēn-, -ˌnīˈz-\ *n* -S [*nephaline* + *-ization*] : the transformation of a rock into one having nepheline as an essential mineral

**ne·phe·li·um** \nəˈfēlēəm, neˈ-\ *n, cap* [NL, fr. LL *nephelion*, a plant, prob. burdock, fr. Gk *nephelion* small cloud, dim. of *nephelē* cloud] : a genus of Asiatic and Australian trees (family Sapindaceae) having terminal panicles of small flowers succeeded by fruits with a sweet edible pulp and a warty crust — see RAMBUTAN

**neph·e·log·no·sy** \ˌnefəˈlägnəsē\ *n* -ES [*nephel-* + *-gnosy*] : scientific observation of clouds

**neph·e·lom·e·ter** \ˌnefəˈlämədə(r)\ *n* [ISV *nephel-* + *-meter*] : an instrument for measuring cloudiness: as **a** : a set of barium chloride or barium sulfate standards used for estimating the turbidity of a fluid and thereby the number of bacteria in suspension **b** : an instrument for determining the concentration or particle size of suspensions by means of transmitted or reflected light **c** : TURBIDIMETER — **neph·e·lo·met·ric** \ˌnefələˈme·trik\ *also* **neph·e·lo·met·ri·cal** \-rəkəl\ *adj* — **neph·e·lo·met·ri·cal·ly** \-k(ə)lē\ *adv* — **neph·e·lom·e·try** \ˌnefəˈlämə·trē\ *n* -ES

**neph·e·lo·scope** *also* **neph·e·le·scope** \ˈnefələˌskōp\ *n* [*nepheloscope* fr. *nephel-* + *-scope*; *nephelescope* fr. Gk *nephelē* cloud + E *-scope*] : an instrument for demonstrating cloud formation in the laboratory by expansion of moist air

**neph·ew** \ˈne(ˌ)fyü, *chiefly Brit* -ˌvyü\ *n* -S [ME *nevew* nephew, grandson, fr. OF *neveu*, fr. L *nepot-, nepos* grandson, nephew, descendant; akin to OE *nefa* grandson, nephew, OHG *nevo* grandson, kinsman, ON *nefi* nephew, kinsman, Gk *nepodes* children, Skt *napāt* grandson, descendant] **1 a** (1) : the son of a brother or sister (2) : the son of a brother-in-law or sister-in-law **b** : an illegitimate son of an ecclesiastic **2** *obs* **a** : a lineal descendant ⟨on that day Adam shall see all his ~s together —John Trapp⟩; *esp* : GRANDSON ⟨among the ancient Greeks the name of the grandfather was commonly given to the ~ —Richard Bentley †1742⟩ **b** : GRANDNEPHEW **c** : COUSIN ⟨Henry the Fourth, grandfather to this King, depos'd his ~ Richard, Edward's son —Shak.⟩

**neph·ew·ship** \-ˌship\ *n* : the relationship of a nephew

**neph·i·la** \ˈnefələ\ *n, cap* [NL, fr. Gk *nēn* to spin + NL *-phila* — more at NEEDLE] : a genus of large elongate brightly marked mainly tropical spiders of the family Argiopidae — see SILK SPIDER

**neph·i·lim** \ˈnefəˌlim, -ləm\ *n, pl in constr, usu cap* [Heb *Nĕphīlīm*] : a biblical race of giants or demigods ⟨the *Nephilim* were on the earth in those days —Gen 6:4 (RSV)⟩

**nephite** \ˈnēˌfīt, ˈneˌ-\ *n* -S *usu cap* [*Nephi*, son of the Jewish prophet Lehi in the *Book of Mormon* (1 Nephi 1) + E *-ite*] *Mormonism* : a member of a people descended from Nephi, a son of the Jewish prophet Lehi who led a colony from Jerusalem to America about 600 B.C., organized as a church by the risen Christ, and exterminated by the Lamanites leaving the scriptures recorded in the Book of Mormon

**nepho-** *comb form* [ISV, fr. Gk, fr. *nephos* — more at NEBULA] : cloud ⟨*nephology*⟩

**nepho·gram** \ˈnefəˌgram\ *n* [*nepho-* + *-gram*] : a photograph of clouds

**nepho·graph** \-raf, -råf\ *n* [ISV *nepho-* + *-graph*] : an instrument for photographing clouds

**ne·phol·o·gy** \neˈfäləjē\ *n* -ES [*nepho-* + *-logy*] : a branch of meteorology dealing with clouds

**neph·o·scope** \ˈnefəˌskōp\ *n* [ISV *nepho-* + *-scope*] : an instrument for observing the direction of motion and velocity of clouds

**nepho·tet·tix** \ˌnefəˈtedˌiks\ *n, cap* [NL, fr. *nepho-* + Gk *tettix* cicada] : a genus of leafhoppers including one (*N. apicalis*) that transmits a virus causing dwarf disease of rice

**nephr-** *or* **nephro-** *comb form* [LL *nephr-* & NL *nephro-*, fr. Gk *nephr-, nephro-*, fr. *nephros* — more at NEPHRITIS] **1** : kidney ⟨*nephric*⟩ ⟨*nephrology*⟩ **2** : nephric and ⟨*nephroabdominal*⟩ ⟨*nephrogastric*⟩

**-nephra** *pl of* -NEPHROS

**ne·phrec·to·mize** \nəˈfrektəˌmīz, neˈ-\ *vb* -ED/-ING/-S *vt* : to perform nephrectomy upon ~ *vi* : to remove a kidney

**ne·phrec·to·my** \-mē\ *n* -ES [ISV *nephr-* + *-ectomy*] : the surgical removal of a kidney

**neph·ric** \ˈnefrik\ *adj* [*nephr-* + *-ic*] : of or relating to the kidneys : RENAL

**ne·phrid·i·al** \nəˈfridēəl\ *adj* [*nephridium* + *-al*] : of or relating to a nephridium

**nephridial gland** *n* : NEPHRIDIUM

**ne·phrid·io·blast** \-ēəˌblast\ *n* [*nephridio-* (fr. *nephridium*) + *-blast*] : a single large coelomic cell that is the precursor of a nephridium in some worms

**ne·phrid·io·duct** \-ˌdəkt\ *n* [*nephridio-* (fr. *nephridium*) + *duct*] : the duct of a nephridium connecting nephrostome and nephridiopore and often serving as a common excretory and genital outlet

**ne·phrid·io·pore** \-ˌpō(ə)r\ *n* [*nephridio-* (fr. *nephridium*) + *-pore*] : the excretory orifice of a nephridium

**ne·phrid·io·stome** \-ˌstōm\ *n* -S [*nephridio-* (fr. *nephridium*) + *-stome*] : NEPHROSTOME

**ne·phrid·i·um** \nəˈfridēəm\ *n, pl* **nephrid·ia** \-ēə\ [NL, fr. *nephr-* + *-idium*] **1** : an excretory organ that is characteristic of various coelomate invertebrates (as annelid worms, mollusks, brachiopods, and some arthropods), occurs paired in each body segment or as a single pair serving the whole body, typically consists of a tube opening at one end into the coelom by a nephrostome and discharging at the other end by a nephridiopore on the exterior of the body, is often lengthened and convoluted, and has glandular walls **2** : any of various primarily excretory structures; *esp* : NEPHRON

**neph·rite** \ˈneˌfrīt\ *n* -S [G *nephrit*, fr. *nephr-* + *-it* -ite] : a compact tremolite or actinolite constituting the less valuable kind of jade and formerly worn as a remedy for kidney diseases

**¹ne·phrit·ic** \nəˈfridˌik, (ˈ)neˈf-\ *adj* [LL *nephriticus*, fr. Gk *nephritikos*, fr. *nephritis* + *-ikos* -ic] **1** : arising from, originating in, or affecting the kidneys **2** : of, relating to, or affected with nephritis

**²nephritic** \"\ *n* -S : a person affected with nephritis

**nephritic wood** *n* **1** : the wood of the rosilla tree formerly used in an infusion for kidney diseases **2** : the wood of the East Indian horseradish tree formerly used in an infusion for kidney diseases

**ne·phri·tis** \nəˈfrīdəs, neˈf-\ *n, pl* **nephrit·i·des** \-ridəˌdēz\ *also* **nephri·tis·es** [LL, fr. Gk, fr. *nephr-* (fr. *nephros* kidney) + *-itis*; akin to ME *nere* kidney, OHG *nioro* kidney, testicle, ON *nȳra* kidney, Lanuvian *nebrundines* testicles] : inflammation of the kidney affecting the structure (as of the glomerulus or parenchyma), being acute or chronic, and caused by infection, degenerative process, or vascular disease ⟨parenchymatous ~⟩ ⟨glomerular ~⟩ — distinguished from *nephrosclerosis* and *nephrosis*; compare BRIGHT'S DISEASE

**nephro-** — see NEPHR-

**neph·ro·blast** \ˈnefrəˌblast\ *n* [*nephr-* + *-blast*] : NEPHRIDIOBLAST

**neph·ro·calcinosis** \ˌne(ˌ)frō+\ *n* [NL, fr. *nephr-* + *calcinosis*] : a condition marked by calcification of the tubules of the kidney

**neph·ro·coel** *or* **neph·ro·coele** \ˈnefrəˌsēl\ *n* -S [*nephr-* + *-coele*] : the cavity of a nephrotome

**neph·ro·cy·ta·ry** \ˌnefrəˈsīdˌərē\ *adj* [*nephrocyte* + *-ary*] : of or relating to a nephrocyte

**neph·ro·cyte** \ˈnefrəˌsīt\ *n* -S [ISV *nephr-* + *-cyte*] : an excretory cell; *specif* : a cell that has the ability to store up substances of an excretory nature

**neph·ro·gen·ic** \ˌnefrəˈjenik\ *also* **ne·phrog·e·nous** \nəˈfräjənəs, (ˈ)neˈf-\ *adj* [*nephr-* + *-genic* or *-genous*] **1** : originating in the kidney : caused by factors originating in the kidney ⟨~ hypertension⟩ **2** : developing into or producing kidney tissue ⟨strands of ~ cells⟩

**neph·ro·gonaduct** \ˌne(ˌ)frō+\ *n* [*nephr-* + *gonoduct*] : a nephridium that serves as a gonoduct

**neph·roid** \ˈneˌfrȯid\ *adj* [Gk *nephroeidēs* like a kidney, fr. *nephr-* + *-oeidēs* -oid] : RENIFORM

**ne·phrol·e·pis** \nəˈfräləpəs, neˈ-\ *n, cap* [NL, fr. *nephr-* + *-lepis*] : a small genus of mainly tropical ferns (family Polypodiaceae) having large pinnate fronds, the pinnae articulated at the rachis, and the sori on the upper branches of the free veins — see SWORD FERN

**neph·ro·lith** \ˈnefrəˌlith\ *n* -S [ISV *nephr-* + *-lith*] : RENAL CALCULUS

**neph·ro·li·thi·a·sis** \ˌnefrə+\ *n, pl* **nephrolithiases** [NL, fr. *nephr-* + *lithiasis*] : a condition marked by the presence of renal calculi

**neph·ro·lith·ic** \ˌnefrəˈlithik\ *adj* [ISV *nephrolith* + *-ic*] : of or relating to renal calculi

**neph·ro·li·thot·o·my** \ˌnefrələˈthädəmē\ *n* -ES [ISV *nephrolith* + *-o-* + *-tomy*] : the surgical operation of removing a calculus from the kidney

**ne·phrol·o·gist** \nəˈfräləjəst, neˈ-\ *n* -S [ISV *nephrology* + *-ist*] : a specialist in nephrology

**ne·phrol·o·gy** \-jē\ *n* -ES [ISV *nephr-* + *-logy*] : the science that deals with the kidneys, esp. their structure, functions, or diseases

**ne·phro·ma** \nəˈfrōmə, neˈ-\ *n, pl* **nephromas** \-məz\ *also* **nephroma·ta** \-mədə\ [NL, fr. *nephr-* + *-oma*] : a malignant tumor of the renal cortex

**neph·ro·mere** \ˈnefrəˌmi(ə)r\ *n* -S [*nephr-* + *-mere*] : a segment of the mesoblast giving rise to a part of the kidney

**neph·ro·mix·i·um** \ˌnefrəˈmiksēəm\ *n, pl* **nephromix·ia** \-ēə\ [NL, fr. *nephr-* + *-mixium* (perh. fr. Gk *mixis* act of mixing, fr. *mignynai* to mix) — more at MIX] : a nephridium that functions as an excretory organ and a genital duct

**neph·ron** \ˈneˌfrän\ *also* **neph·rone** \-rōn\ *n* -S [G *nephron*, fr. Gk *nephros* kidney — more at NEPHRITIS] : a single excretory unit; *esp* : such a unit in the vertebrate kidney typically consisting of a Malpighian corpuscle, proximal convoluted tubule, loop of Henle, distal convoluted tubule, collecting tubule, and vascular and supporting tissues and discharging by way of a renal papilla into the renal pelvis

**ne·phrop·a·thy** \neˈfräpəthē\ *n* -ES [ISV *nephr-* + *-pathy*] : an abnormal state of the kidney; *esp* : one associated with or secondary to some other pathologic process ⟨diabetic ~⟩

**neph·ro·pexy** \ˈnefrəˌpeksē\ *n* -ES [ISV *nephr-* + *-pexy*] : surgical fixation of a floating kidney

**neph·ro·pore** \-ˌpō(ə)r\ *n* -S [*nephr-* + *-pore*] : NEPHRIDIOPORE

**neph·rops** \ˈneˌfräps\ *n, cap* [NL, fr. *nephr-* + *-ops*] : a genus of lobsters including the Norway lobster

**ne·phrop·si·dae** \neˈfräpsəˌdē\ *n pl, cap* [NL, fr. *Nephrops* + *-idae*] *in some classifications* : a family of crustaceans coextensive with Homaridae

**neph·rop·to·sis** \ˌneˌfräpˈtōsəs, ˌnefrəpˈtō-\ *n, pl* **nephroptoses** \-ōˌsēz\ [NL, fr. *nephr-* + *-ptosis*] : abnormal mobility of the kidney : floating kidney

**ne·phror·rha·phy** \ne'frȯrəfē\ *n* -ES [ISV *nephr-* + *-rrhaphy*] **:** the fixation of a floating kidney by suturing it to the posterior abdominal wall

**-neph·ros** \ˌnefrəs, -ˌfräs\ *also* **-neph·ron** \-ən,-ˌän\ *n comb form, pl* **-nephroi** *also* **-nephra** [NL, fr. Gk *nephros*] **:** kidney ⟨*pronephros*⟩

**neph·ro·sclerosis** \ˌne(ˌ)frō+\ *n* [NL, fr. *nephr-* + *sclerosis*] **:** hardening of the kidney; *specif* **:** a condition that is characterized by sclerosis of the renal arterioles with reduced blood flow and contraction of the kidney, that is associated usu. with hypertension, and that terminates in renal failure and uremia

**ne·phro·sis** \nə'frōsəs, ne'-\ *n, pl* **nephro·ses** \-ō,sēz\ [NL, fr. *nephr-* + *-osis*] **:** noninflammatory degeneration of the kidneys chiefly affecting the renal tubules — distinguished from *nephritis, nephrosclerosis*

**neph·ro·stome** \'nefrə,stōm\ *also* **neph·ro·stom** \-täm\ *or* **ne·phros·to·ma** \nə'frästəmə, ne'-\ *n, pl* **nephrostomes** \-tōmz\ *also* **nephrostoms** \-tämz\ *or* **neph·ro·sto·ma·ta** \ˌnefrə'stōməd·ə\ [NL *nephrostoma*, fr. *nephr-* + *-stoma*] **:** the ciliated funnel-shaped coelomic opening of a typical nephridium — **neph·ro·stomic** \ˌnefrə¦stōmik, -täm-\ *adj*

**¹ne·phrot·ic** \nə'fräd·ik, ne'-\ *adj* [fr. *nephrosis*, after such pairs as E *narcosis: narcotic*] **:** of, relating to, or affected by nephrosis

**²nephrotic** \"\ *n* -S **:** one that is affected with nephrosis

**neph·ro·tome** \'nefrə,tōm\ *n* -S [*nephr-* + *-tome*] **:** the modified part of a somite of a vertebrate embryo that develops into a segmental excretory tubule of the primitive kidney

**ne·phrot·o·my** \nə'fräd·əmē, ne'-\ *n* -ES [NL *nephrotomia*, fr. *nephr-* + *-tomia* -tomy] **:** surgical incision of a kidney (as for the extraction of a stone)

**neph·ro·toxic** \ˌnefrō+\ *adj* [ISV *nephr-* + *toxic*] **:** poisonous to the kidney ⟨a ~ serum⟩ **:** sufficient to poison the kidney ⟨a ~ dose⟩ **:** resulting from or marked by poisoning of the kidney ⟨~ nephritis⟩ — **neph·ro·toxicity** \ˌne(ˌ)frō+\ *n* -ES

**neph·thy·tis** \nef'thīd·əs, 'nefthəd-·\ *n* [NL, fr. Gk *Nephthys*, Egyptian goddess] **1** *cap* **:** a small genus of tropical western African creeping or twining rhizomatous herbs (family Araceae) that usu. have long-petioled sagittate leaves and include some (as *N. afzelii*) that are cultivated as ornamental foliage plants **2** *pl* **nephthytis a :** any plant of the genus *Nephthytis* **b :** any of several plants that are confused with or have formerly been included among members of the genus *Nephthytis*

**¹nepid** \'nepəd, 'nēp-\ *adj* [NL *Nepidae*] **:** of or relating to the Nepidae

**²nepid** \"\ *n* -S [NL *Nepidae*] **:** an insect of the family Nepidae

**nep·i·dae** \'nepə,dē\ *n pl, cap* [NL, fr. *Nepa*, type genus + *-idae*] **:** a family of true bugs comprising the water scorpions — see NEPA, RANATRA

**nepi·on·ic** \ˌnepē¦änik, ˌnēp-\ *adj* [Gk *nēpios* infant + E *-onic* (as in *embryonic*)] **:** IMMATURE, LARVAL ⟨~ forms of many of the common larger fossils —*Jour. of Geol.*⟩

**ne plus ul·tra** \ˌnē,plə'səl·trə; ˌnā,plü'sül·trə, -ˌträ\ *n, pl* **ne plus ultras** [NL, no further] **1 a :** the highest point capable of being reached or attained **:** the summit of achievement **:** ACME ⟨the *ne plus ultra* of original philosophy —O.W.Holmes †1935⟩ ⟨the most sophisticated people in the *ne plus ultra* of civilized society —Edith Hamilton⟩ **b :** the highest degree of a quality or state ⟨found a small clerical job in the town — the *ne plus ultra* of humiliation —Van Wyck Brooks⟩ **2** *archaic* **:** a prohibition against or obstacle to further advance or achievement ⟨her fancy of no limit dreams, no *ne plus ultra* bounds her schemes —Hannah More⟩

**nep·man** \'nepmən, -ˌman\ *n, pl* **nepmen** [Russ, fr. *nep* New Economic Policy (fr. *Novaya Ekonomicheskaya Politika* New Economic Policy) + *-man* (prob. fr. G *mann* man, fr. OHG *man*) — more at MAN] **:** one of a group of small private traders and merchants appearing briefly in Russia during the third decade of the 20th century as a result of a temporary relaxation by the Communist government of its ban on private enterprise

**nepo·tal** \'nepəd·ᵊl, ne'pōd-·\ *adj* [L *nepot-, nepos* + E *-al*] **:** of, relating to, or resembling a nephew

**nepote** \'ne,pōt, 'nē,-\ *n* -S [L *nepot-, nepos*] *Scot* **:** NEPHEW

**ne·pot·ic** \(ˈ)ne¦päd·ik, nə'-\ *adj* [fr. *nepotism*, after such pairs as E *despotism: despotic*] **1 :** of or relating to nepotism **:** disposed to nepotism **2 :** NEPOTAL

**nep·o·tism** \'nepə,tizəm\ *n* -S [F *népotisme*, fr. It *nepotismo*, fr. *nipote, nepote* nephew (fr. L *nepot-, nepos* grandson, nephew) + *-ismo* -ism — more at NEPHEW] **:** favoritism shown to nephews and other relatives (as by giving them positions because of their relationship rather than on their merits) ⟨continued some of the earlier traditions . . . of ~, creating the duchy of Parma for his vicious illegitimate son —R.A.Hall b.1911⟩ ⟨British administration at the beginning of the 19th century was honeycombed with ~ —C.J.Friedrich⟩

**nep·o·tist** \-pəd·əst, -pətə-\ *n* -S [*nepotism* + *-ist*] **:** one who practices nepotism

**nep·o·tis·tic** \ˌnepə¦tistik\ *or* **nep·o·tis·ti·cal** \-stəkəl\ *adj* **:** of or relating to nepotism or nepotists

**ne·pou·ite** \nə'pü,īt\ *n* -S [ISV *nepou-* (fr. *Népoui*, New Caledonia, its locality) + *-ite*] **:** a mineral $(Ni,Mg)_3Si_2O_5(OH)_4$ consisting of a hydrous nickel magnesium silicate

**nepped** *past of* NEP

**nep·pi·ness** \'nepēnəs\ *n* -ES **:** the quality or state of being neppy

**nepping** *pres part of* NEP

**nep·py** \'nepē\ *adj* -ER/-EST [³*nep* + *-y*] **:** having neps **:** containing many neps ⟨~ cotton⟩ ⟨~ yarns⟩

**neps** *pl of* NEP, *pres 3d sing of* NEP

**¹nep·tic·u·lid** \(ˈ)nep¦tikyələd, ¦neptə¦kyül-\ *adj* [NL *Nepticulidae*] **:** of or relating to the Nepticulidae

**²nepticulid** \"\ *n* -S [NL *Nepticulidae*] **:** a moth of the family Nepticulidae

**nep·ti·cu·li·dae** \ˌneptə'kyülə,dē\ *n pl, cap* [NL, fr. *Nepticula*, type genus (fr. LL *nepticula* little granddaughter, dim. of L *neptis* granddaughter) + *-idae* — more at NIECE] **:** a family of minute and widely distributed moths whose larvae occur as leaf miners on many deciduous trees

**nep·tune** \'nep,t(y)ün *sometimes* -p,chün\ *n* -S [after *Neptune*, Roman god of waters, fr. L *Neptunus*] **1** *usu cap* **:** OCEAN, SEA ⟨full often hath she . . . sat with me on *Neptune's* yellow sands —Shak.⟩ **2 :** a copper or brass plate or pan used in trade with the natives of Africa **3** *or* **neptune green** *often cap N* **:** a light to moderate green that is bluer and stronger than surf green

**neptune's cup** *also* **neptune's goblet** *n, usu cap N* **:** either of two very large cup-shaped sponges (*Poterion neptuni* and *P. amphitritae*) sometimes four feet high

**neptune shell** *n* **:** a large whelk (*Neptunea decemcostata*) of the eastern coast of northern No. America distinguished by 10 raised reddish bands surrounding the body whorl of the drab-colored shell

**¹nep·tu·ni·an** \(ˈ)nep¦t(y)ünēən *sometimes* -¦chü-\ *adj* [L *neptunius* Neptunian (fr. *Neptunus*) + E *-an*] **1** *usu cap* **:** of or relating to the god Neptune, the planet Neptune, or the ocean **2 a :** formed by the agency of water **b :** of or relating to neptunism or the neptunists

**²neptunian** \"\ *n* -S **:** NEPTUNIST

**nep·tun·ism** \'ˌ=ˌ=nizəm\ *n* -S [ISV *neptun-* (fr. L *Neptunus*) + *-ism*] **:** the theory of the neptunists

**nep·tun·ist** \-ˌnəst\ *n* -S [ISV *neptun-* (fr. L *Neptunus*) + *-ist*] **:** one holding the now obsolete theory that all of the rocks of the earth's crust were formed by the agency of water — compare PLUTONIST

**nep·tun·ite** \-ˌnīt\ *n* -S [Sw *neptunit*, fr. L *Neptunus* Neptune + Sw *-it* -ite] **:** a mineral $(Na,K)_2(Fe,Mn)TiSi_4O_{12}$ consisting of a silicate of iron, manganese, potassium, sodium, and titanium

**nep·tu·ni·um** \nep't(y)ünēəm *sometimes* -p'chü-\ *n* -S [NL, fr. ISV *Neptune*, the planet Neptune (fr. L *Neptunus*, the god Neptune) + NL *-ium*] **:** a radioactive metallic element of the actinide series that is similar chemically to uranium, that was discovered as a short-lived isotope by spontaneous emission of an electron from uranium 239 produced in turn by neutron bombardment of uranium 238, and that is obtained as the longest-lived isotope in nuclear reactors as a by-product in the production of plutonium — symbol *Np;* see ELEMENT table

**neptunium series** *n* **:** a radioactive series that does not now occur in nature and that begins with plutonium of mass number 241 and continues to americium, to the longest-lived member of the series neptunium of mass number 237, and eventually to the stable end product bismuth

**ne·ral** \'ni,ral, 'nē,-\ *n* -S [ISV *nerol* + *-al*] **:** the cis form of citral

**¹ne·re·id** \'nirēəd\ *n* -S *usu cap* [L *Nereid-, Nereis*, fr. Gk *Nērēid-, Nērēis, Nēreid-, Nēreis*, fr. *Nēreus* Nereus, god of the sea + Gk *-id-, -is* fem. patronymic suffix] **1 :** any of the 50 or 100 sea nymphs held in Greek mythology to be the daughters of Nereus and Doris and attendants on Poseidon and represented as riding sea horses and other sea monsters and usu. as having the human form **2 :** an often malevolent nymph of Greek folklore dwelling in springs or trees as well as in the sea

**²nereid** \"\ *adj* [NL *Nereidae*] **:** of or relating to the Nereidae

**³nereid** \"\ *n* -S [NL *Nereidae*] **:** a worm of the family Nereidae

**ne·re·idae** \nə'rēə,dē\ *n pl, cap* [NL, fr. *Nereis*, type genus + *-idae*] **:** a large family of predaceous marine polychaete worms that have an elongated many-segmented body with large complex parapodia on most segments and a well-defined head with paired tentacles and palps, four prostomial eyes, eight peristomial cirri, and large jaws which bite transversely and that include burrowing and free-swimming forms — see NEREIS

**ne·re·idi·for·mia** \ˌnirē,idə'fȯrmēə, nə,rēəd-\ *n pl, cap* [NL, fr. *Nereid-, Nereis*, genus of polychaete worms + *-iformia* (fr. L, neut. pl. of *-iformis* -iform)] *in some classifications* **:** a division of polychaete worms nearly equivalent to Errantia

**ne·re·is** \'nirēəs\ *n* [NL *Nereid-, Nereis*, fr. L, Nereid] **1** *cap* **:** the type genus of Nereidae comprising usu. large, often dimorphic, and frequently greenish polychaete worms — see CLAM WORM **2** *pl* **nereides :** any marine worm of the genus *Nereis*

**ne·reo·cys·tis** \ˌnirēō'sistəs\ *n, cap* [NL, fr. *nereo-* (fr. Gk *Nēreus* Nereus) + *-cystis*] **:** a monotypic genus of probably annual brown algae (family Laminariaceae) of the northern Pacific that have a stipe which sometimes exceeds 100 feet in length, is hollow in its upper part, and terminates in a large spherical float supporting dependent long thin dichotomously branched laminae and that have been used as a source of potash — see SEA-OTTER'S-CABBAGE

**ne·ri** \'nā(ˌ)rē\ *n pl, usu cap* [It, lit., blacks, pl. of *nero* black, fr. L *nigr-, niger*] **:** a political faction of the Guelphs in Tuscany, Italy, about 1300 opposed to the Bianchi

**ne·ri·ne** \nə'rī(ˌ)nē\ *n* [NL, fr. L *Nerine* Nereid, fr. Gk *Nēreus* Nereus] **1** *cap* **:** a genus of southern African bulbous herbs (family Amaryllidaceae) with strap-shaped leaves and showy red flowers resembling lilies — see GUERNSEY LILY **2** -S **:** any plant of the genus *Nerine*

**ne·ri·ta** \nə'rīd·ə\ *n* [NL, fr. L, sea snail, fr. Gk *nēritēs, nēritēs*, fr. *Nēreus* Nereus] **1** *cap* **:** the type genus of Neritidae comprising marine snails with the shell short and smooth or spirally ridged and with a thick usu. toothed outer lip and a toothed operculum **2** -S **:** any mollusk of the genus *Nerita* — see BLEEDING TOOTH — **neri·toid** \nə'rī,tȯid, 'nerə,-\ *adj*

**ner·ite** \'ne,rīt\ *n* -S [NL *Nerita*] **:** NERITID

**ne·rit·ic** \nə'rid·ik\ *adj* [ISV *nerit-* (perh. fr. NL *Nerita*) + *-ic*] **:** of, relating to, or constituting the belt or region of shallow water adjoining the seacoast and usu. considered to extend from low-tide mark to a depth of 100 fathoms ⟨the ~ zone⟩ ⟨a characteristic ~ fauna⟩ — compare OCEANIC, PELAGIC

**¹ne·ri·tid** \nə'rīd·əd, -rid·əd\ *adj* [NL *Neritidae*] **:** of or relating to the Neritidae

**²neritid** \"\ *n* -S [NL *Neritidae*] **:** a snail of the family Neritidae

**ne·rit·i·dae** \nə'rid·ə,dē\ *n pl, cap* [NL, fr. *Nerita*, type genus + *-idae*] **:** a family of operculate snails (suborder Rhipidoglossa) with turbinate shells having the aperture shaped like a half-moon and a columella resembling a shelf — see NERITA, NERITINA

**ner·i·ti·na** \ˌnerə'tīnə, -tēnə\ *n* [NL, fr. L *nerita* sea snail + NL *-ina*] **1** *cap* **:** a genus of ornately marked and brightly colored snails (family Neritidae) chiefly inhabiting fresh and brackish waters **2** -S **:** any snail of the genus *Neritina*

**ne·ri·um** \'nirēəm\ *n, cap* [NL, fr. L, oleander, fr. Gk *nērion*] **:** a small genus of tropical Old World shrubs (family Apocynaceae) having coriaceous verticillate leaves and large red or white fragrant flowers — see OLEANDER

**nernst effect** \'ne(ə)rn|zt-, 'nərn|, |(t)st-\ *n, usu cap N* [after Walther H. *Nernst* †1941 Ger. physicist & chemist] **:** a transverse electromotive force produced when a metal through which a flow of heat occurs is placed in a magnetic field and observed when the magnetic lines of force are perpendicular to the thermal flux

**nernst heat theorem** *n, usu cap N* **:** a theorem in thermodynamics: no change in entropy is involved in a physical or chemical process taking place in the vicinity of the absolute zero of temperature

**nernst lamp** *n, usu cap N* **:** an electric incandescent lamp whose filament or rod consists of a mixture of magnesia with oxides of the rare earth metals that on being raised to a high temperature (as by a glowing platinum spiral) becomes luminous and conducting and may be kept thus by the passage of a comparatively weak current and without a vacuum

**ne·ro an·ti·co** \ˌnā(ˌ)rō,an·'tē(ˌ)kō, rō,än-·\ *n* [It, lit., ancient black] **:** an ornamental black marble found in fragments among Roman ruins and believed to have come from ancient Laconia

**nerol** \'ne,rōl, 'ni,-, -rȯl\ *n* -S [ISV *ner-* (fr. *neroli oil*) + *-ol*] **:** a liquid unsaturated alcohol $C_{10}H_{17}OH$ that has a rose scent, that occurs in many essential oils (as neroli, petitgrain, and rose oils), that is prepared from its stereoisomer geraniol, and that is used in perfumery esp. in rose and orange blossom scents — compare CITRAL

**Nerol** \"\ *trademark* — used for a dye; see DYE table I (under *Acid Black 26B*)

**ne·rol·i·dol** \ne'rōlə,dōl, -räl-, -dȯl\ *n* -S [ISV *nerol* + *-ide* + *-ol*] **:** a liquid acyclic sesquiterpenoid tertiary alcohol $C_{15}H_{25}OH$ that has a floral odor, that is isomeric with farnesol, and that occurs in many essential oils (as neroli oil and the oil from Peru balsam)

**ner·o·li oil** \'nerəlē-\ *n* [F *néroli*, fr. It *neroli*, fr. Anna Maria de la Tremoille, princess of *Nerole* fl 1670] **:** a fragrant pale yellow essential oil that darkens on standing, that is obtained from the flowers esp. of the sour orange, and that is used chiefly in cologne and other perfumes and as a flavoring material — called also *orange-flower oil*

**ne·ro·ni·an** \nə'rōnēən, nē'-\ *or* **ne·ron·ic** \-'ränik\ *adj, usu cap* [*neronian* fr. L *neronianus*, fr. *Neron-, Nero* Nero †A.D.68 Rom. emperor + L *-anus, -ianus* -an; *neronic* fr. L *Neron-, Nero* + E *-ic*] **1 :** resembling Nero in some characteristic (as moral depravity) **2 :** of or relating to Nero or his times

**ne·ro·nize** \'nērō,nīz, 'nir-\ *vt* -ED/-ING/-S *often cap* [L *Neron-, Nero* + E *-ize*] **:** to tyrannize over in the manner of Nero

**ner ta·mid** \ˌnā(ə)rtä'mēd\ *n, usu cap N&T* [Heb *nēr tāmīdh*, lit., eternal light] **:** a light that hangs in front of and above the ark in the synagogue and is symbolic of the light of truth and the presence of God

**ner·thri·dae** \'nərthrə,dē\ [NL, fr. *Nerthra*, genus of toad bugs + *-idae*] *syn of* GELASTOCORIDAE

**nerts** \'nərts, -ōts,-əits\ *n pl* [by alter.] *slang* **:** NUT 6b

**nerv-** *or* **nervi-** *or* **nervo-** *comb form* [ME *nerv-*, fr. L, fr. *nervus* sinew, nerve] **1 :** nerve ⟨*nervate*⟩ ⟨*nerviduct*⟩ **2 :** nervous and ⟨*nervo*muscular⟩

**ner·val** \'nərvəl\ *adj* [L *nervalis*, fr. *nervus* nerve + *-alis* -al] **:** of or relating to nerves or nervous tissue **:** NEURAL

**¹ner·vate** \'nər,vāt\ *vt* -ED/-ING/-S [*nerve* + *-ate*, v. suffix] *archaic* **:** NERVE, INSPIRIT, SUPPORT

**²nervate** \"\ *also* **ner·vat·ed** \-ˌād·əd\ *adj* [*nervate* prob. fr. (assumed) NL *nervatus*, fr. L *nervus* sinew, nerve + *-atus* -ate (adj. suffix); *nervated* prob. fr. (assumed) NL *nervatus* + E *-ed*] **:** NERVED

**ner·va·tion** \nər'vāshən\ *n* -S [prob. fr. (assumed) NL *nervation-, nervatio*, fr. (assumed) NL *nervatus* nervate + L *-ion-, -io* -ion] **:** an arrangement or system of nerves; *often* **:** VENATION

**ner·va·ture** \'nərvə,chü(ə)r, -ˌchər\ *n* -S [prob. fr. (assumed) NL *nervatura*, fr. (assumed) NL *nervatus* nervate + L *-ura* -ure] **:** NERVATION

**¹nerve** \'nərv, -ōv,-əiv\ *n* -S [L *nervus* sinew, nerve; akin to Gk *neuron* sinew, nerve, string, Skt *snāvan* sinew, Gk *nēn* to spin — more at NEEDLE] **1 a :** SINEW, TENDON — used in the phrase *to strain every nerve* **b :** a sinew or tendon taken (as for a bowstring or for thread) from an animal **2 :** one of the filamentous bands of nervous tissue that connect parts of the nervous system with the other organs of the body and conduct nervous impulses to or away from these organs and that are made up of nerve fibers together with protective and supportive structure with the fibers of larger nerves being gathered into funiculi surrounded by a perineurium and the funiculi being enclosed in a common epineurium **3 a :** the mainspring of action, drive, force, or vitality **:** the center or source of energy or direction ⟨develops and finds the ~ of its own style —Milton Klonsky⟩ ⟨proved again and again that he himself was the heart and ~ of the whole undertaking⟩ **b :** power of endurance, self-command, equilibrium, or control **:** FORTITUDE, HEART, STAMINA, STRENGTH ⟨knew that now he was to face some trial of mind and ~ —Gilbert Parker⟩ **c :** BOLDNESS, DARING ⟨true leadership begins when a statesman . . . has the ~ to dwell on distasteful facts —Fremont Rider⟩; *often* **:** presumptuous audacity or hardihood **:** BRASS, EFFRONTERY, ¹GALL 3 ⟨the ~ of her⟩ **4 a :** a sore or sensitive point **:** a touchy subject or aspect ⟨touched the pocketbook ~⟩ **b nerves** *pl* **:** nervous disorganization or collapse **:** HYSTERIA ⟨went all to pieces with ~*s*⟩ **5 :** VEIN 3a ⟨magnesium deficiency causes a light yellow discoloration of the old leaves except for the parenchyma along the ~*s* —Charles Coster⟩ **6 :** the sensitive pulp of a tooth **7 :** VEIN 3c **8 :** the aggregate of the physical properties (as firmness, strength, and elasticity) characteristic of crude rubber **:** rubbery quality ⟨low-grade soft rubbers lack ~⟩ **syn** see TEMERITY

**²nerve** \"\ *vt* -ED/-ING/-S **:** to give strength, vigor, or courage to **:** supply with physical or moral force ⟨this feeling . . . *nerved* him to break through the awe-inspiring aloofness of his captain —Joseph Conrad⟩ **syn** see ENCOURAGE

**nerve block** *n* **:** an interruption of the passage of impulses through a nerve (as with pressure or narcotization); *sometimes* **:** BLOCK ANESTHESIA

**nerve canal** *n* **:** PULP CANAL

**nerve cavity** *n* **:** PULP CAVITY

**nerve cell** *n* **:** one of the cells that constitute nervous tissue, that have the property of transmitting and receiving nervous impulses, and that are typically composed in higher animals and man of somewhat reddish or grayish protoplasm with a large nucleus containing a conspicuous nucleolus, irregular cytoplasmic granules, and cytoplasmic processes which are highly differentiated as frequently multiple dendrites or usu. solitary axons and which conduct impulses toward and away from the nerve cell body **:** NEURON; *sometimes* **:** a nerve cell body exclusive of its processes **:** the major structural element of the gray matter of the brain and spinal cord, the ganglia, and the retina

**nerve center** *n* **1 :** CENTER 2e **2 :** the essential part of a body or system **:** the place or source of leadership, control, or influence ⟨the political and economic *nerve center* of the archipelago —R.S.Kain⟩

**nerve cord** *n* **:** a cord of nervous tissue; *specif* **:** the pair of closely united ventral longitudinal nerves with their segmental ganglia that is characteristic of many elongate invertebrates (as earthworms)

**nerved** \-vd\ *adj* [¹*nerve* + *-ed*] **1 :** having nerves; *esp* **:** having nerves of a specified character — often used in combination ⟨fan-*nerved*⟩ **2 :** showing courage or strength **:** BOLD, POISED ⟨broad hand ~ and vital in bronze as if in actual flesh —Dymphna Cusack & Florence James⟩

**nerve ending** *also* **nerve end** *n* **:** the structure in which the distal end of the axon of a nerve fiber terminates

**nerve fiber** *n* **:** an axon or dendrite covered with both a medullary sheath and a neurilemma (as in the peripheral nervous system), with a medullary sheath only (as in the central nervous system), or with a neurilemma only (as in the sympathetic system), or not covered at all (as in the gray matter)

**nerve gas** *n* **:** a war gas that is absorbed into the body through the skin, ingested, or inhaled and that has a paralyzing or other harmful effect esp. on the nervous and respiratory systems

**nerve impulse** *also* **nervous impulse** *n* **:** the progressive alteration in the protoplasm of a nerve fiber that follows stimulation of the fiber, is accompanied by a wave of alteration of electrical potential, and serves to transmit a record of sensation from a receptor or an instruction to act to an effector

**nerve·less** \'=ləs\ *adj* **1 :** destitute of strength or courage **:** FEEBLE, POWERLESS ⟨a weak, ~ fool, devoid of energy and promptitude —Nathaniel Hawthorne⟩ **2 :** lacking nerves or nervures **3 :** exhibiting control or balance **:** COOL, POISED ⟨surely one of the most ~ champions in the history of the tournament —*New Yorker*⟩ — **nerve·less·ly** *adv* — **nerve·less·ness** *n* -ES

**nerve·let** \'=lət\ *n* -S [¹*nerve* + *-let*] **:** a little nerve

**nerve net** *n* **:** a network (as in various lower invertebrates and possibly the wall of the vertebrate intestine) that consists of primitive nerve cells each of which appears continuous with adjacent cells without intervening synapses and that conducts stimulation in all directions with a decrement

**nerve of lan·ci·si** \-län'chēzē\ *usu cap L* [after Giovanni M. *Lancisi* †1720 Ital. anatomist] **:** STRIA LONGITUDINALIS

**nerve of wris·berg** \-'riz,bərg, *Ger* -'vris,berk\ *usu cap W* [after Heinrick A. *Wrisberg* †1808 Ger. anatomist] **:** GLOSSOPALATINE NERVE

**nerve-racking** *or* **nerve-wracking** \'=ˌ=ˌ=\ *adj* **:** extremely trying on the nerves

**nerve ring** *n* **:** a ring of nervous tissue; *esp* **:** a ring of concentrated nervous tissue about the pharynx of various invertebrate animals

**nerveroot** \'=ˌ=\ *n* **:** MOCCASIN FLOWER

**nerves** *pl of* NERVE, *pres 3d sing of* NERVE

**nerve sheath** *n* **:** NEURILEMMA

**nerve trunk** *n* **:** a bundle of nerve fibers enclosed in a connective tissue sheath

**nervi** *pl of* NERVUS

**nervi-** — see NERV-

**ner·vi·duct** \'nərvə,dəkt\ *n* [*nerv-* + *duct*] **:** a bony or cartilaginous passage for a nerve

**nervier** *comparative of* NERVY

**nerviest** *superlative of* NERVY

**ner·vii** \'nərvē,ī, 'nervē,ē\ *n pl, usu cap* [L] **:** a Celtic-German people of Belgium almost exterminated by Julius Caesar

**ner·vi·ly** \'nərvəlē, -ōv-,-əiv-, -li\ *adv* **:** in a nervy manner

**ner·vi·muscular** \ˌnərvə, -vē+\ *or* **ner·vo·muscular** \-(ˌ)vō+\ *adj* [*nerv-* + *muscular*] **:** NEUROMUSCULAR

**¹ner·vine** \'nər,vēn *sometimes* -vīn\ *adj* [*nerv-* + *-ine*] **:** affecting the nerves **:** tending to soothe nervous excitement

**²ner·vine** \'nər,vēn, ,=ˈ=\ *n* -S **:** a nerve tonic

**ner·vi ner·vo·rum** \ˌnər,vī,nər'vōrəm, ¦ner,vē,ner-\ *n pl* [NL, lit., nerves of nerves] **:** small nerve filaments innervating the sheath of a larger nerve

**ner·vi·ness** \'nərvēnəs, -ōv-,-əiv, -vin-\ *n* -ES **:** the quality or state of being nervy ⟨the scramble and ~ of competitive living —George Farwell⟩

**nerv·ing** \-viŋ,-vēŋ\ *n* -S [¹*nerve* + *-ing*] **:** the removal of part of a nerve trunk in chronic inflammation to destroy sensation in the parts supplied and thus cure lameness (as in a horse)

**nerv·ish** \-vish,-vēsh\ *adj, dial* **:** NERVOUS

**nervo-** — see NERV-

**ner·von** \'nər,vän\ *also* **ner·vone** \-vōn\ *n* -S [ISV *nerv-* + *-on* or *-one*] **:** a crystalline cerebroside $C_{48}H_{91}NO_8$ found together with a hydroxy derivative in the brain

**ner·von·ic acid** \(ˈ)nər¦vänik-\ *n* [*nervonic* ISV *nervon* + *-ic*] **:** a crystalline unsaturated fatty acid $C_{23}H_{45}COOH$ obtained from nervon by hydrolysis and also found in some fish-liver oils — called also *selacholeic acid*

**ner·vose** \'nər,vōs, ,=ˈ=\ *adj* [L *nervosus* sinewy, vigorous, energetic] **1** *obs* **:** of, relating to, affecting, or consisting of nerves **2** *of a leaf* **:** having nerves **:** NERVED, VEINED

**ner·vos·i·ty** \ˌnər'väsəd·ē\ *n* -ES [L *nervositat-, nervositas* strength, thickness, fr. *nervosus* + *-itat-, -itas* -ity] **:** NERVOUSNESS

**ner·vous** \ˈnərvəs, -ōv-,-əiv-\ *adj* [ME, fr. L *nervosus* sinewy, vigorous, energetic, fr. *nervus* sinew, nerve + *-osus* -ose — more at NERVE] **1 a** *archaic* **:** having strong sinews **:** VIGOROUS **b** *obs* **:** having abundant tendons — used of animals and meat **2 :** manifesting vigor of mind **:** marked by strength of thought, feeling, or style **:** highly organized **:** FORCIBLE, SPIRITED ⟨the texture of her writing is compact and ~ —G.F.Whicher⟩ ⟨vivid pages in simple, ~, racy language —Carl Van Doren⟩ **3 :** of, relating to, or made up of nervous tissues ⟨the ~ layer of the eye⟩ **4 a :** of or relating to the nerves **:** originating in or affected by the nerves ⟨~ energy⟩ ⟨~ excitement⟩ **b :** exhibiting, suggesting, or originating in undue irritability **:** JERKY, JUMPY, UNSTEADY ⟨a hurried and ~ conclave —G.G. Coulton⟩ ⟨in the ~ atmosphere thus created, a tragic event occurred —*Amer. Guide Series: Wash.*⟩ **c :** TIMID, APPREHENSIVE ⟨permitted a ~ smile to flit across her face —Louis Bromfield⟩ — often used with *of* in British speech ⟨we were ~ of broaching it —Harry Lauder⟩ **d** *archaic* **:** affecting or used as medication for the nerves ⟨a ~ draught⟩ **5 a :** tending to produce nervousness or agitation **:** CRITICAL, DIFFICULT ⟨the moment was ~ — as far as the private secretary knew, quite the most critical moment in the records of American diplomacy —Henry Adams⟩ **b :** appearing or acting unsteady, irregular, or erratic — used of inanimate things ⟨climbed carefully into his ~ kayak —Farley Mowat⟩ **syn** see VIGOROUS

**nervous breakdown** *also* **nervous prostration** *n* **1 :** NEURASTHENIA **2 :** a case of neurasthenia ⟨she had a *nervous breakdown* last year⟩

**nervous fluid** *n* **:** a fluid formerly supposed to circulate through nerves and function as the essential agent in transmitting nerve impulses

**ner·vous·ly** *adv* **:** in a nervous manner

**nervous nel·lie** \-ˈnelē, -li\ *n, usu cap 2d N* [*nervous* + *Nellie*, dim. of *Ellen, Eleanor*, or *Helen*] **:** a timid or ineffectual person ⟨the *nervous Nellies*, who always come into a bull market too late, pushed prices too high —Burton Crane⟩

**ner·vous·ness** *n* -ES **:** the quality or state of being nervous

**nervous system** *n* **:** the bodily system that in vertebrates is made up of brain and spinal cord, nerves, ganglia, and parts of the receptor organs and that receives and interprets stimuli and transmits impulses to the effector organs — see AUTONOMIC NERVOUS SYSTEM, CENTRAL NERVOUS SYSTEM

**ner·vule** \ˈnər(ˌ)vyül\ *n* -S [prob. fr. (assumed) NL *nervulus*, fr. L *nervus* sinew, nerve + *-ulus*] **1 :** a small nerve **2 :** NERVURE

**ner·vu·lose** \ˈnərvyəˌlōs\ *adj* [*nervule* + *-ose*] **:** minutely nerved

**ner·vu·ra·tion** \ˌnərvyəˈrāshən\ *n* -S [*nervure* + *-ation*] **:** the neuration of an insect's wing

**ner·vure** \ˈnərvyər, -ˌvyů(ə)r\ *n* -S [F, fr. MF *nerveure* leather strap used to strengthen a shield, fr. *nerf* sinew, fr. L *nervus* sinew, nerve] **:** VEIN 3c

**ner·vus** \ˈnərvəs, ˈnerv-\ *n, pl* **ner·vi** \ˈnərˌvī, ˈne(ə)rˌvē\ [L] **:** NERVE

**nervus ter·mi·na·lis** \-ˌtərməˈnaləs, -nāl-; -ˌtərməˈnäl-\ *n* [NL, lit., terminal nerve] **:** a slender ganglionated nerve associated with the olfactory nerves in most vertebrates from fishes to man

**nervy** \ˈnərvē, -ōv-,-əiv-, -vi\ *adj* -ER/-EST [¹*nerve* + *-y*] **1** *archaic* **:** SINEWY, STRONG ⟨his ~ knees —John Keats⟩ **2 a :** showing calm courage **:** BOLD, INTREPID ⟨all good tacklers, and ~, no matter how much they may be outclassed —Paul Withington⟩ **b :** marked by effrontery or presumption **:** BRASH, IMPUDENT ⟨unwelcome, and knowing he was unwelcome, he was ~ enough to come anyway⟩ **3 :** marked by nervousness **:** EXCITABLE, JERKY ⟨smoked one cigarette after another; he was very ~ and couldn't sit still —Christopher Isherwood⟩ **4** *of rubber* **:** having nerve

**NES** *abbr, often not cap* not elsewhere specified

**ne·science** \ˈne|sh(ē)ən(t)s, |sēn- *also* ˈnē|\ *n* -S [LL *nescientia*, fr. L *nescient-, nesciens* (pres. part. of *nescire* not to know, fr. *ne-*, negative prefix + *scire* to know) + *-ia* -y — more at NO, SCIENCE] **1 :** lack of knowledge or awareness **:** IGNORANCE ⟨his apparent ~ of contemporary literature was not a pose —A.T.Quiller-Couch⟩ **2 :** a conviction or doctrine that ultimate or immaterial realities cannot be known through the rational processes of the mind **:** AGNOSTICISM

**¹ne·scient** \-ənt\ *adj* [L *nescient-, nesciens*] **:** exhibiting or characterized by nescience **:** IGNORANT, AGNOSTIC **syn** see IGNORANT

**²nescient** \"\ *n* -S **:** AGNOSTIC

**nese** \ˈnēz\ *n* -S [ME *nese, neose;* akin to MD *nēse, neuse* nose, MLG *nese* and prob. to OE *nasu* nose — more at NOSE] *now chiefly Scot* **:** NOSE

**¹nesh** \ˈnesh\ *adj* [ME *nesshe, nesche*, fr. OE *hnesce;* akin to OHG *nascōn* to nibble, eat dainties, Goth *knasqus* soft, fine, tender, Gk *kneōron, kneōros* spurge flax, Skt *kiknasa* particles of ground grain, groats, L *ciner-, cinis* ashes — more at INCINERATE] **1** *chiefly dial* **:** SOFT, JUICY, TENDER ⟨~ grass in the spring⟩ **2** *chiefly dial* **a :** DELICATE, RETIRING **b :** GENTLE, KINDLY **c :** extremely fastidious or dainty **d :** TIMID

**²nesh** \"\ *vi* -ED/-ING/-ES [ME *nesshen, neschen* to make soft, become soft, fr. OE *hnescian*, fr. *hnesce*, adj.] *dial Eng* **:** to act timidly

**nes·khi** *or* **nes·ki** \ˈneskē\ *or* **nas·khi** \ˈnas-\ *n* -S *usu cap* [Ar *naskhī*, fr. *nasakha* to copy] **:** the ordinary cursive Arabic script used in writing scientific and religious books — compare KUFIC

**neso-** *comb form* [NL, fr. Gk *nēso-*, fr. *nēsos;* akin to Gk *nēchein, nēchesthai* to swim, L *nare* — more at NOURISH] **:** island ⟨*Nesogaean*⟩

**neso·gae·an** *or* **neso·ge·an** \ˌnēsəˈjēən, ˌnes-\ *adj, usu cap* [NL *Nesogaea* Polynesia (fr. *neso-* + *-gaea*) + E *-an*] **:** POLYNESIAN 3

**ne·so·kia** \nəˈsōkēə\ *n, cap* [NL] **:** a genus of burrowing Indian scaly-tailed murine rats including important vectors of plague

**neso·silicate** \ˌnē(ˌ)sō, ˌne(- + \ *n* [prob. fr. *neso-* + *silicate*] **:** a mineral silicate (as olivine) that contains independent tetrahedral silicon-oxygen anionic groups $SiO_4$ **:** ORTHOSILICATE — compare INOSILICATE

**ne·sot·ra·gus** \nəˈsä·trəgəs\ *n, cap* [NL, fr. *neso-* + Gk *tragos* goat — more at TRAGEDY] **:** a genus of very small antelopes of southeastern Africa comprising the Sunis and closely related to the royal antelopes

**nes·pe·lem** \ˈnespəˌlem, -ˌləm\ *or* **nes·pe·lim** \-ˌlim, -ˌləm\ *n, pl* **nespelem** *or* **nespelems** *or* **nespelim** *or* **nespelims** *usu cap* **1 a :** a Salishan people of northeastern Washington **b :** a member of such people **2 :** a dialect of Okanagon

**nes·que·ho·nite** \ˌneskwəˈhōˌnīt\ *n* -S [*Nesquehoning*, Pa. + E *-ite*] **:** a mineral $MgCO_3.3H_2O$ consisting of a colorless hydrous magnesium carbonate in prismatic crystals

**ness** \ˈnes\ *n* -ES [ME *naisse, nasse*, fr. OE *naess, naessa, ness;* akin to ON *nes* ness, MD *nesse, nes*, MLG *nes, ness* ness, OE *nasu* nose — more at NOSE] **:** CAPE, HEADLAND, PROMONTORY

**-ness** \nəs *sometimes esp when an unstressed syllable precedes & esp in the pl* ,nes; *see* BUSINESS\ *n suffix* -ES [ME *-nes, -ness, -nesse*, fr. OE *-nes, -ness, -nyss, -nys;* akin to OS *-nissi, -nussi* -ness, MD *-nisse, -nesse*, OHG *-nissa, -nassī, -nussī*, Goth *-inassus* (*-n-, -in-* being orig. part of the stem)] **:** state **:** condition **:** quality **:** degree ⟨good*ness*⟩ ⟨great*ness*⟩ ⟨sick*ness*⟩

**ness·ber·ry** \ˈnes- — *see* BERRY\ *n, sometimes cap* [Helge *Ness* †1928 Am. horticulturist born in Norway + E *berry*] **:** a hybrid bramble with fruit of superior flavor but inferior picking and shipping qualities produced by interbreeding dewberries and red raspberries and grown to a limited extent in the southern U.S.

**nes·sel·rode pie** \ˈnesəlˌrōd-\ *n, usu cap N* [after Count Karl R. *Nesselrode* †1862 Russ. statesman] **:** cream pie filled with mixed preserved fruits and topped with shaved chocolate

**nesselrode pudding** *n, usu cap N* **:** a frozen pudding containing chestnuts and maraschino

**ness·ler·iza·tion** \ˌneslərəˈzāshən, -ˌrīˈz-\ *n* -S *sometimes cap* **:** the process of nesslerizing

**ness·ler·ize** \ˈneslәˌrīz\ *vt* -ED/-ING/-S *sometimes cap* [Julius *Nessler* †1905 Ger. agricultural chemist + E *-ize*] **:** to treat or test with Nessler's reagent

**ness·ler's reagent** *or* **nessler's solution** \ˈneslə(r)z-\ *n, usu cap N* [after Julius *Nessler*] **:** an alkaline solution of potassium mercuric iodide used in chemical analysis esp. in a delicate test for ammonia in aqueous solution (as when obtained from water, blood, urine) with which it forms a yellowish brown color or precipitate

**nessler tube** *n, usu cap N* [after Julius *Nessler*] **:** a narrow glass cylinder with a flat bottom used in colorimetry (as in nesslerization) for comparing the colors of liquids

**¹nest** \ˈnest\ *n* -S *often attrib* [ME, fr. OE; akin to MD & OHG *nest*, L *nidus*, OIr *net* nest, Skt *nīḍa* resting place, nest; all from a prehistoric IE compound whose first constituent is represented by Skt *ni* down and whose second constituent is akin to the root of E *sit* — more at NETHER] **1 a :** the bed, receptacle, or location prepared by a bird for holding its eggs and for hatching and rearing its young **b :** the settled and often concealed place in which the eggs of animals (as insects, fishes, or turtles) are laid and hatched and the young are reared **2 a :** a place of rest, retreat, or lodging **:** HOME, SHELTER ⟨a cozy little blanketed ~ which she had arranged and furnished herself —Zane Grey⟩ **b :** the place of resort of persons of like character or purpose esp. regarded as bad or hostile **:** DEN, HANGOUT ⟨the ~ of Saracen marauders . . . in the Alpine passes —R.W.Southern⟩ **3 a :** the family, group, or swarm of animals occupying a nest **b :** the persons frequenting a place of resort **4 a :** a group of similar things **:** AGGREGATION ⟨it had become a ~ of empty paint jars —John Updike⟩ ⟨rammed into a ~ of sampans —Chesley Wilson⟩ ⟨right up into a ~ of giant mountains —Helen MacInnes⟩ **b :** a center or home of practices or habits of thought of a particular kind ⟨felt most strongly that, in practice, the Court of Rome was a ~ of abuses —G.G.Coulton⟩ **5 :** a group of objects made to fit close together or graduated in size to fit one within another ⟨a ~ of picnic plates⟩ — compare NEST OF TABLES **6 :** a receptacle or locating device shaped to hold something ⟨a ~ to receive the Continental-type spare tire mounting —Jeff Taylor⟩ ⟨there is a sudden rush of air into the bilges under the tube ~ —E.L.Beach⟩ **7 :** a small isolated mass of ore or mineral within another formation **8 a :** a compact group of devices (as pulleys, gears, springs) working together **b :** a group of things (as boilers or tubes in a water-tube boiler) **c :** a group of holes or pins for locating work in a jig or die **9 :** an isolated collection or clump of cells in tissue of a different structure ⟨a ~ of sarcomatous cells in the liver⟩ **10 :** an emplaced group of weapons ⟨a ~ of machine guns⟩

nest of measuring spoons

**²nest** \"\ *vb* -ED/-ING/-S [ME *nesten*, fr. *nest*, n.] *vi* **1 :** to build or occupy a nest **:** settle down in or as if in a nest ⟨birds ~ in many places⟩ **2 :** to fit compactly together or within one another ⟨to solve the schools' storage problem, the chairs stack easily, the tables ~ —*Time*⟩ ~ *vt* **1 :** to fit or settle into a bed or suitable receptacle **:** adjust into a protective place ⟨~ their jelly bottles in green tissue paper —John Haverstick⟩ ⟨the old method of ~*ing* a fragile product in a great mass of loose cushioning material —*Modern Packaging*⟩ **2 :** to pack or fit compactly together (as in a stack or a close or graduated series) ⟨cooking pans and racks ~*ed* under an aluminum dome —*New Yorker*⟩ **3 :** to assemble (as boiler tubes or piles) in a group **4 :** to arrange (tobacco) so that the better bundles are exposed to view in a warehouse

**nest·able** \-təbəl\ *adj* **:** capable of being nested

**nest·age** \-tij\ *n* -S **:** a place or group of nests or a nest

**nest box** *n* **:** a box provided for the nesting of domesticated animals (as hens or rabbits)

**nest egg** *n* **1 :** a natural or artificial egg left in the nest of a domestic fowl to induce her to continue to lay there **2** *archaic* **:** something used as an inducement, lure, or decoy **3 a :** a fund of money accumulated as a reserve or as a basis for further acquisition ⟨a retirement-fund *nest egg*, built up over a 15-year period —E.R.Leibert⟩ **b :** a nucleus or accumulation intended to promote further growth or development ⟨will have a *nest egg* of 128 — only five less than half the 266 needed to win —H.H.Martin⟩

**nest·er** \-tə(r)\ *n* -S **1 :** one that nests (as a bird) ⟨enough fish to make the kingfishers constant ~*s* in their banks —John Masefield⟩ **2** *West* **:** a homesteader or squatter who takes up rangeland for a farm ⟨not all of the ~*s* stayed to prove up, but enough did to settle the West —Seth Agnew⟩

**nest fungus** *n* **:** a fungus of the family Nidulariaceae

**nes·tle** \ˈnesəl\ *vb* **nestled; nestled; nestling** \-s(ə)liŋ\ **nestles** [ME *nestlen*, fr. OE *nestlian*, fr. *nest* + *-lian* -le] *vi* **1** *archaic* **a :** to make or occupy a nest **:** settle in a nest **b :** to make one's home **:** take up abode **2 a :** to settle snugly or comfortably **:** take up a cozy, warm, or affectionate position ⟨*nestled* quietly into the cushions⟩ ⟨the infant *nestled* at his mother's breast⟩ **b :** to press or lie close **:** CUDDLE ⟨she had *nestled* down with him, that his head might lie upon her arm —Charles Dickens⟩ **3 :** to lie embosomed, embedded, or sheltered **:** seem at home or naturally located ⟨settlements *nestled* in narrow valleys and ravines —J.F.Embree & W.L. Thomas⟩ **4** *dial chiefly Eng* **:** to be restless **:** FIDGET ~ *vt* **1 :** to settle, shelter, or house in or as if in a nest ⟨*nestled* himself into the warm bed⟩ ⟨*nestled* the monkey's body in the crook of his arm —Joseph Whitehill⟩ **2 :** to press or snuggle close or affectionately ⟨*nestled* her shoulder close against him⟩

**nes·tler** \ˈnes(ə)lə(r)\ *n* -S **:** one that nestles **:** NESTLING

**nest·ling** \ˈnes(t)liŋ\ *n* -S [ME, fr. *nest* + *-ling*] **1 :** a young bird that has not abandoned the nest **2 a :** a young animal still living in the parental nest **b :** a young child

**nest of tables :** a set of small tables graduated in size so that they fit one beneath another

nest of tables

**nes·tor** \ˈnestə(r); -ˌstȯ(ə)r; -ō(ə)\ *n* [after *Nestor*, legendary Greek hero known for long life and wisdom (fr. L & Gk; L, fr. Gk *Nestōr*)] **1** -S *often cap* **:** a wise elder counselor **:** a grand old man **:** one regarded as patriarch or leader in his field ⟨the *Nestor* of that great-statured generation —J.R. Chamberlain⟩ ⟨the ~ of American philosophy —D.D.Runes⟩ **2** *cap* [NL, fr. L] **:** a genus of large parrots of New Zealand and the Papuan subregion that include the kaka and the kea and with related forms constitute a subfamily of Psittacidae or in some classifications a separate family **3** -S [by alter.] **:** NESTER 2 ⟨horse-and-cow-men, when they got to timbered country, found ~*s* and sodbusters, who were their natural enemies —W.F.Harris⟩

**¹nes·to·ri·an** \neˈstōrēən\ *n* -S *usu cap* [ME, fr. LL *Nestorianus*, fr. *Nestorius* †ab451 patriarch of Constantinople + L *-anus* -an] **1 :** a member of the Church of the East that originated in the ancient Persian Empire, rejected the condemnation of Nestorius by the Council of Ephesus in 431, and survives among Assyrians in Iraq, Iran, Syria, and the U.S. **2 :** an adherent of Nestorianism **3 :** ASSYRIAN 3

**²nestorian** \(ˈ)═ˌ═══\ *adj, usu cap* **:** of or relating to the Nestorians, to Nestorius, or to Nestorianism

**nestorian alphabet** *n, usu cap N* **:** a Syriac alphabet widely spread by Nestorian missionaries

**nes·to·ri·an·ism** \═ˈ═══ˌnizəm\ *n* -S *usu cap* **1 :** Nestorian Christianity **2 :** the doctrines imputed to Nestorius or the Nestorians; *esp* **:** the doctrine that a divine and a human personality were joined in Jesus Christ in perfect harmony of action but remained distinct with the corollary that Mary should not be called the Mother of God

**nestorian syriac** *n, cap N & S* **1 :** an eastern dialect of Syriac **2 :** NEO-SYRIAC

**nes·to·rine** \ˈnestəˌrīn, -rēn\ *adj* [NL *Nestor* + E *-ine*] **:** of or relating to the genus *Nestor* or the parrots belonging to it

**nests** *pl of* NEST, *pres 3d sing of* NEST

**nes·ty** \ˈnesti\ *Scot var of* NASTY

**¹net** \ˈnet, *usu* -ed·+V\ *n* -S *often attrib* [ME *net, nett, nette*, fr. OE *net, nett;* akin to OS *net, netti* net, MD *net, nette*, OHG *nezzi*, ON *net, nōt*, Goth *nati* net, L *nodus* knot, OIr *nascim* I bind, and prob. to L *nassa* fish basket and perh. to Skt *nahyati* he binds; basic meaning: to knot, weave] **1 a :** a meshed arrangement of threads, cords, or ropes that have been twisted, knotted, or woven together at regular intervals **b :** any of various devices made of net and used esp. for catching fish, birds, or insects **c :** something made of net and used esp. for protecting, confining, carrying, or dividing (as a cargo net or tennis net) **2 :** something designed to entrap or ensnare ⟨a man that flatters his neighbor spreads a ~ for his feet —Prov 29:5 (RSV)⟩ ⟨the engineer cannot escape the ~ of circumstances in which he is caught —W.P.Webb⟩ **3 a :** a machine-twisted fabric in fine to coarse geometric meshes made usu. of silk, rayon, nylon, or cotton and used for dresses, curtains, veils, or trimmings **b :** a handmade or machine-made background fabric for lace usu. in fine geometric meshes **4 :** something resembling a net in reticulation **:** a network of lines, fibers, or figures ⟨a perfect ~ of steamer, bus and air service —Frederick Arnold⟩ **5 a :** a three-sided structure that consists of poles and netting enclosing a wicket and that is used in cricket for batting and bowling practice **b :** a three-sided structure enclosed in netting and used as a goal in hockey or lacrosse — often used in pl. **c :** a return of the ball in a racket game that goes into the net **6 a :** a rigging of ropes and twine on a free balloon that supports the weight of the basket and distributes the load over the entire upper surface of the envelope **b :** a rectangular net of cordage used to restrain the envelope of a kite, balloon, or airship during inflation and before the car is attached **7 a :** a group of communications stations operating under unified control on assigned frequencies and in accordance with a plan for the systematic handling and relay of radio traffic ⟨Army radio ~⟩ **b :** NETWORK 5 **8 :** a device made usu. of canvas stretched in a frame and used for catching persons leaping from a building or other structure

**²net** \"\ *vb* **netted; netted; netting; nets** *vt* **1 :** to cover or enclose with or as if with a net ⟨to leave his favorite tree . . . after . . . *netting* it to keep off the birds —Maria Edgeworth⟩ ⟨how dense a fold of danger ~*s* him round —Alfred Tennyson⟩ **2 :** to make in the style of or by means of network ⟨is *netting* herself the sweetest cloak you can conceive —Jane Austen⟩ **3 :** to catch as if in a net **:** capture by stratagem or wile ⟨and now I am here, *netted* and in the toils —Sir Walter Scott⟩ **4 a :** to use nets in for catching fish ⟨*netted* the wallow and brought out scores of small fish —Francis Birtles⟩ **b :** to catch by means of a net ⟨*netted* 15 tons of smelt in 10 minutes —*Amer. Guide Series: Mich.*⟩ **5 :** to cover with or as if with a network ⟨her high plump cheeks were *netted* with little purple veins —Marguerite Steen⟩ **6 :** to hit (a ball) into the net for the loss of a point in a racket game ~ *vi* **1 :** to make nets or netting ⟨was *netting* away as if nothing unusual had occurred —Elizabeth C. Gaskell⟩ **2 :** to hit a ball into the net for the loss of a point in a racket game **3 :** to combine into a communications net or network

**³net** \"\ *adj* [ME, fr. MF — more at NEAT (bright)] **1** *archaic* **:** NEAT, TRIM **2** *obs* **:** CLEAN, BRIGHT **3 :** free from all charges or deductions: as **a :** remaining after the deduction of all charges, outlay, or loss ⟨~ earnings⟩ ⟨~ proceeds⟩ — opposed to *gross* **b :** excluding all tare or tret ⟨~ weight⟩ **4 a :** free from adulteration **:** PURE ⟨~ wine⟩ **b :** excluding all nonessential or extraneous considerations **:** BASIC, FUNDAMENTAL ⟨the ~ effect is one that disturbs many scholars —C.V.Newsom⟩ ⟨the ~ result is a huge canvas of small-town life —C.J. Rolo⟩

**⁴net** \"\ *vt* **netted; netted; netting; nets 1 a :** to make by way of profit **:** CLEAR ⟨*netted* $8000 a year from the restaurant⟩ **b :** to produce by way of profit **:** YIELD ⟨the restaurant *netted* $8000 a year⟩ **2 :** to get possession, control, use, or benefit of **:** GAIN ⟨war experiences which *netted* him just about all the decorations there are —Clarence Woodbury⟩ ⟨*netting* us less security than we would otherwise enjoy —Sidney Hook⟩

**⁵net** \"\ *n* -S **1 :** a net amount, profit, weight, or price ⟨reduced taxes . . . partly accounted for the high ~ —*Time*⟩ **2 :** the score of a golfer in a handicap match after deducting his handicap from his gross **3 :** the fundamental point **:** ESSENCE, GIST ⟨the ~ of all these articles is that competition is dying —Raymond Moley⟩

**⁶net** \"\ *vt* **netted; netted; netting; nets** [MF *netir*, fr. OF, fr. *net* clean, pure, bright — more at NEAT] *dial chiefly Eng* **:** WASH, RINSE

**NET** *abbr, often not cap* not earlier than

**net area** *n* [³*net*] **:** the part of the cross-sectional area of a masonry unit effective in carrying load

**net assets** *n pl* **1 :** the excess of value of resources over liabilities to creditors — called also *net worth* **2 :** ADMITTED ASSETS

**net ball** \ˈ═ˌ═\ *n* **1 :** a ball that on the service (as in tennis and volleyball) strikes the top of the net and lands in the service court but must be served over — compare ²LET 2 **2 :** a ball that during play in tennis is hit into the net for loss of point

**netball** \ˈ═ˌ═\ *n* [¹*net* + *ball*] **:** a game that resembles basketball and that is played with a soccer ball between 2 teams of 7 players each on a hard court 100 feet long and 50 feet wide

**net blotch** *n* [¹*net*] **:** a disease of barley characterized by spots on the leaves and caused by a fungus (*Helminthosporium teres*)

**net earnings** *n pl* [³*net*] **:** NET INCOME

**net·ful** \ˈnetˌfu̇l\ *n* -S **:** as much or as many as will fill a net ⟨a ~ of fish⟩

**neth·er** \ˈnethə(r)\ *adj* [ME *nether, nethere, nithere*, fr. OE *nithera*, fr. *nither, nithor*, adv., down, downward; akin to OS *nithiri*, adj., nether, *nithar*, adv., down, OHG *nidari, nidaro*, adj., nether, *nidar*, adv., down, ON *nethri, netharri*, adj., nether, *nithr*, adv., down; all fr. a Gmc word that is a compar. of a word akin to Skt *ni* down; akin to OE *in* — more at IN] **1 :** situated down or below **:** lying beneath or in the lower part **:** LOWER, UNDER ⟨wandered onward till they reached the ~ margin of the heath —Thomas Hardy⟩ ⟨her ~ lip crept up between her upper and lower teeth —F.V.W.Mason⟩ ⟨caught between the ~ millstone of higher labor costs and the upper millstone of . . . rigidly set price ceilings —Clark Kerr⟩ ⟨her first contact with the ~ side of the smooth social surface —Edith Wharton⟩ **2 :** situated or believed to be situated beneath the surface of the earth ⟨captured her and carried her off to the ~ world to be his wife —S.V.McCasland⟩

**neth·er·land** \-lənd\ *adj, usu cap* **:** NETHERLANDS

**neth·er·land·er** \ˈnethə(r)ˌlandə(r), -ˌlən-, -ˌlaan-, ═ˈ═ˈla(a)n-\ *n* -S *cap* [*Netherlands*, country in Europe (trans. of D *Nederlanden*, pl. of *Nederland*) + E *-er*] **:** a native or inhabitant of the Netherlands

**¹neth·er·land·ish** \-dish, -dēsh\ *adj, usu cap* [*Netherlands* + E *-ish*] **1 a :** of, relating to, or characteristic of the Netherlands **b :** of, relating to, or characteristic of the people of the Netherlands **2 :** of, relating to, or characteristic of the language of the Netherlands

**²netherlandish** \"\ *n* -ES *cap* **:** the Germanic language of the Netherlanders

**neth·er·lands** \ˈnethə(r)lən(d)z\ *adj, usu cap* [fr. the *Netherlands*, country of Europe] **:** of or from the Netherlands **:** of the kind or style prevalent in the Netherlands **:** DUTCH, NETHERLANDISH

**nethermore** \ˈ═ˌ═\ *adj* [ME, fr. *nether* + *more*] **:** LOWER ⟨the heavens expelled them; nor them the ~ abyss receives —H.W. Longfellow⟩

**nethermost** \ˈ═ˌmōst, *esp Brit also* -ˌməst\ *adj* [ME *nethermast*, fr. *nether* + *-mast*, *-most* -most] **:** LOWEST ⟨a grin of malice which would have held its own in the ~ hell —Bram Stoker⟩

**neth·er·stock** \ˈ═ˌstäk\ *n* [*nether* + *stock* (stocking)] **:** STOCKING; *specif* **:** a 16th century stocking reaching above the knee and worn with upperstocks

**neth·er·ward** \-ˌwə(r)d\ *adj* [*nether* + *-ward*] **:** DOWNWARD ⟨in the ~ black of the night —Walt Whitman⟩

**neth·er·wards** \-dz\ *adv* [alter. (influenced by such words as *afterwards, downwards*) of earlier *netherward*, fr. ME *netherward, nitherward*, fr. OE *nitherweard, nitherweardes;* OE *nitherweard*, fr. *nither* down + *-werd, -weard* -ward; OE *nitherweardes*, fr. *nither* down + *-weardes* -wards — more at NETHER] **:** DOWNWARD

netherstock: *1* trunk hose, *2* upperstock, *3* netherstock

**netherworld** \ˈ═ˌ═\ *n* [*nether* + *world*] **1 :** the world of the dead ⟨journeys to the ~ to plead for his wife's return —*Time*⟩ **2 :** UNDERWORLD

⟨sheds a withering light on the ~ of deceit, subversion, and espionage —R.M.Nixon⟩
**ne·thi·nim** \ˌnetēˈnēm\ *n pl, usu cap* [Heb *nĕthīnīm*, lit., those given] **:** servants performing the lowest menial services about an ancient Jewish tabernacle and temple
**net income** *n* **:** the balance of gross income remaining after deducting related costs and expenses usu. for a given period and losses allocable to the period
**net interest** *n* **:** PURE INTEREST
**net–knot** \ˈ=,=\ *n* [¹*net*] **:** KARYOSOME
**netlayer** \ˈ=,==\ *n* **:** a small naval vessel equipped to lay and repair harbor defense nets
**netleaf** \ˈ=,=\ *or* **netleaf plantain** *n, pl* **netleafs** *or* **netleaf plantains :** a common rattlesnake plantain (*Goodyera pubescens*)
**net lease** *n* [³*net*] **:** a lease requiring the lessee to assume all operating expenses (as maintenance, insurance, taxes) in addition to the payment of rent
**netlike** \ˈ=,=\ *adj* **:** resembling a net
**N et M** \ˌeˌnedˈem\ *abbr, often not cap N & M* [L *nocte et mane*] night and morning
**netmaker** \ˈ=,==\ *n* [ME, fr. *net* + *maker*] **:** a maker of nets
**net·man** \ˈnetˌman, -ˌmən\ *n, pl* **netmen 1 :** a worker who takes care of fishing nets **2 :** a tennis player; *esp* **:** the partner in a doubles match who stays near the net when his teammate serves
**net national product** *n* **:** the net value of the goods and services produced in a nation during a specific period (as a year) computed by subtracting from the gross national product charges for depreciation of capital assets — compare NATIONAL INCOME
**net necrosis** *n* **:** a necrosis of the phloem of the potato tuber caused by frost or the leaf roll virus in which the pith and cortex contain a broken netlike pattern of necrotic cells
**ne·top** \ˈnēˌtäp\ *n* -s [of Algonquian origin; akin to Narraganset *netoup* my friend, companion, Abnaki *nidanbé*] *chiefly NewEng* **:** FRIEND — often used in salutation to an Indian by the American colonists
**net plankton** *n* **:** plankton consisting of small and usu. microscopic organisms that are large enough to be retained by a net of number 25 mesh silk bolting cloth — compare NANNOPLANKTON
**net premium** *n* [³*net*] **:** an insurance premium consisting of the amount required to pay the insurance liability on its becoming due without paying any expenses or contingent charges
**net quick assets** *n pl* [³*net* + *quick assets*] **:** the excess of quick assets over current liabilities
**Ne·trop·sin** \nəˈträpsən\ *trademark* — used for an antibiotic obtained from bacteria of the genus *Streptomyces*
**nets** *pl of* NET, *pres 3d sing of* NET
**net sales** *n pl* **:** the balance of gross sales remaining after deducting trade discounts, returned sales, and sales allowances
**net silk** *n* [¹*net*] *Brit* **:** THROWN SILK
**nets·man** \ˈnetsmən\ *n, pl* **netsmen :** one who uses a net (as in fishing)
**ne·tsu·ke** \ˈnetskē, -ˌskā, -səˌkā\ *n* -s [Jap] **:** a small object carved in wood or ivory or wrought in metal, pierced with holes, and used by the Japanese as a toggle to fasten a small pouch or purse to the kimono sash
**nett** *Brit var of* NET
**net·ta·ble** \ˈnedˌəbəl, -etə-\ *adj* **:** capable of being netted
**net·ta·pus** \ˈnedˌəpəs\ *n, cap* [NL, fr. Gk *nētta*, *nēssa* duck + NL *-pus* — more at ANAS] **:** a genus of small chiefly tropical Old World geese with the legs so short as to be nearly useless on land — see PYGMY GOOSE
**net tare** *n* [³*net*] **:** CLEAR TARE
**net·ta·stom·i·dae** \ˌned·əˈstäməˌdē\ *n pl, cap* [NL, fr. *Nettastoma*, type genus (fr. Gk *nētta* duck + NL *-stoma*) + *-idae*] **:** a family of slender fragile-bodied deep-sea eels (order Apodes) that have an elongated upper jaw and thin black-pigmented skin
**netted** *past of* NET
**netted melon** *or* **net melon** *n* **:** a melon (*Cucumis melo reticulatus*) that is a variety of the muskmelon and has a thin rind with reticulated surface and deep green sweet flesh — called also *nutmeg melon*
**net tender** *n* **:** a small naval vessel that tends the openings in a harbor defense net
**net·ter** \ˈned·ə(r), -etə-\ *n* -s [ME, netmaker, fr. *net* + *-er*] **:** one that makes or uses nets (as for fishing)
**¹net·ting** \ˈnetiŋ\ *n* -s [ME, prob. fr. MD or MLG *netten* to wet + ME *-ing*; akin to OHG *nezzen* to wet, Goth *natjan*, denominative causatives fr. a root represented by OHG *naz*, *nazz* wet, MD *nat*; perh. akin to Gk *noteros* wet, damp — more at NOURISH] *dial Eng* **:** URINE
**²net·ting** \ˈned·|iŋ, -et|, |ēŋ\ *n* -s [¹*net* + *-ing*] **1 :** NETWORK: as **a :** a network of ropes used on a ship (as for stowing away sails or hammocks) **b :** a material of crossed, twisted, or knotted cords, threads, ropes, or wires with open spaces between **c :** the reticulation on the surface of a melon **2** [fr. gerund of ²*net*] **:** the act or process of making a net or network **3** [fr. gerund of ²*net*] **:** the act, process, or right of fishing with a net
**netting knot** *n* **:** SHEET BEND
**net·ti·on** \ˈned·ēˌän\ *n, cap* [NL, fr. Gk *nēttion* duckling, dim. of *nētta* duck] *in some classifications* **:** a genus of ducks comprising the common European teal, the American green-winged teal, and several related birds that are now usu. included in *Anas*
**¹net·tle** \ˈned·ᵊl, -etᵊl\ *n* -s *often attrib* [ME *nettle*, *netle*, fr. OE *netle*, *netel*, *netele*; akin to MD *netel* nettle, OHG *nazza*, *nezzila*, ON *nötr*, MIr *nenaid*, Gk *adikē* nettle, and perh. to OE *net*, *nett* net — more at NET] **1 :** a plant of the genus *Urtica* or the family Urticaceae **2 :** any of numerous prickly or stinging plants not of the family Urticaceae — usu. used with preceding modifier
**²nettle** \ˈ"\ *vb* **nettled; nettled; nettling** \-d·ᵊliŋ, -t(ᵊ)liŋ\ **nettles** [ME *netlen*, *nettyllen*, fr. *netle*, *nettle*, n.] *vt* **1 a :** to whip or sting with nettles **b :** to cause to be stung by nettles **2 :** to arouse displeasure, impatience, or anger in **:** PROVOKE, VEX ⟨ashamed at having been *nettled* by so minor a cause —Edwin O'Connor⟩ **3 :** to stir up **:** INCITE ~ *vi* **:** to become irritated, vexed, or provoked **syn** see IRRITATE
**³nettle** \ˈ"\ *or* **knet·tle** \ˈ"\ *or* **knit·tle** \ˈnid·ᵊl, -itᵊl\ *n* -s [alter. of earlier *knettel*, fr. ME *knittel*, fr. OE *cnyttels* string, sinew, fr. *cnyttan* to knit, bind, tie — more at KNIT] **1 :** a small line made of rope yarn and used esp. for hammock clews or seizings **2 nettles** *pl* **:** halves of yarns in the end of a rope twisted up for pointing
**nettle butterfly** *n* **:** any of several butterflies (as the red admiral) whose larvae feed on nettles
**nettle cell** *n* **:** NEMATOCYST
**nettle family** *n* **:** URTICACEAE
**nettlefish** \ˈ==,=\ *n* **:** JELLYFISH
**nettlehead** \ˈ==,=\ *n* **:** a virus disease of the hop characterized by leaves that curl and cluster so as to resemble those of a nettle (*Urtica dioica*)
**nettle-leaved goosefoot** *or* **nettleleaf goosefoot** \ˈ==,=-\ *n* **:** an annual European goosefoot (*Chenopodium murale*) with coarsely dentate leaves that is widespread in the U.S. and southern Canada
**net·tler** \ˈned·ᵊlə(r), -et(ᵊ)lə-\ *n* -s **:** one that nettles
**nettle rash** *n* **:** an eruption on the skin caused by or resembling the condition produced by stinging with nettles **:** URTICARIA
**net·tle·some** \ˈned·ᵊlsəm, -etᵊl-\ *adj* [²*nettle* + *-some*] **1 :** readily nettled **:** IRRITABLE ⟨was not the least ~ of his countrymen —*Life of Quin*⟩ **2 :** causing vexation **:** IRRITATING ⟨will anticipate such ~ problems as traffic rules for orbiting spacecraft —*Newsweek*⟩
**nettle tree** *n* **1 :** a tree of the genus *Celtis* (esp. *C. australis*) **2 :** a tree of the genus *Laportea*; *esp* **:** AUSTRALIAN NETTLE TREE **3 :** a tree of the genus *Trema*
**net·tling** \ˈned·liŋ, -et(ᵊ)liŋ\ *n* -s [³*nettle* + *-ing*] **1 :** a process resembling splicing by which two ropes are joined end to end so as to form one rope **2 :** a process of tying together the ends of yarns in pairs so as to prevent tangling
**nettling cell** *n* [fr. pres. part. of ²*nettle*] **:** NEMATOCYST
**net·tly** \ˈned·ᵊlē, -etᵊlē, -ᵊli\ *adj* -ER/-EST **1 :** having a profusion of nettles **2 :** NETTLESOME
**net ton** *n* **:** TON 1b
**net tonnage** *n* **:** the gross tonnage of a ship less deductions for space occupied by crew's quarters, machinery for navigation, engine room, and fuel
**net tracery** *n* **:** window tracery (as in 14th-century Gothic work) in which the openings are of nearly the same size and of approximately the same form
**net·ty** \ˈned·|ē, -et|, |i\ *adj* -ER/-EST **:** NETLIKE
**net–veined** \ˈ=,=\ *adj* **1** *of a leaf* **:** having netted or reticulated veins **2 :** having a fine network of veins ⟨a *net-veined* wing⟩
**net weaver** *n* **:** any of various sedentary spiders (as of the family Theridiidae) that spin irregular webs in which the threads cross in all directions
**net–winged** \ˈ=,wiŋd\ *adj* **:** having wings with a fine network of veins **:** NEUROPTEROID
**¹network** \ˈ=,=\ *n, often attrib* [¹*net* + *work*] **1 :** a fabric or structure of threads, cords, or wires that cross each other at regular intervals and are knotted or secured at the crossings ⟨ribbons, lace and embroidery wrought together in a most curious piece of ~ —Joseph Addison⟩ **2 :** a system of lines or channels that interlace or cross like the fabric of a net ⟨a ~ of highways⟩ ⟨a ~ of rivers⟩ ⟨a ~ of veins⟩ ⟨a ~ of roots⟩ ⟨a ~ of nerves⟩ **3 :** an interconnected or interrelated chain, group, or system ⟨a ~ of secret agents⟩ ⟨a ~ of alliances⟩ ⟨a ~ of beliefs⟩ **4 :** a system of electrical conductors in which conduction takes place between certain points by more than one path **5 a :** a group of local radio or television stations linked by wire or radio relay for the usu. simultaneous broadcasting or televising of the same program **b :** a radio or television company that produces programs to be relayed to local stations for broadcast by radio or television ⟨sold the show to a big ~⟩ **syn** see SYSTEM
**²network** \ˈ"\ *vt* **:** to cover with or as if with a network ⟨a continent . . . so ~*ed* with navigable rivers and canals —*Lamp*⟩
**net worth** *n* **:** NET ASSETS
**neuf·châ·tel** \ˌn(y)üshaˈtel, ¦nə(r)sh-, ¦nōsh-\ *or* **neufchâtel cheese** *n* -s *usu cap N* [F *neufchâtel*, fr. *Neufchâtel*, France] **:** a small soft unripened cheese made from whole or skim milk with or without cream and often with condiments added — compare CREAM CHEESE 1
**neuk** \ˈnyük\ *chiefly Scot var of* NOOK
**neu·ma** \ˈn(y)ümə\ *n* -s [ML] **:** NEUME
**neu·mat·ic** \n(y)üˈmad·ik\ *adj* [F *neumatique*, fr. ML *neumaticus*, fr. *neumat-*, *neuma* + L *-icus* -ic] **:** consisting of or characterized by neumes
**neume** *also* **neum** *or* **pneume** \ˈn(y)üm\ *n* -s [*neume*, *neum*, fr. F, fr. MF, fr. ML *neuma*, *pneuma* (also, group of notes sung to a final syllable as long as the breath lasts), fr. Gk *pneuma* breath; *pneume* fr. ML *pneuma* — more at PNEUMATIC] **1 :** a symbol in the musical notation of the middle ages derived from the Greek system of accents, indicating from one to usu. four notes, and showing only relative pitch **2 :** one of the square symbols in the plainsong notation of the Roman Catholic Church **3 :** PNEUMA 2a — **neu·mic** \-mik\ *adj*
**neur-** *or* **neuro-** *comb form* [*neur-* fr. Gk, nerve, sinew, fr. *neuron*; *neuro-* fr. NL, fr. Gk, nerve, sinew, fr. *neuron* — more at NERVE] **1 :** neural tissue **:** nerve ⟨*neuro*anatomy⟩ ⟨*neuro*sarcoma⟩ ⟨*neuro*trophy⟩ **2 :** neural ⟨*neur*ectoderm⟩ ⟨*neuro*cyte⟩ ⟨*neuro*malacia⟩ ⟨*Neuro*ptera⟩ **3 :** neural and ⟨*neuro*cardiac⟩ ⟨*neuro*psychic⟩ ⟨*neuro*vascular⟩
**-neu·ra** \ˈn(y)ürə, -ürə\ *n comb form, pl* **-neura** [NL, fr. Gk *neuron* nerve] **:** one or ones having (such) nerves or veins — in taxonomic names ⟨*Dasyneura*⟩ ⟨*Streptoneura*⟩
**neu·rad** \ˈn(y)ü(ˌ)rad\ *adv* [*neur-* + *-ad*] **:** toward the neural side — opposed to *hemad*; compare HEMAL 2
**neu·ral** \ˈn(y)ürəl, -ür-\ *adj* [*neur-* + *-al*] **1 :** of, relating to, or affecting a nerve or the nervous system **2 :** situated in the region of or on the same side of the body as the neural axis — used of vertebrate anatomical relations as an equivalent to *dorsal*; opposed to *hemal* — **neu·ral·ly** \-rəlē\ *adv*
**neural arch** *n* **:** the cartilaginous or bony arch on the dorsal side of a vertebra **:** the series of neural arches forming the canal in which the spinal cord is situated
**neural axis** *n* **:** CEREBROSPINAL AXIS
**neural canal** *n* **1 :** the canal formed by the series of vertebral neural arches **2 :** the neurocoele of the vertebrate embryo
**neural cavity** *n* **:** the cavity comprising the spinal canal and the interior of the cranium
**neural crest** *n* **:** the ridge of a neural fold giving rise to the spinal ganglia and various autonomic structures
**neural fold** *n* **:** the lateral longitudinal fold on each side of the neural plate that by folding over and fusing with the opposite fold gives rise to the neural tube
**neu·ral·gia** \n(y)üˈraljə, n(y)əˈ-\ *n* -s [NL, fr. *neur-* + *-algia*] **:** an acute paroxysmal pain radiating along the course of one or more nerves usu. without demonstrable changes in the nerve structure — compare NEURITIS — **neu·ral·gic** \-jik\ *adj*
**neu·ral·gi·form** \-jəˌfȯrm\ *adj* [NL *neuralgia* + E *-form*] **:** resembling neuralgia or that of neuralgia ⟨~ pains⟩
**neural gland** *n* **:** a glandular mass in ascidians that lies in close relation to the nerve ganglion and is possibly homologous with the pituitary body of vertebrates
**neural groove** *n* **1 :** the longitudinal hollow that separates the neural crest from the main body of the neural plate **2 :** MEDULLARY GROOVE
**neu·ral·gy** \n(y)əˈraljē, -ji\ *n* -ES [NL *neuralgia*] *dial* **:** NEURALGIA
**neural lamina** *n* **:** one of the medullary folds
**neural plate** *n* **1 :** a thickened plate of ectoderm along the dorsal midline of the early vertebrate embryo that gives rise to the neural tube and crests **2 :** one of the bony plates in the middorsal part of the carapace of most turtles
**neural process** *n* **:** the lateral half of the neural arch of a vertebra equivalent to the pedicle and lamina together
**neural ridge** *n* **:** NEURAL CREST — compare NEURAL PLATE
**neural shield** *n* **:** any of a number of horny shields above the neural plates on the carapace of turtles
**neural spine** *n* **:** the median dorsal spine of a vertebra **:** SPINOUS PROCESS
**neural tube** *n* **:** the hollow longitudinal tube formed by infolding and subsequent fusion of the opposite neural folds in the vertebrate embryo
**neur·aminic acid** \ˌn(y)ür+-\ *n* [ISV *neur-* + *aminic*] **:** an amino acid $C_9H_{17}NO_8$ of carbohydrate character occurring in the form of acyl derivatives — see SIALIC ACID
**neur·apophysis** \"+\ *n, pl* **neurapophyses** [NL, fr. *neur-* + *apophysis*] **1 :** NEURAL PROCESS **2 :** NEURAL SPINE
**neur·asthenia** \"+\ *n* [NL, fr. *neur-* + *asthenia*] **:** a syndrome marked by ready fatigability of body and mind, usu. by worrying and depression, and often by headache and by gastrointestinal and circulatory disturbances
**¹neur·asthenic** \"+\ *adj* [NL *neurasthenia* + E *-ic*] **:** of, relating to, or having neurasthenia ⟨before the ~ tendencies of the patient are developed —*Jour. Amer. Med. Assoc.*⟩ — **neu·ras·then·i·cal·ly** \-nək(ə)lē, -nēk-, -li\ *adv*
**²neurasthenic** \ˈ"\ *n* -s **:** one affected with neurasthenia
**neu·ra·tion** \n(y)üˈrāshən, n(y)ə-\ *n* -s [*neur-* + *-ation*] **:** VENATION — used esp. of the veins of an insect's wing
**neur·axial** \(ˈ)n(y)ür+\ *adj* [*neur-* + *axial*] **:** of or relating to a neuraxis
**neur·axis** \"+\ *n* [NL, fr. *neur-* + *axis*] **1 :** AXON **2 :** CEREBROSPINAL AXIS
**neur·axon** \"+\ *also* **neur·axone** \"+\ *n* [NL *neuraxon*, fr. *neur-* + *axon*] **:** NEURAXIS
**neur·ectoblast** \"+\ *n* [*neur-* + *ectoblast*] **:** embryonic ectoderm destined to produce neural tissue
**neur·ectoderm** \"+\ *n* [*neur-* + *ectoderm*] **:** ectoderm destined to give rise to neural tissues
**neu·rec·to·my** \n(y)üˈrektəmē\ *n* -ES [*neur-* + *-ectomy*] **:** the excision of part of a nerve
**neur·enteric** \ˌn(y)ür+\ *adj* [*neur-* + *enteric*] **:** being or relating to a canal that in embryos of many vertebrates and tunicates temporarily connects the neural tube and the primitive intestine
**neu·rer·gic** \(ˈ)n(y)üˈrərjik\ *adj* [*neur-* + *erg-* + *-ic*] **:** of or relating to the action of a nerve
**neu·ri·lem·ma** *also* **neu·ri·lema** *or* **neu·ro·lemma** \ˌn(y)ürəˈlemə\ *n* -s [NL, fr. *neur-* + Gk *eilēma* covering, coil, fr. *eilein* to wind (akin to Gk *eilyein* to enfold, wrap); influenced by Gk *lemma* peel, rind, fr. *lepein* to peel, husk — more at VOLUBLE, LEPER] **1 :** the delicate nucleated outer sheath of a nerve fiber **2 :** PERINEURIUM — **neu·ri·lem·mal** \¦==¦leməl\ *or* **neu·ri·lem·mat·ic** \-ləˈmad·ik\ *or* **neu·ri·lem·ma·tous** \-ˈlemad·əs\ *adj*
**neu·ri·lem·mo·ma** *or* **neu·ri·le·mo·ma** \ˌ==ləˈmōmə\ *n, pl* **neu·ri·lem·mo·mas** \-məz\ *or* **neu·ri·lem·mo·ma·ta** \-məd·ə\ *or* **neurilemomas** *or* **neurilemomata** [NL, fr. *neurilemma* or *neurilema* + *-oma*] **:** a tumor of the sheath of a peripheral nerve
**neu·ril·i·ty** \n(y)üˈriləd·ē, -ətē, -i\ *n* -ES [*neur-* + ¹*-ile* + *-ity*] **:** the special properties and functions of the nerves
**neu·rine** \ˈn(y)üˌrēn, ˈn(y)ürən\ *also* **neu·rin** \ˈn(y)ürən\ *n* -s [ISV *neur-* + *-ine* or *-in*] **:** a syrupy poisonous quaternary ammonium hydroxide $CH_2{=}CHN(CH_3)_3OH$ that has a fishy odor, that is obtained esp. from animal sources (as brain, bile, egg yolk), and that is formed by dehydration of choline (as by boiling with barium hydroxide solution and in the putrefaction of flesh)
**neu·ri·no·ma** \ˌn(y)ürəˈnōmə\ *n, pl* **neurino·mas** \-məz\ *or* **neurinoma·ta** \-məd·ə\ [NL, fr. *neur-* + *-inoma* (as in L *carcinoma*)] **:** a nerve tumor supposed to be derived from the neurilemma
**neu·rite** \ˈn(y)üˌrīt\ *n* -s [ISV *neur-* + *-ite*] **:** AXON
**¹neu·rit·ic** \(ˈ)n(y)üˈrid·ik, n(y)əˈ-, -itik, -ēk\ *adj* [NL *neuritis* + E *-ic*] **:** of, relating to, or affected by neuritis
**²neuritic** \ˈ"\ *n* -s **:** an individual affected with neuritis
**neu·ri·tis** \n(y)üˈrīd·əs, n(y)əˈ-, -ītəs\ *n, pl* **neuritides** *or* **neuritises** [NL, fr. *neur-* + *-itis*] **:** an inflammatory or degenerative lesion of a nerve characterized by pain, sensory disturbances, paralysis, muscle atrophy, and impaired or lost reflexes in the part innervated — compare NEURALGIA
**neu·ro-** *in pronunciations below*, ¦==¦n(y)ü(ˌ)rō *or* ¦n(y)ürō *or* ¦n(y)ürə\ — see NEUR-
**neu·ro·anatomic** \¦==+\ *also* **neu·ro·anatomical** \"+\ *adj* [*neuroanatomy* + *-ic* or *-ical*] **:** of or relating to the structure of nervous tissue or the nervous system
**neu·ro·anatomist** \"+\ *n* **:** a specialist in neuroanatomy
**neu·ro·anatomy** \"+\ *n* [*neur-* + *anatomy*] **1 :** the study of the structure of nervous tissue and the nervous system **2 :** the structural makeup of nervous tissue and the nervous system
**neu·ro·bio·tac·tic** \"+¦bīəˈtaktik\ *or* **neu·ro·bio·tac·ti·cal** \-təkəl\ *adj* [*neurobiotactic* fr. NL *neurobiotaxis*, after such pairs as NL *chemotaxis*: E *chemotactic*; *neurobiotactical* fr. *neurobiotactic* + *-al*] **:** of, relating to, or involving neurobiotaxis — **neu·ro·bio·tac·ti·cal·ly** \-tək(ə)lē\ *adv*
**neu·ro·bio·taxis** \"+¦bīōˈtaksəs\ *n* [NL, fr. *neur-* + *bi-* + *-taxis*] **:** a hypothetical directed and oriented shift of nerve cells in the course of phylogeny toward a region of maximum stimulation that has been held to explain cephalization and brain evolution
**neu·ro·blast** \ˈn(y)ürəˌblast\ *n* [ISV *neur-* + *-blast*] **:** a cellular precursor of a nerve cell; *esp* **:** an undifferentiated embryonic nerve cell — **neu·ro·blas·tic** \¦==¦blastik\ *adj*
**neu·ro·blas·to·ma** *pronunc at* NEURO- + ˌblaˈstōmə\ *n, pl* **neuroblasto·mas** \-məz\ *or* **neuroblastoma·ta** \-məd·ə\ [NL, fr. ISV *neuroblast* + NL *-oma*] **:** a malignant tumor formed of embryonic ganglion cells
**neu·ro·canal** \"+\ *n* [*neur-* + *canal*] **:** the central canal of the spinal cord
**neurocele** *var of* NEUROCOELE
**neu·ro·central** \¦== *at* NEURO- +\ *adj* **1** [*neur-* + *central*] **:** of, relating to, or situated between the neural arch and the centrum of a vertebra **2** [NL *neurocentrum* + E *-al*] **:** of, relating to, or being a neurocentrum
**neu·ro·centrum** \"+\ *n* [NL, fr. *neur-* + *centrum*] **:** the dorsal element of a vertebra that unites with its fellow of the opposite side to form a neural arch from which the vertebral spine is developed
**neu·ro·chondrite** \"+\ *n* [*neur-* + *chondr-* + *-ite*] **:** NEUROCENTRUM
**neu·ro·chord** \ˈn(y)ürə+ˌ-\ *n* [*neur-* + *chord*] **:** a prominent strand of nervous tissue **:** a nerve cord: as **a :** the primitive chordate central nervous system (as in a lancelet) **b :** one of the very large longitudinal nerve fibers of various segmented worms
**neu·ro·circulatory** \¦== *at* NEURO- +\ *adj* [*neur-* + *circulatory*] **:** of or relating to both the nervous and circulatory systems
**neurocirculatory asthenia** *n* **:** CARDIAC NEUROSIS
**neu·ro·coele** *or* **neu·ro·coel** *also* **neu·ro·cele** \ˈn(y)ürəˌsēl\ *n* -s [*neur-* + *-coele*] **:** the cavity or system of cavities in the interior of the vertebrate central nervous system comprising the central canal of the spinal cord and the ventricles of the brain — **neu·ro·coe·li·an** \¦==¦sēlēən\ *adj*
**neu·ro·cranium** \¦== *at* NEURO- +\ *n* [NL, fr. *neur-* + *cranium*] **:** the portion of the skull that encloses and protects the brain — compare BRANCHIOCRANIUM, SPLANCHNOCRANIUM
**neu·ro·crine** \ˈn(y)ürəkrən; -ˌkrin, -rīn, -rēn\ *adj* [*neur-* + *endocrine*] **:** of, relating to, or being a hormonal substance that influences the activity of the nerves ⟨~ synaptic transmission⟩ — **neu·ro·crin·ism** \-ˌkrəˌnizəm, -ˌkrī-, -ˌkrē-\ *n* -s
**neu·ro·cutaneous** \¦== *at* NEURO- +\ *adj* [*neur-* + *cutaneous*] **:** of, relating to, or affecting the skin and nerves ⟨~ syndrome⟩
**neu·ro·cyte** \ˈn(y)ürəˌsīt\ *n* [*neur-* + *-cyte*] **:** the cell body of a neuron; *broadly* **:** NEURON
**neu·ro·cy·to·ma** \ˌ== *at* NEURO- + ˌsīˈtōmə\ *n, pl* **neurocytomas** \-məz\ *or* **neurocytoma·ta** \-məd·ə\ [NL, fr. *neur-* + *cyt-* + *-oma*] **:** any of various tumors of nerve tissue arising in the central or sympathetic nervous system
**neu·ro·dendrite** \¦== *at* NEURO- +\ *or* **neu·ro·dendron** \"+\ *n* [*neurodendrite* fr. *neur-* + *dendrite*; *neurodendron*, NL, fr. *neur-* + *-dendron*] **:** DENDRITE 3
**neu·ro·dermatitic** \"+\ *adj* [NL *neurodermatitis* + E *-ic*] **:** of, relating to, or exhibiting neurodermatitis
**neu·ro·dermatitis** \"+\ *n* [NL, fr. *neur-* + *dermatitis*] **:** a chronic allergic disorder of the skin characterized by patches of an itching lichenoid eruption and occurring esp. in persons of nervous and emotional instability
**neu·ro·ectoderm** \"+\ *n* [*neur-* + *ectoderm*] **:** embryonic ectoderm destined to give rise to nervous tissue — **neu·ro·ectodermal** \"+\ *adj*
**neu·ro·effector** \"+\ *adj* [*neur-* + *effector*] **:** of, relating to, or involving both neural and effector components
**neu·ro·endocrine** \"+\ *adj* [*neur-* + *endocrine*] **:** NEUROCRINE
**neu·ro·epidermal** \"+\ *adj* [*neur-* + *epidermal*] **:** relating or giving rise to the central nervous system and epidermis
**neu·ro·epithelial** \"+\ *adj* **1** [NL *neuroepithelium* + E *-al*] **:** of or relating to neuroepithelium **2** [*neur-* + *epithelial*] *of a cell* **:** having qualities of both neural and epithelial cells
**neu·ro·epithelium** \"+\ *n* [NL, fr. *neur-* + *epithelium*] **1 :** the part of the embryonic ectoderm that gives rise to the nervous system **2 :** the modified epithelium of an organ of special sense
**neu·ro·fibril** \"+\ *n* [NL *neurofibrilla*] **:** one of a system of many minute fibrils in a neuron believed by some to be conducting elements
**neu·ro·fibrilla** \"+\ *n* [NL, fr. *neur-* + *fibrilla*] **:** NEUROFIBRIL
**neu·ro·fibrillary** \"+\ *adj* [NL *neurofibrilla* + E *-ary*] **:** of or relating to neurofibrils ⟨~ network⟩
**neu·ro·fibroma** \"+\ *n* [NL, fr. *neur-* + *fibroma*] **:** a fibroma originating in the fibrous tissue of a nerve sheath
**neu·ro·fibromatosis** \"+\ *n* [NL, fr. *neurofibromat-*, *neurofibroma* + *-osis*] **:** a condition marked by the presence of many neurofibromas chiefly in the subcutaneous tissues
**neu·ro·formative system** \"+-\ *n* [*neur-* + *formative*] **:** NEUROMOTOR SYSTEM
**neu·ro·gen** \ˈn(y)ürəjən, -ˌjen\ *n* -s [*neur-* + *-gen*] **:** a hypothetical specific primary organizer that induces formation of neural structures in an embryo
**neu·ro·gen·ic** \¦==¦jenik\ *adj* [*neur-* + *-genic*] **1 a :** originating in nervous tissue ⟨a ~ tumor⟩ **b :** induced, controlled, or modified by nervous factors ⟨~ intestinal lesions⟩ ⟨a ~ suckling reflex⟩; *esp* **:** disordered because of abnormally altered neural relations ⟨the ~ kidney⟩ **2 a :** constituting the neural component of a bodily process ⟨~ factors in disease⟩ **b** *of cardiac muscular contraction* **:** taking place or viewed as

taking place in ordered rhythmic fashion under the control of a net of nerve cells scattered in the cardiac muscle — compare MYOGENIC 2 — **neu·ro·gen·i·cal·ly** \-nək(ə)lē\ *adv*

**neu·rog·e·nous** \(ˈ)n(y)u̇ˈräjənəs\ *adj* [*neur-* + *-genous*] : NEUROGENIC

**neu·ro·glandular** \ˌ==+ *at* NEURO- +\ *adj* [*neur-* + *glandular*] **1** : of or relating to a gland with its nerves and their nerve centers **2** : having the properties of both nervous and glandular tissue ⟨the pituitary body is ~⟩

**neu·rog·lia** \n(y)u̇ˈräglēə; ˌn(y)u̇rəˈglīə, -lēə\ *n* -s [NL, fr. *neur-* + MGk *glia* glue — more at CLAY] : sustentacular tissue that fills the interstices and supports the essential elements of nervous tissue esp. in the brain, spinal cord, and ganglia, is of ectodermal origin, and is composed of a network of fine fibrils and of flattened stellate cells with numerous radiating fibrillar processes — compare MICROGLIA — **neu·rog·li·al** \(ˈ)n(y)u̇ˈräglēəl\ *or* **neu·rog·li·ar** \-ə(r)\ *adj*

**neu·rog·li·o·ma** \n(y)u̇ˌrägliˈōmə\ *n* [NL, fr. *neuroglia* + *-oma*] : a tumor developed from neuroglia cells : GLIOMA

**neu·rog·li·o·sis** \-ˈōsəs\ *n, pl* **neuroglio·ses** \-ˌsēz\ [NL, fr. *neuroglia* + *-osis*] : a condition marked by the development of multiple neurogliomas throughout the nervous system

**neu·ro·gram** \ˈn(y)u̇rəˌgram\ *n* [*neur-* + *-gram*] : the postulated modified neural structure resulting from activity and serving to retain whatever has been learned : a neural engram — **neu·ro·gram·mic** \ˌ==ˈgramik\ *adj*

**neu·ro·graphic** \ˌ==+\ *adj* : of or relating to neurography

**neu·rog·ra·phy** \n(y)u̇ˈrägrəfē\ *n* -ES **1** [NL *neurographia*, fr. *neur-* + *-graphia* -graphy] : a description of the nervous system **2** [*neur-* + *-graphy*] **a** : the postulated formation of neurograms **b** : the postulated system of engrams present in an individual's brain

**neu·ro·hormonal** \ˌ== *at* NEURO- +\ *adj* [*neur-* + *hormonal*] : involving both neural and hormonal mechanisms ⟨~ factors in certain forms of heart disease⟩

**neu·ro·hormone** \"+\ *n* [ISV *neur-* + *hormone*] : a hormone produced by or acting on nervous tissue

**neu·ro·humor** \"+\ *n* [*neur-* + *humor*] : a substance liberated at a nerve ending that participates in the transmission of a nerve impulse

**neu·ro·humoral** \"+\ *adj* : of or relating to neurohumors

**neurohumoral theory** *n* : a theory in physiology: transmission of nerve impulses are due to chemical mechanisms — compare CHEMICAL MEDIATION THEORY

**neu·ro·hypnotic** \"+\ *adj* : HYPNOTIC 2

**neu·ro·hypnotism** \"+\ *n* [*neur-* + [1]*hypnotic* (soporific) + *-ism*] : HYPNOTISM

**neu·ro·hypophysis** \"+\ *n* [NL, fr. *neur-* + *hypophysis*] : the portion of the pituitary body derived from the embryonic brain and made up of the infundibulum and of the posterior lobe which is associated with the secretion of various hormones (as one regulating the renal mechanism that controls the salt and water balance of the body) — compare ADENOHYPOPHYSIS

**neu·roid** \ˈn(y)u̇ˌrȯid, ˈn(y)u̇ˌ-\ *adj* [*neur-* + *-oid*] **1** : resembling a nerve or nerve tissue **2** : of or relating to the transmission of excitation through tissues without nerve fibers

**neu·ro·keratin** \ˌ== *at* NEURO- +\ *n* [ISV *neur-* + *keratin*] : a pseudokeratin present in nerve tissue (as in the sheath of the axis cylinder of medullated nerve fibers)

**neu·ro·kyme** \ˈn(y)u̇rəˌkīm\ *n* -s [*neur-* + Gk *kyma* wave — more at CYME] : the kinetic energy of neural activity

**neurolemma** *var of* NEURILEMMA

**neu·ro·log·i·cal** \ˌn(y)u̇rəˈläjəkəl, -jēk-\ *or* **neu·ro·log·ic** \-jik, -jēk\ *adj* [*neurology* + *-ical* or *-ic*] : of or relating to neurology ⟨combined with the study of basic ~ sciences —*Jour. Amer. Med. Assoc.*⟩

**neu·rol·o·gist** \n(y)u̇ˈräləjəst, n(y)əˈ-\ *n* -s : one specializing in neurology; *esp* : a physician skilled in the diagnosis and treatment of disease of the nervous system — distinguished from *psychiatrist*

**neu·rol·o·gize** \-ˌjīz\ *vt* -ED/-ING/-S [*neurology* + *-ize*] : to attempt an explanation of behavioral phenomena in neural terms

**neu·rol·o·gy** \-ˌjē, -ji\ *n* -ES [NL *neurologia*, fr. Gk *neuro-* nerve, sinew (fr. *neuron*) + NL *-logia* -logy — more at NERVE] : the scientific study of the nervous system esp. in respect to its structure, functions, and abnormalities

**neu·ro·lymphomatosis** \ˌ== *at* NEURO- +\ *n* [NL, fr. *neur-* + *lymphomatosis*] : a disease of the avian leukosis complex that is marked by mononuclear cell infiltration of peripheral nerves esp. of the legs and wings of chickens approaching maturity, that results in flaccid paralysis, and that is sometimes held due to a specific virus infection — called also *fowl paralysis, range paralysis*

**neu·rol·y·sis** \=ˈräləsəs\ *n* [NL, fr. *neur-* + *-lysis*] **1** : the breaking down of nerve substance (as from disease or exhaustion) **2** : the operation of freeing a nerve from adhesions

**neu·ro·lyt·ic** \ˌn(y)u̇rəˈlid·ik\ *adj* [fr. NL *neurolysis*, after such pairs as NL *histolysis*: E *histolytic*] : of, relating to, or causing neurolysis

**neu·ro·ma** \n(y)u̇ˈrōmə\ *n, pl* **neuro·mas** \-məz\ *or* **neuro·ma·ta** \-məd·ə\ [NL, fr. *neur-* + *-oma*] **1** : a tumor or mass growing from a nerve and usu. consisting of nerve fibers **2** : a mass of nerve tissue in an amputation stump resulting from abnormal regrowth of the stumps of severed nerves — called also *amputation neuroma, pseudoneuroma*

**neu·ro·mast** \ˈn(y)u̇rəˌmast\ *n* -s [*neur-* + Gk *mastos* hillock, breast — more at MEAT] : one of the characteristic sensory organs of the lateral lines of fishes and various other lower vertebrates consisting of a cluster of sensory cells connected with nerve fibers — **neu·ro·mas·tic** \ˌ==ˈmastik\ *adj*

**neu·ro·mere** \ˈn(y)u̇rəˌmi(ə)r\ *n* -s [*neur-* + *-mere*] **1** : a metameric segment of the vertebrate nervous system ⟨the ~s of the spinal cord are identified by the exits of the spinal nerves⟩ **2** : a primitive nerve ganglion of an invertebrate

**neu·rom·er·ism** \n(y)u̇ˈräməˌrizəm\ *n* -s : metamerism of the nervous system

**neu·ro·motor** \ˌ== *at* NEURO- +\ *adj* [*neur-* + *motor*] : relating to efferent nervous impulses

**neu·ro·motorium** \"+\ *n* [NL, fr. *neur-* + *motorium*] : NEUROMOTOR SYSTEM

**neuromotor system** *also* **neuromotor apparatus** *n* : a system of noncontractile cytoplasmic fibrils that is often associated with a motorium in various protozoans and may be analogous to the nervous system of higher forms

**neu·ro·muscular** \ˌ== *at* NEURO- +\ *adj* [ISV *neur-* + *muscular*] : of, relating to, or involving both nerves and muscles or nervous and muscular tissue

**neuromuscular spindle** *n* : MUSCLE SPINDLE

**neu·ro·my·al** \ˌ== *at* NEURO- + ˈmīəl\ *also* **neu·ro·my·ic** \-īik\ *adj* [*neur-* + *my-* + *-al* or *-ic*] : NEUROMUSCULAR

**neu·ro·myelitis** \"+\ *n* [NL, fr. *neur-* + *myelitis*] **1** : inflammation of the medullary substance of the nerves **2** : inflammation of both spinal cord and nerves

**neu·ron** \ˈn(y)u̇ˌrän, ˈn(y)u̇ˌ-\ *also* **neu·rone** \-ˌrōn\ *n* -s [NL *neuron*, fr. Gk, nerve, sinew — more at NERVE] **1** *archaic* : the brain and spinal cord **2** : a nerve cell esp. with all its processes — **neu·ro·nal** \ˈn(y)u̇rənəl, (ˈ)n(y)u̇ˈrōnᵊl\ *or* **neu·ron·ic** \(ˈ)n(y)u̇ˈränik\ *adj*

**neuron doctrine** *or* **neuron theory** *n* : a theory in anatomy and physiology: the nervous system is composed of nerve cells each of which is a structural unit in contact with other units but not in continuity, a genetic unit derived from a single embryonic neuroblast, a functional unit or unit of conduction with the nervous pathways being chains of such units, and a trophic unit with the nerve processes degenerating when severed from the cell body and being replaced by outgrowths from the cell body

**neu·ro·neuronal** \ˌ== *at* NEURO- +\ *adj* [*neur-* + *neuronal*] : between nerve cells or nerve fibers ⟨~ synapses⟩

**neu·ron·ism** \ˈn(y)u̇rəˌnizəm\ *n* -s [NL *neuron* + E *-ism*] : a theory in psychology that stresses the brain neurons as the vehicles of mental processes

**neu·ron·ist** \-ˌnəst\ *n* -s : one who accepts neuronism

**neu·ron·i·tis** \ˌn(y)u̇rəˈnīd·əs, -ītəs\ *n* -ES [NL, fr. *neuron* + *-itis*] : inflammation of neurons; *esp* : neuritis involving nerve roots and nerve cells within the spinal cord

**neu·ro·no·pha·gia** \n(y)u̇rəˌrōnōˈfājēə\ *also* **neu·ro·noph·a·gy** \ˌn(y)u̇rəˈnäfəjē\ *n, pl* **neuronophagias** *also* **neuronophagies** [*neuronophagia*, NL, fr. *neuron* + *-o-* + *-phagia*; *neuronophagy*, ISV, fr. NL *neuron* + *-o-* + ISV *-phagy*] : destruction of neurons by phagocytic cells

**neu·ro·path** \ˈn(y)u̇rəˌpath\ *n* -s [*neur-* + *-path*] : a person subject to nervous disorders or to neuroses

**neu·ro·path·ic** \ˌ==ˈpathik -thēk\ *adj* [*neur-* + *-pathic*] : of or relating to neuropathy : being or having nervous disease — **neu·ro·path·i·cal·ly** \-thək(ə)lē -thēk, -li\ *adv*

**neu·ro·pathologic** \ˌ== *at* NEURO- +\ *or* **neu·ro·pathological** \"+\ *adj* [*neuropathology* + *-ic* or *-ical*] : of, relating to, or involving neuropathology

**neu·ro·pathologist** \"+\ *n* : a specialist in neuropathology

**neu·ro·pathology** \"+\ *n* [ISV *neur-* + *pathology*] : pathology of the nervous system

**neu·rop·a·thy** \n(y)u̇ˈräpəthē, n(y)əˈ-\ *n* -ES [ISV *neur-* + *-pathy*] : any of various abnormal states of the nervous system or nerves esp. when involving degenerative changes; *also* : a systemic condition (as muscular atrophy) that stems from a primary degeneration of the nervous system

**neu·ro·phile** \ˈn(y)u̇rəˌfīl\ *or* **neu·ro·phil·ic** \ˌ==ˈfilik\ *adj* [*neurophile*, ISV *neur-* + *-phile*; *neurophilic* fr. *neur-* + *-philic*] : NEUROTROPIC

**neu·ro·physiologic** \ˌ== *at* NEURO- +\ *or* **neu·ro·physiological** \"+\ *adj* [*neur-* + *physiologic* or *physiological*] : of or relating to neurophysiology

**neu·ro·physiologist** \"+\ *n* : a specialist in neurophysiology

**neu·ro·physiology** \"+\ *n* [ISV *neur-* + *physiology*] : physiology of the nervous system

**neu·ro·pil** \ˈn(y)u̇rəˌpil\ *also* **neu·ro·pile** \-ˌpīl\ *n* -s [ISV *neur-* + *-pil*, *-pile* (fr. Gk *pilos* felt) — more at PILE (hair)] **1** : a feltwork of delicate unmyelinated nerve fibers interrupted by numerous synapses and found in concentrations of nervous tissue esp. throughout the vertebrate central nervous system and esp. in parts of the brain where it is highly developed and constitutes with interspersion of myelinated fibers the reticular formations **2** : a delicate terminal branch of a nerve fiber — **neu·ro·pi·lar** \ˌ==ˈpīlə(r)\ *adj*

**neu·ro·plasm** \ˈ==ˌplazəm\ *n* [*neur-* + *-plasm*] : the ground cytoplasm of a nerve cell — contrasted with *neurofibril* — **neu·ro·plasmatic** \ˌ==+\ *or* **neu·ro·plasmic** \"+\ *adj*

**neu·ro·po·di·al** \ˌn(y)u̇rəˈpōdēəl\ *adj* [NL *neuropodium* + E *-al*] : of or relating to a neuropodium

**neu·ro·po·di·um** \ˌ==ˈdēəm\ *n, pl* **neuropo·dia** \-ēə\ [NL, fr. *neur-* + *-podium*] **1** : one of the delicate terminal branches of an axon **2** *also* **neu·ro·pod** \ˈ==ˌpäd\ : the ventral lobe of a parapodium

**neu·rop·o·dous** \n(y)u̇ˈräpədəs\ *adj* [*neur-* + *-podous*] : having ventrally directed limbs or limbs with neuropodia — used of certain annelid worms

**neu·ro·pore** \ˈn(y)u̇rəˌpō(ə)r\ *n* [*neur-* + *pore*] : an opening from the exterior into the neurocoele

**neu·ro·psychiatric** \ˌ== *at* NEURO- +\ *adj* [*neur* + *psychiatric*] : of or relating to neuropsychiatry

**neu·ro·psychiatrist** \"+\ *n* : a specialist in neuropsychiatry

**neu·ro·psychiatry** \"+\ *n* [*neur-* + *psychiatry*] **1** : a combined field of neurology and psychiatry **2** : psychiatry that is an outgrowth of or a branch of neurology

**neu·ro·psychological** \"+\ *adj* [*neur-* + *psychological*] : of or relating to neuropsychology

**neu·ro·psychologist** \"+\ *n* [*neur-* + *psychologist*] : a specialist in neuropsychology

**neu·ro·psychology** \"+\ *n* [*neur-* + *psychology*] : a science that attempts to correlate psychological and neurological facts

**neu·rop·ter** \n(y)u̇ˈräptə(r)\ *n* -s [NL *Neuroptera*] : NEUROPTERON

**neu·rop·tera** \-tərə\ *n pl, cap* [NL, fr. *neur-* + *-ptera*] : an order of usu. net-winged insects that have holometabolous development and that include the lacewings, ant lions, and related insects — see MEGALOPTERA — **neu·rop·ter·an** \(ˈ)==ˈ==tərən\ *adj or n* — **neu·rop·ter·ous** \-rəs\ *adj*

**neu·rop·ter·is** \=ˈ==tərəs\ *n, cap* [NL, fr. *neur-* + *-pteris*] : a genus of fossil seed ferns represented by abundant fronds and stems from the Devonian to the Triassic

**neu·rop·ter·ist** \-rəst\ *n* -s [NL *Neuroptera* + E *-ist*] : a student of the neuropterous insects

[1]**neu·rop·ter·oid** \(ˈ)=ˈ==ˌrȯid\ *adj* [NL *Neuroptera* + E *-oid*] : resembling or related to the Neuroptera

[2]**neuropteroid** \"\ *n* -s [NL *Neuropteroidea*] : an insect of the superorder Neuropteroidea

**neu·rop·ter·oi·dea** \=ˌ==ˈrȯidēə\ *n pl, cap* [NL, fr. *Neuroptera*, order of insects + *-oidea*] : a superorder of insects including the orders Neuroptera, Mecoptera, Trichoptera, Lepidoptera, Diptera, and Siphonaptera

**neu·rop·ter·ol·o·gy** \-ˈräləjē\ *n* -ES [NL *Neuroptera* + E *-o-* + *-logy*] : a branch of entomology dealing with the Neuroptera

**neu·rop·ter·on** \=ˈ==ˌrän\ *n* -s [NL, sing. of *Neuroptera*] : an insect of the order Neuroptera

**neu·ro·retinitis** \ˌ== *at* NEURO- +\ *n* [NL, fr. *neur-* + *retinitis*] : inflammation of the optic nerve and the retina

**neu·ro·secretion** \"+\ *n* [ISV *neur-* + *secretion*] **1** : a secretion produced by nerve cells **2** : the act or process of producing a neurosecretion

**neu·ro·secretory** \"+\ *adj* : relating to or promoting neurosecretion

**neu·ro·sis** \n(y)u̇ˈrōsəs, n(y)əˈ-\ *n, pl* **neuro·ses** \-ˌsēz\ [NL, fr. *neur-* + *-osis*] **1** : a functional disorder of the central nervous system usu. manifested by anxiety, phobias, obsessions, or compulsions but frequently displaying signs of somatic disorder involving any of the bodily systems with or without other subjective or behavioral manifestations and having its most probable etiology in intrapsychic or interpersonal conflict ⟨somatic changes such as induced by drugs or by fatigue may act as precipitating, and constitutional factors as predisposing, influences in ~⟩ ⟨it is the feeling of isolation, of being shut out, which is the painful sting of every ~ —Erich Fromm⟩ ⟨a ~ or a neurotic fantasy always relates to a reality, and a neurotic expression of a reality is likely to have more force than a "normal" one —Lionel Trilling⟩ **2** : individual or group behavior that is characterized by rigid adherence to an idealized concept of the personal or social organism esp. when that concept is significantly at variance with reality and that results in interpersonal, cultural, or political conflict and in the development of discomforting intraorganismal tensions ⟨the atmosphere of conformity, induced by our present ~⟩

**neu·ro·some** \ˈn(y)u̇rəˌsōm\ *n* -s [ISV *neur-* + *-some* (body)] **1** : the cell body of a neuron **2** : one of various small particles in the cytoplasm of a neuron

**neu·ro·spon·gi·um** \ˌn(y)u̇rəˈspənjēəm, -ˈspän-\ *n, pl* **neu·rospon·gia** \-ēə\ [NL, fr. *neur-* + *-spongium*] **1** : a network of fibrils in the cytoplasm of a nerve cell **2** : the inner reticular stratum of the retina

**neu·ros·po·ra** \n(y)u̇ˈräspərə\ *n, cap* [NL, fr. *neur-* + *-spora*] : a genus of ascomycetous fungi (family Sphaeriaceae) used extensively in genetic research, having black perithecia and persistent asci, and including some forms that have salmon pink or orange spore masses and cause severe damage in bakeries

**neu·ro·surgeon** \ˌ== *at* NEURO- +\ *n* [*neur-* + *surgeon*] : a surgeon specializing in neurosurgery

**neu·ro·surgery** \"+\ *n* [*neur-* + *surgery*] : surgery of the brain, spinal cord, nerves, or other nervous structures

**neu·ro·surgical** \"+\ *adj* [*neur-* + *surgical*] : of, relating to, or performed by means of neurosurgery

**neu·ro·syphilis** \"+\ *n* [NL, fr. *neur-* + *syphilis*] : syphilis of the central nervous system

**neu·ro·tendinous** \"+\ *adj* [*neur-* + *tendinous*] : of or relating to a nerve and tendon; *esp* : being any of various nerve endings in tendons

[1]**neu·rot·ic** \(ˈ)n(y)u̇ˈräd·ik, n(y)əˈr-, -ätik, -ēk\ *n* -s [Gk *neur-* nerve, sinew (fr. *neuron*) + E *-otic* (as in *narcotic*, n.) — more at NERVE] **1** *archaic* : a drug acting esp. noxiously on the nervous system **2** [[2]*neurotic*] : an emotionally unstable individual or one affected with a neurosis

[2]**neurotic** \"\ *adj* [fr. NL *neurosis*, after such pairs as NL *narcosis*: E *narcotic*] **1 a** : of or relating to the nerves : seated in the nerves ⟨a ~ disorder⟩ **b** : being a neurosis : NERVOUS ⟨a ~ disease⟩ **2 a** : affected with, relating to, or characterized by neurosis ⟨a ~ person has become estranged from large parts of this world —Karen Horney⟩ **b** : tending to respond to present life situations on the basis of their resemblance to early childhood experiences or on the basis of an idealized concept of the self rather than in terms of the requirements of immediate reality ⟨the very nature of the ~ disorder is tied to pride —G.W.Allport⟩ ⟨the assumption that the ~ behavior as observed in animals is the counterpart of that observed in man —*Diseases of the Nervous System*⟩

**neu·rot·i·cal·ly** \-ək(ə)lē, -ēk-, -li\ *adv* : in a neurotic manner : as a result of or as though affected by neurosis ⟨an embittered pedant, ~ conscious of his personal dignity —*Contemporary Rev.*⟩

**neu·rot·i·cism** \=ˈräd·əˌsizəm, -ätə-\ *n* -s [[2]*neurotic* + *-ism*] : a neurotic condition, character, or trait ⟨imputation of ~ to the intelligentsia as a group —Philip Rahv⟩ ⟨the apparently *normal* world of men and women whose ~s are concealed, even from themselves, by their adherence to fixed behavior patterns —*Tomorrow*⟩

**neu·roto·gen·ic** \n(y)u̇ˌräd·əˈjenik\ *adj* [[1]*neurotic* + *-o-* + *-genic*] : tending to produce neurosis ⟨~ effects⟩

**neu·rot·oid** \=ˈräd·ˌȯid\ *adj* [[1]*neurotic* + *-oid*] : resembling or simulating neurosis ⟨~ behavior⟩

**neu·ro·tome** \ˈn(y)u̇rəˌtōm\ *n* -s [*neur-* + *-tome*] : NEUROMERE

**neu·rot·o·my** \n(y)u̇ˈräd·əmē\ *n* -ES [*neur-* + *-tomy*] **1** : the dissection or cutting of nerves **2** : the division of a nerve (as to relieve neuralgia)

**neu·ro·toxic** \ˌ== *at* NEURO- +\ *adj* [*neur-* + *toxic*] : toxic to the nerves or nervous tissue ⟨~ snake venom⟩ — **neu·ro·toxicity** \"+\ *n*

**neu·ro·toxin** \"+\ *n* [ISV *neur-* + *toxin*] : a poisonous protein complex that is present in various snake venoms and that exerts its principal effect as a nervous system depressant

**neu·ro·trope** \ˈn(y)u̇rəˌtrōp\ *n* -s [prob. fr. F or G; F, adj., neurotropic, fr. G *neurotrop*, fr. *neuro-* neur- + *-trop* -trope] : a neurotropic agent

**neu·ro·troph·ic** \ˌ== *at* NEURO- + ˈträfik, -rōf-\ *adj* [ISV *neur-* + *-trophic*] **1** : relating to or dependent on the influence of nerves on the nutrition of tissue **2** [prob. by alter.] : NEUROTROPIC

**neu·ro·trop·ic** \ˌ==ˈträpik, -rōp-\ *adj* [ISV *neur-* + *-tropic*] **1** : having an affinity for nerve tissue ⟨~ drugs⟩ ⟨~ poisons⟩ ⟨~ stains⟩ **2** : localizing selectively in nerve tissue ⟨~ viruses⟩ ⟨~ infectious agents⟩ — compare ORGANOTROPIC, PANTROPIC

**neu·rot·ro·pism** \n(y)u̇ˈrä·trəˌpizəm\ *n* [ISV *neur-* + *tropism*] : the quality or state of being neurotropic

**neu·ro·tubule** \ˌ== *at* NEURO- +\ *n* [*neur-* + *tubule*] : one of the tubular elements sometimes considered to be a fundamental part of the nerve-cell axon

**neu·ro·vascular** \"+\ *adj* [*neur-* + *vascular*] : of, relating to, or involving both nerves and blood vessels

**neu·ro·vegetative** \"+\ *adj* [*neur-* + *vegetative*] : SYMPATHETIC 6

**neu·ru·la** \ˈn(y)u̇rələ\ *n, pl* **neuru·las** \-ləz\ *or* **neuru·lae** \-ˌlē, -ˌlī\ [NL, fr. *neur-* + *-ula*] **1** : an early embryo consisting of an elongated gastrula in which nervous tissue is beginning to differentiate **2** : the stage of embryonic development at which neural tissue is beginning to differentiate and in which the neural tube is formed — **neu·ru·lar** \-lə(r)\ *adj* — **neu·ru·la·tion** \ˌ==ˈlāshən\ *n* -s

**neu·si·ok** \ˈn(y)üsēˌäk\ *n, pl* **neusiok** *or* **neusioks** *usu cap* **1** : an Indian people of uncertain linguistic affiliation south of the lower Neuse river in No. Carolina **2** : a member of the Neusiok people

**neus·tic** \ˈn(y)üstik\ *or* **neus·ton·ic** \(ˈ)=ˈstänik\ *adj* [*neustic*, ISV *neuston* + *-ic*; prob. orig. formed as G *neustisch*; *neustonic* fr. *neuston* + *-ic*] : of, relating to, or being neuston

**neus·ton** \ˈn(y)üˌstän\ *n* -s [G, fr. Gk, neut. of *neustos* swimming, verbal of *nein* to swim; akin to L *nutrire* to nourish — more at NOURISH] : minute organisms that float in the surface film of water

[1]**neus·tri·an** \ˈn(y)üstrēən\ *adj, usu cap* [ML *Neustria*, northwestern portion of the Frankish empire + E *-an*] **1** : of, relating to, or characteristic of Neustria, the northwestern portion of the Frankish empire including most of the territory between the Loire and the Scheldt **2** : of, relating to, or characteristic of the people of Neustria

[2]**neustrian** \"\ *n* -s *cap* : a native or inhabitant of Neustria

**neut** *abbr* **1** neuter **2** neutral

[1]**neu·ter** \ˈn(y)üd·ə(r), -ütə-\ *adj* [ME *neutre*, fr. MF & L; MF *neutre*, fr. L *neuter*, fr. *ne-* (negative prefix) + *uter* which of two — more at NO, WHETHER] **1 a** : belonging to, connected with, or constituting the gender that ordinarily includes most words or grammatical forms referring characteristically to things that are neither masculine nor feminine ⟨a ~ noun⟩ ⟨the ~ gender⟩ ⟨a ~ ending⟩ **b** : neither active nor passive : INTRANSITIVE; *also* : restricted to mere existence or state — used of verbs and verb forms **2** : taking no side : free from marked bias or partiality : NEUTRAL ⟨the man who stands ~ is considered an offender with him who lifts his hand against his captain —C.B.Nordhoff & J.N.Hall⟩ **3** : belonging to neither of two usu. opposed classes **4 a** : having no generative organs : SEXLESS **b** : having imperfectly developed or nonfunctional generative organs either permanently or seasonally ⟨the worker bee is ~⟩ — **neu·ter·ly** *adv* — **neu·ter·ness** *n* -ES

[2]**neuter** \"\ *n* -s **1 a** : a noun, pronoun, adjective, or inflectional form or class of the neuter gender **b** : the neuter gender **2 a** : one that is neutral **b** *usu cap* : NEUTRAL 1b **3 a** : an imperfectly developed female of various social insects (as ants and honeybees) that performs labors of the community : WORKER **b** : a spayed or castrated animal (as a cat)

[3]**neuter** \"\ *vt* -ED/-ING/-S : CASTRATE, ALTER

[1]**neu·tral** \ˈn(y)ü·trəl\ *adj* [MF, fr. (assumed) ML *neutralis*, fr. L, of neuter gender, fr. *neutr-*, *neuter* neuter + *-alis* -al] **1 a** : not engaged on either side : not siding with or assisting either of two or more contending parties **b** *of a state or power* : lending no active assistance to either or any belligerent **2** : of or belonging to a neutral state or power : not involved in hostilities ⟨~ territory⟩ **3 a** : being neither one thing nor the other : belonging to neither of two usu. opposed or contrasted classes : not decided or pronounced as to characteristics : MIDDLING, INDIFFERENT ⟨a ~ character without marked virtues or vices⟩ **b** (1) : totally lacking in saturation : ACHROMATIC, HUELESS (2) : not decided in color : nearly achromatic : of low saturation **c** (1) : NEUTER 4 (2) : lacking stamens or pistils **d** (1) : neither acid nor basic : neither acid nor alkaline; *specif* : having a pH value of 7.0 ⟨a ~ solution contains both hydrogen ions and hydroxide ions at the same concentration, 1.00x10⁻⁷ —Linus Pauling⟩ (2) : NORMAL 10c ⟨a ~ salt⟩ (3) : neither degressive nor progressive ⟨~ burning of propellants in which the total surface remains nearly constant⟩ **e** (1) : not electrically charged ⟨a ~ particle⟩ (2) : being at an arbitrary zero of electrical potential (3) : being at a potential midway between extremes **f** : being the position in which a propelling mechanism although itself revolving freely transmits no motion to the parts to be driven **g** (1) : neither distinctively physical nor distinctively mental ⟨~ stuff⟩ ⟨~ entities⟩ (2) : common to the knowing mind and the object known **h** : being neither milk nor meat nor prepared with dairy products or meat derivatives : PAREVE **i** *usu cap* : TRANSITION **4 a** (1) *of the tongue or lips* : being in a rest position intermediate between extreme positions to which movable (2) *of the tongue* : lying low in the mouth and having no effort-produced arching ⟨the ~ articulation of either vowel of \əˈbəv\ *above*⟩ (3) *of the lips* : open and with the corners of the mouth neither closely approximated nor widely separated ⟨the ~ articulation of the vowel of *hut* or *art*⟩ **b** *of a vowel* : produced with the tongue in a position of rest : having brief duration : not of strongly defined or readily perceptible quality : UNSTRESSED ⟨either ~ vowel of \əˈbəv\ *above*⟩ ⟨the ~ vowel schwa⟩ — **neu·tral·ly** \-rəlē, -li\ *adv* — **neu·tral·ness** \-lnəs\ *n* -ES

[2]**neutral** \"\ *n* -s **1 a** : a person, party, ship, or nation that takes or belongs to one who takes no part in a contest between others : one that exhibits neutrality **b** *usu cap* (1) **neutrals** *pl* : an Iroquoian people of the region about Lake Erie in Canada and the U.S. (2) a member of such people **2** : a neutral color **3** : a neutral substance: as **a** : NEUTRAL LARD **b** : NEUTRAL OIL 2 **4 a** : an electrically neutral point, wire, conductor, bus bar, or other element **b** : a neutral position of driving and driven parts of a machine : a position of disengagement (as of gears from the motive power) ⟨when the transmission is in ~, it means simply that the flow of power is

cut off in the transmission so that rotation of the clutch shaft is not transmitted to the main shaft —Joseph Heitner⟩
**neutral axis** *n* **:** the line in a beam or other member subjected to a bending action in which the fibers are neither stretched nor compressed or where the longitudinal stress is zero
**neutral brandy** *n* **:** brandy of 170 proof or over but of less than 190 proof used chiefly for fortifying wines or as a base for various fruit-flavored brandies — compare NEUTRAL SPIRITS
**neutral conductor** *n* **:** the intermediate conductor in a three-wire electrical system usu. grounded or maintained at zero potential
**neutral corner** *n* **:** either of the two diagonally opposite corners of a boxing ring that are not appropriated to one or the other of the contestants
**neutral dye** *n* **1 :** a dye capable of dyeing fibers (as cotton) directly in a neutral or faintly alkaline bath **2 :** a salt formed by interaction of an acid dye (as eosin) and a basic dye (as methylene blue) — called also *neutral stain*
**neutral flame** *n* **:** a flame resulting from the burning of gases supplied in the proper proportions for perfect combustion (as approximately equal volumes of acetylene and oxygen)
**neutral gray** *n* **:** GRAY 3a
**neutral gray G** *n* **:** a direct dye — see DYE table I (under *Direct Black 3*)
**neu·tral·ism** \ˈn(y)ütrəˌlizəm\ *n* -s [ˈ*neutral* + *-ism*] **1 a :** NEUTRALITY **b :** a policy or the advocacy of neutrality esp. in international affairs (as with respect to a conflict between world powers) **c :** the practice or an attitude of neutrality; *also* **:** the expression of neutral sentiments **2 :** NEUTRAL MONISM
**neu·tral·ist** \-ləst\ *n* -s **1 :** a professor or practicer of neutrality **2 :** one that favors the neutralization of a state or region — **neu·tral·is·tic** \¦==¦listik\ *adj*
**neu·tral·i·ty** \n(y)üˈtraləd·ē, -ətē, -i\ *n* -ES [MF or ML; MF *neutralité* state or condition of being neutral, fr. ML *neutralitat-, neutralitas*, fr. (assumed) ML *neutralis* neutral + L *-itat-, -itas* -ity — more at NEUTRAL] **1** *archaic* **:** a party that is neutral **:** a combination of neutral powers or states — used with *the;* see ARMED NEUTRALITY **2 a :** the quality or state of being neutral **:** a condition of being uninvolved in contests or controversies between others or of refraining from taking part on either side of such contest or controversy **b :** the condition of a state or government that refrains from taking part directly or indirectly in a war between other powers **c :** a condition of immunity from invasion or use by belligerents in the course of operations against each other that is sometimes guaranteed by treaty (as to a nation or of a waterway) **3 :** the particular character conveyed to something belonging to a state (as a citizen or place) by the maintenance of neutrality by that state during hostilities ⟨insisted on recognition of the ~ of the port⟩ **4 :** the quality or state of being intermediate, falling between extremes, or belonging to neither one nor the other of two well-defined categories or classes ⟨a solution of perfect ~ is neither acid nor basic⟩ **5 :** the quality or state of being neuter
**neu·tral·i·za·tion** \ˌn(y)ütrələˈzāshən, -ˌlīˈ-\ *n* -s [*neutralize* + *-ation*] **1 :** an act or process of neutralizing **2 :** the quality or state of being neutralized **3 :** the absence in some contexts of a phonetic or grammatical contrast found elsewhere or formerly in a language (as the contrast between final \s\ and \z\ after \t\ in English or between the nominative and accusative neuter case in Latin)
**neutralization number** *also* **neutralization value** *n* **:** a number indicating the degree of acidity or alkalinity of a substance determined by finding the amount of alkali or acid required for neutralization; *specif* **:** the weight in milligrams of potassium hydroxide required to neutralize the acid in one gram of an oil (as a hydrocarbon oil)
**neu·tral·ize** \ˈn(y)ütrəˌlīz\ *vb* -ED/-ING/-S *see -ize in Explan Notes* [ˈ*neutral* + *-ize*] *vt* **1 :** to make chemically neutral ⟨~ an acid with a base⟩ **:** destroy the peculiar properties or effect of ⟨stimulated the adrenals to secrete a hormone that *neutralized* rheumatism —G.W.Gray b. 1886⟩ **2 :** to destroy the peculiar properties or opposite dispositions of **:** reduce to inefficiency **:** counteract the activity or effect of ⟨*neutralized* his effort by a show of force⟩ ⟨*neutralizing* these arguments with consummate skill⟩ **3 :** to make void of electricity or electrically inert by combining equal positive and negative quantities **4 :** to invest (as a country) with conventional or obligatory neutrality conferring inviolability under international law by belligerents **5 :** to reduce or destroy the combat effectiveness of (as an enemy force or an artillery installation) **6 :** to make (a color) neutral by blending with the complement **7 :** to make inoperative (a phonetic or grammatical contrast found elsewhere or formerly) ⟨with many speakers the \t\-\d\ opposition in *latter: ladder* is *neutralized*⟩ ~ *vi* **1 :** to prevent regeneration by inserting a device to balance signal feedback from the output to the input of an electronic device **2 :** to undergo neutralization
**syn** COUNTERACT, NEGATIVE: NEUTRALIZE indicates an equalizing, making ineffectual or inoperative, or nullifying by an opposing force, power, agency, or effect ⟨a quinine that can *neutralize* his venom; it is called courage —Elmer Davis⟩ ⟨*neutralize* the effects of propaganda with counterpropaganda so as to render the international environment favorable —Earl Latham⟩ ⟨our esteem for facts has not *neutralized* in us all religiousness —William James⟩ COUNTERACT may indicate merely neutralizing or counterbalancing; it is often used in situations in which the good and bad or the beneficial and deleterious are opposed ⟨these two principles have often sufficed, even when *counteracted* by great public calamities and by bad institutions, to carry civilization rapidly forward —T.B. Macaulay⟩ ⟨frequently visited the Choctaws, in an effort to *counteract* the influence of the French and to win them to an alliance with the English —W.J.Ghent⟩ NEGATIVE indicates an annulling, contradicting, making futile, useless, or ineffective, or vitiating by an opposing force, effect, or trend ⟨as if the wind might blow it over, thus *negativing* the idea of solidity —Arnold Bennett⟩ ⟨it is only in literature that the paradoxical and even mutually *negativing* anecdotes in the history of a human heart can be juxtaposed and annealed by art into verisimilitude and credibility —William Faulkner⟩
**neu·tral·iz·er** \-zə(r)\ *n* -s **:** one that neutralizes: as **a :** any of various devices that neutralize or eliminate some unwanted or side effect (as static from radio, excess acidity from a solution) **b :** a worker who neutralizes something (as a product of acid hydrolysis by suitable treatment with a base) as his regular work **c :** a worker who cleans metal objects in an acid bath **d :** a chemical solution used to terminate the action of a permanent waving solution **e :** ˈCLOCKER 3
**neutral lard** *n* **:** lard of high quality that is rendered at temperatures not exceeding 131° F from leaf fat or back fat of a hog and is used esp. in the manufacture of oleomargarine
**neutral money** *n* **:** money that functions in such a manner as to leave economic results unchanged from those of a barter economy
**neutral monism** *n* **:** a philosophical monism that takes primordial reality to be neither mind nor matter but something more fundamental than either of these
**neutral oil** *n* **1 :** an oil that is neither acid nor alkaline **2 :** a lubricating oil of low or medium viscosity (as prepared from paraffin-base petroleum without chemical treatment)
**neutral orange** *n* **:** BITTERSWEET ORANGE
**neutral point** *n* **:** the temperature at which the thermoelectric power of two metals is zero and which is midway between the temperature of the cold junction and the corresponding temperature of inversion
**neutral position** *n* **1** *or* **neutral line :** the position of the brushes of a dynamoelectric machine for least sparking **2 :** a position in amateur wrestling in which neither contestant has advantage over his opponent — compare ADVANTAGE POSITION
**neutral red** *n* **1** *sometimes cap N&R* **:** a basic phenazine dye used chiefly as a biological stain and acid-base indicator **2 :** a dark red to purplish red that is lighter and stronger than plum violet or sultana and paler than wild cherry
**neutrals** *pl of* NEUTRAL
**neutral shoreline** *n* **:** a shoreline the major features of which are not a result of either submergence or emergence of the adjacent land
**neutral spirits** *n pl but sing or pl in constr* **:** ethyl alcohol of 190 or higher proof used esp. for blending other alcoholic liquors — compare NEUTRAL BRANDY
**neutral spore** *n* **:** MONOSPORE
**neutral stain** *n* **:** NEUTRAL DYE 2
**neutral tint** *n* **1 :** a gray pigment of various shades used by artists **2 :** a color approximating to gray; *specif* **:** a nearly neutral slightly purplish black that is very slightly bluer and lighter than lamp black or sooty black
**neutral wire** *n* **:** the wire in a three-wire distribution system usu. required to be grounded for safety of both linemen and householders
**neutral zone** *n* **1 :** the position on the armature of a direct-current machine where the magnetic flux from the field poles is zero, being midway between the poles at no load **2 a :** a space between the two lines of scrimmage in American football equivalent to the length of the ball that may not be encroached upon by either team until the ball is put in play **b :** the portion of an ice hockey rink between the attacking and defensive zones — see ICE HOCKEY illustration
**neu·tret·to** \n(y)üˈtred·(ˌ)ō\ *n* -s [*neutron* + It *-etto* (dim. suffix)] **:** a neutral meson
**neu·tri·no** \n(y)üˈtrē(ˌ)nō\ *n* -s [It, fr. *neutrone* neutron (prob. fr. E *neutron*) + *-ino* (dim. suffix)] **:** an uncharged elementary particle that comes in two forms associated respectively with the electron and the muon, that is a lepton with one-half quantum unit of spin and is believed to be massless, and that interacts very weakly with matter after its creation in the process of particle decay
**neutro-** *comb form* [LL, fr. L *neutr-, neuter* of neuter gender — more at NEUTER] **1 :** neutral ⟨*neutro*phile⟩ ⟨*neutro*ceptor⟩ **2 :** neutrophil ⟨*neutro*penia⟩
**neu·tro·cep·tor** \ˌn(y)ütrōˌseptə(r)\ *n* -s [*neutro-* + *receptor*] **:** a receptor for stimuli that are not necessarily either harmful or beneficial — compare NOCICEPTOR
**neu·tro·clu·sion** \¦==¦klüzhən\ *n* -s [*neutro-* + *occlusion*] **:** the condition in which the anteroposterior occlusal relations of the teeth are normal
**neu·tro·cyte** \ˈn(y)ütrəˌsīt\ *n* -s [*neutro-* + *-cyte*] **:** NEUTROPHIL — **neu·tro·cyt·ic** \¦==¦sid·ik\ *adj*
**neu·tron** \ˈn(y)üˌträn\ *n* -s [prob. fr. ˈ*neutral* + *-on*] **:** an uncharged elementary particle that has a mass nearly equal to that of the proton, that by itself is unstable with an average lifetime of 1013 seconds, that can be stabilized when joined to a proton, and that is present in all known atomic nuclei except the lightest hydrogen nucleus
**neu·tro·pe·nia** \ˌn(y)ütrəˈpēnēə\ *n* -s [NL, fr. *neutro-* + *-penia*] **:** leukopenia in which the decrease in white blood cells is chiefly in neutrophils — **neu·tro·pe·nic** \¦==¦nik\ *adj*
**neu·tro·phil** \ˈn(y)ütrəˌfil\ *or* **neu·tro·phile** \-ˌfīl\ *n* -s [*neutrophil* or *neutrophile*, adj.] **:** the chief phagocytic leukocyte of the blood having fine cytoplasmic granules that stain indifferently with the acid or basic dye fraction of common blood stains
**neu·tro·phile** \-ˌfīl\ *also* **neu·tro·phil** \-ˌfil\ *or* **neu·tro·phil·ic** \¦==¦filik\ *adj* [*neutrophile, neutrophil*, ISV *neutro-* + *-phile* or *-phil* (adj. comb. forms); *neutrophilic*, ISV *neutrophi* + E *-ic*] **:** staining indifferently with acid or basic dyes — used chiefly of cells or cell parts
**neu·tro·phil·ia** \-=ˈfilēə\ *n* -s [NL, fr. ISV *neutrophil* + NL *-ia*] **:** leukocytosis in which the increase in white blood cells is chiefly in neutrophils
**neu·tro·phil·ine** \-ˈfiˌlēn, -lən\ *also* **neu·tro·phil·in** \-lən\ *n* -s [*neutrophil* + *-ine* or *-in*] **:** a substance produced by the liver that is believed to stimulate the release of leukocytes from the bone marrow into the circulation
**neu·troph·i·lous** \n(y)üˈträfələs\ *adj* [ISV *neutrophil* (adj.) + E *-ous*] **1 :** NEUTROPHILE **2 :** preferring or thriving in an environment without excess of either acid or base
**neu·wi·der green** \(ˈ)nȯiˌvēdə(r)-\ *n, often cap N* [part trans. of G *neuwieder grün*, fr. *neuwieder* of Neuwied (fr. *Neuwied*, Germany) + G *grün* green] **:** a light yellowish green to green
**neu·wied blue** \(ˈ)nȯiˌvēd-\ *n, often cap N* [fr. *Neuwied*, Germany; prob. trans. of G *neuwieder blau*] **:** BREMEN BLUE
**ne·vada** \nəˈvadə, -ädə, -ādə\ *adj, usu cap* [fr. *Nevada*, state in the western U.S., fr. Sierra *Nevada*, mountain range in Calif., fr. Sp, lit., snow-covered mountain range, fr. *sierra* mountain range + *nevada*, fem. of *nevado* snow-covered, prob. fr. L *nivatus* cooled with snow, fr. *niv-, nix* snow + *-atus* -ate — more at SNOW] **:** of or from the state of Nevada ⟨a *Nevada* mine⟩ **:** of the kind or style prevalent in Nevada **:** NEVADAN
**nevada bluegrass** *n, usu cap N* [*nevada* + *blue grass*] **:** a tall bluegrass (*Poa nevadensis*) of the Mohave desert and adjacent mountain slopes having a large panicle with appressed branches
ˈ**ne·vadan** \nəˈvadᵊn, -äd-, -ād-\ *also* **ne·vadi·an** \-dēən\ *adj, usu cap* [*Nevada* state + E *-an*] **1 :** of, relating to, or characteristic of Nevada or Nevadans **2 :** of or relating to mountain-making movements of the American Mesozoic era — see GEOLOGIC TIME table
²**nevadan** \"\ *also* **nevadian** \"\ *n* -s *cap* **:** a native or resident of the state of Nevada
**ne·va green** \ˈnēvə-\ *n* [*neva* (origin unknown) + *green*] **:** a strong yellow green to brilliant yellowish green
**ne·val** \ˈnēvəl\ *adj* [NL *nevus* + E *-al*] **:** of or relating to a nevus ⟨~ cells⟩
**nevar** *var of* NEWAR
**né·vé** \(ˈ)nāˈvā\ *n* -s [F (Swiss dial.), fr. L *niv-, nix* snow] **:** the partially compacted granular snow that forms the surface part of the upper end of a glacier; *broadly* **:** a field of granular snow — called also *firn*
ˈ**nev·el** *also* **nev·ell** \ˈnevəl\ *vt* **nevelled; nevelled; nevelling; nevels** *also* **nevells** [perh. fr. obs. E *neve* fist (fr. ME) + E *-el* (as in *pommel*) — more at NIEVE] *chiefly Scot* **:** to beat with the fists
²**nevel** *var of* NEBEL
**névé line** *n* **:** a line or zone marking the lower limit of the névé on a glacier
**nev·er** \ˈnevə(r)\ *adv* [ME *never, nevere*, fr. OE *nǣfre*, fr. *ne* not, no + *ǣfre* ever — more at NO, EVER] **1 :** not ever **:** not at any time **:** at no time ⟨~ saw his equal⟩ — often used to form emphatic double negatives ⟨I ~ had no trouble with him before⟩ **2 :** not in any degree **:** not in the least **:** not in any way **:** not under any condition — used in emphatic negation ⟨~ fear⟩ ⟨he had ~ a cent⟩ ⟨~ the wiser for his experience⟩ ⟨answered him to ~ a word —Mt 27:14 (AV)⟩
**neverland** \ˈ==ˌ=\ *n* [short for *never-never land*] **:** NEVER-NEVER 1
**nevermind** \¦==¦=\ *n* [fr. the phrase *never mind*] **:** a serious affair **:** matter of concern **:** strict attention — used in negative constructions ⟨that's no ~ of theirs⟩ ⟨not paying nobody no ~ —Stetson Kennedy⟩
**nevermore** \¦==¦=\ *adv* [ME *nevermore, nevermor, nevermar*, fr. *never* + *more, mor, mar* more] **:** never again **:** at no time hereafter ⟨quoth the raven, "*Nevermore*" —E.A.Poe⟩
**never-never** \¦==¦==\ *n* -s [short for *never-never land*, prob. fr. redupl. of *never* + *land*] **1** *or* **never-never land** *also* **never-never country a** *Austral* **:** sparsely settled country in the northern and western part of Queensland **b :** a remote or sparsely settled region **:** a barren or frontier area **c :** an ideal or imaginary place or region **2 :** an illusory existence **3** [redupl. of *never*] *Brit* **:** a system of installment purchase
**never-say-die** \¦==ˌ=¦=\ *adj* [fr. the phrase *never say die*] **:** INDOMITABLE ⟨a *never-say-die* spirit⟩
**never so** *adv* [ME, fr. OE *nǣfre swā*, fr. *nǣfre* never + *swā* so — more at NEVER, SO] **:** to an exceptional or unheard-of degree or extent **:** ESPECIALLY, PARTICULARLY ⟨though he offered *never so* much money for our help⟩
**nevertheless** \¦==ə¦=\ *adv* [ME *never the lesse*, fr. *never* + *the* (adv.) + *lesse, less* less (adv.)] **:** in spite of that **:** NOTWITHSTANDING **:** YET
**never-was** \¦==ˌ=\ *n, pl* **never-weres** [fr. the phrase *never was*] **:** one that has attained no rank, success, or eminence
**nev·ey** *or* **nev·vy** \ˈnevē, -vi\ *dial var of* NEPHEW
**ne·vile and win·ther's acid** \ˈnāvəl, ˈvintə(r)z-\ *n, usu cap N&W* [after R.H.C. *Nevile*, 19th cent. chemist and Adolph *Winther*, 20th cent. Ger. chemist] **:** a crystalline phenolic sulfonic acid $HOC_{10}H_6SO_3H$ made by sulfonation of alpha-naphthol and used as a dye intermediate; 1-naphthol-4-sulfonic acid
**ne·vo·carcinoma** \¦nēvō+\ *n* [NL, fr. *nevo-* (fr. *nevus*) + *carcinoma*] **:** a carcinoma developing from a nevus
**ne·void** *also* **nae·void** \ˈnēˌvȯid\ *adj* [NL *nevus* or L *naevus* + E *-oid*] **:** resembling a nevus ⟨a ~ tumor⟩ **:** accompanied by nevi or similar superficial lesions ⟨idiocy with ~ lesions⟩
**nev·oy** \ˈnevi\ *Scot var of* NEPHEW
**ne·vus** *also* **nae·vus** \ˈnēvəs\ *n, pl* **ne·vi** *also* **nae·vi** \-ˌvī\ [NL *nevus*, fr. L *naevus*] **:** a congenital pigmented area on the skin **:** BIRTHMARK, MOLE; *esp* **:** a tumor made up chiefly of blood vessels (as dilated arteries, veins, or capillaries) — see BLUE NEVUS
**nev·yansk·ite** \nevˈyan(t)ˌskīt\ *n* -s [G *newjanskit*, fr. *Newjansk* Nevyansk, U.S.S.R. + G *-it* -ite] **:** iridosmine containing over 40 percent of iridium and occurring in tin-white scales
ˈ**new** \ˈn(y)ü; *in geographical names, before a stressed syllable often* ˌn(y)ə (*as in* n(y)əˈyȯ(ə)rk *for* "*New York*") *or* +*V* n(y)əw (*as in* nyəˈwiŋglənd *for* "*New England*")\ *adj* **newer** \ˈn(y)üə(r); -ü(ə)r, -üə\ **newest** \-üəst\ [ME *new, newe*, fr. OE *nīwe, nēowe, nīewe;* akin to MD *nieuwe, niewe, nūe* new, OS & OHG *niuwi*, ON *nȳr*, Goth *niujis*, OIr *nūe*, W *newydd*, L *novus*, Gk *neos*, Skt *nava, navya*, Lith *naujas*, OSlav *novŭ* and prob. to the root of E *now*] **1 :** having existed or having been made but a short time **:** having originated or occurred lately **:** not early or long in being **:** RECENT, FRESH, MODERN — opposed to *old* ⟨a ~ coat⟩ ⟨a ~ regime⟩ ⟨~ fashions⟩ **2 a :** having been seen or known but a short time although perhaps existing before **:** recently manifested, recognized, or experienced **:** NOVEL ⟨a ~ crop for this region⟩; *broadly* **:** STRANGE, UNFAMILIAR ⟨~ doctrines⟩ ⟨~ concepts⟩ ⟨liked to visit ~ places⟩ **b :** being other than the former or old **:** having freshly come into a relation (as use, connection, or function) ⟨turn a ~ leaf⟩ ⟨the ~ teacher⟩ ⟨a ~ product⟩ **c** *of land* **:** undergoing or about to undergo cultivation for the first time ⟨broke 10 acres of ~ ground that winter⟩ **d :** being the first or earliest available of the current season's crop ⟨~ potatoes⟩ ⟨~ peas are sometimes ready by July 4⟩ **3 :** having been in a relationship, position, or condition but a short time and usu. lacking full adaptation thereto ⟨a ~ member⟩ ⟨~ from school⟩ ⟨~ to the plow⟩ **4 a :** beginning or appearing as the recurrence, resumption, or repetition of a previous act or thing ⟨a ~ year⟩ ⟨a ~ start⟩ ⟨a ~ edition⟩ **b :** RENOVATED, RECREATED, REGENERATED ⟨rest had made him a ~ man⟩ **5 :** different or distinguished from a person, place, or thing of the same kind or name that has longer or previously existed ⟨the ~ reservoir⟩ ⟨the ~ theology⟩ **6 a :** not of ancient lineage **:** of a family previously unknown or undistinguished **:** having recently acquired an improved status (as of rank or wealth) ⟨a ~ family⟩ ⟨the ~ rich⟩ **b :** of dissimilar origin and usu. of superior quality to or capable of causing improvement in what preexists ⟨introducing ~ blood into an ancient but outworn line⟩ ⟨try a ~ strain of hybrid corn⟩ **7** *usu cap, of a language* **:** MODERN; *esp* **:** having been in use after medieval times
**syn** NEW, NOVEL, NEWFASHIONED, NEWFANGLED, NEOTERIC, MODERN, MODERNISTIC, ORIGINAL, and FRESH can apply to something very recently come into existence, employment, or recognition. NEW implies that the thing was not known, thought of, manufactured, or experienced before its advent or has only recently been acquired, employed, put to use, and so on ⟨a *new* invention⟩ ⟨a *new* type of adding machine⟩ ⟨a *new* movie star⟩ ⟨a *new* experience⟩ ⟨a *new* pan⟩ ⟨a *new* baby⟩ ⟨a *new* president⟩ NOVEL applies to something that is not only new but also markedly out of the ordinary in its type of newness often to the point of seeming strange or startling ⟨built a *novel* fort of parallel log walls filled with earth —*Amer. Guide Series: Minn.*⟩ ⟨vacationists who like *novel* activities can sail to a remote part of the islands . . . for buried treasure —L.A. Werden⟩ ⟨the book was *novel* to the point of seeming bizarre —W.L.Sperry⟩ ⟨in a *novel* and highly photogenic setting —Rome's new, deluxe depot —Arthur Knight⟩ ⟨the experiment of appointing as a teacher of law one who had never practiced the profession was *novel*—Samuel Williston b. 1861⟩ NEWFASHIONED suggests a newness of form, style, or character that challenges curiosity or that has been only recently popularly accepted ⟨the type of old-fashioned scholarship . . . the type of *newfashioned* criticism —S.E.Hyman⟩ ⟨the *newfashioned* girl in light, comfortable clothes⟩ NEWFANGLED is disparaging in suggesting unnecessary or objectionable and usu. ingenious novelty ⟨its villages have avoided any incongruous *newfangled* type of building —S.P.B.Mais⟩ ⟨quite a modern hostelry for its time. It had such *newfangled* doodads as mechanical dishwashers and potato peelers —Green Peyton⟩ ⟨the empress Tzu Hsi, who again seized the reins of government and revoked all the *newfangled* regulations —Olga Lang⟩ MODERN and the now rare or literary NEOTERIC imply a belonging to the present time in a broad sense or to the present era, often suggesting up-to-dateness and sometimes novelty ⟨Pineville is even more *modern* in appearance, most of its residences having been rebuilt after a destructive cyclone in 1923 —*Amer. Guide Series: La.*⟩ ⟨telephone line, house, and highway, although giving the *modern* touch, are far from being truly up-to-date —G.R.Stewart⟩ ⟨pianoforte compositions. In these, Bach is more *modern* than Haydn, Mozart or even Beethoven —*Encyc. Americana*⟩ ⟨*modern* English dates from the 16th century⟩ ⟨the *modern* era in geology covers many thousands of years⟩ ⟨a girl anxious to be considered *modern*, not oldfashioned⟩ ⟨*neoteric* brass playing by a group of young men who are obviously fond of J. S. Bach —Wilder Hobson⟩ MODERNISTIC, sometimes interchangeable with MODERN, usually adds to MODERN a contemptuous suggestion of the ephemerally novel ⟨his adoption of many *modernistic* harmonic procedures makes his works tantalizing by the very incongruity of their essence and their idiom —Nicolas Slonimsky⟩ ⟨the jury . . . felt called upon to point out that Conway's work was "in no way *modernistic*, though distinctly modern" —*Time*⟩ ⟨when I refer to modern music, I do not mean necessarily "*modernistic*" music, much of which is a pale afterglow of the great and original modernism of yesteryear —Virgil Thomson⟩ ORIGINAL applies to what is or produces something new, novel, and the first of its kind ⟨the Aztec character was perfectly *original* and unique —W.H. Prescott⟩ ⟨the would-be *original* veers perilously towards the extravagant and the eccentric —J.L.Lowes⟩ ⟨an interesting and *original* mind that despised imitation⟩ FRESH in this connection applies to what is new and still retaining a first liveliness, energy, virginal quality, and so on ⟨a *fresh* and vital painting⟩ ⟨a lively and *fresh* active mind⟩ ⟨a *fresh* point of view upon an old problem⟩
²**new** \"\ *n* -s [ME *new, newe*, fr. OE *nīwe*, fr. *nīwe, nēowe, nīewe*, adj.] **1 :** a new thing **:** something new ⟨the ~ ever supplants the old⟩; *esp* **:** the first phase (in the ~ of the moon) **2 :** FRESHNESS, NEWNESS ⟨wear the ~ off these shoes⟩
³**new** \"\ *adv* [ME *new, newe*, fr. OE *nīwe*, fr. *nīwe, nēowe, nīewe*, adj.] **:** NEWLY, RECENTLY, ANEW, AFRESH ⟨grass ~ washed by rain⟩ — often used in combination ⟨*new*-mown⟩
**ne·war** *also* **ne·var** *or* **ni·war** \nəˈwär\ *n, pl* **newar** *or* **newars** *usu cap* **:** one of the Mongoloid Nepalese
**ne·wa·ri** \nəˈwärē\ *n* -s *usu cap* **:** the Tibeto-Burman language of the Newars
**new·ark** \ˈn(y)üə(r)k\ *adj, usu cap* [fr. *Newark*, N.J.] **:** of or from the city of Newark, N.J. ⟨the *Newark* parks⟩ **:** of the kind or style prevalent in Newark
**newark charging system** *n, usu cap N* **:** a system of charging library books in which when a book is lent the date of issue or the date due is stamped on the book card, on a plate in the book, and on the borrower's card and the borrower's name or number also is recorded on the book card which is filed until the book is returned and the return is recorded on the borrower's card
**new·ark·er** \-kə(r)\ *n* -s *cap* [*Newark*, N.J. + E *-er*] **:** a native or resident of Newark, N.J.
**new art** *n, usu cap N&A* [trans. of F *art nouveau*] **:** ART NOUVEAU
**new bedford** *adj, usu cap N&B* [fr. *New Bedford*, Mass.] **:** of or from the city of New Bedford, Mass. ⟨the *New Bedford* harbor⟩ **:** of the kind or style prevalent in New Bedford
**new·bery·ite** \ˈn(y)üb(ə)rēˌīt, -ˌber-\ *n* -s [G *newberyit*, fr. J. Cosmo *Newbery*, 19th cent. Australian mineralogist + G *-it* -ite] **:** a mineral $HMgPO_4.3H_2O$ consisting of an acid magnesium phosphate occurring as white orthorhombic crystals in guano

**new birth** *n* : REGENERATION 2

**new blood** *n* : an agent that is expected to convey vitality or superior qualities to or renew them in something (as a natural strain or an organization) ⟨as retirements provide openings for *new blood* in the directorate⟩

**new blue** *n* [prob. trans. of G *neublau*] **1** : any of several blue pigments: as **a** : cobalt blue containing chromium **b** : ULTRAMARINE 1b **c** : any of various iron blue pigments **2** : any of several blue dyes — see DYE table I (under *Basic Blue 6*) **3** : FRENCH BLUE

[1]**newborn** \ˈ=ˌ=\ *adj* [ME *new born*] **1 a** : recently born ⟨a ~ kitten⟩ **b** : affecting or relating to the newborn ⟨the ~ period⟩ ⟨~ disorders⟩ **2** : born anew ⟨~ and whole in spirit⟩

[2]**newborn** \"\ *n, pl* **newborn** *or* **newborns** : a newborn individual : NEONATE

**new bronze** *n* : a moderate brown that is yellower, lighter, and less strong than bay, yellower and slightly lighter than auburn, and lighter and slightly yellower and stronger than chestnut brown — called also *Brussels brown, cowboy*

**new broom** *n* [fr. the proverb "a *new broom* sweeps clean"] : a person recently established in a position of authority and vigorous in exercise of his duties

**new bruns·wick** \-ˈbrənz(ˌ)wik\ *adj, usu cap N&B* [fr. *New Brunswick*, province of Canada] : of or from the province of New Brunswick : of the kind or style prevalent in New Brunswick

**new bruns·wick·er** \-kə(r)\ *n -s cap N&B* [*New Brunswick*, province of Canada + E *-er*] **1** : a native or resident of New Brunswick province, Canada **2** [*New Brunswick*, N.J. + E *-er*] : a native or resident of New Brunswick, N.J.

**new brunswick green** *n, often cap B* : CHROME GREEN 1b

**new·burg** *or* **new·burgh** \ˈn(y)üˌbərg, -əg, -əig\ *adj, usu cap* [prob. fr. (*lobster*) *newburg*] : made of cream, butter, sherry or Madeira, and yolks of eggs or dressed with a rich sauce ⟨a *Newburg* sauce⟩ — usu. used postpositively with the names of seafoods ⟨shrimp *Newburg*⟩

**new·cal** \ˈn(y)ükəl\ *or* **new·ca'd** \-kəd\ *adj* [[3]*new* + *cal* (short for *calved*) or *ca'd* (contr. of *calved*)] *chiefly Scot, of a cow* : newly calved

[1]**new caledonian** *adj, usu cap N&C* [*New Caledonia*, Fr. island and territory in the southwest Pacific + E *-an*] : of or from New Caledonia : of the kind or style prevalent in New Caledonia

[2]**new caledonian** *n, cap N&C* : a native or inhabitant of New Caledonia

**new caledonian pine** *n, usu cap N&C* : a very tall columnar araucaria (*Araucaria columnaris*) of New Caledonia and the New Hebrides that is often confused with Norfolk Island pine

**new candle** *n* : CANDLE 4b

[1]**new·cas·tle** \ˈ=ˌkasəl, -aas-,-ais-,-ȧs-; *the Brit places are locally often* =ˈ==\ *adj* **1** *or* **newcastle-upon-tyne** \-ˌ=ˌ=ˈtīn\ *usu cap N&T* [fr. *Newcastle* upon Tyne, England] : of or from Newcastle upon Tyne, England : of the kind or style prevalent in Newcastle upon Tyne **2** *or* **newcastle-under=lyme** \-ˌ==ˈlīm\ *usu cap N&L* : of or from Newcastle under Lyme, England : of the kind or style prevalent in Newcastle under Lyme **3** *usu cap* [fr. *Newcastle*, New So. Wales] : of or from Newcastle, New So. Wales : of the kind or style prevalent in Newcastle

[2]**newcastle** \"\ *n -s usu cap* [prob. fr. *Newcastle* upon Tyne, England] **1** : an old English round dance for eight participants **2** [by shortening] : NEWCASTLE DISEASE

**newcastle disease** *n, usu cap N* [fr. *Newcastle* upon Tyne] : a virus disease of domestic fowl and other birds resembling bronchitis or coryza but in later stages distinguished by nervous invasion leading to incoordination, tremors, and twitching of the head and being esp. destructive of young birds although all ages may be attacked — called also *avian pneumoencephalitis*; compare INFECTIOUS LARYNGOTRACHEITIS

**newcastle thorn** *n, usu cap N* [prob. fr. *Newcastle*, a name or place name] : COCKSPUR THORN

**new christian** *n, sometimes cap N & usu cap C* [prob. trans. of Sp *cristiano nuevo*] : MARRANO

**new chum** *n, chiefly Austral* : a recent immigrant esp. from the British Isles : NEWCOMER

**new cocoa** *n* : a grayish brown that is yellower and slightly lighter than chestnut and slightly yellower and lighter than coconut — called also *mahal, Natal brown*

**new·comb** \ˈn(y)ükəm\ *also* **newcomb ball** *n -s usu cap N* [prob. fr. the name *Newcomb*] : a game resembling volleyball in which a ball is thrown back and forth across a net by the opposing players by whom it has been caught

**newcome** \ˈ=ˌ=\ *adj* [ME *newcum, new-cumen*, fr. OE *nīwcumen*, fr. *nīwe*, adv., new + *cumen*, past part. of *cuman* to come — more at NEW, COME] : recently come

**new·com·er** \-mə(r)\ *n* : one that has recently arrived: as **a** : IMMIGRANT **b** : NOVICE 2 **c** : something that is advancing toward a position of greater prominence or eminence

**new connexion** *usu cap N&C* **1** : a former division of the General Baptists of England founded in 1770 **2** : a former division of British Methodists formed in 1797

**new covenant** *n* : a new promise of redemption by God to men as individuals rather than as a nation and on the basis of grace rather than law ⟨Christ is . . . the mediator of a *new covenant* —*Interpreter's Bible*⟩

**new critic** *n, usu cap N&C* : a practitioner of the New Criticism

**new criticism** *n, usu cap N&C* : an analytic literary criticism focusing intensively upon the language, imagery, and emotional or intellectual tensions in particular literary works (as poems) in an attempt to explain their total formal aesthetic organization — usu. used with *the*

**new-cut** \ˈ=ˌ=\ *n* [[1]*new* + *cut*, n.] : card game played in England in the 16th and 17th centuries

**new-day** \ˈ=ˌ=\ *adj* [[1]*new* + *day*, n.] : current, modern, or stylish at the time in question : UP-TO-DATE ⟨*new-day* society⟩ ⟨various *new-day* conveyances⟩

**new deal** *n* [so called fr. the supposed resemblance to the situation of freshness and equality of opportunity provided by a fresh deal in a card game] : a fundamental revaluation and reorganization (as of a government's duties and responsibilities) designed to have far-reaching and usu. liberalizing effects ⟨it will require a complete *new deal* to solve the problem⟩

**new dealer** *n* [*new deal* + *-er*] : a political liberal in government service : a proponent or supporter of a governmental new deal

**new-deal·ish** \ˈ=ˈ=lish\ *adj* [*new deal* + *-ish*] : suited to a new deal esp. in liberal or radical tendencies

**new deal·ism** \-ˌlizəm\ *n, pl* **new dealisms** [*new deal* + *-ism*] : political orientation based on the use of new deal techniques in government : advocacy of a governmental new deal

**new delhi** *adj, usu cap N&D* [fr. *New Delhi*, India] : of or from New Delhi, the capital of India : of the kind or style prevalent in New Delhi

**new duck disease** *n* : ANATIPESTIFER INFECTION

**new dunker** *n, usu cap N&D* : a member of the Church of God organized in 1848 and distinguished from other Dunker churches chiefly by insistence on a Biblical name for the church

**new egyptian** *n, cap N&E* : the language of Egypt under the 18th to 21st dynasties

**new·el** \ˈn(y)üwəl\ *n -s* [ME *nowell*, fr. MF *nouel, noiel* stone of a fruit, newel, fr. OF, stone of a fruit, fr. LL *nucalis* like a nut, fr. L *nuc-, nux* nut + *-alis* -al — more at NUT] **1** *or* **newel-post** \ˈ==ˌ=\ **a** : an upright post or the upright made of the inner or smaller ends of the steps about which the steps of a circular staircase wind **b** : the principal post at the foot of a stairway with straight flight or a secondary one at a landing — see HOLLOW NEWEL **2** : a cylindrical pillar terminating a wing wall of a bridge or viaduct

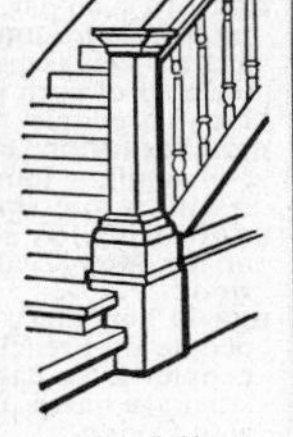
newel 1b

**newel stair** *n* : a stair with newels at the angles to receive the ends of the strings; *also* : a spiral stair in which the inner or smaller ends of the steps are engaged in a solid vertical core

**new·el·ty** \ˈn(y)üəltē, -ti\ *n -es* [ME *newelte*, alter. (influenced by *new, newl* new) of *novelte* novelty — more at NEW, NOVELTY] *chiefly dial* : NOVELTY

**new empire** *adj, usu cap N&E* : of or belonging to the late period of Mayan culture from about A.D.980 to about 1450 — compare OLD EMPIRE

**new england** *adj, usu cap N&E* [fr. *New England*, northeast section of U.S.] : of or from New England : of the kind or style prevalent in New England

**new england aster** *n, usu cap N & E* : a common perennial aster (*Aster novae-angliae*) of eastern No. America having showy purplish flowers and being one of the parents of the Michaelmas daisies

**new england boiled dinner** *n, usu cap N&E* : BOILED DINNER

**new england boxwood** *n, usu cap N&E* : FLOWERING DOGWOOD

**new england clam chowder** *n, usu cap N&E* : clam chowder made of minced clams, salt pork, onions, potatoes, and milk — compare MANHATTAN CLAM CHOWDER

**new england colonial** *n* [*New England* + *colonial*, adj.] : architecture of or based on the style typical of colonial New England characterized by the saltbox house and the Cape Cod cottage

**new englander** *n, cap N&E* [*New England* + E *-er*] : a native or resident of New England

**new england hemlock** *n, usu cap N&E* : EASTERN HEMLOCK

**new en·gland·ish** \-dish — *see* [1]NEW\ *adj, usu cap N&E* [*New England* + E *-ish*] : like or like that of New England : typical or suggestive of New England

**new en·gland·ism** \-ˌdizəm\ *n, pl* **new englandisms** *usu cap N&E* [*New England* + E *-ism*] **1** : the traits, ideas, or attitudes distinctive of native New Englanders **2** : a locution or pronunciation characteristic of New England

**new eng·land·ly** *adv, usu cap N&E* [*New England* + E *-ly*] : in the manner of a New Englander ⟨thinks and acts *New Englandly*⟩

**new england pine** *n, usu cap N&E* : WHITE PINE 1a

**new england short o** *n, usu cap N&E* : a vowel short in duration, of a quality that varies from \ō\-like to \ȯ\-like to \ə\=like, and less and less used in New England in some or all of approximately 50 consonant-final monosyllables and their compounds and derivatives that in other dialects have the vowel of *no* (as in *coat, road, stone, whole, wholly*)

**new england theology** *n, usu cap N&E* : the modified Calvinism originated by Jonathan Edwards (1703–58)

**new english** *n, cap N&E* : Modern English

**newer** *comparative of* NEW

**newest** *superlative of* NEW

[1]**new·fan·gle** \ˈn(y)üˈfaŋgəl, -aiŋ-\ *adj* [ME *newefangel*, fr. *newe* new + *-fangel* (fr. OE *fangen*, past part. of *fōn* to take, seize) — more at NEW, PACT] : NEWFANGLED

[2]**newfangle** \"\ *n -s archaic* : a newfangled thing

[3]**newfangle** \"\ *vt* -ED/-ING/-S *archaic* : to make newfangled ⟨not . . . to ~ the scripture —John Milton⟩

**new·fan·gled** \-ld\ *adj* [ME *newe fangled*, fr. *newefangel* + *-ed*] **1** : attracted to new or novel things or modes : given to new theories or fashions ⟨he was not sufficiently ~ to please the crowd⟩ **2** : newly made or of the newest fashion : NOVEL, UP-TO-THE-MINUTE ⟨swore he'd never wear those ~ pajamas⟩ **syn** see NEW

**new·fan·gled·ly** *adv* : in a newfangled style or manner

**new·fan·gled·ness** *n* -ES : the quality or state of being newfangled

**new·fan·gle·ment** \=ˈ=gəlmənt\ *n -s* : a novelty or a newfangled thing ⟨tired of all these changes and ~s⟩

**newfashioned** \ˈ=ˈ==\ *adj* [[3]*new* + *fashioned*, past part. of [2]*fashion*] **1** : made in a new fashion or form : lately come into fashion **2** : following the newest fashions : UP-TO-DATE **syn** see NEW

**new·fie** \ˈn(y)üfē, -fi\ *n -s usu cap* [by shortening and alter.] **1** : NEWFOUNDLANDER **2** : NEWFOUNDLAND 2

**new fire ceremony** *also* **new fire** *n* [*new fire ceremony* fr. *new fire* (fr. [1]*new* + *fire*) + *ceremony*] : a ceremony that recurs in many cultures, is symbolic of new life, the new year, or rebirth, and involves the extinguishing of all household fires and their rekindling on the hearths from a newly kindled ceremonial fire

**newfish** \ˈ=ˌ=\ *n, New South Wales* : AUSTRALIAN SALMON

**new forest pony** *n, usu cap N&F&P* [fr. *New Forest*, region of southern England] **1** : a British breed of hardy largeheaded ponies of the New Forest region of southern England 12 to 14 hands high with short neck, sturdy shoulders, and deep body that make excellent surefooted saddle ponies when trained **2** : a pony of the New Forest breed

**newfound** \ˈ=ˌ=\ *adj* [ME *newe founde*, fr. *newe, new*, adv., new + *founde*, past part. of *finden* to find — more at NEW, FIND] : newly found, uncovered, or made evident ⟨his ~ aggressiveness⟩

**new foundation** *n, usu cap N&F, Church of England* : the status of having been founded at the Reformation with a new organization — compare OLD FOUNDATION

[1]**new·found·land** \ˈn(y)üfən(d)lənd; ˈ==ˌland, -laa(ə)nd, ˌ==ˈ=; nyüˈfaun(d)lənd, n(y)əˈ-\ *adj, usu cap* [fr. *Newfoundland*, province of Canada] : of or from the province of Newfoundland : of the kind or style prevalent in Newfoundland

[2]**newfoundland** \"\ *n, usu cap* **1** : a breed of very large vigorous highly intelligent dogs that are believed to have been developed in Newfoundland during the 17th century by crossing dogs of European fishermen and possibly introducing some native blood, are vigorous swimmers, stand 26 to 28 inches high, weigh from 110 to 150 pounds, have a strong massive build with large broad head, decided stop, and squarish muzzle, and develop a coarse flat dense coat that is usu. black though black and white or bronze sometimes appear **2** *also* **newfoundland dog** -s : a dog of the Newfoundland breed

**newfoundland caribou** *n, usu cap N* : a large caribou (*Rangifer caribou terraenovae*) that is a variety of the woodland caribou confined to Newfoundland

**new·found·land·er** \-də(r)\ *n -s cap* [*Newfoundland* + E *-er*] **1** : a native or resident of Newfoundland, Canada **2** : a Newfoundland boat

**new franc** *n* : the franc established as the French legal unit of value effective Jan. 1, 1960 — see MONEY table

**new fuchsine** *n, often cap N&F* : a dye closely related to fuchsine — see DYE table I (under *Basic Violet 2*)

**new greek** *n, usu cap N&G* : Greek as used by the Greeks for literature and for speech since the end of the medieval period — compare GREEK, LATE GREEK, MIDDLE GREEK

**newground** \ˈ=ˌ=\ *n, chiefly South & Midland* : a piece of land recently cleared and put under cultivation

**newgrowth** \ˈ=ˌ=\ *n* : NEOPLASM

**new guinea** *adj, usu cap N&G* [fr. *New Guinea*, island of eastern Malay Archipelago] : of or from the island of New Guinea : of the kind or style prevalent in New Guinea

**new guinea butter bean** *n, usu cap N&G* : SNAKE GOURD

[1]**new guinean** *adj, usu cap N&G* [*New Guinea*, island + E *-an*] **1** : of, relating to, or characteristic of the island of New Guinea **2** : of, relating to, or characteristic of the people of New Guinea

[2]**new guinean** *n, cap N&G* : a native or inhabitant of New Guinea

**new guinea wood** *or* **new guinea walnut** *n, usu cap N&G* : the light gray to brown wood of a tree (*Dracontomelum mangiferum*) of the family Anacardiaceae that is native to the southern Pacific islands, has black markings and a high figure, and is used esp. in veneers

[1]**new hampshire** *adj, usu cap N&H* [fr. *New Hampshire*, state in the northeastern U.S.] : of or from the state of New Hampshire ⟨a *New Hampshire* road⟩ : of the kind or style prevalent in New Hampshire

[2]**new hampshire** *also* **new hampshire red** *n, usu cap N&H&R* [*new hampshire* fr. *New Hampshire* state; *new hampshire red* fr. *new hampshire* + (*rhode island*) *red*] **1** : a breed of general purpose domestic fowls that were developed chiefly in New Hampshire by selection from Rhode Island Red, resemble members of the parent breed but are always single-combed, and are noted for rapid maturing and for heavy winter egg production **2** : a bird of the New Hampshire breed

**new hamp·shire·man** \-*pronunc at* HAMPSHIRE +mən\ *n, pl* **new hampshiremen** *cap* [*New Hampshire* + E *man*] : NEW HAMPSHIRITE

**new hamp·shir·ite** \-ˌīt\ *n, cap N&H* [*New Hampshire* + E *-ite*] : a native or resident of the state of New Hampshire

**new ha·ven** \-ˈhāvən\ *adj, usu cap N&H* [fr. *New Haven*, Conn.] : of or from the city of New Haven, Conn. ⟨*New Haven* schools⟩ : of the kind or style prevalent in New Haven

**new ha·ven·er** \-v(ə)nə(r)\ *n -s cap N&H* [*New Haven*, Conn. + E *-er*] : a native or resident of New Haven, Conn.

**new haven theology** *n, usu cap N&H* : TAYLORISM

**new hebrew** *n, cap N & H* : ISRAELI HEBREW

**new humanism** *n* [ˈ*new* + *humanism*] : a 20th century doctrine marked by a belief in moderation, the dignity of the human will, a sense of permanent values, and a dualistic order of existence

**new humanist** *n* : one who advocates or accepts new humanism

**new·ing** \ˈnyüən, -üiŋ\ *n -s* [ME *neweinge* novelty, something new, fr. *newing*, gerund of *newen* to renew, fr. OE *nīwian*, fr. *nīwe, nēwe*, adj., new — more at NEW] *now dial Brit* : NEWS — usu. used in pl.

**new·ish** \ˈn(y)üish, -ēsh\ *adj* [ˈ*new* + *-ish*] : rather new : not yet showing signs of use or wear

**new israel** *n, usu cap N&I* : the Christian fellowship of believers : the Christian Church

**new jersey** *adj, usu cap N&J* [fr. *New Jersey*, state in the eastern U.S.] : of or from the state of New Jersey ⟨*New Jersey* truck farms⟩ : of the kind or style prevalent in New Jersey

**new jerseyite** *n, cap N&J* [*New Jersey* + E *-ite*] : a native or resident of the state of New Jersey

**new jersey pine** *n, usu cap N&J* : JERSEY PINE

**new jersey tea** *n, usu cap N&J* [so called fr. its leaves having been used as a substitute for tea during the Am. Revolution] : a low deciduous shrub (*Ceanothus americanus*) of the eastern U.S. with ovate to ovate-oblong dull green leaves and with small white flowers borne in large terminal panicles in summer

**new jerusalem** *n, usu cap N&J* [fr. the phrase "the holy city, *New Jerusalem*" (Rev 21: 2); trans. of LL *Jerusalem nova*, trans. of Gk *Hierousalēm kainē*] : the abode of the redeemed

**new je·ru·sa·lem·ite** \-*pronunc at* JERUSALEM +ˌīt\ *n, pl* **new jerusalemites** *usu cap N&J* [*New Jerusalem* (*Church*) church holding the doctrines taught by Emanuel Swedenborg †1772 Swed. philosopher and religious writer (fr. *New Jerusalem* + *church*) + E *-ite*] : SWEDENBORGIAN

**new latin** *n, cap N&L* : Latin as used since the end of the medieval period; *esp* : Latin as used in scientific description and classification — compare LATE LATIN, LATIN, MEDIEVAL LATIN

**new learning** *n, usu cap N&L* **1** : learning of the 15th and 16th centuries based on the study of the Bible and the classics (as Greek) in the original **2** : the learning and doctrines of the English Reformation

**new licht** \ˈnyüˌlikt\ *n, usu cap N&L* [Sc, lit., new light] : a member of one of the parties in the Scottish Secession Churches both Burgher and Antiburgher that supported the principle of voluntarism in opposition to the Auld Lichts

**new light** *n, usu cap N&L* : a person who accepts new usu. more modern or more liberal religious views, doctrines, or methods: as **a** : a member of a group favoring revivalism and emotionalism in religion (as in Congregational, Presbyterian, and Baptist Churches) during and following the American revival movement of 1740–42 — compare OLD LIGHT **b** : NEW LICHT **c** : DISCIPLE 2

**newlight** \ˈ=ˌ=\ *n* [*new light*; fr. its association with [1]*campbellite*] : CRAPPIE

**new·lins** \ˈnyülənz\ *adv* [alter. of earlier *newlingis*, fr. ME, fr. *new* (adj.) + *-lingis, -linges* -lings] *archaic Scot* : NEWLY

**new look** *n* : the changed appearance or makeup of something into which radical innovations have been recently introduced ⟨this year's car has a *new look*⟩ ⟨the *new look* of current Broadway plays⟩ ⟨a military *new look* to suit world conditions⟩

**new·ly** \ˈn(y)ülē, -li\ *adv* [ME *newly, newliche*, fr. OE *nīwlīce*, fr. *nīwe*, adj., new + *-līce* -ly — more at NEW] **1** : LATELY, RECENTLY ⟨~ blossomed trees⟩ **2** : ANEW, AFRESH ⟨a ~ floored stable⟩ **3** : in a new way ⟨a house ~ furnished⟩ ⟨a thought ~ expressed⟩

**newlywed** \ˈ==ˌ=\ *n -s* [*newly* + *wed* (past part.)] : one recently married

**new man** *n* [fr. the phrase "put on the *new man*" (Eph 4: 24 —AV); trans. of LL *novus homo*, trans. of Gk *kainos anthrōpos*] : man as regenerated by religious conversion or experience

**new·man·ism** \ˈn(y)üməˌnizəm\ *n -s usu cap* [John Henry *Newman* †1890 Eng. theologian + E *-ism*] : the theological and ecclesiastical views taught by John Henry Newman while a member of the Church of England in which he argued that the language of the Thirty-nine Articles admits of a Catholic interpretation by distinguishing between the corruptions against which they were directed and the doctrines they did not oppose

**new·man·ite** \-ˌnīt\ *n -s usu cap* [John Henry *Newman* + E *-ite*] : a follower of John Henry Newman : an adherent of Newmanism

**new·mar·ket** \ˈn(y)üˌmärkət, -mȧk-, *usu* -əd·+V\ *n* [fr. *Newmarket*, England] **1** *sometimes cap* : a long close-fitting coat worn in the 19th century **2** *usu cap* : a card game of English origin equivalent to the U.S. game of Michigan

[1]**new mexican** *adj, usu cap N&M* [*New Mexico* state + E *-an*] : of, relating to, or characteristic of New Mexico or New Mexicans

[2]**new mexican** *n, cap N&M* : a native or resident of the state of New Mexico

**new mexican locust** *n, usu cap N&M* : a thorny shrub or small tree (*Robinia mexicana*) of dry rocky uplands of the southwestern U.S. and adjacent Mexico that is an important browse plant

**new mexican piñon** *n, usu cap N&M* : a nut pine (*Pinus edulis*)

**new mexico** *adj, usu cap N&M* [fr. *New Mexico*, state in the southwestern U.S.] : of or from the state of New Mexico ⟨a *New Mexico* pueblo⟩ : of the kind or style prevalent in New Mexico : NEW MEXICAN

**new-mint** \ˈ=ˈ=\ *vt* [[3]*new*] : to coin anew; *specif* : to give a fresh meaning to (as a word or phrase)

**new-model** \ˈ=ˈ==\ *vt* [prob. fr. *New Model*, the English parliamentary army as reorganized in 1645] : REORGANIZE, REMODEL

**new moon** *n* [ME *newe mone, newe moone*, fr. OE *nīwe mōna*] **1 a** : the moon's phase when it is in conjunction with the sun so that its dark side is turned toward the earth — see MOON illustration **b** : the moon's dark appearance when at the new moon phase **c** : the position in the orbit when the moon is new **d** : the thin crescent moon seen in the western evening sky shortly after sunset a few days after the actual occurrence of the new moon phase **2 a** : the day when the new moon is first seen **b** : ROSH HODESH

**new negro** *n, usu cap 2d N* : a Negro brought from Africa to the New World as a slave

**new·ness** *n* -ES [ME *newnes*, fr. OE *nīwnes*, fr. *nīwe*, adj., new + *-nes* -ness — more at NEW] : the quality or state of being new ⟨the ~ of this system⟩

**new norse** *n* : LANDSMÅL

**new order** *n* : a reorganized and usu. fundamentally reoriented basis of action

**new orleanian** *n -s cap N&O* [*New Orleans*, La. + E *-an*] : ORLEANIAN

**new or·leans** \=ˈȯrlēənz, -lənz, -lyənz, -ˈō(ə)l-, *chiefly by outsiders* ˌ=ˈ=ˈlēnz\ *adj, usu cap N&O* [fr. *New Orleans*, La.] : of or from New Orleans ⟨the *New Orleans* Mardi Gras⟩ : of the kind or style prevalent in New Orleans

**new orleans molasses** *n* : a molasses that is comparatively light in color and rich in sugar

**new philharmonic pitch** *n* : a tuning standard of 435 to 439 vibrations per second for A above middle C adopted in Britain at the end of the 19th century to replace the old philharmonic pitch

**new platonism** *n, usu cap N&P* : NEOPLATONISM

**new·port** \ˈn(y)üˌpō(ə)r|t, -ȯ(ə)r|, |, -ōə|, -ȯ(ə)|, *usu* |d·+V\ *adj, usu cap* **1** [*Newport*, Monmouthshire, England] : of or from the county borough of Newport, Monmouthshire, England : of the kind or style prevalent in Newport, Monmouthshire **2** [*Newport*, Isle of Wight, England] : of or from Newport, county seat of the Isle of Wight, England : of the kind or style prevalent in Newport, Isle of Wight **3** [*Newport*, R.I.] : of or from the city of Newport, Rhode Island : of the kind or style prevalent in Newport, Rhode Island

**new realism** *n* : a form of realism that was developed at the beginning of the 20th century in opposition to idealism, that emphasizes the distinction between the object and the act of sensation, and that holds the objective world to exist independently of the knowing mind and to be directly knowable — compare CRITICAL REALISM, MONISM

**new realist** *n* **:** an advocate of new realism

**¹new-rich** \'=;=\ *n* [trans. of F *nouveau riche*] **:** NOUVEAU RICHE

**²new-rich** \"\ *adj* **1 :** recently become rich **2 :** typical of a new-rich person ⟨*new-rich* snobbery⟩

**¹news** \'n(y)üz\ *n pl but sing or pl in constr, often attrib* [ME *newes*, fr. pl. of *new*, *newe*, adj., new; prob. trans. of MF *nouvelles*] **1 :** a report of a recent event **:** new information **:** fresh tidings ⟨gave the bad ~⟩ ⟨wanted to tell her as quickly as he could his evil ~ —Pearl Buck⟩ **2 a :** what is reported in a newspaper, news periodical, or news broadcast **b :** matter that is interesting to newspaper readers or news broadcast audiences **:** matter that is suitable for news copy **3** [by shortening] **a :** NEWSBOARD **b :** NEWSPRINT **c :** NEWSPAPER **d :** NEWSCAST

**²news** \"\ *vb* -ED/-ING/-ES *vt* **:** to tell or repeat as news ⟨it is being ~*ed* about that the report is inaccurate⟩ ~ *vi* **:** to tell or repeat news **:** GOSSIP ⟨were ~*ing* over the teacups⟩

**news agency** *n* **1 :** the place of business of a newsagent **2 :** a commercial organization that collects and supplies news to subscribing newspapers, periodicals, and news broadcasters — compare PRESS ASSOCIATION

**newsagent** \'=,=\ *n* [¹*news* + *agent*] **:** a dealer in newspapers and magazines

**news analyst** *n* **:** COMMENTATOR b

**newsbeat** \'=,=\ *n* **:** BEAT 7 e

**news bell** *n, now dial Eng* **:** a singing in the ears supposed to portend news

**newsboard** \'=,=\ *n* **1** *chiefly Brit* **:** a bulletin board for posting news **2 :** paperboard made chiefly from repulped newspapers

**newsboat** \'=,=\ *n* **:** a boat that puts out to passing ships to supply and receive news

**newsbook** \'=,=\ *n* **:** a publication popular in 17th century England consisting of one or two sheets folded octavo to make 8 or 16 pages and containing domestic news

**newsboy** \'=,=\ *n* **:** a person that delivers or sells newspapers at retail **:** CARRIER 2e

**newsbreak** \'=,=\ *n* **:** a newsworthy event

**news case** *n* **:** either of a pair of type cases one containing lowercase letters and the other uppercase letters

**newscast** \'=,=\ *n* [¹*news* + broad*cast*] **:** a radio or television broadcast of news

**news·cast·er** \-tə(r)\ *n* -s [¹*news* + broad*caster*] **:** a person engaged to broadcast news **:** COMMENTATOR

**¹newscasting** \'=,==\ *n* [¹*news* + broad*casting*] **:** the broadcasting of news

**²newscasting** \"\ *adj* **:** of or relating to the broadcasting of news

**new school** *n, usu cap N&S* **:** the more liberal of two parties into which the Presbyterian Church in the U.S. was divided about 1825, later organized as a separate church from 1838 to 1869 when a reunion was effected with the more conservative party

**newsclip** \'=,=\ *n* **:** ⁴CLIP 2a

**news conference** *n* **:** PRESS CONFERENCE

**news dealer** *n* **:** a seller of newspapers and periodicals

**news feature** *n* **:** FEATURE 4b(1)

**newsgirl** \'=,=\ *n* **:** a girl that sells or delivers newspapers to individual customers

**newshawk** \'=,=\ *n* **:** NEWSHOUND

**newshound** \'=,=\ *n* **:** a reporter for a newspaper, news periodical, or news agency

**new side** *adj, usu cap N&S* **:** of, relating to, or constituting a more liberal division among American Presbyterians resulting from a great religious awakening in the colonies beginning about 1734, favoring revivalism and employing its methods, and separating from Old Side Presbyterians in 1741 but reuniting with them in 1758

**newsie** *var of* NEWSY

**newsier** *comparative of* NEWSY

**newsies** *pl of* NEWSY

**newsiest** *superlative of* NEWSY

**new silver** *n* **:** a yellowish gray that is greener and less strong than sand and greener and duller than natural — compare OLD SILVER

**news·i·ness** \'n(y)üzēnəs, -zin-\ *n* -ES **:** the quality or state of being newsy

**newsing** *pres part of* NEWS

**news·less** \'n(y)üzləs\ *adj* **:** lacking news **:** not receiving or producing news — **news·less·ness** *n* -ES

**newsletter** \'=,==\ *n* **1 :** a circular letter formerly written or printed for the dissemination of news **2 :** a printed sheet, pamphlet, or small newspaper containing news or information of current interest to or bearing upon the interests of a special group ⟨the Commerce Department is planning to begin publication in January of a semimonthly, four-page ~ containing all information stemming from the department which might be useful to small businessmen —*Newsweek*⟩

**newsmagazine** *n* **:** a periodical typically published weekly and devoted chiefly to summarizing and analyzing current news

**news·man** \'n(y)üzmən, -,man,-,maa(ə)n\ *n, pl* **newsmen 1** *archaic* **:** a bearer of news **2 :** one who gathers, reports, or comments on the news **:** REPORTER, CORRESPONDENT

**newsmonger** \'=,==\ *n* **:** a gossipy person **:** one active in gathering and repeating news

**new south wales** *adj, usu cap N&S&W* [fr. *New South Wales*, Australia] **:** of or from the state of New South Wales, Australia **:** of the kind or style prevalent in New South Wales

**¹news·pa·per** \'n(y)üz,pāpə(r), -üs,pā-\ *n, often attrib* [¹*news* + *paper*] **1 :** a paper that is printed and distributed daily, weekly, or at some other regular and usu. short interval and that contains news, articles of opinion (as editorials), features, advertising, or other matter regarded as of current interest **2 :** an organization engaged in composing and issuing a newspaper **3 :** newsprint or the paper making up newspapers ⟨wrap the dirty shoes in ~⟩ ⟨sketching on unprinted ~⟩

**²newspaper** \"\ *vi* **:** to do newspaper work (as running a newspaper or reporting or editing news)

**newspaperboy** \'=,==,=\ *n* **:** NEWSBOY

**news·pa·per·ish** \-p(ə)rish\ *adj* **:** like or like that of a newspaper ⟨a brisk ~ style⟩

**news·pa·per·man** \-,man, -aa(ə)n\ *n, pl* **newspapermen 1 a :** a person regularly employed as writer or editor on the editorial staff of a newspaper or news agency **b :** one who writes professionally for newspapers, news periodicals, or news agencies **2 :** one who owns or runs a newspaper or news agency

**newspaper post** *n* **:** the postal service of the British Post Office providing for special rates on newspapers that are registered as such with the General Post Office and that thus constitute a classification of mail corresponding to second class in the U.S.

**newspaperwoman** \'=,==,==\ *n, pl* **newspaperwomen :** a woman engaged in newspaper work

**news·pa·po·ri·al** \,n(y)üz,pā,pōrēəl, -üspə',-, -;pòr-\ *adj* [irreg. (influenced by *-or*) fr. ¹*newspaper* + *-ial*] **:** of or relating to newspapers **:** suitable to a newspaper ⟨~ items⟩ ⟨~ labors⟩

**newsprint** \'=,=\ *n* **:** cheap machine-finished paper made chiefly from groundwood with a little chemical pulp to give strength and used mostly for newspapers

**new-sprung** \'=;=\ *adj* [³*new* + *sprung*, past. part. of *spring*] **:** recently come into being

**newsreader** \'=,==\ *n, Brit* **:** NEWSCASTER

**newsreel** \'=,=\ *n* **:** a short motion-picture film portraying or dealing with current events

**newsroom** \'=,=\ *n* **1 :** a room or place where newspapers or periodicals are sold **2 :** a reading room primarily devoted to newspapers and periodical literature **3 :** the office, offices, or portion of an office in which news is processed by a newspaper, news agency, or radio or television station

**news service** *n* **:** NEWS AGENCY 2

**news-sheet** \'n(y)üz(h),shēt, *usu* -ēd-+V\ *n* **:** NEWSPAPER, NEWSLETTER

**news·stand** \'=,=\ *n* **:** a place (as a counter or an outdoor stall) where newspapers and periodicals are sold

**news stick** *n* **:** a composing stick permanently set to a fixed measure

**new star** *n* [prob. trans. of It *nuova stella* or NL *nova stella*] **1 :** NOVA **2 :** a star that is newly formed

**new stone age** *n, usu cap N&S&A* **:** the Neolithic age

**new style** *adj, usu cap N&S* **:** using or according to the Gregorian calendar — abbr. *N.S.*

**new suit** *n* **:** a suit when bid for the first time in the current auction of a bridge game

**news vendor** *n* **:** a seller of newspapers

**newsweekly** \'=,==\ *n* **:** a periodical issued weekly and devoted primarily to current events of general interest or of interest to a special group ⟨the leading theatrical ~⟩

**newsworthiness** \'=,===\ *n* **:** the quality or state of being newsworthy

**newsworthy** \'=,==\ *adj* **:** sufficiently interesting to a general public to warrant reporting in the news

**¹newsy** \'n(y)üzē, -zi\ *adj* -ER/-EST [¹*news* + *-y* (adj. suffix)] **1 a :** filled with news ⟨a ~ letter⟩ **b :** given to gossip ⟨a ~ old aunt⟩ **2 :** likely to give rise to news **:** designed to attract attention — often used of styles in women's dress ⟨a ~ new cut about the shoulder⟩

**²newsy** *or* **news·ie** \"\ *n, pl* **newsies** [*news*boy + *-y* or *-ie* (dim. n. suffix)] **:** NEWSBOY

**newt** \'n(y)üt, *usu* -üd·+V\ *n* -S [ME *newte*, alter. (resulting from incorrect division of *an ewte*) of *ewte*, *evete* — more at EFT] **:** any of various small semiaquatic salamanders esp. of the genus *Triturus* **:** EFT, TRITON

newt

**new·take** \'nyü,tāk\ *n, Brit* **:** a field of moorland newly placed under cultivation

**new testament** *n, cap N&T* [ME *newe testament*, trans. of LL *novum testamentum* new testament, new covenant, trans. of Gk *kainē diathēkē* new covenant (2 Cor 3: 6)] **:** the covenant of God with man embodied in the coming of Christ and the teaching of Christ and his followers as set forth in the Bible — abbr. *N. T.*

**new thought** *n, cap N&T* **:** a mental healing movement embracing a number of small groups and organizations devoted generally to such ideas as spiritual healing, the creative power of constructive thinking, and personal guidance from an inner presence

**new·ton** \'n(y)üt°n\ *n* -S [after Sir Isaac *Newton* †1727 Eng. natural philosopher and mathematician] **:** the unit of force in the mks system of physical units that is of such size that under its influence a body whose mass is one kilogram would experience an acceleration of one meter per second per second ⟨one ~ equals $10^5$ dynes⟩

**¹new·to·ni·an** \(')n(y)ü;tōnēən\ *adj, usu cap* [Sir Isaac *Newton* + E *-an*] **:** of, relating to, or following Sir Isaac Newton, his discoveries, or doctrines

**²newtonian** \"\ *n* -S *usu cap* **1** *also* **new·ton·ist** \'n(y)üt°nəst\ **:** a follower of Sir Isaac Newton **2** [by shortening] **:** NEWTONIAN TELESCOPE

**newtonian fluid** *or* **newtonian liquid** *n, usu cap N* **:** a fluid whose viscosity does not change with rate of flow

**newtonian force** *n, usu cap N* **:** any of the forces that like gravitation are subject to the inverse-square law

**new·to·ni·an·ism** \n(y)ü'tōnēə,nizəm\ *n* -S *usu cap* [¹*newtonian* + *-ism*] **:** the doctrine of the universe as expounded in Newton's *Principia*; *esp* **:** Newton's mathematical theory of universal gravitation

**newtonian mechanics** *n pl but sing or pl in constr, usu cap N* **:** classical mechanics

**newtonian physics** *n pl but sing or pl in constr, usu cap N* **:** classical physics

**newtonian potential** *n, usu cap N* **:** a potential in a field of force obeying the inverse-square law; *esp* **:** GRAVITATIONAL POTENTIAL

**newtonian telescope** *n, usu cap N* **:** a reflecting telescope including a spherical or paraboloidal primary mirror and a flat reflecting surface (as of a mirror or prism) set at 45 degrees to the optical axis to reflect the light to a focus at the side of the telescope tube

**newton's disk** *n, usu cap N* [after Sir Isaac *Newton*] **:** a disk divided into sectors of proper relative dimensions bearing the different colors of the spectrum so that fusion of the colors by rotation gives a white or gray

**newton's first law of motion** *usu cap N* **:** LAW OF MOTION 1

**newton's law of cooling** *usu cap N* **:** a statement in physics: the rate at which an exposed body changes temperature through radiation is approximately proportional to the difference between its temperature and that of its surroundings

**newton's rings** *n pl, usu cap N* **:** colored rings due to light interference that are seen about the contact of a convex lens with a plane surface or of two lenses differing in curvature

**newton's second law of motion** *usu cap N* **:** LAW OF MOTION 2

**newton's third law of motion** *usu cap N* **:** LAW OF MOTION 3

**new town** *n, usu cap N&T* **:** any of several recent British urban developments that constitute small and essentially self-sufficient cities with accommodations for about 20,000 persons each and a planned ordering of residential, industrial, and commercial development

**new wheat disease** *or* **new wheat poisoning** *n* **:** BLUE COMB

**new woman** *n* **:** a woman esp. of the late 19th century actively resisting traditional controls and seeking to fill a complete role in the world

**new world** *n, usu cap N&W* **:** the western hemisphere; *esp* **:** the continental landmass of No. and So. America

**new-world monkey** *n* [*New World*] **:** a platyrrhine monkey

**new world porcupine** *n, usu cap N&W* **:** any of numerous more-or-less arboreal porcupines constituting a family (Erethizontidae) restricted to No. and So. America

**new world vulture** *n, usu cap N&W* **:** a bird of the family Cathartidae

**new year** *n* [ME *newe yere*] **1 a** *often cap N&Y* (1) **:** the calendar year following the current Gregorian year; *also* **:** the Gregorian calendar year just begun (2) **:** the year following the current year in any calendar **b** *usu cap N&Y* **:** NEW YEAR'S DAY; *also* **:** New Year's Day and succeeding days at the beginning of the new year **2** *usu cap N&Y* **:** the first day and traditionally also the second day of Tishri, the first month of the Jewish civil year — called also *Rosh Hashanah*

**new-year** \'=,=\ *also* **new year's** *adj, often cap N&Y* [ME *newyere*, *new yeer*, *new yeres*, *newe yeers*, fr. *newe yere*, n.] **:** of, relating to, or suitable for the commencement of the year ⟨*new-year* resolutions⟩ ⟨a *new year's* party⟩

**new year's day** *or* **new year's** *n, usu cap N&Y&D* [*new year's day* fr. ME *new yeres day*, *newe yeersday*; *new year's*, short for *new year's day*] **:** the first day of the calendar year observed as a legal holiday in many countries (as the U.S., Canada, Scotland)

**new year's eve** *n, usu cap N&Y&E* [ME *newe yeres even*] **:** the eve of New Year's Day

**new york** \(')n(y)ü;yò(ə)rk, -ò(ə)k *sometimes* nə'y-\ *adj* **1** *or* **new york city** *usu cap N&Y&C* [fr. *New York* or *New York City*, N. Y.] **:** of or from New York, N.Y. ⟨a *New York* skyscraper⟩ ⟨*New York City* police⟩ **:** of the kind or style prevalent in New York **2** *or* **new york state** *usu cap N&Y & often cap S* [fr. *New York*, *New York State*, middle Atlantic state of the U.S.] **:** of or from the state of New York ⟨*New York* freeways⟩ **:** of the kind or style prevalent in New York

**new york aster** *n, usu cap N&Y* **:** an erect perennial herb (*Aster novibelgii*) of northeastern No. America with slender lanceolate leaves and showy violet-rayed heads

**new york cut** *adj, usu cap N&Y, of beef sirloin* **:** cut with the hipbone included

**new york dressed** *adj, usu cap N&Y, of poultry* **:** killed, bled, and picked for marketing but with head, feet, and viscera intact — compare FULL-DRESSED

**new york·er** \n(y)ü'yòrkər, -ò(ə)kə(r *sometimes* nə'-\ *n, cap N&Y* [*New York* (city or state) + E *-er*] **:** a native or resident of the city or state of New York

**new york·ese** \,n(y)ü,yòr'kēz, -ēs\ *n, usu cap N&Y* [*New York* City + E *-ese*] **:** the speech or an item of the speech (as of vocabulary or pronunciation) characteristic of New York City

**new york fern** *n, usu cap N&Y* **:** a slender shield fern (*Dryopteris noveboracensis*) of moist woods in eastern No. America

**new york point** *n, usu cap N&Y* **:** an embossed system of writing for the blind that is now largely disused, is similar to braille but employs a cell two dots high and variable up to four dots in width arranged in accommodation to the frequency of letter occurrence, and provides for mathematical expression and a full musical notation

**new york weasel** *n, usu cap N&Y* **:** a common weasel (*Mustela frenata noveboracensis*) widely distributed in the eastern U.S. that is a variety of the No. American long-tailed weasel

**new york weevil** *n, usu cap N&Y* **:** PEACH WEEVIL

**new-yorky** \n(y)ü'yòrkē\ *adj, usu cap N&Y* [*New York* (city or state) + E *-y* (adj. suffix)] **:** suggestive of or like that of New York ⟨*New-Yorky* sophistication⟩

**¹new zea·land** \(')n(y)ü;zēlənd\ *adj, usu cap N&Z* [fr. *New Zealand*, Brit. dominion in the south Pacific ocean] **1 :** of or from New Zealand **:** of the kind or style prevalent in New Zealand **2 :** of, relating to, or being the biogeographic region or subregion of the Australian region that includes New Zealand and a few adjacent islands

**²new zealand** \"\ *n, usu cap N&Z* **1 :** an American breed of medium-sized white or reddish tan domestic rabbits **2** *pl* **new zealands :** an animal of the New Zealand breed

**new zealand beech** *n, usu cap N&Z* **:** any of several tall New Zealand trees of the genus *Nothofagus* some of which yield useful timber

**new zealand birch** *n, usu cap N&Z* **:** NEW ZEALAND BEECH

**new zealand blue cod** *n, usu cap N&Z* **:** smoked Australian freshwater catfish

**new zealand bramble** *n, usu cap N&Z* **:** a leafless prickly bramble (*Rubus australis*) of New Zealand that forms impenetrable thickets — called also *bush lawyer*, *wait-a-bit*

**new zealand broom** *n, usu cap N&Z* **:** a leguminous plant of the genus *Carmichaelia* (esp. *C. australis*)

**new zealand bur** *n, usu cap N&Z* **:** a creeping mat-forming New Zealand plant (*Acaena microphylla*) that is sometimes cultivated for its grayish to rosy bronze foliage and showy crimson spines

**new zealand cotton** *n, usu cap N&Z* **:** a fiber from the bast of the ribbon tree

**new zea·land·er** \-də(r)\ *n, cap N&Z* [*New Zealand* + E *-er*] **:** a native or inhabitant of New Zealand

**new zealand flax** *or* **new zealand hemp** *n, usu cap N&Z* **1 :** a tall New Zealand herb (*Phormium tenax*) having erect, sword-shaped leaves and scarlet or yellow flowers **2 :** the strong fiber from the leaves of New Zealand flax used chiefly for cordage, twine, and mattings

**new zealand frog** *n, usu cap N&Z* **:** a rare frog (*Liopelma hochstetteri*) peculiar to New Zealand and the only amphibian known from that region

**new zealand honeysuckle** *n, usu cap N&Z* **:** REWA-REWA

**new zealand pepper tree** *n, usu cap N&Z* **:** an aromatic and pungent evergreen tree (*Drimys axillaris*) with pinnate leaves and greenish flowers succeeded by red berrylike drupes

**new zealand spinach** *n, usu cap N&Z* **:** a coarse annual chiefly Australasian herb (*Tetragonia expansa*) of the family Aizoaceae used as a potherb

**new zealand tea tree** *n, usu cap N&Z* **:** a tea tree (*Leptospermum scoparium*) of New Zealand and Australia

**new zealand white pine** *n, usu cap N&Z* **:** KAHIKATEA

**nex·al** \'neksəl\ *adj* [L *nexum* + E *-al*] **:** of, relating to, or constituting the contract of nexum

**¹next** \'nekst, *before a consonant* " *or* 'neks\ *adj* [ME *next*, *nexte*, fr. OE *nēhst*, *nīehst*, *nȳhst*, superl. of *nēah*, *nēh* nigh — more at NIGH] **1 :** being the nearest **:** having nothing similar intervening: as **a :** adjoining in a series **:** immediately preceding or following in order (as of place, rank, relation, or time) ⟨the ~ verse⟩ ⟨the ~ house⟩ ⟨is ~ in line⟩ ⟨the ~ day⟩ ⟨~ Monday⟩ **b :** following that approaching or in progress ⟨cannot go this Christmas, but I hope to go ~⟩ ⟨our ~ job will be clearing the land⟩ **c :** first in nearness without implication of succession or contiguity **:** first located, appearing, happening, or otherwise made relevant ⟨his ~ neighbor was five miles away⟩ **2** *archaic* **:** most pressing, convenient, ready, direct, or available **3** *slang* **a :** aware of what is happening or planned ⟨~ to their schemes⟩ **b :** INTIMATE, CLOSE ⟨planned to be ~ to her to learn the scandal when it broke⟩ **4** *of a suit in euchre* **:** of the same color as the exposed or otherwise indicated suit — **next·ness** *n* -ES

**²next** \"\ *adv* [ME *next*, *nest*, fr. OE *nīehst*, *nēhst*, *nȳhst* next, last, nearly, superl. of *nēah*, *nēh* near, nigh — more at NIGH] **1 :** in the time, place, or order nearest or immediately succeeding ⟨~ we drove home⟩ **:** in next order (as of place, rank, relation, or time) ⟨the ~ widest horizon he knew —C.S.Forester⟩ ⟨my ~ newest dress⟩ — compare NEAR **2 :** on the first occasion to come ⟨when ~ we meet⟩

**³next** \"\ *prep* [ME *nexte*, *nest*, fr. OE *nēahst*, *nēhst*, *nȳhst*, fr. *nīehst*, *nēhst*, *nȳhst*, adv.] **:** nearest or adjacent to (as in place or order) ⟨a mad dog . . . will fly upon and bite anyone that comes ~ him —Daniel Defoe⟩ ⟨one ~ himself in power —John Milton⟩

**next best** *n* **:** SECOND BEST

**next friend** *n* [trans. of AF *prochein ami*] **:** a person that is admitted to or appointed by a court as a special guardian to act for the benefit of an infant, a married woman, or any person not sui juris (as in a suit at law) **:** PROCHEIN AMI, GUARDIAN AD LITEM

**next·ly** *adv* **:** in the next place **:** so as to be or come next

**next of kin** *n, pl* **next of kin 1 :** a person in the nearest degree of relationship by blood to another person ⟨divided among children and other *next of kin* —G.B.Shaw⟩ **2 :** STATUTORY NEXT OF KIN **3 :** a person closely related to another person by blood, marriage, or court decision ⟨*next of kin* are being notified of his death⟩

**¹next to** *prep* [ME, fr. *next* (adj.) + *to*] **:** immediately following or adjacent to (as in space, time, or importance) ⟨*next to* the best flavor of all⟩ ⟨the top news *next to* the war⟩

**²next to** *adv* **:** very nearly **:** ALMOST, PRACTICALLY ⟨*next to* impossible to win⟩ ⟨had *next to* no food left⟩

**next ways** *adv* [irreg. (influenced by the *ways* in *a good ways*, *a great ways*) fr. the phrase obs. E *next way* nearest way] **:** by the shortest way or route **:** DIRECTLY

**nex·um** \'neksəm\ *n* -S [L, fr. neut. of *nexus*, past part. of *nectere* to bind] *Roman law* **:** a formal contract of loan with coin and balance in the presence of five witnesses under which the obligor could be seized and held in bondage for failure to perform

**nex·us** \'neksəs\ *n, pl* **nexuses** *or* **nexus** *see sense 4* [L, fr. *nexus*, past part. of *nectere* to bind — more at ANNEX] **1 :** CONNECTION, INTERCONNECTION, TIE, LINK **2 :** a connected group or series **3 :** a predicative relation or a construction consisting of grammatical elements either actually or felt as so related — compare JUNCTION, RANK **4** *pl* **nexi** \-k,sī\ [L, fr. *nexus* (past part.)] *Roman law* **:** a person bound by a contract of nexum

**nez percé** *or* **nez perce** \'nez'pərs\ *n, pl* **nez percé** *or* **nez percés** *or* **nez perce** *or* **nez perces** *usu cap N&P* [F, lit., pierced nose] **1 a :** a Shahaptian people of central Idaho and adjacent parts of Washington and Oregon **b :** a member of such people **2 :** a language of the Nez Percé people

**NF** *abbr* **1** near face **2** no funds **3** nonferrous **4** nonfundable **5** not fordable

**NFD** *abbr, often not cap* no fixed date

**NFS** *abbr* not for sale

**NG** *abbr* **1** national guard **2** nitroglycerin **3** \(')en¦jē\ no good; not good

**nga·dju** \əŋ'gä(,)jü\ *also* **ngadju dayak** *n, pl* **ngadju** *or* **ngadjus** *also* **ngadju dayak** *or* **ngadju dayaks** *usu cap N&D* **1 a :** a Dayak people inhabiting the interior of Borneo **b :** a member of such people **2 :** the Austronesian language of the Ngadju people

**ngai camphor** \əŋ'gī-\ *n* [*ngai*, prob. native name in Borneo] **:** a camphor found in various essential oils (as the oil of the Asiatic woody shrub *Blumea balsamifera*); levorotatory borneol

**ngaio** \'nī(,)ō\ *n* -S [Maori] **:** a small tree (*Myoporum laetum*) of the New Zealand coast with edible fruit and light tough wood

**nga·la** \əŋ'gälə\ *n, pl* **ngala** *or* **ngalas** *usu cap* **1 a :** a Bantu people of French Equatorial Africa **b :** a member of such people **2 :** a Bantu language of the Ngala people **3 :** a trade language based on Ngala (sense 2) and widely used in the Belgian Congo

**n'gana** *var of* NAGANA

**nga·na·sa·ni** *also* **nga·na·sa·ne** \ˌəŋ,gänə'sänē\ *n, pl* **nga-nasani** *or* **nganasanis** *also* **nganasane** *or* **nganasanes** *cap* **1 :** a Samoyed people inhabiting the Taimyr peninsula of Siberia **2 :** a member of the Nganasani people

**ngan·dong man** \əŋ'gän,dȯŋ\ *n, usu cap N* [fr. *Ngandong,* fossil site near Trinil, south central Java] **:** SOLO MAN

**nga·ba·ka** \əŋ'bäkə\ *n, pl* **ngbaka** *or* **ngbakas** *usu cap* **1 a :** a people of the northwest Congo **b :** a member of such people **2 :** an Adamawa-Eastern language of the Ngbaka people

**nge·ge** \əŋ'gāgē\ *n pl* **ngege** *or* **ngeges** [native name in East Africa] **:** an important African cichlid food fish (*Tilapia esculenta*) — compare TILAPIA

**NGF** *abbr* naval gunfire

**ngo·ko** \əŋ'gō(,)kō\ *n* -s *usu cap* **:** a dialect of Javanese used in speaking to inferiors

**ngo·lok** \əŋ'gō,läk\ *n, pl* **ngolok** *or* **ngoloks** *usu cap* **1 :** a nomadic Tibetan people **2 :** a member of the Ngolok people

**ngo·ni** \əŋ'gōnē\ *or* **ngu·ni** \-günē\ *n, pl* **ngoni** *or* **ngonis** *or* **nguni** *or* **ngunis** *usu cap* **1 a :** a prominent people of the region of Lake Nyasa in south central Africa **b :** a member of such people **2 a :** a group of closely related Bantu languages consisting of Zulu, Xhosa, and Swazi **b :** a dialect of Zulu more or less mixed with adjoining languages spoken in Nyasaland and Tanganyika

**ngt** *abbr* night

**ngwa·na** \əŋ'gwänə\ *n, pl* **ngwana** *or* **ngwanas** *usu cap* **:** KINGWANA

**ngwa·to** \əŋ'gwä(,)tō\ *n, pl* **ngwato** *or* **ngwatos** *usu cap* **:** a Bantu-speaking people of Bechuanaland in south central Africa

**NH** *abbr* **1** never hinged **2** nonhygroscopic

**nham·bi·qua·ra** *or* **nham·bi·cua·ra** \ˌnyambə'kwärə, nē,am-\ *usu cap, var of* NAMBICUARA

**nhang** \'nyaŋ, nē'aŋ\ *n, pl* **nhang** *or* **nhangs** *usu cap* **:** GIAI

**NHP** *abbr, often not cap* nominal horsepower

**ni** *abbr* night

**NI** *abbr* naval intelligence

**Ni** *symbol* nickel

**ni·a·cin** \'nīəsən\ *n* -s [*nicotinic acid* + *-in*] **:** NICOTINIC ACID

**ni·a·cin·a·mide** \ˌnīə'sinə,mīd\ *n* [*niacin* + *amide*] **:** NICOTINAMIDE

**ni·ag·a·ra** \nī'ag(ə)rə, -aig-, *attributively* (')≈'≈(≈)≈\ *n* -s *often cap* [fr. *Niagara* Falls waterfall of the Niagara river between Ontario, Canada and New York State] **:** an overwhelming flood **:** TORRENT ⟨a ~ of curses⟩ ⟨a ~ of cheap fiction⟩

**niagara green** *n, often cap N* [fr. *Niagara* Falls or *Niagara* river] **:** a light bluish green that is greener and duller than average aqua green (sense 1), greener and paler than average turquoise green, and greener and stronger than robin's-egg blue (sense 2)

**ni·ag·a·ran** \-rən\ *adj, usu cap* [*Niagara* River + E *-an*] **:** of or relating to a division of the American Silurian — see GEOLOGIC TIME table

**nia·mey** \nē'ä(,)mā, ¦nē(,)ä¦mā\ *adj, usu cap* [fr. *Niamey,* Niger Republic] **:** of or relating to Niamey, capital of the Niger Republic **:** of the kind or style prevalent in Niamey

**ni·aou·li** \nē'aùlē\ *n* -s [native name in New Caledonia] **:** a small irregular evergreen tree (*Melaleuca viridiflora*) of the southwestern Pacific islands that is closely related to the Indian cajeput and similarly used

**ni·as** \'nē,äs\ *n* -ES *usu cap* **:** the Austronesian language of the Niasese people

**ni·a·sese** \ˌnēə'sēz, -ēs\ *n, pl* **niasese** *usu cap* [*Nias,* island in the Indian ocean + E *-ese*] **1 :** a people inhabiting the island of Nias west of Sumatra **2 :** a member of the Niasese people

**ni·as·san** \'nēəsən\ *n* -s *cap* [*Nias,* island in the Indian ocean, west of Sumatra + E *-an*] **:** an Indonesian native or inhabitant of Nias and adjacent islands

**¹nib** \'nib\ *n* -s [prob. alter. of *neb*] **1 :** BILL, BEAK, NEB **2 a :** the sharpened point of a quill pen **b :** each of the two divisions of a pen point **c :** a pen point (as of gold or steel) intended for insertion into a holder **3 :** a small pointed or projecting part: as **a :** the scorer of an auger bit **b :** the tip of a caliper or a scriber **c :** a sharp tip (as a diamond) on a cutting tool **d :** a small lug (as on a roofing tile) **e :** the tongue of a buckle **f :** TOOTH 3e **4** *dial Eng* **a :** one of the handles which project from a scythe snath **b :** one of the shafts on the pole of a wagon **5 a :** a cacao seed with germ removed **b :** COFFEE BEAN **6 a :** a tiny knot or lump (as in raw silk or wool or in a woven or knitted fabric) **b :** a small lump or particle in a film (as of paint or varnish) **c :** irregularly twisted or lumpy leaves of oolong tea

**²nib** \"\ *vt* **nibbed; nibbed; nibbing; nibs :** to furnish with a nib; *esp* **:** to mend the point of (a pen)

**³nib** \"\ *vb* [prob. by shortening] *dial chiefly Eng* **:** NIBBLE

**nibbana** *usu cap, var of* NIRVANA

**nib·ber** \'nibə(r)\ *n* -s [¹*nib* & ²*nib* + *-er*] **:** one that nibs: as **a :** one who puts nibs on buckles **b :** a worker who cuts nibs from hosiery **c :** a machine for crushing cacao beans; *also* **:** its operator

**¹nib·ble** \'nibəl\ *vb* **nibbled; nibbled; nibbling** \-b(ə)liŋ\ **nibbles** [origin unknown] *vt* **1 :** to bite lightly or gently **:** eat in small bits ⟨leaves had been *nibbled* away by deer⟩ **2 :** to take away or conserve bit by bit **3 a :** to trim or shape (glass) by breaking off small bits **b :** to cut (as metal) with a nibbling machine ~ *vi* **1 a :** to take gentle or cautious bites ⟨a cracker to ~ on⟩ ⟨fish *nibbled* at the bait⟩ **b :** to make small attempts **:** deal with or attack something cautiously or timidly — used with *at* ⟨legislation was *nibbling* away at the worst abominations of . . . housing —F.L.Allen⟩ **2 :** to make petty criticisms **:** CARP, TRIFLE — used with *at*

**²nibble** \"\ *n* -s **1 :** an act of nibbling **:** a small or cautious bite or an attempt to take such a bite **2 :** a bit (as of food) such as might be taken in a small bite **:** a trifling quantity

**³nibble** \"\ *chiefly dial var of* NIPPLE

**nib·bler** \-b(ə)lə(r)\ *n* -s **:** one that nibbles: as **a :** CUNNER **b** *also* **nibbling machine :** a machine for cutting sheets or plates of metal by punching a succession of overlapping holes along the desired contour

**¹nib·by** \'nibē, -bi\ *n* -ES [¹*nib* + *-y*] *chiefly Scot* **:** a hooked staff such as is used by a shepherd

**²nibby** \"\ *adj* -ER/-EST [¹*nib* + *-y*] *dial* **:** INQUISITIVE, NOSY

**nib·lick** *also* **nib·lic** \'niblik, -lēk\ *n* -s [origin unknown] **:** an iron golf club with a wide deeply slanted face used for short shots out of sand or long grass or for shots where quick loft and little roll is desired — called also *number eight iron;* see IRON illustration

**ni·bong** \'nē,bȯŋ\ *or* **ni·bung** \-bəŋ\ *n* -s [Malay] **:** a Malay feather palm (*Oncosperma fasciculata*)

**nibs** \'nibz\ *n pl but sing or pl in constr* [perh. alter. of *nabs*] **:** a person of importance or authority **:** CHIEF, BOSS — used chiefly in *his nibs* as if a title of honor

**ni·cae·an** \(')nī¦sēən\ *adj, usu cap* [*Nicaea,* ancient city, Asia Minor (fr. L) + E *-an*] — more at NICENE] **:** NICENE

**²nicaean** \"\ *n* -s **1** *cap* **:** a native or inhabitant of Nicaea **2** *usu cap* **:** a 4th or 5th century adherent of the Nicene Creed

**nic·a·ra·gua** \ˌnikə'rägwə, -räg- *sometimes* -gyəwə, *chiefly Brit* -rag-\ *adj, usu cap* [fr. *Nicaragua,* republic, Central America] **:** of or from Nicaragua **:** of the kind or style prevalent in Nicaragua **:** NICARAGUAN ⟨Nicaragua coffee⟩

**¹nic·a·ra·guan** \-gwən, -gyəw-\ *adj, usu cap* [*Nicaragua,* republic, Central America + E *-an*] **:** of or relating to Nicaragua or its inhabitants

**²nicaraguan** \"\ *n* -s *cap* **:** a native or resident of Nicaragua

**nicaragua wood** *n, usu cap N* **:** BRAZILETTE

**nic·a·rao** \ˌnikə'raù\ *n, pl* **nicarao** *or* **nicaraos** *usu cap* [prob. fr. AmerSp] **1 :** a Uto-Aztecan people of southwestern Nicaragua **2 :** a member of the Nicarao people

**nic·colic** \'nikə(,)lik; ni'kälik, -kōl-\ *or* **nic·co·lous** \'nikələs\ *adj* [NL *niccolum* nickel + E *-ic, -ous*] **:** composed of or containing nickel

**nic·co·lite** \'nikə,līt\ *n* -s [NL *niccolum* nickel (prob. fr. Sw *nickel*) + E *-ite* — more at NICKEL] **:** a mineral NiAs of a pale copper red color and metallic luster usu. occurring massive and composed essentially of a nickel arsenide (hardness 5–5.5, sp. gr. 7.33–7.67)

**niccolo** *var of* NICOLO

**¹nice** \'nīs\ *adj* -ER/-EST [ME, foolish, wanton, fr. OF, simpleminded, stupid, fr. L *nescius* ignorant, not knowing, fr. *nescire* not to know — more at NESCIENCE] **1** *obs* **a :** LEWD, WANTON, DISSOLUTE **b :** COY, MODEST, DIFFIDENT, RETICENT **2 a :** showing fastidious, particular, or finical tastes ⟨too ~ about his food to like camp cooking⟩ ⟨an animal ~ about its diet⟩ **b :** satisfying a dainty palate **:** pleasing delicate tastes ⟨the ~ dishes at the banquet⟩ **3 :** marked by refinement and culture, refined tastes, or wise discrimination ⟨the popular ear, none too ~ to distinguish between sense and fustian —V.L.Parrington⟩ **4 :** showing, marked by, or requiring meticulous choice, tactful handling, careful consideration, or precise and scrupulous conduct ⟨a diplomatic mission requiring ~ judgment⟩ ⟨the highest standards which a man of . . . the *nicest* sense of honor might impose —B.N.Cardozo⟩ **5 :** requiring, marked by, or capable of delicate discrimination, precision, closely accurate measurement, subtle analysis, or minute treatment ⟨the balance was ~ enough . . . to make both parties appeal for popular support —G.G.Coulton⟩ ⟨a ~ question of ethics⟩ ⟨~ measurements with a micrometer⟩ **6** *obs* **a :** lacking vigor, strength, or endurance **b :** lacking significance **:** TRIVIAL ⟨the letter was not ~ but full of charge —Shak.⟩ **7 :** pleasant and satisfying: as **a :** COMPLAISANT, AFFABLE, AGREEABLE, CONSIDERATE ⟨the duty of being ~ to one's mother-in-law —F.D.Roosevelt⟩ ⟨what a ~ fellow you are, and we all thought you so nasty —George Meredith⟩ **b :** ENJOYABLE, ATTRACTIVE, PLEASING, DELIGHTFUL ⟨a ~ time at the party⟩ ⟨~ and warm by the fire⟩ ⟨we have four ~ bedrooms upstairs to make them comfortable —Willa Cather⟩ **c :** very good **:** well-executed **:** well-conducted **:** OUTSTANDING ⟨a ~ bit of satire⟩ ⟨a ~ shot bringing down the bird⟩ **d :** well-intentioned **:** BENIGN ⟨~ people support charities⟩ **e :** MILD, CLEMENT, PLEASING ⟨the ~ weather of late spring⟩ ⟨the ~ old days of the past⟩ **f :** well or appropriately dressed **:** NEAT, PERSONABLE, COMELY ⟨always a ~ dresser⟩ ⟨a *nice*-looking American businessman with a quiet calm manner and a friendly face —Dorothy C. Fisher⟩ **g :** FITTING, APPROPRIATE, SUITABLE ⟨the ~ clothes she wears⟩ ⟨not a ~ word for use in church⟩ **h** — used with *and* as an intensive ⟨blankets are ~ and dry⟩ ⟨this soup is ~ and hot⟩ **8 :** most inappropriate **:** UNPLEASANT, UNATTRACTIVE **:** MEAN, TREACHEROUS — used ironically ⟨a chronic alcoholic is certainly a ~ one to talk about temperance⟩ ⟨a ~ friend, who would have me . . . cover myself with eternal infamy —J.A.Froude⟩ ⟨got himself in a ~ fix⟩ **9 :** marked by conformity to convention: as **a :** given to accustomed practices **:** established in conventional normal ways of life **:** not unusual, bizarre, wild, morbid, wayward ⟨unpopular with the *nicer* people of the town⟩ **b :** not marked by sexual license **:** VIRTUOUS, CHASTE **c :** not profane, indecent, or obscene **:** PROPER

**syn** DAINTY, FASTIDIOUS, FINICAL, PARTICULAR, FUSSY, SQUEAMISH, PERNICKETY: NICE implies fine discrimination in perception and evaluation ⟨a *nice* taste in literature —Compton Mackenzie⟩ NICE may indicate a tender or squeamish disinclination to countenance the questionable or raw ⟨boycotted by the respectables, who were too *nice* to accept socially those whose business they tolerated —W.A.White⟩ DAINTY may describe a tendency to pick and choose with delicate sensibility and, sometimes, to reject disdainfully ⟨*dainty* feeders who expect perfection —A.W.Long⟩ ⟨the tough jargon of the East Side no less than the *dainty* discourse of the Four Hundred —C.H.Grandgent⟩ FASTIDIOUS implies a meticulously careful judgment, often with disdainful rejection of what does not meet with very high standards occas. set capriciously ⟨a *fastidious* critic both of the written and the spoken word, hating anything which savored of the fantastic or the turgid —John Buchan⟩ ⟨the *fastidious* author could never satisfy himself, and the result is a production more remarkable for high polish than warmth of poetic feeling —Richard Garnett †1906⟩ ⟨the *fastidious* lady whom it was most difficult to please —L.P.Smith⟩ FINICAL describes an affected, capricious fastidiousness that sometimes seems composed partly of a determination to be displeased or dissatisfied ⟨I am possibly a trifle overscrupulous about the conventions, but you must contrive to forgive a *finical* old friend —Elinor Wylie⟩ PARTICULAR may indicate a demand that all details satisfy an exacting standard ⟨every year it used to get a nice coat of paint —Papa was very *particular* about the paint —Lillian Hellman⟩ ⟨they wear gloves, hats and stockings, and are usually *particular* about grooming because they were brought up in the stricter times —Agnes M. Miall⟩ FUSSY may blend the suggestions of FINICAL and PARTICULAR with a hint of querulousness ⟨a busy, *fussy* sort of man, much concerned with regulating everything —A.M.Young⟩ ⟨so *fussy* about the punctilious observance of orders that almost any brakeman would take a chance once in a while, from natural perversity —Willa Cather⟩ SQUEAMISH describes a sensitive or prudish readiness to be nauseated, disgusted, or antagonized by whatever does not satisfy one's delicate standards or preferences ⟨his conditioning had made him not so much pitiful as profoundly *squeamish.* The mere suggestion of illness or wounds was to him not only horrifying, but even repulsive and rather disgusting —Aldous Huxley⟩ ⟨not *squeamish* about the soft fleshy mud creeping round his ankles, or about the things which slid from under his feet —Audrey Barker⟩ PERNICKETY is deprecatory in indicating exasperating crusty fussiness ⟨the grammarian, the purist, the *pernickety* stickler for trifles —Brander Matthews⟩ **syn** see in addition CORRECT, DECOROUS

**²nice** \"\ *adv* **:** NICELY

**³nice** \'nēs\ *adj, usu cap* [fr. *Nice,* seaport of France] **:** of or from the city of Nice, France **:** of the kind or style prevalent in Nice

**nice·ish** \'nīsish\ *adj* [¹*nice* + *-ish*] **:** fairly nice **:** rather pleasant or agreeable ⟨seemed to be ~ people⟩ ⟨~ income⟩

**nice·ling** \'nīsliŋ\ *n* -s [¹*nice* + *-ling*] **1 :** an overfastidious person **2 :** one who makes fine distinctions

**¹nice·ly** \'nīslē, -li\ *adv* [ME, foolishly, fr. *nice* (adj.) + *-ly*] **1 :** PRECISELY ⟨~ calculated stroke⟩ **2 :** SCRUPULOUSLY **3 :** SATISFACTORILY, AGREEABLY, PLEASANTLY

**²nicely** \"\ *adj, chiefly dial* **:** being in good health **:** WELL

**ni·cene** \'nī,sēn, ≈'≈\ *adj, usu cap* [ME, fr. LL *Nicenus, Nicaenus,* fr. L *Nicea, Nicaea* Nicaea, fr. Gk *Nikaia*] **1 :** of or relating to Nicaea or Nice, an ancient city of Asia Minor **2 :** of or relating to a confession of Christian faith formulated and decreed by the First Council of Nicaea in A.D. 325 in opposition to Arianism and reaffirmed by the First Council of Constantinople in A.D. 381 or to one of the later forms of this confession

**nice nelly** *or* **nice nellie** \≈'nelē\ *n, usu cap 2d N* [prob. fr. ¹*nice* + *Nelly, Nellie,* the name] **1 :** PRUDE ⟨I'm no *nice Nelly* —Ethel Merman⟩ **2 :** a euphemistic term or expression

**nice-nelly** *or* **nice-nellie** \≈¦≈≈\ *adj, often cap 2d N* [*nice Nelly* or *nice Nellie*] **:** overly delicate **:** PRUDISH, EUPHEMISTIC ⟨*nice-nelly* . . . terms for the sexual and excretory functions —George Devereux⟩

**nice-nel·ly·ism** \(')nī'snelē,izəm\ *n* -s *often cap 2d N* **1 :** PRUDERY, PRUDISHNESS **2 :** EUPHEMISM

**nice·ness** \'nīsnəs\ *n* -ES **:** the quality or state of being nice ⟨scrutinize his conduct with a ~ —J.A.Froude⟩ ⟨revolt against formal and philistine ~ —Max Eastman⟩

**ni·ce·ni·an** \nī'sēnēən\ *also* **ni·cen·ist** \'nī,sēnəst, ≈'≈≈\ *n* -s *usu cap* [*Nicene* + *-ian* or *-ist*] **:** NICAEAN 2

**niceno-** *comb form, usu cap* [*Nicene*] **:** Nicene and ⟨*Niceno*-Constantinopolitan⟩

**nicer** *comparative of* NICE

**nicest** *superlative of* NICE

**ni·ce·ty** \'nīsəd·ē, -ətē, -i\ *n* -ES [ME *nicete* (also, foolishness), fr. MF *niceté* foolishness, fr. *nice* (adj.) + *-té* -ty] **1 :** the quality or state of being nice **:** NICENESS **2 :** a dainty, delicate, or elegant thing or feature ⟨enjoy the *niceties* of civilized life⟩ **3 :** an expression, act, mode of treatment, distinction involving delicacy or subtlety **:** a minute distinction, point, or detail ⟨*niceties* of workmanship⟩ ⟨~ of a problem⟩ **4 :** delicacy or exactness of perception or discrimination **:** PRECISION, ACCURACY ⟨depicted the scene with the greatest ~⟩ ⟨the ~ of a trained eye and hand⟩ **5 :** the quality of demanding delicacy and accuracy of treatment ⟨a question of great ~⟩ **6 a :** delicacy of taste or feeling **:** FASTIDIOUSNESS **b :** excessive fastidiousness **:** SQUEAMISHNESS, PRUDISHNESS — **to a nicety** *adv* **:** PRECISELY, ACCURATELY

**¹niche** \'nich *sometimes* 'nish *or* 'nēsh\ *n* -s [F, fr. MF, fr. *nicher* to nest, fr. OF *nichier,* fr. (assumed) VL *nidicare,* fr. L *nidus* nest — more at NEST] **1 :** a recess in a wall: **a :** a hollowed space in a wall made esp. for a statue, bust, or other ornament **b :** a vaulted passage or alcove made usu. within the thickness of a wall **c :** a space provided at the side of a roadway (as of a tunnel, bridge, highway) for emergency use **2 :** a covert or retreat resembling a niche in its formation or privacy **3 :** a place, condition of life or employment, or position suitable for the capabilities or merits of a person or qualities of a thing ⟨his poetry fills a ~ of its own⟩ **4 :** CRATER 1d **5 a :** the sum of the physical and biotic life-controlling factors (as climate, food sources, water supply, enemies); *also* **:** a site or habitat supplying these factors characteristically necessary for the successful existence of an organism or species in a given habitat **b :** the role of an organism in an ecological community involving esp. its way of life and its effect on the environment (as through its relations to other biotic factors and to abiotic factors) **c :** MICROHABITAT — not used technically

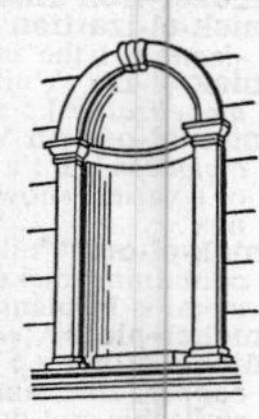
niche 1a

**²niche** \"\ *vb* -ED/-ING/-S [partly fr. ¹*niche* and partly fr. F *nicher* to nest] *vt* **1 :** to place in or as if in a niche: as **a :** to put into a position to attract attention or veneration ⟨safely *niched* as classics⟩ **b :** to settle snugly or cozily **c :** SECRETE **2 :** to construct as or furnish with a niche ~ *vi* **:** to settle or grow in a niche **:** NESTLE

**ni·chi·ren** \ˌnichə'ren\ *n* -s *cap* [after *Nichiren* †1282 Jap. religious teacher and founder of the sect] **:** a Japanese Buddhist sect based doctrinally on the Saddharma-pundarika Sutra and noted historically for its militant nationalism

**nich·ol·son's hydrometer** \'nikəlsənz-\ *n, usu cap N* [after Wm. *Nicholson* †1815 Eng. scientist] **:** a hydrometer with a submerged pan for determining the specific gravities of solids by weighing them in water and in air

**nich·ols terrace** \'nikəlz-\ *n, usu cap N* [after Mark L. *Nichols b*1888 Am. agricultural engineer] **:** a broad-channel terrace with a wide bank constructed along a contour usu. on gently sloping land

**nicht** \'nikt\ *Scot var of* NIGHT

**¹nick** *vt* -ED/-ING/-S [ME *nicken,* fr. OE *niccan,* fr. *nic, nicc,* adv., not I, no, contr. of *ne* not + *ic* I — more at NO, I] **:** to say nay to **:** DENY

**²nick** \'nik\ *n* -s [ME *nyke,* prob. alter. of *nocke* nock — more at NOCK] **1 a :** a cut made or occurring in a surface or edge **:** NOTCH; *usu* **:** a small sharp-edged cut made typically with one blow or stroke and without intention ⟨the razor had bad ~*s*⟩ ⟨~*s* in the table⟩ **b** *chiefly Scot* **:** a gap or slight opening in a range of hills **c :** a notch on the belly of a piece of type — compare GROOVE; — see TYPE illustration **2 a** *archaic* **:** a cut (as in a stick) serving as a tally **b** *obs* **:** RECKONING, ACCOUNT **c :** a particular point or place considered as marked by a cut **:** a precise or critical moment ⟨help came in the ~ of time⟩ **d** [fr. the obs. phrase *nick and froth*] *obs* **:** a false bottom in a beer mug **3 a :** the exact mark aimed at ⟨just what he needed, mum; it was in the ~ —Joyce Cary⟩ ⟨his rejoinder hit the ~⟩ **b :** the junction line of wall and floor in court tennis, squash, handball **c** [³*nick* (to breed)] **:** an individual superior to either parent; *also* **:** a mating that produces such offspring **4 :** the sound produced by a slight or brief impact **:** TICK **5** *Austral* **:** physical condition **:** SHAPE ⟨in great ~⟩ **6 a** *also* **nick point :** a place of abrupt change in a stream gradient **b :** a sharp angle cut at the base of a cliff (as by waves and currents or by shore ice) — compare NIP 5

**³nick** \"\ *vb* -ED/-ING/-S *vt* **1 a :** to make a nick in **:** NOTCH ⟨~ a tree⟩ ⟨~ a steel bar before sawing⟩ **b :** to injure by denting or chipping the surface or edge of ⟨~ a knife blade⟩ ⟨~ a china cup⟩ ⟨~ a table leg⟩ **2 a :** to score by making a nick on a tally **b :** to jot down **:** RECORD, SCORE **3** *obs* **:** to tally with **:** correspond to **:** copy closely **4** [partly short for ²*nickname*] *obs* **:** to fix a fitting name upon **:** NICKNAME **5** *obs* **a :** to provide (a beer mug) with a false bottom **b :** CHEAT, DEFRAUD **6 a :** to cut off or cut out **:** cut short ⟨cold weather ~*ed* steel and automobile output —*Time*⟩ **b :** to cut into slightly **:** wound lightly ⟨bullet ~*ed* his leg⟩ ⟨~*ed* himself while shaving⟩ **c :** to make a crosscut on the underside of (the tail of a horse) to effect a higher carrying position **:** cut beneath the tail of (a horse) **7 :** to hit, grasp, or catch precisely at the right point or time ⟨~ an opportunity⟩ ⟨~ a secret⟩ ⟨~ a train⟩ **8 a** *slang Brit* **:** to catch off guard **:** ARREST **b** *slang Brit* **:** STEAL **c :** to take from as payment or loan **:** CHARGE ⟨complained they were being ~*ed* as high as $30 a ton more for special steels —*Time*⟩ ~ *vi* **1 :** to make petty attacks **:** SNIPE, HACK ⟨people who ~ at the American system —*Saturday Rev.*⟩ **2** *of a ball in court games* **:** to strike the wall and floor simultaneously **3 :** to outrun and take the inner course from another (as in racing) **:** cut in **4 :** to complement one another genetically **:** breed together and produce offspring of good quality

**nickar nut** *var of* NICKER NUT

**nick-eared** \'≈,≈\ *adj* [²*nick*] **:** CROP-EARED 1

**¹nick·el** \'nikəl\ *n* -s *often attrib* [prob. fr. Sw, short for *kopparnickel* niccolite, part trans. of G *kupfernickel,* prob. fr. *kupfer* copper (fr. OHG *kupfar*) + *nickel* goblin, demon, fr. *Nickel,* nickname for *Nikolaus* Nicholas — more at COPPER] **1 :** a nearly silver-white hard malleable ductile ferromagnetic metallic element capable of a high polish and resistant to corrosion that occurs native esp. in meteorites and combined in minerals (as garnierite and pentlandite associated with pyrrhotite and chalcopyrite), that is usu. obtained by roasting, smelting, sintering to the oxide, reducing to the metal, and refining by electrolysis or by formation and decomposition of nickel carbonyl, that is closely related chemically to cobalt and iron forming a monoxide and characteristic green bivalent salts, and that is used chiefly in alloys (as nickel steel and nickel silver) and as a catalyst (as Raney nickel) esp. in hydrogenation — symbol *Ni;* see ELEMENT table **2 a** *also* **nick·le** \"\ **:** the U.S. 5-cent piece regularly containing 25 percent nickel and 75 percent copper **b :** the Canadian 5-cent piece **3 a :** five cents **b :** a trifling sum of money ⟨not worth a ~⟩ **4 :** a nearly neutral, slightly reddish, medium gray

**²nickel** *vt* **nickeled** *or* **nickelled; nickeled** *or* **nickelled; nickeling** *or* **nickelling** \-k(ə)liŋ\ **nickels :** to plate with nickel

**nick·el·age** \-kəlij\ *n* -s [ISV ¹*nickel* + *-age*] **:** the art, act, or process of nickel plating

**nickel bloom** *or* **nickel ocher** *n* [*nickel bloom* trans. of G *nickelblüte; nickel ocher* trans. of NL *ochra niccoli*] **:** ANNABERGITE

**nickel carbonyl** *or* **nickel tetracarbonyl** *n* **:** a volatile flammable poisonous liquid compound $Ni(CO)_4$ obtained by passing carbon monoxide over finely divided nickel and readily decomposed by heating

**nickel-chromium stainless steel** *n* **:** a stainless steel containing 8 percent of nickel and 18 percent of chromium that is strong and ductile and suitable for chemical processing equipment

**nickeled** *or* **nickelled** *adj* **:** NICKEL-PLATED, SHINY

**nickel glance** *n* [G *nickelglanz,* fr. *nickel* + *glanz* glance (mineral sulfide)] **:** GERSDORFFITE

**nickel green** *n* **:** a dark grayish green that is bluer, lighter, and stronger than average ivy, yellower than persian green, and yellower and lighter than hemlock green — called also *frosty green*

**nickel gymnite** *n* **:** GENTHITE

**nick·el·ic** \ni'kelik, 'nikəl-\ *adj* [¹*nickel* + *-ic*] **:** of, relating to, or containing nickel — used esp. of compounds in which this element is regarded as having a higher valence than two

**nick·el·if·er·ous** \ˌnikə'lif(ə)rəs\ *adj* [¹*nickel* + *-iferous*] **:** containing nickel ⟨~ pyrrhotite⟩

**¹nick·el·ine** \'nikə,līn, -lēn\ *adj* [¹*nickel* + *-ine*] **:** consisting of nickel

**²nick·el·ine** \ˌnikə'lēn\ *n* -s [F, fr. *nickel* (fr. Sw) + *-ine*] **:** any of several varieties of nickel silver

**nickel-iron** \≈¦≈≈\ *n* [prob. part trans. of G *nickeleisen,* fr. *nickel* + *eisen* iron] **:** an alloy of nickel and iron (Ni,Fe) occurring native terrestrially in pebbles, grains, and fine scales and in meteorites as fine borders about and intimate intergrowths with kamacite

**nickel–iron alkaline battery** *n* : EDISON BATTERY
**nick·el·iza·tion** \ˌnikələ'zāshən, -ˌlī'z-\ *n* -s [¹*nickel* + *-ization*] : the act or process of plating with nickel
**nick·el·ize** \'nikəˌlīz\ *vt* -ED/-ING/-S [back-formation fr. *nickelization*] : NICKEL
**nick·el·ode·on** \ˌnikə'lōdēən\ *n* -s [prob. blend of ¹*nickel* + *melodeon*] **1** : a theater affording a motion-picture exhibition or a variety show for an admission price of five cents **2** : JUKEBOX
**nick·el·ous** \'nikələs\ *adj* [¹*nickel* + *-ous*] : of, relating to, or containing nickel — used esp. of compounds in which this metal is bivalent ⟨light green ~ hydroxide⟩
**nickel–plate** \ˌ=='=\ *vt* : to electroplate with nickel
**nickel silver** *n* : a silver-white alloy that consists essentially of copper, zinc, and nickel usu. in the proportion 3:1:1, that is malleable and ductile and not affected by exposure to the air, and that is used for tableware, keys, and restaurant and hospital equipment — called also *German silver*
**nickel–skutterudite** \ˌnikəl+\ *n* : a mineral $(Ni,Co)As_3$ consisting of a tri-arsenide of nickel and cobalt having more nickel than cobalt and isomorphous with skutterudite, smaltite, and chloanthite
**nickel steel** *n* : steel containing nickel
**nickel sulfate** *n* : a salt $NiSO_4$ obtained usu. as the green or blue crystalline hexahydrate and used chiefly in nickel-plating baths — called also *single nickel salt*
¹**nick·el·type** \'nikəlˌtīp\ *n* [¹*nickel* + electro*type*] : a nickel-faced electrotype made usu. by first electrodepositing nickel and then thinly coating on the back with copper prior to backing with lead — called also *steelfaced electrotype*
²**nickeltype** \"\ *vt* : to make a nickeltype from (a printing surface) ~ *vi* : to be reproducible by nickeltyping
¹**nick·er** \'nikə(r)\ *n* -s [ME *niker*, fr. OE *nicor*; akin to MD *nicker* water sprite, OHG *nihhus* water monster, water sprite, *nicchessa* mermaid, ON *nykr* water monster, L *noegeum* white upper garment, OIr *nigim* I wash, Gk *nizein*, *niptein* to wash, Skt *nejana* act of washing, *nenēkti* he washes] : a fabulous water monster : WATER SPRITE, NIX
²**nicker** \"\ *n* -s [³*nick* + *-er*] : one that nicks: as **a** : one of the 18th century night brawlers of London noted for breaking windows with halfpence **b** : an operator of a machine for making cuts on the curved edges of shoe vamps, uppers, tongues, tips, and piping so that the edges may be folded under smoothly — called also *snipper*
³**nicker** \"\ *vi* **nickered; nickered; nickering** \-k(ə)riŋ\ **nickers** [perh. alter. of ¹*neigh*] **1** : to neigh gently : WHICKER **2** : SNICKER
⁴**nicker** \"\ *n* -s **1** : NEIGH **2** : SNICKER
⁵**nicker** \"\ *n, pl* **nicker** *or* **nickers** [perh. fr. ²*nicker*] *slang Brit* : one pound sterling
**nick·er nut** *also* **nicker** *or* **nicker–seed** *or* **nick·ar nut** \'nikə(r)(-)\ *n* -s [*nicker*, prob. fr. obs. *nicker* marble, modif. of D *knikker*, fr. *knikken* to crack, snap, fr. MD *cnicken*, prob. of imit. origin like MLG *knicken* to crack, snap, MHG *knacken* to make a cracking noise — more at KNACK] : the very hard shiny gray seed of bonduc (sense 2)
**nicker tree** *n* **1** : BONDUC 2 **2** *dial* : KENTUCKY COFFEE TREE
**nick·ey** \'nikē\ *n* -s [perh. fr. *Nicholas*, name of frequent occurrence among Cornishmen who first brought it to the Isle of Man] : a lug-sailed fishing boat common on the Manx fishing grounds
**nick·ing** \'nikiŋ\ *n* -s [fr. gerund of ³*nick*] **1** : gouged or notched carving frequent on cabinetwork of the 17th and early 18th centuries — called also *gouge carving, notch carving* **2** : localized constriction of a retinal vein by the pressure from an artery crossing it seen esp. in arterial hypertension

nickey

**nickle** *var of* NICKEL
**nicknack** *or* **nicnac** *var of* KNICKKNACK
¹**nick·name** \'nikˌnām\ *n* [ME *nekename*, an additional name, alter. (resulting from incorrect division of *an ekename*) of *ekename*, fr. *eke* (n.) + *name*] **1** : a usu. descriptive name (as Shorty, Tex) given instead of or in addition to the one belonging to a person, place, or thing **2** : a familiar form of a proper name (as Bill, Tommy)
²**nickname** \"\ *vt* **1** : to misapply the name of (one person or thing) to another : MISNAME, MISCALL ⟨psychical research is so often *nicknamed* ghost hunting —A.G.N.Flew⟩ **2** : to give a nickname to : call by a nickname
**nick·name·less** \-ləs\ *adj* : having no nickname
**nick·nam·er** \-mə(r)\ *n* [²*nickname* + *-er*] : one who invents or applies a nickname ⟨the ~ of genius called this brand of genius "pig philosophy" —T.H.Huxley⟩
**nick off** *vi* [prob. fr. ³*nick*] *Austral* : to go away : DEPART
**nick point** *n* : NICK 6a
**nicks** *pres 3d sing of* NICK, *pl of* NICK
**nickstick** \'=,=\ *n* [²*nick* or ³*nick* + *stick*] : a stick on which a reckoning is kept by notches : TALLY
**nick·um** \'nikəm\ *n* -s [perh. alter. & contr. of the phrase *nick them* or *nick him*, fr. ³*nick* (cheat) + *them* or *him*] **1** *slang* : SHARPER **2** *Scot* : SCAMP, WAG
**nicky** \'nikē\ *n* -ES [perh. fr. ²*nick* + *-y*] *dial chiefly Eng* : a bundle of wood
**nic·o·bar·ese** \ˌnikəˌbä'rēz, -ēs\ *n, pl* **nicobarese** *usu cap* [*Nicobar* islands, Bay of Bengal + E *-ese*] **1 a** : the people of the Nicobar islands in the Bay of Bengal **b** : a member of such people **2** : the Mon-Khmer language of the Nicobarese people
**nicobar pigeon** *n, usu cap N* [fr. *Nicobar* islands] : a green pigeon (*Caloenas nicobarica*) of the Malayan and Polynesian islands
**nic·o·de·mite** \ˌnikə'dēˌmīt\ *n* -s *usu cap* [*Nicodemus*, the Jewish ruler who came to Jesus by night (fr. L, fr. Gk *Nikodēmos*) (John 3:1–21) + E *-ite*] : a secret follower or adherent; *specif* : a 16th century Protestant Christian who to escape persecution concealed his Protestantism while living in a Roman Catholic country
**nic·o·la·i·tan** \ˌnikə'lāət°n\ *n* -s *usu cap* [ME *Nicholaite* Nicolaitan (fr. Gk *Nikolaitēs* follower of Nicolaus, fr. *Nikolaos* Nicolaus, a reputed heretic + *-itēs* -ite) + E *-an*] **1** : one of a group reproved in Rev 2:6, 14–15 and generally associated with those who were rebuked for eating things offered to idols and for fornication **2** : one of a group of 3d century antinomian Gnostics **3** [ML *Nicolaitae*, pl., Nicolaitans, heretics (fr. Gk *Nikolaitai*, pl. of *Nikolaitēs*) + E *-an*] : one of the married or concubinary clergy in the medieval period; *also* : an opponent of clerical celibacy
¹**nic·o·lo** \'nikəˌlō\ *n* -s [It] : a large 17th century reed bombardon
²**nicolo** \"\ *also* **nic·co·lo** \"\ *n* -s [obs. It *niccolo*, prob. dim. of OIt *onice* onyx, fr. L *onych-*, *onyx* onyx] : a variety of onyx having a faint bluish layer over black
**nic·ol prism** \'nikəl-\ *also* **nicol** *n* -s *usu cap N* [after William *Nicol* †1851 Brit. physicist who invented it] : a device used for the production or analysis of polarized light consisting of the two parts of a rhombohedron of clear calcite bisected obliquely at a particular angle and subsequently cemented together with a transparent cement of which the refractive index lies between that of calcite for the ordinary ray which is totally reflected at the cement interface and the maximum refractive index of calcite for the extraordinary ray which is alone transmitted, both rays being plane-polarized at right angles to each other
**nic·o·sia** \ˌnikə'sēə\ *adj, usu cap* [fr. *Nicosia*, Cyprus] : of or from Nicosia, the capital of Cyprus : of the kind or style prevalent in Nicosia
**nicotia** *n* -s [NL, fr. Jean *Nicot* †1600 Fr. diplomat and scholar who introduced tobacco into France + NL *-ia*] *obs* : NICOTINE, TOBACCO
**ni·co·tian** \ni'kōshən\ *n* -s [MF *nicotiane*, prob. fr. NL *nicotiana* (in *herba nicotiana* Nicot's herb, tobacco), fem. of *nicotianus*, adj., of Nicot fr. Jean *Nicot* †1600 + L *-ianus* -an] **1** *obs* : TOBACCO **2** *archaic* : a user of tobacco
**ni·co·ti·ana** \niˌkōshē'anə, -'ä-,-'ā-\ *n* [NL, prob. fr. *nicotiana* (in *herba nicotiana*)] **1** *cap* : a genus of American and Asiatic herbs or shrubs (family Solanaceae) having viscid foliage and tubular flowers with a cleft or divided calyx and a many-seeded capsule — see TOBACCO **2** -s : FLOWERING TOBACCO
**nicotin–** *or* **nicotino–** *comb form* [*nicotin-* fr. *nicotine*; *nicotino-* fr. *nicotine* + *-o-*] **1** : nicotine : tobacco ⟨*nicotin*ism⟩ ⟨*nicotino*phobe⟩ **2** [*nicotin-* ISV, fr. *nicotinic*; *nicotino-* ISV *nicotinic* + *-o-*] : nicotinic acid ⟨*nicotin*amide⟩ ⟨*nicotino*nitrile⟩
**nic·o·ti·na** \ˌnikə'tēnə\ *n* -s [NL, fr. Jean *Nicot* †1600 + L *-ina* (fem. of *-inus* -ine, adj. suffix)] *archaic* : NICOTINE
**nic·o·tin·amide** \ˌnikə'tēnəˌmīd, -ˌməd\ *n* [ISV *nicotin-* + *amide*] : a bitter crystalline basic amide $C_5H_4NCONH_2$ that is a member of the vitamin B complex and is interconvertible with nicotinic acid in the living organism, that occurs naturally usu. as a constituent of coenzymes, and that is used similarly to nicotinic acid; the amide of nicotinic acid — called also *niacin*; see PYRIDINE NUCLEOTIDE
**nic·o·tin·ate** \-ēˌnāt\ *n* -s [*nicotin*ic + *-ate*] : a salt or ester of nicotinic acid
**nic·o·tine** \'nikəˌtēn, ˌ=='=\ *n* -s [F, fr. NL *Nicotiana* + F *-ine*] **1 a** : a very poisonous volatile weakly basic liquid alkaloid $C_{10}H_{14}N_2$ that constitutes the chief active principle of tobacco, that darkens on exposure, that causes an acrid burning sensation in the mouth, that is obtained usu. as a by-product of the tobacco industry, and that is used as an insecticide in various forms (as the free alkaloid or as a solution of the sulfate) **2** : FLOWERING TOBACCO
**nic·o·tined** \-ēnd\ *adj* **1** : full of, stained with, or saturated with tobacco smoke ⟨~ fingers⟩ **2** : drugged with nicotine
**nic·o·tine·less** \-ēnləs\ *adj* : lacking nicotine
**nic·o·tin·ian** *also* **nic·o·tin·ean** \ˌnikə'tēnēən, -tin-\ *adj* [*nicotine* + *-an*] : relating to or caused by use of tobacco
**nic·o·tin·ic** \-tēnik, -tin-\ *adj* [ISV *nicotin-* + *-ic*] **1** : of or relating to nicotine or nicotinic acid **2** : producing a transitory stimulation followed by paralysis in autonomic ganglion cells ⟨~ effect⟩ ⟨a ~ drug⟩ — compare MUSCARINIC
**nicotinic acid** *n* : a crystalline acid $C_5H_4NCOOH$ that is a member of the vitamin B complex occurring usu. in the form of a complex of nicotinamide in various animal and plant parts (as blood, liver, yeast, bran, legumes), is made by oxidation of nicotine, quinoline, or methylethy pyridine, and is effective in preventing and treating human pellagra and blacktongue of dogs; 3-pyridine-carboxylic acid — called also *niacin*
**nic·o·tin·ism** \'nikəˌtēˌnizəm, ˌ=='=ˌ==\ *n* -s [ISV *nicotin-* + *-ism*] : the effect of the excessive use of tobacco
**nic·o·tin·ize** \-tēˌnīz\ *vt* -ED/-ING/-S [*nicotin-* (fr. *nicotine*) + *-ize*] : to drug with nicotine
**nic·o·ti·no·yl** \ˌnikə'tēnəwəl, -tin-\ *or* **nic·o·ti·nyl** \-tēn°l\ *n* -s [*nicotin-* + *-yl*] : the radical $NC_5H_4CO-$ of nicotinic acid
**nic·o·tin·uric acid** \ˌnikəˌtē'nyu̇rik-\ *n* [ISV *nicotinuric*, fr. *nicotin-* + *-uric*] : a crystalline acid $NC_5H_4CONHCH_2COOH$ found in the urine of some animals as a product of the metabolism of nicotinic acid; *N*-nicotinoyl-glycine
**nic·tate** \'nikˌtāt\ *vi* -ED/-ING/-S [L *nictatus*, past part. of *nictare* — more at CONNIVE] : WINK — **nictation** *n* -s
**nic·ti·tant** \'niktətənt\ *adj* [*nictitate* + *-ant*] : adapted for winking ⟨~ membrane of a snake⟩
**nic·ti·tate** \'niktəˌtāt *sometimes probably by* t-dissimilation ÷-kə-\ *vi* -ED/-ING/-S [alter. (influenced by L freq. verbs in *-itare*) of *nictate*] : WINK — **nic·ti·ta·tion** \ˌ=='tāshən\ *n* -s
**nictitating membrane** *n* [*nictitating* fr. pres. part. of *nictitate*] : a thin membrane found in many animals at the inner angle or beneath the lower lid of the eye and capable of extending across the eyeball
**nictitating spasm** *n* : clonic spasm of the eyelid
**nic·u·ri** \ˌnikə'rē\ *n* -s [prob. fr. Pg, modif. of Tupi *aricuri*] : OURICURY
**NID** *abbr* naval intelligence department; naval intelligence division
**ni·dal** \'nīd°l\ *adj* [L *nidus* nest + E *-al*] : of or relating to a nidus
**nida·men·tal** \ˌnīdə'ment°l\ *adj* [L *nidamentum* materials for a nest (fr. *nidus* nest) + E *-al* — more at NEST] : relating to or producing a capsule or covering for an egg or mass of eggs
**ni·da·tion** \nī'dāshən\ *n* -s [L *nidus* nest + E *-ation*] **1** : the development of the epithelial membrane lining the inner surface of the uterus following menstruation **2** : IMPLANTATION 1b
**nida·to·ry** \'nīdəˌtōrē, 'nid-\ *adj* [L *nidus* nest + E *-atory*] : of or relating to a nest
**nid·der·ing** *or* **nid·er·ing** \'nid(ə)riŋ\ *n* -s [*niddering*, alter. of *nidering*, alter. of ME *nithing*] *archaic* : COWARD
**nid·dick** \'nidik\ *n* -s [origin unknown] *dial Eng* : the nape of the neck
**nid·dle** \'nid°l\ *vi* -ED/-ING/-S [origin unknown] *chiefly Scot* : to move quickly
**niddle–noddle** \ˌnid°lˌnäd°l\ *adj* [redupl. & alter. of ²*noddle*] : having an unstably nodding head
**nid·dy nod·dy** \ˌnidēˌnädē\ *n* [perh. fr. obs. *niddy-noddy* to nod to and fro unsteadily, by redupl. & alter. of ¹*nod*] : a hand reel for yarn
**nide** \'nīd\ *n* -s [L *nidus* nest] *chiefly Brit* : a family or group of pheasants
¹**nidge** \'nij\ *vi* -ED/-ING/-S [origin unknown] : SHAKE, QUIVER
²**nidge** *var of* NIG
**nid·get** \'nijət\ *n* -s [alter. of earlier *nidiot*, alter. (from incorrect division of *an idiot*) of ¹*idiot*] *archaic* : IDIOT, FOOL
**nidi** *pl of* NIDUS
**ni·dic·o·lous** \(')nī'dikələs\ *adj* [L *nidi-* (fr. *nidus* nest) + E *-colous*] **1** : reared for a time in a nest : ALTRICIAL — compare NIDIFUGOUS **2** : living in a nest; *esp* : sharing the nest of another kind of animal ⟨some beetles are ~ with ants⟩
**nid·i·fi·cant** \'nidəfəkənt, (')nī'dif-\ *adj* [L *nidificant-*, *nidificans*, pres. part. of *nidificare*] : building a nest
**nid·i·fi·cate** \'nidəfəˌkāt, nī'dif-\ *vi* -ED/-ING/-S [L *nidificatus*, past part. of *nidificare*] : to build a nest
**nid·i·fi·ca·tion** \ˌnidəfə'kāshən, (ˌ)nīˌdif-\ *n* -s [ML *nidification-*, *nidificatio*, fr. L *nidificatus* (past part.) + *-ion-*, *-io* -ion] : the act or process of nidificating : the construction of a nest — **nid·i·fi·ca·tion·al** \-shən°l, -shnəl\ *adj*
**ni·dif·u·gous** \(')nī'difyəgəs\ *adj* [L *nidi-* (fr. *nidus* nest) + E *-fugous* (as in *lucifugous*)] : leaving the nest soon after hatching : PRECOCIAL — compare NIDICOLOUS
**nid·i·fy** \'nidəˌfī\ *vi* -ED/-ING/-ES [L *nidificare*, fr. *nidi-* (fr. *nidus* nest) + *-ficare* -fy — more at NEST] : to build a nest
**nid–nod** \'nidˌnäd\ *vi* [redupl. & alter. of ¹*nod*] : to nod repeatedly from drowsiness
**ni·dol·o·gist** \nī'däləjəst\ *n* -s [L *nidus* nest + E *-ologist*] : one who specializes in the study of birds' nests
**ni·dol·o·gy** \-jē\ *n* -ES [L *nidus* nest + E *-ology*] : the study of birds' nests
**ni·dor** \'nīˌdȯ(ə)r, -ˌdər\ *n* -s [L; akin to OE *hnītan* to thrust, gore, knock, encounter, *gehnǣst* collision, battle, ON *hnīta* to strike, *hnīta* to weld, *hnissa* smell from cooking, unpleasant taste, MIr *cned* wound, Gk *knizein* to scratch, tickle, tease, *knisma* scratch, *knismos* irritation, itching, *knisa*, *knisē* smell of burnt sacrifice, nidor, Latvian *kniest* to itch and to L *ciner-*, *cinis* ashes — more at INCINERATE] : a strong smell : REEK; *esp* : the smell of cooking or burning meat or fat
**ni·dor·ous** \'nīdərəs\ *adj* [LL *nidorosus* steaming, reeking, fr. L *nidor* + *-osus* -ous] : rankly odorous : smelling of or like burning or decaying animal matter
**nid·u·lant** \'nijələnt\ *adj* [L *nidulant-*, *nidulans*, pres. part. of *nidulari*] : EMBEDDED, NESTLING; *specif* : lying free in a cavity
**nid·u·lar·ia** \ˌnijə'la(a)rēə\ *n, cap* [NL, fr. L *nidulus* small nest + NL *-aria*] : a genus of fungi (the type of the family Nidulariaceae) having a sessile globose peridium opening by a lacerate mouth
**nid·u·lar·i·a·ce·ae** \-ˌla(a)rē'āsēˌē\ *n pl, cap* [NL, fr. *Nidularia*, type genus + *-aceae*] : a family of small fungi (order Nidulariales) comprising the bird's-nest fungi and having the spores formed in peridioles borne in the peridium like eggs in a nest — compare SPHAEROBOLACEAE — **nid·u·lar·i·a·ceous** \ˌ=ˌ==ˌ=='āshəs\ *adj*
**nid·u·lar·i·a·les** \ˌ=ˌ==ˌ=ē'ā(ˌ)lēz\ *n pl, cap* [NL, fr. *Nidularia* + *-ales*] : a small order of basidiomycetous fungi (subclass Homobasidiomycetes) usu. including the families Nidulariaceae and Sphaerobolaceae
**nid·u·late** \'nijəˌlāt\ *adj* [L *nidulatus*, past part. of *nidulari* to make a nest, fr. *nidulus* small nest, dim. of *nidus* nest — more at NEST] : NIDULANT
**nid·u·la·tion** \ˌnijə'lāshən\ *n* -s [obs. E *nidulate* to make a nest (fr. L *nidulatus*, past part.) + E *-ion*] : nest building : NESTING
**nid·u·li·tes** \-'līd·(ˌ)ēz\ *n, cap* [NL, fr. L *nidulus* small nest + NL *-ites*] : a genus of hollow ovoidal calcareous fossils that have walls with a honeycomb structure and are often considered to belong among or to be related to the Porifera but are sometimes treated as calcareous algae
**nid·u·lus** \'nijələs\ *n, pl* **niduli** [NL, fr. L, small nest] : CENTER 2e
**ni·dus** \'nīdəs\ *n, pl* **ni·di** \-ˌdī\ *or* **ni·dus·es** [NL, fr. L, nest] **1** : a nest for the eggs of insects, spiders, small animals **2 a** : a breeding place; *esp* : a place or substance in an animal or plant where the germs of a disease or other organisms lodge and multiply **b** : a place of development for spores or seeds **c** : a group of regenerative epithelial cells of the insect ventriculus **3 a** : a place where something originates or is fostered or develops ⟨hysterical symptoms often grow from an organic ~, congenital or acquired —D.N.Parfitt⟩ **b** : a place where something is settled, lodged, or located
**niece** \'nēs\ *n* -s [ME *nece*, fr. AF *nece* niece & OF *niece* granddaughter, niece, fr. LL *neptia*, fr. L *neptis* granddaughter; akin to L *nepos*, grandson, nephew — more at NEPHEW] **1** *obs* : a female descendant or relative; as **a** : GRANDDAUGHTER **b** : GRANDNIECE **2 a** : a daughter of one's brother or sister **b** : a daughter of one's brother-in-law or sister-in-law
**niece·less** \-sləs\ *adj* : having no niece
**nief** *var of* NEIF
**ni·el·lat·ed** \nē'eˌlād·əd\ *or* **ni·elled** \-eld\ *adj* [*niellated* fr. It *niellato* (past part. of *niellare* to inlay with niello, fr. *niello*) + E *-ed*; *nielled*, perh. fr. F *nieller* to inlay with niello (fr. *nielle* niello, fr. It *niello*) + E *-ed*] : NIELLOED
**ni·el·list** \-eləst\ *n* -s : a maker of or worker in niello
¹**ni·el·lo** \-e(ˌ)lō\ *n, pl* **niel·li** \-ˌlē\ *or* **niellos** [It, fr. ML *nigellum*, fr. neut. of L *nigellus* blackish, dark, dim. of *niger* black] **1** : any of several metallic alloys of sulfur with silver, copper or lead having a deep black color **2** : the art, process, or method of decorating metal with incised designs filled with niello; *also* : work of this kind **3** : an object decorated with niello **4** : an impression on paper taken from the engraved or incised surface before niello has been inlaid
²**niello** \"\ *vt* -ED/-ING/-S : to inlay or ornament with niello
**niel·sen method** \'nēlsən-\ *n, usu cap N* [after Holger *Nielsen* †1955 Dan. army officer who originated it] : BACK PRESSURE-ARM LIFT METHOD
**nie·mann–pick disease** \'nēˌmänˈpik-\ *n, usu cap N&P* [after Albert *Niemann* †1921 Ger. surgeon and Ludwig *Pick* †1944 Ger physician] : a familial disease of infants characterized by gastrointestinal disturbances, malnutrition, and enlargement of the spleen, liver, and lymph nodes, and marked by abnormalities of the blood-forming organs
**nie·nock** \'nēnək\ *n* -s *often cap* [origin unknown] : AMERICAN LOTUS
**nientsi** *usu cap, var of* NENTSI
**nie·pa** \'nēpə\ *n* -s [prob. fr. the native name in East India] **1** : an East Indian tree (*Samadera indica*) whose bark contains a bitter principle similar to quassia **2** *also* **niepa bark** : the bark of the niepa tree
**nie·rem·ber·gia** \ˌnirəm'bərjēə, -rgēə\ *n* [NL, fr. Juan E. *Nieremberg* †1658 Span. Jesuit naturalist and author + NL *-ia*] **1** *cap* : a genus of tropical American creeping herbs (family Solanaceae) having solitary white or purple flowers and a slender corolla tube bearing five exserted stamens at its apex **2** -s : any plant of the genus *Nierembergia* — called also *cupflower*
**nies·hout** \'nēsˌhau̇t\ *n* -s [Afrik, fr. *nies* to sneeze (fr. D *niezen*) + *hout* wood (fr. D)] : SNEEZEWOOD
¹**nietz·sche·an** \'nēchēən\ *adj, usu cap* [Friedrich W. *Nietzsche* †1900 Ger. philosopher and poet + E *-an*] : of or relating to the philosopher Nietzsche or to Nietzscheanism
²**nietzschean** \"\ *n* -s *usu cap* : an adherent to Nietzscheanism : an advocate of the ideas of Nietzsche
**nietz·sche·an·ism** \-əˌnizəm\ *or* **nietz·sche·ism** \-chēˌizəm\ *n* -s *usu cap* [*nietzscheanism* fr. ¹*nietzschean* + *-ism*; *nietzscheism* fr. F. W. *Nietzsche* + E *-ism*] : the philosophical theories of Nietzsche advocating the overcoming of both a threatening nihilism and a slave morality as exemplified for him in historical Christianity through a reevaluation of all values on the basis of a will to power epitomized in his doctrine of the superman and the idea of the eternal recurrence of all things
¹**nieve** \'nēv\ *also* **nief** \'nēf\ *n* -s [ME *neve*, *nefe*, fr. ON *hnefi*] **1** *chiefly dial* : a person's hand **2** *chiefly dial* : FIST
²**nieve** \"\ *n* -s [AF *neife*, *niefe*, *nief*, fem. of (assumed) *neif*, *naif* neif — more at NEIF] : a female neif
**nie·ve pen·i·ten·te** \nē'āvāˌpenə'tentā, 'nyāv-\ *n, pl* **nie·ves peniten·tes** \-vās . . . tās\ [Sp, lit., penitent snow; fr. the illusion of kneeling human figures] : a jagged sometimes curved pinnacle of ice or névé produced by uneven melting of a snowbank or of the surface of a glacier; *also* : an assemblage of such pinnacles — compare SERAC
**nie·ve·ta** \ˌnēə'vēd·ə, nyə-'-\ *n* -s [AmerSp, fr. *nieve* snow, fr. L *niv-*, *nix* — more at SNOW] : a low Californian herb of the genus *Cryptantha* (family Boraginaceae) with small white flowers like forget-me-nots
**niev·ie–niev·ie–nick–nack** \'nēvē'nēvē'nikˌnak\ *n* -s [prob. fr. redupl. of *nievie* (dim. of ¹*nieve*) + *nick-nack*, alter. of *knickknack*] : a child's guessing game
¹**nif·fer** \'nifə(r)\ *vb* -ED/-ING/-S [perh. alter. of ¹*nieve*] *chiefly Scot* : EXCHANGE, TRADE
²**niffer** \"\ *n* -s *chiefly Scot* : BARGAIN, DICKER, EXCHANGE
**niff–naff** \'nifˌnaf\ *vi* -ED/-ING/-S [origin unknown] *dial Brit* : TRIFLE
**niff–naf·fy** \-ˌnafi\ *adj, Scot* : TRIFLING
**ni·fle** \'nīfəl, 'nif-\ *or* **nif·fle** \'nif-\ *n* -s [ME *nifle*] *chiefly dial* : a trivial or worthless person or thing
¹**nif·ty** \'niftē, -ti\ *adj* -ER/-EST [origin unknown] : very good : very attractive : SMART, STYLISH ⟨~ clothes⟩ ⟨a ~ blond⟩ : well-executed ⟨a ~ right to the jaw⟩ : SPLENDID ⟨a ~ show⟩ : HANDY ⟨a ~ little machine⟩ : CLEVER, ADEPT ⟨~ hands of a third baseman —John McNulty⟩
²**nifty** \"\ *n* -ES : something that is nifty; *esp* : a clever or neatly turned phrase or joke ⟨hurled a few fistfuls of crackling *nifties* at them —Bob Hope⟩
¹**nig** \'nig\ *n* -s [by shortening] : NIGGER
²**nig** \"\ *vi* **nigged; nigged; nigging; nigs** [short for *renig*] : RENEGE, REVOKE
³**nig** \"\ *or* **nidge** *vt* **nigged** *or* **nidged; nigged** *or* **nidged; nigging** *or* **nidging; nigs** *or* **nidges** [origin unknown] : to dress (stone) with a sharp-pointed hammer
**ni·gel·la** \nī'jelə\ *n* [NL, fr. LL, black caraway, fr. fem. of L *nigellus* blackish, dark — more at NIELLO] **1** *cap* : a genus of erect annual European herbs (family Ranunculaceae) having dissected leaves and blue or white flowers — see LOVE-IN-A-MIST **2** -s : any plant of the genus *Nigella*
¹**niger** *n* -s [prob. modif. (influenced by L *niger*, adj., black, dark) of Sp *negro*] *obs* : NEGRO
²**ni·ger** \'nījə(r)\ *also* **niger morocco** *n* -s [fr. *Niger* river, West African river flowing through Nigeria] : leather from Nigerian goats used chiefly for fine bookbinding
³**niger** \"\ *adj, usu cap* [fr. *Niger* Republic, western Africa] : of or relating to the Niger Republic : of the kind or style prevalent in the Niger Republic
**niger–congo** \ˌ=='(ˌ)=\ *n, usu cap N&C* [fr. *Niger*, river of West Africa + *Congo*, river of central Africa] : a language family that consists of the West-Atlantic, Mande, Gur, Kwa, Ijo, Central, and Adamawa-Eastern branches and that is spoken by most of the indigenous peoples of west, central, and south Africa
**ni·ge·ria** \(')nī'jirēə\ *adj, usu cap* [fr. *Nigeria*, state in West Africa] : of or from Nigeria : of the kind or style prevalent in Nigeria : NIGERIAN
¹**ni·ge·ri·an** \='==\ *n* -s *cap* [*Nigeria*, West Africa + E *-an*] : a native or inhabitant of Nigeria
²**nigerian** \(')='==\ *adj, usu cap* : of or relating to Nigeria
**ni·ger·ite** \'nījəˌrīt\ *n* -s [*Nigeria*, its locality + E *-ite*] : a mineral $(Zn,Fe,Mg)(Sn,Zn)_2(Al,Fe)_{12}O_{22}(OH)_2$ consisting of an oxide and hydroxide of aluminum, iron, tin, zinc, and magnesium

**ni·ge·rois** \ˌnēzhərˈwä, -ˌzher-\ *n, pl* **nigerois** \-wä(z)\ *cap* [(assumed) F, fr. *Niger*, country in western Africa + F *-ois* -ese, fr. L *-ensis*] **:** a native or inhabitant of the Republic of Niger

**niger seed** *n* [prob. fr. *Niger* river, West Africa, where it originated] **:** the seed of ramtil that yields a valuable oil

**niger-seed oil** *n* [*niger seed*] **:** a drying oil obtained from the seeds of ramtil and used in food, soap, and paints

**¹nig·gard** \ˈnigə(r)d\ *n* -s [ME *nigart, nigard, niggard*, prob. fr. earlier *nig* niggard (of Scand origin) + *-art, -ard*; akin to ON *hnøggr* niggardly, stingy, *hnøggva, hnyggja* to humble, bring down; akin to OE *hnēaw* niggardly, stingy, OHG *hniuwan* to crush, Gk *knyein* to scratch, *knoos, knous* grating noise of an axle, sound of footsteps, *knuos* itch, Latvian *knūt, knūst* to itch and to L *ciner-, cinis* ashes — more at INCINERATE] **:** a person meanly close and covetous **:** MISER

**²niggard** \"\ *adj* [ME *nigart*, adj. & n.] **1 :** NIGGARDLY, STINGY ⟨~ storekeepers who refused to pay . . . his modest monthly honorarium —Ben Riker⟩ ⟨cold, unappreciative, very ~ in even modified praise —Arnold Bennett⟩ **2 :** resulting from or displaying niggardliness **:** SCANTY ⟨the shop-windows' show is ~ and shabby —W.C.Brownell⟩

**³niggard** *vb* -ED/-ING/-S *vi, obs* **:** to act niggardly ~ *vt, obs* **:** to treat in a niggardly manner

**nig·gard·li·ness** \-dlēnə̇s\ *n* -ES **:** the quality or state of being niggardly

**¹nig·gard·ly** \-lē, -li\ *adj* [¹*niggard* + *-ly*] **1 :** grudgingly loath to part with money or possessions or to grant favors ⟨they were not ~, these tramps, and he who had money did not hesitate to share it —W.S.Maugham⟩ ⟨so ~ about entry to their country —Bernard Pares⟩ **2 :** provided in meanly limited supply **:** SCANTY ⟨the country has been handicapped by ~ transport resources —V.H.Whitney⟩ **syn** see STINGY

**²niggardly** \"\ *adv* [²*niggard* + *-ly*] **:** in the manner of a niggard ⟨the people of our respective states . . . cannot afford to deal ~ with their universities —L.M.Chamberlain⟩

**nig·gard·ness** *n* -ES [²*niggard* + *-ness*] **:** NIGGARDLINESS

**¹nig·ger** \ˈnigə(r)\ *n* -s *often attrib* [alter. of *neger* or ¹*niger*] **1 a :** NEGRO — usu. taken to be offensive **b :** a member (as an East Indian, a Filipino, an Egyptian) of any very dark-skinned race — usu. taken to be offensive **2 :** any of several dark-colored insect larvae (as of some ladybugs and of the turnip sawfly) **3 :** COTTON SPINNER **4 :** a steam-operated capstan for warping river steamboats over snags and shallows **5 :** a long-toothed power-propelled lever arm used to position logs on a carriage (as in a sawmill)

**²nigger** \"\ *vt* -ED/-ING/-S **:** to divide (a log) by burning — usu. used with *off* ⟨~*ed* off into lengths —Conrad Richter⟩

**nigger baby** *n, Southwest* **:** either of two herbs: **a :** a sanicle (*Sanicula bipinnatifida*) with purple flowers **b :** a blue-eyed grass (*Sisyrinchium bellum*) with purplish blue flowers — usu. used in pl.

**nigger bug** *n* **:** NEGRO BUG

**nigger chaser** *n* **:** a small firework that shoots about on the ground

**nigger daisy** *n* **:** BLACK-EYED SUSAN 1

**niggerfish** \ˈ==ˌ=\ *n* **:** CONEY 5a

**niggergoose** \ˈ==ˌ=\ *n, pl* **niggergeese :** CORMORANT

**niggerhead** \ˈ==ˌ=\ *n* **1 :** a dark-colored mound or clump of vegetation (as a hummock of tundra or a tussock of sedge in a permafrost bog) found in far northern regions (as Alaska) **2 :** a strong black chewing tobacco **:** NEGROHEAD **3 a :** a hard dark-colored nodule or boulder **b :** a coral boulder broken off and thrown to the surface by wind and wave action (as on the Great Barrier reef) **4 :** a large blackish smooth-shelled freshwater mussel (*Quadrula ebena*) used in button making and sometimes producing valuable pearls **5 a** (1) **:** any of various plants of the genus *Rudbeckia* (2) **:** a ribgrass (*Plantago lanceolata*) (3) **:** a wild peony (*Paeonia brownii*) of the western U.S. (4) **:** the common greenbrier (*Smilax rotundifolia*) of eastern No. America (5) **:** PURPLE CONEFLOWER **b** *Austral* (1) **:** the spiny head of a saltwort (2) **:** NEGROHEAD BEECH **6 a :** a drum on a windlass **b :** BOLLARD **7** *Canad* **:** SCOTER **8 a :** a small wire nail driven into the furniture of a form on a cylinder press to produce a black mark on the feed-gauge edge of the printed sheet as a guide for trimming and folding **b** (1) **:** a mark made by a niggerhead (2) **:** a similar mark used as a collating mark

**niggerhead cactus** *n* **:** BISNAGA

**nigger heaven** *n, slang* **:** the highest balcony or row of seats in a theater

**nigger in the woodpile :** something (as a concealed motive or obscure factor) contrary to appearances in a situation

**nigger pine** *n* **:** JERSEY PINE

**nigger-shooter** \ˈ==ˌ==\ *n* **:** SLINGSHOT

**niggertoe** \ˈ==ˌ=\ *n* **1** *South* **:** any of various herbs (as of the genera *Gaillardia, Coreopsis*, and *Rudbeckia*) having flower heads with black or dark-colored disks **2 :** BRAZIL NUT

**niggerweed** \ˈ==ˌ=\ *n* **:** JOE-PYE WEED

**niggerwool** \ˈ==ˌ=\ *n* **:** a sedge (*Carex filifolia*) of the western Great Plains of No. America that is used for mulch in erosion control

**nig·gery** \ˈnigərē\ *adj* [¹*nigger* + *-y*] **:** characteristic of a Negro

**nigging** *pres part of* NIG

**nig·gle** \ˈnigəl\ *vb* **niggled; niggled; niggling** \-g(ə)liŋ\ **niggles** [origin unknown] *vi* **1 a :** TRIFLE ⟨didn't ~ with . . . prepositions but printed the lecture title as it was received —*Newsweek*⟩ **b :** to work meticulously; *esp* **:** to spend too much effort on minor details **2 :** to find fault constantly in a petty way **:** CARP ⟨she haggles, she ~s, she wears out our patience —Virginia Woolf⟩ **3 :** GNAW ⟨a tiny *niggling* noise like a mouse —Ruth Park⟩ ⟨the question which had *niggled* insistently at his brain —J.E.Macdonnell⟩ ~ *vt* **:** to give stingily or in tiny portions ⟨it seems greedier to me to . . . ~ it out in tiny bits —Florence Bullock⟩

**nig·gler** \-g(ə)lə(r)\ *n* -s **:** one that niggles ⟨the ~s . . . take great pride in their discovery of a trifling error and go to immense lengths to point it out —Philip Wylie⟩

**nig·gli·ite** \ˈniglēˌīt\ *n* -s [Paul *Niggli* †1953 Swiss mineralogist + E *-ite*] **:** a mineral PtTe₃(?) consisting of a telluride of platinum found in Griqualand East

**niggling** *adj* [fr. pres. part. of *niggle*] **1 :** PETTY ⟨impatient with small patterns and regular meters, which they find ~ and hampering —Louise Bogan⟩ **2 a :** METICULOUS ⟨begin some ~ task, usually the preparation of a very careful drawing —*Lancet*⟩ **b :** overelaborate or feeble in execution ⟨the brushwork trailed off in ~ strokes —*Atlantic*⟩ — **nig·gling·ly** *adv*

**nig·gly** \ˈnig(ə)lē\ *adj* -ER/-EST [*niggle* + *-y*] **:** NIGGLING

**niggun** *var of* NIGUN

**¹nigh** \ˈnī\ *adv* -ER/-EST [ME *nigh, neigh, neih, neh*, adv. & adj., fr. OE *nēah, nēh*; akin to OS *nāh*, adv. & adj., nigh, MD *nā*, prep. & adv., OHG *nāh*, adv. & adj., nigh, prep., nigh, after, ON *nā-* (in composition) nigh, Goth *nehw, ˈnehwa*, adv., nigh, and perh. to Skt *naśati* he attains, reaches — more at ENOUGH] **1 :** near in place, time, or relationship — often used with *on, onto*, or *unto* ⟨served . . . for ~ on forty years —M.S.Tisdale⟩ ⟨my end draws ~; 'tis time that I were gone —Alfred Tennyson⟩ **2 :** NEARLY, ALMOST ⟨the already ~ obliterated records of childhood —Osbert Sitwell⟩

**²nigh** \"\ *adj* -ER/-EST [ME *nigh, neigh, neih, neh*, fr. OE *nēah, nēh*, adj. & adv.] **1 :** CLOSE ⟨man in . . . friend, brother, ~*est* neighbor —Walt Whitman⟩ — often used predicatively ⟨vow that my heart, when death is ~ —Sidney Lanier⟩; often used with a preposition ⟨some so silent, dark, and ~ to death —Walt Whitman⟩ **2** *chiefly dial* **:** DIRECT, SHORT ⟨took a ~ cut through the hill paths home —J.H. Stuart⟩ **3 :** ⁴NEAR 3b **4** *chiefly dial* **:** STINGY

**³nigh** \"\ *prep* [ME *nigh, neigh, neih, neh*, fr. OE *nēah, nēh*, prob. fr. *nēah, nēh*, adv.] **:** NEAR ⟨everyone wanted to be next and ~ me —Padraic Colum⟩

**⁴nigh** \"\ *vb* -ED/-ING/-S [ME *nighen, neighen, neihen, neghen*, fr. *nigh, neigh, neih*, adv.] *vt* **:** to draw or come near to **:** APPROACH ⟨strapped, noosed, ~*ing* his hour —A.E.Housman⟩ ~ *vi* **:** to draw near

**nigh-hand** \ˈ=ˌ=\ *adv* [ME *nigh hand, neih hond*, fr. OE *nēh hand*, fr. *nēh*, adv., nigh + *hand*] **1 :** near at hand **:** close by ⟨living *nigh-hand* to where the new house was to be built —A.H.Bullen⟩ **2 :** NEARLY, ALMOST ⟨wasn't it enough for you to *nigh-hand* kill one o' my horses —Samuel Lover⟩

**nigh·ly** *adv* [ME *neli*, fr. OE *nēalīce*, fr. *nēah*, adv. & adj., nigh + *-lice* -ly] **:** NEARLY, ALMOST

**nigh·ness** *n* -ES [ME, fr. *nigh* (adj.) + *-ness*] **:** the quality or state of being nigh

**¹night** \ˈnīt, *usu* -īd·+V\ *n* -s [ME *night, niht*, fr. OE *niht, næht, neaht*; akin to MD *nacht* night, OS & OHG *naht*, ON *nōtt, nātt*, Goth *nahts* night, OIr *in-nocht* tonight, W *nos* night, L *noct-, nox*, Gk *nykt-, nyx*, Skt *nakt, nakti*, Lith *naktis*, OSlav *noštĭ*] **1 :** the part of the solar day when the sun is beneath the horizon; *esp* **:** the time from dusk to dawn when no light of the sun is visible ⟨had an exhausting ~ alone in the woods⟩ ⟨extra pay for working at ~⟩ ⟨dine, drink, dance, or gamble by ~ —T.H.Fielding⟩ — compare DAY **2 a :** an evening or night taken as an occasion or point of time ⟨saw the opera on the opening ~⟩ ⟨saw the satellite on the third ~⟩ **b** (1) **:** an evening set aside for a particular purpose ⟨it was bingo ~ and everybody was at the movies —Theodora Keogh⟩ (2) **:** an evening program ⟨hold an amateur ~⟩ ⟨plan a ladies' ~ for the men's next club meeting⟩ **c :** the evening following a particular day ⟨Christmas ~⟩ ⟨their wedding ~⟩ ⟨election ~⟩ — compare EVE **3 a :** DARKNESS ⟨under cover of ~ swooped in among the cumbersome ships of the line —Frank Yerby⟩ **b :** a condition or period felt to resemble the darkness of night; *specif* **:** a period of dreary inactivity or affliction **:** mental or moral darkness ⟨the glories of Roman civilization were lost in a gloomy ~ of ignorance, superstition, and barbarism —R.A.Hall b.1911⟩ **c :** the beginning of darkness **:** NIGHTFALL ⟨rainbow at ~, sailors' delight⟩ ⟨waited until it was ~⟩ **4 a :** the period between sunset or the evening meal and bedtime ⟨went bowling every ~⟩ ⟨Thursday evening is their maid's ~ out⟩ **b :** the period between nightfall or 6 p.m. and midnight ⟨the ~ of May 1⟩ **c :** the period between bedtime and morning usu. spent in bed ⟨slept quietly all ~⟩ **d :** a time for sexual intercourse **e :** a period of gainful employment coming during or chiefly during the night ⟨began his ~ at eleven and got off at seven⟩ ⟨paid the lecturer $500 a ~⟩ **5** *archaic* **:** TONIGHT — used with *the* **6 :** a night's rest ⟨the patient had a good ~⟩

**²night** \"\ *vi* -ED/-ING/-S [ME *nighten*, fr. *night*, n.] **:** to remain during the night **:** to spend the night

**³night** \"\ *adj* [¹*night*] **1 :** of, relating to, or associated characteristically with the night ⟨~ poetry⟩ ⟨~ air⟩ **2 :** intended for use at night ⟨a ~ lamp⟩ ⟨the ~ bell⟩ **3 :** existing, occurring, or carried out during the night ⟨the ~ view of the city⟩ ⟨~ noises⟩ ⟨~ baseball⟩ **4 a** (1) **:** working at night ⟨a ~ nurse⟩ ⟨the ~ clerk⟩ (2) **:** of or relating to work done at night ⟨posted the ~ hours⟩ **b :** operating at night ⟨the ~ train⟩ **5 :** active or effective at night ⟨a ~ fly⟩

**night adder** *n* **:** any of several nocturnal African vipers (genus *Causus*) with greatly enlarged venom glands extending along the neck

**night and day** *adv* [ME, fr. OE *nǣht & dæg*] **:** CONTINUALLY

**night ape** *n* **1 :** any of several small nocturnal Central and So. American monkeys of the genus *Aotes* with whitish ruff, long nonprehensile tail, short ears, and very large yellow eyes — called also *owl monkey* **2 :** BUSH BABY

**night ark** *n, Brit* **:** a small chicken house with a slatted floor often measuring six by three feet

**night bird** *n* **1 :** a bird associated with night: as **a :** OWL **b :** NIGHTINGALE **c :** MOORHEN **d :** MANX SHEARWATER **2 :** NIGHTHAWK 2

**night-blind** \ˈ=ˌ=\ *adj* [back-formation fr. *night blindness*] **:** afflicted with night blindness

**night blindness** *n* **:** NYCTALOPIA

**night-blooming cereus** \ˈ=ˌ==-\ *n, pl* **night-blooming cereuses :** any of several night-blooming cacti: as **a :** a slender sprawling or climbing cactus (*Selenicereus grandiflorus*) that has ribbed stems and yellow spines and is often cultivated for its very large showy white strongly-scented flowers which are followed by yellow red-streaked fruits **b :** any of several cacti of the genera *Cereus* and *Hyalocereus* with flexuous climbing angled branches and large fragrant white flowers

**night blue** *n* **:** a dark grayish blue that is greener and paler than indigo

**night bolt** *n* **1 :** the bolt of a night latch **2 :** an auxiliary bolt on the inside of a door to prevent opening from the outside except by a key

**nightcap** \ˈ=ˌ=\ *n* [ME *night cappe*, fr. ¹*night* + *cappe* cap] **1 a :** a cloth cap worn with nightclothes **b** *or* **nightcap wig** *archaic* **:** a close-fitting wig **2 :** a cloud resting about the summit of a mountain or hill **3 :** something usu. soporific (as hot cocoa or toddy) taken at bedtime **4 :** the final race or contest of a day's sports; *esp* **:** the final game of a baseball doubleheader

nightcap 1a

**nightcaps** *n pl but sing or pl in constr* [pl. of *nightcap*] **:** WOOD ANEMONE a

**night cart** *n* **:** a cart for removing night soil

**night chair** *n* **:** CLOSESTOOL

**nightchurr** \ˈ=ˌ=\ *n* -s **:** the European goatsucker

**nightclothes** \ˈ=ˌ=\ *n pl* **1 :** garments worn in bed ⟨left me in total darkness, to scramble into my ~ as I could —Jane W. Carlyle⟩ **2** *obs* **:** informal evening wear

**night cloud** *n* **:** STRATUS

**¹nightclub** \ˈ=ˌ=\ *n* **:** a restaurant open at night usu. serving liquor, having a floor show, and providing music and space for dancing

**²nightclub** \"\ *vi* **:** to patronize nightclubs ⟨*nightclubbed* until the early hours . . . with a long-haired blond —*Associated Press*⟩ — **nightclubber** \"+ə(r)\ *n*

**night court** *n* **:** a criminal court in a large city that sits at night (as for summary disposition of criminal charges and the granting of bail)

**night crawler** *n* **:** EARTHWORM; *esp* **:** a large earthworm found on the surface of the soil usu. at night and used for fish bait

**night crow** *n* [ME *nihtcrowe, night crowe*, fr. *niht, night* night + *crowe* crow] **:** a bird that cries in the night; *esp* **:** NIGHT HERON

**night dial** *n* **1 :** a dial showing time by the moon's shadow — called also *moondial* **2 :** a clockface made luminous at night by a light from behind or by radioluminescent paint

**nightdress** \ˈ=ˌ=\ *n* **1 :** NIGHTGOWN **2 :** NIGHTCLOTHES

**night·ed** \ˈnīd·ə̇d\ *adj* [fr. past part. of obs. *night* to become night, grow dark, benight, fr. ME *nighten* (also, to spend the night) — more at NIGHT (v.)] **1 :** DARKENED, CLOUDED **2 :** BENIGHTED

**night editor** *n* **:** an editor in charge of the final makeup of a morning paper

**night effect** *n* **:** a shifting of the apparent direction of arrival of radio waves received with a direction finder that is sometimes accompanied by other irregularities of wave behavior and is most commonly observed at night

**night emerald** *n* **:** chrysolite or olivine having by artificial light a color resembling emerald and being used as a gem

**night·ery** \ˈnīd·ərē\ *n* -ES **:** NIGHTCLUB

**nightfall** \ˈ=ˌ=\ *n* **:** the close of the day **:** DUSK

**night fighter** *n* **:** a fighter plane equipped with searchlights or radar and used at night as an interceptor

**nightflit** \ˈ=ˌ=\ *n* [prob. fr. ¹*night* + *flit* (v.)] **:** WOODCOCK

**night-flowering catchfly** \ˈ=ˌ==-\ *n* **:** a European herb (*Silene noctiflora*) naturalized in No. America and having fragrant white or pink night-blooming flowers

**nightfowl** \ˈ=ˌ=\ *n* **:** NIGHT BIRD

**nightgear** \ˈ=ˌ=\ *n* **:** NIGHTCLOTHES 1

**night glass** *n* **:** a telescope having a low f-number to increase the light-gathering power for use at night

**night glasses** *n pl* **:** binoculars of similar design to the night glass

**nightgown** \ˈ=ˌ=\ *n* [ME *nightgoun*, fr. ¹*night* + *goun* gown] **1** *archaic* **:** a loose gown suitable for wear on evenings at home **:** DRESSING GOWN ⟨found him . . . wrapped in a tartan ~ —Sir Walter Scott⟩ **2 :** a garment resembling a dress or shirt designed for wear in bed ⟨she rose in her pale ~ —W.B. Yeats⟩ ⟨stockinet ~s are comfortable . . . for the baby —Benjamin Spock⟩

**night green** *n* [so called because it retains its greenness at night even under a dim gaslight] **:** a strong yellowish green that is paler than shamrock green and greener and less strong than Cyprus green

**nighthawk** \ˈ=ˌ=\ *n* **1 a :** any of several No. American goatsuckers of the genus *Chordeiles* related to the whippoorwill; *specif* **:** a goatsucker (*C. minor*) common in the eastern U.S. that is marbled black, brown, and ocherous with white on the wings, throat, and in the male also on the tail and that feeds on insects which it secures on the wing principally at twilight flying at a considerable height and often diving almost vertically **b :** the European nightjar **c :** any of several large petrels of the genera *Pterodroma* and *Priofinus* inhabiting southern seas **d** *Austral* **:** MOREPORK 1 **2 :** a person who habitually stays up or goes about late at night **3 :** an independent taxicab operated chiefly at night **4 :** a ranch hand who works at night on the range; *specif* **:** a hand who herds the saddle horses at night

**night heron** *n* **:** any of various nocturnal or crepuscular herons of *Nycticorax* and related genera found in most temperate and tropical regions; *esp* **:** a heron (*N. nycticorax*) that ranges from southern Europe to India and northern Africa — see BLACK-CROWNED NIGHT HERON, YELLOW-CROWNED NIGHT HERON

**night hitch** *n* [¹*night* + *hitch* (v.); fr. its use on night duty] **:** BUNKER SUIT

**night horn** *n* [prob. trans. of G *nachthorn*] **:** COR-DE-NUIT

**night·ie** *also* **nighty** \ˈnīd·ē\ *n, pl* **nighties** [*nightgown* + *-ie* or *-y*] **:** NIGHTGOWN 2; *esp* **:** one for a woman or child

**nighting** *pres part of* NIGHT

**night·in·gale** \ˈnīˌtᵊnˌgāl, |d·ən,-, |tən,- *sometimes* |d·iŋ,g- *or* |d·ēŋ,g- *or* |ti- *or* |tē-\ *n* -s [ME *nihtegale, nightingale*, fr. OE *nihtegale*, fr. *niht* night + *-gale* (fr. *galan* to sing); akin to OS *nahtigala* nightingale, MD *nachtegale*, OHG *nahtagala* — more at NIGHT, YELL] **1 :** any of several Old World thrushes of the genus *Luscinia*: as **a :** a thrush (*L. megarhyncha*) common in Great Britain that is about six inches long and russet brown above with the rump and tail lighter and the under parts whitish and that is noted for the sweet song of the male often heard at night during the breeding season **b :** a similar but larger thrush (*L. luscinia*) of eastern Europe **2 :** any of various birds that sing at night

**night intruder** *n* **:** an airplane equipped with navigation and radar equipment for flying into enemy territory at night

**night intrusion** *n* **:** the air tactic of interdicting enemy supply lines at night

**nightjar** \ˈ=ˌ=\ *n* [¹*night* + *jar* (pound); fr. its harsh sound] **:** a common grayish brown European nocturnal bird (*Caprimulgus europaeus*) that is speckled and barred with dark brown and buff and in the male has white markings on wing tips and outer tail feathers; *broadly* **:** GOATSUCKER — used esp. of Old World forms

**night jasmine** *n* **1 :** HURSINGHAR **2 :** a tropical shrub (*Cestrum nocturnum*) with tubular yellow flowers

**night kaka** *n* **:** KAKAPO

**night key** *n* **:** a key for operating a night latch

**night latch** *or* **night lock** *n* **:** a door lock having a spring bolt operated from the outside by a key and from the inside by a knob

**night·less** \ˈnītlə̇s\ *adj* **:** having no night — **night·less·ness** *n* -ES

**night letter** *also* **night lettergram** *n* **:** a telegram sent at night at a reduced rate per word

**night life** *n* **:** the activity of pleasure-seekers at night (as in nightclubs)

**night lifer** *n* [*night life* + *-er*] **:** a person taking part in night life **:** NIGHTCLUBBER ⟨the *night lifers* . . . listen to the best Negro bands and pay feverish prices for liquor —Earl Brown⟩

**night-light** \ˈ=ˌ=\ *n* **:** a light kept burning at night

**night line** *n* **:** a fishline set overnight

**¹nightlong** \ˈ=ˌ=\ *adj* [¹*night* + *long*] **:** lasting the whole night ⟨a ~ festivity⟩

**²nightlong** \"\ *adv* **:** through the whole night ⟨working ~ to save whom they could —*Newsweek*⟩

**¹night·ly** \ˈnītlē, -li\ *adj* [ME *nightly, nihtlich*, fr. OE *nihtlīc*, fr. *niht*, n., night + *-līc* -ly] **1 :** of or relating to the night or every night ⟨peering into the ~ murk —*Springfield (Mass.) Union*⟩ **2 :** happening, done, or used by night or every night ⟨giving five-minute ~ analyses of the news —*Current Biog.*⟩

**²nightly** \"\ *adv* [ME, fr. *nightly*, adj.] **:** every night ⟨gathered ~ to listen to the band concerts⟩; *also* **:** at or by night

**night·man** \ˈnītmən, *in sense 2* -ˌman *or* -ˌmaa(ə)n\ *n, pl* **nightmen 1 :** a man who empties privies by night **2** *usu* **night man :** a man whose work is at night; *specif* **:** NIGHT WATCHMAN 1

**¹night·mare** \ˈnītˌma(a)|(ə)r, -me|, |ə\ *n* [ME, fr. ¹*night* + *mare* (spirit)] **1 :** an evil spirit formerly thought to oppress people during sleep: as **a :** INCUBUS **b :** SUCCUBUS **c :** a hag sometimes believed to be accompanied by nine attendant spirits ⟨the ~, with her whole ninefold, seems to make it the scene of her gambols —Washington Irving⟩ **2 :** a frightening dream accompanied by a sense of oppression or suffocation that usu. awakens the sleeper **3 a :** something producing a feeling of burden, agitation, anxiety, or terror **:** a source of trouble or worry ⟨the worst ~s were the bridges high above rushing torrents —Dillon Ripley⟩ ⟨the ~ of the surgeon dealing with battle wounds is infection —C.L.Boltz⟩ **b :** APPREHENSION, WORRY ⟨the life of a hotel man here is precarious and full of ~s —Sam Schneider⟩ **4 :** an experience, situation, or work of imagination having the monstrous character of a nightmare ⟨their existence would be one living ~ of hideous watchfulness and dread —*Blue Bk.*⟩ ⟨signs that we dwellers in the modern ~ love one another —F.A.Swinnerton⟩ ⟨an enormous imitation palace . . . a ~ of pretentiousness —John Hersey⟩ **syn** see FANCY

**²nightmare** \"\ *adj* **1 :** of or relating to a nightmare ⟨a ~ obsession in some current poetry⟩ **2 :** NIGHTMARISH ⟨began a ~ existence in an iron lung —*N.Y. Times Book. Rev.*⟩ ⟨years that seemed to pass with ~ speed —William DuBois⟩

**night·mar·ish** \-ma(a)rish, -mer-, -rēsh\ *adj* **:** resembling or suggestive of a nightmare ⟨had a ~ memory of certain doorknobs . . . horrible in color and in shape —Royal Cortissoz⟩ ⟨paints a ~ picture —Henry Hazlitt⟩ — **night·mar·ish·ly** *adv* — **night·mar·ish·ness** *n* -ES

**night monkey** *n* **:** NIGHT APE

**night owl** *n* **:** a person who keeps late hours at night **:** NIGHTHAWK

**night parrot** *n* **1 :** KAKAPO **2 :** a nearly extinct nocturnal terrestrial parrot (*Geopsittacus occidentalis*) of western Australia

**night partridge** *or* **night peck** *n* [*night partridge* fr. ¹*night* + *partridge; night peck* fr. ¹*night* + *peck* (v.)] **:** WOODCOCK

**night piece** *n* **:** a work (as a picture, composition, or writing) dealing with night

**night rail** *n* **:** a woman's loose robe or gown formerly worn as a nightgown or dressing gown

**night raven** *n* [ME, fr. OE *niht-hræfn*, fr. *niht* night + *hræfn* raven] **:** a bird that cries at night; *esp* **:** NIGHT HERON

**night rider** *n* **:** one that rides at night; *esp* **:** a member of a secret band who ride masked at night doing acts of violence for the purpose of punishing or terrorizing

**night-riding** \ˈ=ˌ==\ *n* **:** activity of or resembling that of night riders

**night-robe** \ˈ=ˌ=\ *n* **:** NIGHTGOWN ⟨in her *night-robe* loose she lay reclined —Sir Walter Scott⟩

**night rocket** *n* **:** DAME'S VIOLET

**nights** \ˈnīts\ *adv* [ME *nightes*, fr. OE *nihtes*, adverbial gen. of *niht* night — more at NIGHT] **:** in the nighttime repeatedly ⟨he had written it ~ and over weekends —*Current Biog.*⟩ **:** on any night ⟨gets little sleep ~⟩

**night-scented stock** \ˈ=ˌ==-\ *n* **:** an annual or biennial stock (*Matthiola bicornis*) having very fragrant lilac or purplish flowers followed by forked elongated seed pods

**night school** *n* **:** school held in the evening; *specif* **:** a course offered (as by a university or high school) for people in working life and often stressing vocational training and recreational activities as well as general education — compare ADULT EDUCATION

**nightshade** \ˈ=ˌ=\ *n* [ME *nighteschede, nightschode*, fr. OE *nihtscada*, prob. fr. *niht* night + *sceadu* shade; akin to MD *nachtschade* nightshade, OHG *nahtscato* — more at SHADE] **1 :** any plant of the genus *Solanum*: as **a :** BLACK NIGHTSHADE **b :** BITTERSWEET 2a **2 :** BELLADONNA 1 **3 :** HENBANE 1a

**nightshade family** *n* **:** SOLANACEAE
**night shift** *n* **1 :** a shift worked chiefly at night (as between 10 p.m. and 8 a.m.) **2 :** the workers on a night shift
**nightshirt** \ˈ=,=\ *n* **:** a nightgown resembling a shirt
**nightside** \ˈ=,=\ *n* **:** the staff that works on a morning edition of a newspaper — contrasted with *dayside*
**night singer** *n* **:** a bird that sings at night; *specif* **:** SEDGE WARBLER
**night soil** *n* **:** human excrement collected for fertilizing the soil
**night song** *n* **:** COMPLINE
**night sparrow** *n* **:** CHIPPING SPARROW
**night spot** *n* **:** NIGHTCLUB
**nightstand** \ˈ=,=\ *n* **:** NIGHT TABLE
**nightstick** \ˈ=,=\ *n* [so called fr. its being originally carried by night] **:** a policeman's club
**nightstock** \ˈ=,=\ *n* **:** DAME'S VIOLET
**nightstool** \ˈ=,=\ *n* **:** CLOSESTOOL

nightshirt

**night sweat** *n* **:** profuse sweating during sleep that is sometimes a symptom of febrile disease
**night table** *n* **:** a small bedside table or stand — called also *nightstand*
**night terror** *n* **:** a sudden awakening in dazed terror occurring in children and often preceded by a sudden shrill cry uttered in sleep
**nighttide** \ˈ=,=\ *n* **1 :** NIGHTTIME **2 :** a flood tide occurring during the night
**nighttime** \ˈ=,=\ *n* [ME, fr. ¹*night* + *time*] **:** the time from dusk to dawn
**night vision** *n* **:** ability to see in dim light (as provided by moon and stars)
**nightwalker** \ˈ=,==\ *n* [ME, fr. ¹*night* + *walker*] **1 a :** a person who roves about at night esp. with criminal intent **b :** a prostitute who walks the street at night **2 a :** an animal active at night **b** *chiefly North* **:** NIGHT CRAWLER

night table

**night warbler** *n* **:** SEDGE WARBLER
**night watchman** *n* **1 :** a watchman on duty by night **2 :** a member of a night watch
**nightwear** \ˈ=,=\ *n* **:** NIGHTCLOTHES 1
**night willow herb** *n* **:** an evening primrose (*Oenothera biennis*)
**nightworks** \ˈ=,=\ *n pl* **:** the parts of a lock mechanism which make the lock inoperable from the outside except by a key
**nighty** *var of* NIGHTIE
**nig·nay** \ˈnig,nā\ *also* **nig·nye** \-nī\ *n* -s [origin unknown] *chiefly Scot* **:** TRIVIALITY, TRIFLE
**nig·ra** \ˈnigrə\ *n* -s [by alter.] **:** NEGRO — often taken to be offensive
**ni·gran·i·line** \nīˈgranˈələn\ *n* [ISV *nigr-* (fr. L *nigr-, niger* black) + *aniline*] **:** a dark blue basic compound yielding blue salts with acids that is formed from emeraldine as an intermediate in the production of aniline black
**nig·ra scale** \ˈnigrə-\ *n* [NL *nigra* (specific epithet of *Saissetia nigra*, species of coccid), fr. L, fem. of *niger* black, dark] **:** a coccid (*Saissetia nigra*) that is a serious pest on cotton, coffee, and other plants of warm temperate regions
**ni·gre** \ˈnīgə(r), ˈnig-\ *n* -s [prob. alter. of obs. E *nigger*, fr. E ¹*nigger*] **:** a dark-colored water solution of soap and impurities formed during manufacture of soap by settling from the neat soap
**ni·gres·cence** \nīˈgresˈn(t)s\ *n* -s [*nigrescent* + *-ence*] **1 :** a process of becoming black or dark **2 :** BLACKNESS, DARKNESS; *specif* **:** darkness of complexion
**ni·gres·cent** \(ˈ)nī;gresˈnt\ *adj* [L *nigrescent-, nigrescens*, pres. part. of *nigrescere* to become black, fr. *nigr-, niger* black] **:** BLACKISH
**nig·ri·cant** \ˈnigrəkənt\ *adj* [L *nigricant-, nigricans*, pres. part. of *nigricare* to be blackish, fr. *nigr-, niger* black] **:** BLACKISH
**nig·ri·fy** \ˈnigrəfī\ *vt* -ED/-ING/-ES [LL *nigrificare* to blacken, fr. L *nigr-, niger* black + *-ficare* -fy] **:** BLACKEN
**ni·grine** \ˈnīgrən\ *n* -s [G *nigrin*, fr. L *nigr-, niger* black + G *-in* -ine] **:** a mineral consisting of black ferruginous rutile
**ni·gri·tian** \nəˈgrishən\ *adj, usu cap* [*Nigritia*, former name of the Sudan (fr. L *nigr-, niger* black) + E *-an*] **:** SUDANESE
**nig·ri·tude** \ˈnigrə,tüd, -ə,tyüd\ *n* -s [L *nigritudo*, fr. *nigr-, niger* black + *-tudo* -tude] **:** intense darkness **:** BLACKNESS
**ni·gro·man·cer** \ˈnīgrə,man(t)sə(r)\ *archaic var of* NECROMANCER
**ni·grom·e·ter** \nīˈgrämədə(r)\ *n* [*nigro-* (fr. L *nigr-, niger* black) + *-meter*] **:** an instrument for measuring degree of blackness (as of paints or dyes)
**ni·gro·sine** \ˈnīgrə,sēn, -sən\ *also* **ni·gro·sin** \-sən\ *n* -s *often cap* [L *nigr-, niger* black + E *-ose* + *-ine* or *-in*] **:** any of several azine dyes closely related to the indulines: as **a** *or* **nigrosine base B** *usu cap N & both Bs* **:** an oil-soluble bluish black dye obtained as the free base by heating aniline and aniline hydrochloride with nitrobenzene or nitrophenol in the presence of iron and used chiefly in coloring waxes, shoe polish, plastics, and lacquers and as wood stains — see DYE table I (under *Solvent Black 7*) **b** *or* **nigrosine spirit soluble** *usu cap N & both Ss* **:** a chloride of the free base that is soluble in alcohol and is used similarly — see DYE table I (under *Solvent Black 5*) **c** *or* **nigrosine water soluble** *usu cap N&W&S* **:** a water-soluble sulfonation product of the free base or of its chloride used chiefly in dyeing leather and paper and as a biological stain — see DYE table I (under *Acid Black 2*)
**ni·grous** \ˈnīgrəs\ *adj* [L *nigr-, niger* black + E *-ous*] **:** BLACK
**nigs** *pl of* NIG, *pres 3d sing of* NIG
**ni·gua** \ˈnēgwə\ *n* -s [Sp, fr. Taino] **:** CHIGOE
**ni·gun** *or* **nig·gun** \nēˈgün\ *n, pl* **ni·gu·nim** *or* **nig·gu·nim** \,nēgüˈnēm\ [LHeb *niggūn*, fr. Heb *naggēn* to play an instrument] **:** MELODY; *specif* **:** a traditional synagogal or folk melody
**ni·hil de·bet** \ˈnī,hilˈdē,bet\ *n* [L, he owes nothing] **:** a legal plea of the general issue in an action of debt on a simple contract or on a specialty when the deed is the only inducement to the action
**nihil di·cit** \-ˈdī,sit\ *n* [L, he says nothing] **1 :** a refusal or neglect by the defendant to plead or answer **2 :** a judgment rendered against a defendant charged with nihil dicit
**nihil ha·bet** \-ˈhā,bet\ *n* [L, he has nothing] **:** a return by a sheriff or other officer made on a scire facias or other writ indicating that the defendant has no property within reach of the process, and the defendant has not been served
**ni·hil·ian·ism** \nīˈhilyə,nizəm\ *n* -s [L *nihil* nothing + E *-ianism* (as in *pelagianism*) — more at NIL] **:** a doctrine that the human nature of Christ was nothing having true subsistence
**ni·hi·lism** \ˈnīə,lizəm, ˈnihə-, ˈnēə-, *sometimes* ˈnīhə- *or* ˈnēhə-\ *n* -s [G *nihilismus*, fr. L *nihil* nothing + G *-ismus* -ism] **1 a :** a viewpoint that all traditional values and beliefs are unfounded and that all existence is consequently senseless and useless **:** a denial of intrinsic meaning and value in life **b :** a doctrine that denies or is taken as denying any objective or real ground of truth; *specif* **:** an ethical doctrine that denies any objective ground of moral principles — called also *ethical nihilism, moral nihilism* **2 a :** a doctrine that no reality exists **b :** a profession of nihilistic delusions **3 :** an annihilation (as by mystical contemplation) of desires and self-consciousness **4 a** [Russ *nigilizm*, fr. F *nihilisme*, fr. G *nihilismus*] (1) **:** a doctrine or belief that conditions in the social organization are so bad as to make destruction desirable for its own sake independent of any constructive program or possibility (2) *usu cap* **:** the program or doctrine of a Russian party or succession of parties of the 19th and 20th centuries who proposed various schemes of revolutionary reform and resorted to terrorism and assassination **b :** revolutionary propaganda **:** TERRORISM **5 :** scepticism as to the therapeutic value of a drug or method ⟨therapeutic ~⟩ **6 :** the advocacy or practice of nihilism **7 :** a nihilistic belief, act, or utterance
¹**ni·hi·list** \-ləst\ *n* -s *sometimes cap* [F *nihiliste*, fr. L *nihil* nothing + F *-iste* -ist] **1 :** an advocate of nihilism **2** [Russ *nigilist*, fr. F *nihiliste*] **:** a member of a Russian nihilistic party resorting to terrorism
²**nihilist** \"\ *or* **ni·hi·lis·tic** \¦==¦listik\ *adj* **:** of, relating to, or characterized by nihilism — **ni·hi·lis·ti·cal·ly** \-tək(ə)lē\ *adv*
**nihilist cipher** *n, usu cap N* [¹*nihilist*; fr. its use by the Russian nihilists] **:** a substitution method replacing each letter by its row and column numbers in an alphabet square
**nihilistic delusion** *n* **:** the belief that oneself, a part of one's body, or the real world does not exist or has been destroyed
**ni·hil·i·ty** \nīˈhilədē\ *n* -ES [F *nihilité*, fr. MF, fr. ML *nihilitat-, nihilitas*, fr. L *nihil* nothing + *-itat-, -itas* -ity] **1 :** NOTHINGNESS **2 :** a thing amounting to nothing **:** NULLITY, TRIFLE
**nihil ob·stat** \-ˈäbz,tat, -b,st-\ *n* [L, nothing hinders] **1 :** the certification by an official censor of the Roman Catholic Church that a book has been examined and found to contain nothing opposed to faith and morals **2 :** authoritative or official approval ⟨the surest road to fame was . . . through the imprimatur and *nihil obstat* of a foreign critic —P.H.Odegard⟩
**ni·i·ga·ta** \ˌnēəˈgäd·ə\ *adj, usu cap* [fr. *Niigata*, Japan] **:** of or from the city of Niigata, Japan **:** of the kind or style prevalent in Niigata
**nij·me·gen** \ˈnī,māgən\ *adj, usu cap* [fr. *Nijmegen*, Netherlands] **:** of or from the city of Nijmegen, Netherlands **:** of the kind or style prevalent in Nijmegen
**ni·kau** \ˈnē,kaů\ *or* **nikau palm** *n* -s [Maori *nikau*] **:** a graceful pinnate-leaved New Zealand palm (*Kentia sapida*)
**nik·eth·amide** \nəˈkethə,mīd, -,məd\ *n* [*nik-* (alter. of *nic-* in *nicotinic acid*) + *diethyl* + *amide*] **:** a bitter viscous liquid or crystalline compound $C_5H_4NCON(C_2H_5)_2$ used chiefly in aqueous solution as a respiratory stimulant; *N,N*-diethyl= nicotinamide
**nik·ko** \ˈni(,)kō\ *n* -s *often cap* [prob. fr. *Nikko*, Japan] **:** CHINA BLUE
**nikko fir** *n, usu cap N* [fr. *Nikko*, village in central Japan] **:** a Japanese evergreen tree (*Abies homolepis*) widely cultivated for ornament and having deeply grooved branchlets, cones that are purple when young, and leaves slightly bifid at the apex
**ni·ko·la·ev** \ˌnikəˈlīəf\ *adj, usu cap* [fr. *Nikolaev*, U.S.S.R.] **:** of or from the city of Nikolaev, U.S.S.R. **:** of the kind or style prevalent in Nikolaev
¹**nil** \ˈnil\ *n* -s [L, nothing, contr. of *nihil, nihilum*, prob. fr. *ne-* (negative prefix) + *hilum* small thing, trifle — more at NO] **1 :** NOTHING, ZERO ⟨reducing to almost ~ the relevant collection work —John Fiddler⟩ **2** *chiefly Brit* **:** a score of nothing ⟨a game won by a goal to ~⟩ ⟨a *nil*-all draw⟩
²**nil** \"\ *adj* **:** NONEXISTENT — usu. used predicatively ⟨tuition fees are ~ or nominal —B.K.Sandwell⟩
³**nil** \"\ *n* -s [short for *nilgai*] **:** a male nilgai
**nil di·cit** \-ˈdī,sit\ *n* [L, he says nothing] **:** NIHIL DICIT
**nile** \ˈnīl *esp before pause or consonant* -īəl\ *or* **nile green** *n* -s *often cap N* [fr. *Nile* river, Africa] **:** a variable color averaging a pale yellow green that is greener and stronger than smoke gray and greener and deeper than oyster gray — called also *boa, eau de Nile*
**nile bird** *n, usu cap N* [fr. *Nile*, river in Africa] **1** *dial Eng* **:** WRYNECK **2 :** CROCODILE BIRD
**nile blue** *n* [fr. *Nile*, river in Africa] **1** *often cap N* **:** a light bluish green, greener and deeper than average aqua green (sense 1), bluer and paler than average turquoise green, and bluer and stronger than robin's-egg blue (sense 2) **2** *or* **nile blue A** *usu cap N & sometimes cap B* **:** an oxazine dye used chiefly in the form of the sulfate as a biological stain (as for staining neutral fat red in the presence of dilute sulfuric acid)
**nile crocodile** *n, usu cap N* **:** a widely distributed and dangerous African crocodile (*Crocodylus niloticus*)
**nile goose** *n, usu cap N* **:** EGYPTIAN GOOSE
**nile perch** *n, usu cap N* **:** a large predacious food fish (*Lates nilotica*) of the rivers and lakes of northern and central Africa that may exceed 200 pounds in weight — called also *capitaine*
**nil·gai** *also* **nil·ghai** \ˈnil,gī\ *n, pl* **nilgais** *or* **nilgai** *also* **nilghais** *or* **nilghai** [Hindi *nīlgāw* blue bull (fem. *nīlgāī*), fr. Skt *nīla* dark blue + *go* bull, cow — more at ANILINE, COW (animal)] **:** a large bluish gray antelope (*Boselaphus tragocamelus*) of India, the male of which has short horns, a black mane, and a bunch of long hair on the throat — called also *blue bull*
**nil·gi·ri nettle** *or* **nil·ghi·ri nettle** \ˈnilgərē-\ *n, usu cap 1st N* [fr. *Nilgiri* Hills, India] **:** any of several plants (genus *Girardinia*) of the family Urticaceae; *esp* **:** an East Indian fiber plant (*G. palmata*) with stinging foliage and stems that yield a strong fiber useful for cordage
**nil grade** *n* **:** ZERO GRADE
¹**nill** \ˈnil\ *vb* -ED/-ING/-S [ME *nilen, nellen*, fr. OE *nyllan, nellan*, fr. *ne* not + *wyllan* to wish — more at NO, WILL] *vi, archaic* **:** to be unwilling ⟨will you ~ you, I will marry you —Shak.⟩ ~ *vt, archaic* **:** not to will **:** REFUSE, REJECT, PREVENT
²**nill** \"\ *dial Eng var of* NEEDLE
**nil·ly-will·y** \¦nilē¦wilē\ *adv* [by alter.] **:** WILLY-NILLY
**ni·lo-hamite** \¦nī(,)lō+\ *n, usu cap N&H* [¹*nilotic* + *hamite*] **:** a member of a group of East African pastoral peoples including esp. the Masai and others linguistically, traditionally, and otherwise culturally affiliated with these
**ni·lo-hamitic** \"+\ *n, usu cap N&H* [¹*nilotic* + *hamitic*] **:** the eastern branch of the Nilotic languages
**ni·lom·e·ter** \nīˈläməd·ə(r)\ *n, often cap* [modif. (influenced by E *-meter*) of NL *nilometrion*, fr. Gk *neilometrion*, fr. *Neilos* Nile, river in Africa + *-metrion* (fr. *metron* measure) — more at MEASURE] **:** a gauge for measuring the height of water in the Nile esp. during its flood; *specif* **:** a graduated scale cut on a natural rock or in the stone wall of a pit communicating with the river — **ni·lo·met·ric** \ˌnīlə¦me·trik\ *adj, often cap*
**ni·lot** \ˈnī,lät, -lət\ *n, pl* **ni·lo·tes** \nīˈlōd·(,)ēz, -ō,tēz\ *usu cap* [modif. (influenced by E *-ot* as in *cypriot*) of Gk *Neilōtēs* in the Nile, on the Nile, fr. *Neilos* Nile] **:** a native of the region of the Upper Nile
¹**ni·lot·ic** \(ˈ)nī¦läd·ik, -ät|, ¦ēk\ *adj, usu cap* [L *niloticus* of the Nile, fr. *nilotis*, fem. adj. (fr. Gk *neilōtis*, fr. *Neilos* Nile) + *-icus* -ic] **1 :** of or relating to the Nile or the peoples dwelling in the territory directly drained by it ⟨the *Nilotic* year⟩; *specif* **:** of or relating to the Dinka, Luo, Nuer, Shilluk and linguistically related peoples who constitute a distinctive negroid race or subrace characterized particularly by extreme height **2 :** of, relating to, or constituting the Nilotic group of Sudanic languages
²**nilotic** \"\ *n* -s *usu cap* **1 :** a member of a Nilotic people **2 :** a group of languages spoken in the Nile valley above Khartoum and southeastward into Kenya and Tanganyika, divided into western containing Acholi, Alur, Dinka, Lango, Luo, Nuer, and Shilluk and eastern containing Bari, Karamojong, Masai, Nandi, and Teso, and variously considered as a family or as a branch of the Chari-Nile family **3 :** the western division only of the Nilotic languages in distinction to the eastern branch called Nilo-Hamitic
**nils** *pl of* NIL
¹**nim** \ˈnim\ *vb* **nimmed; nimmed; nimming; nims** [fr. earlier *nim* to take, fr. ME *nimen*, fr. OE *niman* — more at NIMBLE] *vt* **:** STEAL, FILCH ⟨this snuff-box . . . *nimm'd* two nights ago in the park —John Gay⟩ ⟨a kirtle that I would not have *nimmed* from a hedge—E.G.Bulwer-Lytton⟩ ~ *vi, archaic* **:** THIEVE
²**nim** \"\ *n* -s [prob. fr. ¹*nim*] **:** any of various games in which counters are laid out in one or more piles of agreed numbers, each of two players in turn draws one or more counters, and the object is to take the last counter, force the opponent to take it, or take the most or the fewest counters
³**nim** *var of* NEEM
**nimb** \ˈnim *also* -mb\ *n, pl* **nimbs** \-mz\ [L *nimbus*] **:** NIMBUS, HALO ⟨with an aureate ~ —Thomas Hardy⟩
**nimbed** \-md\ *also* **nim·bat·ed** \-m,bād·əd\ *adj* [*nimb* + *-ed* or *-ated* (fr. *-ate* + *-ed*)] **:** having a nimbus esp. around the head ⟨apostles, martyrs, and saints all ~ with glory —Daniel Rock⟩
¹**nim·ble** \ˈnimbəl\ *adj* **nim·bler** \-b(ə)lə(r)\ **nim·blest** \-b(ə)ləst\ [ME *nymel, nemel*, fr. OE *numol* holding much, quick at grasping, *næmel* receptive, both from *niman* to take; akin to OHG *neman* to take, ON *nema*, Goth *niman*, L *numerus* number, Gk *nemein* to distribute, pasture, manage, *nomos* pasture, district, *nomos* usage, custom, law, Av *nəmah* loan; basic meaning: to assign] **1 a :** marked by quick light movement **:** moving easily or dexterously **:** AGILE, LIVELY ⟨~ fingers⟩ ⟨a ~ rabbit⟩ ⟨a ~ leap⟩ ⟨a ~ climber⟩ ⟨a ~ well= schooled colt with a smooth, powerful, effortless stride —G.F. T.Ryall⟩ ⟨a ~, fast-moving shovel —*Steel*⟩ **b** *of money* **:** circulating rapidly ⟨~ shilling⟩ ⟨a ~ sixpence is better than a slow shilling —*North Carolina Folklore*⟩ **2 a :** marked by quick, alert, clever conception, comprehension, or resourcefulness ⟨~ mind⟩ ⟨~ tongue⟩ ⟨her lines combine the closest observation and the *nimblest* imagination —Louis Untermeyer⟩ ⟨the amiability of these Italians, aided by their sharp and ~ wits, caused them to overflow with plausible suggestions —Nathaniel Hawthorne⟩ ⟨writes ~ dialogue —Bernard Hollowood⟩ **b :** marked by ready sensitive responsiveness ⟨a ~ listener⟩ ⟨nothing like playacting to make you ~ in your feelings —Mary Austin⟩ ⟨disinclination of every ~ spirit to bruise itself against walls —*Nation*⟩ **syn** see AGILE
²**nimble** \"\ *vi* **nimbled; nimbled; nimbling; \-b(ə)liŋ\ nimbles** *archaic* **:** to move or act nimbly
**nimble kate** \¦==¦kāt\ *n, usu cap K* [so called fr. its climbing habits] **:** BUR CUCUMBER 1
**nimbleness** *n* -ES **:** the quality or state of being nimble
**nimble will** \ˈ==¦wil\ *n, often cap W* [so called fr. its rapid spreading] **:** a slender branching American grass (*Muhlenbergia schreberi*) of some value for grazing in the central U.S.
**nim·bly** \-blē,-bli\ *adv* [ME *nemely*, fr. *nemel* nimble + *-ly*] **:** in a nimble manner ⟨~ scaling an iron gate —Charles Dickens⟩ ⟨speaks crisply, ~, and neatly —Francis Fergusson⟩
**nimbo-** *comb form* [NL *nimbus*] **:** nimbus and ⟨*nimbo*stratus⟩
**nim·bo·ran** \ˈnimbə,ran\ *n, pl* **nimboran** *or* **nimborans** *usu cap* **1 :** a Papuan people of Netherlands New Guinea **2 :** a member of the Nimboran people
**nim·bose** \ˈnim,bōs\ *adj* [L *nimbosus*, fr. *nimbus* + *-osus* -ose] **:** CLOUDY, STORMY
**nim·bo·stratus** \¦nim(,)bō+\ *n* [NL, fr. *nimbo-* + *stratus*] **:** a low dark gray rainy cloud layer
**nim·bus** \ˈnimbəs\ *n, pl* **nim·bi** \-(,)bī\ *or* **nimbus·es** [L, rainstorm, cloud; akin to Pahlavi *namb* dew, mist and perh. to L *imber* rain, *nebula* mist — more at IMBRICATE] **1 a :** a luminous vapor, cloud, or atmosphere about a god or goddess when on earth **b :** a cloud or atmosphere (as of romance) about a person or thing ⟨before the ~ of idolatry enveloped him —*N.Y.Herald Tribune Bk. Rev.*⟩ **2 :** an indication in an art work (as a painting) of radiant light or glory around or above the head of a sacred or venerated personage; *specif* **:** a circle, disk, rectangle, triangle, or rayed structure about the head of a drawn or sculptured divinity, saint, or sovereign — see AUREOLE 2 **3 a :** the rain cloud characterized by its uniform grayness and extending over the entire sky in seasons of continued rain **b :** a cloud from which rain is falling
**nim·bused** \-bəst\ *adj* **:** furnished with or surrounded by a nimbus ⟨they were ~ . . . by the last light of a sun that had set —Hugh MacLennan⟩
**ni·mi·e·ty** \niˈmīəd·ē\ *n* -ES [LL *nimietas*, fr. *nimie-* (fr. L *nimius* too much, adj., fr. *nimis*, adv.) + *-tas* -ty; perh. akin to L *ne-* not and to L *minor* — more at NO, MINOR] **:** EXCESS, REDUNDANCY ⟨Edwardian ~ made poems drowsier, pictures bigger . . . meals heavier than ever before —*Times Lit. Supp.*⟩
**niminy** *adj* [by shortening] **:** NIMINY-PIMINY
**niminy–piminy** \¦nimənē¦pimənē\ *adj* [prob. alter. of *namby-pamby*] **:** MIMINY-PIMINY ⟨the . . . press is already too *niminy= piminy*, too nice altogether, too refined —*Persuasion*⟩
**nim·i·ous** \ˈnimēəs\ *adj* [ME *nymyos*, fr. L *nimius*] **:** EXCESSIVE, EXTRAVAGANT ⟨the author . . . is never ~; there is nothing in excess —Sydney Smith⟩
**nimmed** *past of* NIM
**nim·mer** \ˈnimə(r)\ *n* -s [¹*nim* + *-er*] **:** THIEF, PILFERER
**nimming** *pres part of* NIM
**nim·ra·vus** \nimˈrävəs\ *n, cap* [NL] **:** a genus of Oligocene and Miocene No. American saber-toothed tigers that is usu. made type of a distinct subfamily
**nim·rod** \ˈnim,räd\ *n* -s [fr. *Nimrod*, son of Cush, described as a mighty man and hunter (Gen 10:8–9)] **1** *usu cap, obs* **:** TYRANT **2** *sometimes cap* **:** HUNTER ⟨some more squirrel hunters than any other kind of ~s in Alabama —*Ala. Dept. of Conservation*⟩ — **nim·rod·ian** \(ˈ)nim¦rädēən, -rōd-\ *adj, sometimes cap*
**nims** *pres 3d sing of* NIM, *pl of* NIM
**nim·shi** \ˈnim(p)shē\ *n* [prob. alter. of E dial. *nimshie* flighty girl] *North* **:** a silly person **:** FOOL
**nim tree** *n* [Hindi *nīm* — more at NEEM] **:** MARGOSA
**nin·com** *or* **nin·cum** \ˈninkəm, -iŋk-\ *n* -s [by shortening] **:** NINCOMPOOP
**nin·com·poop** \ˈninkəm,püp *also* -iŋk-\ *n* -s [origin unknown] **:** FOOL, SIMPLETON ⟨compelled to vote for dummies and ~s —G.B.Shaw⟩ — **nin·com·poop·ery** \-üpərē, -ri, ,==ˈ===\ *n* -ES
¹**nine** \ˈnīn *sometimes for emphasis, as by telephone operators*, -īən\ *adj* [ME *nyne, nigen*, fr. OE *nigon*; akin to OHG & Goth *niun* nine, ON *nīu*, L *novem*, Gk *ennea*, Skt *nava*] **:** being one more than eight in number ⟨~ years⟩ — see NUMBER table
²**nine** \"\ *pron, pl in constr* [ME *nyne*, fr. OE *nigone*, fr. *nigon*, adj.] **:** nine countable persons or things not specified but under consideration and being enumerated ⟨~ are here⟩ ⟨~ were found⟩
³**nine** \"\ *n* -s [ME, fr. *nyne*, adj. & pron.] **1 :** one more than eight **:** three threes **:** the square of three **2 a :** nine units or objects ⟨a total of ~⟩ **b :** a group or set of nine ⟨arranged by ~s⟩ **3 a :** the numerable quantity symbolized by the arabic numeral 9 **b :** the figure 9 **4 :** nine o'clock — compare BELL table, TIME illustration **5 :** the ninth in a set or series: as **a :** a playing card marked to show that it is ninth in a suit **b :** an article of clothing of the ninth size ⟨wears a ~⟩ **6 :** something having as an essential feature nine units or members: as **a :** a playing team of nine members; *esp* **:** a baseball team **b :** the first or last 9 holes of an 18-hole golf course ⟨fired a two= under-par 33 on the front ~ and held his advantage in the back ~ —*Vancouver (Canada) Sun*⟩ — **to the nines** *also* **up to the nines :** to the highest point, degree, or mark ⟨dressed *to the nines* —*Harper's Bazaar*⟩ ⟨the paper . . . is done *to the nines* with a sensitiveness worthy of its subject —Leonard Bacon⟩ ⟨garnished *up to the nines* —C.E.Montague⟩
**nine-banded armadillo** \ˈ=,==-\ *n* **:** PEBA
**ninebark** \ˈ=,=\ *n* **:** an American white-flowered shrub of the genus *Physocarpus* having bark which separates into many thin layers
**nine days' wonder** *n* **:** an object or event that creates a short= lived sensation ⟨those political explosions . . . that make a *nine days' wonder* till something fresh comes along —Mary Deasy⟩ ⟨a *nine days' wonder*, fated to sink swiftly into obscurity —*Times Lit. Supp.*⟩
**nine-eyes** \ˈ=,=\ *n pl but sing or pl in constr, also* **nine-eyed eel** \ˈ=,=-\ [fr. its numerous spiracles] **:** LAMPREY
¹**ninefold** \ˈ=¦=\ *adj* **1 :** having nine parts or aspects **2 :** being nine times as large, as great, or as many as some understood size, degree, or amount ⟨a ~ increase⟩
²**ninefold** \"\ *adv* **:** to nine times as much or as many **:** by nine times ⟨increased ~⟩
**nineholes** \ˈ=,=\ *n pl but sing in constr* **1 :** a game in which balls or marbles are rolled into nine holes in the ground or through arches in a board **2 :** a difficult situation — usu. used in the phrase *in the nineholes*
**nine-killer** \ˈ=,==\ *n* [trans. of D *negendoder* or G *neuntöter*; fr. the belief that it kills nine birds a day] **:** SHRIKE
**nine-men's morris** *n* **:** morris played with nine counters
**nine mile fever** *n, usu cap N&M* [fr. *Nine Mile* Creek, Mont., where it was first recognized] **:** a rickettsial disease identical with or closely related to Q fever that affects man and various mammals in parts of the northwestern U.S.
**nine·pence** *Brit* ˈnīnpən(t)s *sometimes* -īmp-, *US* " *or* -īn,pen-\ *n, pl* **ninepence** *or* **ninepences 1 :** the sum of nine usu. British pennies **2 :** an old Irish shilling worth in England about nine British pennies **3 :** the old Spanish real formerly worth in New England about 12½ cents
**nine·pen·ny** \-pənē, -ni; -,penē\ *adj* **:** costing or having the value of ninepence
**ninepenny morris** *n* **:** NINE-MEN'S MORRIS
**ninepin** \ˈ=,=\ *n* **1 :** a pin used in ninepins **2 ninepins** *pl but sing in constr* **:** a bowling game played with nine wooden pins **:** tenpins played without the headpin
**ninepin block** *n* **:** a fairlead shaped like a ninepin
**nine-spined stickleback** \ˈ=,=-\ *n* **:** a stickleback (*Pungitius pungitius*) of both Europe and America

ninepins set up ready for play

¹**nine·teen** \(ˈ)nīn¦tēn, -īnt¦tēn *sometimes* -īnt·ēn\ *adj* [ME *nynetene, nigentene*, fr. OE *nigontiene, nigontȳne, nigontēne* (akin to OHG *niunzehan*, ON *nītjān*), fr.

*nigon* nine + *-tīene, -tȳne, -tēne* (fr. *tīen, tȳn, tēn* ten) — more at NINE, TEN] **:** being one more than 18 in number ⟨~ years⟩ — see NUMBER table; used prepositively to designate various years of the 20th century ⟨the *nineteen*-eighties⟩ ⟨the early *nineteen*-hundreds⟩

2**nineteen** \"\ *pron, pl in constr* [ME *nynetene, nigentene,* fr. *nynetene, nigentene* nineteen, adj.] **:** nineteen countable persons or things not specified but under consideration and being enumerated ⟨~ are here⟩ ⟨~ were found⟩

3**nineteen** \"\ *n* -s **1 :** 10 and nine **2 a :** 19 units or objects ⟨a total of ~⟩ **b :** a group or set of 19 **3 :** the numerable quantity symbolized by the arabic numerals 19 **4 :** the nineteenth in a set or series; *esp* **:** an article of clothing of the nineteenth size ⟨wears a ~⟩ **5 :** something having as an essential feature nineteen units or members **6** [so called from the fact that no hand can score exactly 19] **:** a score of zero in cribbage

**nineteen order** *n* **:** a train order for which the engineer or other member of a train crew does not have to sign — compare THIRTY-ONE ORDER

1**nine·teenth** \-ēn(t)th\ *adj* [ME *nyntenthe,* adj. & n., alter. (influenced by *nynetene* nineteen) of *nyentethe,* fr. OE *nigontēotha,* fr. *nigontīene, nigontȳne, nigontēne* nineteen + *-otha, -tha* -th] **1 :** being number 19 in a countable series ⟨the ~ day⟩ — see NUMBER table **2 :** being one of 19 equal parts into which something is divisible ⟨a ~ share of the money⟩

2**nineteenth** \"\ *n, pl* **nineteenths** \-ēn(t)s,-ēn(t)ths\ **1 :** number 19 in a countable series ⟨the ~ of the month⟩ **2 :** the quotient of a unit divided by 19 **:** one of 19 equal parts of something ⟨one ~ of the total⟩ **3 a :** a musical interval of two octaves and a fifth **b :** an organ stop sounding pitches two octaves and a fifth above the keys used

**nineteenth hole** *n* **:** the locker room or other convivial gathering place of golfers after play on the course

1**nine·ti·eth** \'nīntēəth, -ti\ *adj* [ME *nyntithe,* fr. OE *nigontigotha,* fr. *nigontig* ninety + *-otha, -tha* -th] **1 :** being number 90 in a countable series ⟨the ~ day⟩ — see NUMBER table **2 :** being one of 90 equal parts into which something is divisible ⟨a ~ share of the money⟩

2**ninetieth** \"\ *n* -s **1 :** number 90 in a countable series **2 :** the quotient of a unit divided by 90 **:** one of 90 equal parts of something ⟨one ~ of the total⟩

1**nine·ty** \'nīntē, -ti\ *adj* [ME *nynety, nigenti,* fr. OE *nigontig,* short for *hundnigontig,* fr. *hundnigontig,* n., group of 90, fr. *hund* hundred + *nigon* nine + *-tig* group of ten — more at EIGHTY] **:** being one more than 89 in number ⟨~ years⟩ — see NUMBER table

2**ninety** \"\ *pron, pl in constr* **:** ninety countable persons or things not specified but under consideration and being enumerated ⟨~ are here⟩ ⟨~ were found⟩

3**ninety** \"\ *n* -ES **1 :** nine tens **:** twice 45 **:** three times 30 **:** five times 18 **:** six fifteens **:** fourscore and 10 **2 a :** 90 units or objects ⟨a total of ~⟩ **b :** a group or set of 90 **3 :** the numerable quantity symbolized by the arabic numerals 90 **4 :** the 90th in a set or series **5 :** something having as an essential feature 90 units or numbers **6 nineties** *pl* **a :** the numbers 90 to 99 inclusive ⟨a golf score in the *nineties*⟩ ⟨all his grades in that subject are in the *nineties*⟩ **b** (1) **:** the members of a series or set of successive numbers that end in 90 to 99 inclusive ⟨the *nineties* of the preceding century⟩ ⟨lives in the *nineties* in the next block⟩ (2) *usu cap* **:** the years of the last decade of the 19th century ⟨the Gay *Nineties*⟩ ⟨the so-called decadent romantics of the *Nineties* —*Publ's Mod. Lang. Assoc. of Amer.*⟩ **c :** the portion of a continuum lying between 90 and 100 on a scale of measurement or segmentation ⟨temperatures in the high *nineties* tomorrow⟩ ⟨a man in his *nineties*⟩ ⟨overcoats selling in the *nineties*⟩

**ninety-day wonder** *n* **:** a person commissioned as an officer in one of the armed services after 90 days or a relatively short length of training

1**ninety-eight** \¦==¦=\ *adj* **:** being one more than 97 in number ⟨*ninety-eight* years⟩ — see NUMBER table

2**ninety-eight** \"\ *pron, pl in constr* **:** ninety-eight countable persons or things not specified but under consideration and being enumerated ⟨*ninety-eight* are here⟩ ⟨*ninety-eight* were found⟩

3**ninety-eight** \"\ *n* **1 :** eight and 90 **:** two times 49 **:** seven times 14 **2 a :** 98 units or objects ⟨a total of *ninety-eight*⟩ **b :** a group or set of 98 **3 :** the numerable quantity symbolized by the arabic numerals 98

1**ninety-eighth** \¦==¦=\ *adj* **1 :** being number 98 in a countable series ⟨the *ninety-eighth* day⟩ — see NUMBER table **2 :** being one of 98 equal parts into which something is divisible ⟨a *ninety-eighth* share of the money⟩

2**ninety-eighth** \"\ *n* **1 :** number 98 in a countable series **2 :** the quotient of a unit divided by 98 **:** one of 98 equal parts of something

1**ninety-fifth** \¦==¦=\ *adj* **1 :** being number 95 in a countable series ⟨the *ninety-fifth* day⟩ — see NUMBER table **2 :** being one of 95 equal parts into which something is divisible ⟨a *ninety-fifth* share of the money⟩

2**ninety-fifth** \"\ *n* **1 :** number 95 in a countable series **2 :** the quotient of a unit divided by 95 **:** one of 95 equal parts of something

1**ninety-first** \¦==¦=\ *adj* **1 :** being number 91 in a countable series ⟨the *ninety-first* day⟩ — see NUMBER table **2 :** being one of 91 equal parts into which something is divisible ⟨a *ninety-first* share of the money⟩

2**ninety-first** \"\ *n* **1 :** number 91 in a countable series **2 :** the quotient of a unit divided by 91 **:** one of 91 equal parts of something

1**ninety-five** \¦==¦=\ *adj* **:** being one more than 94 in number ⟨*ninety-five* years⟩ — see NUMBER table

2**ninety-five** \"\ *pron, pl in constr* **:** ninety-five countable persons or things not specified but under consideration and being enumerated ⟨*ninety-five* are here⟩ ⟨*ninety-five* were found⟩

3**ninety-five** \"\ *n* **1 :** five and 90 **:** five times 19 **2 a :** 95 units or objects ⟨a total of *ninety-five*⟩ **b :** a group or set of 95 **3 :** the numerable quantity symbolized by the arabic numerals 95

1**ninety-four** \¦==¦=\ *adj* **:** being one more than 93 in number ⟨*ninety-four* years⟩ — see NUMBER table

2**ninety-four** \"\ *pron, pl in constr* **:** ninety-four countable persons or things not specified but under consideration and being enumerated ⟨*ninety-four* are here⟩ ⟨*ninety-four* were found⟩

3**ninety-four** \"\ *n* **1 :** four and 90 **:** two times 47 **2 a :** 94 units or objects ⟨a total of *ninety-four*⟩ **b :** a group or set of 94 **3 :** the numerable quantity symbolized by the arabic numerals 94

1**ninety-fourth** \¦==¦=\ *adj* **1 :** being number 94 in a countable series ⟨the *ninety-fourth* day⟩ — see NUMBER table **2 :** being one of 94 equal parts into which something is divisible ⟨a *ninety-fourth* share of the money⟩

2**ninety-fourth** \"\ *n* **1 :** number 94 in a countable series **2 :** the quotient of a unit divided by 94 **:** one of 94 equal parts of something

**nine·ty·ish** \'nīntēish, -ti·ish\ *adj* **:** resembling what was current in the 1890s ⟨the tale of macabre horror is definitely ~ —F.B.Millett⟩

1**ninety-nine** \¦==¦=\ *adj* **:** being one more than 98 in number ⟨*ninety-nine* years⟩ — see NUMBER table

2**ninety-nine** \"\ *pron, pl in constr* **:** ninety-nine countable persons or things not specified but under consideration and being enumerated ⟨*ninety-nine* are here⟩ ⟨*ninety-nine* were found⟩

3**ninety-nine** \"\ *n* **1 :** nine and 90 **:** three times 33 **:** nine times 11 **2 a :** 99 units or objects ⟨a total of *ninety-nine*⟩ **b :** a group or set of 99 **3 :** the numerable quantity symbolized by the arabic numerals 99 — often used with *and* instead of a hyphen

1**ninety-ninth** \¦==¦=\ *adj* **1 :** being number 99 in a countable series ⟨the *ninety-ninth* day⟩ — see NUMBER table **2 :** being one of 99 equal parts into which something is divisible ⟨a *ninety-ninth* share of the money⟩

2**ninety-ninth** \"\ *n* **1 :** number 99 in a countable series **2 :** the quotient of a unit divided by 99 **:** one of 99 equal parts of something

1**ninety-one** \¦==¦=\ *adj* **:** being one more than 90 in number ⟨*ninety-one* years⟩ — see NUMBER table

2**ninety-one** \"\ *pron, pl in constr* **:** ninety-one countable persons or things not specified but under consideration and being enumerated ⟨*ninety-one* are here⟩ ⟨*ninety-one* were found⟩

3**ninety-one** \"\ *n* **1 :** one and 90 **2 a :** seven times 13 **:** 91 units or objects ⟨a total of *ninety-one*⟩ **b :** a group or set of 91 **3 :** the numerable quantity symbolized by the arabic numerals 91

1**ninety-second** \¦==¦==\ *adj* **1 :** being number 92 in a countable series ⟨the *ninety-second* day⟩ — see NUMBER table **2 :** being one of 92 equal parts into which something is divisible ⟨a *ninety-second* share of the money⟩

2**ninety-second** \"\ *n* **1 :** number 92 in a countable series **2 :** the quotient of a unit divided by 92 **:** one of 92 equal parts of something

1**ninety-seven** \¦==¦==\ *adj* **:** being one more than 96 in number ⟨*ninety-seven* years⟩ — see NUMBER table

2**ninety-seven** \"\ *pron, pl in constr* **:** ninety-seven countable persons or things not specified but under consideration and being enumerated ⟨*ninety-seven* are here⟩ ⟨*ninety-seven* were found⟩

3**ninety-seven** \"\ *n* **1 :** seven and 90 **2 a :** 97 units or objects ⟨a total of *ninety-seven*⟩ **b :** a group or set of 97 **3 :** the numerable quantity symbolized by the arabic numerals 97

1**ninety-seventh** \¦==¦==\ *adj* **1 :** being number 97 in a countable series ⟨the *ninety-seventh* day⟩ — see NUMBER table **2 :** being one of 97 equal parts into which something is divisible ⟨a *ninety-seventh* share of the money⟩

2**ninety-seventh** \"\ *n* **1 :** number 97 in a countable series **2 :** the quotient of a unit divided by 97 **:** one of 97 equal parts of something

1**ninety-six** \¦==¦=\ *adj* **:** being one more than 95 in number ⟨*ninety-six* years⟩ — see NUMBER table

2**ninety-six** \"\ *pron, pl in constr* **:** ninety-six countable persons or things not specified but under consideration and being enumerated ⟨*ninety-six* are here⟩ ⟨*ninety-six* were found⟩

3**ninety-six** \"\ *n* **1 :** six and 90 **:** two times 48 **:** three times 32 **:** four times 24 **:** six times 16 **:** eight times 12 **:** eight dozen **2 a :** 96 units or objects ⟨a total of *ninety-six*⟩ **b :** a group or set of 96 **3 :** the numerable quantity symbolized by the arabic numerals 96

1**ninety-sixth** \¦==¦=\ *adj* **1 :** being number 96 in a countable series ⟨the *ninety-sixth* day⟩ — see NUMBER table **2 :** being one of 96 equal parts into which something is divisible ⟨a *ninety-sixth* share of the money⟩

2**ninety-sixth** \"\ *n* **1 :** number 96 in a countable series **2 :** the quotient of a unit divided by 96 **:** one of 96 equal parts of something

1**ninety-third** \¦==¦=\ *adj* **1 :** being number 93 in a countable series ⟨the *ninety-third* day⟩ — see NUMBER table **2 :** being one of 93 equal parts into which something is divisible ⟨a *ninety-third* share of the money⟩

2**ninety-third** \"\ *n* **1 :** number 93 in a countable series **2 :** the quotient of a unit divided by 93 **:** one of 93 equal parts of something

1**ninety-three** \¦==¦=\ *adj* **:** being one more than 92 in number ⟨*ninety-three* years⟩ — see NUMBER table

2**ninety-three** \"\ *pron, pl in constr* **:** ninety-three countable persons or things not specified but under consideration and being enumerated ⟨*ninety-three* are here⟩ ⟨*ninety-three* were found⟩

3**ninety-three** \"\ *n* **1 :** three and 90 **:** three times 31 **2 a :** 93 units or objects ⟨a total of *ninety-three*⟩ **b :** a group or set of 93 **3 :** the numerable quantity symbolized by the arabic numerals 93

1**ninety-two** \¦==¦=\ *adj* **:** being one more than 91 in number ⟨*ninety-two* years⟩ — see NUMBER table

2**ninety-two** \"\ *pron, pl in constr* **:** ninety-two countable persons or things not specified but under consideration and being enumerated ⟨*ninety-two* are here⟩ ⟨*ninety-two* were found⟩

3**ninety-two** \"\ *n* **1 :** two and 90 **:** two times 46 **:** four times 23 **2 a :** 92 units or objects ⟨a total of *ninety-two*⟩ **b :** a group or set of 92 **3 :** the numerable quantity symbolized by the arabic numerals 92

**nin·e·vite** *or* **nin·i·vite** \'ninə,vīt\ *n* -s *usu cap* [*Nineveh, Ninive,* ancient capital of Assyria + E *-ite*] **:** an inhabitant of the ancient Assyrian city of Nineveh

**ningle** *n* -s [alter. (resulting fr. incorrect division of *an ingle*) of *ingle*] *obs* **:** CATAMITE

**ning·po** \'niŋ¦pō\ *adj, usu cap* [fr. *Ningpo,* China] **:** of or from the city of Ningpo, China **:** of the kind or style prevalent in Ningpo

**nin·gre·ton·go** \,niŋgrə¦täŋ(,)gō\ *n* -s *usu cap N&T* [prob. fr. Taki-Taki, fr. E *nigger* + *tongue*] **:** TAKI-TAKI

**nin·hy·drin** \nin'hīdrən\ *n* -s [fr. *Ninhydrin,* a trademark] **:** a poisonous crystalline mild oxidizing agent $C_9H_4O_2(OH)_2$ used chiefly as an analytical reagent; 1,2,3-indan-trione hydrate or triketo-hydrindene hydrate

**ninhydrin reaction** *n* **:** a reaction of ninhydrin with amino acids or related amino compounds used for the colorimetric determination of amino acids, peptides, or proteins by measuring the intensity of the blue to violet to red color formed or for the quantitative determination of alpha-amino acids by measuring the amount of carbon dioxide produced

**nin·ny** \'ninē, -ini\ *n* -ES [perh. by shortening and alter. fr. *an innocent*] **:** FOOL, SIMPLETON ⟨don't stand there fiddling like a ~ —Paul Gallico⟩ — **nin·ny·ish** \-ish\ *adj*

**nin·ny·ham·mer** \-,hamə(r)\ *n* **:** NINNY

**nin·ny·watch** \-,wäch\ *n* [origin unknown] *dial Brit* **:** DISTURBANCE, COMMOTION

**ni·non** \'nē,nō", ='=\ *n* -s [prob. fr. F *Ninon,* nickname for *Anne*] **:** a smooth sheer fabric made in a plain close weave and novelty open weaves usu. of silk, rayon, or nylon and used esp. for women's clothing and curtains

**ni·nox** \'nī,näks\ *n, cap* [NL] **:** a large genus of owls having bristly feet and long wings and ranging from Madagascar to Australian and Indo-Malayan regions

1**ninth** \'nīn(t)th\ *adj* [ME *nynthe,* adj. & n., alter. (influenced by *nyne, nigen* nine) of *nithe,* fr. OE *nigotha* (akin to OS *niguōtho,* MLG *negede*), fr. *nigon* nine + *-otha, -tha* -th — more at NINE] **1 :** being number nine in a countable series ⟨the ~ day⟩ — see NUMBER table **2 :** being one of nine equal parts into which something is divisible ⟨a ~ share of the money⟩

2**ninth** \"\ *n, pl* **ninths** \-īn(t)s,-īn(t)ths\ **1 :** number nine in a countable series ⟨the ~ of the month⟩ **2 :** the quotient of a unit divided by nine **:** one of nine equal parts of something ⟨one ~ of the total⟩ **3 a :** a musical interval embracing an octave and a second **b :** a tone at this interval **c :** NINTH CHORD

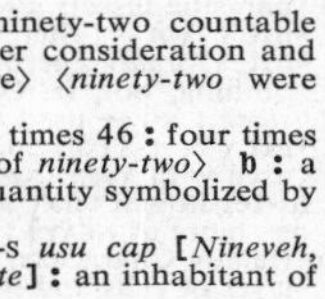

ninth 3a

3**ninth** \"\ *adv* **1 :** in the ninth place **2 :** with eight exceptions ⟨the nation's ~ largest city⟩

**ninth chord** *n* **:** a dominant seventh chord with the ninth added **:** a chord composed of four superposed thirds

**ninth cranial nerve** *or* **ninth nerve** *n* **:** GLOSSOPHARYNGEAL NERVE

**ninth·ly** \-īn(t)thlē, -li\ *adv* **:** in the ninth place ⟨~ and lastly, they were wholly unintelligible —Rudyard Kipling⟩

**ninth of ab** *usu cap N&A* [¹*ab*] **:** TISHAH B'AB

**nin·ut** \'ninət\ *n* -s [origin unknown] *Brit* **:** MAGPIE 1a

**ni·o·bate** \'nīə,bāt\ *n* -s [NL *niobium* + E *-ate*] **:** a salt of niobic acid — called also *columbate*

**ni·o·bic** \(')nī¦ōbik\ *adj* [NL *niobium* + E *-ic*] **:** of, relating to, or containing niobium — used esp. of compounds in which this element is pentavalent

**niobic acid** *n* **:** a gelatinous hydrated form $Nb_2O_5.nH_2O$ of niobium pentoxide that reacts with alkalies to yield salts (as sodium niobate $NaNbO_3$) — called also *columbic acid*

**ni·o·bite** \'nīə,bīt\ *n* -s [G *niobit,* fr. NL *niobium* + G *-it* -ite] **:** COLUMBITE

**ni·o·bi·um** \nī'ōbēəm\ *n* -s [NL, fr. *Niobe,* daughter of Tantalus + NL *-ium* — so called fr. its occurrence in tantalite] **:** a platinum-gray ductile chiefly pentavalent metallic element of brilliant luster that occurs combined in columbite and various other rare minerals but almost always associated with tantalum which it closely resembles chemically and from which it is separated as a by-product and that is used esp. in alloys (as in small amounts in stainless steels to inhibit intergranular corrosion) — called also *columbium;* symbol *Nb;* see ELEMENT table

**niobium pentoxide** *n* **:** a compound $Nb_2O_5$ obtained as a white infusible powder

**ni·o·bous** \(')nī¦ōbəs\ *adj* [NL *niobium* + *-ous*] **:** of, relating to, or containing niobium — used esp. of compounds in which this element has a lower valence than in niobic compounds

**ni·o·ta** \nē'ōd·ə\ *or* **niota bark** *n* -s [Malayalam *ñoṭṭa*] **:** NIEPA 2

1**nip** \'nip\ *vb* **nipped** *or archaic* **nipt; nipped** *or archaic* **nipt; nipping; nips** [ME *nippen;* akin to MD *nīpen* to nip, ON *hnippa* to prod, Gk *knips,* an insect, *skniptein* to nip, *konis* dust — more at INCINERATE] *vt* **1 a :** to catch hold of and squeeze tightly between two surfaces, edges, or points **:** compress esp. by pinching or biting **:** CLAMP ⟨the dog *nipped* him on the leg⟩ ⟨*nipped* his grandson between his knees —Ethel Anderson⟩ ⟨a little gold ring . . . *nipped* to the top of an ear —Christopher Rand⟩ **b :** to secure or stop (as a cable or rope) with seizing **c** *obs* **:** to close up (a glass vessel or tube) by pressing together the heated mouth or neck **2 a :** to sever by or as if by pinching sharply or biting ⟨choosing a slender cigar . . . he *nipped* it carefully and lit it —Ann Bridge⟩ ⟨*nipped* out pieces from the ends of the bar —L.A.Werden⟩ ⟨salient, in danger of being *nipped* off anytime —Earle Birney⟩; *specif* **:** to pinch or clip off (as a bud or shoot) in horticulture ⟨in the spring the blooms are *nipped,* allowing the bulb to retain the full nourishment of the plant juices —*Amer. Guide Series: La.*⟩ **b :** to destroy the growth, progress, maturing, or fulfillment of ⟨his designs were . . . *nipped* in their infancy —T.L.Peacock⟩ — often with *in the bud* ⟨the political leaders would . . . ~ the conspiracy in the bud —William Clark⟩ **:** check sharply ⟨government fiscal policy was used to ~ a downswing —J.R. Chamberlain⟩ **c :** to diminish by cutting off bits ⟨the Atlantic . . . nibbling away at the rocks, *nipping* off a bit here and swallowing a valley there —Alastair Borthwick⟩ **3 :** to censure sharply or bitingly ⟨when her brother whom she despised grew sentimental . . . she *nipped* him —Rose Feld⟩ **4 a :** to make numb with cold **:** CHILL ⟨the wind . . . *nipped* him to the bone —Rudyard Kipling⟩ **b :** to cause injury to (vegetation) **:** BLIGHT ⟨see if this frost has not *nipped* my fruit trees —James Boswell⟩ **c :** to affect painfully and closely ⟨these tidings ~ me and I hang the head —Shak.⟩ **5 :** to seize suddenly and forcibly **:** SNATCH; *esp* **:** STEAL ⟨whoever *nipped* the whiskey, *nipped* the money, too —Mark Twain⟩ **6 a :** to apply momentary mechanical pressure to (as a book or something mounted) so as to compact the leaves or promote adhesion — compare SMASH 4 **b :** to shape up (the raised bands on the backbone of a leather-covered book) with band nippers **7 :** to beat (an opponent) by a very small margin of score, distance, or time ⟨*nipped* him by 6 in. at the tape —*Time*⟩ — *vi, chiefly Brit* **:** to move briskly, nimbly, or quickly ⟨~ up there and fetch me down a book —James Ronald⟩: as **a :** JUMP, HOP ⟨*nipping* in and out of buses and taxis —Alan Moorehead⟩ ⟨*nipping* on a tram —Richard Llewellyn⟩ **b** (1) **:** HURRY ⟨~ back here with the key —Dodie Smith⟩ (2) **:** hurry away — used with *off* ⟨we *nipped* off while they was milking —Audrey Barker⟩ (3) **:** DART ⟨*nipping* in under his host's arm —Elizabeth Bowen⟩ **c :** to make a quick trip **:** HOP 2b ⟨shall I ~ out and buy one —Alan Paton⟩ **d :** INTERRUPT, INTRUDE — used with *in* or *into* ⟨*nipped* in with a neat query —*Punch*⟩

2**nip** \"\ *n* -s **1 :** something (as a quality or element of a thing) that nips: as **a :** a sharp, biting comment **:** 2DIG 1b ⟨many a privy ~ has he given him —Andrew Marvell⟩ **b :** a sharp, stinging cold ⟨the ~ of the air had startled her —Willa Cather⟩; *esp* **:** a frost that checks or destroys the growth of vegetation ⟨some tender slip saved with care from Winter's ~ —John Milton⟩ **c :** a biting or pungent flavor: (1) *Scot* **:** TANG ⟨cheese with a ~⟩ (2) **:** PIQUANCY ⟨a scholar with a ~ in his words —H.J.Laski⟩ **2 :** a compression between two surfaces, edges, or points: as **a :** a sharp bite **:** PINCH ⟨the . . . ~s of the timid black widow spider —Donald Carlisle⟩ **b :** a pinch of a coal seam **c** (1) **:** the pressure of a rope when it is bent around or held by something (2) **:** a sharp bend or turn in a rope where chafing occurs ⟨in calm weather the ~ of a cable is usually freshened every 24 hours —*Manual of Seamanship*⟩ **d :** the crushing pressure on a ship caught in the ice **e** (1) **:** the region of a calender or other squeezing or crushing device where the rolls or jaws are closest together (2) **:** the line of contact of any pair of the rolls used in papermaking (as press and calender rolls) between which the paper passes (3) **:** the distance between the corrugations of a pair of rollers (as those used in flour milling) in the course of rotation **3 a :** a sly thief **:** CUTPURSE, PICKPOCKET ⟨punishment of foists and ~s caught in the act was prompt —*Times Lit. Supp.*⟩ **4 :** a small portion **:** 3BIT ⟨wrapped a loaf of bread and a ~ of cheese in the blanket —A.B.Mayse⟩ **5 :** a low cliff often with a narrow platform at its base cut by waves and currents in an initial stage of their activity

3**nip** \"\ *n* -s [alter. of 1*nep*] *dial chiefly Eng* **:** CATNIP

4**nip** \"\ *n* -s [prob. short for *nipperkin*] **:** a small quantity of liquor **:** SIP ⟨might take a little ~ now and then —Hamilton Basso⟩ ⟨gin at threepence a ~ —Fred Majdalany⟩

5**nip** \"\ *vi* **nipped; nipped; nipping; nips :** to take liquor in nips **:** TIPPLE ⟨getting higher all the time by *nipping* at . . . bottles filled with martinis —Daniel Curley⟩

6**nip** \"\ *n or adj, usu cap* [by shortening] **:** NIPPONESE — usu. used disparagingly

**ni·pa** \'nēpə\ *n* [prob. fr. It, fr. Malay *nipah* an East Indian palm] **1** -s **:** an alcoholic beverage made from the fermented sap of an Australasian palm **2** *cap* [NL, fr. Malay *nipah*] **:** a monotypic genus of creeping semiaquatic palms whose sap is a source of nipa and of sugar, whose seeds are edible, and whose long strong pinnate leaves are extensively used in thatching and basketry **3** -s **a** *or* **nipa palm :** any palm of the genus *Nipa* **b :** thatch made of nipa leaves ⟨a row of ~ huts⟩

**nip and tuck** \¦nipən·¦tək\ *adj (or adv)* **:** so close that the lead or advantage shifts rapidly from one contestant to another **:** neck and neck ⟨the race was *nip and tuck* for a time —*Our Dumb Animals*⟩ ⟨until about the 25th lap, it was a *nip and tuck* go —*Illustrated Speedway News*⟩

**nipcheese** \'=,=\ *n* **1** *slang* **:** a ship's purser ⟨that's our ~ —Frederick Marryat⟩ **2** *slang* **:** MISER ⟨the old ~ . . . has been wasting his time —T.B.Costain⟩

**nip draw** *n* **:** a short draw shot used in billiards when the cue ball and first object ball are in close proximity

**nip·e·cot·ic acid** \¦nipə¦käd·ik-\ *n* [ISV, prob. blend of *nicotinic* and *piperidine*] **:** a crystalline heterocyclic amino acid $HNC_5H_9COOH$ obtained by hydrogenation of nicotinic acid; 3-piperidine-carboxylic acid

**nip·is·sing** \'nipəsiŋ\ *n, pl* **nipissing** *or* **nipissings** *usu cap* **1 a :** an Algonkian people of southeastern Ontario **b :** a member of such people **2 :** the Algonquian language of the Nipissing people

**nip·kow disc** \'nip(,)kō-\ *n, usu cap N* [after Paul G. *Nipkow* †1940 Ger. television pioneer] **:** a mechanical television scanner consisting of a rotating disk with small holes upon its periphery through which narrow beams of light pass

1**nip·per** \'nipə(r)\ *n* -s [1*nip* + *-er*] **1 :** any of various devices for nipping: as **a :** small pincers that are used for gripping, breaking, or cutting — usu. used in pl. **b :** long slender-nosed pliers or pincers used for seizing the end of a key in a lock to turn it — usu. used in pl. **c :** a device for squeezing tar from rope yarn **d nippers** *pl* **:** handcuffs or leg irons **e :** a grab for seizing heavy objects (as large stones) for hauling or hoisting **f nippers** *pl* **:** EYEGLASSES; *specif* **:** PINCE-NEZ **g nippers** *pl* **:** a nail or cuticle cutter with short curved blades **h :** a short selvagee or sennit for securing a nautical hemp cable temporarily to a messenger to assist in the raising of an anchor **i** (1) **:** a power press that compresses the leaves of books during the binding process by means of momentary pressure (2) **:** a small hand press used to compress single books or mounted material **2 a :** an incisor of a horse; *esp* **:** one of the middle four incisors **b :** one of the large claws or pincers of a crab or lobster **3** *chiefly Brit* **a :** a boy employed as a helper (as of a carter or hawker) **b :** CHILD, KID ⟨from fat, solemn babies . . . to ~s of nine or ten —Gavin Casey⟩ **4 a :** CUNNER **b** *b or*

**nipper crab :** a European crab (*Polybius henslowii*) **c** *Austral* (1) : PRAWN (2) : SNAPPING SHRIMP **5 a** (1) : a workman who assists miners (as by distributing drill steel or carrying blasting powder) (2) : one that tends ventilation doors in a mine (3) : BRAKEMAN 1a(2) **b :** a workman who holds up railroad ties to the rails with a bar or other tool while the rails are being spiked in place **6 :** a thick band or mitten worn by deep-sea fishermen to protect the hand from the lines

2**nip·per** \"\ *vt* -ED/-ING/-S : to secure (a ship's cable) with nippers : RACK 7

**nip·per·kin** \ˈnipə(r)kən\ *n* -S [origin unknown] **1 :** a liquor container or vessel with a capacity of a half pint or less **2 :** a quantity of liquor contained in or able to be contained in a nipperkin

**nip·pi·ly** \ˈnipəlē\ *adv* : in a nippy manner : BRISKLY, NIMBLY ⟨a panther could not have moved more ~ —P.G.Wodehouse⟩

**nip·pi·ness** \-pēnəs\ *n* -ES : the quality or state of being nippy : AGILITY

1**nipping** *adj* [fr. pres. part. of 1*nip*] : that nips : SHARP, CAUSTIC, CHILLING ⟨in her most ~ tones —Harriet B. Stowe⟩ ⟨there was a ~ wind on deck —Robert Grant †1940⟩

2**nipping** *n* -S [fr. gerund of 1*nip*] : the act or process of holding ties up to the rails in track laying

**nippingly** *adv* : in a nipping manner

**nippitate** *adj* [fr. *nippitaty, nippitate,* n.] *obs, of liquor* : strong and good : EXCELLENT

**nippitaty** *also* **nippitate** *or* **nippitato** *or* **nippitatum** *n* [origin unknown] *obs* : particularly good and strong liquor; *esp* : good ale

1**nip·ple** \ˈnipəl\ *n* -S [earlier *neble, nible,* prob. dim. of *neb, nib*] **1 a :** a more or less conical eminence surmounting the mammary gland in all higher mammals that contains the terminal and usu. fused parts of the lactiferous ducts of the gland and is the part of the breast or udder from which the young animal draws milk in suckling : TEAT — called also *mammilla, pap* **b :** any papilla marking the outlet of a gland **2 :** any of various devices resembling a nipple in appearance or function: as **a :** an artificial teat through which an infant sucks milk from a nursing bottle **b :** a device (as a stopcock) with an orifice through which the discharge of a liquid can be regulated **c :** a hollow conical projection on the percussion lock of a firearm on which the cap is placed and through which fire from the exploding cap is conveyed to the charge **3 a :** any eminence or protuberance (as the crest of a mountain) resembling or suggesting the nipple of a breast **b :** a small projection through which oil or grease is injected into machinery **4 :** a pipe coupling consisting of a short piece of tubing usu. with an external screw thread at each end

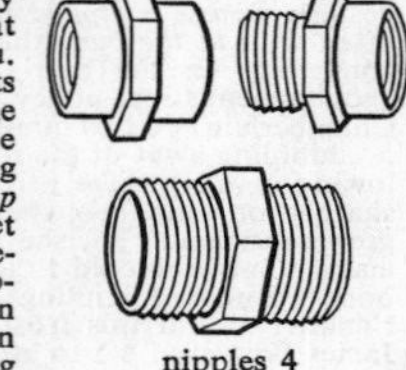

nipples 4

2**nipple** \"\ *vt* **nippled; nippled; nip·pling** \-p(ə)liŋ\ **nipples :** to provide with a nipple : cover with or as if with nipples ⟨a rain of fire *nippling* the water —H.D.Skidmore⟩

**nipplewort** \ˈ==,=\ *n* [so called fr. its use as a medication for nipples] : a slender branching annual herb (*Lapsana communis*) with loose-panicled small heads of yellow flowers

1**nip·pon·ese** \ˌnipəˈnēz, -ēs\ *adj, usu cap* [*Nippon* (Japan) + E *-ese*] : JAPANESE

2**nipponese** \"\ *n, pl* **nipponese** *cap* : JAPANESE

**nip·pon·ism** \ˈ==,nizəm\ *n* -S *usu cap* : JAPANISM

**nip·pon·ize** \-,nīz\ *vt* -ED/-ING/-S *often cap* : JAPANIZE

**nip·po·strongylus** \ˌni(ˌ)pō+\ *n, cap* [NL, fr. *nippo-* (fr. *Nippon*) + *Strongylus*] : a genus of strongyloid nematode worms that comprise intestinal parasites of rodents and are much used in biological research

**nip·py** \ˈnipē, -pi\ *adj* -ER/-EST **1 :** marked by a tendency to nip : NIPPING, SNAPPISH, MORDANT ⟨a narrower and *nippier* breed —G.D.Brown⟩ ⟨the dialogue got much *nippier* —J.P. O'Donnell⟩ **2 :** brisk, quick, or nimble in movement : SNAPPY ⟨~ little chaps —Rudyard Kipling⟩ ⟨in good physical trim and exceptionally . . . ~ on his feet —Tyrone Guthrie⟩ ⟨an excellent pony . . . ~, fast, and intelligent —*Farmer's Weekly (So. Africa)*⟩ ⟨a . . . ~ little car —A.J.Liebling⟩ **3 :** PUNGENT, SHARP ⟨~ cheese⟩ ⟨~ cider⟩ **4 :** CHILLY, CHILLING ⟨a canter on a ~ fall day —Henry Cavendish⟩

**ni pr** *or* **ni pri** *abbr* [L *nisi prius*] unless before

**nip roll** *n* : one of a pair or set of rolls for squeezing materials (as in a wringer)

**nips** *pres 3d sing of* NIP, *pl of* NIP

**nipt** \ˈnipt\ *archaic past of* NIP

**nip·ter** \ˈniptə(r)\ *n* -S [MGk *niptēr*, fr. Gk, washbasin, fr. *niptein, nizein* to wash — more at NICKER] : the ceremony of foot washing on Maundy Thursday in the Eastern Orthodox Church — compare MAUNDY 1

**nip-up** \ˈni,pəp\ *n, pl* **nip-ups 1 :** KIP-UP ⟨doing *nip-ups* and handsprings during meetings with his top military aides —R.L. Taylor⟩ **2 :** STUNT, CAPER ⟨vaudeville came back with a *nip-up* that made news —*Newsweek*⟩

**nir·gran·tha** \nirˈgräntə, -iə'-, -ran-\ *n, pl* **nirgrantha** *or* **nirgranthas** *usu cap* [Skt, free from ties, fr. *nir-, nis-* out, without + *grantha* tying, fr. *grathnāti* he ties] : JAIN

**nirles** \ˈnirlz\ *n pl* [origin unknown] *chiefly Scot* : an eruption resembling measles or chicken pox — usu. used with *the* ⟨suffering from the ~⟩

**nir·ma·na·ka·ya** \nirˈmänəˈkäyə, -iə'-\ *n* -S [Skt *nirmāṇakāya* body of magic transformation, fr. *nirmāṇa* measuring, creating, magical creation (fr. *nir- nis-* out + *māti* he measures) + *kāya* body, fr. *cinoti* he piles in order — more at MEASURE, POET] : the historically manifested body of Buddha in the doctrine of trikaya

**nir·va·na** \nirˈvänə, niə'-, nə(r)'-, -anə\ *n* -S [Skt *nirvāṇa*, lit., blowing out, fr. *nir- nis-* out + *vāti* it blows — more at WIND] **1** *usu cap* **a** *Hinduism, Jainism, Buddhism* : the state of freedom from karma, extinction of desire, passion, illusion, and the empirical self, and attainment of rest, truth, and unchanging being : SALVATION — contrasted with *samsara* **b** *also* **nib·ba·na** \niˈbänə\ [*nibbana* fr. Pali *nibbāna*, fr. Skt *nirvāṇa*] *Buddhism* : the state of enlightenment in which karma is transcended, desire, hatred, delusion and the empirical self are extinguished, and rest, harmony, and unchanging being are attained **c** *Jainism* : the state of omniscient passive peace attained by a soul liberated from matter, the effects of karma, and the course of samsara **2** *often cap* **a :** a place or state of rest, harmony, or pleasure : OBLIVION, PARADISE ⟨his old roommate of the clipping shack was in an alcoholic ~ —Herman Wouk⟩ **b :** a goal hoped for but apparently unattainable : DREAM ⟨that ~ of the . . . weatherman: a foolproof system of forecasting—*Newsweek*⟩

**nirvana principle** *n* : the psyche's characteristic tendency to reduce inner tensions and approach an inorganic state as if responding to the death instinct

**nir·va·nic** \(ˈ)=ˈvänik, -an-\ *adj* : of, relating to, or resembling nirvana ⟨~ calm⟩

**nis·an** *or* **nis·san** \ˈnisᵊn, (ˈ)nēˈsän\ *n* -S *usu cap* [Heb *Nīsān*, fr. Assyr-Bab] : the 7th month of the civil year or the 1st month of the ecclesiastical year in the Jewish calendar — see MONTH table

**ni·sei** \(ˈ)nēˈsā\ *n, pl* **nisei** *also* **niseis** *often cap* [Jap, lit., second generation, fr. *ni* second + *sei* generation] : a son or daughter of issei parents who is born and educated in America and esp. in the U.S. — distinguished from *kibei*; compare SANSEI

**ni·sha·da** \niˈshädə\ *n* -S *usu cap* [Skt *niṣāda*, fr. *Niṣāda*, name of a wild non-Aryan tribe] : a member of a low caste in India : the offspring of a Brahman and a Sudra

**ni·shi·no·mi·ya** \ˌnēˌshē(ˌ)nōˈmēyə\ *adj, usu cap* [fr. *Nishinomiya*, city in western Japan] : of or from the city of Nishinomiya, Japan : of the kind or style prevalent in Nishinomiya

**ni·si** \ˈnī,sī, ˈnē(,)sē\ *adj* [L, unless, fr. *ne-* not + *si* if — more at NO] : not final or absolute — used in law to denote that a rule, decree, or order shall take effect at a given time unless before that time it is modified or avoided by cause shown or further proceedings or by the fulfillment of some condition therein named ⟨the decree is ~ and not absolute —*Economist*⟩ ⟨a rule ~⟩ — compare DECREE NISI

**ni·sin** \ˈnīsən\ *n* -S [origin unknown] : a crystalline antibiotic that is produced by lactic acid bacteria, is active esp. against bacteria of the genus *Clostridium*, and causes spoilage in dairy products

**nisi pri·us** \-ˈprīəs\ *n* [ME, fr. ML, lit., unless before (words introducing a clause in the writ)] **1 a :** a cause involving issues of fact that being begun in the courts of Westminster was appointed to be tried there in an Easter or Michaelmas term by a jury from the county wherein the cause of action arose unless before the day appointed the judges of assize came into the county in question and there tried the cause **b :** an issue of fact triable at the assizes **2 a** (1) : a writ commanding the sheriff to provide a jury at the Court of Westminster on a day certain unless the judges of assize previously come to the county from which the jury is to be returned (2) : the clause in this writ introduced by the words *nisi prius* (3) : the authority or commission conferred by this clause on the judges of assize **b :** an action tried or to be tried in an English court under such a writ **c** (1) : the trial of such causes by the judges of assize (2) : the trial of issues of fact in civil causes or other such court business (as the trial of causes before the judges of the King's Bench Division in London) **3 a :** a court of record in the U.S., Great Britain, and other English-speaking countries that tries an issue of fact before a jury and a single judge **b :** the proceedings in such a court — compare *in banc* at BANC

**nis·ka** \ˈniskə\ *n, pl* **niska** *or* **niskas** *usu cap* **1 a :** a Tsimshian people or group of peoples of the Nass river valley and contiguous Pacific coast, British Columbia, Canada **b :** a member of any of such peoples **2 :** the language of the Niska people

**nis·nas** \ˈnisnəs\ *n, pl* **nisnas** [Ar *nisnās*] : a guenon (*Cercopithecus griseoviridis*) of northeastern Africa or a monkey of a related species

**ni·spe·ro** \ˈnēspə,rō\ *n* -S [AmerSp *níspero*, fr. Sp, medlar, fr. (assumed) VL *nespilus*, fr. L *mespilus, mespilum*, fr. Gk *mespilon*] **1 :** any of various plants of the genus *Achras* found in Spanish America; *esp* : SAPODILLA **2 :** LOQUAT

**nis·qual·li** *also* **nis·qual·ly** \niˈskwälē, ˈniz,kw-\ *n, pl* **nisqualli** \"\ *or* **nisquallis** *usu cap* **1 a :** a Salishan people of Puget Sound, Wash. **b :** a member of such people **2 :** the language of the Nisqually people

**nis·se** \ˈnisə\ *n, pl* **nisser** *or* **nisses** [Sw or Dan or Norw, alter. of *Nils* (Saint) Nicholas] : a friendly goblin or brownie of Scandinavian folklore that frequents farm buildings : KOBOLD ⟨~ . . . a harmless creature, dressed in red blouse and pantaloons and wearing a red cap —*Nat'l Geographic*⟩

**nis·sen hut** \ˈnisᵊn-\ *n, usu cap N* [after Lieut. Col. Peter N. *Nissen* †1930 Brit. mining engineer and inventor] : a barrel-shaped prefabricated shelter of corrugated iron with cement floor

**nissl bodies** \ˈnisəl-\ *or* **nissl corpuscles** *or* **nissl granules** *or* **nissl's bodies** *or* **nissl's corpuscles** *or* **nissl's granules** *n pl, usu cap N* [after Franz *Nissl* †1919 Ger. neurologist] : discrete bodies of variable size that are found in the cytoplasm of nerve cells and that stain deeply with methylene blue

**nissl substance** \"-\ *n, usu cap N* : the material of Nissl bodies

**ni·sus** \ˈnīsəs\ *n, pl* **nisus** [L, fr. *nisus*, past part. of *niti* to bear down, strive; akin to L *conivēre, connivēre* to close the eyes — more at CONNIVE] **1 :** a conative state or condition : STRIVING, INCLINATION ⟨a ~ or energizing towards a presented object —L.P.Hickok⟩ ⟨this ~ towards individuality —R.H. Gault & D.T.Howard⟩ ⟨a ~ towards large generalizing —George Saintsbury⟩ **2 :** a tendency or principle in reality according to some philosophers exhibited in the emergence of higher levels of existence (as life, mind, deity) ⟨there is a ~ in space-time which, as it has borne its creatures forward through matter and life to mind, will bear them forward to some higher level of existence —Samuel Alexander⟩

1**nit** \ˈnit, *usu* -id·+V\ *n* -S [ME *nite, nitte*, fr. OE *hnitu*; akin to OHG *hniz* nit, Gk *konid-, konis*] : the egg of a louse or other parasitic insect; *also* : the insect itself when young

2**nit** \"\ *n* -S [alter. of *nut*] *chiefly Scot* : NUT; *esp* : HAZELNUT

3**nit** \"\ *adv* [perh. fr. Yiddish, not, no, fr. MHG *niht, nit* nothing, not, fr. OHG *niwiht, neowiht* — more at NAUGHT] *slang* : NO — used as a negative response

4**nit** \"\ *n* -S [origin unknown] *Austral* : GUARD, WATCH — usu. used with *keep* ⟨keep ~ in the corridor⟩

**ni·tel·la** \nīˈtelə\ *n, cap* [NL, fr. L *nitēre* to shine + NL *-ella* — more at NEAT] : a genus of delicate branching stoneworts (family Characeae) differing from *Chara* in lacking a cortical layer of cells and in having the leaves all branched

**ni·ter** *also* **ni·tre** \ˈnīd·ə(r), -ītə-\ *n* -S [ME *nitre* natron, fr. MF, fr. L *nitrum*, fr. Gk *nitron*, fr. Egypt *ntry*] **1** *usu nitre, obs* : NATRON **2 a :** potassium nitrate esp. occurring naturally (as in desert deposits in northern Chile) **b :** SODIUM NITRATE; *esp* : CHILE SALTPETER **c** *archaic* : NITRATE 1 **3** *usu nitre, obs* : a supposed nitrous substance or element occurring esp. diffused through the air **4** *usu nitre* : ETHYL NITRITE ⟨spirit of ~⟩ — compare ETHYL NITRITE SPIRIT **5 :** SUGAR SAND

**niter-blue** \ˈ==ˈ=\ *vt* : to make (steel) blue by immersing in a molten niter mixture

**niter cake** *n* : SODIUM BISULFATE; *esp* : a caked form obtained as a by-product in the original manufacture of nitric acid from sodium nitrate and sulfuric acid or in the manufacture of hydrochloric acid from common salt and sulfuric acid

**ni·te·rói** *or* **ni·te·roi** \ˌnēdəˈrȯi\ *adj, usu cap* [fr. *Niterói*, city in southeast Brazil] : of or from the city of Niterói, Brazil : of the kind or style prevalent in Niterói

**nit·ery** \ˈnīd·ərē, -itə-, -ri\ *n* -ES [nite (alter. of *night*) + *-ery*] : NIGHTCLUB

**nit fly** *n* : a horse botfly (*Gasterophilus intestinalis*)

**nit grass** *n* : an annual grass (*Gastridium ventricosum*) of the family Gramineae that is native to the Mediterranean region but adventive in some parts of the southern U.S. and has small shining spikelets

1**nith·er** \ˈnith̲ə(r)\ *vt* -ED/-ING/-S [ME *nitheren*, fr. OE *nitherian*; akin to OHG *nideren* to lower, debase, ON *nithra* to lower; all fr. a prehistoric NGmc-WGmc verb derivative fr. the root of OE *nither* down — more at NETHER] *chiefly Scot* **1 :** DEBASE, HUMILIATE **2 :** BLAST, BLIGHT ⟨~*ed* plants⟩

2**nither** \"\ *vi* -ED/-ING/-S [prob. of Scand origin] *chiefly Scot* : to shiver or tremble esp. with cold

3**nither** \"\ *dial var of* NEITHER

**nithing** *n* -S [ME, fr. OE *nīthing*, fr. ON *nīthingr*, fr. *nīth* scorn, contumely + *-ingr* -ing; ON *nīth* akin to OE *nīth* envy, hatred, strife, OHG *nīd* envy, hatred, Goth *neith* envy and perh. to L *nitēre* to shine — more at NEAT] **1** *obs* : COWARD, SCOUNDREL, POLTROON **2** *obs* : NIGGARD

**nit·id** \ˈnid·əd\ *also* **nit·i·dous** \-d·əs\ *adj* [L *nitidus* — more at NEAT] : BRIGHT, GLOSSY, LUSTROUS ⟨Nereids beneath the ~ moon —P.B.Rice⟩ ⟨terse ~ language —Frederico de Onís⟩ ⟨apex with a depressed, glabrous, *nitidous* flange —*Pan-Pacific Entomologist*⟩

**ni·tid·i·ty** \niˈtidəd·ē\ *n* -ES : the quality or state of being nitid : BRILLIANCY, SHEEN

1**ni·tid·u·lid** \nəˈtijələd\ *adj* [NL *Nitidulidae*] : of or relating to the Nitidulidae

2**nitidulid** \"\ *n* -S : a beetle of the family Nitidulidae

**nit·i·du·li·dae** \ˌnid·əˈd(y)üləˌdē\ *n pl, cap* [NL, fr. *Nitidula*, type genus (fr. LL, fem. of *nitidulus* natty, dim. of L *nitidus* bright, neat) + *-idae*] : a family of small beetles having 5-jointed tarsi and antennae ending in a 3-jointed clavate expansion, including some that are believed to be vectors of the oak wilt fungus, and having larvae that develop usu. in decaying vegetation but sometimes attack healthy plants

**nit·i·nat** \ˈnid·əˌnat\ *n, pl* **nitinat** *or* **nitinats** *usu cap* **1 a :** a subdivision of the Nootka **b :** a member of such subdivision **2 :** the dialect of the Nitinat people

**ni·to** \ˈnē(ˌ)tō\ *n* -S [Tag *nitò*] : any of several climbing ferns (genus *Lygodium*) whose stems are used in the Philippines for making hats and baskets

**ni·ton** \ˈnīd·ˌän, ˈnē-\ *n* -S [L *nitēre* to shine + ISV *-on*; fr. its phosphorescent properties — more at NEAT] : RADON 1

**nitr-** *or* **nitro-** *comb form* [L & Gk; L *nitrum* natron, fr. Gk *nitron* — more at NITER] **1 :** nitrate ⟨*nitro*bacteria⟩ ⟨*nitrogen*⟩ **2 a :** containing nitrogen in combined form esp. when derived from an acid (as nitric acid) ⟨*nitr*amide⟩ ⟨*nitro*hydrochloric acid⟩ **b** *usu nitro-* : containing the univalent group $-NO_2$ composed of one nitrogen and two oxygen atoms united through nitrogen to (1) carbon or nitrogen; (2) oxygen; or (3) a central atom — in names respectively of (1) organic compounds ⟨*nitro*benzene⟩ ⟨*nitro*methane⟩ ⟨*nitr*amines⟩; (2) organic nitrates ⟨*nitro*glycerin⟩ ⟨*nitro*cellulose⟩; (3) coordination complexes ⟨*nitro*-pentammine-cobalt ion $[Co(NO_2)(NH_3)_5]^{++}$⟩ — compare ISONITRO-, NITRITO-, NITRYL

**ni·tra·mide** \nīˈtra,mīd ˈnī·trə,m-, -,məd\ *n* [ISV *nitr-* + *amide*] : a crystalline weakly acid compound $NH_2NO_2$ that is made from a nitro-carbamate (as nitro-urethane) or from nitro-urea and that decomposes on heating into nitrous oxide; the amide of nitric acid

**ni·tra·mine** \ˌnī·trəˈmēn, nīˈtramən\ *n* [ISV *nitr-* + *amine*] **1 :** any of a class of compounds characterized by the grouping $>NNO_2$ consisting of a nitro group attached to nitrogen and regarded either as *N*-nitro derivatives of amines or as organic derivatives of nitramide; *esp* : TETRYL **2 :** NITRAMIDE

**nitraniline** *var of* NITROANILINE

1**ni·trate** \ˈnī,trāt, -,trət, *usu* -d·+V\ *n* -S [F, fr. *nitr-* + *-ate*] **1 :** a salt or ester of nitric acid, most of the salts being soluble in water and some of them (as the sodium, potassium, and calcium salts) constituting the principal source of nitrogen for higher plants **2 :** sodium nitrate or potassium nitrate used as a fertilizer **3 :** cellulose nitrate or its products (as a plastic)

2**ni·trate** \-,trāt, *usu* -ād·+V\ *vt* -ED/-ING/-S : to treat or combine with nitric acid or a nitrate; *esp* : to convert (an organic compound) into a nitro compound or a nitrate (as by treating with a mixture of nitric acid and sulfuric acid)

**nitrate group** *or* **nitrate ion** *n* : the univalent group or anion $NO_3$ or $-ONO_2$ characteristic of nitric acid and nitrates

**nitrate of iron :** a dark red chiefly ferric sulfate liquid made usu. by oxidizing a solution of ferrous sulfate with nitric acid and used as a mordant in dyeing

**nitrate of lime :** calcium nitrate esp. for use as a fertilizer

**nitrate of potash :** potassium nitrate esp. for use as a fertilizer

**nitrate of soda :** SODIUM NITRATE

**ni·tra·tine** \ˈnī·trə,tēn, -,tən\ *n* -S : native sodium nitrate : CALICHE 1

**ni·tra·tion** \nīˈtrāshən\ *n* -S : the process of nitrating

**nitrato-** *comb form* [ISV *nitrate*] : containing the nitrate group — esp. in names of coordination complexes ⟨ammonium hexa-*nitrato*-cerate $(NH_4)_2[Ce(NO_3)_6]$⟩

**ni·tra·tor** \ˈnī,trād·ə(r)\ *n* -S : one that nitrates: as **a :** an acid-resistant vessel with cooling equipment used for the nitration of organic substances **b :** one who tends a nitrator

**nitre** *var of* NITER

**ni·tri·ary** \ˈnī·trē,erē\ *n* -ES [F *nitrière*, fr. L *nitraria* natron bed, fr. *nitrum* natron + *-aria* -ary — more at NITER] : an artificial bed of refuse animal matter for the manufacture of niter by nitrification

**ni·tric** \ˈnī·trik, -ēk\ *adj* [F *nitrique*, fr. *nitr-* + *-ique* -ic] : derived from nitrogen — used esp. of compounds in which this element has a higher valence than in corresponding nitrous compounds ⟨~ oxide⟩

**nitric acid** *n* [trans. of F *acide nitrique*] : a corrosive liquid inorganic acid $HNO_3$ made usu. by the catalytic oxidation of ammonia or by the action of sulfuric acid on nitrates and used chiefly as an oxidizing agent (as in rocket propellants), in nitrations, and in the manufacture of fertilizers, explosives, dyes, nitroparaffins, and a variety of other organic compounds : AQUAFORTIS — see AQUA REGIA, FUMING NITRIC ACID

**nitric anhydride** *n* : NITROGEN PENTOXIDE

**nitric bacterium** *n* : a bacterium (as a member of the genus *Nitrobacter*) that oxidizes nitrites to nitrates

**nitric oxide** *n* : a colorless poisonous gas NO that is obtained by oxidation of nitrogen or ammonia in making nitric acid or by reduction of nitrous acid and that turns brown in air by oxidation to nitrogen dioxide; nitrogen monoxide — called also *nitrogen(II) oxide*

**ni·trid·a·tion** \ˌnī·trəˈdāshən\ *n* -S : conversion into a nitride : NITRIDING

1**ni·tride** \ˈnī,trīd, -,trəd\ *n* -S [ISV *nitr-* + *-ide*] : a binary compound of nitrogen with a more electropositive element (as boron, silicon, and most metals)

2**ni·tride** \-,trīd\ *vt* -ED/-ING/-S : to convert into a nitride; *esp* : to treat (steel) by the process of nitriding

**nitriding** *n* -S [fr. gerund of 2*nitride*] : a process of casehardening steel by impregnating with nitrogen usu. by being heated in ammonia gas between 900 and 1000°F

**ni·trid·ize** \-,dīz\ *vt* -ED/-ING/-S [1*nitride* + *-ize*] : to combine with nitrogen; *also* : to change (a compound) by increasing the proportion of the electronegative part or to deprive (an atom or ion) of electrons by means of nitrogen — compare OXIDIZE

**nitrido-** *comb form* [1*nitride*] : NITRILO- — esp. in names of inorganic compounds ⟨*nitrido*-tri-sulfuric acid $N(SO_3H)_2$⟩

**ni·tri·fac·tion** \ˌnī·trəˈfakshən\ *n* -S [*nitr-* + *-i-* + *-faction*] : formation of niter

**ni·trif·er·ous** \(ˈ)nīˈtrif(ə)rəs\ *adj* [*nitr-* + *-iferous*] : containing or yielding niter

**ni·tri·fi·able** \ˌnī·trəˈfīəbəl\ *adj* [*nitrify* + *-able*] : capable of nitrification

**ni·tri·fi·ca·tion** \ˌ==fəˈkāshən\ *n* -S [F, fr. *nitrifier* to nitrify, after such pairs as F *amplifier* to amplify: *amplification*] : the process of nitrifying; *specif* : the oxidation by bacteria of ammonium salts to nitrites and the further oxidation of nitrites to nitrates wherever the proper conditions of temperature, air, moisture, and alkalinity allow the nitrobacteria to act (as in all productive soils and in the heaps of waste organic matter formerly used in manufacturing potassium nitrate) — see NITROGEN CYCLE, NITROGEN FIXATION 2; compare DENITRIFICATION

**ni·tri·fier** \ˈ==,fī(ə)r, -iə\ *n* -S : one that nitrifies

**ni·tri·fy** \-,fī\ *vt* -ED/-ING/-ES [F *nitrifier*, fr. *nitre* niter + *-ifier* -ify] **1 :** to combine or impregnate with nitrogen or a nitrogen compound **2 :** to convert by oxidation into nitric acid or nitrous acid or their salts : subject to or produce by nitrification — compare NITROSIFY

**ni·trile** \ˈnī·trəl; -,trēl, -trīl\ *n* -S [ISV *nitr-* + *-ile*] : any of a class of compounds characterized by the presence of the trivalent nitrogen radical N≡ and derivable from oxygen-containing acids by complete removal of the elements of water from their ammonium salts; *usu* : a compound (as acetonitrile, benzonitrile) that is characterized by the presence of the cyanogen group, is derivable from a carboxylic acid or its amide, and yields the acid on complete hydrolysis : an organic cyanide

**nitrile rubber** *n* : any of a class of synthetic rubbers that are made by copolymerizing butadiene and acrylonitrile, are characterized by good resistance to swelling caused by oils, solvents, and greases, and are used esp. in hose for carrying oils and gasoline, in tank linings, and in gaskets

**nitrilo-** *comb form* [ISV *nitrile*] : containing the trivalent radical N≡ characteristic of nitriles — esp. in names of organic compounds ⟨*nitrilo*-tri-acetic acid $N(CH_2COOH)_3$⟩

**ni·trite** \ˈnī,trīt, *usu* -īd·+V\ *n* -S [*nitr-* + *-ite*] : a salt or ester of nitrous acid

**nitrite group** *or* **nitrite ion** *n* : the univalent group or anion $NO_2$ or ONO characteristic of nitrous acid and nitrites in which it is united through oxygen and hence is isomeric with the nitro group

**nitrito-** *comb form* [*nitrite*] : containing the nitrite group — esp. in names of coordination complexes ⟨*nitrito*-pentammine-cobalt ion $[Co(ONO)(NH_3)_5]^{++}$⟩ — compare NITR- 2b

**ni·tri·toid** \ˈnī·trə,tȯid\ *adj* [ISV *nitrite* + *-oid*] : resembling a nitrite or being something (as poisoning) caused by a nitrite ⟨a severe ~ crisis may follow arsphenamine injection⟩

1**ni·tro** \ˈnī·(ˌ)trō\ *adj* [*nitr-*] : containing or being the univalent group $-NO_2$ united through nitrogen — used esp. of organic compounds in which the group is united to carbon or nitrogen; compare NITR- 2b, NITRITE GROUP, NITRYL

2**nitro** \"\ *n* -S : any of various nitrated products: as **a** [by shortening] : NITROGLYCERIN **b** [short for *nitrocellulose*] : CELLULOSE NITRATE **c :** NITRO POWDER

**ni·tro-** *in pronunciations below*, ˈ==ˌnī·(ˌ)trō *or* -·,trə\ — see NITR-

**ni·tro·amine** \ˈ==+\ *n* [*nitro-* + *amine*] : a nitro derivative of an amine; *esp* : NITRAMINE 1

**ni·tro·an·i·line** \"+\ *also* **ni·tran·i·line** \(ˈ)nīˈtranᵊlən *sometimes* -,īn *or* -,ēn\ *n* [ISV *nitr-* + *aniline*] : a nitro derivative of aniline: as **a :** the bright yellow crystalline para mono derivative $H_2NC_6H_4NO_2$ made usu. from *para*-nitro-chlorobenzene by reaction with ammonia or from acetanilide by nitration and hydrolysis and used chiefly as an intermediate for azo and azoic dyes **b :** the orange-yellow crystalline ortho isomer made similarly to the para derivative **c :** the yellow crystalline meta isomer made usu. from *meta*-dinitrobenzene by partial reduction and used chiefly as a dye intermediate

**ni·tro·bac·ter** \ˌ⸗⸗ˌbaktə(r)\ *n* [NL, fr. *nitr-* + *-bacter*] **1** *cap* **:** a genus of rod-shaped nonmotile bacteria (family Nitrobacteriaceae) occurring in soil, securing energy for growth by oxidizing nitrites to nitrates, and growing poorly on organic media **2** -s **:** any bacterium of the genus *Nitrobacter* **:** NITRIC BACTERIUM

**ni·tro·bacteria** \¦⸗⸗+\ *n pl* [NL, fr. *nitr-* + *bacteria*] **1 :** the soil bacteria concerned in nitrification **2 :** NITRIC BACTERIA — compare NITROSOBACTERIA

**ni·tro·bacteriaceae** \"+\ *n pl, cap* [NL, irreg. fr. *Nitrobacter*, type genus + *-aceae*] **:** a family of Eubacteriales (order Pseudomonadales) comprising rod-shaped or rarely spherical bacteria capable of using carbon dioxide as a source of carbon and obtaining energy by oxidation of ammonia or nitrites — compare THIOBACTERIACEAE

**ni·tro·bar·ite** \"+\ *n* [*nitr-* + *baryta* + *ite*] **:** native barium nitrate

**ni·tro·benzene** \"+\ *n* [ISV *nitr-* + *benzene*] **:** a poisonous insoluble oil $C_6H_5NO_2$ of slightly yellow color and sweetish odor that is made by nitration of benzene and that is used chiefly as a solvent, mild oxidizing agent, and starting material in making aniline and other dye intermediates

**ni·tro·calcite** \"+\ *n* [*nitr-* + *calc-* + *-ite*] **:** native calcium nitrate $Ca(NO_3)_2.4H_2O$ occurring as an efflorescence (as on old walls and in limestone caves)

**ni·tro·cellulose** \"+\ *n* [ISV *nitr-* + *cellulose*] **:** nitrated cellulose **:** CELLULOSE NITRATE ⟨~ lacquers⟩ — **ni·tro·cel·lulosic** \"+\ *adj*

**ni·tro·chloroform** \"+\ *n* [*nitr-* + *chloroform*] **:** CHLOROPICRIN

**ni·tro·cotton** \"+\ *n* **:** cellulose nitrate made from cotton; *esp* **:** GUNCOTTON

**ni·tro·ethane** \"+\ *n* [ISV *nitr-* + *ethane*] **:** a volatile liquid nitroparaffin $C_2H_5NO_2$ obtained usu. along with the nitropropanes and used as an industrial solvent and in chemical synthesis

**ni·tro·form** \ˈnī·trəˌfȯrm\ *n* [ISV *nitr-* + *-form* (as in *chloroform*)] **:** a crystalline explosive compound $CH(NO_2)_3$ analogous to chloroform; trinitro-methane

**ni·tro·furan** \¦⸗⸗ *at* NITRO- +\ *n* [*nitr-* + *furan*] **:** any of several derivatives of furan containing a nitro group in the alpha or 2- or 5-position and used as antibacterial agents

**ni·tro·fu·ra·zone** \ˌ⸗⸗ˈfyu̇rəˌzōn\ *n* -s [*nitr-* + *fur-* + semicarb*azone*] **:** a pale yellow crystalline compound $O_2NC_4H_2\text{-}OCH{=}NNHCONH_2$ used chiefly externally as a bacteriostatic or bactericidal dressing (as for wounds and infections); 5-nitro-2-furfural semicarbazone

**ni·tro·ga·tion** \ˌnī·trəˈgāshən\ *n* -s [*nitr-* + irr*igation*] **:** fertilization of the soil with nitrogen by the addition of anhydrous ammonia from pressure tanks to the irrigation water

**ni·tro·gelatin** *or* **ni·tro·gelatine** \¦⸗⸗ *at* NITRO- +\ *n* [ISV *nitr-* + *gelatin*] **:** BLASTING GELATIN

**ni·tro·gen** \ˈnī·trəjən, -rēj-\ *n* -s [F *nitrogène*, fr. *nitr-* + *-gène* -gen] **:** a common nonmetallic element that in the free form is normally a colorless odorless tasteless insoluble inert diatomic gas comprising 78 percent of the atmosphere by volume, obtained industrially by fractional distillation of liquid air, and used chiefly as an inert atmosphere (as in industrial processes) and that in the combined form has a wide range of valences (as from −3 in ammonia to +5 in nitric acid and nitrates) and is a constituent of biologically important compounds (as proteins, nucleic acids, alkaloids) and hence of all living cells as well as of industrially important substances (as cyanides, fertilizers, dyes, antibiotics) — symbol *N;* see ELEMENT table, NITROGEN CYCLE, NITROGEN FIXATION

**ni·tro·gen·ate** \-jəˌnāt, nīˈträjəˌ-, *usu* -ād·+V\ *vt* -ED/-ING/-S **:** to combine with nitrogen **:** NITROGENIZE — **ni·tro·gen·a·tion** \ˌnī·trəjəˈnāshən, nīˌträjəˈ-\ *n* -s

**nitrogen balance** *n* **1 :** the difference between nitrogen intake and nitrogen excretion in the animal body, a greater intake resulting in a positive balance and an increased excretion causing a negative balance — see NITROGEN EQUILIBRIUM **2 :** the net loss or gain of soil nitrogen resulting from the removal of nitrogen (as by cropping, leaching, denitrification, and soil erosion) and the addition of nitrogen (as through fertilizers and nitrogen fixation by organisms)

**nitrogen base** *or* **nitrogenous base** *n* **:** a basic derivative of ammonia (as hydroxylamine); *esp* **:** an organic derivative (as methylamine, pyridine)

**nitrogen chloride** *n* **:** NITROGEN TRICHLORIDE

**nitrogen cycle** *n* **:** a continuous series of natural processes by which nitrogen passes through successive stations in air, soil, and organisms involving principally decay, nitrogen fixation, nitrification, and denitrification

**nitrogen dioxide** *n* **:** a suffocating poisonous strongly oxidizing gas that is reddish brown and has the formula $NO_2$ at 150°C but becomes paler on being cooled because it dimerizes to nitrogen tetroxide, that is usu. obtained in an equilibrium mixture with nitrogen tetroxide by oxidation (as of nitric oxide or ammonia), by reduction of nitric acid, or by decomposition of lead nitrate, and that is used in either gaseous or liquefied form chiefly in making concentrated nitric acid, in nitration processes, and as an oxidizing agent (as in rocket propellants) — called also *nitrogen(IV) oxide*

**nitrogen equilibrium** *n* **:** nitrogen balance when intake and excretion of nitrogen are equal

**nitrogen family** *n* **:** the related elements nitrogen, phosphorus, arsenic, antimony, and bismuth forming a subdivision of group V of the periodic table

**nitrogen fixation** *n* **1 :** the conversion of free nitrogen into combined forms useful as such or as starting materials for fertilizers, explosives, and a variety of chemicals by any of several industrial processes (as the synthesis of ammonia, the synthesis of calcium cyanamide, the synthesis of nitric oxide and nitrogen dioxide from nitrogen and oxygen of the air at very high temperatures produced in an electric arc or by combustion of natural gas) — compare CYANAMIDE PROCESS, SYNTHETIC AMMONIA PROCESS **2 :** the metabolic assimilation of atmospheric nitrogen by heterotrophic bacteria (as free-living members of the genera *Azotobacter* and *Clostridium* in soil or symbiotic rhizobia in root nodules of leguminous plants) the nitrogen being utilized in the presence of carbohydrate to build bacterial protein and released for plant use by nitrification in the soil on the death of the bacteria that initially fix it

**nitrogen fixer** *n* **:** any of various soil organisms involved in the process of nitrogen fixation

**nitrogen–fixing** \¦⸗⸗⸗¦⸗⸗\ *adj* [*nitrogen* + *fixing*, fr. pres. part. of [1]*fix*] **:** having the power of nitrogen fixation ⟨*nitrogen-fixing* bacteria⟩; *broadly* **:** contributing to the process of nitrogen fixation ⟨*nitrogen-fixing* plants⟩

**ni·tro·gen·iza·tion** \nīˌträjənəˈzāshən, ˌnī·trəjə-, -ˌnīˈz-\ *n* -s **:** the process of nitrogenizing

**ni·tro·gen·ize** \nīˈträjəˌnīz, ˈnī·trəjə,-\ *vt* -ED/-ING/-S **:** to combine or impregnate with nitrogen or its compounds

**nitrogen monoxide** *n* **1 :** NITROUS OXIDE **2 :** NITRIC OXIDE

**nitrogen mustard** *n* **:** any of a group of toxic blistering compounds that are analogous in composition to mustard gas but with nitrogen replacing sulfur and that typically are chlorinated tertiary alkylamines; *esp* **:** an amine $CH_3N(CH_2CH_2Cl)_2$ used in the form of its crystalline hydrochloride in treating neoplastic diseases (as Hodgkin's disease and leukemia); methyl-bis-(2-chloroethyl)-amine

**ni·trog·e·nous** \(ˈ)nīˈ¦träjənəs\ *adj* [*nitrogen* + *-ous*] **:** of, relating to, or containing nitrogen in combined form (as in nitrates or proteins) ⟨~ fertilizers such as ammonium nitrate and tankage⟩ ⟨~ feeds⟩

**nitrogenous equilibrium** *n* **:** NITROGEN EQUILIBRIUM

**nitrogen oxide** *n* **:** any of several oxides of nitrogen some of which are formed in a mixture as toxic fumes by the action of nitric acid on oxidizable material (as organic substances or metals) or by the decomposition of nitrates or nitro compounds and are used as catalysts in the chamber process of making sulfuric acid: as **a :** NITROUS OXIDE **b :** NITRIC OXIDE **c :** NITROGEN TRIOXIDE **d :** NITROGEN DIOXIDE **e :** NITROGEN PENTOXIDE

**nitrogen pentoxide** *n* **:** a white crystalline unstable compound $N_2O_5$ obtainable by oxidation of nitrogen dioxide with ozone or by dehydration of nitric acid and yielding nitric acid on combination with water with evolution of much heat; di-nitrogen pentoxide — called also *nitric anhydride, nitrogen(V) oxide*

**nitrogen peroxide** *n* **:** the oxide nitrogen dioxide as such, as its dimer nitrogen tetroxide, or as a mixture of these two

**nitrogen tetroxide** *n* **1 :** a colorless poisonous gas $N_2O_4$ that is obtained by cooling nitrogen dioxide, that condenses to a colorless or pale yellow liquid at 21°C, and that freezes to colorless crystals at −11°C **2 :** a brown liquid produced commercially and containing both nitrogen tetroxide and nitrogen dioxide

**nitrogen trichloride** *n* **:** a pungent volatile explosive yellow oil $NCl_3$ formerly used in bleaching and aging flour

**nitrogen trioxide** *n* **:** a compound $N_2O_3$ obtained at a low temperature as a deep blue unstable liquid that readily decomposes into nitric oxide and nitrogen dioxide; di-nitrogen trioxide — called also *nitrogen(III) oxide, nitrous anhydride*

**ni·tro·glycerin** *or* **ni·tro·glycerine** \¦⸗⸗ *at* NITRO- +\ *n* [ISV *nitr-* + *glycerin;* prob. orig. formed as F *nitroglycérine*] **:** a heavy oily explosive poisonous liquid compound $C_3H_5(ONO_2)_3$ that is almost colorless when pure and has a sweet taste, that is obtained by nitrating glycerol, that burns quietly in the open air but explodes on heating in a closed vessel or esp. on percussion with the formation of about 10,000 times its own volume of gas, and that is used chiefly in making dynamites and propellant explosives (as blasting gelatin) and in medicine as a vasodilator (as in angina pectoris) — compare *glyceryl trinitrate*

**ni·tro·guanidine** \"+\ *n* [ISV *nitr-* + *guanidine*] **:** a crystalline smokeless flashless propellant $HN{=}C(NH_2)NHNO_2$ obtained usu. by treating guanidine nitrate with concentrated sulfuric acid and used as a component in military smokeless powder (as in guns requiring rapid firing without overheating the barrel of the gun)

**ni·tro·hydrochloric acid** \"+-\ *n* [*nitr-* + *hydrochloric*] **:** AQUA REGIA

**ni·trol·amine** \¦nī·ˌtrōl, -ōl+\ *n* [G *nitrolamin*, fr. *nitro-* (fr. *nitros-*) + *-lamin* (fr. *hydroxylamin* hydroxylamine)] **:** any of a class of compounds obtained by the action of amines or ammonia on nitrosates, nitrosites, or nitrosochlorides

**ni·tro·lic acid** \(ˈ)nīˈ¦trōlik, -rälik-\ *n* [*nitr-* + *-ol* + *-ic*] **:** any of a class of weak acids of the general formula $RC({=}NOH)\text{-}NO_2$, that are formed by the action of nitrous acid on primary nitroparaffins $RCH_2NO_2$ and that react with alkalies to give intensely red-colored solutions of their salts ⟨aceto-*nitrolic acid* $CH_3C({=}NOH)NO_2$⟩ — compare PSEUDONITROLE

**ni·tro·lim** \ˈnī·trəˌlim\ *or* **ni·tro·lime** \-ˌlīm\ *n* -s [*nitrolim* alter. of *nitrolime*, fr. *nitr-* + *-lime*] **:** CALCIUM CYANAMIDE — used chiefly commercially

**ni·tro·magnesite** \¦⸗⸗ *at* NITRO- +\ *n* [*nitr-* + *magnes*ium + *-ite*] **:** native magnesium nitrate $Mg(NO_3)_2.6H_2O$ occurring as an efflorescence in limestone caverns

**ni·tro·mersol** \ˌ⸗⸗ˈmərˌsȯl, -ōl\ *n* -s [*nitr-* + *mer*cury + cre*sol*] **:** a brownish yellow to yellow solid organic mercurial $C_7H_5HgNO_3$ that is a derivative of *ortho*-cresol used chiefly in the form of a solution of its sodium salt as an antiseptic and disinfectant

**ni·trom·e·ter** \nīˈträməd·ə(r)\ *n* [*nitr-* + *-meter*] **:** an apparatus for collecting and measuring the volume of gaseous nitrogen or other gas that is liberated from a substance during analysis — **ni·tro·met·ric** \¦⸗⸗ *at* NITRO- +¦me·trik\ *adj*

nitrometer

**ni·tro·methane** \¦⸗⸗ *at* NITRO- +\ *n* [ISV *nitr-* + *methane*] **:** a liquid nitroparaffin $CH_3NO_2$ that boils at 101°C, that is obtained usu. along with the nitropropanes, and that is used chiefly as an industrial solvent, as a rocket monopropellant, and in chemical synthesis

**ni·tro·muriatic acid** \"+-\ *n* [*nitr-* + *muriatic*] **:** AQUA REGIA

**nitro musk** *n* **:** any of several synthetic musks (as musk ambrette, musk ketone, musk xylene) that are nitro derivatives of substituted benzenes

**ni·tro·naphthalene** \¦⸗⸗ *at* NITRO- +\ *n* [ISV *nitr-* + *naphthalene*] **:** either of two yellow crystalline compounds $C_{10}H_7NO_2$: **a :** the alpha or 1-isomer made by direct nitration of naphthalene and used in making alpha-naphthylamine **b :** the beta or 2-isomer made indirectly (as by nitration of tetrahydronaphthalene followed by dehydrogenation)

**ni·trone** \ˈnī·ˌtrōn\ *n* -s [*nitr-* + *-one*] **:** any of a class of compounds that contain the grouping $>C{=}N(O)-$ consisting of carbon and oxygen attached to nitrogen and that are made from alkyl or aryl derivatives of hydroxylamine by interaction with aldehydes or ketones or from nitroso compounds and derivatives of diazomethane ⟨phenyl-*N*-methyl-nitrone $C_6H_5\text{-}CH{=}N(O)\text{-}CH_3$ ⟨oxime-*nitrone* tautomerism⟩

**ni·tron·ic acid** \(ˈ)nīˈ¦tränik-\ *n* [*nitronium* + *-ic*] **:** a tautomeric form of a nitroparaffin characterized by the isonitro group $={NO(OH)}$

**ni·tro·ni·um** \nīˈtrōnēəm\ *n* -s [NL, fr. *nitr-* + *-onium*] **:** NITRYL; *esp* **:** the nitryl cation $NO_2^+$ ⟨~ perchlorate $NO_2\text{-}ClO_4$⟩

**ni·tro·paraffin** \¦⸗⸗ *at* NITRO- +\ *n* [ISV *nitr-* + *paraffin*] **:** a nitro derivative (as nitromethane, nitropropane) of any member of the methane series, the mononitro derivatives of the lower members of the series being dense liquids of pleasant odor that form crystalline salts with alkalies

**ni·tro·phenol** \"+\ *n* [ISV *nitr-* + *phenol*] **1 :** a nitro derivative of phenol: as **a :** a yellow crystalline compound $O_2N\text{-}C_6H_4OH$ used chiefly in organic synthesis — called also *ortho-nitrophenol* **b :** a colorless to yellowish isomeric compound $O_2NC_6H_4OH$ used chiefly as an acid-base indicator, as a fungicide, and in organic synthesis — called also *para-nitrophenol* **2** *usu* **nitro phenol :** a nitro derivative of any of the class of phenols

**ni·troph·i·lous** \(ˈ)nīˈ¦träfələs\ *adj* [ISV *nitr-* + *-philous*] **:** preferring or thriving in a soil rich in nitrogen

**ni·tro·phyte** \ˈnī·trəˌfīt\ *n* -s [ISV *nitr-* + *-phyte*] **:** a plant requiring a soil rich in nitrogen — **ni·tro·phyt·ic** \¦⸗⸗¦fid·ik\ *adj*

**nitro powder** *n* **:** an explosive powder made from nitrated organic materials (as guncotton, smokeless powder)

**ni·tro·propane** \¦⸗⸗ *at* NITRO- +\ *n* **:** either of two liquid nitroparaffins $C_3H_7NO_2$ made usu. by hot vapor-phase nitration of propane and used chiefly as industrial solvents and in chemical synthesis: **a :** the primary derivative $CH_3CH_2CH_2NO_2$ — called also *1-nitropropane* **b :** the secondary derivative $CH_3CH(NO_2)CH_3$ — called also *2-nitropropane*

**ni·tro·prussiate** \"+\ *n* [ISV *nitr-* + NL *prussia* Prussian blue + ISV *-ate*] **:** NITROPRUSSIDE

**ni·tro·prusside** \"+\ *n* -s [ISV *nitr-* + NL *prussia* Prussian blue + ISV *-ide*] **:** a salt containing the anion $[Fe(CN)_5NO]^{--}$ composed of five cyanogen groups and one nitrosyl group coordinated with iron; penta-cyano-nitrosyl-ferrate — see SODIUM NITROPRUSSIDE

**nitros-** *or* **nitroso-** *comb form* [NL *nitrosus* nitrous] **:** containing the univalent group —NO composed of one nitrogen and one oxygen atom — esp. in names of organic compounds ⟨*nitroso*benzene $C_6H_5NO$⟩ ⟨*nitros*amines⟩; compare ISONITROSO-, NITROSYL 1, NITR- 2b

**ni·tros·amine** \ˌnī·trōsəˈmēn, -ōˈsamən\ *n* -s [*nitros-* + *amine*] **:** any of a class of neutral compounds formed from secondary amines by action of nitrous acid and characterized by the grouping $>NNO$ consisting of a nitroso group attached to nitrogen; an *N*-nitroso-amine

[1]**ni·tro·sate** \ˈnī·trəˌsāt, -ˌsət\ *n* -s [G *nitrosat*, contr. of *nitrosonitrat*, fr. *nitros-* + *nitrat* nitrate] **:** any of a class of compounds obtained by the action of nitrogen dioxide on unsaturated hydrocarbons (as terpenes)

[2]**nitrosate** \-ˌsāt\ *vt* -ED/-ING/-S [*nitros-* + *-ate* (vb. suffix)] **:** to introduce the nitroso group into (a compound) **:** convert into a nitroso compound

**ni·tro·sa·tion** \ˌ⸗⸗ˈsāshən\ *n* -s [ISV *nitros-* + *-ation*] **:** the process of converting into a nitroso compound

**ni·tros·i·fy** \nīˈtrōsəˌfī\ *vt* -ED/-ING/-ES [NL *nitros*us nitrous + E *-ify*] **:** to convert by oxidation into nitrous acid or nitrites — compare NITRIFY

**ni·tro·site** \ˈnī·trəˌsīt\ *n* -s [G *nitrosit*, contr. of *nitrosonitrit*, fr. *nitros-* + *nitrit* nitrite] **:** any of a class of compounds obtained by the action of nitrous acid or nitrogen trioxide on unsaturated hydrocarbons (as terpenes)

**ni·tro·so** \nīˈtrō(ˌ)sō\ *adj* [*nitros-*] **:** containing or being the univalent group —NO — used esp. of organic compounds; compare NITRO, NITROS-, NITROSYL 1

**ni·tro·so·bacteria** \⸗¦⸗⸗+\ *n pl* [NL, fr. *nitros*us nitrous + *-o-* + *bacteria*] **:** the nitrobacteria that oxidize ammonia to nitrites **:** NITROUS BACTERIA

**ni·tro·so·chloride** \"+\ *n* [*nitros-* + *chloride*] **:** any of a class of crystalline compounds obtained by the action of nitrosyl chloride or of alkyl nitrites and hydrochloric acid on unsaturated hydrocarbons (as terpenes) and characterized by the grouping $>CCl{-}C(NO)<$ or $>CCl{-}C({=}NOH)<$

**ni·tro·so·coc·cus** \⸗ˌ⸗⸗ˈkäkəs\ *n, cap* [NL, fr. *nitros*us nitrous + *-o-* + *-coccus*] **:** a genus of large nonmotile spherical bacteria (family Nitrobacteriaceae) comprising a single species (*N. nitrosus*) that oxidizes ammonia compounds to nitrites in the soil or on suitable media

**ni·tro·som·o·nas** \ˌnī·(ˌ)trōˈsämənəs, -ˌnas\ *n, cap* [NL, fr. *nitros*us + *-o-* + *-monas*] **:** a genus of ellipsoidal autotrophic soil bacteria (family Nitrobacteriaceae) that obtain energy for growth by oxidizing ammonia to nitrites and grow poorly on organic matter

**ni·tro·so·phenol** \nī·¦trō(ˌ)sō+\ *n* [ISV *nitros-* + *phenol*] **:** a nitroso derivative of phenol; *esp* **:** the unstable pale yellow to light brown crystalline para derivative $ONC_6H_4OH$ that is tautomeric with quinone oxime, is made from phenol by reaction with nitrous acid, and is used as a dye intermediate

**ni·tro·so·sulfuric acid** \"+-\ *n* [*nitros-* + *sulfuric*] **:** NITROSYLSULFURIC ACID

**ni·tro·starch** \ˈnī·trə+,-\ *n* [ISV *nitr-* + *starch*] **:** a high explosive that is similar to cellulose nitrate, that is obtained as a white powder by nitrating starch, and that is used chiefly in blasting and demolition explosives — called also *starch nitrate*

**ni·tro·syl** \-ˌsil, -ēl\ *n* -s [ISV *nitros-* + *-yl*] **1 :** the nitroso group, radical, or cation — used esp. in names of inorganic compounds ⟨~ chloride⟩ and coordination complexes; compare NITROPRUSSIDE **2 :** a compound of the nitrosyl radical with a metal analogous to a carbonyl ⟨cobalt tricarbonyl ~ $Co(CO)_3NO$⟩

**nitrosyl chloride** *n* **:** an orange-red corrosive gaseous compound NOCl that has an odor like chlorine, that is present in aqua regia but is made usu. by reaction of nitric oxide with chlorine or of nitric acid with common salt, and that is used chiefly in bleaching flour and in chemical synthesis

**nitrosylsulfuric acid** \ˌ⸗⸗ˌ⸗+-\ *n* [ISV *nitrosyl* + *sulfuric*] **:** a crystalline acid $NOHSO_4$ that is formed by the reaction of nitrogen oxides or fuming nitric acid with sulfuric acid or sulfur dioxide (as in the manufacture of sulfuric acid by the chamber process) and that is used chiefly in the form of a straw-colored corrosive oily liquid containing over half sulfuric acid in making dyes and dye intermediates (as by diazotization); nitrosyl hydrogen sulfate

**ni·tro·toluene** \¦⸗⸗ *at* NITRO-+\ *n* [ISV *nitr-* + *toluene*] **:** a nitro derivative of toluene or a mixture of such derivatives: as **a :** the yellow liquid ortho mono derivative $CH_3C_6H_4NO_2$ made by nitration of toluene and used chiefly as an intermediate for azo dyes **b :** the colorless crystalline solid para isomer obtained along with the ortho derivative and used similarly

**ni·trous** \ˈnī·trəs\ *adj* [NL *nitrosus*, fr. L, full of natron, fr. *nitrum* natron + *-osus* -ous — more at NITER] **1 :** of, relating to, containing, or impregnated with niter **:** of the nature of or like niter ⟨~ powder⟩ ⟨Priestley's name for nitric oxide was ~ air⟩ **2 :** of, relating to, or containing nitrogen — used esp. of compounds in which this element has a lower valence than in corresponding nitric compounds ⟨~ oxide⟩ ⟨~ acid⟩

**nitrous acid** *n* **:** an unstable acid $HNO_2$ known only in pale blue solutions and esp. in the form of its salts and used chiefly in diazotization processes

**nitrous anhydride** *n* **:** NITROGEN TRIOXIDE

**nitrous bacterium** *n* **:** a bacterium that oxidizes ammonia to nitrites **:** one of the nitrosobacteria

**nitrous ether** *n* **:** ETHYL NITRITE

**nitrous oxide** *n* **:** a colorless gas $N_2O$ that is obtained usu. by heating ammonium nitrate, that when inhaled produces incoordination of movement and loss of sensibility to pain preceded by exhilaration and sometimes laughter, and that is used chiefly as an anesthetic (as in dentistry) and in preparing whipped cream and other food aerosols; di-nitrogen monoxide — called also *laughing gas, nitrogen(I) oxide*

**nitrous vitriol** *n* **:** strong sulfuric acid in which nitrogen oxides have been absorbed in the Gay-Lussac tower in the chamber process of making sulfuric acid — see GLOVER TOWER

**ni·trox·yl** \nīˈträksəl\ *n* [ISV *nitr-* + *oxy-* + *-yl*] **:** NITRYL

**ni·tryl** \ˈnī·tril, -rēl\ *n* -s [ISV *nitr-* + *-yl*] **:** the nitro group, radical, or cation — esp. in names of inorganic compounds ⟨~ chloride $NO_2Cl$⟩

**nits** *pl of* NIT

**nit·ta·ny turkey** \ˈnit(ᵊ)nē, -ni-\ *n, usu cap N* [fr. *Nittany* valley, Pennsylvania] **:** a domesticated strain of the native wild turkey developed in Pennsylvania and being smaller and darker than the domestic Bronze turkey which it considerably resembles

**nit·ta tree** \ˈnid·ə-\ *n* [perh. fr. Mandingo *nete* leguminous mimosa] **:** any of several Old World tropical trees of the genus *Parkia* (as *P. biglobosa* and *P. filicoidea*)

**nit·ter** \ˈnid·ə(r)\ *n* -s [[1]*nit* + *-er*] **:** an insect (as a botfly) that deposits nits on horses

**nit·ty** \ˈnid·ē, -i\ *adj* -ER/-EST [[1]*nit* + *-y*] **:** full of or infested with nits

**nitweed** \ˈ⸗ˌ⸗\ *n* [[1]*nit* + *weed;* fr. its minute leaves] **:** ORANGE GRASS

**nit·wit** \ˈnit·ˌ⸗\ *n* [prob. fr. G dial. *nit* not (fr. OHG *niwiht*, *neowiht* nothing) + E *wit* — more at NAUGHT] **:** an empty-headed or stupid person ⟨convention that the characters of farce should be ~s devoid of feeling —Eric Keown⟩

**nit·witted** \(ˈ)⸗¦⸗⸗\ *adj* **:** EMPTY-HEADED, STUPID, SILLY

**nitzsch·ia** \ˈnichēə\ *n, cap* [NL, fr. Christian L. *Nitzsch* †1837 Ger. naturalist + NL *-ia*] **:** a genus (the type of the family Nitzschiaceae) of mostly solitary and free-floating diatoms that are elongate with rhomboidal cross section

**nitzsch·i·a·ce·ae** \ˌ⸗⸗ēˈāsēˌē\ *n pl, cap* [NL, fr. *Nitzschia*, type genus + *-aceae*] **:** a family of diatoms (order Pennales) having the features of the genus *Nitzschia*

[1]**niu·e·an** \(ˈ)n(y)üˈ(w)āən\ *adj, usu cap* [*Niue* Island, south central Pacific ocean + E *-an*] **1 a :** of, relating to, or characteristic of the island of Niue **b :** of, relating to, or characteristic of the people of Niue **2 :** of, relating to, or characteristic of the Polynesian language of the Niuean people

[2]**niuean** \"\ *n* -s *usu cap* **1 :** a Polynesian of Niue Island **2 :** the Polynesian language of the Niuean people

**ni·val** \ˈnīvəl\ *adj* [L *nivalis*, fr. *niv-*, *nix* snow + *-alis* -al — more at SNOW] **:** characterized by, abounding with, or living in or under snow **:** of or relating to a region of perennial snow ⟨~ flora⟩ ⟨~ climate⟩

**ni·va·tion** \nīˈvāshən\ *n* -s [L *niv-*, *nix* snow + E *-ation*] **:** erosion of rock or soil caused by the alternate thawing and freezing of meltwater beneath and at the margins of snowbanks

**ni·veau** \(ˈ)nē¦vō\ *n, pl* **ni·veaux** \"\ [F, fr. MF *niveau, nivel*, alter. of *livel* — more at LEVEL] **:** a level or plateau (as of existence or achievement) esp. in a progression ⟨cultural ~ and religious level —Joachim Wach⟩ ⟨the life history and achievement ~ of the patient-to-be —*Scientific Monthly*⟩

**niv·en·ite** \ˈnivəˌnīt\ *n* -s [William *Niven* †1937 Am. mineralogist + E *-ite*] **:** a velvet-black variety of uraninite containing cerium and yttrium

**niv·e·ous** \ˈnivēəs\ *adj* [L *niveus*, fr. *niv-*, *nix* snow] **:** of or relating to snow **:** resembling snow (as in whiteness) **:** SNOWY ⟨~ rock⟩ ⟨a ~ landscape⟩

**niv·er** \ˈnivə(r)\ *dial var of* NEVER

**niwar** *usu cap, var of* NEWAR

[1]**nix** \ˈniks\ *n* -ES [G, fr. OHG *nihhus* — more at NICKER] **:** a supernatural creature orig. in Germanic folklore and conceived of in many forms but usu. as having the form of a woman or as half human and half fish, dwelling in fresh water usu. in a beautiful palace, and usu. unfriendly to man ⟨haunting, penetrating, pining as voice of ~ or siren —Walter de la Mare⟩ — called also *nixie*

[2]**nix** \"\ *n* -ES [G *nichts* nothing, fr. MHG *nihtes*, gen. of *niht*

nothing, fr. OHG *niwiht, neowiht* — more at NAUGHT] **1** *slang* **:** NOTHING **:** NO ONE ⟨what a man means to say signifies ~ in politics —*Emporia (Kans.) Gazette*⟩ **2 :** 2NIXIE

**3nix** \"\ *adv, slang* **:** NO — used to express disagreement or the withholding of permission ⟨if I were to say ~ on the books he'd be miserable —*Everybody's Mag.*⟩

**4nix** \"\ *vt* -ED/-ING/-ES *slang* **:** VETO, FORBID, PROHIBIT, BAN, REJECT, CANCEL ⟨~*ed* a request for a $2500 business loan —Carl Sifakis⟩ ⟨tried to ~ the idea of a lie-detector test —Barbara Graham⟩

**1nix·ie** \ˈniksē, -si\ *n* -S [G, female nix, fr. OHG *nicchessa*, fem. of *nihhus* nix] **:** 1NIX

**2nixie** *also* **nixy** \"\ *n, pl* **nixies** [2*nix* + *-ie, -y*] **:** a piece of mail that is undeliverable because illegibly or incorrectly addressed

**3nixie** *also* **nixy** \"\ *vt* **nixied; nixied; nixying; nixies :** to stamp (a piece of mail) as a nixie and dispatch to sender or to dead-letter office

**nix·ta·mal** \ˌnēshtəˈmäl\ *n, pl* **nixtamal** \"\ *or* **nixtama·les** \-(ˌ)läs\ [MexSp, fr. Nahuatl, fr. *nextli* ashes + *tamalli* tamale] **:** limed kernels of corn that is ready to be ground into masa

**ni·yo·ga** \nēˈyōgə\ *n* -S [Skt, order, duty, fr. *niyunakti* he orders, enjoins, fr. *ni-* down, into + *yunakti* he yokes, joins — more at NETHER, YOKE] *Hindu law* **:** an appointed task; *specif* **:** the appointment of a brother or any near kinsman to raise up issue to a deceased childless husband by marrying his widow

**ni·zam** \nəˈzäm, (ˈ)nī¦-, -zam\ *n* [Hindi *nizām* order, arrangement, governor, fr. Ar *nizām*] **1** *pl* **nizams :** one of the sovereigns of Hyderabad, India reigning from 1713 to 1950 **2** *pl* **nizam** [Turk, fr. Ar *nizam*] **:** a Turkish soldier

**ni·zam·ate** \-ˌmāt\ *n* -S [*nizam* + *-ate*] **:** the territory or office of the nizam

**nizh·ni ta·gil** \ˈnizhnētəˈgil\ *adj, usu cap N&T* [fr. *Nizhni Tagil*, U.S.S.R.] **:** of or from the city of Nizhni Tagil, U.S.S.R. **:** of the kind or style prevalent in Nizhni Tagil

**nizy** \ˈnizē, -zi\ *n* -ES [perh. fr. 1*nice* + *-y*] *dial chiefly Brit* **:** FOOL, LUNKHEAD

**nja·ve** \ˈnyävə\ *or* **dja·ve** \ˈjä-\ *n* -S [native name in Africa] **:** a very large tropical African tree (*Mimusops njave*) that has a termite-resistant wood somewhat resembling mahogany, a slightly acid edible fruit, and a seed rich in a fat that resembles shea butter

**njo·ro·an** \nyəˈrōən\ *adj, usu cap* [fr. *Njoro*, Bantu stock in Kenya + E *-an*] **:** of or relating to a Neolithic culture of Kenya characterized by polished stone axes and extended burial in cemeteries

**nk** *abbr* neck

**NK** *abbr* not known

**nko·le** \ən̩ˈkōlə\ *n, pl* **nkole** *or* **nkoles** *usu cap* **:** NYANKOLE

**NL** *abbr* **1** *often not cap* new line **2** night letter **3** *often not cap* [L *non licet*] it is not permitted **4** *often not cap* [L *non liquet*] it is not clear **5** *often not cap* [L *non longe*] not far **6** north latitude

**NLO** *abbr* naval liaison officer

**NLT** *abbr* **1** net long ton **2** night letter **3** *often not cap* not later than **4** *often not cap* not less than

**NM** *abbr, often not cap* **1** nautical mile **2** night message **3** no mark; not marked **4** [L *nocte et mane*] night and morning

**NME** *abbr* national military establishment

**NMT** *abbr, often not cap* not more than

**NN** *abbr, often not cap* **1** names **2** nomen novum **3** nomen nudum **4** notes **5** not to be noted **6** nouns

**NN** *symbol* place for the insertion of two or more usu. given names of a person (as in a ceremonial statement)

**NNE** *abbr* north-northeast

**NNW** *abbr* north-northwest

**1no** \ˈnō; *when expressing disgust, impatience, or strong disagreement* ˈnö, ˈnä, ˈnȧ, (*esp. when reduplicated*) ˈnə, ˈʔm̩ʔm̩, ˈʔəʔə, *or* ˈʔãⁿ, ˈʔãⁿ\ *adv* [ME *no, na*, fr. OE *nō, nā*, fr. *ne* not, no + *ā, ō* ever, always; akin to OS & OHG *ni, ne* not, ON *ne, nē*, Goth *ni*, OIr *ni, nī*, L *ne-* not (negative prefix), *nē* not, Gk *nē-*, Skt *na, nā*, OSlav *ne* — more at AYE (ever)] **1 a** *chiefly Scot* **:** NOT ⟨have walked forty miles and yet am ~ wearied —Hugh Mitchell⟩ ⟨and he's ~ rightly young either —John Buchan⟩ **b** — used as a function word to express the negative of an alternative choice or possibility ⟨whether he was satisfied or ~ —H.J.Laski⟩ ⟨shall we write a letter or ~ —J.H.Robinson †1936⟩ **2 :** in no respect or degree **:** not at all — used in comparisons ⟨regard criticism . . . as ~ better than blasphemy —Elmer Davis⟩ ⟨is ~ more serious than the rest of them⟩ ⟨your experience was ~ different from mine⟩ **3 :** not so — used to express negation, dissent, denial, or refusal in answer to a question or request ⟨are you going? *No*, I am not going⟩ ⟨~, you can't have any more candy⟩ or to introduce a statement correcting or contradicting a preceding statement ⟨~, that's not the way the accident happened⟩ **4** — used with a following adjective to imply a meaning expressed by the opposite positive statement ⟨express his opinions in ~ uncertain terms —B.W.Bond⟩ ⟨a teacher of ~ mean ability —L.W.Fox⟩ ⟨an item of ~ small importance —B.H. Hibbard⟩ **5** — used as a function word to emphasize a following negative or to introduce a more emphatic, explicit, or comprehensive statement ⟨none is righteous, ~, not one —Rom 3:10 (RSV)⟩ ⟨had the ambition, ~, the conviction, that he would . . . be a great singer —Hans Herbert⟩ **6** — used as an interjection to express surprise, doubt, or incredulity ⟨~, that's impossible⟩ ⟨~, you couldn't have been the one responsible⟩

**2no** \ˈnō\ *adj* [ME *no, non, na, nan*, fr. OE *nān* — more at NONE] **1 a :** not any ⟨let there be ~ strife between you and me —Gen 13:8 (RSV)⟩ ⟨and ~ birds sing —John Keats⟩ ⟨with ~ dancing in the streets or ritual bonfires —Mollie Panter-Downes⟩ ⟨wanted ~ part of army routine —Georg Meyers⟩ ⟨show little or ~ concern for the . . . rest of the population —Vera M. Dean⟩ ⟨~ two of the rugged, scarecrow figures were dressed alike —F.V.W.Mason⟩ **b :** hardly any **:** very little ⟨in ~ time other families followed —John Mason Brown⟩ ⟨it's ~ distance from the house to the store⟩ **2 :** not a **:** quite other than a **:** far from being a — usu. used to modify a predicate noun ⟨whether this is true . . . I don't know; I'm ~ anatomist —Deems Taylor⟩ ⟨that goodness is ~ name and happiness ~ dream —Lord Byron⟩ ⟨this was ~ Bohemia, but a workshop in the woods —*Amer. Guide Series: N.H.*⟩ ⟨it was ~ job to pull the elk cows out of the water —F.B.Gipson⟩ **3 :** not any possible — used to modify a gerund that follows a finite form of the verb *to be* ⟨there's ~ speaking a word but you fly into a passion —Fanny Burney⟩ ⟨there's ~ accounting for tastes⟩ **4 :** that is absent, lacking, or nonexistent ⟨frankly confide to yourself these opinions or rather ~ opinions of mine —Thomas Jefferson⟩ — usu. used in combination ⟨thoroughly frightened with certain *no*-persons called ghosts —Henry Fielding⟩ ⟨a dog such as I have described, whatever be this breed or his *no*-breed —William Carnegie⟩ — **no dice 1** *of a cast of dice* **:** not valid **:** VOID **2** *slang* — used chiefly in the predicate to emphasize a negative attitude, result, or expectation ⟨tried for a scholarship but it was *no dice*⟩ ⟨to such a proposition I can only say *no dice*⟩

**3no** \"\ *n, pl* **noes** *or* **nos 1 :** an act or instance of refusing or denying by the use of the word *no* **:** DENIAL ⟨my wooing mind shall be expressed in russet yeas and honest kersey ~*es* —Shak.⟩ ⟨the Everlasting *No* —Thomas Carlyle⟩ **2 a :** a negative vote or decision ⟨110 ayes were cast and only 16 ~*es*⟩ **b** *noes or nos pl* **:** persons voting in the negative ⟨the chairman asked the ~*es* to raise their right hands⟩

**4no** *or* **noh** \"\ *n, pl* **no** *or* **noh** *often cap* [Jap *nō*, lit., talent, ability] **:** classic Japanese dance-drama that is heroic in subject and in the use of measured chants and movements — called also *nogaku*

**no** *abbr* **1** north **2** nose **3** [L *numero*, abl. of *numerus*] number

**NO** *abbr* **1** name of **2** natural order **3** naval officer **4** non-official **5** no orders **6** not out

**No** *symbol* nobelium

**noa** \ˈnōə\ *adj* [Hawaiian, Tahitian, & Maori] **:** charged with little or no supernatural power **:** free or freed from taboo **:** COMMON, PROFANE

**1no-account** \ˈ≈,≈\ *or* **no-count** \ˈ≈,≈\ *adj* [fr. the phrase *of no account*] *chiefly dial* **:** worthless and lazy **:** of no account **:** TRIFLING ⟨those *no-account* relatives of his⟩

**2no-account** \"\ *or* **no-count** \"\ *n* -S **:** a worthless or shiftless person

**no·a·chi·an** \(ˈ)nō¦ākēən\ *also* **no·a·chic** \-kik\ *adj, usu cap* [Heb *Noah* Noah, patriarch who built an ark to save his family and representative living creatures from the Flood (Gen 5:28–10:32) + E *-an* or *-ic*] **1 :** of or relating to the patriarch Noah or his time **2 :** ANCIENT, ANTIQUATED

**no·a·chite** \ˈnōəˌkīt\ *n* -S [perh. fr. F, fr. Heb *Noah* Noah + F *-ite*] **1 :** a Freemason who has taken the 21st degree of the Scottish rite — called also *Prussian Knight* **2 :** FREEMASON

**no·ah's ark** \ˈnōəz-\ *n, usu cap N* [so called fr. the supposed similarity to Noah's ark (Gen 6:14–20)] **1** *also* **noah's ark shell :** ARK SHELL; *esp* **:** a common ark shell (*Arca noae*) **2 :** a series of straight parallel narrow bands of cloud that by perspective appear to spring from common points on opposite sides of the horizon and to arch and spread apart as they approach the zenith **3 :** a set of toys representing Noah's ark and the animals in it **4 a :** LADY'S SLIPPER 1 **b :** a monkshood (*Aconitum napellus*)

**noap** *dial Brit var of* 1NOPE

**1nob** \ˈnäb\ *n* -S [prob. alter. of 1*knob*] **1** *slang* **:** HEAD 1 **2** *slang* **:** a blow on the head **3 :** a jack of the same suit as the starter scoring in cribbage one point for the holder

**2nob** \"\ *vb* **nobbed; nobbed; nobbing; nobs** *vt* **:** to strike (as a person) in the head ~ *vi* **:** to strike blows at or on the head ⟨*nobbed* away without connecting once⟩

**3nob** \"\ *n* -S [perh. fr. 1*nob*] *chiefly Brit* **:** one in a superior position in life or of superior attainments (as in a field of specialization) **:** SWELL, TOFF

**4nob** \"\ *var of* KNOB

**NOB** *abbr* naval operating base

**no ball** *n* [fr. the umpire's call "no ball"] **:** a bowled ball in a cricket game that because ruled unfair by the umpire cannot take a wicket, does not count as a ball in the over, and counts one run if not otherwise scored from — compare EXTRA

**no-ball** \ˈ≈ˌ≈\ *vt* [*no ball*] **:** to declare a delivery by (a cricket bowler) to be a no ball

**nob·bily** \ˈnäbəlē\ *adv* **:** in a nobby manner

**1nob·ble** \ˈnäbəl\ *vt* **nobbled; nobbled; nobbling** \-b(ə)liŋ\ **nobbles** [perh. alter. of 2*nab* + *-le*] **1** *Brit* **:** to incapacitate (a racehorse) esp. by drugging **2** *slang Brit* **a :** to win over to one's side (as by bribery or flattery) **b :** STEAL, TAKE **c :** SWINDLE, CHEAT

**2nobble** \"\ *vt* -ED/-ING/-S [2*nob* + *-le*] *dial chiefly Eng* **:** to strike on the head

**1nob·bler** \-b(ə)lə(r)\ *n* -S [1*nobble* + *-er*] **1** *Brit* **:** one that nobbles horses **2** *Brit* **:** SWINDLER

**2nobbler** \"\ *n* -S [origin unknown] *Austral* **:** a drink of liquor or beer

**3nobbler** \"\ *n* -S [2*nobble* + *-er*] **1** *slang Brit* **:** a blow on the head **:** KNOCKOUT **2** *slang Brit* **:** 2NOBBY 1

**nobbly** *var of* KNOBBLY

**nob·but** \ˈnäbət\ *adv* [ME *no but*, fr. *no* (adv.) + *but*] **1** *dial Brit* **:** ONLY, JUST ⟨tha's ~ had one marriage —Eric Knight⟩ **2** *dial Brit* **:** nothing but ⟨~ warts o' trees —Marjorie Whitaker⟩

**1nob·by** *also* **knob·by** \ˈnäbē, -bi\ *adj* -ER/-EST [3*nob* + *-y*] **:** of the first quality or style **:** of the finest design or finish **:** EXCELLENT, SMART, STYLISH

**2nobby** \"\ *n* -ES [perh. fr. 2*nob* + *-y*] **1 :** a stick sometimes used by anglers for killing fish **2 :** a small fishing boat used off the Isle of Man

**no-being** \ˈ≈,≈≈\ *n* [2*no* + *being*] **:** the negation of being **:** NONEXISTENCE

**no·bel·ist** \nōˈbeləst\ *n* -S *often cap* [*Nobel* (*Prize*), a prize usu. awarded annually for the encouragement of men and women who work for the interests of humanity (after Alfred B. *Nobel* †1896 Swed. manufacturer, inventor, and philanthropist, who left his entire estate for the establishment of such prizes) + E *-ist*] **:** a winner of a Nobel Prize

**no·bel·i·um** \nōˈbelēəm\ *n* -S [NL, fr. Alfred B. *Nobel* + NL *-ium*] **:** a radioactive element produced artificially (as by bombardment of curium with ions of carbon) — symbol *No*; see ELEMENT table

**nob·i·le of·fi·ci·um** \ˈnäbəlēəˈfishēəm\ *n* [L, noble office] *Scots law* **:** the equitable discretion of the Court of Sessions to afford relief in cases where none is possible at law

**no·bil·i·ary** \nōˈbilēˌerē, -lyərē\ *adj* [*nobility* + *-ary*] **:** of or relating to the nobility

**no·bi·li's ring** \ˈnōbəlēz-, ˈnōb-\ *n, usu cap N* [after Leopoldo *Nobili* †1835 It. physicist] **:** one of the colored rings formed upon a metal plate by electrolytic deposition (as of copper or lead peroxide) — usu. used in pl.

**no·bi·li·tate** \nōˈbiləˌtāt\ *vt* -ED/-ING/-S [L *nobilitatus*, past part. of *nobilitare*, fr. *nobilis* famous, noble] **:** ENNOBLE — **no·bi·li·ta·tion** \≈,≈≈ˈtāshən\ *n* -S *archaic*

**no·bil·i·ty** \nōˈbilədē, -ətē, -i\ *n* -ES [ME *nobilite*, fr. MF *nobilité*, fr. L *nobilitat-, nobilitas*, fr. *nobilis* famous, noble + *-itat-, -itas* -ity] **1 :** the quality or state of being noble: as **a :** the condition of possessing characteristics or properties of a very high kind or order **:** superiority in excellence, value, or importance ⟨the ~ of gold⟩ ⟨the ~ of his prose⟩ **b :** superiority of mind or of character **:** commanding moral worth or excellence **:** EMINENCE ⟨a man of true ~⟩ **c :** the quality or state of being of noble or high birth or of exalted rank or station either inherited or acquired **:** preeminence or distinction by rank or title ⟨in many Continental countries . . . ~, once conferred, extends to every member of the family in all generations —Valentina Heywood⟩ **2 a :** the body of persons forming the noble class in a country or state **:** ARISTOCRACY; *specif* **:** the British peerage — usu. used with *the* ⟨a street where many of the ~ reside —Samuel Johnson⟩ **b :** a noble class or a body of nobles — used with *a* ⟨the Venetians were a ~ of merchants —C.C.Clarke⟩ **3 :** a manifestation of noble spirit

**nobill** \ˈ≈,≈\ *vt* [fr. the phrase *no bill* (of indictment)] **:** to release from charges by failing to find a true bill ⟨the grand jury ~*ed* her after the murder⟩

**no-bill** \ˈ≈,≈\ *n* -S [prob. fr. 2*no* + *waybill*] *slang* **:** a nonunion railroad employee

**1noble** \ˈnōbəl\ *adj* **nobler** \-b(ə)lə(r)\ **noblest** \-b(ə)ləst\ [ME, fr. OF, fr. L *nobilis* knowable, known, well known, famous, noble, fr. OL *gnobilis*; akin to L *noscere* (OL *gnoscere*) to come to know — more at KNOW] **1 a** *of a person* **:** possessing outstanding qualities (as of eminence, dignity) **:** ILLUSTRIOUS **b** *of a deed* **:** FAMOUS, NOTABLE **2 :** having the power of transmitting by inheritance some recognized preeminence founded on hereditary succession **:** of high birth or exalted rank **:** of, belonging to, or constituting the nobility **:** HIGHBORN, ARISTOCRATIC ⟨my sire is of a ~ line —S.T.Coleridge⟩ **3 a :** possessing very high or excellent qualities or properties **:** belonging to a kind that is considered exceptionally fine ⟨~ wines⟩ **b :** very good or excellent **:** superior of its kind ⟨inherited a ~ estate⟩ **4 :** outstanding or impressive esp. by reason of grandeur, largeness, magnificence ⟨a ~ cathedral⟩ ⟨these ~ edifices⟩ **5 :** possessing, characterized by, arising from, or indicating superiority or commanding excellence of mind or character, or high ideals or morals **:** LOFTY ⟨a man of ~ nature⟩ **6 :** resisting chemical action **:** chemically inert or inactive esp. toward oxygen **:** relatively stable ⟨a ~ metal⟩ ⟨a ~ gas⟩ ⟨a ~ patina⟩ **syn** see GRAND, MORAL

**2noble** \"\ *n* -S [ME, partly fr. *noble*, adj., and partly fr. MF *noble*, fr. *noble*, adj.] **1 :** a person of noble rank or birth **:** a member of the nobility **:** NOBLEMAN, PEER **2 a** (1) **:** an old English gold coin first issued by Edward III as equivalent to 6*s* 8*d* and orig. weighing a little over 138 grains but reduced to 128, then to 120 grains, and then debased by Henry IV to 108 grains — see RYAL (2) **:** a corresponding unit of value ⟨half-*noble* and quarter-*noble* coins were issued⟩ **b** (1) **:** a Scottish gold coin similar to the English noble (as one issued by David II another by James VI) (2) **:** a silver coin, the half-mark piece of James VI, worth 6*s* 8*d* **3** *slang* **:** a captain of strikebreakers or an overseer in charge of strikebreaking operations

**noble art** *or* **noble science** *n* [*noble art* short for *noble art of boxing; noble science* short for *noble science of defense*] **:** BOXING

**noble cane** *n* **:** any of various sugarcanes that are considered to represent the highest development of the species and are characterized by thick barrel-shaped internodes, large soft-rinded juicy stalks, and high sugar content

**noble fir** *n* **:** a valuable evergreen timber tree (*Abies procera*) attaining a height of 250 feet in the Cascade mountains being distinguished by cones with taper pointed bracts that project beyond and are reflexed over the scales, and yielding a useful timber resembling that of spruce — called also *Oregon larch*

**noble gas** *n* **:** INERT GAS 2

**noble hawk** *n* **:** FALCON 1b — used in the technical language of falconry

**noble liverwort** *n* **:** a hepatica (*Hepatica triloba*)

**no·ble·man** \ˈnōbəlmən\ *n, pl* **noblemen** [1*noble* + *man*] **1 :** a man of noble rank **:** one belonging to the nobility **:** NOBLE, PEER **2 noblemen** *pl* **:** the pieces as distinguished from the pawns in chess

**no·ble·man·ly** \-nlē\ *adj* **:** of, relating to, or befitting a nobleman

**noble metal** *n* [ME *noble metall*] **:** a metal (as gold, silver, or platinum) or alloy relatively superior in resistance to corrosion or oxidation — opposed to *base metal*; compare PRECIOUS METAL

**noble-minded** \ˈ≈≈¦≈≈\ *adj* **:** having or characteristic of an honorable, upright, and generous mind ⟨a *noble-minded* reply⟩ — **no·ble-mind·ed·ly** *adv* — **no·ble-mind·ed·ness** *n* -ES

**no·ble·ness** *n* -ES [ME *nobilnes*, fr. *nobil, noble* noble + *-nes* -ness] **1 :** the quality or state of being noble: as **a :** elevation of mind, character, or station **b** *obs* **:** SPLENDOR, GRANDEUR **2** *obs* **a :** 2NOBLE 1 **b :** NOBILITY 2a

**noble pine** *n* **:** PIPSISSEWA

**nobler** *comparative of* NOBLE

**noble rot** *n* [trans. of F *pourriture noble*] **1 :** an alteration of various wine grapes that is caused by the action of a fungus on the grapes when allowed to hang on the vine until overripe and that is responsible for the characteristic flavor of sauternes and related wines **2** *also* **noble mold :** the imperfect fungus (*Botrytis cinerea*) that causes noble rot

**no·blesse** \nōˈbles\ *n* -S [ME *noblesse, noblesce*, fr. OF *noblesce*, fr. *noble*] **1 :** noble birth or condition **:** NOBILITY 1c **2 :** NOBILITY 2b; *esp* **:** the members of the French nobility

**noblesse oblige** \-ōˈblēzh\ *n* [F, lit., nobility obligates] **:** the obligation of honorable, generous, and responsible behavior that is a concomitant of high rank or birth

**noblest** *superlative of* NOBLE

**noblewoman** \ˈ≈≈,≈≈\ *n, pl* **noblewomen :** a woman of noble rank **:** PEERESS

**no·bly** \ˈnōb(ə)lē, -li\ *adv* [ME *nobly, nobliche*, fr. *noble* (adj.) + *-ly, -liche* -ly] **1 :** with greatness of soul **:** GALLANTLY ⟨a deed ~ done⟩ **2 :** SPLENDIDLY, MAGNIFICENTLY ⟨a ~ planned work⟩ ⟨~ clad attendants⟩ **3 :** of noble extraction ⟨~ born⟩

**1no·body** \ˈnōˌbädē, -(ˌ)bədē, -di\ *pron* [ME *no body*] **:** no person **:** not anybody

**2nobody** \"\ *n* **:** a person of no influence, importance, social standing, or other outstanding quality

**no-bond resonance** *n* [2*no* + *bond*, n.] **:** HYPERCONJUGATION

**nob·ut** \ˈnäbət\ *var of* NOBBUT

**no·cake** \ˈnōˌkāk\ *n* [of Algonquian origin; akin to Narraganset *nokehick* parched corn meal, lit., it is soft, Natick *nookhic*] **:** Indian corn parched and pounded into a powder

**no·car·dia** \nōˈkärdēə\ *n* [NL, fr. Edmond I. E. *Nocard* †1903 Fr. veterinarian and biologist + NL *-ia*] **1** *cap* **:** a genus of aerobic actinomycetes (family Actinomycetaceae) that form limited mycelia which tends to break up into rod-shaped cells, develop neither conidia nor endospores but occas. form spores by fragmentation of the parent cell, and include various pathogens as well as some soil-dwelling saprophytes **2** -S **:** any organism of the genus *Nocardia*

**no·car·di·o·sis** \nōˌkärdēˈōsəs\ *n, pl* **nocardio·ses** \-ˈōˌsēz\ [NL, fr. *Nocardia* + *-osis*] **:** actinomycosis caused by actinomycetes of the genus *Nocardia* and characterized by production of spreading granulomatous lesions — compare MADUROMYCOSIS

**nocence** *also* **nocency** *n, pl* **nocences** *also* **nocencies** [LL *nocentia*, fr. L *nocent-, nocens* (pres. part.) + *-ia -y*] *obs* **:** GUILT

**no·cent** \ˈnōsᵊnt\ *adj* [ME, fr. L *nocent-, nocens* harmful, criminal, fr. pres. part. of *nocēre* to harm, hurt — more at NOXIOUS] **1 :** doing harm or having a tendency to harm **:** HURTFUL, HARMFUL ⟨a ~ dose⟩ **2** *archaic* **:** GUILTY, CRIMINAL — opposed to *innocent*

**no·cer·ite** \ˈnōsəˌrīt, nōˈchā,-\ *n* -S [*Nocera*, Italy, its locality + E *-ite*] **:** a mineral $Ca_3Mg_3F_8O_2$ that is a calcium magnesium oxyfluoride

**nocht** \ˈnäkt\ *chiefly Scot var of* NAUGHT

**noci-** *comb form* [L *nocēre* to hurt, harm + E *-i-*] **:** pain ⟨*noci*perception⟩

**no·ci·cep·tive** \¦nōsē¦septiv\ *adj* [*noci-* (fr. L *nocēre* to hurt) + *receptive*] **1** *of a stimulus* **:** PAINFUL, INJURIOUS **2 :** of, induced by, or responding to a nociceptive stimulus — used esp. of receptors or protective reflexes

**no·ci·cep·tor** \-tə(r)\ *n* -S [*noci-* + *receptor*] **:** a receptor for injurious or painful stimuli **:** a pain sense organ — compare NEUTROCEPTOR

**no·ci·fen·sor** \-ˈfen(t)sə(r)\ *adj* [*noci-* + *-fensor* (prob. fr. *defense* + *-or*)] **:** of, relating to, or constituting a system of cutaneous nerve fibers believed to mediate diffuse pain sensations

**no·ci·perception** \¦nōsē+\ *n* [*noci-* + *perception*] **:** perception of injurious stimuli

**no·ci·perceptive** \"+\ *adj* **:** of or relating to nociperception

**no·cive** \ˈnōsiv\ *adj* [MF or L; MF *nocif*, fr. L *nocivus*, fr. *nocēre* to hurt + *-ivus* -ive — more at NOXIOUS] **:** HARMFUL, INJURIOUS ⟨~ effects of insecticides⟩

**1nock** \ˈnäk\ *n* -S [ME *nocke, nokke*; akin to OE *hnocc* penis, MD *nocke* tip, summit, end of a yardarm, ON *hnuka* to sit cowering, *hnykill* clew of yarn, tumor, Sw *nock, nocke* pin, peg, end of a yardarm, OIr *cnocc* lump, hill, L *nux* nut — more at NUT] **1 a** (1) **:** either of two tips of horn fastened on the ends of a bow and having notches for holding the string (2) **:** one of the notches cut in these or in the bow itself **b** (1) **:** the part of an arrow having a notch for the bowstring whether as formerly a thick bulbous wooden end containing the notch or as now usu. an attached fixture (as of horn or plastic) **:** the butt end of any arrow (2) **:** the notch itself — see ARROW illustration **2** *obs* **:** the cleft between the buttocks **3** [prob. fr. D *nok*, fr. MD *nocke* tip, summit] **:** the upper fore corner of a boom sail or a staysail when cut with a square tack

**2nock** \"\ *vt* -ED/-ING/-S **:** to make a notch in or fit into or by means of a notch: as **a :** to slip (the eye of a bowstring) into a bow nock in bracing a bow **b :** to fit (an arrow) on the string of a bow **c :** to furnish (an arrow or bow) with a nock

**nock·erl** \ˈnäkər(ə)l\ *n, pl* **nock·erln** \-ln\ [G dial. (Austria), dim. of *nock*, a kind of mountain, dumpling; akin to MD *nocke* tip, summit] **:** a rich light dumpling

**nock·et** \ˈnäkət\ *var of* NACKET

**nocking point** *n* [*nocking*, gerund of 2*nock*] **:** the commonly reinforced point on a bowstring where an arrow is nocked

**no-count** *var of* NO-ACCOUNT

**noct-** *or* **nocti-** *or* **nocto-** *comb form* [*noct-* fr. NL, fr. L *noct-, nox*; *nocti-* fr. L, fr. *noct-, nox*; *nocto-* fr. *noct-* + *-o-* — more at NIGHT] **:** night **:** during the night ⟨*noct*ambulation⟩ ⟨*nocti*florous⟩ ⟨*nocto*vision⟩

**noc·tam·bu·lant** \(ˈ)näk¦tambyələnt\ *adj* [*noctambul*ation + *-ant*] **1 :** NOCTAMBULOUS **2 :** walking by night ⟨a ~ rogue⟩

**noc·tam·bu·la·tion** \ˌnäkˌtambyəˈlāshən\ *or* **noc·tam·bu·lism** \ˈ≈ˈ≈≈ˌlizəm\ *n* -S [*noctambulation* fr. *noct-* + *ambulation*; *noctambulism*, prob. fr. F *noctambulisme*, fr. *noctambule* + *-isme* -ism] **1 :** SOMNAMBULISM **2 :** a stroll by night

**noc·tam·bule** \näkˈtamˌbyül\ *n* -S [F, fr. NL *noctambulo*] **:** SOMNAMBULIST

**noc·tam·bu·lic** \(ˈ)näk¦tambyəlik\ *also* **noc·tam·bu·lis·tic** \(ˌ)näkˌtambyəˈlistik\ *adj* [*noctambulic* fr. *noctambule* + *-ic*; *noctambulistic* fr. *noctambulist* + *-ic*] **:** of or relating to noctambulism

**noc·tam·bu·list** \ˈ≈ˈ≈≈ləst\ *n* -S [*noctambul*ation + *-ist*] **:** one who walks at night esp. in his sleep

**noctambulo** *n, pl* **noctambulones** *or* **noctambuloes** *or* **noctambulos** [NL, fr. *noct-* + *-ambulo* (fr. L *ambulare* to walk) — more at AMBLE] *obs* **:** SOMNAMBULIST

**noc·tam·bu·lous** \(')näk¦tambyələs\ *adj* [*noctambul*ation + *-ous*] : of, relating to, or given to walking by night ⟨given way to ~ habits —*Times Lit. Supp.*⟩

**noc·ti·diurnal** \¦näktə+\ *adj* [*noct-* + *diurnal*] : comprising a sequence of day and night

**noc·til·io** \näk'tilē,ō\ *n, cap* [NL, fr. *noct-* + *-ilio* (as in *Vespertilio*)] : a genus (the type of the family Noctilionidae) of tropical American fish-eating mastiff bats

**noc·ti·lu·ca** \,näktə'lükə\ *n* [NL, fr. L, moon, lantern, fr. *nocti-* noct- + *-luca*, fr. *lucēre* to shine — more at LIGHT (n.)] **1** -s *obs* : PHOSPHOR 2 **2** *cap* [NL, fr. L, moon] : a genus of marine plantlike flagellates (order Dinoflagellata) that are unusually large, complex in structure, and bioluminescent and that when present in numbers are responsible for much of the phosphorescence of the sea **3** *pl* **noctilucas** \-kəz\ *or* **noctilu·cae** \-ü,sē\ : any organism of the genus *Noctiluca*

**noc·ti·lu·cence** \¦==¦lüs°n(t)s\ *n* -s [NL *noctiluca* + E *-ence*] : BIOLUMINESCENCE

**noc·ti·lu·cent** \-°nt\ *adj* **1** [fr. *noctilucence*, after such pairs as E *translucence*: *translucent*] : BIOLUMINESCENT **2** [*noct-* + *lucent*] : visible or glowing at night — see NOCTILUCENT CLOUD

**noctilucent cloud** *n* : a luminous cloud seen at night at a height of about 275,000 feet

**noc·ti·lu·cine** \,=='lü,sēn, -,sən\ *n* -s [F, fr. NL *Noctiluca*, genus of flagellates + F *-ine*] : an extract from luminous organisms to which their luminescence has been attributed — compare LUCIFERIN

**noc·ti·lu·cous** \¦==¦lükəs\ *adj* [NL *noctiluca* (phosphor) + E *-ous*] : shining at night : PHOSPHORESCENT

**noc·tiv·a·gant** \(')näk¦tivəgənt\ *adj* [L *noctivag*us night-wandering (fr. *noct-*, *nox* night + *vagus* wandering) + E *-ant* — more at NIGHT, VAGARY] : going about in the night : night-wandering

**noc·tiv·a·ga·tion** \,näk,tivə'gāshən\ *n* -s [*noctivag*ant + *-ation*] : a roving or going about in the night

**noctivagator** *n* -s [*noctivagat*ion + *-or*] *obs* : NIGHT-WALKER

**noc·tiv·a·gous** \(')näk¦tivəgəs\ *adj* [L *noctivagus*] : NOCTIVAGANT

**noc·to·graph** \'näktə,graf, -råf\ *n* [*noct-* + *-graph*] : a writing frame for the blind

**noc·to·vis·ion** \'näktə,vizhən\ *n* [*nocto-* + tele*vision*] : television in which the use of infrared rays makes it possible to transmit the image of a subject not visible to the eye (as because of darkness or fog)

**noc·tua** \'näkchəwə\ *n, cap* [NL, fr. L, night owl, owl; akin to L *nox* night] : a large and widely distributed genus (the type of the family Noctuidae) of moths having larvae that are cutworms

**noc·tu·ary** \'näkchə,werē\ *n* -ES [L *noctu*, adv., by night + E *-ary;* akin to L *nox* night] *archaic* : a journal of nocturnal incidents

1**noc·tu·id** \'näkchəwəd\ *adj* [NL *Noctuidae*] : of or relating to the Noctuidae

2**noctuid** \"\ *n* -s : a moth of the family Noctuidae

**noc·tu·i·dae** \näk'tüə,dē\ *n pl, cap* [NL, fr. *Noctua*, type genus + *-idae*] : a large nearly cosmopolitan family of medium-sized stout-bodied dull-colored night-flying moths with usu. naked larvae that include many destructive agricultural pests (as the cutworms and armyworms) — see NOCTUA, OWLET MOTH; compare BOLLWORM, COTTON LEAFWORM, DAGGER MOTH, UNDERWING

**noc·tule** \'näk,chül\ *n* -s [prob. fr. NL *noctula* (used as specific epithet), fr. LL *noctula* small owl, dim. of L *noctua* owl] : PIPISTRELLE

**noc·tu·ria** \näk'türēə\ *n* -s [NL, fr. *noct-* + *-uria*] : urination at night esp. when excessive — called also *nycturia*

1**noc·turn** \'näk,tərn\ *n* -s [ME *nocturne*, fr. MF, fr. ML *nocturna*, fr. fem. of L *nocturnus* nocturnal] *Roman Catholicism* : one of the three principal divisions of the office of matins, formerly sung or recited between midnight and 4 o'clock in the morning, but now often on the preceding afternoon or evening

2**nocturn** \(')=¦=\ *adj* [MF or L; MF *nocturne*, fr. L *nocturnus*] *archaic* : NOCTURNAL

1**noc·tur·nal** \(')näk¦tərn°l, -tən-\ *adj* [MF or LL; MF *nocturnal*, *nocturnel*, fr. LL *nocturnalis*, fr. L *nocturnus* of night, nocturnal + *-alis* -al; akin to L *nox* night — more at NIGHT] **1** : of or relating to night : done, held, or occurring in the night ⟨~ darkness⟩ ⟨a ~ journey⟩ **2 a** : active at night — used of animals and sometimes plants that perform most of their functions (as feeding, breeding, or blooming) at night; compare DIURNAL **b** : characterized by nocturnal activity ⟨a ~ form of filariasis⟩ ⟨a ~ flower⟩ **3** : suggestive of or having the character of a nocturne **4** *of a sign of the zodiac* : EVEN 5a — **noc·tur·nal·ly** \-°lē, -°li\ *adv*

2**nocturnal** \"\ *n* -s **1** : NIGHT PIECE; *specif* : a play in which the action takes place to a considerable extent on a darkened stage **2** : one that is abroad or active at night : NIGHTWALKER **3** : an astrolabe formerly used for finding the time at night or determining latitude

**nocturnal emission** *n* : an involuntary discharge of semen during sleep often accompanied by an erotic dream — see WET DREAM

**noc·tur·nal·ity** \,nak,tər'naləd·ē\ *also* **noc·tur·nal·ism** \näk'tərn°l,izəm\ *n, pl* **nocturnalities** *also* **nocturnalisms** : the condition of being nocturnal ⟨many rodents exhibit strict ~⟩

**noc·turne** \'näk,tərn, -tən\ *n* -s [F, adj., nocturnal, fr. L *nocturnus*] **1** : a musical night piece; *esp* : a dreamy pensive composition for the piano **2** : a painting of a scene at night : NIGHT PIECE

**noc·u·ous** \'näkyəwəs\ *adj* [L *nocuus*, fr. *nocēre* to harm, hurt — more at NOXIOUS] : likely to cause injury : HARMFUL, DAMAGING ⟨~ grubs in the soil⟩ ⟨a ~ stimulus⟩ — **noc·u·ous·ly** *adv*

1**nod** \'näd\ *vb* **nodded; nodded; nodding; nods** [ME *nodden;* akin to OHG *hnotōn* to shake, ON *hnjotha* to rivet, clinch, L *cinis* ashes — more at INCINERATE] *vi* **1** : to incline the head with a quick motion : make a quick downward motion of the head whether as a sign (as of assent, salutation, or command) or involuntarily (as from drowsiness) ⟨her cousin *nodded* in agreement⟩ ⟨sat *nodding* by the fire⟩ **2** : to incline or sway from the vertical as though ready to fall ⟨the *nodding* debris that once was a city⟩ **3** : to bend or sway the upper part downward or forward with a quick motion : bob gently ⟨the plumes that ~ on his helmet⟩ **4** : to be for the moment inattentive, inaccurate, or careless : make a slip or error in a moment of abstraction ~ *vt* **1** : to incline (as the head) or bend downward or forward; *specif* : to make a quick downward motion of (the head) as a sign or involuntarily ⟨*nodded* his head in approval⟩ **2** : to bring, invite, or send by a nod ⟨~ one back⟩ **3** : to signify by a nod ⟨~ approbation⟩ **4** : to cause to bend : SWAY

2**nod** \"\ *n* -s : the act of one that nods or an instance of nodding: as **a** : NAP **b** : a signal of approval or victory **c** : a careless or inattentive fault : SLIP, LAPSE

3**nod** \"\ *n* -s [prob. back-formation fr. 1*noddle*] *dial Eng* : the nape of the neck

**nod·al** \'nōd°l\ *adj* [1*node* + *-al*] : being, relating to, or located at or near a node or nodes — **nod·al·ly** \-°lē\ *adv*

**no·dal·i·ty** \nō'daləd·ē\ *n* -ES : the quality or state of being nodal

**nodal point** *n* : NODE; *esp* : either of two points so located on the axis of a lens or optical system that any incident ray directed through one will produce a parallel emergent ray directed through the other

**nodal slide** *n* : a device for locating the nodal points of a lens or lens system

**no·dat·ed** \'nō,dād·əd\ *adj* [L *nodat*us (past part. of *nodare* to make knotty, knot, fr. *nodus* knot) + E *-ed* — more at NODE] : having or forming a node ⟨a ~ hyperbola⟩

**nod·der** \'nädə(r)\ *n* -s : one that nods

**nodding** *adj* [fr. pres. part. of 1*nod*] **1** : bending downward or forward : PENDULOUS, DROOPING ⟨a plant with ~ flowers⟩ **2** : DROWSY ⟨the ~ bees⟩ — **nod·ding·ly** *adv*

**nodding acquaintance** *n* **1** : a very slight or superficial knowledge or understanding of something ⟨had no more than a *nodding acquaintance* with economic theory⟩ **2** : a person with whom one is on terms of casual and distant civility

**nodding cap** *or* **nodding pogonia** *n* : a slender tuberous woodland orchid (*Triphora trianthophora*) of eastern No. America having a pale pink or whitish nodding flower with three-lobed lip

**nodding catchfly** *n* : a perennial European sticky herb (*Silene nutans*)

**nodding ladies' tresses** *n pl but sing or pl in constr* : SCREW AUGER

**nodding lily** *n* **1** : MEADOW LILY **2** : TURK'S-CAP LILY b

**nodding mandarin** *n* : a No. American disporum (*Disporum maculatum*) with yellow purple-spotted flowers

**nodding onion** *n* : a widely distributed No. American bulbous herb (*Allium cernuum*) with white to deep rose flowers — called also *wild onion*

**nodding thistle** *n* : MUSK THISTLE

**nodding trillium** *n* : a No. American trillium (*Trillium cernuum*) with whitish or creamy to pinkish or roseate nodding flowers nearly hidden under the leaves

1**nod·dle** \'näd°l\ *n* -s [ME *nodel, nodle*] **1 a** *obs* : the back of the head **b** *chiefly dial* : the nape of the neck **2** : HEAD, PATE, BRAIN

2**noddle** \"\ *vb* **noddled; noddled; noddling** \-d(°)liŋ\ **noddles** [1*nod* + *-le*] : NOD

**nod·dy** \'nädē, -di\ *n* -ES [prob. short for obs. *noddypoll*, alter. (influenced by 1*nod*) of *hoddypoll*] **1** : a stupid person : DUNCE, SIMPLETON, FOOL **2 a** *also* **noddy tern** : any of several stout-bodied terns of the genera *Anoüs* and *Micranous* chiefly of tropical and subtropical seas; *esp* : a dark sooty brown tern (*A. stolidus*) common on the southern Atlantic and Gulf coasts of the U.S. **b** *Midland* : RUDDY DUCK **c** : FULMAR **d** : RAZORBILL **3 a** : an old card game resembling cribbage **b** : JACK 1c(1) **4** [prob. fr. 1*nod* + *-y*] **a** : a small usu. 2-wheeled one-horse hackney vehicle formerly used in Ireland and Scotland **b** : an inverted pendulum consisting of a short vertical flat spring that supports a rod having a bob at the top and used for measuring slight horizontal vibrations

**node** \'nōd\ *n* -s [L *nodus* knot, node — more at NET] **1** : a complication or difficulty (as in a drama) : PREDICAMENT, ENTANGLEMENT **2** : a thickened or swollen enlargement (as on the trunk of a tree) : KNOB, PROTUBERANCE **a** : a pathological swelling or enlargement (as one in the neighborhood of a joint affected by rheumatism or gout or a firm tumor) **b** : a body part resembling a knot; *esp* : a discrete mass of one kind of tissue enclosed in tissue of a different kind ⟨the lymph ~*s* of the intestinal wall⟩ **3** : either of the two points where the orbit of one celestial body intersects a specific reference plane (as the ecliptic in the solar system or the plane of the sky for a double star system) — see ASCENDING NODE, DESCENDING NODE **4** : a point at which subsidiary parts originate or center: **a** : the often swollen or otherwise modified point on a stem or similar structure at which a leaf or leaves are inserted **b** : a point at which a curve intersects itself in such a manner that the branches have different tangents **c** : a point in an electrical network at which several branches come together **5** : a point, line, or surface of a vibrating system that is constantly free or relatively free from vibratory motion (as the middle point of a stretched vibrating string constrained to vibrate in two equal segments or a point in a conductor at which the current or voltage remains zero or at a minimum)

**nod·ed** \-dəd\ *adj* : having or divided into nodes

**node of ran·vier** \-rän'vyā\ *usu cap R* [after Louis A. *Ranvier* †1922 Fr. histologist] : a constriction in the medullary sheath of a medullated nerve fiber

**nodi** *pl of* NODUS

**no·di·ak** \'nōdē,ak\ *n* -s [prob. native name in New Guinea] : the 3-toed echidna (*Zaglossus bruijnii*) of New Guinea

**nod·i·cal** \'nädəkəl, 'nōd-\ *adj* [*node* + *-ical*] : of or relating to astronomical nodes : measured from node to node ⟨the ~ revolution of the moon⟩

**nodical month** *n* : the mean time of the moon's revolution in its orbit from ascending node to ascending node equal to 27 days, 5 hours, 5 minutes, 35.8 seconds of mean solar time — called also *draconic period*

**no·di·corn** \'nōdə,kȯrn\ *adj* [prob. fr. F *nodicorne*, fr. *nodi-* (fr. L *nodus* knot) + *-corne*, fr. L *-cornis* -corn] : having nodose antennae

**no·dif·er·ous** \(')nō¦dif(ə)rəs\ *adj* [ISV *nod-* (fr. L *nodus* knot, node) + *-iferous*] : producing or having nodes

**no·di·form** \'nōdə,fȯrm\ *adj* [*node* + *-iform*] : resembling a node

**no·do·sa·ria** \,nōdə'sa(a)rēə\ *n, cap* [NL, fr. L *nodosus* knotty + NL *-aria*] : a genus of foraminiferans having the shell composed of chambers arranged in a straight or gently curved line — **no·do·sa·ri·an** \¦==¦sa(a)rēən\ *adj or n* — **no·do·sar·oid** \-(a),rȯid\ *adj*

**no·do·saur** \'nōdə,sȯ(ə)r\ *n* -s [NL *Nodosaurus*] : a dinosaur of the genus *Nodosaurus*

**no·do·sau·rus** \,=='sȯrəs\ *n, cap* [NL, fr. L *nodus* node, knot + NL *-saurus*] : a genus of heavily armored No. American Upper Cretaceous dinosaurs somewhat resembling gigantic horned toads

**no·dose** \(')nō¦dōs\ *also* **no·dous** \'nōdəs\ *adj* [L *nodosus*, fr. *nodus* knot, node + *-osus* -ose, -ous — more at NET] : having numerous or conspicuous protuberances : KNOTTY, KNOBBED ⟨~ antennae⟩ ⟨~ leaf petioles⟩

**no·dos·i·ty** \nō'däsəd·ē\ *n* -ES [F or It or LL; F *nodosité* & It *nodosita*, fr. LL *nodositat-*, *nodositas* knottiness, fr. L *nodosus* knotty + *-itat-*, *-itas* -ity] **1** : the quality or state of being nodose **2** : PROTUBERANCE, SWELLING, NODE ⟨a surface dotted with *nodosities*⟩

**nods** *pres 3d sing of* NOD, *pl of* NOD

**nod·u·lar** \'näjələ(r)\ *adj* [*nodule* + *-ar*] **1** : of, relating to, characterized by, or having nodules ⟨~ vaginitis⟩ **2** : occurring in the form of nodules ⟨a ~ ore⟩ ⟨~ graphites⟩ **3** : infested with nodular worms ⟨a section of ~ intestine⟩

**nodular disease** *also* **nodule disease** *n* : infestation with or disease caused by nodular worms of the genus *Oesophagostomum* esp. in sheep

**nodular iron** *n* : cast iron in which the graphite is present as tiny nodules of characteristic structure

**nodular worm** *also* **nodule worm** *n* **1** : any of several nematode worms (genus *Oesophagostomum*) that are parasitic in the large intestine of ruminants and swine where they cause swellings of the intestinal wall resembling abscesses **2** : a filarial worm (*Onchocerca gibsoni*) causing nodular swellings in the skin and subcutaneous tissues of Australian cattle

**nod·u·late** \-jə,lāt\ *vb* -ED/-ING/-S [prob. back-formation fr. *nodulated*, adj.] *vt* **1** : NODULIZE **2** : to cause the formation of nodules on or in ⟨some rhizobia are capable of *nodulating* several different legumes⟩ ~ *vi* : to form or multiply in nodules — used of symbiotic nitrogen-fixing bacteria

**nod·u·lat·ed** \-ād·əd\ *adj* [*nodule* + *-ated*] **1 a** : having nodules; **b** *of a leguminous plant* : having nodules containing symbiotic bacteria on the roots **2** : NODULAR 2

**nod·u·la·tion** \¦==¦lāshən\ *n* -s [*nodulat*ed (adj.) + *-ion*] **1** : the process of becoming or condition of being nodular or nodulated **2** : NODULE

**nod·ule** \'nä,jül\ *n* -s [L *nodulus* small knot, dim. of *nodus* knot, node — more at NET] **1** *obs* : a small quantity of medicinal material tied up in a bag or bit of cloth **2** : a small rounded mass of irregular shape : a little lump: as **a** : a small rounded lump of a mineral or mineral aggregate ⟨a ~ of ironstone⟩ **b** (1) : a plant bud or gemma (2) : a thickening on the valve of a diatom (3) : one of the swellings on the roots of a leguminous plant that contains symbiotic bacteria **c** : the nodulus of the cerebellum **d** : a small abnormal knobby protuberance (as of tumorous growth or of calcification near an arthritic joint)

**nod·uled** \-ld\ *adj* : having or occurring in the form of nodules

**nod·u·lize** \'näjə,līz\ *vt* -ED/-ING/-S : to convert (as finely divided ores) into nodules

**nod·u·lose** \¦==¦lōs\ *also* **nod·u·lous** \'==,ləs\ *adj* [*nodule* + *-ose* or *-ous*] : having minute nodules : finely knobby — see ROOT illustration

**nod·u·lus** \'näjələs\ *n, pl* **nodu·li** \-jə,lī\ [L, small knot] : NODULE; *esp* : a prominence on the inferior surface of the cerebellum forming the anterior end of the vermis

**no·dus** \'nōdəs\ *n, pl* **no·di** \-ō,dī\ [L, knot, node] : NODE: as **a** : COMPLICATION, DIFFICULTY **b** : a center or central point **c** : a hinge on the front margin of the wings of insects of the order Odonata

**NOE** *abbr* not otherwise enumerated

**noe·genesis** \¦nōē+\ *n* [NL, fr. Gk *noē-* (as in *noēma*, understanding, thought, *noēsis* intelligence, understanding) + *genesis*] : a schema for the production of knowledge including three processes: (1) observation; (2) discovery of relations; and (3) the bringing to mind or the creation of ideas that stand in a given relation to given ideas

**no·e·ge·ne·tic** \¦nōējə¦ned·ik\ *adj* [fr. NL *neogenesis*, after E *genesis: genetic*] : of, relating to, or involving noegenesis

**noek·kel·ost** \'nəkə,lōst\ *or* **nok·kel·ost** \'näkə,lȯst\ *n* -s [Norw *nøkkelost*, fr. *nøkkel* key + *ost* cheese; fr. its being modeled after cheese from Leiden, Holland, that was marked with the crossed keys of Leiden's escutcheon] : a dark cheese made from whole or partly skimmed milk and spiced with cumin, caraway, or cloves, or all three

**no·el** \nō'el\ *n* -s [F *noël*, fr. L *natalis* birthday, fr. *natalis*, adj., natal — more at NATAL] **1** : a Christmas carol **2** : the Christmas season

**no·e·ma** \nō'ēmə\ *n, pl* **noema·ta** \-məd·ə\ [NL, fr. Gk *noēma* perception, thought understanding, mind, fr. *noein* to perceive, think] *in Husserlian philos* : the objective aspect of or the content within an intentional experience — distinguished from *noesis*

**no·e·ma·tach·o·graph** \nō,ēmə'takə,graf, -råf\ *n* [Gk *noēma* thought, understanding + E *tacho-* + *-graph*] : an instrument for measuring complex reaction time

**no·e·ma·ta·chom·e·ter** \nō,ēməd·ə'kämməd·ə(r)\ *n* [ISV *noema-* (fr. Gk *noēma* thought, understanding) + *tacho-* + *-meter*] : an instrument for measuring simple reaction time

**no·e·mat·ic** \¦nōē¦mad·ik\ *adj* [prob. fr. G *noematisch*, fr. LGk *noēmatikos* rational, fr. Gk *noēmat-*, *noēma* thought, understanding + *-ikos* -ic] : of, relating to, or involved in noema

**noes** *pl of* NO

**no·e·sis** \nō'ēsəs\ *n* -ES [Gk *noēsis*, fr. *noein* to perceive, think] **1** : purely intellectual apprehension: **a** *Platonism* : the highest kind of knowledge or knowledge of the eternal forms or ideas — contrasted with *dianoia* **b** *in Husserl* : the subjective aspect of or the act in an intentional experience — distinguished from *noema* **2** : cognition esp. when occurring through direct knowledge

1**no·et·ic** \(')nō¦ed·ik\ *adj* [Gk *noētikos*, fr. *noētos* (verbal of *noein* to perceive, fr. *noos*, *nous* mind) + *-ikos* -ic] : of, relating to, or characterized by noesis ⟨~ experiences⟩: as **a** : apprehended only by the intellect ⟨~ truths⟩ **b** : given to purely intellectual or abstract reasoning ⟨a ~ thinker⟩

2**noetic** \"\ *n* -s **1** : one that is noetic **2** : the logical doctrine of axioms or of the laws of thought — often used in pl.

**no-fines concrete** *n* [*no-fines*, fr. 2*no* + *fines*] : porous concrete made without the use of fine aggregate

1**nog** \'näg *sometimes* 'nȯg\ *n* -s [origin unknown] : a wooden peg, pin, or block of the size of a brick; *esp* : a small block built into a wall as a hold for nails

2**nog** \"\ *vt* **nogged; nogged; nogging; nogs** : to fill in (as between scantling) with brickwork ⟨~ partitions⟩

3**nog** *also* **nogg** \"\ *n* -s [origin unknown] **1** : a strong ale formerly brewed in Norfolk, England **2** [by shortening] : EGGNOG **3** : any of various mixed drinks usu. containing beaten egg, milk, or both and often spirits ⟨a brandy ~⟩ ⟨a prune ~⟩

4**nog** \'näg\ *n* -s [by shortening] *dial Brit* : NOGGIN

**no·gai** \'nō,gī\ *n, pl* **nogai** *or* **nogais** *usu cap* [of Altaic origin; akin to Tatar & Kirghiz *Nogai*] **1 a** : a nomad Tatar people of the northeastern Caucasus **b** : a member of such people **2** : a Turkic language of the Nogai people

**no·ga·ku** \'nō,gäkü\ *n, pl* **nogaku** [Jap *nōgaku*, fr. *nō* no (drama) + *gaku* music] : 4NO

**no·gal** \nō'gäl\ *n* -ES [Sp, walnut tree, fr. LL *nucalis* like a nut — more at NEWEL] *chiefly Southwest* : a walnut, pecan, or hickory tree

**nog·gin** \'nägən\ *also* **nag·gin** \'nag-\ *n* -s [origin unknown] **1 a** : a small mug or cup **b** : a small usu. wooden pail **2** : a small quantity of drink usu. equivalent to a gill ⟨a ~ of milk⟩ **3** : a person's head

**nogging** *n* -s [fr. gerund of 2*nog*] **1** : rough brick masonry used to fill in the open spaces of a wooden frame **2** *also* **nogging piece** : a horizontal reinforcement or furring strip between vertical studs

**no-go gage** \'=,=-\ *n* [*no-go*, fr. the phrase *no go*] : a limit gage that will not go in or on the part being tested or will not screw on more than a given number of turns — compare GO GAGE

1**no-good** \'=¦=\ *adj* [fr. the phrase *no good*] : having no virtue, value, or chance of success : WORTHLESS, HOPELESS, USELESS ⟨he was *no-good* at anything tedious⟩ ⟨it's *no-good* to argue⟩ ⟨see what that *no-good* dog has done⟩

2**no-good** \'=,=\ *n* : a no-good person or thing

**noh** *var of* NO

**no-hit** \'=¦=\ *adj* [fr. the phrase *no hit*] : of, relating to, or being a baseball game in which the pitcher allows the opposition no base hits

**no-hit·ter** \'nō'hid·ə(r)\ *n* : a no-hit game in baseball

**no-holds-barred** \'='='=\ *adj* [fr. the phrase *no holds barred*] : free from hampering rules or conventions ⟨the discussion on a *no-holds-barred* basis⟩

**no-hoper** \'nō'hōpə(r)\ *n* [fr. the phrase *no hope* + *-er*] *Austral* : a shiftless individual without ideals or ambitions

**nohow** \'nō,hau̇\ *adv* [2*no* + *how*] **1** : in no manner or way : not at all ⟨could ~ make out the writing⟩ ⟨was ~ equal to the task⟩ — often used dial. following another negative ⟨couldn't see him ~⟩ **2** *chiefly Midland* : ANYWAY ⟨where are you going ~⟩ **3** *chiefly dial* : in a state of confused disorder : out of sorts — usu. used with *all* ⟨was all ~ at the thought of going⟩

**NOHP** *abbr* not otherwise herein provided

**NOIBN** *abbr* not otherwise indexed by name

**no·ib·wood** \'nōib,wu̇d\ *also* **noib** *n* -s [*noib* (of unknown origin)] : BETHABARA

**NOIC** *abbr* naval officer in charge

**noil** \'nȯi(ə)l\ *n* -s [origin unknown] : short fiber removed during the combing of a textile fiber (as wool, silk, camel's hair) and spun into yarn for cloth ⟨whereas silk ~ is often waste, that of camel's hair is the best part of the fleece⟩

**noint** \'nȯint\ *vb* -ED/-ING/-S [ME *nointen*, prob. alter. of *anointen* — more at ANOINT] *archaic* : ANOINT

**noir** \'nwär\ *n* -s [F, fr. *noir*, adj., black, fr. L *niger*] : the black numbers in roulette when a bet is made on them

1**noise** \'nȯiz\ *n* -s [ME, fr. OF, noise, noisy strife, quarrel, fr. L *nausea* seasickness, nausea — more at NAUSEA] **1** : loud, confused, or senseless shouting or outcry : din or uproar of persons **2 a** (1) : sound or a sound that lacks agreeable musical quality or is noticeably loud, harsh, or discordant ⟨~ results from irregular vibrations and produces an unpleasant sound —Henry Melnik⟩ ⟨~ represents sounds in which the energy is more or less uniformly distributed over a considerable frequency range without a definite pitch being present —F.E.Terman⟩ (2) : the din or loud persistent incoherent sound that is a feature of most communities or activities ⟨the ~ of a rookery⟩ ⟨far away from city ~ and disorder⟩ **b** : any sound that is undesired or that interferes with something to which one is listening (as a hum or the scratching of a needle produced by a sound recording or reproducing system) **c** : an unwanted signal that enters an electronic communication system (as telephone, radio, television) or that is created in it and that tends to interfere with the desired signals ⟨a hissing sound in a telephone receiver, static in a radio receiver, and snow in a television receiver are forms of ~⟩ **3** *obs* : general or common talk or discussion : RUMOR; *esp* : evil or slanderous report **4 a** : sound or a sound that is not regarded as unpleasing or that has a pleasing melodious quality ⟨the tinkling ~*s* of the brook⟩ ⟨the ~ of heavenly choirs⟩ **b** *obs* : a company of musicians

2**noise** \"\ *vb* -ED/-ING/-S [ME *noisen*, fr. *noise*, n.] *vt* : to spread by rumor or report — usu. used with *abroad* or *about* ⟨it was *noised* about that the troops were to be returned home⟩ ⟨a rumor is being *noised* abroad⟩ ~ *vi* **1** : to talk much or loudly **2** : to make a noise or outcry

**noise factor** *or* **noise figure** *n* : the ratio of the noise output of an electronic device to that of a similar ideal device

**noise field intensity** *n* : the electromagnetic field intensity produced by waves of an interfering character in radio reception

**noise·ful** \'nȯizfəl\ *adj* [ME, fr. *noise* + *-ful*] : full of noise: as **a** : full of, abounding in, or making sounds : NOISY **b** *obs* : full of evil report—**noise·ful·ly** \-fəlē\ *adv*

**noise·less** \-zləs\ *adj* [1*noise* + *-less*] **1** : making or causing no noise or stir : free from noise : SILENT, QUIET ⟨kittens on ~ feet⟩ **2 a :** making less noise than is typical of its kind **b** of a typewriter : having a type-bar action that is quieter than that of a standard typewriter — **noise·less·ly** adv — **noise·less·ness** n -ES

**noiseless recording** n : a method of film recording in which the average density of the unmodulated track of the negative is decreased during silent and soft passages in order to reduce background noise

**noise limiter** n : an electronic device that eliminates some types of noise (as one due to strong pulses of interference) in radio receivers

**noisemaker** \ˈ=,==\ n : one that makes noise; specif : any of several devices (as a horn, clapper, rattle) used to make noise at a celebration or merrymaking — **noisemaking** \ˈ=,==\ n or adj

**noiseproof** \ˈ=¦=\ adj : SOUNDPROOF

**noise spectrum** n : the array of frequencies involved in noise

**[1]noi·sette** \nwəˈzet\ n -S [F, hazel nut, fr. MF, fr. OF, dim. of nois, noix nut, fr. L nuc-, nux — more at NUT] **1 :** a small rounded morsel of food: as **a :** a small piece of lean meat (as the eye of a chop or a small slice of tenderloin) **b :** a small potato ball browned in butter **2** or **noisette brown** [noisette, fr. F, adj., hazel, light brown, fr. noisette hazel nut] : HAZEL 4

**[2]noisette** \"\ adj [F] : prepared with, consisting principally of, or dressed with browned butter ⟨a ~ sauce⟩ ⟨cutlets ~⟩

**noi·sette rose** \nwəˈzet\ also **noisette** n -S usu cap N [after Philippe Noisette, brother of Louis Claude Noisette †1849 Fr. horticulturist] : any of various hardy garden roses supposedly descended from a hybrid between the China rose (Rosa chinensis) and the moss rose (R. centifolia muscosa)

**nois·i·ly** \ˈnȯizəlē, -li\ adv : in a noisy manner : so as to produce usu. disturbing noise

**nois·i·ness** \-zēnəs\ n -ES : the quality or state of being noisy

**noi·some** \ˈnȯisəm\ adj [ME noysome, fr. noy annoy (alter. of anuy, anoi) + -some — more at ANNOY (n.)] **1 :** NOXIOUS, HARMFUL, UNWHOLESOME, DESTRUCTIVE ⟨a ~ environment⟩ **2 :** offensive to the smell or other senses : DISGUSTING, DISTASTEFUL ⟨foul breath is ~ —Shak.⟩ **3** obs : ANNOYING — **noi·some·ly** adv — **noi·some·ness** n -ES

**noisy** \ˈnȯizē, -zi\ adj -ER/-EST [[1]noise + -y] **1 :** making or given to making noise : CLAMOROUS, VOCIFEROUS ⟨the ~ crowd⟩ ⟨never rode in a noisier car⟩ **2 :** full of or characterized by the presence of noise ⟨that ~ night⟩ ⟨such a ~ office⟩ **3 :** tending to attract attention usu. by reason of showiness, gaudiness, or brightness of color : LOUD ⟨a ~ sweater⟩

**noisy friarbird** n : FRIARBIRD 1

**noisy pitta** n : DRAGOON BIRD

**no·ki** \ˈnōkē\ n -S [prob. the native name in So. Africa] : a rock rat (Petromys typicus)

**nokkelost** var of NOEKKELOST

**no·ko** \ˈnō(,)kō\ n -S usu cap : NGOKO

**no·li me tan·ge·re** \ˈnōlē¦māˈtäŋgə,rā\ n, pl **noli me tangeres** [L, do not touch me] **1 :** a warning against touching or interference **2 a :** a person or thing not to be touched or meddled with **b** [so called fr. Christ's warning to Mary Magdalene in the Vulgate (John 20:17)] : a painting representing Christ's appearance to Mary Magdalene after the Resurrection

**no·li·na** \nōˈlīnə\ n [NL, after P. C. Nolin 18th cent. Fr. botanist and cleric] **1** cap : a genus of perennial plants (family Liliaceae) of the southern U.S. and Mexico that resemble yuccas and have a thick woody trunk often much dilated at its base and narrow rigid finely serrate leaves which have been used as a source of a hard cordage fiber **2** -S : any plant of the genus Nolina : BEAR GRASS

**no·li·tion** \nōˈlishən\ n -S [prob. fr. F, fr. MF, fr. L nolle not to will, to be unwilling (fr. ne- not + velle to will, wish, be willing) + MF -ition (as in volition) — more at NO, WILL] : adverse action of will : UNWILLINGNESS — opposed to volition

**noll** \ˈnōl\ n -S [ME noll, nolle, fr. OE knoll, knol top, crown of the head; akin to MD nolle, nol top, crown or back of the head, OHG knol, nol top, knel top, crown of the head and to OE hnecca neck — more at NECK] dial Eng : HEAD

**nol·le** \ˈnälē\ vt -ED/-ING/-S [short for nolle pros] : NOL-PROS

**nolle pros** \-ˈpräs\ vt **nolle prossed; nolle prossed; nolle prossing; nolle prosses** [nolle prosequi] : NOL-PROS

**nolle pros·e·qui** \-ˈpräsə,kwī\ n, pl **nolle prosequis** [L, to be unwilling to pursue] : an entry on the record of a legal action denoting that the prosecutor or plaintiff will proceed no further in his action or suit either as a whole or as to some count or as to one or more of several defendants — abbr. nol pros; compare NON PROSEQUITUR

**noll-kholl** \ˈnōl,kōl\ n -S [D knolkool, fr. knol turnip + kool cabbage] India : KOHLRABI

**no·lo** \ˈnō(,)lō\ n -S [by shortening] : NOLO CONTENDERE

**nolo con·ten·de·re** \-kən·ˈtendərē\ n, pl **nolo contenderes** [L, I do not wish to contend] : a plea by the defendant in a criminal prosecution that without admitting guilt subjects him to a judgment of conviction as in case of a plea of guilty but does not preclude him from denying the truth of the charges in a collateral proceeding

**nol-pros** \ˈnälˈpräs\ vt **nol-prossed; nol-prossed; nol-prossing; nol-prosses** [nolle prosequi] : to discontinue by entering a nolle prosequi

**nom** abbr **1** nomenclature **2** nominal **3** nominative

**no·ma** \ˈnōmə\ n -S [NL, fr. L nome spreading ulcer, fr. Gk nomē pasturage, food from pasturing, spreading ulcer; akin to Gk nemein to distribute, pasture — more at NIMBLE] : a spreading invasive gangrene chiefly of the lining of cheek and lips most often occurring in persons severely debilitated by disease or profound nutritional deficiency

**[1]no·mad** also **no·made** \ˈnō,mad\ n -S [L nomad-, nomas, fr. Gk; akin to Gk nemein to pasture, distribute] **1 :** a member of a people that has no fixed residence but wanders from place to place usu. seasonally and within a well-defined territory for the purpose of securing its supply of food either by gathering of plants and hunting of animals, by using suitable grounds for quick crops, or esp. by finding grazing lands and water for its herds — compare MIGRANT **2 :** an individual that roams about aimlessly or without a fixed pattern of movement

**[2]nomad** \"\ adj : being a nomad : ROVING, NOMADIC ⟨~ herdsmen⟩

**no·mad·ic** \(ˈ)nō¦madik, -dēk\ adj [Gk nomadikos pastoral, wandering, fr. nomad-, nomas nomad + -ikos -ic] **1 :** of, relating to, or characteristic or suggestive of a people of nomads or their way of life ⟨a ~ tribe⟩ ⟨the ~ habits of the Bedouins⟩ **2 :** roaming about from place to place aimlessly or without a fixed pattern of movement : VAGRANT ⟨many ownerless dogs are ~ —E.M.Pullar⟩ ⟨girls . . . make up from one eighth to one third of the ~ group —W.C.Naw⟩

**no·mad·i·dae** \nōˈmadə,dē\ n pl, cap [NL, fr. Nomada, type genus (fr. Gk nomad-, nomas nomad) + -idae] : a family of small bees resembling wasps — see CUCKOO BEE

**no·mad·ism** \ˈnō,ma,dizəm\ n -S **1 :** the mode of life of a nomadic people ⟨pastoral ~⟩ **2 :** the mode of life or behavior of an individual that roams about aimlessly or without any fixed pattern of movement; specif : VAGRANCY ⟨sometimes a roaming instinct — the trait of ~ —appears —J.A.O'Brien⟩ ⟨incidence of ~ — about twice as frequent in the broken home group —Nathan Blackman⟩

**no·mad·ize** \-dīz\ vb -ED/-ING/-S [[1]nomad + -ize] vi : to live the life of a nomad : roam about ~ vt : to make nomadic ⟨nomadized by evacuation from the bombed cities —Foreign Affairs⟩

**no man** n [ME no man, naman, non man, nan man, fr. OE nān man, fr. nān no, none + man — more at NONE] **1 :** no person : NOBODY **2** usu **no-man** \ˈ=,=\ [[2]no + man] : a man who is accustomed or inclined to disagree in an independent manner or to decline requests in a firm resolute way ⟨surrounded by a number of no-men to resist me at every point —Sir Winston Churchill⟩ — compare YES-MAN

**no·man·cy** \ˈnōmən(t)sē\ n -ES [obs. F nomancie, alter. of onomancie — more at ONOMANCY] : divination by letters

**no-man's-land** \ˈ=,=,=\ n [no man's (gen. of no man) + land] **1 a :** an area of unowned, unclaimed, or uninhabited land ⟨a no-man's-land of bottomlands and islands aggregating up to forty square miles —N.Y.Times⟩ ⟨many metropolitan areas will become a kind of no-man's-land should they become heavily contaminated —R.E.Lapp⟩ ⟨staring down into a no-man's-land where once had stood busy streets —S.P.B.Mais⟩ **b :** a belt of ground between the most advanced elements of opposing armies : an area in a theater of operations not controlled by either side **2 :** an area of anomalous, ambiguous, or indefinite character ⟨lived in a no-man's-land between slavery and freedom —World⟩ ⟨the no-man's-land between political theory, theology, and political history —Richard Mayne⟩ ⟨the no-man's-land that was neither wholly good nor wholly evil —Nigel Dennis⟩

**nom·arch** \ˈnä,märk\ n -S [Gk nomarchēs, nomarchos (also, governor of a region or province), fr. Gk nomos district + -archēs, -archos -arch — more at NIMBLE] **1 :** the chief magistrate of a nome in ancient Egypt **2** [NGk nomarchēs, fr. Gk] : the chief administrator of a nomarchy in modern Greece

**nom·archy** \-,mə(r)kē\ n -ES [NGk nomarchia, fr. Gk nomarchia province or district of a nomarch, fr. nomos district + -archia -archy] : a province or department of modern Greece : NOME

**no·mar·thra** \nōˈmärthrə\ [NL, fr. Gk nomos law + arthron joint — more at NIMBLE, ARTHR-] syn of PHOLIDOTA

**nombles** var of NUMBLES

**nom·bril** \ˈnämbrəl\ or **nombril point** n -S [MF nombril, lit., navel, fr. OF, prob. alter. of lombril, fr. le the + ombril navel, fr. (assumed) VL umbiliculus, dim. of L umbilicus navel — more at LA, NAVEL] : the center point of the lower half of an armorial escutcheon — called also navel; see POINT illustration

**nom de guerre** \,nämdəˈga(a)r, -ger\ n, pl **noms de guerre** \-m(z)d-\ [F, lit., war name] : a fictitious name : PSEUDONYM ⟨drawings . . . shall be signed with a device or nom de guerre —Pencil Points⟩

**nom de plume** \,nämdəˈplüm\ n, pl **noms de plume** \-m(z)d-\ also **nom de plumes** \-m(z)\ [F, pen name; prob. coined in E] : a pseudonym assumed by a writer : PEN NAME ⟨the author hid under a nom de plume⟩

**[1]nome** \ˈnōm\ n -S [Gk nomos place of pasturage, district, province — more at NIMBLE] **1 :** a province of ancient Egypt **2** [NGk nomos, fr. Gk] : a province or department of modern Greece : NOMARCHY

**[2]nome** \"\ n -S [Gk nomos (also, usage, custom, melody) — more at NIMBLE] : a musical composition of ancient Greece intended either for instrumental performance alone or to be accompanied by a recitation of epics

**no·me·i·dae** \nōˈmēə,dē\ n pl, cap [NL, fr. Nomeus, type genus + -idae] : a family of usu. small fishes most of which are found in the open sea

**no·men** \ˈnōmən\ n, pl **nom·i·na** \ˈnämənə, ˈnōm-\ [L — more at NAME] **1 :** NAME ⟨no longer a ~ of bitter sarcasm —Gertrude Atherton⟩ **2 :** the name of the gens being the second of the three usual names of a person among the ancient Romans — compare AGNOMEN, COGNOMEN, PRAENOMEN **3 :** a grammatical form with the functions of a noun : NOUN, SUBSTANTIVE

**no·men·cla·tive** \ˈnōmən,klād·iv\ adj [[1]nomenclature + -ive] : of or relating to name or the act of naming ⟨the family connection might seem a little remote . . . for such ~ prominence —M.D.Geismar⟩

**no·men·cla·tor** \-d·ə(r)\ n -S [L, slave in ancient Rome who attended a candidate for office to tell him the names of influential persons whom they met, slave who told his master the names of the other slaves, fr. nomen name + -clat- (fr. calare to call) + -or — more at CLAIM] **1 :** a book containing collections or lists of words : VOCABULARY **2 a :** a person who calls persons or things by their names **b** archaic : one who announces the names of guests or of persons generally **3 :** one who gives names to or invents names for things : a classifier of objects under appropriate names ⟨the ~ of the English Gothic styles —Tudor Edwards⟩

**no·men·cla·to·ri·al** \nō¦menklə¦tōrēəl\ adj : NOMENCLATURAL — **no·men·cla·to·ri·al·ly** \-ēəlē\ adv

**no·men·cla·tur·al** \¦nōmən¦klāch(ə)rəl\ adj : relating to or connected with nomenclature — **no·men·cla·tur·al·ly** \-rəlē\ adv

**[1]no·men·cla·ture** \ˈnōmən,klāchə(r) sometimes nōˈmenkləch-\ n -S [L nomenclatura act of calling by name, list of names, fr. nomenclator + -ura -ure] **1 a :** NAME, APPELLATION, DESIGNATION ⟨the patricians — mainly of Etruscan origin and ~ —R.A.Hall b.1911⟩ ⟨the generally accepted ~ of Theileria was proposed —John Legg⟩ ⟨whose main obsession was his ~ —Sydney (Australia) Bull.⟩ ⟨an example of the odd ~ of coal patches —Amer. Guide Series: Pa.⟩ ⟨has a magnitude of ~ second to none —St. Clair McKelway⟩ ⟨the changing ~ of her streets is even more baffling —Cornelia O. Skinner⟩ **b :** the collective names given to or borne by places in a particular area or region ⟨whose names are preserved in the village ~ of the Danelaw —F.M.Stenton⟩ **2 :** the act or process or an instance of naming ⟨by an odd quirk of ~ —Green Peyton⟩ ⟨problems of ~⟩ ⟨~ . . . is at its simplest the task of assigning a name to each distinct species —R.I.Smith⟩ **3 a :** LIST, CATALOG ⟨no more than an annotated ~ of the rich and varied writings —R.L.Bruckberger⟩ **b** obs : VOCABULARY, DICTIONARY, GLOSSARY **4 a :** a system or set of names, designations, or symbols used by a person or group ⟨the following ~ is used in the paper —A.W.Cochardt⟩ ⟨employs a very strange ~⟩ ⟨most textual critics have refused to adopt this ~ —B.M. Metzger⟩ **b :** a system or set of names or designations used in a particular science, discipline, or art and formally adopted or sanctioned by the usage of its practitioners : TERMINOLOGY ⟨the course includes a survey of the nature of law; its subject matter . . . and ~ —College of William & Mary Catalog⟩ ⟨the standard ~ of diseases and operations —Jour. Amer. Med. Assoc.⟩ ⟨reflects changes in the aircraft ~ —William Wallrich⟩ ⟨the ~s of politics and law —E.J.Kimble⟩ **c :** an international vocabulary of New Latin names of kinds and groups of kinds of animals and plants standardized under rules set up by international commissions sponsored by the basic biological taxonomic disciplines — see BINARY NOMENCLATURE, BINOMIAL NOMENCLATURE; compare FAMILY, GENUS, ORDER, SPECIES; -ACEAE, -ALES, -IDAE, -INAE; TAXONOMY **d :** a set of chemical names that may be systematic (as according to decisions of the International Union of Pure and Applied Chemistry) or not and that aims to tell the composition and often the structure of a given compound by naming the elements, groups, radicals, or ions present and employing suffixes denoting function (as -ic and -ate for acids and salts, -ane, -ol, -one for hydrocarbons and some of their derivatives, -ine for organic bases), prefixes denoting composition (as hypo-, per-, chloro-, Greek numerical prefixes), configuration prefixes (as cis-, syn-, xylo-, meso-), operational prefixes (as cyclo-, dehydro-, deoxy-, homo-), arabic numbers or Greek letters for indicating structure (as positions of substituents), or Roman numerals for indicating oxidation state — see GENEVA SYSTEM, STOCK SYSTEM; compare STRUCTURAL FORMULA

**[2]nomenclature** \"\ vt -ED/-ING/-S : NAME, DESIGNATE

**no·men·cla·tur·ist** \¦nōmən¦klāch(ə)rəst\ n -S : NOMENCLATOR 3

**no·men con·ser·van·dum** \ˈnōmən,kän(t)sə(r)ˈvandəm\ n, pl **nom·i·na con·ser·van·da** \ˈnämənə, . . . də\ [L, name to be preserved] : a name that should not be changed; specif : a biological generic name or other taxon to be preserved by special sanction in exception to the usual rules (as of priority)

**nomen no·vum** \-ˈnōvəm\ n, pl **nomina no·va** \-və\ [L, new name] : a taxonomic name for a plant or animal substituted for an untenable one

**nomen nu·dum** \-ˈnüdəm\ n, pl **nomina nu·da** \-də\ [L, naked name, mere name] : a proposed taxonomic name invalid because the group designated is not described or illustrated sufficiently for recognition, having no nomenclatural status, and consequently capable of being used as though never previously proposed

**nomes** pl of NOME

**no·me·us** \nōˈmēəs\ n, cap [NL, fr. Gk, herdsman; akin to G nemein to distribute, pasture — more at NIMBLE] : a genus (the type of the family Nomeidae) of fishes including the man-of-war fish

**no·mia** \ˈnōmēə\ n, cap [NL, fr. Gk nomios of shepherds, pastoral; akin to Gk nomeus shepherd, herdsman] : a genus of bees (family Halictidae) some of which are important pollinators of legumes

**[1]nom·ic** \ˈnämik, ˈnōm-\ adj [Gk nomos nome, melody, custom + E -ic — more at NIMBLE] : relating to a musical nome

**[2]nomic** \"\ adj [Gk nomikos, fr. nomos usage, custom, law + -ikos -ic — more at NIMBLE] **1 :** having the general force of natural law : generally valid ⟨a ~ statement⟩ **2 a :** CUSTOMARY, ORDINARY, CONVENTIONAL **b** of spelling : ORTHOGRAPHIC, NONPHONETIC

**[3]no·mic** \ˈnōmik\ n -S [no metal in composition] : NEAR-PRINT

**nomina** pl of NOMEN

**nomina conservanda** pl of NOMEN CONSERVANDUM

**[1]nom·i·nal** \ˈnämənᵊl sometimes -mnəl\ adj [ME nominalle, fr. ML nominalis, fr. L, of or relating to a name, fr. nomin-, nomen name + -alis -al — more at NAME] **1 a :** of, relating to, or being a noun : SUBSTANTIVAL **b :** of, relating to, or being a word that is otherwise characteristically an adjective or adverb but that takes a noun construction in a given context (as good in "the good die young" **2** [[2]nominal] : of or relating to the nominalists **3 a :** of, relating to, being, or consisting in a name ⟨the Russian system of ~ brevity —Irwin Ross⟩ **b :** bearing or mentioning the name of a specific person ⟨~ shares⟩ **c :** containing or being a set of names ⟨~ lists of priests —Robert Graves⟩ ⟨taxable males as revealed by the ~ rolls —M.D.W.Jeffreys⟩ **4 a** (1) : existing or being something in name or form but usu. not in reality : FORMAL, OSTENSIBLE — distinguished from actual ⟨a large majority of indifferent and lukewarm ~ Christians —Emil Brunner⟩ ⟨was both the ~ and the real head of his party⟩ ⟨that sign of the ~ virgin —J.H. Wheelwright⟩ ⟨we'll consider that the jewelry had only a ~ value —Erle Stanley Gardner⟩ ⟨the budget continued in ~ balance —Collier's Yr. Bk.⟩ ⟨the plaintiff is only a ~ party and not the real party in interest —D.C.Cook & Myer Feldman⟩ ⟨the ~ spokesman for a continent in travail —Time⟩ ⟨the pleasure derived from them . . . is practically ~ —Herbert Spencer⟩ (2) : measured in money as distinct from actual purchasing power ⟨~ wages⟩ — compare REAL **b :** being so small, slight, or negligible as scarcely to be entitled to the name : TRIFLING, INSIGNIFICANT ⟨parts are supplied at a ~ cost —R.S.Casey & J.W.Perry⟩ ⟨will pay a ~ price when it suits him —Walter Lippmann⟩ **c :** not known to exist except as a name ⟨a ~ species⟩ — compare NOMINATE **5 a :** APPROXIMATE, RATED ⟨although described as 4 inch by 4 inch, which is the ~ size, a piece which has been dried and dressed on four sides is actually 3⅝ by 3⅝ inch —Amer. Builder Catalog Directory⟩ ⟨the ~ voltage of a circuit, or system, is a value assigned to a circuit, or system of a given voltage class, for the purpose of convenient designation —Electrical Engineering⟩ **b** of a price : based on opinions of value expressed by buyers and sellers rather than on actual transactions when there is little or no trading in a particular commodity — **nom·i·nal·ly** \-ᵊlē, -mnəl-, -i\ adv

**[2]nominal** \"\ n -S **1 :** an individual that exists or is something in name or form but not in reality ⟨the Republican side . . . includes a lot of ~s —R.H.Rovere⟩ **2 :** a note from which a scale or other series of musical tones is named

**nominal account** n : any one of the income or expense accounts — compare MIXED ACCOUNT, REAL ACCOUNT

**nominal damages** n pl : a small or token sum awarded to a person who has been wronged but who has not shown such an injury as to be entitled to compensatory damages

**nominal definition** n : a statement giving the meaning of a name, word, or expression ⟨a purely nominal definition, completely lacking in operational utility —Morris Watnick⟩ — contrasted with real definition

**nominal essence** n, Lockeanism : an abstract complex idea that has been given a distinct general name ⟨the nominal essences of things, expressed by their common name, rest upon the experienced resemblances that cause objects to fall into different groups and to receive different appellations —B.A.G. Fuller⟩ — contrasted with real essence

**nom·i·nal·ism** \-ᵊl,izəm, -mnə,li-\ n -S **1 a :** a theory that there are no universal essences in reality and that the mind can frame no single concept or image corresponding to any universal or general term; specif : a theory advanced by the medieval thinker Roscellinus that universal terms such as indicate genus or species and all general collective words or terms such as animal, man, tree, air, city, nation, wagon have no objective real existence corresponding to them but are mere words, names, or terms or mere vocal utterances and that only particular individual things and events exist — compare CONCEPTUALISM, REALISM **b :** a logical or mathematical theory excluding from its language any names or variables for such abstract or higher level entities as classes — contrasted with platonism **2 :** a sociological doctrine or theory that holds that society is merely an aggregate of discrete individuals and that it has no superorganic reality — contrasted with realism

**no·mi·nal·ist** \-ᵊləst, -,ləst\ n -S [prob. fr. F nominaliste, fr. MF, fr. nominal nominalist (fr. ML nominalis, fr. L nominalis, adj., of or relating to a name) + -iste -ist — more at NOMINAL] : an advocate of nominalism

**nom·i·nal·is·tic** \¦==nᵊl¦istik, ¦==¦listik, -tēk\ adj : of, relating to, or advocating nominalism — **nom·i·nal·is·ti·cal·ly** \-tək(ə)lē\ adv

**nom·i·nal·ize** \ˈnämənᵊl,īz, -mnə,līz\ vt -ED/-ING/-S [[1]nominal + -ize] : to convert into or use as a noun ⟨nominalized able into ability⟩ ⟨~s the adjective poor into the poor⟩

**nominal partner** n : a person who holds himself out as a partner or permits a partner to hold him out as a copartner though in fact he is not a partner

**nominal rate** n : a rate of interest used in adding compound interest to a principal sum when interest is compounded other than annually — compare EFFECTIVE RATE

**nominal sentence** n : an equational sentence

**nominal value** n : PAR VALUE

**nomina nova** pl of NOMEN NOVUM

**nomina nuda** pl of NOMEN NUDUM

**[1]nom·i·nate** \ˈnämənət, -mə,nāt, usu -d·+V\ adj [L nominatus (past part.)] **1** Roman & civil law : having a special or certain name : being a contract involving the delivery of property for which the actual property or similar property was to be returned (as in the case of a loan, deposit, or pledge) — distinguished from innominate **2 :** appointed to an office — chiefly used in Scots law of a tutor appointed by a father or since 1886 by a mother in a will or some other sufficient writing **3 :** being the first named and by rule a tautonymic subdivision of a species ⟨Icterus cucullatus cucullatus is a ~ race⟩ ⟨the ~ race of this oriole —Condor⟩

**[2]nom·i·nate** \ˈnämə,nāt, usu -ād·+V\ vt -ED/-ING/-S [L nominatus, past part. of nominare, fr. nomin-, nomen name — more at NAME] **1 a :** to call by some name or title : DESIGNATE, NAME, DENOMINATE ⟨the first of the commonly so nominated explorers of the American Arctic —Vilhjalmur Stefansson⟩ **b :** to mention by name : give the name of : call or name off ⟨~ . . . all the islets of the sound would entail a couple of hours' work —A.A.MacGregor⟩ ⟨becomes more and more difficult to ~ the real criminals —R.H.S.Crossman⟩ **2 a** (1) : to appoint to an office or place ⟨the person nominated by the deceased's will as his executor —Edward Jenks⟩ (2) : to propose by name for office as a preliminary to appointment upon approval or confirmation by some person or body ⟨the President . . . shall ~, and, by and with the advice and consent of the Senate, shall appoint ambassadors —U.S.Constitution⟩ **b** (1) : to propose, select, or formally enter by any of various methods (as the caucus, the convention, the primary, or petition) as a candidate for public office (2) : to propose or enter as a candidate for a nonpublic office ⟨nominated for club chairman but lost by a few votes⟩ **3** obs : FIX, SPECIFY ⟨let the forfeit be nominated —Shak.⟩ **4 :** to put forward or propose formally or informally for some honor, eminence, or status ⟨do not share the taste that ~s these poems for greatness —A.S.Stein⟩ ⟨~ him as the best model football player of 1952 —Eddie Beachler⟩ **5 a** (1) : to select (as a bull) for the serving of a particular female (2) : to request service for (as a mare) from a particular male : offer to book service for — used with to ⟨the mare should be nominated to a stallion whose qualities complement her own⟩ **6 :** to enter (a horse) in a race **syn** see DESIGNATE

**nom·i·nate·ly** adv : by name

**no·mi·na·tim** \,näməˈnād·əm\ adv [L, fr. nomin-, nomen name] : by name : EXPRESSLY

**nom·i·na·tion** \,näməˈnāshən\ n -S [ME nominacioun, fr. MF nomination, fr. L nomination-, nominatio, fr. nominatus (past part.) + -ion-, -io -ion] **1 :** the act, process, or an instance of nominating: as **a** (1) : an act or right of designating by name for an office or duty : APPOINTMENT ⟨won for the crown the right of ~ to all benefices⟩ (2) : the act or an instance of proposing by name for offices as a preliminary to appointment upon approval or confirmation by some person or body ⟨the senate approved all the president's ~s⟩ (3) : the act, process, or an instance of proposing, selecting, or formally entering by any of various methods as a candidate for a public or nonpublic office ⟨the process whereby party members select the person they wish to bear the party emblem in the race . . . is called ~ —O.P.Field, P.S.Sikes, & J.E.Stoner⟩ **b** *Church of England* : the naming of a clergyman by a patron to the rightful authority for presentation in cases where patronage does not include the legal rights of a presenter **2** : the state of being nominated ⟨competition for the ~ was very keen⟩ — often used in the phrase *in nomination* ⟨kind enough to put my name in ~ for this job —Rolfe Humphries⟩ **3** *archaic* **a** : NAME, DENOMINATION **b** : assignment of a name **4** : the part of the Roman legal formula that designates by name the judex or the recuperatores **5** : the preliminary entry in a race of a horse by name

1**nom·i·na·tive** *in sense 1 usu* 'nām(ə)nəd·iv *or* -nətiv; *in other senses* " *or* 'nāmə,nād·\|iv *or* -āt\| *or* \|ēv *also* \|əv\\ *adj* [ME *nominatif*, fr. L *nominativus*, fr. *nominatus* (past part.) + *-ivus* -ive] **1 a** : marking typically the subject of a verb ⟨Latin *filius* in *filius amat matrem suam*, "the son loves his mother", is in the ~ case⟩ — used esp. in the grammar of languages that have relatively full inflection **b** *of a word or word group* : being the subject of a verb even when the relation is not marked by any inflective element (as *John* in *John sees Henry*) **c** : of or relating to the nominative case ⟨a ~ ending⟩ **2** : nominated or appointed by nomination **3** : bearing a person's name : NOMINAL ⟨~ shares⟩

2**nom·i·na·tive** \\'nām(ə)nəd·iv\\ *n* -s : the nominative case of a language or a form in the nominative case

**nominative absolute** *also* **nominative independent** *n* : a construction in English consisting of a noun in the common case or a pronoun in the nominative case joined with a predicate that does not include a finite verb and functioning usu. as a sentence modifier but also sometimes capable of being construed as the modifier of a particular word in the sentence (as *her head erect* in "she walked along, her head erect" or *he being absent* in "he being absent, no business was transacted")

**nom·i·na·tive·ly** \\-d·ə̇vlē\\ *adv* : in the manner of a nominative

**nom·i·na·tor** \\'nāmə,nād·ə(r), -ātə-\\ *n* -s [LL, fr. L *nominatus* (past part.) + *-or*] **1** : one that nominates **2** : a person in whose name a horse is entered for a race

**no·mi·na·tum** \\,nāmə'nād·əm\\ *n, pl* **nomina·ta** \\-d·ə\\ [L, neut. of *nominatus*, past part of *nominare* to name — more at NOMINATE] : the thing that is named by a sign, word, or linguistic expression ⟨the ~ of a proper name is the object itself which is designated thereby —Herbert Feigl & W.S. Sellars⟩ — compare DESIGNATUM

**nom·i·nee** \\,nāmə'nē\\ *n* -s [2*nominate* + *-ee*] **1** : a person named as the recipient in an annuity or grant **2** : a person named for any office, duty, or position **3** : a person in whose name a stock or registered bond certificate is registered but who is not the actual owner

**nom·i·ny** \\'nāməni\\ *n* -ES [prob. fr. L *in nomine* in the name] **1** *dial Eng* : a formulaic or conventional piece of rhyming doggerel; *also* : RIGMAROLE **2** *dial Eng* : a long-winded speech

**no·mism** \\'nō,mizəm\\ *n* -s [Gk *nomos* custom, usage, law + E *-ism* — more at NIMBLE] : ethical or religious basing of conduct on the observance of moral law : LEGALISM

**no·mis·ma** \\nō'mizmə\\ *n, pl* **nomisma·ta** \\-əd·ə\\ [Gk, something established by usage, current coin, money, fr. *nomizein* to use customarily, fr. *nomos* usage, custom] : the Byzantine solidus

**no·mis·tic** \\(')nō¦mistik\\ *adj* : based on or conforming to moral law

**no·mi·us** \\'nōmēəs\\ *n, cap* [NL] : a genus of ground beetles (family Carabidae) one of which (*N. pygmaeus*) occurs in parts of Europe and No. America and produces a strong offensive odor

**nom·la·ki** \\nām'lākē\\ *n, pl* **nomlaki** *or* **nomlakis** *usu cap* **1** : a Wintun people of the lower Sacramento river valley, Calif. **2** : a member of the Nomlaki people

**nom nov** *abbr* nomen novum

**nom nud** *abbr* nomen nudum

**nomo-** *comb form* [Gk, fr. *nomos* — more at NIMBLE] : usage : law ⟨*nomology*⟩

**no·mo·ca·non** \\,nōmə'kā,nōn\\ *n* -s *often cap* [MGk *nomokanōn*, fr. *nomo-* + LGk *kanōn* canon, rule, fr. Gk, measuring rod, rule, standard — more at CANON] : a collection of the ecclesiastical laws of the ancient Eastern Orthodox Church and the Byzantine imperial laws that pertained to the administration of the church

**no·moc·ra·cy** \\nō'mākrəsē\\ *n* -ES [*nomo-* + *-cracy*] : government in accordance with a system of law

**no·mo·genesis** \\¦nōmə+\\ *n* [NL, fr. *nomo-* (fr. Gk) + L *genesis*] : a theory of evolution that regards evolutionary change as due to inherent orderly processes fundamental to organic nature and independent of environmental influences

**nom·o·gram** \\'nāmə,gram, 'nōm-\\ *or* **nom·o·graph** \\-raf\\ *n* [ISV *nomo-* + *-gram* or *-graph*] : a graphic representation of numerical relations by any of various systems; *specif* : a graph that enables one by the aid of a straightedge to read off the value of a dependent variable when the value of two or more independent variables are given ⟨if the viscosity of a slag is known at one temperature, the entire viscosity-temperature relationship for the liquid slag can be ascertained from the ~ . . . which readily gives the viscosity of a liquid slag at any desired temperature if the viscosity is known at a particular temperature —*Kent's Mech. Engineers' Handbook*⟩

**no·mog·ra·pher** \\nō'mägrəfə(r)\\ *n* -s [Gk *nomographos* one who drafts laws (fr. *nomo-* + *-graphos* -grapher) + E *-er*] : a writer or maker of laws : one who is expert in nomography

**nom·o·graph·ic** \\¦nāmə¦grafik, ¦nōm-\\ *adj* **1** : of or relating to nomography **2** : of, being, or relating to a nomogram ⟨~ chart⟩ — **nom·o·graph·i·cal·ly** \\-fə̇k(ə)lē\\ *adv*

**no·mog·ra·phy** \\nō'mägrəfē\\ *n* -ES [Gk *nomographia*, fr. *nomo-* + *-graphia* -graphy] **1** : the art of or a treatise on drafting laws **2** : the theory, making, and use of nomograms

**nom·o·log·i·cal** \\¦nāmə¦läjə̇kəl, ¦nōm-\\ *adj* **1** : of or relating to nomology **2** : of, relating to, or in accordance with laws : LAWLIKE ⟨~ statements⟩

**no·mol·o·gy** \\nō'mäləjē\\ *n* -ES [*nomo-* + *-logy*] : the science of the laws of the mind

**nom·o·pel·mous** \\¦nāmə¦pelməs, ¦nōm-\\ *adj* [*nomo-* + *-pelmous*] : having a separate and simple tendon to flex the hallux ⟨~ birds⟩

1**no more** *n* [ME *nomare*, *nomore*, *namare*, *namore*, fr. OE *nā māre*, fr. *nā* no + *māre* more — more at NO, MORE] : nothing more : nothing further ⟨it is a fantasy and *no more* —D.W. Brogan⟩ ⟨will hear *no more* of this nonsense⟩

2**no more** *adv* [ME *namare*, *namore* (adv. & n.)] **1 a** : no longer ⟨those stately homes stand *no more*⟩ **b** : no longer in existence : DEAD, DEPARTED ⟨the glory of his house is *no more*⟩ ⟨the great leader is *no more*⟩ **2** : to no greater extent : in no greater degree ⟨can *no more* attempt to do intricate law-business than to play the piano —W.M.Thackeray⟩ **3** : NEVERMORE ⟨these fields and hills shall see thee *no more*⟩ **4** : NEITHER ⟨he won't hear of it. *No more* will I —W.C.Williams⟩ ⟨*no more* you'll have to, if you don't want —William Faulkner⟩

3**no more** *adj* [ME *namore*, *nomore* (adj. & n.)] : not any more ⟨there's *no more* milk or bread in the house⟩

**no·mos** \\'nō,mäs\\ *n, pl* **no·moi** \\-mȯi\\ [Gk — more at NIMBLE] : LAW ⟨natural slavery and slavery according to ~ — C.J.O'Neil⟩

**nom·o·thet·ic** \\¦nāmə¦thed·ik\\ *adj* [Gk *nomothetikos* of or relating to legislation, legislative, fr. *nomothetēs* lawgiver (fr. *nomo-* + *-thetēs* one who establishes, fr. *tithenai* to establish, place, set) + *-ikos* -ic — more at DO] : relating to, involving, or dealing with the abstract, recurrent, universal : formulating general statements or scientific laws — contrasted with *idiographic*

**noms de guerre** *pl of* NOM DE GUERRE

**noms de plume** *pl of* NOM DE PLUME

**-no·my** \\nəmē, -mi\\ *n comb form* -ES [ME *-nomie*, fr. OF, fr. L *-nomia*, fr. Gk, fr. *-nomos* distributing, arranging + *-ia* -y; akin to Gk *nemein* to distribute, manage — more at NIMBLE] : system of laws governing or sum of knowledge regarding a (specified) field ⟨astro*nomy*⟩ ⟨agro*nomy*⟩

1**non-** \\(¦)nän *sometimes* ¦nən\\ *prefix* [ME, fr. MF, fr. L *non* not, fr. OL *noenum*, fr. *ne-* not + *oinom*, neut. of *oinos* one — more at NO, ONE] : not : reverse of : absence of ⟨*non*academic⟩ ⟨*non*conformity⟩ ⟨*non*breakable⟩ ⟨*non*productive⟩ ⟨*non*intervention⟩ ⟨*non*-Arabic⟩ ⟨*non*-Mormon⟩

2**non-** *or* **nona-** *comb form* [L *non-*, fr. *nonus* ninth — more at NOON] : ninth : nine ⟨*non*agon⟩ ⟨*non*ane⟩

**non·ability** \\¦= *at* NON- +\\ *n* **1** : lack of ability or capacity; *specif* : lack of legal capacity (as in bringing suit) **2** : a plea or exception raising a lack of legal capacity

**non·abrasive** \\"+\\ *adj* : not abrasive

**non·absorbable** \\"+\\ *adj* : not capable of being absorbed ⟨~ silk sutures⟩

**non·academic** \\(¦)=+\\ *adj* : not academic: as **a** : other than academic : TECHNICAL, PROFESSIONAL, PRACTICAL ⟨children in need of ~ training⟩ **b** (1) : not conforming to the rules of a literary or artistic school (as one characterized by conservatism or strict adherence to tradition) (2) *of art* : NONREPRESENTATIONAL **c** : not connected with or foreign to academic life, atmosphere, or activity ⟨prefers to move in ~ circles⟩ ⟨the ~ world of competitive industry⟩

**non·acceptance** \\¦=+\\ *n* : failure or refusal to accept

**non·access** \\(')= *at* NON- +\\ *n* : the nonexistence of opportunity for sexual intercourse esp. between husband and wife or the absence of such intercourse

**non·achromatic** \\(¦)=+\\ *adj* [1*non-* + *achromatic*] : CHROMATIC

**non·acid** \\(')=+\\ *adj* : not acid : destitute of acid properties ⟨a ~ radical⟩

**non·a·co·sane** \\,nänə'kō,sān\\ *n* -s [ISV *nonacos-* (fr. 2*non-* + *-cos-* — fr. *eicosa-*) + *-ane*] : a paraffin hydrocarbon $C_{29}H_{60}$; *esp* : the crystalline normal hydrocarbon $CH_3(CH_2)_{27}CH_3$

**non·activistic** \\(¦) *at* NON- + \\ *adj* : not activist

**non·adaptive** \\¦= *at* NON-+\\ *adj* : not serving to adapt the individual to his environment ⟨~ traits⟩

**non·a·dec·ane** \\,nänə'de,kān\\ *n* -s [ISV *nonadec-* (fr. 2*non-* + *deca-*) + *-ane*] : a paraffin hydrocarbon $C_{19}H_{40}$; *esp* : the crystalline normal hydrocarbon $CH_3(CH_2)_{17}CH_3$

**non·adherence** \\¦= *at* NON-+\\ *n* : a lack of adherence

**non·adhesive** \\"+\\ *adj* : not adhesive

**non·adjacent** \\"+\\ *adj* : not adjacent

**non·adjustable** \\"+\\ *adj* : not adjustable

**non·adjustive** \\"+\\ *adj* [1*non-* + *adjustive*] : tending to produce maladjustment ⟨~ behavior⟩

**nonadministrative** \\"+\\ *adj* : not administrative

**non·admitted asset** \\"+-\\ *n* : an asset of an insurer not permitted by state regulations to be reckoned in determining the financial condition of an insurance company (as past-due accounts, furniture, and fixtures) — compare ADMITTED ASSET

**non·aesthetic** \\"+\\ *adj* : not aesthetic

1**non·age** \\'nänij, 'nōn-, *sometimes* 'nən- *or* -nēj\\ *n* [ME, fr. MF, fr. *non-* 1non- + *age*, fr. OF *aage*, *eage* — more at AGE] **1** : the condition of being under 21 and consequently not of age to manage one's property and affairs : the condition of not being of the required legal age to enter into some particular transaction (as marriage) — compare FULL AGE, MINOR 2 **2 a** : a period of youth, childhood, or infancy ⟨the brook we leaped so nimbly in our ~ —R.S.Hillyer⟩ ⟨these slight novels of his ~ —*Time*⟩ **b** : IMMATURITY ⟨bored with the ~ of her contemporaries —*Newsweek*⟩

2**no·nage** \\'nōnij, 'nän-, -nēj\\ *n* -s [ML *nonagium*, fr. L *nonus* ninth + ML *-agium* -age (fr. OF *-age*)] : the ninth part of movable goods of a decedent sometimes payable to the clergy

**nonaged** *adj* [1*nonage* + *-ed*] *obs* : belonging to the period of nonage : YOUTHFUL, MINOR

1**nona·ge·nar·i·an** \\,nänəjə'nerēən, ,nōn-, -na(a)r-, -nār-\\ *n* -s [L *nonagenarius* containing or consisting of ninety (fr. *nonageni* ninety each — fr. *nonaginta* ninety — + *-arius* -ary) + E *-an*, n. suffix] : a person who is 90 or more and less than 100 years old

2**nonagenarian** \\¦===¦===\\ *adj* : 90 or more and less than 100 years old

**nona·ges·i·mal** \\¦==¦jesəməl\\ *adj* [L *nonagesimus* ninetieth (fr. *nonaginta* ninety, fr. *nona-* — akin to L *novem* nine — + *-ginta* — akin to L *-ginti* in *viginti* twenty) + E *-al* — more at NINE, VICENARY] : NINETIETH

**non·aggression** \\¦= *at* NON-+\\ *n* : forbearance or refrainment from aggression ⟨proposed an all-European ~ treaty —*N. Y. Times*⟩ ⟨~ and arbitration of all disputes —*Rev. of Reviews*⟩

**non·a·gon** \\'nänə,gän, *sometimes* -ə̇gən\\ *n* -s [2*non-* + *-gon*] : a plane polygon of nine angles and therefore nine sides

nonagon

**non·agreement** \\¦= *at* NON-+\\ *n* : a lack of agreement

**non·agricultural** \\(¦)=+\\ *adj* : not agricultural: as **a** : being other than agricultural : not being a product of agriculture **b** : not devoted to or engaged in agriculture ⟨the primitive ~ people of Cuba —*Amer. Antiquity*⟩

**nona·hydrate** \\¦nänə+\\ *n* [2*non-* + *hydrate*] : a chemical compound with nine molecules of water

**non·alcoholic** \\(¦)= *at* NON-+\\ *adj* : not containing alcohol

**non·allelic** \\¦=+\\ *adj* [1*non-* + *allelic*] *of genes* : not behaving as alleles toward one another

**non·alphabetic** \\(¦)=+\\ *adj* : not alphabetic

**non·amino** \\¦=+, (')=+\\ *adj* [1*non-* + *amino*] : not in the form of the amino group ⟨~ nitrogen⟩

**non·analytic** \\(¦)=+\\ *adj* : not analytic

**no·nane** \\'nō,nān, 'nä,-\\ *n* -s [ISV 2*non-* + *-ane*] : any of several liquid isomeric paraffin hydrocarbons $C_9H_{20}$; *esp* : the normal hydrocarbon $CH_3(CH_2)_7CH_3$ obtained esp. from petroleum

**non·a·no·ic acid** \\¦nänə¦nōik-\\ *n* [*nonanoic* ISV *nonane* + *-oic*] : PELARGONIC ACID — used in the system of the International Union of Pure and Applied Chemistry

**no·na·nol** \\'nōnə,nȯl, 'nän-, -nōl\\ *n* -s [*nonane* + *-ol*] : any of five isomeric liquid water-insoluble alcohols $C_9H_{19}OH$ derived from normal nonane; *esp* : the fragrant primary or 1-isomer $CH_3(CH_2)_7CH_2OH$ that occurs as an ester in sweet orange oil — compare NONYL ALCOHOL

**non·antigenic** \\(¦)= *at* NON-+\\ *adj* : not antigenic

**non·apparent easement** \\¦=+-\\ *n* : an easement not involving any permanent visible sign of its existence (as an easement of a way or of drawing a net upon a shore) — distinguished from *apparent easement*

**non·appearance** \\"+\\ *n* [ME *noun apperaunce*, fr. *noun-*, *non-* 1non- + *apperaunce* appearance — more at APPEARANCE] : default of appearance (as in court) to prosecute or defend : failure to appear

**non·aquatic** \\"+\\ *adj* : not aquatic : not restricted to living in water or at the waterside

**non·aqueous** \\(')=+\\ *adj* : not aqueous : of, relating to, or having the characteristics of a liquid other than water ⟨a ~ solvent such as benzene⟩ : made from, with, or by means of a liquid other than water ⟨~ solutions⟩

**non·arcing** *or* **non·arcking** \\"+\\ *adj* [1*non-* + *arcing*, pres. part. of *arc*, v.] : not capable of readily maintaining an electric arc ⟨~ metals of the zinc group⟩

**non·aromatic** \\(¦)=+\\ *adj* : not aromatic

**non·assessable** \\¦=+\\ *adj* [1*non-* + *assessable*] : exempting the owner from further contributions to the capital or business of an issuing corporation and when fully paid for entailing no further liability on the part of the owner either to the corporation or its creditors ⟨~ stock⟩

**nonassessable mutual** *n* : a mutual company issuing policies not subject to assessment

**non as·sump·sit** \\¦nänə'səm(p)sə̇t, ¦nōn-\\ *n* [NL, he did not undertake] : a general plea or denial in an action of assumpsit

**non·athletic** \\¦= *at* NON-+\\ *adj* : not athletic

**non·attendance** \\"+\\ *n* : neglect or failure to attend ⟨school authorities complained of the child's ~⟩

**non·attributive** \\"+\\ *adj* : not attributive — **non·attributively** \\"+\\ *adv*

**non·automotive** \\(¦)=+\\ *adj* : not automotive

**non·bank** \\(')=+\\ *adj* [1*non-* + *bank*, n.] : being or done by someone other than a bank : not being or done by a bank ⟨~ borrowing⟩ ⟨~ lenders⟩ ⟨~ investors⟩

**non·bearing partition** \\"+-\\ *or* **nonbearing wall** *n* [*nonbearing* fr. 1*non-* + *bearing*, pres. part. of *bear*, v.] : a dividing wall that supports no vertical weight other than its own weight

**non·being** \\"+\\ *n* : absence or lack of being : NONEXISTENCE, VOID

**non·believer** \\¦= *at* NON-+\\ *n* **1** : a person who does not believe or have faith in something ⟨a ~ in ghosts⟩ **2** : a person without religious beliefs : ATHEIST

**non·belligerency** \\"+\\ *n* [1*non-* + *belligerency*] **1** : the status of not being at war : the status of not being a belligerent **2** : the status or attitude of a country that refrains from direct participation in a war but openly favors and usu. gives unneutral aid in varying degree and kind to one of the belligerents ⟨after the fall of France the United States shifted to ~ and intervention —A.P.Whitaker⟩

1**non·belligerent** \\"+\\ *adj* [1*non-* + *belligerent*, adj.] : being a nonbelligerent

2**nonbelligerent** \\"\\ *n* : a country whose status or attitude is one of nonbelligerency

**non·beverage** \\(')= *at* NON-+\\ *adj* [1*non-* + *beverage*] : not used as a beverage : not suitable for use as a beverage ⟨~ products⟩

**non·biting** \\"+\\ *adj* : not given to or characterized by biting

**non·board** \\"+\\ *adj* [1*non-* + *board*, n.] : not being a member of a rate-making association or bureau ⟨a ~ insurance firm⟩

**non·book** \\"+\\ *adj* [1*non-* + *book*, n.] : being something other than a book : being a manuscript, microfilm, map, or other library holding that is not a book ⟨housing and arrangement of ~ materials —W.H.Jesse⟩

**non·brachiating** \\"+\\ *adj* : not brachiating

**non·breeding** \\"+\\ *adj* : not breeding ⟨~ mice⟩ : gone beyond the time for breeding

**non·broody** \\"+\\ *adj* : not broody ⟨~ hens⟩

**non·business** \\"+\\ *adj* : not related to business

**non·calcarea** \\¦=+\\ *n pl, cap* [NL, fr. 1*non-* + *Calcarea*] *in some classifications* : a class of Porifera including all sponges not placed in Calcarea

**non·calcareous** \\"+\\ *adj* : not calcareous

**non·callable** \\(')=+\\ *adj* : not capable of or susceptible to being called

**non·cancelable** \\"+\\ *adj* [1*non-* + *cancelable*] : guaranteed renewable from year to year ⟨a ~ accident policy⟩

**non·canonical** \\¦=+\\ *adj* : not forming part of or being a canon ⟨~ writings⟩

**non·carbohydrate** \\(¦)=+\\ *n* : a substance that is not a carbohydrate; *esp* : one (as an aglycon) combined with a carbohydrate (as a sugar) — compare GLYCOSIDE

**non·carnivorous** \\¦=+\\ *adj* : not carnivorous

**noncarrying** \\(')=+\\ *adj* [1*non-* + *carrying*, pres. part. of *carry*, v.] : keeping within the range 0 to 9 by adding or dropping tens ⟨in ~ addition and subtraction 3+9=2 and 3−9=4⟩ — see 2ADDITIVE 3

**non·cash** \\"+\\ *adj* [1*non-* + *cash*, n.] : other than cash ⟨~ income⟩

**non·caste** \\"+\\ *adj* [1*non-* + *caste*] : being of no caste or rank

1**nonce** \\'nän(t)s, *sometimes* 'nən-\\ *n* -s [ME *nones*, fr. *nanes*, alter. (resulting from incorrect division of *then anes* in such phrases as *to then anes* for the one purpose, fr. *to* + *then* — dat. sing. neut. of *the*, def. art. — + *anes* one purpose) of *anes* one purpose, alter. (prob. influenced by *anes* once) of *ane*, dat. sing. neut. of *an* one, fr. OE *ān* — more at ONE, ONCE] : the one, particular, or present occasion, purpose, or use — **for the nonce** *adv* **1** *dial chiefly Eng* : for the particular or express purpose ⟨had an anger fit *for the nonce* —*Ballad Book*⟩ **2 a** *archaic* : for the one, single, or particular occasion **b** : for the time being ⟨we had changed characters *for the nonce* — W.H.Hudson †1922⟩ ⟨*for the nonce*, conditions were reasonably normal —P.G.Wodehouse⟩

2**nonce** \\"\\ *adj* : occurring, used, or made only once or for a special occasion ⟨the words which he cites . . . represent mainly ~ loans —C.E.Reed⟩ ⟨even factitious and ~ names have been listed —F.G.Cassidy⟩ ⟨chose one of four societies as a ~ police —*Jour. of the Royal Anthrop. Inst. of G. Brit. & Ire.*⟩ ⟨~ uses⟩

**non·cellular** \\(')= *at* NON- +\\ *adj* : not made up of or divided into cells : ACELLULAR

**non·centric** \\"+\\ *adj* : not centric

**nonce word** *n* : a word (as *ringday* in "four girls I know have become engaged today: this must be ringday") coined and used apparently to suit one particular occasion sometimes independently by different writers or speakers but not adopted into use generally ⟨Coleridge coined *mammonolatry* in 1820 as a *nonce word*⟩ ⟨I still think I heard it, though so seldom that it had more or less the air of a *nonce word* —S.T.Byington⟩

**non·cha·lance** \\¦nänshə¦län(t)s, -ȧn(t)s; '==,lən(t)s\\ *n* -s [F, fr. OF, fr. *nonchalant* (pres. part. of *nonchaloir* to disregard, make light of), after such pairs as OF *abundant: abundance*] : an attitude marked by or reflecting lack of concern, anxiety, or excitement esp. under circumstances that might be expected to provoke such feelings : a display or air of jaunty unconcern or indifference : IMPERTURBABILITY, POISE, SANGFROID ⟨just takes a little practice, ~, and stability —T.H.Fielding⟩ ⟨the ~ of boys who are sure of a dinner —R.W.Emerson⟩

**non·cha·lant** \\-nt\\ *adj* [F, fr. OF, fr. pres. part. of *nonchaloir* to disregard, make light of, fr. *non-* 1non- + *chaloir* to be of interest to, concern, fr. L *calēre* to be warm — more at LEE] : marked by or reflecting an attitude of nonchalance : having a manner or air of jaunty unconcern or indifference : UNRUFFLED, IMPERTURBABLE ⟨a hastily assumed air of ~ confidence —J.B.Priestley⟩ ⟨drove the car with ~ abandon⟩ ⟨~ amid the booming of guns and the rattle of machine-gun fire⟩ **syn** see COOL

**non·cha·lant·ly** *adv* : in a nonchalant manner

**non·cha·lant·ness** *n* -ES : the quality or state of being nonchalant

**non·charitable** \\(')= *at* NON- +\\ *adj* : not charitable

**non·chemical** \\"+\\ *adj* : not chemical

**non·chitinous** \\"+\\ *adj* : not chitinous

**non·circular** \\"+\\ *adj* : not circular : ECCENTRIC

**non·citizen** \\"+\\ *n* : a person who is not a citizen; *esp* : a person residing in the U.S. but not a citizen thereof ⟨the legal right to employ a ~ —*Veteran's Guide*⟩

**non·claim** \\"+\\ *n* [ME *noun cleime*, fr. *noun-*, *non-* 1non- + *cleime*, *claim*, *claime* claim] : neglect or failure to make a demand within the time limited by law

**non·classical** \\"+\\ *adj* : not classical

**non·clerical** \\"+\\ *adj* : not clerical ⟨a ~ democracy⟩

**non·climax** \\"+\\ *adj* [1*non-* + *climax*, n.] : not having a climax : not being in a climactic environment

**non·clotting** \\"+\\ *adj* : not clotting

**non·cognitive** \\"+\\ *adj* [1*non-* + *cognitive*] : not based on or incapable of being reduced to empirical factual knowledge ⟨~ statements⟩

**non·cognitivism** \\"+\\ *n* [*noncognitive* + *-ism*] : a theory holding that ethical statements cannot be reduced without remainder to empirical cognitive statements by reason of the emotive or imperative elements in their content; *specif* : EMOTIVISM

**non·cognitivist** \\"+\\ *n* [*noncognitive* + *-ist*] : an advocate of noncognitivism in ethics

**non·collectible** \\¦=+\\ *adj* : not collectible

**non·colloid** \\(')=+\\ *n* [1*non-* + *colloid*, n.] : CRYSTALLOID

**non·com** \\(')= *at* NON- + ¦käm\\ *n* -s *often attrib* [by shortening] : NONCOMMISSIONED OFFICER ⟨most of the ~*s* were killed and wounded —Marjory S. Douglas⟩ ⟨with the ~ marks still on him —William Chamberlain⟩

**non·combat** \\(')=+\\ *adj* [1*non-* + *combat*, n.] : not involving combat ⟨~ service⟩ : not combatant

1**non·combatant** \\¦=+, (')=+\\ *n* [1*non-* + *combatant*] : a person (as a chaplain or a member of the medical services) whose military or naval duties do not include fighting; *also* : CIVILIAN

2**noncombatant** \\"\\ *adj* **1** : not usu. engaged in or assigned to combat or combat duties ⟨~ personnel⟩ **2** : not designed for or normally used in combat ⟨~ stores⟩ **3** : not constituting or directly forwarding combat ⟨~ operations⟩

1**non·combustible** \\¦=+\\ *adj* : not combustible : incapable of catching fire and burning when subjected to fire ⟨asbestos and carbon dioxide are ~⟩ — compare INCOMBUSTIBLE

2**noncombustible** \\"\\ *n* : a noncombustible substance

**non·commensurable** \"+\ *adj* : not commensurable : INCOMMENSURABLE

**non·commercial** \"+\ *adj* : not commercial: as **a** : not used in commerce : having no commercial importance ⟨a ~ species of fish —H.P.Clemens⟩ **b** : not commercially motivated ⟨their friendly ~ attitude —*Atlantic*⟩ ⟨the ~ theater⟩

**non·commissioned** \"+\ *adj* : not having a commission

**noncommissioned officer** *n* : a subordinate officer in a branch of the armed services appointed usu. on the basis of examination from enlisted personnel and holding one of various grades (as corporal, sergeant, petty officer)

¹**non·committal** \"+\ *n* [¹*non-* + *committal*] : the state of being noncommittal to a particular position or point of view : refusal to commit oneself

²**noncommittal** \"\ *adj* **1** : taking no clear position or giving no clear indication of attitude, feeling, or point of view : RESERVED ⟨finally consent to sign the brief and ~ communiqué —A.L.Funk⟩ ⟨soft-spoken in a ~ sort of way —L.C.Stevens⟩ ⟨her tone was friendly but ~ —Helen Howe⟩ ⟨did not greet him with flowery excitement but with a ~ "hello" —Sinclair Lewis⟩ ⟨elicited a ~ grunt —C.G.D.Roberts⟩ **2** : having no clear, sharply defined, or distinctive character, meaning, or significance ⟨a ~ word that might be used of anything from babies to furnaces —J.C.Swaim⟩ ⟨pitched in the null, ~ surroundings of a rehearsal room —Osbert Sitwell⟩ ⟨the exterior of the house was equally ~ —Jean Stafford⟩ — **non·com·mit·tal·ly** \-ᵊlē, -i\ *adv*

**non·com·mit·tal·ism** \-ᵊl,izəm\ *n* -s : a noncommittal position or policy

**non·communicable** \¦= at NON-+\ *adj* : not capable of being communicated; *specif* : not transmissible by direct contact ⟨a ~ disease⟩

**non·communicant** \"+\ *n* : a person who is not a communicant : one who does not receive Communion; *specif* : one who does not attend church

**non·communion** \"+\ *n* : neglect or refusal to receive Communion

**non·communist** \(ˈ)= at NON-+\ *adj* **1** : not communist : being other than communist ⟨~ labor leaders⟩ **2** *usu* **non-communist** *usu cap C* : affirming or certifying to nonmembership in the Communist party ⟨*non-Communist* oaths⟩

**non·comoquer** \(¦)=+\ *n* [MexSp, fr. Sp *non-* ¹non- + MexSp *comoquer*] : an ace or king that can be combined in panguingue and other Mexican forms of rummy with other cards of the same rank (as the ace of spades and two aces of hearts) — compare COMOQUER

**non·compearance** \¦=+\ *n, Scots law* : default in appearing in court

**non·competent** \(ˈ)=+\ *adj* : not competent; *specif* : not legally qualified or capable ⟨declared ~ by the government —F.B.Gipson⟩

**non·competing** \¦=+\ *adj* : not competing

**non·competitive** \"+\ *adj* : not competitive: as **a** : not subject to competition : not filled by competitive examinations ⟨~ positions⟩ **b** : lacking competitive spirit or not motivated by a spirit of competition ⟨stimulate ~ interest in games —*Atlantic*⟩

**non·complementary** \(¦)=+\ *adj* : not complementary

**non·compliance** \¦=+\ *n* : failure or refusal to comply

**non·com·pos** \(ˈ)nän¦kämpəs\ *n, pl* **noncompos·es** *or* **non·compos·ses** \-səz\ [L *non compos* (in the phrase *non compos mentis*)] : a person who is non compos mentis

**non compos** \"\ *adj* [L *non compos* (in the phrase *non compos mentis*)] : non compos mentis ⟨they'll say you're *non compos* —Kenneth Roberts⟩

**non compos men·tis** \-pəˈsmentəs\ *adj* [L, lit., not having mastery of one's mind] : not of sound mind : wholly lacking mental capacity to understand the nature, consequences, and effect of a situation or transaction

**non·compound** \(ˈ)= at NON-+\ *adj* : not compound

**non·compounder** \¦=+\ *n* : **1** one that does not compound **2** *usu cap* : one of the Jacobites who desired the unconditional restoration of James II of England after his abdication

**noncon** *abbr* nonconformist

**non·concentric** \¦= at NON- +\ *adj* : not concentric

**non·concur** \¦= at NON-+\ *vb* [¹*non-* + *concur*] *vt, archaic* : to refuse to concur in : dissent from ~ *vi* : to refuse to concur ⟨moved to ~ with the lower board —*Springfield (Mass.) Union*⟩ ⟨*nonconcurred* in the Senate's adjournment resolution —H.W.Sparrow⟩

**non·concurrence** \"+\ *n* [¹*non-* + *concurrence*] : the act or an instance of nonconcurring

**non·concurrency** \"+\ *n* [¹*non-* + *concurrency*] : the state of being nonconcurrent

**non·concurrent** \"+\ *adj* [¹*non-* + *concurrent*] : having unlike provisions or application to a loss ⟨a ~ insurance policy⟩

**non·condensing engine** \"+-\ *or* **noncondensing turbine** *n* : a steam engine or turbine not provided with a condenser

**non·conducting** \"+\ *adj* : not conducting ⟨~ material⟩

**non·conductor** \"+\ *n* [¹*non-* + *conductor*] : a substance that conducts heat, electricity, or sound only in very small degree

**non·confidence** \(ˈ)=+\ *n* : lack of confidence; *esp* : lack of confidence in a government by a parliamentary body ⟨the cabinet fell as a result of a formal vote of ~⟩

¹**nonconform** *adj* [¹*non-* + *conform*, adj.] *obs* : NONCONFORMING

²**non·conform** \¦= at NON-+\ *vi* [¹*non-* + *conform*, v.] : to fail to conform

**nonconformable** *adj* [¹*non-* + *conformable*] *obs* : NONCONFORMING — **non·conformably** \"+\ *adv*

**non·conformance** \"+\ *n* [¹*non-* + *conformance*] : failure to conform ⟨~ to the established traditions —Bernard Taper⟩

**non·conformer** \"+\ *n* [¹*non-* + *conformer*] : one that does not conform ⟨a natural-born ~ —*Newsweek*⟩

**non·conforming** \"+\ *adj* [¹*non-* + *conforming*, pres. part. of *conform*] : not conforming : declining conformity ⟨pressures on ~ individuals —*New Yorker*⟩; *esp* : not conforming to the established church ⟨~ ministers⟩ ⟨~ sects⟩

**non·conformism** \"+\ *n* [*nonconformist* + *-ism*] : the principles or practices of nonconformity ⟨their individualism . . . constantly drives them to ~ —Janet Flanner⟩ ⟨their vociferous ~ —Norman Lewis⟩ ⟨deeply averse to excitement and ~ —Robert Pick⟩

¹**non·conformist** \"+\ *n* [¹*non-* + *conform*, v. + *-ist*] **1 a** : a person who does not conform to an established church or its doctrine, discipline, or polity ⟨Lutheran churchmen and Swedish ~*s* cooperate —N.G.Sahlin⟩ **b** *often cap* (1) : one of the clergymen numbering about 2000 who left the Church of England in 1662 rather than submit to the Act of Uniformity (2) : a member of a religious body separated from the Church of England : DISSENTER ⟨a desire to bring *Nonconformists* within the established church —*Brit. Book News*⟩ **2 a** : a person who fails or refuses to conform to some norm : one who deviates from a generally accepted or socially approved way or pattern of thought or behavior ⟨the Bureau of Naval Personnel soon returned these ~*s* to a civilian status —A.A.Ageton⟩ **b** : a person who dissents on principled grounds from an established or conventional creed, rule, or practice : one who displays a courageous independence of thought in refusing to conform blindly or timidly to a prevailing dogma or orthodoxy ⟨whoso would be a man must be a ~ —R.W.Emerson⟩ ⟨those who have done most for the world . . . have been the dissenters and ~*s* —R.J.McCracken⟩ **3** : a natural object that does not conform or behave according to rule or in a manner typical of its kind ⟨gallium is a ~ among metals —L.J.Briggs⟩ ⟨type of variable star had been recognized as a ~ since 1946 —J.M.Chamberlain⟩

²**nonconformist** \"\ *adj* **1 a** : nonconforming to an established church **b** *often cap* : relating to a member of or being a religious body separated from the Church of England ⟨~ ministers gathered⟩ ⟨a poor, *Nonconformist* family —*Time*⟩ **2** : nonconforming to some norm or socially approved pattern of thought or behavior or to an established creed, rule, or practice ⟨whose rabidly ~ deportment has made them legendary figures —*New Yorker*⟩ ⟨also ~, also biased by abnormality —Edmund Wilson⟩ ⟨the old, stubborn, ~ spirit of the earliest settlers —R.M.Coates⟩

**non·conformity** \¦= at NON-+\ *n* [¹*non-* + *conformity*] **1 a** (1) : failure or refusal to conform to an established church : the principles or practices of religious nonconformists ⟨the early church was hostile to all ~⟩ (2) *often cap* : neglect or refusal esp. by Protestant dissenters to conform to the Church of England or its doctrine, discipline, or polity : the movement, doctrines, or principles of English Protestant dissent ⟨*Nonconformity* reached its height of political power . . . round the beginning of the century —D.W.Brogan⟩ (3) *often cap* : the body of English nonconformists ⟨efforts on behalf of persecuted *Nonconformity* —Douglas Bush⟩ ⟨made many friends in the circles of prosperous ~ —John Buchan⟩ **b** : refusal to conform to an established or conventional creed, rule, or practice ⟨totalitarian orthodoxy hates defiant ~ —A.E.Stevenson †1965⟩ ⟨the world . . . with its tenor of ~ —Mary Webb⟩ **2** : absence of agreement or correspondence ⟨the striking ~ of his ideas and his practice⟩ **3** : a surface of contact between sedimentary rocks and underlying eroded igneous or metamorphic rocks upon which they were deposited : a depositional contact; *also* : an unconformity occurring between two nonparallel sequences of strata

**non·conscious** \(ˈ)=+\ *adj* : not conscious ⟨~ psychic processes —A.A.Brill⟩

**non·consumable** \¦=+\ *adj* : not consumable

**non·contagious** \"+\ *adj* : not contagious ⟨a ~ disease⟩

**non·content** \"+\ *n* [¹*non-* + *content*, n.] : a member of the British House of Lords who gives a negative vote

**non·contentious** \"+\ *adj* : not contentious

**non·continuous** \"+\ *adj* : not continuous : DISCONTINUOUS

**noncontinuous easement** *n* : DISCONTINUOUS EASEMENT

**non·contraband** \(ˈ)=+\ *adj* : not being contraband

**non·contractile** \¦=+\ *adj* : not contractile

**non·contradiction** \(¦)=+\ *n* : absence of logical contradiction

**non·contradictory** \"+\ *adj* : not contradictory

**non·contributory** \¦=+\ *adj* : making or involving no contribution: as **a** : involving, related to, or constituting a pension plan whereby the employer pays the total cost **b** : making no contribution to a medical diagnosis ⟨the past history was ~ —*Seminar*⟩

**non·convulsive** \"+\ *adj* : not convulsive

**non·cooperation** \"+\ *n* : failure or refusal to cooperate; *specif* : refusal through civil disobedience (as by nonpayment of taxes or by boycott of courts, legislative councils, schools) of a people to cooperate with the government of a country — used esp. of the policy of Gandhi and his followers in India — **non·cooperationist** \"+\ *n*

**non·cooperative** \"+\ *adj* : of, relating to, or characterized by noncooperation

**non·cooperator** \"+\ *n* : one who practices noncooperation

**non·corroding** \" +\ *adj* : not corrodible

**non·crystalline** \(ˈ)=+\ *adj* : not crystalline

**noncum** *abbr* noncumulative

**non·cumulative** \(ˈ)= at NON-+\ *adj* [¹*non-* + *cumulative*] : not entitled to future payments of dividends or interest passed when normally due ⟨~ stock⟩ ⟨~ income bonds⟩

**non·current** \"+\ *adj* : not current

**non·cyclic** *or* **non·cyclical** \"+\ *adj* : not cyclic

**non·da** \ˈnändə\ *also* **nonda plum** *n* -s [*nonda* native name in southeast Queensland, Australia] **1** : an edible fruit of an Australian tree that resembles a plum **2** : the tree (*Parinarium nonda*) that bears nondas

**non·deciduata** \¦nän+\ *n pl, cap* [NL, fr. ¹*non-* + *Deciduata*] : mammals having a nondeciduate placenta — used as if it were a taxon

**non·deciduate** \¦= at NON-+\ *adj* [¹*non-* + *deciduate*] *of a placenta* : having the fetal and maternal tissues but superficially associated so that no maternal tissue is lost at parturition (as in ungulates and whales)

**non·deductibility** \"+\ *n* [¹*non-* + *deductibility*] : the condition of being nondeductible

**non·deductible** \"+\ *adj* [¹*non-* + *deductible*] : not deductible; *esp* : not deductible for income tax purposes ⟨~ losses⟩

**non·delegable** \(ˈ)=+\ *adj* : not capable of being delegated

**non·delinquent** \¦= +\ *n* : one that is not a delinquent

**non·delivery** \¦=+\ *n* : neglect or failure to deliver

**non·democratic** \(¦)=+\ *adj* : not democratic : not believing in or practicing democratic ideals and principles

**non·denominational** \¦=+\ *adj* : not restricted to a denomination ⟨a ~ church⟩

**non·denominationalism** \"+\ *n* : the principle of being nondenominational or of not emphasizing denominationalism

**nondeposition** \"+\ *n* : no deposition

¹**non·de·script** \¦nändə¦skript\ *adj* [¹*non-* + L *descriptus*, past part. of *describere* to describe — more at DESCRIBE] **1** *archaic* : not hitherto described **2** : lacking distinguishing characteristics or a distinctive character : belonging or appearing to belong to no particular class or kind : not easily described : UNCLASSIFIABLE, INDETERMINATE, INDESCRIBABLE ⟨clad in ~ gray clothes and battered black hat —Rex Ingamells⟩ ⟨a section of ~ row houses —*Amer. Guide Series: Va.*⟩ ⟨a ~ mixture of styles in the worst possible taste —G.B.Shaw⟩

²**nondescript** \"\ *n* -s **1** *archaic* : something (as a species of plant or mineral) not hitherto described **2** : someone or something lacking distinguishing characteristics or a distinctive character : an individual not easily classified or of no particular class or kind ⟨the famous turquoise eyes had washed out to a milky ~ —Budd Schulberg⟩ ⟨a wizened old ~ —Norman Douglas⟩ ⟨the rush of prospectors, middlemen, gamblers, outlaws, and ~*s* —*Amer. Guide Series: Nev.*⟩ ⟨ranging from the landlord to the lowest stable ~ —Charles Dickens⟩ ⟨cattle in the region, 80 percent of which were crossbred ~*s* —*Farmer's Weekly (So. Africa)*⟩ **3** : the bottom or near the bottom grade of marketable tobacco

**non·deteriorative** \¦= at NON- +\ *adj* : not deteriorative

**non de·ti·net** \(ˈ)nän¦detᵊn,et\ *n, pl* **non detinets** [L, he does not detain] : the general issue in an action of detinue putting in issue only the question of detainer

**non·detonating** \(ˈ)= at NON- +\ *adj* : not detonating : reacting by deflagration

**non·development** \¦=+\ *n* : a failure or lack of development

**non·diffusible** \"+\ *adj* : not diffusible

**non·diffusing** \"+\ *adj* : not diffusing

**non·digestible** \"+\ *adj* : not digestible

**non·directional** \"+\ *adj* : not directional : OMNIDIRECTIONAL ⟨a ~ beacon⟩

**non·directive** \"+\ *adj* [¹*non-* + *directive*] **1** : of or relating to psychotherapy or counseling in which the counselor refrains from interpretive or associative comment but usu. by repeating phrases used by the client encourages him to express, clarify, and restructure his problems — contrasted with *directive* **2** : of or relating to interviewing (as by an anthropologist of a native informant) which avoids direct questioning and prompts the person being interviewed to talk freely, informally, or spontaneously ⟨prolonged . . . ~ interviews —B.J.Siegel⟩

**non·disclosure** \"+\ *n* : a failure to reveal facts bearing upon a transaction

**non·disjunction** \"+\ *n* [ISV ¹*non-* + *disjunction*] *n* : the failure of two homologous chromosomes to separate during reduction division — **non·disjunctional** \"+\ *adj*

**non·distinctive** \"+\ *adj* [¹*non-* + *distinctive*] *of a speech sound* : having no signaling value : NONFUNCTIONAL

**non·distribution** \(¦)=+\ *n* : a lack or absence of distribution

**non·divided** \¦=+\ *adj* : not divided

**non·do** \ˈnän(,)dō\ *n* -s [origin unknown] : a perennial herb (*Levisticum canadense*) of the eastern U.S. having an aromatic root

**non·dollar** \(ˈ)= at NON- +\ *adj* [¹*non-* + *dollar*] **1** : being an area where the U.S. dollar is not used as a basis for exchange and currencies usu. cannot be converted freely into dollars ⟨~ countries⟩ **2** : not consisting in or composed of dollars ⟨a ~ loan⟩ ⟨~ currencies⟩

**non·dormant** \"+\ *adj* [¹*non-* + *dormant*] : being in such a condition that germination is possible ⟨~ seeds⟩ or being in active vegetative growth ⟨~ plants⟩

**non·dramatic** \¦=+\ *adj* : not dramatic

**non·drying** \(ˈ)=+\ *adj* : not drying

**nondrying oil** *n* : a natural or synthetic oil (as olive oil) characterized by low unsaturation and consequent inability to solidify readily when exposed in a thin film to the air

**non·dualism** \"+\ *n* [¹*non-* + *dualism*] **1** : a doctrine of classic Brahmanism holding that the essential unity of all is real whereas duality and plurality are phenomenal illusion and that matter is materialized energy which in turn is the temporal manifestation of an incorporeal spiritual eternal essence constituting the innermost self of all things **2** : any of various monistic or pluralistic theories of the universe

**non·durables** \"+\ *or* **nondurable goods** *n pl* : consumer goods or producer goods (as textiles, food, clothing, petroleum, chemical products) that are serviceable for a comparatively short period of time or that are consumed or destroyed in a single usage

¹**none** \ˈnən\ *pron, sing or pl in constr* [ME *noon, none*, pron. & adj., fr. OE *nān*, fr. *ne* not + *ān* one — more at NO, ONE] **1 a** : not any ⟨~ of them were intellectually absorbing enough —Winthrop Sargeant⟩ ⟨~ of our scholars has written a monograph on him —Norman Douglas⟩ ⟨~ of our creeds are entirely free from guesswork —M.R.Cohen⟩ **b** : NEITHER ⟨of which ~ of the two can really be responsible —*Science & Culture*⟩ **2 a** : one that is not or lacks the requisite qualities of the thing or person mentioned ⟨how to make a brave or wise man of one that is ~⟩ **b** *archaic* : one that is not at all the thing or person mentioned — used in the phrase *none of* ⟨thou art ~ of my brother —*Ballad Book*⟩ **3** : not one : NO ONE, NOBODY ⟨~ is said to be left now —Stark Young⟩ ⟨~ is immune from the feeling and need for individuality —John Sirjamaki⟩ ⟨in the morning ~ was visible —*Time*⟩ ⟨~ were deeper in that labyrinthine ambition —G.K.Chesterton⟩ **4** : not any such thing or person ⟨half a loaf is better than ~⟩ **5** : no part : NOTHING ⟨had ~ of the condescension of the foreigner —Walter Lippmann⟩ ⟨seemed to want ~ of it —*Time*⟩ ⟨will have ~ of this theory —R.S.Bourne⟩ ⟨a sluttish sort and I want ~ of her —Marcia Davenport⟩

²**none** \"\ *adj* [ME *noon, none*, pron. & adj., fr. OE *nān*] *archaic* : not any : NO ⟨thou shalt have ~ other gods before me —Deut 5:7 (AV)⟩

³**none** \"\ *adv* [ME *noon, none* not at all, fr. *noon, none*, pron. & adj.] **1** : by no means : not at all ⟨the authenticity of many . . . is ~ too clear —A.L.Kroeber⟩ ⟨~ too prosperous, it sought to save itself —*Amer. Guide Series: Pa.*⟩ **2** : in no way : to no extent — often used in substandard speech with another negative ⟨ain't heard her ~ this morning —Burl Ives⟩

⁴**none** \ˈnōn\ *n* -s *often cap* [LL *nona*, fr. L, ninth hour of the day counting from sunrise — more at NOON] **1** : a canonical hour that according to ancient Roman and Eastern reckoning is the ninth hour **2** : a religious office formerly recited at 3 p.m. but now in the Roman Catholic Church often somewhat earlier

**non·economic** \(¦)= at NON-+\ *adj* : not economic: as **a** : being other than economic ⟨~ kinds of motivation —Harold Koontz & Cyril O'Donnell⟩ ⟨over any ~ issue such as the union shop —*U.S. Code*⟩ **b** : having no economic importance or implication ⟨a number of . . . ~ plants —*Encyc. Americana*⟩

**non·economist** \¦= +\ *n* : one that is not an economist

**non·eczematous** \¦=+\ *adj* : not eczematous

¹**non·effective** \"+\ *adj* **1** : not effective **2** : not fit or available for military or naval duty

²**noneffective** \"\ *n* : a soldier or sailor unavailable for regular duty because of unfitness (as from sickness or wounds)

**non·effervescent** \(¦)=+\ *adj* : not effervescent

**non·ego** \(ˈ)=+\ *n* [¹*non-* + *ego*; trans. of G *nicht-ich*] : the external world or object of knowledge as contrasted with the subject or ego — used esp. in the idealistic doctrines of Fichte and Schelling

**nonelastic** \¦=+\ *adj* : not elastic

**non·electrolyte** \¦=+\ *n* [¹*non-* + *electrolyte*] : a substance (as sugar or benzene) that is not appreciably ionized (as in aqueous solution) and therefore is a poor conductor of electricity : a nonpolar substance

**non·empirical** \"+\ *adj* : not empirical ⟨~ intuition⟩

**no·nene** \ˈnō,nēn, ˈnä,-\ *n* -s [ISV ²*non-* + *-ene*] : any of four liquid straight-chain hydrocarbons $C_9H_{18}$ of the ethylene series

**non·ent** \(ˈ)nä¦nent\ *n* -s [ML *nonent-, nonens*, fr. L *non* not + ML *ent-, ens* ens — more at NON-, ENS] : something that does not exist

**non·entanglement** \¦= at NON- +\ *n* : abstention from becoming entangled ⟨policy of ~ —*Amer. Scholar*⟩ or condition of not being entangled ⟨his ~ in that scandalous affair⟩

**non·entitative** \(ˈ)=+\ *or* **non·en·ti·tive** \"+¦entəd·iv\ *adj* [*nonentitative* fr. ¹*non-* + *entitative*; *nonentitive* fr. *nonentity* + *-ive*] : NONEXISTENT

**non·entity** \(ˈ)=at NON+\ *n* **1** : something that does not exist or exists only in the imagination ⟨the whole realm of *nonentities*, such as "the round square" . . . "Apollo", "Hamlet" —Herbert Feigl & W.S.Sellars⟩ ⟨in one day . . . high-heaped money-wages became fairy-money and ~ —Thomas Carlyle⟩ **2** : the quality or state of not existing : NONEXISTENCE **3 a** : a person who is totally undistinguished or unimpressive in mind, character, or achievement : one of small or mediocre talents ⟨manifested by hacks and *nonentities* put in nomination —*New Republic*⟩ ⟨there can be no leaders if all the followers are *nonentities* —W.L.Sullivan⟩ ⟨becoming a moral ~ —Lionel Trilling⟩ **b** : something of no consequence or significance : something totally lacking in distinction ⟨this building therefore sinks . . . a ~, into the dismal swamp of buildings around it —Lewis Mumford⟩ **c** : the condition of being a nonentity ⟨his shrunken figure relapsed into drab ~ —Gerald Beaumont⟩ ⟨emerging from the unfathomable abyss of ~ —H.L. Mencken⟩ ⟨after five and a half months of political ~ —*Time*⟩

**non·en·tres** *or* **non·en·tresse** \(ˈ)nä¦nen·trəs\ *n, pl* **nonentreses** *or* **nonentresses** [ME (Sc) *none entress*, fr. *none-*, *non-* ¹non- + *entress, entres* entrance, entry, fr. ME *entren* to enter + *-ess, -es, -esse* (as in *duresse* duress, restraint) — more at ENTER] *Scots feudal law* : failure of an heir to land to make an entry thereon and to obtain investiture of the feu from the superior; *also* : the feudal casualty arising from such failure

**non·entry** \(ˈ)=at NON-+\ *n* [ME (Sc) *nonentree*, fr. ME ¹*non-* + *entree, entre* entry — more at ENTRY] **1** : the fact of not entering **2** *Scots feudal law* : NONENTRES

**non·episcopal** \¦=+\ *adj* : not episcopal

**non·eruptive** \"+\ *adj* : not eruptive

**nones** \ˈnōnz\ *n pl but sing or pl in constr* [ME *nonys*, fr. L *nonae*, fr. fem. pl. of *nonus* ninth — more at NOON] **1** : the ninth day before the ides according to ancient Roman reckoning — compare CALENDS **2** *often cap* [pl. of ⁴*none*] : ⁴NONE

**none-so-pretty** \¦=(,)=¦=+\ *n, pl* **none-so-pretties** **1** : a decorative braid or tape used in the late 18th century **2 a** : LONDON PRIDE 1 **b** : LOBEL'S CATCHFLY

¹**non·essential** \¦=at NON-+\ *adj* : not essential : not of prime or central importance ⟨~ to the integral meanings of poetry —*Publ's Mod. Lang. Assoc. of Amer.*⟩ ⟨guard carefully against unnecessary uniformity in ~ matters —E.P.Cubberley⟩

²**nonessential** \"\ *n* : something that is not essential

**nonessential clause** *n* : NONRESTRICTIVE CLAUSE

**non est fac·tum** \ˈnä,nestˈfaktəm, ˈnō,-\ *n, pl* **non est factums** [NL, it was not done] : the plea of the general issue in an action of debt on bond or other specialty and on any written instrument in some states

**non est in·ven·tus** \-inˈventəs\ *n, pl* **non est inventuses** [ME, fr. ML, he has not been found] : the return of a sheriff on a writ when the defendant or person to be served or arrested is not found in his jurisdiction

¹**none·such** \ˈnən¦səch\ *or* **non·such** \"*sometimes* ˈnän-\ *n* -ES [¹*none* + *such*] **1** : a person or thing without an equal in some respect or category : one that has no match or rival : PARAGON, NONPAREIL ⟨the team's ~ . . . began throwing his famous passes —*New Yorker*⟩ ⟨only a ~ could go through a schedule like that —G.F.T.Ryall⟩ ⟨made him a ~ in New York politics —*Atlantic*⟩ **2** *also* **nonesuch clover** : BLACK MEDIC

²**nonesuch** \"\ *or* **nonsuch** \"\ *adj* : UNEQUALED, UNRIVALED, MATCHLESS ⟨a ~ hero of space opera —J.F.McComas⟩

**nonesuch chest** *var of* NONSUCH CHEST

**no·net** \nōˈnet\ *n* -s [It *nonetto*, fr. *nono* ninth (fr. L *nonus*) + *-etto* (as in *duetto* duet) — more at NOON] : a combination of nine instruments or voices; *also* : a musical composition for such a combination

**nonetheless** \¦=='=\ *adv* [fr. the phrase *none the less*] : NEVERTHELESS ⟨there is ~ that risk —Henry Wynmalen⟩ ⟨~, the presentation . . . is so reasonable one cannot resist being convinced despite the method of reasoning —A.D.Kossoff⟩

**non·ethical** \(ˈ)⸗ *at* NON- +\ *adj* **:** not ethical

**non·etymological** \(¦)⸗+\ *adj* **:** not etymological

**non-euclidean** *also* **non-euclidian** \¦⸗*at* NON-+\ *adj, often cap E* [prob. trans. of G *nichteuklidisch*] **:** not euclidean; *specif* **:** not assuming all the axioms and postulates assumed in the *Elements* of Euclid

**non·exempt** \"+\ *adj* **:** not exempt ⟨~ property⟩

**non·existence** \"+\ *n* **1 :** absence of existence **:** the negation of being **2 :** something that has no existence

**1non·existent** \"+\ *adj* **:** not having existence

**2nonexistent** \"\ *n* **:** one that does not exist

**non·expendable** \¦⸗+\ *adj* [1*non-* + *expendable*] **:** not consumed in use and not losing identity in use ⟨~ tooling such as dies, jigs, and templates —P.T.Sherwood⟩

**non·explosive** \"+\ *adj* **:** not explosive ⟨a ~ gas⟩

**non·extant** \(ˈ)⸗+, ¦⸗+\ *adj* **:** not extant; *esp* **:** no longer existing or accessible through loss or destruction ⟨its ~ original was written on vellum —G.B.Saul⟩

**non·fabricated** \(ˈ)⸗+\ *adj* **:** not fabricated

**non·farm** \(ˈ)⸗+\ *adj* [1*non-* + *farm*, n.] **:** not of or related to a farm: as **a :** not engaged in, devoted to, or derived from farming ⟨~ jobs⟩ ⟨approximately one half of the rural population . . . was classed as ~ —Alexander Heard⟩ **b :** not composed of or belonging to farm families ⟨farmers have failed to make clear beyond all doubt to ~ America —*Country Gentleman*⟩ ⟨~ homes⟩ **c :** of or relating to commodities other than agricultural ⟨~ prices⟩

**non·fat** \"+\ *adj* **:** lacking fat **:** having fat removed

**non·fea·sance** \nänˈfēzᵊn(t)s\ *n* -S [1*non-* + obs. E *feasance* performance, doing, fr. AF *fesance*, fr. MF, *faisance*, act, fr. OF, fr. *fais-* (stem of *faire* to do, fr. L *facere*) + *-ance* — more at DO] **:** omission to do esp. what ought to be done

**non·febrile** \(ˈ)⸗*at* NON-+\ *adj* **:** not febrile

**non·feeding** \"+\ *adj* **:** not feeding

**non·ferrous** \"+\ *adj* **:** not containing, including, or relating to iron ⟨~ metal⟩ **:** relating to metals other than iron

**non·fibrous** \"+\ *adj* **:** not fibrous

**non·fiction** \"+\ *n* **:** literary works other than novels or stories ⟨the best-selling ~ of that spring —*Current Biog.*⟩

**non·fictional** \"+\ *adj* **:** not fictional

**non·figurative** \"+\ *adj* **:** NONOBJECTIVE ⟨~ art⟩

**non·filamentous** \(¦)⸗+\ *adj* **1 :** not having the form of a thread **2 :** not made up of filamentous parts

**non·filterable** \(ˈ)⸗+\ *adj* **:** not filterable

**non·financial** \¦⸗+\ *adj* **:** being or relating to an enterprise or economic activity (as manufacturing, trade, or public utilities) other than financial **:** not engaged in the banking or insurance business ⟨~ corporations⟩ ⟨controlled 49 percent of all the ~ corporate wealth of the country —P.H.Douglas⟩

**non·fissionable** \(ˈ)⸗+\ *adj* **:** not fissionable

**non·flagellated** \"+\ *adj* **:** not flagellated

**non·flam** \(ˈ)⸗+¦flam\ *adj* [by shortening] **:** not flammable

**non·flammable** \"+\ *adj* [1*non-* + *flammable*] **:** not flammable **:** incapable of being easily ignited and of burning with extreme rapidity

**non·flowering** \"+\ *adj* **:** producing no flowers; *specif* **:** lacking a flowering stage in the life cycle — used esp. of liverworts, mosses, ferns, and fern allies

**non·forfeiture** \"+\ *n* **:** no forfeiture

**non·forfeiture benefit** \"+-\ *or* **nonforfeiture value** *n* **:** a benefit (as in cash or insurance) received by a policyholder who after making premium payments for at least the minimum period as provided wishes to discontinue further premium payments

**nonforfeiture law** *n* **:** a law requiring life insurance companies within certain limitations to grant surrender values on policies for which premium payments have been discontinued

**non·fossiliferous** \(¦)⸗+\ *adj* **:** not fossiliferous

**non·fraternal** \¦⸗+\ *adj* **:** not fraternal **:** not connected with a fraternal order or association

**non·freezing** \"+\ *adj* **:** not subject to freezing **:** resistant to freezing

**non·fulfillment** \¦⸗+\ *n* **:** a lack of fulfillment

**non·functional** \(ˈ)⸗+\ *adj* **:** not functional: as **a :** having no function **:** serving or performing no useful purpose ⟨there is no merit in ~ footnotes —G.W.Sherburn⟩ ⟨spending an extra hundred thousand dollars for ~ . . . decorations —Paul Woodring⟩ **b :** not performing or able to perform its regular function

**non·fundable** \"+\ *adj* **:** not capable of being funded

**non·game** \"+\ *adj* [1*non-* + *game*, n.] **:** not hunted for food, sport, or fur ⟨~ birds⟩

**non·generic** \¦⸗+\ *adj* **:** not generic

**non·genetic** \¦⸗+\ *adj* **:** not genetic

**non·genic** \(ˈ)⸗+\ *adj* **:** not genic

**non·glandular** \"+\ *adj* **:** not glandular

**non·government** \(ˈ)⸗+\ *adj* **:** not belonging to or affiliated with the government

**non·governmental** \(¦)⸗+\ *adj* **:** not governmental

**non grata** *see* PERSONA NON GRATA\ *adj* [L (in *persona non grata*)] **:** not approved **:** UNWELCOME ⟨a sign informed us that the public was *non grata* at the gathering —*New Yorker*⟩

**non·gregarious** \¦⸗*at* NON-+\ *adj* **:** not gregarious

**non·halation** \"+\ *adj* **:** ANTIHALATION

**non·hardening** \(ˈ)⸗+\ *adj* **:** not hardening

**non·hardy** \(ˈ)⸗+\ *adj* **:** not capable of enduring low winter temperatures — compare TENDER

**non·harmonic** \¦⸗+\ *adj* **:** not harmonic; *specif* **:** not belonging to the essential musical harmony ⟨a ~ note⟩

**non·heritable** \(ˈ)⸗+\ *adj* **:** not heritable

**non·historical** \¦⸗+\ *adj* **:** not historical

**non·homogeneous** \(¦)⸗+\ *adj* **:** not homogeneous

**non·homologous** \¦⸗+\ *adj* **:** being of unlike genic constitution — used of chromosomes of one set containing nonallelic genes

**non·human** \(ˈ)⸗+\ *adj* **1 :** being other than a human being ⟨~ animals⟩ ⟨the great world of ~ spirits —*Amer. Mercury*⟩ **2 :** not belonging or appropriate to or produced by human beings ⟨a babel of ~ noises —*N.Y. Times*⟩

**non·hygroscopic** \(¦)⸗+\ *adj* **:** not hygroscopic

**no·ni** \ˈnō(ˌ)nē\ *n* -S [Hawaiian & Marquesan] *central Polynesia & Hawaii* **:** INDIAN MULBERRY 1

**no·nil·lion** \nōˈnilyən\ *n* -S *often attrib* [F, fr. MF, fr. L *nonus* ninth + MF *-illion* (as in *million*) — more at NOON] — see NUMBER table

**non·immigrant** \(ˈ)⸗*at* NON-+\ *n* **:** an alien (as a foreign tourist, government official, or student) who enters the U.S. for a temporary period or a resident alien returning from a temporary stay abroad

**1non·immune** \¦⸗+\ *adj* **:** not immune **:** being a nonimmune

**2nonimmune** \"\ *n* **:** one that lacks immunity to a particular disease **:** SUSCEPTIBLE

**non·importation** \(¦)⸗+\ *n, often attrib* **:** cessation or prohibition of the import of goods from another country esp. as employed against Great Britain by the American colonies in the Revolutionary era in retaliation for the Townshend Acts and by the U.S. in the Napoleonic era as a measure of reprisal for British violations of American neutral rights ⟨~ associations made effective use of an economic boycott —*Amer. Guide Series: N.C.*⟩ ⟨the device of ~ was tried, in resistance to British political and economic aggression —J.C.Fitzpatrick⟩

**non·inbred** \(ˈ)⸗+\ *adj* **:** free from or not produced by inbreeding

**non·inductive** \¦⸗+\ *adj* **:** having negligible inductance ⟨a ~ electrical resistor⟩ — **non·inductively** \"\ *adv* — **non·in·duc·tiv·i·ty** \(¦)⸗+ˌin,dəkˈtivəd·ē, -ətē, -i\ *n*

**non·industrial** \¦⸗+\ *adj* **:** not industrial

**non·infectious** \"+\ *adj* **:** not infectious

**non·inflammable** \"+\ *adj* **:** not inflammable **:** NONFLAMMABLE

**non·inflammatory** \"+\ *adj* **:** not inflammatory

**non·inflationary** \"+\ *adj* **:** not inflationary

**non·inflectional** \"+\ *adj* **:** not inflectional

**non·inherent** \"+\ *adj* **:** not inherent

**non·inheritable** \"+\ *adj* **:** not inheritable

**non·institutional** \(¦)⸗+\ *adj* **:** not institutional

**non·intercourse** \(ˈ)⸗+\ *n* **:** suspension or absence of dealings or relations ⟨diplomatic ~ between the two states continued 25 years⟩; *esp* **:** suspension by one country of commercial relations with another esp. as employed during the Napoleonic era by the U.S. against Great Britain and France in retaliation for their violations of American neutral rights

**non·interference** \(¦)⸗+\ *n* **:** the fact or an instance of refraining from interference

**non·intersecting** \"+\ *adj* **:** not intersecting

**non·intervention** \"+\ *n, often attrib* [1*non-* + *intervention*] **1 :** the state or habit of not intervening **:** refusal or failure to intervene; *esp* **:** a systematic policy or practice of refraining from interference in the affairs of other states ⟨had to preserve the legal fiction of ~ —*Collier's Yr. Bk.*⟩ ⟨the outworn doctrine of ~ —*New Republic*⟩ ⟨a ~ pact⟩ ⟨~ is overwhelmingly supported by our people⟩ **2 :** an instance of nonintervention ⟨advocated ~ in the civil war across the border⟩

**1non·interventionist** \"+\ *n* [ISV *nonintervention* + *-ist*] **:** one who does not intervene or favors nonintervention ⟨the God of the Deists was . . . a ~ —W.L.Sperry⟩; *esp* **:** one who favors nonintervention in the affairs of another country ⟨the trend of his votes revealed him as a ~ —*Current Biog.*⟩

**2noninterventionist** \"\ *adj* **:** implementing or favorable to nonintervention ⟨~ policies⟩ ⟨turned from a ~ stand to one of internationalism —*Current Biog.*⟩

**non·intoxicant** \¦⸗+\ *n* **:** a beverage that does not intoxicate

**non·intoxicating** \"+\ *adj* **:** not conducive to intoxication

**non·intrusion** \"+\ *n* **:** absence of intrusion **:** refusal to intrude; *specif* **:** the principle historically upheld by the Church of Scotland that a minister may not be settled in a parish against the will of the people — **non·in·tru·sion·ism** \-ˌnizəm\ *n* — **non·in·tru·sion·ist** \-ˌnəst\ *n*

**non in·ven·tus** \¦näˌninˈventəs, ¦nōˌ-\ *n, pl* **non inventuses** [L, not found] **:** NON EST INVENTUS

**non·involvement** \¦⸗*at* NON-+\ *n* **:** refusal to become involved or committed **:** the condition of not being involved or committed ⟨much to be said . . . for ~ in the affairs of the Orient —*Saturday Rev.*⟩

**1non·ionic** \"+\ *adj* **:** not ionic **:** NONPOLAR

**2nonionic** \"\ *n* -S **:** a nonionic substance; *esp* **:** NONIONIC DETERGENT

**nonionic detergent** *n* **:** any of a class of synthetic detergents (as long-chain ether derivatives or esters of alcohols or phenols) that are neither anionic nor cationic but produce electrically neutral colloidal particles in solution

**non·irrigated** \(ˈ)⸗+\ *adj* **:** not irrigated

**nonis** *pl of* NONI

**non·isobaric** \(¦)⸗*at* NON-+\ *adj* **:** not directly associated with any definite form of isobars or isobaric gradients

**non·issuable** \(ˈ)⸗+\ *adj* **:** not being of such a nature as to raise a fact in issue determinative of the merits of a case ⟨a ~ plea⟩

**non·joinder** \"+\ *n* **:** the omission of a necessary party, plaintiff, or defendant to a suit at law or in equity

**non·ju·ran·cy** \(ˈ)nänˈju̇rənsē\ *n* -ES [1*nonjurant* + *-cy*] **:** the state of being a nonjuror **:** nonjuring principles

**1non·ju·rant** \(ˈ)⸗¦ju̇rənt\ *adj* [1*non-* + L *jurant-*, *jurans*, pres. part. of *jurare* to swear — more at JURY] **:** NONJURING **:** relating to or characteristic of nonjurors

**2nonjurant** \"\ *n* -S **:** NONJUROR

**non·juridical** \¦⸗*at* NON-+\ *adj* **:** not juridical

**non·ju·ring** \(ˈ)nän¦ju̇riŋ, -rēŋ\ *adj* [1*non-* + L *jurare* to swear + E *-ing*] **:** not swearing allegiance — used esp. of a member of a party in Great Britain that would not swear allegiance to William and Mary or to their successors

**non·juror** \(ˈ)⸗*at* NON-+\ *n* [1*non-* + *juror*] **:** a person refusing to take an oath (esp. of allegiance, supremacy, or abjuration): **a :** one of the beneficed clergy in England and Scotland refusing to take an oath of allegiance to William and Mary or to their successors after the revolution of 1688 **b :** one of the Scotch Presbyterians refusing to take an oath of abjuration as involving recognition of episcopacy

**non·laminated** \"+\ *adj* **:** not laminated

**non·lateral** \"+\ *adj* **:** not lateral ⟨~ oral sound⟩

**non·laying** \"+\ *adj* **:** not laying ⟨~ hens⟩

**non·ledger assets** \"+-\ *n pl* [*nonledger* fr. 1*non-* + *ledger*, n.] **1 :** assets (as interest, rent, premiums), receivable in the current year but not received as of a given date **2 :** excess of market values of investments over book values

**non·legal** \"+\ *adj* **:** not legal; *specif* **:** not being within the province of the law so as to be either required as legal or forbidden as illegal

**non·legato** \¦⸗+\ *adv* (*or adj*) [1*non-* + *legato*] **:** with breaks between successive tones **:** with a bow stroke for each tone — used as a direction in music esp. for a bowed instrument

**non·legislative** \(ˈ)⸗+\ *adj* **:** not legislative

**non·lethal** \"+\ *adj* **:** not lethal

**non·letterpress** \"+\ *adj* **:** not consisting of or printed by letterpress

**non·lexical** \"+\ *adj* **:** not lexical

**non·life** \"+\ *n* **:** absence of life ⟨somewhere along the road . . . life and ~ seem to merge —*Treasury of Science*⟩

**non·linear** \"+\ *adj* **:** not linear

**non·linearity** \(¦)⸗+\ *n* [1*non-* + *linearity*] **:** the failure of an output signal in an electronic reproducing system to reproduce an input signal faithfully

**non·linguist** \(ˈ)⸗+\ *n* [1*non-* + *linguist*] **:** one not versed or accomplished in language

**non·linguistic** \¦⸗+\ *adj* **1 :** not consisting of or related to language **2 :** lacking ability to learn or use foreign languages ⟨we are a ~ people, and most of our professors are unable to deliver lectures in a foreign tongue —*Survey Graphic*⟩

**non li·quet** \(ˈ)nänˈlīkwət, (ˈ)nōn-, -lik-\ *n, pl* **non liquets** [L, it is not clear] **:** an expression or condition of doubt or uncertainty as to the facts or where the truth lies ⟨questions which can be answered only with a *non liquet* —Louis Infield⟩ — used by Roman judges in rendering a decision in a doubtful case or in asking leave to be excused

**non·liquid** \(ˈ)⸗*at* NON-+\ *adj* **:** not liquid

**non·literary** \"+\ *adj* **:** not literary

**1non·literate** \"+\ *adj* **1 :** having no written language ⟨primitive people are above all ~ people —A.L.Kroeber⟩ **2 :** characterized by a lack of written language, simple technology, and relatively simple social organization **:** PRELITERATE, PRIMITIVE ⟨~ cultures⟩

**2nonliterate** \"\ *n* **:** a person having no written language ⟨ethnological fieldwork with ~*s*⟩

**non·liturgical** \¦⸗+\ *adj* **:** not liturgical

**non·living** \(ˈ)⸗+\ *adj* **:** not having or characterized by life ⟨~ matter⟩

**non-load-bearing tile** \(ˈ)⸗+-\ *n* **:** tile (as partition tile or furring tile) not capable of carrying superimposed loads for use in masonry construction

**non·local** \(ˈ)⸗+\ *adj* **:** not local

**non·localized vector** \(ˈ)⸗+-\ *n* **:** a vector that requires for its description only its magnitude and direction

**non·logical** \(ˈ)⸗+\ *adj* **:** not based on or derived from a process of reasoning or logic **:** based on or proceeding from insight, intuition, or the unconscious ⟨~ actions⟩ ⟨his cardinal doctrine is that most human behavior is ~ —H.J.Muller⟩ — compare ILLOGICAL

**non·luminescent** \(¦)⸗+\ *adj* **:** not luminescent

**non·luminous** \(ˈ)⸗+\ *adj* **:** lacking luminosity **:** not luminous

**non·lustrous** \"+\ *adj* **:** not lustrous

**non·magnetic** \¦⸗+\ *adj* **:** lacking magnetic qualities

**non·mailable** \(ˈ)⸗+\ *adj* **1 :** being in an unfit condition for mailing ⟨a hole in the paper as the result of poor erasing should render a paper ~ —Virginia Reva⟩ **2 :** not lawful to mail ⟨had the right to declare particular issues of the paper ~ —O.K.Fraenkel⟩

**non·malignant** \¦⸗+\ *adj* **:** not malignant

**non·mammalian** \"+\ *adj* **:** not mammalian

**non·man** \(ˈ)⸗+\ *n, pl* **nonmen :** a being that is not a man ⟨a man who is completely dehumanized by snobbery, a ~, a monster —E.R.Bentley⟩

**non·mandatory** \"+\ *adj* **:** not mandatory

**non·marine** \¦⸗+\ *adj* **:** not marine ⟨~ sandstone⟩

**non·market** \(ˈ)⸗+\ *adj* [1*non-* + *market*, n.] **:** not relating to or characteristic of a market

**non·marketable** \"+\ *adj* [1*non-* + *marketable*] **:** capable of being cashed at or before maturity only by the registered holder or one authorized to act for him ⟨~ securities⟩

**non·master** \"+\ *n* **:** a player in a U. S. contract-bridge tournament having too few master points to qualify for masters' tournaments

**non·matching** \"+\ *adj* **:** not matching

**non·material** \¦⸗+\ *adj* **:** not material: as **a :** being spirit or soul **:** IMMATERIAL, SPIRITUAL ⟨finds no evidence in man of a ~ faculty which . . . can be filled up with knowledge like a tank —Albert Lynd⟩ **b :** CULTURAL, INTELLECTUAL, AESTHETIC ⟨there are few ~ compensations for these material hardships —*Report: (Canadian) Royal Commission on Nat'l Development*⟩ **c :** of or relating to those aspects of a culture that constitute its ideological superstructure **:** not directly serving the sustenance and maintenance of life ⟨the ~ elements of a culture⟩ ⟨the beliefs and theories of the hated infidel, his ~ culture —H.E.Barnes & H.P.Becker⟩

**non·mechanical** \"+\ *adj* **:** not mechanical

**non·medical** \"+\ *adj* **:** not medical

**nonmedical insurance** *n* **:** life, accident, or health insurance issued without medical examination of the applicant

**non·medullated** \(ˈ)⸗+, ¦⸗+\ *adj* **:** not medullated

**non·member** \(ˈ)⸗+\ *n* **:** an individual that is not a member

**nonmember bank** *n* **1 :** a bank that is not a member of the Federal Reserve system **2 :** a bank that is not a member of a clearinghouse association

**non·membership** \(ˈ)⸗+\ *n* **:** the state or status of a non-member

**non·mental** \"+\ *adj* **:** not mental

**non·metal** \"+\ *n* [1*non-* + *metal*] **:** a chemical element (as boron, carbon, phosphorus, nitrogen, oxygen, sulfur, chlorine, argon) that is not classed as a metal because it does not exhibit most of the typical metallic properties **:** an element that in general is characterized chemically by the ability to form anions, acidic oxides and acids, and stable compounds with hydrogen — compare METALLOID

**1non·metallic** \¦⸗+\ *adj* [1*non-* + *metallic*] **1 :** not metallic (as in luster or other physical properties) **2 :** of, relating to, or being a nonmetal ⟨~ elements⟩

**2nonmetallic** \"\ *n* -S **:** a mineral or other naturally occurring substance (as rock or clay) that is not used for extraction of its metal content

**non·metameric** \(¦)⸗+\ *adj* **:** not divided into or originating from metameric segments ⟨a ~ nervous system⟩

**non·metered** \(ˈ)⸗+\ *adj* [1*non-* + *metered*, past part. of *meter*] **:** used for nonmetered mail ⟨~ permit⟩ ⟨~ postage⟩

**nonmetered mail** *n* **:** mail for which postage is paid by the batch at the time of mailing according to special permits for batches of identical pieces of any one class of mail and which bears indicia printed by some device other than a postage meter

**non·metrical** \"+\ *adj* **:** not metrical

**non·migratory** \"+\ *adj* **:** not migratory

**non·military** \(ˈ)⸗+\ *adj* **:** not military

**non·miscible** \"+\ *adj* **:** not miscible

**non·modifying** \"+\ *adj* **:** not modifying

**non·moral** \"+\ *adj* **1 :** neither moral nor immoral **:** not in the sphere of morals or ethics **:** AMORAL ⟨make religion ~, a matter of inner experience and personal attitude —J.H.Randall⟩ **2 :** not moralistic **:** having no moral ⟨a ~ story⟩

**non·motile** \"+\ *adj* **:** not motile

**non·muscular** \"+\ *adj* **:** not muscular

**non·mutant** \"+\ *adj* **:** not mutant

**non·nasal** \(ˈ)⸗+\ *adj* **:** not nasal

**1non·native** \"+\ *adj* **:** not native: as **a :** not being an aborigine; *esp* **:** being a member of the colonizing or dominant race or nation ⟨the ~ population of South Africa⟩ **b :** not born in the place or region to which reference is had ⟨relatively large proportions of ~ population —W.C.Bagley⟩

**2nonnative** \"\ *n* **:** an individual who is not a native ⟨to ~*s* of his state —Vance Packard⟩

**non·natural** \"+\ *adj* [1*non-* + *natural*] **1 :** not natural: as **a** *or* **non·naturalistic** \(¦)⸗+\ **:** not dependent on, explainable in terms of, or reducible to natural or empirical observable characteristics but existing objectively as a spiritual or metaphysical reality apprehended by a priori intuition ⟨~ properties⟩ **:** INTUITIONIST ⟨*nonnaturalistic* ethics⟩ **b :** not conforming to the natural interpretation **:** FORCED ⟨a ~ way of viewing things⟩ **2** *or* **nonnaturalistic :** of, relating to, or having the characteristics of nonnaturalism or nonnaturalists

**non·naturalism** \(ˈ)⸗+\ *n* [1*non-* + *naturalism*] **1 :** an art style that avoids representation of the objects and appearances of the natural world **:** an abstract or nonobjective art style **2 :** an ethical theory opposed to naturalism; *esp* **:** INTUITIONISM

**non·naturalist** \"+\ *n* [1*non-* + *naturalist*] **:** an advocate or supporter of nonnaturalism

**non·naturals** \"+\ *n pl* [*nonnatural*] **:** the six things held in old medicine to be necessary to health

**non·necessity** \¦⸗+\ *n* **1 :** the condition of being unnecessary ⟨a certificate of ~⟩ **2 :** something that is unnecessary

**non·negotiable** \"+\ *adj* **:** not negotiable

**non·nitrogenous** \"+\ *adj* **:** not containing nitrogen

**non·normative** \(ˈ)⸗+\ *adj* **:** not based upon or employing a norm **:** OBJECTIVE ⟨analyzing political data in ~ empirical statements of verifiable relationships about the political behavior of men —Avery Leiserson⟩

**non·notification** \(¦)⸗+\ *n* [1*non-* + *notification*] **:** a sale to a finance company or factor of an account receivable without informing the debtor who continues to remit to the vendor

**non·novelist** \(ˈ)⸗+\ *n* **:** one that is not a novelist

**non·nucleated** \(ˈ)⸗+\ *adj* **:** not nucleated

**non·ny-non·ny** \¦nänē¦nänē, -äni\ [origin unknown] *archaic* — used as a refrain esp. in songs of the Elizabethan era

**non·objective** \¦⸗ *at* NON-+\ *adj* [1*non-* + *objective*] **:** representing or intended to represent no concrete object of nature or natural appearance **:** NONREPRESENTATIONAL, ABSTRACT ⟨~ art⟩ ⟨~ paintings⟩ — **non·objectivity** \(¦)⸗+\ *n*

**non·objectivism** \¦⸗+\ *n* **:** the theory or practice of nonobjective painting

**non·objectivist** \"+\ *n* **:** an adherent or supporter of nonobjectivism

**non·obligatory** \¦⸗+, (ˈ)⸗+\ *adj* **:** not obligatory

**non·observance** \¦⸗+\ *n* **:** a lack of observance **:** failure to observe

**non·ob·stan·te** \ˌnänəbˈstantē, ˌnōn-\ *n* -S [ME *non obstante*, fr. L, notwithstanding, being no hindrance; fr. the medieval English use in statutes and letters patent of the L words *non obstante aliquo statuto in contrarium* notwithstanding any statute to the contrary] **1 :** a license from the crown to do a thing notwithstanding any statute to the contrary **2** *obs* **a :** a dispensation from or relaxation of a law or rule **b :** an exception to a rule

**non obstante** \"\ *prep* [L] **:** NOTWITHSTANDING — abbr. *non obst.*

**non obstante ve·re·dic·to** \-ˌverəˈdik(ˌ)tō\ [ML] **:** notwithstanding a verdict — used of a judgment entered by order of the court on motion of one party for that party notwithstanding a verdict for the other party (as when the record shows that the party for whom the verdict was rendered is not entitled to judgment as a matter of law) ⟨refer to judgment *non obstante veredicto* —Richard Hartshorne b.1888⟩

**non·occurrence** \¦⸗ *at* NON-+\ *n* **:** an absence or lack of occurrence

**non·official** \"+\ *adj* **:** not official: as **a :** not relating to, proceeding from, or approved by officials **:** having no official status ⟨~ points of view —*Atlantic*⟩ ⟨the panel of ~ advisers —*Manchester Guardian Weekly*⟩ **b :** UNOFFICIAL — **non·officially** \"+\ *adv*

**no·no·ic acid** \nōˈnōik-\ *n* [*nonoic* fr. *non*ane + *-oic*] **:** any of the numerous monocarboxylic acids $C_8H_{17}COOH$ (as pelargonic acid) derived from the nonanes

**non·olfactory** \(¦)⸗ *at* NON-+\ *adj* **:** not olfactory

**no-nonsense** \ˈ⸗¦⸗⸗\ *adj* [fr. the phrase *no nonsense*] **:** tolerating no nonsense **:** not frivolous **:** SERIOUS, BUSINESSLIKE ⟨the somber *no-nonsense* manner of a prosecuting attorney —Russell Baker⟩ ⟨a warmhearted, *no-nonsense* patrolman —*Lamp*⟩

**1non·op** \(ˈ)nä¦näp\ *n, pl* **nonops** [short for *nonoperator*] **1 :** NONOPERATOR **2 :** a union composed of nonoperators ⟨the 17 ~*s* previously reached such an agreement with the Eastern railroads —*Progressive Labor World*⟩

**2nonop** \"\ *adj* [by shortening] **:** NONOPERATING ⟨agreed to the union shop for their ~ unions —*Americana Annual*⟩

**non·opaque** \(¦)⸗ *at* NON-+\ *adj* **:** not opaque

**non·operating** \(ˈ)⸗ *at* NON-+\ *adj* [1*non-* + *operating*] **:** not operating: as **a :** of or relating to railroad employees (as telegraph operators, train dispatchers, signalmen) not directly engaged in train operation ⟨~ unions⟩ ⟨~ railroad workers⟩

**b** : arising from the minor operations of a business : AUXILIARY, SUPPLEMENTARY ⟨~ profits⟩

**non·operator** \"+\ *n* [1*non-* + *operator*] : a nonoperating railroad employee

**non·operculate** \¦=+\ *adj* : not operculate

**non·optical** \(ˈ)=+\ *adj* : not optical

**non·organic** \¦=+\ *adj* : not organic

**non·palatal** \(ˈ)=+\ *adj* : not palatal

**non·par** \(ˈ)=+\ *adj* [1*non-* + *par*, n.] : being a bank that has not agreed to pay all checks drawn on it at par and so cannot join the par clearance system of the Federal Reserve system

**non·parallel** \"+\ *adj* : not parallel

**non·parametric** \(¦)=+\ *adj* : not involving the estimation of parameter values of a distribution function ⟨~ methods⟩

**non·parasitic** \"+\ *adj* : not parasitic; *esp* : not caused by parasites — **non·parasitically** \"+\ *adv*

**1non·pa·reil** \¦nänpə¦rel *sometimes* ¦nən- *or* -rī(ə)l *or* -rā(ə)l *or* -rē(ə)l *or, by British printers* ˈnänprəl *or* ˈnämp-\ *adj* [MF, fr. *non-* 1non- + *pareil* equal, fr. (assumed) VL *pariculus*, fr. L *par* equal — more at PAIR] : having no equal : PEERLESS ⟨a lover's triumph in the ~ beauty of his mistress —Robert Lynd⟩

**2nonpareil** \"\ *n* -s **1** : an individual of unequaled excellence : PARAGON ⟨the very ~ of tidiness and cleanliness —Eric Linklater⟩ ⟨~*s* whose conduct was a model for all time —Maurice Collis⟩ ⟨a virtuoso, a master, a ~ —S.H.Adams⟩ **2** [F *nonpareille*, fr. fem. of *nonpareil*, adj.] **a** : an old size of type (approximately 6 point) between agate and minion **b** : 6-point interlinear space or spacing material **3** [F *nonpareille*, fr. fem. of *nonpareil*, adj.] **a** : a small flat disk of chocolate covered with very small white pellets of sugar **b** : sugar in the form of small pellets of various colors used in covering candy or decorating cakes or cookies **4** : PAINTED BUNTING

**non·participant** \¦= *at* NON-+\ *n* [1*non-* + *participant*, n.] : one who does not participate

**non·participating** \"+\ *adj* : not participating; *specif* : not participating or not giving the right to participate in surplus or profit

**non·participation** \"+\ *n* : an absence or lack of participation

**1non·partisan** \(ˈ)=+\ *adj* : not partisan: as **a** : not affiliated with or committed to the support of a particular political party : politically independent ⟨labor will continue playing its ~ role of helping friends, opposing enemies —Sam Stavisky⟩ **b** : viewing matters or policies without party bias : OBJECTIVE, IMPARTIAL ⟨expected to be ~ in foreign affairs —Norman Hill & Eugene Haugse⟩ **c** : held or organized with all party designations or emblems absent from the ballot ⟨legislation to substitute ~ for partisan election of judges —G.R.Winters⟩ **d** : composed, appointed, or elected without regard to the political party affiliations of members ⟨a ~ ticket⟩ ⟨a ~ board⟩ ⟨a ~ commission⟩ — **non·partisanship** \"+\ *n*

**2nonpartisan** \"\ *n* : a person who is nonpartisan

**nonpartisan ballot** *n* : a ballot bearing no party designations

**nonpartisan primary** *n* : a direct primary in which all qualified voters may participate without regard to political affiliations and may vote usu. for two nominees for each office who are the two receiving the highest vote and whose names are placed on the ballot without any party designation

**non·party** \(ˈ)= *at* NON-+\ *adj* : not party: **a** : not affiliated with any political party ⟨~ delegates to a congress⟩ **b** : not based upon or representing political parties ⟨a ~ regime —*Atlantic*⟩ **c** : not actuated by party spirit : NONPARTISAN ⟨the ~ report by British members of Parliament —*Manchester Guardian Weekly*⟩

**non·passerine** \"+\ *adj* : not passerine — used esp. of birds of the order Coraciiformes

**1non·past** \ˈ=¦=\ *adj* [1*non-* + *past*] *of a verb* : lacking inflection for a past tense : PRESENT : present and future

**2nonpast** \"\ *n* : a verb form or set of verb forms lacking inflection for a past tense

**non·paternity** \¦=+\ *n* : the condition of not being the father of a particular child ⟨comparative blood tests established his ~ beyond question⟩

**non·pathogenic** \(¦)=+\ *adj* : not capable of inducing disease — compare AVIRULENT

**non·payment** \(ˈ)=+\ *n* [ME *nonpayement*, fr. 1*non-* + *payement* payment] : neglect or failure to pay ⟨imprisonment for ~ of ordinary debts —Edward Jenks⟩

**non·pecuniary** \¦=+\ *adj* : not consisting of money ⟨~ compensation allowable under law —*U. S. Code*⟩

**non·performance** \"+\ *n* : neglect or failure to perform

**non·periodic** \(¦)=+\ *adj* : not periodic

**non·peripteral** \¦=+\ *adj* : being without a row of columns ⟨a ~ temple⟩

**non·perishable** \(ˈ)=+\ *adj* [1*non-* + *perishable*] : processed or packaged to withstand prolonged storage — used esp. of foods; distinguished from *fresh* ⟨~ staples⟩

**non·permanent** \"+\ *adj* : not permanent; *specif* : being any one of six member states of the United Nations elected by the General Assembly for two-year terms as members of the Security Council who are not eligible for immediate reelection

**non·personal** \"+\ *adj* : not personal

**non·petaloid** \"+\ *adj* : not petaloid

**non·philatelic** \(¦)=+\ *adj* : not philatelic

**non·philosophic** \"+\ *adj* : not philosophic

**non·phonemic** \(¦)=+\ *adj* : not phonemic

**non·phonetic** \"+\ *adj* : not phonetic

**non·physical** \(ˈ)=+\ *adj* : not physical : INTANGIBLE

**non·physiological** \(¦)=+\ *adj* : not physiological

**non·pictorial** \¦=+\ *adj* : not pictorial

**non·pigmented** \(ˈ)=+\ *adj* : not pigmented

**non·placental** \¦=+\ *adj* : lacking a placenta ⟨~ mammals⟩ : not involving a placenta ⟨~ gaseous exchange⟩

**non pla·cet** \(ˈ)nänˈplāsət, (ˈ)nōn-\ *n, pl* **non placets** [L, it does not please] : a negative vote or expression of disapproval — used in ecclesiastical assemblies and in the legislative assemblies of some universities

**non–placet** \"\ *vt* -ED/-ING/-S [*non placet*] : to vote negatively on : REJECT, VETO ⟨the *non-placeted* ambassador to the Vatican —E.A.Peers⟩

**non·plastic** \(ˈ)= *at* NON- +\ *adj* : not plastic

**1non·plus** \(ˈ)nän¦pləs\ *n, pl* **nonpluses** *or* **nonplusses** [L *non plus* no more] : a state of bafflement or perplexity : inability to proceed or decide : QUANDARY, DILEMMA ⟨reducing the young man to a ~ —Leigh Hunt⟩ ⟨appear to be at a ~ —George Borrow⟩

**2non·plus** *adj, obs* : NONPLUSSED, PERPLEXED

**3non·plus** \(ˈ)nän¦pləs\ *vt* **nonplussed** *also* **nonplused**; **nonplussed** *also* **nonplused**; **nonplussing** *also* **nonplusing**; **nonplusses** *also* **nonpluses** : to cause to be at a loss as to what to say, think, or do : reduce to a state of total incapacity to act or decide : PERPLEX, BAFFLE, STUMP ⟨this turn of events *nonplusses* me —J.R.Perkins⟩ ⟨*nonplussed* by the disclosure —*Newsweek*⟩ ⟨for a moment the girl was *nonplussed* —A.R. Williams⟩ **syn** see PUZZLE

**non·poisonous** \(ˈ)= *at* NON-+\ *adj* : not poisonous

**non·polar** \"+\ *adj* : not polar: **a** : relating to or being a combination in which two or more atoms with incomplete electron shells make up for their instability by sharing electrons and thus achieve completed outer shells which neither could attain individually : COVALENT **b** : lacking a dipole : having a low dielectric constant : NONIONIC

**non·political** \¦=+\ *adj* : not political: as **a** : not influenced by or concerned with political considerations or issues ⟨our foundations are clearly ~ —L.U.Hauke⟩ ⟨~ experts appointed by Congress to serve as counselors —*Tomorrow*⟩ ⟨on a ~ tour inspecting the drought devastation —*Atlantic*⟩ **b** : NONPARTISAN ⟨appoint a ~ commission to cooperate with similar bodies in the states —*Rev. of Reviews*⟩ **c** : not interested in or concerned with politics : APOLITICAL ⟨the large ~ element in the population⟩

**non·porous** \(ˈ)=+\ *adj* [1*non-* + *porous*] : not porous; *specif* : not possessing vessels extending along the grain that appear as pores ⟨~ wood⟩

**non·positive** \"+\ *adj* : not positive : NEGATIVE, PRIVATIVE

**non·possession** \¦=+\ *n* : an absence or lack of possession

**non·possessor** \"+\ *n, usu cap* [1*non-* + *possessor*] : a member of a 16th century monastic movement within the Russian Orthodox Church, dedicated to prayer and meditation, to simplicity of life and dissociation from worldly affairs esp. as achieved through a life of solitude, and to the ideal of poverty to the extent of preferring to own no property either singly or collectively and particularly opposing the established custom of monasteries' owning farms worked by secular laborers

**non pos·su·mus** \(ˈ)nänˈpäs(y)əməs, (ˈ)nōn-\ *n, pl* **non possumes** [L, we cannot] : a statement expressing inability to do something ⟨had been compelled to express a *non possumus* —*Canadian Mining Jour.*⟩

**non·precipitation** \¦= *at* NON-+\ *n* : an absence or lack of precipitation

**non·pregnant** \(ˈ)=+\ *adj* : not pregnant

**non·prehensile** \¦=+\ *adj* : not prehensile

**non·prescription drug** \¦=+-\ *or* **nonprescription medicine** *n* : a drug or medicine that can be bought without a doctor's prescription — see PROPRIETARY 6c

**non·pressure** \(ˈ)=+\ *adj* : not having pressure

**non·principled** \(ˈ)=+\ *adj* : having no concern with or awareness of principles : AMORAL ⟨not exactly unprincipled, but ~ —Joseph Furphy⟩

**non·printing** \"+\ *adj* : not printing

**non·producer** \¦=+\ *n* : one that is not productive ⟨they carry the load, while the ~*s* ride —*Atlantic*⟩

**non·productive** \"+\ *adj* **1** : failing to produce or yield : UNPRODUCTIVE ⟨consisted of four vines, all ~ —*Current Biog.*⟩ ⟨a ~ oil well⟩ **2** : not directly productive : not creating exchangeable values ⟨~ labor⟩ **3** *of a cough* : not effective in raising mucus or exudate from the respiratory tract : DRY — **non·productively** \"+\ *adv* — **non·productiveness** \"+\ *n*

**1non·professional** \"+\ *adj* : not professional: as **a** : having no profession ⟨the ~ . . . wives of their male colleagues —H.M.Parshley⟩ **b** : not belonging to or trained in a particular profession ⟨will not be read by very many ~ citizens —B.F. Wright⟩ **c** : engaging in or practicing some craft or art without previous training or professional status : AMATEUR ⟨~ actors⟩ — **non·professionally** \"+\ *adv*

**2nonprofessional** \"\ *n* : a person who is not a professional: as **a** : a person who does not belong to or possess training in a particular profession ⟨a book is of great value if it can give the ~ a clear, intelligible answer —Lise Meitner⟩ **b** : a person who engages in or practices some craft or art without previous training or professional status ⟨build a cast of ~*s* around an established cast —*Current Biog.*⟩

**non·professionalism** \"+\ *n* : an absence or lack of professionalism

**non·profit** \(ˈ)=+\ *adj* [1*non-* + *profit*, n.] **1** : not conducted or maintained for the purpose of making a profit ⟨a ~ agency supported by endowments and private contributions —*Current Biog.*⟩ **2** : not based on the profit motive : not organized on capitalistic principles : SOCIALIST ⟨decreed the creation of a ~ society —*Time*⟩

**non·profitable** \"+\ *adj* : not profitable

**non·progressive** \¦=+\ *adj* : not progressive

**non·proportional** \"+\ *adj* : not proportional

**non·propositional** \(¦)=+\ *adj* : not propositional

**non·proprietary** \¦=+\ *adj* : not proprietary

**non·pros** \(ˈ)=+¦präs\ *vt* **nonprossed**; **nonprossed**; **nonprossing**; **nonprosses** [fr. *non pros*, abbr. of *non prosequitur*] : to enter a non prosequitur against

**non pro·se·qui·tur** \¦nän(ˌ)prōˈsekwəd·ə(r), ¦nōn-\ *n, pl* **non prosequiturs** [LL, he does not prosecute] : a judgment entered against the plaintiff in a suit in which he does not appear to prosecute — abbr. *non pros.*; compare NOLLE PROSEQUI

**non·protein** \(ˈ)= *at* NON-+\ *n, often attrib* **1** : a substance that is not a protein — compare PROSTHETIC **2** : any or the sum of all of the plant or animal nitrogenous constituents (as asparagine of plants or urea and uric acid of urine or various extractives of muscle) that are less complex in structure than proteins ⟨~ nitrogen⟩

**non·proven** \"+\ *adj* : not established by proof : not proved ⟨what is ~ is its value —Anne Fremantle⟩

**non·psychiatric** \(¦)=+\ *adj* : not psychiatric

**non·public** \(ˈ)=+\ *adj* : not public

**non·pungent** \"+\ *adj* [1*non-* + *pungent*] : UNPOINTED, BLUNT ⟨flexible ~ fin rays⟩

**non·quota** \"+\ *adj* [1*non-* + *quota*, n.] **1** : not included in or subject to a quota : of or relating to a nonquota immigrant ⟨~ visas⟩ **2** : exceeding a quota ⟨a penalty tax on his ~ cotton —*Time*⟩

**nonquota immigrant** *n* : an immigrant not subject to the quota restrictions imposed by various U. S. immigration laws

**non·radially** \(ˈ)=+\ *adv* : not radially

**non·radioactive** \(¦)=+\ *adj* : not radioactive

**non·random** \"+\ *adj* : not random — **non·randomness** \"+\ *n*

**non·rational** \"+\ *adj* : not based on, guided by, or employing reason : not rational : IRRATIONAL ⟨they fight from ~ causes of a lower kind —Norman Angell⟩ ⟨there is a great deal that is ~ in modern cultures —*American Anthropologist*⟩

**non·reactive** \¦=+\ *adj* [1*non-* + *reactive*] : having no inductance or capacitance — used of a circuit offering only ohmic resistance to a current

**nonreactive load** *n* : a load consisting of ohmic resistance only

**non·reader** \(ˈ)= *at* NON-+\ *n* : a person who lacks the ability or desire to read; *specif* : a child in school whose progress in learning to read is exceedingly slow

**non·realistic** \(¦)=+\ *adj* : not realistic: as **a** : not viewing matters in their true light : not practical : IMPRACTICAL, VISIONARY ⟨a ~ point of view⟩ **b** : not characterized by realism in conception and portrayal ⟨a ~ style⟩

**non·reciprocal** \¦=+\ *adj* : not reciprocal or reciprocating

**non·reciprocity** \(¦)=+\ *n* : the absence of reciprocity

**non·recognition** \"+\ *n* : absence of recognition : failure or refusal to recognize ⟨the doctrine of ~ of governments established by revolutionary means⟩

**non·recourse** \(¦)=+\ *adj* [1*non-* + *recourse*, n.] : not giving a holder the right to sue the borrower or endorser for a deficiency or loss — used esp. of price-support loans to farmers made by the Commodity Credit Corporation

**nonrecourse loan** *n* : a loan by which a lender agrees to accept the collateral security in lieu of repayment from the borrower if he is unable to pay or if the value of the security falls below the amount of the loan : a loan in which a lender under an endorsement without recourse discounts commercial paper for an endorser and agrees to accept the security and to hold the party primarily liable responsible and not the immediate endorser

**non·rectilinear** \"+\ *adj* : not rectilinear

**non·recurrent** \¦=+\ *adj* : not recurrent

**non·recurring** \"+\ *adj* : not recurring

**non·reducing** \"+\ *adj* : not reducing; *specif* : not readily reducing Fehling solution or a similar reagent

**non·reflexive** \"+\ *adj, of a pronoun* : not reflexive

**non·regent** \(ˈ)=+\ *n* : a Master of Arts at an English university whose regency has expired

**non·regulation** \(¦)=+\ *adj* : not being in accordance with regulations ⟨a ~ uniform⟩

**non·reimbursable** \"+\ *adj* : not reimbursable

**non·religious** \¦=+\ *adj* **1** : not religious : not having a religious character : SECULAR ⟨the ~ nature of the art —*Nat'l Geographic*⟩ ⟨the state is not irreligious; it is simply ~ —W.L.Sperry⟩ **2** : having no religion : IRRELIGIOUS ⟨a ~ individual may see little but show and outward circumstance in all this business —*Amer. Mercury*⟩

**non·removable** \"+\ *adj* : not removable

**non rep** *abbr* [L *non repetatur*] not to be repeated

**1non·repatriable** \¦= *at* NON-+\ *adj* : being not repatriable; *specif* : displaced and stateless or not capable of being repatriated for any of a variety of reasons (as unwillingness to return to one's former country) ⟨a plan to rehabilitate and resettle these ~ victims of German action —Eli Ginzberg⟩

**2nonrepatriable** \"\ *n* -S : a person who is nonrepatriable

**non·representational** \(¦)=+\ *adj* : not representing or imitating external reality or the objects of nature : ABSTRACT, NONFIGURATIVE, NONOBJECTIVE ⟨~ art⟩ — **non·representationalism** \"+\ *n*

**non·representative** \"+\ *adj* : not representative: as **a** : not typical or characteristic ⟨rendered them ~ of the great majority —*Popular Science Monthly*⟩ **b** : NONREPRESENTATIONAL ⟨stressing ~ design —Thomas Munro⟩

**non·residence** \(ˈ)=+\ *also* **non·residency** \"+\ *n* [*nonresidence* fr. ME *noun residense*, fr. *noun-*, *non* 1non- + *residense*, *residence* residence; *nonresidency* fr. 1*non-* + *residency*] : the state or fact of being nonresident

**1non·resident** \"+\ *adj* [1*non-* + *resident*] **1** : not residing in a particular place or a place referred to by implication ⟨a ~ student⟩; *specif* : having one's permanent residence away from one's benefice, charge, or estate ⟨a ~ clergyman⟩ **2** : of or relating to a nonresident ⟨nearly four hundred ~ licenses were sold —*Alaska Sportsman*⟩

**2nonresident** \"\ *n* : a nonresident person ⟨most of the land is owned by ~*s* —J.L.Christian⟩

**non·residenter** \"+\ *n* [1*nonresident* + *-er*] : NONRESIDENT

**non·residential** \(¦)=+\ *adj* : not residential

**non·resistance** \¦=+\ *n* [1*non-* + *resistance*] : the principles or practice of a nonresistant : passive obedience or submission

**1non·resistant** \"+\ *adj* [1*non-* + *resistant*] : not resistant: as **a** : practicing or adhering to nonresistance ⟨pacifist and ~ in attitude and program —G.F.Hershberger⟩ **b** : not capable of resisting : incapable of offering opposition (as to a disease) : SUSCEPTIBLE ⟨~ strains of mice⟩

**2nonresistant** \"\ *n* : a person who maintains or acts on the theory that no resistance should be made to constituted authority even when unjust or oppressive; *also* : one who holds that violence should never be resisted by force

**non·resister** \¦=+\ *n* : NONRESISTANT

**non·resisting** \"+\ *adj* : not resisting : NONRESISTANT

**non·restraint** \"+\ *n* : an absence or lack of restraint

**non·restricted** \"+\ *adj* : not restricted : not subject to restrictions

**non·restrictive** \"+\ *adj* : not restrictive; *specif* : not limiting the reference of a modified word or phrase

**nonrestrictive clause** *n* : a descriptive clause that adds information but is so loosely attached to the main clause as to be not essential to the definiteness of its meaning and to be marked off from it by commas (as in "the aldermen, *who were present*, assented")

**non·retractable** \"+\ *adj* : not retractable

**non·retractile** \"+\ *adj* : not retractile

**non·returnable** \"+\ *adj* : not returnable; *specif* : not returnable to the vendor or dealer ⟨the ~ beer bottle⟩

**non·return valve** \"+-\ *n* : CHECK VALVE

**non·revenue** \(ˈ)=+\ *adj* [1*non-* + *revenue*] **1** : not productive of revenue ⟨~ equipment⟩ **2** : not arising from current revenue

**nonreversible** \¦=+\ *adj* : not reversible

**non·rhythmic** \(ˈ)=+\ *adj* : not rhythmic

**1non·rigid** \"+\ *adj* [1*non-* + *rigid*] : maintaining form by pressure of contained gas ⟨a ~ airship⟩

**2nonrigid** \"\ *n* -s : an airship of nonrigid type

**non·rotatable** \(¦)=+\ *adj* : that does not rotate

**non·ruminant** \(ˈ)+\ *adj* : not ruminant

**non·ruminantia** \¦=+\ *n pl, cap* [NL, fr. 1*non-* + *Ruminantia*] *in some classifications* : the Artiodactyla exclusive of the Ruminantia

**non·sacred** \(ˈ)= *at* NON- +\ *adj* : not sacred

**non·sapi·ens** \(ˈ)nän¦sapēənz, -sāp- *also* -ēˌenz *or* -ēˌen(t)s\ *adj* [1*non-* + NL *sapiens* (specific epithet of *Homo sapiens*) fr. L *sapient-*, *sapiens* wise — more at SAPIENT] : of, relating to, or being any of the extinct men that are usu. treated as distinct from recent man at a species or higher level

**non·scheduled** \(ˈ)= *at* NON- +\ *adj* [1*non-* + *scheduled*, past part. of *schedule*] : licensed to carry passengers or freight by air between authorized points as frequently as demand requires and not on a regular schedule ⟨a ~ airline⟩ ⟨~ service⟩

**non·school** \ˈ=+¦-\ *adj* **1** : not being in school **2** : not connected with school

**non·scientific** \(¦)=+\ *adj* : not scientific: as **a** : not based on fact or empirical methods of inquiry : not being in conformity with the methods or principles of science ⟨~ theories⟩ **b** : not having the professional status of a scientist : not trained in science ⟨the ~ reader⟩

**non·scientist** \(ˈ)=+\ *n* : a person who is not a scientist or who lacks training in the sciences

**non·seasonal** \"+\ *adj* : not seasonal

**non·secretor** \¦=+\ *n* [1*non-* + *secretor*] : an individual who lacks water-soluble group-specific substances

**non·secretory** \"+\ *adj* : not secretory

**non·sectarian** \"+\ *adj* : not having a sectarian character : not restricted to or dominated by a particular religious group ⟨~ colleges⟩ ⟨religious training in a ~ atmosphere⟩

**non·segregated** \(ˈ)=+\ *adj* : UNSEGREGATED ⟨not one of us ever spent a day in a ~ school —F.A.Perry⟩

**non·segregation** \(¦)=+\ *n* : the absence of segregation esp. of individuals or groups from a larger group or from society ⟨a defiant enclave of ~ in segregated Virginia —*Time*⟩ — compare DESEGREGATION, INTEGRATION

**non·selective** \¦=+\ *adj* : not selective

**non–self–governing** \(¦)=+\ *adj* : not self-governing : not independent ⟨*non-self-governing* territories⟩

**1non·sense** \ˈnänˌsen(t)s, -ˌsən-\ *n* **1 a** : something that is not sense or has no sense : words or language having no meaning or conveying no intelligible ideas ⟨apples harvest — the words are now ~; they have lost their grammar —Charlton Laird⟩ **b** : something written or said that is absurd or contrary to good sense : TWADDLE, DRIVEL ⟨a lot of ~ has been uttered —R.A. Lester⟩ ⟨no throaty oratorical ~ was there —W.A.White⟩ **c** (1) : conduct or a course of action that is absurd or contrary to good sense : a piece of absurdity ⟨this, of course, makes ~ of the liberation policy —*New Statesman & Nation*⟩ ⟨this attitude is, manifestly, ~ —Allan Sangster⟩ ⟨the ~ that the ragged rebels spoke of as their War for Independence —F.V. W.Mason⟩ (2) : an instance of nonsensical action ⟨if this did happen to be just a ~ —Nigel Balchin⟩ ⟨dispelling his many ~*s* —*Amer. Anthropologist*⟩ **d** : a concrete object whose acceptance or use is contrary to good sense ⟨an Eskimo cloak makes perfect sense in the Arctic regions, though it . . . is ~ in Guayaquil —Gustave Weigel⟩ ⟨never pay any attention to the ~ of omens —George Meredith⟩ **2 a** : things of no importance or value : TRIFLES, FOLDEROL, FRILLS ⟨the raincoats are classic, without any ~ —*New Yorker*⟩ **b** : foolish, affected, impudent or frivolous conduct or manner : FOOLING, HUMBUG ⟨the Indians of those regions would stand no ~ —S.E.Morison & H.S.Commager⟩ ⟨were taught to recite poetry when asked and no ~ —Katherine A. Porter⟩ ⟨a brisk old lady with no ~ about her —Jean Stafford⟩

**2nonsense** \"\ *adj* **1** *archaic* : NONSENSICAL **2 a** : being a verse (as *ibbety, bibbety, sibbety, sab*) consisting of words or syllables arranged primarily with regard to meter and not to sense **b** : being a poem or other literary composition of humorous or whimsical character typically with odd, grotesque, or anomalous themes, characters, and actions and often marked by the use of words coined for the purpose that sometimes have an evocative character but no precise or generally accepted meaning ⟨limericks and other types of ~ poetry⟩ **3** : being a simulated unit of speech (as a word or syllable) fabricated by arbitrary grouping of speech sounds or symbols and pronounced to provide a test as of ability to apprehend speech sounds or word or syllable boundaries ⟨ˈshkrȯgˌthyəmpth is a ~ word⟩ ⟨a linguistic response like the ~ syllable provides . . . a highly differentiable but easily recognizable response —J.B.Carroll⟩

**non·sen·si·cal** \(ˈ)nän¦sen(t)sə̇kəl, -sēk-\ *adj* **1 a** : being nonsense or full of nonsense : UNMEANING, ABSURD, FOOLISH, PREPOSTEROUS ⟨asked a ~ question —W.F.de Morgan⟩ ⟨refused to modify his opinions, even when the plain facts made them ~ —Douglas Stewart⟩ **b** : characterized by or revealing absurd or foolish speech, thoughts, or acts ⟨subjected to strains and stresses by their ~ wives —*Irish Digest*⟩ **2 a** : NONSENSE 3 ⟨if ~ syllables are used as test material —G.A.Miller⟩ **b** : NONSENSE 2 ⟨represented by a few light ~ sketches —Marc Slonim⟩ — **non·sen·si·cal·i·ty** \ˌ=(ˌ)==ˈkaləd·ē, -ətē, -i\ *n* -ES — **non·sen·si·cal·ly** \-sə̇k(ə)lē, -ēk-, -li\ *adv* — **non·sen·si·cal·ness** \(ˈ)=¦sen(t)sə̇kəlnə̇s, -sēk-\ *n* -ES

**non·sensitive** \(ˈ)ˌ= *at* NON- +\ *adj* : not sensitive; *specif* : not involving or related to the national security ⟨employees in ~ jobs may not be dismissed as security risks —*Time*⟩
**non·septate** \"+\ *adj* : not septate
**non se·qui·tur** \(ˈ)nänˈsekwəd·ə(r), ˈnōn-, -sākwə̇,tu̇(ə)r\ *n, pl* **non sequiturs** [L, it does not follow] : an inference that does not follow from the premises; *specif* : a fallacy resulting from a simple conversion of a universal affirmative proposition or from the transposition of a condition and its consequent
**non·settler** \(ˈ)ˌ= *at* NON- +\ *n* [¹non- + settler] : a domestic animal (as a cow) persistently failing to conceive or settle to service or insemination
**non·sexual** \"+\ *adj* : not sexual
¹**non·significant** \ˌ=+\ *n* [¹non- + significant, n.] : ²NULL 2
²**nonsignificant** \"\ *adj* [¹non- + significant, adj.] : not significant: as **a** : having slight or no importance : INSIGNIFICANT ⟨cluttered up with ~ features —R.A.Hall b.1911⟩ **b** : having or conveying no meaning ⟨inserted ~ symbols —W.W.R.Ball⟩
**non·silicate** \(ˈ)=+\ *n* : a substance that is not a silicate
**non·sked** \"+ˌsked\ *n* -s [by shortening & alter. fr. *non-scheduled*] : an air transport carrier that offers service at irregular times, at less frequent intervals, and often at lower fares than certificated scheduled service; *also* : a nonscheduled transport plane
¹**non·skid** \(ˈ)=+\ *adj* [¹non- + skid, n. or skid, v.] **1** : designed to reduce or prevent skidding **2** *of an automobile tire* : having the tread corrugated or otherwise specially constructed to resist skidding
²**nonskid** \"\ *n* : a nonskid tire
**non·slaveholding** \"+\ *adj* : not allowing slavery or not inhabited by slaveholders ⟨the ~ North⟩ ⟨~ states⟩
**non·slip** \"+\ *adj* [¹non- + slip, n. or slip, v.] : designed to reduce or prevent slipping ⟨~ concrete⟩
**non·smoker** \"+\ *n* : a person who does not smoke
**non·social** \"+\ *adj* : having no social character; *specif* : not directed toward others ⟨~ behavior⟩
**non·solid** \"+\ *adj* : not solid
**non·spatial** \"+\ *adj* : not spatial
**non·speaking** \"+\ *adj* : involving no spoken lines ⟨~ part in a play⟩
**non·specialist** \"+\ *n* : a person who is not a specialist in a particular subject
**non·specific** \ˌ=+\ *adj* : not specific; *esp* : not caused by a specific agent ⟨~ adenitis⟩ ⟨~ enteritis⟩
**non·spectral** \(ˈ)=+\ *adj* [¹non- + spectral] : not being in the spectrum; *esp* : purple in the range from red to violet
**non·speculative** \"+\ *adj* : not speculative
**non·spillable** \"+\ *adj* : not spillable
**non·spore–forming** \"+\ *adj* : not producing spores
**non·sporting** \"+\ *adj* **1** : lacking the qualities characteristic of a gundog or hunting dog ⟨the Newfoundland is a ~ breed that has contributed valuable characteristics to various of the retrievers⟩ **2** *of a plant or animal variety* : not giving rise to sports : not subject to frequent mutation
**non·staining** \"+\ *adj* : not staining ⟨a ~ medicine⟩ : incapable of being stained ⟨~ elements in cells⟩
**non·standard** \"+\ *adj* **1** : not standard **2** *of language* : not conforming in pronunciation, grammatical construction, idiom, or choice of word to the usage generally characteristic of educated native speakers of the language ⟨the common core of ~ words and phrases in folk speech —A.R.Dunlap⟩ — compare SUBSTANDARD
**non·stellar** \"+\ *adj* : not stellar; *specif* : being a celestial object (as an asteroid) that resembles a star but is not a star
**non·stock** \"+\ *adj* [¹non- + stock, n.] : not organized for profit and so having no stock outstanding ⟨~ corporations⟩
**non·stoichiometric** \(ˌ)=+\ *adj* : not stoichiometric
¹**non·stop** \(ˈ)=+\ *adj* [¹non- + stop, n.] : made without a stop ⟨a ~ journey⟩; *specif* : made without intermediate landings between takeoff and destination ⟨a ~ flight⟩ **2** : made or held without a pause or interruption ⟨a ~ dive-bombing attack⟩ ⟨a ~ performance⟩ ⟨a 25-hour ~ conference —*Time*⟩
²**nonstop** \"\ *adv* : without a stop ⟨rushed ~ through his Latin —Bruce Marshall⟩
**non·striated** \(ˈ)=+\ *adj* : being without striations
**nonstriated muscle** *n* : SMOOTH MUSCLE
**nonstriker** \"+\ *n* [¹non- + striker] : a batsman in cricket who is in but is not receiving the bowling — compare STRIKER
**non·structural** \"+\ *adj* : not structural
**non·subjective** \ˌ=+\ *adj* : not subjective
**non·subscriber** \"+\ *n* : a person who does not subscribe; *specif* : one who refuses to subscribe to a confession of faith or covenant (as the National Covenant of 1638 in the Church of Scotland)
**nonsuch** *var of* NONESUCH
**non·such chest** *also* **none·such chest** \ˈnən,səch-\ *n* [perh. fr. *Nonsuch* palace, Cheam, Surrey] : a chest popular in the later 16th and early 17th centuries with front panels decorated in inlay of architectural design
**non·sugar** \ˈ= *at* NON- +\ *n* : a substance that is not a sugar; *esp* : AGLYCON
¹**non·suit** \(ˈ)ˌ= *at* NON- +\ *n* [ME, fr. AF *nounsuyte*, fr. *noun-* ¹non- + OF *suite, sieute* following, pursuit — more at SUIT] : a judgment given against a plaintiff because of his failure to prosecute his case or his inability to establish a prima facie case at the trial
²**nonsuit** \"\ *adj* [ME *non suit*, fr. *nonsuit*, n.] *archaic* : NONSUITED
³**nonsuit** \"\ *vt* [¹nonsuit] **1** : to determine, adjudge, or record (a plaintiff) as having terminated a suit by default or failure to establish a good cause of action : subject to a nonsuit — used in strict common-law practice only of the termination of the suit on motion of the defendant against a defaulting plaintiff but in modern practice of other terminations of a case not on the merits (as by a nolle prosequi); compare DISCONTINUANCE **2** *obs* : to deny the suit of
**non·superconducting** \(ˌ)=+\ *adj* : not superconducting
**non·superimposable** \"+\ *adj* : not capable of being superimposed
**non·support** \ˌ=+\ *n* **1** : lack of support : failure to support ⟨use the threat of ~ . . . to bring recalcitrants in his party to heel —R.H.Rovere⟩ **2** : failure on the part of one under obligation either by contract or by statutory liability to provide maintenance or means of sustenance
**non·surgical** \(ˈ)=+\ *adj* : not surgical
**non·syllabic** \ˌ=+\ *adj* : not constituting a syllable or the nucleus of a syllable: **a** *of a consonant* : accompanied in the same syllable by a vowel ⟨\n\ is syllabic in \ˈbätᵊnē\ *botany*, ~ in \ˈbätnē\⟩ **b** *of a vowel* : having vowel quality less prominent than that of another vowel in the syllable ⟨the second vowel of a falling diphthong, as \i\ in \ȯi\, is ~⟩
**non·symbiotic** \(ˌ)=+\ *adj* : not living or occurring in a state of mutualism or symbiosis — **non·symbiotically** \"+\ *adv*
**non·symmetrical** \ˌ=+\ *adj* : UNSYMMETRICAL
**non·sync** \(ˈ)=+ˌsiŋk\ *n* -s [short for *nonsynchronous turntable*, fr. *nonsynchronous* not synchronous (fr. ¹non- + *synchronous*) + *turntable*] : an accessory pair of ordinary phonograph turntables and pickups in a sound-on-film reproducing system used to provide musical interludes and background music for silent films
**non tan·to** \(ˈ)nänˈtän·(,)tō, (ˈ)nōn-, -tȧn-\ *adv (or adj)* [It, lit., not so much] : NON TROPPO — used as a direction in music
**nontaster** \ˈ= *at* NON- +\ *n* : a person unable to taste the chemical phenylthiourea
**non–tax–paid** \(ˈ)=+\ *adj* : not having had the tax paid ⟨contained eighty gallons of *non-tax-paid* liquor —*Beam v. Georgia*⟩
**non·technical** \(ˈ)=*at* NON- +\ *adj* : not technical: as **a** : not related to technique or to technical skills or subjects ⟨~ training⟩ ⟨the ~ aspects of a performance⟩ **b** : not employing the words, expressions, or meanings peculiar or largely confined to a particular occupation or science ⟨~ language⟩ : written or phrased in a plain manner easily comprehended by laymen ⟨an excellent ~ guide —D.H.Kupfer⟩ — **nontechnically** *adv*
**non·temporal** \"+\ *adj* : not temporal
**non·tenure** \"+\ *n* [AF *nountenure*, fr. *noun-* ¹non- + MF *tenure*] : a former plea in bar made by a defendant in a real action setting up that he did not hold the land : a plea denying a demise or letting
**non·term** \"+\ *n* : the vacation between two terms of a law-court

**non·terminal** \"+\ *adj* : not terminal
**non·theatrical** \ˌ=+\ *adj* : not theatrical: as **a** : not designed for or presented in a theater ⟨tended to be more dramatic in his ~ works —Irving Kolodin⟩ **b** : of or relating to a moving picture esp. on film of substandard size that is designed primarily for showing in the home, classroom, or assembly hall ⟨the wholly ~ film tends to be of two- to three-reel length —Raymond Spottiswoode⟩
**non·theistic** \"+\ *adj* : not theistic
**non·tidal** \(ˈ)=+\ *adj* : not tidal
**non·tournament** \"+\ *adj* : not involving tournament play
**non·toxic** \"+\ *adj* : not toxic; *often* : free from toxicity for an indicated organism or a warm-blooded vertebrate at concentrations normally employed ⟨~ insecticides⟩
**non·traditional** \ˌ=+\ *adj* : not traditional; *specif* : not conforming to tradition ⟨~ practices⟩ ⟨~ designs⟩
**nontransferable** \(ˌ)=+\ *adj* : not transferable
**non·transparency** \ˌ=+\ *n* : the quality or state of being not transparent
**non·transparent** \(ˌ)=+\ *adj* : not transparent
**non·tron·ite** \ˈnän·trə,nīt\ *n* -s [F *nontronite*, fr. *Nontron*, town in southwest France + F *-ite*] : a pale yellow or greenish clay mineral that consists chiefly of hydrous iron silicate and is classed as montmorillonite in which iron has replaced more or less of the aluminum
**non·tropical** \(ˈ)ˌ= *at* NON- +\ *adj* : not tropical
**nontropical sprue** *n* : CELIAC DISEASE
**non trop·po** \(ˈ)nänˈträ(,)pō, (ˈ)nōn-, -trō-, -trȯ-\ *adv (or adj)* [It, lit., not too much] : without excess — used as a direction in music ⟨*non troppo* presto⟩
**non·trump** \(ˈ)ˌ= *at* NON- +\ *adj* [¹non- + trump, n.] : not having a trump ⟨a ~ hand⟩ : not being trumps ⟨a ~ suit⟩
**non·umbilicate** \(ˌ)=+\ *adj* : characterized by lack or closure of the umbilicus ⟨~ shells⟩
**non·uniform** \(ˈ)=+\ *adj* [¹non- + uniform] : not uniform — **non·uniformly** \"+\ *adv*
**non·uniformist** \"+\ *n* [nonuniform + -ist] : a person who believes that past changes in the structure of the earth have proceeded from cataclysms or processes more violent than are now operating — called also *nonuniformitarian*
**non·uniformitarian** \(ˌ)=+\ *n* [nonuniformity + -arian] : NONUNIFORMIST
**non·uniformity** \"+\ *n* [¹non- + uniformity] : the fact, condition, or an instance of being nonuniform : absence of uniformity ⟨such *nonuniformities* are greater with the faster heating process —F.O.Hess⟩ ⟨~ of composition⟩
¹**non·union** \(ˈ)=+\ *adj* [¹non- + union, adj.] **1** : not belonging to or affiliated with a trade union ⟨~ carpenters⟩ **2** : not recognizing or favoring trade unions or trade unionists ⟨a ~ contractor⟩
²**nonunion** \"\ *n* [¹non- + union, n.] : lack of union : failure to unite; *specif* : failure of the fragments of a broken bone to knit together
**non·unionism** \"+\ *n* [¹nonunion + -ism] : the theories, opinions, or practices of those who do not support trade unions
**non·unionist** \"+\ *n* [¹non- + unionist] : a person who does not belong to a trade union
**nonunion shop** *n* **1** : an establishment in which the employer recognizes no labor union and excludes from employment anyone affiliated with a labor union **2** : a shop in which a labor union forbids its members to accept employment
**non·uple** \ˈnä,n(y)üpəl, =ˈ==; ˈnänəp-\ *adj* [F, fr. MF, fr. L *nonus* ninth + MF *-ple* (as in *quadruple*) — more at NOON] **1** : consisting of nine : being nine times as great or as many : NINEFOLD **2** : taken by nines or in groups of nine
**non·u·plet** \-plət\ *n* -s [L *nonus* ninth + E *-plet* (as in *triplet*)] : a combination of nine of a kind **2** : a group of nine musical notes to be performed in the time of eight or six
**non·use** \(ˈ)ˌ= *at* NON- +\ *n* **1** : failure to use ⟨influence consumers in their use or ~ of citrus products —*Consumers' Use of & Opinions About Citrus Products*⟩ **2** : the fact or condition of not being used ⟨difficult to explain its ~ by scholars⟩
¹**non·user** \"+\ *n* [¹non- + -user (as in ²misuser)] : neglect or omission to use : failure to exercise a legal right or privilege
²**nonuser** \"\ *n* [¹non- + user] : one who is not a user
**non·vascular** \"+\ *adj* : not vascular
**non·venomous** \"+\ *adj* : not venomous
**non·verbal** \"+\ *adj* : not verbal: as **a** : being other than verbal ⟨the various ~ elements which are background to conversation —David Abercrombie⟩ **b** : involving, using, or requiring minimal or no use of language ⟨~ tests⟩ ⟨animal communication is always ~ —Stuart Chase⟩ **c** : ranking low in verbal skill : lacking facility in the use and comprehension of words ⟨simplified spelling for ~ types —W.H.Auden⟩ ⟨rural students . . . often come from ~ background —Julia F. Sherbourne⟩
**non·vernalized** \"+\ *adj* : not vernalized; *specif* : not subjected to low temperatures in early stages of germination to hasten flowering and fruiting ⟨~ seeds⟩
**non·viable** \"+\ *adj* : not viable : not capable of living, growing, or developing and functioning successfully ⟨a ~ theory⟩ ⟨~ embryos⟩
**non·vibratile** \"+\ *adj* : not vibratile
**non·vibratory** \"+\ *adj* : not vibratory
**non·vintage** \"+\ *adj* [¹non- + vintage, n.] : undated and usu. blended to approximate a standard ⟨a ~ wine⟩
**non·violence** \"+\ *n* : abstention on principled grounds from all use of violence; *also* : the ideal, doctrine, or principle of such abstention from all use of violence ⟨complete ~ is complete absence of ill will against all —D.M.Brown⟩ ⟨exalt ~, which . . . they consider the sublime ethics —Albert Schweitzer⟩
**non·violent** \"+\ *adj* : abstaining on principled grounds from all use of violence : not carried on or done with the use of violence : PEACEFUL ⟨extolled the method of ~ struggle —W.J. Ehrenpreis⟩ ⟨by methods of . . . passive resistance and ~ sabotage —Edmond Taylor⟩
**non·viscous** \"+\ *adj* : not viscous
**non·vocal** \"+\ *adj* : not vocal
**non·volatile** \"+\ *adj* : not volatile; *esp* : not volatilizing readily ⟨a ~ acid⟩
**nonvolatile vehicle** *n* : the liquid portion of a paint aside from its volatile thinner and water
**non·voting** \(ˈ)=*at* NON- +\ *adj* **1** : not voting : not exercising the right to vote ⟨the ~ element in the population⟩ **2** : not entitled to vote ⟨~ preferred stock⟩
**non vult con·ten·de·re** \ˌnän,vəltkənˈtendə,rē, ˌnōn-\ *or* **non vult** *n, pl* **non vult contenderes** *or* **non vults** [L *non vult contendere* he does not wish to contend] : NOLO CONTENDERE
**non·war** \(ˈ)= *at* NON- +\ *adj* : not serving or used for military purposes ⟨~ industries⟩ ⟨~ products⟩
¹**non·white** \"+\ *n* : a person who is not of the white race ⟨thousands of ~s —D.T.Bogue⟩
²**nonwhite** \"\ *adj* : of or relating to a race that is not white ⟨47 percent of the ~ population . . . were under 20 years of age —H.W.Odum⟩
**non·worker** \(ˈ)=+\ *n* **1** : a person who does not work ⟨the rule is that ~s shall not eat⟩ **2** : a person (as a self-employed man) who is not an employee
**non·woven** \"+\ *adj* : made without weaving; *esp* : having textile fibers bonded together by adhesive resins, rubber, or plastic or felted together under pressure ⟨~ fabrics⟩
**non·yl** \ˈnä,nil, ˈnō,-, -ᵊl\ *n* -s [ISV *nonane* + *-yl*] : an alkyl radical $C_9H_{19}$ derived from a nonane; *esp* : the normal radical $CH_3(CH_2)_7CH_2$—
**nonyl alcohol** *n* : any of several alcohols $C_9H_{19}OH$ derived from the nonanes; *esp* : primary or 1-nonanol
**non·yl·ene** \ˈnänᵊl,ēn, ˈnō-\ *n* -s [ISV *nonyl* + *-ene*] : any of several liquid isomeric hydrocarbons $C_9H_{18}$ of the ethylene series
**no·nyl·ic acid** \nōˈnilik-\ *n* [*nonylic* ISV *nonyl* + *-ic*] : NONOIC ACID
**non·zero** \(ˈ)ˌ= *at* NON- +\ *adj* : not being or involving zero
**noo** \ˈnü\ *dial var of* NOW
**noo-** *comb form* [LGk *noo-*, fr. Gk *noos, nous*] : mind ⟨*noo*scopic⟩
¹**noo·dle** \ˈnüdᵊl\ *n* -s [perh. alter. of ¹noddle] **1** : a stupid person : SIMPLETON, BLOCKHEAD, NINNY **2** : NODDLE, HEAD ⟨try to get this into your ~⟩
²**noodle** \"\ *n* -s [G *nudel*] : a food paste shaped typically in ribbon form and made with egg

³**noodle** \"\ *vt* **noodled; noodled; noodling** \-d(ə)liŋ\ **noodles** [prob. fr. G *nudeln*, fr. *nudel*, n.] : to feed (geese) forcibly with a fattening mixture in the form of an elongated roll
⁴**noodle** \"\ *vb* -ED/-ING/-S [origin unknown] *vt*. *chiefly Midland* : to catch (fish) with the bare hands or with a crude hook held in the hand : GUDDLE ~ *vi*, *chiefly Midland* : to fish with the bare hands
⁵**noodle** \"\ *vb* -ED/-ING/-S [imit.] *vi* **1** : to prelude or improvise on an instrument in an informal or desultory manner ⟨background of soft *noodling* by a clarinet⟩ ⟨went to the piano and *noodled* around until the tune came back to him⟩ **2** : to work over or elaborate the lines (as of a drawing) so as to impair the spontaneity and freedom ~ *vt* : to work over (a drawing) ⟨*noodled* letters are more closely related to printing types than to handwriting —Percy Seitlin⟩
**noo·dle·dom** \-ᵊldəm\ *n* -s **1** : the world of fools **2** : FOOLISHNESS, STUPIDITY
**noodlehead** \ˈ==,=\ *n* : NOODLE, BLOCKHEAD
**noo·goo·ra burr** \nüˈgürə\ *n, usu cap N* [*noogoora* (of unknown origin) + *burr*] : a European cocklebur (*Xanthium pungens*) that is a noxious weed in Australia
**nook** \ˈnu̇k\ *n* -s [ME *noke, nok*, perh. of Scand origin; akin to Norw dial. *nok* hook] **1** *chiefly Scot* : a corner of a rectangular piece (as of paper or cloth) or surface (as a field) **2** *obs* : a projecting piece of land : PROMONTORY **3** *chiefly Scot* : a projecting corner of a building or of an obstruction (as a hedge) **4 a** : an interior angle formed by two meeting walls : RECESS ⟨chimney ~⟩ **b** : a remote, secluded, sheltered, or out-of-the-way place or part ⟨odd ~s and corners of knowledge⟩ ⟨searched every ~ and cranny⟩ ⟨resting in a shady ~⟩
**nooked** \ˈnu̇kt\ *adj, chiefly dial* : having corners or angles — often used in combination ⟨four-*nooked* sheet⟩
**nook·er·y** \ˈnu̇k(ə)rē\ *n* -ES : a snug or cozy place or room
**nook·let** \-klət\ *n* -s : a little nook
**nook·sack** *or* **nook·sak** \ˈnu̇k,sak\ *also* **noot·sack** *or* **noot·sak** \ˈnüt,-, ˈnu̇t,-\ *n, pl* **nooksack** *or* **nooksacks** *or* **nooksak** *or* **nooksaks** *usu cap* **1 a** : a Salishan people of the Nooksack river valley, Washington **b** : a member of such people **2** : the language of the Nooksack people
**nook shaft** *n* : a column set in a reentering angle (as that made by the parts of a compound pier) differing from an angle shaft in standing free and being therefore usu. larger
**nook–shot·ten** \ˈnu̇k,shätᵊn\ *adj* [*nook* + obs. E *shotten*, past part. of E *shoot*] *chiefly dial* : jutting out at numerous angles : JAGGED ⟨a *nook-shotten* coastline⟩
¹**nooky** \ˈnu̇kē, -ki\ *adj* -ER/-EST [*nook* + *-y*, adj. suffix] **1** : full of nooks **2** : like a nook
²**nooky** \"\ *n* -ES [prob. fr. *nook* + *-y*, n. suffix forming diminutives] : SEXUAL INTERCOURSE — usu. considered vulgar
**no·olog·i·cal** \ˌnōəˈläjəkəl\ *adj* [*noology* + *-ical*] : relating to mind or to mental character ⟨~ anthropology⟩
**no·ol·o·gy** \nōˈäləjē\ *n* -ES [LGk *noo-* (fr. Gk *noos, nous* mind) + E *-logy*] : the study of mind : the science of phenomena regarded as purely mental in origin
¹**noon** \ˈnün\ *n* -s *often attrib* [ME, ninth hour of the day counting from sunrise, noon, midday, fr. OE *nōn* ninth hour of the day counting from sunrise, fr. L *nona*, fr. fem. of *nonus* ninth; akin to Skt *navama* ninth, L *novem* nine — more at NINE] **1** *obs* : ⁴NONE **2** : the middle of the day : the time when the sun is on the meridian : twelve o'clock in the daytime : MIDDAY ⟨several hours before ~⟩ ⟨a ~ meal⟩ ⟨the ~ line on a sundial⟩ **3** : MIDNIGHT — used chiefly in the phrase *noon of night* **4** : the highest point : CULMINATION ⟨~ of life⟩
²**noon** \"\ *vi* -ED/-ING/-S **1** *chiefly dial* : to take a rest or stop for a meal at noon **2** : to reach the culmination
**noonday** \ˈ=,=\ *n* : MIDDAY ⟨seek for it . . at broad ~ —Virginia Woolf⟩ ⟨~ heat⟩
**no one** *pron* : no person : NOBODY, NONE ⟨we saw *no one*⟩ ⟨*no one* will believe it⟩
**no. 1** *adj, usu cap N* : NUMBER ONE
**noonflower** \ˈ=,==\ *n* : GOATSBEARD 1
**noon·ing** \ˈnüniŋ\ *n* -s [¹noon + -ing] **1** *chiefly dial* : NOONTIME **2** *chiefly dial* : a meal eaten at noon **3** *chiefly dial* : a period at noon for eating or resting
**noonlight** \ˈ=,=\ *n* : the light of noon : the brightest daylight
**noon·stead** \ˈnün,sted\ *n, chiefly dial* : the position of the sun at noon
**noon·tide** \-,tīd\ *n* [ME *none-tyde*, fr. OE *nōntīd* ninth hour of the day counting from sunrise, fr. *nōn* + *tīd* time — more at NOON, TIDE] **1** : the time of noon : MIDDAY **2** : the highest or culminating point ⟨the bright ~ of southern gastronomy was somewhere in the past —Lucius Beebe⟩
**noon·time** \-tīm\ *n, often attrib* [ME *none tyme*, fr. *none, noon* noon + *tyme, time* time] : MIDDAY, NOONTIDE
**no·oscop·ic** \ˌnōəˈskäpik\ *adj* [*noo-* + *-scopic*] : of or relating to the examination of the mind
¹**noose** \ˈnüs\ *n* -s [prob. fr. Prov *nous* knot, fr. L *nodus* — more at NET] **1** : a loop with a running knot (as in a hangman's halter or a lariat) that binds closer the more it is drawn **2** : TIE, BOND, SNARE ⟨matrimonial ~⟩ **3** : the free end of a bowstring fastened to the bow nock by a timber hitch — compare EYE 2d(5)
²**noose** \"\ *vt* -ED/-ING/-S **1** : to secure by or as if by a noose : catch or capture in a noose : put a noose round : ENTRAP ⟨~ a snake⟩ **2** : to execute by hanging : HANG **3** : to furnish with a noose : make a noose in or of : pass (as a rope) around something so as to make a noose
**noot·ka** \ˈnu̇tkə, ˈnüt-\ *n, pl* **nootka** *or* **nootkas** *usu cap* **1 a** : a Wakashan people of Vancouver Island and the Cape Flattery region in northwestern Washington **b** : a member of such people **2** : the Wakashan language of the Nootka people
**nootka cypress** *or* **nootka sound cypress** *n, usu cap N&S* [*Nootka Sound*, Vancouver Island, British Columbia] : YELLOW CEDAR 1a
**noot·kan** \-kən\ *adj, usu cap* [*Nootka* + E *-an*] : belonging or relating to the Nootka people
**nootsack** *or* **nootsak** *usu cap, var of* NOOKSACK
**NOP** *abbr* **1** not otherwise provided for **2** not our publication
**no·pal** \ˈnōpəl\ *n* -s [Sp, fr. Nahuatl *nopalli*] : a cactus of the genus *Nopalea* (as the cochineal fig); *broadly* : PRICKLY PEAR
**no·pa·lea** \nōˈpālēə\ *n, cap* [NL, fr. Sp *nopal*] : a genus of cacti differing from *Opuntia* with which it is sometimes combined by the erect petals and scarlet flowers with stamens that are much longer than the petals
**no·pal·ry** \ˈnōpəlrē\ *n* -ES : a plantation of nopal for raising the cochineal insect
**no–par** \ˈ=ˈ=\ *or* **no–par–value** *adj* [fr. the phrase *no par* or *no par value*] : having no nominal value ⟨*no-par* share⟩ ⟨*no-par* common stock⟩
¹**nope** \ˈnōp\ *n* -s [earlier *nowpe*, prob. alter. (resulting from incorrect division of *an owpe*) of obs. E *owpe*, prob. alter. of E dial. ¹*alp*] *dial Brit* : BULLFINCH
²**nope** \"\ *adv* [alter. of ¹no] : definitely not : NO — not often in formal use; compare YEP
**no·pi·nene** \ˈnōpə,nēn\ *n* -s [ISV *nopin-* (as in *nopinic acid* $C_{10}H_{16}O_3$) (prob. anagram of *pinon-* — in *pinonic acid*) + *-ene* — more at PINONIC ACID] : a terpene $C_{10}H_{16}$ associated with alpha-pinene in turpentine oils and hyssop oil : a liquid bicyclic that is usu. levorotatory in its natural oils and that isomerizes to alpha-pinene (as on heating) — called also *beta-pinene, 2(10)-pinene*
**no place** *adv* [fr. the phrase *no place*] : NOWHERE
¹**nor** \nə(r), (ˌ)nȯ(ə)r, (ˌ)nȯ(ə), *in R speech in the southern US also* (ˌ)när\ *conj* [ME, contr. of *nother* nor, neither, fr. *nother*, pron. & adj., not either of two, neither — more at NEITHER] **1** : or not — used to introduce the second member ⟨neither here ~ there⟩ or last member ⟨does not drink, smoke, ~ gamble⟩ or second and each following member ⟨not be done by you ~ by me ~ by anyone⟩ of a series of two or more items of which each is negated **2 a** — used with *neither* as a negative correlative ⟨neither good ~ bad⟩; also used archaically to imply a negative in a preceding member ⟨thou ~ I have made the world —Alfred Tennyson⟩ **b** — used archaically to introduce both alternatives in a negative statement ⟨~ bits ~ bridles can his rage sustain —John Dryden⟩ **3** : and not — often used with inversion of subject and predicate after an affirmative that is equivalent to or implies a negative ⟨the crisis . . . was serious; ~ was it really serious —Ernest Barker⟩ ⟨forbear, ~ carry out the scheme you've planned —W.S.

Gilbert› **4** *chiefly dial* : AND, OR — used with a negative (as *not, never, no*) ‹it cannot ~ it will not come to good —Shak.›

**²nor** \"\ *conj* [ME, perh. fr. ¹*nor*] *dial* : THAN ‹did you ever . . . see a poorer place ~ this place —Donn Byrne›

**nor-** *comb form* [ISV, fr. ¹*normal*] **1** : parent compound from which (a specified compound) may be regarded as derived (as by removal of side chains from a ring system) — esp. in names of terpenes ‹*nor*bornane› **2** : compound of normal structure isomeric with the one to the name of which it is prefixed ‹*nor*leucine› **3** : homologue lower by one methylene group — esp. in names of steroids and alkaloids ‹*nor*cholane› ‹*nor*nicotine›

**nor** *abbr* **1** normal **2** north; northern

**nor·adrenaline** \¦nȯr+\ *n* [ISV *nor-* + *adrenaline*] : NOREPINEPHRINE

**no·rate** \nō'rāt, ˌ=ˈ=\ *vb* -ED/-ING/-S [alter. of *narrate*] *vt* **1** *chiefly South & Midland* : to spread (news) by word of mouth **2** *chiefly South & Midland* : to make deprecating statements about (a person) ~ *vi, chiefly South & Midland* : GOSSIP

**no·ra·tion** \nō'rāshən\ *n* -S [alter. of *narration*] *Midland* : RUMOR

**nor·berg·ite** \'nȯr,bər,gīt\ *n* -S [Sw *norbergit*, fr. Norberg, Västmanland, Sweden, its locality + Sw *-it* -ite] : a mineral $Mg_3SiO_4(F,OH)_2$ of the humite group composed of a magnesium silicate with fluorine and hydroxyl

**nor·bert·ine** \'nȯ(r)bə(r)d·ən\ *adj or n, usu cap* [St. *Norbert* †1134 Ger. ecclesiastic + E *-ine*, adj. suffix] : PREMONSTRATENSIAN

**nor·bornane** \(')nȯr+\ *n* [*nor-* + *bornane*] : a bicyclic crystalline hydrocarbon $C_7H_{12}$ that is the parent compound of various terpenoids (as camphor and fenchone) and that is obtained by adding ethylene to cyclopentadiene under heat and pressure and then hydrogenating; 1,4-methano-cyclohexane; bicyclo[2.2.1]heptane — called also *norcamphane*

**nor·camphane** \"+\ *n* [*nor-* + *camphane*] : NORBORNANE

**nord·cap·er** \'nȯ(r)d,kāpə(r)\ *n* -S [D *noordkaper*, fr. *Noordkaap* North Cape, northern Norway + D *-er*] : RIGHT WHALE

**nor·den·skiol·dine** \'nȯ(r)dᵊn,shəldən\ *n* -S [Norw *nordenskiöldin*, fr. Baron Nils A.E. *Nordenskjöld* †1901 Swed. geologist + Norw *-in* -ine] : a mineral $CaSn(BO_3)_2$ consisting of a calcium tin borate

**nord·hau·sen acid** \'nȯ(r)d,hau̇zᵊn-\ *n, usu cap N* [fr. *Nordhausen*, city in central Germany where it was orig. manufactured] : OLEUM 2

**¹nor·dic** \'nȯrdik, 'nȯ(ə)d-, -dēk\ *adj, usu cap* [F *nordique*, fr. *nord* north (fr. OF, fr. OE *north*) + *-ique* -ic — more at NORTH] **1** : of or relating to the Germanic peoples of northern Europe **2** : of or relating to a physical type characterized by tall stature, long head, light skin and hair, and blue eyes, occurring most frequently in northern Europe, and regarded by some as a racial division of the Caucasian : TEUTONIC — compare ALPINE, MEDITERRANEAN **3** : ARYAN 3a **4** : of or relating to Norway, Sweden, Denmark, Iceland, and Finland

**²nordic** \"\ *n* -S *cap* **1** : a native of northern Europe **2 a** : a person representative of the Nordic physical type **b** : a member of the hypothetical Nordic division of the Caucasian race **3** : a member of the Norwegian, Swedish, Danish, Icelandic, or Finnish peoples : SCANDINAVIAN

**nordic combined** *n, pl* **nordic combineds** *usu cap N* : a competitive ski event consisting of both ski jumping and cross-country racing — compare ALPINE COMBINED

**nor·di·cism** \'nȯ(r)də,sizəm\ *n* -S *usu cap* **1** : the belief in or the doctrine of the superiority of the hypothetical Nordic racial type and its cultural capacities — compare ARYANISM **2** : qualities or traits regarded as distinctive of the hypothetical Nordic race

**nor·di·cist** \-,səst\ *n* -S : a believer in the doctrine of Nordic preeminence and supremacy

**nor·di·hy·dro·guai·a·ret·ic acid** \¦nȯ(r),dī¦hīdrō¦g(w)īə¦red·ik-\ *n* [*nordihydroguaiaretic* fr. *nor-* + *dihydr-* + *guaiaretic* (in *guaiaretic acid* $C_{20}H_{24}O_4$) (ISV *guaia-* — fr. NL *Guaiacum* — + *ret-* — fr. Gk *rhētinē* resin — + *-ic*)] : a crystalline derivative $[(HO)_2C_6H_3CH_2CH(CH_3)-]_2$ of pyrocatechol obtained esp. from the creosote bush or made synthetically and used in trace amounts as an antioxidant to prevent rancidity of lard and other fats or oils — abbr. *NDGA*

**nord·mann's fir** \'nȯrdmənz-\ *n, usu cap N* [after A. von *Nordmann* †1866 Russ. naturalist] : an ornamental evergreen tree (*Abies nordmanniana*) native to the Caucasus region having rigid horizontal branches

**nord·mark·ite** \'nȯrd,mär,kīt\ *n* -S [*Nordmark*, Sweden, its locality + E *-ite*] : a variety of staurolite containing manganese

**nor·ephedrine** \¦nȯr, (')nȯr+\ *n* [*nor-* + *ephedrine*] : a crystalline compound $C_6H_5CHOHCH(CH_3)NH_2$ known in three optically isomeric forms of which the levoratatory form occurs naturally with ephedrine; 1-phenyl-2-amino-1-propanol — called also *phenylpropanolamine*

**nor·epinephrine** \¦nȯr+\ *n* [*nor-* + *epinephrine*] : a crystalline compound $(HO)_2C_6H_3CH(OH)CH_2NH_2$ that occurs in the levoratatory form as a hormone with epinephrine and that has a strong vasoconstrictor action and mediates transmission of sympathetic nerve impulses but lacks or exhibits weakly most other epinephrine effects (as on cardiac output or blood-sugar concentration) — called also *arterenol, noradrenaline;* compare SYMPATHIN

**¹nor·folk** \'nȯr¦fək, 'nȯ(ə)|; *in sense 2 also* |,fōk *sometimes* |,fōk\ *adj, usu cap* [fr. *Norfolk*, county in eastern England] **1** : of or from the county of Norfolk, England : of the kind or style prevalent in Norfolk **2** [fr. *Norfolk*, city in southeast Virginia] : of or from the city of Norfolk, Virginia ‹*Norfolk* shipyards› : of the kind or style prevalent in Norfolk

**²nor·folk** \'nȯrfək, 'nȯ(ə)f-\ *n* -S *often cap* [fr. *Norfolk*, county in eastern England] : NORFOLK JACKET

**norfolk island pine** *n, usu cap N&I* [fr. *Norfolk Island*, island in the southern Pacific ocean administratively attached to Australia] : an evergreen tree (*Araucaria excelsa*) of Australia and Norfolk Island with whorls of horizontal branches densely set with deep green awl-shaped leaves that in its native home grows to 200 feet but is often grown in pots and there seldom exceeds a few feet in height

**norfolk jacket** *n, often cap N* [fr. Norfolk, county in eastern England] : a single-breasted usu. loose-fitting jacket with four box pleats, one at each side of the front and back, and a belt that typically runs through them

Norfolk jacket

**norfolk plover** *n, usu cap N* [fr. *Norfolk*, county in eastern England] : STONE CURLEW

**norfolk spot** *n, usu cap N* [fr. *Norfolk*, city in southeast Virginia] : SPOT 7

**norfolk trotter** *n, usu cap N&T* [fr. *Norfolk*, county in eastern England] : HACKNEY 2a

**norfolk turkey** *n, usu cap N* [fr. *Norfolk*, county in eastern England] : a medium-sized greenish black turkey that has pink feet which turn slaty black with age and that is sometimes considered to constitute a distinct breed

**norfolk wherry** *n, usu cap N* [fr. *Norfolk*, county in eastern England] : WHERRY 2

**no·ri** \'nōrē\ *n* -S [Jap] : AMANORI

**no·ria** \'nōrēə\ *n* -S [Sp, fr. Ar *nā'ūrah*] : a Persian wheel of the bucket type

**nor·ie** \'nȧri\ *n* -S [origin unknown] *chiefly Scot* : a cormorant (*Phalacrocorax carbo*)

**nor·i·mon** \'nȧrə,män\ *n* -S [Jap *norimono*, fr. *nori* riding + *mono* thing] : a Japanese covered litter carried by men

**nor·it** \'nȯrət\ *n* -S [fr. *Norit*, a trademark] : a commercially produced activated carbon that is used as an adsorbent (as for decolorizing sugar solutions or isolating vitamins or antibiotics)

**nor·ite** \'nȯ,rīt\ *n* -S [Norw *norit*, fr. *Norge* Norway + Norw *-it* -ite] : a variety of gabbro consisting of a granular aggregate of basic plagioclase, orthorhombic pyroxene, and usu. some magnetite — **nor·it·ic** \(')nȯ¦rid·ik\ *adj*

**no·ri·to** \'nōrə,tō\ *n pl* [Jap] : Shinto ritualistic prayers

**nor·land** \'nȯrlənd\ *n* [contr. of *northland*] **1** *chiefly dial* : the land in the north : north country **2** *chiefly Scot* : NORLANDER

**nor·land·er** \-də(r)\ *n* -S *chiefly dial* : a person from the north country : NORTHERNER

**nor·leucine** \(')nȯ(r)+\ *n* [ISV *nor-* + *leucine*] : a crystalline amino acid $CH_3(CH_2)_3CH(NH_2)COOH$ isomeric with leucine and usu. made synthetically; alpha-amino-caproic acid

**norm** \'nȯ(ə)rm, 'nȯ(ə)m\ *n* -S [L *norma* carpenter's square, pattern, rule] **1** : an authoritative rule or standard : MODEL, TYPE, PATTERN; *specif* : a hypothetical mineral composition of a rock calculated according to certain definite rules and usu. differing widely from the actual mineral composition or mode **2** : a standard of conduct or ethical value : a principle of right action : MAXIM; *esp* : an imperative statement asserting or denying that something ought to be done or has value ‹~*s* or ideals or values that are not held, that don't become peoples' interests, will be peculiarly valueless, no matter what inherent validity they may possess —Lucius Garvin› **3** : an ideal standard binding upon the members of a group and serving to guide, control, or regulate proper and acceptable behavior ‹no society lacks ~*s* governing conduct —R.K.Merton› **4** : AVERAGE ‹$10,000 per annum is the ~ in this community›: as **a** : a set standard of development or achievement usu. derived from the average or median achievement of a large group ‹these students . . . scored above the national ~*s* for teachers college graduates —*Education Digest*›; *specif* : a production quota set for a worker **b** : the average score of a specified class of persons on a specified test ‹grade ~› ‹age ~› **c** : a pattern or trait taken or estimated to be typical in the behavior of a social group because most frequently observed ‹studies aimed at establishing the ~*s* of sexual behavior among the middle classes› **syn** see AVERAGE

**norm-** *or* **normo-** *comb form* [ISV, fr. ¹*normal*] : normal ‹*norm*ergy› ‹*normo*blast› ‹*normo*tension›

**nor·ma** \'nȯrmə\ *n, pl* **nor·mae** \-r,mē\ [L, carpenter's square, pattern, rule] **1** : RULE, MODEL, STANDARD, NORM **2** *anthrop* **a** : a standard position for viewing a part (as the skull); *also* : an aspect of a bodily part (as the cranium) **b** : a line or pattern indicating the contour of the cranium

**¹nor·mal** \'nȯrməl, 'nȯ(ə)m-\ *adj* [in sense 1, fr. L *normalis* according to a square, forming a right angle, fr. *norma* carpenter's square, pattern, rule (prob. fr. Gk *gnōmona*, accus. of *gnōmōn* interpreter, discerner, pointer on a sundial, carpenter's square) + *-alis* -al; in senses 2–7 and 9–10, fr. LL *normalis* according to rule, fr. L, according to a square; in sense 8, trans. of F *normale* (in *école normale* normal school) — more at GNOMON] **1** : forming a right angle : PERPENDICULAR **2** : according to, constituting, or not deviating from an established norm, rule, or principle : conformed to a type, standard, or regular pattern : not abnormal : REGULAR ‹~ word order of subject and verb› ‹~ working hours› ‹~ pronunciation› **3 a** : unaffected by or not exposed to any particular infection or experimental treatment ‹a ~ control animal› **b** : occurring naturally and not because of disease, inoculation, or any experimental treatment ‹~ immunity› **4 a** : of, relating to, or characterized by average intelligence or development : free from intellectual defect **b** : free from mental disorder : having neither neurosis, personality disorder, nor psychosis : SANE **c** : characterized by balanced, well-integrated functioning of the organism as a whole within the limits imposed by the environment and in accord with the pattern of one's biological endowment **5** : relating to or conforming with long-run expectations or to a permanent standard deviations from which on the part of individual economic phenomena are to be regarded as self-corrective ‹a ~ price corresponds to long-run costs of production› **6 a** : approximating the statistical norm or average ‹a ~ infant mortality rate› ‹~ rainfall of the region› **b** : consistent with the social norm ‹~ married life› **7** : average over many years at a particular place and for a definite time, a certain day, or some other specified period — used of a meteorological element **8** : of or relating to the training of teachers ‹~ college› ‹~ department› **9** : of, relating to, or characterized by full ablaut grade **10 a** *of a solution* : having a concentration of one gram equivalent of solute per liter ‹~ hydrochloric acid› — abbr. *N* **b** : being an assumed fundamental compound (as an acid from which the known acids are obtained by dehydration) ‹~ sulfuric acid $S(OH)_6$› — compare ORTH- 3a **c** : containing neither basic hydroxyl nor acid hydrogen ‹~ silver phosphate $Ag_3PO_4$› — used of a compound (as a salt, ester, or amide) **d** : not associated ‹~ liquids› ‹~ molecules› **e** : having a straight-chain structure ‹~ pentane› ‹~ butyl alcohol› — abbr. *n;* used of an aliphatic hydrocarbon, one of its derivatives, or an alkyl radical; compare IS- 2b **f** : CIS — used esp. of stereoisomeric compounds containing two fused saturated rings; contrasted with *allo* ‹the allo and ~ forms of steroids› **syn** see REGULAR

**²normal** \"\ *n* -S **1** *math* **a** : PERPENDICULAR: (1) : a line perpendicular to the tangent line to a curve at a point of the curve (2) : a plane perpendicular to the tangent plane to a surface at a point on the surface **b** : the intercept on the normal line between a curve and the x-axis **2** : one that is normal: as **a** : a normal person or organism **b** : a normal level (as of temperature, pressure, rainfall, price) : MEAN, AVERAGE **c** : NORMAL SCHOOL **3** : a form or state regarded as the norm : STANDARD

**normal barrage** *n* : a standing barrage which is to be fired in an attack and for which batteries are habitually laid on a target line with the barrage being fired on call from the appropriate area

**normal curve** *n* : a bell-shaped curve representing a Gaussian distribution (as of random error)

**nor·mal·cy** \'nȯ(r)məlsē, -si\ *n* -ES : the state, condition, or fact of being normal : NORMALITY ‹a return to ~ after war›

**normal dispersion** *n* : dispersion (as of light by an optical grating) in which the separation of components in any one spectrum increases continuously and almost uniformly with the wavelength, the separation being a monotonic function of the dispersion variable

**normal distribution** *n* : GAUSSIAN DISTRIBUTION

**normal dropper** *n* : DROPPER 4b

**normal equation** *n* : any of a set of simultaneous equations involving experimental unknowns and derived from a larger number of observation equations in the course of least-squares adjustment of observations

**normal fault** *n* : an inclined fault in which the hanging wall has slipped down relative to the footwall

**normal form** *n, logic* : a canonical or standard fundamental form of a statement to which others can be reduced; *esp* : a compound statement in the propositional calculus consisting of nothing but a conjunction of disjunctions whose disjuncts are either elementary statements or negations thereof

**normal honey** *n* : honey produced from floral nectars as distinguished from that produced from honeydew

**normal horizontal separation** *n* : the horizontal separation measured in a direction at right angles to the strike of a faulted stratum

**nor·mal·i·ty** \nȯ(r)'malәd·ē, -әtē, -i\ *n* -ES [prob. fr. F *normalité*, fr. *normal* according to or constituting an established norm, normal (fr. LL *normalis* according to rule) + *-ité* -ity — more at NORMAL] **1** : the quality or state of being normal : conformity with the norm ‹~ of human behavior› ‹~ of structure in an organism› **2** *of a solution* : concentration expressed in gram equivalents of solute per liter **3** : conformity (as of statistical data) to the Gaussian distribution law

**nor·mal·iza·tion** \,nȯ(r)məlә'zāshən, -,lī-\ *n* -S [*normalize* + *-ation*] : the act or process of making normal ‹~ of diplomatic relations›

**nor·mal·ize** \'nȯ(r)mə,līz\ *vt* -ED/-ING/-S *see -ize in Explan Notes* [¹*normal* + *-ize*] : to make normal : make conform to or reduce to a norm or standard: **a** : to secure uniformity and destroy coarse structure and strains in (metal) esp. by heating to a temperature at which recrystallization takes place or (in steel) by heating above the upper transformation temperature and then cooling in still air — compare HEAT-TREAT **b** : to make (a text, dialect, or language) regular as to spelling and inflection by using consistently only one symbol or group of symbols for each phoneme and only one of several variants for each grammatical form

**nor·mal·iz·er** \-zә(r)\ *n* -S : one that normalizes; *specif* : one that heat-treats metal to relieve internal strains and strengthen it during or after the annealing process

**nor·mal·ly** \-lē, -li\ *adv* **1** : in a normal manner ‹acting ~ in spite of his anxiety› : to a normal degree ‹~ educated person› **2** : COMMONLY, USUALLY ‹the ~ stabilizing middle class —E.B. George› : in normal circumstances : under normal conditions ‹contract ~ would have expired in January›

**normal minor scale** *n* : NATURAL MINOR SCALE

**normal moisture capacity** *n* : FIELD CAPACITY

**normalness** *n* -ES : NORMALITY

**normal overlap** *n* : an individual normal in phenotype although possessing a genotype that should cause deviation from normal — compare PENETRANCE

**normal pitch** *n* : the distance between points of intersection of the line of action of gear teeth with the working faces of two adjacent teeth

**normal place** *n* : the apparent position of a planet or comet at a specified time as ascertained from a considerable number of observations

**normal pressure** *n* : standard pressure usu. taken to be equal to that of a column of mercury 760 millimeters in height, the mercury being 0° C and gravity being that at 45 degrees latitude : one atmosphere

**normal saline solution** *also* **normal salt solution** *n* : PHYSIOLOGICAL SALINE

**normal school** *n* [trans. of F *école normale;* fr. the fact that the first school so named in France was intended to serve as a model for other teacher training schools] : a school for the training chiefly of elementary schoolteachers commonly state-supported and usu. offering a two-year course to high school graduates — compare TEACHERS COLLEGE

**normal state** *n* : GROUND STATE

**normal tax** *n* : a basic rate of taxation (as on income) applied to large groups of taxpayers to which varying surtaxes may be added for smaller subgroups

**normal valence** *n* : the usually accepted valence of a chemical element or of an atom or radical ‹the *normal valence* of oxygen is −2›

**normal volume** *n* : the volume of a gas at 0° C and 760 millimeters pressure as ascertained either by direct observation or by calculations in accordance with the laws of Boyle and Charles

**¹nor·man** \'nȯrmən, 'nȯ(ə)m-\ *n* -S *cap* [ME, fr. OF *normant*, fr. ON *Northmann-, Northmathr* Norwegian, Scandinavian, fr. *northr* north + *mann-, mathr* man — more at NORTH, MAN] **1** : a native or inhabitant of Normandy: **a** : one of the Scandinavians who conquered Normandy in the 10th century **b** : a member of the Norman-French people who conquered England in 1066 under William the Conqueror **2** : NORMAN-FRENCH

**²norman** \"\ *adj, usu cap* : of, relating to, or characteristic of Normandy or the Normans ‹*Norman* castle›

**³norman** \"\ *n* -S [origin unknown] **1** : a heavy wooden or iron bar to insert into a hole in a bitt or stanchion in order to guide or secure a cable or rope **2** : a pin used in a hole for any of various purposes (as a fid through a rudderhead)

**norman architecture** *n, usu cap N* **1** : a Romanesque style first appearing in and near Normandy about A.D. 950 **2** : architecture resembling or imitating this style

**norman crimson** *or* **norman red** *n, often cap N* : vermilion or a color resembling it

**nor·mand** \'nȯrmənd\ *n* -S *cap* [ME *Normand, Normant*, fr. MF, Norman] : a modern descendant of the Normans or Norman-French : a native of Normandy

**normande sauce** \(')nȯr¦mänd-\ *or* **nor·man·dy sauce** \'nȯ(r)məndē-\ *n, often cap N* [*normande sauce* fr. F *normande* (in *sauce normande* normande sauce) (fem. of *normand*, adj., Norman, fr. *Normand*, n., Norman, fr. OF *Normant*) + E *sauce; normandy sauce* fr. *Normandy*, region of northwest France + E *sauce*] : a white sauce made of fish stock, flavored with wine, and enriched with cream and yolks of eggs

**norman-french** \¦=¦=\ *n* -ES *cap N&F* **1 a** : the French language used by the medieval Normans **b** : the modern dialect of Normandy **2** : LAW FRENCH

**nor·man·ism** \'nȯ(r)mə,nizəm\ *n* -S *usu cap* **1** : the quality or traits distinctive of the Normans; *also* : partiality for Norman culture or civilization **2** : a Norman idiom or expression

**nor·man·iza·tion** \,nȯ(r)mənə'zāshən\ *n* -S *often cap* [*normanize* + *-ation*] : the act or process of making Norman ‹~ of England after the Conquest›

**nor·man·ize** \'nȯ(r)mə,nīz\ *vt* -ED/-ING/-S *see -ize in Explan Notes, often cap* [¹*Norman* + *-ize*] : to make Norman in quality, traits, or culture; *also* : to bring under the military or civil control of Normans

**nor·man·nic** \(')nȯr¦manik\ *adj, usu cap* : relating to or characteristic of the Normans

**nor·ma·tive** \'nȯ(r)məd·iv, -ət|\ *adj* [F *normatif*, fr. *norme* norm (fr. L *norma* carpenter's square, pattern, rule) + *-atif* -ative — more at NORMAL] **1** : of, relating to, or dealing with norms, their nature, or mode of discovery and existence ‹~ discipline› **2** : explicating, inferring, or discovering a norm ‹a ~ judgment› ‹~ statements› **3** : creating, prescribing, or imposing a norm ‹a ~ law› **4 a** : REGULATIVE, HEURISTIC ‹guiding ~ principles› **b** : PRESCRIPTIVE, DIDACTIC ‹governing, ~ rules› ‹~ grammar› **5** : relating to norms of mineral composition — **nor·ma·tive·ly** \|əvlē, -li\ *adv* — **nor·ma·tive·ness** \|ivnəs\ *n* -ES

**normative currency** *n* : a currency system in which the unit is based upon a metallic standard — compare FREE CURRENCY

**normative science** *n* : a science that tests or evaluates and not merely describes or generalizes facts; *specif* : the group comprising logic, ethics, and aesthetics

**normative truth** *n* : the truth about values that is presumably not determinable simply by the existence or nonexistence of things or by logic alone without reference to something further (as the human will or objective ideals) — called also *aesthetic truth, ethical truth, ideal truth*

**nor·mer·gic** \(')nȯr¦mərjik\ *adj* : having the degree of sensitivity toward an allergen typical of age group and community — distinguished from *hyperergic* and *hypoergic*

**nor·mer·gy** \'nȯ(r)mə(r)jē\ *n* -ES [ISV *norm-* + all*ergy*] : the quality or state of being normergic

**normo-** — see NORM-

**nor·mo·blast** \'nȯ(r)mə,blast\ *n* [ISV *norm-* + *-blast*] : an immature red blood cell containing hemoglobin and a pycnotic nucleus and normally present in bone marrow but appearing in the blood in many anemias — compare ERYTHROBLAST — **normo·blas·tic** \¦=¦blastik\ *adj*

**nor·mo·chro·mia** \,nȯ(r)mə'krōmēə\ *n* -S [NL, fr. *norm-* + *-chromia*] : the condition of red blood cells that contain a normal amount of hemoglobin whatever their other deficiencies

**nor·mo·chro·mic** \¦=¦krōmik\ *adj* [*normochromia* + *-ic*] **1** *of blood* : having a normal color **2** *of anemia* : accompanied by normal color of the red blood cells : not marked by decrease in the hemoglobin content of the individual red blood cells

**nor·mo·cyte** \'nȯ(r)mə,sīt\ *n* -S [ISV *norm-* + *-cyte*] : a red blood cell normal in size and in hemoglobin content

**nor·mo·cyt·ic** \¦=¦sid·ik\ *adj* **1** *of blood* : containing red blood cells that are normal in size and usu. also in hemoglobin content **2** *of anemia* : marked by the presence of diminished numbers of normal red blood cells in the circulating blood

**nor·mo·splanchnic** \¦nȯ(r)mō+\ *adj* [ISV *norm-* + *splanchnic;* orig. formed as It *normosplancnico*] : having average or intermediate body-build — distinguished from *macrosplanchnic* and *microsplanchnic*

**nor·mo·tension** \"+\ *n* [*norm-* + *tension*] : normal blood pressure

**¹nor·mo·ten·sive** \¦nȯ(r)mō¦ten(t)siv\ *adj* [*normotension* + *-ive*] : having a blood pressure typical of the age group and community to which one belongs — compare HYPERTENSIVE

**²normotensive** \"\ *n* -S : a person with normal blood pressure

**norms** *pl of* NORM

**norn** \'nȯ(ə)rn\ *n* -S *often cap* [ON] : a goddess presiding over personal destiny : a fate of Norse mythology ‹blinks and croaks like a toad or a *Norn* —R.P.Warren› — usu. used in pl. ‹buy something you cannot afford as a gesture of defiance at the *Norns* —Frank Sullivan›

**nor·nicotine** \(')nȯ(r)+\ *n* [*nor-* + *nicotine*] : a liquid alkaloid $C_9H_{12}N_2$ found in tobacco and obtained from nicotine by demethylation; 3-α-pyrrolidyl-pyridine

**nor·roy** \'nä,rȯi\ *n* -S *usu cap* [ME *norrey*, prob. fr. MF *nord* north (fr. OF, fr. OE *north*) + *rey, roy* king, fr. L *reg-, rex* — more at NORTH, ROYAL] **1** : NORROY KING OF ARMS **2** : NORROY AND ULSTER KING OF ARMS

**norroy and ulster king of arms** *also* **norroy and ulster** *usu cap N&U&K&Arms* [*Ulster*, former province in northern Ireland] **:** a king of arms having jurisdiction in England north of the river Trent and in Northern Ireland — compare COLLEGE OF ARMS, CLARENCEUX KING OF ARMS, GARTER KING OF ARMS; see NORROY KING OF ARMS, ULSTER KING OF ARMS

**norroy king of arms** *usu cap N&K&A* **:** one of the English kings of arms, having jurisdiction north of the river Trent and since 1943 given an expanded jurisdiction and called *Norroy and Ulster King of Arms;* compare COLLEGE OF ARMS, CLARENCEUX KING OF ARMS, GARTER KING OF ARMS, ULSTER KING OF ARMS

**¹norse** \ˈnȯ(ə)rs, ˈnȯ(ə)s\ *n, pl* **norse** *cap* [prob. fr. obs. D *noorsch*, adj., Norwegian, Scandinavian (now *noors* Norwegian), alter. of obs. D *noordsch*, adj., northern (now *noords*), fr. D *noord* north + *-sch* -ish; akin to OE *north* and to OE *-isc* -ish — more at NORTH, -ISH] **1** *norse pl* **a :** SCANDINAVIANS **b :** NORWEGIANS **2 a :** NORWEGIAN 2 **b :** any of the western Scandinavian dialects or languages **c :** the Scandinavian group of Germanic languages

**²norse** \"\ *adj, usu cap* **1 :** of or relating to ancient Scandinavia or the language of its inhabitants ⟨*Norse* mythology⟩ **2 :** of or relating to Norway or the Norwegians **:** NORWEGIAN

**¹norse-american** \ˌ≈¦≈≈≈\ *adj, usu cap N&A* **:** Norwegian and American; *specif* **:** of, relating to, or being an American of Norwegian origin or descent

**²norse-american** \"\ *n, cap N&A* **:** an American of Norwegian origin or descent

**nor·sel** \ˈnȯrsəl\ *n* -s [alter. of ME *nostul, nostylle*, fr. OE *nostle* fillet, band; akin to OHG *nestila, nestilo* bow, band, shoelace — more at LANYARD] **:** a short line for fastening fishnets or fishhooks

**nor·sel·ler** \-lər\ *n* -s **:** one that attaches norsels to fishnets

**norse·man** \ˈnȯrsmən, ˈnȯ(ə)s-\ *n, pl* **norsemen** *cap* **1 :** one of the ancient Scandinavians — called also *Northman* **2 :** SCANDINAVIAN; *specif* **:** NORWEGIAN

**nor·ski** *or* **nor·skie** *or* **nor·sky** \ˈnȯrskē\ *n, pl* **norskis** *or* **norskies** *usu cap* [*norskie, norsky* fr. Norw *norsk*, adj., Norwegian (fr. ONorw, prob. contr. of — assumed — ONorw *norrœnsk*, fr. ONorw *norrœnn*, adj., Norwegian — akin to OE *northerne* northern — + *-sk* -ish, akin to OE *-isc* -ish) + E *-ie* or *-y; norski* alter. of *norskie, norsky* — more at NORTHERN, -ISH] **:** a Norwegian or Norwegian-American — used as a nickname

**nor·te** \ˈnȯrtā\ *n* -s [Sp, north wind, north, fr. MF *nord* north, fr. OF, fr. OE *north*] **:** a strong northerly wind esp. in Mexico or Central America **:** NORTHER

**nor·te·amer·i·ca·no** \ˌnȯ(r)tāə,merəˈkä(,)nō\ *n* -s [Sp, adj. & n., fr. *norte* north + *americano* American] **:** NORTH AMERICAN 2

**¹north** \ˈnȯ(ə)rth, ˈnȯ(ə)th\ *adv* [ME, fr. OE; akin to OHG *nord* north, ON *northr* north, Umbrian *nertru* left, Gk *nerteros* lower, infernal; basic meaning: left] **:** to, toward, or in the north **:** NORTHWARD

**²north** \"\ *adj* [ME, fr. OE *north-*, fr. *north*, adv.] **1 a :** situated toward or at the north ⟨the ~ entrance⟩ ⟨the ~ country⟩ **b** [ME, fr. OE *northan-*, fr. *northan*, adv.; akin to ON *northan* from the north; derivative fr. the root of E ¹*north*] **:** coming from the north ⟨the ~ wind⟩ **2 :** in the direction of the left side of a church looking from the nave toward the altar or chancel

**³north** \"\ *n* -s [ME, fr. *north*, adv.] **1 a :** the direction of the north terrestrial pole **:** the direction to the left of one facing east **:** the direction to the left of one facing the sunrise when the sun is near one of the equinoxes **b :** the part of the sky lying to the left of an observer facing east **c :** the cardinal point directly opposite to south — abbr. *N;* see COMPASS CARD **d :** the direction along any meridian toward that pole of the earth viewed from which the earth's rotation is counterclockwise — compare MAGNETIC NORTH **e :** the direction on the celestial sphere to the left when one faces the direction of its apparent rotation **:** the direction to the left when one faces the direction of revolution around the sun of the earth and the principal planets **2** *usu cap* **a :** regions or countries lying to the north of a specified or implied point of orientation (as in the U. S. the states lying in general north of Mason and Dixon's Line and the Ohio river) **b :** something (as people, culture, or institutions) characteristic of the North ⟨the *North* favored certain legislative proposals⟩ **3 :** the north wind **4** *often cap* **a :** the one of four positions at 90-degree intervals that lies toward the north **b :** a person (as a bridge player) occupying such a position in the course of a specific activity

**⁴north** \"\ *vb* -ED/-ING/-S [¹*north*] **:** to move or veer toward the north

**northabout** \ˈ≈≈,≈\ *adv (or adj)* **:** about in tacking so as to head north; *broadly* **:** toward the north **:** NORTHWARD

**¹north african** *adj, usu cap N&A* [*North Africa*, the countries of northern Africa + E *-an*] **1 :** of, relating to, or characteristic of North Africa — often used specif. of the region including Morocco, Algeria, Tunisia, Libya, and Egypt **2 :** of, relating to, or characteristic of the North Africans

**²north african** *n, cap N&A* **:** a native or inhabitant of North Africa — usu. used specif. of the natives and inhabitants of Morocco, Algeria, Tunisia, Libya, and Egypt

**north america** *adj, usu cap N&A* [fr. *North America*, continent in the western hemisphere] **:** of or from the continent of North America **:** of the kind or style prevalent in North America **:** NORTH AMERICAN

**¹north american** *n, cap N&A* [*North America* + E *-an*, n. suffix] **1 :** a native or inhabitant of North America **2** [trans. of Sp *norteamericano*] **:** a native or inhabitant of the U. S. as distinguished esp. from the Latin natives or inhabitants of Mexico, Central America, the West Indies, and So. America — compare ANGLO-AMERICAN

**²north american** *adj, usu cap N&A* [*North America* + E *-an*, adj. suffix] **1 :** of, relating to, or characteristic of North America **2 :** of, relating to, or characteristic of the people of North America **3** [trans. of Sp *norteamericano*] **:** of, relating to, or characteristic of the people of the U. S. as distinguished esp. from the Latin peoples of Mexico, Central America, the West Indies, and So. America ⟨a strong sensitive face, too quick and mobile to be *North American* —Thurston Scott⟩

**north american blastomycosis** *n, usu cap N&A* **:** blastomycosis that involves esp. the skin, lymph nodes, and lungs and that is caused by infection with a fungus (*Blastomyces dermatitidis*)

**north american indian** *n, usu cap N&A&I* **:** an Indian of the North American continent; *esp* **:** an Indian of the U. S. and Canada

**north·amp·ton** \(ˈ)nȯ(r)ˈtham(p)tən, -(r)thˈha-\ *adj, usu cap* [fr. *Northampton*, city and county in central England] **:** of or from the city of Northampton, England **:** of the kind or style prevalent in Northampton

**north·amp·ton·shire** \-n,shi(ə)r, -,shiə, -,shə(r)\ *or* **northampton** *adj, usu cap* [fr. *Northamptonshire, Northampton*, county in central England] **:** of or from the county of Northampton, England **:** of the kind or style prevalent in Northampton

**north arabic** *n, usu cap N&A* **:** a group of Semitic dialects spoken in northern and central Arabia from the 4th century onward, one of which forms the basis of classical and modern Arabic

**northbound** \ˈ≈,≈\ *adj* **:** traveling or headed in a northerly direction ⟨~ traffic⟩ — compare EASTBOUND

**north briton** *n, cap N&B* **:** SCOT

**¹north by east** **:** a compass point that is one point east of due north **:** N 11° 15′ E — abbr. *N b E, N by E;* see COMPASS CARD

**²north by east** *adv (or adj)* **1 :** toward north by east **2 :** from north by east

**¹north by west** **:** a compass point that is one point west of due north **:** N 11° 15′ W — abbr. *N b W, N by W;* see COMPASS CARD

**²north by west** *adv (or adj)* **1 :** toward north by west **2 :** from north by west

**north carolina** *adj, usu cap N&C* [fr. *North Carolina*, south Atlantic state of the U.S., fr. ²*north* + *Carolina*, English colony from which No. and So. Carolina were formed — more at CAROLINIAN] **:** of or from the state of North Carolina ⟨the *North Carolina* coast⟩ **:** of the kind or style prevalent in North Carolina **:** NORTH CAROLINIAN

**north carolina bay** *n, usu cap N&C* **:** a mountain magnolia (*Magnolia fraseri*)

**north carolina pine** *n, usu cap N&C* **1 a :** SHORTLEAF PINE **b :** the wood of shortleaf pine **2 a :** LOBLOLLY PINE **b :** the wood of loblolly pine **3 :** JERSEY PINE

**¹north carolinian** *n, cap N&C* [*North Carolina* (state) + E *-an*, n. suffix] **:** a native or resident of North Carolina

**²north carolinian** *adj, usu cap N&C* [*North Carolina* (state) + E *-an*, adj. suffix] **1 :** of, relating to, or characteristic of the state of North Carolina **2 :** of, relating to, or characteristic of the people of North Carolina

**north celestial pole** *n* **:** NORTH POLE 1a

**north central** *adj, usu cap N&C* **:** of, relating to, or characteristic of the states of the Mississippi valley and the Great Lakes region lying north of the Ohio river and the southern boundaries of Kansas and Missouri and between the eastern boundaries of Montana, Wyoming, and Colorado and the western boundary of Pennsylvania

**north-countryman** \ˈ≈¦≈≈≈\ *n, pl* **north-countrymen** *cap N* [*north country* (fr. ME *north cuntree*, fr. ²*north* + *cuntree* country) + *man*] *Brit* **:** a native or inhabitant of the northern counties of England

**north dakota** *adj, usu cap N&D* [fr. *North Dakota*, northwestern state of the U. S., fr. ²*north* + *Dakota (territory)*, former region of the U. S. including No. & So. Dakota — more at DAKOTA] **:** of or from the state of North Dakota ⟨the *North Dakota* plains⟩ **:** of the kind or style prevalent in North Dakota **:** NORTH DAKOTAN

**¹north dakotan** *adj, usu cap N&D* [*North Dakota* (state) + E *-an*] **1 :** of, relating to, or characteristic of the state of North Dakota **2 :** of, relating to, or characteristic of the people of North Dakota

**²north dakotan** *n, cap N&D* **:** a native or resident of the state of North Dakota

**¹north·east** \(ˈ)nȯr¦thēst, -ȯ(ə)¦-, *usual nautical pronunciation* (ˈ)nȯ¦rēst\ *adv* [ME *northest*, fr. OE *northēast*, fr. ¹*north* + *ēast* adv., east] **:** to, from, or in the northeast **:** NORTHEASTWARD

**²northeast** \"\ *n* [ME *northest*, fr. *northest*, adv.] **1 a :** the general direction between north and east **b :** the part of the northern sky lying east of the observer's meridian **c :** the point of the compass midway between the cardinal points north and east **:** the point directly opposite to southwest — abbr. *NE;* see COMPASS CARD **2** *usu cap* **a :** regions or countries lying to the northeast of a specified or implied point of orientation **b :** something (as people or institutions) characteristic of the Northeast ⟨the *Northeast* was solidly against the bill⟩ **3 :** the northeast wind

**³northeast** \"\ *adj* [ME *northest*, fr. *northest*, adv.] **1 :** coming from the northeast ⟨the ~ wind⟩ **2 :** situated toward or at the northeast ⟨the ~ section of land⟩

**¹northeast by east** **:** a compass point that is one point east of due northeast **:** N 56° 15′ E — abbr. *NE b E, NE by E;* see COMPASS CARD

**²northeast by east** *adv (or adj)* **1 :** toward northeast by east **2 :** from northeast by east

**¹northeast by north** **:** a compass point that is one point north of due northeast **:** N 33° 45′ E — abbr. *NE b N, NE by N;* see COMPASS CARD

**²northeast by north** *adv (or adj)* **1 :** toward northeast by north **2 :** from northeast by north

**north·east·er** \-tə(r)\ *n* [³*northeast* + *-er*] **:** a storm, strong wind, or gale coming from the northeast ⟨a good ~, which usually means three days of wind and rain —J.P.Marquand⟩ ⟨a partial shelter from the sweep of the seas if a ~ should blow up —C.G.D.Roberts⟩

**¹north·east·er·ly** \-tərlē, -li, *-R* -təl- *sometimes* -tᵊl-\ *adv (or adj)* [fr. ³*northeast*, after E ²*easterly*] **1 :** from the northeast ⟨the wind blew ~⟩ ⟨~ gales⟩ **2 :** toward the northeast ⟨voyaging ~ for several days⟩ ⟨a ~ voyage⟩

**²northeasterly** \"\ *n* **:** a wind from the northeast

**north·east·ern** \-tə(r)n, *-R also* -tᵊn\ *adj* [²*northeast* + *-ern* (as in *eastern*)] **1** *often cap* **:** of, relating to, originating or dwelling in, or characteristic of a region (as of the U. S.) conventionally designated Northeast ⟨~ seaports⟩ ⟨~ schools⟩ **2 :** situated toward or coming from the northeast ⟨the ~ suburbs of a city⟩

**north·east·ern·er** *R* -tə(r)nər, *-R* -tənə(r *also* -tᵊnə(r\ *n, usu cap* **:** a native or inhabitant of a northeastern region (as of the U. S.)

**north·east·ern·most** \-n,mōst, *esp Brit also* -,məst\ *adj* **:** farthest to the northeast **:** most northeastern

**¹north·east·ward** \-twə(r)d\ *adv (or adj)* **:** toward the northeast **:** in a northeast direction

**²northeastward** \"\ *n* **:** NORTHEAST ⟨to the ~⟩

**north·east·ward·ly** \-dlē\ *adv (or adj)* **:** toward or from the northeastward **:** NORTHEASTERLY

**north·east·wards** \-dz\ *adv* **:** NORTHEASTWARD

**northed** *past of* NORTH

**¹north·er** \ˈnȯrthər, ˈnȯ(ə)thə(r\ *vi* -ED/-ING/-S [¹*north* + *-er* (as in ¹*batter*)] **:** to turn, veer, or shift to the north — used chiefly of the wind

**²norther** \"\ *n* -s [²*north* + *-er*, n. suffix] **:** a northerly wind; *esp* **:** a sudden strong north wind over the Plains or such a wind in Texas and on the Gulf of Mexico and western Caribbean sea — compare BLUE NORTHER, NORTE

**north·er·li·ness** \-thə(r)lēnəs\ *n* -ES **:** the situation of being northerly

**¹north·er·ly** \-lē, -li\ *adj* [fr. ²*north*, after E ²*east:* ¹*easterly*] **1 :** situated or directed toward the north **:** NORTHERN ⟨~ slopes of hills⟩ ⟨~ flight of birds⟩ ⟨the color characterizes the peculiar ~ atmosphere —Dorothy Adlow⟩ **2 :** blowing from the north ⟨the wind's much more ~ —David Beaty⟩

**²northerly** \"\ *adv* **1 :** from the north ⟨the wind blew ~⟩ **2 :** toward the north ⟨streets running ~⟩

**³northerly** \"\ *n* -ES **:** a wind from the north ⟨the morning ~ was making up —G.W.Brace⟩

**north·er·most** \-thə(r),mōst, *esp Brit also* -,məst\ *adj* [fr. ²*north*, after such pairs as E ²*east: eastermost*] **:** NORTHERNMOST

**¹north·ern** *R* ˈnȯrthərn *sometimes* -thən, *-R* ˈnȯ(ə)thən\ *adj* [ME *northerne*, fr. OE; akin to OHG *nordrōni* northern, ON *norrœnn* Norwegian; derivative fr. the root of E ¹*north*] **1** *often cap* **a :** of, relating to, originating or dwelling in, or characteristic of a region (as of the U.S. or England) conventionally designated North ⟨~ factories⟩ ⟨the ~ autumn⟩ **b :** of, relating to, or typical of northern dialect **2 a :** lying toward the north ⟨the ~ lakes⟩ ⟨~ suburbs⟩ **b :** coming from the north ⟨a ~ snowstorm⟩ **3** *of a sign of the zodiac* **:** situated north of the equator

**²northern** \"\ *n* -s **1** *usu cap* **a :** an inhabitant of the North **:** NORTHERNER **2** *or* **northern dialect** *usu cap N* **:** the dialect of English spoken in the part of the U. S. that lies north of a line running northwest from central New Jersey across the northern tier of counties in Pennsylvania and through northern Ohio, Indiana, and Illinois **3 :** ⁴PIKE 1a

**northern anchovy** *n* **:** a large-mouthed anchovy (*Engraulis mordax*) of the Pacific coast of No. America much used for bait and sometimes as food

**northern anthracnose** *n* **:** a disease of clovers (as red and crimson clovers) in No. America, Asia, and Europe caused by a fungus (*Kabatulla caulivora*) of the family Tuberculariaceae causing sunken linear brown lesions on the stems and petioles

**northern athapaskan** *n, usu cap N&A* **:** DÉNÉ

**northern baptist** *n, cap N&B* **:** AMERICAN BAPTIST

**northern barracuda** *n* **:** a small barracuda (*Sphyraena borealis*) of the Atlantic coast of the U. S. from Cape Fear to Cape Cod

**northern bedstraw** *n* **:** a stoloniferous perennial No. American bedstraw (*Galium boreale*) sometimes used as an ornamental and having several-veined leaves in fours and white flowers

**northern black currant** *n* **1 :** an erect unarmed shrub (*Ribes hudsonianum*) of northern No. America **2 :** the edible black fruit of the northern black currant — called also *quinsyberry*

**northern catfish** *n* **:** a catfish that constitutes a northern subspecies (*Ictailurus lacustris lacustris*) of the channel catfish

**northern cattle grub** *n* **:** the larva of a warble fly (*Hypoderma bovis*) — see BOMB FLY

**northern dusky wing** *n* **:** a common No. American butterfly (*Thorybes pylades*) of the family Hesperidae

**northern eider** *n* **:** a No. American duck that constitutes a subspecies (*Somateria mollissima borealis*) of the European eider

**north·ern·er** *R* ˈnȯrthə(r)nər, *-R* ˈnȯthənə(r\ *n* -s *usu cap* **:** a native or inhabitant of the North; *esp* **:** a native or inhabitant of the northern states of the U. S.

**northern fowl mite** *n* **:** a parasitic mite (*Ornithonyssus sylviarum*) of the family Laelaptidae that is a serious pest of poultry, pigeons, and other birds in both Europe and No. America — called also *fowl mite*

**northern fox grape** *n* **:** FOX GRAPE c

**northern hartebeest** *n* **:** an African hartebeest (*Alcelaphus buselaphus*) also found in Arabia

**northern hemisphere** *n* **:** the half of the earth that lies north of the equator

**northern ireland** *adj, usu cap N&I* [fr. *Northern Ireland*, division of the United Kingdom of Great Britain and Northern Ireland occupying the northeast section of the island of Ireland] **:** of or from Northern Ireland, a division of the United Kingdom of Great Britain and Northern Ireland **:** of the kind or style prevalent in Northern Ireland

**north·ern·ize** \-thə(r),nīz\ *vt* -ED/-ING/-S *sometimes cap* **:** to imbue with qualities native to or associated with residents of northern U. S.

**northern lights** *n pl* **:** AURORA BOREALIS

**north·ern·ly** \-thə(r)nlē, -li\ *adv (or adj)* **:** NORTHERLY

**northern mammoth** *n* **:** WOOLLY MAMMOTH

**northern masked chafer** *n* **:** a beetle (*Cyclocephala borealis*) of the family Lucanidae the grubs of which feed on turf roots

**north·ern·most** \-n,mōst, *esp Brit also* -,məst\ *adj* **:** farthest to the north **:** most northern

**northern muskellunge** *n* **:** CHAUTAUQUA MUSKELLUNGE

**northern paiute** *n, usu cap N&P* **1 a :** a group of Shoshonean peoples in western Nevada, southeastern Oregon, and northeastern California **b :** a member of any such peoples **2 :** any of the dialects of the Shoshonean language family spoken by the Northern Paiute peoples

**northern phalarope** *n* **:** a phalarope (*Lobipes lobatus*) breeding in the arctic regions of the Old and New Worlds and often occurring in large flocks far out at sea

**northern pike** *also* **northern pickerel** *n* **:** ⁴PIKE 1a

**northern pine** *n* **1 :** SCOTCH PINE **2 :** WHITE PINE 1a **3 :** the wood of northern pine

**northern porgy** *n* **:** SCUP a

**northern rat flea** *n* **:** a common and widely distributed flea (*Nosopsyllus fasciatus*) parasitic on rats

**northern red oak** *n* **:** RED OAK 1a

**northern shrike** *n* **:** a shrike (*Lanius borealis*) occurring in northern No. America — called also *butcher-bird*

**northern sucker** *n* **:** a sucker (*Catostomus catostomus*) of northern No. America reaching a length of two and a half feet and being from the Great Lakes northward a valuable food fish

**northern tehuelche** *n, usu cap N&T* **:** PUELCHE

**northern union football** *n, usu cap N&U* [*Northern Union*, unofficial name of *The Northern Rugby Football Union*, football league that was formed in the North of England in 1895 and changed its name to The Rugby Football League in 1922] **:** RUGBY LEAGUE FOOTBALL

**northern water thrush** *n* **:** a No. American water thrush (*Seiurus noveboracensis*)

**northern white cedar** *n* **:** AMERICAN ARBORVITAE

**northern white pine** *n* **:** WHITE PINE 1 a

**northern whiting** *n* **:** a whiting (*Menticirrhus saxatilis*) of the east coast of the U. S. closely resembling the king whiting but having a filament extending from the first spine of the dorsal fin

**northers** *pres 3d sing of* NORTHER, *pl of* NORTHER

**north geographical pole** *n* **:** NORTH POLE 1b

**north germanic** *n, cap N&G* **:** a subdivision of the Germanic languages that includes Icelandic, Faeroese, Norwegian, Swedish, Danish — see INDO-EUROPEAN LANGUAGES table

**north·ing** \ˈnȯr¦th¦iŋ, ˈnȯ(ə)|, |th|, |ēŋ\ *n* -s [¹*north* + *-ing*] **1 :** difference in latitude to the north from the last preceding point of reckoning ⟨the problem is to determine differences of ~ between distant points by means of angular observations at each end of the base line —L.G.Trorey⟩ **2 :** northerly progress **:** a going northward ⟨our progress was slow, but we made steady ~ —Deneys Reitz⟩ ⟨the captains decided to make as much ~ as they could —Bernard DeVoto⟩

**north·land** \ˈnȯrth,land, ˈnȯ(ə)th-, -aa(ə)nd, -,lənd\ *n, often cap* [ME, fr. OE, fr. ¹*north* + *land*] **:** land in the north **:** the north of a country ⟨my stay in the *Northland* was ended —W.E. Ekblaw⟩ ⟨when winter closes in over the ~ —Melvin Beck⟩

**north light** *n* **1 :** light admitted to a room (as a studio) that comes solely from the north and in the northern hemisphere is preferred by artists because it is there more neutral in color and less productive of variation than light from any other direction **2 :** a window or skylight furnishing a north light

**north·man** \-thmən\ *n, pl* **northmen** **1** *cap* **:** NORSEMAN **2** *often cap* **:** a native or inhabitant of a northern region (as of northern Europe or northern Canada)

**north·most** \-th,mōst, *esp Brit also* -,məst\ *adj* **:** NORTHERNMOST

**north·ness** *n* -ES **:** the quality or state of being north

**¹north-northeast** \(¦)≈¦≈¦≈\ *adv (or adj)* [ME *north northest*, fr. ¹*north* + *northest* northeast] **1 :** toward north-northeast **2 :** from north-northeast

**²north-northeast** \"\ *n* **:** a compass point that is two points east of due north **:** N 22° 30′ E — abbr. *NNE;* see COMPASS CARD

**¹north-northwest** \(¦)≈¦≈¦≈\ *adv (or adj)* [ME *north northwest*, fr. ¹*north* + *northwest*, adv.] **1 :** toward north-northwest **2 :** from north-northwest

**²north-northwest** \"\ *n* [ME *north northwest*, fr. *north northwest*, adv.] **:** a compass point that is two points west of due north **:** N 22° 30′ W — abbr. *NNW;* see COMPASS CARD

**north oscan** *adj, usu cap N&O* **:** of or being a group of Italic languages comprising Paelignian, Marrucinian, and Vestinian

**north polar distance** *n* **:** the angular distance of a celestial body measured along its hour circle from the north celestial pole

**north pole** *n* [ME] **1 a :** the zenith of the heavens as viewed from the north terrestrial pole **b** *often cap N&P* **:** the northernmost point of the earth **:** the northern extremity of the earth's axis — see ZONE illustration **2** *of a magnet* **:** the pole that points toward the north when the magnet is freely suspended

**norths** *pl of* NORTH, *pres 3d sing of* NORTH

**north-seeking pole** *n* **:** NORTH POLE 2

**north semitic** *n, cap N&S* **:** NORTHWEST SEMITIC

**north star** *n, usu cap N&S* [ME *north sterre*] **:** POLESTAR

**north temperate** *adj, often cap N&T* **:** of or relating to the north temperate zone of the earth lying between the tropic of Cancer and the arctic circle — see ZONE illustration

**north terrestrial pole** *n* **:** NORTH POLE 1b

**north·um·ber** \nȯ(r)ˈthəmbə(r)\ *n* -s *cap* [ME *Northhumbre*, fr. OE *Northhymbre* (pl.), fr. ¹*north* + *-hymbre* (fr. *Humbre* Humber, river in eastern England)] **:** an inhabitant of ancient Northumbria

**north·um·ber·land** \nȯ(r)ˈthəmbə(r)lənd\ *adj, usu cap* [fr. *Northumberland*, county in northeast England] **:** of or from the county of Northumberland, England **:** of the kind or style prevalent in Northumberland **:** NORTHUMBRIAN

**¹north·um·bri·an** \(ˈ)nȯ(r)ˈthəmbrēən\ *adj, usu cap* [*Northumber* + *-an*] **1 a :** of, relating to, or characteristic of ancient Northumbria **b :** of, relating to, or characteristic of the people of Northumbria **c :** of, relating to, or characteristic of the Old English dialect of Northumbria **2 a :** of, relating to, or characteristic of Northumberland **b :** of, relating to, or characteristic of the people of Northumberland **c :** of, relating to, or characteristic of the modern English dialect of Northumberland

**²northumbrian** \"\ *n* -s *cap* **1 :** a native or inhabitant of ancient Northumbria **2 :** a native or inhabitant of Northumberland **3 a :** the Old English dialect of Northumbria **b :** the modern English dialect of Northumberland

**northumbrian burr** *n, usu cap N* **:** a uvularly trilled *r* said to be characteristic of some Northumbrian speech

**nor·thup·ite** \ˈnȯ(r)thə,pīt\ *n* -s [C. H. *Northup*, 19th cent. Am. mineral collector who first obtained it + E *-ite*] **:** a mineral $Na_3MgCl(CO_3)_2$ composed of a magnesium sodium carbonate with chloride and occurring in colorless octahedral crystals

¹**north·ward** \'nȯrthwərd, 'nȯ(ə)thwəd\ *adv (or adj)* [ME, fr. OE *northweard*, fr. ¹*north* + *-weard* -ward] **:** toward the north ⟨sailing ~⟩ ⟨a journey ~⟩ ⟨the ~ flight of birds⟩
²**northward** \"\ *n* -s **:** northward direction or part ⟨sailing to the ~⟩
**north·ward·ly** \-dlē, -li\ *adv (or adj)* **:** in a northern direction ⟨the seabed extending ~ approximately 250 feet —*Bahamas Acts*⟩ ⟨a ~ wind⟩
**north·wards** \-dz\ *adv* [ME *northwardis*, fr. OE *northweardes*, fr. *northweard* northward + *-es* -s (adv. suffix)] **:** NORTHWARD
¹**north·west** \(')nȯr¦thwest, -ō(ə)¦-, *usual nautical pronunciation* (')nȯr¦w- *or* -ō(ə)¦w-\ *adv* [ME, fr. OE, fr. ¹*north* + *west*, adv.] **:** to, toward, or in the northwest **:** NORTHWESTWARD
²**northwest** \"\ *n* [ME, fr. *northwest*, adv.] **1 a :** the general direction between north and west **b :** the part of the northern sky lying west of the observer's meridian **c :** the point of the compass midway between the cardinal points north and west **:** the point directly opposite to southeast — abbr. *NW;* see COMPASS CARD **2** *usu cap* **a :** regions or countries lying to the northwest of a specified or implied point of orientation **b :** something (as people or institutions) characteristic of the Northwest **3 :** the northwest wind
³**northwest** \"\ *adj* [ME, fr. *northwest*, adv.] **1 :** coming from the northwest ⟨a ~ storm⟩ **2 :** situated toward or at the northwest ⟨the ~ passage⟩
¹**northwest by north :** a compass point that is one point north of due northwest **:** N 33° 45′ W — abbr. *NW b N, NW by N;* see COMPASS CARD
²**northwest by north** *adv (or adj)* **1 :** toward northwest by north **2 :** from northwest by north
¹**northwest by west :** a compass point that is one point west of due northwest **:** N 56° 15′ W — abbr. *NW b W, NW by W;* see COMPASS CARD
²**northwest by west** *adv (or adj)* **1 :** toward northwest by west **2 :** from northwest by west
**northwest coast indian** *n, usu cap N&C&I* **:** a member of any of the peoples living along the Pacific coast from northern California to Alaska and comprising the Haida, Tlingit, Tsimshian, Bellabella, Kwakiutl, Nootka, Chinook, and Makah
**north·west·er** \-tə(r)\ *n* [³*northwest* + *-er*] **1 :** a storm or gale from the northwest **:** a strong northwest wind **2** *usu cap* **:** an employee of a fur-trading company formerly operating in western Canada
¹**north·west·er·ly** \-tərlē, -li, *–R* -təl- *sometimes* -tᵊl-\ *adv (or adj)* [fr. ³*northwest*, after E *west: westerly*] **1 :** from the northwest ⟨winds blowing ~⟩ ⟨~ frosts —*Spectator*⟩ **2 :** toward the northwest ⟨steered the ship ~⟩ ⟨journeyed ~ all day⟩
²**northwesterly** \"\ *n* **:** a wind from the northwest
**north·west·ern** \-tə(r)n, *–R also* -tᵊn\ *adj* [²*northwest* + *-ern* (as in *western*)] **1** *often cap* **:** of, relating to, originating or dwelling in, or characteristic of a region (as of the U.S.) conventionally designated Northwest ⟨~ forests⟩ ⟨~ folklore⟩ **2 :** situated toward or coming from the northwest ⟨the ~ counties⟩
**northwestern anthracnose** *n* **:** APPLE ANTHRACNOSE
**northwestern apple box** *n* **:** a nailed paper-lined wooden fruit box designed to produce little or no compression of contents
**north·west·ern·er** *R* -tə(r)nər, *–R* -tənə(r *also* -tᵊnə(r\ *n, usu cap* **:** a native or inhabitant of a northwestern region (as of the U.S.)
**northwest semitic** *n, cap N&S* **:** a division of the Semitic languages consisting of Aramaic and Canaanitic languages
**northwest shipworm** *n, often cap N* **:** a large destructive shipworm (*Bankia setacea*) of the Pacific coast of No. America
¹**north·west·ward** \-twə(r)d\ *adv (or adj)* [ME, fr. ¹*northwest* + *-ward*] **:** toward the northwest **:** in a northwest direction
²**northwestward** \"\ *n* -s **:** NORTHWEST ⟨to the ~⟩

northwestern apple box

**north·west·ward·ly** \-dlē\ *adv (or adj)* **:** toward or from the northwest **:** NORTHWESTERLY
**north·west·wards** \-dz\ *adv* **:** NORTHWESTWARD
**nor·valine** \(')nȯ(r)+\ *n* [ISV *nor-* + *valine*] **:** a crystalline amino acid $C_2H_5CH_2CH(NH_2)COOH$ isomeric with valine and usu. made synthetically; alpha-aminovaleric acid
¹**nor·ward** \'nȯrwərd\ *adv (or adj)* [by contr.] **:** NORTHWARD
²**norward** \"\ *n* -s **:** NORTHWARD
**nor·way** \'nȯr,wā, 'nȯ(ə),-\ *adj, usu cap* [fr. *Norway*, country in northwest Europe] **:** of or from Norway **:** of the kind or style prevalent in Norway **:** NORWEGIAN
**norway haddock** *n, usu cap N* **:** ROSEFISH
**norway iron** *n, usu cap N* **:** a high grade of wrought iron produced in Sweden but usu. finished in and exported from Norway
**norway lobster** *n, usu cap N* **:** a lobster (*Nephrops norvegicus*) of European seas resembling the American lobster but much slenderer
**norway maple** *n, usu cap N* **:** a European maple (*Acer platanoides*) with dark green or often reddish or red-veined leaves that is much planted for shade in the U.S.
**norway pine** *n, usu cap N* **1 :** RED PINE 1a **2 :** the wood of Norway pine
**norway rat** *n, usu cap N* **:** BROWN RAT
**norway spruce** *n, usu cap N* **:** a widely cultivated spruce (*Picea abies*) native to northern Europe and having pyramidal shape, spreading branches and pendulous branchlets, dark foliage, and long pendulous cones
¹**nor·we·gian** \(')nȯ(r)¦wējən\ *adj, usu cap* [ML *Norvegia, Norwegia* Norway + E *-an*, adj. suffix] **1 a :** of, relating to, or characteristic of Norway **b :** of, relating to, or characteristic of the Norwegians **2 :** of, relating to, or characteristic of the Norwegian language
²**norwegian** \"\ *n* -s *cap* [ML *Norvegia, Norwegia* Norway + E *-an*, n. suffix] **1 a :** a native or inhabitant of Norway **b :** a person of Norwegian descent **2 :** the Germanic language of the Norwegian people — see LANDSMÅL, RIKSMÅL; INDO-EUROPEAN LANGUAGES table
**norwegian elkhound** *n* **1** *usu cap N&E* **:** a Norwegian breed of medium-sized compact short-bodied dogs having a very heavy gray coat tipped with black and developed for herding sheep, guarding farms, hunting, and for draft purposes **2** *usu cap N & often cap E* **:** a dog of the Norwegian Elkhound breed
**norwegian saltpeter** *n, usu cap N* **:** CALCIUM NITRATE
**norwegian whist** *n, usu cap N* **:** whist in which each player in turn offers to win or lose tricks, bidding grand or nullo, there being no trumps
**nor·wich** \'nȯr,wich, 'närij\ *adj, usu cap* [fr. *Norwich*, county borough in eastern England] **:** of or from the county borough of Norwich, England **:** of the kind or style prevalent in Norwich
**norwich terrier** *n, usu cap N* **:** a terrier of a small active low-set English breed with rather long straight wiry coat of red, black and tan, or grizzle
**nos** *pl of* NO
**nos-** *or* **noso-** *comb form* [prob. fr. LL *noso-*, fr. Gk *nos-, noso-*, fr. *nosos*] **:** disease ⟨*nosetiology*⟩ ⟨*nosogeography*⟩
**NOS** *abbr* not otherwise specified
¹**nose** \'nōz\ *n* -s [ME, fr. OE *nosu;* akin to OE *nasu* nose, OHG *nasa*, ON *nös*, L *nasus*, Skt *nāsā*] **1 a :** the prominent part of the face of man or other mammals that bears the nostrils and covers the anterior part of the nasal cavity; *broadly* **:** this part together with the nasal cavity ⟨his ~ is stopped up with a cold⟩ ⟨people who speak through their ~*s*⟩ **b :** the anterior part of the head above or projecting beyond the mouth; SNOUT, PROBOSCIS, MUZZLE ⟨hit the shark over the ~ with an oar⟩ **2 a :** the sense of smell **:** OLFACTION; *also* **:** ability to track by scent ⟨this dog has a good ~⟩ **b :** SCENT; *esp* **:** AROMA ⟨the ~ of well-cured leafy hay⟩ **c :** the bouquet of an alcoholic beverage **3 :** the vertebrate olfactory organ consisting essentially of a moist layer of sensory epithelium derived from invaginated embryonic ectoderm and in intimate contact with terminations of the olfactory nerve, lying in higher vertebrates in the upper part of the nasal cavity and in fishes in small sacs on each side of the head, and communicating with the external environment through the nares **4 a :** the front or forward end or projection of something ⟨I pushed on, the ~ of my car headed for the tropics —Francis Birtles⟩ **b :** the projecting or working end of a tool or a machine part (as a spindle) ⟨a quarter-inch radius is specified for the ~ of this lathe tool⟩ ⟨pliers with a long ~⟩ **c :** the end of a projectile that is forward in flight ⟨could blow half a dozen men to pieces by dropping a cartridge on the point of that ~ —Wirt Williams⟩ **d :** the forward end of an airplane; *specif* **:** the part of a fuselage or nacelle projecting in front **e :** the distal end of a gooseberry, currant, apple, or other fruit **f :** the projecting edge of a molding or stair tread **5 a :** the stem of a boat **b :** the protective metal covering a boat's stem **6 a :** an anticlinal flexure plunging downward at one end and opening broadly at the other **b :** a buttress of usu. overhanging rock **7 :** the nose regarded as a symbol of officious or prying concern, interest, or intervention ⟨a clever fellow . . . with his ~ in all sorts of dark corners —H.J.Laski⟩ ⟨why can't he keep his big ~ out of things —James Jones⟩ **8 :** the knack for discovering or the instinct for recognizing or discerning **:** FLAIR ⟨anyone with a ~ for it might scent out a drama even in the meager information just provided —E.R.Bentley⟩ ⟨has an unerring ~ for humbug of any sort —Frank O'Connor⟩ ⟨a ~ for news⟩ ⟨one of the keener ~*s* for hit tunes —R.G.Hubler⟩ **9 a :** the approximate length of the nose (as of a horse) ⟨won the race by a ~⟩ **b :** an extremely narrow margin of victory ⟨won the election by a ~⟩ — compare HEAD, NECK — **nose to the grindstone :** in a state of hard, monotonous, servile, or unremitting work ⟨his demanding wife and large growing family are keeping his *nose to the grindstone*⟩ — **on the nose** *adv (or adj)* **1 :** to a prescribed or specified measure or limit of size or time **:** on the button **:** EXACTLY, PRECISELY ⟨ended the broadcast at 12 *on the nose*⟩ ⟨the 1.5314 inches dimension checked out *on the nose*⟩ **2 :** to win — used of horse or dog racing bets ⟨bet $10 on the favorite *on the nose*⟩ — **through the nose** *adv* **:** with the resonance characteristic of a stopped-up or defective nose ⟨*m* pronounced *through the nose* sounds like *b*⟩ — **under the nose of :** in plain sight of; *esp* **:** in bold and successful defiance of ⟨carried off the floating vote *under the very nose of* the conservative candidate⟩
²**nose** \"\ *vb* -ED/-ING/-S *vt* **1 :** to perceive the odor of **:** detect by or as if by smell **:** SCENT **:** smell out **2** *archaic* **:** to treat insolently **:** deal irreverently or disrespectfully with **:** BEARD **3 a :** to push or move with the nose ⟨the dog *nosed* the door open⟩ ⟨wolves or foxes had *nosed* aside some of the rocks —Farley Mowat⟩ **b :** to push or make (one's way) with the nose ⟨the plane . . . ~*s* its way into the whirling mass of clouds —Nona B. Brown⟩ **c :** to advance the nose, prow, or forward end into **:** push ahead in ⟨our craft . . . *nosed* the first strong swell —J.R.Perkins⟩ **4 :** to touch or rub with the nose **:** thrust the nose against or into in affection or curiosity **:** NUZZLE ⟨as he sat despairing his dog came up and *nosed* him⟩ **5 :** to round off or bevel the end of (as a log for skidding) **6 a :** to defeat by the length of a nose in a horse race **b :** to defeat by a narrow margin in a sport or contest ~ *vi* **1 :** to use the nose in examining, smelling, or showing affection **:** SCENT, SNIFF, NUZZLE **2 :** to pry or search impertinently **3 :** to move ahead esp. slowly or cautiously ⟨the cars had begun to move again, *nosing* out into the main road —Maurice Duggan⟩ ⟨had been *nosing* along the shores in pinnace, yacht, or bark —*Amer. Guide Series: Md.*⟩ **4 :** to dip or run in the form of a geological nose — **nose around :** to sniff around **:** EXPLORE ⟨plant auditors may also be found *nosing around* scrap heaps to see whether material is being wasted —Hugh Morrow⟩ — **nose into :** to poke or pry into with or as if with the nose ⟨she was *nosing into* everything around here —Edwin Lanham⟩
**no·se·an** \'nōzēən\ *n* -s [obs. G *nosian* (now *nosean*), fr. Karl W. *Nose* †1835 Ger. geologist + G *-ian*] **:** NOSELITE
**nose ape** *n* **:** PROBOSCIS MONKEY
**nose bag** *n* **:** a usu. canvas bag that is used for feeding an animal (as a horse) and that is fastened on top of the head and covers the muzzle — called also *feed bag*
**noseband** \'⸗,⸗\ *n* **:** the part of a headstall that passes over a horse's nose — see BRIDLE illustration
**nose bit** *n* **:** a wood bit similar to a gouge or pod bit but having a cutting edge on one side of its boring end
**nosebleed** \'⸗,⸗\ *n* [¹*nose* + *bleed*, v.] **1 a :** bleeding from the nose — called also *epistaxis* **b :** an attack of nosebleed ⟨had a severe ~⟩ **2** [ME *noseblede* yarrow, fr. ¹*nose* + *blede*, *bleden* to bleed] **a :** either of two red-flowered plants: (1) **:** a trillium (*Trillium erectum*) (2) **:** INDIAN PAINTBRUSH **b** [so called fr. its use in folk medicine to check epistaxis] **:** YARROW

nose bag

**nose bot** *or* **nose fly** *n* **:** a widely distributed botfly (*Gasterophilus haemorrhoidalis*) parasitic in the larval stage on horses and mules
**noseclip** \'⸗,⸗\ *n* **:** a small clamp usu. of rubber or plastic worn to keep water out of a swimmer's nose
**nose cone** *n* **:** a protective cone constituting the forward end of a rocket or missile and capable of withstanding the heat caused by reentry into the earth's atmosphere
**nosed** \'nōzd\ *adj* [¹*nose* + *-ed*] **1 :** having a nose esp. of a specified kind — usu. used in combination ⟨thick, snub-*nosed*, ankle-high shoes —Robert Shaplen⟩ **2** *obs* **:** keen of scent
**nose dive** *n* **1 :** the downward nose-first plunge of an airplane or other flying object (as a kite) ⟨a pilot must have altitude in order to get out of a *nose dive* —E.J.David⟩ **2 :** a sudden extreme drop (as of prices) ⟨the blue chips were seriously off, and speculative favorites had gone into a *nose dive* —J.K. Galbraith⟩
**nose–dive** \'⸗,⸗\ *vi* [*nose dive*] **:** to plunge headlong
**nose down** *vi* **:** to head down **:** depress the nose ⟨the airplane *nosed down* out of the overcast⟩ ~ *vt* **:** to turn, point, or direct (an airplane's nose) down **:** head (an airplane) down ⟨she *nosed* the airplane *down* —Robert Craig⟩
**nose drops** *n pl* **:** a medicated liquid instilled into the nostrils with a medicine dropper
**no–see–um** \nō'sēəm\ *n* -s [fr. the group of words (as supposedly spoken by American Indians) *no see um* you don't see them] **:** BITING MIDGE
**nose flute** *n* **:** a flute played by blowing through the nostrils
**nosegay** \'⸗,⸗\ *n* [ME, fr. ¹*nose* + *gay*, n.] **1 a :** a small bunch of flowers suitable to be worn on the person **:** POSY **b :** something likened to a bouquet: as (1) **:** an expression of compliment or praise (2) **:** a collection of lovely things ⟨this ~ of 18 sprightly short stories —James Kelly⟩ **2** *archaic* **:** an odorous object or its scent
**nose glasses** *n pl* **:** PINCE-NEZ
**nose–heavy** \'⸗,⸗⸗\ *adj* **:** having the center of gravity located forward of the center of lift so that the nose tends to drop when the longitudinal control is released in level flight ⟨a *nose-heavy* airplane⟩ — compare TAIL-HEAVY
**nosehole** \'⸗,⸗\ *n, dial chiefly Eng* **1 :** NOSTRIL **2 :** BYE HOLE
**nose iron** *n* **:** an adjustable pivot assembly in a weighing scale for changing the multiplication of a lever
**nose leaf** *n* **:** an expansion of skin resembling a leaf on the nose of various bats that is believed to have a delicate tactile function
**nose·less** \'nōzləs\ *adj* [ME *noseles*, fr. ¹*nose* + *-les* -less] **:** having no nose — **nose·less·ly** *adv* — **nose·less·ness** *n* -ES
**nose line** *n* **:** a line drawn on the profile of a stairway following the outer edges of the treads and marking the slope of the stairway — compare NOSING
**no·se·lite** \'nōzə,līt\ *n* -s [G *noselith*, fr. Karl W. *Nose* †1835 Ger. geologist who described it + G *-lith* -lite] **:** a grayish, bluish, or brownish mineral $Na_5Al_3Si_3O_{12}(SO_4)$ that is a sodium aluminosilicate and sulfate related to hauynite
**no·se·ma** \nō'sēmə\ *n, cap* [NL, fr. Gk *nosēma* disease, fr. *nosein* to be sick, fr. *nosos* disease] **:** a genus (the type of the family Nosematidae) of microsporidian protozoans that includes various parasites of insects and other invertebrates — see NOSEMA DISEASE; compare GLUGEA
**nosema disease** *n* **:** a disease of bees caused by a microsporidian (*Nosema apis*) that invades the stomach and midgut causing dysentery and varying degrees of paralysis in the affected host
**nose–nippers** \'⸗,⸗⸗\ *n pl* **:** PINCE-NEZ
**nose of wax :** a pliant person or thing **:** one readily influenced or turned in any direction ⟨am neither an untrue man . . . nor a mere *nose of wax* to be twisted this way and that —Sir Walter Scott⟩
**nose out** *vt* **1 :** to discover by prying **:** ferret out **:** smell out ⟨found that detectives were *nosing out* divorce evidence⟩ ⟨our horses were able to *nose out* the trail despite the darkness⟩ **2 :** to defeat by a narrow margin ⟨he was *nosed out* in the primary⟩
**nose over** *vi* **:** to turn over by pivoting on the nose (as in a faulty airplane landing)
**nosepiece** \'⸗,⸗\ *n* **1 :** a piece of armor for protecting the nose **:** NASAL **2 :** NOSEBAND **3 a :** the endpiece of a microscope body to which an objective is attached **b :** a revolving holder for two or more microscope objectives **4 :** the bridge of a pair of eyeglasses
**noseprint** \'⸗,⸗\ *n* **:** an impression of the bare surface of an animal's nose used to identify a particular individual by means of the unique pattern of pores and lines — compare FINGERPRINT
**nose putty** *n* **:** a material used in plastic alteration of the nose (as in theatrical makeup)
**nos·er** \'nōzə(r)\ *n* -s **1** *archaic* **:** a blow or fall on the nose **2** *archaic* **:** a wind full in one's face
**nose ring** *n* **1 :** a ring worn in the nose for ornament **2 :** a ring fixed in the nose of an animal in order to control it (as to prevent a pig from rooting or to lead a bull)
**noses** *pl of* NOSE, *pres 3d sing of* NOSE
**nose stiffener** *n* **:** BOW STIFFENER
**nose·thirl** \'nōz,thərl\ *n* -s [ME — more at NOSTRIL] *chiefly dial* **:** NOSTRIL
**nose–thumbing** \'⸗,⸗⸗\ *n* **:** the placing of thumb to nose in derision or contempt
**nose up** *vi* **:** to head up **:** elevate the nose ⟨the airplane *nosed up* into the sky⟩ ~ *vt* **:** to turn, point, or direct (an airplane's nose) up **:** head (an airplane) up
**nosewheel** \'⸗,⸗\ *n* **:** a landing-gear wheel located under the nose of an airplane
**nosewing** \'⸗,⸗\ *n* **:** a nasal ala ⟨laughed . . . slyly, rubbing her ~ with a finger —Thomas Wolfe⟩
**nose·wise** \'nōz,wīz\ *adj* **1** *archaic* **:** CONCEITED **2** *obs* **:** keen-scented
¹**nosey** \'nōzē\ *n* -s [¹*nose* + *-y*, adj. suffix] *archaic* **:** a person having a conspicuous nose
²**nosey** *var of* NOSY
**nosey par·ker** \-'pärkər\ *n, often cap P* [prob. fr. a name *Nosey Parker*, fr. *nosy* (used as a nickname) + *Parker* (the surname)] **:** a meddlesome prying busybody
**no–show** \'⸗'⸗\ *n* [¹*no* + *show*, v. (as in *show up*)] **:** a person who reserves space on a train, a ship, or esp. an airplane but neither uses nor cancels the reservation
**no side** *n* [²*no* + *side*, n. (one of the contesting parties in a game)] **:** the end of a Rugby game
**nos·i·ly** \'nōzəlē\ *adv* **:** in a nosy manner
**nos·i·ness** \-zēnəs\ *n* -ES **:** the quality or state of being nosy
**nos·ing** \'nōziŋ\ *n* -s [¹*nose* + *-ing*] **1 a :** the usu. rounded edge of a stair tread that projects over the riser **b :** any of various similar rounded projections (as of molding) **2 a :** the end of a bridge pier **b :** the transverse horizontal motion of a locomotive that exerts a lateral force on the track

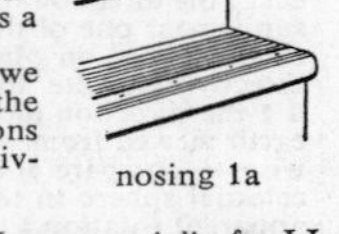
nosing 1a

**nos·ism** \'nō,sizəm, 'nä,-\ *n* -s [L *nos* we + E *-ism* — more at US] **1** *archaic* **:** the conceit or pride of a group of persons **2** *archaic* **:** the practice of using *we* in giving one's opinions
**noso-** — see NOS-
**nos·o·co·mi·al** \,näsə¦kōmēəl\ *adj* [NL *nosocomialis*, fr. LL *nosocomium* hospital (fr. LGk *nosokomeion*, fr. Gk *nosokomos* one that tends the sick, fr. *nos-* + *-komos*, akin to Gk *kamnein* to work) + L *-alis* -al — more at COMA] **:** originating or taking place in a hospital ⟨~ infection⟩
**noso·geographic** \,näsō+\ *or* **noso·geographical** \"+\ *adj* **:** of or relating to nosogeography
**noso·geography** \"+\ *n* [ISV *nos-* + *geography*] **:** the geography of disease **:** GEOMEDICINE
**nos·o·graph·ic** \,näsə¦grafik\ *adj* [prob. fr. (assumed) NL *nosographicus*, fr. NL *nosographia* nosography + L *-icus* -ic] **:** of or relating to nosography
**no·sog·ra·phy** \nō'sägrəfē\ *n* -ES [prob. fr. NL *nosographia*, fr. *nos-* + L *-graphia* -graphy] **:** a description or classification of diseases
**nos·o·log·ic** \,näsə¦läjik\ *or* **nos·o·log·i·cal** \-jəkəl\ *adj* [*nosologic* prob. fr. (assumed) NL *nosologicus*, fr. NL *nosologia* nosology + L *-icus* -ic; *nosological* prob. fr. (assumed) NL *nosologicus* + E *-al*] **:** relating to a classification of diseases — **nos·o·log·i·cal·ly** \-jək(ə)lē\ *adv*
**no·sol·o·gist** \nō'säləjəst *sometimes* nō'zä-\ *n* -s [prob. fr. (assumed) NL *nosologistes*, fr. NL *nosologia* nosology + L *-istes* -ist] **:** a specialist in nosology
**no·sol·o·gy** \-jē, -ji\ *n* -ES [prob. fr. NL *nosologia*, fr. *nos-* + L *-logia* -logy] **:** a branch of medical science that deals with orderly relating or classification of diseases; *sometimes* **:** a classification or list of diseases or a treatise comprising such a classification
**nos·o·psyl·lus** \,näsə'siləs\ *n, cap* [NL, fr. *nos-* + *-psyllus* (fr. Gk *psylla* flea) — more at PSYLLA] **:** a genus of fleas that includes the northern rat flea (*N. fasciatus*)
**nos·tal·gia** \nə'stalj(ē)ə, nä'- *sometimes* nō'- *or* nȯ'- *or* -täl-\ *n* -s [NL (trans. of G *heimweh*), fr. Gk *nostos* return home + NL *-algia;* akin to OE *genesan* to survive, OHG *ginesan* to survive, Goth *ganisan* to get well, be saved, Skt *nasate* he approaches, joins] **1 a** *archaic* **:** a severe melancholia caused by protracted absence from home or native place **b :** HOMESICKNESS **2 :** a wistful or excessively sentimental sometimes abnormal yearning for return to or return of some real or romanticized period or irrecoverable condition or setting in the past ⟨~ for his more impressionable youth⟩ ⟨felt a sudden pang of ~ for German music⟩ — **nos·tal·gic** \nə'staljik, (')nä¦s-, -jēk *sometimes* (')nō¦s- *or* (')nȯ¦s- *or* -täl-\ *adj or n* — **nos·tal·gi·cal·ly** \-jək(ə)lē, -jēk-, -li\ *adv*
**nos·tal·gy** \nə'staljē, nä'-\ *n* -ES [NL *nostalgia*] *archaic* **:** NOSTALGIA
**nos·toc** \'nä,stäk\ *n* [NL] **1** *cap* **:** a widely distributed genus (the type of the family Nostocaceae) of blue-green algae having filaments enveloped and united by a gelatinous substance into a generally spherical colony living on damp ground or in the water — see STAR JELLY, WITCHES'-BUTTER **2** -s **:** any plant of the genus *Nostoc*
**nos·to·ca·ce·ae** \,nästə'kāsē,ē\ *n pl, cap* [NL, fr. *Nostoc*, type genus + *-aceae*] **:** a family of minute freshwater blue-green algae (order Hormogonales) consisting of moniliform filaments and reproducing by hormogonia — see ANABAENA — **nos·to·ca·ceous** \¦⸗⸗¦kāshəs\ *adj*
**nos·to·ca·les** \,nästə'kā(,)lēz\ *n pl, cap* [NL, fr. *Nostoc* + *-ales*] *in some classifications* **:** an order equivalent to Hormogonales
**nos·tra·da·mus** \,nästrə'dāməs, ,nōstrə'däməs\ *n* -ES *usu cap* [after *Nostradamus* †1566 Fr. physician and astrologer] **:** one professing to foretell future events ⟨one does not have to be a *Nostradamus* to predict tomorrow's weather —*Domestic Commerce*⟩
**nos·tril** \'nä¦strəl *sometimes* 'nō¦ *or* |(,)stril\ *n* -s [ME *nostrill*, *nosethirl*, fr. OE *nosterl*, *nosthyrl*, *nosthyrel*, fr. *nosu* nose + *thyrel* hole — more at NOSE, THIRL] **1 a :** an external naris; *broadly* **:** a naris with the adjoining passage on the same side of the nasal septum **:** the anterior part of a nasal fossa with its naris **b :** the fleshy lateral wall of the nose **:** a nasal ala **2 :** a small hole for passage of combustion air or waste gas in any of various industrial furnaces
**nos·triled** *or* **nos·trilled** \-ld\ *adj* **:** having nostrils
**nostril fly** *n* **:** a fly of the family Oestridae; *esp* **:** SHEEP BOTFLY
**nos·tril·i·ty** \nä'strilәd·ē\ *n* -ES **:** prominence of nostril
**nos·trum** \'nästrəm *sometimes* 'nōs-\ *n* -s [L, neut. of *noster* our, ours, fr. *nos* we — more at US] **1 :** a remedy or medicine of

secret composition recommended by its preparer but usu. lacking general repute or acceptance : a dubious specific ⟨remedies which can have no possible value as medicine, as in the case of a ~ offered for the treatment of diabetes at $12 a pint —*Encyc. Americana*⟩ **2 :** a questionable remedy or scheme : CURE-ALL, PANACEA ⟨have never been able to believe wholeheartedly in any simple ~ by which all ills are to be cured —Bertrand Russell⟩ ⟨identify this spiritually impotent but socially powerful ~ with Christianity —H.N.Fairchild⟩

**no·su** \'nō(,)sü\ *n, pl* **nosu** *or* **nosus** *usu cap* **1 :** a Tibeto-Burman people of the high plateaus and mountains of southwest Szechwan, former eastern Sikang and northern Yunnan — called also *Lolo* **2 :** a member of the Nosu people

**nosy** *or* **nosey** \'nōzē, -zi\ *adj* **nosier; nosiest** [[1]*nose* + *-y*] **1** *archaic* **a :** bad-smelling **b :** FRAGRANT **2 :** of prying or inquisitive disposition or quality : INTRUSIVE **syn** see CURIOUS

[1]**not** \'nät, *usu* -äd·+V\ *or* **-nt** *or* **-n't** \(ə)n(t), (ᵊ)n(t)\ *also* **-not** \(')nät *sometimes* -ˌnət, *usu* -d·+V\ *adv* [ME, alter. of *nought*, fr. *nought*, pron. — more at NAUGHT] **1 a** — used as a function word to turn an expression consisting of a word or group of words into an implicitly opposite expression ⟨~ pregnant⟩ ⟨~ in sight⟩ ⟨the team did ~ win⟩ ⟨if he will ~ go⟩ ⟨the telephone is ~ ringing⟩ ⟨will ~ pay the bill⟩ ⟨there has ~ been time —Lois M. Miller⟩ ⟨a faint smell of disinfectant, but it did ~ reek of the stuff —Phil Stong⟩ ⟨we could ~ defend the Philippines —James Forrestal⟩ ⟨recommend that we ~ offend against charity —G.H.Dunne⟩ ⟨may insist that prefabricated products be ~ used in the buildings they work in —T.W.Arnold⟩ ⟨can*not* read or write —Vicki Baum⟩ ⟨yield ~ to temptation⟩ **b :** NO ⟨my cold is ~ worse than yesterday⟩ ⟨was ~ less fortunate in marriage —T.B.Macaulay⟩ ⟨there were ~ cleaner windows . . . in the whole street —Charles Dickens⟩ ⟨should like to know how language evolved from what was ~ language —C.F.Hockett⟩ **c :** in no manner or degree : in no way : NOWISE ⟨~ at all satisfactory⟩ ⟨~ near so expensive⟩ ⟨it is certainly ~ the viewpoint of the minister —C.F.Hunter⟩ ⟨thou shalt ~ kill⟩ **d** — used as a function word to stand for the opposite of a preceding group of words ⟨changes in the environment are sometimes beneficial to the animals and sometimes ~ —W.H.Dowdeswell⟩ ⟨the little girl used to sit very quiet and be good and the little boy used ~ —James Stephens⟩ ⟨if ~, you'll be sorry⟩ and often correlatively ⟨will he be here or ~⟩ ⟨whether you need to make decisions or ~ —W.J. Reilly⟩ **e** — used esp. with *think* to negate a following noun clause ⟨I do*n't* think it will rain⟩ ⟨do*n't* think I'll go⟩ or without a verb to introduce a clause ⟨~ that it matters⟩ ⟨~ that it doesn't matter⟩ ⟨~ that my congratulations to her would not have been tempered with misgivings —Walter de la Mare⟩ ⟨the poem is bad, ~ because it is didactic —S.E.Hyman⟩ ⟨~ to go is a mistake⟩ **f** — used without modifying the meaning of an expression containing another negative ⟨could*n't* stand it no longer —Mark Twain⟩; compare DOUBLE NEGATIVE **2** — used as a generalized negative function word to express an unspecified degree of comparative difference varying from almost identical to almost opposite ⟨today is ~ Wednesday⟩ ⟨in better light you can see the cloth is ~ black⟩ ⟨~ a full cup, please⟩ ⟨five dollars does*n't* count in that place⟩ ⟨the question is ~ as simple as it seems —A.G.Hays⟩ ⟨will be found that it is ~ so easy as it seems —J.A.Powell⟩ ⟨in the auditorium there were many ~ idolaters who found their admiration mixed with apprehension —John Mason Brown⟩ ⟨the holdups he took part in were ~ carefully planned —Croswell Bowen⟩ ⟨was ~ merely a man of words —*Quarterly Jour. of Speech*⟩ ⟨he's ~ all there⟩ ⟨try ~ to hurt me so much⟩ ⟨~ paying careful attention to the warnings⟩ ⟨charged with ~ assuming full responsibility⟩ ⟨after your ~ heavy body shrunken in death —Amy Lowell⟩ **3 :** not even : not so much as ⟨~ a red cent⟩ ⟨~ a dog would bark at him —Washington Irving⟩ ⟨five wounded and ~ a man killed —S.C.Williams⟩ **4 :** NEVER ⟨ten years old and ~ been to a circus⟩ **5 :** OTHERWISE ⟨whalers were more often than ~ three or four years away from port —Sacheverell Sitwell⟩ **6 :** slightly less than : somewhat less than : HARDLY ⟨while ~ as interesting as similar works —E.C.Carter⟩ — usu. used with an intensive (as *very, quite, always, wholly*) and sometimes with *half* ⟨the clergy and elders . . . by and large, are ~ very helpful —John Cogley⟩ ⟨for the armed forces, life is ~ quite as trying as it is for the civilian —Emily Hahn⟩ ⟨the canvasses by other writers have ~ been as revealing —Harold Fields⟩ ⟨the irony of this ~ altogether heartening disclosure —*Sat. Eve. Post*⟩ ⟨the conditions today are ~ half bad⟩ **7** — used as a function word before a negative word to express an intentionally unemphatic affirmation ⟨~ dishonest⟩ ⟨~ implausibly⟩ ⟨~ atypical⟩ ⟨~ inconsistent with law —*U.S.Code*⟩ ⟨~ unreasonable or unexpected —*Atlantic*⟩ **8** — used as the first element of the correlatives *not only . . . but* ⟨will have brought about ~ only the defect of evil, but some permanent good —Julian Huxley⟩ ⟨effective ~ only in terminating an unlawful conspiracy, but in limiting price increases —T.W.Arnold⟩; of the correlatives *not only . . . but also* ⟨~ only the spelling of the words, but also the grammatical forms become conventionalized —William Chomsky⟩; of the correlatives *not . . . but* ⟨~ a country town but a metropolis —Leslie Stephen⟩ ⟨our most significant contribution to general culture, however, was made ~ in modern times but in Saxon times —Kemp Malone⟩; of the correlatives *not . . . nor* ⟨~ for wealth nor for fame did he strive —J.A.Powell⟩ ⟨did ~ speak nor stir —B.A.Williams⟩; or of the correlatives *not . . . or* ⟨such quotations do ~ discredit or impair the sincerity —William Hard⟩ ⟨~ folded bud, or wave that laps a shore —Phyllis McGinley⟩ — **not a little :** to a considerable extent or degree ⟨*not a little* embarrassed by the lack of adequate references —R.W.Chapman⟩ — **not half** *Brit* : not at all

[2]**not** \'nät, *usu* -äd·+V\ *n* -S : NEGATION, NEGATIVE

[3]**not** \"\ *prep* : other than : EXCEPT ⟨nobody ~ a professor has the remotest idea —W.L.Sullivan⟩

[4]**not** *or* **nott** \"\ *adj* [ME, close-cropped, fr. OE *knot*] *dial Eng* : POLLED

[5]**not** *or* **nott** \"\ *n* -S *dial Eng* : a hornless sheep, cow, or steer

[1]**not-** *or* **noto-** *comb form* [NL, fr. Gk *nōt-*, *nōto-*, fr. *nōtos*, *nōton* back — more at NATES] : back : back part ⟨*noto*chord⟩ ⟨*not*algia⟩

[2]**not-** *or* **noto-** *comb form* [NL, fr. Gk *notos* south wind, south, southwest; akin to Gk *noteros* damp — more at NOURISH] : south : southern ⟨*Not*alian⟩ ⟨*Noto*therium⟩

**-not** \(ˌ)nät, 'nät, ˌnət, *usu* -d·+V\ *adv comb form* [[1]*not*] : not ⟨can*not*⟩

**nota** *pl of* NOTUM

**no·ta be·ne** \ˌnōd·ə'benē, -ōtə-, -ni *sometimes* -bēn-; ˌnōˌtä'be(ˌ)nā, -tȧ'-\ [L, mark well] — used to call attention to something important ⟨whom, *nota bene*, I had never seen —Joseph Conrad⟩

**no·ta·bilia** \ˌnōd·ə'bilēə, -bēl-, -lyə\ *n pl* [L, neut. pl. of *notabilis*] : things worthy of note ⟨collected ~ into groups —G.U.Yule⟩

**no·ta·bil·i·ty** \ˌnō|d·ə'biləd·ē, |tə-, -lətē, -i, *in sense 1* " *or* ˌnä|\ *n* -ES [[1]*notable* + *-ity*] **1** *archaic* : the industry or management appropriate to a housewife **2 :** a notable or prominent person ⟨all the *notabilities* gave balls —Lady Hanson⟩

[1]**no·ta·ble** \'nō|d·əbəl, |tə-, *in sense 3* " *or* 'nä|\ *adj* [ME, fr. MF, fr. L *notabilis*, fr. *notare* to note + *-abilis* -able — more at NOTE] **1 a** (1) **:** worthy of note : STRIKING, CONSPICUOUS, REMARKABLE ⟨~ chiefly for its sublime unreality —G.B. Hurff⟩ ⟨wins the ~ distinction of being feared by all —H.A. Overstreet⟩ ⟨the ~ increase in joint production of films —*College English*⟩ ⟨the clock kept time with ~ accuracy —*New Yorker*⟩ ⟨the most ~ exception to this statement —Alfred Cobban⟩ ⟨~ for their endurance . . . and resignation —W.C. Huntington⟩ (2) **:** being of much weight, scope, or significance : IMPORTANT, MEMORABLE ⟨a ~ intrigue was set in motion —Claudia Cassidy⟩ ⟨appeared as chief counsel in many ~ cases⟩ ⟨~ deposits were found in other parts of the area⟩ **b** (1) **:** noteworthy for excellence, quality, merit, or high rank or standing : DISTINGUISHED, PROMINENT ⟨had aid and comfort from that ~ scholar —Leonard Bacon⟩ ⟨attended by the most ~ persons of the community⟩ ⟨his conduct toward the one that survived was very ~ —Nancy Mitford⟩ ⟨based on the journal of that ~ trader —*Amer. Guide Series: Ore.*⟩ ⟨a ~ technique wedded to an austere and searching subject —Hollis Alpert⟩ ⟨married into a ~ family⟩ (2) **:** NOTORIOUS ⟨a ~ criminal⟩ ⟨cleaned out a crew of ~ horse thieves —S.H.Holbrook⟩ **2 :** capable of being noted : OBSERVABLE ⟨other important events . . . were ~ throughout 1948 —*Collier's Yr. Bk.*⟩ **3** *archaic* **a :** efficient or capable in performance of housewifely duties ⟨~ mothers, who knew what it was to keep children whole and sweet —George Eliot⟩ **b :** of or relating to household management — **no·ta·ble·ness** *n* -ES

[2]**notable** \"\ *n* -S **1 :** a prominent or conspicuous figure : a person of note : NOTABILITY ⟨~*s* from princes to publishers have been involved —Al Brannon⟩ ⟨has been a ~ in the cafeterias, diners, barrooms —Joseph Mitchell⟩ **2 a :** a person of high social rank : a member of the wealthy or upper class ⟨employed as domestic servants in the homes of ~*s* —J.F. Embree & W.L.Thomas⟩ **b notables** *pl, often cap* : a group of prominent persons usu. of the aristocracy summoned esp. in monarchical France or regions under its political influence to act as a deliberative body ⟨an assembly of *Notables* decided in favor of the establishment in Mexico of a monarchy —W.S. Robertson⟩

**no·ta·bly** \-blē,-bli\ *adv* [ME, fr. [1]*notable*] **1 :** in a notable manner : to an extreme or considerable degree : REMARKABLY, STRIKINGLY ⟨club operators are ~ close-mouthed on sales figures —Mitchell Gordon⟩ ⟨became apparent that the seasons vary ~ in length —Benjamin Farrington⟩ ⟨American English has tended to be ~ euphemistic —Thomas Pyles⟩ ⟨beef consumption was ~ higher —*Dun's Rev.*⟩ ⟨were both ~ stubborn —Hugh MacLennan⟩ **2 :** ESPECIALLY, PARTICULARLY ⟨neither comfortable nor ~ uncomfortable —Andy Logan⟩ ⟨other powers, ~ Britain and the United States —C.A.Fisher⟩ ⟨continued to be produced, ~ in recent years —I.M.Price⟩ **3 :** in a manner likely to attract attention : NOTICEABLY, CONSPICUOUSLY ⟨could not really be called united, with so many countries ~ absent —Mollie Panter-Downes⟩

**no·ta·canth** \'nōd·əˌkan(t)th\ *n* -S [NL *Notacanthus*, type genus of Notacanthidae, fr. [1]*not-* + Gk *akantha* thorn, spine — more at ACANTH-] : a fish of the family Notacanthidae

**no·ta·can·thid** \ˌ==='kan(t)thəd\ *n* -S [NL *Notacanthidae*] : NOTACANTH

**no·ta·can·thi·dae** \-n(t)thəˌdē\ *n pl, cap* [NL, fr. *Notacanthus*, type genus + *-idae* — more at NOTACANTH] : a small family of deep-sea fishes (order Heteromi) resembling eels and having long dorsal and anal fins with both spines and soft rays

**no·ta·can·thous** \¦==¦kan(t)thəs\ *adj* [[1]*not-* + Gk *akantha* + E *-ous*] : having spines on the back

**no·tae·al** \(')nō¦tēəl\ *adj* [NL *notae*um + E *-al*] : of or relating to a notaeum

**no·tae ti·ro·ni·a·nae** \'nōd·ˌētəˌrōnē'āˌnē, -ōd·ˌī-, -āˌnī\ *n pl, cap T* [NL, characters of Tiro, after M. Tullius *Tiro*, secretary of Cicero] : a system of shorthand employed in ancient Rome

**no·tae·um** *or* **no·te·um** \nō'tēəm\ *n, pl* **no·taea** *or* **no·tea** \-ēə\ [NL, fr. Gk *nōtaios* of the back, fr. *nōton*, *nōtos* back — more at NATES] : the upper surface of a bird's body

**no·tal** \'nōd·ᵊl, -ōtᵊl\ *adj* [[1]*not-* + *-al*] **1 :** of or belonging to the back : DORSAL **2** [NL *not*um + E *-al*] : of or belonging to a notum

**no·ta·lian** \(')nō¦tālēən, -lyən\ *adj, usu cap* [NL *Notalia* south temperate marine biogeographic realm (fr. [2]*not-* + *-alia*) + E *-an*] : of, relating to, or being the south temperate marine biogeographic realm that is bounded by the southern isocrymes of 68° and 44° F

**no·tam** \'nōˌtam\ *n* -S [*no*tice to *a*ir*m*en] : a notice providing pilots with general information essential for the safe and efficient operation of airplanes (as the establishment or condition of or change in any aeronautical facility, service, procedure, or hazard)

**no·tan** \'nō'tän\ *n* -S [Jap *nōtan*] : the combination of lights and darks esp. as used in Japanese art : the design or pattern of a work of art as seen in flat areas of dark and light values only — compare CHIAROSCURO

**no·tan·dum** \nō'tandəm\ *n, pl* **notan·da** \-də\ *also* **notandums** [L, neut. of *notandus*, gerundive of *notare* to note — more at NOTE] : something to be noted or an entry of it : NOTE, MEMORANDUM

**no·tar** \'nōd·ər\ *n* [ME, alter. of *notary*] *archaic Scot* : NOTARY

**no·tar·i·al** \(')nō¦ta(a)rēəl\ *adj* [*notary* + *-al*] : of, relating to, or characteristic of a notary : done, executed, framed, or taken by a notary ⟨~ documents⟩ — **no·tar·i·al·ly** \-əlē\ *adv*

**no·ta·ri·za·tion** \ˌnōd·ərə'zāshən, -ōtə-, -ˌrī'-\ *n* -S [*notarize* + *-ation*] **1 :** the act of a notary in authenticating a document or verifying it under oath **2 :** the act or an instance of causing a document to be authenticated by a notary or to be verified under oath before him **3 :** the notarial certificate appended to a document

**no·ta·rize** \'==ˌrīz\ *vt* -ED/-ING/-S [*notary* + *-ize*] **1 :** to acknowledge or attest as a notary public ⟨~ a legal paper⟩ **2 :** to cause (a document) to be acknowledged, attested before, or authenticated by a notary public

**no·ta·ry** \-ˌrē, -ri\ *n* -ES [ME, fr. L *notarius* stenographer, secretary, fr. *notarius* of shorthand, fr. *nota* mark, shorthand character + *-arius* -ary] **1** *obs* **a :** CLERK, SECRETARY **b :** NOTER, OBSERVER **2 a** *or* **notary public** *pl* **notaries public** *or* **notary publics** [ME, fr. *notary* + *public*, adj.] : a public officer appointed in the U. S. usu. by the governors of the states and in England where he is still nominally an ecclesiastical official by the Archbishop of Canterbury to take acknowledgment of or otherwise attest or certify deeds and other writings or copies of them usu. under official seal to make them authentic and to take affidavits, depositions, and protests of negotiable paper **b :** a French official who draws up and records documents and instruments of legal importance and certifies to copies of judgments and records and to protests of commercial paper, who is appointed by the president of the Republic, and who cannot serve as advocate or engage in any other business **c :** an official in Quebec who draws up and records instruments, examines titles, and does noncontentious legal business

**no·ta·ry·ship** \'===ˌship\ *n* : the office, tenure, or dignity of a notary

[1]**no·tate** \'nōˌtāt, *usu* -ād·+V\ *adj* [L *nota* mark + E *-ate*] : marked with spots or lines

[2]**notate** \"\ *vt* -ED/-ING/-S [back formation fr. *notation*] : to put into notation

**no·ta·tion** \nō'tāshən\ *n* -S [L *notation-*, *notatio*, fr. *notatus* (past part. of *notare* to note, denote) + *-ion-*, *-io* -ion — more at NOTE] **1** *obs* : etymological explanation or denotation **2 a :** ANNOTATION, NOTE ⟨damage, according to the constable's ~*s*, consisted of broken front bumper —Richard Joseph⟩ ⟨if a letter refers to an enclosure, add the appropriate ~ to the closing lines —D.D.Lessenberry & T.J.Crawford⟩ **b :** an act of noting : OBSERVATION **3 a :** the act, process, method, or an instance of representing by a system or set of marks, signs, figures, or characters **b :** a system of characters, symbols, or abbreviated expressions used in an art or science to express technical facts, quantities, or other data **4 a** (1) **:** the act, process, or system of recording music or musical details by means of written notes or symbols to indicate pitch, rhythm, tempo, harmonic combinations, style, and specific directions for performance (2) **:** musical notes and symbols **b :** the representation of dance movements by means of written symbols **c :** the recording of chess moves **d :** the system of signs and symbols used in symbolic logic — compare TRUTH table **5 :** the act or an instance of recording (as natural appearances or states of mind) through artistic or literary means ⟨swift ~*s* of a light quite different from that of the Caribbean —Virgil Barker⟩ ⟨exact ~ of qualities, tones, rapports of colors and forms —Meyer Schapiro⟩ ⟨the whole purport of literature . . . is the ~ of the heart —Thornton Wilder⟩

**no·ta·tion·al** \(')=¦tāshənᵊl, -shnəl\ *adj* : of or relating to notation

**no·ta·tive** \'nōd·əd·iv, -ōtətiv\ *adj* [L *notat*us + E *-ive*] : suggesting the characteristics or things denoted

**no·ta·tor** \(')nō¦tād·ə(r), -ātə-\ *n* -S [L *notat*us (past part. of *notare* to note) + E *-or* — more at NOTE] : a specialist in musical or dance notation

**no·tau·lix** \nō'tȯ(ˌ)liks\ *n, pl* **notauli·ces** \-ˌləˌsēz\ [NL, fr. [1]*not-* + LL *aulic-*, *aulix* furrow, MS error for *aulac-*, *aulax*, fr. Gk *aulak-*, *aulax*] : a longitudinal furrow in the anterior part of the mesonotum of various insects

**not–being** \'=¦==\ *n* : the state of not being

[1]**notch** \'näch\ *n* -ES [perh. alter. (resulting from incorrect division of *an otch*) of (assumed) *otch*, fr. MF *oche*] **1 a :** a V-shaped indentation or hollow (as in a surface or edge) **b** (1) **:** a slit or cut made in something esp. to serve as a mark or record : NICK ⟨supposed to be three ~*es* on the butt of his business six-shooter —Green Peyton⟩ (2) **:** a run in cricket **c :** UNDERCUT **d :** a half-moon (as in a thumb index) cut in book leaves at the fore edge to provide space for an identification guide **e :** a space cut out in the safety roller of lever escapements and in the staff of duplex escapements of watches to permit passage of a safety finger piece during impulse to the balance **f** (1) **:** a small V-shaped cut or one of several cuts along the edge of clothing patterns to be used as an aid in assembling a garment (2) **:** a V-shaped angle at the joining of lapel and collar on a garment **2 :** a narrow passage between two mountains or other elevations : a deep close pass : DEFILE, GAP ⟨the most historic of nine ~*es* . . . which are scattered through these mountains —*Ford Times*⟩ — often used in place names ⟨Crawford *Notch*⟩ **3 :** a degree, step, or peg ⟨his voice rose another ~ —Earle Birney⟩ ⟨this book . . . is ~*es* above the usual product —Louise D. Rich⟩

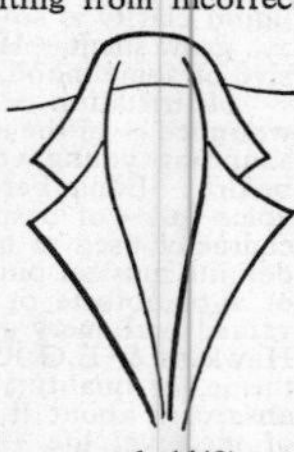

notch 1f(2)

[2]**notch** \"\ *vb* -ED/-ING/-ES *vt* **1 a** *obs* : to cut (the hair) unevenly or poorly **b** (1) **:** to cut or make a notch in : INDENT ⟨fitted together by ~*ing* the ends —*Amer. Guide Series: Minn.*⟩ ⟨the much steeper continental slope, ~*ed* by the mouths of the gorges —R.E.Coker⟩ (2) **:** to score, mark, or record by or as if by means of a notch ⟨~*ed* another kill on the butt of his gun⟩ (3) **:** to score, gain, or achieve successfully ⟨~*ed* his second victory against three losses —*N.Y.Times*⟩ ⟨wrote the thesis which ~*ed* him his M.D. —Sydney (*Australia*) *Bulletin*⟩ ⟨~*ed* his thirteenth consecutive perfect performance —*Postal Service News*⟩ ⟨~*ed* himself a place in Spanish history —Hamilton Basso⟩ **c :** to make an undercut in ⟨~ a tree⟩ **2 :** to fit (the arrow) to the string : NOCK **3 a :** to fasten or insert by means of a notch ⟨logs being ~*ed* into each other at the corners —*Amer. Guide Series: Texas*⟩ **b :** to give a particular shape or form to by making notches — used with *into* **4 :** to change the position of (a control device) step by step ~ *vi* : to make or form a notch ⟨the path ~*ed* into the jungle wall —William Faulkner⟩

**notch block** *n* : SNATCH BLOCK

**notchboard** \'=ˌ=\ *n* : a board that receives the ends of the steps in a staircase

**notch carving** *n* : NICKING

**notched** \'nächt\ *adj* [partly fr. past part. of [2]*notch*, partly fr. [1]*notch* + *-ed*] **1 :** having a notch : INDENTED, SERRATED ⟨a ~ collar⟩ ⟨a ~ log⟩ ⟨a medicinal tablet . . . which is ~ down the middle —Richard Joseph⟩ ⟨brow . . . already ~ with care —Julian Maclaren-Ross⟩ ⟨a leaf with ~ edges⟩ **2** *archaic* : having the hair cut unevenly

**notched binding** *n* : the fastening of sets of single leaves (as of books or magazines) with a series of glue-filled grooves at the backbone edge rather than by sewing

**notched falcon** *n* : any of several So. American kites (genus *Harpagus*) having the maxilla doubly toothed

**notched wrack** *n* : a common rockweed (*Fucus serratus*) of the northern Atlantic

**notch·er** \'nächə(r)\ *n* -S : one who cuts notches: as **a :** UNDERCUTTER **b :** an operator of a machine for notching tin plate to facilitate the flanging and seaming operations in the making of tin cans **c :** an instrument for making notches

**notch graft** *n* : a graft similar to a cleft graft except that a slit in the stock is made with a saw and the scion is inserted in the slit

**notch grafting** *or* **notch graftage** *n* : the process of making a notch graft

**notching** *n* -S [fr. gerund of [2]*notch*] **1 a :** the act or an instance of making notches : an act of cutting into small hollows **b :** a method of joining (as timbers or scantling) by notching (as at the ends) and overlapping or interlocking the notched portions; *also* : a joint so formed **c :** the removal of a wedge of bark above a bud (as on a branch of an apple tree) to induce the formation of a branch from the bud **2 :** a small hollow formed by notching : NOTCH

**notchweed** \'=ˌ=\ *also* **notchwort** \'=ˌ=\ *n* : STINKING GOOSEFOOT

**notchwing** \'=ˌ=\ *n* : a European moth (*Peronia caudana*) of the family Tortricidae

**not content** *n, pl* **not contents** [[1]*not* + *content*, adj.] : NONCONTENT

[1]**note** \'nōt, *usu* -ōd·+V\ *n* -S [ME, use, profit, benefit, fr. OE *nutu;* akin to OE *nēotan* to use, enjoy — more at NEAT] *dial Eng* : a cow's lactation period

[2]**note** \"\ *vt* -ED/-ING/-S [ME *noten*, fr. OF *noter*, fr. L *notare*, fr. *nota* note, mark] **1 a** (1) **:** to record or fix in the mind or memory : take due or special notice of : notice or observe with care ⟨must be *noted* that some southern Negroes were able to rise —Mercer Cook⟩ ⟨please ~ that payment in full is enclosed⟩ ⟨*noted* the fine stature of the Indian males —*Amer. Guide Series: Oreg.*⟩ ⟨pleased to ~ that I will be summoned to appear in court —Oris Turner⟩ (2) **:** to record or preserve in writing : make a note of ⟨*noted* on the margin his disagreement with the writer⟩ — often used with *down* ⟨*noted* down his impressions of the city⟩ (3) *archaic* : to set down in or provide with notes esp. musical notes (4) **:** to make a notarial memorandum of nonpayment of (a negotiable bill) on presentation (5) **:** to make notes in; *also* : ANNOTATE ⟨*noted* cases for the attorney general —John Buchan⟩ **b :** to recognize the existence or presence of : PERCEIVE, OBSERVE ⟨in these brilliant and gifted inhabitants . . . one may ~ a number of characteristics —W.K.Ferguson⟩ ⟨edema is likely to be *noted* first in the legs —Morris Fishbein⟩ ⟨too good and simple himself to ~ what was implied —Mary Austin⟩ ⟨one ~*s* the scars pocking the buildings —H.L.Matthews⟩ ⟨quick to ~ a shadow of pain across his pale features —W.J.Locke⟩ **2** *obs* : DENOTE, SIGNIFY **3 a :** to call attention to in speech or writing : make separate or special mention of : REMARK ⟨the odds, someone *noted*, were stacked . . . in favor of the house —T.H.White b. 1915⟩ ⟨~*s* with gallant approval the civilizing influences of British administrators —Hal Lehrman⟩ ⟨the magazine *noted* his understanding of international problems —*Current Biog.*⟩ **b :** to indicate or show ⟨records fail to ~ what became of him⟩ ⟨on this occasion she was merely *noted* as a member of the company —F.C.Schang⟩ ⟨scales that can ~ the absence of a dime in a batch of thousands —*Buick Mag.*⟩ **4** *obs* : CHARGE, ACCUSE, BRAND — usu. used with *of, for,* or *with* **syn** see SEE

[3]**note** \"\ *n* -S [L *nota* note, mark, character, brand] **1 a** (1) **:** a

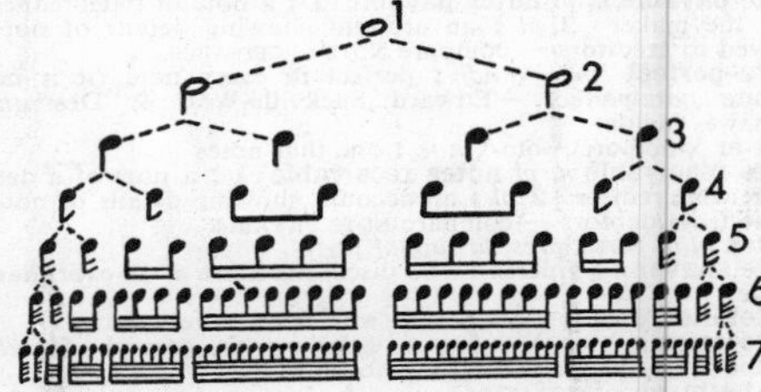


relative duration of notes 1b(1): *1* whole, *2* half, *3* quarter, *4* eighth, *5* sixteenth, *6* thirty-second, *7* sixty-fourth notes

melody or song ⟨mine ear is much enamored of thy ~ —Shak.⟩ (2) **:** a tone of definite pitch (as of a musical instrument or the voice) (3) **:** CRY, CALL, SOUND ⟨heard the iron on the roof give an uneasy warning ~ —Eve Langley⟩ ⟨not even the loon, in whose voice there is a human ~ —Charlton Laird⟩ (4) **:** the musical call or song of a bird ⟨you know its ~: the liquid clarity is so perfect that when it sings the other birds . . . grow silent —Harold Laski⟩ (5) **:** a tone of voice expressive of some mood, attitude, or emotion ⟨her voice carried a ~ of irritation —Louis Bromfield⟩ ⟨would cry with the wounded ~ of the utterly betrayed —Mary Austin⟩ ⟨her deep-sounding young voice with a ~ in it he had never heard before —Edna Ferber⟩ ⟨a wild anxiety had come into her voice—a ~ of desperate pleading —O.E.Rölvaag⟩ **b** (1) **:** a character used to indicate relative duration by its shape and definite musical pitch by its position on the staff (2) **:** a key of a pianoforte or similar instrument **c :** ODOR, SMELL ⟨a valued perfumery synthetic with a lily-of-the-valley ~ —J.E. Hawkins & E.G.Rietz⟩ **2 a** (1) **:** a characteristic feature, theme, or quality **:** ELEMENT, MOTIF ⟨there was such a ~ of absurdity about it —T.B.Costain⟩ ⟨those are the main ~*s* of medieval life —G.G.Coulton⟩ ⟨the essential ~*s* of his satire —F.R.Leavis⟩ ⟨a fixed ~ of my father's life —Van Wyck Brooks⟩ ⟨two ~*s* of gentility our family maintained —R.M.Lovett⟩ ⟨a strong ~ of realism —Ellen L. Buell⟩ ⟨there isn't a ~ in you which I don't know —Thomas Hardy⟩ (2) **:** an identifying or dominant theme, characteristic, or motif ⟨the hard, varnished, cosmopolitan cleverness which is the ~ of the hour —Sinclair Lewis⟩ ⟨strikes at once the ~ of his career —H.E.Scudder⟩ (3) **:** a concrete object that sets the tone or constitutes an identifying or characteristic feature ⟨vast ranches whose one modern ~ is an occasional oil derrick —*Amer. Guide Series: Texas*⟩ (4) **:** MOOD, TONE, TENOR ⟨hadn't intended to end on this ~ —F.R.Leavis⟩ ⟨answered on the same detached ~ —Francis King⟩ ⟨began . . . on a ~ of urgency —Christine Weston⟩ ⟨inject a ~ of intimacy into their contacts —T.B.Costain⟩ **b** *archaic* **:** STIGMA, REPROACH **3 a** (1) **:** an abstract of particulars recorded in the conveyance by fine (2) *Scots law* **:** a short and concise statement used as a pleading of an action or defense and setting forth without argument the statutes or cases relied upon **b** (1) **:** a brief writing intended to assist the memory or to serve as the basis for a fuller statement **:** MEMORANDUM, MINUTE ⟨made a ~ on a piece of paper —Barnaby Conrad⟩ (2) **:** a condensed record of a speech, lecture, lesson, or discussion made at the time of listening ⟨takes extensive ~*s* in all his classes⟩ (3) **:** an artist's rough sketch esp. of a detail **c** (1) **:** a brief remark by way of explanation or information **:** a comment or explanation (as penciled in the margin of a page) **:** a critical explanation or illustrative observation (2) **:** a printed comment or reference that is set apart from the main text and usu. in smaller type — see FOOTNOTE, SHOULDER NOTE, SIDENOTE; compare REFERENCE MARK (3) **:** explanatory printed comment on a work of art ⟨program ~*s* for a concert⟩ ⟨~*s* on a record album⟩ **d** (1) *archaic* **:** ACCOUNT, BILL (2) **:** a written or printed paper acknowledging a debt and promising payment **:** a written promise to pay ⟨has my ~ for $1000⟩ (3) **:** a bank note or other form of paper that is current money ⟨deposited the sum in ~*s* and coin⟩ (4) *obs* **:** a signed receipt **:** VOUCHER **e** (1) **:** a short informal letter (2) **:** a formal diplomatic communication regularly bearing the signature of the person who sends it, addressed personally to the minister or other official to whom it is sent, usually written in the first person although sometimes in the third, and typically used for the most important correspondence — compare AIDE-MÉMOIRE, MEMORANDUM, NOTE VERBALE (3) **:** any of a number of diplomatic communications of varying character or formality **f** (1) **:** a short account, essay, or sketch ⟨not attempting in this brief ~ to recount again the public battles of that far-off time —Bruce Bliven b.1889⟩; *specif* **:** a communication (as to a scholarly or technical journal) usu. considerably shorter in length than an article and severely restricted in scope or subject matter ⟨a brief ~ . . . reported the find of an association of human burials and artifacts —G.W.Hewes⟩ (2) **:** an often informal record of impressions or incidents — usu. used in pl. ⟨~*s* on a journey to the headwaters of the Amazon⟩ (3) **:** a brief item in a newspaper or magazine **:** JOTTING ⟨financial ~*s*⟩ ⟨household ~*s*⟩ ⟨social ~*s*⟩ **4 a :** DISTINCTION, REPUTATION, EMINENCE ⟨other animal stories of ~ —Ellen L. Buell⟩ ⟨a figure of almost international ~ —John Buchan⟩ **b :** OBSERVATION, NOTICE, HEED — usu. used with *take* ⟨took full ~ of all that had happened⟩ **c :** KNOWLEDGE, INFORMATION ⟨his popularity has long been a matter of ~ —*Current Biog.*⟩ **5 :** an incident or situation of an unexpected, startling, or disagreeable character ⟨wasn't that a ~ for a chief officer to swallow —Sam Ross⟩ ⟨that's a hell of a ~ —Ernest Hemingway⟩ **syn** see CHARACTER, SIGN

**notebook** \ˈ≈,≈\ *n* **1 :** a book in which notes or memoranda are recorded **2 :** a book with blank leaves used by students for taking notes during a class or lecture

**note broker** *n* **:** a broker who deals in short-term negotiable instruments (as acceptances, bills, or notes)

**notecase** \ˈ≈,≈\ *n, Brit* **:** a pocketbook for banknotes **:** WALLET

**note col·lec·tive** \ˈnōt,kȯ,lekˈtēv\ *n, pl* **notes collectives** \-ōts,kȯ,lekˈtēv\ [F] **:** a formal diplomatic communication addressed by two or more states to one or more states that is usu. signed and not merely initialed by the representatives of the states presenting it

**not·ed** \ˈnōd·əd, -ōtəd\ *adj* [ME, fr. past part. of *noten* to note] **1 :** well-known by reputation **:** EMINENT, CELEBRATED ⟨a ~ educator⟩ ⟨a ~ landmark⟩ ⟨a ~ beauty⟩ ⟨a ~ racehorse⟩ **2 :** provided with musical notes or score — **not·ed·ly** *adv* — **not·ed·ness** *n* -ES

**note di·plo·ma·tique** \ˈnōt,diplə,maˈtēk\ *n, pl* **notes diplomatiques** \-ōts,diplə,maˈtēk\ [F] **:** a formal diplomatic communication signed and not merely initialed and understood to speak for and under the direction of the government presenting it

**notehead** \ˈ≈,≈\ *or* **noteheading** \ˈ≈,≈≈\ *n* **:** a sheet of writing paper that has a printed or engraved heading and is usu. somewhat smaller than a letterhead; *also* **:** the heading itself

**noteholder** \ˈ≈,≈≈\ *n* **:** a person who holds a note

**not·e·laea** \,näd·əˈlēə\ *n, cap* [NL, fr. ²*not-* + Gk *elaia* olive tree — more at OLIVE] **:** a small genus of chiefly Australian trees or shrubs (family Oleaceae) most of which have very hard wood

**note·less** \ˈnōtləs\ *adj* **1 :** not noted or not noticed **:** UNDISTINGUISHED ⟨some ~ Gaelic poet —W.B.Yeats⟩ **2 :** devoid of musical notes or tones **:** UNMUSICAL — **note·less·ly** *adv* — **note·less·ness** *n* -ES

**note·let** \-lət\ *n* -S **:** a little or short note

**note·man** \-mən, -,man\ *n, pl* **notemen :** a member of a surveying party who keeps the records of the data secured

**note of exclamation** *also* **note of admiration :** EXCLAMATION POINT

**note of hand :** PROMISSORY NOTE

**note of interrogation :** QUESTION MARK

**notepaper** \ˈ≈,≈≈\ *n* **:** writing paper of a quality, size, or fold suitable for notes, letters, memoranda

**note payable** *n, pl* **notes payable 1 :** a note of indebtedness of the maker **2** *pl* **:** an account showing details of notes owed to creditors — compare NOTE RECEIVABLE

**note–perfect** \ˈ≈ˈ≈≈\ *adj* **:** perfect in every note ⟨it is not quite *note-perfect* —Edward Sackville-West & Desmond Shawe-Taylor⟩

**not·er** \ˈnōd·ə(r), -ōtə-\ *n* -S **:** one that notes

**note receivable** *n, pl* **notes receivable 1 :** a note of a debt due the creditor **2** *pl* **:** an account showing details of notes due from debtors — compare NOTE PAYABLE

**notes** *pl of* NOTE, *pres 3d sing of* NOTE

**note shaver** *n* **:** a person who discounts notes at an exorbitant rate

**notetaker** \ˈ≈,≈≈\ *n* **:** a person who takes notes

**note–taking** \ˈ≈,≈\ *n* [³*note* + *taking,* fr. gerund of *take*] **:** the act or process of taking notes

**no·teum** *var of* NOTAEUM

**note ver·bale** \ˈ;ver'bäl\ *n, pl* **notes verbales** \ˈ;nōt(s)\≈ˈbäl(z)\ [F, lit., verbal note] **:** a diplomatic note that is more formal than an aide-mémoire and less formal than a note, is drafted in the third person, and is never signed

**noteworthily** \ˈ≈,≈≈\ *adv* **:** in a noteworthy manner

**noteworthiness** \ˈ≈,≈≈\ *n* -ES **:** the quality or state of being noteworthy

**noteworthy** \ˈ≈,≈\ *adj* **:** worthy of note **:** REMARKABLE, NOTABLE ⟨made ~ contributions in diverse fields —M.R. Cohen⟩ ⟨the damage to the promenade . . . was ~ —J.A. Steers⟩

**not-go gage** \ˈ≈ˈ≈\ *n* **:** NO-GO GAGE

**not guilty** *adj* — used as the term of general issue to deny the whole indictment in legal actions

**noth-** *or* **notho-** *comb form* [NL, fr. Gk *noth-, notho-,* fr. *nothos* bastard, spurious, born of unequal parents] **:** bastard **:** spurious **:** hybrid ⟨*Nothar*ctus⟩ ⟨*Notho*saurus⟩

¹**no·tharc·tid** \nəˈthärktəd\ *adj* [NL *Notharctidae,* family including *Notharctus*] **:** of or relating to *Notharctus* or a closely related genus

²**notharctid** \"\ *or* **no·tharc·tine** \-tīn, -tən\ *n* -S **:** a lemur of *Notharctus* or a closely related genus

**no·tharc·tus** \-ˌtəs\ *n, cap* [NL, fr. *noth-* + Gk *arktos* bear — more at ARCTIC] **:** a genus of primitive No. American Eocene lemurs with large orbits and 40 teeth of which the incisors are not procumbent, that is related to *Adapis,* and known from the No. American Eocene

¹**noth·er** \ˈnəthə(r)\ *pron* [ME, alter. (resulting fr. incorrect division of *an other, none other*) of *other,* pron.] *chiefly dial* **:** OTHER

²**nother** \"\ *adj* [ME, alter. (resulting fr. incorrect division of *an other, none other*) of *other,* adj.] *chiefly dial* **:** OTHER

¹**noth·ing** \ˈnəthiŋ, -thēŋ\ *pron* [ME *nothing, nathing, non thing,* fr. OE *nāthing, nān thing,* fr. *nān* no + *thing* — more at NONE] **1 :** not any thing **:** no thing ⟨~ in the . . . document precludes the existence of regional arrangements —Vera M. Dean⟩ ⟨leaving ~ to chance —Fred Majdalany⟩ ⟨the dead feel ~, hear ~ —Carson McCullers⟩ ⟨had done little or ~ toward solving the really fundamental problem —*Collier's Yr. Bk.*⟩ ⟨just say ~ —Lilian Balch⟩ **2 :** no share, element, or part ⟨wrote ~ of an acceptance message in advance —J.A.Huston⟩ ⟨~ of him that doth fade —*Shak.*⟩ **3 a :** one that is of no interest, value, or consequence to a person ⟨she's ~ to me, and I am ~ to her —Thomas Hardy⟩ ⟨the work he does . . . is ~ to him —T.P.Whitney⟩ **b :** no gain or advantage — often used in the phrase *nothing in it* ⟨there was ~ in it for him —L.C.Douglas⟩ **c :** no point or element of advantage **:** no superiority of condition — usu. used in the phrase *have nothing on* ⟨palaces had . . . ~ on her lovely thatched cottage —*No. Amer. Rev.*⟩ **d :** no substance or reality ⟨there's ~ to that story⟩ **e :** no complexity or difficulty ⟨the inexperienced hunter, who, after having killed a dozen or so of the animals . . . begins to think there is ~ in it —James Stevenson-Hamilton⟩ ⟨there's ~ to it if you know how⟩ **f :** no money or resources ⟨lived . . . on next to ~ —Ellen Glasgow⟩ ⟨left with ~⟩ **g :** no incriminating or damning evidence — usu. used in the phrase *have nothing on* ⟨the police had ~ on him⟩ — **for nothing** *adv* **1 :** to no purpose **:** in vain ⟨not born in the hills of Tennessee *for nothing* —W.C.Fridley⟩ **2 :** for no reason ⟨crying *for nothing* at all⟩ **3 :** without cost or payment ⟨delight of impressions given by nature *for nothing* —Henry Adams⟩ — **in nothing flat** *adv* **:** in the shortest possible time ⟨the rain swallowed up the tail light *in nothing flat* —E.S. Gardner⟩ ⟨put away her sandwiches *in nothing flat* —*New Yorker*⟩ — **nothing but :** nothing other than **:** ONLY ⟨has *nothing but* the clothes on his back⟩ — **nothing doing 1 :** by no means **:** definitely no ⟨*nothing doing* was the substance of his reply⟩ **2 :** no result or accomplishment ⟨there was *nothing doing* —W.R.Frye⟩ — **nothing for it :** no alternative ⟨*nothing for it* but to ride away . . . for the doctor —D.M. Davin⟩ ⟨there is *nothing for it,* but to keep her under close watch —Henry Wynmalen⟩ — **nothing if not :** above all **:** EXTREMELY ⟨*nothing if not* persistent —J.D.Carr⟩

²**nothing** \"\ *adv* [ME *nothing, nathing,* fr. OE *nāthing, nān thing,* fr. *nāthing, nān thing,* pron.] **:** not at all **:** in no degree ⟨that he should become a deity is ~ surprising —A.M. Young⟩ ⟨~ daunted, they dive into the icy water —G.W. Long⟩ — **nothing like** *adv* **:** NOWHERE NEAR **:** not nearly ⟨is *nothing like* as big as it looks on the map —Harry Gilroy⟩

³**nothing** \"\ *n* -S [¹*nothing*] **1 a :** no thing at all **:** something that does not exist ⟨an emissary of the primeval ~ —Thomas Carlyle⟩ ⟨~ cannot become an object of consciousness —Herbert Spencer⟩ **b** (1) **:** the absence of all magnitude or quantity **:** ZERO (2) **:** the symbol naught **:** CIPHER **c :** something that is characterized by utter absence of determination **:** perfect indistinguishableness ⟨pure ~⟩ **d** *obs* **:** utter insignificance **:** NOTHINGNESS ⟨find the emptiness of all things and the ~ of what is past —Sir Thomas Browne⟩ **2 a** (1) **:** something of no or slight value or significance **:** TRIFLE, BAGATELLE ⟨a little ~ of a dress —Lois Long⟩ ⟨love at first sight is a romantic ~ —Walter Le Beau⟩ ⟨so badly damaged that they looked like ~ —J.P.Blank⟩ (2) **:** a trifling or inane remark ⟨the glories of silent appreciation were shattered by garrulous ~*s* —William Beebe⟩ ⟨having drinks and saying sweet ~*s* —Hugh Gaitskell⟩ **b :** a person or other living individual who is supremely insignificant or inconsequential **:** one with no claim to note **:** NULLITY ⟨his wife . . . is strictly a ~ —*New Yorker*⟩ ⟨the bull . . . had temporarily become a ~ —Jean Stafford⟩ — **no nothing :** nothing at all ⟨no drama, no astonishing shots—*no nothing* —*New Yorker*⟩

**noth·ing·ar·i·an** \,≈≈ˈerēən\ *n* -S [¹*nothing* + *-arian*] **:** a person of no belief, creed, or particular sect

¹**noth·ing·ly** *adj* [³*nothing* + *-ly*] **:** VALUELESS, INEFFECTUAL

²**nothingly** \"\ *n* -ES **:** CIPHER

**noth·ing·ness** *n* -ES **1 :** the quality or state of being nothing: as **a :** absence of being **:** NONEXISTENCE ⟨the smoke . . . was snatched and scattered into ~ —Gordon Webber⟩ **b :** utter insignificance, worthlessness, or futility ⟨would be intimidated into meek ~ —Sinclair Lewis⟩ **c :** DEATH ⟨human reason cannot conceive of ~, yet men fear it —*Time*⟩ ⟨cannot believe in ~ being the destined end of all —T.B.Cabell⟩ **d :** the state or quality of utter indistinguishableness **:** total absence of determination or particularity **2 :** something that is utterly insignificant or valueless **3 :** EMPTINESS, VOID ⟨beyond the window was only a gray ~ —Hugh MacLennan⟩ ⟨ran behind a great green wall into ~ —Ira Wolfert⟩ **4 :** the conceptualization or reification of the affective content in an emotional experience (as of anxiety) that is negatively colored ⟨~ is . . . a distinctive metaphysical entity —J.A.Franquiz⟩; *also* **:** MEANINGLESSNESS ⟨the utter ~ of not being —Jean Wahl⟩

**nothing off** [²*nothing*] — used as an order to a steersman to keep the ship close to the wind

**notho-** — see NOTH-

**notho·cli·nal** \ˌnäthəˈklīnᵊl\ *adj* **:** of, relating to, or constituting a nothocline

**notho·cline** \ˈ≈≈,klīn\ *n* -S [*noth-* + *cline*] **:** a gradation of forms resulting from interspecific hybridization **:** a hybrid cline

**noth·o·fa·gus** \,≈≈ˈfāgəs\ *n, cap* [NL, fr. *noth-* + *Fagus*] **:** a genus of timber trees of the cooler parts of the southern hemisphere differing from the genus *Fagus* in the chiefly evergreen smaller leaves and in the flowers of both sexes being solitary or in threes — see EVERGREEN BEECH, NEW ZEALAND BEECH

**noth·o·lae·na** \-ˈlēnə\ *n, cap* [NL, fr. *noth-* + L *laena* cloak, fr. Gk *chlaina*] **:** a genus of rock-inhabiting ferns (family Polypodiaceae) of very diverse habit and with pinnate, bipinnate, or tripinnate fronds that are silky, hairy, tomentose, or farinose

**noth·o·saur** \ˈ≈≈,sȯ(ə)r\ *n* -S [NL *Nothosauria*] **:** a reptile or fossil of the suborder Nothosauria

**noth·o·sau·ria** \,≈≈ˈsȯrēə\ *n pl, cap* [NL *Nothosaurus* + *-ia*] **:** a suborder of primitive chiefly marine European Triassic reptiles (order Sauropterygia) —see NOTHOSAURUS — **noth·o·sau·ri·an** \;≈≈;sȯrēən\ *adj or n*

**noth·o·sau·rus** \,≈≈ˈsȯrəs\ *n, cap* [NL, fr. *noth-* + *-saurus*] **:** a genus of extinct reptiles (suborder Nothosauria) resembling the plesiosaurs but having longer and more slender limbs less completely modified for swimming

**noth·o·scor·dum** \-ˈskȯrdəm\ *n, cap* [NL, fr. *noth-* + Gk *skordon* garlic] **:** a genus of bulbous plants (family Liliaceae) that resemble the related onions and are sometimes cultivated for their terminal umbels of showy flowers — see CROW POISON

¹**no·tice** \ˈnōd·əs, -ōtəs\ *n* -S [ME *notyce,* fr. MF *notice* acquaintance, fr. L *notitia,* fr. *notus* (past part. of *noscere* to become acquainted with) + *-itia* -ice — more at KNOW] **1 a** (1) **:** formal or informal warning or intimation of something **:** ANNOUNCEMENT ⟨subject to change without ~ —*Dun's Rev.*⟩ ⟨was ~ that Britain meant to crack down on violence —*Time*⟩ ⟨give ~ of the fat and wrinkles coming to the young bride —H.M.Parshley⟩ (2) **:** a warning, announcement, or intimation given a specified time before the event to take place ⟨evacuating a school building . . . in a minute's ~ —Rose Bernadette⟩ ⟨upon reasonable ~, these charges are subject to adjustment —*Bull. of Bates Coll.*⟩ ⟨ready to leave at short ~⟩ ⟨allow me ten minutes' ~⟩ (3) **:** notification by one of the parties to an agreement or relation (as by an employer to a laborer) of intention of terminating it at a specified time ⟨tenants' right freely to give ~ —Store Bolin⟩ (4) **:** a communication of intelligence or of a claim or demand often required by statute or contract and prescribing the manner or form of giving it ⟨a ~ to quit leased premises⟩ (5) **:** the condition of being warned or notified — usu. used in the phrase *on notice* ⟨are on ~ that their military supply centers . . . would no longer be a privileged sanctuary —*N.Y.Times*⟩ ⟨putting all . . . court personnel on ~ that fundamental rights had to be observed —E.E.Nobleman⟩ **b :** INFORMATION, INTELLIGENCE ⟨~ of any errors . . . should be addressed —*Federal Guide (Australia)*⟩ ⟨give ~ of a poet —H.A.Larrabee⟩ **c** (1) *archaic* **:** KNOWLEDGE (2) **:** actual knowledge of a pertinent legal fact — called also *actual notice, express notice* (3) **:** knowledge of a particular fact (as the terms of a lease when one knows a tenant is in possession) capable of being acquired by the exercise of reasonable care on the part of the person legally chargeable with it — called also *implied notice* (4) **:** knowledge of a particular fact (as from deeds recorded in a public registry office) imputed by a positive rule of law to a person regardless of his actual knowledge — called also *constructive notice* **d** *obs* **:** NOTION, IDEA **2 a** (1) **:** ATTENTION, HEED, OBSERVATION ⟨first attracted ~ with his short novel⟩ ⟨will be brought under the ~ of the police —Priscilla Hughes⟩ ⟨the first . . . to receive ~ from history —W.J.Entwistle & W.A.Morison⟩ — often used in the phrase *take notice* ⟨doubted whether she would take much ~ —Gerard Bourke⟩ ⟨you sit up and take ~⟩ (2) **:** the condition of being noticed ⟨brought him into public ~ —Gearoid O'Sullivan⟩ **b :** polite or favorable attention **:** FAVOR, RESPECT, CIVILITY ⟨she had very little ~ from any but him —Jane Austen⟩ **3 :** a written or printed announcement or bulletin ⟨one sees crude ~*s* of patent medicines —*Amer. Guide Series: Fla.*⟩ ⟨inserted a ~ in the newspaper⟩ ⟨all the societies put up printed ~*s* of their activities —S.P.B.Mais⟩ **4 a :** a critical account or commentary on a play or other public performance ⟨the stage play received . . . glowing ~*s* —C.J.Rolo⟩ ⟨opened to enthusiastic ~*s* —*Current Biog.*⟩ **b :** BOOK REVIEW ⟨presume that your book . . . is not out yet though I have heard rumors of ~*s* —O.W.Holmes †1935⟩ ⟨a collection of book ~*s* —*Brit. Book News*⟩ **c :** critical examination **:** REVIEW, EVALUATION ⟨the books under ~ . . . are a valuable addition —*Times Lit. Supp.*⟩ ⟨considered 2,179 publications and selected 887 for ~ —L.H.Evans⟩

²**notice** \"\ *vb* -ED/-ING/-S [in sense 1a, fr. ME *notysen* to notify, fr. *notyce;* in other senses fr. ¹*notice*] *vt* **1 a** *archaic* **:** NOTIFY, INTIMATE **b :** to give notice of the scheduling of (a legal proceeding) by placing on a court calendar ⟨hearing on the motion was *noticed* for February 14 —Caryl Chessman⟩ **2 a :** to comment or remark upon **:** make mention of **:** refer to ⟨the city merchant's house . . . that is *noticed* in another chapter —Elizabeth Montizambert⟩ ⟨three of the four men *noticed* by name —H.M.Reichard⟩ **b :** to write a notice of **:** REVIEW ⟨asked me to ~ the volume —O.W.Holmes †1935⟩ ⟨*noticed* in these pages when it came out last year —*Times Lit. Supp.*⟩ **3 a :** to pay polite or favorable attention to **:** treat with attention or civility **:** GREET, RECOGNIZE ⟨were *noticed* only by a curtsey —Jane Austen⟩ **b** (1) **:** to take notice of with the senses **:** pay attention to **:** SEE, SENSE, NOTE ⟨*noticed* a strange odor in the room⟩ ⟨some attractive feature that can be *noticed* —Agnes M. Miall⟩ ⟨doesn't ~ a word —Charles Dickens⟩ ⟨began to ~ other men —*Time*⟩ ⟨barely *noticed* the clock strike midnight —Erle Stanley Gardner⟩ (2) **:** to take notice of with the mind **:** MARK ⟨the first thing that we ~ is that our thought moves with . . . incredible rapidity —J.H.Robinson †1936⟩ ⟨worth while to ~ that belief in the supernatural presupposes a belief in natural law —W.R.Inge⟩ **4 :** to give a formal notice or notification to **:** serve a notice on ⟨~ a tenant⟩ **~** *vi* **:** to take notice **syn** see SEE

**no·tice·abil·i·ty** \,nōd·əsəˈbiləd·ē, -ōtə-, -lətē, -i\ *n* -ES **:** the quality or state of being noticeable

**no·tice·able** \ˈ≈≈bəl\ *adj* **1 :** worthy of notice **:** likely to attract attention **:** CONSPICUOUS ⟨~ for the variety and harmony of its coloring —O. Elfrida Saunders⟩ **2 :** capable of being observed ⟨gives the water a ~, but not unpleasant taste —*Amer. Guide Series: Mich.*⟩

**syn** REMARKABLE, PROMINENT, OUTSTANDING, CONSPICUOUS, SALIENT, SIGNAL, STRIKING, ARRESTING: NOTICEABLE applies to whatever is worthy of notice or unlikely to escape notice ⟨the influence of northern architecture and farming methods is still *noticeable* —*Amer. Guide Series: La.*⟩ REMARKABLE applies to that which commands attention or comment as extraordinary or exceptional ⟨a sudden and *remarkable* transformation of feeling —W.A.Swanberg⟩ ⟨the *remarkable* belief of some primitive peoples which associates twins with water and especially with rain —J.G.Frazer⟩ PROMINENT describes that which stands out from its setting or environment and demands notice as superior or more important ⟨the 25-foot cylindrical marble shaft, surmounted with draped flags and an eagle, occupies a *prominent* position in a traffic island on the main street —*Amer. Guide Series: Pa.*⟩ ⟨his inflammatory speeches against the Hitler regime won him a *prominent* place on the Nazi blacklist —*Americana Annual*⟩ OUTSTANDING, close to PROMINENT in meaning and connotation, heightens the notion of rising above or excelling others ⟨fortunate, too, in the men of *outstanding* ability who planned our resources and our campaigns —Clement Attlee⟩ ⟨trout appeared at several points along the main stream and have steadily increased in number, until the Au Sable is known as the *outstanding* trout stream in the state —*Amer. Guide Series: Mich.*⟩ CONSPICUOUS describes that which thrusts itself into notice and is unlikely to be overlooked or ignored ⟨*conspicuous* natural features like mountain ranges, waterfalls, and high cliffs overlooking rivers and lakes —*Amer. Guide Series: N.Y.*⟩ ⟨did not loom up in a room as such formidable and *conspicuous* pieces of furniture as the older pianos —A.E.Wier⟩ SALIENT may suggest a demanding attention as esp. significant ⟨days rich in *salient* news —C.E. Montague⟩ ⟨whoever called Africa the dark continent was guilty of a half truth. The *salient* point about South Africa is its brightness —N.F.Busch⟩ SIGNAL describes what is entitled to notice and remark as extraordinarily indicative or significant ⟨this work is not intelligible unless we appreciate a few *signal* facts in the history of psychoanalytic theory —Abram Kardiner⟩ ⟨even to do the very trifling thing will be of *signal* value, provided he catches hold of the underlying idea —H.A. Overstreet⟩ STRIKING suggests that which forcefully, powerfully, and suddenly calls attention ⟨everyone agreed that the most *striking* feature of the Plains was the absence of trees —R.H.Brown⟩ ⟨a *striking* figure. Handsome, graceful, cool, he personally led his soldiers to battle —F.P.Gaines⟩ ARRESTING indicates a being able to bring about a focusing of absorbed interest ⟨her magnificent agate-green eyes must at any age have been *arresting:* they seemed to concentrate the light of the intellect as a powerful lens does the sun —Edmund Wilson⟩ ⟨it is an *arresting* thought that murderers' skulls so often show quite normal shaped heads while the skulls of poets, scientists, lawyers and the rest are often abnormal in shape —S.P.B.Mais⟩

**no·tice·ably** \-blē, -li\ *adv* **:** in a noticeable manner

**notice board** \ˈ≈≈,≈\ *n, chiefly Brit* **:** a board displaying a notice or warning; *specif* **:** BULLETIN BOARD

**noticed** *past of* NOTICE

**notice of dishonor :** a notice by the holder to the drawer and each endorser of a negotiable bill or note that has been dishonored with failure to give such notice to any person liable generally discharging the obligation of that person

notice board

**notices** *pl of* NOTICE, *pres 3d sing of* NOTICE

**noticing** *pres part of* NOTICE

**no·tid·a·ni** \nōˈtidə,nī\ *n pl, cap* [NL, fr. pl. of *Notidanus*] *in some classifications* : an order of sharks that comprises forms with embolomerous vertebrae and 6 or 7 pairs of gill slits, includes Hexanchidae and sometimes Chlamydoselachidae — see NOTIDANOIDEA

**no·tid·a·noi·dea** \=,=='nȯidēə\ *n pl, cap* [NL, fr. *Notidanus* + *-oidea*] : a suborder of Pleurotremata equivalent to the order Notidani

**no·tid·a·nus** \-ˌnəs\ [NL, fr. Gk *nōtidanos* small shark, fr. *nōt-* not- + *idanos* comely, fr. *idein* to see — more at WIT] *syn of* HEXANCHUS

**no·ti·fi·a·ble** \ˌnōd·əˌfīəbəl, -ōtə-\ *adj* [*notify* + *-able*] : requiring notice to be given; *specif* : required by law to be reported to official health authorities ⟨~ diseases⟩

**no·ti·fi·ca·tion** \ˌ==ˌfə'kāshən\ *n* -S [ME *notificacioun*, fr. MF *notification*, fr. ML *notification-*, *notificatio*, fr. LL *notificatus* (past. part. of *notificare* to make known) + L *-ion-* *-io* -ion — more at NOTIFY] **1** : the act or an instance of notifying : INTIMATION, NOTICE; *esp* : the act of giving official notice or information **2** : a written or printed matter that gives notice **3** : the notifying of a borrower's debtors that their accounts have been sold or assigned and that they are requested to make payment to the finance company or bank making the loan ⟨a loan on the ~ basis⟩

**notified** *adj* [fr. past part. of *notify*] *archaic* : CELEBRATED, NOTORIOUS

**no·ti·fier** \'nōd·əˌfī(ə)r, -ōtə-, -īə\ *n* -S : one that notifies

**no·ti·fy** \-ˌfī\ *vb* -ED/-ING/-ES [ME *notifien*, fr. MF *notifier* to make known, fr. LL *notificare*, fr. L *notus* (past. part. of *noscere* to come to know) + *-ificare* -ify — more at KNOW] *vt* **1** *obs* **a** : to take notice of : OBSERVE **b** : to point out : INDICATE, DENOTE **2 a** : to give notice of : make known : DECLARE, PUBLISH ⟨Her Majesty's pleasure not to disallow this act is *notified* in the *Gazette* —*Bahamas Acts*⟩ **b** : to report the occurrence of (a communicable disease or an individual suffering from such disease) in a community to public-health or other authority ⟨~ any cow which . . . appears to be affected with tuberculosis —*Control of Certain Diseases of Dairy Cows*⟩ **3** : to give notice to : inform by notice ⟨*notified* the citizens to meet at the city hall⟩ ~ *vi* : to give notice **syn** see INFORM

**noting** *pres part of* NOTE

**no·tion** \'nōshən\ *n* -S [L *notion-*, *notio* idea, conception, act of coming to know, fr. *notus* + *-ion-*, *-io* -ion] **1 a** (1) : a mental apprehension or picture of whatever may be known or imagined : the meaning or content assigned by the mind to a term : CONCEPTION, IDEA ⟨my ~ of the country gentleman of the 17th century —T.B.Macaulay⟩ ⟨have no adequate ~ of what we mean by causation —Edward Sapir⟩ ⟨outraged her mother's ~*s* of economic and amorous propriety —*N.Y.Times*⟩ ⟨her ~ of a delta was a lot of channels and islands —C.S. Forester⟩ (2) *obs* : a form, character, or sense in which a thing is taken or exists (3) *obs* : CONNOTATION, MEANING (4) : PHRASE, TERM ⟨the meaning of the ~ *law*⟩ **b** : a general or universal concept ⟨introduced the ~ of organism into the world of minute beings —A.N.Whitehead⟩ ⟨the ~ of an established body of alphabetical symbols —Charlton Laird⟩ ⟨arriving at the ~ of law —Irving Babbitt⟩ **c** (1) *Lockeanism* : a complex idea that has its original and constant existence in the thoughts of men rather than in the reality of things (2) *Berkeleianism* : a conception that in distinction from an idea has no corresponding sense impression but nevertheless has something real corresponding to it (as minds and their operations, including God) ⟨it must be owned at the same time that we have some ~ of soul, spirit, and the operations of the mind, such as willing, loving, hating, inasmuch as we know or understand the meaning of these words —George Berkeley⟩ (3) [trans. of G *begriff*] *Hegelianism* : the organized unity of a differentiated whole corresponding to some universal; *specif* : the dialectical synthesis of Being and Essence approaching the Absolute Idea (4) *Kantianism* : a pure concept of reason — compare NOUMENON **2 a** : an idea, theory, or belief held by someone ⟨had a vague ~ that some supervision should be exercised —Robertson Davies⟩ ⟨disliked this ~ of begging of strange people —Pearl Buck⟩ ⟨this ~ of a basically honest mankind —L.A.Fiedler⟩ ⟨man's ~*s* about his history have altered tremendously —L.C.Eiseley⟩ **b** (1) : an inclination, whim, or fancy ⟨it's a queer ~ of the old gentleman —George Meredith⟩ — often used in the phrase *take a notion* ⟨took the ~ of having a ball in costume —Winston Churchill⟩ ⟨rocks their ancestors had taken a ~ to —Willa Cather⟩ (2) : a perverse, crotchety, or flighty idea or fancy ⟨don't go getting any ~*s* into your head —Maeve Brennan⟩ ⟨get ~*s* before he was fifty —Jean Stafford⟩ ⟨some of it was just ~*s* that the poor woman had got into her head —B.A.Williams⟩ **c** *dial chiefly Brit* : a fondness for one of the opposite sex **3 a** *obs* : MIND, INTELLECT **b** : UNDERSTANDING, KNOWLEDGE, INKLING ⟨has not the least ~ of what it's all about⟩ ⟨has no more ~ of how to run a business than a child⟩ ⟨had no ~ . . . that you analysed people like that —Walter de la Mare⟩ **4 a** : an ingenious device : any of various small articles or wares : KNICKKNACK **b notions** *pl* : small articles usu. sold in one department of a store (as findings for sewing, ribbons, buttons, small personal and clothing items) **syn** see IDEA

**no·tion·al** \-shənᵊl, -shnəl\ *adj* [*notion* + *-al*] **1 a** : having an abstract or speculative character : not based on fact or empirical investigation : THEORETICAL ⟨distinguishes between . . . ~ assent and apprehension and real assent and apprehension —*Times Lit. Supp.*⟩ ⟨a ~ figure of cost is given to them so that they may determine their production costs —*Packet Foods*⟩ ⟨more ~ than empirical⟩ **b** *archaic* : given to speculation or holding speculative views **2** : existing in the mind only : VISIONARY, IMAGINARY, UNREAL ⟨is fictional only, as furnishing . . . a repository and ~ vehicle for the later transfer of title —*McLean v. Keith*⟩ **3 a** : given to, marked by, or reflecting foolish or fanciful moods or ideas : WHIMSICAL, CROTCHETY ⟨subject to all the ~ vagaries of childhood —Gerald Beaumont⟩ ⟨ships weren't ~ —Richard Hallet⟩ ⟨both reactionary and ~ to reject so much of modern history —L.P.Curtis⟩ **b** *dial* : being of the opinion ⟨I'm ~ that there is something queer afoot —S.H.Adams⟩ **4 a** : of, relating to, or being a notion or idea ⟨can improve ~ comprehension —J.T.Clark⟩ **b** (1) : carrying a full meaning of its own : having descriptive value in presenting an idea of a thing or quality ⟨*has* is ~ in *he has luck*, relational in *he has gone*⟩ (2) : of or representing what exists or occurs in the world of things as distinguished from syntactic categories ⟨sex is a ~, gender a syntactic category⟩ — **no·tion·al·i·ty** \ˌnōshə'naləd·ē\ *n* -ES — **no·tion·al·ly** \'nōshənᵊlē, -shnəl-, -i\ *adv*

**no·tion·al·ist** \'nōshənᵊləst, -shnəl-\ *n* -S *archaic* : THEORIST

**no·tion·ary** \'nōshəˌnerē\ *adj, archaic* : NOTIONAL

**no·tion·ate** \-ˌnət, *usu* -əd·+V\ *adj* [*notion* + *-ate*] **1** *chiefly dial* : FANCIFUL, NOTIONAL **2** *chiefly dial* : HEADSTRONG, STUBBORN

**no·tion·ist** \-nəst\ *n* -S *archaic* : a person whose religious opinions are characterized by extravagance

**no·tion·less** \'nōshənləs\ *adj* : devoid of any notion or idea

**no·tiony** \-nē\ *adj, chiefly dial* : given to notions : WHIMSICAL, FANCIFUL, CROTCHETY ⟨it'll keep time . . . it's just ~ —*Chapel Hill (N.C.) News Leader*⟩ ⟨wildflowers . . . are shy, ~ little things —H.H.Martin⟩

**no·tio·sorex** \ˌnōshēō+\ *n, cap* [NL, fr. *notio-* southern (fr. L *notius*, fr. Gk *notios*, fr. *notos* south wind, south) + *Sorex* — more at NOT-] : a genus of shrews of the southern U.S. and Mexico having only 28 teeth

**notio·thau·mi·dae** \-'thȯməˌdē\ *n pl, cap* [NL, fr. *Notiothauma*, type genus (fr. *notio-* + Gk *thauma* wonder) + *-idae* — more at THEATER] : a family of primitive insects (order Mecoptera) containing a single Chilean species (*Notiothauma reedi*)

**no·ti·tia** \nō'tish(ē)ə\ *n, pl* **notiti·ae** \-shēˌē\ [LL, fr. L, acquaintance, knowledge — more at NOTICE] : a list or register esp. of ecclesiastical sees or districts

**noto-** — see NOT-

**no·to·cen·tral** \ˌnōd·ōˌsen·trəl\ *or* **no·to·cen·trous** \-rəs\ *adj* [NL *notocentrum* + E *-al* or *-ous*] : of, relating to, or being a notocentrum

**no·to·cen·trum** \ˌ=='=·trəm\ *n* [NL, fr. 1*not-* + *centrum*] : the centrum of a vertebra when formed by the dorsal arches (as in a toad or frog)

**no·to·chord** \'nōd·əˌkȯrd, -ōtə-, -ȯ(ə)d\ *n* [1*not-* + L *chorda* cord — more at CORD] : a longitudinal flexible rod of cells that acts as a specific inductor of neural plate formation, that in the lowest chordates (as amphioxus and the lampreys) and in the embryos of the higher vertebrates forms the supporting axis of the body, being almost obliterated in the adult of the higher vertebrates as the bodies of the vertebrae develop, and that arises as an outgrowth from dorsal lip of the blastopore extending forward between epiblast and hypoblast in the middorsal line — **no·to·chord·al** \ˌ==ˌkȯrdᵊl, -ȯ(ə)d-\ *adj*

**1no·to·don·tid** \ˌnōd·əˌdäntəd\ *adj* [NL *Notodontidae*] : of or relating to the Notodontidae

**2notodontid** \"\ *n* -S : a moth of the family Notodontidae

**no·to·don·ti·dae** \ˌ=='däntəˌdē\ *n pl, cap* [NL, fr. *Notodonta*, type genus (fr. 1*not-* + *-odonta*) + *-idae*] : an extensive family of moths which resemble the Noctuidae but are distinguished from them chiefly by the venation of the forewings and whose larvae are usu. naked and often of grotesque form with humps, spines, or fleshy processes — compare LOBSTER MOTH, PUSS MOTH

**1no·to·don·toid** \ˌ==ˌ=ˌtȯid\ *adj* [NL *Notodontidae* + E *-oid*] : resembling or related to the Notodontidae

**2notodontoid** \"\ *n* -S : a notodontoid moth

**no·to·ed·res** \ˌ=='eˌdrēz\ *n, cap* [NL, fr. 1*not-* + Gk *hedra* seat, abode — more at SIT] : a genus of mites (family Sarcoptidae) containing mange mites that attack various mammals

**no·to·ed·ric** \ˌ==ˌedrik\ *adj* [NL *Notoedres* + E *-ic*] **1** : of or relating to the genus *Notoedres* **2** : caused by mites of the genus Notoedres

**no·to·gae·an** *or* **no·to·ge·an** \ˌ==ˌjēən\ *also* **no·to·gae·al** *or* **no·to·ge·al** \-ēəl\ *or* **no·to·gae·ic** *or* **no·to·ge·ic** \-ēik\ *adj, usu cap* [NL *Notogaea*, *Notogea* south temperate terrestrial biogeographic realm (fr. 2*not-* + *-gaea*, *-gea*) + E *-an*, *-al*, *-ic*] : of, relating to, or being a biogeographic realm that includes the Australian and New Zealand regions and the islands of the southwestern Pacific

**1no·tom·ma·tid** \nə'tämәd·əd\ *adj* [NL *Notommatidae*] : of or relating to the Notommatidae

**2notommatid** \"\ *n* -S : a rotifer of the family Notommatidae

**no·tom·mat·i·dae** \ˌnōd·ə'mad·əˌdē\ *n pl, cap* [NL, fr. *Notommata*, type genus (fr. 1*not-* + Gk *ommat-*, *omma* eye) + *-idae* — more at OPTIC] : a large family of rotifers (order Monogononta) including many typical and common forms that usu. have a nearly cylindrical body with a slender posterior foot ending in two toes

**no·to·mys** \'nōd·əˌmis\ *n, cap* [NL, fr. 2*not-* + *-mys*] : a genus of jerboa rats

**no·to·nec·tal** \ˌnōd·əˌnektəl\ *adj* [NL *Notonectidae* + E *-al*] : of or relating to the Notonectidae

**no·to·nec·tid** \ˌ=='=təd\ *n* -S [NL *Notonectidae*] : a bug of the family Notonectidae

**no·to·nec·ti·dae** \-təˌdē\ *n pl, cap* [NL, fr. *Notonecta*, type genus (fr. 1*not-* + *-necta* swimmer, fr. Gk *nēktēs*, fr. *nēchein* to swim) + *-idae* — more at NESO-] : a family of aquatic carnivorous insects (order Hemiptera) having the back strongly convex and the hind legs long and resembling oars and habitually swimming back downward

**no·to·po·di·al** \ˌ==ˌpōdēəl\ *adj* [NL *notopodium* + E *-al*] : of or relating to a notopodium

**no·to·po·di·um** \ˌ=='pōdēəm\ *also* **no·to·pod** \'==ˌpäd\ *n, pl* **notopo·dia** \ˌ=='podēə\ *also* **notopods** [NL *notopodium*, fr. 1*not-* + *-podium*] : the dorsal lobe or branch of a parapodium

**1no·top·ter·id** \nə'täptərəd, -ˌrid\ *adj* [NL *Notopteridae*] : of or relating to the Notopteridae

**2notopterid** \"\ *n* -S : a fish of the family Notopteridae

**no·top·ter·i·dae** \ˌnōˌtäp'terəˌdē\ *n pl, cap* [NL, fr. *Notopterus*, type genus (fr. 1*not-* + *-pterus*) + *-idae*] : a small family of freshwater fishes (order Isospondyli) of West Africa and southeastern Asia having the dorsal fin when present short and high, the anal fin long and confluent with the caudal, and the air bladder complex

**1no·top·ter·oid** \nə'täptəˌrȯid\ *adj* [NL *Notopteridae* + E *-oid*] : resembling or related to the Notopteridae

**2notopteroid** \"\ *n* -S : a notopteroid fish

**notorhynchus** *syn of* NOTORYNCHUS

**no·to·ri·e·ty** \ˌnōd·ə'rīəd·ē, ˌnōtə'rīətē, -i\ *n* -ES [MF or ML; MF *notorieté*, fr. ML *notorietat-*, *notorietas*, fr. *notorie-* (fr. *notorius*) + L *-tat*, *-tas* -ty] **1** : the quality or state of being notorious: as **a** : the condition of being publicly or generally known ⟨a fact of such ~ hardly requires documentation⟩ **b** : the condition of being an object of wide or general attention, interest, and comment ⟨the ~ surrounding the awards dates back only to 1949 —*Advertising Age*⟩ ⟨won favorable ~ as counsel —C.B.Swisher⟩ **c** : the condition of being an object of wide or general attention, interest, and comment but for something reprehensible or scandalous ⟨enjoys a most unenviable ~ —J.C.Snaith⟩ ⟨reputation is to ~ what real turtle is to mock —Douglas Jerrold⟩ ⟨certain personalities . . . whose fame would better be described by another word . . . ~ —*Phoenix Flame*⟩ ⟨the city's ~ for corrupt and incompetent government —R.E.Merriam⟩ **2** : a notorious person; *esp* : one notorious for something sensational or scandalous ⟨love to have notabilities and *notorieties* under one roof —*Times Lit. Supp.*⟩ **syn** see FAME

**no·to·ri·ous** \(')nōˌtōrēəs, nəˌ-, -ȯr-\ *adj* [ML *notorius*, irreg. fr. LL *notorium* information, indictment, fr. neut. of (assumed) LL *notorius*, adj., making known, fr. L *notus* (past part. of *noscere* to come to know) + *-orius* -ory — more at KNOW] **1 a** (1) : being or constituting something commonly known : well known ⟨iron is a ~ conductor of heat—Lewis Mumford⟩ ⟨the ~ mass-energy relation —P.W.Bridgman⟩ ⟨the possession must be open and ~ —C.S.Lobingier⟩ ⟨contradicted by multiple and ~ documentation —G.G.Coulton⟩ ⟨in mathematics it is ~ that we start from absurdities to reach a realm of law —Havelock Ellis⟩ (2) : well known or celebrated for a particular quality or trait ⟨the tapeworms are ~ in this respect —W.H.Dowdeswell⟩ ⟨it is ~ for its ability to dive instantly —Ralph Hoffmann⟩ ⟨novelists are ~ for their howlers —V.S. Pritchett⟩ ⟨~ as a sane level-headed man —Arnold Bennett⟩ **b** (1) : widely and unfavorably known as an individual of a specified kind or class ⟨a ~ chiseler⟩ ⟨a ~ gangster⟩ ⟨a ~ gambler⟩ ⟨this bird is a ~ destroyer of poultry⟩ (2) : widely and unfavorably known or discussed for something reprehensible or scandalous or for some negative quality or trait ⟨an area ~ for soot, smog, and dust —*Pliotron*⟩ ⟨this scandal made the little town ~ —*Amer. Guide Series: Mich.*⟩ ⟨his front was a ~ law firm —George Carter⟩ ⟨the most ~ of Confederate prisons —W.B.Hesseltine⟩ **2** *obs* : CONSPICUOUS, EVIDENT, MANIFEST — **no·to·ri·ous·ly** *adv* — **no·to·ri·ous·ness** *n* -ES

**no·tor·nis** \nə'tȯrnəs\ *n* [NL, fr. 2*not-* + NL *-ornis*] **1** *cap* : a genus of flightless birds of New Zealand related to the gallinules **2** *pl* **notornis** : any bird of the genus *Notornis*

**no·to·ryc·tes** \ˌnōd·ə'rikˌtēz\ *n, cap* [NL, fr. 2*not-* + Gk *oryktēs* digger, fr. *oryssein* to dig — more at ROUGH] : a genus of small burrowing Australian marsupials comprising solely the marsupial mole

**1no·to·ryc·tid** \ˌ==ˌ=təd\ *adj* [NL *Notoryctidae* (family including *Notoryctes*), fr. *Notoryctes* + *-idae*] : of or relating to the genus *Notoryctes*

**2notoryctid** \"\ *n* -S : MARSUPIAL MOLE

**no·to·ryn·chus** \ˌ=='riŋkəs\ *n, cap* [NL, irreg. fr. 1*not-* + *-rhynchus*] : a genus of cow sharks with seven pairs of external gill openings

**no·to·stig·ma** \-'stigmə\ *n pl, cap* [NL, fr. 1*not-* + *-stigma* (neut. pl. of *-stigmus*, fr. Gk *stigma* mark, brand) — more at STIGMA] *in some classifications* : a subclass of centipedes distinguished by seven dorsal unpaired tracheal spiracles — compare ANAMORPHA

**no·tos·tra·ca** \nə'tästrəkə\ *n pl, cap* [NL, fr. 1*not-* + *-ostraca*] : an order of small freshwater crustaceans (subclass Branchiopoda) having a shield-shaped carapace, sessile paired eyes, vestigial antennae, and 40 to 63 pairs of trunk appendages — see TRIOPS — **no·tos·tra·can** \-kən\ *adj or n*

**no·to·the·ri·um** \ˌnōd·ə'thirēəm\ *n, cap* [NL, fr. 2*not-* + NL *-therium*] : a genus of gigantic herbivorous diprotodont marsupials of the Pleistocene of Australia

**no·to·tre·ma** \ˌnōd·ə·'trēmə\ *n, cap* [NL, fr. 1*not-* + *-trema*] : a genus consisting of the marsupial frogs

**no·to·ungulata** \ˌnōd·ˌō+\ *n pl, cap* [NL, fr. 2*not-* + *Ungulata*] : an order of extinct New World herbivorous mammals widely distributed in So. America from the Paleocene to the Pleistocene

**1no·to·un·gu·late** \ˌ=ˌ=ˌəŋgyələt, -ˌlāt, *usu* -d·+V\ *or* **no·tun·gu·late** \(')nōˌtəŋ-\ *adj* [NL *Notoungulata*] : of or relating to the Notoungulata

**2notoungulate** \"\ *or* **notungulate** \"\ *n* : a mammal or fossil of the order Notoungulata

**no·tour** \'nōd·ər\ *adj* [ME, fr. MF *notoire*, fr. ML *notorius* — more at NOTORIOUS] *chiefly Scot* : NOTORIOUS, INFAMOUS

**notour bankrupt** *n* **1** *Scots law* : a debtor who has fled to a sanctuary to escape imprisonment for debt **2** *Scots law* : a debtor who is declared bankrupt

**not out** *adj, of a batsman in cricket* : not dismissed (as after an opponent's unsuccessful appeal to an umpire) : with innings uncompleted (as at the end of a day's play)

**not–out** \'=ˌ=\ *n* -S : a batsman in cricket who is not out

**not proved** *or* **not proven** *adj, Scots law* — used as a verdict of acquittal brought in by a jury who find the evidence insufficient for conviction of guilt

**no·tro·pis** \'nō·trəpəs\ *n, cap* [NL, irreg. fr. 1*not-* + Gk *tropis* keel of a ship, fr. *trepein* to turn — more at TROPE] : a genus of No. American fishes (family Cyprinidae) comprising typical shiners

**1no–trump** \'=ˌ=\ *adj* [2*no* + *trump*] : being without trumps; *specif* : being a bid or contract to play or a hand suitable to play without any suit being trumps

**2no–trump** \"\ *also* **no–trumps** *n, pl* **no–trump** *or* **no–trumps** **1** : a bridge bid, declaration, or contract that names no suit as trumps and that outranks the suit bids **2** : a hand played without any suit named as trumps

**no–trump·er** \-pə(r)\ *n* [1*no-trump* + *-er*] : a no-trump bridge hand or contract or a hand considered strong enough for a no-trump bid or declaration

**nots** *pl of* NOT

**not–self** \'=ˌ=\ *n* : something that is other than or objective to the self : NONEGO ⟨the world is in some manner a *not-self*, whose nature is both like and unlike my own —Weston La Barre⟩

**nott** \'nät, *usu* -äd·+V\ *dial var of* NOT

**not·ta·way** \'näd·əˌwā\ *n, pl* **nottaway** *or* **nottaways** *usu cap* [Algonquian *nadowa*, perh. fr. *natowe* rattlesnake] **1 a** : an extinct Iroquoian people of southeastern Virginia **b** : a member of such people **2** : a language of the Nottaway people

**not·ting·ham** \'näd·iŋəm, 'nätiŋ- *sometimes* -ŋˌham\ *adj, usu cap* [fr. *Nottingham*, city and county of north central England] **1** : of or from the city of Nottingham, England : of the kind or style prevalent in Nottingham **2** : NOTTINGHAMSHIRE

**nottingham lace** *n, usu cap N* : any of the various flat laces and nets machine-made orig. at Nottingham, England and used for curtains, dresses, tablecloths

**not·ting·ham·shire** \-ˌshi(ə)r, -ˌshiə, -ˌshə(r)\ *or* **not·ting·ham** *adj, usu cap* [fr. *Nottinghamshire*, *Nottingham* county in north central England] : of or from the county of Nottingham, England : of the kind or style prevalent in Nottingham

**not·tur·no** \nə'tu̇r(ˌ)nō, nō'-\ *n, pl* **nottur·ni** \-(ˌ)nē\ [It, adj., of night, fr. L *nocturnus* — more at NOCTURNAL] **1** : an 18th century piece for an instrumental group composed in several movements and resembling the serenade or divertimento **2** : NOCTURNE

**no·tum** \'nōd·əm\ *n, pl* **no·ta** \-ōd·ə\ [NL, fr. Gk *nōton* back — more at NATES] : a back part or surface of an animal; *specif* : the dorsal surface of a thoracic segment of an insect

**no·tun·gu·la·ta** \nōˌtəŋgyə'läd·ə, -lād·ə\ [NL, fr. 2*not-* + *Ungulata*] *syn of* NOTOUNGULATA

**notungulate** *var of* NOTOUNGULATE

**-no·tus** \ˌnōd·əs, -ōtəs\ *n comb form* [NL, fr. Gk *nōtos*, *nōton* back — more at NATES] : one having a (specified) kind of back — in generic names of animals ⟨Campo*notus*⟩ ⟨Pycno*notus*⟩

**1notwithstanding** \ˌ==ˌ==\ *prep* [ME *notwithstonding*, fr. 1*not* + *withstonding*, pres. part. of *withstonden* to withstand] : without prevention or obstruction from or by : in spite of ⟨~ its wide distribution, it is an animal seldom encountered —James Stevenson-Hamilton⟩ — often used after its substantive and in this position still sometimes taken as a negative present participle joined with the substantive in a nominative absolute construction ⟨anything in the Constitution or laws of any state to the contrary ~ —*U.S. Constitution*⟩

**2notwithstanding** \"\ *adv* [ME *notwithstonding*, fr. *notwithstonding*, prep.] : NEVERTHELESS, HOWEVER, YET ⟨you are welcome ~ —Shak.⟩

**3notwithstanding** \"\ *conj* [ME *notwithstonding*, fr. *notwithstonding*, prep.] : ALTHOUGH ⟨unknown to most, ~ he had lived here many years⟩

**nouak·chott** \'nwäkˌshät, nə'wä-, -shȯt, (=ˌ)='=\ *adj, usu cap* [fr. *Nouakchott*, Mauritania] : of or relating to Nouakchott, the capital of Mauritania : of the kind or style prevalent in Nouakchott

**nou·gat** \'nügət, *usu* -əd·+V; -ˌgä\ *n* -S [F, fr. Prov, fr. OProv *nogat*, fr. *noga* nut (fr. L *nuc-*, *nux*) + *-at* -ate; akin to OE *hnutu* nut — more at NUT] : a confection made by mixing nuts or sometimes fruit pieces in a sugar paste whose composition is varied to give either a chewy or a brittle consistency

**nou·ga·tine** \ˌnügəˌtēn\ *n* -S [*nougat* + *-ine*] : a chocolate with a nougat center

**nought** *var of* NAUGHT

**noughts–and–crosses** \'=='==\ *n pl but sing in constr, chiefly Brit* : TICKTACKTOE

**noughty** \'nȯd·ē, -i\ *adj* [ME, fr. *nought* naught + *-y*] *chiefly Scot* : WORTHLESS

**nould** \ˌnəd, (ˌ)nu̇d\ *vb* [ME *nolde*, fr. OE, 1st & 3d sing. past indic. of *nillan* to be unwilling — more at NILL] *archaic* : would not

**nou·me·ite** \'nümēˌīt, ='māˌīt\ *also* **nou·me·a·ite** \nü'māəˌīt\ *n* -S [*Nouméa*, New Caledonia + E *-ite*] : GARNIERITE; *esp* : a dark green unctuous variety of garnierite

**nou·me·nal** \'nümənəl, 'nau̇m-\ *adj* : of or relating to the noumenon or noumena — contrasted with *phenomenal* ⟨these elemental, unconscious and ~ needs —A.L.Rowse⟩ — **nou·me·nal·ly** \-nəlē\ *adv*

**nou·me·nal·ism** \-ˌlizəm\ *n* -S : the doctrine of the existence of things-in-themselves

**nou·me·nal·ist** \-ˌləst\ *n* -S : an adherent of noumenalism

**nou·me·non** \'nüməˌnän, 'nau̇m-\ *n, pl* **noume·na** \-ˌnə\ [G, fr. Gk *nooumenon* that which is conceived, thought, fr. neut. of pres. pass. part. of *noein* to conceive, think, fr. *nous* mind] **1** *Kantianism* **a** : an object that is conceived by reason and consequently thinkable but is not knowable by the senses : THING-IN-ITSELF **b** : an unknowable object (as God or the soul) whose existence is theoretically problematic **2** : an object of purely rational apprehension as opposed to an object of perception

**noun** \'nau̇n\ *n* -S *often attrib* [ME *nowne*, fr. AF *noun* name, noun, fr. OF *nun*, *non*, *nom*, fr. L *nomen* — more at NAME] **1** : a word that is the name of a subject of discourse (as a person, animal, plant, place, thing, substance, quality, idea, action, or state) and that in languages with grammatical number, case, and gender is inflected for number and case but has inherent gender **2** : a word except a pronoun used in a sentence as subject or object of a verb, as object of a preposition, as the predicate after a copula, or as a name in an absolute construction — see COMMON NOUN, COUNT NOUN, MASS NOUN, PROPER NOUN

**noun·al** \-nᵊl\ *adj* : of, relating to, or of the nature, function, or quality of a noun — **noun·al·ly** \-ᵊlē\ *adv*

**noun equivalent** *n* : a word group (as *to err* in "to err is human") or a word (as *they* in "they are hungry") not otherwise a noun in a syntactic function that is ordinarily performed by a noun

**noun of multitude** : a noun that is collective

**nouns** \'nau̇nz\ *interj* [alter. of *wounds*, fr. pl. of *wound*, n.] *archaic* — a mild oath

**noup** \'nüp\ *n* -S [ON *nūpr*, *gnūpr* peak; perh. akin to OE *hnutu* nut — more at NUT] *Scot* : a high steep promontory

**nou·rice** \'nürəs\ *chiefly Scot var of* NURSE

**nour·ish** \'nər·|ish, 'nə·r|, |ēsh, *chiefly in pres part* |əsh\ *vb* -ED/-ING/-ES [ME *nurishen*, *norishen*, *norissen*, fr. OF *norriss-*, stem of *norrir*, fr. L *nutrire*; akin to L *nare*, *natare* to swim, Gk *nan* to flow, *nein* to swim, *noteros* damp, Skt *snauti* it drips, *snāti* he bathes] *vt* **1 a** : to bring up : RAISE, NUR-

TURE, REAR ⟨to save my boy, to ~ and bring him up —Shak.⟩ ⟨it was for Chaucer, ~*ed* in other literatures . . . to make rapid advances on the road of English poetry —H.S.Bennett⟩ ⟨~*ed* in the old bootlegger days . . . demanded his cut from every pie —George Carter⟩ **b** *archaic* : to bring up (an animal) : RAISE ⟨episcopal visitors were recording . . . that it was scandalous to ~ hunting dogs in monasteries —G.G. Coulton⟩ **2** : to promote or stimulate the growth or development of : BUILD UP, STRENGTHEN ⟨has ~*ed* in us the dream of liberty —Liston Pope⟩ ⟨no occasions to exercise the feelings nor ~ passion —L.O.Coxe⟩ **3** : BREAST-FEED, SUCKLE ⟨wish she would not see fit to sit down and ~ her baby in my poor old bachelor drawing room —H.G.Wells⟩ **4 a** : to furnish or sustain with food or nutriment ⟨the human body can be ~*ed* on any food —R.W.Emerson⟩ ⟨the rain which ~*ed* the bushes —Laura Krey⟩ ⟨the heart speeds up and the blood pressure rises to better ~ the tissues —H.G.Armstrong⟩ **b** : to provide with sustenance ⟨the glow of a fire ~*ed* by partially dried logs —P.A.Talbot⟩ ⟨this great work ~*ed* American lawyers —Howard M. Jones⟩ **c** : to provide for : MAINTAIN, SUPPORT ⟨thou shalt dwell in the land of Goshen . . . and there will I ~ thee —Gen. 45:10–11 (AV)⟩ ⟨welfare committees whose task it is to ~ the social life of old people —M.A.Abrams⟩ ⟨their profits flow into the underworld and ~ other criminal activities —Beverly Smith⟩ **5 a** *archaic* : to grow or let grow (one's hair) ⟨~*ed* two locks, which graceful hung behind in equal curls —Alexander Pope⟩ **b** *archaic* : to cultivate (as plants or trees) ⟨it's a' for the apple he'll ~ the tree —Robert Burns⟩ **6** : to cherish or keep alive (as a feeling or plan) ⟨~*ed* the hope that something might come of it later —L.C.Douglas⟩ ⟨~ a shrewd distrust of anybody who looked like a big tycoon —F.L.Allen⟩ ⟨for many years had ~*ed* the project of a trip abroad⟩ ~ *vi* **1** *obs* : to furnish nourishment ⟨grains and roots ~ more than the leaves —Francis Bacon⟩ **2** : to receive nourishment : be fed ⟨thrives and ~*es* where poverty prevails —M.O.Purcell⟩ **syn** see FEED

**nour·ish·able** \-shəbəl\ *adj* [ME, fr. *nurishen* + *-able*] **1** *obs* : capable of giving nourishment **2** : capable of receiving nourishment

**nour·ish·er** \-shə(r)\ *n* -s [ME *norysshher*, fr. *norishen* + *-er*] : one that nourishes

**nourishing** *adj* [ME *norissching*, fr. pres. part. of *norishen*] : giving nourishment : NUTRITIOUS — **nour·ish·ing·ly** *adv*

**nour·ish·ment** \-mənt\ *n* -s [ME *norysshement*, fr. MF *norrissement*, fr. *norriss-* (stem of *norrir*) + *-ment*] **1** : something that nourishes : FOOD, NUTRIMENT, SUSTENANCE ⟨takes little ~ between breakfast and dinner⟩ ⟨the soil was poor and gave almost no ~ to the plants⟩ ⟨a few books provided his only intellectual ~⟩ **2** : the act of nourishing or the state of being nourished ⟨devoted himself to the ~ of education⟩

**nour·i·ture** \-əchə(r), -ēch-, -,chu̇(ə)r, -ùə\ *n* -s [ME *noriture*, fr. MF *nourreture*, partly fr. *norrir* to nourish, partly fr. ML *nutritura* upbringing, fr. LL, nursing, suckling, fr. L *nutritus* (past part. of *nutrire* to nourish) + *-ura* -ure] **1** : NOURISHMENT **2** *obs* : NURTURE

**nous** \'nüs, 'nau̇s\ *n* -ES [Gk *noos, nous* mind] **1 a** : an intelligent purposive principle controlling and ordering the world of matter : the highest intellect : MIND, REASON **b** *Platonism* (1) : a purely teleological and completely immaterial principle (2) : the capacity for the highest intuitive and immediate insight **c** *Aristotelianism* : reason regarded either as passive (as in sense perception) or as active and creative **d** *Neoplatonism* : the divine reason as the first emanation or creation of God **2** : mental quickness : ALERTNESS, COMMON SENSE ⟨may be full of erudite theories but is liable to go astray from lack of practical sense and ordinary ~ —Jacquetta & Christopher Hawkes⟩

**nout** \'nōt, 'nȯt\ *dial Eng var of* NAUGHT

**nou·ther** \'nōthə(r)\ *dial var of* NEITHER

**nou·veau** \(')nü¦vō\ *adj* [F, new, fr. OF *novel* — more at NOVEL] : newly arrived or developed : IMMATURE, RAW ⟨the Hollywood rich were flamboyantly ~ in the 1920's —Budd Schulberg⟩ ⟨the ~ society of his adopted home —John Farrelly⟩

**nouveau riche** \,nü,vō'rēsh\ *n, pl* **nou·veaux riches** \"\ [F, fr. *nouveau* + *riche* rich (of Gmc origin; akin to OE *rice* rich)] : a person of newly acquired wealth but limited education or culture : PARVENU ⟨had made his money quickly, and the curse of the *nouveau riche* had fallen upon him —Leslie Charteris⟩ ⟨the typical inferiority complex of the *nouveaux riches*: the desire to possess foreign culture through wealth —J.D.Hart⟩

**nou·velle** \(')nü'vel\ *n* -s [F, trans. of It *novella*] : NOVELLA 2

**nov-** *or* **novo-** *comb form* [L *novus* new — more at NEW] : new ⟨*Nov*anglian⟩

**no·va** \'nōvə\ *n, pl* **no·vas** \-vəz\ *or* **no·vae** \-,vē, -,vī\ [NL, fem. of L *novus* new] : a star that suddenly increases its light output tremendously (as 10,000 times or more within a few days) and then fades away less rapidly and reaches its former obscurity in a few months or years — see RECURRENT NOVA, SUPERNOVA

**no·va·chord** \'nōvə,kȯrd, -ō(ə)d\ *n* [fr. *Novachord*, a trademark] : a musical instrument resembling a piano and electrically producing and controlling by means of vacuum tubes musical tones ranging in quality from those of the piano and organ to those of stringed and woodwind instruments

**no·vac·u·lite** \nə'vakyə,līt\ *n* -s [L *novacula* razor (fr. — assumed — L *novare* to shave, whet + L *-cula*, suffix denoting an instrument) + E *-ite*; akin to Skt *kṣṇauti* he whets, ON *snöggr* shorn, bald, OE *besnythian* to deprive, MHG *snœde* contemptible, ON *snauthr* bereft, poor, OE *-heord* hair of a woman's head — more at HURDS] : a very hard fine-grained siliceous rock used for whetstones and thought to be of sedimentary origin

**no·va·lia** \nō'vālēə\ *n pl* [L, pl. of *novale* fallow land, land ploughed for the first time, fr. *novus* new — more at NEW] *Scots law* : lands newly reclaimed for improvement or agriculture; *specif* : lands not liable for teinds

¹**no·van·gli·an** \nō'vaŋglēən, -aiŋ-\ *also* **no·van·gli·can** \-ləkən, -ēk-\ *adj, usu cap* [*novanglian* fr. NL *Nova Anglia* New England + E *-an*; *novanglican* fr. NL *novanglicus* of New England (fr. *Nova Anglia* + L *-icus* -ic) + E *-an*] **1** : of, relating to, or characteristic of New England **2** : of, relating to, or characteristic of the people of New England ⟨rather admire this stolid self-reliance and Novanglian assumption —Bayard Taylor⟩

²**novanglian** \"\ *also* **novanglican** \"\ *n* -s *cap* : a native or inhabitant of New England

**novarsenobenzene** \(¦)nōv+\ *or* **nov·ar·se·no·ben·zol** \-,zōl, -ōl\ *n* [*novarsenobenzene* fr. *nov-* + *arsenobenzene*; *novarsenobenzol* fr. *nov-* + *arsen-* + *benzol*] : NEOARSPHENAMINE

**no·va sco·tia** \¦nōvə¦skōshə\ *adj, usu cap N&S* [fr. *Nova Scotia*, province of southeastern Canada] : of or from the province of Nova Scotia : of the kind or style prevalent in Nova Scotia : NOVA SCOTIAN

¹**nova sco·tian** \¦==¦skōshən\ *adj, usu cap N&S* [*Nova Scotia*, province of Canada + E *-an*] **1** : of, relating to, or characteristic of Nova Scotia **2** : of, relating to, or characteristic of the people of Nova Scotia

²**nova scotian** \"\ *n* -s *cap* : a native or inhabitant of the province of Nova Scotia, Canada

**no·vate** \nō'vāt, '=,=, *usu* -ād+V\ *vt* -ED/-ING/-S [L *novatus*, past part. of *novare* to make new, fr. *novus* new — more at NEW] : to replace (an old obligation) by a new obligation

**no·va·tian** \nō'vāshən\ *n* -s *usu cap* [ME, fr. LL *novatianus*, fr. *Novatianus*, 3d cent. antipope and founder of the sect] : one of an early Christian schismatic sect existing from A.D. 251 to the 6th or 7th century that denied that the church should restore lapsed Christians to membership and advocated a rigidly purist conception of church membership

**no·va·tian·ism** \-,nizəm\ *n* -s *usu cap* [*Novatian, Novatianus*, 3d cent. sectarian + E *-ism*] : the denial of the church's right to restore lapsed Christians to membership

**no·va·tian·ist** \-,nəst\ *n* -s *usu cap* : NOVATIAN

**no·va·tion** \nō'vāshən\ *n* -s [LL *novation-, novatio*, fr. L *novatus* + *-ion-, -io* -ion] **1** : INNOVATION **2** : the substitution of a new legal obligation for an old one (as by a substitution of a new contract, a new debtor, or a new creditor for an old one) — see DELEGATION

**no·va·tor** \-ād·ə(r)\ *n* -s [L, renewer, fr. *novatus* + *-or*] : INNOVATOR

¹**nov·el** \'nävəl\ *n* -s [ME, fr. MF *novele*, fr. fem. of *novel* new, fr. L *novellus*, fr. *novus* new] **1 a** *chiefly dial* : NEWNESS, NOVELTY **b** *obs* : a piece of news **2** [It *novella*] **a** *archaic* : NOVELLA 1 — usu. used in pl. **b** : an invented prose narrative of considerable length and a certain complexity that deals imaginatively with human experience through a connected sequence of events involving a group of persons in a specific setting **c** : the literary type constituted by such narratives ⟨the ~ is the chief literary form of the present day⟩ **3** *usu cap* [NL *novella*, fr. LL *novellae constitutiones*, lit., new statutes] : a Roman imperial enactment issued supplementary to a code; *esp* : one of a collection of statutes of Justinian and his immediate successors promulgated subsequent to the Justinian Code ⟨the nine collations, the legal standard of modern tribunals, consist of ninety-eight *Novels* —Edward Gibbon⟩

²**novel** \"\ *adj* [ME, fr. MF] **1** : not resembling something formerly known : having no precedent : NEW ⟨the great geographical discoveries posed ~ practical problems in navigation —S.F.Mason⟩ ⟨the opportunity to experiment in providing four-year courses on ~ lines —James Britton⟩ **2** : original or striking in conception or style : STRANGE, UNUSUAL ⟨if a man cannot write what is new, at least he can write what is ~ —Richard Hallet⟩ ⟨the feverish search for the ~ and the disquieting, the odd, and the macabre —Bernard Smith⟩ **syn** see NEW

**novel assignment** *n* [²*novel*] *law* : a new assignment or specification of the cause of action set forth in a previous assignment (as with more certainty or particularity is required)

**novel disseizin** *n* [ME, fr. AF *novele disseisine*] : an ancient remedy in English law, abolished in 1833, for the recovery of land from which the owner had been recently disseized

**nov·el·ese** \¦nävə'lēz, -ēs\ *n* -s : a style characteristic of bad novels; *esp* : a style marked by the use of trite expressions ⟨the revolting ~ that the English translator spreads upon the page —J.M.Barzun⟩

**nov·el·esque** \-esk\ *adj* : suitable for or resembling a novel

**nov·el·ette** *also* **nov·el·et** \¦nävə¦let\ *n* -s **1 a** : a brief novel or long short story ⟨is also buying ~*s* of around 15,000 words —Iris Litt⟩ ⟨all of it is short; nothing exceeding ~ length —Richard Sullivan⟩ **b** *Brit* : a light usu. sentimental romantic novel ⟨was a great reader of ~*s* and had romantic ideas —Flora Thompson⟩ ⟨weeping over a sentimental ~ —F.M. Ford⟩ **2** [G *novellette*, fr. *novelle* novel (fr. It *novella*) + *-ette* — more at NOVELLA] : a romantic piano piece of free form characteristically containing a number of contrasting sections

**nov·el·et·tish** \-ed·ish\ *adj* **1** : of, relating to, or characteristic of a novelette **2** : CHEAP, SENTIMENTAL ⟨its situations and dialogue are at times ~, its humour stilted and elementary —T.R.Fyvel⟩ ⟨a mawkish schoolgirl with a crude, ~ mind —*Times Lit. Supp.*⟩

**nov·el·et·tist** \-d·əst\ *n* -s : one who writes novelettes

**nov·el·ish** \'nävəlish\ *adj* [¹*novel* + *-ish*] : NOVELISTIC

**nov·el·ism** \-,lizəm\ *n* -s [¹*novel* + *-ism*] **1** *obs* : INNOVATION **2** : the writing of novels ⟨the text itself . . . is rarely much beyond talented facility and expert ~ —*New Republic*⟩

**nov·el·ist** \-ləst\ *n* -s [¹*novel* + *-ist*] **1** *obs* : one who likes novelty : INNOVATOR **2** *archaic* : a bearer of news : NEWSMONGER **3** : a writer of novels ⟨the ~ is concerned with the nature of man's constant experience as it can be illustrated in character —Douglas Grant⟩

**nov·el·is·tic** \¦==¦listik\ *adj* : of, relating to, or characteristic of a novel ⟨slowness . . . is an element essential to the ~ form — as opposed to the dramatic or short-story form —R.C. Hutchinson⟩ ⟨the ~ fashions he parodied and superseded —William Irvine⟩ — **nov·el·is·ti·cal·ly** \-tək(ə)lē\ *adv*

**nov·el·i·za·tion** \,nävələ'zāshən, -,lī'-\ *n* -s : the act or process of novelizing ⟨~*s* of successful films which were not originally based on novels —J.T.Farrell⟩ ⟨the mere skillful ~ of a chapter in a psychiatry casebook —Clifton Fadiman⟩

**nov·el·ize** \'==,līz\ *vt* -ED/-ING/-S **1** : to convert into the form of a novel ⟨that queer, clumsy mongrel species . . . the *novelized* play —*Nation*⟩ ⟨comb Hollywood for its outstanding scenarios and ~ them —*Newsweek*⟩ **2** : to treat as fiction : FICTIONALIZE ⟨what he sees he ~*s* into a string of anecdotes —*Saturday Rev.*⟩ ⟨*novelized* biography and history⟩

**no·vel·la** \nō'velə\ *n, pl* **novel·las** \-ləz\ *or* **novel·le** \-(,)lā\ *see numbered senses* [It, fr. fem. of *novello* new, fr. L *novellus*, fr. *novus* new — more at NEW] **1** *pl* ***novelle*** : a story with a compact and pointed plot ⟨found the plots of several of his plays in Italian *novelle*⟩ **2** *pl usu* ***novellas*** : a short novel : a work of fiction intermediate in length and complexity between a short story and a novel ⟨is not a major work of fiction, but as a ~ it is a gem —*Newsweek*⟩ — called also *nouvelle*

**nov·el·ly** \'näv(ə)lē, -li\ *adv* [²*novel* + *-ly*] : in a novel manner

**novel news** *or* **novel paper** *n* [¹*novel*] : a paper similar to newsprint but often somewhat more bulky that is used in pulp magazines

**nov·el·ty** \'nävəltē, -ti\ *n* -ES *often attrib* [ME *novelte*, fr. MF *noveleté*, fr. *novel* + *-té* -ty] **1** : something novel : a new or unusual thing or event ⟨men in uniform are no ~ to a city which considers itself the army's home town —Green Peyton⟩ ⟨found it a ~ and a satisfaction to work on the soil —Martha Sharp⟩ ⟨~ seekers⟩ ⟨the ballet season produced only two *novelties*⟩ ⟨a ~ song⟩ **2** : the quality or state of being novel : recentness of origin or introduction : NEWNESS ⟨a general uncritical acceptance of ~ as advance —Howard M. Jones⟩ ⟨the ~ of space travel⟩ ⟨the charm of ~⟩ ⟨~ appeal⟩ **3 a** : a small manufactured article intended mainly for decoration or adornment and marked by unusual or novel design ⟨a ~ shop⟩ ⟨~ goods⟩ ⟨factories that manufacture paper, wooden *novelties*, and snowplows —*Amer. Guide Series: Mich.*⟩ — usu. used in pl. **b** : a short-lived fashion : an article (as a fabric or garment) of unusual or fancy design created for a special season or occasion ⟨~ sweaters⟩

**novelty siding** *n* : DROP SIDING

¹**no·vem·ber** \nə'vembə(r), (')nō¦v-\ *n* -s *usu cap* [ME *novembre*, fr. OF, fr. L *november* (ninth month), fr. *novem* nine — more at NINE] : the eleventh month of the Gregorian calendar — abbr. *Nov.*; see MONTH table

²**november** \"\ *usu cap* — a communications code word for the letter *n*

**no·vem·decillion** \¦nō,vem+\ *n, often attrib* [L *novemdecim* nineteen (fr. *novem* nine + *-decim*, fr. *decem* ten) + E *-illion* (as in *million*) — more at TEN] — see NUMBER table

**no·ve·na** \nō'vēnə\ *n* -s [ML, fr. L, fem. of *novenus* nine each, ninefold, fr. *novem*] *Roman Catholicism* : a nine days' devotion for a religious intention

¹**nov·e·nary** \'nävə,nerē, nō'vēnərē, -ri\ *adj* [L *novenarius*, fr. *novenus* + *-arius* -ary] : of or relating to the number nine : based on the number nine

²**novenary** \"\ *n* -ES [*novena* + *-ary*] : NOVENA

**no·ver·cal** \nə'vərkəl\ *adj* [L *novercalis*, fr. *noverca* stepmother + *-alis* -al — more at ANEROID] : of, relating to, or characteristic of a stepmother ⟨of true ~ type, dragon and devil —Robert Browning⟩

¹**nov·go·rod·i·an** \¦nävgə¦rädēən, -rōd-\ *adj, usu cap* [*Novgorod*, city of northwest U.S.S.R. + E *-ian*] **1** : of, relating to, or characteristic of Novgorod, U.S.S.R. **2** : of, relating to, or characteristic of the people of Novgorod

²**novgorodian** \"\ *n* -s *cap* : a native or resident of Novgorod, U.S.S.R.

**nov·ice** \'nävəs\ *n* -s [ME *novice, novis*, fr. MF *novice*, fr. ML *novicius*, fr. L, new, inexperienced, fr. *novus*] **1 a** : one who has entered a religious house and is on probation : a postulant who has received the habit in a religious house and is under training **b** : one newly received into the church or one newly converted to the Christian faith **2** : one who has no previous training or experience in a specific field or activity : BEGINNER, TYRO ⟨a ~ in cooking who had never prepared a meal⟩ ⟨a ~ who was teaching his first class⟩ ⟨a ~ at bridge⟩ **3** : an animal that has never won a first prize in show competition

**syn** NOVITIATE, APPRENTICE, PROBATIONER, POSTULANT, NEOPHYTE: NOVICE and the less common NOVITIATE may designate any inexperienced beginner in a trade, career, or way of life, especially in a religious order ⟨superiors instructing *novices*⟩ ⟨her book shows the uneven hand of a *novice* at writing —Rose Feld⟩ ⟨to show the Communist *novitiate* as a human being with idealistic impulses —Daniel Bell⟩ APPRENTICE may apply to a beginner placed, sometimes formally, under a master or supervisor for training or instruction ⟨while still an *apprentice*, he had made his first attempt at engraving —R.C.Smith⟩ ⟨the breathless, the fructifying adoration of a young *apprentice* in the atelier of some great master of the Renaissance —Van Wyck Brooks⟩ PROBATIONER indicates a beginner on trial in which he must demonstrate aptitude ⟨the *probationer* is not allowed to take part in assemblies or to sit as a judge —*Current Biog.*⟩ POSTULANT designates a candidate on probation, especially for admission to a religious order ⟨a master in the field of diplomacy but a *postulant* in democratic politics —M. W.Straight⟩ NEOPHYTE is applicable to one, often eager and unsophisticated, newly connected with or entered into a group, society, faith, or pursuit ⟨the old philosopher of Monticello was more than pleased with this ardent *neophyte*, who offered to purchase books for him in Europe —Van Wyck Brooks⟩ ⟨in many states it is almost impossible to differentiate between the *neophyte* and the confirmed criminal —C.R.Cooper⟩

**nov·ice·ship** \-və(sh),ship *also* -vəs-,sh-\ *n* : NOVITIATE

**no·vi·lla·da** \,nōvē'yädə\ *n* -s [Sp, fr. *novillo*] : a bullfight in which novilleros fight immature, overage, or defective bulls ⟨the best bullfight to see first would be a ~ —Ernest Hemingway⟩

**no·vi·lle·ro** \-'ye(ə)(,)rō\ *n* -s [Sp, fr. *novillo*] : an aspiring bullfighter who has not yet attained the rank of matador

**no·vi·llo** \nō'vē(,)(y)ō\ *n* -s [Sp, young bull, fr. L *novellus* new — more at NOVEL] : a bull used in a novillada ⟨sell me like a ~ to the butcher —Budd Schulberg⟩

**no·vi·tiate** *also* **no·vi·ciate** \nō'vish(ē)ət, nə'-, -shē,āt, *usu* -d·+V\ *n* -s [F *noviciat*, fr. ML *noviciatus, novitiatus*, fr. *novicius, novitius* novice + L *-atus* -ate] **1 a** : the probationary period or state of a novice in a religious order ⟨monks were to be admitted first for a ~ of one year —K.S.Latourette⟩ **b** : a period or state of initiation or apprenticeship in an activity or occupation ⟨some of these early works were hung in the Paris Salon during his ~ —W.H.Downes⟩ ⟨the musician's long ~ of practicing mechanical scales and octaves —M.B. Smith⟩ **2 a** : a novice in a religious order or priesthood ⟨entered the Sisters of Charity Convent . . . as a ~ —*Newsweek*⟩ ⟨must pass some time as a ~ in a Buddhist monastery —John Gunther⟩ ⟨~*s* to the Druidic priesthood required twenty years' training —C.W.Ferguson⟩ **b** : APPRENTICE, BEGINNER ⟨the ~ at this business of motoring south —Jack Westeyn⟩ ⟨has little to offer a person already knowledgeable about India, but it provides a pleasant sojourn for the ~ —Marguerite A. Brown⟩ **3** : a place where novices are trained and housed ⟨all their German, Czech and Austrian ~*s* were closed, the buildings confiscated —Anne Fremantle⟩ **syn** see NOVICE

**nov·i·ty** \'nävəd·ē, -ətē, -i\ *n* -ES [ME *novitee*, fr. MF *novité*, fr. L *novitat-, novitas*, fr. *novus* new + *-tat-, -tas* -ty — more at NEW] : NOVELTY

**novo-** — see NOV-

**no·vo·bi·o·cin** \,nō(,)vō'bīəsən\ *n* -s [prob. fr. *nov-* + antibiotic + streptomycin] : an acid antibiotic $C_{31}H_{36}N_2O_{11}$ that is produced by actinomycetes of the genus *Streptomyces* (as *S. niveus* or *S. spheroides*) and is active esp. against gram-positive bacteria (as staphylococci)

**No·vo·cain** \'nōvə,kān\ *trademark* — used for a preparation containing procaine hydrochloride

**no·vo·caine** \'nōvə,kān\ *n* -s [ISV *nov-* + *cocaine*; orig. formed as G *novokain*] : procaine or its hydrochloride

**no·vo·da·mus** \,nō(,)vō'dāməs, -,vō'-\ *n* -ES [L (*de*) *novo damus* we grant anew] *Scots law* : a clause sometimes added to a grant, charter, or deed granting anew certain rights, privileges, or estates and thereby confirming or validating them; *also* : the written instrument containing such a grant

**no·vo·si·birsk** \¦nō(,)vōsə¦birsk\ *adj, usu cap* [fr. *Novosibirsk*, U.S.S.R.] : of or from the city of Novosibirsk, U.S.S.R. : of the kind or style prevalent in Novosibirsk

¹**now** \(¦)nau̇\ *adv* [ME, fr. OE *nū*; akin to OHG *nū*, *nu* now, ON *nū*, Goth *nu*, L *nunc*, Gk *ny, nyn*, Skt *nū, nu*] **1 a** : at the present time : at this moment ⟨he is busy ~⟩ ⟨is ~ abroad⟩ ⟨is ~ writing a new play⟩ ⟨he teaches ~⟩ **b** : in the time immediately before the present : very lately : a moment ago ⟨was here just ~⟩ ⟨we were thinking of you just ~⟩ **c** : in the time immediately to follow : without delay : FORTHWITH ⟨steps to correct this weakness must be taken ~⟩ ⟨must write ~ or it will be too late⟩ **2** — used with the sense of present time weakened or lost to express command, request, or admonition ⟨~ hear this⟩ ⟨~ be a good boy and do as I tell you⟩ ⟨~ don't get me angry⟩ **3** — used with the sense of present time weakened or lost to introduce an important point or indicate a transition from one idea to another ⟨~, this central cord is present in all the vertebrate animals we have so far mentioned —W.E.Swinton⟩ ⟨~ this point of view . . . seems to me absolutely unhistorical —Edmund Wilson⟩ **4** : SOMETIMES ⟨full of pathos and humor, ~ gay, ~ sad —H.H.Reichard⟩ ⟨the foothills roll along on either side, ~ bare and ~ wooded —*Amer. Guide Series: Vt.*⟩ **5** : under the present conditions : in view of the existing circumstances ⟨after his quick victory over his last opponent, he is ~ favored to defeat the champion⟩ ⟨since my plan has failed, we must ~ try his⟩ **6** : at the time under consideration : at the time referred to ⟨the people ~ proceeded to give him almost every important honor within their gift —E.M.Coulter⟩ ⟨the ore is loaded in chutes from towering trestled docks —Meridel Le Sueur⟩ **7** : reckoning to the present time : by this time ⟨spurned as the lowest form of wit for several centuries ~ —Esther K. Sheldon⟩ ⟨a good many years ago ~, when I was a soldier —John Connell⟩

²**now** \"\ *conj* [ME, fr. OE *nū*, fr. *nū*, adv.] : seeing that : in view of the fact that : SINCE ⟨~ he is better, he can return to school⟩ — often followed by *that* ⟨~ that I have seen her, I can understand your feeling for her⟩

³**now** \'nau̇\ *n* -s [ME, fr. ¹*now*] : the present time or moment : PRESENT ⟨the ~ is that which limits and determines the before and after of time —W.A.Gerhard⟩ ⟨about three times as large as any dining alcove of ~ —Sylvia T. Warner⟩

⁴**now** \"\ *adj* [ME, fr. ¹*now*] : of or relating to the present time : EXISTING ⟨was working for the ~ judge —*Time*⟩ ⟨the father of the ~ king⟩

¹**now·a·days** \'nau̇(ə),dāz\ *also* **now·a·day** \-,dā\ *adv* [*nowadays* fr. ME *now a dayes*, fr. ¹*now* + *a dayes* adays; *nowaday* fr. ME, fr. ¹*now* + *aday*, fr. ¹*a-* + *day*] : in these days : at the present time ⟨it is solely by their language that the upper classes ~ are distinguished —Nancy Mitford⟩

²**nowadays** \"\ *also* **nowaday** \"\ *adj* : of or relating to the present time ⟨the tendency of the *nowaday* producer —Johnston Forbes-Robertson⟩

³**nowadays** \"\ *n* : the present time ⟨the land of ~ that we never discover —Booth Tarkington⟩

**now and again** *or* **now and then** *adv* : from time to time : OCCASIONALLY ⟨*now and again* . . . our grandmother would put the good book back on the shelf —Rumer Godden⟩ ⟨as they drove along, the beautiful scenery *now and then* attracted his attention⟩

**now·a·nights** \-,nīts\ *adv* [¹*now* + *anights*] : on present nights ⟨outspread ~ across the high dark coast road —Max Beerbohm⟩

**no·way** \'nō,wā\ *adv* [ME *na wai*, fr. *na* no + *wai* way] **1** : in no way whatever : not at all ⟨is ~ to blame⟩ **2** *dial* : ANYHOW ⟨me and my wife ain't got much longer to live, ~ —Erskine Caldwell⟩ ⟨you ain't goin' to git in ~, so you've got all the time there is —T.S.Stribling⟩

**no·ways** \-āz\ *adv* [ME *nanes weies, nanwais, naways*, fr. gen. of *nan wei, nan wai* no way, fr. *nan* no, none + *wai* way] : NOWAY

**nowed** \'nüəd, 'nau̇d\ *adj* [modif. (influenced by E *-ed*) of MF *noué*, past. part. of *nouer* to knot, fr. L *nodare*, fr. *nodus* knot — more at NET] *heraldry* : twisted into a knot : KNOTTED

¹**now·el** *or* **now·ell** \nō'el, 'nōəl\ *n* -s [ME, fr. MF *noel*] : NOEL

²**now·el** \'nōəl, 'nau̇əl\ *n* -s [ME *nowell* newel — more at NEWEL] **1** : the core of a mold for casting a large hollow object **2** : the bottom part of a mold or of a flask, in distinction from the cope : DRAG

¹**no·where** \'nō,(h)we(ə)r, -wa(ə)|, |ə; *when a stressed syllable, as "else," follows, sometimes* -ōwə(r)\ *adv* [ME *nowher*, fr.

OE *nāhwær*, fr. *nā* no + *hwær* where, anywhere — more at WHERE] **1 a :** not anywhere **:** not in or at any place ⟨the book is ~ to be found⟩ ⟨the discovered gold ~⟩ ⟨has property everywhere and a home ~⟩ **b :** to no place ⟨has gone ~ for months⟩ ⟨the team will get ~ this year⟩ **2 :** not in any part of a book **:** in no written work or writer ⟨this word is ~ used by Shakespeare⟩ ⟨these facts are ~ stated⟩ **3 :** far behind **:** out of the running ⟨is ~ when it comes to the race for class president⟩ ⟨a dazzling exhibition of grace and beauty that left her rivals ~ —*Current Biog.*⟩

²**nowhere** \"\ *n* **1 :** a place that does not exist ⟨as if all truth was gone out, and night and ~ had the world —Horace Bushnell⟩ **2 :** an unknown or undeveloped place **:** WILDERNESS ⟨lost forever in the ~ of South America —Marcia Davenport⟩ ⟨the lumbermen, construction workers and miners who are carving towns out of ~ in Canada —Bill Wolf⟩ **3 :** a state of not existing or of not being known to exist ⟨out of the ~ into the here came trouble —W.A.White⟩ ⟨an officer appeared from ~ to strike the soldier sharply —Kenneth Roberts⟩ ⟨a gossipy, clucking crowd materialized from ~ —Anne S. Mehdevi⟩ **4 :** a state of being unknown **:** OBSCURITY ⟨starting from ~, he became a leading politician in a few years⟩ ⟨came out of ~ to become a big-league star⟩ **5 :** an inhabited place ⟨many miles from ~, on a dismal desert island —E.O.Hauser⟩ ⟨found a cattleman with a broken leg miles from ~ —Ellen Buell⟩

**nowhere near** *adv* **:** not nearly **:** not by a great deal ⟨purposes *nowhere near* as good —J.R.Wiggins⟩ ⟨operates at *nowhere near* its theoretical efficiency —*Collier's Yr. Bk.*⟩

**no·wheres** \|(ə)rz, |əz\ *adv* [*nowhere* + *-s*] *chiefly dial* **:** NOWHERE

**no whit** *adv* [²*no* + *whit*] **:** not at all **:** not in the least

**nowhither** \'=,==, =ˈ==\ *adv* [ME *nowhider*, fr. OE *nāhwider*, fr. *nā* no + *hwider* whither, anywhither — more at WHITHER] **:** to or toward no place **:** NOWHERE ⟨allures us into byways leading ~ —J.B.Cabell⟩

**nowise** \'=,=\ *adv* [ME *nawise*, *no wise*, fr. *na*, *no* no + *wise*, n.] **:** in no manner or degree **:** not at all ⟨the human values that we have taken for granted are ~ different from those of the past —Norman Foerster⟩

**nown** \'nōn\ *archaic var of* OWN

**now·ness** \'naůnəs\ *n* -ES [¹*now* + *-ness*] **:** the quality or state of existing at or belonging to the present time ⟨concerned with the present moment, the ~ of life —Alwyn Berland⟩

**nows** *pl of* NOW

**nows and nans** \'nüzᵊn'nanz\ *adv* [alter. of *nows and thens*] *Scot* **:** OCCASIONALLY ⟨Tam drank *nows and nans* —J.M.Barrie⟩

¹**nowt** \'nōt\ *dial Eng var of* NAUGHT

²**nowt** \'naůt, 'nōt\ *n, pl* **nowt** *often attrib* [ME, fr. ON *naut* — more at NEAT] **1** *chiefly Scot* **:** OX, BULLOCK — usu. used in pl. **2** *chiefly Scot* **:** BLOCKHEAD, LOUT

**now·ther** \'nōthə(r)\ *dial var of* NEITHER

**nowy** \'naůē, 'nōē\ *adj* [F *noué*, fr. L *nodatus* having a knot, fr. *nodus* knot + *-atus* -ate — more at NET] *of a cross* **:** expanded into a circle at the junction of the arms

**noxa** \'näksə\ *n, pl* **nox·ae** \-,sē, -sī\ [NL, fr. LL, that which has caused damage, fr. L, damage, offense — more at NOXIOUS] **:** something that exerts a harmful effect on the body

**nox·ae de·di·tio** \'näk,sēdē'dishē,ō, -,sīd-, -did-ē,ō\ *n* [LL, lit., surrender of that which has caused damage] **:** NOXAL SURRENDER

**nox·al** \'näksəl\ *adj* [LL *noxalis*, fr. *noxa* + L *-alis* -al] **:** of or relating to damage or an injury caused by another's chattel

**noxal action** *n* [LL *noxalis actio*] **:** an action brought against someone for damage or injury done by a person or animal belonging to him

**noxal surrender** *n* [trans. of LL *noxae deditio*] **:** the surrender of a person or thing that has done damage to the damaged person in satisfaction of his damage or injury; *also* **:** the right (as among the Romans and in medieval Europe) to make this surrender in full satisfaction of damages

**nox·ious** \'näkshəs\ *adj* [L *noxius*, fr. *noxa* damage, offense, harm; akin to L *nocēre* to harm, *nec-*, *nex* violent death, Gk *nekros* dead body, Skt *naśyati* he disappears, perishes] **1 :** harmful or destructive to man or to other organisms ⟨dust, fumes, effluvia, sometimes ~ for human organisms —Lewis Mumford⟩ ⟨the ~ wastes in the stream killed the fish⟩ ⟨~ weeds that prevent the growth of food plants⟩ **2 :** having or regarded as capable of having a harmful influence on thought or behavior **:** INJURIOUS, PERNICIOUS ⟨a ~ book⟩ ⟨a ~ doctrine⟩ ⟨a ~ system of education⟩ **3 :** DISTASTEFUL, OBNOXIOUS ⟨this ~ political scandal —H.L.Ickes⟩ ⟨have outgrown their ~ reputation —John Marks⟩ ⟨the Transcendentalists and their ~ crew —Van Wyck Brooks⟩ **syn** see PERNICIOUS

**nox·ious·ly** *adv* **:** in a noxious manner

**nox·ious·ness** *n* -ES **:** the quality or state of being noxious

**no·yade** \(')nwä¦yäd, (')nwī¦äd\ *n* -S [F, fr. *noyer* to drown, fr. LL *necare*, fr. L, to kill, fr. *nec-*, *nex* violent death] **:** an execution by drowning **:** a mass drowning

**noyance** *n* -S [ME *noiaunce*, short for *anoiaunce* annoyance] *obs* **:** ANNOYANCE

**no·yau** \(')nwä¦yō, (')nwī¦yō\ *n, pl* **no·yaux** \-ō(z)\ [by shortening] **:** CRÈME DE NOYAU

**no·zi** \'nōzē\ *n, pl* **nozi** *or* **nozis** *usu cap* **:** YANA

¹**noz·zle** \'näzəl\ *n* -S [dim. of *nose*] **1 :** a socket on a candlestick or sconce into which the lower end of a candle fits **2 a :** a projecting vent of something **:** a small spout or other projecting part with an opening ⟨the ~ of a bellows⟩ ⟨the ~ of a gun⟩ **b :** a short tube or duct that usu. tapers or has a constriction, often forms the vent of a hose or pipe, and is used to direct the flow of fluid or to increase the velocity of flow ⟨delivery of fuel to an injection ~ at each engine cylinder —William Landon⟩ ⟨the ~ is that part of the rocket motor in which the gases are accelerated to high velocities —G.P. Sutton⟩ **c :** any of several channels through which steam or gas is conveyed to the rotor vanes of a turbine **3** *slang* **:** NOSE ⟨longed to clout him in the ~ —J.H.Wheelwright⟩

²**nozzle** \"\ *vb* **nozzled**; **nozzled**; **nozzling** \-z(ə)liŋ\ **nozzles** *vt* **1 :** to furnish with a nozzle or something resembling a nozzle **2 :** to press the nose against ⟨pawing and *nozzling* some remnants of fodder —J.L.Allen⟩ **3 :** to spray or eject through or as if through a nozzle ⟨seemed as though every gun . . . *nozzled* a cone of fire at it —H.M.Forgy⟩ ~ *vi* **:** to nose about ⟨hungry birds will force their way into broken reeds . . . to spatter and ~ for food —*Pall Mall Mag.*⟩

**noz·zle·man** \-mən\ *n, pl* **nozzlemen :** one who works with a stream of water or sand projected through a nozzle (as in firefighting, hydraulic mining, sandblasting)

**np** *abbr* nil

**NP** *abbr* **1** net proceeds **2** neuropsychiatric **3** *often not cap* new paragraph **4** nickel-plated **5** nisi prius **6** *often not cap* nonparticipating **7** *often not cap* no paging **8** *often not cap* no place **9** no protest **10** notary public **11** noun phrase

**Np** *symbol* neptunium

**n paper** *n, usu cap N* **:** paper containing significant imperfections and graded below M paper — compare P PAPER

**NPD** *abbr* north polar distance

**NPF** *abbr, often not cap* not provided for

**NPL** *abbr* nonpersonal liability

**NPN** *abbr* nonprotein nitrogen

**NPNA** *abbr* no protest nonacceptance

**NP or D** *abbr, often not cap* no place or date

**NPT** *abbr* normal pressure and temperature

**NPV** *abbr* no par value

**nr** *abbr* **1** near **2** number

**NR** *abbr, often not cap* **1** net register **2** [L *non repetatur*] not to be repeated **3** no risk

**NRAD** *abbr, often not cap* no risk after discharge

**n-radiation** \'=,==ˈ==\ *n, usu cap N* **:** X rays emitted when an electron becomes an N electron in an atom

**nrit·ta** \en'rid·ə\ *n* -S [Skt *nṛtta* dance] **:** a purely abstract type of bharata natya dance in southern India

**nrit·ya** \en'rityə\ *n* -S [Skt *nṛtya* dance, play] **:** a narrative type of bharata natya dance in southern India

**nrml** *abbr* normal

**NRT** *abbr, often not cap* net register ton

**n's** *or* **ns** *pl of* N

**NS** *abbr* **1** national society **2** near side **3** new school **4** new series **5** new side **6** new style **7** nickel steel **8** [F *Notre Seigneur*] Our Lord **9** not specified **10** not sufficient **11** nuclear ship **12** numismatic society

**nsam·bya** \en'sämbyə\ *n* -S [native name in Uganda, eastern Africa] **1 :** an African timber tree (*Markhamia platycalyx*) of the family Bignoniaceae having yellow flowers and tough durable wood **2 :** the wood of the nsambya tree used chiefly for poles and construction work

**NSF** *abbr* not sufficient funds

**NSJC** *or* **NSJC** *abbr* [L *Noster Salvator Iesus (Jesus) Christus*] Our Savior Jesus Christ

**NSO** *abbr* naval staff officer

**NSP** *abbr* navy standard part

**NSPF** *abbr* not specifically provided for

**n star** *n, usu cap N* **:** a star of spectral type N — see SPECTRAL TYPE table

**nstd** *abbr* nested

**nt** *abbr* **1** net **2** neuter **3** night

**NT** *abbr* **1** net ton **2** new terms **3** new translation

**-n't** *or* **-nt** \ᵊn(t), n(t)\ *adv comb form* [by contr.] **:** not ⟨*isn't*⟩ ⟨*needn't*⟩ ⟨*can't*⟩

**NTC** *abbr, often not cap* negative temperature coefficient

**ntfy** *abbr* notify

**nth** \'en(t)th\ *adj* [*n* + *-th*] **1 :** numbered with some unspecified or indefinitely large ordinal number ⟨a polynomial of the ~ degree⟩ ⟨hunting up the ~ decimal of pi —Lucius Garvin⟩ ⟨fascinated . . . by the consideration of space to the ~ dimension —Peter Watson⟩ **2 :** EXTREME, UTMOST ⟨all the components of dullness and boringness to the ~ degree —S.H.Adams⟩ ⟨never quite attains the ~ power of enthusiasm —William Beebe⟩ ⟨the art of photography raised to its ~ power —Margaret A. Barnes⟩

**nthn** *abbr* northern

**ntla·kya·pa·muk** \,entlə'kyäpə,mək\ *n, pl* **ntlakyapamuk** *or* **ntlakyapamuks** *usu cap* **:** THOMPSON

**NTM** *abbr, often not cap* net ton mile

**NTO** *abbr* not taken out

**NTP** *abbr* **1** normal temperature and pressure **2** no title page

**NTS** *abbr* not to scale

**n-tu·ple** \'en·,t(y)üpəl, =ˈ==; 'entəp-\ *adj* [*n* + *-tuple* (as in *quintuple*)] **:** multiple in the degree denoted by *n* — **n-tu·ply** *adv*

¹**nu** \'n(y)ü\ *n* -S [Gk *ny*, of Sem origin; akin to Heb *nūn* nun] **:** the 13th letter of the Greek alphabet — symbol N or ν; see ALPHABET table

²**nu** \'nü\ *or* **nu-tzu** \-'dzü\ *n, pl* **nu** *or* **nus** *or* **nu-tzu** *or* **nu-tzus** *usu cap* [Chin (Pek) *Nu⁴ Tzu³*] **1 :** the Tibeto-Burman inhabitants of the upper Salween river region in Yunnan **2 :** a member of any of various Tibeto-Burman groups of the upper Salween region related to the Nu and including the Chingpaw and Lisu

**NU** *abbr* **1** name unknown **2** national union **3** number unobtainable

¹**nu·ance** \'n(y)ü,än(t)s, =ˈ= *also* -äⁿs *sometimes* 'n(y)üən-\ *n* -S [F, fr. MF, shade of color, fr. *nuer* to make shades of color (fr. *nue* cloud, fr. L *nubes*) + *-ance*; akin to Gk *nythos* dark, W *nudd* mist, Av *snaotha* clouds and perh. to Gk *nan* to flow — more at NOURISH] **1 a :** a shade of difference **:** minute variation **:** delicate gradation **:** subtle distinction ⟨the play of surfaces, the dance of subtle lights and shadows, the ~*s* of color, tones, atmosphere —Lewis Mumford⟩ ⟨~*s* of flavor and fragrance cannot be described accurately —Scott Seegers⟩ ⟨a quick ear for ~*s* in mood —Irwin Edman⟩ **b :** a subtle expressive variation in a musical performance (as in tempo, dynamic intensity, or timbre) that is not indicated in the score ⟨the jazz world's increasing preoccupation with melodic and harmonic ~*s* —Wilder Hobson⟩ **2 :** a subtle or implicit quality, aspect, or device **:** NICETY ⟨a sense of the ~*s* of plain words —E.F.Goldman⟩ ⟨its vernacular shape may have given it a ~ of humor —R.A.Hall⟩ ⟨captures both the essence and the ~*s* of different theological positions —*Rev. of Religion*⟩ ⟨a very singular ~ of a boy's character — the one which decides what he will or will not consider to be sneaking —W.F. De Morgan⟩ **3 :** sensibility to, awareness of, or ability to express delicate shadings (as of meaning, feeling, or value) **:** extreme finesse ⟨form of acting, which has no ~ or restraint — *Current Biog.*⟩ ⟨a performance of remarkable pliability and ~ —Irving Kolodin⟩

²**nuance** \"\ *vt* -ED/-ING/-S **:** to give nuances to **:** express or perform with nicety or precision **:** depict in delicate gradations (as of colors or tones) ⟨it is not color as such that lends enchantment to a painting, it is the manner in which it is *nuanced* —Frederic Taubes⟩ ⟨an individually *nuanced* pronunciation —Edward Sapir⟩ ⟨the treatment of the first movement is excessively *nuanced* —B.A.Haggin⟩

¹**nub** \'nəb\ *n* -S [alter. of *knub*] **1 :** KNOB, LUMP, PROTUBERANCE **2** [by shortening] **:** NUBBIN ⟨a ~ of corn⟩ ⟨a ~ of pencil⟩ ⟨a ~ of land⟩ ⟨puffed at the ~ of his cigarette —Lionel Shapiro⟩ ⟨saw a fawn standing at a ~ of grass —Jack Kerouac⟩ **3 :** CORE, CRUX, GIST, KERNEL, POINT ⟨the ~ of an argument⟩ ⟨the ~ of a problem⟩ ⟨if this is the ~ of the book —W.W.Howells⟩ **4 :** a small bunch of fibers usu. made on the card, dyed, and interspersed in yarn during spinning ⟨jacket of tobacco-colored wool dotted with fat black ~*s* —Lois Long⟩ — **to the nub** *or* **to a nub** *adv* **:** to a state of fatigue or exhaustion **:** to the condition of being worn out ⟨worn *to a nub* doing the extra work the baby entails —Alma K. Reck⟩ ⟨danced me clean down *to the nub* last time —Ross Santee⟩

²**nub** \"\ *vt* **nubbed**; **nubbed**; **nubbing**; **nubs** [perh. fr. ¹*nub*] **1** *dial Eng* **:** NUDGE **2** *obs* **:** to execute by hanging

³**nub** \"\ *vt* **nubbed**; **nubbed**; **nubbing**; **nubs** [¹*nub*] **:** to provide with nubs ⟨*nubbed* silk⟩ ⟨*nubbed* weaves⟩ ⟨*nubbed* pottery⟩

**nu·ba** \'nübə\ *n, pl* **nuba** *or* **nubas** *usu cap* [LL *Nuba*, sing. of L *Nubae* Nubians] **1 a :** any of numerous diverse peoples constituting a loose community in the Nuba hills of So. Kordofan believed by some to be related to the Nubians **b :** a member of any such people **2 :** any of several languages spoken by the Nuba people — compare NUBIAN

**nub·bin** \'nəbən\ *n* -S [¹*nub*] **1 :** something (as a fruit) that is small of its kind, stunted, undeveloped, or imperfect ⟨made cider of the ~*s*⟩ ⟨blackberry ~*s*⟩ ⟨found some potato ~*s* about the size of small marbles —Ross Santee⟩; *esp* **:** a small or imperfect ear of Indian corn **2 :** something that remains after a large part has been removed or worn away **:** a small piece or chunk **:** STUB, STUMP ⟨drew spider webs with a ~ of pink chalk — Jean Stafford⟩ ⟨a ~ of coal⟩ **3 :** NUB 3 ⟨further questions before you get to the ~ and ask your victim how he or she actually intends to vote —Stewart Alsop⟩ ⟨the ~ of hard intelligence in their opponents' argument —John Chamberlain⟩

**nubbin disease** *n* **:** CUCUMBER MOSAIC

**nubbing cheat** *n* [*nubbing* fr. gerund of ²*nub*] *obs* **:** GALLOWS

**nub·ble** \'nəbəl\ *n* -S [dim. of ¹*nub*] **1 :** a small knob or lump **:** NUB ⟨a ~ of sod —W.D.Edmonds⟩ **2 :** a small hill **3 :** ISLET

**nub·bly** *also* **knub·bly** \'nəb(ə)lē, -li\ *adj* -ER/-EST [*nubble* or *knubble* + *-ly*] **1 :** having or like nubbles **:** KNOBBY, LUMPY ⟨~ steel walls —R.M.Hodesh⟩ ⟨sharp, ~ grains provide more cutting points —*advt*⟩ ⟨little ~ reefs —D.C.Peattie⟩ ⟨a ~ magenta carpet —Alexander Laing⟩ **2 :** NUBBY 2

**nub·by** *also* **knub·by** \'nəbē, -bi\ *adj* -ER/-EST [¹*nub* or *knub* + *-y*] **1 :** NUBBLY 1 ⟨thin ~ shoulders —Shirley A. Grau⟩ ⟨~ branches sprouting fan-sized leaves —D.W.Dresden⟩ **2** *of a textile* **:** having nubs ⟨enabling the fabric stylist to create all sorts of ~ and slubby effects —J.B.Goldberg⟩

**nu·bec·u·la** \n(y)ü'bekyələ\ *n, pl* **nubecu·lae** \-yə,lē\ [NL, fr. L, little cloud, dim. of *nubes* cloud] *med, archaic* **:** a cloudy formation (as in urine) or speck (as in the eye)

**nu·bia** \'n(y)übēə\ *n* -S [alter. (influenced by NL *-ia*) of earlier *nube*, fr. Sp, cloud, nubia, fr. L *nubes* cloud] **:** a woman's lightweight knitted or crocheted scarf for the head and shoulders

¹**nu·bi·an** \'n(y)übēən\ *adj, usu cap* [*Nubia*, region in Nile valley, northeastern Africa + E *-an*, adj. suffix] **1 a :** of, relating to, or characteristic of Nubia **b :** of, relating to, or characteristic of the Nubians **2 :** of, relating to, or characteristic of a Nubian language

²**nubian** \"\ *n* -S *usu cap* [*Nubia*, region in Nile valley + E *-an*, n. suffix] **1 :** one of the people of Nubia; *esp* **:** a member of one of the group of negroid tribes who were early Christianized and formed a powerful empire between Egypt and Ethiopia from the 6th to the 14th centuries when they were conquered by the Arabs and converted to the Muslim religion **2 a :** any of several languages spoken in central and northern Sudan esp. by the Nuba people and including some dialects that are extremely distantly related if at all **b :** a branch of the Chari-Nile language family containing the Nubian language of the Nuba people **c :** CUSHITIC **3 a** *also* **nubian horse :** an Arabian horse from Nubia **b** *also* **nubian goat :** a breed of long-legged roman-nosed brown or black goats of northern Africa the does of which are relatively heavy milkers; *also* **:** a goat of this breed — compare ANGLO-NUBIAN

**nu·bile** \'n(y)übəl\ *adj* [F, fr. L *nubilis*, fr. *nubere* to marry — more at NUPTIAL] **:** of marriageable condition or age **:** physically suited for or desirous of sexual relationship — used esp. of girls or young women ⟨~ provincial schoolgirls —Janet Flanner⟩ ⟨an excessively ~ young woman —Anthony West⟩

**nu·bil·i·ty** \n(y)ü'bilad·ē\ *n* -ES [F *nubilité*, fr. *nubile* + *-ité* -ity] **:** the quality or state of being nubile

**nu·bi·lous** \'n(y)übələs\ *adj* [L *nubilus*, fr. *nubes* cloud — more at NUANCE] **1 :** CLOUDY, FOGGY, MISTY ⟨trade-wind clouds which are constantly piling up in ~ traffic jams —S.E.Morison⟩ **2 :** OBSCURE, VAGUE ⟨some ~ notions about an ideal society⟩

**nubs** *pl of* NUB, *pres 3d sing of* NUB

**nub yarn** *n* [¹*nub*] **:** a yarn with nubs; *specif* **:** KNOP YARN

**nu·ca·ment** \'n(y)ükəmənt\ *n* -S [L *nucamenta* fir cones, lit., things shaped like nuts, fr. *nuca-* (fr. *nuc-*, *nux* nut) + *-menta*, pl. of *-mentum* -ment — more at NUT] **:** AMENT

**nu·cel·lar** \(')n(y)ü¦selə(r)\ *adj* [NL *nucellus* + E *-ar*] **:** of or relating to a nucellus ⟨~ seedling⟩

**nu·cel·lus** \n(y)ü'seləs\ *n, pl* **nucel·li** \-e,lī\ [NL, fr. L *nucella* small nut, fr. *nuc-*, *nux* nut + *-ella* -el] **:** a mass of thin-walled parenchymatous cells that composes the central and chief part of the body of an ovule and that contains the embryo sac and is surrounded by one or more integuments

**nu·cha** \'n(y)ükə\ *n, pl* **nu·chae** \-ü,kē\ [ML, nape, fr. Ar *nukhā'* spinal marrow] **1 a** *obs* **:** SPINAL CORD **b :** ¹NAPE **2** [NL, fr. ML, nape] **:** the hind part of the thorax of an insect bearing the petiole of the abdomen

¹**nu·chal** \-ükəl\ *adj* [in sense 1, fr. *nucha* + *-al*; in other senses, fr. (assumed) NL *nuchalis*, fr. NL *nucha* + L *-alis* -al] **1 :** of, relating to, or lying in the region of the nape **2 :** situated on the back of the prothorax of an insect immediately behind the head **3 :** of or relating to a nucha

²**nuchal** \"\ *n* -S **:** a nuchal element (as a scale or bone)

**nu·che fly** \'nüchā-\ *n* [*nuche* fr. AmerSp] **:** HUMAN BOTFLY

**nu·ci·form** \'n(y)üsə,fȯrm\ *adj* [F *nuciforme*, fr. *nuc-* (fr. L *nuc-*, *nux* nut) + *-iforme* -iform] **:** like a nut in shape

**nucle-** *or* **nucleo-** *also* **nuclei-** *comb form* [F *nuclé-*, *nucléo-*, *nucléi-*, fr. NL *nucleus*] **1 :** nucleus **:** nuclear ⟨*nucleo*fugal⟩ ⟨*nuclei*form⟩ ⟨*nucleo*gony⟩ **2 :** nucleic acid ⟨*nucleo*protein⟩

**nu·cle·al** \'n(y)üklēəl\ *adj* [ISV *nucle-* + *-al*; orig. formed as F *nucléal*] **:** NUCLEAR

**nucleal reaction** *or* **nucleal stain :** FEULGEN REACTION

**nu·cle·ar** \'n(y)üklēə(r), *chiefly in substand speech* -kyələ(r)\ *adj* [ISV *nucle-* + *-ar*; orig. formed as F *nucléaire*] **1 :** of or relating to a nucleus **:** constituting or like a nucleus ⟨annexation of the suburban fringe by the ~ metropolis —W.H.Wickwar⟩ ⟨the oldest or ~ parts of the continents —O. D. von Engeln⟩ ⟨~ budding⟩ **2 a :** *of an atom or group of atoms* **:** attached directly to a nucleus or ring in a molecule **b :** ¹CENTRAL 1 — used of an atom or ion in a coordination complex **3 a :** of or relating to the atomic nucleus ⟨~ particle⟩ ⟨~ forces⟩ ⟨~ physics⟩ ⟨~ scientist⟩ ⟨~ structure⟩ **b :** of or relating to atomic energy ⟨~ inventions⟩ ⟨~ studies⟩: as (1) **:** being, involving, or relating to a weapon or missile that utilizes atomic energy (as in the atom bomb) ⟨~ attack⟩ ⟨~ device⟩ ⟨~ war⟩ (2) **:** being, propelled by, produced by, or relating to atomic power (as that produced by a reactor) ⟨~ airplane⟩ ⟨~ engineering⟩ ⟨~ propulsion⟩ ⟨~ ship⟩ ⟨~ submarine⟩

**nuclear bomb** *n* **:** ATOM BOMB 2

**nuclear chemistry** *n* **:** RADIOCHEMISTRY 1

**nuclear cycle** *n* **:** the cyclic nuclear changes (as between haplophase and diplophase) characteristic of the life cycles of various fungi and algae and occurring in many without accompanying marked changes in form and mode of life

**nuclear emulsion** *n* **:** a photographic emulsion for recording the track of a nucleon or other ionizing particle as a definite arrangement of developed silver grains

**nuclear energy** *n* **:** ATOMIC ENERGY

**nuclear exclusion clause** *or* **nuclear clause** *n* **:** a clause in a fire or similar insurance policy excluding loss from nuclear reaction or from nuclear radiation or radioactive contamination

**nuclear family** *n* **:** a family group consisting of father, mother, and children — opposed to *extended family*

**nuclear fission** *n* **:** FISSION 4

**nuclear fuel** *n* **:** FUEL 1c

**nuclear fusion** *n* **:** FUSION 2g

**nuclear isomer** *n* **:** ISOMER 2

**nuclear magneton** *n* **:** a unit of magnetic moment of a nuclear particle involving the mass of the proton instead of the electron and equaling 1/1837 Bohr magneton

**nuclear membrane** *n* **:** the boundary of a nucleus variously interpreted as an organized physical structure or a visible interface or colloidal phase boundary — see CELL illustration

**nuclear plate** *n* **:** EQUATORIAL PLATE

**nuclear-powered** \¦==¦=,=\ *adj* **:** utilizing atomic power (as for propulsion) ⟨*nuclear-powered* submarine⟩

**nuclear reaction** *n* **:** REACTION 4b

**nuclear reactor** *n* **:** REACTOR 4b

**nuclear reticulum** *or* **nuclear network** *n* **:** the diffuse intermeshed granular threads that represent the chromosomes in the resting or metabolic nucleus

**nuclear sap** *n* **:** KARYOLYMPH

**nuclear spindle** *n* **:** the spindle-shaped figure formed in mitosis — compare MITOSIS

**nu·cle·ase** \'n(y)üklē,ās, -āz\ *n* -S [ISV *nucleic* (in *nucleic acid*) + *-ase*; orig. formed as G *nuklease*] **:** any of the enzymes found in plants and animals that promote hydrolysis of nucleic acids (as into nucleotides) — see DEOXYRIBONUCLEASE, RIBONUCLEASE

¹**nu·cle·ate** \'n(y)üklē,āt\ *vb* -ED/-ING/-S [L *nucleatus*, past part. of *nucleare* to become kernelly, hard, fr. L *nucleus* kernel, dim. of *nuc-*, *nux* nut — more at NUT] *vt* **1 :** to form into a nucleus **:** CLUSTER ⟨almost no community life or social solidarity, the *nucleating* factors being rooming houses, bars, pool rooms —J.H.Burma⟩ ⟨business establishments are compactly *nucleated* —H.W.H.King⟩ ⟨vague but tremendous expectations were gradually *nucleated* in certain symbolic demands —*Yale Rev.*⟩ **2 :** to act as a nucleus for (as crystallization or precipitation) ⟨light-diffusing crystals whose precipitation is *nucleated* by submicroscopic silver particles formed photographically within the glass —S.D.Stookey⟩ ⟨an oasis *nucleated* by a hamlet —P.K.Hitti⟩; *also* **:** to cause (as particles) to nucleate ~ *vi* **:** to form a nucleus **:** CLUSTER ⟨new communities *nucleating* as the boundaries of older ones⟩

²**nu·cle·ate** \-ēət, -ē,āt\ *adj* [L *nucleatus*, fr. *nucleus* kernel + *-atus* -ate] **:** having a nucleus or nuclei ⟨~ cells⟩

³**nucleate** \"\ *n* -S [ISV *nucleic* (in *nucleic acid*) + *-ate*] **:** a salt or ester of a nucleic acid

**nu·cle·a·tion** \,n(y)üklē'āshən\ *n* -S **:** the process of nucleating or clustering ⟨the ~ of communities in villages and cities —A.J.Bruwer⟩: as **a :** the formation of nuclei (as in a supersaturated vapor or the free air) ⟨kept a continuous record of atmospheric ~ for several years —*Science*⟩ **b :** the action of a nucleus in starting a process (as condensation, crystallization, or precipitation) ⟨pearlitic structure . . . is formed by a process of ~ and growth —Frederick Seitz⟩ **c :** the process of seeding a cloud for the production of rain

**nu·cle·a·tor** \'=ˌ=ˌād·ə(r)\ *n* -S **:** one that nucleates

**nuclei** *pl of* NUCLEUS

**nuclei-** — see NUCLE-

**nu·cle·ic acid** \n(y)ü'klē¦ik-, -lā|, ¦ēk-\ *n* [*nucleic* ISV *nucle-* + *-ic*; orig. formed in G] **:** any of two groups of complex acids that are found in all living cells esp. in combination as nucleoproteins, that are polynucleotides yielding on partial hydrolysis less highly polymerized nucleotides, nucleosides, and finally purine bases, pyrimidine bases, a pentose sugar, and phosphoric acid — see DEOXYRIBONUCLEIC ACID, RIBONUCLEIC ACID

**nu·cle·in** \'n(y)üklēən\ *n* -S [ISV *nucle-* + *-in*; orig. formed as G *nuklein*] **1 :** NUCLEOPROTEIN **2 :** NUCLEIC ACID

**nu·cle·in·ation** \ˌn(y)üklēəˈnāshən\ *n* -s [*nuclein* + *-ation*] **:** the deposition of nucleic acids on the chromosomes during the stage of prophase coiling
**nucleo-** — see NUCLE-
**nu·cleo·centrosome** \¦n(y)üklē,ō+\ *n* [*nucle-* + *centrosome*] **:** an intranuclear division center (as in some protozoans)
**nu·cleo·cytoplasmic** \"+\ *adj* [*nucle-* + *cytoplasmic*] **:** of or relating to nucleus and cytoplasm
**nucleocytoplasmic ratio** *n* **:** the more or less constant proportionality between the volume of nucleus and cytoplasm characteristic of any given type of cell
**nu·cle·og·o·ny** \ˌn(y)üklēˈägənē\ *n* -ES [*nucle-* + *-gony*] **:** nuclear division accompanied by cytoplasmic growth but not by cell division
**nu·cleo·histone** \¦n(y)üklē,ō+\ *n* [ISV *nucle-* + *histone*] **:** a nucleoprotein derived from a histone
[1]**nu·cle·oid** \ˈn(y)üklē,ȯid\ *adj* [*nucle-* + *-oid*] **:** resembling a nucleus
[2]**nucleoid** \"\ *n* -s [ISV *nucle-* + *-oid*] **:** a body (as in some bacteria) resembling a nucleus in composition and behavior but not proved to be such
**nucleol-** *or* **nucleolo-** *comb form* [ISV, fr. NL *nucleolus*] **:** nucleolus ⟨*nucleolo*centrosome⟩ ⟨*nucleol*oid⟩
**nu·cle·o·lar** \n(y)üˈklēələ(r) *also* ¦n(y)üklē¦ōlə(r)\ *adj* [ISV *nucleol-* + *-ar*; prob. orig. formed as F *nucléolaire*] **:** of, relating to, or constituting a nucleolus ⟨~ proteins⟩
**nucleolar organizer** *also* **nucleolar zone** *n* **:** NUCLEOLUS ORGANIZER
**nu·cle·o·lat·ed** \n(y)üˈklēə,lād·əd, ˈn(y)üklēə,-\ *also* **nu·cle·o·late** \-,lāt, -lət\ *adj* [*nucleolated* fr. NL *nucleolus* + E *-ate* + *-ed*; *nucleolate* ISV *nucleol-* + *-ate*] **:** having a nucleolus or nucleoli
**nu·cle·ole** \ˈn(y)üklē,ōl\ *n* -s [NL *nucleolus*] **:** NUCLEOLUS
**nu·cle·o·li·nus** \ˌn(y)üklēōˈlīnəs\ *n, pl* **nucleoli·ni** \-ī,nī\ [NL, dim. of *nucleolus*] **:** a differentiated body within a nucleolus
**nu·cle·o·lo·centrosome** \n(y)ü¦klēə,lō+\ *n* [ISV *nucleol-* + *centrosome*; prob. orig. formed as G *nucleolozentrosom*] **:** NUCLEOCENTROSOME
**nu·cle·o·loid** \n(y)üˈklēə,lȯid\ *adj* [*nucleol-* + *-oid*] **:** resembling a nucleolus
**nu·cle·o·lus** \n(y)üˈklēələs\ *n, pl* **nucleo·li** \-ē,ə,lī\ [NL, fr. L, small kernel, dim. of *nucleus* kernel — more at NUCLEUS] **1 :** an organized body of predominantly protein structure that is typical of the metabolic nucleus, is variously regarded as a center of synthetic activity or as a storage organelle, and is usu. absent during mitosis being formed anew after each division in contact with the nucleolus organizer of the SAT-chromosome **:** PLASMOSOME — see CELL illustration **2 :** any differentiated nuclear body other than a chromosome (as an endosome, karyosome, or nucleocentrosome)
**nucleolus organizer** *n* **:** the part of a SAT-chromosome that is associated with and possibly responsible for nucleolus reorganization following nuclear division
**nu·cle·ol·y·sis** \ˌn(y)üklēˈäləsəs\ *n* [NL, fr. *nucle-* + *-lysis*] **:** KARYOLYSIS
**nu·cle·ome** \ˈn(y)üklē,ōm\ *n* -s [ISV *nucle-* + *-ome*; orig. formed as F *nucléome*] **:** the entire nuclear content of a protoplast
**nu·cle·om·e·ter** \ˌn(y)üklēˈäməd·ə(r)\ *n* [*nucle-* + *-meter*] **:** a sensitive counting device for nuclear particles
**nu·cle·on** \ˈn(y)üklē,än\ *n* -s [ISV *nucle-* + *-on*] **:** a proton or neutron esp. in the atomic nucleus — **nu·cle·on·ic** \¦==¦änik\ *adj*
**nu·cle·on·ics** \ˌ==ˈäniks\ *n pl but sing or pl in constr* [*nucleon* + *-ics*] **:** a branch of physical science that deals with nucleons or with all phenomena of the atomic nucleus esp. in their practical applications
**nu·cle·o·phil·ic** \¦n(y)üklēə¦filik\ *adj* [*nucle-* + *-philic*] **:** having an affinity for atomic nuclei **:** donating electrons to atomic nuclei **:** ANIONOID — contrasted with *electrophilic* ⟨~ reagents⟩ ⟨~ displacement reactions⟩
**nu·cle·o·plasm** \ˈn(y)üklēə,plazəm\ *n* -s [ISV *nucle-* + *-plasm*; prob. orig. formed as G *nucleoplasma*] **1 :** the protoplasm of a nucleus — distinguished from *cytoplasm* **2 :** KARYOLYMPH — **nu·cle·o·plas·mat·ic** \¦===,plaz¦mad·ik\ *or* **nu·cle·o·plas·mic** \¦===¦plazmik\ *adj*
**nu·cleo·protamine** \¦n(y)üklē,ō+\ *n* [*nucle-* + *protamine*] **:** a nucleoprotein derived from a protamine
**nu·cleo·protein** \"+\ *n* [ISV *nucle-* + *protein*] **:** any of a class of conjugated proteins that are combinations of a protein and a nucleic acid, that occur in all living cells in the nuclei or the cytoplasm, and that constitute either the whole or the essential portion of genes and viruses (as tobacco mosaic virus)
**nu·cle·o·sid·ase** \ˈn(y)üklēə,sī,dās\ *n* -s [ISV *nucleoside* + *-ase*] **1 :** an enzyme that promotes the hydrolysis of a nucleoside **2 :** a phosphorylase that promotes reversibly the reaction of a nucleoside with phosphate forming a base and a phosphate of ribose or deoxyribose — called also *nucleoside phosphorylase*
**nu·cle·o·side** \-,sīd\ *n* -s [ISV *nucle-* + *-ose* + *-ide*] **:** a crystalline compound formed by partial hydrolysis of a nucleic acid or a nucleotide and consisting typically of a glycosylamine derived from ribose or deoxyribose and one of the purine bases adenine or guanine or one of the pyrimidine bases cytosine, uracil, or thymine — see ADENOSINE, CYTIDINE, GUANOSINE, THYMIDINE, URIDINE
**nucleoside phosphorylase** *n* **:** NUCLEOSIDASE 2
**nu·cle·o·tid·ase** \ˈn(y)üklēə,tī,dās\ *n* -s [*nucleotide* + *-ase*] **:** a phosphatase that promotes hydrolysis of a nucleotide (as into a nucleoside and phosphoric acid)
**nu·cle·o·tide** \-,tīd\ *n* -s [ISV *nucle-* + *-t-* + *-ide*] **1 :** a compound that is formed by partial hydrolysis of a nucleic acid or occurs free in tissues, that is an ester of a nucleoside and a phosphoric acid, and that may consist of one or more units of phosphate-pentose-nitrogen base — see ADENYLIC ACID, CYTIDYLIC ACID, GUANYLIC ACID, THYMIDYLIC ACID, URIDYLIC ACID **2 :** any of various compounds chemically related to those obtained from nucleic acids and including some coenzymes (as coenzyme A, the pyridine nucleotides, riboflavin phosphate)
**nu·cleo·toxic** \¦n(y)üklēō+\ *adj* [*nucle-* + *toxic*] **:** toxic to the nuclei of cells ⟨c-mitotic agents are basically ~⟩
**nu·cle·us** \ˈn(y)üklēəs\ *n, pl* **nu·clei** \-ē,ī\ *also* **nucleuses** [NL, fr. L, kernel, dim. of *nuc-*, *nux* nut — more at NUT] **1 a :** the relatively small, brighter, and denser portion of a galaxy, of the head of a comet, or of another celestial body **b :** the hot faint central star of a planetary nebula **2 :** a central point, part, group, or mass about which gathering, concentration, or accretion takes place **:** a center for subsequent increase or growth ⟨the ~ of masters and students that should grow into a university —H.O.Taylor⟩ ⟨a ~ of fact beneath the incrustation of fable over famous names —Edward Clodd⟩ ⟨enough patients . . . to form the ~ of a new practice —O.S.J.Gogarty⟩ ⟨not primarily boarding schools but rather day schools with a ~ of boarders —J.B.Conant⟩ ⟨frontiers of pioneer settlement have appeared around the margins of the original ~es —P.E.James⟩: as **a :** an element of the protoplasm of most plant and animal cells that is regarded as an essential agent in their metabolism, growth, and reproduction and in the transmission of hereditary characters and that typically consists of a more or less rounded mass of nucleoplasm made up of a hyaline ground substance in which is suspended a network rich in nucleoproteins from which the mitotic chromosomes and one or more nucleoli condense, the whole being enclosed by a nuclear membrane — see MACRONUCLEUS, MICRONUCLEUS; compare COENOCYTE, ENERGID, PROTOPLAST; KARYOLYMPH, LININ; MEIOSIS, MITOSIS; CELL illustration **b :** the earliest formed part of a shell, operculum, or other similar structure **c :** a visceral mass containing the stomach and other organs of some tunicates **d :** MADREPORITE **e :** FOCUS 8 **f :** the hilum of a starch granule **g :** CORE 1 k **h :** a mass of gray matter or group of nerve cells in the central nervous system **i :** a small mass of bees and combs of brood used in forming a new colony or in rearing queens **j :** a characteristic and stable complex of atoms or groups in a molecule; *esp* **:** a ring system **:** RING ⟨the naphthalene ~⟩ — compare BENZENE RING **k :** a particle on which metal forms and grows (as in solidification, condensation, recrystallization, or transformation from one solid crystalline form to another) **l :** a particle upon which water vapor condenses in free air — called also *kern* **m :** the positively charged central portion of an atom that comprises nearly all of the atomic mass but occupies only a very small fraction of the volume and that consists of protons and neutrons except in the case of hydrogen which consists of one proton only — see ATOMIC NUMBER, MASS NUMBER **n** (1) **:** the peak of energy in the utterance of a syllable (2) **:** the syllable that is the seat of maximum stress in a stress group **o :** HEAD 25 **syn** see CENTER
**nucleus dor·sa·lis** \-dȯrˈsāləs, -sal-, -sāl-\ *n, pl* **nuclei dorsa·les** \-a(,)lēz, -ā(,)lēz, -ä(,)lās\ [NL, lit., dorsal nucleus] **:** an elongated longitudinal strand of neurons in the spinal cord with its axons passing into the direct cerebellar tract
**nucleus of pan·der** \-ˈpandə(r)\ *usu cap P* [after Christian H. *Pander* †1865 Russ. zoologist] **:** the expanded upper end of the flask-shaped mass of white yolk in a bird's egg
**nucleus pul·po·sus** \-,pəlˈpōsəs\ *n, pl* **nuclei pulpo·si** \-ō,sī\ [NL, lit., pulpy nucleus] **:** an elastic pulpy mass lying in the center of each intervertebral fibrocartilage and regarded as a remnant of the notochord
**nu·clide** \ˈn(y)ü,klīd\ *n* -s [*nucleus* + *-ide* (irreg. fr. Gk *eidos* species, form) — more at IDOL] **:** a species of atom characterized by the constitution of its nucleus and hence by the number of protons, the number of neutrons, and the energy content **:** an atom of specified atomic number and mass number — compare ISOBAR, ISOTONE, ISOTOPE, RADIOISOTOPE ⟨the different isotopes of an element are composed of ~s having the same atomic number but different mass numbers⟩ — **nu·clid·ic** \(ˈ)n(y)ü¦klidik\ *adj*
**nucquedah** *var of* NAKHODA
**nu·cu·la** \ˈn(y)ükyələ\ *n* [NL, fr. L, nutlet, fr. *nuc-*, *nux* nut + *-ula* -ule] **1** *cap* **:** the type genus of Nuculidae **2** -s **a :** a mollusk of the genus *Nucula* **b :** a nut shell or beaked cockle
**nu·cu·la·na** \-yə,lanə, -lānə, -länə\ *n, cap* [NL, fr. *Nucula* + *-ana* (fr. L, neut. pl. of *-anus* -an)] **:** the type genus of Nuculanidae comprising various beaked cockles
**nu·cu·lan·i·dae** \ˌ==ˈlanə,dē\ *n pl, cap* [NL, fr. *Nuculana*, type genus + *-idae*] **:** a family of marine bivalve mollusks (order Protobranchia) related to and formerly included in Nuculidae but distinguished by a shell that is produced posteriorly and considerably elongated — see BEAKED COCKLE
**nu·cu·la·ni·um** \ˌn(y)ükyəˈlānēəm\ *also* **nu·cu·lane** \ˈ==,lān\ *n, pl* **nucula·nia** \-ēə\ *also* **nuculanes** [*nuculanium* fr. NL, fr. L *nucula* nutlet + connective *-n-* + NL *-ium*; *nuculane* fr. NL *nuculanium*] **:** an indehiscent fleshy fruit (as the grape) resembling a berry except in being superior
**nu·cule** \ˈn(y)ü,kyül\ *n* -s [F, nutlet, fr. L *nucula*] **1 :** NUTLET **2 :** the female reproductive organ in plants of the family Characeae
[1]**nu·cu·lid** \ˈn(y)ükyələd\ *adj* [NL *Nuculidae*] **:** of or relating to the Nuculidae
[2]**nuculid** \"\ *n* -s [NL *Nuculidae*] **:** a mollusk of the family Nuculidae
**nu·cu·li·dae** \n(y)üˈkyüləd·ē\ *n pl, cap* [NL, fr. *Nucula*, type genus + *-idae*] **:** a large widely distributed family of marine bivalve mollusks (order Protobranchia) having a small nutlike equivalve shell and very large labial palps and including the typical nut shells — see NUCULANIDAE
[1]**nu·cu·loid** \ˈn(y)ükyə,lȯid\ *adj* [NL *Nucula* + E *-oid*] **:** resembling or related to the Nuculidae
[2]**nuculoid** \"\ *n* -s **:** a nuculoid mollusk
**nu·da** \ˈn(y)üdə\ *n pl, cap* [NL, fr. L, neut. pl. of *nudus* naked] **:** a class of ctenophores without tentacles including but one genus (*Beroë*)
**nuda pacta** *pl of* NUDUM PACTUM
[1]**nude** \ˈn(y)üd\ *adj* -ER/-EST [L *nudus* naked — more at NAKED] **1 a :** lacking some essential particular **:** being without consideration **:** NAKED, UNSUPPORTED **b** *Roman & civil law* **:** having no cause — compare NUDUM PACTUM **2 :** devoid of some natural, conventional, or customary covering, furnishing, or adornment ⟨a ~ hillside⟩ ⟨a broad ~ valley —R.L.Stevenson⟩ **3 a :** devoid of clothing **:** UNCLOTHED **b :** UNDRAPED — used of an artistic representation of a human figure esp. in sculpture and painting **4 :** of the color nude **syn** see BARE
[2]**nude** \"\ *n* -s **1 a :** a picture or other representation of an unclothed undraped human figure **b :** an unclothed person **2 :** the condition of being unclothed or undraped — usu. used with *the* **3 :** a brownish pink that is slightly yellower, lighter, and stronger than atmosphere
**nude·ly** *adv* **:** in a nude manner
**nude matter** *n* **:** MATTER IN PAIS 1
**nude·ness** *n* -ES **:** the quality or state of being nude
**nude pact** *n* [trans. of ML *nudum pactum*] **:** NUDUM PACTUM
**nude tan** *n* **:** a moderate yellowish pink that is duller and much yellower than coral pink and yellower and duller than peach pink
[1]**nudge** \ˈnəj\ *vb* -ED/-ING/-S [perh. of Scand origin; akin to Icel *nugga* to push, rub, ON *gnaga* to gnaw — more at GNAW] *vt* **1 :** to touch or push gently (as with the elbow) usu. to call attention or convey an intimation **2 :** to prod lightly **:** urge into action ⟨needled and *nudged* and worried him till finally he consented —Ellery Sedgwick⟩ **3 :** to ease along **:** assist in maneuvering ⟨impudent little tugboats . . . *nudged* our ship out of its slip —June W. Brown⟩ **4 :** to get close to **:** NEAR ⟨its circulation is *nudging* the four million mark —Bennett Cerf⟩ ⟨defense in the old protective sense is *nudging* the impossible —*Sydney (Australia) Bull.*⟩ ~ *vi* **:** to give a nudge ⟨well-polished automobiles . . . ~ into a parking space —*Amer. Guide Series: N. Y. City*⟩ ⟨the annual supply vessel should ~ through the bay ice —*Nat'l Geographic*⟩
[2]**nudge** \"\ *n* -s **:** a slight push, poke, or jog (as with the elbow) ⟨he felt a sharp ~ in his side —Scott Fitzgerald⟩ ⟨some further ~s toward integrity —R.W.McEwen⟩
**nudg·er** \-jə(r)\ *n* -s **:** one that nudges
**nudi-** *comb form* [LL, fr. L *nudus* naked] **:** naked **:** bare ⟨*Nudi*branchia⟩ ⟨*nudi*ped⟩
[1]**nu·di·branch** \ˈn(y)üdə,braŋk\ *adj* [back-formation fr. obs. *nudibranchial*, fr. NL *Nudibranchia* + E *-al*] **:** of or relating to the Nudibranchia
[2]**nudibranch** \"\ *n* -s [NL *Nudibranchia*] **:** a mollusk of the suborder Nudibranchia
**nu·di·bran·chia** \ˌ==ˈbraŋkēə\ *n pl, cap* [NL, fr. *nudi-* + *-branchia*] **:** a suborder of Opisthobranchia comprising numerous highly varied marine gastropod mollusks lacking a shell in the adult state and without true ctenidia and typically having a body suggesting that of a slug usu. with brightly colored often branching respiratory cerata on the back — **nu·di·bran·chi·an** \¦==¦braŋkēən\ *adj* — **nu·di·bran·chi·ate** \-ēət, -ē,āt\ *adj or n*
**nu·di·bran·chi·a·ta** \ˌ==,braŋkēˈād·ə, -ˈäd·ə\ *syn of* NUDIBRANCHIA
**nu·di·caudate** \¦n(y)üdə+\ *adj* [ISV *nudi-* + *caudate*] **:** having a hairless tail
**nu·di·caul** \ˈn(y)üdə,kȯl\ *or* **nu·di·cau·lous** \¦==¦kȯləs\ *adj* [*nudicaul* fr. (assumed) NL *nudicaulis*, fr. *nudi-* + L *caulis* stem; *nudicaulous* fr. *nudi-* + *caul-* + *-ous* — more at COLE] **:** having leafless stems
**nu·di·flo·rous** \¦n(y)üdə¦flōrəs\ *adj* [fr. (assumed) NL *nudiflorus*, fr. *nudi-* + LL *-florus* -florous] **:** having flowers naked and esp. without hairs or glands
[1]**nu·di·ped** \ˈn(y)üdə,ped\ *adj* [F *nudipède*, fr. LL *nudiped-*, *nudipes*, fr. *nudi-* + L *ped-*, *pes* foot — more at FOOT] **:** having feet without a natural covering (as of hair or feathers)
[2]**nudiped** \"\ *n* -s [*nudi-* + *-ped*] **:** a nudiped animal
**nud·ish** \ˈn(y)üdish\ *adj* **:** nearly nude **:** approaching nudity
**nud·ism** \-ü,dizəm\ *n* -s [ˈ*nude* + *-ism*] **:** the cult or custom of going unclothed as a social practice
[1]**nud·ist** \-dəst\ *n* -s [ˈ*nude* + *-ist*] **:** an advocate or practitioner of nudism
[2]**nudist** \"\ *adj* **:** of or relating to nudists or nudism
**nu·di·ty** \ˈn(y)üdəd·ē, -ətē, -i\ *n* -ES [F or LL; F *nudité*, fr. LL *nuditat-*, *nuditas*, fr. L *nudus* + *-itat-*, *-itas* -ity] **1 :** the quality or state of being nude **2 :** a nude figure esp. as depicted in art
**nud·nick** *or* **nud·nik** \ˈnüdnik\ *n* -s [Yiddish *nudnik*, fr. Russ *nudnyĭ* tiresome, boring (fr. *nuda* need, boredom) + Yiddish *-nik* (n. suffix denoting a person engaged in or connected with something specified), fr. Pol & Russ; akin to OSlav *nužda* need, OE *nēd* — more at NEED] **:** a person who is a bore **:** NUISANCE, PEST
**nu·dum pac·tum** \¦nüˌdu̇mˈpäkˌtu̇m\ *n, pl* **nu·da pac·ta** \-üdəˈpäktə\ [ML, naked pact] **:** a pact or agreement not enforceable by action because lacking in or bare of certain legal essentials or formalities: as **a** *Roman law* **:** a pact or agreement not in the form required for a binding stipulation **b** *common law* **:** a promise unenforceable for lack of the required consideration **c** *civil law* **:** a promise unenforceable for lack of a lawful motive
**nu·er** \ˈnüə(r)\ *n, pl* **nuer** *or* **nuers** *usu cap* **1 a :** a numerous and widespread Nilotic people in the Sudan and on the Ethiopian border **b :** a member of such people **2 :** a Nilotic language of the Nuer people
**nuernberg** *usu cap, var of* NUREMBERG
**nu·ga·cious** \(ˈ)n(y)ü¦gāshəs\ *adj* [L *nugac-*, *nugax* trifling + E *-ous*] **:** TRIFLING, TRIVIAL — **nu·ga·cious·ness** *n* -ES
**nu·gac·i·ty** \n(y)üˈgasəd·ē\ *n* -ES [LL *nugacitas*, fr. L *nugac-*, *nugax* trifling (fr. *nugae* trifles, jokes) + *-itas* -ity] **1 :** TRIVIALITY **2 :** something frivolous or trivial ⟨hummed the scrambled fragments of two or three *nugacities* —Robertson Davies⟩
**nugation** *n* -s [ML *nugation-*, *nugatio*, fr. L *nugatus* (past part. of *nugari* to trifle, joke, fr. *nugae* trifles, jokes) + *-ion*, *-io* -ion] *obs* **:** the act or an instance of trifling
**nu·ga·to·ry** \ˈn(y)ügə,tōrē, -tȯr-, -ri\ *adj* [L *nugatorius*, fr. *nugatus* + *-orius* -ory] **1 :** having little or no consequence **:** WORTHLESS **2 :** having no force **:** INVALID **syn** see VAIN
**nug·gar** \nəˈgär\ *n* -s [Ar *nuqqār*] **:** a cargo boat used on the Nile

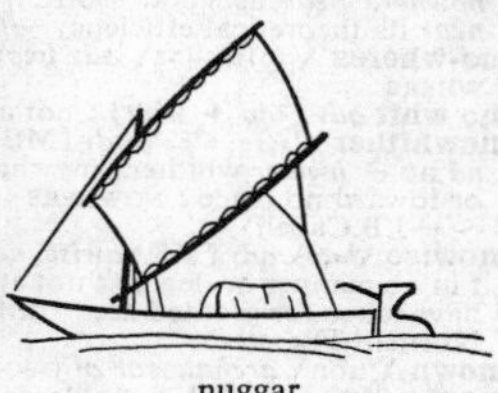

nuggar

**nug·get** \ˈnəgət, *usu* -əd·+V\ *n* -s [origin unknown] **1 a :** a solid lump; *esp* **:** a native lump of precious metal ⟨a ~ of gold⟩ ⟨a few ~s of uranium —Harrison Smith⟩ **b :** something resembling a gold nugget ⟨~s of wisdom —C.J. Rolo⟩ ⟨odd ~s of information —*Newsweek*⟩ **2** *Austral* **:** a sturdy and thickset person or animal **3 :** BRONZE YELLOW
**nugget gold** *n* **:** a strong yellow that is redder and deeper than yolk yellow, gamboge, or light chrome yellow
**nug·gety** \-gəd·ē\ *adj* **1 :** having or resembling a nugget **:** occurring in nuggets; *also* **:** covered with small rocks **2** *Austral* **:** short and thickset **:** COMPACT ⟨a sardonic ~ old prospector —George Farwell⟩
**nuik** \ˈnyük\ *chiefly Scot var of* NOOK
[1]**nui·sance** \ˈn(y)üsᵊn(t)s\ *n* -s [ME *nusaunce*, fr. AF *nusaunce*, *nuisance*, fr. OF *nuisir* to hurt, harm (fr. L *nocēre*) + *-aunce*, *-ance* -ance — more at NOXIOUS] **1 :** HARM, INJURY ⟨relieving the ~ of poisonous fumes from rural factories —*Collier's Yr. Bk.*⟩ **2** *law* **:** an offensive, annoying, unpleasant, or obnoxious thing or practice **:** a cause or source of annoyance that although often a single act is usu. a continuing or repeated invasion or disturbance of another's right — see PRIVATE NUISANCE, PUBLIC NUISANCE **3 :** a person that annoys usu. by obtrusion **:** PEST ⟨he was a perfect ~, running through the house slamming doors⟩ **4 a :** a vexing, difficult, or distressing practice or state of things ⟨the ~ of litter in the countryside —*Manchester Guardian Weekly*⟩ **b :** something that is disagreeable or troublesome **:** ANNOYANCE ⟨timber was cheap, in fact, a ~ to those who wanted farms —S.H.Holbrook⟩ ⟨motels . . . accessible without the ~ of city traffic —*Look*⟩
[2]**nuisance** \"\ *adj* **1 :** possessing the ability to annoy, distress, or hamper ⟨burn off the ~ scrub growth —Frank Cameron⟩ ⟨the ~ strikes in public services that seriously injured the tourist season —W.H.Chamberlin⟩ **2 :** constituting a nuisance — used esp. of wild animals ⟨transfer of ~ beavers⟩
**nuisance tax** *n* **:** an excise tax levied on a wide range of miscellaneous commodities and borne mostly by the consumer (as the American excises on electric light bulbs, musical instruments, television sets, telephone services)
**nuisance value** *n* **:** value, importance, or usefulness arising from a capacity to annoy, frustrate, harass, or injure ⟨atolls and islands having a high *nuisance value* —W.V.Pratt⟩ ⟨the business of the minor parties is to develop so great a *nuisance value* that one of the major parties will take over their programs —H.S.Commager⟩ ⟨alert to opportunities to institute representative suits solely for their *nuisance value* —G.B.Hurff⟩
**nu·ku·hi·van** \ˌnükəˈhēvən\ *n* -s *usu cap* [*Nuku Hiva* Island, Marquesas islands + E *-an*] **:** the Polynesian language of Nukuhiva **:** MARQUESAN
**nul** \ˈnəl\ *adj, sometimes* -ER/-EST [F, fr. MF] *law* **:** not any **:** NO
[1]**null** \ˈnəl\ *adj* [MF *nul*, lit., none, not any, fr. L *nullus*, fr. *ne-* not + *ullus* any (akin to *unus* one) — more at NO, ONE] **1 a :** having no legal or binding force or validity **:** of no efficacy **:** INVALID, VOID — often used in the phrase *null and void* **b :** capable of being regarded as void **:** voidable at the option of an injured party **2 :** amounting to nothing **:** NIL, NONEXISTENT ⟨the ~ uselessness of the wireless transmitter that lacks a receiving station —Fred Majdalany⟩ **3 a :** having no value **:** of no consequence **:** INSIGNIFICANT ⟨news as ~ as nothing —Emily Dickinson⟩ **b :** lacking distinction, character, or personality ⟨the scene . . . was pitched in the ~, noncommittal surroundings of a rehearsal room —Osbert Sitwell⟩ **4 a :** having no members **:** EMPTY ⟨the ~ class⟩ **b** (1) **:** having the character or value of zero ⟨the ~ element⟩ (2) **:** having a zero radius ⟨a ~ sphere⟩ **5 :** indicating usu. by a zero reading on a scale when current or voltage is zero — used of an instrument **6 :** of, being, or relating to zero ⟨the photoelectric current through a load resistor produces a voltage drop that is balanced by a potentiometer, thus giving a ~ reading for each condition of balance —*Jour. of Research*⟩ **7 :** relating to the null of a radio receiver
[2]**null** \"\ *n* -s **1 a :** ZERO 2a(1) ⟨a *null*-reading instrument⟩ ⟨the various signals can combine so that a substantial ~ in transmission exists at certain frequencies —B.D.Loughlin⟩ **b :** a condition of a radio receiver existing when minimum or zero signal is received and resulting from adjustment of parts (as rotation of the directional antenna or tuning of the circuit) **2 :** a meaningless letter or code group introduced to impede cryptanalysis
[3]**null** \"\ *vt* -ED/-ING/-S [ML *nullare*, fr. L *nullus* null, adj.] **1 :** to reduce to nothing **:** DESTROY, EXPUNGE, OBLITERATE **2 :** to make void **:** ANNUL, NULLIFY ⟨the first election he ~*ed* because its irregularity was glaring —Edmund Burke⟩ ⟨election ~*ed* by the courts⟩
[4]**null** \"\ *n* -s [by alter.] **:** KNUR
[5]**null** \"\ *n* -s [by alter.] **:** KNURL 1; *esp* **:** a raised convex boss or ornament on a flat surface on a piece of furniture
[6]**null** \"\ *vt* -ED/-ING/-S [back-formation fr. *nulling*] **:** KNURL
[7]**null** \"\ *n* -s [³*null*] **1 :** NULLO **2 :** a game of skat played without a trump suit in which the bidder undertakes to lose every trick
**nul·la** \ˈnələ\ *n* -s [by shortening] **:** NULLA-NULLA
**nul·la bo·na** \ˌnələˈbōnə\ *n* [NL, no goods] **:** the return made upon a writ of fieri facias or execution by a sheriff or other officer when he has found no leviable goods
**nul·lah** *also* **nul·la** \ˈnələ\ *or* **nal·lah** *or* **nal·la** \ˈnalə\ *n* -s [Hindi *nālā*, prob. of Dravidian origin; akin to Tamil *ñeḷḷal* hollow, pit, Kanarese *naḷḷu* nullah] **:** a watercourse that is often dry **:** GULLY, RAVINE
**null and void** *adj* **:** having no force, binding power, or validity **:** utterly invalid
**nul·la–nul·la** \ˈnələˈnələ\ *n* [native name in Australia] **:** a hardwood club of a type used by the Australian aborigines
**nulled** \ˈnəld\ *adj* [by alter.] **:** KNURLED
**null hypothesis** *n* [¹*null*] **:** the assumption that any observed difference between two samples of a statistical population is purely accidental and not due to a systematic cause
**nulli-** *comb form* [LL, fr. L *nullus*] **:** none **:** null ⟨*nulli*fidian⟩ ⟨*nulli*form⟩ ⟨*nulli*parous⟩
**nul·li·bic·i·ty** \ˌnələˈbisəd·ē\ *also* **nul·li·bi·e·ty** \-bīəd·ē\ *n* -ES [L *nullibi* nowhere (fr. *nullus* null + *ibi* here, there) + E *-icity* (as in *simplicity*) or *-ety* (as in *society*); akin to Gk *itha-* here, Skt *iha* here, L *ita* thus — more at NULL, ITERATE] **:** the quality or state of being nowhere

**nul·li·bist** \'nələbəst\ *n* -s [L *nullibi* nowhere + E *-ist*] **:** one who denies that the soul exists in space

**nul·li·fi·ca·tion** \,nələfə'kāshən\ *n* -s [LL *nullification-, nullificatio,* fr. *nullificatus* (past part. of *nullificare* to nullify) + L *-ion-, -io* -ion] **1 :** the act of nullifying or the state of being nullified **2 :** the action of a state of impeding or attempting to prevent the operation and enforcement within its territory of a law of the U. S. — **nul·li·fi·ca·tion·ist** \-sh(ə)nəst\ *n* -s

**nul·li·fi·ca·tor** \'===,kād·ə(r)\ *n* -s **:** NULLIFIER

**¹nul·li·fid·i·an** \,nələ'fidēən\ *n* -s [LL *nulli-* + L *fides* faith + E *-an* — more at FAITH] **1 :** a person of no faith or religion **:** SKEPTIC, UNBELIEVER **2 :** one lacking in faith **:** DISBELIEVER

**²nullifidian** \;==;===\ *adj* **:** having no faith or religion **:** SKEPTICAL

**nul·li·fi·er** \'nələ,fī(ə)r, -īə\ *n* -s **:** one that nullifies; *specif* **:** one maintaining the right of nullification against the U. S. government

**nul·li·fy** \-fī\ *vt* -ED/-ING/-ES [LL *nullificare,* fr. *nulli-* + L *-ficare* -fy] **1 :** to make null; *specif* **:** to make legally null and void ⟨we are asked to ~ legislation as an undue encroachment upon the sphere of individual liberty —B.N.Cardozo⟩ **2 :** to make of no value or consequence **:** reduce to nothing **:** EFFACE ⟨the lightning *nullified* the meager table lamp —R.A.W. Hughes⟩ ⟨the small gains made in the Colony were *nullified* by the Revolution —*Amer. Guide Series: N. C.*⟩

**syn** INVALIDATE, NEGATE, ANNUL, ABROGATE: although these five verbs are almost interchangeable, NULLIFY and INVALIDATE carry the most general and inclusive meanings. NULLIFY means to counteract completely the force, effectiveness, or value of something ⟨the earlier devices for *nullifying* the effects of the Fifteenth Amendment were becoming outworn —Helen Sullivan⟩ ⟨at least 19 international cartels which threaten to *nullify* efforts to reduce trade barriers —*Current Biog.*⟩ ⟨a lack of . . . confidence tends to *nullify* and destroy the results of enormous effort in technical and interpretative development —A.E.Wier⟩ INVALIDATE carries this general sense but adds the idea of rendering unacceptable by reason of legal or official requirements or condition not adequately met ⟨a priest of wisdom with a flaw in his ordination and an *invalidating* clause in his commission —W.L.Sullivan⟩ ⟨so many reservations, explicit and implicit, as to *invalidate* that pact from the outset —Vera M. Dean⟩ ⟨we do not say that we have met with an instance which *invalidates* the mathematical proposition that the sum of the three angles of a Euclidean triangle is 180 degrees —A.J. Ayer⟩ NEGATE suggests a canceling out or a nullification of one thing by another of two mutually exclusive things ⟨excellent clauses regarding the employment of children, they are *negated* not only by the negligence and venality of some local officials but also by the sheer facts of existence among the poor —George Woodcock⟩ ⟨the discovers he has appended his signature to contracts which *negate* each other —Richard Maney⟩ ⟨shock may temporarily *negate* the effects of drinking —Theodore Loveless⟩ ANNUL suggests a rendering ineffective by depriving of the power to function or rendering nonexistent, often officially or legally ⟨the two opposing electricities, so proportioned and so disposed that each of them *annuls* the actions which the other would produce outside the block if it were by itself —K.K.Darrow⟩ ⟨mystery does not *annul* meaning but enriches it —Reinhold Niebuhr⟩ ⟨war, as it becomes more and more total, practically *annuls* the difference as to injury and exposure to danger which formerly existed between armed forces and noncombatants —H.M.Huber⟩ ⟨the Emancipation Proclamation *annulled* all prior laws regarding slaves⟩ ABROGATE is much like *annul* but has a stronger association with a legal or official purposeful act ⟨the military clique *abrogated* the existing constitution —*Americana Annual*⟩ ⟨the Council of Ministers . . . has the power to *abrogate* actions of the constituent republics which contravene laws or decrees of the central government —F.A.Ogg & Harold Zink⟩ ⟨his audience had reached the point where it had *abrogated* all desire to think about anything —Nigel Dennis⟩

**nul·li·gravida** \,nələ+\ *n* [NL, fr. *nulli-* + L *gravida* pregnant woman — more at GRAVIDA] **:** a woman who has never been pregnant — compare NULLIPARA

**nul·ling** \'nəliŋ\ *n* -s [alter. of *knurling*] **:** KNURLING; *esp* **:** a quadrant-shaped decorative detail carved on moldings (as in Jacobean architecture)

**nul·lip·a·ra** \(,)nə'lipərə\ *n, pl* **nulliparas** \-rəz\ *also* **nul·lipa·rae** \-pə,rē\ [NL, fr. *nulli-* + *-para*] **:** a woman who has never borne a child — compare NULLIGRAVIDA — **nul·lip·a·rous** \(;)nə;lipərəs\ *adj*

**nul·li·pennate** \;nələ+\ *adj* [*nulli-* + *pennate*] **:** having no flight feathers

**nul·li·pen·nes** \,nələ'pe,nēz\ [NL, fr. *nulli-* + *-pennes* (fr. L *penna* feather, wing); akin to Gk *pteron* wing, feather — more at FEATHER] *syn of* APTERYGIFORMES

**nul·li·plex** \'nələ, pleks\ *adj* [*nulli-* + *-plex* -fold — more at SIMPLE] **:** homozygously recessive at a specified locus or for a specified factor — used of a polyploid ⟨~ for color intensifiers⟩

**nul·li·pore** \'nələ,pō(ə)r\ *n* -s [ISV *nulli-* + *-pore*] **:** any of several lime-secreting coralline algae formerly thought to be animals — **nul·lip·o·rous** \(;)nə;lipərəs, ;nələ;pōrəs\ *adj*

**nul·li·some** \'nələ,sōm\ *n* -s [*nulli-* + *-some*] **:** NULLISOMIC

**¹nul·li·so·mic** \;nələ;sōmik\ *adj* [ISV *nulli-* + *-somic*] **:** having two less than the diploid number of chromosomes due to loss of one chromosome pair

**²nullisomic** \"\ *n* -s **:** a nullisomic individual

**nul·li·ty** \'nələd·ē, -ətē, -i\ *n* -ES [MF *nullité,* fr. ML *nullitat-, nullitas,* fr. LL *nulli-* + L *-itat-, -itas* -ity] **1 a** (1) **:** the state or fact of being legally null or void **:** INVALIDITY (2) **:** a case of nullity (3) **:** a nullifying or invalidating fact or circumstance **b** (1) *Eng law* **:** the total absence of legal effect or existence (2) **:** a judicial declaration of the invalidity of a marriage ab initio **:** ANNULMENT **c :** any act or proceeding void of legal effect either absolutely (as in English law) or relatively (as sometimes in the civil law) **2 a :** the state of being null or nothing **:** want of efficacy or force **:** NOTHINGNESS ⟨a haunting and growing sense of the ~ of human life —Edmund Wilson⟩ **b :** a mere nothing **:** NONENTITY ⟨a diplomacy that results in pure *nullities* —R.H.Rovere⟩ ⟨taken a nice ~ as an individual character —Sidney Alexander⟩

**nul·li·us fi·li·us** \,nə;lēəs'fēlēəs, ;nülēəs-\ *n* [NL] **:** an illegitimate child **:** a bastard having no heritable rights in common law

**nullius ju·ris** \-'jürəs\ *adj* [ML] **:** having no standing in law **:** without legal effect or validity

**null method** *n* **:** a method of measurement in which an unknown quantity (as of electric current) is compared (as in a Wheatstone bridge) with a known quantity of the same kind and found equal by zero response of the detector

**nul·lo** \'nə(,)lō\ *n* -s [alter. of ³*null*] **1 a :** a bid in a card game by which a player undertakes to win no tricks **b :** a condition of play in which each trick counts against instead of for the player winning it **2 :** ⁷NULL 2

**nulls** *pl of* NULL, *pres 3d sing of* NULL

**nul tiel record** \-'tēl-\ *n* [AF, lit., no such record] **:** a plea alleging the record on which the action is founded does not exist

**nul tort** *n* [AF, lit., no wrong] **:** a former plea of the general issue in the real action of novel disseizin whereby the defendant denies he did anything wrong

**num** *abbr* **1** number **2** numeral

**¹numb** \'nəm\ *adj* -ER/-EST [ME *nomen,* fr. *nome, nomen* (past part. of *nimen* to take), fr. OE *numen,* past part. of *niman* to take — more at NIMBLE] **1 a :** devoid of sensation esp. due to cold **:** BENUMBED ⟨my right cheek has been ~ all day —Jack London⟩ ⟨had to lay him down again and rest her ~ arms —Elsie Singmaster⟩ **b :** devoid of emotion **:** DESENSITIZED, INDIFFERENT ⟨prisoners . . . ~ from suffering and anguish —E.M.Lustgarten⟩ ⟨personally, I am ~, and can't rouse . . . interest in anybody —Anthony Boucher⟩ **c :** devoid of skill or sensitivity ⟨he is tough, ~, and simple-minded —J.W.Aldridge⟩ **2 :** NUMBING ⟨it was a listless and ~ gray day —Edith Sitwell⟩ **3 :** characterized by numbness ⟨a deep sensation of cold . . . a ~ feeling —R.S.Woodworth⟩

**²numb** \"\ *vb* -ED/-ING/-S *vt* **:** to make numb **:** DEADEN ⟨fatigue ~*ed* his legs —William Chamberlain⟩ ⟨his body was ~*ed* with fear —Liam O'Flaherty⟩ ⟨the ~*ing* hand of officialdom —*Britain Today*⟩ ~ *vi* **:** to become numb ⟨tried to shield his face . . . but his jaw ~*ed* and his teeth ached —Andrew Hamilton⟩

**numb** *abbr* numbered

**num·bat** \'nəm,bat\ *n* -s [native name in Australia] **:** BANDED ANTEATER

**numbed** \'nəmd\ *adj* [short for *benumbed*] **:** made inert or insensitive — **numbed·ly** \-mədlē, -md-\ *adv*

**¹num·ber** \'nəmbə(r)\ *n* -s [ME *noumbre, nombre,* fr. OF *nombre,* fr. L *numerus* — more at NIMBLE] **1 a :** an arithmetical total **:** sum of the units involved **:** AGGREGATE ⟨~ of desks in the room⟩ ⟨~ of people in the hall⟩ ⟨owing to the ~ of prior

### CARDINAL NUMBERS[1]

| NAME[2] | SYMBOL arabic[3] | SYMBOL roman[4] |
|---|---|---|
| naught *or* zero *or* cipher | 0 | |
| one | 1 | I *or* i *also* j[5] |
| two | 2 | II *or* ii |
| three | 3 | III *or* iii |
| four | 4 | IV *or* iv *also* IIII |
| five | 5 | V *or* v |
| six | 6 | VI *or* vi |
| seven | 7 | VII *or* vii |
| eight | 8 | VIII *or* viii |
| nine | 9 | IX *or* ix |
| ten | 10 | X *or* x |
| eleven | 11 | XI *or* xi |
| twelve | 12 | XII *or* xii |
| thirteen | 13 | XIII *or* xiii |
| fourteen | 14 | XIV *or* xiv |
| fifteen | 15 | XV *or* xv |
| sixteen | 16 | XVI *or* xvi |
| seventeen | 17 | XVII *or* xvii |
| eighteen | 18 | XVIII *or* xviii |
| nineteen | 19 | XIX *or* xix |
| twenty | 20 | XX *or* xx |
| twenty-one | 21 | XXI *or* xxi |
| twenty-two | 22 | XXII *or* xxii |
| twenty-three | 23 | XXIII *or* xxiii |
| twenty-four | 24 | XXIV *or* xxiv |
| twenty-five | 25 | XXV *or* xxv |
| twenty-six | 26 | XXVI *or* xxvi |
| twenty-seven | 27 | XXVII *or* xxvii |
| twenty-eight | 28 | XXVIII *or* xxviii |
| twenty-nine | 29 | XXIX *or* xxix |
| thirty | 30 | XXX *or* xxx |
| thirty-one | 31 | XXXI *or* xxxi |
| thirty-two *etc* | 32 | XXXII *or* xxxii |
| forty | 40 | XL *or* xl *also* XXXX |
| forty-one | 41 | XLI *or* xli |
| forty-two *etc* | 42 | XLII *or* xlii |
| fifty | 50 | L *or* l |
| sixty | 60 | LX *or* lx |
| seventy | 70 | LXX *or* lxx |
| eighty | 80 | LXXX *or* lxxx *also* XXC |
| ninety | 90 | XC *or* xc *also* LXXXX |
| one hundred | 100 | C *or* c |
| one hundred and one *or* one hundred one *etc* | 101 | CI *or* ci |
| one hundred and two | 102 | CII *or* cii |
| one hundred and fifty | 150 | CL *or* cl |
| two hundred | 200 | CC *or* cc |
| three hundred | 300 | CCC *or* ccc |
| four hundred | 400 | CD *or* cd *also* CCCC |
| five hundred | 500 | D *or* d *also* IↃ[6] |
| six hundred | 600 | DC *or* dc *also* IↃC |
| seven hundred | 700 | DCC *or* dcc *also* IↃCC |
| eight hundred | 800 | DCCC *or* dccc |
| nine hundred | 900 | CM *or* cm |
| one thousand *or* ten hundred *etc* | 1,000[7] | M *or* m *also* CIↃ |
| two thousand *etc* | 2,000 | MM *or* mm |
| five thousand | 5,000 | $\overline{V}$[6] |
| ten thousand | 10,000 | $\overline{X}$ |
| one hundred thousand | 100,000 | $\overline{C}$ |
| one million | 1,000,000 | $\overline{M}$ |

### ORDINAL NUMBERS[8]

| NAME[9] | SYMBOL[10] |
|---|---|
| first | 1st |
| second | 2d *or* 2nd |
| third | 3d *or* 3rd |
| fourth | 4th |
| fifth | 5th |
| sixth | 6th |
| seventh | 7th |
| eighth | 8th |
| ninth | 9th |
| tenth | 10th |
| eleventh | 11th |
| twelfth | 12th |
| thirteenth | 13th |
| fourteenth | 14th |
| fifteenth | 15th |
| sixteenth | 16th |
| seventeenth | 17th |
| eighteenth | 18th |
| nineteenth | 19th |
| twentieth | 20th |
| twenty-first | 21st |
| twenty-second | 22d *or* 22nd |
| twenty-third | 23d *or* 23rd |
| twenty-fourth | 24th |
| twenty-fifth | 25th |
| twenty-sixth | 26th |
| twenty-seventh | 27th |
| twenty-eighth | 28th |
| twenty-ninth | 29th |
| thirtieth | 30th |
| thirty-first | 31st |
| thirty-second *etc* | 32d *or* 32nd |
| fortieth | 40th |
| forty-first | 41st |
| forty-second *etc* | 42d *or* 42nd |
| fiftieth | 50th |
| sixtieth | 60th |
| seventieth | 70th |
| eightieth | 80th |
| ninetieth | 90th |
| hundredth *or* one hundredth | 100th |
| hundred and first *or* one hundred and first *etc* | 101st |
| hundred and second | 102d *or* 102nd |
| two hundredth | 200th |
| three hundredth | 300th |
| four hundredth | 400th |
| five hundredth | 500th |
| six hundredth | 600th |
| seven hundredth | 700th |
| eight hundredth | 800th |
| nine hundredth | 900th |
| thousandth *or* one thousandth | 1,000th |
| two thousandth *etc* | 2,000th |
| ten thousandth | 10,000th |
| hundred thousandth *or* one hundred thousandth | 100,000th |
| millionth *or* one millionth | 1,000,000th |

### DENOMINATIONS ABOVE ONE MILLION

*American system*[11]

| NAME[12] | VALUE IN POWERS OF TEN | NUMBER OF ZEROS[13] | NUMBER OF PERIODS OF 0's AFTER 1,000[12] |
|---|---|---|---|
| billion[14] | $10^{9}$ | 9 | 2 |
| trillion[14] | $10^{12}$ | 12 | 3 |
| quadrillion | $10^{15}$ | 15 | 4 |
| quintillion | $10^{18}$ | 18 | 5 |
| sextillion | $10^{21}$ | 21 | 6 |
| septillion | $10^{24}$ | 24 | 7 |
| octillion | $10^{27}$ | 27 | 8 |
| nonillion | $10^{30}$ | 30 | 9 |
| decillion | $10^{33}$ | 33 | 10 |
| undecillion | $10^{36}$ | 36 | 11 |
| duodecillion | $10^{39}$ | 39 | 12 |
| tredecillion | $10^{42}$ | 42 | 13 |
| quattuordecillion | $10^{45}$ | 45 | 14 |
| quindecillion | $10^{48}$ | 48 | 15 |
| sexdecillion | $10^{51}$ | 51 | 16 |
| septendecillion | $10^{54}$ | 54 | 17 |
| octodecillion | $10^{57}$ | 57 | 18 |
| novemdecillion | $10^{60}$ | 60 | 19 |
| vigintillion | $10^{63}$ | 63 | 20 |
| centillion | $10^{303}$ | 303 | 100 |

*British system*[11]

| NAME | VALUE IN POWERS OF TEN | NUMBER OF ZEROS[13] | POWERS OF 1,000,000[12] |
|---|---|---|---|
| milliard | $10^{9}$ | 9 | — |
| billion | $10^{12}$ | 12 | 2 |
| trillion | $10^{18}$ | 18 | 3 |
| quadrillion | $10^{24}$ | 24 | 4 |
| quintillion | $10^{30}$ | 30 | 5 |
| sextillion | $10^{36}$ | 36 | 6 |
| septillion | $10^{42}$ | 42 | 7 |
| octillion | $10^{48}$ | 48 | 8 |
| nonillion | $10^{54}$ | 54 | 9 |
| decillion | $10^{60}$ | 60 | 10 |
| undecillion | $10^{66}$ | 66 | 11 |
| duodecillion | $10^{72}$ | 72 | 12 |
| tredecillion | $10^{78}$ | 78 | 13 |
| quattuordecillion | $10^{84}$ | 84 | 14 |
| quindecillion | $10^{90}$ | 90 | 15 |
| sexdecillion | $10^{96}$ | 96 | 16 |
| septendecillion | $10^{102}$ | 102 | 17 |
| octodecillion | $10^{108}$ | 108 | 18 |
| novemdecillion | $10^{114}$ | 114 | 19 |
| vigintillion | $10^{120}$ | 120 | 20 |
| centillion | $10^{600}$ | 600 | 100 |

[1]The cardinal numbers are used in simple counting or in answer to "how many?" The words for these numbers may be used as nouns (he counted to *twelve*), as pronouns (*twelve* were found), or as adjectives (*twelve* boys)

[2]In formal contexts the numbers one to one hundred and in less formal contexts the numbers one to nine are commonly written out, while larger numbers are given in numerals. In nearly all contexts a number occurring at the beginning of a sentence is usually written out. Numerals are invariably used for dates except in very formal contexts

[3]The arabic numerals were first used in India and were introduced to the West by the Arabs. They are sometimes called *Hindu numerals* or *Hindu-Arabic numerals.* In an early form arabic numerals are called *gobar numerals*

[4]The roman numerals are built up on seven basic symbols: I, V, X, L, C, D, and M according to the following rules:

1. A symbol following one of equal or greater value adds its value (II=2)
2. A symbol preceding one of greater value subtracts its value (IV=4; XL=40)
3. When a symbol stands between two of greater value, its value is subtracted from the second and the remainder is added to the first (XIV=14; LIX=59)
4. Of two equivalent ways of representing a number, that in which the symbol of larger denomination precedes is preferred (XIV, not VIX, for 14; XLV, not VL, for 45); in modern usage a short form by subtraction is preferred to a long form by addition (IV rather than IIII for 4, although IIII is seen on some clock faces; IX for 9 rather than VIIII; MCM for 1900 rather than MDCCCC)

[5]In medieval roman numerals the symbol for 1 was J and in modern times the lowercase j for a final i may be found, as in medical prescriptions (ij=2; vj=6)

[6]Several methods were employed in expressing the larger numbers in roman numerals, but none of them frequently since there was little use for the larger numbers themselves. The apostrophus Ↄ was used in ancient and medieval times following I to express 500 and repeated after the IↃ to express larger numbers, as IↃↃ for 5,000 and IↃↃↃ for 50,000. To represent numbers twice as great as these, C was repeated as many times before the stroke I as the Ↄ was after it as CCIↃↃ for 10,000 and CCCIↃↃↃ for 100,000. A straight line over a letter was sometimes used, esp. in medieval times, to indicate multiples of a thousand

[7]Arabic numerals from 1,000 to 9,999 are often written without commas (1000, 9999). Year numbers are always written without commas (1783)

[8]The ordinal numbers are used to show the order or succession in which such items as names, objects, and periods of time are considered (the *twelfth* month; the *fourth* row of seats; the *18th* century)

[9]Each of the terms for the ordinal numbers excepting *first* and *second* is used in designating one of a number of parts into which a whole may be divided (a *fourth;* a *sixth;* a *tenth*) and as the denominator in fractions designating the number of such parts constituting a certain portion of a whole (one *fourth;* three *fifths;* five *sixths;* seven *tenths*). The fractions when used as nouns are usually written as two words, although they are often hyphenated as nouns and regularly hyphenated as adjectives (a *two-thirds* majority; a *three-fourths* vote). When fractions are written in numerals, the cardinal symbols are used (¼, ⅗, ⅚)

[10]The arabic symbols for the cardinal numbers may be read as ordinals in certain contexts (January 1=January first; August 15=August fifteenth; 1 Chronicles=First Chronicles; 2 Samuel =Second Samuel). The roman numerals are sometimes read as ordinals (Henry IV=Henry the Fourth; the *Argonaut II*= the *Argonaut the Second*); sometimes they are written with the ordinal suffixes (XIXth Dynasty, XXth Dynasty)

[11]The American system of numeration for denominations above one million was modeled on the French system but more recently the French system has been changed to correspond to the German and British systems. In the American system each of the denominations above 1,000 millions (the American *billion*) is 1,000 times the one preceding (one trillion=1,000 billions; one quadrillion=1,000 trillions). In the British system the first denomination above 1,000 millions (the British *milliard*) is 1,000 times the preceding one, but each of the denominations above 1,000 milliards (the British *billion*) is 1,000,000 times the preceding one (one trillion=1,000,000 billions; one quadrillion=1,000,000 trillions)

[12]The names of the denominations in the American system correspond to the number of periods of zeros (groups of three zeros) that come after 1,000 (the numeral for one billion [1,000,000,000] contains two [bi-]; and the numeral for one trillion [1,000,000,000,000] contains three [tri-]. The names of the British denominations correspond to the values expressed in powers of one million (one billion=a million to the 2d power; one trillion=a million to the 3d power)

[13]For convenience in reading large numerals the thousands, millions, etc., are usually separated by commas (21,530; 1,155,465) or by half spaces (1 155 465). Serial numbers (as a social security number or the engine number of a car) are often written with hyphens (583-695-20), spaces, or other devices.

[14]The usual French term for the American billion is *milliard,* the British term is *milliard,* and the German is *Milliarde.* The British billion (1,000 milliards or 1,000,000 millions) is equivalent to the American trillion.

applications, he shortly withdrew —J.C.Archer⟩ **b :** an ascertainable total **:** the possibility of numbering ⟨the sands of the seashore are beyond ~⟩ ⟨times without ~⟩ **c :** an allotted total **:** COMPLEMENT ⟨the whole ~ of Senators —*U.S.Constitution*⟩ **d :** a total of units of a particular kind ⟨an enormous ~ of languages —J.B.Carroll⟩ ⟨there is a limited ~ of such laboratories —P.D.Close⟩ ⟨the city is . . . continuing to draw increasing ~s of visitors —H.W.H.King⟩ ⟨archery clubs have been established . . . and their ~ is growing rapidly —*Amer. Guide Series: Minn.*⟩ **e :** an unspecified total **:** SEVERAL ⟨a ~ of solutions have been proposed —S.H.Hofstadter⟩ ⟨the . . . concern occupies a ~ of brick buildings —*Amer. Guide Series: N.H.*⟩ ⟨collection which he has exhibited a ~ of times —Mary Zimmer⟩; *esp* **:** quite a few ⟨a ~ of instances⟩ **2 a :** a select company ⟨I want to be in that ~ when the saints go marching in —*When the Saints Go Marching In*⟩ **b** *obs* (1) **:** a designated class **:** CATEGORY ⟨a mineral . . . of the ~ of bitumens —A. Cooper⟩ (2) **:** a specified group of people ⟨this happy ~ that have endured shrewd days and nights with us —Shak.⟩ (3) **:** a numerous group **:** MULTITUDE; *specif* **:** PROLETARIAT ⟨the ~ may be hanged, but not be crowned —Alexander Pope⟩ **3 :** the enumerative aspect of things existing in countable units ⟨a weak sense of time and ~ —G.T.Trewartha & Wilbur Zelinsky⟩ **4 a :** an abstract unit in a numerical series ⟨seven is his lucky ~⟩ ⟨a ~ divisible by two⟩ **b numbers** *pl* **:** the art of computation **:** ARITHMETIC ⟨teach children their ~s⟩ ⟨from simple ~s to the calculus —*Brit. Book News*⟩ **5 a :** distinction of word form to denote reference to one or to more than one or in some languages also to two usu. expressed by an inflectional change; *also* **:** the distinctive form itself (as of noun, adjective, or verb) or one of the groups of forms so distinguished — compare PLURAL, SINGULAR **b** (1) *obs* **:** tuneful cadence **:** RHYTHM ⟨in full harmonic ~ joined —John Milton⟩ (2) **numbers** *pl, archaic* **:** musical sounds **:** NOTES ⟨~s which thou warblest —Rachel M. Praed⟩ **c numbers** *pl* (1) **:** symmetry of cadence **:** PERIOD ⟨melodic ~s of the classic orators⟩ (2) **:** metrical structure **:** METER ⟨most by ~s judge a poet's song —Alexander Pope⟩ (3) **:** metrical lines **:** VERSES ⟨these ~s will I tear, and write in prose —Shak.⟩ **6 a :** a written word, symbol, or group of symbols representing a number ⟨spell out ~s under three digits —Kate L. Turabian⟩; *specif* **:** NUMERAL ⟨the code employs letters as well as ~s⟩ **b :** a numerical label or designation: as (1) **:** a digit or group of digits used as a means of identification ⟨house ~⟩ ⟨catalog ~⟩ ⟨stamped a ~ on each ball —Millen Brand⟩; *specif* **:** LICENSE PLATE ⟨the victim remembered the ~ of the getaway car⟩ — symbol # ⟨apartment #32⟩ (2) **:** an allotted position in a numerical sequence ⟨take ~ two position in column —Wirt Williams⟩; *specif* **:** relative position on a promotion roster ⟨for the grounding of his ship . . . he was reduced ten ~s —Allan Westcott⟩ (3) **:** an individual identified by position in a sequence or by a numerical label ⟨opened fire on ~ three —*Oxford Bk. of English Talk*⟩ ⟨tackled on the line of scrimmage by ~ 22⟩ ⟨to the keeper I was just a new ~, another dirty blanket to issue —Gilbert Millstein⟩ — compare OPPOSITE NUMBER (4) **:** the specified position of an article in a series with respect to established criteria (as of size or quality) ⟨~ nine shoe⟩ ⟨~ one manila⟩ ⟨a ~ two can of tomatoes⟩ — compare ²COUNT 8a (5) **:** a telephone number ⟨dialed a ~ on the interoffice telephone —Hamilton Basso⟩ (6) **:** a numerical value obtained as the result of a chemical test and used in characterizing the substance tested ⟨the iodine ~ of a fatty oil⟩ **7 :** a large supply **:** QUANTITY, SWARM ⟨squaretails in ~ —Stewart Holbrook⟩ — usu. used in pl. ⟨~s of this shark sometimes attack shoals of sardines —J.L.B.Smith⟩ ⟨individuals of great wealth will certainly not exist in any ~s in another decade or so —*Persuasion*⟩ ⟨~s of beauties major and minor —F.R.Leavis⟩ **8 numbers** *pl* **a :** a numerous group **:** MANY ⟨~s died on the way —Marjory S. Douglas⟩ **b :** a numerical preponderance ⟨there is safety in ~s⟩ **c :** units of population ⟨their ~s outstrip their resources —Barbara Ward⟩ ⟨the graduate school doubled its ~s —C.F.Smith⟩ **9 a :** a single issue of a periodical ⟨a year's subscription brings you 12 ~s⟩ ⟨his article will appear in the February ~⟩ **b :** one that is singled out from a group: as (1) **:** one of a company of people **:** PERSON ⟨two . . . stokers as ammunition ~s —*The Crowsnest*⟩; *esp* **:** GIRL ⟨a cute ~ in a yellow dress —R.L. Strout⟩ ⟨a blondined ~ . . . draped in silver fox —Margaret Long⟩ (2) **:** a musical or literary selection ⟨a catchy little ~ in waltz time —A.E.Stevenson b. 1900⟩ ⟨contains perhaps half a dozen ~s that are among the best things he ever wrote —Robert Collet⟩ (3) **:** an item of merchandise offered for sale ⟨put that black velvet ~ with the sequins on the blonde dummy —Bennett Cerf⟩ ⟨the new nylon ~ which he calls an armored vest —*New Yorker*⟩ ⟨costs a lot of money to bring out any new toy ~ —*Marketing Toys*⟩ ⟨a more modestly priced blanket is an all-wool ~ —Hamilton Basso⟩ (4) **:** BOOK ⟨novel . . . was going to turn out to be one of those amnesia ~s —E.J.Fitzgerald⟩ **:** PLAY ⟨supported this cheery little ~ for just fifteen performances —Deems Taylor⟩ **c :** a feature or episode in a theatrical production ⟨the tango ~ late in Act I —*Theatre Arts*⟩ ⟨my ~s are just an extension of the speaking part —Murray Schumach⟩ **10 :** information about or insight into a person's ability or character ⟨the other side had his ~ and was riding him —Mary Deasy⟩ ⟨she was incapable of subterfuge and it didn't take him long to get her ~⟩ **11 numbers** *pl but sing or pl in constr* **a :** a form of lottery played in the U.S. in which one may select any three digits from 001 to 999 and bet on them to appear in a specified order or in any combination and in which the winning numbers and order are determined by figures regularly published in newspapers (as clearinghouse or stock market receipts, pari-mutuel payoffs, or the cards in an article on contract bridge) — called also *number pool, numbers game* **b :** POLICY 2a

**syn** NUMBER, NUMERAL, FIGURE, DIGIT, and INTEGER can mean in common a character by which an arithmetical value is designated. NUMBER may refer to a character or to a word ⟨the *number* forty-five⟩ ⟨the *number* 45⟩ or to a character with an affix ⟨the ordinal *numbers* 2d, 3d, and 4th⟩ NUMERAL applies to the characters as numbers as distinguished from the words standing for the same numbers ⟨a license plate with both letters and the *numerals* 13249⟩ ⟨the Roman numerals V, VI, and XLII⟩ FIGURE stresses the characters as characters, usu. arabic ⟨write the numbers in *figures* wherever possible to save space⟩ ⟨his salary went into five *figures*⟩ DIGIT refers expressly to one of the characters in Arabic notation ⟨if you include 0, Arabic numerals consist of 10 *digits,* though some authorities exclude 0 as a digit⟩ INTEGER, in this connection, is an arithmetical term for a whole number, one that is not or does not contain a fraction ⟨11½ is not an *integer*⟩ **syn** see in addition SUM

— **any number :** quite a few ⟨laid out with *any number* of trees of different species —B.C.Cronwright⟩ — **by the numbers** *adv* **1 :** in unison to a specific count or cadence **2 :** in a systematic, routine, or mechanical manner — **have one's number on it :** believed to be or to have been destined by fate to cause the death of one — usu. used of a projectile ⟨as a bullet⟩

²**number** \"\ *vb* **numbered; numbered; numbering** \-b(ə)riŋ\ **numbers** [ME *noumbren, nombren,* fr. OF *nombrer,* fr. L *numerare,* fr. *numerus* number] *vt* **1 a :** to ascertain the number of **:** COUNT ⟨~s his friends by the hundreds⟩ **b** *archaic* **:** to determine by mathematical processes **:** COMPUTE ⟨was desirous of accurately ~*ing* the interval of time from one . . . festival to another —Thomas Taylor⟩ **c** *obs* **:** to gauge the amount of **:** ESTIMATE ⟨poets cannot think, speak, cast, write, sing, ~ . . . his love —Shak.⟩ **2 :** to claim as part of a total **:** INCLUDE ⟨it is only by accident that I am ~*ed* among American philosophers —George Santayana⟩ ⟨writers resident in Texas ~*ed* none of note whose literary work was not incidental —*Amer. Guide Series: Texas*⟩ ⟨prudence . . . is ~*ed* with the cardinal virtues —H.O.Taylor⟩ **3 :** to restrict to a limited or definite number ⟨doctors told him his days were ~*ed* —H.E.Starr⟩ **4 :** to assign a number to esp. as a means of identification ⟨~ the pages of a book⟩ ⟨stay on ~*ed* highways⟩ ⟨we use letters to ~ the rows of seats in an assembly room —D.E.Smith⟩ ⟨five thousand dollars of the stolen money was in ~*ed* bills —E.S. Gardner⟩ **5** *archaic* **a :** to report the number of **:** ENUMERATE ⟨the quantities of . . . furnitures following so royal an army, what pen can ~ —Robert Johnson⟩ — often used with *up* ⟨you ~*ed* up the acts of trust —R.H.Hutton⟩ **b :** to check over one by one **:** TELL ⟨let my brother ~ his beads devoutly —Philip Massinger⟩ **c :** APPORTION, DIVIDE ⟨days of this life's pilgrimage . . . to ~ wisely —J.W.Warter⟩ ⟨my . . . fellows I ~*ed* into two companies —William Morris⟩ **6** *archaic* **:** to experience the passage of (an interval of time) ⟨I since then have ~*ed* o'er some thrice three years —Alfred Tennyson⟩; *esp* **:** to reach or have (a specified age) in years ⟨of as able body as when he ~*ed* thirty —Shak.⟩ **7 :** to comprise in number **:** TOTAL ⟨they were a miscellaneous lot . . . ~*ing* in all some 20 or 30 —R.W.Southern⟩ ⟨his extensive collection . . . ~*ing* many thousand specimens —Witmer Stone⟩ ~ *vi* **1 :** to reach a total **:** COUNT ⟨controls . . . literally ~ in the thousands —Harold Koontz & Cyril O'Donnell⟩ **2 :** to call off numbers in sequence ⟨*neng, song, sam,* she ~*ed* in Siamese —Kathryn Grondahl⟩; *esp* **:** to call off one's number as a member of a squad or group ⟨men fall in in single rank and ~ from the right in fours —*Fire Service Drill Bk.*⟩ — often used with *off* ⟨lined up and ~*ed* off⟩ **syn** see COUNT

³**number** *comparative of* NUMB

**num·ber·able** \-bərəbəl\ *adj* **:** capable of being numbered

**number agreement** *n* **:** grammatical concord in form (as singular, dual, or plural) of adjective with noun, finite verb with subject, or pronoun with antecedent

**number-board** \ˈ==,=\ *n* **:** SLATE 3b

**number eight iron** *n* **:** NIBLICK

**num·ber·er** \-bərə(r)\ *n* -s **:** one that numbers

**number field** *or* **number system** *n* **:** the aggregate of all numbers of a given type (as integers, irrationals, complex numbers, vectors) which can be combined by addition or multiplication to obtain a result of the same type

**number five iron** *n* **:** MASHIE

**number four iron** *n* **:** MASHIE IRON

**numbering machine** *n* **:** a device for the rapid stamping or printing of usu. consecutive numbers on successive pages, sheets, or discrete items

**num·ber·less** \-bə(r)ləs\ *adj* **:** too many to be counted **:** INNUMERABLE ⟨the possible combinations are ~ —Alfred Marshall⟩

numbering machine

¹**number one** *n* **:** one's own interests or welfare **:** ONESELF ⟨he's very careful of *number one*⟩ ⟨never neglects a chance to exploit a personal advantage on the theory that you've got to look out for *number one*⟩

²**number one** *adj* **1 :** first in rank, importance, or influence **:** FOREMOST ⟨America's *number one* woman golfer —*Providence (R.I.) Evening Bull.*⟩ ⟨declared stamp collecting to be "the nation's *number one* hobby" —H.M.Ellis⟩ ⟨public enemy *number one*⟩ **2 :** of highest or of high quality **:** A1 2 ⟨a real *number one* dinner⟩

**number one iron** *n* **:** DRIVING IRON 2

**number plate** *n* **:** a plate or tab bearing an identifying number; *specif* **:** LICENSE PLATE

**number pool** *n* **:** NUMBER 11

**numbers** *pl of* NUMBER, *pres 3d sing of* NUMBER

**number seven iron** *n* **:** PITCHER 4

**numbers game** *also* **numbers pool** *or* **numbers racket** *n* **:** NUMBER 11

**number sign** *n* **:** a sign # used before a numeral to denote number ⟨#2 pencil⟩ ⟨apartment #32⟩ ⟨catalog #6954⟩

**number six iron** *n* **:** MASHIE NIBLICK

**number theory** *n* **:** advanced arithmetic devoted to the study of the properties of numbers

**number three iron** *n* **:** MID-MASHIE

**number two iron** *n* **:** MIDIRON

**numbest** *superlative of* NUMB

**numbfish** \ˈ=,=\ *n* [¹*numb* + *fish;* fr. the numbing effect of its shocks] **:** ELECTRIC RAY

**numbing** *adj* [fr. pres. part. of ²*numb*] **:** causing numbness **:** DEADENING, STUPEFYING ⟨a deep ~ hurt way down inside me —Billie Hamlet⟩ ⟨the significance of the title . . . is explained at ~ length —Wolcott Gibbs⟩ — **numb·ing·ly** *adv*

**num·bles** *also* **nom·bles** \ˈnəmbəlz\ *n pl* [ME *noumbles, nombles,* fr. MF *nombles,* pl. of *nomble* muscle from the thigh of a deer, fillet of beef, pork loin, modif. of L *lumbulus* small loin, fr. *lumbus* loin + *-ulus* -ule — more at LOIN] **:** certain edible viscera (as the heart, lights, liver) of an animal (as a deer) **:** UMBLES — compare GIBLET 1

**numb·ly** *adv* **:** in a numb manner **:** INSENSIBLY, DULLY ⟨his . . . arms hung down ~ —Peter Schmid⟩ ⟨the men . . . stared up at him ~ —Irwin Shaw⟩

**numb·ness** *n* -ES [¹*numb* + *-ness*] **1 :** reduced sensibility to touch ⟨patients subsequently experienced a feeling of ~ . . . in the thighs —*Jour. Amer. Med. Assoc.*⟩ **2 :** reduced sensitivity to perception or emotion **:** STUPOR ⟨a drowsy ~ pains my sense, as though of hemlock I had drunk —John Keats⟩ ⟨slipped from her waking ~ into complete oblivion —Mary Webb⟩

**numbrous** *adj* [MF *nombreux,* fr. *nombre* number + *-eux* -ous — more at NUMBER] *obs* **:** NUMEROUS

**numbs** *pres 3d sing of* NUMB

**numbskull** *var of* NUMSKULL

**num·dah** \ˈnəmdə\ *or* **nam·mad** *or* **na·mad** \ˈnəməd\ *n* -s [Hindi *namdā,* fr. Per *namad,* fr. MPer *namat;* akin to Av *nəmata-* brushwood] **:** a thick felted rug of India and Persia usu. made of pounded goat's hair and embroidered with bird or floral designs in colored wool yarn — compare DRUGGET

**nu·men** \ˈn(y)ümən\ *n, pl* **nu·mi·na** \-mənə\ [L, nod, divine will, numen; akin to MHG *nucken* to nod off, MLG *nucke* sudden push, L *nuere* to nod, Gk *neuein* to nod, *nyssein, nyttein* to prick, sting, Skt *navate, nauti* he moves, turns] **1 a :** a spirit believed by animists to inhabit a natural object or phenomenon ⟨said to have set up one of the stones . . . and to have poured oil on the top of it as an offering to the indwelling ~ —E.O.James⟩ **b :** a presiding spirit **:** a local deity ⟨the ~ that exercised watch and ward over the whole household —J.B. Noss⟩ **2 :** a dynamic or creative force **:** GENIUS ⟨the strange and powerful ~ which, he felt, used him as its tabernacle —Aldous Huxley⟩

**nu·me·ni·us** \n(y)üˈmēnēəs\ *n, cap* [NL, fr. LGk *noumēnios,* a bird, perh. the curlew, fr. Gk *noumēnia, neomēnia* new moon, first of the month, fr. *ne-* + *mēn* month + *-ia* — more at MOON] **:** a genus of birds (family Scolopacidae) consisting of the curlews

**nu·mer·a·ble** \ˈn(y)üm(ə)rəbəl\ *adj* [L *numerabilis,* fr. *numerare* to count + *-abilis* -able — more at NUMBER] **:** capable of being counted ⟨the small ~ band of runaway planets —A.N.Whitehead⟩

¹**nu·mer·al** \ˈn(y)üm(ə)rəl\ *adj* [MF, fr. LL *numeralis,* fr. L *numerus* number + *-alis* -al — more at NUMBER] **1 :** of, relating to, or expressing numbers ⟨~ adjective⟩ ⟨used the letters of their alphabet for ~ symbols —D.E.Smith⟩ **2 :** consisting of numbers or numerals ⟨~ cipher⟩ — **nu·mer·al·ly** \-rəlē, -li\ *adv*

²**numeral** \"\ *n* -s **1 :** NUMBER 6 **2 numerals** *pl* **:** the numbers designating by year a school or college class ⟨carried a banner with the class ~s on it in the reunion parade⟩ ⟨won ~s in basketball, baseball, and track⟩ — compare LETTER 6 **syn** see NUMBER

**nu·mer·ate** \ˈn(y)ümə,rāt\ *vt* -ED/-ING/-S [L *numeratus,* past part. of *numerare* to count] **:** to give a detailed list of **:** ENUMERATE ⟨might have been illuminating had he *numerated* the mistakes made by each side —Mary K. Hammond⟩

**nu·mer·a·tion** \,==ˈrāshən\ *n* -s [ME *numeracion,* fr. L *numeration-, numeratio,* fr. *numeratus* (past part. of *numerare* to count) + *-ion-, -io* -ion] **1 a :** a system or process of enumeration ⟨the positional system which came . . . to supersede the clumsy ~ of the Romans —*Times Lit. Supp.*⟩ **b :** the application of enumerative processes **:** COMPUTATION ⟨study of African or American Indian languages shows systems of ~, often on a decimal scale —D.J.Struik⟩ **c :** an act or instance of counting or of applying numbers to something **:** CENSUS, NUMBERING ⟨make an exact ~ of the inhabitants of Ireland —Edmund Burke⟩ ⟨a fourteenth century Arabic ~ is written in the lower outer corner . . . of the leaves —Jack Finegan⟩ **2 :** arithmetical skill; *esp* **:** the art of reading off in words numbers set down in figures

¹**nu·mer·a·tive** \ˈn(y)ümərəd·iv, -mə,rād·-\ *adj* [*numerate* + *-ive*] *archaic* **:** of or relating to number or numeration ⟨a ~ noun interposed between it and the substantive —R.K.Douglas⟩

²**numerative** \"\ *n* **:** CLASSIFIER 2

**nu·mer·a·tor** \ˈn(y)ümə,rād·ə(r), -ātə-\ *n* -s [F *numérateur,* fr. LL *numerator* one that counts, fr. L *numeratus* (past part. of *numerare* to count) + *-or*] **1 :** the part of a fraction that is above the line and signifies the number of parts of the denominator taken **:** DIVIDEND **2** [LL] **:** one that numbers

**nu·mer·ic** \(ˈ)n(y)üˈmerik\ *adj* [back-formation fr. *numerical*] **:** NUMERICAL 1

**nu·mer·i·cal** \-rəkəl, -rēk-\ *adj* [L *numerus* number + E *-ical*] **1 a :** of or relating to numbers ⟨~ analyst⟩ ⟨~ superiority of the enemy⟩ **b :** denoting a number ⟨letters of the alphabet were employed as ~ signs —William Chomsky⟩ **c :** expressed in figures rather than letters ⟨spies . . . used a very simple ~ cipher, which changed every day —Alexander d'Agapeyeff⟩ ⟨the ~ proportions of hybrid crosses —Lancelot Hogben⟩ ⟨~ equation⟩ **d :** designated by number ⟨conscious of his ~ standing in every class —Harry Levin⟩ **e :** of or relating to ability to think in or work with numbers ⟨~ skill⟩ ⟨the ~ factor of a test⟩ — compare VERBAL **2 a** *archaic* **:** of a corresponding type **:** INDISTINGUISHABLE, SAME ⟨many of these ~ postures . . . are found in statues of the ancients —John Bulwer⟩ **b** *obs* **:** IDENTICAL ⟨in a river we swim in the same place, though not in the same ~ water —Robert Burton⟩ ⟨probably that very ~ book . . . kept in the temple —Thomas Fuller⟩

**numerical aperture** *n* **:** a quantity that indicates the resolving power of a microscope objective and that is numerically equal to the product of the index of refraction of the medium in front of the objective and the sine of the angle which the most oblique ray entering it makes with the optical axis

**nu·mer·i·cal·ly** \-rək(ə)lē, -rēk-, -li\ *adv* **1 a :** in respect to number **:** in numbers ⟨a ~ inferior but intellectually potent group —K.S.Davis⟩ **b :** according to number ⟨copy . . . is filed ~ —E.M.Robinson⟩ **c :** in figures ⟨if a date is written ~ —Marjorie E. Skillin & R.M.Gay⟩ **2 :** in a precisely similar way **:** INDISTINGUISHABLY ⟨the emotion . . . is not ~ identical —John Dewey⟩

**numerical rating system** *n* **:** a system of establishing insurance premium rates for substandard lives on the basis of numerical weights for various impairments

**numerical value** *n* **1 a :** a quantitative value assigned to a letter of the alphabet ⟨exegetical rule . . . according to which every Hebrew letter has a *numerical value* —S.A.Binion⟩ **b :** a sum obtained by adding together the numerical equivalents of the letters in a word or phrase ⟨if two names had the same *numerical value,* this fact showed some relation between the individuals —D.E.Smith⟩ — compare GEMATRIA **2 :** ABSOLUTE VALUE

**nu·mer·ist** \ˈn(y)ümərəst\ *n* -s [L *numerus* number + E *-ist*] *archaic* **:** NUMEROLOGIST

**nu·mer·o·log·i·cal** \,n(y)ümərəˈläjəkəl\ *adj* **:** of or relating to numerology

**nu·mer·ol·o·gist** \,n(y)üməˈräləjəst\ *n* -s **:** a specialist in numerology ⟨bets $2000 on a horse, after consulting his private ~ —Malcolm Cowley⟩

**nu·mer·ol·o·gy** \-jē, -ji\ *n* -ES [L *numerus* number + *-o-* + *-logy*] **:** the study of the occult significance of numbers — compare GEMATRIA

**nu·mer·os·i·ty** \,n(y)üməˈräsəd·ē\ *n* -ES [MF *numerosité* numerousness, fr. LL *numerositat-, numerositas,* fr. L *numerosus* numerous + *-itat-, -itas* -ity] **1 :** NUMEROUSNESS ⟨the earliest scales of measurement were scales of ~ —scales for the counting of pebbles or cattle or warriors —S.S.Stevens⟩ **2** *archaic* **:** melodic flow **:** RHYTHM

**nu·mer·ous** \ˈn(y)üm(ə)rəs\ *adj* [MF *numereux,* fr. L *numerosus,* fr. *numerus* number + *-osus* -ous — more at NUMBER] **1 a :** consisting of great numbers of units **:** existing in abundance **:** MANY, PLENTIFUL ⟨decked out with . . . ~ ribbons and a thousand other joyous trifles —Osbert Sitwell⟩ ⟨mutation . . . has occurred ~ times under natural conditions —Theodosius Dobzhansky⟩ ⟨legends regarding buried treasure . . . are as ~ as they are improbable —Thomas Barbour⟩ **b :** consisting of a great number of individuals **:** LARGE, MULTITUDINOUS ⟨it was too bad that the family was ~: each man got only one share . . . instead of two —Ernest Beaglehole⟩ ⟨this species has become infinitely more ~ during the past five or six years —Thomas Heinitz⟩ **c** *archaic* **:** of or relating to a great number of individuals ⟨the birds begun at four o'clock . . . a music ~ —Emily Dickinson⟩ **2** *archaic* **:** musically cadenced **:** RHYTHMICAL ⟨blank verse . . . falling occasionally almost into ~ prose —Henry Hallam⟩

**nu·mer·ous·ly** *adv* **:** in large numbers **:** ABUNDANTLY ⟨letters have been arriving ~ of late —Virgil Thomson⟩

**nu·mer·ous·ness** *n* -ES **:** the quality or state of being numerous ⟨~ of kinsfolk⟩

**nu·me·rus clau·sus** \ˌnüməˌrüˈsklauˌsüs\ *n* [NL, lit., closed or restricted number] **:** a quantity fixed as the maximal number or percentage (as of applicants of a particular race or class) admissible to an academic institution

**nu·mi·da** \ˈn(y)ümədə\ *n, cap* [NL, fr. L *Numida* Numidian, fr. Gk *Nomada*] **:** the type genus of Numididae comprising the domesticated guinea fowls and closely related African wild guinea fowls

¹**nu·mid·i·an** \(ˈ)n(y)üˈmidēən\ *adj, usu cap* [L *Numidianus,* fr. *Numidia* + *-ianus* -ian] **:** of or relating to Numidia, an ancient country of No. Africa nearly coextensive with modern Algeria

²**numidian** \"\ *n* -s *cap* **1 :** a native or inhabitant of ancient Numidia **2 :** the Berber language of the Numidian people

**numidian alphabet** *n, usu cap N* **:** LIBYAN ALPHABET

**numidian crane** *n, usu cap N* **:** DEMOISELLE 2a

**nu·mid·i·dae** \n(y)üˈmidə,dē\ *n pl, cap* [NL, fr. *Numida,* type genus + *-idae*] **:** a family of African and Madagascan birds that are closely related to the pheasants and peacocks and often included with them in the family Phasianidae and that comprise the guinea fowls — see NUMIDA

**numina** *pl of* NUMEN

¹**nu·mi·nous** \ˈn(y)ümənəs\ *adj* [L *numin-, numen* numen + E *-ous* — more at NUMEN] **1 a :** of, relating to, or characteristic of a numen **:** SUPERNATURAL ⟨a single dark and ~ power ruling the world —Aldous Huxley⟩ **b :** dedicated to or hallowed by association with a deity **:** SACRED ⟨a ~ wood⟩ **c :** having talismanic properties **:** MAGICAL ⟨all quests are concerned with some ~ object, the waters of life, the Grail, buried treasure —W.H.Auden⟩ **2 a :** filled with a sense of the presence of divinity **:** HOLY ⟨the holiest, most ~ moment in the Mass — the moment of transubstantiation —V.C.Aldrich⟩ **b :** inspiring reverence ⟨as beautiful and as ~ as a cathedral —C.E.Raven⟩ **3 a :** appealing to the higher emotions or to the aesthetic sense **:** SPIRITUAL ⟨when tradition has lost its . . . ~ authority —George Santayana⟩ ⟨the candle was a graceful . . . and ~ method of illumination —*New Yorker*⟩ **b :** beyond understanding or description **:** MYSTERIOUS, INCOMPREHENSIBLE ⟨emphasizes the ~ aspect of writing —*Times Lit. Supp.*⟩

²**numinous** \"\ *n* -ES [G *numinos,* fr. L *numin-, numen* numen] **:** an unseen but majestic presence that inspires both dread and fascination and constitutes the nonrational element characteristic of vital religion **:** a psychic revelation of deity producing religious awe and ecstasy — usu. used with *the* ⟨African Bushmen, awed by the presence of the ~ at a given place . . . throwing a few grains into a hole in the hallowed ground —Joachim Wach⟩ ⟨the unanimity of prophets and seers regarding their experiences of the ~ —William Telfer⟩

**nu·mis·mat·ic** \ˌn(y)üməzˈmad·ik, -məsˈ-, -at|, |ēk\ *also* **nu·mis·mat·i·cal** \|ək·əl, |ēk-\ *adj* [*numismatic* fr. F *numismatique,* fr. L *numismat-, numisma, nomismat-, nomisma* money, coin (fr. Gk *nomismat-, nomisma* custom, usage, currency, coin) + F *-ique; numismatical* fr. L *numismat-, numisma* + E *-ical;* akin to Gk *nomos* custom, usage, law — more at NIMBLE] **1 :** of or relating to numismatics ⟨will accept any dime but would prefer it to be of some ~ value —J.M.Hageman⟩ **2 :** of or relating to currency **:** MONETARY ⟨cowrie shells because of their ~ . . . significance were given the technical name of *Cypraea moneta* —*Numismatist*⟩

**nu·mis·mat·i·cal·ly** \|ək(ə)lē, |ēk-, -li\ *adv* **:** from a numismatic point of view **:** with regard to numismatics ⟨coins in this ~ and historically interesting series —*Numismatist*⟩

**nu·mis·mat·ics** \,==ˈmad·iks\ *n pl but sing in constr* [F *numismatique*, fr. *numismatique*, adj.] **1 :** the study of coins, tokens, medals, paper money, and objects closely resembling them in form or purpose **2 :** the collecting of numismatic objects

**nu·mis·ma·tist** \n(y)ü'mizmədəst, -ism-, -ətəst\ *n* -s [L *numismat-, numisma* + E *-ist*] **1 :** a specialist in numismatics **2 :** a collector of numismatic objects : a coin collector

**nu·mis·ma·tol·o·gist** \n(y)ü,mizmə'täləjəst, -ism-\ *n* -s [*numismatology* + *-ist*] : NUMISMATIST

**nu·mis·ma·tol·o·gy** \-jē\ *n* -ES [*numismatic* + *-ology*] : NUMISMATICS

**num·ma·ry** \'nəmərē\ *adj* [L *nummarius*, fr. *nummus* coin, money (fr. Gk *nomimos* customary, lawful) + *-arius* -ary; akin to Gk *nomos* custom, usage, law — more at NIMBLE] : of, relating to, or dealing with money or coins

**num·mi·form** \'nəmə,fȯrm\ *adj* [F *nummiforme*, fr. L *nummus* coin + F *-forme* -form] : NUMMULAR

**num·mu·lar** \'nəmyələ(r)\ *adj* [F *nummulaire*, fr. L *nummulus* (dim. of *nummus* coin) + F *-aire* -ar] **1 :** circular or oval in shape ⟨~ lesions⟩ **2 a :** marked by circular or oval lesions ⟨~ dermatitis⟩ **b :** forming circular or oval drops ⟨~ sputum⟩

**num·mu·la·ria** \,nəmyə'la(a)rēə\ *n, cap* [NL, fr. L *nummulus*, dim. of *nummus* coin + NL *-aria*] : a genus of mostly saprophytic fungi (family Xylariaceae) forming generally amorphous crustose round or discoid black stromata — see BLISTER CANKER

**num·mu·lary** \'nəmyə,lerē\ *adj* [L *nummularius* of or relating to money changing, fr. *nummulus* some money, money (dim. of *nummus* coin) + *-arius* -ary] *archaic* : NUMMARY

**num·mu·line** \'nəmyə,līn, -,lən\ *adj* [*nummulite* + *-ine*] : NUMMULITIC

**num·mu·lite** \'nəmyə,līt\ *n* -s [NL *Nummulites*] : a foraminifer or fossil of the family Nummulitidae — **num·mu·lit·ic** \;==;lid·ik\ *adj*

**num·mu·li·tes** \,nəmyə'līd·(,)ēz\ *n, cap* [NL, fr. L *nummulus* (dim. of *nummus* coin) + NL *-ites* -ite] : the type genus of the family Nummulitidae

**nummulitic limestone** *n* : the most widely distributed and distinctive formation of the Eocene in Europe, Asia, and northern Africa attaining a thickness of thousands of feet and being composed chiefly of the remains of foraminifers (esp. of the genus *Nummulites*)

**num·mu·lit·i·dae** \,nəmyə'lid·ə,dē\ *n pl, cap* [NL, fr. *Nummulites*, type genus + *-idae*] : a family of foraminifers that are mostly extinct, have a calcareous symmetrical usu. lenticular or discoidal shell composed of numerous chambers spirally or concentrically arranged, and form whole strata in some Eocene and Oligocene deposits of eastern and southern Asia and the Mediterranean region from their shelly remains

**num·mu·li·toid** \;==;lī,tȯid\ *adj* [NL *Nummulites* + E *-oid*] : resembling or related to the genus *Nummulites*

**num·mu·loi·dal** \;==;lȯid°l\ *adj* [*nummulite* + *-oidal*] : shaped like a nummulite

**num·nah** \'nəmnə\ *n* -s [Hindi *namdā* — more at NUMDAH] : a felt or sheepskin pad placed between a horse's back and the saddle to prevent chafing ⟨a soft . . . ~ under the saddle has been known to cure some buckjumpers —W.A.Kerr⟩

**nu movable** *n* [*nu* fr. Gk *ny*] : a nu inserted in ancient and modern Greek at the end of vowel-final words of certain classes when followed by a vowel-initial word or by a pause or inserted in poetry even before an immediately following word with a single initial consonant to provide two consonants to make a preceding short vowel long in position — compare MOVABLE 5

**num·skull** *or* **numb·skull** \'nəm,skəl\ *n* [¹*numb* + *skull*] **1 :** a dull or stupid person : BONEHEAD, DUNCE ⟨the moment he sits down at the piano only a ~ wouldn't know he was a genius —Robert Rice⟩ **2 :** a thick or muddled head ⟨the wooden sound of ~s being soundly hit —Edith Sitwell⟩ — **num·skulled** \-ld\ *adj*

¹**nun** \'nən\ *n* -s *except sense 2c(1)* [ME, fr. OE *nunne*, fr. LL *nonna* nun, child's nurse; of baby-talk origin like Gk *nanna*, *nenna* female relative, aunt, W *nain* grandmother, Alb *nanë* mother, child's nurse, Russ *nyanya* child's attendant, Skt *nanā* mother, little mother] **1 a** *obs* : a priestess of a pagan deity ⟨prohibited all but the emperor and vestal ~s to be buried within the city —John Houghton⟩ **b :** a woman belonging to a religious order ⟨in primitive Buddhism there were four ecclesiastical orders: monks, ~s, devout laymen, and devout laywomen —*Religions in Japan*⟩; *esp* : a woman living in a convent under vows of poverty, chastity, and obedience ⟨a convent of ~s vowed to contemplation who . . . never went outside the convent walls —L.P.Smith⟩ **2 a** *dial Eng* : BLUE TIT **b** *chiefly Brit* : SMEW **c (1)** *usu cap* : a German breed of domestic pigeons **(2) :** a bird of this breed that is white with a colored head, tail, and wing tips and has a semicircular crest of white feathers curving forward from the back of the head **d :** a weaverbird of the genus *Lonchura* **3 :** NUN MOTH **4** [by shortening] : NUN BUOY

²**nun** \"\ *vt* **nunned; nunned; nunning; nuns :** to confine in or as if in a nunnery

³**nun** \'nün, 'nùn\ *n* -s [Heb *nūn*] **1 :** the 14th letter of the Hebrew alphabet — symbol ג; see ALPHABET table **2 :** the letter of the Phoenician alphabet or of any of various other Semitic alphabets corresponding to the Hebrew nun

**nun·a·tak** \'nənə,tak\ *n* -s [Esk] : a hill or mountain completely surrounded by glacial ice

**nun bird** *n* : any of several dark-colored So. American puffbirds of the genus *Monasa* having white around the face and throat

**nun buoy** *n* : a red metal buoy made of two cones joined at the base and usu. marking the starboard side of a channel approached from the sea — see BUOY illustration

**nun·cheon** *also* **nun·chion** \'nùnshən, 'nən-, -nch-\ *or* **nunch** \'nùnsh, 'nən-, -nch\ *n, pl* **nuncheons** *also* **nunchions** *or* **nunches** [*nuncheon, nunchion* fr. ME *nonechench, noneschench*, lit., noon drink, fr. *none* noon + *schench* drink, cup, fr. OE *scenc*; akin to OE *scencan* to pour out drink, give to drink, OHG *skenken* to pour out, ON *skakkr* crooked, askew; *nunch* short for *nuncheon, nunchion* — more at NOON, SHANK] *dial chiefly Eng* : a light midmorning or midafternoon snack consisting typically of bread, cheese, and beer

**nun·ci·ate** \'nən(t)sēət\ *n* -s [L *nuncius, nuntius* messenger, message + E *-ate*] *archaic* : one that proclaims : NUNCIO

**nun·ci·a·ture** \'nən(t)sēə,chù(ə)r\ *n* -s [It *nunciatura, nunziatura*, fr. *nunciato, nunziato* (past part. of *nunciare, nunziare* to announce, proclaim) (fr. L *nunciatus, nuntiatus*, past part. of *nunciare, nuntiare* to announce, relate, inform, fr. *nuncius, nuntius* messenger, message) + *-ura* -ure (fr. L)] **1 :** the office or period of office of a papal nuncio **2 :** an official delegation from the pope to a foreign power ⟨negotiations . . . for establishing an apostolic ~ in Washington and an American embassy accredited to the Vatican —*N.Y.Times*⟩

**nun·cio** \'nən(t)sē,ō, 'nùn|, |shē,ō, |chē,ō\ *n* -s [It *nuncio, nunzio*, fr. L *nuncius, nuntius* messenger, message] **1 a :** a top-ranking diplomatic envoy of the pope accredited to a civil government — distinguished from *legate a latere*; compare APOSTOLIC DELEGATE, INTERNUNCIO **b** *obs* : MESSENGER ⟨she will attend it better in thy youth, than in a ~'s of more grave aspect —Shak.⟩ **2 :** a member of the former Polish diet

**nun·cle** \'nəŋkəl\ *n* -s [alter. (resulting fr. incorrect division of *an uncle*) of *uncle*] *chiefly dial* : UNCLE

**nunc pro tunc** \,nùŋk,prō'tùŋk\ [NL] : now for then — used of a legal entry, judgment, or decree made currently to have effect as of an earlier date when it ought to have been made, done, or recorded

**nun·cu·pate** \'nəŋkyə,pāt\ *vt* -ED/-ING/-S [L *nuncupatus*, past part. of *nuncupare* to name, declare, dedicate, contr. of *nomen capere*, fr. *nomen* name + *capere* to take — more at NAME, HEAVE] **1** *obs* **a :** to inscribe to by way of compliment : DEDICATE ⟨*nuncupating* my litany to your ladyship —John Bastwick⟩ **b :** to utter solemnly : PRONOUNCE ⟨they do here . . . ~ this deliberate vow —Edmund Burke⟩ **2 :** to declare (a will) publicly : PROCLAIM ⟨how doth that will appear . . . in whose presence did he ~ it —Isaac Barrow⟩

**nun·cu·pa·tion** \,==ˈpāshən\ *n* -s [L *nuncupation-, nuncupatio*, fr. *nuncupatus* (past part. of *nuncupare* to name, declare) + *-ion-, -io* -ion] : an oral will ⟨the dying seaman made a ~ in favor of his mother⟩

**nun·cu·pa·tive** \'==,pād·iv, (')nəŋ¦kyüpəd·iv, (')nən¦-\ *adj* [ML *nuncupativus*, fr. LL, so-called, fr. L *nuncupatus* (past part. of *nuncupare* to name, declare) + *-ivus* -ive] **1 :** stated verbally : ORAL — used chiefly of a will **2** *archaic* : DESIGNATIVE ⟨participles substantive or ~ —T.F.Middleton⟩ — **nun·cu·pa·tive·ly** \-d·ə̇vlē\ *adv*

**nuncupative will** *n* [trans. of ML *testamentum nuncupativum*] **1** *Roman law* : a will consisting orig. in the simple oral declaration of the testator's testamentary dispositions in the presence of seven witnesses and later in such a declaration made before a magistrate **2 a :** a will primarily evidenced by the testator's oral declaration to a witness of his testamentary dispositions as distinguished from one primarily evidenced by a written disposition **b** *English law* : an oral will made by a person in extremis

**nuncupatory** *adj* [prob. fr. (assumed) NL *nuncupatorius*, fr. ML, naming, fr. L *nuncupatus* (past part. of *nuncupare* to name, declare) + *-orius, -ory*] **1** *obs* : ORAL **2** *obs* : DEDICATORY

**nun·di·nal** \'nəndən°l\ *adj* [L *nundinalis*, fr. *nundinae* nundine + *-alis* -al] : of or relating to a nundine

**nundinal letter** *n* : one of the first eight letters of the alphabet used by the ancient Romans in the Sabine calendar after adoption of the seven-day week, the first seven letters being repeated consecutively in one column to designate days of the week and all eight in a parallel column to mark the recurrence of market days under an older eight-day cycle

**nun·di·na·tion** \,nəndə'nāshən\ *n* -s [F, fr. L *nundination-, nundinatio*, fr. *nundinatus* (past part. of *nundinari* to trade, market, fr. *nundinae* nundine) + *-ion-, -io* -ion] *archaic* : an act or instance of bartering : SALE ⟨the ~ of indulgences —Isaac Taylor⟩

**nun·dine** \'nən,dīn, -,dən\ *n* -s [L *nundinae*, pl., market time, lit., nine days, fr. *nundinus* of nine days, alter. of *novem dies* nine days, fr. *novem* nine + *dies* day; fr. its being held every ninth day of the Roman calendar — more at NINE, DEITY] : a market day held every ninth day according to ancient Roman reckoning

**nung** \'nùŋ\ *n, pl* **nung** *or* **nungs** *usu cap* **1 :** a Thai-speaking group of peoples known by a variety of names with slight phonetic variations and mainly found in Kwangsi province of China but also in northern Vietnam — compare GIAI **2 a :** a Tibeto-Burman people related to the Chingpaw in north Burma but having a more archaic language **b :** a member of such people

**nun·hood** \'nən,hùd\ *n* -s [¹*nun* + *-hood*] : the status or calling of a nun

**nun·let** \'nənlət\ *n* -s [¹*nun* + *-let*] : any of several small So. American puffbirds of the genus *Nonnula*

**nunlike** \'=,=\ *adj* : resembling or characteristic of a nun or her habit ⟨~ serenity⟩ ⟨~ coif⟩

**nun moth** *n* : a European tussock moth (*Lymantria monacha*) that often damages coniferous forest trees

**nun·na·ri** \'nənərē\ *or* **nunnari root** *n* -s [*nunnari* prob. native name in India] : INDIAN SARSAPARILLA

**nun·na·tion** \,nə'nāshən\ *n* -s [NL *nunnation-, nunnatio*, fr. Ar *nūn*, letter n of the Arabic alphabet + L *-ation-, -atio* -ation] : the addition of a final *n* in declension of nouns (as in Arabic)

**nunned** *past of* NUN

**nun·nery** \'nən(ə)rē, -ri\ *n* -ES [ME *nunnerie*, fr. ¹*nun* + *-erie* -ery] **1 :** an establishment housing a community of nuns : CONVENT **2 :** an order of nuns : SISTERHOOD

**nun·ni** \'nənē\ *n, pl* **nunni** *or* **nunnis** [Sechuana *nōné*] : BLESBOK

**nunning** *pres part of* NUN

**nun·nish** \'nənish\ *adj* : of, relating to, or characteristic of a nun

**nun·ny·watch** \'nən-\ *var of* NINNYWATCH

**nun of the visitation** *usu cap N & V, Roman Catholicism* : a member of a religious order founded by St. Jane Frances de Chantal under the direction of St. Francis de Sales in 1610 at Annecy, Savoy, and now chiefly devoted to teaching

**nuns** *pl of* NUN, *pres 3d sing of* NUN

**nun·ship** \'nən,ship\ *n* [¹*nun* + *-ship*] : NUNHOOD

**nun's veiling** *n* : a fine sheer clothing fabric in plain weave usu. made of worsted, silk, or cotton

**nun·ti·us** \'nənshēəs\ *n, pl* **nun·tii** \-ē,ī\ [L — more at NUNCIO] : NUNCIO 1a

**nu·pe** \'nüpā\ *n, pl* **nupe** *or* **nupes** *usu cap* **1 a :** a Negro people of west central Nigeria **b :** a member of such people **2 :** a Kwa language of the Nupe people

**Nu·per·caine** \'n(y)üpə(r),kān\ *trademark* — used for dibucaine

**nu·phar** \'n(y)üfə(r)\ *n, cap* [NL, fr. Ar *nūfar*, short for *naynūfar* — more at NENUPHAR] : a genus of water lilies (family Nymphaeaceae) having flowers with showy usu. yellow sepals and minute petals that resemble stamens or scales, leaves with a deep sinus, and a cylindrical creeping rootstock — see SPATTERDOCK

**nupson** *n* [*nup* of unknown origin + *son*] *obs* : FOOL, SIMPLETON

¹**nup·tial** \'nəpshəl, -pchəl, *chiefly in substandard speech* |əwəl\ *adj* [L *nuptialis*, fr. *nuptiae* wedding (fr. *nuptus*, past part. of *nubere* to marry a man) + *-alis* -al; akin to Gk *nymphē* bride, nymph, OSlav *smibiti* to couple] **1 :** of or relating to marriage or the marriage ceremony ⟨the ~ day⟩ ⟨a ~ hymn⟩ **2 a :** capable of breeding ⟨several large ~ males⟩ **b :** characteristic of the breeding season ⟨~ coloration⟩ **c :** concerned with or preliminary to copulation ⟨~ behavior⟩

²**nuptial** \"\ *n* -s : MARRIAGE, WEDDING ⟨must employ you in some business against our ~ —Shak.⟩ — usu. used in pl. ⟨preparations . . . for the approaching ~s —W.H.Prescott⟩

**nuptial father** *n, archaic* : one who represents the bride's father at a wedding

**nuptial flight** *n* : a flight of sexually mature social insects (as bees) in which mating takes place and which is usu. a prelude to the forming of a new colony; *esp* : the mass flight and mating of winged sexual forms of ants after leaving the parent nest

**nup·ti·al·i·ty** \,nəpshē'aləd·ē, ,nəp'shal-\ *n* -ES [F *nuptialité*, fr. *nuptial* of marriage (fr. L *nuptialis*) + *-ité* -ity] : the marriage rate ⟨~ . . . being very high in the general rural population —B.W.Gussman⟩

**nuptial plumage** *also* **nuptial dress** *n* : the specialized plumage assumed by the males of many birds while the gonads are enlarging prior to the start of the annual breeding period and characterized by greater brilliance of color and form than that of the nonbreeding males — called also *breeding plumage*; compare ECLIPSE PLUMAGE

**nuque** \'n(y)ük\ *n* -s [MF, fr. ML *nucha* — more at NUCHA] : the back of the neck

**nu·ra·ghe** \nü'rägā\ *n, pl* **nura·ghi** \-gē\ *or* **nuraghes** [It (Sardinian dial.), perh. fr. *Nura, Nurra*, locality in Nuoro province, central Sardinia, Italy] : a large stone structure of Sardinia built in the shape of a truncated cone and held to date from the bronze age ⟨the *nuraghi* . . . are easily the equal of the sphinx in mystery and grandeur —P.E.Deutschman⟩ — **nuraghic** *adj*

**nur·em·berg** \'n(y)ùrəm,bərg\ *or* **nürn·berg** *or* **nurn·berg** *or* **nuern·berg** \'nüern,berk\ *adj, usu cap* [fr. *Nuremberg*, city in southern Germany] : of or from the city of Nuremberg, Germany : of the kind or style prevalent in Nuremberg

**nuremberg violet** *n, often cap N* : MANGANESE VIOLET

¹**nurse** \'nərs, 'nəs, 'nəis\ *n* -s *often attrib* [ME *nurse, norse, nurice*, fr. OF *norrice, nurice*, fr. LL *nutricia*, fr. L, fem. of *nutricius, nutritius* nourishing — more at NUTRITIOUS] **1 a :** a woman who suckles and takes care of an infant that is not her own : WET NURSE **b :** a woman who takes care of a young child : DRY NURSE **2 a :** a person who looks after or gives advice to another **b :** something that serves as a fostering agency or influence ⟨time is a ~ and breeder of all good —Shak.⟩ **3 a :** a person skilled in caring for and waiting on the infirm, the injured, or the sick; *specif* : one esp. trained to carry out such duties under the supervision of a physician **b :** a person esp. trained to assist a physician or dentist (as in an operating room) **4 :** NURSE TREE **5 a :** a worker form of a social insect (as an ant or bee) that cares for the young **b :** an asexual zooid that produces and carries the blastozooids in some ascidians (as of the genus *Doliolum*) **c :** a female mammal used to suckle the young of another female usu. of her own kind — usu. used with following noun ⟨~ doe⟩ ⟨~ cow⟩ **6 :** the act of nursing the balls in billiards — **to nurse** *adv* **1** *or* **at nurse :** under the care of a nurse ⟨would send for the baby, though I entreated him . . . to put it out *to nurse* —Charlotte Brontë⟩ **2 :** under the control of trustees ⟨put his estate *to nurse* —Tobias Smollett⟩

²**nurse** \"\ *vb* -ED/-ING/-S [alter. (influenced by ¹*nurse*) of ME *nurshen* to nourish, contr. of *nurishen* — more at NOURISH] *vt* **1 a :** to nourish at the breast : SUCKLE ⟨four women were unable to ~ their infants —J.P.Greenhill⟩ ⟨keep the kittens alive till the mother can ~ them —Eleanor B. Simmons⟩ **b :** to take nourishment from the breast of : suck milk from ⟨possible for a baby to contract tuberculosis from *nursing* its mother —L.H.Brevard⟩ ⟨the foal should not be permitted to ~ the mare when she is hot and sweating —James Law & M.S. Shahan⟩ **2 :** to bring up : REAR, EDUCATE ⟨for we were *nursed* upon the selfsame hill —John Milton⟩ **3 a :** to promote the growth, development, or progress of ⟨anything to ~ the arts and bring them into the homes of the . . . people —M.R. Cohen⟩ ⟨the policy of attracting original work and *nursing* authors of promise —*Times Lit. Supp.*⟩ **b :** to cultivate (a plant) with care ⟨*nursed* the long rows of vines that were their livelihood —Margaret Evans⟩ **c :** to manage (as a business) with care or economy ⟨on his hundreds of thousands of dollars — *nursed* into millions — a substantial Boston family had been built —J.A.Michener⟩ **d :** to take charge of and watch over in the manner of a nurse ⟨to ensure that performers arrive on time he ~s them from show to show —Don Everitt⟩ ⟨trout are hatched and *nursed* to planting age —*Amer. Guide Series: Wash.*⟩ **e :** to cause to develop ⟨fancied it to be their interest . . . to ~ the embers of the old enmity into a flame —Edward Edwards⟩ **4 a :** to care for and wait on (as an injured or infirm person) : ATTEND ⟨great-grandfather was bedridden . . . and my mother *nursed* him —Ellen Glasgow⟩ **b :** to attempt a cure of (as an ailment) by care and treatment ⟨would stay in her room and ~ a sick headache —Louis Auchincloss⟩ ⟨had been pitched against a bridge . . . and was *nursing* a painfully bruised arm —Llewellyn Howland⟩ **5 :** to hold in one's heart or mind : keep in memory or consideration ⟨had spent the night watches in *nursing* his wrath —John Buchan⟩ ⟨did not ~ the idea that her life was at an end —Arnold Bennett⟩ ⟨*nursed* a plan to invade the South and forcibly liberate the slaves —B.B.Stutler⟩ **6 :** to hold or grasp carefully or firmly ⟨~ my fat briefcase on my knees and go through my papers —Christopher Morley⟩ ⟨took her hands again and *nursed* them against my cheek —Mary Austin⟩ **7 a :** to use, handle, or drive carefully so as to conserve energy or avoid injury ⟨trying to ~ a gigantic crippled plane back over many hundreds of miles of open ocean —J.A.Michener⟩ **b :** to use with forethought and care so as to conserve or stretch out ⟨~s his time so that he may keep his brain in rested condition for decisions —*Atlantic*⟩ **c :** to consume slowly so as to conserve or stretch out ⟨like to ~ a drink . . . and watch the people around us —Dwight Taylor⟩ ⟨~s a cup of coffee and a doughnut until it is morning —Norman Mailer⟩ **8** *chiefly Brit* : to attract or sustain the favorable attention of usu. by personal contacts and the dispensing of favors in order to sustain electoral support ⟨is busy *nursing* his constituency and calculating how he can be reelected —W.E.Binkley⟩ **9 :** to keep (billiard balls) close together and in good position for a series of caroms ~ *vi* **1 a :** to give suck **b :** to feed at the breast : SUCK **2 :** to act or serve as a nurse

**syn** CULTIVATE, NURTURE, FOSTER, CHERISH: NURSE implies careful sustaining of an infant, person, thing, or notion. CULTIVATE is likely to differ from NURSE in suggesting methods of sustaining and protecting the useful in the plant world; it implies sedulous and steady care but lacks the human warmth suggested in many of the other words in this group ⟨spinning theories of fiction is my favorite amusement . . . a good habit to *cultivate* —Ellen Glasgow⟩ ⟨whatever physical gifts she may have are carefully *cultivated* —Lafcadio Hearn⟩ ⟨the morbid curiosity *cultivated* in Browning by his father's tasks and inclinations —Ruth R. Chapman⟩ NURTURE places stress on giving that which sustains and affording a safe environment pointing toward a certain development or course ⟨men who have not been *nurtured* in dissecting rooms and other laboratories —C.S.Peirce⟩ ⟨had been *nurtured* in sentiments opposed to the institution of human servitude —R.P.Warren⟩ FOSTER may suggest the relationship of foster parent to child in implying caring for, encouraging, sustaining, and maintaining growth ⟨such a sentiment is *fostered* by all those agencies of the mind and spirit which may serve to gather up the traditions of the people —Felix Frankfurter⟩ ⟨the pope . . . used his powers to *foster* abuses that brought wealth to the Roman court —G.M.Trevelyan⟩ ⟨we must *foster* on every campus the principle of individualism as contrasted with docile receptivity —C.M. Fuess⟩ CHERISH implies fondness or love for something with incidental nurturing of it ⟨a cause which is embraced and *cherished* by so vast a portion of American society —Kenneth Roberts⟩

³**nurse** \"\ *n* -s [earlier *nuse*, fr. ME *nusse*] : NURSE SHARK

**nurse cell** *n* : a cell of a type present in the ovary of many animals that supplies nourishment to the developing egg cell and is commonly believed to be a rudimentary egg cell

**nurse-child** \'=,=\ *n* : a child under the care or supervision of a nurse

**nurse crop** *n* : a crop planted with another presumably to shelter it from competition with weeds or other undesirable plants — compare COMPANION CROP, NURSE GRASS

**nursed** *past of* NURSE

**nurse-father** *n* [prob. trans. of MF *pere nourricier*] *obs* : a foster father

**nurse frog** *n* : OBSTETRICAL TOAD

**nurse-garden** *n, obs* : NURSERY 4

**nurse graft** *n* : a plant graft in which the stock is intended to remain united with the scion only temporarily usu. until the latter establishes roots of its own

**nurse grass** *n* : a quick-growing grass planted to shade and protect other grass and to help suppress weeds — compare NURSE CROP

**nursehound** \'=,=\ *n* [³*nurse* + *hound*] : a European dogfish (*Scyliorhinus canicula*)

**nursekeeper** \'=,==\ *n, archaic* : a nurse for the sick

**nurseling** *var of* NURSLING

¹**nursemaid** \'=,=\ *n* [¹*nurse* + *maid*] **1 :** one who is regularly employed to look after children **2 :** one who guards or takes care ⟨became to his people a combination oracle and ~ —M.R. Werner⟩ ⟨was the ~ to . . . polo ponies —James Jones⟩

²**nursemaid** \"\ *vt* -ED/-ING/-S : to watch over or take care of in a solicitous manner ⟨grateful to a conductor who ~s six soloists —Virgil Thomson⟩ ⟨that engine . . . was greased and cleaned and ~*ed* —C.S.Forester⟩ ⟨in the midst of the school crossing . . . ~*ing* moppets —R.M.Stern⟩

**nurs·er** \'nərsər\ *n* -s **1 :** one that nurses ⟨known as a ~ of nickels⟩ **2 :** NURSING BOTTLE

**nur·sery** \'nərs(ə)rē, 'nə̄s-, 'nəis-, -ri\ *n* -ES *often attrib* [ME *norserie*, fr. *norse* nurse + *-erie* -ery] **1** *obs* : attentive care ⟨thought to set my rest on her kind ~ —Shak.⟩ : FOSTERAGE **2 :** a place designed for the care or training of children: **a :** a child's bedroom **b :** a room or apartment in a house set aside for the use of children **c :** a room or place in a public building (as a church) where children are temporarily cared for in their parents' absence by trained attendants **d :** DAY NURSERY **e :** NURSERY SCHOOL **3 a :** something that fosters, develops, or promotes ⟨the inland seas became the first *nurseries* of seamanship and commerce —W.G.East⟩ ⟨an equal claim to be noticed as a ~ of the arts —*Times Lit. Supp.*⟩ **b :** a place in which persons are trained or educated ⟨the chancery became a ~ of clever and unscrupulous churchmen —E.A.Freeman⟩ ⟨France at this time . . . was a ~ for good surgeons —Harvey Graham⟩ **4 :** an area where trees, shrubs, or plants are grown for transplanting, for use as stocks for budding and grafting, or for sale **5 :** a place where young animals are cared for: as **a :** a pond, trough, or box in which young fish are kept until the yolk sac is absorbed **b :** BROODER 2a **6 :** a handicap race for 2-year-olds

**nurserymaid** \'=(=),=\ *n* : NURSEMAID

**nur·sery·man** \'=(=)mən\ *n, pl* **nurserymen :** one whose occupation is the scientific cultivation of trees, shrubs, and plants

**nursery rhyme** *n* : a tale in rhymed verse for children

**nursery school** *n* : a school for children usu. under five years of age — compare KINDERGARTEN

**nursery stock** n : young plants grown in a nursery
**nurses** pl of NURSE, pres 3d sing of NURSE
**nurse's aide** n : a worker who assists trained nurses in a hospital by performing nonspecialized services (as making beds or giving baths)
**nurse shark** n [³nurse] 1 : GREENLAND SHARK 2 : any of various sharks of a widely distributed family (Orectolobidae); esp : GATA 3 : a large pale Australian sand shark (Carcharias arenarius)
**nurse-tender** \'=,==\ n, chiefly Irish : a nurse who cares for the sick
**nurse tree** n : a tree that protects or fosters the growth of other young trees
**nursing** n -s [fr. gerund of ²nurse] 1 : the profession of a nurse ⟨modern schools of ~⟩ 2 : the varied activities that constitute the duties of a nurse ⟨proper ~ is no easy job⟩
**nursing anemia** or **nursing sickness** n : an abnormality of ranch-reared nursing mink that is marked by extreme emaciation, loss of appetite, and death and is apparently due to dietary deficiencies superimposed on the strain of milk production
**nursing bottle** n : a bottle to which a rubber nipple is attached and which is used in supplying food to infants — called also feeding bottle
**nursing chair** n : an armless chair with a low seat
**nursing home** n 1 chiefly Brit : a private hospital 2 : a private home or other place where maintenance and personal or nursing care are provided for three or more persons who are unable to care for themselves properly
**nursing sister** n, Brit : GRADUATE NURSE
**nur·sle** \'nərsəl\ vt -ED/-ING/-S [prob. alter. (influenced by ²nurse) of ²nuzzle] : to bring up : NURTURE ⟨nursled . . . under a regime of religious liberty —S.R.Gardiner⟩
**nurs·ling** also **nurse·ling** \'nərsliŋ, 'nəs-, 'nəis-, -lēŋ\ n -s [¹nurse + -ling] 1 : one that is solicitously cared for and fostered ⟨was the child and ~ of that Burgundian court —Sarah Austin⟩ 2 : a nursing child or other young nursing mammal; esp : one that is suckled by another than its mother
**nur·tur·al** \'nərchərəl\ adj : of, relating to, or resulting from nurture

nursing bottle

**¹nur·ture** \'nərchər, 'nəchə(r, 'nəichə(r\ n -s [ME nurture, norture, fr. MF norriture, norreture, fr. LL nutritura act of nursing or suckling, fr. L nutritus (past part. of nutrire to suckle, nourish) + -ura -ure — more at NOURISH] 1 a : the breeding, education, or training that one receives or possesses : UPBRINGING ⟨the poverty she lived in was utterly unbefitting her gentle ~ —George Meredith⟩ b obs : moral training 2 : something that nourishes : FOOD ⟨fed him well and nourished himself and took ~ for the road —R.D.Blackmore⟩ 3 : the process of bringing up : TUTELAGE ⟨the best moral atmosphere for the ~ of creative scientists —Weston La Barre⟩ 4 : the sum of the influences modifying the expression of the genetic potentialities of an organism — compare NATURE
**²nurture** \"\ vt **nurtured; nurtured; nurturing** \-ch(ə)riŋ\ **nurtures** [ME nurturen, norturen, fr. nurture, norture, n.] 1 : to supply with food, nourishment, and protection ⟨was not nurtured by the best of mothers—O.W.Holmes †1894⟩ 2 a : to train by or as if by instruction : EDUCATE ⟨will ask for the financial support of the alumni whom they have nurtured —C.M.Fuess⟩ b obs : to give moral training to : DISCIPLINE 3 : to further the development of : promote the growth of : FOSTER ⟨~ your mind with great thoughts —Benjamin Disraeli⟩ **syn** see NURSE
**nur·ture·less** \-chə(r)ləs\ adj : lacking nurture or nourishment
**nur·tur·er** \-ch(ə)rə(r)\ n -s : one that nurtures
**nus** pl of NU
**nu·sai·ri** \nü'sīrē\ n -s usu cap [Ar Nuṣayrīyah Nusairis] : a member of a syncretistic religious sect of northern Syria that lives in comparative isolation and mingles religious beliefs from Islamic, Christian, and native sources — called also Ansarie
**¹nut** \'nət, usu -əd·+V\ n -s [ME nute, note, fr. OE hnutu; akin to OHG nuz, hnuz nut, ON hnot, MIr cnū, L nuc-, nux] 1 a (1) : a hard-shelled dry fruit or seed having a more or less distinct separable rind or shell and interior kernel or meat — used to include various forms (as peanuts and Brazil nuts) not botanically true nuts (2) : the kernel of a nut b : a dry indehiscent one-seeded fruit (as an acorn, hazelnut, or chestnut) with a woody pericarp developing from an inferior syncarpous ovary — see FRUIT illustration 2 : something resembling a nut in the difficulty it represents: as a : a problem to be solved — often used with to crack ⟨communications were a tough ~ —John Dos Passos⟩ ⟨many hard ~s to crack in developing satisfactory processes —J.P.Baxter b. 1893⟩ b : an undertaking to be shouldered — usu. used with to crack ⟨climbed the lower slopes but the summit proved too hard a ~ to crack⟩ c : a person to be conciliated ⟨tried to convince him but he was a tough old ~⟩ 3 : a perforated block that is usu. a small piece of metal of square or hexagonal section, that has an internal screw thread, and that is used on a bolt or screw for tightening or holding something or for transmitting motion 4 : a projection on the shank of an anchor to secure the stock in place 5 a : the ridge in a stringed musical instrument over which the strings pass on the upper end of the fingerboard nearest the head and pegbox b : the movable piece at the lower end of a bow (as a violin bow) by which the hairs may be tightened 6 **nuts** pl a slang : a source of joy and pleasure : DELIGHT — usu. used with the ⟨they thought this one was the ~s when they built it —Calder Willingham⟩ ⟨it's the ~s — you can splash around all you want to —Better Homes & Gardens⟩ b : NONSENSE — often used interjectionally to express disapproval or annoyance; sometimes considered vulgar ⟨~s to you and your friends⟩ c : TESTES — usu. considered vulgar 7 slang : a person's head ⟨you get this in your ~ —Richard Llewellyn⟩ ⟨should think there was something wrong in his ~ —H.J.Laski⟩ 8 a slang Austral : LARRIKIN b (1) : one whose thinking or conduct is eccentric ⟨his contemporaries sometimes considered him just a prodigiously talented ~ —Time⟩ (2) : one who is or seems to be mentally unbalanced ⟨a ~ got into the . . . reception and started screaming obscenities —Toni Howard⟩ (3) : one who is overenthusiastic about a particular matter (as a hobby) ⟨some golf ~ who had ranged the world collecting out-of-the-way golf courses —E.J.Kahn⟩ c slang Brit : a smartly or sprucely dressed person 9 : a rounded cake or biscuit (as a doughnut or spice nut) 10 : the complete expense involved — usu. used of the costs of a stage or television production 11 : EN ⟨indent one ~⟩ — **for nuts** adv, slang chiefly Brit : at all ⟨may be good at lessons, but she can't sew for nuts —Flora Thompson⟩ ⟨they can't write for nuts either —S.M.Lipset⟩ — **off one's nut** : CRAZY ⟨we're all rude to each other and if we weren't we'd go off our nuts —H.E.Bates⟩

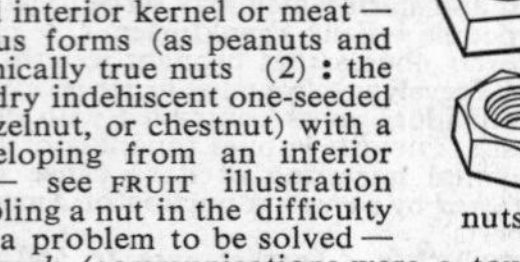
nuts 3

**²nut** \"\ adj [ME nute, note, fr. OE hnut-, fr. hnutu nut, n.] 1 : of, relating to, or characteristic of a nut : having nuts ⟨my little ~ tree⟩ 2 : serving as a receptacle for nuts ⟨~ dish⟩
**³nut** \"\ vi **nutted; nutted; nutting; nuts** [¹nut] : to gather or seek nuts — usu. used in the form nutting
**nu·tant** \'n(y)üt°nt\ adj [L nutant-, nutans, pres. part. of nutare to nod, sway] : DROOPING, NODDING ⟨the equestrian statue . . . rode under the ~ trees —Malcolm Lowry⟩
**nu·tate** \'n(y)ü,tāt\ vi -ED/-ING/-S [L nutatus, past part. of nutare to nod, sway] : to exhibit nutation
**nu·ta·tion** \n(y)ü'tāshən\ n -s [L nutation-, nutatio, fr. nutatus (past part. of nutare to nod, sway, rock, freq. of nuere to nod) + -ion-, -io -ion — more at NUMEN] 1 : the act of nodding; esp : an involuntary nodding of the head 2 : a small inequality in the motion of precession : a libratory motion of the earth's axis like the nodding of a top due to joint action of the sun and moon by which its inclination to the plane of the ecliptic varies with a period of about 19 years and with a range of only a few seconds of arc so that the celestial poles describe wavy rather than circular parallels round the poles of the ecliptic 3 : a more or less rhythmical change in the position of growing plant organs due to variation in growth rates on different sides of the growing apex : an autonomic movement — compare CIRCUMNUTATION 4 : the vibratory displacement of the axis of a precessing top or gyroscope from the cone-shaped figure traced by the axis during precession
**nu·ta·tion·al** \-shən°l, -shnəl\ adj : of or relating to nutation
**nut bone** n : a large transversely extended sesamoid bone behind the joint between the coronary bone and coffin bone in the foot of a horse
**nutbreaker** \'=,==\ n [trans. of G nussbrecher] : NUTCRACKER 2
**nut-brown** \'=¦=\ adj : brown as a nut
**nut brown** n : a color of brown nuts (as hazel, chestnut, or walnut)
**nut·burg·er** \'nət,bərgər\ n [¹nut + -burger] : a patty containing ground nuts
**nutcake** \'=,=\ n [¹nut + cake] 1 NewEng : DOUGHNUT 2 : a cake containing nuts
**nut coal** n [by shortening] 1 : CHESTNUT COAL 2 : bituminous coal of medium size having varying top and bottom limits in different localities and ranging between top sizes of 1½ to 2 inches and bottom sizes of ¾ to 1½ inches
**¹nutcracker** \'=,==\ n [¹nut + cracker] 1 a : an implement for cracking nuts b : something resembling a nutcracker ⟨squeezed in the ~ of taxes and inflation —Jour. of Accountancy⟩ 2 a [trans. of G nussbrecher] : a European bird (Nucifraga caryocatactes) of the family Corvidae that is dark brown spotted with white b : CLARK NUTCRACKER

nutcracker 1a

**²nutcracker** \"\ adj : suggestive of or resembling the jaws of a nutcracker esp. from lack of teeth ⟨a thin young man with a ~ nose and jaw —David Garnett⟩
**nutfall** \'=,=\ n : the normal or precocious dropping of nuts from a tree
**nutgall** \'=,=\ n : a nutlike gall; esp : a gall produced on oak
**nut grass** n 1 : any of several aggressively weedy sedges of the genus Cyperus; esp : a perennial sedge (C. rotundus) of wide distribution having slender rootstocks that bear small edible nutlike tubers 2 : any of several American sedges of the genus Scleria
**nut·hatch** \'nət,hach\ n [alter. (influenced by ¹hatch) of ME nuthak, alter. (influenced by hak hack) of notehache, fr. note nut + hache ax, hatchet (fr. OF, battle-ax); fr. its way of breaking nuts for food — more at NUT, HACK, HASH] : any of various birds of the family Sittidae that are chiefly small with long wings and a short tail, creep over the trunk and branches of trees, and have character and habits intermediate between the titmice and the creepers — see RED-BREASTED NUTHATCH, WHITE-BREASTED NUTHATCH
**nuth·er** \'nəthə(r)\ dial var of NEITHER
**nuthook** n [¹nut + hook] 1 obs : a hook at the end of a pole to pull down boughs for gathering nuts 2 obs Brit : CONSTABLE
**nut·job·ber** \'nət,jäbə(r)\ n [¹nut + jobber (fr. ⁴job + -er)] dial Brit : NUTHATCH
**nut·let** \'nətlət\ n -s [¹nut + -let] 1 : a small nut 2 : a small nutlike fruit (as of many plants of the family Boraginaceae) 3 : the stone of a drupelet
**nutlike** \'=,=\ adj 1 : resembling a nut; often : being or having the characteristics of a nut 2 : suggesting or like that of a nut : NUTTY ⟨a ~ flavor⟩
**nut margarine** n : margarine made principally from coconut and peanut oils churned with soured whole or skimmed milk and salt
**nutmeat** \'=,=\ n [¹nut + meat] : the kernel of a nut
**¹nut·meg** \'nət,meg, -māg\ n -s often attrib [ME notemuge, part trans., part modif. of OF nois muguete, nois muguede nutmeg, alter. of nois muscade, fr. OProv noz muscada, fr. noz nut (fr. L nuc-, nux) + muscada, fem. of muscat musky — more at NUT, MUSCAT] 1 a : a hard aromatic spheroidal seed that is widely used as a spice — see ³MACE b or **nutmeg tree** : a small evergreen tropical tree (Myristica fragrans) native to the Molucca islands but widely cultivated for its spherical yellow drupaceous fruits which yield mace and nutmeg 2 : any of various trees related to or in some respect resembling the nutmeg: as a : any of several trees of the genus Myristica having seeds that resemble but are generally inferior to the true nutmegs b : a Central and So. American banak (Virola koschnii) yielding a timber used for veneer and plywood c : CALIFORNIA NUTMEG d : NUTMEG HICKORY e : a western African tree (Pycnanthus kombo) of the family Myristicaceae with a somewhat aromatic arillode and seed which is of importance primarily as a source of oil 3 : DARK BEAVER
**²nutmeg** \"\ or **nut·meg·ger** \-gə(r)\ n -s cap [nutmeg short for wooden nutmeg; fr. the notion that wooden or imitation nutmegs came from Connecticut and were examples of Yankee inventiveness; nutmegger fr. Nutmeg State, nickname of the state of Connecticut (fr. the phrase wooden nutmeg state) + E -er] : a native or resident of Connecticut — used as a nickname
**nutmeg apple** n : the fruit of the nutmeg tree
**nutmeg butter** n : a soft yellowish or orange fat of nutmeg odor obtained from nutmegs and used chiefly in ointments
**nutmeg family** n : MYRISTICACEAE
**nutmeg flower** n : a European annual herb (Nigella sativa) with small black aromatic seeds sometimes used as a flavoring agent and insect repellent
**nutmeg geranium** n : a cultivated pelargonium (Pelargonium odoratissimum) with round fragrant leaves and small white flowers
**nutmeg hickory** n : a hickory (Carya myristicaeformis) of the southern U. S. and Mexico having a nutmeg-shaped fruit
**nutmeg liver** n : a liver appearing mottled like a nutmeg when cut because of congestion and associated with impaired circulation esp. from heart or lung disease
**nutmeg melon** n : NETTED MELON
**nutmeg oil** n : either an oil or a fat obtained from nutmegs: a : a colorless or pale yellow essential oil of nutmeg odor distilled from nutmegs and used chiefly in flavoring and in medicine as a local stimulant — called also myristica oil b : NUTMEG BUTTER
**nutmeg pigeon** n : any of several pigeons of the genus Ducula (syn. Myristicivora) of the East Indies and Australia that feed on wild nutmegs
**nutmeg shell** n [so called fr. its rough, warty surface] : a marine snail of the genus Cancellaria
**nut of bahera** : a myrobalan that is the fruit of a tall East Indian tree (Terminalia belerica) and that is used in tanning and dyeing and in folk medicine
**nut oil** n [prob. trans. of D noot olie] : an oil obtained from nuts: as a : WALNUT OIL b : TUNG OIL c : PEANUT OIL
**nut palm** n : an Australian cycad (Cycas media) having edible seeds
**nutpecker** \'=,==\ n [¹nut + pecker] : NUTHATCH
**nutpick** \'=,=\ n [¹nut + pick] : a small sharp-pointed table implement for extracting the kernels from nuts
**nut pine** n : a pine with edible seeds: as a : any of several piñons (as Pinus edulis or P. cembroides) b : STONE PINE 2 c : SWISS PINE
**nut plate** n : a nut with an extended flat base so that it may be secured to a surface and made captive
**nu·tria** \'n(y)ütrēə\ n -s [Sp nutria, nutra coypu, otter, modif. of L lutra otter; akin to Gk hydros water snake — more at OTTER] 1 a : COYPU 1 b : the fur of the coypu that is usu. light brown but occas. black, is durable, and is plucked and blended to imitate beaver 2 : an olive gray that is paler than the color rat and redder and darker than stone gray — called also beaverpelt, grège
**nu·tri·cial** \(')n(y)ü¦trishəl\ adj [L nutricius, nutritius nourishing, nursing + E -al — more at NUTRITIOUS] : of or relating to nursing or rearing ⟨~ castration in worker bees⟩
**nu·tri·cism** \'n(y)ü·trə,sizəm\ n -s [prob. fr. (assumed) NL nutricismus, fr. L nutric-, nutrix nurse + -ismus -ism — more at NUTRITIOUS] : symbiosis in which one organism is nourished or protected by the other without apparently being of reciprocal benefit : COMMENSALISM
**nu·tri·culture** \'n(y)ü·trə+,-\ n [nutrient solution + culture] : HYDROPONICS
**¹nu·tri·ent** \'n(y)ü·trēənt\ adj [L nutrient-, nutriens, pres. part. of nutrire to nourish — more at NOURISH] : furnishing nourishment : promoting growth : NUTRITIOUS ⟨feed avidly on water hyacinths, but they do not make good fodder and are not ~ —Thomas Barbour⟩ ⟨magnesium is the ~ element in plant growth —Market Growers Jour.⟩
**²nutrient** \"\ n -s : a nutritious substance or component; esp : a chemical element or inorganic compound (as a nitrate) taken in by a green plant and used in organic synthesis
**nu·tri·fy** \-rə,fī\ vb -ED/-ING/-ES [LL nutrificare, fr. L nutrire to nourish + -ficare -fy] vt, archaic : NOURISH ~ vi, archaic : to supply nourishment
**nu·tri·lite** \'n(y)ü·trə,līt\ n -s [nutrition + -lite (as in metabolite)] : a substance (as a vitamin or growth factor) required in small quantities for normal metabolism and growth and obtained by an organism in its food
**nu·tri·ment** \'n(y)ü·trəmənt\ n -s [L nutrimentum, fr. nutrire to nourish + -mentum -ment] : something that nourishes : something that promotes growth and repairs the natural waste of animal or vegetable life : ALIMENT, FOOD, NOURISHMENT
**nu·tri·men·tal** \¦==¦ment°l\ adj [ME, fr. LL nutrimentalis, fr. L nutrimentum nourishment + -alis -al] : NUTRITIOUS
**nu·tri·tial** \(')n(y)ü¦trishəl\ adj [L nutritius, nutricius nourishing + E -al — more at NUTRITIOUS] : NUTRICIAL
**nu·tri·tion** \n(y)ü'trishən\ n -s [MF, fr. LL nutrition-, nutritio, fr. nutritus (past part. of nutrire to nourish) + -ion-, -io -ion] : the act or process of nourishing or being nourished; specif : the sum of the processes by which an animal or plant takes in and utilizes food substances in animals typically involving ingestion, digestion, absorption, and assimilation
**nu·tri·tion·al** \(')=¦shən°l, -shnəl\ adj : of, relating to, or functioning in nutrition — **nu·tri·tion·al·ly** \-°lē, -əlē, -i\ adv
**nutritional anemia** n : anemia which results from inadequate intake or assimilation of nutrients or other elements essential to the production of red blood cells and hemoglobin (as hypochromic anemia)
**nutritional deficiency** n : an inadequate supply of essential nutrients (as vitamins and minerals) in the diet resulting in malnutrition or disease
**nutritional encephalomalacia** n : CRAZY CHICK DISEASE
**nutritional roup** n : avitaminosis of poultry
**nu·tri·tion·ist** \=¦=sh(ə)nəst\ n -s : a specialist in the study of nutrition
**nu·tri·tious** \(')n(y)ü¦trishəs\ adj [L nutritius, nutricius, fr. nutric-, nutrix nurse + -ius -ious — more at NOURISH] : promoting growth and repairing natural waste : NOURISHING, NUTRITIVE — **nu·tri·tious·ly** adv
**nu·tri·tious·ness** n -ES : the quality or state of being nutritious
**¹nu·tri·tive** \'n(y)ü·trəd·|iv, -ət|\ adj [ME nutritif, fr. MF & LL; MF nutritif, fr. LL nutritivus, fr. L nutritus (past part. of nutrire to nourish) + -ivus -ive — more at NOURISH] 1 : of, relating to, or concerned in nutrition ⟨the ~ functions⟩ 2 : affording nourishment : NUTRITIOUS ⟨~ food⟩ — **nu·tri·tive·ly** \|əvlē, -li\ adv
**²nutritive** \"\ n -s [ME, fr. nutritif nutritive, adj.] : a nutritive substance : a nourishing food
**nu·tri·tive·ness** \|ivnəs\ n -ES : the quality or state of being nutritive
**nutritive plasma** n : TROPHOPLASM
**nutritive polyp** n : GASTROZOOID
**nutritive ratio** n : the ratio of digestible protein to other digestible nutrients in a foodstuff or ration ⟨the nutritive ratio of shelled corn is about 1 to 10⟩
**nu·tri·to·ry** \'n(y)ü·trə,tōrē\ adj [LL nutritorius, fr. L nutritus (past part. of nutrire to nourish) + -orius -ory] : NUTRITIVE
**nu·tri·ture** \'n(y)ü·trə,chü(ə)r, -,chər\ n -s [It nutritura, fr. LL, fr. L nutritus + -ura -ure] : NOURISHMENT
**nut rush** n 1 : a sedge of the genus Scleria having hard bony achenes 2 : NUT GRASS 1
**nuts** \'nəts\ adj [fr. pl. of ¹nut] 1 : eagerly enthusiastic : fervently ardent : KEEN, WILD ⟨everyone seems ~ about it —Lois Long⟩ ⟨she was ~ about the boy next door⟩ 2 : CRAZY, DEMENTED ⟨thought I would go ~ waiting around —Polly Adler⟩ ⟨she thought I was ~ but she liked me —Agnes de Mille⟩
**nutsch filter** \'nüch-\ or **nutsch** n -ES sometimes cap N [G nutsch, nutsche, lit., sucking bottle, fr. nutschen to suck, of imit. origin] : a filter of a simple type adapted to batch operation; esp : such a filter operated by suction
**nut sedge** n : NUT GRASS
**¹nutshell** \'=,=\ n [ME nut schell, fr. ¹nut + schell shell — more at SHELL] 1 : the shell or hard external covering in which the kernel of a nut is enclosed 2 a obs : something of little or no value ⟨don't stake your life against a ~ —Jeremy Collier⟩ b : something of little or small compass, size, amount, or length ⟨a little ~ of people here —Owen Wister⟩ ⟨seven of these ~s of poems —Times Lit. Supp.⟩ — **in a nutshell** adv : in or within a small compass or limit : in a very brief statement : in a few words ⟨explained the situation in a nutshell⟩
**²nutshell** \"\ vt : to state or sum up in a few words ⟨he ~ed the whole plan for them⟩
**nut shell** n : a marine bivalve mollusk of the family Nuculidae or sometimes of the related Nuculanidae — see NUCULA
**nutsy** \'nətsē\ adj -ER/-EST [nuts + -y, adj. suffix] : LUNATIC
**nut·tall blister beetle** \'nəd·,ȯl-\ n, usu cap N [after Thomas Nuttall †1859 Am. botanist and ornithologist born in England] : a metallic green and copper-colored blister beetle (Lytta nuttallii) that feeds on bean and pea plants
**¹nut·tal·lia** \nə'talēə\ [NL, fr. Thomas Nuttall †1859 Am. botanist and ornithologist + NL -ia] syn of MENTZELIA
**²nuttallia** \"\ n, cap [NL, fr. George H. F. Nuttall †1937 Am. biologist + NL -ia] : a genus sometimes treated as a subgenus of Babesia and comprising tick-borne protozoan parasites of mammals — compare BABESIIDAE
**nut·tal·li·a·sis** \,nəd·°l'īəsəs\ or **nut·tal·li·o·sis** \nə,talē'ōsəs\ n, pl **nuttallia·ses** \-ī,sēz\ or **nuttallio·ses** \-ō,sēz\ [NL, fr. ²Nuttallia + -iasis or -osis] : infection with or disease caused by protozoans of the genus Nuttallia — compare PIROPLASMOSIS
**nuttall oak** or **nuttall's oak** n, usu cap N [after Thomas Nuttall †1859 Am. botanist and ornithologist] : a large tree (Quercus nuttallii) of Missouri, Mississippi, and Texas having dark brownish gray bark and a nut with a thin-walled cup that has cinereous-puberulent scales
**nut·ted** \'nəd·əd\ adj [¹nut + -ed] : furnished with or secured by a nut
**nut·ter** \'nəd·ə(r)\ n -s [³nut + -er] : a gatherer of nuts
**nut·tery** \'nəd·ərē\ n -ES [¹nut + -ery] : a place where nut trees grow; also : a place for storing nuts
**nut·ti·ly** \'nəd·|°lē, -əl|, |°li, |əl-\ adv : in a nutty manner
**nut·ti·ness** \|ēnəs, |in-\ n -ES : the quality or state of being nutty
**nutting** pres part of NUT
**nut·ty** \|ē, |i\ adj -ER/-EST [¹nut + -y, adj. suffix] 1 : having or producing nuts ⟨the pine . . . letting fall its ripe ~ cones —Cyril Connolly⟩ 2 a : NUTS 1 ⟨most sixteen-year-olds are ~ about cars⟩ b : CRACKBRAINED, ECCENTRIC; also : mentally unbalanced ⟨the projects in progress that summer seemed fairly ~ —Bruce Bliven b.1916⟩ ⟨the cranks who send ~ letters to editors —C.W.Morton⟩ ⟨all as ~ as fruitcakes —Nancy Hale⟩ 3 : full of a pleasant zest : STIMULATING ⟨the fine ~ flavor of American politics —D.C.Coyle⟩ ⟨his thoughts, many of them thin, diffuse, abstract, others ~ . . . phrased in a rare flowing antique style —V.W.Brooks⟩ 4 Brit : spruce in appearance 5 : having a flavor like that of nuts ⟨poured a fine old ~ sherry⟩ ⟨chewed at a strip of rich ~ blubber —Rudyard Kipling⟩
**nut weevil** n : a weevil (as of the genus Balaninus) whose larva lives in nuts
**nux vom·i·ca** \'nəks'vämēkə\ n, pl **nux vomica** [NL, lit., emetic nut] 1 : the poisonous seed of an Asiatic tree (Strychnos nux-vomica) that contains several alkaloids but chiefly strychnine and brucine 2 : the tree that yields nux vomica — see FALSE ANGOSTURA BARK
**nu·zi** \'nüzē\ n -s usu cap [fr. Nuzi, ancient city south of Kirkuk, northeastern Iraq, where cuneiform tablets in this dialect were discovered] : a dialect of Akkadian in use at Nuzi
**nuz·zer** \'nəzə(r)\ n -s [Hindi nazr, fr. Ar] : a ceremonial offering to a superior in India

**1nuz·zle** \ˈnəzəl\ *vb* **nuzzled; nuzzled; nuzzling** \-z(ə)liŋ\ **nuzzles** [earlier *nosill, nousle,* fr. ME *noselen* to bring the nose towards the ground, fr. 1*nose* + *-elen, -len* -le] *vi* **1 :** to work with or as if with the nose **:** root, rub, or snuff with the nose ⟨feedboxes where once horses had *nuzzled* —H.P.Kishbaugh⟩ ⟨carp in the shadows . . . *nuzzling* for crumbs under lily pads —Amy Lowell⟩ ⟨felt a nose *nuzzling* at his shoulder —George Orwell⟩ **2 :** to poke, press, or rub against something ⟨two tugs *nuzzled* up gently to the bow . . . and began to push —Vernon Pizer⟩ **3 :** to lie close or snug **:** associate intimately **:** NESTLE ~ *vt* **:** to root, rub, or touch with or as if with the nose **:** NUDGE, PUSH, THRUST ⟨horses stopped by the fence and began *nuzzling* the snow —Ellen Glasgow⟩ ⟨*nuzzled* her face into her pillow —Maritta Wolff⟩ ⟨*nuzzling* his lips against her hair —Adria Langley⟩ ⟨*nuzzled* his shoulder blades more comfortably into the pillows —Olive H. Prouty⟩

**2nuzzle** \"\ *vt* -ED/-ING/-S [origin unknown] **1** *obs* **:** to bring up or train in a practice **:** NURTURE ⟨possessed with blind zeal, and *nuzzled* with superstition —Robert Burton⟩ **2** *chiefly Brit* **:** to make snug **:** nestle with **:** NURSE

**NV** *abbr* **1** new version **2** nonvoting

**NVM** *abbr* **1** Nativity of the Virgin Mary **2** nonvolatile matter

**NVR** *abbr* no voltage release

**NW** *abbr* **1** naked weight **2** net weight **3** northwest; northwestern

**NWG** *abbr* national wire gauge

**NY** *abbr* **1** navy yard **2** new year **3** no year

**nya·la** \ˈnyälə\ *n, pl* **nyalas** *or* **nyala** [Tsonga & Venda] **1 :** a harnessed antelope (*Tragelaphus angasi*) of southeastern Africa with a shaggy black mane on the male underside — called also *inyala* **2 :** a grayish chestnut rather shaggy antelope (*Tragelaphus buxtoni*) of some central eastern mountains of Africa

**nyam·we·zi** \nyämˈwāzē\ *n, pl* **nyamwezi** *or* **nyamwezis** *usu cap* **1 :** a Bantu-speaking people of the Unyamwezi region of western Tanganyika comprising one of the two largest communities of the territory **2 :** a Bantu language of the Nyamwezi people

**nyan·ja** \ˈnyanjə\ *n, pl* **nyanja** *or* **nyanjas** *usu cap* **1 a :** a people of Nyasaland who live chiefly around Lake Nyasa, the lower shores of the Shire river, and Lake Shirwa **b :** a member of such people **2 :** a Bantu language of the Nyanja people

**nyan·ko·le** \nyäŋˈkōlā\ *n, pl* **nyankole** *or* **nyankoles** *usu cap* **1 :** the Bantu-speaking peoples of the kingdom of Ankole in Uganda presumed to be cognate with the Nyoro and other neighboring peoples **2 :** a Bantu language of the Nyankole peoples

**1ny·asa** \(ˈ)nīˈasə, nēˈa-, ˈnya-\ *adj, usu cap* [fr. *Nyasa*land, southeastern Africa] **1 :** of, relating to, or characteristic of Nyasaland ⟨*Nyasa* Africans⟩ ⟨*Nyasa* Europeans⟩ **2 :** of, relating to, or characteristic of the people of Nyasaland

**2nyasa** \"\ *n* -S *cap* [fr. *Nyasa*land, southeastern Africa] **:** a native or inhabitant of Nyasaland

**ny·asa·land·er** \-ə,landə(r)\ *n* -S *usu cap* [*Nyasaland,* southeastern Africa + E *-er*] **:** NYASA

**nyaya** \ˈnyäyə\ *n* -S *usu cap* [Skt *nyāya* rule, model, maxim, logic, fr. *ni* down, back (i.e., to an original model) + *eti* he goes — more at NETHER, ISSUE] **:** an orthodox philosophical system in Hinduism dealing primarily with logic and epistemological analysis

**nych·them·er·al** *also* **nyc·them·er·al** \(ˈ)nikˈthem(ə)rəl\ *adj* [*nychthemeron, nycthemeron* + *-al*] **:** of or relating to a nychthemeron

**nych·them·er·on** *also* **nyc·them·er·on** \=ˈ=mə,rän\ *n, pl* **nychthem·era** \-m(ə)rə\ *or* **nychthemerons** [Gk *nychthēmeron,* fr. *nykt-, nyx* night + *-hēmeron* (fr. *hēmera* day) — more at NIGHT, HEMERA] **:** a full period of a night and a day

**nyct-** *or* **nycti-** *or* **nycto-** *comb form* [NL, fr. L, fr. Gk *nykt-, nykti-, nykto-,* fr. *nykt-, nyx* night — more at NIGHT] **:** night ⟨*Nyct*anthes⟩ ⟨*nycti*tropic⟩ ⟨*nycto*phobia⟩

**nyc·ta·gi·na·ce·ae** \,niktəjəˈnāsē,ē\ *n pl, cap* [NL, fr. *Nyctagin-, Nyctago,* type genus (obs. syn. of *Mirabilis*) (fr. *nyct-* + *-agin-, -ago* — as in *Plantagin-, Plantago* —) + *-aceae*] **:** a family of chiefly American herbs and rarely shrubs or trees (order Caryophyllales) having apetalous flowers with an involucre simulating a calyx and fruit enclosed by the persistent base of the perianth — **nyc·ta·gi·na·ceous** \ˌ=ˌ=ˌ=ˈnāshəs\ *adj*

**nyc·ta·lope** \ˈniktə,lōp\ *n* -S [MF, fr. Gk *nyktalōp-, nyktalōps*] **:** one affected with nyctalopia

**nyc·ta·lo·pia** \,=ˈlōpēə\ *n* -S [NL, fr. ML, fr. L *nyctalops* unable to see at twilight (fr. Gk *nyktalōp-, nyktalōps,* fr. *nykt-* nyct- + *alaos* blind + *-ōp-, ōps* eye) + *-ia* -y — more at EYE] **1 :** a defect of vision characterized by reduced visual capacity in faint light or at night — called also *night blindness* **2 :** HEMERALOPIA — **nyc·ta·lop·ic** \ˌ=ˌ=ˈläpik\ *adj*

**nyc·tea** \ˈniktēə\ *n, cap* [NL, fr. *nyct-* + L *-ea* (neut. pl. suffix)] **:** a genus of birds (family Strigidae) consisting of the snowy owl

**nyc·tem·era** \nikˈtem(ə)rə\ *n, cap* [NL, fr. Gk *nyktēmeron, nychthēmeron* night and day; prob. fr. the black-and-white color of the moths] **:** a genus of Australian and New Zealand black-and-white moths — see MAGPIE MOTH b

**nyc·te·reu·tes** \,niktəˈrüd·ēz\ *n, cap* [NL, fr. Gk *nyktereutēs* one who hunts or fishes by night, fr. *nykt-* nyct- + *ereutēs* collector, exactor, fr. *ereuein* to search, investigate, ask; akin to ON *raun* attempt, examination, *reyna* to test, experience] **:** a genus of mammals (family Canidae) consisting of the raccoon dogs

**1nyc·te·ribi·id** \ˌniktəˈribēəd\ *adj* [NL *Nycteribiidae*] **:** of or relating to the Nycteribiidae

**2nycteribiid** \"\ *n* -S [NL *Nycteribiidae*] **:** an insect of the family Nycteribiidae

**nyc·te·ri·bi·idae** \,niktərəˈbīə,dē\ *n pl, cap* [NL, fr. *Nycteribia,* type genus (fr. Gk *nykteris* bat + NL *-bia*) + *-idae*] **:** a family consisting of the bat flies

**1nyc·ter·is** \ˈniktərəs\ *n, cap* [NL, fr. Gk *nykteris* bat, fr. *nykt-, nyx* night — more at NIGHT] **:** a genus (the type of the family Nycteridae) of African and Asiatic bats comprising the hollow-faced bats

**2nycteris** \"\ [NL, fr. Gk *nykteris* bat] *syn of* LASIURUS

**-nycteris** \"\ *n comb form* [NL, fr. *Nycteris*] **:** bat — in generic names

**nycthemeral** *var of* NYCHTHEMERAL

**nycthemeron** *var of* NYCHTHEMERON

**nycti-** — see NYCT-

**nyc·tic·o·rax** \nikˈtikə,raks\ *n, cap* [NL, fr. Gk *nyktikorax* long-eared owl, fr. *nykt-* nyct- + *korax* raven — more at RAVEN] **:** a genus of herons consisting of the typical night herons

**nyc·tim·e·ne** \nikˈtimənē\ *n, cap* [NL, fr. L *Nyctimene,* Lesbian king's daughter who was transformed into an owl, fr. Gk *Nyktimenē*] **:** a genus of East Indian fruit bats — see HARPY BAT 1

**nyc·ti·nas·tic** \ˌniktəˈnastik\ *adj* **:** of, relating to, or caused by nyctinasty — **nyctinastically** *adv*

**nyc·ti·nas·ty** \ˈ=ˌ=,nastē\ *n* -ES [ISV *nyct-* + *-nasty;* prob. orig. formed as G *nyktinastie*] **:** a nastic movement (as the opening and closing of some flowers) that is associated with diurnal changes of temperature or light intensity

**nyc·ti·pelagic** \ˌniktə+\ *adj* [ISV *nyct-* + *pelagic*] **:** bathypelagic and appearing at the surface only at night ⟨~ fauna⟩

**nyc·ti·pi·the·cus** \,niktəpəˈthēkəs, -təˈpithəkəs\ [NL, fr. *nyct-* + *-pithecus*] *syn of* AOTES

**nyc·ti·trop·ic** \ˌniktəˈträpik\ *adj* [ISV *nyct-* + *-tropic*] **:** exhibiting nyctitropism

**nyc·tit·ro·pism** \nikˈti·trə,pizəm\ *n* -S [ISV *nyct-* + *-tropism*] **:** a sleep movement in plants characterized by response to a stimulus that is greatest or exclusively from one direction — compare NYCTINASTY

**nycto-** — see NYCT-

**nyc·turia** \nikˈtürēə, -k·ˈtyü-\ *n* -S [NL, fr. *nyct-* + *-uria*] **:** NOCTURIA

**NYD** *abbr, often not cap* not yet diagnosed

**nye** \ˈnī\ *n* -S [ME *neye, nye,* fr. MF *nyee, niee* brood, flock, fr. OF, fr. *ni* nest, fr. L *nidus* — more at NEST] *chiefly Brit* **:** a brood or flock of pheasants

**ny·lon** \ˈnī,län\ *n* -S *often attrib* [coined word] **1 :** any of numerous synthetic materials consisting of polyamides that are made from a dicarboxylic acid (as adipic acid or sebacic acid) and a diamine (as hexamethylenediamine) or from an omega-amino acid or its lactam (as caprolactam), that can be formed from a melt or solution into fibers, filaments, bristles, or sheets (as by extrusion through spinnerets and drawing or by casting), that are characterized when cold-drawn by toughness, elasticity, and strength, and that are used chiefly in making yarn, fabrics, cordage, resins, and plastics (as for molded products requiring high resistance to wear, heat, or chemicals) ⟨gears made of ~⟩ ⟨~ rope⟩ ⟨~ cord tires⟩ **2 a :** a quick-drying fiber made from nylon in filament and staple form and often blended with other fibers in fabrics ⟨~ velvet⟩ **b :** yarn or fabric made from nylon ⟨~ hosiery⟩ ⟨~ tricot⟩ **3 a :** an article made of nylon fibers **b nylons** *pl* **:** stockings made of nylon

**ny·loned** \-nd\ *adj* **:** wearing nylon stockings ⟨crossing her ~ legs —William Sansom⟩

**nylon salt** *n* **:** a white crystalline salt made by mixing dicarboxylic acid and the diamine in the first step of nylon manufacture

**nymph** \ˈnim(p)f\ *n, pl* **nymphs** \-m(p)fs, -mps\ [ME *nimphe,* fr. MF, nymph, fr. L *nympha* bride, nymph, fr. Gk *nymphē* — more at NUPTIAL] **1** *Greek & Roman mythol* **:** one of the minor divinities of nature that are represented as beautiful maidens dwelling in the mountains, forests, meadows, and waters — compare NAIAD, NEREID, OCEANID, OREAD, WOOD NYMPH 1 ⟨she fled as if she were a startled ~ —E.A.Peeples⟩ **2 a :** GIRL **b :** a woman of loose morals **3 a :** any of various hemimetabolic insects in an immature stage: as (1) **:** a late larva (as of a true bug) in which wing pads and rudiments of the genitalia are present; *broadly* **:** any insect larva that differs chiefly in size and degree of differentiation from the imago (2) **:** NAIAD 2 **b :** a mite or tick in the first 8-legged form that immediately follows the last larval molt **c :** a nymphal stage in the life cycle of an insect or acarid **4 :** NYMPH PINK **5 :** an artificial fly of a type made in imitation of the larval stage of the Ephemeridae

**nymph-** *or* **nympho-** *also* **nymphi-** *comb form* [F *nymph-,* fr. L, fr. Gk, fr. *nymphē*] **1 :** nymph ⟨*nympho*lepsy⟩ **2 :** nymphae ⟨*nympho*tomy⟩ ⟨*nymph*itis⟩ **3 :** nymphaea ⟨*nympho*ides⟩ **4 :** nympha ⟨*nymph*osis⟩

**nym·pha** \ˈnim(p)fə\ *n, pl* **nym·phae** \-),fē\ [L — more at NYMPH] **1 :** NYMPH 3 **2** *nymphae pl* [NL, fr. L, pl. of *nympha* nymph] **:** LABIA MINORA **3** [NL, fr. *nymphae* labia minora] **:** one of the thickened marginal processes behind the beak of many bivalves where the ligament is attached

**1nym·phaea** \nimˈfēə\ *n* [NL, fr. L, water lily, fr. Gk *nymphaia;* akin to Gk *nymphē* bride, nymph] **1** *cap* **:** the type genus of the family Nymphaeaceae including numerous typical water lilies with sometimes fragrant flowers that have four green sepals and numerous petals which are as large as the sepals in the outer whorls and diminish centrally to the size and appearance of stamens and occur in white, pink to red, blue, and yellow in various members of the genus **2** -S **:** any plant of the genus *Nymphaea*

**2nymphaea** \"\ [NL, fr. L, water lily] *syn of* NUPHAR

**nym·phae·a·ceae** \,nim(p)fēˈāsē,ē\ *n pl, cap* [NL, fr. *Nymphaea,* type genus + *-aceae*] **:** a family of aquatic plants (order Ranales) having long-stalked often peltate leaves, large flowers with 3 to 5 sepals and numerous petals and stamens, and polycarpellary indehiscent fruit and comprising the water lilies — see NELUMBO, NUPHAR, NYMPHAEA, VICTORIA — **nym·phae·a·ceous** \ˌ=ˌ=ˈāshəs\ *adj*

**nym·phae·um** *also* **nym·phe·um** \nimˈfēəm\ *n, pl* **nym·phaea** \-ēə\ [F *nymphaeum,* fr. L, lit., shrine of nymphs, fr. Gk *nymphaion,* fr. *nymphē* nymph] **:** a Roman building or room containing a fountain, adorned with plants and sculpture, and serving as a place of rest

**nymph·al** \ˈnim(p)fəl\ *adj* [F, fr. MF, fr. *nymphe* nymph + *-al*] **:** of, relating to, or being a nymph **:** consisting of nymphs ⟨during the ~ period the mite may molt one or more times —Nathan Banks⟩ ⟨the first ephemerids . . . crack their ~ shucks —Richard Salmon⟩ ⟨will result in lower ~ populations —*Biol. Abstracts*⟩

**1nym·pha·lid** \nimˈfaləd, -fāl-, -fäl-\ *adj* [NL *Nymphalidae*] **:** of or relating to the Nymphalidae

**2nymphalid** \"\ *n* -S **:** a butterfly of the family Nymphalidae

**nym·phal·i·dae** \nimˈfalə,dē\ *n pl, cap* [NL, fr. *Nymphalis,* type genus + *-idae*] **:** a widely distributed family of butterflies mostly of medium or large size and distinguished by having the forelegs much reduced in size in both sexes so that they are useless in walking and are carried folded on the breast, usu. absent tarsal claws, larvae that are usu. spiny or provided with fleshy processes, and pupae that are usu. of angular outline and hang suspended by the tip of the tail — see FOUR-FOOTED BUTTERFLY

**nym·pha·lis** \nimˈfaləs, -fāl-, -fäl-\ *n, cap* [NL, fr. L, nymphal, fr. *nympha* nymph + *-alis* -al — more at NYMPH] **:** a widely distributed genus of nymphalid butterflies

**nym·phe·an** \ˈnim(p)fēən, nimˈf-\ *adj* [*nymph* + *-an*] **:** of or appropriate to nymphs **:** inhabited by nymphs ⟨~ grace and beauty —G.W.Cable⟩

**nymph·et** \(ˈ)nimˈfet, ˈnim(p)fət\ *n* -S [MF *nymphette,* fr. *nymphe* nymph + *-ette* -et — more at NYMPH] **1 :** a young nymph ⟨the ~*s* sporting there —Michael Drayton⟩ **2 :** a sexually precocious girl **:** a loose young woman

**nymph·id** \-fəd\ *n* -S [*nymph* + *-id,* n. suffix] **:** NYMPH 3

**nym·phi·dae** \ˈnim(p)fə,dē\ *n pl, cap* [NL, fr. *Nymphes,* type genus (fr. L *nympha* nymph) + *-idae*] **:** a small family of primitive neuropterous insects related to the ant lions and confined to the Australian region

**nym·phip·a·ra** \nimˈfipərə\ [NL, fr. *nymph-* + *-para* (fr. L, neut. pl. of *-parus* -parous)] *syn of* PUPIPARA

**nymph·ish** \ˈnim(p)fish\ *adj* **:** of, relating to, or resembling a nymph

**nymphlike** \ˈ=,=\ *adj* **:** resembling a nymph (as in grace or beauty)

**nym·pho** \ˈnim(p)(,)fō\ *n* -S [by shortening] **:** NYMPHOMANIAC

**nympho-** — see NYMPH-

**nym·phoi·des** \nimˈfȯidēz\ *n, cap* [NL, fr. *nymph-* + L *-oides* -oid] **:** a genus of aquatic herbs (family Menyanthaceae) mostly of tropical regions and having floating round or cordate leaves and small yellow or white umbellate flowers — see FLOATING HEART

**nym·pho·lep·sy** \ˈnim(p)fə,lepsē\ *n* -ES [*nymph-* + *-lepsy*] **1 :** a species of demoniac enthusiasm supposed by the ancients to seize one possessed or bewitched by a nymph **2 :** a frenzy of emotion (as for some unattainable ideal)

**1nym·pho·lept** \-pt\ *n* -S [Gk *nympholēptos* caught by nymphs, raptured, frenzied, fr. *nymphē* nymph + *lēptos,* verbal of *lambanein* to take, seize — more at NUPTIAL, LATCH] **:** one seized with nympholepsy ⟨the ~*s* of old —Augustine Birrell⟩

**2nympholept** \"\ *adj* **:** NYMPHOLEPTIC

**nym·pho·lep·tic** \ˌ=ˈleptik\ *adj* [Gk *nympholēptos* + E *-ic*] **:** of, relating to, or affected with nympholepsy

**nym·pho·ma·nia** \,nim(p)fəˈmānēə\ *n* [NL, fr. *nymph-* + LL *mania*] **:** excessive desire by a female for sexual activity usu. based on feelings of personal inadequacy — called also *uteromania;* compare SATYRIASIS

**1nym·pho·ma·ni·ac** \-ē,ak\ *n* **:** one affected by nymphomania

**2nymphomaniac** \ˌ=ˌ=ˌ=ˌ=\ *also* **nym·pho·ma·ni·a·cal** \ˌnim(p)fōməˈnīəkəl\ *or* **nym·pho·man·ic** \ˌnim(p)fəˈmanik\ *adj* [*nymphomaniac* fr. *nymphomaniac,* n.; *nymphomaniacal* fr. 1*nymphomaniac* + *-al; nymphomanic* fr. *nymphomania* + *-ic*] **:** of, affected with, or characterized by nymphomania

**nym·pho·sis** \nimˈfōsəs\ *n, pl* **nympho·ses** \-ō,sēz\ [NL, fr. *nymph-* + *-osis*] **:** the change of an insect into a nymph

**nymph pink** *n* **:** a moderate to strong pink that is bluer and darker than hermosa pink or peachblossom (sense 1)

**nymphs** *pl of* NYMPH

**nymss** \ˈnim(p)s\ *n* -ES [native name in Egypt] **:** an ichneumon (*Herpestes ichneumon*)

**nyo·ro** \ˈnyō(,)rō\ *n, pl* **nyoro** *or* **nyoros** *usu cap* **1 :** a Bantu-speaking people of Uganda constituting a socially and economically complex society organized as a kingdom and presumed to be cognate with the Nyankole and other neighboring peoples **2 :** a Bantu language of the Nyoro people

**NYP** *abbr* not yet published

**NYR** *abbr* not yet returned

**ny·ro·ca** \nəˈrōkə\ [NL, fr. Russ *nyrok* diver (duck), fr. *nyryat* to dive; akin to Lith *nerti* to dive, thread — more at NARROW] *syn of* AYTHYA

**nys·i·us** \ˈnisēəs\ *n, cap* [NL] **:** a large and widely distributed genus of bugs (family Lygaeidae) that includes the false chinch bugs

**nys·sa** \ˈnisə\ *n, cap* [NL, perh. fr. Gk, meta, post] **:** a small genus of American and Asiatic trees (family Nyssaceae) having flowers with imbricate petals and a single or 2-cleft style — see BLACK GUM, TUPELO

**nys·sa·ce·ae** \nəˈsāsē,ē\ *n pl, cap* [NL, fr. *Nyssa* + *-aceae*] **:** a family of dicotyledonous trees (order Myrtales) containing the sour gums and having alternate leaves without stipules, inconspicuous greenish flowers in small heads, a 1- or 2-locular ovary, and the fruit a drupe

**nys·tag·mic** \nəˈstagmik\ *adj* [ISV *nystagm-* (fr. NL *nystagmus*) + *-ic*] **:** of, relating to, characterized by, or constituting nystagmus

**nys·tag·moid** \-g,mȯid\ *adj* [NL *nystagmus* + E *-oid*] **:** resembling that which is characteristic of nystagmus ⟨the eyes may show rapid lateral ~ movements —W.S.Weidorn⟩

**nys·tag·mus** \-gməs\ *n* -ES [NL, fr. Gk *nystagmos* drowsiness; akin to Gk *nystazein* to doze, sleep, Lith *snusti* to doze off and perh. to Gk *nythos* dark — more at NUANCE] **:** a rapid involuntary oscillation of the eyeballs occurring normally with dizziness during and after bodily rotation or abnormally after injuries (as to the cerebellum or the vestibule of the ear)

**nys·ta·tin** \ˈnistəd·ən\ *n* -S [*New York State,* where it was developed + E *-in*] **:** a pale yellow crystalline antibiotic isolated from cultures of a soil actinomycete (*Streptomyces noursei*) that is active against fungi and is useful esp. in the treatment of moniliasis (as of the mouth, skin, or intestines)

**ny·tril** \ˈnī·trəl\ *n* -S [*vi*nylidene di*nitrile*] **:** a synthetic fiber composed chiefly of a long-chain polymer of vinylidene dinitrile

**-nyx·is** \ˈniksəs\ *n comb form, pl* **-nyx·es** \-k,sēz\ [NL, fr. Gk *nyxis* act of pricking, of stabbing; akin to Gk *nyssein, nyttein* to prick, sting — more at NUMEN] **:** puncture ⟨pyro*nyxis*⟩ ⟨sclero*nyxis*⟩

**¹o** \ˈō\ *n, pl* **o's** *or* **os** \ˈōz\ *often cap, often attrib* **1 a :** the 15th letter of the English alphabet **b :** an instance of this letter printed, written, or otherwise represented **c :** a speech counterpart of orthographic *o* (as long *o* in *code,* short *o* in *cod,* or *o* in *cord*) **2 :** a printer's type, a stamp, or some other instrument for reproducing the letter *o* **3 :** someone or something arbitrarily or conveniently designated *o* esp. as the 14th or when j is used for the 10th the 15th in order or class **4 :** something having the shape of the capital letter O ⟨made an enthusiastic *O* with his thumb and forefinger —John Dos Passos⟩ ⟨the Roman girl's eyes widened, her mouth formed an *O* —F.V.W.Mason⟩; *esp* **:** ZERO ⟨wrote a couple of *O's*⟩

**²o** *usu cap, var of* OH

**³o** *abbr, often cap* **1** object **2** oblast **3** observation; observer **4** occident; occidental **5** ocean **6** [L *octarius*] pint **7** October **8** [L *oculus*] eye **9** off **10** office; officer **11** official **12** ohm **13** oil **14** old **15** only **16** opening **17** operation **18** [L *optimus*] best **19** order **20** [L *ordinis*] of the order of **21** [L *ordo*] order **22** ordnance **23** oriental **24** original **25** [L *os*] bone **26** out **27** outfield **28** outlet **29** over **30** overcast **31** owner

**⁴o** *symbol, cap* **1** octavo **2** oxygen

**¹o-** *or* **oo-** *comb form* [Gk *ōi-, ōio-,* fr. *ōion* egg — more at EGG] **:** egg ⟨oidium⟩ ⟨oology⟩; *specif* **:** ovum ⟨oogenesis⟩ ⟨oogonium⟩

**²o-** *abbr* ortho-

**¹-o** \(ˌ)ō\ *n suffix* -s [perh. fr. ¹*oh*] **:** one that is or that constitutes or that has the qualities of or that is in some way associated with ⟨boyo⟩ ⟨bucko⟩ — chiefly in informal or nonstandard speech; often in place of the missing element in a shortened word ⟨compo⟩ ⟨combo⟩; in writing sometimes attached to its base by a hyphen ⟨daddy-o⟩ or sometimes attached to the reduplicated final consonant of its base ⟨kiddo⟩

**²-o** \"\ *interj suffix* [prob. fr. ¹*oh*] — in interjections formed from other parts of speech ⟨cheerio⟩ ⟨righto⟩, esp. imitative words ⟨smacko⟩ ⟨bango⟩

**-o-** [ME, fr. OF, fr. L, fr. Gk, thematic vowel of many nouns and adjectives in combination] — used as a connective vowel orig. to join two elements of Greek origin and being either identical with ⟨chrysoprase⟩ or analogous to ⟨Anglo-Saxon⟩ an original Greek stem vowel or simply inserted ⟨jazzophile⟩ ⟨dramatico-musical⟩; compare -I-

**o'** *also* **o** \ə\ *prep* [in sense 1 fr. ME *o, o-,* alter. of *on;* in sense 2 fr. ME *o, o-,* alter. of *of*] **1** *chiefly dial* **:** ON **2 :** OF — now chiefly in dial. use except in a few set phrases (as *o'clock*)

**OA** *abbr* **1** on account **2** open account **3** overall

**OAA** *abbr* old-age assistance

**oaf** \ˈōf\ *n* -s [of Scand origin; akin to ON *alfr* elf — more at ELF] **1** *obs* **a :** CHANGELING 2b(2) **b :** a deformed or mentally defective child **2 :** a stupid person **:** SIMPLETON, DUMBBELL, BOOB ⟨numerous readers who may not be such ~s as they suppose —F.L.Allen⟩ **3 :** a big clumsy slow-witted fellow **:** LOUT, LUMMOX

**oaf·ish** \-fish, -ēsh\ *adj* **:** having the qualities typical of an oaf **:** STUPID, LOUTISH ⟨~ remarks⟩ — **oaf·ish·ly** *adv* — **oaf·ish·ness** *n* -ES

**¹oa·hu·an** \ōˈähüən,-hwən\ *n* -s *cap* [*Oahu,* Hawaii + E *-an* n. suffix] **:** a native or resident of Oahu, the chief island of the state of Hawaii

**²oahuan** \"\ *adj, usu cap* [*Oahu,* Hawaii + E *-an,* adj. suffix] **:** of, relating to, or characteristic of Oahu or Oahuans

**oak** \ˈōk\ *n, pl* **oaks** *or* **oak** *often attrib* [ME *ook, ok,* fr. OE *āc;* akin to OHG *eih* oak, ON *eik,* Gk *aigilōps* havergrass, Turkey oak and perh. to L *aesculus,* an oak] **1 a :** a tree or shrub of *Quercus* or the related genus *Lithocarpus* **b** (1) **:** the tough hard durable wood of an oak tree; *esp* **:** such wood (as of the white oak, red oak, bur oak, cork oak, English oak) having a distinct pattern produced by prominent medullary rays (2) **:** furniture made of this wood ⟨bought ~ for the living room⟩ **c :** the leaves of an oak used as a decoration ⟨a wreath of ~⟩ ⟨hung with ~⟩ **2 a :** any of various plants resembling oaks (as in foliage) — usu. used with a qualifying adjective or other attributive word; see POISON OAK, SILK OAK **b** *Austral* **:** CASUARINA 2 **3 :** a moderate to strong brown that is yellower and slightly darker than Vassar tan and yellower and slightly lighter than Arabian brown — called also *briar*

**oak apple** *n* [ME *oke appil,* fr. *oke* oak + *appil* apple; fr. its shape — more at APPLE] **:** an oak gall resulting from the presence of a larva of one of the cynipid wasps (esp. *Amphibolips concluentus* or *Andricus californicus*)

**oak beauty** *n* **:** a British moth (*Amphidasis prodomaria*) of the family Geometridae whose larva feeds on the oak

**oak blight** *n* **:** a black plant louse (*Anoecia querci*) that lives on the small branches of oak trees and on the dogwood

**oak borer** *n* **:** any of several cerambycid beetles with larvae that excavate galleries in the heartwood of oak and hickory

**oak brown** *n* **:** a moderate brown that is yellower, stronger, and slightly lighter than bay, yellower and stronger than auburn, and stronger and slightly yellower than chestnut brown

**oak chestnut** *n* **:** a tree of the genus *Castanopsis*

**oak·en** \ˈōkən\ *adj* [ME *oken,* fr. *ok* oak + *-en*] **1 a :** made of oak wood ⟨an ~ door⟩ ⟨~ paneling⟩ **b** *archaic* **:** made of oak leaves or oak twigs ⟨around her head an ~ wreath was seen —William Falconer⟩ **2** *archaic* **:** belonging to or coming from an oak tree ⟨a fall of ~ leaves —Richmond Lattimore⟩ **3** *archaic* **:** consisting of oak trees ⟨with breezes from our ~ glades —Alfred Tennyson⟩

**oakenshaw** \ˈ==ˌ=\ *n* [*oaken* + *shaw*] **:** an oak grove ⟨when winds were in the ~s —A.E.Housman⟩

**oak family** *n* **:** FAGACEAE

**oak fern** *n* [trans. of L *dryopteris*] **:** a widely distributed fern (*Thelypteris dryopteris*) of the family Polypodiaceae chiefly of damp acid woodlands of boreal and alpine parts of the northern hemisphere that has a slender subterraneous rhizome and delicate solitary triangular fronds

**oak fungus** *n* **:** SHOESTRING FUNGUS

**oak gall** *n* **:** a gall on oak caused by the presence of insect larvae esp. of the family Cynipidae

**oak green** *n* **:** AUCUBA GREEN

**oakie** *usu cap, var of* OKIE

**oak lace bug** *n* **:** a bug (*Corythucha arcuata*) of the family Tingidae that feeds on North American oaks

**oak·land** \ˈōklənd\ *adj, usu cap* [fr. *Oakland,* Calif.] **:** of or from the city of Oakland, Calif. ⟨*Oakland* canneries⟩ **:** of the kind or style prevalent in Oakland

**oak·land·er** \-də(r)\ *n* -s *cap* [*Oakland* + E *-er*] **:** a native or resident of Oakland, Calif.

**oakleaf brown** \ˈ==ˌ=\ *n* **:** FEUILLE MORTE

**oak leaf miner** *n* **:** a larva of any of several insects that tunnels in oak leaves

**oak leather** *n* **1 :** a mycelial mat formed in decaying oak wood **2** *or* **oak-tanned leather** \ˈ==-\ **:** leather tanned with tannin derived from oak bark alone or from oak bark and other materials

**oak-leaved goosefoot** *also* **oak leaf goosefoot** *n* **:** an annual European goosefoot (*Chenopodium glaucum*) that has leaves farinose beneath with inflated white hairs and greenish flowers in axillary or terminal spikes and that is common as a weed in the northern part of the U.S. and Canada

**oak·ling** \ˈōkliŋ, -lēŋ\ *n* -s [*oak* + *-ling*] **:** a young or small oak tree

**oak looper** *n* **:** a larva of a geometrid moth (*Lambdina somniaria*)

**oakmoss** \ˈ==ˌ=\ *n* **:** any of several lichens that grow on oak trees and yield a resin used in perfumery

**oak of cap·pa·do·cia** \-ˌkapəˈdōsh(ē)ə\ *usu cap C* [*cappadocia* fr. *Cappadocia,* ancient country in extreme eastern Asia Minor] **:** SEA RAGWEED

**oak of jerusalem** *or* **oak of paradise** *usu cap J&P* **:** JERUSALEM OAK

**oak opening** *n* **:** an open usu. even-aged stand of white oak or bur oak in a turf of native grasses forming a characteristic natural plant community adjoining or interspersed by prairie in much of Illinois and southern Wisconsin prior to the establishment of settlements and agriculture

**oak pruner** *or* **oak twig pruner** *n* **:** a twig pruner (*Hypermallus villosus*) that is sometimes abundant on oak

**oak root fungus** *n* **:** SHOESTRING FUNGUS

**oak scale** *n* **:** any of several scales attacking oaks

**oak toad** *n* **:** a small toad (*Bufo quercicus*) of Georgia and neighboring coastal states

**oa·kum** \ˈōkəm\ *n* -s [ME *okum,* fr. OE *ācumba* hurds, tow, lit., off-combings, fr. *ā-* (separative and perfective prefix) + *-cumba* (akin to OE *camb* comb) — more at ABEAR, COMB] **:** loosely twisted fiber usu. of hemp or jute impregnated with tar or with a tar derivative (as creosote or asphalt) and used in caulking seams (as of the wood hulls and decks of ships) and in packing joints (as of pipes, caissons)

**oak wilt** *n* **:** a destructive disease of oak trees caused by a fungus (*Chalara quercina*) characterized by wilting and by yellow and red discoloration of the foliage that begins at the top or at the branch extremities and usu. progresses downward and inward and that is often accompanied or followed by defoliation

**oakwood** \ˈ==ˌ=\ *n* **:** a moderate brown that is lighter, stronger, and slightly yellower than auburn, lighter, stronger, and slightly redder than chestnut brown, and yellower and slightly stronger than toast brown

**oak worm** *n* **:** any of several lepidopterous insect larvae that feed on oak leaves — usu. used with a qualifying term ⟨red-humped *oak worm*⟩

**oaky** \ˈōkē\ *adj* -ER/-EST [*oak* + *-y,* adj. suffix] **:** of, relating to, or having the characteristics of oak trees

**oam** \ˈōm\ *n* -s [perh. fr. (assumed) ME *oom;* akin to ON *eimr* steam, vapor — more at EMBER] *Scot* **:** warm vaporous air

**O and R** *abbr* ocean and rail

**o antigen** \ˈō-\ *n, usu cap O* [G, fr. ohne hauch antigen, fr. *ohne hauch* without breath + *antigen*] **:** SOMATIC ANTIGEN

**o antiphon** *n, usu cap O&A* [²*o;* fr. the fact that it opens with O (as O Adonai)] **:** GREAT ANTIPHON

**OAP** *abbr* old-age pension

**¹oar** \ˈō(ə)r, ˈȯ(ə)r, ˈōə, ˈȯə\ *n* -s [ME *oor, or,* fr. OE *ār;* akin to ON *ār* oar] **1 a :** a long rather heavy wooden pole with a broad fairly flat blade at one end that is used for propelling and steering or stopping a boat and that is usu. held in place in an oarlock at the side of a boat or sometimes at the stern (as of a gondola) so that the shorter usu. narrower end can be readily grasped and manipulated by a rower in the boat in such a way that the blade can be dipped into and pulled against and raised from the water or otherwise manipulated so as to propel or steer or stop the boat **b** *archaic* **:** something (as an arm, the wing of a bird) used for propulsion through water or air and suggestive in its action of an oar **2 a** *archaic* **:** ROWBOAT — usu. used in pl. and often with *pair* ⟨went into a pair of ~s that was ready —Edward Hyde⟩ **b** *or* **oars** *pl but sing in constr* **:** OARSMAN **c oars** *pl but sing or pl in constr* **:** the position of holding a boat's oars horizontal and at right angles with the boat's sides and with the blade ends parallel with the water — often used as a command to prepare to row or to rest from rowing **3 :** a stick or pole or paddle used for stirring something (as mash) — **lay on one's oars** *or* **lay on the oars :** to lie on one's oars — **lie on one's oars** *or* **lie on the oars** *or* **rest on one's oars** *or* **rest on the oars 1 :** to take the position of oars **2 :** to cease effort **:** take it easy **:** REST, RELAX ⟨had not been content entirely to *rest on his oars* during that ten days —F.W.Crofts⟩ — **put one's oar in** *also* **shove one's oar in** *or* **stick one's oar in :** to offer usu. unwanted advice or assistance **:** take part in another's affairs usu. without being asked or wanted **:** be meddlesome **:** INTERFERE ⟨had to *put their oar in* all the time —Robert Westerby⟩ ⟨was trying to *stick his oar in* —J.G.Cozzens⟩ ⟨wasn't afraid to *shove in his oar* now and again —Elizabeth Goudge⟩

**²oar** \"\ *vb* -ED/-ING/-S *vt* **1 :** to propel with or as if with oars **:** ROW ⟨~*ed* the boat forward⟩ **2** *archaic* **:** to manipulate (as one's arm) like an oar ~ *vi* **:** to go along by or as if by using oars ⟨~*ing* slowly over the water⟩ ⟨a lazy troupe of rooks flapped over the sky, cawing as they ~*ed* along —Richard Church⟩

**oar·age** \-rij, -rēj\ *n* -s [¹*oar* + *-age*] **1** *archaic* **:** the action of oaring **2** *archaic* **a :** rowing equipment **:** oars and oar fittings **b :** something resembling oars in appearance or movement ⟨the ~ of the wings of a single great bird —C.E.Montague⟩

**oared shrew** *n* [so called fr. its fringed feet] **:** the European water shrew

**oar feather** *n* **:** REMEX

**oarfish** \ˈ==ˌ=\ *n* **1 :** any of several fishes of the genus *Regalecus* that have narrow soft delicate bodies ranging from 20 to 30 feet in length, a dorsal fin running the entire length of the body with red-tipped anterior rays rising above the head, and ventral fins reduced to long filaments, that lack a caudal fin, and that are found off the coasts of Europe and Asia and the Pacific coast of America **2 :** a fish of the family Lophotidae that resembles the oarfish

**oar-footed** \ˈ=ˌ==\ *adj* **:** having feet adapted for swimming

**oarlock** \ˈ=ˌ=\ *n* [ME *orlok,* fr. OE *ārloc,* fr. *ār* oar + *loc* lock — more at LOCK] **:** a usu. U-shaped device or arrangement for supporting and holding an oar in place **:** ROWLOCK: as **a :** a metal fork or stirrup pivoted in the gunwale or on an outrigger **b :** a single pin swiveling in the gunwale or on an outrigger and passing through a hole in the oar or having the oar attached (as by a grommet) to it **c :** a pair of pins set vertically in the gunwale or on an outrigger **d :** a U-shaped notch in the gunwale

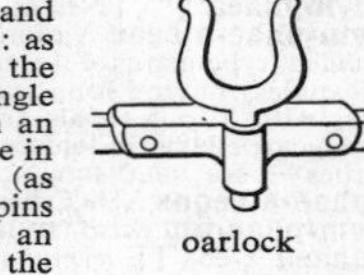

oarlock

**oars·man** \ˈō(ə)rzmən, ˈȯ(ə)rz-, ˈōəz-,ˈȯəz- *also* **oar·man** \ˈ=mən\ *n, pl* **oarsmen** *also* **oarmen** [*oarsman* fr. *oar's* (gen. of ¹*oar*) + *man*] **:** one that rows **:** ROWER; *esp* **:** one that is skilled in rowing

**oars·man·ship** \-ˌship\ *n* **:** skill in rowing

**oarweed** \ˈ=ˌ=\ *n* [E dial. *oare, ore* seaweed (fr. ME *ware,* fr. OE *wār*) + E *weed;* akin to OE *wīr* myrtle, MD *wier* seaweed, and prob. to ON *visk* wisp — more at WHISK] **:** any of several large brown algae esp. of the genus *Laminaria* including some used as a source of iodine and other chemicals, as fertilizer, and sometimes as food

**oary** \ˈōrē, ˈȯrē, -ri\ *adj* [¹*oar* + *-y*] **1** *archaic* **a :** resembling or having the qualities or function of oars **b :** widely outspread ⟨~ wings⟩ **2** *archaic* **:** equipped with oars

**OAS** *abbr* on active service

**oa·sal** \(ˈ)ōˌāsəl\ *or* **oa·se·an** \-sēən\ *adj* [*oasis* + *-al* or *-an*] **:** OASITIC

**OASI** *abbr* old-age and survivors insurance

**oa·sis** \ōˈāsəs, ˈōəsəs\ *n, pl* **oa·ses** \-ˌsēz\ [LL, fertile land in the Libyan desert, fr. Gk, prob. of Hamitic origin; akin to Coptic *wahe*] **1 :** a small isolated fertile area (as in the midst of a sandy desert) that is surrounded by general aridity or barrenness and that is typically marked by trees or other greenery and that has a water supply furnished by local springs or wells or by local seepage or by water flowing from a distant source either naturally or through artificial irrigation **2 :** something (as a place of refuge or a time of relaxation) existing or occurring in an isolated way (as in the midst of surrounding dreariness or monotony or tiresomeness) and affording welcome refreshment or relief or contrast ⟨an ~ of calm in a troubled and turbulent universe —Douglas MacArthur⟩ ⟨an ~ of prosperity in an increasingly impoverished world —P.G.Worsthorne⟩ ⟨a lovely intellectual ~ —Green Peyton⟩ **3 :** any of numerous small dark roundish spots on the planet Mars at the intersection of its canals

**oa·sit·ic** \ˌōəˈsid·ik\ *adj* [*oasis* + *-itic*] **:** of, relating to, or resembling an oasis ⟨an ~ place, full of coolness and tranquility, perfect for relaxing⟩

**oast** \ˈōst\ *or* **oasthouse** \ˈ=ˌ=\ *n* -s [*oast* fr. ME *ost,* fr. OE *āst;* akin to MD *eest, est* kiln, L *aestus* heat, *aestas* summer — more at EDIFY] **:** a kiln or group of kilns often of a distinctive conical shape and used for drying hops, malt, or tobacco

**¹oat** \ˈōt, *usu* ōd·+V\ *n* -s *often attrib* [ME *ote,* fr. OE *āte*] **1 a** (1) **:** a plant of the genus *Avena; esp* **:** a cereal grass (*Avena sativa*) that is an important grain crop in temperate regions through its wide cultivation as a source of food for both human beings and animals (2) *usu* **oats** *pl but sing or pl in constr* **:** a crop of oats ⟨~s can be grown further north than wheat⟩; *also* **:** a field or plot of growing oats ⟨the ~s are doing well⟩ **b** *usu* **oats** *pl but sing or pl in constr* **:** oat seed; *esp* **:** the seed of the cultivated oat plant **2** *archaic* **:** a crude reed instrument made of an oat straw **:** an oaten pipe

**²oat** \"\ *vt* -ED/-ING/-S *archaic* **:** to feed (a horse) with oats

**oatcake** \ˈ=ˌ=\ *n* **:** a thin flat cake made of oatmeal mixed with water, milk, or buttermilk and cooked on a griddle or in an oven

**-o·ate** \əˌwāt, *usu* -ād·+V\ *n suffix* -s [*-oic* + *-ate*] **:** salt or ester of a carboxylic acid with a name ending in *-oic* ⟨caproate⟩ ⟨octanoate⟩

**oat·en** \ˈōtᵊn\ *adj* [ME *oten,* fr. *ote* + *-en*] **1 :** made of oat grain or of oatmeal ⟨~ bread⟩ **2 :** made of oat straw or of an oat stem ⟨a shepherd playing on an ~ pipe⟩ ⟨~ thatch⟩ **3 :** of or relating to oat plants ⟨~ hay⟩ ⟨~ chaff⟩

oat 1a (1)

**oat·er** \ˈōd·ə(r)\ *n* -s **:** HORSE OPERA

**oat grass** *n* **1 :** WILD OAT 1a **2 :** one of several grasses of the genera *Danthonia* and *Trisetum* **3 a** *Austral* **:** ULLA GRASS **b :** an Australian forage grass (*Anisopogon avenaceus*)

**¹oath** \ˈōth\ *n, pl* **oaths** \-ths,-t͟hz\ [ME *ooth, oth,* fr. OE *āth;* akin to OHG *eid* oath, ON *eithr,* Goth *aiths;* all prob. fr. a prehistoric Gmc word of Celt origin; akin to MIr *ōeth* oath] **1 a** (1) **:** a solemn usu. formal calling upon God or a god to witness to the truth of what one says or to witness to the fact that one sincerely intends to do what one says (2) **:** a usu. formal affirmation made solemn by being coupled with the invocation of something viewed as sacred or of something highly revered (3) **:** a usu. formal affirmation that is in some way made solemn without such an appeal or without such an invocation **b :** something (as the truth of what one says, a promise that one makes) that is corroborated by an oath **c :** a form of expression used in taking an oath **2 a :** an irreverent or thoughtless or otherwise profane use (as in giving vent to anger, expressing ill will or annoyance, expressing surprise, corroborating a trivial statement) of the name of something viewed as sacred (as the name of God, Christ) **b :** a word or phrase identical with or derived from or in some other way involving the name of something viewed as sacred that is used in such an irreverent or thoughtless or otherwise profane way — **under oath** *or* **on oath** *also* **upon oath :** under the solemn obligation of an oath ⟨was *under oath* to tell all he knew⟩

**²oath** \"\ *vb* -ED/-ING/-S *archaic* **:** SWEAR

**oathay** \ˈ=ˌ=\ *n, Brit* **:** unthreshed oats used as hay

**oath helper** *n, Old Eng law* **:** one brought into court to swear to the truth of his principal's oath in a wager of law

**oath of calumny** [trans. of LL *juramentum calumniae*] **:** an oath taken by a plaintiff or defendant that attests to the plaintiff's or defendant's good faith and to his conviction that there exists a good ground of action

**oatmeal** \ˈ=ˌ=\ *n* [ME *ote-mele,* fr. *ote* oat + *mele* meal — more at OAT, MEAL] **1 a** (1) **:** meal made by grinding oats from which the husks have been removed (2) **:** ROLLED OATS **b :** porridge made from ground or rolled oats **2 :** a grayish yellow that is greener and paler than chamois, paler and very slightly greener than old ivory, and paler and slightly redder than crash **3 :** a fabric (as of wool, cotton) with a rough pebbled surface made with fine warp yarns and coarse filling yarns

**oatmeal paper** *or* **oatmeal wallpaper** *n* **:** a wallpaper that is given a coarse surface by the addition of sawdust to the fiber finish

**oat nematode** *n* **:** an Old World plant-parasitic nematode (*Heterodera major* or *Heterodera avenae*) that is destructive to the roots of oats, barley, and several other cereals and that has become established in parts of Canada

**oat opera** *n* **:** HORSE OPERA

**oats** *pl of* OAT, *pres 3d sing of* OAT

**¹oaves** \ˈōvz, -vəs\ *dial Eng var of* EAVES

**²oaves** \ˈōvz\ *archaic pl of* OAF

**ob-** *prefix* [ME, fr. OF, fr. L, to, toward, against, over, completely, fr. *ob* to, before, against, on account of — more at EPI-] **1 :** inward ⟨obimbricate⟩ **2 :** incompletely ⟨obrotund⟩ ⟨obround⟩ **3 :** in reverse order ⟨obdiplostemonous⟩ **4 :** inverse ⟨obovate⟩ ⟨obconic⟩ ⟨obcordate⟩

**ob** *abbr* **1** [L *obiit*] he died **2** obiter **3** oblong **4** oboe **5** [L *obolus*] halfpenny **6** observation **7** obstetrics

**OB** *abbr* **1** opening of books **2** ordered back **3** order of battle **4** outboard **5** outward bound

**oba** *also* **ob·ba** \ˈōbə\ *n* -s [native name in western Nigeria] **:** a ruler of any of several African peoples of western Nigeria — used as a form of address

**ob·am·bu·late** \äˈbambyəˌlāt, əˈ-\ *vi* [L *obambulatus,* past part. of *obambulare* to walk to or before, fr. *ob-* to, against, over + *ambulare* to walk — more at OB-, AMBLE] *archaic* **:** to walk about **:** WANDER

**oban** \ˈōˌbän\ *or* **obang** \-aŋ\ *n* -s [Jap *ōban,* prob. fr. Chin (Pek) *hung² p'ai²* customs clearance, lit., red seal] **:** a large oval Japanese gold coin of the 16th to 19th centuries that varied in size and weight

**obb** *abbr* obbligato

**ob·ben·ite** \ˈäbəˌnīt\ *n* -s *usu cap* [*Obbe* Philipszoon †1568 Du. religious leader + connective *-n-* + E *-ite*] **:** a member of an Anabaptist group arising in the 16th century

**¹ob·bli·ga·to** *also* **ob·li·ga·to** \ˌäbləˈgäd·(ˌ)ō, -lē-, -ä(ˌ)tō\ *adj* [It *obbligato* (past part. of *obbligare* to obligate), fr. L *obligatus,* past part. of *obligare* to obligate — more at OBLIGATE] **:** obligatory and not to be omitted — used as a musical direction ⟨accompaniment ~⟩; distinguished from *ad libitum*

**²obbligato** *also* **obligato** \"\ *n, pl* **obbliga·tos** \-ōz\ *also* **obbliga·ti** \-d·(ˌ)ē, -(ˌ)tē\ **1 :** a prominent part of semi-independent melodic character accompanying a solo voice or principal melody and usu. played by a single instrument ⟨a song with violin ~⟩ **2 :** an accompaniment to something; *esp* **:** an attendant sound ⟨arrived with a flourish accompanied by an ~ of honking geese and barking dogs⟩

**obcaecation** *n* -s [obs. F *obcecation,* fr. MF, fr. LL *obcaecation-, obcaecatio, occaecation-, occaecatio* act of hiding, fr. L *obcaecatus, occaecatus* (past part. of *obcaecare, occaecare* to blind, fr. *ob-, oc-* toward, against, over + *caecare* to blind, fr. *caecus* blind) + *-ion-, -io* -ion — more at OB-, CECUM] *obs* **:** BLINDNESS

**ob·clavate** \(ˈ)äb+\ *adj* [ISV *ob-* + *clavate*] **:** inversely clavate

**ob·clude** \äbˈklüd\ *vt* -ED/-ING/-S [alter. (influenced by *ob-*) of *occlude*] **:** to hide from view **:** OCCLUDE

**ob·compressed** \ˌäb+\ *adj* [*ob-* + *compressed*] **:** flattened vertically or anteriorly rather than laterally

**ob·conic** \(ˈ)äb+\ *also* **ob·conical** \"+\ *adj* [*ob-* + *conic* or *conical*] **:** conical with the apex below or forming the point of attachment ⟨a moss with an ~ capsule⟩

**ob·cordate** \"+\ *adj* [*ob-* + *cordate*] *of a leaf* **:** heart-shaped with the notch apical **:** inversely cordate — compare RETUSE

**ob·cuneate** \"+\ *adj* [*ob-* + *cuneate*] **:** inversely cuneate

**ob·deltoid** \"+\ *adj* [*ob-* + *deltoid*] **:** inversely deltoid **:** triangular with downward pointing apex

**ob·diplostemonous** \(ˈ)äb+\ *adj* [prob. fr. (assumed) NL *obdiplostemonus,* fr. NL *ob-* + (assumed) NL *diplostemonus* diplostemonous — more at DIPLOSTEMONOUS] **:** having the stamens in two whorls with those of the outer whorl opposite the petals — compare DIPLOSTEMONOUS — **ob·diplostemony** \"+\ *n* -ES

**obdt** *abbr* obedient

**ob·duce** \äbˈd(y)üs\ *vt* -ED/-ING/-S [L *obducere,* fr. *ob-* toward, over + *ducere* to draw, lead — more at OB-, TOW] **:** to cover with **:** draw over **:** envelop in

**obduction** *n* -s [L *obduction-, obductio,* fr. *obductus* (past part. of *obducere* to obduce) + *-ion-, -io* -ion] **:** an act or instance of drawing or laying something (as a covering) over

**ob·du·ra·cy** \ˈäbd(y)ərəsē, äbˈd(y)ůrə-, əbˈ-, -si\ *n* -ES [¹*obdurate* + *-cy*] **:** the quality or state of or an instance of being obdurate

**¹ob·du·rate** \-rət, *usu* -əd·+V\ *adj* [ME *obdurat,* fr. L *obduratus,* past part. of *obdurare* to harden, fr. *ob-* toward, over + *durare* to harden — more at OB-, DURE] **1 a :** hardened in feelings esp. against moral or mollifying influences : stubbornly persistent in wrongdoing ⟨that ~ old sinner⟩ **b** : resistant to persuasion or softening influences : INFLEXIBLE, UNYIELDING ⟨~ in his determination⟩ ⟨remaining ~ to her husband's advances —Edith Wharton⟩ **2** : hard and resistant : HARSH, RUGGED, ROUGH ⟨wringing a livelihood from that ~ soil⟩ — **ob·du·rate·ly** *adv* — **ob·du·rate·ness** *n* -ES

**²obdurate** \-,rāt, *usu* -ād.+V\ *vt* -ED/-ING/-S [L *obduratus*, past part. of *obdurare* to harden] : to make obdurate; *esp* : to make stubbornly persistent in ill-doing — **ob·du·ra·tion** \,äbd(y)ə'rāshən\ *n* -S

**¹ob·dure** \äb'd(y)u̇(ə)r, -u̇ə\ *vb* -ED/-ING/-S [L *obdurare* to harden] *archaic* : HARDEN

**²obdure** \"\ *adj* [*ob-* + *dure*, adj.] *archaic* : OBDURATE

**obe** \'ōb\ *n* -S [Gk (Laconian dial.) *ōba*; akin to Gk *oiē* village] : a subdivision of a phyle or clan in ancient Laconia

**obe·ah** \'ōbēə\ *also* **obi** \'ōbē\ *n* -S [of African origin; akin to Edo $o^3bi^1$ poison, Twi $a^1bi^1a^3$, a creeper used in making medicine and charms] **1** *often cap* : a system of belief that is probably of Ashanti origin, has long been practiced but is of increasingly declining influence among Negroes chiefly of the British West Indies, the Guianas, and the southeastern U.S., and is characterized by the use of sorcery and magic ritual — compare VOODOOISM **2 a** : a charm or fetish used in obeah **b** : the influence of obeah ⟨put ~ on a person⟩

**obeah man** *also* **obeah doctor** *n* : an adept or leader in the practice of obeah : WITCH DOCTOR

**obe·che** *also* **obe·chi** \ō'bēchē\ *n* -S [native name in Nigeria] **1** : a large West African tree (*Triplochiton scleroxylon*) with soft white to pale yellow wood — called also *arere, samba* **2** : the wood of the obeche — used esp. for veneering

**obe·di·ence** \ō'bēdēən(t)s, ə'-\ *n* -S [ME, fr. OF, fr. L *oboedientia*, fr. *oboedient-, oboediens* (pres. part. of *oboedire* to obey) + *-ia* -y — more at OBEY] **1** : the act or fact of obeying or the quality or state of being obedient : compliance with that which is required by authority : subjection to rightful restraint **2 a** : JURISDICTION, CONTROL, RULE — now used chiefly of the spiritual authority of the Roman Catholic Church over its members **b** : a sphere of jurisdiction : an ecclesiastical or sometimes a secular dominion **3** *dial chiefly Eng* : BOW, CURTSY **4** [ML *obedientia*, fr. L *oboedientia* obedience] **a** : an official position or specific assigned task or responsibility within a monastic establishment; *also* : the part of such an establishment devoted to the activities of a particular function **b** : conformity to the rule of a monastic order and to the will of its superior **c** : a specific and usu. written precept or injunction from a superior in a religious order to one of the congregation ⟨hoping that his abbot will place him under ~ to use his singular talents —J.A.O'Brien⟩ **5** : a system of dog training designed to develop the intelligent response of the animal to the demands of his handler by means of a graded series of specific problem situations of increasing difficulty ⟨goes big for ~ . . . running all five classes off in the first day —*All-Pets Mag.*⟩

**obe·di·en·cer** \-nsə(r)\ *n* -S [ME, fr. *obedience* + *-er*] *archaic* : OBEDIENTIARY

**obe·di·en·cy** \-nsē, -si\ *n* -ES [L *oboedientia* (fr. *oboedient-, oboediens*) + *-ia* -y] : OBEDIENCE 1

**obe·di·ent** \-nt\ *adj* [ME, fr. OF, fr. L *oboedient-, oboediens*, pres. part. of *oboedire* to obey] **1 a** : submissive to the restraint, control, or command of authority : willing to obey ⟨an ~ child⟩ ⟨the most modest . . . of little men, and as ~ to his wife —W.M.Thackeray⟩ **b** : SUBJECT, SUBSERVIENT ⟨that Germany would become an ~ sovietized state under the tight grip of the Soviet Union —*Collier's Yr. Bk.*⟩ **2 a** : conformable or conforming to the control of an indicated agent ⟨drifting ~ to winds and tides⟩ ⟨~ instruments of his will —Max Lerner & Edwin Mims⟩ **b** : acting in conformance to an indicated situation ⟨~ to his nature he pried into everything⟩
**syn** DOCILE, TRACTABLE, AMENABLE, BIDDABLE: OBEDIENT suggests due and accustomed recognition of and compliance with the commands of recognized authority ⟨as second in command, Abercromby proved himself an *obedient* and trustworthy officer —Stanley Pargellis⟩ ⟨he seemed to have lost all power of will; he was like an *obedient* child —W.S.Maugham⟩ DOCILE may stress a disposition to submit, either to due guidance and control or to imposition and oppression ⟨that is a question which you must excuse my child from answering. Not, sir, from want of will, for she is *docile* and obedient —W.H.Hudson †1922⟩ ⟨a state which dwarfs its men in order that they may be more *docile* instruments in its hands —Howard M. Jones⟩ TRACTABLE suggests characteristics that make for easy guiding, leading, ordering, or managing ⟨they are the tamest, the most abject creatures that we can possibly imagine: mild, peaceable, and *tractable*, they seem to have no will or power to act but as directed by their masters —William Bartram⟩ ⟨a wave of rebelliousness ran through the countryside. Bulls which had always been *tractable* suddenly turned savage —George Orwell⟩ AMENABLE indicates a disposition to be agreeable or complaisant and a lack of assertive independent or stubborn truculence ⟨strikingly individual, never *amenable* to group coercion, expressing their convictions freely and ready to uphold their views by the code of the duel —V.L.Parrington⟩ ⟨she therefore tackled her brother, anticipating a curt refusal, but determined nevertheless to stick to her point. Hermann, however, proved quite *amenable*, and admitted his liability without discussion —J.D.Beresford⟩ BIDDABLE, often applied to children, indicates a ready, constant inclination to follow orders, requests, and suggestions ⟨well-behaved children, *biddable*, meek, neat about their clothes, and always mindful of the proprieties —Willa Cather⟩ ⟨so used to being *biddable* that words and wishes said and shown by older folks were still like orders to her —A.B.Guthrie⟩

**²obedient** \"\ *n* -S : an obedient person

**obe·di·en·tial** \ə,bēdē'enchəl\ *adj* [ML *obedientialis*, fr. *obedientia* rule of obedience, obedience (fr. L *oboedientia* obedience) + L *-alis* -al] : according to a rule of obedience — **obe·di·en·tial·ly** \-ch(ə)lē\ *adv*

**obe·di·en·tia·ry** \-ch(ə)rē, -ri\ *n* -ES [ML *obedientiarius*, fr. *obedientia* obedience + *-arius* -ary — more at OBEDIENCE] **1** *obs* : one owing or yielding obedience : SUBJECT **2** : one of the minor officials in a medieval monastery appointed by the abbot

**obe·di·ent·ly** *adv* [ME, fr. ¹*obedient* + *-ly*] : in an obedient manner ⟨procured fire, which ~ to human purpose cooks and gives warmth —A.N.Whitehead⟩

**obedient plant** *n* [so called fr. the fact that its blossoms will remain for some time in the direction in which they are moved] : FALSE DRAGONHEAD 1

**obei·sance** \ō'bāsᵊn(t)s, ə'-, -bēs-\ *n* -S [ME *obeisaunce*, fr. MF *obeissance*, fr. *obeissant* (fr. OF) + *-ance*] **1** *obs* : OBEDIENCE 1, 2 **2 a** : a movement of the body (as a bending or prostration) or other gesture made in token of respect or submission : BOW, CURTSY ⟨after making his ~s he approached the altar⟩ **b** : an attitude of respect : DEFERENCE, HOMAGE ⟨an author could hardly ask for more than this cultivated ~ —Wolcott Gibbs⟩ **syn** see HONOR

**obei·sant** \-ᵊnt\ *adj* [ME *obeisaunt*, *obeisant*, fr. OF *obeissant*, pres. part. of *obeir* to obey — more at OBEY] **1** *obs* : OBEDIENT **2 a** : DEFERENTIAL **b** : SERVILE, OBSEQUIOUS **c** : bowing in homage — **obei·sant·ly** *adv*

**o-be-joyful** \'ō(,)bē'jȯifəl\ *n* -S *slang* : intoxicating drink

**obe·lia** \ō'bēlyə, -lēə\ *n* [NL, prob. fr. Gk *obelias*, a cake, fr. *obelos* spit (rod used in baking)] **1** *cap* : a genus of small delicate colonial hydroids having a medusa that lacks a velum and being widely distributed in temperate seas and a common colonial hydrozoan about wharves and pilings **2** -S : a member of the genus *Obelia; broadly* : any colonial hydroid of similar form

**obe·li·al** \-lēəl\ *also* **obe·li·ac** \-ē,ak\ *adj* [*obelion* fr. NL *obelion* + E *-al*; *obeliac* fr. NL *obelion* + E *-ac* (fr. L *-acus*, adj. suffix, fr. Gk *-akos*)] : of or relating to the obelion

**obe·li·on** \-lē,än, -ēən\ *n, pl* **obe·lia** \-ēə\ [NL, fr. Gk *obelos* spit, pointed pillar + *-ion*, n. suffix] : a point on the sagittal suture that lies between two small openings through the superior dorsal aspect of the parietal bones and is used in craniometric determinations — see CRANIOMETRY illustration

**ob·e·lis·cal** \,äbə'liskəl\ *adj* [L *obeliscus* obelisk + E *-al*] : of, relating to, or being an obelisk

**ob·e·lis·coid** *or* **ob·e·lis·koid** \-,skȯid\ *adj* : shaped like an obelisk

**¹ob·e·lisk** \'==,lisk\ *n* -S [MF *obelisque*, fr. L *obeliscus*, fr. Gk *obeliskos* small spit, obelisk, dim. of *obelos* spit, pointed pillar, obelus] **1** : an upright, 4-sided, and usu. monolithic pillar that gradually tapers as it rises and terminates in a pyramid ⟨Cleopatra's Needle and the Washington Monument are ~s⟩ **2** : OBELUS **b** : DAGGER 1b(1) **3** : a decorative feature (as on a lamp base or on a chandelier) having a tall slender tapering form

**²obelisk** \"\ *vt* -ED/-ING/-S : to mark or designate with an obelisk

**ob·e·lism** \-,lizəm\ *n* -S [MGk *obelismos*, fr. Gk *obelizein* to obelize + *-ismos* -ism] : the act of obelizing

**ob·e·lize** *also* **ob·e·lise** \-,līz\ *vt* -ED/-ING/-S [Gk *obelizein*, fr. *obelos* obelus + *-izein* -ize] : to designate or annotate with an obelus; *esp* : so to mark as doubtful or spurious

**ob·e·lus** \-ləs\ *n, pl* **ob·e·li** \-,lī\ [LL, fr. Gk *obelos* obelus, lit., spit, pointed pillar] : a symbol — or ÷ used in ancient manuscripts (as of the Septuagint) to mark the beginning of a suspected passage — compare METOBELUS

obelisk

**obe·rea** \ō'birēə\ *n, cap* [NL] : a widely distributed genus of beetles (family Lamiidae) having larvae that are stem borers in various woody plants — see RASPBERRY CANE BORER

**obe·rek** \ō'berək\ *n* -S [Pol] : a Polish folk dance characterized by acrobatics for the man and marching steps for both partners

**ober·hau·sen** \'ōbə(r),hau̇zᵊn\ *adj, usu cap* [fr. *Oberhausen*, Germany] : of or from the city of Oberhausen, Germany : of the kind or style prevalent in Oberhausen

**ober·re·al·schu·le** \-(r)rā'äl,shülə\ *n, pl* **oberrealschu·les** \-ləz\ *or* **oberrealschu·len** \-lən\ [G, fr. *ober* upper (fr. OHG *obaro*) + *realschule*; akin to OHG *ubar* over — more at OVER, REALSCHULE] : a German secondary school preparing students for the university and emphasizing modern languages and natural sciences rather than Latin or Greek — compare GYMNASIUM

**obese** \ō'bēs\ *adj* [L *obesus*, fr. past part. of *obedere* to eat away, devour, fr. *ob-* toward, over + *edere* to eat — more at OB-, EAT] **1 a** *of a person* : excessively corpulent : having a graceless and often unhealthy excess of flesh : afflicted with obesity **b** : bloated out : unusually rounded or full ⟨an ~ pie cooling on the sill⟩ ⟨opened his ~ billfold⟩ **2** : suitable to or like that typical of an obese person ⟨a burst of ~ laughter⟩ **syn** see FAT

**obe·si·ty** \ō'bēsəd.ē, -bes-, -ətē, -i\ *n* -ES [L *obesitas*, fr. *obesus* obese + *-itas* -ity] : a bodily condition marked by excessive generalized deposition and storage of fat : CORPULENCE

**obex** \'ō,beks\ *n* -ES [L *obic-, obex*, fr. *obicere, objicere* to throw in the way, to hinder — more at OBJECT] **1** : OBSTACLE **2** [NL, fr. L, obstacle] : a thin triangular lamina of gray matter in the roof of the fourth ventricle of the brain

**obey** \ō'bā, ə'-\ *vb* -ED/-ING/-S [ME *obeien*, fr. OF *obeir*, fr. L *oboedire* to listen to, obey, fr. *ob-* to, toward, over + *-oedire* (fr. *audire* to hear) — more at OB-, AUDIBLE] *vt* **1** : to fit one's conduct to and perform as directed or requested by ⟨~ one's parents⟩ ⟨~*ing* a superior's order⟩ **2** : to submit to or accord with: **a** : to rule one's conduct in accordance with ⟨the fiercest rebel against society . . . ~s most of its conventions —H.J. Muller⟩ ⟨~*ed* his sense of justice even when it ran counter to his own interests —E.M.Violette⟩ **b** : to act or react in conformity with ⟨the ship ~*ed* the helm⟩ ⟨concluded that by analogy electrical force also ~*ed* the inverse square law —S.F. Mason⟩ ~ *vi* **1** *obs* : to accord with orders or requests and do as told or asked — used with *to* ⟨~*ed* to the king's command⟩ **2** : to perform or behave as directed often without question or attempt at independent decision : be obedient ⟨a people gentle, submissive, prompt to ~ —Agnes Repplier⟩
**syn** MIND, COMPLY: OBEY is the general term indicating to accord with another's commands or wishes ⟨*obey* one's father⟩ ⟨*obey* orders⟩ It may suggest lack of questioning or attempting independent judgment ⟨hear and *obey*⟩ ⟨the submissive way of one long accustomed to *obey* under coercion —Charles Dickens⟩ OBEY is wider in application than MIND or COMPLY since it may be used in reference to laws, principles, moral forces, abstractions ⟨what *obeys* reason, is free —John Milton⟩ ⟨*obey* at all costs the call of what was felt as truth —Havelock Ellis⟩ As a synonym for *obey* MIND is likely to be used in connection with children or juniors; it often suggests admonition to an inferior, ward, or charge ⟨*mind* your mother⟩ ⟨children refusing to *mind* their teachers⟩ COMPLY may suggest a yielding or giving in to another's wishes or orders or to rules or requirements, perhaps through complaisance or lack of strong opinion ⟨should you think ill of that person for *complying* . . . without waiting to be argued into it —Jane Austen⟩ ⟨on being invited by the brute to go outside, what could he do but *comply* —Arnold Bennett⟩

**obey·able** \-əbəl\ *adj* : capable of being obeyed ⟨~ laws⟩

**obey·ance** \-ən(t)s\ *n* -ES : an act or the custom of obeying : OBEDIENCE ⟨~ of laws⟩

**obey·er** \-ə(r)\ *n* -S : one that obeys

**obfirm** *also* **obfirmate** *vt* -ED/-ING/-S [*obfirm* fr. L *obfirmare*, *offirmare*, fr. *ob-, of-* to, against, over + *firmare* to make firm; *obfirmate* fr. L *obfirmatus*, *offirmatus*, past part. of *obfirmare*, *offirmare* to make firm — more at OB-, FIRM] *obs* : to make obdurate

**obfirmation** *n* -S [ML *obfirmation-, obfirmatio*, fr. L *obfirmatus*, *offirmatus* + *-ion-, -io* -ion] *obs* : confirmation in ill-doing : OBDURACY

**ob·fusc** \(')äb'fəsk, əb'f-\ *adj* [by shortening] : OBFUSCATED

**ob·fus·ca·ble** \äb'fəskəbəl, əb'-\ *adj* : capable of being obfuscated

**¹ob·fus·cate** \(')äb'fə,skāt, əb'f-, -,skət, *usu* -d.+V\ *adj* [LL *obfuscatus, offuscatus*, past part. of *obfuscare*, *offuscare* to darken] : OBFUSCATED

**²obfuscate** \'äbfə,skāt, əb'f; 'äb(,)fə,-; *usu* -ād.+V\ *vt* -ED/-ING/-S [LL *obfuscatus, offuscatus*, past part. of *obfuscare*, *offuscare* to darken, fr. L *ob-, of-* over, completely + *fuscare* to darken, fr. *fuscus* dark brown, blackish — more at OB-, DUSK] **1** : CONFUSE, BECLOUD; *esp* : to cause confusion in the mind of ⟨to give the reader all the facts and yet ~ him as to meaning⟩ **2** : to make obscure: **a** : to make difficult of comprehension or interpretation ⟨the small facts could not be ignored without *obfuscating* the main dramatic purpose⟩ **b** : to make unnecessarily complex usu. to the point of confusion ⟨his use of symbolism became a mere mechanical device for *obfuscating* the commonplace and intelligible⟩ **3** : to throw into shadow : make difficult to see : DARKEN **syn** see OBSCURE

**obfuscated** *adj* : confused and baffled ⟨this ~ Indian⟩

**ob·fus·ca·tion** \,äb(,)fə'skāshən\ *n* -S [LL *obfuscation-, obfuscatio, offuscation-, offuscatio*, fr. *obfuscatus, offuscatus* + L *-ion-, -io* -ion] **1** : the quality or state of being obfuscated **2** : an act or instance of obfuscating something

**ob·fus·ca·tor** \äb'fə,skād.ə(r), əb'-; 'äb(,)fə,-\ *n* -S : one that obfuscates

**ob·fus·ca·to·ry** \äb'fəskə,tōrē, əb'-; 'äb(,)fə,skād.ərē, -ri\ *adj* [²*obfuscate* + *-ory*] : tending to obfuscate : CONFUSING, OBSCURING

**ob·fusque** \äb'fəsk, əb'-\ *vt* -ED/-ING/-S [MF *obfusquer*, fr. LL *obfuscare, offuscare*] : OBFUSCATE

**ob·fus·ti·cat·ed** \äb'fəstə,kād.əd, əb'-\ *adj* [alter. of *obfuscated*] *dial* : OBFUSCATED, CONFUSED, BEWILDERED

**¹obi** *var of* OBEAH

**²obi** \'ōbē\ *n* -S [Jap] : a broad Japanese sash wound around the waist over the main kimono and tied at the back

**obis·po** \ō'bi(,)spō, ə'-\ *n* -ES [Sp, lit., bishop, fr. LL *episcopus*; fr. the resemblance of its head to a bishop's mitre — more at BISHOP] : SPOTTED EAGLE RAY

**obispo pine** *n* : BISHOP PINE

**obit** \'ōbət, 'äb- *also chiefly in sense 3* ō'bit\ *n* -S [ME, fr. MF, fr. L *obitus*, fr. *obitus*, past part. of *obire* to die, fr. *ob-* to, over, completely + *ire* to go — more at OB-, ISSUE] **1** *obs* **a** : a person's death : DECEASE **b** : a funeral solemnity : OBSEQUIES; *specif* : a requiem mass and office of the dead **2** *archaic* : a service for the soul of a deceased person (as by an institution in memory of its founder) on his deathday : a regularly recurrent memorial service **3** : a notice or record of a person's death and the date thereof; *esp* : OBITUARY 1

**obital** *adj* [*obit* + *-al*] *obs* : OBITUARY

**¹obi·ter** \'ōbəd.ə(r) *sometimes* 'äb-\ *adv* [L, fr. *ob-* + *iter* way, journey, fr. *ire* to go] : in passing : INCIDENTALLY

**²obiter** \"\ *n* -S [by shortening] : OBITER DICTUM

**obiter dic·tum** \,==='diktəm\ *n, pl* **obiter dic·ta** \-tə\ [LL] **1** : an incidental and collateral opinion uttered by a judge and therefore not material to his decision or judgment and not binding — compare RESPONSA PRUDENTIUM **2** : an incidental or casually interjected remark, reflection, comment, or opinion

**obit·u·al** \ō'bichəwəl, ə'-\ *adj* [L *obitus* death + E *-al*] : OBITUARY

**obit·u·ar·ist** \-chə,werəst, -chər-\ *n* -S : a writer of obituaries or the writer of an obituary

**obit·u·a·rize** \-chəwə,rīz, -chə,r-\ *vi* -ED/-ING/-S [*obituarist* + *-ize*] : to write an obituary

**¹obit·u·ary** \-chə,werē, -chər-, -ri\ *n* -ES [ML *obituarium*, fr. L *obitus* death + *-arium*] **1 a** : a record or notice of a person's death **b** : a usu. short account of the significant aspects and accomplishments of a person's life published (as in a newspaper) upon the person's death **2** : something suggesting an obituary in signaling or seeming to signal the end or death of an enterprise or plan

**²obituary** \"\ *adj* : of, relating to, or recording the death of a person or persons

**obj** *abbr* object; objection; objective

**¹ob·ject** \'äbjikt, -jēkt *sometimes* -,jekt\ *n* -S [ME, fr. L *objectus*, fr. *objectus*, past part. of *objicere*, *obicere* to throw in the way, hinder, object, fr. *ob-* to, toward, against + *-jicere*, *-icere* (fr. *jacere* to throw) — more at OB-, JET] **1** : something that is put or may be regarded as put in the way of some of the senses : something visible or tangible ⟨observed an ~ in the distance⟩ **2** : something that arouses feelings (as of pity, amusement, disgust) in an observer : SIGHT, SPECTACLE **3 a** : something (as an end, aim, or motive) by which the mind or any of its activities is directed : something on which the purposes are fixed as the end of action or effort : something that is sought for : final cause ⟨let our ~ be, our country, our whole country, and nothing but our country —Daniel Webster⟩ ⟨the attainment of wealth was the ~ of his every effort⟩ **b** (1) : something that is set or may be regarded as set before the mind so as to be apprehended or known ⟨an ~ of fear⟩ ⟨such ~s of study⟩ (2) : something of which the mind by any of its activities takes cognizance, whether a thing external in space and time or a conception formed by the mind itself ⟨the opinion that the four main kinds of ~s are cultural objects, other minds, physical objects, and data of our minds —Jørgen Jørgensen⟩ — sometimes distinguished from *ego, self-consciousness*, and *subject* (3) : the totality of external phenomena constituting the not-self — compare INTENTION **4** *obs* : REPRESENTATION, APPEARANCE, SHOW **5 a** : a noun or noun equivalent denoting in verb constructions that on or toward which the action of a verb is directed either actually or as conceived (as *ball* in *I struck the ball* and *what had happened* in *I saw what had happened*) and either immediately (as *thanks* in *I give thanks*) or less immediately (as *you* in *I give you thanks*) **b** : a noun or noun equivalent having with an adjective or adverb a relation analogous to that of object with verb (as *trouble* in *worth the trouble* and *brother* in *like his brother*) **c** : a noun or noun equivalent in a prepositional phrase (as *table* in *on the table* and *city* in *from the city*) **syn** see INTENTION

**²ob·ject** \əb'jekt\ *vb* -ED/-ING/-S [ME *objecten*, fr. L *objectus*, past part. of *objicere*, *obicere* to throw in the way, to object] *vt* **1** *archaic* **a** : to set before or against : bring into opposition : OPPOSE, INTERPOSE **b** : to bring or place in view : EXPOSE **c** : to offer as supportive evidence : bring forward as an argument or reason **2** : to offer in opposition (as by way of accusation or reproach) : adduce as an objection or adverse reason ⟨~*ed* that the statement was misleading⟩ **3** *obs* **a** : to expose to danger or other hazard **b** : IMPUTE ~ *vi* **1** : to oppose something with words or argument — usu. followed by *to* ⟨~*ed* vigorously to their statements⟩ **2** : to feel aversion or distaste for something ⟨any honest man will ~ to such a policy⟩
**syn** PROTEST, REMONSTRATE, EXPOSTULATE, KICK: OBJECT focuses attention on the fact of voiced dislike, aversion, or dissent without implication about its manner or content ⟨*objecting* as a matter of principle⟩ ⟨*objecting* because the evidence was unclear⟩ PROTEST may suggest uttered objection delivered either with orderly formality or with emotion ⟨the bill was passed despite the arguments of the *protesting* senators⟩ ⟨he went here and there swearing and *protesting* against every delay in the work —Sherwood Anderson⟩ REMONSTRATE may apply to utterance blending objection and desire to persuade, influence, or convince ⟨now and then a well-meaning friend of Sir Austin's ventured to *remonstrate* on a dangerous trial he was making in developing any new plan of Education for a youth —George Meredith⟩ EXPOSTULATE may suggest earnest explanation of something objected to coupled with urgent insistence on change ⟨I resolved, for Johnny's sake, to protest, and that very evening drew Gibbings aside and *expostulated* with him —A.T.Quiller-Couch⟩ KICK, often considered colloquial, suggests strenuous or recalcitrant objecting ⟨employees *kicking* about the new regulations⟩ ⟨the crew *kicking* about their food⟩ ⟨newspaper editorials *kicking* about the delay⟩

**ob·ject·able** \-təbəl\ *adj* [²*object* + *-able*] *archaic* : OBJECTIONABLE

**ob·ject·ant** \-tənt\ *n* -S : one that objects (as to military service or some matter in a legal proceeding)

**object ball** *n* : the ball that is first struck by the cue ball in pool or billiards; *also* : any ball that may be hit by the cue ball

**object color** *n* : color that is perceived as belonging to an object and is classifiable as bulky color for interiors of non-opaque objects or as surface color

**ob·jec·tee** \,äb,jek'tē, əb,jek'tē\ *n* -S [²*object* + *-ee*] : one that is objected to

**object glass** *n* : OBJECTIVE 5

**ob·jec·ti·fi·a·ble** \əb'jektə,fīəbəl\ *adj* [*objectify* + *-able*] : capable of being made objective

**ob·jec·ti·fi·ca·tion** \=,==fə'kāshən\ *n* -S [fr. *objectify*, after such pairs as E *identify: identification*] **1** : an act or instance or the process of making objective ⟨Schopenhauer declared . . . that, in contemplating works of art, we contemplate the ~ of will —John Dewey⟩ **2 a** : the state of being objectified **b** : something that is objectified

**ob·jec·ti·fy** \=='==,fī\ *vt* -ED/-ING/-ES [¹*object* + *-ify*] **1 a** : to cause to become or to assume the character of an object **b** : to render objective; *specif* : to give the status of external or independent reality to (something in the mind) **2** : to externalize visually (as in hallucinatory vision)

**ob·jec·tion** \əb'jekshən\ *n* -S [ME *objeccioun*, fr. MF *objection*, fr. LL *objection-, objectio*, fr. L *objectus* (past part. of *objicere*, *obicere* to object) + *-ion-, -io* -ion — more at OBJECT] **1** : an act of objecting ⟨prevent action by ~⟩ **2 a** : something that is or may be presented in opposition : adverse reason or argument : reason for objecting or opposing ⟨presented his ~s in a formal report⟩ **b** : a feeling of disapproval ⟨I have no ~ to going⟩ **3** *obs* : presentation or representation to the view or to the mind

**ob·jec·tion·abil·i·ty** \=,==sh(ə)nə'biləd.ē, -ətē, -i\ *n* : the quality or state of being objectionable

**¹ob·jec·tion·able** \=='=sh(ə)nəbəl\ *adj* : open to objection : OFFENSIVE, UNPLEASING, DISTASTEFUL — **ob·jec·tion·able·ness** \-bəlnəs\ *n* -ES — **ob·jec·tion·ably** \-blē, -li\ *adv*

**²objectionable** \"\ *n* -S : an objectionable individual

**ob·jec·tion·al** \-shənᵊl, -shnəl\ *adj* **1** : of or relating to objection **2** : OBJECTIONABLE

**ob·jec·ti·val** \,äbjək'tīvəl, -,jek-\ *adj* [¹*objective* + *-al*] : of, relating to, or constituting an object in grammar

**ob·jec·ti·vate** \əb'jektə,vāt, äb-\ *vt* -ED/-ING/-S [¹*objective* + *-ate*] : OBJECTIFY — **ob·jec·ti·va·tion** \=,=='vāshən\ *n* -S

**¹ob·jec·tive** \əb'jektiv, äb-, -tēv *also* -əv\ *adj* [It *obiettivo*, fr. ML *objectivus*, fr. L *objectus* object + *-ivus* -ive — more at OBJECT] **1 a** : of or relating to an object of action or feeling : forming an object of attraction or a final cause **b** : contained in, constituting, or having the status of an object: as (1) : existing only in relation to mind : relating to the thing known considered merely in its relation to the knowing subject or to the thing willed or desired in its relation to the agent willing or desiring (2) **:** existing independent of mind **:** relating to an object as it is in itself or as distinguished from consciousness or the subject (3) **:** belonging to nature or the sensible world **:** publicly or intersubjectively observable or verifiable esp. by scientific methods **:** independent of what is personal or private in our apprehension and feelings **:** of such nature that rational minds agree in holding it real or true or valid ⟨his first impression was disproved by ~ reality⟩ (4) *of a symptom of disease* **:** perceptible to persons other than an affected individual **c :** emphasizing or expressing the nature of reality as it is apart from self-consciousness **:** treating events or phenomena as external rather than as affected by personal reflections or feelings **d :** expressing or involving the use of facts without distortion by personal feelings or prejudices ⟨an ~ analysis⟩ ⟨~ tests⟩ **2 :** perceptible to the senses or derived from sense perception ⟨~ data⟩ **3 :** belonging or relating to an object to be delineated ⟨an ~ line⟩ ⟨~ planes⟩ **4** *of a lens* **:** nearest the object — see PRISM BINOCULAR illustration **5 a :** relating to, characteristic of, or being the case which follows a verb used transitively or a preposition **:** being the case that denotes the relation of object; *also* **:** relating to the relation itself **b :** expressing a relation that resembles that of an object to its verb ⟨the ~ genitive *member's* in *a member's expulsion from the club*⟩ **c :** taking an object or noun complement — used of an adjective or adverb (as *worth* in *worth his salt* and *like* in *like his mother*) and of a transitive verb in contrast to an intransitive verb **syn** see FAIR, MATERIAL

[2]**objective** \"\ *n* -s **1 :** something toward which effort is directed **:** an aim or end of action **:** GOAL, OBJECT **2 :** something that is objective; *specif* **:** something external to the mind **3 a :** the objective case that in modern English replaces the Old English accusative and dative **b :** a word in the objective case **4 :** a strategic position to be attained, the purpose to be satisfied (as the destruction of the effectiveness of an enemy's force), or the designated terrain feature to be reached by a military or naval operation **5 :** a lens or system of lenses that forms an image of the object on a screen (as in a camera or projector) or in the focal plane of an eyepiece (as in a telescope or microscope) **syn** see INTENTION

**objective complement** *or* **objective predicate** *n* **:** a noun, adjective, or pronoun used in the predicate as complement to a factitive verb or a verb of choosing, naming, thinking and as qualifier of its direct object (as *chairman* in *make John chairman*, *angry* in *make him angry*, and *red* in *paint his nose red*)

**objective correlative** *n* **:** something (as a situation or chain of events) that symbolizes or renders objective an emotion and may be employed in creative writing to evoke a desired emotional response in the reader

**objective idealism** *n* **:** the acceptance of nature as ultimately ideal or spiritual and existing independently of any subjects; *specif* **:** the philosophy of F.W.J. von Schelling according to which nature is visible intelligence and intelligence invisible nature — contrasted with *subjective idealism*

**objective line** *n* **:** a line drawn on the geometrical plane to be represented

**ob·jec·tive·ly** \əb'jektəvlē, äb-, -li\ *adv* **:** in an objective manner **:** with objectivity

**ob·jec·tive·ness** \-tivnəs, -tēv- *also* -əv-\ *n* -ES **:** OBJECTIVITY

**objective plane** *n* **:** the plane tangent to the ground at a military objective

**objective prism** *n* **:** a transparent prism of small apex angle but large size that is placed in front of the objective of a telescope to cause all stars and other objects to appear as short spectra in the focal plane where they may be photographed together on a single plate of the field

**objective test** *n* **:** a test designed to exclude as far as possible the subjective element on the part of both those taking and grading it by presenting a number of factual questions to be answered by one word or a check mark instead of verbal expression and organization of material — compare ESSAY EXAMINATION

**objective time** *n* **:** time that is an objectively determinable order in which durations are measured and an absolute present is indifferent — contrasted with *subjective time;* called also *public time*

**ob·jec·tiv·ism** \əb'jektə,vizəm, äb-\ *n* -s **1 a** (1) **:** any of various philosophical theories that stress the external elements of reality to the relative neglect of the mental (2) **:** a theory that asserts human knowledge to have objective validity **b :** any theory or system of analysis that stresses objectivity through the rigid exclusion of data that do not admit of quantitative treatment — compare BEHAVIORISM **2 :** an ethical theory considering the moral good to be objective and independent of personal or merely human feelings: **a :** such a theory considering the moral good to be something natural and observable without a special faculty or insight **b :** such a theory (as in intuitionism) considering the moral good to be something nonnatural **3 :** the theory or practice of objective art or literature

**ob·jec·tiv·ist** \-ˌvəst\ *n* -s **:** an adherent or advocate of objectivism

**ob·jec·tiv·is·tic** \=ˌ==ˌvistik, -ēk\ *adj* **:** of or relating to objectivism

**ob·jec·tiv·i·ty** \ˌäb(ˌ)jek'tivəd·ē, -ˌjək-, -vətē, -i\ *n* -ES **1 :** the quality, state, or relation of being objective ⟨his completely unimpassioned ~⟩ **2 :** objective reality

**ob·jec·ti·vi·za·tion** \əbˌjektəvə'zāshən, äb-, -ˌvī'z-\ *n* -s **:** the act or process of making or becoming objective

**ob·jec·tiv·ize** \əb'jektəˌvīz, äb-\ *vt* -ED/-ING/-S [[2]*objective* + *-ize*] **:** OBJECTIFY

**ob·ject·ize** \'äb(ˌ)jekˌtīz, -ˌjək-\ *vt* -ED/-ING/-S [[1]*object* + *-ize*] **:** OBJECTIFY

**object language** *n* **1 :** a language dealing with objects or entities outside itself or referring to things, events, and their properties **2 :** a language that is being talked about or is an object of investigation by another language — compare METALANGUAGE

**ob·ject·less** \'äbjəktləs, -ˌjek-\ *adj* **:** lacking an object **:** having no clear-cut purpose or intent ⟨~ rambles⟩ — **ob·ject·less·ly** *adv* — **ob·ject·less·ness** *n* -ES

**object lesson** *n* **1 :** a lesson in which a material object is made the basis of instruction **2 :** something that teaches by exemplifying a principle in concrete form

**object libido** *n* [part trans. of G *objekt libido*] **:** erotic desire directed toward another individual than the self — compare EGO-LIBIDO

**object matter** *n* **:** SUBJECT MATTER

**object of art** [by trans.] **:** OBJET D'ART

**ob·jec·tor** \əb'jektə(r)\ *n* -s [[2]*object* + *-or*] **:** one that objects (as to a proposition or measure)

**objects** *pl of* OBJECT, *pres 3d sing of* OBJECT

**object space** *n* **:** the space in relation to an optical system in which are located the objects to be imaged by the system — compare IMAGE SPACE

**ob·jet d'art** \ˌóbˌzhā'där, -då(r\ *n, pl* **ob·jets d'art** \"\ [F, lit., art object] **1 :** an article of artistic worth **2 :** BIBELOT, CURIO, TRINKET

**ob·ji·cient** \əb'jishənt\ *n* -s [L *objicient-, objiciens, obicient-, obiciens*, pres. part. of *objicere, obicere* to object — more at OBJECT] **:** OBJECTOR

**ob·ju·ra·tion** \ˌäbjə'rāshən\ *n* -s [L *objur*are to bind by oath (fr. *ob-* + *jurare* to swear) + E *-ation* — more at JURY] **:** a binding or charging by or as if by oath

**ob·jur·gate** \'äbjə(r)ˌgāt\ *vt* -ED/-ING/-S [L *objurgatus*, past part. of *objurgare* to scold, blame, fr. *ob-* against, over + *jurgare* to quarrel, blame, bring a lawsuit, fr. *jur-, jus* law + *-gare* (fr. *agere* to drive, lead, act, do) — more at OB-, JUST, AGENT] **:** to decry vehemently ⟨*objurgated* the custom of garnishing poems with archaisms —T.R.Weiss⟩ **:** to castigate with harsh or violent language **:** VITUPERATE **syn** see EXECRATE

**ob·jur·ga·tion** \ˌäbjə(r)'gāshən\ *n* -s [MF or L; MF, fr. L *objurgation-, objurgatio*, fr. *objurgatus* + *-ion-, -io* -ion] **:** an act or instance of objurgating **:** a harsh or violent reproof

**ob·jur·ga·tive** \əb'jərgəd·iv\ *adj* **:** OBJURGATORY — **ob·jur·ga·tive·ly** \-d·əvlē\ *adv*

**ob·jur·ga·tor** \'äbjə(r)ˌgād·ə(r)\ *n* -s **:** one that objurgates

**ob·jur·ga·to·ri·ly** \əbˌjərgəˌtōrəlē, (ˌ)äb-\ *adv* **:** in an objurgatory manner

**ob·jur·ga·to·ry** \əb'jərgəˌtōrē\ *adj* [L *objurgatorius*, fr. *objurgatus* (past part. of *objurgare* to objurgate) + *-orius* -ory] **:** constituting objurgation ⟨~ speeches⟩ **:** expressing rebuke ⟨relapse from her official ~ tone —George Eliot⟩

**ob·jur·ga·trix** \ˌäbjərˌgā·triks\ *n, pl* **objurgatri·ces** \ˌ=='gā·trəˌsēz; əbˌjərgə·'trī(ˌ)sēz, ˌäb-\ [ML, fem. of L *objurgator* scolder, fr. *objurgatus* + *-or*] *archaic* **:** COMMON SCOLD

**obl** *abbr* **1** obligation **2** oblique **3** oblong

**OBL** *abbr* order bill of lading

**ob·lanceolate** \(')äb+\ *adj* [*ob-* + *lanceolate*] **:** inversely lanceolate ⟨an ~ leaf⟩ — see LEAF illustration

**ob·last** \'äˌblást, 'óˌ-\ *n, pl* **oblasts** \-sts\ *also* **oblasti** \-stē\ [Russ *oblast'* province, oblast, fr. OSlav, fr. *ob-* (fr. *ob* to, on) + *vlast'* dominion, government; akin to L *ob* to, before, against and to Lith *veldėti* to rule — more at EPI-, WIELD] **:** a governmental subdivision of the U. S. S. R. corresponding to an autonomous province or state

**oblat** \óblå\ *n* -s [F, fr. ML *oblatus* oblate, n., fr. L *oblatus*, suppletive past part. of *offerre* to carry to, offer] **:** OBLATE

**ob·la·ta** \ä'bläd·ə, -ād·ə\ *n pl* [ML, oblates, neut. pl. of *oblatus* oblate, n.] *archaic* **:** old debts or gifts to the crown remaining unpaid to the English Exchequer; *also* **:** the entries for them in the rolls of the Exchequer

[1]**ob·late** \ä'blāt, ə'-, *usu* -ād·+V\ *vt* -ED/-ING/-S [L *oblatus* (suppletive past part. of *offerre* to carry to, offer) fr. *ob-* to, towards + *latus* carried (suppletive past part. of *ferre* to carry) — more at OB-, BEAR, TOLERATE] **:** OFFER; *esp* **:** to make an oblation of

[2]**ob·late** \(')äˌblāt, (')ōˌ-, ə'blāt, *usu* -ād· + V\ *adj* [prob. fr. (assumed) NL *oblatus*, lit., carried forward, stretched, fr. L, suppletive past part. of *offerre*] **:** flattened or depressed at the poles ⟨an ~ leaf⟩ ⟨~ teapot⟩ ⟨~ spheroid⟩ — opposed to *prolate* — **ob·late·ly** *adv*

[3]**oblate** \"\ *n* -s [ML *oblatus*, fr. L, suppletive past part. of *offerre*] **1** *Roman Catholicism* **:** one offered or devoted to the monastic life or to some special religious service or work: **a :** a child dedicated in his or her early years by the parents to the monastic life **b :** one of a class of persons who have offered themselves and their property to a monastery in which they live **2** *usu cap, Roman Catholicism* **:** a member of one of the religious orders devoted to a particular work

**oblate ellipsoid of revolution** [[2]*oblate*] **:** the ellipsoid of revolution obtained by revolving an ellipse about its minor axis

**ob·late·ness** *n* -ES [[2]*oblate* + *-ness*] **:** oblate state or character; *specif* **:** ELLIPTICITY 1 ⟨~ of a planet⟩

**ob·la·tio** \ä'blāshēˌō, -(ˌ)shō\ *n* -s [LL, oblation] *Roman civil law* **:** a tender of something (as a payment) due

**ob·la·tion** \ə'blāshən, ō'b-, ä'b-\ *n* -s [ME *oblacioun*, fr. MF *oblation*, fr. LL *oblation-, oblatio*, fr. L *oblatus* (suppletive past part. of *offerre* to carry to, offer) + *-ion-, -io* -ion] **1 a :** a religious or ritualistic offering usu. of something without life in contrast to a sacrifice of living things **b** *usu cap* **:** the act of offering the eucharistic elements to God in a Christian communion service **2 :** something offered or presented in worship or sacred service **:** OFFERING, SACRIFICE **3 :** an offering made to a church ⟨offering her ~*s* for aid to the poor⟩ **4** *usu cap* **:** one of several loaves of leavened bread offered by members of an Eastern Orthodox church for use in the Eucharist

**ob·la·tion·al** \-shənᵊl, -shnəl\ *adj* **:** OBLATORY

**ob·la·tion·ary** \-shəˌnerē, -ri\ *n* -ES [ML *oblationarius*, fr. LL *oblation-, oblatio* oblation + L *-arius* -ary] **:** an ecclesiastic who receives the oblations offered in the celebration of the Eucharist

**ob·la·to·ry** \'äbləˌtōrė, -tȯr-, -ri\ *adj* [ML *oblatorius*, fr. L *oblatus* + *-orius* -ory] **:** of or relating to oblation

**ob·lec·ta·tion** \ˌäˌblek'tāshən\ *n* -s [MF or L; MF, fr. L *oblectation-, oblectatio*, fr. *oblectatus* (past part. of *oblectare* to delight, fr. *ob-* to, over, completely + *lactare*, freq. of *lacere* to allure) + *-ion-, -io* -ion — more at OB-, DELIGHT] **:** PLEASURE, SATISFACTION, DELIGHT ⟨~ of the senses⟩

**obleege** \ə'blēj\ *chiefly dial var of* OBLIGE

**ob·ley** \'äblē, -li\ *n* -s [ME, fr. MF *oublee*, fr. ML *oblata*, fem. of *oblatus* offering, oblate — more at OBLATE] **:** a small flat cake or wafer; *esp* **:** a wafer of altar bread

**ob·li·ga·bil·i·ty** \ˌäbləgə'biləd·ē, -lēg-\ *n* **:** the quality or state of being obligable

**ob·li·ga·ble** \'==gəbəl\ *adj* [*oblig*ation + *-able*] **:** subject to or involving obligation

**ob·li·gant** \-gənt\ *n* -s [L *obligant-, obligans*, pres. part. of *obligare* to oblige — more at OBLIGE] **:** OBLIGOR

[1]**ob·li·gate** \-gət, -ləˌgāt\ *adj* [ME *obligat*, fr. L *obligatus*, past part. of *obligare*] **1 a** *obs* **:** placed under obligation **:** BOUND **b :** restricted to a particular condition of life ⟨an ~ parasite⟩ ⟨~ anaerobes⟩ **2 :** completely unavoidable **:** ESSENTIAL, NECESSARY ⟨the presence of mycorrhiza appears ~ to the healthy growth of many plants⟩ ⟨following an ~ course of development⟩ — **ob·li·gate·ly** *adv*

[2]**obligate** \'äbləˌgāt, *usu* -ād·+V\ *vt* -ED/-ING/-S [L *obligatus*, past part. of *obligare* to oblige — more at OBLIGE] **1** *obs* **:** BIND, FASTEN **2 a :** to pledge as security **b :** to assign or commit (as funds) to meet a particular obligation ⟨the treasury had *obligated* anticipated receipts from the new tax⟩ **3 a :** to constrain or bind to some course of action (as by legal measures, moral or social considerations, or force of circumstances) ⟨*obligated* to pay alimony⟩ ⟨community life ~*s* each of us to certain restraints and conformities⟩ **b :** OBLIGE 3a ⟨hoping to ~ enough of his colleagues to put over the measure⟩ ⟨I don't like to be *obligated* to anybody⟩ **4 :** to put under a promise, vow, or oath esp. as part of a ceremony of initiation into an organization

**ob·li·ga·tion** \ˌ=='gāshən\ *n* -s [ME *obligacioun*, fr. OF *obligation*, fr. L *obligation-, obligatio*, fr. *obligatus* + *-ion-, -io* -ion] **1 :** an act of obligating oneself to a course of action **:** a putting under a promise, vow, or oath (as in initiation into an organization) **2 a :** an obligating factor or instrument **:** something (as a promise, vow, or demand of ideals or conscience) that binds or constrains to a course of action **:** the obligating power inherent in such a factor or instrument ⟨the ~*s* of conscience⟩ **b :** a bond with a condition annexed and a penalty for nonfulfillment; *broadly* **:** a formal and binding agreement or acknowledgment of a liability to pay a specified sum or do a specified thing **c :** an investment security ⟨corporate bonds and other ~*s*⟩ **3 a :** something that one is bound to do or forbear **:** an imperative duty (as imposed by promise, religion, conscience, ideals, or social standards) **b :** a duty arising by contract **:** a legal liability **4 a :** a condition or feeling of being bound legally or ethically **b :** a condition or feeling of social indebtedness (as for kindnesses and favors granted) ⟨their repeated assistance left him with an intolerable sense of ~⟩ **5 :** money committed to a particular purpose **:** LIABILITY, ENCUMBRANCE **6** *Roman & civil law* **:** a legal relationship or tie in accordance with which one party is able to compel another in a personal action and under the existing circumstances to do or not to do a specified act (as to pay money or transfer property) or to refrain from specified conduct and which arises out of a contract, quasi contract, delict, or quasi delict

**syn** DUTY and OBLIGATION are often interchangeable but OBLIGATION can apply to what one must do or refrain from doing usu. by an immediate constraint inherent in position, occupation, relationship, or belief ⟨the *obligation* of the courts to refuse to enforce any legislation which violates freedom of speech —Zechariah Chafee⟩ ⟨Christians differ in their understanding of religious *obligation* —J.C.Swaim⟩ ⟨one of the most compelling *obligations* of the good citizen —John Lodge⟩ ⟨one's *obligation* to provide for one's family⟩ whereas DUTY can suggest less immediate compulsion but a greater general compulsion on moral or ethical grounds ⟨one's *duty* to one's family⟩ ⟨considered that every one owed a certain *duty* to society —A.C.Benson⟩ ⟨the *duty* of self-preservation —W.R. Inge⟩ ⟨still has his *duty* to his mother —Mary Austin⟩ **syn** see in addition DEBT

**ob·li·ga·tion·al** \ˌ==ˌgāshənᵊl, -shnəl\ *adj* **:** of, relating to, or constituting an obligation; *specif* **:** qualified to create a legal or financial obligation ⟨an ~ authority⟩

**ob·li·ga·tive** \'==ˌgād·iv\ *adj* [L *obligat*us (past part. of *obligare* to oblige) + E *-ive*] **1 :** entailing an obligation **:** OBLIGATORY ⟨an ~ contract⟩ **2 :** OBLIGATE 1b **3 a :** characterized by or relating to the obligative mood **b :** containing a form in the obligative mood

**obligative mood** *n* **:** modal expression of obligation or propriety (as in "the door *should* be closed")

**obli·gato** *var of* OBBLIGATO

**ob·li·ga·tor** \'äbləˌgād·ə(r)\ *n* -s [ML, fr. L *obligatus* + *-or*] **1 :** OBLIGOR **2 :** OBLIGER

**oblig·a·to·ri·ly** \əˌbligəˌtōrəlē, ˌäbləg-,-lēg-, -tȯr-, -li, *chiefly Brit* ˌäbləˌgāt(ə)rəli\ *adv* **:** in an obligatory manner **:** so as to be obligatory ⟨they are infinitesimally small, living things, ~ parasitic —W.A.Hagan⟩

**ob·li·ga·to·ri·ness** \-rēnəs, -rin-\ *n* -ES **:** the quality or state of being obligatory

**oblig·a·to·ry** \ə'bligəˌtōrē, 'äbləg-,-lēg-, -tȯr-, -ri, *chiefly Brit* ˌäbləˌgātəri *or* -ā·tri\ *adj* [ME, fr. MF *obligatoire*, fr. LL *obligatorius*, fr. L *obligatus* + *-orius* -ory] **1 a :** demanded or required by existing obligations esp. of a moral or legal nature; *specif* **:** binding in law or conscience **b :** imposing or constituting duty or obligation — often used with *on* or *upon* ⟨obedience is ~ on a soldier⟩ **2 :** relating to or used to create or enforce an obligation ⟨a writ ~⟩ **3 :** having to be coped with (as by studying, acting, paying) **:** REQUIRED ⟨physical education is ~⟩ ⟨an ~ contribution⟩ **4 :** OBLIGATE 1b

**ob·li·ga·tum** \ˌäblə'gäd·əm, -ād·əm\ *n, pl* **obliga·ta** \-äd·ə, -ād·ə\ [NL, lit., obligation, fr. L, neut. of *obligatus*, past part. of *obligare*] **:** a proposition that is not self-contradictory and that is assumed for argument in scholastic disputation

**oblige** \ə'blīj\ *vb* -ED/-ING/-S [ME *obligen*, fr. OF *obliger*, fr. L *obligare*, fr. *ob-* to, against, over + *ligare* to bind, tie — more at OB-, LIGATURE] *vt* **1 :** to constrain (as another or oneself) by physical, moral, or legal force **:** put under obligation to do or to forbear from doing something ⟨necessity *obliged* him to this crime⟩ ⟨we *obliged* ourselves to settle our father's bills⟩ ⟨the soldiers were *obliged* to retreat⟩ ⟨the law ~*s* everyone to pay his taxes⟩ **2 a** *obs* **:** to pledge as security **:** PAWN, MORTGAGE **b** *obs* **:** to bind as subject to a penalty (as by a bond) **c :** to make (oneself) liable to punishment under the law **3 a :** to bind by a favor or service performed **:** place under obligation by helping or favoring **:** make indebted by such treatment ⟨you will ~ me greatly if you get there early⟩ **b :** to do a favor or minor service for ⟨always seeking to ~ his friends⟩ **c** *obs* **:** PLEASE, ACCOMMODATE, GRATIFY **d** *dial* **:** to work for esp. in a domestic capacity ⟨used to ~ a few favored neighbors on festive occasions⟩ **e :** to make a loan to ⟨can you ~ me with a few dollars⟩ **~** *vi* **:** to do something as or as if a favor ⟨the sun *obliged* somewhat fitfully —Mollie Panter-Downes⟩: as **a :** to perform by way of entertainment ⟨the quartet will ~ with a song⟩ **b** *dial* **:** to work for someone esp. in a domestic capacity ⟨she *obliged* for the cottagers in summer⟩

**syn** OBLIGE, ACCOMMODATE, FAVOR all signify to do a service or perform a courtesy. OBLIGE suggests the doing of something that is so pleasing or so esp. convenient for someone else that it could be thought to, though does not necessarily, create an obligation ⟨*oblige* a friend by lending him money⟩ ⟨the hotel *obliged* by serving them meals at odd hours with no extra charge⟩ ⟨*oblige* me by retiring for the night —George Meredith⟩ ACCOMMODATE, often interchangeable with *oblige*, usu. suggests the putting of oneself to some inconvenience or sacrifice to oblige; in its very common use in business it frequently suggests a practical or commercial motive above that of goodwill ⟨*accommodate* a friend with the loan of a car⟩ ⟨keep exotic foods in stock to *accommodate* special customers⟩ FAVOR usu. confines the service or courtesy to one of goodwill ⟨*favor* one's friends with many small kindnesses⟩ ⟨*favor* an audience with an encore⟩ although it has come, in this sense, to suggest often a supercilious or patronizing quality in the action ⟨*favor* common people around him with a cold smile⟩ ⟨*favor* his admirers with a glance⟩ ⟨*favor* his parents with a yearly letter⟩ **syn** see in addition FORCE

**obliged** \-jd\ *adj* **1 :** full of appreciation **:** OBLIGATED **2 a :** FATED, SURE ⟨it's ~ to rain soon⟩ **b :** FORCED ⟨~ to continue on foot⟩ — **oblig·ed·ly** \-jədlē, -li\ *adv* — **oblig·ed·ness** \-jədnəs\ *n* -ES

**ob·li·gee** \ˌäbləˌjē\ *n* -s [*oblige* + *-ee*] **1 a :** one to whom another is obligated **:** one toward whom another has undertaken an obligation **:** one in a position to enforce a legal duty owed by another — opposed to *obligor* **b :** a person whose interests are protected under a surety bond **2 :** one who is obliged — opposed to *obliger*

**oblige·ment** \ə'blījmənt\ *n* -s [F, fr. *obliger* to oblige + *-ment*] **:** an obligation or accommodation esp. resulting from a service or favor

**oblig·er** \-jə(r)\ *n* -s **:** one that obligates or obliges

**obliging** *adj* [fr. pres. part. of *oblige*] **1** *archaic* **:** OBLIGATING, OBLIGATORY **2 :** willing to do services or favors **:** accommodating to others **:** HELPFUL, COOPERATIVE ⟨was very ~ and offered to do anything in his power —Bram Stoker⟩ **syn** see AMIABLE

**oblig·ing·ly** *adv* **:** in an obliging manner **:** PLEASANTLY, COOPERATIVELY

**oblig·ing·ness** *n* -ES **:** the quality or state of being obliging

**ob·li·gis·tic** \ˌäbləˌjistik\ *adj* [NL *oblig*atum + E *-istic*] **:** of or relating to the obligata of scholastic disputation ⟨an ~ proposition⟩

**ob·li·gor** \ˌäbləˌgȯ(ə)r, -ȯ(ə)\ *n* -s [*oblige* + *-or*] **1 :** one that binds himself or gives his bond to another **:** one that places himself under a legal obligation — opposed to *obligee* **2 a :** a surety or surety company that writes a bond **b :** the person bonded under a surety bond

**obliquate** *vt* -ED/-ING/-S [L *obliquatus*, past part. of *obliquare* to bend aside, turn aside, fr. *obliquus* oblique] *obs* **:** to turn or bend aside or to one side — **obliquation** *n* -s *obs*

[1]**oblique** \ə'blēk, ō'-, -līk\ *adj* [ME *oblike*, fr. L *obliquus*, fr. *ob-* to, towards, over + *-liquus* (akin to L *liquis* oblique); akin to L *ulna* elbow — more at OB-, ELL] **1 a :** neither perpendicular nor parallel **:** having a slanting direction or position **:** INCLINED **b** *of a solid* **:** having the axis not perpendicular to the base **2 a :** not straightforward **:** INDIRECT, OBSCURE ⟨~ glances⟩ ⟨~ accusations⟩ ⟨~ perspective⟩ **b :** DEVIOUS, UNDERHAND, PERVERSE, SINISTER ⟨behaving in a curiously ~ manner⟩ **c** (1) **:** SKEW ⟨an ~ arch⟩ ⟨~ bridges⟩ (2) *of a leaf* **:** having the two sides of the blade unequal esp. at the base **3 :** not direct in descent **:** COLLATERAL **4** *of a muscle* **:** situated obliquely and having one end that is not inserted on bone ⟨the ~ muscles of the eye or abdomen⟩ **5 :** taken from an airplane with the camera axis intentionally directed horizontally or downward but not vertically — used of a photograph of the surface of the earth — **oblique·ly** *adv* — **oblique·ness** *n* -ES

[2]**oblique** \"\ *n* -s **1 :** an oblique thing (as a line or photograph) **2 :** any of several oblique muscles: as **a :** one of the thin flat muscles forming the middle and outer layers of the lateral walls of the abdomen and having aponeuroses that extend medially to ensheathe the rectus muscles and fuse in the midventral line in the linear alba **b** (1) **:** a long thin muscle that is inserted on the upper part of the eyeball and that moves the eye downward and laterally — called also *superior oblique* (2) **:** a short muscle that is inserted slightly in front of and below the superior oblique and that moves the eye upward and laterally — called also *inferior oblique* **3 :** DIAGONAL 4 **4 :** a printed letter characterized by essentially the same form and degree of inclination as italic **5 a :** OBLIQUE CASE **b :** an inflection of an oblique case

[3]**oblique** \ə'blīk, ō'-\ *vi* -ED/-ING/-S [F *obliquer*, fr. L *obliquare* to bend aside, turn aside, fr. *obliquus* oblique] *of a military formation* **:** to march or advance obliquely at an angle of about 45 degrees to the original front formerly by oblique steps but now by direct steps with the participants half-faced to right or left and marching forward

**oblique angle** *n* **:** an acute or obtuse angle — distinguished from *right angle*

**oblique case** *n* **:** a grammatical case other than the nominative and vocative

**oblique coordinates** *n pl* **:** Cartesian coordinates that are not rectangular

**oblique drawing** *n* **:** a projective drawing of which the frontal lines are given in true proportions and relations and all others at suitable angles other than 90 degrees without regard to the rules of linear perspective

**oblique fault** *n* **:** a geological fault whose trend is oblique to the strike

**oblique helicoid** *n* **:** a helicoid whose generating half line maintains a constant oblique angle with the helix axis
**oblique lamination** *n* **:** CROSS-BEDDING
**oblique·ly** *adv* **:** in an oblique way or direction
**oblique·ness** *n* -ES **:** the quality or state of being oblique
**oblique projection** *n* **1 :** a representation in a mechanical drawing of an object usu. placed with its front face or with two of its principal axes parallel to a plane of projection by means of lines of projection that make angles of other than 90 degrees with the plane **2 :** a map projection not centered upon one of the poles or on the equator and not using the equator or a meridian as a center line of orientation
**oblique sailing** *n* **:** the movement of a vessel when it sails upon a course making an oblique angle with the meridian
**oblique section** *n* **:** a section in a mechanical drawing that is neither a cross section nor a longitudinal section
**oblique sphere** *n* **:** the celestial sphere and its analogous terrestrial sphere when oriented so the heavenly bodies rise and set at angles other than a right angle (as for an observer at any point on the earth except the poles and the equator)
**oblique triangle** *n* **:** a triangle that is not a right triangle
**ob·liq·ui·tous** \ə'blikwəd·əs, ō'-, -ətəs\ *adj* **:** exhibiting or characterized by obliquity
**ob·liq·ui·ty** \-wəd·ē, -ətē, -i\ *n* -ES [ME *obliquitee*, fr. MF *obliquité*, fr. L *obliquitat-, obliquitas*, fr. *obliquus* oblique + *-itat-, -itas* -ity — more at OBLIQUE] **1 a :** deviation from moral rectitude or sound thinking **b** *obs* **:** deviation from ordinary rules **2 a** (1) **:** the quality or state of being oblique **:** deviation from parallelism or perpendicularity (2) **:** the amount of such deviation **:** DIVERGENCE **b** *or* **obliquity of the ecliptic :** the angle between the planes of the earth's equator and orbit having a mean value of 23°26′40″.16 in 1960 and diminishing 0″.47 per year **3 a :** indirectness or deliberate obscurity of speech or conduct **b :** an obscure or confusing statement ⟨hiding their thoughts behind such *obliquities*⟩
**ob·lit·er·a·ble** \ə'blid·ərəbəl, ō'-, ä'-, -itər-\ *adj* **:** capable of being obliterated
[1]**ob·lit·er·ate** \-rət\ *adj* [L *obliteratus, oblitteratus*, past part. of *obliterare, oblitterare*] **1 :** blotted out **:** OBLITERATED **2 :** FAINT, INDISTINCT, OBSCURE — used esp. of markings on an insect
[2]**obliterate** \-,rāt, *usu* -ād·+V\ *vb* -ED/-ING/-S [L *obliteratus, oblitteratus*, past part. of *obliterare, oblitterare*, prob. fr. *ob-* to, against, over + *litera, littera* letter — more at OB-, LETTER] *vt* **1 :** to remove from significance and bring to nothingness: as **a :** to make undecipherable or imperceptible by obscuring, covering, or wearing or chipping away ⟨a dimness . . . envelops consciousness as mist ~*s* a crag —Emily Dickinson⟩ ⟨only copper so worn that even the stamp is *obliterated* —Amy Lowell⟩ **b :** to remove utterly from recognition, cognizance, consideration, or memory ⟨a successful love crowned all other successes and *obliterated* all other failures —J.W.Krutch⟩ **c** (1) **:** to remove from existence **:** make nonexistent **:** destroy utterly all traces, indications, significance of ⟨many of our monuments . . . seem to shout for a friendly zeppelin to ~ them —W.R.Inge⟩ (2) **:** to cause to disappear (as a body part, scar, or the lumen of a duct) **:** REMOVE ⟨possible to ~ the gall bladder by electrosurgical methods⟩ **2 :** to withdraw utterly from attention and make as inconspicuous as if nonexistent ⟨those hero-worshipers who ~ themselves —Robert Lynd⟩ **3 :** CANCEL ~ *vi* **:** to become obliterated **syn** see ERASE
**ob·lit·er·at·ing·ly** *adv* **:** in an obliterating manner **:** so as to obliterate
**ob·lit·er·a·tion** \ə,blid·ə'rāshən, ō,-, ä,-, -litə-\ *n* -S [L *obliteration-, oblitteratio*, fr. *obliteratus, oblitteratus* + *-ion-, -io* -ion] **1 :** an act or instance of obliterating **2 :** the state of being obliterated **:** EXTINCTION
**ob·lit·er·a·tive** \ə'==,rād·iv, -rə|, |t|, |ēv *also* |əv\ *adj* **:** inducing or characterized by obliteration: as **a :** causing or accompanied by collapse or closure of a lumen (as of a blood vessel) ⟨~ endarteritis⟩ **b :** tending to make inconspicuous ⟨the characteristic ~ shading of fishes⟩ ⟨~ behavior⟩ — **ob·lit·er·a·tive·ly** \|əvlē, -li\ *adv*
**ob·lit·er·a·tor** \-,rād·ə(r), -ātə-\ *n* -S [LL *obliterator, oblitterator*, fr. L *obliteratus, oblitteratus* + *-or*] **:** one that obliterates; *esp* **:** a device for canceling postage stamps
**ob·li·ves·cence** \,äblə'vesᵊn(t)s\ *n* -S [alter. (influenced by *-escence*) of *obliviscence*] **:** an act or the process of forgetting
**ob·liv·i·al** \ə'blivēəl\ *adj* [L *oblivialis*, fr. *oblivion-, oblivio* oblivion + *-alis* -al] **:** OBLIVIOUS **:** causing oblivion — **ob·liv·i·al·i·ty** \=,==ʹaləd·ē\ *n* -ES
**ob·liv·i·ate** \=ʹ==,āt\ *vt* -ED/-ING/-S [L *oblivion-, oblivio* oblivion + E *-ate*] **:** FORGET
**ob·liv·i·on** \ə'blivēən, ō'-, ä'-\ *n* -S [ME, fr. MF, fr. L *oblivion-, oblivio*, fr. *oblivisci* to forget (perh. fr. *ob-* to, over, completely + *levis* smooth) + *-ion-, -io* -ion — more at OB-, LIME] **1 :** an act of forgetting or the fact of having forgotten **:** FORGETFULNESS, OBLIVIOUSNESS ⟨seeking ease and the ~ of sleep⟩ **2 :** the quality or state of being forgotten ⟨contentedly accepted his political ~⟩ **3 :** official ignoring of offenses **:** general pardon **:** AMNESTY ⟨an act of ~⟩
**ob·liv·i·on·ize** \-,nīz\ *vt* -ED/-ING/-S **:** to relegate to oblivion
**ob·liv·i·ous** \ə'blivēəs, ō'-, ä'-\ *adj* [ME, fr. L *obliviosus*, fr. *oblivion-, oblivio* oblivion + *-osus* -ous] **1 :** lacking remembrance, memory, or mindful attention **:** characterized by forgetfulness ⟨~ old age⟩ — usu. used with *of* ⟨~ of past slights⟩ **2** *archaic* **:** relating to or associated with forgetfulness **3 :** lacking active conscious knowledge or awareness **:** UNNOTICING, UNAWARE — usu. used with *of* or *to* ⟨~ to the risk she ran⟩ ⟨~ of the surrounding crowds⟩ **syn** see FORGETFUL
**ob·liv·i·ous·ly** *adv* **:** without remembrance or awareness **:** in an oblivious manner
**ob·liv·i·ous·ness** *n* -ES **:** the quality or state of being oblivious
**ob·li·vis·cence** \,äblə'visᵊn(t)s\ *n* -S [L *oblivisci* to forget + E *-ence*] **:** FORGETFULNESS
**ob·lo·cu·tor** \,äblə'kyüd·ə(r)\ *n* -S [L, fr. *oblocutus* (past part. of *obloqui* to speak against) + *-or* — more at OBLOQUY] **:** DISPUTER, GAINSAYER, DETRACTOR — used chiefly in law
[1]**ob·long** \'ä,blȯŋ *also* -läŋ\ *adj* [ME *oblonge*, fr. L *oblongus* elongated, somewhat long, fr. *ob-* toward, over, completely + *longus* long — more at OB-, LONG] **:** deviating from a square or circular form through elongation: **a :** rectangular with adjacent sides unequal **b :** rectangular with the normally horizontal dimension the greater — used of a plane surface or of an object with a principal plane surface ⟨an ~ sheet of paper⟩ ⟨~ tables⟩ — **ob·long·ly** *adv* — **ob·long·ness** *n* -ES
[2]**oblong** \"\ *n* -S **:** an oblong figure ⟨a border of silver ~*s*⟩
**ob·lon·ga·ta** \,ä,blȯŋ'gäd·ə\ *n*, *pl* **oblonga·tas** \-äd·əz\ *or* **oblonga·tae** \-äd·ē\ [NL, lit., oblong, fem. of *oblongatus*, past part. of *oblongare* to elongate, fr. L *oblongus* oblong] **:** MEDULLA OBLONGATA
**ob·long·atal** \,ä,blȯŋ'gäd·ᵊl *also* -läŋ-\ *adj* [NL *oblongata* + E *-al*] **:** of, relating to, occurring or originating in, or affecting the medulla oblongata
**ob·long·at·ed** \(')ä,blȯŋ,gād·əd *also* -läŋ-\ *adj* [NL *oblongatus* (past part. of *oblongare* to prolong, elongate) + E *-ed*] **:** PROLONGED, ELONGATED
**ob·long·ish** \'ä,blȯŋish, -ŋēsh *also* -läŋ-\ *adj* **:** somewhat oblong
**ob·lo·qui·al** \ä'blōkwēəl,ə'-\ *adj* **:** relating to or constituting obloquy
**obloquious** *adj*, *obs* **:** characterized by obloquy
**ob·lo·quy** \'äbləkwē, -kwi\ *n* -ES [LL *obloquium*, fr. L *obloqui* to speak against, fr. *ob-* toward, against + *loqui* to speak — more at OB-] **1 a :** a strongly and often intemperately condemnatory utterance **:** defamatory or calumnious language **:** abusive or slanderous reprehension **:** CALUMNY ⟨names . . . mentioned with ~ and detraction —Joseph Addison⟩ **b** *obs* **:** a calumnious utterance **2 a :** the condition of one that is subjected to or deserving of obloquy **:** a blending of ill fame, hatred, and contempt on the one hand with distress and shame on the other ⟨living out his days in the ~ of one who had betrayed a solemn trust⟩ **b** *obs* **:** a cause or source of reproach **:** DISGRACE **syn** see ABUSE, DISHONOR
**ob·mu·tes·cence** \,ämyə'tesᵊn(t)s\ *n* [L *obmutescere* to become mute (fr. *ob-* to, toward + *mutescere* to become mute, fr. *mutus* mute) + E *-ence* — more at OB-, MUTE] **:** a becoming or keeping silent or mute

**ob·neb·u·late** \äb'nebyə,lāt, əb-\ *vt* -ED/-ING/-S [*ob-* + L *nebula* mist, cloud + E *-ate* — more at NEBULA] **:** BECLOUD, BEFOG
**ob·nounce** \=ʹnaùn(t)s\ *vi* -ED/-ING/-S [L *obnunciare, obnuntiare*, lit., to announce, fr. *ob-* to, toward + *nunciare, nuntiare* to report, relate — more at NUNCIATURE] **:** to tell of an ill omen
**ob·nox·i·e·ty** \,äb,näk'sīəd·ē\ *n* -ES [ML *obnoxietas*, fr. L *obnoxius* obnoxious + *-tas* -ty] **:** LIABILITY
**ob·nox·ious** \əb'näkshəs, äb'-\ *adj* [L *obnoxiosus* subjected, submissive, fr. *obnoxius* subject to harm (fr. *ob-* to, toward + *noxius* harmful, noxious) + *-osus* -ous — more at OB-, NOXIOUS] **1 a** *archaic* **:** subject to the authority or power of another **:** exposed or open to a particular action or influence **b** *obs* **:** SUBMISSIVE, OBSEQUIOUS **2 :** subject, liable, exposed, or open (as to a hurtful influence) — used with *to* ⟨actions ~ to censure⟩ **3 :** deserving of censure **:** REPREHENSIBLE **4** [influenced in meaning by L *noxius*] *obs* **:** HARMFUL, NOXIOUS **5 :** forming an object of dislike or disgust **:** OFFENSIVE, ODIOUS, OBJECTIONABLE ⟨thoroughly ~ views⟩ ⟨~ to his associates⟩ **syn** see HATEFUL
**ob·nox·ious·ly** *adv* **:** in an obnoxious manner **:** so as to be obnoxious
**ob·nox·ious·ness** *n* -ES **:** the quality or state of being obnoxious
**ob·nu·bi·late** \äb'n(y)übə,lāt, əb'-\ *vt* -ED/-ING/-S [L *obnubilatus*, past part. of *obnubilare* to cover with clouds, fr. *ob-* to, over + *nubilus* cloudy, fr. *nubes* cloud — more at OB-, NUANCE] **1 :** to cover or obscure by or as if by clouds **:** BECLOUD ⟨vision *obnubilated* by fatigue⟩ **2 a :** to make cloudy of mind ⟨*obnubilated* by scholastic philosophy⟩ **b :** to induce torpor in ⟨~ with drugs⟩ **syn** see OBSCURE
**ob·nu·bi·la·tion** \=,==ʹlāshən\ *n* -S [LL *obnubilation-, obnubilatio*, fr. L *obnubilatus* (past part. of *obnubilare*) + *-ion-, -io* -ion] **:** the quality or state of being or making something be cloudy or obscure ⟨~ of the intellect⟩
[1]**oboe** \'ō(,)bō\ *n* -S [It, fr. F *hautbois*, fr. MF — more at

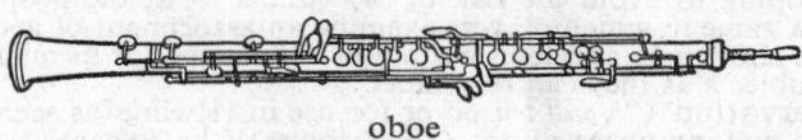

oboe

HAUTBOIS] **1 :** a nontransposing orchestral woodwind instrument having a conical body with a slightly flaring end, a double reed mouthpiece, a range from B-flat below to third G above middle C, and a nasal and penetrating tone quality and forming the highest and chief member of a family of double-reed instruments — compare BASSOON, ENGLISH HORN **2 :** an organ reed stop that gives a tone resembling that of an oboe **3 :** a chanter in a bagpipe
[2]**oboe** \"\ *usu cap* — a communications code word for the letter *o*
[3]**oboe** \"\ *n* -S *usu cap* [prob. so called fr. its being a key word for the letter O] **:** a radar blind-bombing and navigation system in which one airplane flies a circular course while two ground stations measure the distance to a radar beacon in the plane
**oboe da cac·cia** \,ō(,)bōdə'kächə, ,ōbə,wäd-\ *n*, *pl* **oboi da caccia** \,ōbə,wēd-\ *or* **oboe da caccias** \-chəz\ [It, lit., oboe of the hunt] **:** an alto oboe that is the forerunner of the modern English horn
**oboe d'a·mo·re** \,ō(,)bōdə'mōrē, ,ōbə,wäd-\ *n*, *pl* **oboi d'amore** \,ōbə,wēd-\ *or* **oboe d'amores** \-r,ēz\ [It, lit., oboe of love, prob. trans. of F *hautbois d'amour*] **:** a mezzo-soprano oboe having a pear-shaped bell and a rich somber tone **2** *or* **oboe d'a·mour** \,ō(,)bōdə'mü(ə)r\ *pl* **oboe d'a·mours** \-rz\ [modif. (influenced by [1]*oboe*) of F *hautbois d'amour*] **:** a pipe-organ oboe stop having a veiled and pathetic tone
**obo·ist** *or* **oboe·ist** \'ō(,)bōəst, -,bəwəst\ *n* -S [*oboist* prob. fr. It *oboista*, fr. *oboe* + *-ista* -ist (fr. L); *oboeist* fr. *oboe* + *-ist*] **:** an oboe player
**obol** \'äbəl, 'ōb-əl\ *n* -S [L *obolus*, fr. Gk *obolos*, lit., nail; akin to Gk *obelos* spit, pointed pillar, obelus] **1 :** a unit of weight of ancient Greece equivalent in the Attic standard to ⅙ drachma or 11¼ grains or 0.71 grams **2 :** an ancient Greek coin equal to ⅙ drachma **3 a :** OBOLE **b :** any of several old small coins of the European continent
**ob·ole** \'ä,bōl\ *n* -S [F, fr. L *obulus*] **:** the medieval half denier of France
**ob·o·lus** \'äbələs\ *n*, *pl* **obo·li** \-,lī\ [L] **:** OBOL 2, 3
**ob·omegoid** \,äb+\ *adj* [*ob-* + *omegoid*] **:** obversely omegoid
**obon·go** \ō'bäŋ(,)gō\ *n*, *pl* **obongo** *or* **obongos** *usu cap* **:** ABONGO
**ob·ovate** \(')äb+\ *adj* [*ob-* + *ovate*] **:** inversely ovate **:** ovate with the narrower end basal ⟨an ~ leaf⟩ — see LEAF illustration
**ob·ovoid** \"+\ *adj* [*ob-* + *ovoid*] **:** ovoid with the broad end toward the apex ⟨an ~ fruit⟩
**ob·pyramidal** \,äb+\ *adj* [ISV *ob-* + *pyramidal*] **:** inversely pyramidal — compare CUNEATE
**ob·pyriform** \(')äb+\ *adj* [*ob-* + *pyriform*] **:** inversely pyriform
**ob·rep·tion** \ä'brepshən\ *n* -S [L *obreption-, obreptio* act of creeping upon, stealing upon, deceiving, fr. *obreptus* (past part. of *obrepere* to steal upon, surprise, deceive, fr. *ob-* to, toward, over + *repere* to creep) + *-ion-, -io* -ion — more at OB-, REPTILE] *canon & Scots law* **:** the obtaining of or attempting to obtain a dispensation from ecclesiastical authority or a gift from the sovereign by fraud — distinguished from *subreption*
**ob·rep·ti·tious** \,ä,brep'tishəs\ *adj* [LL *obrepticius, obreptitius*, fr. L *obreptus* (past part. of *obrepere*) + *-icius, -itius* -itious] **:** marked by obreption **:** done or obtained by trickery or by concealing the truth — **ob·rep·ti·tious·ly** *adv*
**o'bri·en potatoes** \ō'brīən-\ *n pl*, *usu cap O&B* [prob. fr. the name *O'Brien*] **:** diced potatoes sautéed in butter and dressed with chopped sweet pepper
**ob·ro·gate** \'äbrə,gāt, *usu* -ād·+V\ *vt* -ED/-ING/-S [L *obrogatus*, past part. of *obrogare* to obrogate, fr. *ob-* toward, against + *rogare* to ask, propose, propose a law — more at OB-, RIGHT] **:** to modify or repeal (a law) in whole or in part by passing a new law — compare ABROGATE 1 — **ob·ro·ga·tion** \,==ʹgāshən\ *n*
**ob·rok** \ä'bräk, ə'brȯk\ *n* -S [Russ, fr. *ob-* (fr. *ob* to, on) + *rok* regulation, term, fate, lot; akin to L *ob* to, before, against and to OE *regn-* might, ON *rögn*, pl., the decreeing powers, gods, Goth *ragin* counsel, decision, Skt *racayati* he completes, builds — more at EPI-] **:** a yearly tax formerly paid by a Russian peasant engaged in trade
**ob·ro·tund** \,äbrə,tənd\ *adj* [LL *obrotundus*, fr. L *ob-* to, over, completely + *rotundus* round — more at OB-, ROUND] **:** nearly spherical but with one diameter slightly exceeding the others **:** OBROUND
**ob·round** \(')äb+\ *adj* [*ob-* + *round*] **:** having the form of a flattened cylinder with the sides parallel and the ends hemispherical
**obs** *abbr* **1** obscure **2** observation; observatory; observed **3** obsolete **4** obstacle **5** obstruction
**ob·scene** \əb'sēn, (')äb¦s-\ *adj* -ER/-EST [MF, fr. L *obscenus, obscaenus*; prob. fr. a prehistoric Latin compound whose first constituent is akin to L *ob* to, before, against and whose second constituent is akin to L *caenum* filth, Sw dial. *hven* swamp, Latvian *svīns* dirtied — more at EPI-] **1 a :** disgusting to the senses usu. because of some filthy, grotesque, or unnatural quality ⟨~ fungi clothed the wall of that dank cavern⟩ ⟨dressed in ~ rags⟩ **b :** grossly repugnant to the generally accepted notions of what is appropriate **:** SHOCKING ⟨death under the stars is ~ somehow —*Infantry Jour.*⟩ **2 :** offensive or revolting as countering or violating some ideal or principle: as **a :** abhorrent to morality or virtue **:** stressing or reveling in the lewd or lustful; *specif* **:** inciting or designed to incite to lust, depravity, indecency ⟨the dance often becomes flagrantly ~ and definitely provocative —Margaret Mead⟩ ⟨a sly and ~ humor, the whispering and important lecheries of an old worn-out rake —Thomas Wolfe⟩ **b :** marked by violation of accepted language inhibitions and by the use of words regarded as taboo in polite usage ⟨~ chantey —Sinclair Lewis⟩ **c :** repulsive by reason of malignance, hypocrisy,

cynicism, irresponsibility, crass disregard of moral or ethical principles ⟨the ~ little counterdemonstration lewdly exulting in the forthcoming deaths —T.R.Ybarra⟩ ⟨the debate . . . was almost ~ in its irresponsibility —*New Republic*⟩ **syn** see COARSE
**ob·scene·ly** *adv* **:** to an obscene degree **:** in an obscene manner
**ob·scene·ness** \-nnəs\ *n* -ES **:** OBSCENITY 1a
**ob·scen·i·ty** \əb'senəd·ē, äb'-, -sēn-, -əti, -i\ *n* -ES [F *obscenité*, fr. L *obscenitat-, obscenitas, obscaenitat-, obscaenitas*, fr. *obscenus, obscaenus* obscene + *-itat-, itas* -ity] **1 a :** the quality or state of being obscene ⟨the ~ of a writing may lie as much in intent as in wording⟩ **b** *archaic* **:** FILTHINESS, FOULNESS **2 :** something (as an utterance or act) that is obscene — usu. used in pl. ⟨*obscenities* in the public press⟩
[1]**ob·scu·rant** \əbz'kyürənt, äb-, -b'sk-\ *n* -S [F, fr. L *obscurant-, obscurans*, pres. part. of *obscurare* to obscure] **:** one who obscures esp. by striving to prevent enlightenment or to hinder the progress of knowledge and wisdom — compare OBSCURANTISM
[2]**obscurant** \"\ *or* **ob·scu·ran·tic** \,äbzkyə'rantik, -bsk-\ *adj* **1 :** tending to make obscure **2 :** of or relating to obscurants or obscurantism
**ob·scu·ran·tism** \əbz'kyürən,tizəm, äb-, -b'sk-; ,äbzkyə'ran-, -bsk-\ *also* **ob·scu·ran·ti·cism** \,äbzkyə'rantə,sizəm, -bsk-\ *n* -S [*obscurantism* fr. F *obscurantisme*, fr. *obscurant* + *-isme* -ism; *obscuranticism* fr. *obscurantic* + *-ism*] **1 :** deprecation of or positive opposition to enlightenment or the spread of knowledge; *esp* **:** a policy (as in art or social science) of deliberately making something obscure or withholding knowledge from the general public **2 a :** a style (as in literature or art) characterized by haziness and lack of sharp definition **b :** an act or instance of obscurantism **:** an obscure utterance or one intended to confuse ⟨legal ~*s*⟩
[1]**ob·scu·ran·tist** \əbz'kyürəntəst, äb-, -b'sk-; ,äbzkyə'ran-, -bsk-\ *n* -S [[1]*obscurant* + *-ist*] **:** a practitioner of or believer in obscurantism
[2]**obscurantist** \=ʹ===, ¦==¦==\ *adj* **1 :** of, relating to, or constituting obscurantism ⟨~ doctrines⟩ **:** affected by obscurantism ⟨an American society made sterile and ~ by big business —H.N.Smith⟩ **2 :** being or characteristic of an obscurantist ⟨a notably ~ leader⟩
**ob·scu·ra·tion** \,äbzkyə'rāshən, -bsk-\ *n* -S [ME, fr. L *obscuration-, obscuratio*, fr. *obscuratus* (past part. of *obscurare* to obscure) + *-ion-, -io* -ion] **:** an act of obscuring or the quality or state of being obscured
**ob·scu·ra·tive** \əbz'kyürəd·iv, äb-, -b'sk-\ *adj* [L *obscuratus* (past part. of *obscurare*) + E *-ive*] **:** tending to obscure
[1]**ob·scure** \əbz'kyü(ə)r, (')äbz¦k-, -b'sk-, -b¦sk-, -üə\ *adj*, *sometimes* -ER/-EST [ME, fr. MF *obscur*, fr. L *obscurus*, fr. *ob-* to, against, over + *-scurus* (akin to OHG *scūr* covered place, shelter, OFris *skūre* barn, shed, Icel *skūrr* sheltering roof, Gk *keuthein* to conceal, *skytos* skin, leather — more at OB-, HIDE] **1 :** lacking or inadequately supplied with light **:** DARK, DIM, GLOOMY ⟨the ~ dusk of the shuttered room⟩ **2 :** not readily perceived: as **a** *of a place* **:** withdrawn from the centers of human activity **:** REMOTE, RETIRED, SECRET ⟨these ~ regions⟩ ⟨settled in an ~ country village⟩ **b :** not readily understood **:** lacking clarity or legibility **:** not clearly expressed **:** ABSTRUSE ⟨an ~ reference⟩ ⟨an ~ writing⟩ **c :** lacking showiness, worth, or prominence by which the attention might be attracted **:** INCONSPICUOUS, HUMBLE ⟨such ~ everyday people⟩ ⟨an ~ Roman poet⟩ ⟨this ~ cottage housed an unnoticed genius⟩ **d :** lacking clarity or distinctness of form or outline **:** FAINT, INDISTINCT ⟨~ markings on the wing of a butterfly⟩ ⟨a delicate pattern of ~ lines⟩ **e :** indistinctly or imperfectly felt or apprehended ⟨an ~ pulse⟩ ⟨sounds ~ in the distance⟩ **3 :** of or relating to darkness **:** frequenting or enveloped in darkness **:** UNSEEN ⟨the ~ powers of evil⟩ ⟨standing ~ in the deepest shade⟩ **4 :** constituting the unstressed vowel \ə\ or having unstressed \ə\ as its value
**syn** DARK, VAGUE, ENIGMATIC, CRYPTIC, AMBIGUOUS, EQUIVOCAL: OBSCURE may apply to communication the meaning of which is hidden or veiled, often through some defect of expression, sometimes through abstruse or arcane nature ⟨there are more *obscure* poems written and printed every year than clear ones —R.B.West⟩ ⟨the communiqué was apt to be *obscure* as to its sense, so that the priests might have to clarify it —W.W.Howells⟩ DARK may refer to what is imperfectly revealed and hence somewhat mysterious, perhaps with ominous or sinister suggestion ⟨they hunt for clues to our present duty and future destiny among the *dark* sayings of Daniel, Micah, and the Book of Revelations —Brand Blanshard⟩ VAGUE may describe that which lacks clear distinctness as not susceptible to definitive formulation or as imperfectly conceived or not definitively thought out ⟨much *vaguer* and indeed obscure allegory —Rex Warner⟩ ⟨only a *vague*, genial theory as a policy with inadequate preparation, and lacking a clear-cut, definitive, and detailed plan —R.E.Danielson⟩ ⟨a *vague* sense of obligation was replaced by an exacting set of rules —R.W.Southern⟩ ENIGMATIC refers to what puzzles by suggestive unclarity of allusion or ramification ⟨this *enigmatic* utterance —Jack London⟩ ⟨fell to conjecturing the meaning of Farfrae's *enigmatic* words about not daring to ask her what he fain would —Thomas Hardy⟩ CRYPTIC may describe that which is purposefully darkly enigmatic or esoteric ⟨a very *cryptic* text —S.F.Mason⟩ ⟨that *cryptic* unintelligibility, the sibylline phrase, which, if it has a meaning, sometimes guards it all too well from the bewildered reader —*Amer. Guide Series: Mass.*⟩ AMBIGUOUS applies to communication admitting of more than one interpretation ⟨most words are *ambiguous* as regards their plain sense, especially in poetry —I.A.Richards⟩ ⟨the title of this chapter is *ambiguous* —A.S.Eddington⟩ EQUIVOCAL may describe whatever admits of false interpretation, often purposefully phrased or delivered as an expedient to deceive or evade ⟨to veil the matter, with utterances capable of more *equivocal* meaning —H.O.Taylor⟩ ⟨the Moral Law speaks in *equivocal* tones to those who listen most scrupulously for its dictates —L.P.Smith⟩ **syn** see in addition DARK
[2]**obscure** \"\ *vt* -ED/-ING/-S [L *obscurare*, fr. *obscurus* obscure] **1 :** to make obscure: as **a :** to make dim **:** DARKEN ⟨the soot on the lampshade *obscured* the light⟩ **b :** to conceal or hide from view as by or as if by covering wholly or in part **:** make difficult to discern ⟨the fine sunburn somewhat *obscured* the inherent transparency of his complexion —Elinor Wylie⟩; *also* **:** DISGUISE ⟨no dukedom even, however high-sounding and traditional, could ~ for him native idiocy —Osbert Sitwell⟩ **c :** to dim in glory or significance **:** OVERSHADOW ⟨in the shadow of Emerson and Thoreau, the wit of Back Bay is in danger of being *obscured* —V.L.Parrington⟩ **d :** to make unintelligible or vague **:** make difficult to understand ⟨too much use of symbolism *obscured* his poetic thought⟩ **e :** to make (as a sound or line) indistinct or undefined ⟨writing *obscured* by age and mildew⟩; *also* **:** to make indistinct in logical or rational order ⟨reasoning *obscured* by emotion⟩ **f :** to make (as the judgment) weak **:** IMPAIR ⟨her blood being stirred . . . her judgment was slightly *obscured* —Arnold Bennett⟩ **2 :** to use unstressed \ə\ for (an item of spelling) or instead of (another vowel in a variant spelling or gradational form)
**syn** OBSCURE, DIM, BEDIM, DARKEN, ECLIPSE, CLOUD, BECLOUD, FOG, BEFOG, OBFUSCATE, OBNUBILATE: of these terms OBSCURE, DIM, BEDIM, and DARKEN all suggest the effect obtained by the lessening or the removal of illumination — the making of an object difficult to see clearly or the weakening or impairing of the ability to see with the eye or the mind. OBSCURE stresses the indistinctness, often concealment, of the object or idea or the unclearness of the vision or the comprehension ⟨there are readers of human papers who . . . like the ordinary, average day, with its good human humdrum; they do not want to have its nature denied or *obscured* —C.E.Montague⟩ ⟨the faded yellow building, its original austerity of line somewhat *obscured* by a comfortable porch —*Amer. Guide Series: Vt.*⟩ DIM and BEDIM stress the diminishing of light or of clarity, intensity, or luster or the consequent diminishing of capacity to see, distinguish, or comprehend; BEDIM is usually found in a more literary context than DIM ⟨celestial tears *bedimm'd* her large blue eyes —Lord Byron⟩ ⟨the old patriotic glow began to *dim* its ineffectual fires —Howard M. Jones⟩ DARKEN, although like

DIM and BEDIM suggesting a diminishing of illumination, is much richer metaphorically in suggesting strongly the alteration of an object or the impairment of clear or normal vision or mental comprehension by reason of confusion, ignorance, or evil ⟨the yearly migrations of passenger pigeons . . . literally *darkening* the sky —*Amer. Guide Series: Mich.*⟩ ⟨his intellect was indeed *darkened* by many superstitions and prejudices —T.B.Macaulay⟩ ⟨evils enough to *darken* all his goodness —Shak.⟩ ECLIPSE may stand alone in suggesting the effect of an actual astronomical eclipse, the partial or total darkening or concealment of one object by another and, hence, the overshadowing or supplanting of one object by another ⟨in the English field, Anglo-Saxon never *eclipsed* the study of Shakespeare or Milton —A.L.Guérard⟩ CLOUD, BECLOUD, FOG, BEFOG, OBFUSCATE, and OBNUBILATE all suggest the obstruction or impairment of vision by clouds, fog, or other vapor or, in figurative extension, the making of the mental perception or object of that perception murky or confused. CLOUD and BECLOUD stress the obscuring of the object, or the murky view of the object; BECLOUD is somewhat more literary than CLOUD ⟨the beginnings of our physical universe are necessarily *beclouded* in the swirling mists of countless ages past —F.L. Whipple⟩ ⟨smoke *clouding* the prospect before us⟩ ⟨the actual issues *clouded* by prejudice and politics⟩ ⟨reasoning *clouded* by hysteria⟩ FOG and BEFOG are applied possibly more frequently than CLOUD and BECLOUD to matters of the understanding or mental comprehension and usu. suggest a greater obstruction or impairment of clear vision of eye and mind and, so, a greater and more unnecessary indistinctness, illogicality, or confusion; BEFOG is somewhat more literary than FOG ⟨the willfully created misunderstandings that so often *befog* the American political scene —Carl Sandburg⟩ ⟨the landscape *fogged* by the smoke from the forest fire⟩ ⟨eyes *fogged* by sleep⟩ ⟨a mind *befogged* by fatigue⟩ ⟨truth *fogged* by the imperfections of human sight⟩ ⟨a text *fogged* by careless scholarship⟩ OBFUSCATE found usu. in a literary context suggests strongly an avoidable, often willful, obscuring of an object or confusing of the mind by darkening or illogicality ⟨the process, not of enlightening but of *obfuscating* the mind —H.D.Thoreau⟩ OBNUBILATE confines itself in modern usage chiefly to a nontechnical medical use to designate the radical impairing of the mental faculties to the point of torpor ⟨*obnubilate* the patient with thiopentone and then wake him up with some cerebral stimulant —*Lancet*⟩

**³obscure** \"\ *n* -s [¹*obscure*] **:** something (as an unknown place, the darkness of night, or a part in a picture) that is obscure **:** OBSCURITY

**obscured** *past of* OBSCURE

**ob·scur·ed·ly** \əbz'kyu̇rədlē, äb-, -b'sk-\ *adv* **:** so as to be obscure **:** in an obscure manner

**obscure glass** *n* **:** sheet glass made translucent or opaque (as by roughening one side) ⟨used *obscure glass* panels to enclose the patio⟩

**ob·scure·ly** *adv* **:** in an obscure manner **:** INDISTINCTLY, VAGUELY

**ob·scure·ment** \əbz'kyu̇(ə)rmənt, äb-, -b'sk-, -u̇əm-\ *n* -s [F, fr. *obscurer* to obscure (fr. L *obscurare*) + *-ment*] **:** OBSCURATION

**ob·scure·ness** *n* -ES **:** the quality or state of being obscure

**ob·scur·er** \-rə(r)\ *n* -s **:** one that obscures

**ob·scu·ri·fy** \-rə,fī\ *vt* -ED/-ING/-ES [¹*obscure* + *-ify*] **:** to make obscure

**obscuring** *pres part of* OBSCURE

**ob·scur·ing·ly** *adv* **:** so as to obscure **:** to an obscuring degree ⟨fog drifted ~ into the valley⟩

**ob·scu·ri·ty** \əbz'kyu̇rəd·ē, äb-, -b'sk-, -ətē, -i\ *n* -ES [MF & L; MF *obscurité*, fr. L *obscuritat-, obscuritas*, fr. *obscurus* obscure + *-itat-, -itas* -ity] **1 :** the quality or state of being obscure, inconspicuous, unknown, uncomprehended, or imperspicuous **2 :** someone or something obscure ⟨these silly *obscurities* mar his writing⟩

**obsd** *abbr* observed

**ob·se·crate** \'äbsə,krāt\ *vt* -ED/-ING/-S [L *obsecratus*, past part. of *obsecrare* to beseech, pray, fr. *ob-* toward, over + *sacrare* to consecrate, fr. *sacr-, sacer* sacred — more at OB-, SACRED] *archaic* **:** BESEECH, SUPPLICATE, BEG

**ob·se·cra·tion** \,==ˈkrāshən\ *n* -s [ME *obsecracioun*, fr. L *obsecration-, obsecratio*, fr. *obsecratus* (past part. of *obsecrare* to beseech) + *-ion-, -io* -ion] **1 :** SUPPLICATION; *specif* **:** a supplicatory prayer mentioning in its appeal things or events held to be sacred ⟨"through thy victory over death, O Lord, deliver us" is an ~⟩ **2 :** DEESIS

**ob·sede** \əb'sēd\ *vt* -ED/-ING/-S [F *obséder*, fr. L *obsidēre* to sit at, possess — more at OBSESS] **:** OBSESS

**ob·se·quence** \'äbsəkwən(t)s\ *n* -s [L *obsequentia*, fr. *obsequent-, obsequens*, (pres. part. of *obsequi* to yield) + *-ia*] **:** OBSEQUIOUSNESS, COMPLIANCE

**¹ob·se·quent** \'äbsəkwənt\ *adj* [L *obsequent-, obsequens*, pres. part.] **1** *obs* **:** YIELDING, SUBMISSIVE, OBSEQUIOUS **2 a** *of a stream* **:** flowing in a direction opposite to that of the dip of the local strata and joining a subsequent valley developed along the strike of poorly resistant beds **b :** produced by differential erosion of fault blocks and facing in a direction opposite to that of a previous fault scarp — used of fault-line scarps and cliffs

**²obsequent** \"\ *n* -s **:** an obsequent stream

**ob·se·qui·al** \əb'sēkwēəl, äb-\ *adj* **:** of or relating to obsequies **:** FUNEREAL

**ob·se·qui·ence** \-ēən(t)s\ *n* -s [by alter. (influence of *obsequious*)] **:** OBSEQUENCE

**ob·se·qui·ous** \-ēəs\ *adj* [ME, fr. L *obsequiosus*, fr. *obsequium* compliance (fr. *obsequi* to yield, fr. *ob-* to, toward, over + *sequi* to follow) + *-osus* -ose — more at OB-, SUE] **1 a :** exhibiting ready and proper compliance to the will of another **:** prompt and dutiful in attendance on the wishes of one in authority **b** *obs* **:** dutiful in regard to the dead and in the proper and appropriate performance of obsequies **2 :** meanly or servilely attentive **:** compliant to excess **:** exhibiting a servile and sycophantic complaisance ⟨an ~ toady⟩ ⟨fawning ~ behavior⟩ **syn** see SUBSERVIENT

**ob·se·qui·ous·ly** *adv* **:** in an obsequious manner

**ob·se·qui·ous·ness** *n* -ES [ME *obsequiousnesse*, fr. *obsequious* + *-nesse* -ness] **:** the quality or state of being obsequious

**ob·seq·ui·ty** \əb'sekwəd·ē, äb-, -sēk-\ *n* -ES [*obsequious* + *-ity*] **:** OBSEQUIOUSNESS

**ob·se·qui·um** \äb'sēkwēəm\ *n, pl* **obsequ·ia** \-ēə\ [L, lit., compliance] **:** the customary respectful behavior due from a freedman to his patron or former master under ancient Roman law including freedom from lawsuit by the freedman except with the consent of the praetor and the duty to support the patron when needy

**ob·se·quy** \'äbsəkwē, -wi\ *n* -ES [ME *obsequie, obseque*, fr. MF, fr. ML *obsequiae*, alter. (influenced by L *exsequiae* funeral rites) of L *obsequia* obsequies, pl. of *obsequium* compliance — more at EXEQUY] **1 :** the last duty or service to a person rendered after his death; *esp* **:** a rite or ceremony relating to burial — usu. used in pl. **2** [ME, fr. L *obsequium*] *obs* **:** COMPLIANCE, OBSEQUIOUSNESS; *also* **:** RITUAL

**ob·serv·abil·i·ty** \əb,zərvə'biləd·ē, -zȯv-, -zəiv-, -lətē, -i\ *n* **:** capacity for or possibility of being observed

**¹ob·serv·able** \əb'zərvəbəl, -zȯv-, -zəiv-\ *adj* [F, fr. L *observabilis*, fr. *observare* to observe + *-abilis* -able — more at OBSERVE] **1 :** requiring or suitable to be observed, regarded, or kept ⟨a very ~ old custom⟩ ⟨forms ~ in social intercourse⟩ **2 a :** deserving of observation **:** NOTEWORTHY **b** *obs* **:** REMARKABLE, NOTABLE **3 :** capable of being observed **:** DISCERNIBLE, DETECTABLE, NOTICEABLE ⟨an ~ decline in health⟩ ⟨an ~ phenomenon⟩ — **ob·serv·able·ness** \-bəlnəs\ *n* -ES — **ob·serv·ably** \-blē, -li\ *adv*

**²observable** \"\ *n* -s **1** *archaic* **:** something noteworthy or unusual **2 :** an event that is perceptible directly or indirectly (as by the medium of instruments) through the senses **:** PHENOMENON ⟨such ~s as size, energy, momentum, or viscosity⟩

**ob·serv·ance** \-vən(t)s\ *n* -s [ME *observaunce*, fr. OF *observance*, fr. LL *observantia*, fr. L, regard, respect, fr. *observant-, observans* (pres. part. of *observare*) + *-ia*] **1 a :** something (as an act of religious or ceremonial nature) that is carried out in accord with prescribed forms **:** a customary practice, rite, or ceremony **b :** a rule or set of regulations governing members of a religious order **c** *usu cap, Roman Catholicism* **:** the ordinances governing the strict Franciscans **2 a :** the performance of a customary rite (as of ceremony or religion) ⟨do the ~ due to sprightly May —John Dryden⟩ ⟨our customary Sabbath ~s⟩ **b :** an act or the practice of paying due heed to something established (as a rule, law, custom) **:** an attending, participating in, or following with care ⟨~ of the speed laws⟩ **3** *archaic* **:** respectful and dutiful service or attention (as to a person) **:** deferential courtesy **4 :** an act or instance of observing **:** ATTENTION, OBSERVATION ⟨~ of life⟩

**ob·serv·an·cy** \-nsē\ *n* -ES [LL *observantia*] **:** OBSERVANCE

**observandum** *n, pl* **observanda** [L, neut. of *observandus*, gerundive of *observare*] *obs* **:** a thing to be observed

**¹observant** *n* -s [ME, fr. L *observant-, observans*, pres. part. of *observare* to observe] **1** *obs* **:** OBSERVER **2** *obs* **:** an assiduous or obsequious servant or attendant

**²ob·serv·ant** \əb'zərvənt, -zȯv-, -zəiv-\ *adj* [F, fr. pres. part. of *observer* to observe, fr. L *observare*] **1 :** taking notice **:** viewing or noticing attentively **:** ATTENTIVE ⟨~ spectators⟩ ⟨an ~ habit of mind⟩ **2** *archaic* **:** RESPECTFUL, DEFERENTIAL **3 :** attentive in observing **:** REGARDFUL, MINDFUL — used with *of* ⟨~ of rules⟩ ⟨carefully ~ of the niceties of life⟩ **4** *obs* **:** OBSERVABLE **5 :** CAREFUL, HEEDFUL ⟨~ to avoid offense⟩ — **ob·serv·ant·ly** *adv* — **ob·serv·ant·ness** *n* -ES

**¹ob·ser·va·tion** \,äbsə(r)'vāshən, -bzə-\ *n* -s [MF, fr. L *observation-, observatio*, fr. *observatus* (past part. of *observare* to observe) + *-ion-, -io* -ion — more at OBSERVE] **1** *obs* **:** something (as an ordinance, rite, or custom) that must be observed **:** OBSERVANCE 1a **2 :** OBSERVANCE 2a **3 :** an act or the faculty of observing or taking notice **:** an act of seeing or fixing the mind upon something **4 a :** an act of recognizing and noting some fact or occurrence (as in nature) often involving the measurement of some magnitude with suitable instruments ⟨made an ~ of the sun's altitude⟩ ⟨temperature ~s⟩ **b :** a record so obtained **5 :** an expression of a judgment upon what one has observed; *broadly* **:** REMARK, STATEMENT, UTTERANCE ⟨a very childish ~⟩ **6 :** a conclusion drawn from observing **:** VIEW, REFLECTION **7** *obs* **:** deferential courtesy **:** HEED **8 :** the condition of one that is seen, examined, or noticed ⟨stooping to avoid the risk of ~⟩ ⟨under ~ at the hospital⟩ **9 :** a game in which players examine an assortment of articles for a short time and then write down the names of as many of the objects as they can remember

**²observation** \"\ *adj* **:** used for or for use in viewing (as scenery) or in making observations ⟨an ~ tower⟩ ⟨the ~ car⟩

**ob·ser·va·tion·al** \-shənᵊl, -shnəl\ *adj* **:** of, relating to, or based on observation — sometimes distinguished from *experimental* — **ob·ser·va·tion·al·ly** \-ᵊlē, -əl|, |i\ *adv*

**ob·ser·va·tion·al·ism** \-ᵊl,izəm, -ə,l-\ *n* -s **:** a theory that knowledge is based on observation

**observation battalion** *n* **:** a military artillery unit that performs sound, flash, and radar ranging and furnishes topographic and meteorological data

**observation equation** *n* **:** an equation expressing a measured value of some function of one or more unknown quantities

**observation kite** *n* **:** WAR KITE

**ob·serv·a·tive** \əb'zərvəd·iv, -zȯv-, -zəiv-\ *adj* [L *observatus* (past part. of *observare* to observe) + E *-ive*] **:** OBSERVANT

**ob·ser·va·tor** \'äbzər,vād·ər, -bsə-, -zə(r),vād·ə(r), -ātə-\ *n* -s [MF *observateur*, fr. L *observator*, fr. *observatus* (past part. of *observare*) + *-or*] **:** OBSERVER

**ob·serv·a·to·ri·al** \əb;zərvə;tōrēəl, -zȯv-, -zəiv-, -tȯr-\ *adj* **:** of or relating to an observer or an observatory

**¹ob·serv·a·to·ry** \-'==,tōrē, -tȯr-, -ri\ *n* -ES [prob. fr. (assumed) NL *observatorium*, fr. L *observatus* (past part. of *observare* to observe) + *-orium*] **1 :** a building or place given over to or equipped for observation of natural phenomena (as in astronomy, magnetism, meteorology, ornithology); *also* **:** an institution whose primary purpose is making such observations **2 :** a situation, position, or place (as a building or elevated chamber) affording or commanding a wide view **:** LOOKOUT

**²observatory** \"\ *adj* [L *observatus*, past part. + E *-ory*] **:** relating to observation esp. when scientific

**¹ob·serve** \əb'zərv, -zȯv, -zəiv\ *vb* -ED/-ING/-S [ME *observen*, fr. MF *observer*, fr. L *observare* to watch, guard, observe, fr. *ob-* to, over, completely + *servare* to keep, guard, observe — more at OB-, CONSERVE] *vt* **1 :** to take notice of by appropriate conduct **:** conform one's action or practice to **:** HEED, OBEY ⟨~ rules⟩ ⟨*observing* common decencies⟩ **2** *obs* **:** to give heed to (as in deference) **:** WORSHIP, HONOR **3 :** to inspect or take note of as an augury, omen, or presage ⟨*observed* the sacred geese⟩ ⟨*observed* the stumble of his horse and turned back⟩ **4 :** to celebrate or solemnize (as a ceremony, rite, or festival) after a customary or accepted form ⟨we always *observed* birthdays at home⟩ ⟨~ the Sabbath⟩ **5 :** to see or sense esp. through directed, careful, analytic attention ⟨in order to get fresh light on this subject, I have *observed* my own children carefully —Bertrand Russell⟩ ⟨keeping an ear pricked to ~ the movements of the viceroy —Victoria Sackville-West⟩ **6 :** to come to realize or know esp. through consideration of noted facts ⟨have *observed* that profane men living in ships . . . develop traits of profound resemblance —Joseph Conrad⟩ ⟨as we trace . . . the development of the Greek mind, we can ~ their intellect and their moral sense expanding —G.L.Dickinson⟩ **7 :** to express as a result of observation **:** utter as a remark **:** say in a casual or incidental way **:** REMARK **8 :** to make an observation on or of **:** ascertain by scientific observation ⟨~ phenomena⟩ ⟨*observed* the height of the sun⟩ ~ *vi* **1 a :** to take notice **:** be attentive **b :** to make observations **:** WATCH **2 :** REMARK, COMMENT — usu. used with *on* or *upon* **syn** see KEEP, SEE

**²observe** \"\ *n* -s *Scot* **:** REMARK, OBSERVATION ⟨a clever ~⟩

**ob·serv·ed·ly** \-vədlē, -li\ *adv* **:** to a significant degree **:** NOTABLY

**ob·serv·er** \-və(r)\ *n* -s **:** one that observes: as **a :** a keeper of or adherent to something established (as a law, custom, regulation, rite, or vow) **:** one that conforms to an accepted, usual, or traditional practice **b :** one that pays attention to something; *esp* **:** one engaged in or trained in the methods of close and exact observation ⟨an astronomical ~⟩ **c :** one that makes a remark **d** *obs* **:** a dutiful attendant or sycophantic follower **e :** a representative sent to observe and listen but not to participate officially in a gathering **f** (1) **:** one that accompanies the pilot of an airplane in order to make observations during flight (2) **:** an officer or other person that ascends in a captive balloon (as to reconnoiter or observe) (3) **:** an aeronautical rating for a member of an air crew with a special duty (as navigator, radar operator, bombardier) other than piloting — called also *aircraft observer* **g :** a subject in introspective analysis who describes his experiences under physical conditions arranged by an experimenter

**observing** *adj* **1 :** attentive to what passes **:** OBSERVANT **2 :** engaged in making observations — **ob·serv·ing·ly** *adv*

**ob·sess** \əb'ses, äb-\ *vt* -ED/-ING/-ES [L *obsessus*, past part. of *obsidēre* to sit at, possess, besiege, fr. *ob-* toward, against, over + *sedēre* to sit — more at OB-, SIT] **1** *obs* **:** BESIEGE, INVEST **2 a** *archaic* **:** HAUNT, POSSESS, BESET **b :** to occupy an undue or disproportionate place in the mind of **:** trouble continuously in mind ⟨he was ~*ed* by details⟩

**ob·sess·ed·ly** \-sədlē, -stlē, -li\ *adv* **:** in an obsessed manner

**ob·sess·ing·ly** *adv* **:** to an obsessing degree **:** so as to obsess

**ob·ses·sion** \əb'seshən, äb-\ *n* -s [L *obsession-, obsessio*, fr. *obsessus* (past part. of *obsidēre* to besiege) + *-ion-, -io* -ion] **1** *obs* **:** SIEGE **2 :** the act of a devil or a spirit in besetting a person or impelling him to action from without **:** the fact of being so beset or impelled — distinguished from *possession* **3 a :** a persistent and disturbing intrusion of or anxious and inescapable preoccupation with an idea or feeling esp. if known to be unreasonable — compare COMPULSION **b :** an emotion or idea causing such intrusion

**ob·ses·sion·al** \-shənᵊl, -shnəl\ *adj* **:** relating to, characterized by, or constituting an obsession **:** OBSESSIVE ⟨the ~ character of his response⟩ — **ob·ses·sion·al·ly** \-ᵊlē, -əlē, -li\ *adv*

**obsessional neurosis** *n* **:** an obsessive-compulsive neurosis in which obsessive thinking predominates with little need to perform compulsive acts

**ob·ses·sion·ist** \-sh(ə)nəst\ *n* -s **:** one that is obsessed

**¹ob·ses·sive** \-'sesiv, -sēv *also* -səv\ *adj* [*obsession* + *-ive*] **1 a :** tending to provoke obsession **b :** excessive in some quality (as interest, concern, urgency) to or nearly to the point of abnormality ⟨an ~ nurse⟩ ⟨our ~ need for quick solutions —A.E.Stevenson b.1900⟩ **2 :** relating to, characterized by, or constituting obsession — **ob·ses·sive·ly** \-səvlē, -li\ *adv* — **ob·ses·sive·ness** \-sivnəs, -sēv- *also* -səv-\ *n* -ES

**²obsessive** \"\ *n* -s **:** a person that is obsessed **:** an obsessional neurotic

**¹obsessive-compulsive** \=;===;==\ *adj* **:** relating to or characterized by obsessions and compulsions esp. as symptoms of a neurotic state — compare ANANKASTIC

**²obsessive-compulsive** \"\ *n* -s **:** a person affected with an obsessive-compulsive neurosis

**obsessive-compulsive neurosis** *or* **obsessive-compulsive reaction** *n* **:** a psychoneurotic disorder in which the patient is beset with obsessions or compulsions or both and suffers extreme anxiety or depression through failure to think the obsessive thoughts or perform the compelling acts

**ob·ses·sus** \əb'sesəs\ *n* -ES [ML, fr. L, past part. of *obsidēre* to possess, besiege — more at OBSESS] *archaic* **:** a person believed to be possessed by an evil spirit

**ob·sid·i·an** \əb'sidēən, äb-\ *n* -s [NL *obsidianus*, fr. L *Obsidianus* lapis (MS var. of *Obsianus* lapis), lit., stone of Obsidian, fr. *Obsidius* (MS var. of *Obsius*), Roman traveler named by Pliny as its discoverer + *-ianus* -ian] **:** volcanic glass that is generally black, banded, or spherulitic and has a marked conchoidal fracture, a bright luster, and a composition similar to rhyolite but usu. with more water

**ob·sid·i·an·ite** \-ə,nīt\ *n* -s [ISV *obsidian* + *-ite*] **:** a material composed of small approximately spherical balls of natural glass that are usu. black, green, or brown

**ob·sid·i·o·nal** \əb'sidēənəl\ *adj* [L *obsidionalis*, fr. *obsidion-, obsidio* siege (fr. *obsidēre* to besiege + *-ion-, -io* -ion) + *-alis* -al — more at OBSESS] **1 :** of or relating to a siege **2** *of a piece of money* **:** issued for use during a siege

**obsidional crown** *n* [trans. of L *corona obsidionalis*] **:** a crown bestowed in ancient Rome upon a general who raised the siege of a beleaguered place or upon one who held out against a siege

**ob·sid·i·o·nary** \='===,nerē\ *adj* [L *obsidion-, obsidio* + E *-ary*] **:** OBSIDIONAL 2

**ob·sid·i·ous** \='==əs\ *adj* [L *obsidium* siege (fr. *obsidēre* to besiege + *-ium*, n. suffix) + E *-ious*] **:** BESETTING

**ob·sig·na·tion** \,äb(,)sig'nāshən\ *n* -s [LL *obsignation-, obsignatio*, fr. L, action of sealing, fr. *obsignatus* (past part. of *obsignare* to mark upon, fr. *ob-* + *signare* to mark) + *-ion-, -io* -ion — more at SIGN] **:** a formal ratification (as by an official seal)

**obsn** *abbr* observation

**ob·so·lesce** \,äbsə'les\ *vi* -ED/-ING/-S [L *obsolescere*] **:** to be or become obsolescent

**ob·so·les·cence** \,=='lesᵊn(t)s\ *n* -s [*obsolescent* + *-ence*] **1 a :** the process of becoming obsolete or the condition of being nearly obsolete ⟨the gradual ~ of machinery⟩ ⟨reduced to ~⟩ **b :** the process of becoming or condition of being vestigial or nonfunctional ⟨the ~ of the wings of some strictly terrestrial birds⟩ **2 :** a factor included in depreciation to cover decline in value of fixed assets due to invention of new and better processes or machines, changes in demand, in design, or in the art, and other technical or legal changes but not to cover physical deterioration

**ob·so·les·cent** \;=='lesᵊnt\ *adj* [L *obsolescent-, obsolescens*, pres. part. of *obsolescere*] **1 :** going out of use **:** falling into disuse esp. as unable to compete with something more recent ⟨animal transport is largely ~⟩ **2 :** becoming obsolete; *esp* **:** VESTIGIAL — **ob·so·les·cent·ly** *adv*

**¹ob·so·lete** \;äbsə;lēt, *usu* -ēd·+V\ *adj* [L *obsoletus*, past part. of *obsolescere* to grow old, fall into disuse, perh. fr. *ob-* to, toward + *-solescere* (fr. *solēre* to be accustomed) — more at OB, INSOLENT] **1 :** no longer active or in use **:** DISUSED, NEGLECTED: as **a :** formerly but no longer current ⟨an ~ word⟩ ⟨an ~ construction⟩ **b :** of a kind or style no longer current **:** OUTMODED ⟨~ equipment⟩ ⟨an ~ theory⟩ **c** (1) *of a postage or revenue stamp* **:** no longer issued by a post office **:** no longer on sale as a postal or revenue item (2) *of a piece of currency* **:** no longer legal tender because demonetized or issued by an authority that is no longer in existence **d** *of a business firm* **:** gone out of existence **:** having ceased to conduct business **2 :** worn out **:** reduced to a trace **:** EFFACED: as **a** *of a plant or animal part* **:** indistinct or imperfect as compared with a corresponding part in related organisms **:** REDUCED, RUDIMENTARY, VESTIGIAL ⟨spotting and ridges ~⟩ **b** *of a lesion or an infective process* **:** DIMINISHED, INDISTINCT, EFFACED **3 :** regarded as out of date whether currently in use or not ⟨this model makes all other cars ~⟩ ⟨the colonial system is ~⟩ **syn** see OLD

**²obsolete** \"\ *vt* -ED/-ING/-S [L *obsoletus*, past part. of *obsolescere*] **:** to make obsolete

**³obsolete** \"\ *n* -s [¹*obsolete*] **:** something that is obsolete (as a word or phrase)

**ob·so·lete·ly** *adv* **:** in an obsolete manner **:** so as to be out of date or fashion

**ob·so·lete·ness** *n* -ES **:** the quality or state of being obsolete

**ob·so·le·tion** \,äbsə'lēshən\ *n* -s [¹*obsolete* + *-ion*] **:** the act of becoming or condition of being obsolete

**ob·so·let·ism** \'==,lēd·,izəm\ *n* -s **1 :** something (as a custom or a word) that is obsolete **2 :** OBSOLETENESS

**obsr** *abbr* observer

**ob·sta·cle** \'äbz(,)tikəl, -,tək-, -tēk-; 'äb(,)stik-, -,stək-, -stēk-\ *n* -s *often attrib* [ME, fr. MF, fr. L *obstaculum*, fr. *obstare* to stand before, hinder, fr. *ob-* to, against + *stare* to stand — more at OB-, STAND] **1 :** something that stands in the way or opposes **:** something that hinders progress **:** a physical or moral impediment or obstruction **:** HINDRANCE **2** *obs* **:** OPPOSITION, RESISTANCE

**syn** OBSTACLE, OBSTRUCTION, IMPEDIMENT, BAR, and SNAG can signify, in common, something which hampers or stops action or progress. OBSTACLE applies to anything which stands in one's way or stops passage ⟨the removal of an *obstacle* in the throat —F.D.Smith & Barbara Wilcox⟩ ⟨the poverty of some of the . . . districts is an *obstacle* to good education —B.K.Sandwell⟩ ⟨those *obstacles*, placed in the path of westward-marching pioneers by nature, must be surmounted before the continent was settled —R.A.Billington⟩ OBSTRUCTION stresses a blocking of the way or passage ⟨can only be used in straight stretches of water where there are no *obstructions* —W.H.Dowdeswell⟩ ⟨science deals with a psychological complex much as it deals with an *obstruction* in the bowels —Albert Dasnoy⟩ ⟨circumvent the *obstructions* placed in the way of emigration —*Amer. Guide Series: N.Y.*⟩ IMPEDIMENT, often interchangeable with OBSTACLE, usu. suggests something that hinders or delays as by entangling ⟨the rugged hills of the peninsula were no *impediment* to the discharge of his clerical duties —*Amer. Guide Series: Maine*⟩ ⟨the most important *impediment* . . . to reform, perhaps, is the number and diversity of the plans which have been submitted as possible cures —R.M.Dawson⟩ ⟨the increasing *impediments* to international trade —D.W.Brogan⟩ BAR implies something interposed as between a person and his goal ⟨there were, of course, no *bars* against immigration in those days —Paul Blanshard⟩ ⟨difference in language should be no *bar* to friendship⟩ SNAG applies to an obstacle or a delay encountered suddenly and unexpectedly ⟨his plan to build hit its first *snag* in the building code⟩ ⟨the operations were constantly running into legal *snags* which delayed progress considerably⟩

**²obstacle** *adj, obs* **:** OBSTINATE

**³obstacle** *pronunc at n*\ *vt* -ED/-ING/-S [obs. F *obstacler*, fr. F *obstacle*, n., fr. MF] **:** to resist or harass with obstacles

**obstacle course** *n* **:** a military training area filled with obstacles (as hurdles, fences, walls, ditches) that must be surmounted

**obstacle sense** *n* **:** the enhanced sensitivity that some blind persons exhibit to the presence of a large mass being approached

**ob·stet·ric** \əbz'te·trik, əb'st-, (')äbz;t-, (')äb;st-, -rēk\ *or* **ob·stet·ri·cal** \-rəkəl, -rēk-\ *adj* [*obstetric* prob. fr. (assumed) NL *obstetricus*, fr. L *obstetric-, obstetrix* midwife, lit., one who stands before (i.e., to receive the child), fr. *obstare* to stand before; *obstetrical* fr. L *obstetric-, obstetrix* + E *-al* — more at OBSTACLE] **:** of or relating to obstetrics **:** belonging to or associated with pregnancy and childbirth ⟨~ shock⟩ ⟨the ~ canal⟩ — **ob·stet·ri·cal·ly** \-rək(ə)lē, -rēk-, -li\ *adv*

**obstetrical toad** *n* **:** either of two rather small toads (*Alytes obstetricans* and *A. cisternasi*) of central and southwestern Europe the male of which takes up and fastens about his

hind legs the strings of eggs laid by the female and carries them about until they hatch
**ob·stet·ri·cate** \ə'=·trə,kāt\ *vb* -ED/-ING/-S [LL *obstetricatus*, past part. of *obstetricare* to act as midwife, fr. L *obstetric-, obstetrix* midwife] *vi, archaic* : to function as a midwife ~ *vt, obs* : to attend (a woman) as a midwife at childbirth
**obstetric forceps** *n* : a forceps for grasping the fetal head or other part to facilitate delivery in difficult labor

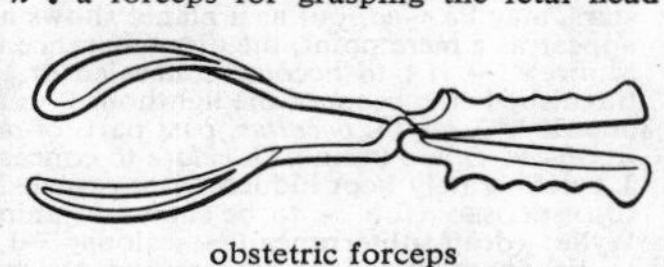
obstetric forceps

**ob·ste·tri·cian** \,äbz,te'trishən, ,äb,st-, -bztə-, -bstə-\ *n* -S [*obstetrics* + *-an*] : a physician or veterinary specializing in obstetrics
**ob·stet·rics** \əbz'te·triks, -b'st-; äbz't-, -b'st-\ *n pl but sing or pl in constr* [*obstetric* + *-s*, pl. suffix] : a branch of medical science that deals with birth and with its antecedents and sequels
**ob·stet·rist** \-rəst\ *n* -S [*obstetrics* + *-ist*] : OBSTETRICIAN
**ob·sti·na·cy** \'äbztənəsē, -bst-, -si\ *n* -ES [ME, fr. ML *obstinatia*, fr. L *obstinatus* (past part. of *obstinare* to be set upon, be obstinate) + *-ia* -y] **1 a** : the quality or state of being obstinate : fixedness in will, opinion, or resolution : firm and usu. unreasonable adherence to an opinion, purpose, or system : STUBBORNNESS, PERTINACITY, PERSISTENCY **b** : the quality or state of being difficult to remedy, relieve, or subdue ⟨the ~ of tuberculosis⟩ ⟨the ~ of this evil⟩ **2** : an instance of being obstinate : an obstinate action or stand ⟨irritated by his neighbor's petty *obstinacies*⟩
**ob·sti·nance** \-nən(t)s\ *or* **ob·sti·nan·cy** \-nənsē\ *n, pl* **obstinances** *or* **obstinancies** [ML *obstinantia*, fr. L *obstinant-, obstinans* (pres. part. of *obstinare*) + *-ia* -y] : OBSTINACY
[1]**ob·sti·nate** \-nət, *usu* -əd·+V\ *adj* [ME *obstinat*, fr. L *obstinatus*, past part. of *obstinare* to be set upon, be obstinate, fr. *ob-* to, over + *-stinare* (akin to *stare* to stand) — more at OB-, STAND] **1** : pertinaciously adhering to an opinion, purpose, or course : not yielding to reason, arguments, or other means **2** : not yielding readily : not easily subdued or removed ⟨these ~ fever⟩ ⟨these ~ obstructions⟩
**syn** OBSTINATE, DOGGED, STUBBORN, PERTINACIOUS, MULISH, STIFF-NECKED, PIGHEADED, and BULLHEADED can mean, in common, fixed or unyielding in one's course, purpose, opinion, and so on. OBSTINATE implies persistent adherence to an opinion, purpose, or course, suggesting unreasonableness or perversity rather than steadfastness ⟨a man so *obstinate* as to resist the strongest arguments can never be brought to repentance, for he can never be persuaded of his errors —Leslie Stephen⟩ ⟨so stupid and so *obstinate* that it was impossible to get him to do or understand anything —Anthony Trollope⟩ ⟨not courageous, only quarrelsome; not determined, only *obstinate*; not masterful, only domineering —G.B. Shaw⟩ DOGGED adds the idea of downright or tenacious persistence, usu. connoting stolid determination or unwavering purpose ⟨the immense amount of planning, of *dogged* study; the tireless, constant activity, the ability to get what he was after —Adria Langley⟩ ⟨the dull, *dogged*, unspectacular heroism which was needed for fighting filth and ignorance and disease —Louis Bromfield⟩ ⟨*dogged* hope and resolution for a peaceful union of nations —Laurence Stapleton⟩ STUBBORN implies the unyielding adherence of OBSTINATE and the stolid determination of DOGGED, carrying strongly the idea of fixedness of character, in a person, that resists attempts to change his purpose, course, or opinion or, in a thing, that makes it hard to work with or manipulate ⟨the *stubborn* resistance which he met showed that the temper of the people was not easily broken —J.R.Green⟩ ⟨his *stubborn* refusal to accept the consequences of his own discoveries —J.B.Conant⟩ ⟨she was so *stubborn* that she wouldn't adjust her opinions —Sinclair Lewis⟩ ⟨man and beast joined against *stubborn* nature and her grudging soil —Ann F. Wolfe⟩ PERTINACIOUS stresses a sticking to a chosen pursuit, purpose, and so on, with an unusual, often annoying, persistence ⟨a *pertinacious* newsman⟩ ⟨a *pertinacious* mosquito⟩ MULISH suggests the unreasonable obstinacy of a mule ⟨in refusing to accept ardent suitors who were urged upon her, she was obstinately *mulish* —*Fashion Digest*⟩ ⟨a *mulish* determination to make the worst of everything —T.S.Eliot⟩ ⟨there is a *mulish* quality about vellum that renders it difficult to cope with —Edith Diehl⟩ STIFF-NECKED, even more than OBSTINATE or STUBBORN, stresses inflexibility, suggesting a haughtiness or arrogance that will not be directed ⟨*stiff-necked* in his determination to wage a national campaign rather than a series of local campaigns —*Newsweek*⟩ ⟨the *stiff-necked* secretaries of Cromwell's army who had been glad to stand in pillories and suffer their ears to be cropped rather than put bread in the mouths of priests —V.W.Brooks⟩ PIGHEADED and BULLHEADED, terms of severe reproach, suggest a particularly perverse or stupid kind of obstinacy, PIGHEADED stressing rather imperviousness to reason, BULLHEADED stressing rather headstrong determination ⟨too . . . *pigheaded* to listen to reason —Dashiell Hammett⟩ ⟨a *pigheaded* refusal to budge from an untenable political position⟩ ⟨a *bullheaded* driving at a private goal no matter who else is hurt along the way⟩
[2]**ob·sti·nate** \-,nāt\ *vt* -ED/-ING/-S [ME *obstinaten*, fr. L *obstinatus*, past part. of *obstinare* to be obstinate] : to make obstinate
**ob·sti·nate·ly** *adv* [ME *obstinatly*, fr. [1]*obstinat* + *-ly*] : in an obstinate manner : with obstinacy
**ob·sti·nate·ness** *n* -ES : the quality or state of being obstinate
**ob·sti·na·tion** \,äbztə'nāshən, -bat-\ *n* -S [ME *obstinacioun*, fr. MF *obstination*, fr. L *obstination-, obstinatio*, fr. *obstinatus* (past part. of *obstinare*) + *-ion-, -io* -ion] : OBSTINACY
**ob·sti·pate** \'äbztə,pāt, -bst-\ *vt* -ED/-ING/-S [back-formation fr. *obstipation*] : to bind up : constipate severely
**ob·sti·pa·tion** \,==,'pāshən\ *n* -S [LL *obstipation-, obstipatio* close pressure, fr. L *ob-* + *stipare* to press together + *-ion-, -io* -ion — more at STIFF] : BLOCKAGE ⟨~ of a body passage⟩; *specif* : severe and obstinate constipation
**ob·strep·er·ate** \əbz'trepə,rāt, äb-, -b'st-\ *vi* -ED/-ING/-S [*obstreperous* + *-ate*] *archaic* : to make a noise
**ob·strep·er·ous** \-p(ə)rəs\ *adj* [L *obstreperus*, fr. *obstrepere* to make noise against, fr. *ob-* to, against + *strepere* make noise; akin to OE *thræft* quarrel, discord, MLG *drevelinge* vain chatter, ON *thrapt* chatter; all of imit. origin — more at OB-] **1** : marked by or engaging in aggressive noisiness : LOUD, CLAMOROUS ⟨~ roaring⟩ **2** : stubbornly defiant : resisting control or restraint often with a show of noisy disorder : TURBULENT, UNMANAGEABLE ⟨an ~ crew⟩ ⟨~ elephants —Faubion Bowers⟩ **syn** see VOCIFEROUS
**ob·strep·er·ous·ly** *adv* : in a loud, clamorous, or disorderly manner : REBELLIOUSLY
**ob·strep·er·ous·ness** *n* -ES : the quality or state of being obstreperous
**obstriction** *n* -S [LL *obstriction-, obstrictio*, fr. L *obstrictus* (past part. of *obstringere* to bind, obligate, fr. *ob-* to, over + *stringere* to draw tight, bind) + *-ion-, -io* -ion — more at OB-, STRAIN] *obs* : the condition of being obligated : OBLIGATION
**ob·strop·o·lous** \əbz'träpələs, äb-, -b'st-\ *dial var of* OBSTREPEROUS
**ob·struct** \əbz'trəkt, äb-, -b'st-\ *vb* -ED/-ING/-S [L *obstructus*, past part. of *obstruere* to build against, block up, fr. *ob-* to, against + *struere* to pile up, build — more at OB-, STRUCTURE] *vt* **1** : to block up : stop up or close up : place an obstacle in or fill with obstacles or impediments to passing ⟨traffic ~*ing* the street⟩ ⟨veins ~*ed* by clots⟩ **2** : to be or come in the way of : hinder from passing, action, or operation : IMPEDE, RETARD ⟨unwise rules ~ legislation⟩ ⟨constant interruptions ~ our progress⟩ **3** : to cut off from sight : shut out ⟨the high wall ~*ed* the view⟩ ~ *vi* : to place obstacles in the way : IMPEDE **syn** see HINDER
**ob·struc·tion** \-kshən\ *n* -S [L *obstruction-, obstructio* fr. *obstructus* (past part. of *obstruere* to obstruct) + *-ion-, -io* -ion] **1** : an act of obstructing or the condition of being obstructed: as **a** : a condition of being clogged or blocked ⟨intestinal ~⟩ ⟨respiratory ~ due to thyroid disease⟩ **b** *obs* : arrest of vital functions : DEATH **c** : a delay or attempted delay of business by dilatory parliamentary tactics in a deliberative body (as a legislature) — compare FILIBUSTER 2 **d** : the illegal hindrance of the progress of an opponent in a game (as soccer) by remaining in the path he wants to follow **2** : something that obstructs or impedes : IMPEDIMENT, HINDRANCE ⟨removing ~s from the path⟩ ⟨this was the major ~ to the success of our plan⟩ **syn** see OBSTACLE
**ob·struc·tion·ism** \-,nizəm\ *n* -S [*obstructionist* + *-ism*] : the practice of an obstructionist : deliberate interference with progress or business
**ob·struc·tion·ist** \-nəst\ *n* -S *often attrib* : one that hinders progress : one that deliberately and often by indirect or delaying tactics obstructs business (as in a legislative body) — **ob·struc·tion·is·tic** \=,==;nistik\ *adj*
[1]**ob·struc·tive** \əbz'trəktiv, äb-, -b'st-, -ēv *also* -əv\ *adj* [L *obstructus* + E *-ive*] **1** : tending to obstruct : presenting obstacles : HINDERING **2** : of, relating to, or characterized by obstruction — **ob·struc·tive·ly** \-tə̇vlē\ *adv* — **ob·struc·tive·ness** \-tivnəs, -tēv- *also* -təv-\ *n* -ES
[2]**obstructive** \"\ *n* -S : an obstructive person or thing
**obstructive jaundice** *n* : jaundice due to obstruction of the biliary passages (as by gallstones or tumor)
**ob·struc·tor** \əbz'trəktə(r), äb-, -b'st-\ *n* -S : one that obstructs
[1]**ob·stru·ent** \'äbztrəwənt -bst-\ *adj* [L *obstruent-, obstruens*, pres. part. of *obstruere* to obstruct — more at OBSTRUCT] **1** *archaic* : causing obstruction : blocking up **2** *phonetics* : characterized by stoppage or friction
[2]**obstruent** \"\ *n* -S : a speech sound in the articulation of which the breath passage is obstructed completely or to the point of producing friction : STOP, FRICATIVE — compare RESONANT
**obstruse** *adj* [L *obstrusus*, MS var. of *abstrusus* concealed — more at ABSTRUSE] *obs* : ABSTRUSE
**ob·stu·pe·fy** \äbz't(y)üpə,fī, -b'st-\ *vt* [L *obstupefacere*, fr. *ob-* to, against, over + *stupefacere* to stupefy — more at OB-, STUPEFY] : STUPEFY
**obt** *abbr* **1** obedient **2** [L *obiit*] he died
**ob·tain** \əb'tān, äb-\ *vb* -ED/-ING/-S [ME *obteinen*, fr. MF & L; MF *obtenir*, fr. L *obtinēre* to take hold of, fr. *ob-* to, completely + *-tinēre* (fr. *tenēre* to hold) — more at OB-, THIN] *vt* **1 a** : to gain or attain possession or disposal of usu. by some planned action or method ⟨ability to doubt until evidence is ~*ed* —John Dewey⟩ ⟨~*ing* the information easily⟩ **b** : to bring about or call into being : EFFECT ⟨~ quiet for their annual meetings —*Amer. Guide Series: N.Y.City*⟩ **2** *obs* : HOLD, KEEP, POSSESS, OCCUPY ⟨he who ~s the monarchy of heaven —John Milton⟩ **3** *obs* : to arrive at : ATTAIN, REACH ~ *vi* **1** *archaic* : SUCCEED **2** *obs* : ATTAIN, ARRIVE — used with *to* or *unto* **3** : to have a firm footing : become recognized or established : be prevalent or general ⟨the custom ~s of going to the seashore in summer⟩ ⟨a greater degree of free expression than usually ~s in film production —Roger Manvell⟩ **syn** see GET
**ob·tain·able** \-nəbəl\ *adj* : capable of being obtained : AVAILABLE
**ob·tain·al** \-nᵊl\ *n* -S [*obtain* + *-al*] : OBTAINMENT
**ob·tain·er** \-nə(r)\ *n* -S : one that obtains
**ob·tain·ment** \-mənt\ *n* -S **1** : the act or process of obtaining **2** : something that is obtained
**obtd** *abbr* obtained
**ob·tect** \əb'tekt\ *also* **ob·tect·ed** \-təd\ *adj* [*obtect* fr. L *obtectus*, past part. of *obtegere* to cover up, fr. *ob-* to, over + *tegere* to cover; *obtected* fr. L *obtectus* + E *-ed* — more at OB-, THATCH] : enclosed in or characterized by enclosure in a firm chitinous case or covering ⟨an ~ pupa⟩ ⟨~ metamorphosis⟩ — compare EXARATE
**ob·tem·per** \əb'tempər\ *vt* [MF *obtemperer*, fr. L *obtemperare*, fr. *ob-* to, over + *temperare* to temper, mingle properly — more at OB-, TEMPER] *Scots law* : SUBMIT, COMPLY, OBEY
**ob·tem·per·ate** \-,rāt\ *vt* [ME *obtemperat*, fr. L *obtemperatus*, past part. of *obtemperare* to comply, obey] *archaic* : OBEY
**obtend** *vt* [L *obtendere* to stretch before, draw out, pretend, fr. *ob-* to, toward + *tendere* to stretch — more at OB-, TEND] **1** *obs* : to offer as a reason : PRETEND **2** *obs* : OPPOSE
**ob·ten·e·brate** \äb'tenə,brāt\ *vt* -ED/-ING/-S [LL *obtenebratus*, past part. of *obtenebrare* to darken, fr. L *ob-* to, toward, over + *tenebrare* to darken, fr. *tenebrae* darkness — more at OB-, TEMERITY] : to darken by or as if by shadowing
**ob·ten·tion** \əb'tenchən, äb-\ *n* -S [F, fr. L *obtentus* (past part. of *obtinēre* to take hold of) + F *-ion* — more at OBTAIN] : an act or instance of obtaining : OBTAINMENT
**ob·test** \äb'test\ *vb* [MF *obtester*, fr. L *obtestari*, fr. *ob-* to, toward + *testari* to be a witness — more at OB-, TESTAMENT] *vt* **1** : BESEECH, SUPPLICATE **2** : to call to witness : invoke as a witness ~ *vi* **1** : SUPPLICATE **2** : PROTEST
**ob·tes·ta·tion** \,=,te'stāshən\ *n* -S [L *obtestation-, obtestatio*, fr. *obtestatus* (past part. of *obtestari*) + *-ion-, -io* -ion] : an act of obtesting : solemn supplication or adjuration
**obtrect** *vt* -ED/-ING/-S [L *obtrectare* to detract from, fr. *ob-* + *-trectare* (fr. *tractare* to draw, handle, manage, treat) — more at TREAT] *obs* : SLANDER — **obtrectation** *n* -S *obs* — **obtrectator** *or* **obtrector** *n* -S *obs*
**ob·trude** \əb'trüd, äb-\ *vb* -ED/-ING/-S [L *obtrudere*, fr. *ob-* to, toward, against + *trudere* to thrust — more at OB-, THREAT] *vt* **1** : to thrust out : push or extend into sight : EXTRUDE ⟨the snail slowly *obtruded* his tentacle⟩ **2** : to thrust forward, present, or call to notice without warrant or request ⟨not a man to ~ his beliefs casually⟩ ⟨forced to ~ ourselves into their party⟩ ~ *vi* : to thrust oneself or some other matter upon attention : INTRUDE ⟨do what we may our childhood background will ~⟩
**ob·trud·er** \-də(r)\ *n* -S : one that obtrudes
**ob·truncate** \(')äb+\ *vt* [L *obtruncatus*, past part. of *obtruncare* to cut off, fr. *ob-* toward, against, over + *truncare* to cut off, fr. *truncus* trunk — more at OB-, TRUNCATE] : to cut the head or top from
**ob·tru·sion** \əb'trüzhən, äb-\ *n* -S [LL *obtrusion-, obtrusio* fr. L *obtrusus* (past part. of *obtrudere* to obtrude) + *-ion-, -io* -ion] **1** : an act of obtruding : a thrusting upon others by force or unsolicited **2** : something that is obtruded
**ob·tru·sive** \əb'trüs\iv, (')äb¦t-, -üz\, \ēv *also* \əv\ *adj* [L *obtrusus* + E *-ive*] **1** : thrust out : PROTRUDING ⟨a sharp ~ edge⟩ **2 a** : disposed to obtrude : FORWARD, PUSHING, INTRUSIVE ⟨~ behavior⟩ **b** : undesirably or unattractively noticeable or showy ⟨hats will be less ~ this season⟩ ⟨the propaganda was occasionally ~⟩ **syn** see IMPERTINENT
**ob·tru·sive·ly** \ə̇vlē, -li\ *adv* : in an obtrusive manner : so as to be obtrusive
**ob·tru·sive·ness** \ivnə̇s, \ēv *also* \əv-\ *n* -ES : the quality or state of being obtrusive
**ob·tund** \äb'tənd\ *vt* -ED/-ING/-S [ME *obtunden*, fr. L *obtundere* to beat against, to dull — more at OBTUSE] : to reduce the edge or violence of : DULL, BLUNT ⟨~*ed* reflexes⟩ ⟨agents that ~ pain⟩
[1]**ob·tund·ent** \(')=¦təndənt\ *adj* [L *obtundent-, obtundens*, pres. part. of *obtundere*] : blunting irritation or lessening pain
[2]**obtundent** \"\ *n* -S : an agent that blunts pain or dulls sensibility
**ob·tu·rate** \'äbt(y)ə,rāt\ *vt* -ED/-ING/-S [L *obturatus*, past part. of *obturare* to stop up, fr. *ob-* toward, over + *-turare* (akin to *tumēre* to swell) — more at OB-, THUMB] : OBSTRUCT, CLOSE; *esp* : to stop (a gun breech) so as to prevent the escape of gas in firing — **ob·tu·ra·tion** \,==\'rāshən\ *n* -S
**ob·tu·ra·tor** \'==,rād·ə(r)\ *n* -S *often attrib* [NL, fr. L *obturatus* + *-or*] : one that closes or stops up an opening: **a** : either of two muscles arising from the obturator membrane and adjacent bony surfaces: (1) *or* **obturator ex·ter·nus** \-ek'stərnəs\ : a muscle arising from the outer surface of the membrane and being inserted into the trochanteric fossa of the femur (2) *or* **obturator in·ter·nus** \-in'tərnəs\ : a muscle arising from the inner surface of the membrane and being inserted into the greater trochanter of the femur **b** : a prosthetic device that usu. has the form of a plate and is designed to bridge an unnatural opening (as a fissure of the palate) **c** : a device for preventing the escape of gas through the breech mechanism of a breech-loading gun **d** : a hooded swelling of the placenta that fits over the nucellus in some plants
**obturator artery** *n* : an artery that passes out through the obturator canal and dividing into two branches is distributed to the muscles and fasciae of the hip and thigh
**obturator canal** *n* : the small patent opening of the obturator foramen through which nerves and vessels pass
**obturator foramen** *n* : an opening that is situated between the pubic and ischial parts of the innominate bone and that is largely closed by the obturator membrane — see OBTURATOR CANAL
**obturator membrane** *n* : a firm fibrous membrane covering most of the obturator foramen and serving as origin of the obturator muscles
**obturator nerve** *n* : a branch of the lumbar plexus arising from the second, third, and fourth lumbar nerves and supplying the hip and knee joints, adductor muscles of the thigh, and skin
**obturator vein** *n* : a tributary of the internal iliac vein that accompanies the obturator artery
**ob·turbinate** \(')äb+\ *adj* [ISV *ob-* + *turbinate*] : inversely turbinate
**ob·tuse** \əb't(y)üs, (')äb¦-\ *adj, sometimes* -ER/-EST [L *obtusus*, past part. of *obtundere* to beat against, to dull, fr. *ob-* to, against + *tundere* to beat — more at OB-, STUTTER] **1** : lacking acuity of sensibility or perceptions : having neither delicate feelings nor alert awareness : DENSE ⟨too ~ to take a hint⟩ ⟨a dull ~ person⟩ **2 a** *of an angle* : exceeding 90 degrees but being less than 180 degrees — see ANGLE illustration **b** : not pointed or acute : BLUNT ⟨an ~ contour⟩ **c** *of a leaf* : blunt or rounded at the free end **d** : OBTUSE-ANGLED **3** : not causing an acute impression : MILD ⟨an ~ pain⟩ **syn** see DULL
**obtuse-angled** \-;==\ *also* **obtuse-angular** \-;===\ *adj* : having one or more angles that are obtuse
**obtuse bisectrix** *n* : the bisectrix of the obtuse angle formed by the axes of a biaxial crystal — called also *second mean line*
**ob·tuse·ly** *adv* : in an obtuse manner : so as to be obtuse
**ob·tuse·ness** *n* -ES : the quality or state of being obtuse
**obtusi-** *comb form* [NL, fr. L *obtusus*, past part.] : obtusely ⟨*obtusi*rostrate⟩ ⟨*obtusi*folious⟩
**ob·tu·sion** \äb't(y)üzhən\ *n* -S [LL *obtusion-, obtusio*, fr. L *obtusus* (past part. of *obtundere*) + *-ion-, -io* -ion] : a blunting or a condition of being blunted
**ob·tu·si·ty** \-üsəd·ē\ *n* -ES [ML *obtusitas*, fr. L *obtusus* + *-itas* -ity] : OBTUSENESS; *esp* : human density and insensitivity
**ob-ugrian** \(')äb+\ *n* -S *usu cap O&U* [*Ob*, river in Siberia + *Ugrian*] : a member of an Ostyak and Vogul people of Siberia that is of Finno-Ugrian ethnic classification, has a primitive hunting and fishing economy, and is closest linguistic ally to the Magyar peoples
**ob·um·brant** \(')ä¦bəmbrənt\ *adj* [L *obumbrant-, obumbrans*, pres. part. of *obumbrare* to overshadow] : OVERHANGING ⟨~ hackle feathers⟩
[1]**obumbrate** *adj* [L *obumbratus*, past part. of *obumbrare* to overshadow, fr. *ob-* to, over + *umbrare* to shade, fr. *umbra* shadow — more at OB-, UMBRAGE] *obs* : darkened by or as if by shadow
[2]**ob·um·brate** \ä'bəm,brāt\ *vt* -ED/-ING/-S [L *obumbratus*, past part. of *obumbrare*] **1** : SHADE, DARKEN, CLOUD **2** *archaic* : ADUMBRATE — **ob·um·bra·tion** \,ä,bəm'brāshən\ *n* -S
**obus** \ōbüs, -üz; ˈōbəs\ *n, pl* **obus** \"\ *or* **obus·es** \ˈōbəsəz\ [F, fr. G *haubitze* howitzer — more at HOWITZER] : an artillery shell
**obv** *abbr* obverse
**ob·vallate** \(')äb+\ *adj* [L *obvallatus*, past part. of *obvallare* to surround with a wall, fr. *ob-* toward, over + *vallare* to surround with a wall, fr. *vallum* wall, rampart — more at OB-, WALL] : surrounded by or as if by a wall ⟨~ papillae⟩
**ob·ve·la·tion** \,äbvə'lāshən\ *n* -S [L *obvelare* to cover over, hide (fr. *ob-* toward, over + *velare* to cover, fr. *velum* covering, veil) + E *-ation* — more at OB-] : VEILING, CONCEALING — compare REVELATION
**ob·ven·tion** \äb'venchən\ *n* -S [ME *obvencioun*, fr. MF *obvention*, fr. L *obvention-, obventio* income, revenue, fr. L *obventus* (past part. of *obvenire* to come about, fr. *ob-* to, toward + *venire* to come) + *-ion-, -io* -ion — more at OB-, COME] : something that comes casually (as an incidental advantage or an occasional religious offering)
[1]**ob·verse** \əb'vərs, (')äb¦v-, -vōs,-vəis\ *adj* [L *obversus*, past part. of *obvertere* to turn towards] **1** : facing the observer or opponent — opposed to *reverse* **2** : having the base or end next the attachment narrower than the top or free end ⟨an ~ tool⟩ ⟨an ~ leaf⟩ **3** : constituting a counterpart or complement — **ob·verse·ly** *adv*
[2]**ob·verse** \'äb,vərs, äb'vərs, -vōs,-vəis\ *n* -S [L *obversus*, past part. of *obvertere*] **1 a** : the side of a coin, token, medal, or currency note that is considered the front and that bears the principal device and lettering; *broadly* : a front or principal surface **b** : the more conspicuous of two possible sides, things, or cases ⟨the ~ of this situation⟩ **2 a** : a counterpart necessarily involved in or answering to a fact or truth **b** *logic* : a proposition which may be inferred immediately from another and in which the quality of the given proposition is changed, the subject term remains unaltered, and the predicate is the negative of that given ⟨the ~ of "all *A* is *B*" is "no *A* is not *B*"⟩ **syn** see CONVERSE
**ob·ver·sion** \äb'vərzhən, -vōzh-, -vəizh- *also* -shən\ *n* -S [L *obversion-, obversio*, fr. *obversus* (past part. of *obvertere*) + *-ion-, -io* -ion] *logic* : the operation of immediate inference that gives the obverse
**ob·vert** \='vərt, -vōt, -vəit\ *vt* -ED/-ING/-S [L *obvertere* to turn towards, fr. *ob-* to, toward + *vertere* to turn — more at OB-, WORTH] **1** : to turn so as to present a different surface to view : to change the appearance or seeming of **2** : to subject (a proposition in logic) to obversion
**ob·ver·tend** \'äbvə(r),tend\ *n* -S [L *obvertendus*, gerundive of *obvertere* to obvert] : a proposition upon which the operation of obversion is performed
**ob·vi·a·ble** \'äbvēəbəl\ *adj* [*obviate* + *-able*] : capable of being obviated
**ob·vi·ate** \'äbvē,āt, *usu* -ād·+V\ *vt* -ED/-ING/-S [LL *obviatus*, past part. of *obviare* to meet, withstand, oppose, fr. L *obviam* in the way] **1** : to meet or anticipate and dispose of : make unnecessary ⟨~ the necessity of going⟩ **2** *obs* : OPPOSE **syn** see PREVENT
**ob·vi·a·tion** \,==ˈāshən\ *n* -S [ME *obviacioun*, fr. LL *obviation-, obviatio*, fr. *obviatus* + *-ion-, -io* -ion] : an act or instance of obviating or being obviated
[1]**ob·vi·a·tive** \'äbvē,ād·iv\ *adj* [*obviate* + *-ive*] *of a grammatical form* : denoting the second of two third persons referred to in a context (as in the construction in some languages corresponding to "he held *his* [another's] horse") — compare PROXIMATE
[2]**obviative** \"\ *n* -S : an obviative grammatical form
**ob·vi·ous** \'äbvēəs *in rapid speech often* 'ävē-\ *adj* [L *obvius*, fr. *obviam* in the way, towards, about to, fr. *ob* to, before, against + *viam*, accus. of *via* way, road — more at EPI-, VIA] **1 a** *obs* : presenting itself in the way : occurring often **b** *archaic* : being in the way or to the front : OPPOSITE, FRONTING **c** : so placed as to be easily or inevitably perceived or noticed ⟨an ~ light switch⟩ **2** *archaic* : liable or exposed to some effect (as injury or mockery) : OPEN, SUBJECT **3** : capable of easy perception: **a** : readily perceived by the senses : hard not to perceive, sense, or grasp ⟨the invisible as opposed to the ~ —M.R.Cohen⟩ **b** : readily and easily perceived by the sensibilities or mind : requiring very little insight or reflection to perceive, recognize, or comprehend ⟨all was taken in at a glance; the fell purpose . . . was ~ —Herman Melville⟩ **c** : easily understood : requiring no thought or consideration to understand or analyze : so simple and clear as to be unmistakable ⟨poetry, in fact, whatever else it may or may not be, must be poetry—a sound, if ~, conclusion —C.D.Lewis⟩ **d** : disappointingly simple and easy to discover or interpret : wanting in any challenging or interesting complexity or ingenuity ⟨the devices . . . are rather too ~ —Henry Adams⟩ **syn** see EVIDENT
**ob·vi·ous·ly** *adv* : in an obvious manner : CERTAINLY
**ob·vi·ous·ness** *n* -ES : the quality or state of being obvious
**ob·vo·lute** \'äbvə,lüt *also* -əl,yüt, *usu* -üd·+V\ *adj* [L *obvolutus*, past part. of *obvolvere*] : OVERLAPPING, CONTORTED, CONVOLUTE
**ob·volve** \äb'välv\ *vt* -ED/-ING/-S [L *obvolvere* to roll around, wrap around, fr. *ob-* to, over + *volvere* to roll — more at OB-, VOLUBLE] *archaic* : ENWRAP
**oc** *abbr* ocean
**OC** *abbr* **1** of course **2** office copy **3** officer candidate

4 officer commanding 5 officer in charge 6 officer's cook 7 official classification 8 old charter 9 old crop 10 on center 11 *often not cap* only child 12 open charter 13 open cover 14 *often not cap* [L *opere citato*] in the work cited 15 order canceled 16 original cover 17 outing club 18 overcharge 19 oxygen consumed

**oca** *or* **oka** \'ōkə\ *n* -s [Sp *oca,* fr. Quechua *ókka*] **:** either of two So. American wood sorrels (*Oxalis crenata* and *O. tuberosa*) cultivated for their edible tubers

**oc·a·ri·na** \,äkə'rēnə\ *n* -s [It, dim of *oca* goose, fr. LL *auca,* fr. (assumed) VL *avica,* backformation fr. L *avicula* small bird, dim. of *avis* bird — more at AVIARY] **:** a simple wind instrument or toy of the flute class having a mouthpiece and finger holes and usu. made of terracotta in various sizes — called also *sweet potato*

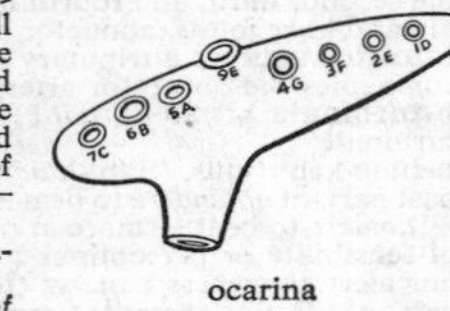
ocarina

**occ** *abbr* 1 occasional; occasionally 2 occulting

**oc·ca·mism** *usu cap, var of* OCKHAMISM

**occam's razor** *usu cap O, var of* OCKHAM'S RAZOR

**oc·ca·nee·chi** \,äkə'nēchē\ *n, pl* **occaneechi** *or* **occaneechis** *usu cap* **1 :** an extinct Siouan people formerly found on the middle island in the Roanoke river, Virginia **2 :** a member of the Occaneechi people

**¹oc·ca·sion** \ə'kāzhən\ *n* -s [ME *occasioun,* fr. MF or L; MF *occasion,* fr. L *occasion-, occasio,* fr. *occasus* (past part. of *occidere* to fall down, fr. *ob-* + *cadere* to fall) + *-ion-, -io* -ion — more at CHANCE] **1 :** a situation or set of circumstances favorable to a particular purpose or development **:** a timely chance **:** OPPORTUNITY ⟨rose to the ~⟩ ⟨was equal to the ~⟩ ⟨took ~ by the forelock⟩ ⟨only those living in exceptionally fortunate localities had ~ to grow surplus products —Samuel Van Valkenburg & Ellsworth Huntington⟩ ⟨while the new science has achieved wonders in medicine and surgery, it has also produced and spread ~*s* for diseases and weaknesses —John Dewey⟩ **2 a :** something that produces an effect or brings about an event ⟨a formula that has been the ~ for a considerable amount of misunderstanding —I.A.Richards⟩ ⟨any ~ which prompts a mind to ask some fundamental question —Hunter Mead⟩ ⟨an ~ of sin⟩ **b :** something that helps to bring about an event or produce an effect without directly causing it **:** a contributing or incidental cause ⟨the birthday . . . was merely the ~, not the cause, of the guests' effusions —Lillian Ross⟩ ⟨the specific ~ of the poem is not known —C.S.Kilby⟩ ⟨a casual mention of the house by a friend was the ~ of their buying it⟩ ⟨an inspiring teacher was the ~ of his great achievements in science⟩ **3 :** a circumstance, occurrence, or state of affairs that provides ground or reason for something ⟨there is no ~ for alarm: it is a very mild illness⟩ ⟨his graduation with honors is ~ for celebration⟩ **4 a :** a particular occurrence **:** HAPPENING, INCIDENT ⟨well adapted for treatment as a row of detached episodes or ~*s* —Percy Lubbock⟩ ⟨everybody has been terribly kind since my recent sad ~ —Thomas Kelly⟩ **b :** a particular time at which something takes place **:** a time marked by some happening ⟨on the ~ of his daughter's wedding⟩ ⟨on the ~ of the signing of the peace treaty⟩ **5 a :** a need arising from a particular circumstance **:** EXIGENCY, REQUIREMENT ⟨there had been no ~ for being so definite —Sherwood Anderson⟩ ⟨knowledge for which he will never have any ~ —C.H. Grandgent⟩ **b** *archaic* **:** a personal want or need — usu. used in pl. ⟨my purse, my person, my extremest means lie all unlock'd to your ~*s* —Shak.⟩ **6 occasions** *pl* **:** something that one has to do **:** necessary affairs **:** BUSINESS ⟨minded his own ~*s* and was content to let other folk mind theirs —S.H. Adams⟩ ⟨going about their lawful or unlawful ~*s* all over the seven seas —Douglas Bush⟩ **7 a :** a religious ceremonial; *specif* **:** a Scottish communion service **b :** a special event or ceremony **:** CELEBRATION ⟨he liked the ~ —the Changing of the Guard at St. James's Palace, parties, and balls, and such things as that —Basil Taylor⟩ ⟨sat in the big parlor as though this was an ~ —Agnes S. Turnbull⟩ **syn** see CAUSE, OPPORTUNITY — **on occasion** *adv* **:** now and then **:** OCCASIONALLY ⟨he lives in the country, though he visits the city *on occasion*⟩

**²occasion** \"\ *vt* -ED/-ING/-S **1 :** to give occasion to **:** bring about **:** give rise to **:** CAUSE ⟨a violent storm ~*ed* a new delay of two weeks —Oscar Handlin⟩ ⟨social and commercial intercourse will ~ movement of language —Charlton Laird⟩ **2 :** to cause to do something ⟨was almost at the end of his financial resources, which fact ~*ed* him to turn away from a pretentious hotel —Zane Grey⟩

**¹oc·ca·sion·al** \-zhən³l, -zhnəl\ *adj* **1 :** occurring or operating on a particular occasion **:** proceeding from the occasion ⟨the cabinet has ~ special meetings to deal with urgent matters⟩ ⟨a budget must be able to meet ~ demands as well as regular ones⟩ **2 :** acting as the occasion or contributing cause of something ⟨nothing else ~ of my long silence —D.G. Rossetti⟩ **3 :** written for a particular occasion or to celebrate a particular event or anniversary ⟨an ~ essay⟩ ⟨an ~ poem⟩ ⟨~ verse⟩ **4 :** met with, appearing, or occurring irregularly and according to no fixed or certain scheme **:** INFREQUENT ⟨takes an ~ vacation⟩ ⟨sees an ~ visitor⟩ ⟨runs into an ~ storm⟩ **5 :** acting in a specified capacity on a particular occasion or from time to time ⟨an ~ speaker⟩ ⟨an ~ chauffeur⟩ ⟨an ~ fisherman⟩ **6 :** designed or constructed to be used as the occasion demands ⟨an ~ chair⟩ ⟨an ~ table⟩

**²occasional** \"\ *n* -s **:** something occasional —usu. used in pl. ⟨the furniture department has a good selection of ~*s*⟩

**occasional cause** *n* **1 a :** a mental state (as desire or decision) considered as the occasion but not the real cause of a physical phenomenon (as bodily behavior) **b :** a physical phenomenon considered similarly as the occasion of a mental state — compare OCCASIONALISM **2 :** a circumstance that precedes an effect and that without being the real cause is the occasion of its action

**oc·ca·sion·al·ism** \-zhən³l,izəm, -zhnə,li-\ *n* -s [ISV ¹*occasional* + *-ism*] **:** a doctrine held by the Cartesian philosophers Geulincx and Malebranche that mind and matter are inherently incapable of affecting each other and that their apparent reciprocal action must therefore be due to the intervention of God who on the occasion of a change in one produces a corresponding change in the other — compare OCCASIONAL CAUSE

**oc·ca·sion·al·ist** \-₋ləst\ *n* -s [ISV ¹*occasional* + *-ist*] **:** an adherent of occasionalism

**oc·ca·sion·al·is·tic** \ə¦kāzhən³l¦istik, -zhnə¦li-\ *adj* **:** of or relating to occasionalism or occasionalists

**oc·ca·sion·al·i·ty** \ə,kāzhə'nalәdē\ *n* -ES **:** the quality or state of being occasional

**oc·ca·sion·al·ly** \ə'kāzhən³lē, -zhnəlē, -i *sometimes* -zhənl-\ *adv* **1 :** now and then **:** here and there **:** SOMETIMES ⟨open areas are only ~ interrupted by clumps of aspen —*Amer. Guide Series: Nev.*⟩ **2** *dial chiefly Eng* **:** on a particular occasion **:** for the occasion

**oc·ca·sion·er** \-nə(r)\ *n* -s **:** one that occasions

**occasions** *pl of* OCCASION, *pres 3d sing of* OCCASION

**oc·ci·dent** \'äksədənt *also* -d³nt *or* -,dent\ *n* -s [ME, west, fr. MF, fr. L *occident-, occidens,* fr. pres. part. of *occidere* to fall down, go down, set — more at OCCASION] **1** *obs* **:** the part of the firmament or of the world where the sun sets — compare ORIENT **2** *cap* **:** WEST 2 ⟨sailed for the *Occident*⟩

**¹oc·ci·den·tal** \¦==¦dent³l\ *adj* [ME, fr. L *occidentalis,* fr. *occident-, occidens* + *-alis* -al] **1** *often cap* **:** of, relating to, or situated in the Occident **:** WESTERN — compare ORIENTAL **2 a** *often cap* **:** of, relating to, or having the characteristics of Occidentals ⟨~ culture⟩ ⟨~ art⟩ **b :** of, relating to, or characteristic of the western U. S. ⟨the ~ plane tree⟩ **3 :** of inferior grade, luster, or value ⟨~ agate⟩ — compare ORIENTAL 2a — **oc·ci·den·tal·ly** \-³lē, -i\ *adv*

**²occidental** \"\ *n* -s *usu cap* **:** a member of one of the indigenous peoples of the Occident ⟨the *Occidental* regards much oriental and primitive music as mere noise —Thomas Munro⟩

**oc·ci·den·tal·ism** \,==¦dent³l,izəm\ *n* -s *usu cap* **:** the characteristic features of occidental peoples or culture

**oc·ci·den·tal·ist** \-₋ləst\ *n* -s *often cap* **:** one who favors occidental culture

**oc·ci·den·tal·iza·tion** \,==,dent³lə'zāshən\ *n* -s *often cap* **:** the process of occidentalizing or the state of being occidentalized

**oc·ci·den·tal·ize** \,==¦dent³l,īz\ *vt* -ED/-ING/-S *sometimes cap* **:** to make occidental **:** cause to conform to western standards or culture ⟨served to widen the gulf between the small *occidentalized* intelligentsia and the great mass of the people —Virginia Thompson & Richard Adloff⟩

**occipit-** *or* **occipito-** *comb form* [ML *occipit-* & NL *occipito-,* fr. L *occipit-, occiput*] **1 :** occiput ⟨*occipit*ad⟩ **2 :** occipital and ⟨*occipito*nasal⟩

**oc·cip·i·tad** \(')äk¦sipə,tad\ *adv* [*occipit-* + *-ad*] **:** toward the occiput

**¹oc·cip·i·tal** \(')äk¦sipəd·³l, -ət³l\ *adj* [MF, fr. ML *occipitalis,* fr. L *occipit-, occiput* occiput + *-alis* -al — more at OCCIPUT] **1 :** of or relating to the occiput or an occipital part **2 :** lying near or oriented toward the occiput — **oc·cip·i·tal·ly** \-³lē, -i\ *adv*

**²occipital** \"\ *n* -s **1 :** OCCIPITAL BONE **2 :** a part or structure lying near or on the occiput (as certain scales on reptiles)

**occipital arch** *n* **:** a part of the insect cranium between the occipital and postoccipital sutures

**occipital artery** *n* **:** a branch of the external carotid supplying the muscles and other structures of the back of the neck and head

**occipital bone** *n* **:** a compound bone that forms the posterior part of the skull and surrounds the foramen magnum, bearing the condyle or condyles for articulation with the atlas, in higher vertebrates being usu. composed of four more or less completely united elements and in man much curved and of trapezoid outline, ending in front of the foramen magnum in the basilar process, and bearing on its outer surface behind the foramen magnum the two curved transverse superior and inferior nuchal lines besides a median crest and protuberance

**occipital condyle** *n* **1 :** an articular surface on the occipital bone by which the skull articulates with the atlas **2 :** a projection of the border of the postocciput of the insect head to which the lateral neck plates articulate

**occipital crest** *n* **1 :** either of the two ridges connecting the occipital protuberances and foramen magnum **2 :** a transverse ridge at the upper posterior border of the skull of many animals between the occipital and parietal segments **3 :** a crest of feathers on the back of the head of certain birds

**occipital foramen** *n* **1 :** FORAMEN MAGNUM **2 :** an opening at the back of an insect's head through which the alimentary canal and other organs pass to the thorax

**occipital ganglion** *n* **:** one of the paired ganglia of the stomodaeal nervous system of an insect that are located just behind the brain

**oc·cip·i·ta·lis** \äk,sipə'taləs, -tāl-, -täl-\ *n* -ES [NL, fr. ML, occipital] **:** the posterior muscular part of the occipitofrontalis

**occipital lobe** *n* **:** the posterior lobe of the cerebral hemisphere that is indistinctly separated from the parietal lobe in front and the temporal lobe below and has the form of a 3-sided pyramid

**occipital plate** *n* **:** a scute on the back of the head of certain reptiles

**occipital point** *n* **:** the point on the occiput farthest removed from the glabella

**occipital protuberance** *n* **:** either of two prominences on the occipital bone: **a :** a prominence on the outer surface of the occipital bone midway between the upper border and the foramen magnum that gives attachment to the ligamentum nuchae — called also *external occipital protuberance* **b :** a prominence similarly situated on the inner surface of the occipital bone — called also *internal occipital protuberance*

**occipital sinus** *n* **:** a venous sinus lodged in a groove on the internal occipital crest

**oc·cip·i·to·fron·ta·lis** \äk¦sipəd·ō+\ *n* [NL, fr. *occipit-* + *frontalis* frontal] **:** a fibrous layer covering each side of the vertex of the skull from the eyebrow to the occiput and continuous anteriorly and posteriorly with the frontalis and occipitalis muscles respectively — called also *epicranius*

**oc·cip·i·to·mas·toid** \"+\ *adj* [*occipit-* + *mastoid*] **:** of, relating to, lying between, or distributed to the occipital and mastoid bones ⟨~ suture⟩

**oc·cip·i·to·pa·ri·e·tal index** \"+ . . .-\ *n* [*occipitoparietal* ISV *occipit-* + *parietal*] **:** the ratio of the breadth of the skull between the asterions to its greatest breadth multiplied by 100

**oc·ci·put** \'äksə(,)pət, *usu* -d·+V\ *n, pl* **occiputs** \-ts\ *or* **oc·cip·i·ta** \äk'sipəd·ə\ [L *occipit-, occiput,* back-formation (influenced by L *capit-, caput* head) fr. *occipitium* back part of the head, occiput, fr. *ob-* + *-cipitium* (fr. *capit-, caput* head) — more at HEAD] **1 :** the back part of the head of a vertebrate or insect — see DOG illustration **2 :** the back part of the skull

**oc·ci·sion** \äk'sizhən\ *n* -s [ME *occisioun,* fr. MF *occision,* fr. L *occision-, occisio,* fr. *occisus* (past part. of *occidere* to kill, fr. *ob-* + *caedere* to cut, strike, kill) + *-ion-, -io* -ion — more at CONCISE] **:** SLAUGHTER ⟨applauded their pitiless ~ —R.S.Ellery⟩

**oc·clude** \ə'klüd\ *vb* -ED/-ING/-S [L *occludere,* fr. *ob-* + *claudere* to shut, close — more at CLOSE] *vt* **1 :** to shut or stop up so as to prevent the passage of something **:** CLOSE, OBSTRUCT ⟨a thrombus *occluding* a coronary artery⟩ ⟨an *occluded* bronchus⟩ ⟨sank ships to ~ the harbor⟩ **2 :** to bar the passage of **:** shut in or out ⟨concern with the mechanics of pronunciation ~*s* comprehension of the author's ideas —A.S.Artley⟩ ⟨the dandy's world is friendly, formal, and heartless, *occluding* the imagination —Cyril Connolly⟩ **3 :** to bring (upper and lower teeth) into occlusal relations **4 :** to take in and retain (a substance) in the interior rather than on an external surface **:** SORB ⟨proteins in precipitating may ~ alcohol⟩ — used esp. of metals sorbing gases ⟨palladium ~*s* large volumes of hydrogen⟩ **5 :** to cut off from contact with the surface of the earth and force aloft by the convergence of a cold front upon a warm front ⟨an *occluded* cyclone⟩ ⟨*occluded* warm air⟩ ⟨an *occluded* low⟩ ~ *vi* **1 :** to close with the cusps fitting together ⟨his teeth do not ~ properly⟩ **2 :** to become cut off from contact with the earth's surface ⟨the cyclone ~*s* and is left behind by the storm below —T.M.Longstreet⟩

**occluded front** *n* **:** OCCLUSION 1 c (2) — see FRONT illustration

**oc·clud·ent** \-d³nt\ *adj* [L *occludent-, occludens,* pres. part. of *occludere*] **:** serving to occlude

**occlus-** *or* **occluso-** *comb form* [prob. fr. (assumed) NL *occlus-,* fr. L *occlusus,* past part. of *occludere* to occlude] **1 :** occlusion ⟨*occlus*al⟩ ⟨*occluso*meter⟩ **2 :** occlusal and ⟨*occluso*gingival⟩

**oc·clu·sal** \ə'klüs³l\ *adj* [*occlus-* + *-al*] **:** of or relating to the grinding or biting surface of a tooth or occlusion of the teeth ⟨~ surface⟩ ⟨~ relationship⟩ ⟨an ~ neurosis⟩

**oc·clu·sion** \-üzhən\ *n* -s [prob. fr. (assumed) NL *occlusion-, occlusio,* fr. L *occlusus* (past part. of *occludere* to occlude) + *-ion-, -io* -ion] **1 :** the act of occluding or the state of being occluded **:** a shutting off or obstruction of something ⟨a coronary ~⟩ ⟨the silting up and ~ of the mouth of the river⟩ ⟨the ~ of sources of information⟩: as **a :** a blocking of the central passage of one reflex by preoccupation of nerve relays with the passage of another **b** (1) **:** the complete obstruction of the breath passage in the articulation of a stop (2) **:** the complete obstruction of the mouth passage in the articulation of a nasal consonant **c** (1) **:** the meteorological process of occluding (2) **:** something that has been occluded; *specif* **:** the front formed by a cold front overtaking a warm front and lifting the warm air above the earth's surface **2 a :** the bringing of the opposing surfaces of the teeth of the two jaws into contact; *also* **:** the relation between the surfaces when in contact **b :** the transient approximation of the edges of a natural opening ⟨~ of the eyelids⟩ **3 :** SORPTION; *esp* **:** sorption of gases

**¹oc·clu·sive** \-üsiv, -sēv *also* -sev\ *adj* [ISV *occlus-* + *-ive*] **1 :** serving to occlude ⟨an ~ dressing for a wound⟩ ⟨~ arterial disease⟩ **2 :** characterized by occlusion

**²occlusive** \"\ *n* -s **1 :** STOP 9 **2 :** a nasal consonant

**oc·clu·sor** \-üsə(r)\ *n* -s [NL, fr. L *occlusus* (past part. of *occludere*) + NL *-or*] **:** a body part that closes or blocks another ⟨~ muscles⟩ ⟨the operculum forms an effective ~ of the snail's shell⟩

**occn** *abbr* occasion

**¹oc·cult** \ə'kəlt, 'ä,kəlt\ *vb* -ED/-ING/-S [L *occultare,* fr. *occultus,* past part. of *occulere* to cover up] *vt* **1 :** to hide from sight **:** CONCEAL ⟨the lids lowered again, ~*ing* the old eyes' softened gleam —*MacLean's Mag.*⟩ ⟨if his ~*ed* guilt do not itself unkennel in one speech —Shak.⟩ **2 :** to conceal or extinguish the light of by intervention **:** ECLIPSE ⟨planets, like stars, may be ~*ed;* but as a planet shows a disk, and does not appear as a mere point, the disappearance is gradual —Patrick Moore⟩ ~ *vi* **:** to become concealed or to have its light extinguished ⟨the beam of the lighthouse ~*s* at regular intervals⟩

**²occult** \"\ *adj* [L *occultus,* past part. of *occulere* to cover up, fr. *ob-* + *-culere* (akin to L *celare* to conceal) — more at HELL] **1 :** deliberately kept hidden **:** not revealed to others **:** SECRET, UNDISCLOSED ⟨too ~ to be shown to uninitiate eyes —Elinor Wylie⟩ ⟨deep subterranean ~ jealousy —J.C.Powys⟩ **2 :** not to be apprehended or understood **:** demanding more than ordinary perception or knowledge **:** ABSTRUSE, MYSTERIOUS, RECONDITE ⟨as far as the general public was concerned, the museum was an esoteric, ~ place —Aline B. Saarinen⟩ ⟨~ matters like nuclear physics, radiation effects and the designing of rockets —Robert Bendiner⟩ ⟨the ~ properties of the ductless glands —W.R.Inge⟩ **3 a :** hidden from view **:** not able to be seen **:** CONCEALED ⟨the silica may appear in crystalline form . . . or it may remain ~ in the groundmass —G.W. Tyrrell⟩ **b** *archaic* **:** of or relating to lines drawn in dots or meant to be erased **4 :** of, relating to, or dealing in matters regarded as involving the action or influence of supernatural agencies or some secret knowledge of them ⟨deals in the ~ arts⟩ ⟨an ~ fortune-teller⟩ **5 :** not manifest or detectable by clinical methods alone ⟨~ carcinoma⟩ ⟨~ infection⟩; *esp* **:** not present in macroscopic amounts ⟨~ blood in the feces⟩ — compare GROSS — **oc·cult·ly** *adv*

**³occult** \"\ *n* -s **:** something mysterious or supernatural — usu. used with *the* ⟨he is a student of the ~⟩

**oc·cul·ta·tion** \,ä(,)kəl'tāshən\ *n* -s [ME *occultacion* concealment, fr. L *occultation-, occultatio,* fr. *occultatus* (past part. of *occultare* to conceal) + *-ion-, -io* -ion] **1 :** the state of being hidden from view or lost to notice **:** disappearance from the public eye ⟨his fame was already emerging from the ~ of changing fashion —*Times Lit. Supp.*⟩ **2 :** the shutting off of the light of a celestial body by the intervention of some other celestial body; *esp* **:** an eclipse of a star or planet by the moon

**occult balance** *n* **:** an asymmetrical mode of composition (as in flower arrangement or Chinese and Japanese painting)

**oc·cult·er** \ə'kəltə(r), 'ä,k-\ *n* -s [¹*occult* + *-er*] **:** an occulting opaque object

**occulting** *adj* [fr. pres. part. of ¹*occult*] **:** of or relating to any of various devices for cutting off from view a light or light-giving body ⟨an ~ disk located in the optical system of the coronagraph blacks out . . . the face of the sun to establish a perpetual, artificial, total eclipse —*Christian Science Monitor*⟩

**occulting light** *n* **:** a navigational light whose beam is interrupted at regular intervals by a brief period of darkness

**oc·cult·ism** \ə'kəl,tizəm, 'ä(,)kə-\ *n* -s [ISV ²*occult* + *-ism*] **:** occult theory or practice **:** a belief in hidden or mysterious powers and the possibility of subjecting them to human control ⟨~*s,* incantations, glimpses of the beyond, intimations of another world —L.P.Smith⟩ ⟨a kind of experimental ~ which relied on psychic phenomena for its proofs —*Times Lit. Supp.*⟩

**oc·cult·ist** \-₋təst\ *n* -s [ISV ²*occult* + *-ist*] **:** an adherent of occultism **:** one thought to be proficient in occult practices

**occult mineral** *n* **:** a mineral molecule shown by calculation of chemical analyses to be present in a rock (as plagioclase in orthoclase) but not actually seen under the microscope

**oc·cult·ness** *n* -ES **:** the quality or state of being occult

**occult spavin** *n* **:** spavin in which there is pronounced lameness without apparent enlargement on the hock joint

**oc·cu·pance** \'äkyəpən(t)s\ *n* -s [fr. *occupant,* after such pairs as E *assistant: assistance*] **:** OCCUPANCY ⟨the sequent ~ of the valleys and their adjacent benchlands —*Geog. Rev.*⟩

**oc·cu·pan·cy** \-nsē, -si\ *n* -ES [*occupant* + *-cy*] **1 a :** the taking and holding possession of real property under a lease or tenancy at will **b :** the act of taking possession of something that has no owner (as a waif or derelict) and thus acquiring title to it **2 a :** the act of becoming an occupant or the condition of being an occupant ⟨between successive human *occupancies,* the caves were often used by wild animals —R.W. Murray⟩ ⟨the essential quality of his existence consists in his ~ of this world of symbols and ideas —L.A.White⟩ ⟨ten years of uninterrupted ~ of this position⟩ **b :** the condition of being occupied ⟨though the village site showed two levels of ~, the temple mound showed three —*Amer. Guide Series: Tenn.*⟩ ⟨ghetto-slums which were both substandard and homogeneous in their ~ —Charles Abrams⟩ **3 :** the particular use or type of use to which property (as a building or part of a building) is put ⟨residential ~⟩ ⟨industrial ~⟩ ⟨storage ~⟩ **4 :** an occupied building or part of a building (as an apartment or office)

**oc·cu·pant** \-nt\ *n* -s [MF, fr. pres. part. of *occuper* to take possession of — more at OCCUPY] **1 a :** one who takes the first possession of something that has no owner and thereby acquires title by occupancy **b :** one who takes possession under title, lease, or tenancy at will **2 a :** one who occupies a particular place or premises **:** TENANT, RESIDENT ⟨the influence of sudden variations in temperature . . . on the ~*s* of a small pond —W.H.Dowdeswell⟩ ⟨the only year-around ~*s* of snowcapped Mount Washington —R.S.Monahan⟩ ⟨the human body has fascinated, pleased and frightened its ~*s* for many an age —R.M.Yoder⟩ **b :** one who holds a particular post ⟨a study of the ~*s* of the supreme court bench⟩ ⟨the first ~ of the post of assistant to the president⟩ **3 :** one who has the actual use or possession of something ⟨limped hurriedly to grab a table whose ~*s* had scarcely risen fully to their feet —William Sansom⟩

**oc·cu·pa·tion** \,äkyə'pāshən\ *n* -s [ME *occupacioun,* fr. MF *occupation,* fr. L *occupation-, occupatio,* fr. *occupatus* (past part. of *occupare* to take possession of, occupy, employ) + *-ion-, -io* -ion — more at OCCUPY] **1 a :** an activity in which one engages **:** a way of passing the time ⟨declared she had always plenty of ~ for herself while he was away —William Black⟩ ⟨bathing or loafing on the beaches are obviously a major ~ hereabouts —Ann Panners⟩ **b :** the principal business of one's life **:** a craft, trade, profession or other means of earning a living **:** EMPLOYMENT, VOCATION ⟨his ~ is farming⟩ ⟨has gone from one ~ to another without settling down to any⟩ ⟨writing has been his ~ for many years⟩ **2 :** the function or use of something ⟨if the ~ of steamboats be a matter of such general notoriety —John Marshall⟩ ⟨it is . . . the great ~ of the graphic arts to give us first of all order and variety in the sensuous plane —Roger Fry⟩ **3 a :** the actual possession and use of real estate (as by lease) **:** OCCUPANCY, TENANCY ⟨this fairly old house . . . was otherwise in doctors' and dentists' ~ —Elizabeth Bowen⟩ ⟨the last of the historic private houses in the metropolis . . . still in the ~ of its hereditary owner —*Sydney (Australia) Bull.*⟩ **b :** the possession or settlement of a place or area **:** TENURE ⟨many relics of this early Indian ~ have been found —*Amer. Guide Series: N. H.*⟩ ⟨from this section westward evidences of ancient human ~ are many —*Amer. Guide Series: Texas*⟩ **c :** the holding of an office or position ⟨it is only . . . the ~ . . . of two offices at the same time that offends public policy —W.D.Miller⟩ **d** *Brit* **:** land held by a tenant **:** HOLDING **4 :** the act or process of occupying or taking possession of a place or area **:** SEIZURE ⟨the fate of New Spain depended on forestalling England's ~ of that waterway —R.A.Billington⟩ **5 a :** the usu. temporary holding and control of a country or a part of a country by a foreign military force ⟨the ~ of the divided capital city —*Current Biog.*⟩ **b** *often cap* **:** the military force occupying a country or the policies carried out by such a force ⟨the broad program of the ~ was being carried out without disturbance —*Collier's Yr. Bk.*⟩ ⟨the *Occupation* removed this requirement in order to decrease the sense of regimentation —Hugh & Mabel Smythe⟩ **syn** see WORK

**¹oc·cu·pa·tion·al** \¦==¦pāshən³l, -shnəl\ *adj* **:** of or relating to occupation or an occupation ⟨~ troops⟩ ⟨~ choice⟩ — **oc·cu·pa·tion·al·ly** \-³lē, -əlē, -i\ *adv*

**²occupational** \"\ *n* -s **:** OCCUPATION STAMP

**occupational disease** *n* **1 :** an illness caused by factors arising from one's occupation ⟨dermatitis is often an *occupational disease*⟩ **2 :** an exaggerated or harmful attitude, tendency, or type of behavior associated with a particular occupation ⟨to diagnose the ills of our liberal arts colleges has become almost an *occupational disease* among college presidents —J.B. Conant⟩

**occupational neurosis** *n* **:** a condition that is caused by overuse of a muscle or set of muscles in repetitive performance of an operation (as in milking or dancing) and that is marked by loss of ability to constrain the muscles to perform the particular operation involved

**occupational therapist** *n* **:** one trained in or engaged in the practice of occupational therapy

**occupational therapy** *n* **:** therapy by means of mental or physical activity; *specif* **:** prescribed creative activity carried out under supervision for its effect in promoting recovery or rehabilitation following disease or injury

**occupation bridge** *n* **:** a bridge connecting the parts of an estate separated by a railroad, highway, or canal

**occupation currency** *n* **:** currency issued by the occupying power of a conquered country

**occupation day** *n, usu cap O&D* **:** July 25 observed in Puerto Rico as a holiday commemorating the anniversary of the landing of American troops at Guanica in 1898

**occupation stamp** *n* **:** a postage stamp issued for use in a country occupied by forces of a foreign country

**oc·cu·pa·tive** \ˈäkyə,pād·iv\ *adj* [L *occupatus* (past part. of *occupare* to take possession of, occupy, employ) + E *-ive*] **1 :** held by occupation ⟨an ~ field⟩ **2 :** of or relating to an occupation ⟨Smith is an ~ name⟩

**oc·cu·pi·able** \ˈäkyə,pīəbəl, ,=ˈ===\ *adj* **:** capable of being occupied or fit for occupancy ⟨an ~ room⟩

**oc·cu·pied** \ˈäkyə,pīd\ *adj* [ME *occupyed*, fr. past part. of *occupien* to occupy] **1 :** held by occupation ⟨an ~ country⟩ ⟨an ~ area⟩ ⟨an ~ house⟩ **2 :** engaged in activity **:** BUSY, EMPLOYED ⟨a constantly ~ person⟩ **3 :** taken up **:** FILLED ⟨has few ~ days⟩ **4 :** technically published whether valid or not

**oc·cu·pi·er** \-ī(ə)r, -īə\ *n* -s [ME, fr. *occupien* to occupy + *-er*] **:** one that occupies a place ⟨the region is not burdened with unpalatable space ~*s* —W.S.Hopkins⟩: as **a** *Brit* **:** one who holds possession of property as owner or tenant ⟨the hovels which still exist under the name of cottages almost always belong to the ~*s* themselves —G.E.Fussell⟩ ⟨the present ~*s* of the . . . mansion do not follow the generous custom of the owners in admitting the public —Elizabeth Montizambert⟩ **b :** a member of a foreign military force occupying a country or part of a country ⟨joined the resistance movement against the ~*s*⟩

**oc·cu·py** \ˈäkyə,pī\ *vt* -ED/-ING/-ES [ME *occupien* to take possession of, occupy, employ, modif. of MF *occuper*, fr. L *occupare*, fr. *ob-* + *-cupare* (akin to L *capere* to seize) — more at HEAVE] **1 :** to engage the attention or energies of **:** BUSY, EMPLOY ⟨the deeper issues which have *occupied* modern thinkers —A.N.Whitehead⟩ ⟨had to be given extra work to ~ her —Jean Stafford⟩ ⟨was *occupied* in national service throughout that period —*Current Biog.*⟩ **2 a :** to fill up (a place or extent) ⟨*occupies* an attractive site along the bay shore —*Amer. Guide Series: Mich.*⟩ ⟨the center of the house was *occupied* by a magnificent mahogany staircase —R.M.Lovett⟩ **b :** to take up (a specified time) ⟨they must have *occupied* tens of thousands of years —W.H.Dowdeswell⟩ ⟨a ten-day race meet *occupies* the last week of July and the first week of August —*Amer. Guide Series: Md.*⟩ **3 a :** to take possession of by conquest **:** SEIZE ⟨the enemy troops, in a massive attack, quickly *occupied* the eastern half of the country⟩ **b :** to take up residence in **:** settle in ⟨the area was discovered in 1820 and was *occupied* soon after by pastoralists —H.W.H.King⟩ **c :** to maintain possession or control of by military occupation ⟨second-grade troops, useful mainly to ~ parts of the country that have already been pacified —Brian Crozier⟩ **4 a :** to hold possession of ⟨*occupied* a ridge from which they dominated the crossroads⟩ **b :** to hold a particular position or office ⟨~ the newly created office of chancellor —*Current Biog.*⟩ ⟨the woman *occupied* . . . a position very like that of the father in our society —Abram Kardiner⟩ **5 :** to reside in as an owner or tenant ⟨*occupies* the house that his grandfather built fifty years ago⟩ ⟨*occupies* the apartment on a two-year lease⟩ **6** *archaic* **:** USE ⟨bind me fast with new ropes that never were *occupied* —Judg 16:11 (AV)⟩ **7** *obs* **:** to have sexual intercourse with **8** *archaic* **:** to use in commerce **:** trade with **:** INVEST ⟨~ thy merchandise —Ezek 27:9 (AV)⟩

**oc·cur** *R* əˈkər, +V -kər·; *-R* əˈkə, + *suffixal vowel* əˈkər· *also* əˈkər, + *vowel in a word following without pause* əˈkər· *or* əˈkə *also* əˈkər\ *vi* **occurred; occurred; occurring; occurs** [L *occurrere*, fr. *ob-* + *currere* to run — more at CURRENT] **1 :** to be found or met with **:** APPEAR ⟨this bird ~*s* in the Middle Atlantic states throughout the year —F.C.Lincoln⟩ **2 :** to present itself **:** come to pass **:** take place **:** HAPPEN ⟨successful marriages do not ~, but are created —Katharine F. Gerould⟩ **3 :** to come to mind **:** suggest itself ⟨something *occurred* to him which he had never thought of before —Louis Bromfield⟩ **4 :** to fall on the same day as another festival — used esp. of Christian festivals; compare CONCUR **syn** see HAPPEN

**oc·cur·rence** \əˈkər·ən(t)s *also* əˈkərə-\ *n* -s [prob. fr. ¹*occurrent*, after such pairs as E *abstinent*: *abstinence*] **1 :** something that takes place; *esp* **:** something that happens unexpectedly and without design **:** HAPPENING ⟨a happy ~⟩ ⟨a disastrous ~⟩ ⟨an unusual ~⟩ **2 a :** the action or process of happening or taking place ⟨the ~ of a genuine dispute —R.M.Dawson⟩ **b :** the action or process of being met with or coming into view **:** APPEARANCE ⟨the ~ of mammal remains falls sharply throughout the summer —*Ecology*⟩ ⟨a fish of regular ~ along the southern coast of California⟩ **:** the fact of being met with or of taking place **3 :** the presence of a natural form or material at a particular place; *also* **:** the mineral, rock, or deposit thus occurring ⟨evidence of oil ~⟩ ⟨the ~ of shallow coal beds in this region⟩ **4 :** the occurring of Christian festivals

**syn** INCIDENT, EPISODE, EVENT, CIRCUMSTANCE: OCCURRENCE is a general term for taking place or happening and lacks much connotational range; it may suggest a happening without plan, intent, or volition ⟨*occurrences* which we not only do not, but cannot perceive —Bertrand Russell⟩ INCIDENT may suggest either a trivial happening unworthy of attention or a more consequential or unusual happening having some effect ⟨his unexpected appearances and disappearances were *incidents* in the house —Willa Cather⟩ ⟨the faculty for myth . . . seizes with avidity upon any *incidents*, surprising or mysterious —W.S. Maugham⟩ EPISODE stresses the notion that the occurrence in question has an apartness or unity by itself, with no implication about the significance, or lack of it, of the occurrence ⟨the dumb creation lives a life made up of discrete and mutually irrelevant *episodes* —Aldous Huxley⟩ EVENT is more likely than others in this set to suggest a happening or occurrence of moment or significance or a happening logically ensuing from or giving rise to another happening ⟨assassination was an *event* of daily occurrence —T.B.Macaulay⟩ ⟨it is, in fact, almost a routine incident in a distinguished career. In the case of Mark Twain it became a historic *event* —Van Wyck Brooks⟩ ⟨*events* acting upon us in unexpected, abrupt, and violent ways —John Dewey⟩ CIRCUMSTANCE in the general sense here involved indicates specific or detailed incident ⟨stood reflecting on the *circumstances* of the preceding hours —Thomas Hardy⟩

¹**oc·cur·rent** \-nt\ *adj* [MF, fr. L *occurrent-, occurrens*, pres. part. of *occurrere* to occur] **1 a :** presently occurring **:** CURRENT **b :** happening by the way **:** INCIDENTAL **2 :** of or relating to an occurrent (sense 2)

²**occurrent** \"\ *n* -s **1** *archaic* **:** OCCURRENCE **2 :** something that occurs as distinguished from that which continues to exist **:** an alterable state — contrasted with *continuant*

**ocean** \ˈōshən\ *n* -s *often attrib* [ME *occean*, fr. OF, fr. L *oceanus* fr. Gk *ōkeanos* ocean, great river believed to encompass the earth] **1 :** the whole body of salt water that covers nearly three fourths of the surface of the globe, that has an average depth of about 13,000 feet and a maximum reported depth of 35,040 feet, that contains on the average 3½ percent of dissolved salts comprising mainly common salt with smaller amounts of magnesium and calcium salts, that has a density of 1.026, and that has a floor sometimes level or gently undulating and sometimes quite irregular with narrow elongated depressions called trenches and with elevations of various shapes and sizes (as ridges, rises, seamounts and swells) — called also *sea* **2 :** one of the large bodies of water into which the great ocean is regarded as divided (as the Atlantic, Pacific, Indian, Arctic, and Antarctic) **3 :** an immense expanse **:** an apparently unlimited space or quantity ⟨that mighty tropical ~ of foliage —William Beebe⟩ ⟨first began navigating the ~ of air —H.L.Smith b.1906⟩ ⟨disappeared into an ~ of official silence —Darrell Berrigan⟩

**ocea·nar·i·um** \,ōshəˈna(a)rēəm, -ner-, -nār-\ *n, pl* **oceanariums** \-mz\ *or* **oceanar·ia** \-ēə\ [*ocean* + *-arium*] **:** a large marine aquarium

**ocean basin** *n* **:** BASIN 3e — compare CONTINENTAL PLATEAU

**ocean bug** *n* **:** an insect of *Halobates* or related genera (order Hemiptera) found on the surface of the sea far from land

**ocean deep** *n* **:** a part of an ocean basin in which the depth greatly exceeds the average for the basin as a whole

**oceanfront** \ˈ==,=\ *n, often attrib* **:** the waterfront of a resort town or area situated along the ocean

**oceangoing** \ˈ==,==\ *adj* **:** of, relating to, or suitable for travel on the ocean ⟨~ commerce⟩ ⟨an ~ ship⟩

**ocean green** *n* **:** a light yellowish green that is yellower and paler than apple green (sense 2) or crayon green and paler than pistachio

¹**oce·an·i·an** \,ōshēˈanēən, -ˈān-\ *adj, usu cap* [F *océanien*, fr. *Oceania*, region of the central and south Pacific + F *-en, -ien* -an] **1 :** of, relating to, or characteristic of the region of Oceania comprising the islands and archipelagoes of the central and south Pacific **2 :** of, relating to, or characteristic of the people of Oceania

²**oceanian** \"\ *n* -s *cap* **:** a native or inhabitant of Oceania

**oce·an·ic** \-ˈanik, -nēk\ *adj* [F *océanique*, fr. MF *oceanique*, fr. *ocean*, *occean* ocean + *-ique* -ic] **1 a :** of, relating to, occurring in, living in, or frequenting the ocean ⟨~ currents⟩ ⟨~ depths⟩ ⟨~ rock⟩ ⟨~ birds⟩ **b :** affected by or produced by the ocean ⟨a wet, windy, ~ climate —C.D.Forde⟩ **c :** resembling the ocean esp. in immensity of size or extent ⟨October gives the grain belt an ~ vastness of gold —W.W.Haines⟩ ⟨the ~ violence of his rage against the miseries of man's life —Walter McElroy⟩ **2** *usu cap* **:** OCEANIAN **3 :** of, relating to, constituting, or living in the open sea as distinguished from littoral or neritic regions ⟨~ waters⟩ ⟨~ life⟩ — compare ABYSSAL, PHOTIC **4** *usu cap* **:** relating to, belonging to, or characterizing the Austronesian family of languages or the Melanesian and Polynesian divisions of that family

**oceanic area** *n* **:** the ocean as contrasted with the neritic zone consisting of a photic zone which extends down as far as light penetrates with a twilight zone as its lower limit and an abyssal zone which extends thence to the bottom

**oceanic bonito** *n* **:** any of several bonitos (as of the genus *Katsuwonus*); *esp* **:** SKIPJACK 2a(2)

**oceanic island** *n* **:** an island in the ocean far from any continent — compare CONTINENTAL ISLAND

**oce·a·nid** \ōˈsēənəd\ *n* -s *usu cap* [Gk *ōkeanid-, ōkeanis*, fr. *Okeanos* Oceanus, deity identified as a great river believed to encompass the earth + Gk *-id-, -is*, fem. patronymic suffix] **:** an ocean nymph

**oce·an·i·ty** \,ōshēˈanəd·ē\ *n* -ES [ISV *ocean* + *-ity*] **1 :** the quality or state of being oceanic **2 :** the degree to which a climate has oceanic qualities — compare CONTINENTALITY

**ocean lane** *n* **:** LANE 3a

**ocean liner** *n* **:** a liner for navigating the ocean

**ocean marine insurance** *n* **:** insurance against risks incident to transportation by sea — compare INLAND MARINE INSURANCE, MARINE INSURANCE

**ocea·nod·ro·mous** \,ōshəˈnädrəməs\ *adj* [*ocean* + *-o-* + *-dromous*] *of a fish* **:** migratory in salt water

**ocean·og·ra·pher** \,ōshəˈnägrəfə(r)\ *n* -s [*oceanography* + *-er*] **:** a specialist in oceanography

**ocean·o·graph·ic** \,ōshənəˈgrafik\ *or* **ocean·o·graph·i·cal** \-fəkəl\ *adj* [*oceanographic* ISV *oceanography* + *-ic*; *oceanographical* fr. *oceanography* + *-ical*] **:** of or relating to oceanography — **ocean·o·graph·i·cal·ly** \-fək(ə)lē\ *adv*

**ocean·og·ra·phy** \,ōshəˈnägrəfē\ *n* -ES [ISV *ocean* + *-o-* + *-graphy*] **:** a science that deals with the ocean and its phenomena — see BIOLOGICAL OCEANOGRAPHY, DYNAMIC OCEANOGRAPHY, PHYSICAL OCEANOGRAPHY

**ocean·ol·o·gy** \-ˈäləjē\ *n* -ES [*ocean* + *-o-* + *-logy*] **:** OCEANOGRAPHY

**ocean perch** *n* **:** ROSEFISH

**ocean pout** *n* **:** EELPOUT

**oceans** *pl of* OCEAN

**ocean sea** *n, often cap O&S* **:** OCEAN 1

**ocean spray** *n* **:** a white-flowered shrub (*Holodiscus discolor*) of western U. S. — called also *arrowwood, creambush*

**ocean station vessel** *n* **:** a ship assigned to a specific station at sea to take weather observations, assist aircraft in determining position, and help in rescue operations

**ocean sunfish** *n* **1 :** a large usu. gray or brown marine fish (*Mola mola*) that has a deep compressed body truncated behind, no pelvic fins, and very long dorsal and anal fins nearly adjoining the short caudal fin and that is widely distributed in warm and temperate seas — called also *headfish* **2 :** SHARPTAIL OCEAN SUNFISH

**ocean tramp** *n* **:** TRAMP 6

**ocean whitefish** *n* **:** a large showy brownish food and sport fish (*Caulolatilus princeps*) found along the warmer parts of the Pacific coast from Peru to central California — see BLANQUILLO

**oc·el·lana** \,äsəˈlanə\ *n, pl* **ocel·lanae** \-a,nē\ [NL, fr. *ocellus* + *-ana* (fr. L, fem. of *-anus* -an)] **:** STEMMA

**ocel·lar** \ōˈselə(r)\ *adj* [prob. fr. (assumed) NL *ocellaris*, fr. NL *ocellus* + L *-aris* -ar] **1 :** of, relating to, or connecting with an ocellus **2 :** of or relating to a type of rock structure characterized by radiated aggregates resembling eyes

**ocellar center** *n* **:** an aggregation of ganglia in the ocellar pedicel of an insect

**ocellar pedicel** *n* **:** a slender stalk consisting of nerve fibers that connect the ocellus in an insect with the forebrain

**ocel·lat·ed** \ōˈse,lād·əd, ˈäsə,-\ *also* **ocel·late** \-,lāt, -lət\ *adj* [*ocellated* prob. fr. (assumed) NL *ocellatus* ocellated (fr. NL *ocellus* + L *-atus* -ate) + E *-ed*; *ocellate* prob. fr. (assumed) NL *ocellatus*] **1 :** having ocelli **2 :** resembling an ocellus **:** EYELIKE ⟨an ~ spot⟩

**ocellated argus** *n* **:** ARGUS 2; *esp* **:** an argus (*Rheinartia ocellata*) of southeastern Asia that is predominantly brown with in the male elaborate spotting in black, white, and buff, a long pointed tail patterned with nonmetallic ocelli, and a large occipital crest

**ocellated blenny** *n* **:** a dusky brown blenny (*Blennius ocellaris*) of the Mediterranean and western European coastal waters that has the body barred with dark crossbars and a round black white-bordered spot on the dorsal fin

**ocellated lizard** *n* **:** a moderately large lizard (*Lacerta ocellata*) found in parts of southern Europe and No. Africa and having black-edged blue spots on the sides

**ocellated turkey** *n* **:** a wild turkey (*Agriocharis ocellata*) of Yucatan, Honduras, and Guatemala that is slightly smaller than the common turkey and has the tail feathers margined with rich coppery color and ocellated with greenish blue

**oc·el·la·tion** \,äsəˈlāshən\ *n* -s [prob. fr. (assumed) NL *ocellation-, ocellatio*, fr. (assumed) NL *ocellatus* + L *-ion-, -io* -ion] **1 :** the state of being ocellated **2 :** an ocellus or eyelike spot

**oc·el·loc·u·lar** \,äsəˈläkyələ(r)\ *adj* [*ocellus* + *ocular*] **:** lying or extending between the compound eye and the median simple eye of an insect ⟨~ distance⟩

**ocel·lus** \ōˈseləs\ *n, pl* **ocel·li** \-e,lī, -e(,)lē\ [NL, fr. L, small eye, dim. of *oculus* eye — more at EYE] **1 a :** a minute simple eye or eyespot found in many organisms; *specif* **:** one of usu. three simple eyes in an insect located in a triangle between the compound eyes **b :** one of the elements of a compound eye **2 :** a spot of color encircled by a band of another color **:** an eyelike spot ⟨a butterfly with a striking ~ on its wing⟩

**oce·lot** \ˈōsə,lät, ˈäs- *sometimes* -lət, *usu* -d·+V\ *n* -s [F, fr. Nahuatl *ocelotl* jaguar] **1 :** a medium-sized American wildcat (*Felis pardalis*) ranging from Texas to Patagonia and having a tawny yellow or grayish coat that is dotted and striped with black **2 :** the fur or pelt of the ocelot

ocelot

**och** \ˈäk\ *interj* [ScGael & IrGael] *Irish & Scot* — used to express regret or surprise

¹**ocher** *or* **ochre** \ˈōkə(r)\ *n* -s [ME *oker*, fr. MF *ocre*, fr. L *ochra*, fr. Gk *ōchra*, fr. *ōchros* yellow, pale] **1 a :** an earthy usu. red or yellow and often impure iron ore that is extensively used as a pigment; *also* **:** any of various ferruginous clays — compare HEMATITE, LIMONITE **b :** an earthy metallic oxide ⟨tungstic ~⟩ **2 :** the color of ocher, esp. of yellow ocher **:** OCHER YELLOW **3 :** any of various chiefly yellow to orange pigments prepared from the natural ochers (as by washing, grinding, and sometimes calcining) — see BURNT OCHER; compare SIENNA, UMBER

²**ocher** *or* **ochre** \"\ *vt* **ochered** *or* **ochred; ochered** *or* **ochred; ochering** *or* **ochring** \-k(ə)riŋ\ **ochers** *or* **ochres** **:** to color with ocher

**ocher brown** *n* **:** a moderate orange that is yellower and deeper than honeydew, yellower and darker than Persian orange, and duller than mikado orange — called also *brown ocher, doubloon, golden ocher, Roman ocher*

**ocher·ish** *or* **ochre·ish** \ˈōk(ə)rish\ *adj* **:** resembling or suggesting ocher (as in color) **:** somewhat like ocher

**ocher orange** *n* **:** a strong orange that is yellower and stronger than pumpkin, deeper and slightly redder than cadmium orange, and redder and deeper than cadmium yellow — called also *burnt Roman ocher, orange ocher, Spanish ocher, Tangier*

**ocher·ous** \ˈōk(ə)rəs\ *or* **ochre·ous** \", ˈōkrēəs\ *also* **ochrous** \ˈōkrəs\ *adj* [¹*ocher* + *-ous* or *-eous*] **1 :** of or relating to ocher **:** containing or resembling ocher **2 :** of the color ocher yellow

**ocher red** *n* **:** a dark reddish orange that is yellower, less strong, and slightly darker than average lacquer and redder and slightly darker than burnt sienna — called also *jaded rose*

**ochery** \ˈōk(ə)rē\ *or* **ochry** \ˈōkrē\ *or* **ochrey** \ˈōk(ə)rē\ *adj* [¹*ocher* + *-y*] **:** OCHEROUS

**ocher yellow** *n* **:** YELLOW OCHER

**och·i·dore** \ˈäkə,dō(ə)r\ *n* -s [origin unknown] **:** SHORE CRAB

**och·loc·ra·cy** \äkˈläkrəsē\ *n* -ES [Gk & MF; MF *ochlocratie*, fr. Gk *ochlokratia*, fr. *ochlos* crowd, mob + *-kratia* -cracy] **:** government by the mob **:** mob rule

**och·lo·crat** \ˈäklə,krat\ *n* -s [F *ochlocrate*, back-formation fr. *ochlocratie* & *ochlocratique*] **:** a partisan of ochlocracy

**och·lo·crat·ic** \ˈ==ˈkrad·ik\ *or* **och·lo·crat·i·cal** \-d·əkəl\ *adj* [*ochlocratic* fr. F *ochlocratique*, fr. MF, fr. *ochlocratie* + *-ique* -ic; *ochlocratical* fr. F *ochlocratique* + E *-al*] **:** of or relating to ochlocracy — **och·lo·crat·i·cal·ly** \-d·ək(ə)lē\ *adv*

**och·lo·pho·bia** \,äkləˈfōbēə\ *n* [NL, fr. Gk *ochlos* crowd + NL *-phobia*] **:** morbid fear of crowds

**och·lo·pho·bist** \-bəst\ *n* -s [NL *ochlophobia* + E *-ist*] **:** one who is afflicted with ochlophobia

**och·na** \ˈäknə\ *n, cap* [NL, fr. Gk *ochnē, onchnē* pear tree; prob. akin to Gk *achras*, a wild pear tree (prob. *Pyrus amygdaliformis*) — more at ACHRAS] **:** a genus (the type of the family Ochnaceae) of African and Asiatic trees and shrubs having yellow flowers with coriaceous petaloid sepals and numerous stamens

**och·na·ce·ae** \äkˈnāsē,ē\ *n pl, cap* [NL, fr. *Ochna*, type genus + *-aceae*] **:** a family of tropical trees, shrubs, or rarely herbs (order Parietales) having thick shining parallel-veined leaves and paniculate flowers with elongated anthers — **och·na·ceous** \(ˈ)äkˈnāshəs\ *adj*

**ocho·an** \ōˈchōən\ *adj, usu cap* [*Ochoa*, locality in southeastern New Mexico + E *-an*] **:** of or relating to a subdivision of the American Permian — see GEOLOGIC TIME table

**och·one** \äˈkōn\ *interj* [ScGael & IrGael *ochōn*] *Irish & Scot* — used as an exclamation of regret or grief

**och·o·to·na** \,äkəˈtōnə\ *n, cap* [NL, fr. Mongolian *ochodona* pika] **:** the type genus of Ochotonidae comprising the pikas

**och·o·ton·i·dae** \-ˈtänə,dē\ *n pl, cap* [NL, fr. *Ochotona*, type genus + *-idae*] **:** a family of short-eared lagomorph mammals that comprises the pikas and various extinct related forms

**ochra·ceous** \ōˈkrāshəs\ *adj* [prob. fr. (assumed) NL *ochraceus*, fr. L *ochra* ocher + *-aceus* -aceous] **:** OCHEROUS

**ochre** *var of* OCHER

**ochrea** *var of* OCREA

**ochroid** \ˈō,krȯid\ *adj* [Gk *ōchroeidēs* pallid, fr. *ōchros* yellow, pale + *-eidēs* -oid] **:** resembling ocher or yellow ocher in color

**och·ro·ma** \äˈkrōmə\ *n, cap* [NL, fr. Gk *ōchrōma* pallor, fr. *ōchros* yellow, pale] **:** a genus of tropical American trees (family Bombacaceae) having very light wood and seeds enveloped in silky floss — see BALSA

**ochro·no·sis** \,ōkrəˈnōsəs\ *n, pl* **ochrono·ses** \-nō,sēz\ [NL, fr. Gk *ōchros* yellow, pale + NL *-nosis* (irreg. — influenced by NL *-osis* — fr. Gk *nosos* disease)] **:** a rare familial condition often associated with alkaptonuria and marked by pigment deposits in cartilages, ligaments, and tendons

**ochro·not·ic** \ˈ==ˈnäd·ik\ *adj* [fr. *ochronosis*, after such pairs as E *narcosis*: *narcotic*] **:** of, relating to, or marked by ochronosis ⟨~ arthritis⟩

**ochrous** *var of* OCHEROUS

**ochry** *var of* OCHERY

¹**ocht** \ˈäkt\ *chiefly Scot var of* AUGHT

²**ocht** \"\ *Scot & Irish var of* OUGHT

**oc·i·mene** \ˈäsə,mēn\ *n* -s [ISV *ocim-* (fr. NL *Ocimum*) + *-ene*] **:** an acyclic terpene hydrocarbon $C_{10}H_{16}$ that occurs in several essential oils (as basil oil) and that resinifies readily in air and isomerizes on heating

**oc·i·mum** \ˈäsəməm\ *n, cap* [NL, fr. L, basil, fr. Gk *ōkimon*] **:** a large genus of mints (family Labiatae) found chiefly in warm climates and having flowers with a reflexed calyx and a very short corolla tube — see BASIL 1, HOLY BASIL, SWEET BASIL

**-ock** \ək *or, in many words,* ik *or* ēk\ *n suffix* -s [ME *-oc, -ok*, fr. OE *-uc, -oc*] **:** small one ⟨bittock⟩ ⟨lassock⟩

**ock·ham·ism** *or* **oc·cam·ism** \ˈäkə,mizəm\ *n* -s *usu cap* [William of *Ockham* (or *Occam*) †1349? Eng. scholastic philosopher + E *-ism*] **:** the philosophy developed by Ockham and consisting essentially of a revival of nominalism

**ock·ham·ist** *or* **oc·cam·ist** \-məst\ *also* **ock·ham·ite** \-,mīt\ *or* **oc·cam·ite** *n* -s *usu cap* [William of *Ockham* (or *Occam*) + E *-ist* or *-ite*] **:** an adherent of Ockhamism

**ock·ham·is·tic** *or* **oc·cam·is·tic** \ˈ==ˈmistik\ *adj, usu cap* **:** of or relating to Ockham or his philosophy

**ock·ham's razor** *or* **oc·cam's razor** \ˈäkəmz-\ *n, usu cap O* **:** the philosophic rule that entities should not be multiplied unnecessarily

**o'clock** \əˈkläk\ *adv* [contr. of *of the clock*] **1 :** according to the clock **:** by the clock ⟨the time is three ~⟩ **2 :** on a clock dial imagined in a horizontal position with the observer at the center facing the numeral 12 or in a vertical position in front of and facing the observer with the numeral 12 at the top — used for indicating position or direction ⟨the pilot saw a plane approaching at eleven ~⟩ ⟨a bullet hit the target at three ~⟩

**oco·nee bells** \əˈkōnē-\ *n pl but sing or pl in constr* [prob. fr. *Oconee* river, central Georgia] **:** a stemless perennial herb (*Shortia galacifolia*) that has crenate-dentate glossy leaves

**oco·te** \ōˈkōtā\ *or* **ocote pine** *n* -s [MexSp, fr. Nahuatl *ocotl* torch] **:** a resinous Mexican pine (*Pinus montezumae*) with prominently ridged young shoots

**oco·tea** \əˈkōd·ēə\ *n, cap* [NL, fr. a native name in Guiana] **:** a genus of tropical trees and shrubs (family Lauraceae) having alternate coriaceous leaves and small panicled flowers — see STINKWOOD

**ocotea cymbarum oil** *n, usu cap 1st O* [NL *Ocotea cymbarum* (species name of a Brazilian tree) + E *oil*] **:** an essential oil obtained by steam distillation from the wood of Brazilian trees (*Ocotea cymbarum*) and used chiefly as a source of safrole and as a substitute for sassafras oil in technical but not medicinal preparations

**oco·ti·llo** \,ōkəˈtē(,)(y)ō\ *also* **oco·ti·lla** \-ē(y)ə\ *n* -s [MexSp, dim. of *ocote*] **1 :** a desert shrub (*Fouquieria splendens*) of southwestern U.S. and Mexico characterized by naked thorny branches that after the rainy season put forth foliage and clusters of scarlet flowers **2 :** an ashy gray Mexican

shrub (*Gochnatia hypoleuca*) of the family Compositae that is used for making charcoal
**-oc·ra·cy** \'äkrəsē, -si\ — see -CRACY
**-ocrat** — see -CRAT
**oc·rea** *or* **och·rea** \'äkrēə, 'ōk-\ *n, pl* **ocre·ae** *or* **ochre·ae** \-ē,ē\ [NL, fr. L *ocrea* greave, legging; perh. akin to L *ocris* stony mountain — more at MEDIOCRE] **:** a tubular sheath around the base of the petiole consisting of a single stipule in the red clover or of a pair of coherent stipules in the buckwheat family (Polygonaceae)
**oc·re·ate** \-ēət, -ē,āt\ *adj* [NL *ocreatus*, fr. L, wearing greaves or leggings, fr. *ocrea* + *-atus* -ate] **:** provided with ocreae
**OCS** *abbr or n* -s **:** officer candidate school
**OCS** *abbr* Old Church Slavonic
**oct** *abbr* octavo
**octa-** *or* **octo-** *also* **oct-** *comb form* [Gk *okta-*, *oktō-*, *okt-* (fr. *oktō*) & L *octo-*, *oct-* (fr. *octo*) — more at EIGHT] **1 :** eight ⟨*Octacnemus*⟩ ⟨*octamerous*⟩ ⟨*octoploid*⟩ ⟨*octose*⟩ **2 :** containing eight atoms, groups, or equivalents ⟨*octaacetate*⟩
**oc·ta·acetate** \'äktə+\ *n* [*octa-* + *acetate*] **:** an acetate containing eight acetate groups ⟨sucrose ~⟩
**oc·ta·chord** \'äktə,kȯrd\ *n* [L *octachordos* with eight strings, fr. Gk *oktachordos*, fr. *okta-* octa- + *-chordos* stringed — more at -CHORD] **1 :** a musical instrument having eight strings **2 :** a system of eight tones (as the diatonic octave)
**oc·tac·ne·mus** \,äk,tak'nēməs\ *n, cap* [NL, fr. *octa-* + *-cnemus*] **:** a genus of deep-sea tunicates of the order Ascidiacea found in the south Pacific ocean
**oc·ta·co·sane** \,äktə'kō,sān\ *n* -s [ISV *octacos-* (fr. *octa-* + *-cos-* — fr. *eicosa-*) + *-ane*] **:** a solid paraffin hydrocarbon $C_{28}H_{58}$; *esp* **:** the normal hydrocarbon $CH_3(CH_2)_{26}CH_3$
**oc·tad** \'äk,tad\ *n* -s [Gk *oktad-*, *oktas* number eight, body of eight men, fr. *okta-* octa- + *-ad-*, *-as* -ad] **:** a group or arrangement of eight; *esp* **:** a group of eight figures representing consecutive powers of ten in ancient mathematical notation
**oc·ta·dec·a·di·e·no·ic acid** \,äktə¦dekə¦dīə¦nōik-\ *n* [*octadecadienoic* ISV *octadecadiene* $C_{18}H_{34}$ (ISV *octadeca-* — fr. *octa-* + *deca-* — + *-diene*) + *-oic*] **:** any of several unsaturated fatty acids $C_{17}H_{31}COOH$ some of which (as linoleic acid) occur in fats and oils
**oc·ta·dec·ane** \,äktə'de,kān\ *n* [ISV *octadec-* (fr. *octa-* + *deca-*) + *-ane*] **:** any of numerous isomeric hydrocarbons $C_{18}H_{38}$ of the paraffin series; *esp* **:** the crystalline normal hydrocarbon $CH_3(CH_2)_{16}CH_3$
**oc·ta·dec·a·no·ic acid** \¦==¦dekə¦nōik-\ *n* [*octadecanoic* ISV *octadecane* + *-oic*] **:** STEARIC ACID
**oc·ta·dec·a·nol** \,==¦dekə,nȯl, -nōl\ *n* [*octadecane* + *-ol*] **:** any of several alcohols $C_{18}H_{37}OH$ derived from normal octadecane; *esp* **:** STEARYL ALCOHOL
**oc·ta·dec·e·no·ic acid** \,äktə¦dekə¦desə¦nōik-\ *n* [*octadecenoic* ISV *octadecene* $C_{18}H_{36}$ (ISV *octadec-* — fr. *octa-* + *deca-* — + *-ene*) + *-oic*] **:** any of several unsaturated fatty acids $C_{17}H_{33}COOH$ some of which (as oleic acid, vaccenic acid) occur in fats and oils
**oc·ta·dec·yl** \,äktə'desəl\ *n* [ISV *octadecane* + *-yl*] **:** an alkyl radical $C_{18}H_{37}$ derived from an octadecane by removal of one hydrogen atom; *esp* **:** the normal radical $CH_3(CH_2)_{16}$-$CH_2$–
**oc·ta·drachm** *or* **oc·to·drachm** \'äktə,dram\ *n* [Gk *oktadrachmos* worth eight drachmas, fr. *okta-* octa- + *drachmē* drachma — more at DRAM] **:** an ancient Greek coin weighing or worth eight drachmas
**oc·ta·gon** \'äktə,gän *sometimes* -tēgən\ *n* -s [L *octagonum*, *octogonum*, fr. Gk *oktagōnon*, fr. neut. of *oktagōnos* octagonal, fr. *okta-* octa- + *-gōnos* (fr. *gōnia* angle); akin to Gk *gony* knee — more at KNEE] **1 :** a plane polygon of eight angles and therefore eight sides — see AREA table **2 :** an octagonal object ⟨the central ~ was covered by a dome —E.H. Short⟩

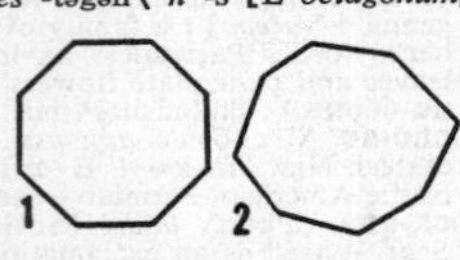

octagons: *1* regular, *2* irregular

**oc·tag·o·nal** \(')äk¦tagənᵊl, -taig-\ *adj* [alter. (influenced by *octagon*) of earlier *octogonal*, fr. MF, fr. *octogone* octagon (fr. L *octagonum*, *octogonum*) + *-al*] **:** having eight sides ⟨built a mansion in the shape of an octagon, which started quite a fashion for ~ houses —*Time*⟩ — **oc·tag·o·nal·ly** \-ᵊlē, -ᵊli\ *adv*
**oc·ta·he·dral** \,äktə¦hēdrəl\ *adj* [*octahedron* + *-al*] **:** having eight plane faces **:** of, relating to, or formed in octahedrons ⟨~ crystals⟩
**octahedral cleavage** *n* **:** cleavage of minerals parallel to the octahedral faces
**octahedral iron ore** *n* **:** MAGNETITE
**oc·ta·he·drite** \,äktə'hē,drīt\ *n* -s [F *octaédrite*, fr. *octaèdre* octahedron (fr. Gk *oktaedron*) + *-ite*] **1 :** ANATASE **2 :** an iron meteorite having plates of kamacite with narrow selvages of taenite and interstitial plessite constituting a very intimate mixture of kamacite and taenite — compare WIDMANNSTAETTEN FIGURES
**oc·ta·he·dron** \,äktə'hēdrən\ *n, pl* **octahedrons** \-nz\ *also* **octahe·dra** \-rə\ [Gk *oktaedron*, fr. neut. of *oktaedros* octahedral, fr. *okta-* octa- + *hedra* seat — more at SIT] **:** a solid bounded by eight plane faces

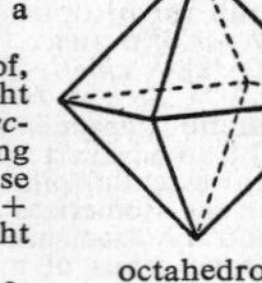
octahedron

**oc·tal** \'äktᵊl\ *adj* [*octa-* + *-al*] **1 :** of, relating to, or based on the number eight ⟨~ notation⟩ ⟨~ coding⟩ **2** *of an electronic tube* **:** having eight connecting pins arranged symmetrically on the base
**oc·ta·mer** \'äktəmə(r)\ *n* -s [*octa-* + *-mer*] **:** a polymer formed from eight molecules of a monomer
**oc·tam·er·ous** \(')äk'tam(ə)rəs\ *or* **oc·tom·er·ous** \-täm-\ *adj* [*octa-* + *-merous*] **:** having eight parts or having organs arranged in eights ⟨an ~ flower⟩
**¹oc·tam·e·ter** \(')äk¦tamədə(r), -mətə-\ *adj* [LL, fr. LGk *oktametros*, fr. Gk *okta-* octa- + *metron* measure — more at MEASURE] **:** having eight metrical feet
**²octameter** \"\ *or* **oc·tom·e·ter** \-¦täm-\ *n* **:** a line consisting of eight metrical feet (as in Poe's "Deep into the darkness peering, long I stood there wond'ring, fearing")
**oc·ta·meth·yl·py·ro·phos·phor·a·mide** \,äktə,methəl,pīrō,fäs'fȯrə,mīd\ *n* [*octamethyl-* (fr. *octa-* + *methyl*) + *pyrophosphoramide* (fr. *pyrophosphor-* — in *pyrophosphoric acid* — + *amide*)] **:** SCHRADAN
**oc·ta·nal** \'äktə,nal\ *n* -s [ISV *octane* + *-al*] **:** a liquid aldehyde $CH_3(CH_2)_6CHO$ of powerful characteristic odor found in the essential oils of many plants — called also *caprylaldehyde*
**oc·tan·dria** \äk'tandrēə\ *n pl, cap* [NL, fr. *octa-* + *-andria*] *in some classifications* **:** a class of plants comprising all those having flowers with eight stamens — **oc·tan·dri·an** \(')=¦==ən\ *adj* — **oc·tan·dri·ous** \-əs\ *adj*
**oc·tane** \'äk,tān *sometimes* =¦=\ *n* -s [ISV *octa-* + *-ane*] **1 :** any of several isomeric liquid paraffin hydrocarbons $C_8H_{18}$: as **a :** the normal hydrocarbon $CH_3(CH_2)_6CH_3$ found in petroleum **b :** ISOOCTANE b **2 :** OCTANE NUMBER ⟨100-*octane* gasoline⟩ **3 :** motor fuel as rated by octane number ⟨*octane*-propelled vehicles⟩ ⟨100-*octane* cracking plants⟩
**octane number** *or* **octane rating** *n* **:** a number that is used to measure the antiknock properties of a liquid motor fuel and that represents the percentage by volume of isooctane (sense b) in a reference fuel consisting of a mixture of isooctane and normal heptane and matching in knocking properties the fuel being tested, the higher the number the less likely being the fuel to detonate
**oc·tan·gu·lar** \(')äk¦tangyələ(r)\ *adj* [L *octangulus* octagonal (fr. *oct-* — fr. *octo* eight — + *angulus* angle) + E *-ar* — more at EIGHT, ANGLE] **:** OCTAGONAL
**oc·ta·no·ate** \,äktə'nōə,wāt, -ōə,āt\ *n* -s [ISV *octanoic* (in *octanoic acid*) + *-oate*] **:** CAPRYLATE
**oc·ta·no·ic acid** \¦äktə¦nōik-\ *n* [*octanoic* ISV *octane* + *-oic*] **:** CAPRYLIC ACID — used in the nomenclature adopted by the International Union of Pure and Applied Chemistry
**oc·ta·nol** \'äktə,nȯl, -nōl\ *n* -s [*octane* + *-ol*] **:** any of four liquid alcohols $C_8H_{17}OH$ derived from normal octane: as **a :** the primary alcohol $CH_3(CH_2)_6CH_2OH$ having a penetrating odor, occurring free or in the form of esters in oils from plant seeds and fruits, and used chiefly in organic synthesis and in perfumes — called also *1-octanol*, *n-octyl alcohol* **b :** a viscous oily secondary alcohol $CH_3(CH_2)_5CH(OH)CH_3$ having an aromatic odor, made by heating the sodium soap of castor oil, and used chiefly as a solvent, in organic synthesis, and in perfumes — called also *2-octanol*
**oc·ta·no·yl** \¦äktə¦nōəl; äk'tanə,wil, -,wēl\ *n* -s [ISV *octanoic* (in *octanoic acid*) + *-yl*] **:** CAPRYLYL
**oc·tant** \'äktənt\ *n* -s [L *octant-*, *octans* half quadrant, fr. *octo* eight] **1 a :** the position or aspect of a celestial body (as the moon or a planet) when halfway between conjunction or opposition and quadrature **b :** an instrument used for observing altitudes of a celestial body from a moving ship or aircraft and having a maximum angle of 45 degrees between its reflecting mirrors — compare SEXTANT **2 a :** one of the eight regions into which three usu. orthogonal planes meeting in a point divide all three-dimensioned space around it **b :** any of the eight parts into which a space is divided by three coordinate planes
**oc·ta·phyllite** \¦äktə+\ *n* [*octa-* + *phyllite*] **:** any of various micas (as biotite) in which there are eight cations for every ten oxygen and two hydroxyl ions — compare HEPTAPHYLLITE
**oc·ta·pla** \'äktəplə\ *n* -s *often cap* [LGk *oktapla*, fr. Gk, neut. pl. of *oktaplous*, *oktaploos* eightfold, fr. *okta-* octa- + *-plous*, *-ploos* -fold (as in *diploos* double) — more at DOUBLE] **:** an edition or work in eight texts or versions in parallel columns; *esp* **:** an edition of a portion of the Old Testament compiled by Origen in the 3d century A.D. and consisting of the Hebrew text and seven Greek versions of it — compare HEXAPLA
**octaploid** *var of* OCTOPLOID
**oc·ta·pod·ic** \¦äktə¦pädik\ *adj* [*octapody* + *-ic*] **:** having eight metrical feet
**oc·tap·o·dy** \äk'tapədē\ *n* -ES [*octa-* + *-pody* (as in *dipody*)] **:** OCTAMETER
**oc·tarch** \'äk,tärk\ *adj* [*octa-* + *-arch*] **:** having eight xylem groups ⟨~ roots⟩
**oc·tarchy** \'äk,tärkē\ *n* -ES [*octa-* + *-archy*] **1 :** a government by eight persons **2 :** a confederacy of Anglo-Saxon kingdoms considered as having eight rulers — compare HEPTARCHY
**oc·ta·stich** \'äktə,stik\ *also* **oc·tas·ti·chon** \äk'tastə,kän\ *n, pl* **octastichs** \-ks\ *also* **octasti·cha** \-stəkə\ [LGk *oktastichon*, neut. of *oktastichos* consisting of eight lines, fr. Gk *okta-* octa- + *stichos* line; akin to Gk *steichein* to go — more at STAIR] **:** a verse unit of eight lines
**oc·ta·stroph·ic** \¦äktə¦sträfik\ *adj* [*octa-* + *strophic*] **:** having eight strophes
**oc·ta·style** *also* **oc·to·style** \'äktə,stīl\ *adj* [L *octastylos*, fr. Gk *oktastylos*, fr. *okta-* octa- + *-stylos* -style] **:** marked by columniation with eight columns across the front — compare DISTYLE
**oc·ta·sty·los** \,==¦stī,läs\ *n* -ES [L *octastylos*, adj.] **:** an octastyle building
**oc·ta·teuch** \'äktə,tük, -ə,tyük\ *n* -s *often cap* [LL *octateuchus*, fr. Gk *oktateuchos*, fr. *okta-* octa- + *teuchos* vessel, case for holding a roll of papyrus; akin to Gk *teuchein* to make, build — more at DOUGHTY] **:** a collection of eight books; *esp* **:** the first eight books of the Old Testament
**oc·ta·val** \(')äk¦tāvəl, 'äktəv-\ *adj* **:** of or relating to an octave
**oc·ta·valent** \¦äktə+\ *adj* [*octa-* + *valent*] **:** having a valence of eight
**oc·ta·vary** \'äktə,verē\ *n* -ES [NL *octavarium*, fr. ML *octava* octave + NL *-arium*] **:** a Roman Catholic service book containing collects and lections for use within festival octaves
**¹oc·tave** \'äktəv, -tēv, -,tāv\ *n* -s [ME, fr. ML *octava*, fr. L,

octave 3a

fem. of *octavus* eighth, fr. *octo* eight — more at EIGHT] **1 a :** the eighth day counting the festival day after a church festival **b :** the eight day period beginning with the festival day **2 a :** a stanza of eight lines **:** OTTAVA RIMA **b :** the first two quatrains or first eight verses of a sonnet — called also *octet*; compare SESTET **3 a :** a musical interval embracing eight diatonic degrees **b :** a tone or note at this interval **c :** the harmonic combination of two tones an octave apart **d :** the whole series of notes, tones, or digitals comprised within this interval and forming the unit of the modern scale **e :** an organ stop giving tones an octave above those corresponding to the digitals **4 :** a parry or guard position in fencing defending the lower outside target in which the hand is to the right in a position of supination with the tip of the blade directed at the opponent's knee — compare SECONDE **5 :** a group of eight ⟨an ~ of oarsmen⟩ **6** *in a spectrum of vibrations* **:** an interval analogous to the musical octave and being such that the frequencies at its beginning and end are to each other as 1 : 2 ⟨the visible or photic portion of the 60 or more ~s of the electromagnetic spectrum of radiant energy, extending from wireless waves to cosmic rays, constitutes about 1 ~ and has wavelengths ranging from the red end of the spectrum (7700A) to the extreme violet end (about 4000A) —Charles Sheard⟩ **7 a :** a cask for wine holding ⅛ pipe **b :** a unit of liquid capacity equal to ⅛ pipe or 13½ gallons **8** *archaic* **:** a series of eight chemical elements in order of increasing atomic weights
**²octave** \"\ *adj* **1 :** consisting of eight units **2 :** sounding or producing sounds at the octave ⟨an ~ organ stop⟩
**octave flute** *n* **1 :** PICCOLO **2 :** a 4-foot flute stop in a pipe organ
**octave species** *n* **:** a specific arrangement of the whole-step and half-step intervals comprising the diatonic scale of the octave **:** MODE, SCALE
**oc·ta·vo** \äk'tā(,)vō, -tä(-\ *n* -s [L, abl. of *octavus* eighth — more at OCTAVE] **:** the size of a piece of paper cut eight from a sheet; *also* **:** paper or a page of this size — abbr. *8vo*; symbol *8°*; see BOOK tables
**oc·tene** \'äk,tēn\ *n* -s [ISV *octa-* + *-ene*] **:** any of the four oily liquid straight-chain octylenes
**oc·ten·ni·al** \(')äk¦tenēəl\ *adj* [LL *octennium* period of eight years (fr. L *oct-* — fr. *octo* eight — + *-ennium*, fr. *annus* year) + E *-al* — more at EIGHT, ANNUAL] **1 :** happening every eighth year **2 :** lasting for a period of eight years
**oc·tet** *also* **oc·tette** \(')äk¦tet, *usu* -ed·+V\ *n* -s [*octa-* + *-et* or *-ette*; trans. of It *ottetto*] **1 a :** a musical composition for eight parts (as eight instruments or voices) **b :** a group of eight singers or players in joint performance **2 :** OCTAVE 2b **3 :** a group of eight electrons in the outer valence shell of an atom that are considered to constitute a stable arrangement and to be present in pairs which may or may not be shared with another atom — compare COVALENCE, LEWIS-LANGMUIR THEORY
**oc·til·lion** \äk'tilyən\ *n* -s *often attrib* [F, fr. MF, fr. *octo-* + *-illion* (as in *million*)] — see NUMBER table
**octine** *var of* OCTYNE
**octo-** — see OCTA-
**oc·to·ate** \'äktə,wāt\ *n* -s [*octoic* (in *octoic acid*) + *-ate*] **:** a salt or ester of an octoic acid: as **a :** CAPRYLATE **b :** ETHYLHEXOATE
**oc·to·bass** \'äktə,bās\ *n* [F *octobasse*, *octabasse*, fr. *octa-* + *basse* bass, contrabass, fr. fem. of *bas* low, of little height — more at BASE] **:** a huge contrabass having three strings stopped by finger keys and pedals
**oc·to·ber** \äk'tōbə(r)\ *n* -s *usu cap* [ME *octobre*, fr. OF, fr. L *october* (eighth month), fr. *octo* eight] **1 :** the tenth month of the Gregorian calendar — abbr. *Oct.*; see MONTH table **2** *Brit* **:** ale made in October ⟨sent down to the storehouse for a bottle of rum and a bottle of *October* —B.M.Carew⟩
**oc·to·brist** \-brəst\ *n* -s *usu cap* [*octobr-* (fr. *october*) + *-ist*; trans. of Russ *oktyabrist*] **1 :** a member of a moderately liberal political party in czarist Russia whose principles of constitutional government and measures of reform were expressed in an imperial manifesto of October, 1905 **2** [trans. of Russ *oktyabrenok*; fr. the Russian Communist revolution that began on October 25, 1917, Old Style (November 7, New Style)] **:** a member of a Russian Communist youth organization with members between the ages of 8 and 10 — compare PIONEER
**oc·to·co·ral·lia** \,äktōkə'ralēə\ [NL, fr. *octa-* + L *corallia*, pl. of *corallium* coral] *syn of* ALCYONARIA
**oc·tode** \'äk,tōd\ *n* -s [ISV *octa-* + *-ode*] **:** a vacuum tube with eight electrodes comprising a cathode, an anode, a control grid, and five additional electrodes that are usu. grids
**oc·to·de·cil·lion** \,äktōdə'silyən\ *n, often attrib* [L *octodecim* eighteen + E *-illion* (as in *million*)] — see NUMBER table
**oc·to·dec·i·mo** \,äktə'desə,mō\ *n* -s [L, abl. of *octodecimus* eighteenth, fr. *octodecim* eighteen, fr. *octo* eight + *-decim* (fr. *decem* ten) — more at TEN] **:** EIGHTEENMO — symbol *T;* see BOOK tables
**oc·to·don** \'äktə,dän\ *n* [NL *Octodont-*, *Octodon*, fr. *octa-* + *-odont-*, *-odon* -odon] **1** *cap* **:** a genus (the type of the family Octodontidae) of small long-eared social rodents of western So. America having combs of long stiff hairs at the base of the claws **2** -s **:** any rodent of the genus *Octodon* **:** DEGU
**¹oc·to·dont** \'äktə,dänt\ *adj* [NL *Octodont-*, *Octodon*] **1 :** having eight teeth **2 :** of or relating to the genus *Octodon* or the family Octodontidae
**²octodont** \"\ *n* -s [NL *Octodont-*, *Octodon*] **:** an octodont rodent
**octodrachm** *var of* OCTADRACHM
**oc·to·echos** \,äktə'ē,käs\ *n* -ES [NGk *oktōēchos*, *oktaēchos*, fr. Gk *okta-* octa- + *ēchos* sound — more at ECHO] **:** a liturgical book of the Eastern Orthodox Church attributed to St. John of Damascus and containing all hymns to be used at offices throughout the whole week
**¹oc·to·foil** \'äktə,fȯil\ *adj* [*octa-* + *foil*, n.] **:** having eight leaves ⟨a temple column of ~ plan⟩
**²octofoil** \"\ *n* **1 :** an octofoil figure ⟨the chancel E window has an ~ above three cusped lights —Nikolaus Pevsner⟩ **2 :** DOUBLE QUATREFOIL
**¹oc·to·ge·nar·i·an** \,äktəjə'na(a)rēən, -tōj-, -ner-, -nār-\ *n* -s [L *octogenarius* containing or consisting of eighty + E *-an*, n. suffix] **:** a person who is 80 or more but less than 90 years old
**²octogenarian** \¦=====¦==\ *adj* **:** 80 or between 80 and 90 years old
**oc·to·ge·nar·i·an·ism** \,===¦=rēə,nizəm\ *n* -s **:** the state of being an octogenarian
**oc·tog·e·nary** \(')äk¦täjə,nerē\ *adj* [L *octogenarius* containing or consisting of eighty, fr. *octogeni* eighty each (fr. *octoginta* eighty, fr. *octo* eight + *-ginta* — akin to L *-ginti* in *viginti* twenty) + *-arius* -ary — more at VICENARY] **1 :** OCTOGENARIAN **2 :** based on the number 80
**oc·to·gyn·ia** \,äktə'jinēə\ *n pl, cap* [NL, fr. *octa-* + *-gynia*] *in some classifications* **:** an order of plants having flowers with eight pistils
**oc·to·ic acid** \äk'tōik-\ *n* [*octoic* fr. *octane* + *-oic*] **:** any of the monocarboxylic acids $C_7H_{15}COOH$ derived from the octanes: as **a :** CAPRYLIC ACID **b :** ETHYLHEXOIC ACID
**oc·toid** \'äk,tȯid\ *adj* [*octa-* + *-oid*] **:** being a gear tooth form that is commonly used for generated bevel gear teeth and that closely approximates the involute
**octomerous** *var of* OCTAMEROUS
**octometer** *var of* OCTAMETER
**oc·to·nar·ius** \,äktə'na(a)rēəs\ *n, pl* **octonar·ii** \-ē,ī\ [L *octonarius*, adj.] **:** an eight-foot verse (as of four iambic or trochaic dipodies)
**¹oc·to·nary** \'äktə,nerē\ *n* -ES [L *octonarius*, adj., containing or consisting of eight, fr. *octoni* eight each (fr. *octo* eight) + *-arius* -ary] **:** a stanza or group of eight verses; *esp* **:** one of the stanzas of the 119th Psalm
**²octonary** \"\ *adj* [L *octonarius*, adj.] **:** of or relating to the number eight **:** consisting of eight **:** in sets of eight
**oc·to·noc·u·lar** \¦äktə¦näkyələ(r)\ *adj* [L *octoni* eight each + E *ocular*] **:** having eight eyes
**oc·to·pal** \'äktəpəl\ *adj* [*octopus* + *-al*] **:** resembling or having the characteristics of an octopus ⟨all the slow ~ movements of her temper —Thomas Wolfe⟩
**oc·to·pe·an** \,äktə'pēən, (')äk¦täp-\ *or* **oc·to·pine** \'äktə,pīn, -,pən\ *adj* [*octopus* + *-an* or *-ine*] **:** of, relating to, or like an octopus
**oc·toph·thal·mous** \,äk,täf'thalməs\ *adj* [*octa-* + *-ophthalmous* (fr. Gk *ophthalmos* eye) — more at OPHTHALMIA] **:** having eight eyes
**¹oc·to·ploid** *also* **oc·ta·ploid** \'äktə,plȯid\ *adj* [ISV *octa-* + *-ploid*] **:** eightfold in appearance or arrangement; *specif* **:** having a chromosome number eight times the basic chromosome number — **oc·to·ploi·dy** \'==,plȯidē\ *n* -ES
**²octoploid** \"\ *n* -s **:** an octoploid individual
**¹oc·to·pod** \'äktə,päd\ *adj* [Gk *oktōpod-*, *oktapod-*, *oktōpous*, *oktapous*, fr. *okta-* octa- + *pod-*, *pous* foot — more at FOOT] **1 :** having eight feet, limbs, or arms **2** [NL *Octopoda*] **:** of or relating to the Octopoda
**²octopod** \"\ *n* [partly fr. ¹*octopod*, partly fr. NL *Octopoda*] **:** an individual having eight limbs; *specif* **:** OCTOPUS
**oc·top·o·da** \äk'täpədə\ *n pl, cap* [NL, fr. Gk *oktōpoda*, *oktapoda*, neut. pl. of *oktōpod-*, *oktapod-*, *oktōpous*, *oktapous* octopod] **:** an order of cephalopod mollusks (subclass Dibranchia) comprising the octopuses, argonauts, and related mollusks that have eight arms with sessile suckers devoid of horny rims and that often have vestiges of an internal shell but have an external shell only in the argonaut — **oc·top·o·dan** \(')=¦==dᵊn\ *adj or n*
**oc·to·pod·i·dae** \,äktə'pädə,dē\ *n pl, cap* [NL, fr. *Octopod-*, *Octopus*, type genus + *-idae*] **:** a family of mollusks comprising the typical octopuses that are comparatively large eight-armed cephalopods with a small saclike body, a large head armed with a strong beak, highly developed eyes, and the arms united at the base by a membrane and usu. provided with two rows of suckers by which they cling to the sea bottom or hold their prey
**oc·top·o·dous** \(')äk¦täpədəs\ *adj* [Gk *oktōpod-*, *oktapod-*, *oktōpous*, *oktapous* octopod + E *-ous*] **:** OCTOPOD
**oc·to·pole** *also* **oc·tu·pole** \'äktə,pōl\ *n* [*octopole* fr. *octa-* + *pole*; *octupole* alter. (influenced by *quadrupole*) of *octopole*] **:** a system composed of eight electric charges arranged as four dipoles or two quadrupoles
**oc·to·pus** \'äktəpəs *sometimes* -tə,pùs\ *n* [NL *Octopod-*, *Octopus*, fr. Gk *oktōpod-*, *oktapod-*, *oktōpous*, *oktapous* octopod] **1 a** *cap* **:** a genus formerly including all of the common octopuses but now restricted to a few typical forms and being the type of the family Octopodidae **b** *pl* **octopuses** \-səz\ *or* **octo·pi** \-tə,pī\ *also* **oc·top·o·des** \äk'täpə,dēz, -tōp-\ **:** any mollusk of this genus; *broadly* **:** any member of the order Octopoda usu. excepting the paper nautilus **2** *pl* **octopuses** *or* **octopi :** something that resembles or is thought to resemble an octopus esp. in having many branches centrally directed or in exerting control over others by many means ⟨an ~ of a corporation which lends, buys, produces, and sells —*Atlantic*⟩
**oc·to·roon** \¦äktə¦rün\ *n* -s [*octa-* + *-roon* (as in *quadroon*)] **:** a person of one-eighth Negro ancestry
**oc·tose** \'äk,tōs\ *n* -s [*octa-* + *-ose*] **:** any of a class of synthetic monosaccharides $C_8H_{16}O_8$ containing eight carbon atoms in the molecule
**oc·to·spore** \'äktə,spō(ə)r\ *n* [ISV *octa-* + *spore*] **:** one of eight carpospores commonly produced by red algae of the family Bangiaceae — **oc·tos·po·rous** \(')äk¦täspərəs, ¦äktə¦spōrəs\ *adj*
**oc·tos·ti·ate** \(')äk¦tästēət, -ē,āt\ *adj* [NL *Octostiatae*, fr. *octa-* + *-ostiatae* (fr. fem. pl. of *-ostiatus* having a specified number of ostia, fr. *ostium* + L *-atus* -ate)] **1 :** having eight ostia **2 :** belonging to a group of spiders having eight cardiac ostia
**octostyle** *var of* OCTASTYLE
**¹oc·to·syllabic** \¦äktə, ¦äktō+\ *adj* [LL *octosyllabus*, *octasyllabus* octosyllabic (fr. Gk *oktasyllabos*, fr. *okta-* octa- + *-syllabos*, fr. *syllabē* syllable) + E *-ic* — more at SYLLABLE] **:** having eight syllables or composed of verses having eight syllables ⟨an ~ line⟩ ⟨an ~ poem⟩
**²octosyllabic** \"\ *n* -s **:** a verse of eight syllables
**¹oc·to·syllable** \"+\ *adj* [part trans. of LL *octosyllabus*, *octasyllabus*] **:** OCTOSYLLABIC
**²octosyllable** \"\ *n* **:** a word or line of eight syllables
**oc·troi** \'äk,trȯi, (')äk¦trwä\ *n* -s [F, fr. MF, fr. *octroyer*] **1 :** a concession or privilege granted by an absolute sovereign and serving as a limitation on his authority **2 a :** a tax on commodities brought into a town or city esp. in certain Euro-

pean countries **:** a municipal customs **b :** the agency for collecting such a tax or the city entrance at which it is collected

**oc·troy** \'äk,trȯi\ *vt* -ED/-ING/-S [MF *octroyer*, fr. OF *otreier*, fr. ML *auctorizare* to authorize, warrant, consent — more at AUTHORIZE] **:** to grant or concede as a privilege ⟨such charters, or constitutions, are said to be ~*ed*, or issued by royal fiat —R.G.Gettell⟩

**oc·tuor** \'äktüȯr\ *n* -S [F, fr. *octa-* + *-uor* (as in *quatuor*)] **:** OCTET

[1]**oc·tu·ple** \'äk,t(y)üpəl, ═'══; 'äktəp-\ *adj* [L *octuplus*, fr. *oct-* (fr. *octo* eight) + *-uplus* (as in *quadruplus* quadruple) — more at EIGHT] **1 :** consisting of eight **:** being eight times as great or as many **:** EIGHTFOLD **2 :** taken by eights or in groups of eight

[2]**octuple** \"\ *n* -S **:** a sum eight times as great as another **:** an eightfold amount **:** the eighth multiple

[3]**octuple** \"\ *vb* **octupled; octupled; octupling** \-p(ə)liŋ\ **octuples** *vt* **:** to make eight times as much or as many ~ *vi* **:** to increase or grow to eight times as much or as many

**octuple press** *n* **:** a rotary newspaper press that prints 64 pages per revolution

**oc·tup·let** \(')äk¦təplət, -¦t(y)üp-, 'äktəp-, *usu* -əd.+V\ *n* -S [[1]*octuple* + *-et*] **1 :** a combination of eight of a kind **2 a :** a group of eight musical notes or tones to be performed in the time of six of the same value

[1]**oc·tu·pli·cate** \(')äk¦t(y)üpləkət, -lə,kāt\ *adj* [L *octuplicatus* eightfold, fr. *octuplus*, after L *quadruplus* quadruple: *quadruplicatus* (past part. of *quadruplicare* to quadruple, quadruplicate)] **:** made in eight identical copies **:** EIGHTFOLD

[2]**octuplicate** \"\ *n* -S **1 :** an eighth thing like seven others of the same kind **2 :** eight copies all alike — used with *in* ⟨typed in ~⟩

[3]**oc·tu·pli·cate** \═'═plə,kāt\ *vt* -ED/-ING/-S **:** to multiply by eight **:** OCTUPLE **:** reproduce seven times; *specif* **:** to make at one time an original and seven carbon copies of

**octupole** *var of* OCTOPOLE

**oc·tyl** \'äkt[ə]l\ *n* -S [ISV *octane* + *-yl*] **:** an alkyl radical $C_8H_{17}$ derived from an octane: as **a :** the normal radical $CH_3(CH_2)_6CH_2$— **b :** the radical $CH_3(CH_2)_3CH(C_2H_5)CH_2$— having a branched chain; 2-ethyl-hexyl

**octyl alcohol** *n* **:** any of several alcohols $C_8H_{17}OH$ derived from the octanes; *esp* **:** OCTANOL a — compare ISOOCTYL ALCOHOL

**oc·tyl·ene** \'äktə,lēn\ *n* -S [ISV *octyl* + *-ene*] **:** any of numerous isomeric hydrocarbons $C_8H_{16}$ belonging to the ethylene series and including the octenes — compare DIISOBUTYLENE

**oc·tyne** *also* **oc·tine** \'äk,tīn\ *n* -S [ISV *octa-* + *-yne* or *-ine*] **:** any of four straight-chain hydrocarbons $C_8H_{14}$ of the acetylene series

**ocul-** *or* **oculo-** *comb form* [L *ocul-*, fr. *oculus* — more at EYE] **1 :** eye ⟨*oculo*motor⟩ **2 :** ocular and ⟨*oculo*auditory⟩ ⟨*oculo*facial⟩

[1]**oc·u·lar** \'äkyələ(r)\ *adj* [LL *ocularis* of the eyes, fr. L *oculus* eye + *-aris* -ar] **1 a :** done or carried out by means of the sight ⟨~ measurement⟩ ⟨~ inspection⟩ ⟨the density of the vegetation as determined by ~ estimate —*Ecology*⟩ **b** (1) **:** addressed to or perceived by the eye **:** received by actual sight **:** VISIBLE ⟨be sure of it; give me the ~ proof —Shak.⟩ ⟨~ evidence for my belief that those books were written and were published —Max Beerbohm⟩ (2) **:** based on what has been seen ⟨~ testimony⟩ **c :** of or relating to the sense of sight **:** VISUAL ⟨of wondrous ~ excitement to any art-minded provincial youth —Janet Flanner⟩ ⟨this correction of ~ illusions was a practice of Greek architects —Benjamin Farrington⟩ **2 a :** of, relating to, or connected with the eye ⟨~ diseases⟩ ⟨~ muscles⟩ **b :** used by or expressed by the eye ⟨the ~ dialect needs no dictionary —R.W.Emerson⟩ ⟨~ approval⟩ **c :** resembling or suggesting an eye in form or function ⟨spindly balusters, ~ windows —Frederic Beck⟩

[2]**ocular** \"\ *n* -S **1 :** EYE ⟨stick an eyeglass in his ~ —W.S. Gilbert⟩ **2 :** EYEPIECE 1 ⟨the perfect ~ exists only in the astronomer's wistful imagination —*Times Lit. Supp.*⟩ **3 :** an ocular scale or shield (as in certain reptiles)

**oc·u·lar·i·um** \,äkyə'la(a)rēəm\ *n, pl* **ocular·ia** \-ēə\ [ML, fr. L *oculus* eye + *-arium*] **:** a slit for vision in a barrel helm

**oc·u·lar·ly** *adv* **1 :** by means of the eyes or the sight ⟨expressed her feelings ~⟩ **2 :** to the sight ⟨~ demonstrated ~⟩

**ocular micrometer** *n* **1 :** MICROMETER EYEPIECE **2 :** EYEPIECE MICROMETER

**ocular sclerite** *n* **:** a narrow circular strip of the insect cranium surrounding the compound eye

**ocular spectrum** *n* **:** AFTERIMAGE

**ocular spot** *n* **:** a pigmented organ or part believed to be sensitive to light

**oc·u·late** \'äkyələt, -yə,lāt\ *adj* [LL *oculatus* having ornaments resembling eyes, fr. L, having eyes, fr. *oculus* eye + *-atus* -ate] **:** having spots or holes resembling eyes **:** OCELLATED

**oc·u·lau·di·to·ry** \¦äkyə¦lȯdə,tōrē\ *adj* [*ocul-* + *auditory*] **:** combining the sense of sight and that of hearing

**oc·u·li·na** \,äkyə'līnə\ *n, cap* [NL, fr. L *oculus* eye + NL *-ina*] **:** a genus (the type of the family Oculinidae) of tropical aporose corals comprising the typical ivory corals — **oc·u·lin·id** \-lənəd\ *n* -S — **oc·u·lin·oid** \¦══¦li,nȯid\ *adj*

**oc·u·list** \'äkyələst\ *n* -S [F *oculiste*, fr. MF, fr. L *oculus* eye + MF *-iste* -ist] **1 :** OPHTHALMOLOGIST **2 :** OPTOMETRIST

**oc·u·li sunday** \'äkyə,lī-\ *n, cap O&S* [L *oculi*, pl. of *oculus* eye; from the fact that the introit for the day, Ps 24: 15 (Vulgate), begins with the word *oculi*] **:** the third Sunday in Lent

**oculo-** — see OCUL-

**oc·u·lo·gy·ric** \¦äkyəlō¦jīrik\ *also* **oc·u·lo·gy·ral** \-rəl\ *adj* [*oculogyric* fr. *ocul-* + *gyr-* (fr. Gk *gyros* circle) + *-ic*; *oculogyral* fr. *ocul* + *gyral* — more at GYRE] **:** relating to or involving circular movements of the eyeballs

**oculogyric crisis** *n* **:** a spasmodic attack that occurs in some nervous diseases and is marked by fixation of the eyeballs in one position usu. upward

[1]**oc·u·lo·motor** \¦äkyəlō+\ *adj* [*ocul-* + *motor*] **1 :** moving or tending to move the eyeball **2 :** involving movement of the eyeball ⟨~ palsies⟩

[2]**oculomotor** \"\ *n* **:** an oculomotor part; *esp* **:** OCULOMOTOR NERVE

**oculomotor nerve** *n* **:** either nerve of the 3d pair of cranial nerves that are motor nerves with some associated autonomic fibers, arise from the midbrain, and supply muscles of the eye except the superior oblique and the lateral rectus with motor fibers and the ciliary body and iris with autonomic fibers by way of the ciliary ganglion

**oc·u·lus** \'äkyələs\ *n, pl* **ocu·li** \-yə,lī\ [L, lit., eye — more at EYE] **1 :** an architectural member resembling or suggesting an eye: as **a :** the central boss of a volute **b :** a round opening in a dome **c :** OEIL-DE-BOEUF **2 :** EYE **3 :** a painted or metal image of a human eye placed on the bow or other part of a boat (as in ancient Egypt)

**oculus mun·di** \-'mən,dī\ *n, pl* **oculi mundi** [L, eye of the world] **:** OPAL

**ocyp·o·da** \ō'sipədə\ *syn of* OCYPODE

**ocyp·o·de** \-də\ *n* [NL, irreg. fr. Gk *ōkypod-*, *ōkypous* swift-footed, fr. *ōkys* swift + *pod-*, *pous* foot; akin to L *ocior* swifter, Skt *āśu* swift, and perh. to L *acer* sharp — more at EDGE, FOOT] **1** *cap* **:** a genus (the type of the family Ocypodidae) of square-bodied, long-legged, and swift-running crabs that are related to the fiddler crabs and live in holes in the sand along the seashore **2** -S **:** a ctenophore of the genus *Ocypode* — **oc·y·po·di·an** \¦äsə¦pōdēən\ *adj or n* — **ocyp·o·doid** \ō'sipə,dȯid\ *adj*

**ocyr·oe** \ō'sirəwē\ *n, cap* [NL, fr. Gk *ōkyroēs* swift-flowing, fr. *ōkys* swift + *-roēs* (akin to *rhein* to flow) — more at STREAM] **:** a genus (coextensive with the family Ocyroidae) of ctenophores of the Gulf of Mexico and the Caribbean sea that swim by means of a large winglike process on each side of the body

[1]**od** *also* **odd** \'äd\ *interj, often cap* [euphemism for *God*] — a mild oath

[2]**od** \'äd, 'ōd\ *n* -S [G, coined 1850 by Baron Carl-Ludwig von Reichenbach †1869 Ger. chemist and natural philosopher] **:** a force or natural power formerly held by some to reside in certain individuals and things and to underlie hypnotism and magnetism and some other phenomena

**OD** \(')ō'dē\ *abbr or n* -S **1 :** OFFICER OF THE DAY **2 :** OLIVE DRAB **:** an olive drab uniform **3 :** a doctor of optometry

**OD** *abbr* **1** [L *oculus dexter*] right eye **2** on demand **3** on duty **4** ordinary seaman **5** ordnance datum **6** outside diameter; outside dimensions **7** overdraft; overdrawn

**oda** *or* **odah** \'ōdə, ō'dä\ *n, pl* **odas** *or* **oda** *or* **odahs** *or* **odah** [Turk *oda* room, chamber] **1 :** a room in a harem **2 :** ODALISQUE

**odac·i·dae** \ō'dasə,dē\ *n pl, cap* [NL, fr. *Odac-*, *Odax*, type genus + *-idae*] **:** a family of labroid fishes that is usu. made coextensive with the genus *Odax*

[1]**odal** *or* **odel** *also* **odhal** *or* **odhall** \'ōd[ə]l\ *n* -S [ON *ōthal* — more at ATHELING] **:** alodium owned by individuals or families belonging to Teutonic and esp. Scandinavian peoples in the premedieval or medieval period

[2]**odal** \'ōd[ə]l\ *adj* **:** of, relating to, or constituting odal ⟨~ soil⟩

**oda·lisque** *also* **oda·lisk** *or* **oda·lisc** \'ōd[ə]l,isk\ *n* -S [F *odalisque*, alter. of *odalique*, fr. Turk *odalık*, fr. *oda* room + *-lık*, n. suffix] **:** a female slave or concubine in a harem

**odal·ler** \'ōd[ə]lə(r)\ *n* -S **:** an owner of odal

**odax** \'ō,daks\ *n, cap* [NL, fr. Gk, adv., by biting, irreg. (influence of *odous* tooth), fr. the stem of *daknein* to bite — more at TOOTH, TONGS] **:** a genus of marine fishes of Australian and New Zealand seas that resemble sparid fishes but have a jaw with the front margin modified into a sharp cutting edge that replaces teeth — see ODACIDAE

[1]**odd** \'äd\ *adj, usu* -ER/-EST [ME *odde*, fr. ON *oddi* point of land, triangle, odd number (as in such compounds as *odda-mathr* odd man, *oddatala* odd number); akin to OE *ord* point of a weapon, OHG *ort*, ON *oddr*, and prob. to Lith *usnis* thistle, hawthorn, Alb *usht* ear of grain] **1 a :** that is without its corresponding mate **:** that lacks its complementary match **:** that is unpaired ⟨found two pairs of shoes and an ~ shoe in the closet⟩ ⟨lost a glove somewhere and was unable to match the ~ one⟩ **b** (1) **:** that exists alone or is present alone in contrast with others that are paired or coupled or grouped **:** that is left over ⟨four of them began playing bridge, and the ~ player drew up a chair and watched⟩ ⟨came without his wife and so turned out to be the ~ guest at the party⟩ (2) **:** that exists alone or is present alone as something that forms or that is designed to form part of a complete set or series **:** that is separated from an actual or contemplated complete set or series ⟨had in his possession only two or three ~ volumes of the original 12-volume set⟩ **c** *chiefly dial* **:** that is the only one **:** SINGLE ⟨just for this ~ night —Margery Sharp⟩ **d** *obs* **:** excelling in a unique way **:** CHOICE **2 a** (1) **:** being somewhat though insignificantly more than the indicated round number or than the indicated approximate quantity or extent or degree — used formerly with a preceding *and* ⟨the eighty and ~ pigeons —Matthew Arnold⟩ but now usu. used immediately following the numerical adjective and usu. connected with it by a hyphen ⟨a book of 300-*odd* pages⟩ ⟨was 40-*odd* years old⟩ (2) **:** increased by the addition of a fraction of one of the indicated units — now usu. used following the substantive qualified by a numerical adjective ⟨will cost 23 dollars ~⟩ **b** (1) **:** that constitutes a remainder in comparison with an expressed or implied unitary amount (as of money) **:** that is left over as a remainder ⟨used most of the check for necessary expenses and spent the ~ dollars on his hobby⟩ (2) **:** that does not total up to any very considerable amount **:** that does not constitute any very considerable unitary amount ⟨had some ~ change in his pocket⟩ ⟨some ~ nickels and dimes⟩ **c** *archaic* **:** SOME, SEVERAL — used to indicate an indefinite usu. small number of unitary amounts of lesser extent than an immediately preceding unitary amount ⟨two thousand ~ hundred cavalry —R.T.Wilson⟩ ⟨three thousand and ~ hundred clouds —Henry Petowe⟩ **3 a :** being any member of a sequence of positive integers beginning with one and counting by twos **:** not divisible exactly by two — opposed to EVEN **b :** having an odd number as one of a series ⟨read every other ~ page of the book⟩ **c :** marked by an odd number of units (as of measurement) ⟨needed two *odd*-length boards, one of 3 feet and one of 5 feet⟩ **4 :** that exists or occurs or is produced in addition to or apart from what is regular or planned in advance or taken into account: as **a** (1) **:** that is a scrap or fragment ⟨swept up the ~ bits of metal left on the floor⟩ (2) **:** that is one of several or many mixed or varied usu. unrelated things **:** MISCELLANEOUS ⟨rummaged around and picked up a few ~ things we needed⟩ (3) **:** HAPHAZARD, RANDOM, SCATTERED ⟨collected ~ bits of information⟩ ⟨found a few ~ references to the book⟩ **b** (1) **:** that occurs at an irregular or indefinitely determined time ⟨the matter was brought up at one of the club's ~ sessions⟩ (2) **:** that occurs largely by chance **:** that occurs unpredictably **:** ACCIDENTAL, FORTUITOUS ⟨an ~ stroke of luck⟩ (3) **:** that occurs at some indefinitely indicated time **:** that comes along at some time or other ⟨told her he would see her again some ~ day⟩ (4) **:** that occurs sporadically or in an isolated way **:** that crops up or materializes from time to time **:** happening or becoming available now and then **:** OCCASIONAL, STRAY ⟨manages to get in some reading at ~ moments⟩ ⟨at ~ moments as a boy he was set to hoeing the family garden —*Current Biog.*⟩ **c** (1) **:** that does not form part of a regular schedule (as of work) **:** that is done or engaged in or attended to over and above a regular program or routine **:** INCIDENTAL ⟨does ~ chores around the house, potters ineffectually round the garden —Geoffrey Gorer⟩ ⟨try to supplement their pensions by taking on ~ jobs —M.A.Abrams⟩ (2) **:** that is engaged to do miscellaneous work esp. requiring little training or skill ⟨hired a couple of ~ hands for the farm⟩ ⟨had begun life as an ~ boy in various steelworks —R.W.Pickford⟩ **d :** that is produced over and above what comes from a regular source **:** EXTRA ⟨hoped to make a few ~ dollars during his summer vacation⟩ **e :** CASUAL 4 b (2) ⟨wear ~ jackets and slacks —Richard Joseph⟩ **5 :** that has an out-of-the-way location **:** SECLUDED, REMOTE ⟨found it in some ~ corner of the house⟩ **6 :** that differs markedly from what is usual or ordinary or accepted **:** that is hardly or not at all the expected or normal thing **:** PECULIAR: as **a** (1) **:** strange in behavior or action ⟨a very ~ way to show gratitude⟩ ⟨has ~ little habits⟩ (2) **:** eccentric or mentally unbalanced ⟨there must have been something ~ about the man, or he wouldn't have buried himself alive —G.K.Chesterton⟩ **b** (1) **:** strange in appearance ⟨had an ~ look in her eyes⟩ (2) **:** grotesque or freakish in appearance ⟨was one of the ~*est* creatures I had ever seen⟩ **c** (1) **:** altogether unusual **:** most uncommon **:** quite extraordinary **:** SINGULAR, CURIOUS, QUEER ⟨it's ~ you didn't know⟩ ⟨an ~ assortment of buildings —André Maurois⟩ (2) **:** BAFFLING, MYSTERIOUS, INEXPLICABLE ⟨suffered an ~ impulse to get up and kick his chair over —Mary Austin⟩ ⟨the young man had an ~ effect on her, making her almost giddily loquacious —Harriet La Barre⟩ **syn** see STRANGE

[2]**odd** \"\ *adv* [ME *odde*, fr. *odde*, adj.] *archaic* **:** ODDLY

[3]**odd** \"\ *n* -S [[1]*odd*] **1 a :** a stroke in golf that when played will be one more than the number of strokes played for a hole by one's opponent **b :** a stroke deducted from a weaker opponent's golf score for a hole **2 :** ODD TRICK 1

[1]**oddball** \'═,═\ *n* [[1]*odd* + *ball*] **:** one whose behavior is eccentric or otherwise peculiar ⟨talked like an ~, and he had a funny look in his eyes —Everett Wilson⟩

[2]**oddball** \'═,═\ *adj* **:** ECCENTRIC, PECULIAR, ODD ⟨the downtown ~ rendezvous —Jules Griffon⟩

**odd-come-short** \¦═(,)═'═\ *n, pl* **odd-come-shorts 1** *archaic* **a :** a cast-off garment or piece of cloth **b** *odd-come-shorts pl* **:** ODDS AND ENDS **2** *archaic* **:** some day or other

**odd-come-shortly** \¦═(,)═¦══\ *n, pl* **odd-come-shortlys** *or* **odd-come-shortlies** *archaic* **:** some day or other ⟨one of these *odd-come-shortlies* —W.F.De Morgan⟩

**odd court** *n* **:** the left half court in a singles racket game — compare EVEN COURT

**odder** *comparative of* ODD

**oddest** *superlative of* ODD

**odd-eyed** \'═¦═\ *adj* **:** having the two eyes of different colors ⟨an *odd-eyed* cat⟩

**odd fellow** *n, usu cap O & F* **:** a member of one of the major benevolent and fraternal orders

**odd fish** *n, pl* **odd fish :** ODDBALL

**odd function** *n* **:** a function changed by reversing the sign of its argument: $f(-x)=-f(x)$

**odd·ish** \'ädish, -dēsh\ *adj* **:** somewhat odd

**odd·i·ty** \'ädəd-ē, -ətē, -i\ *n* -ES **1 :** something odd: as **a :** a peculiar quality or trait or feature **:** PECULIARITY, ECCENTRICITY ⟨an ~ of character⟩ ⟨the *oddities* of this particular pilot —J.A.Michener⟩ ⟨any *oddities* in his behavior will be commented upon —Robert Graves⟩ **b** (1) **:** an eccentric or otherwise peculiar individual ⟨had all sorts of *oddities* visiting me —H.J.Laski⟩ (2) **:** something strange or grotesque or freakish (as in appearance) ⟨among *oddities* of the sea are the opalescent squid and the sea squirt —*Amer. Guide Series: Wash.*⟩ (3) **:** something unique or curiously unusual or anomalous **:** CURIOSITY ⟨a good piece of steak is an ~ —Green Peyton⟩ **c :** a strange event **:** peculiar occurrence ⟨the *oddities* of history⟩ ⟨meeting her there was a real ~⟩ **2 :** the quality or state of being odd ⟨the ~ of the situation⟩ ⟨saw for myself one example of his ~ —S.P.B.Mais⟩ ⟨the ~ of our own temperaments —Virginia Woolf⟩

**odd-job** \'═¦═\ *vi* [fr. the n. phrase *odd job*] **:** to work at odd jobs esp. those requiring little training or skill ⟨gone in to work in town, *odd-jobbing* —Paul Annixter⟩

**odd-job·ber** \(')═¦jäbə(r)\ *n* [*odd job* + *-er*] **:** ODD-JOBMAN

**odd-job·man** \-mən\ *n, pl* **odd-jobmen** [*odd job* + *man*] **:** one that works at odd jobs

**odd-leg caliper** \'═,═-\ *n* **1 :** a caliper having the points of its legs bent in the same direction for measurements on stepped surfaces or similar surfaces **2 :** HERMAPHRODITE CALIPER

odd-leg caliper

**odd legs** *n pl but sing in constr* **:** ODD-LEG CALIPER

**odd·ling** \'ädliŋ, -lēŋ\ *n* -S **1** *chiefly dial* **:** a mildly eccentric individual **2 oddlings** *pl, Brit* **:** ODDS AND ENDS

**odd lot** *n* **:** a number or quantity other than the usual unit in transactions; *specif* **:** a quantity of less than 100 shares of stock — compare ROUND LOT

**odd·ly** \'ädlē, -li\ *adv* [ME *oddely*, fr. *odde* odd + *-ly* — more at ODD] **:** in an odd manner ⟨seem to have acted ~ —Nigel Balchin⟩ ⟨was quite happy, ~ enough⟩ or to an odd extent ⟨sensed that he was ~ disturbed —Wilson Collison⟩

**odd man** *n* **1 :** one that casts or may cast a decisive vote when a vote is otherwise tied **2 a :** a player (as in the game of odd man wins) whose coin shows a face different from two other coins tossed or matched **b :** ODD MAN OUT 2 **3** [*odd* (*job*)] **a** *chiefly Brit* (1) **:** one that does odd jobs (2) **:** DAY LABORER **b :** FLOATER 4 b, 4 d

**odd man out** *n* **1 :** a method or game of choosing or eliminating one of a number of persons (as by matching coins) **2 a :** an individual singled out from others (as by matching coins) **b :** one that by choice or circumstances does not share in the ordinary affairs of others

**odd man wins** *n* **:** a gambling game in which three players match coins and declare the winner the one whose coin does not match the others

**odd mark** *n, dial Eng* **:** a portion of arable land lying fallow in preparation for seeding

**odd·ment** \'ädmənt\ *n* -S [[1]*odd* + *-ment*] **1 oddments** *pl* **:** ODDS AND ENDS ⟨clawing the ~*s* out of his pockets —Verne Athanas⟩ **2 a :** something left over or remaining or isolated (as a garment or piece of goods from a larger stock, a book from a complete set) ⟨an ~ sale⟩ — usu. used in pl. ⟨a display of ~*s*⟩ **b :** a garment designed for casual or otherwise informal wear ⟨frivolous ~*s* for summer —*New Yorker*⟩ — usu. used in pl. **3** *chiefly Brit* **a :** a page (as the title page) of a book that does not carry the actual text or other central material — usu. used in pl. **b oddments** *pl* **:** pages of a book remaining over after complete sections are made up **4 :** something odd **:** ODDITY — usu. used in pl. ⟨a museum where were gathered those ~*s* that rich men seem disposed to accumulate —Agnes M. Cleaveland⟩ ⟨various ~*s* of humanity —G.F. Whicher⟩ ⟨explains some nice ~*s* of behavior —Russel Lynes⟩

**odd·ness** *n* -ES [ME *oddenesse*, fr. *odde* odd + *-nesse* -ness] **1 :** the quality or state of being odd ⟨comical in their ~ —George Meredith⟩ **2 :** an instance of oddness ⟨were warned off by his ~*es* —Thomas Hughes⟩

**odd or even** *or* **odd and even** *or* **odds or evens** *n* **:** one of several games of chance or skill in which there is guessing or betting as to whether a certain number will be odd or even: as **a :** a game in which one player selects and holds an odd or even number of counters (as beans) and the other guesses which it is **b :** a game of betting on casts of dice or turns of a wheel **c :** a simplified form of fan-tan (sense 1) **d :** a mathematical game similar to nim in which the object is to take or leave an odd number of counters

**odd-pinnate** \'═¦═¦═\ *adj, of a compound leaf* **:** having leaflets on each side of the petiole and having a single leaflet at the tip of the petiole — see LEAF illustration

[1]**odds** \'ädz\ *n pl but sometimes sing in constr* [[1]*odd* + *-s*] **1 a** *archaic* **:** INEQUALITIES, DISPARITIES ⟨death looks down with nods and smiles and makes the ~ all even —W.M.Praed⟩ **b** *obs* **:** degree of unlikeness ⟨a manifest ~ between the bigness of the diameter —John Locke⟩ **2 a :** amount of difference by which one thing exceeds or falls short of another **:** amount in excess or defect ⟨won the election by considerable ~⟩ **b** (1) **:** difference favoring one of two opposed things **:** balance of advantage or weight of opposition ⟨the overwhelming ~ it affords the sportsman over bird and animal —Richard Jefferies⟩ ⟨one man's determination to win through despite heavy ~ —Robert Nicholas⟩ ⟨has managed to beat the ~ against him —Frank O'Leary⟩ ⟨would assume that the ~ were against him —Gilbert Highet⟩ (2) *archaic* **:** the state or fact of being in an advantageous position (3) **:** difference in the way of advantage or disadvantage or of benefit or detriment **:** significant difference **:** IMPORTANCE **:** advantage to be gained **:** PROFIT, BENEFIT, USE, PERCENTAGE ⟨it makes no ~ what you do⟩ ⟨she'll do it anyway, so what's the ~ of telling her not to⟩ ⟨it was little ~ what they sang, for they were all singing out of tune —Michael McLaverty⟩ ⟨what's the ~, if thinking so makes them happy —Flora Thompson⟩ **c** (1) **:** the probability that one thing is so rather than another or that one thing will happen rather than another **:** balance of probability **:** greater likelihood **:** CHANCES ⟨the night is clear and the ~ are that it'll stay that way until morning —H.D.Cooper⟩ ⟨the ~ are against it⟩ (2) **:** the ratio of probability that one thing is so rather than another or that one thing will happen rather than another ⟨it is even ~ which makes the more noise —Claudia Cassidy⟩ **3 :** DISAGREEMENT, DISSENSION, VARIANCE — now usu. used with *at* ⟨was at ~ with everything she represented —Cliff Farrell⟩ ⟨were at moral ~ among themselves —*Time*⟩ **4 a** (1) **:** an advantage (as a head start in a footrace) given to a less skilled or otherwise weaker competitor ⟨allowed ~ to the other team⟩ (2) **:** special favor **:** special treatment or consideration **:** PARTIALITY ⟨I ask no ~ of them, no more than I do of the dirt I walk on —H.C.Kimball⟩ **b** (1) **:** the advantage of an unequal wager that is granted by one making a bet to one accepting the bet and that is made proportionate to and is designed to equalize the assumed chances favoring the one or the other of the bettors ⟨offered him ~ of 3 to 1 but he refused to take the bet⟩ (2) **:** the ratio assumed to exist or actually arrived at (as by preliminary placement of bets) with regard to the probabilities of winning or losing and used as a basis for placing bets; *specif* **:** the ratio existing between the amount to be paid off for a winning bet and the amount of the bet placed ⟨the horse was running at ~ of 6 to 1⟩ — **by all odds** *also* **by long odds** *or* **by odds** *adv* **:** from every viewpoint **:** in every way **:** without question **:** far and away ⟨was *by all odds* the outstanding public question in the United States —*New Republic*⟩ ⟨is *by long odds* the most rigidly intellectual —G.W.Johnson⟩ ⟨social life centered in the palace of the governor, *by odds* the most pretentious and stately house in town —C.G.Bowers⟩

[2]**odds** \"\ *vt, past or past part* **oddsed**; *pres 3d sing* **odds** *dial Eng* **:** to make some adjustment in (as by altering)

**odds and ends** *n pl* **1 a :** small often trifling items that are usu. varied and often unrelated **:** miscellaneous things **:** miscellaneous articles ⟨*odds and ends* found lying around the attic⟩ ⟨threw some *odds and ends* into a suitcase⟩ **b :** miscellaneous small matters (as of business) to be attended to ⟨have some *odds and ends* to do tomorrow morning⟩ **2 :** miscellaneous

bits or fragments or scraps or remnants or leftovers ⟨*odds and ends* of information⟩ ⟨*odds and ends* of food⟩
**odds bobs** *or* **odds bob** *often cap O, var of* ODS-BOBS
**odds fish** *also* **odsfish** \'=;=\ *interj, often cap O* [gen. of ¹*od*, *odd* + *fish*] — a mild oath
¹**odds–on** \'=;=\ *adj* [*odds* + *on*, adv.] **1 a** : that is more likely to win or that is viewed as being more likely to win than not ⟨an *odds-on* favorite at the racetrack⟩ : having or viewed as having a better than even chance to win ⟨an *odds-on* political candidate⟩ **b** : that is viewed as being more likely to be so or more likely to turn out so than not ⟨the book is an *odds-on* best seller⟩ ⟨an *odds-on* candidate for reform school —*Newsweek*⟩ fairly sure : quite probable ⟨it's *odds-on* she did it —Ngaio Marsh⟩ **2** : that does not involve much risk : fairly good ⟨an *odds-on* chance of getting out⟩ : fairly safe : pretty sure ⟨if you were given the opportunity to make a fresh start, it is an *odds-on* bet you'd wind up in much the same sort of job —Stanley Frank⟩
²**odds–on** \"\ *n* -s : favorable odds — usu. used with *at* ⟨won the chief event and at *odds-on*⟩
**odd trick** *n* **1** : the first trick in excess of six won by the same side in whist **2** : each trick in excess of six won by declarer's side at bridge or by either side at whist or bridge-whist
**ode** \'ōd\ *n* -s [MF or LL; MF, fr. LL *ode, oda*, fr. Gk *aoidē* (Attic *ōidē*), fr. *aeidein* (Attic *aidein*) to sing; akin to OHG *farwāzan* to deny, Gk *audē* voice, sound, speech, Toch A & Toch B *wätk-* to command, Skt *vadati* he says, sings, plays music] **1** : a lyric poem usu. marked by particular exaltation of feeling and style and typically marked by varying length of line and by complexity of stanza forms **2 a** : one of nine scriptural canticles used in the morning office of the Eastern Church on certain days **b** : one of nine hymns of a canon (sense 10)
¹**-ode** \,ōd\ *n comb form* -s [F, fr. Gk *-ōdēs*, prob. fr. the stem of *ozein* to smell — more at ODOR] : thing that resembles ⟨plac*ode*⟩
²**-ode** \"\ *n comb form* -s [Gk *-odos*, fr. *hodos* — more at CEDE] **1** : way : path : road ⟨electr*ode*⟩ **2** : electrode ⟨di*ode*⟩
**-o·dea** \'ōdēə\ *n pl comb form* [NL, fr. Gk *-ōdēs* -ode] : animals belonging to or resembling — in names of higher taxa (as orders, suborders) ⟨Blatto*dea*⟩ ⟨Embi*odea*⟩
**odel** *var of* ODAL
**oden·se** \'ō<u>th</u>ənsə\ *adj, usu cap* [fr. *Odense*, Denmark] : of or from the city of Odense, Denmark : of the kind or style prevalent in Odense
**-o·des** \'ō(,)dēz\ *n comb form* [NL, fr. Gk *-ōdēs* -ode] : animal or plant resembling — in generic names ⟨Goni*odes*⟩
**odes·sa** \ō'desə\ *adj, usu cap* [fr. *Odessa*, U.S.S.R.] : of or from the city of Odessa, U.S.S.R. : of the kind or style prevalent in Odessa
**odes·san** \-sᵊn\ *n* -s *cap* [*Odessa* + E *-an*] : a native or resident of Odessa, U.S.S.R.
**ode·um** \ō'dēəm, 'ōdēəm\ *also* **ode·on** \'ōdē,än, -ən\ *n, pl* **ode·ums** \-mz\ *also* **odeons** \-nz\ *or* **odea** \-ēə\ [L & Gk; L *odeum*, fr. Gk *ōideion*, fr. *ōidē* song, ode — more at ODE] **1** : a relatively small typically circular roofed theater of ancient Greece and Rome used chiefly for competitions in music and poetry that were attended by the public **2** : a contemporary theater or concert hall
**odhal** *or* **odhall** *var of* ODAL
¹**od·ic** \'ädik, 'ōd-\ *adj* [ISV ²*od* + *-ic*] : of or relating to od
²**od·ic** \'ōdik\ *adj* [*ode* + *-ic*] : of, relating to, or forming an ode ⟨~ stanzas⟩
**-odies** *pl of* -ODY
**odif·er·ous** \(')ō¦dif(ə)rəs\ *adj* [ME *odeferus*, contr. of *odoriferous* — more at ODORIFEROUS] **1** : ODORIFEROUS ⟨the ~ principles of natural musk —*Swiss Industry & Trade*⟩ **2** : having a strong gamy often acrid odor ⟨the long ~ line of baggage camels —A.R.Griffin⟩
**odin·ic** \(')ō¦dinik\ *adj, usu cap* [*Odin*, the chief god of the ancient Scandinavians (fr. ON *Óthinn*) + E *-ic*] : of or relating to the god Odin
**odin·ism** \'ōdᵊn,izəm\ *n* -s *usu cap* [*Odin* + E *-ism*] : worship of Odin : the Odinic cult
**odin·ist** \-,nəst\ *n* -s *usu cap* [*Odin* + E *-ist*] : a worshiper of Odin
**odi·om·e·ter** \,ōdē'ämәd·ə(r)\ *n* [*odio-* (irreg. fr. *odor*) + *-meter*] : an olfactometer measuring the greatest dilution of an odorous vapor detectable by smell
**odi·ous** \'ōdēəs\ *adj* [ME, fr. MF *odieus*, fr. L *odiosus*, fr. *odium* + *-osus* -ous] : exciting or deserving odium : HATEFUL ⟨was in some mysterious way ~ and unlovable —Joseph Conrad⟩ ⟨the ~ feelings he must have —John Galsworthy⟩ ⟨his cruelty to such a charming woman made him ~ to her —Jane Austen⟩ — **odi·ous·ly** *adv* — **odi·ous·ness** *n* -ES
**od·ist** \'ōdəst\ *n* -s [*ode* + *-ist*] : a writer of odes
**odi·um** \'ōdēəm\ *n* -s [L; akin to L *odi* I hate, OE *atol* terrible, horrible, ON *atall* fierce, loathsome, Gk *odyssasthai* to be angry, Arm *ateam* I hate, and perh. to L *odor* — more at ODOR] **1 a** : the state or fact of being subjected to widespread or deep hatred and severe condemnation and often loathing or contempt usu. as a result of a despicable act or blameworthy situation ⟨these three artists had finally started losing their ~ —Janet Flanner⟩ **b** : hatred and condemnation often marked by loathing or contempt and usu. directed toward one guilty of or held responsible for some despicable act or situation : DETESTATION ⟨was compelled to . . . face the ~ —John Buchan⟩ ⟨heaps ~ on those responsible for the defeat —*Americas*⟩ ⟨would risk the ~ that would come from overthrowing him —*N.Y.Times*⟩ **2 a** (1) : the qualities of something (as a despicable act or situation) that excite hatred and condemnation and often loathing or contempt : HATEFULNESS ⟨has endeavored to remove that ~ —Elmer Davis⟩ (2) : a mark of disgrace or reproach : STIGMA ⟨the whole ~ fell on the girl —Margaret Mead⟩ ⟨shift the burden and the ~ of decision —G.B.Sansom⟩ **b** : great disrepute or infamy attached to something : OPPROBRIUM ⟨prizefighting had not yet escaped the ~ which clung to it throughout the bareknuckle days —F.R.Dulles⟩ ⟨no ~ attached to those who didn't go to football games —John Reed⟩ ⟨eliminate the ~ attaching to the word —William James⟩ **3** : an object of widespread or deep hatred and condemnation ⟨other ~*s* were abolished —Mark Harris⟩ **syn** see DISHONOR
**odium the·o·lo·gi·cum** \'=,==,thēə'läjəkəm\ *n* [NL, lit., theological hatred] : bitterness developed during or typical of controversy about religion and giving rise to an unyielding refusal to continue a discussion ⟨the *odium theologicum* which prevented any real understanding —*Times Lit. Supp.*⟩
**odly** *abbr* orderly
**odo·ben·i·dae** \,ōdō'benə,dē\ *n pl, cap* [NL, fr. *Odobenus*, type genus + *-idae*] : a small family of marine mammals (suborder Pinnipedia) that are related to the seals, have a thick tough nearly hairless skin underlaid by a thick layer of blubber and the upper canines enlarged into tusks, and include the walruses and extinct related forms
**odo·be·nus** \-'bēnəs\ *n, cap* [NL, fr. Gk *odōn* tooth + *bainein* to walk; fr. the belief that walruses use their tusks in sequence — more at TOOTH, COME] : the type genus of Odobenidae comprising the walruses
**odo·coi·le·us** \-'kōilēəs\ *n, cap* [NL, fr. Gk *odōn* tooth + *koilos* hollow — more at CAVE] : a genus including the Virginia deer, mule deer, black-tailed deer, and related American species
**odo·graph** \'ōdə,graf\ *n* [*odo-* (as in *odometer*) + *-graph*] **1** : an instrument for automatically plotting the course and distance traveled by a vehicle **2** : a device for recording the length and rapidity of stride and the number of steps taken by a walker
**odom·e·ter** \ō'dämәd·ə(r)\ *n* [F *odomètre*, modif. of Gk *hodometron, hodometros* instrument for measuring distance, fr. *hodos* way, road + *metron* measure — more at CEDE, METER] **1** : an instrument attached to a vehicle to measure the distance traversed ⟨some speedometers are equipped with a trip ~ which registers distance traveled up to 999.9 miles —Ernest Venk & William Landon⟩ **2** : a wheel used by surveyors that registers the miles and rods traversed
**-o·don** \ə,dän, ō,-, -,dən\ *n comb form* -s [NL, fr. Gk *odōn* tooth — more at TOOTH] : animal having teeth of a (specified) kind — chiefly in the names of genera in zoology ⟨Iguan*odon*⟩ ⟨mast*odon*⟩
**odo·na·ta** \,ōdᵊn'ād·ə, -'äd·ə; ō'dänəd·ə\ *n pl, cap* [NL, irreg. fr. Gk *odōn* tooth + NL *-ata*] : an order of insects containing the dragonflies and damselflies and characterized by aquatic larvae that are nymphs or naiads and by predaciousness in both adult and larval forms
¹**odo·nate** \'ōdᵊn,āt, -,ət\ *n* -s *sometimes cap* [NL *Odonata*] : an insect of the order Odonata ⟨nymphs of certain of the larger ~*s* . . . capture and eat small fish —*Biol. Abstracts*⟩
²**odonate** \"\ *adj* : of or relating to the Odonata ⟨~ larvae⟩ ⟨~ nymphs⟩ ⟨~ life⟩
**odo·na·tol·o·gist** \,ōdᵊnə'täləjəst\ *n* -s : a specialist in odonatology
**odo·na·tol·o·gy** \-jē\ *n* -ES [NL *Odonata* + E *-o-* + *-logy*] : the study of the Odonata
**odont-** *or* **odonto-** *comb form* [F, fr. Gk, fr. *odont-, odōn* — more at TOOTH] : tooth ⟨*odont*itis⟩ ⟨*odonto*cete⟩ ⟨*odonto*geny⟩ ⟨*odonto*logy⟩ ⟨*odonto*rrhagia⟩
**-o·dont** \ə,dänt, ō,d-\ *adj comb form* [Gk *odont-, odōn* tooth] : having or being teeth of a (specified) nature ⟨heter*odont*⟩ ⟨loph*odont*⟩
**-o·don·ta** \ə'däntə, ō,d-\ *n comb form, pl* **-odonta** [NL, fr. Gk *odont-, odōn* tooth] : animal or animals having teeth of a (specified) nature — in names of zoological taxa ⟨Bun*odonta*⟩ ⟨Creo*donta*⟩ ⟨Heter*odonta*⟩ ⟨Labyrinth*odonta*⟩
**odon·tal·gia** \,ō,dän'talj(ē)ə\ *n* -s [NL, fr. Gk *odontalgia*, fr. *odont-* + *-algia* -algia] : TOOTHACHE
**odon·tal·gic** \¦ō,dän¦taljik\ *adj* [F *odontalgique*, fr. *odontalgie* odontalgia (fr. Gk *odontalgia*) + *-ique* -ic] : of or relating to toothache
**odon·tas·pid·i·dae** \(,)ō,dän·,ta'spidə,dē\ *also* **odon·tas·pi·dae** \,ō,dän·'taspə,dē\ [NL, fr. *Odontaspid-*, *Odontaspis* + *-idae*] *syn of* CARCHARIIDAE
**odon·tas·pis** \,ō,dän·'taspəs\ [NL, fr. *odont-* + Gk *aspis* shield — more at ASPID-] *syn of* CARCHARIAS
**-o·don·tes** \ə'dän·,tēz, ō'd-\ *n comb form, pl* **-odontes** [NL, fr. Gk *odontes*, pl. of *odōn* tooth — more at TOOTH] : animal or animals having teeth of a (specified) nature — in names of zoological taxa ⟨Gymn*odontes*⟩ ⟨Pri*odontes*⟩
**odon·tia** \ō'dänch(ē)ə\ *n, cap* [NL, fr. *odont-* + *-ia*; fr. its conical spines] : a widely distributed genus of fungi (family Hydnaceae) including some that are pathogens of economic plants — see STELLATE-CRYSTAL FUNGUS
¹**-o·don·tia** \ə'dänch(ē)ə, ō'd-\ *n comb form, pl* **-odontia** [NL, fr. Gk *odont-, odōn* tooth] : animal or animals having teeth of a (specified) nature — in taxonomic names in zoology ⟨An*omodontia*⟩ ⟨Apl*odontia*⟩ ⟨Dicyn*odontia*⟩
²**-odontia** \"\ *n comb form* -s [NL, fr. *odont-* + *-ia*] : form, condition, or mode of treatment of the teeth ⟨macr*odontia*⟩ ⟨sapr*odontia*⟩ ⟨orth*odontia*⟩ — compare -ODONT
**odon·ti·a·sis** \,ō,dän·'tīəsəs\ *n, pl* **odontia·ses** \-,sēz\ [NL, fr. Gk *odontian* to cut teeth (fr. *odont-, odōn* tooth) + NL *-sis*] : cutting of the teeth : TEETHING
**-odonties** *pl of* -ODONTY
**odon·ti·tis** \,ō,dän·'tīd·əs\ *n, pl* **odon·tit·i·des** \-'tid·ə,dēz\ [NL, fr. *odont-* + *-itis*] : inflammation of a tooth
**odon·to·blast** \ō'däntə,blast\ *n* [ISV *odont-* + *-blast*] : one of the elongated radially arranged outer cells of the dental pulp that secrete the dentin of a tooth — **odon·to·blas·tic** \-¦==¦blastik\ *adj*
**odon·to·cer·i·dae** \=,==sera,dē\ *n pl, cap* [NL, fr. *Odontocera*, type genus (fr. *odont-* + Gk *keras* horn) + NL *-idae* — more at HORN] : a small family of widely distributed caddis flies
¹**odon·to·ce·te** \ō,däntə'sē,tē\ [NL, fr. *odont-* + L *cete*, pl. of *cetus* whale] *syn of* ODONTOCETI
²**odon·to·cete** \'=,==,sēt\ *also* **odon·to·ce·tous** \=¦==¦sēd·əs\ *adj* : of or relating to the Odontoceti
**odon·to·ce·ti** \=,=='sē,tī\ *n pl, cap* [NL, fr. *odont-* + L *ceti*, pl. of *cetus* whale — more at CETE] : a suborder of Cetacea comprising the toothed whales — compare MYSTICETI
**odon·to·clast** \='==,klast\ *n* -s [*odont-* + *-clast*] : one of the large multinucleate cells that are active during the absorption of the roots of the milk teeth
**odon·to·gen·ic** \=¦==¦jenik\ *adj* [*odont-* + *-genic*] **1** : forming or capable of forming teeth ⟨~ tissues⟩ **2** : containing or arising from odontogenic tissues ⟨an ~ tumor⟩
**odon·to·glos·sum** \=,=='gläsəm, -lòs-\ *n* [NL, fr. *odont-* + *-glossum* (fr. Gk *glōssa* tongue) — more at GLOSS] **1** *cap* : a large genus of showy tropical American epiphytic orchids having flowers with the tip not spurred and distinct from the column and including many that are cultivated and of great diversity in form and color **2** -s : any plant of the genus *Odontoglossum*
**odon·tog·na·thae** \,=,dän·'tägnə,thē\ *n pl, cap* [NL, fr. *odont-* + *-gnathae*] : a superorder of extinct toothed birds (subclass Neornithes) — **odon·tog·na·thous** \¦=,=;==thəs\ *also* **odon·to·gnath·ic** \¦ō,dän,tō¦nathik\ *adj*
**odon·to·graph** \ō'däntə,graf\ *n* [ISV *odont-* + *-graph*] : an instrument for marking or laying off the outlines of gear teeth
**odon·tog·ra·phy** \,ō,dän·'tägrəfē\ *n* -ES [*odont-* + *-graphy*] : scientific description of the teeth (as of their gross structure); *also* : a treatise on this subject
¹**odon·toid** \ō'dän·,tȯid\ *adj* [Gk *odontoeidēs*, fr. *odont-* + *-oeidēs* -oid] **1** : having the form of a tooth : TOOTHLIKE **2** : of or relating to the odontoid process
²**odontoid** \"\ *n* -s : ODONTOID PROCESS
**odontoid ligament** *n* : any of the three ligaments that pass from the odontoid process to the margins of the foramen magnum
**odontoid process** *n* : a toothlike process that projects from the anterior end of the centrum of the axis vertebra, serves as a pivot on which the atlas vertebra rotates, and is morphologically the centrum of the atlas though detached from that vertebra and more or less perfectly united with the next one behind
**odon·tol·cae** \,ō,dän·'täl,sē\ *n pl, cap* [NL, fr. *odont-* + *-olcae* (fr. Gk *holkos, holkē* furrow) — more at SULCUS] *in some classifications* : a superorder of Aves including *Hesperornis* and related genera of extinct aquatic birds with teeth set in a groove
**odon·to·lite** \ō'däntᵊl,īt\ *n* -s [F, fr. *odont-* + *-lite*] : a mineral consisting of fossil bone or tooth made bright blue by phosphate of iron — called also *bone turquoise, fossil turquoise*
**odon·tol·o·gist** \,ō,dän·'täləjəst, ,ä,d-\ *n* -s : a specialist in odontology
**odon·tol·o·gy** \-jē, -ji\ *n* -ES [F *odontologie*, fr. *odont-* + *-logie* -logy] : a science that treats of the teeth, their structure and development, and their diseases
**odon·to·lox·ia** \ō,däntə'läksēə\ *n* -s [NL, fr. *odont-* + Gk *loxos* slanting, crosswise + NL *-ia*] : irregularity of the teeth
**odon·to·ma** \,ō,dän·'tōmə, ,ä,d-\ *n, pl* **odonto·mas** \-məz\ *also* **odontoma·ta** \-məd·ə\ [NL, fr. *odont-* + *-oma*] : a tumor originating from a tooth and containing dental tissue (as enamel, dentin, cementum)
**odon·tom·e·ter** \-'tämәd·ə(r)\ *n* [*odont-* + *-meter*] : ODONTOGRAPH
**odon·toph·o·ral** \,ō,dän·¦täf(ə)rəl\ *also* **odon·toph·o·rine** \-fə,rīn, -,rən\ *adj* : of or relating to an odontophore
**odon·to·phore** \ō'däntə,fō(ə)r\ *n* -s [ISV *odont-* + *-phore*] **1** : a usu. more or less protrusible structure in the mouths of most mollusks except the bivalves that supports the radula **2** : RADULA
**odon·toph·o·rous** \¦=,dän·¦täf(ə)rəs\ *adj* : having an odontophore
**odon·toph·o·rus** \,ō,dän·'täf(ə)rəs\ *n, cap* [NL, fr. *odont-* + *-phorus*] : a genus of Central and South American crested partridges that resemble quails and are placed in a distinct subfamily of Phasianidae or sometimes isolated in a distinct family
**odon·top·te·ris** \,ō,dän·'täptərəs\ *n, cap* [NL, fr. *odont-* + Gk *pteris* fern; akin to Gk *pteron* wing, feather — more at FEATHER] : a genus of fossil seed ferns found in the coal measures of the Carboniferous that have pinnatifid fronds with indistinct midribs and veins not forming a network
**odon·top·ter·yx** \-tə(,)riks\ *n, cap* [NL, fr. *odont-* + *-pteryx*] : a genus of serrate-jawed totipalmate birds from the Lower Eocene of England
**odon·to·rhyn·chous** \ō¦däntə¦riŋkəs\ *adj* [*odont-* + *rhynch-* + *-ous*] : LAMELLIROSTRAL
**odon·tor·mae** \,ō,dän·'tȯr(,)mē\ *n pl, cap* [NL, alter. of *Odontotormae*] *in some classifications* : a higher group coextensive with the family Ichthyornithidae
**odon·tor·ni·thes** \,ō,dän·'tȯrnə,thēz, -,tȯr'nī(,)thēz\ *n pl, cap* [NL, fr. *odont-* + Gk *ornithes*, pl. of *ornis* bird — more at ERNE] *in some classifications* : a group of Mesozoic toothed birds comprising the Odontolcae and the Odontormae — **odon·tor·nith·ic** \¦=,dän,tȯr¦nithik\ *adj*
**odon·to·sis** \,ō,dän·'tōsəs, ,ä,d-\ *n, pl* **odonto·ses** \-,sēz\ [NL, fr. *odont-* + *-sis*] : DENTITION
**odon·to·syl·lis** \,ō,dän·,tō+\ *n, cap* [NL, fr. *odont-* + *Syllis*] : a genus of polychaete worms (family Syllidae) that are bioluminescent during the breeding period
**odon·tot·o·my** \,ō,dän·'täd·əmē\ *n* -ES [*odont-* + *-tomy*] : the operation of cutting into a tooth
**odon·to·tor·mae** \ō,dän·,tō'tȯr(,)mē\ *n pl, cap* [NL, fr. *odont-* + *-tormae* (fr. Gk *tormos* socket) — more at TERM] *syn of* ODONTORMAE
**-o·don·ty** \ə,däntē, ō,d-, -ti\ *n comb form* -ES [*odont-* + *-y*] : condition of having a (specified) type of tooth formation — chiefly in terms employed in anthropometry ⟨selen*odonty*⟩
**odor** \'ōdə(r)\ *n* -s *see -or in Explan Notes* [ME *odour*, fr. OF, fr. L *odor*; akin to L *olēre* to smell, Gk *ozein* to smell, *odmē, osmē* smell, odor, Lith *uosti* to smell, and perh. to Sw *os* odor, ill-smelling gas] **1 a** : a quality of something that affects the sense of smell : SCENT, FRAGRANCE, AROMA ⟨one . . . system classifies all ~*s* according to six fundamental sensations or combinations of sensations: namely, spicy, flowery, fruity, resinous, foul and burnt —F.J.Gruber⟩ **b** : one of a class of sensations resulting from adequate chemical stimulation of the receptors for the sense of smell : SMELL ⟨emit an ~⟩ ⟨a sweet ~⟩ ⟨a disagreeable ~⟩ ⟨the ~ of a bakery —William Black⟩ ⟨the penetrating, acid ~ of hardwood smoke —Rufus Jarman⟩ ⟨a new ~ . . . the sweet, intense smell of overripe fruit —William Beebe⟩ **2 a** : a characteristic or predominant quality : FLAVOR ⟨the ~ of earnestness is not good for melodrama —E.R.Bentley⟩ ⟨an ~ of . . . unsavory politics —G.F. Cronkhite⟩ ⟨a faint ~ of romance —*Nation*⟩ **b** : REPUTE, ESTIMATION ⟨another . . . committee in equally bad ~ as regards the propriety of its procedures —R.D.Leigh⟩ **3** *archaic* : something (as incense, spice, a flower) that emits a sweet or pleasing scent : PERFUME ⟨throw in . . . all sorts of spices and sweet ~*s* —James Maxwell⟩ **syn** see SMELL
¹**odor·ant** \'ōdərənt\ *adj* [ME *odoraunt*, fr. MF *odorant*, fr. L *odorant-, odorans*, pres. part. of *odorare* to perfume, fr. *odor*, n.] : ODOROUS, ODORIFEROUS
²**odorant** \"\ *n* -s : an odorous substance ⟨~*s* used as warning agents in natural gas⟩
**odor·ate** \-rət\ *adj* [L *odoratus*, past part. of *odorare*] *archaic* : SCENTED
**odored** \'ōdə(r)d\ *adj* : having an odor : SCENTED — used chiefly in combination ⟨ill-*odored*⟩
**odo·ri** \ō'dȯr,ē\ *n* -s [Jap, dancing, dance] : any lively Japanese folk or theater dance characterized by rapid footwork — distinguished from *mai*
**odor·if·er·ous** \¦ōdə¦rif(ə)rəs\ *adj* [L *odorifer* odoriferous (fr. *odor* + *-i-* + *-fer* -ferous) + E *-ous* — more at ODOR] **1** : bearing or yielding an odor : ODOROUS ⟨the constituents of perfumes . . . the vehicle or solvent, the fixative, and the ~ elements —R.N.Shreve⟩ : as **a** : sweet-smelling : FRAGRANT, BALMY ⟨~ flowers⟩ ⟨~ spices⟩ **b** : ill-smelling : MALODOROUS ⟨~ stockyards⟩ ⟨~ fumes⟩ **2** : morally offensive ⟨~ legislation⟩ — **odor·if·er·ous·ly** *adv* — **odor·if·er·ous·ness** *n* -ES
**odor·im·e·ter** \,ōdə'rimәd·ə(r)\ *n* [*odor* + *-i-* + *-meter*] : ODOROMETER
**odor·im·e·try** \-mə·trē\ *n* -ES [ISV *odor* + *-i-* + *-metry*] : the measurement of the intensity of odors
**odor·i·phore** \ō'dȯrə,fō(ə)r\ *n* -s [*odor* + *-i-* + *-phore*] : OSMOPHORE
**odor·i·vec·tor** \-,vektə(r)\ *n* [*odor* + *-i-* + L *vector* bearer — more at VECTOR] : a substance that gives rise to an odor
**odor·iza·tion** \,ōdərə'zāshən, -,rī'z-\ *n* -s : the act or process of odorizing ⟨*reodorization* of rubber and leather articles —A.C.Morrison⟩; *esp* : the act or process of odorizing gas ⟨odor tests should be made on the gas at the point of ~ —*Chem. Abstracts*⟩
**odor·ize** \'ōdə,rīz\ *vt* -ED/-ING/-S [*odor* + *-ize*] : to make odorous : SCENT, PERFUME ⟨~ a room⟩ ⟨~ industrial products to mask bad smells⟩; *specif* : to add a characteristic detectable odor to (a relatively odorless domestic fuel gas) as a safety measure ⟨some city and state utility regulatory bodies have made it mandatory to ~ natural, propane, and butane gases supplied in their territories —H.A.Gollamer⟩
**odor·less** \'ōdə(r)ləs\ *adj* : lacking an odor : INODOROUS, SCENTLESS ⟨~ gas⟩ ⟨~ flowers⟩
**odorless phosphate** *n* : BASIC SLAG
**odor of sanctity** [trans. of ML *odor sanctitatis*] **1** : a fragrance held to proceed from the person, clothing, or domicile of a saint during life or after death ⟨died in the *odor of sanctity* and . . . was canonized —Charles Speroni⟩ **2 a** : an appearance of or reputation for goodness and righteousness ⟨the *odor of sanctity* that seemed to cling about his every utterance —Kenneth Roberts⟩ **b** : SANCTIMONIOUSNESS
**odor·om·e·ter** \,ōdə'rämәd·ə(r)\ *n* [*odor* + *-o-* + *-meter*] : an instrument for measuring the intensity of odors of substances in varying concentrations in air — compare OSMOSCOPE
**odor·o·phore** \ō'dȯrə,fō(ə)r\ *n* -s [*odor* + *-o-* + *-phore*] : a substance that produces an odor : ODORANT
**odor·ous** \'ōdərəs\ *adj* [L *odorus*, fr. *odor*, n.] : having or emitting an odor : SCENTED ⟨~ materials . . . captured by the mucous lining of the nostrils —F.A.Geldard⟩: as **a** : FRAGRANT ⟨the ~ air of the orchard —H.W.Longfellow⟩ ⟨~ gums from the East —Oscar Wilde⟩ ⟨fresh, moist, ~ bread —Della Lutes⟩ **b** : MALODOROUS ⟨grievances of the men . . . ~ salt junk and weevily hardtack —H.A.Chippendale⟩ — **odor·ous·ly** *adv*
**odorous house ant** *or* **odorous ant** *n* : a common No. American ant (*Tapinoma sessile*) that emits a characteristic odor and that frequently invades buildings
**odors** *pl of* ODOR
**odour** \'ōdə(r)\ *chiefly Brit var of* ODOR
**ods** *pl of* OD
**ODs** *pl of* OD
**ods-bobs** \(')ädz'bäbz\ *interj, often cap* [prob. euphemism for *God's body*] *archaic* — a mild oath
**ods·bod·i·kins** \(')ädz'bädəkənz, -dēk-\ *also* **ods bodkins** \-'bädkənz\ *interj, often cap* [prob. euphemism for *God's bodykins*] *archaic* — a mild oath
**ods·bud** \-'bəd\ *also* **od's–buds** *interj, often cap* [euphemism for *God's blood*] *archaic* — a mild oath
**odsfish** *often cap, var of* ODDS FISH
**od·so** \'äd¦sō\ *interj, sometimes cap* [euphemism for obs. *Godso*, by folk etymology fr. It *cazzo*, lit., penis — more at CATSO] — used typically as a mild oath or as an expression of surprise
**odum** \ō'düm\ *n* -s [native name in western Africa] : IROKO
**-o·dus** \ədəs\ *n comb form* [NL *-odont-, -odus*, fr. Gk *odont-, odous* tooth — more at TOOTH] : animal having teeth of a (specified) kind — in generic names in zoology ⟨Gyr*odus*⟩
**-o·dy** \,ōdē, -di\ *n comb form* -ES [Gk *-ōdia*, fr. *-ōdēs* -ode + *-ia* -y] : process of becoming like : metamorphosis into (something specified) — chiefly in botanical terms ⟨sepal*ody*⟩
**od·yl** *or* **od·yle** \'äd°l, 'ōd-\ *n* -s [ISV ²*od* + Gk *hylē* forest, wood, material — more at -YL] : OD
**odyl·ic** \(')ō¦dilik\ *adj* : of or relating to odyl
**odylic force** *n* : OD
**od·yl·ism** \'äd°l,izəm, 'ōd-\ *n* -s : the theory of od
**od·y·ne·rus** \,ädə'nīrəs\ *n, cap* [NL, fr. Gk *odynēros* painful, fr. *odynē* pain; akin to Gk (Homeric) *edmenai* to eat — more at EAT] : a genus of solitary wasps having a very short abdominal peduncle and often resembling yellow jackets in coloration
**-o·dyn·ia** \ə'dinēə, ō'd-\ *n comb form* -s [NL, fr. Gk, state of pain, fr. *odynē* pain + *-ia* -y] : pain ⟨crym*odynia*⟩ ⟨neur*odynia*⟩ ⟨om*odynia*⟩ — **-odyn·ic** \(')ō¦dinik, ə'd-\ *adj comb form*
**od·ys·se·an** \¦ädə¦sēən\ *adj, usu cap* [*Odyssey* + E *-an*] : of, relating to, or having the characteristics of Homer's *Odyssey*
**od·ys·sey** \'ädəsē, -si\ *n* -s [fr. the *Odyssey*, long epic poem recounting the adventures of Odysseus on his way home from the siege of Troy and attributed to Homer, Greek poet who prob. lived *ab* 8th cent. B.C., fr. L *Odyssea*, fr. Gk *Odysseia*, fr. *Odysseus*, its hero + Gk *-ia* -y] **1** : a long wandering : a series of adventurous journeys usu. marked by many changes

of fortune ⟨the journey of these unwilling adventurers ... is certainly one of the strangest ~s in modern fiction —James Stern⟩ ⟨his ~ up and down the land as a journeyman printer —W.A.White⟩ ⟨the ~ of man through time —*Think*⟩ **2 :** an extensive intellectual or spiritual wandering or quest ⟨everyone's philosophic ~ —Anthony Nemetz⟩ ⟨the course of his political ~ —Sidney Hook⟩ ⟨the random and voracious reading ~s of your childhood —J.H.Burns⟩ ⟨the emotional ~ of an intelligent and romantic young girl —*Times Lit. Supp.*⟩ ⟨less a historical novel than the story of a spiritual ~ —Ann F. Wolfe⟩

**od·zooks** \äd'zu̇ks, -üks\ *also* **od·zook·ers** \-kə(r)z\ *interj, sometimes cap* [*od* (euphemism for *God*) + *-zooks* or *-zookers* (origin unknown)] — a mild oath

**oe** \'ō\ *n* -s [Faroese *óthi*, fr. *óthur* mad, furious, fr. ON *ōthr* — more at WOOD] **:** a violent whirlwind off the Faroe islands

**OE** *abbr* **1** Old English **2** *often not cap* omissions excepted

**oec-** *or* **oeco-** — see EC-

**oe·can·thus** \ē'kan(t)thəs\ *n, cap* [NL, fr. ²*ec-* + *-anthus*] **:** a genus of Orthoptera that includes the tree crickets

**-oe·cia** \'ēs(h)ēə\ *n pl comb form* [NL, fr. Gk *oikia* building, house, dwelling, fr. *oikos* house + *-ia* -y — more at VICINITY] **:** plants of a (specified) type — in names of botanical taxa ⟨*Monoecia*⟩ ⟨*Dioecia*⟩

**oe·ci·a·cus** \ē'sīəkəs\ *n, cap* [NL, fr. Gk *oikiakos* member of a household, fr. *oikiakos* of a house, fr. *oikia* house] **:** a genus of bugs related to the bedbugs and including a parasite (*O. vicarius*) of swallows

**oe·cist** \'ēsəst\ *or* **oe·kist** \-kəst\ *n* -s [Gk *oikistēs*, fr. *oikos* house + *-istēs* -ist] **:** COLONIZER

**oe·ci·um** \'ēs(h)ēəm\ *n, pl* **oe·cia** \-s(h)ēə\ [NL, fr. ²*ec-* + *-ium*] **:** OVICELL

**oecoid** *var of* ECOID

**oecology** *var of* ECOLOGY

**oe·con·o·mus** \ē'känəməs\ *n, pl* **oecono·mi** \-,mī\ [LL, fr. Gk *oikonomos* steward — more at ECONOMY] **:** a steward or manager of the temporalities of a diocese, college, or religious society

¹**oe·coph·o·rid** \ē'käfərəd\ *adj* [NL *Oecophoridae*] **:** of or relating to the Oecophoridae

²**oecophorid** \"\ *n* -s **:** a moth of the family Oecophoridae

**oe·co·phor·i·dae** \,ēkə'fȯrə,dē, fär-\ *n pl, cap* [NL, fr. *Oecophora*, type genus (fr. ²*ec-* + *-phora*) + *-idae*] **:** a large family of small mostly inconspicuous moths whose larvae feed on leaves and flowers

**oecumenical** *var of* ECUMENICAL

**oe·cus** \'ēkəs\ *n, pl* **oe·ci** \'ē,sī\ [L, fr. Gk *oikos* house — more at VICINITY] **:** an apartment, room, or hall in an ancient Roman dwelling house

**oedema** *var of* EDEMA

¹**oe·de·me·rid** \,ēdə'mirəd\ *adj* [NL *Oedemeridae*] **:** of or relating to the Oedemeridae

²**oedemerid** \"\ *n* -s [NL *Oedemeridae*] **:** a beetle of the family Oedemeridae

**oe·de·mer·i·dae** \,=='merə,dē\ *n pl, cap* [NL, fr. *Oedemera*, type genus (fr. Gk *oidein* to swell + *mēros* thigh) + NL *-idae* — more at EDEMA, MEMBER] **:** a family of soft-bodied elongate beetles that have heteromerous tarsi, usu. strikingly colored adults which frequent flowers, and larvae which feed on decaying wood and sometimes are injurious to damp timbers of wharves, bridges, and mines

**oe·dic·ne·mus** \,ē(,)dik'nēməs\ [NL, *oidi-* (fr. Gk *oidein* to swell) + *-cnemus* (fr. Gk *knēmē* shinbone) — more at HAM] *syn of* BURHINUS

**oed·i·pal** \'edəpəl, 'ēd-\ *adj, often cap* [*Oedipus* (*complex*) + *-al*] **:** of, relating to, characterized by, or resulting from the Oedipus complex

**oed·i·pe·an** \,==='pēən\ *adj, usu cap* [*Oedipus*, Theban hero + E *-ean*] **:** of or relating to Oedipus or the Oedipus complex

**oed·i·pus** \'==pəs\ *adj, usu cap* [*Oedipus* (*complex*)] **:** OEDIPAL

**oedipus complex** *also* **oedipus** \"\ *n, pl* **oedipus complexes** *also* **oedipuses** *usu cap O* [G *Ödipuskomplex*, after *Ödipus* (Oedipus), Theban hero of ancient Greek legend who slew his father and married his mother, fr. L *Oedipus*, fr. Gk *Oidipous*] **1 :** the positive esp. libidinal feelings that a child develops usu. between the ages of three and six toward the parent of the opposite sex and that are largely repressed because of the fear of retaliation by the parent of the same sex who is viewed as a rival and toward whom unconscious hostility is generated — used esp. of the male child; see ELECTRA COMPLEX **2 :** the unresolved oedipal feelings persisting into adult life that are conceived as a source of personality disorder

**oe·do·go·ni·a·ce·ae** \,ēdə,gōnē'āsē,ē\ *n pl, cap* [NL *Oedogonium*, type genus + *-aceae*] **:** a family (usu. coextensive with the order Oedogoniales but sometimes placed in Chaetophorales) of filamentous green algae having a characteristic method of growth that gives rise to series of narrow cells at various intervals in the filaments and developing large zoospores with a crown of cilia and also oogonia and antheridia that are sometimes on the same plant but frequently on separate plants with the male plants being often of only a few cells and attached to the female filaments — **oe·do·go·ni·a·ceous** \;==;==;'āshəs\ *adj*

**oe·do·go·ni·a·les** \-'ā(,)lēz\ *n pl, cap* [NL, fr. *Oedogonium* + *-ales*] **:** an order of simple or branched filamentous freshwater green algae (class Chlorophyceae) with zoospores having many flagella and oogamous reproduction

**oe·do·go·ni·um** \,=='gōnēəm\ *n, cap* [NL, fr. Gk *oidos* swelling, tumor + *gonos* offspring, seed + NL *-ium* — more at ATTER, GON-] **:** a genus (the type of the family Oedogoniaceae) of freshwater green algae that have long unbranched filaments usu. free-floating when mature but attached by special basal cells when young

**oeil-de-boeuf** \,ərdə'bə(r)f, ,ɔ̄d-, ,əid-, ,äd-, -bɔ̄f, œydəbœf\ *n, pl* **oeils-de-boeuf** \"\ [F, lit., eye of an ox] **:** a circular or oval window

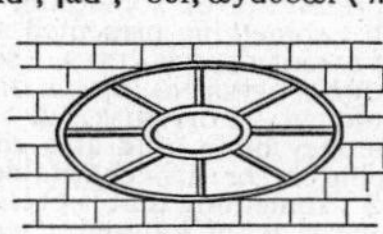
oeil-de-boeuf

**oeil·lade** \,ə(r)'yäd, ɔ̄'y-,əi'y-,ā'y-, œ'yäd\ *n, pl* **oeillades** \-d(z)\ [F, fr. MF, fr. *oeil* eye (fr. L *oculus* eye) + *-ade* — more at EYE] **:** a glance of the eye; *esp* **:** OGLE

**oekist** *var of* OECIST

**oen-** *or* **oeno-** *also* **en-** *or* **eno-** *comb form* [L *oen-*, *oeno-*, fr. Gk *oin-*, *oino-*, fr. *oinos* — more at WINE] **:** wine ⟨*oenin*⟩ ⟨*oenology*⟩ ⟨*oenopoetic*⟩

**oenanthaldehyde** *var of* ENANTHALDEHYDE

**oenanthate** *var of* ENANTHATE

¹**oe·nan·the** \ē'nan(,)thē\ *n, cap* [NL, fr. L, a kind of dropwort, a bird (perh. the wheatear), fr. Gk *oinanthē*, fr. *oin-* oen- + *anthē* bloom, blossom, fr. *anthos* flower — more at ANTHOLOGY] **:** a genus of Old World herbs (family Umbelliferae) having compound umbels of white flowers without carpophores — see WATER DROPWORT

²**oenanthe** \"\ *n, cap* [NL, fr. L, a bird (perh. the wheatear)] **:** a small genus of Old World passerine birds comprising the wheatears

¹**oe·nan·thic acid** \(')ē;nan(t)thik-\ *n* [ISV *oenanth-* (fr. L *oenanthe* wild grape) + *-ic* — more at ENANTHIC ACID] **:** an acid or mixture of acids obtained by hydrolysis of an oenanthic ester

²**oenanthic acid** *var of* ENANTHIC ACID

**oenanthic ester** *also* **oenanthic ether** *n* **1 :** an oily liquid that is obtained in the distillation of wine and that is held to be responsible for the flavor characteristic of wines in general and to consist of a mixture of esters **2 :** the ethyl ester of enanthic acid

**oe·ne·is** \ē'nēəs\ *n, cap* [NL] **:** a genus of alpine and arctic butterflies belonging to the family Satyridae

**oe·nin** *also* **enin** \'ēnən\ *n* -s [ISV *oen-* + *-in*; prob. orig. formed as G *önin*] **:** an anthocyanin pigment occurring in the skin of the blue grape and forming a dark red or reddish brown crystalline chloride $C_{23}H_{25}ClO_{12}$

**oe·no·car·pus** \,ēnə'kärpəs\ *n, cap* [NL, fr. *oen-* + *-carpus*] **:** a genus of So. American pinnate-leaved palms that have a slender spadix which resembles a broom, a woody double caducous spathe, and edible black or purplish oily fruit — see BACABA

**oe·noch·oe** \ē'näkə(,)wē\ *also* **oi·noch·oe** \ȯi'n-\ *n, pl* **oenochoes** \-ə,wēz\ *or* **oenocho·ae** \-ə,wē\ [Gk *oinochoē*, fr. *oino-* oen- + *choē* action of pouring out, drink offering, fr. *chein* to pour — more at FOUND] **:** an ancient Greek wine pitcher or jug usu. with a trefoil-shaped mouth

oenochoe

**oe·no·cyte** \'ēnə,sīt\ *n* -s [ISV *oen-* + *-cyte*] **:** one of the large straw-colored cells that are segmentally arranged in connection with the fat bodies and tracheae of most insects and that may have important secretory functions — **oe·no·cyt·ic** \;==;sid·ik\ *adj*

**oe·no·cy·toid** \,==='sī,tȯid\ *n* -s [*oenocyte* + *-oid*] **:** a large blood cell resembling an oenocyte and occurring in insects

**oe·nol·o·gist** \ē'näləjəst\ *n* -s **1 :** FERMENTOLOGIST **2 :** one versed in enology

**oenology** *var of* ENOLOGY

**oe·no·mel** \'ēnə,mel\ *n* -s [LL *oenomeli*, fr. Gk *oinomeli*, fr. *oino-* oen- + *meli* honey — more at MELLIFLUOUS] **1 :** an ancient Greek beverage of wine and honey **2 :** something resembling oenomel ⟨memories to my thinking make a better ~ —Elizabeth B. Browning⟩

**oe·no·phile** \-,fīl\ *or* **oe·noph·i·list** \ē'näfələst\ *n* -s [*oen-* + *-phile*, *-philist*] **:** a lover or connoisseur of wine

**oe·no·thera** \,ēnə'thirə, ē'näthərə\ *n, cap* [NL, fr. L *oenothera*, *onothera*, a plant of the genus *Epilobium*, fr. Gk *oinothēras*, *onothēras*] **:** a genus of mostly No. American annual or biennial herbs (family Onagraceae) having usu. nocturnal yellow flowers with erect buds and terete seeds in two rows in a capsule — see EVENING PRIMROSE, KNEIFFIA

**oe·no·therapy** \,ēnə+\ *n* [*oen-* + *therapy*] **:** a use of wine for therapeutic purposes

¹**o'er** \'ō(ə)r, 'ȯə, 'ō(ə)r, 'ō(ə)\ *adv* [by contr.] **:** OVER

²**o'er** \"\ *prep* [by contr.] **:** OVER

**oer·li·kon** \'ərlə,kän\ *n* -s *usu cap* [fr. *Oerlikon*, suburb of Zurich, Switzerland, noted for its gun manufacturing] **:** any of several automatic aircraft or antiaircraft cannon shooting 20 millimeter greased ammunition

**oer·sted** \'ər,sted\ *n* -s [after Hans Christian *Oersted* †1851 Dan. physicist] **:** the cgs electromagnetic unit of magnetic intensity equal to the intensity of a magnetic field in a vacuum in which a unit magnetic pole experiences a mechanical force of one dyne in the direction of the field — used instead of *gauss* after official adoption in 1932

**oes** *pl of* O *or of* OE

**oesophag-** — see ESOPHAG-

**oesophageal** *var of* ESOPHAGEAL

**oesophageal ganglion** *n* **:** OCCIPITAL GANGLION

**oe·soph·a·go·stome** \ə'säfəgə,stōm, ē's-\ *n* -s [NL *Oesophagostomum*] **:** a nematode worm of the genus *Oesophagostomum*

**oe·soph·a·go·sto·mi·a·sis** \=,==(,)gästə'mīəsəs\ *n, pl* **oesophagostomiases** [NL, fr. *Oesophagostomum* + *-iasis*] **:** infestation with or disease caused by nematode worms of the genus *Oesophagostomum* **:** NODULAR DISEASE

**oe·soph·a·gos·to·mum** \=,=='gästəməm\ *n, cap* [NL, fr. *esophag-* + *-stomum*] **:** a genus of nematode worms (family Strongylidae) comprising the nodular worms of ruminants and swine and other worms affecting primates including man, esp. in Africa

**oesophagus** *var of* ESOPHAGUS

**oestradiol** *var of* ESTRADIOL

**oes·trel·a·ta** \e'streləd·ə, ē's-\ [NL, fr. Gk *oistrēlatos* driven by a gadfly, fr. *oistros* gadfly + *-elatos* (fr. *elan* to drive) — more at IRE, ELASTIC] *syn of* HERODROMA

**oes·tri·a·sis** \e'strīəsəs, ē's-\ *n, pl* **oestria·ses** \-,sēz\ [NL, fr. ¹*Oestrus* + *-iasis*] **:** infestation with or disease caused by botflies of the genus *Oestrus*

¹**oes·trid** \'estrəd, 'ēs-\ *adj* [NL *Oestridae*] **:** of or relating to the Oestridae

²**oestrid** \"\ *n* -s **:** a fly of the family Oestridae

**oes·tri·dae** \-trə,dē\ *n pl, cap* [NL, fr. ²*Oestrus*, type genus + *-idae*] **:** a family of two-winged flies consisting of the botflies and formerly including also the warble flies

**oestrin** *var of* ESTRIN

**oestriol** *var of* ESTRIOL

**oestrogen** *var of* ESTROGEN

**oestrone** *var of* ESTRONE

**oes·tro·scope** \'estrə,skōp, 'ēs-\ *n* [²*oestrus* + *-o-* + *-scope*] **:** a device for determining the existence of estrus in cattle by measuring the viscosity of the cervical mucus

**oestrous** *or* **oestral** *or* **oestrual** *var of* ESTROUS

**oestruation** *var of* ESTRUATION

¹**oes·trus** \'estrəs, 'ēs-\ *n* [L, gadfly, fr. Gk *oistros* gadfly, desire, frenzy — more at IRE] **1** -ES *archaic* **:** a biting or tormenting fly **2** *cap* [NL, fr. L] **:** the type genus of *Oestridae* comprising the sheep botfly

²**oestrus** *or* **oestrum** *var of* ESTRUS

**oeu·vre** \'ə(r)v(rᵊ), 'ɔ̄v-, -vrə, *F* œvr(ᵊ) *or* -v(rə)\ *n, pl* **oeuvres** \"\ [F *œuvre* work (something produced by labor), fr. L *opera*, fr. pl. of *opus* work — more at OPERATE] **:** a substantial body of work constituting the lifework of a writer, an artist, or a composer ⟨even without an ~, some dramatists can effect a satisfying unity and significance of pattern in single plays —T.S.Eliot⟩ ⟨the ~ of one and the same painter sometimes is divided into two strata —Wolfgang Born⟩ ⟨the most popular of all the music in the Wagnerian ~ —P.H.Lang⟩

¹**of** \,əv; *esp before a consonant* -ə; *after an unstressed or lightly stressed vowel sometimes* v (*as in* thəsīdēəvābz *for "this idea of Abe's"*), *or, before a voiceless consonant*, f (*as in* thəsīdēəftämz *for "this idea of Tom's"*), *or, before* f, *without pronunciation* (*as in* thəsīdēəfredz *for "this idea of Fred's"*); *when emphatic, as when it is the last or the first word in a sentence*, ;əv *or* ;äv\ *prep* [ME, of, off, fr. OE (also adv., away, off); akin to OHG *aba*, prep., off, away from, & adv., off, away, down, ON *af*, prep., off, from, Goth *af* from, away from, since, L *ab* from, Gk *apo* away from, off, Skt *apa* away, off] **1** *obs* — used as a function word to indicate the place or thing from which anything moves, comes, goes, or is directed or impelled ⟨with the least drawing blood ~ another —Samuel Purchas⟩ **2** *archaic* — used as a function word to indicate an anterior condition from which a transition has been made ⟨I, ~ brute, human; ye, ~ human, gods —John Milton⟩ **3 :** at an interval or in a direction with respect to — used to indicate something from which position or reckoning is defined ⟨north ~ the lake⟩ ⟨the arrow went wide ~ the mark⟩ ⟨passed within a foot ~ the rock⟩ ⟨waited upwards ~ an hour⟩ ⟨within a few hours ~ birth⟩ ⟨I know you ~ old, you don't fool me⟩ **4** — used as a function word to indicate something from which a person or thing is delivered ⟨cured him ~ being late⟩ ⟨eased ~ her pain⟩ ⟨rid the barn ~ rats⟩ or with respect to which someone or something is made destitute ⟨robbed ~ his sleep⟩ ⟨stripped ~ all his titles⟩ ⟨relieved ~ his command⟩ **5 a :** from by birth or descent ⟨born ~ a royal house⟩ ⟨he is ~ a well-to-do family⟩ **b :** from as the place of birth, production, or distribution **:** having as its base of operation, point of initiation, or source of issuance or derivation ⟨~ or relating to Italy, its language, or its people⟩ **c :** from as cause or occasion **:** in regard to ⟨I wish him joy ~ her —Shak.⟩ ⟨vote yes . . . because they are frightened ~ their skins —John Gunther⟩ **d :** from as possessor, seller, loser, giver ⟨buy our eggs ~ a farmer⟩ ⟨held his lands ~ the duke⟩ **e :** from as one that is looked to for something ⟨asked a favor ~ me⟩ ⟨too much to expect ~ a child⟩ **f :** from undergoing or coping with — used with *it* ⟨had a hard time ~ it at school⟩ ⟨make a good job ~ it⟩ **6** — used as a function word to indicate the cause, motive, or reason by which a person or thing is actuated or impelled ⟨die ~ shame⟩ ⟨this milk tastes ~ garlic⟩ ⟨dead ~ violence⟩ ⟨afraid ~ his own shadow⟩ ⟨went ~ their own free will⟩ ⟨did it ~ necessity⟩ **7** — used as a function word to indicate the agent or doer of an act or action (1) archaically after such participles as *loved, ordained, forgotten* ⟨despised and rejected ~ men —Isa 53:3 (AV)⟩, (2) after an adjective or adjective phrase characterizing the act or conduct ⟨it was kind ~ him to offer it⟩, and (3) after a noun indicating the maker or doer often with the force of a subjective genitive ⟨plays ~ Shakespeare⟩ ⟨the mercy ~ the Lord⟩ ⟨the ruins ~ time⟩ **8** *archaic* — used as a function word to indicate the means or instrument by which an action is carried out ⟨it is pouring ~ rain⟩ ⟨pave it ~ gold⟩ **9** — used as a function word to indicate the material, parts, or elements composing something or the contents held by something ⟨throne ~ gold⟩ ⟨company ~ 20 men⟩ ⟨distance ~ five miles⟩ ⟨genus ~ mammals⟩ ⟨cup ~ water⟩ **10 a** — used as a function word to indicate a particular example belonging to the class denoted by the preceding noun ⟨the city ~ Rome⟩ ⟨month ~ August⟩ ⟨goes under the name ~ charity⟩ ⟨the crime ~ murder⟩ **b** — used as a function word to indicate simple or definitional apposition ⟨great barn ~ a house⟩ ⟨that fool ~ a husband⟩ ⟨jewel ~ a woman⟩ **11 :** relating to **:** with reference to **:** as regards **:** ABOUT ⟨stories ~ his travels⟩ ⟨the truth ~ the matter⟩ ⟨judge ~ the case⟩ ⟨dreaming ~ home⟩ ⟨think ~ a way out⟩ ⟨complaining ~ the heat⟩ ⟨test ~ skill⟩ **12** — used as a function word indicating the object of an action denoted or implied by the preceding noun ⟨love ~ nature⟩ ⟨care ~ children⟩ ⟨creation ~ the world⟩ ⟨the polishing ~ a diamond⟩ ⟨pursuit ~ happiness⟩ ⟨knowledge ~ the past⟩ **13** — used as a function word (1) idiomatically after some adjectives implying action or process or perception ⟨fruitful ~ results⟩ ⟨sparing ~ words⟩ ⟨greedy ~ gain⟩ ⟨neglectful ~ his duties⟩ or (2) chiefly dial. after verbs and participles ⟨felt ~ his head⟩ ⟨ever trying ~ something new —Adrian Bell⟩ ⟨stop pestering ~ your father⟩ **14 :** in respect to ⟨slow ~ speech⟩ ⟨light ~ step⟩ ⟨forty years ~ age⟩ ⟨problems difficult ~ solution⟩ **15** — used as a function word to indicate a quality or possession characterizing or distinguishing a subject ⟨a fellow ~ infinite jest —Shak.⟩ ⟨men ~ goodwill⟩ ⟨persons ~ refinement⟩ ⟨boy ~ ten years⟩; used with *all* to indicate a temporary quality or condition ⟨all ~ a tremble⟩ ⟨all ~ a sweat⟩; used with a following noun denoting or implying action usu. with a possessive ⟨wine ~ choice⟩ ⟨rulers ~ their own choosing⟩ ⟨girl ~ his dreams⟩ ⟨boat ~ his own design⟩ **16 a** — used as a function word indicating the aggregate or whole that includes the part or quantity denoted by the preceding word ⟨most ~ the army⟩ ⟨many ~ those present⟩ ⟨ton ~ coal⟩ ⟨three glasses ~ beer⟩ ⟨first years ~ life⟩ **b** — used as a function word to indicate a whole or quantity from which some is removed or expended by the action of the preceding verb ⟨gave generously ~ his time⟩ ⟨partook ~ the morning meal⟩ **17 a** — used as a function word indicating a possessive relationship ⟨gates ~ heaven⟩ ⟨courage ~ the pioneers⟩ ⟨lateness ~ the hour⟩ ⟨cube ~ six⟩ ⟨member ~ parliament⟩ or close association in time ⟨in the days ~ the Roman emperors⟩ ⟨knights ~ yore⟩; used often with a following possessive ⟨a friend ~ mine⟩ ⟨an acquaintance ~ the colonel's⟩ ⟨through no fault ~ his⟩ **b** — used as a function word to indicate such relationships as ruler and subject, owner and property ⟨king ~ England⟩ ⟨Mary ~ Scotland⟩ ⟨chiefs ~ state⟩ ⟨captain ~ Company A⟩ ⟨head ~ the household⟩ **18** — used as a function word to indicate a point or space in time relating either to a single or to a usual action or occurrence ⟨he died ~ a Monday⟩ ⟨likes to visit a bar ~ an evening⟩ ⟨plays golf ~ a Sunday⟩ **19** — used as a function word indicating position before the clock hour ⟨ten minutes ~ eight⟩ ⟨twenty-five ~ five⟩ ⟨quarter ~ ten⟩ **20 a** *now dial* **:** ON ⟨a plague ~ all cowards —Shak.⟩ ⟨fell flat ~ his back in the grass —F.B.Gipson⟩ **b** *chiefly Brit* **:** IN ⟨continue her full membership ~ the Commonwealth —*Brit. Information Services*⟩ **c** *chiefly dial* **:** WITH ⟨what's the matter ~ her⟩

²**of** \ə(v)\ *verbal auxiliary* [by alter.] **:** HAVE — used esp. in written dialogue to represent a supposed dial. or substand. speech ⟨meant to ~ written you —Christopher La Farge⟩ ⟨hadn't ought to ~ fooled with figures —Delos Avery⟩ ⟨told you we should ~ quit —William English⟩

**OF** *abbr* **1** Old French **2** oxidizing flame

**ofay** \(')ō;fā\ *n* -s [origin unknown] **:** a white person ⟨stays in Harlem and learns to hate ~s —*New Republic*⟩

**ofc** *abbr* office

**ofcl** *abbr* official

**ofcr** *abbr* officer

¹**off** \'ȯf *also* 'äf\ *adv* [ME *of*, fr. OE — more at OF] **1 a :** from a place or position ⟨march ~⟩ ⟨fly ~⟩ ⟨send a letter ~⟩; *specif* **:** in a direction away from land ⟨ship stood ~ to sea⟩ **b :** so as to prevent close approach ⟨drove the dogs ~⟩ ⟨fighting ~ drowsiness⟩ ⟨buy ~ an enemy⟩ **c :** from a course **:** in a slanting or oblique direction **:** ASIDE ⟨turned ~ into a bypath⟩ ⟨veered ~ to avoid collision⟩ ⟨his drive fell ~ to the left of the green⟩; *specif* **:** away from the wind ⟨ship eased ~ a point or two⟩ **d :** into an unconscious state **:** into sleep ⟨dozed ~ for a while⟩ ⟨must have dropped ~⟩ **2 :** to a state or condition of separateness **:** so as not to be supported ⟨rolled to the edge of the table and ~⟩ or covering or enclosing ⟨blew the lid ~⟩ ⟨took his coat ~⟩ or attached ⟨the handle came ~⟩ ⟨peeled ~ the skin⟩ ⟨married ~ two daughters⟩ or united ⟨surface marked ~ into squares⟩ **3 a :** to a state of discontinuance ⟨shut ~ an engine⟩ ⟨turn ~ the water⟩ ⟨break ~ a conversation⟩ or exhaustion ⟨drain ~ excess fluid⟩ ⟨drink ~ a glass at one draft⟩ or completion ⟨the weather has cleared ~⟩ ⟨coat of paint to finish it ~⟩ ⟨smooth ~ the corners⟩ ⟨sweep ~ the porch steps⟩ ⟨rattle ~ a string of clichés⟩ ⟨run ~ a series of racing heats⟩ ⟨play ~ a tie⟩ **b :** into a state of relief resulting from an orgasm ⟨go ~⟩ ⟨dream ~⟩ — not often in formal use **4 :** in absence from or suspension of regular work or service ⟨take time ~ for lunch⟩ ⟨ask for a day ~⟩ **5 :** at a distance in space or time ⟨stood ten paces ~⟩ ⟨Christmas is only two weeks ~⟩ ⟨lives ~ in the hills⟩ **6 :** OFFSTAGE ⟨turns and goes ~ left⟩ ⟨knocking is heard ~⟩ **7** *substand* — used as a function word with *and* to express abruptness or unexpectedness or directness of an action ⟨he ~ and bought a whole new outfit⟩ ⟨~ and busted him in the jaw⟩; compare HAUL OFF — **off with** — used interjectionally to express a command or exhortation that something be taken off or away or cast aside ⟨off with the old, on with the new⟩ ⟨*off with his* head⟩

²**off** \"\ *prep* [ME *of* — more at OF] **1 a** — used as a function word to indicate a supporting surface or a position of rest, attachment, or union from which separation is made ⟨take it ~ the table⟩ ⟨eat ~ a plate⟩ ⟨bullet glanced ~ the wall⟩ ⟨took the property ~ his hands⟩ ⟨cut two yards ~ the roll of cloth⟩ **b :** down from ⟨stepped ~ the train⟩ **2 a :** from the charge or possession of ⟨bought it ~ a wandering peddler⟩ ⟨had his wallet stolen ~ him⟩ **b :** from as a source of supply **:** at the expense of ⟨lived ~ the county⟩ ⟨lived ~ his sister⟩ ⟨got two runs ~ the first pitcher⟩ ⟨made his living ~ the tourists⟩ ⟨liked the money he made ~ it —Will Rogers b.1911⟩ **c :** so as to consume ⟨dined ~ oysters and champagne⟩ **3 :** to seaward of ⟨two miles ~ shore⟩ **4** — used as a function word to indicate something that one has been or is normally but is not now occupied with or engaged upon ⟨~ duty⟩ ⟨recently gone ~ smoking⟩ **5 a** — used as a function word to indicate a standard or level from which there is a reduction or falling away ⟨~ his usual tennis form⟩ ⟨fifteen percent ~ the list price⟩ ⟨two seconds ~ the track record⟩ **b :** diverging from (a main course) ⟨two points ~ the wind⟩ ⟨~ center⟩ ⟨~ balance⟩ ⟨kept getting ~ the subject⟩ ⟨got ~ the route at the park⟩ ⟨a street opening ~ the avenue⟩ **:** situated or occurring apart from (a principal place or proceeding) ⟨little shop just ~ Main Street⟩ ⟨speaking ~ the record⟩ — used often in combination ⟨*off*-Broadway play⟩ ⟨talks . . . to imaginary people that are carefully *off*-camera —*Newsweek*⟩ — **off the mark** *adv* (*or adj*) **:** away from the main point or focal center

³**off** \"\ *adj* [¹*off*] **1 a :** more removed or distant **:** opposite to the main part or side ⟨went round to the ~ side of the building⟩ ⟨the ~ side of the medal was blank⟩ **b :** situated to one side **:** not main or principal ⟨~ street⟩ ⟨~ branch of the river⟩ **c :** being on the side away from the shore **:** SEAWARD ⟨keeping the buoy on her ~ side⟩ **d :** being or relating to the side of an animal, team, or vehicle that is farther from the driver as he walks or rider as he mounts **:** RIGHT ⟨~ horse in a team⟩ ⟨~ leg⟩ ⟨~ wheel⟩ — opposed to *near* **e :** of or relating to the side of the cricket field opposite to that on which the batsman stands ⟨an ~ hit⟩ ⟨an ~ play⟩ ⟨an ~ stroke⟩ **2 a :** set in motion **:** started on the way ⟨~ on one of his tirades⟩ ⟨~ on a spree⟩ **b :** not taking place or staying in effect ⟨the picnic is ~⟩ ⟨in case of a tie all bets are ~⟩ **c** *bridge* **:** having lost or destined to lose ⟨the spade finesse was ~⟩ **d :** off side (sense 3) **e :** not flowing **:** checked from flowing by a closed valve or opened switch ⟨repairs made while the current is ~⟩ ⟨the lever is in the ~ position⟩ ⟨hot water is ~⟩ **f** *of a braking device* **:** not applied **:** RELEASED,

INOPERATIVE 3 a : not corresponding to fact : divergent or erring from a true line or exact figure ⟨~ in his reckoning⟩ ⟨your guesses are way ~⟩ b : not being up to normal condition or usual efficiency : not being at one's best ⟨every performer has his ~ days⟩ c : not entirely sane : mentally unstable : ODD, ECCENTRIC ⟨the poor fellow is a little ~⟩ ⟨psychiatrists . . . understand that a person can be ~ on one topic and fully normal in others —Ruth P. Randall⟩ d : REMOTE, SLIGHT ⟨only an ~ chance of his being right⟩ e : not familiar or well-known : not well advertised ⟨suspicious of ~ brands⟩ 4 a : taken or spent off duty or in relaxation ⟨reading on his ~ days⟩ b : marked by a falling off or by less than ordinary activity or productiveness or amount of business : SLACK ⟨~ season in European travel⟩ 5 a : slightly tinged with some other hue or with gray ⟨~ shades⟩ ⟨an ~ kind of blue —C. B.Kelland⟩ b : being of inferior quality ⟨~ grade of oil⟩ : detracting from quality ⟨trying to keep butter free from any ~ odors⟩; *also* : TAINTED ⟨this cream is ~⟩ c : being at a lower level ⟨industrial stocks were 1.12 points ~ for the day⟩ ⟨railroad traffic was ~ 5 percent⟩ — opposed to *up* d *of a racetrack* : not being in good condition : not fast ⟨ran his best races on ~ tracks⟩ e *of a bridge hand* : short of the ideal or normal requirement ⟨~ by two aces⟩ 6 : having completed a pressrun whether or not removed from the press ⟨form is ~⟩ 7 : conditioned or circumstanced esp. as to material welfare ⟨not rich but comfortably ~⟩ ⟨thought he was just as well ~ without a wife⟩ ⟨the house was badly ~ for paint⟩ 8 *of an animal's age* : more than a specified number of years — distinguished from *rising* ⟨a mare four ~ but not yet rising five⟩ 9 : relating to the sale of liquor that is to be consumed away from the premises ⟨an ~ license⟩

**4off** \"\ *vb* -ED/-ING/-S [1off] *vt* : to take off : DOFF ~ *vi* 1 *of a ship* : to move away from shore : start out to sea 2 a : to go away : DEPART — used chiefly as an imperative ⟨~, or I shoot⟩ b : to get or be off — used chiefly as an imperative ⟨~, ye lendings —Shak.⟩

**5off** \"\ *n* -s [3off] 1 : the condition or state of being off ⟨their engagement had its ~s and ons⟩ 2 : the side of a cricket field bisected by a straight line passing through both middle stumps from boundary to boundary opposite to that on which the batsman stands — compare LEG, ON; see CRICKET illustration

**off** *abbr* 1 offered 2 office; officer; official 3 officinal

**of·fal** \ˈȯfəl, ˈäf-\ *n* -s [ME, fr. *of* off + *fal*, *fall* fall — more at OFF, FALL] 1 : material that is left as waste or by-product of a process of preparation or manufacture: as a : the stalks and dust from tobacco leaves b : less valuable portions (as the belly, head, and shoulders) of a hide c : the by-products of milling (as of wheat or barley) used esp. for stock feed d : the parts of a butchered animal that are removed in dressing, that consist largely of the viscera (as brain, heart, sweetbreads, liver) and the trimmings (as tail, hooves, blood, skin, head meat), and that are used as edible products or as raw material in the manufacture of by-products e : small or inferior or unmarketable fish 2 a : a dead or slaughtered animal or parts of it considered inedible by nature or through tainting b : something thrown away as worthless : RUBBISH, GARBAGE c : worthless, vicious, or outcast persons ⟨~ of the jails and brothels —T.B.Macaulay⟩ **syn** see REFUSE

**of·fa·ly** \ˈäfəlē, -li\ *adj, usu cap* [fr. County *Offaly*, Ireland] : of or from County Offaly, Ireland : of the kind or style prevalent in County Offaly

**off and on** *adv* 1 : with interruptions or intermissions : INTERMITTENTLY ⟨the war lasted *off and on* for thirty years⟩ ⟨rained *off and on* all evening⟩ 2 : on different tacks alternately toward and away from the land ⟨the ship stood *off and on* until morning⟩

**off-axis reflector** \(ˈ)=ˌ==-\ *n* : HERSCHELIAN TELESCOPE

**off-balance** \ˈ=ˌ==\ *adj (or adv)* 1 : not well proportioned : out of balance ⟨the plans are *off-balance*⟩ ⟨their military is *off-balance*⟩ 2 : not standing, sitting, or resting in normal physical equilibrium ⟨caught *off-balance* and knocked down —Jack Dempsey⟩ 3 a : upset from or in a state of being upset by confusion : UPSETTING ⟨the *off-balance* presentation of alternatives —S.L.Payne⟩ ⟨keep us *off-balance*⟩ b : into a state of surprise from the unexpected ⟨may turn us momentarily *off-balance* by saying one thing when he means another —R.B.West⟩

**off-bar** \ˈ=ˌ=\ *vb* : to bar off

**off-bear** \ˈ=ˌ=\ *vt* : to take away (as bricks from a molding bench or boards or slabs from a saw)

**off-bearer** \ˈ=ˌ==\ *n* : a worker who removes partly processed or completed products from a machine, conveyor belt, power saw, or other equipment and piles them, packs them, or trucks them away

**1offbeat** \ˈ=ˌ=\ *n* [3off + beat] : the part of a musical measure other than the principally accented one — compare DOWNBEAT

**2offbeat** \ˈ=ˌ=\ *adj* [fr. the phrase *off beat*] : diverging from the main stream of current fashion : UNCONVENTIONAL, UNORTHODOX ⟨~ advertising⟩ ⟨~ style of comedy⟩

**off-board** \ˈ=ˌ=\ *adj* : OVER-THE-COUNTER ⟨*off-board* market for securities⟩

**offbreak** \ˈ=ˌ=\ *n* : a bowled ball in cricket that breaks from the off side to the leg side

**1offcast** \ˈ=ˌ=\ *adj* [1off + *cast*, past part. of *cast* (after *cast off*)] : cast off : DISCARDED, REJECTED

**2offcast** \"\ *n* : CASTOFF

**off-center** \ˈ=ˌ==\ *or* **off-centered** \ˈ=ˌ==\ *adj* 1 : having an axis (as of rotation or equilibrium) deviating from the geometrical center ⟨*off-center* revolving disk⟩ ⟨*off-center* placing of a letterhead⟩ ⟨an *off-centered* postage stamp⟩ 2 : not entirely normal or sound : not perfectly balanced : UNSTABLE, ECCENTRIC ⟨suspicion that existentialism is *off-center* . . . has elevated experiences that all of us have occasionally into permanent and decisive qualities of life —Charles Frankel⟩

**off-color** \ˈ=ˌ==\ *or* **off-colored** \ˈ=ˌ==\ *adj* 1 a : not having the right or standard color : not colorless ⟨*off-color* diamond⟩ ⟨*off-color* paper⟩ ⟨*off-color* show dog⟩ ⟨*off-colored* racial mixtures⟩ b : not being up to a required standard : not being in sound condition or good health ⟨feeling *off-color* and out of sorts⟩ 2 : being of doubtful propriety : not socially acceptable : DUBIOUS ⟨*off-color* reputation⟩ : RISQUÉ ⟨*off-color* anecdotes⟩

**offcome** \ˈ=ˌ=\ *n* -s [3off + come] *chiefly Scot* 1 : OUTCOME 2 : EXCUSE

**1offcut** \ˈ=ˌ=\ *n* [3off + cut (after *cut off*)] : something that is cut off: as a : a portion cut from a sheet of paper to reduce it to the press size b : a part of a printed sheet cut off and folded separately c : an odd or waste piece of lumber ⟨plywood ~s⟩

**2offcut** \ˈ=ˌ=\ *adj* [1off + *cut*, past part. of *cut* (after *cut off*)] : not being of the usual or standard sizes ⟨~ lumber⟩

**offed** *past of* OFF

**of·fen** \ˈȯfən\ *prep* [alter. of *off from*] *substand* : OFF

**of·fen·bach** \ˈäfən,bäk, ˈȯf-, -äk\ *adj, usu cap* [fr. *Offenbach*, Germany] : of or from the city of Offenbach, Germany : of the kind or style prevalent in Offenbach

**of·fend** \əˈfend\ *vb* -ED/-ING/-S [ME *offenden*, fr. MF *offendre*, fr. L *offendere*, fr. *of-* (fr. *ob-* to, toward, against) + *fendere* to strike — more at OB-, DEFEND] *vi* 1 *obs* : TRIP, STUMBLE 2 a : to transgress the moral or divine law : SIN ⟨if it be a sin to covet honor, I am the most ~ing soul alive —Shak.⟩ b : to act in violation of a law, rule, or code : do wrong — used often with *against* ⟨that only those . . . who will never again ~ against the law should be paroled —Fred Finsley⟩ 3 a : to cause difficulty or discomfort or injury ⟨took off his shoe and removed the ~ing pebble⟩ b : to cause dislike, anger, or vexation ⟨take care that your dog does not . . . ~ on the common staircase —Agnes M. Miall⟩ ⟨a fabric of brick and asbestos that would not ~ in that landscape —Bryan Morgan⟩ ~ *vt* 1 a : VIOLATE, TRANSGRESS ⟨a contract not ~ing a statute . . . might still be in restraint of trade —C.A. Cooke⟩ ⟨at the risk of ~ing the canons of reviewing —J.N.L. Baker⟩ b *obs* : to strike against : ATTACK, ASSAIL c : to cause pain to : HURT, INJURE ⟨tasteless billboards that ~ the eye⟩ ⟨the horse . . . develops . . . bony growths around the joints that have been ~ed —R.R.Dykstra⟩ 2 *obs* : to oppose or obstruct in duty : cause to sin ⟨if thy right eye ~ thee, pluck it out —Mt 5:29 (AV)⟩ 3 : to cause to feel vexed or resentful : hurt the feelings of ⟨some people might be ~ed at mentioning a novelist in church —Compton Mackenzie⟩ ⟨friend of my youth may remember something in a different shape and be ~ed with my book —W.B.Yeats⟩

**syn** AFFRONT, INSULT, OUTRAGE: OFFEND indicates causing vexation, resentment, or hurt feelings or occas. violating notions of what is proper or right ⟨begged pardon for having displeased her. In a softened tone she declared herself not at all *offended* —Jane Austen⟩ ⟨hurt and *offended* by Ivy's rudeness —Willa Cather⟩ ⟨an old man asks her to become his mistress: she is not much *offended* morally, nor is she horrified —E.K. Brown⟩ AFFRONT indicates treating with incivility, lack of consideration, rudeness, or contempt, either with willful intent or deliberate indifference to courtesy ⟨a vigor, resolution, and at times an arrogance, which *affronted* his contemporaries —*New Republic*⟩ ⟨further *affronted* every soldier by saying that as things stand, England's only defense was the navy —Anthony West⟩ INSULT indicates a deliberate, insolent, wanton causing of another's shame, hurt pride, or humiliation ⟨he would *insult* them flagrantly; he would fling his hands in the air and thunder at their ignorance —Louis Auchincloss⟩ OUTRAGE applies to flagrant, egregious offense calling forth extreme feelings ⟨*outraged* at the aspersions upon the character of his old friend —S.H.Adams⟩ ⟨deputies, *outraged* because they thought Mendès was appealing over their heads to the people, broke into an angry roar —*Time*⟩

**of·fend·ed·ly** *adv* : in an offended manner

**of·fend·er** \əˈfendə(r)\ *n* -s 1 : one that offends : one that violates a law, rule, or code of conduct : one that commits an offense : WRONGDOER, TRANSGRESSOR ⟨the ruler should have a power . . . to pardon some ~s —John Locke⟩ 2 : something that causes injury or annoyance

**of·fense** *or* **of·fence** \əˈfen(t)s, ˈȯ,f-, ˈä,f-\ *n* -s [ME, fr. MF, fr. L *offensa*, fr. fem. of *offensus*, past part. of *offendere* to offend — more at OFFEND] 1 a *obs* : act of stumbling ⟨for a rock of ~ to both the houses of Israel —Isa 8:14 (AV)⟩ b *archaic* : a cause or occasion of sin : STUMBLING BLOCK ⟨woe unto the world because of ~s —Mt 18:7 (AV)⟩ 2 *obs* : DISFAVOR, DISGRACE 3 *archaic* : INJURY, DAMAGE 4 : something that outrages the moral or physical senses : NUISANCE ⟨~ to the public conscience⟩ ⟨such chord successions are an ~ to the ear⟩ 5 a : the act of attacking : ATTACK, ASSAULT ⟨weapons of ~⟩ b : an athletic team in possession of the ball or puck 6 a : the act of displeasing, affronting, or angering ⟨no ~ intended and none taken, I hope⟩ ⟨his words have given great ~ at court⟩ b : the state of being displeased, insulted, or morally outraged ⟨likely to take ~ at the least word of criticism⟩ 7 a : a breach of moral or social conduct : SIN, TRANSGRESSION, MISDEED ⟨tolerant of his youthful ~s⟩ b : an infraction of law : CRIME, MISDEMEANOR ⟨nor shall any person be subject for the same ~ to be twice put in jeopardy —*U. S. Constitution*⟩; *sometimes* : a misdemeanor not indictable but subject to summary punishment ⟨a record of petty ~s⟩

**syn** RESENTMENT, UMBRAGE, PIQUE, DUDGEON, HUFF: OFFENSE (or OFFENCE), commonly as the object of *give* or *take*, refers to the hurt displeasure one feels at a slight, insult, or indignity ⟨some demon of contradiction impelled her to find a point of *offense* everywhere —Ellen Glasgow⟩ ⟨could say things that from anyone else would sound outrageous, but he phrased them so amusingly, and was so lacking in malice, that he never gave *offense* —V.G.Heiser⟩ ⟨this tiny breath of genuine criticism had given deep *offense* —E.M.Forster⟩ RESENTMENT may apply to a feeling longer lasting, deeper, and marked by more indignation and smoldering ill will than OFFENSE ⟨actuated in great measure by *resentment* at not having received leave of absence to visit his dying wife, he made very serious charges against the personal character of his commandant —Edward Breck⟩ ⟨requited their hospitality by robbing them of much of their supplies. So fierce was their *resentment* that Hudson was forced to put from shore —*Amer. Guide Series: Maine*⟩ UMBRAGE, chiefly in the phrase *to take umbrage*, may suggest blended hurt pride, jealousy, suspicion of another's motives, and ill will ⟨a man took *umbrage* at being called a certain kind of fool —W.F.Hambly⟩ ⟨although the rector was not inclined to take *umbrage* at the treatment they had received, he showed . . . that he was quite aware that it was not what might have been considered due to them —Archibald Marshall⟩ PIQUE applies to the roiled displeasure of one taking offense or irritation at a petty cause that wounds vanity or shakes composure ⟨a ridiculous sense of *pique* at being left out, like a child shut out from a room in which a vitally interesting game is being played —H.G.Wells⟩ ⟨fits of jealous *pique* when one or the other rated special questioning —*Newsweek*⟩ DUDGEON, usu. used with *in*, suggests an irate fit of indignation ⟨this offended Mr. Barrow, who retired in *dudgeon* to the remotest part of the field —Dorothy Sayers⟩ ⟨sometimes the employer, flanked by his lawyer, will in a *dudgeon* refuse to sit in the same room with the union representatives —Dorothy Bromley⟩ HUFF, also usu. used with *in*, suggests a peevish or petulant fit of anger, often short-lived, at some petty cause ⟨at the first hint that we were tired of waiting and that we should like the show to begin, he was off in a *huff* —Henry James †1916⟩ ⟨read the letter, flew into a rage, and left the country in a *huff* —Virginia Woolf⟩

**of·fense·less** \-ləs\ *adj* : incapable of offending or attacking : INOFFENSIVE — **of·fense·less·ly** *adv*

**of·fen·sible** \əˈfen(t)səbəl\ *adj* [MF, fr. LL *offensibilis* liable to stumble, fr. L *offensus* (past part. of *offendere* to stumble, offend) + *-ibilis* -ible — more at OFFEND] 1 *obs* : OFFENSIVE, HARMFUL, INJURIOUS 2 : liable to be offended

**1of·fen·sive** \əˈfen(t)siv, ˈȯ,f-, ˈä,f-, -sēv *also* -səv\ *adj* [MF or ML; MF *offensif*, fr. ML *offensivus*, fr. L *offensus* (past part. of *offendere*) + *-ivus* -ive] 1 : making attack : relating to or characterized by attack : AGGRESSIVE : fitted for or used in attacking ⟨~ weapons⟩ ⟨~ maneuver⟩ ⟨~ strength⟩ — opposed to *defensive* 2 a *obs* : causing injury or damage : HARMFUL b : giving painful or unpleasant sensations : NAUSEOUS, OBNOXIOUS, REVOLTING ⟨~ odor of garbage⟩ 3 : causing displeasure or resentment : giving offense : INSULTING, AFFRONTING ⟨loud, ~ behavior⟩ ⟨~ advertising⟩ ⟨it's ~ to a gentleman's feelings when his word isn't believed —Dorothy Sayers⟩ 4 *obs* : OFFENDING, TRANSGRESSIVE, SINFUL

**syn** LOATHSOME, REPULSIVE, REPUGNANT, REVOLTING: OFFENSIVE describes what is disagreeable or nauseating or painful because of outrage to taste and sensibilities or affronting insultingness ⟨her head thrown back, her face discolored, her eyes bulging, her mouth wet and yawning: a sight horribly *offensive* —Arnold Bennett⟩ ⟨bad manners and a blatancy that, for some reason, seemed much more *offensive* than any mere peasant crudeness of their parents —Edmund Wilson⟩ ⟨his jeering voice had an *offensive*, deliberately insulting tone —O.E.Rölvaag⟩ LOATHSOME applies to what is foul or corrupt to the point of being quite disgusting or abhorrent ⟨upon the bed, before that whole company, there lay a nearly liquid mass of *loathsome* — of detestable putrescence —E.A.Poe⟩ ⟨picturing on many pages of his immortal comedy of hell, purgatory, and paradise the most horrible monsters and tortures, and the most *loathsome* and noisome abominations —C.W.Eliot⟩ REPULSIVE describes whatever produces strong physical disgust or aversion ⟨there was something *repulsive* about his touch. I shrank from his hand; my flesh revolted —Jack London⟩ ⟨rats, mice, dogs, cats, and such *repulsive* substitutes for food —J.L.Motley⟩ REPUGNANT describes what is highly offensive as in conflict with one's nature, principles, or tastes ⟨intensely *repugnant* to human nature, being a condition of chronic terror that at last became unbearable —G.B.Shaw⟩ ⟨if violence was incompatible with the character of a Virginia gentleman, how much more *repugnant* must it appear to the ideal of pure womanhood —Ellen Glasgow⟩ REVOLTING applies to what is offensive or repulsive and calls forth a determination to resist, rebel, or escape, esp. on the part of a person of delicate sensibilities ⟨his whole body shivered and started into awe-inspiring movement, monstrous and inhuman, *revolting* as a spectacle of degrading vice and yet pitiful in its helplessness —Liam O'Flaherty⟩ ⟨the maneuvers of selfishness and duplicity must ever be *revolting* —Jane Austen⟩

**2offensive** \"\ *n* -s 1 : the state or posture of one that is attacking : aggressive attitude : act of the attacking party ⟨took the ~⟩ — opposed to *defensive* 2 : a sustained or large-scale attack ⟨~ aimed at the enemy's capital⟩ : an aggressive action or movement ⟨an economic ~ can often prevent the necessity for a . . military defense —W.H. Draper⟩

**of·fen·sive·ly** \-sәvlē, -li\ : in an offensive manner ⟨~ conceited⟩ ⟨smelling ~ of cheap perfume⟩

**of·fen·sive·ness** \-sivnəs, -sēv- *also* -səv-\ *n* -ES : the quality or state of being offensive ⟨the ~ of his continual bragging⟩

**1of·fer** \ˈȯfə(r), ˈäf-\ *vb* **offered; offered; offering** \-f(ə)riŋ\ **offers** [ME *offren*, *offeren*, in sense 1, fr. OE *offrian*, fr. LL *offerre*, fr. L, to present, tender, proffer, offer, fr. *of-* (fr. *ob-* to, toward, against) + *ferre* to carry; in other senses, fr. OF *offrir*, fr. L *offerre* — more at OB-, BEAR] *vt* 1 a : to present as an act of worship or devotion : SACRIFICE ⟨to the Catholic church where she would ~ a candle or so to his recovery —F.M.Ford⟩ b : to utter (as a prayer) in devotion — often used with *up* ⟨~ed up prayers of thanksgiving⟩ 2 a : to present for acceptance or rejection : hold out : TENDER, PROFFER ⟨~ a bribe⟩ ⟨~ a bill to the legislature⟩ ⟨~ed his hand in marriage⟩ ⟨was ~ed a job⟩ b : to present in order to meet a requirement ⟨candidates for the degree may ~ English as one of their foreign languages⟩ 3 a : to bring or put forward for action or consideration : PROPOSE, SUGGEST ⟨~ an opinion⟩ ⟨~ a proposition⟩ ⟨~ed himself as a candidate for governor⟩ b : to declare one's readiness or willingness — used with an infinitive object ⟨~ed to help me⟩ ⟨~ed to join in the search⟩ 4 a : to try or begin to exert ⟨~ed stubborn resistance⟩ ⟨don't shoot unless they ~ violence⟩ b : UNDERTAKE, ATTEMPT — used with an infinitive object ⟨~ed to strike him with his cane⟩ ⟨~ed to kiss her⟩ ⟨a young bruiser . . . can hardly ~ to beat up on an old man —W.L.Gresham⟩ 5 : to make available or accessible : SUPPLY, AFFORD ⟨summit ~s a magnificent panorama⟩ ⟨stream ~ing excellent fishing⟩ ⟨the college ~s courses in Russian⟩; *esp* : to place (merchandise) on sale ⟨~s a range of cameras at reasonable prices⟩ 6 : to present in performance or exhibition ⟨~ a new comedy⟩ 7 : to propose as payment : BID ⟨~ed me $10 for it⟩ ~ *vi* 1 : to present something as an act of worship or devotion : make an offering or sacrifice : SACRIFICE ⟨in no other country . . . do people pray and ~ as much as they do in Tibet —Heinrich Harrer⟩ 2 *archaic* : to make an attempt — used with *at* 3 : to come to hand : present itself ⟨buying land whenever opportunity ~ed⟩ 4 : to make a proposal; *esp* : to propose marriage 5 *Brit* : to be or to become available ⟨free choice to get work where work is ~ing —*Sydney (Australia) Bull.*⟩ ⟨corn that is ~ing is quite suitable —*Farmer's Weekly* (*So. Africa*)⟩

**syn** OFFER, PROFFER, TENDER, PRESENT, and PREFER can mean, in common, to put something before another for acceptance. OFFER in itself usu. implies no more than the common meaning ⟨*offer* a cigarette⟩ ⟨*offer* a helping hand⟩ ⟨*offer* a solution to a problem⟩ ⟨*offer* to help out in a crisis⟩ ⟨*offer* a good evening's entertainment⟩ PROFFER, more literary than OFFER, adds, or throws stress on, the idea of voluntariness, spontaneity, or courtesy on the part of the doer or subject of the verb ⟨*proffer* one's hand to a lady⟩ ⟨*proffer* hospitality to strangers in trouble⟩ ⟨sympathy should be *proffered* to the bereaved —Alexander MacDonald⟩ TENDER, a term with a legal currency implying an offering of something according to the terms of the law for approval or acceptance, in general use adds to OFFER the idea of the modesty, humility, or gentleness of the doer or subject of the verb ⟨*tender* your resignation⟩ ⟨*tender* your services⟩ ⟨*tender* your friendship⟩ PRESENT can carry a strong suggestion of formalness or a ceremoniousness or outward show in the act of offering or can suggest the character of a gift in the thing offered ⟨*present* a prize to a winning team⟩ ⟨*presented* the Davy-Faraday Laboratory to the Royal Institution —S.F.Mason⟩ ⟨the analysis of experimental science *presented* in this foreword —J.B.Conant⟩ ⟨words by which one scholar can *present* clearly to another the results of an investigation on this complex subject —E.S. McCartney⟩ PREFER in the sense of PROFFER or PRESENT is current only in legal use, though it is common in literary works up to the late nineteenth century ⟨the government of which the victim is a subject may justly *prefer* a claim —*Encyc. Americana*⟩ ⟨has *preferred* some serious charges —Reginald Bretnor⟩ ⟨I don't *prefer* any claim to being the soul of romance —Charles Dickens⟩

**2offer** \"\ *n* -s [ME *offre*, fr. MF, fr. OF, fr. *offrir*] 1 : an act of offering: as a : a presenting for acceptance : PROFFER ⟨refused all ~s of assistance⟩ ⟨considering job ~s from several firms⟩; *specif* : a proposal of marriage ⟨if she was still single it was not for lack of ~s⟩ b : an undertaking upon terms that embodies a promise given in consideration and in exchange for another's stipulated act or forbearance or designated reciprocal promise and that calls for acceptance or rejection by that other — compare CONTRACT 2 *obs* : OFFERING 3 : a price named by one proposing to buy : BID ⟨had several good ~s for his house⟩ 4 a : ATTEMPT, TRY ⟨made an ~ to catch the ball⟩ b : an action or movement indicating a purpose or intention of doing something ⟨halfhearted ~ of resistance⟩ ⟨made an ~ of jumping out of the car⟩ 5 : a small knob on a deer's antler : a rudimentary tine — **on offer** *adv (or adj)* : on sale : for sale

**of·fer·able** \-f(ə)rəbəl\ *adj* : capable of being offered

**of·fer·ee** \ˌȯfəˈrē, ˌäf-\ *n* -s : one to whom an offer is made ⟨a contract is formed when there is mutual assent between an offeror and an ~ —*College & Univ. Business*⟩

**of·fer·er** *or* **of·fer·or** \ˈȯf(ə)rə(r)\ *n* -s [ME *offerer*, fr. *offeren* to offer + *-er* — more at OFFER] 1 : one that offers : one that makes an offer or an offering ⟨~ of a bribe⟩ ⟨~ of a sacrifice⟩ 2 *now usu* **offeror** : one that communicates an offer (as of purchase) to another ⟨*offeror* and offeree have agreed on terms of the contract⟩

**of·fer·ing** \-f(ə)riŋ, -rēŋ\ *n* -s [ME *offring*, *offering*, fr. OE *offrung*, fr. *offrian* to offer, sacrifice + *-ung* -ing — more at OFFER] 1 : the act of one who offers : PROFFERING: as a : a presenting of something as an act of worship or devotion b : something presented as an expiation or atonement for sin : SACRIFICE, OBLATION — see BURNT OFFERING, DRINK OFFERING, GUILT OFFERING, HEAVE OFFERING, PEACE OFFERING, SIN OFFERING, WAVE OFFERING 2 : GIFT, PRESENT; *esp* : a gift made in money or in kind at a church service for the support of the church or its charitable, missionary, or other activities 3 : something that is presented or made available for purchase ⟨large ~ of long-term securities⟩ ⟨~s for last month on the wool market⟩ or patronage ⟨~s of an opera company⟩ ⟨latest ~s of the leading novelists⟩ ⟨~s of a television network⟩ 4 : an opportunity for instruction or study in a specific subject provided by an educational institution ⟨several new ~s in the history department⟩

**offering plate** *n* : a plate for collecting offerings from the members of a church congregation

**offering price** *n* [*offering* fr. pres. part. of 1*offer*] : the price quoted for a commodity or service in a schedule of prices or price list

offering plate

**of·fer·to·ry** \ˈȯfə(r),tōrē, ˈäf-, -tȯr-, -ri\ *n* -ES [ML *offertorium*, fr. *offertus* (past part. of LL *offerre* to offer) + L *-orium* -ory — more at OFFER] 1 *often cap* a : a part of a eucharistic service in which bread and wine are offered to God before they are consecrated b : prayers said by the priest when making the offerings 2 *often cap* : an antiphon, anthem, or other musical selection sung or played during a liturgy or during a religious service in which an offering is received from the congregation 3 a : an offering received from the congregation in a Christian worship service during the playing or singing of the offertory b : a collection of money taken at a religious service

**offerture** *n* -s [MF, fr. ML *offertura*, fr. *offertus* + L *-ura* -ure] 1 *obs* : act of offering (as in worship) 2 *obs* : PROPOSAL, OVERTURE

**off-face** \ˈ=ˌ=\ *adj* : OFF-THE-FACE

**off-flavor** \ˈ=ˌ==\ *n* : a flavor that is not natural or up to standard owing to deterioration or contamination ⟨*off-flavors* of cream⟩

**off-glide** \ˈ=ˌ=\ *n* : a glide produced by the movement of the vocal organs from the articulatory position of a speech sound

to a position of inactivity or to the articulatory position of an immediately following speech sound — compare ON-GLIDE
**off-go** \'ˌ-ˌ-\ *n* [³*off* + *go* (after *go off*)] **:** a going or starting off **:** START
**offgoing** \'ˌ-ˌ-, -'-ˌ-\ *n* [³*off* + *going*] **:** a going off **:** DEPARTURE, REMOVAL
¹**offgrade** \'ˌ-'-\ *adj* [fr. the phrase *off grade*] **:** varying from and inferior to a standard grade ⟨~ fruit⟩ ⟨~ ore⟩
²**offgrade** \"\ *n* **:** a product (as lumber) that is below standard
¹**offhand** \'ˌ-'-\ *adv* [²*off* + *hand*] **1 :** without previous study or preparation **:** EXTEMPORE ⟨couldn't give the figures ~⟩ ⟨reasons she would give ~ if you asked her why she read novels —Bernard DeVoto⟩ **2 :** from a standing position **:** without a support or rest ⟨fire ~ with . . . accuracy in . . . deer shooting —Claude Parmalee⟩
²**offhand** \"\ *adj* **1 a :** done or made offhand **:** EXTEMPORANEOUS; IMPROMPTU ⟨~ excuses⟩ **b :** showing no premeditation or preparation **:** CASUAL, INFORMAL ⟨bored, ~ manner⟩ ⟨grumbled about the ~, grudging service —*Time*⟩ ⟨her clothes usually gave an ~ effect⟩ **2 a :** shaped by hand without the use of molds ⟨~ glassworking⟩ **b :** done with a workpiece held in the hand ⟨~ grinding⟩ ⟨~ polishing⟩ **3 :** fired from a standing position ⟨rifle too heavy for ~ shooting⟩
**offhanded** \'ˌ-ˌ-\ *adj* **:** OFFHAND ⟨trying to sound ~ and reassuring —H.L.Davis⟩ — **off·hand·ed·ly** *adv* — **off·hand·ed·ness** *n*
**off-hour** \'ˌ-ˌ-\ *n* **1 :** a period of time spent off duty or away from work **2 a :** a period of time other than rush hour ⟨cut-rate tickets for *off-hour* travelers —William White⟩ or regular business hours ⟨a small store depends on customers during *off-hours*⟩ **b :** a time when one is not up to one's usual standard
¹**of·fice** \'ȯfəs, 'äf-\ *n* -s [ME, fr. OF, fr. L *officium* service, kindness, activity, duty, office, alter. of (assumed) *opificium*, fr. *opus* work + *-i-* + *-ficium* (fr. *facere* to do, make) — more at OPERATE, DO] **1 a :** a special duty, charge, or position conferred by an exercise of governmental authority and for a public purpose **:** a position of authority to exercise a public function and to receive whatever emoluments may belong to it ⟨qualified to hold public ~⟩ **b :** a position of responsibility or some degree of executive authority **c :** the fact or state of holding a public position of authority ⟨permitting . . . Socialism to be corrupted by ~ —*Times Lit. Supp.*⟩ **2** [ME, fr. OF, fr. LL *officium*, fr. L] **:** a set form of prayer or other religious service drawn up by church authority and sanctioned as the approved usu. obligatory form to be used by particular individuals (as clerics) or on particular occasions: as **a** *often cap* **:** the service of the breviary **:** DIVINE OFFICE ⟨a priest reciting his ~⟩ **b :** the rites or one of the rites of the missal ⟨the ~ of the mass⟩ **c :** a prayer service (as evensong) used in churches of the Anglican communion **3 a :** a religious or social ceremonial observance **:** RITE **b offices** *pl* **:** rites for the dead **4 a :** something that one ought to do or must do **:** an assigned or assumed duty, task, or role ⟨his ~ was merely to . . . point the way to new achievements —Frank Thilly⟩ ⟨to suppose she would shrink . . . from the ~ of a friend —Jane Austen⟩ **b :** something that is done or performed by a particular thing **:** the proper or customary action of something **:** FUNCTION ⟨the sentence through its ~ of assertion —R.M.Weaver⟩ ⟨numbed ears refused their proper ~ of conveying meanings to the mind —Kenneth Roberts⟩ **c :** something that a person does for another **:** SERVICE ⟨light the lights for them, the last ~ of welcome that she would ever be able to do here —*New Yorker*⟩ **d** INQUEST OF OFFICE **5 :** a place where a particular kind of business is transacted or a service is supplied: as **a :** a place in which the functions (as consulting, record-keeping, clerical work) of a public officer are performed **b :** the directing headquarters of an enterprise or organization ⟨continuing point of contact of the new student with the college ~ —*Official Register of Harvard Univ.*⟩ ⟨directives to branch factories were sent out from the New York ~⟩ **c :** the place in which a professional man (as a physician or lawyer) conducts his professional business **6 offices** *pl, chiefly Brit* **:** the apartments, attached buildings, or outhouses (as kitchens, pantries, laundries, stables) in which the activities attached to the service of a house are carried on ⟨3 bedrooms, bathroom and compact ~*s* —*Country Life*⟩ **7 :** the company whose place of business is in an office; *specif, Brit* **:** an insurance company **8 a** *Brit* **:** a principal branch or division of governmental administration **:** DEPARTMENT ⟨War *Office*⟩ ⟨Colonial *Office*⟩ **b :** a branch or subdivision of governmental administration that ranks (in the national government) below the department ⟨Patent *Office*⟩ ⟨*Office* of Education⟩ **9** *slang* **:** PRIVY **10** *slang* **:** a private usu. covert signal, warning, or cue ⟨in case the boss gives you the ~ that the cops . . . are going to investigate —John Scarne & Clayton Rawson⟩ **syn** see FUNCTION
²**office** \"\ *vb* -ED/-ING/-S *vt, obs* **:** to appoint to or place in office ~ *vi* **:** to maintain or occupy a professional or business office ⟨the old Vienna doctors have always had the habit of *officing* in their homes —Ernst Waldinger⟩
**office-bearer** \'ˌ-ˌ-\ *n, Brit* **:** OFFICEHOLDER, OFFICER
**office-block ballot** \'ˌ-ˌ-\ *or* **office-group ballot** \'ˌ-ˌ-\ *n* **:** an Australian ballot on which the names of candidates with or without party labels are grouped under the titles of the offices to be filled — compare INDIANA BALLOT, MASSACHUSETTS BALLOT
**office boy** *n* **:** a boy employed for errands and odd jobs in a business office
**office copy** *n* **1 :** an authenticated or certified copy of an official or legal record **2 :** a copy made or kept to be used in an office
**office found** *n* **:** the return of a verdict by an inquest of office
**officeholder** \'ˌ-ˌ-\ *n* **:** one holding a public office esp. in the civil service
**office hours** *n pl* **:** the hours set for business, work, or professional service in an office
**office lawyer** *n* **:** a lawyer whose practice is largely work carried on in his office rather than litigated cases requiring trials or hearings in the courts
**of·fice·less** \'ȯfəsləs, 'äf-\ *adj* [ME *officeles*, fr. *office* + *-les* -less] **:** lacking an office **:** not holding an office
**office lock** *n* **:** a door lock having the keyhole above the knob
**office machine** *n* **:** BUSINESS MACHINE
**office of arms 1 :** a body of officers of arms of a nation organized as a corporate body or as a division of the government **2** *usu cap 1st O&A* **:** the office in Dublin, terminated March 31, 1943, of which Ulster king of arms was head, having charge of heraldic matters in the island of Ireland
**office premium** *n* **:** GROSS PREMIUM
¹**of·fi·cer** \'ȯfəsə(r), 'äf- *sometimes* -fs-\ *n* -s [ME, fr. MF *officier*, fr. ML *officiarius*, fr. L *officium* office + -arius -ary — more at OFFICE] **1 a** *obs* **:** one charged with a duty **:** AGENT **b :** one charged with administering and maintaining the law (as a constable, bailiff, sheriff) ⟨~*s* of the peace⟩ ⟨the ~ on duty at a traffic corner⟩ **c :** a chief official engaged in domestic management or service in a large household or a college ⟨~*s* of the royal household⟩ **2 :** one who holds an office **:** one who is appointed or elected to serve in a position of trust, authority, or command esp. as specif. provided for by law ⟨~*s* of state⟩ ⟨~ in the foreign service⟩ ⟨~ of a bank⟩ ⟨the club held a meeting to elect its ~*s* for the year⟩ — distinguished from *employee* and sometimes from *official* **3 a :** one who holds a position of authority or command in the armed forces; *specif* **:** one who holds a commission ⟨separate clubs for ~*s* and enlisted men⟩ — see NONCOMMISSIONED OFFICER, PETTY OFFICER, WARRANT OFFICER **b :** the master or any of the mates of a merchant or passenger ship ⟨the ~*s'* rooms opened off the dining room —H.A.Chippendale⟩ **4 a :** a member of an honorary order in a grade above the lowest ⟨~ of the Legion of Honor⟩ **b** *in the Salvation Army* **:** a person trained and commissioned to engage in paid full-time service — see SALVATIONIST; compare LOCAL OFFICER
²**officer** \"\ *vt* -ED/-ING/-S **1 :** to furnish with officers **:** appoint officers over ⟨supply and ~ a militia⟩ **2 :** to command or direct as an officer ⟨veterans ~*ed* the recruits⟩ ⟨the troops were well ~*ed*⟩

office lock

**officer at arms** *obs* **:** OFFICER OF ARMS
**of·fi·cer·less** \'ȯfəsə(r)ləs, 'äf-\ *adj* **:** lacking officers
**officer of arms** [ME *officers of armes*] **:** any officer of whatever specific rank (as king of arms, herald, or pursuivant) having the duties of a herald or having supervision over officers who have such duties
**officer of the day :** the officer who acting directly under the commanding officer of a military organization or installation is responsible on an assigned day for overseeing the guard, preserving order, protecting property, enforcing inspection regulations, and guarding prisoners
**officer of the deck :** the officer in charge of a naval vessel for an assigned period (as a 4-hour watch) who is stationed on the bridge while at sea or on the quarterdeck while in port, who represents the commanding officer, and who for the duration of such duty is superior to all other officers except the executive officer
**officer of the watch :** the officer representing the engineering officer for an assigned period and serving in the engine room
**of·fi·cer·ship** \'ˌ-ˌ-ˌship\ *n* **:** the post or rank of an officer
**offices** *pl of* OFFICE, *pres 3d sing of* OFFICE
**office seeker** *n* **:** one who tries to gain public office ⟨after a few weeks of heading off *office seekers* he will move into the White House —*Nation*⟩
¹**of·fi·cial** \ə'fishəl, ō'f-\ *n* -s [ME, fr. MF, fr. ML *officialis*, fr. LL, adj.] **1** *or* **official principal :** a person appointed (as by an archbishop, bishop, dean, chapter, archdeacon) to exercise jurisdiction in an ecclesiastical court **2 a :** one who holds or is invested with an office **:** OFFICER ⟨government ~*s*⟩ **b :** a person authorized to act for a government, corporation, organization, or for another person esp. in administering or directing in a subordinate capacity ⟨~*s* of a sports contest⟩ ⟨railroad ~*s*⟩ **3 :** OFFICIAL STAMP
²**official** \"\ *adj* [LL *officialis*, fr. L *officium* duty, office + *-alis* -al — more at OFFICE] **1** *obs* **:** performing a function or service **2 :** belonging or relating to an office, position, or trust **:** connected with holding an office ⟨~ duties⟩ ⟨~ routine⟩ **3 :** holding an office or serving in a public position **:** authorized to perform a service ⟨~ messenger⟩ ⟨president's ~ representative⟩ **4 a :** derived from the proper office or officer or authority **:** made or communicated by virtue of authority **:** AUTHORIZED, AUTHORITATIVE ⟨~ statement⟩ ⟨~ biography⟩ **b :** prescribed or recognized as authorized ⟨~ ballot⟩ ⟨~ language of a region⟩ ⟨~ architecture⟩ ⟨~ record for the mile⟩; *specif* **:** described by the U.S. Pharmacopeia or the National Formulary ⟨~ species of a plant genus⟩ **5 :** befitting or characteristic of a person in office or acting in his capacity of an officer **:** FORMAL ⟨was extended an ~ greeting⟩ ⟨~ condolences⟩ ⟨faults to which ~ writing is especially prone —Ernest Gowers⟩ **6 :** serving in a legislature of a British dependency by virtue of nomination by the governor from the public service of the colony — compare UNOFFICIAL 1c
**official at bat** *or* **official time at bat :** AT BAT 2
**of·fi·cial·dom** \-dəm\ *n* -s **:** officials as a class or as a body ⟨the kind of ~ which characterized the Roman Empire —K.S. Latourette⟩ ⟨referring to all ~ — executives, legislators and judges —D.R.Richberg⟩ ⟨people are informed of only so much as ~ decides they need to be told —Arthur Krock⟩
**of·fi·cial·ese** \ə'fishə'lēz, -lēs\ *n* -s **:** the characteristic language of official statements **:** wordy, pompous, or obscure language ⟨handbooks which would fortify civil servants against the reduction of ~ —C.J.Rolo⟩
**of·fi·cial·ism** \-'ˌ-ˌlizəm\ *n* -s **:** action characteristic of an official **:** official system or routine **:** BUREAUCRACY, RED-TAPEISM ⟨where there is ~ every human relation suffers —E.M. Forster⟩
**of·fi·ci·al·i·ty** \əˌfishē'alədē, ˌōˌf-\ *n* -ES [F *officialité*, fr. LL *officialitat-, officialitas*, fr. *officialis* + L *-itat-, -itas* -ity] **1 :** the ecclesiastical charge, office, court, or jurisdiction of an official principal **2 :** the state or fact of being official **:** OFFICIALISM **3 :** OFFICIALS
**of·fi·cial·iza·tion** \əˌfishələ'zāshən, ōˌf-, -ˌlī'z-\ *n* -s **:** the process of becoming or being made official **:** act of placing under the control of officials
**of·fi·cial·ize** \ə'fishəˌlīz\ *vt, see -ize in Explan Notes* [²*official* + *-ize*] **:** to make official **:** subject to official routine **:** bring under public control
**of·fi·cial·ly** \-sh(ə)lē, -li\ *adv* **1 :** with official authorization **:** FORMALLY ⟨the bridge will be ~ opened next week⟩ **2 :** in an official capacity ⟨~ responsible for the disaster, as the man charged . . . with the security of all frontiers —Robert Graves⟩ **3 :** PROFESSEDLY, PUBLICLY, OSTENSIBLY ⟨this is the dry season; ~, no rain should fall —Marjory J. Douglas⟩ — often contrasted with *actually*
**official oath** *n* **:** the promissory oath required by law of an officer upon qualifying for his office in which he promises faithfully to perform the duties of the office and makes all other declarations or promises required by law — compare JUDICIAL OATH
**official principal** *n* **:** OFFICIAL 1
**official receiver** *n* **:** RECEIVER 2b(4)
**official stamp** *n* **:** a postage stamp for use by government officials on government mail
**of·fi·ci·ant** \ə'fishēənt\ *n* -s [ML *officiant-, officians*, pres. part. of *officiare* to officiate] **:** an officiating priest or minister
¹**of·fi·ci·ary** \-shēˌerē, -ri\ *n* -ES [ML *officiarius* — more at OFFICER] **1 :** OFFICER, OFFICIAL **2 :** a body of officers or officials
²**officiary** \"\ *adj* [L *officium* office + E *-ary* — more at OFFICE] **:** connected with, derived from, or having a title or rank in virtue of holding an office ⟨~ earl⟩
¹**of·fi·ci·ate** \ə'fishēˌāt, ō'f-, *usu* -ād+V\ *vb* -ED/-ING/-S [ML *officiatus*, past part. of *officiare*, fr. LL *officium* (ecclesiastical) office — more at OFFICE] *vi* **1 a :** to perform a prescribed religious service or ceremony ⟨~ at a Communion service⟩ ⟨~ at a coronation⟩ ⟨~ at a wedding⟩ **b :** to carry through a prescribed or traditional ceremony **:** perform a social duty ⟨~ as toastmaster at a banquet⟩ ⟨~ as hostess at a formal dinner⟩ **2 a :** to act in an official capacity **:** fill a position ⟨asked her to ~ temporarily as his personal secretary⟩ **b :** to act as an official at a sports contest ~ *vt* **1 :** to carry out (an official duty or function) **2 :** to serve as a leader or celebrant of (a ceremony) **3 :** to administer the rules of (a game or sport) esp. as a referee or umpire
²**officiate** \-ēət\ *n* -s [L *officium* + E *-ate*] **:** a body of officials
**of·fi·ci·a·tion** \əˌfishē'āshən\ *n* -s **:** the act or term of officiating **:** performance of a ceremony ⟨no provisions for a civil marriage, hence some kind of religious ~ is obligatory —Alfred Werner⟩
**of·fi·ci·a·tor** \-'ˌ-ˌād·ə(r)\ *n* -s [ML, fr. *officiatus* + L *-or*] **:** one that officiates
¹**of·fic·i·nal** \ə'fisᵊnəl, ˌȯfə'sīnᵊl, ˌäf-\ *adj* [ML *officinalis* of a storeroom, fr. *officina* storeroom (fr. L, workshop, alter. of *opificina*, fr. *opific-, opifex* artisan — fr. *opus* work + *-i-* + *-fic-, -fex*, fr. *facere* to do, make — + *-ina*, fr. fem. of *-inus* -ine) + L *-alis* -al — more at OPERATE, DO] **1 a :** kept in stock by druggists **:** available without special preparation or compounding **:** not magistral ⟨~ drugs⟩ ⟨~ medicines⟩ **b :** OFFICIAL 4b **2** *of a plant* **:** MEDICINAL ⟨~ herbs⟩ ⟨~ rhubarb⟩ — **of·fic·i·nal·ly** \-əlē, -li\ *adv*
²**officinal** \"\ *n* -s **:** an officinal drug, medicine, or plant
**officing** *pres part of* OFFICE
**of·fi·cious** \ə'fishəs\ *adj* [L *officiosus*, fr. *officium* service, kindness, duty, office + *-osus* -ous — more at OFFICE] **1 a** *obs* **:** eager to serve or help **:** KIND, OBLIGING ⟨~ humility of a heart devoted to the assistance merely of the inquisitive —Laurence Sterne⟩ **b** *obs* **:** DUTIFUL **c** *obs* **:** OFFICIAL, FORMAL **2 :** volunteering one's services where they are neither asked nor needed **:** MEDDLESOME ⟨a college . . . should excise ~ administration . . . in order to let learning happen —F.N. Davis⟩ ⟨shouting orders and generally making an ~ nuisance of himself⟩ **3 :** having a connection with official matters or duties merely through the position of the speaker or doer or the nature of the matters or duties **:** of an informal or unauthorized nature **:** UNOFFICIAL ⟨~ conversation between foreign ministers⟩ — opposed to *official* **syn** see IMPERTINENT
**of·fi·cious·ly** *adv* **:** in an officious manner ⟨nothing so fatal as to strive too directly or too ~ for an abstract quality like beauty —Herbert Read⟩

**of·fi·cious·ness** *n* -ES **:** officious quality or behavior
**off·ing** \'ȯfiŋ, 'äf-, -fēŋ\ *n* -s [¹*off* + *-ing*] **1 a :** the part of the open sea that is in sight of but a safe distance from the shore ⟨ships lay in the ~ waiting for a favorable wind⟩ **b :** a position or course near to but safely clear of the land ⟨steered southwest to get a good ~ . . . when he was sufficiently offshore . . . set course for the Canaries —S.E.Morison⟩ **c :** the act of anchoring offshore ⟨decided to make an ~ at the African village . . . to do some trading —H.A.Chippendale⟩ **2 :** the near or foreseeable future ⟨a wedding was in the ~ —D.R. Morris⟩ or the near distance ⟨a waiter hovered in the ~⟩
**off·ish** \'ȯfish *also* 'äf- *or* -fēsh\ *adj* [¹*off* + *-ish*] **1 :** inclined to stand off **:** stiffly or rudely unapproachable in manner **2 :** somewhat off in health or quality — **off·ish·ly** \-fəshlē, -fēsh-\ *adv* — **off·ish·ness** \-fishnəs, -fēsh-\ *n* -ES
**off-key** \'ˌ-'-\ *adj* **1 :** varying in pitch from the proper notes of a melody ⟨his *off-key*, squeaky voice . . . as he hummed his favorite hymn —Lynn Montross⟩ ⟨band . . . caterwauling away . . . more stridently *off-key* than ever —*Time*⟩ **2 :** INCONGRUOUS, UNACCOUNTABLE, ANOMALOUS ⟨symbols are sometimes *off-key*; his details of plot are occasionally eccentric —Gene Baro⟩ ⟨sensed something *off-key* about the disastrous fire —Denis Daly⟩
**offlap** \'ˌ-ˌ-\ *n* [³*off* + *lap*] **:** the progressive withdrawal of a sea from the land; *also* **:** the arrangement of the strata deposited on the floor of such a sea during its regression — compare ONLAP, OVERLAP
**off-let** \'ˌ-ˌ-\ *n* -s [³*off* + *let* (after *let off*)] **:** a pipe or channel for letting off water or other fluid
**off-license** \'ˌ-ˌ-\ *n, Brit* **:** a license to sell liquor to be consumed off the premises; *also* **:** an establishment so licensed
**off limits** *adj* **:** not to be entered or patronized by a designated class (as military personnel, students, athletes in training) ⟨*off limits* section of town⟩ ⟨the casino was declared *off limits* to the airmen at the base⟩
**off-line** \'ˌ-'-\ *adj* [²*off* + *line*] **:** located at a point not in the immediate area served by a particular railroad ⟨*off-line* ticket agent⟩ ⟨*off-line* destination⟩
**off-list** \'ˌ-'-\ *adj* [²*off* + *list*] *of merchandise* **:** bought and sold below the list price
**off-load** \'ˌ-ˌ-\ *vb* [trans. of Afrik *aflaai*] **:** UNLOAD
**off-lying** \'ˌ-ˌ-\ *adj* [¹*off* + *lying* (after *lie off*)] **1 :** situated off the shore ⟨*off-lying* islands⟩ or off the main part ⟨*off-lying* apartment for servants⟩ **2 :** OUTLYING, REMOTE ⟨*off-lying* provinces⟩
**off-mike** \'ˌ-'-\ *adj* [²*off* + *mike*] **:** recorded or transmitted at less than normal volume **:** distant from or turned away from the microphone ⟨background of *off-mike* voices⟩
**off'n** \'ȯfən\ *prep* [alter. of *off from*] *dial* **:** off from **:** OFF
**off-odor** \'ˌ-ˌ-\ *n* **:** an odor that is not natural or up to standard owing to deterioration or contamination ⟨the butter smelled of fish and other *off-odors*⟩
**off of** *prep* **:** OFF
**off-peak** \'ˌ-ˌ-\ *adj* [²*off* + *peak*] **:** not at the maximum ⟨the *off-peak* load of a power plant⟩
**off-presser** \'ˌ-ˌ-\ *n* [³*off* + *presser* (after *press off*, v.)] **:** an operator of a machine designed for pressing a particular part (as collar, sleeves, top of trousers) of a garment
¹**offprint** \'ˌ-ˌ-\ *n* [trans. of G *abdruck*] **:** an excerpt (as a magazine article) separately printed
²**offprint** \"\ *vt* **:** to reprint as an offprint
**offr** *abbr* officer
**offs** *pres 3d sing of* OFF, *pl of* OFF
**offsaddle** \'ˌ-ˌ-\ *vb* [trans. of Afrik *afsaal*] *chiefly Brit* **:** UNSADDLE
**off-sale** \'ˌ-'-\ *adj, of a license* **:** permitting sale of alcoholic beverages only in sealed containers for off-premises consumption
**off·scape** \'ȯfˌskāp *also* 'äf-\ *n* [³*off* + *-scape*] **:** the distant part of a landscape; *specif* **:** the visible surroundings of a tract to be landscaped ⟨plantings . . . will be used along the roadside to screen objectionable ~*s* —B.D.Tallamy⟩
**offscour** \'ˌ-'-\ *vt* [¹*off* + *scour*] **:** to scour off **:** CLEANSE
**offscouring** \'ˌ-ˌ-\ *n* -s [³*off* + *scouring* (after *scour off*, v.)] **1 :** something that is scoured off **:** cast-off filth **:** REFUSE **2 :** someone driven off from society **:** SCUM, OUTCAST — usu. used in pl. ⟨~*s* of the nation, but they were hardy men —C.B. Kelland⟩
**offscreen** \'ˌ-'-\ *adj* [²*off* + *screen*] **:** taking place or produced out of the viewer's sight ⟨~ voice⟩ ⟨~ violence⟩
**off-season** \'ˌ-ˌ-\ *n* **:** a time of suspended or reduced activity ⟨springtime, once considered an *off-season*, has become a thriving vacation period —Bert Pierce⟩
¹**offset** \'ˌ-ˌ-\ *n, pl* **offsets** [³*off* + *set*, n. (after *set off*, v.)] **1 a** *archaic* **:** OUTSET, START **b :** CESSATION — opposed to *onset* ⟨rapid regular beating of the heart . . . characterized by sudden onset and sudden ~ —H.J.Stewart⟩ **2 a** (1) **:** a short prostrate lateral shoot arising from the base of the parent plant (as a houseleek) (2) **:** a small bulb arising from the base of a mother bulb **b :** a lateral or collateral branch of a family or race **:** OFFSHOOT **c :** a spur from a range of hills or mountains **d :** a short drift or crosscut driven from a main level or gangway of a mine **3 a :** a horizontal ledge on the face of a wall, pier, or buttress formed by a diminution of its thickness above **b :** a level terrace on a bank or hillside **c :** horizontal displacement in faulting of strata from previous alignment **:** STRIKE SLIP **d :** an abrupt change in the dimension or profile of an object (as a bowl) or the part set off by such change **4 :** something that sets off to advantage or embellishes something else **:** FOIL **5 a :** an abrupt bend in an object (as a pipe or rod) by which one part is turned aside out of line but nearly parallel with the rest; *also* **:** the part thus bent aside **b :** a short distance measured usu. at right angles from a line (as to a boundary in computing the area of an irregular-shaped piece of land or to a continuation of a line parallel to itself at some distance away to avoid an obstruction) **c :** the distance of any point in a ship's structure from one of the three reference planes measured normal to that plane **6 :** something that serves to counterbalance or to compensate for something else ⟨the ~ of a century of industry was the universal ugliness —Sacheverell Sitwell⟩; *specif* **:** either of two equivalent items on the two sides of an account ⟨these agencies . . . borrow money in order to relend it, and have ~*s* consisting of debts owed them —*New Republic*⟩ **7 :** OFFSET WELL **8** [fr. past part. of ²*offset*] **a :** unintentional transfer of ink (as from the surface of a freshly printed sheet to the back of the sheet placed on top of it); *also* **:** the ink or image so transferred — called also *setoff* **b** *or* **offset lithography :** a printing process in which an inked impression (usu. from a dampened planographic surface) is first made on a rubber-blanketed cylinder and then transferred to the paper being printed — compare DRY OFFSET, LITHOGRAPHY, PHOTO-OFFSET, PLANOGRAPHY **9 :** a rip current running out from or along a beach **:** SEA PUSS **10 :** difference in value or direction **:** DEVIATION, DISCREPANCY ⟨modern man cannot divest himself of his desire to act in the old way . . . the result is an ~ between his desires and his possibilities —W.P.Webb⟩
²**offset** \'ˌ-'-\ *vb* [¹*off* + *set*, v.] *vt* **1 a :** to place over against **:** BALANCE ⟨~ items of deposit and withdrawal⟩ **b :** COUNTERBALANCE, COMPENSATE ⟨had speed enough to ~ his opponents' greater weight⟩ **2 :** to form an offset in (as a wall, rod, pipe) **3** *geol* **:** to move horizontally to one side out of alignment by faulting **4 :** to transfer (an inked impression) from one surface to another by contact ~ *vi* **:** to receive an unintentionally transferred impression **:** set off ⟨interleaving to prevent *offsetting*⟩
³**offset** \"\ *adj* [fr. past part. of ²*offset*] **1 :** placed or moved out of line or out of the center ⟨fishing rod with ~ handle⟩ ⟨~ wheels⟩ **2 :** neither parallel nor intersecting — used esp. of the axes of gears or pulleys **3 :** printed by the offset method ⟨an ~ postage stamp⟩
**offset arch** *n* **:** CORBEL ARCH

offset screwdriver

**offset screwdriver** *n* **:** a screwdriver with the blade at right angles to the shaft for use where a straight screwdriver cannot reach the screwhead

**offset sheet** *n* : SLIP SHEET
**offset tool** *n* : a cutting tool whose cutting edge is not in line with the shank
**offset well** *n* : an oil well drilled opposite another oil well on an adjoining property
**off-shade** \ˈ=ˌ=\ *adj* : imperfectly matching an original or desired color ⟨least mistake in the quantities of dyed wool means *off-shade* yarn —*Dyestuffs*⟩
**off-shears** \ˈ=ˌ=\ *adj* [²*off* + *shears*] *Austral* : of or relating to sheep that have been shorn ⟨*off-shears* sale⟩ ⟨*off-shears* dipping⟩
**offshoot** \ˈ=ˌ=\ *n* [³*off* + *shoot*] **1** : a branch of a main stem **2 a** : a lateral branch (as of a mountain range) **b** : a collateral or derived branch, descendant, or member : OUTGROWTH ⟨the Roman law and its ~*s*⟩ ⟨American culture began as an ~ of Europe —Peter Viereck⟩ **c** : a minor or secondary activity or product ⟨devoted to fiction, and these nonfictional pieces are . . . ~*s* of this activity —J.T.Farrell⟩
**¹offshore** \ˈ=ˈ=\ *adv* [²*off* + *shore*] **1** : from the shore ⟨a breeze blowing ~⟩ : at a distance from the shore ⟨a boat sailing along ~⟩ **2** : outside the country : ABROAD ⟨purchasing weapons ~⟩
**²offshore** \ˈ"\ *adj* **1** : coming or moving away from the shore ⟨an ~ breeze⟩ ⟨an ~ current⟩ **2 a** : situated off the shore or within a zone generally considered to extend to three miles from low-water line ⟨~ bar⟩ ⟨~ islands⟩ ⟨~ oil reserves⟩ **b** : distant from the shore ⟨~ navigation⟩ ⟨~ fishing⟩ **c** : placed or made abroad ⟨~ procurement⟩
**offshore bar** *n* : BARRIER 2b(1)
**off side** *adv* (*or adj*) **1** : illegally in advance of the ball or puck: as **a** : beyond or across the line of scrimmage in football before the ball is snapped **b** : in the opponent's territory in field hockey or soccer in advance of a teammate having the ball when less than two opponents are between ball and goal line **2** : in poor taste : OFF-COLOR ⟨comedy line cut out as being *off side*⟩ **3** : in such position as to cause a finesse to lose ⟨the queen is *off side*⟩
**offside** \ˈ=ˌ=\ *n* [³*off* + *side*] **1 a** *chiefly Brit* : the right side (as of a horse or a vehicle) **b** : the far or inferior side ⟨into the rough surroundings of Chicago's ~ —*Science*⟩ **2** [*off side*] : an instance of being off side in a game ⟨five-yard penalty for ~⟩
**off·sid·er** \ˈ=ˌsīdə(r)\ *n*, *Austral* : HELPER, ASSISTANT, ASSOCIATE, FOLLOWER ⟨wanted him as ~ on the boat —Vance Palmer⟩ ⟨an ~ of the governor, too —Thomas Wood †1950⟩
**off-sorts** \ˈ=ˌ=\ *n pl* [²*off* + *sorts*] : the less desirable parts of the fleece separated during wool-sorting
**off soundings** *adv* : offshore beyond the 100 fathom line
**offspin** \ˈ=ˌ=\ *n* [³*off* + *spin*] : spin imparted to a bowled ball in cricket that tends to cause it to break from the off side to the leg side
**off·spring** \ˈȯf,spriŋ *also* ˈäf-\ *n*, *pl* **offspring** *also* **offsprings** [ME *ofspring*, fr. OE, fr. *of* off + *springan* to spring — more at OF, SPRING] **1** : something that springs from an animal or plant reproducing its kind : YOUNG, PROGENY, CHILD, ISSUE ⟨a mother of numerous ~⟩ **2** : something that comes into being as a result : PRODUCT ⟨atomic bomb is the ~ of 20th century physics —I.I.Rabi⟩ **3** *obs* **a** : GENERATION **b** : ancestral stock : RACE **c** : LINEAGE, DESCENT **d** : SOURCE, ORIGIN
**offstage** \ˈ=ˈ=\ *adv* (*or adj*) [²*off* + *stage*] **1** : off or away from the stage : out of sight of the audience ⟨the actual murder is carried out ~⟩ ⟨voices heard ~⟩ **2** : in private life ⟨known ~ as a kindly man⟩ **3** : behind the scenes : out of the public view : UNOFFICIALLY ⟨much of the important work of the conference was done ~⟩
**off-street** \ˈ=ˌ=\ *adj* [²*off* + *street*] : located outside the boundary lines of any street ⟨an *off-street* parking facility⟩
**off stump** *n* : the outside stump farther from the batsman in cricket — compare LEG STUMP
**offtake** \ˈ=ˌ=\ *n* [³*off* + *take* (after *take off*, v.)] **1** : the act of taking off: as **a** : the taking off or purchase of goods **b** : the amount of goods purchased during a given period **2** : a channel or passage for taking or leading off (as a liquid or gas) ⟨~ of a distilling flask⟩
**off-taste** \ˈ=ˌ=\ *n* : an unwanted taste imparted by spoilage or contamination
**off-the-face** \ˌ=ˌ=ˈ=\ *adj*, *of a woman's hat* : brimless or having a brim that does not shade the face
**off theory** *n* : a cricket strategy in which a concentration of fielders is placed on the off side esp. in the slips and the bowling aimed generally at or outside of the off stump — compare LEG THEORY
**off-trail** \ˈ=ˌ=\ *adj* (*or adv*) [²*off* + *trail*] : UNUSUAL, UNCONVENTIONAL, UNHACKNEYED ⟨the plot, which is an odd and *off-trail* one —Anthony Boucher⟩ ⟨interesting *off-trail* body designs —Roger Huntington⟩
**offtype** \ˈ=ˌ=\ *adj* [²*off* + *type*] : not true to type : markedly deviating from the normal or standard ⟨~ individuals cropping out within a breed of rabbits⟩
**off·ward** \ˈȯfwə(r)d *also* ˈäf-\ *also* **off·wards** \-dz\ *adv* [¹*off* + *-ward*, *-wards*] : off or away from something as to direction or position; *specif* : off or away from the shore ⟨the deck was canting ~⟩
**off-wheeler** \ˈ=ˌ==\ *n* [*off wheel* right wheel + *-er*] : a wheelhorse on the right side
**off-white** \ˈ=ˌ=\ *n* : a color (as cream, oyster, beige) closely resembling white but having a slight tinge of gray or of a pale hue : a yellowish or grayish white ⟨cloths handwoven in *off-white* with wide borders —*New Yorker*⟩
**off year** *n* : a year characterized by or noted for diminished activity or inferior production: as **a** : a year in which there are no national elections; *esp* : a year in which no president is elected — compare MIDTERM **b** : the year of light bearing in biennial-bearing fruit trees
**of·lag** \ˈō,fläg\ *n* -s [G, short for *offizierslager* officers' camp] : a German prison camp for officers
**ofo** \ˈō(,)fō\ *n*, *pl* **ofo** *or* **ofos** *usu cap* **1 a** : a Siouan people of the Yazoo river valley, Mississippi **b** : a member of such people **2** : the language of the Ofo people
**OFr** *abbr* Old French
**oft** \ˈȯft\ *adv*, *sometimes* -ER/-EST [ME, fr. OE *oft*; akin to OHG *ofto* often, ON *opt*, Goth *ufta*] : OFTEN — now used chiefly in compound adjectives ⟨an ~ neglected factor⟩ ⟨~ quoted statement⟩
**¹of·ten** \ˈȯfən, -ftən\ *adv*, *usu* -ER/-EST [ME, alter. of *oft*] : on many occasions : in many instances or places ⟨numerous plates ~ in color⟩ : not seldom : FREQUENTLY ⟨are ~ puzzled and sometimes annoyed by the ways of other peoples —W.A. Parker⟩ ⟨in the sense in which the Dialect Society ~*est* employs the word *dialect* —Louise Pound⟩ ⟨now and then he finds adventure by imagining it, ~*er* he transforms his own experience —Walter Lippmann⟩
**²often** \ˈ"\ *adj* [ME, fr. *often*, adv.] *archaic* : frequently occurring : FREQUENT ⟨use a little wine for . . . thine ~ infirmities —1 Tim 5:23 (AV)⟩
**of·ten·ness** \-n(n)əs\ *n* -ES : FREQUENCY
**of·tens** \-nz\ *adv* [¹*often* + *-s*] *dial chiefly Eng* : OFTEN
**oftentimes** \ˈ==ˌ=\ *also* **oftentime** \ˈ==ˌ=\ *adv* [ME, alter. of *ofttime*, *ofttimes*] : OFTEN
**oft·time** \ˈȯf(t)ˌtīm\ *adv* [ME, fr. *oft* + *time*] *archaic* : OFTEN
**oft·times** \-mz\ *adv* [ME, fr. *oft* + *times*] : OFTEN
**OG** *abbr* **1** officer of the guard **2** original gum **3** outside guard
**o gage** *n*, *usu cap O* [²*oh*, *o*] : a gage of track in model railroading in which the rails are approximately 1¼ inches apart
**ogalala** *usu cap*, *var of* OGLALA
**og·co·ce·phal·i·dae** \ˌägkōsəˈfaləˌdē\ *n pl*, *cap* [NL, fr. *Ogcocephalus*, type genus + *-idae*] : a small family of sluggish spiny bottom-dwelling marine fishes (order Pediculati) with broad flat head and body, slender tapering tail, small mouth and feeble teeth, a short illicium, and jugular pelvic fins resembling limbs by means of which they crawl about — see BATFISH
**og·co·ceph·a·lus** \ˌägkōˈsefələs\ *n*, *cap* [NL, irreg. fr. Gk *onkos* bulk + NL *-cephalus*; akin to Gk *enenkein* to carry — more at ENOUGH] : the type genus of the family Ogcocephalidae comprising various typical batfishes
**og·do·ad** \ˈägdō,ad\ *n* -s *usu cap* [Gk *ogdoad-*, *ogdoas*, fr. *ogdoos* eighth (fr. *oktō* eight) + *-ad-*, *-as*, fem. suffix denoting descent from or connection with — more at EIGHT] **1** *Gnosticism* : a group of eight divine beings or of eight aeons **2** *Gnosticism* : the seat of rule of the higher archon and his son
**¹ogee** *also* **OG** \(ˈ)ōˌjē\ *n* -s [fr. obs. E *ogee* ogive, modif. of F *ogive*; fr. the use of such moldings in ogives — more at OGIVE] **1 a** : a molding with a profile in the form of a letter S : CYMA RECTA, CYMA REVERSA **b** : a reverse curve like the profile of an ogee molding **2** : an ogee arch

ogee 1a

**²ogee** *also* **OG** \ˈ"\ *adj* **1** : having the outline of an ogee molding ⟨an ~ bracket foot⟩ — see FOOT illustration **2** : having an outline composed of two contrasted ogee curves meeting in a point at the apex ⟨an ~ arch⟩ ⟨an ~ doorhead⟩ — see ARCH illustration
**ogee·chee lime** \ōˈgēchē-\ *n*, *usu cap O* [fr. *Ogeechee* river, Ga.] **1** : the acid olive-shaped drupe of a tupelo (*Nyssa ogeche*) of the southern U. S. **2** : a tree whose fruits are Ogeechee limes
**ogee clock** *or* **OG clock** *n* : a 19th century U. S. shelf clock with S-curve molding
**ogeed** \(ˈ)ōˌjēd\ *adj* [¹*ogee* + *-ed*] : shaped like an ogee or like two meeting contrasted ogees
**og·ham** *or* **og·am** *also* **og·um** \ˈägəm, ˈȯg-\ *n* -s [IrGael & MIr; IrGael *ogham*, fr. MIr *ogom*, *ogum*] **1** *sometimes cap* : a system of alphabetic writing which is known principally from inscriptions in Old Irish running vertically up rough standing memorial stones that date from at least as early as the 5th century and are found in the British Isles esp. in southern Ireland and which in its typical form had 15 consonant symbols consisting of lines touching or crossing an edge of the stone and five vowel symbols consisting of notches on the edge **2** : a letter of the ogham alphabet **3** : an inscription in ogham characters **4** : the form of Old Irish appearing in ogham inscriptions

n q r i s c z e f t ng u l d g o b h m a

ogham

**ogham·ic** *or* **ogam·ic** \ōˈgamik\ *adj* **1** : of, relating to, characteristic of, or constituting ogham ⟨~ characters⟩ ⟨the ~ alphabet⟩ **2** : inscribed or written in ogham
**og·ham·ist** \ˈägəməst, ˈȯg-\ *n* -s : one that practices inscribing or writing in ogham ⟨embellishments by an ~ no longer bound by practical tradition —Howard Meroney⟩
**ogham stone** *n* : a usu. roughly worked upright stone placed over a grave in ancient Ireland and having at least one sharp edge on which a memorial inscription in ogham is cut
**oghuz** \ōˈgüz\ *n*, *pl* **oghuz** *usu cap* : GHUZ
**ogi·val** \(ˈ)ōˌjīvəl\ *adj* [F, fr. *ogive* + *-al*] **1** : of, relating to, or having the form of an ogive **2** : characterized by the use of pointed arches and ribbed vaulting : GOTHIC **3** : shaped like an ogee or like two meeting contrasted ogees ⟨an ~ chair arm⟩
**ogive** \(ˈ)ōˌjīv\ *n* -s [F, fr. MF *ogive*, *augive*, perh. fr. *auge* trough (fr. L *alveus* tub, trough) + *-ive* — more at ALVEOLUS] **1 a** : a diagonal arch or rib across a Gothic vault **b** : a pointed arch **c** : a contour like that of a pointed arch **2 a** : the curve determining the shape of the head of modern pointed projectiles that is struck on a line perpendicular to the axis of the projectile on a radius expressed in calibers **b** : the ogival head of a projectile **3** : a graph each of whose ordinates represents the sum of all the frequencies up to and including a corresponding frequency in a frequency distribution **4** : OGEE 1a
**ogived** \-vd\ *adj* : shaped like an ogive
**og·la·la** \ägˈlälə\ *or* **og·a·la·la** \ˌägə'-\ *n*, *pl* **oglala** *or* **oglalas** *or* **ogalala** *or* **ogalalas** *usu cap* **1 a** : a Teton Dakota people **b** : a member of such people **2** : the language of the Oglala people
**¹ogle** \ˈōgəl *sometimes* ˈäg-\ *vb* **ogled**; **ogled**; **ogling** \-g(ə)liŋ\ **ogles** [prob. fr. LG *oegeln*, freq. of *oegen* to look at, fr. *oog* eye; akin to OHG *ouga* eye — more at EYE] *vi* : to glance coquettishly or provocatively : look with amorous invitation or challenge ⟨subject to temptation to ~ at young ladies —Lucius Garvin⟩ ~ *vt* **1** : to eye amorously : glance at admiringly, provocatively, or enticingly ⟨lounged in front of a sidewalk cafe, *ogling* the women who passed —Steve Nelson⟩ **2** : to look at esp. with greedy or interested attention ⟨was still *ogling* the drinks on the next table —William DuBois⟩
**²ogle** \ˈ"\ *n* -s **1** *slang* : EYE ⟨y'll 'ave to clap a beefsteak on that ~ of yours —G.B.Shaw⟩ **2** : an amorous or coquettish glance ⟨gave him two or three ~*s* accompanied by . . . a captivating smile —T.L.Peacock⟩
**ogler** \-g(ə)lə(r)\ *n* -s : one that ogles
**oglio** *archaic var of* OLIO
**og·mic** \ˈägmik\ *adj* [irreg. fr. *ogham* + *-ic*] : OGHAMIC
**ogre** \ˈōgə(r)\ *n* -s [F, prob. fr. L *Orcus*, god of the underworld] **1** : a hideous giant represented in fairy tales and folklore as feeding on human beings : MONSTER ⟨he was going to strike her in terror, thinking her an ~ from his dreams, when she spoke —Liam O'Flaherty⟩ **2** : a dreaded person or object : someone or something very difficult to cope with ⟨the ~ of nonuniformity of laws comes up again and again —*Motor Transportation in the West*⟩
**ogre·ish** *also* **ogrish** \ˈōg(ə)rish, -rēsh\ *adj* : resembling or befitting an ogre — **ogre·ish·ly** *adv*
**ogress** \ˈōgrəs\ *n* -ES [F *ogresse*, fr. *ogre* + *-esse* -ess] **1** *heraldry* : a roundel sable : GUNSTONE, PELLET **2** : a female ogre
**ogyg·i·an** \ōˈjijēən\ *adj*, *usu cap* [L *ogygius* Ogygian (fr. Gk *ōgygios*, fr. *Ōgygos*, *Ōgygēs*, ancient legendary king of Boeotia) + E *-an*] **1** : of or relating to the legendary Greek King Ogyges or to a deluge said to have taken place in his reign **2** : ANCIENT, PRIMEVAL
**¹oh** *or* **o** \ˈō(ō)\ *interj*, *usu cap when spelled o* [ME *o*] **1** — used to express various emotions (as astonishment, pain, or desire) **2** — used in direct address ⟨*Oh*, *porter! Come here, please*⟩
**²oh** \ˈō\ *or* **o** *n* -s *usu cap when spelled o* [¹*o*; fr. the similarity of the symbol for zero (0) to the letter O] : ZERO ⟨the number is three six ~ seven (3607)⟩
**OH** *abbr* **1** open hearth **2** overhead
**ohe·lo** \ōˈhā(ˌ)lō\ *n* -s [Hawaiian *ʻohelo*] : an endemic Hawaiian blueberry (*Vaccinium reticulatum*) with a shining fleshy rather astringent red or yellow berry
**OHG** *abbr* Old High German
**oh hell** *or* **oh pshaw** *n* : a card game for three to six players in which a player scores only if he has correctly predicted the exact number of tricks he will win
**ohia** \ōˈhēə\ *n* -s [Hawaiian *ʻōhiʻa*] **1** *or* **ohia-lehua** \=ˌ===-ˈ==\ [*ohia-lehua* fr. Hawaiian *ʻōhiʻa-lehua*, fr. *ʻōhiʻa* + *lehua* fruit of the lehua tree] *Hawaii* : LEHUA **2** *also* **ohia-ai** \=ˈ==ˈī\ [*ohia-ai* fr. Hawaiian *ʻōhiʻa-ʻai*, fr. *ʻōhiʻa* + *ʻai* food plant] *Hawaii* : MALAY APPLE
**ohi·an** \ōˈhīən\ *n* -s *cap* [*Ohio* state + *-an*] : OHIOAN
**ohio** \ōˈhī(ˌ)ō\ *adj*, *usu cap* [fr. *Ohio*, north central state of the U. S., fr. the *Ohio* river, perh. fr. Iroquois *oheo* beautiful] : of or from the state of Ohio ⟨*Ohio* clay products⟩ : of the kind or style prevalent in Ohio : OHIOAN
**¹ohio·an** \ōˈhīəwən\ *adj*, *usu cap* [*Ohio* state + E *-an*] **1** : of, relating to, or characteristic of the state of Ohio **2** : of, relating to, or characteristic of the people of Ohio
**²ohioan** \ˈ"\ *n* -s *cap* : a native or resident of the state of Ohio
**ohio buckeye** *n*, *usu cap O* : a buckeye (*Aesculus glabra*) that occurs chiefly in the central U. S. and has gray bark which is much-furrowed and broken into scaly plates and leaves which have usu. five finely toothed leaflets more or less glabrous beneath
**ohio curcuma** *n*, *usu cap O* : GOLDENSEAL
**ohio horsemint** *n*, *usu cap O* : a stiff hairy perennial mint (*Blephilia ciliata*) having showy purple irregular flowers
**ohm** \ˈōm\ *n* -s [after Georg Simon *Ohm* †1854 Ger. physicist] **1** : the practical mks unit of electric resistance that is equal to the resistance of a circuit in which a potential difference of one volt produces a current of one ampere or to the resistance in which one watt of power is dissipated when one ampere flows through it and that is taken as standard in the U. S. **2** : a unit of electrical resistance equal to 1.00049 ohms that was formerly taken as the standard in the U. S. — called also *international ohm* **3** : the cgs unit of acoustic resistance, reactance, and impedance corresponding to a pressure amplitude of one dyne per square centimeter per cubic centimeter per second of flux (volume-velocity) amplitude — called also *acoustic ohm*
**ohm·age** \-mij\ *n* -s : the resistance of a conductor expressed in ohms
**ohm-ammeter** \ˈ=ˈ=ˌ==\ *n* : a combined ohmmeter and ammeter
**ohm·ic** \ˈōmik\ *adj* [ISV *ohm* + *-ic*] **1** : of or relating to an ohm : measured in ohms **2** : relating to a material or an electrical contact for which the electrical resistance is not dependent on the applied voltage
**ohmic resistance** *n* : electrical resistance as distinguished from inductive or capacitive reactance
**ohm·me·ter** \ˈō(m),mēd·ə(r), -ētə-\ *n* [ISV *ohm* + *-meter*] : an instrument for indicating directly resistance in ohms
**OHMS** *abbr* On Her Majesty's Service; On His Majesty's Service
**ohm's law** *n*, *usu cap O* [after G. S. *Ohm*] **1** : a law in electricity: the strength or intensity of an unvarying electrical current is directly proportional to the electromotive force and inversely proportional to the resistance of the circuit **2** : a statement in acoustics: the human ear in perceiving a complex sound receives not a sensation of a single sound but sensations of the separate components of the complex wave causing the sound
**oho** \ōˈhō\ *interj* [ME] — used to express various emotions (as taunting or amused surprise)
**ohone** \äˈkōn\ *var of* OCHONE
**OHV** *abbr*, *often not cap* overhead valve
**OIC** \ˌō,ī'sē, ˈȯik\ *n* [*Ohio Improved Chester White*] **1** : a breed of low set white lard-type swine developed in Ohio by selection from a strain of the Chester White breed **2** -s : any hog of the OIC breed
**-o·ic** \ˈōik, ˈōēk\ *adj suffix* [*-o-* + *-ic*] : containing carboxyl or a derivative of it — in names of acids and related compounds ⟨capr*oic*⟩ ⟨hex*oic*⟩ ⟨napth*oic*⟩; *esp* : containing carboxyl in place of methyl ⟨hexan*oic* acid⟩
**¹-oid** \ˌȯid\ *n suffix* -s [L *-oides*, fr. *-oīdes*, adj. suffix] : something resembling a (specified) object or having a (specified) quality ⟨cylindr*oid*⟩ ⟨glob*oid*⟩ ⟨hyperbol*oid*⟩
**²-oid** \"\ *adj suffix* [MF *-oide* & L *-oīdes*, fr. Gk *-oeidēs*, fr. *-o-* + *-eidēs*, fr. *eidos* form, shape, kind — more at WISE] : resembling : having the form or appearance of ⟨asbest*oid*⟩ ⟨Caucas*oid*⟩ ⟨crystall*oid*⟩ ⟨granit*oid*⟩ ⟨intellectual*oid*⟩
**-oi·dal** \ˈȯidᵊl\ *adj suffix* [¹*-oid* + *-al*] : -OID ⟨asbest*oidal*⟩
**-oi·dea** \ˈȯidēə\ *or* **-oi·da** \-də\ *or* **-oi·dei** \-dē,ī\ *n pl suffix* [*-oidea*, NL, fr. L *-oīdes* -oid + *-ea*, neut. pl. of *-eus* -eous; *-oida*, NL, fr. L *-oīdes*; *-oidei*, NL, fr. L *-oīdes* + *-ei*, masc. pl. of *-eus* -eous] : animals characterized by or of the nature of — in names of higher taxa in zoology ⟨Echin*oidea*⟩ ⟨Hydr*oida*⟩ ⟨Gan*oidei*⟩
**oid·i·oid** \ōˈidē,ȯid\ *adj* [NL *Oidium* + E *-oid*] **1** : of, relating to, or resembling fungi of the genus *Oidium* **2** : producing oidia
**oid·i·o·my·co·sis** \ō,idēō,mīˈkōsəs\ *n* [NL, fr. *Oidium* + *-o-* + NL *-mycosis*] : infection with or disease caused by fungi of the genus *Oidium*
**oid·i·um** \ōˈidēəm\ *n* [NL, fr. *o-* + *-idium*] **1 a** *cap* : a genus of imperfect fungi (family Moniliaceae) including many now considered to represent conidial stages of various powdery mildews — compare BLASTOMYCETES, THRUSH **b** *pl* **oid·ia** \-ēə\ : a fungus of this genus **c** *pl* **oidia** : one of the small conidia borne in chains by various fungi (as members of the genus *Oidium*) — called also *arthrospore* **2** *pl* **oidia** : a powdery mildew caused by a fungus of the genus *Oidium* esp. in the grape — compare OIDIOMYCOSIS
**oiko-** — see ²EC-
**¹oi·ko·mo·nad** \ˌȯikəˈmō,nad\ *adj* [NL *Oikomonad-*, *Oikomonas*] : of or relating to the genus *Oikomonas* or to the family Oikomonadidae
**²oikomonad** \"\ *n* -s : a protozoan of the genus *Oikomonas* or the family Oikomonadidae
**oi·kom·o·nas** \ȯiˈkämənəs\ *n*, *cap* [NL, fr. ²*ec-* + *-monas*] : a cosmopolitan genus (the type of the family Oikomonadidae) of minute uniflagellate protozoans common in stagnant water, soil, and sewage
**oi·ko·plast** \ˈȯikə,plast\ *n* -s [²*ec-* + *-plast*] : one of the ectodermal cells that secrete the gelatinous layer in the Appendicularia
**oi·ko·pleu·ra** \ˌȯikəˈplürə\ *n*, *cap* [NL, fr. ²*ec-* + *-pleura*] : a cosmopolitan genus of small tunicates (order Larvacea) with egg-shaped body and long tail
**¹oil** \ˈȯi(ə)l *dial* ˈī(ə)l, *esp before pause or consonant* \əl\ *n* -s *often attrib* [ME *olie*, *oile*, fr. OF, fr. L *oleum* olive oil, oil, fr. Gk *elaion*, fr. *elaia* olive — more at OLIVE] **1 a** : any of various substances that typically are unctuous viscous combustible liquids or solids easily liquefiable on warming and are not miscible with water but are soluble in ether, naphtha, and often alcohol and other organic solvents, that leave a greasy not necessarily permanent stain (as on paper or cloth), that may be of animal, vegetable, mineral, or synthetic origin, and that are used according to their types chiefly as lubricants, fuels and illuminants, as food, in soap and candles, and in perfumes and flavoring materials — compare ESSENTIAL OIL, FAT, FATTY OIL, MINERAL OIL **b** : PETROLEUM **2** : a substance of an oily consistency: as **a** : a cosmetic preparation containing oil ⟨bath ~⟩ ⟨hair ~⟩ ⟨sunburn ~⟩ **b** : NITROGLYCERIN **3 a** : an oil color used by an artist ⟨paints in ~*s*⟩ **b** : a painting done in oil colors ⟨suggests that his best ~*s* retain the sharp conviction of his sketches —J.T.Soby⟩ **4** : unctuous or flattering speech : smooth or persuasive utterance ⟨it's just the old ~ —Harris Downey⟩ **5** *slang Austral* : INFORMATION **6 oils** *pl* : stocks or bonds of oil companies
**²oil** \"\ *vb* -ED/-ING/-S [ME *oilen*, fr. *oile*, n.] *vt* **1** *obs* : to anoint ceremonially with oil (as a king at coronation) **2 a** : to smear or rub over with oil : furnish or feed with oil : LUBRICATE ⟨carefully ~*ed* the bearings of the machine⟩ ⟨liberal contributions ~*ed* the campaign machinery⟩ **b** : to spray oil on (as a dirt road) **3** : to make bland or smooth ⟨I learned to use a soft voice to ~ my words —Lillian Smith⟩ **4** : to turn into or make of the consistency of oil (as grease by melting) ~ *vi* **1 a** : to become like oil in consistency **b** : to separate with the formation of an oily portion (as butter fat) — used with *off* ⟨cream poured into hot coffee ~*s off*⟩ **2** : to take on fuel oil — used chiefly of ships and locomotives — **oil the hand** *or* **oil the palm** : BRIBE, TIP ⟨a cop whose *palm* I'd *oiled* —Polly Adler⟩
**oil and gas lease** *n* : a deed by which a landowner authorizes exploration for and production of oil and gas on his land usu. in consideration of a royalty
**oil bag** *n* : a canvas bag containing cotton, oakum, or other absorbent material soaked with oil that is sometimes dropped with a sea anchor to create an oil slick tending to reduce surface wave violence
**oil bath** *n* : a bath of oil: as **a** : a volume of oil in which a solid is submerged (as for lubrication, preservation, or tempering) **b** : the container for oil so used **c** : a stream of oil flowing upon a cutting tool to cool it
**oil beetle** *n* : a beetle of *Meloe* or a related genus having a swollen body and short elytra that overlap instead of meeting in a straight line, passing through more than the usual number of larval instars, and emitting a yellowish liquid from the leg joints when disturbed
**oilbird** \ˈ=ˌ=\ *n* : a nocturnal bird (*Steatornis guácharo*) of northern So. America and Trinidad that is related to the goatsuckers and in some characters to the owls, nests in caverns, feeds chiefly on oily fruits of various nut palms, is believed to employ a form of echo-location comparable to that of bats, and has fatty young from which an oil is extracted for use instead of butter — called also *guacharo*
**oil-break switch** *n* : a switch in which the contacts are immersed in oil — compare AIR-BREAK SWITCH
**oil burner** *n* **1** : a burner equipped to vaporize or atomize fuel oil, mix it with air and ignite the mixture, and direct the flame upon the surface to be heated **2** : a ship whose boilers are oil-fired **3** : a gasoline engine that consumes an excessive amount of oil
**oil cake** *n* : the solid residue that remains after expressing or

extracting most of the oil from various seeds (as of cotton, hemp, flax, and soybeans) and that is then often ground to make oil meal

**oilcan** \'ˌ=,=\ *n* **:** a can for oil; *esp* **:** a can equipped with a slender spout for lubricating machinery

**oilcloth** \'=,=\ *n* **1 a :** cotton cloth coated with a dull or glossy finish that usu. contains oil, clay, and colored pigment and used for waterproof coverings **b :** an article (as a tablecloth) made of this material **2 :** a floor covering made of a strong open canvas treated with linseed-oil paint, smoothed with pumice, and printed from blocks as in calico printing — compare LINOLEUM

oilcan

**oil color** *n* **1 :** a pigment used for oil paint **2 :** OIL PAINT **3 :** a concentrated dispersion of a colored pigment in linseed oil or other drying oil

**oil column** *or* **oil crane** *n* **:** a vertical pipe with control valve and spout for supplying oil to the tenders of oil-burning locomotives

**oil cup** *n* **:** a cup connected with a bearing as a lubricator and usu. having a wick, valve, or other means for regulating the delivery of oil

**oil·dom** \'ȯi(ə)ldəm\ *n* -S [¹*oil* + *-dom*] **1 a :** a petroleum region **2 :** the petroleum industry

**oiled** *adj* **1 a :** lubricated with oil **b :** polished, dressed, or impregnated with oil **c :** coated or treated with oil or an oil compound ⟨~ silk⟩ ⟨~ paper⟩ **2** *slang* **:** DRUNK ⟨thoroughly ~ and very talkative —*Amer. Mercury*⟩

**oil–electric** \ˌ=ˈ=ˌ=\ *adj* **:** DIESEL-ELECTRIC

**oil·er** \'ȯilə(r)\ *n* -S **1 a :** one who is employed to do routine oiling and greasing of mechanical equipment (as in a mill, factory, power plant, railroad yard, or on a vessel) **b :** one who works oil or grease into hides or skins to soften and protect the leather **2 :** an oilcan, oil cup, or other receptacle or device for applying oil to mechanical bearing surfaces **:** LUBRICATOR **3 :** a producing oil well **4 a :** a ship using oil as fuel **b :** an oil cargo ship **:** TANKER **5 oilers** *pl* **:** OILSKINS **6 :** a device that automatically applies an oil or insecticide to the hide of a domestic animal that rubs against it

**oilfeeder** \'=,==\ *n, Brit* **:** a force-feed oilcan

**oil field** *n* **:** a region rich in petroleum deposits; *esp* **:** a region containing numbers of producing oil wells

**oil·field·er** \'ȯil,fēldə(r)\ *n* **:** a worker in an oil field

**oilfish** \'=,=\ *n* **:** ESCOLAR

**oil gas** *n* **:** gas (as blau gas or Pintsch gas) made usu. by vaporizing and cracking a petroleum distillate (as a heavy oil) — compare CARBURETED WATER GAS, GAS OIL

**oil geologist** *n* **:** PETROLEUM GEOLOGIST

**oil gilding** *or* **oil gold** *n* **:** gilding on a surface coated with oil paint and size

**oil gland** *n* **:** a gland that secretes oil; *specif* **:** UROPYGIAL GLAND

**oil groove** *n* **:** a groove in the bearing surface of a machine part that distributes lubricating oil injected through an oilhole

**oil–harden** \'=,==\ *vt* **:** to quench (steel) in oil for the purpose of hardening

**oil heater** *n* **:** a heater that burns fuel oil

**oilhole** \'=,=\ *n* **:** a small hole through which oil is injected to lubricate a mechanical bearing surface

**oilhole drill** *also* **oil drill** *n* **:** a twist drill having oilholes through which a lubricant is fed to its cutting edge while drilling

**oilier** *comparative of* OILY

**oiliest** *superlative of* OILY

**oil·i·ly** \'ȯiləlē\ *adv* **:** in an oily manner **:** UNCTUOUSLY ⟨waddled forward, smiling ~ —John Buchan⟩

**oil–immersion lens** *n* **:** IMMERSION LENS

**oil·i·ness** \'ȯilēnəs, -lin-\ *n* -ES **:** the quality or state of being oily

**oiling** *pres part of* OIL

**oil–in–water** \ˌ==ˈ==\ *adj* **:** consisting of oil dispersed in water ⟨*oil-in-water* emulsions⟩

**oil length** *n* **:** the ratio of drying oil to resin in a varnish or similar coating expressed usu. as the number of gallons of oil per 100 pounds of resin ⟨varnishes are usually classified as to *oil length* as well as to the major types of oil and resin used —S.B.Levinson⟩ — compare LONG-OIL, SHORT-OIL

**oil·less** \'ȯilləs\ *adj* **:** lacking oil **:** not lubricated with oil **:** not requiring oil — **oil·less·ness** *n* -ES

**oilless bearing** *n* **:** a bearing that does not require oil; *esp* **:** one in which a lubricant (as powdered graphite) is incorporated in the material of which the bearing is made

**oil·let** \'ȯilət\ *n* -S [ME *oilet* — more at EYELET] *archaic* **:** ¹EYELET 2

**oil·man** \'=,man, -ˌmaa(ə)n, -ˌmən\ *n, pl* **oilmen 1 :** an entrepreneur or leader in the petroleum industry **2 :** one who sells or delivers oil

**oil meal** *n* **:** a meal made by grinding oil cake and fed to livestock or used as fertilizer

**oil mill** *n* [ME, fr. *oile* + *mill*] **1 :** a machine that crushes seeds (as cottonseed or soybeans) to extract their oil **2 :** a factory using oil mills

**oil nut** *n* **1 :** BUFFALO NUT **2 :** any of several nuts and seeds yielding oil: as **a :** COCONUT **b :** the fruit of the oil palm **c :** BUTTERNUT; *esp* **:** this nut with its husks used while still soft and immature for pickling whole

**oil of catechumens :** holy oil used in baptism, ordination, consecration of churches, and coronation of rulers

**oil of hartshorn :** BONE OIL 1

**oil of philosophers :** PHILOSOPHERS' OIL

**oil of the sick :** holy oil used in extreme unction

**oil of vitriol :** concentrated sulfuric acid

**oil·om·e·ter** \ȯi'lämədə(r)\ *n* [¹*oil* + *-o-* + *-meter*] **1 :** OLEOMETER **2 :** a reservoir for oil **:** an oil tank

**oil paint** *n* **:** paint in which a drying oil is the vehicle

**oil painting** *n* **1 a :** the act or art of painting in oil colors **b :** a picture painted in oils **2 :** painting that uses pigments orig. ground in oil

**oil palm** *n* **:** a palm of the genus *Elaeis*; *esp* **:** AFRICAN OIL PALM

**oil pan** *n* **:** the lower section of the crankcase used as a lubricating-oil reservoir on an internal-combustion engine

**oilpaper** \'=,==\ *n* **:** paper made translucent and waterproof by soaking in oil ⟨dim light . . . streamed in through ~ windows —J.H.Cutler⟩

**oil plant** *n* **:** a plant that yields oil: as **a :** SESAME **b :** CASTOR-OIL PLANT

**oil pool** *n* **:** ¹POOL 3

**oil press** *n* **:** a press for expressing oil (as from nuts, olives, seeds)

**oil process** *n* **:** a photographic printing process in which a layer of gelatin is sensitized with a bichromate solution, exposed under a negative, soaked in water, and inked with an oily printing ink by a brush, the unexposed portions of the gelatin swelling in the water and repelling the oily ink while the exposed portions tanned by the light action remain unswollen and accept the ink

**¹oilproof** \'=,=\ *adj* [¹*oil* + *proof*] **:** impervious to oil

**²oilproof** \"\ *vt* **:** to make oilproof

**oil red** *n, often cap O&R* **:** any of several oil-soluble red dyes — see DYE table I (under *Solvent Red 26 and 27*)

**oil ring** *n* **1 :** a seal engravers' finger ring having a small receptacle containing a mixture of oil and diamond dust used in replenishing the engraving tool **2 :** RING OILER **3 :** a piston ring designed to secure proper distribution of lubricating oil over the length of cylinder wall traversed by the piston

**oil rock** *n* **:** the stratum usu. of sandstone, limestone, or shale from which petroleum is produced

**oils** *pl of* OIL, *pres 3d sing of* OIL

**oil sand** *n* **:** a porous sandstone from which petroleum is obtained by drilled wells

**oil seal** *n* **:** a device (as a gland with packing) for preventing the escape or entrance of oil

**oilseed** \'=,=\ *n* **1 :** any of various seeds grown largely for oil; as **a :** CASTOR BEAN **b :** SESAME **c :** COTTONSEED **d :** LINSEED **e :** RAPESEED **2 a :** GOLD OF PLEASURE **b :** the seed of gold of pleasure yielding cameline oil

**oil shale** *n* **:** shale from which oil may be produced by distillation

**oil shark** *n* **:** any of several sharks from whose livers oil is obtained: as **a :** BASKING SHARK **b :** SOUPFIN SHARK

**oilskin** \'=,=\ *n* **1 :** an oiled cloth (as of cotton, linen, silk) used for waterproof coverings and garments **2 :** an oilskin raincoat **3 oilskins** *pl* **:** an oilskin suit usu. consisting of coat and trousers

**oil–skinned** \"+d\ *adj* **:** dressed in or protected with oilskin

**oil slick** *n* **:** a film of oil floating on water

**oil–soluble** \'=,===\ *adj* **:** soluble or dispersible in oils **:** FAT-SOLUBLE ⟨*oil-soluble* dyes⟩ ⟨*oil-soluble* resins⟩

**oil spot** *n* **1 :** one of the pale transparent areas on the upper leaf surface in the early stages of downy mildew of the grape **2 :** OLEOCELLOSIS

**oilstock** \'=,=\ *n* **:** a vessel for holding holy oil

**¹oilstone** \'=,=\ *n* [¹*oil* + *stone*] **1 :** a whetstone for use with oil **2 :** stone from which oilstones may be made

**²oilstone** \"\ *vt* **:** to sharpen with an oilstone **:** polish with oilstone powder or oilstone slips

**oilstove** \'=,=\ *n* **:** a stove that burns oil (as kerosine)

**oil switch** *n* **:** a switch in which the contacts are immersed in oil

**oil tanning** *n* **:** the conversion of hides into leather by impregnation with oil — see ¹CHAMOIS 2b

**oil–temper** \'=,==\ *vt* **:** to harden (steel) by quenching in oil after heating

**oiltight** \'=,=\ *adj* **:** so tight as to prevent the passage of oil ⟨~ joints⟩ — **oil·tight·ness** *n*

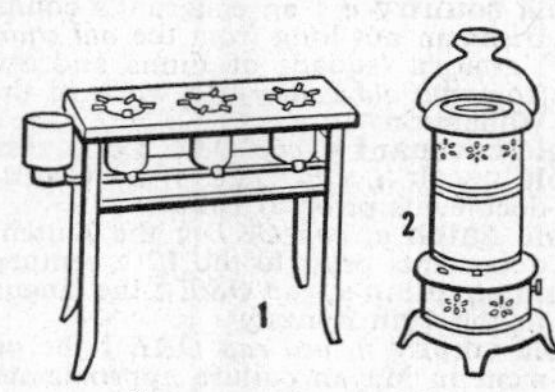

oilstoves: *1* for cooking, *2* for heating

**oil transfer process** *n* **:** a photographic printing process in which an image in oily ink produced in the oil process is transferred to another support (as paper) by contact and pressure

**oil tube** *n* **:** VITTA 1

**oil varnish** *n* **:** a varnish consisting of a solution of natural or synthetic resins in a drying oil (as linseed oil or tung oil)

**oilway** \'=,=\ *n* **:** a channel by which oil may reach a part to be lubricated

**oil well** *n* **:** a well from which petroleum is obtained

**¹oily** \'ȯilē, -li\ *adj* -ER/-EST [¹*oil* + *-y*] **1 :** of, relating to, or consisting of oil **:** containing oil **:** having the nature or qualities of oil **2 :** covered or impregnated with oil **:** GREASY ⟨rid of rubbish and ~ rags —*My Weekly Reader*⟩ **3 :** unctuously ingratiating or insinuating **:** PLAUSIBLE, SMOOTH, SUAVE ⟨an ~, sycophantic press agent —Lee Rogow⟩

**²oily** \"\ *adv* **:** OILILY ⟨of ~ smooth texture⟩

**oily bean** *or* **oily grain** *n* **:** SESAME

**oil yellow** *n* **1** *often cap O&Y* **a :** any of several oil-soluble yellow dyes — see DYE table I (under *Solvent Yellow*) **b** *or* **oil yellow II :** a carcinogenic azo dye $C_6H_5N_2C_6H_4N(CH_3)_2$ formerly used in coloring butter and oils; *para-*dimethyl-aminoazobenzene — called also *butter yellow, methyl yellow;* see DYE table I (under *Solvent Yellow 2*) **2 :** a moderate greenish yellow that is greener and duller than citron yellow and deeper than linden green

**oily–tongued** \ˌ==ˈ=\ *adj* **:** excessively smooth-spoken **:** UNCTUOUS

**oi·me** *also* **oi·mee** \ȯi'mā\ *interj* [It *oimè, ohimè,* fr. *ohi* alas + *me* me] *archaic* — used to express grief or lamentation

**-oin** \əwən, ə̇wən, ˌōin, 'ōən\ *n suffix* -S [ISV *-o-* + *-in*] **:** acyloin ⟨*acetoin*⟩

**¹oink** \'ȯiŋk\ *n* -S [imit.] **:** the natural grunt of a hog

**²oink** \"\ *vi* -ED/-ING/-S **:** to utter the natural grunt of a hog

**oinochoe** *var of* OENOCHOE

**oint** \'ȯint\ *vt* -ED/-ING/-S [ME *ointen,* fr. MF *oint,* past part. of *oindre,* fr. L *ungere, unguere*] *chiefly dial* **:** ANOINT

**oint·ment** \'ȯintmənt\ *n* -S [ME, alter. (influenced by *ointen* to anoint) of *oignement, oinement,* fr. OF *oignement,* fr. (assumed) VL *unguimentum,* alter. of L *unguentum,* fr. *unguent-, unguens,* pres. part. of *unguere* to anoint, smear; akin to OHG *ancho, anko* butter, OIr *imb,* W *ymenyn* butter, Skt *añjati, anakti* he salves] **:** a salve or unguent for application to the skin; *specif* **:** a semisolid medicinal preparation usu. having a base of fatty or greasy material (as petrolatum, lard, wool fat) — see SIMPLE OINTMENT

**o'io** \'ō(ˌ)ē,ō\ *n* -S [Hawaiian *'ō'io*] *Hawaii* **:** BONEFISH

**oi·ti·ci·ca** \ˌȯid·ə'sēkə\ *n* -S [Pg, fr. Tupi] **:** any of several So. American trees; *esp* **:** a tall tree (*Licania rigida*) of northeastern Brazil having a fruit like the pecan with a kernel that yields oiticica oil

**oiticica oil** *n* **:** a drying oil obtained from the kernels of the fruit of the oiticica tree that is similar to tung oil in many properties and is used chiefly in varnishes, paints, and printing inks

**ojib·wa** *or* **ojib·way** \ō'jib,wā\ *n, pl* **ojibwa** *or* **ojibwas** *or* **ojibway** *or* **ojibways** *usu cap* [Ojibwa *ojib-ubway* moccasin with a puckered seam (such as the Ojibwa traditionally wore), lit., to roast till puckered up] **1 a :** an Indian people of the region around Lake Superior and westward **b :** a member of such people **2 :** an Algonquian language of the Ojibwa, Salteaux, Ottawa, and Algonquian peoples — called also *Chippewa*

**¹OK** *or* **okay** *also* **okey** *or* **okeh** \(')ō¦kā\ *adj* [abbr. of *oll korrect,* alter. of *all correct*] **:** all right ⟨an *OK* battery commander —John Phillips⟩ ⟨will print anything however bad which is politically *OK* —George Orwell⟩ ⟨there are people, nice people, *okay* people, who do their own housework, cooking, and serving —Laura Hobson⟩

**²OK** *or* **okay** *also* **okey** *or* **okeh** \"\ *adv* **:** all right **:** YES ⟨*OK,* Doctor, I'll let you know —John Hersey⟩ ⟨*okay, okay,* but be good to him —C.O.Gorham⟩

**³OK** *or* **okay** *also* **okey** *or* **okeh** \"\ *vt* **OK'd** *or* **okayed; OK'd** *or* **okayed; OK'ing** *or* **okaying; OK's** *or* **okays :** APPROVE, AUTHORIZE, SANCTION ⟨read and *OK'd* every script —Sam Balter⟩ ⟨all right, I'll *okay* that —James Hilton⟩ ⟨*okehs* easing small business tax —*Sacramento (Calif.) Bee*⟩

**⁴OK** *or* **okay** *also* **okey** *or* **okeh** \"\ *n* -S **:** APPROVAL, ENDORSEMENT, SANCTION, AUTHORIZATION ⟨he gets the *OK* of the Production Code censors —Joseph Wechsberg⟩ ⟨an ad presented to the publisher for *okey* —*Publishers' Weekly*⟩

**¹oka** *var of* OCA

**²oka** \'ōkə\ *n* -S *usu cap* [CanF, fr. *Oka,* village in Quebec, Canada, where it is made] **:** a Trappist cheese made by Trappist monks in Quebec

**OKA** *abbr, often not cap* otherwise known as

**oka·na·gon** \ˌōkə'nägən\ *n, pl* **okanagon** *or* **okanagons** *usu cap* **1 a :** a Salishan people of the Okanagon river valley of Washington and British Columbia **b :** a member of such people **2 :** a language of the Okanagon, Colville, Nespelem, Sanpoil, and Senijextee people

**oka·pi** \ō'käpē\ *n* -S [native name in Africa] **:** a mammal (*Okapia johnstoni*) discovered in the deep forests of the Belgian Congo in 1900 and closely related to and in many respects resembling the giraffe but being somewhat smaller than an ox, having a relatively short neck, a coat of solid reddish chestnut on the body, the cheeks yellowish white, and the upper parts of the legs ringed with cream and purplish black

okapi

**oka·ya·ma** \ˌōkə'yämə\ *adj, usu cap* [fr. *Okayama,* Japan] **:** of or from the city of Okayama, Japan **:** of the kind or style prevalent in Okayama

**¹oke** \'ōk\ *or* **oka** \'ōkə\ *n* -S [F, NGk & Turk; F *oque,* fr. NGk & Turk; NGk *oka,* fr. Turk *okka,* fr. Ar *ūqīyah,* prob. fr. Gk *oungia, ounkia* ounce, fr. L *uncia* — more at OUNCE] **:** any of three units of weight varying around 2.8 pounds and used respectively in Greece, Turkey, and Egypt

**²oke** \'ōkā\ *n* -S [by shortening & alter.] **:** OKOLEHAO

**oken·ite** \'ōkə,nīt\ *n* -S [G *okenit,* fr. Lorenz *Oken* †1851 Ger. naturalist + G *-it* -ite] **:** a compact or fibrous mineral $CaSi_2O_4(OH)_2.H_2O$ consisting of a whitish hydrous calcium silicate

**okey·doke** \ˌōkē¦dōk\ *or* **okey·dokey** \-dōkē\ *adv* (*or adj*) [redupl. of ²*OK*] *slang* **:** all right

**okie** *also* **oakie** \'ōkē\ *n* -S *usu cap* [fr. *Ok*lahoma + *-ie*] **:** a migrant agricultural worker; *esp* **:** such a worker from Oklahoma — compare ARKIE

**¹oki·na·wan** \ˌōkə¦näwən, -naůən\ *adj, usu cap* [*Okinawa,* island and island group of the Ryukyu islands, between the East China sea and the Pacific ocean + E *-an*] **1 :** of, relating to, or characteristic of the island of Okinawa **2 :** of, relating to, or characteristic of the people of Okinawa

**²okinawan** \"\ *n* -S *cap* **:** a native or inhabitant of Okinawa

**okla·bar** \'ōklə,bär\ *n* -S *usu cap* [fr. ¹*okla*homa + *bar*] **1 :** a breed of autosexing gold or silvery barred domestic fowls developed in Oklahoma and notable for fast feathering and good meat conformation **2** *often cap* **:** a bird of the Oklabar breed

**¹okla·ho·ma** \ˌōklə¦hōmə\ *adj, usu cap* [fr. *Oklahoma,* state in the southwestern U. S., fr. Choctaw *okla humma, okla homma* red people] **:** of or from the state of Oklahoma ⟨an *Oklahoma* Indian⟩ **:** of the kind or style prevalent in Oklahoma **:** OKLAHOMAN

**²oklahoma** \"\ *n* -S *usu cap* **1 :** a form of rummy related to canasta **2** *or* **oklahoma gin :** a form of gin rummy in which the rank of the first upcard determines the minimum count on which one may knock

**oklahoma city** *adj, usu cap O&C* [fr. *Oklahoma City,* Okla.] **:** of or from Oklahoma City, the capital of Oklahoma **:** of the kind or style prevalent in Oklahoma City

**¹okla·ho·man** \-mən\ *adj, usu cap* [*Oklahoma* + E *-an*] **1 :** of, relating to, or characteristic of the state of Oklahoma **2 :** of, relating to, or characteristic of the people of Oklahoma

**²oklahoman** \"\ *n* -S *cap* **:** a native or resident of Oklahoma

**oklahoma plum** *n, usu cap O* **:** a low shrub (*Prunus gracilis*) with white flowers and globose red fruit

**oko·le·hao** *also* **oko·le·hau** \ˌōkəlā'hau̇\ *or* **okulehau** *n* -S [Hawaiian *'ōkolehao* iron try-pot still, okolehao, lit., iron buttocks] *Hawaii* **:** an alcoholic liquor distilled from ti or taro roots

**okou·me** *or* **oku·me** \ˌōkə'mā\ *n* -S [F *okoumé,* fr. native name in Africa] **:** GABOON 2a

**okra** *also* **okro** \'ōkrə, *chiefly in southern U. S.* -rē *or* -ri\ *n* -S [of African origin; akin to Twi *ŋ̀kʷrūmā̃* okra] **1 :** a tall annual (*Hibiscus esculentus*) widely cultivated in the southern U. S. and the West Indies for its mucilaginous green pods that are pickled or used as the basis of soups and stews **2 :** the pods of the okra **3 :** ¹GUMBO 2a

**ok·vik** \'äkvik\ *adj, usu cap* [fr. *Okvik,* site on Punuk Island, S.E. of St. Lawrence Island in the Bering sea] **:** of or belonging to an early phase of the Old Bering Sea culture in northern Alaska and northeastern Siberia that produced an art style in which patterns suggesting scrolls are noticeable

okra

**ol** *abbr* oleum

**OL** *abbr* **1** occupational level **2** [L *oculus laevus*] left eye **3** overflow level **4** overhead line **5** overload **6** Old Latin

**¹-ol** \ˌȯl, ˌōl\ *n suffix* -S [ISV, fr. *alcohol*] **:** chemical compound containing hydroxyl ⟨hydr*ol*⟩ — esp. in names of alcohols and phenols ⟨glycer*ol*⟩ ⟨methan*ol*⟩ ⟨cres*ol*⟩

**²-ol** — see -OLE; not used systematically

**³-ol** *also* **-ole** \ˌōl, ˌȯl\ *n comb form* -S [ISV, fr. L *oleum* oil — more at OIL] **:** hydrocarbon of the benzene series esp. in a commercial mixture containing homologous hydrocarbons ⟨xyl*ol*⟩ — not used systematically; compare -ENE

**ol·a·ca·ce·ae** \ˌälə'kāsē,ē\ *n pl, cap* [NL, fr. *Olac-, Olax,* type genus + *-aceae*] **:** a family of tropical trees or shrubs (order Santalales) having simple leaves and small flowers with a one-celled ovary followed by a one-seeded fruit — **ol·a·ca·ceous** \ˌ==ˈkāshəs\ *adj*

**OL and T** *abbr* owners, landlords, and tenants

**ola·tion** \ō'lāshən\ *n* -S [¹*-ol* + *-ation*] **:** the formation of polynuclear coordination complexes by means of hydroxyl groups as bridges

**olax** \'ō,laks\ *n, cap* [NL, fr. LL *olax* odorous, fr. *olēre* to smell; fr. the unpleasant odor of the wood — more at ODOR] **:** a genus (the type of the family Olacaceae) of evergreen trees and shrubs distributed through the tropics of Asia, Africa, and Australia and having distichous leaves and small racemose flowers with three stamens

**ol·cha** \'ōlchə\ *n, pl* **olcha** *or* **olchas** *usu cap* **1 :** a Tungusic people living near the mouth of the Amur river in Asia — compare TUNGUS **2 :** a member of the Olcha people

**¹old** \'ōld, *before a consonant often* 'ōl\ *adj* -ER/-EST [ME *ald, old,* fr. OE *eald, ald;* akin to OS *ald* old, OHG *alt* old, ON *aldr* age, *ala* to bring up, nourish, Goth *alds* period of time, age (of a person), *altheis* old, *alan* grown up, L *alere* to feed, nourish, *alescere* to grow, *altus* high, Gk *aldēskein* to grow, *analtos* insatiable, Skt *anala* fire (lit., the insatiable one), *ṛdhnoti* he flourishes, succeeds; basic meaning: to grow, nourish] **1 a :** dating from the remote past **:** ANCIENT ⟨beautiful ~ Japanese traditions —Lafcadio Hearn⟩ **b :** persisting from an earlier time **:** CHRONIC ⟨~ pains keep . . . gnawing at your heart —Joseph Conrad⟩ **c :** of long standing **:** having a status strengthened by the passage of time ⟨an ~ friend⟩ ⟨~ residents of the vicinity —John De Meyer⟩ ⟨comes from an ~ family⟩ **2 a :** distinguished from an object of the same kind by being of an earlier date ⟨new . . . standards for ~ jobs —Bruce Payne⟩ ⟨the ~ name was readopted at the time of incorporation —*Amer. Guide Series: Pa.*⟩ ⟨how slow this ~ moon wanes —Shak.⟩; *specif, usu cap* **:** belonging to an early period in the development of a language or literature and preceding a middle period **b :** constituting an earlier geographic entity ⟨the ~ Roman Empire⟩ ⟨repeatedly toured the ~ Northwest —E.S.Bates⟩ **c** *of a holiday* **:** celebrated on the Old Style date ⟨*Old Christmas*⟩ ⟨*Old Midsummer Day*⟩ **3 a :** having existed for a specified period of time ⟨a little girl three years ~⟩ ⟨a gambrel roofed house over 200 years ~⟩ ⟨the campaign was scarcely two days ~ —P.W.Thompson⟩ **b :** exceeding a specified age ⟨~ geese retailed at 47¢ lb.⟩ **4 a :** performed in or descriptive of the distant past ⟨~ sacrifices to the Cretan bulls⟩ ⟨mentioned in ~ histories⟩ **b :** of, relating to, or characteristic of antiquity or of a past era **:** ANTIQUE, BYGONE ⟨interpreting ~ writers in their own tongue —Benjamin Farrington⟩ ⟨~ Hitchcock chairs⟩ ⟨rural simplicity and innocence because in ~ days, as now, this region lay apart from the active life . . . near the sea —Samuel Van Valkenburg & Ellsworth Huntington⟩ **c :** stemming from or reminiscent of a past era ⟨tenacity of ~ opinion —H.T. Buckle⟩ ⟨giving new meanings to ~ words —M.R.Cohen⟩ ⟨chandeliers, which are merely ~, as opposed to antique —*New Yorker*⟩ **d :** famed through the ages ⟨the ~ historical lands of Europe —Mark Pattison⟩ **5 a :** advanced in years **:** nearing the end of the normal life span ⟨an ~ man with a long white beard⟩ ⟨a tall ~ virgin pine . . . spared by fire and woodcutter —*Amer. Guide Series: Minn.*⟩ **b :** exhibiting the physical or mental characteristics of age ⟨looked ~ at 20 because of prolonged suffering⟩ ⟨wake up . . . in a world where no one was conventional or stuffy or ~ —Margery Sharp⟩ **6 :** having a knowledge or ability gained through long practice **:** EXPERIENCED ⟨~ in the ways of conspirators —Max Peacock⟩ **7 a :** identified with an earlier period ⟨the ~ democratic objection to despotism —G.K.Chesterton⟩ ⟨ministers . . . who spoke the ~ tongue —Oscar Handlin⟩ ⟨the grandfather's clock still stands in the same ~ place⟩ ⟨retained all of his ~ alertness and charm —F.J.Mather⟩ **b :** during an earlier period **:** FORMER ⟨hundreds of his ~ students were present —L.M.Crosbie⟩ ⟨the badge . . . is treasured among ~ members of our squadron —L.G.Pine⟩ **8 a :** deteriorated or mellowed by or as if by time or use **:** AGED, WORN ⟨~ books⟩ ⟨~ wine⟩ ⟨~ pasture⟩ ⟨marks the northern end of an ~ sea wall —H.Lovegrove⟩ — often used to express disparagement ⟨give mamma that dirty ~ stick⟩, generalized affection ⟨good ~ Santa Claus⟩ ⟨our little ~ wobbledy calf —Eugene Field⟩ ⟨a great ~ establishment —Sinclair Lewis⟩, familiarity ⟨fifty years ago, there was only one kind of pneumonia — just plain ~ pneumonia —R.J.Huebner⟩ ⟨back to the same ~ grind⟩, personalization ⟨the ~ stomach did a buck and wing —P.G.Wodehouse⟩, or as an intensive ⟨having a high ~ time⟩ esp. of *any* ⟨come any ~ time, I'll be home all day⟩ ⟨not any ~ ink will print well —Séan Jennett⟩ **b :** well advanced toward reduction to baselevel — used of topography and topographic features or their age ⟨a wide, nearly level floor . . . characterizes an ~ valley —W.J.Miller⟩ **c** *obs* **:** dressed in old clothes **:** SHABBY ⟨the rest were ragged, ~, and beggarly —Shak.⟩ **d :** no longer in use **:** DISCARDED ⟨the profitable . . . reworking of ~ tailings —*Amer. Guide Series: Nev.*⟩ **e :** of a grayish or dusty tone — used of a color

**syn** ANCIENT, VENERABLE, ANTIQUE, ANTIQUATED, ANTEDILUVIAN, ARCHAIC, OBSOLETE: OLD is a general term opposed to *young* or *new*, describing whatever has had a long life or existence. ANCIENT, often opposed to *modern*, applies to what has been in existence from the remote past; it may suggest possession of valuable characteristics (as rarity or wisdom) accruing from age, describe an aspect of the distant now dead past, or be used to indicate hoary antiquity ⟨some illustrious line so *ancient* that it has no beginning —Edward Gibbon⟩ ⟨the civilization of China is *ancient* —Havelock Ellis⟩ ⟨poets of *ancient* Greece⟩ ⟨*ancient* pre-Inca Peruvians —Current Biog.⟩ ⟨the decrepit manager who was too *ancient* and incompetent for more serious employment —Ellen Glasgow⟩ VENERABLE usu. implies respect or veneration ⟨*venerable* men, you have come down to us from a former generation —Daniel Webster⟩ ⟨the ruins, Etruscan, Roman, Christian, *venerable* with a threefold antiquity —Nathaniel Hawthorne⟩ but sometimes emphasizes decrepitude ⟨a *venerable* Hudson whose driver makes periodic stops to wield a screwdriver and siphon gasoline —Claudia Cassidy⟩ ANTIQUE is a close synonym of ANCIENT; it is likely to apply to something old-fashioned that has acquired value through rarity or nostalgic charm ⟨a savor of the *antique*, primeval world and the earliest hopes and victories of mankind —Laurence Binyon⟩ ⟨*antique* monsters, older than Italy and Greece, than Babylon and Carthage —Llewelyn Powys⟩ ⟨such prosperous cities had already in Leland's day outgrown their *antique* suits of stone armor —G.M.Trevelyan⟩ ⟨an *antique* clock⟩ ANTIQUATED usu. applies to what is discredited or deprecated as outmoded ⟨we are apt to scorn our neighbor because his rate of motion is faster or more sluggish than our own. He is *antiquated* if he clings to the values of yesterday —A.L.Guérard⟩ ⟨as *antiquated* as the powdered periwig of an eighteenth century courtier —Waldemar Kaempffert⟩ ANTEDILUVIAN carries an even stronger sense of deprecation ⟨up-to-date models of scientific inquiry have steadily replaced the *antediluvian* constructions of an earlier generation —Ethel Albert⟩ ARCHAIC applies to what belongs to or has the characteristics of an earlier period ⟨when new opinions have overthrown the *archaic* institutions, they will create new institutions in harmony with themselves —S.M.Crothers⟩ ⟨Portugal at this time, *archaic* in its chivalry, had the most resplendent court in Europe —Francis Hackett⟩ ⟨*methinks* is an *archaic* construction⟩ OBSOLETE applies to what has been entirely displaced or superseded ⟨*obsolete* as the feudal baron —J.C.Snaith⟩ ⟨the relationship between the English king and the English people is a relationship far more modern and far better fitted to the needs of the times than the *obsolete* language and the *obsolete* trappings of the court suggest —D.W.Brogan⟩ ⟨instructing his civil officers in California to regard General Kearny's orders as *obsolete* —Irving Stone⟩

[2]**old** \"\ *n* -s [ME *ald, old,* fr. *ald, old,* adj.] **1** *obs* **:** an advanced stage **:** OLD AGE ⟨they must not be gelded . . . in the ~ of the moon —Richard Surflet & Gervase Markham⟩ **2 :** an earlier time or period ⟨in days of ~ when knights were bold —Edward Thomas⟩ **3 :** one that is of a specified age — usu. used in combination ⟨had come to the park when she was a five-year-*old* —W.A.White⟩ ⟨for 14 and 15 year ~*s* the reduction has been about 38 percent —*Amer. Child*⟩ ⟨entered a promising two-year-*old* in the Derby⟩ — **of old** *adv* **:** in times past **:** FORMERLY ⟨more . . . committees than *of old* were appointed —Allan Nevins⟩ ⟨still must the poet as *of old* . . . starve, freeze, and fashion verses —Edna S. V. Millay⟩

[3]**old** \ˈōl(d)\ *adv* [[1]*old*] **:** of old **:** ANCIENTLY — used chiefly in combination ⟨*old*-established⟩

**old adam** *n, usu cap A* [after the Biblical *Adam,* the first man and first sinner] **:** unregenerate man ⟨grant that the *old Adam* in this child may be so buried —*Bk. of Com. Prayer*⟩ ⟨the *old Adam* in me . . . rises and asserts himself —R.W. Jackson⟩ — called also *old man*

**old age** *n* [ME] **1 :** the final stage of the normal life span **:** SENESCENCE ⟨for purposes of the conference *old age* was considered to be 65 years or over —*Progressive Labor World*⟩ **2 :** the final stage in a cycle of erosion — compare ADOLESCENCE, INFANCY, MATURITY ⟨plains that illustrate the extreme of erosional *old age* —V.C.Finch & G.T.Trewartha⟩

**old-age** \'=¦=\ *adj* [*old age*] **1 :** of or relating to senescence ⟨*old-age* pension⟩ **2 :** of or relating to the final stage in an erosion cycle ⟨there is abundant evidence of an *old-age* topography in the summit area —*Jour. of Geol.*⟩

**old-age and survivors insurance** *n* **:** national insurance under the U. S. government providing retirement benefits at age 65 and payments to survivors upon death of the insured — compare SOCIAL SECURITY

**old akkadian** *n, cap O&A* **:** the Akkadian language exemplified in texts before 1900 B.C.

**old american** *n, usu cap O&A* **:** an American descended from white ancestors who for three or more generations have been born in the U. S.

**old armenian** *n, cap O&A* **:** the Armenian language exemplified in documents from the 5th century through the medieval period

**old army game** *n* **1 :** a game or device whereby an inexperienced or unwary person is fleeced or victimized — used esp. from time to time of various gambling games (as craps, poker, blackjack) **2 :** the practice of shifting responsibility to another esp. when faced with an unpleasant situation

**old assyrian** *n, cap O&A* **:** the dialect of Akkadian used in Assyria from 2000 B.C. to 1500 B.C.

**old babylonian** *n, cap O&B* **:** the dialect of Akkadian used in Babylonia from 2000 B.C. to 1500 B.C.

**old believer** *n, usu cap O&B* [trans. of Russ *Starover*] **:** RASKOLNIK

**old belt** *n* [fr. the *Old Belt,* the piedmont area of Virginia and North Carolina] **:** a flue-cured tobacco produced mostly in north-central No. Carolina

**old ber·ing sea** \-'beriŋ-, -'biriŋ-\ *adj, usu cap O&B&S* [fr. the *Bering sea,* part of the northern Pacific ocean] **:** of or belonging to an Eskimo culture of northern Alaska and northeastern Siberia about A.D. 100–500 characterized esp. by fossil-ivory implements

**old blue** *n* **:** a pale blue that is redder and duller than average powder blue, greener and less strong than Sistine, and greener and paler than average cadet gray — called also *bleu passé*

**old boy** *n* **1** *usu cap O&B* **:** OLD NICK **2 a :** an often sprightly or waggish old man ⟨that incorrigible broth of an *old boy* —Peter Forster⟩ **b :** a man of a past era or of established prestige ⟨not in the nature of these tough *old boys* to give way —O.S.Nock⟩ ⟨I find the *old boys* . . . too long-winded —O.W. Holmes†1935⟩ **3** *chiefly Brit* **:** a graduate of a boys' school **:** ALUMNUS ⟨heard a headmaster say that the test of a school was the quality of the *old boys* —*Manchester Guardian Weekly*⟩

**old brain** *n* **:** ARCHIPALLIUM

**old bulgarian** *n, cap O&B* **:** OLD CHURCH SLAVONIC

**old catholic** *n, usu cap O&C* **1 :** a member of a separate religious communion formed by members of the Roman Catholic Church who rejected the dogma of papal infallibility as adopted by the Vatican Council of 1870 **2 :** a member of an American communion that retains most of the doctrines and customs of the Roman Catholic Church but has rejected the ecclesiastical authority of the Roman Catholic hierarchy

**old cedar** *n* **:** CASTILIAN BROWN

**old china** *n* **1 :** a moderate blue that is greener and duller than average copen or Dresden blue and redder and less strong than azurite blue **2 :** a grayish blue that is redder and paler than electric, less strong and slightly redder than copenhagen, and redder and stronger than Gobelin

**old christmas** *n, usu cap C, chiefly Midland* **:** January 6 **:** TWELFTHNIGHT

**old church slavonic** *or* **old church slavic** *n, cap O&C&S* **:** the Slavic language used in the Bible translation of Cyril and Methodius and later continued as the liturgical language of many of the Eastern churches

**old-clothes·man** \ˈōl(d)ˈklō(th)z,man, -,maa(ə)n, -mən\ *n, pl* **old-clothesmen :** a dealer in secondhand clothing

**old coral** *n* **:** JASPER RED

**old country** *n* **:** an emigrant's country of origin ⟨big-talking Irishman not long from the *old country* —Mari Sandoy⟩; *esp* **:** EUROPE ⟨squads of Finns and Swedes were brought over from the *old country* to work in the granite quarries —S.T. Williamson⟩

**old covenant** *n, cap O&C* **:** OLD TESTAMENT

**old czech** *n, cap O&C* **:** the Czech language exemplified in documents prior to 1620

**old dutch** *n, cap O&D* **:** the Dutch language exemplified in documents prior to the 12th century

**old egyptian** *n, cap O&E* **:** the language of Egypt from the 1st to the 10th dynasty

**old empire** *n, usu cap O&E* **:** the period of highest development in Mayan culture approximately A.D. 200–600 — compare NEW EMPIRE

[1]**old·en** \ˈōldən\ *adj* [ME, fr. [2]*old* + *-en* (adj. suffix)] **1 :** of or relating to a bygone era **:** ANCIENT, QUAINT ⟨Denmark in very ~ times was a wooded country —Erik Schacke⟩ ⟨in the ~ days, water wheels were used to drive some of the machinery —L.D.Stamp⟩ ⟨a style which resembles that of the ~ chronicles —P.J.Searles⟩ **2 :** advanced in years **:** OLD ⟨assented to the judgment of an ~ rabbinic teacher —Leonard Bernstein⟩

[2]**olden** \"\ *vb* -ED/-ING/-S [[1]*old* + *-en* (v. suffix)] *vi* **:** to grow old **:** AGE ⟨saw an ~*ing* flaccid face —Maurice Walsh⟩ ~ *vt archaic* **:** to make older ⟨experience . . . had ~*ed* him —W.M. Thackeray⟩

**ol·den·burg** \ˈōldən,bərg\ *adj, usu cap* [fr. *Oldenburg,* Germany] **:** of or from the city of Oldenburg, Germany **:** of the kind or style prevalent in Oldenburg

**old english** *n, cap O&E* **1 a :** the language of the English people from the time of the earliest documents in the 7th century to about 1100; *specif* **:** WEST SAXON — distinguished from *Middle English;* called also *Anglo-Saxon;* see INDO-EUROPEAN LANGUAGES table **b :** English of any period prior to Modern English **2 :** BLACK LETTER **3 a :** a style of architecture popular esp. for residences in 16th century England and featuring heavy half-timbering **b :** a contemporary adaptation of 16th century English architecture

**old english alphabet** *n, cap O&E* **:** ANGLO-SAXON ALPHABET

**old english brown** *n, often cap E* **:** a dark grayish to dark yellowish brown — called also *broncho, Indian brown*

**old english game** *n, usu cap O&E&G* **:** a class of game fowls characterized by conventional form and now bred almost wholly for show — compare MODERN GAME

**old english sheepdog** *n* **1** *usu cap O&E&S* **:** an English breed of medium-sized sheep and cattle dogs believed to trace back to the Roman occupation of the British Isles, having no tail or a very short one, a square large skull, nose tapered but blunt-ended, body short and compact with deep brisket and well-sprung ribs, forelegs straight, and hind legs well-muscled, being in length and height from about 21 to 26 inches each, and having a profuse, shaggy, blue-gray and white coat that often obscures the eyes and hangs from the body almost to the ground **2** *usu cap O&E, sometimes cap S* **:** a dog of the Old English Sheepdog breed — called also *bobtail*

**ol·den·lan·dia** \,ōldən'landēə\ *n, cap* [NL, fr. H.B.*Oldenland* †*ab*1699 Dan. physician and botanist + NL *-ia*] **:** a large genus of chiefly tropical herbs (family Rubiaceae) with usu. elongated leaves and crowded axillary or terminal cymes of small flowers — see CLUSTERED BLUET

**older** *comparative of* OLD

**oldest** *superlative of* OLD

**oldest profession** *n* **:** PROSTITUTION

**old ewe disease** *n* **:** PREGNANCY DISEASE

**old face** *n, chiefly Brit* **:** OLD STYLE 2

**old·fan·gled** \ˈōl(d)¦faŋgəld\ *adj* **:** OLD-FASHIONED

**old-farrand** \(')=¦==\ *adj* **:** AULD-FARRANT

**old-fashion** \'=¦=\ *adj, archaic* **:** OLD-FASHIONED

[1]**old-fashioned** \'=¦==\ *adj* **1 a :** of, relating to, or characteristic of a past era **:** ANCIENT, ANTIQUATED ⟨wears an *old-fashioned* black bow tie —Green Peyton⟩ ⟨*old-fashioned* houses, with their ornamental cornices and high gables —*Amer. Guide Series: Mich.*⟩ ⟨men with the *old-fashioned* hellfire in their sermons —*Atlantic*⟩ ⟨suggested reviving *old-fashioned* home and classroom discipline with physical punishment —*N.Y. Times*⟩ **b :** adhering to traditions or standards of a past era **:** CONSERVATIVE ⟨my mother's family . . . more *old-fashioned*, more pious, and in a word more Victorian even than the English county families of the time —Harold Nicolson⟩ **c :** reminiscent of the past **:** NOSTALGIC, QUAINT ⟨two editions, one of them bound in *old-fashioned* blue gingham —H.H.Reichard⟩ ⟨attendants carried *old-fashioned* bouquets —*Springfield (Mass.) Union*⟩ **2 :** out of date **:** supplanted by something more modern **:** OBSOLETE ⟨thirty *old-fashioned* propeller planes —J.A.Michener⟩ ⟨*old-fashioned* methods for making maple sugar —Murray Schumach⟩ ⟨propaganda — the *old-fashioned* name for psychological warfare —George Fischer⟩ **3** *dial chiefly Eng* **:** of a mature or intelligent nature **:** KNOWING ⟨the collie . . . had turned on him an *old-fashioned* eye —John Buchan⟩ **4 :** growing wild **:** of early hybrid origin — used esp. of a rose — **old-fash·ioned·ly** *adv*

[2]**old-fashioned** \"\ *adv* [[1]*old-fashioned*] **1** *dial chiefly Eng* **:** in a knowing way **:** QUIZZICALLY **2 :** in an outmoded way **:** QUAINTLY ⟨a dress . . . cut kind of *old-fashioned* —J.B. Benefield⟩

[3]**old-fashioned** \"\ *n* -s [*old-fashioned (cocktail)*] **1 :** a cocktail usu. made of whiskey, bitters, sugar, a twist of lemon peel, and a small amount of water or soda, served with ice, and often garnished with fruit (as orange, pineapple, maraschino cherry) **2 :** a short broad glass usu. with a flared top, a sham bottom, and a capacity of seven or eight ounces

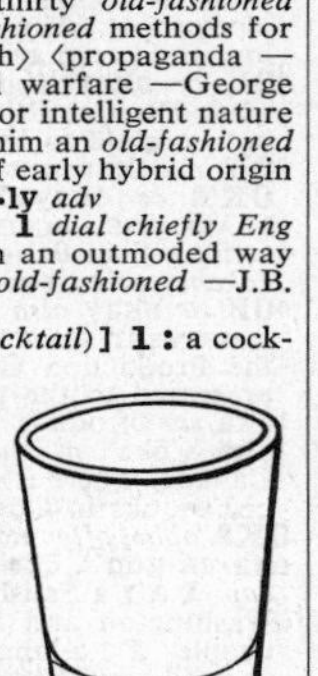

old-fashioned 2

**old-fash·ioned·ness** *n* -ES **:** the quality or state of being old-fashioned

**old field** *n* **1 :** land exhausted by cultivation and no longer tilled **2 :** a field that has produced a particular crop (as alfalfa) for many years

**old-field birch** *n* **:** AMERICAN GRAY BIRCH

**old-field clover** *n* **:** RABBIT-FOOT CLOVER

**old-field colt** \'=,=-\ *or* **old-fields colt** \ˈōl(d),fēldz-\ *n* **:** WOODS COLT

**old-field lark** *n, chiefly South & Midland* **:** MEADOWLARK 1

**old-field pine** *n* **1 :** LOBLOLLY PINE 1 **2 :** SAND PINE **3 :** SHORTLEAF PINE **4 :** JERSEY PINE

**old-field school** *n* **:** a rural elementary school often built in an exhausted corn or tobacco field and common in the South before the Civil War

**old flemish** *n, cap O&F* **:** the Flemish language exemplified in documents prior to the 12th century

**old foundation** *n, usu cap O&F, Church of England* **:** the status of having been founded prior to the Reformation — compare NEW FOUNDATION

**old franconian** *n, cap O&F* **:** the Franconian dialects in use before 1100

**old frankish** *n, cap O&F* **:** OLD FRANCONIAN

**old french** *n, cap O&F* **:** the French language from the time of the earliest documents preserved until the time of Modern French or approximately from the 9th to the 16th century; *esp* **:** French from the 9th to the 13th century as distinguished from Middle French of the 14th to the 16th century

**old frisian** *n, cap O&F* **:** the Frisian language exemplified in documents prior to the 16th century

**old fustic** *n* **1 :** any of several trees of the family Moraceae; *esp* **:** FUSTIC 1a — see MACLURIN, MORIN **2 :** [6]LIME 3

**old german baptist brethren** *n pl, usu cap O&G&B&B* **:** Dunkers withdrawing from the Church of the Brethren in 1881 in protest over Sunday schools, higher education, missions, and church societies — called also *Old Order Dunkers*

**old girl** *n, chiefly Brit* **:** a graduate of or former student at a girls' school **:** ALUMNA

**old glory blue** *n* [fr. *Old Glory,* nickname for the flag of the U.S.] **:** a moderate purplish blue that is redder and stronger than marine blue, duller than average cornflower, and redder and darker than gentian blue

**old glory red** *n* **:** a vivid red that is yellower and duller than apple red or carmine and duller and very slightly bluer than scarlet

**old gold** *n* **1 :** a variable color averaging a dark yellow that is redder and slightly darker than average antique gold (sense 1) and redder, stronger, and slightly lighter than mustard (sense 3 a) **2 :** a light olive that is less strong than citrine

**old gooseberry** *n, usu cap O&G* **:** OLD NICK

**old growth** *n* **1 :** a mature or overmature forest growth more or less uninfluenced by human activity — called also *virgin forest* **2 :** a stand consisting mainly of mature trees

**old guard** *n, often cap O&G* [fr. the *Old Guard,* the imperial French guard created by Napoleon I in 1804; trans. of F *Vieille Garde*] **:** a group of established prestige and influence ⟨the *old guard* of the socially elect —F.L.Allen⟩ ⟨among physicists . . . he had become the leader of the *Old Guard* —Bertrand Russell⟩; *esp* **:** a dominant usu. conservative element of a political party ⟨proceeded to undermine . . . the caucus, which the *Old Guard* of that day dominated —H.R. Penniman⟩

**old guard·ism** \-'gär,dizəm\ *n, often cap O&G* **:** conservatism esp. in politics

**old guardist** *n, often cap O&G* **:** a member or supporter of a conservative group **:** DIEHARD

**old·ham** \ˈōldəm\ *adj, usu cap* [fr. *Oldham,* England] **:** of or from the county borough of Oldham, England **:** of the kind or style prevalent in Oldham

**old·ham·ite** \ˈōldə,mīt\ *n* -s [Thomas *Oldham* †1878 Irish geologist + E *-ite*] **:** a mineral CaS consisting of sulfide of calcium and found in meteorites

**old·ham's coupling** \ˈōldəmz-\ *n, usu cap O* [fr. the name *Oldham*] **:** a coupling for parallel shafts slightly out of line consisting of a disk on the end of each shaft and an intermediate disk having two mutually perpendicular feathers on opposite sides that engage slots in the respective shaft disks

**old hand** *n* **1 :** one having knowledge or ability gained through long experience **:** VETERAN ⟨viewed it with the lenient, slightly bored cynicism of an *old hand* —Francis Hackett⟩ ⟨even *old hands* had to gear up anew for these new jobs —J.A.Conway⟩; *esp* **:** one having detailed knowledge of a geographical area due to extended residence or activity there ⟨an *old* China *hand*⟩ **2** *Austral* **:** an ex-convict; *esp* **:** one of the early immigrants to Australia

**old harry** *n, usu cap O&H* **:** OLD NICK

**old hat** *adj* **1 a :** that is behind the times **:** OLD-FASHIONED, REACTIONARY ⟨in today's climate suffragism seems *old hat* —Helen B. Woodward⟩ ⟨the very young still regarded the rather young as *old hat* —R.L.Duffus⟩ **b :** lacking in freshness **:** HACKNEYED, TRITE ⟨a buyer's main problem is . . . dropping the trend before it becomes *old hat* —*Fashion Accessories*⟩ ⟨accustomed to dismiss Dutch 17th century painting as *old hat* —Emily Genauer⟩ **2 :** inferior to present methods or practices **:** DATED, OBSOLETE ⟨the company's microwave loop . . . (coaxial cable is *old hat* now) —*New Yorker*⟩ ⟨such crude methods are *old hat* —R.G.Spivack⟩

**old helio** *n* **:** MADDER VIOLET

**old high german** *n, cap O&H&G* **:** High German exemplified in documents prior to the 12th century — see INDO-EUROPEAN LANGUAGES table

**old home week** *n* **1** *often cap O&H&W* **:** a week of special festivities during which a community invites former residents to return for a reunion ⟨the social activities of an *Old Home Week* —Agnes Repplier⟩ **2 :** a reunion of former associates marked by special warmth or cordiality ⟨a little knot of alumni having an *old home week* in the stadium parking lot⟩

**old house borer** *n* **:** a cerambycid beetle (*Hylotrupes bajulus*) orig. European but now established in the U. S. whose larvae feed on dry coniferous wood and frequently do serious damage to old rafters and flooring

**old hunker** *n, usu cap O&H* **:** [2]HUNKER 1

**old icelandic** *n, cap O&I* **:** Icelandic spoken or written from the 9th century to the 16th century — compare OLD NORSE; see INDO-EUROPEAN LANGUAGES table

**old identity** *n, Austral* **:** an old and well-known inhabitant of a locality

**old·ie** *also* **oldy** \ˈōldē, -di\ *n, pl* **oldies** [[1]*old* + *-ie, -y*] **:** something trite **:** an old chestnut ⟨take the ~, "Never use a preposition to end a sentence with" —C.E.Borklund⟩; *esp* **:** a popular song of an earlier day ⟨students favor ~*s*, such as "When Irish Eyes Are Smiling" —Kathryn Murray⟩

**old indo-aryan** *or* **old indic** *n, cap O&I&A* **:** SANSKRIT

**old injun** *n* **:** OLD-SQUAW

**old ionic** *n, cap O&I* **:** the Greek dialect of the Homeric epics

**old iranian** *n, cap O&I* **:** any Iranian language in use in the period B.C.

**old irish** *n, cap O&I* **:** the Irish in use between the 7th and 11th centuries — compare IRISH GAELIC; see INDO-EUROPEAN LANGUAGES table

**old·ish** \ˈōldish, -dēsh\ *adj* **:** somewhat elderly

**old italian book hand** *n, usu cap I* **:** SEMICURSIVE

**old ivory** *n* **:** a grayish yellow that is duller and slightly greener than chamois, slightly redder and stronger than crash, and darker and very slightly greener than flax

**old lady** *n* **1 a :** WIFE ⟨my *old lady* . . . said when we were first hooked up it was usually the bills —Adela R. St. Johns⟩ — not often in formal use **b :** MOTHER ⟨used to fight with my *old lady* about taking a bath once a week —L.M.Uris⟩ — not often in formal use **2 :** OLD MAID 2

**old lag** *n* [[5]*lag*] *chiefly Brit* **:** HABITUAL CRIMINAL

**old·land** \ˈōld,land, -lənd\ *n* **:** an extensive area of ancient crystalline rocks reduced to low relief by long erosion

**old lang syne** *n* **:** AULD LANG SYNE

**old latin** *n, cap O&L* **:** the Latin used in the early inscriptions and in the literature prior to the classical period

**old lavender** *n* **1 :** a pale violet that is paler than dusty lavender and redder and duller than dusty periwinkle blue **2 :** a dark grayish purple that is bluer and less strong than raisin black, redder and less strong than average purple wine, and redder and duller than average orchid taupe

**old light** *n, usu cap O&L* **1 :** AULD LICHT **2 :** a member of a conservative group in colonial America (as in a Baptist, Congregationalist, or Presbyterian church) opposed to revivalism and emotionalism in religion — compare NEW LIGHT

**old-line** \'=¦=\ *adj* [fr. the phrase *old line*] **1 a :** having a reputation or authority based on seniority **:** ESTABLISHED, EXPERIENCED ⟨*old-line* bankers, remembering 1929, shuddered at the shaky loans their young executives . . . were willing to make —H.H.Martin⟩ ⟨there is not a single *old-line* movie company that doesn't now have some business connection with television —T.M.Pryor⟩ ⟨he is an *old-line* Yankee⟩ **b :** out of date **:** OLD-FASHIONED ⟨endorsement of the *old-line* and supposedly discredited control —S.H.Adams⟩ **2 :** adhering to old policies or practices **:** CONSERVATIVE, TRADITIONAL ⟨the *old-line* purchasing agent who . . . defies improvements —G.W.H.Ahl⟩ ⟨*old-line* political parties . . . had lost the confidence of the public —A.P.Whitaker⟩ ⟨earned . . . the displeasure of the *old-line* Humanists —G.C.Sellery⟩ **3 :** of or relating to a legal-reserve insurance company established prior to the rise of fraternal benefit societies ⟨most *old-line* policies cannot be turned in for cash till after the third year —*Time*⟩

**old-line company** *n* **:** a nonfraternal insurance company that writes an absolute contract, collects a fixed level premium, and accumulates the legal reserve

**old liner** *n* [*old line* + *-er*] **:** [2]CONSERVATIVE 2, 3

**old low franconian** *or* **old low frankish** *n, cap O&L&F* **:** the Germanic dialects of the lower Rhine valley used prior to about 1100

**old low german** *n, cap O&L&G* **:** Low German exemplified in documents prior to the 12th century

**old maid** *n* **1 :** SPINSTER 3 **2 :** a prim nervous person of either sex who frets over inconsequential details **:** FUSSBUDGET **3 :** a simple game of matching cards which is played with a pack with one queen removed and in which the player holding the odd queen at the end of the game is an "old maid" **4 a** *West Indies* **:** [1]PERIWINKLE 1c **b :** a common garden zinnia (*Zinnia elegans*)

**old maidhood** *n* **:** the status or condition of being an old maid

**old–maidish** \ˈ=ˌ=ˈ=\ *adj* [*old maid* + *-ish*] **:** characteristic of an old maid **:** FUSSY, OLD-WOMANISH — **old–maid·ish·ly** *adv*

**old–maid·ish·ness** *n* -ES **:** the prim conservatism of an old maid

**old–maid's–bonnet** \ˈ=ˌ=ˌ==\ *n* **:** WILD LUPINE

**old–maid's–nightcap** \ˈ=ˌ=ˌ=\ *n* **:** SPOTTED CRANESBILL

**old–maid's–pink** \ˈ=ˌ=ˈ=\ *n* **1 :** CORN COCKLE **2 :** SOAPWORT 1

**old man** *n* **1 a :** HUSBAND ⟨a married woman steppin out on her *old man* —James Jones⟩ — not often in formal use **b :** FATHER ⟨my *old man* was not any great shakes as a parent —Damon Runyon⟩ — not often in formal use **c** *usu cap O&M* **:** BOSS ⟨was not wholly satisfied with the way the *Old Man* was running the department —H.S.Commager⟩; *esp* **:** COMMANDING OFFICER ⟨the *Old Man* pointed her head for Nantucket Sound —H.A. Chippendale⟩ — not often in formal use **2 a :** one having the skill or status acquired through long experience **:** recognized authority ⟨the great *old man* of Eurasian archaeology —O.J. Maenchen-Helfen⟩ **b :** a senior member or former member of an organization (as a military unit) ⟨the *old men* who had fought in the regiment's first two battles —Dan Levin⟩ **c** (1) **:** a tribal elder or sage ⟨the *old man* . . . presides at ceremonials —C.D.Forde⟩ (2) *usu cap O&M* **:** CULTURE HERO ⟨marks on the birch tree . . . inflicted in a moment of anger by *Old Man* —W.D.Wallis⟩ **d** (1) **:** OLD ADAM ⟨put off . . . the *old man*, which is corrupt according to the deceitful lusts —Eph 4: 22 (AV)⟩ (2) **:** GOD **3** *Austral* **:** a full-grown male kangaroo **4 a :** SOUTHERNWOOD **b :** ROSEMARY **5** *dial Eng* **:** the last sheaf of the harvest sometimes shaped into a human effigy and buried **6 :** a drilling post for use with a ratchet, electric, or pneumatic drill

**old–man–and–woman** \ˈ=ˈ==ˈ==\ *n* -S **:** HOUSELEEK

**old–man cactus** *n* **:** a Mexican cactus (*Cephalocereus senilis*) having its joints crowned by drooping white hairs

**old–man fern** *n* **:** an Australasian tree fern (*Dicksonia antarctica*) with very large tripinnate fronds

**old man saltbush** *n* **:** a tall Australian shrub (*Atriplex nummularia*)

**old–man's–beard** \ˈ=ˌ=ˈ=\ *n* **1 :** any of several clematises: as **a :** an American virgin's bower (*Clematis virginiana*) **b :** a European traveler's-joy (*C. vitalba*) **2 a :** SPANISH MOSS **b :** BEARD LICHEN **3 :** FRINGE TREE **4** *dial Eng* **:** any of several plants of the genus *Equisetum*

**old–man's–flannel** \ˈ=ˌ=ˈ==\ *n* **:** MULLEIN

**old–man's–pepper** \ˈ=ˌ=ˈ==\ *n* **:** YARROW

**old–man's–root** \ˈ=ˌ=ˈ=\ *n* **:** the American spikenard (*Aralia racemosa*)

**old master** *n* **1 :** a superior artist or craftsman of established reputation; *esp* **:** a distinguished painter of the 16th, 17th, or early 18th century **2 :** a work by an old master — **old masterly** *adv*

**old–mine** \ˈ=ˈ=\ *adj* **:** having a deep crown and cut in an obsolete style that gives it less sparkle than the modern brilliant — used of a diamond ⟨a Victorian diamond necklace with thirty-eight *old-mine* diamonds —*N. Y. Herald Tribune*⟩

**old moss** *or* **old moss green** *n* **:** a light olive color that is greener, stronger, and slightly deeper than citrine, deeper than grape green, and redder and duller than average willow green — called also *lizard bronze, moss*

**old ned** \-ˈned\ *n, usu cap N* [prob. fr. *Old Ned*, nickname for the devil] *Midland* **:** home-cured hog meat and esp. salt pork or bacon

**old·ness** *n* -ES [ME *oldnes*, fr. OE *ealdnes*, fr. *eald* old + *-nes* -ness — more at OLD] **:** AGE, ANTIQUITY

**old nick** *n, usu cap O&N* **:** the personification of evil **:** DEVIL, SATAN — called also *Old Boy, Old Gooseberry, Old Harry, Old One, Old Scratch, Old Serpent*

**old norse** *n, cap O&N* **:** the North Germanic language of the Scandinavian peoples prior to about A.D. 1350; *specif* **:** the western branch of Old Norse including Old Norwegian and Old Icelandic — see INDO-EUROPEAN LANGUAGES table

**old north french** *n, cap O&N&F* **:** the northern dialects of Old French including esp. those of Normandy and Picardy

**old norwegian** *n, cap O&N* **:** the Norwegian language before the Reformation

**old olive** *n* **:** OLIVE BROWN

**old one** *n, usu cap both Os* **1 :** OLD NICK **2 :** the creator or chief deity in many primitive religions

**old order amish** *n, usu cap both Os&A* **:** a member of the Old Order Amish Mennonite Church adhering strictly to the older forms of worship and attire

**old order brethren** *n pl, usu cap both Os&B* **:** YORKER BRETHREN

**old order dunkers** *n pl, usu cap both Os&D* **:** OLD GERMAN BAPTIST BRETHREN

**ol·do·wan** \ˈäldəwən\ *adj, usu cap* [*Oldoway* gorge, Tanganyika + E *-an*] **:** of or belonging to a Lower and Middle Pleistocene culture of East Africa characterized by crude pebble choppers, scrapers, and hand axes

**old persian** *n, cap O&P* **:** one of the two ancient languages composing Old Iranian and known from cuneiform inscriptions from the 6th and 5th centuries B.C. — compare AVESTAN

**old pink** *n* **:** a light brown that is yellower, stronger, and slightly darker than blush and redder, stronger, and slightly lighter than cork

**old provençal** *n, cap O&P* **:** the Provençal language exemplified in documents from the 11th to the 16th centuries

**old prussian** *n, cap O&P* **1 :** a member of an early people related to the Lithuanians and inhabiting the shores of the Baltic sea east of the Vistula **:** BORUSSIAN **2 :** the Baltic language of the Old Prussian people

**old rail** *n, slang* **:** a veteran or retired railroad employee

**old red** *n* **:** BURNT CARMINE

**old red sandstone** *n, usu cap O&R&S* **:** a thick series of fragmental chiefly sandstone rocks of nonmarine origin, predominantly red in color, and representing the Devonian system in some parts of Great Britain and elsewhere in northwestern Europe

**old regime** *n* **:** ANCIEN REGIME

**old ritualism** *n, usu cap O&R* **:** the doctrines and practices of the Raskolniks

**old ritualist** *n, usu cap O&R* **:** RASKOLNIK

**old rose** *n* **:** a variable color averaging a grayish red that is bluer and paler than bois de rose, bluer and lighter than blush rose, and bluer and paler than appleblossom or Pompeian red

**old roseleaf** *n* **:** a dark red that is yellower and less strong than cranberry and yellower and paler than average garnet or average wine — called also *chocolate maroon, Cuyahoga red*

**old russian** *n, cap O&R* **:** the Russian language exemplified in documents of the 12th to 15th centuries

**olds** *pl of* OLD

**old salt** *n* **:** an experienced sailor **:** a seafaring man ⟨nothing pleases the *old salts* more than a yarn with the boys on the dock —Anthony Anable⟩

**old saxon** *n, cap O&S* **:** the language of the Saxons of northwest Germany between the Rhine and Elbe rivers until about the 12th century — compare LOW GERMAN; see INDO-EUROPEAN LANGUAGES table

**old scandinavian** *n, cap O&S* **:** OLD NORSE

**old school** *n* **1 :** adherents to the conservative policies and practices of the past ⟨the charming self-portrait of a gentleman of the *old school* —Frank Meyer⟩ ⟨of the *old school* that believed the only way to make money was by hard work⟩ **2** *usu cap O&S* **:** adherents to conservative theology or practice and opponents of innovation; *specif* **:** OLD LIGHT 2

**old school baptist** *n, usu cap O&S&B* **:** PRIMITIVE BAPTIST

**old school tie** *n, sometimes cap O&S&T* **1 a :** a necktie displaying the colors of an English public school ⟨entitled to wear the very best of *old school ties*, the Etonian pale blue and black —*Fortune*⟩ **b :** an attitude of conservatism, aplomb, and upper-class solidarity associated with English public school graduates ⟨the traditional prejudice against the British, their aristocratic society and their *old school ties* —*Atlantic*⟩ **c :** a graduate of an English public school ⟨to the *old school ties* the dictators seem ignorant uneducated rebels —G.B.Shaw⟩ **2 :** CLANNISHNESS, CLIQUISM ⟨the War and Navy departments each accumulated growing prestige which fostered the spirit of the *old school tie* —Beirne Lay⟩

**old scratch** *n, usu cap O&S* **:** OLD NICK

**old serpent** *n, usu cap O&S* [ME] **:** OLD NICK

**old–shoe** \ˈ=ˈ=\ *adj* **:** characterized by familiarity or freedom from restraint **:** COMFORTABLE, UNPRETENTIOUS ⟨*old-shoe* and easy to talk with —Ernie Pyle⟩

**old side** *adj, usu cap O&S* **:** of or relating to a conservative element among Presbyterians in colonial America favoring stricter adherence to a confession of faith and opposing the more revivalistic methods — compare NEW SIDE

**old silver** *n* **:** a nearly neutral slightly yellowish medium gray that is darker than gull (sense 2a) or agate gray and very slightly redder than flint gray — compare NEW SILVER, SILVER

**old slavic** *or* **old slavonic** *n, cap O&S* **:** OLD CHURCH SLAVONIC

**old sledge** *n* **:** SEVEN-UP

**old soldier** *n, slang* **:** an emptied liquor bottle

**old–squaw** \ˈ=ˈ=\ *n* **:** a common sea duck (*Clangula hyemalis*) of the more northern parts of the northern hemisphere of which the adult male is marked with sharply contrasted black and white and has the middle tail feathers very long and slender and the female is plainer and lacks the long tail feathers — called also *old injun, oldwife*

**old stager** *n, chiefly Brit* **:** OLD HAND 1

**old·ster** \ˈōl(d)stə(r), -(d)st-\ *n* -S **1 :** an experienced hand ⟨∼s pass it down faithfully to each newcomer —Elmont Waite⟩; *specif* **:** a midshipman of four years' standing in the British navy — distinguished from *youngster* **2 :** an aging or elderly person ⟨gray-bearded ∼s go swaggering down the boulevards —Hubert Herring⟩ ⟨the accumulated wisdom and lore of the ∼s —E.A.Hoebel⟩

**old stone age** *n, usu cap O&S&A* **:** the Paleolithic period

**old story** *n* **:** something well established **:** an idea or object no longer a novelty ⟨by the time Virginia was first settled secular schools were an *old story* in England —G.W.Johnson⟩

[1]**old style** *n* **1 :** something belonging to or characteristic of an earlier period **2 :** a style of type resembling an 18th century design of William Caslon and distinguished by graceful irregularity among individual letters, slanted ascender serifs, and but slight contrast between light and heavy strokes

(as in this example of Old Style)

— contrasted with *modern*

[2]**old style** *adj, usu cap O&S* **:** using or according to the Julian calendar — abbr. *O.S.*

**old testament** *n, cap O&T* [ME, trans. of LL *Vetus Testamentum*, trans. of Gk *Palaia Diathēkē*] **:** the covenant of God with the Hebrews as set forth in the Bible — abbr. *O.T.;* called also *Old Covenant*

**old–time** \ˈ=ˈ=\ *adj* **1 :** of, relating to, or characteristic of an earlier period ⟨an *old-time* community sing⟩ ⟨loved the conservative *old-time* ways —Van Wyck Brooks⟩ ⟨using the *old-time* . . . mule-power grinding mills —*Amer. Guide Series: N. C.*⟩ **2 :** of long standing **:** EXPERIENCED, VETERAN ⟨many *old-time* bowlers are back bowling this year —*Deerfield (Wisc.) Independent*⟩ ⟨*old-time* summer residents —*N. Y. Times*⟩

**old–tim·er** \ˈ=ˈtīmə(r)\ *n* -S **1 a :** OLD HAND, VETERAN ⟨the stranger must compete with the *old-timers* already established —Justina Hill⟩ ⟨the eternal friction between *old-timer* and rookie —Dixon Wecter⟩ **b :** OLDSTER 2 ⟨service for . . . *old-timers* beyond retirement age —W.R.Wood⟩ **2 :** something that is old-fashioned **:** ANTIQUE ⟨a collar . . . one of those hard-boiled *old-timers* which calls for gold collar buttons front and rear —F.C.Othman⟩

**old–timey** *also* **old–timy** \ˈ=ˈtīmē\ *adj* **:** of a kind or style prevalent in or reminiscent of an earlier period **:** OLD-TIME ⟨hollyhocks and *old-timey* roses —C.F.Saunders⟩ ⟨our *old-timey*, crotchety operetta . . . from London —*New Yorker*⟩

**old tuberculin** *n* **:** tuberculin prepared by boiling, filtering, and concentrating a broth culture of tubercle bacilli and orig. introduced as a proposed curative agent for tuberculosis

**old welsh** *n, cap O&W* **:** the Welsh language exemplified in documents prior to about 1150 — see INDO-EUROPEAN LANGUAGES table

**oldwench** \ˈ=ˌ=\ *n* **:** QUEEN TRIGGERFISH

**old wife** *n, pl* **old wives** [ME] **:** a prattling old woman **:** GOSSIP ⟨a mishmash of *old wives'* tales —J.N.Leonard⟩

**oldwife** \ˈ=ˌ=\ *n, pl* **oldwives** [perh. so called fr. the large belly] **:** any of several fishes: as **a :** the European black sea bream (*Cantharus lineatus*) **b :** any of several triggerfishes; *esp* **:** QUEEN TRIGGERFISH **c :** LONGFIN POMPANO **d :** [1]SPOT 7 **e :** [2]ALEWIFE 1a **f :** MENHADEN **g :** an Australian fish (*Enoplosus armatus*) resembling a perch **2 :** OLD-SQUAW

**old wine** *n* **:** a variable color averaging a dark red that is yellower and paler than average wine or average garnet and yellower, less strong, and slightly darker than cranberry

**old witchgrass** *n* **:** WITCHGRASS 2

**old woman** *n* **1 a :** WIFE — not often in formal use **b :** MOTHER — not often in formal use **2** *chiefly dial* **:** BEACH WORMWOOD

**old–wom·an·ish** \ˈ=ˈwu̇mənish\ *adj* **:** OLD-MAIDISH

**old–woman's–bitter** \ˈ=ˌ==ˈ==\ *n* **:** a tropical American fiddlewood (*Citharexylum fruticosum*)

**old wood** *n* **:** a grayish red that is bluer and darker than bois de rose and yellower and deeper than appleblossom

**old world** *n, usu cap O&W* **:** EASTERN HEMISPHERE; *specif* **:** the continent of Europe ⟨renaissance . . . in the countries of the *Old World* —Hellmut Lehmann-Haupt⟩

**old–world** \ˈ=ˈ=\ *adj* [*Old World*] **:** OLD-FASHIONED, PICTURESQUE ⟨the *old-world*, vacillating, pathetically likable headmaster of the school —Leslie Rees⟩ ⟨as quaint . . . as any *old-world* continental city —Arnold Bennett⟩

**old–world monkey** *n* **:** a catarrhine monkey; *esp* **:** a monkey of the family Cercopithecidae widely distributed in the warmer parts of the Old World

**old world porcupine** *n, usu cap O&W* **:** a porcupine of the family Hystricidae; *esp* **:** a rather bulky short-tailed terrestrial porcupine of the common widely distributed genus *Hystrix*

**olé** \ōˈlā\ *n* -S [Sp *ole, olé*, fr. Ar *wa-llāh*, fr. *wa-* and + *allāh* God] **:** [2]BRAVO ⟨the generous approbation and shouted ∼s of these warm Mexican people —George Sklar⟩ — often used interjectionally in applauding a superior performance

**ole–** *or* **oleo–** *also* **olei–** *comb form* [F *olé-, oléo-*, fr. L *ole-*, fr. *oleum* — more at OIL] **1 :** oil ⟨*olei*ferous⟩ ⟨*ole*in⟩ ⟨*oleo*graph⟩ ⟨*oleo*cyst⟩ **2 a :** olein ⟨*oleo*-di-stearin⟩ **b :** oleic acid ⟨*ole*oyl⟩

[1]**–ole** *also* **–ol** \ˌōl, ˈōl, ˌōl, ˈōl\ *n comb form* -S [ISV, fr. L *oleum* oil — more at OIL] **1 :** chemical compound containing a five-membered ring usu. heterocyclic ⟨imidaz*ole*⟩ ⟨pyrr*ole*⟩ **2** *usu -ole* **:** chemical compound not containing hydroxyl — esp. in names of ethers ⟨anis*ole*⟩ ⟨phenet*ole*⟩

[2]**–ole** — see -OL

[3]**–ole** \ˌōl\ *n suffix* -S [F, fr. L *-olus, -olum, -ola*, dim. suffix] **:** little one ⟨ven*iole*⟩

[1]**olea** \ˈōlēə\ *n, cap* [NL, fr. L, olive tree, olive, fr. Gk *elaia* — more at OLIVE] **:** a genus (the type of the family Oleaceae) of trees or shrubs having simple entire leaves, axillary flowers with induplicate calyx lobes, and oily drupaceous fruit — see MAIRE, OLIVE

[2]**olea** *pl of* OLEUM

**ole·a·ce·ae** \ˌōlēˈāsēˌē\ *n pl, cap* [NL, fr. *Olea*, type genus + *-aceae*] **:** a family of shrubs and trees (order Oleales) having opposite or rarely alternate exstipulate leaves, tetramerous flowers, and the fruits a berry, drupe, or capsule

**ole·a·ceous** \ˌ=ˈāshəs\ *adj* [NL *Oleaceae* + E *-ous*] **:** of or relating to the Oleaceae

**ole·a·ci·na** \ˌōlēəˈsīnə\ *n, cap* [NL, prob. fr. L *oleaceus* oily (fr. *ole-* + *-aceus* -aceous) + NL *-ina*] **:** a genus of West Indian carnivorous land snails (suborder Stylommatophora) having elongate usu. smooth glassy brownish shells and feeding primarily on other snails

**ole·a·cin·i·dae** \-sinəˌdē\ *n pl, cap* [NL, fr. *Oleacina*, type genus + *-idae*] **:** a family of carnivorous land snails (suborder Stylommatophora) that feed chiefly on other snails — see EUGLANDINA

**ole·ag·i·nous** \ˌōlēˈajənəs\ *adj* [MF *oleagineux*, fr. L *oleaginus, oleagineus* of an olive tree, of an olive, fr. *olea* olive tree, olive, fr. Gk *elaia* — more at OLIVE] **1 :** resembling or having the properties of oil ⟨∼ liquid⟩ ⟨an ∼ smear⟩ **:** containing or producing oil **:** OILY ⟨∼ matter keeps his wavy black hair slick —Darrell Berrigan⟩ ⟨the crop of winter ∼ seeds —Kay Boyle⟩ **2 :** characterized by suave urbanity or sickly sentimentality ⟨∼ disc-plugging crooners —Bernard Hollowood⟩

**ole·ag·i·nous·ly** *adv* **:** in an oily manner **:** UNCTUOUSLY

**ole·ag·i·nous·ness** *n* -ES *archaic* **:** the quality or state of being oily ⟨the ∼ of urinous spirits —Robert Boyle⟩

**ole·a·les** \ˌōlēˈā(ˌ)lēz\ *n pl, cap* [NL, fr. *Olea* + *-ales*] **:** an order of dicotyledonous woody plants including the single family Oleaceae and being often included in the order Gentianales

**ole·an·der** \ˌōlēˈandə(r)\ *n* -S [ML *oleander*, alter. of *arodandrum, lorandrum*, prob. alter. of L *rhododendron* — more at RHODODENDRON] **:** a plant of the genus *Nerium*; *specif* **:** an ornamental evergreen shrub (*Nerium oleander*) that is native to the East Indies but widely cultivated and naturalized in warm regions and that has narrow entire leaves and clusters of fragrant white to red flowers

**oleander aphid** *n* **:** an aphid (*Aphis nerii*) that infests foliage and flower buds of oleander

**oleander fern** *n* **:** a tropical fern (*Oleandra neriiformis*) of the family Polypodiaceae having coriaceous fronds that resemble oleander leaves

**oleander scale** *n* **:** any of several scales injurious to the oleander, orange, and lemon; *esp* **:** a common greenhouse scale (*Aspidiotus hederae*)

**ole·an·drin** \ˌōlēˈandrən\ *n* -S [ISV *oleander* + *-in*] **:** a poisonous crystalline glycoside $C_{32}H_{48}O_9$ found in oleander leaves and resembling digitalis in its action

**ole·a·no·lic acid** \ˌōlēəˈnōlik-\ *n* [ISV *olea-* (fr. L *olea* olive tree, olive) + connective *-n-* + *-olic* — more at OLEA] **:** a crystalline triterpenoid acid $C_{29}H_{47}COOH$ derived from beta-amyrin and occurring free or in the form of saponins or other glycosides (as in olive leaves, clove buds, sugar beets)

**ole·ar·ia** \ˌōlēˈa(a)rēə\ *n, cap* [NL, fr. Adam Ölschläger (Latinized *Olearius*) †1671 Ger. traveler + NL *-ia*] **:** a large genus of Australasian shrubs or low trees (family Compositae) with alternate leaves and rather large heads of flowers having white or purple rays, the pappus capillary, and the receptacle without chaff

**o'lea·ry** \ōˈlirē, -ler-\ *n* -ES *usu cap O&L* [prob. alter. of ME *a-lery, aliri* crossed (used of the legs)] **:** a game in which a child bounces a ball and executes prescribed movements (as crossing one leg over the ball) at certain words of an accompanying verse

**ole·as·ter** \ˌōlēˈastə(r)\ *n* -S [L, fr. *olea* olive tree, olive — more at OLEA] **1 :** any of several plants of the genus *Elaeagnus*; *esp* **:** RUSSIAN OLIVE **2 :** a wild tree of the commonly cultivated olive

**oleaster family** *n* **:** ELAEAGNACEAE

**ole·ate** \ˈōlēˌāt, -ēət\ *n* -S [F *oléate*, fr. *olé-* ole- + *-ate*] **1 :** a salt or ester of oleic acid **2 :** a liquid or semisolid preparation of a medicinal dissolved in an excess of oleic acid ⟨mercury ∼⟩ ⟨∼ of quinine⟩

**olec·ra·nal** \ōˈlekrənᵊl, ˌōləˈkrānᵊl\ *adj* [NL *olecranon* + E *-al*] **:** of, belonging to, or relating to the olecranon

**olec·ra·non** \-rəˌnän, -rā,-\ *n* -S [NL, fr. Gk *ōlekranon*, fr. *ōlenē* elbow + *kranion* head, skull — more at ELL, CRANIUM] **:** the large process of the ulna that projects behind the elbow joint, forms the bony prominence of the elbow, and receives the insertion of the triceps muscle — see FUNNY BONE 1

**ole·fi·ant gas** \ˌōləˈfīənt-; ōˈlefēənt-, ōˈlef\ *n* [part trans. of F *gaz oléfiant*, fr. *gaz* gas + *oléfiant*, fr. *olé-* ole- + *-fiant*, pres. part. of *-fier* -fy] *archaic* **:** ETHYLENE

**ole·fin** *also* **olefine** \ˈōləfən, -əˌfēn\ *n* -S [ISV *olefiant* (*gas*) + *-in, -ine*] **:** an unsaturated open-chain hydrocarbon containing at least one double bond; *esp* **:** a member of the ethylene series **:** ALKENE — compare CYCLOOLEFIN, DIOLEFIN, TRIOLEFIN

**ole·fin·ic** \ˌ==ˈfinik\ *adj* **:** of, relating to, or being an olefin **:** ETHYLENIC ⟨∼ bonds⟩ ⟨∼ terpenes⟩

**olei–** — see OLE-

**ole·ic** \(ˈ)ōˈlēik\ *adj* [*ole-* + *-ic*] **1 :** relating to, derived from, or contained in oil **2 :** of or relating to oleic acid or its derivatives ⟨∼ esters⟩

**oleic acid** *n* **:** a liquid unsaturated fatty acid $CH_3(CH_2)_7CH{=}CH(CH_2)_7COOH$ that occurs in the form of glycerides in vegetable oils (as olive oil) and animal fats and oils (as depot fats), that is usu. obtained commercially from inedible tallow or grease as a colorless to red or brown oil, that yields stearic acid on hydrogenation and azelaic acid and pelargonic acid on cleavage by oxidation, and that is used chiefly in making textile soaps, synthetic detergents, lubricants (as for textile fibers), sulfonated oils and cosmetics, and in compounding rubber; *cis*-9-octadecenoic acid — see ELAIDIC ACID, RED OIL

**olei·cul·ture** \ˈōlēə+ˌ-\ *n* [F *oléiculture*, fr. L *olea* olive + F *-i-* + *culture* — more at OLEA, CULTURE] **:** the production, processing, and marketing of olives

**ole·if·er·ous** \ˌōlēˈif(ə)rəs\ *adj* [*ole-* + *-ferous*] **:** producing oil ⟨∼ seeds⟩

**ole·in** \ˈōlēən\ *n* -S [F *oléine*, fr. *olé-* ole- + *-ine*] **1 :** an ester of glycerol and oleic acid; *esp* **:** TRIOLEIN **2** *also* **ole·ine** \", -ēˌēn\ **a :** the liquid portion of any fat — distinguished from *stearin* **b :** SULFONATED OIL **c :** commercial oleic acid ⟨white ∼⟩ — compare RED OIL 1a

**ole·nel·lid** \ˌōləˈneləd\ *n* -S [NL *Olenellidae* family of trilobites, fr. NL *Olenellus*, type genus + *-idae*] **:** a trilobite of the genus *Olenellus*

**ole·nel·lus** \-ləs\ *n, cap* [NL, dim. of *Olenus*] **:** a genus of Lower Cambrian trilobites having a large spine on the fifteenth thoracic segment

**olent** \ˈōlənt\ *adj* [L *olent-, olens*, pres. part. of *olēre* to smell — more at ODOR] *archaic* **:** having a scent **:** ODOROUS

**ole·nus** \ˈōlēnəs\ *n, cap* [NL, after *Olenus*, character in Greco-Roman mythology who was changed into a stone pillar, fr. L, fr. Gk *Ōlenos*] **:** a genus of trilobites from the Upper Cambrian of Europe having 12–15 thoracic segments, pleurae with sharp back-bent extremities, and a small pygidium

**oleo** \ˈōlēˌō\ *n* -S [in sense 1, short for *oleomargarine*; in sense 2, fr. *ole-*; in sense 3, short for *oleograph*] **1 a :** OLEOMARGARINE **b :** OLEO OIL **2** *or* **oleo gear :** a shock-absorbing device that utilizes the damping action produced by the flow of a column of liquid through an orifice of variable area **3 a :** OLEOGRAPH **b :** a backdrop for a television scene

**oleo–** — see OLE-

**oleo·calcareous** \ˌōlēō+\ *adj* [ISV *ole-* + *calcareous*] **:** consisting of or containing a mixture of oil and lime

**ole·o·cel·lo·sis** \ˌōlēōˌseˈlōsəs\ *n, pl* **oleocello·ses** \-ˈlōˌsēz\ [NL, fr. *ole-* + ISV *cell* + NL *-osis*] **:** a spotting of citrus fruits by oil liberated from the oil glands of the rind — called also *green spot*

**ole·o·cyst** \ˈōlēōˌsist\ *n* [*ole-* + *-cyst*] **:** a diverticulum of the nectocalyx in various Calycophora that contains oil

**ole·o·graph** \ˈōlēōˌgraf, -räf\ *n* [ISV *ole-* + *-graph*] **1 :** a chromolithograph printed on canvas or other cloth to imitate an oil painting **2 :** the peculiar form or figure assumed by a drop of oil when placed on water or some other immiscible liquid — **oleographic** *adj*

**ole·og·ra·phy** \ˌōlēˈägrəfē\ *n* -ES [ISV *ole-* + *-graphy*] **1 :** the art or process of producing oleographic pictures **2 :** a process of identifying oils by their oleographs

**oleo–gum–resin** \ˈ=ˌ=ˈ=ˈ==\ *n* [*ole-* + *gum* + *resin*] *n* **:** a solid plant exudation (as asafetida or myrrh) consisting of a mixture of volatile oil, gum, and resin

**oleo·margaric** \ˈ+\ *adj* **:** of, relating to, or containing oleomargarine

**oleo·margarine** *also* **oleo·margarin** \"+\ *n* [F *oléomargarine*, fr. *oléo-* ole- + *margarine* — more at MARGARINE] **1 :** OLEO OIL **2 :** MARGARINE

**ole·om·e·ter** \ˌōlēˈämәd·ə(r)\ *n* [ISV *ole-* + *-meter*; prob. orig. formed as F *oléomètre*] **1 :** a hydrometer for determining the specific gravity of oils **2 :** an apparatus (as a Soxhlet extractor) for determining the percentage of oil in a material

**oleo oil** *n* **1 :** a yellow oil of buttery consistency expressed usu. from edible tallow and used in making margarine and soap and in lubrication — compare OLEOSTEARIN **2 :** any of various oils (as a hydrogenated vegetable oil) used in making margarine

**ole·o·phil·ic** \ˌōlēōˌfilik\ *adj* [*ole-* + *-philic*] **:** having or relating to strong affinity for oils **:** HYDROPHOBIC — compare LIPOPHILIC

**ole·o·pho·bic** \-fōbik\ *adj* [*ole-* + *-phobic*] **:** having or relating to a lack of strong affinity for oils **:** HYDROPHILIC

**ole·o·plast** \ˈōlēōˌplast\ *n* -s [ISV *ole-* + *-plast*] **:** ELAIOPLAST

**ole·op·tene** \ˌōlēˈäpˌtēn\ *n* -s [ISV *ole-* + Gk *ptēnos* winged — more at ELEOPTENE] **:** ELEOPTENE

**oleo·refractometer** \ˌōlēō+\ *n* [ISV *ole-* + *refractometer;* prob. orig. formed as F *oléoréfractomètre*] **:** a refractometer for use with oils

**oleo·resin** \"+\ *n* [ISV *ole-* + *resin*] **1 :** a natural plant product (as copaiba, elemi) consisting essentially of essential oil and resin; *esp* **:** TURPENTINE 1 b — compare BALSAM **2 :** a solid, liquid, or semiliquid preparation extracted (as from capsicum, cubebs, ginger) usu. by means of ether or acetone and consisting essentially of fatty or essential oil holding resin in solution

**oleo·resinous** \"+\ *adj* [ISV *oleoresin* + *-ous*] **1 :** of, relating to, or containing oleoresin ⟨the ~ exudation of the balsam fir⟩ **2 :** made of drying oils and resins usu. cooked — used esp. of a varnish or a paint vehicle

**ole·o·sac·cha·rum** \ˌōlēōˈsakərəm\ *n, pl* **oleosaccha·ra** \-rə\ [NL, fr. *ole-* + L *saccharum* sugar — more at SACCHARINE] **:** a homogeneous mixture used in pharmacy that is made by triturating sugar with a small amount of essential oil

**ole·o·some** \ˈōlēōˌsōm\ *n* -s [ISV *ole-* + *-some*] **:** a fat or fatty inclusion in cytoplasm

**oleo·stearin** *also* **oleo·stearine** \ˌōlēō+\ *n* [ISV *ole-* + *stearin, stearine*] **:** a solid residue of tallow remaining after removal of oleo oil or tallow oil and used chiefly in lard substitutes

**oleo strut** \ˈōlē,ō-\ *n* [*ole-* + *strut*] **:** a cylindrical strut with a built-in telescopic shock absorber that damps or absorbs rectilinear shock (as in an aircraft landing gear) by forcing oil up through an orifice in the bottom of a hollow piston into an air-compression chamber

oleo strut: *1* inner cylinder, *2* orifice, *3* oil, *4* outer cylinder

**oleo·thorax** \ˌōlēō+\ *n* [NL, fr. *ole-* + *thorax*] **:** a state in which oil is present in the pleural cavity usu. as a result of injection — compare PNEUMOTHORAX

**ole·ous** \ˈōlēəs\ *also* **ole·ose** \-ē,ōs\ *adj* [L *oleosus,* fr. *ole-* + *-osus* -ous, -ose] *archaic* **:** OILY

**oleo·vitamin** \ˌōlēō+\ *n* [*ole-* + *vitamin*] **:** a preparation containing one or more fat-soluble vitamins or derivatives in oil (as a fish-liver oil or an edible vegetable oil) ⟨~ A⟩ ⟨synthetic ~ D⟩

**ole·o·yl** \ōˈlēə,wil\ *n* -s [*ole-* + *-yl*] **:** the radical $C_{17}H_{33}CO$– of oleic acid

**ol·er·a·ceous** \ˌäləˈrāshəs\ *adj* [L *oleraceus, holeraceus,* fr. *oler-, olus, holer-, holus* potherb + *-aceus* -aceous; akin to L *helvus* light-bay-colored — more at YELLOW] **:** having the qualities of a potherb ⟨~ plants⟩

**ol·eri·culture** \ˈälərə, ōˈlerə+,-\ *n* [L *oler-, olus, holer-, holus* + E *-i-* + *culture*] **:** a branch of horticulture that deals with the production, storage, processing, and marketing of vegetables

**ol·eri·culturist** \,==+\ *n* -s **:** a specialist in olericulture

**olés** *pl of* OLÉ

**-oles** *pl of* -OLE

[1]**ole·threu·tid** \ˌōləˈthrüd·əd\ *adj* [NL *Olethreutidae*] **:** of or relating to the Olethreutidae

[2]**olethreutid** *n* -s **:** a moth of the family Olethreutidae

**ole·threu·ti·dae** \-ˈthrüd·əˌdē\ *n pl, cap* [NL, fr. *Olethreutes,* type genus (fr. Gk *olethreuein* to slay, destroy, fr. *olethros* destruction) + *-idae*] **:** a large family of small moths including the codling moth and the oriental peach moth

**ole·um** \ˈōlēəm\ *n, pl* **olea** \-ēə\ *or* **oleums** [L — more at OIL] **1** *pl* **olea :** OIL — used chiefly in phrases that are the Latin names of oils ⟨~ thae piperitae⟩ **2** *pl* **oleums :** a heavy oily strongly corrosive liquid that consists of a solution of sulfur trioxide in anhydrous sulfuric acid, that fumes in moist air and reacts violently with water with the evolution of heat, and that is used chiefly in sulfonation and sulfation processes, in mixed acid for nitration, and in petroleum refining — called also *fuming sulfuric acid* ⟨the strength of ~ is designated as percent by weight of free sulfur trioxide: thus 20% ~ contains 20% $SO_3$ and 80% $H_2SO_4$ by weight —B.M.Carter⟩

**ole·yl** \ōˈlēəl\ *n* -s [*ole-* + *-yl*] **1 :** OLEOYL **2 :** the univalent radical $C_{17}H_{33}CH_2$– derived from oleyl alcohol

**oleyl alcohol** *n* **:** an oily liquid unsaturated compound $C_{17}H_{33}CH_2OH$ found in fish oils and other marine-animal oils that is made by reduction or hydrogenation of esters of oleic acid and is used chiefly in making surface-active agents and plasticizers; *cis*-9-octadecen-1-ol

**ol·fac·tion** \älˈfakshən\ *n* -s [L *olfactus, olefactus* (past part. of *olfacere, olefacere* to smell) + E *-ion* — more at OLFACTORY] **1 :** the sense of smell **2 :** the act or process of smelling

**ol·fact·ive** \(ˈ)älˈfaktiv\ *adj* [L *olfactus, olefactus* + E *-ive*] **:** OLFACTORY

**ol·fac·tol·o·gy** \,äl,fakˈtäləjē\ *n* -ES [L *olfactus* smell (fr. *olfactus, olefactus,* past part. of *olfacere, olefacere*) + E *-o-* + *-logy*] **:** the scientific study of smells or of the sense of smell

**ol·fac·tom·e·ter** \ˌälˈfakˈtäməd·ə(r)\ *n* [ISV *olfacto-* (fr. L *olfactus* smell) + *-meter*] **:** an instrument for measuring the sensitivity of the sense of smell

**ol·fac·to·met·ric** \älˌfaktəˈme·trik\ *adj* **:** of, relating to, or marked by the use of olfactometry — **ol·fac·to·met·ri·cal·ly** \-rək(ə)lē\ *adv*

**ol·fac·tom·e·try** \,äl,fakˈtäməˌtrē\ *n* -ES [ISV *olfacto-* + *-metry*] **:** the testing and measurement of the sensitivity of the sense of smell

**ol·fac·to·ri·ly** \(ˈ)älˈfakt(ə)rəlē, (ˈ)ōlˌ-\ *adv* **:** in respect to the sense of smell

**ol·fac·to·ry** \-rē, -ri\ *adj* [L *olfactorius,* fr. *olfactus, olefactus* (past part. of *olfacere, olefacere,* fr. *olēre* to smell + *facere* to make, do) + *-orius* -ory — more at ODOR, DO] **:** of, relating to, or connected with the sense of smell ⟨~ receptors⟩

**olfactory area** *n* **1 :** the sensory area for olfaction lying in the hippocampal convolution **2 :** the area of nasal mucosa in which the olfactory organ is situated

**olfactory bulb** *n* **:** a bulbous anterior projection of the olfactory lobe in which the olfactory nerves terminate, being esp. well developed in lower vertebrates (as many fishes)

**olfactory capsule** *n* **:** NASAL CAPSULE

**olfactory cell** *n* **:** a sensory cell specialized for the reception of sensory stimuli caused by odors; *specif* **:** one of the spindle-shaped nerve cells buried in the nasal mucous membrane of vertebrates, each having a round nucleus and two slender processes of which the inner constitutes an olfactory nerve fiber and the short outer one is modified peripherally to form the actual sensory receptor — see OLFACTORY ORGAN

**olfactory gyrus** *n* **:** either a lateral or a medial gyrus by which the olfactory tract on either side communicates with the olfactory area of the brain

**olfactory lobe** *n* **:** a lobe of the brain that projects forward from the anterior lower part of each cerebral hemisphere, is continuous anteriorly with the olfactory nerve and well developed in most vertebrates, but is reduced to a narrow elongated body in man — see OLFACTORY BULB; BRAIN illustration

**olfactory nerve** *also* **olfactory** *n* -ES **:** either of the first pair of cranial nerves, being a sensory nerve, arising from the olfactory cells as discrete bundles of nonmedullated fibers that pass in small groups (in man, about 20) through the cribriform plate of the ethmoid and terminate in the olfactory bulb, and serving to conduct sensory stimuli from the olfactory organ to the brain

**olfactory organ** *n* **:** an organ of chemical sense that receives stimuli interpreted as odors from volatile and soluble substances in low dilution, that lies in the walls of the upper part of the nasal cavity, and that forms a mucous membrane continuous with the rest of the lining of the nasal cavity and made up of tall columnar supporting cells containing golden brown pigment interspersed with olfactory cells the outer processes of which project between the supporting cells as small vesicles surmounted by delicate sensory filaments and the inner ends of which are continuous with fibers of the olfactory nerves

**olfactory pit** *n* **1 :** an olfactory organ having the form of a small depression (as in amphioxi and various invertebrates) **2 :** a depression on the head of an embryo that becomes converted into a nasal passage — called also *nasal sac*

**ol·fac·ty** \älˈfaktē\ *n* -ES [L *olfactus* smell + E *-y* — more at OLFACTOLOGY] **:** an arbitrary unit used in olfactometry for measuring the strength of an odorous stimulus

**olib·a·num** \ōˈlibənəm\ *n* -s [ME, fr. ML, fr. Ar *al-lubān* the frankincense] **:** FRANKINCENSE 1

**-o·lic** \ˈōlik, ˈäl-, -lēk\ *adj suffix* [ISV *-ol* + *-ic*] **1 :** containing a triple bond — in names of acids ⟨propi*olic* acid⟩ **2 :** containing hydroxyl and carboxyl — in names of hydroxy acids ⟨olean*olic* acid⟩

**ol·id** \ˈäləd\ *adj* [L *olidus,* fr. *olēre* to smell — more at ODOR] **:** having a strong disagreeable smell **:** FETID

**olifant** *var of* OLIPHANT

**olig-** *or* **oligo-** *comb form* [ML, fr. Gk, fr. *oligos;* akin to Gk *loigos* ruin, havoc, OIr *líach* miserable, unhappy, Lith *liga* sickness, Arm *ałkat* poor, scant, and perh. to Gk *liazesthai* to bend, recoil, sink — more at LESS] **1 :** few ⟨*Oligo*chaeta⟩ ⟨*oligo*gene⟩ ⟨*oligo*myodian⟩ **:** few things ⟨*oligo*phagous⟩ **2** *med* **:** deficiency **:** insufficiency ⟨*oligo*chromemia⟩ ⟨*olig*uria⟩ **3 :** little **:** small ⟨*oligo*lecithal⟩

**ol·i·garch** \ˈäləˌgärk, -gäk\ *n* -s [Gk *oligarchēs,* fr. *olig-* + *-archēs* -arch] **:** a member or supporter of an autocratic clique ⟨bureaucratic ~s in striped pants or khaki —Edmond Taylor⟩; *esp* **:** a member of a political oligarchy ⟨the factional violence between democrats and ~s with which the Greek cities of the late fifth and early fourth centuries were sadly familiar —G.R.Morrow⟩

**ol·i·gar·chal** \ˌ==ˈgärkəl\ *adj* **:** OLIGARCHIC

**ol·i·gar·chic** \ˌäləˈgärkik, -gák-, -kēk\ *or* **ol·i·gar·chi·cal** \-kəkəl, -kēk-\ *adj* [Gk *oligarchikos,* fr. *oligarchia* + *-ikos* -ic, -ical] **:** of, relating to, characteristic of, or supporting oligarchy — **ol·i·gar·chi·cal·ly** \-kək(ə)lē\ *adv*

**ol·i·gar·chy** \ˈ==ˌgärkē, -gák-, -ki\ *n* -ES [Gk *oligarchia,* fr. *olig-* + *-archia* -archy] **1 a** (1) **:** despotic power exercised by a privileged clique ⟨a plutocratic ~ exercising all the old kingly powers —G.B.Shaw⟩ — compare ARISTOCRACY (2) **:** government by the few ⟨democracy and ~ shade into each other and are chiefly distinguished by the degree of the citizens' participation in government —D.D.McKean⟩ **b :** autocratic control of any group or organization by a small faction ⟨the alarming growth of economic ~ resulting from corporate concentration —C.C.Rodee⟩ **2 a :** a group or organization that is controlled by a privileged few ⟨high schools are *oligarchies* . . . or whatever you like, but not democracies —*Saturday Rev.*⟩ **b :** the faction in control of such a group or organization ⟨rival *oligarchies* supporting similar programs within the same party —H.R.Penniman⟩ ⟨the Millennium — old domination of the landowning and merchant ~ —D.M.Friedenberg⟩

**ol·i·ge·mia** \ˌäləˈgēmēə, -ˈjē-\ *n* -s [NL, fr. Gk *oligaimia,* fr. *olig-* + *-aimia* -emia] **:** a condition in which the total volume of the blood is reduced — **ol·i·ge·mic** \ˌ==ˈ=mik\ *adj*

**ol·i·gist** \ˈäləjəst\ *or* **oligist iron** *n* -s [F *oligiste,* fr. Gk *oligistos* least, superl. of *oligos* small, few — more at OLIG-] **:** HEMATITE — **ol·i·gis·tic** \ˌ==ˈjistik\ *or* **ol·i·gis·ti·cal** \-təkəl\ *adj*

**ol·i·go·cene** \ˈäləgōˌsēn, əˈligə,-\ *adj, usu cap* [ISV *olig-* + *-cene;* orig. formed as G *oligozän*] **:** of or relating to a subdivision of the Tertiary — see GEOLOGIC TIME table

**ol·i·go·chae·ta** \ˌäləgōˈkēd·ə, ə,ligəˈ-\ *n pl, cap* [NL, fr. *olig-* + *-chaeta*] **:** a class or in former classifications an order of Chaetopoda comprising hermaphroditic terrestrial and aquatic annelids distinguished from the polychaetes by possession of compact localized gonads and simple direct life histories without formation of a trochophore and by lack of parapodia and head specialization — see ARCHIOLIGOCHAETA, NEOLIGOCHAETA

[1]**ol·i·go·chaete** *also* **ol·i·go·chaet** *or* **ol·i·go·chete** \ˈäləgōˌkēt, əˈligə,-\ *adj* [NL *Oligochaeta*] **:** of or relating to the Oligochaeta

[2]**oligochaete** *also* **oligochaet** *or* **oligochete** \"\ *n* -s **:** an annelid worm of the class Oligochaeta

**ol·i·go·chae·to·log·i·cal** \ˌäləgōˌkēd·əlˈäjəkəl, ə,ligəˌkē-\ *adj* **:** of or relating to oligochaetology

**ol·i·go·chae·tol·o·gy** \ˌäləgōkēˈtäləjē, ə,ligəkē'-\ *n* -ES [NL *Oligochaeta* + E *-o-* + *-logy*] **:** a branch of zoology that deals with the oligochaete worms

**ol·i·go·chro·me·mia** \ˌäləgōkrōˈmēmēə, ə,ligək-\ *n* -s [NL, fr. *olig-* + *chrom-* + *-emia*] **:** deficiency of hemoglobin in the blood

**ol·i·go·chronometer** \ˌäləgō, əˌligə+\ *n* [ISV *olig-* + *chronometer*] **:** an instrument for measuring very small time intervals

**ol·i·go·clase** \ˈäləgōˌklās, əˈligə,-\ *n* -s [G *oligoklas,* fr. *oligo-* olig- + *-klas* -clase] **:** a mineral of the plagioclase series — compare FELDSPAR

**ol·i·go·cy·the·mia** \ˌäləgōˌsīˈthēmēə, ə,ligə,s-\ *n* -s [NL, fr. *olig-* + *cyt-* + *-hemia*] **:** absolute deficiency in the number of red blood cells present in the body — compare ANEMIA — **ol·i·go·cy·the·mic** \ˌäləgōˌsīˈthēmik, ə,ligə,-\ *adj*

**ol·i·go·dac·tyl·ism** \ˌäləgōˈdaktəˌlizəm, ə,ligəˈ-\ *also* **ol·i·go·dac·tyly** \-ˌlē\ *n, pl* **oligodactylisms** *also* **oligodactylies** [*olig-* + *-dactylism, -dactyly*] **:** a deficiency of fingers or toes

**ol·i·go·den·dro·cyte** \ˌäləgōˈdendrəˌsīt, ə,ligəˈ-\ *n* -s [ISV *olig-* + *dendr-* + *-cyte*] **:** a neuroglial cell resembling an astrocyte but small with few and slender processes having few branches

**ol·i·go·den·drog·lia** \ˌäləgō,denˈdräglēə, ə,ligə,de-\ *n* -s [NL, fr. *olig-* + *dendr-* + *-glia*] **:** neuroglia made up of oligodendrocytes that is often prominent in pathologic states

**ol·i·go·den·dro·gli·o·ma** \ˌäləgō,dendrō,glīˈōmə, ə,ligə,de-\ *n, pl* **oligodendrogliomas** *or* **oligodendrogliomata** [NL, fr. *oligodendroglia* + *-oma*] **:** a tumor of the nervous system composed of oligodendroglia

**ol·i·go·dynamic** \ˌäləgō, əˌligə+(,)==ˈ=\ *adj* [ISV *olig-* + *dynamic;* orig. formed as G *oligodynamisch*] **1 :** active in very small quantities ⟨an ~ germicide⟩ **2 a :** produced by very small quantities ⟨~ action of finely divided silver in disinfecting water⟩ **b :** of or relating to the action of such quantities **3 :** of, relating to, or being produced by the specific activity of an oligodynamic substance ⟨the ~ action of some pyridine derivatives on pathogenic microorganisms⟩

**ol·i·go·gene** \ˈäləgōˌjēn, əˈligə,-\ *n* [*olig-* + *gene*] **:** a gene that alone or with a few other genes controls the inheritance of a qualitative character or one showing typical Mendelian distribution — see POLYGENE; compare PARTICULATE INHERITANCE — **ol·i·go·gen·ic** \ˌäləgōˈjenik, əˌligəˈ-\ *adj*

**ol·i·go·hydramnios** \ˌäləgō, əˌligə+,==ˈ==\ *n* [NL, fr. *olig-* + *hydramnios*] **:** deficiency of amniotic fluid sometimes resulting in embryonic defect through adherence between embryo and amnion

**ol·i·go·lecithal** \"+\ *adj* [ISV *olig-* + *lecithal*] **:** MICROLECITHAL

**ol·i·go·menorrhea** \"+\ *n* [NL, fr. *olig-* + *menorrhea*] **:** abnormally infrequent or scanty menstrual flow

**ol·i·gom·era** \ˌäləˈgämərə\ *n pl, cap* [NL, fr. *olig-* + *-mera* (fr. Gk *meros* part) — more at MERIT] *in some classifications* **:** a division of invertebrate animals having the body divided into few or obscure segments

**ol·i·go·my·o·di·an** \ˌäləgō,mīˈōdēən, ə,ligə,-\ *adj* [*olig-* + Gk *myōdēs* muscular (fr. *mys* mouse, muscle + *-ōdēs* -ode) + E *-ian* — more at MOUSE] **:** having few syringeal muscles

**ol·i·go·nephric** \ˌäləgō, əˌligə+\ *adj* [*olig-* + *nephric*] *of an insect* **:** having few Malpighian tubes

**ol·i·go·neu·ri·el·i·dae** \ˌäləgō,n(y)ürēˈelə,dē, ə,ligə,n-\ *n pl, cap* [NL, fr. *Oligoneuriella,* type genus (dim. of *Oligoneuria,* genus of mayflies, fr. *olig-* + *neur-* + *-ia*) + *-idae*] **:** a large and widely distributed family of mayflies

**ol·i·go·nite** \ˈäləgōˌnīt, əˈligə,-\ *n* -s [G *oligonit,* fr. Gk *oligon* (neut. sing. of *oligos* little) + G *-it* -ite — more at OLIG-] **:** a manganiferous variety of siderite

**ol·i·goph·a·gous** \ˌäləˈgäfəgəs\ *adj* [*olig-* + *-phagous*] **:** eating only a few specific kinds of food — used esp. of an insect subsisting on a few usu. related plants — compare MONOPHAGOUS — **ol·i·goph·a·gy** \ˌ==ˈgäfəjē\ *n* -ES

**ol·i·go·phre·nia** \ˌäləgōˈfrēnēə, ə,ligəˈ-\ *n* -s [NL, fr. *olig-* + *-phrenia*] **:** mental deficiency **:** FEEBLEMINDEDNESS

[1]**ol·i·go·phren·ic** \ˌäləgōˌfrenik, əˌligəˌ-\ *adj* **:** of, relating to, or exhibiting mental deficiency

[2]**oligophrenic** *n* -s **:** a mentally deficient person

**ol·i·go·pod** \ˈäləgōˌpäd, əˈligə,-\ *adj* [*olig-* + *-pod*] *of an insect larva* **:** having thoracic legs fully developed and the abdomen completely segmented ⟨carabid beetles have ~ larvae⟩

**ol·i·gop·o·list** \ˌäləˈgäpələst\ *n* -s **:** a member of an oligopolistic industry or market

**ol·i·gop·o·lis·tic** \ˌ==ˌgäpəˈlistik\ *adj* **:** of or relating to an oligopoly

**ol·i·gop·o·ly** \ˌ==ˈgäpəlē\ *n* -ES [*olig-* + *monopoly*] **:** a market situation in which each of a limited number of producers is strong enough to influence the market but not strong enough to disregard the reaction of his competitors — compare DUOPOLY, MONOPOLY

**ol·i·gop·so·nist** \ˌäləˈgäpsənəst\ *n* -s **:** a member of an oligopsonistic industry or market

**ol·i·gop·so·nis·tic** \ˌ==ˌgäpsəˈnistik\ *adj* **:** of or relating to an oligopsony

**ol·i·gop·so·ny** \ˌ==ˈgäpsənē\ *n* -ES [*olig-* + Gk *opsōnia* purchase of victuals, catering — more at DUOPSONY] **:** a market situation in which each of a limited number of buyers is strong enough to influence the market but not strong enough to ignore the reaction to such influence by his competitors — compare DUOPSONY, MONOPSONY

**ol·i·go·pyrene** \ˌäləgō, əˌligə+\ *adj* [ISV *olig-* + *pyrene;* prob. orig. formed as G *oligopyren*] **:** containing less than the normal amount of chromatin — used of a sperm cell; compare APYRENE, EUPYRENE

**ol·i·go·saccharide** \"+\ *n* [ISV *olig-* + *saccharide;* orig. formed as G *oligosaccharid*] **:** any of the saccharides that contain a known small number of constituent monosaccharide units and include esp. the disaccharides, trisaccharides, and tetrasaccharides — compare POLYSACCHARIDE

**ol·i·go·saprobic** \"+\ *adj* [ISV *olig-* + *saprobic;* orig. formed as G *oligosaprobisch*] **:** living in or being a highly oxygenated aquatic environment in which little organic material and a minimum of fermentation is present — compare MESOSAPROBIC, POLYSAPROBIC

**ol·i·go·siderite** \"+\ *n* [F, fr. *olig-* + *siderite*] **:** a meteorite characterized by the presence of only a small amount of metallic iron

**ol·i·go·spermatic** \"+\ *adj* [*olig-* + *spermatic*] **:** affected with or exhibiting oligospermia

**ol·i·go·sper·mia** \ˌäləgōˈspərmēə, ə,ligəˈ-\ *n* -s [NL, fr. *olig-* + *-spermia*] **:** scantiness of semen or of living spermatozoa in the semen

**ol·i·got·ri·cha** \ˌäləˈgä·trəkə\ *n pl, cap* [NL, fr. *olig-* + *-tricha*] **:** a suborder of Spirotricha comprising ciliated protozoans having the body ciliation reduced to a few large bristles or entirely absent and including numerous free-living aquatic forms (as the tintinnids) as well as the cellulose-digesting ciliates of the ruminant stomach — compare OPHRYOSCOLECIDAE, TINTINNIDAE — **ol·i·got·ri·chous** \ˌ==ˈ==kəs\ *adj*

**ol·i·go·trich·i·da** \ˌäləgōˈtrikədə, ə,ligəˈ-\ [NL, fr. *olig-* + *trich-* + *-ida*] *syn of* OLIGOTRICHA

**ol·i·go·troph·ic** \ˌäləgōˈträfik, əˌligəˌ-\ *adj* [ISV *olig-* + *-trophic;* orig. formed as G *oligotrophisch*] *of a lake* **:** deficient in plant nutrients and usu. having abundant dissolved oxygen with no marked stratification — compare DYSTROPHIC, EUTROPHIC

**ol·i·go·trop·ic** \-ˈräpik\ *adj* [ISV *olig-* + *-tropic*] **:** visiting only a few kinds of flowers for nectar — used of a bee; compare MONOTROPIC, POLYTROPIC

**ol·i·go·zo·ic** \-ˈzōik\ *adj* [ISV *olig-* + *-zoic*] **:** containing few kinds or small numbers of animals — used of a habitat

**ol·i·go·zo·o·sper·mia** \ˌäləgō,zōəˈspərmēə, ə,ligə,z-\ *n* -s [NL, fr. *olig-* + *zo-* + *-spermia*] **:** OLIGOSPERMIA

**ol·i·gu·ria** \ˌäləˈg(y)ürēə\ *n* -s [NL, fr. *olig-* + *-uria*] **:** reduced excretion of urine

**olin·ia** \ōˈlinēə\ *n, cap* [NL, fr. Johan Henrik *Olin* 18th cent. Swed. botanist + NL *-ia*] **:** a small genus (coextensive with the family Oliniaceae of the order Myrtales) of African shrubs with opposite coriaceous leaves, small flowers in branched cymes, and drupaceous fruits — see HARD PEAR 1

**olio** \ˈōlē,ō\ *n* -s [modif. of Sp *olla* — more at OLLA] **1 :** OLLA PODRIDA **2 a :** a miscellaneous mixture **:** HODGEPODGE ⟨an incredibly bourgeois ~ of fancy stonework, stained glass, and light-opera staircases —R.H.Rovere⟩ **b :** a miscellaneous collection (as of literary or musical selections) ⟨a rich ~ of literary fare —Ray Corsini⟩ **3 :** vaudeville numbers performed usu. in front of the curtain between acts or as a variety bill at the end of a burlesque or minstrel show ⟨the ~ consisted of clog dancing, acrobatic acts —C.F.Wittke⟩

**ol·i·phant** *or* **ol·i·fant** \ˈäləfənt\ *n* -s [F *olifant,* fr. OF *olifant, oliphant* elephant, ivory, horn made of ivory — more at ELEPHANT] **:** a hunter's horn made from an elephant tusk

**ol·i·prance** \ˈäləprən(t)s\ *n* [ME *olipraunce*] *archaic* **:** boisterous merrymaking **:** FROLIC

**olis·thops** \ˈäləs,thäps, əˈlis-\ *n, cap* [NL, fr. Gk *olisthos* slippery (akin to *olisthanein* to slip) + NL *-ops* — more at SLIDE] **:** a genus of Pacific scarid fishes including the Australian herring-cale

[1]**ol·i·to·ry** \ˈäləˌtōrē\ *adj* [L *olitorius, holitorius,* fr. *olitor, holitor* vegetable gardener, fr. *olus, holus* potherb — more at OLERACEOUS] *archaic* **:** of, relating to, or produced in a kitchen garden

[2]**olitory** \"\ *n* -ES *archaic* **:** KITCHEN GARDEN

**oli·va** \ōˈlīvə\ *n, cap* [NL, fr. L, olive — more at OLIVE] **:** a genus of carnivorous marine snails (the type of the family Olividae) — see OLIVE SHELL

**ol·i·va·ceous** \ˌäləˈvāshəs\ *adj* [*olive* + *-aceous*] **1 :** resembling an olive **2 :** of the olive color or olive green ⟨~ markings on a bird⟩

**ol·i·vary** \ˈäləˌverē, -ri\ *adj* [L *olivarius,* fr. *oliva* olive + *-arius* -ary] **1 :** shaped like an olive **2 :** of or relating to an olivary body

**olivary body** *n* **1 :** INFERIOR OLIVE **2 :** SUPERIOR OLIVE

[1]**ol·ive** \ˈäləv, -lēv\ *n* -s [ME, fr. OF, fr. L *oliva,* fr. (assumed) OGk *elaiwa* (whence Gk *elaia*), prob. of non-IE origin; akin to the source of Arm *eul* oil] **1 a :** a plant of the genus *Olea; specif* **:** a tree (*Olea europaea*) cultivated for its fruit from antiquity in Asia Minor and southern Europe and more recently elsewhere and having a trunk that is often gnarled, leaves resembling the willow, and yellow flowers **b :** any of various shrubs and trees resembling the olive — compare WILD OLIVE **2 :** the oblong or ovoid drupaceous fruit of the olive tree that is eaten as a pickle or relish either when unripe and green or when bluish black and ripe and that yields a valuable oil **3 :** the hard yellow often attractively variegated wood of the olive tree used esp. in turnery **4 :** OLIVE BRANCH **5 :** something that is shaped like an olive: as **a :** a small slice of meat seasoned, rolled up, and cooked — usu. used in pl. ⟨~s of veal⟩ **b :** OLIVARY BODY **6 :** any of several colors resembling that of the unripe fruit of the olive tree that are yellow to yellow green in hue, of medium to low lightness, and of moderate to low saturation **7 a :** OLIVE SHELL **b :** OLIVE FLY

olive: *1* flowering branch, *2* fruit

[2]**olive** \"\ *adj* **1 :** of the color olive or olive green **2** *of a complexion* **:** approaching closer in color to olive than the average complexion

[3]**oli·ve** \ōˈlēvā\ *n, pl* **olive** *or* **olives** *usu cap* [Sp, of AmerInd origin] **1 a :** an Indian people of northeastern Mexico **b :** a member of such people **2 :** a language of the Olive people that is of unknown relationship

**olive acanthus** *n, archit* **:** an acanthus with lobes resembling olive leaves

**olive–backed thrush** \ˈ==,=-\ *or* **olive back** *n* **:** a common thrush (*Hylocichla ustulata*) of northern No. America migrating to the tropics that is brownish olive above and whitish beneath and has a ring about the eye and the sides of the head buff and the chest buff marked with black — compare GRAY-CHEEKED THRUSH

**olive branch** *n* [ME] **1 a :** a branch of the olive tree esp. when used as an emblem of peace ⟨making their submission through a boy clad in ash-color and bearing an *olive branch* —E.K.Chambers⟩ **b :** an offer or gesture of conciliation or goodwill ⟨his belief that the *olive branch* should be extended by loyal Democrats to . . . dissident party members —J.N. Popham⟩ **2 :** CHILD ⟨the rest of his letter is only about . . . his expectation of a young *olive branch* —Jane Austen⟩

**olive brown** *n* **:** any of a group of colors intermediate in hue between yellowish browns and olives; *typically* **:** a moderate olive that is lighter and very slightly redder than the color autumn — called also *bronze nude, old olive*

**olive drab** *n* **1 :** a variable color averaging a grayish olive that is greener, lighter, and slightly stronger than average covert brown and redder, lighter, and slightly stronger than bronzesheen **2 a :** a wool or cotton fabric of an olive drab color used esp. for making uniforms **b :** a uniform of this fabric

**olive family** *n* **:** OLEACEAE

**olive fruit fly** *n* **:** a small acalyptrate fly (*Dacus oleae*) of the family Trypetidae whose larva is a pest of the olive in Europe

**olive G** *n, usu cap O* **:** a sulfur dye — see DYE table I (under *Sulfur Green 11*)

**olive gray** *n* **:** a variable color averaging a grayish yellow green that is yellower and paler than average sage green or palmetto and yellower and duller than mermaid or celadon

**olive green** *n* **:** a variable color that is greener, lighter, and stronger than average olive color

**olive gum** *n* **:** a gummy exudation from the olive tree used as a drug by the ancients and now used as a perfume

**olive hole** *n* **:** a hole in a jeweled watch bearing whose sharp corners have been ground off to reduce the friction between the sides of the hole and the pivot that turns in it

**olive knot** *n* **:** a bacterial disease of the olive caused by a bacterium (*Pseudomonas savastonoi*) and characterized by small or large excrescences on leaves, branches, or even the main trunk — called also *olive tubercle*

**olive lace bug** *n* **:** a lace bug (*Froggattia olivina*) injurious to olives in Australia

**ol·i·vel·la** \\,älə'velə\\ *n* [NL, dim. of L *oliva* olive — more at OLIVE] **1** *cap* **:** a genus of small marine shining snails (family Olividae) having an operculum and a small smooth shining shell formerly used by some Indians of the Pacific coast of No. America as money and for ornament — compare OLIVE SHELL **2** -s **:** any shell or animal of the genus *Olivella*

**olive mangrove** *n* **:** BLACK MANGROVE

**olive moth** *n* **:** a moth (*Prays oleellus*) of the family Yponomeutidae with a larva that feeds on the buds, leaves, and fruits of olives

**oliv·en·ite** \\ō'livə,nīt, 'äləvə,-\\ *n* -s [G *olivenit*, fr. *olive* (fr. L *oliva*) + *-it* -ite] **:** a mineral $Cu_2(AsO_4)(OH)$ consisting of a basic arsenate of copper that is olive green, dull brown, or yellowish in color

**olive oil** *n* **:** a pale yellow to yellowish green nondrying oil obtained from the pulp of olives usu. by expression and used chiefly as a salad oil and in cooking, in toilet soaps, as an emollient, and as a wool oil — compare SULFUR OIL

**olive-oil castile soap** *n* **:** CASTILE 1

**olive plum** *n* **1 :** the fruit of a shrub or tree of the genus *Elaeodendron* (family Celastraceae) having simple leathery leaves, small greenish or white flowers in axillary clusters, and a drupaceous fruit **2 :** a tree of the genus *Elaeodendron*

**ol·i·ver** \\'äləvə(r)\\ *n* -s [prob. fr. the name *Oliver*] **1 :** an old form of smith's hammer worked by means of a treadle and normally held off the work by a spring pole **2 :** a device consisting of a pair of swages held together by a spring handle

**¹ol·i·ve·ri·an** \\,älə'virēən\\ *n* -s *usu cap* [*Oliver* Cromwell †1658 Eng. general and statesman + E *-ian*] **:** an adherent or partisan of Oliver Cromwell

**²oliverian** \\''==''==\\ *adj, usu cap* **:** CROMWELLIAN 1

**oliver's bark** *n, usu cap O* [fr. the name *Oliver*] **:** the dried bark of a tree (*Cinnamomum oliveri*) of New So. Wales and Queensland used as a substitute for cinnamon

**olives** *pl of* OLIVE

**olive scab** *n* **:** a disease of the olive caused by a fungus (*Cycloconium oleaginum*) and characterized by blotches on the leaves and peduncles

**olive scale** *n* **:** any of several scales that attack olives: as **a :** an armored scale (*Parlatoria oleae*) that is a serious pest in California **b :** BLACK SCALE 1

**ol·i·ves·cent** \\,älə'vesᵊnt\\ *adj* [²*olive* + *-escent*] **:** verging on olive in color

**olivesheen** \\'==,=\\ *n* **:** a dark grayish yellow that is greener and stronger than California green and greener, less strong, and slightly darker than honey or yellowstone

**olive shell** *n* **:** any of numerous chiefly tropical marine gastropod mollusks of the genus *Oliva* or the family Olividae having an elongate smooth highly polished shell with a very short spire, a narrow mouth notched in front, a plicate columella, a large foot, and a mantle that envelops the shell — compare OLIVELLA

**olive-sided flycatcher** \\'=,==-\\ *n* **:** a medium-sized flycatcher (*Nuttallornis borealis*) of eastern No. America

**ol·i·vet** \\,älə'vet\\ *n* -s [*olivette* dim. of *olive* — more at OLIVE] **:** an imitation pearl esp. of a kind made for trading with primitive peoples in Africa

**olive terra verte** *n* **:** AUCUBA GREEN

**olive tree** *n* [ME] **1 :** OLIVE 1 **2 :** TUPELO 1

**olive-tree agaric** *n* **:** a red luminescent mushroom (*Pleurotus phosphoreus*) of Europe

**ol·i·vette** *also* **ol·i·vet** \\,älə'vet\\ *n* -s [F *olivette*, dim. of *olive*] **:** a theatrical floodlight consisting of a 1000-watt bulb in an open-front metal box usu. mounted on a telescopic pipe stand or hung from a batten

**olive tubercle** *n* **:** OLIVE KNOT

**olive wood** *n* **1 :** the wood of the olive tree **2 a :** OLIVE PLUM 2 **b :** the wood of the olive plum **3 :** American-grown black ash esp. when quartersawed for veneer **4 :** a grayish yellowish brown that is darker and slightly redder than deer and slightly redder and darker than acorn — called also *brun doré, collie*

**olive yellow** *n* **:** a variable color averaging a dark greenish yellow that is greener, stronger, and very slightly darker than chartreuse green

**oliv·i·dae** \\ō'livə,dē\\ *n pl, cap* [NL, fr. L *Oliva*, type genus + NL *-idae*] **:** a family of burrowing snails (suborder Stenoglossa) with cylindrical, glossy, and often brightly colored shells

**ol·i·vif·er·ous** \\,älə'vif(ə)rəs\\ *adj* [L *olivifer* oliviferous (fr. *oliva* olive + *-fer* -ferous) + E *-ous* — more at OLIVE] **:** producing olives

**oliv·i·form** \\ō'livə,fȯrm\\ *adj* [ISV ¹*olive* + *-iform*] **:** shaped like an olive or an olive shell

**ol·i·vine** \\'älə,vēn, -,vən\\ *n* -s [G *olivin*, fr. *olive* + *-in* -ine — more at OLIVENITE] **1 a :** a mineral $(Mg,Fe)_2SiO_4$ consisting of a silicate of magnesium and iron and comprising the isomorphous series forsterite-fayalite that is used in making refractories; *broadly* **:** a member of the isomorphous system $(Mg,Fe,Mn,Ca)_2SiO_4$ including forsterite, fayalite, tephroite, and a hypothetical calcium orthosilicate — see PERIDOT **b :** DEMANTOID **2 :** a light yellowish green that is yellower and paler than apple green (sense 2), lighter and stronger than pistachio, and deeper than ocean green

**ol·i·vin·ic** \\,==='vinik\\ *or* **ol·i·vi·nit·ic** \\,äləvə'nid·ik\\ *adj* [ISV *olivine* + *-ic* or *-itic*] **:** relating to, resembling, or containing olivine

**¹ol·la** \\'älə, 'ō(l)yə, 'ō(l)yə\\ *n* -s [Sp, fr. L *aulla, aula, olla* pot — more at OVEN] **1** *chiefly Southwest* **:** a large earthenware jar with a globular body often having a wide mouth and looped handles and used esp. as a stewpot or as a container for water **2** *chiefly Southwest* **:** OLLA PODRIDA 1

**²ol·la** \\'älə\\ *n* -s [Pg *ola*, fr. Malayalam *ōla*] **1 :** a leaf or strip from the leaf of the talipot palm used in India for writing paper **2 :** a document written on olla

**ol·la po·dri·da** \\,äləpə'drēdə, ,ō(l)yə-, ,ō(l)yə-\\ *n, pl* **olla podridas** \\-ēdəz\\ *also* **ollas podridas** \\-yəzp-\\ [Sp, lit., rotten pot] **1 :** a highly seasoned soup or stew made of one or more meats and several vegetables usu. including chick-peas cooked in an olla **2 :** OLIO 2

**ol·lav** *or* **ol·lave** *or* **ol·lamh** \\'äləv\\ *n* -s [IrGael *ollamh*, fr. MIr *ollam*] **:** a learned man in ancient Ireland

**olluco** *var of* ULLUCO

**olm** \\'ōlm\\ *n* -s [G, fr. OHG] **:** an elongated European cave-dwelling aquatic salamander (*Proteus anguinus*) with permanent external gills and small eyes covered by the skin

**¹ol·mec** \\'äl,mek\\ *also* **ol·me·ca** \\äl'mākə\\ *n, pl* **olmec** *or* **olmecs** *also* **olmeca** *or* **olmecas** *usu cap* [Sp *olmeca*, of AmerInd origin] **:** an ancient people of the Isthmus of Tehuantepec in southern Mexico antedating or being contemporary with the Mayas

**²olmec** \\''\\ *adj, usu cap* **:** of or relating to an early culture of southeastern Mexico characterized by stone and jade carvings **:** LA VENTA

**ol·o·gist** \\'äləjəst\\ *n* -s [fr. *-ologist* (as in *geologist, psychologist*)] **:** SPECIALIST

**ol·o·graph** \\'älə,graf, -räf\\ *n* [by alter.] **:** HOLOGRAPH

**ol·o·gy** \\'äləjē\\ *n* -ES [fr. *-ology* (as in *geology, psychology*)] **:** a branch of knowledge **:** SCIENCE ⟨at least a dozen *ologies* will be represented on any one expedition nowadays —S.A. Korff⟩

**olo·liu·qui** \\,ōlə'l(y)ükē\\ *n* -s [Sp *ololiuque*, fr. Nahuatl *ololiuhqui*, lit., one that covers, fr. *ololoa* to cover] **:** a woody stemmed Mexican vine (*Rivea corymbosa*) of the family Convolvulaceae having small fleshy fruits with single seeds resembling lentils that are used by the Indians for medicinal, narcotic, and religious purposes

**olo·na** \\,ōlə'nä\\ *n* -s [Hawaiian *olonā*] **1 :** a Hawaiian shrub (*Touchardia latifolia*) of the family Urticaceae with erect stems, large thick leaves, and small flowers in globose clusters **2 a :** the strong bark fiber of the olona used for making fishnets and ropes resistant to sea water **b :** a cord made from this fiber

**olo·nets** \\ə'lōnəts\\ *also* **ol·nets** \\'äl,nets\\ *n, usu cap* [fr. *Olonets*, town on Lake Ladoga in northwestern Russia] **:** a dialect of Karelian spoken east of Lake Ladoga

**olor** \\'ō,lō(ə)r\\ *n, cap* [NL, fr. L, swan — more at AUK] **:** a genus of swans with no frontal knob including the whistling and trumpeter swans

**olo·ro·so** \\,ōlə'rō(,)sō\\ *n* -s [Sp, fr. *oloroso*, adj., fragrant, fr. *olor* odor (fr. L, fr. *olēre* to smell) + *-oso* -ous (fr. L *-osus*) — more at ODOR] **:** a sherry of golden color and medium sweetness

**ölöt** \\'ü'lüt\\ *n, pl* **ölöt** *or* **ölöts** *usu cap* **1 :** a Mongol people of Chinese Turkestan and Mongolia **2 :** a member of the Ölöt people

**olp** \\'älp\\ *also* **olph** \\'älf\\ *dial Eng var of* ¹ALP

**ol·pe** \\'älpē\\ *n, pl* **olpes** \\-ēz\\ *or* **ol·pae** \\-ē\\ [Gk *olpē*; akin to Gk *elpos* oil — more at SALVE] **:** either of two ancient Greek containers: **a :** a leather flask for oils or other liquids **b :** a wine pitcher resembling the oenochoe but more cylindrical in body

**ol·pid·i·a·ce·ae** \\äl,pidē'āsē,ē\\ *n pl, cap* [NL, fr. *Olpidium*, type genus + *-aceae*] **:** a family of fungi (order Chytridiales) in which each thallus develops into a single sporangium

**ol·pid·i·as·ter** \\=,==='astə(r)\\ *n, cap* [NL, fr. *Olpidium* + *-aster*] **:** a genus of fungi (family Olpidiaceae) resembling *Olpidium* but having a sporangium without a neck

**ol·pid·i·um** \\äl'pidēəm\\ *n, cap* [NL, fr. Gk *olpid-, olpis* leather flask; akin to Gk *elpis* oil — more at SALVE] **:** a genus of fungi (family Olpidiaceae) having a sporangium with a neck and retaining the spores in a sac until fully matured

**-ols** *pl of* -OL

**ol·y·koek** *also* **ol·y·cook** \\'älə,kük\\ *n* -s [D *oliekoek*, fr. *olie* oil (fr. MD, fr. L *oleum*) + *koek* cake — more at OIL, COOKIE] *North* **:** DOUGHNUT

**olym·pia** \\ō'limpēə\\ *adj, usu cap* [fr. *Olympia*, Wash.] **:** of or from Olympia, capital of the state of Washington ⟨*Olympia* residents⟩ **:** of the kind or style prevalent in Olympia

**olym·pi·ad** \\ə'limpē,ad\\ *n* -s *often cap* [MF *Olympiade*, fr. L *Olympiad-, Olympias*, fr. Gk, fr. *Olympia*, plain in Elis in the northwestern Peloponnesus where the ancient Olympian games took place (fr. *Olympos*, a mountain in Elis + Gk *-ia* -y) + Gk *-ad-, -as*, fem. suffix denoting descent from or connection with] **1 :** one of the four-year intervals between Olympian games by which time was reckoned in ancient Greece ⟨the city was taken on the third month, on the day of the fast, upon the hundred and seventy-ninth ~ —R.L.Odom⟩ **2 a :** a quadrennial celebration of the modern Olympic Games ⟨India, in the past five ~s, has won 20 contests without defeat —*Amateur Athlete*⟩ **b :** OLYMPIC GAMES ⟨national ~s⟩

**¹olym·pi·an** \\-ēən\\ *adj, usu cap* [L *Olympius* Olympian (fr. Gk *Olympios*, fr. *Olympia*) + E *-an*] **1 :** of or relating to the ancient Greek region of Olympia **2 a :** of, relating to, or constituting the Olympian games **b :** ²OLYMPIC 2

**²olympian** \\''\\ *n* -s **1** *cap* **:** a native or inhabitant of ancient Olympia **2** *usu cap* **:** a participant in Olympic Games ⟨two American *Olympians* and other red-capped, blue-jacketed competitors —*Newsweek*⟩

**³olympian** \\''\\ *adj, usu cap* [L *Olympius* Olympian (fr. Gk *Olympios*, fr. *Olympos* Olympus, mountain in Thessaly that was considered the abode of the chief gods of ancient Greece) + E *-an*] **1 :** of or relating to Mount Olympus in Thessaly ⟨*Olympian* deities⟩ **2 :** befitting or characteristic of the gods conceived as inhabiting Mount Olympus **:** displaying majestic omniscience or detachment **:** LOFTY, SUPERLATIVE ⟨verdicts based on *Olympian* detachment and austere standards —Richard Watts⟩ ⟨lies in *Olympian* beauty gazing upon it all with . . . serene composure —C.B.Tinker⟩

**⁴olympian** \\''\\ *n* -s *usu cap* **1 :** one of the gods conceived as inhabiting Mount Olympus ⟨something lofty and sinister like an *Olympian's* caprice —Joseph Conrad⟩ **2 :** a being of lofty detachment or superior attainments ⟨side by side with these *Olympians* are the less conspicuous who are glad for modest honors —C.M.Fuess⟩

**olympian blue** *n, often cap O* [³*Olympian*] **:** MATELOT 2

**olympian games** *n pl, usu cap O* [¹*Olympian*] **:** a Panhellenic festival dedicated to Zeus, originating in 776 B.C. and held every fourth year in the first month after the summer solstice, and consisting of contests in sports, music, and literature with the victor's prize a crown of wild olive, a palm branch, and the right to erect a statue in the central enclosure of the sacred precincts — compare AGON a

**olympian green** *n, often cap O* [³*Olympian*] **:** MALACHITE GREEN 3

**olym·pi·an·ism** \\-ēə,nizəm\\ *n* -s *usu cap* [³*Olympian* + *-ism*] **:** worship of the Olympian gods

**olym·pi·an·ly** *adv, usu cap* [³*Olympian* + *-ly*] **:** in an Olympian manner ⟨the accident was *Olympianly* disregarded except by the butler —Jean Stafford⟩

**olympia oyster** *n, usu cap 1st O* **:** a small flavorful native oyster (*Ostrea lurida*) of the Puget Sound area of the Pacific coast of No. America

**¹olym·pic** \\ō'limpik, -pēk\\ *adj, often cap* [L *Olympicus*, fr. Gk *Olympikos*, fr. *Olympos* Mt. Olympus + Gk *-ikos* -ic] **:** ³OLYMPIAN

**²olympic** \\''\\ *adj, often cap* [L *Olympicus*, fr. Gk *Olympikos*, fr. *Olympia*, region in Elis + Gk *-ikos* -ic] **1 :** ¹OLYMPIAN 1 **2 :** of or relating to the Olympic Games

**olympic blue** *n, often cap O* [¹*Olympic*] **:** COBALT BLUE 2

**olympic games** *n pl, usu cap O&G* [²*Olympic*] **1 :** OLYMPIAN GAMES **2 :** a modified revival of the Olympian games originating in Athens in 1896, held once every four years, and consisting of international athletic contests — called also *Olympics*

**olym·pics** \\-ks\\ *n pl, usu cap* [²*olympic* + *-s*] **:** OLYMPIC GAMES

**olyn·thi·an** \\ō'lin(t)thēən\\ *n* -s *cap* [*Olynthus*, town in ancient Macedonia + E *-an*] **:** a native or inhabitant of Olynthus in ancient Macedonia

**olyn·thus** \\ō'lin(t)thəs\\ *n* -ES [NL, fr. Gk *olynthos* fig] **:** a young calcareous sponge immediately after fixation of the free larva where it resembles a vase in form and has a simple and asconoid body wall — compare ASCON

**om** *also* **aum** \\'ōm\\ *interj* [Skt *om*] — used in Hinduism, Sikhism, and Lamaism as a mantra in mystical contemplation of ultimate reality

**om-** *or* **omo-** *comb form* [MF *omo-*, fr. Gk *ōm-, ōmo-*, fr. *ōmos* — more at HUMERUS] **1 :** shoulder ⟨*om*arthritis⟩ **2 :** of or relating to the shoulder and ⟨*omo*hyoid⟩

**OM** *abbr* **1** old measurement **2** outer marker

**-o·ma** \\'ōmə\\ *n suffix, pl* **-omas** \\-məz\\ *or* **-oma·ta** \\-məd·ə, -ətə\\ [L *-omat-, -oma*, fr. Gk *-ōmat-, -ōma*] **1 :** tumor of a (specified) kind ⟨aden*oma*⟩ ⟨melan*oma*⟩ ⟨hygr*oma*⟩ or of a consisting predominantly of a (specified) kind of cell or tissue ⟨fibr*oma*⟩ ⟨my*oma*⟩ ⟨myelocyt*oma*⟩ or occurring in a (specified) organ ⟨nephr*oma*⟩ **2 :** -OME

**oma·dhaun** \\'ämə,thȯn\\ *n* -s [IrGael *amadān*] *chiefly Irish* **:** FOOL, IDIOT, SIMPLETON

**oma·gua** \\ō'mä(g)wə\\ *n, pl* **omagua** *or* **omaguas** *usu cap* **1 a :** a Tupian people of western Brazil and Peru **b :** a member of such people **2 :** the language of the Omagua people

**¹oma·ha** \\'ōmə,hȯ, -hä\\ *also* **ma·ha** \\mə'>\\ *n, pl* **omaha** *or* **omahas** *also* **maha** *or* **mahas** *usu cap* [Omaha, lit., those going upstream or against the wind] **1 a :** a Siouan people in the Missouri river valley in northeastern Nebraska **b :** a member of such people **2 :** a dialect of Dhegiha

**²omaha** \\''\\ *adj, usu cap* [fr. *Omaha*, city in eastern Nebraska, fr. *Omaha* (Siouan people)] **:** of or from the city of Omaha, Nebr. ⟨an *Omaha* packinghouse⟩ **:** of the kind or style prevalent in Omaha

**oma·han** \\-,hȯn, -hän\\ *n* -s *cap* [*Omaha*, Nebraska + E *-an*] **:** a native or resident of Omaha, Nebr.

**oman** \\(')ō'män\\ *adj, usu cap* **:** Muscat and Oman

**¹oma·ni** \\ō'mänē\\ *n* -s *cap* [Ar *'umānīy*, fr. *'umān* Oman] **:** a native or inhabitant of Muscat and Oman

**²omani** *adj, usu cap* **:** of, relating to, or characteristic of Muscat and Oman or its people

**omao** \\ō'maù\\ *n* -s [Hawaiian] **:** a thrush (*Phaeornis obscurus*) of Hawaii

**omar·ian** \\ō'märēən\\ *n* -s *usu cap* [*Omar* Khayyám †*ab*1123 Pers. poet and astronomer + E *-an*] **:** a student or admirer of the poetry of Omar Khayyám

**omar stanza** \\'ō,mär-\\ *n, usu cap O* [after *Omar* Khayyám] **:** RUBAIYAT STANZA

**oma·sal** \\(')ō'māsəl\\ *adj* [*omasum* + *-al*] **:** of or relating to the omasum

**oma·si·tis** \\,ōmə'sīd·əs\\ *n* -ES [NL, fr. *omasum* + *-itis*] **:** inflammation of the omasum

**oma·sum** \\ō'māsəm\\ *n, pl* **oma·sa** \\-sə\\ [NL, fr. L, tripe of a bullock] **:** the division between the reticulum and the abomasum in the stomach of a ruminant — called also *manyplies, psalterium*

**o·mayyad** *usu cap, var of* UMAYYAD

**¹om·bre** *also* **om·ber** \\'ämbə(r)\\ *n, pl* **ombres** *also* **ombers** [alter. of *umber*] **:** a European grayling (*Thymallus thymallus*)

**²om·bre** *also* **om·ber** *or* **hom·bre** \\'ämbə(r)\\ *n* -s [F or Sp; F *hombre*, fr. Sp, lit., man — more at HOMBRE] **:** a 3-handed card game played throughout Europe in the 17th and 18th centuries and still played in Spain; *also* **:** the player in this game who elects to name the trump and oppose the other 2 players

**³om·bré** *or* **om·bre** \\(')ōⁿ'brā, (')äm'b-\\ *adj* [F *ombré*, past part. of *ombrer* to shade, fr. It *ombrare*, fr. *ombra* shade, shadow, fr. L *umbra* — more at UMBRAGE] **:** SHADED — used esp. of fabrics with a dyed or woven design in which the color is graduated from light to dark and often into stripes of varying shades of one or more colors ⟨some hats are of ~ blues and lavenders —Lois Long⟩

**⁴ombré** *or* **ombre** \\''\\ *n* -s **1 :** an ombré design **2 :** a fabric with an ombré design ⟨a gray leaf-and-fern pattern printed on a pink-to-red ~ —Lois Long⟩

**om·bres chi·noises** \\,ämbrə,shēn'wäz\\ *n pl, sometimes cap* [F, lit., Chinese shadows] **:** shadows of puppets or persons thrown upon a transparent screen and used as characters in a dramatic presentation

**ombrette** *var of* UMBRETTE

**ombro-** *comb form* [Gk, fr. *ombros* — more at IMBRICATE] **:** rain ⟨*ombro*logy⟩

**om·bro·graph** \\'ämbrə,graf\\ *n* [ISV *ombro-* + *-graph*] **:** a self-registering rain gage

**om·brol·o·gy** \\äm'bräləjē\\ *n* -ES [*ombro-* + *-logy*] **:** a branch of meteorology that deals with rain

**om·brom·e·ter** \\äm'brämәd·ə(r)\\ *n* [Gk *ombros* rain + E *-meter*] **:** RAIN GAGE

**om·bro·phile** \\'ämbrə,fīl\\ *n* -s [ISV *ombro-* + *-phile*] **:** an ombrophilous plant

**om·broph·i·lous** \\(')äm'bräfələs\\ *also* **om·bro·phil·ic** \\,ämbrə'filik\\ *adj* [*ombrophilous* ISV *ombro-* + *-philous*; *ombrophilic* fr. *ombrophilous* + *-ic*] *of a plant* **:** capable of withstanding or thriving in the presence of much rain — **om·broph·i·ly** \\äm'bräfəlē\\ *n* -ES

**om·bro·phobe** \\'ämbrə,fōb\\ *n* -s [ISV *ombro-* + *-phobe*] **:** an ombrophobous plant

**om·broph·o·bous** \\(')äm'bräfəbəs\\ *adj* [ISV *ombro-* + *-phobous*] *of a plant* **:** incapable of withstanding long-continued rain — **om·broph·o·by** \\-==bē\\ *n* -ES

**om·bu** \\äm'bü\\ *n* -s [Sp *ombú*, fr. Guarani *umbú*] **:** a large herbaceous So. American tree (*Phytolacca dioica*) having an immensely broad trunk, soft spongy wood, and dark green oval leaves

**om·deh** *also* **om·da** \\'ämdə\\ *n* -s *sometimes cap* [Ar *'umdah* column, authority] **:** the leader of an Egyptian village ⟨the tendency of village ~s . . . to back the winning horse —*Economist*⟩

**om·dur·man** \\,ämdə(r)'man\\ *adj, usu cap* [fr. *Omdurman*, city in Sudan] **:** of or from the city of Omdurman, Sudan **:** of the kind or style prevalent in Omdurman

**-ome** \\,ōm\\ *n suffix* -s [NL *-omat-, -oma*, fr. L *-omat-, -oma* -oma] **:** abstract entity **:** group **:** mass **:** stem ⟨caul*ome*⟩ ⟨mest*ome*⟩

**¹omega** \\ō'megə, -'mēgə, -'māgə *sometimes* 'ōmigə *or* 'ōmegə *or* 'ō,megə, ō,māgə\\ *n* -s [Gk *ō mega*, lit., large o] **1 :** the 24th and last letter of the Greek alphabet — symbol Ω or ω; see ALPHABET table **2 :** the last (as in sequence, order, classification) **:** ENDING ⟨between her alpha and ~, a span of fifty years —Jean Stafford⟩ — compare ALPHA

**²omega** \\''\\ *or* **ω** *adj* **:** of, relating to, or being an end group or position ⟨~ oxidation of fatty acids⟩ ⟨ω-chloro-styrene $C_6H_5CH{=}CHCl$⟩

**omega·tron** \\=='==,trän\\ *n* -s [*omega* + *-tron*] **:** a small instrument utilizing the principle of the cyclotron for the measurement of the masses of atomic particles

**omegoid** \\ō'me,gȯid, -'mē,-, -'mā,-\\ *adj* [*omega* + *-oid*] **:** having the form of the Greek capital letter omega

**om·e·let** *also* **om·e·lette** \\'äm(ə)lət, *usu* -əd·+V\\ *n* -s [F *omelette*, fr. MF, alter. of *amelette*, alter. of *alumette*, alter. (influenced by *-ette*) of *alumelle*, lit., blade (of a sword or knife), fr. OF *alemele, alemele*, alter. of *lemelle, lemele*, fr. L *lamella* small metal plate, dim. of *lamina* thin plate] **:** eggs beaten to a froth, cooked without stirring until set, and served in a half-round form by folding one half over the other ⟨cheese ~⟩ ⟨jelly ~⟩

**¹omen** \\'ōmən\\ *n* -s [L *omin-, omen*] **:** an occurrence or phenomenon believed to portend or show the character of a future event **:** AUGURY, FORETOKEN, PRESAGE ⟨priests took ~s before the warriors went into battle —Ralph Linton⟩ ⟨the ghostly bidding of the cloud, the ~ of thunder —C.P.Aiken⟩

**²omen** \\''\\ *vt* -ED/-ING/-S **:** to divine or to foreshow by signs or portents **:** have omens or premonitions regarding **:** AUGUR, PRESAGE ⟨the blazing red of the setting sun ~ed fine weather⟩

**oment-** *or* **omento-** *comb form* [*omentum*] **:** omentum ⟨*oment*itis⟩ ⟨*omento*pexy⟩

**omen·tal** \\(')ō'mentəl\\ *adj* [*omentum* + *-al*] **:** of, relating to, or formed from an omentum

**omen·to·pexy** \\ō'mentə,peksē\\ *n* -ES [ISV *oment-* + *-pexy*] **:** the operation of suturing the omentum esp. to another organ ⟨nephro-*omentopexy*⟩

**omen·tu·lum** \\ō'menchələm\\ *n, pl* **omentu·la** \\-lə\\ [NL, fr. L *omentum* + *-ulum*] **:** LESSER OMENTUM

**omen·tum** \\ō'mentəm\\ *n, pl* **omen·ta** \\-tə\\ *or* **omentums** [L, fr. *o-* (akin to L *-uere* to put on) + *-mentum* — more at EXUVIAE] **:** a free fold of peritoneum or one connecting or supporting viscera or other abdominal structures — see GREATER OMENTUM, LESSER OMENTUM; compare MESENTERY

**omer** \\'ōmə(r)\\ *n* -s [Heb *'ōmer*] **1 :** an ancient Hebrew unit of dry capacity equal to ¹⁄₁₀ ephah or about ½ peck **2 a :** a wave offering of a sheaf or omer measure of barley representing the first reaping of the grain harvest and presented to the priest in a temple ceremony on the second day of the Passover **b :** a period of seven weeks between the second day of the Passover and Shabuoth during which in traditional Judaism various restrictive laws (as the prohibition of festivities except on Rosh Hodesh and Lag b'Omer) are in force and each day is formally counted in the evening service ⟨hast commanded us concerning the counting of the ~ —*Jewish Daily Prayer Book*⟩

**om·i·cron** *also* **om·i·kron** \'äma,krän, *chiefly Brit* ō'mīkrən\ *n* -s [Gk *o mikron*, lit., small o] **:** the 15th letter of the Greek alphabet — symbol O or o; see ALPHABET table

**om·i·nate** \'äma,nāt\ *vb* -ED/-ING/-S [L *ominatus*, past part. of *ominari*, fr. *omin-*, *omen* omen] *vt* **1** *archaic* **:** to prophesy from signs and omens **:** AUGUR **2** *archaic* **:** to be a portent or omen of ~ *vi* **1** *obs* **:** to utter prophecies or forebodings **2** *obs* **:** to serve as a prophecy

**omination** *n* -s [L *omination-*, *ominatio*, fr. *ominatus* + *-ion-*, *-io -ion*] *obs* **:** the act of prophesying

**om·i·nous** \'ämənəs\ *adj* [L *ominosus*, fr. *omin-*, *omen* + *-osus -ose*] **1 :** of or relating to an omen **:** being or exhibiting an omen ⟨the continual wars and revolutions so ~ of the future —Margaret Parton⟩ **2 :** indicative of future misfortune or calamity **:** causing anxiety and fear **:** potentially disastrous ⟨the ~ waves of cloud seemed to advance with terrific speed —O.E.Rölvaag⟩ ⟨a dead and ~ silence prevailed everywhere —J.A.Froude⟩ ⟨the ~ sounds the motor was making —Herbert Passin⟩

**syn** PORTENTOUS, FATEFUL, INAUSPICIOUS, UNPROPITIOUS: OMINOUS applies to that which shows a menacing, threatening, and frightful character foreshadowing evil or tragic developments, sometimes rather vague ⟨there was something *ominous* about it, and in intangible ways one was made to feel that the worst was about to come —Jack London⟩ ⟨they formed together an *ominous* cloud charged with forces of uncertain magnitude, but of the reality of which Italy had already terrible experience —J.A.Froude⟩ PORTENTOUS is now likely to indicate the prodigious, huge, impressive, marvelous, or monstrous, and only secondarily to suggest the character of a portent, a forewarning of calamity to come ⟨in the midst of a *portentous* silence, the consul unrolled his papers, evidently intending to produce an effect by the exceeding bigness of his looks —Herman Melville⟩ ⟨something quivered in every fiber of his being, like moonlit ripples on the sea. He felt at the same time a *portentous* stillness and an immense enterprise —H.G.Wells⟩ FATEFUL may imply an especial importance, often solemn, decreed by fate; it is often simply a synonym for *momentous* ⟨the moving, *fateful* story of his death —H.O.Taylor⟩ ⟨the hour seemed awful to them, and the hearts within them burned as though of *fateful* matters their souls were newly learned —William Morris⟩ ⟨six thousand years ago, the Nile, the begetter of water and grain, was as *fateful* to the fellah as it is today —Mary Lindsay⟩ INAUSPICIOUS and UNPROPITIOUS may suggest the presence of distinctly unfavorable signs or may be simply synonyms for *unlucky* or *unfavorable* ⟨while my words with *inauspicious* thunderings shook Heaven —P.B.Shelley⟩ ⟨*unpropitious* weather⟩ ⟨an *unpropitious* attitude for a politician seeking reelection to take⟩

**om·i·nous·ly** *adv* **:** in an ominous manner ⟨the steps to the veranda sagged ~ under his weight —Harold Sinclair⟩ ⟨the night sky glowed ~ red —O.S.Nock⟩

**om·i·nous·ness** *n* -ES **:** the quality or state of being ominous

**omis·si·bil·i·ty** \ō,misə'biləd·ē\ *n* -ES **:** the quality or state of being omissible

**omis·si·ble** \ō'misəbəl\ *adj* [L *omissus* (past part. of *omittere*) + E *-able*] **:** that may be omitted **:** subject to or suitable for omission

**omis·sion** \ō'mishən,ə'm-\ *n* -s [ME *omissioun*, fr. LL *omission-*, *omissio*, fr. L *omissus* (past part. of *omittere*) + *-ion-*, *-io -ion*] **1 a :** apathy toward or neglect of duty **:** lack of action ⟨allowed themselves to be engulfed . . . through ~ or commission —*N. Y. Times Mag.*⟩ — compare COMMISSION 5 **b :** something neglected or left undone ⟨pondered many ~*s* that night in the rectory's best bedroom —J.D.Beresford⟩ **2 :** the act of omitting whether by leaving out or by abstention from inserting or by failure to include or perform; *also* **:** the state of being omitted ⟨the ~ of clues essential to understanding —J.H. Wheelock⟩ ⟨when the ~ was discovered, they would send somebody —Margaret Kennedy⟩

**omis·sive** \ō'misiv\ *adj* [L *omissus* (past part. of *omittere*) + E *-ive*] **:** leaving out **:** failing or neglecting to do **:** OMITTING — **omis·sive·ly** *adv*

**omit** \ō'mit, ə'm-, *usu* -id.+V\ *vt* **omitted; omitted; omitting; omits** [ME *omitten*, fr. L *omittere*, fr. *ob-* to, against, over + *mittere* to send — more at OB-, SMITE] **1 :** to leave out or leave unmentioned **:** fail to insert, include, or name ⟨if you ~ the industrial areas . . . this way of life is pastoral, parochial, picturesque —W.G.Hardy⟩ ⟨will not wish to ~ this valuable book from his reading —Harry Schwartz⟩ **2 :** to fail to perform or make use of **:** leave alone or undone **:** FORBEAR ⟨nor could I think well of the man who should ~ an occasion of testifying his respect —Jane Austen⟩ ⟨most visitors ~ to walk round the walls in their hurry —S.P.B.Mais⟩ **3** *obs* **:** to leave unnoticed or unregarded ⟨~ him not; blunt not his love nor lose the good advantage of his grace —Shak.⟩ **4** *obs* **:** to refrain or cease from keeping **:** let go ⟨traitors . . . having sense of beauty do ~ their mortal natures —Shak.⟩ **syn** see NEGLECT

**omittance** *n* -s [*omit* + *-ance*] *obs* **:** OMISSION

**-om·ma** \'ämə\ *n comb form* [NL *-ommat-*, *-omma*, fr. Gk *ommat-*, *omma* eye; akin to Gk *ōps* eye — more at EYE] **:** one having (such) an eye or (such or so many) eyes — in generic names in zoology ⟨Lox*omma*⟩

**om·mas·tre·phes** \ə'mastrə,fēz\ *n, cap* [NL, fr. Gk *omma* eye + *strephein* to turn — more at STROPHE] **:** a widely distributed genus (type of the family Ommastrephidae) of extremely active cephalopods (order Decapoda) having a cylindrical body, large rhombic terminal fins, and short strong arms

**om·ma·te·al** \'ämə'tēəl\ *adj* [*ommate*um + *-al*] **:** of, relating to, or having compound eyes

**om·ma·te·um** \,=='tēəm\ *n, pl* **omma·tea** \-ēə\ [NL, fr. Gk *ommat-*, *omma* eye] **:** COMPOUND EYE

**om·ma·tid·i·al** \'ämə'tidēəl\ *adj* [*ommatid*ium + *-al*] **:** of, relating to, or having ommatidia

**om·ma·tid·i·um** \,==='ēəm\ *n, pl* **ommatid·ia** \-ēə\ [NL, fr. Gk *ommat-*, *omma* eye + NL *-idium*] **:** one of the elements corresponding to a small simple eye or ocellus that make up the compound eye of an arthropod and that typically consist of an external corneal lens beneath which is a crystalline cone and below it a rhabdom which is enclosed in a sensitive retinula protected by pigment

**om·ma·tin** \'äməd·ən\ *n* -s [Gk *ommat-*, *omma* eye + E *-in*] **:** an ommochrome (as a brown pigment in the eye of the fruit fly) of low molecular weight

**om·mat·o·phore** \ə'mad·ə,fō(ə)r\ *n* -s [prob. fr. (assumed) NL *ommatophorus*, fr. Gk *ommat-*, *omma* eye + NL *-o-* + *-phorus -phore*] **:** a movable peduncle bearing an eye ⟨a snail probing with his eyes at the end of their ~*s*⟩ — **om·ma·toph·o·rous** \'ämə'täf(ə)rəs\ *adj*

**ommiad** *usu cap, var of* UMAYYAD

**om·mo·chrome** \'ämə,krōm\ *n* [*ommo-* (fr. Gk *omma* eye) + *-chrome*] **:** any of various pigments derived from tryptophan and found esp. in the eyes of insects

**omn-** *or* **omni-** *comb form* [ME *omni-*, fr. MF, fr. L, fr. *omnis* all] **:** all **:** universal **:** universally **:** without restriction ⟨*omni*meter⟩ ⟨*omni*present⟩ ⟨*omn*ist⟩

**om·ne·i·ty** \äm'nēəd·ē\ *n* -ES [L *omne* (neut. of *omnis* all) + E *-ity*] **:** the state of being all-comprehensive **:** ALLNESS

**om·ni·bearing** \'ämnə,-nē+,-\ *n* [*omn-* + *bearing*] **:** the bearing of an omnidirectional radio range station from an airplane usu. expressed in terms of magnetic rather than true north

**1om·ni·bus** \'ämnə,bəs,-nē-, -,bəs\ *n* -ES [F, fr. L, for all, dat. pl. of *omnis* all; perh. akin to L *ops* wealth — more at OPULENT] **1 :** a public vehicle usu. automotive and 4-wheeled and designed to carry a comparatively large number of passengers **:** BUS **2 :** OMNIBUS BILL ⟨this bill is an ~ and is being reviewed at length by the author —E.H.Wilson⟩ **3 :** BUSBOY ⟨little ~*es* in white suits moved about gathering up papers or napkins dropped by careless diners —H.S.Harrison⟩ **4 :** a book containing reprints of a number of works (as of a single author or on a single subject or related subjects)

**2omnibus** \"\ *adj* **:** of, relating to, or providing for many things or classes at once **:** containing or including many items ⟨meager appropriation in view of the ~ nature of its assignment —*Nation's Business*⟩ ⟨a sort of ~ tribute, touching on the natives, the huts, the palm trees, . . . hookworm, dysentery —R.L.Taylor⟩

**omnibus bill** *n* **:** a legislative bill that includes a number of miscellaneous provisions or appropriations ⟨a tough *omnibus bill* he could dump as a single package —*Time*⟩

**omnibus box** *n* **:** a large box in a theater or opera house adapted to contain many persons

**omnibus clause** *n* **:** a clause or section (as of a contract or statute) intended to cover various items not otherwise specifically covered; *esp* **:** a clause in an automobile insurance policy that extends protection to others than the named insured

**om·ni·competence** \'ämnə,-nē+\ *n* [fr. *omnicompetent*, after E *competent: competence*] **:** the quality or state of being omnicompetent ⟨they act on an identical assumption of ~ —Hannah Arendt⟩

**om·ni·competent** \"+\ *adj* [*omn-* + *competent*] **:** having jurisdiction or legal capacity to act in all matters ⟨too little aware of the peril in a monopoly of political and economic power in the hands of the ~ state —Reinhold Niebuhr⟩

**om·ni·directional** \"+\ *adj* [ISV *omn-* + *directional*] **1 :** receiving or sending radiations equally well in all directions ⟨~ radio transmitter⟩ ⟨~ antenna⟩ **2** *of a microphone* **:** not directional

**omnidirectional radio range** *or* **omnidirectional range** *n* **:** OMNIRANGE

**om·ni·far·i·ous** \'ämnə'fa(a)rēəs, -fer-, -fār-\ *adj* [LL *omnifarius*, fr. L *omni-* omn- + *-farius* (as in *bifarius* twofold) — more at BIFARIOUS] **:** of all varieties, forms, or kinds ⟨his ~ reading . . . craved books of poetry and chivalry —E.A.Weeks⟩ — **om·ni·far·i·ous·ly** *adv* — **om·ni·far·i·ous·ness** *n* -ES

**om·nif·ic** \(')äm'nifik\ *adj* [ML *omnificus*, fr. L *omni-* omn- + *-ficus -fic*] **:** being all-creating **:** OMNIFICENT

**om·nif·i·cence** \äm'nifəsən(t)s\ *n* -s [fr. *omnificent*, after such pairs as E *benevolent: benevolence*] **:** the quality or state of being omnificent

**om·nif·i·cent** \-nt\ *adj* [*omn-* + *-ficent* (as in *magnificent*)] **:** creating all that comes into existence **:** unlimited in creative power

**om·ni·fy** \'ämnə,fī\ *vt* -ED/-ING/-ES [*omn-* + *-fy*] **:** to make universal **:** ENLARGE

**om·nig·e·nous** \(')äm'nijənəs\ *adj* [L *omnigenus*, fr. *omni-* omn- + *genus* kind — more at KIN] **:** composed of or containing all varieties

**om·ni·graph** \'ämnə,graf, -rȧf\ *n* [*omn-* + *-graph*] **:** a device for automatically producing dot-and-dash sounds of the telegraph code used in instructing radiotelegraph operators

**om·nil·e·gent** \(')äm'nilәjənt\ *adj* [*omn-* + L *legent-*, *legens*, pres. part. of *legere* to read — more at LEGEND] **:** reading or having read everything **:** characterized by encyclopedic reading ⟨no historians have been more ~, more careful of the document —George Saintsbury⟩

**om·nim·e·ter** \äm'nimәd·ә(r)\ *n* [*omn-* + *-meter*] **:** a theodolite having a microscope rigidly attached to the telescope so that the vertical angular movement of the telescope can be observed through the microscope

**om·ni·phib·i·ous** \'ämnə'fibēəs\ *adj* [*omn-* + *-phibious* (as in *amphibious*)] *of an airplane* **:** able to land on any surface (as water, snow, ice, or land)

**om·nip·o·tence** \äm'nipəd·ən(t)s, əm'-, -ətən- *also* -ət°n-\ *n* [LL *omnipotentia*, fr. L *omnipotent-*, *omnipotens* + *-ia -y*] **1 a :** the quality or state of being omnipotent **:** almighty or unlimited power **b :** an agency or force of unlimited power and influence ⟨I could not share the popular faith in the ~ of education —M.R.Cohen⟩ **2** *cap* **:** DEITY 1b

**om·nip·o·ten·cy** \-nsē, -si\ *n* -ES [ME *omnipotencie*, fr. LL *omnipotentia*] **:** OMNIPOTENCE

**1om·nip·o·tent** \-nt\ *adj* [ME, fr. MF, fr. L *omnipotent-*, *omnipotens*, fr. *omni-* omn- + *potent-*, *potens* potent — more at POTENT] **1** *often cap* **:** ALMIGHTY 1a ⟨lift up our mind in contemplation of the aid of the *Omnipotent* Deity —P.N.Ure⟩ **2 a** *obs* **:** ARRANT ⟨this is the most ~ villain that ever cried "Stand!" to a true man —Shak.⟩ **b :** having virtually unlimited authority or influence **:** ALL-POWERFUL **:** possessing infinite capacity ⟨for five years this man was the ~ leader of the Roman mob —J.A.Froude⟩ ⟨enjoy smoothly functioning and ~ libraries —H.N.Southern⟩

**2omnipotent** \"\ *n* -s **1 :** one who is omnipotent **2** *cap* **:** 2ALMIGHTY

**om·nip·o·tent·ly** *adv* **:** in an omnipotent manner **:** with unlimited power

**om·ni·pres·ence** \'ämnə'prez°n(t)s\ *n* [ML *omnipraesentia*, fr. *omnipraesent-*, *omnipraesens* omnipresent + L *-ia -y*] **:** the quality or state of being omnipresent **:** UBIQUITY ⟨find some positive value in life to pose against the ~ of death —Joseph Frank⟩ ⟨the ~ of scholarship as a background —R.P.Blackmur⟩

**om·ni·pres·ent** \,==='prez°nt\ *adj* [ML *omnipraesent-*, *omnipraesens*, fr. L *omni-* omn- + *praesent-*, *praesens* present — more at PRESENT] **:** present in all places at all times **:** UBIQUITOUS ⟨an ~ Deity⟩ ⟨had always been conscious of poverty as . . . an ~ reality which ate its way into the marrow of life —Christine Weston⟩ ⟨the most ~ sign without words . . . is the red and green traffic light —Stuart Chase⟩ — **om·ni·pres·ent·ly** *adv*

**om·ni·range** \'ämnə, -nē+,-\ *n* [*omnirange* fr. *omn-* + *range*] **:** a system of radio navigation in which any bearing relative to a special radio transmitter on the ground may be chosen and flown by an airplane pilot

**om·ni·science** \äm'nishən(t)s\ *also* **om·ni·scien·cy** \-nsē, -si\ *n, pl* **omnisciences** *also* **omnisciencies** [ML *omniscientia*, fr. L *omni-* omn- + *scientia* knowledge — more at SCIENCE] **:** the quality or state of being omniscient: **a :** infinite knowledge ⟨in ~ . . . there is only an unmediated timeless knowledge —J.R.Everett⟩ **b :** universal or complete learning or knowledge ⟨a company should possess enough humility to deny ~ and to invite help and advice —L.H.Bristol⟩

**1om·ni·scient** \(')=='nishənt\ *adj* [NL *omniscient-*, *omnisciens*, back-formation fr. ML *omniscientia*] **1 :** having infinite awareness, understanding, and insight **:** knowing all things **:** infinitely wise ⟨would take an ~ Deity to know what you're talking about —Edith Wharton⟩ **2 :** possessed of universal or complete knowledge **:** exhaustively learned ⟨was as ~ as the scholarship and science of his day permitted —O.S.J. Gogarty⟩ — **om·ni·scient·ly** *adv*

**2omniscient** \"\ *n* -s **1 :** a being or person that is omniscient **2** *cap* **:** 2GOD

**om·ni·scope** \'ämnə,skōp\ *n* [*omn-* + *-scope*] **:** PERISCOPE

**om·nist** \'ämnəst\ *n* -s [*omn-* + *-ist*] **:** one that believes in all religions

**om·ni·tude** \'ämnə,tüd, -ə,tyüd\ *n* -s [*omn-* + *-tude*] **:** TOTALITY, UNIVERSALITY ⟨no other metropolitan area so reflects American civilization's ~ —D.W.Lantis⟩

**om·ni·um** \'ämnēəm\ *n* -s [L, of all, gen. pl. of *omnis* all — more at OMNIBUS] **1 :** the total of the different stocks and other items formerly offered by the British government for the capital subscribed in funding a loan or for a unit of subscribed capital **2** *Brit* **:** the total of the items in any fund or stock made up by combination of various independent constituents **3 :** WHATNOT

**omnium-gath·er·um** \-'gathərəm\ *n* -s [L *omnium* + E *gather* + L *-um* (inflectional ending of many neuter nouns and of the neuter of many adjectives)] **:** a miscellaneous collection of a variety of things or persons **:** a confused mixture **:** HODGEPODGE ⟨at least part of the *omnium-gatherum* of my research —G.T.Hellman⟩; *also* **:** a place for holding such a collection ⟨an *omnium-gatherum*, stocked to meet all common family wants —*Atlantic*⟩

**om·ni·verse** \'ämnə,vərs, -vəs, -vəis\ *n* -s [*omn-* + *-verse* (as in *universe*)] **:** a universe that is spatiotemporally four-dimensional

**om·niv·o·ra** \äm'nivərə\ *n pl* [NL, fr. L, neut. pl. of *omnivorus* omnivorous] **1** *cap, in some esp former classifications* **:** a group comprising the pigs and the hippopotamuses **2** *often cap* **a :** omnivorous animals **b :** man and swine — used when it is desired to stress fundamental similarities of habits and physiology

**om·ni·vore** *also* **om·ni·vor** \'ämnə,vō(ə)r\ *n* -s [NL *Omnivora*] **:** one that is omnivorous

**om·niv·o·rous** \(')äm'niv(ə)rəs\ *adj* [L *omnivorus*, fr. *omni-* omn- + *-vorus -vorous*] **1 :** eating everything; *esp* **:** feeding on both animal and vegetable substances ⟨only a very few insects appear to be normally . . . ~ —C.T.Brues⟩ — compare CARNIVOROUS **2 :** avidly taking in everything as if devouring or consuming ⟨became an ~ reader of the classics —T.S. Lovering⟩ ⟨an expression of ~ but benevolent curiosity —A.J. Liebling⟩ ⟨an ~ collector of antiques⟩ — **om·niv·o·rous·ly** *adv* — **om·niv·o·rous·ness** *n* -ES

**omnivorous leaf tier** *n* **:** a tortricid moth (*Cnephasia longana*) whose larva is a pest on many plants (as strawberry, flax, and cultivated flowers) in Europe and parts of the western U. S.

**omo-** — see OM-

**om·odyn·ia** \,ōmō'dinēə, ,äm-\ *n* -s [NL, fr. *om-* + *-odynia*] **:** pain in the shoulder

**1omo·hyoid** \,ōmō, ,ämō+\ *adj* [*om-* + *hyoid*] **:** of or relating to the shoulder and the hyoid bone; *specif* **:** being a muscle that arises from the upper border of the scapula and is inserted in the body of the hyoid bone

**2omohyoid** \"+\ *n* **:** an omohyoid muscle

**omo·hy·oi·de·us** \,==,hī'ȯidēəs\ *n, pl* **omohyoi·dei** \-ē,ī\ [NL, fr. *om-* + *hyoides* hyoid bone + L *-eus -eous* — more at HYOID BONE] **:** OMOHYOID

**omoi·de·um** \ō'mȯidēəm\ *n* -s [NL, fr. *om-* + *-oideum* (fr. L *-oides -oid* + *-eum*, neut. of *-eus -eous*)] **:** the pterygoid bone of a bird

**omo·pho·ri·on** \,ōmə'fōrēən, ,äm-\ *n, pl* **omopho·ria** \-ēə\ [LGk *ōmophorion*, fr. Gk *ōm-* om- + LGk *-phorion* (fr. Gk *pherein* to bear, carry) — more at BEAR] **:** the distinctive vestment of bishops of the Eastern Church corresponding to the pallium of the Western Church but made in two forms and worn in one form or the other by all bishops during the celebration of liturgical offices

**omo·plate** \'ōmə,plāt, 'äm-; ō'mäplə,tē\ *n* [MF, fr. Gk *ōmoplatē*, fr. *ōm-* om- + *platē* blade of an oar; akin to Gk *platys* flat, broad — more at PLACE] **:** SCAPULA

**omo·pla·tos·co·py** \,ōmōplə'täskəpē, ,äm-; ō,mäp-\ *n* -ES [MGk *ōmoplatoskopia*, fr. Gk *ōmoplatē* + *-o-* + *-skopia -scopy*] **:** SCAPULIMANCY

**omos·te·gite** \ō'mästə,jīt\ *n* -s [*om-* + *-stegite*] **:** the part of a crustacean's carapace covering the thorax

**omo·sternum** \,ōmō, ,ämō+\ *n* [NL, fr. *om-* + *sternum*] **1 :** a median bony element of the sternum of amphibians extending forward from the ventral ends of the precoracoids and bearing the episternum at its anterior end **2 :** an interarticular cartilage or bone between the sternum and each clavicle in many mammals

**OMPA** \,ō,empē'ā\ *n* -s [*o*ctamethyl*p*yrophosphor*a*mide] **:** SCHRADAN

**om·pha·cite** \'äm(p)fə,sīt\ *n* -s [G *omphazit*, fr. Gk *omphakitēs* green stone, fr. *omphak-*, *omphax* unripe grape + *-itēs -ite*] **:** a mineral consisting of a grass-green granular or foliated pyroxene found in the rock eclogite

**omphal-** *or* **omphalo-** *comb form* [Gk, fr. *omphalos* — more at NAVEL] **1 :** umbilicus ⟨*omphal*oid⟩ ⟨*omphalo*skepsis⟩ **2 :** umbilical and ⟨*omphalo*mesenteric⟩

**om·pha·lia** \äm'fālēə\ *n, cap* [NL, fr. *omphal-* + *-ia*] **:** a genus of fungi (family Agaricaceae) having white spores, small caps usu. with a central indentation, and a very narrow fragile stipe

**om·phal·ic** \(')äm'falik\ *adj* [*omphal-* + *-ic*] **:** of or relating to the umbilicus

**om·pha·li·on** \äm'fālēən\ *n* -s [NL, fr. Gk, small navel, dim. of *omphalos* navel] **:** the center of the umbilicus

**om·pha·li·tis** \,äm(p)fə'līd·əs\ *n, pl* **ompha·lit·i·des** \-lid·ə,dēz\ [NL, fr. *omphal-* + *-itis*] **1 :** inflammation of the umbilicus **2 :** avian navel ill **:** MUSHY CHICK

**om·pha·lo·di·um** \,=='lōdēəm\ *or* **omphalode** \'==,lōd\ *n, pl* **omphalo·dia** \-'lōdēə\ *or* **ompha·lodes** \-,lōdz\ [NL *omphalodium*, fr. Gk *omphalōdēs* like a navel (fr. *omphal-* + *-ōdēs -ode*) + NL *-ium*] **:** the scar at the hilum of a seed; *also* **:** HILUM

**om·pha·loid** \'==,lȯid\ *adj* [*omphal-* + *-oid*] **:** resembling an umbilicus **:** UMBILICATE

**om·pha·lo·mesenteric** \'äm(p)fə(,)lō+\ *adj* [*omphal-* + *mesenteric*] **:** of or relating to the umbilicus and mesentery ⟨the ~ arteries of an embryo⟩

**omphalomesenteric duct** *n* **:** VITELLINE DUCT

**om·pha·lo·phlebitis** \'äm(p)fə(,)lō+\ *n* [NL, fr. *omphal-* + *phlebitis*] **:** NAVEL ILL

**om·pha·lo·pleure** \'äm(p)fəlō,plù(ə)r\ *n* -s [*omphal-* + *-pleure* (fr. *-pleura*)] **:** an embryonic membrane constituted in part of the yolk sac wall

**om·pha·lopsy·chite** \,äm(p)fəlō'sī,kīt, -'läpsə,k-\ *n* -s [*omphal-* + *psyche* + *-ite*] **:** one who stares fixedly at his navel to induce a mystical trance — often used of the hesychasts

**om·pha·los** \'äm(p)fə,läs, -ləs\ *n, pl* **ompha·li** \-,lī, -,lē\ [Gk, lit., navel] **1 :** a central part **:** FOCAL POINT ⟨come to a sort of ~ of the whole projected history —George Saintsbury⟩ **2** *also* **om·pha·lus** \-ləs\ [NL, fr. Gk *omphalos*] **:** UMBILICUS

**om·pha·lo·skep·sis** \,äm(p)fəlō'skepsəs\ *n* -ES [*omphal-* + Gk *skepsis* act of viewing, examination; akin to Gk *skeptesthai* to view — more at SPY] **:** meditation while staring fixedly at one's navel practiced by Eastern mystics as an aid toward inducing a mystical trance

**om·rah** \äm'rä\ *n* -s [Hindi *umrā*, fr. Ar *umarā'*, pl. of *amīr* ruler, commander] **:** a lord or grandee of a Muslim court in India

**OMS** *abbr* output per man shift

**omsk** \'ōmzk, 'äm-, -m(p)sk\ *adj, usu cap* [fr. *Omsk*, city in the western part of Asiatic Russia, U.S.S.R.] **:** of or from the city of Omsk, U.S.S.R. **:** of the kind or style prevalent in Omsk

**omu·ta** \'ōmə,tä\ *adj, usu cap* [fr. *Omuta*, city in northwest Kyushu, Japan] **:** of or from the city of Omuta, Japan **:** of the kind or style prevalent in Omuta

**1on** \(')ȯn, (')än, *in the southeastern US sometimes* (')ōn\ *prep* [ME, prep. & adv., fr. OE *an*, *on*, prep. & adv.; akin to OHG *ana*, prep. & adv., on, at, ON *ā*, prep. & adv., Goth *ana*, prep. & adv., on, at, L *an-* (in *anhelare* to pant) Gk *ana*, prep & adv., up, on, Skt *ana*, prep. & adv., after] **1 a —** used as a function word to indicate position over and in contact with that which supports from beneath ⟨the book is ~ the table⟩ ⟨was built ~ an island⟩ ⟨kept his hands ~ the desk⟩ **b —** used as a function word to indicate presence within ⟨rode there ~ a train⟩ ⟨booked passage ~ an ocean liner⟩ **c —** used as a function word to indicate situation along a whole surface ⟨a streak ~ the wall running from top to bottom⟩ or at any particular point on a surface ⟨there wasn't a mark ~ it⟩ or to indicate situation at the projecting usu. supporting edge or point or end of something ⟨their clothes hung ~ a couple of nails in the wall⟩ or situation inside of something (as clothing) worn by or covering the principal object of attention ⟨found a knife ~ him⟩ **2 —** used as a function word to indicate contiguity or dependence; esp. (1) contact and support from elsewhere than beneath ⟨a fly ~ the ceiling⟩ ⟨hanging ~ the wall⟩; (2) location closely adjoining something ⟨a town situated ~ the river⟩ or location very near some point of a narrowly extended area (as a street) ⟨lives ~ the principal street of the town⟩; (3) imminence or beginning (as of some action or activity) ⟨the storm is ~ us⟩; (4) connection or employment or activity with or in or with regard to something ⟨works ~ the committee⟩ ⟨is now ~ the third problem⟩ ⟨will be ~ duty⟩ ⟨has long been successful ~ the stage⟩; (5) engagement in doing something ⟨are now ~ a tour around the country⟩; (6) source or support or basis on which something (as an action, opinion) turns or rests ⟨learned it ~ good authority⟩ ⟨his reliance ~ her⟩ ⟨will do it ~ one condition⟩ **3 a —** used as a function word to indicate position with regard to place, direction, or time; esp. (1) position with regard to a point of the compass ⟨~ the west are rolling plains⟩; (2) position near a specified part of something ⟨~ the side of the house is a garden⟩; (3) occurrence during the course of a specified day ⟨will see them ~ Monday⟩ or of some other divisions of time ⟨said she would write ~ the morrow⟩ or at a set time ⟨trains leave here every hour ~ the hour⟩; (4) occurrence at the same time as or following or as a result of something ⟨will send a check ~ receipt of the book⟩ ⟨will do it ~ your arrival⟩ ⟨was uneasy ~ arriving home and finding no one there⟩ **b —** used as a function word to indicate location in or progress along something taken as a standard ⟨is ~ the right road⟩ ⟨a boat keeping ~ course⟩ **4 a —** used as a function word to indicate involvement in a specified condition or process ⟨the house is ~ fire⟩ ⟨beer ~ tap⟩ ⟨merchandise ~ sale⟩ ⟨business is ~ an upturn⟩ **b —** used as a function word to indicate participation in a condition of privilege ⟨has been ~ sick leave〉 or subjection to a condition of restriction 〈is ~ probation〉 **5** — used as a function word to indicate manner 〈did it ~ the sly〉 〈cut it ~ the bias〉 **6** — used as a function word to indicate the object of action or motion; esp. (1) the object of action or motion coming esp. down from above so as to touch or strike the surface or cover the upper part 〈watched the rain fall ~ the earth〉 〈put a lid ~ the jar〉; (2) the object of action or motion directed up to or against the object 〈crept up ~ him〉 〈marched ~ the ancient fortress〉; (3) the object of action or motion directed toward the object without actual physical contact 〈smiled ~ her〉 〈blamed it ~ them〉 〈was always bent ~ fighting〉; (4) the object of some emotion 〈had pity ~ them〉 or formality 〈served an injunction ~ him〉 or obligation 〈a charge ~ an overdue book〉; (5) the object in connection with which payment, computation of interest, reduction, or similar settlement is made 〈paid off a substantial sum ~ the mortgage〉 〈creditors received about 75 cents ~ the dollar〉 〈a rebate of 15 cents ~ a ton〉 〈an inroad ~ supplies〉 **7 a :** with regard to : with reference or relation to : ABOUT 〈agreed ~ a price〉 〈a monopoly ~ wheat〉 〈a satire ~ society〉 〈at variance ~ what to do〉 **b** *chiefly dial* : OF 〈be not jealous ~ me —Shak.〉 **8** — used as a function word to indicate means or agency 〈cut her finger ~ a knife〉 〈playing the latest hits ~ the piano〉 〈heard it ~ the radio〉 **9** — used as a function word to indicate reduplication or succession in a series 〈trouble ~ trouble followed his involvement with her〉 〈loss ~ loss〉 **10** — used as a function word to indicate an object of reference; esp. (1) an object having some advantage or disadvantage 〈is very talented but has nothing ~ her brother who is a real genius〉 〈his brother has two inches ~ him in reach〉; (2) an object subjected to expense or cost 〈drinks are ~ the house〉 〈the joke was ~ me〉; (3) an object that bears some stress or strain 〈long hours began to tell ~ him〉; (4) an object subjected to indicated annoyance 〈the fire went out ~ him〉 〈don't try to pull that ~ me〉 or discomfiture or some other unwanted or detrimental thing

[2]**on** \"\ *adv* [ME, prep. & adv., fr. OE *an, on,* prep. & adv.] **1 :** in or into the position of being in contact with the upper surface of something or of being supported from beneath by the upper surface 〈the plates are ~〉 〈put a jazz recording ~〉 **2 :** in or into the position of being attached to or covering a surface 〈has suspenders ~〉 〈put a clean shirt ~〉 〈keep your hat ~〉 **3 a** (1) **:** toward a point that lies ahead in space or time : FORWARD, ONWARD 〈spent a day there and then went ~ to the next town〉 〈from here ~ you'll need help〉 (2) **:** at a more advanced point in space or time 〈will do it later ~〉 〈did not see her until well ~ in the evening〉 〈was well ~ in years〉 **b :** with forward movement or action : in constant progression : without break : CONTINUOUSLY 〈read ~ late into the night〉 〈spoke ~ without hesitation〉 〈slept peacefully ~〉 **c :** in succession : from one to another : in continuance 〈a tradition handed ~ through the centuries〉 〈pass the note ~〉 **4 a :** in or into action or operation 〈the radio was ~〉 〈turn the lights ~〉 : in or into a functioning state : in or into a state of activity 〈the water is ~〉 〈the electricity finally came ~〉 **b :** in or into a position designed to set something into action or otherwise produce some activity 〈the light switch is ~〉 〈had a large fish ~〉 : in or into an operative position 〈the brake is ~〉 **5 :** in or into the process of doing something : in or into engagement in some function or activity 〈two speeches had already been given and he was told he would be ~ next〉 〈has worked two nights and will also be ~ tomorrow night〉 〈a well-known star will be ~ in the role when the show opens〉 **6 a :** with an indicated part turned toward a point of contact, approach, or observation 〈the two cars smashed together head ~〉 〈the boats collided bows ~〉 **b :** with direction toward something 〈didn't want to play but preferred simply to look ~〉 **7 :** in a condition of being decided upon or planned for or regarded as something that must be done 〈has nothing particular ~ for tonight〉 **8 :** in or into a state of being aware of something 〈wasn't ~ to what had happened〉 : in or into a knowledgeable state about something 〈quickly got ~ to what they were trying to do〉 — usu. used with *to* **9 :** in a state of being willing to participate in something 〈told them about the plan and asked if they were ~〉 **10** *printing* : UP 〈printed eight ~〉 **11 :** on base in baseball

[3]**on** \"\ *adj* **1** *cricket* : that sends the ball to the on 〈an ~ hit〉 〈an ~ drive〉 **2** *cricket* : that is on the on side of the wicket 〈an ~ stroke〉 **3 :** permitted to flow by means of an opened valve or closed switch : FLOWING 〈the water was ~〉

[4]**on** \"\ *n* -s **:** the side of the wicket on which a batsman stands in the game of cricket or the corresponding side of the field — compare OFF; see CRICKET illustration

[1]**-on** \,än\ *n suffix* -s [ISV, alter. of *-one*] **:** chemical compound not a ketone or other oxo compound 〈nerv*on*〉 — sometimes distinguished from *-one*

[2]**-on** \"\ *n suffix* -s [fr. *-on* (in *anion, cation,* & *ion*)] **1 :** elementary particle 〈nucle*on*〉 **2 :** unit : quantum 〈magnet*on*〉 〈phot*on*〉

[3]**-on** \"\ *n suffix* -s [NL, fr. Gk, neut. of *-os* (nom. sing. masc. ending of many adjectives)] **:** inert gas 〈rad*on*〉

**ON** *abbr* **1** octane number **2** order notify

**ona** \'ōnə\ *n, pl* **ona** *or* **onas** *usu cap* **1 a :** a Chonan people of Tierra del Fuego off the southern tip of So. America — compare FUEGIAN **b :** a member of such people **2 :** the language of the Ona people

**on-again, off-again** \'=,=,='=,=\ *adj* [fr. the phrase *on again, off again*] **:** occurring suddenly and irregularly and vanishing quickly : becoming briefly existent and then disappearing in an intermittent unpredictable way : FITFUL, SPASMODIC 〈*on-again, off-again* fads〉 〈troubled with *on-again, off-again* headaches〉 〈months of *on-again, off-again* negotiations —Kennett Love〉

**on·a·ger** \'änəjə(r)\ *n* -s [ME, wild ass, fr. L *onager, onagrus,* fr. Gk *onagros,* fr. *onos* ass + *agros* (fr. *agros* field) — more at ASS, ACRE] **1 :** a small pale-colored kiang having a broad dorsal stripe and being usu. treated as a natural variety but sometimes considered to constitute a distinct species (*Equus onager*) **2** [LL, fr. L] **:** an ancient and medieval heavy catapult used for hurling heavy stones and made up basically of a strong lever with a receptacle at one end for the stones and of ropes twisted so as to pull the lever back under great strain until suddenly released

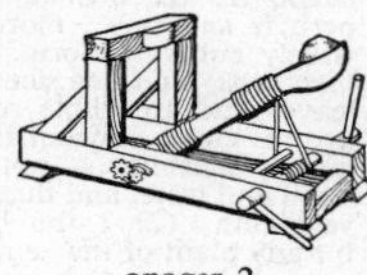

onager 2

**onagra** \ō'nagrə, 'änəg-\ [NL, fr. Gk, oleander] *syn of* OENOTHERA

**on·a·gra·ce·ae** \,änə'grāsē,ē\ *n pl, cap* [NL, fr. *Onagra* + *-aceae*] **:** a large widely distributed family of plants of the order Myrtales having an inferior ovary, 2 or 4 petals, 1 to 8 stamens, and a simple style — **on·a·gra·ceous** \,änə;grāshəs\ *adj*

**on and off** *adv (or adj)* **:** off and on 〈we've been living together *on and off* —Paul Scott〉

**on and on** *adv (or adj)* **:** at great often tedious length 〈talked *on and on*〉

**onan·ism** \'ōnə,nizəm\ *n* -s [prob. fr. (assumed) NL *onanismus,* fr. *Onan,* son of Judah described in Gen 38: 9 as practicing coitus interruptus + L *-ismus* -ism] **1 :** COITUS INTERRUPTUS **2 :** MASTURBATION **3 :** self-gratification 〈the kind of intellectual ~ to which he was dedicated — Esther P. Shiverick〉 — **onan·is·tic** \,ōnə'nistik\ *adj*

**onan·ist** \'ōnənəst\ *n* -s [ISV *onanism* + *-ist*] **:** one that practices onanism

**onc-** *or* **onco-** *also* **onch-** *or* **oncho-** *or* **onci-** *comb form* [NL, fr. Gk *onkos* barbed hook — more at ANGLE] **1 :** barb : hook 〈*Onc*orhynchus〉 〈*Onci*dium〉 〈*onch*ium〉 〈*Oncho*cerca〉 **2 :** barbed 〈*Onci*cola〉

[1]**once** \'wən(t)s\ *adv* [ME *ones, anes,* fr. gen. of *on, an* one — more at ONE] **1 :** one time and no more : just one time : one time only 〈visited her father ~ a month〉 〈spoke to her ~ and didn't see her again〉 〈have read it only ~〉 **2 a :** at any one time : in any possible contingency : under any circumstances whatsoever 〈don't ~ let them know〉 〈couldn't ~ succeed in doing what was asked〉 **b :** at all : ONLY, MERELY, JUST 〈if you thought about it ~, you'd see I'm right〉 **c :** EVER 〈if they ~ lose hope, their failure is certain〉 〈didn't ~ guess the truth〉 — usu. used in negative or conditional clauses **3 a :** at some indefinite time in the past : at one time : FORMERLY 〈~ knew her well, but had now forgotten her name〉 〈was ~ very happy〉 **b** *archaic* : at some indefinite time in the future : at some future time : SOMEDAY **4** *obs* **a :** one time for all times : once and finally : once and for all 〈if I have him not, I am resolved to die a maid, that's ~ —John Dryden〉 **b :** in short : in a word : by way of summing up **5 :** by one degree of relationship 〈is a cousin ~ removed〉 〈lives a life only ~ removed from that of animals〉 **6** *dial* — used as a vague sentence expletive esp. in imperative constructions 〈come here ~〉 〈hand me that hammer ~〉 — **once and a while** [by alter.] **:** once in a while 〈*once and a while* to think of my first love —R.D.Blackmore〉 — **once and for all** *or* **once for all 1 :** once and finally : once and decisively : once and be done with it 〈make up your mind *once and for all*〉 : DEFINITIVELY : with such finality as to preclude reservation or modification 〈deciding to settle the matter *once for all*〉 **2 :** for the last time : one time to end all times 〈I'm telling you *once and for all*〉 — **once in a way** *also* **once and a way** *chiefly Brit* : once in a while : one time by way of exception 〈for we were permitted to hear, for *once in a way,* the pizzicato accompaniment —*Manchester Guardian Weekly*〉 — **once in a while :** now and then : occasionally but not often : from time to time : at infrequent intervals : SOMETIMES 〈spend most of their time at home and go out *once in a while*〉 — **once upon a time :** once at some indefinite time in the past usu. long ago 〈had *once upon a time* known them well〉 〈*once upon a time* there was a beautiful princess〉

[2]**once** \"\ *adj* **:** that once was : FORMER 〈the ~ province of Britain —J.N.Pomeroy〉

[3]**once** \"\ *n* -s **:** one single time : one sole time 〈thought it was only the ~ —Anne D. Sedgwick〉 〈please listen to me just this ~〉 : one time at least : one time by way of exception 〈for ~ you seem to know what I'm talking about〉 — **all at once** *adv* **1 :** all at the same time 〈seemed happy and sad *all at once*〉 **2 :** with great suddenness : suddenly and unexpectedly 〈*all at once* there was a clatter of dishes〉 — **to once** *adv, dial* : at once

[4]**once** \"\ *also* **once that** *conj* **:** when once : if once : at the moment when : as soon as 〈~ the job is finished, we'll have nothing to worry about〉 〈*once that* he finds out, you'll have to be careful〉

**once-accented octave** *n* **:** ONE-LINE OCTAVE

**once and again** *adv* **1 a :** once and once more 〈spoke to her *once and again*〉 **b :** two or more times 〈have heard it said *once and again*〉 **2 :** now and again : from time to time : OCCASIONALLY, SOMETIMES 〈*once and again* this sort of thing is bound to happen〉

**once-born** \'=,=\ *adj* **:** not having been or not needing to be regenerated spiritually

**once more** *or* **once again** *adv* [*once more* fr. ME *ones more,* fr. *ones* once + *more; once again* fr. [1]*once* + *again*] **:** one more time 〈decided to try *once more*〉

**once or twice** *adv* [ME *ones or twies,* fr. *ones* once + *or* + *twies* twice] **:** a couple of times : a few times : OCCASIONALLY 〈have seen her *once or twice* during the past month〉

**once-over** \'=,==\ *n* -s [fr. the phrase *once over*] **:** a single swift examination or consideration or treatment of something : rapid survey; *esp* : a swift comprehensive appraising glance 〈gave every new applicant the *once-over*〉 〈as she walked in she got the *once-over*〉

[1]**once-over-lightly** \;=,=;=='==\ *n* -ES [fr. the phrase *once over lightly*] **:** ONCE-OVER; *esp* : an esp. casual or cursory or gingerly once-over 〈had given political problems the *once-over-lightly* —Sigrid Arne〉

[2]**once-over-lightly** \;=,=;='==\ *adj* **:** swift and usu. casual or cursory or gingerly 〈gets the *once-over-lightly* treatment —Sidney Hyman〉

**once·er** \'wən(t)sə(r)\ *n* -s [[1]*once* + *-er*] **:** one that does or has done something only once

**oncet** \'wənzt, -n(t)st\ *substand var of* ONCE

**onch-** *or* **oncho-** *or* **onci-** — see ONC-

**on·chi·di·idae** \,äŋkə'dīə,dē\ *n pl, cap* [NL, fr. *Onchidium,* type genus + *-idae*] **:** a family of slugs (suborder Stylommatophora) — see ONCHIDIUM

**on·chid·i·um** \äŋ'kidēəm, än'-\ *n, cap* [NL, fr. *onc-* + *-idium*] **:** a genus (the type of the family Onchidiidae) of chiefly Indo-Pacific marine air-breathing slugs that live chiefly on rocky shores between tide levels or in mangrove swamps

**on·chi·um** \'äŋkēəm\ *n, pl* **on·chia** \-ēə\ [NL fr. *onc-* + *-ium*] **:** one of the hooks or rasps located in the buccal cavity of various nematode worms and serving to grasp and break up prey

**on·cho·cer·ca** \,äŋkə'sərkə\ *n, cap* [NL, fr. *onc-* + *-cerca* (fr. Gk *kerkos* tail)] **:** a genus of long slender filarial worms (family Dipetalonematidae) that are parasites of subcutaneous and connective tissues of mammals with their adults enclosed in fibrous nodules and their larvae free in the tissues — see ONCHOCERCIASIS — **on·cho·cer·cal** \;==;=kəl\ *adj*

**on·cho·cer·ci·a·sis** *also* **on·co·cer·ci·a·sis** \,äŋkō,sər'kīəsəs\ *n, pl* **onchocerciases** \-ə,sēz\ [NL, fr. *Onchocerca* + *-iasis*] **:** infestation with or disease caused by filarial worms of the genus *Onchocerca*; *esp* : a disease of man caused by a worm (*O. volvulus*) native to Africa but now present in parts of tropical America, transmitted by several biting flies, and marked by subcutaneous nodules containing adult worms and migration of larvae through the tissues causing local irritation and itching and when the eyes are involved sometimes blindness — compare CRAW-CRAW

**on·cho·cer·co·ma** \-'kōmə\ *n* -s [NL, fr. *Onchocerca* + *-oma*] **:** the subcutaneous nodule of onchocerciasis that contains encysted parasites

**on·cho·cer·co·sis** \-'kōsəs\ *n, pl* **onchocerco·ses** \-ō,sēz\ [NL, fr. *Onchocerca* + *-osis*] **:** ONCHOCERCIASIS

**on·cho·sphere** *also* **on·co·sphere** \'äŋkō,sfi(ə)r\ *n* [ISV [1]*onco-* + *sphere*] **:** the hexacanth embryo that is the earliest differentiated stage of a cyclophyllidean tapeworm

**on·ci·co·la** \än'sikələ\ *n, cap* [NL, fr. *onc-* + *-cola*] **:** a genus of small acanthocephalan worms having the adults parasitic in the intestines of dogs and coyotes and the infective larvae encysted in turkeys and armadillos

**on·cid·i·um** \än'sidēəm\ *n* [NL, fr. *onc-* + *-idium;* fr. the shape of the labellum] **1** *cap* **:** a genus of showy tropical American epiphytic or terrestrial orchids with the column short and winged and the labellum usu. at right angles to it **2** -s **:** any plant of the genus *Oncidium* — called also *butterfly plant*

[1]**onco-** *or* **oncho-** *comb form* [NL, fr. Gk *onkos* bulk, mass; akin to Gk *enenkein* to carry — more at ENOUGH] **1 :** tumor 〈*onco*logy〉 **2 :** bulk : mass 〈*oncho*sphere〉 〈*onco*meter〉

[2]**onco-** — see ONC-

**on·co·chaeta** \,äŋkō+\ *n, pl* **oncochaetae** *or* **oncochaetas** [NL, fr. *onc-* + *-chaeta*] **:** a hair or bristle with a hooked tip 〈*onchochaetae* on the thorax of a fly〉

**on·co·cyte** \'äŋkō,sīt\ *n* -s [[1]*onco-* + *-cyte*] **1 :** an acidophilic granular cell esp. of the parotid gland **2 :** a tumor cell

**on·co·gen·ic** \¦äŋkō¦jenik\ *also* **on·cog·e·nous** \(')äŋ¦käjənəs, (')än'-\ *adj* [[1]*onco-* + *-genic* or *-genous*] **:** relating to tumor formation : tending to cause tumors 〈~ tars〉

**on·cog·e·ny** \äŋ'käjənē, än'-\ *n* -ES [[1]*onco-* + *-geny*] **:** the process of tumor formation

**on·co·graph** \'äŋkə,graf, -ràf\ *n* [ISV [1]*onco-* + *-graph*] **:** a recording device attached to an oncometer — **on·cog·ra·phy** \äŋ'kägrəfē, än'-\ *n* -ES

**on·co·log·ic** \¦äŋkə¦läjik\ *adj* **:** of or relating to oncology

**on·col·o·gist** \äŋ'käləjəst, än'-\ *n* -s **:** a specialist in oncology

**on·col·o·gy** \-jē\ *n* -ES [ISV [1]*onco-* + *-logy*] **:** the study of tumors

**on·col·y·sis** \-ləsəs\ *n* [NL, fr. [1]*onco-* + *-lysis*] **:** the destruction of tumor cells — **on·co·lyt·ic** \¦äŋkə¦lid·ik\ *adj*

**oncome** \'=,=\ *n* [ME, fr. *on* + *come, cume* action of coming, fr. *comen, cumen* to come (after *comen on* to come on) — more at COME] **1** *chiefly Scot* : ONSET, BEGINNING **2** *chiefly Scot* : an attack of disease

**on·co·melania** \,äŋkō+\ *n, cap* [NL, perh. fr. [1]*onco-* + *Melania*] **:** a genus of amphibious operculate snails (family Bulimidae) of Asiatic and Pacific island freshwaters that is sometimes extended to include *Katayama, Schistosomophora,* and possibly other genera and that comprises forms which are intermediate hosts of the blood fluke (*Schistosoma japonicum*)

**oncomer** \'=,==\ *n* [*on* + *comer* (after *come on,* v.)] **:** COMER 2 〈~*s* being developed for our international teams —*Lawn Tennis & Badminton*〉

**on·com·e·ter** \äŋ'kämədə(r), än'-\ *n* [ISV [1]*onco-* + *-meter*] **:** an instrument for measuring variations in size or volume of the internal organs of the body

[1]**oncoming** \'=,==\ *adj* [[2]*on* + *coming,* adj. (after *come on,* v.)] **1 a :** coming nearer in space or time : moving forward upon one : APPROACHING 〈blinded by the lights of an ~ car〉 〈during the ~ year〉 **b :** that is to be : FUTURE 〈not for just a few of our ~ citizens, but also for all present citizens —L.L. Medsker〉 〈discussed the ~ visit〉 **2 :** RISING, EMERGENT 〈~ generations began to seek new goals —Hunter Mead〉

[2]**oncoming** \'=,==, ='==\ *n* -s [*on* + *coming,* n. (after *come on,* v.)] *archaic* : APPROACH

**on·co·pel·tus** \,äŋkō'peltəs\ *n, cap* [NL, perh. fr. *onc-* + *-peltus* (fr. Gk *peltē* small shield) — more at PELTA] **:** a genus of lygaeid bugs including the common milkweed bug (*O. fasciatus*)

**on·cop·era** \äŋ'käpərə, än'-\ *n, cap* [NL, perh. fr. *onc-* + Gk *pēra* pouch] **:** a genus of moths (family Hepialidae) whose caterpillars are serious pests on grass in Australia and Tasmania

**on·co·rhyn·chus** \,äŋkō'riŋkəs\ *n, cap* [NL, fr. *onc-* + *-rhynchus*] **:** a genus of salmons that are related to those of the genus *Salmo* but have a greater number of anal rays, branchiostegals, pyloric caeca, and gill rakers and that include commercially important fishes of the north Pacific and of the coastal streams of both America and Asia

**oncosphere** *var of* ONCHOSPHERE

**oncost** \'=,=\ *n* -s [ME *oncost, uncost,* fr. MD *oncost* extra charge, fr. *on-* un- (akin to OE *un-*) + *cost* expense, charge, prob. fr. OF — more at UN-, COST] *Brit* : indirect expense : OVERHEAD

**on·cot·ic pressure** \(')än¦käd·ik-, (')äŋ\ *n* [*oncotic* prob. ISV [1]*onco-* + *-tic* (as in *osmotic*)] **:** the pressure exerted by plasma proteins on the capillary wall and made up of the osmotic and imbibition pressures of the hydrophilic colloid systems in which these proteins exist

**on·cot·o·my** \äŋ'kädəmē, än'-\ *n* -ES [NL *oncotomia,* fr. [1]*onco-* + *-tomia* -tomy] **:** surgical incision of a swelling (as an abscess or tumor)

**onct** *like* ONCET\ *substand var of* ONCE

**on·dat·ra** \än'datrə\ *n, cap* [NL, fr. F, muskrat, fr. Huron] **:** a genus of rodents (family Cricetidae) comprising the muskrats

**ondé** *var of* UNDÉ

**ondes mu·si·cales** \ōⁿdmüzēkäl\ *or* **ondes martenot** \ōⁿdmärtənō\ *n, pl* **ondes musicales** *like sing*\ *or* **ondes martenot** *like sing*\ *often cap O&M* [*ondes musicales* fr. F, lit., musical waves; *ondes martenot* fr. F, lit., Martenot waves, after Maurice *Martenot b*1898 Fr. musician, its inventor] **:** a melodic electrophone capable of producing quarter tones and eighth tones

**on·dine** \(')än¦dēn, (')ȯn¦-, (')ōⁿ¦-\ *n* -s [F, fr. NL *undina* — more at UNDINE] **1 :** UNDINE **2 :** a pale green that is bluer, lighter, and slightly less strong than celadon gray and duller than spray green

**on·ding** \'än,diŋ\ *n* -s [[2]*on* + *ding,* v. (to beat) (after the verb phrase *ding on*)] *chiefly Scot* : a heavy fall of rain or snow 〈the rain was such an ~ by now —Maristan Chapman〉

**on-dit** \(')ōⁿ¦dē\ *n, pl* **on-dits** \-ē(z)\ [F, fr. *on dit* they say, it is said] **:** a piece of gossip : vague rumor : REPORT 〈the *on-dits* and surreptitious tales that float about —*Saturday Rev.*〉 〈there were incredible *on-dits* —Clare Sheridan〉

**on·di·um mar·te·not** \'ändēəm,märtᵊn'ō\ *n, often cap O&M* [*ondium* fr. *ond-* (fr. *ondes musicales*) + *-ium* (as in *harmonium*)] **:** ONDES MUSICALES

**on·do·graph** \'ändə,graf, -ràf\ *n* [F *ondographe,* fr. *onde* wave (fr. L *unda*) + *-o-* + *-graphe* -graph — more at WATER] **:** an instrument for autographically recording the wave forms of varying electrical currents and esp. rapidly varying alternating currents

**on·du·le** \'ändə;lā, -njə-\ *n* -s [F *ondulé* wavy, fr. past part. of *onduler* to wave, ripple, back-formation fr. *ondulation* wave, concentric wave-motion in a liquid or gas, prob. fr. (assumed) NL *undulation-, undulatio* concentric wave motion in a liquid or gas — more at UNDULATION] **:** a wavy weaving pattern produced by a special reed that alternately spreads and converges a small group of warp threads

**ondy** *var of* UNDÉ

[1]**one** \¦wən\ *adj* [ME *oon, on,* fr. OE *ān;* akin to OHG *ein* one, ON *einn,* Goth *ains,* L *unus* one, Gk *oinē* ace on dice, Skt *eka* one, and perh. to L *is* he, that — more at ITERATE] **1 a :** being a single unit or entire being or thing and no more — see NUMBER table **b :** existing alone in a specified sphere 〈there is ~ apple in the basket〉 **2 a** (1) **:** being a particular unit or entire being or thing singled out (as by way of contrast, difference) from two or more identical or similar units or beings or things 〈spent ~ day of our vacation exploring the forest〉 〈have mentioned ~ important point out of the several that will have to be considered〉 〈went from ~ side to the other〉 (2) **:** being an individual that is preeminently what is indicated 〈is really ~ fine person〉 **b :** existing as at least a single unit or being or thing : that is at least something : one at any rate : one in any case 〈well, that's ~ thing you can be proud of〉 〈that's ~ consolation, anyway〉 **3 a** (1) **:** existing as something actually or virtually the same as something else : that is identical with or substantially the same as something else 〈the writer and his principal character are ~〉 〈~ and the same substance〉 (2) **:** single in kind : quite the same : EQUAL 〈are of ~ age〉 (3) **:** that is not marked by any notable differences from something else : that amounts to the same thing 〈it's all ~ to me what you do〉 (4) **:** that is commonly shared by two or more individuals 〈~ plague was on you all —1 Sam 6:4 (AV)〉 **b** (1) **:** constituting a unified entity made up of or formed from or produced by two or more components or sources 〈combined the elements in such a way as to form ~ substance〉 〈cried out with ~ voice〉 (2) **:** that is so united to or merged with something else as to form a single harmonious whole with it : that is at one : that is in agreement : UNITED 〈is ~ with you in all you do〉 **4 :** existing or occurring as something not definitely fixed or placed (as in time) 〈will see you again ~ day〉 or as something merely mentioned with little or no specifying description : a certain 〈~ John Doe got up and made a speech〉 — compare [2]A 4 d **5 :** that is the only individual of an indicated or implied kind 〈was the ~ person she wanted to marry〉

[2]**one** \"\ *pron* [ME *oon, on,* fr. OE *ān,* fr. *ān,* adj.] **1 a :** a certain indefinitely indicated person or thing usu. of a kind mentioned or under consideration 〈saw ~ of his classmates〉 〈had several current novels and let her borrow ~〉 **b** (1) **:** an individual of a vaguely indicated group : anyone at all : anyone in a general way 〈~ wouldn't like to see that happen〉 (2) — sometimes used as a 3d-person substitute for a pronoun of the first person (as *I, we*) 〈~ supposes you will come〉 **2 :** something of an indicated or implied kind: as **a :** JOKE, LAUGH 〈that's ~ on you〉 **b :** BLOW, SOCK 〈got ~ on the jaw which he remembered for a long time —John Masefield〉 **3** *chiefly Midland* : one or the other — used after the second of two alternatives to indicate the necessity of a choice between the two 〈stay in bed or go to school, ~〉 — **by one and one** *archaic* : one by one — **in one** *adv* **:** in or into a single whole : TOGETHER 〈is a source of information and pleasure, all *in one*〉 — **one by one** *also* **one after one** *adv* **:** with one following the other : one after another : one at a time : SINGLY, SUCCESSIVELY 〈came into the room *one by one*〉

[3]**one** \", *in sense 1c(2)* ,wən\ *n* -s [ME *oon, on,* fr. OE *ān,* fr. *ān,* adj. & pron.] **1 a :** the first whole number above zero and below two : the number denoting unity **b :** a single unit or entire being or thing and no more 〈has the ~ but will need another〉 **c** (1) **:** a particular unit or entire being or thing singled out (as by way of contrast, difference) from two or more identical or similar units or beings or things 〈this is the ~ that is best〉 (2) **:** an individual of a particular kind 〈that's really a splendid ~〉 **2 a :** the numerable quantity symbolized by the arabic numeral 1 **b :** the figure 1 **c :** the letter I **3 :** one o'clock — compare BELL table, TIME illustration **4 a :** a domino with one spot on one of its halves **b :** a die with one spot on the uppermost side **c :** an article of clothing of the first size; *esp* : a baby's shoe of the first size 〈wears a ~〉 **5 a :** a pound note **b :** a one-dollar bill **6** *cap* : the ulti-

mate being : the first principle of all things : the Absolute : GOD **7 a :** DEVOTEE, FAN ⟨was a ~ for football —Naomi G. Royde-Smith⟩ **b :** an extraordinary or unique or eccentric individual ⟨you're quite the ~⟩ ⟨you are a ~, aren't you⟩

**⁴one** \'wən\ *vt* **oned; oned; oneing; ones** [ME *onen*, fr. *oon, on*, adj. — more at ¹ONE] : UNITE ⟨prayer . . . ~*s* the soul to God —Walter Lippmann⟩

**-one** \,ōn\ *n suffix* -s [ISV, fr. Gk *-ōnē* (fem. patronymic suffix)] **1 :** ketone or oxo compound not a true ketone — in names of specific organic compounds ⟨acet*one*⟩ ⟨pentan*one*⟩ ⟨5-pyrazol*one*⟩ **2 :** chemical compound containing oxygen esp. in a carbonyl or analogous group (as sulfonyl) — in names of classes of compounds ⟨ket*one*⟩ ⟨lact*one*⟩ ⟨sulf*one*⟩ **3 :** ¹-ON

**one-a-cat** *var of* **one old cat**

**one and all** *pron* [ME *oon and al*] : each one individually and jointly ⟨I greet you, *one and all*⟩

**one-and-thirty** \¦=¦==\ *n, archaic* : THIRTY-ONE

**one another** *pron* [ME *oon . . . another*] : EACH OTHER ⟨were madly in love with *one another* —C.G.Norris⟩ ⟨they all knew *one another*⟩

**one-arm** \'=¦=\ *adj* : marked by the use of chairs having one arm extended and broadened in such a way as to support a tray of food ⟨ate in . . . *one-arm* joints —Saul Bellow⟩

**one-armed bandit** *also* **one-arm bandit** \¦=¦=-\ *n* [so called fr. the handle that is pulled to make the wheels spin] : SLOT MACHINE 2

**one-base hit** \'=,=-\ *or* **one-bagger** \'=ˈbagə(r), -ˈbaag-, -ˈbaig-\ *n* : a base hit that enables a batter to reach first base safely — called also *single*

**one-berry** \'wən-— *see* BERRY\ *n* **1 :** HACKBERRY **2 :** PARTRIDGEBERRY 1 **3 :** JACK-IN-THE-PULPIT

**one-crop** \'=¦=\ *adj* : marked by the raising of only one kind of crop on the same land over a long time ⟨*one-crop* farming⟩

**one-dimensional** \¦=(,)=¦=(=)=\ *adj* : lacking depth : SUPERFICIAL ⟨seems rather *one-dimensional* and unimportant —Merle Miller⟩ ⟨the characters are *one-dimensional* stereotypes —Anthony Boucher⟩ ⟨too often give us only *one-dimensional* news —Elmer Davis⟩

**one-egg** \¦=¦=\ *adj* : MONOZYGOTIC ⟨*one-egg* twins⟩

**one-eighty** \,=ˈ==\ *n* -s : a complete turn of 180 degrees ⟨did a *one-eighty* and crashed —*Infantry Jour.*⟩

**one-eye** \'=,=\ *also* **one-eyed card** \'=,=-\ *n* : one of three face cards (as the jack of hearts or jack of spades or king of diamonds) that in a standard pack of playing cards carry a profile view

**one-eyed** \'=¦=\ *adj* [ME *oon-eyed*, fr. *oon* one + *eyed*] **1 :** having one eye : having the sight of only one eye **2 :** lacking breadth of vision : narrow in outlook ⟨our naive submission to the *one-eyed* methodology of the physical sciences —Lewis Mumford⟩ — **one-eyed·ness** \¦=¦ī(d)dnəs\ *n* -ES

**one-eyed cat** \ˌwənə¦kat, ¦wə,nīd¦k-\ *n* : ONE OLD CAT

**one-flowered wintergreen** *or* **one-flowered pyrola** \'=,=-\ *n* : a delicate perennial herb (*Moneses uniflora*) of the family Ericaceae that resembles the wintergreen and has a solitary white terminal flower

**one·fold** \'wən¦fōld\ *adj* : constituting a single undivided whole ⟨simple counterpoint in which the many sounds are ~ —*Encyc. Britannica*⟩

**one-foot pitch** *n* : the pitch of a one-foot stop on a pipe organ

**one-foot stop** *n* : a pipe-organ stop sounding pitches three octaves higher than the notes indicate — compare EIGHT-FOOT STOP

**one-for-one** \¦==¦=\ *adj* : ONE-TO-ONE ⟨a *one-for-one* correspondence between symbols and syllables —Kenneth Croft⟩

**one-gallus** *or* **one-gallused** \'=¦==\ *adj, Midland* : low-class and often ignorant and backward

**one·gite** \ˈōˈne,gīt, ˈäni,g-\ *n* -s [G *onegit*, fr. Lake *Onega*, northwest U.S.S.R., its locality + G *-it* -ite] : a pale amethyst gemstone penetrated by needles of goethite

**oneg shab·bat** \ˌō,neg(,)shäˈbät\ *n, pl* **oneg shabbat** *often cap O&S* [NHeb *ʿōneg shabbāt*, lit., Sabbath delight] : a Jewish social gathering held on Saturday afternoon or Friday evening and typically marked by talks and community singing

**one-handed** \'=¦==\ *adj* [ME *oon handyd*, fr. *oon* one + *-handyd, -handed* having (such or so many) hands (fr. *hand* + *-ed*)] **1 :** having or using only one hand ⟨said he could beat him up *one-handed*⟩ **2** *or* **one-hand a :** designed for or requiring the use of only one hand ⟨a *one-hand* alphabet for the use of deaf-mutes⟩ **b :** effected by the use of only one hand ⟨made an amazing *one-handed* catch of the ball⟩

**one-horse** \'=¦=\ *adj* **1 a :** designed to be drawn by only one horse ⟨a *one-horse* wagon⟩ **b :** using or owning only one horse ⟨a *one-horse* farm⟩ **2 a** (1) **:** that falls woefully below usual or expected standards : most inferior or inadequate : distinctly below par : SECOND-RATE ⟨put on an art exhibition that was pretty much a *one-horse* affair⟩ ⟨elected a *one-horse* committee⟩ ⟨a *one-horse* newspaper⟩ ⟨*one-horse* lawyer struggling to get along —Hamilton Basso⟩ (2) **:** that lacks substance and force : that is of little real importance or consequence : TRIVIAL ⟨advanced some kind of *one-horse* theory⟩ ⟨a *one-horse* argument⟩ **b :** that is small in size and limited in resources and narrowly provincial in outlook, atmosphere, and development : JERKWATER, INSULAR ⟨stop overnight in a *one-horse* town⟩

**one-hundred-percent** \,=¦===¦=\ *adv (or adj)* : HUNDRED-PERCENT

**one-hundred-percenter** \,=,==pə(r)ˈsentə(r)\ *n* -s : HUNDRED-PERCENTER

**one-hundred-percentism** \-pə(r)ˈsent-,izəm\ *n* -s : HUNDRED-PERCENTISM

**onei·da** \ōˈnīdə\ *n, pl* **oneida** *or* **oneidas** *usu cap* [Iroquois *Oneyóde'*, lit., standing rock] **1 a :** an Iroquoian people orig. living near Oneida Lake in the state of New York **b :** a member of such people **2 :** the language of the Oneida people

**one-ideaed** *or* **one-idea'd** \ˌwə,nī¦dēəd\ *adj* : having or possessed by only one idea ⟨her *one-ideaed* peasant mind was as inaccessible as a closed iron safe —Joseph Conrad⟩ ⟨sneered at him as a *one-ideaed* abolitionist —David Donald⟩

**oneing** *pres part of* ONE

**oneir-** *or* **oneiro-** *also* **onir-** *or* **oniro-** *comb form* [Gk *oneir-, oneiro-*, fr. *oneiros, oneiron*; akin to Arm *anurǰ* dream] : dream ⟨*oneiro*logy⟩

**onei·ric** \ōˈnīrik\ *adj* [*oneir-* + *-ic*] **1 :** of or relating to dreams ⟨those ~ images which have had so profound an effect on certain kinds of twentieth-century art —J.T.Soby⟩ **2 :** DREAMY **2 :** ANAGOGIC 2

**onei·ro·crit·ic** \ōˌnīrōˌkrid·ik\ *n* -s [Gk *oneirokritikos*, adj.] : an interpreter of dreams

**onei·ro·crit·i·cal** \-d·əkəl\ *adj* [Gk *oneirokritikos* oneirocritical (fr. *oneir-* + *kritikos* able to discern or judge) + E *-al* — more at CRITIC] : of, relating to, or specializing in the interpretation of dreams — **onei·ro·crit·i·cal·ly** \-k(ə)lē\ *adv*

**onei·ro·crit·i·cism** \-d·ə,sizəm\ *n* [fr. *oneirocritical*, after E *critical: criticism*] : the interpreting of dreams

**onei·ro·crit·ics** \-d·iks\ *n pl but usu sing in constr* [modif. (influenced by E *-ics*) of Gk *oneirokritika*, fr. neut. pl. of *oneirokritikos*, adj.] : ONEIROCRITICISM

**onei·ro·man·cy** \ōˈnīrō,man(t)sē\ *n* -ES [*oneir-* + *-mancy*] : divination by means of dreams

**one-legged** \'=¦=(=)\ *adj* **1 :** having only one leg ⟨a *one-legged* veteran⟩ **2 :** lacking some important part or element so as to be faulty or altogether ineffective ⟨a *one-legged* law⟩

**one-line octave** *n* [so called fr. the one accent mark of the symbol C′ representing middle C] : the musical octave that begins on middle C — see PITCH illustration

**one-lung** \'=¦=\ *adj* **1** *or* **one-lunged** \'=¦ləŋd\ **:** having only one lung **2** *slang* **:** having only one cylinder ⟨a *one-lung* jalopy⟩ ⟨a *one-lung* motorboat⟩

**one-lung·er** \'=¦ləŋə(r)\ *n* -s **1** *slang* **:** a one-cylinder engine **2** *slang* **:** a vehicle or craft powered by a one-cylinder engine

**one-man** \'=¦=\ *adj* **:** of or relating to just one individual (as a man): as **a :** consisting of only one individual ⟨a *one-man* government⟩ ⟨a *one-man* staff⟩ ⟨a *one-man* committee⟩ ⟨a *one-man* band⟩ **b** (1) **:** done, presented, or produced by only one individual ⟨a *one-man* stage play⟩ (2) **:** that features the work of a single artist (as a painter) and that is usu. exhibited by the artist ⟨a *one-man* show of oils⟩ **c** (1) **:** designed for or limited to one individual ⟨a *one-man* job⟩ ⟨a small *one-man* boat⟩ or operation by one individual ⟨a *one-man* typesetting machine⟩ (2) **:** managed or controlled by only one individual ⟨a *one-man* business⟩ (3) **:** originating with or supported by or dependent upon only one individual ⟨started a *one-man* revolution⟩ ⟨a *one-man* political movement⟩ **d :** that obeys or is friendly toward only one individual ⟨a *one-man* dog⟩ ⟨a *one-man* horse that no one else could ride⟩

**one-many** \'=¦==\ *adj, of a relation in logic* **:** constituted so that if the first term is given any of many things can be the second term whereas if the second term is given only one thing can be the first term ⟨the relation "father-child" is *one-many*⟩ — compare MANY-ONE, ONE-ONE

**one·ness** \'wənnəs\ *n* -ES **1 :** the quality or state or fact of being one: as **a** (1) **:** SINGLENESS ⟨a ~ of purpose⟩ (2) **:** UNIQUENESS ⟨the ~ of man⟩ **b :** WHOLENESS, INTEGRITY ⟨achieving a ~ of personality⟩ **c :** HARMONY, CONCORD ⟨a ~ of thoughts and desires⟩ **d :** SAMENESS, IDENTITY ⟨numerical ~⟩ **e :** UNITY, UNION ⟨physical and spiritual ~ with each other⟩ **2** *archaic* **:** SOLITARINESS

**one-night stand** \'=,=-\ *also* **one-night·er** \ˈwənˈnīd·ə(r)\ *n, pl* **one-night stands** *also* **one-nighters 1 :** a performance (as of a play, concert) given and designed to be given (as by a traveling group of actors, musicians) only once in separate localities : a single night's performance ⟨the television show was considerably more wearing for him than *one-night stands* —Harold Brown⟩ **2 a :** a locality (as a city, town) used for one-night stands ⟨these cities became *one-night stands* for road companies —*Amer. Guide Series: N.Y.*⟩ **b :** a stopover for a one-night stand ⟨making *one-night stands* all over the Midwest —R.J.Donovan⟩

**one-o'clock** \'==¦=\ *n* **:** DANDELION 1

**one old cat** \ˌwənə¦kat, ¦wə,nōl¦k-\ *or* **one o' cat** *also* **one-a-cat** \ˌwənə¦k-\ *n* **:** a ball game in which a batter hits a ball and then tries to run from home base to the single other base and back home again without being put out by the other players

**one-one** \'=¦=\ *adj* **1** *of a relation in logic* **:** constituted so that one term is given only one thing can be the other term ⟨in a monogamous society the relation "husband-wife" is *one-one*⟩ — compare MANY-ONE, ONE-MANY **2 :** ONE-TO-ONE ⟨a *one-one* correlation between the names of things and the things named —W.E.Johnson⟩

**one·o·ta** \ˌōnēˈōd·ə\ *adj, usu cap* [*Oneota*, village in eastern Minnesota] **:** of, relating to, or constituting a culture of the Upper Mississippi phase of the Mississippi culture pattern that in some areas has been definitely related to the Siouan peoples

**one-over-one** \,=¦==¦=\ *n* **1 :** a forcing bid in contract bridge of one in a suit made in response to a partner's opening bid of one in a suit **2 :** a system of bidding in contract bridge in which the one-over-one bid is an essential

**one over the eight** *Brit* **:** one drink too many

**one-part code** *n* **:** a code having code groups assigned in alphabetical or numerical order to an alphabetically and logically arranged list of plaintext segments — compare TWO-PART CODE

**one-piece** \'=¦=\ *adj* **:** that consists of or is made in a single undivided piece ⟨a *one-piece* bathing suit⟩ — **one-piec·er** \'=¦pēsə(r)\ *n* -s

**one-point perspective** *n* **:** PARALLEL PERSPECTIVE

**one-pound·er** \'=ˈpaundə(r)\ *n* **:** a gun firing a one-pound shot or shell

**on·er** \'wənə(r)\ *n* -s [*one* + *-er*] *Brit* **:** something unique or extraordinary

**oner·ous** \ˈänərəs, ˈōn-\ *adj* [ME, fr. MF *onereus*, fr. L *onerosus*, fr. *oner-, onus* burden + *-osus* -ose; akin to Skt *anas* cart and perh. to Gk *ania* grief] **1 a :** that involves, imposes, or constitutes much oppressive or irksome work, effort, difficulty, or responsibility : heavily demanding : TROUBLESOME, BURDENSOME ⟨~ duties⟩ ⟨an ~ political system⟩ ⟨an ~ task⟩ **b :** that involves, imposes, or constitutes a legal burden ⟨~ property⟩ ⟨an ~ option⟩ **2 :** of or relating to something done or given for an equivalent ⟨an ~ grant⟩

**syn** ONEROUS, BURDENSOME, OPPRESSIVE, and EXACTING can mean, in common, imposing great trouble, labor, or hardship. ONEROUS implies laboriousness or heaviness and usu. connotes irksomeness ⟨an unending, tiring, *onerous* job⟩ ⟨the tyranny of a majority might be more *onerous* than that of a despot —A.N. Whitehead⟩ ⟨a permanent agreement which should remove *onerous* taxes —*Encyc. Americana*⟩ BURDENSOME usu. implies both mental and physical strain ⟨a *burdensome* responsibility⟩ ⟨the *burdensome* customs regulations and the unfair tax laws —Allan Nevins & H.S.Commager⟩ ⟨a *burdensome* bureaucratic structure —*Current Biog.*⟩ OPPRESSIVE adds to BURDENSOME the idea of distress to spirit or body, usu. implying extreme harshness or severity and suggesting excessive impositions, cruelty, or tyranny ⟨the utter solitude and silence were *oppressive* —Herman Melville⟩ ⟨*oppressive* taxes⟩ ⟨others who have lived under *oppressive* governments get into the fixed habit of not telling the truth to government officials —M.R.Cohen⟩ ⟨one distant universal enemy is less *oppressive* than a thousand unchecked pilferers and plotters at home —George Santayana⟩ EXACTING implies great demands, suggesting rigor, sternness, or extreme fastidiousness rather than oppression ⟨aristocrats subjected themselves as proudly and willingly to the *exacting* discipline of the warrior —Edith Hamilton⟩ ⟨the pity of it was that even the least *exacting* husband should so often desire something more piquant than goodness —Ellen Glasgow⟩ ⟨an *exacting* standard for the economic system —J.M.Clark⟩ ⟨*exacting* specifications⟩

**oner·ous·ly** *adv* **:** in an onerous manner

**oner·ous·ness** *n* -ES **:** the quality or state of being onerous

**onery** *var of* ORNERY

**ones** *pl of* ONE, *pres 3d sing of* ONE

**-ones** *pl of* -ONE

**one-seat·er** \'wənˈsēd·ə(r)\ *n* **:** SINGLE-SEATER

**one-seed juniper** *n* **:** a small hardy drought-resistant tree (*Juniperus monosperma*) used for hedges and windbreaks esp. in the southern U.S.

**one·self** *also* **one's self** \(,)wən *sometimes* (,)wənz + *pronunc at* SELF\ *pron* **1 :** a person's self : the self of one : one's own self — compare HIMSELF, HERSELF; used (1) reflexively as object of a preposition or direct or indirect object of a verb ⟨one is a long time finding out how different others are from ~ —Van Wyck Brooks⟩ ⟨one can easily fool ~⟩ ⟨willingness to sacrifice ~ —E.P.Cubberley⟩ ⟨one must buy ~ whatever is necessary⟩; (2) for emphasis in apposition with *one* or sometimes *who, that,* or a noun ⟨if one does not have the information ~, one can ask others⟩; (3) for emphasis instead of *one* or instead of *one oneself* as subject of a verb ⟨an undertaking which is so much bigger than anything ~ would even try to engage in —H.J. Morgenthau⟩ or as predicate nominative ⟨one can trust only one person and that is ~⟩ or in comparisons after *than* or *as* ⟨one usually associates with people of the same age as ~⟩ **2 :** one's normal, healthy, or sane condition : one's normal, healthy, or sane self ⟨in such a place one could not be ~⟩ ⟨after a short interval one will come to ~⟩

**¹one-shot** \'=¦=\ *adj* **1 a :** that is complete or effective through being done or used or applied only once and that does not require repetition ⟨a *one-shot* cure⟩ ⟨a *one-shot* riveting machine⟩ **b :** that is successful in only one try ⟨those *one-shot* Johnnies who make a lucky strike and then spend the rest of their lives trying to repeat —Hamilton Basso⟩ **2 a** (1) **:** that is not followed and is not designed to be followed by something else of the same kind : that is not open to repetition or subsequent modification ⟨a *one-shot* sale⟩ ⟨a *one-shot* business deal⟩ (2) **:** that is limited to just one time, occasion, or instance ⟨a *one-shot* criminal⟩ ⟨a *one-shot* bank robbery⟩ ⟨a *one-shot* job in a nightclub⟩ (3) **:** existing or occurring only once ⟨a *one-shot* affair⟩ **b** (1) **:** that is not followed and is not designed to be followed by a second issue : that does not appear as one of a series ⟨books and pamphlets are usually produced as *one-shot* publications⟩ (2) **:** that is not one of a series of productions of the same kind : performed or produced or put on just once ⟨a *one-shot* television program⟩

**²one-shot** \"\ *also* **one-shot·ter** \'=¦shäd·ə(r)\ *n* -s **1 :** something that is not followed and is not designed to be followed by something else of the same kind: as **a :** a book or other publication that is not to be published in successive issues **b :** a program (as a theater production) that is put on and designed to be put on only once **2** *usu one-shotter* **:** one that performs an act or that functions only once

**one-shot camera** *n* **:** a color camera in which three color-separation negatives are made with a single exposure by using semitransparent reflectors to divide the beam that has passed through the lens so as to form three geometrically identical images on three plates or films through three different color filters

**one-sided** \'=¦==\ *adj* **1 a :** having or existing or occurring on one side only : having one side prominent or more developed ⟨a *one-sided* leaf⟩ **b :** limited to one side : PARTIAL, UNJUST, UNFAIR ⟨a *one-sided* interpretation⟩ **2 :** UNILATERAL ⟨a *one-sided* decision⟩ — **one-sid·ed·ly** *adv* — **one-sid·ed·ness** *n* -ES

**¹one-step** \'=,=\ *n* **1 :** a ballroom dance popular in the early 20th century and marked by quick walking steps backward and forward in 2/4 time **2 :** a piece of music for the one-step

**²one-step** \"\ *vi* **:** to dance the one-step

**one-sucker** *n* **:** a tobacco produced in western Kentucky and north central Tennessee and suckered only once or topped only just before cutting and used in the manufacture of chewing tobacco

**one-suiter** \'=ˈsüd·ə(r)\ *n* -s **:** a man's wardrobe case designed to hold one suit and accessories

**¹onetime** \'=,=\ *adj* **:** FORMER, SOMETIME, QUONDAM ⟨a ~ professor of history⟩

**²onetime** \"\ *adv* **:** FORMERLY ⟨said they ~ knew him very well⟩

**one-to-one** \¦=tə¦=, -də-\ *adj* **1 :** correlating uniquely and wholly and exactly ⟨a *one-to-one* correspondence between the sounds of a language and the symbols used to represent the sounds⟩ **2 :** ONE-ONE 1

**one-track** \'=¦=\ *adj* **1 a :** that lacks flexibility and nimbleness and can handle only one thing at a time ⟨is an unimaginative person and has a *one-track* mind⟩ **b :** marked by often narrowly constricted attention to or absorption in just one thing ⟨a *one-track* party member⟩ **2 :** that lacks variety or breadth : limited in scope : UNDIVERSIFIED ⟨areas where *one-track* farming has been the rule —A.J.Bruwer⟩

**one-two** \'=¦=\ *n* **1 :** a fencing attack made by simulating a disengagement and followed by delivery of a thrust in the original line if the adversary's parry is drawn **2** *or* **one-two punch** \'=¦=-\ **:** delivery of two short blows in rapid succession in boxing; *esp* **:** delivery of a jab with the left hand followed at once by a hard straight blow with the right

**one-upmanship** *n* **:** the art or practice of going a friend or competitor one better or keeping one jump ahead of him (as by appearing to have better information, connections, possessions, or experience) ⟨a branch of *one-upmanship* that involves playing off one milieu off against another —Edmund Wilson⟩

**¹one-way** \'=¦=\ *adj* **1 a** (1) **:** that moves in only one direction ⟨*one-way* traffic⟩ ⟨a *one-way* stream of time —A.J.Toynbee⟩ (2) **:** that exists on one side only : ONE-SIDED ⟨was pretty much a *one-way* conversation —G.K.Wynne⟩ : UNILATERAL ⟨a *one-way* agreement⟩ **b :** that allows or provides for or is limited to movement in only one direction ⟨a *one-way* path along which there can be no retreat —S.A.Coblentz⟩ ⟨a *one-way* plane ticket⟩; *esp* **:** that is limited to vehicles moving in only one direction ⟨a *one-way* street⟩ **2 :** that functions in only one of two or more possible ways ⟨a *one-way* radio for receiving but not transmitting broadcast signals⟩

**²one-way** \"\ *or* **one-way disc plow** *n* **:** a disc plow that has relatively small discs set at a sharp angle in the same direction and that is designed to turn soil only partially

**onfall** \'=,=\ *n* [*on* + *fall*, n.; prob. trans. of G *anfall*] **:** ATTACK, ASSAULT ⟨intend to make an ~ —J.H.Wheelwright⟩

**onflow** \'=,=\ *n* [*on* + *flow*, n. (after the verb phrase *flow on*)] **:** the action or fact of flowing on : onward flow

**onga-onga** \ˌäŋgəˌäŋgə\ *n* -s [Maori] **:** a New Zealand shrubby nettle (*Urtica ferox*) with copious stinging hairs

**on·ge** *or* **on·gi** \ˈänjē\ *n, pl* **onge** *or* **onges** *or* **ongi** *or* **ongis** *usu cap* **1 :** a people of the Andaman islands in the Bay of Bengal **2 :** a member of the Onge people

**on-glaze** \'=¦=\ *adj* [prob. fr. the phrase *on glaze*, fr. ¹*on* + *glaze*, n.] **:** OVERGLAZE

**on-glide** \'=,=\ *n* [*on* + *glide*, n.] **:** a glide produced by the movement of the vocal organs to the articulatory position of a speech sound from a position of inactivity or from the articulatory position of an immediately preceding speech sound — compare OFF-GLIDE

**¹ongoing** \'=,==\ *n* [*on* + *going*, n. (after *go on*, v.)] **1 ongoings** *pl* **:** GOINGS-ON ⟨the ~*s* in the Orient —*Forbes*⟩ **2 :** the action of going on : the action of continued forward movement : PROGRESS, DEVELOPMENT ⟨throughout this entire period of the world's ~ —P.W.Sinks⟩

**²ongoing** \"\ *adj* [²*on* + *going*, adj. (after *go on*, v.)] **:** that is going on: **a :** that is actually in process ⟨~ and contemplated research on language —*Amer. Anthrop. Assoc. Bull.*⟩ ⟨~ activities of the world —S.H.Horton⟩ **b :** that is continuously moving forward : making progress : GROWING, DEVELOPING ⟨the long ~ history of Christian thought —W.L.Sperry⟩ ⟨~ human society exacts a high degree of conformity —Bernard Rosenberg⟩ — **on·go·ing·ness** *n* -ES

**on·gole** \ˈäŋ,gōl, ˈäŋ,-\ *n, usu cap* [fr. *Ongole*, town in southeast India] **:** NELLORE

**onhanger** \'=,==\ *n* [*on* + *hanger* (after *hang on*, v.)] **:** HANGER-ON

**-on·ic** \ˈänik, -nēk\ *adj suffix* [ISV, fr. *-onic* (in *gluconic acid*)] **:** containing carboxyl esp. when formed by oxidizing the aldehyde group of an aldose sugar ⟨ald*onic* acid⟩ ⟨hex*onic* acid⟩ ⟨lact*onic*⟩

**onio·ma·nia** \ˌōnēōˈmānēə\ *n* [NL, fr. Gk *ōnios* to be bought, for sale (fr. *ōnos* price) + LL *mania* — more at VENAL] **:** a mania for buying things — **onio·ma·ni·ac** \-ē,ak\ *n*

**¹on·ion** \ˈənyən, *dial* ˈiŋə(r)n\ *n* -s *often attrib* [ME *onion, union*, fr. MF *oignon*, fr. L *union-, unio*, perh. fr. *unus* one — more at ONE] **1 a** (1) **:** a widely cultivated orig. Asiatic plant (*Allium cepa*) that has slender hollow tubular leaves and an edible rounded bulb made up of close concentric easily separable layers, that has a notably strong sharp smell and taste, and that is widely used as a vegetable (2) **:** the bulb of this plant **b :** any plant of the genus *Allium* including several that are cultivated for their showy heads of flowers **2** *obs* **:** a rounded knob or similar projection; *esp* **:** BUNION — **off one's onion** *also* **off one's onions** *chiefly Brit* **:** FOOLISH, CRAZY ⟨thought he was a trifle *off his onion* —Walter Murdoch⟩

onion 1a(2)

**²onion** \"\ *vt* -ED/-ING/-S **:** to apply an onion to

**onion couch** *or* **onion twitch** *n* **:** TALL OAT GRASS

**onion flute** *n* **:** KAZOO

**onion fly** *n* **1 :** a dipterous insect of the family Anthomyiidae whose larva feeds on onion bulbs; *esp* **:** an orig. European insect (*Hylemya antiqua*) now widely distributed in America **2 :** an insect (*Tritoxa flexa*) of the family Otitidae with habits like those of the onion fly — called also *black onion fly*

**onion foot** *n, pl* **onion foots :** BUN FOOT

**oniongrass** \'==,=\ *n* **:** MELIC GRASS

**onion maggot** *n* **:** the larva of the onion fly

**onion mildew** *n* **1 :** a downy mildew of the onion **2 :** a fungus (*Peronospora destructor*) that causes onion mildew

**onion red** \'==¦=\ *or* **onionpeel** \'==,=\ *n* **:** a grayish red that is bluer and deeper than Pompeian red, bluer and darker than bois de rose, and deeper than livid brown

**onion set** *n* **:** a small onion bulb planted in the spring to produce an early crop esp. of green onions

**onionskin** \'==,=\ *n* **:** a thin strong translucent paper of very light weight

**onionskin pink** *n* **:** a light brown that is stronger and slightly redder and darker than alesan, stronger and slightly yellower and darker than blush, lighter, stronger, and slightly redder than French beige; and redder, stronger, and slightly lighter than cork

**onion smudge** *or* **onion scab** *n* **1 :** a common fungus disease of the onion characterized by black concentric internal rings or smutty spots on the surface of the bulb scales **2 :** the fungus (*Colletotrichum circinans*) that causes onion smudge

**onion smut** *n* **1 :** a fungus disease of the onion that is esp. destructive to seedlings and is characterized by elongate blackish blisters on the scales and leaves **2 :** the fungus (*Urocystis cepulae*) that causes onion smut

**onion thrips** *also* **onion louse** *n* **:** a minute widely distributed thrips (*Thrips tabaci*) that is often very injurious to the foliage of onions and in some regions to tobacco

**on·iony** \ˈənyənē\ *adj* **:** flavored with or tasting or smelling of onions ⟨~ soup⟩ ⟨an ~ breath⟩

**onir-** *or* **oniro-** — see ONEIR-

**onis·coi·dea** \ˌänəˈskȯidēə, ˌōn-\ *n pl, cap* [NL, fr. *Oniscus* + *-oidea*] **:** a suborder of Isopoda that includes all terrestrial isopods and a few that are to some extent aquatic — **onis·coi·de·an** \ˌ⸗⸗ˈ⸗dēən\ *adj or n*

**onis·cus** \ōˈniskəs\ *n, cap* [NL, fr. L, wood louse fr. Gk *oniskos*, fr. *onos* wood louse, ass + *-iskos*, dim. n. suffix — more at ASS, -ISH] **:** a genus (the type of the family Oniscidae) comprising isopods that cannot roll into a ball and formerly including most of the known isopods but now restricted to a few chiefly Old World terrestrial forms with flattened body, large eyes, and 3-jointed antennal flagella

**oni·um** \ˈōnēəm, ˈōnyəm\ *adj* [*-onium*] **:** characterized by a cation that is usu. complex (as oxonium, pyridinium, or a substituted ammonium) — compare QUATERNARY AMMONIUM COMPOUND

**-o·ni·um** \"\ *n suffix* -s [ISV, fr. NL *ammonium*] **:** an ion having a positive charge — in names of complex cations containing hydrogen or one or more organic radicals coordinated to a central atom ⟨*oxonium*⟩ ⟨*phosphonium*⟩ ⟨*sulfonium*⟩; compare -IUM 1b

**on·kos** \ˈäŋkəs\ *n, pl* **on·koi** \-ˌkȯi\ *or* **onkos·es** \-ˌkəsəz\ [Gk, lit., bulk, mass — more at ONCO-] **:** a topknot worn on the mask in ancient Greek tragedy

**onlap** \ˈ⸗ˌ⸗\ *n* [*on* + *lap*, n.] **1 :** progressive submergence of land by an advancing sea **2 :** the arrangement of strata deposited on the floor of an advancing sea during its advance — compare OFFLAP, OVERLAP

**¹onlay** \(ˈ)⸗ˈ⸗\ *vt* [²*on* + *lay*] **:** to lay on; *specif* **:** to mount (an onlay) on a surface

**²onlay** \ˈ⸗ˌ⸗\ *n* **1 :** material mounted on a surface usu. so as to be in relief and usu. for decorative effect; *esp* **:** a thin ornamental piece of leather mounted on the surface of a leather bookbinding **2 :** INLAY 2b

**on–license** \ˈ⸗ˌ⸗⸗\ *n* **:** a license to sell liquor for consumption on the premises

**on·li·est** \ˈōnlēəst\ *adj* [¹*only* + *-est*] *dial* **:** ONLY ⟨couldn't see anything to cause a loving father to let go his ~ daughter —Miriam Michelson⟩

**on limits** *adj* **:** available or approved for military personnel

**on·li·ness** \ˈōnlēnəs\ *n* -ES **:** the quality or state of being the only one of an indicated or implied kind or category ⟨was an only child and was lonely in his ~⟩

**onload** \ˈ⸗ˌ⸗\ *vb* [²*on* + *load*] **:** LOAD ⟨~*ing* cargo⟩

**onlooker** \ˈ⸗ˌ⸗⸗\ *n* [*on* + *looker* (after *look on*, v.)] **:** one that looks on ⟨curious ~*s*⟩; *esp* **:** a passive spectator ⟨a crowd of indifferent ~*s*⟩

**onlooking** \ˈ⸗ˌ⸗⸗\ *adj* [²*on* + *looking*, pres. part. of *look* (after *look on*, v.)] **:** that looks on ⟨walked by the ~ crowd⟩

**¹on·ly** \ˈōnlē, -li\ *adj* [ME *only*, *oonly*, fr. OE *ānlīc*, fr. *ān* one + *-līc* -ly — more at ONE] **1 :** that is unequaled (as in quality, rank) **:** unquestionably the best or the most outstanding **:** PEERLESS ⟨was convinced that the team was the ~ one⟩ **:** that alone is worth serious consideration ⟨the ~ actor on Broadway⟩ **2** *dial chiefly Eng* **:** that is without companions or associates **:** LONE, ISOLATED **3 :** being one or more of which there exist no others of the same class or kind **:** alone in an indicated or implied category ⟨is the ~ authority you can really rely on⟩ ⟨said she was the ~ one for him⟩ ⟨was the ~ book deserving to be read⟩ **:** SOLE, SINGLE ⟨was an ~ child⟩ ⟨had an ~ brother⟩ ⟨is the ~ known species⟩ ⟨the ~ begotten son⟩

**²only** \"\ *adv* [ME *only*, *oonly*, fr. *only*, *oonly*, adj.] **1 a :** as a single solitary fact or instance or occurrence **:** as just the one simple thing and nothing more or different **:** SIMPLY, MERELY, JUST ⟨has ~ lost one election —George Orwell⟩ ⟨if ~ she had yellow hair —Jean Stafford⟩ ⟨saw my father three times ~ —T.B.Costain⟩ ⟨has ~ two dollars⟩ **b :** EXCLUSIVELY, SOLELY ⟨will tell it ~ to you⟩ ⟨is ~ known to scholars —Stephen Spender⟩ **2 a :** at the very least **:** without going any further than necessary ⟨it was ~ too true⟩ ⟨it was ~ too probable that my inquiries would be reported —Allen Upward⟩ **b :** by that much indeed **:** all the more as a matter of fact ⟨such significance ~ adds to the value of such literature —Herbert Read⟩ ⟨the risk ~ makes the whole thing more interesting⟩ **3 a :** in the final outcome **:** at last **:** as a final result ⟨it will ~ make you sick⟩ ⟨a period of personal rule which ~ ended with revolution —R.A.Billington⟩ **b :** with nevertheless the final outcome or result ⟨won a great deal, ~ to lose it all later on⟩ **4 :** as recently as ⟨saw her ~ last week⟩ **:** in the immediate past ⟨I ~ just talked to her⟩

**³only** \"\ *conj* [ME *only*, *oonly*, fr. *only*, *oonly*, adv.] **1 a :** with the qualification or restriction that **:** BUT ⟨you may go, ~ come back early⟩ **b :** and yet **:** HOWEVER ⟨they look very nice, ~ we can't use them⟩ **2 :** were it not that **:** if it weren't for the fact that **:** EXCEPT ⟨he would have come over, ~ we never expected you as early as this —J.G.Cozzens⟩

**⁴only** \"\ *prep* [²*only*] *chiefly dial* **:** EXCEPT

**onmarch** \ˈ⸗ˌ⸗\ *n* [*on* + *march*, n. (after the verb phrase *march on*)] **:** a march onward ⟨the ~ of history —*Science*⟩

**on·mun** \ˈȯnmən\ *or* **en·mun** \ˈunm-\ *n* -s *often cap* [Korean] **:** HANKUL

**ono** \ˈō(ˌ)nō\ *n, pl* **ono** *or* **onos** [Hawaiian, Marquesan, & Tahitian] **:** WAHOO

**on·o·bry·chis** \ˌänəˈbrīkəs\ *n, cap* [NL, fr. Gk *onobrychis*, a leguminous plant, fr. *onos* ass + *-brychis* (fr. *brykein*, *brychein* to eat greedily, gnash the teeth) — more at ASS, BRUXISM] **:** a genus of Old World herbs of the family Leguminosae having pinnate leaves, pink or white racemose flowers, and flat unjointed pods

**ono·centaur** \ˈänə+\ *n* [LL *onocentaurus*, a wild animal inhabiting waste places, fr. Gk *onokentauros*, fr. *onos* ass + *kentauros* centaur] **:** a mythological creature having the head and arms and upper torso of a human being and the body and legs of an ass

**on·o·clea** \ˌänəˈklēə\ *n, cap* [NL, fr. Gk *onokleia* anchusa] **:** a genus of ferns (family Polypodiaceae) of cold temperate regions having fronds that are broad and pinnatifid or that consist of segments rolled up into berrylike structures enclosing the sori — **on·o·cle·oid** \ˌänəˈklēˌȯid\ *n or adj*

**on·o·man·cy** \ˈänəˌman(t)sē, ōˈnämənsē\ *n* -ES [obs. F *onomancie*, fr. MF, irreg. fr. Gk *onoma* name + MF *-mancie* -mancy] **:** divination from the letters of a name

**on·o·ma·si·o·log·ic** \ˌänəˌmāsēəˈläjik, -āzē-\ *or* **on·o·ma·si·o·log·i·cal** \-jəkəl\ *adj* **:** relating to the gathering or comparison of lists of words that designate similar or associated concepts

**on·o·ma·si·ol·o·gy** \ˌ⸗⸗ˌ⸗⸗ˈäləjē\ *n* -ES [Gk *onomasia* name, expression (fr. *onomazein* to call, name) + E *-o-* + *-logy*] **:** the study of words and expressions having similar or associated concepts and a basis (as social, regional, occupational) for being grouped

**on·o·mas·tic** \ˌänəˈmastik\ *adj* [Gk *onomastikos*, fr. *onomazein* to name, fr. *onoma* name — more at NAME] **1 :** of, relating to, or consisting of a name or names ⟨published an ~ study⟩ **2** *of a signature* **:** written in the handwriting of the author of a letter or document or in the handwriting of one subscribing to a letter or document the body of which is in the handwriting of another person

**on·o·mas·ti·con** \ˌänəˈmastəˌkän, -ˌkən\ *n* -s [NL, fr. Gk *onomastikon*, fr. neut. of *onomastikos* onomastic] **1 a :** a collection or listing of words esp. in a specialized field (as science or commerce) **b :** a work containing such a collection or listing **:** WORDBOOK, LEXICON **2 a :** a collection or listing of proper names of persons or places usu. with etymologies **b :** a work containing such a collection or listing

**on·o·mas·tics** \-stiks\ *n pl but usu sing in constr* [modif. (influenced by E *-ics*) of F *onomastique*, fr. *onomastique* onomastic, fr. Gk *onomastikos*] **1 a :** the science or study of the origins and forms of words esp. as used in a specialized field (as science or commerce) ⟨a course in ~⟩ **b :** the science or study of the origin and forms of proper names of persons or places ⟨any student of ~ and of surnames in particular —Otto Springer⟩ **2 :** the system underlying the formation and use of words esp. for proper names or of words used in a specialized field ⟨according to rules of Indo-European ~ —E.E.Herzfeld⟩

**onomato-** *comb form* [LL, fr. Gk, fr. *onomat-*, *onoma*] **:** name **:** word ⟨*onomato*mania⟩

**on·o·ma·tol·o·gy** \ˌänəməˈtäləjē *sometimes* ōˌnäm-\ *n* -ES [F *onomatologie*, fr. *onomato-* + *-logie* -logy] **:** ONOMASTICS

**on·o·mato·mania** \ˌänəˌmadəˈmānēə *sometimes* ōˌnäməd- *or* ˌänəˌmäd-\ *n* [NL, fr. *onomato-* + LL *mania*] **:** uncontrollable obsession with words or names or their meanings or sounds; *esp* **:** a mania for repeating certain words or sounds

**onoma·tope** \ˈänəməˌtōp, ōˈnäm-\ *n* -s [irreg. fr. *onomatopoeia*] **:** an onomatopoeic word ⟨fondness of comic-strip artists for ~*s* —H.L.Mencken⟩

**on·o·mat·o·poe·ia** \ˌänəˌma|dəˈpēə, |tə- *sometimes* ōˌnämə| *or* ˌänəˌmä| *or* -pēyə\ *n* -s [LL, fr. Gk *onomatopoiia*, fr. *onomato-* + *-poiia* (fr. *poiein* to make + *-ia* -y) — more at POET] **1 a :** formation of words in imitation of natural sounds **:** the naming of a thing or action by a more or less exact reproduction of the sound associated with it (as *buzz*, *hiss*, *bobwhite*) **:** the imitative or echoic principle in language — compare BOWWOW THEORY **b :** a word so formed ⟨the international stock of ~*s* —Leo Spitzer⟩ **2 :** the use of words whose sound suggests the sense ⟨a study of the poet's ~⟩ — **on·o·mat·o·poe·ian** \-ˈpē(y)ən\ *adj*

**on·o·mat·o·poe·ic** \-ēik\ *also* **on·o·mat·o·poe·i·cal** \-ēəkəl\ *adj* [*onomatopoeia* fr. F *onomatopéique*, fr. *onomatopée* onomatopoeia (fr. LL *onomatopoeia*) + *-ique* -ic; *onomatopoeical* fr. *onomatopoeic* + *-al*] **:** of, relating to, or characterized by onomatopoeia **:** imitative in origin **:** ECHOIC ⟨~ words⟩ ⟨~ imitation of noises —Cecil Sprigge⟩ — **on·o·mat·o·poe·i·cal·ly** \-k(ə)lē\ *adv*

**on·o·mat·o·po·et·ic** \ˌ⸗⸗ˌ⸗⸗pōˈed·ik, ⸗ˌ⸗⸗⸗-\ *adj* [fr. MGk *onomatopoiēsis*, after L *poesis* poetry, poem: *poeticus* poetic — more at POESY] **:** ONOMATOPOEIC ⟨independently developed in more than one place as an ~ term —Harry Hoijer⟩ — **on·o·mat·o·po·et·i·cal·ly** \-k(ə)lē\ *adv*

**on·o·mat·o·py** \ˌänəˈmad·əpē\ *n* -ES [LL *onomatopoeia*] **:** ONOMATOPOEIA ⟨the possibility that ~ has produced in different languages similar but genetically unrelated words —George Herzog⟩

**on·on·da·ga** \ˌänənˈdȯgə, -dägə *or, prob by* n*-dissimilation*, ˌänəˈd-\ *n, pl* **onondaga** *or* **onondagas** *usu cap* [Iroquois *Onōtáge'*, principal village of the Onondaga people, lit., on top of the hill] **1 a :** an Iroquoian people in and about Onondaga county in the central part of the state of New York **b :** a member of such people **2 :** the language of the Onondaga people — **on·on·da·gan** \ˌ⸗⸗ˈ⸗gən\ *adj, usu cap*

**ono·nis** \ōˈnōnəs\ *n, cap* [NL, fr. Gk *onōnis* restharrow] **:** a genus of European herbs (family Leguminosae) that resemble clovers and have red or yellow solitary or clustered flowers — see RESTHARROW

**on·o·por·don** \ˌänəˈpȯrdᵊn, -ˌdän\ *n, cap* [NL, fr. Gk *onopordon* pellitory, fr. *onos* ass + *-pordon* (fr. *pordē* expulsion of intestinal gas); akin to Gk *perdesthai* to break wind — more at ASS, FART] **:** a genus of Eurasian herbs (family Compositae) with tomentose prickly foliage and large heads of purplish flowers — see COTTON THISTLE

**on·os·mo·di·um** \ˌänäzˈmōdēəm, -nəˈsm-\ *n, cap* [NL, irreg. fr. Gk *onosma*, a boraginaceous plant, fr. *onos* ass + *-osma* (fr. *osmē* odor) — more at ODOR] **:** a genus of No. American perennial herbs (family Boraginaceae) with hispid foliage and small yellowish or greenish flowers — see FALSE GROMWELL

**on-plant** \ˈ⸗ˌ⸗\ *adj* [¹*on* + *plant*, n.] **:** IN-PLANT

**onroll** \ˈ⸗ˌ⸗\ *n* [*on* + *roll*, n. (after the verb phrase *roll on*)] **:** a rolling forward or onward

**onrush** \ˈ⸗ˌ⸗\ *n* [*on* + *rush*, n. (after the verb phrase *rush on*)] **1 :** a rushing forward or onward ⟨the ~ of industrialization created a serious housing shortage —Nels Anderson⟩ **2 :** ONSET, ONSLAUGHT ⟨the first ~ of some sudden grief —Laura Krey⟩

**onrushing** \ˈ⸗ˌ⸗⸗\ *adj* **:** rushing forward rapidly or impetuously

**-ons** *pl of* -ON

**on-sale** \ˈ⸗ˌ⸗\ *adj* **1** *of a license* **:** that permits sale and consumption of alcoholic beverages on the premises ⟨secured an *on-sale* license for his restaurant⟩ **2 a :** authorized to sell ⟨an *on-sale* retailer⟩ or buy ⟨*on-sale* patrons⟩ alcoholic beverages under the conditions of an on-sale license **b :** sold ⟨*on-sale* liquor⟩ or licensed ⟨an *on-sale* restaurant⟩ under the conditions of an on-sale license

**¹onset** \ˈ⸗ˌ⸗\ *n* [*on* + *set*, n. (after *set on*, v.)] **1 :** ATTACK, ASSAULT ⟨unable to withstand the ~ of the army⟩ **2 a :** BEGINNING, COMMENCEMENT, START ⟨the ~ of winter⟩ **b :** the initial existence or symptoms of a disease ⟨the ~ of scarlet fever⟩ **c :** the initial formation of a speech sound ⟨the ~ of a voiceless consonant⟩ **3 :** ELECTRONOGRAPHY

**²on·set** \ˈänˌset, -ˌsȯt\ *n* [*on* + *set*, n.] *chiefly Scot* **:** a farmhouse with its outbuildings

**onsetter** \ˈ⸗ˌ⸗⸗\ *n* [*on* + *setter* (after *set on*, v.)] **:** CAGER 1a

**¹onshore** \(ˈ)⸗ˈ⸗\ *adv* [¹*on* + *shore*, n.] **1 :** toward or onto the shore ⟨a breeze blowing ~⟩ **:** near the shore ⟨a boat sailing along ~⟩ **2 :** within the country **:** DOMESTICALLY ⟨does all his business ~⟩

**²onshore** \"\ *adj* **1 :** coming or moving toward or onto the shore ⟨an ~ breeze⟩ ⟨an ~ current⟩ **2 a :** situated on or near the shore ⟨~ oil reserves⟩ ⟨~ fishing⟩ **b :** placed or made within the country **:** DOMESTIC ⟨~ purchases⟩

**on side** *adv (or adj)* **1 :** not off side **:** in a position legally to play the ball or puck or to receive it from a teammate **2 :** in a position to make a finesse in a card game successful ⟨the king is *on side*⟩

**onside kick** \ˈ⸗ˌ⸗-\ *n* **:** a free kick (as a kickoff) in football that a kicker deliberately aims only slightly beyond the defensive restraining line in the hope of recovering the ball which becomes free after crossing the restraining line

**on·slaught** \ˈȯnˌslȯt, ˈän-, *usu* -ȯd·+V\ *n* -s [alter. (influenced by E *on* and obs. E *slaught* slaughter, fr. ME, fr. OE *sleaht*) of earlier *anslaight*, modif. of D *aanslag* act of striking, fr. MD *aenslach* act of striking, attack, fr. *aen* on, at + *slach* blow, stroke; akin to OE *an*, *on* on and to OE *slēan* to strike, beat — more at ON, SLAY, SLAUGHTER] **1 :** an esp. fierce attack ⟨the tremendous ~ across the Rhine —Sir Winston Churchill⟩ ⟨an ~ of disease⟩ ⟨less resilient under his wife's verbal ~*s* —D.G.Gerhaty⟩

**onst** *like* ONCE\ *dial var of* ONCE

**onstage** \(ˈ)⸗ˈ⸗\ *adv (or adj)* [¹*on* + *stage*, n.] **:** on a part of the stage visible to the audience **:** toward the central part of the stage ⟨is ~ almost continuously —Philip Hamburger⟩ ⟨began to walk ~⟩ ⟨has good ~ diction⟩

**on·stead** \ˈänzˌted, -nˌst-, -ˌtəd, -ˌstəd\ *n* [*on* + *stead*, n.] *Scot* **:** a farmhouse with its outbuildings

**on-stream** *adj* [fr. the phrase *on stream*] **:** moving through or flowing (as in a pipe or filter) in the desired operational direction ⟨*on-stream* chemical reactions⟩ ⟨the *on-stream* time for a filter varies widely —D.P.Thornton⟩

**on stream** *adv* **:** in operation **:** into operation ⟨a new polypropylene plant will go *on stream*⟩

**ont-** *or* **onto-** *comb form* [NL, fr. LGk *onto-*, fr. Gk *ont-*, *ōn*, pres. part. of *einai* to be — more at IS] **1 :** being **:** existence ⟨*ontic*⟩ **2 :** individual living thing **:** living organism ⟨*ontogeny*⟩

**-ont** \ˌänt\ *n comb form* -s [Gk *ont-*, *ōn*, pres. part. of *einai* to be] **:** cell **:** organism ⟨*gamont*⟩

**¹on·tar·i·an** \(ˈ)änˈterēən, -ta(a)r-, -tār-\ *adj, usu cap* [*Ontario*, province of southern and central Canada + E *-an*, adj. suffix] **1 :** of, relating to, or characteristic of the province of Ontario in south central Canada **2** [Lake *Ontario*, lake lying between the state of New York and the Canadian province of Ontario + E *-an*, adj. suffix] **:** of, relating to, or characteristic of Lake Ontario lying between the state of New York and Canada

**²ontarian** \"\ *also* **on·tar·io·an** \⸗ˈ⸗⸗ˌōən\ *n* -s *cap* [*Ontario* (province) + E *-an*, n. suffix] **:** a native or inhabitant of the province of Ontario in Canada

**on·tar·io** \⸗ˈ⸗⸗ˌō\ *adj, usu cap* **:** of or from the province of Ontario **:** of the kind or style prevalent in Ontario **:** ONTARIAN

**ontario violet** *n, often cap O* **:** a pale purplish blue that is redder and paler than hydrangea blue and redder and deeper than starlight blue — called also *blue lavender*

**on·thoph·a·gus** \änˈthäfəgəs\ *n, cap* [NL, fr. Gk *onthos* dung + NL *-phagus* (fr. Gk *-phagos* -phagous)] **:** a widely distributed genus of scarabaeid beetles

**on·tic** \ˈäntik\ *also* **on·tal** \-tᵊl\ *adj* [*ont-* + *-ic* or *-al*] **:** of, relating to, or having real being or existence **:** NOUMENAL ⟨~ aspects of experience —Fritz Kaufmann⟩ ⟨the alleged ~ status of moral values —Ernest Nagel⟩ — distinguished from *phenomenal* — **on·ti·cal·ly** \-tək(ə)lē\ *adv*

**on·to** \ˈȯntə, ˈän-, -ntü, -n·(ˌ)tü, +V *often* -ntəw\ *prep* [²*on* + *to*] **1 a :** to a position or point on or upon ⟨slipped away from the chair ~ the floor —C.D.Lewis⟩ ⟨water splashed down from the roof ~ my hat —Joseph Wechsberg⟩ ⟨jumped off the boat and ~ the dock⟩ ⟨climbed out ~ the roof⟩ **b** *chiefly dial* **:** in position on ⟨the coat has big buttons ~ it —Delia H. Pugh⟩ **2 :** in or into a state of awareness or knowledgeability about ⟨he's a shrewd bird and he's ~ me —Mark Schorer⟩ ⟨was ~ something that should have been pursued further —Bosley Crowther⟩ — compare ²ON 8

**onto·genesis** \ˌäntə+\ *n* [NL, fr. *ont-* + L *genesis*] **:** ONTOGENY

**on·to·ge·net·ic** \ˌäntəjəˈned·ik\ *adj* [ISV, fr. NL *ontogenesis*, after such pairs as LL *antithesis: antitheticus* antithetical] **1 :** of or relating to ontogeny **2 :** based on visible morphological characters and not necessarily indicative of natural evolutionary relationships ⟨an ~ key to the Lygaeidae⟩ **3 :** appearing in the course of ontogenetic development **:** INDIVIDUAL ⟨~ traits⟩ ⟨an ~ modification⟩ — **on·to·ge·net·i·cal·ly** \-d·ək(ə)lē\ *adv*

**on·to·gen·ic** \ˌäntəˈjenik\ *adj* [ISV *ontogeny* + *-ic*] **:** ONTOGENETIC — **on·to·gen·i·cal·ly** \-enək(ə)lē\ *adv*

**on·tog·e·nist** \änˈtäjənəst\ *n* -s **:** a student of ontogeny

**on·tog·e·ny** \-jənē\ *n* -ES [ISV *ont-* + *-geny*] **:** the biological development or course of development of an individual organism — distinguished from *phylogeny*

**on·to·log·i·cal** \ˌäntᵊlˈäjəkəl, ˌäntəˈlä-\ *also* **on·to·log·ic** \-jik\ *adj* [*ontological* fr. *ontologic* + *-al*; *ontologic* prob. fr. (assumed) NL *ontologicus*, fr. NL *ontologia* ontology + L *-icus* -ic] **1 :** of or relating to ontology **2 :** of or relating to being or existence; *esp* **:** based upon or drawn from analysis of the nature of being ⟨the ~ argument for the existence of God⟩ — **on·to·log·i·cal·ly** \-jək(ə)lē\ *adv*

**on·tol·o·gism** \änˈtäləˌjizəm\ *n* -s [ISV *ontology* + *-ism*] **1 :** a philosophical method that analyzes reality on ontological principles (as from a consideration of the categories) **2 :** a theory in philosophy: the order of intellectual apprehension follows the order of real being and knowledge of God is immediate and intuitive

**on·tol·o·gist** \-jəst\ *n* -s [*ontology* + *-ist*] **1 :** a specialist in ontology **2 :** an advocate or adherent of ontologism — **on·tol·o·gis·tic** \(ˌ)änˌtäləˈjistik\ *adj*

**on·tol·o·gize** \änˈtäləˌjīz\ *vt* -ED/-ING/-S [ISV *ontology* + *-ize*] **:** to convert into ontological entities or express ontologically

**on·tol·o·gy** \-jē\ *n* -ES [NL *ontologia*, fr. *ont-* + *-logia* -logy] **1 a** (1) **:** a science or study of being; *specif* **:** a branch of metaphysics relating to the nature and relations of being (2) **:** a particular system according to which problems of the nature of being are investigated **b :** FIRST PHILOSOPHY **2 :** a theory concerning the kinds of entities and specif. the kinds of abstract entities that are to be admitted to a language system

**onus** \ˈōnəs\ *n* -ES [L — more at ONEROUS] **1 a :** something (as a task, duty, responsibility) that involves considerable difficulty or annoyance or necessitates rather strenuous effort or results in notable strain or fatigue **:** BURDEN ⟨the job of caring for his dependents was a real ~⟩ ⟨believe it to be the ~ on every man to add . . . to the sum total of human knowledge —Douglas Carruthers⟩ **b :** something distasteful or objectionable and difficult to bear: as (1) **:** a disagreeable necessity of doing something ⟨free of all ~ of retort or comment —Richard Blaker⟩ (2) **:** BLAME ⟨tried to shift the ~ for causing the war onto the other country⟩ ⟨adroitly transfer the ~ from the accused to the accusers —Eugene Lyons⟩ (3) **:** STIGMA ⟨excusing himself ahead of time so that the ~ would be less if his failure was realized —Norman Mailer⟩ **2** *or* **onus pro·ban·di** \-prōˈbanˌdī, -ndē\ **:** BURDEN OF PROOF ⟨put forth a theory that left the ~ squarely on him⟩

**onwaiting** \ˈ⸗ˌ⸗⸗\ *n* [*on* + *waiting*, gerund of *wait* (after the verb phrase *wait on*)] *Scot* **:** the act of awaiting

**¹on·ward** \ˈȯnwə(r)d, ˈän-\ *also* **on·wards** \-dz\ *adv* [ME *onward*, fr. ²*on* + *-ward*] **:** toward or at a point lying ahead in space or time **:** FORWARD, AHEAD ⟨moved ~ into the forest⟩ ⟨the bridge was farther ~ along that road⟩ ⟨from the 6th century ~⟩

**²onward** \"\ *adj* **:** directed or moving onward **:** FORWARD ⟨the difficult and dangerous ~ path which we must tread —Sir Winston Churchill⟩ ⟨the ~ course of events⟩ ⟨the ~ march of agricultural settlement —B.K.Sandwell⟩

**on·ward·ness** *n* -ES **:** the quality or state of being directed forward or of moving forward ⟨~ that he found among these youthful liberals —Francis Biddle⟩

**ony** \ˈänē\ *dial var of* ANY

**onych-** *or* **onycho-** *comb form* [L *onych-*, fr. Gk *onych-*, *onycho-*, fr. *onych-*, *onyx* — more at ONYX] **:** nail of the finger or toe ⟨*onych*auxis⟩ **:** claw ⟨*Onycho*phora⟩

**on·y·cha** \ˈänəkə\ *n* -s [ME, fr. LL, fr. Gk, acc. of *onych-*, *onyx* aromatic substance, onyx, nail of the finger or toe] **:** an ingredient of the incense anciently used in some religious ceremonies of the Jews

**on·ych·aux·is** \ˌänəˈkȯksəs\ *n, pl* **onychauxes** [NL, fr. *onych-* + *-auxis* (fr. Gk *auxein* to increase) — more at EKE] **:** overgrowth of the nails

**onych·ia** \ōˈnikēə\ *n* -s [NL, fr. *onych-* + *-ia*] **:** inflammation of the matrix of the nail leading to suppuration and loss of the nail

**-onychia** \"\ *n comb form* -s [NL, fr. *onych-* + *-ia*] **:** condition of the nails of the fingers or toes ⟨leuk*onychia*⟩

**on·y·chi·tis** \ˌänəˈkīdəs\ *n, pl* **ony·chit·i·des** \-kidəˌdēz\ [NL, fr. *onych-* + *-itis*] **:** ONYCHIA

**onych·i·um** \ōˈnikēəm\ *n, pl* **onych·ia** \-ēə\ [NL, fr. Gk *onychion* little claw, dim. of *onych-*, *onyx* nail of the finger or toe, claw] **:** EMPODIUM

**-onychium** \"\ *n comb form* -s [NL, fr. Gk *onychion* little claw] **:** fingernail **:** toenail **:** region of the fingernail or toenail ⟨*eponychium*⟩ ⟨*hyponychium*⟩

**on·y·chog·a·le** \ˌänəˈkägə(ˌ)lē\ *syn of* ONYCHOGALEA

**on·y·cho·ga·lea** \ˌänəkōˈgālēə\ *n, cap* [NL, fr. *onych-* + Gk *galē*, *galeē* weasel, ferret — more at GALEA] **:** a genus of marsupials comprising the nail-tailed wallaby

**on·y·cho·gryposis** \ˌänəkō+\ *n* [NL, fr. *onych-* + *gryposis*] **:** an abnormal state of the nails (as in acromegaly) characterized by marked hypertrophy and increased curvature

**on·y·choid** \ˈänəˌkȯid\ *adj* [*onych-* + *-oid*] **:** resembling a fingernail in shape or texture

**on·y·chol·y·sis** \ˌänəˈkäləsəs\ *n* [NL, fr. *onych-* + *-lysis*] **:** a loosening of a nail from the nail bed beginning at the free edge and proceeding to the root

**on·y·cho·ma·de·sis** \ˌänəkōməˈdēsəs\ *n* -ES [NL, fr. *onych-* + Gk *madēsis* loss of hair, fr. *madan* to be bald, be moist; akin to L *madēre* to be wet — more at MEAT] **:** loosening and shedding of the nails

**on·y·cho·mycosis** \ˌänəkō+\ *n* [NL, fr. *onych-* + *mycosis*] **:** a fungous disease of the nails

**onych·o·mys** \ōˈnikəməs\ *n, cap* [NL, fr. *onych-* + *-mys*] **:** a genus of rodents (family Cricetidae) comprising the No. American grasshopper mice

**on·y·cho·pha·gia** \ˌänəkōˈfāj(ē)ə\ *n* -s [NL, fr. *onych-* + *-phagia*] **:** NAIL-BITING

**on·y·choph·a·gy** \ˌänəˈkäfəjē\ *n* -ES [NL *onychophagia*, fr. *onych-* + *-phagia* -phagy] **:** NAIL-BITING

**on·y·choph·o·ra** \ˌänəˈkäfərə\ *n pl, cap* [NL, fr. *onych-* + *-phora*] **:** a class of Arthropoda or an independent phylum comprising small elongated velvety-skinned terrestrial invertebrate animals of damp dark habitats in warm regions that are in some respects intermediate between annelid worms and typical arthropods, that have an unsegmented vermiform body, numerous pairs of short unsegmented legs with terminal bifid claws, and a head bearing a pair of segmented antennae, a pair of oral papillae on which slime glands open, a pair of simple eyes, and a pair of jaws resembling blades, that possess a hemocoel as a body cavity, and that breathe by means of tracheae and excrete by means of nephridia — **on·y·choph·oran**

\ˌ==ˌ==rən\ *adj or n* — **on·ycho·phore** \ōˈnikəˌfō(ə)r, ˈänəkō,-\ *n* -s — **on·y·choph·o·rous** \ˌänəˈkäfərəs\ *adj*

**on·y·chor·rhex·is** \ˌänəkəˈreksəs\ *n, pl* **onychorrhexes** [NL, fr. *onych-* + *-rrhexis*] **:** longitudinal ridging and splitting of the finger and toe nails

**on·y·cho·schiz·ia** \ˌänəkōˈskitsēə, -izēə\ *n* -s [NL, fr. *onych-* + *-schizia* (fr. Gk *schizein* to split) — more at SCHISM] **:** a condition of the nails marked by lamination in two or more layers and by scaling away in thin flakes

**on·y·cho·sis** \ˌänəˈkōsəs\ *n, pl* **onycho·ses** \-ōˌsēz\ [NL, fr. *onych-* + *-osis*] **:** a disease of the nails

**on–year** \ˈ=ˌ=\ *n* **:** a year marked by the regular or expected or full occurrence of something ⟨looked forward to a good yield from his biennial fruit trees during their *on-year*⟩

**onyg·e·na** \ōˈnijənə\ *n, cap* [NL, irreg. fr. Gk *onyx* nail of the finger or toe, claw, hoof + NL *-gena* (fr. Gk *-genēs* born) — more at -GEN] **:** a genus (the type of the family Onygenaceae) of ascomycetous fungi that have stalked capitate ascocarps and occur typically on decaying animal materials (as hooves or feathers)

**-o·nym** \əˌnim\ *n comb form* -s [ME *-onyme*, fr. L *-onymum*, fr. Gk *-ōnymon*, fr. neut. of *-ōnymos*, adj. comb. form (as in *homōnymos* having the same name) — more at HOMONYMOUS] **:** name **:** word ⟨all*onym*⟩ ⟨hyp*onym*⟩

**on·y·mous** \ˈänəməs\ *adj* [back-formation fr. *anonymous*] **:** bearing a name; *esp* **:** giving or bearing the author's name ⟨an ~ article in a magazine⟩ — opposed to *anonymous* — **on·y·mous·ly** *adv*

**-on·y·my** \ˈänəmē, -mi\ *n comb form* -ES [L *-onymia*, fr. Gk *-ōnymia*, fr. *-ōnymos* (as in *homōnymos*) + *-ia* -y] **1 :** kind of name or word **:** kind or set of names or words ⟨hydr*onymy*⟩ **2 :** study of a (specified) kind of names or words ⟨anthrop*onymy*⟩

**¹onyx** \ˈäniks, -nēks *sometimes* ˈōn-\ *n* -ES [ME *onix, oniche*, fr. OF & L; OF *onix, oniche*, fr. L *onych-, onyx*, fr. Gk, nail of the finger or toe, claw, onyx — more at NAIL] **1 a :** a chalcedony that has straight parallel alternating bands of color (as white and black or white and brown) and that is used esp. in making cameos — compare SARDONYX **b :** BLACK ONYX **2** *or* **onyx marble :** ALABASTER 1b

**²onyx** \"\ *adj* **:** of the color jet black ⟨the ~ night sky —Flora Lewis⟩ ⟨~ days of the depression —Maurice Zolotow⟩

**-onyx** \ˌäniks, ˌōniks, ᵊniks, -nēks\ *n comb form* [NL, fr. Gk *onych-, onyx* nail of the finger or toe, claw] **:** one having (such) nails or claws — chiefly in generic names of animals ⟨Cole*onyx*⟩

**onyx·is** \ōˈniksəs\ *n* -ES [NL, irreg. fr. Gk *onych-, onyx*] **:** an ingrowing of the nail

**on·za** \ˈōnzə, -n(ˌ)sä, -n(ˌ)thä\ *n* -s [Sp, lit., ounce, fr. L *uncia* ounce, twelfth part — more at OUNCE] **:** an old Spanish gold doubloon

**oo** \ˈōˌō\ *n* -s [Hawaiian *ʻōʻō*] **:** an Hawaiian honey eater of the genus *Moho*; *esp* **:** a bird (*M. nobilis*) having yellow axillary tufts used in native featherwork after the extinction of the mamo until it too became extinct

**OO** *abbr* **1** order of **2** ordnance office; ordnance officer **3** or order

**oo-** — see O-

**o–o–a–a** \ˌōˈōˌäˌä, ˌōəˈ-\ *n* -s [Hawaiian *ʻōʻō-ʻāʻā*, fr. *ʻōʻō* oo + *ʻaʻa* dwarf] **:** a bird of the family Meliphagidae (*Moho braccatus*) confined to the island of Kauai

**oo·blast** \ˈōəˌblast\ *n* [*o-* + *-blast*] **1 :** a cellular precursor of an ovum **2 :** a tube by which the diploid nucleus resulting from fertilization in red algae is carried to an auxiliary cell — called also *connecting filament*

**oo·blas·te·ma filament** \ˌōəˌblaˈstēmə-\ *n* [NL *ooblastema* fertilized ovum, fr. *o-* + *blastema*] **:** OOBLAST 2

**oo·capt** \ˈōəˌkapt\ *n* -s [*o-* + *-capt*, fr. Gk *kaptein* to gulp down — more at HEAVE] **:** a muscular enlargement of the beginning of the oviduct of various worms that serves to draw the egg into the oviduct

**oo·cyesis** \ˌōə +\ *n, pl* **oocyeses** [NL, fr. *o-* + *cyesis*] **:** extrauterine pregnancy in an ovary

**oo·cyst** \ˈōəˌsist\ *n* [ISV *o-* + *-cyst*] **:** ZYGOTE; *specif* **:** a sporozoan zygote undergoing sporogenous development

**oo·cys·ta·ce·ae** \ˌōəsəˈstāsēˌē\ *n pl, cap* [NL, fr. *Oocystis*, type genus (fr. *o-* + *-cystis*) + *-aceae*] **:** a family of free-floating green algae (order Chlorococcales) which are unicellular or colonial with an indefinite number of cells and in which the cells are often retained within the distended gelatinized wall of the old mother cell — **oo·cys·ta·ceous** \ˌōəsəˈstāshəs\ *adj*

**oo·cyte** \ˈōəˌsīt\ *n* -s [ISV *o-* + *-cyte*] **:** an egg before maturation **:** a female gametocyte or macrogametocyte

**OOD** *abbr* officer of the deck

**oo·din·i·um** \ˌōəˈdinēəm\ *n, cap* [NL, fr. *o-* + *Dinoflagellata* + *-ium*] **:** a genus of parasitic dinoflagellates occurring esp. on marine and freshwater fish

**oo·dles** \ˈüdᵊlz\ *also* **oo·dlins** \ˈüdlənz\ *n pl but sometimes sing in constr* [*oodles* perh. alter. of *huddles*, pl. of ²*huddle*; *oodlins* perh. alter. of *huddlings*, pl. of *huddling*, fr. gerund of ¹*huddle*] **:** a great quantity **:** ABUNDANCE, HEAP, LOT ⟨~ of money⟩ ⟨jolly picnics and ~ of good food —E.J.Fitzgerald⟩ ⟨~ of eyelet cottons are blossoming out all over the place this spring —*Christian Science Monitor*⟩

**ooe·cial** \(ˈ)ōˈēsh(ē)əl\ *adj* **:** of or relating to an ooecium

**ooe·ci·um** \(ˈ)ōˈēs(h)ēəm\ *n, pl* **ooe·cia** \-ēə\ [NL, fr. *o-* + *oecium*] **:** an ovicell of a bryozoan

**oof** *var of* OUF

**oof·tish** \ˈüftish\ *or* **oof** *n, pl* **ooftishes** *or* **oofs** [*ooftish* fr. Yiddish *uf tish* on (the) table; *oof* short for *ooftish*] *slang* **:** MONEY

**oofy** \ˈüfi\ *adj* -ER/-EST [*oof* + *-y*] *slang* **:** RICH, WEALTHY

**oo gage** \ˌdəbəlˈō-\ *n, usu cap both Os* [so called fr. its being smaller than O gage] **:** a gage of track in model railroading in which the rails are approximately ¾ inch apart

**oo·gamete** \ˌōə+\ *n* [*o-* + *gamete*] **:** a female gamete; *specif* **:** a relatively large nonmotile gamete containing reserve material for use by the developing zygote that results when a sperm fuses with such a gamete

**oog·a·mous** \(ˈ)ōˈägəməs\ *adj* [*o-* + *-gamous*] **1** *of sexual reproduction* **:** characterized by fusion of a small actively motile male gamete and a large immobile female gamete — compare ANISOGAMOUS, HETEROGAMOUS, ISOGAMOUS **2 :** having oogamous reproduction — **oog·a·my** \ōˈägəmē\ *n* -ES

**oo·genesis** \ˌōə+\ *n* [NL, fr. *o-* + *genesis*] **:** formation and maturation of the egg

**oo·genetic** \"+\ *adj* [*o-* + *genetic*] **:** of or relating to oogenesis

**oog·e·ny** \ōˈäjənē\ *n* -ES [*o-* + *-geny*] **:** OOGENESIS

**oo·glea** *or* **oo·gloea** \ˌōəˈglēə\ *n* -s [NL *o-* + *gloea*] **:** EGG CEMENT

**oo·go·ni·al** \ˌōəˈgōnēəl\ *adj* **:** of or relating to an oogonium

**oo·go·ni·um** \ˌōəˈgōnēəm\ *n* [NL, fr. *o-* + *gonium*] **1 :** the female sexual organ in oogamous algae and fungi that corresponds to the archegonium of ferns and mosses but is unicellular in structure and lacks differentiation into neck and venter and that contains one or more eggs which after fertilization develop into oospores — compare ANTHERIDIUM **2 :** one of the descendants of a primordial germ cell that give rise to oocytes

**¹ooid** \ˈōˌōid\ *or* **ooi·dal** \(ˈ)ōˈōidᵊl\ *adj* [Gk *ōioeidēs*, fr. *ōi-* o- + *-eidēs* -oid] **:** shaped like an egg

**²ooid** \"\ *n* -s [¹*ooid*] **:** one of the individual spherical concretionary bodies that characterize an oolite

**ook** *var of* OUK

**oo·kinesis** \ˌōə+\ *n, pl* **ookineses** [NL, fr. *o-* + *-kinesis*] **:** the nuclear phenomenon incidental to maturation and fertilization of an egg

**oo·ki·nete** \ˌōəˈkīˌnēt, -ˌkəˈnēt, -ˌkīˈnēt\ *n* -s [*o-* + Gk *kinētos* moving — more at KINETIC] **:** a motile zygote in various protozoans (as the malaria parasite)

**oo·kinetic** \"+\ *adj* **:** of or relating to ookinesis

**oolachan** *var of* EULACHON

**oo·lem·ma** \ˌōəˈlemə\ *n* -s [NL, fr. *o-* + Gk *lemma* rind, husk — more at LEMMA] **:** a membrane surrounding an egg: **a :** ZONA PELLUCIDA **b :** VITELLINE MEMBRANE

**oo·lite** \ˈōəˌlīt\ *n* -s [prob. fr. F *oolithe* (fr. *o-* + *-lithe* -lite), trans. of G *rogenstein*, lit., roe stone] **:** a rock consisting of small round grains that resemble the roe of fish, are cemented together, and consist of small concretions which usu. are of calcium carbonate forming a variety of limestone but sometimes are of silica or iron oxide — **oo·lit·ic** \ˌōəˈlidik\ *adj*

**oolitic limestone** *n* **:** calcareous oolite quarried chiefly for building purposes

**oo·log·i·cal** \ˌōəˈläjəkəl\ *also* **oo·log·ic** \-jik\ *adj* **:** of or relating to oology — **oo·log·i·cal·ly** \-jək(ə)lē\ *adv*

**ool·o·gist** \ōˈäləjəst\ *n* -s **1 :** one specializing in oology **2 :** a collector of birds' eggs

**ool·o·gize** \-ˌjīz\ *vi* -ED/-ING/-S **1 :** to study oology **2 :** to hunt for birds' nests and eggs

**ool·o·gy** \-jē\ *n* -ES [*o-* + *-logy*] **:** a branch of zoology that treats of eggs and esp. of the collection of birds' eggs and the study of their shape and coloration

**oo·long** \ˈüˌlȯŋ *also* -läŋ\ *n* -s [Chin *wu¹ lung²*, lit., black dragon, fr. *wu¹* black + *lung²* dragon] **:** a tea that is partially fermented before drying and combines the characteristics of black and green teas

**oom·an** \ˈümən\ *dial var of* WOMAN

**oo·man·cy** \ˈōəˌman(t)sē\ *also* **oo·man·tia** \ˌōəˈmantēə\ *n, pl* **oomancies** *also* **oomantias** [*oomancy* fr. *o-* + *-mancy*; *oomantia*, NL, fr. *o-* + *-mantia* -mancy] **:** divination by means of eggs

**oom·e·ter** \ōˈäməd·ə(r)\ *n* [*o-* + *-meter*] **:** an instrument for measuring eggs — **oo·met·ric** \ˌōəˈmetrik\ *adj* — **oom·e·try** \ōˈäməˌtrē\ *n* -ES

**oomiak** *also* **oomiack** *var of* UMIAK

**oom·pah** \ˈüm(ˌ)pä, ˈum-\ *n* -s [imit.] **:** an insistent or monotonous bass accompaniment in a band or orchestra

**oomph** \ˈüm(p)f\ *n* -s [prob. imit. of an appreciative *mm* uttered by a man at the sight of an attractive woman] **1 :** personal charm or magnetism **:** ATTRACTIVENESS, GLAMOUR ⟨a magician lends all his own ~ to the spell he is making —W.W.Howells⟩ ⟨the singer with the extra special and highly individual ~ in his voice —Margaret Hinxman⟩ ⟨had a lot of friends, but very little political ~ —Volta Torrey⟩ ⟨type of book . . . may not possess that curious ~ which spells "Sales Appeal" —R.E.Danielson⟩ **2 :** SEX APPEAL ⟨a girl liberally endowed with ~ —P.G.Wodehouse⟩ **3 :** SPIRIT, VITALITY, ENTHUSIASM, ANIMATION ⟨sings with her accustomed ~ two arias —Roland Gelatt⟩ ⟨lack of meat is sapping British ~ needed to keep the export drive in high gear —*Wall Street Jour.*⟩

**oo·mycete** \ˌōə+\ *n* -s [NL *Oomycetes*] **:** a fungus of the subclass Oomycetes

**oo·my·ce·tes** \ˌōəˌmīˈsēdˌēz\ *n pl, cap* [NL, fr. *o-* + *-mycetes*] **:** a subclass of parasitic or saprophytic fungi (class Phycomycetes) that includes water molds, white rusts, and downy mildews and that is distinguished from the Zygomycetes by having the gametangia usu. differentiated into antheridia and oogonia and by producing oospores as a result of the sexual process — **oo·my·ce·tous** \-d·əs\ *adj*

**oo·my·ceti·dae** \ˌōəˌmīˈsēd·əˌdē, -sed-\ [NL, fr. *Oomycetes* + *-idae*] *syn of* OOMYCETES

**¹oon** \ˈün\ *dial Brit var of* OVEN

**²oon** \"\ *dial Brit var of* ONE

**oo·nop·i·dae** \ˌōəˈnäpəˌdē\ *n pl, cap* [NL, fr. *Oonops*, type genus (irreg. fr. Gk *ōion* egg + NL *-ops*) + *-idae* — more at EGG] **:** a family of small hunting spiders (suborder Dipneumonomorphae) having six eyes or none and six spinnerets

**oons** \ˈünz\ *interj* [alter. of *wounds*, fr. pl. of *wound*, n.] — used as a mild oath

**¹oont** \ˈünt\ *dial Eng var of* WANT

**²oont** \"\ *n* -s [Hindi *ūṭ*, fr. Skt *uṣṭra*] *India* **:** CAMEL

**¹oop** \ˈüp\ *dial var of* UP

**²oop** \ˈüp\ *vt* -ED/-ING/-S [origin unknown] *Scot* **:** BIND, UNITE

**oo·pak** *also* **oo·pack** \ˈüˌpak\ *n* -s [fr. *Hupeh*, province in east central China] **:** any of several black teas grown in the Hupeh province of China

**ooph·a·gous** \(ˈ)ōˈäfəgəs\ *adj* [*o-* + *-phagous*] **:** living or feeding on eggs — used of insects or reptiles

**oophor-** *or* **oophoro-** *comb form* [NL *oophoron*] **:** ovary **:** ovarian ⟨*oophor*ectomy⟩ ⟨*oophoro*tomy⟩

**oo·phore** \ˈōəˌfō(ə)r\ *n* -s [*o-* + *-phore*] **:** OOPHYTE — **oo·pho·ric** \ˌōəˈfōrik\ *adj*

**oo·pho·rec·to·mize** \ˌōəfəˈrektəˌmīz\ *vt* -ED/-ING/-S [*oophorectomy* + *-ize*] **:** OVARIECTOMIZE

**oo·pho·rec·to·my** \-ˌmē\ *n* -ES [ISV *oophor-* + *-ectomy*] **:** OVARIECTOMY

**oo·pho·ri·tis** \ˌōəfəˈrīd·əs\ *n* -ES [NL, fr. *oophor-* + *-itis*] **:** inflammation of one or both ovaries **:** OVARITIS

**ooph·o·ron** \ōˈäfəˌrän\ *n* -s [NL, fr. *o-* + Gk *-phoron* -phore] **:** OVARY

**oo·phyte** \ˈōəˌfīt\ *n* -s [*o-* + *-phyte*] **:** the sexual generation in the life cycle of an archegoniate plant (as a moss, fern, liverwort) **:** the stage in which sexual organs are developed — compare GAMETOPHYTE, SPOROPHYTE — **oo·phyt·ic** \ˌōəˈfidik\ *adj*

**oo·plasm** \ˈōəˌplazəm\ *n* -s [*o-* + *-plasm*] **:** the cytoplasm of an egg — **oo·plas·mic** \ˌōəˈplazmik\ *adj*

**oo·plast** \ˈōəˌplast\ *n* -s [*o-* + *-plast*] **:** OOSPHERE

**oo·pod** \ˈōəˌpäd\ *n, pl* **oop·o·da** \ōˈäpədə\ [*o-* + *pod-*] **:** any of the pieces composing the ovipositor or sting of an insect — **oop·o·dal** \(ˈ)ōˈäpədᵊl\ *adj*

**oo·porphyrin** \ˌōə+\ *n* [ISV *o-* + *porphyrin*] **:** a pale brown pigment in eggshells (as of the domestic hen)

**oops** \ˈ(w)u̇(ə)p(s) *also* ˈwə(ˌ)p(s) *or* ˈ(w)üp(s) *or* ˈ(w)ōp\ *interj* [origin unknown] — used typically to express mild apology, surprise, or dismay (as when one drops an object or makes a faux pas)

**oo·pu·hue** \ˌōˌōpəˈhüē\ *n* -s [Hawaiian *ʻoʻopu-hue*, fr. *ʻoʻopu* fish + *hue* gourd] *Hawaii* **:** GLOBEFISH

**oor** \(ˈ)ür\ *chiefly Scot var of* OUR

**oo·ra·li** *or* **u·ra·li** \üˈrälē\ *n* -s [Carib *urali, urari, kurari*] **:** CURARE

**oorial** *var of* URIAL

**oorie** *var of* OURIE

**oo·scope** \ˈōəˌskōp\ *n* [*o-* + *-scope*] **:** an instrument for viewing the interior of an egg

**oos·co·py** \ōˈäskəpē\ *n* -ES [*o-* + *-scopy*] **:** use of an ooscope; *also* **:** OOMANCY

**oo·some** \ˈōəˌsōm\ *n* -s [ISV *o-* + *-some*; orig. formed as It *oosoma*] **:** a disk-shaped mass of protoplasm near the posterior pole of an insect egg

**oo·sorp·tion** \ˌōəˈsȯrpshən\ *n* -s [*o-* + *resorption*] **:** resorption of ripe or developing eggs that constitutes a physiological response of a parasitic hymenopteran to the absence of the appropriate host — **oo·sorp·tive** \-ptiv\ *adj*

**oo·sperm** \ˈōəˌspərm\ *n* [*o-* + *sperm*] **:** a fertilized egg **:** ZYGOTE, OOSPORE

**oo·sphere** \-ˌsfi(ə)r\ *n* [ISV *o-* + *sphere*] **:** an unfertilized egg **:** a female gamete that is fully mature and ready for fertilization **:** OVUM 1 a — used esp. of lower plants

**oos·po·ra** \ōˈäspərə\ *n, cap* [NL, fr. *o-* + *-spora*] **:** a genus of imperfect fungi (order Moniliales) comprising parasitic and saprophytic forms with short hyphae, sparse mycelium, and usu. globose conidia — see ACHORION; compare OIDIUM

**oo·spore** \ˈōəˌspō(ə)r\ *n* [ISV *o-* + *spore*] **:** ZYGOTE; *esp* **:** a resting spore produced by heterogamous fertilization that ultimately produces the sporophytic generation of a plant — compare ZYGOSPORE — **oo·spo·ric** \ˌōəˈspōrik\ *adj* — **oospo·rous** \ˌōəˈspōrəs, (ˈ)ōˈäspər-\ *adj*

**oo·spor·if·er·ous** \ˌōəˌspōˈrif(ə)rəs\ *adj* [*oospore* + *-iferous*] **:** bearing or producing oospores

**oos·te·gite** \ōˈästəˌjīt\ *n* -s [*o-* + *-stegite*] **:** a platelike expansion of the basal segment of a thoracic appendage in many crustaceans that helps to form a receptacle for the eggs — **oos·te·git·ic** \(ˌ)ōˌästəˈjid·ik\ *adj*

**oos·te·go·pod** \ōˈästəgōˌpäd\ *n* -s [*oostegite* + *-o-* + *-pod*] **:** a modified thoracic leg bearing an oostegite in a crustacean

**oot** \ˈüt\ *chiefly Scot var of* OUT

**oo·the·ca** \ˌōəˈthēkə\ *n, pl* **oothe·cae** \-ē(ˌ)sē\ [NL, fr. *o-* + *-theca*] **:** a firm-walled and distinctive egg case (as of many mollusks or of a cockroach) — **oo·the·cal** \ˌōəˈthēkəl\ *adj*

**oo·tid** \ˈōəˌtid\ *n* -s [irreg. (influenced by *spermatid*) fr. *o-* + *-id*] **:** an egg cell after meiosis — compare SPERMATID

**oo·type** \ˈōəˌtīp\ *n* -s [*o-* + *-type*] **:** the part of the oviduct of most flatworms in which the eggs are furnished with a shell

**¹ooze** \ˈüz\ *n* -s [ME *wose*, fr. OE *wāse* mud, mire; akin to ON *veisa* slime, stagnant water, L *virus* slimy liquid, poison — more at VIRUS] **1 :** a soft deposit on the bottom of a body of water ⟨to tread the ~ of the salt deep —Shak.⟩: as **a :** soft mud or slime typically in the bed of a river or estuary **:** earth so wet as to flow gently or easily yield to pressure **b :** a soft deposit that resembles mud, covers large areas of the ocean bottom, and is composed largely or mainly of the shells or other hard parts of minute organisms (as foraminiferans, radiolarians, and diatoms) **2 :** a stretch or piece of muddy ground **:** a marsh or bog that results from the flow of a spring, stream, or brooklet **3** *archaic* **:** SEAWEED

**²ooze** \"\ *n* -s [ME *wose*, fr. OE *wōs*] **1 :** JUICE, SAP ⟨dyed . . . threads in the ~ she wrung from herbs —George McMillan⟩ **2 a :** a decoction of vegetable material used for tanning leather **:** tanning liquor **b :** OOZE LEATHER **3 :** the action of oozing **:** gentle flow ⟨bleeding in the form of a profuse ~ from surgical wounds —*Anesthesia Digest*⟩ **4 :** something that oozes **:** a slow stream

**³ooze** \"\ *vb* -ED/-ING/-S [ME *wosen*, fr. *wose* ooze (juice)] *vi* **1 :** to pass slowly or in small amounts through the pores or small openings of a body **:** flow slowly through interstices ⟨blood appears to have *oozed* from a varicose vein —Morris Fishbein⟩ ⟨water *oozed* from the ground —Harry Gilroy⟩ ⟨sweet potatoes baked in the peeling until the juice ~s out —*Amer. Guide Series: N.C.*⟩ ⟨a weak tear *oozed* from each eye —Agnes S. Turnbull⟩ **2 a :** to pass through or as if through small openings or crevices ⟨we could hear the wind . . . ~ through the briar thickets —J.H.Stuart⟩ ⟨a voice ~s from a slit of a door —Francis Aldor⟩ ⟨the clatter of typewriters *oozed* from every transom —Herbert Hoover⟩ **b :** to move slowly or imperceptibly ⟨what they skim off ~s across the floor —R.A.W.Hughes⟩ ⟨the crowd began to ~ forward —Bruce Marshall⟩ **3 a :** to exude moisture; *specif* **:** to exude blood **b :** to exude something in a way suggestive of the emitting of moisture — usu. used with *with* ⟨a writing that ~s with hostility⟩ ⟨a person *oozing* with good cheer⟩ **4 :** to escape slowly and quietly — often used with *out* or *away* ⟨courage *oozing* out at his finger tips —A.T.Weaver⟩ ⟨satisfaction would ~ away —*Times Lit. Supp.*⟩ ⟨failure *oozed* out of the very pores of his skin —Ellen Glasgow⟩ ~ *vt* **1 :** to emit or give out slowly (as air or liquid) ⟨thick steaks *oozing* blood —Marcia Davenport⟩ **2 :** to exude or give off in a way suggestive of the emitting of moisture ⟨popular songs which ~ optimism —J.T.Farrell⟩ ⟨his voice *oozing* sarcasm —Walter Goodman⟩ ⟨*oozing* charm from every pore —*Irish Digest*⟩ **syn** see EMIT

**ooze leather** *n* [²*ooze*] **:** leather usu. made from calfskins by the vegetable tanning process and having a soft sueded finish on the flesh side

**oo·zooid** \ˌōə+\ *n* -s [*o-* + *zooid*] **:** a sexually produced compound tunicate larva that by budding gives rise to blastozooids

**oozy** \ˈüzē, -zi\ *adj* -ER/-EST [ME *wosie*, fr. *wose* ooze, mud + *-ie* -y] **1 :** containing or composed of ooze **:** resembling ooze **:** MUDDY, MIRY **2** [³*ooze* + *-y*] **:** exuding moisture **:** damp with exuded or deposited moisture **:** SLIMY

**op** *abbr* **1** opera **2** operation; operative; operator **3** opposite **4** opus

**OP** *abbr* **1** observation plane **2** observation post **3** old prices **4** open policy **5** opposite prompt; opposite prompter **6** out of print **7** outpost **8** overprint **9** overproof

**opa·cate** \ōˈpāˌkāt, ˈōpəˌk-\ *vt* -ED/-ING/-S [L *opacatus*, past part. of *opacare* to shade, darken, fr. *opacus* shaded, dark — more at OPAQUE] **:** to make opaque **:** DARKEN, DIM

**opaci·fi·ca·tion** \ōˌpasəfəˈkāshən, ōˌpakə-\ *n* -s [fr. *opacify*, after such pairs as E *amplify*: *amplification*] **:** an act or the process of becoming or rendering opaque ⟨~ of the cornea following ulceration⟩ ⟨~ of the bile passages for roentgenographic examination⟩

**opaci·fi·er** \=ˈ==ˌfī(ə)r\ *n* -s **:** a constituent or additive (as of an enamel, a paint, a glass) that tends to opacify the system of which it is a part

**opaci·fy** \-ˌfī\ *vb* -ED/-ING/-ES [ISV *opaci-* (fr. L *opacus*) + *-fy*] *vt* **:** to cause (as glass or enamel) to become opaque ~ *vi* **:** to become opaque ⟨~*ing* gradually in the heat of the furnace⟩

**opa·cim·e·ter** \ˌōpəˈsiməd·ə(r)\ *n* [ISV *opaci-* + *-meter*] **:** an instrument (as a turbidimeter or a nephelometer) for measuring opacity

**opac·i·ty** \ōˈpasəd·ē, -sətē, -i\ *n* -ES [F *opacité*, fr. L *opacitat-, opacitas*, fr. *opacus* shaded, dark + *-itat-, -itas* -ity] **1 :** the quality or state or an instance of being shaded or obscure **:** DARKNESS, OBSCURITY **2 a :** the quality or state of a body that renders it impervious to the rays of light **:** lack of transparency or translucency **b :** degree of nontransparency ⟨titanium dioxide has the greatest ~ and tinctorial strength of all white pigments —Andries Voet⟩ **c :** the property of a photographic image that causes partial absorption of rays of light **d :** the capacity of matter to obstruct by absorption or reflection the transmission of forms of radiant energy in addition to light (as radio waves, infrared radiation, sound) ⟨the ~ to ultrasound of porous media —A.B.Wood⟩; *also* **:** a measure of this capacity **:** the reciprocal of the transmissivity **3 a :** obscurity of sense **:** lack of clearness **:** UNINTELLIGIBLENESS **b :** mental dimness or obtuseness **:** DULLNESS **4 :** an opaque spot on a normally transparent structure (as the cornea or lens of the eye)

**opa·cous** \ōˈpākəs\ *adj* [L *opacus*] *archaic* **:** OPAQUE

**opah** \ˈōpə\ *n* -s [Ibo *úbà*] **:** a large marine elliptical fish (*Lampris regius* syn. *L. luna*) that is nearly cosmopolitan in warm and temperate seas and that has brilliant colors and rich oily red flesh

**opa·ka·pa·ka** \ˌōpəkəˈpäkə\ *n* -s [Hawaiian *ʻōpakapaka*] **:** any of several brightly colored chiefly Hawaiian snappers of the genus *Pristipomoides* including some that are important food fishes

**opal** \ˈōpəl\ *n* -s *often attrib* [L *opalus*, fr. Skt *upala* stone, jewel, upper millstone; perh. akin to Skt *upari* over — more at OVER] **1 :** a mineral $SiO_2 \cdot nH_2O$ that is a hydrated amorphous silica softer and less dense than quartz and typically with definite and often marked iridescent play of colors — see BLACK OPAL, HARLEQUIN OPAL **2 a :** OPAL GLASS **b :** OPALINE

**opal blue** *n* **1 :** a grayish blue that is redder and paler than electric, greener and paler than copenhagen, and redder and lighter than Gobelin **2 :** NATIONAL BLUE

**opal·esce** \ˌōpəˈles\ *vi* -ED/-ING/-S [back-formation fr. *opalescence* & *opalescent*] **:** to emit or exhibit a play of colors like those of an opal

**opal·es·cence** \ˌōpəˈlesᵊn(t)s\ *n* -s [*opal* + *-escence*] **:** the quality or state of being opalescent ⟨that mother-of-pearl ~ which shimmers in the hollowness of certain seashells —J.C. Powys⟩

**opal·es·cent** \ˌōpəˈlesᵊnt\ *adj* [*opal* + *-escent*] **1 :** reflecting an iridescent light **:** having a milky iridescence **2 :** having a colored smooth surface that gives the effect of cloudiness and diffusion due to the intentional presence of fissures, striae, and bubbles ⟨~ glass⟩

**opal·es·cent·ly** *adv* **:** as if opalescent **:** so as to appear opalescent

**opal·esque** \ˌōpəˈlesk\ *adj* [*opal* + *-esque*] **:** suggesting opal **:** OPALESCENT

**opaleye** \ˈ==ˌ=\ *n* [*opal* + *eye*] **:** any of several fishes of the family Girellidae; *esp* **:** a small green shorefish (*Girella nigricans*) of the California coast that feeds chiefly on seaweeds and is a minor food fish — called also *greenfish*

**opal glass** *n* **:** a translucent or opaque glass; *esp* **:** a milky white glass that is prepared by adding impurities (as fluorine compounds) which disperse as crystallites within the matrix of glass and that is used esp. for ornamental pressed glass and for diffusing light without serious loss of lighting efficiency — compare MILK GLASS

**opal gray** *n* **:** a reddish gray that is duller and slightly yellower than evenglow and yellower and duller than mist gray

**opa·li·na** \ˌōpəˈlīnə, -lēnə\ *n, cap* [NL, fr. L *opalus* opal + NL *-ina*] **:** a genus (the type of the family Opalinidae) of large flattened multinucleate protociliates that are endozoic in the rectum of amphibians

**¹opal·ine** \ˈōpəˌlīn, -lēn\ *adj* [*opal* + *-ine*] **:** resembling opal esp. in appearance **:** OPALESCENT

**²opal·ine** \ˌōpəˈlēn\ *n* -s **1 :** any of several minerals related to or resembling opal **2 a :** a French decorative opalescent glassware developed in the late 18th century **b :** MILK GLASS **3 :** an opaline color or surface

**opaline green** *n* **:** a very light green

**¹opa·linid** \ˌōpəˈlīnəd, -lēn-,-lin-\ *adj* [NL *Opalinidae*, family of protociliates, fr. *Opalina*, type genus + *-idae*] **:** of or relating to the genus *Opalina* or the family Opalinidae

**²opalinid** \"\ *n* -s [NL *Opalinidae*] **:** PROTOCILIATE

**opal·iza·tion** \ˌōpələ'zāshən, -ˌlī'z-\ *n* -s **:** the process of opalizing

**opal·ize** \'ōpəˌlīz\ *vt* -ED/-ING/-S **1 :** to replace with or convert into opal ⟨*opalized* trunks of trees, most of them of prehistoric species —*Nat'l Geographic*⟩ **2 :** to make opalescent ⟨~ glass⟩

**opal lamp** *n* **:** an incandescent electric lamp with a bulb of opal glass

**opal matrix** *n* **:** a matrix of opal

**opal·oid** \'ōpəˌlȯid\ *adj* [*opal* + *-oid*] **:** milky and translucent **:** OPALINE

**¹opaque** \(')ō¦pāk\ *adj, sometimes* -ER/-EST [alter. (influenced by F *opaque*) of earlier *opake*, fr. L *opacus* shaded, dark, perh. fr. *op-*, *ob* to, before — more at EPI-] **1** *archaic* **:** lacking illumination **2 :** neither reflecting nor emitting light — not in current technical use **3 a :** impervious to the rays of visible light **:** not transparent or translucent ⟨his eyes were light, large, and bright, but it was that kind of brightness which belongs to an ~, and not to a transparent body —Anthony Trollope⟩ **b :** impervious to forms of radiant energy other than visible light (as infrared radiation or radio waves) ⟨organic compounds containing iodine or bromine are also ~ to roentgen rays —C.H.Thienes⟩ **4 a :** hard to understand, solve, or explain **:** not simple, clear, or lucid ⟨how ~ and incredible the past seems to us —L.P.Smith⟩ **b :** impervious to reason **:** STUPID, DULL, DENSE ⟨too ~ to recognize the insult⟩ **syn** see DARK

**²opaque** \"\ *n* -s **:** something that is opaque **:** an opaque medium or space: as **a :** an opaque paint or other preparation for blocking out portions of a photographic negative or print **b :** an opaque photographic print — contrasted with *transparency*

**³opaque** \"\ *vt* -ED/-ING/-S **1 :** to make opaque **2 :** to apply opaque to (as parts of a photographic negative or positive)

**opaque·ly** *adv* **:** in an opaque manner

**opaque·ness** \ō'pāknəs\ *n* -ES **:** the quality or state of being opaque

**opaque projector** *n* **:** a projector for projection by reflected light of an image of an opaque object or of a picture or other graphic matter on an opaque support

**opaqu·er** \ō'pākə(r)\ *n* -S **:** a worker who applies photographic opaque

**opa·ta** \ō'pädə\ *n, pl* **opata** *or* **opatas** *usu cap* [Pima, lit., hostile people] **1 a :** a Taracahitian people or group of peoples of the northeastern part of the state of Sonora, Mexico **b :** a member of such people or group of peoples **2 :** the language of the Opata people

**op cit** *abbr* opere citato; opus citatum

**¹ope** \'ōp\ *adj* [ME, alter. of ¹*open*] **:** OPEN

**²ope** \"\ *vb* -ED/-ING/-S [ME *open*, alter. of *openen* to open] **:** OPEN

**³ope** \"\ *n* -s [¹*ope*] **1** *archaic* **a :** APERTURE, OPENING **b :** OPPORTUNITY **2** *dial chiefly Eng* **:** a narrow covered passage between houses

**-ope** \ˌōp\ *n comb form* -s [F, fr. LL *-op-*, *-ops* having (such) eyes, fr. Gk *ōp-*, *ōps* eye, face — more at EYE] **:** one having eyes with a (specified) defect ⟨hypermetr*ope*⟩

**opeg·ra·pha** \ō'pegrəfə\ *n, cap* [NL, fr. Gk *opē* hole, opening (akin to Gk *ōp-*, *ōps*) + *graphē* writing, fr. *graphein* to write — more at CARVE] **:** a genus of crustaceous lichens occurring chiefly on bark and forming markings like writing or hieroglyphics

**opei·do·scope** \ō'pīdəˌskōp\ *n* [Gk *opa* (acc.) voice + *eidos* form + E *-scope* — more at VOICE, IDOL] **:** an instrument consisting essentially of a tube across one end of which is stretched a thin flexible membrane bearing a small mirror and used for exhibiting upon a screen by rays reflected from the mirror vibratory motions caused by sounds

**ope·let** \'ōplət\ *n* -S [¹*ope* + *-let*] **:** a bright-colored European actinian (*Anemonia sulcata*) with permanently expanded tentacles

**ope·lu** \'ōpəˌlü\ *n* -s [Hawaiian *'ōpelu*] **1** *Hawaii* **:** JAPANESE MACKEREL **2** *Hawaii* **:** a common Pacific mackerel scad (*Decapterus sanctae-helenae*) much used as bait

**¹open** \'ōpən, *esp before consonants* -pᵊm\ *adj* **opener** \-p(ə)nə(r)\ **openest** \-p(ə)nəst\ [ME, fr. OE; akin to OHG *offan* open, ON *opinn*; all fr. a prehistoric NGmc-WGmc past part. of a verb derived from the root of OE *ūp* up] **1 :** so arranged or governed as to permit ingress, egress, or passage: as **a :** having no enclosing or confining barrier **:** free from fences, boundaries, or other restrictive margins ⟨an ~ village⟩ ⟨the ~ moor⟩ **b** (1) **:** adjusted in a position that permits passage **:** not shut or fast ⟨an ~ door⟩ ⟨these ~ gates⟩ (2) **:** having a movable barrier so adjusted ⟨the house is ~⟩ **c** (1) **:** not stopped by a finger ⟨the four ~ strings of a violin⟩ (2) **:** unstopped by the hand or by a mute ⟨~ horn⟩ (3) **:** produced by an open string or on a wind instrument by the lip without the use of slides, valves, or keys ⟨~ tone or note⟩ (4) **:** having clarity and resonance unimpaired by undue tension or constriction of the throat ⟨an ~ vocal tone⟩ **2 a :** completely free from concealment **:** exposed to general or particular perception or knowledge ⟨now lay ~ all your plans⟩ ⟨an ~ ballot⟩ ⟨~ total war⟩ **b :** free from reserve or pretense **:** natural, forthright, and free **:** not concealing or intending to conceal one's thoughts or actions ⟨very ~ about his plans⟩ ⟨~ and uninhibited in speech⟩ ⟨a very ~ manner⟩ **3 a :** having no roof, lid, or other covering ⟨an ~ boat⟩ **b :** having no protective or concealing cover **:** BARE, NAKED ⟨~ wiring⟩ ⟨laying the arm ~ to the bone⟩ **c** (1) *obs, of the face* **:** UNCOVERED, UNABASHED (2) **:** not covered with wool or enshrouding hair ⟨a ewe with an ~ face⟩ **d :** lacking some immaterial protection **:** LIABLE, SUBJECT ⟨~ to infection⟩ ⟨~ to challenge⟩ **e** (1) **:** not covered, enclosed, or scabbed over ⟨an ~ lesion⟩ ⟨an ~ running ulcer⟩ (2) **:** not involving or encouraging a covering (as by bandages or overgrowth of tissue) or enclosure ⟨~ treatment of burns⟩ (3) **:** shedding the infective agent to the exterior ⟨~ tuberculosis⟩ **f** (1) **:** not completely enclosed by defining lines ⟨an ~ drawing⟩ (2) **:** not defined by a figure or outline — used in the phrase *open color* **g** (1) **:** lacking covers or parts that restrict ventilation **:** not enclosed ⟨an ~ motor⟩ (2) **:** FREE 13e **h :** using a plain language text in conjunction with code or cipher: as (1) **:** using a concealment cipher (2) **:** using a jargon code **4 a :** requiring no special status, identification, or permit for entry or participation **:** generally available or known ⟨this house is ~ to all that need help⟩ ⟨an ~ Communion service⟩ ⟨an ~ secret⟩ **b :** not restricted to a particular group or category of participants ⟨~ to the public⟩ ⟨~ bowling⟩ **c :** enterable by both amateur and professional contestants ⟨an ~ golf tournament⟩ **d :** enterable by competitors of different classes ⟨~ to dogs of all breeds⟩ **5 :** fit to be traveled over or through **:** presenting no serious obstacle to passage or view: as **a :** free from hampering obstructions ⟨an ~ stretch of road⟩ **b :** free from woods, buildings, or large rocks ⟨an ~ field⟩ ⟨~ country⟩ **c :** presenting no surface impediment (as ice) or underwater hazard (as shoals) to the passage of a boat **d** (1) **:** unobstructed by congestion ⟨~ sinuses⟩ (2) **:** not constipated ⟨~ bowels⟩ **e** (1) **:** relatively free from snow and cold ⟨~ winter⟩ (2) **:** not foggy or misty ⟨as the sun warmed the air patches of ~ water began to appear⟩ (3) **:** not frozen solid ⟨an ~ harbor⟩ **6 a** *obs* **:** lying or sailing in full view **b :** having a visible opening between ⟨steer so as to keep the two spires ~⟩ **7 a :** spread out **:** UNFOLDED **:** having the parts or surfaces laid back in an expanded position **:** not drawn together, folded, or contracted ⟨an ~ letter⟩ ⟨left the book ~⟩ ⟨an ~ rose⟩ **b :** removed from a carcass by splitting down the mid-ventral line and along the inner surfaces of each limb and cured and dressed flat ⟨an ~ hide⟩ **8 a** *obs* **:** uttered with the mouth open **b** (1) *of a vowel* **:** LOW 1a (5) (2) *of one of two vowels constituting a pair because similar in articulation or orthography or in both* **:** formed with the tongue in a lower position ⟨Italian has an ~ *e*⟩ (3) **:** characterized by moderate lip-rounding (4) *of a consonant* **:** formed with the articulating organs narrowed without contact or with loose contact (as \s\ or \k\) **:** CONTINUANT, SPIRANT, FRICATIVE — contrasted with *stopped* **9 a** (1) **:** available to use **:** ACCESSIBLE, SUITABLE, USABLE **:** free and unoccupied ⟨keep an hour ~ on Friday⟩ ⟨the invitation is still ~⟩ ⟨there are only two courses ~ to us⟩ (2) **:** not now pregnant ⟨an ~ heifer⟩ **b :** available for consideration or decision **:** adjustable according to the requirements of circumstances **:** not finally closed or determined ⟨an ~ question⟩ ⟨an ~ verdict⟩ **c :** kept available for future custom ⟨an ~ pattern⟩ ⟨~ stocks⟩ **d :** remaining available for use or filling until canceled ⟨an ~ order for four more⟩ **:** OPERATIVE **:** not terminated or liquidated **e :** legally available for hunting, fishing, and similar sports ⟨an ~ season on deer⟩ ⟨an ~ brook⟩ **f :** unoccupied and undefended by military forces and divested of any military installation and when so proclaimed and acknowledged immune under international law from enemy bombardment ⟨an ~ city⟩ **10 :** characterized by ready accessibility and usu. cooperative attitude: as **a :** generous in giving **b :** willing to hear and consider or to accept and deal with **:** RESPONSIVE ⟨~ to suggestion⟩ ⟨~ to an offer⟩ **c :** permitting the registration of a high-grade animal conforming to breed type as well as of an animal having both sire and dam registered ⟨an ~ studbook⟩ **d :** accessible to the influx of new factors (as new members and ideas or foreign goods) ⟨an ~ class system⟩ ⟨an ~ market⟩ **e :** tolerant of internal change (as by social mobility, reforms, and the development of new ideas, values, and customs) and permissive of diversity in social, religious, and political institutions ⟨an ~ society⟩ **11 :** having openings, interruptions, interstices, or spaces ⟨~ banks⟩ ⟨*open*-grained lumber⟩: as **a :** light, porous, and friable so as to be easily tilled and receptive to water infiltration ⟨~ soil⟩ **b :** sparsely distributed **:** SCATTERED ⟨~ population⟩ **c** (1) **:** having relatively wide spacing between words or lines ⟨~ type⟩ ⟨~ printed matter⟩ (2) **:** having each leaf separate and distinct from the others after the bolts are opened or trimmed off ⟨the ~ signatures of a book⟩ **d :** having the warp threads of a shed always divided into two sections and never coming together as one section **e :** having cambium between the xylem and phloem portions — used of a vascular bundle **f** (1) **:** widely apart — used of dancers or the position of their feet (2) **:** having the participants well separated — used of a dance or dance figure **g :** characterized by open-chain structure **h :** GRANULAR, HARD ⟨soap in an ~ condition⟩ — used in soap manufacturing **12 :** ready to operate **:** actively functioning **:** ACTIVE ⟨the store is ~ from 9 to 5⟩ ⟨an ~ microphone⟩ **13 a** (1) **:** characterized by lack of effective control or regulation of various commercial enterprises (as amusements) ⟨notorious as an ~ town⟩ (2) **:** not repressed by legal controls ⟨~ gambling⟩ **b :** using a minimum of physical restrictions and custodial restraints upon the freedom of movement of inmates ⟨an ~ prison⟩ **c :** not yielding to usu. controlling factors **:** free from checking or hampering restraints ⟨an ~ economy⟩ ⟨faced with ~ inflation⟩ **d :** relatively unguarded by opponents in a sports competition ⟨~ ice⟩ ⟨~ court⟩ **14** *of an expression in logic* **:** containing one or more free variables **15 :** not crossed ⟨an ~ pulley belt⟩ ⟨~ eccentric rods⟩ **16 :** characterized by a free development of chess pieces in front of the pawns **17 a :** having been opened by a first ante, bet, or bid ⟨an ~ pot in poker⟩ ⟨the bidding is ~⟩ **b** (1) **:** having cards properly exposed ⟨the dummy is the ~ hand⟩ (2) **:** played or to be played with cards exposed **c :** interrupted or incomplete by a break in card sequence ⟨an ~ straight⟩ **18 a** *of punctuation* **:** characterized by omission of commas when possible without ambiguity **b** *of the punctuation of a letter* **:** characterized by the omission of punctuation marks at the end of the lines of the heading and after the complimentary close — opposed to *close* **syn** see FRANK, LIABLE

**²open** \"\ *vb* **opened** \-pənd,-pᵊmd\ **opened** \"\ **opening** \-p(ə)niŋ, -pniŋ\ **opens** \-pənz,-pᵊmz\ [ME *openen*, fr. OE *openian*; akin to OHG *offanōn* to open, ON *opna*; all fr. a prehistoric NGmc-WGmc denominative fr. the root of OE ¹*open*] *vt* **1 a :** to move (as a door or lid) from its shut position ⟨~ the windows⟩ ⟨slowly ~*ed* her eyelids⟩ ⟨~ a switch⟩ **b :** to make available for entry or passage by turning back (as a barrier), removing (as a cover), or clearing away (as an obstruction) ⟨the janitor ~*s* the building at 7 o'clock⟩ ⟨~*ing* the road after the flood⟩ ⟨~ your heart to mercy⟩: as (1) **:** to free (a body passage) of an occluding agent ⟨used cathartics to ~ the bowels⟩ ⟨an inhalator for ~*ing* congested nasal passages⟩ (2) **:** to make available for or active in a regular function ⟨plan to ~ a new store soon⟩ ⟨at what time do you ~ your office⟩; *also* **:** to make accessible for a particular purpose ⟨~*ed* new land for settlement⟩ (3) **:** to declare (as a public building or park) to be open to the public usu. by a formal ceremony **2 a :** to expose to view **:** DISCLOSE, REVEAL, UNBOSOM **b** *archaic* **:** INTERPRET, EXPOUND **c :** to make more discerning or responsive **:** ENLIGHTEN **d :** to bring into view or come in sight of by changing position so as to remove an intervening object from the line of sight ⟨sailed on until we ~*ed* a bay⟩ **3 a :** to make one or more openings in **:** cut or break into ⟨~*ed* the boil⟩ ⟨planned to ~ the tombs of the ancient kings⟩ **b :** to loosen and make less compact usu. by separating the constituent parts ⟨~ the soil by cultivating⟩ ⟨~*ed* the matted wool by shaking vigorously⟩ **c :** to salt out — used in soap manufacturing **4 :** to spread out **:** UNFOLD, UNROLL, EXTEND ⟨the rose ~*s* its dewy petals⟩ ⟨~*ed* the book near the middle⟩ **5 a :** to enter upon **:** BEGIN ⟨~*ed* the meeting⟩ ⟨will ~ his campaign soon⟩ **b** (1) **:** to make the statement by which the trial of (a case) is begun and put before the court (2) **:** to be the first to speak in summing up or arguing (a case) **c :** to commence action in a card game by making (a first bid), putting a first bet in (the pot), or playing (a specified card or suit) as first lead **6 :** to restore or recall (as an order, rule, judgment) from a finally determined state to a state in which the parties are free to prosecute or oppose by further legal proceedings **7 :** to shift the feet so as to assume (an open stance) in golf or batting ~ *vi* **1 a :** to become open **:** UNCLOSE ⟨the door ~*ed* slowly⟩ **b :** to open a door or other barrier or make open a closed place usu. so as to give admittance ⟨~ in the name of the law⟩ **c :** to have the doors opened for admittance of the public ⟨the store ~*s* at 9⟩ **2 a :** to spread out **:** EXPAND ⟨the buds are beginning to ~⟩ **b :** to separate or come apart usu. with an effect of spreading out ⟨the wound ~*ed* under the strain⟩ ⟨the book ~*ed* to my place⟩ **c :** to expand into view **:** become disclosed **:** spread out in the sight esp. so that elements come to be seen as distinct ⟨a lovely vista ~*ed* before us⟩ **3 :** to become enlightened or responsive ⟨my heart ~*s* to your words⟩ **4 a :** to give access ⟨an arch ~*s* into the dining room⟩ **b :** to have an opening, passage, or outlet ⟨all the rooms ~ onto a long hall⟩ **c :** to open in an indicated direction ⟨the door ~*s* toward the hall⟩ **5 :** to bark on first finding scent **:** give tongue to a scent trail ⟨the dog ~*ed* almost at once⟩ **6 :** to bare or make plain one's mind, feelings, or knowledge by speaking **:** speak out **:** be open in speech ⟨finally ~*ed* freely on the subject⟩ **7 a :** to begin action **:** commence in some course or activity ⟨the artillery ~*ed* on the enemy⟩ ⟨the stock ~*ed* at par⟩ **b :** to commence by a first incident (as a performance of a drama, a concert, or a day's hunting) ⟨the opera season ~*s* Friday⟩ **c :** to make a bet, bid, or lead in commencing a round or hand of a card game — **open one's eyes 1 :** to cause one to stare with wonder or amazement **2 :** to awaken one to a knowledge or realization of something usu. unpleasant — **open one's heart 1 :** to disclose one's intimate thoughts or feelings **2 :** to behave with generosity — **open one's mouth 1 :** to begin speaking **2 :** to give power of speech **:** induce to speak (as by bribery) **3 :** to speak indiscreetly or disclose confidential matters in speech — **open one's shoulders** *cricket* **:** to use the long handle in batting — **open ranks :** to execute a movement in infantry drill in which the third rank stands fast and the others take a varying number of steps forward or back from it — **open the books :** to resume use of corporation or other record books after temporary closing: as **a :** to reopen stock transfer books after they have been closed because of a forthcoming stockholders' meeting or other purpose **b :** to begin to accept subscriptions to a new offering ⟨*the books will be opened* for the new Treasury issue⟩

**³open** \"\ *adv* [ME, fr. ¹*open*] **:** in an open manner

**⁴open** \"\ *n* -s [ME, in sense 1 fr. *openen* to open; in other senses fr. ¹*open*] **1 :** OPENING **2 :** open and unobstructed space: as **a :** land without trees, buildings, or obstructions ⟨finally broke out of the forest into the ~⟩ **b :** countryside free from hedges or fences **c** (1) **:** cultivated land as distinguished from some protected place (as a greenhouse) ⟨grapes grown in the ~ have a distinctive tang⟩ (2) **:** outdoors as distinguished from inside ⟨spent the day in the ~⟩ **d :** open water esp. of the ocean or a lake **3 :** a style of type characterized by letters in outline

LIKE THIS

**4 :** a break in an electric circuit **5 :** an open contest, competition, or tournament (as in a sport)

**open·able** \'ōp(ə)nəbəl\ *adj* **:** capable of being opened

**open-access** \¦==¦=,=\ *adj, Brit* **:** OPEN-SHELF

**open account** *n* **1 :** CURRENT ACCOUNT 1a **2 :** an account with a debtor or creditor having a balance due or payable

**open air** *n* **:** the space where air is unconfined; *esp* **:** out of doors ⟨exercise in the *open air*⟩

**open-air** \¦==¦=\ *adj* [*open air*] **1 :** taking place, done, existing in, or characteristic of the open air **:** OUTDOOR ⟨an *open-air* meeting⟩ **2 :** plein air

**open-and-shut** \¦ōp(ə)nən¦shət\ *adj* **1 :** perfectly simple **:** OBVIOUS **2** *chiefly dial* **:** partly cloudy **:** alternately overcast and clear

**open-and-shut block** *n* **:** a football block preceded by a side step to gain position and used by a lineman or a wingback to block inwardly a tackler who is on his outside shoulder

**open-and-shut case** \¦==¦=-\ *n* [so called fr. the fact that it may be closed as soon as opened] **:** a case open to no doubts as to the legal principles to be applied and the necessary result

**open arc lamp** *n* **:** an arc lamp operated in the open air — compare ENCLOSED ARC LAMP

**open arms** *n pl* **:** an eager or warm welcome ⟨greeted them with *open arms*⟩

**open-arse** \'==,=\ *n* [ME *openers*, fr. OE *openærs*, fr. *open* + *ærs*, *ears* ass; fr. the large open disk between the lobes of the calyx — more at ASS] *dial Brit* **:** ¹MEDLAR 1

**open back** *n* **:** HOLLOW BACK

**openband** \'==,=\ *adj, of a twist in textile manufacture* **:** right-hand or Z-shaped — compare CROSSBAND

**openbeak** \'==,=\ *n* **:** OPENBILL

**openbill** \'==,=\ *n* **:** a stork of the genus *Anastomus* characterized by a grooved bill with the upper and lower parts touching only at the base and tip

**open book** *n* **:** something that is widely or fully known **:** a thing completely free from mystery or concealment ⟨her life is an *open book*⟩

**open-book examination** *n* **:** a written examination during which an examinee is permitted to consult references (as a text book, dictionary, or anthology) to answer questions calling for organization, analysis, or judgment, rather than memorization

**open bridle** *n* **:** a bridle having no blinders

**open caisson** *n* **:** a small cofferdam that is set in place, pumped dry, and filled with concrete to form a foundation (as for a pier)

**¹opencast** \'==,=\ *n, chiefly Brit* **:** ¹OPENCUT 1

**²opencast** \"\ *adv (or adj), chiefly Brit* **:** ²OPENCUT ⟨~ mining⟩

**open chain** *n* **:** an arrangement of atoms represented in a structural formula by a chain whose ends are not joined so as to form a ring — opposed to *closed chain*

**open charge** *n* **:** a charge placed against a defendant usu. to enable the police to gain time for the discovery of further evidence so that another more serious charge may be made

**open check** *n, Brit* **:** an unindorsed check payable to the order of the bearer

**open circuit** *n* **:** an electrical circuit in which the continuity is broken so that current does not flow

**open cluster** *n* **:** a cluster of stars in which all the individual members may be discerned with an optical aid and which is much less compact and has fewer members than a globular cluster; *often* **:** a galactic cluster

**open commission** *n* **:** a commission to take testimony in which the witnesses to be examined are not named or in which the scope of the inquiry is not limited to specific questions

**open communion** *n* **:** Communion open to all Christians and not restricted to those of a particular denomination or those meeting a specific qualification (as baptism by immersion) — opposed to *close communion*

**open compound** *n* **:** a compound whose word components are separated by a space in printing or writing — compare SOLID COMPOUND

**open couplet** *n* **:** a couplet the sense of which requires completion by what follows

**open court** *n* **1 :** a court that is in session and lawfully organized and engaged in the transaction of official business as distinguished from a court taking evidence in camera or from a judge in chambers or elsewhere exercising his powers as a magistrate rather than as a court **2 :** a session of court at the transactions of which the public are free to be present

**open craps** *n* **:** craps in which a house or banker undertakes to cover all bets at its established odds but also permits players to bet among themselves

**open cure** *n* **:** hot vulcanization of rubber in the presence of steam

**¹opencut** \¦==¦=\ *n* **1 :** a mine working in which excavation is performed from the surface — compare STRIP MINE **2 :** a trench for the passage of a roadway or railway through an obstruction (as a hill) — distinguished from *tunnel*

**²opencut** \"\ *adv (or adj)* **:** with the surface exposed to the air or worked from the exposed surface ⟨an ~ iron mine⟩ ⟨a copper mine worked ~⟩

**open-delta connection** *n* **:** a usu. temporary or emergency connection of a three-phase electrical circuit in which one of the three transformers is omitted and its load carried by the two transformers — called also *V-connection*

**open diapason** *n* **:** a pipe organ foundation stop having a full sonorous tone and consisting usu. of metal pipes of 8-foot pitch open at the top

**open door** *n* **1 a :** a recognized right of admittance (as to the presence or attention of a superior) **:** freedom of access **b :** free and unhampered opportunity or a source of such ⟨education is an *open door* to advancement⟩ **2 :** a policy giving all nations equal opportunity for commercial and other intercourse with a country controlled by more powerful states and abolishing special concessions to a favored nation

**open-door** \¦==¦=\ *adj* [*open door*] **1 :** done or carried on with or as if with the doors open **:** PUBLIC **2 :** of, relating to, or sustaining the open door in foreign relations ⟨trade was on an *open-door* basis⟩ ⟨an *open-door* policy was initiated⟩

**open-eared** \¦==¦=\ *adj* **1 :** attentive to what is heard **2 :** responsive to appeal, suggestion, or other utterance

**opened** *past of* OPEN

**open-end** \¦==¦=\ *adj* **:** organized, formulated, or constituted to contain possibilities for various contingencies whether unspecified, merely inferable, or definitely stated: as **a :** permitting additional debt to be incurred under the original indenture subject to specified conditions ⟨an *open-end* bond issue⟩ — compare OPEN-END MORTGAGE **b :** offering for sale or having issued outstanding capital shares redeemable upon demand usu. at liquidating value or at a slight discount ⟨an *open-end* investment company⟩ — opposed to *closed-end* **c :** calling for the filling by a particular contractor of all government needs for a specific product during a specified period ⟨an *open-end* contract⟩ **d :** having blank spaces for the insertion of commercials ⟨*open-end* transcription for a new TV program⟩ **e** *usu* **open-ended** \¦==¦==\ **:** having no fixed set of alternative replies and permitting spontaneous and unguided responses for expression (as of attitudes, opinions, and intent) ⟨an *open-ended* question⟩ ⟨*open-ended* interview⟩

**open-end mortgage** *n* **:** a mortgage under which additional funds may be borrowed without making a new mortgage — contrasted with *closed mortgage*

**open-end straight** *n* **:** four cards in poker sequence (as 4, 5, 6, 7) that can be filled at either end

**open end wrench** *n* **:** a wrench with jaws having a fixed width of opening at one or both ends of the handle

open end wrench

**¹open·er** \'ōp(ə)nə(r)\ *n* -s [²*open*] **:** one that opens ⟨a can ~⟩: as **a** *obs* **:** APERIENT **b :** a machine in which textile fiber (as cotton) is loosened and partially cleaned **c open-**

**ers** *pl* **:** cards of sufficient value for a player to open the betting in a poker game **d :** the first item on a multiple bill (as of vaudeville acts) or of a series (as of professional baseball games)
²**opener** *comparative of* OPEN
**openest** *superlative of* OPEN
**open-eyed** \¦⸗¦⸗\ *adj* **1 :** having the eyes open (as in surprise or amazement) ⟨watching in *open-eyed* wonder⟩ **2** *also* **open-eye :** characterized by alert vigilance and attention **:** WATCHFUL, DISCERNING ⟨a policy of *open-eyed* awareness⟩
**open-faced** *or* **open-face** \¦⸗¦⸗\ *adj* **:** having an open face: as **a** *of a watch* **:** having the face or dial covered only with a glass — compare HUNTING CASE **b :** having a frank, ingenuous, or undisguised face **c :** lacking a top covering — used of a made dish (as a pie or sandwich) **d :** BAREFACED
**open-field** \¦⸗¦⸗\ *adj* **1 :** of, relating to, or constituting a system of agriculture widely practised in medieval Europe and based upon dividing the arable land into unenclosed strips usu. subject to a 3-year rotation and upon distributing it among different cultivators **2** *of a football player* **:** notably capable of gaining yardage in a broken field ⟨an *open-field* runner⟩
**open field** *n* **1 :** BROKEN FIELD **2 :** an unhampered chance ⟨given an *open field* to experiment⟩
**open file** *n* **:** a chess file void of pawns; *also* **:** a file with neither pieces nor pawns on it
**open-file** \¦⸗¦⸗\ *adj* **:** not restricted as to circulation or possession ⟨*open-file* reports⟩
**open fire** *n* **1 :** a fire (as in a fireplace) that is not wholly enclosed by a stove or furnace **2 :** a fire in a forge in which combustion takes place on the top of the fuel
**open-fire** \¦⸗¦⸗\ *adj, ceramics* **:** exposed to direct contact with the fire as opposed to muffled firing
**open flash** *n* **:** a method of taking flashlight pictures by leaving the camera shutter open while the lamp is flashed and then closing it
**open flow** *n* **:** the total flow produced by an oil or gas well in a given time with the main valve wide open
**open form** *n* **:** a crystal form (as a prism) whose faces do not completely enclose a space
**open frame** *n* **:** a frame in which a bowler scores neither a strike nor a spare
**open furrow** *n* **:** a furrow not filled by a furrow slice
**open fuse** *n* **:** a fuse not enclosed in a cartridge
**open gait** *n* **:** the gait of a trotting horse that places his hind feet outside the forward ones in action
**open gate** *n* **:** a slalom obstacle placed at right angles to the vertical descent of a ski slope — compare CLOSED GATE
**open-grained** *or* **open grain** \¦⸗¦⸗\ *adj* **:** having a coarse texture; *esp* **:** having large pores ⟨*open-grained* woods⟩
**openhanded** \¦⸗¦⸗⸗\ *adj* **1 :** generous in giving **:** MUNIFICENT **2** *obs* **:** ready to accept bounty **3 :** OBVIOUS, BRAZEN ⟨~ extortion⟩ **syn** see LIBERAL
**open·hand·ed·ly** *adv* **:** in an openhanded manner **:** GENEROUSLY
**open·hand·ed·ness** *n* **:** GENEROSITY, MUNIFICENCE
**open-handled** \¦⸗¦⸗⸗\ *adj* **:** OPEN 7b
**open harmony** *n* **:** an arrangement of the note or tones of a musical chord in which the three upper parts encompass an octave or more — called also *open position;* compare CLOSE HARMONY
**open hawse** *n* **:** an arrangement of starboard and port anchor cables in which the cables run directly to the anchors — compare FOUL HAWSE
**open-headed** \¦⸗¦⸗⸗\ *adj* **:** trained and pruned without a central leader and with the center open in order to facilitate spraying and other operations and provide superior exposure to sunlight ⟨*open-headed* apple trees⟩
**openhearted** \¦⸗¦⸗⸗\ *adj* **1 :** candidly straightforward **:** freely communicative **:** FRANK **2 :** responsive to emotional appeal **:** generously kind — **open·heart·ed·ly** *adv* — **open·heart·ed·ness** *n* -ES
**open hearth** *n* **1 :** the shallow hearth of a reverberatory

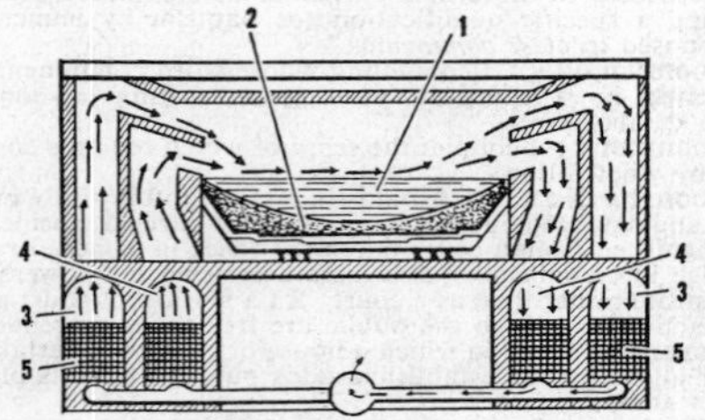

cross section of an open hearth 2: *1* molten steel, *2* lining, *3* air, *4* gas, *5* checker

melting furnace heated by hot gases above it **2 :** an open-hearth furnace
**open-hearth** \¦⸗¦⸗\ *adj* [*open hearth*] **:** of, relating to, involving, or produced by an open hearth ⟨*open-hearth* steel⟩ ⟨an *open-hearth* ladle⟩
**open-hearth process** *n* **:** a process of making steel in a furnace of the regenerative reverberatory type from pig iron usu. charged molten by adding to it with lime and other slag-forming constituents either steel scrap or iron ore or both
**open hole** *n* **:** an oil well or portion of an oil well that has not been cased
**open house** *n* **1 :** ready and usu. informal hospitality or entertainment ⟨kept *open house* for the young people of the neighborhood⟩ **2 a :** an occasion when a person or institution (as a club) entertains a large number of guests often by general rather than specific invitation **b :** an occasion or period during which an organization puts its special features (as products) on public display
**open ice** *n* **:** ice on navigable waters sufficiently broken up to permit passage of a ship
**open·ing** \ˈōp(ə)niŋ, -pnēŋ\ *n* -S [ME, fr. gerund of *openen* to open] **1 a :** an act or instance of making or becoming open ⟨the slow ~ of the door⟩ ⟨the ~ of distant markets⟩ **b :** an act or instance of beginning **:** a first step toward starting or activating (as of an enterprise) ⟨the ~ of two new stores helped the neighborhood⟩; *esp* **:** a formal and usu. public event by which something new is put officially into operation ⟨the mayor spoke at the ~ of the new bridge⟩ **2 :** something that is open: as **a** (1) **:** BREACH, APERTURE ⟨planned the ~*s* for the doors and windows⟩ (2) **:** an open width **:** SPREAD, SPAN **b :** an indentation of water into land **:** STRAIT, BAY, GULF **c :** an area without trees or with scattered usu. mature trees that occurs as a break in a forest — compare OAK OPENING **d :** two pages that face one another in a book **e :** the daily beginning of trading on an exchange; *also* **:** the prices of the initial transaction in a particular stock or commodity futures contract on an exchange **3 :** something that constitutes a beginning **:** an initial stage, instance, part, or event ⟨the ~ of his speech⟩: as **a :** a lawyer's statement of his case prior to adducing evidence **b :** the first phase of a game (as of chess or cards); *specif* **:** a planned series of moves made at the beginning of a game of chess or checkers — compare END GAME, MIDDLE GAME **c :** the introductory and often burlesque part of a pantomime — compare HARLEQUINADE **d :** a first performance (as of a play or an artist) **4 a :** something (as a circumstance) that constitutes an opportunity or occasion ⟨waiting for an ~ to tell his story⟩ **b :** a professional or business vacancy **:** an opportunity for employment ⟨there are always ~*s* for qualified engineers⟩ **c :** a scoring opportunity in a sports competition esp. as a result of a mistake or lapse by the opponent
**opening bid** *n* **:** ORIGINAL BID
**opening bit** *n* **:** BROACH, REAMER
**opening day** *n* **:** the first of a sequence of days related by some common factor ⟨the *opening day* of deer season⟩ ⟨a baseball park filled on *opening day*⟩
**opening die** *n* **:** a screw-cutting die head that automatically opens to clear the cut thread at the end of each run
**opening gun** *n* **:** the initial event of a sequence of related events ⟨the *opening gun* of the campaign⟩
**opening material** *n, ceramics* **:** material (as grog or sand) not affected by water that is added to plastic clay to increase the rate of drying and reduce shrinkage
**open interest** *n* **:** the total in physical units of outstanding long and short futures contracts on a commodity exchange
**open-jaw** \¦⸗¦⸗\ *or* **open-jaw ticket** *n* **:** a round trip ticket having a terminal point that is not the originating point — used esp. in respect to air transportation
**open joint** *n* **:** the depression in a case-bound book between the shoulder of the backbone and the edge of the cover board that forms the joint — compare TIGHT JOINT
**open juncture** *or* **open internal juncture** *n* **:** a juncture between two consecutive sounds in speech having less mutual assimilation than a close juncture and less hiatus than a terminal juncture
**open-kettle** \¦⸗¦⸗⸗\ *adj* **1 :** consisting of or made by evaporation of sap or the juice of sugarcane in open pans ⟨*open-kettle* molasses⟩ **2 :** canned by the hot-pack method
**open letter** *n* **:** a letter of protest or appeal intended for the general public and printed in a newspaper or periodical
**open-letter proof** *n* **:** a proof (as of an engraving) with title or other inscription in outline letters
**open listing** *n* **:** a system whereby two or more real-estate brokers are given the right to sell property for a commission to be paid to the broker making the sale but permitting the owner to sell it himself if possible with no obligation to pay the broker — compare MULTIPLE LISTING
**open·ly** \ˈōpənlē, -pᵊnl-, -li\ *adv* [ME, fr. OE *openlīce*, fr. ¹*open* + *-līce* -ly] **:** in an open manner **:** freely and without concealment
**open market** *n* **:** a freely competitive market in which any buyer or seller may trade and in which prices are determined by competition
**open-market** \¦⸗¦⸗⸗\ *adj* [*open market*] **1 :** of, relating to, or occurring in an open market ⟨*open-market* operations⟩ **2 :** arrived at through or resulting from freely competitive bidding ⟨an *open-market* price⟩ ⟨*open-market* exchange rates⟩
**open-minded** \¦⸗¦⸗⸗\ *adj* **:** receptive of arguments or ideas **:** free from rigidly fixed preconceptions **:** UNPREJUDICED ⟨an *open-minded* curiosity that made him receptive to new ideas —V.L.Parrington⟩ — **open-mind·ed·ly** *adv* — **open-mind·ed·ness** *n* -ES
**openmouthed** \¦⸗¦⸗\ *adj* **1 :** having the mouth widely open (as for gasping, seizing, or crying out) **2 :** struck with amazement or wonder **3 :** urgent or determined in speech or protest **:** CLAMOROUS, VOCIFEROUS — **open·mouthed·ly** \-¦mau̇thədlē, -t͟hədlē,-thtlē,-t͟hdlē\ *adv* — **open·mouthed·ness** \-thədnəs, -t͟hədn-, -th(t)n-, -t͟h(d)n-\ *n* -ES
**openmouthed grunt** *n* **:** FRENCH GRUNT
**open·ness** \ˈōpənnəs, -pmnəs\ *n* -ES **:** the quality or state of being open ⟨the unusual ~ of that winter⟩ ⟨behaved with perfect ~⟩
**open newel** *n* **:** HOLLOW NEWEL
**open-newel stair** *n* **:** a stair having successive flights or a continuous spiral surrounding a space left open between the strings
**open note** *n* **1 :** a musical note with an outline head instead of with a solid one (as a half note) **2 :** a natural harmonic of the fundamental tone of the instrument occurring in the playing of a brass wind instrument — called also *open tone*
**open order** *n* **1 :** a military formation in which the units are separated by considerable intervals **:** EXTENDED ORDER **2 :** an order to buy securities or commodity futures that remains effective until filled or canceled — compare DAY ORDER **3 :** an order for merchandise expressed in very general terms so that the seller has considerable latitude in selecting the articles actually provided ⟨sent an *open order* for 60 better-class suits⟩
**open-pit** \¦⸗¦⸗\ *n or adj or adv* **:** OPENCUT
**open plan** *n* **:** the disposition of interior space in a building (as a dwelling) without distinct or conventional barriers between areas designed for different uses
**open policy** *n* **:** a continuous policy of marine insurance that is terminable by either party after notice, covers specific shipments automatically, and has the premiums determined by the values reported
**open-pollinated** \¦⸗¦⸗⸗,⸗\ *adj* **:** pollinated by natural agencies (as wind or insects) without direct human control or intervention ⟨*open-pollinated* and hybrid sweet corns⟩
**open port** *n* **1 :** a port open to foreign commerce **2 :** a port free from ice the year round
**open position** *n* **:** OPEN HARMONY
**open price** *n* **:** a price at which goods or commodities are sold or are to be sold and which is filed by businesses at a central point of registration and open to all businesses concerned
**open primary** *n* **:** a primary in which the voter is not required to indicate party affiliation — compare CLOSED PRIMARY
**open question** *n* **1 a :** a matter that is undecided or unsettled ⟨it's an *open question* whether the landlord is responsible⟩ **b :** a matter on which a political party has not taken a positive stand **2 :** a question that is so phrased as to encourage an expression of opinion as distinguished from a simple negative or affirmative
**open rate** *n* **1 :** a railroad rate included in a published tariff **2 :** a rate charged by publishers for advertising space that is subject to discounts for volume purchased or frequency of use
**open reduction** *n* **:** realignment of a fractured bone after incision into the fracture site — compare ¹REDUCE 7
**open rein** *n* **:** DIRECT REIN
**open riser** *n* **:** the space between two adjacent stairs when not closed by a solid riser
**opens** *pres 3d sing of* OPEN, *pl of* OPEN
**open-sand** \¦⸗¦⸗\ *adj, of a foundry mold or casting* **:** made entirely of sand or in sand without a flask or cover
**open sandwich** *n* **:** a sandwich lacking a top covering of bread
**open score** *n* **:** a musical choral or orchestral score in which each part has a staff to itself — compare CLOSE SCORE
**open sea** *n* **1 :** the part of the sea not enclosed between headlands or included in narrow straits **:** the main sea **2 :** the part of the sea outside the territorial jurisdiction or maritime belt of any country — compare MARE CLAUSUM
**open secret** *n* **:** a matter that is ostensibly secret but generally known
**open section** *n* **:** a railway Pullman accommodation providing seats that are not enclosed for day use and upper and lower berths closed off with curtains for night use
**open ses·a·me** \,⸗⸗ˈsesəmē, -mi\ *n, sometimes cap O* [fr. *open sesame*, the magical command used to open the door of the robbers' den by Ali Baba in the *Arabian Nights* tale of *Ali Baba and the Forty Thieves*] **:** something that unfailingly brings about a desired end ⟨believe that education is for them . . . an *open sesame* to a good life —E.O.Melby⟩
**open setting** *n* **:** arrangement of ceramic ware in a kiln so that it is exposed to the fire and is not in a muffle
**open-shelf** \¦⸗¦⸗\ *adj* **:** of, used in, or constituting a system of library organization in which books are so shelved as to permit direct examination and selection by patrons ⟨an *open-shelf* room⟩ ⟨the *open-shelf* idea⟩
**open shop** *n* **:** an establishment in which eligibility for employment and retention on the payroll are not determined by membership or nonmembership in a labor union though there may be an agreement by which a union is recognized as sole bargaining agent — compare CLOSED SHOP
**open-shop·per** \¦⸗¦shäpə(r)\ *n* **:** an operator of an open shop or an advocate of open shops
**openside** \¦⸗¦⸗\ *adj* **:** having one side left unobstructed for the accommodation of large work ⟨an ~ punchpress⟩
**openside planer** *n* **:** a planer having the crossrail supported by a housing on one side only
**open sight** *n* **:** a firearm rear sight having an open notch instead of a peephole or a telescope
**open-stack** \¦⸗¦⸗\ *adj* **:** OPEN-SHELF
**open stance** *n* **:** a preparatory position (as in baseball batting or golf) in which the left foot of a right-handed person is drawn back farther from the line of play than the right — contrasted with *closed stance*
**open station** *n* **:** a railway station to which freight can be shipped COD — contrasted with *prepaid station*
**open string** *n* **:** a string in stairs having its upper edge cut to fit underneath the steps, and its ends overlapping the edge
**open syllable** *n* **:** a syllable ended by a vowel or diphthong
**open-tank** \¦⸗¦⸗\ *adj* **:** of, relating to, or constituting a nonpressure process of treating wood with chemicals (as creosote and oil) to guard against decay
**open-timbered** *or* **open-timber** \¦⸗¦⸗⸗\ *adj* **:** having the timbers exposed ⟨an *open-timbered* gable⟩
**open-timbered roof** *n* **:** a timber roof of which the constructional parts together with the under side of the covering or its lining are treated ornamentally and left to form the ceiling of an apartment below
**open-to-buy** \¦⸗⸗⸗¦⸗\ *n* [fr. the phrase *open to buy*] **:** the portion of a budget allotment remaining available for additional purchases at any given moment of a budgetary period ⟨an *open-to-buy* is an amount which is budgeted for the placement of purchase orders —H.D.Broehm⟩
**open tone** *n* **:** OPEN NOTE 2
**open traverse** *n* **:** a surveying traverse that fails to terminate where it began and therefore does not completely enclose a polygon — compare ERROR OF CLOSURE 2
**open tunnel** *n* **:** a square dance figure with a space between the outstretched arms of joined couples for the passage of other couples
**open turn** *n* **:** a turn in dancing made with the partners in open position
**open up** *vi* **1 :** to commence firing **2 a :** to become communicative **b** *of a hound* **:** to give tongue **3 :** to spread out in or come into view ⟨the road *opens up* ahead⟩ **4 :** to turn toward an audience or camera **5 :** to launch an offensive esp. in competitive sport ⟨*open up* with forward passes⟩ ⟨*open up* with a series of quick punches⟩ ~ *vt* **1 :** to cut into; *esp* **:** to open surgically **2 a :** to make plain or visible **:** DISCLOSE ⟨her account *opened up* a whole new line of investigation⟩ **b :** to bring into view ⟨means to place his drive so as to *open up* the green for his approach —Paul Gallico⟩ **3 :** to make available ⟨new opportunities were *opened up* as the population grew⟩ **4 :** to force (a defense) to spread itself thin ⟨split the line to *open up* this defense —Jim Tatum⟩
**open valley** *n* **:** a roofing valley laid with a broad open gutter with the slates, tiles, or shingles lapping over the edges of the metal
**open verdict** *n* **:** a verdict on a preliminary investigation finding the fact of a crime but not stating the criminal or finding the fact of a violent death without disclosing the cause
**open water** *n* **:** water less than one tenth of which is covered with floating ice
**open-well stair** *n* **:** OPEN-NEWEL STAIR
**openwork** \ˈ⸗⸗,⸗\ *n, often attrib* **:** work so constructed or manufactured as to show openings through its substance **:** work that is perforated or pierced ⟨an ~ sweater⟩ ⟨balconies decked with wrought-iron ~⟩ — **open-worked** \ˈ⸗⸗,⸗\ *adj*
**o·pe·pe** \ˈōpəpē\ *n* -S [Yoruba *òpepe*] **:** a large African forest tree (*Sarcocephalus diderrichii*) that yields a strong hard durable yellow to golden brown lumber
¹**op·e·ra** \ˈōpərə, ˈäp-\ *pl of* OPUS
²**op·e·ra** \ˈäp(ə)rə\ *n* -S [It, work, opera, fr. L, work, pains; akin to L *oper-, opus* work — more at OPERATE] **1 :** a drama in which music is the essential factor comprising songs with orchestral accompaniment (as *recitative, aria, chorus*) and orchestral preludes and interludes — compare MUSIC DRAMA **2 :** the score of a musical drama **3 a :** the performance of an opera or a house where operas are performed ⟨a season of ~⟩ ⟨heard it at the ~⟩ **b :** an organization that produces and performs operas **4 :** musical drama as a form of art ⟨the origin of ~⟩ ⟨French ~⟩ **5** [by shortening] **a :** OPERA PUMP **b :** OPERA SLIPPER **6 :** a showy unrealistic literary or theatrical production — see HORSE OPERA, SOAP OPERA, SPACE OPERA
³**opera** \"\ *adj* **:** used or suitable for use at or in an opera ⟨~ chairs⟩; *esp* **:** of a formal style suitable for wear at the opera ⟨an ~ cloak⟩
**opé·ra bal·let** \,äp(ə)rə+*pronunc at* ²BALLET; *or* ȯpārȧbȧlā\ *n* [F] **:** an opera in which ballet dancing constitutes a principal feature
**op·er·a·bil·i·ty** \,äp(ə)rəˈbilәd·ē\ *n* **:** the quality or state of being operable — compare RESECTABILITY
**op·er·a·ble** \ˈäp(ə)rəbəl\ *adj* [LL *operabilis* working, efficacious, fr. L *operari* to work + *-abilis* -able] **1 :** fit, possible, or desirable to use **:** PRACTICABLE ⟨a highly ~ machine⟩ **2 :** suitable for surgical treatment ⟨an ~ cancer⟩ — compare RESECTABLE — **op·er·a·bly** \-blē\ *adv*
**opéra bouffe** \,äp(ə)rəˈbüf, ȯpārȧbüf\ *n* [F, fr. It *opera buffa*] **:** a light comic opera having a light or sentimental subject and characterized by parody or burlesque
**opéra-bouffe** \"\ *adj* [*opéra bouffe*] **:** fit for opéra bouffe **:** being a parody of the thing specified ⟨*opéra-bouffe* revolutions⟩
**ope·ra buf·fa** \,äp(ə)rəˈbüfə, ,ȯpərä ˈbüffä\ *n* [It] **:** an Italian comic opera particularly of the 18th century of farcical character with dialogue in recitative
**opé·ra co·mique** \,äp(ə)rə,käˈmēk, ȯpārȧkȯmēk\ *n* [F] **:** an opera characterized by spoken dialogue interspersed between the set arias and ensemble numbers — compare GRAND OPERA
**opera glass** \ˈ⸗(⸗)⸗,⸗\ *n* **:** a small binocular optical instrument similar to the field glass and adapted for use at the opera or theater — often used in pl.

opera glasses

**opera hat** *n* **:** a man's hat worn with evening dress having a narrow brim and a high cylindrical crown with slightly concave sides and consisting usu. of a dull silky fabric stretched over a steel frame that may be collapsed by a spring device
**opera house** *n* **:** a theater devoted principally to the performance of operas; *broadly* **:** THEATER
**op·er·ance** \ˈäpərən(t)s\ *n* -S [fr. ¹*operant*, after such pairs as E *expectant: expectance*] **:** the act of operating or working something **:** OPERATION
**op·er·an·cy** \-nsē\ *n* -ES [¹*operant* + *-cy*] **:** the quality or state of being operative **:** OPERATION
**op·er·and** \ˈäpə,rand\ *n* -S [L *operandum*, neut. of gerundive of *operari* to work, operate — more at OPERATE] **1 :** a quantity upon which a mathematical operation is performed or which arises from an operation **2** *logic* **a :** something that is operated on by an operator **b :** the scope of an operator
¹**op·er·ant** \ˈäpərənt\ *adj* [L *operant-, operans*, pres. part. of *operari*] **1 :** functioning or tending to produce effects **:** EFFECTIVE ⟨an ~ conscience⟩ **2 :** of, relating to, or being a behavioral operant ⟨~ conditioning⟩
²**operant** \"\ *n* -S **1 :** one that operates **:** OPERATIVE, OPERATOR **2 :** behavior or responses that operate on the environment to produce rewarding and reinforcing effects
**ope·ra om·nia** \,ōpərəˈämnēə, ¦äp-\ *n pl* [L, lit., all works] **:** the complete works of a writer
**opera pink** *n* **:** a light yellowish pink that is redder and less strong than light apricot and darker than petal pink
**opera pump** *n* **:** a woman's low-cut, high-heeled shoe usu. cut from a single piece of leather or fabric and untrimmed
**operas** *pl of* OPERA
**ope·ra se·ria** \,äp(ə)rəˈsirēə\ *n* [It] **:** an 18th century opera with a heroic or legendary subject chiefly characterized musically by the highly stylized treatment and preponderant use of the aria and recitative
**opera slipper** *n* **1 :** OPERA PUMP **2 :** a man's house slipper cut low on both sides at the shank
**op·er·at·able** \ˈäpə,rād·əbəl, ,⸗⸗ˈ⸗⸗⸗\ *adj* **:** possible to operate or to operate on **:** OPERABLE
**op·er·ate** \ˈäpə,rāt *sometimes* ˈä,prāt; *usu* -ād·+V\ *vb* -ED/-ING/-S [L *operatus*, past part. of *operari* to work, fr. *oper-, opus* work, labor; akin to Skt *apas* work, OHG *uoben* to put to work, be active, OE *efnan* to perform, ON *efna*] *vi* **1 :** to perform a work or labor **:** exert power or influence **:** produce an effect ⟨a plain reason ~*s* on the mind of a learned hearer⟩ ⟨factors *operating* against our success⟩ ⟨this remark

opera slipper 2

*operated* to close the meeting in disorder⟩ **2 :** to produce or take an appropriate effect **:** issue in the result designed ⟨the drug *operated* quickly⟩ **3 a :** to perform an operation or series of operations ⟨a mill for *operating* on the crude ore⟩ **b :** to perform surgery ⟨the doctor ~*s* from 8 to 10⟩ **c :** to carry on a military or naval action or mission **d :** to function through the use of a specified agent ⟨the tractor ~*s* on diesel oil⟩ **4 :** to trade or speculate in securities or commodities **:** act as a dealer or broker in the markets ⟨*operated* largely in cotton futures⟩ **5 :** to follow a course of conduct or way of life, esp. one that is irregular or antisocial ⟨*operated* as a salesman⟩ ⟨crooked gamblers *operating* on the Atlantic liners⟩ **~** *vt* **1 :** to cause to occur **:** bring about by or as if by the exertion of positive effort or influence **:** INITIATE ⟨such influences may ~ remarkable changes⟩ **2 a :** to cause to function usu. by direct personal effort **:** WORK ⟨~ a car⟩ ⟨*operating* a drill press⟩ **b :** to manage and put or keep in operation whether with personal effort or not ⟨*operated* a grocery store⟩ **3 :** to perform surgery on ⟨not all surgeons will ~ malignant growths⟩ ⟨the *operated* limb regained strength slowly⟩ **syn** see ACT

**¹op·er·at·ic** \ˌäpəˈrad·ik, -rat|, |ēk\ *adj* [fr. *opera*, after such pairs as E *drama: dramatic*] **:** of, relating to, resembling, or suitable to opera — **op·er·at·i·cal·ly** \|ək(ə)lē, |ēk-, -li\ *adv*

**²operatic** \"\ *n* -s **1 operatics** *pl but sing or pl in constr* **a :** the performance or production of opera **b :** noisily histrionic behavior ⟨no excuse for such ~*s*⟩ **2 :** an operatic recording

**operating** *adj* [fr. pres. part. of *operate*] **1 :** engaged in some form of operation **:** FUNCTIONAL ⟨an ~ motor⟩; *esp* **:** engaged in active business (as manufacture, transportation, merchandising) **2 a :** arising out of or concerned with the current operations of a concern engaged in transportation or manufacturing as distinct from its financial transactions and its permanent improvements ⟨~ expense⟩ ⟨~ personnel⟩ **b :** of or dealing with profit and loss or income and expenses ⟨an ~ statement⟩ **3 :** used for or in operations ⟨the ~ room in a hospital⟩

**op·er·a·tion** \ˌäpəˈrāshən\ *n* -s [ME *operacioun*, fr. MF *operation*, fr. L *operation-, operatio*, fr. *operatus* (past part. of *operari* to work) + *-ion, -io* -ion — more at OPERATE] **1 a** *obs* **:** a doing or performing esp. of action **:** WORK, DEED **b :** a doing or performing of a practical work or of something involving practical application of principles or processes often experimentally or as part of a series of actions ⟨the mechanical ~*s* involved in sculpture⟩ ⟨practice until you can go through the whole ~ without hesitation or thinking⟩ **2 a :** an exertion of power or influence **:** FUNCTIONING, WORKING ⟨depending on the ~*s* of the intelligence⟩ ⟨the ~ of a drug⟩ **b :** the quality or state of being functional or operative — usu. used with *in* or *into* ⟨the plant has been in ~ for several weeks⟩ ⟨the new line will be put into ~ soon⟩ **c :** method or manner of functioning ⟨a machine of very simple ~⟩ ⟨the ~ of the circulation⟩ **3 a :** capacity for action or functioning **:** EFFICACY, POTENCY — archaic except in legal usage **b** *archaic* **:** result of the action or existence (as of a disease, an activity) **:** INFLUENCE **4** *obs* **a :** PRODUCTION, CREATION **b :** a product of creative activity **5 :** actual energy or activity viewed as expressing the agent's nature or natures ⟨the ~ of the Holy Spirit⟩ **6 :** a procedure carried out on a living body for the purpose of altering an existing esp. abnormal state or condition by means of instruments (as in surgery) or the hands of a surgeon (as by manipulation of joints) — compare BLOODLESS SURGERY, ELECTROSURGERY **7 a :** a process whereby one quantity or expression is derived from another or others **b** *logic* (1) **:** TRANSFORMATION (2) **:** a function or correlation when conceived as a process of proceeding from one or more entities to another according to a definite rule **c :** the checking of the applicability of a given term or concept to a concrete situation by means of observation and usu. manipulation ⟨determining the acidity of a liquid by indicators constitutes an ~⟩ **8 a :** a military or naval action, mission, or maneuver, including its planning and execution — often used in combination with a designating code word **b operations** *pl* **:** the office on the flight line of an airfield where pilots file clearances for flights and which controls flying from the field **c operations** *pl* **:** the staff agency (as in a U.S. air headquarters) for transacting the principal planning and operating functions of a headquarters and its subordinate units **9 a :** a business transaction esp. when speculative ⟨continued his ~*s* in cotton futures⟩ **b :** the whole process of planning for and operating a business or other organized unit ⟨the ~ of a large household⟩ ⟨the ~ of a steel mill⟩ **c :** a phase of a business or of business activity ⟨the new forge shop has proved a valuable addition to our ~*s*⟩ **10 :** the operating of or putting and maintaining in action of something (as a machine or an industry) ⟨careful ~ of a motor car⟩ ⟨problems in the ~ of a railroad⟩

**op·er·a·tion·al** \ˌäpəˈrāshənᵊl, -shnəl\ *adj* **1 :** of or relating to operation or an operation **2 :** concerned with, involving, or based on operations ⟨~ symbols⟩ ⟨an ~ definition⟩ — see OPERATIONAL CALCULUS **3 a :** of, engaged in, or connected with execution of military or naval operations in campaign and battle as distinguished from training, testing, observation ⟨an ~ leave⟩ ⟨~ patrols⟩ **b :** ready for or in condition to undertake a destined function ⟨the new pool should be ~ in a few weeks⟩; *esp* **:** serviced in readiness for action ⟨the fleet is fully manned and ~⟩

**operational calculus** *n* **:** a branch of mathematics that subjects to algebraic operations symbols of operation as well as of magnitude

**operational fatigue** *n* **:** COMBAT FATIGUE

**op·er·a·tion·al·ism** \ˌäpəˈrāshənᵊlˌizəm, -shnəˌli-\ *n* -s **:** the view that the concepts or terms used in nonanalytic scientific statements must be definable in terms of identifiable and repeatable operations

**op·er·a·tion·al·ist** \-ᵊləst, -əl-\ *n* -s **:** an advocate or adherent of operationalism

**op·er·a·tion·al·ly** \ˌ¦äpə¦rāshənᵊl|ē, -shnəl|, |i\ *adv* **1 :** in an operational condition or manner **:** so as to be operational **2 :** in respect to operation **:** as observed in actual use or function ⟨reported the machine ~ satisfactory⟩ ⟨a well-trained staff that is ~ adequate⟩

**operational research** *n, chiefly Brit* **:** OPERATIONS RESEARCH

**op·er·a·tion·ism** \-shəˌnizəm\ *n* -s **:** OPERATIONALISM

**op·er·a·tion·is·tic** \ˌ¦äpəˌrāshə¦nistik\ *adj* **:** of or relating to operationalism **:** OPERATIONAL

**operations analysis** *n* **:** the systematic examination of a tactic or other military procedure usu. by mathematical and statistical methods to determine its efficiency and to devise or indicate possible improvements

**operations research** *n* **:** the application of scientific and esp. mathematical methods to the study and analysis of complex problems (as of industrial, governmental, or military activity) that are not traditionally considered to fall within the field of profitable scientific inquiry

**¹op·er·a·tive** \ˈäp(ə)rəd·|iv, ˈäpəˌrā|, |t|, |ēv *also* |əv\ *adj* [MF *operatif*, fr. L *operatus* (past part. of *operari* to work) + MF *-if* -ive — more at OPERATE] **1 :** producing an appropriate or designed effect **:** EFFICACIOUS ⟨an ~ dose⟩ ⟨an ~ word⟩ **2 :** having the power of acting **:** exerting force or influence **:** OPERATING ⟨an ~ motive⟩ ⟨an ~ force⟩ **3 a :** involving or having to do with physical operations (as of the hands or of machines) ⟨~ arts⟩ ⟨~ skills⟩ **b :** engaged in or doing work **:** occupied in productive labor **:** WORKING ⟨an ~ craftsman⟩ ⟨~ freemasons working at their craft⟩ **4 :** based upon or consisting of an operation or operations ⟨~ surgery⟩ ⟨~ dentistry⟩ — **op·er·a·tive·ly** \|əvlē, -li\ *adv* — **op·er·a·tive·ness** \|ivnəs, |ēv- *also* |əv-\ *n* -ES

**²operative** \"\ *n* -s **:** one that operates **:** OPERATOR: as **a :** a person engaged in an occupation or profession; *esp* **:** a skilled or semiskilled employee in industry (as in a mill or factory) **:** ARTISAN, MECHANIC ⟨machine ~*s*⟩ ⟨wool ~*s*⟩ **b :** a secret agent **:** PRIVATE DETECTIVE

**op·er·a·tize** \ˈäp(ə)rəˌtīz\ *vt* -ED/-ING/-s [fr. *opera*, after such pairs as E *drama: dramatize*] **:** to convert (as a drama) into opera

**op·er·a·tor** \ˈäpəˌrād·ə(r), -ātə- *sometimes* ˈäˌprā-\ *n* -s [LL, worker, fr. L *operatus* + *-or*] **1 :** one that produces a physical effect or engages himself in the mechanical aspect of any process or activity: as **a :** one (as an operative surgeon or dentist) that performs surgical operations **b** (1) **:** a worker who operates a usu. specified machine or device as his regular trade ⟨loom ~*s*⟩; *broadly* **:** one that uses or operates a machine or device professionally or otherwise — sometimes used to distinguish the user of fixed devices from the driver of automotive devices (2) **:** DRIVER 1b ⟨~*s* of motor vehicles⟩ **c :** a person in charge of a telephone switchboard, connecting and disconnecting the lines and routing calls; *also* **:** a supervisor of such persons **d :** a person who transmits or receives telegraphic or radio messages or who operates electronic communications equipment (as radar or computer installation) **2 a** *obs* **:** MAKER, CREATOR **b** (1) *obs* **:** a maker of quack medicines or of shoddy or fraudulent articles; *broadly* **:** MOUNTEBANK, FRAUD (2) **:** a shrewd and skillful person who knows how to evade or circumvent restrictions, controls, or difficulty **:** one that is smooth and highly expert in some line **3 a** (1) **:** a dealer or speculator in stocks or commodities (2) **:** a person who regularly or professionally engages in some usu. financial activity esp. on a large scale ⟨an important ~ around the gambling houses⟩ **b :** a person that actively operates a business (as a mine, a farm, or a store) whether as owner, lessor, or employee **4 a :** a mathematical symbol denoting an operation to be performed ⟨$\frac{d}{dx}$ is the differentiating ~⟩ **b :** something that performs a logical operation or forms a symbol denoting such an operation (as a quantifier or a sentential connective) **c :** FUNCTION WORD ⟨a preposition, auxiliary, or conjunction is an ~⟩ **5 :** HYPNOTIST

**¹op·er·a·to·ry** \ˈäp(ə)rəˌtōrē\ *adj* [*operate* + *-ory*] **:** OPERATIVE

**²operatory** \"\ *n* -ES [ML *operatorium*, fr. L *operatus* + *-orium* -ory] **:** a working space (as of a dentist or engineer) **:** LABORATORY, SURGERY

**oper·cle** \ōˈpərkəl, ˈōpər-\ *n* -s [L *operculum* cover — more at *operculum*] **:** OPERCULUM; *specif* **:** the upper posterior and usu. the largest bone of the operculum of a fish

**oper·cled** \-kəld\ *adj* [*opercle* + *-ed*] **:** OPERCULATE

**¹oper·cu·lar** \(ˈ)ō¦pərkyələr\ *adj* [*operculum* + *-ar*] **:** of, relating to, or resembling an operculum

**²opercular** \"\ *n* -s **:** an opercular part; *esp* **:** the opercle of a fish

**opercular bones** *n pl* **:** the bony plates attached in and supporting the gill cover in most fishes and being usu. the opercle, preopercle, subopercle, and interopercle

**¹oper·cu·late** \-lət, -ˌlāt\ *also* **oper·cu·lat·ed** \-ˌlād·əd\ *adj* [*operculum* + *-ate*] **:** having an operculum

**²operculate** \"\ *n* -s **:** an operculate gastropod

**operculi-** *comb form* [NL *operculum*] **:** operculum ⟨*operculi*ferous⟩ ⟨*operculi*form⟩

**oper·cu·lum** \ōˈpərkyələm\ *n, pl* **opercu·la** \-lə\ *also* **oper·culums** [NL, fr. L, cover, lid, fr. *operire* to cover, shut (fr. *op-, ob* to, before + — assumed — *verire* to shut) + *-culum*, suffix denoting instrument — more at EPI-, WEIR] **1 :** a lid or covering flap (as of a moss capsule, of an ascus, of a pyxidium in a seed plant, or of the pitcher in some pitcher plants) **2 :** a part of the cerebrum bordering the lateral fissure and concealing the island of Reil **3 :** a body process or part that suggests a lid: as **a :** the horny or shelly plate that develops on the posterior dorsal surface of the foot in many gastropod mollusks (as in Streptoneura) and serves to close the shell when the animal is retracted **b :** the two or more movable plates of the shell of a barnacle **c :** the first pair of abdominal appendages of a king crab which are united and cover the other pairs **d :** one of the small plates covering the orifice of a trachea or lung sac in a spider **e :** the fold of integument usu. supported by bony plates that protects the gills in most fishes and some amphibians **:** GILL COVER — see FISH illustration **f :** the principal bony plate of the gill cover **:** OPERCLE **g :** a flap that covers the mouth of some bryozoans **h :** a circular lid at one end of the egg of various invertebrates

**ope·re ci·ta·to** \ˌōpəˌrākəˈtād·(ˌ)ō, -ˌsīˈtād-\ *adv* [L] **:** in the work quoted — abbr. *op. cit.* or *o.c.*

**op·er·et·ta** \ˌäpəˈred·ə, -etə *sometimes* äˈpre-\ *also* **op·er·ette** \¦äpə¦ret, *usu* -ed·+V\ *n* -s [It., fr. *opera* + *-etta* ette] **1** *archaic* **:** LIGHT OPERA **2 :** a light musical-dramatic production having usu. a romantic plot and containing spoken dialogue and dancing scenes; *also* **:** the musical score of such a work

**op·er·et·tist** \ˌäpəˈred·əst, äˈpre-\ *n* -s **:** one that composes operettas

**op·er·ose** \ˈäpəˌrōs\ *adj* [L *operosus*, fr. *oper-, opus* work + *-osus* -ose — more at OPERATE] **1 :** wrought with labor **:** requiring or involving effort ⟨an ~ affair⟩ **2 :** DILIGENT, BUSY, INDUSTRIOUS — **op·er·ose·ly** *adv* — **op·er·ose·ness** *n* -ES

**op·er·os·i·ty** \ˌäpəˈräsəd·ē\ *n* -ES [L *operositas*, fr. *operosus* + *-itas* -ity] **:** OPEROSENESS

**operous** *adj* [L *operosus*] *obs* **:** OPEROSE

**opes** *pres 3d sing of* OPE, *pl of* OPE

**-opes** *pl of* -OPE

**opg** *abbr* opening

**¹ophe·lia** \ōˈfēlyə, əˈf-, -lēə\ *n, cap* [NL, prob. fr. Gk *ophis* serpent + *helos* marsh + NL *-ia* — more at HELODES] **:** a genus of small littoral burrowing polychaete worms with rudimentary parapodia of which the dorsal cirri are modified into gills

**²ophelia** \"\ *n* -s *often cap* [prob. fr. *Ophelia*, feminine proper name] **:** a grayish reddish purple to purplish red

**ophe·lim·i·ty** \ˌäfəˈlimədˌē, ˌōf-\ *n* -ES [It *ofelimità*, fr. Gk *ōphelimos* useful, helpful (fr. *ōphelein* to help, fr. *ophelos* advantage, help) + It. *-ità* -ity; akin to Skt *ā* toward and to Skt *phalam* fruit, profit — more at ACHARYA] **:** economic satisfaction ⟨the seller's net ~ varies with the price⟩

**ophi-** *or* **ophio-** *comb form* [Gk, fr. *ophis* snake — more at ANGUIS] **1 :** snake **:** serpent ⟨*ophio*phagous⟩ ⟨*ophio*latrous⟩ **2 a :** thing suggesting a snake ⟨*ophi*calcite⟩ **b :** being or resembling a snake in respect to a (specified) structure or quality ⟨*ophio*cephalus⟩

**ophi·an** \ˈäfēən, ˈōf-\ *n* -s *usu cap* [LGk *ophianoi*, pl., fr. Gk *ophis* + *-anoi*, pl. of *-anos* -an] **:** ²OPHITE

**ophic** \ˈäfik, ˈōf-\ *adj* [irreg. fr. *ophi-* + *ic*] **:** of or relating to snakes ⟨~ worship⟩

**ophi·cal·cite** \¦äfə, ¦ōfə+\ *n* [*ophi-* + *calcite*] **:** crystalline limestone or marble spotted with greenish serpentine **:** VERD ANTIQUE — called also *ophiolite*

**ophi·ce·phal·i·dae** \ˌäfəsəˈfaləˌdē, ˌōf-\ *n pl, cap* [NL, fr. *Ophicephalus*, type genus (fr. *ophi-* + *-cephalus*) + *-idae* — more at -CEPHALIC] **:** a family of elongated cylindrical carnivorous labyrinth fishes comprising the snakehead mullets of eastern Asia and Africa and usu. made coextensive with a suborder of Percomorphi

**oph·ich·thy·i·dae** \ˌäˌfikˈthīəˌdē, ˌōˌf-\ *n pl, cap* [NL, fr. *Ophichthys, Ophicthys*, type genus (irreg. fr. *ophi-* + *-ichthys*) + *-idae*] **:** a family of slender tropical eels comprising the snake eels

**ophi·cleide** \ˈäfəˌklīd, ˈōf-\ *n* -s [F *ophicléide*, fr. *ophi-* + Gk *kleid-, kleis* key — more at CLEID-] **1 :** a deep-toned brass wind musical instrument of the key bugle class, consisting of a large tapering tube bent double and provided with finger keys **2 :** a powerful organ reed stop of 8-foot or 16-foot pitch — **ophi·clei·de·an** \¦==ˈklīdēən\ *adj*

ophicleide

**ophi·cleid·ist** \ˈ==ˌklīdəst\ *n* -s **:** one who plays the ophicleide

**ophid·ia** \ōˈfidēə\ *n pl* [NL, irreg. fr. Gk *ophis* snake + NL *-ia* — more at ANGUIS] *syn of* SERPENTES

**¹ophid·i·an** \ōˈfidēən\ *adj* [NL *Ophidia* + E *-an*] **:** of, relating to, or resembling that of snakes **:** SNAKELIKE — **ophid·i·an·ly** *adv*

**²ophidian** \"\ *n* -s **:** SNAKE 1

**¹ophid·i·id** \ōˈfidēəd; ¦äfə¦dīəd, ¦ōf-\ *adj* [NL *Ophidiidae*] **:** of or relating to the Ophidiidae

**²ophidiid** \"\ *n* -s **:** a fish of the family Ophidiidae

**ophi·di·idae** \ˌäfəˈdīəˌdē, ˌōf-\ *n pl, cap* [NL, fr. *Ophidion*, type genus (fr. L *ophidion*, fish resembling the conger, fr. Gk, dim. of *ophis*) + *-idae*] **:** a family of elongate compressed somewhat eel-shaped fishes comprising the cusk eels and with related forms constituting a suborder of Percomorphi

**ophid·io·batrachia** \ōˌfidē(ˌ)ō+\ *or* **ophio·batrachia** \ˌäfē(ˌ)ō, ˌōf- +\ [*Ophidiobatrachia*, NL, fr. Gk *ophidion* + NL *Batrachia*; *Ophiobatrachia*, NL, fr. *ophi-* + *Batrachia*] *syn of* GYMNOPHIONA

**¹ophid·i·oid** \ōˈfidēˌȯid; ¦äfə¦dīˌȯid, ¦ōf-\ *adj* [NL *Ophidiidae* + E *-oid*] **:** like or related to the family Ophidiidae

**²ophidioid** \"\ *n* -s **:** an ophidioid fish

**ophi·ob·o·lus** \ˌäfēˈäbələs, ˌōf-\ *n, cap* [NL, fr. *ophi-* + Gk *-bolos* throwing, casting, fr. *ballein* to throw — more at DEVIL] **:** a genus of fungi (family Pleosporaceae) characterized by spindle-shaped several-septate ascospores — see TAKE-ALL

**ophio·ce·phal·i·dae** \ˌäfē(ˌ)ōsəˈfaləˌdē, ˌōfē-\ *syn of* OPHICEPHALIDAE

**ophio·glos·sa·ce·ae** \ˌäfē(ˌ)ō(ˌ)gläˈsāsēˌē, ˌōf-\ *n pl, cap* [NL, fr. *Ophioglossum*, type genus + *-aceae*] **:** a family of eusporangiate ferns (order Ophioglossales) that are more or less succulent and have a stem and usu. a single frond with thin sheathing stipules and sporophylls forming a spike or panicle, the sporangia opening by transverse slits — see OPHIOGLOSSUM — **ophio·glos·sa·ceous** \¦==(ˌ)=(¦)=¦sāshəs\ *adj*

**ophio·glos·sa·les** \ˌ==(ˌ)=(ˌ)gläˈsā(ˌ)lēz\ *n pl, cap* [NL, fr. *Ophioglossum* + *-ales*] **:** an order of Filicineae coextensive with the family Ophioglossaceae

**ophio·glos·sum** \ˌ===ˈgläsəm\ *n, cap* [NL, fr. *ophi-* + *-glossum*, fr. Gk *glōssa* tongue — more at GLOSS (explanation)] **:** the type genus of the family Ophioglossaceae comprising the adder's-tongues and having a solitary simple frond with netted venation and a terminal spike formed of two rows of coalescent sporangia

**ophi·ol·a·try** \ˌäfēˈäləˌtrē, ˌōf-\ *n* -ES [*ophi-* + *-latry*] **:** the worship of or attribution of divine or sacred nature to snakes

**ophi·o·lite** \ˈäfēəˌlīt, ˈōf-\ *n* -s [F *ophiolithe*, fr. *ophi-* + *lithe* -lite] **1** *obs* **:** SERPENTINE **2 :** OPHICALCITE — **ophi·o·lit·ic** \¦===¦lid·ik\ *adj*

**ophi·o·log·i·cal** \¦äfēə¦läjəkəl, ¦ōf-\ *adj* [*ophiology* + *-ical*] **:** of or relating to ophiology

**ophi·ol·o·gy** \ˌ==ˈäləjē *also* **ophi·dol·o·gy** \ˌäfəˈdä-, ˌōf-\ *n* -ES [*ophiology* fr. *ophi-* + *-logy*; *ophidology* fr. NL *ophido-* (irreg. fr. Gk *ophis* serpent) + E *-logy*] **:** a branch of herpetology concerned with the study of snakes

**ophio·mor·pha** \ˌ==əˈmȯrfə\ [NL, fr. *ophi-* + *-morpha*] *syn of* GYMNOPHIONA

**ophio·mor·phic** \¦==¦=fik\ *adj* [*ophi-* + *-morphic*] **1 :** snakelike in form **2** [NL *Ophiomorpha* + E *-ic*] **:** of or relating to the Gymnophiona

**ophi·on** \ˈōfīˌän; ˈäfēˌän, ˈōf-\ *n* [NL, fr. Gk *ophiōn*, a fabulous animal of Sardinia] **1** *cap* **:** a widely distributed genus of ichneumon flies that have a compressed abdomen and are parasitoid on the caterpillars of various moths in which they lay a single egg **2** -s **:** any insect of the genus *Ophion* — **ophi·o·nine** \ōˈfīəˌnīn; ˈäfēə-, ˈōfēə-\ *adj or n*

**ophi·oph·a·gous** \¦äfē¦äfəgəs, ¦ōfē-\ *adj* [Gk *ophiophagos*, fr. *ophi-* + *-phagos* -phagous] **:** feeding on snakes

**ophio·pluteus** \¦äfē(ˌ)ō, ¦ōf- +\ *n* [NL, fr. *ophi-* + *pluteus*] **:** the pluteus of a brittle star

**ophio·po·gon** \ˌ===ˈpōˌgän\ *n, cap* [NL, fr. *ophi-* + *-pogon*] **:** a genus of stoloniferous scapose grass-leaved herbs (family Liliaceae) having racemes or spikes of white, blue, violet, or lilac flowers with the ovary inferior — see LILYTURF

**ophio·sau·rus** \-ˈsȯrəs\ *syn of* OPHISAURUS

**ophi·os·to·ma** \ˌ==ˈästəmə\ [NL, fr. *ophi-* + *-stoma*] *syn of* CERATOSTOMELLA

**-o·phis** \əfəs\ *n comb form* [Gk *ophis* snake — more at *anguis*] **:** snake **:** serpent — in generic names esp. in herpetology ⟨Hydr*ophis*⟩

**ophi·sau·rus** \ˌäfəˈsȯrəs, ˌōf-\ *n, cap* [NL, fr. *ophi-* + *-saurus*] **:** a genus of lizards comprising the glass snakes

**ophism** \ˈäˌfizəm, ˈōˌf-\ *n* -s **1** *usu cap* **:** the doctrines and rites of the Ophites **2 :** serpent worship or the use of serpents as magical agencies **:** OPHIOLATRY — compare SNAKE DANCE

**¹ophite** \-ˈfīt\ *n* -s [L, fr. Gk *ophitēs* (*lithos*), lit., serpentine stone, fr. *ophitēs* like a snake, fr. *ophis*] **:** any of various usu. green and often mottled or blotched rocks (as a serpentine or serpentine marble)

**²ophite** \"\ *n* -s *usu cap* [LL *Ophitae*, pl., fr. LGk *Ophitai*, pl., fr. Gk *ophis* snake + *-itae*, pl. of *-ites* -ite — more at ANGUIS] **:** a member of a Gnostic sect or group of sects including the Naassenes and Perates that revered the serpent as the symbol of the hidden divine wisdom and as having befriended Adam and Eve by persuading them to eat of the tree of knowledge

**ophit·ic** \(ˈ)ä¦fid·ik, (ˈ)ō¦-\ *adj* [¹*ophite* + *-ic*] **:** having a rock fabric in which lath-shaped plagioclase crystals are enclosed wholly or in part in later formed augite ⟨diabase has an ~ structure⟩

**ophi·ura** \ˌäfē(y)ˈu̇rə, ˌōf-\ *n, cap* [NL, fr. *ophi-* + *-ura*] **:** a very large and widely distributed genus of brittle stars

**ophi·urae** \-ˌu̇ˌrē\ [NL, pl. of *Ophiura*] *syn of* OPHIUROIDEA

**ophi·uran** \-¦==¦=rən\ *adj or n* [NL *Ophiura* + E *-an*] **:** OPHIUROID

**¹ophi·urid** \¦==¦=rəd\ *adj* [NL *Ophiurida*] **:** of or relating to the Ophiurida; *broadly* **:** OPHIUROID

**²ophiurid** \"\ *n* -s **:** a member of the order Ophiurida **:** a typical brittle star; *broadly* **:** OPHIUROID

**ophi·uri·da** \ˌ==ˈ=rədə\ *n pl, cap* [NL, fr. *Ophiura* + *-ida*] **:** an order or other division of Ophiuroidea comprising brittle stars with simple unbranched arms

**¹ophi·uroid** \¦==¦=ˌrȯid\ *adj* [NL *Ophiuroidea*] **:** of or relating to the Ophiuroidea

**²ophiuroid** \"\ *n* -s **:** an echinoderm of the subclass Ophiuroidea **:** BRITTLE STAR, BASKET STAR

**ophi·uroi·dea** \ˌ== (y)əˈrȯidēə\ *n pl, cap* [NL, fr. *Ophiura* + *-oidea*] **:** a subclass or class of Echinodermata comprising the brittle stars and basket stars and being distinguished from Asteroidea by the slender flexible arms that are sharply marked off from the central disc, contain neither intestinal ceca nor prolongations of the gonads, and lack ambulacral grooves and by the location of the madreporite on the ventral surface adjacent to the mouth — see EURYALIDA, OPHIURIDA

**ophry·on** \ˈäfrēˌän, ˈōf-\ *n* -s [NL, fr. Gk *ophrys*, brow, eyebrow — more at BROW] **:** a craniometric point in the median line of the forehead and immediately above the orbits — see CRANIOMETRY illustration

**ophryo·sco·lec·i·dae** \¦äfrē(ˌ)ōskōˈlesəˌdē, ¦ōf-\ *n pl, cap* [NL, fr. *Ophryoscolec-, Ophryoscolex*, type genus (fr. Gk *ophrys* + NL *-o-* + *-scolec-, -scolex*) + *-idae*] **:** a large family of oligotrichous ciliates that are endocommensals in the stomach of ruminants where they break down starches and probably cellulose and presumably contribute protein to their hosts

**ophrys** \ˈäfrəs, ˈōf-\ [NL, fr. Gk, brow, eyebrow, a plant with two leaves] *syn of* LISTERA

**ophthalm-** *or* **ophthalmo-** *comb form* [Gk, fr. *ophthalmos* eye — more at OPHTHALMIA] **1 :** eye **:** eyeball ⟨*ophthalmo*tomy⟩ ⟨*ophthalm*ectomy⟩ **2 :** of or affecting the eyes ⟨*ophthalmo*carcinoma⟩ ⟨*ophthalm*algia⟩

**-oph·thal·ma** \ˌäfˈthalmə, ÷ˌäpˈth-\ *or* **-oph·thal·mia** \-mēə\ *n pl comb form* [-*ophthalma*, NL, fr. Gk, neut. pl. of adj. comb. form *-ophthalmos* having a (specified) eye, fr. *ophthalmos*; *-ophthalmia*, NL, fr. Gk *ophthalmos* + NL *-ia*] **:** ones having a (specified) eye — used in higher taxa esp. of arthropods ⟨Edri*ophthalma*⟩ ⟨Pod*ophthalmia*⟩

**oph·thalm·encephalon** \(¦)äf¦thalm, ÷(¦)äp¦th- + \ *n* [NL, fr. *ophthalm-* + *encephalon*] **:** the neural visual apparatus including the retinas, the optic nerves, and the parts of the brain functioning in vision

**oph·thal·mia** \äfˈthalmēə, ÷ äpˈth-\ *n* -s [ME *obtalmia*, fr. LL *ophthalmia*, fr. Gk, fr. *ophthalmos* eye, prob. fr. *op-* (root of *opsesthai* to be going to see) + *-thalmos*, alter. of *thalamos* chamber, room — more at OPTIC, THALAMUS] **:** an inflammation of the conjunctiva or of the eyeball

**-oph·thal·mia** \ˌäfˈthalmēə, ÷ˌäpˈth-\ *n comb form* -s [NL, fr. Gk, fr. *ophthalmos* eye + *-ia* -y] **:** condition of having (such) eyes ⟨micr*ophthalmia*⟩

**ophthalmia neo·na·to·rum** \-ˌnēənəˈtōrəm\ *n* [NL] **:** acute inflammation of the eyes in the newborn from infection during passage through the birth canal

**oph·thal·mi·a·ter** \äfˈthalmēˌād·ə(r), ÷äpˈth-\ *n* -s [*ophthalm-* + Gk *iatēr* healer, fr. *iasthai* to heal — more at IATRIC] **:** OCULIST

**oph·thal·mic** \(ˈ)äf¦thalmik, -mēk, ÷ (ˈ)äp¦th-\ *adj* [Gk *ophthalmikos* fr. *ophthalm-* + *-ikos* -ic] **1 :** of, relating to, or

near the eye : OCULAR **2** : for use on or in the eye ⟨an ~ ointment⟩
**ophthalmic artery** *n* : a branch of the internal carotid following the optic nerve through the optic foramen into the orbit and supplying the eye and adjacent structures
**ophthalmic ganglion** *n* : CILIARY GANGLION
**ophthalmic glass** *n* : glass similar to optical glass but annealed in rolled sheets and used primarily for spectacle lens blanks
**ophthalmic nerve** *n* : the first division of the trigeminal nerve, arising from the gasserian ganglion and by its branches supplying sensory fibers to the lachrymal gland, eyelids, ciliary muscle, nose, forehead, and adjoining parts
**ophthalmic optician** *n, Brit* : OPTOMETRIST
**ophthalmic vein** *n* : either of two veins, a superior and an inferior, that pass from the orbit through the superior orbital fissure to the cavernous sinus
**oph·thal·mite** \⸗ˈ⸗,mīt\ *n* -s [*ophthalm-* + *-ite*] : an eyestalk of a crustacean
**oph·thal·mi·tis** \ˌ⸗ˌ⸗ˈmīd·əs, -ˌthəl-\ *n* -ES [NL, fr. *ophthalm-* + *-itis*] : OPHTHALMIA
**oph·thal·mo·diastimeter** \äf¦thal(ˌ)mō, ÷äp¦th-\ *n* [*ophthalm-* + *diastimeter*] : an instrument for adjusting the distance between the eyes and lenses (as of spectacles)
**ophthalmodynamometer** \"+\ *n* [ISV *ophthalm-* + *dynamometer*; prob. orig. formed as F *ophtalmodynamomètre*] : an instrument used to determine the nearest point to which the two eyes can be made to converge
**oph·thal·mo·graph** \äf'thalmə,graf, -räf, ÷äp'th-\ *n* [*ophthalm-* + *-graph*] : an instrument that photographs the movements of the eyes during reading
**oph·thal·mo·leu·ko·scope** *also* **oph·thal·mo·leu·co·scope** \(ˌ)äf,thalmə'lükə,skōp, ÷ (ˌ)äp,th-\ *n* [*ophthalm-* + *leuc-* + *-scope*] : an apparatus for testing the color sense by means of colors produced by polarized light
**oph·thal·mo·log·ic** \(¦)äf¦thalmə¦läjik, ÷(¦)äp¦th-, ¦⸗-thəl-, -jēk, *by l-dissimilation* ÷-ˌthamə-\ *also* **oph·thal·mo·log·i·cal** \-jəkəl, -jēk-\ *adj* : of or relating to ophthalmology — **oph·thal·mo·log·i·cal·ly** \-jək(ə)lē, -jēk-, -li\ *adv*
**oph·thal·mol·o·gist** \ˌäf,thal'mäləjəst, ÷ˌäp,th-, -ˌthəl-, *by l-dissimilation* ÷-ˌthə'm-\ *n* -s : a physician that specializes in the study and treatment of defects and diseases of the eye — compare OPTICIAN, OPTOMETRIST
**oph·thal·mol·o·gy** \-jē,-ji\ *n* -ES [*ophthalm-* + *-logy*] : a branch of medical science concerned with the structure, functions, and diseases of the eye — compare OPTOMETRY
**oph·thal·mom·e·ter** \ˌ⸗,thal'mäməd·ə(r), -ˌthəl-\ *n* [ISV *ophthalm-* + *-meter*] : an instrument for measuring the eye; *specif* : an instrument for measuring the size of a reflected image on the convex surface of the cornea of the eye by which its principal meridians and the presence and amount of astigmatism may be determined
**oph·thal·mo·met·ric** \(¦)äf¦thalmə¦me·trik, ÷(¦)äp,th-\ *or* **oph·thal·mo·met·ri·cal** \-rəkəl\ *adj* : of, relating to, or by means of an ophthalmometer or ophthalmometry
**oph·thal·mom·e·try** \ˌ⸗ˌ⸗'mämə·trē, -ˌthəl-\ *n* -ES [ISV *ophthalm-* + *-metry*] : the measuring of the corneal curvatures of the eye and of their deviations from normal (as in astigmatism) usu. by means of an ophthalmometer
**oph·thal·mo·phore** \⸗'thalmə,fō(ə)r\ *also* **oph·thal·mo·pho·ri·um** \(ˌ)⸗ˌ⸗mə'fōrēəm\ *n, pl* **ophthalmophores** \-,fō(ə)rz\ *also* **ophthalmopho·ria** \-'fōrēə\ [*ophthalmophore* fr. *ophthalm-* + *-phore*; *ophthalmophorium* fr. NL, fr. E *ophthalmophore*] : OMMATOPHORE — **oph·thal·moph·o·rous** \¦⸗¦⸗¦mäfərəs, -ˌthəl-\ *adj*
**oph·thal·mo·ple·gia** \(ˌ)⸗,thalmə'plēj(ē)ə\ *n* -s [NL, fr. *ophthalm-* + *-plegia*] : paralysis of the muscles of the eye — **oph·thal·mo·ple·gic** \¦⸗¦⸗¦plējik\ *adj*
**oph·thal·mo·pod** \⸗'⸗⸗,päd\ *n* -s [*ophthalm-* + *-pod*] : EYESTALK
**ophthalmo-reaction** \⸗¦⸗(ˌ)mō+\ *n* [ISV *ophthalm-* + *reaction*] : a serological diagnostic reaction involving the use of a test antigen (as tuberculin) on the mucous membrane of the eye, a positive response indicative of infection being signalized by hyperemia, swelling, and lacrimation
**oph·thal·mo·sau·rus** \(ˌ)⸗ˌ⸗mə'sórəs\ *n, cap* [NL, fr. *ophthalm-* + *-saurus*] : a genus of Jurassic and Lower Cretaceous ichthyosaurs of England having no or only a few small teeth
**oph·thal·mo·scope** \⸗'⸗mə,skōp\ *n* [ISV *ophthalm-* + *-scope*; prob. orig. formed as G *ophthalmoskop*] : an instrument for viewing the interior of the eye consisting of a concave mirror with a hole in the center through which the observer examines the eye, a source of light that is reflected into the eye by the mirror, and lenses in the mirror which can be rotated into the opening in the mirror to neutralize the refracting power of the eye being examined and thus make the image of the fundus clear — **oph·thal·mo·scop·ic** \(¦)⸗¦⸗⸗¦skäpik\ *adj* — **oph·thal·mo·scop·i·cal·ly** \-pək(ə)lē\ *adv*
**oph·thal·mos·co·py** \ˌäf,thal'mäskəpē, -ˌthəl-, ÷ˌäp(ˌ)th-\ *n* -ES [ISV *ophthalm-* + *-scopy*] : examination of the eye with an ophthalmoscope
**oph·thal·mo·trope** \⸗'thalmə,trōp\ *n* -s [*ophthalm-* + *-trope*] : a mechanical eye for demonstrating the movement of the eye muscles
**oph·thal·mo·tropometer** \(¦)⸗¦thalmō +\ *n* [*ophthalm-* + *tropometer*] : an instrument for measuring ocular movements
**-oph·thal·mus** \äf'thalməs, ÷ˌäp'th-\ *n comb form* [NL, fr. Gk *-ophthalmos*, fr. *ophthalmos* eye — more at OPHTHALMIA] **1** : one having a (specified) kind of eye — in generic names usu. of arthropods ⟨*Megophthalmus*⟩ **2** -ES : eyes of a (specified) form or in a (specified) state ⟨*megalophthalmus*⟩
**-o·pia** \'ōpēə\ *n comb form* [NL, fr. Gk *-ōpia*, fr. *ōps* eye, face + *-ia* -y — more at EYE] **1** *also* **-o·py** \ˌōpē, -pi\ *pl* **-o·pias** *also* **-opies** [NL *-opia*] **a** : vision : condition of having (such) vision ⟨*diplopia*⟩ ⟨*amblyopy*⟩ **b** : possession of an eye or eyes with a (specified) defect ⟨*anopia*⟩ **2** : one having a (specified) kind of eye — in generic names in zoology ⟨*Heteropia*⟩
**opi·an·ic acid** \¦ōpē¦anik-\ *n* [*opiane*, obs. syn. of *narcotine* (fr. *opium* + *-ane*) + *-ic*] : a bitter crystalline aldehyde acid $C_6H_2(OCH_3)_2(CHO)COOH$ obtained by the oxidation of narcotine and hydrastine
**¹opi·ate** \'ōpēət, -ē,āt, *usu* -d·+V\ *adj* [ML *opiatus*, fr. L *opium* + *-atus* -ate] **1** : containing or mixed or impregnated with opium **2 a** : inducing sleep : SOMNIFEROUS, NARCOTIC **b** : causing rest, dullness, or inaction
**²opiate** \"\ *n* -s **1** : a medicine containing or derived from opium and tending to induce sleep and to alleviate pain **2** : a synthetic drug capable of producing or sustaining addiction similar to that characteristic of morphine and cocaine : NARCOTIC — used esp. in modern law **3** : something that induces rest or inaction or quiets uneasiness ⟨price fixing is a most dangerous ~ —T.W.Arnold⟩
**³opiate** \-ē,āt, *usu* -ād·+V\ *vt* -ED/-ING/-S [*opium* + *-ate*, vb. suffix] **1 a** : to subject to the influence of an opiate : put to sleep **b** : to diminish the force, intensity, or sensitiveness of : DEADEN **2** : to impregnate or mix with opium
**opi·at·ic** \¦ōpē¦ad·ik\ *adj* : of, relating to, or like opiates
**-opies** *pl of* -OPY
**opifice** *n* -s [L *opificium*, fr. *opific-* *opifex* workman, irreg. fr. *opus* work + *-fic*, *-fex* (fr. *facere* to do, make) — more at OPERATE, DO] *obs* : LABOR, WORKMANSHIP; *also* : a piece of work
**opif·i·cer** \ə'pifəsə(r)\ *n* -s [L *opific-* *opifex* + E *-er*] : ARTIFICER, WORKMAN, MAKER
**opi·hi** \ō'pē(ˌ)hē\ *n* -s [Hawaiian *'opihi*] *Hawaii* : any of several edible limpets (genus *Helcioniscus*)
**opil·ia** \ō'pilēə\ *n, cap* [NL, perh. fr. *Opilio*, genus of arachnids — more at OPILIONEA] : a small genus (the type of the family Opiliaceae) of Old World tropical climbing shrubs
**opil·i·a·ce·ae** \ˌ⸗ˌ⸗'āsē,ē\ *n pl, cap* [NL, fr. *Opilia*, type genus + *-aceae*] : a family of tropical shrubs or trees (order Santalales) having coriaceous leaves, small flowers, and drupaceous fruit — **opil·i·a·ceous** \ˌ⸗¦⸗¦āshəs\ *adj*
**opil·i·o·nea** \ō,pilē'ōnēə\ *or* **opil·i·o·nes** \-,nēz\ *or* **opil·i·o·ni·na** \-ə'nīnə\ [NL, fr. *Opilion-*, *Opilio*, genus of arachnids, fr. L *opilion-*, *opilio* shepherd, fr. *ovis* sheep + *-pilion-*, *-pilio* driver (fr. *pellere* to drive) — more at EWE, FELT] *syn of* PHALANGIDA
**opil·i·o·nine** \⸗'⸗⸗ə,nīn, -ˌnən\ *adj or n* [NL *Opilionina*] : PHALANGID

**opinable** *adj* [L *opinabilis*, fr. *opinari*, to have an opinion, think + *-abilis* -able — more at OPINE] **1** *obs* : being a matter of opinion **2** *obs* : capable of being opined : constituting an object of opinion
**op·i·nant** \'äpənənt, ō'pīn-\ *n* -s [F, fr. pres. part. of *opiner* to opine, fr. L *opinari*] : OPINER
**¹opin·a·tive** \ō'pīnəd·iv\ *adj* [LL *opinativus* expressing a conjecture, fr. L *opinatus* (past part. of *opinari*) + *-ivus* -ive] **1** *obs* : OBSTINATE, OPINIONATED **2** : of, relating to, or constituting opinion : UNCERTAIN — **opinatively** *adv, obs*
**²opinative** \"\ *n* -s : an opinionated person
**opinator** *n* -s [L, fr. *opinatus* + *-or*] *obs* : OPINER, THEORIST
**opine** \ō'pīn, ə'p-\ *vb* -ED/-ING/-S [MF *opiner*, fr. L *opinari* to have an opinion, think; perh. akin to L *optare* to choose, desire, *option-*, *optio* free choice, Gk *epiopsesthai* to be going to choose] *vt* **1** : to express in form as one's opinion : give a formal opinion about : STATE ⟨*opined* that the weather would improve⟩ **2** : to have, hold, or form an opinion about ⟨some things we know, some we only ~⟩ ~ *vi* : to form or express opinions ⟨you may ~ about anything under the sun⟩
**opin·er** \-nə(r)\ *n* -s : one that opines
**oping** *pres part of* OPE
**opin·i·ate** \ō'pinē,āt, ə'p-\ *vt* -ED/-ING/-S [irreg. fr. *opinion* + *-ate*] **1** *archaic* : OPINE, SUPPOSE **2** *archaic* : to establish in an opinion **3** *archaic* : to declare an opinion on
**opin·i·a·tive** \ō'pinē,ād·iv, ə'p-\ *adj* [MF *opiniatif*, irreg. fr. *opinion* + *-atif* -ative] : OPINIONATIVE — **opin·i·a·tive·ness** *n* -ES
**¹opiniatre** *also* **opiniastre** *or* **opiniaster** *adj* [MF *opinionastre*, *opiniatre*, fr. *opinion*] *obs* : OPINIONATED
**²opiniatre** *also* **opiniastre** *or* **opiniaster** *n* -s *obs* : an opinionated person
**³opiniatre** *vb* -ED/-ING/-S [F *opiniâtrer*, fr. *opiniâtre* opiniated, fr. MF *opiniatre*] *vt, obs* : to obstinately maintain (an opinion) or persist in (a course of action) ~ *vi, obs* : to obstinately maintain an opinion or persist in a course of action
**opiniatrety** *also* **opiniatry** *n* -ES [*opiniatrety* fr. F *opiniâtreté*, fr. *opiniâtre* + *-té* -ty; *opiniatry* fr. F *opiniastrie*, fr. MF *opiniastre* + *-ie* -y] *obs* : the quality or state of being opinionated : mental obstinacy or inflexibility
**opin·i·cus** \ō'pinəkəs\ *n* -ES [origin unknown] **1** : a fabulous beast represented esp. in heraldry much like a griffon but with a short tail **2** : an insignia bearing or consisting of an opinicus

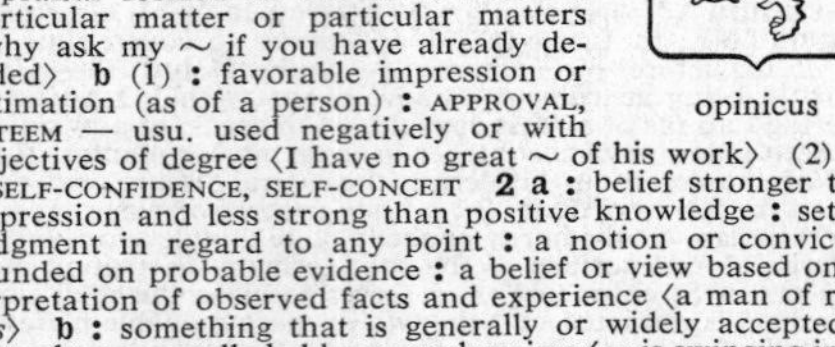
opinicus

**¹opin·ion** \ə'pinyən *sometimes* ō'p-\ *n* -s [ME, fr. MF, fr. L *opinion-*, *opinio*; akin to L *opinari*] **1 a** : a view, judgment, or appraisal formed in the mind about a particular matter or particular matters ⟨why ask my ~ if you have already decided⟩ **b** (1) : favorable impression or estimation (as of a person) : APPROVAL, ESTEEM — usu. used negatively or with adjectives of degree ⟨I have no great ~ of his work⟩ (2) *obs* : SELF-CONFIDENCE, SELF-CONCEIT **2 a** : belief stronger than impression and less strong than positive knowledge : settled judgment in regard to any point : a notion or conviction founded on probable evidence : a belief or view based on interpretation of observed facts and experience ⟨a man of rigid ~s⟩ **b** : something that is generally or widely accepted as factual : a generally held or popular view ⟨~ is swinging in his favor⟩ **c** : a view or belief that is not demonstrable as fact ⟨this is only my ~ of course⟩ **3 a** : a formal expression by an expert (as a professional authority) of his thought upon or judgment or advice concerning a matter ⟨decided to obtain a medical ~ of the case⟩ **b** : the formal expression (as by a judge, court, referee) of the legal reasons and principles upon which a legal decision is based; *also* : the judgment or decision so based **4** *obs* : estimation in which one is held by others; *esp* : favorable reputation **5** *obs* : EXPECTATION, ANTICIPATION **6** *Platonism* : conjecture or belief based on experience and perception
**syn** VIEW, BELIEF, CONVICTION, PERSUASION, SENTIMENT: these nouns have in common the sense of a more or less clearly formulated idea or judgment which one holds as true. OPINION implies a conclusion concerning something on which ideas may differ, not, however, excluding a careful consideration or weighing of evidence or pros and cons, but usu. stressing the subjectivity and disputability of the conclusion ⟨opposing political *opinions*⟩ ⟨a man of strong likes and dislikes but few *opinions*⟩ ⟨a dissenting *opinion* handed down by a Supreme Court judge⟩ ⟨to prefer to deal in facts rather than *opinions*⟩ VIEW is an opinion or set of opinions usu. more or less colored by individual feeling, sentiment, or bias ⟨the political *views* of the opposing party⟩ ⟨expressed her *views* on the role of education in the integration of home and community life —*Current Biog.*⟩ ⟨to air one's *views*⟩ BELIEF differs from *view* or *opinion* in implying a conclusion or set of interrelated conclusions not necessarily formulated by the individual but often constituting a dogma, doctrine, or proposition already formulated prior to the individual's acceptance or adoption of it; it emphasizes the individual's assent to the conclusion or his assurance of its truth ⟨religious *beliefs*⟩ ⟨old customs and old *beliefs* —Wilfrid Goatman⟩ ⟨to hold the *belief* that man has certain inalienable rights⟩ CONVICTION is a belief held strongly because one has no doubts about its truth ⟨the *conviction* that where one was born and lives is the best place in the world —E.L.Ullman⟩ ⟨along with that faith have lost the old . . . *conviction* that most people are good and that evil is merely an accident —Malcolm Cowley⟩ ⟨a man of many positive *convictions*⟩ PERSUASION suggests a belief or set of beliefs held strongly, often predominantly though by no means exclusively on nonlogical or nonrational grounds ⟨Christians of all *persuasions* —*Current Biog.*⟩ ⟨the childish *persuasion* that we have the only rational way of doing things —Gustave Weigel⟩ ⟨an artist who is not of the contemporary *persuasion* —*Sydney (Australia) Bull.*⟩ SENTIMENT, rather infrequent today in this sense, suggests a more or less settled opinion, often involving feelings or emotions ⟨a speech in which he expressed an apparent reversal of his known conservative *sentiments* —A.L. Funk⟩ ⟨to express strong *sentiments* on a political issue⟩
— **be of the opinion** : to hold as an opinion : THINK
**²opinion** \"\ *vb* -ED/-ING/-S *chiefly dial* : OPINE
**opin·ion·able** \-nəbəl\ *adj* [²*opinion* + *-able*] : admitting of opinion : having no single provable solution
**opin·ion·al** \-nəl\ *adj* : of, relating to, or constituting opinion
**opin·ion·ate** \-nət, -ˌnāt\ *adj* [¹*opinion* + *-ate*, adj. suffix] **1** *obs* : grounded on opinion : lacking firm factual bases **2** *obs* : OPINIONATED — **opin·ion·ate·ly** *adv*
**²opin·ion·ate** \-ˌnāt, *usu* -ād·+V\ *vt* -ED/-ING/-S [¹*opinion* + *-ate*, vb. suffix] : OPINE
**opin·ion·at·ed** \-ˌnād·əd, -ātəd\ *adj* [¹*opinionate* + *-ed*] **1** *obs* : having or holding a specified opinion : OPINIONED; *specif* : CONCEITED **2** : stiff in opinion : firmly or unduly adhering to one's own opinion or to preconceived notions : OBSTINATE — **opin·ion·at·ed·ly** *adv* — **opin·ion·at·ed·ness** *n* -ES
**opin·ion·a·tive** \-ˌnād·iv\ *adj* [*opinion* + *-ative*] **1** *obs* **a** : based on opinion : CONJECTURAL, IMAGINARY **b** : PROUD, CONCEITED **2** : of, relating to, or consisting of opinion or belief : DOCTRINAL **3** : unduly attached to one's own opinions : tending to be opinionated — **opin·ion·a·tive·ly** \-d·əvlē\ *adv* — **opin·ion·a·tive·ness** \-d·ivnəs\ *n* -ES
**opin·ion·a·tor** \-ˌnād·ə(r)\ *n* -s [²*opinionate* + *-or*] : an expresser, holder, or creator of opinion
**opin·ioned** \ə'pinyənd *sometimes* ō'p-\ *adj* [¹*opinion* + *-ed*] **1** : having or holding an opinion : possessed of a usu. specified opinion ⟨are we so hardly ~ as to hear no arguments⟩ **2** : having a usu. favorable opinion with respect to a particular thing ⟨arrogant fellows very well ~ of themselves⟩ **3** : OPINIONATED ⟨a biased and ~ editorial⟩
**opin·ion·ist** \-nəst\ *n* -s **1** : one who holds an unusual or heretical belief or opinion : SECTARY **2** : a person holding a specified opinion
**opin·ion·naire** *also* **opin·ion·aire** \ə¦pinyə¦na(a)(ə)r, -ne(, |ə\ *n* -s [*opinion* + question*naire*] : a questionnaire designed to elicit views on matters of opinion from which generalizations may be abstracted
**opinion poll** *n* : a recording of the replies to a question or set of questions of opinion given by a small percentage of the members of a group or of the general public and used as a basis for gauging group opinion or public opinion on a particular issue
**opinions** *pl of* OPINION, *pres 3d sing of* OPINION
**opio-** *comb form* [Gk *opion* opium — more at *opium*] : opium ⟨*opiomania*⟩ ⟨*opiophagous*⟩
**opio·phile** \'ōpēə,fīl\ *n* -s [*opio-* + *-phile*] : a user of opium
**opip·a·rous** \ō'pipərəs\ *adj* [L *opiparus*, fr. *ops* riches + *parare* to provide, prepare — more at OPULENT, PARE] *archaic* : SUMPTUOUS — **opip·a·rous·ly** *adv, archaic*
**op·i·som·e·ter** \ˌäpə'säməd·ə(r)\ *n* [fr. Gk *opisō* backwards + E *-meter*; akin to Gk *opisthen*] : an instrument used for measuring curved lines (as on a map) and consisting essentially of a screw with a wheel-shaped nut that is made to rotate forward along the curved lines and then backward to its original position on the screw along a straight scale

opisometer

**opisth-** *or* **opistho-** *comb form* [Gk, fr. *opisthen*, *opithen* behind, in the rear; akin to Gk *epi* on, upon — more at EPI-] **1** : having something (specified) located dorsally or posteriorly ⟨*opisth*otic⟩ ⟨*opisth*andric⟩ **2** : dorsal or posterior ⟨*opisth*aptor⟩ ⟨*opistho*dome⟩
**op·is·thap·tor** \¦äpəs¦thaptə(r)\ *n* [NL, fr. *opisth-* + *haptor*] : the posterior and usu. complex adhesive organ of a monogenetic trematode
**opis·the·nar** \ə'pisthə,när, -ā(r)\ *n* [NL, fr. Gk, fr. *opisth-* + *thenar*] : the back of the hand
**opis·thi·on** \ə'pisthē,än\ *n, pl* **opis·thia** \-ēə\ *or* **opisthions** [NL, fr. Gk, neut. of *opisthios* hinder, fr. *opisthen*] : the median point of the posterior border of the foramen magnum
**¹opis·tho·branch** \ə'pisthə,braŋk\ *adj* [NL *Opisthobranchia*] : of or relating to the Opisthobranchia
**²opisthobranch** \"\ *n* -s : a mollusk of the order Opisthobranchia
**opis·tho·bran·chia** \ˌ⸗ˌ⸗⸗'braŋkēə\ *n pl, cap* [NL, fr. *opisth-* + *-branchia*] *zool* : a large order of Euthyneura comprising marine gastropod mollusks having the gills when present posterior to the heart and having no operculum — compare STREPTONEURA; see NUDIBRANCHIA, TECTIBRANCHIA — **opis·tho·bran·chi·ate** \⸗¦⸗⸗¦braŋkēət, -ē,āt\ *adj or n*
**opis·tho·bran·chi·a·ta** \ˌ⸗ˌ⸗⸗,⸗⸗'äd·ə, -ād·ə\ *syn of* OPISTHOBRANCHIA
**opis·tho·coe·la** \ˌ⸗ˌ⸗⸗'sēlə\ *n pl, cap* [NL, fr. neut. pl. of *opisthocoelus* hollow behind — more at OPISTHOCOELOUS] : a suborder of Salientia comprising frogs and toads having short free ribs and vertebrae that are concave behind but not in front and including the families Discoglossidae and Pipidae — **opis·tho·coe·lan** \-lən\ *n* -s — **opis·tho·coe·lid** \⸗¦⸗⸗¦sēləd\ *adj or n*
**opis·tho·coe·lia** \ˌ⸗ˌ⸗⸗'sēlēə\ [NL, fr. *opisthocoelus* + *-ia*] *syn of* SAUROPODA
**opis·tho·coe·li·an** \⸗¦⸗⸗¦lēən\ *adj* [NL *opisthocoelus* + E *-ian*] : OPISTHOCOELOUS
**opis·tho·coe·lous** \-ləs\ *adj* [NL *opisthocoelus*, fr. *opisth-* + Gk *koilos* hollow — more at CAVE] : of, relating to, or being a vertebra that is concave behind with the anterior end of the centrum flat or convex and the posterior concave
**opis·tho·come** \ə'pisthə,kōm\ *n* -s [NL *Opisthocomus*, fr. LGk *opisthokomos* wearing the hair long behind, from Gk *opisth-* + *komē* hair] : HOATZIN
**op·is·tho·co·mi** \ˌäpəs'thäkə,mī\ *n pl, cap* [NL, pl. of *Opisthocomus*] : a suborder of Galliformes constituted by the hoatzin
**opis·tho·com·i·dae** \ə,pisthə'kämə,dē\ *n pl, cap* [NL, fr. *Opisthocomus*, type genus + *-idae*] : a family of birds coextensive with the suborder Opisthocomi
**opis·tho·cra·ni·on** \-'krānē,än\ *n* -s [NL, fr. LGk *opisthokranion*, fr. Gk *opisth-* + *kranion* skull — more at CRANIUM] : the posteriormost point in the midsagittal plane of the occiput
**opis·tho·det·ic** \⸗¦⸗⸗¦ded·ik\ *adj* [Gk *opisthodetos* tied behind (fr. *opisth-* + *detos*, verbal of *dein* to tie, bind) + E *-ic* — more at DIADEM] : situated behind the beak — used of the ligament of a bivalve mollusk — compare PROSODETIC
**opis·tho·dome** \⸗'⸗⸗,dōm\ *n* [Gk *opisthodomos*, fr. *opisth-* + *domos* house — more at TIMBER] : a back chamber; *esp* : the part of the naos of a classical temple farthest from the main entrance
**op·is·thod·o·mos** \ˌäpəs'thädəməs, -ˌmäs\ *or* **op·is·thod·o·mus** \-məs\ *n* -ES [*opisthodomos*, Gk; *opisthodomus*, L, fr. Gk *opisthodomos*] : OPISTHODOME
**opis·tho·dont** \ə'pisthə,dänt\ *adj* [*opisth-* + *-odont*] : having back teeth only ⟨~ snakes⟩
**opis·tho·gastric** \ə¦pisthə+\ *adj* [F *opisthogastrique*, fr. *opisth-* + *gastrique* gastric] : situated behind the stomach
**opis·tho·glos·sa** \ˌ⸗ˌ⸗⸗'gläsə, -lȯsə\ *n pl, cap* [NL, fr. *opisth-* + *-glossa*] : a division of Salientia comprising amphibians with the tongue attached in front and free behind — **opis·tho·glos·sal** \⸗¦⸗⸗¦gläsəl, -lȯs-\ *or* **opis·tho·glos·sate** \-sət, -ˌsāt\ *adj*
**¹opis·tho·glyph** \⸗'⸗⸗,glif\ *or* **opis·tho·glyph·ous** \⸗¦⸗⸗¦glifəs\ *also* **opis·tho·glyph·ic** \-fik\ *adj* [*opisthoglyph* fr. NL *Opisthoglypha*; *opisthoglyphous* fr. NL *Opisthoglypha* + E *-ous*; *opisthoglyphic* fr. NL *Opisthoglypha* + E *-ic*] : of or relating to the Opisthoglypha : having teeth of the type characteristic of this group
**²opisthoglyph** \"\ *n* -s : an opisthoglyph snake
**op·is·thog·ly·pha** \ˌäpəs'thägləfə, ə,pisthə'glifə\ *n pl, cap* [NL, neut. pl. of *opisthoglyphus*, carved behind, fr. *opisth-* + Gk *-glyphos*, fr. *glyphein* to carve — more at CLEAVE] : a group of snakes having one or a few posterior maxillary teeth grooved to conduct venom from the enlarged upper labial glands and comprising the families Homalopsidae, Elachistodontidae and Boigidae — compare PROTEROGLYPHA
**opis·tho·gnath·i·dae** \ə,pisthə'nathə,dē, -ˌthäg'n-\ *n pl, cap* [NL, fr. *Opisthognathus*, type genus, (fr. *opisth-* + *-gnathus*) + *-idae*] : a family of large-mouthed percoid fishes with a large naked head and the body covered with small cycloid scales — see JAWFISH
**op·is·thog·na·thism** \ˌäpəs'thägnə,thizəm\ *n* -s [ISV *opisth-* + *gnathism*] : the condition of being markedly opisthognathous
**op·is·thog·na·thous** \¦⸗⸗¦⸗⸗thəs\ *adj* [*opisth-* + *-gnathous*] **1** : having retreating jaws — opposed to *prognathous* **2** : having the mouthparts ventral and posterior to the cranium — used esp. of hemipterons
**opis·tho·go·ne·a·ta** \ə,pisthə,gōnē'äd·ə, -ād·ə\ *n pl, cap* [NL, fr. *opisth-* + Gk *gonē* genitalia (fr. Gk *gignesthai* to be born) + NL *-ata* — more at KIN] : a primary division of Arthropoda comprising forms with single posterior genital aperture and including the insects and centipedes or sometimes only the latter
**opis·tho·go·ne·ate** \⸗¦⸗⸗¦⸗⸗ət, -ˌāt\ *adj* [*opisth-* + Gk *gonē* + E *-ate*] **1** : having the genital opening near the hind end of the body — distinguished from *progoneate* **2** [NL *Opisthogoneata*] : of or relating to the Opisthogoneata
**opis·tho·graph** \ə'pisthə,graf\ *n* [L *opisthographus* written on the back, fr. Gk *opisthographos*, fr. *opisth-* + *-graphos* -graph] : an ancient manuscript or tablet written or inscribed upon both the back and the front — **opis·tho·graph·ic** \⸗¦⸗⸗¦grafik\ *or* **opis·tho·graph·i·cal** \-fəkəl\ *adj* — **op·is·thog·ra·phy** \ˌäpəs'thägrəfē\ *n* -ES
**opis·tho·gyrate** \ə¦pisthə+\ *adj* [*opisth-* + *gyrate*] : curving toward the posterior ⟨a bivalve shell with ~ umbones⟩ — compare PROSOGYRATE
**opis·tho·mere** \⸗'⸗⸗,mi(ə)r\ *n* -s [*opisth-* + *-mere*] : any of several terminal plates of the abdomen of the female earwig that unite to form a horny sclerite
**opis·tho·mi** \-ˌmī\ *n pl, cap* [NL, pl. of *opisthomus* with the shoulder behind fr. *opisth-* + Gk *ōmos* shoulder — more at HUMERUS] : a small order of freshwater carnivorous fishes of Africa and southern Asia that resemble eels and have modified tubular nostrils and highly developed olfactory organs — **opis·tho·mous** \-məs\ *adj*
**opis·tho·neph·ros** \ˌ⸗ˌ⸗⸗'ne,fräs\ *n, pl* **opis·tho·neph·roi** \-ˌfrȯi\ [NL, fr. *opisth-* + Gk *nephros* kidney — more at

NEPHRITIS] **:** the adult kidney of animals (as some amphibians) that are commonly considered mesonephric as adults, resembling but not identical to the embryonic mesonephros

**opis·tho·par·ia** \ə,pisthə'pa(a)rēə\ *n pl, cap* [NL, fr. *opisth-* + *-paria* (fr. Gk *pareia* cheek)] **:** an order of trilobites including those in which the angles or spines are borne by the free cheeks — **opis·tho·par·i·an** \⸗;⸗⸗;pa(a)rēən\ *n or adj*

**opis·thor·chi·a·sis** \ə,pis,thȯ(r)'kīəsəs\ *n* -ES [NL, fr. *Opisthorchis* + *-iasis*] **:** infestation with or disease caused by liver flukes of the genus *Opisthorchis*

**¹op·is·thor·chi·id** \¦äpəs¦thȯ(r)kēəd\ *adj* [NL *Opisthorchiidae*] **:** of or relating to the Opisthorchiidae

**²opisthorchiid** \"\ *n* -S **:** a trematode of the family Opisthorchiidae

**opis·thor·chi·idae** \ə,pis,thȯ(r)'kīə,dē\ *n pl, cap* [NL, fr. *Opisthorchis*, type genus + *-idae*] **:** a family of digenetic trematodes that are parasitic as adults in the bile ducts of various birds and mammals including man, that are ingested with fish as encysted metacercaria and freed in the digestive tract to make their way into the liver, and that are distinguished by the absence of a cirrus pouch and the presence of the ovary anterior to the testes — see CLONORCHIS, OPISTHORCHIS

**op·is·thor·chis** \,äpəs'thȯ(r)kəs\ *n, cap* [NL, fr. *opisth-* + Gk *orchis* testicle — more at ORCHIS] **:** the type genus of Opisthorchiidae including several trematodes that are casual or incidental parasites of the human liver

**opis·tho·so·ma** \ə,pisthə'sōmə\ *n, pl* **opisthosomata** [NL, fr. *opisth-* + *-soma*] **:** the posterior portion of the body of an arthropod esp. when unsegmented or when the segmentation is obscured

**opis·tho·somal** \ə¦pisthə+\ *also* **opis·tho·somatic** \"+\ *adj* **1 :** of, relating to, or lying in the posterior region of the body **2 :** forming an opisthosoma ⟨an ~ mass⟩

**opis·tho·the·lae** \⸗,⸗⸗'thē(,)lē\ *n pl, cap* [NL, fr. *opisth-* + *-thelae* (fr. Gk *-thēlai*, fr. *thēlē* nipple)] *in some classifications* **:** a large suborder of Araneida containing spiders that have nonsegmented abdomens and the first pair of spinnerets unbranched — compare LIPHISTIOMORPHAE

**¹op·is·thot·ic** \¦äpəs¦thäd·ik\ *adj* [*opisth-* + *-otic*] **:** of, relating to, or constituting the posterior and inferior of the bony elements of the capsule of the internal ear

**²opisthotic** \"\ *n* -S **:** an opisthotic bone or cartilage

**opis·tho·ton·ic** \ə¦pisthə¦tänik\ *adj* [Gk *opisthotonikos*, fr. *opisthotonos* + *-ikos* -ic] **:** characteristic of or affected with opisthotonos ⟨an ~ posture⟩

**op·is·thot·o·nos** \,äpəs'thätᵊnəs, -ᵊn,äs\ *n* -ES [Gk, drawn backwards, fr. *opisth-* + *tonos* stretching — more at TONE] **:** a condition of tetanic spasm of the muscles of the back, causing the head and lower limbs to bend backward and the trunk to arch forward

**op·is·thot·o·nus** \-ᵊnəs\ *n* -ES [NL, fr. Gk *opisthotonos*] **:** OPISTHOTONOS

**opi·um** \'ōpēəm\ *n* -S *often attrib* [ME, fr. L, fr. Gk *opion* poppy juice, opium, dim. of *opos* vegetable juice, sap; perh. akin to L *sucus, succus* juice, sap — more at SUCCULENT] **1 :** a drug that consists of the dried milky juice of the opium poppy obtained from incisions made in the unripe capsules of the plant, that has a brownish yellow color, a faint smell, and a bitter and acrid taste, that is a stimulant narcotic poison usu. producing a feeling of well-being, hallucinations, and drowsiness terminating in coma or death if the dose is excessive, that was formerly much used in medicine to soothe pain but is now often replaced by derivative alkaloids (as morphine or codeine) or synthetic substitutes, that is smoked as an intoxicant with baneful effects, and that on continued use in any form causes an addiction which is difficult to break and eventually results in physical and mental deterioration **2 :** something having an effect like that of opium **:** STUPEFIER

**opi·um·ism** \-,mizəm\ *n* -S **1 :** the habitual use of opium **2 :** the state resulting from habitual use of opium

**opium poppy** *n* **:** a variable erect annual Eurasian poppy (*Papaver somniferum*) that has cordate leaves with wavy toothed margins and large usu. white or lavender and sometimes double flowers on long stiff peduncles and that has been cultivated since antiquity as the source of opium, for its edible oily seeds, or for ornament — see ⁶MAW, POPPY SEED OIL

**op·leg·nath·i·dae** \,ä(,)pleg'nathə,dē\ *n pl, cap* [NL, fr. *Oplegnathus*, type genus (fr. Gk *hoplē* hoof + NL *-gnathus*) + *-idae*] **:** a small family of short deep-bodied marine percoid fishes with small mouths and the teeth fused into a plate or beak — see PARROT FISH

**opn** *abbr* **1** operation **2** opinion

**opng** *abbr* opening

**opo-** *comb form* [Gk, fr. *opos* — more at OPIUM] **:** juice **:** sap ⟨*opo*therapy⟩

**op·o·bal·sam** \,äpə'bȯlsəm\ *or* **op·o·bal·sa·mum** \-'balsəməm\ *n* [L *opobalsamum*, fr. Gk *opobalsamon*, fr. *opo-* + *balsamon* balsam — more at BALM] **:** BALM OF GILEAD 2 a

**op·o·del·doc** \-'del,däk\ *n* -S [NL *oppodeltoch*, prob. fr. *opo-* + *-deltoch* (origin unknown)] **1** *obs* **:** a medical plaster for external use **2 :** any of various soap liniments; *esp* **:** an unofficial camphorated soap liniment of a soft semisolid consistency

**opop·a·nax** \ə'päpə,naks\ *n* [L, fr. Gk, fr. *opo-* + *panax*] **1** *also* **opop·o·nax** \"\ -ES **a :** an odorous gum resin formerly used in medicine and believed to be obtained from Hercules' allheal **b :** BISABOL **2 a** *cap* **:** a genus of southern European herbs (family Umbelliferae) having compound umbels of yellow flowers and fruit with numerous oil tubes **b** -ES **:** a plant of the genus *Opopanax; specif* **:** HERCULES' ALLHEAL **3** -ES **:** HUISACHE

**¹opor·to** \ō'pōrd·(,)ō\ *adj, usu cap* [fr. *Oporto*, Portugal] **:** of or from the city of Oporto, Portugal **:** of the kind or style prevalent in Oporto

**²oporto** \"\ *n* -S *often cap* [¹*oporto*] *archaic* **:** ⁹PORT 1

**opos·sum** \ə'päsəm, ō'p-\ *n, pl* **opossums** *also* **opossum** *often attrib* [fr. *âpäsûm* (in some Algonquian language of Virginia), lit., white animal] **1 a :** any of various American marsupials of the family Didelphidae; *esp* **:** a common omnivorous largely nocturnal and arboreal mammal (*Didelphis virginiana*) of the eastern U. S. that is naturalized on the Pacific coast, is about 2½ feet long including the scaly prehensile tail, has coarse grayish fur mingled with whitish hairs and an abdominal pouch to which the young are transferred at birth, reputedly feigns death when startled or alarmed, and is esteemed as food in some sections **b :** the pelt or fur of an opossum ⟨an ~ coat⟩ **2** *Austral* **:** any of several phalangers that somewhat resemble the true opossums

opossum

**opossum mouse** *n* **:** any of several small Australian phalangers (genus *Cercaërtus* syn. *Dromicia*) that resemble mice

**opossum rat** *n* **:** any of several small So. American marsupials of the genus *Caenolestes*

**opossum shrimp** *n* **:** a small crustacean of the order Mysidacea with females that carry their eggs in a pouch between the legs

**opossum tree** *n* **1 :** OPOSSUM WOOD **2 :** LIQUIDAMBAR

**opossum wood** *n* **1 a :** SILVER BELL **b :** the close-grained hard pinkish wood of the silver bell **2 :** an Australian timber tree (*Quintinia sieberi*)

**op·o·therapy** \¦äpə+\ *n* [ISV *opo-* + *therapy*] **:** ORGANOTHERAPY

**opp** *abbr* **1** opportunity **2** opposed; opposite

**OPP** *abbr* out of print at present

**op·pen·auer oxidation** \'äpə,naù(ə)r, -aùə-\ *n, usu cap 1st O* [after Rupert V. Oppenauer 20th cent. Austrian chemist] **:** the oxidation of a saturated or unsaturated secondary alcohol (as cholesterol) to the corresponding ketone by reaction with acetone or other ketone in the presence of aluminum *tert*-butoxide or aluminum isopropoxide — compare MEERWEIN-PONNDORF REACTION

**op·pen·heim·er** \'äpən,hīmə(r)\ *n* -S [G, of *Oppenheim*, fr. *Oppenheim*, town in Hesse, Germany] **:** a white table wine of the Rhine wine group from Rheinhessen, Germany

**¹op·pi·dan** \'äpədən, -dᵊn\ *n* -S [L *oppidanus*, fr. *oppidanus*, adj.] **1 :** a resident of a town **:** TOWNSMAN **2** *obs* **a :** an inhabitant of a university town not a member of the university **b :** a university student living in the town rather than at a college **3 :** a student at Eton College living in a residence owned by the school but situated in the town outside the limits of the original foundation — compare COLLEGER

**²oppidan** \"\ *adj* [L *oppidanus*, fr. *oppidum* + *-anus* -an] **:** of or relating to a town or to town as opposed to country

**op·pi·dum** \-dəm\ *n, pl* **oppi·da** \-də\ [L, fortified town, barriers of a circus; prob. fr. *ob* to, before, in the way of + *ped-*, *pes* foot — more at EPI-, FOOT] **:** an ancient Roman provincial town lacking self-government; *esp* **:** one having walls and fortifications and serving as a provincial strong point

**op·pig·no·rate** *or* **op·pig·ne·rate** \ə'pignə,rāt\ *vt* -ED/-ING/-S [L *oppignoratus, oppigneratus*, past. part. of *oppignorare, oppignerare* to pawn, fr. *ob-* + *pignorare, pignerare* to pledge — more at PIGNORATION] *archaic* **:** PLEDGE, PAWN

**op·pi·late** \'äpə,lāt\ *vt* -ED/-ING/-S [L *oppilatus*, past part. of *oppilare* to stop up, fr. *ob-* + *pilare* to ram down, thrust, fr. *pila* mortar; akin to L *pinsere* to pound, crush — more at PESTLE] *archaic* **:** to stop up **:** fill with obstructions **:** block up **:** OBSTRUCT

**op·pi·la·tion** \,⸗⸗'lāshən\ *n* -S [L *oppilation-, oppilatio*, fr. *oppilatus* + *-ion-, -io* -ion] *archaic* **:** an act of oppilating or the state of being oppilated **:** OBSTRUCTION

**op·pi·la·tive** \'⸗⸗,lād·iv\ *adj* [L *oppilatus* + E *-ive*] *archaic* **:** tending to oppilate **:** OBSTRUCTIVE, CONSTIPATING

**op·po** \'ä(,)pō\ *n* -S [prob. fr. *opposite* (in *opposite number*) + *-o*] *Brit* **:** FRIEND, COMPANION; *esp* **:** SWEETHEART

**oppone** *vb* -ED/-ING/-S [L *opponere* — more at OPPONENT] *obs* **:** OPPOSE

**op·po·nen·cy** \ə'pōnənsē\ *n* -ES [²*opponent* + *-cy*] **1 :** OPPOSITION, ANTAGONISM **2** *archaic* **:** the action of maintaining an opposing argument in or opening an academic disputation (as in trying for a degree) by proposing objections to a tenet

**op·po·nens** \ə'pō,nenz\ *n, pl* **op·po·nen·tes** \,äpə'nen·(,)tēz\ *or* **opponens** [NL, fr. L, pres. part. of *opponere* to oppose] **:** any of several muscles of the hand or foot that tend to draw one of the lateral digits across the palm or sole toward the others

**¹op·po·nent** \ə'pōnənt\ *n* -S [L *opponent-, opponens*, pres. part. of *opponere* to place against, oppose, fr. *ob-* + *ponere* put, place — more at POSITION] **1 a :** one that opposes a tenet or thesis in a disputation, argument, or other verbal controversy **b** *archaic* **:** one that opens an academic disputation by attacking a thesis or proposition — distinguished from *respondent, defendant* **2 :** one that opposes **:** ADVERSARY, FOE **3 :** a muscle that opposes or serves to counteract and limit the action of another **:** ANTAGONIST

**²opponent** \"\ *adj* [L *opponent-, opponens*] **1 :** OPPOSING, ADVERSE, ANTAGONISTIC **2 :** situated in front **:** OPPOSITE

**op·por·tune** \¦äpə(r)¦tün, -(r)¦tyün\ *adj* [ME, fr. MF *opportun*, fr. L *opportunus*, fr. the phrase *ob portum* (*veniens*) coming to harbor, fr. *ob* to, towards + *portum*, accus. of *portus* harbor, port — more at PORT] **1 a :** fit, suitable, or convenient for a particular occurrence ⟨made his bid for power at an ~ moment⟩ ⟨couldn't have chosen a more ~ spot⟩ **b :** occurring at a suitable time **:** TIMELY ⟨this most ~ assistance⟩ ⟨~ words of reassurance⟩ **2** *obs* **:** ADVANTAGEOUS, HELPFUL, USEFUL **3** *obs* **:** open or liable to **:** EXPOSED **syn** see SEASONABLE

**op·por·tune·ly** *adv* **:** at a suitable time or place **:** so as to be opportune

**op·por·tune·ness** \-n(n)əs\ *n* -ES **:** the quality or state of being opportune

**op·por·tun·ism** \-ü,nizəm\ *n* -S [It *opportunismo*, fr. *opportuno* opportune (fr. L *opportunus*) + *-ismo* -ism] **:** the art, policy, or practice of taking advantage of opportunities or circumstances, esp. with little regard for principles or ultimate consequences

**¹op·por·tun·ist** \-,nəst\ *n* -S [F *opportuniste*, fr. *opportunisme* opportunism, fr. It *opportunismo*] **:** one who practices opportunism ⟨an aristocracy of ~s who sought power for no end except their own —Victor Canning⟩

**²opportunist** \"\ *or* **op·por·tun·is·tic** \¦⸗⸗¦⸗¦nistik, -tēk\ *adj* **:** of, relating to, or having the characteristics of an opportunist **:** marked by opportunism ⟨the rare kind of honesty that refuses to be ~ —E.B.Barrett⟩ ⟨is superbly *opportunistic*, taking advantage of every break —Alfred Bester⟩ — **op·por·tun·is·ti·cal·ly** \-tək(ə)lē, -tēk-, -li\ *adv*

**op·por·tu·ni·ty** \,äpə(r)'tünəd·ē, -(r)·'tyü-, -nətē, -i\ *n* -ES [ME *opportunite*, fr. MF *opportunité*, fr. L *opportunitat-, opportunitas*, fr. *opportunus* + *-itat-, -itas* -ity] **1 a :** a combination of circumstances, time, and place suitable or favorable for a particular activity or action ⟨the many small rivers . . . offered unlimited *opportunities* for water transport —*Amer. Guide Series: R. I.*⟩ ⟨artists are given ~ to do creative work —*Amer. Guide Series: N. H.*⟩ **b :** an advantageous circumstance or combination of circumstances esp. when affecting security, wealth, or freedom (as from constraint) **:** a time, place, or condition favoring advancement or progress ⟨to strike out in search of new *opportunities* in new surroundings —H.S.Truman⟩ ⟨sons of poor and ignorant farmers, blacksmiths, tanners and backwoodsmen, with few *opportunities* —E.G.Conklin⟩ **2** *obs* **:** FITNESS, COMPETENCY **3 :** the quality or state of being opportune **:** TIMELINESS **4** *archaic* **:** convenience or advantage of situation **5** [by confusion] *obs* **:** IMPORTUNITY

**syn** OCCASION, CHANCE, BREAK, TIME: OPPORTUNITY indicates a combination of circumstances facilitating a certain action or inviting a certain decision ⟨it was deemed advisable to continue the case . . . in order that we might have an *opportunity* of giving to the whole subject a more deliberate consideration —R.B.Taney⟩ OCCASION is likely to convey the notion of the period or time at which an opportunity is offered; since this may be fleeting, OCCASION may suggest a combination of circumstances that are urgent and quite likely to evoke action or that have evolved it ⟨afterward she can explain . . . as *occasion* shall require —F.W.Maitland⟩ ⟨so long as a child is with adults, it has no *occasion* for the exercise of a number of important virtues —Bertrand Russell⟩ CHANCE is close to OPPORTUNITY in this sense ⟨the most challenging *opportunity* of all history — the *chance* to help create a new society —Wendell Willkie⟩ It may suggest a situation arising accidentally ⟨in war lay the greatest *chance* of his life —H.L.Mencken⟩ or a fair situation arising in an equitable allotment of things ⟨only those who have a special cause to plead will hold that . . . children of the poor [have] the same *chances* as those of the well-to-do —John Dewey⟩ BREAK, formerly a slang term and more common in the U. S. than in England, suggests a turn of luck or an opportunity offered by luck or by an act of kindliness from one with power or influence ⟨not a single day of storm, not one day of flat calm, only a few days of variables did he experience. He had all the *breaks* —S.E. Morison⟩ ⟨Communist promises of a better *break* for the common people —A.E.Stevenson b. 1900⟩ TIME may be used as a synonym for opportune time or occasion ⟨an adversary of no common prowess was watching his *time* —T.B.Macaulay⟩

**opportunity cost** *n* **:** the monetary or other advantage surrendered for something in order to acquire it in competition with other potential users ⟨the *opportunity cost* method is clearly applicable in determining the value of a property that can be shifted to another use —M.S.Kendrick⟩ ⟨by putting such things as leisure, safety, and agreeableness of work into the utility scales of the individuals, the disutility of any occupation can be represented as an *opportunity cost* —B.E.Lippincott⟩

**opportunity school** *n* **:** a school designed to meet the special needs of particular groups (as adult illiterates, foreigners seeking competency in a language, or persons requiring vocational retraining)

**oppos** *pl of* OPPO

**op·pos·abil·i·ty** \ə,pōzə'biləd·ē, -lətē, -i\ *n* **:** the quality or state of being opposable

**op·pos·able** \ə'pōzəbəl\ *adj* **1 :** capable of being opposed or resisted **2 :** capable of being placed opposite something else ⟨the thumb is ~ to the forefinger⟩

**opposal** *n* -S [ME *opposaille*, fr. *opposen* to oppose + *-aille* -al] **1** *obs* **a :** a putting of questions **:** EXAMINATION **b :** something that poses or puzzles **2** *obs* **:** OPPOSITION

**op·pose** \ə'pōz\ *vb* -ED/-ING/-S [in sense 1, fr. ME *opposen*, fr. MF *opposer;* in other senses, fr. F *opposer*, fr. MF, modif. (influenced by *poser* to put, place) of ML *opponere*, fr. L, to place against or opposite, to adduce in contradiction (perfect stem *oppos-*), fr. *ob-* + *ponere* to put, place — more at POSITION, POSE] *vt* **1** *obs* **:** to confront with hard or searching questions or objections **2 a :** to place opposite ⟨uncertain which of two *opposed* doors he should enter⟩ **b** (1) **:** to place the ball of (a first digit) against the corresponding part of a second digit of the same hand or foot ⟨some monkeys ~ the great toe as freely as the thumb⟩ (2) **:** to bring the palmar surfaces of (the forepaws) into contact ⟨various rodents ~ the paws in handling food⟩ **3 :** to place over against something so as to provide resistance, counterbalance, or contrast ⟨principles that may be *opposed* to this modern confusion —Irving Babbitt⟩ ⟨to ~ one military force to another⟩ ⟨diametrically *opposed* political beliefs⟩ ⟨concreteness as *opposed* to abstraction —L. E.Lynch⟩ **4 :** to offer resistance to, contend against, or forcefully withstand ⟨~ the enemy⟩ ⟨~ a congressional bill⟩ ⟨*opposed* every tendency toward nationalism —E.R.Dobson⟩ **5** *obs* **:** to lay (as oneself) open **:** EXPOSE ~ *vi* **:** to offer opposition to something **syn** see CONTEST

**opposed** *adj* [fr. past part. of *oppose*] **1 :** set or placed in opposition **:** OPPOSITE, CONTRARY, ADVERSE **2 a** *of two engine cylinders* **:** opposite to each other **:** placed on opposite sides of a common crankshaft **b** *of an engine* **:** having cylinders so placed

**op·pose·less** \ə'pōzləs\ *adj* [*oppose* + *-less*] **:** IRRESISTIBLE

**op·pos·er** \-zə(r)\ *n* -S **:** one that opposes; *specif* **:** one that formally seeks to prevent registration of a trademark

**opposing** *adj* [fr. pres. part. of *oppose*] **1 :** opposite in position **2 :** active in or offering opposition — **op·pos·ing·ly** *adv*

**opposing train** *n* **:** a train that is moving in a direction opposite to and toward another train on the same track

**¹op·po·site** \'äpəzət, -psət, *usu* -əd·+V\ *n* -S [ME, fr. MF, fr. *opposite*, adj.] **1** *obs* **a :** the opposed point of the heavens **b :** OPPOSITION 1 **2 :** one that opposes: as **a :** one taking an opposite position (as on a public question) or exhibiting opposite qualities or characteristics ⟨though twins they were complete ~s in temperament⟩ **b** *archaic* **:** ANTAGONIST, OPPONENT **c :** the person occupying the position opposite to one's own in square dancing **3 a :** something that is opposed to some other usu. specified thing ⟨vice and virtue are ~s⟩ **b :** ANTONYM ⟨what is the ~ of good⟩ **4 a :** a proposition in logic that is characterized by opposition (sense 2a(2)) **b opposites** *pl* **:** CONTRARY TERMS

**²opposite** \"\ *adj* [ME, fr. MF, fr. L *oppositus*, past part. of *opponere* to place against — more at OPPOSE] **1 a :** set over against something that is at the other end or side of an intervening line or space **:** FACING: as (1) *of two sides of a quadrilateral* **:** not adjacent **:** sharing no point at which the intervening space is zero (2) *of two angles formed by the intersection of a pair of lines* **:** having contact only at the apex, sharing no common side, and usu. having a combined magnitude of other than 180 degrees (3) *of two points on the circumference of a circle* **:** terminating the same diameter **b** (1) **:** situated in pairs on an axis each being separated from the other by half the circumference of the axis — used esp. of leaves; compare PHYLLOTAXY (2) *of floral parts* **:** SUPERPOSED (3) **:** situated side by side ⟨bordered pits ~⟩ — distinguished from *alternate* **2 a :** OPPOSED, HOSTILE ⟨belonged to the ~ faction⟩ ⟨~ sides of the question⟩ **b :** diametrically different **:** CONTRARY, ANTAGONISTIC, ANTONYMIC ⟨~ meanings⟩ **3 :** being the other of a matching or contrasting pair **:** corresponding or complementary in position, function, or nature ⟨his courtesy toward all members of the ~ sex⟩ ⟨the chess king is set up on a square of the ~ color⟩

**syn** CONTRADICTORY, CONTRARY, ANTITHETICAL *or* ANTITHETIC, ANTIPODAL *or* ANTIPODEAN, ANTONYMOUS: OPPOSITE may apply to ideas, statements, conditions, or forces marked by sharp, unmistakable contrast, conflict, or antagonism ⟨the reaction against the follies of the old rationalism has led them to the *opposite* extreme of irrationalism —M.R.Cohen⟩ ⟨self-interest and sympathy, *opposite* in quality —John Dewey⟩ CONTRADICTORY applies to statements or tendencies that completely negate each other; it may imply that if one is true or valid, the other must be untrue or invalid ⟨the reconciliation of the seemingly *contradictory* facts, that the power of the many over production is at once paramount and small —W.H. Mallock⟩ ⟨*contradictory* predictions are being made, some gloomy, some optimistic —J.T.Farrell⟩ CONTRARY suggests extreme, perhaps diametrical, divergence or opposition ⟨foolishly began to teach matters *contrary* to the faith, and in the end was condemned as a heretic —H.O.Taylor⟩ ⟨*contrary* to general opinion young pilots are not the safest —H.G. Armstrong⟩ ⟨this hypothesis is not only unfounded but *contrary* to all reasonable assumptions —Edward Westermarck⟩ ANTITHETICAL *or* ANTITHETIC may stress diametrical opposition, the contrast involved being useful to highlight a certain significance or nature ⟨a combination of *antithetical* elements which are at eternal war with one another —W.S.Gilbert⟩ ⟨the *antithetic* consciousness of alienation from, and of communion with, the unseen power which surrounds us —W.R.Inge⟩ ANTIPODAL and ANTIPODEAN indicate a diametrical opposition and also a remoteness, as though located at opposite poles of the earth ⟨hunters, like pipe smokers, are recruited from two *antipodal* types of men — gentlemen and worthless loafers — D.C.Peattie⟩ ⟨two men *antipodean* in all their tastes⟩ ANTONYMOUS refers to words expressing opposite meanings ⟨*hot* and *cold* are *antonymous*⟩

**³opposite** \"\ *adv* **:** on opposite sides **:** in an opposed position

**⁴opposite** \"\ *prep* [²*opposite* & ³*opposite*] **1 :** across an intervening space from and usu. facing or on the same level with ⟨make a check ~ a name⟩ ⟨live ~ the post office⟩ **2 :** in a role complementary to ⟨played ~ the leading man⟩

**opposite lady** *n* **:** the woman of the couple opposite a man in a square dance set — compare CORNER LADY, PARTNER

**opposite–leaved** \¦⸗(⸗)⸗¦⸗\ *adj* **:** having opposite leaves

**op·po·site·ly** *adv* **:** in an opposite position **:** so as to be opposite

**op·po·site·ness** *n* -ES **:** the quality or state of being opposite

**opposite number** *n* **1 :** a member of a system or class who holds relatively the same position as a particular member in a corresponding system or class ⟨the Secretary of State and his *opposite number*, the Minister of Foreign Affairs⟩ ⟨union executives met their *opposite numbers* in industry⟩ **2 :** a corresponding or comparable establishment, area, implement, publication, word, esp. in a different country or language

**opposite tide** *n* **:** high tide at a corresponding place on the opposite side of the earth accompanying a high tide at any given place — compare DIRECT TIDE

**oppositi-** *comb form* [L *oppositus*] **:** situated opposite **:** having the corresponding parts opposite ⟨*oppositi*folious⟩ ⟨*oppositi*sepalous⟩

**op·po·si·tion** \,äpə'zishən\ *n* -S [ME *opposicioun*, fr. ML *opposition-, oppositio*, fr. L, act of opposing, fr. *oppositus* (past part. of *opponere* to place against) + *-ion-, -io* -ion — more at OPPOSE] **1 :** a configuration in which one celestial body is opposite another in the sky or in which the elongation is near or equal to 180 degrees — see CONFIGURATION **2 a** (1) *obs* **:** a setting of one rhetorical proposition against another **:** a counter proposition (2) **:** the relation that occurs between two propositions in logic having the same subject and predicate but differing in quantity, in quality, or in both and that is usu. considered to occur in the four forms of contrariety, subcontrariety, subalternation, and contradiction **b** *obs* **:** OPPOSITE, CONTRARY, CONTRAST **3 :** an act of setting opposite or over against or the condition of being so set **4 a :** hostile or contrary action or condition **:** action designed to constitute a barrier or check ⟨offered strong ~ to the advance of the enemy⟩ ⟨a child's automatic ~ to maturity⟩ ⟨held up a hand in ~ to oncoming traffic⟩ **b :** a position of the king in chess preventing the advance of the enemy king either directly or obliquely **c :** a position of one's blade when crossed with that of one's opponent such that the latter cannot hit in the line of engagement **d** (1) **:** refusal of a creditor to assent to the debtor's discharge in a bankruptcy proceeding (2) **:** a formal action for preventing the registration of a trademark **5 a :** something that opposes; *specif* **:** the aggregate of those in opposition to a particular thing (as a political policy or party) **b** *often cap* **:** a political party that actively opposes the party in power and is prepared to replace it if opportunity offers ⟨Her Majesty's Loyal *Opposition*⟩ ⟨last election saw considerable strengthening of the ~⟩ **6 :** movement of diagonally opposite limbs (as in various complex reflexes and some dance patterns) **7 :** the relationship of partial difference between two partially similar elements of a language (as oral versus nasal with *b* and *m* or singular versus plural with *man's* and *men's*)

**op·po·si·tion·al** \¦==¦zishən°l, -shnəl\ *adj* **1 :** relating to or constituting opposition ⟨~ activities⟩ **2 :** acting in opposition to one another ⟨~ alleles⟩

**op·po·si·tion·ary** \-shə,nerē\ *adj* : OPPOSITIONAL 1

**op·po·si·tion·ism** \-,nizəm\ *n* -s : a policy of opposition (as in politics)

**op·po·si·tion·ist** \-,nəst\ *n* -s : a member of an opposition or one who advocates or practices oppositionism

**op·po·si·tion·less** \-nləs\ *adj* : lacking opposition

**op·po·si·tious** \¦==¦zishəs\ *adj* [*opposition* + *-ous*] : inclined to oppose : determined in opposition

**op·pos·i·tive** \ə'päzəd·iv, -ətiv\ *adj* [L *oppositus* (past part. of *opponere* to set against) + E *-ive* — more at OPPOSE] : tending to oppose : functioning in the expression of contrariety — **op·pos·i·tive·ly** \-əvlē, -li\ *adv*

**op·po·sure** \ə'pōzhə(r)\ *n* -s [*oppose* + *-ure*] : OPPOSITION

**op·press** \ə'pres\ *vt* -ED/-ING/-ES [ME *oppressen*, fr. MF *oppresser*, fr. ML *oppressare*, fr. L *oppressus*, past part. of *opprimere* to press down, fr. *ob-* + *-primere* (fr. *premere* to press) — more at PRESS] **1 a** *archaic* : to put down : SUPPRESS, QUELL **b :** to crush, burden, or trample down by or as if by abuse of power or authority : treat with unjust vigor or with cruelty ⟨rulers that ~ the people⟩ **2 a :** to burden spiritually or mentally as if by pressure : weigh heavily upon : weigh down ⟨~*ed* by a sense of failure⟩ ⟨~*ed* by prolonged sultry weather⟩ **b** *obs* : HARASS, DISTRESS **3** *archaic* **a :** to press upon with physical violence : injure by physical pressure : CRUSH, TRAMPLE **b :** to overpower in or as if in battle : overwhelm by numbers **c :** OVERCOME — used of sleep, death, or other vital phenomena **4** *obs* **a :** to take unawares **b :** RAPE, RAVISH **syn** see DEPRESS, WRONG

**oppressed** *adj* [fr. past part. of *oppress*] : subjected to debruising

**op·press·ible** \ə'presəbəl\ *adj* : subject to oppression : unable to resist oppression

**op·pres·sion** \ə'preshən\ *n* -s [MF, fr. L *oppression-*, *oppressio*, fr. *oppressus* + *-ion-*, *-io* -ion] **1 a :** unjust or cruel exercise of authority or power esp. by the imposition of burdens; *esp* : the unlawful, excessive, or corrupt exercise of power other than by extortion by any public officer so as to harm anyone in his rights, person, or property while purporting to act under color of governmental authority **b :** something that so oppresses : EXACTION ⟨unfair taxes and other ~*s*⟩ **2 a :** the act of weighing down (as a person, his mind or spirits) ⟨the continued ~ of the heat⟩ **b :** the condition of being weighed down (as by misfortune) **3 :** an act of pressing down : PRESSURE, WEIGHT **4 :** a sense of heaviness or obstruction in the body or mind : DEPRESSION, DULLNESS, LASSITUDE ⟨an ~ of spirits⟩ ⟨an ~ of the lungs⟩

**op·pres·sive** \ə'presiv, -sēv *also* -səv\ *adj* [ML *oppressivus*, fr. L *oppressus* + *-ivus* -ive] **1 :** unreasonably burdensome : unjustly severe, rigorous, or harsh : constituting oppression ⟨~ legislation⟩ ⟨~ taxes⟩ ⟨~ exactions⟩ **2 :** using or depending upon oppression : TYRANNICAL ⟨an ~ ruler⟩ **3 :** overpowering or depressing to the spirit or senses : hard to be borne ⟨~ grief⟩ ⟨an ~ climate⟩ ⟨to ease the soul of one ~ weight —Alexander Pope⟩ **syn** see ONEROUS

**op·pres·sive·ly** \-sə̇vlē, -li\ *adv* : in an oppressive manner : so as to oppress

**op·pres·sive·ness** \-sivnə̇s, -sēv-\ *n* -ES : the quality or state of being oppressive

**op·pres·sor** \-sə(r)\ *n* -s [ME, fr. AF *oppressour*, fr. L *oppressor* crusher, destroyer, fr. *oppressus* + *-or*] : one that oppresses esp. when in a position of public authority ⟨the orphan pines while the ~ feeds —Shak.⟩

**op·pro·bri·ate** \ə'prōbrē,āt\ *vt* -ED/-ING/-S [ML *opprobriatus*, past part. of *opprobriare*, fr. L *opprobrium*] : to regard or speak of as opprobrious

**op·pro·bri·ous** \-ēəs\ *adj* [ME, fr. MF or LL; MF *opprobrieux*, fr. LL *opprobriosus*, fr. L *opprobrium* + *-osus* -ous] **1 :** expressive of opprobrium : conveying or intended to convey disgrace : SCURRILOUS, CONTUMELIOUS — used chiefly of utterances ⟨~ language⟩ **2 :** deserving of opprobrium : INFAMOUS, DESPICABLE ⟨this ~ monument to human greed⟩ ⟨this dark, ~ den of shame —John Milton⟩ — **op·pro·bri·ous·ly** *adv* — **op·pro·bri·ous·ness** *n* -ES

**op·pro·bri·um** \-ēəm\ *n* -s [L, fr. *opprobrare* to reproach, fr. *ob-* + *probrum* disgraceful act, infamy, reproach, fr. *prober* guilty, subject to reproach; akin to Gk *propherein* to bring forward, reproach — more at FOR, BEAR] **1 :** something that gives occasion for disgrace or reprobation : opprobrious behavior **2** *obs* : opprobrious utterance **3 a :** public or known disgrace or ill fame that ordinarily follows from or is attached to conduct considered grossly wrong or vicious : INFAMY ⟨I can name four from thereabouts who have been in the pen. To only one . . . who . . . turned out to be truly criminal, does ~ attach —Oliver La Farge⟩ **b :** contempt or distaste usu. mingled with reproach and an implication of inferiority ⟨*cold storage* was once a term of ~⟩ ⟨there has always been ~ attached to ignorance of grammar —Charlton Laird⟩ **syn** see DISHONOR

**op·pro·bry** \ə'prōbrē\ *n* -ES [ME, fr. L *opprobrium*] *archaic* : OPPROBRIUM

**op·pugn** \ə'pyün\ *vb* -ED/-ING/-S [ME *oppugnen*, fr. L *oppugnare*, fr. *ob-* + *pugnare* to fight — more at PUGNACIOUS] *vt* **1 a :** to fight against **b** *obs* : WITHSTAND **2 :** to call in question : challenge the accuracy, propriety, probity, or other quality of : CONTROVERT ~ *vi* : stand in opposition : CONTEND

**op·pug·nan·cy** \ə'pəgnənsē, -si\ *n* -ES [LL *oppugnantia*, fr. L *oppugnant-* *oppugnans* + *-ia* -y] : OPPOSITION, HOSTILITY, RESISTANCE

**¹op·pug·nant** \-nənt\ *adj* [L *oppugnant-*, *oppugnans*, pres. part. of *oppugnare*] : HOSTILE, OPPOSING, ANTAGONISTIC

**²oppugnant** \"\ *n* -s : OPPONENT, ANTAGONIST

**op·pug·nate** \-,nāt\ *vt* -ED/-ING/-S [L *oppugnatus*, past part. of *oppugnare*] *archaic* : OPPUGN

**op·pug·na·tion** \,ä(,)pəg'nāshən\ *n* -s [L *oppugnation-*, *oppugnatio*, fr. *oppugnatus* + *-ion-*, *-io*, -ion] : ATTACK, OPPOSITION

**op·pugn·er** \ə'pyünə(r)\ *n* -s : one that oppugns

**oppy** *abbr* opportunity

**opr** *abbr* operate; operator

**oprich·nik** \ä'prichnik\ *n*, *pl* **oprich·ni·ki** \-nəkē\ *or* **oprichniks** [Russ., fr. *oprichina* corps of life-guards of Ivan IV] : a member of an imperial Russian police force

**op·ry** \'äprē, -ri\ *dial var of* OPERA

**-ops** \,äps\ *n comb form* [Gk *-ōp-*, *-ōps*, fr. *ōp-*, *ōps* eye, face — more at EYE] **1** *pl* **-ops** *or* **-opses :** organism with a (specified) kind of eye or face — chiefly in generic names ⟨megal*ops*⟩ ⟨Sty*lops*⟩ ⟨Selen*ops*⟩ **2 :** organism resembling a (specified) thing — in generic names usu. combined with the names of other genera ⟨Echin*ops*⟩ ⟨Dryobalan*ops*⟩

**-op·sia** \'äpsēə\ *or* **-op·sy** \,äpsē, -si\ *n comb form*, *pl* **-opsias** *or* **-opsies** [*-opsia* fr. NL, fr. Gk, fr. *opsis* appearance, vision + *-ia* -y; *-opsy* fr. Gk *-opsia* — more at *-opsis*] : vision of a (specified) kind or condition ⟨an*opsia*⟩ ⟨hemi*opsia*⟩

**op·si·math** \'äpsə,math\ *n* -s [Gk *opsimathēs* late in learning, fr. *opse*, *opsi* late (akin to Gk *epi* on, to) + *-mathēs*, fr. *manthanein* to learn — more at EPI-, MATHEMATICAL] : a person who begins to learn late in life

**op·sin** \'äpsən\ *n* -s [prob. back-formation fr. *rhodopsin*] : any of various colorless proteins formed together with retinene by the action of light on a visual pigment (as rhodopsin or porphyropsin)

**-op·sis** \'äpsə̇s\ *n comb form* [NL, fr. Gk, fr. *opsis* appearance, vision — more at OPTIC] **1 a :** organism resembling or having a part that resembles a (specified) thing — in generic names ⟨Chil*opsis*⟩ ⟨Ampel*opsis*⟩ **b** *pl* **-opses :** structure resembling a (specified) thing ⟨cary*opsis*⟩ **2** *pl* **-opses :** -OPSIA

**op·sis·form** \'äpsə̇s,fȯrm\ *also* **op·sis·type** \-,tīp\ *n* [Gk *opsis* + E *form*, *type*] : a rust fungus that lacks uredinia — compare EU-FORM

**opson-** *or* **opsono-** *comb form* [*opsonin*] : opsonin ⟨*opson*ic⟩ ⟨*opsono*therapy⟩ ⟨*opsono*philic⟩

**op·son·ic** \(')äp¦sänik, -nēk\ *adj* [*opson-* + *-ic*] : of, relating to, or involving opsonin ⟨an ~ test⟩

**opsonic index** *n* : the ratio of the phagocytic index of a tested serum to that of normal serum taken as the unit

**op·son·i·fi·ca·tion** \(,)äp,sänəfə'kāshən\ *n* -s [*opson-* + *-i-* + *-fication*] : the action or the effect of opsonins in making bacteria more readily phagocytized

**op·so·nin** \'äpsənən\ *n* -s [L *opsonium* relish (fr. Gk *opsōnion* victuals, money for victuals, fr. *opsōnein* to purchase victuals + E *-in* — more at DUOPSONY] : a constituent of blood serum that makes foreign cells (as invading pathogenic bacteria) more susceptible to the action of the phagocytes

**op·so·nize** \-,nīz\ *vt* -ED/-ING/-S : to modify (as a bacterium) by the action of opsonins

**op·so·no·cytophagic test** \¦äpsə,nō+-\ *n* [*opson-* + *cytophagic*] : a test for immunity to or infection by a pathogenic organism (as of brucellosis or whooping cough) based on the assumption that the serum of an immune or infected individual contains specific opsonins capable of facilitating phagocytosis of the organism in question

**-op·sy** \,äpsē, ,əp-, -si\ *n comb form* -ES [Gk *-opsia*] **1 :** -OPSIA **2 :** examination ⟨bi*opsy*⟩

**opt** \'äpt\ *vi* -ED/-ING/-S [F *opter* to choose, desire, fr. L *optare* — more at OPINE] **1 :** to make a choice of citizenship; *esp* : to choose between a former citizenship and that of a new sovereign state made of a territory transferred by treaty ⟨~*ed* to retain his nationality⟩ **2 a :** to decide to do one of two or more alternatively possible things ⟨~*ed* to go to Europe⟩ **b :** to decide in favor of one or more alternatively available things or courses ⟨give the people an opportunity to ~ for statehood —Rupert Emerson⟩ ⟨would still ~ for a good jazz band⟩

**opt** *abbr* **1** operate **2** optative **3** optical; optician; optics **4** option; optional

**optable** *adj* [L *optabilis* desirable, fr. *optare* + *-abilis*, -able] *obs* : worthy to be chosen : DESIRABLE

**op·tant** \'äptənt\ *n* -s [G & Dan, fr. L *optant-*, *optans*, pres. part. of *optare* to choose] : one who opts

**op·tate** \'äp,tāt\ *vi* -ED/-ING/-S [L *optatus*, past part. of *optare*] : OPT 2 — **op·ta·tion** \äp'tāshən\ *n* -s

**¹op·ta·tive** \'äptəd·iv, -ətiv; (')äp¦tād·iv, -ātiv\ *adj* [MF *optatif*, fr. LL *optativus*, fr. L *optatus* + *-ivus* -ive] **1 a :** of, relating to, characterizing, or being a mood of verbs in Greek and other related languages that is expressive of wish or desire and various related distinctions **b :** characterizing or being a sentence that is expressive of wish or hope and marked as optative by the subjunctive mood and by word order (as in *Heaven help him*) **2 :** expressing desire or wish — **op·ta·tive·ly** \-d·ə̇vlē, -tə̇v-, -li\ *adv*

**²optative** \"\ *n* -s **1 a :** the optative mood **b :** a verb or verbal form denoting the optative mood **2 :** something to be desired

**¹op·tic** \'äptik, -tēk\ *adj* [MF *optique*, fr. ML *opticus*, fr. Gk *optikos*, fr. *optos* (verbal of *opsesthai* to be going to see) + *-ikos* -ic; akin to Gk *opsis* sight, appearance, vision, *ōps* eye, face, *ommat-*, *omma* eye — more at EYE] **1 a :** of or relating to vision ⟨~ phenomenon⟩ **b :** dependent chiefly on vision for orientation ⟨man is basically an ~ animal⟩ — compare OSMATIC **2 a :** of or relating to the eye : OCULAR ⟨the ~ axis⟩ **b :** affecting the eye or an optic structure **3** *archaic* : relating to optics : OPTICAL

**²optic** \"\ *n* -s [in sense 1, prob. trans. of It *ottica*, fr. L *optice*, fr. Gk *optikē*, fr. fem. of *optikos*; in other senses, fr. ¹*optic*] **1** *obs* : OPTICS **2 :** an organ of sight : EYE — not used technically **3 :** any of the lenses, prisms, or mirrors of an optical instrument ⟨the ~*s* of this instrument⟩ ⟨interchangeable ~*s* of quartz, glass, rock salt —R.A.Sawyer⟩

**op·ti·cal** \-təkəl, -tēk-\ *adj* [in sense 1, fr. ²*optic* + *-al*; in other senses, fr. ¹*optic* + *-al*] **1 a :** relating to the science of optics **b :** dealing with or expert in optics **2 :** relating to vision : OCULAR, VISUAL ⟨an ~ illusion⟩ **3 a :** designed or constructed to aid the vision ⟨an ~ magnifier⟩ **b :** acting by means of light or in accord with the principles of optics

**optical activity** *n* : ability to rotate the plane of polarization of light — compare OPTICAL ROTATION

**optical anomaly** *n* : an apparent lack of harmony between the crystal form of a mineral and its optical properties

**optical antipode** *n* : ENANTIOMORPH 2

**optical axis** *n* **1 a :** a straight line perpendicular to the front of the cornea of the eye and extending through the center of the pupil **b :** the axis of symmetry of a radially symmetrical optical system **2 :** OPTIC AXIS 1

**optical bench** *n* : a horizontal rod or movable track that is fitted with movable clamps, is usu. provided with a linear scale, and is used for the convenient location and adjustment of light sources, optical devices, and screens employed in the observation and measurement of optical phenomena

**optical bleach** *n* : FLUORESCENT BRIGHTENER

**optical calcite** *n* : calcite suitable for use in optical instruments

**optical center** *n* **1 :** a point on the axis of a lens that is so located that any ray of light passing through it in passing through the lens suffers no net deviation and that may be within, without, or on either surface of the lens **2 :** the part of a flat surface (as a printed page or sheet) that appears to the eye to be in the center esp. when not coincident with the geometric center

**optical constant** *n* : any of several quantities characteristic of the optical behavior of a substance (as the refractive index, absorption coefficient, or reflectivity for a specified wavelength)

**optical contact** *n* : juxtaposition of two surfaces (as of glass) with a separation small compared to the wavelength of light so that interference fringes are not observable

**optical correction** *n* : a slight modification of geometrically correct lines (as of a building) for the purpose of making them appear correct to the eye

**optical density** *n* : DENSITY 5

**optical double star** *also* **optical double** *or* **optical pair** *n* : DOUBLE STAR 2 — compare PHYSICAL DOUBLE STAR

**optical electron** *n* : VALENCE ELECTRON

**optical flat** *n* : FLAT 6 a

**optical gage** *n* : a gage (as a micrometer comparator) that makes no direct contact with the object measured but measures an optical image of it

**optical glass** *n* : flint or crown glass of extreme purity and well-defined optical characteristics that is used chiefly for making lenses, prisms, and other optical forms

**optical haze** *n* : a condition of impaired atmospheric transparency resulting when the juxtaposition of air masses of different densities over a heated surface induces irregular refraction

**optical inversion** *n* : INVERSION 5 a

**optical isomer** *n* : one of two or more forms of a compound exhibiting optical isomerism

**optical isomerism** *n* : stereoisomerism in which the isomers have different effects on polarized light and in which asymmetry of the molecule as a whole or the presence of one or more asymmetric atoms is held to be responsible for such effects — compare ASYMMETRIC CARBON ATOM, DIASTEREOISOMERISM, ENANTIOMORPHISM, GEOMETRIC ISOMERISM

**optical lever** *n* : an arm or lever the displacement of which is measured by an attached mirror and a fixed telescope and scale commonly used for measuring small lengths

**op·ti·cal·ly** \'äptək(ə)lē, -tēk-, -li\ *adv* [*optical* + *-ly*] **1 :** by means of sight : with or to the eye ⟨as viewed ~⟩ ⟨an ~ accurate measurement⟩ **2 :** with reference to or by means of optics or to optical properties ⟨vitamins measured ~⟩ ⟨~ ground surfaces⟩ — compare OPTICALLY ACTIVE

**optically active** *adj* : capable of rotating the plane of polarization of light to the right or left : either dextrorotatory or levorotatory ⟨*optically active* substances may be divided into two classes depending upon whether activity is due to crystal structure —R.L.Shriner & Roger Adams⟩ — see ASYMMETRIC CARBON ATOM

**optically inactive** *adj* : INACTIVE c (2)

**optical maser** *n* : LASER

**optical microscope** *n* : a microscope in which light rays are seen directly by the observer as distinguished from one (as an electron microscope) in which some transformation or system of indirect viewing is used

**optical path** *n* : the path followed by a ray of light through an optical system

**optical printer** *n* : an apparatus for transferring a photographic picture or sound image from one film to another by means of various optical elements and devices that permit changing the size of the image and the production of special effects (as fades, dissolves, wipes) not usu. possible with contact printing

**optical pyrometer** *n* : a pyrometer that measures temperature by means of determining the intensity of the light of a particular wavelength emitted by a hot body

**optical rotation** *n* : the angle through which the plane of polarization of polarized light that traverses an optically active substance is rotated depending on the nature of the substance, on the length of the layer of the substance traversed, and on the wavelength of the light

**optical section** *n* : a plane in a translucent object (as a slip of tissue or a cell) brought into view by adjustment of the focus of a microscope

**optical square** *n* : a small hand instrument used by surveyors for laying off a right angle by means of two mirrors set at an angle of 45 degrees

**optical system** *n* : a combination of lenses, mirrors, and prisms that constitutes the optical part of an optical instrument (as a microscope or telescope)

**optical train** *n* : OPTICAL SYSTEM

**optical wedge** *n* : a graded sheet or block (as of glass or film on which is coated a layer of neutral or colored substance varying progressively in transmittance with distance along the sheet) for reducing the intensity of light or radiation gradually or in steps

**optic angle** *n* **1 a :** the angle formed by the optical axes of the two eyes when directed to the same point **b :** VISUAL ANGLE **2 :** the angle between the optic axes of a biaxial crystal

**optic atrophy** *n* : degeneration of the optic nerve

**optic axis** *n* **1 :** a line in a doubly refracting medium that is parallel to the direction in which all components of plane-polarized light travel with the same speed **2 :** OPTICAL AXIS 1

**optic capsule** *n* : either of a pair of cartilaginous capsules that develop around the eyes of elasmobranch fishes and of embryos of higher vertebrates

**optic chiasma** *also* **optic chiasm** *n* : the X-shaped partial decussation on the undersurface of the hypothalamus through which the optic nerves are continuous with the brain

**optic cup** *n* : the optic vesicle after invaginating to form a two-layered cup from which the retina and pigmented layer of the eye will develop

**optic disk** *n* : the nearly circular light-colored area at the back of the retina where the optic nerve enters the eyeball

**optic foramen** *n* : the passage in the sphenoid bone traversed by the optic nerve and ophthalmic artery — see OPTIC GROOVE

**optic groove** *n* : a narrow transverse groove that lies near the front of the superior surface of the body of the sphenoid bone, is continuous with the optic foramen, and houses the optic chiasma

**op·ti·cian** \äp'tishən\ *n* -s [F *opticien*, fr. ML *optica* optics + F *-ien* -ian] **1** *archaic* : one skilled in optics **2 a :** a maker of or dealer in optical items and instruments **b :** one that grinds spectacle lenses to prescription and dispenses spectacles — compare OCULIST, OPTOMETRIST

**op·ti·cist** \'äptəsə̇st\ *n* -s : a specialist in optics

**optic lobe** *n* **1 :** either of the anterior pair of corpora quadrigemina of a mammal **2 :** either of the corpora bigemina of a lower vertebrate **3 :** a lateral lobe of the forebrain of some arthropods containing the visual centers of the compound eyes

**optic nerve** *also* **op·tic** \'äptik, -tēk\ *n* -s [*optic nerve* trans. of MF *nerf optique*, trans. of ML *nervus opticus*; *optic* fr. ¹*optic*] : either of the second pair of cranial nerves being a sensory nerve, arising from the ventral part of the diencephalon, forming in higher vertebrates an optic chiasma before passing to the eye and spreading over the anterior surface of the retina, and serving to conduct visual stimuli from the retina to the brain; *sometimes* : the portion of this nerve lying between the retina and the optic chiasma — see EYE illustration; OPTIC TRACT

**optic neuritis** *n* : inflammation of the optic nerve

**optico-** *comb form* [F, fr. Gk *optikos* — more at OPTIC] **1 :** optical and ⟨*optico*chemical⟩ **2 :** relating or belonging to the eye : ocular ⟨*optico*pupillary⟩ **3 :** optic and ⟨supra*opticohypophyseal*⟩ ⟨*optico*chiasmatic⟩

**op·ti·coel** \'äptə,sēl\ *n* -s [blend of *optic* and *-coel* (fr. Gk *koilos* hollow) — more at CAVE] : the cavity of the optic vesicle

**op·ti·con** \-,kän\ *n* -s [NL, fr. Gk *optikon*, neut. of *optikos* optic] : an external enlargement of the optic lobe of the insect brain that is the innermost of the ganglionic masses connected with the compound eye

**-op·ti·con** \-,kən, -,kän\ *n comb form* -s [*stereopticon*] : stereopticon ⟨pan*opticon*⟩ ⟨sci*opticon*⟩

**optic orientation** *also* **optical orientation** *n* : the relation between the principal vibration directions of a crystal and the crystallographic axes

**optic papilla** *n* : a slight elevation that is nearly coextensive with the optic disk and is produced by the thick bundles of the fibers of the optic nerve in entering the eyeball

**optic placode** *n* : LENS PLACODE

**optic radiation** *n* : any of several neural radiations concerned with the visual function; *esp* : one made up of fibers from the pulvinar and lateral geniculate body to the cuneus and other parts of the occipital lobe

**optic rod** *n* : RHABDOM

**¹op·tics** \'äptiks, -tēks\ *n pl but usu sing in constr* [ML *optica*, fr. Gk *optika*, fr. neut. pl. of *optikos* optic] : a science that deals with light, its genesis and propagation, the effects that it undergoes and produces, and other phenomena closely associated with it — see GEOMETRICAL OPTICS, PHYSICAL OPTICS

**²optics** *pl of* OPTIC

**optic sign** *n* : the distinctive character of the double refraction of a crystal

**optic stalk** *n* : the constricted part of the optic vesicle by which it remains continuous with the embryonic forebrain

**optic thalamus** *n* : either of two masses of nerve tissue in the floor of the diencephalon from which the optic nerves take their origin

**optic tract** *n* : the portion of each optic nerve between the chiasma and the diencephalon proper

**optic vesicle** *n* : an outpouching of each lateral wall of the forebrain of a vertebrate embryo from which the essential nervous structures of the eye develop

**optima** *pl of* OPTIMUM

**op·ti·ma·cy** \'äptəməsē\ *n* -ES [NL *optimatia*, fr. L *optimat-*, *optimas* optimate + *-ia* -y] *archaic* : the best people : ARISTOCRACY

**op·ti·mal** \-məl\ *adj* [*optimum* + *-al*] : most desirable or satisfactory : OPTIMUM ⟨~ concentration of a drug⟩ — **op·ti·mal·i·ty** \,==¦malədē\ *n* -ES — **op·ti·mal·ly** \'==məlē\ *adv*

**op·ti·mal·ize** \'==mə,līz\ *vt* -ED/-ING/-S : to make optimal; *specif* : to bring (as an industrial plant) to a peak of economic efficiency esp. by the use of precise analytical methods

**op·ti·me** \'äptə,mē\ *n* -s [fr. the L phrase *optime disputasti* you have argued very well] : a student at Cambridge University, England, prior to the 20th century obtaining honors but failing to get placed among the wranglers in the mathematical tripos

**op·tim·e·ter** \äp'timəd·ə(r)\ *n* [*optic* + *-meter*] : an instrument for measuring the accuracy of gage blocks or similar devices by means of an optical lever

**op·ti·mism** \'äptə,mizəm\ *n* -s [F *optimisme*, fr. L *optimum* that which is best, (fr. neut. of *optimus* best) + F *-isme* -ism; akin to L *ops* power, wealth, help — more at OPULENT] **1 a :** a doctrine that this world is the best possible world based on the argument that God being all-wise must know all possible worlds, being all-powerful must be able to create whichsoever he might choose, and being all-good must choose the best — used orig. in reference to this doctrine as formulated by Leibniz **b :** a doctrine or opinion that reality is essentially good, completely good, or as good as it conceivably could be **c :** a doctrine that the goods of life overbalance the pain and evil of it and that life is preponderantly good — compare PESSIMISM **2 a :** the quality of being the best or for the best **b :** the best possible or conceivable condition **3 :** an inclination to put the most favorable construction upon actions and happenings, to minimize adverse aspects, conditions, and possibilities, or to anticipate the best possible outcome **:** a cheerful and hopeful temperament

**op·ti·mist** \-ˌməst\ *n* -s [F *optimiste*, fr. L *optimum* + F *-iste* -ist] **:** one given to optimism; *esp* **:** an adherent of philosophical optimism — opposed to *pessimist*

**op·ti·mis·tic** \ˌ==ˈmistik, -tēk\ *also* **op·ti·mis·ti·cal** \-təkəl, -tēk-\ *or* **op·ti·mist** \ˈ==ˌməst\ *adj* [*optimist* + *-ic* or *-ical*] **1 :** of or relating to optimism **:** tending or conforming to the opinion that all events are ordered for the best **2 :** anticipating the best often to an unwise extent or on scanty evidence **:** notably hopeful **:** SANGUINE ⟨an ~ view⟩ — **op·ti·mis·ti·cal·ly** \ˌ==ˈmistək(ə)lē, -tēk-, -li\ *adv*

**op·tim·i·ty** \äpˈtiməd·ē\ *n* -ES [LL *optimitat-*, *optimitas* fr. *optimus* + *-itat-*, *-itas* -ity] **:** the condition or fact of being best or for the best

**op·ti·mi·za·tion** \ˌäptəməˈzāshən, -ˌmīˈz-\ *n* -s **:** an act of optimizing or the fact of being optimized

**1op·ti·mize** \ˈ==ˌmīz\ *vb* -ED/-ING/-S [back-formation fr. *optimist*] *vi* **:** to be optimistic ⟨*optimizing* about the future⟩ ~ *vt* **:** to make the best of **:** treat optimistically

**2optimize** \"\ *vt* [*optimum* + *-ize*] **:** OPTIMALIZE **:** to make as perfect, effective, or functional as possible ⟨~ the distribution of raw materials⟩

**1op·ti·mum** \-məm\ *n*, *pl* **opti·ma** \-mə\ *also* **optimums** [L, neut. of *optimus* best — more at OPTIMISM] **1 :** the amount or degree of something that is most favorable to some end; *esp* **:** the most favorable condition (as of temperature, light, moisture, food) for the growth and reproduction of an organism **2 a :** greatest degree (as of growth, activity, or effectiveness) attained under implied or specified conditions ⟨this pest reaches its ~ further south⟩ **b :** a period of warmer and drier climate than that of the present ⟨the post-Wisconsin ~ of the northern hemisphere is considered to have occurred between 6000 B.C. and 3000 B.C.⟩

**2optimum** \"\ *adj* **1 :** most favorable or most conducive to a given end esp. under fixed conditions ⟨~ temperature for incubation⟩ ⟨question is one of combining these various techniques to ~ advantage —H.V.R.Iengar⟩ **2 :** greatest or best possible under a restriction expressed or implied ⟨~ safe speed⟩ ⟨an ~ return on capital⟩

**opting** *pres part of* OPT

**1op·tion** \ˈäpshən\ *n* -s [F, fr. L *option-*, *optio* free choice — more at OPINE] **1 :** an act of choosing **:** exercise of the power of choice ⟨at the student's ~ and with the professor's permission —*Loyola Univ. Bull.*⟩ ⟨hard to make one's ~ between such alternatives⟩ **2** *obs* **:** expression of a desire **:** WISH **3 a :** the power or right to choose (as between alternatives) **:** freedom of choice ⟨have an ~ . . . between accepting its findings or sticking to what we call traditional grammar —W.N. Francis⟩ **b :** a right formerly belonging to an archbishop of the Church of England to select any one dignity or benefice in the gift of a suffragan bishop consecrated or confirmed by him for bestowal by himself when next vacant **c** (1) **:** a privilege of demanding fulfillment of a contract on any day within a specified limit (2) **:** a right (as a put or call) to buy or sell designated securities or commodities at a specified price during the period of the contract **d :** a right of an insured person to choose the form in which various payments due him on a policy shall be made or applied **4 :** something that is offered for choice or that is chosen; *esp*, *chiefly Brit* **:** ELECTIVE **syn** see CHOICE

**2option** \"\ *vt* -ED/-ING/-S **:** to grant or take an option (as to purchase or rent) on ⟨~*ed* a building site to an out-of-state company⟩ ⟨ready to ~ the film rights from the author⟩

**1op·tion·al** \-shənᵊl, -shnəl\ *adj* **:** involving or depending on the exercise of an option **:** left to the discretion of the one concerned **:** not compulsory or obligate ⟨an ~ activity⟩ ⟨formal dress is ~⟩ — **op·tion·al·i·ty** \ˌäpshəˈnaləd·ē\ *n* -ES — **op·tion·al·ly** \ˈäpshənᵊlē, -shnəlē, -li\ *adv*

**2optional** \"\ *n* -s **1 :** something that is optional **2** *chiefly Brit* **:** ELECTIVE

**op·tion·al·ize** \ˈäpshənᵊlˌīz, -shnəˌlīz\ *vt* -ED/-ING/-S **:** to make optional

**optional pass** *n* **:** an offensive maneuver in football in which the quarterback may select the receiver for a pass or may himself run with the ball

**optional referendum** *n* **:** a referendum held in an area and on a subject (as a piece of legislation) that the legislature may deem advisable

**optional writ** *n* **:** an original legal writ that gives a defendant a choice either of doing some act that immediately provides a remedy to the plaintiff or of defending his own action **:** PRAECIPE

**op·tion·ary** \ˈäpshəˌnerē\ *adj* **:** OPTIONAL

**op·tion·ee** \ˌäpshəˈnē\ *n* -s [*1option* + *-ee*] **:** the grantee in an option contract

**op·tion·or** \ˈäpshənə(r); ˌ==ˈnȯ(ə)r, -ȯ(ə)\ *n* -s [*1option* + *-or*] **:** the grantor in an option contract

**option play** *n* **:** a football play (as an optional pass) in which an offensive player reacts to the situation rather than according to a predetermined pattern

**op·tive** \ˈäptiv\ *adj* [L *optivus* chosen; akin to L *option-*, *optio* free choice — more at OPINE] *Roman law* **:** chosen or appointed to an office or trust by an interested person — compare DATIVE, NOMINATIVE, TESTAMENTARY

**opto-** *comb form* [Gk *optos*, verbal of *opsesthai* to be going to see — more at OPTIC] **1 :** vision ⟨*optometer*⟩ **2 :** eye ⟨*optoblast*⟩ ⟨*optotype*⟩ **3 :** optic **:** optic and ⟨*optokinetic*⟩ ⟨*optocoele*⟩

**op·to·gram** \ˈäptəˌgram\ *n* [ISV *opto-* + *-gram*, orig. formed as G *optogramm*] **:** an image of an external object fixed on the retina by the photochemical action of light on the visual purple

**op·to·kinetic** \ˌäp,tō+\ *adj* [*opto-* + *kinetic*] **:** of, relating to, or involving movements of the eyes

**op·tom·e·ter** \äpˈtämәd·ә(r)\ *n* [*opto-* + *-meter*] **:** an instrument for measuring the power and range of vision

**op·to·met·ric** \ˌäptəˈme·trik, -rēk\ *also* **op·to·met·ri·cal** \-rəkəl, -rēk-\ *adj* **:** of or relating to optometry

**op·tom·e·trist** \äpˈtämə·trəst\ *n* -s **:** a specialist in optometry **:** REFRACTIONIST — compare OPTICIAN

**op·tom·e·try** \-rē, -ri\ *n* -ES [ISV *opto-* + *-metry*] **1 :** measurement of visual powers (as by use of an optometer) **2 :** an art or occupation consisting of the examination of the eye for defects and faults of refraction and the prescription of correctional lenses and exercises but not including the use of drugs or surgery — compare OPHTHALMOLOGY

**op·to·mo·tor reaction** \ˌäptəˈmōd·ə(r)-\ *n* [*opto-* + *-motor* (as in *locomotor*, *vasomotor*)] **:** a reflex involving turning of head or body in response to moving stripes of differing luminosity

**op·to·phone** \ˈäptəˌfōn\ *n* [*opto-* + *-phone*] **:** an instrument by which light variations are converted into sound variations so that a blind person is enabled by its use to locate and estimate varying degrees of light through the ear and thus even to read printed matter

**op·to·type** \-ˌtīp\ *n* [NL *optotypus*, fr. *opto-* + *typus* type, fr. L, character — more at TYPE] **:** type of different size used in testing the acuity of vision — usu. used in pl.

**opts** *pres 3d sing of* OPT

**op·u·lence** \ˈäpyələn(t)s\ *also* **op·u·len·cy** \-nsē, -si\ *n*, *pl* **opulences** *also* **opulencies** [L *opulentia*, fr. *opulentus* + *-ia* -y] **1 :** WEALTH, RICHES, AFFLUENCE **2 a :** PLENTY, PROFUSION, AMPLITUDE **b :** showy florid fullness (as of utterance or musical style)

**op·u·lent** \-nt\ *adj* [L *opulentus*, fr. *ops* power, wealth, help; akin to Skt *apnas* possession, property, Gk *ompnē* food, prosperity, L *oper-*, *opus* work — more at OPERATE] **:** exhibiting or characterized by opulence: as **a :** having a large estate or property **:** WEALTHY, AFFLUENT **b :** amply or plentifully provided or fashioned **:** LUXURIANT, PROFUSE, LAVISH ⟨~ blossoms⟩ ⟨an ~ bosom⟩ **syn** see LUXURIOUS, RICH

**op·u·lent·ly** *adv* **:** with opulence **:** in an opulent manner

**opun·tia** \ōˈpənch(ē)ə, -ntēə\ *n* [NL, fr. L, a plant, fr. fem. of *opuntius* of Opus, fr. *Opunt-*, *Opus* Opus, ancient city of Locris, Greece, fr. Gk *Opount-*, *Opous*] **1** *cap* **:** a very large genus of cacti comprising the prickly pears, being native to America but naturalized in most warm regions, having flat or terete joints usu. studded with tubercles that bear sharp spines, prickly hairs, or both, and producing mostly yellow flowers followed by pulpy edible fruits **2** -s **:** any cactus of the genus *Opuntia*

**opun·ti·a·les** \=ˌ=chēˈā(ˌ)lēz, -tēˈā-\ *n pl*, *cap* [NL, fr. *Opuntia* + *-ales*] **:** an order of succulent dicotyledonous plants coextensive with the family Cactaceae

**opun·ti·oid** \=ˈ=chēˌȯid, -tē,-\ *adj* [NL *Opuntia* + E *-oid*] **:** resembling a prickly pear

**opus** \ˈōpəs, *chiefly Brit* ˈäp-\ *n*, *pl* **opera** \ˈōpərə, ˈäp-\ *also* **opuses** [L *oper-* *opus* — more at OPERATE] **:** WORK: as **a :** a musical composition or set of compositions usu. numbered in the order of its issue — abbr. *op* **b :** EMBROIDERY — used in combination; see OPUS ANGLICANUM

**opus an·gli·ca·num** \-ˌaŋgləˈkānəm, -ka-,-kā-\ *n*, *pl* **opera anglica·na** \-nə\ [ML, lit., English work] **:** fine English medieval embroidery having pictorial designs following early paintings and being used esp. for ecclesiastical vestments

**opus ci·ta·tum** \-kəˈtād·əm, -ˌsīˈtäd-\ *n*, *pl* **opera cita·ta** \-d·ə\ [NL] **:** the work quoted from — abbr. *op cit*

**opus·cu·lar** \(ˈ)ōˌpəskyələ(r)\ *adj* **:** of or relating to an opuscule

**opus·cule** \ōˈpə(ˌ)skyül\ *also* **opus·cle** \ōˈpəsəl\ *n* -s [*opuscule* fr. F, fr. L *opusculum*; *opuscle* fr. L *opusculum*] **:** a small or petty work **:** OPUSCULUM

**opus·cu·lum** \ōˈpəskyələm\ *n*, *pl* **opuscu·la** \-lə\ [L, dim. of *opus*] **:** a minor work (as of literature) — usu. used in pl.

**opus la·te·ri·ci·um** \-ˌlad·əˈrikēəm, -ishē-\ *or* **opus la·te·ri·ti·um** \-ˌlad·əˈridēəm, -ishē-\ *n*, *pl* **opera lateri·cia** *or* **opera lateri·tia** \-ēə\ [L *opus latericium*, lit., work of brick] **:** masonry of bricks or tiles of baked clay laid in mortar and much used in Greco-Roman building for the facing of walls in stone masonry

**opus li·tho·stra·tum** \-ˌlithəˈsträd·əm, -rā-\ *n*, *pl* **opera lithostra·ta** \-d·ə\ [NL, lit., work paved with stone] **:** a facing or covering of stone

**opus mu·si·vum** \-müˈsēvəm; -myüˈsīvəm, -ˈzī-\ *n*, *pl* **opera musi·va** \-və\ [LL, lit., mosaic work] **:** mosaic decoration of walls often employing glass or enamel

**opus ope·ran·tis** \-ˌäpəˈrantəs\ *n*, *pl* **opera operan·tes** \-n·ˌtēz\ [ML, lit., work of the worker] **:** the efficacy of the agent — compare EX OPERE OPERANTIS

**opus ope·ra·tum** \-ˌäpəˈräd·əm, -rā-\ *n*, *pl* **opera opera·ta** \-d·ə\ [ML, lit., work done] **:** the efficacy of the action — compare EX OPERE OPERATO

**opus qua·dra·tum** \-kwäˈdräd·əm, -rā-\ *n*, *pl* **opera quadra·ta** \-d·ə\ [NL, lit., squared work] **:** Roman masonry of squared blocks

**opus sec·ti·le** \-ˈsektəlē\ *n*, *pl* **opera sec·til·ia** \-ˌsekˈtilēə\ [NL, lit., cut work] **:** stone inlay or tiling using pieces cut to follow the outline of the design

**opus tes·se·la·tum** \-ˌtesəˈlād·əm,-lā-\ *n*, *pl* **opera tessela·ta** \-d·ə\ [NL, lit., checkered work] **:** mosaic work employing cubes in simple geometric arrangements

**opus ver·mi·cu·la·tum** \-və(r)ˌmikyəˈlād·əm, -lā-\ *n*, *pl* **opera vermicula·ta** \-d·ə\ [NL, lit., work in the form of worms] **:** mosaic work employing small stones arranged in patterns of curving lines or in pictorial designs

**-opy** — see -OPIA

**oquas·sa** \ōˈkwäsə\ *n*, *pl* **oquassa** *or* **oquassas** [fr. *Oquassa* (Rangeley lake), lake in western Maine] **:** a small rather slender trout (*Salvelinus oquassa*) found in the Rangeley lakes of Maine

**1or** \ə(r), (ˌ)ȯ(ə)r, (ˌ)ȯ(ə), *in southern US also* (ˌ)ä(r)\ *conj* [ME *other*, *or*, fr. OE *oththe*, *oththa*, *eththa*; akin to OHG *eddo*, *odo*, *odar* or, ON *etha*, Goth *aiththau*] **1** — used as a function word to indicate (1) an alternative between different or unlike things, states, or actions ⟨wolves ~ bears are never seen in that part of the country⟩ ⟨sick ~ well, he should not be here⟩ ⟨eat ~ go hungry is all the same to him⟩; (2) choice between alternative things, states, or courses ⟨will you have tea ~ coffee⟩ ⟨decide to study medicine ~ law⟩ ⟨to be, ~ not to be: that is the question —Shak.⟩; (3) the synonymous, equivalent, or substitutive character of two words or phrases ⟨fell over a precipice ~ cliff⟩ ⟨the off ~ far side⟩ ⟨lessen ~ abate⟩; (4) correction or greater exactness of phrasing or meaning ⟨these essays, ~ rather rough sketches⟩ ⟨the present king had no children — ~ no legitimate children —Max Peacock⟩; (5) approximation, doubt, or uncertainty ⟨will be Tuesday ~ Wednesday before he arrives⟩ ⟨in five ~ six days⟩ ⟨it's scarlet fever ~ diphtheria⟩; (6) succession by turns ⟨one ~ the other will watch over him all night⟩; (7) the operation or logical connective symbolized by v or by +; compare TRUTH TABLE **2** *archaic* **:** EITHER — used with a second paired *or* ⟨no man can ~ foretoken or forefend —Walter de la Mare⟩ **3 :** or else **:** OTHERWISE ⟨do what I say, ~ you'll suffer the consequences⟩ ⟨pay ~ I'll sue⟩ **4** *archaic* **:** WHETHER — used with a second paired *or* ⟨~ rich or poor —*Baltimore (Md.) Sun*⟩ **5 :** on another occasion **:** as another instance **:** AGAIN ⟨~, an electron may serve merely to measure —L.A.White⟩

**2or** \"\ *prep* [ME *ar*, *or*, prep. & conj., fr. *ar*, *or*, adv., early, earlier, before, fr. ON *ār* early — more at ERE] *chiefly dial* **:** BEFORE

**3or** \"\ *conj* [ME *ar*, *or*] **1** *chiefly dial* **:** sooner than **:** UNTIL, BEFORE, ERE ⟨~ the porter was at the gate, the boy was in the hall —*Ballad Book*⟩ **2** *chiefly dial* **:** THAN

**4or** \ˈȯ(ə)r, ˈȯ(ə)\ *n* -s [MF, gold, fr. L *aurum* — more at ORIOLE] **1 :** a heraldic metal conventionally supposed to be the color of gold but in practice also represented as any of various shades of yellow **2 :** the color gold or the color yellow represented in drawing or engraving by small dots — compare TINCTURE

**5or** \"\ *adj* **:** being of the heraldic metal or **:** GOLDEN, YELLOW

**1-or** \ə(r) *sometimes* ˌȯ(ə)r *or* ˌȯ(ə)\ *n suffix* -s [ME *-or*, *-our*, fr. OF *-eor*, *-eur* & L *-or*; OF *-eor*, *-eur*, partly fr. L *-or*; partly fr. L *-ator*, fr. *-atus* -ate + *-or*] **:** one that does a (specified) thing ⟨grant*or*⟩ ⟨alternat*or*⟩ ⟨occlus*or*⟩ ⟨elevat*or*⟩

**2-or** \"\ *n suffix* -s [ME *-or*, *-our*, fr. OF *-eur*, fr. L *-or*] **:** condition **:** activity ⟨demean*or*⟩

**or** *abbr* **1** oriental **2** original

**OR** *abbr* **1** official receiver **2** on request **3** operating room **4** operations room **5** ordered recorded **6** other ranks **7** owner's risk

**1ora** \ˈōrə\ *n*, *pl* **oras** \-rəz\ *also* **orae** \ˈōˌrē, ˈōrˌī\ [OE *ōra*, of Scand origin; akin to ON *aur-*, *eyrir* ounce (usu. of silver), money (in pl.) — more at EYRIR] **:** a money of account introduced into England by the Danish invaders and valued in A.D. 920 at 2½ shillings and in the Domesday Book of 1086 at 20*d* sterling

**2ora** *pl of* OS

**ora** *abbr* oratorio

**ora·bas·su** \ˌōrəˈbaˌsü\ *n* -s [Tupi *oyapussá*] **:** any of several So. American titi monkeys of the genus *Callicebus*

**or·ache** *or* **or·ach** \ˈärəch\ *n*, *pl* **oraches** [ME *arage*, *orage*, fr. MF *arache*, modif. of L *atriplic-*, *atriplex*, fr. Gk *atraphaxys*] **:** a plant of the genus *Atriplex*; *esp* **:** GARDEN ORACHE

**1or·a·cle** \ˈȯrəkəl, ˈär-, -rēk-\ *n* -s [ME, fr. MF, fr. L *oraculum*, fr. *orare* to speak + *-culum*, suffix denoting means, place, or instrument — more at ORATION] **1 a** (1) **:** a revelation received from the God of Judaism and Christianity **:** a divine revelation (2) **:** a typically ambiguous or enigmatic revelation or utterance believed to issue from a divinity through a medium (as a priest or priestess) thought to be inspired **b :** an authoritative or wise expression **:** an answer delivered with an aspect of oracular certainty ⟨could utter ~*s* of Delphian ambiguity —Thomas Hardy⟩ **2 a** (1) **:** a medium by which a pagan god reveals hidden knowledge or makes known the divine purpose (2) **:** a medium of communication from the Hebraic or Christian God **:** an expounder or interpreter of God's will **b :** a place where a divine revelation or an utterance believed to issue from a divinity is given **3 a :** a person of great authority or wisdom whose opinions or judgments are regarded with great respect **:** one who is considered or professes to be infallible ⟨a systematic philosopher, not a dabbler or ~ —W.W.Austin⟩ **b :** something (as a scientific instrument) on which one can rely for guidance or direction **:** an infallible guide ⟨electronic computers are rapidly becoming the ~*s* of industry —*Time*⟩

**2oracle** \"\ *vb* **oracled; oracled; oracling** \-kliŋ\ **oracles** *archaic* **:** to proclaim or speak as an oracle

**oracle bone** *n* **:** a bone used in early China esp. during the Shang dynasty 1765–1123 B.C. in divination by writing a question upon it, heating it, and divining the answer from the resultant cracks

**orac·u·lar** \ȯˈrakyələ(r), äˈr-, əˈr-\ *adj* [L *oraculum* oracle + E *-ar* — more at ORACLE] **1 :** of, relating to, or being an oracle **:** used to forecast or divine **:** FORECASTING, DIVINING ⟨~ bone inscriptions —Chung-Yuan Chang⟩ ⟨~ instruments —Nathaniel Micklem⟩ ⟨able by ~ means to expose a witch —*Notes & Queries on Anthropology*⟩ **2 :** resembling an oracle esp. in solemnity of delivery or obscurity of thought ⟨the ~ sayings of Victorian poets —René Wellek & Austin Warren⟩ — **orac·u·lar·ly** *adv* — **orac·u·lar·ness** *n* -ES

**orac·u·lar·i·ty** \=ˌ==ˈlarəd·ē\ *n* -ES **:** the quality, state, or an instance of being oracular

**orac·u·late** \=ˈ==ˌlāt\ *vb* -ED/-ING/-S [L *oraculum* + E *-ate*] **:** ORACLE

**orac·u·lous** \-ləs\ *adj* [L *oraculum* + E *-ous*] *archaic* **:** ORACULAR — **orac·u·lous·ly** *adv*, *archaic*

**orad** \ˈōrˌad, ˈōˌr-\ *adv* [L *or-*, *os* mouth + E *-ad*] **:** toward the mouth or oral region

**orae serratae** *pl of* ORA SERRATA

**1oral** \ˈōrəl, ˈȯr-, ˈär-\ *adj* [L *or-*, *os* mouth + E *-al*; akin to OE *ōr* beginning, origin, *ōra* border, bank, shore, ON *ōss* mouth of a river, L *ora* edge, border, MIr *ā* (gen. sing.) mouth, Skt *ās*] **1 a :** uttered by the mouth or in words **:** not written **:** SPOKEN ⟨~ traditions⟩ ⟨~ delivery⟩ ⟨~ testimony⟩ **b :** using lip movement and voice articulation **:** conducted or delivered by the spoken word ⟨~ reading⟩; *specif* **:** emphasizing lip reading and the development of vocal expression rather than the use of manual signs in teaching the deaf ⟨~ teacher⟩ ⟨~ method⟩ ⟨~ system⟩ **2 a** (1) **:** of, relating to, or belonging to the mouth **:** BUCCAL ⟨the ~ mucous membrane⟩ (2) **:** given or taken through or by way of the mouth ⟨doses for ~ administration⟩ (3) **:** acting on the mouth ⟨~ diseases⟩ ⟨a skillful ~ surgeon⟩ **b :** articulated between lips and uvula and with the velum raised so that there is no nasal resonance ⟨~ speech sounds⟩ ⟨an ~ consonant⟩ **c** (1) **:** being the surface on which the mouth is situated ⟨the ~ surface of a starfish⟩ (2) **:** relating to or located on an oral surface ⟨the water-vascular system is chiefly ~⟩ — opposed to *aboral* **3 a :** of, relating to, or characterized by the first stage of psychosexual development in which libidinal gratification is derived from intake (as of food), by sucking, and later by biting **b :** of, relating to, or characterized by personality traits of passive dependency and aggressiveness — compare ANAL, GENITAL — **oral·ly** \-rəlē, -li\ *adv*

**2oral** \"\ *n* -s **1 :** an oral part (as a plate or valve) **2 :** an oral examination — usu. used in pl. ⟨had to clear this hurdle before reaching your ~*s* —Francis Biddle⟩

**oral arm** *n* **:** one of the prolongations of the distal end of the manubrium of a jellyfish

**oral disc** *n* **1 :** LOPHOPHORE **2 :** the more or less flattened upper or free end of the body bearing the mouth in its center and tentacles near or at its border in most polyps **3 :** the sucker-bordered mouth of some trematode worms

**ora·le** \ōˈrā(ˌ)lē\ *n* -s [ML, fr. L *or-*, *os* mouth + *-ale*, neut. of *-alis* -al] **:** FANON d

**oral·er** \ˈōrələ(r), ˈȯr-,ˈär-\ *n* -s [*1oral* + *-er*] **:** one who bets (as on a race) by word of mouth without giving or receiving any ticket or slip

**oral groove** *n* **:** a depressed peristome resembling a groove

**oral hood** *n* **:** a prolongation of the metapleural folds surrounding the mouth in an amphioxus and bearing the oral cirri

**oral·ism** \ˈōrəˌlizəm, ˈȯr-,ˈär-\ *n* -s **:** advocacy or use of the oral method of teaching the deaf

**oral·ist** \-ləst\ *n* -s **:** a practicer of oralism

**oral·i·ty** \ōˈraləd·ē, ȯˈr-,äˈr-\ *n* -ES **:** the quality or state of being oral

**oral law** *n* **1 :** law handed down and perpetuated by word of mouth rather than by writing **2** *usu cap O&L* **:** MISHNAH

**oral lobe** *n* **:** a labial palp of a bivalve mollusk

**oral method** *n* **:** a method of instructing the deaf by which they are taught to speak and to understand the speech of others by lipreading

**oral·o·gy** \ōˈraləjē, ȯˈr-,äˈr-\ *n* -ES [irreg. fr. *1oral* + *-logy*] **:** STOMATOLOGY

**oral plate** *also* **oral membrane** *n* **:** STOMODAEUM

**oral surgeon** *n* **:** one that specializes in oral surgery

**oral surgery** *n* **1 :** a branch of dentistry that deals with the diagnosis and treatment of oral conditions requiring surgical intervention **2 :** a branch of surgery that deals with conditions of the jaws and mouth structures requiring surgery

**oran** \ōˈrän\ *adj*, *usu cap* [*Oran*, Algeria] **:** of or from the city of Oran, Algeria **:** of the kind or style prevalent in Oran

**or/and** \ˈȯ(ə)(r)ənd\ *conj* **:** AND/OR

**orang** *also* **ourang** *n* -s [by shortening] **:** ORANGUTAN

**1or·ange** \ˈȯrənj, ˈär-, -rēnj, *in rapid speech esp in pl or in compounds* -rnj\ *n* -s [ME *orenge*, *orange*, fr. MF, fr. OProv *auranja*, fr. Ar *nāranj*, fr. Per *nārang*, fr. Skt *nāraṅga*, of Dravidian origin; akin to Tamil *naru* fragrant] **1 a :** any of various globose to subglobose tropical or subtropical fruits that are technically berries with a reddish yellow leathery aromatic rind containing many oil glands and used extensively in confectionery, preserves, and cookery and with a usu. sweet but acid juicy edible pulp rich in minerals and vitamin C — see MANDARIN ORANGE, NAVEL ORANGE, SOUR ORANGE, SWEET ORANGE **b :** any of various rather small evergreen and often spiny trees of the genus *Citrus* (as *C. aurantium*, *C. sinensis*, or *C. reticulata*) that have pointed ovate unifoliate leaves, hard yellow wood, and usu. fragrant white flowers and that produce fruits which are oranges — see TRIFOLIATE ORANGE **2 a :** the evergreen orange tree usu. not over 30 feet in height with oval unifoliolate leaves, hard yellow wood, and a fragrant white blossom **b :** any of several trees or fruits resembling the orange **3** [*2orange*] **a :** any of a group of colors about midway between red and yellow in hue, of medium lightness, and of moderate to high saturation **b :** a hue midway between red and yellow that is evoked in the normal observer under normal conditions by radiant energy of the wavelength 610 millimicrons **c :** a pigment or dye producing an orange color — see DYE table I (under *Acid Orange*), ORANGE G, ORANGE II **4 :** a roundel tenné

orange 2 (flowering branch)

**2orange** \"\ *adj* **1 :** of or relating to an orange **2 :** being of the color orange ⟨an ~ ribbon⟩

**3orange** \"\ *adj*, *usu cap* [fr. *Orange*, princely family of Europe to which belong William III of England and the present reigning family of the Netherlands] **1 :** of or relating to the Orange family or house in the Netherlands **2 :** of or relating to the Orangemen **:** being or relating to those belonging to or in sympathy with them

**or·ange·ade** \ˌȯrənˈjād, ˌär-, -rēn-, *in rapid speech* (ˈ)ȯrn- *or* (ˈ)ärn-\ *n* [F, fr. *orange* + *-ade*] **:** a beverage of orange juice sweetened and mixed with plain or carbonated water

**or·ange·a·do** \ˌȯrənˈjä(ˌ)dō, ˌär-, -rēn-\ *n* -s [prob. modif. (influenced by *1orange*) of Sp *naranjado*, *naranjada*, fr. *naranja* orange (fr. Ar *nāranj*) + *-ado* -ate (fr. L *-atus*) or *-ada*, fem. of *-ado* — more at ORANGE] *archaic* **:** candied orange peel

**orange aphid** *n* **:** COTTON APHID

**orange aurora** *n* **:** AURORA 3

**orange basketworm** *n* **:** a grub that is the larva of a small moth (*Platoeceticus gloveri*), lives on the orange tree, and forms an oval larval case

**orange bat** *or* **orange horseshoe bat** *n* **:** a common bat (*Rhinonycteris aurantius*) of northwest Australia with soft fur that is bright orange on the male and pale yellow on the female

**orange berry** *n* **1 :** LIMEBERRY **2 :** EUROPEAN CRANBERRY

**orangebird** \ˈ=(=)ˌ=\ *n* **:** a Jamaican tanager (*Spindalis zena nigricephala*) with a bright orange breast

**orange bitters** *n pl but usu sing in constr* **:** an orange-flavored bitters; *esp* : one made in England from the bitter Seville orange and used chiefly as a cocktail ingredient

**orange blossom** *n* **1** : a white fragrant blossom that is the flower of the orange and is a favorite flower at weddings and a source of a fragrant oil used as an ingredient of eau de cologne **2** : BIRTHROOT **3** : MEXICAN ORANGE **4** : a cocktail consisting of gin, orange juice, and sugar or sometimes honey shaken with ice and strained before serving

**orange–blossom orchid** *n* : an orchid (*Sarcochilus falcatus*) of Australia having white flowers with purple and orange markings on the lip

**orange chrome** *n* : CHROME ORANGE

**orange chrome yellow** *n* : CHROME ORANGE

**orange chromide** *n* : CHROMIDE

**orange creeper** *n* : a very showy Brazilian woody vine (*Pyrostegia venusta*) of the family Bignoniaceae commonly cultivated for its showy crimson-orange flowers in hanging panicles

**orange–crowned warbler** \ˈ≈(≈),≈-\ *n* : a small grayish green and yellowish American warbler (*Vermivora celata*) having a concealed orange crown patch

**orangecup lily** \ˈ≈(≈),≈-\ *n* : WOOD LILY 1b

**orange daisy** *or* **orange fleabane** *n* : a perennial herb (*Erigeron aurantiacus*) of Turkestan with nearly double orange-yellow flower heads

**orange dog** *n* : the larva of the orange-tree butterfly (*Papilio cresphontes*)

**orange drink** *n* : a still beverage consisting of orange oils, citric acid, sugar, and water

**orange fin** *n, Brit* : a young sea trout : a sea trout smolt

**orange flower** *n* **1** : ORANGE BLOSSOM **2** : MEXICAN ORANGE **3** : MOCK ORANGE

**orange–flower oil** *n* : NEROLI OIL

**orange–flower water** *n* : a saturated solution of neroli oil used in pharmaceutical preparations and toilet water

**orange fly** *n* : any of several small flies whose larvae burrow in oranges; *esp* : MEXICAN FRUITFLY

**orange fruit moth** *n* : any of several moths able to pierce oranges and other fruits

**orange G** *n, usu cap O* : an acid azo dye made by coupling diazotized aniline and G acid and used chiefly in dyeing wool and leather and as a biological stain — see DYE table I (under *Acid Orange 10*)

**orange grass** *n* : a No. American weed (*Hypericum gentianoides*) with wiry stems, minute leaves resembling scales, and small bright yellow flowers

**orange hawkweed** *n* : a European hawkweed (*Hieracium aurantiacum*) that has flower heads with bright orange-red rays and is troublesome as a weed esp. in northeastern No. America

**or·ange·ism** \ˈȯrənˌjizəm, ˈär-, -rēn-\ *n* -s *usu cap* [³*orange* + *-ism*] : attachment to the principles of the society of Orangemen : the tenets or practices of the Orangemen

**orange jessamine** *or* **orange jasmine** *n* : an East Indian shrub or small tree (*Murraya paniculata*) with evergreen pinnate leaves and fragrant white bell-shaped flowers

**orange lead** *n* : ORANGE MINERAL

**orange leaf rust** *n* : a rust of wheat and other grasses caused by a fungus (*Puccinia triticina*), characterized by orange-colored pustules on the leaves, resulting in decreased yield and quality of grain, and involving as alternate host of the parasite a meadow rue or related plant

**orange lily** *n* : either of the two European lilies (*Lilium croceum* and *L. bulbiferum*) having erect bright orange or orange-red flowers

**oran·ge·lo** \ȯˈranjəˌlō\ *n* -s [blend of *orange* and *pomelo*] : a hybrid citrus fruit produced by crossing an orange and a pomelo

**orange madder** *n* : MADDER ORANGE

**orange maggot** *n* : the larva of an orange fly

**or·ange·man** \ˈ≈(≈)mən, -ˌman, -ˌmaa(ə)n\ *n, pl* **orangemen** *usu cap* [William III †1702 king of England and prince of *Orange* + E *man*] **1** : a member of a secret society organized in the north of Ireland in 1795 to defend the reigning sovereign of Great Britain, to support the Protestant religion, and to maintain the laws of the kingdom **2** : a Protestant Irishman esp. of Ulster

**orange margined blue** \ˈ≈(≈),≈≈-\ *n* : any of several lycaenid butterflies of the genus *Lycaeides*

**orange melon** *n* : MANGO MELON

**orangemen's day** *n, usu cap O&D* : July 12 observed in northern Ireland as a holiday commemorating the Battle of Aughrim in 1691 and the Battle of the Boyne in 1690

**orange milkweed** *n* : BUTTERFLY WEED

**orange milkwort** *n* : an annual bog herb (*Polygala lutea*) of the pine barrens of the southeastern U. S. with yellow-orange spikes of irregular flowers

**orange mineral** *n* : a pigment that is similar in composition to red lead but lighter in color and is usu. obtained by roasting white lead

**orange ocher** *n* : OCHER ORANGE

**orange oil** *n* : an essential oil from orange peel or orange flowers: as **a** : a yellow to deep orange oil obtained from the peel of the sweet orange and used chiefly as a flavor and perfume — called also *sweet orange oil* **b** : a similar but bitter pale yellow or yellowish brown oil from the peel of the sour orange — called also *bitter orange oil*

**orange I** *n* : an acid dye — see DYE table I (under *Acid Orange 20*)

**orange peel** *n* **1** : the peel of an orange **2** : a rough surface resembling that of an orange that may occur with a fast-drying coating (as shellac or lacquer) or with some ceramic glazes **3** : a strong orange color that is yellower, lighter, and stronger than pumpkin and slightly redder and darker than cadmium orange

**orange–peel bucket** *n* : a bucket having three or more crescent-shaped jaws resembling segments of orange peel hinged to a single support at the top

orange-peel bucket

**orange pekoe** *n* **1 a** : a tea formerly made from the tiny leaf and end bud of the spray **b** : a similar small-leaved tea of India and Ceylon obtained by screening fired tea **2** : a good grade of India or Ceylon tea; *esp* : one made from the first and second leaves of the shoot

**orange plume** *n* : YELLOW FRINGED ORCHID

**orange puppy** *n* : ORANGE DOG

**orange quit** *n* : a Jamaican honeycreeper (*Glossiptila ruficollis*)

**orange R** *n, usu cap O* : an acid dye — see DYE table I under *Acid Orange 8*

**or·ange·rie** *like* ORANGERY\ *n* -s [F — more at ORANGERY] : ORANGERY

**orange rockfish** *n* : a rockfish (*Sebastodes pinniger*) found from Puget Sound to southern California that becomes two feet long, is olive gray blotched with orange shading to grayish white below, and is a common market fish

**orangeroot** \ˈ≈(≈),≈\ *n* [²*orange* + *root*] **1** : GOLDENSEAL **2** : BUTTERFLY WEED 1

**orange–rufous** \ˌ≈(≈)ˈ≈≈\ *adj* : of any of several colors averaging a strong orange that is deeper than pumpkin and redder and darker than cadmium orange

**orange rust** *n* **1** : either of two diseases of raspberries and blackberries caused by two rusts (*Gymnoconia peckiana* and *Kunkelia niteus*) and characterized by retarded growth and curled and distorted usu. small leaves lacking in green color and with bright red or orange powder on the under surfaces; *also* : the fungus causing either disease **2** : a strong yellowish brown that is redder, stronger, and slightly darker than buckthorn brown and redder and deeper than centennial brown

**or·ange·ry** \ˈȯrənjrē, ˈär-, -rēnj-, -ri, -rnj-\ *n* -ES [F *orangerie*, fr. *orange* + *-erie* -ery — more at ORANGE] **1** : a greenhouse or other protected place for raising oranges in cool climates **2** *obs* **a** : orange perfume **b** : orange-scented snuff

**oranges** *pl of* ORANGE

**oranges and lemons** *n pl but sing or pl in constr* : an old singing game played like London Bridge

**orange scab** *n* : citrus scab of the orange

**orange scale** *n* : any of several scales that infest orange trees: as **a** : PURPLE SCALE **b** : GLOVER SCALE **c** : RED SCALE **d** : BROWN SCALE

**orange shellac** *n* : SHELLAC 1

**orange sneezeweed** *n* : WESTERN SNEEZEWEED

**orange spoon** *n* : a teaspoon that tapers to a sharp point or teeth and that is used for citrus fruits and melons

orange spoon

**orangespotted sunfish** \ˈ≈(≈),≈≈-\ *or* **orangespot sunfish** \ˈ≈(≈),≈-\ *n* : a very small orange-marked sunfish (*Lepomis humilis*) widely distributed in silty waters of the central U. S.

**orange star** *n* : a star of spectral type K

**orange stick** *n* : a thin stick like a pencil usu. of orangewood with pointed and rounded ends for manicuring

**orange–sucker** \ˈ≈(≈),≈≈\ *n* : ORANGE FRUIT MOTH

**orange swallowwort** *n* : BUTTERFLY WEED 1

**orange–tawny** \ˌ≈(≈)ˈ≈≈\ *adj* : of any of several colors averaging the color Mars orange

**orange tip** *n* : any of several small pierid butterflies in which the males or both males and females usu. have a conspicuous orange blotch at the tip of the forewing

**orange tortrix** *n* : a tortricid moth (*Argyrotaenia citrana*) whose larva infests oranges and also feeds on several fruit trees and various other cultivated and wild plants esp. in California

**orange–tree butterfly** *n* : a large black and yellow butterfly (*Papilio cresphontes*) — see ORANGE DOG

**orange II** *n* : an acid azo dye made by coupling diazotized sulfanilic acid with beta-naphthol and used chiefly in dyeing wool and leather, in making pigments (as for wallpaper), and as a biological stain — see DYE table I (under *Acid Orange 7*)

**orange vermilion** *n* : a strong reddish orange that is yellower and paler than poppy or paprika and slightly yellower and lighter than scarlet vermilion

**orange wine** *n* : a wine variously made by fermenting orange juice or orange peel

**orangewood** \ˈ≈(≈),≈\ *n* : the wood of the orange tree used esp. in turnery and carving

**orange worm** *n* : the larva of any of several moths that are pests on oranges; *esp* : ORANGE TORTRIX

**orang laut** \ˈōrəŋˌlau̇t\ *n, pl* **orang laut** *or* **orang lauts** *usu cap O&L* [Malay, fr. *orang* person, man + *laut* sea] : BAJAU

**orangs** *pl of* ORANG

**orang·utan** *or* **orang·ou·tan** *or* **orang·ou·tang** *also* **oran·utan** *or* **ou·rang·ou·tang** \əˈraŋəˌtaŋ, ōˈr-, ȯˈr-, -raiŋəˌtaiŋ *sometimes* ≈ˈ≈yü,- *or* ≈ˈ≈≈,tan *or* -,taa(ə)n *or* ˌō,≈-ˈ(y)ü,≈ *or* ˌō,≈ˈ≈,≈ *or* ˌōrəŋˈ(y)üt°n *or with* n *instead of* ŋ *after the vowel of the second syllable*\ *n* -s [Malay *orang hutan*, fr. *orang* man, person + *hutan* forest] : a largely herbivorous arboreal anthropoid ape (*Pongo pygmaeus*) of low swampy forests of Borneo and Sumatra that is about two thirds as large as the gorilla with the adult male standing four feet high and weighing up to 250 pounds, is distinguished by its small ears, brown skin, long sparse reddish brown hair, and very long arms, and has the face, hands, and feet naked and the cheeks in old males flattened and expanded

orangutan

**or·angy** *or* **or·ang·ey** \ˈȯrənjē, ˈär-, -rēn-, -ji, *in rapid speech* -rnj-\ *adj, sometimes* **orang·i·er**; **orang·i·est** [¹*orange* + *-y*] **1** : resembling or suggestive of an orange (as in flavor or color) ⟨an ~ pink —Tamara T. Rice⟩ **2** *of a color of gems* : having the orange component strong ⟨~ yellow is midway between orange yellow and yellow⟩

**oran·ian** \ōˈrānēən\ *adj, usu cap* [*Oran*, seaport and department in northwestern Algeria + E *-ian*] : of or relating to an Upper Paleolithic culture of western Algeria and Morocco typified by tiny crescent-backed blades

**orans** \ˈōr,anz\ *n, pl* **oran·tes** \ōˈran·(ˌ)tēz\ [ML or NL] : ORANT

**orant** \ˈōrənt\ *or* **oran·te** \ōˈran·(ˌ)tē\ *n* -s [*orant* fr. ML or NL *orant-, orans*, fr. L, pres. part. of *orare* to pray; *orante* fr. It, fr. ML or NL *orant-, orans* — more at ORATION] **1** : a female figure in the posture of prayer in ancient Greek art **2** : a usu. female figure standing with outstretched arms as if in prayer used in early Christian art as a symbol of the faithful dead

**ora·on** \ˈōrä,ōn\ *n, pl* **oraon** *or* **oraons** *usu cap* **1** : KURUKH **2** : the Kurukh language

**ora·ri·on** \ōˈrarē,ōn\ *or* **orar·i·um** \ōˈra(a)rēəm, -rer-, -rär-\ *n, pl* **oraria** \-rēə\ [MGk & LL; MGk *ōrarion*, fr. LL *orarium*, fr. L *or-, os* mouth + *-arium* -ary — more at ORAL] : a stole worn hanging over the left shoulder by a deacon in the Eastern Church

**oras** *pl of* ORA

**ora ser·ra·ta** \ˌōrəsəˈräd·ə, -räd·ə\ *n, pl* **orae serra·tae** \ˌōr,īsəˈräd·,ī, ˌōr,ēsəˈräd·,ē\ [NL, lit., serrated margin] : the dentate border of the retina

**orate** \ōˈrāt, ōˈr-, ˈ≈,≈, *usu* -ād·+V\ *vb* -ED/-ING/-S [back-formation fr. *oration*] *vi* **1** : to deliver an oration ⟨~ in the sonorous periods of a rhetoric long forgotten —Patrick Balfour⟩ **2** : to talk in a declamatory, grandiloquent, or impassioned manner : HARANGUE ⟨love to hear him ~ with waving hands about the racial sins of his native land —Ben Burns⟩ ⟨go around *orating* about pure Southern womanhood —James Street⟩ ~ *vt* : to talk to in a declamatory, grandiloquent, or impassioned manner : HARANGUE ⟨*orated* the Italian people into that tragic aggression —Herbert Hoover⟩

¹**ora·tion** \ōˈrāshən, əˈr-\ *n* -s [in sense 1, fr. ME *oracione*, fr. LL *oration-, oratio*, fr. L, speech, language, style, harangue, oration, fr. *oratus* (past part. of *orare* to recite a ritual, plead, pray, speak) + *-ion-, -io* -ion; in other senses, fr. L *oration-, oratio*; akin to Gk *ara, arē* prayer, Russ *orat'* to yell, cry, and perh. to Skt *āryati* he acknowledges, praises; basic meaning: to speak, call] **1** *archaic* : PETITION, PRAYER ⟨the bells tolled the hour of ~ —Washington Irving⟩ **2** : an elaborate discourse delivered in public and treating an important subject in a formal and dignified manner; *esp* : a formal discourse on some special occasion (as a funeral or an anniversary) **3** *dial Eng* : CLAMOR, UPROAR

²**oration** \"\ *vi* -ED/-ING/-S : to deliver an oration

**ora·tio obli·qua** \ōˌräd·ē,ōəˈblēkwə\ *n* [L, indirect speech] : discourse that is indirect : a paraphrase rather than an exact quotation

**or·a·tor** \ˈȯrəd·ə(r), ˈär-, -ətə- *also* -ˌtō(ə)r *or* -ō(ə)\ *n* -s [ME *oratour*, fr. MF or L; MF *orateur*, fr. L *orator*, fr. *oratus* (past part. of *orare*) + *-or*] **1 a** *obs* : ADVOCATE, PLEADER **b** : PETITIONER, SUPPLIANT **c** : the petitioner or plaintiff in a bill of information or petition in a court of justice esp. in chancery **2 a** : a public speaker : one who delivers an oration; *esp* : one distinguished for his skill and power as a public speaker ⟨might have been a spouter who thought he was an ~ —W.A.White⟩ **b** (1) : an officer of an English university who represents the university on public occasions, writes addresses and letters of a public nature, and presents candidates for honorary degrees (2) : a college or high school student selected to deliver an oration at commencement or other public occasion **c** : one of the officers of the Masonic order and some other secret societies

**or·a·to·ri·al** \ˌȯrəˈtōrēəl, ˌär-, -tȯr-\ *adj* [L *oratorius* oratorial (fr. *orator*) + E *-al*] : ORATORICAL

¹**or·a·to·ri·an** \-rēən\ *n* -s *usu cap* [*Oratory* of St. Philip Neri + E *-an*] : a member of the Oratory of St. Philip Neri established in Rome in 1564 as a religious society of diocesan priests that live a community life but do not make special vows

²**oratorian** \"\ *adj, usu cap* : of or relating to the Oratorians

**or·a·tor·i·cal** \ˌ≈≈ˈtȯrəkəl, -tär-, -rēk-\ *also* **or·a·tor·ic** \-rik, -rēk\ *adj* [*orator* & *oratory* + *-ical*, *-ic*] : of, relating to, or suggestive of an orator or oratory : RHETORICAL ⟨the pomp and glitter of ~ prose —Pedro Salinas⟩ ⟨the letters grow more ~ —T.L.Robertson⟩ ⟨harangued his men in an ~ way —Robert Graves⟩ **2** : given to oratory — **or·a·tor·i·cal·ly** \-rək(ə)lē, -rēk-, -li\ *adv*

**or·a·to·rio** \ˌȯrəˈtōrē,ō, ˌärə-, -tȯr-\ *n* -s [It, fr. the *Oratorio* di San Filippo Neri (Oratory of St. Philip Neri) in Rome, where musical religious services similar to mystery plays were held in the 16th century] **1** : a musical composition having a libretto based usu. on a religious or scriptural subject and consisting typically of recitatives, arias, choruses, orchestral interludes and accompaniment, and sometimes spoken dialogue or narration but having no action, scenery, or costume **2** : a performance of such a composition

¹**or·a·to·ry** \ˈ≈≈,tōrē, -tȯr-, -ri\ *n* -ES [ME *oratorie*, fr. LL *oratorium*, fr. L *oratus* (past part. of *orare* to pray) + *-orium* -ory — more at ORATION] **1** : a place of orisons or prayer; *esp* : a chapel or small room set apart for private devotions **2** *often cap* : an establishment or house of the Oratorians

²**oratory** \"\ *n* -ES [L *oratoria*, fr. fem. of *oratorius* oratorial — more at ORATORIAL] **1** : the art of an orator : the art of speaking in public eloquently or effectively : the exercise of rhetorical skill in discourse : ELOQUENCE ⟨a student of ~⟩ **2** : an example or instance of rhetorical speech or art : the substance of such speech ⟨his ~ was pure bombast⟩ ⟨campaign ~⟩ ⟨your general's speeches . . . are admirable as ~ but damnably unhistorical —Robert Graves⟩

**or·a·trix** \ˈȯrə,triks, ˈär-\ *n, pl* **or·atrices** \ˌ≈≈ˈtrī(ˌ)sēz\ [L, fem. of *orator* — more at -TRIX] : a female orator

¹**orb** \ˈȯ(ə)rb, ˈō(ə)b\ *n* -s [AF *orbe*, fr. OF *orbe* blind, without light, fr. L *orbus* orphaned, bereft, blind — more at ORPHAN] : a detail in medieval architecture of uncertain character but prob. a recessed panel surrounded by moldings (as one member of a blind arcade or one of the spaces between the ribs of a Gothic vault)

²**orb** \"\ *n* -s [MF *orbe*, fr. L *orbis* circle, disk, orb; akin to L *orbita* track, rut] **1 a** : any of the azure transparent spheres in old astronomy surrounding the earth one within the other and carrying the heavenly bodies in their revolutions **b** (1) : a globular celestial object (as the sun or moon, a planet or star) ⟨the celestial ~s revolve with uniform circular movements —G.C.Sellery⟩ (2) : EARTH ⟨solid, ironical, rolling ~ —Walt Whitman⟩ **c** (1) : a spherical body : something of globular shape : GLOBE ⟨skewering the smaller ~s where they cowered amid their leaves —A.B.Mayse⟩ (2) : EYE ⟨her sightless ~s —Arnold Bennett⟩ (3) : a sphere surmounted by a cross symbolizing kingly power and justice and forming part of the English regalia (4) : a similar sphere on top of a scepter or crown **d** *archaic* (1) : a collective whole : WORLD (2) : a sphere of action : STATION ⟨in our ~s we'll live so round and safe —Shak.⟩ **2 a** : something circular (as a disk, wheel, ring) : CIRCLE ⟨the wheeling ~ of change —Alfred Tennyson⟩ **b** (1) *obs* : a period of time marked off by the revolution of a heavenly body (2) *archaic* : the orbit or the plane of the orbit of a planet or other heavenly body

orb 1c (3)

³**orb** \"\ *vb* -ED/-ING/-S *vt* **1** : to form into a disk or circle : round out **2** *archaic* : ENCIRCLE, SURROUND, ENCLOSE ~ *vi* : to move in an orbit

**ORB** *abbr* **1** omnidirectional radio beacon **2** owner's risk of breakage

**orbed** \ˈȯ(ə)rbd, ˈō(ə)bd, *in poetry often* -bəd\ *adj* [¹*orb* + *-ed*] : having the form of an orb : ROUND

**or·bic** \ˈȯrbik, ˈō(ə)b-, -bēk\ *or* **or·bi·cal** \-bəkəl, -bēk-\ *adj* [*orbic* fr. L *orbicus*, fr. *orbis* + *-icus* -ic; *orbical* fr. L *orbicus* + E *-al*] : ORBICULAR

**or·bi·cel·la** \ˌȯ(r)bəˈselə\ *n, cap* [NL, fr. L *orbis* orb, circle + L *cella* cell — more at ORB, CELL] : a genus of usu. massive star corals with the zooids widely separated

**or·bic·u·lar** \ȯ(r)ˈbikyələ(r)\ *adj* [ME *orbiculer*, fr. MF or LL; MF *orbiculaire*, fr. LL *orbicularis* circular, fr. L *orbiculus* small disk + *-aris* -ar — more at ORBICULE] **1 a** : resembling or having the form of an orb : SPHERICAL, CIRCULAR ⟨nearly ~ in shape —P.S.Barnhart⟩ **b** : containing rounded bodies consisting of minerals in generally radial or tangential groupings usu. in successive concentric zones ⟨~ rocks⟩ **c** : encircling a part or opening ⟨an ~ ligament⟩ **2** : COMPLETE, ROUNDED, INTEGRAL ⟨an ~ system of political thought⟩ — **or·bic·u·lar·i·ty** \ˌ≈ˌ≈≈ˈlarəd·ē\ *n* -ES — **or·bic·u·lar·ly** *adv*

**or·bi·cu·lar·is** \ȯ(r)ˌbikyəˈla(a)rəs, -lär-\ *n, pl* **orbicula·res** \-(ˌ)rēz\ [NL, fr. LL *orbicularis*, adj.] : a muscle encircling an orifice ⟨the ~ that encircles the opening of the orbit⟩

**orbicularis oris** \-ˈōrəs\ *n, pl* **orbiculares oris** [NL, lit., orbicularis of the mouth] : a muscle made up of several layers of fibers passing in different directions that encircles the mouth and controls most movements of the lips (as compressing, closing, or pursing movements)

**orbicular ligament** *n* : ANNULAR LIGAMENT b

**or·bic·u·late** \ȯ(r)ˈbikyələt, -ˌlāt, *usu* |d·+V\ *adj* [L *orbiculatus*, fr. *orbiculus* + *-atus* -ate] : having the form of an orb : circular or nearly circular in outline : ORBICULAR ⟨an ~ leaf⟩ — see LEAF illustration — **or·bic·u·late·ly** *adv*

**or·bi·cule** \ˈȯ(r)bə,kyül\ *n* -s [L *orbiculus* small disk, dim. of *orbis* disk, circle — more at ORB] : a more or less spherical body found in some granites and other rocks, varying in size from a pellet visible only under the microscope to a sphere 10 feet or more in diameter, and having its constituents arranged in concentric shells

**orbier** *comparative of* ORBY

**orbiest** *superlative of* ORBY

¹**or·bit** \ˈȯrbət, ˈō(ə)b-, *usu* -əd·+V\ *n* -s [L *orbita* track, rut, orbit] **1** [ML *orbita*, fr. L] **a** : the bony cavity perforated for the passage of nerves and blood vessels that occupies the lateral front of the skull immediately beneath the frontal bone on each side and encloses and protects the eye and its appendages — called also *eye socket* **b** : the skin around the eye of a bird **2 a** : a path described by a celestial body, an artificial satellite, or a spacecraft in its revolution around another body ⟨the ~ of the earth around the sun⟩ ⟨the ~ of a spacecraft around the moon⟩; *also* : one complete revolution of an orbiting body ⟨a spacecraft making two ~s of the moon⟩ **b** : the course of an orbiting airplane **c** (1) : the usu. curved path of a body in a field of force (as the path of an electron in the presence of a nucleus, or of a charged particle in electric and magnetic fields, or of the earth in the sun's gravitational field) (2) : a state of a particle as determined by its energy, angular momentum, and other factors as it moves in a force field — used esp. of an electron in the presence of a nucleus **3** : range or sphere of activity, experience, influence, or interest ⟨Roman political power swept the Mediterranean world into its ~ —Benjamin Farrington⟩ ⟨within the ~ of my curiosity —Alec Waugh⟩ **4** : BALL, ORB **syn** see RANGE

²**orbit** \"\ *vb* -ED/-ING/-S *vt* **1** : to revolve in an orbit around ⟨a satellite ~*ing* the earth⟩ **2** : to send up and make revolve in an orbit ⟨~ a satellite⟩ ~ *vi* : to travel in circles : CIRCLE ⟨a plane ~*ing* over a landing field⟩

¹**or·bit·al** \ˈȯ(r)bəd·°l, -bət°l\ *adj* [¹*orbit* + *-al*] **1** : of or relating to an orbit ⟨~ revolution⟩ **2** : OCULAR ⟨an ~ scale⟩

²**orbital** \"\ *n* -s **1** : a solution of the Schrödinger wave equation describing a possible mode of motion of a single electron in an atom or molecule **2** : the state that is described by the orbital

**orbital arch** *n* : the curved upper edge of the orbit of the eye

**or·bi·tale** \ˌȯ(r)bəˈta(ˌ)lē, -ā(ˌ)lē, -ä(ˌ)lē\ *n* -s [NL, fr. ML *orbita* orbit + L *-ale*, neut. of *-alis* -al — more at ORBIT] : the lowest point on the lower edge of the cranial orbit

**orbital electron** *n* **:** one of the electrons that according to the theory of Rutherford and Bohr revolve in an orbit about the nucleus of an atom

**orbital fissure** *n* **:** either of two openings transmitting nerves and blood vessels to or from the orbit with a superior lying between the greater and the lesser wing of the sphenoid bone and an inferior between the greater wing of the sphenoid and the maxilla

**orbital fossa** *n* **:** a depression in the front of the carapace of a crustacean from which the eyestalk arises

**orbital index** *n* **:** the ratio of the length of the orbital cavity measured from the dacryon to the farthest opposite border to its greatest height (as determined by a line at right angles to the preceding) multiplied by 100 — see CHAMAECONCH, HYPSICONCH, MESOCONCH

**orbital lobe** *n* **:** the part of the lower surface of the frontal lobe of the brain that overlies the orbits

**orbital moment** *n* **:** the angular momentum of an atomic electron corresponding to its supposed motion in an orbit

**orbital nerve** *n* **:** ZYGOMATIC NERVE

**orbital point** *n* **:** ORBITALE — see CRANIOMETRY illustration

**orbital process** *n* **:** a process of the palatine bone that forms part of the floor of the orbit

**orbital quantum number** *n* **:** AZIMUTHAL QUANTUM NUMBER

**or·bi·te·lous spider** \ˌȯ(r)bəˈtēləs-\ *n* [*orbitelous* fr. NL *Orbitelae*, tribe of Argiopidae (fr. L *orbis* circle, disk, orb + *tela* web) + E *-ous* — more at ORB, TOIL] **:** ORB WEAVER

**or·bit·er** \ˈȯ(r)bəd·ə(r), -ətə-\ *n* -S **:** one that orbits; *esp* **:** a man-made satellite ⟨the successful achievement of space ~s —J.B.Medaris⟩

**¹or·bi·toid** \ˈȯ(r)bəˌtȯid\ *adj* [NL *Orbitoides*] **:** of or relating to the genus *Orbitoides*

**²orbitoid** \"\ *n* -S **:** a member of the genus *Orbitoides*

**or·bi·toi·des** \ˌ==ˈtȯi(ˌ)dēz\ *n, cap* [NL, fr. L *orbita* orbit + *-oides* -oid — more at ORB] **:** a genus of Upper Cretaceous to Miocene foraminiferans similar to *Nummulites* but characterized by radially arranged chambers and several layers of small chambers superimposed on both surfaces of the layer of large chambers

**or·bi·to·li·na** \ˌ=bəd·əˈlīnə, -lēnə\ *n, cap* [NL, fr. *Orbitolites* + *-ina*] **:** a genus of foraminiferans very abundant in the Cretaceous having a bowl-shaped or depressed conic siliceous test with agglutinated sandy particles

**or·bit·o·lite** \ȯ(r)ˈbid·ᵊlˌīt\ *n* -S [NL *Orbitolites*] **:** a fossil of the genus *Orbitolites*

**or·bi·to·li·tes** \ˌȯ(r)bəd·əˈlīd·(ˌ)ēz\ *n, cap* [NL, fr. L *orbita* track, rut, orbit + NL *-o-* + *-lites* -lite — more at ORB] **:** a genus of foraminiferans of the Eocene that form thin, broad, circular disks containing numerous small chambers disposed concentrically about a few spirally wound primordial chambers

**¹or·bi·to·sphenoid** \ˌȯ(r)bəd·(ˌ)ō+\ *also* **or·bi·to·sphenoi·dal** \"+\ *adj* [¹*orbit* + *-o-* + *sphenoid, sphenoidal*] **:** being or relating to a paired element of the skull between the presphenoid and frontal that in man forms the lesser wing of the sphenoid

**²orbitosphenoid** \"\ *n* -S **:** an orbitosphenoid bone or process

**or·bito·stat** \ˈȯ(r)bəd·əˌstat, =ˈbid·ə,-\ *n* -S [ISV ¹*orbit* + *-o-* + *-stat*] **:** a device used for measuring the axis of the cranial orbit

**orbits** *pl of* ORBIT, *pres 3d sing of* ORBIT

**or·bi·ty** \ˈȯ(r)bəd·ē\ *n* -ES [MF *orbité*, fr. L *orbitat-, orbitas*, fr. *orbus* orphaned, childless, bereft + *-itat-, -itas* -ity — more at ORPHAN] *archaic* **:** CHILDLESSNESS

**orb·less** \ˈȯrbləs, ˈȯ(ə)b-\ *adj* [²*orb* + *-less*] **:** lacking an orb

**orbs** *pl of* ORB, *pres 3d sing of* ORB

**orb-spider** \ˈ=ˌ==\ *n* **:** ORB WEAVER

**or·bu·li·na** \ˌȯ(r)byəˈlīnə, -lēnə\ *n, cap* [NL, fr. L *orbis* circle, disk + *-ulus* -ule + NL *-ina*] **:** a genus of minute foraminiferans having a globular unilocular shell

**orb weaver** *n* [²*orb*] **:** a spider of the family Argiopidae — compare GEOMETRIC SPIDER

**orb web** *n* **:** a web made by an orb weaver

**orby** \ˈȯrbē, ˈȯ(ə)bē, -bi\ *adj* -ER/-EST [²*orb* + *-y*] *archaic* **:** having the course of an orb **:** like an orb **:** REVOLVING

**orc** \ˈȯ(ə)rk, ˈȯ(ə)k\ *n* -S [MF *orque*, fr. L *orca*, a whale, prob. fr. Gk *oryga*, acc. of *oryx*, a whale] **1 :** a grampus or some other sea animal supposed to resemble it **2 :** a giant, ogre, or other mythical creature usu. of horrid form or aspect

**ORC** *abbr* owner's risk of chafing

**¹or·ca** \ˈȯrkə\ [NL, fr. L, a whale] *syn of* ORCINUS

**²orca** \"\ *n* -S [NL *Orca*] **:** KILLER WHALE

**¹or·ca·di·an** \(ˈ)ȯ(r)ˈkādēən\ *n* -S *cap* [L *Orcades* Orkney islands + E *-ian*] **:** a native or inhabitant of the Orkney islands

**²orcadian** \"\ *adj, usu cap* **1 :** of or relating to the Orkney islands **2 :** of or relating to the people of the Orkneys

**or·ca·nette** *also* **or·ca·net** *or* **or·cha·net** \ˈȯ(r)kəˌnet\ *n* -S [MF *orcanette*, alter. of OF *arquenet*, dim. of *arcanne, alcanne* henna, fr. ML *alchanna* — more at ALKANNA] **:** ALKANET 1b, 2

**or·ce·in** \ˈȯ(r)sēən\ *n* -S [F *orcéine*, fr. *orcine* orcin + *-éine* -ein] **:** a purple nitrogenous dye that is the essential coloring matter of cudbear and archil and is obtained from orcinol by action of aqueous ammonia and atmospheric oxygen

**orch** *abbr* orchestra

**or·chard** \ˈȯrchərd, ˈȯ(ə)chəd\ *n* -S [ME, fr. OE *ortgeard, orceard* fr. L *hortus* garden + OE *geard* enclosure, yard — more at YARD] **1 :** a plantation or enclosure containing fruit trees, nut-bearing trees, or sugar maples; *also* **:** the trees of such a plantation **2** *archaic* **:** a grove of wild fruit-bearing trees

**orchard bush** *n, chiefly Brit* **:** open woodland of tropical uplands in which the individual trees are more or less uniformly distributed

**orchard fruit** *n* **:** TREE FRUIT

**orchard grass** *n* **:** a widely grown tall stout hay and pasture grass (*Dactylis glomerata*) growing in tufts with loose open panicles — called also *cocksfoot, cockspur*

**orchard heating** *n* **:** the protection of fruit trees in bloom or fruit from frost injury by means of numerous small heaters utilizing as fuel crude oil, coke, coal, or wood or by large heaters burning oil and supplying radiant heat — compare SMUDGE

**orchard house** *n* **:** a greenhouse for raising fruit trees

**or·chard·ing** \ȯ(r)chə(r)diŋ\ *n* -S **1 :** the cultivation of orchards **2 :** orchard land **:** ORCHARDS

**or·chard·ist** \-dəst\ *n* -S **:** a person who is engaged in orcharding

**or·chard·man** \dmən\ *n, pl* **orchardmen :** ORCHARDIST

**orchard oriole** *n* **:** an oriole (*Icterus spurius*) of eastern No. America smaller than the Baltimore oriole with the adult male a rich chestnut with a black head, neck, and upper back

**orchectomy** *var of* ORCHIECTOMY

**or·chel·la weed** \ȯrˈchelə\ *n* **:** ARCHIL 2

**or·che·sis** \ȯ(r)ˈkēsəs\ *n* -ES [Gk *orchēsis* action or art of dancing, fr. *orcheisthai* to dance + *-sis*] **:** the art of dancing in the Greek chorus

**or·che·sog·ra·phy** \ˌȯ(r)kəˈsägrəfē\ *n* -ES [F *orchésographie*, fr. MF *orchesographie*, fr. Gk *orchēsis* dancing + MF *-o-* + *-graphie* -graphy] **:** CHOREOGRAPHY

**or·ches·tia** \ȯ(r)ˈkestēə\ *n, cap* [NL, fr. Gk *orchēstēs* dancer (fr. *orcheisthai* to dance, leap) + NL *-ia*] **:** a genus (the type of the family Orchestiidae) of semiterrestrial amphipod crustaceans comprising the widely distributed beach fleas of sandy seacoasts

**¹or·ches·ti·id** \(ˈ)=ˈkestēəd\ *adj* [NL *Orchestiidae*, family of crustaceans, fr. *Orchestia*, type genus + *-idae*] **:** of or relating to the genus *Orchestia* or the family Orchestiidae

**²orchestiid** *n* -S **:** an orchestiid crustacean

**or·ches·tra** \ˈȯ(r)kəstrə *also* -ˌkes-\ *n* -S [L, fr. Gk *orchēstra*, fr. *orcheisthai* to dance; akin to Skt *rghāyati* he raves, rages, trembles and perh. akin to Gk *ornynai* to urge on, incite, call forth — more at RISE] **1 a :** a circular space used by the chorus in front of the proscenium in an ancient Greek theater — see THEATER illustration **b :** a corresponding semicircular space in a Roman theater used for the seats of persons of distinction **2 a :** a large group of players of musical instruments including typically strings, woodwinds, brasses, and percussion organized esp. for performing one of the larger forms of concert music (as a symphony) or for accompanying an oratorio or other dramatic work (as a ballet or opera) or for playing light or popular music ⟨symphony ~⟩ ⟨pops ~⟩ **b :** a small group of musicians organized specif. to play for dining and dancing ⟨a small 4-piece ~⟩ **c** (1) **:** a space in a modern theater or other public hall that is used by a band of instrumental performers and that is commonly just in front of the stage and at or below the level of the auditorium floor (2) **:** the forward section of seats on the main floor of a theater (3) **:** the main floor of a theater

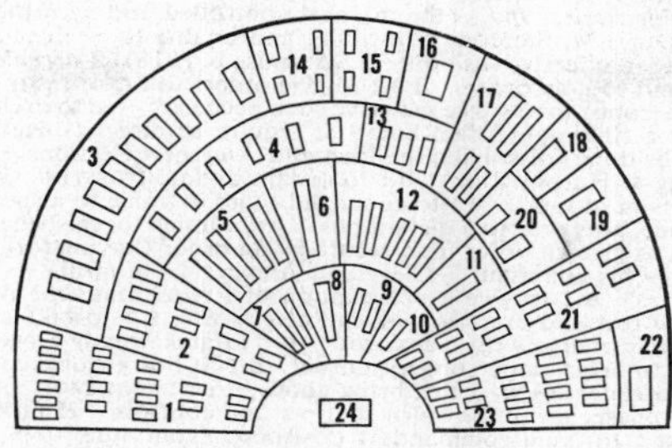


orchestra: typical arrangement: *1* first violins, *2* cellos, *3* basses, *4* French horns, *5* bassoons, *6* contrabassoons, *7* oboes, *8* English horn, *9* flutes, *10* piccolo, *11* bass clarinet, *12* clarinets, *13* trumpets, *14* percussion, *15* timpani, *16* chimes, *17* trombones, *18* tuba, *19* piano, *20* saxophones, *21* violas, *22* harp, *23* second violins, *24* podium

**orchestra bells** *n pl* **:** GLOCKENSPIEL 2

**orchestra circle** *n* **:** PARQUET CIRCLE

**or·ches·tral** \(ˈ)ȯ(r)ˈkestrəl *sometimes* ˈ=ˌkəs-\ *adj* [*orchestra* + *-al*] **1 a :** of, relating to, or designed for an orchestra ⟨seek new ~ works in Paris —*Current Biog.*⟩ ⟨~ concerts⟩ ⟨~ programs⟩ **b :** imitating a specified orchestral instrument — used in the names of organ stops ⟨~ oboe⟩ **2 :** suggestive of an orchestra or its characteristic musical qualities or effects ⟨a poem of ~ sweep and grandeur⟩ — **or·ches·tral·ly** \-trəlē, -li\ *adv*

**or·ches·tra·less** *pronunc at* ORCHESTRA + ləs\ *adj* **:** having no orchestra

**orchestral organ** *n* **:** SOLO ORGAN

**orchestra pit** *n* **:** a pit underneath the forestage from which an orchestra plays

**or·ches·trate** \ˈȯ(r)kəˌstrāt, *usually* -ād.+V\ *vb* -ED/-ING/-S [F *orchestrer* to orchestrate (fr. *orchestre* orchestra, fr. L *orchestra*) + E *-ate*] *vt* **1 :** to compose or arrange (music) for an orchestra **:** provide with orchestration ⟨~ a ballet⟩ ⟨~ a waltz⟩ **2 :** to arrange, develop, organize, or combine so as to achieve a desired or maximum effect ⟨must ~ the best thoughts of mankind —K.F.Leidecker⟩ ⟨the teller of tall tales . . . who would always ~ his facts —H.A.L. Craig⟩ ⟨separate periods of time are *orchestrated* according to the novel's needs —Bernard DeVoto⟩ ~ *vi* **:** to arrange or compose music for an orchestra ⟨~s very well⟩

**or·ches·tra·tion** \ˌ==ˈstrāshən\ *n* -S [F, fr. *orchestrer* + *-ation*] **1 :** the arranging of music for an orchestra; *specif* **:** the treatment of a composition with regard to the structure, manipulation, compass, and timbre of the orchestral instruments and their effective combination, the proper distribution of the harmony, and the writing of orchestral scores — compare INSTRUMENTATION **2 :** harmonious organization, integration, or combination ⟨an exquisite ~ of activity —G.W.Gray b. 1886⟩ ⟨develop a world community through ~ of cultural diversities —L.K.Frank⟩

**or·ches·tra·tor** *also* **or·ches·trat·er** \ˈ==ˌstrād·ə(r), -ātə-\ *n* -S **:** a person that arranges music for orchestral use or provides with orchestration

**or·ches·trelle** \ˌȯ(r)kəˈstrel\ *n* -S [*orchestra* + F *-elle*, dim. suffix] **:** a reed organ of the late 19th and early 20th centuries constructed on the principle of the mechanical player piano and designed to imitate the effect of an orchestra

**or·ches·tric** \(ˈ)ȯ(r)ˈkestrik\ *adj* [*orchestra* + *-ic*] **:** ORCHESTRAL

**or·ches·tri·na** \ˌȯ(r)kəˈstrēnə\ *n* -S [*orchestra* + *-ina*] **:** ORCHESTRION

**or·ches·tri·on** \ȯ(r)ˈkestrēən\ *n* -S [*orchestra* + *-ion* (as in *melodion*)] **:** a mechanical device provided with different stops capable of imitating a variety of musical instruments

**or·chid** \ˈȯrkəd, ˈȯ(ə)k-\ *n* -S [NL *Orchidaceae*] **1 :** a plant of the family Orchidaceae **2 :** a variable color averaging a light purple **3 :** PRAISE, COMMENDATION, COMPLIMENT — usu. used in pl. ⟨an unsung editor deserves some of the ~s —S.L.A. Marshall⟩ ⟨extended ~s to industry for its encouragement of such students —*Ethyl News*⟩

**or·chi·da·ce·ae** \ˌ=kəˈdāsēˌē\ *n pl, cap* [NL, fr. *Orchid-, Orchis*, type genus + *-aceae*] **:** a very large family of highly specialized perennial herbaceous monocotyledonous plants (order Orchidales) that have entire sheathing or scalelike leaves, tuberous or bulbous or thickened roots, and extremely complex usu. showy flowers with a calyx of three often petaloid sepals, a corolla of three petals of which one forms a distinctive and often spurred labellum, a column consisting of the variously fused style, stigma, and stamen, the pollen usu. aggregated into pollinia which adhere to visiting insects, and an inferior ovary and that reproduce by minute seeds lacking endosperm and containing chlorophyll — see ORCHID, ORCHIS

**or·chi·da·cean** \ˌ==ˈdāshən\ *n* -S [NL *Orchidaceae* + E *-an*] **:** a plant of the family Orchidaceae

**or·chi·da·ceous** \ˌ=ˈ=ˈshəs\ *adj* [NL *Orchidaceae* + E *-ous*] **1 :** of, relating to, or resembling the Orchidaceae or an orchid **2 a :** SHOWY, OSTENTATIOUS ⟨from the modern standpoint she was a very ~ writer —*N.Y. Herald Tribune*⟩ **b :** marked by or displaying a showy or luxurious beauty ⟨an ~ lady of no definite profession —William Du Bois⟩ — **or·chi·da·ceous·ly** *adv*

**or·chi·da·les** \ˌ==ˈ=(ˌ)lēz\ *n pl, cap* [NL, fr. *Orchid-, Orchis* + *-ales*] **:** an order of monocotyledonous plants with irregular flowers, an inferior compound ovary, and minute seeds that lack endosperm — see BURMANNIACEAE, ORCHIDACEAE

**orchid cactus** *n* **:** a cactus of the genus *Epiphyllum*

**or·chi·dec·to·my** \ˌȯ(r)kəˈdektəmē\ *n* -ES [irreg. fr. Gk *orchis* testicle + E *-ectomy*] **:** ORCHIECTOMY

**orchid family** *n* **:** ORCHIDACEAE

**orchid fly** *n* **:** CATTLEYA FLY

**orchid gray** *n* **:** a variable color averaging a grayish purple that is redder, lighter, and stronger than telegraph blue, bluer and stronger than mauve gray, and bluer and paler than average rose mauve

**orchid haze** *n* **:** a light purplish gray that is stronger and very slightly bluer than lilac gray

**-or·chi·dism** \ˈȯ(r)kəˌdizəm\ *n comb form* -S [NL *-orchidismus*, irreg. fr. Gk *orchis* testicle + L *-ismus* -ism] **:** -ORCHISM ⟨*cryptorchidism*⟩

**or·chid·ist** \ˈȯ(r)kədəst\ *n* -S **:** a cultivator of orchids

**orchid mist** *n* **:** a variable color averaging a grayish purplish pink that is bluer and paler than cameo pink and bluer, stronger, and slightly lighter than dawn pink

**or·chid·ol·o·gist** \ˌȯ(r)kəˈdäləjəst\ *n* -S **:** a specialist in orchidology

**or·chid·ol·o·gy** \-jē, -ji\ *n* -ES [*orchid* + *-o-* + *-logy*] **:** a branch of botany or horticulture which treats of orchids

**or·chi·do·pexy** \ˈȯ(r)kədōˌpeksē\ *n* -ES [irreg. fr. Gk *orchis* testicle + E *-pexy*] **:** surgical fixation of a testis

**orchid peat** *n* **:** the stipes, roots, and other parts of ferns chopped up and used for potting ferns, orchids, and epiphytes

**orchid pink** *n* **:** a variable color averaging a light purplish pink

**orchid rose** *n* **:** a variable color averaging a deep purplish pink that is redder and less strong than amaranth pink

**orchid taupe** *n* **:** a variable color averaging a dark grayish purple that is redder and paler than average purple wine, bluer and paler than raisin black, and bluer, lighter, and stronger than old lavender (sense 2)

**orchid tint** *n* **:** a pale purplish pink that is bluer and paler than mauve pink

**orchid tree** *n* **:** MOUNTAIN EBONY

**or·chi·ec·to·my** \ˌȯ(r)kēˈektəmē\ *also* **or·chec·to·my** \ȯ(r)ˈkektəmē\ *n* -ES [Gk *orchis* testicle + E *-ectomy* — more at ORCHIS] **:** excision of a testis

**or·chil** *var of* ARCHIL

**or·chil·la weed** *n* \ȯrˈchilə\ **:** ARCHIL 2

**or·chi·o·pexy** \ˈȯ(r)kēōˌpeksē\ *n* -ES [Gk *orchis* testicle + E *-o-* + *-pexy*] **:** ORCHIDOPEXY

**or·chis** \ˈȯrkəs\ *n* [NL *Orchid-, Orchis*, fr. L *orchis* orchid, fr. Gk, testicle, orchid; fr. the shape of the roots; akin to MIr *uirgge* testicle, Alb *herdhe* testicle, Av *ərəzi-* scrotum] **1** *cap* **:** a genus (the type of the family Orchidaceae) of terrestrial or epiphytic herbs having fleshy tubers or rootstocks and spicate flowers with a spurred lip and having the pollinia borne in a common pouch — see MALE ORCHIS, SALEP **2** -ES **:** ORCHID; *specif* **:** any plant of the genus *Orchis*

**-or·chism** \ˈȯ(r)ˌkizəm\ *n comb form* -S [NL *-orchismus*, fr. Gk *orchis* testicle + L *-ismus* -ism] **:** a (specified) form or condition of the testes ⟨*cryptorchism*⟩

**or·chit·ic** \(ˈ)ȯ(r)ˈkid·ik\ *adj* [NL *orchitis* + E *-ic*] **:** of, producing, or affected with orchitis

**or·chi·tis** \ȯ(r)ˈkīd·əs\ *n* -ES [NL, fr. Gk *orchis* testicle + NL *-itis*] **:** inflammation of a testis

**or·cin** \ˈȯrsən\ *n* -S [ISV *orcin* + *-in*] **:** ORCINOL

**or·cin·ol** \-ˌnȯl, -nōl\ *n* -S [ISV *orcin* + *-ol*] **:** a crystalline dihydroxy phenol $CH_3C_6H_3(OH)_2$ obtained from various lichens (as of the genera *Roccella* and *Lecanora*), from extract of aloes, and synthetically from some derivatives of toluene; 5-methyl-resorcinol

**or·ci·nus** \ȯ(r)ˈsīnəs\ *n, cap* [NL, fr. L *orca*, a whale + *-inus* -ine — more at ORC] **:** the genus consisting of the killer whale

**orcs** *pl of* ORC

**ord** *abbr* **1** ordained **2** order **3** orderly **4** ordinal **5** ordinance **6** ordinary **7** ordnance

**ORD** *abbr* owner's risk of damage

**or·dain** \ȯrˈdān, ȯ(ə)ˈ-\ *vb* -ED/-ING/-S [ME *ordeinen*, fr. OF *ordener* (3d sing. pres. *ordeine*), fr. LL & L; LL *ordinare* to ordain (a clergyman), fr. L, to put in order, arrange, appoint, fr. *ordin-, ordo* order — more at ORDER] *vt* **1 :** ARRANGE, ORDER, REGULATE, MANAGE, CONDUCT ⟨a boy not yet fit to ~ his life —Oliver La Farge⟩ ⟨whether federal or state organs shall ~ the legal relations of citizens —Abe Shayes⟩ **2 a** (1) **:** to invest with ministerial or sacerdotal functions **:** introduce into the office of the Christian ministry by the laying on of hands or by other forms **:** set apart by the ceremony of ordination — compare CONSECRATE (2) **:** to invest with regal functions by a religious ceremony ⟨~*ed* king in Westminster Abbey —F.M. Stenton⟩ **b :** to establish by appointment, decree, or law **:** CONSTITUTE, INSTITUTE, ENACT ⟨the plan was ~*ed* by the governor and judges —*Amer. Guide Series: Mich.*⟩ ⟨~*ed* a form of government closely resembling an absolute monarchy —E.O. Hauser⟩ **c :** to predestine or destine as part of a divine plan, by the force of circumstances, or as necessary in the nature of things **:** FATE ⟨truly ~*ed* to be one of the world's great crossroads —H.F.Bain⟩ ⟨~*ed* to be hewers of wood and drawers of water —*Newsweek*⟩ ⟨the end is ~*ed* by fate —C.H.Rickword⟩ **d :** to order by fiat or by virtue of great or supreme authority **:** COMMAND, DECREE ⟨~*ed* that the best gumtrees were to be left standing —Rex Ingamells⟩ ⟨cannot ~ that so many tons of steel be produced —F.A.Ogg & Harold Zink⟩ ~ *vi* **:** to issue an order **:** DECREE, COMMAND ⟨so great Jove ~s⟩ **syn** see DICTATE

**or·dain·er** \-nə(r)\ *n* -S [ME *ordeinour*, fr. OF *ordeneor*, fr. *ordener* + *-eor* -or] **1 :** one that ordains **2 :** *often cap* **:** one of a commission of 21 nobles and prelates appointed under Edward II in 1310 to frame ordinances esp. for regulating the king's household

**or·dain·ment** \-nmənt\ *n* -S **:** appointment or ordinance esp. by divine power or fate **:** ORDINATION

**¹or·deal** \(ˈ)ȯrˈdēl, (ˈ)ȯ(ə)ˈ-, *esp before pause or consonant* -ēəl\ *n* -S [ME *ordal*, fr. OE *ordāl, ordēl*; akin to OFris *ordēl, urdêl* judgment, verdict, ordeal, OS *urdēli* judgment, verdict, OHG *urteili, urteil*; all fr. a prehistoric WGmc compound derived fr. a compound verb represented by OHG *irteilen* to render a verdict, judge, bestow, distribute, fr. *ir-*, perfective prefix + *teilen* to divide, render a verdict — more at ABEAR, DEAL] **1 :** a primitive means used to determine guilt or innocence by submitting the accused to dangerous or painful tests believed to be under divine or superhuman control with escape from injury ordinarily taken as a vindication of innocence ⟨~ by battle⟩ ⟨~ by fire⟩ ⟨~ by water⟩ **2 :** something that tests or is used to test character or endurance **:** a severe trial **:** a trying experience ⟨recover from the ~ of that climb —John Hunt & Edmund Hillary⟩ ⟨the ~ of watching the last dollars disappear —Irving Stone⟩ ⟨an encounter with the headmaster could be something of an ~ —A.F.Fforde⟩

**²ordeal** \"\ *adj* **:** of or relating to trial by ordeal

**ordeal bark** *n* [so called fr. its use as an ordeal poison] **:** the poisonous bark of a West African tree (*Erythrophloeum guineense*) of the family Leguminosae **:** SASSY BARK

**ordeal bean** *n* **:** CALABAR BEAN

**ordeal tree** *n* **1 :** a poisonous Madagascan tree (*Tanghinia venenifera*) having fruit resembling plums and poisonous seeds **2 :** ORDEAL BARK **3 :** a southern African tree (*Acocanthera venenata*) **4 :** a poisonous central African shrub (*Strychnos densiflora*)

**¹or·der** \ˈȯrdər, ˈȯ(ə)də(r)\ *n* -S [MF *ordre, order*, fr. OF *ordene, ordne, ordre*, fr. ML & L; ML *ordin-, ordo* order (in ecclesiastical senses), fr. L (in other senses); akin to L *ordiri* to lay the warp, begin to weave, begin, and perh. to Gk *arariskein* to fit together, fasten, suit — more at ARM] **1 a** (1) **:** one of the nine grades of angels in medieval theology; *also* **:** an analogous class of supernatural beings ⟨an ~ of spirits who abuse and persecute those they possess —Ralph Linton⟩ (2) *sometimes cap* **:** any of the several grades of the Christian ministry — see MAJOR ORDER, MINOR ORDER (3) **orders** *pl* **:** the office and dignity of a person in the Christian ministry ⟨in deacon's ~s⟩ (4) **:** ORDINATION — usu. used in pl. ⟨received ~s⟩ (5) *often cap* **:** a ritually prescribed form of service (as for the administration of a sacrament) ⟨the ~ of baptism⟩ **b** (1) **:** a religious body typically an aggregate of separate communities living under a distinctive rule, discipline, or constitution **:** a monastic brotherhood or society (2) **:** any of several knightly fraternities bound by a discipline both religious and military and typically originating in the era of the crusades (3) **:** a society patterned on the knightly fraternities of the middle ages but typically founded by a sovereign, a prince, or a national legislature for the conferring of honorary distinction (4) **:** the badge, medal, or other insignia of such a society; *also* **:** a military decoration for bravery or distinguished service (5) **:** a fraternal society or other association of private character ⟨the Masonic *Order*⟩ ⟨the *Order* of Gregg Artists is the largest and best-known shorthand organization in the world —Florence E. Ulrich⟩ ⟨a secret ~ of conspirators⟩ **c** (1) **:** one of the classes comprising a hierarchical or stratified society **:** a social class or grouping ⟨there are two main ~s, the natural aristocracy and the common people —C.J.Friedrich⟩ — often used in the phrases *higher orders, lower orders* ⟨the lower ~s of whites were all but beyond the reach of democracy —Van Wyck Brooks⟩ (2) **:** a narrowly delimited group of persons having a common interest and forming a distinct class by profession, special privileges, or other common interests ⟨the first two ~s, the clergy and the nobility —D.W.S.Lidderdale⟩ ⟨the ~ of baronets⟩ (3) **:** the totality of social, political, and cultural arrangements prevailing in a particular place and time **:** a particular sociopolitical

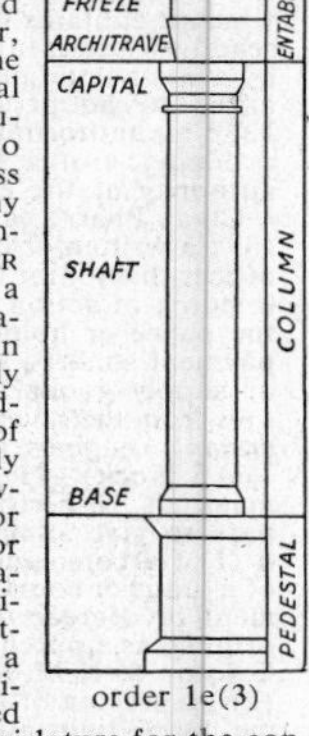


order 1e(3)

system ⟨inclined to oppose radical changes in the established ~ —*Amer. Guide Series: Maine*⟩ ⟨symbols of the decaying ~*s* they headed —Claude Pepper⟩ ⟨the ceremonies are part of the traditional ~ —*Brit. Book News*⟩ **d** (1) *archaic* **:** a rank, row, or series of objects (2) **:** level or degree of importance, quality, or value **:** RANK ⟨a world power of the first ~ —S.L.Sharp⟩ ⟨the productions booked for these communities were of a low ~ —*Amer. Guide Series: Mich.*⟩ ⟨realism of the highest ~ —A.L.Guérard⟩ (3) **:** a category, type, class, or kind of thing of distinctive character or rank ⟨there is an ~ of mind which is perpetually modern —Edith Hamilton⟩ ⟨cultivated after his fashion the ~ of verse —*Times Lit. Supp.*⟩ ⟨in the same ~ of ideas —O.G.Frazer⟩ ⟨in emergencies of this ~ —R.B.Westerfield⟩ ⟨revolutions are a different ~ of events —John Strachey⟩ ⟨presents a problem of the severest ~ —J.B.Gallagher⟩ **e** (1) **:** a style of building (2) **:** a type of column and entablature that with its forms, proportions, and mode of decoration is the unit of a style ⟨Corinthian ~⟩ ⟨Doric ~⟩ (3) **:** a columnar treatment based on the classic orders **f** (1) **:** arrangement of objects in position or of events in time (2) **:** DEGREE ⟨conics are curves of the second ~⟩ (3) **:** number of columns or of rows in a determinant (4) **:** number of successive differentiations ⟨a derivative of the third ~⟩ (5) **:** ORDER OF MAGNITUDE 2 **g** (1) **:** degree or grade in a series based on size or quantity ⟨lines, of the ~ of one third of an inch in diameter —R.E.Coker⟩ (2) **:** general or approximate size, quantity, or level of magnitude or a figure indicative thereof ⟨a population of the ~ of 40,000 —W.G.East⟩ ⟨all explosions were divided into two general types — low ~ and high ~ —H.A.Holsinger⟩ ⟨at a date of the ~ of 50,000 years ago —R.C.Murphy⟩ ⟨the time period is of the ~ of a thousand years —A.N.Whitehead⟩ **h :** a category of taxonomic classification ranking above the family and below the class and in botany characteristically having a name ending in *-ales* (as Rosales) and often being made up of several families — see NATURAL ORDER **i :** position in a sequence of interference of diffraction phenomena ⟨a grating spectrum of the third ~⟩ **j** (1) **:** a sequential arrangement of mathematical elements (2) **:** a degree, type, level, or rank within an order ⟨a predicate of a higher ~⟩ **k :** the broadest category in soil classification ⟨zonal ~⟩ ⟨intrazonal ~⟩ **l :** a class of consonants whose common characteristic is that they have the same place of articulation ⟨the bilabials \p\, \b\, \m\ belong to the same ~⟩ **2 a** (1) **:** the manner in which one thing succeeds another **:** sequence or succession in space or time ⟨let me tell of these events in their ~⟩ ⟨were issued in a strange ~ —Edward Sackville-West & Desmond Shawe-Taylor⟩ (2) **:** sequence in respect of value, importance, or some other criterion ⟨good to know the goods in their ~ —R.M.Hutchins⟩ ⟨osmium, iridium and platinum in that ~ are the three heaviest metals known —W.R.Jones⟩ ⟨necessary to establish some ~ of importance —G.P.Wibberley⟩ ⟨the children came in proper ~, first the oldest, then their juniors⟩ (3) **:** the sequence of constituents as a device for conveying meaning (as in *Cain* [subject] *killed* [predicate] *Abel* [object]) **b** (1) **:** the totality of arrangements composing some sphere of action or being **:** a system functioning according to some definite laws or rules ⟨the contemporary economic ~⟩ ⟨our political ~⟩ ⟨should take the lead in reconstructing the social ~ —Paul Woodring⟩ ⟨whose loyalty to the English ~ of things was suspect —*Amer. Guide Series: Mich.*⟩; *also* **:** a prevailing mode, style, or trend ⟨the new ~ in literary criticism⟩ (2) *obs* **:** customary mode of procedure **:** established usage (3) **:** the customary, established, or prescribed mode of procedure in debate or other business (as of a deliberative or legislative body or a public meeting) ⟨rose to a point of ~⟩ ⟨a book on the rules of ~⟩ (4) **:** the condition of being in conformity with such a mode of procedure — usu. used in the phrases *in order*, *out of order* ⟨your motion is out of ~⟩ ⟨the amendment was inconsistent with the resolution and hence out of ~ —Walter Goodman⟩ (5) **:** the attentive, orderly, or decorous behavior or state appropriate to the conduct of deliberative or legislative business ⟨will the meeting please come to ~⟩ — compare CALL TO ORDER **c** (1) **:** the manner in which something is ordered **:** ARRANGEMENT, FORMATION, ARRAY ⟨the troops retired in good ~⟩ ⟨in his ~ of battle his center . . . was pushed forward —Tom Wintringham⟩ (2) **:** regular or harmonious arrangement or disposition **:** SYSTEM, PATTERN, METHOD ⟨there was a feminine ~ in the arrangement —Jean Stafford⟩ ⟨a world whose lack of ~ . . . must inspire them with a certain fear —Herbert Read⟩ ⟨the stuff of our lives is . . . a tangled web, yet in the end there is ~ —Havelock Ellis⟩ (3) **:** a condition in which everything is so arranged as to play its proper part ⟨a lover of ~⟩ ⟨values rank and station and ~ above other things in politics —R.G.F.Robinson⟩ ⟨the sense of ~ we associate with the medieval world —Wallace Fowlie⟩ (4) **:** the rule of law or proper authority **:** freedom from disturbance **:** public quiet ⟨restore ~ in a lawless community⟩ ⟨the victory of ~ . . . must be assured at all costs —*Times Lit. Supp.*⟩ (5) *archaic* **:** provision or disposition to achieve some end — usu. used in the phrase *take order* (6) **:** state or condition with regard to quality, functioning, or repair ⟨a square grand piano in good ~ —D.D.Martin⟩ ⟨found the equipment in the worst possible ~⟩ ⟨erect and maintain in good ~ a gate —*Farmer's Weekly* (*So. Africa*)⟩ (7) **:** a sound, proper, orderly, or functioning condition ⟨the finances and plans of the . . . institute have been set in ~ —W.G.Penfield⟩ ⟨the telephone is out of ~⟩ ⟨her usually cast-iron digestion was out of ~ —D.G.Gerahty⟩ ⟨had his place put in ~ —Everett Lloyd⟩ ⟨his passport is not in ~⟩ (8) **:** the condition of being proper, appropriate, or required by the circumstances — used in the phrases *in order*, *out of order* ⟨this retraction is in ~ —Alexander MacDonald⟩ ⟨your suggestion is completely out of ~⟩ ⟨technically, his conviction was in ~ —S.H.Adams⟩ ⟨nominations for president are now in ~⟩ (9) **:** ORDER ARMS **d :** a condition of the tobacco leaf in the curing process in which it contains sufficient moisture to be pliable and handled readily without breaking **3 a** (1) **:** a rule or regulation made by a competent authority ⟨the Board of Aldermen will also be asked to adopt an ~ —*Springfield* (*Mass.*) *Daily News*⟩ (2) **:** an authoritative mandate usu. from a superior to a subordinate **:** INJUNCTION, INSTRUCTION ⟨refusal to recognize the authority of the emperor amounted to a refusal to take ~*s* —Clyde Pharr⟩ ⟨an executive ~⟩ ⟨under ~ to sail for home⟩ (3) **:** a written or oral directive from a senior military or naval officer to a junior telling him what to do but giving him certain freedom of action in complying **b** (1) **:** a direction by which the payee or holder of negotiable paper prescribes to whom payment shall be made (2) **:** a commission to purchase, sell, or supply goods **:** a direction in writing to furnish supplies ⟨~*s* from the seven canners had been too small —*Pacific Fisherman*⟩ ⟨engines built to the ~ of the Ministry of Supply —O.S.Nock⟩ (3) **:** a formal written authorization to deliver materials, to perform work, or to do both **c :** a direction or pass to give admittance (as to a building or entertainment) **d** (1) **:** a command or direction of a court (2) **:** a direction of a judge or court entered in writing and not entered in a judgment or decree **4 a** (1) **:** the merchandise, goods, or items ordered as a purchase ⟨should receive your ~ promptly —S.A. Taintor & K.M.Monro⟩ ⟨the ~ arrived in good condition⟩ (2) **:** a serving of food ordered in a public eating place ⟨bring me my ~ right away⟩ ⟨one ~ of mashed potatoes⟩; *also* **:** an oral or written direction to serve such food ⟨the waitress will take your ~ now⟩ **b :** an assigned or requested undertaking ⟨this is a large ~, which would seem to require a much longer book —K.E.Poole⟩ ⟨trying to move loose horses through snow was almost as tall an ~ —H.L.Davis⟩ — **in order that** *conj* **:** THAT ⟨invite you *in order that* you may see for yourself⟩ — **in order to 1** *obs* **:** in regard or reference to **2 :** for the purpose of **:** as a means to ⟨ran *in order to* get home in time⟩ — **on the order of :** after the fashion of **:** LIKE ⟨something *on the order of* a state park —W.D.Hartley⟩ ⟨much *on the order of* Great Lakes bulk carriers —*Ships and the Sea*⟩ — **to order** *adv* **:** in fulfillment of an order given ⟨shoes made *to order*⟩

[2]**order** \"\ *vb* **ordered; ordered; ordering** \-d(ə)riŋ\ **orders** [ME *ordren*, fr. *ordre*, n.] *vt* **1 a** (1) **:** to arrange or dispose according to some plan or with reference to some end **:** put in a particular order **:** arrange in a series or sequence ⟨~*s* the arts and sciences according to their value in his Christian system —H.O.Taylor⟩ (2) *archaic* **:** to draw up in battle array **:** ARRAY, MARSHAL (3) **:** to put in order **:** make neat or orderly ⟨~*ed* her dress —D.C.Peattie⟩ **b :** to manage by rule or regulation ⟨~*ed* his affairs to the tempo of an earlier day —*Amer. Guide Series: Ind.*⟩ ⟨the marshal controlled and ~*ed* the hall —Doris M. Stenton⟩ ⟨unwilling and unable to ~ their economy in effective fashion —E.S.Furniss b. 1918⟩ **2** *archaic* **:** to admit to holy orders **3 a :** to give orders to **:** COMMAND ⟨~*ed* the troops to advance⟩ ⟨twelve such pence are ~*ed* to exchange for a shilling —Adam Smith⟩ **:** require or direct (something) to be done ⟨dissolving the Diet and ~*ing* new elections —F.A. Ogg & Harold Zink⟩ **b :** to ordain by fate **:** DESTINE ⟨it was so ~*ed* of God⟩ **c :** to command to go or come to a specified place ⟨was ~*ed* to a distant post⟩ ⟨~*ed* home for misbehavior⟩ **d :** to give an order for **:** secure by an order ⟨having forgotten to ~ his chauffeur —Cleveland Amory⟩ ⟨~ a meal⟩ ⟨~ groceries⟩ **e :** to give a prescription of **:** PRESCRIBE ⟨the doctor ~*ed* rest and exercise⟩ **4** *dial chiefly Eng* **a :** to take a particular course with **:** deal with **b :** to make ready **:** PREPARE **c :** to bring (a person) into order **5 :** to bring (tobacco leaf) into order ~ *vi* **1 :** to bring about order **:** REGULATE, DIRECT ⟨a renascence of the spirit that ~*s* and controls —H.G.Wells⟩ **2 a :** to issue commands **:** COMMAND ⟨your turn to ~ next week⟩ **b :** to give or place an order ⟨be sure to ~ before it's too late⟩ **3 :** to become the object of an order ⟨slacks are ~*ing* with renewed strength —*Women's Wear Daily*⟩

**syn** ORDER, ARRANGE, MARSHAL, ORGANIZE, SYSTEMATIZE, METHODIZE can mean to put (a number of things) in their proper places or into a fit place, esp. in an interrelation or organization. ORDER in the sense of to put in a given sequence is somewhat archaic; in more general current use it means to put into an interrelationship thought of as reasoned or effective or to dispose so that system is achieved or confusion or friction is eliminated ⟨the ceremony is not well *ordered;* in fact there is here no single ceremony but a group of separate little rituals —C.L.Jones⟩ ⟨life as it came to him without conscious *ordering* —Virginia Woolf⟩ ⟨free to *order* their affairs as they choose —W.L.Sperry⟩ ⟨trees, lawns, terraces, rock gardens, paved walks, and many benches, all cleverly *ordered* in harmonious composition —*Amer. Guide Series: N. Y. City*⟩ ARRANGE is usu. used to apply to a putting of things in a proper, fit, or pleasing sequence or relationship, often by straightening up or adjusting to fixed circumstantial things, sometimes, however, suggesting contrivance or manipulation of things to a given end ⟨*arrange* the articles on a desk⟩ ⟨each of us *arranges* the world according to his own notion of the fitness of things —Joseph Conrad⟩ ⟨made his bed and *arranged* his room —Willa Cather⟩ ⟨the distressingly difficult task of *arranging* a peaceful world —K.F.Mather⟩ ⟨*arrange* things so that Father could go to Santa Fe —Mary Austin⟩ MARSHAL implies an assembling and arranging (of things, or sometimes diverse elements of a thing) esp. in preparation for or to facilitate a particular move or operation ⟨resources of the government have been *marshaled* in support of science —A.T.Waterman⟩ ⟨*marshals* his facts and arguments with lucidity and detachment —*Times Lit. Supp.*⟩ ⟨*marshaled* the evidence in his client's behalf —H.D.Hazeltine⟩ ⟨*marshal* a case before going into court⟩ ORGANIZE implies an arrangement in which several or many parts function in smooth interrelation ⟨our most successful historians . . . can *organize* their materials clearly and cogently —W.G.Carleton⟩ ⟨man, as a highly *organized* whole —H.J.Muller⟩ ⟨*organized* the hospital work of the Crimean war —G.B.Shaw⟩ ⟨the daily routine was gradually *organized* after a fashion —André Maurois⟩ SYSTEMATIZE implies arrangement according to a predetermined scheme ⟨if grammar was to become a rational science, it had to *systematize* itself through principles of logic —H.O.Taylor⟩ ⟨everything was *systematized* to an extraordinary extent. There was a way for doing everything, or rather sixteen, or thirty-six, or some other consecrated number of ways, each distinct and defined and each with a name —Laurence Binyon⟩ METHODIZE differs from SYSTEMATIZE in suggesting more the imposition of orderly procedure than a fixed scheme ⟨modern criticism has developed a number of specialized procedures of its own and *methodized* them, sometimes on the analogy of scientific procedure —S.E. Hyman⟩ **syn** see in addition COMMAND

**order arms** *n* [fr. the imper. phrase *order, arms*] **:** a position in the manual of arms in which the rifle is held vertically at the right side with the butt on the ground — often used as a command

**order bill of lading :** a negotiable receipt and contract between carrier and shipper by which legal possession of the shipment may be ordered by endorsement from person to person — compare STRAIGHT BILL OF LADING

**orderboard** \'==,=\ *n* **:** a manual signal used at railroad stations, a vertical position of the signal indicating that there are no orders, a horizontal position indicating to the crew of an approaching train that train orders must be picked up

**order book** *n* **1 :** a book in which orders from customers are entered **:** a specially printed book for making multiple copies of orders including one for the customer **2** *often cap O&B* **:** a calendar of future business of a session of the English House of Commons or other legislative body of the British Commonwealth — called also *order paper*

**order buyer** *n* **:** a buyer who purchases (as produce or livestock) for another's account

**ordered** *adj* **:** characterized by order: as **a :** marked by system, regularity, or discipline **:** carefully regulated or managed ⟨theirs was an ~ life —C.B.Flood⟩ ⟨my quiet, ~ house —L.P. Smith⟩ **b :** marked by a regular or harmonious arrangement or disposition **:** arranged or disposed so as to form a pattern ⟨the trim and ~ landscape —Oscar Handlin⟩ ⟨society before the industrial revolution . . . was ~ and relatively stable —R.C.Beatty⟩ ⟨the ~ structure of crystals —J.L.Hoard & Seymour Galler⟩ **c** *of a solid solution* **:** characterized by a regular arrangement of solvent and solute atoms

**ordered lattice** *n* **:** the crystal lattice of a substitutional alloy in which the substituted atoms occur in a regular order of spacing

**or·der·er** \'ȯ(r)dərə(r)\ *n* -s [alter. of ME *orderour*, fr. *ordren* to order + *-our* -or — more at ORDER] **:** one that orders

**order-in-council** \'==='==\ *n, pl* **orders-in-council :** an order having the full force of law that is issued by the British monarch acting by and with the advice of the Privy Council or by a governor-general acting by and with the advice of the privy council or similar body of a member nation of the British Commonwealth usu. as a means of giving legal effect to a decision of the cabinet in areas not involving parliamentary action ⟨the promulgation of *orders-in-council* both in pursuance of royal prerogative and under authority of statute —F.A.Ogg & Harold Zink⟩

**ordering** *n* -s [ME, fr. gerund of *ordren* to order] **:** the act, an instance, or the result of ordering: as **a :** MANAGEMENT, REGULATION ⟨determined to have the ~ of things in its hands —John Buchan⟩ **b :** mode or product of ordering **:** ARRANGEMENT ⟨the polity is a certain ~ of the inhabitants of the polis —C.H.McIlwain⟩ ⟨the distinction between the two ~*s* of knowledge —C.W.Berenda⟩ **c :** the process of applying water to tobacco either as steam, moist air, or spray to make it soft and pliable for handling

**or·der·less** \'ȯ(r)də(r)ləs\ *adj* **:** lacking order, regularity, or system **:** DISORDERLY

**or·der·li·ness** \-lēnəs, -lin-\ *n* -ES **:** the quality or state of being orderly

[1]**or·der·ly** \-lē, -li\ *adv* [ME, fr. *ordre, order* + *-ly* (adv. suffix)] **:** in or according to due order **:** REGULARLY, METHODICALLY, DULY ⟨will find the following lessons ~ arranged —Whitcomb Crichton⟩

[2]**orderly** \"\ *adj* [[1]*order* + *-ly* (adj. suffix)] **1 a** (1) **:** arranged, disposed, or organized in some order, pattern, or sequence **:** conforming to a plan **:** well ordered **:** REGULAR ⟨the city plan is ~ —*Amer. Guide Series: Mich.*⟩ ⟨~ rows of shacks —*Amer. Guide Series: Fla.*⟩ (2) **:** not disordered **:** NEAT, TIDY ⟨found the room and its belongings in ~ condition⟩ **b :** governed by law or system **:** not haphazard **:** REGULATED, SYSTEMATIC ⟨gives rise to ~ involuntary motor responses —H.G.Armstrong⟩ ⟨a series of ~ actions at regular hours —Ellen Glasgow⟩ **c :** characterized by methodical ways or procedures **:** systematic in action or thought ⟨an ~ mind⟩ ⟨an ~ person⟩ **d :** reflecting or exhibiting a methodical mind or temper ⟨admired his ~ ways⟩ **2 :** having regard for good order, authority, or rule **:** not unruly **:** PEACEFUL, QUIET ⟨thrifty, ~ New England —Allan Nevins & H.S.Commager⟩ ⟨the parts of provincial Africa which lay near the desert were less ~ —James Bryce⟩ **3 :** relating to or charged with the transmission of military orders

**syn** ORDERLY, METHODICAL, SYSTEMATIC can apply to what follows closely a set arrangement, design, or pattern. ORDERLY implies an observance of due sequence or proper arrangement as in the disposition of things, in the observance of rules, in keeping a place free from litter, or in the making of a plan or the following of a scheme ⟨an *orderly* setting of a table⟩ ⟨an *orderly* election⟩ ⟨an *orderly* household⟩ ⟨an *orderly* housekeeper⟩ ⟨an *orderly* mind⟩ METHODICAL implies the careful observance of an order of things or actions that is worked out, usu. carefully, in advance or that is logical or inevitable ⟨a *methodical* search for the facts⟩ ⟨a *methodical* course of instruction⟩ ⟨a *methodical* cleaning up of a yard⟩ ⟨a *methodical* housekeeper following a more or less fixed routine⟩ SYSTEMATIC comes close to METHODICAL but puts stress upon the integrity and completeness of the order adopted or followed ⟨a *systematic* course in astronomy⟩ ⟨a cold-blooded and *systematic* destruction of one's enemies⟩ ⟨a *systematic* devotee of physical exercise⟩ ⟨a *systematic* workman⟩

[3]**orderly** \"\ *n* -ES **1 :** a soldier who attends a superior officer to carry his orders or to give other service; *also* **:** a soldier detailed to look after a room or otherwise assist in a hospital ward **2 :** a hospital attendant who does routine or heavy work (as cleaning, carrying supplies, or moving patients to surgery)

**orderly book** *n, Brit* **:** a book kept at a military headquarters in which orders and instructions received from higher authority are recorded

**orderly officer** *n* **1** *Brit* **:** OFFICER OF THE DAY **2** *Brit* **:** ORDERLY

**orderly room** *n* **:** a room in barracks sometimes occupied by the first sergeant that contains the company, troop, or battery records and is used for company business

**orderly sergeant** *n, archaic* **:** FIRST SERGEANT

**order of a reaction :** a number that relates the rate of a chemical reaction with the concentrations of the reacting substances **:** the sum of all the exponents of the terms expressing concentrations of the molecules or atoms determining the rate of the reaction — compare FIRST-ORDER REACTION, SECOND-ORDER REACTION, THIRD-ORDER REACTION, ZERO-ORDER REACTION; MOLECULARITY

**order of battle 1 :** a particular disposition given to troops or ships **2 :** a tabular compilation by unit showing organization, commanders, movements, and other details over an extended time

**order of business 1 :** the precedence or priority under the rules or practice of a deliberative or legislative body in which different proceedings, reports, motions, and general business will be considered or will take place **2 :** a program or sequence of different matters or classes of business arranged in the order in which they are to be taken up by an assembly **3 :** a matter or problem calling for attention or solution **:** TASK ⟨the problem of congestion is the first *order of business* with the commission —S.H.Hofstadter⟩

**order of contact :** a numerical measure of contact equal to or less than the number of points that coincide

**order of magnitude 1 :** ORDER ⟨two explosions of the same low *order of magnitude*⟩ **2 :** a range of magnitude extending from some value to ten times that value ⟨two quantities are of the same *order of magnitude* if one is no larger than ten times the other, but if one is one hundred times the other it is larger by two *orders of magnitude*⟩

**order of service :** the arrangement of the various parts of a religious service in Protestant Christianity

**order of the day 1 a :** the order of business appointed for an assembly for a given day **:** AGENDA ⟨*order of the day* will include three conferences, rosary in common, confessions —*Springfield* (*Mass.*) *Union*⟩; *esp* **:** the order of business appointed for a legislative body for a given day ⟨the House . . . proceeded to the *order of the day* —Christopher Morley⟩ **b :** a stage of a bill or other matter that the House of Commons or other legislative body of the British Commonwealth has ordered to be taken under consideration on a particular day **2 :** a statement issued by a commander to his troops usu. in commemoration of some achievement **3 :** the salient, characteristic, or dominant custom, theme, feature, or activity of a particular time **:** HALLMARK; KEYNOTE ⟨lavishness is the *order of the day* —Betty Pepis⟩ ⟨minuets, cancan, and ballet were the *order of the day* —*N.Y. Times*⟩ ⟨expansionism was the *order of the* new *day* —R.H.Brown⟩

**order of worship :** the arrangement of the various parts of a worship service within Protestant Christianity

**order paper** *n, often cap O&P* **:** ORDER BOOK 2

**order pro confesso** *n* **:** an order in U.S. equity practice that takes a bill as confessed for want of appearance or want of answer

**orders** *pl of* ORDER, *pres 3d sing of* ORDER

**order up** *vt* **1 :** to summon up for active military duty **:** call up ⟨*ordered up* all the militia regiments⟩ **2 :** to direct an opposing dealer to take (the trump) into his hand and discard in euchre — compare ASSIST 3a

**or·di·na·ble** \'ȯ(r)d(ᵊ)nəbəl\ *adj* [ML *ordinabilis*, fr. L *ordinare* to put in order, arrange, appoint + *-abilis* -able — more at ORDAIN] **:** capable of being ordered or arranged

[1]**or·di·nal** \'ȯrd(ᵊ)nəl, 'ȯ(ə)d-\ *n* -s [ME, fr. ML *ordinale*, fr. LL, neut. of *ordinalis*, adj.] **1** *usu cap* **a :** a book containing directions for Roman Catholic services every day in the year **b :** a collection of forms to be used in the Anglican Communion in the consecration of bishops and the ordination of priests and deacons **2** [LL *ordinalis*, fr. *ordinalis*, adj.] **:** ORDINAL NUMBER **3 :** the divisor in a fraction as spoken or written out (as *hundredth* in *one hundredth* or *hundredths* in *three hundredths*

[2]**ordinal** \"\ *adj* [LL *ordinalis*, fr. *ordin-*, *ordo* order + *-alis* -al — more at ORDER] **1 :** being of a specified order or rank (as sixth) in a numberable series **2 :** of or relating to an order ⟨family and ~ names . . . of fishes are badly jumbled in the text —*N. Y. Herald Tribune Bk. Rev.*⟩

**ordinal number** *n* **:** a number designating the place (as first, second, third) occupied by any item in an ordered sequence — distinguished from *cardinal number;* see NUMBER table

**or·di·nance** \'ȯrd(ᵊ)nən(t)s, 'ȯ(ə)d-\ *n* -s [ME *ordinaunce*, fr. MF & ML; MF *ordenance*, lit., art of ordering, arranging, fr. ML *ordinantia*, fr. L *ordinant-*, *ordinans* (pres. part. of *ordinare* to put in order, arrange, appoint + *-ia* -y — more at ORDAIN] **1 a :** an authoritative decree or direction **:** ORDER ⟨our swift ~*s* on their way over the whole earth —Walt Whitman⟩ **b :** a public enactment, rule, or law promulgated by governmental authority: as (1) **:** one of a number of laws or regulations issued at various periods of English history without the assent of one of the three powers (Crown, House of Lords, and House of Commons) necessary to an act of Parliament (2) **:** a regulation or decree promulgated in Great Britain by any authority less than the sovereign enacting power (3) **:** any of several acts of the U. S. Congress under the Articles of Confederation (4) **:** a local law or regulation enacted by a city council or other similar body under powers delegated to it by the state **2 a :** the act or an instance of ordering or arranging **:** DIRECTION, DISPENSATION, CONTROL ⟨insistence upon a higher and rational ~ throughout the world —G.G.Coulton⟩ **b :** something ordained or decreed by fate or a deity **:** a decree or disposition of divine or providential origin ⟨an ~ of the Christian God —G.F.Hudson⟩ **c** *obs* **:** ordained or appointed place or condition **3 a :** established rule, policy, or practice ⟨a positive ~ . . . that there should be no sketching until lessons were done —Arnold Bennett⟩ **b :** an established and fully authoritative religious ceremony, rite, or usage that is not considered a sacrament **syn** see LAW

**or·di·nand** \'ȯrdə,nand\ *n* -s [LL *ordinandus*, gerundive of *ordinare* to ordain — more at ORDAIN] **:** a person about to be ordained

[1]**or·di·nant** \-d(ᵊ)nənt\ *adj* [L *ordinant-*, *ordinans*, pres. part.] **:** that ordains, decrees, or regulates

[2]**ordinant** \"\ *n* -s [LL *ordinant-*, *ordinans*, pres. part.] **:** a person who ordains

**or·di·nar·i·ate** \,ȯ(r)dᵊn'erēət, -ē,āt\ *n* -s [[1]*ordinary* + *-ate*] **1 :** the administrative division of a particular Roman Catholic diocese or archdiocese **2 :** a group of members of an Eastern rite in communion with the Pope who are subject to the personal jurisdiction of an appointed prelate (as a titular bishop) of the same rite — see MILITARY ORDINARIATE

**or·di·nar·i·ly** \ˌȯ(r)dᵊnˌerəlē, -li *sometimes* -dəˌne- *or* -dˌne-\ *adv* **:** in an ordinary manner: as **a :** in the ordinary course of events **:** USUALLY ⟨~ took notice of such things —Ross Annett⟩ ⟨were ~ sung in the court by the minstrel —R.A. Hall b. 1911⟩ **b :** to the usual extent **:** MODERATELY ⟨could afford, if he was ~ conscientious, to keep an assistant priest —G.G.Coulton⟩ **c :** in a commonplace or inferior way **:** without distinction ⟨two apartments . . . very ~ furnished —Walt Whitman⟩

**or·di·nar·i·ness** \ˈȯ(r)dᵊnˌerēnəs, -rin- *sometimes* -dəˌne- *or* -dˌne-\ *n* -ES **:** the quality or state of being ordinary: as **a :** routine or commonplace character ⟨the ~ of our sun which has accomplished the creation of life —*Think*⟩ **b :** everyday or typical quality or character ⟨either too pretty or too brutal; it lacks ~ —Virginia Woolf⟩

**¹or·di·nary** \-rē, -ri\ *n* -ES [ME *ordinarie*, fr. AF & ML; AF, fr.

ordinary 2d

ML *ordinarius*, fr. L *ordinarius*, adj.] **1 a** (1) *often cap* **:** a prelate exercising actual ecclesiastical jurisdiction over a specified territory ⟨the local ~ of a province is an archbishop⟩ (2) **:** a clergyman appointed formerly in England to give spiritual assistance to condemned criminals and to prepare them for the ordeal of the death penalty **b** (1) *civil & Scots law* **:** a judge having jurisdiction in his own right; *specif* **:** a lord ordinary in Scotland (2) **:** a judge of probate in some states of the U. S. **c** *obs* **:** the persons formerly employed to care for warships when laid up **d** *obs* **:** a courier in regular service; *also* **:** MAIL **e :** the second rank in the sea exploring program of the Boy Scouts of America **2 a** (1) *obs* **:** regular provision or allowance (as of food) (2) *Brit* **:** a meal served to all comers at a fixed price in distinction from one where each dish is separately charged for ⟨lunching . . . on the very excellent ~ —Elizabeth Montizambert⟩ (3) *chiefly Brit* **:** a tavern or eating house where regular meals are served; *also* **:** the dining room in such a house **b** (1) **:** regular, customary, or ordinary condition or course of things **:** such as is ordinarily met with or experienced — usu. used in the phrase *out of the ordinary* ⟨nothing out of the ~ —Glenway Wescott⟩ (2) **:** someone or something of ordinary or routine character ⟨the little *ordinaries* of life⟩ **c** (1) **:** a heraldic charge or bearing (as the bend, chevron, chief, cross, fess, pale, or saltire) of simple form and in constant use — see SUBORDINARY (2) **:** a book containing a collection of coats of arms arranged by design — compare ARMORY **d :** an early bicycle with a very large and a very small wheel as distinguished from a safety bicycle **e** *Brit* **:** common stock or a share of it **3** *often cap* **a :** an ecclesiastical order of service; *specif* **:** the parts of the mass that do not vary from day to day **b :** the part of a missal containing the ordinary of the mass — **by ordinary** *adv* **:** in the ordinary course of events **:** ORDINARILY ⟨*by ordinary* retained the elaborately cordial manner he had brought —Shelby Foote⟩ — **in ordinary 1 :** regularly attending or serving — used in titles ⟨the royal sculptor *in ordinary* —*Springfield* (*Mass.*) *Union*⟩ ⟨physician *in ordinary* —*Notes & Queries*⟩ **2** *of a ship* **:** laid up (as for repairs)

**²ordinary** \"\ *adj, sometimes* -ER/-EST [ME *ordinarie*, fr. L *ordinarius*, fr. *ordin-*, *ordo* order + *-arius* -ary — more at ORDER] **1 a** (1) **:** occurring or encountered in the usual course of events **:** not uncommon or exceptional **:** not remarkable **:** ROUTINE, NORMAL ⟨the ~ experience common to everyone —W.V. Houston⟩ ⟨a spring van, ~ in shape but singular in color —Thomas Hardy⟩ ⟨the ~ traffic had been stopped . . . to allow of the passage of troops and guns —H.G.Wells⟩ (2) *obs* **:** being of frequent occurrence **:** COMMON, ABUNDANT (3) *archaic* **:** commonly experienced or practiced **b :** characterized by common quality, merit, rank, or ability **:** lacking in excellence, superior merit, uncommon appeal, or distinctive characteristics ⟨just ~ people, with no more authority or judgment than they had themselves —Rose Macaulay⟩ ⟨not the ~ rice, but rice which has been specially planted and tended —J.G.Frazer⟩ **c :** being of a poor or mediocre quality **:** SECOND-RATE, INFERIOR ⟨a very ~ wine⟩ **d :** not advanced or honorary ⟨an ~ examination⟩ ⟨an ~ degree⟩ **e :** of or relating to life insurance sold in amounts of $1000 or more with premiums payable annually, semiannually, or quarterly — compare INDUSTRIAL LIFE INSURANCE **2 a :** having or constituting immediate or original jurisdiction as opposed to that which is delegated **:** having jurisdiction of his own right or by virtue of office; *also* **:** belonging to such jurisdiction **b** *Brit* **:** constituting the common-law branch of the Chancery Court

**syn** see COMMON

**ordinary care** *or* **ordinary diligence** *or* **ordinary prudence** *n* **:** the care that an average reasonable man exercises to prevent harm to the person or property of others and failure to exercise which when under a duty to do so constitutes actionable negligence on the part of one causing such harm

**ordinary differential equation** *n* **:** DIFFERENTIAL EQUATION

**ordinary lay** *n* **:** a lay of a wire rope in which the twist of the strands is the reverse of that of the wires

**ordinary life insurance** *n* **:** life insurance for which premiums are payable as long as the insured lives

**ordinary negligence** *n* **:** a failure to exercise or an absence of such care and diligence as a person of ordinary care, precaution, and diligence would exercise under the same or similar circumstances that is one of the three degrees of negligence recognized both at common law and in the civil law in many jurisdictions and in some jurisdictions is the only degree of negligence recognized — compare GROSS NEGLIGENCE, SLIGHT NEGLIGENCE

**ordinary of the season :** an established Christian service or any part of it appointed for any ordinary Sunday or weekday from the octave of Epiphany to the first Sunday in Lent and from Trinity to Advent

**ordinary point** *n* **:** any point on a curve that is not a singular point

**ordinary ray** *n* **:** the part of a ray divided in two by double refraction that follows the ordinary laws of refraction because its speed is the same in all directions through the doubly refracting medium

**ordinary's court** *n* **:** ORDINARY 1b(2)

**ordinary seaman** *n* **:** a seaman of some experience but not as skilled as an able-bodied seaman

**¹or·di·nate** \ˈȯrd(ᵊ)nət, ˈȯ(ə)d-, -dᵊnˌāt, *usu* -d.+V\ *adj* [ME *ordinat*, fr. L *ordinatus*, past part. of *ordinare* to put in order, arrange — more at ORDAIN] **:** arranged in rows ⟨~ markings⟩

**²or·di·nate** \-dᵊnˌāt\ *vt* -ED/-ING/-S [L *ordinatus*, past part. of *ordinare*] *archaic* **:** ORDER, ORDAIN

**³or·di·nate** \-d(ᵊ)nət, -dᵊnˌāt, *usu* -d.+V\ *n* -S [NL (*linea*) *ordinate* (*applicata*) & (*linea*) *ordinatim* (*applicata*), lit., line applied in an orderly manner; NL *ordinate*, *ordinatim*, adv., fr. L *ordinatus*, past part.] **:** the vertical coordinate of a point in a plane Cartesian coordinate system obtained by measuring parallel to the y-axis — compare ABSCISSA

**or·di·na·tion** \ˌȯ(r)dᵊnˈāshən\ *n* -S [in sense 1, fr. ME *ordinacioun*, fr. LL *ordination-*, *ordinatio*, fr. *ordinatus* (past part. of *ordinare* to ordain) + L *-ion-*, *-io* -ion; in sense 2, fr. L *ordination-*, *ordinatio*, fr. *ordinatus* (past part. of *ordinare* to put in order, arrange) + *-ion-*, *-io* -ion — more at ORDAIN] **1 :** the act or an instance of ordaining or state of being ordained **:** APPOINTMENT; *specif* **:** the admission into the Christian ministry **2 :** DISPOSITION, ARRANGEMENT, ORDERING ⟨a sign . . . of God's ~ of the world —Isaac Rosenfeld⟩

**or·di·na·tor** \ˈ==ˌād·ə(r)\ *n* -S [in sense 1, fr. LL, fr. *ordinatus* + L *-or*; in sense 2, fr. L, fr. *ordinatus* + *-or*] **1 :** one that ordains into the Christian ministry **2 :** one that orders ⟨an ~ of states and a guide to destinies —H.B.Alexander⟩

**or·di·nee** \ˌȯ(r)dᵊnˈē\ *n* -S [LL *ordinare* to ordain + E *-ee* — more at ORDAIN] **:** one who has been or is being ordained

**ordines** *pl of* ORDO

**ord·nance** \ˈȯrdnən(t)s, ˈȯ(ə)d-\ *n* -S *often attrib* [ME *ordinaunce*, fr. MF *ordenance*, lit., act of ordering, arranging — more at ORDINANCE] **1 a :** military supplies including weapons, ammunition, combat vehicles, and the necessary maintenance tools and equipment **b :** a service of the army charged with the duty of procuring by purchase or manufacture and distributing the necessary ordnance for the army and organized militia and of establishing and maintaining arsenals and depots for their manufacture and safekeeping ⟨*Ordnance* had to start pretty close from scratch —*Time*⟩ ⟨*Ordnance* Corps⟩ **2 :** heavy firearms discharged from mounts **:** CANNON, ARTILLERY

**ord·nance·man** \ˈ==ˌ=\ *n, pl* **ordnancemen :** a person who is engaged in the testing, assembling, storing, maintenance, or transportation of ordnance equipment

**ordnance officer** *n* **1 :** an officer of an ordnance corps or department; *also* **:** a staff officer who advises and assists the commander in ordnance matters **2 :** GUNNERY OFFICER

**ordnance stores** *n pl* **:** ORDNANCE

**or·do** \ˈȯr(ˌ)dō\ *n, pl* **ordos** \-ōz\ *or* **or·di·nes** \-rdəˌnēz\ *usu cap* [ML, fr. L, order — more at ORDER] **:** an annual publication containing the list of offices and feasts of the Roman Catholic Church for each day of the year

**or·don·nance** \ˈȯ(r)dənən(t)s\ *n* -S [F, alter. of MF *ordenance*, lit., act of ordering, arrangement — more at ORDINANCE] **1 :** disposition of the parts of a composition with regard to one another and the whole **:** ARRANGEMENT, STRUCTURE ⟨there are design and ~ in it —C.D.Lewis⟩ **2** [F (*compagnie d'*) *ordonnance*, lit., ordinance company; fr. the *Ordonnance Royale* (Royal Ordinance) of 1437 which created the first standing army of France] **:** a company of French men-at-arms **3 a :** DECREE, LAW, ORDER ⟨the ~s of France are so unfavorable to strangers —Tobias Smollett⟩ **b :** an orderly compilation of a body of law on a particular subject (as of prizes and captures at sea)

**¹or·do·vi·cian** \ˌȯ(r)dəˈvishən\ *adj, usu cap* [*Ordovices*, ancient people in northern Wales (fr. L) + E *-ian*] **:** of or relating to the period between the Cambrian and the Silurian — called also *Lower Silurian*; see GEOLOGIC TIME table

**²ordovician** \"\ *n* -S *usu cap* **:** the Ordovician period or system of rocks

**or·dure** \ˈȯrjər, ˈȯ(ə)jə(r\ *n* -S [ME, filth, excrement, fr. MF, fr. *ord* filthy, foul (fr. L *horridus* horrid) + *-ure* — more at HORRID] **1 :** EXCREMENT **2 :** something (as pornographic material) that is morally degrading ⟨these ~s are rapidly depraving the public taste —Thomas Jefferson⟩

**¹ore** \ˈō(ə)r, ˈȯ(ə)r, ˈōə, ˈȯ(ə)\ *n* -S *often attrib* [ME *oor*, *or*, fr. OE *ār* brass, copper, ore; akin to OHG *ēr* bronze, ON *eir* bronze, copper, Goth *aiz* bronze, L *aes* bronze, copper, money, Skt *ayas* metal, iron] **1 a :** a natural or native mineral that can usu. be profitably mined and treated for the extraction of any of its constituents ⟨iron ~⟩ ⟨copper ~⟩ **b :** a source from which valuable matter is extracted **c :** an unrefined condition or material **2 :** PRECIOUS METAL

**²ore** \"\ *n* -S [OE *ōra* — more at ORA] **:** ORA

**³ore** \ˈœrə, ˈōrə\ *n, pl* **öre** [Dan & Norw *øre* & Sw *öre*, fr. L *aureus*, a gold coin — more at AUREUS] **1 :** a Danish and Norwegian unit of value equal to 1/100 krone; *also* **:** a coin representing this unit — see MONEY table **2 :** a Swedish unit of value equal to 1/100 krona; *also* **:** a coin representing this unit — see MONEY table

**ore-** *or* **oreo-** *comb form* [L, fr. Gk, fr. *ore-*, *oros* mountain, hill — more at RISE] **:** mountain ⟨*Oreophasis*⟩ ⟨*Oreortyx*⟩ ⟨*Oreamnos*⟩ — compare ¹ORO-

**ore·ad** \ˈōrēˌad, -ēəd\ *n* -S *often cap* [L *Oread-*, *Oreas*, fr. Gk *Oreiad-*, *Oreias*, fr. *oreios* of a mountain (fr. *oros* mountain) + *-ad-*, *-as*, fem. suffix denoting descent from or connection with] **:** one of the nymphs of mountains and hills

**ore·am·nos** \ˌōrēˈamnəs\ *n, cap* [NL, fr. *ore-* + Gk *amnos* lamb — more at YEAN] **:** a genus of ruminant mammals consisting of the mountain goat

**ore body** *n* **:** a more or less solid mass of ore that may consist of low-grade as well as high-grade ore and that is of different character from the adjoining rock

**ore bridge** *n* **:** a large gantry crane for loading or unloading ore at stockpiles

**orec·tic** \ōˈrektik\ *adj* [Gk *orektikos* appetitive, fr. *orektos* stretched out, longed for (fr. *oregein* to stretch, reach for, desire) + *-ikos* -ic — more at RIGHT] **:** of or relating to the desires; *specif* **:** impelling to gratification **:** APPETITIVE ⟨the ~ mechanism . . . does not consist simply of a number of instincts —C.E. Spearman⟩

**orec·to·lob·i·dae** \ōˌrektəˈläbəˌdē\ *n pl, cap* [NL, fr. *Orectolobus*, type genus + *-idae*] **:** a large family of chiefly Pacific and tropical sharks including the carpet shark, having two dorsal fins, a well-developed fleshy barbel at the anterior margin of the nostril, and small teeth with several cusps, and being mostly small often brilliantly marked bottom dwellers of shallow waters

**orec·tol·o·bus** \ōˌrekˈtäləbəs, ˌȯrˌe-\ *n, cap* [NL, fr. Gk *orektos* stretched out + NL *-lobus*] **:** the type genus of the family Orectolobidae

**ore dressing** *n* **:** mechanical treatment (as of low-grade ore) to separate a metallic or other valuable mineral from gangue rock and sometimes from other minerals that includes preparation (as by crushing or grinding) and concentration (as by gravity separation, flotation, magnetic separation) — compare METALLURGY

**oregano** [AmerSp *orégano*, fr. Sp, wild marjoram, fr. L *origanum* — more at ORIGANUM] *var of* ORIGANUM

**or·e·gon** \ˈȯrēgən, ˈär-, -rəg-, *chiefly by outsiders* -ˌgän\ *adj, usu cap* [*Oregon*, state in the northwestern U. S., fr. the *Oregon* river, former name for the Columbia river in southwestern Canada and northwestern U. S.] **:** of or from the state of Oregon **:** of the kind or style prevalent in Oregon **:** OREGONIAN

**oregon alder** *n, usu cap O* **:** RED ALDER

**oregon ash** *n, usu cap O* **1 :** a timber tree (*Fraxinus oregona*) of western No. America **2 :** the hard light wood of the Oregon ash tree

**oregon balsam** *n, usu cap O* **1 :** a liquid oleoresin obtained from the Douglas fir **2 :** a mixture of rosin and turpentine **3** *also* **oregon balsam fir :** DOUGLAS FIR

**oregon boat** *n, usu cap O* **:** a heavy iron shackle attached to the ankle and foot of a prisoner to prevent escape (as while being transported)

**oregon box** *n, usu cap O* **:** a low evergreen shrub (*Pachistima myrsinites*) of western No. America with tiny reddish brown flowers — called also *goatbrush*, *mountain lover*

**oregon cedar** *n, usu cap O* **:** PORT ORFORD CEDAR

**oregon char** *n, usu cap O* **:** DOLLY VARDEN 2

**oregon cliff brake** *n, usu cap O* **:** a No. American fern (*Pellaea densa*) with wiry light brown stipes that is cultivated for ornament — called also *pod fern*

**oregon crab apple** *n, usu cap O* **:** a small tree (*Malus fusca*) of western No. America having white flowers

**oregon fir** *or* **oregon douglas fir** *n, usu cap O&D* **:** DOUGLAS FIR

**oregon grape** *also* **oregon holly grape** *n, usu cap O* **:** either of two small evergreen shrubs (*Mahonia aquifolium* or *M. nervosa*) that have stiff pinnate dark green leaves tending to turn bronzy in winter, fascicled racemes of usu. yellow flowers, and globose blue berries, are native to the Pacific coast from northern California to British Columbia, and are cultivated in many temperate areas as shade-tolerant ornamentals — called also *hollygrape*, *holly-leaved barberry*, *mountain grape*

**oregon graperoot** *n, usu cap O* **:** BERBERIS 2

**¹or·e·go·nian** \ˌȯrəˈgōnēən, ˌär-, -rēˈg-, -nyən\ *n* -S *cap* [*Oregon* state + E *-ian*] **:** a native or resident of the state of Oregon

**²oregonian** \"==ˈ=(=)=\ *adj, usu cap* **:** of, relating to, or characteristic of Oregon or Oregonians

**oregon jargon** *n, usu cap O & J* **:** CHINOOK JARGON

**oregon jay** *n, usu cap O* **:** a crestless jay (*Perisoreus canadensis obscurus*) of northwestern No. America resembling the typical Canada jay but brownish

**oregon larch** *n, usu cap O* **1 :** WESTERN LARCH **2 :** NOBLE FIR

**oregon lily** *n, usu cap O* **:** a slender bulbous herb (*Lilium columbianum*) of western No. America with scattered leaves and showy orange-red purple-spotted flowers

**oregon maple** *n, usu cap O* **:** a large-leaved maple (*Acer macrophyllum*) of the Pacific coast of No. America

**oregon myrtle** *n, usu cap O* **:** CALIFORNIA LAUREL

**oregon oak** *or* **oregon white oak** *n, usu cap 1st O* **:** an oak (*Quercus garryana*) of western No. America with light-gray bark and obovate pinnatifid leaves — called also *Garry oak*

**oregon pine** *n, usu cap O* **:** DOUGLAS FIR

**oregon robin** *n, usu cap O* **:** VARIED THRUSH

**oregon triton** *n, usu cap O* **:** a large whelk (*Argobuccinum oregonensis*) of the Pacific coast of No. America with a heavy hairy epidermis covering the shell

**oreide** *var of* OROIDE

**ore·jón** \ˌȯrəˈhōn\ *n, pl* **orejón** \"\ *or* **ore·jo·nes** \-ō(ˌ)nās\ *usu cap* [Sp, lit., big ear, aug. of *oreja* ear, fr. L *auricula* external ear — more at AURICLE] **1 :** any of various No. American or So. American Indian peoples known to distend the earlobes with metal or wooden disks or ornaments: as **a :** ²COTO **b :** CHANÉ **c :** a Witotoan people of southern Colombia and eastern Ecuador **d :** a Coahuiltec people of Texas **e :** any of several peoples of the northwest coast of the U. S. **2 :** a member of any of the Orejón peoples

**orel** \ȯrˈyȯl, ōˈrel\ *adj, usu cap* [fr. *Orel*, U.S.S.R.] **:** of or from the city of Orel, U.S.S.R. **:** of the kind or style prevalent in Orel

**ore·less** \ˈō(ə)rləs, ˈȯ-\ *adj* **:** having no ore

**or else** *conj* **:** if not — see ¹ELSE 2a

**oren·da** \ōˈrendə\ *n* -S [Wyandot] **:** extraordinary invisible power believed by the Iroquois Indians to pervade in varying degrees all animate and inanimate natural objects as a transmissible spiritual energy capable of being exerted according to the will of its possessor ⟨a successful hunter's ~ overcomes that of his quarry⟩

**oreo-** — *see* ORE-

**oreo·car·ya** \ˌōrē(ˌ)ōˈka(a)rēə\ *n, cap* [NL, fr. *ore-* + *-carya* (fr. Gk *karyon* nut) — more at CAREEN] **:** a genus of perennial herbs (family Boraginaceae) that resemble forget-me-nots, have leafy stems and small white or yellow flowers in one-sided spikes or racemes, and are found in the western U. S. and adjacent Mexico — see WHITE FORGET-ME-NOT

**¹ore·odon** \ˈōrēəˌdän, ōˈr-\ [NL, fr. *ore-* + *-odon*] *syn of* MERYCOIDODON

**²oreodon** \"\ *n* -S [NL *Oreodon*] **:** an ungulate mammal of the genus *Merycoidodon*

**¹ore·odont** \-nt\ *adj* [NL *Oreodontidae*] **:** of or relating to the Merycoidodontidae

**²oreodont** \"\ *n* -S **:** an ungulate mammal of the family Merycoidodontidae

**ore·odon·ti·dae** \ˌōrēōˈdäntəˌdē, ōˌr-\ [NL, fr. *Oreodont-*, *Oreodon*, type genus + *-idae*] *syn of* MERYCOIDODONTIDAE; see MERYCOIDODON

**oreo·doxa** \ˌōrēōˈdäksə\ *n, cap* [NL, fr. *ore-* + Gk *doxa* glory, splendor — more at DOXOLOGY] **:** a small genus of tropical So. American palms that is closely related to *Roystonea* and in some classifications includes the royal palm

**oreography** *var of* OROGRAPHY

**oreo·pha·sine** \ˌōrēōˈfāˌsīn\ *adj* [NL *Oreophasinae*, subfamily of Cracidae, fr. *Oreophasis*, type genus + *-inae*] **:** of or relating to the genus *Oreophasis*

**oreo·pha·sis** \ˌ===ˈ=səs\ *n, cap* [NL, fr. *ore-* + Gk *Phasis*, a river (now Rion) in Colchis (now western Georgia, U.S.S.R.), the etymon of Gk *phasianos* pheasant] **:** a genus of curassows including the mountain curassow

**ore·or·tyx** \ˌōrēˈȯrdˌiks\ *n, cap* [NL, fr. *ore-* + Gk *ortyx* quail; akin to Skt *vartaka*, *vartika* quail] **:** a genus of birds (family Perdicidae) comprising the mountain quail of the western U. S.

**ore·ot·ra·gus** \ˌōrēˈä·trəgəs\ *n, cap* [NL, fr. *ore-* + Gk *tragos* male goat — more at TRAGEDY] **:** a genus of antelopes comprising the klipspringer

**oreo·troch·i·lus** \ˌōrēōˈträkələs\ *n, cap* [NL, fr. *ore-* + L *trochilus* wren — more at TROCHILUS] **:** a genus of hummingbirds found near the snow line in the So. American Andes

**ore pocket** *n* **:** a bin for temporary storage of ore in a mine

**ores** *pl of* ORE

**ore shoot** *n* **:** a usu. large and more or less vertical rich body of ore

**ore te·nus** \ˌōrēˈtenəs\ *adv* [L, by mouth] **:** by spoken word **:** ORALLY ⟨pleading done *ore tenus*⟩

**-o·rex·ia** \ōˈreksēə, əˈ-\ *n comb form* -S [NL, fr. Gk *orexis* desire, appetite, longing + L *-ia* -y] **:** desire **:** appetite ⟨cyn*orexia*⟩ ⟨par*orexia*⟩

**orex·is** \-səs\ *n* -ES [L, fr. Gk, fr. *oregein* to stretch, reach for, desire + *-sis* — more at RIGHT] **:** the feeling and striving aspect of mind as contrasted with the intellectual **:** DESIRE, APPETITE

**orey-eyed** \ˌōrēˈīd\ *adj* [*orey* of unknown origin] **:** very angry **:** WILD-EYED ⟨this bad steer . . . was an *orey-eyed* old devil —F.B.Gipson⟩ ⟨sure can make me *orey-eyed* —Helen Rich⟩

**orf** \ˈȯ(ə)rf\ *n* -S [alter. of E dial. *hurf*, prob. of Scand origin; akin to ON *hrūfa* crust on a wound, scab — more at DANDRUFF] *Brit* **:** SORE MOUTH 1

**ORF** *abbr* **1** owner's risk of fire **2** owner's risk of freezing

**orfe** \ˈȯ(ə)rf\ *n* -S [G *orf*, *orfe*, fr. OHG *orvo*, fr. L *orphus*, a sea fish, fr. Gk *orphos*, *orphōs*; perh. akin to OE *eorp*, *earp* dark, dusky, OHG *erpf* brown, ON *jarpr* brown, Gk *orphnos* dark] **:** an ide of a golden variety that is often stocked in ornamental pools; *broadly* **:** ²IDE

**or·fe·vre·rie** \ȯrfevrərē\ *n* -S [F *orfèvrerie*, fr. *orfèvre* goldsmith (fr. OF *orfevre*, fr. *or* gold + *fevre* smith, fr. L *fabr-*, *faber*) + *-erie* -ery — more at OR, DAFT] **:** goldsmith's or jeweler's work **:** gold or silver plate **:** JEWELRY

**orf·gild** \ˈȯrfˌgild\ *n* -S [OE *orf* cattle + *gield*, *geld*, *gild* tax, tribute; akin to OE *ierfe* inheritance — more at ORPHAN, GELD] **:** a fine imposed for taking away cattle and payable under old English law by the hundred to which the wrongdoer belonged

**orfray** *or* **orfrey** *var of* ORPHREY

**org** *abbr* **1** organic **2** organization; organized

**¹or·gan** \ˈȯrgən, ˈȯ(ə)g- *sometimes* -gᵊn\ *n* -S [ME, partly fr. OE *organa*, fr. L *organum*, fr. Gk *organon*, lit., tool, instrument; partly fr. OF *organe*, fr. L *organum*; akin to Gk *ergon* work — more at WORK] **1 a** *archaic* **:** a musical instrument ⟨the harp . . . the solemn pipe, and dulcimer, all ~s of sweet stop —John Milton⟩; *esp* **:** a wind instrument ⟨praise him with stringed instruments and ~s —Ps 150: 4 (AV)⟩ **b :** any of several large musical instruments producing sustained tones and played by means of a keyboard: (1) **:** a wind instrument consisting of sets of pipes sounding by compressed air, controlled by manual and pedal keyboards, and capable of producing a variety of musical timbres and orchestral effects — called also *pipe organ* (2) **:** REED ORGAN (3) **:** an instrument in which the sound and resources of the pipe organ are approximated by means of electronic devices **c :** one of various similar cruder instruments (as the barrel organ) **d :** a division of a pipe organ consisting of a group of stops with their actions and usu. an independent keyboard set on a single wind-chest — see CHOIR ORGAN, ECHO ORGAN, GREAT ORGAN, SOLO ORGAN, SWELL ORGAN **2 a :** a differentiated structure (as a heart, kidney, leaf, flower) in an animal or plant made up of various cells and tissues and adapted for the performance of some specific function and grouped with other structures sharing a common function into systems — see HOLLOW ORGAN **b :** the bodily parts performing a particular function or cooperating in a particular activity — usu. used in pl. ⟨speech ~s⟩ ⟨visual ~s⟩ **c :** PENIS **3 :** an instrumentality exercising some function or accomplishing some end ⟨the political cartoon is one of the greatest ~s of propaganda —A.C.W.Harmsworth⟩; *specif* **:** a governmental instrumentality operating as a part of a larger organization ⟨the cabinet's function as a general ~ of government without special regard to the king's wishes —*Times Lit. Supp.*⟩ **4 :** a publication (as a newspaper or magazine) expressing the view of a single person or a special group or specif. serving a special group ⟨a newspaper that is the official ~ of the government⟩; *broadly* **:** PERIODICAL ⟨newspaper and magazine clippings should be accompanied by the name of the ~ from which they are taken —*Western Folklore*⟩ **syn** see MEAN

**²organ** \"\ *vt* **organed** \-nd,-ŋd\ **organed** \"\ **organing** \-gəniŋ\ **organs** \-gənz,-gəŋz\ **:** to play on an organ

**³organ** \"\ *n* -s [by alter.] *dial chiefly Eng* **:** ORIGAN

**organ-** *or* **organo-** *comb form* [ME, fr. ML, fr. L *organum* — more at ¹ORGAN] **1 a :** organ ⟨*organ*elle⟩ ⟨*organo*genesis⟩ ⟨*organo*nymy⟩ **b :** organic substance or life ⟨*organo*genic⟩ **2 a :** organic **:** organic and ⟨*organo*chemical⟩ ⟨*organo*mineral⟩ **b :** organometallic ⟨*organo*tin⟩ ⟨*organo*arsenic⟩ ⟨*organo*phosphorus⟩

**or·ga·nal** \'ȯ(r)gənᵊl\ *adj* [*organ*um + *-al*] **:** of or being an organum ⟨an ~ voice⟩ ⟨the ~ parts⟩

**organ beater** *n* **:** a medieval organist

**organbird** \'==,=\ *n* **1 :** a Tasmanian magpie (*Gymnorhina hyperleuca*) whose discordant notes suggest an organ out of tune **2 :** a wren (*Leucolepis arada*) of northern So. America

**organ cactus** *var of* ORGAN-PIPE CACTUS

**organ coral** *n* **:** ORGAN-PIPE CORAL

**or·gan·dy** *also* **or·gan·die** \'ȯ(r)gəndē, -di, *chiefly Brit sometimes* ='gan-\ *n, pl* **organdies** [F *organdi*] **:** a very fine transparent plain-woven muslin with a temporary or permanent finish for crispness made orig. of cotton and now imitated in other fibers and used esp. for clothing, curtains, and trimmings

**or·gan·elle** \¦ȯ(r)gə¦nel\ *also* **or·gan·el·la** \,==ˈnelə\ *n* -s [NL *organella*, fr. *organ-* + *-ella*] **:** a specialized part of a cell (as a cilium or a cytopharynx) performing functions analogous to those of the organs of many-celled animals — compare ORGANOID 1

**or·gan·ette** \¦ȯ(r)gə¦net\ *n* -s [¹*organ* + *-ette*] **1 :** a small portable organ sometimes mechanically played **2 :** a large accordion

**organ genus** *n* **:** a genus of fossil plants diagnosed on the basis of single organs or restricted groups of connected organs — compare FORM GENUS

**organ-grinder** \'==,==\ *n* **:** one that cranks a hand organ; *esp* **:** an itinerant street musician who grinds a barrel organ

**organ gun** *n* **:** a piece of ordnance with several chambers or barrels arranged side by side

**¹or·gan·ic** \(ˈ)ȯ(r)¦ganik, -nēk\ *adj* [L *organicus*, fr. Gk *organikos*, fr. *organon* tool, instrument, organ + *-ikos* -ic — more at ORGAN] **1** *archaic* **:** serving as an instrument or means **:** INSTRUMENTAL **2** [F *organique*, fr. MF, fr. LL *organicus*, fr. Gk *organikos*] **a :** of or relating to an organ or a system of organs; *specif* **:** relating to or affecting the internal organs of the body ⟨~ changes in emotion⟩ **b :** consisting of or containing organs ⟨the ~ structure of animals and plants⟩ **c :** produced by an organ ⟨~ pleasure⟩; *specif* **:** having origin in demonstrable somatic pathology ⟨~ psychoses⟩ — compare FUNCTIONAL **d :** affecting the structure of the organism ⟨an ~ disease⟩ — compare FUNCTIONAL **3 a** (1) **:** of, relating to, or derived from living organisms ⟨~ evolution⟩ ⟨~ matter⟩ **:** being, composed of, or containing matter of plant or animal origin ⟨~ remains in the Silurian rocks⟩ ⟨a highly ~ soil⟩ (2) **:** relating to, produced with, or based on the use of organics as fertilizers without employment of chemically formulated fertilizers or pesticides ⟨~ farming⟩ ⟨~ vegetables⟩ **b :** exhibiting characters or qualities peculiar to living organisms ⟨~ growth⟩ ⟨~ nature⟩; *broadly* **:** forming or belonging to the animate world ⟨the powers of the atom bomb to effect strict ~ and inorganic destruction —W.D.Pardridge⟩ ⟨~ life⟩ **4 a :** being, containing, or relating to carbon compounds esp. in which hydrogen is attached to carbon whether derived from living organisms or not — usu. distinguished from *inorganic* or *mineral* ⟨~ solvents⟩ ⟨~ pigments⟩ **b :** being in the form of such a carbon compound ⟨~ nitrogen in proteins⟩ **5 a** (1) **:** forming an integral element of a whole **:** FUNDAMENTAL, INHERENT, VITAL ⟨incidental music rather than ~ parts of the action —Francis Fergusson⟩ (2) **:** involving or inherent in the basic character or structure (as of a nation or church) **:** CONSTITUTIONAL, ORGANIZATIONAL ⟨the ~ union of what had been two denominations⟩ (3) **:** belonging etymologically to the structure of a word ⟨~ *t* in *dental*⟩ ⟨~ *d* in *hound* contrasted with *d* in *sound* [L *sonus*]⟩ (4) **:** assigned to and constituting a permanent part of a military organization (as a regiment) under its table of organization and equipment **b** (1) **:** constituting a whole whose parts are mutually dependent or intrinsically related **:** having systematic coordination **:** ORGANIZED ⟨an overall perceivable pattern into which the parts can be fitted to make an ~ whole —Irving Stone⟩ (2) **:** forming a complex entity in which the whole is more than the sum of the individual parts and the parts have a life and character deriving from their participation in the whole **:** having the character of an organism ⟨form and content . . . wrought into a unique ~ whole outside of which neither element has any relevant meaning —Carlos Lynes⟩ ⟨in such an ~ society the concept of individual liberty was virtually unknown —H.J.Laski⟩ **6 a :** arising and developing in a manner resembling the growth of a living plant or animal ⟨~ form in poetry⟩ ⟨the romantic principle asserts that form is an ~ event, proceeding from the intuitive experience of the artist —Kathleen Raine⟩ ⟨many new coinages in modern Hebrew stem from the normal ~ structure of the language —William Chomsky⟩ **:** having the character of a natural outgrowth ⟨an ~ connection between the Koran and the Old and New Testaments —Norman Cousins⟩ **b** (1) **:** having a form suggesting natural growth as opposed to one that is calculated and contrived ⟨~ crystal formations⟩ (2) **:** having a form growing out of inherent factors (as function, site) rather than convention ⟨a clear ~ architecture . . . whose function is clearly recognizable in the relation of its forms —Walter Gropius⟩ **7 :** being or relating to the law by virtue of which a government or organization exists as such **:** incorporated or involved in the organization of a state, political organism, or other organized association ⟨their nation has written the separation of church and state into its ~ law —Paul Blanshard⟩ ⟨the purpose of the weather bureau as defined in its ~ act is to provide meteorological information —F.W.Reichelderfer⟩ **8 :** interpreting something (as human society) as having the characteristics of a living plant or animal **:** ORGANISMIC ⟨an ~ concept of the novel⟩ ⟨the ~ theory of the state⟩

**²organic** \"\ *n* -s **:** an organic substance **:** as **a :** a fertilizer consisting only of matter or products of plant or animal origin **b :** a pesticide whose active component is an organic compound or mixture of organic compounds

**or·gan·i·cal** \-nəkəl, -nēk-\ *adj* [L *organicus* + E *-al*] *archaic* **:** ORGANIC

**or·gan·i·cal·ly** \-k(ə)lē, -li\ *adv* **:** in an organic manner ⟨~ diseased⟩ ⟨smaller combines consisting of ~ linked plants —*Economist*⟩

**organic base** *n* **:** a basic compound containing carbon; *esp* **:** an organic nitrogen base (as an amine)

**organic chemistry** *n* **:** a branch of chemistry that deals chiefly with hydrocarbons and their derivatives — compare INORGANIC CHEMISTRY

**or·gan·i·cism** \ȯ(r)'ganə,sizəm\ *n* -s [ISV ¹*organic* + *-ism*] **:** a theory interpreting something as organic in character: as **a :** a theory that disease is always associated with a structural lesion of an organ **b :** a theory holding in contrast to vitalism on the one hand and mechanism on the other that life and living processes are the manifestation of an activity possible only in virtue of the state of autonomous organization of the system rather than because of its individual components — compare HOLISM, OBJECTIVE IDEALISM, PHILOSOPHY OF ORGANISM **c :** a conception of society as a superindividual organism constituted of ideas, beliefs, and volitions or as an entity analogous to a biological organism and subject to the same stages of birth, maturity, and death

**or·gan·i·cist** \-səst\ *n* -s [ISV ¹*organic* + *-ist*] **:** an advocate of organicism ⟨the ~ believes that every actual event in the world is a more or less concealed organic process —S.C. Pepper⟩ — **or·gan·i·cis·tic** \(¦)ȯ(r)¦ganə¦sistik\ *adj*

**or·ga·nic·i·ty** \,ȯ(r)gə'nisəd·ē\ *n* -ES [¹*organic* + *-ity*] **:** the quality or state of being organic

**organic mechanism** *n* **:** PHILOSOPHY OF ORGANISM

**organic memory** *n* **:** the permanent modification of an organism by stimulation and activity; *also* **:** MNEME

**organic pigment** *n* **:** an insoluble coloring matter consisting essentially of a dye that is itself insoluble or has been converted into an insoluble product ⟨the expression "lakes and toners" has come to be used synonymously with *organic pigments* —E.R.Allen⟩ — distinguished from *mineral pigment;* see DYE table I, ⁴LAKE 1b, TONER a

**organic selection** *n* **:** a process by which acquired individual characters are sometimes considered to protect heritable variations while these are still insufficiently developed to be perpetuated by natural selection

**organic sensation** *n* **:** a sensation (as hunger, nausea) arising from internal organs

**organic soil** *n* **:** soil composed mostly of plant material

**organic synthesis** *n* **:** the synthesis of organic compounds including pharmaceuticals and dyes

**organing** *pres part of* ORGAN

**organise** *Brit var of* ORGANIZE

**or·ga·nism** \'ȯ(r)gə,nizəm\ *n* -s [*organ-* + *-ism*] **1 :** organic structure **:** ORGANIZATION ⟨the man of large and imperious physical ~ —Havelock Ellis⟩ **2 :** something felt to resemble a living plant or animal: as **a** (1) **:** an entity having an existence independent of or more fundamental than its elements and having distinct members or parts whose relations and powers or properties are determined by their function in the whole ⟨the nation is not merely the sum of individual citizens at any given time, but it is a living ~, a mystical body . . . of which the individual is an ephemeral part —Joseph Rossi⟩ (2) **:** a being in which every part is at once a means and an end to every other **b :** something arising and developing in an organic manner ⟨whether the whole of reality is an ~ or a machine —Weston LaBarre⟩ **3 :** an individual constituted to carry on the activities of life by means of parts or organs more or less separate in function but mutually dependent **:** a living being **syn** see SYSTEM

**or·ga·nis·mic** \¦ȯ(r)gə¦nizmik\ *also* **or·ga·nis·mal** \-məl\ *adj* **1 :** of or belonging or relating to an organism esp. as a functional whole **2 :** of or relating to organicism or organic mechanism **:** HOLISTIC ⟨the ~ theory of the state⟩ — **or·ga·nis·mi·cal·ly** \-mək(ə)lē\ *adv*

**organismic psychology** *n* **:** the study of man as a psychosomatic unity

**or·gan·ist** \'ȯ(r)gənəst\ *n* -s [MF or ML; MF *organiste*, fr. ML *organista*, fr. L *organum* organ + *-ista* -ist — more at ORGAN] **:** a musician who plays an organ **:** an organ player

**or·ga·nis·tic** \¦ȯ(r)gə¦nistik\ *adj* [¹*organ* + *-istic*] **1 :** suitable for performance on an organ **2 :** ORGANISMIC 2

**or·ga·nis·trum** \,ȯ(r)gə'nistrəm\ *n* -s [ML, fr. L *organum* organ — more at ORGAN] **:** HURDY-GURDY 1

**or·gan·ist·ship** \'ȯ(r)gənəs(t),ship\ *n* **:** the position of organist (as of a church)

**or·gan·ite** \'ȯ(r)gə,nīt\ *n* -s [ISV *organ-* + *-ite*] **:** ORGANELLE

**or·ga·niz·able** \'ȯ(r)gə,nīzəbəl, ,==ˈ===\ *adj* **:** capable of being organized

**or·ga·ni·za·tion** \,ȯ(r)g(ə)nə'zāshən, ,ȯ(r)gə,nī'z-\ *n* -s *often attrib* [ME *organizacion*, fr. MF or ML; MF *organisation*, fr. ML *organization-, organizatio*, fr. *organizatus* (past part. of *organizare*) + L *-ion-, -io* -ion] **1 a :** the act or process of organizing ⟨the ~ of his material into an outline⟩ **b :** the formation of fibrous tissue from a clot or exudate by invasion of connective tissue cells and capillaries from adjoining tissues accompanied by phagocytosis of superfluous material and multiplication of connective tissue cells — compare GRANULATION **c :** the unification and harmonizing of all elements of a work of art **:** COMPOSITION **2 :** something organized: **a :** an organic being or system **:** ORGANISM **b :** a group of people that has a more or less constant membership, a body of officers, a purpose, and usu. a set of regulations ⟨representative of a local business ~⟩ ⟨tax exemption for religious and charitable ~*s*⟩; *specif* **:** a military command consisting of two or more units **3 a :** a state or manner of being organized **:** organic structure **:** purposive systematic arrangement **:** CONSTITUTION ⟨a group with a high degree of ~⟩ ⟨genius . . . implies an unusually subtle . . . ~ of the personality —E. R.Bentley⟩; *specif* **:** the administrative and functional structure of an organization (as a business, political party, military unit) including the established relationships of personnel through lines of authority and responsibility with delegated and assigned duties **b :** a body of administrative officials; *specif* **:** the usu. professional and full-time body of officials directing the affairs of a political party — **or·ga·ni·za·tion·al** \¦ȯ(r)-g(ə)nə¦zāshən°l, ¦ȯ(r)gə,nī¦z-, -shnəl\ *adj* — **or·ga·ni·za·tion·al·ly** \-°l|ē, -əl|, |i\ *adv*

**organization center** *n* **:** the point (as the chordamesoderm of the dorsal lip of the vertebrate blastopore) in a developing embryo that serves as a focus about which the embryo differentiates

**organization man** *n* **:** a man who subordinates individualism to conformity with the standards and requirements of an organization

**or·ga·nize** \'ȯ(r)gə,nīz\ *vb* -ED/-ING/-S *see -ize in Explan Notes* [ME *organysen*, fr. MF or ML; MF *organiser*, fr. ML *organizare*, fr. L *organum* organ + *-izare* -ize — more at ORGAN] *vt* **1 a :** to cause to develop an organic structure ⟨around it the egg is *organized* as a unitary organism —C.H.Waddington⟩ **b :** to make ready for embryonic differentiation and development **:** act in the manner of an inductor in relation to **2 a :** to arrange or constitute into a coherent unity in which each part has a special function or relation ⟨~ his knowledge in a coherent system of thought —J.S.Schapiro⟩ ⟨these practical proposals are *organized* by a philosophy of natural law —F.S.Cohen⟩ **b :** to unify into a coordinated functioning whole **:** put in readiness for coherent or cooperative action ⟨paused to ~ his thoughts⟩ ⟨wake and ~ the hikers for the day's climb⟩ ⟨~ a defense before the invasion⟩ **:** INTEGRATE ⟨was poorly *organized* and revealed an unevenness in logical procedure which is a common identifying mark of schizophrenia —Miriam G. Siegel⟩ **:** RALLY ⟨active in *organizing* sentiment . . . against the British government —R.E.Moody⟩ **c** (1) **:** to set up an administrative and functional structure for **:** provide with or establish as an organization ⟨~ a congregation and erect a church⟩ ⟨~ a company to manufacture his invention⟩ ⟨~ a territory⟩ (2) **:** to associate in an organization ⟨*organized* the dairymen into a marketing cooperative⟩ (3) **:** UNIONIZE ⟨~ the white-collar workers⟩ ⟨~ the factory⟩ ⟨~ the garment industry⟩ **3 :** to sing the organum to (a cantus firmus) **4 :** to arrange by systematic planning and coordination of individual effort ⟨helped to ~ games and entertainment among the passengers —*Current Biog.*⟩ ⟨~ short courses for teacher-librarians —*Times Lit. Supp.*⟩ ⟨~ a traveling art exhibition⟩ ⟨~ a tour of the campus for new students⟩ ⟨~ the attack⟩ ⟨~ a strike⟩ **5 :** to put in a state of order ⟨tried to ~ the torrent of emotions . . . seething inside her —Barnaby Conrad⟩ **:** arrange in an orderly manner ⟨~ the chairs for the rehearsal⟩ **~** *vi* **1 :** to sing the organum **2 :** to undergo organization ⟨an *organized* clot in the femoral vein⟩ ⟨sometimes the exudate of pneumonia ~*s* instead of being resolved⟩ **3 :** to arrange elements into a whole of interdependent parts ⟨began *organizing* for victory by kicking the commander in chief . . . upstairs to the vice-royalty —O.S.J.Gogarty⟩ **4 a :** to form an organization ⟨prohibiting an armed group from *organizing* on its soil —*Collier's Yr. Bk.*⟩ **b** (1) **:** to establish or found a labor union ⟨that workers had a right to ~⟩ (2) **:** to persuade workers to join or form a workers group into a union ⟨spent his early years as a union employee *organizing*⟩ **syn** see FOUND, ORDER

**organized** *adj* **1 :** exhibiting the characters of an organism esp. in being differentiated to perform various vital functions ⟨the amoeba is in fact a highly ~ animal⟩ ⟨production of ~ life in an infusion depends chiefly on airborne spores⟩ **2 a :** having a formal organization to coordinate or carry out joint activities ⟨~ baseball⟩ ⟨~ crime⟩ **b :** having a politically defined area and formal governmental institutions usu. as a result of action by a higher authority ⟨~ county⟩ ⟨~ territory of the U. S.⟩ **3 :** affiliated by membership in an organization ⟨~ labor⟩ ⟨~ medicine⟩ ⟨an estimated 8 million ~ bowlers in the U. S. —Victor Kalman⟩ **4** *slang* **:** INTOXICATED

**organized militia** *n* **:** a former body of U. S. militia under the concurrent jurisdiction of both the state and the federal governments and now constituted as a National Guard

**or·ga·niz·er** \'ȯ(r)gə,nīzə(r)\ *n* -s **:** one that organizes: as **a :** one who travels in various localities for the purpose of establishing new branches of a lodge or similar organization **b :** a union employee who organizes new locals of a particular labor union **c :** something that acts as an inductor in a developing embryo — compare ORGANIZATION CENTER

**or·gan·less** \'ȯ(r)gənləs\ *adj* **:** lacking organs

**organ meat** *n* **:** any edible part of a slaughter animal that consists of or forms part of an internal organ (as the liver, kidney, heart, or brain) — distinguished from *meat*

**organ neurosis** *n* **:** a somatic conversion in which intrapsychic conflict affects or is thought to affect a bodily organ — compare CONVERSION HYSTERIA

**organo-** — see ORGAN-

**or·gano·chlorosilane** \¦ȯ(r)gə(,)nō, ȯ(r)¦ganō+\ *n* [*organ-* + *chlorosilane*] **:** CHLOROSILANE 2

**organ of bo·ja·nus** \-bō'yānəs\ *usu cap B* [after Ludwig H. Bojanus †1827 Ger. anatomist] **:** one of a pair of nephridial excretory organs of bivalve mollusks situated on each side of the body just below the pericardium

**organ of cor·ti** \-'kȯrd·ē, -r,tē\ *usu cap C* [after Alfonso *Corti* — more at ARCH OF CORTI] **:** a complex epithelial structure in the cochlea that in mammals is the chief if not the only part of the ear by which sound is directly perceived and that rests on the internal surface of the basilar membrane and contains two spiral rows of minute rods of Corti which arch over a spiral tunnel of Corti and support on the inner side a single row of columnar hair cells and on the outer side several rows having their bases surrounded by arborizations derived from the ganglion cells of the spiral ganglion of the cochlear nerve

**organ of jacobson** *usu cap J* **:** JACOBSON'S ORGAN

**organ of johnston** *usu cap J* **:** JOHNSTON'S ORGAN

**organ of tö·mös·va·ry** \-'tə(r)məsh,värē, -'tōm-\ *usu cap T* [fr. the name *Tömösvary*] **:** either of a pair of cephalic sensory organs of unknown function in many myriopods

**or·gano·gel** \ȯ(r)'ganə,jel\ *n* [ISV *organ-* + *gel*] **:** a gel formed by the coagulation of an organosol

**or·gano·genesis** \,ȯ(r)gə(,)nō, ȯ(r),ganə+\ *n* [NL, fr. *organ-* + *genesis*] **:** the origin and development of organs in plants and animals — called also *morphogenesis* — **or·gano·genetic** \"+\ *adj* — **or·gano·genetically** \"+\ *adv*

**or·gano·genic** \"+¦jenik\ *adj* [*organ-* + *-genic*] **:** derived from organic substances

**or·ga·nog·e·nist** \,ȯ(r)gə'näjənəst\ *n* -s **:** an expert in organogenesis

**or·ga·nog·e·ny** \-jənē\ *n* -ES [ISV *organ-* + *-geny*] **1 :** ORGANOGENESIS **2 :** the study of organogenesis

**or·gano·graph·ic** \¦ȯ(r)gənō¦grafik, ȯ(r)¦ganə¦-\ *adj* **:** of or relating to organography

**or·ga·nog·ra·phy** \,ȯ(r)gə'nägrəfē\ *n* -ES [*organ-* + *-graphy*] **:** description of the organs of animals or plants esp. of the externally recognizable members of the plant body — compare MORPHOLOGY 1

**¹or·gan·oid** \'ȯ(r)gə,nȯid\ *adj* [ISV *organ-* + *-oid;* prob. orig. formed in G] **:** resembling an organ in structural appearance or qualities — used esp. of abnormal masses (as tumors or galls)

**²organoid** \"\ *n* -s **1 :** a morphologically differentiated part of a cell (as a Golgi body or a mitochondrion) **:** ORGANELLE **2 :** any of various minute organized body structures (as a stinging hair or a nematocyst) — compare ORGANELLE

**or·gano·lep·tic** \¦ȯ(r)gənō¦leptik, ȯ(r)¦ganə¦-\ *adj* [F *organoleptique*, fr. *organ-* + Gk *lēptikos* disposed to take or accept, fr. *lēptos*, verbal of *lambanein* to take, seize + *-ikos* -ic — more at LATCH] **1 :** affecting or making an impression upon one or more of the organs of special sense **2 a :** of, relating to, or involving the employment of the sense organs — used esp. of subjective testing (as of flavor, odor, appearance) of food and drug products **b :** relating to or determined by organoleptic examination ⟨~ grade of milk⟩ — **organoleptically** *adv*

**or·gano·log·ic** \-¦läjik\ *or* **or·gano·log·i·cal** \-jəkəl\ *adj* **:** of or relating to organology

**or·ga·nol·o·gy** \,ȯ(r)gə'näləjē\ *n* -ES [ISV *organ-* + *-logy*] **:** the study of the organs of animals and plants; *esp* **:** SPLANCHNOLOGY

**or·gano·mercurial** \¦ȯ(r)gə(,)nō, ȯ(r)¦ganō+\ *n* [*organ-* + *mercurial*] **:** an organic compound or a pharmaceutical preparation containing mercury

**or·gano·metallic** \"+\ *adj* [ISV *organ-* + *metallic*] **:** of, relating to, or constituting an organic compound of a metal or sometimes of a metalloid or a nonmetal (as phosphorus) **:** METALLO-ORGANIC; *esp* **:** of, relating to, or being a compound in which the metal is attached directly to carbon

**or·ga·non** \'ȯ(r)gə,nän\ *n* -s [Gk, lit., tool, instrument — more at ORGAN] **:** an instrument for acquiring knowledge; *specif* **:** a body of methodological doctrine comprising principles for scientific or philosophic procedure or investigation

**or·gano·phil·ic** \¦ȯ(r)gənō¦filik, ȯ(r)¦ganə¦-\ *also* **or·gano·phile** \'===,fīl, ='==-\ *adj* [*organ-* + *-philic* or *-phile*] **:** of, relating to, or having a strong affinity for organic compounds — used esp. of colloids that swell and form solvates in organic liquids commonly used as solvents; compare HYDROPHILIC

**or·ganophy·ly** \,ȯ(r)gə'näfəlē; 'ȯ(r)gənō,fīlē, ȯ(r)'ganə,-\ *n* -ES [*organ-* + *phyl-* + *-y*] **:** phylogeny of organs

**or·ga·no pie·no** \,ȯ(r)gə(,)nōpē'ä(,)nō, -pē'e-\ *adv* [It] **:** with full organ — used as a direction in music

**or·gano·plas·tic** \¦ȯ(r)gə(,)nō¦plastik, ȯ(r)¦ganə¦-\ *adj* [ISV *organ-* + *-plastic;* prob. orig. formed as F *organoplastique*] *biol* **:** producing organs

**or·ga·nos·co·py** \,ȯ(r)gə'näskəpē\ *n* -ES [ISV *organ-* + *-scopy*] **:** examination of the bodily organs

**or·gano·silicon** \¦ȯ(r)gə(,)nō, ȯ(r)¦ganō+\ *adj* [*organ-* + *silicon*] **:** of, relating to, or constituting an organic compound of silicon esp. when the silicon is attached directly to carbon (as in silicones)

**or·gano·sol** \ȯ(r)'ganə,säl, -sōl\ *n* [*organ-* + *sol*] **:** a sol in which an organic liquid forms the dispersion medium; *esp* **:** a dispersion of a powdered thermoplastic resin (as a vinyl resin) in a liquid mixture containing a volatile thinner as well as a plasticizer that is considerably less viscous than a plastisol and is used similarly

**or·gano·therapeutic** \¦ȯ(r)gə(,)nō, ȯ(r)¦ganə+\ *adj* [*organ-* + *therapeutic*] **:** of, relating to, or used in organotherapy

**or·gano·therapy** \"+\ *n* [ISV *organ-* + *therapy*] **:** a treatment of disease by the administration of animal organs or of their extracts

**or·gano·trophic** \"+¦träfik, -rōf-\ *adj* [*organ-* + *-trophic*] **:** relating to the formation and nutrition of living organs

**or·gano·trop·ic** \"+¦träpik\ *adj* [*organ-* + *-tropic*] **:** attracted to, localizing in, or entering the body by way of the visceral and abdominal organs or occas. the somatic tissue ⟨an ~ disease⟩ ⟨~ viruses⟩ — compare NEUROTROPIC — **or·gano·trop·i·cal·ly** \-pək(ə)lē\ *adv* — **or·ga·not·ro·pism** \,ȯ(r)gə'nä·trə,pizəm\ *n* -s — **or·ga·not·ro·py** \-pē\ *n* -s

**organ-pipe cactus** *or* **organ cactus** *n* **:** any of several tall upright cacti of the southwestern U. S. and adjacent Mexico: as **a :** SAGUARO **b :** a cactus (*Lemaireocereus marginatus* or *Pachycereus marginatus*) branching near the base to form several ridged upright stems and bearing 2-inch flowers that are red without and greenish white within

**organ-pipe coral** *n* **:** an alcyonarian coral of the genus *Tubipora* having a usu. red or purple skeleton consisting of a mass of parallel cylindrical tubes united at intervals by horizontal plates and being found in tropical parts of the Indian ocean and the Pacific ocean

**organ point** *n* **:** PEDAL POINT

**organ rest** *n* **:** CLARION 5

**organs** *pl of* ORGAN, *pres 3d sing of* ORGAN

**or·ga·num** \'ȯ(r)gənəm, ÷='gan-, ÷='gän-\ *n* -s [ML, fr. L, organ — more at ORGAN] **1 :** ORGANON **2 a :** a polyphonic voice part accompanying the cantus firmus note against note in parallel motion, usu. at a fourth, fifth, or octave above or below **b :** part writing or singing of this nature in two, three, or four parts — called also *diaphony*

**or·ga·ny** \'ȯ(r)gənē\ *n* -ES [modif. of L *origanum* — more at ORIGANUM] **:** ORIGAN

**or·gan·za** \ȯ(r)'ganzə\ *n* -s *often attrib* [prob. alter. of *Lorganza*, a trademark] **:** a sheer dress fabric in plain weave usu. made of silk, rayon, or nylon and with more body and stiffness than organdy

**or·gan·zine** \'ȯ(r)gən,zēn\ *n* -s *often attrib* [F or It; F *or-*

*gansin,* fr. It *organzino,* prob. fr. *Urgench,* town in Soviet Central Asia where it was first manufactured + It *-ino* -ine] **:** a raw silk yarn formed from two or more twisted strands doubled and twisted in the reverse direction when plied that is used for warp threads in fine fabrics — compare ¹TRAM

**or·gasm** \'ȯ(r),gazəm\ *n* -s [NL *orgasmus,* fr. Gk *orgasmos,* fr. *organ* to grow ripe, swell, be lustful; akin to Gk *orgē* impulse, anger, OIr *ferc, ferg* anger, Skt *ūrj, ūrjā* nourishment, power, strength] **1 a :** intense or paroxysmal emotional excitement **b :** an instance or outburst of such excitement **2 a** *obs* **:** a condition of turgescence and physiologic excitement of a body part or organ **b** (1) **:** the climax of sexual excitement typically occurring toward the end of coitus; *specif* **:** the sudden release of tensions developed during coitus usu. accompanied in the male by ejaculation (2) **:** an instance of the occurrence of such a climax

**or·gas·mic** \(')ȯ(r)¦gazmik\ *adj* **1 :** like or suggestive of an orgasm **2 :** tending to produce an orgasm

**or·gas·tic** \-astik\ *adj* [fr. *orgasm,* after such pairs as E *sarcasm: sarcastic*] **:** of, relating to, or being an orgasm

**or·geat** \'ȯr,zhä\ *n* -s [F, fr. MF, fr. *orge* barley, fr. L *hordeum* — more at HORDEUM] **1 :** a nonalcoholic drink prepared from the sweetened juice of almonds and other flavorings (as orange blossom essence, rose water) and usu. served cold **2 :** a sweet almond-flavored nonalcoholic syrup used as a cocktail ingredient or food flavoring — called also *sirop d'orgeat*

**or·gia** \'ȯ(r)jēə, -)gēə\ *n, pl* **orgia** *also* **orgias** [L, pl. — more at ORGY] **:** ORGY 1, 2

**or·gi·ast** \'ȯ(r)jē,ast\ *n* -s [Gk *orgiastēs,* fr. *orgiazein* to celebrate orgies, fr. *orgia* orgies — more at ORGY] **:** one who celebrates orgies

**or·gi·as·tic** \¦ȯ(r)jē¦astik, -a(a)s,- -tēk\ *also* **or·gi·as·ti·cal** \-tə̇kəl, -tēk-\ *adj* [Gk *orgiastikos,* fr. (assumed) *orgiastos* (verbal of *orgiazein*) + *-ikos,* -ic] **1 :** tending to produce wild emotion ⟨~ music⟩ **2 :** of or having the character or quality of an orgy — **or·gi·as·ti·cal·ly** \-tə̇k(ə)lē, -tēk-, -li\ *adv*

**orgn** *abbr* organization

**or·gone** \'ȯr,gōn\ *n* -s [prob. fr. *orgasm* + *-one* (as in *hormone*)] **:** a vital energy held to pervade nature and to be accumulable for use by the human body by sitting in a specially designed box

**orgue** \'ȯ(ə)rg\ *n* -s [F, lit., organ, fr. L *organum* — more at ORGAN] **:** one of a number of long thick timbers pointed and shod with iron and formerly suspended over or in the vaulted passage behind a gateway to be let down in case of attack

**or·gu·i·nette** \¦ȯ(r)gə¦net\ *n* -s [irreg. (influence of F *orgue*) fr. ¹*organ* + *-ette*] **:** a small portable reed organ mechanically played by turning a crank

**or·gu·lous** \'ȯ(r)g(y)ələs\ *also* **or·gil·lous** \-gəl-\ *adj* [ME *orgeilus, orgulous,* fr. OF *orgueilleus, orguilleus,* fr. *orgueil, orguil* pride (of Gmc origin; akin to OHG *urguol* remarkable, distinguished) + *-eus* -ous] **1 :** PROUD, HAUGHTY ⟨such ~ vaunting is best cured by bloodletting —E.G.Bulwer-Lytton⟩ **2 :** SHOWY, SPLENDID ⟨the organ began — an ~ roll — and the academic procession passed slowly down the aisle —J.P. Bishop⟩ — **or·gu·lous·ly** *adv*

**or·gy** *also* **or·gie** \'ȯrjē, 'ȯ(ə)j-, -ji\ *n, pl* **orgies** [MF *orgie,* fr. L *orgia,* pl., fr. Gk *orgia;* akin to Gk *ergon* work — more at WORK] **1 :** secret ceremonial rites held in honor of any of various deities (as of ancient Greece) and characterized by ecstatic or frenzied singing and dancing — usu. used in pl. **2 :** a ritual observance or ceremony **3 :** drunken revelry **:** CAROUSAL **4 a :** a manifestation of excessive indulgence in some predilection ⟨an ~ of speechmaking⟩ ⟨indulge in an ~ of destruction⟩ **b :** a riotous display ⟨an ~ of pink stucco⟩

**or·ham·wood** \'ȯrəm,=\ *n* [*orham* prob. modif. of F *orme* elm (fr. L *ulmus*) + E *wood* — more at ELM] **:** AMERICAN ELM

**ori-** *comb form* [MF, fr. LL, fr. L *or-, os* mouth — more at ORAL] **1 :** mouth ⟨*orifice*⟩ **2 :** mouth and ⟨*orifacial*⟩

**-oria** *pl of* -ORIUM

**-o·ri·al** \¦ōrēəl,¦ȯr-\ *adj suffix* [ME *-oriale,* fr. L *-orius* -ory + ME *-ale* -al] **:** of, belonging to, or connected with ⟨gress*orial*⟩ ⟨insess*orial*⟩

¹**orib·a·tid** \ō'ribəd-əd, ¦ōrə¦bad-·\ *or* **orib·a·toid** \ō'ribə,tȯid, ¦ōrə¦bad·,ȯid\ *adj* [*oribatid* fr. NL *Oribatidae; oribatoid* fr. NL *Oribatoidea*] **:** of or relating to the Oribatoidea

²**oribatid** \"\ *n* -s [NL *Oribatidae*] **:** a mite of the superfamily Oribatoidea

**ori·bat·i·dae** \,ōrə'bad·ə,dē\ *n pl, cap* [NL, fr. *Oribata,* type genus + *-idae*] *in some classifications* **:** a family of mites coextensive with the superfamily Oribatoidea

**ori·ba·toi·dea** \,ōrəbə'tȯidēə\ *n pl, cap* [NL, fr. *Oribata* (perh. fr. Gk *oreibatēs* mountain-ranging, fr. *oros* mountain + *-batēs,* fr. *bainein* to go) + *-oidea* — more at ORIENT, COME] **:** a superfamily of small oval eyeless nonparasitic mites having a heavily sclerotized integument with a leathery appearance

**or·i·bi** \'ȯrəbē\ (*also* **ou·re·bi** \'u̇rə-\ *n* -s [Afrik *oribi,* prob. fr. Hottentot (Nama dial.) *arab*] **:** any of several small antelopes (genus *Ourebia*) of southern and eastern Africa that are tawny yellow above and white below and have straight annulated horns about five inches long

**or·i·chalc** *or* **or·i·chalch** \'ȯrə,kalk\ *n* -s [L *orichalcum,* fr. Gk *oreichalkos,* lit., mountain copper, fr. *oros* mountain + *chalkos* copper — more at ORIENT, CHALC-] **1 :** a yellow metallic substance considered precious by the ancient Greeks **2 :** brass rich in zinc

**or·i·chal·cum** \,ȯrə'kalkəm\ *n* -s [L] **:** ORICHALC

**ori·el** \'ōrēəl, 'ȯr-\ *n* -s [ME, porch, gallery, oriel, fr. MF *oriol* porch, gallery, prob. fr. ML *auleolum* niche, small chapel, dim. of *aula* court, hall, fr. L — more at AULA] **:** a large bay window of semihexagonal or semisquare plan projecting from the face of a wall and supported by a corbel or bracket

oriel

**ori·en·cy** \'ōrēənsē, 'ȯr-\ *n* -ES [²*orient* + *-cy*] **:** the quality or state of being orient **:** BRILLIANCY

¹**ori·ent** \'ōrēənt, 'ȯr-, -ē,ent\ *n* -s [ME, fr. MF, fr. L *orient-, oriens,* fr. pres. part. of *oriri* to rise, come forth — more at RISE] **1** *archaic* **:** the part of the firmament or of the world where the sun rises **:** EAST 1 — compare OCCIDENT **2** *usu cap* **:** EAST 2 ⟨sailed for the *Orient*⟩ **3** *archaic* **:** DAWN, SUNRISE **4 a :** a pearl of great luster **b :** the luster or sheen of a pearl **5 :** a moderate to strong blue that is redder than average Prussian blue

²**orient** \"\ *adj* [ME, fr. MF, *orient,* n.] **1** *archaic* **:** ORIENTAL 1 **2 a :** LUSTROUS, SPARKLING ⟨~ gems⟩ **b** *archaic* **:** GLOWING, RADIANT ⟨with ~ colors waving —John Milton⟩ **3** *archaic* **:** RISING ⟨the ~ moon —P.B.Shelley⟩

³**ori·ent** \-ē,ent *sometimes when no syllable-increasing suffix follows* -ēənt\ *vt* -ED/-ING/-s [F *orienter,* fr. MF, fr. *orient,* n.] **1 a :** to cause to face or point toward the east; *specif* **:** to build (as a church or temple) with the longitudinal axis pointing eastward and the chief altar at the eastern end **b :** to define the position of in relation to the east **c :** to set or arrange in any determinate position in relation to the points of the compass **d :** to ascertain the bearings of ⟨determined to get some distance up the ridge above the hut, to ~ myself with the country —Elyne Mitchell⟩ **2 :** to set right by adjusting to facts or principles **:** put into correct position or relation **:** acquaint with the existing situation ⟨will help freshmen to ~ themselves to college and to life —*advt*⟩ **3 :** to direct toward **:** place in relation to ⟨~ youth to the responsibilities of military service —*Amer. Child*⟩ **4 a :** to direct to a given position in a chemical compound esp. about a nucleus ⟨the ~*ing* effect of the nitro group⟩ **b :** to ascertain the relative positions of atoms or groups in (a compound) **c :** to cause the axes of the molecules of (as a fiber or material) to assume the same direction ⟨~ a fiber by stretching⟩ ⟨highly ~*ed* cellulose⟩ **5 :** to place (a crystal) so that its crystallographic axes lie in conventionally fixed directions **6 :** to rotate (a map attached to a plane table) until the line of direction between any two of its points is parallel to the corresponding direction in nature

¹**ori·en·tal** \¦ōrē¦entᵊl, ¦ȯr-\ *adj* [ME, fr. MF, fr. L *orientalis* of or belonging to the East, fr. *orient-, oriens,* n., orient + *-alis* -al] **1** *often cap* **:** of, relating to, or situated in the Orient — compare OCCIDENTAL **2 a :** of superior grade, luster, or value — used of pearls and other precious stones; compare OCCIDENTAL 3 **b :** GLOWING **c** *sometimes cap* **:** being corundum or sapphire but simulating another gem in color ⟨~ amethyst⟩ ⟨~ aquamarine⟩ ⟨~ emerald⟩ **3** *often cap* **:** of, relating to, or having the characteristics of Orientals ⟨maintain . . . an ~ politeness and a set smile which nothing can dispel or penetrate —Joseph Chiari⟩ **4** *usu cap* **:** of, relating to, or constituting the biogeographic realm or region that includes Asia south and southeast of the Himalayas and the Malay archipelago west of Wallace's line — **ori·en·tal·ly** \-ᵊlē, -ᵊli\ *adv*

²**oriental** \"\ *n* -s *usu cap* **1 orientals** *pl, obs* **:** oriental languages **2 :** a member of one of the indigenous peoples of the Orient (as a Chinese, Indian, or Japanese)

³**ori·en·tal** \,ōre,en·'täl\ *n, pl* **ori·en·ta·les** \-ä,lās\ *usu cap* [AmerSp, fr. Sp, adj., easterner, fr. L *orientalis*] **:** URUGUAYAN

**oriental arborvitae** *n, usu cap O* **:** an Asiatic shrub or small tree (*Thuja orientalis*) having branchlets in vertical planes — compare AMERICAN ARBORVITAE

**oriental beetle** *n, usu cap O* **:** a small beetle (*Anomala orientalis*) of the family Scarabaeidae now established in the U. S. and having a larva that feeds on the roots of grasses and sugar cane

**oriental bezoar** *n, usu cap O* **:** a bezoar composed chiefly of resinous organic matter arranged in concentric layers about a hard foreign nucleus and found in the bezoar goat or the gazelle

**oriental bittersweet** *n* **:** a vigorous European climber (*Celastrus orbiculatus*) naturalized esp. in eastern No. America and having suborbicular to broadly obovate leaves with crenate teeth

**oriental blue** *n* **:** a strong blue that is redder and darker than Sèvres and redder and duller than cerulean blue (sense 1b) — compare ORIENT BLUE

**oriental bole** *n* **:** ²BOLE 3

**oriental cockroach** *also* **oriental roach** *n, sometimes cap O* **:** a dark or blackish brown medium-sized cockroach (*Blatta orientalis*) prob. originating in Asia but now nearly cosmopolitan in warm and temperate areas esp. about dwellings — called also *Asiatic cockroach, blackbeetle*

**oriental export porcelain** *n, usu cap O* **:** LOWESTOFT WARE 2

**oriental fruit fly** *n* **:** a trypetid fly (*Dacus dorsalis*) that attacks many fruits, vegetables, and other plants in Hawaii, Formosa, the Philippines, and the Malay archipelago

**oriental green** *n* **:** a moderate to strong green

**ori·en·ta·lia** \,ōrēən·'tālyə, ,ȯr-, -ē,en-, -lēə\ *n pl, usu cap* [NL, fr. L, neut. pl. of *orientalis* oriental — more at ORIENTAL] **:** materials (as literary, artistic, archaeological products and remains) relating to the Orient

**ori·en·tal·ism** \-'entᵊl,izəm\ *n* -s *often cap* **1 :** a trait, custom, or habit of expression characteristic of oriental peoples **2 :** learning in oriental subjects **3 a :** an oriental turn of thought adopted by a western thinker **b :** a characteristic of oriental art or culture appearing in western practice

**ori·en·tal·ist** \-ᵊləst\ *n* -s *often cap* [*orientalism* + *-ist*] **:** a specialist in oriental subjects ⟨a very learned ~ —*Modern Language Notes*⟩

**ori·en·tal·i·ty** \-,en·'taləd·ē, -,en-·\ *n* -ES **:** the quality or state of being oriental

**ori·en·tal·iza·tion** \-,entᵊlə'zāshən, -ᵊl,ī'z-\ *n* -s *often cap* **:** the act or process of orientalizing or becoming orientalized

**ori·en·tal·ize** \-'entᵊl,īz\ *vb* -ED/-ING/-s *often cap* [¹*oriental* + *-ize*] *vt* **:** to make oriental **:** give oriental qualities or characteristics to ⟨left the West far more *Orientalized* than the East was Hellenized —Elmer Davis⟩ ~ *vi* **1 :** to become oriental **:** adopt oriental traits or attitudes **2 :** to pursue oriental studies

**oriental moth** *n, usu cap O* **:** an Asiatic moth (*Cnidocampa flavescens*) of the family Eucleidae now established in eastern No. America and having a larva that feeds on fruit and some shade trees

**oriental mustard** *n* **:** INDIAN MUSTARD

**oriental peach moth** *or* **oriental fruit moth** *n, sometimes cap O* **:** a small moth (*Grapholitha molesta*) prob. native to Japan but now of nearly cosmopolitan distribution and having a larva that is injurious to the twigs and fruit of orchard trees and esp. to the peach

**oriental pearl** *n* **1 :** a true or natural marine pearl **2 :** SLATE GRAY

**oriental plane** *n, usu cap O* **:** a Eurasian shade tree (*Platanus orientalis*) with broad 5- to 7-lobed leaves and globose bristly fruiting heads produced in clusters of 3 to 7

**oriental poppy** *n, usu cap O* **:** an Asiatic perennial poppy (*Papaver orientale*) commonly cultivated and having stiff coarse heavily haired leaves and bright scarlet, pink, orange, or salmon-colored flowers

**oriental rat flea** *n* **:** a flea (*Xenopsylla cheopis*) that is widely distributed on rodents and is a vector of plague

**oriental red** *n* **:** GOYA

**oriental rice borer** *n* **:** a crambid moth (*Chilo simplex*) with a larva that is destructive to rice in southern and eastern Asia

**oriental roller** *n, usu cap O* **:** a tumbler pigeon originating in Asia Minor and having a longer head and tail than ordinary tumblers

**oriental rug** *or* **oriental carpet** *n, usu cap O* **:** a handwoven or hand-knotted one-piece rug or carpet made in the Orient esp. in Asia and usu. having a pile produced by knotting one or several tufts of colored woolen or silk yarn around one or usu. two warps of cotton or wool with a woof shot being passed over each row

**oriental sore** *n, sometimes cap O* **:** leishmaniasis of the skin caused by a protozoan (*Leishmania tropica*), marked by persistent granulomatous and ulcerating lesions, and distributed widely in the Orient and in tropical regions

**oriental spruce** *n* **:** an evergreen tree (*Picea orientalis*) of the Caucasus and Asia Minor that is used as an ornamental and has pendulous branchlets with brown pubescence

**oriental topaz** *n* **:** a yellow corundum used as a gem

**orientalwood** \,==¦==,=\ *or* **oriental walnut** *n, often cap O* **:** AUSTRALIAN WALNUT

**ori·en·tate** \'ōrēən,tāt, 'ȯr-, -ē,en-; ,=='en,tāt; *usu* -ād·+V\ *vb* -ED/-ING/-s [F *orienter* (fr. MF) + E *-ate* — more at ORIENT] *vt* **:** ORIENT ⟨when they come to London, colonials ~ themselves by Piccadilly Circus —Ngaio Marsh⟩ ~ *vi* **1 :** to face or turn to the east

**ori·en·ta·tion** \,==ən·'tāshən *also* -,en-·\ *n* -s **1 a :** the directing or placing of something so as to face the east; *esp* **:** the building of a church or temple on an east-west axis with the chancel and main altar to the east **b :** the placing of a building in any determined relation to the points of the compass **2 a :** the act of determining one's bearings or settling one's sense of direction ⟨witnessed the bee's momentary pause for ~ before it headed back to the hive⟩ **b :** the settling of a sense of direction or relationship in moral or social concerns or in thought or art ⟨reflection conducive to the individual's intellectual and spiritual ~ —*College English*⟩ ⟨America has quite a different ~ toward new music —Ernst Krenek⟩ **3 :** choice or adjustment of associations, connections, or dispositions ⟨development toward a money ~ —W.E.Moore⟩ ⟨nations widely different in their political ~ —J.G.Colton⟩ **4 :** introduction to an unfamiliar situation **:** guidance in experience or activity of a new kind ⟨the ~ program set up for the benefit of new employees —*Dun's Rev.*⟩ **5 :** the change of position exhibited by some protoplasmic bodies within the cell in relation to external influences (as light or heat) or in relation to one another **6 a :** the relative positions of atoms or groups in a chemical compound esp. about a nucleus **b :** the determination of such positions — compare ³ORIENT 4 **7** *psychiatry* **:** awareness of the existing situation with reference to time, place, and identity of persons — **ori·en·ta·tion·al** \¦==(,)=¦tāshənᵊl, -shnəl\ *adj*

**ori·en·ta·tor** \-ād·ə(r), -ātə-\ *n* -s **:** an apparatus in which a man seated in a partly enclosed box or cage can be subjected to the motions and stresses experienced by an airplane pilot in flight

**orient blue** *n* **1 :** a grayish blue that is redder and paler than electric, greener than copenhagen, and redder, lighter, and stronger than Gobelin — compare ORIENTAL BLUE **2 :** ORIENT 5

**oriented** *adj* [fr. past part. of ³*orient*] **1 :** DIRECTED, RELATED ⟨this book, value-*oriented* throughout, associates itself with these more recent tendencies to seek a common human ethics which will be valid for all mankind —Cornelius Krusé⟩ **2 :** having psychological orientation ⟨on the fourth day she was alert and ~ —Milton Rosenbaum⟩

**ori·ent·er** *or* **ori·en·tor** \'==,entə(r)\ *n* -s **:** one who assists a newcomer in adjusting to a social situation or to the local routine

**orienting** *pres part of* ORIENT

**ori·en·tite** \'==·ən·,tīt; '==·ən-,tīt, -,en-·\ *n* -s [*Oriente,* province in eastern Cuba, its locality, + E *-ite*] **:** a mineral $Ca_4Mn_4Si_5O_{20}.4H_2O$ consisting of a hydrous calcium manganese silicate occurring in small brown orthorhombic crystals (hardness 4.5-5, sp. gr. 3)

**oriently** *adv, obs* **:** in an orient manner **:** CLEARLY, LUSTROUSLY

**orientness** *n* -ES *obs* **:** the quality or state of being orient **:** BRILLIANCY

**orient pink** *n* **:** a moderate yellowish pink that is yellower and paler than coral pink and yellower and less strong than peach pink

**orient red** *n* **:** GOYA

**orients** *pl of* ORIENT, *pres 3d sing of* ORIENT

**orient yellow** *n* **:** CADMIUM YELLOW 2

**-ories** *pl of* -ORY

**or·i·fice** \'ȯrəfə̇s, 'är-\ *n* -s [MF, fr. LL *orificium,* fr. L *or-, os* mouth + *-ficium* (fr. *-ficus* -fic) — more at ORAL] **:** the mouth or opening of something **:** APERTURE, HOLE, VENT ⟨was obviously the ~ of entrance, because its edges were torn and lacerated —Basil Thomson⟩ — see CLAM illustration

**orifice box** *n* **:** a stilling basin under the inlet to a reservoir

**orifice plate** *n* **:** a disk containing a calibrated circular hole bolted between two abutting pipe flanges to regulate flow

**or·i·fi·cial** \¦==¦fishəl\ *adj* **:** of or relating to an orifice

**or·i·flamme** \'ȯrə,flam, 'är-, -laa(ə)m\ *n* -s [ME *oriflamble,* fr. MF *oriflamble, orieflambe,* fr. OF, fr. ML *aurea flamma,* lit., golden flame, fr. L *aurea,* fem. of *aureus* golden (fr. *aurum* gold) + *flamma* flame — more at ORIOLE, FLAME] **:** a banner inspiring lively devotion or courage **:** a bright or glorious ensign or symbol ⟨that gallant and chivalrous spirit that has streamed like an ~ through the storms of centuries —J.L.Lowes⟩

**orig** *abbr* origin; original; originally

**ori·ga·mi** \,ōrə'gämē\ *n* -s [Jap] **1 :** the art or process of Japanese paper folding **2 :** something (as a representation of a bird, insect, flower) made by origami

**or·i·gan** \-rə̇gən\ *also* **or·i·gane** \-,gan, -,gān\ *n* -s [ME *origane,* fr. MF *origan, origane* wild marjoram, fr. L *origanum*] **:** any of various aromatic mints (as wild marjoram)

¹**orig·a·num** \ə'rigənəm, ō'-\ *or* **oreg·a·no** \ə'regə,nō, ō'-\ *n* -s [*origanum,* fr. ME, fr. L, wild marjoram, fr. Gk *origanon; oregano* fr. Sp *orégano,* fr. L *origanum*] **:** any of various fragrant aromatic plants of the families Labiatae and Verbenaceae that are used as seasonings in cookery; *usu* **:** WILD MARJORAM

²**origanum** \"\ *n, cap* [NL, fr. L, wild marjoram] **:** a genus of Eurasian aromatic mints having small erect spikes of flowers arranged in panicles or corymbs and the calyx almost equally 5-toothed — see CRETAN DITTANY, WILD MARJORAM; compare MAJORANA

**origanum oil** *n* **1 :** an essential oil obtained from various herbs of the genus *Origanum* formerly used in medicine and perfumery **2 :** THYME OIL

¹**or·i·geni·an** \¦ȯrə¦jēnēən, ¦är-, -jen-\ *adj, usu cap* [*Origen* †A.D. 254? Christian writer, teacher, and theologian + E *-an*] **:** of, relating to, or attributed to Origen

²**origenian** \"\ *n* -s *usu cap* **:** an adherent or follower of Origen

**or·i·gen·ic** \-¦jenik\ *adj, usu cap* [*Origen* †A.D. 254? Christian writer, teacher and theologian + E *-ic*] **:** ORIGENIAN

**or·i·gen·ism** \'==jə,nizəm, -,je,n-\ *n* -s *usu cap* [*Origen* †A.D. 254? + E *-ism*] **:** the doctrines held by or attributed to the 3d century Christian theologian Origen who sought to work out a complete Christian philosophy based on the Scriptures and developed largely along Platonic lines

¹**or·i·gen·ist** \-,nə̇st\ *n* -s *usu cap* [LL *origenistes,* fr. *Origen* †A.D. 254? Christian writer, teacher and theologian + L *-istes* -ist] **:** an advocate of Origenism

²**origenist** \"\ *or* **or·i·gen·is·tic** \¦==(,)=¦nistik\ *adj, usu cap* [*origenism* + *-ist* or *-istic*] **:** of or relating to Origen or Origenism

**or·i·gin** \'ȯrəjən, 'är-\ *n* -s [ME *origine,* prob. fr. MF, fr. L *origin-, origo,* fr. *oriri* to rise, come forth — more at ORIENT] **1 :** ANCESTRY, PARENTAGE ⟨was of humble ~⟩ **2 a :** rise, beginning, or derivation from a source ⟨had its ~ . . . when a tramp printer established it as a weekly —*Amer. Guide Series: Pa.*⟩ **b :** primary source or cause **:** FOUNTAIN, SPRING ⟨a letter found on his clothes tells us the ~ of the quarrel —George Meredith⟩ **3 :** the more fixed, central, or larger attachment or part of a muscle — compare INSERTION **4 a :** the intersection of the axes of Cartesian coordinates **b :** any arbitrary zero from which a magnitude is reckoned

**syn** SOURCE, INCEPTION, ROOT, PROVENANCE, PROVENIENCE, PRIME MOVER: ORIGIN applies to a person, situation, or condition that marks the beginning of a course or development, to the point at which something rises or starts, or, sometimes, to effective causes ⟨it is probable that the *origin* of language is not a problem that can be solved out of the resources of linguistics alone —Edward Sapir⟩ ⟨the exact *origin* of the pain is not definitely known since it might reasonably be expected to appear in any unyielding tissue or it could arise from distention of the joint cavity itself —H.G.Armstrong⟩ ⟨found the *origin* of faith in an undifferentiated feeling of the Infinite and Eternal —W.R.Inge⟩ SOURCE, often interchangeable with ORIGIN, may center attention on a point of ultimate beginning whence something rises, flows, or emanates ⟨this mystery and meaning of freedom, sin, and grace are the perennial *sources* of the religious life —Reinhold Niebuhr⟩ ⟨the *source* of infection was traced to the feeding to hogs of raw garbage from ships from the Orient —*Americana Annual*⟩ ⟨the probable *sources* of civilization, roughly the three great river valleys of the Nile, the Tigris and Euphrates, and the Indus —R.W.Murray⟩ INCEPTION stresses the notion of an initiating, starting, or beginning point without implication about causes ⟨joining the group at its *inception*⟩ ⟨tin miners, who had to bring coal from south Wales, used the Watt engine from the time of its *inception* —S.F.Mason⟩ ⟨has taken part in the United States atomic energy program since its *inception* in 1942 —*Current Biog.*⟩ ROOT may suggest a first, ultimate, or fundamental source, often one not patently evident ⟨several of the large foundations . . . have been spending hundreds of thousands of dollars to get at the *root* of the trouble —J.M.Barzun⟩ PROVENANCE and PROVENIENCE designate the area, sphere, or group in which something has originated or from which it is derived ⟨any layman who is sufficiently interested in the cheese he eats to inquire about its *provenance* must have noticed how much a monastery background improves a cheese —*New Yorker*⟩ ⟨relatively recent words of scientific *provenance, e.g.,* appendicitis, iodine, quinine, and so on —H.L.Mencken⟩ ⟨the African *provenience* of northern Negroes —M.J.Herskovits⟩ PRIME MOVER may refer to an ultimate and original source of motive power that sets a thing moving; of personal agents it may refer to an inciter or instigator ⟨wind as the *prime mover* in impelling a sailing ship⟩ ⟨a committee on general education, in the organization of which your headmaster was a *prime mover* —A.W.Griswold⟩ ⟨evidence was also obtained implicating Heath as the *prime mover* in the affair and immediately upon Daniel's return the former was arrested —D.D.Martin⟩

¹**orig·i·nal** \ə'rijənᵊl, -jnəl\ *n* -s [ME, fr. MF, fr. ML *originale,* fr. L *originale,* adj., original, neut. of *originalis*] **1** *archaic* **:** the source or cause from which something arises **b :** PARENTAGE **c :** AUTHOR, ORIGINATOR **2** *archaic* **:** ORIGIN 2 **3 a :** a model, pattern, or archetype that is copied **b** (1) **:** a primary manuscript from which copies are made (2) **:** a direct impression produced by a typewriter esp. when made simultaneously with one or more carbon copies **c** (1) **:** the person or thing represented in a photograph or an artist's work (2) **:** a picture or work of art from which copies are made **4 :** a work composed firsthand **:** an artist's independent or spontaneous product ⟨caught up on their mail or . . .

wrote an ~ against the rainy season —Budd Schulberg) **5 a :** a person of fresh initiative or inventive capacity **:** INNOVATOR ⟨an ~ among popular pianists, combining jazz and romantic techniques in an unusually effective manner —Douglas Watt⟩ **b** *archaic* **:** ECCENTRIC 3 **6 :** a postage stamp from an original issue, as distinguished from a reprint or a reissue

**²original** \"\ *adj* [ME, fr. MF, fr. L *originalis*, fr. *origin-*, *origo* origin + *-alis* -al] **1 a :** of or relating to a rise or beginning **:** existing from the start **:** INITIAL, PRIMARY, PRISTINE ⟨~ plans called for many films to be made simultaneously —Cecile Starr⟩ ⟨the forests were in large part ~ —J.M. Mogey⟩ **b :** constituting a source, beginning, or first reliance ⟨the ~ account of the mutiny . . . as recorded by two of the survivors —F.R.Dulles⟩ **2 a :** taking independent rise **:** having spontaneous origin **:** not secondary, derivative, or imitative **:** FRESH, NEW ⟨gives us, as all good poetry does, an ~ angle of vision —C.D.Lewis⟩ **b :** gifted with powers of independent thought, direct insight, or constructive imagination **:** CREATIVE, FERTILE, GERMINAL, INVENTIVE ⟨esteemed as an ~ American composer⟩ **c :** constituting the product or model from which copies are made ⟨found the ~ manuscript, of which copies had long been current⟩ **syn** see NEW

**original bid** *n* **:** the first bid made in the auction in a card game — called also *opening bid*

**original bill** *n* **:** the initial bill of an equity proceeding not already before the court between the same parties standing in the same interests and consisting of a statement of the cause of complaint and petition for relief

**original contract** *n* **:** SOCIAL CONTRACT

**original cost** *n* **1 :** HISTORICAL COST 2 **2** *in public utility practice* **:** the cost of a property to that owner who first devoted it to public service **3** *in real estate practice* **:** the cost of a property to a present owner regardless of cost to a prior owner

**original gum** *n* **:** the intact adhesive gum on a postage stamp considered as evidence of the stamp's mint condition — abbr. *O.G.;* called also *full gum*

**orig·i·nal·i·ty** \ə,rijə'naləd-ē, -lətē, -i\ *n* -ES [F *originalité*, fr. *original*, adj. + *-ité* -ity] **1** *archaic* **:** the quality or state of being authentic or genuine **2 a :** freshness of aspect or design **:** independence or newness of style or character ⟨modern Brazilian architecture . . . is full of ~ and, above all, vitality —William Tate⟩ **b :** the power of independent thought or perception **:** capacity for constructive imagination or significant innovation **:** creative ability ⟨the directness of blunt truth and . . . a bardic ~ and vigor —C.B.Taylor⟩ **3 a** *patent law* **:** creation of a useful device, design, or process not before known or created **b** *copyright law* **:** novelty in the form of expression rather than in subject matter

**original jurisdiction** *n* **:** jurisdiction of first instance **:** authority of a court that takes cognizance of a controversy at the inception of legal proceedings therein

**orig·i·nal·ly** \ə'rijənᵊl|ē, -jnəl|, |i\ *adv* **1** *archaic* **:** by origin or derivation **:** from the first **:** INHERENTLY ⟨power ~ the people's⟩ **2 :** in the beginning **:** in the first place **:** INITIALLY, PRIMARILY **3 :** in a fresh or original manner ⟨rebinding of single books demanding . . . ~ designed covers —Edith Diehl⟩

**original minor scale** *n* **:** NATURAL MINOR SCALE

**original package doctrine** *n* **:** a doctrine whereby goods and commodities imported from one state of the U.S. into another or from a foreign country are usu. protected from being subject to the laws of the state of importation until sale is made by the importer so long as they are contained in the original unbroken individual package, container, or receptacle accepted from the shipper by the carrier and delivered in the same form to the importer

**original process** *n* **:** an original writ or summons issued by authority of a court as the foundation of and first step in a lawsuit, including always a notice to the defendant when to appear to make his defense and often an order to arrest the defendant, seize or attach his property, or garnishee a claim due from a third person to the defendant or an order that the defendant do or refrain from doing a specified act or that an officer of the court do a specified act in connection with the suit — distinguished from *final process* and *mesne process*

**original sin** *n* [ME, trans. of ML *peccatum originale*] **:** hereditary sin or defect often held in Christian theology to be transmitted from one generation to the next and inherited by each person as a consequence of the original sinful choice made by the first man of the human race — compare ACTUAL SIN

**original writ** *n* [ME, trans. of ML *breve originale*] **1 :** a writ issued under the great seal by which in English law the jurisdiction of the court was laid in beginning personal actions until the summons was substituted by the Judicature Act of 1873 — compare JUDICIAL WRIT, PRAECIPE **2 :** ORIGINAL PROCESS

**orig·i·nant** \ə'rij(ə)nənt\ *adj* [*origin* + *-ant*] *archaic* **:** ARISING, ORIGINATING

**¹orig·i·nary** \-jə,nerē\ *adj* [LL *originarius*, fr. L *origin-*, *origo* origin + *-arius* -ary — more at ORIGIN] **1** *obs* **:** NATIVE, ORIGINATING **2** *archaic* **:** constituting a source or cause

**²originary** *n* -s [LL *originarii* (pl.), fr. pl. of *originarius*, adj.] *obs* **:** ABORIGINE

**orig·i·nate** \ə'rijə,nāt, *usu* -ād·+V\ *vb* -ED/-ING/-S [prob. back-formation fr. *origination*] *vt* **1 :** to cause the beginning of **:** give rise to **:** INITIATE ⟨have *originated* a mass of legend —*Irish Digest*⟩ **2 :** to start (a person or thing) on a course or journey ⟨freight is *originated* at the dock⟩ ~ *vi* **:** to take or have origin **:** be derived **:** ARISE, BEGIN, START ⟨a retractor muscle that ~s on the body wall⟩ ⟨the train *originated* in Washington⟩ **syn** see SPRING

**originating company** *n* **:** DIRECT-WRITING COMPANY 1

**originating notice** *or* **originating summons** *n, Eng law* **:** a notice the service of which begins a legal proceeding — see ADJOURNED SUMMONS

**orig·i·na·tion** \ə,rijə'nāshən\ *n* -s [L *origination-*, *originatio*, fr. *origin-*, *origo* origin + *-ation-*, *-atio* -ation] **1** *obs* **:** DERIVATION, ETYMOLOGY **2 :** a coming into existence **:** BEGINNING, RISE ⟨a custom that has its ~ far back in time⟩ **3 :** ORIGIN 3 **4 :** a bringing into existence **:** CREATION, INVENTION, MAKING, PRODUCTION ⟨a representative legislature with annual meetings and the ~ of laws —C.G.Bowers⟩

**orig·i·na·tive** \ə'rijə,nād·iv\ *adj* **:** having ability to originate **:** CREATIVE, FERTILE, INVENTIVE ⟨the very greatest and most remarkable ~ geniuses —H.S.Hartfield⟩

**orig·i·na·tor** \ə'rijə,nād-ə(r), -ātə-\ *n* -s **:** one that originates

**or·i·gin·ist** \'ȯrəjənəst, 'är-\ *n* -s **1** *obs* **:** FOUNDER, ORIGINATOR **b :** a historian of origins **2 :** a theorist about origins

**origin of coordinates** [trans. of F *origine des coordonnées*] **:** the point of intersection of coordinate axes

**ori·hon** \'ōrē,hän\ *n* -s [Jap, prob. fr. *ori* fold + *hon* book, volume] **:** a strip of paper, papyrus, or vellum that is accordion-folded so as to divide the writing or printing which appears on one side into pages or columns and that sometimes has laced-on covers

**oril·lon** \ōrēyōⁿ\ *or* **oril·lion** \ə'rilyən\ *n* -s [F *orillon*, lit., little ear, dim. of *oreille* ear, fr. L *auricula*, dim. of *auris* ear — more at EAR] *archaic* **:** a projection built out at the corner of a bastion between flank and face from which to defend the flank

**ori·nasal** \¦ōrə, ¦ȯrə, ¦ärə+\ *adj* [*ori-* + *nasal*] **1 :** of or relating to the mouth and nose **2 :** pronounced (as a French nasal vowel) through both mouth and nose

**o ring** \'ō-\ *n, usu cap O* **:** a flat ring of synthetic rubber used as a gasket in sealing a joint against high pressures

**ori·no·co crocodile** \¦ōrə¦nō(,)kō-\ *n, usu cap O* [fr. *Orinoco* river, Venezuela] **:** a ferocious narrow-snouted crocodile (*Crocodylus intermedius*) of the Orinoco river and drainage basin

**ori·ole** \'ōrē,ōl, 'ȯr- *also* -ēəl\ *n* -s [F *oriol*, fr. OF, fr. ML *oryolus*, fr. L *aureolus* golden, dim. of *aureus* golden, fr. *aurum* gold; akin to Lith *auksas* gold, Arm *os-ki* gold and prob. to L *aurora* dawn — more at EAST] **1 :** any of various usu. brightly colored Old World birds constituting the family Oriolidae — see FIG-BIRD, GOLDEN ORIOLE **2 :** any of various American birds of the family Icteridae **3 :** LEATHER 4

**ori·ol·i·dae** \,==ōlə,dē, -'äl-\ *n pl, cap* [NL, fr. *Oriolus*, type genus (fr. ML *oryolus*) + *-idae*] **:** a family of passerine birds related to the crows and consisting of the Old World orioles most of which inhabit tropical and subtropical regions

**ori·on** \ə'rīən, ō'-, ō'- *sometimes* 'ōrēən *or* 'ōrē-\ *n* -s [ME *Orion*, constellation of seven stars located east of Taurus on the equator, fr. L, fr. Gk *Ōriōn*] **:** HOLLAND BLUE

**ori·sha** \'ōrə,shä\ *n, pl* **orisha** *or* **orishas** [Yoruba] **:** a Yoruba deity or spirit

**oris·mo·log·i·cal** \ə¦rizmə¦läjəkəl\ *or* **oris·mo·log·ic** \-jik\ *adj* [*orismological* fr. *orismology* + *-ical*; *orismologic* ISV *orismolog-* (fr. *orismology*) + *-ic*] **:** of or relating to orismology

**or·is·mol·o·gy** \,ȯrəz'mälə jē, ,är-\ *n* -ES [Gk *horismos* definition (fr. *horizein* to limit, define) + E *-logy* — more at HORIZON] **:** the science of defining technical terms **:** TERMINOLOGY

**or·i·son** \'ȯrəsən, 'är-, -rəzən\ *n* -s [ME, fr. OF, fr. LL *oration-*, *oratio*, fr. L, speech, oration — more at ORATION] **1 :** PRAYER ⟨nymph, in thy ~s be all my sins remembered —Shak.⟩ **2 :** mystical contemplation ⟨the steps of the ladder . . . in the art of contemplation are called, in technical terms, the degrees of ~ —Evelyn Underhill⟩

**-o·ri·um** \'ōrēəm, 'ȯr-\ *n suffix, pl* **-o·ri·ums** \-ēəmz\ *or* **-o·ria** \-ēə\ [L, fr. neut. of *-orius* -ory] **1 :** place for ⟨*natatorium*⟩ **2 :** thing used for ⟨*haustorium*⟩

**ori·ya** \ō'rē(y)ə\ *n, pl* **oriya** *or* **oriyas** *usu cap* **1 a :** a chiefly Hindu people of Orissa, India **b :** a member of such people **2 :** the Indic language of Orissa

**or·khon turk** \'ȯr,kän-\ *n, usu cap O&T* [fr. *Orkhon* river, northern Mongolia] **:** one of a Turkish tribe in the 8th century occupying the drainage of the Orkhon river in north central Mongolia, practicing intensive irrigation agriculture and using a runic alphabet derived from Aramaic

**ork·ney** \'ȯrknē\ *adj, usu cap* [fr. *Orkney* islands, northeastern Scotland] **:** of or from the Orkney islands constituting the county of Orkney, Scotland **:** of the kind or style prevalent in the Orkneys **:** ORKNEYAN

**¹ork·ney·an** \'ȯrknēən, ='==\ *adj, usu cap* [*Orkney* islands + E *-an* (adj. suffix)] **1 :** of, relating to, or characteristic of the Orkney islands **2 :** of, relating to, or characteristic of the people of the Orkney islands

**²orkneyan** \"\ *n* -s *cap* [*Orkney* islands + E *-an* (n. suffix)] **:** a native or inhabitant of the Orkney islands

**orkney skiff** *n, usu cap O* **:** a beamy clinker-built fishing skiff used off the Orkney islands of Scotland

**ORL** *abbr* owner's risk of leakage

**orle** \'ȯr(ə)l\ *n* -s [MF, lit., border, hem, fr. *orler* to put a hem on, fr. (assumed) VL *orulare*, fr. (assumed) VL *orula* border, hem, fr. L *ora* border, rim, coast — more at ORAL] **1** *heraldry* **a :** a number of small charges arranged so as to form a border within the edge of the field ⟨an ~ of martlets⟩ **b :** a border within and parallel to but not touching the edge of the field **c :** the wreath or chaplet surmounting or encircling the helmet of a knight and bearing the crest **2 :** a narrow fillet at the top of a shaft separating it from the bell of the capital or at the bottom above the molding of the base — **in orle** *adv* **:** in the form of an orle round the escutcheon leaving the middle of the field vacant or occupied by something else — used of bearings on the shield

**or·lean** \'ȯrlēən, ȯr'lē(ə)n\ *n* -s [F *orléane*, by folk etymology (influence of *Orléans*, city in north central France) fr. NL *orellana* (specific epithet of *Bixa orellana*), after Francisco de *Orellana* †1549 Span. soldier and explorer who discovered the Amazon on the banks of which annatto is common] **:** ANNATTO 1a

**¹or·lea·nian** \(')ȯ(r)¦lēnyən, -ēnēən\ *adj, usu cap* [New *Orleans*, La. + E *-ian* (adj. suffix)] **1 :** of, relating to, or characteristic of New Orleans, La. **2 :** of, relating to, or characteristic of the people of New Orleans

**²orleanian** \"\ *n* -s *cap* [New *Orleans* + E *-ian* (n. suffix)] **:** a native or resident of New Orleans

**or·lean·ist** \'ȯ(r)lēənəst, 'ȯ(r)lyən-, ȯ(r)'lē(ə)n-\ *n* -s *usu cap* [F *orléaniste*, fr. *Orléans*, cadet branch of the Valois and Bourbon houses of France + *-iste* -ist] **:** an adherent or supporter of the Orleans family in its claim to the throne of France on the ground of descent from a younger brother of Louis XIV and usu. of the moderate conservative policies associated with it — compare LEGITIMIST

**orl fly** \'ȯr(ə)l-\ *n* [E dial. *orl* alder (fr. ME *oryelle*, alter. of *alder*, *aller*) + E *fly* — more at ALDER] **:** a British alderfly (*Sialis lutaria*)

**or·lo** \'ȯr(,)lō\ *n* -s [It, lit., border, hem, fr. *orlare* to hem, fr. (assumed) VL *orulare*] **1 :** ORLE 2 **2 :** the smooth surface between two flutes of a shaft **3 :** the surface between two grooves of a triglyph **4 :** a flat plinth of any width

**or·loff** \'ȯr,läf, -lȯf, ='=\ *n* -s *usu cap* [after Count Aleksei Grigorievich *Orlov* †1808 Russ. nobleman who started the breed] **:** a Russian breed of trotting horses evolved by interbreeding Dutch, Frisian, and Arabian horses and including a large heavy harness horse that is usu. black and a lighter speedier horse that is commonly gray and is sometimes used for racing

**Or·lon** \'ȯr,län, 'ȯ(ə)l-\ *trademark* **1** — used for an acrylic fiber made in filament or staple form, characterized often by its high bulk and soft warm hand, used esp. in bulky suitings, in knitted goods, and because of its resistance to sunlight in curtains and awnings, and often blended with other fibers in fabrics **2 :** a yarn or fabric made of Orlon fiber

**or·lop deck** \'ȯr,läp-\ *n* [*orlop* fr. ME *overlop* deck of a single-decker, fr. MLG *overlōp*, lit., something that overleaps, fr. *over* + *lōp* leap, fr. *lōpen* to leap, run; akin to OHG *ubar* over and to MD *lōpen* to run — more at OVER, LEAP] **1 :** the deck below the lower deck **:** the lowest continuous deck in a ship having more than three decks — see DECK illustration **2 :** the lowest deck in a ship

**or·mer** \'ȯ(r)mə(r)\ *n* -s [F dial. (Isle of Guernsey), prob. fr. *or-* (fr. L *auris* ear) + *mer* sea, fr. L *mare*; fr. the shape of the shell — more at EAR, MARINE] **:** ABALONE

**or·mo·lu** \'ȯ(r)mə,lü\ *n* -s *often attrib* [F *or moulu*, lit., ground gold] **1** *archaic* **:** gold ground for use in gilding; *also* **:** metal gilded with ground gold **2 :** a brass made to imitate gold and used in mounts for furniture and for other decorative purposes — called also *mosaic gold* **3 :** something pretending to more than its real value or quality **:** something showy rather than genuine ⟨some ~ vocal numbers —Nat Hentoff⟩ ⟨fiction relating inordinate and ~ violence —*Times Lit. Supp.*⟩

**ormolu varnish** *n* **:** a varnish used to give the appearance of gold

**or·mo·sia** \ȯ(r)'mōzh(ē)ə\ *n, cap* [NL, fr. Gk *hormos* chain, necklace + NL *-ia*; fr. the use of its berries as beads — more at SERIES] **:** a genus of shrubs and trees (family Leguminosae) chiefly of So. America and Central America with pink to reddish wood — see JUMBY BEAN, NECKLACE TREE

**¹or·na·ment** \'ȯ(r)nəmənt\ *n* -s [ME *ornament*, *ornement*, fr. OF *ornement*, fr. L *ornamentum*, fr. *ornare* to furnish, embellish + *-mentum* -ment — more at ORNATE] **1** *archaic* **:** a useful accessory (as of clothing, furniture) **:** ADJUNCT; *esp* **:** an article or object used in a church service **2 a :** something that lends grace or beauty **:** a decorative part or addition **:** a structural component or applied detail that embellishes ⟨the profiles and the carved ~s of the moldings —D.S.Robertson⟩ **b :** a manner, quality, or trait that adorns or beautifies ⟨the various devices of poetical ~ —*Encyc. Americana*⟩ **3 :** a person whose virtues or graces add luster to his place, time, or society ⟨the greatest teachers and ~s of our species —T.L. Peacock⟩ ⟨the greatest mathematician of his age and an ~ of the academies of Berlin and St. Petersburg —Paul Koelner⟩ **4 :** the act of adorning or beautifying **:** DECORATION, ORNAMENTATION ⟨indulged in excessive ~⟩ **5 :** an embellishing note or notes (as a trill, appoggiatura, mordent) not belonging to the essential musical harmony or melody and indicated by the composer or esp. in the 16th to 18th centuries introduced by the performer for a decorative effect **:** GRACE — called also *embellishment, fioritura*

**²or·na·ment** \-,ment, -mənt — *see* ²-MENT\ *vt* -ED/-ING/-S **:** to provide with ornament **:** DECORATE, EMBELLISH ⟨touched nothing that he did not ~ with his learning and injure with his theories —Harvey Graham⟩ **syn** see ADORN

**¹or·na·men·tal** \¦ȯ(r)nə¦mentᵊl\ *adj* **:** having decorative quality or value ⟨encourages the useful rather than the ~ public virtues —Ellen Glasgow⟩ — **or·na·men·tal·i·ty** \,==,mən-'taləd-ē, -,men-·, -ləd-ē, -i\ *n* -ES — **or·na·men·tal·ly** \¦==¦mentᵊlē, -ᵊli\ *adv* — **or·na·men·tal·ness** \,=='mentᵊlnəs\ *n* -ES

**²ornamental** \"\ *n* -s **:** a decorative object; *esp* **:** a plant cultivated for its beauty rather than for use

**or·na·men·tal·ism** \,=='mentᵊl,izəm\ *n* -s **:** a tendency to ornamental display

**or·na·men·tal·ist** \-ᵊləst\ *n* -s **:** one who uses ornamentation freely

**or·na·men·ta·tion** \,ȯ(r)nəmən'tāshən, -,men-\ *n* -s [²*ornament* + *-ation*] **1 :** the act or process of ornamenting or the state of being ornamented ⟨an effort at ~ which did little to conceal the poverty of his imagination⟩ **2 :** a decorative device **:** EMBELLISHMENT; *collectively* **:** ORNAMENTS **3 :** characteristic markings or sculpture on the body of an animal

**or·na·ment·er** \'==,mentə(r)\ *n* -s **:** one that ornaments or decorates

**or·na·ment·ist** \-,mentəst, -,mən-\ *n* -s **:** a designer or maker of ornaments

**ornaments rubric** *n* **:** a rubric in the Book of Common Prayer concerning objects used in service taken from an act of Elizabeth I directing the retention of usage established in the second year of the reign of Edward VI

**ornary** *var of* ORNERY

**¹or·nate** \(')ȯr¦nāt, (')ȯ(ə)¦-, *usu* -ād-+V\ *adj* [ME *ornat*, fr. L *ornatus*, past part. of *ornare* to furnish, embellish; akin to L *ordinare* to order, arrange — more at ORDAIN] **1 :** marked by elaborate rhetoric or florid style ⟨~ poems can be more satisfactorily translated than simple ones —Walter Silz⟩ ⟨is clear and simple rather than ~ and pompous —*Times Lit. Supp.*⟩ **2 :** elaborately ornamented **:** amply or excessively decorated ⟨the most ~ carving and gold of the baroque churches —Lewis Mumford⟩

**syn** ORNATE, ROCOCO, BAROQUE, FLAMBOYANT, FLORID can mean, in common, elaborately and often pretentiously decorated or designed. ORNATE can apply to anything heavily adorned or ornamented or conspicuously embellished ⟨the extremely *ornate* gingerbread architecture of the eighties and nineties, when fanciful scrollwork trim, cupolas, and brackets were in vogue —*Amer. Guide Series: Ariz.*⟩ ⟨elaborate and *ornate* rituals —A.M.Young⟩ ⟨stately town houses, *ornate* with hand-carved woodwork, sparkling chandeliers, elaborate fireplaces, and imported rugs —*Amer. Guide Series: Ark.*⟩ ⟨a prose simple or *ornate* as the situation demands —William Peden⟩ ROCOCO, applying orig. to an elaborate playful and fanciful 18th century French decorative design, can apply to any similarly elaborate decoration, esp. with an ornateness of design (as of furniture, mirror frames) marked by proliferating curves and scrolls, shellwork, and general fancifulness and often extending to anything regarded as over-elaborately decorated ⟨the long *rococo* halls, giddy with plush and whorled designs in gold, were peopled with Roman fragments, white and disassociated; a runner's leg, the chilly half-turned head of a matron stricken at the bosom —Djuna Barnes⟩ ⟨the extreme refinement and delicacy of 12th century taste is a little saccharine, a little *rococo*, with just a hint of something meretricious verging on the tawdry —T.K. Whipple⟩ ⟨doesn't mind getting caught out with a *rococo* phrase or an overstuffed image —*Los Angeles* (*Calif.*) *Times*⟩ BAROQUE, often loosely interchangeable with ROCOCO but from a style of architecture prior to the rococo, suggests more an extravagant massive strength, often grotesqueness, of decorative quality, stressing the ingenious, varied, bizarre, or contorted, often in overintricate interrelationship ⟨a *baroque* style, it has been called by critics who admired this funeral sumptuousness, this glittering bric-a-brac, this aesthetic perversity —Claude Vigée⟩ ⟨a landscape of truly *baroque* invention, richly variegated and unfailing in its calculated surprises —*Times Lit. Supp.*⟩ ⟨*baroque* poetry with its frigid vehemence, its exhibitionistic forcefulness and false dynamism, its arbitrary twisting and distortions, its carefully arranged denaturalizing of living speech into a dead language, its strained mannerisms and calculated artificialities —H.L.Davis⟩ ⟨poetry is *baroque*. Baroque is tragic, massive and mystical. It is elemental. It demands depth and insight —W.S.Maugham⟩ FLAMBOYANT can suggest an ornateness but stresses more an excess of color or bold, daring, conspicuous display ⟨a flair for *flamboyant* clothes, including red slacks —*Time*⟩ ⟨a man of *flamboyant* egotism, given to pomposities of speech and absurdities of prose —*New Yorker*⟩ ⟨he indulges in *flamboyant* gestures and exaggerated strutting —Howard Barnes⟩ ⟨the worker's reaction was characterized more by a serious eagerness than a *flamboyant* enthusiasm —Samuel Liss⟩ FLORID suggests an overelaboration of rich color, figure of speech, ornamental flourish, and so on, implying showiness and conspicuous embellishment ⟨she would put on the *florid* costume, fix the gold circlets into the lobes of her ears, slip the garish imitation topaz onto her forefinger —William Fifield⟩ ⟨*florid* oriental imagery —Douglas Bush⟩ ⟨*florid* verbiage —H.G.Wells⟩ ⟨contrasting with the simplicity of these gardens was the exotic, *florid* display of fruit and vegetable stands —*Buick Mag.*⟩

**²ornate** *vt* -ED/-ING/-ES [ME *ornaten*, fr. L *ornatus*, past part. of *ornare*] *obs* **:** ADORN

**ornate aphid** *n* **:** an aphid (*Myzus ornatus*) widely distributed in northern Europe and now established in California that is a pest of numerous plants

**or·nate·ly** *adv* [ME *ornatly*, fr. *ornat* ornate + *-ly*] **:** in an ornate manner

**or·nate·ness** *n* -ES **:** the quality or state of being ornate

**or·na·ture** \'ȯrnə,chu̇(ə)r, -,chər\ *n* -s [MF, fr. LL *ornatura* ornament, fr. L *ornatus*, past part. + *-ura* -ure] **:** ORNAMENTATION

**or·neri·ness** \'ȯ(r)n(ə)rēnəs, 'än(-, -rinəs\ *n* -ES [*ornery* + *-ness*] **:** bad temper **:** PERVERSITY

**or·nery** *or* **on·ery** *or* **or·na·ry** \'ȯrn(ə)rē, 'ȯ(ə)n-, 'än-, -ri\ *adj, often* -ER/-EST [alter. of *ordinary*] **1** *chiefly dial* **a :** of inferior quality **:** COMMON **b :** LAZY, SHIFTLESS **2 a :** having a touchy disposition **:** inclined to be short-tempered **:** CANTANKEROUS ⟨he's been ~ all day⟩ ⟨the sorrel was an ~ cuss and threw anybody that tried to ride him⟩ **b :** independent and individualistic sometimes to the point of seeming eccentric ⟨Yankees are an ~ lot, but they're all right at heart⟩ **syn** see CONTRARY

**ornify** *vt* -ED/-ING/-ES [L *ornare* to embellish + E *-ify*] *obs* **:** ADORN

**or·nis** \'ȯrnəs, 'ȯ(ə)n-\ *n, pl* **orni·thes** \ȯ(r)'nī(,)thēz\ [G, fr. Gk, bird] **:** the birdlife of a region **:** AVIFAUNA

**-ornis** \"\ *n comb form, pl* **-ornithes** \ȯ(r)'nī(,)thēz\ [NL, fr. Gk *ornis* — more at ERNE] **:** bird ⟨*Heliornis*⟩ ⟨*Archaeornithes*⟩

**ornith-** *or* **ornitho-** *comb form* [L, fr. Gk, fr. *ornith-*, *ornis*] **:** bird ⟨*ornithichnite*⟩ ⟨*ornithography*⟩

**or·nith·ic** \(')ȯ(r)¦nithik\ *adj* [Gk *ornithikos*, fr. *ornith-* + *-ikos* -ic] **:** of, relating to, or characteristic of birds

**or·nith·ichnite** \¦ȯ(r)nəth+\ *n* [*ornith-* + *ichnite*] **:** the fossil footprint of a bird

**or·ni·thine** \'ȯ(r)nə,thēn\ *n* -s [ISV *ornith-* (in *ornithuric acid*) + *-ine*] **:** a crystalline or syrupy basic amino acid $H_2N(CH_2)_3CH(NH_2)COOH$ formed together with urea by hydrolysis of arginine (as by arginase) and in turn converted by reaction with ammonia and carbon dioxide into citrulline and then arginine; α,δ-diamino-valeric acid

**or·nith·is·chia** \,ȯ(r)nə'thiskēə\ *n pl, cap* [NL, fr. *ornith-* + *-ischia* (fr. Gk *ischion* hip joint) — more at ISCHIUM] **:** an order of archosaurian reptiles comprising herbivorous dinosaurs with tetraradiate pelves and including many bizarre forms (as the armored dinosaurs of the suborders Stegosauria and Ankylosauria and the horned dinosaurs of the suborder Ceratopsia) — **or·nith·is·chi·an** \¦=='=skēən\ *adj or n*

**or·ni·tho·ceph·a·lus** \¦ȯ(r)nə(,)thō'sefələs, ȯ(r),nithə's-\ *n, cap* [NL, fr. *ornith-* + *-cephalus*] **:** the first discovered and best known genus of pterodactyls (type of the family Ornithocephalidae)

**or·ni·tho·cop·ros** \-'käprəs, -,präs\ *n* -ES [NL, fr. *ornith-* + Gk *kopros* dung — more at COPR-] **:** the dung of birds **:** GUANO

**or·nith·o·delph** \ȯ(r)'nithə,delf\ *or* **or·nith·o·del·phi·an** \=,=='delfēən\ *n* -s [*ornithodelph* fr. NL *Ornithodelphia*; *ornithodelphian* fr. NL *Ornithodelphia* + E *-an*] **:** MONOTREME

**or·nith·o·del·phes** \=,=='del(,)fēz\ *or* **or·nith·o·del·phia** \-lfēə\ [NL, fr. *ornith-* + *-delphes* or *-delphia* (fr. Gk *delphys* womb) — more at DOLPHIN] *syn of* PROTOTHERIA

**or·nith·o·del·phi·an** \ˌ=ˌ=ˈ=ˈfēən\ *or* **or·nith·o·del·phic** \-fik\ *or* **or·nith·o·del·phous** \-fəs\ *adj* [NL *Ornithodelphia* + E *-an* or *-ic* or *-ous*] : MONOTREMATOUS

**or·ni·thod·o·ros** \ˌȯ(r)nəˈthädərəs\ *n, cap* [NL, fr. *ornith-* + Gk *doros* leather bag; akin to Gk *derma* skin — more at DERM-] : a genus of ticks (family Argasidae) containing forms that act as carriers of relapsing fever as well as Q fever

**or·ni·thod·o·rus** \"\ [NL] *syn of* ORNITHODOROS

**or·ni·tho·fauna** \ȯ(r)ˈnithə, ˈȯ(r)nə(ˌ)thō+\ *n* [NL, fr. *ornith-* + *fauna*] : the birds of a region or habitat : AVIFAUNA

**or·ni·tho·gae·an** *or* **or·ni·tho·ge·an** \"+ˈjēən\ *adj, usu cap* [NL, fr. *ornith-* + *-gaea, -gea* + E *-an*] : [1]NEW ZEALAND 2

**or·ni·thog·a·lum** \ˌȯ(r)nəˈthägələm\ *n* [NL, fr. Gk *ornithogalon* star-of-Bethlehem, fr. *ornith-* + *-galon* (fr. *gala* milk) — more at GALAXY] **1** *cap* : a large genus of Old World bulbous herbs (family Liliaceae) with basal leaves resembling grass and naked scapes bearing clusters of white, yellow, or greenish flowers with spreading perianth segments and flattened filaments — see STAR-OF-BETHLEHEM **2** -S : any plant of the genus *Ornithogalum*

**or·ni·thoid** \ˈȯ(r)nəˌthȯid\ *adj* [ISV *ornith-* + *-oid*] : resembling a bird : BIRDLIKE

**or·ni·tho·les·tes** \ȯ(r)ˌnithəˈle(ˌ)stēz, ˌȯ(r)nəthōˈl-\ *n, cap* [NL, fr. *ornith-* + Gk *lēistēs* robber; akin to L *lucrum* gain — more at LUCRE] : a genus of small light-boned carnivorous dinosaurs of the Jurassic with small skull, slender neck, and long slim fingers

**or·ni·tho·log·i·cal** \ȯ(r)ˌnithəˈläjəkəl, ˌȯ(r)nəthəˈl-, -jēk-\ *or* **or·ni·tho·log·ic** \-jik, -jēk\ *adj* : of or relating to ornithology — **or·ni·tho·log·i·cal·ly** \-jək(ə)lē, -jēk-, -li\ *adv*

**or·ni·thol·o·gist** \ˌȯ(r)nəˈthäləjəst\ *n* -S : a specialist in ornithology

**or·ni·thol·o·gy** \-jē, -ji\ *n* -ES [NL *ornithologia*, fr. *ornith-* + *-logia* -logy (fr. L)] **1** : a branch of zoology that deals with birds **2** : a treatise on ornithology

**or·nith·o·man·cy** \ȯ(r)ˈnithəˌman(t)sē\ *n* -ES [Gk *ornithomanteia*, fr. *ornith-* + *-manteia* -mancy] : divination by observation of the flight of birds : AUGURY

**or·ni·tho·mimid** \ȯ(r)ˌnithəˈmīməd, ˌȯ(r)nəthōˈm-, -ˈmim-\ *n* -S [NL *Ornithomimidae*, fr. *Ornithomimus* + *-idae*] : a dinosaur of the genus *Ornithomimus* or of the family Ornithomimidae

**or·ni·tho·mi·mus** \-ˈmīməs\ *n, cap* [NL, fr. *ornith-* + *-mimus*] : a genus (the type of the family Ornithomimidae) of small slender theropod dinosaurs of the Upper Cretaceous having toothless jaws and a birdlike skeleton

**or·ni·tho·my·zous** \ȯ(r)ˌnithəˈmīzəs, ˌȯ(r)nəthōˈm-\ *adj* [ISV *ornith-* + *myzo-* + E *-ous*] : parasitic on birds

**or·ni·thon** \ˈȯ(r)nəˌthän, ȯ(r)ˈnīˌth-\ *n* -S [L, fr. Gk *ornithōn*, fr. *ornith-*, *ornis* bird — more at ERNE] : AVIARY

**or·ni·tho·pap·pi** \ȯ(r)ˌnithəˈpaˌpī, ˌȯ(r)nəthōˈp-, -apē\ [NL, fr. *ornith-* + *-pappi* (fr. Gk *pappos* grandfather) — more at PAPA] *syn of* ARCHAEORNITHES

**or·ni·thoph·i·lous** \ˌȯ(r)nəˈthäfələs\ *adj* [*ornith-* + *-philous*] **1** : having a fondness for birds : bird-loving **2** : pollinated by birds

**or·nith·o·pod** \ȯ(r)ˈnithəˌpäd\ *n* -S [NL *Ornithopoda*] : a dinosaur of the suborder Ornithopoda

[1]**or·ni·thop·o·da** \ˌȯ(r)nəˈthäpədə\ *n pl, cap* [NL, fr. *ornith-* + *-poda*] : a suborder of the order Ornithischia comprising bipedal dinosaurs having distinctly digitigrade hind limbs usu. with only three functional toes which are blunt and having also hollow limb bones, a fourth trochanter on the femur, and no dermal armor

[2]**ornithopoda** \"\ [NL, fr. *ornith-* + *-poda*] *syn of* ORNITHISCHIA

**or·ni·thop·o·dous** \ˌ=ˌ=ˈ=ˌ=dəs\ *adj* [NL [2]*Ornithopoda* + E *-ous*] : of or relating to the Ornithischia

**or·ni·thop·ter** \ˈȯ(r)nəˌthäptə(r), ˌ=ˈ=ˌ=\ *n* -S [ISV *ornith-* + *-pter* (as in *helicopter*)] : a heavier-than-air airplane deriving its chief support and propulsion from flapping wings

**or·ni·thop·tera** \ˌȯ(r)nəˈthäpt(ə)rə\ *n, cap* [NL, fr. *ornith-* + *-ptera*] : a genus of large butterflies of the Malay archipelago closely related to the genus *Papilio* and having the females much larger and much less brightly colored than the males

**or·ni·tho·rhyn·chous** \ȯ(r)ˌnithəˈriŋkəs, ˌȯ(r)nəthōˈr-\ *adj* [NL *ornithorhynch*us + E *-ous*] : having a beak like that of a bird

**or·ni·tho·rhyn·chus** \ȯ(r)ˌnithəˈriŋkəs, ˌȯ(r)nəthōˈr-\ *n* [NL, fr. *ornith-* + *-rhynchus*] **1** *cap* : a genus (coextensive with the family Ornithorhynchidae) of egg-laying mammals including only the platypus **2** -ES : PLATYPUS

**or·ni·tho·scop·ic** \ȯ(r)ˌnithəˈskäpik, ˌȯ(r)nəthōˈs-\ *adj* : of or relating to ornithoscopy

**or·ni·thos·co·pist** \ˌȯ(r)nəˈthäskəpəst\ *n* -S : one that practices ornithoscopy

**or·ni·thos·co·py** \-pē\ *n* -ES [Gk *ornithoskopia*, fr. *ornithoskopos* predicting by observing the flight of birds (fr. *ornith-* + *skopos* observer — fr. *skopein* to view, watch —) + *-ia* -y — more at SPY] **1** : ORNITHOMANCY **2** : BIRD-WATCHING ⟨would alternate ~ with entomology —Rose Macaulay⟩

**or·ni·tho·sis** \ˌȯ(r)nəˈthōsəs\ *n, pl* **ornitho·ses** \-ˌsēz\ [NL, fr. *ornith-* + *-osis*] : PSITTACOSIS — used esp. of the form of the disease originating in birds other than psittacines

**or·ni·thot·ic** \ˌ=ˌ=ˈthäd·ik\ *adj* [fr. NL *ornithosis* after such pairs as NL *narcosis*: E *narcotic*] : of or relating to ornithosis

**or·ni·tho·tom·i·cal** \ȯ(r)ˌnithəˈtäməkəl, ˌȯ(r)nəthōˈt-\ *adj* [*ornithotomy* + *-ical*] : of or relating to ornithotomy

**or·ni·thot·o·mist** \ˌȯ(r)nəˈthäd·əməst\ *n* -S : a specialist in ornithotomy

**or·ni·thot·o·my** \-mē\ *n* -ES [ISV *ornith-* + *-tomy*] : the anatomy or dissection of birds

**or·nith·uric acid** \ȯ(r)ˌnəˈthyu̇rik-\ *n* [*ornithuric* ISV *ornith-* + *-uric*] : a crystalline acid $C_6H_5CONH(CH_2)_3CH(NHCOC_6H_5)COOH$ secreted in the urine of birds and reptiles

[1]**oro-** *comb form* [Gk *oros* mountain — more at RISE] : mountain ⟨orography⟩ ⟨orogenesis⟩ ⟨orophyte⟩ : elevation ⟨orometer⟩

[2]**oro-** *comb form* [L *or-*, *os* mouth — more at ORAL] : mouth ⟨oropharynx⟩ : mouth and ⟨oroanal⟩ ⟨orofacial⟩

**oro·anal** \ˈōr(ˌ)ō+\ *adj* [[2]*oro-* + *anal*] : functioning both as mouth and anus ⟨the ~ orifice of the starfish⟩

**oro·ban·cha·ce·ae** \ˌōrōˌbaŋˈkāsēˌē\ *n pl, cap* [NL, fr. *Orobanche*, type genus + *-aceae*] : a family of widely distributed brown or yellow leafless root-parasitic herbs (order Polemoniales) with axillary or spicate 2-lipped flowers and a 1-celled ovary

**oro·ban·cha·ceous** \ˌ=ˌ=ˌ=ˈkāshəs\ *adj* [NL *Orobanchaceae* + E *-ous*] : of or relating to the family Orobanchaceae

**oro·ban·che** \ˌ=ˌ=ˈbaŋ(ˌ)kē\ *n, cap* [NL, fr. L, broomrape, fr. Gk *orobanchē* dodder, broomrape, fr. *orobos* bitter vetch, chick-pea + *anchein* to strangle — more at ERS, ANGER] : a large genus (the type of the family Orobanchaceae) of root-parasitic herbs native to the Old World and western America that have fleshy yellowish white and spicate bracted flowers — see BROOMRAPE

**oro·bathymetric** \ˈōr(ˌ)ō+\ *adj* [[1]*oro-* + *bathymetric*] : of or relating to the representation of submerged mountains by depth contours ⟨~ charts of the north Atlantic —*Geog. Jour.*⟩

**oro·chi** \ōˈrōchē\ *also* **oro·chon** \-ōchən\ *or* **oro·kon** \-ōkən\ *n, pl* **orochi** *or* **orochis** *usu cap* **1** : a Tungus people dwelling near the mouth of the Amur that encoffins its dead on platforms **2** : a member of the Orochi people

**oro·crat·ic** \ˈōrəˈkrad·ik\ *adj* [[1]*oro-* + *-cratic*] : of or relating to a degree of roughness of the earth's surface comparable to that now existing

**oro·facial** \ˈōrə+\ *adj* [[2]*oro-* + *facial*] : of or relating to the mouth and face ⟨~ abnormalities⟩

**oro·gen** \ˈōrəjən, -ˌjen\ *also* **oro·gene** \-ˌjēn\ *n* -S [G *orogen*, back-formation fr. *orogenie* orogeny] **1** : a mountain mass that is a unit with respect to origin or uplift **2** : a region of mountain-making disturbance — compare KRATOGEN

**oro·gen·ic** \ˌ=ˈjenik\ *also* **oro·ge·net·ic** \-jəˈned·ik\ *adj* [in sense 1, ISV *orogeny* + *-ic* or *-etic*; in sense 2, ISV *orogen* + *-ic* or *-etic*] **1** : of, relating to, or produced by orogeny **2** : of, relating to, or characteristic of an orogen — **oro·gen·i·cal·ly** \-ˈjenək(ə)lē\ *adv*

**orog·e·ny** \ōˈräjənē\ *also* **oro·genesis** \ˌōrō+\ *n, pl* **orogenies** *also* **orogeneses** [ISV [1]*oro-* + *-geny*] : the process of mountain making esp. by folding of the earth's crust; *also* : a sequence of mountain-making movements closely associated in time and place — compare DIASTROPHISM, EPEIROGENY

**oro·graph** \ˈōrəˌgraf, -räf\ *n* [ISV [1]*oro-* + *-graph*] : a machine used in making topographical maps that is operated by being pushed across country and that records both distances and elevations

**oro·graph·ic** \ˈōrəˈgrafik\ *also* **oro·graph·i·cal** \-fəkəl\ *adj* [[1]*oro-* + *-graphic*, *-graphical*] : of or relating to mountains esp. with respect to their location, distribution, and accompanying phenomena — **oro·graph·i·cal·ly** \-fək(ə)lē\ *adv*

**orographic rain** *n* : the rain produced when a mountain deflects moisture-laden wind upward

**orog·ra·phy** \ōˈrägrəfē\ *n* -ES [ISV [1]*oro-* + *-graphy*; prob. orig. formed as F *orographie*] : a branch of physical geography that deals with mountains and mountain systems : OROLOGY

**oro·hip·pus** \ˌōrōˈhipəs\ *n, cap* [NL, fr. [1]*oro-* + *-hippus*] : a genus of very small American Eocene horses having four complete toes in front and three behind and having the tubercles of the molar teeth partially fused into a set of ridges

**oro·hydrographic** *or* **oro·hydrographical** \ˈōrō+\ *adj* [*orohydrographic* ISV *orohydrography* + *-ic*; *orohydrographical* fr. *orohydrography* + *-ical*] : of or relating to orohydrography

**oro·hydrography** \"+\ *n* [ISV [1]*oro-* + *hydrography*] : a branch of hydrography that deals with the relations of mountains to drainage

**oro·hydrologic** *or* **oro·hydrological** \"+\ *adj* [[1]*oro-* + *hydrologic, hydrological*] : OROHYDROGRAPHIC

**oro·hydrology** \"+\ *n* [[1]*oro-* + *hydrology*] : OROHYDROGRAPHY

**oro·ide** \ˈōrəˌwīd\ *or* **ore·ide** \-rēˌīd\ *n* -S [F *oréide*, prob. fr. *or* gold (fr. MF) + *-éide* (fr. Gk *eidos* form) — more at OR, WISE] : an alloy chiefly of copper and zinc or tin that resembles gold in color and brilliancy and is used in making cheap jewelry

**oro·kai·va** \ˌōrəˈkīvə\ *n, pl* **orokaiva** *or* **orokaivas** *usu cap* **1** : a people of Papua **2** : a member of the Orokaiva people

**oro·ke** \əˈrōkē\ *n, pl* **oroke** *or* **orokes** *usu cap* **1** : a Tungus people of Sakhalin Island related to the Orochi of the Amur river mouth region **2** : a member of the Oroke people

**oro·ko·lo** \ˌōrəˈkō(ˌ)lō\ *n, pl* **orokolo** *or* **orokolos** *usu cap* **1 a** : a Papuan people of Papua **b** : a member of such people **2** : the language of the Orokolo people

**orokon** *usu cap, var of* OROCHI

**or·o·log·i·cal** \ˌōrəˈläjəkəl\ *adj* : of or relating to orology — **or·o·log·i·cal·ly** \-k(ə)lē\ *adv*

**orol·o·gist** \ōˈräləjəst\ *n* -S : a specialist in orology

**orol·o·gy** \-jē\ *n* -ES [[1]*oro-* + *-logy*] : the science of mountains : OROGRAPHY

**orom·e·ter** \ōˈrämədˑə(r)\ *n* [[1]*oro-* + *-meter*] : an aneroid barometer having a second scale that gives the approximate elevation above sea level of the place where the observation is made

**oro·met·ric** \ˌōrəˈme·trik\ *adj* [[1]*oro-* + *-metric*] **1** : of or relating to orometry **2** : of or relating to an orometer

**orom·e·try** \ōˈräməˑtrē\ *n* -ES [ISV [1]*oro-* + *-metry*] : the measurement of mountains

**oron·chon** \ōˈränchən\ *or* **orun·chun** \-rən-\ *n, pl* **oronchon** *or* **oronchons** *or* **orunchun** *or* **orunchuns** *usu cap* **1** : a hunting people dwelling in Siberia and in small numbers over the border in Manchuria **2** : a member of the Oronchon people

**oro·no·co** *or* **oro·no·ko** \ˌōrəˈnō(ˌ)kō\ *also* **oro·noo·ko** \-nü(-\ *n* -S [perh. fr. *Orinoco* river, Venezuela; fr. the fact that it originated in South America] : a variety of tobacco

**or·o·pe·sa** \ˌōrəˈpāsə\ *n* -S [fr. *Oropesa*, British trawler that first used it] : one of a pair of torpedo-shaped floats towed one on each side by a minesweeper at a fixed distance to suspend the ends of the steel rope used to tear submerged mines from their moorings

**oro·pharyngeal** \ˈōr(ˌ)ō+\ *adj* [[2]*oro-* + *pharyngeal*] **1** : of or relating to the oropharynx **2** : of or relating to the mouth and pharynx

**oro·pharynx** \"+\ *n* [[2]*oro-* + *pharynx*] : the lower part of the pharynx that is continuous with the mouth and can be seen by direct vision

**oroph·i·lous** \(ˈ)ōˈräfələs\ *adj* [[1]*oro-* + *-philous*] : preferring or thriving in a subalpine environment

**oro·phyte** \ˈōrəˌfīt\ *n* -S [[1]*oro-* + *-phyte*] : a subalpine plant

**oro·sius** \ōˈrōzh(ē)əs, -ōsh(ē)əs, -ōzēəs, -ōsēəs\ *n, cap* [NL] : a genus of jassids of the Australian region that includes one (*O. argentatus*) which is a vector of several plant virus diseases

**orot·ic acid** \(ˈ)ōˈräd·ik-\ *n* [*orotic* prob. fr. *orot-* (fr. Gk *oros* whey) + *-ic* — more at SERUM] : a crystalline acid $C_4H_4N_2O_4$ that was first found in milk, is a growth factor for various microorganisms (as *Lactobacillus bulgaricus*), and is a precursor of the pyrimidines of nucleotides; 4-uracilcarboxylic acid

**oro·ti·ña** \ˌōrəˈtēnyə\ *n, pl* **orotiña** *or* **orotiñas** *usu cap* **1** : a Chorotegan people of western Costa Rica **2** : a member of the Orotiña people

**oro·tund** \ˈōrəˌtənd, ˈär-, ˈōr-\ *adj* [modif. of L *ore rotundo*, lit., with round mouth] **1** : marked by fullness, strength, and clearness of sound : SONOROUS — used esp. of the human voice ⟨an ~ voice like a preacher's or an actor's —Kenneth Roberts⟩ **2** : unduly full and strong in delivery or style : MAGNILOQUENT, POMPOUS, BOMBASTIC ⟨the surging and ~ utterances of *Leaves of Grass* —J.L.Lowes⟩ ⟨~ speeches about the full dinner pail —F.L.Allen⟩ **syn** see RESONANT

**oro·tun·di·ty** \ˌ=ˌ=ˈtəndəd·ē, -ndətē, -i\ *n* -ES : the quality or state of being orotund : orotund mode of intonation ⟨the ~ of the title —Francis Hackett⟩ ⟨orchestral ~ —Virgil Thomson⟩

**oroya fever** \əˈrȯiə-\ *n, usu cap O* [*oroya* fr. La *Oroya*, town in Peru where the disease causing it originally appeared] : the acute first stage of bartonellosis characterized by high fever and severe anemia

**orp** \ˈōrp\ *vi* -ED/-ING/-S [prob. back-formation fr. *orpit*] *chiefly Scot* : to fret morosely

[1]**or·phan** \ˈōrfən, ˈȯ(ə)f-, *dial* -nt\ *n* -S [LL *orphanus*, fr. Gk *orphanos*; akin to OE *ierfe* inheritance, OHG *erbi*, ON *arfi*, Goth *arbi*, OIr *orbe* inheritance, L *orbus* orphaned, bereft, Skt *arbha* small, weak] **1 a** : a child deprived by death of both father and mother : parentless child **b** : HALF-ORPHAN **c** : a young animal that has lost its mother by death or desertion ⟨pails for feeding calves, bottles and rubber nipples for feeding ~s —*Better Feeding of Livestock*⟩ **2** : one deprived of some protection or advantage ⟨~s of the storm⟩ ⟨internationalists who are ~s of the . . . national organization —*New Republic*⟩

[2]**orphan** \"\ *adj* [LL *orphanus* orphan, n.] : that is an orphan ⟨a home for a delicate . . . ~ boy —Flora Thompson⟩ ⟨the ~ pigs . . . drink their synthetic milk —*Farmer's Weekly So. Africa*⟩

[3]**orphan** \"\ *vt* **orphaned; orphaned; orphaning** \-f(ə)niŋ\ **orphans** **1** : to cause to become an orphan : deprive of parents ⟨as a boy on a Texas farm he had been ~*ed* by violence —*Saturday Rev.*⟩ ⟨~*ed* in babyhood, brought up . . . in public institutions —*Times Lit. Supp.*⟩ **2** : to deprive of some protection or advantage ⟨millions were ~*ed* when he died —*New Republic*⟩ ⟨~*ed* of their Primate —*Sunday Independent (Dublin)*⟩

**or·phan·age** \ˈōrf(ə)nij, ˈȯ(ə)f-, -fnēj\ *n* -S [[1]*orphan* + *-age*] **1** : ORPHANHOOD ⟨unemployment, widowhood and ~ —*New Republic*⟩ **2** : an institution for the care of orphans or homeless children : an orphan asylum ⟨the ~ was considered a step forward in treating underprivileged children —N.K.Teeters & J.O.Reinemann⟩

**or·phan·cy** \-fənsē\ *n* -ES [[1]*orphan* + *-cy*] *archaic* : ORPHANHOOD

**orphaned mission** *n* : a Christian mission cut off by war or some grave world crisis from the assistance of supporting missionary organizations

**or·phan·hood** \-fənˌhu̇d\ *n* : the quality or state of being an orphan ⟨draw from him the facts . . . including his place of abode, his ~ —Theodore Bonnet⟩

**or·phan·ism** \-fəˌnizəm\ *n* -S : ORPHANHOOD

**or·phan·ize** \-nīz\ *vt* -ED/-ING/-S [[1]*orphan* + *-ize*] : to make an orphan of

**orphans' court** *n* : a court existing in some states of the U.S. orig. established to probate wills and grant letters of administration, appoint guardians for minors, and protect orphans and their property and now usu. given additional probate jurisdiction — called also *prerogative court* compare PROBATE COURT

**or·phar·i·on** \ȯ(r)ˈfa(a)rēən\ *or* **or·phe·o·re·on** \ˌȯ(r)fēˈōrēən\ *or* **or·phe·ri·an** \ȯ(r)ˈfirēən\ *n* -S [*orpharion* prob. fr. *Orpheus*, poet and musician in Greek mythology + *Arion*, 7th cent. B.C. semilegendary Greek poet; *orpheoreon* or *orpherian* alter. of *orpharion* — more at ARION] : an old musical instrument of the cittern family having six to nine pairs of metal strings played with a plectrum

orpharion

**or·phe·an** \ˈȯ(r)fēən, (ˈ)=ˈ=\ *adj, usu cap* [L *Orpheus* (fr. Gk *Orpheios*, fr. *Orpheus*, poet and musician in Greek mythology) + E *-an*] : of, relating to, or resembling Orpheus or his music : ORPHIC 3 ⟨~ lyre⟩

**or·phé·on** \ȯrfāōⁿ\ *n, pl* **orphéons** \-ōⁿ(z)\ [F, fr. *Orphée* Orpheus, fr. L *Orpheus*] : a French male choral society

**or·phe·on·ist** \ȯ(r)fēənəst\ *n* -S [F *orphéoniste*, fr. *orphéon* + *-iste* -ist] : a member of an orphéon

[1]**or·phic** \ˈȯrfik, ˈȯ(ə)f-, -fēk\ *also* **or·phi·cal** \-fəkəl, -fēk-\ *adj* [*orphic* fr. L *Orphicus*, fr. Gk *Orphikos*, fr. *Orpheus*, Thracian poet and musician in Greek mythology who was a favorite of the muses and who symbolized the spirit of music + *-ikos* -ic; *orphical* fr. L *Orphicus* + E *-al*] **1** *usu cap* : of or relating to Orpheus or the literature, rites, or doctrines ascribed to him ⟨the Eleusinian, the Dionysian, and the *Orphic* rites were the most important mystery religions of Greece —G.E.Mylonas⟩ ⟨*Orphic* cults . . . influenced the sublime mysticism of Plato —Nathaniel Micklem⟩ ⟨the *Orphic* brotherhoods, wandering evangelists of a new life —E.D.Soper⟩ **2** *sometimes cap* : ESOTERIC ⟨~ doctrine⟩ ⟨~ expression⟩ : MYSTIC, ORACULAR ⟨~ sayings⟩ ⟨plunged into a sort of youthful ~ response to existence —Louise Bogan⟩ ⟨his critical style is often ~ . . . in its immaculate ardor —*N.Y. Herald Tribune Bk. Rev.*⟩ **3** : resembling the music or song ascribed to Orpheus : ENTRANCING ⟨the imagination sings ~ songs from the center of existence —Stephen Spender⟩ — **or·phi·cal·ly** \-fək(ə)lē, -li\ *adv*

[2]**orphic** \"\ *n* -S **1** : an Orphic song or hymn **2** [*orphism* + *-ic*] : an adherent of the Orphic rites or doctrines

**or·phi·cism** \ˈȯ(r)fəˌsizəm\ *n* -S *usu cap* [[1]*orphic* + *-ism*] : ORPHISM

[1]**or·phism** \ˈȯ(r)ˌfizəm\ *n* -S *usu cap* [*Orpheus*, poet and musician in Greek mythology who was regarded as founder of the mysteries + E *-ism*] : the religion of the Orphic mysteries with its initiating rites, doctrines of original sin and salvation, and belief in the purification of the soul through a cycle of reincarnation

[2]**orphism** \"\ *n* -S *often cap* [F *orphisme*, fr. *Orphée* Orpheus + *-isme* -ism] : an art movement or practice growing out of cubism about 1912 that is typified by the work of the French painter Delaunay and is characterized by an effort to achieve lyrical emphasis in totally abstract composition by means of brilliant color

**or·phist** \ˈȯrfəst, ˈȯ(ə)f-\ *n* -S *often cap* [F *orphisme* + E *-ist*] : an adherent or follower of the art theory, method, or practice of Orphism

**or·phrey** *or* **or·fray** *or* **or·frey** \ˈȯrfrē\ *n* -S [ME *orfrey*, *orfray*, fr. MF *orfreis*, fr. ML *aurifrigium*, fr. *auri-* + L *Phrygium*, neut. of *Phrygius* Phrygian] **1 a** : elaborate embroidery (as of gold) **b** : a piece of such embroidery **2** : an ornamental border or embroidered band esp. on an ecclesiastical vestment

**or·pi·ment** \ˈȯ(r)pəmənt\ *n* -S [ME, fr. MF, fr. L *auripigmentum*, fr. *auri-* + *pigmentum* pigment — more at PIGMENT] **1 a** : an orange to yellow mineral $As_2S_3$ consisting of arsenic trisulfide and frequently associated with realgar **b** : artificially produced arsenic trisulfide **2** *or* **orpiment yellow** : a light to brilliant yellow that is darker than empire yellow — called also *king's yellow, mineral yellow, Montpellier yellow, patent yellow, quercitron, realgar yellow, royal yellow, Turner's yellow, Verona yellow, Veronese yellow, yellow daisy*

**orpiment orange** *n* : a strong to vivid orange that is yellower than Big Four yellow

**orpiment red** *n* : DUTCH ORANGE

**or·pine** \ˈȯrpən\ *n* -S [ME *orpin*, fr. MF, fr. *orpiment*; prob. fr. the yellow blossoms of a common species (*Sedum acre*)] : a glabrous Eurasian sedum (*Sedum telephium*) having clustered erect stems bearing terminal cymes of reddish purple flowers and numerous fleshy alternate leaves, occurring in No. America in cultivation or locally as an escape, and formerly used in folk medicine; *broadly* : SEDUM 2

**orpine family** *n* : CRASSULACEAE

**orping** *pres part of* ORP

**or·ping·ton** \ˈȯ(r)piŋtən\ *n* [fr. *Orpington*, Kent, England, where the breed originated] **1** *usu cap* : an English breed of large deep-chested broad-backed domestic fowls with short unfeathered legs and usu. single combs that occurs in several color varieties of both standard and bantam types of which the buff is perhaps best known **2** -S *often cap* : a bird of the Orpington breed — usu. used with a qualifying term indicating the color variety

**or·pit** \ˈȯrpət\ *adj* [origin unknown] *Scot* : FRETFUL

**orps** *pres 3d sing of* ORP

**or·ra** *or* **or·row** \ˈärə\ *adj* [origin unknown] **1** *Scot* **a** : ODD, OCCASIONAL ⟨an ~ job here and there⟩ **b** : consisting of odds and ends : MISCELLANEOUS **2** *Scot* : not occupied or employed ⟨your ~ hours⟩ **3** *Scot, of a person* : IDLE, WORTHLESS

**orra man** *n, Scot* : a farm laborer hired to do odd jobs

**or·rery** \ˈȯrərē, ˈärə-\ *n* -ES [after Charles Boyle †1731 4th Earl of Orrery] **1** : an apparatus that illustrates the relative positions and motions of bodies in the solar system by rotation and revolution of balls moved by wheelwork **2** : a mechanical device incorporated into a clock to indicate the relative movements of some planets and satellites

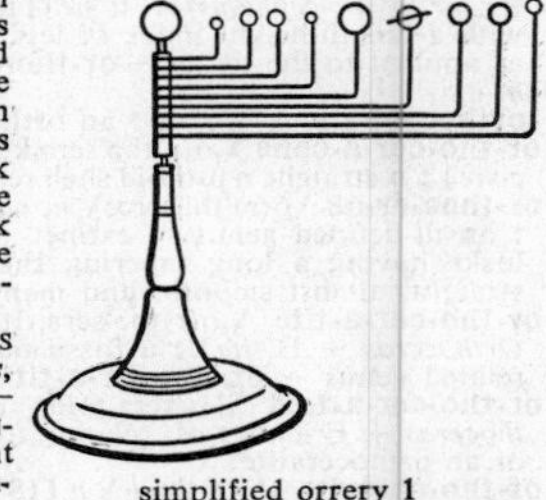

simplified orrery 1

[1]**or·ris** \ˈȯrəs, ˈär-\ *n* -ES [prob. alter. of ME *ireos*, fr. OIt, modif. of L *iris* — more at IRIS] **1** : FLORENTINE IRIS **2** : the fragrant rootstock of the Florentine iris

[2]**orris** \"\ *n* -ES [perh. alter. (influenced by *arras*) of earlier *orfrays*, pl. of *orfray* orphrey] : gold or silver lace or braid used on 18th century clothing; *also* : such lace or braid used as a galloon for upholstery

**orris oil** *also* **orrisroot oil** *n* : a yellowish semisolid fragrant essential oil containing free myristic acid and irones as its principal components, obtained from the roots of the Florentine iris, and used chiefly as a flavoring material and in perfumes

**orrisroot** \ˈ=ˌ=\ *n* [[1]*orris* + *root*] : the fragrant rootstock of any of several European plants of the genus *Iris* (esp. *I. pallida*) used in pulverized form in perfumery and medicine and as an ingredient of sachet and tooth powders

**ors** *pl of* OR

**-ors** *pl of* -OR

**ORS** *abbr* owner's risk of shifting

**or·sat apparatus** \ˈȯrsət-, -ˌsat-\ *n, usu cap O* [*orsat* of unknown origin] : an apparatus for gas analysis that consists essentially of a measuring burette, a connected series of pipettes containing selective absorbents, and usu. a combustion pipette

**orse** *abbr* otherwise

**or·seille** \(')ȯr¦sā(ə)l, -sā,-sel\ *or* **or·selle** \-sel,-sā\ *n* -s [F *orseille*] : ARCHIL

**or·sel·lin·ic acid** \¦ȯ(r)sə¦linik-\ *n* [*orsellinic* ISV *orsellin-* (fr. *orselle* + *-in*, chemical suffix) + *-ic*] : a crystalline acid $C_6H_2(OH)_2(CH_3)COOH$ found chiefly in combination in certain lichens; 4,6-dihydroxy-*ortho*-toluic acid — called also *ortho-orsellinic acid;* compare LECANORIC ACID

1**ort** \'ȯ(ə)rt\ *n* -s [ME, prob. fr. MD *orte*] **1** : a morsel left at a meal : LEAVING, REFUSE — usu. used in pl. ⟨ate their meals without forks and covered up the ~*s* with rushes —Frederic Harrison⟩ **2** : SCRAP, BIT — usu. used in pl. ⟨ideological ~*s* and fragments —David Daiches⟩

2**ort** \"\ *vt* -ED/-ING/-S [prob. fr. MD *orten* to leave over, fr. *orte* leftover, ort] *chiefly Scot* : to select by rejecting what is unsatisfactory

**or·tal·i·dae** \ȯ(r)'talə,dē\ [NL, fr. *Ortalis*, type genus + *-idae*] *syn of* OTITIDAE

**or·ta·lis** \'ȯ(r)d·ᵊləs\ *n*, *cap* [NL, fr. Gk, fowl; akin to Gk *ornis* bird — more at ERNE] : a genus of guans comprising the chachalacas

**ort·er·de** \'ȯrd·,erdə\ *n* -s [G, fr. *ort* site, place (fr. OHG, point) + *erde* earth (fr. OHG *erda*) — more at ODD, EARTH] : a soil horizon in which there is little or no cementation between the iron and the organic matter

**or·tet** \'ȯr,tet, ='=\ *n* -s [L *ort*us origin + E *-et;* akin to L *origin-*, *origo* origin — more at ORIGIN] : the original plant from which the members of a clone have descended — compare RAMET

**orth-** *or* **ortho-** *comb form* [ME, fr. MF, straight, right, true, fr. L, fr. Gk, fr. *orthos;* akin to Goth ga*wrisqan* to bring fruit, Skt *ūrdhva* upright, high, *vardhate* he increases] **1 a** : straight : upright : vertical ⟨*ortho*ceras⟩ ⟨*orth*al⟩ ⟨*ortho*grade⟩ ⟨*ortho*symmetric⟩ **b** : exact : parallel ⟨*ortho*diagram⟩ ⟨*ortho*-cousin⟩ ⟨*orth*odome⟩ **2** : correct : corrective ⟨*orth*ometry⟩ ⟨*orth*odontia⟩ **3 a** : an acid in the highest hydrated or hydroxylated form known either in the free state or in salts or esters ⟨*ortho*arsenic acid⟩ ⟨*ortho*formic acid⟩ — compare META- 4 c, PYR- 2a **b** (1) : the relation of two neighboring positions in the benzene ring (2) *ortho-*, *usu ital* : a derivative in which two substituting groups occupy such positions — abbr. *o-* ⟨*ortho*-xylene or *o*-xylene is 1,2-dimethyl-benzene⟩; compare META- 4b, PARA- 2b **4** : derived from igneous rock — in the name of a metamorphic rock ⟨*ortho*gneiss⟩ ⟨*ortho*site⟩; compare PARA-

**or·thal** \'ȯrthəl\ *adj* [*orth-* + *-al*] *of mastication* : effected by vertical motion — compare PALINAL, PROAL, PROPALINAL

**or·tha·nil·ic acid** \¦ȯ(r)thə¦nilik-\ *n* [*orth-* + sulf*anilic* acid] : a crystalline sulfonic acid $H_2NC_6H_4SO_3H$ isomeric with sulfanilic acid; *ortho*-amino-benzenesulfonic acid

**or·the·zia** \ȯ(r)'thēzh(ē)ə\ *n*, *cap* [NL, prob. fr. J. A. D*orthes* †1794 Fr. physician + NL *-ia*] : a genus of coccids (the type of the family Ortheziidae) including species that attack greenhouse plants throughout the world

**or·thi·an** \'ȯ(r)thēən\ *adj* [Gk *orthios* steep, high-pitched, fr. *orthos* straight + E *-an*] : characterized by high pitch — used of a style of singing or a tune

**or·thic** \'ȯrthik\ *adj* [*orth-* + *-ic*] : of or relating to the altitudes of a triangle

**or·thi·con** \'ȯ(r)thə,kän\ *n* -s [ISV *orth-* + *-icon* (fr. *iconoscope*)] : a camera tube similar to but more sensitive than an iconoscope in which the charges are scanned by a low-velocity beam to eliminate the secondary emission that reduces picture quality at low light levels

**or·thid** \'ȯrthəd\ *n* -s [NL *Orthidae*, fr. *Orthis* + *-idae*] : a brachiopod of the genus *Orthis* or of the family Orthidae

**or·this** \-əs\ *n*, *cap* [NL, fr. Gk *orthos* straight; fr. the valves being hinged along a straight line] : a genus (the type of the family Orthidae) of articulate brachiopods abundant in the Paleozoic

**or·thite** \-,thīt\ *n* -s [G *orthit*, fr. *orth-* + *-it* -ite; fr. the fact that it forms straight radii] : allanite esp. when occurring in slender prismatic crystals — **or·thit·ic** \(')=¦thid·ik\ *adj*

1**or·tho** \'ȯr(,)thō, 'ȯ(ə)(,)-\ *adj* [*orth-*] **1** : derived from or being an acid in the highest hydrated or hydroxylated form known — compare ORTH- 3a **2** : relating to, characterized by, or being two neighboring positions in the benzene ring — compare ORTH- 3b **3** : of, relating to, or being a diatomic molecule (as of hydrogen) in which the nuclei of the atoms are spinning in the same direction — opposed to *para* ⟨*ortho*-para conversion⟩

2**ortho** \"\ *adj* [by shortening] : ORTHOCHROMATIC

**ortho-** — see ORTH-

**or·tho·arsenate** \¦ȯ(r)(,)thō+\ *n* [*orthoarsen*ic (in *orthoarsenic acid*) + *-ate*] : a salt or ester of orthoarsenic acid

**or·tho·arsenic acid** \"+...-\ *n* [*orth-* + *arsenic acid*] : the arsenic acid $H_3AsO_4 \cdot \frac{1}{2}H_2O$

**or·tho·axis** \¦o(r)(,)thō+\ *n* [*orth-* + *axis*] : the diagonal or lateral axis that is at right angles with the vertical axis in the monoclinic system of crystallization

**or·tho·benzoquinone** \"+\ *n* [*orth-* + *benzoquinone*] : QUINONE 1b — written systematically with ital. *ortho-* or *o-*

**or·tho·boric acid** \"+...-\ *n* [*orth-* + *boric acid*] : BORIC ACID a

**or·tho·carbonic acid** \¦ȯ(r)(,)thō+...-\ *n* [ISV *orth-* + *carbonic*] : a hypothetical acid $H_4CO_4$ or $C(OH)_4$ known in the form of its esters

**orthocarbonic ester** *n* : an ester of orthocarbonic acid; *esp* : the liquid tetraethyl ester $C(OC_2H_5)_4$ of pleasant odor made by reaction of sodium ethoxide with chloropicrin

**or·tho·carpus** \¦ȯ(r)thə+\ *n*, *cap* [NL, fr. *orth-* + *-carpus*] : a genus of chiefly Californian herbs (family Scrophulariaceae) having alternate leaves and showy varicolored flowers and having the 4-cleft calyx and bilabiate corolla both tubular — see OWL'S CLOVER

**or·tho·center** *also* **or·tho·centre** \"+\ *n* [ISV *orth-* + *center*, *centre*] : the common intersection of the three altitudes of a triangle or of the several altitudes of a polyhedron provided these latter exist and meet in a point

1**or·tho·cephalic** \¦ȯ(r)(,)thō+\ *or* **or·tho·ceph·a·lous** \¦ȯ(r)thə¦sefələs\ *adj* [NL *orthocephal*us orthocephalic person (fr. *orth-* + *-cephalus*) + E *-ic*] : having a relatively low head with a length-height index of less than 75 or of less than 63 as applied to the living — **or·tho·ceph·a·ly** \,ȯ(r)thə'sefəlē\ *n* -ES

2**orthocephalic** \"\ *n* -s : an orthocephalic person

**or·tho·cer·a·cone** \,ȯ(r)thə'serə,kōn\ *n* [NL *Orthoceras* + E *cone*] : a straight nautiloid shell resembling that of *Orthoceras*

**or·thoc·er·as** \ȯ(r)'thäsərəs\ *n*, *cap* [NL, fr. *orth-* + *-ceras*] : an ill-defined genus of extinct nautiloid cephalopod mollusks having a long tapering shell that is nearly or quite straight, almost smooth, and many-chambered

**or·tho·cer·a·tite** \,ȯ(r)thə'serə,tīt\ *n* -s [NL *Orthocerat-*, *Orthoceras* + E *-ite*] : a fossil nautiloid of *Orthoceras* or a related genus — **or·tho·cer·a·tit·ic** \¦==,==¦tid·ik\ *adj*

**or·tho·cer·a·toid** \¦==¦serə,tȯid\ *adj* [NL *Orthocerat-*, *Orthoceras* + E *-oid*] : of, relating to, or resembling *Orthoceras* or an orthoceratite

**or·tho·chlorite** \¦ȯ(r)thə+\ *n* [ISV *orth-* + *chlorite*] : a distinctly crystalline form of chlorite (as clinochlore) — opposed to *leptochlorite*

**or·tho·chromatic** \"+\ *adj* [ISV *orth-* + *chromatic;* prob. orig. formed as F *orthochromatique*] **1** : of, relating to, or producing tone values of light and shade in a photograph that correspond to the tones in nature **2** *of a photographic material* : sensitive to all colors except red

**or·tho·clase** \'ȯ(r)thə,klās, -āz\ *n* -s [G *orthoklas*, fr. *orth-* + *-klas* -clase] : a mineral $KAlSi_3O_8$ consisting of a monoclinic polymorph of common potassium feldspar with sodium often in place of some of the potassium and occurring usu. colorless to white, cream-yellow, or flesh-red (hardness 6, sp. gr. 2.57) — see FELDSPAR, MOONSTONE

**or·tho·clas·tic** \¦==¦klastik\ *adj* [G *orthoklastisch*, fr. *orth-* + *-klastisch* -clastic] : cleaving in directions at right angles to each other — used orig. of the monoclinic feldspars

**ortho-cousin** \¦ȯ(r)thə+\ *n* : PARALLEL COUSIN

**or·tho·cra·nic** \¦ȯ(r)thə¦krānik\ *adj* [G *orthokran* (fr. *orth-* + Gk *kranion* skull) + E *-ic* — more at CRANIUM] : ORTHOCEPHALIC — **or·tho·cra·ny** \-nē\ *n* -ES

**or·tho·cresol** \¦ȯ(r)thə+\ *n* [ISV *orth-* + *cresol*] : the ortho isomer of cresol — written systematically with ital. *ortho-* or *o-*

**or·tho·diagonal** \¦ȯ(r)(,)thō+\ *n* [ISV *orth-* + *diagonal*] : ORTHOAXIS

**or·tho·diagram** \¦ȯ(r)thə+\ *n* [ISV *orth-* + *diagram*] : a tracing showing the outer contours and exact size of an organ (as the heart) made by illuminating the edge of the organ with parallel X rays through a small movable aperture and marking the outer edge of the shadow cast upon a fluoroscopic screen

**or·tho·diagraphic** \"+\ *adj* [*orth-* + *diagraphic*] : of, relating to, or by means of orthodiagrams — **or·tho·diagraph·ically** \"+\ *adv*

**or·tho·dichlorobenzene** \"+\ *n* [*orth-* + *dichlorobenzene*] : a volatile oily liquid compound $C_6H_4Cl_2$ made by chlorination of benzene and used chiefly as a solvent and cleaner, heat-transfer medium, and insecticide — written systematically with ital. *ortho-* or *o-*

**or·tho·dolichocephalic** \¦ȯ(r)(,)thō+\ *adj* [*orth-* + *dolichocephalic*] : having a relatively long head of medium height

**or·tho·dome** \'ȯ(r)thə,dōm\ *n* [ISV *orth-* + *dome*] : the dome of a crystal having planes parallel to the orthoaxis — compare BRACHYDOME, CLINODOME, MACRODOME

**or·tho·don·tia** \,ȯ(r)thə'dänch(ē)ə\ *n* -s [NL, fr. *orth-* + *-odontia*] : ORTHODONTICS

**or·tho·don·tic** \¦==¦däntik, -tēk\ *adj* [ISV *orthodont-* (fr. NL *orthodontia*) + *-ic*] : of or relating to orthodontics ⟨~ studies⟩ : involving the methods of orthodontics ⟨~ care of facial abnormalities⟩

**or·tho·don·tics** \,=='=tiks, -tēks\ *n pl but sing or pl in constr* [NL *orthodont*ia + E *-ics*] : a branch of dentistry that deals with irregularities of the teeth and abnormalities of their relations with surrounding parts and with the correction of these esp. by means of braces and mechanical aids

**or·tho·don·tist** \¦==¦=təst\ *n* -s [NL *orthodont*ia + E *-ist*] : a specialist in orthodontics

1**or·tho·dox** \'ȯ(r)thə,däks\ *adj* [MF or LL; MF *orthodoxe*, fr. LL *orthodoxus*, fr. LGk *orthodoxos*, fr. Gk *orthodoxein* to have the right opinion, fr. *ortho-* straight, right, true + *-doxein* (fr. *doxa* opinion, belief, reputation) — more at ORTH-, DOXOLOGY] **1** : marked by conformity to doctrines or practices esp. in religion that are held as right or true by some authority, standard, or tradition ⟨the simple security of the old ~ assumptions has vanished —A.N.Whitehead⟩: as **a** : conforming to the Christian faith as formulated in the church creeds and confessions ⟨an ~ Christian⟩ **b** : according to or congruous with the doctrines of Scripture as interpreted in some standard (as the creed of a church or decree of a council) ⟨~ belief⟩ ⟨an ~ book⟩ — contrasted with *heretical* and *heterodox* **2** *usu cap* : of, relating to, or characterizing a particular religious organization or group (as the Eastern Orthodox Church, the Sunnites of Islam, Hindus acknowledging the authority of the Vedas, or the conservative Friends as distinguished from the Hicksite Friends) **3 a** : of, relating to, or characterizing the dominant or officially approved form of something ⟨~ Marxism⟩ ⟨the ~ form of a text⟩ ⟨~ economic theory⟩ ⟨the ~ approach⟩ **b** : CONSERVATIVE ⟨very ~ in her belief and practices⟩ ⟨simple, dark, ~ clothes —*English Digest*⟩ **c** : CONVENTIONAL ⟨~ routes to Europe —*Geog. Jour.*⟩ ⟨~ in treatment and subject —Charles Lee⟩ —**or·tho·dox·ness** *n* -ES

2**orthodox** \"\ *n*, *pl* **orthodox** *or* **orthodoxes** [ML *orthodoxus*, fr. LL, orthodox, adj.] **1** : one that is orthodox **2** *usu cap* : a member of the Eastern Orthodox Church

**or·tho·dox·al** \¦==¦däksəl\ *adj* [LL *orthodox*us + E *-al*] : ORTHODOX — **or·tho·dox·al·i·ty** \,==,='saləd·ē\ *n* -ES — **or·tho·dox·al·ly** \¦==¦=səlē\ *adv*

**or·tho·dox·ian** \,=='däksēən\ *n* -s : an adherent of or believer in orthodoxy

**or·tho·dox·i·cal** \¦==¦däksəkəl\ *adj* [LL *orthodox*us + E *-ical*] : ORTHODOX — **or·tho·dox·i·cal·ly** \-k(ə)lē\ *adv*

**or·tho·dox·ism** \'==,däk,sizəm\ *n* -s : ORTHODOXY — often used disparagingly

**orthodox jew** *n*, *usu cap O&J* : an adherent of Orthodox Judaism

**orthodox judaism** *n*, *cap O&J* : Judaism that adheres to Biblical law as interpreted in the authoritative rabbinic tradition as the final and complete revelation of divine law and that seeks to observe all the practices commanded in it — compare CONSERVATIVE JUDAISM, RECONSTRUCTIONISM, REFORM JUDAISM

**or·tho·dox·ly** *adv* : in an orthodox manner

**orthodox sunday** *n*, *usu cap O&S* : FEAST OF ORTHODOXY

**or·tho·doxy** \'ȯ(r)thə,däksē, -si\ *n* -ES [LL *orthodoxia*, fr. Gk, right opinion, fr. *orthodoxein* to have the right opinion + *-ia* -y] **1** : the quality or state of being orthodox : conformity to an official formulation of truth esp. in religious belief or practice ⟨make it my object to teach thinking, not ~ —Bertrand Russell⟩ — contrasted with *heresy* and *heterodoxy* **2** : an orthodox belief or practice ⟨the new astronomy . . . one factor in shaking traditional *orthodoxies* —Douglas Bush⟩ **3** *usu cap* [MGk *orthodoxia*, fr. Gk] : the system of faith, practice, and discipline of the Eastern Orthodox Church

**or·tho·drom·ic** \¦==¦drämik\ *adj* : of or relating to orthodromy

**or·tho·drom·ics** \,=='=miks\ *n pl but sing or pl in constr* [F *orthodromique*, fr. *orthodromie* orthodromy + *-ique* -ic] : ORTHODROMY

**or·thodro·my** \'ȯ(r)thə,drōmē, ȯ(r)'thädrəmē\ *n* -ES [F *orthodromie*, fr. *orthodrom-* (fr. Gk *orth-* + *-dromos* -drome) + *-ie* -y] : the act or art of great-circle sailing

**or·tho·ep·ic** \¦ȯ(r)thə¦wepik\ *also* **or·tho·ep·i·cal** \-pəkəl\ *adj* : of or relating to orthoepy ⟨~ evidence —Harold Whitehall⟩ ⟨the terminology of civic administration seems to abound in ~ pitfalls —J.T.Winterich⟩ — **or·tho·ep·i·cal·ly** \-pək(ə)lē\ *adv*

**or·tho·epist** \'ȯ(r)thə,wepəst, ȯ(r)'thōəp-\ *n* -s : a person who is skilled in orthoepy — **or·tho·epis·tic** \¦ȯ(r)thə,we¦pistik, (¦)ȯ(r)¦thōə¦p-\ *adj*

**or·tho·epy** \'ȯ(r)thə,wepē, ȯ(r)'thōəpē\ *n* -ES [NL *orthoepia*, fr. Gk *orthoepeia*, fr. *orth-* + *-epeia* (fr. *epos* word, speech) — more at VOICE] **1** : the customary pronunciation of a language **2** : the study of the pronunciation of a language

**ortho ester** *n* [1*ortho*] : an ester of an ortho acid; *esp* : an ester $RC(OR')_3$ (as orthoformic ester) of an ortho-carboxylic acid

**or·tho·ferrosilite** \¦ȯ(r)(,)thō+\ *n* [*orth-* + *ferrosilite*] : a mineral $FeSiO_3$ consisting of iron silicate in the orthorhombic form — compare CLINOFERROSILITE, FERROSILITE

**or·tho·for·mic acid** \¦ȯrthə¦fȯrmik-\ *n* [ISV *orth-* + *-form* + *-ic*] : a hypothetical acid $HC(OH)_3$ known in the form of its esters

**orthoformic ester** *n* : an ester of orthoformic acid; *esp* : the liquid triethyl ester $HC(OC_2H_5)_3$ of pungent odor made by reaction of sodium ethoxide with either chloroform or carbon tetrachloride and used in making acetals

**or·tho·genesis** \,ȯ(r)thə+\ *n* [NL, fr. *orth-* + *genesis*] **1** : variation of organisms in successive generations along some predestined line resulting in progressive evolutionary trends independent of natural selection or other external factors — called also *determinate evolution;* compare ORTHOSELECTION **2 a** : the theory that social evolution takes place in the same direction and through the same stages in every culture despite differing external conditions **b** : variation of culture in a particular direction in accordance with internal predetermining factors rather than through external contact

**or·tho·genetic** \¦ȯ(r)thə+\ *adj* [ISV *orthogenet-* (fr. NL *orthogenesis*) + *-ic*] : of, relating to, or exhibiting orthogenesis ⟨the theory of ~ evolution —B.R.Redman⟩ — **or·tho·genetically** \"+\ *adv*

**or·tho·gen·ic** \¦==¦jenik\ *adj* [ISV *orthogenesis* + *-ic*] **1** : ORTHOGENETIC **2** [*orth-* + *-genic*] : of, relating to, or devoted to the rehabilitation of emotionally disturbed mentally retarded children

**or·tho·geosyncline** \¦ȯ(r)thə+\ *n* [*orth-* + *geosyncline*] : a linear geosyncline between cratons — compare PARAGEOSYNCLINE

**or·thog·na·thism** \ȯ(r)'thägnə,thizəm\ *or* **or·thog·na·thy** \-nəthē\ *n*, *pl* **orthognathisms** *or* **orthognathies** [*orthognathism* ISV *orthognath*ous + *-ism; orthognathy* ISV *orthognath*ous + *-y*] : the quality or state of being orthognathous

**or·thog·na·thous** \(')ȯ(r)¦thägnəthəs\ *also* **or·thognath·ic** \¦ȯ(r)thə(g)¦nathik, -,thäg¦n-\ *adj* [*orthognathous* ISV *orth-* + *-gnathous; orthognathic* fr. *orth-* + *gnathic*] : having straight jaws : not having the lower parts of the face projecting

**or·tho·gneiss** \'ȯ(r)thə+,-\ *n* [G *orthogneis*, fr. *orth-* + *gneis* gneiss — more at GNEISS] : gneiss derived from an igneous rock

1**or·thog·o·nal** \(')ȯ(r)¦thägənᵊl\ *adj* [MF, fr. L *orthogonius* orthogonal (fr. Gk *orthogōnios*, fr. *orth-* + *-gōnios*, fr. *gōnia* angle) + MF *-al* — more at -GON] **1** : lying or intersecting at right angles : RECTANGULAR, RIGHT-ANGLED ⟨wind and sea may displace the ship's center of gravity along three ~ axes —C.C.Shaw⟩ ⟨in ~ cutting, the cutting edge is perpendicular to the direction of tool travel —M.E.Merchant & Hans Ernst⟩ **2 a** : mutually perpendicular ⟨two vector functions the integral of whose scalar product throughout space is zero are ~⟩ **b** : completely independent ⟨two statistical variables having zero correlation are ~⟩ ⟨mental ability may be classified into several ~ . . . factors —O.D.Duncan⟩ — **or·thog·o·nal·ly** \-gənᵊlē,-gnəlē\ *adv*

2**orthogonal** \"\ *n* -s : an imaginary line at right angles to wave crests in oceanography

**orthogonal functions** *n pl* : two mathematical functions such that with suitable limits the definite integral of their product is zero

**or·thog·o·nal·i·ty** \(,)ȯ(r),thägə'naləd·ē\ *n* -ES [ISV *orthogonal-* (fr. 1*orthogonal*) + *-ity*] : the quality or state of being orthogonal

**or·thog·o·nal·ize** \='=gənᵊl,īz\ *vt* -ED/-ING/-S [1*orthogonal* + *-ize*] : to make orthogonal

**orthogonal projection** *n* : ORTHOGRAPHIC PROJECTION 1

**orthogonal system** *n* : a system of curves or surfaces consisting of two families whose components where they intersect are mutually perpendicular (as the lines of force and the equipotential surfaces in an electrostatic field)

**orthogonal trajectory** *n* : a mathematical curve which cuts every curve of a given set at right angles

**or·tho·grade** \'ȯ(r)thə,grād\ *adj* [*orth-* + *-grade*] : walking with the body upright or vertical — compare PRONOGRADE

**or·tho·graph** \-raf,-ráf\ *n* [fr. *orthographic*, after such pairs as E *autographic: autograph*] : an orthographic projection plan, elevation, or section esp. of a building

**or·thog·ra·pher** \ȯ(r)'thägrəfə(r)\ *n* -s [LL *orthograph*us orthographer (fr. L *orth-* + LL *-graphus* -grapher) + E *-er*] : a person who is skilled in orthography : an expert in spelling

**or·tho·graph·ic** \¦ȯ(r)thə¦grafik, -fēk\ *also* **or·tho·graph·i·cal** \-fəkəl, -fēk-\ *adj* [*orthography* + *-ic* or *-ical*] **1** : characterized by perpendicular lines or right angles : ORTHOGONAL **2 a** : of or relating to orthography **b** : correct in spelling : spelled in the traditional way of writing — **or·tho·graph·i·cal·ly** \-fək(ə)lē, -fēk-, -li\ *adv*

**orthographic projection** *n* **1** : projection in which the projecting lines are perpendicular to the plane of projection — called also *orthogonal projection* **2** : a map projection of one half the globe as it would appear to a camera centered on any point desired from an infinite distance being true to scale at the center only

**or·thog·ra·phist** \ȯ(r)'thägrəfəst\ *n* -s : a specialist in orthography

**or·thog·ra·phize** \-,fīz\ *vt* -ED/-ING/-S [*orthography* + *-ize*] **1 a** : to spell correctly or according to usage **b** : to correct in regard to spelling **2** : to devise a writing system for (a language)

**or·thog·ra·phy** \ȯ(r)'thägrəfē, -fi\ *n* -ES [ME *ortografie*, fr. MF, fr. L *orthographia*, fr. Gk, fr. *orth-* + *-graphia* (fr. *graphein* to write + *-ia* -y) — more at CARVE] **1 a** : the art of writing words with the proper letters according to standard usage : correct spelling — opposed to *cacography* **b** : a method of representing the sounds of a language by written or printed symbols; *also* : a complete set of such symbols **2** : the part of language study that treats of the letters and of the art of spelling **3** [L *orthographia*, fr. Gk] : ORTHOGRAPHIC PROJECTION

**or·tho·hexagonal axes** \¦ȯ(r)(,)thō+. . .-\ *n pl* [*orthohexagonal* fr. *orth-* + *hexagonal*] : a set of orthogonal axes with a fixed ratio ($1{:}\sqrt{3}$) between two of them used occas. in descriptions of and in calculations for hexagonal or trigonal crystals

**ortho-hydrogen** \¦ȯ(r)thə+\ *n* : molecular hydrogen in which the two hydrogen nuclei are spinning in the same direction — compare PARA-HYDROGEN ⟨ordinary hydrogen gas comprises an equilibrium mixture of three parts of *ortho-hydrogen* (with parallel nuclear spin) to one part of para-hydrogen (with antiparallel nuclear spin) —Otto Reinmuth⟩

**or·tho·kinesis** \"+\ *n* [NL, fr. *orth-* + *kinesis*] : random movement (as of a planarian) in response to a stimulus

**or·tho·metopic** \"+\ *adj* [*orth-* + *metopic*] : having or characterized by a vertical forehead

**or·tho·metric** \"+\ *adj* [ISV *orth-* + *metric*] : ORTHOGONAL

**or·thom·e·try** \ȯ(r)'thämə·trē\ *n* -ES [*orth-* + Gk *-metria* measurement, meter, fr. *metrein* to measure + *-ia* -y — more at MEASURE] : the art of correct versification

**or·tho·mor·pha** \,ȯrthə'mȯrfə\ *n*, *cap* [NL, fr. *orth-* + *-morpha*] : a genus of millipedes containing the common European greenhouse millipede (*O. gracilis*)

**or·tho·mor·phic** \¦==¦=fik\ *adj* [F *orthomorphique*, fr. *orth-* + *-morphique* -morphic] : CONFORMAL 2

**or·tho·mor·phism** \¦==¦=,fizəm\ *n* -s [F *orthomorphisme*, prob. fr. *orthomorphique* + *-isme* -ism] : CONFORMALITY

**or·tho·nec·ti·da** \,=='nektədə\ *n pl*, *cap* [NL, fr. *orth-* + *nect-* + *-ida*] : an order or other division of Mesozoa comprising a number of rare parasites of the tissues and cavities of various invertebrates that alternate between an asexual plasmodial generation and a sexual generation resembling the nematogens of dicyemids but having numerous internal cells — compare DICYEMIDA

**ortho nitraniline orange** *n*, *often cap both Os & N* [1*ortho*] : an organic pigment — see DYE table I (under *Pigment Orange 2*)

**ortho nitroaniline** \¦ȯ(r)(,)thō+\ *n* [ISV *orth-* + *nitroaniline*] : NITROANILINE b

**or·tho·non** \'ȯ(r)thə,nän, -,nən\ *n* -s [*orth-* + *nonhalation*] : a photographic material sensitive only to violet and blue — compare COLOR-BLIND 2

**or·tho·panchromatic** \¦ȯ(r)(,)thō+\ *adj* [ISV *orth-* + *panchromatic*] *of a panchromatic material* : having a color sensitivity most nearly matching that of the eye

**or·tho·pe·dic** *also* **or·tho·pae·dic** \¦ȯ(r)thə¦pēdik, -dēk\ *adj* [F *orthopédique*, fr. *orthopédie* orthopedics (fr. *orth-* + *-péd-* — fr. Gk *paid-*, *paîs* child — + *-ie* -y) + *-ique* -ic — more at FEW] **1** : of, relating to, or employed in orthopedics **2** : involving or affected by deformities or crippling ⟨an ~ condition⟩ ⟨~ children⟩

**or·tho·pe·dics** *also* **or·tho·pae·dics** \,=='=diks, -dēks\ *n pl but sing or pl in constr* [*orthopedic*, *orthopaedic* + *-s*] : the correction or prevention of deformities esp. of the skeletal structures in children

**or·tho·pe·dist** *also* **or·tho·pae·dist** \-dəst\ *n* -s [F *orthopédiste*, fr. *orthopédie* orthopedics + *-iste* -ist] : one that practices orthopedics

**or·tho·periodic acid** \¦ȯ(r)(,)thō+. . .-\ *n* [*orth-* + *periodic acid*] : PERIODIC ACID a

**or·tho·pho·ria** \,ȯ(r)thə'fōrēə\ *n* -s [NL, fr. *orth-* + *-phoria*] : a normal condition of balance of the ocular muscles of the two eyes in which their visual lines meet at the object toward which they are directed

**or·tho·phosphate** \¦ȯ(r)thə+\ *n* [*orthophosph*oric acid + *-ate*] : a salt or ester of orthophosphoric acid — called also *phosphate*

**or·tho·phosphoric acid** \"+. . .-\ *n* [*orthophosphoric* ISV *orth-* + *phosphoric*] : PHOSPHORIC ACID 1a — distinguished from *metaphosphoric acid* and *pyrophosphoric acid*

**or·tho·pinacoid** \¦ȯ(r)thə+\ *n* [ISV *orth-* + *pinacoid*] : a pinacoid whose planes are parallel to the ortho and vertical axes in a monoclinic crystal

**or·thop·nea** *also* **or·thop·noea** \ȯ(r)'thäpnēə *also* ,ȯ(r),thäp'nēə *or* ,ȯ(r)thə'n-\ *n* -s [L *orthopnoea*, fr. Gk *orthopnoia*, fr. *orth-* + *-pnoia* -pnea] : inability to breathe except in an upright position (as in congestive heart failure) — **or·thop·ne·ic** *also* **or·thop·noe·ic** \¦ȯ(,)¦=¦ik\ *adj*

**or·thop·o·da** \ȯ(r)'thäpədə\ [NL, fr. *orth-* + *-poda*] *syn of* ORNITHISCHIA

**or·tho·praxy** \'ȯ(r)thə,praksē\ *n* -ES [*orth-* + Gk *praxis* doing, practice + E *-y* (as in *orthodoxy*) — more at PRAXIS] **:** correctness of practice or a body of practices accepted or recognized as correct ⟨religious ~⟩

**or·tho·psychiatric** *also* **or·tho·psychiatrical** \¦ȯ(r)(,)thō+\ *adj* **:** of or relating to orthopsychiatry

**or·tho·psychiatrist** \"+\ *n* **:** a specialist in orthopsychiatry

**or·tho·psychiatry** \"+\ *n* [*orth-* + *psychiatry*] **:** prophylactic psychiatry concerned esp. with incipient mental and behavioral disorders in childhood and youth — compare MENTAL HYGIENE

**or·thop·ter** \(')ȯ(r)'thäptə(r)\ *n* -S [F *orthoptère*, fr. *orth-* + *-ptère* (as in *hélicoptère* helicopter) — more at HELICOPTER] **1 :** a flying machine propelled by flapping of wings **:** a mechanical bird **2** [F *orthoptère*, fr. NL *Orthoptera*] **:** ORTHOPTERON

**or·thop·tera** \ȯ(r)'thäptərə\ *n pl, cap* [NL, fr. *orth-* + *-ptera*; fr. the straight and narrow wings] **:** an order of Insecta comprising insects with mouthparts fitted for chewing, two pairs of wings or none, and an incomplete metamorphosis: **a** *in some esp. former classifications* **:** a very large order including the cockroaches, mantises, grasshoppers and crickets, stick insects, and certain related forms and sometimes also the earwigs **b :** an order including the mantises, grasshoppers and crickets, stick insects, and certain related forms and comprising the suborders Manteodea, Grylloblattodea, Saltatoria, and Phasmatodea **c** *in some classifications* **:** an order coextensive with Saltatoria

**or·thop·ter·al** \(')=¦=tərəl\ *or* **or·thop·ter·an** \-rən\ *or* **or·thop·ter·ous** \-rəs\ *adj* **:** of or relating to the Orthoptera

**orthopteran** \"\ *n* -S [NL *Orthoptera* + E *-an*] **:** ORTHOPTERON

**or·thop·ter·ist** \=¦=tərəst\ *n* -S [NL *Orthoptera* + E *-ist*] **:** ORTHOPTEROLOGIST

**¹or·thop·ter·oid** \=¦=tə,rȯid\ *adj* [NL *Orthoptera* + E *-oid*] **1 :** resembling or related to the Orthoptera **2** [NL *Orthopteroidea*] **:** of or relating to the Orthopteroidea

**²orthopteroid** \"\ *n* -S **:** an orthopteroid insect

**or·thop·ter·oi·dea** \(,)=,=tə'rȯidēə\ *n pl, cap* [NL, fr. *Orthoptera* + *-oidea*] *in some classifications* **:** a superorder or other division of Insecta that includes Orthoptera together with various other groups (as Phasmatodea, Dermaptera, and Diploglossata)

**or·thop·ter·o·log·i·cal** \(¦)=¦=tərə¦läjəkəl\ *adj* [*orthopterology* + *-ical*] **:** of or relating to orthopterology

**or·thop·ter·ol·o·gist** \(,)=,==ˈräləjəst\ *n* -S **:** a specialist in orthopterology

**or·thop·ter·ol·o·gy** \-jē\ *n* -ES [NL *Orthoptera* + E *-logy*] **1 :** the study of the Orthoptera **2 :** a treatise on the Orthoptera

**or·thop·ter·on** \=¦=tərən, -,rän\ *n, pl* **orthoptera** \-,rə\ [NL, sing. of *Orthoptera*] **:** an insect of the order Orthoptera

**or·thop·tic** \(')=¦thäptik\ *adj* [ISV *orth-* + *optic*] **:** of or relating to orthoptics

**or·thop·tics** \=¦=tiks\ *n pl but sing or pl in constr* [*orthoptic* + *-s*] **:** the treatment or the art of treating defective visual habits, defects of binocular vision, and muscle imbalance (as strabismus) by reeducation of visual habits, exercise, and visual training

**or·thop·tist** \(')=¦=təst\ *n* -S [*orthoptics* + *-ist*] **:** a person who is trained in or practices orthoptics

**or·tho·quartzite** \¦ȯ(r)thō+\ *n* [*orth-* + *quartzite*] **:** a quartzite of sedimentary origin

**or·tho·quinone** \"+\ *n* [*orth-* + *quinone*] **1 :** QUINONE 1b **2 :** the ortho isomer of a quinone

**or·thor·ha·pha** *syn of* ORTHORRHAPHA

**or·tho·rhombic** \¦ȯ(r)thə+\ *adj* [ISV *orth-* + *rhombic*] **:** of, relating to, or characterized by the orthorhombic system of crystallization **:** RHOMBIC, PRISMATIC, TRIMETRIC

**orthorhombic system** *n* **:** a crystal system characterized by three unequal axes at right angles — see CRYSTAL SYSTEM illustration

**or·thor·rha·pha** \ȯ(r)'thȯrəfə\ *n pl, cap* [NL, fr. *orth-* + *-rrhapha* (fr. Gk *rhaphē* seam, fr. *rhaptein* to sew together) — more at WRAP] **:** a large suborder of Diptera that usu. includes the Nematocera and many of the Brachycera but is sometimes restricted to the more primitive families of Brachycera and that is distinguished by a pupal case opening by a T-shaped cleft behind the head or by a transverse slit between the seventh and eighth abdominal segments — **or·thor·rha·phous** \(')=¦==fəs\ *adj*

**or·tho·scope** \'ȯ(r)thə,skōp\ *n* [ISV *orth-* + *-scope*; prob. orig. formed as G *orthoskop*] **:** an instrument for examining the superficial parts of the eye through a layer of water which neutralizes the corneal refraction

**or·tho·scop·ic** \¦==¦skäpik\ *adj* [ISV *orth-* + *-scopic*] **:** giving an image in correct and normal proportions **:** giving a flat field of view

**or·tho·selection** \¦ȯ(r)thə+\ *n* [*orth-* + *selection*] **:** natural selection promoting the progress and continuance of an adaptive trend in biological evolution and thus simulating orthogenesis — **or·tho·selective** \"+\ *adj*

**or·tho·silicate** \¦ȯ(r)(,)thō+\ *n* [ISV *orth-* + *silicate*] **:** a silicate containing the group $SiO_4$ in which the ratio of silicon to oxygen is 1 to 4 **:** a salt or ester (as ethyl silicate) of orthosilicic acid **:** NESOSILICATE

**or·tho·silicic acid** \"+...-\ *n* [*orthosilicic* ISV *orth-* + *silicic*] **:** a weak acid $H_4SiO_4$ or $Si(OH)_4$ known only in solution and in the form of salts or esters

**or·tho·sis** \ȯ(r)'thōsəs\ *n, pl* **ortho·ses** \-ō,sēz\ [NL, fr. Gk *orthōsis* straightening, fr. *orthoun* to straighten, fr. *orthos* straight — more at ORTH-] **:** corrective treatment of maladjusted or neurotic individuals

**or·tho·site** \'ȯ(r)thə,sīt\ *n* -S [F, fr. *orthose* orthoclase (fr. *orth-* + *-ose*) + *-ite*] **:** a granular igneous rock composed essentially of orthoclase

**or·tho·somatic** \¦ȯ(r)(,)thō+\ *adj* [*orth-* + *somatic*] **:** having the body straight ⟨~ insect larvae⟩

**or·tho·stat·ic** \'ȯ(r)thə+\ *adj* [ISV *orth-* + *-static* (fr. Gk *statos* — verbal of *histanai* to cause to stand — + *-ikos* -ic) — more at STAND] **:** of, relating to, or caused by erect posture

**orthostatic albuminuria** *n* **:** albuminuria that occurs only when a person is in an upright position and disappears when he lies down for a short time

**or·tho·stereoscope** \"+\ *n* [*orth-* + *stereoscope*] **:** a stereoscopic binocular microscope that presents erect images in true perspective — **or·tho·stereoscopic** \"+\ *adj*

**or·tho·stereoscopy** \¦ȯ(r)(,)thō+\ *n* [*orth-* + *stereoscopy*] **:** a process of stereoscopic photography for producing a three-dimensional visual image that is a full-sized true-to-scale reproduction of the original object in all three dimensions and that appears at the same distance from the eye as the original object

**or·thos·ti·chous** \(')ȯ(r)¦thästəkəs\ *adj* [*orthostichy* + *-ous*] **:** arranged in vertical ranks

**or·thos·ti·chy** \=¦=kē\ *n* -ES [ISV *orth-* + Gk *stichos* row + ISV *-y* — more at STICH] **:** a hypothetical line passing through the bases of leaves or scales situated directly above one another on an axis; *also* **:** the arrangement of leaves or scales in such lines — compare PARASTICHY, PHYLLOTAXY

**¹or·tho·style** \'ȯ(r)thə+,-\ *n* [*orth-* + *-style* (as in *peristyle*)] **:** an arrangement of architectural columns in a straight row

**²orthostyle** \"\ *adj* **:** of or relating to an orthostyle

**or·tho·symmetric** *or* **or·tho·symmetrical** \¦ȯ(r)(,)thō+\ *adj* [*orth-* + *symmetric*, *symmetrical*] **:** ORTHORHOMBIC

**or·tho·telluric acid** \"+...\ *n* [*orth-* + *telluric acid*] **:** TELLURIC ACID a

**ortho–tolidine** \¦ȯ(r)(,)thō+\ *n* **:** TOLIDINE a

**or·tho·tone** \'ȯ(r)thə,tōn\ *adj* [Gk *orthotonos* with the unmodified accent, fr. *ortho-* orth- + *tonos* accent, tone — more at TONE] **:** having or retaining an independent accent **:** not enclitic or proclitic — used esp. of some indefinite Greek pronouns and adverbs when used interrogatively

**or·thot·o·nus** \ȯ(r)'thätᵊnəs\ *n* -ES [NL, fr. *orth-* + L *tonus* tension, tone — more at TONE] **:** tetanic spasm characterized by rigid straightness of the body

**or·tho·top·ic** \¦ȯ(r)thə¦täpik\ *adj* [*orth-* + heterotopic] **:** of or relating to the grafting of tissue in a natural position ⟨~ transplant⟩ — compare HETEROTOPIA

**or·tho·triaene** \¦ȯ(r)thō+\ *n* [*orth-* + *triaene*] **:** a tetraradiate sponge spicule having one long and three short rays

**or·tho·trop·ic** \¦ȯ(r)thə¦träpik\ *adj* [*orth-* + *-tropic*] **:** having the longer axis more or less vertical — compare PLAGIOTROPIC — **or·tho·trop·i·cal·ly** \-pək(ə)lē\ *adv*

**or·thot·ro·pism** \ȯ(r)'thä·trə,pizəm\ *n* [*orth-* + *tropism*] **:** the tendency of a plant to have the longer axis more or less vertical

**or·thot·ro·pous** \(')ȯ(r)'thä·trəpəs\ *adj* [ISV *orth-* + *-tropous*] **:** having the ovule straight so that the chalaza, hilum, and micropyle are in the same axial line — compare AMPHITROPOUS, ANATROPOUS, CAMPYLOTROPOUS

**or·tho·type** \'ȯ(r)thə,tīp\ *n* [*orth-* + *type*] **:** a genotype designated as such in the first publication of a generic name — **or·tho·typ·ic** \¦==¦tipik\ *adj*

**or·tho–xylene** \¦ȯ(r)thō+\ *n* [*orth-* + *xylene*] **:** XYLENE 1a — written systematically with ital. *ortho-* or *o-*

**or·thros** \'ȯr,thrȯs\ *or* **or·thron** \-thrȯn\ *n, pl* **orthroses** *or* **orthrons** *often cap* [*orthros* fr. LGk, fr. Gk, dawn, sunrise; *orthron* fr. MGk or NGk, alter. of LGk *orthros*; akin to Gk *orthos* straight, upright — more at ORTH-] **:** the morning office in the Eastern Orthodox Church somewhat corresponding to the Latin lauds

**orting** *pres part of* ORT

**or·to·lan** \'ȯ(r)dᵊlən\ *n* -S [F or It; F *ortolan*, fr. It *ortolano* ortolan, gardener, fr. L *hortolanus* gardener, fr. *hortulus* small garden (dim. of *hortus* garden) + *-anus* -an — more at YARD] **1 :** a European bunting (*Emberiza hortulana*) that is about six inches long, has a greenish gray head, brown and black wings and back, yellowish breast, and buff abdomen, and is commonly netted and fattened for a table delicacy **2 a** *Brit* **:** WHEATEAR **b :** SORA **c :** BOBOLINK

**orts** *pl of* ORT, *pres part of* ORT

**ort·stein** \'ȯrt,stīn\ *n* [G, fr. *ort* site, place (fr. OHG, point) + *stein* stone (fr. OHG)] — more at ODD, STONE] **:** HARDPAN

**or·ty·gan** \'ȯ(r)d·əgən\ *n* -S [Gk *ortyg-*, *ortyx* quail + E *-an*] **:** one of several East Indian birds of the genus *Turnix*

**or·ty·gian** \(')ȯ(r)¦tij(ē)ən\ *adj, usu cap* [in sense 1, fr. *Ortygia* Delos, smallest island of the Cyclades, south Aegean Sea + E *-an*; in sense 2, fr. *Ortygia*, island near the southeastern coast of Sicily + E *-an*] **1 :** of or relating to the Greek island of Delos held in antiquity to be the birthplace of Apollo and Artemis ⟨*Ortygian* Artemis⟩ **2 :** of or relating to the Sicilian island of Ortygia on which modern Syracuse is built ⟨beneath the *Ortygian* shore —P.B.Shelley⟩

**orunchun** *usu cap, var of* ORONCHON

**orus·si·dae** \ō'rəsə,dē\ *n pl, cap* [NL, fr. *Orussus*, type genus (fr. Gk *oryssein* to dig) + *-idae* — more at ROUGH] **:** a hymenopterous family including the parasitic wood wasps

**or·vi·etan** \,ȯ(r)vē'ātᵊn\ *n* -S [F *orviétan*, fr. It *orvietano*, fr. *Orvieto*, city in central Italy where it was invented + *-ano* -an (fr. L *-anus*)] **:** a counterpoison formerly in vogue

**ORW** *abbr* owner's risk of becoming wet

**ory** \'ō(ə)rē, 'ȯ(-, -ri\ *adj* [¹*ore* + *-y* (adj. suffix)] *archaic* **:** resembling or containing metallic ore

**¹-ory** \(ə)rē, -ri, ,ȯr-\ *n suffix* -ES [ME *-orie*, fr. L *-orium*, fr. neut. of *-orius*, adj. suffix] **:** one that relates to or is used for: as **a :** place of or for ⟨reformat*ory*⟩ ⟨observat*ory*⟩ **b :** something that serves for ⟨cremat*ory*⟩

**²-ory** \"\ *adj suffix* [ME *-orie*, *-oire*, fr. MF & L; MF *-orie* *-oire*, fr. OF, fr. L *-orius*] **1 :** of, relating to, or characterized by ⟨observat*ory*⟩ ⟨gustat*ory*⟩ **2 :** containing, involving, or conveying ⟨amendat*ory*⟩ ⟨compuls*ory*⟩ **3 :** serving for, producing, or maintaining ⟨classificat*ory*⟩ ⟨equilibrat*ory*⟩

**oryct-** *or* **orycto-** *comb form* [NL, fr. Gk *oryktos* formed by digging, dug, verbal of *orychein*, *oryssein* to dig — more at ROUGH] **:** fossil **:** mineral ⟨*oryct*ology⟩ ⟨*orycto*gnosy⟩

**oryc·ter·o·pus** \ə,rik'terəpəs, ,ȯr,i-\ *n, cap* [NL, fr. Gk *oryktēr* miner (fr. *oryssein*, *orychein* to dig) + NL *-pus*] **:** a genus (coextensive with the family Orycteropodidae and sole recent representative of the order Tubulidentata) that comprises the aardvarks

**oryc·tognos·tic** \ə¦riktə(g)¦nästik\ *also* **oryc·tognos·ti·cal** \-stəkəl\ *adj* [*oryct-* + *-gnostic*, *-gnostical*] **:** of or relating to oryctognosy — **oryc·tognos·ti·cal·ly** \-stək(ə)lē\ *adv*

**oryc·tog·no·sy** \ə,rik'tägnəsē, ,ȯr,i-\ *n* -ES [*oryct-* + *-gnosy*] **:** MINERALOGY

**oryc·tol·a·gus** \-äləgəs\ *n, cap* [NL, fr. *oryct-* + Gk *lagōs* hare] **:** a genus comprising the common European rabbits

**oryc·to·log·ic** \ə¦riktə¦läjik\ *also* **oryc·to·log·i·cal** \-jəkəl\ *adj* **:** of or relating to oryctology

**oryc·tol·o·gist** \-ləjəst\ *n* -S **:** a specialist in oryctology

**oryc·tol·o·gy** \ə,rik'täləjē, ,ȯr,i-\ *n* -ES [prob. fr. (assumed) NL *oryctologia*, fr. Gk *oryktos* formed by digging, dug, verbal of *oryssein* to dig + NL *-logia* -logy] **:** MINERALOGY

**orys·si·dae** \ō'risə,dē\ [NL, fr. *Oryssus* (syn. of *Orussus*) (fr. Gk *oryssein*) + *-idae* — more at ROUGH] *syn of* ORUSSIDAE

**oryx** \'ōriks, 'ȯr-,'är-\ *n* [NL, fr. L, a gazelle, fr. Gk, pickax, leucoryx, fr. *oryssein*] **1** *cap* **:** a genus of large African antelopes having in both sexes long cylindrical nearly straight horns ribbed in their basal half and projecting backward in nearly exact continuation of the plane of the forehead and nose **2** *pl* **oryxes** *also* **oryx :** any antelope of the genus *Oryx*

**oryz-** *or* **oryzo-** *also* **oryzi-** *comb form* [NL, fr. L *oryza* rice, fr. Gk — more at RICE] **:** rice ⟨*oryzi*vorous⟩ ⟨*Oryzo*mys⟩

**ory·za** \ō'rīzə\ *n, cap* [NL, fr. L, rice] **:** a small genus (family Gramineae) of tropical cereal grasses having perfect flowers with six stamens — see RICE

**ory·ze·nin** \-zənən\ *n* -S [*oryzen-* (irreg. fr. Gk *oryza* rice) + *-in*] **:** a glutelin found in the seeds of rice

**or·y·ziv·o·rous** \¦ȯrə¦ziv(ə)rəs\ *adj* [*oryz-* + *-vorous*; prob. orig. formed as F *orizivore*] **:** feeding on rice

**ory·zo·mys** \ō'rīzəməs\ *n, cap* [NL, fr. *oryz-* + *-mys*] **:** a genus of cricetid rodents including the rice rats

**or·y·zop·sis** \,ȯrə'zäpsəs\ *n, cap* [NL, fr. *oryz-* + *-opsis*] **:** a genus of American tufted grasses with open panicles composed of one-flowered spikelets remotely suggesting rice — see MOUNTAIN RICE, SILK GRASS

**ory·zo·rictes** \ō,rīzə'rik(,)tēz\ *n, cap* [NL, fr. *oryz-* + Gk *oryktēs* digger, fr. *orychein*, *oryssein* to dig — more at ROUGH] **:** a genus of Malagasy insectivores comprising the rice tenrecs

**¹os** \'äs\ *n, pl* **os·sa** \-sə\ [L *oss-*, *os* — more at OSSEOUS] **:** BONE

**²os** \"\ *n, pl* **ora** \'ōrə\ [L *or-*, *os* — more at ORAL] **:** MOUTH, ORIFICE

**³os** *also* **ose** \'ōs\ *n, pl* **osar** \'ō,sär\ *also* **oses** [Sw *ås* mountain ridge, fr. ON *áss* — more at HUMERUS] **:** ESKER

**OS** \'ō'es\ *vt* **OSed; OSed; OSing; OSes** [abbr. of *order sheet* or *on sheet*] **:** to record the time of arrival and departure of (a train) by telegraphing the information prefixed by the signal OS and the office call ⟨turned to the key to ~ his first train out —*Trains*⟩

**OS** *abbr* **1** [L *oculus sinister*] left eye **2** off stage **3** old school **4** old series **5** old side **6** old style **7** one side **8** only son **9** on sale **10** on sample **11** on schedule **12** on sheet **13** on side **14** ordinary seaman **15** original series **16** out of stock **17** outside **18** outside sentinel **19** outsize **20** outstanding

**Os** *symbol* osmium

**o's** *or* **os** *pl of* O

**osage** \(')ō¦sāj\ *n, pl* **osage** *or* **osages** *usu cap* [Osage *Wazhazhe*] **1 a** (1) **:** a Siouan people of the Osage and Missouri river valleys, Missouri (2) **:** a member of such people **b :** the language of the Osage people **2 :** OSAGE ORANGE

**osage apple** *n* ... *also* **osage orange** *n, usu cap 1st O* **1 a** *also* **osage apple :** an ornamental American tree (*Maclura pomifera*) of the family Moraceae having dark green glossy leaves, milky sap, hard bright orange-colored wood that yields a dye, and imperfect flowers **b :** the wood of the osage orange **c :** the yellowish green tubercled globular fruit of the osage orange tree consisting of the united fleshy calyxes of the pistillate flowers **2** *usu cap 1st O & often cap 2d O* **:** the yellow coloring matter that is extracted from the wood of the osage orange tree and is similar to old fustic — see DYE table I (under *Natural Yellow 8*)

**osa·gi·an** \-jēən\ *adj, usu cap* [*Osage* river, eastern Kansas and western and central Missouri + E *-an*] **:** of or relating to the division of the Mississippian geologic period between the Kinderhook and the Meramec — see GEOLOGIC TIME table

**osa·ka** \ō'säkə\ *adj, usu cap* [fr. *Osaka*, city in west central Honshu, Japan] **:** of or from the city of Osaka, Japan **:** of the kind or style prevalent in Osaka

**OS and D** *abbr* over, short, and damaged

**osa·zone** \'ōsə,zōn, 'äs-\ *n* -S [ISV ²*-ose* + *az-* + *-one*; prob. orig. formed as G *osazon*] **:** any of a class of basic compounds that contain two adjacent hydrazone groupings and are made from an alpha-diketone and hydrazine, an alkyl- or aryl-hydrazine, or from an alpha-hydroxy aldehyde or ketone (as glucose or benzoin) and an aryl-hydrazine; *esp* **:** PHENYLOSAZONE

**osc** *abbr* oscillate; oscillating; oscillator

**os cal·cis** \-'kalsəs\ *n, pl* **ossa calcis** [L, bone of the heel] **:** CALCANEUS

**os·can** \'äskən, 'ōs-\ *n* -S *cap* [L *Oscus* Oscan + E *-an*] **1 :** one of a people of ancient Italy occupying Campania **2 :** the language of the Oscan people and orig. of the Samnites preserved in inscriptions of various kinds written in an alphabet of Etruscan origin — compare SAMNITE, UMBRIAN

**¹os·car** \'äskə(r), 'ōs-\ *n* -S [after *Oscar* Pierce, 20th cent. Am. wheat and fruit grower] **1** *usu cap* **a :** any of a number of golden statuettes awarded annually by a professional organization for notable achievement in motion pictures **b :** any annual award for notable achievement **2** [by rhyming slang fr. John S. H. *Oscar* Asche †1936 Australian actor] *Austral* **:** MONEY, CASH

**²oscar** \"\ *usu cap* [fr. the name *Oscar*] — a communications code word for the letter *o*

**os·cil·late** \'äsə,lāt, *usu* -ād·+V\ *vb* -ED/-ING/-S [L *oscillatus*, past part. of *oscillare* to swing, fr. *oscillum* swing] *vi* **1 a :** to swing backward and forward like a pendulum **:** move to and fro **:** VIBRATE ⟨the completed statue . . . was placed upon a turntable base that slowly ~*s*, completing a 90-degree arc every hour —*Amer. Guide Series: Minn.*⟩ ⟨rocker arms on all other overhead valve engines ~ on stationary tubular shafts —H.F.Blanchard & Ralph Ritchen⟩ **b :** to travel back and forth between two points ⟨he ~*s* regularly between his comfortable home . . . and his downtown office-laboratory —Gladwin Hill⟩ **2 a :** to vary the state or condition **:** FLUCTUATE ⟨the snow line ~*s* with the seasons, descending below ten thousand feet in winter —C.D.Forde⟩ ⟨diaries showing how he *oscillated* between wealth and poverty —E.V.Lucas⟩ **b :** to vary between opposing attitudes, beliefs, feelings, or theories **:** think or act in a fickle manner **:** SHILLY-SHALLY ⟨men have *oscillated* in their opinions —W.E.Swinton⟩ **3 :** to vibrate or vary above and below a mean value ⟨bank rate oscillating between 2½ percent and 6½ percent —W.M.Dacey⟩ ⟨a polynomial which ~*s* greatly between the observed values —J.G.Kemeny⟩ ~ *vt* **:** to cause to oscillate ⟨~ the crankshaft slightly to locate dead center —H.F.Blanchard & Ralph Ritchen⟩ **syn** see SWING

**oscillating current** *n* **:** electric current consisting of oscillations

**oscillating wave** *n* **:** GREGARIOUS WAVE

**os·cil·la·tion** \,äsə'lāshən\ *n* -S [L *oscillation-*, *oscillatio* action of swinging, fr. *oscillatus* (past part. of *oscillare* to swing) + *-ion-*, *-io* -ion] **1 :** the action or fact of oscillating **:** a swinging or moving backward and forward like a pendulum **:** VIBRATION ⟨stays can be effectively used to prevent aerodynamic ~*s* in new bridges —D.B.Steinman⟩ ⟨vibration in aircraft occurs principally as a result of ~*s* from the motor and propeller —H.G.Armstrong⟩ ⟨a diatomic molecule . . . can absorb vibrational energy by ~ of the atoms within the molecule —F.H.Getman⟩ **2 a :** a periodic variation or fluctuation between conditions ⟨famines due to excessive storminess and violent ~*s* of rain and drought, heat and cold —Ellsworth Huntington⟩ ⟨major prosperities and depressions are not to be explained by the process and mechanism of business cycles (endogenous ~*s*) —Clark Warburton⟩ ⟨men get tired of everything, of heaven no less than of hell; and that all history is nothing but a record of the ~*s* of the world between these two extremes —G.B.Shaw⟩ **b :** the change back and forth between opposing beliefs, opinions, or theories **:** variation in attitudes, policies, principles, or purposes often for fickle reasons ⟨fruitless ~*s* or the decision to make no decision will destroy his days —J.B.Conant⟩ ⟨a lover's instant ~ from black to white, from hate to love —Clemence Dane⟩ **3 :** a flow of electricity changing periodically from a maximum to a minimum or from positive to negative when an electrical system with capacitance and inductance is disturbed from equilibrium **4 :** the variation of a mathematical function between limits; *specif* **:** the difference between the greatest and least values of a function **5 a :** a single swing from one extreme limit to the other of an oscillating body **b :** one of the periodic variations of an oscillating variable (as the electron current in a radio tube) — compare HARMONIC OSCILLATION — **os·cil·la·tion·al** \¦==¦lāshənᵊl, -shnəl\ *adj*

**oscillation circuit** *n* **:** a circuit designed to produce electric oscillations

**oscillation ripple** *or* **oscillation ripple mark** *n* **:** a symmetrical ripple on a bedding plane or on a sea or lake floor with sharp crest and broadly rounded trough formed by gregarious waves — compare CURRENT RIPPLE

**os·cil·la·tor** \'==,lād·ə(r), -ātə-\ *n* -S [NL, fr. L *oscillatus* (past part. of *oscillare*) + NL *-or*] **:** one that oscillates: as **a :** an instrument for measuring rigidity by the torsional oscillations of a weighted wire **b :** a device for producing electric oscillations; *specif* **:** a radio-frequency or audio-frequency generator esp. of a nonrotating type

**os·cil·la·to·ria** \,äsəlā'tōrēə\ *n, cap* [NL, fr. fem. of *oscillatorius* oscillatory] **:** a genus of blue-green algae that is the type of the family Oscillatoriaceae

**os·cil·la·to·ri·a·ce·ae** \,===,tōrē'āsē,ē\ *n pl, cap* [NL, fr *Oscillatoria*, type genus + *-aceae*] **:** a family of blue-green algae (order Hormogonales) growing as slender filaments often in tangled masses in water or on damp rocks or soil, forming slimy layers on soil, commonly exhibiting oscillating movements, and reproducing only asexually by hormogonia — **os·cil·la·to·ri·a·ceous** \¦===¦==¦āshəs\ *adj*

**os·cil·la·to·ri·a·les** \,===,==ə'(,)lēz\ [NL, fr. *Oscillatoria* + *-ales*] *syn of* HORMOGONALES

**os·cil·la·to·ry** \'äsələ,tōrē, -tȯr-, -ri\ *adj* [NL *oscillatorius*, fr. L *oscillatus* (past part. of *oscillare*) + *-orius* -ory] **:** characterized by oscillation **:** VIBRATORY

**oscillatory circuit** *n* **:** a circuit containing capacity and inductance such that a single voltage impulse would give rise to a damped alternating current

**oscillatory current** *n* **:** OSCILLATING CURRENT

**oscillatory discharge** *n* **:** an electric discharge in a circuit having sufficient capacitative reactance to result in damped alternating surges of electricity

**os·cil·lo·gram** \ä'silə,gram\ *n* [ISV *oscillo-* (fr. L *oscillare*) + *-gram*] **:** an autographic record made by an oscillograph or oscilloscope

**os·cil·lo·graph** \-raf, -räf\ *n* [F *oscillographe*, fr. *oscillo-* (fr. L *oscillare*) + *-graphe* -graph] **:** an instrument that produces in the form of a continuous curve a permanent record (as a graph or a photograph) of periodic or irregular variations in an electrical quantity (as voltage) and often indirectly in some related quantity (as sound pressure) by means of a moving element (as a galvanometer needle or a vibrating beam of cathode rays) — compare OSCILLOSCOPE — **os·cil·lo·graph·ic** \=¦==¦grafik\ *adj* — **os·cil·lo·graph·i·cal·ly** \-fək(ə)lē\ *adv* — **os·cil·log·ra·phy** \,äsə'lägrəfē\ *n* -ES

**os·cil·lom·e·ter** \,äsə'lämәd·ə(r)\ *n* [ISV *oscillo-* (fr. L *oscillare*) + *-meter*] **1 :** an instrument for measuring the angle through which a ship rolls or pitches at sea **2 :** an instrument for measuring the changes in pulsations in the arteries esp. of the extremities — **os·cil·lo·met·ric** \¦äsəlō¦me·trik\ *adj* — **os·cil·lom·e·try** \,äsə'lämə·trē\ *n* -ES

**os·cil·lo·scope** \ä'silə,skōp\ *n* [ISV *oscillo-* (fr. L *oscillare*) + *-scope*] **:** an instrument in which the variations in a fluctuating electrical quantity (as voltage) are not recorded but appear temporarily as a visible wave form on the fluorescent screen of a cathode-ray tube; *broadly* **:** OSCILLOGRAPH — **os·cil·lo·scop·ic** \=¦==¦skäpik\ *adj*

**os·cine** \'äs'n, 'ä,sīn\ *adj* [NL *Oscines*] **:** relating to or having the character of the Oscines

**os·ci·nel·la** \,äsə'nelə\ *n, cap* [NL, fr. L *oscin-*, *oscen* singing bird used in divination + *-ella*] **:** a genus of chloropid flies containing the frit fly

**os·ci·nes** \'äsə,nēz\ *n pl, cap* [NL, fr. L, pl. of *oscin-*, *oscen* singing bird used in divination, fr. *os-* (fr. *ob* to, before, against) + *-cin-*, *-cen* (fr. *canere* to sing) — more at EPI-,

CHANT] *in some classifications* : a suborder or superfamily of birds equivalent to the suborder Passeres

**os·cin·i·dae** \ə'sinə,dē\ [NL, fr. *Oscinis* (syn. of *Oscinella*) (fr. L *oscin-, oscen* singing bird used in divination) + *-idae*] *syn of* CHLOROPIDAE

**os·ci·nine** \'äsə,nīn, -,nən\ *adj* [NL *Oscines* + E *-ine*] : OSCINE

**os·cin·o·so·ma** \,äsənō'sōmə\ [NL, fr. L *oscin-, oscen* singing bird used in divination + NL *-o-* + *-soma*] *syn of* OSCINELLA

**os·ci·tan·cy** \'äsəd·ənsē\ *n* -ES [*oscitant* + *-cy*] **1 a** : drowsiness usu. demonstrated by yawns **b** : DULLNESS, SLUGGISHNESS **2** : the act of gaping or yawning

**os·ci·tant** \-nt\ *adj* [L *oscitant-, oscitans*, pres. part. of *oscitare* to yawn, fr. *os* mouth + *citare* to put in motion — more at CITE] : yawning with drowsiness; *also* : LAZY, STUPID

**os·ci·ta·tion** \,äsə'tāshən\ *n* -S [L *oscitation-, oscitatio* action of yawning, fr. *oscitatus* (past part. of *oscitare* to yawn) + *-ion-, -io* -ion] **1** : the act of being inattentive **2** : the condition of being drowsy

**os·co-umbrian** \'ä(,)skō+\ *n, cap O&U* [*osco-* (fr. L *Oscus* Oscan) + *umbrian*] : a subdivision of the Italic branch of the Indo-European language family containing the closely related languages of Oscan and Umbrian

**os cox·ae** \-'käk,sē\ *n, pl* **ossa coxae** [L, bone of the hip] : INNOMINATE BONE

**os·cu·lant** \'äskyələnt\ *adj* [NL *osculant-, osculans*, fr. L, pres. part. of *osculari* to kiss] **1** : intermediate in character : forming a connecting link between two groups **2** : adhering closely : EMBRACING

**os·cu·lar** \'äskyələ(r)\ *adj* [NL *oscularis*, fr. L *osculum* little mouth, kiss + *-aris* -ar] **1** : of, relating to, or concerned with kissing ⟨~ muscles⟩ **2 a** : of or relating to an osculum **b** : of or relating to a mouth — **os·cu·lar·i·ty** \,äskyə'larəd·ē\ *n* -ES

**os·cu·late** \'äskyə,lāt, *usu* -ād·+V\ *vb* -ED/-ING/-S [L *osculatus*, past part. of *osculari* to kiss, fr. *osculum* little mouth, kiss, dim. of *os* mouth — more at ORAL] *vt* **1** : KISS **2** *math* : to have contact of the second or higher order with ~ *vi* : to have characters in common with two groups

**os·cu·la·tion** \,==ˈlāshən\ *n* -S [L *osculation-, osculatio*, fr. *osculatus* (past part. of *osculari*) + *-ion-, -io* -ion] : the act of kissing; *also* : KISS

**¹os·cu·la·to·ry** \'äskyələ,tōrē\ *n* -ES [ML *osculatorium*, fr. L *osculatus* (past part. of *osculari*) + *-orium* -ory] : PAX 1

**²osculatory** \"\ *adj* [prob. fr. (assumed) NL *osculatorius*, fr. L *osculatus* (past part. of *osculari*) + *-orius* -ory] : of, relating to, or characterized by kissing

**os·cule** \'ä,skyül\ *n* -S [F, fr. NL *osculum*] : OSCULUM

**os·cu·lom·e·ter** \,äskyə'lämәd·ә(r)\ *n* [*oscul-* (fr. *osculate*) + *-o-* + *-meter*] : a graduated series of circular arcs for determining by superposition the curvature at any point on a curve; *also* : an instrument used for a similar purpose

**os·cu·lum** \'äskyələm\ *n, pl* **oscula** [NL, fr. L, little mouth, kiss] : one of the excurrent orifices of a sponge

**¹ose** \'ōs\ *n* -S [ISV, fr. *²-ose*] : GLYCOSE

**²ose** *var of* OS

**¹-ose** \,ōs, *in some words* ¦ō| *or* 'ō|, *or* |z\ *adj suffix* [ME, fr. L *-osus*] : full of : having : possessing the qualities of ⟨clad*ose*⟩

**²-ose** \,ōs *also* ,ōz\ *n suffix* -S [F, fr. *glucose*] **1** : carbohydrate ⟨amyl*ose*⟩; *esp* : sugar ⟨fruct*ose*⟩ ⟨pent*ose*⟩ **2** : primary hydrolysis product ⟨prote*ose*⟩

**³-ose** \,ōs\ *n suffix* -S [NL *-osis*] : -OSIS 4 ⟨chytridi*ose*⟩

**osete** *cap, var of* OSSET

**osi·an·dri·an** \,ōzē'andrēən, ,ōsē'-\ *also* **osi·an·drist** \-rəst\ *n* -S *usu cap* [Andreas *Osiander* †1552 Ger. Lutheran theologian + E *-an* or *-ist*] : an adherent of the doctrine that in justification by faith the believer is actually made righteous by an indwelling of Christ in him and not merely declared righteous by imputation

**oside** \'ō,sīd, 'ōsəd\ *n* -S [ISV, fr. *-oside*] : GLYCOSIDE

**-o·side** \,ō,sīd; ə,sīd, əsəd\ *n suffix* -S [ISV *²-ose* + *-ide*] : glycoside or similar compound ⟨gangli*oside*⟩ ⟨heter*oside*⟩ — compare -IDE 2b

**¹osier** \'ōzhə(r)\ *n* -S [ME, fr. MF *osier, osiere*, fr. ML *auseria* osier bed] **1** : any of various willows whose pliable twigs are used for furniture and basketry: as **a** : a European willow (*Salix viminalis*) — called also *velvet osier* **b** : ALMOND WILLOW **c** : GOLDEN WILLOW **d** : PURPLE WILLOW **2** : an osier rod used in basketry; *esp* : a coarse unstripped rod used for making hampers **3** : any of several American dogwoods

**²osier** \"\ *adj* : made of, covered with, or containing osiers

**osi·ered** \-(r)d\ *adj* : covered or adorned with osiers

**osier willow** *n* **1** : OSIER 1 **2** : a willow used as an osier rod

**osiery** \-ərē\ *n* -ES : an area where osiers are grown; *also* : work made of osiers

**osi·ri·an** \ō'sīrēən\ *adj, usu cap* [*Osiris*, Egyptian god of the underworld (fr. L *Osirid-, Osiris*, fr. Gk, fr. Egypt *Ws'r*) + E *-an*] : of or relating to the ancient Egyptian god Osiris

**osi·ride** \ō'sīrəd\ *adj* [L *Osirid-, Osiris* Osiris] : OSIRIAN — used esp. of a pillar against which is set an image of Osiris

**osi·ri·fi·ca·tion** \ō,sīrəfə'kāshən\ *n* -S [fr. *osirify*, after such pairs as E *deify: deification*] : the act or state of being osirified

**osi·ri·fy** \ō'sīrə,fī\ *vt* -ED/-ING/-ES [*Osiris* + E *-fy*] : to identify as or with Osiris

**osi·rism** \ō'sī,rizəm\ *n* -S *usu cap* [*Osiris* + E *-ism*] : the worship of Osiris

**-o·sis** \'ōsəs\ *n suffix, pl* **-o·ses** \'ō,sēz\ *or* **-o·sis·es** [ME, fr. L, fr. Gk *-ōsis*, fr. *-ō-* (medial vowel characteristic of derivatives of certain verbs) + *-sis*] **1 a** : action : process : condition ⟨hypn*osis*⟩ **b** : abnormal or diseased condition ⟨leuk*osis*⟩ **2** : increase : formation ⟨leukocyt*osis*⟩ **3** : arrangement ⟨pteryl*osis*⟩ **4** [NL, fr. L] : disease caused by a (specified) fungus ⟨chytridi*osis*⟩

**os·lo** \'äz(,)lō, 'äs(-\ *adj, usu cap* [fr. *Oslo*, Norway] : of or from Oslo, the capital of Norway : of the kind or style prevalent in Oslo

**oslo breakfast** *or* **oslo meal** *n, usu cap O* : a mid-morning or mid-afternoon meal of uncooked protective foods (as whole wheat bread, butter, milk, cheese, raw fruit or vegetable)

**os·lo·ite** \'äzlō,īt, 'äsl-\ *n* -S *cap* [*Oslo* + E *-ite*] : a native or resident of Oslo, Norway

**osm-** *or* **osmo-** *comb form* [NL, fr. Gk *osm-*, fr. *osmē* — more at ODOR] **1** : odor : smell ⟨*Osmo*rhiza⟩ **2 a** : osmium ⟨*osm*ic⟩ **b** *osmo-* : osmous ⟨*osmo*cyanide⟩

**-os·ma** \'äzmə *also* 'äsmə\ *n comb form* [NL, fr. Gk *osmē*] : one having (such) an odor — in generic names of plants ⟨Bar*osma*⟩ ⟨Copr*osma*⟩

**os·ma·gogue** \'äzmə,gäg\ *adj* [*osm-* + *-agogue* (fr. LL *-agogus* promoting the expulsion of) — more at -AGOGUE] : stimulating to the sense of smell

**os·man·li** \äz'manlē, ä'sm, -män-\ *also* **os·man** \'äzmən; äz'män, ä'sm-\ *n* -S *cap* [Turk *osmanlı*, fr. *Osman, Othman* †1326 founder of the Ottoman Empire] **1** : a Turk of the western branch of the Turkish peoples **2** : TURKISH 1

**os·man·thus** \äz'man(t)thəs\ *n, cap* [NL, fr. *osm-* + *-anthus*] : a widely distributed genus of evergreen shrubs or trees (family Oleaceae) with inconspicuous bisexual flowers, sometimes foliage resembling holly, and a drupaceous fruit with a hard woody endocarp — see DEVILWOOD

**os·mate** \'äzmət, -z,māt\ *n* -S [ISV *osmic* + *-ate*] : a salt or ester of osmic acid

**os·matic** \(')äz¦mad·ik\ *or* **os·mic** \'äzmik\ *adj* [*osmatic* fr. *osm-* + *-atic* (as in *aquatic*); *osmic* fr. *osm-* + *-ic*] : depending chiefly on the sense of smell for orientation ⟨the dog is a strongly ~ animal⟩ — compare OPTIC

**os·mer·i·dae** \äz'merə,dē\ *n pl, cap* [NL, fr. *Osmerus*, type genus + *-idae*] : a family (order Isospondyli) to which the true smelts belong

**os·me·rus** \äz'mirəs\ *n, cap* [NL, fr. Gk *osmēros* odorous, fr. *osmē* odor] : a genus of smelts of the type of the family Osmeridae

**os·me·sis** \äz'mēsəs\ *n* -ES [NL, fr. Gk *osmēsis*, fr. *osmasthai* to smell, perceive by smell (fr. *osmē* odor) + *-sis*] : OLFACTION — **os·met·ic** \(')=¦med·ik\ *adj*

**os·me·te·ri·um** *also* **os·ma·te·ri·um** \,äzmə'tirēəm\ *n, pl* **osmete·ria** *also* **osmate·ria** \-ēə\ [NL, irreg. fr. Gk *osmē* odor] : a protrusile forked process that emits a disagreeable odor, is borne on the first thoracic segment of the larvae of many butterflies of the family Papilionidae, and is probably a defensive organ

**os·mia** \'äzmēə\ *n, cap* [NL, fr. *osm-* + *-ia*] : a cosmopolitan genus of solitary bees (family Megachilidae) including several that are important pollinators of economic plants

**os·mic** \'äzmik\ *adj* [ISV *osm-* + *-ic*] : of, relating to, or derived from osmium — used esp. of compounds in which this element exhibits a relatively high valence; compare OSMOUS

**osmic acid** *n* [ISV *osmic* + *acid*] **1** : a hypothetical acid $H_2OsO_4$ known esp. in the form of salts (as potassium osmate $K_2OsO_4.2H_2O$) obtainable from osmium tetroxide in alkaline solution **2** : OSMIUM TETROXIDE

**os·mics** \'äzmiks\ *n pl but sing in constr* [*osm-* + *-ics*] : a science that deals with the sense of smell : the study of odors

**os·mi·dro·sis** \,äzmə'drōsəs\ *n, pl* **osmidro·ses** \-ō,sēz\ [NL, fr. *osm-* + *-idrosis*] : BROMIDROSIS

**os·mio·phil** \'äzmēə,fil\ *or* **os·mio·phil·ic** \¦===¦filik\ *also* **os·mio·phile** \'===,fīl\ *adj* [*osmium* + *-o-* + *-phil, -phile* or *-philic*] : reacting specif. to the presence of osmium tetroxide usu. by the formation of a black deposit — **os·mio·phil·ia** \,==='filēə\ *n* -S — **os·mi·oph·i·ly** \,äzmē'äfəlē\ *n* -ES

**osmious** *var of* OSMOUS

**os·mi·rid·i·um** \,äzmə'ridēəm\ *also* **os·mi·irid·i·um** \-mə-,ī'-\ *n* -S [G *osmiridium*, fr. *osm-* + *iridium*, fr. NL] : IRIDOSMINE

**os·mi·um** \'äzmēəm\ *n* -S [NL, fr. Gk *osmē* odor + NL *-ium*; fr. the strong characteristic smell of osmium tetroxide] : a hard brittle blue-gray or blue-black high-melting polyvalent metallic element that is one of the platinum metals, that is the heaviest metal known, that occurs in platinum ores principally alloyed with iridium in iridosmine, and that is used chiefly as a catalyst and in hard alloys esp. with platinum or ruthenium (as for pen nibs and phonograph needles) — symbol *Os*; see ELEMENT table

**osmium dioxide** *n* [ISV *osmium* + *dioxide*] : a brown or black solid $OsO_2$ obtainable by oxidation of osmium or reduction of osmium tetroxide

**osmium lamp** *n* : an incandescent lamp with a filament of osmium or an osmium alloy — compare TUNGSTEN LAMP

**osmium oxide** *n* [ISV *osmium* + *oxide*] : an oxide of osmium: **a** : OSMIUM DIOXIDE **b** : OSMIUM TETROXIDE

**osmium tetroxide** *n* [ISV *osmium* + *tetroxide*] : a crystalline compound $OsO_4$ that has a poisonous irritating pungent vapor, that is usu. made by oxidizing osmium, and that is used chiefly as a catalyst, as an oxidizing and hydroxylating agent (as in the conversion of olefins to glycols), and as a stain for fatty substances in cytology

**¹osmo-** *comb form* [*¹osmose*] : osmosis : osmotic ⟨*osmo*meter⟩

**²osmo-** — see OSM-

**os·mo·graph** \'äzmə,graf, -räf\ *n* [*¹osmo-* + *-graph*] : an instrument for recording the height of the liquid in an endosmometer or for registering osmotic pressures

**os·mom·e·ter** \äz'mämәd·ә(r)\ *n* [*¹osmo-* + *-meter*] : an apparatus for measuring osmotic pressure

**os·mo·met·ric** \¦äzmə¦me·trik\ *adj* [*osmometry* + *-ic*] : of or relating to osmometry — **os·mo·met·ri·cal·ly** \-rәk(ә)lē\ *adv*

**os·mom·e·try** \äz'mämə·trē\ *n* -ES [ISV *¹osmo-* + *-metry*] : the measurement of osmotic pressure ⟨determination of the molecular weight of proteins by ~⟩

**osmond** *var of* OSMUND

**¹os·mo·phil·ic** \¦äzmə¦filik\ *also* **os·mo·phile** \'==,fīl\ *adj* [*osmophilic* fr. *¹osmo-* + *-philic*; *osmophile* ISV *¹osmo-* + *-phile*] : living or thriving in a medium of high osmotic pressure ⟨~ yeasts that ferment maple syrup⟩

**²osmophilic** \"\ *also* **osmophile** \"\ *adj* [*osm-* + *-philic* or *-phile*] : of, relating to, constituting, or containing cellular lipoids that become blackened with a precipitate of osmium when exposed to osmium tetroxide

**os·mo·phore** \'äzmə,fō(ə)r\ *n* -S [ISV *osm-* + *-phore*] : a group or radical (as hydroxyl, cyanogen, the aldehyde group) to whose presence in a molecule the odor of a compound is attributed — compare CHROMOPHORE — **osmophoric** *adj*

**os·mo·receptor** \¦äzmō+\ *n* [*¹osmo-* + *receptor*] : a sensory endorgan that is stimulated by changes in osmotic pressure

**os·mo·regulation** \"+\ *n* [ISV *¹osmo-* + *regulation*] : regulation of osmotic pressure esp. in the body of a living organism

**os·mo·regulator** \"+\ *n* [ISV *¹osmo-* + *regulator*] : a body mechanism concerned with the maintenance of constant osmotic pressure relationships — **os·mo·regulatory** \"+\ *adj*

**os·mo·rhi·za** \,äzmə'rīzə\ *n, cap* [NL, fr. *osm-* + *-rhiza*] : a genus of American and Asiatic white-flowered herbs (family Umbelliferae) with decompound leaves and fleshy aromatic roots

**¹os·mo·scope** \'äzmə,skōp\ *n* [*osm-* + *-scope*] : an instrument for detecting and for measuring odors — compare ODOROMETER

**²osmoscope** \"\ *n* [*¹osmo-* + *-scope*] : an apparatus for carrying out osmosis

**¹os·mose** \'äz,mōs, 'ä,sm-\ *n*'-s [fr. obs. *endosmose* endosmosis & obs. *exosmose* exosmosis — more at ENDOSMOSIS, EXOSMOSIS] : OSMOSIS 1

**²osmose** \"\ *vb* -ED/-ING/-S *vt* : to subject to osmosis : DIALYZE ~ *vi* : to diffuse by osmosis

**os·mo·sis** \äz'mōsəs, ä'sm-\ *n, pl* **osmo·ses** \-ō,sēz\ [alter. (influenced by Gk *-sis*) of *¹osmose*] **1** : the flow or diffusion that takes place through a semipermeable membrane (as of a living cell) typically separating either a solvent (as water) and a solution or a dilute solution and a concentrated solution and thus bringing about conditions for equalizing the concentrations of the components on the two sides of the membrane because of the unequal rates of passage in the two directions until equilibrium is reached; *esp* : the passage of solvent in distinction from the passage of solute; compare ABSORPTION 1c, DIALYSIS, ELECTROOSMOSIS, ENDOSMOSIS, EXOSMOSIS, IMBIBITION 2 a, SAP, TURGOR **2** : a process of absorption, interaction, or diffusion suggestive of the flow of osmotic action ⟨owing to the usual mysterious news ~, had already heard about it —Agnes S. Turnbull⟩: as **a** : an interaction or interchange (as of cultural groups or traits) by mutual penetration esp. through a separating medium **b** : a usu. effortless often unconscious absorption or assimilation (as of ideas or influences) by a seemingly general permeation ⟨absorbing democratic habits and ideals as by ~ —H.G.Rickover⟩ ⟨working alongside pupils in higher grades, the bright student gets advanced learning practically by ~ —Gertrude Samuels⟩ ⟨acquired his ideas through thought processes, not through social ~ —Roscoe Drummond⟩ ⟨a kind of cultural ~, the unconscious absorption of Oriental influences through seemingly trivial contacts —Edmond Taylor⟩

**os·mo·tac·tic** \¦äzmə¦taktik\ *adj* [fr. *osmotaxis*, after such pairs as E *hypotaxis: hypotactic*] : of or relating to osmotaxis

**os·mo·tax·is** \,===ˈtaksəs\ *n* [NL, fr. *¹osmo-* + *-taxis*] : a taxis in which a difference of osmotic pressure is the directing factor

**os·mot·ic** \(')äz¦mäd·ik, (')ä¦sm-, -ät|, |ēk,\ *adj* [fr. *endosmotic*] : of, relating to, or having the property of osmosis — **os·mot·i·cal·ly** \|ək(ə)lē\ *adv*

**osmotic pressure** *n* : the pressure produced by or associated with osmosis and dependent on molar concentration and absolute temperature: as **a** : the maximum pressure that develops in a solution separated from a solvent by a membrane permeable only to the solvent **b** : the pressure that must be applied to a solution to just prevent osmosis — compare OSMOMETRY

**os·mous** \'äzməs\ *also* **os·mi·ous** \-mēəs\ *adj* [*osmous* fr. *osm-* + *-ous*; *osmious* ISV *osmium* + *-ous*] : of, relating to, or derived from osmium — used esp. of compounds in which this element exhibits a relatively low valence; compare OSMIC

**¹os·mund** *also* **os·mond** \'äzmənd\ *n* -S [ME *osmunde*, fr. OF *osmonde*] **1** *obs* : any of various ferns (as the male fern) **2** : a fern of the genus *Osmunda*; *esp* : ROYAL FERN

**²osmund** *also* **osmond** \"\ *n* -S [ME *osmond*, fr. MLG *osemunt*, fr. OSw *osmunder*] : a superior iron formerly imported into England from Sweden and used esp. for making arrowheads, fishhooks, and clockworks; *also* : a piece of this iron

**os·mun·da** \äz'məndə\ *n* [NL, fr. ML, osmund, fr. OF *osmonde*] **1** *cap* : the type genus of Osmundaceae comprising rather large ferns with creeping rhizomes, stipes winged at the base, and naked glabrose sporangia borne on modified pinnae — see CINNAMON FERN, ROYAL FERN **2** -S : any fern of the genus *Osmunda*

**os·mun·da·ce·ae** \,äzmən'dāsē,ē\ *n pl, cap* [NL, fr. *Osmunda*, type genus + *-aceae*] : a large family of widely distributed ferns with naked sori and brightly stalked annulate sporangia that open longitudinally — **os·mun·da·ceous** \¦==¦dāshəs\ *adj*

**osmund brake** *n* : ROYAL FERN

**osmund furnace** *n* [*²osmund*] : a high forge intermediate in development between the Catalan forge and the blast furnace and formerly used for making a wrought iron for wire

**os·mun·dine** \äz'mən,dēn\ *n* -S [NL *Osmunda* + E *-ine*] : material prepared from the roots of various ferns (primarily *Osmunda cinnamomea* and *O. claytonia*) and used in the potting of orchids

**osmund iron** *n* [ME *osmonde iren* (trans. of OSw *osmundsiærn*), fr. *osmonde, osmond* osmund + *iren* iron] : OSMUND; *also* : iron made in the osmund furnace

**os·na·brück** *or* **os·na·bruck** *or* **os·na·brueck** \'äznə,brůk\ *adj, usu cap* [fr. *Osnabrück*, city in northwest Germany] : of or from the city of Osnabrück, Germany : of the kind or style prevalent in Osnabrück

**os·na·burg** \'äznə,bərg\ *n* -S [irreg. fr. *Osnabrück*, Germany] : a rough coarse durable cotton fabric in plain weave made orig. of flax and used in the gray for bagging and industrial purposes and in various finishes usu. for upholstery, sportswear, and curtains

**oso·berry** \'ōsə— *see* BERRY\ *n* [Sp *oso* bear (fr. L *ursus*) + E *berry* — more at ARCTIC] **1** : the blue-black fruit resembling cherries of a shrub (*Osmaronia cerasiformis*) of the family Rosaceae of Oregon and California **2** : a plant bearing osoberries

**osone** \'ō,sōn\ *n* -S [ISV *²-ose* + *-one*; orig. formed as G *oson*] : a compound that contains two alpha carbonyl groups and is obtained by hydrolyzing an osazone ⟨xylose ~ $HOCH_2$-$(CHOH)_2COCHO$⟩

**oso·triazole** \¦ōsō+\ *n* [ISV *oso-* (fr. *²-ose*) + *triazole*] : a vicinal triazole usu. made by boiling an osazone solution with dilute copper sulfate solution and useful in forming crystalline derivatives of carbohydrates

**OSP** *abbr, often not cap* [L *obiit sine prole*] he died without issue

**os·phra·di·al** \(')äs¦frādēəl\ *adj* [*osphradium* + *-al*] : of or relating to the osphradium

**os·phra·di·um** \-'==əm\ *n, pl* **osphra·dia** \-ēə\ [NL, fr. MGk *osphradion* nosegay, dim. of LGk *osphra* smell; akin to Gk *ozein* to smell — more at ODOR] : a single or paired sense organ connected with one of the visceral ganglia and situated near the gill of most aquatic mollusks that is supposed to be olfactory or to test the purity of the water passing to the gills

**-os·phre·sia** \äs'frēzh(ē)ə, (,)äs-\ *also* **-os·phra·sia** \'-rāzh-\ *n comb form* -S [NL, fr. Gk *osphrēsis* sense of smell & Gk *osphrasia* odor; akin to Gk *ozein* to smell] : sense of smell ⟨an*osphresia*⟩ ⟨an*osphrasia*⟩

**os·phre·sis** \äs'frēsəs\ *n* -ES [NL, fr. Gk *osphrēsis*] : OLFACTION

**os·phret·ic** \(')äs¦fred·ik\ *adj* [Gk *osphrētikos*, fr. *osphrētos* capable of being smelled + *-ikos* -ic; akin to Gk *ozein* to smell] : OLFACTORY

**os·phro·men·i·dae** \,äsfrə'menə,dē\ *n pl, cap* [NL, fr. *Osphromenus*, type genus (fr. Gk *osphromenos*, aor. part. of *osphrainesthai* to smell, catch the scent of) + *-idae*; fr. a resemblance of certain organs to another supposed by the namer to be an organ of smell; akin to Gk *ozein* to smell] *in some classifications* : a family of freshwater fishes of southeastern Asia and Africa including the gouramis and a number of favored aquarium fishes and usu. included in the same family (Anabantidae) as the genus *Anabas*

**os·prey** \'äsprē, 'ä,sprā\ *n* -S [ME *ospray*, fr. (assumed) MF *osfraie*, fr. L *ossifraga* sea eagle — more at OSSIFRAGE] **1** : a large harmless hawk (*Pandion haliaetus*) found in most countries of the world that is a dark brown color above and mostly pure white below, builds a bulky nest often occupied year after year, and feeds on fish that it captures by hovering and diving — called also *fish hawk* **2** : a feather trimming (as an aigrette) used for millinery

**ossa** *pl of* OS

**¹osse** *or* **oss** \'äs\ *vb* **ossed; ossed; ossing; osses** [ME *ossen* to prophesy, presage] *dial Eng* : ATTEMPT, VENTURE, DARE

**²osse** *n* -S [obs. *osse*, v., to prophesy, presage, fr. ME *ossen*] *obs* : a prophetic or ominous utterance

**osse-** *or* **osseo-** *comb form* [NL, fr. L *osse-* (in *osseus*)] **1** : bone ⟨*osse*in⟩ **2** : osseous and ⟨*osseo*cartilaginous⟩

**os·se·in** \'äsēən\ *n* -S [ISV *osse-* + *-in*] : the chief organic substance of bone tissue that remains as a residue after removal of the mineral matters from cleaned degreased bone by dilute acid and is used in making gelatin : the collagen of bones

**os·se·let** \'äs(ə)lət\ *n* -S [F, lit., small bone, fr. OF, fr. *ossel* bone (fr. *os* bone — fr. LL *ossum*, fr. L *oss-, os* — + *-el*) + *-et*] : an exostosis on the leg of a horse; *esp* : one on the lateral or anterior aspect of the fetlock occurring chiefly in horses subjected to severe strain while young

**os·se·ous** \'äsēəs\ *adj* [L *osseus*, fr. *oss-, os* bone + *-eus* -eous; akin to Gk *osteon* bone, Skt *asthi*] : composed of or resembling bone : BONY — **os·se·ous·ly** *adv*

**osseous fish** *n* : BONY FISH

**osseous labyrinth** *n* : BONY LABYRINTH

**os·set** \'äsət\ *also* **os·ete** *or* **os·sete** \'ä,sēt\ *or* **os·se·ta** \'äsəd·ə\ *or* **os·se·tine** \-d·ən\ *or* **os·se·tian** \ə'sēshən\ *n* -S *cap* [*osset, osete, ossete, osseta, ossetine* fr. Russ *Osetin*, fr. Georgian *Os, Oset'i*, land of the Ossets; *ossetian* fr. *osset* + *-an*, n. suffix] : one of a tall Aryan people of central Caucasus who are possibly immigrants from Persia and are supposed to be descendants of the Alans and who follow a religion that is a mixture of Muhammadanism and Christianity

**¹os·set·ic** \ə'sed·ik\ *also* **os·se·tian** \-sēshən\ *adj, usu cap* [*osset* + *-ic* or *-an*, adj. suffix] : of, relating to, or characteristic of the Ossets

**²ossetic** \"\ *or* **os·sete** \'ä,sēt\ *n* -S *cap* [*ossetic* fr. *ossetic*, adj.; *ossete* fr. *ossete*, var. of *osset*] : the Iranian language of the Ossets

**ossi-** *comb form* [L, fr. *oss-*, *os*] : bone ⟨*ossi*fic⟩

**os·sia** \ō'sēə\ *conj* [It, fr. *o sia* or let it be, fr. *o* or (fr. L *aut*) + *sia* let it be, be it, 3d pers. sing. pres. subj. of *essere* to be, fr. L *esse* — more at EKE, IS] : or else — used as a direction in music to indicate an alternative and usu. simpler form of a passage

**os·si·an·ic** \¦äs(h)ē¦anik\ *adj, usu cap* [*Ossian*, 3d cent. A.D. legendary Irish warrior and bard asserted by James Macpherson to be the author of the alleged Gaelic epic poems of which Macpherson's *Fingal* (1762) and *Temora* (1763) are purported to be English translations + E *-ic*] : of, relating to, or resembling the legendary Irish bard Ossian, the poems ascribed to him, or the rhythmic prose style used by James Macpherson in his alleged translations

**os·si·cle** \'äsəkəl\ *n* -S [L *ossiculum*, dim. of *oss-, os* bone] **1** : any of certain small bones: as **a** : the malleus, incus, or stapes of the ear **b** : one of the small plates of bone in the sclerotic of some reptiles and birds **2** : any of various small calcareous bodies: as **a** : one of the numerous small calcareous pieces of the skeleton of many echinoderms **b** : one of the parts of the gastric mill of the stomach of some crustaceans

**os·sic·u·lar** \ə'sikyələ(r)\ *adj* [LL *ossicularis*, fr. L *ossiculum* + *-aris* -ar] : of, relating to, or resembling ossicles

**os·sic·u·late** \-yələt, -yə,lāt\ *or* **os·sic·u·lat·ed** \-,lād·əd\ *adj* [*ossiculate* fr. NL *ossiculatus*, fr. L *ossiculum* + *-atus* -ate; *ossiculated* fr. NL *ossiculatus* + E *-ed*] : having ossicles

**os·si·cu·lec·to·my** \,äsəkyə'lektəmē\ *n* -ES [ISV *ossicul-* (fr. L *ossiculum*) + *-ectomy*] : the surgical removal of an auditory ossicle

**os·si·cu·lot·o·my** \-'läd·əmē\ *n* -ES [L *ossiculum* + E *-o-* + *-tomy*] : the surgical division of one or more of the auditory ossicles

**os·sic·u·lum** \ə'sikyələm\ *n, pl* **ossicu·la** \-lə\ [L] : OSSICLE

**os·sif·ic** \ə'sifik\ *adj* [prob. fr. (assumed) NL *ossificus*, fr. L *ossi-* + *-ficus* -fic] : tending to form bone : making bone

**os·si·fi·ca·tion** \,äsəfə'kāshən\ *n* -S [prob. fr. (assumed) NL *ossification-, ossificatio*, fr. (assumed) NL *ossificatus* (past part. of *ossificare* to ossify) + L *-ion-, -io* -ion] **1 a** : the process of bone formation usu. beginning at particular centers in each prospective bone and involving the activities of special osteoblasts that segregate and deposit inorganic bone substance about themselves — see ENDOCHONDRAL OSSIFICATION, INTERMEMBRANOUS OSSIFICATION **b** : an instance of this process **2 a** : the condition of being altered into a hard bony substance ⟨~ of the muscular tissue⟩ **b :** a mass or particle of ossified tissue **:** a calcareous deposit in the tissues ⟨~s in the aortic wall⟩ **3 a :** the process of becoming hardened, indifferent, and insensitive to the feelings of others; *also* **:** a state of callousness ⟨the emotional ~ which the poet must escape —J.M.O'Brien⟩ **b :** the process of becoming molded or set in a conventional pattern; *also* **:** a state of unimaginative conformity ⟨continue its present course of ~ into a new dogmatism —Paul Woodring⟩ ⟨a way of life that . . . might remain in a state of cosy ~ until doomsday —Norman Lewis⟩

**os·sif·i·ca·tory** \ä'sifəkə,tōrē\ *adj* [fr. *ossification*, after such pairs as E *commendation: commendatory*] **:** of or involving ossification ⟨some ~ processes of the immature skull —E.A. Hooton⟩

**ossified** *adj* [fr. past part. of *ossify*] **1** *of tissues* **:** changed to bone or something resembling bone **:** hardened by deposits of mineral matter of any kind **2 :** set in a conventional form **:** FIXED, HARDENED, ULTRACONSERVATIVE ⟨bitterly criticized the organization for being ~⟩

**os·si·fi·er** \'äsə,fī(ə)r\ *n* -s **:** one that ossifies

**os·si·frage** \'äsəfrij\ *n* -s [L *ossifraga* sea eagle, fr. fem. of *ossifragus* bone-breaking, fr. *ossi-* + *-fragus* (fr. *frangere* to break) — more at BREAK] **1 :** LAMMERGEIER **2 :** OSPREY

**os·si·fy** \'äsə,fī\ *vb* -ED/-ING/-ES [prob. fr. (assumed) NL *ossificare*, fr. L *ossi-* + *-ficare* -fy] *vi* **1 :** to form or be transformed into bone ⟨additional cartilages ~ with age⟩ **2 :** to become callous or hardened **:** become set in a conventional pattern ⟨so easy for the mind to ~ and generous ideals to end in stale platitudes —John Buchan⟩ ~ *vt* **1 :** to change (as cartilage) into bone ⟨osteoblasts ~ the tissue⟩ **2 :** to make callous, rigid, or inactive **:** mold firmly in a conventional pattern **:** HARDEN ⟨guilds that won freedom by combination and then *ossified* it into monopoly —D.C.Coyle⟩

**ossing** *pres part of* OSSE

**os·su·ary** \'äshə,werē\ *n* -ES [LL *ossuarium*, fr. L, neut. of *ossuarius* of bones, fr. OL *ossua* (pl. of *oss-*, *os* bone) + L *-arius* -ary — more at OSSEOUS] **1 :** a depository (as a vault, room, urn) for the bones of the dead **2 :** a communal burial place (as of American Indians)

**-ost** \,äst *also* ,ȯst\ *n comb form* -S [Gk *osteon*] **:** bone ⟨actin*ost*⟩

**ost** *abbr* osteopathic

**OST** *abbr, often not cap* ordinary spring tides

**o star** *n, usu cap O* **:** a star of spectral type O — see SPECTRAL TYPE table

**os·tar·i·o·phy·san** \ä,sta(a)rēō'fīsᵊn\ *n* -s [NL *Ostariophysi* + E *-an*] **:** a fish of the order Ostariophysi

**os·tar·i·o·phy·se·ae** \-'īsē,ē\ *or* **os·tar·i·o·phy·si·na** \-'īsᵊnə\ [NL, fr. *ostario-* (fr. Gk *ostarion* small bone) + *-physeae*, *-physina* (fr. Gk *physa* bellows, bladder)] *syn of* OSTARIOPHYSI

**os·tar·i·o·phy·si** \-ī,sī\ *n pl, cap* [NL, fr. *ostario-* (fr. Gk *ostarion* small bone, dim. of *osteon* bone) + *-physi* (fr. Gk *physa* bellows, bladder) — more at PUSTULE] **:** a large order or other division of teleost fishes (as the characin, carp, catfish) having the anterior four vertebrae strongly modified and often grown together and supporting a chain of small bones which connect the air bladder with the ear — **os·tar·i·o·phys·i·al** \¦==¦==fizēəl\ *adj* — **os·tar·i·o·phy·sine** \-fī,sīn\ *adj* — **os·tar·i·o·phy·sous** \-fīsəs\ *adj*

**oste-** *or* **osteo-** *comb form* [NL, fr. Gk, fr. *osteon* — more at OSSEOUS] **:** bone ⟨*oste*al⟩ ⟨*osteo*myelitis⟩

**os·te·al** \'ästēəl\ *adj* [ISV *oste-* + *-al*] **1 :** sounding like bone under percussion **2 :** of or relating to bone ⟨~ development⟩ **:** like bone ⟨the ~ part of the cartilage⟩ **:** affecting or involving bone or the skeleton ⟨~ lesions in leukemia⟩

**os·te·ich·thy·es** \,ästē'ikthē,ēz\ *n pl, cap* [NL, fr. *oste-* + Gk *ichthyes*, pl. of *ichthys* fish — more at ICHTHUS] *in some classifications* **:** a class or other category of fishes including the lungfishes, crossopterygians, teleosts, and esp. formerly the arthrodires and ostracoderms and distinguished from other forms resembling fish by the presence of true bone in their skeleton — compare CHONDRICHTHYES

**os·te·in** \'ästēən\ *n* -s [ISV *oste-* + *-in*] **:** OSSEIN

**os·te·it·ic** \¦ästē¦id·ik\ *adj* [*osteitis* + *-ic*] **:** relating to or characterized by osteitis

**os·te·i·tis** \,==ˈīd·əs\ *n, pl* **os·te·it·i·des** \-'id·ə,dēz\ [NL, fr. *oste-* + *-itis*] **:** inflammation of bone

**osteitis de·for·mans** \-dē'fȯr,manz\ *n* [NL, deforming osteitis] **:** a chronic disease of bones characterized by their great enlargement and rarefaction with bowing of the long bones and deformation of the flat bones — called also *Paget's disease*

**osteitis fi·bro·sa** \-fī'brōsə\ *n* [NL, fibrous osteitis] **:** a disease of bone that is characterized by fibrous degeneration of the bone and the formation of cystic cavities and that results in deformities of the affected bones and sometimes in fracture

**os·tend** \ä'stend\ *vt* -ED/-ING/-S [ME *ostenden*, fr. L *ostendere* to show] **:** to show clearly **:** EXHIBIT, MANIFEST ⟨seemed to me somewhat to ~ his relationship with the . . . household —H.H.Johnston⟩

**os·ten·si·bil·i·ty** \ä,sten(t)sə'biləd·ē\ *n* -ES **:** the quality or state of being ostensible

**os·ten·si·ble** \ä'sten(t)səbəl, ə'- *sometimes* ȯ'-\ *adj* [F, fr. L *ostensus* (past part. of *ostendere* to show, fr. *os-* — fr. *ob* to, before, against — + *tendere* to stretch) + F *-ible* -able — more at EPI-, THIN] **1 a :** capable of being shown **:** prepared to be exhibited **:** PRESENTABLE ⟨send me two letters—one confidential, another ~ —Jeremy Bentham⟩ **b :** open to view **:** CONSPICUOUS ⟨the ~ validity of his predictions regarding the past war —S.H.Croog⟩ ⟨have different ~ properties —C.H. Whitely⟩ **2 :** professing genuineness and sincerity but often concealing the real aspects behind a plausible facade ⟨the sketches of Stratford-on-Avon . . . the ~ reason for his trip, duly appeared —F.J.Mather⟩ ⟨organized a company whose ~ purpose was to provide an adequate supply of water —Sidney Warren⟩ **syn** see APPARENT

**ostensible authority** *or* **ostensible agency** *n* **:** authority or agency by estoppel arising when a principal has intentionally or negligently caused a third person to believe and rely upon the apparent authority of his supposed agent even though it has not been given

**ostensible partner** *n* **:** one who holds himself out as a member of an actual partnership or one apparently existing or concurring to the partners or apparent partners representing him as such though as between themselves he is no partner **:** a partner by estoppel and liable as such to those relying thereon

**os·ten·si·bly** \-blē, -li\ *adv* **:** in an ostensible manner **:** to all outward appearances ⟨~ this is a brief statement about a little pale yellow deer —C.S.Kilby⟩ ⟨had been ~ frank as to his purpose while really concealing it —Thomas Hardy⟩

**os·ten·sion** \ä'stenchən\ *n* -s [ME *ostensioun*, fr. MF *ostension*, fr. L *ostension-*, *ostensio*, fr. *ostensus* (past part. of *ostendere* to show) + *-ion-*, *-io* -ion] **1 :** an act or process of showing, pointing out, or exhibiting **2 :** exposition of the Host

**os·ten·sive** \-en(t)siv\ *adj* [LL *ostensivus*, fr. L *ostensus* (past part. of *ostendere* to show) + *-ivus* -ive] **1 :** manifestly or immediately demonstrative **:** DEICTIC ⟨the ~ and syntactical rules are relatively independent of each other —Max Black⟩ **2 :** OSTENSIBLE 2 — **os·ten·sive·ly** \-səvlē\ *adv*

**ostensive definition** *n* **:** a definition accomplished by exhibiting and characterizing the thing to be defined or by pointing out and characterizing the cases or instances to be covered

**ostensive reduction** *n* **:** DIRECT REDUCTION

**os·ten·so·ri·um** \,ästən'sōrēəm\ *or* **os·ten·so·ry** \ä'sten(t)sərē\ *n, pl* **ostenso·ria** \-ēə\ *or* **ostensories** [ML *ostensorium*, fr. L *ostensus* (past part. of *ostendere* to show) + *-orium* -ory] *Roman Catholicism* **:** MONSTRANCE

**os·tent** \ä'stent\ *n* -s [in sense 1, fr. L *ostentum*, fr. neut. of *ostentus*, past part. of *ostendere* to show; in other senses, fr. L *ostentus*, n., fr. *ostentus*, past part. of *ostendere* to show] **1 :** a significant sign **:** PORTENT ⟨the night waxed wan, as though with an awed sense of such ~ —Thomas Hardy⟩ **2 :** the act of showing or displaying **:** APPEARANCE, MANIFESTATION ⟨be merry and employ your chiefest thoughts to courtship and such fair ~s of love —Shak.⟩ **3 :** excessive display **:** OSTENTATION 1 a ⟨the city of glorious ~ and vanity —Christopher Morley⟩

**os·ten·tate** \'ästən,tāt\ *vt* -ED/-ING/-S [L *ostentatus*, past part. of *ostentare*, fr. *ostentus*, past part. of *ostendere* to show] **:** to display ostentatiously ⟨the front door *ostentated* a brass plate —Israel Zangwill⟩

**os·ten·ta·tion** \,ä¦stən·'tāshən *sometimes* ,ȯ¦ *or* ¦,sten-\ *n* -s [ME *ostentacioun*, fr. MF *ostentation*, fr. L *ostentation-*, *ostentatio*, fr. *ostentatus* (past part. of *ostentare* to display ostentatiously) + *-ion-*, *-io* -ion] **1 a :** the act of making an ambitious display **:** vain and unnecessary show esp. for the purpose of attracting attention, admiration, or envy **:** PRETENTIOUSNESS ⟨a woman brought up in the traditions of a modesty so proud that it scorns ~ —Arnold Bennett⟩ ⟨most city editors . . . do their work without bluster or ~ —Stanley Walker⟩ **b :** overly elaborate embellishment esp. in art **:** FLORIDITY ⟨architecture . . . characterized by ~ and ornamental frills of the Victorian era —*Amer. Guide Series: Texas*⟩ ⟨stepped over the . . . boundary which divides wealth from ~, eloquence from pedantry, art from technique —Gilbert Highet⟩ ⟨interpret the inmost thoughts of the composer, and to reproduce them without sentimentality and ~ —A.E.Wier⟩ **2** *archaic* **:** the act of exhibiting or showing **:** DISPLAY ⟨maintain a mourning ~ —Shak.⟩

**os·ten·ta·tious** \¦==(,)=¦tāshəs\ *adj* [fr. *ostentation*, after such pairs as E *contention: contentious*] **:** characterized by, fond of, or evincing ostentation **:** attracting attention often by gaudiness or show **:** overly elaborate or ornate **:** CONSPICUOUS, EXAGGERATED ⟨a very ~ method of gaining her attention —Robertson Davies⟩ ⟨the cold philanthropies, the ~ public charities —Oscar Wilde⟩ ⟨embarrassed by the too ~ piety of our family —R.M.Lovett⟩ ⟨went ahead with plans to build an ~ skyscraper —Christopher Rand⟩ ⟨accumulated an ~ wardrobe of fifty suits —Greer Williams⟩

**os·ten·ta·tious·ly** *adv* **:** in an ostentatious manner **:** for the purpose of attracting attention **:** PRETENTIOUSLY ⟨crooked ~ picturesque streets —W.B.Yeats⟩ ⟨eccentricity—sometimes ~ cultivated —H.S.Commager⟩

**os·ten·ta·tious·ness** *n* -ES **:** the quality or state of being ostentatious

**ostentative** *adj* [*ostentate* + *-ive*] *obs* **:** OSTENTATIOUS

**ostentive** *or* **ostentous** *adj* [*ostent* + *-ive* or *-ous*] *obs* **:** OSTENTATIOUS

**osteo-** — see OSTE-

**os·teo·arthritic** \¦ästēō+,=¦==\ *adj* [*osteoarthritis* + *-ic*] **:** of, relating to, or affected with degenerative arthritis

**os·teo·arthritis** \"+,=¦==\ *n* [NL, fr. *oste-* + *arthritis*] **:** DEGENERATIVE ARTHRITIS

**os·teo·arthropathy** \"+,=¦===\ *n* [ISV *oste-* + *arthropathy*; prob. orig. formed as F *ostéoarthropathie*] **:** a disease of joints or bones; *specif* **:** a condition marked by enlargement of the terminal phalanges, thickening of the joint surfaces, and curving of the nails and sometimes associated with chronic disease of the lungs

**os·te·o·blast** \'ästēə,blast\ *n* [ISV *oste-* + *-blast*; prob. orig. formed in G] **:** a bone-forming cell — see OSSIFICATION 1 a

**os·te·o·blas·tic** \¦===¦blastik\ *adj* [ISV *osteoblast* + *-ic*] **1 :** relating to or involving the formation of bone **2 :** of or relating to osteoblasts

**osteochondr-** *or* **osteochondro-** *comb form* [ISV *oste-* + *chondr-*] **:** bone and cartilage ⟨*osteochondro*pathy⟩ ⟨*osteochondr*ous⟩

**os·te·o·chon·drop·a·thy** \,ästēō,kän'dräpəthē\ *n* -ES [*osteochondr-* + *-pathy*] **:** a disease involving both bone and cartilage

**os·te·o·chon·dro·sis** \-rōsəs\ *n, pl* **osteochondro·ses** \-ō,sēz\ [NL, fr. *osteochondr-* + *-osis*] **:** a disease of children in which an ossification center esp. in the epiphyses of long bones undergoes degeneration followed by calcification — **os·te·o·chon·drot·ic** \¦==,=¦dräd·ik\ *adj*

**os·te·o·chon·drous** \¦===¦kändrəs\ *also* **os·te·o·chon·dral** \-əl\ *adj* [*osteochondr-* + *-ous* or *-al*] **:** relating to or composed of bone and cartilage

**os·te·oc·la·sis** \,ästē'äkləsəs\ *n* -ES [NL, fr. *oste-* + *-clasis*] **:** the breaking of a bone as a step in the surgical correction of a deformity

**os·te·o·clast** \'ästēə,klast\ *n* -s [ISV *oste-* + *-clast*; orig. formed as G *osteoklast*] **1 :** one of the large multinucleate cells in developing bone that are considered to function in the dissolution of unwanted bone (as in the formation of canals or the healing of fractures) **2 :** an instrument for performing osteoclasis — **os·te·o·clas·tic** \¦===¦klastik\ *adj*

**os·te·o·col·la** \,ästēō'kälə\ *n* -s [modif. (influenced by Gk *kolla* glue) of NL *osteocollus*, fr. *oste-* + *-collus* (fr. Gk *kolla* glue); fr. a belief that it could be used to join broken bones — more at PROTOCOL] **:** a cellular incrustation of calcium carbonate on stems and roots of plants

**os·te·o·com·ma** \-'kämə\ *n* -s [NL, fr. *oste-* + Gk *komma* piece, stamp, clause — more at COMMA] **:** a metameric segment of the vertebrate skeleton

**os·teo·cranium** \¦ästēō+\ *n* [NL, fr. *oste-* + ML *cranium*] **:** the bony cranium; *esp* **:** the parts of the cranium that arise in membrane bone — distinguished from *chondrocranium*

**os·te·o·cyte** \'ästēə,sīt\ *n* -s [*oste-* + *-cyte*] **:** a cell that is characteristic of adult bone and isolated in a lacuna of the bone substance

**os·teo·dentin** *also* **os·teo·dentine** \¦ästēō+\ *n* [*oste-* + *dentin*] **:** a modified dentine approaching true bone in structure and found chiefly in the teeth of fishes — **os·teo·dentinal** \"+\ *adj*

**os·te·o·derm** \'ästēə,dərm\ *n* [ISV *oste-* + *-derm*] **:** a bony plate in the skin (as of a crocodile) — **os·te·o·der·mal** \¦===¦dərməl\ *adj*

**os·te·o·der·ma·tous** \¦===¦dərməd·əs\ *also* **os·te·o·dermous** \-məs\ *adj* [*osteodermatous* fr. *oste-* + *-dermatous*; *osteodermous* fr. *osteoderm* + *-ous*] **:** having the skin more or less ossified; *also* **:** having osteoderms

**os·teo·dystrophia** \¦ästēō+\ *n* [NL, fr. *oste-* + *dystrophia*] **:** OSTEITIS ⟨~ fibrosa⟩ ⟨~ deformans⟩

**os·teo·dystrophic** \"+(,)=¦==\ *adj* **:** of, relating to, or marked by osteodystrophy

**os·teo·dystrophy** \"+\ *also* **os·teo·dystrophia** \"+\ *n* [NL *osteodystrophia*, fr. *oste-* + *dystrophia*] **:** defective ossification of bone usu. associated with disturbed calcium and phosphorus metabolism and renal insufficiency

**os·teo·fibrosis** \"+,=¦==\ *n* [NL, fr. *oste-* + *fibrosis*] **:** fibrosis of bone

**os·teo·fibrous** \"+\ *adj* [*oste-* + *fibrous*] **:** composed of bone and fibrous connective tissue

**os·teo·gen·e·sis** \,ästēō'jenəsəs\ *n* [NL, fr. *oste-* + L *genesis*] **:** development and formation of bone **:** OSSIFICATION

**osteogenesis im·per·fec·ta** \-,impə(r)'fektə\ *n* [NL, imperfect osteogenesis] **:** FRAGILITAS OSSIUM

**os·te·o·gen·ic** \¦ästēə¦jenik\ *also* **os·te·o·ge·net·ic** \-ēōjə¦ned·ik\ *adj* [*osteogenic* ISV *oste-* + *-genic*; *osteogenetic* fr. *oste-* + *-genetic*] **1 :** bone-producing **2 :** originating in bone

**os·te·og·e·nous** \¦ästē¦äjənəs\ *adj* [*oste-* + *-genous*] **:** OSTEOGENIC 1

**¹os·te·o·glos·sid** \¦ästēō¦gläsəd\ *adj* [NL *Osteoglossidae*] **:** of or relating to the Osteoglossidae

**²osteoglossid** \"\ *n* -s [NL *Osteoglossidae*] **:** a fish of the family Osteoglossidae

**os·te·o·glos·si·dae** \,===ˈgläsə,dē\ *n pl, cap* [NL, fr. *Osteoglossum*, type genus + *-idae*] **:** a family of very large tropical freshwater fishes (suborder Osteoglossoidea) consisting of the piraruсu and related forms and having the head naked and largely encased in bone and the scales large, bony, and composed of pieces resembling mosaic

**os·te·o·glos·soi·dea** \,===,glä'sȯidēə\ *n pl, cap* [NL, fr. *Osteoglossum* + *-oidea*] **:** a suborder of Isospondyli comprising the Osteoglossidae and a few related fishes chiefly of the tropical southern hemisphere

**os·te·o·glos·sum** \,===ˈgläsəm\ *n, cap* [NL, fr. *oste-* + *-glossum* (fr. Gk *glōssa* tongue) — more at GLOSS] **:** a genus of fishes that is the type of the family Osteoglossidae

**os·te·og·ra·phy** \,ästē'ägrəfē\ *n* -ES [*oste-* + *-graphy*] **:** descriptive osteology

**¹os·te·oid** \'ästē,ȯid\ *adj* [ISV *oste-* + *-oid*] **1 :** resembling bone **2 :** having a bone skeleton ⟨~ fishes⟩

**²osteoid** \"\ *n* -s [*oste-* + *-oid*] **:** uncalcified bone matrix

**¹os·te·o·lep·id** \¦ästēō¦lepəd\ *adj* [NL *Osteolepidae*] **:** of or relating to the Osteolepidae

**²osteolepid** \"\ *n* -s [NL *Osteolepidae*] **:** a fish of the family Osteolepidae

**os·te·o·lep·i·dae** \,===ˈlepə,dē\ *n pl, cap* [NL, fr. *Osteolepis*, type genus + *-idae*] **:** a widely distributed family of freshwater Paleozoic fishes (order Rhipidistia) having slender elongated bodies, large rhombic scales, and a well-ossified cranium and commonly considered to be on the direct ancestral line of the amphibians

**os·te·o·lep·i·form** \¦===ˈlepə,fȯrm\ *adj* [NL *Osteolepiformes*] **:** RHIPIDISTID

**os·te·o·lep·i·for·mes** \,===,==ˈfȯr,mēz\ [NL, fr. *Osteolepis* + *-formes*] *syn of* RHIPIDISTIA

**os·te·ol·e·pis** \,ästē'äləpəs\ *n, cap* [NL, fr. *oste-* + *-lepis*] **:** the type genus of Osteolepidae comprising fossil fishes chiefly from the Middle Devonian of Scotland

**os·te·ol·e·poid** \¦=¦älə,pȯid\ *adj* [NL *Osteolepis* + E *-oid*] **:** belonging to or like members of the family Osteolepidae

**os·te·o·lite** \'ästēō,līt\ *n* -s [G *osteolith*, fr. *oste-* + *-lith* -lite] **:** a mineral consisting of a massive impure earthy apatite

**os·te·o·log·ic** \¦ästēə¦läjik\ *or* **os·te·o·log·i·cal** \-jəkəl\ *adj* [*osteologic* ISV *osteology* + *-ic*; *osteological* fr. *osteology* + *-ical*] **:** of or relating to osteology — **os·te·o·log·i·cal·ly** \-jək(ə)lē\ *adv*

**os·te·ol·o·gist** \,ästē'äləjəst\ *n* -s [*osteology* + *-ist*] **:** a specialist in osteology

**os·te·ol·o·gy** \-jē\ *n* -ES [NL *osteologia*, fr. Gk, description of bones, fr. *oste-* + *-logia* -logy] **1 :** a branch of anatomy dealing with the bones **2 :** the features comprised in the bony structure and organization of an organism or any of its parts ⟨the ~ of a cat⟩ ⟨the ~ of the head⟩

**os·te·ol·y·sis** \,ästē'äləsəs\ *n* [NL, fr. *oste-* + *-lysis*] **:** dissolution of bone esp. when associated with resorption

**os·te·o·lyt·ic** \¦ästēō¦lid·ik\ *adj* **:** characteristic of or marked by osteolysis

**os·te·o·ma** \,ästē'ōmə\ *n, pl* **osteomas** \-məz\ *or* **osteomata** \-məd·ə\ [NL, fr. *oste-* + *-oma*] **:** a benign tumor composed of bone tissue

**os·teo·malacia** \¦ästēō+\ *n* [NL, fr. *oste-* + *malacia*] **:** a disease of the bones characterized by softening, caused by a deficiency of minerals (as calcium and phosphorus) and of vitamin D, affecting adults of man and domestic animals, and representing the counterpart of rickets in immature animals

**os·te·o·ma·toid** \,ästē¦ōmə,tȯid\ *adj* [NL *osteomat-*, *osteoma* osteoma + E *-oid*] **:** resembling an osteoma

**os·te·o·ma·tous** \-məd·əs\ *adj* [NL *osteomat-*, *osteoma* osteoma + E *-ous*] **:** of, relating to, or being an osteoma

**os·te·o·met·ric** \¦ästēə¦me·trik\ *or* **os·te·o·met·ri·cal** \-rəkəl\ *adj* **:** of or relating to osteometry

**os·te·om·e·try** \,ästē'ämə·trē\ *n* -ES [ISV *oste-* + *-metry*; prob. orig. formed as F *ostéométrie*] **:** the measurement of bones; *esp* **:** anthropometric measurement of the human skeleton

**os·teo·myelitic** \¦ästēō+\ *adj* [*osteomyelitis* + *-ic*] **:** of, caused by, or affected by osteomyelitis

**os·teo·myelitis** \"+\ *n* [NL, fr. *oste-* + *myelitis*] **:** an inflammatory disease of bone that may involve the marrow, cortex, or periosteum, that is caused by an infectious agent that reaches the site by way of the blood from a source in adjacent tissue or through a penetrating injury (as a laceration or compound fracture), and that produces death of tissue with separation of the devitalized portion from the viable tissue by the formation of a sequestrum

**-os·te·on** \'ästē,än\ *n comb form* -S [NL, fr. Gk *osteon* bone — more at OSSEOUS] **:** bone **:** bone part ⟨loph*osteon*⟩

**os·te·o·path** \'ästēə,path\ *n* -s [back-formation fr. *osteopathy*] **:** a practitioner of osteopathy

**os·te·o·path·ic** \¦===¦pathik\ *adj* [*osteopathy* + *-ic*] **:** of, relating to, or by means of osteopathy — **os·te·o·path·i·cal·ly** \-thək(ə)lē\ *adv*

**os·te·op·a·thist** \,ästē'äpəthəst\ *n* -s [*osteopathy* + *-ist*] **:** OSTEOPATH

**os·te·op·a·thy** \-thē, -thi\ *n* -ES [NL *osteopathia*, fr. *oste-* + L *-pathia* -pathy] **1 :** a disease of bone **2 :** a system of medical practice based on the theory that diseases are due chiefly to a loss of structural integrity in the tissues and that this integrity can be restored by manipulation of the parts supported by the use of medicines, surgery, proper diet, and other therapy

**os·teo·periostitis** \¦ästēō+\ *n* [NL, fr. *oste-* + *periostitis*] **:** inflammation of a bone and its periosteum

**os·te·o·pe·tro·sis** \,ästēōpə'trōsəs\ *n* [NL, fr. *oste-* + *petr-* + *-osis*] **:** an abnormal thickening and hardening of bone often with the development of bands of varying density in the long bones and sometimes with partial occlusion of the marrow cavities **2 a :** a hereditary disorder that affects the bones of human beings and that is marked by extreme density and hardness and abnormal fragility — called also *marble bones* **b :** a hereditary bone disease of rabbits that is marked by enlargement and faulty development of the skeletal parts **c :** a disease of the avian leukosis complex of chickens marked by great enlargement and excessive calcification of the long bones esp. of the legs and by more or less complete obliteration of the marrow cavities and varying degrees of anemia — called also *marble bone*

**os·te·o·pe·trot·ic** \¦===¦träd·ik\ *adj* **:** characteristic of or marked by osteopetrosis

**os·te·o·phage** \'ästēə,fāj\ *n* [ISV *oste-* + *-phage*] **:** OSTEOCLAST 1

**os·te·o·pha·gia** \,ästēō'fājēə\ *n* -s [NL, fr. *oste-* + *-phagia*] **:** the eating or chewing of bones by herbivorous animals (as cattle) craving phosphorus

**os·te·o·phyte** \'ästēə,fīt\ *n* -s [ISV *oste-* + *-phyte*] **:** a small pathological bony outgrowth — **os·te·o·phyt·ic** \¦===¦fid·ik\ *adj*

**os·teo·plast** \'===,plast\ *n* -s [ISV *oste-* + *-plast*] **:** OSTEOBLAST

**os·te·o·plas·tic** \¦===¦plastik\ *adj* [ISV *osteoplasty* + *-ic*] **1 :** of or relating to the replacement of bone ⟨an ~ operation⟩ **2** [ISV *osteoplast* + *-ic*] **:** OSTEOBLASTIC

**os·te·o·plas·ty** \'===,plastē\ *n* -ES [ISV *oste-* + *-plasty*] **:** plastic surgery on bone; *esp* **:** replacement of lost bone tissue or reconstruction of defective bony parts

**os·teo·porosis** \¦ästēō+\ *n, pl* **osteoporoses** [NL, fr. *oste-* + *porosis*] **1 :** a condition characterized by decrease in bone mass with decreased density and enlargement of bone spaces producing porosity and fragility and resulting from disturbances of nutrition and mineral metabolism **2 :** a progressive metabolic disease of grazing animals (as horses and mules) marked by withdrawal of mineral matter from the bones causing enlargement, softening, and porosity of the bones esp. of the head

**os·teo·porotic** \"+\ *adj* [fr. *osteoporosis*, after such pairs as E *narcosis: narcotic*] **:** characteristic of or marked by osteoporosis

**os·te·op·sath·y·ro·sis** \,ästēäp,sathə'rōsəs\ *n, pl* **osteopsathyroses** [NL, fr. *oste-* + Gk *psathyros* friable, crumbling + NL *-osis*; akin to Gk *psēphos* pebble — more at SAND] **:** FRAGILITAS OSSIUM

**os·teo·radionecrosis** \¦ästēō+\ *n* [NL, fr. *oste-* + *radionecrosis*] **:** necrosis of bone following irradiation

**os·teo·sarcoma** \"+\ *n* [NL, fr. *oste-* + *sarcoma*] **:** a sarcoma derived from bone or containing bone tissue

**os·teo·sclereid** \"+\ *n* [*oste-* + *sclereid*] **:** one of the sclereids forming the hypodermal layer in many fruits and seeds and occurring also in the leaves of certain xerophytes — called also *bone cell*; compare MACROSCLEREID

**os·teo·sclerosis** \"+\ *n* [NL, fr. *oste-* + *sclerosis* (fr. ML *scliros*is)] — more at SCLEROSIS] **:** OSTEOPETROSIS 1

**os·teo·sclerotic** \"+\ *adj* [fr. *osteosclerosis*, after E *sclerosis: sclerotic*] **:** of, relating to, or affected by osteopetrosis

**¹os·te·os·tra·can** \¦ästē¦ästrəkən\ *adj* [NL *Osteostraci* + E *-an*] **:** of or relating to the Cephalaspida

**²osteostracan** \"\ *n* -s **:** CEPHALASPID

**os·te·os·tra·ci** \,===ˈästrə,sī\ [NL, fr. *oste-* + *-ostraci* (fr. Gk *ostrakon* shell) — more at OYSTER] *syn of* CEPHALASPIDA

**os·teo·synthesis** \¦ästēō+\ *n* [ISV *oste-* + *synthesis*] **:** the operation of uniting the ends of a fractured bone by mechanical means (as by a metal plate)

**os·te·o·tome** \'ästēə,tōm\ *n* -s [NL *osteotomus*, fr. *oste-* + *-tomus* -tome] **:** strong nippers or a chisel without a bevel used in surgical and other procedures on bone

**os·te·ot·o·my** \ˌästēˈädəmē\ *n* -ES [prob. fr. (assumed) NL *osteotomia*, fr. NL *oste-* + *-tomia* -tomy] **:** a surgical operation of dividing a bone or of cutting a piece out of it to correct a deformity

**os·te·o·tribe** \ˈästēə,trīb\ *n* -S [*oste-* + *-tribe*] **:** a rasp used for removing carious bone

**os·te·ria** \ˌästəˈrēə, ˌōs-\ *n* -S [It, fr. *oste* innkeeper, fr. L *hospit-, hospes* host, stranger, guest — more at HOST] **1 :** a wayside inn ⟨stopped for the night at a small ~ —J.H.Shorthouse⟩ **2 :** RESTAURANT ⟨a sandwich and wine at an ~ near the job —*N. Y. Times Mag.*⟩

**os·ter·ta·gia** \ˌästə(r)ˈtājēə\ *n, cap* [NL, fr. Robert von *Ostertag* †1940 Ger. veterinarian and parasitologist + NL *-ia*] **:** a genus of slender brown nematode worms (family Trichostrongylidae) parasitic in the abomasum of ruminants where their presence in numbers is associated with gastritis, scouring, or general unthriftiness

**-os·te·us** \ˈästēəs\ *n comb form* [NL, fr. Gk *osteon* bone — more at OSSEOUS] **:** one having (such) a bone or bones — in generic names esp. of fishes ⟨*Coccosteus*⟩

**ostiak** *usu cap, var of* OSTYAK

**os·ti·al** \ˈästēəl\ *adj* [*ostium* + *-al*] **:** of or relating to an ostium

**os·ti·ary** \ˈästē,erē\ *n* -ES [L *ostiarius*, fr. *ostium* door, mouth of a river + *-arius* -ary] **1 :** DOORKEEPER **2** *obs* **:** a mouth of a river

**os·ti·ate** \ˈästēət, -ē,āt\ *adj* [*ostium* + *-ate*] **:** having an ostium

**¹osti·na·to** \ˌästəˈnäd·(,)ō, -tē¦-, ¦ōs-, ¦ös-, -nä(,)tō\ *adj* [It, stubborn, fr. L *obstinatus* obstinate] **:** relating to any frequently repeated motif or passage in any part of a musical composition or to the use of such repetition

**²ostinato** \"\ *n* -S **1 a :** a musical figure repeated persistently at the same pitch throughout a composition **b :** the use of such repetition **2 :** GROUND BASS

**os·ti·o·lar** \ˈästēələ(r), -ē,ōl-\ *adj* **:** of, relating to, or being an ostiole

**os·ti·o·late** \-lət, -,lāt\ *adj* **:** having ostioles

**os·ti·ole** \ˈästē,ōl\ *n* -S [NL *ostiolum*, fr. L, small door, dim. of *ostium*] **:** a small aperture, orifice, or pore: as **a :** the mouth of the perithecium or other spore fruit in a fungus or lichen **b :** an orifice of an odoriferous gland in various Hemiptera **c :** the opening of the conceptacle in various fucoid seaweeds **d :** one of the small inhalant orifices of a sponge

**os·ti·um** \ˈästēəm\ *n, pl* **os·tia** \-ēə\ [NL, fr. L, door, mouth of a river; akin to Russ *ust'e* mouth of a river, Skt *oṣṭha* lip, L *or-, os* mouth — more at ORAL] **:** an entrance or opening: as **a :** either end of a Fallopian tube **b :** one of the lateral slits in the heart of an arthropod by which the blood enters from the pericardium

**ostler** *var of* HOSTLER

**os·tler·ess** \ˈäslərəs\ *n* -ES **:** a female hostler

**ost·men** \ˈōstmən\ *n pl, cap* [ME, fr. ON *austmenn*, pl. of *austmathr*, fr. *austr* to the east + *mathr* man — more at EAST, MAN] **:** Scandinavians anciently settled along the east coast of Ireland

**¹os·tom·a·tid** \äˈstäməd·əd\ *adj* [NL *Ostomatidae*] **:** of or relating to the Ostomatidae

**²ostomatid** \"\ *n* -S [NL *Ostomatidae*] **:** a beetle of the family Ostomatidae

**os·to·mat·i·dae** \ˌästəˈmad·ə,dē\ *n pl, cap* [NL, fr. *Ostomat-, Ostoma*, type genus (irreg. fr. Gk *osteon* bone) + *-idae*] **:** a family of beetles most of which are useful predators

**-os·to·sis** \ˈäˈstōsəs\ *n comb form, pl* **-osto·ses** *or* **-ostosises** \-ō,sēz\ [NL, fr. Gk *-ostōsis*, fr. *osteon* bone + *-ōsis* -osis] **:** ossification of a (specified) part or to a (specified) degree ⟨*hyperostosis*⟩ ⟨*ectostosis*⟩

**ostrac-** *or* **ostraco-** *comb form* [NL, fr. Gk *ostrak-, ostrako-*, fr. *ostrakon*] **:** shell ⟨*Ostracoidea*⟩ ⟨*Ostracophori*⟩

**ostraca** *pl of* OSTRACON

**-os·tra·ca** \ˈästrəkə *also* ˈōs-\ *n pl comb form* [NL, fr. Gk *-ostraka* (neut. pl. of *-ostrakos*, fr. *ostrakon* shell) — more at OYSTER] **:** ones having (such) a shell — in names of taxa chiefly of crustaceans ⟨*Arthrostraca*⟩ ⟨*Conchostraca*⟩

**os·tra·cea** \äˈstrāshēə\ [NL, irreg. fr. *Ostrea* + *-acea*] *syn of* OSTRAEACEA

**¹os·tra·cean** \(ˈ)ä¦strāshən\ *adj* [NL *Ostracea* + E *-an*] **:** of or relating to the Ostraeacea

**²ostracean** \"\ *n* -S **:** an oyster of the suborder Ostraeacea

**os·tra·ceous** \-shəs\ *adj* [NL *Ostracea* + E *-ous*] **:** of or relating to the Ostraeacea

**os·tra·ci·idae** \ˌästrəˈsīə,dē\ [NL, fr. *Ostracion* + *-idae*] *syn of* OSTRACIONTIDAE

**os·tra·ci·on** \äˈstrās(h)ē,än\ *n, cap* [NL *Ostraciont-, Ostracion*, irreg. fr. Gk *ostrakion* small shell, dim. of *ostrakon* shell] **:** a genus of boxfishes that is the type of the family Ostraciontidae, is now restricted to forms found chiefly in East Indian waters, and is characterized by a carapace of more or less quadrangular section

**os·tra·ci·on·ti·dae** \ˌ==ˈäntə,dē\ *n pl, cap* [NL, fr. *Ostraciont-, Ostracion*, type genus + *-idae*] **:** a family of marine fishes (order Plectognathi) comprising the boxfishes

**os·tra·cism** \ˈästrə,sizəm *also* ˈöst-\ *n* -S [Gk *ostrakismos*, fr. *ostrakizein* + *-ismos* -ism] **1 :** a method of temporary banishment by popular vote and without a trial or special accusation practiced in ancient Greek cities to remove a person considered dangerous to the state **2 :** exclusion by general consent from common privileges or social acceptance ⟨met part of her expenses by waiting on tables — a task she thought would mean social ~ —*Current Biog.*⟩

**os·tra·cite** \ˈästrə,sīt\ *n* -S [L *ostracites*, a precious stone, fr. Gk *ostrakitēs* earthen, fr. *ostrakon* earthen vessel, shell] **:** a fossil oyster

**os·tra·cize** *also* **os·tra·cise** \ˈästrə,sīz *also* ˈöst-\ *vt* -ED/-ING/-S [Gk *ostrakizein* to banish by voting with potsherds, fr. *ostrakon* earthen vessel, potsherd, shell + *-izein* -ize — more at OYSTER] **1 a :** to banish from society **:** cast out from social or political favor or fellowship ⟨she was ever afterward *ostracized* in her home city —A.F.Harlow⟩ **b :** to get rid of **:** ABOLISH ⟨when we really become civilized we will certainly ~ smoky cities —C.C.Furnas⟩ **2 :** to exile by ostracism **:** banish temporarily by a popular vote **syn** see BANISH

**os·tra·ciz·er** \-zə(r)\ *n* -S **:** one that ostracizes

**os·tra·cod** \ˈästrə,käd\ *n* -S [NL *Ostracoda*] **:** one of the Ostracoda

**os·tra·co·da** \ˌästrəˈkōdə, äˈstrakədə\ *n pl, cap* [NL, fr. Gk *ostrakōdēs* testaceous, fr. *ostrakon* potsherd, shell] **:** a subclass of crustacea comprising small active mostly freshwater forms having the body enclosed in a bivalve shell composed of right and left valves, the body segmentation obscured, the abdomen rudimentary, and only seven pairs of appendages — **os·tra·co·dan** \-dᵊn\ *adj* — **os·tra·co·dous** \-dəs\ *adj*

**¹os·tra·co·derm** \ˈästrəkō,dərm\ *adj* [NL *Ostracodermi*] **:** of, relating to, or having characteristics of the Ostracodermi

**²ostracoderm** \"\ *n* -S [NL *Ostracodermi*] **:** one of the Ostracodermi

**os·tra·co·der·mi** \ˌ===ˈdər,mī\ *n pl, cap* [NL, fr. *ostrac-* + *-dermi* (fr. Gk *derma* skin) — more at DERM-] **1** *in some classifications* **:** a suborder of Plectognathi comprising the boxfishes **2** *in some classifications* **:** an order or other category comprising the Agnatha except the Cyclostomi and some of the Placodermi that are known only from imperfect remains found in Ordovician, Silurian, and Devonian rocks, that lack jaws and limb girdles as well as paired fins homologous with those of recent fishes, that in most forms show the very broad anterior part of the body to be encased in a bony armor, and that have the slender scaly posterior part ending in an unsymmetrical tail

**os·tra·coi·dea** \ˌästrəˈkȯidēə\ [NL, fr. *ostrac-* + *-oidea*] *syn of* OSTRACODA

**os·tra·con** *or* **os·tra·kon** \ˈästrə,kän\ *n, pl* **ostra·ca** *or* **ostra·ka** \-rəkə\ [Gk *ostrakon*] **1 :** a potsherd used as a ballot in the ancient Athenian practice of ostracism **2 :** a fragment of pottery or limestone containing a written inscription ⟨that the Hebrews . . . wrote freely on papyrus, parchment and potsherds is apparent from large finds of *ostraca* —I.M. Price⟩

**os·tra·co·phore** \ˈästrəkō,fō(ə)r\ *n* -S [NL *Ostracophori*] **:** one of the Ostracophori — **os·tra·coph·o·rous** \ˌästrəˈkäf(ə)rəs\ *adj*

**os·tra·coph·o·ri** \ˌästrəˈkäfə,rī\ [NL, fr. *ostrac-* + *-phori* (fr. Gk *-phoroi*, pl. of *-phoros* -phorous)] *syn of* OSTRACODERMI **2**

**os·trae·a·cea** \ˌästrēˈāshēə\ *n pl, cap* [NL, irreg. fr. *Ostrea* + *-acea*] **:** a suborder of Eulamellibranchia including the common oysters and related mollusks

**ostre-** *or* **ostrei-** *or* **ostreo-** *comb form* [L *ostre-*, fr. *ostrea*] **:** oyster ⟨*ostrei*form⟩ ⟨*ostre*oid⟩ ⟨*ostreo*phagous⟩

**os·trea** \ˈästrēə\ *n, cap* [NL, fr. L, oyster — more at OYSTER] **:** the type genus of Ostreidae including those oysters (as the European oyster) that retain eggs in the parent's gills during early stages of development — compare CRASSOSTREA — **os·tre·a·ceous** \¦ästrē¦āshəs\ *adj*

**os·tre·ger** \ˈästrəjə(r)\ *n* -S [ME *ostringer*, fr. MF *otrucher, ostricier*, fr. *ostour, ostor* hawk, fr. ML *auceptor*, alter. (influenced by L *avis* bird) of L *acceptor*, alter. (influenced by L *accipere* to take, accept) of *accipiter* — more at ACCIPITER, ACCEPT, AVIARY] **:** a falconer who keeps goshawks

**os·trei·culture** \ˈästrēə+,-\ *n* [ISV *ostre-* + *culture*] **:** oyster culture — **os·trei·culturist** \,===+\ *n*

**os·tre·i·dae** \äˈstrēə,dē\ *n pl, cap* [NL, fr. *Ostrea*, type genus + *-idae*] **:** a family of bivalve mollusks (suborder Ostraeacea) being usu. attached by the lower valve and including the common edible oysters

**os·tre·i·form** \ˈästrēə,fȯrm, äˈs-\ *adj* [ISV *ostre-* + *-form*] **:** shaped like an oyster

**os·treo·dynamometer** \¦ästrēō+\ *n* [*ostre-* + *dynamometer*] **:** a device for detection of the movements of an oyster within its shell and used esp. in connection with water pollution investigations

**os·tre·oid** \ˈästrē,ȯid\ *adj* [ISV *ostre-* + *-oid*] **:** resembling an oyster

**os·tre·oph·a·gous** \¦ästrē¦äfəgəs\ *adj* [*ostre-* + *-phagous*] **:** feeding on oysters

**¹os·trich** \ˈästrich, ˈōs-, -rē| *sometimes* |j\ *n* -ES [ME *ostriche*, fr. OF *ostrusce*, fr. (assumed) VL *avis struthio*, fr. L *avis* bird + LL *struthio* ostrich — more at AVIARY, STRUTHIO] **1 a :** a swift-footed flightless ratite bird of the genus *Struthio* having a downy neck and head, a body covered with soft feathers, thighs nearly bare, two-toed feet, and valuable wing and tail plumes for which it has been domesticated: as (1) **:** an ostrich (*S. camelus*) of the more arid parts of Africa and Arabia that is the largest of existing birds attaining a height of six or eight feet and a weight of 300 lbs. (2) **:** an ostrich (*S. c. australis*) of southern Africa (3) **:** an ostrich (*S. c. molybdophanes*) of eastern Africa **b :** RHEA **2** [so called fr. a popular belief that the ostrich when pursued hides his head and believes himself to be unseen] **:** a person whose behavior is thought to resemble that ascribed to the ostrich **:** one having qualities or habits suggesting an ostrich ⟨we must live as men and not as ~*es* —F.D.Roosevelt⟩ ⟨tried to play ~, pretended not to see —B.H.Williams⟩ ⟨between the positions of the alarmist and the ~ is a broad middle ground —*Scientific Monthly*⟩

**²ostrich** \"\ *adj* **:** of, relating to, or resembling an ostrich **:** OSTRICHLIKE ⟨overcoming the traditional ~ attitude of the public —*Newsweek*⟩ ⟨the uphill fight against . . . ~ isolationism —W.H.Hale⟩

**³ostrich** \"\ *vi* -ED/-ING/-ES **:** to hide one's head **:** deliberately avoid seeing, recognizing, or understanding

**ostrich fern** *n* **1 :** a tree fern (*Pteretis struthiopteris*) of the north temperate zone that has graceful arched bipinnatifid fronds growing in a circle from an erect rootstock and pinnate sporophylls having segments like a necklace and resembling ostrich plumes **2 :** a fern of the genus *Pteretis*

**os·trich·ism** \|,chizəm, |,ji-\ *n* -S **:** the deliberate avoidance or ignorance of conditions as they exist **:** SELF-DELUSION ⟨~ will not, of course, save one single American —Pearl Buck⟩ ⟨perhaps the lack of fear is a result of what might be called ~ —John Gunther⟩

**ostrich leather** *n* **:** strong durable leather from the skins of ostriches readily identified by quill holes and used principally for shoes and handbags

**ostrichlike** \ˈ==,=\ *adj* **:** marked or characterized by self-delusion into a sense of security by deliberately refraining from seeing or understanding ⟨our assumptions as to the sources of the criticism have been . . . based upon wishful or ~ thinking —Paul Woodring⟩

**ostrich-plume hydroid** *n* **:** a colonial hydroid of a common genus (*Aglaophenia*) characterized by pinnate branching colonies resembling feathers or ferns

**os·tro·goth** \ˈästrə,gäth\ *n, cap* [LL *Ostrogothi, Ostrogothae*, pl., of Gmc origin; prob. fr. a Gothic compound whose first constituent is akin to ON *austr* to the east and whose second constituent is the same as the source of LL *Gothi* Goths — more at EAST, GOTH] **:** a member of the eastern division of the Goths that conquered Italy toward the end of the fifth century A.D. — called also *East Goth;* compare VISIGOTH — **os·tro·goth·i·an** \¦==¦gäthēən\ *adj, usu cap* — **os·tro·goth·ic** \-thik\ *adj, usu cap*

**os·trya** \ˈästrēə\ *n, cap* [NL, fr. Gk, hop hornbeam; prob. akin to Gk *ostrakon* shell and to Gk *drys* tree — more at OYSTER, TREE] **:** a small widely distributed genus of trees (family Betulaceae) having fruit resembling cones with membranous inflated bracts — see HOP HORNBEAM

**os·ty·ak** *also* **os·ti·ak** \ˈästē,ak\ *n* -S *cap* [Russ *Ostyak*, fr. Ostyak *āsyakh* dwellers on the Ob river, fr. *Ās* Ob river, U.S.S.R.] **1 :** a member of any of a group of the Paleo-Asiatic nomadic Finnic peoples of the Ural mountain regions and western Siberia **2 :** the Finno-Ugric language of the Ostyak people — see URALIC LANGUAGES table

**ostyak samoyed** *n, cap O&S* **1 :** one of the people of mixed Samoyed and Ostyak stock in Siberia **2 :** the Uralic language of the Ostyak Samoyed people — see URALIC LANGUAGES table

**o substance** *n, usu cap O* **:** an antigen characteristic of red blood cells of persons of blood group O

**os·we·go bass** \äˈswē(,)gō-\ *n, usu cap O* [*Oswego* river, central New York] **1 :** LARGEMOUTH BLACK BASS **2 :** SMALLMOUTH BLACK BASS

**oswego tea** *n, usu cap O* **:** a No. American mint (*Monarda didyma*) with showy bright scarlet irregular flowers — called also *bee balm, fragrant balm, mountain mint*

**ot-** *or* **oto-** *comb form* [Gk *ōt-, ōto-*, fr. *ōt-, ous* — more at EAR] **:** ear ⟨*otitis*⟩ ⟨*otology*⟩ ⟨*otoscope*⟩ ⟨*otosteal*⟩ **:** ear and ⟨*oto*laryngology⟩

**OT** *abbr* **1** occupational therapy **2** oiltight **3** old terms **4** old tuberculin **5** on time **6** on track **7** on truck **8** overtime

**ot·acariasis** \¦ōd·+\ *n* [NL, fr. *ot-* + *acariasis*] **:** infestation with or disease caused by ear mites **:** EAR MANGE, CANKER 7a

**¹ot·acoustic** \¦ōd·+\ *n* -S [Gk *ōtakoustein* to listen, eavesdrop (fr. *ōt-* ot- + *akoustos* heard, audible) + E *-ic* — more at ACOUSTIC] **:** an otacoustic instrument

**²otacoustic** \"\ *adj* [F *otacoustique*, fr. Gk *ōtakoustein* to listen, eavesdrop + F *-ique* -ic] **:** assisting the sense of hearing

**ota·go** \ōˈtä(,)gō\ *adj, usu cap* [fr. *Otago*, New Zealand] **:** of or from the provincial district of Otago, New Zealand **:** of the kind or style prevalent in Otago provincial district

**ota·hei·tan** \¦ōd·ə¦hātᵊn\ *adj or n, usu cap* [fr. *Otaheite* (now Tahiti), island in the southern Pacific + E *-an*] **:** TAHITIAN

**ota·hei·te apple** \,==ˈhād·(,)ē-\ *n, usu cap O* [fr. *Otaheite* Tahiti] **1 :** a Polynesian tree (*Spondias cytherea*) having a fruit with sweet edible flesh and turpentine-flavored rind **2 :** the fruit of the Otaheite apple **3 :** MALAY APPLE

**otaheite arrowroot** *n, usu cap O* **:** a starch obtained from the root of the pia; *also* **:** a root or plant yielding such starch

**otaheite gooseberry** *n, usu cap O* **1 :** a tropical African and Asiatic tree (*Phyllanthus acidus*) of the family Euphorbiaceae **2 :** the acid edible fruit of the Otaheite gooseberry

**otaheite orange** *n, usu cap 1st O* **:** a small bush (*Citrus taitensis*) sometimes grown as a pot plant and having oblong to elliptic crenulate leaves, flowers colored pink on the outside, and a lemon-shaped fruit

**otal·gia** \ōˈtalj(ē)ə\ *n* -S [NL, fr. Gk *ōtalgia*, fr. *ōt-*, ot- + *-algia*] **:** pain in the ear **:** EARACHE

**otal·gic** \-jik\ *n* -S [Gk *ōtalgikos*, adj., having an earache, fr. *ōtalgia* + *-ikos* -ic] **:** a remedy for earache

**otar·ia** \ōˈta(a)rēə\ *n, cap* [NL, fr. *ot-* + *-aria*] **:** the type genus of *Otariidae* comprising the sea lions of the southern So. American coast

**ota·ri·idae** \,ōd·əˈrīə,dē\ *n pl, cap* [NL, fr. *Otaria*, type genus + *-idae*] **:** a family of Pinnipedia consisting of the eared seals and sometimes ranked as a subfamily (Otariinae) of Phocidae — **ota·rine** \ˈōd·ə,rēn, -,rən\ *or* **otar·i·ine** \(ˈ)ō¦ta(a)rē,īn, -ēən\ *adj* — **otar·i·oid** \-ē,ȯid\ *adj or n*

**ota·ru** \ōˈtä(,)rü\ *adj, usu cap* [fr. *Otaru*, Japan] **:** of or from the city of Otaru, Japan **:** of the kind or style prevalent in Otaru

**ota·ry** \ˈōd·ərē\ *n* -ES [NL *Otaria*] **:** EARED SEAL

**ota·te** \ōˈtäd·(,)ā\ *n* -S [Sp, fr. Nahuatl *otlatl*] **:** a giant grass (*Guadua amplexifolia*) used by Mexicans for making baskets

**ota·vite** \ōˈtä,vīt\ *n* -S [G *otavit*, fr. *Otavi*, town in South-West Africa + G *-it* -ite] **:** a mineral $CdCO_3$ consisting of cadmium and isostructural with calcite

**OTB** *abbr* open to buy

**otbd** *abbr* outboard

**OTC** *abbr* **1** officer in tactical command **2** officers' training camp; officers' training corps

**-ote** \,ōt, -,ət\ *n suffix* -S [L & Gk; L *-otes*, fr. Gk *-ōtēs*] **:** inhabitant **:** native ⟨*Capriote*⟩

**othe·o·scope** \ˈōthēə,skōp\ *n* [Gk *ōthein* to push + E *-o-* + *-scope* — more at ENDOSMOSIS] **:** an instrument for exhibiting the pressure exerted by light or other radiation in an exhausted vessel — compare RADIOMETER

**¹oth·er** \ˈəthə(r)\ *adj* [ME, adj., n., pron., & adv., fr. OE *ōther*, adj., n., & pron.; akin to OHG *andar* other, ON *annarr*, Goth *anthar*, Skt *antara*, Lith *añtras*] **1 a :** being the one (as of two or more) left **:** not being the one (as of two or more) first mentioned or of primary concern **:** REMAINING ⟨carrying the load in one hand and holding on with the ~⟩ **b :** being the ones distinct from the one or those first mentioned or understood — used with a plural noun ⟨these cars being somewhat smaller than ~ European cars⟩ **c :** SECOND — now chiefly used with *every* ⟨every ~ day it rained⟩ **2 a :** not the same **:** DIFFERENT ⟨any ~ man would have done better⟩ **b :** DIFFERENT, DISTINCT — used after the noun and with *than* ⟨all parts of the house ~ than the windows were in good condition⟩ **3 :** MORE, ADDITIONAL ⟨thou shalt have no ~ gods before me —Exod 20:3 (AV)⟩ — often used after the noun and with *than* ⟨no clothes ~ than those he was wearing⟩ **4 a :** just past ⟨the ~ evening⟩ ⟨the ~ day it rained⟩ **b :** FORMER ⟨in ~ times⟩

**²other** \"\ *n* -S [ME] **1 a :** one that remains of two or more ⟨one stayed and the ~ went away⟩ ⟨after he left the ~*s* played cards⟩ **b** *obs* **:** second one **2 :** a different one ⟨each gust of wind came after the ~ with clocklike regularity⟩ ⟨some businesses survived and ~*s* went into bankruptcy⟩ **3 :** an additional one ⟨some are successful and ~*s* are not⟩ **4 :** something else that exists as an opposite of or as excluded by something else ⟨the nonego being the ~ of the ego⟩ ⟨the objective world being the ~ of self-consciousness⟩

**³other** \"\ *pron, sometimes pl in constr* [ME] **1** *obs* **a :** one of two that remains ⟨priest and people interchangeably pray each for ~ —Anthony Sparrow⟩ **b :** each preceding one **2** *obs* **:** a different one ⟨every one taketh before ~ his own supper —1 Cor 11:21 (AV)⟩⟨I have pleased some and displeased ~ —Robert Wilkinson⟩ **3 :** an additional one ⟨hardly a day passes in which we do not have some visitor or ~ —Jane Austen⟩ ⟨~ of the Protestant clergy —F.G.Lee⟩ **4** *chiefly Scot* **:** one another ⟨we know not ~ — oceans are between —Thomas Campbell⟩

**⁴other** \"\ *adv* [ME] **:** OTHERWISE **1** — used with *than* ⟨not being able to sell the product ~ than by reducing the price⟩

**¹other-directed** \¦==¦==\ *adj* [⁴*other* + *directed*] **:** determined or motivated by contemporary trends and pressures and not by inner decision ⟨an *other-directed* personality⟩ — **oth·er-di·rect·ed·ness** *n*

**²other-directed** \"\ *n* -S **:** an other-directed person

**other-direction** \¦===¦==\ *n* **:** a sense of direction based on contemporary trends and pressures

**othergates** \ˈ==,=\ *adv* [ME, fr. *other* + *gates*, gen. of *gate* way — more at GATE] *chiefly dial* **:** in another manner **:** OTHERWISE ⟨he would have tickled you ~ than he did —Shak.⟩

**other-group** \ˈ==,=\ *n* **:** OUTGROUP

**otherguess** *adj* [alter. of *othergates*, fr. *othergates*, adv.] *obs* **:** DIFFERENT

**other half** *n* **1 :** a segment of the population radically different economically and often socially from that to which one belongs or with which a context is associated ⟨see how the *other half* lives⟩; *esp* **:** PROLETARIAT **2 :** SPOUSE

**other insurance** *n* **:** DOUBLE INSURANCE

**oth·er·ness** *n* -ES [¹*other* + *-ness*] **1 :** the quality or state of being other; *also* **:** a thing that is other ⟨externality and ~ —Lionel Stanford⟩ **2 :** the quality or state of being different ⟨struck with a sense of ~, of unfamiliarity —A.C.Danto⟩

**oth·er·some** \ˈəthə(r)səm\ *pron* [ME *other sum*, fr. *other* + *sum* some — more at SOME] *chiefly dial* **:** some others ⟨some folks do and ~ don't⟩

**otherways** \ˈ==,=\ *adv* [ME *other wayes*, fr. *other* + *wayes*, gen. of *way*] *chiefly dial* **:** OTHERWISE

**otherwhere** \ˈ==,=\ *adv* **:** in or to some other place **:** ELSEWHERE

**otherwhile** \ˈ==,=\ *also* **otherwhiles** \ˈ==,=\ *adv* [ME *otherwhil, otherwhiles*, fr. *other* + *whil* while or *whiles*, gen. of *whil* — more at WHILE] **1** *chiefly dial* **:** at another time **2** *chiefly dial* **:** SOMETIMES, OCCASIONALLY

**¹oth·er·wise** \ˈəthə(r),wīz\ *adv* [ME, fr. OE (*on*) *ōthre wīsan* in other manner] **1 :** in a different way or manner **:** DIFFERENTLY ⟨he could not act ~⟩ **2 :** in different circumstances **:** under other conditions ⟨~ he might have won⟩ **3 :** in other respects ⟨weak but ~ well⟩

**²otherwise** \"\ *adj* **1 :** DIFFERENT ⟨if conditions were ~⟩ **2 :** under different circumstances ⟨their political enemies were also their ~ friends⟩

**oth·er·wise·ness** *n* -ES **:** the quality or state of being otherwise

**otherworld** \¦==¦=\ *n* [¹*other* + *world*] **:** a world beyond death or beyond the world of present reality

**otherworldliness** \¦==¦===\ *n* **:** the quality or state of being otherworldly; *also* **:** an otherworldly characteristic

**otherworldly** \¦==¦==\ *also* **otherworld** \¦==¦=\ *adj* **1 a :** of or relating to a world other than the actual world **:** TRANSMUNDANE, TRANSCENDENTAL **b :** concerned with the world to come **:** devoted to preparing for the world to come **c :** morbidly spiritual **:** selfishly ascetic **2 :** devoted to intellectual or imaginative pursuits often to the extent of weakening the hold on or slighting practical everyday living

**othman** *usu cap, archaic var of* OTTOMAN

**othon·na** \ōˈthänə\ *n, cap* [NL, fr. L, a plant of Syria, fr. Gk] **:** a genus of southern African herbs or shrubs (family Compositae) with smooth often fleshy leaves and heads of yellow flowers of which the discoid ones are sterile

**oti** \ōˈtē\ *n, pl* **oti** *or* **otis** *usu cap* [Pg *oti, oti*, of AmerInd origin] **1 a :** an extinct group of peoples of southern Brazil — called also *Chavanté* **b :** a member of such a group of peoples **2 :** the language of the Otí group of peoples

**OTI** *abbr* official test insecticide

**otic** \ˈōd·ik, ˈäd-\ *adj* [Gk *ōtikos*, fr. *ōt-* ot- + *-ikos* -ic] **:** of, relating to, or in the region of the ear **:** AURICULAR, AUDITORY

**¹-ot·ic** \¦äd·ik, ¦ät|, |ēk\ *adj suffix* [Gk *-ōtikos*, fr. *-ōtos*, suffix used to form adjectives derived fr. certain verbs & *-ōtēs*, suffix used to form agent nouns derived fr. certain verbs + *-ikos* -ic] **1 a :** of, relating to, or characterized by a (specified) action, process, or condition ⟨*holocoenotic*⟩ **b :** having an abnormal or diseased condition of a (specified) kind ⟨*aphosphorotic*⟩ **2 :** showing an increase or a formation of (something specified) ⟨*leukocytotic*⟩ **3 :** of, relating to, or characterized by having a disease caused by a (specified) fungus ⟨*blastomycotic*⟩ — often used to form adjectives corresponding to nouns in *-osis*

**²-otic** \¦ōd·ik, ¦ä|, |t|, |ēk\ *adj comb form* [Gk *ōtikos* of the ear] **1 :** of or relating to a (specified) part of the ear ⟨*epiotic*⟩ ⟨*entotic*⟩ **2 a :** of or relating to an area having a (specified) spatial relationship to the ear ⟨*parotic*⟩ ⟨*periotic*⟩ **b :** of or relating to a bone having a (specified) spatial relationship to the ear ⟨*prootic*⟩ ⟨*sphenotic*⟩

**otic ganglion** *n* **:** a small autonomic ganglion on the mandibular nerve just below the foramen ovale

**otic vesicle** *n* **:** the sacular invagination of ectoderm from which the vertebrate ear develops

**otid·i·dae** \ōˈtidə,dē\ *n pl, cap* [NL, fr. *Otid-, Otis*, type genus + *-idae*] **:** a family of Old World birds comprising the bustards and constituting the suborder Otides, being of the order Gruiformes, and formerly classed with the Charadriiformes

— **otid·i·form** \ˈ≈≈ˌfȯrm\ *adj* — **oti·dine** \ˈōd·əˌdēn, -ˌdən\ *adj*
**otid·i·phaps** \ōˈtidəˌfaps\ *n, cap* [NL, fr. Gk *ōtid-, ōtis* bustard + NL *-i-* + Gk *phaps* wild pigeon] **:** a genus of large terrestrial pigeons of New Guinea and adjacent islands
**otid·i·um** \-dēəm\ *n, pl* **otidia** [NL, fr. *ot-* + *-idium*] **:** the otocyst of a mollusk
¹**oti·o·rhyn·chid** \ˌōshē(ˌ)ōˈriŋkəd\ *adj* [NL *Otiorhynchidae*] **:** of or relating to the Otiorhynchidae
²**otiorhynchid** \"\ *n* -s **:** a weevil of the family Otiorhynchidae
**oti·o·rhyn·chi·dae** \ˌ≈≈(ˌ)≈ˈriŋkəˌdē\ *n pl, cap* [NL, fr. *Otiorhynchus* type genus (fr. Gk *ōtion* ear — dim. of *ōt-, ous* ear — + NL *-rhynchus*) + *-idae* — more at EAR] **:** an extensive family of weevils often regarded as a subfamily of the family Curculionidae in which the mandibles of the pupa have a deciduous process that leaves a scar in the adult
**oti·ose** \ˈōshēˌōs, ˈōd·ēˌōs\ *adj* [L *otiosus*, fr. *otium* ease, leisure + *-osus* -ose] **1 :** being at leisure or ease **:** IDLE, UNEMPLOYED **2 :** without profit **:** STERILE, FUTILE ⟨an ~ undertaking⟩ **3 :** lacking use or effect **:** FUNCTIONLESS ⟨~ letters in an alphabet⟩ ⟨~ lines in a play⟩ **4** *of a deity* **:** remote and aloof **:** not concerned with the details of the world **syn** see VAIN
**oti·ose·ly** *adv* **:** in an otiose manner
**oti·ose·ness** *n* -ES **:** the quality or state of being otiose
**oti·os·i·ty** \ˌ≈≈ˈäsəd·ē, -ətē, -i\ *n* -ES [alter. of earlier *ociosity*, fr. MF *ociosité*, fr. LL *otiositat-, otiositas*, fr. L *otiosus* + *-itat-, -itas* -ity] **:** the quality or state of being otiose
**otis** \ˈōd·əs\ *n, cap* [L, bustard, fr. Gk *ōtis*, fr. *ōt-, ous* ear; fr. its long ear feathers — more at EAR] **:** a genus of typical bustards that includes the great bustard and is the type of the family Otididae
**otit·ic** \ōˈtid·ik\ *adj* [NL *otitis* + E *-ic*] **:** of, associated with, or relating to otitis
¹**otit·id** \(ˈ)ōˌtid·əd\ *adj* [NL *Otitidae*] **:** of or relating to the Otitidae
²**otitid** \"\ *n* -s **:** a fly of the family Otitidae
**otit·i·dae** \ōˈtid·əˌdē\ *n pl, cap* [NL, fr. *Otites*, type genus (origin unknown) + *-idae*] **:** a family of acalyptrate flies that includes numerous robust flies usu. with spotted or banded wings, frequently with metallic colors, and with larvae which usu. feed on decaying vegetable matter
**oti·tis** \ōˈtīd·əs\ *n, pl* **otit·i·des** \≈ˈtid·ə(ˌ)dēz\ [NL, fr. *ot-* + *-itis*] **:** inflammation of the ear
**otitis ex·ter·na** \-ekˈstərnə\ *n* [NL] **:** inflammation of the external ear
**otitis me·dia** \-ˈmēdēə\ *n* [NL] **:** inflammation of the middle ear marked by pain, fever, dizziness, and abnormalities of hearing — see AERO-OTITIS MEDIA
**oto** *or* **otoe** \ˈōd·(ˌ)ō\ *n, pl* **oto** *or* **otos** *or* **otoe** *or* **otoes** *usu cap* [perh. fr. Iowa-Oto *wat'ota*, lit., lechers; fr. the seduction of one chief's daughter by another chief's son] **1 a :** a Siouan people in the Platte and Missouri river valleys of Nebraska **b :** a member of such people **2 :** a dialect of Chiwere
**oto-** — see OT-
**oto·bi·us** \ōˈtōbēəs\ *n, cap* [NL, fr. *ot-* + *-bius*] *in some classifications* **:** a genus of argasid ticks that includes the spinose ear tick of southwestern U. S. and Mexico and that is often considered inseparable from *Ornithodoros*
**oto·cephalic** \ˌōd·ə+\ *adj* [ISV *ot-* + *-cephalic*] **:** of, relating to, or exhibiting otocephaly
**oto·ceph·a·ly** \ˌ≈≈ˈsefəlē\ *n* -ES [ISV *ot-* + *-cephaly*] **:** abnormal and deficient development of the head
**oto·co·ni·al** \ˌ≈≈ˈkōnēəl\ *adj* [fr. NL *otoconium* + E *-al*] **:** of or relating to otoconia
**oto·co·ni·um** \ˌ≈≈ˈnēəm\ *n, pl* **otoco·nia** \-nēə\ [NL, fr. *ot-* + *-conium* (fr. Gk *konis, konia* ashes, dust — more at INCINERATE)] **:** a vertebrate otolith
**oto·cy·on** \ˌ≈≈ˈsīˌän\ *n, cap* [NL, fr. *ot-* + Gk *kyōn* dog — more at HOUND] **:** a monotypic genus of the family Canidae that includes only the long-eared fox of southern Africa
**oto·cyst** \ˈōd·əˌsist\ *n* [ISV *ot-* + *-cyst*; orig. formed as F *otocyste*] **1 :** one of the supposed auditory organs of many invertebrates that contains a fluid and otoliths **:** STATOCYST **2 :** OTIC VESICLE — **oto·cys·tic** \ˌ≈≈ˈsistik\ *adj*
**oto·dec·tes** \ˌ≈≈ˈdekˌtēz\ *n, cap* [NL, fr. *ot-* + *-dectes*] **:** a genus of mites that have suckers on the legs, live in the ears of dogs, cats, and a few other mammals, and often cause ear mange — **oto·dec·tic** \ˌ≈≈ˈdektik\ *adj*
**otodectic mange** *n* [NL *Otodectes* + E *-ic*] **:** ear mange caused by mites of the genus *Otodectes*
**otog·e·nous** \(ˈ)ōˈtäjənəs\ *or* **oto·gen·ic** \ˌōd·əˈjenik\ *adj* [ISV *ot-* + *-genous, -genic*] **:** originating in the ear ⟨~ sepsis⟩
**oto·laryngological** \ˌōd·ō+\ *adj* **:** of or relating to otolaryngology ⟨a ~ examination⟩ ⟨~ disorders⟩
**oto·laryngologist** \"+\ *n* **:** a specialist in otolaryngology
**oto·laryngology** \"+\ *n* [*ot-* + *laryng-* + *-ology*] **:** a branch of medicine that deals with the ear, nose, and throat and their disorders and diseases
**oto·lite** \ˈōd·ᵊlˌīt\ *n* -s [by alter.] **:** OTOLITH — **oto·lit·ic** \ˌ≈≈ˈid·ik\ *adj*
**oto·lith** \ˈōd·ᵊlˌith\ *n* [F *otolithe*, fr. *ot-* + *lithe* -lith] **:** a calcareous concretion in the internal ear of a vertebrate or in the otocyst of an invertebrate that is esp. conspicuous in many teleost fishes where they form hard bodies and in most of the higher vertebrates where they are represented by masses of small calcareous otoconia — **oto·lith·ic** \ˌ≈≈ˈithik\ *adj*
**oto·lith·i·dae** \ˌōd·ᵊlˈithəˌdē\ *n pl, cap* [NL, fr. *Otolithus*, type genus (fr. *ot-* + Gk *lithos* stone) + *-idae*] *syn of* SCIAENIDAE
**oto·log·ic** \ˌōd·əˈläjik\ *also* **oto·log·i·cal** \-jəkəl\ *adj* **:** of or relating to otology — **oto·log·i·cal·ly** \-jək(ə)lē\ *adv*
**otol·o·gist** \ōˈtäləjəst\ *n* -s **:** a specialist in otology
**otol·o·gy** \-jē, -ji\ *n* -ES [ISV *ot-* + *-logy*] **:** a science that deals with the ear and its diseases — distinguished from *audiology*
**oto·mac** \ˌōd·əˈmäk\ *or* **oto·ma·co** \-ä(ˌ)kō\ *or* **oto·mak** \-äk\ *n, pl* **otomac** *or* **otomaco** *or* **otomak** *or* **otomacs** *or* **otomacos** *or* **otomaks** *usu cap* [Sp *otomaco*, of AmerInd origin] **1 a :** an extinct aboriginal people of southern Venezuela **b :** a member of such people **2 :** the language of the Otomac people
**oto·man·gue·an** \ˌōd·əˈmäŋ(ˌ)gāən\ *n* -s *usu cap* [blend of *Otomian* and ²*Mangue* + *-an*] **:** a language stock of Mexico and Guatemala comprising the Otomian, Popolocan, Triquean, and Chorotigan language families
**oto·mi** \ˌōd·əˈmē\ *n, pl* **otomi** *or* **otomis** *usu cap* [Sp *otomí*, of AmerInd origin] **1 a :** an Otomian people of the states of Guanajuato, Hidalgo, Querétaro, and México, Mexico **b :** a member of such people **2 :** the language of the Otomi people
**oto·mi·an** \ˌōd·əˈmēən, ōˈtōmē-\ *n* -s *usu cap* [*Otomi* + *-an*] **1 a :** an Indian people of central Mexico **b :** a member of such people **2 :** a language family comprising Otomi, Pame, Mazahua, and Matlatzinca
**oto·mycosis** \ˌōd·əˌmīˈkōsəs\ *n* [NL, fr. *ot-* + *mycosis*] **:** disease of the ear produced by the growth of fungi in the external auditory canal
**oto·mycotic** \ˌ≈≈+\ *adj* [*ot-* + *mycotic*] **:** of, relating to, or affected by otomycosis
**oto·plas·ty** \ˈ≈≈ˌplastē\ *n* -ES [ISV *ot-* + *-plasty*] **:** plastic surgery of the external ear
**oto·rhinolaryngology** \ˌ≈≈+\ *n* [ISV *ot-* + *rhin-* + *laryng-* + *-ology*] **:** OTOLARYNGOLOGY
**otor·rhea** *also* **otor·rhoea** \ˌōd·əˈrēə\ *n* -s [NL, fr. *ot-* + *-rrhea, -rrhoea*] **:** a discharge from the external ear
**oto·salpinx** \ˌōd·ō+\ *n, pl* **otosalpinges** [NL, fr. *ot-* + *salpinx*] **:** EUSTACHIAN TUBE
**oto·sclerosis** \ˌ≈≈+\ *n* [NL, fr. *ot-* + *sclerosis*] **:** growth of spongy bone in the inner ear where it gradually obstructs the vestibular or cochlear window or both and causes progressively increasing deafness
**oto·sclerotic** \ˌ≈≈+\ *adj* [*ot-* + *sclerotic*] **:** of, relating to, or affected by otosclerosis
**oto·scope** \ˈōd·əˌskōp\ *n* [ISV *ot-* + *-scope*] **:** an instrument fitted with lighting and magnifying lens systems and used to facilitate visual inspection of the auditory canal and ear drum — **oto·scop·ic** \ˌ≈≈ˈskäpik\ *adj* — **otos·co·py** \ōˈtäskəpē\ *n* -ES
**oto·sis** \ōˈtōsəs\ *n, pl* **oto·ses** \-ˌtōˌsēz\ [NL, fr. *ot-* + *-osis*] **:** mishearing or misinterpretation of spoken sounds; *also* **:** alteration in word forms due to it
**oto·sphe·nal** \ˌōd·əˈsfēnᵊl\ *n* -s [*ot-* + *sphen-* + *-al*] **:** BASIOCCIPITAL
**ot·osteal** \(ˈ)ōd·+\ *adj* [*ot-* + *osteal*] **:** of or relating to the bones of the ear
**otos·te·on** \ˈ≈ˈ≈≈ˌän\ *n* -s [NL, fr. *ot-* + *-osteon*] **1 :** OTOLITH **2 :** any of the auditory ossicles
**OTS** *abbr* officers' training school
**ottar** *var of* ATTAR
**ot·ta·va** \ōˈtävə\ *adv (or adj)* [It, octave, fr. ML *octava* — more at OCTAVE] **:** at an octave higher than written if placed above the staff or lower than written if placed below the staff — abbr. *8va*; used as a direction in music, sometimes as *all' ottava*; compare ⁵LOCO
**ottava al·ta** \-ˈältə\ *adj (or adv)* [It, lit., high octave] **:** intended to be played one octave higher than written — used as a direction in music
**ottava bas·sa** \-ˈbäsə\ *adj (or adv)* [It, lit., low octave] **:** intended to be played one octave lower than written — used as a direction in music
**ottava ri·ma** \-ˈrēmə\ *n, pl* **ottava rimas** [It, lit., eighth rhyme] **:** a stanza of eight lines of heroic verse or sometimes (as in the Italian prototype) hendecasyllabic verse with three rhymes of which the first six lines rhyme alternately and the last two form a couplet (as *a b a b a b c c*)
**ot·ta·vi·no** \ˌōd·əˈvē(ˌ)nō\ *n* -s [It, dim. of *ottava* octave; fr. its playing an octave higher than a flute] **:** PICCOLO 1
¹**ot·ta·wa** \ˈäd·əwə, ˈätə-\ *n, pl* **ottawa** *or* **ottawas** *usu cap* [F *Outouan*, of Algonquian origin; akin to Ojibwa *atāwe* to trade, Cree *atāweu* trader] **1 a :** an Algonquian people of southern Ontario, Canada, and Michigan **b :** a member of such people **2 :** a dialect of Ojibwa
²**ottawa** \"\ *adj, usu cap* [fr. *Ottawa*, Ontario, Canada] **:** of or from Ottawa, the capital of Canada **:** of the kind or style prevalent in Ottawa
**ot·ta·wan** \-wən\ *n* -s *cap* [*Ottawa*, Ontario + E *-an*] **:** a native or resident of Ottawa, Canada
¹**ot·ter** \ˈäd·ə(r), ˈätə-\ *n, pl* **otter** *or* **otters** *often attrib* [ME *oter*, fr. OE *otor*, *oter*; akin to MD & MLG *otter*, OHG *ottar*, ON *otr* otter, Gk *hydros* water snake, Skt *udra*, an aquatic animal, Gk *hydōr* water — more at WATER] **1 a :** any of several aquatic fish-eating mustelid mammals chiefly of the nearly cosmopolitan genus *Lutra* that are from two to four feet long with the tail long and flattened, the legs short, the feet completely webbed and with claws, the ears small, and the whiskers very bristly and that have dark brown fur highly valued for its beauty and durability and when dressed resembling beaver — compare SEA OTTER **b :** the fur or pelt of an otter **2 a (1) :** fishing tackle consisting of a short plank weighted at one end so as to stand in the water to which flies or bait are attached and whose movements are controlled by lines in the hands of the fisherman ashore **(2) :** OTTER BOARD **b :** PARAVANE **3 :** the larva of a ghost moth (*Hepialus humuli*) that is very injurious to hopvines **4** *or* **otter brown :** a dark grayish yellowish brown that is slightly yellower and deeper than seal and less strong, slightly redder, and darker than sepia brown — called also *loutre, perique, pickaninny*

otter 1 a

²**otter** \"\ *vb* -ED/-ING/-S *vi* **:** to hunt the otter ~ *vt* **:** to fish with an otter
**otter board** *n* **:** one of the two large boards or metal plates that keep the net of an otter trawl spread and that are attached to each side of the mouth of the net and are caused to flare apart by pressure of the water
**otter canoe** *n* **:** a long shallow boat used by Alaskans in hunting the sea otter
**otter civet** *n* **:** MAMPALON
**otterhound** \ˈ≈≈ˌ≈\ *n* **:** a British hound of complex ancestry that in many respects resembles the bloodhound, that has a wiry shaggy coat, long pendulous ears, and a scowling expression, and that is a good water dog with a keen scent although slow and usu. hunted on foot
**otter sheep** *n* **:** ANCON SHEEP
**otter shell** *also* **otter-shell clam** *or* **otter's shell** *n* **:** any of several bivalve mollusks of the genus *Lutraria* that resemble those of the genus *Mya* but have shells which are more porcelaneous
**otter shrew** *n* **:** an African insectivorous mammal (*Potamogale velox*) about the size of a stoat but similar in form and habits to an otter
**otter trawl** *n* **:** a trawl using otter boards to spread the net and drawn usu. by trawlers that handle the fish caught
**otter trawler** *n* **:** a person or boat fishing with an otter trawl
**otto** *var of* ATTAR
**ot·to cycle** \ˈäd·(ˌ)ō, ˈä(ˌ)tō-\ *n, usu cap O* [after Nikolaus A. *Otto* †1891 Ger. technician and inventor] **:** a four-stroke cycle for internal-combustion engines of the type used in automobiles wherein the first stroke consists of the suction into the cylinder of the explosive charge (as gas and air), the second stroke consists of the compression, ignition, and explosion of the charge, the third stroke consists of the expansion of the gases, and the fourth stroke consists of the expulsion of the products of combustion from the cylinder
**otto engine** *n, usu cap O* **:** an engine using the Otto cycle
¹**ot·to·man** \ˈäd·əmən, ˈätə-\ *adj, usu cap* [F, adj. & n., prob. fr. It *ottomano*, fr. Turk *osmani*, fr. *Osman, Othman* †1326, founder of the Ottoman Empire] **:** of or relating to the Turks or Turkey **:** TURKISH ⟨the *Ottoman* Empire⟩
²**ottoman** \"\ *n* -s [F *Ottoman*] **1** *cap* **:** TURK **2** [F *ottomane*, fr. fem. of *ottoman*, adj.] **a :** an upholstered often overstuffed seat or couch usu. without a back **b :** an overstuffed footstool **3** [F *ottoman*, fr. *ottoman*, adj.] **:** a heavy pliable clothing fabric usu. with a silk or rayon warp covering a cotton or wool weft characterized by pronounced crosswise ribs of regular or varying size

ottoman 2 b

**ot·to·mane·an** \ˌ≈≈ˈmānēən, ˌ≈≈-ˈmanēən\ *adj, usu cap* [²*ottoman* + *-ean*] **:** OTTOMANIC
**ot·to·man·ic** \ˌ≈≈ˈmanik\ *adj, usu cap* [²*Ottoman* + *-ic*] **:** of or relating to the Ottomans or their empire
**ottoman red** *n, usu cap O* **:** vermilion or a color resembling it
**ottoman turkish** *n, cap O&T* **:** TURKISH 1
**ot·to·ni·an** \(ˈ)äˈtōnēən\ *adj, usu cap* [G *Ottonen* Ottos, kings of Germany and Holy Roman Emperors (*Otto* I †973, *Otto* II †983, *Otto* III †1002) + E *-ian*] **:** of, relating to, or characteristic of the reigns (936–1002) of the first three Ottos of Germany and the Holy Roman Empire or of the arts that flourished in Germany in this period ⟨*Ottonian* bronze doors in Hildesheim and Augsburg —*Art Bull.*⟩
**otto of rose** *or* **otto of roses :** ATTAR OF ROSES
**ot·tre·lite** \ˈä·trəˌlīt\ *n* -s [F *ottrélite*, fr. *Ottrez*, Belgium, its locality + F *-lite*] **:** a gray to black mineral occurring in small scales in certain schists and being a variety of chloritoid
**OTU** *abbr* operational training unit
**otu·ke** \ˌōd·əˈkā\ *n, pl* **otuke** *or* **otukes** *usu cap* [Sp *otuke*, *otuque, otuki, otuqui*, of AmerInd origin] **1 a :** a people of northern Paraguay **b :** a member of such people **2 :** the language of the Otuke people
**otu·ki·an** \ˌōd·əˈkēən\ *adj, usu cap* **:** of, relating to, or constituting a branch of the Bororoan language family
**otus** \ˈōd·əs\ *n, cap* [NL, fr. Gk *ōtos*, fr. *ous* ear — more at EAR] **:** a genus of rather small-eared owls (family Strigidae) that are usu. predominantly insectivorous and nocturnal — see SCOPS OWL, SCREECH OWL
**o–type star** \ˈōˌtīp-\ *n, usu cap O* **:** a star of spectral type O — see SPECTRAL TYPE table
**ou** \ˈō\ *dial Brit var of* ¹OH
**oua·ba·gen·in** \ˌwäbəˈjenən; wäˈbäjənən, -ˌnēn\ *n* -s [*ouabain* + *-genin*] **:** a cardiac hexahydroxy steroidal lactone $C_{23}H_{34}O_8$ obtained by hydrolysis of ouabain
**oua·ba·in** \wäˈbīən, ˈwäbəən\ *n* -s [ISV *ouabaïo* + *-in*; prob. orig. formed as F *ouabaïne*] **:** a very toxic crystalline steroidal glycoside $C_{29}H_{44}O_{12}$ obtained from the seeds of an African shrub (*Strophanthus gratus*) or from the wood of trees of the genus *Acocanthera* (as *A. schimperi*) that yields rhamnose and ouabagenin on hydrolysis and that is used similarly to digitalis and in Africa as an arrow poison — called also *g-strophanthin, strophanthin-g*
**oua·baio** \wäˈbī(ˌ)ō\ *n* -s [F *ouabaïo*, fr. Somali *waba yo*] **:** either of two southern African trees (*Acocanthera ouabaio* and *A. venenata*) from which ouabain is obtained
**oua·ga·dou·gou** \ˌwägəˈdü(ˌ)gü\ *adj, usu cap* [fr. *Ouagadougou*, Upper Volta] **:** of or from Ouagadougou, capital of the Upper Volta **:** of the kind or style prevalent in Ouagadougou
**oua·ka·ri** *or* **ua·ka·ri** \wäˈkärē\ *n* -s [Tupi] **:** any of several So. American monkeys of the genus *Cacajao* that are related to the sakis but have short tails like those of baboons and long silky mostly whitish or yellowish hair
**oua·na·niche** \ˌwänəˈnēsh, -nish\ *also* **ouananiche salmon** *n, pl* **ouananiche** *also* **ouananiche salmon** [CanF *ouananiche*, fr. Montagnais *wananish*, dim. of *wanans* salmon] **:** a small landlocked salmon of Lake St. John, Canada, and neighboring waters
**ouanga** *var of* WANGA
**ou·bli·ette** \ˌüblēˈet\ *n* -s [F, fr. MF, fr. *oublier* to forget (fr. OF *oblider*, fr. — assumed — VL *oblitare*, fr. L *oblitus*, past part. of *oblivisci* to forget) + *-ette* — more at OBLIVION] **:** a dungeon with an opening only at the top and often a concealed pit below the floor ⟨human animals thrust away in the ~s —V.L.Parrington⟩
¹**ouch** \ˈau̇ch\ *n* -ES [ME *ouche*, alter. (resulting from incorrect division of *a nouche*) of *nouche*, fr. MF *nosche, noche, nouche*, of Gmc origin; akin to OS *nuska, nuskia* clasp, brooch, MD *nusche*, OHG *nusca* clasp, brooch; akin to OE *net* — more at NET] **1** *obs* **:** a clasp or brooch for a garment **2 a :** a bezel or other setting for a precious stone ⟨thou shalt make them to be set in ~es of gold —Exod 28:11 (AV)⟩ **b :** a buckle or brooch set with precious stones **3 :** a necklace, bracelet, jewel, or other personal ornament ⟨your brooches, pearls, and ~es —Shak.⟩ ⟨left her golden chains and ~es —Charles Kingsley⟩
²**ouch** \"\ *interj* [origin unknown] — used to express sudden pain or displeasure
**oucht** \ˈäkt\ *Scot var of* OUGHT
**oud** \ˈüd\ *n* -s [Ar *'ūd*, lit., wood] **:** a musical instrument of southwest Asia and northern Africa resembling a mandolin ⟨hypnotized by the tinkling of an ~ —Truman Capote⟩
**oued** *var of* WADI
**ouf** \ˈau̇f\ *also* **oof** \ˈüf, ˈu̇f\ *interj* [origin unknown] — used to express discomfort, aversion, or impatience
**ough** \ˈük, ˈu̇k\ *interj* [origin unknown] — used to express pain or disgust
¹**ought** *archaic past of* OWE
²**ought** \ˈȯt, *usu* -d·+V\ *verbal auxiliary* [ME *aghten, aughten, oughten* to be obliged to, owe, fr. *aghte, aughte, oughte* possessed, owned, owed (past indic. & subj. of *aghen, aughen, owen* to possess, own, owe), fr. OE *āhte*, 1st & 3rd pers. sing. past ind. of *āgan* to possess, own, owe — more at OWE] — used to express moral obligation, duty, or necessity ⟨~ to follow the dictates of our conscience⟩ ⟨~ to pay our debts⟩ or what is correct, advisable, or expedient ⟨you ~ to take care of yourself⟩ ⟨this suit ~ to be pressed⟩ or what is naturally expected or logically sound ⟨~ to be able to understand this book⟩ ⟨if our reasoning is correct, the result ~ to be infinity⟩
**syn** OUGHT, SHOULD, MUST, and HAVE can all function as verbal auxiliaries meaning to be bound (to do or be or not do or be). HAVE with *got* can be used interchangeably with some of these. OUGHT and SHOULD are often interchangeable and imply the compulsion of obligation, OUGHT more commonly suggesting duty or moral constraint, SHOULD applying more to the obligation of fitness, propriety, or expediency ⟨it *ought* not to be very difficult —Nevil Shute⟩ ⟨*ought* to fulfill our obligations⟩ ⟨the stopper is small enough so that it *ought* to fit in the bottle⟩ ⟨*should* not try to evade responsibilities⟩ ⟨the car *should* be around at noon⟩ ⟨*should* make the five o'clock train⟩ MUST, though sometimes stressing extremely strong obligation, usu. implies the compulsion of necessity, whether physical or moral ⟨number three of my suggestions is that a new federal labor law *must* outlaw unfair bargaining practices —A.E. Stevenson b.1900⟩ ⟨the employees *must* contribute 40 percent of the entire premium for all benefits provided under this plan —*U.S.Code*⟩ ⟨again and again he went to performances of what *must* have been his favorite play —*Time*⟩ ⟨to qualify for a college degree you *must* pass certain examinations⟩ HAVE and *have got* are interchangeable with MUST in meaning although *have got* occurs more frequently in spoken than literary English ⟨to qualify for a college degree you *have* to pass certain examinations⟩ ⟨the man I wished to see *had* to leave before I came⟩ ⟨the speeder *has* got to pay a fine⟩ ⟨we *have* got to come into court — the high court of public opinion — with clean hands —*Newsweek*⟩
³**ought** \ˈäkt\ *vt* -ED/-ING/-S [ME *aghten, aughten, oughten*] **1** *chiefly Scot* **:** OWE **2** *chiefly Scot* **:** POSSESS ⟨there's naebody but you and me that ~ the name —R.L.Stevenson⟩
⁴**ought** \ˈȯt, *usu* -d·+V\ *n* -s [²*ought*] **:** moral obligation **:** DUTY ⟨the ethical ~ voices or expresses . . . what would, upon reflection, be regarded as binding upon any normal person within a given social system —H.D.Aiken⟩ — contrasted with *is*
⁵**ought** *var of* AUGHT
**ought·lins** \ˈäktlənz\ *adv* [⁵*ought* + *-lins*, alter. of *-lings*] *Scot* **:** in the least degree
**ought·ness** *n* -ES [⁴*ought* + *-ness*] **:** the quality or state of being morally obligatory ⟨to each such duty belongs a feeling of ~ —W.H.Kilpatrick⟩ — contrasted with *isness*
**oughtn't** \ˈȯtᵊn(t)\ [by contr.] **:** ought not
**Oui·ja** \ˈwējə, -jē-\ *trademark* — used for a board that has the letters of the alphabet and other signs written on it and that is used together with a planchette to seek messages of spiritualistic or telepathic origin
**ouistiti** *var of* WISTITI
**ouk** \ˈük\ *n* -s [ME (Sc dial.) *ouke*, alter. of *wouke*, fr. OE *wucu* — more at WEEK] *Scot* **:** WEEK
**oul** \ˈōl\ *or* **ould** \ˈōl(d)\ *Irish var of* OLD
**ou·led na·il** \ülednäˈēl, ˈü,ledˈnī(ə)l, ˈü,ledˈnā(ə)l\ *n, pl* **ouled nails** *usu cap O&N* [F, fr. *Ouled Naïl*, a confederation of nomadic peoples in Algeria] **:** an Arab prostitute and dancing girl of the No. African cities usu. dressed in a brightly colored bespangled costume and ornamental often feathered headdress
¹**ounce** \ˈau̇n(t)s\ *n* -s [ME *unce, ounce*, fr. MF *unce*, fr. L *uncia* twelfth part, ounce, inch, fr. *unus* one — more at ONE] **1 :** any of various units of weight based on the ancient Roman unit equal to 1/12 Roman pound: as **a :** a unit equal to 1/12 troy pound **b :** a unit equal to 1/16 avoirdupois pound — see MEASURE table **2 :** a small portion or quantity ⟨if any of them had used a grain of common sense or an ~ of resolution —Dan Wickenden⟩ **3 :** FLUIDOUNCE **4 :** ONZA **5 :** a unit of thickness for leather equal to 1/64 inch or 0.397 millimeter
²**ounce** \"\ *n* -s [ME *unce, once*, fr. OF *once*, alter. (by false division, the *l* of *lonce* being taken as the definite article, and *lonce* as *l'once* the lynx), of *lonce*, fr. (assumed) VL *lyncea, luncea*, fr. L *lync-, lynx* lynx — more at LYNX] **1** *archaic* **:** any of various moderate-sized wildcats (as the ocelot or lynx) ⟨tigers, ~s, pards, gamboled before them —John Milton⟩ **2 :** SNOW LEOPARD **3** *archaic* **:** CHEETAH **4 :** a heraldic representation of a leopard
**ounce metal** *n* **:** an alloy composed of one ounce each of tin, zinc, and lead to one pound of copper
**ouph** *or* **ouphe** \ˈau̇f, ˈüf\ *n* -s [prob. alter. of *auf*] **:** ELF
¹**our** [ME *ure, oure*, fr. OE *ūre* (suppletive gen. of *wē* we); akin to OHG *unsēr* of us, ON *vār*, Goth *unsara* of us, *uns, unsis* us — more at US] *obs possessive of* WE
²**our** \(ˈ)är, (ˈ)au̇(ə)r, (ˈ)au̇ə, (ˈ)ä(r, *esp in the South* ˈau̇wə(r\ *adj* [ME *ure, oure*, fr. OE *ūre*; akin to OHG *unsēr* our, ON *vārr*, Goth *unsar*; derivative fr. the root of E *us*] **1 a :** of or relating to us or ourselves or ourself as possessors or possessor **:** due to us **:** inherent in us **:** associated or connected with us ⟨bumped ~ heads⟩ ⟨defending ~ rights⟩ ⟨all ~ rela-

tives⟩ **b :** of or relating to us or ourselves as authors, doers, givers, or agents **:** effected by us **:** experienced by us as subject **:** that we are capable of ⟨criticized all ~ words and actions⟩ ⟨kept ~ promise⟩ ⟨was angry because of ~ being late⟩ ⟨did ~ very best⟩ **c :** of or relating to us as object of an action **:** experienced by us as object ⟨expected ~ being chosen for the job⟩ ⟨~ injuries didn't amount to much⟩ **d :** that we have to do with or are supposed to possess or to have knowledge or a share of or some special interest in ⟨we like golf and we know ~ game⟩ **e :** that is esp. significant for us **:** that brings us good fortune or prominence — used with *day* or sometimes with other words indicating a division of time ⟨today was really ~ day: everything went fine⟩ **2 :** that we have in mind or are speaking of or to ⟨we seem to have digressed from ~ topic⟩ ⟨~ readers will be interested, we feel sure⟩ or that has some other special relation to us ⟨~ man was not so successful⟩

**³our** \ˈō(ə)r, ˈōə\ *dial Eng var of* OVER

**ou·ral green** \ˈu̇rəl-\ *n, often cap O* [*Oural* perh. fr. F, Ural mountains in northwestern Asia] **:** a light yellowish green to very pale green

**ourang** *var of* ORANG

**ourangoutang** *var of* ORANGUTAN

**ourebi** *var of* ORIBI

**ou·ri·cu·ry** *also* **ou·ri·cu·ri** \ˌu̇rəkəˈrē\ *or* **ari·cu·ri** \ˌär-\ *n* -ES [Pg *ouricuri, ouricuri, aricuri, aricuri,* fr. Tupi] **1 :** a straight-trunked Brazilian palm (*Syagrus coronata*) of the family Palmae having a large thick crown of wax-covered leaves — called also *urucuri iba* **2 :** an important Brazilian feather palm (*Attalaea excelsa*) whose large oily nuts are burned for their smoke in curing Para rubber

**ouricury oil** *n* **:** a yellowish edible fatty oil obtained from the kernels of the fruit of the ouricury palm

**ouricury wax** *n* **:** a hard brown wax exuded by the leaves of the ouricury palm that is similar in properties and uses to carnauba wax — called also *licury wax*

**ou·rie** \ˈüri\ *adj* [ME (northern dial.) *ouri,* perh. of Scand origin; akin to ON *ūrigr* wet, fr. *ūr* drizzling rain + *-igr* -y — more at URINE] **1** *chiefly Scot* **:** DEPRESSING, DISMAL **2** *chiefly Scot* **:** shivering with cold

**our-lady's-bedstraw** \ˈ=ˈ==ˈ=,=\ *n, usu cap O&L* **:** YELLOW BEDSTRAW

**our-lady's-mint** \=ˈ==ˈ=\ *n, usu cap O&L* **:** SPEARMINT

**our-lady's-thistle** \=ˈ==ˈ==\ *n, usu cap O&L* **:** MILK THISTLE 1

**our lord's candle** *n, usu cap O&L* **:** any of various yuccas with tall spikes of flowers (esp. *Yucca whipplei*)

**ourn** \ˈau̇(ə)rn, ˈau̇ən, ˈär(ə)n, ˈau̇wə(r)n\ *pron* [ME *ouren, ourn,* fr. *ure, oure* our + *-n* (as in *min* mine — more at OUR)] *dial* **:** OURS

**ou·rou·par·ia** \ˌü(ˌ)rüˈpa(a)rēə\ [NL, fr. Galibi *y-ourou-pari,* a species of *Uncaria*] *syn of* UNCARIA

**-ourous** — see -UROUS

**ours** \ˈau̇(ə)rz, ˈau̇əz, ˈärz, ˈäz, ˈau̇wə(r)z\ *pron, sing or pl in constr* [ME *ures, oures,* fr. *ure, oure* our + *-s* -'s] **1 :** our one or our ones — used without a following noun as a pronoun equivalent in meaning to the adjective *our* ⟨your house is large and ~ is small⟩ ⟨~ is a federal system —Stephen Duggan⟩; often used after *of* to single out one or more members of a class belonging to or connected with a group including the one speaking or writing ⟨a friend of ~⟩ or merely to identify something or someone as belonging to or connected with a group including the one speaking or writing without any implication of membership in a more extensive class ⟨that house of ~⟩ ⟨that indifferent manner of ~⟩ ⟨the tremendous growth that is surely ahead in this country of ~ —C.F.Craig⟩ **2 :** something belonging to us **:** what belongs to us ⟨the victory is ~⟩ ⟨~ is the right to do what we please⟩ ⟨it was all ~⟩

**our·sel** \u̇rˈsel\ *pron* [by shortening] *Scot* **:** OURSELF

**our·self** \=ˈ=, ˌ==ˈ=\ *pron* [ME *oure self*] **1 :** MYSELF — used to refer to the single-person subject when *we* is used instead of *I* (as in editorial style or as in the formal style often used by heads of state) ⟨we ~ will obey our own law⟩ **2 :** the self that each one of us separately possesses **:** the individual self that each one of us separately is ⟨the being which is ~ —Wallace Fowlie⟩

**our·sels** \u̇rˈselz\ *pron* [by contr.] *Scot* **:** OURSELVES

**our·selves** \=ˈ=, ˌ==ˈ=\ *pron pl* [ME *oure selven, our selfs*] **1 :** those identical ones that are we **:** the selves that belong to us **:** the selves that are ours — used (1) reflexively as object of a preposition or direct or indirect object of a verb ⟨we're doing it solely for ~⟩ ⟨busying ~ only with what concerns us⟩ ⟨we're getting ~ a new home⟩; (2) for emphasis in apposition with *we* or *who* ⟨we ~ will never go⟩ ⟨we can speak with some certainty, we who have ~ had the same experience⟩; (3) for emphasis instead of nonreflexive *us* as object of a preposition or direct or indirect object of a verb ⟨this pleases ~ but no one else⟩; (4) for emphasis instead of *we* or instead of *we ourselves* as predicate nominative ⟨the only ones that want to do it are ~⟩ or in comparisons after *than* or *as* ⟨no one knows more about it than ~⟩ or as part of a compound subject ⟨our children and ~ will be glad to come⟩ or archaically or dialectally as only subject of a verb ⟨~ were country folk —Elizabeth Dye⟩; (5) in absolute constructions ⟨~ hardly able to see what was happening, they shut the door in our face⟩ **2 :** our normal, healthy, or sane condition ⟨we were groggy for a moment but quickly came to ~⟩**:** our normal, healthy, or sane selves ⟨we had been ill, but today we are again ~⟩

**-ous** \əs\ *adj suffix* [ME, partly fr. OF *-ous, -os, -eus, -eux,* fr. L *-osus;* partly fr. L *-us* (final portion of the nom. sing. masc. form of adjectives such as *fatuus* foolish, *fuscus* brown)] **1 :** full of **:** abounding in **:** having **:** possessing the qualities of ⟨*clamorous*⟩ ⟨*glamorous*⟩ ⟨*cystous*⟩ ⟨*lymphous*⟩ **2 :** having a valence lower than in compounds or ions named with an adjective ending in *-ic* ⟨*ferrous* iron⟩ ⟨*sulfurous* acid⟩ — compare ²-ITE — **-ous·ly** *adv suffix*

**ouse** \ˈau̇s\ *chiefly Scot var of* OX

**ousel** *var of* OUZEL

**oushak** *var of* USHAK

**ou·sia** \ˈüzēə, ˈüsēə, ˈüzh(ē)ə, ˈüsh(ē)ə\ *n* -S [Gk, fr. *ous-* (stem of *ōn,* pres. part. of *einai* to be) + *-ia* -y — more at IS] **1 :** true being **:** ENTITY, ESSENCE, SUBSTANCE **2 :** HYPOSTASIS 2a

**oust** \ˈau̇st\ *vt* -ED/-ING/-S [AF *ouster* fr. OF *oster,* fr. LL *obstare* to ward off, fr. L, to stand before or against, to thwart, hinder, fr. *ob-* to, toward, against + *stare* to stand — more at OB-, STAND] **1 a :** to put out of possession **:** eject, dispossess from, or deprive of an inheritance (as land or buildings) ⟨the castles and burghs which had slowly ~*ed* him from his inheritance —W.C.Dickinson⟩ **b :** to take away (as a right or authority) **:** BAR, REMOVE **2 :** to eject from a position or place **:** turn out **:** EXPEL ⟨a newfangled apparatus which might ~ them from their jobs —Langston Day⟩ ⟨was ~*ed* from office by a military junta —*Current Biog.*⟩ **3 :** to drive out of use **:** take the place of ⟨must be careful that quantity does not ~ quality —Ralph Vaughan Williams⟩ ⟨colored slides virtually ~*ed* black-and-white —*Geog. Jour.*⟩ **syn** see EJECT

**oust·er** \-tə(r)\ *n* -S [AF, fr. *ouster,* to oust] **1 a :** a wrongful ejection or dispossession of a person from a freehold or other inheritance or from a right or franchise — compare EVICTION **b :** a judgment removing a public or corporate officer or depriving a corporation of a franchise or right (as a charter) **2 :** an ejection from a position or place **:** EXPULSION ⟨the ~ of the manager failed to stop the team's losing streak⟩ ⟨called for the ~ of the man responsible for the blunder⟩

**¹out** \ˈau̇t, *usu* ˈau̇d·+V\ *adv* [ME, fr. OE *ūt;* akin to OHG *ūz* out, ON & Goth *ūt* out, L *us*que continually, Gk *hy*bris wantonness, arrogance, insolence, *hys*teros latter, Skt *ud, ut* up, out; basic meaning: up, out] **1 a :** in a direction away from a particular point or place ⟨started ~ from home⟩ ⟨looked ~ across the valley⟩ **b :** away from one's own country or part of the world **:** ABROAD ⟨went ~ for a short visit and stayed for five years⟩ ⟨was sent ~ as ambassador at a critical time⟩ **c :** away from a particular place, region, or country ⟨said the current storm . . . would move ~ by tonight —*Springfield (Mass.) Daily News*⟩ ⟨left the river with their captives and struck ~ overland —I.B.Richman⟩ **d :** away from one's own control or possession ⟨lent ~ his money on mortgages⟩ ⟨gave ~ the manuscript to be typed⟩ **e :** away from one's usual place of residence, practice, or business ⟨dines ~ once a week⟩ ⟨goes ~ every evening⟩ ⟨~ to lunch⟩ **f :** in a direction away from the shore ⟨the tide is going ~⟩ ⟨they rowed ~ to the ship⟩ **g :** away from a job or task ⟨took time ~ for a cigarette⟩ **2 a** (1) **:** out of the usual or proper place or position ⟨threw his shoulder ~⟩ ⟨laughing his sides ~⟩ ⟨the time has been that, when the brains were ~, the man would die —Shak.⟩ (2) **:** out of the necessary or expected place or position ⟨left ~ two lines⟩ ⟨left ~ the most important part of his argument⟩ **b :** away from or contrary to one's normal or usual state of mind or manner of behavior ⟨greatly put ~ by the bad news⟩ ⟨the two friends fell ~ over a trivial matter⟩ **c :** beyond the usual or proper limits ⟨the edge of the house juts ~ over the cliff⟩ ⟨the point of the nail sticks ~⟩ ⟨his shirttails hang ~⟩ **d :** so as to protrude or stick out ⟨~ at elbows⟩ ⟨~ at the knees⟩ **e :** at odds ⟨he is ~ with his friend over a girl⟩ **f :** out of pocket ⟨by the end of the evening, he was $20 ~⟩ **g :** not in accord with the facts ⟨this story is ludicrously ~ in its geography —B.R.Elliott⟩ ⟨the introductory note . . . by an error in arithmetic, is ~ by twenty years —*Times Lit. Supp.*⟩ **h :** not in agreement ⟨the trial balance was ~ $10⟩ **3 a** (1) **:** in or into the open **:** out of an enclosed space (as a building or container) ⟨he went ~ about an hour ago⟩ ⟨the whole town turned ~ to greet him⟩ ⟨he took ~ his wallet⟩ ⟨she poured ~ the tea⟩ (2) **:** out of a place or position tenaciously held to ⟨drag him ~⟩ ⟨smoke him ~⟩ ⟨crowd him ~⟩ (3) **:** out of a situation or place felt to be confining or unendurable ⟨tried to break ~⟩ ⟨changed his mind afterward and asked to be let ~⟩ **b :** into activity, use, or accessibility ⟨war broke ~⟩ ⟨opened ~ a new route to the West⟩ ⟨the new models are coming ~ next week⟩ **c :** EXTERNALLY ⟨cleaned the house inside and ~⟩ **d :** in the open **:** OUTDOORS ⟨it was nice ~ . . . with the sky all so blue —J.T.Farrell⟩ ⟨it's a lovely day ~ —James Jones⟩ ⟨camp ~⟩ **e** (1) **:** in or into active military service or training ⟨the army was ordered ~ —Marjory S. Douglas⟩ ⟨has been ~ on maneuvers⟩ (2) **:** on a journey or expedition ⟨has been ~ fishing for a week⟩ ⟨has been ~ on a business trip⟩ (3) **:** in or into active rebellion ⟨he was a bitter rebel, and boasted that his grandfather had been ~ in '98 —G.B. Shaw⟩ (4) **:** not at work **:** on strike ⟨ten thousand or more workers are ~ —Warner Bloomberg⟩ **f :** on the exterior or outer side ⟨insulated the roof to keep the heat ~⟩ ⟨closed the windows to keep the rain ~⟩ **g :** to or toward the outside ⟨turned his pockets inside ~⟩ ⟨went to the window and looked ~⟩ **h :** out of jail or prison ⟨he's only been ~ a week, but he's already in trouble⟩ **i :** not on the shelf **:** in circulation ⟨the book you want is ~⟩ **4 a :** at or to a distance away from a given point ⟨the nearest school is three miles ~⟩ ⟨hit the ball 400 feet ~⟩ **b :** at or to a distance away from land **:** at sea ⟨when they were three days ~, the weather turned fine⟩ ⟨an island far ~ in the ocean⟩ **c :** at a relatively far distance ⟨motioned to the shortstop to play ~⟩ **d :** around the circuit of the first nine holes of a golf course ⟨he went ~ in 39⟩ **5 a :** from or among a group ⟨sorting out the negatives and selecting ~ certain cards —R.S.Casey & J.W.Perry⟩ **b :** into sections or parts ⟨portioned ~ the meat among the five of them⟩ ⟨laid ~ the day's work for his two assistants⟩ **6 a :** FREELY, OPENLY ⟨was too frightened to speak ~⟩ **b :** so as to be audible **:** ALOUD ⟨cried ~ to attract his friend's attention⟩ ⟨called ~ a greeting⟩ **c :** in or into print or public circulation ⟨the evening paper isn't ~ yet⟩ ⟨there's a warrant ~ against him⟩ **d :** in or into open view ⟨the moon is ~ tonight⟩ ⟨the sun came ~ from behind the clouds⟩ **e :** in or into leaf, blossom, or fruit ⟨the roses are just ~⟩ ⟨the apples are starting to come ~⟩ **f :** in or into society ⟨wear the same clothes and makeup as girls who are already ~ and go to grown-up parties —Helen Eustis⟩ **g :** in an unfurled or extended state ⟨broke ~ the topsail⟩ **7 a :** to a point of exhaustion or depletion ⟨talked herself ~⟩ ⟨cried herself ~⟩ ⟨pumped the well ~⟩ ⟨the cow is milked ~⟩ **b :** to a point of completion or satisfaction ⟨might as well have your sleep ~ —Ellen Glasgow⟩ ⟨deeply satisfied, the way you feel when you have had a chance to say your say all ~ —Dorothy C. Fisher⟩ ⟨fight it ~ on this line if it takes all summer —U.S.Grant⟩ **c :** in or into a state of extinction, inactivity, or nonexistence ⟨the fire is ~⟩ ⟨put ~ the light⟩ ⟨a custom that is going ~⟩ ⟨a species that is on its way ~⟩ **d :** to a solution or result ⟨work ~ the problem in your own way⟩ ⟨the addition comes ~ wrong each time⟩ **e :** to a conclusion (as to adulthood or to a predetermined size or weight) ⟨grow ~ livestock⟩ **8 a :** at an end ⟨before the year is ~⟩ ⟨now that the summer is ~⟩ **b :** in or into an insensible or unconscious state ⟨the glassy eyes and vague expression of a man who was . . . ~ on his feet —S.H.Adams⟩ ⟨after three drinks he was ~ cold⟩ **c :** out of commission **:** in or into a useless state ⟨only the one plane coming in — actually half a plane — with two of its engines ~ —Saul Levitt⟩ **d** (1) **:** so as to retire a batter or batsman or so as to be retired ⟨put him ~ on three straight pitches⟩ ⟨bowled him ~⟩ ⟨popped ~ to the infield⟩ (2) **:** out of participation in a poker pot ⟨count me ~⟩ ⟨deal me ~⟩ (3) **:** at the winning point of a game (as by having reached or passed the required goal or number of points) **e :** at a stop ⟨the referee called time ~⟩ **f** — used on a two way radio circuit to indicate the end of a communication with no reply expected ⟨over and ~⟩ **9 a :** in an extended manner or to an extended degree ⟨the dog was stretched ~ on the floor⟩ ⟨the last act was terribly drawn ~⟩ **b :** to the fullest possible extent ⟨decked ~ in her best clothes⟩ ⟨clean ~ the attic⟩ ⟨wipe ~ the stain⟩ **c :** in or into competition or determined effort ⟨~ for class president⟩ ⟨intends to go ~ for the football team next year⟩ ⟨~ to win control of the whole industry⟩ **10 a :** out of office or power ⟨voted ~ at the next election⟩ ⟨turned ~ by the new commissioner⟩ **b :** out of season **:** no longer in supply ⟨fresh strawberries are ~ now until next spring⟩ **c :** out of vogue or fashion **:** no longer in request ⟨short skirts are ~⟩ **d :** out of the question **:** so as to be eliminated from consideration ⟨these last two proposals seem definitely ~ —Tom Fitzsimmons⟩ **11** — used as an intensive with numerous verbs ⟨bait ~ the fish lines⟩ ⟨sketch ~ the plans⟩ ⟨write ~ the speech⟩

**²out** \ˈau̇t, *usu* ˈau̇d·+V\ *vb* -ED/-ING/-S [ME *outen,* fr. OE *ūtian,* fr. *ūt,* adv.] *vt* **1 :** to put out **:** eject from a place, office, or possession **:** EXPEL ⟨privately kept ~*ed* vicars as chaplains —Rose Macaulay⟩ **2** *archaic* **:** to make public **:** DISCLOSE, REVEAL **3 :** EXTINGUISH ⟨the lamplighter went his rounds ~*ing* the street lamps —John Bennett⟩ **4 :** to thrust out **:** EXTEND ⟨they ~*ed* oars and pulled hard —Christopher Morley⟩ **5** *slang Brit* **:** knock out **:** render unconscious or kill **6 a :** to put (a batsman) out in cricket **b :** to eliminate in a sports competition ⟨was ~*ed* in a semifinal of the Australian championships —*A.B.C.Weekly*⟩ **7 :** to hit (a ball) out of bounds in tennis or squash **~ *vi*** **1 :** to become known or apparent **:** become public ⟨truth will ~⟩ ⟨murder will ~⟩ ⟨bad blood always ~*s* —Alec Waugh⟩ **2 :** to go out; *esp* **:** go on an outing or excursion **3 :** to hit a tennis ball out of bounds ⟨the Australian ~*ed* and lost the game —*Sydney (Australia) Morning Herald*⟩ — **out with 1 :** to bring out ⟨he *outs with* his money⟩ **2 :** to make known **:** UTTER ⟨he *outs with* the whole story⟩

**³out** \ˈau̇t, *usu* ˈau̇d·+V\ *adj* [ME, fr. *out,* adv.] **1 :** situated or lying on the outside of something **:** EXTERNAL ⟨the ~ edge⟩ **2 :** situated or lying at a distance from a center **:** OUTLYING ⟨the ~ islands⟩ ⟨the ~ parts of the settlement⟩ **3 a :** not in power **:** having no official position or standing ⟨encourage pirating by ~ unions trying to get in —C.O.Gregory⟩ **b :** not having its inning ⟨the ~ side in cricket⟩ **c :** not successful in reaching base ⟨the batter was ~ at first on a close play⟩ ⟨was ~ trying to steal third⟩ **4 :** larger than usual ⟨a dress of an ~ size⟩ **5 :** directed outward or serving to direct something outward **:** OUTGOING ⟨the ~ train⟩ ⟨put the letter in the ~ basket⟩

**⁴out** \(ˌ)au̇t, *usu* (ˌ)au̇d·+V\ *prep* [ME, fr. *out,* adv.] **1 a** — used as a function word to indicate direction from the inside to the outside ⟨peering ~ his window at the river —Hugh MacLennan⟩ **b** — used as a function word to indicate movement or change of position from the inside to the outside ⟨threw his street clothes and luggage ~ a window onto the platform —Joseph Wechsberg⟩ ⟨put the cat ~ the door⟩ **2** — used as a function word to indicate movement or direction away from a center ⟨drove through the streets of town and ~ the dark, wooded road to his house —Nathaniel Benchley⟩ ⟨lives ~ Elm Street⟩; see OUT OF

**⁵out** \ˈau̇t, *usu* ˈau̇d·+V\ *n* -S [¹*out* & ³*out*] **1 :** OUTSIDE ⟨liking not the inside, locked the ~ —Lord Byron⟩ ⟨the width of the building from ~ to ~⟩ **2 :** OUTING **3 a :** one who is without official position or influence **:** a member of a party or group that is out of power — usu. used in pl. ⟨the ~*s* are invariably more emphatic in their advocacy of principles than the ins —C.J.Friedrich⟩ **b out** *pl* **:** the players in a game (as cricket) who are not having their innings **4 :** copy matter (as a word) inadvertently omitted in typesetting **5 :** SHOWING ⟨makes a poor ~ of it when the hub of the house comes down —H.E. Giles⟩ **6 a :** the retiring of a baseball player during his turn at bat ⟨it was the last ~ of the game⟩ **b :** a player so retired ⟨he was an easy ~⟩ **7 outs** *pl, Brit* **:** money paid out esp. in taxes **8 :** an objectionable feature or circumstance **:** BLEMISH ⟨despite all the improvement, rubber still has a number of bad ~*s* —Williams Haynes & E.A.Hauser⟩ **9 :** a ball hit out of bounds in tennis or squash **10 :** an item that is out of stock ⟨the packing list is noted for changes in quantities and ~*s* —D.F.Sellards⟩ **11 a :** a way of avoiding responsibility or escaping from an embarrassing situation **:** a face-saving device ⟨a discreet retirement may provide the easy ~ —Douglass Cater⟩ ⟨can sometimes serve as an easy ~ in cases that might prove to be politically embarrassing —S.K.Padover⟩ **b :** a way out of a difficulty **:** SOLUTION ⟨believe the only ~ for the party is to continue the present system of high, rigid supports on basic farm commodities —W.M.Blair⟩ ⟨a possible ~ for big ships would be their use for mass transportation of tourists —*Newsweek*⟩ — **at outs** *or* **on the outs** *adv* **:** at variance **:** in a state of opposition ⟨was *at outs* with most of the kids on the block —Verne Athanas⟩ ⟨they are bitterly *on the outs*⟩

**out-** *prefix* [ME, fr. *out,* adv.] **:** in a manner that goes beyond, surpasses, or excels ⟨*out*dance⟩ ⟨*out*fight⟩ ⟨*out*run⟩ ⟨*out*bluff⟩ ⟨*out*maneuver⟩

**outact** \(ˈ)=ˈ=\ *vt* [*out-* + *act*] **:** to surpass in acting

**out·age** \ˈau̇d·ij, ˈau̇t|, |ēj\ *n* -S [³*out* + *-age*] **1 a :** a quantity or bulk of something (as of oil or whiskey) lost in transportation or storage **b :** HEADSPACE 3 **2 :** a failure or interruption in the use or functioning of something (as of an electric light bulb or a machine) **3 :** a period during which the supply of electric energy from a generating station or system is interrupted

**out and away** *adv* **:** far and away ⟨*out and away* the best driver I know⟩

**out-and-out** \ˌ==ˈ=\ *adj* (*or adv*) **1 :** free from disguise or concealment **:** OPEN ⟨an *out-and-out* isolationist⟩ **2 :** COMPLETE, THOROUGHGOING ⟨an *out-and-out* fool⟩ ⟨an *out-and-out* attack⟩

**out-and-out·er** \-ə(r)\ *n* [*out-and-out* + *-er*] **1 :** an extreme or outstanding representative of a class or group ⟨the party was split between the moderates and the *out-and-outers*⟩ ⟨an *out-and-outer* as a catcher⟩ **2 :** one who goes to an extreme ⟨an *out-and-outer* in everything he does⟩

**ou·tarde** \üˈtärd\ *n* -S [CanF, fr. F, bustard, fr. (assumed) VL *austarda,* fr. L *avis tarda,* lit., slow bird, fr. *avis* bird + *tarda,* fem. of *tardus* slow — more at AVIARY, TARDY] **:** CANADA GOOSE

**outask** \(ˈ)=ˈ=\ *vt* [¹*out* + *ask*] *dial Eng* **:** to publish the banns of marriage of (a couple) in church for the third time

**¹outback** \(ˈ)=ˈ=\ *adv* [¹*out* + *back*] **:** in or in the direction of the outback ⟨the farther ~ toward the deserts you go the larger your station must be —Margaret I. Ross⟩

**²outback** \ˈ=,=\ *n, sometimes cap, often attrib* **:** the back-country of Australia or New Zealand **:** ¹BUSH 2c ⟨~ life⟩ ⟨~ sheep stations⟩ — usu. used with *the* when not attributive ⟨bringing civilization to the ~⟩

**out·back·er** \-kə(r)\ *n* **:** a native or resident of the outback

**outbalance** \(ˈ)=ˈ==\ *vt* [*out-* + *balance*] **:** OUTWEIGH

**outbellow** \(ˈ)=ˈ==\ *vt* [*out-* + *bellow*] **:** to bellow louder than

**outbid** \(ˈ)=ˈ=\ *vt* [*out-* + *bid*] **1 :** to make a higher bid than **:** offer more than ⟨the rich districts can and do ~ the country school for teachers —W.M.Mason⟩ **2 :** to bid more than (another player) in a card game ⟨~ their opponents for the hand⟩

**outbirth** \ˈ=,=\ *n* [³*out* + *birth*] **:** something that is brought forth **:** PROGENY

**outblaze** \(ˈ)=ˈ=\ *vb* [¹*out* + *blaze*] *vi* **:** to blaze out ⟨the smouldering fire again *outblazed* within him —William Morris⟩ **~ *vt*** [*out-* + *blaze*] **:** to outdo in brilliance of light **:** OUTSHINE ⟨*outblazing* the moon —William Sansom⟩

**outbloom** \(ˈ)=ˈ=\ *vb* [*out-* + *bloom*] *vt* **:** to exceed in bloom ⟨~*ed* all other flowers in the garden⟩ **~ *vi*** [¹*out* + *bloom*] **1 :** to come into bloom ⟨~*ed* in glories manifold —Clinton Scollard⟩ **2 :** to have finished blooming ⟨her azaleas which were famous but all ~*ed* by the time we got there —Catherine Hutter⟩

**outblot** \(ˈ)=ˈ=\ *vt* [¹*out* + *blot*] **:** to blot out

**¹outblowing** \ˈ=ˈ==\ *adj* [¹*out* + *blowing,* pres. part. of ¹*blow*] **:** blowing outward ⟨~ winds⟩

**²outblowing** \"\ *n* [³*out* + *blowing,* gerund of ¹*blow*] **:** a blowing outward ⟨enormous ~*s* of smoke —Arnold Bennett⟩

**outbluff** \(ˈ)=ˈ=\ *vt* [*out-* + *bluff*] **:** to outdo in bluffing ⟨~ the fascist powers —*New Republic*⟩

**¹outboard** \ˈ=,=\ *adj* [⁴*out* + *board,* n.] **1 :** situated or lying outboard ⟨~ rigging⟩ ⟨~ the walls⟩ **2 :** of, relating to, or being a bearing, center, or other support that is used in conjunction with and outside of a corresponding main support usu. in its own independent frame and often on a separate foundation **3 :** having, using, or limited to the use of an outboard motor ⟨~ cruiser⟩ ⟨~ classes⟩

**²outboard** \"\ *adv* [⁴*out* + *board,* n.] **1 :** outside the line of a ship's bulwarks or hull **:** nearer the side than the center **:** in a lateral direction from the hull or from the keel ⟨swing the davits ~⟩ ⟨stand facing ~⟩ — contrasted with *inboard* **2 :** from within outward **:** to or toward the outside ⟨throw a line ~ and catch a fish —*Harper's*⟩ **3 :** in a position closer or closest to either of the wing tips of an airplane **:** in a lateral direction from the longitudinal axis of an airplane

**³outboard** \"\ *n* [¹*outboard*] **1 :** OUTBOARD MOTOR ⟨a 3 h.p. ~⟩ **2 :** a boat with an outboard motor attached ⟨a 16-foot ~⟩

**outboarding** \ˈ=,==\ *n* [³*outboard* + *-ing*] **:** the activity or sport of using or racing boats that are equipped with outboard motors

**outboard motor** *n* **:** a small internal-combustion engine with propeller integrally attached that is temporarily secured to the stern of a small boat

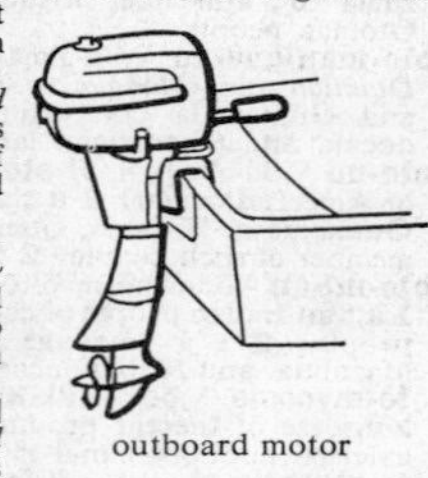

outboard motor

**outbond** \ˈ=,=\ *adj* [³*out* + *bond* (connection)] **:** laid with its longer side parallel to the face of a wall ⟨an ~ brick⟩ — opposed to *inbond*

**outbound** \ˈ=,=\ *adj* [¹*out* + *bound*] **1 :** outward bound ⟨~ traffic⟩ ⟨~ ship⟩ — contrasted with *inbound* **2 :** relating to outward or outbound traffic ⟨an ~ station⟩

**outbox** \(ˈ)=ˈ=\ *vt* [*out-* + *box*] **:** to surpass in boxing ⟨~*ed* bigger and heavier opponents —Sinclair Lewis⟩

**outbranch** \(ˈ)=ˈ=\ *vi* [¹*out* + *branch*] **:** to branch out

**outbrave** \(ˈ)=ˈ=\ *vt* [*out-* + *brave*] **1 :** to face, endure, or resist defiantly ⟨~ defeat⟩ **2** *archaic* **:** to surpass in beauty or showiness of dress **3 :** to exceed in courage ⟨~ the heart most daring on the earth —Shak.⟩

**¹outbreak** \(ˈ)=ˈ=\ *vi* [ME *outbreken,* fr. OE *ūtbrecan,* fr. *ūt* out + *brecan* to break — more at OUT, BREAK] **:** to break out ⟨there *outbroke* the blast of a horn —Stephen Graham⟩

**²outbreak** \ˈ=,=\ *n* [³*out* + *break* (after *break out*)] **1 a :** a bursting forth **:** a sudden or violent breaking out of activity ⟨the ~ of war⟩ ⟨an ~ of new building⟩ ⟨~*s* of experimentation on group effects among the lower animals —W.C.Allee⟩ **b :** a sudden rise in the incidence of a disease esp. to epidemic or near epidemic proportions ⟨an ~ of flu⟩ **c :** a sudden increase in numbers of a harmful or noxious insect or other organism within a particular area ⟨an ~ of locusts⟩ ⟨an ~ center⟩ **2 :** INSURRECTION, REVOLT ⟨a slave ~⟩ ⟨famine conditions led to ~*s* in many cities⟩

**outbreaker** \ˈ=,==\ *n* [³*out* + *breaker*] **:** a breaker distant from the shore

**outbreaking** \ˈ=,==\ *n* [ME *outbreking,* fr. ³*out* + *breking,* gerund of *breken* to break (after *breken out* to break out)] **:** OUTBREAK

**outbreathe** \(ˈ)=ˈ=\ *vb* [¹*out* + *breathe*] **:** EXHALE

**out·breathed** \'=¦bretht\ *adj* [*out (of) breath* + *-ed*] : out of breath

**outbred** \'=¦=\ *adj* [1*out* + *bred*] : subjected to or produced by outbreeding

**outbreed** \(')=¦=\ *vt* [1*out* + *breed*] **1** : to subject to outbreeding — compare CROSSBREED, INBREED **2** [*out-* + *breed*] : to breed faster than ⟨pests sometimes ~ their hosts⟩ **3** : to breed out : eliminate (an unwanted characteristic) through breeding ⟨~ horns⟩

**outbreeding** \'=,==\ *n* [3*out* + *breeding*] **1** : a natural mating of relatively unrelated individuals; *esp* : the mating of an individual of a particular group (as a tribe, people, or social class) with someone outside the group — compare EXOGAMY **2** : a selective breeding of animals on the basis of individual excellence and avoidance of close relationship — compare INBREEDING

**outbuild** \(')=¦=\ *vt* [*out-* + *build*] **1** : to outdo in building ⟨free societies can ~ . . . societies based on tyrannies —Dean Acheson⟩ **2** [1*out* + *build*] : to build outward or outside of ⟨the fish *outbuilt* her shell —R.W.Emerson⟩

**outbuilding** \'=,==\ *n* [3*out* + *building*] : a building (as a stable or smokehouse) separate from but accessory to a main house ⟨a whitewashed edifice of eight rooms, with ample ~*s* —John Buchan⟩ — called also *outhouse*

**outbulk** \(')=¦=\ *vt* [*out-* + *bulk*] : to surpass in bulk

**outburn** \(')=¦=\ *vb* [1*out* + *burn*] *vi* : to burn out : become consumed in burning ~ *vt* [*out-* + *burn*] **1** : to outdo in burning : burn longer than ⟨stars that have ~*ed* the sun⟩ **2** : to dissipate by burning ⟨the sun ~*s* the fog⟩

**1outburst** \(')=¦=\ *vi* [ME *outbersten, outbresten*, fr. *out* + *bersten, bresten* to burst — more at BURST] : to burst out

**2outburst** \'=,=\ *n* [3*out* + *burst* (after *burst out*, v.)] **1** : a bursting out : a violent expression or demonstration of intense feeling ⟨an ~ of rage⟩ ⟨an ~ of affection⟩ **2** : a sudden or intense surge of activity or growth ⟨furious ~*s* of swirling flame —Laurence Binyon⟩ ⟨new ~*s* of creative power —C.E. Montague⟩ ⟨an ~ of vegetative life—Samuel Van Valkenburg & Ellsworth Huntington⟩ **3 a** : ERUPTION ⟨successive volcanic ~*s* which covered the area with dust, pumice, and mudflows —*Biol. Abstracts*⟩ **b** : a cosmic explosion (as of a nova or supernova) ⟨Nova (U) Scorpii has had three ~*s* —*Science*⟩

**out·bye** *also* **out·by** \'aůt¦bī, 'üt¦-\ *adv* [ME (Sc) *out-by*, fr. *out* + *by*] **1** *chiefly Scot* **a** : OUTDOORS, OUTSIDE **b** : a short distance away **c** : far off : far away **2** *chiefly Scot* : toward the shaft or entry of a mine

**outcamp** \'=,=\ *n* [3*out* + *camp*] : an outlying camp : a camp at a distance from a main camp ⟨an ~ which was my base for six weeks —H.H.Finlayson⟩

**outcase** \'=,=\ *n* [3*out* + *case*] : an outer casing (as of a watch)

**1outcast** \(')=¦=\ *vt* [ME *outcasten*, fr. *out* + *casten* to cast — more at CAST] : to cast out

**2outcast** \'=¦=\ *adj* [ME, fr. past part. of *outcasten*] **1** : regarded with contempt : DESPISED ⟨afraid lest she should be mixed up with something low, ~, suspected —Rose Macaulay⟩ **2** : rejected or cast out by society : FRIENDLESS ⟨a rebel, feared and ~ —Lewis Dent⟩ ⟨all alone beweep my ~ state —Shak.⟩ **3** : thrown aside : DISCARDED ⟨~ beliefs⟩

**3outcast** \'=,=\ *n* [ME, fr. *outcast*, adj.] **1 a** : one who is cast out or refused acceptance by society : a friendless or rejected person : CASTAWAY ⟨a social ~⟩ ⟨a political ~⟩ ⟨had no rights and no status and were considered ~*s* —Morris Ploscowe⟩ **b** : something that is cast out ⟨from being a cultural ~ science became a respectable and finally a dominant interest —Douglas Bush⟩ **2** [3*out* + *cast* (after Sc *cast out*)] *Scot* : QUARREL ⟨a bitter black ~ —Robert Burns⟩

**1outcaste** \(')=¦=\ *vt* -ED/-ING/-S [4*out* + *caste*, n.] : to make an outcaste of ⟨~*s* himself if he eats forbidden food⟩ ⟨his wife's family . . . had *outcasted* him —Ela Sen⟩

**2outcaste** \'=,=\ *n* [4*out* + *caste*] **1** *India* : one who has been ejected from his caste for violation of its customs or rules **2** *India* : one who has no caste : one who is considered outside society

**3outcaste** \'=¦=\ *adj* : belonging to no caste

**outclass** \(')=¦=\ *vt* [*out-* + *class*, n.] : to excel or surpass so decisively as to appear of a higher class ⟨said the players of his generation easily ~*ed* the current crop —Stanley Frank⟩ ⟨these new forms . . . ~*ed* the old flat daggers and axes in effectiveness —Jacquetta & Christopher Hawkes⟩

**out-clearing** \'=,==\ *n* [3*out* + *clearing* (after *clear out*)] *Brit* : the checks sent out by a bank for collection during the process of clearing

**outclimb** \(')=¦=\ *vt* [*out-* + *climb*] **1** : to outdo in climbing ⟨~*s* the other children⟩ **2** : to climb beyond ⟨~*s* the other skyscrapers⟩

**out-college** \'=¦==\ *adj* [4*out* + *college*] *chiefly Brit* : residing outside a college ⟨an *out-college* student⟩

**out·come** \'aůt,kəm\ *n* -S [3*out* + *come* (after *come out*, v.)] **1 a** : something that comes out of or follows from an activity or process : CONSEQUENCE, RESULT ⟨this book is the ~ of some 30 years of travel, study and observation —O.S. Nock⟩ ⟨the ~ of the election⟩ ⟨~ of the game⟩ **b** : something that is arrived at on the basis of logic or reason : CONCLUSION ⟨if the principles . . . are accepted, certain ~*s* as to post-school and out-of-school education follow —*General Education in a Free Society*⟩ ⟨it has no positive ~ and suffered from a certain cynicism —H.J.Laski⟩ **2** : OUTLET ⟨offered no ~ for his energy⟩ **syn** see EFFECT

**out·com·er** \-mə(r)\ *n* [3*out* + *comer*] : one who comes from outside : FOREIGNER, STRANGER

**out·com·ing** \-miŋ, -mēŋ\ *n* [3*out* + *coming* (after *come out*)] : RESULT, EMANATION

**1out-country** \'=,==\ *n* [3*out* + *country*] : an outlying area or country

**2out-country** \'=¦==\ *adj* [in sense 1, fr. 4*out* + *country*, in sense 2, fr. 1*out-country*] **1** : ALIEN, FOREIGN ⟨looked down upon *out-country* peoples⟩ **2** : belonging to or characteristic of the country : not urban ⟨his clear, healthy, *out-country* look —*Time*⟩

**out·cri·er** \'=,krī(ə)r, -īə\ *n* [2*outcry* + *-er*] **1** : one who makes an outcry **2** : HUCKSTER

**1outcrop** \'=,=\ *n* [3*out* + *crop* (after *crop out*, v.)] **1 a** : a coming out of bedrock or of an unconsolidated deposit to the surface of the ground **b** : the part of a rock formation that appears at the surface of the ground **2** : a breaking out : a coming to the surface ⟨the recent ~ of unofficial strikes —*Economist*⟩ ⟨recurrent ~*s* of a heavy and pedantic philosophical jargon —*Times Lit. Supp.*⟩

**2outcrop** \(')=¦=\ *vi* **1** : to come out to the surface of the ground ⟨younger rocks ~ progressively towards the west —A.T.Grove⟩ **2** : to come to the surface : become manifest ⟨originality ~*s* in the course of planning —*Psychiatry*⟩

**out·crop·per** \'=,kräpə(r)\ *n* [1*outcrop* + *-er*] : one who works an outcrop

**outcropping** *n* -S : OUTCROP

**1outcross** \'=,=\ *n* [3*out* + *cross*] **1** : a cross between individuals of different strains **2** : the progeny of an outcross

**2outcross** \(')=¦=\ *vt* : to subject to outcrossing

**outcrossing** *n* [fr. gerund of 2*outcross*] : a mating of individuals of different strains but usu. of the same breed

**1outcry** \'=,=\ *n* [ME, fr. *out* + *cry* (after *crien out* to cry out)] **1 a** : a crying out : a loud and excited cry or exclamation : CLAMOR, UPROAR ⟨that ~ of despair —P.B.Shelley⟩ ⟨still she made her ~ for the ring —Alfred Tennyson⟩ **b** : a vehement public protest or demand ⟨the ~ against him reverberated throughout the country —Allan Nevins⟩ ⟨an ~ for more and better cottages —G.E.Fussell⟩ **2 a** : AUCTION ⟨the executor's duty to sell it at public ~ —*Southeastern Reporter*⟩ **b** : a calling out of a price (as in a commodity exchange) ⟨a buyer and seller in the ring can by open ~ mutually agree on a price —*Commodities*⟩

**2outcry** \(')=¦=\ *vb* [ME *outcrien*, fr. *out* + *crien* to cry — more at CRY] *vi* : to cry out ⟨my every pulse *outcries* for love —Evaleen Stein⟩ ~ *vt* [*out-* + *cry*] : to outdo in shouting ⟨~ his competitors⟩

**1outcurve** \'=,=\ *n* [3*out* + *curve*, n. (after *curve out*, v.)] **1** : a curving out **2** : something that curves out; *esp* : a curve in baseball in which the ball breaks away from the batter

**2outcurve** \(')=¦=\ *vb* [1*out* + *curve*, v.] *vt* : to cause to curve outward ~ *vi* : to bend or curve outward

**outdance** \(')=¦=\ *vt* [*out-* + *dance*] : to outdo in dancing ⟨not only ~ the women, they beat them hands down in the music of castanets —Claudia Cassidy⟩

**outdare** \(')=¦=\ *vt* [1*out* + *dare*] **1** : DEFY ⟨~ any danger⟩ **2** [*out-* + *dare*] : to outdo in daring ⟨~*s* all other stuntmen⟩

**outdate** \(')=¦=\ *vt* [1*out* + *date*] : to make out of date : make obsolete ⟨the development of new machinery has *outdated* many plants⟩

**outdated** \'=¦==\ *adj* [1*out* + *dated*] : ANTIQUATED ⟨an ~ directory⟩ ⟨an ~ building⟩

**outdazzle** \(')=¦==\ *vt* [*out-* + *dazzle*] : to surpass in brilliance : OUTSHINE ⟨comes close to *outdazzling* the spotlight —Hamilton Basso⟩

**outdistance** \(')=¦==\ *vt* [*out-* + *distance*] : to go far ahead of (as in a race or competition) : OUTSTRIP ⟨has *outdistanced* all his rivals for the nomination⟩ ⟨threatens to ~ the highest budget of previous years⟩

**outdo** \(')=¦=\ *vt* [*out-* + *do*] **1** : to go beyond in action or performance : EXCEL, SURPASS ⟨it took reptiles to ~ amphibians, and it took mammals to surpass reptiles —Weston La Barre⟩ ⟨*outdid* himself to break the record he had set⟩ ⟨*outdid* him in kindness⟩ **2** : DEFEAT, OVERCOME ⟨*outdid* his enemy by trickery⟩ **syn** see EXCEED

**out·done** \(')=¦=\ *adj* [fr. past part. of *outdo*] *chiefly South & Midland* : PROVOKED, VEXED ⟨grumbled and . . . pretended to be greatly ~ with me —R.P.Warren⟩

**out·door** \(')=¦=\ *also* **out·doors** \(')=¦=\ *adj* [*out-of-door, out-of-doors*] **1 a** : of, belonging to, or characteristic of the outdoors ⟨the fresh and vigorous complexion of an ~ man —I.A.Gordon⟩ ⟨an ~ setting⟩ ⟨an ~ fragrance⟩ **b** : done or performed outdoors ⟨~ sports⟩ ⟨~ exercise⟩ ⟨an ~ concert⟩ **c** : not enclosed : having no roof ⟨an ~ arena⟩ ⟨an ~ theater⟩ **2** : given or administered outside an institution ⟨~ relief⟩ ⟨~ pensions⟩

**1outdoors** \(')=¦=\ *adv* [*out (of) doors*] : out of a building : in or into the open air ⟨stayed ~ until it started to rain⟩ ⟨went ~ to get some fresh air⟩

**2outdoors** \"\ *n pl but sing in constr* **1** : the open air ⟨came in from the ~ at dinner time⟩ **2** : the world away from human habitations ⟨the lure of the great ~⟩ ⟨a man of the ~⟩

**out·doors·man** \-zmən\ *n, pl* **outdoorsmen** **1** : one who lives or prefers to live in the outdoors ⟨simple *outdoorsmen* without much formal education —C.L.Wirth⟩ **2** : one who enjoys outdoor activities (as hunting and fishing) ⟨sells equipment for *outdoorsmen*⟩

**out·doorsy** \-zē, -zi\ *adj* [2*outdoors* + *-y*] : belonging to, characteristic of, or devoted to the outdoors or outdoor life ⟨sounded rugged and ~ —*N.Y. Times*⟩ ⟨our least ~ neighbor has succumbed to the popularity of outdoor picnic ovens —*Better Homes & Gardens*⟩

**outdraft** \'=,=\ *n* [3*out* + *draft*] : an outward draft or current

**outdraw** \(')=¦=\ *vt* [*out-* + *draw*] **1** : to surpass in drawing power : attract a larger audience or following than ⟨basketball ~*s* football in this area⟩ ⟨~*s* all other languages in the city's high schools⟩ **2** : to draw (a gun) more quickly than ⟨~*s* the villainous gunman in a showdown⟩

**outdrink** \(')=¦=\ *vt* [*out-* + *drink*] : to outdo in drinking alcoholic beverages ⟨she can ~ most men⟩

**outdrive** \(')=¦=\ *vt* [*out-* + *drive*] : to drive (a ball) harder or farther than (as in tennis or golf)

**outdrop** \'=,=\ *n* [3*out* + *drop*] : a drop in which a baseball breaks down and away from a right-handed batter

**outdweller** \'=,==\ *n* [3*out* + *dweller*] : one who dwells outside or remote from (a specified place)

**outeat** \(')=¦=\ *vt* [*out-* + *eat*] : to outdo in eating ⟨~*s* people twice his size⟩

**outed** *past of* OUT

**1out·en** \'aůtᵊn\ *prep* [alter. of *out from*] *dial* : out of ⟨hand me an egg ~ the icebox —Elizabeth M. Roberts⟩

**2outen** \"\ *vt* -ED/-ING/-S [1*out* + *-en*] *chiefly dial* : to put out : EXTINGUISH ⟨you might ~ the candles there —Hervey Allen⟩

**1out·er** \'aůd·ə(r), 'aůtə-\ *adj* [ME, fr. *out*, adj. + *-er* (comp. suffix) — more at OUT] **1** : EXTERNAL, OBJECTIVE ⟨~ life⟩ ⟨~ reality⟩ ⟨~ characteristics⟩ — compare INNER 2 **2 a** : situated farther out ⟨~ space⟩ ⟨the ~ line of defense⟩ **b** : away from a center ⟨the satellites of the ~ solar planets—J.T.McIntosh⟩ **c** : situated or belonging on the outside ⟨the two ~ movements of the symphony⟩ ⟨the ~ covering⟩

**syn** OUTWARD, OUTSIDE, EXTERNAL, EXTERIOR: OUTER may retain comparative suggestion and contrast with *inner* ⟨*outer* garments⟩ ⟨*outer* space⟩ ⟨the *outer* line of defenses⟩ OUTWARD, contrasted with *inward*, may be used in relation to trend, direction, or motion ⟨the *outward* push of tourists in search of strange places is spilling over from the accustomed channels —*N.Y. Times*⟩ Both words may describe a surface semblance in contrast to an inner reality ⟨colorless and grey are the *outer* facts of a monk's life —H.O.Taylor⟩ ⟨these twins were alike in many ways, mostly, however, in their *outer* life or manifest behavior —*Biol. Abstracts*⟩ ⟨to give *outward* and objective form to ideas that bubble inwardly and have a fascinating lure in them —H.L.Mencken⟩ ⟨all *outward* actions, every overt thing we do —J.C.Powys⟩ OUTSIDE describes either a position on the outer side or a location or situation beyond borders, bounds, or limits ⟨these ships are completely air-conditioned and their staterooms are all *outside* —Mary G. Reynolds⟩ ⟨in spite of frequent assertions to the contrary, the monks very seldom taught *outside* pupils —G.G.Coulton⟩ ⟨only a relatively small part of the millions that have come from below the ground have remained in the state and most of the larger present-day properties are owned by *outside* companies —*Amer. Guide Series: Nev.*⟩ Like OUTSIDE, EXTERNAL may describe a position, situation, or sphere beyond or away from a thing under consideration ⟨the slavery which would be imposed upon her by her *external* enemies and her internal traitors —F.D.Roosevelt⟩ ⟨a poet only through the demands of an inner being and compulsion, and not through the *external* circumstances of good fortune or bad —H.V.Gregory⟩ It may imply adventitious appearance or semblance unrelated to or different from inner reality ⟨her heart was breaking with grief in spite of her *external* cheerfulness —D.C.Buchanan⟩ EXTERIOR may describe that which is situated on the outer bounds of something; it may also, like OUTER or OUTWARD, describe that which shows or is made apparent ⟨the *exterior* walls are of Lannon stone, an ivory-toned rock of varied shades and fine texture quarried in Wisconsin —*Amer. Guide Series: Mich.*⟩ ⟨the absence of *exterior* demonstration of affection for my mother had no surprise for me —Dixon Wecter⟩

**2outer** \"\ *n* -S : either of the live outside electric wires of a three-wire system as distinguished from the middle or neutral wire

**outer bar** *n* : the junior counsel who have not yet become Queen's or King's Counsel and are not permitted to plead within the bar of the court — compare INNER BAR

**outer closure** *n* : the outer of the two ends of the chamber formed by a stop articulation ⟨the lips, the tongue and teethridge, the tongue and velum, or the glottis may be the *outer closure*⟩ — compare INNER CLOSURE

**outercoat** \'==,=\ *n* : OVERCOAT

**outer-directed** \¦==+\ *adj* : directed in thought and action by external norms : conforming to the values and standards of one's group or society ⟨everything well-adjusted and *outer-directed* —Peter Viereck⟩ — compare INNER-DIRECTED

**outer-direction** \¦==+\ *n* : a sense of direction based on external norms — compare INNER-DIRECTION

**outer ear** *n* : the part of the typical mammalian ear that is continuous with the external surface of the body, that consists of an outer pinna and an inner meatus separated from the middle ear by the tympanic membrane, and that serves to intercept and direct sound waves toward the sensory receptor

**outer form** *n* : a form that prints the side of a sheet on which the first and last pages appear — called also *outside form;* contrasted with *inner form;* compare SHEET IMPOSITION

**1out·er·ly** \'aůd·|ə(r)lē, 'aůt|, |li\ *adv* [ME, fr. *outer* + *-ly* (adv. suffix)] *dial chiefly Eng* : UTTERLY

**2outerly** \"\ *adj* [1*outer* + *-ly* (adj. suffix)] *dial chiefly Eng* : blowing from an outward direction

**outer man** *n* : a person's outward appearance and dress ⟨spent hours in adorning the *outer man*⟩

**out·er·most** \'==,mōst *also chiefly Brit* -məst\ *adj* [1*outer* + *most*] : farthest outward ⟨the ~ corners of the earth —T.D. Durrance⟩

**outer planet** *n* : one of the five principal planets whose orbits are outermost in the solar system ⟨Jupiter, Saturn, Uranus, Neptune, and Pluto are the *outer planets*⟩

**outersole** \¦==¦=\ *n* : OUTSOLE

**outer space** *n* **1** : space immediately outside the earth's atmosphere **2** : interplanetary or interstellar space

**outer table** *n* : the area of the backgammon board separated by the bar from the inner table

**outerwear** \'==,=\ *n* **1** : clothing (as dresses, suits, or sweaters) worn over other clothing **2** : clothing (as coats or jackets) designed for outdoor wear

**outface** \(')=¦=\ *vt* [*out-* + *face*] **1** : to stare down by bold looks : force into silence or submission by self-assurance or impudence ⟨she'd *outfaced* angry mothers at amateur hours —James Reaney⟩ **2** : to confront unflinchingly : DEFY ⟨a people who have *outfaced* the terrors of a total war —H.V. Gregory⟩

**outfall** \'=,=\ *n* [3*out* + *fall* (after *fall out*, v.)] **1 a** : the mouth or outlet of a river, stream, or lake **b** : the lower end of a watercourse or the part of any body of water where it drops away into a larger body **c** : the vent of a drain or sewer **2** : RAID, SORTIE ⟨storms, onslaughts and ~*s* —Sir Walter Scott⟩

**out·fang·thief** \'aůtfəŋ,thēf\ *n* [ME *outfangenthef, outfangthef*, fr. OE *ūtfangenethēof*, fr. *ūt* out + *fangen* (past part. of *fōn* to seize, capture) + *thēof* thief — more at OUT, PACT, THIEF] : the right of a lord under medieval English law to try in his manorial court a thief or other felon dwelling in his manor but caught outside it — distinguished from *infangthief*

**outfield** \'=,=\ *n* [3*out* + *field*] **1 a** : an outlying field : a field distant from a farmhouse **b** : land not regularly cultivated or manured and generally used as pasture **2 a** (1) : LONG FIELD (2) : the area of a cricket field beyond the infield (3) : a fielder stationed beyond the infield **b** (1) : the area of a baseball field beyond the infield and between the foul lines (2) : the defensive positions comprising right field, center field, and left field — contrasted with *infield*

**out·field·er** \-də(r)\ *n* **1** : a fielder stationed in the outfield in cricket **2** : a ballplayer (as in baseball or softball) who covers a position in the outfield

**out·field·ing** \-diŋ, -dēŋ\ *n* : the act or art of playing a position in the outfield

**out·fields·man** \-l(d)zmən\ *n* : an outfielder in cricket

**outfight** \(')=¦=\ *vt* [*out-* + *fight*] : to surpass in fighting : defeat in a fight ⟨decisively *outfought* the challenger⟩ ⟨*outfought* superior forces⟩

**outfighter** \'=,==\ *n* [3*out* + *fighter*] : a boxer who fights without closing in or clinching

**outfighting** \'=,==\ *n* [3*out* + *fighting*] : fighting at long range ⟨was no match for the heavier ship in ~⟩ ⟨the first round was all ~⟩

**1out·fit** \'aůt,fit, *usu* -id·+V\ *n* -S [3*out* + *fit* (after *fit out*)] **1** : the act or process of fitting out or equipping (as for a voyage or expedition) ⟨the ~ of the exploring party took several months⟩ **2 a** : the tools, instruments, or materials comprising the equipment necessary for the practice of a trade or profession or for the carrying out of a particular project ⟨a prospector's ~⟩ ⟨a dentist's ~⟩ ⟨a model plane ~⟩ ⟨a shoeshine ~⟩ **b** : wearing apparel with accessories designed to be worn on a special occasion or in a particular situation or setting ⟨an ~ for a bride⟩ ⟨an ~ for graduation⟩ ⟨an ~ for camp⟩ **c** : physical, mental, or moral endowments or requirements ⟨this addition that the dentist has made to my ~ —O.W.Holmes†1935⟩ ⟨perception is only part of our mental ~ —A.S.Eddington⟩ **3 a** : a group of people traveling together ⟨shared our campfire with a packhorse ~ —Joyce R. Muench⟩ **b** (1) : a team of ranch hands ⟨the whole ~ was commanded by a trail boss —R.A.Billington⟩ (2) : RANCH ⟨almost all the big ~*s* use the stamp iron —S.E.Fletcher⟩ ⟨a dude ~ with a landing field —*Amer. Guide Series: Oregon*⟩ **4** : a group of people working together as a team: as **a** : a political party or group ⟨a small but influential ~ that has the balance of power in the city⟩ **b** : a military unit (as a division, regiment, or company) ⟨enlisted men in line ~*s* all over the world —*Yank*⟩ ⟨a rear echelon ~ —Gene Baro⟩ **c** : a jazz band or combination ⟨the three-piece troubadour ~ —P.E. Deutschman⟩ ⟨this fifteen piece ~ —*Metronome*⟩ **d** : a Navaho social group based on family relationships that presents a united front toward outsiders **5** : an organization engaged in a particular industry or activity ⟨a large manufacturing ~⟩ ⟨worked for a publishing ~⟩ ⟨the university employs more people than any other ~ in the city⟩ **syn** see EQUIPMENT

**2outfit** \"\ *vt* **1** : to furnish with an outfit ⟨*outfitted* expeditions to far-off places —*Amer. Guide Series: Mich.*⟩ **2** : FURNISH, SUPPLY ⟨*outfitting* every family with shoes —*Amer. Guide Series: Vt.*⟩ ⟨required . . . the judge to ~ him legally —Francis Hackett⟩ ~ *vi* : to acquire an outfit ⟨they *outfitted* for the long journey —*Amer. Guide Series: Texas*⟩ **syn** see FURNISH

**outfit car** *n* : CAMP CAR

**out·fit·ter** \-ə(r)\ *n* : one that outfits: as **a** : HABERDASHER **b** : a dealer in equipment and supplies for expeditions or camping trips **c** : a machinist who installs the machinery and mechanical equipment of ships

**outflame** \(')=¦=\ *vt* [*out-* + *flame*] : to exceed in brilliance ⟨~*s* the cities of the land —Vachel Lindsay⟩

**outflank** \(')=¦=\ *vt* [1*out* + *flank*] **1** : to extend beyond or get around the flank of (an opposing force) ⟨the army retreated when it discovered that the enemy ~*ed* it on the right⟩ ⟨~*ed* and surrounded the enemy troops⟩ **2** : to get around : BYPASS ⟨tries to ~ the opposition to his program by an appeal to the people⟩ — **out·flank·er** \-kə(r)\ *n*

**outflaring** \'=,==\ *adj* [1*out* + *flaring*] : FLARING 2a

**outflash** \(')=¦=\ *vb* [*out-* + *flash*] *vt* : to outdo in flashing : OUTSHINE ~ *vi* [1*out* + *flash*] : to flash out

**1outflow** \(')=¦=\ *vi* [1*out* + *flow*] : to flow out

**2outflow** \'=,=\ *n* [3*out* + *flow* (after *flow out*, v.)] **1** : the act or process of flowing out ⟨a dam to stop the ~ of the stream⟩ ⟨the ~ of gold from the country —E.W.Kemmerer⟩ **2** : something that flows out ⟨a river's ~ is usually expressed in cubic feet per second —F.C.Lane⟩

**outflung** \'=¦=\ *adj* [1*out* + *flung*, past part. of *fling* (after *fling out*, v.)] : flung out : thrown wide ⟨~ arms⟩

**outflux** \'=,=\ *n* [3*out* + *flux*] **1** : OUTFLOW **2** : OUTLET

**outfly** \(')=¦=\ *vt* [*out-* + *fly*] : to surpass in speed of flight ⟨in the days when few men even dreamed of ~*ing* the sound of their own voices —Wolcott Gibbs⟩

**outfoot** \(')=¦=\ *vt* [*out-* + *foot*] : to outdo in speed (as in walking, running, or sailing) : OUTSTRIP ⟨~*ed* the other yachts⟩ ⟨~*ed* the secondary to race 58 yards to a touchdown —*Time*⟩

**outfox** \(')=¦=\ *vt* [*out-* + *fox*] : to outdo in trickery : OUTSMART ⟨learning how to ~ new teachers each year is a liberal education in itself —J.P.McEvoy⟩

**out·game** \(')=¦=\ *vt* [*out-* + *game*, adj.] : to surpass in courage or stamina ⟨could outthink, outfight, and ~ the best the enemy could send against them —Foster Hailey⟩ ⟨will ~ and will finally run down and catch any deer —S.P.McCall⟩

**out·gang** \'üt,gaŋ\ *n* -S [ME, fr. OE *ūtgang*, fr. *ūt* out + *gang* act of going — more at OUT, GANG] *chiefly Scot* : DEPARTURE

**outgarth** \'=,=\ *n* [3*out* + *garth*] : an outer yard

**outgas** \(')=¦=\ *vt* [1*out* + *gas*, n.] : to remove adsorbed or occluded gases from usu. by heating ⟨~ a radio tube⟩

**1out·gate** \'aůt,gāt, 'üt,-\ *n* [ME, fr. *out* + *gate* way, road, act of going — more at GATE (way)] **1** *chiefly Scot* : the act of going out : EXITING **2** *chiefly Scot* : a way out : OUTLET

**2outgate** \(')=¦=\ *prep* [fr. obs. *outgate*, adv., outside, prob. fr. 4*out* + *gate* (opening)] *dial* : BEYOND, OUTSIDE ⟨run ~ their wits for a woman —Maristan Chapman⟩

**outgeneral** \(')=¦=(=)=\ *vt* -ED/-ING/-S [*out-* + *general*, n.] : to surpass in generalship : overcome by superior tactics : OUTMANEUVER ⟨you've been ~*ed* and outfought —Kenneth Roberts⟩ ⟨if you ~ the bear you may carry off his pelt —John Burroughs⟩

**1outgiving** \'=,==\ *n* [3*out* + *giving*, gerund of *give* (after *give out*)] : something that is given out; *esp* : a public statement or utterance ⟨examining these opinions and the ~*s* of eminent bankers —F.L.Allen⟩

**2outgiving** \'=¦==\ *adj* [1*out* + *giving*, pres. part. of *give* (after *give out*)] : not holding back : free and easy ⟨cocky, confident, and ~ —Beach Conger⟩ ⟨had an easygoing, ~ personality —Louis Auchincloss⟩

**outgliding** \ˈ=ˌ==\ *adj* [¹*out* + *gliding*, pres. part. of *glide* (after *glide out*, v.)] *of a diphthong or triphthong* **:** concluded with the tongue in a position other than that for the central vowel \ə\ (as in *loud, mine, moist*) — compare CENTERING, UPGLIDING

¹**outgo** \(ˈ)=ˈ=\ *vb* [ME *outgon, outgan*, fr. OE *ūtgān*, fr. *ūt* out + *gān* to go — more at OUT, GO] *vi* **:** to go out ~ *vt* [*out-* + *go*] **1** *archaic* **:** to surpass in swiftness **:** OUTSTRIP **2 :** to go beyond **:** OUTDO ⟨imprinting an ambition and desire in each of them to ~ his fellow —*Times Lit. Supp.*⟩

²**outgo** \ˈ=ˌ=\ *n* [³*out* + *go* (after *go out*)] **1 :** something that goes out ⟨income and ~ of radiant solar energy —R.E.Coker⟩ ⟨inflow and ~ of goods —A.F.Chapin⟩; *specif* **:** EXPENDITURE ⟨the cash budget, which lists merely the cash revenues and ~*es* —William Fellner⟩ **2 a :** the act, action, or process of going out ⟨the ~ of his nature to others was something extraordinary —E.S.Phelps⟩ **b :** DEPARTURE **3 :** OUTLET

**outgoer** \ˈ=ˌ==\ *n* [³*out* + *goer* (after *go out*)] **:** one that goes out ⟨separate ways for ~*s* and incomers —Lew Wallace⟩: as **a :** an outgoing tenant ⟨the ~ could retain use of the farmhouse . . . until the 12th of May —A.D.Rees⟩ **b :** a clay target that is moving away from the shooter

¹**outgoing** \ˈ=ˌ==, =ˈ==\ *n* [ME, fr. ³*out* + *going*, gerund of *gon, goon* to go (after *gon out* to go out) — more at GO] **1 :** the act or action of going out ⟨the ~ of the tide⟩ ⟨couldn't keep up with her incomings and ~*s*⟩ **2 :** something that goes out **:** ISSUE ⟨a mind whose ~*s* in talk showed her to be warmer and more sympathetic —H.S.Canby⟩ **3 outgoings** *pl* **a :** EXPENDITURES, OUTLAYS ⟨the necessary domestic ~*s* of the week —*Times Lit. Supp.*⟩ **b** *Eng law* **:** expenditures (as for rates and taxes) necessary for the upkeep of a property

²**outgoing** \ˈ=ˌ==\ *adj* [¹*out* + *going*, pres. part. of *go* (after *go out*)] **1 a :** going outward **:** DEPARTING ⟨~ correspondence⟩ ⟨an ~ tide⟩ ⟨an ~ ship⟩ **b :** retiring or withdrawing from a place or position ⟨the ~ president⟩ ⟨the ~ sixth grade class⟩ ⟨the ~ generation⟩ **2 :** socially responsive and demonstrative **:** not reserved **:** EXTROVERTED ⟨a boy who was potentially ~ but impeded by fears of his own impulsiveness —Miriam G. Siegel⟩ ⟨as a person he was warm and ~ —E.R.Mowrer⟩ — **out·go·ing·ness** *n* -ES

**outgross** \(ˈ)=ˈ=\ *vt* [*out-* + *gross*] **:** to surpass in gross earnings or sales ⟨~*ed* all other pictures for the year⟩

**outgroup** \ˈ=ˌ=\ *n* [³*out* + *group*] **:** a social group that is distinct from one's own and so usu. an object of hostility or dislike — compare INGROUP

**outgrow** \(ˈ)=ˈ=\ *vt* [*out-* + *grow*] **1 :** to exceed in rate of growth **:** grow faster than ⟨weeds ~ grass⟩ ⟨mankind is ~*ing* food supplies —R.C.Murphy⟩ **2 :** to grow away from or beyond **:** develop to the point of being able to do without ⟨those whom he had *outgrown* socially —Louis Auchincloss⟩ ⟨teen-agers who have *outgrown* children's books —*advt*⟩ **3 :** to grow too large for **:** grow out of ⟨the business *outgrew* the cramped quarters —*Amer. Guide Series: Conn.*⟩ ⟨*outgrew* his new suit⟩

**outgrowth** \ˈ=ˌ=\ *n* [³*out* + *growth*] **1 :** the process of growing out ⟨the effects of added sugars on the ~ of chick heart fibroblasts —*Biol. Abstracts*⟩ **2 :** something that grows directly out of something else **:** OFFSHOOT ⟨an ~ of hair⟩ ⟨a deformed ~⟩ **3 :** something that results from something else **:** CONSEQUENCE ⟨crime is sometimes an ~ of poverty⟩ ⟨the new program is an ~ of cooperation among the colleges of the area⟩

**outguard** \ˈ=ˌ=\ *n* [³*out* + *guard*] **:** a guard that forms the line of observation of an outpost

**outguess** \(ˈ)=ˈ=\ *vt* [*out-* + *guess*] **:** to anticipate correctly the intentions, actions, or movements of ⟨~ the enemy⟩ ⟨~ the pitcher⟩ ⟨~ the stock market⟩

**out guide** *n* [³*out*] **:** a card placed in a file to indicate the location of material that has been temporarily removed

**outgun** \(ˈ)=ˈ=\ *vt* [*out-* + *gun*] **:** to surpass in firepower ⟨will ~ and outspeed every cruiser in the world —H.W.Baldwin⟩

¹**outgush** \(ˈ)=ˈ=\ *vi* [¹*out* + *gush*] **:** to gush out ⟨on either side ~*ed*, with misty spray —John Keats⟩

²**outgush** \ˈ=ˌ=\ *n* [³*out* + *gush* (after *gush out*, v.)] **:** OUTGUSHING

**outgushing** \ˈ=ˌ==\ *n* [³*out* + *gushing*, gerund of *gush* (after *gush out*, v.)] **:** a gushing out **:** a pouring forth ⟨a great ~ of public opprobrium upon his uncalculating head —Donald Davidson⟩

**outhalf** \ˈ=ˌ=\ *n* [³*out* + *half*] **:** STANDOFF HALF

**outhaul** \ˈ=ˌ=\ *n* [³*out* + *haul* (after *haul out*, v.)] **:** a rope used to haul a sail taut along a spar

**outhauler** \ˈ=ˌ==\ *n* [³*out* + *hauler* (after *haul out*, v.)] **:** a rope or line for hauling something out

**outh·er** \ˈau̇thə(r), ˈōth-\ *archaic var of* EITHER

**out–her·od** \(ˈ)=ˈherəd\ *vt* -ED/-ING/-S *usu cap H* [*out-* + *Herod* Antipas †*ab* A.D. 40 ruler of Judea at time of Christ's death, who was depicted as a blustering despot in medieval mystery plays] **:** to exceed in violence or extravagance ⟨*out-Heroding* the preposterous fashion of the times —Sir Walter Scott⟩ — usu. used in the phrase *out-Herod Herod* ⟨a ranting orator who *out-Herods* Herod⟩

**outhit** \(ˈ)=ˈ=\ *vt* [*out-* + *hit*] **:** to get more hits than ⟨~ the other team but lost the ballgame⟩

**out home** *n* [³*out*] **:** OUTSIDE HOME

**outhouse** \ˈ=ˌ=\ *n* [³*out* + *house*] **1 :** OUTBUILDING ⟨a dwelling house in the middle, with kitchens and ~*s* all detached —C.G.Bowers⟩ **2 :** an outdoor toilet **:** PRIVY

**outhousing** \ˈ=ˌ==\ *n* [³*out* + *housing*] **:** a group of outhouses

**outhustle** \(ˈ)=ˈ==\ *vt* [*out-* + *hustle*] **:** to outdo in vigorous and determined effort ⟨it is one thing to be beaten and quite another to be *outhustled* —*Time*⟩

**out·ing** \ˈau̇d·iŋ, ˈau̇t|, |ēŋ\ *n* -S [¹*out* + *-ing*] **1 :** a trip or stay in the open **:** an excursion usu. with a picnic ⟨the annual company ~⟩ ⟨an ~ at the beach⟩ **2 :** an athletic contest or bout ⟨the team's first victory in three ~*s*⟩ ⟨scored a knockout in his first ~ in over a year⟩

**outing flannel** *n* **:** a flannelette sometimes having an admixture of wool

**out island** *n* [³*out*] **:** an island other than the main island of a group (as of the Bahamas)

**outjest** *vt* [*out-* + *jest*] *obs* **:** to overcome by jesting ⟨labors to ~ his heart-struck injuries —Shak.⟩

**outjockey** \(ˈ)=ˈ==\ *vt* [*out-* + *jockey*] **:** OUTMANEUVER

**outjut** \(ˈ)=ˈ=\ *vi* [¹*out* + *jut*] **:** to stick out **:** PROJECT

**outkick** \(ˈ)=ˈ=\ *vt* [*out-* + *kick*] **:** to excel (an opponent) in kicking ⟨~*ed* all others in the second half⟩

**outkitchen** \ˈ=ˌ==\ *n* [³*out* + *kitchen*] **:** a kitchen housed in a separate building ⟨waddling from kitchen to ~ and back again —Caroline Gordon⟩

¹**out·land** \ˈau̇tˌland, -lənd, -ˌlaa(ə)nd\ *n* [ME, fr. OE *ūtland*, fr. *ūt* out + *land* — more at OUT, LAND] **1** *Old Eng & feudal law* **:** the outlying land not kept in demesne but granted to tenants — compare INLAND **2 :** a foreign land or region ⟨the ~*s* were glutting Europe with novelties —H.B.Alexander⟩ ⟨a vast natural buffer zone between her own centers of population and the vigorous pressure of the ~ —*Time*⟩ **3 outlands** *pl* **:** the outlying regions of a country **:** PROVINCES ⟨the man who brought stars to the ~*s* —R.L.Taylor⟩ ⟨in the ~*s*, the Yankees had been strangers —Oscar Handlin⟩

²**outland** \ʺ\ *adj* [ME, fr. *outland*, n.] **1 a :** of or relating to a foreign country or region ⟨the chief ~ interests of the Swedish people lay in their eastern colonies —F.M.Stenton⟩ **b :** belonging to a different region or group **:** ALIEN ⟨had taken up with an ~ man —Maristan Chapman⟩ **2 :** of, relating to, or characteristic of the outlying sections of a country **:** PROVINCIAL ⟨one who peregrinated the country for seasonal jobs and could fascinate children with ~ tales —John Buchan⟩

³**outland** \ʺ\ *adv, South* **:** away from home ⟨on my way ~ — Emmett Gowen⟩

**out·land·er** \-də(r)\ *n* [¹*outland* + *-er*] **:** one who belongs to another region or culture: **a :** a person from another country ⟨insecure in the presence of ~*s* —T.H.Fielding⟩ ⟨~, a wastrel from Europe —B.T.Cleeve⟩ **b :** a person from another state or section ⟨thousands of Californians and ~*s* crowd the Redwood Highway —Anthony Netboy⟩ ⟨the stranger, the ~, the foreigner from New York —Lionel Trilling⟩

**out·land·ish** \au̇tˈlandish, -aa(ə)n-, -dēsh\ *adj* [ME, fr. OE *ūtlendisc*, fr. *ūtland* + *-isc* -ish] **1 :** of or belonging to another country **:** not native **:** FOREIGN ⟨the verdict of ~ readers —John Milton⟩ **2 a :** having a foreign or unfamiliar appearance, manner, or quality ⟨an ~ costume⟩ ⟨an ~ way of talking⟩ ⟨an ~ dish⟩ **b :** BIZARRE, FANTASTIC ⟨introduced ~ or unbelievable people and situations into his work —Lincoln Fitzell⟩ **3 :** remote from civilization or familiarly known regions ⟨no other young men foolish enough to offer to go to such an ~ station —*Geog. Jour.*⟩ **syn** see STRANGE

**out·land·ish·ly** *adv* **:** in an outlandish manner

**out·land·ish·ness** *n* -ES **:** the quality or state of being outlandish

**outlast** \(ˈ)=ˈ=\ *vt* [*out-* + *last*] **:** to last longer than **:** SURVIVE ⟨mummified customs that have long ~*ed* their usefulness —W.R.Inge⟩ **syn** see OUTLIVE

**outlaugh** \(ˈ)=ˈ=\ *vb* [ME *outlaughen*, fr. *out* + *laughen* to laugh — more at LAUGH] *vt* **1** *archaic* **:** to make fun of **:** RIDICULE ⟨his apprehensions of being ~*ed* —Benjamin Franklin⟩ **2** [*out-* + *laugh*] **:** to outdo in laughing ⟨though usually solemn, he ~*ed* all the others at the play⟩ ~ *vi* **:** to laugh out loud ⟨in deep derision ~*s* the foeman —Alice Furlong⟩

¹**out·law** \ˈau̇tˌlȯ\ *n* [ME *outlawe, outlage*, fr. OE *ūtlaga*, fr. ON *ūtlagi*, fr. *ūtlagr*, adj., outlawed, fr. *ūt* out + *-lagr* (fr. *lag-, lög* law) — more at OUT, LAW] **1 a :** a person or thing excluded from the benefit of the law or deprived of its protection **:** a person against whom outlawry has been pronounced **:** a proscribed person or thing ⟨a hunted ~⟩ ⟨the motor vehicle becomes an ~ on the highways if operated without new registration —*Mass. Registry of Motor Vehicles*⟩ **2 a :** a lawless person or a fugitive from the law **:** a person roving and committing acts of violence ⟨gangs of ~*s* made their hideaways in the inadequately policed Indian territory —C.L. Cannon⟩ **b :** a person or organization under a ban or disability ⟨the union declared that those who had gone on strike against its orders were ~*s*⟩ **3 :** an animal (as a horse) that is wild and unmanageable ⟨spoiled horses are ~*s* — they never can be tamed —S.E.Fletcher⟩

²**outlaw** \ʺ\ *vt* -ED/-ING/-S [ME *outlawen*, fr. OE *ūtlagian*, fr. *ūtlaga* outlaw] **1 a :** to deprive of the benefit and protection of law **:** declare to be an outlaw ⟨~ the rebels unless they surrendered immediately⟩ **b :** to make illegal ⟨the type of legislation which ~*ed* dueling —Margaret Mead⟩ ⟨has ~*ed* verbal intimidation on the part of employers —*New Republic*⟩ ⟨a proposal to ~ war⟩ **2 :** to place under a ban or disability ⟨it is neither possible nor convenient to ~ the old vocabulary —A.G.N.Flew⟩ ⟨banned in Boston, ~*ed* in Atlanta —Hamilton Basso⟩ **3 :** to remove from legal jurisdiction or enforcement ⟨~ a debt⟩ ⟨~ a claim⟩ ⟨the case was ~*ed* in 1914 by the Supreme Court under the statute of limitations —H.U. Faulkner⟩

³**outlaw** \ˈ=ˌ=\ *adj* [¹*outlaw*] **1 :** of, relating to, composed of, or dominated by outlaws ⟨an ~ band⟩ ⟨~ country⟩ **2 a :** forbidden by law ⟨an ~ strike⟩ **b :** contrary to the rules of an organization ⟨an ~ baseball league⟩ ⟨playing ~ ball —Oscar Fraley⟩

**out·law·ry** \-rē, -ri\ *n* -ES [ME *outlagerie, outlagarie, outlawerie*, fr. AF *utlagerie* & ML *utlagaria*, fr. ME *outlage* outlaw + OF *-erie* -ery & L *-aria* -ary respectively] **1 a :** the act of outlawing **:** the act or process of putting a person outside the protection of the law ⟨by proscription and bills of ~ —Shak.⟩ — compare FUGITATION **b :** BANISHMENT, EXILE ⟨on his ~ was allowed five days to leave the country —E.A.Freeman⟩ **c :** the act or process of making something illegal ⟨the ~ of war⟩ ⟨the ~ of atomic weapons⟩ **2 :** the state of living outside the law **:** freedom from legal or conventional restraint ⟨whose gay impudence of ~ had in its time set the underworlds of five continents buzzing —Leslie Charteris⟩ ⟨Quincy . . . was liberty, ~, the endless delight of impressions given by nature for nothing —Henry Adams⟩ **3 :** the act of barring a debt, claim, or right (as by operation of a statute of limitations)

¹**outlay** \(ˈ)=ˈ=\ *vt* [¹*out* + *lay*] **1** *archaic* **:** to spread out **:** DISPLAY **2 :** to lay out (money) **:** EXPEND ⟨we *outlaid* 40 billions —*Reader's Digest*⟩

²**outlay** \ˈ=ˌ=\ *n* [³*out* + *lay* (after *lay out*, v.)] **1 :** the act of laying out or expending ⟨make a great ~ of energy seem worth while —*Collier's Yr. Bk.*⟩ **2 :** something that is laid out **:** EXPENDITURE, PAYMENT ⟨an ~ of $10 for food⟩

¹**outleap** \ˈ=ˌ=\ *n* [³*out* + *leap* (after *leap out*, v.)] **:** the act of leaping out **:** OUTBURST

²**outleap** \(ˈ)=ˈ=\ *vb* [¹*out* + *leap*] *vt* **1 :** to leap beyond ⟨~*s* the barriers of the particular to reach a universal truth —Virgilia Peterson⟩ **2** [*out-* + *leap*] **:** to outdo in leaping ~ *vi* **:** to leap out

**outlearn** \(ˈ)=ˈ=\ *vt* [*out-* + *learn*] **:** to surpass in learning ⟨learnt so fast that he *outlearnt* his teacher —Amy Lowell⟩

**out·ler** \ˈütlər\ *n* -S [prob. alter. of *outlier*] *Scot* **:** an animal left unhoused over the winter

¹**out·let** \ˈau̇tˌlet, -lət, -ˌlə\|, *usu* \|d·+V\ *n* [³*out* + *let* (after *let out*, v.)] **1 a :** a means of exit or escape **:** OPENING, VENT ⟨oxidized impurities are expelled through an ~ in the top —*Amer. Guide Series: Pa.*⟩ ⟨an ~ on the Red sea —*Collier's Yr. Bk.*⟩ ⟨~*s* for the surplus population —B.K.Sandwell⟩ **b :** a means of release or satisfaction for an emotion, impulse, or instinctual need ⟨found an ~ for his anger in chopping wood⟩ ⟨singing provided an ~ for her high spirits⟩ ⟨sexual ~*s*⟩ **c :** a medium of expression or publication ⟨a magazine existed . . . that could provide an ~ for the writers who were appearing on every hand —Van Wyck Brooks⟩ **d :** a radio or television station; *esp* **:** a station that transmits network programs locally **2 a :** a stream flowing out of a lake or pond **b :** the channel through which such a stream flows **c :** the lower end of a watercourse where its water flows into a lake or sea **3 a :** a market for a commodity ⟨the farmer has a choice of several ~*s* for his goods —*Marketing*⟩ ⟨must find new ~*s* for their industries⟩ **b :** a retail store ⟨chain ~*s*⟩ ⟨discount ~*s*⟩ ⟨mass ~*s*⟩ ⟨goods usually bought on impulse are located at high traffic points within the ~ —Bud Wilson⟩ **4 :** one or more pairs of terminals giving access to electric wiring (as for attachment of lamps)

²**out·let** \ˈau̇tˌlet, *usu* -ed·+V\ *vt* [¹*out* + *let*] *archaic* **:** to let out

**outlet box** *n* **:** a terminal box for electric wiring or fittings at which the wires terminate for connection to electric fixtures or appliances

**outlie** \(ˈ)=ˈ=\ *vb* [¹*out* + *lie*] *vi* **1 :** to camp out **:** lie outdoors **2 :** to stretch out **:** EXTEND ~ *vt* **:** to lie beyond

**out·li·er** \ˈau̇tˌlī(ə)r\ *n* [³*out* + *lier* (after *lie out*, v.)] **1 a :** one that sleeps outdoors or away from his place of business or duty **b :** an animal outside the fold or enclosure **2 :** something that lies, dwells, or is situated or classed away from a main or related body: as **a :** a minor part of a rock formation separated by erosion from the main body and surrounded by older rocks **b** (1) **:** an outlying island (2) **:** an outlying terrain feature (as a mountain, forest, or plain) **c :** a statistical observation not homogeneous in value with others of a sample

¹**out·line** \ˈau̇tˌlīn\ *n* [³*out* + *line*] **1 a :** a line that marks the outer limits of an object or figure **:** BOUNDARY ⟨in good years the ~ of the cultivated area expands —P.E.James⟩ ⟨the rugged ~*s* of the mountains⟩ **b :** CONTOUR, SHAPE ⟨the original ~ of the house is clearly marked —*Amer. Guide Series: La.*⟩ ⟨the sharpening ~ of her face —Willa Cather⟩ **2 a :** a style of representation or drawing in which contours are marked without shading ⟨paint rapidly in ~ on the stone —F.W.Goudy⟩ ⟨drew a dog in ~⟩ **b :** a sketch in outline ⟨prepared several ~*s* of the suggested mural⟩ **c :** ⁴OPEN 3 **d :** a symbol used to represent a word in shorthand writing ⟨learned how to write shorthand ~*s* for every word she heard —Marie M. Stewart⟩ ⟨my hand was so shaky I could hardly make my ~*s* —Dorothy Sayers⟩ **3 a outlines** *pl* **:** the principal features or general principles of a subject of discussion ⟨shall sketch only the ~*s* of some aspects of American education —J.B.Conant⟩ ⟨agreed on the broad ~*s* of a wage settlement⟩ **b :** a relatively brief and condensed treatment of a particular subject ⟨has written a useful ~ of atomic physics⟩ ⟨an ~ of world history in two volumes⟩ **c :** a summary giving the essential content of a written work ⟨the gist of these books was preserved in a series of small ~*s* —R.W.Southern⟩ **4 a :** a preliminary account or sketch of a projected course of action or study ⟨gave his staff an ~ of his proposed strategy in the coming campaign⟩ ⟨gave the class an ~ of the points he intended to cover⟩ **b :** a brief abstract of the principal points to be covered in an argument or exposition often arranged by heads and subheads ⟨such an ~ as would be required of a student in freshman composition —Archer Taylor⟩ **c :** a synopsis of the plot of a projected piece of writing (as a scenario or play) ⟨the producer gave him a sizable advance on the basis of his ~⟩ **5 :** a fishing line set out overnight **:** TROTLINE

**syn** CONTOUR, PROFILE, SKYLINE, SILHOUETTE: OUTLINE applies to the line marking the outer edge or limit of a thing ⟨the house, built of bricks, was square in *outline* —Elizabeth M. Roberts⟩ ⟨series of natural valleys . . . flanking the western *outlines* of the county —F.S.Williams⟩ ⟨the *outline* of Caprarola palace is a pentagon —George Kish⟩ CONTOUR stresses the shape of a thing, or a visible or particular portion of a thing, as delineated by the outline, esp. involving curving lines ⟨the smooth, though sometimes steep, *contours* of the Coast Range —G.R.Stewart⟩ ⟨glanced up at the pummeled sky and caught sight of a weird, futuristic *contour* —D.B.Dodson⟩ ⟨the chart room, where the changing *contours* of the seabed are automatically recorded —Douglas Willis⟩ PROFILE stresses the sharply outlined shape of something esp. as seen against a lighter background ⟨the beautiful *profile* of the island — William Beebe⟩ ⟨the mountains to the south and east fill the horizon, their *profiles* overlapping one another —*Amer. Guide Series: Vt.*⟩ SKYLINE is the outline or contour of something (as the upper portion of a row of buildings or range of mountains) seen against the sky as background ⟨gracious towers and spires make up the loveliest man-made *skyline* in the world —Sam Pollock⟩ ⟨the region, with its succession of startling contours, jagged *skylines*, sharp pinnacles rising from mountains of solid rock —*Amer. Guide Series: Oregon*⟩ ⟨the *skyline* of Manhattan⟩ SILHOUETTE is the shape of something shadowed, and therefore seen as two-dimensional, with all detail blacked out, blurred, or disregarded ⟨the basilica of Notre Dame de la Garde thrusts a stark *silhouette* in the cobalt sky —Claudia Cassidy⟩ ⟨the *silhouettes* of white sailboats and gray battleships —Jean Stafford⟩ ⟨the ghostly *silhouette* of a submarine gliding under the railway bridge —Stewart Beach⟩

²**outline** \ʺ\ *vt* **1 a :** to draw the outline of ⟨~ the entire figure before beginning to draw in the features⟩ **b :** to set off the outlines of **:** DEFINE ⟨gnarled stump fences ~ the wide fields —*Amer. Guide Series: Vt.*⟩ ⟨a baffling network of paths *outlined* by a very high hedge —J.C.Swaim⟩ **c :** to discover or trace the outline of ⟨~ the exact limits of the lake⟩ ⟨~ the limits of Assyrian conquest⟩ **2 :** to indicate the principal features or different parts of ⟨*outlining* a plan for a future investigation —J.B.Conant⟩ ⟨*outlined* a five-point program for business —*Current Biog.*⟩ — **out·lin·er** \-nə(r)\ *n*

**out·lin·e·ar** \(ˈ)au̇tˈlinēə(r)\ *adj* [¹*outline* + *-ar* (as in *linear*)] **:** of, relating to, or having the characteristics of an outline

**outline map** *n* **:** BASE MAP

**outline stitch** *n* **:** an embroidery stitch used to outline a design; *specif* **:** a stitch made by overlapping backstitches to form a pattern like the twist of a rope

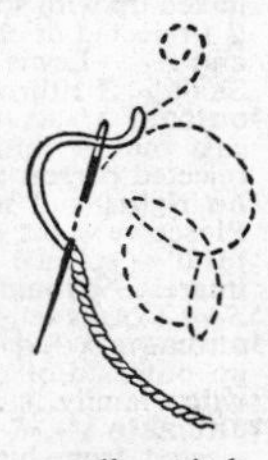
outline stitch

**outlive** \(ˈ)=ˈ=\ *vt* [ME *outleven*, fr. *out-* + *leven, liven* to live — more at LIVE] **1 :** to live beyond or longer than **:** OUTLAST, SURVIVE ⟨has *outlived* the century⟩ ⟨has *outlived* all his friends⟩ ⟨a fiction which has *outlived* any usefulness it may have had —C.S.Lobingier⟩ **2 a :** to survive the effects of **:** live through **:** OVERCOME ⟨the financial support which enabled the small man to ~ a bad harvest —G.G.Coulton⟩ ⟨characters in history whose reputation has *outlived* the vicissitudes of time —*London Calling*⟩ **b :** to live down ⟨repeated the story so often that I have never been able to ~ this joke on myself —David Fairchild⟩

**syn** OUTLAST, SURVIVE: OUTLIVE stresses the fact of continuing alive or in existence longer than another, sometimes through a marked capacity for enduring and surmounting difficulty, sometimes not ⟨*outlived* his brothers⟩ ⟨universities are among the most persistent of human organizations — they *outlive* many political and social changes —J.B.Conant⟩ OUTLAST differs little from OUTLIVE, although it may stress capacity for endurance to a greater degree ⟨their glory is that they have *outlasted* the conditions they observed —A.T.Quiller-Couch⟩ ⟨the sweet sensations of returning health made me happy for a time; but such sensations seldom *outlast* convalescence —W.H.Hudson †1922⟩ SURVIVE may be used of enduring, continuing in existence, or going on after the demise of something else or after some threatening event ⟨the men *surviving* after the wreck⟩ ⟨*surviving* his wife by several years⟩ ⟨a first marriage did not *survive* the long years of wartime separation —H.H.Martin⟩ ⟨a miracle that H.M.S. Marlborough *survives*, and this is due not only to the courage of the men who *survive* that first explosion, but equally to the attitude of the skipper himself —Peter Forster⟩

¹**outlook** \(ˈ)=ˈ=\ *vb* [*out-* + *look*] *vt* **1** *obs* **:** to face down **:** OUTSTARE ⟨~ conquest —Shak.⟩ **2 :** to excel in appearance ⟨a magnificent horse that ~*ed* all the others in the race⟩ ~ *vi* [¹*out* + *look*] **:** to look out ⟨shall be ~*ing*, like a bride newmarried —Robert Browning⟩

²**outlook** \ˈ=ˌ=\ *n* [³*out* + *look* (after *look out*, v.)] **1 a :** a place from which a view can be obtained ⟨has frequent ~*s* affording views of the mountain peaks —*Amer. Guide Series: N.H.*⟩ **b :** a view from a particular place ⟨had as its ~ one of the finest lakes in Europe —Nicholas Monsarrat⟩ **2 :** POINT OF VIEW ⟨a form adapted to the background and ~ of young readers —*Geog. Jour.*⟩ ⟨complete want of sympathy . . . with his entire ~ on life —J.W.Beach⟩ **3 :** the act or state of looking out **:** LOOKOUT ⟨always on the ~ for a better opportunity⟩ **4 :** the prospect for the future ⟨the ~ for steel demand in the U.S. —*Wall Street Jour.*⟩

**outlooker** \ˈ=ˌ==\ *n* [³*out* + *looker* (after *look out*, v.)] **1 :** one who looks out ⟨the outlook was not quite the same — or the ~ was changed —Maurice Hewlett⟩ **2 :** a projecting member that supports the portion of a roof extending beyond the face of a gable

**outlot** \ˈ=ˌ=\ *n* [³*out* + *lot*] **:** a lot situated outside the corporate limits of a town or city

**out loud** *adv* **:** ALOUD

**outlying** \ˈ=ˌ==\ *adj* [¹*out* + *lying*, pres. part. of *lie* (after *lie out*, v.)] **1 :** lying outside prescribed or accepted limits **:** EXTRANEOUS, EXTRINSIC ⟨~ cattle⟩ ⟨~ facts which might not corroborate the facts already organized by the structural hypothesis —S.C.Pepper⟩ **2 a :** situated or lying at a distance away from a center or main body **:** REMOTE ⟨extending library services to ~ regions and rural areas —Helen T. Geer⟩ **b :** situated or lying at the outer end of something ⟨the ~ parts of the apron —Arnold Bennett⟩ ⟨the two ~ wings connected with the main house —*Amer. Guide Series: N.C.*⟩

¹**out·man** \ˈau̇tmən\ *n, pl* **outmen** [ME, fr. *out* + *man*] **:** one living or working outside the limits of a medieval English town

²**outman** \(ˈ)=ˈ=\ *vt* [*out-* + *man*] **:** OUTNUMBER ⟨our own troops would be dangerously *outmanned* —R.H.Rovere⟩

**outmaneuver** \ˌ=ˌ=ˈ==\ *vt* [*out-* + *maneuver*] **1 :** to defeat by greater skill in maneuvering ⟨the political resourcefulness to ~ his antagonists —A.L.Funk⟩ **2 :** to surpass in maneuverability ⟨a plane that can ~ anything in the air⟩

¹**outmarch** \(ˈ)=ˈ=\ *vt* [*out-* + *march*] **:** to surpass in marching **:** outdo in speed or endurance on the march

²**outmarch** \ˈ=ˌ=\ *n* [³*out* + *march*] **:** an outward march

**outmarriage** \ˈ=ˌ==\ *n* [³*out* + *marriage*] **:** marriage outside one's own family, race, or other grouping **:** EXOGAMY — contrasted with *inmarriage*

**outmarry** \(ˈ)=ˈ==\ *vb* [*out-* + *marry*] *vt* **:** to marry a person superior to (oneself) ⟨my grandfather *outmarried* himself more than any man you ever saw —C.E.Craddock⟩ ~ *vi* [¹*out* + *marry*] **:** to marry outside one's own family, race, or other grouping

**outmatch** \(ˈ)=ˈ=\ *vt* [*out-* + *match*] **:** to be superior to **:** OUTDO, SURPASS ⟨can ~ any storyteller in the field —R.M.Dorson⟩

**outmeasure** \(ˈ)=ˈ==\ *vt* [*out-* + *measure*] **:** to surpass in quantity or extent

**out-migrant** \ˈ=ˌ=\ *n* [³*out* + *migrant*] **:** a person who outmigrates

**out-migrate** \(ˈ)=ˈ=ˌ=\ *vi* [¹*out* + *migrate*] **:** to leave one region or community in order to settle in another esp. as part of a substantial and continuing movement of population — compare IN-MIGRATE — **out-migration** \ˈ=+\ *n*

**outmode** \(ˈ)=ˈ=\ *vb* -ED/-ING/-S [*out* (*of*) *mode*] *vt* **:** to make unfashionable or obsolete ⟨the electric trolley ~*s* the horse car —M.S.Rukeyser⟩ ⟨the machine has *outmoded* human slavery —*Nation*⟩ ~ *vi* **:** to become unfashionable or obsolete ⟨equipment ~*s* quicker than hairdos —J.T.Winterich⟩

**out·mod·ed** \-dəd\ *adj* [*out* (*of*) *mode* + *-ed*] **1 :** left behind by change of fashion **:** not in style ⟨the most ridiculous and ~ fashions —Arnold Bennett⟩ **2 :** no longer acceptable or usable **:** OBSOLETE ⟨an ~ building⟩ ⟨~ ideas⟩ ⟨an ~ textbook⟩

**out·most** \ˈau̇tˌmōst *also chiefly Brit* -məst\ *adj* [³*out* + *-most*] **:** OUTERMOST ⟨from the centers of fashion to the ~ periphery of the civilized world —Edward Sapir⟩

**out·ness** *n* -ES [³*out* + *-ness*] **:** the quality or state of being out; *specif* **:** the quality or state of being distinguishable from the perceiving mind by existing in space and possessing materiality **:** EXTERNALITY ⟨are more than thought and have an ~, a reality sui generis —S.T.Coleridge⟩

**outnumber** \(ˈ)=ˈ==\ *vt* [*out-* + *number*] **:** to exceed in number

**out of** *prep* [ME, fr. OE *ūt of*, fr. *ūt* out (adv.) + *of* — more at OUT, OF] **1 a** — used as a function word to indicate direction or movement from an enclosed space to the outside ⟨fell *out of* the crib⟩ ⟨took his hands *out of* his pockets⟩ ⟨hit the ball *out of* the park⟩ ⟨stomped up the aisle and *out of* the church —James Thurber⟩ **b** — used as a function word to indicate removal or situation outside the bounds of a group, association, belief, or condition ⟨voted him *out of* the club⟩ ⟨married *out of* his faith⟩ ⟨born *out of* wedlock⟩ ⟨*out of* the ordinary⟩ **2 a** — used as a function word to indicate a change in quality, state, or form ⟨the patient is *out of* danger⟩ ⟨translated the play *out of* Latin into English⟩ ⟨woke up *out of* a deep sleep⟩ **b** — used as a function word to indicate a quality or state that is not normal, usual, or correct ⟨the trees grew thicker and lower here . . . and many of them were *out of* the vertical —C.S.Forester⟩ ⟨his prices are *out of* line⟩ ⟨the microscope is *out of* focus⟩ ⟨made some remarks that were *out of* line⟩ **c** — used as a function word to indicate a position or state away from what is familiar or expected ⟨*out of* his depth⟩ ⟨*out of* his sphere⟩ ⟨*out of* his class⟩ **3 a** — used as a function word to indicate direction, motion, or distance from a point regarded as a center or starting point ⟨he has gone *out of* town for two days⟩ ⟨they were ten miles *out of* port before they found the stowaway⟩ ⟨the salesmen operate *out of* New York⟩ **b** — used as a function word usu. with a specified number to indicate distance from a place or limit ⟨a suburb two miles *out of* town⟩ ⟨thousands of miles *out of* the earth's gravitational field⟩ **c** — used as a function word to indicate removal or situation away from the effective action of some faculty or agency ⟨the ships fled *out of* range⟩ ⟨he was soon *out of* sight⟩ ⟨*out of* hearing⟩ ⟨*out of* control⟩ **4 a** — used as a function word to indicate origin or birth ⟨many capable performers have been *out of* mares with below average records —F.A. Wrensch⟩ ⟨a farm boy *out of* the Middle West⟩ **b** — used as a function word to indicate basis or source ⟨a farmer who had done well *out of* strawberries —Roy Lewis & Angus Maude⟩ ⟨has made a fortune *out of* steel⟩ ⟨growth must be financed *out of* saving —W.M.Martin b.1906⟩ **c** — used as a function word to indicate cause or motive ⟨acted *out of* reverence rather than *out of* sensibility —R.M.Weaver⟩ ⟨obeys him *out of* fear⟩ ⟨the inflation arose *out of* many different factors⟩ **5 a** — used as a function word to indicate exclusion from or deprivation of an office or position ⟨was forced *out of* his chairmanship⟩ ⟨turned *out of* his post⟩ **b** — used as a function word to indicate the fact or condition of being without something usu. or formerly possessed ⟨the store was *out of* sugar⟩ ⟨he was all *out of* breath when he ran up⟩ ⟨the car is *out of* gas⟩ **6** — used as a function word to indicate choice or selection from among a group ⟨we must select one policy *out of* the many open to us⟩ ⟨only one *out of* three plants survived the frost⟩ — **out of it :** not part of a group, activity, or fashion **:** not in the swim ⟨he couldn't understand a word they were saying and felt hopelessly *out of it*⟩

**out-of-bounds** \ˈ==ˈ=\ *adv* (*or adj*) **:** outside the prescribed area of play **:** off the playing field **:** beyond the sidelines or end lines ⟨ran *out-of-bounds*⟩ ⟨kicked the ball *out-of-bounds*⟩ ⟨beyond the line is *out-of-bounds*⟩

**out-of-date** \ˈ==ˈ=\ *adj* **:** OUTMODED — **out-of-date·ness** *n* -ES

**out-of-door** \ˈ==ˈ=\ *or* **out-of-doors** \ˈ==ˈ=\ *adj* **:** OUTDOOR

**out-of-doors** \ˈ==ˈ=\ *n pl but sing in constr* **:** OUTDOORS

**out of doors** *adv* **:** OUTDOORS

**out of pocket** *adv* **1 :** not in pocket **:** in the position of having lost money ⟨when taxes and drainage rates had been paid, the landlord was *out of pocket* —Henry Williamson⟩ **2 :** out of funds **:** without money ⟨made no effort to order beers, being slightly *out of pocket* —Langston Hughes⟩

**out-of-pocket** \ˈ==ˈ==\ *adj* [*out of pocket*] **1 :** consisting of or requiring an actual cash outlay ⟨*out-of-pocket* expenses⟩ ⟨*out-of-pocket* costs⟩ **2 :** directly attributable to the movement of a particular article of traffic ⟨the *out-of-pocket* cost to the railroad of carrying this freight⟩

**out-of-print** \ˈ==ˈ=\ *n* **:** a title that is out of print

**out-of-round** \ˈ==ˈ=\ *adj* **:** having an imperfectly or unbalanced circular or spherical form or density — **out-of-roundness** \ˈ==ˈ==\ *n*

**out-of-the-way** \ˈ===ˈ=\ *adj* **:** off the beaten track **:** rarely frequented, encountered, or experienced ⟨an *out-of-the-way* restaurant⟩ ⟨an *out-of-the-way* plant⟩ ⟨an *out-of-the-way* book⟩

**out-of-work** \ˈ==ˈ=\ *n* [fr. the phrase *out of work*] **:** one who is unemployed ⟨a ragged, shivering *out-of-work*, who could not even provide for his own family —Edward Scouller⟩

**outpace** \(ˈ)=ˈ=\ *vt* [*out-* + *pace*] **1 :** to surpass in speed ⟨can ~ the fastest of your boasted aeroplanes —Leslie Charteris⟩ **2 :** to go beyond **:** OUTDO ⟨the mining industry was for a time *outpaced* by lumbering —*Amer. Guide Series: Mich.*⟩

**outpage** \ˈ=ˌ=\ *n* [³*out* + *page*] **:** the first right-hand page of a folded book section

**outparish** \ˈ=ˌ==\ *n* [³*out* + *parish*] **:** a parish outside the walls or limits of a town or city; *also* **:** a rural or outlying parish

**outparts** \ˈ=ˌ=\ *n pl* [³*out* + *parts*] *archaic* **:** SUBURBS

**outpass** \(ˈ)=ˈ=\ *vt* [*out-* + *pass*] **1 :** to go beyond **:** EXCEED **2 :** to excel in forwardpassing

**outpatient** \ˈ=ˌ==\ *n* [³*out* + *patient*] **:** a patient who is not an inmate of a hospital but receives diagnosis or treatment in a clinic or dispensary connected with the hospital — distinguished from *inpatient*

**outpayment** \ˈ=ˌ==\ *n* [³*out* + *payment*] **1 :** the act or an instance of paying out **2 :** a payment from — contrasted with *inpayment*

**outpeep** \(ˈ)=ˈ=\ *vi* [¹*out* + *peep*] *archaic* **:** to peep out

**outpension** \ˈ=ˌ==\ *n* [³*out* + *pension*] **:** a public pension granted to one not required to live in a charitable institution — **outpensioner** \ˈ=ˌ=(=)=\ *n*

**outperform** \ˈ=ˈ=\ *vt* [*out-* + *perform*] **:** to do better than ⟨this stock has consistently ~*ed* the market as a whole⟩ ⟨a machine that ~*s* others⟩

**outplace** \(ˈ)=ˈ=\ *vt* [¹*out* + *place*] **:** DISPLACE ⟨grain sorghums are valuable because of drought resistance and this factor has let the sorghums ~ maize —*Biol. Abstracts*⟩

**outplant** \(ˈ)=ˈ=\ *vt* [¹*out* + *plant*] **:** to transplant from a nursery bed, greenhouse, or other location to an outside area

**outplay** \(ˈ)=ˈ=\ *vt* [*out-* + *play*] **:** to excel in playing a game **:** to play more skillfully than ⟨though he ~*ed* his opponent, a series of bad breaks caused him to lose the match⟩

**outpocketing** \ˈ=ˌ===\ *n* -S [³*out* + *pocketing* (after *pocket out* v.)] **:** EVAGINATION

**outpoint** \(ˈ)=ˈ=\ *vt* [*out-* + *point*] **1 :** to sail closer to the wind than **2 a :** to win more points than **b :** to win a decision over (an opponent) in a boxing match by gaining more points **3 :** to get the better of **:** OUTDO

**outpoise** \(ˈ)=ˈ=\ *vt* [*out-* + *poise*] **:** OUTWEIGH

**outpoll** \(ˈ)=ˈ=\ *vt* [*out-* + *poll*] **:** to get more votes than ⟨~*ed* all the other candidates put together⟩

**outport** \ˈ=ˌ=\ *n* [³*out* + *port*] **1 a :** a harbor or port outside the limits of a main port or customhouse jurisdiction **b :** a port other than the main port of a country **2 :** a port of export or departure **3 :** a small fishing village in Newfoundland

**outporter** \ˈ=ˌ==\ *n* [³*out* + *porter*] **1** *Eng* **:** a luggage porter who plies to or from a station or quay **2** [*outport* + *-er*] **:** a native or resident of a Newfoundland fishing village

¹**outpost** \ˈ=ˌ=\ *n* [³*out* + *post*] **1 a :** a security detachment thrown out at some distance from a main body of troops at a halt, in bivouac, or in battle position, to protect it from observation or surprise by the enemy **b :** the post or station of such detachment **c :** a military base established by treaty or agreement in another country ⟨an important U.S. military ~ in the Far East —*Americana Annual*⟩ **2 a :** an outlying settlement ⟨a last-chance ~ at the beginning of the swamp country —B.H.Scott⟩ **b :** the most advanced position or outermost limit of something **:** FRONTIER ⟨at the last ~ of the mind —*Times Lit. Supp.*⟩ ⟨the last ~ of our knowledge of the evolution of man as such —R.W.Murray⟩ ⟨the highest ~ of the trees —G.R.Stewart⟩ **c :** an outlying branch or position of a main organization or group ⟨four Eastern networks, each with an ~ on the West coast —*Time*⟩ **3 :** an oil or gas well near the boundary of an adjoining oil or gas field

²**outpost** \"\ *vt* **:** to guard or place under observation by an outpost detachment ⟨~ the road⟩ ⟨~ the farmhouse⟩

**outpouching** \ˈ=ˌ==\ *n* -S [³*out* + *pouching*, gerund of *pouch* (after *pouch out*, v.)] **:** EVAGINATION

¹**outpour** \(ˈ)=ˈ=\ *vt* [¹*out* + *pour*] **:** to pour out

²**outpour** \ˈ=ˌ=\ *n* [³*out* + *pour* (after *pour out*, v.)] **:** OUTPOURING

**outpouring** \ˈ=ˌ==\ *n* -S [³*out* + *pouring*, gerund of *pour* (after *pour out*)] **1 :** the act of pouring out ⟨~*s* of the spirit —L.P. Smith⟩ ⟨a steady ~ of research work —S.M.Spencer⟩ **2 :** something that pours out or is poured out **:** OUTBURST, OUTFLOW ⟨the ~*s* of lava buried the village⟩ ⟨believes that a work of art is not an oracular ~ —Edmund Wilson⟩

**outpray** \(ˈ)=ˈ=\ *vt* [*out-* + *pray*] **:** to surpass in praying

**outpreach** \(ˈ)=ˈ=\ *vt* [*out-* + *preach*] **:** to outdo in preaching

**outprize** \(ˈ)=ˈ=\ *vt* [*out-* + *prize*] **:** to surpass in value or estimation

**outproduce** \ˈ==ˈ=\ *vt* [*out-* + *produce*] **:** to surpass in production

**outpull** \(ˈ)=ˈ=\ *vt* [*out-* + *pull*] **:** to attract a larger audience than ⟨~*s* all other shows in town⟩

¹**output** \ˈ=ˌ=\ *n* [³*out* + *put* (after *put out*, v.)] **1 :** something that is put out or produced: as **a :** mineral, agricultural, or industrial production ⟨coal ~⟩ ⟨wheat ~⟩ ⟨new car ~⟩ **b :** mental or artistic production ⟨his enormous symphonic ~⟩ ⟨his small literary ~⟩ ⟨a period of great scientific ~⟩ **c :** the amount produced by a person in a given time ⟨the average daily ~ of coal miners⟩ **d** (1) **:** power or energy delivered by a machine or system for storage (as by a storage battery) or for conversion in kind (as by a mechanically driven electric generator or a radio receiver) or for conversion of characteristics (as by a transformer or electronic amplifier) (2) **:** the terminal for the output on an electrical device **e** (1) **:** the information fed out by a computer or accounting machine (2) **:** the recording or printing device or its product (as magnetic tape, punched cards, or printed records) to which such information is transferred **2 :** the act, process, or an instance of putting out

²**output** \(ˈ)=ˈ=\ *vt* [¹*out* + *put*] **:** to put out **:** PRODUCE

**output shaft** *n* **:** a shaft that transmits power from the prime mover to the units or parts to be operated

**outrace** \(ˈ)=ˈ=\ *vt* [*out-* + *race*] **:** to run faster than **:** OUTDISTANCE ⟨inflation is *outracing* production —Eliot Janeway⟩

¹**out·rage** \ˈau̇tˌrāj\ *n* [OE, fr. OF, excess, outrage, fr. *outre* beyond (fr. L *ultra*) + *-age* — more at ULTERIOR] **1 :** an act of violence **:** a brutal attack ⟨arranged ~*s* and assassinations —Anthony West⟩ **2 :** an injury or insult to a person or thing **:** an act or condition that violates accepted standards of behavior or taste ⟨an ~ alike against decency and dignity —John Buchan⟩ ⟨an ~ upon journalism and upon society —F.L.Mott⟩ **3 :** a feeling of anger and resentment aroused by something regarded as an injustice or insult ⟨his sense of ~ overcame his instinct of self-preservation —S.H.Adams⟩ ⟨~ at the harshnesses of the older education —M.B.Smith⟩

²**outrage** \"\ *vt* [ME *outragen*, fr. *outrage*, n.] **1 a :** RAPE ⟨seized the unhappy maiden and brutally *outraged* her —T.B. Macaulay⟩ **b :** to subject to violent injury or gross insult **:** do violence to ⟨an act that *outraged* nature and produced the inevitable tragedy of the play —Louis Auchincloss⟩ ⟨this point-blank refusal *outraged* his sense of justice —J.C.Powys⟩ **2 :** to cause a feeling of anger or violent resentment in ⟨*outraged* by the way this whole matter has been handled —Lister Hill⟩ **syn** see OFFEND

**out·ra·geous** \(ˈ)au̇tˈrājəs\ *adj* [ME, fr. MF *outrageus*, fr. *outrage* + *-eus* -ous] **1 a :** exceeding the limits of what is normal or tolerable ⟨the ~ weather we have been afflicted with —*New Yorker*⟩ **b :** not conventional or matter-of-fact **:** EXTRAVAGANT, FANTASTIC ⟨the text matches the illustrations in this ~ tale —Margaret F. Kieran⟩ ⟨the old ~ gaiety and dash —*Time*⟩ ⟨an ~ scheme⟩ **2 :** violent or unrestrained in action or emotion ⟨know well . . . how formidable a creature you are when you become once ~ —William Cowper⟩ **3 a :** involving or doing violent injury or great harm ⟨an ~ policy of reprisals⟩ ⟨an ~ murder⟩ **b :** extremely offensive **:** showing a disregard for decency or good taste ⟨~ discourtesy⟩ ⟨~ language⟩

**syn** MONSTROUS, HEINOUS, ATROCIOUS: OUTRAGEOUS describes whatever is so flagrantly bad that one's sense of decency or one's power to suffer or tolerate is violated ⟨*outrageous* treatment of prisoners⟩ ⟨the general conviction that patent and *outrageous* crime would bring divine vengeance —H.O.Taylor⟩ ⟨*outrageous* as it was to open a leaden coffin, to see if a woman dead nearly a week were really dead —Bram Stoker⟩ MONSTROUS applies to what is abnormally or fantastically absurd, wrong, or horrible ⟨remarks of such a *monstrous* nature that Mr. Powell had no option but to accept them for gruesome jesting —Joseph Conrad⟩ ⟨the very horror with which men spoke . . . quite plainly indicates that such a wholesale massacre was exceptional, *monstrous* —A.T.Quiller-Couch⟩ ⟨their faces, which were more horrible to human sight than if they had been creatures of a *monstrous* nightmare —J.C.Powys⟩ HEINOUS describes that which excites extremest hatred, loathing, and horror ⟨a murder, and a particularly *heinous* murder, for it involves the violation of hospitality and of gratitude —R.P.Warren⟩ ATROCIOUS may apply to fierce or barbarous merciless cruelty, violence, or contempt of sanctioned values ⟨an *atrocious* murder of a child⟩ ⟨*atrocious* treatment of displaced persons⟩ ⟨*atrocious* acts which can only take place in a slave country —C.R.Darwin⟩ These words are frequently interchangeable and all lend themselves to hyperbolic descriptions of anything deprecated at the moment ⟨*outrageous* service⟩ ⟨a *monstrous* imposition⟩ ⟨a *heinous* blunder⟩ ⟨*atrocious* weather⟩

**out·ra·geous·ly** *adv* [ME, fr. *outrageous* + *-ly*] **:** in an outrageous manner or to an outrageous degree

**out·ra·geous·ness** *n* -ES [ME *oultrageousnes*, fr. *oultrageous*, *outrageous* + *-nes* -ness] **:** the quality or state of being outrageous

**out·rag·er** \ˈau̇tˌrājə(r)\ *n* **:** one that outrages

**ou·trance** \üˈträⁿs\ *n* -S [ME *outraunce*, fr. MF *outrance*, fr. *outrer* to pass beyond, overcome, surpass, carry to excess (fr. *outre* beyond) + *-ance* — more at OUTRAGE] **:** the last extremity — used with *at* or *to*; compare À OUTRANCE

**outrange** \(ˈ)=ˈ=\ *vt* [*out-* + *range*] **1 :** to surpass in range ⟨could ~ guns of the average small destroyer —*Ships and the Sea*⟩ **2 :** to go beyond **:** EXCEL ⟨the poets and the philosophers ~ the historians —A.J.Toynbee⟩

**outrank** \(ˈ)=ˈ=\ *vt* [*out-* + *rank*] **1 a :** to have a higher rank than ⟨~*s* most of his colleagues —*Current Biog.*⟩ **b :** to take precedence over ⟨an invitation to the carnival ~*s* one to class day or proms —*Amer. Guide Series: N. H.*⟩ **2 :** to surpass in importance ⟨peaches now ~ cotton as the chief crop —*Amer. Guide Series: Ark.*⟩ ⟨~*ed* all others as a shipping port for coffee —C.L.Jones⟩

**ou·tray** \üˈtrā\ *vb* [ME *outrayen*, fr. MF *outrer* — more at OUTRANCE] *vt* **1** *archaic* **:** VANQUISH, OVERCOME **2** *archaic* **:** SURPASS, EXCEL ~ *vi*, *archaic* **:** to be immoderate or extravagant **:** commit outrages or excesses

**ou·tré** \(ˈ)üˈtrā\ *adj* [F, fr. past part. of *outrer* to carry to excess — more at OUTRANCE] **:** not conforming to conventional behavior, custom, or style **:** BIZARRE, EXTRAVAGANT ⟨was always so ~ and strange —Samuel Butler †1902⟩ ⟨primitive in style, ~ in pose, and often savage in face —Janet Flanner⟩ — **ou·tré·ness** *n* -ES

¹**outreach** \(ˈ)=ˈ=\ *vb* [*out-* + *reach*] *vt* **1 a :** to surpass in reach ⟨you have to ~ an outfielder to catch a mountain beaver by hand —Irving Petite⟩ **b :** to go beyond **:** EXCEED ⟨the demand for electrical power continues to ~ the supply —*New Republic*⟩ **2 :** to get the better of by trickery **:** OVERREACH ⟨~*ed* his unsuspecting enemies⟩ ⟨~*ed* himself and became tangled in his own plot⟩ ~ *vi* **1 :** to go too far ⟨my foolish and ~*ing* slyness —Owen Wister⟩ **2** [¹*out* + *reach*] **:** to reach out ⟨alert to the ~*ing* trends of his profession —H.A.Overstreet⟩

²**outreach** \ˈ=ˌ=\ *n* [³*out* + *reach* (after *reach out*, v.)] **1 :** the act or process of reaching out ⟨the ~ of the human spirit toward beauty of form —C.S.Kilby⟩ **2 :** an extent or length of reach ⟨away from the ~ of the Ohio floods —Clifton Johnson⟩ ⟨his evangelical ~ was already shortened —W.W. Comfort⟩

**ou·tre·cuid·ance** \ˌüd·ə(r)ˈkwēdᵊn(t)s\ *n* -S [ME *outrecuidaunce*, *utterquidaunce*, fr. MF *outrecuidance*, fr. OF, fr. *outrecuider*, *outrecuidier* to be arrogant, conceited (fr. *outre* beyond + *cuider*, *cuidier* to think, be presumptuous, fr. L *cogitare* to think, think about) + *-ance* — more at OUTRAGE, COGITATE] **:** extreme self-conceit **:** PRESUMPTION

**outrelief** \ˈ=ˌ=\ *n* [³*out* + *relief*] *Brit* **:** relief given to persons living outside an institution **:** outdoor relief

¹**outride** \(ˈ)=ˈ=\ *vb* [*out-* + *ride*] *vt* **1 :** to ride better, faster, or farther than **:** OUTSTRIP ⟨could outwalk them and outdrink them and ~ them —H.W.Van Loon⟩ **2 :** to ride out (a storm) ⟨patience to ~ the intellectual and emotional storms that lie ahead —H.A.Steiner⟩ ⟨a ship strong enough to ~ any storm⟩ ~ *vi* [¹*out* + *ride*] **:** to ride out ⟨*outriding* on the range⟩

²**outride** \ˈ=ˌ=\ *n* [³*out* + *ride* (after *ride out*, v.)] **:** an unstressed syllable or group of syllables added to a foot in sprung rhythm but not counted in the scansion because of its lack of effect upon the rhythmical movement

**outrider** \ˈ=ˌ==\ *n* [³*out* + *rider* (after *ride out*, v.)] **1 a** (1) **:** an attendant on horseback who rides ahead of or next to a carriage ⟨rode in a six-horse coach with liveried lackeys and ~*s* —*Time*⟩ (2) **:** a mounted attendant who escorts race horses to the starting post **b :** one who clears the way for a vehicle or person ⟨a long black limousine with two motorcycle ~*s* —Albert Hubbell⟩ ⟨swept into the headquarters building with ~*s* brushing reporters . . . out of his path —*Time*⟩ **c :** a member of an advance guard or detachment ⟨she is an advanced ~ of feminism —Christopher Rand⟩ **d :** something that precedes or announces the approach of what is to come **:** HARBINGER, PORTENT ⟨are these shadows on so many of our horizons the ~*s* of another long night —Gilbert Highet⟩ ⟨that sugar maple . . . a flaming torch, an ~ of winter —Margaret A. Barnes⟩ **2** *dial* **:** TRAVELING SALESMAN **3 a :** a cowboy who rides on inspection about the range **b :** SCOUT ⟨a hawk, who was acting as ~, observed a truck coming toward them —James Thurber⟩ **4 :** OUTRIDE

**out·rig** \ˈau̇ˌtrig, (ˈ)=ˈ=\ *vt* [back-formation fr. *outrigger*] **:** to equip with outriggers ⟨a craft *outrigged* with pontoons —Geneva J. Yockey⟩

**out·rig·ger** \-gə(r)\ *n* [³*out* + *rigger* (after *rig out*, v.)]

outrigger 1a

**1 a :** a light projecting spar with a shaped log at the end attached to a seagoing canoe (as in the Pacific or Indian oceans) to prevent it from upsetting **b :** a spar or projecting beam run out from a ship's side to help secure the masts or from a mast to extend a rope or sail **c** (1) **:** a projecting support for an oarlock extended from the side of a rowboat or shell to permit greater leverage for the oar (2) **:** a boat so equipped **2 :** a projecting member run out from a main structure to provide additional stability or to support an extension: as **a :** a projection from a building to support hoisting tackle or to hold a flagpole **b :** a projecting or extended section of the frame of a vehicle (as of a truck) **c** (1) **:** a projecting frame usu. of spars, distance pieces, and braces to support the elevator or tail planes of an airplane (2) **:** a projection from the fuselage of a helicopter to support a rotor or a fan

**out·rig·gered** \-gə(r)d\ *adj* **:** furnished with an outrigger

¹**outright** \(ˈ)=ˈ=\ *adv* [ME, fr. ¹*out* + *right* (adv.) — more at RIGHT] **1** *archaic* **:** straight ahead **:** DIRECTLY **2 :** in entirety **:** COMPLETELY ⟨efforts to repeal state civil service laws ~ —F.A.Ogg & P.O.Ray⟩ **3 :** UNRESERVEDLY ⟨was crying ~ now —Donn Byrne⟩ **4 :** on the spot **:** INSTANTANEOUSLY ⟨married her ~ there, while he had the chance —George Meredith⟩ ⟨killed thirty people ~ and injured hundreds —F.L. Allen⟩ **5 :** in one transaction ⟨bought ~ or on a "pay later" plan —Morris Gilbert⟩ ⟨one of the few buildings he ever purchased ~ —*Time*⟩

²**outright** \"\ *adj* **1 a :** going or carried to the full extent **:** not limited or qualified **:** OUT-AND-OUT, THOROUGHGOING ⟨an ~ lie⟩ ⟨~ dishonesty⟩ ⟨an ~ disaster⟩ **b :** given without reservation ⟨an ~ gift⟩ ⟨an ~ bequest⟩ **2** *archaic* **:** proceeding directly onward **3 :** COMPLETE, ENTIRE ⟨the ~ expense⟩ — **out·right·ly** *adv* — **out·right·ness** *n*

**outring** \(ˈ)=ˈ=\ *vb* [¹*out* + *ring*] *vi* **:** to ring out ⟨the bells ~*ing* from the tower⟩ ~ *vt* [*out-* + *ring*] **:** to sound louder than ⟨~*ing* the noise of the hoofs —Theodore Winthrop⟩

**outrival** \(ˈ)=ˈ==\ *vt* [*out-* + *rival*] **:** to outdo in a competition or rivalry ⟨~*s* her brother in the affections of her parents⟩ ⟨~ other nations in economic development⟩

**outroad** \ˈ=ˌ=\ *n* [³*out* + *road*] *archaic* **:** RAID

¹**outroar** \(ˈ)=ˈ=\ *vt* [*out-* + *roar*] **:** to roar louder than ⟨the hurricane ~*ed* them —R.D.Blackmore⟩

²**outroar** \ˈ=ˌ=\ *n* [³*out* + *roar* (after *roar out*, v.)] **:** UPROAR

**outroll** \(ˈ)=ˈ=\ *vt* [¹*out* + *roll*] **:** to roll out **:** UNROLL

**outroom** \ˈ=ˌ=\ *n* [³*out* + *room*] **:** an outer room

**outroot** \(ˈ)=ˈ=\ *vt* [¹*out* + *root*] **:** ERADICATE

¹**outrun** \(ˈ)=ˈ=\ *vb* [ME *outrennen*, fr. ¹*out* + *rennen* to run — more at RUN] *vi*, *archaic* **:** to run out ~ *vt* [*out-* + *run*] **1 a :** to surpass in running **:** run faster than **:** go ahead of ⟨after a ride lasting all day, the Indians *outran* them —W.S. Campbell⟩ ⟨can ~ any other sub —*Time*⟩ **b :** to increase or develop faster than ⟨believes . . . that saving will chronically tend to ~ investment —W.M.Dacey⟩ ⟨multiplication in numbers must inevitably ~ the food supply —R.E.Coker⟩ **c :** to escape from ⟨we'd ~ my past so far, but it would catch up with us some day —J.B.Benefield⟩ ⟨men who had ~ the established law and all the courts —W.P.Webb⟩ **2 :** to go beyond (a particular point or limit) ⟨scientific theory is *outrunning* common sense —A.N.Whitehead⟩ ⟨fashion never permanently ~*s* discretion —Edward Sapir⟩ **3 :** to receive more votes than ⟨*outran* his party's candidates for other state offices⟩ — **outrun the constable :** to go into debt

²**outrun** \ˈ=ˌ=\ *n* [³*out* + *run* (after *run out*, v.)] **1 :** the act of running out ⟨the dog started off in great style on its ~ to collect the sheep —Alastair Robertson⟩ **2 :** a run for cattle or sheep at a distance from the main buildings or head station **3 :** an area into which a skier slides to come to a stop after making a ski jump or run ⟨all steep downhill stretches must have a safe ~ —Walter Prager⟩

**outrunner** \ˈ=ˌ==\ *n* [³*out* + *runner* (after *run out*, v.)] **:** one that runs or goes ahead

¹**outrush** \ˈ=ˌ=\ *n* [³*out* + *rush* (after *rush out*, v.)] **:** the act or an instance of rushing out **:** OUTFLOW ⟨a great ~ of breath —Liam O'Flaherty⟩

²**outrush** \(ˈ)=ˈ=\ *vt* [*out-* + *rush*] **:** to excel (an opposing team) in rushing ⟨~*ed* 104 yards to 78 —J.M.Sheehan⟩

**outs** *pres 3d sing of* OUT, *pl of* OUT

**outsail** \(ˈ)=ˈ=\ *vt* [*out-* + *sail*] **:** to surpass in sailing **:** sail faster than **:** OUTSTRIP ⟨~*ed* the earlier Roman ships —G.S.L. Clowes⟩

**outscore** \(ˈ)=ˈ=\ *vt* [*out-* + *score*] **:** to score more points than ⟨*outscored* their opponents by 20 points⟩

**outscout** \ˈ=ˌ=\ *n* [³*out* + *scout*] **:** SCOUT

**out·scrib·er** \(ˈ)au̇t¦skrībə(r)\ *n* [*out*put + tran*scriber*] **:** a device for transferring data recorded on a magnetic wire by an electronic computer to a medium (as a punched tape) that can be used to actuate a machine for printing the data — compare INSCRIBER

**outsea** \ˈ⸗ˌ⸗\ *n* [³*out* + *sea*] **:** HIGH SEA

**outseam** \ˈ⸗ˌ⸗\ *n* [³*out* + *seam*] **:** PRICKSEAM

**outsee** \(ˈ)⸗¦⸗\ *vt* [*out-* + *see*] **1 :** to surpass in power of vision or insight **2** [¹*out* + *see*] **:** to see beyond (a particular point or limit)

**outsell** \(ˈ)⸗¦⸗\ *vt* [*out-* + *sell*] **1** *archaic* **:** to sell for a higher price than **:** exceed in worth **2 :** to exceed in number of items sold ⟨nonfiction . . . continues to ~ fiction in the bookstores —*Publishers' Weekly*⟩ **3 :** to surpass in selling or salesmanship ⟨~*s* all other salesmen for the company⟩

**outsend** \(ˈ)⸗¦⸗\ *vt* [¹*out* + *send*] *archaic* **:** to send forth **:** EMIT

**outsentry** \ˈ⸗ˌ⸗⸗\ *n* [³*out* + *sentry*] *archaic* **:** a sentry assigned to an outpost

¹**out·sert** \ˈau̇tˌsər|t, -sə̄|, -səi|, *usu* |d.+V\ *n* -s [³*out* + *-sert* (as in *insert*, n.)] **:** a usu. 4-page section (as of a magazine) so imposed and printed that it can be placed outside another signature — compare INSERT

²**out·sert** \(ˈ)au̇t¦sər|t, -sə̄|, -səi|, *usu* |d.+V\ *vt* -ED/-ING/-S [¹*out* + *-sert* (as in *insert*, v.)] **1 :** to place as an outsert ⟨color plates ~*ed* to signatures⟩ **2 :** to add an outsert to ⟨signatures ~*ed* and ready for gathering⟩

**outset** \ˈ⸗ˌ⸗\ *n* [³*out* + *set* (after *set out*, v.)] **1** *Scot* **:** an enclosure of land newly placed under cultivation **2 a :** a setting out (as on a journey, career, course of action, or discussion) **:** BEGINNING, START ⟨one must be clear, from the ~, how limited are the author's aims —S.E.Toulmin⟩ ⟨at the ~ of what might have been a great career —E.F.Edgett⟩ **b :** an initial stage of activity or development ⟨the ~ of any investigation must be occupied by asking obvious questions —Edith C. Rivett⟩ **3 :** an outgoing tidal current **4 :** OUTSERT

¹**outsetting** \ˈ⸗ˌ⸗⸗\ *n* [³*out* + *setting*, gerund of *set* (after *set out*, v.)] **:** the act or process of setting out (as on a journey or expedition) ⟨a full description of the ~ from Gravesend of a detachment of Royal Engineers —*Athenaeum*⟩

²**outsetting** \ˈ⸗ˌ⸗⸗\ *adj* [¹*out* + *setting*, pres. part. of *set* (after *set out*, v.)] **:** setting or flowing out

**outsettlement** \ˈ⸗ˌ⸗⸗⸗\ *n* [³*out* + *settlement*] **:** an outlying settlement

**outsettler** \ˈ⸗ˌ⸗⸗\ *n* [³*out* + *settler*] **:** one who lives in an outlying region

**outshadow** \(ˈ)⸗¦⸗ˌ⸗\ *vt* [*out-* + *shadow*] **:** OVERSHADOW

**outsharp** \(ˈ)⸗¦⸗\ *vt* [*out-* + *sharp*] **:** OUTWIT

**outshine** \(ˈ)⸗¦⸗\ *vb* [*out-* + *shine*] *vt* **1 a :** to surpass in shining **:** shine brighter than ⟨a star that ~*s* the sun⟩ **b :** to excel in splendor or showiness ⟨seeing another, whom she intended to ~, in a more attractive dress than her own —T.L. Peacock⟩ **2 :** EXCEL, OUTDO ⟨would try to ~ his former disciple in wit —Hesketh Pearson⟩ ~ *vi* [¹*out* + *shine*] **:** to shine out ⟨bright *outshining* beams —Shak.⟩

¹**outshoot** \(ˈ)⸗¦⸗\ *vb* [*out-* + *shoot*] *vt* **1 :** to surpass in shooting or making shots ⟨a rifle that ~*s* any other model of its type⟩ ⟨won the tennis match by ~*ing* and outrunning his opponent⟩ **2 :** to shoot or go beyond ⟨tell the philosophers of the day, that I have *outshot* them all —William Cowper⟩ ~ *vi* [¹*out* + *shoot*] **:** to shoot out ⟨up in the tree . . . on an ~*ing* limb —*Hearst's*⟩

²**outshoot** \ˈ⸗ˌ⸗\ *n* [³*out* + *shoot* (after *shoot out*, v.)] **:** something that shoots out; *specif* **:** a pitched baseball that breaks away from a right-handed batter

**outshot** \ˈ⸗ˌ⸗\ *or* **outshut** \ˈ⸗ˌ⸗\ *n* [*outshot* fr. ¹*out* + *shot*, past part. of *shoot* (after *shoot out*, v.); *outshut* alter. of *outshot*] *dial Brit* **:** a projecting section attached to the side of a building **:** LEAN-TO

**outshout** \(ˈ)⸗¦⸗\ *vt* [*out-* + *shout*] **:** to shout louder than ⟨acclaimed only so long as he can personally ~ and outthreaten the rest —Margaret Mead⟩

¹**outside** \(ˈ)⸗¦⸗\ *n* [³*out* + *side*] **1 :** a place or region that is situated beyond an enclosure, boundary, or other limit: as **a :** the world outside an institution ⟨fit an inmate in attitudes and habits for life on the ~ —Garrett Heyns⟩ **b** *Austral* **:** OUTBACK **c** *Alaska* **:** the world outside the territory or state of Alaska **2 a :** an outer side or surface ⟨the ~ of the house needs painting⟩ ⟨the ~ of the door was badly scarred⟩ ⟨walked on the ~ of the path⟩ **b :** the left side of a sword in fencing **c :** the convex aspect of a curve **d :** the side of home plate farther from the batter in baseball ⟨pitched to the batter on the ~⟩ **3 :** an outer manifestation **:** APPEARANCE ⟨he was the fine ~ of a man, the portrait of a gentleman and a soldier —A.W.Long⟩ ⟨the imaginative insides of human reverie can be more thrilling than the heroic ~*s* of action —T.V.Smith⟩ **4 :** the extreme limit of a guess or approximation **:** the utmost extent ⟨the crowd numbered ten thousand at the ~⟩ ⟨estimated that his rate of profit would be ten percent at the ~⟩ ⟨gave him two years to live at the ~⟩ **5 :** one that is without: as **a :** an outside passenger or seat (as in a stagecoach) **b :** a rugby player who is not a forward **6 outsides** *pl* **:** the top and bottom quires of a ream of writing or drawing paper; *broadly* **:** reams made up of such imperfect quires or sheets — compare INSIDE

²**outside** \"\ *adj* **1 a :** of, relating to, or being on the outer side or surface ⟨the ~ edge⟩ ⟨~ qualities⟩ ⟨an ~ lock⟩ **b :** of, relating to, or being on or toward the outer side of a curve or turn ⟨stemming with the ~ ski⟩ ⟨the ~ wheels⟩ **2 a :** situated, belonging, or performed outside a particular place, area, or enclosure ⟨distracted by ~ noises⟩ ⟨take many ~ trips during the school year⟩ ⟨heard little news from the ~ world⟩ **b** *Austral* **:** situated in the outback **c :** connected with or giving access to the outside ⟨asked the switchboard operator for an ~ line⟩ **d** *Eng* **:** done outside a radio or television studio ⟨throughout the summer months the television service specializes in sport and other ~ broadcasts —T.O.Beachcroft⟩ **3 :** MAXIMUM ⟨five millions more than their ~ estimate —F.L.Allen⟩ **4 a :** not included or originating in a particular group or organization **:** EXTRANEOUS ⟨~ influences⟩ ⟨~ pressure⟩ ⟨the ~ public⟩ **b :** not belonging to one's regular occupation, duties, or course of study ⟨~ interests⟩ ⟨~ activities⟩ **c :** done outside of class or class hours ⟨the course demands ten hours a week of ~ preparation⟩ **5 :** barely possible **:** REMOTE ⟨has an ~ chance of scoring an upset and winning the election⟩ **syn** see OUTER

³**outside** \"\ *adv* **1 a :** on or to the outside ⟨waited ~ in the corridor⟩ ⟨carried the lawn furniture ~⟩ **b :** in the open air **:** OUTDOORS **2 :** EXTERNALLY ⟨the car seemed in perfect shape ~⟩

⁴**outside** \"\ *prep* [³*outside*] **1 :** on the outer side of ⟨the American flag ~ my building —William Barrett⟩ ⟨she seemed always ~ her subject —H.J.Laski⟩ **2 :** beyond the limits of ⟨do little of their entertaining ~ their homes —*Amer. Guide Series: Minn.*⟩ ⟨reach ~ the narrow intellectual boundaries imposed by a restricted income in a little village —Flora Rose⟩ ⟨~ the law⟩ **3 :** to the outside of ⟨ran ~ the house⟩ **4 :** EXCEPT 1 ⟨~ these, and a few professional men, there was almost no fancy dress —Arnold Bennett⟩

**outside broker** *n* **:** a stockbroker who is not a member of an exchange

**outside caliper** *n* **:** a caliper for measuring outside dimensions

**outside car** *n, Irish* **:** JAUNTING CAR

**outside clinch** *n* **:** a clinch knot in which the seized end of a line is outside the noose — compare INSIDE CLINCH

**outside finish** *n* **:** the final work on the exterior of a building necessary for its completion (as the adding of corner boards and window casings) — compare INSIDE FINISH

**outside form** *n* **:** OUTER FORM

**outside home** *n* **:** a lacrosse player whose position is on the right side of the opponents' goal next to inside home — called also *out home*

**outside left** *n* **:** the outermost forward on the left of the center in a game (as soccer) in which there are five forwards

**outside loop** *n* **:** a maneuver in which an airplane starting from straight and level flight passes successively through a dive, inverted flight, and a climb and then returns to normal flight

**outside market** *n* **:** ²CURB 9 b

**out·side·ness** *n* -ES **:** the quality or state of being outside ⟨my ~ from current affairs —O.W.Holmes †1935⟩

**outside of** *prep* [³*outside*] **1 :** beyond the limits or compass of ⟨the rapid development of suburban centers *outside of* all our cities —Harrison Smith⟩ **2 :** BESIDES, EXCEPT ⟨*outside of* one servant he is alone in the house⟩

**outside quire** *n* **:** the top quire or the bottom quire of a ream of handmade or moldmade paper

**out·sid·er** \(ˈ)au̇t¦sīdə(r)\ *n* -s [²*outside* + *-er*] **1 a :** a person not recognized or accepted as a member of some group, category, or organization ⟨has lived there for 20 years but is still regarded as an ~⟩ ⟨a political ~⟩ **b :** a person who isolates himself or is felt to be isolated from the world around him ⟨the artist ought to be an ~ —E.M.Forster⟩ **2 :** a contender in a sports event that is not favored to win **3 outsiders** *pl* **:** a pair of long-nosed nippers for grasping the point of a key in the keyhole from the outside **4 :** JAUNTING CAR

**outside right** *n* **:** the outermost forward on the right of the center in a game (as soccer) in which there are five forwards

**outside wire** *n* **:** OUTER

**outsight** \ˈ⸗ˌ⸗\ *n* [³*out* + *sight*] **1 :** the act or capacity of observing **:** the perception of external things ⟨the clear-eyed insight and ~ of the born writer —*New Yorker*⟩ **2** *archaic Scot* **:** movable outdoor goods or property (as plows or cattle)

**outsing** \(ˈ)⸗¦⸗\ *vb* [*out-* + *sing*] *vt* **:** to surpass in singing ⟨a violin that will ~ any instrument yet made by man —H.M. Robinson⟩ ~ *vi* [¹*out* + *sing*] **:** to sing out

**out sister** *n* [³*out*] **:** EXTERN 2

**outsit** \(ˈ)⸗¦⸗\ *vt* [*out-* + *sit*] **1 :** to remain sitting longer than the duration of ⟨*outsat* their pleasure in his company⟩ **2 :** to sit longer than ⟨ready to ~ the negotiators for the other side⟩

¹**outsize** \(ˈ)⸗¦⸗\ *n* [³*out* + *size*] **:** an unusual size (as of an article of clothing); *esp* **:** a size larger than the standard

²**outsize** \"\ *also* **outsized** \(ˈ)⸗¦⸗\ *adj* **1 :** unusually large or heavy ⟨physically he is ~, standing six feet three and weighing 225 pounds —N.M.Clark⟩ ⟨a man whose talent, ego and self-indulgence come in rather ~ proportions —Claudia Cassidy⟩ **2 :** too large ⟨his ~ black homburg resting squarely on both ears —*Newsweek*⟩ ⟨a cheerful rascal in an ~ shirt and undersize pants —J.B.D.Cotter⟩

¹**outskirt** \ˈ⸗ˌ⸗\ *n* [³*out* + *skirt*] **:** a part remote from the center **:** BORDER, FRINGE ⟨a very thinly settled ~ —Edith Wharton⟩ — usu. used in pl. ⟨showed that our sun was not the center of our galaxy but out toward its ~*s* —B.J.Bok⟩ ⟨the ~*s* of the city⟩ ⟨the ~*s* of consciousness⟩

²**outskirt** \(ˈ)⸗¦⸗\ *vt* **1 :** BORDER **2 :** to pass along the border of ⟨~*ed* the lawn⟩

**outskirter** \ˈ⸗ˌ⸗⸗\ *n* **:** one that occupies the outskirts **:** HANGER-ON

**outsleep** \(ˈ)⸗¦⸗\ *vt* [*out-* + *sleep*] **1 :** to sleep later than ⟨fear we shall ~ the coming morn —Shak.⟩ **2** [¹*out* + *sleep*] **:** to sleep through or beyond the end of ⟨*outslept* the storm⟩ ⟨*outslept* his opportunity⟩

**outslick** \(ˈ)⸗¦⸗\ *vt* [*out-* + *slick* (adj.)] **:** to get the better of by trickery or cunning

**outslug** \(ˈ)⸗¦⸗\ *vt* [*out-* + *slug*] **1 :** OUTFIGHT ⟨the trout had *outslugged* him, outwitted him . . . and had got away —Richard Salmon⟩ **2 :** to get more extra-base hits than

**outsmart** \(ˈ)⸗¦⸗\ *vt* [*out-* + *smart* (adj.)] **:** to get the better of ⟨is told that existing society will ~ him if given a chance —*Sydney (Australia) Bull.*⟩; *esp* **:** OUTMANEUVER, OUTWIT ⟨a shrewd criminal who fancied he could ~ the whole world —Louis Bromfield⟩

**outsmell** \(ˈ)⸗¦⸗\ *vt* [*out-* + *smell*] **:** to smell stronger than ⟨his bear's grease *outsmelt* his primroses —Israel Zangwill⟩

**outsoar** \(ˈ)⸗¦⸗\ *vt* [*out-* + *soar*] **:** to soar beyond or above ⟨~ the shadow of war's night —*Times Lit. Supp.*⟩

**outsole** \ˈ⸗ˌ⸗\ *n* [³*out* + *sole*] **:** the outside sole of a boot or shoe

¹**outspan** \(ˈ)⸗¦⸗\ *vb* [¹*out* + *span*; trans. of Afrik *uitspan*] *vi, southern Africa* **:** to unyoke or unharness a draft animal ⟨we *outspanned*, made our beds and then set about preparing supper —*Farmer's Weekly (So. Africa)*⟩ ~ *vt, southern Africa* **:** UNYOKE, UNHITCH

²**outspan** \ˈ⸗ˌ⸗\ *n, southern Africa* **:** a place publicly set aside for use in outspanning or resting animals

**outspeak** \(ˈ)⸗¦⸗\ *vb* [in sense 1, fr. *out-* + *speak*; in other senses, fr. ¹*out* + *speak*] *vt* **1 :** to excel in speaking **:** speak longer, louder, or more forcibly than ⟨though the lawyer for the defense *outspoke* the prosecutor, he lost the case⟩ **2 :** to declare openly or boldly ⟨broke upon him in a loud voice, ~*ing* his contention —Elizabeth M. Roberts⟩ ~ *vi* **:** to speak out ⟨when the rude instinct of our race *outspoke* —Robert Browning⟩

**outspeed** \(ˈ)⸗¦⸗\ *vt* [*out-* + *speed*] **1 :** to outdo in speed **:** go faster than ⟨can ~ any other horse over a short distance⟩ **2 :** to go beyond **:** leave behind ⟨no cruelty horrible enough to ~ her pity —Hugh Walpole⟩

**outspend** \(ˈ)⸗¦⸗\ *vt* [*out-* + *spend*] **1 :** to exceed the limits of in spending ⟨~*s* his income⟩ **2 :** to outdo in spending ⟨promised to ~ the incumbent administration⟩

**outspent** \(ˈ)⸗¦⸗\ *adj* [¹*out* + *spent*] **:** EXHAUSTED

**outspin** \(ˈ)⸗¦⸗\ *vt* [¹*out* + *spin*] **:** to spin (a thread) to its full extent ⟨the thread of life *outspun*⟩

**outspoken** \(ˈ)⸗¦⸗⸗\ *adj* [¹*out* + *spoken*] **1 a :** speaking without fear or reserve **:** direct and open in speech or expression **:** CANDID, FRANK ⟨~ in his assertion of his opinions —H.K. Rowe⟩ ⟨~ in their opposition to slavery —W.L.Sperry⟩ **b :** spoken or expressed without reserve or conventional reticence ⟨won praise for the ~ quality of its language and subject matter —*Current Biog.*⟩ **2** *of a disease* **:** clearly present **:** UNMISTAKABLE ⟨cardiac insufficiency, whether incipient or ~, demands bed rest —R.F.Loeb⟩ — **out·spo·ken·ly** \-nlē, -li\ *adv* — **out·spo·ken·ness** \-n(n)əs\ *n* -ES

**outsport** *vt* [*out-* + *sport*] *obs* **:** to go beyond (a limit) in sportiveness ⟨let's teach ourselves . . . not to ~ discretion —Shak.⟩

¹**outspread** \(ˈ)⸗¦⸗\ *vt* [ME *outspreden*, fr. ¹*out* + *spreden* to spread — more at SPREAD] **:** to spread out **:** EXPAND

²**outspread** \"\ *adj* [fr. past part. of ¹*outspread*] **:** spread out **:** EXTENDED ⟨~ arms⟩ ⟨~ hair⟩

³**outspread** \ˈ⸗ˌ⸗\ *n* [³*out* + *spread* (after *spread out*, v.)] **:** the action or an instance of spreading out ⟨this ~ brought also new problems —D.E.O'Leary⟩

**outspring** \(ˈ)⸗¦⸗\ *vi* [ME *outspringen*, fr. ¹*out* + *springen* to spring — more at SPRING] **:** to spring out

**outstand** \(ˈ)⸗¦⸗\ *vb* [¹*out* + *stand*] *vt* **1** *dial chiefly Eng* **:** to resist stubbornly **:** CONTRADICT **2 :** to endure beyond ⟨I have *outstood* my time —Shak.⟩ ~ *vi* **:** to stand out clearly ⟨he *outstood* in virtue of being a perfect symbol and emblem of the average —Max Beerbohm⟩

**outstanding** \ˈ⸗¦⸗⸗\ *adj* **1 :** standing out or projecting ⟨an ~ skirt that strangely resembled the large lampshade in the drawing room —G.K.Chesterton⟩ **2 a :** UNCOLLECTED, UNPAID ⟨left a balance of ten dollars ~ on his account⟩ **b :** continuing in being **:** UNRESOLVED ⟨one of the long ~ problems of astronomy —*Times Lit. Supp.*⟩ ⟨several ~ issues between the two countries⟩ **c** *of stocks and bonds* **:** publicly issued and sold ⟨has 20,000 shares ~⟩ **3 a :** standing out from a group **:** CONSPICUOUS, PROMINENT ⟨cleanliness is an ~ characteristic of the Acadian housewife —*Amer. Guide Series: La.*⟩ ⟨the ~ subject of discussion —Vera M. Dean⟩ **b :** preeminent in a particular quality or activity **:** EXCELLENT ⟨an ~ painter who has received little recognition⟩ ⟨an ~ student⟩ **syn** see NOTICEABLE

**out·stand·ing·ly** *adv* **:** in an outstanding manner or to an outstanding degree **:** EXTREMELY, REMARKABLY

**outstandings** \ˈ⸗¦⸗⸗\ *n pl* **:** outstanding loans or unsettled accounts ⟨the bank's ~ on real estate mortgages have gone up by over half a million dollars⟩

**outstanding term** *n, Eng law* **:** an estate for a long term of years granted usu. to trustees to secure regular payments to a beneficiary from the tenant of the estate upon which such payments are charged

**outstare** \(ˈ)⸗¦⸗\ *vt* [*out-* + *stare*] **:** to overcome in staring **:** put out of countenance **:** OUTFACE ⟨seem confident that they can ~ the U. S. —*Time*⟩

¹**outstart** \(ˈ)⸗¦⸗\ *vb* [¹*out* + *start*] *vi* **:** to spring out **:** start forth ~ *vt* [*out-* + *start*] **:** to get the start of

²**outstart** \ˈ⸗ˌ⸗\ *n* [³*out* + *start* (after *start out*, v.)] **:** BEGINNING, OUTSET

**outstate** \ˈ⸗ˌ⸗\ *adj* [³*out* + *state* (n.)] **1 :** of, relating to, or situated in a region of a state outside the principal city or largest center of population ⟨small layoffs here and there in the ~ areas —*Wall Street Jour.*⟩ ⟨lost the governorship because the ~ vote went against him⟩ **2** [*out (of) state*] **:** coming from or resident in an outside state ⟨a gorge of unusual natural beauty which few ~ visitors see —M.W.Fishwick⟩ — **out·stat·er** \ˈ⸗ˈstād·ə(r)\ *n*

**outstation** \ˈ⸗ˌ⸗⸗\ *n* [³*out* + *station*] **:** a station (as a sheep run, diplomatic post, or mission) situated in a remote or sparsely settled region ⟨sit . . . at some lonely ~ and shoot three deer before breakfast —*Sydney (Australia) Bull.*⟩ ⟨three nuns waited . . . for a sister reporting in from an ~ —J.A. Michener⟩

**outstay** \(ˈ)⸗¦⸗\ *vt* [*out-* + *stay*] **1 a :** to stay beyond **:** OVERSTAY ⟨~*ed* his welcome⟩ ⟨~*ed* his leave⟩ **b :** to stay longer than ⟨was determined to ~ him —John Buchan⟩ **2 :** to surpass in staying power ⟨~*ed* the favorite by a neck⟩ ⟨a writer who has ~*ed* many who began more brilliantly⟩

**outstep** \(ˈ)⸗¦⸗\ *vt* [*out-* + *step*] **:** to step beyond **:** OVERSTEP ⟨~*s* the moderation of his predecessor in office⟩ ⟨program which it would have been almost blasphemy to ~ —J.C. Stobart⟩

**outstink** \(ˈ)⸗¦⸗\ *vt* [*out-* + *stink*] **:** to smell worse than **:** have a more powerful stench than ⟨~ a skunk⟩

**outstream** \(ˈ)⸗¦⸗\ *vi* [¹*out* + *stream*] **:** to stream out

**out·streat** \(ˈ)⸗¦strēt\ *vi* [¹*out* + obs. *streat* to estreat, short for *estreat* (influenced in meaning by its etymon, obs. F *estrait*, past part. of *estraire* to extract) — more at ESTREAT] *archaic* **:** EXUDE

¹**outstretch** \(ˈ)⸗¦⸗\ *vt* [¹*out* + *stretch*] **1 a :** to stretch out ⟨the image of a kitten erect, one paw ~*ed* as if inviting —Lafcadio Hearn⟩ **b :** to spread out **:** EXTEND ⟨began to paint on the ~*ed* canvas⟩ **2** [*out-* + *stretch*] **:** to stretch beyond ⟨this explanation ~*es* common sense⟩ — **outstretcher** \(ˈ)⸗¦⸗⸗\ *n*

²**outstretch** \ˈ⸗ˌ⸗\ *n* [³*out* + *stretch* (after *stretch out*, v.)] **:** the act or an instance of stretching out ⟨nothing less than poetry's soaring ~ . . . can justify the writing of any novel in verse —*New Republic*⟩

**outstride** \(ˈ)⸗¦⸗\ *vt* [*out-* + *stride*] **:** to outdo in striding **:** stride ahead of ⟨on the utilitarian side . . . American education has *outstridden* the rest of the world —F.P.Corson⟩

**outstrike** *vt* [*out-* + *strike*] *obs* **:** to surpass in striking

**outstrip** \(ˈ)⸗¦⸗\ *vt* [*out-* + *strip*] **1 :** to go faster than ⟨a speed far *outstripping* the fastest rocket plane —R.M.Sutton⟩ **2 a :** to leave behind **:** go ahead of **:** EXCEL, SURPASS ⟨in certain countries knowledge had far *outstripped* wisdom —A.L. Guérard⟩ ⟨the central nervous system . . . has *outstripped* all else —Waldemar Kaempffert⟩ **b :** to exceed in quantity or number ⟨fall into ever greater destitution as their numbers ~ their resources —Barbara Ward⟩ ⟨the demand for mortgage money *outstripped* savings —L.H.Olsen⟩ **syn** see EXCEED

**outstroke** \ˈ⸗ˌ⸗\ *n* [³*out* + *stroke*] **:** an outward stroke; *specif* **:** a stroke in which the piston in a steam or other engine is moving toward the crankshaft — opposed to *instroke*

**outsucken** \(ˈ)⸗¦⸗⸗\ *adj* [⁴*out* + *sucken* (n.)] *Scots law* **:** not astricted to a particular mill for the grinding of corn — compare THIRLAGE

**outsurge** \ˈ⸗ˌ⸗\ *n* [³*out* + *surge*] **:** an outward surge ⟨other ~*s* of steppe peoples went into Europe —J.R.Smith⟩

**outswagger** \(ˈ)⸗¦⸗⸗\ *vt* [*out-* + *swagger*] **:** to outdo in swaggering

**outswear** \(ˈ)⸗¦⸗\ *vt* [*out-* + *swear*] **1 :** to surpass in swearing ⟨can ~ a trooper⟩ **2 :** to get the better of by swearing ⟨we'll outface them and ~ them too —Shak.⟩

**outsweep** \(ˈ)⸗¦⸗\ *vi* [¹*out* + *sweep*] **:** to sweep out ⟨a dress with an ~*ing* skirt⟩

**outsweepings** \ˈ⸗ˌ⸗⸗\ *n pl* [³*out* + *sweepings*, pl. of *sweeping*, gerund of *sweep* (after *sweep out*, v.)] **:** REFUSE

**outsweeten** \(ˈ)⸗¦⸗⸗\ *vt* [*out-* + *sweeten*] **:** to surpass in sweetness ⟨~ honey —Robert Browning⟩

**outswell** \(ˈ)⸗¦⸗\ *vt* [*out-* + *swell*] **:** to exceed in swelling

**outswinger** \ˈ⸗ˌ⸗⸗\ *n* [³*out* + *swinger* (after *swing out*, v.)] **:** a bowled cricket ball that swerves in the air from leg to off — compare INSWINGER

**outtake** \ˈ⸗ˌ⸗\ *n* [³*out* + *take* (after *take out*, v.)] **1 :** a passage outwards **:** FLUE, VENT ⟨the ~ is at the top of the windows —J.E.Rice & H.E.Botsford⟩ **2 :** a discarded film take ⟨from the ~*s* we made a 100-ft. sound-on-film trailer —A.H.Smith⟩

**outtaken** \(ˈ)⸗¦⸗⸗\ *prep* [ME, fr. ¹*out* + *taken*, past part. of *taken* to take (after *taken out* to take out) — more at TAKE] *archaic* **:** EXCEPT

**outtalk** \(ˈ)⸗¦⸗\ *vt* [*out-* + *talk*] **1 :** to surpass in talking ⟨could outwork and ~ them all —Catherine D. Bowen⟩ **2 :** to get the better of by talking ⟨don't let those swabs ~ you —Kenneth Roberts⟩

**outtell** \(ˈ)⸗¦⸗\ *vt* [¹*out* + *tell*] **1 :** to speak out **:** declare openly ⟨all *outtold* their fond imaginations —John Keats⟩ **2 :** to tell completely **3** [*out-* + *tell*] **:** to have more telling effect than ⟨the mere quotation . . . ~*s* all commentary —H. B.Alexander⟩

**outthink** \(ˈ)⸗¦⸗\ *vt* [*out-* + *think*] **1 :** to surpass in thinking **:** to go beyond or transcend by thinking ⟨must ~ the world if they are to outlive it —*Religion in Life*⟩ **2 :** to get the better of by thinking more quickly or adroitly **:** OUTWIT ⟨strives to ~ the buyer rather than to outtalk him —*Concrete Products*⟩

¹**outthrow** \(ˈ)⸗¦⸗\ *vt* [ME *outthrowen*, fr. ¹*out* + *throwen* to throw — more at THROW] **1 :** to throw out ⟨the sheriff grasped one of the *outthrown* arms —Ambrose Bierce⟩ **2** [*out-* + *throw*] **:** to surpass in the length and accuracy of a throw ⟨can ~ any outfielder in the major leagues⟩

²**outthrow** \ˈ⸗ˌ⸗\ *n* [³*out* + *throw* (after *throw out*, v.)] **1 a :** a throwing out **:** OUTBURST ⟨a creative ~ that lasted only a few years⟩ **b :** the act or process of throwing soil away from the crop by the cultivating gangs of a row-crop cultivator; *also* **:** the amount of soil thrown out **2 :** a waste material (as a rag or piece of paper) so made or treated as to be unsuitable for recovery of fibers — usu. used in pl.

¹**outthrust** \(ˈ)⸗¦⸗\ *vb* [ME *outthresten*, fr. ¹*out* + *thresten* to thrust — more at THRUST] *vt* **:** to thrust out ~ *vi* **:** to thrust out ⟨the deep roots, ~*ing* far below the plowshare's reach —George Woodbury⟩

²**outthrust** \ˈ⸗ˌ⸗\ *n* [³*out* + *thrust* (after *thrust out*, v.)] **1 :** a thrusting out **:** an outward pressure **2 :** something that is thrust out **:** PROJECTION ⟨below it was no firm ~ of the mountainside, but eight thousand feet of air —J.R.Ullman⟩

³**outthrust** \ˈ⸗ˌ⸗\ *adj* [¹*out* + *thrust*, past part. of *thrust* (after *thrust out*, v.)] **:** thrust out **:** EXTENDED ⟨an ~ jaw⟩ ⟨an ~ hand⟩

**outthunder** \(ˈ)⸗¦⸗⸗\ *vt* [*out-* + *thunder*] **1 :** to outdo in thundering ⟨in the storm he must ~ the thunder —John Mason Brown⟩ **2 :** to make more noise than **:** overpower in sound ⟨the main thought is ~*ed* by the overtones —J.P. Bishop⟩

**outtire** \(ˈ)⸗¦⸗\ *vt* [*out-* + *tire*] **:** to tire out ⟨would ~ ten horses in a tilting-match —C.E.Robinson⟩

**outtongue** \(ˈ)⸗¦⸗\ *vt* [*out-* + *tongue*] **:** to exceed in eloquence ⟨my services . . . shall ~ his complaints —Shak.⟩

**out-to-out** \¦⸗⸗¦⸗\ *adj* **:** measured from outer edge to outer edge

**outtop** \(ˈ)⸗¦⸗\ *vt* [*out-* + *top*] **:** to surpass in height **:** SURMOUNT ⟨far *outtopping* all the other trees of the forest —J.G. Frazer⟩ ⟨~*s* all other composers of the century⟩

**outtower** \(ˈ)⸗¦⸗⸗\ *vt* [*out-* + *tower*] **:** to tower above **:** surpass in dignity or worth ⟨a moral universe ~*ing* time and passion —H.B.Alexander⟩ ⟨no small man, but ~*ed* by his companion —*Bookman*⟩

**outtrade** \(ˈ)⸗¦⸗\ *vt* [*out-* + *trade*] *vt* **:** to get the better of in a trade ⟨if they tried to ~ him, they'd find their pockets full of bad bills of credit —Kenneth Roberts⟩

**outtravel** \(ˈ)⸗¦⸗⸗\ *vt* [*out-* + *travel*] **1 :** to travel beyond ⟨~ the boundaries of space⟩ **2 :** to travel faster than ⟨~ the news of his coming⟩

**out-tray** \ˈ⸗ˌ⸗\ *n* [³*out* + *tray*] **:** a shallow wood or metal basket usu. on a desk for holding outgoing material (as letters to be posted or memoranda) — distinguished from *in-tray*

**outtrick** \(ˈ)⸗¦⸗\ *vt* [*out-* + *trick*] **:** to get the better of by trickery ⟨deceived and ~*ed* by the Roberts⟩

**outtrump** \(ˈ)⸗¦⸗\ *vt* [*out-* + *trump*] **:** OUTMANEUVER, OUTPLAY

**outturn** \'ˌ=\ *n* [³*out* + *turn* (after *turn out,* v.)] **1 a :** an amount of something (as of a crop or manufactured item) turned out or produced **:** OUTPUT, YIELD ⟨rice was the chief crop . . . and extensive new irrigation works multiplied the ~ —J.S.Furnivall⟩ **b :** a sampling taken at a paper mill from each run on a paper machine **2 a :** the quality or condition of something turned out or produced ⟨oiling of eggs has resulted in greatly improved ~ in the export pack and winter cold storage —*Poultry Farmer (Australia)*⟩ **b :** the condition in which a shipment arrives at its destination ⟨inaugurated special methods of stowing turpentine barrels, in ships bound on long voyages, in order to assure better ~s —*Chem. Markets*⟩

**out-turn** \'ˌ=\ *n* [³*out* + *turn* (after *turn out,* v.)] **:** a moving curling stone which is rotating counterclockwise — compare IN-TURN

**outvalue** \(')=¦=(ˌ)=\ *vt* [*out-* + *value*] **:** to be worth more than ⟨the talk ~s many a novel —Thomas Wood †1950⟩

**outvie** \(')=¦=\ *vt* [*out-* + *vie*] **:** to surpass in a rivalry or competition ⟨*outvying* each other in courtesy⟩ ⟨*outvied* the sun in brilliance⟩

**outvote** \(')=¦=\ *vt* [*out-* + *vote*] **1 :** to cast more votes than **:** defeat by a majority of votes ⟨these two groups can combine to ~ the other members of the board⟩ ⟨the outstate districts can ~ the city⟩ **2 :** to defeat in a contest or on an issue decided by votes ⟨the cabinet must resign if it is *outvoted* —John Gunther⟩

**outwait** \(')=¦=\ *vt* [*out-* + *wait*] **:** to exceed in patience

**outwake** \(')=¦=\ *vt* [*out-* + *wake*] **:** to remain awake longer than **:** OUTWATCH

**out·wale** \'=ˌwāl\ *n* [³*out* + gun*wale*] **:** the outside piece of a gunwale (as of a canoe)

**outwalk** \(')=¦=\ *vt* [*out-* + *walk*] **1 :** to outdo in walking ⟨could ~ those not nearly so old as he was —John Mason Brown⟩ **2 :** to walk past or beyond ⟨~*ed* the furthest city light —*Va. Quarterly Rev.*⟩

**outwall** \'=ˌ=\ *n* [³*out* + *wall*] **1** *archaic* **:** an outer wall or other enclosure **2** *obs* **:** the outer enclosure of a human being (as clothing or the body) ⟨I am much more than my ~ —Shak.⟩

**outwander** \(')=¦==\ *vi* [¹*out* + *wander*] **:** to wander out or away ⟨there is little ~*ing* or outgrowth from the tissues —*Science*⟩

¹**out·ward** \'au̇twə(r)d\ *adj* [ME, fr. OE *ūtanweard, ūteweard, ūtweard,* fr. *ūtan* outside, from outside (fr. *ūt* out), *ūte* out, outside (fr. *ūt* out), & *ūt* out + *-weard* -ward — more at OUT] **1 a :** moving, directed, or turned toward the outside or away from a center ⟨the inward or ~ flow of money —*Jour. of Accountancy*⟩ ⟨the gradual ~ slope of the spur ridges —C.B. Hitchcock⟩ ⟨an ~ journey⟩ **b :** of or relating to a movement toward the outside ⟨the cost of returning a parcel includes postage, generally equivalent to the ~ charge —*Great Britain Post Office Guide*⟩ **2 :** situated or lying on the outside of an enclosure or surface **:** EXTERIOR ⟨found the place where I was to lie . . . close and confined . . . and therefore lay all night in an ~ room —Tobias Smollett⟩ **3 :** of or relating to the body and its surface appearance and clothing as opposed to the mind or spirit **:** BODILY, EXTERNAL ⟨~ man⟩ ⟨~ beauty⟩ ⟨~ form⟩ **4 a :** of or relating to an external act, activity, happening, or condition as distinguished from a mental or emotional process ⟨the chief ~ events of his life⟩ ⟨the new job represented a great improvement in his ~ status⟩ ⟨a feverish ~ display of energy⟩ **b :** of or relating to material objects as opposed to ideal concepts ⟨we alone wore ~ shackles —Mary Johnston⟩ **c :** of or relating to form as distinguished from essence ⟨began to find a recognized place in the ~ pattern of church life —*Eastern Churches Quarterly*⟩ **5** *dial Eng* **:** inclined to drink **:** DISSIPATED **syn** see OUTER

²**outward** \"\ *or* **out·wards** \-dz\ *adv* [*outward* fr. ME, fr. OE *ūtanweard, ūteweard, ūtweard,* fr. *ūtanweard, ūteweard, ūtweard,* adj.; *outwards* fr. ME *outwardes,* fr. OE *ūtweardes,* fr. *ūtweard,* adj. & adv. + *-es* -s] **1 a :** toward the outside **:** away from a center or starting point ⟨the eternally ~ moving stars —*N.Y. Times*⟩ ⟨the city stretches ~ for many miles⟩ **b :** from the soul or mind toward external manifestation **2** *obs* **:** on the outside **:** EXTERNALLY ⟨they have a good cover, they show well ~ —Shak.⟩

³**out·ward** \'au̇twə(r)d\ *n* -s [¹*outward*] **1 :** external form or appearance **:** OUTSIDE ⟨so fair an ~ and such stuff within —Shak.⟩ **2 :** the material world ⟨can perceive the ~ and the inward, nature's good and God's —Robert Browning⟩

**outward-bound** \'=¦=\ *adj* **:** bound in an outward direction or to foreign parts ⟨an *outward-bound* ship⟩ — **outward-bound·er** \-də(r)\ *n*

**outward-flow turbine** \'=ˌ=-\ *n* **:** a water turbine in which the discharge stage of flow is away from the axis

**out·ward·ly** *adv* [ME, fr. *outward,* adj. + *-ly*] **1 a :** on the outside **:** EXTERNALLY ⟨~ visible⟩ ⟨~ apparent⟩ **b :** toward the outside **:** in an outward direction ⟨we see ~ and represent the apparent nature of things —Herbert Read⟩ **2 :** in outward state, behavior, or appearance ⟨his ~ more fortunate fellows —Kenneth Fearing⟩ ⟨~ diffident, inwardly dreamy —Jean S. Untermeyer⟩ ⟨~ a placid island —Patrick Smith⟩

**out·ward·ness** *n* -ES **1 :** the quality or state of being outward **:** EXTERNALITY ⟨the ~ of the world⟩ **2 :** concern with or responsiveness to outward things ⟨hearty showmanship and all-around ~ —F.H.Gervasi⟩

**outwash** \'=ˌ=\ *n, often attrib* [³*out* + *wash* (after *wash out,* v.)] **1 a :** detritus chiefly consisting of gravel and sand carried by running water from the melting ice of a glacier and laid down in stratified deposits **:** glaciofluvial drift **b :** meltwater from a glacier **2 :** soil material washed down a hillside by rainwater and spread upon the more gently sloping adjacent land

**outwash cone** *or* **outwash fan** *n* **:** a cone-shaped or fanlike mass of outwash that is ordinarily found at the margin of a dwindling glacier or shrinking ice sheet

**outwash plain** *also* **outwash apron** *n* **:** a plain constructed of outwash that is ordinarily found on and beyond the distal side of a terminal or recessional moraine and that generally consists of a number of coalescing outwash fans

**outwash train** *n* **:** VALLEY TRAIN

**outwatch** \(')=¦=\ *vt* [*out-* + *watch*] **1 :** to surpass in watching **:** maintain a longer vigil than ⟨~ his companions⟩ **2 :** to maintain a vigil till after the disappearance or end of ⟨~ the moon⟩ ⟨~ the night⟩

**outwear** \(')=¦=\ *vt* [¹*out* + *wear*] **1 :** to wear out or use up **:** consume or destroy by attrition or use **:** EXHAUST ⟨drops of water ~ stone⟩ ⟨the machinery has been *outworn*⟩ ⟨the rowers were *outworn*⟩ **2 a** [*out-* + *wear*] **:** to last longer in use than ⟨a fiber that ~s others⟩ **b :** to grow or develop beyond in course of time **:** OUTGROW, OUTLIVE ⟨in cases where tradition is notoriously *outworn* —W.C.Brownell⟩ **3** *archaic* **:** to take up the time of ⟨with sick longing all the night ~ —John Keats⟩

**outweep** \(')=¦=\ *vt* [¹*out* + *weep*] **1** *archaic* **:** to weep out ⟨like a cloud which had *outwept* its rain —P.B.Shelley⟩ **2** [*out-* + *weep*] **:** to surpass in weeping ⟨can ~ any woman⟩

**outweigh** \(')=¦=\ *vt* [*out-* + *weigh*] **:** to exceed in weight, value, or importance ⟨an ounce of custom ~s a ton of reason —William Hamilton †1856⟩ ⟨no dangers could ~ the advantages of steamboat transportation —*Amer. Guide Series: Ark.*⟩

**outwell** \(')=¦=\ *vb* [¹*out* + *well*] *vt, obs* **:** to pour out ~ *vi* **:** to well out

**outwent** *past of* OUTGO

¹**outwick** \'=ˌ=\ *n* [³*out* + *wick*] **:** a shot in curling in which a player's stone is made to hit the outer edge of another stone so as to drive the latter toward the tee — compare INWICK

²**outwick** \"\ *vi* **:** to make an outwick

¹**outwind** \'=ˌ=\ *n* [³*out* + *wind*] **:** a wind from the sea

²**outwind** \(')=¦=\ *vt* [¹*out* + *wind*] **:** to put out of breath ⟨an ~*ed* runner⟩

**outwing** \(')=¦=\ *vt* [*out-* + *wing*] **1 :** to outstrip or pass in flying **2 :** OUTFLANK

**outwinter** \(')=¦==\ *vb* [¹*out* + *winter*] *vt* **:** to keep (cattle) outdoors in winter ⟨the cost of feeding ~*ed* cattle —T.H. Jackson⟩ ~ *vi* **:** to stay outdoors in winter ⟨the Jersey can ~ provided the climate is not very damp —F.D.Smith & Barbara Wilcox⟩

**outwit** \(')=¦=\ *vt* [*out-* + *wit*] **1 :** to defeat or get the better of by superior cleverness or ingenuity **:** OVERREACH ⟨how best to ~ the youngster and set him to learning when he is not fully aware of it —G.N.Shuster⟩ ⟨three men, caught *outwitting* an innocent pinball machine with a powerful magnet —*Phoenix Flame*⟩ **2** *archaic* **:** to surpass in wisdom ⟨outsee seers and ~ sages —R.W.Emerson⟩ **syn** see FRUSTRATE

**outwith** \'=ˌ=\ *prep* [ME, fr. ¹*out* + *with*] **1** *chiefly Scot* **:** outside of **:** out of **2** *chiefly Scot* **:** EXCEPT

**outwore** *past of* OUTWEAR

¹**outwork** \(')=¦=\ *vt* [¹*out* + *work*] **1 :** to work out **:** COMPLETE ⟨saw, in web unbroken, its history *outwrought* —Thomas Hardy⟩ **2** [*out-* + *work*] *archaic* **:** to surpass in workmanship **3** [*out-* + *work*] **:** to outdo in working **:** work harder or faster than ⟨~s his competitors⟩

²**outwork** \'=ˌ=\ *n* [³*out* + *work*] **1 a :** an outlying point of defense ⟨had been forced to abandon her ~s across the Rhine and the Danube —Richard Koebner⟩ ⟨impairs not only the ~s but the citadel of personality —Walter Moberly⟩ **b :** a small defensive position constructed outside a fortified area **2 :** work done outside the shop or institution from which it is directed or for which it is performed

**outworker** \'=ˌ==\ *n* [³*out* + *worker*] **:** one that works outside the institution or shop by which he is employed

**outworld** \'=ˌ=\ *n* [³*out* + *world*] **:** the outside world

**outworn** \'=¦=\ *adj* [fr. past part. of *outwear*] **1 :** no longer useful or accepted **:** OUTMODED, OBSOLETE ⟨still attempted to cling to the ~ ethics professed at the dawning of the Gilded Age —J.D.Hart⟩ ⟨an ~ road⟩ **2 :** worn out **:** used up **:** EXHAUSTED ⟨an ~ champion pugilist —Stanley Walker⟩

**outwrestle** \(')=¦==\ *vt* [*out-* + *wrestle*] **:** to defeat in wrestling **:** grapple with successfully

**outwrite** \(')=¦=\ *vt* [*out-* + *write*] **1 :** to surpass in ability to write ⟨historian for historian, journalist for journalist, they ~ us —R.H.Rovere⟩ **2** [¹*out* + *write*] **:** to throw off or overcome by writing ⟨*outwrote* his depression⟩

**outwrought** *past of* OUTWORK

**outyell** \(')=¦=\ *vt* [*out-* + *yell*] **:** to yell louder than ⟨women quarreling and trying to ~ each other —H.L.Davis⟩

**outyield** \(')=¦=\ *vt* [*out-* + *yield*] **:** to surpass in yield ⟨fall-sown or winter oats matured earlier and ~*ed* spring oats —*Experiment Station Record*⟩

**ouvarovite** *var of* UVAROVITE

**ou·vert** \(')ü¦ve(ə)r\ *adj* [F, lit., open, fr. OF *overt* — more at OVERT] **1** *ballet* **:** having an open stance or movement **2** *card games* **:** OPEN 17b(2)

**ou·zel** *also* **ou·sel** \'üzəl\ *n* -s [ME *ousel, osel,* fr. OE *ōsle* — more at MERL] **1 :** a European blackbird (*Turdus merula*) **2 :** any of various thrushes or other birds that are related to the ouzel — see RING OUZEL, WATER OUZEL

**ou·zo** \'ü(ˌ)zō\ *n* -s [NGk *ouzon*] **:** a colorless anise-flavored unsweetened Greek liqueur that turns milk-white when mixed with water and ice

**ov-** *or* **ovi-** *or* **ovo-** *comb form* [L *ov-, ovi-,* fr. *ovum* — more at EGG] **1 a :** egg ⟨*ov*ejector⟩ ⟨*ovi*form⟩ ⟨*ovo*mucoid⟩ **b :** ovum ⟨*ovo*cyte⟩ ⟨*ovo*genesis⟩ **2 :** ovally ⟨*ovo*-elliptic⟩

**ov** *abbr* ovum

**OV** *abbr* **1** oil of vitriol **2** over voltage

**ova** *pl of* OVUM

¹**oval** \'ōvəl\ *adj* [ML *ovalis,* fr. LL, of an egg, fr. L *ovum* egg + *-alis* -al] **:** having the shape of an oval **:** broadly elliptical ⟨an ~ ball⟩ — often used in combination ⟨an *oval*-faced child⟩ — **oval·ly** \-vəl(l)ē, -i\ *adv*

²**oval** \"\ *n* -s **1 :** a body or figure generally in the shape of the longitudinal section of an egg **2 :** an object of oval or ellipsoidal shape: as **a :** a cartouche of an Egyptian king **b** (1) **:** a stadium, arena, or athletic field of oval shape (2) **:** RUNNING TRACK, RACETRACK

oval 1

³**oval** \"\ *vb* **ovaled** *or* **ovalled; ovaled** *or* **ovalled; ovaling** \-v(ə)liŋ\ *or* **ovalling; ovals** *vt* **:** to make oval ~ *vi* **:** to become oval

**ov·albumin** \(')ōv+\ *n* [*ov-* + *albumin*] **1 :** the principal albumin of white of egg; *esp* **:** the crystalline part of egg albumins — compare CONALBUMIN **2 :** EGG ALBUMIN

**oval·i·ty** \ō'valəd·ē\ *n* -ES [ISV ¹*oval* + *-ity*] **:** the quality or state of being oval in shape **:** degree of departure from true circularity ⟨~ of a worn gun bore⟩

**oval·ness** \'ōvəlnəs\ *n* -ES **:** OVALITY

**ovalo·cyte** \ō'valəˌsīt, 'ōvəlō,s-\ *n* -s [ISV ¹*oval* + *-o-* + *-cyte*] **:** an oval red blood cell normal in the camel and occurring as a rare hereditary anomaly in man — **ovalo·cyt·ic** \=¦==ˌ=¦sid·ik, ¦==-\ *adj*

**ovalo·cy·to·sis** \ˌ==ˌsī'tōsəs, ˌ==(ˌ)s-\ *n, pl* **ovalocyto·ses** \-ō,sēz\ [NL, fr. ISV *ovalocyte* + NL *-osis*] **:** a hereditary trait in man manifested by the presence in the blood of red blood cells which are oval in shape with rounded ends — compare SICKLEMIA

**oval·oid** \'ōvə,lȯid\ *adj* [²*oval* + *-oid*] **:** approximately oval

**oval window** *n* [trans. of NL *fenestra ovalis*] **:** the oval fenestra of the ear

**ovari-** *or* **ovario-** *also* **ovar-** *comb form* [NL, fr. *ovarium*] **1 :** ovary ⟨*ovar*itis⟩ ⟨*ovari*ectomy⟩ ⟨*ovario*tomy⟩ **2 :** ovarian and ⟨*ovario*-abdominal⟩

**ovar·i·al** \(')ō¦va(a)rēəl, -ver-, -vār-\ *adj* [prob. fr. (assumed) NL *ovarialis,* fr. NL *ovari-* + L *-alis* -al] **:** of, involving, or affecting an ovary ⟨~ function⟩ ⟨~ poisons⟩

**ovar·i·an** \-ēən\ *adj* [prob. fr. (assumed) NL *ovarianus,* fr. NL *ovari-* + L *-anus* -an] **:** of or relating to an ovary

**ovari·ec·to·mize** \(ˌ)ō,va(a)rē'ektə,mīz, ,ovər-\ *vt* -ED/-ING/-S [*ovariectomy* + *-ize*] **:** to remove an ovary surgically from

**ovari·ec·to·my** \-,mē\ *n* -ES [NL *ovariectomia,* fr. *ovari-* + *-ectomia* -ectomy] **:** the surgical removal of an ovary

**ovar·i·ole** \ō'va(a)rē,ōl\ *n* -s [*ovari-* + *-ole*] **:** one of the tubes of which the ovaries of most insects are composed

**ovar·io·testis** \ō¦va(a)rēō+\ *n* [NL, fr. *ovari-* + L *testis*] **:** OVOTESTIS

**ovar·i·ot·o·my** \(ˌ)ō,va(a)rē'äd·əmē\ *n* -ES [NL *ovariotomia,* fr. *ovari-* + *-tomia* -tomy] **1 :** surgical incision of an ovary **2 :** OVARIECTOMY

**ova·ri·tis** \ˌōvə'rīd·əs\ *n, pl* **ova·rit·i·des** \-rid·ə,dēz\ [NL, fr. *ovari-* + *-itis*] **:** inflammation of an ovary **:** OOPHORITIS

**ovar·i·um** \ō'va(a)rēəm\ *n, pl* **ovar·ia** \-ēə\ [NL] *archaic* **:** OVARY

**ova·ry** \'ōv(ə)rē, -ri\ *n* -ES [NL *ovarium,* fr. L *ovum* egg + *-arium* -ary — more at EGG] **1 :** the typically paired essential female reproductive organ that produces eggs and in vertebrates female sex hormones, that occurs in the adult human as an oval flattened body about one inch and one half long suspended from the dorsal surface of the broad ligament of either side, that arises from the Wolffian body, and that consists of a vascular fibrous stroma enclosing developing egg cells which in their later stages with nutricial structures constitute Graafian follicles **2 :** the enlarged rounded usu. basal portion of the pistil or gynoecium of an angiospermous plant that bears the ovules and consists of a single carpel or of several united carpels — see FLOWER illustration

¹**ovate** \'ō,vāt, 'ävət\ *n* -s [modif. of Gk *ouateis,* pl., members of one of three classes of Gaulish bards, prob. of Celt origin; akin to OIr *fāith* seer, poet — more at VATIC] **:** one of a class of bards in Wales graduated in bardic lore and approved by a session of bards

²**ovate** \'ō,vāt, *usu* -ād·+V\ *adj* [L *ovatus,* fr. *ovum* egg + *-atus* -ate] **1 :** shaped like an egg **:** OVAL — often used in combination ⟨*ovate*-oblong⟩ ⟨*ovate*-deltoid⟩ **2 :** having an outline like that of the longitudinal section of an egg with the basal end broader ⟨~ leaves⟩ — see LEAF illustration

**ova·tion** \ō'vāshən\ *n* -s [L *ovation-, ovatio,* fr. *ovatus* (past part. of *ovare* to exult, rejoice) + *-ion-, -io* -ion; akin to Gk *euazein* to shout for joy, *euoi,* interjection used in Dionysiac celebrations] **1 :** a ceremony attending the entering of Rome by a general who had won a victory of less importance than that for which a triumph was granted **2** *archaic* **:** EXULTATION **3 :** enthusiastic popular homage or a public expression of it **:** an enthusiastic popular reception or tribute ⟨received an ~ as he entered the hall⟩

²**ovation** \"\ *vt* -ED/-ING/-S **:** to give an ovation ⟨will all be there . . . to ~ you —Barnaby Conrad⟩

**ova·tion·al** \ō'vāshən°l, -shnəl\ *adj* **:** of or relating to an ovation

**ovc** *abbr* overcast

**ov·e·jec·tor** *also* **ovi·jec·tor** \'ōvə̇,jektə(r), -vē,j-\ *n* -s [ISV *ov-* + *ejector;* orig. formed as F *ovéjecteur*] **:** the terminal highly muscular part of the oviduct of many nematode worms that forces the egg through the genital pore — **ovejectoral** *adj*

**ov·en** \'əvən *sometimes* 'əv°m *or* 'əb°m\ *n* -s [ME, fr. OE *ofen;* akin to OHG *ofan* oven, ON *ofn,* Goth *auhns* oven, L *aulla* pot, Gk *ipnos* oven, Skt *ukha* cooking pot] **1** *obs* **:** FURNACE **2 a :** a chamber of brick or stonework used for baking, heating, or drying **b :** a heated enclosure of varying construction used for such purposes: as (1) **:** a chamber in a stove used for baking or roasting (2) **:** a laboratory hot-air sterilizer

**ovenbird** \'==ˌ=\ *n* [*oven* + *bird;* fr. the shape of their nests] **1 :** any of various So. American passerine birds of the genus *Furnarius* **2 :** an American warbler (*Seiurus aurocapillus*) having olivaceous upper parts with a yellowish brown black-bordered crown, white underparts streaked with black and building a dome-shaped nest placed on the ground

**oven dressed** *adj* **:** ready for cooking **:** FULL-DRESSED ⟨*oven dressed* poultry⟩

**ovendry** \'==¦=\ *adj* [*oven* + *dry,* adj.] **:** dried at a temperature at or above that of boiling water (usu. 100 to 110°C or 212 to 230°F)

**oven–dry** \¦==¦=\ *vt* [*oven* + *dry,* v.] **:** to dry in an oven

**ovenman** \'==,man\ *n, pl* **ovenmen 1 :** a baker who tends an oven **2 :** a worker who bakes parts or products in an oven to harden and strengthen them or to harden their finish

**ovenware** \'==ˌ=\ *n* **:** pottery dishes used for baking and serving food

**oven wood** *n* **:** BRUSHWOOD

¹**over** \'ōvə(r)\ *adv* [ME, adv. & prep., fr. OE *ofer;* akin to OHG *ubari, ubiri,* adv., over, *ubar,* prep., over, ON *yfir,* adv. & prep., Goth *ufar,* prep., over, L *super,* adv. & prep., over, Gk *hyper,* adv. & prep., Skt *upari,* adv. & prep., over, OE *ufan* above] **1 a** (1) **:** from one point to another across an intervening space or barrier ⟨sail ~ to England⟩ ⟨throw the ball ~⟩ ⟨galloped ~ to the scene —H.E.Scudder⟩ ⟨the major called the three ~ —C. G. De Van⟩ (2) **:** so as to pass down or forward and down ⟨went too near the edge and fell ~⟩ (3) **:** from inside to outside across the brim ⟨the soup boiled ~⟩ (4) **:** so as to bring the underside to or toward the top ⟨turned himself ~⟩ ⟨roll a stone ~⟩ ⟨turn the page ~⟩ (5) **:** in the opposite direction ⟨gave the order to put the helm ~ —A. A. & Mary Hoehling⟩ (6) **:** over the side of a ship ⟨put a boat ~ to come and look for you —R.F.Mirvish⟩ ⟨put the ladder ~ —Vincent McHugh⟩ (7) **:** from side to side **:** in diameter **:** ACROSS ⟨the mouth of the cave was about 12 feet ~⟩ (8) **:** so as to pass over a target and beyond ⟨the bullets fell short or went ~⟩ (9) **:** away from a vertical to a prone or inclined position ⟨knocked the boy ~⟩ ⟨the wall fell ~⟩ ⟨the ship heeled ~⟩ (10) **:** to one's home ⟨inviting fifteen or twenty of her friends ~ for fun and games —*N.Y.Times*⟩ **b** (1) **:** on the other side of an intervening space ⟨is ~ in England⟩ (2) **:** at some distance from a particular point **:** AWAY ⟨a fellow a couple of counties ~ —Brad Sebstad⟩ ⟨from two blocks ~ he could hear the thin wail —H.M.Brier⟩ ⟨the bomb hit the next pier ~ —R.O.Bowen⟩ **c** (1) **:** so as to pass or transfer from one person, side, activity, or opinion to another ⟨hand ~ the money⟩ ⟨theater orchestras . . . had gone ~ completely to it —*Amer. Guide Series: Wash.*⟩ ⟨endorsed it ~ to the . . . Housing Corporation —Walter Olivier⟩ ⟨turned it ~ to her daughter —*Amer. Guide Series: Ark.*⟩ ⟨went ~ to the opposition⟩ (2) **:** so as to achieve understanding, acceptance, support, or other desired effect — usu. used with *get* ⟨are not getting ~ to those whom we are addressing —A.T.Weaver⟩ ⟨get your effect and your meaning ~ to the orchestra —Warwick Braithwaite⟩ ⟨wants to get his own message ~ —W.F.Hambly⟩ (3) **:** into one's own possession **:** so as to be in control ⟨the university took it ~ —*Amer. Guide Series: Md.*⟩ ⟨took ~ after a revolt⟩ ⟨took ~ from a firm that had gone into liquidation —*Irish Digest*⟩ — compare TAKE OVER **d :** ASIDE ⟨throwing ~ traditional morality⟩ **2 a :** beyond, above, or in excess of some quantity or limit ⟨boys of twelve and ~⟩ **b** (1) **:** in or to excess **:** beyond the norm ⟨she was ~ canvassed —Peter Heaton⟩ ⟨they were seven minutes ~⟩ (2) **:** INORDINATELY, EXCESSIVELY — often used in combination ⟨on his guard against *over*quick deductions —A.E.Duncan-Jones⟩ ⟨just naturally *over*registers emotion —*Current Biog.*⟩ ⟨*over*conservative traditionalists —John Arlott⟩ **c :** till a later time ⟨leave this new inquiry ~ till Monday —F.W.Crofts⟩ ⟨so glad you can stay ~⟩ **3 a :** ABOVE ⟨the plane was directly ~⟩ **b :** so as to cover, conceal, or affect the whole surface or expanse ⟨the original logs were boarded ~ —*Amer. Guide Series: Ark.*⟩ **4 a :** at an end ⟨those great days are ~ —D.W. Brogan⟩ ⟨it's all ~ between them⟩ ⟨the gathering of the grain and hay was ~ —Gordon Webber⟩ — often used in the phrase *over with* ⟨hurrying to get the business ~ with⟩ **b** — used on a two-way radio circuit to indicate that a particular sentence or message is complete and that a reply is expected **5 a** (1) **:** from beginning to end **:** THROUGH ⟨read it ~ and let me know what you think⟩ (2) **:** in an intensive or comprehensive manner **:** THOROUGHLY ⟨the issue is worked ~ in the most . . . compelling scene of the play —Leslie Rees⟩ ⟨talk the matter ~⟩ **b** (1) **:** for a second or successive time **:** once more **:** AGAIN ⟨this work will have to be done ~⟩ ⟨read the difficult passage twice ~⟩ — often used in the phrase *over again* ⟨asked to recite the verse ~ again⟩ (2) **:** so as to be transformed or changed from a previous state or condition ⟨a man cannot make himself ~⟩

²**over** \"\ *prep* [ME, adv. & prep., fr. OE *ofer* — more at ¹OVER] **1 a** (1) — used as a function word to indicate position higher up than and usu. directly above another object ⟨~ the elm tops in the west —Lucien Price⟩ ⟨towered ~ his diminutive mother⟩ ⟨leaned ~ the rampart⟩ (2) — used as a function word to indicate a surrounding condition or threatening prospect ⟨an atmosphere of doubt and uncertainty hung ~ the town⟩ (3) — used as a function word to indicate that the author's name is subscribed to a writing ⟨sent a letter to the paper ~ his own signature⟩ (4) **:** above the mental capacity or beyond the comprehension of — usu. used in the phrase *over the head of* ⟨his lecture was way ~ the heads of his audience⟩ **b** (1) — used as a function word to indicate submersion above a specified level ⟨~ his waist in water⟩ (2) — used as a function word to indicate extreme or acute embarrassment or difficulty of a specified kind ⟨~ head and ears in debt⟩ **2 a** — used as a function word to indicate the possession or enjoyment of authority, power, or jurisdiction in regard to some thing or person ⟨installed as minister ~ one of the largest congregations in the city⟩ ⟨unfailing in their service of those ~ them —E.R.Hughes⟩ **b** — used as a function word to indicate a relation of superiority, advantage, or preference to another ⟨the relative importance of the abstract ~ the pictorial —C.J. Bulliet⟩ ⟨taking an unprecedented lead ~ the other teams —*Current Biog.*⟩ ⟨this excess of wealth ~ population —W.P. Webb⟩; often used in the phrase *have it over* or *have it all over* ⟨the Britisher in America has it ~ the anthropologist —V.O. Key⟩ **c** — used as a function word to indicate suppression of or release from a passion, infatuation, or other strong feeling ⟨finally got ~ his mad⟩ ⟨never got ~ his love for the baroque —*Current Biog.*⟩ **d** — used as a function word to indicate someone or something that is overcome, circumvented, or disregarded in achieving an objective ⟨we got ~ him —Adrian Bell⟩ ⟨passed ~ the president's veto —*Current Biog.*⟩ **3 a** *archaic* **:** further than **:** BESIDES **b :** more than ⟨cost ~ five dollars⟩ **4 a** (1) **:** upon or down upon so as to rest, cover, or conceal from view ⟨~ which they throw a bridge of flowers —*Amer. Guide Series: La.*⟩ ⟨laid a blanket ~ the sleeping child⟩ ⟨a cap pulled low ~ his eyes⟩ ⟨got some blood ~ your face —Burt Arthur⟩ (2) **:** upon or down upon so as to change or otherwise influence in a pervasive manner ⟨don't know what has come ~ the girl⟩ (3) **:** ON, UPON ⟨bop people ~ the head —Bennett Cerf⟩ ⟨rap a child ~ the knuckles⟩ (4) — used as a function word to indicate change, variation, or difference from some other thing or period ⟨this year's copy contains no innovations ~ those in the past —*Springfield (Mass.) Daily News*⟩ ⟨a drop of three ~ 1956 —*Springfield (Mass.) Daily News*⟩ **b** (1) **:** at or to all the parts of the surface of **:** throughout a specified area ⟨the common toad is found ~ the entire state —*Amer. Guide Series: Minn.*⟩ ⟨packing and shipping concerns who sell the U.S. ~ —*Spokane (Wash.) Spokesman-Rev.*⟩ — often used with intensive *all* ⟨the rumor is all ~ Washington —T.R.Ybarra⟩ ⟨votive chapels sprang up in his honor

all ~ Italy —Norman Douglas⟩ (2) **:** along the length of ⟨~ stony roads that soon wear out the lorries —Michael Barbour⟩ ⟨~ its one-way street system move only the most modern cars —C.B.Hitchcock⟩ (3) — used as a function word to indicate a particular medium or channel of communication ⟨hear one another ~ the air —G.W.Chapman⟩ ⟨spoke to me ~ the telephone⟩ ⟨gave several recitals ~ the . . . network —*Current Biog.*⟩ **c** (1) **:** through every part of **:** all through ⟨the present comtesse . . . showed me ~ it —Ralph Hammond-Innes⟩ (2) — used as a function word to indicate study, review, or examination of something ⟨went ~ his notes in preparation for the quiz⟩ ⟨go ~ the case with the defense attorney⟩ **5 a** — used as a function word to indicate motion that passes above something on the way to the other side or to a place beyond ⟨does a series of tumbles ~ rocky ledges —Y.E.Soderberg⟩ ⟨climb ~ a mountain⟩ ⟨fly ~ a lake⟩ ⟨attack ~ a frontier⟩ ⟨put a boat ~ a ship's side⟩ **b** — used as a function word to indicate position on the other side or beyond ⟨lives in a little shop ~ the way —H.V.Morton⟩ **6 a :** THROUGHOUT, DURING ⟨many times prime minister of his country ~ the past 25 years —Geoffrey Godsell⟩ ⟨lost the use of their eyes through living underground ~ many generations —S.F.Mason⟩ ⟨had written it nights and ~ weekends —*Current Biog.*⟩ **b :** until the end of **:** for a period including ⟨invited us to stay ~ Sunday⟩ ⟨stationed in an isolated post ~ winter⟩ **7 a** — used as a function word to indicate an object of solicitude, interest, consideration, or reference ⟨the Lord watches ~ his own⟩ ⟨laughed ~ my misadventures⟩ ⟨his curiosity ~ the materials and tools —C.D.Gaitskell⟩ ⟨gives way to an intolerable degree of sentimentality ~ some of his women —C.H.Sykes⟩ ⟨am with you ~ this⟩ **b** — used as a function word often with an accompanying concrete word to indicate occupation or activity ⟨spent an hour ~ cards⟩ ⟨deciding to wait ~ a beer —Ralph Ellison⟩ ⟨enjoy an evening with me ~ a bite to eat —Frank O'Leary⟩ **c :** on account of ⟨embittered ~ this fate —L.S.Thompson⟩ ⟨got himself into disgrace ~ some caricatures of military personages —*Times Lit. Supp.*⟩ **8** *card games* **:** next in turn to play after (another card player) — **over a barrel** *adv* **:** at the mercy of one's opponents **:** in a helpless condition ⟨had him *over a barrel*⟩

**³over** \"\ *adj* [ME, alter. (influenced by ¹*over*) of *uvere*, fr. OE *uferra*, compar. of *ofer*, adv. — more at ¹OVER] **1 a :** UPPER, HIGHER, SUPERIOR **b :** COVERING, OUTER **c :** EXCESSIVE ⟨too hasty interpretations and ~ imagination —W.E.Swinton⟩ — often used in combination ⟨*over*activity is not recommended for the patient⟩ **2 a :** REMAINING ⟨that didn't leave me much ~ —Albert Halper⟩ ⟨something ~ to provide for unusual requirements —J.A.Todd⟩ **b :** having an excess or surplus ⟨the cash is said to be ~ —*Twentieth Century Bookkeeping & Accounting*⟩ **3 :** fried on both sides ⟨ordered two eggs ~⟩

**⁴over** \"\ *vt* -ED/-ING/-S [¹*over*] **1** *dial* **:** to get over **:** recover from ⟨whether you ~*ed* a snakebite or not —Conrad Richter⟩ **2** *dial Eng* **:** to bring to an end **:** FINISH **3 :** to leap over **:** CLEAR ⟨~*ed* a stile —A.T.Quiller-Couch⟩ **4** *dial Eng* **:** to be over with ⟨the Sabbath not yet ~*ed* —Charlotte Brontë⟩

**⁵over** *n* -S [¹*over*] **1** [so called fr. the umpire's cry of "*over*" to declare all play for that series at an end] **:** a series of 6 or 8 cricket balls bowled consecutively by one bowler from one end of the wicket **2 overs** *pl, Brit* **:** extra sheets of paper in a ream to allow for spoilage in printing **3 overs** *pl* **:** LUMBERMEN'S OVERS **4 overs** *pl* **:** material that does not pass through any given screen in the milling process **5 :** a shot which strikes or bursts beyond the target

**overabound** \ˌ==ˈ=\ *vi* [ME *overabounden*, fr. ¹*over* + *abounden* to abound] **:** to abound too much **:** be too abundant

**overabundance** \ˌ====\ *n* [ME, fr. ³*over* + *abundance*, *abundaunce* abundance] **:** an excessive abundance **:** SURFEIT, EXCESS, PLETHORA ⟨an ~ of experience with totalitarian governments —John Dean⟩

**overabundant** \ˌ====\ *adj* [¹*over* + *abundant*] **:** surpassingly abundant

**overaccumulation** \ˌ===,==ˈ==\ *n* **:** an undue or excessive accumulation

**overact** \ˌ==ˈ=\ *vt* **1 :** to act or perform (as a part) to excess **:** exaggerate in acting **2** *obs* **:** to outdo in acting **3** *obs* **:** to act upon or influence unduly ~ *vi* **1 :** to act more than is necessary **:** go to excess in action ⟨which muscles of the eyes are . . . ~*ing* —H.G.Armstrong⟩ **2 :** to overact a part

**overaction** \ˌ==ˈ==\ *n* **:** excessive or abnormal action

**overactive** \ˌ==ˈ==\ *adj* **:** excessively or abnormally active ⟨an ~ mind⟩ ⟨~ glands⟩

**overactivity** \ˌ==,=ˈ===\ *n* **:** excessive or abnormal activity

**over against** *prep* **:** as opposed to **:** in contrast with ⟨the failure of Christianity *over against* Islam in successive ages —*Brit. Book News*⟩

**¹overage** \ˌōvə(r)ˈāj\ *adj* [²*over* + *age*, n.] **1 :** too old or regarded as too old to be serviceable or useful ⟨~ warships⟩ ⟨an ~ stand of timber⟩ **2 :** older than is normal for one's position, function, or grade ⟨~ students⟩

**²over·age** \ˈōvərij\ *n* [³*over* + *-age*] **1 :** SURPLUS, EXCESS; *specif* **:** the amount of a product above that recorded as having been shipped or placed in storage **2 :** an excess over a required amount ⟨an ~ was disclosed⟩ — opposed to *shortage* **3 :** the quantity of a pharmaceutical included in a container in excess of the labeled amount (as in an ampul containing a liquid medication intended for injection)

**¹over·all** \ˌōvəˌ(r)ˈȯl\ *adv* [ME *overal*, fr. OE *ofer eall*, fr. *ofer* over + *eall* all] **1 a :** all over **:** EVERYWHERE ⟨man was ripe for civilization and erupted into it ~ —D.S.Stewart⟩ ⟨ships in the fjord were dressed ~ —*London Calling*⟩ **b :** as a whole **:** IN TOTO, GENERALLY ⟨~, the picture quality was good —Cecil McGivern⟩ ⟨~ and in most of its detail the film has remarkable power —*Time*⟩ **2 :** from one extreme point to another of anything including any projections; *specif* **:** from the extreme forward point to the extreme after point of the deck of a ship including overhangs ⟨the boat's dimensions are 34 feet ~ —*Rudder*⟩

**²over·all** \ˈōvəˌrȯl, *chiefly in substand speech* -və(r),hȯ- *in sense 1b*\ *n* -S [²*over* + *all*, pron.] **1 overalls** *pl* **a** *archaic* **:** loose trousers or leggings worn over regular clothes as a protection from bad weather or dirt **b :** close-fitting trousers worn as part of certain British uniforms or for formal riding **c :** trousers made of strong material usu. with a bib and shoulder straps and worn esp. by workmen **2** *chiefly Brit* **:** an outer garment; *esp* **:** a loose-fitting protective garment like a long coat or a smock worn over regular clothing ⟨a laboratory worker in a white ~⟩

overalls 1b

**³over·all** \ˌōvəˌ(r)ˈȯl\ *adj* [²*over* + *all*, pron.] **1 :** including everything between the two extreme points ⟨the ~ length of a ship⟩ **2 a :** taking all units into account **:** TOTAL ⟨~ sales of wholesalers . . . increased 10% —*Americana Annual*⟩ ⟨judge what the ~ demand . . . may be —C.F. Craig⟩ ⟨~ industry growth seems well assured —*Brookmire Investment Reports*⟩ **b :** of or relating to something as a whole **:** viewed as a whole **:** GENERAL ⟨liked the ~ composition and design —Levon West⟩ ⟨the ~ picture . . . was bright —*New Englander*⟩ **:** COMPREHENSIVE ⟨an ~ view of the problem⟩ **3 :** placed over or upon other bearings and therefore hiding them in part — used of a charge

**over·alled** \-vəˌrȯld, -və(r),hȯ-\ *adj* **:** wearing overalls ⟨~ women⟩

**overall pattern** *n* **:** an array of phonetic categories that is necessary and sufficient to account for all phonemes of all dialects of a language

**overall watermark** *n* **:** SHEET WATERMARK

**overambitious** \ˌ==,=ˈ==\ *adj* **:** excessively ambitious ⟨a mother ~ for her precocious child⟩

**over and above** *prep* **:** in addition to **:** BESIDES ⟨provides a financial return *over and above* all direct and indirect costs —R.A.Tybout⟩

**over and over** *adv* **:** one time after another **:** REPEATEDLY

**over-and-under** \ˌ===ˈ==\ *n* -S **:** a 2-barreled firearm whose barrels are fixed one above the other

**overanxious** \ˌ==ˈ==\ *adj* **:** excessively or needlessly anxious

**overarch** \ˌ==ˈ=\ *vt* **1 :** to form an arch over ⟨dense masses ~*ing* the stream —John Muir †1914⟩ **2 :** to be central or decisive in **:** DOMINATE ⟨an utterance which ~*es* the whole conception of the play —R.O.F.Wynne⟩

**overarching** *adj* **1 :** forming an arch overhead ⟨the ~ sky⟩ **2 :** subordinating or encompassing all else **:** ALL-IMPORTANT, DOMINANT ⟨the relation of man's freedom to God's ~ power —Liston Pope⟩ ⟨the ~ thesis of this book⟩ ⟨the ~ fact —*Reporter*⟩ ⟨different aspects of an ~ goal —J.R.Butler⟩

**¹overarm** \ˈ==,=\ *adj* [³*over* + *arm*, n.] **:** done with the arm raised above the shoulder ⟨~ pitching⟩ ⟨~ bowling⟩; *specif* **:** being a swimming stroke in which the arm is lifted out of the water and stretched forward over the shoulder to begin the stroke

**²overarm** \"\ *n* [³*over* + *arm*, n.] **:** a bar extending parallel to and above the arbor of a milling machine with attachments to provide support for the arbor

**overassessment** \ˌ==ˈ===\ *n* **:** the act or an instance of assessing excessively or beyond the norm; *also* **:** the condition of being so assessed

**overattachment** \ˌ===ˈ==\ *n* **:** excessive attachment

**overattentive** \ˌ===ˈ==\ *adj* **:** unduly or excessively attentive

**overawe** \ˌ==ˈ=\ *vt* **:** to make submissive or restrain by awe or fear **:** inspire awe in ⟨~ the English barbarians by his polished Norman manners —Charles Kingsley⟩

**¹overbalance** \ˌ==ˈ==\ *vt* [¹*over* + *balance*] **1 :** to exceed equality with **:** OUTWEIGH ⟨greatly ~*ed* by their concomitant advantages —T.L.Peacock⟩ **2 :** to cause to lose balance **:** put out of balance ⟨implied that it is desirable to ~ the cash budget —William Fellner⟩

**²overbalance** \"\ *n* **1 :** an excess of weight or value **:** something more than an equivalent ⟨an ~ of exports⟩ **2 :** the condition of being out of balance **:** lack of balance **:** INEQUILIBRIUM ⟨keep him from ~, one-sidedness —*Register*⟩

**overbanking** \ˌ==ˈ==\ *n* [³*over* + *banking* (gerund of ²*bank*)] **:** a malfunction in a watch that is caused by premature unlocking of the escape wheel without contact of the fork with the roller jewel and that makes the escapement inoperative — distinguished from *rebanking*

**overbear** \ˌ==ˈ=\ *vt* **1 :** to bring or carry down by superior weight or force **:** OVERWHELM ⟨rushed forth and . . . *overbore* the white-headed giant —William Beebe⟩ **2 a :** to overcome or bend to one's will by force of argument, domineering manner, or other nonphysical means ⟨*overbore* her protests —Josephine Pinckney⟩ ⟨completely *overborne* by his patient —Osbert Sitwell⟩ **b :** to surpass in importance, cogency, or other quality ~ *vi* **:** to bear fruit or offspring to excess

**over·bear·ance** \ˌ==ˈba(a)rən(t)s, -ˈber-\ *n* -S **:** domineering action or behavior **:** IMPERIOUSNESS

**¹overbearing** \ˌ==ˈ==\ *n* [fr. gerund of *overbear*] **:** the behavior of one that overbears another or an instance of such behavior; *esp* **:** dictatorial or arrogant action or conduct ⟨~ and aggression must come to an end —T.E.Goldstein⟩

**²overbearing** \ˌ==ˈ==\ *adj* [fr. pres. part. of *overbear*] **1 a :** OVERPOWERING, OVERWHELMING ⟨combine to create an ~ atmosphere —*Irish Digest*⟩ ⟨a grand alliance of European powers against our ~ greatness —J.H.Plumb⟩ ⟨an ~ preoccupation with economic interest —A.W.Gouldner⟩ **b :** decisively important **:** DOMINANT, PREPONDERATING ⟨the ~ problem of basic American relations with the Soviet Union —T.F.Reynolds⟩ ⟨didn't think it was the ~ consideration here —J.S.Cooper⟩ **2 :** aggressively haughty **:** ARROGANT, DOMINEERING ⟨intolerably . . . ~ in his manner —J.C.Snaith⟩

**syn** see PROUD

**over·bear·ing·ly** \ˌ==ˈ===\ *adv* **:** in an overbearing manner

**overbearingness** \ˌ==ˈ===\ *n* -ES **:** the quality or state of being overbearing

**overbed table** \ˌ==ˈ=-\ *n* [*overbed* fr. ²*over* + *bed*, n.] **:** a narrow rectangular table designed esp. for hospital patients that spans the bed and is typically fitted with casters and a crank for adjusting the height and tilting the top

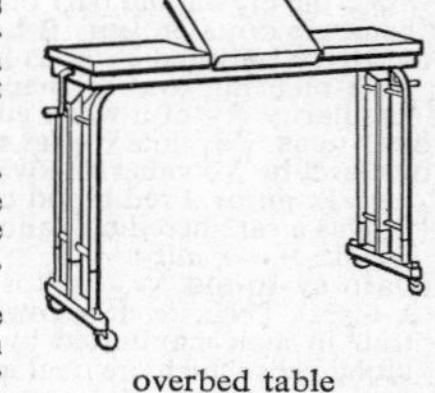

overbed table

**overbelief** \ˈ===,=\ *n* [³*over* + *belief*] **:** belief that is not verifiable or warranted by the evidence ⟨the ~*s* required by the nature . . . of human knowledge —H.J. Muller⟩

**overbend** \ˌ==ˈ=\ *vt* **1 a :** to cause to bend over ⟨more *overbent* than ever by his task —Adrian Bell⟩ **b :** to take a bent position over ⟨brooks *overbent* by arching boughs⟩ **2 :** to bend (as a bow) to excess ~ *vi* **:** to bend or stoop over

**over·berg** \ˌ==ˈ=\ *adj* [²*over* + Afrik *berg* mountain — more at BERG] *Africa* **:** being across a berg **:** TRAMONTANE

**¹overbias** \ˌ==ˈ==\ *n* [³*over* + *bias*] **:** an excessive bias; *specif* **:** an electron-tube grid bias in excess of that required for normal operation

**²overbias** \"\ *vt* **:** to apply an overbias to

**¹overbid** \ˌ==ˈ=\ *vb* [¹*over* + *bid*] *vi* **1 :** to bid in excess of value ⟨~ for stock⟩ **2 a :** to bid more than the trick-winning or scoring capacity of one's hand **b** *Brit* **:** to make a higher bid than the preceding one **:** OVERCALL ~ *vt* **:** to bid beyond or in excess of; *specif* **:** to bid more than the value of (one's hand in cards)

**²overbid** \"\ *n* **:** a bid in excess of a previous bid or of value

**overbit** \ˈ==,=\ *n* **:** a triangular earmark for cattle cut out of the upper side of an animal's ear — see EARMARK illustration

**overbite** \ˈ==,=\ *n* **:** the projection of the upper anterior teeth over the lower in the normal occlusal position of the jaws

**overblouse** \ˈ==,=\ *n* **:** a usu. fitted or belted blouse worn over the waistband of a skirt

**overblow** \ˌ==ˈ=\ *vb* [ME *overblowen*, fr. ¹*over* + *blowen* to blow] *vt* **1 :** to dissipate by or as if by wind **:** blow away **2 :** to cover (as with snow) by blowing or being blown **3 :** to blow (a pipe or other wind instrument) so vigorously as to evoke undesirable overtones that sometimes completely mask the fundamental tone **4 :** to continue to blow in a converter after the impurities have been removed (as carbon from iron or sulfur from copper) completely or below a proper percentage **5 a :** DISTEND, SWELL ⟨whom stout and high living have much *overblown* —Donagh MacDonagh⟩ **b :** to puff up to inflated proportions **:** give a false pathos or bombastic or flamboyant quality to ⟨would have been easy to ~ the story —C.W.Morton⟩ ~ *vi* **1** *of the wind, archaic* **:** to blow too hard to allow light sails (as topsails) to be carried **2 :** to force wind into a wind musical instrument in such a way as to change its pitch typically producing an overtone instead of its fundamental tone

**¹overblown** \ˌ==ˈ=\ *adj* [fr. past part. of *overblow*] **1 :** blown over or away **2 a :** marked by excessively large girth or proportions **:** PORTLY ⟨a handsome, ~ creature —S.J.Perelman⟩ ⟨swamps that helped support his ~ body —Jack Breed⟩ **b** (1) **:** puffed up to inflated proportions ⟨the ~ products of propaganda —*Newsweek*⟩ ⟨empty shuffling of ~ memories —*Saturday Rev.*⟩ ⟨the tale becomes ~ and thin —Amy Loveman⟩ ⟨a corrective power to deflate whatever was ~ —*Listener*⟩ (2) **:** flamboyant, turgid, or bombastic in manner or content **:** PRETENTIOUS ⟨an obsolete and ~ oratory —Bernard De Voto⟩ ⟨as strained, ~, and obvious as a soap opera —Charles Lee⟩ ⟨his climaxes are . . . never maudlin or ~ —*Modern Music*⟩

**²overblown** \"\ *adj* [¹*over* + *blown*, past part. of *blow* (to blossom)] **:** blossomed to excess **:** more than full blown ⟨a rose that already is ~ —C.E.Montague⟩

**overboard** \ˈ==,=, *sometimes* ,==ˈ=\ *adv* [ME *over bord*, fr. OE *ofer bord*, fr. *ofer*, prep., over + *bord* ship's side — more at BOARD] **1 :** over the side of a ship or boat; *esp* **:** from on board a ship into the water ⟨a man fell ~⟩ **2 :** to extremes esp. in approval of someone or something — usu. used in the phrase *go overboard* ⟨tend to go ~ on this subject —*Natural History*⟩ ⟨went ~ for heroes and heroines who don't seem so heroic today —Dwight MacDonald⟩ ⟨go ~ for unattractive girls —J.J.Godwin⟩ ⟨go ~ for passing fads —E.J.Kahn⟩ **3 :** into discard **:** ASIDE ⟨throw theological absolutes ~ —Allan Nevins⟩ ⟨throwing all her moral teachings and inhibitions ~ —Ruth Park⟩

**overboil** \ˌ==ˈ=\ *vi* **:** to boil over or unduly

**overbold** \ˌ==ˈ=\ *adj* **:** excessively bold or forward **:** PRESUMPTUOUS, IMPUDENT ⟨a foolish, ~ act —R.L.Stevenson⟩ — **overboldness** \ˌ==ˈ==\ *n*

**overboot** \ˈ==,=\ *n* **:** OVERSHOE

**overbore** *past of* OVERBEAR

**overborne** \ˌ==ˈ=\ *adj* [fr. past part. of *overbear*] **:** held down by superior force **:** OPPRESSED ⟨art, industry, and commerce, so long crushed and ~ —Francis Parkman⟩

**overbought** *adj* **:** characterized by prices held to be excessively high as a result of heavy buying ⟨price reactions in an ~ market⟩ ⟨an ~ stock⟩ — compare OVERSOLD

**overbowed** \ˌ==ˈ=\ *adj* [¹*over* + *bowed* (furnished with a bow)] **:** equipped with a bow whose drawing weight is too great for the archer

**overbowl** \ˈ==,=\ *n* **:** a throw at bowls that goes beyond the jack

**overbreak** \ˈ==,=\ *n* **:** a caving in of loosened material along the edge of an excavation

**overbred** \ˌ==ˈ=\ *adj* **:** bred too finely or to excess ⟨an ~ family of the nobility⟩

**overbridge** \ˈ==,=\ *n, Brit* **:** OVERPASS

**overbrim** \ˌ==ˈ=\ *vi* **:** to flow over the brim **:** OVERFLOW ~ *vt* **:** to cause to flow over the brim; *also* **:** to flow over the brim of

**overbuild** \ˌ==ˈ=\ *vt* **1 a :** to build too much for **:** build beyond the actual demand of ⟨~ capacity in any phase of industry —C.E.Wilson⟩ **b :** to supply with buildings in excess of actual demand ⟨~ a town⟩ **2 :** to erect a building or structure upon ~ *vi* **:** to build houses in excess of demand ⟨claims that the housing industry is ~*ing*⟩

**overbuilt** \ˌ==ˈ=\ *adj* **:** having too many buildings esp. in relation to the demand ⟨an ~ part of town⟩ **:** faced with an excess of housing in relation to the actual demand ⟨are going to become ~ if we continue to build —*Amer. Builder*⟩

**¹overburden** \ˌ==ˈ==\ *vt* [¹*over* + *burden*, v.] **:** to place an excessive burden on **:** load to excess **:** weigh down ⟨the pauper class which ~*s* the city asylums —Nels Anderson⟩ ⟨~*ed* . . . by a profusion of ornament —Anny Varron⟩ ⟨tree branches ~*ed* with ice⟩

**²overburden** \ˈ==,==\ *n* [in sense 1, fr. ¹*overburden*; in other senses, fr. ³*over* + *burden*, n.] **1 :** excess of burden **2 a :** consolidated or unconsolidated material overlying a deposit of useful geological materials (as a coal seam or an ore body) esp. where mined by open cuts; *also* **:** sedimentary rock overlying older crystalline rocks **b :** loose soil, sand, gravel, or similar material above a bedrock **3 :** the sterile stratum lying above a cultural level at an archaeological site

**over·bur·den·ing·ly** \ˌ==ˈ=(=)=\ *adv* [*overburdening* (pres. part. of ¹*overburden*) + *-ly*] **:** so as to overburden

**overburn** \ˌ==ˈ=\ *vb* **:** to burn too much

**overbuy** \ˌ==ˈ=\ *vb* [ME *overbiggen*, fr. ¹*over* + *biggen*, *byen* to buy] *vt* **1** *obs* **:** to buy at an excessive price **2 a :** to buy in quantities exceeding needs or demand ⟨found that he had *overbought* fertilizer⟩ **b :** to affect injuriously (as by causing price rises) by too much buying esp. in relation to supply ~ *vi* **:** to make purchases that are in excess of needs or demand or are beyond one's means ⟨~*ing* and then holding for an advance in prices —Jules Backman⟩ ⟨~*ing* . . . is often detected and the subscribers warned —A.F.Chapin⟩

**overby** \ˌ==ˈ=\ *adv* [¹*over* + *by*, adv.] *chiefly Scot* **:** a little way over **:** at a short distance ⟨our neighbors ~⟩

**¹overcall** \ˌ==ˈ=\ *vb* [¹*over* + *call*] *vt* **1 :** to make a higher card bid than (the preceding bid) **:** bid higher than (the player who last bid) **2** *Brit* **:** to bid too much **:** OVERBID ~ *vi* **:** to bid over an opponent's bid in bridge when one's partner has not bid or doubled

**²overcall** \"\ *n* **1 a :** a bid in bridge usu. showing meager or limited strength made by a player on the side that did not open the bidding **b :** a bid higher than the preceding bid **2 :** OVERBID

**overcanopy** \ˌ==ˈ===\ *vt* **:** to form a canopy over ⟨great white wings ~*ing* the sparkling water —Lilian S. Taylor⟩

**overcapacity** \ˌ===ˈ=(=)=\ *n* **:** excessive productive capacity in relation to needs or demand ⟨another industry suffering from ~ —*Newsweek*⟩

**overcapitalization** \ˌōvə(r)+\ *n* [³*over* + *capitalization*] **1 :** the act or an instance of overcapitalizing **2 :** the state of being overcapitalized

**overcapitalize** \"+\ *vt* [¹*over* + *capitalize*] **1 :** to put a nominal value on the capital of (a corporation) higher than actual cost or fair market value **2 :** to capitalize (a business enterprise) beyond what the business or the profit-making prospects warrant

**overcareful** \ˌ==ˈ==\ *adj* **:** too careful — **overcarefully** \ˌ==ˈ=(=)=\ *adv*

**overcarry** \ˌ==ˈ==\ *vt* **:** to carry too far **:** carry beyond the proper point

**¹overcast** \ˌ==ˈ=\ *vb* [ME *overcasten*, fr. ¹*over* + *casten* to cast] *vt* **1** *archaic* **:** to cast down **:** OVERTHROW **2 a :** CLOUD, DARKEN, OVERSHADOW ⟨it is the existence of evil . . . which ~*s* life —F.L.Mott⟩ **b :** to cast or cover over **:** OVERSPREAD ⟨the smoke haze that ~ the distant mountains —L.C.Douglas⟩ ⟨something of reverence, ~ with egotism —G.B.Johnson⟩ **3 a** (1) **:** to sew with an overcast stitch from one section of (a book) to the next (2) **:** to reinforce along the back of (a signature) by stitching through half of the leaves (3) **:** to fasten (single leaves) as a group by an overcast stitch at the binding edge **:** WHIPSTITCH **b :** to sew over the edge of; *specif* **:** to sew (raw edges of a seam) with long slanting widely spaced stitches to prevent raveling ~ *vi* **1 :** to become overcast **:** DARKEN **2 :** to make an overbowl at lawn bowls

**²overcast** \ˈ==,=\ *adj* [fr. past part. of ¹*overcast*] **1 a :** clouded over ⟨an ~ night⟩ **b :** DEPRESSED, GLOOMY ⟨his handsome countenance . . . was ~ —Rafael Sabatini⟩ **2** *geol* **:** OVERTURNED ⟨an ~ fold⟩

**³overcast** \"\ *n* [¹*overcast*] **1 :** COVERING ⟨with an ~ of irony —R.M.Coates⟩; *esp* **:** a covering of clouds over the sky ⟨the land rose in pink and violet dales, shading finally into the ~ above the harbor —Norman Mailer⟩ **2 :** an arch or support that carries an overhead passage; *esp* **:** one that carries a passage over another passage in a mine **3 :** sewing that has been overcast

**overcaster** \ˈ==,==\ *n* **:** one who does overcasting by hand or machine — see SERGER

**overcasting** \ˈ==,==\ *n* **:** the act of stitching raw edges of fabric to prevent raveling; *also* **:** the stitching so done

overcasting

**overcatch** \ˌ==ˈ=\ *vt, chiefly dial* **:** OVERTAKE

**overcautious** \ˌ==ˈ==\ *adj* **:** too cautious

**overceiling** \ˌ==ˈ==\ *adj* [²*over* + *ceiling*] **:** being over a ceiling ⟨~ payments⟩

**overcentralized** \ˌ==ˈ===\ *adj* **:** excessively centralized ⟨~ administration⟩

**overcertification** \ˌ==,===ˈ==\ *n* [³*over* + *certification*] **:** the practice or an instance of overcertifying

**overcertify** \ˌ==ˈ===\ *vt* [¹*over* + *certify*] **:** to certify (a check) for an amount in excess of the balance of the deposit account of the drawer

**¹overcharge** \ˌ==ˈ=\ *vb* [ME *overchargen*, fr. ¹*over* + *chargen* to charge] *vt* **1 :** to charge excessively or beyond a due rate or price ⟨may ~ you as much as he likes —G.B.Shaw⟩ **2 :** to fill or load too full **:** CROWD, BURDEN ⟨our language is *overcharged* with consonants —Joseph Addison⟩ ⟨the canvas . . . is rather *overcharged* —Norman Douglas⟩ **3** *obs* **:** to make extravagant accusations against **4 :** EXAGGERATE, OVERDRAW ⟨~ a report⟩ ~ *vi* **:** to make an excessive charge

**²overcharge** \ˈ==,=, ˌ==ˈ=\ *n* **1 :** an excessive charge or burden **2 a :** a monetary charge in excess of the proper, legal, or agreed rate or amount **:** an exorbitant charge **b** (1) **:** an act of charging an excessive amount ⟨increase civil penalties for rent ~*s* —*New Republic*⟩ (2) **:** a sum in excess of the just amount ⟨found and corrected a twenty-five-cent ~ —*Atlantic*⟩

**overcharge claim** *n* : a formal request by a shipper on a carrier for refund of an excess over the lawful charge

1**overcheck** \ˈ=ˌ=\ *n* [3*over* + *check* (checkrein)] : a checkrein passing between the ears of a horse — compare SIDECHECK

2**overcheck** \"\ *n* [3*over* + *check* (pattern in squares)] : a textile design usu. consisting of two checked patterns of different size or color so made that one is superimposed on the other; *also* : a fabric with such a design

**overchurched** \ˌ=ˈ=ˌchərcht\ *adj* [1*over* + *-churched* (fr. *church*, n. + *-ed*)] : having more churches than are needed to serve the population ⟨an ~ community⟩

**overchurching** \ˌ=ˈ=ˌchərchiŋ\ *n* [1*over* + *-churching* (fr. *church*, n. + *-ing*)] : the providing of more churches than are needed to serve the population of a community

**overchute** \ˈ=ˌ=\ *n* : an overhead flume (as one over a stream or canal)

**overcivilized** \ˌ=ˈ=ˌ=ˌ=\ *adj* : too highly civilized ⟨a standardized and ~ minority —Douglas Bush⟩

**overclaim** \ˈ=ˌ=\ *n* : an excessive claim ⟨gross and palpable ~*s* —Raymond Moley⟩

**overclothe** \ˌ=ˈ=\ *vt* : to clothe to excess ⟨babies should never be *overclothed* —Morris Fishbein⟩

**overclothes** \ˈ=ˌ=\ *n pl* : outer garments

**overcloud** \ˌ=ˈ=\ *vt* **1** : to cover or overspread with clouds : OVERCAST, OBSCURE ⟨a dust storm so intense that it ~*ed* the sun⟩ **2 a** : to cast a shadow upon : DARKEN ⟨did much to ~, if they did not embitter, her indulgent husband's early life —Peter Quennell⟩ **b** : to make dim or dull : BECLOUD ⟨if his clear understanding had not been ~*ed* —T.B.Macaulay⟩

1**overcoat** \ˈ=ˌ=\ *n* [3*over* + *coat*, n.] **1** : a coat worn over a suit or other clothing; *esp* : a warm coat for winter wear **2** : a protective coating (as of paint or varnish)

2**overcoat** \ˌ=ˈ=\ *vt* [2*over* + *coat*, v.] : to apply an additional coat (as of paint) to

**overcoating** \ˈ=ˌ=ˌ=\ *n* [in sense 1, fr. 1*overcoat* + *-ing*; in sense 2, prob. fr. 3*over* + *coating*] **1** : heavy material suitable for overcoats **2** : OVERCOAT 2

**overcoil** \ˈ=ˌ=\ *n* : the outer coil of a Bréguet hairspring bent over the spring toward the center

**overcoiler** \"ə(r)\ *n* : a worker who adjusts an overcoil so that it will remain concentric with the balance staff as the spring winds and unwinds

1**over·come** \ˌōvə(r)ˈkəm\ *vb* [ME *overcomen*, fr. OE *ofercuman*, fr. *ofer*, adv., over + *cuman* to come] *vt* **1 a** : to get the better of : SURMOUNT, CONQUER, SUBDUE ⟨search out and ~ the difficulties —George Sampson⟩ ⟨finally *overcame* the opposition of the traditionalists —Helen Sullivan⟩ ⟨the difficulty of language had to be ~ —L.S.B.Leakey⟩ **b** : to affect or influence so strongly as to make physically helpless or emotionally distraught (as from exhaustion or agitation) : OVERPOWER, OVERWHELM ⟨were ~ by fear —H.E.Scudder⟩ ⟨too much ~ to notice what was in it —L.A.G.Strong⟩ ⟨~ by the . . . champagne —Kenneth Roberts⟩ **c** *archaic* : to go beyond : EXCEED, OUTSTRIP **d** *obs* : COMPLETE, ACCOMPLISH **2 a** *archaic* : to come or pass over : spread or flow over **b** *obs* : to come over suddenly ~ *vi* **1** : to gain the superiority : WIN ⟨strong in the faith that truth would ~⟩ **2** *chiefly dial* : to regain consciousness after a swoon **syn** see CONQUER

2**over·come** \ˈō(ə)rˌkəm, ˈōvər-, -ˌkūm\ *n* [3*over* + obs. E *come* action of coming, fr. ME — more at DOWNCOME] **1** *chiefly Scot* : SURPLUS **2** *chiefly Scot* : something (as the burden of a song or a trite phrase) that is often repeated

**over·com·er** \ˌōvə(r)ˈkəmə(r)\ *n* [ME, fr. *overcomen* to overcome + *-er*] : one that overcomes ⟨they're ~*s* by nature —Robertson Davies⟩

**over·compensate** \ˌōvə(r)+\ *vt* : to compensate inordinately or to excess ⟨*overcompensated* the popular teacher and ignored the specialist —H.M.Jones⟩ ~ *vi* : to exhibit overcompensation : overcome through overt behavior a feeling of inferiority ⟨may ~ through disastrous adventures —Jack Weinberg⟩ — **over·compensatory** \"+\ *adj*

**over·compensation** \"+\ *n* : excessive compensation; *specif* : excessive reaction to a feeling of inferiority, guilt, or inadequacy leading to an exaggerated attempt to overcome the feeling

**over·compound** \"+\ *vt* : to add series coils to (a compounded dynamo) beyond those required to maintain a constant terminal voltage with the result that the voltage increases with the current load

**over·confidence** \"+\ *n* : excess of confidence

**over·confident** \"+\ *adj* : marked by or reflecting overconfidence

**overconscientious** \ˌ=ˌ=ˈ=ˌ=\ *adj* : unduly or excessively conscientious

**over·conservative** \ˌōvə(r)+\ *adj* : unduly or extremely conservative

**overcooked** \ˌ=ˈ=\ *adj* [1*over* + *cooked* (past part. of *cook*)] : cooked too much

**overcorrect** \ˌ=ˌ=ˈ=\ *vt* : to apply a correction to in excess of that required (as for satisfactory performance); *specif* : to correct (a lens) beyond the point of achromatism or so that there is aberration of a kind opposite to that of the uncorrected lens — **overcorrection** \ˌ=ˌ=ˈ=\ *n*

1**overcover** \ˌ=ˈ=\ *vt* [ME *overcoveren*, fr. 1*over* + *coveren* to cover] : to cover up : cover completely

2**overcover** \ˈ=ˌ=\ *n* : something that covers over or covers completely ⟨beneath a dense ~ of thick jungle trees —G.H. Johnston⟩ ⟨fishing rods in green baize ~*s* —F.M.Ford⟩

**overcritical** \ˌ=ˈ=ˌ=\ *adj* [1*over* + *critical*] : HYPERCRITICAL

**overcrop** \ˌ=ˈ=\ *vt* [1*over* + *crop*] : to exhaust the fertility of by excessive production without the application of adequate fertilizer to the soil

**overcrossing** \ˈ=ˌ=\ *n* : OVERPASS

**overcrow** \ˌ=ˈ=\ *vt* **1** : to crow, exult, or boast over **2** : to triumph over : OVERBEAR, OVERPOWER

**overcrowd** \ˌ=ˈ=\ *vt* : to cause to be too crowded : fill to the point of discomfort or disadvantage ⟨there is always danger of ~*ing* the attractive business —*Amer. Guide Series: Mich.*⟩ ~ *vi* : to crowd together too much

**overcrowded** *adj* : crowded or filled to excess : CONGESTED ⟨an ~ room⟩ : characterized by overcrowding ⟨live in ~ conditions —*Social Services in Brit.*⟩

**overcrowding** *n* **1** : the act or an instance of crowding too much **2** : the condition of being overcrowded

**overcrust** \ˌ=ˈ=\ *vt* : to cover over with a crust

**overcup oak** \ˈ=ˌ=-\ *n* [*overcup* fr. 3*over* + *cup*, n.] : any of several oaks (as the bur oak) having the acorn deeply immersed in the cup; *esp* : a timber tree (*Quercus lyrata*) of the southern U. S. that has pale scaly bark and lyrate leaves

**overcurious** \ˌ=ˈ=ˌ=\ *adj* **1** *obs* : too finicky or fastidious **2** : too inquisitive — **overcuriously** \ˌ=ˈ=ˌ=\ *adv* — **over·cu·ri·ous·ness** \ˌ=ˈ=ˌ=\ *n*

**overcurrent** \ˈ=ˌ=\ *n* : an electrical current whose intensity is higher than a specified amount

1**overcut** \ˈ=ˌ=\ *n* [3*over* + *cut*] **1** : excessive cutting; *specif* : cutting of timber in excess of the annual growth of the forest **2** : an absence from class (as in a college) in excess of the number customarily allowed **3** : a cut (as in tennis) made with an overhand stroke

2**overcut** \ˌ=ˈ=\ *vb* [1*over* + *cut*] *vt* : to cut excessively; *specif* : to cut timber from (a forest) in excess of the annual growth or in excess of the annual estimate ~ *vi* : to do excessive cutting; *specif* : to cut timber in excess

**overcutter** \ˈ=ˌ=\ *n* [3*over* + *cutter*] : TURRET CUTTER

**overcutting** \ˈ=ˌ=\ *n* [3*over* + *cutting* (gerund of *cut*)] : the effect in disc recording of one groove cutting through the intervening wall into the adjacent groove as the result of excessive excursion of the cutting stylus

**overdamp** \ˌ=ˈ=\ *vt* : to damp in excess ⟨use of a high sensitivity galvanometer greatly ~*ed* —*Physical Rev.*⟩

**overdare** *vi* : to dare too much or rashly : become too daring ~ *vt*, *obs* : to surpass in daring

**overdaring** \ˌ=ˈ=\ *adj* : too daring : FOOLHARDY — **overdaringly** *adv*

1**overdate** \ˈ=ˌ=\ *n* [3*over* + *date*] **1** : a changed date on a coin that has traces of the original date still showing **2** : a coin having an overdate

2**overdate** \"\ *vt* [1*over* + *date*] : to strike (a coin) with an overdate

**overdated** \ˈ=ˌ=\ *adj* [in sense 1, fr. 1*over* + *dated* (past part. of *date*, v.); in sense 2, fr. past part. of 2*overdate*] **1** *archaic* : OUT-OF-DATE : BYGONE **2** : bearing an overdate ⟨~ coins⟩

**overdear** \ˌ=ˈ=\ *adj* [ME *over dere*, fr. 1*over* + *dere* dear] : too dear; *esp* : too costly

**overdeck** \ˌ=ˈ=\ *vt* : to adorn extravagantly : adorn excessively

**overdecorated** \ˌ=ˈ=ˌ=ˌ=\ *adj* : decorated to excess

**overdeepen** \ˌ=ˈ=\ *vt* : to deepen excessively esp. through erosive action (as of water or ice) ⟨the ~*ed* main valleys —A. E.Trueman⟩

**overdeepening** \ˌ=ˈ=(ə)=\ *n* : the process or result of deepening excessively ⟨this ~ amounts at most to only a few hundred feet —*Jour. of Geol.*⟩

**overdelicate** \ˌ=ˈ=ˌ=\ *adj* : unduly or extremely delicate

**over·den** \ˈōvə(r)ˌden\ *n* [PaG *owwerdenn* loft over the threshing floor, fr. *owwer* upper (fr. G *ober*) + *denn* threshing floor, fr. G *tenne*, fr. OHG *tenni* — more at OBERREALSCHULE, DEN] *Northeast* : HAYMOW

**overdependent** \ˌ=ˌ=ˈ=\ *adj* : unduly or extremely dependent

**overdetermination** \ˌ=ˌ=ˌ=ˈ=\ *n* [3*over* + *determination*] : the condition of being overdetermined

**overdetermined** \ˌ=ˌ=ˈ=\ *adj* [1*over* + *determined*] **1** : too determined : too positive or decided ⟨~ insistence that everything . . . can be reduced to sex —Norman Cameron⟩ **2** : having more than one determining psychological factor : affording an outlet for more than a single wish or need ⟨an ~ dream symbol⟩

**overdevelop** \ˌ=ˌ=ˈ=\ *vt* : to develop excessively; *specif* : to subject (as an exposed photographic plate, film, paper) to a developing solution under one or more conditions of excessive time, temperature, agitation, or concentration — **overdevelopment** \ˌ=ˌ=ˈ=\ *n*

**overdiligent** \ˌ=ˈ=ˌ=\ *adj* : extremely diligent

1**overdischarge** \ˌōvə(r)+\ *vt* [1*over* + *discharge*] : to discharge excessively; *specif* : to discharge (a battery) beyond the proper point

2**overdischarge** \"+\ *n* **1** : the act, process, or an instance of overdischarging **2** : the condition of being overdischarged

**overdo** \ˌ=ˈ=\ *vb* [ME *overdon*, fr. OE *oferdōn*, fr. *ofer*, adv., over + *dōn* to do] *vt* **1 a** : to do too much : do to excess : carry too far ⟨if she does housework, she will ~ it —H.A.Overstreet⟩ ⟨~ the social side of pregnancy —Morris Fishbein⟩ **b** : to make excessive use or application of ⟨tend to ~ the wisecrack —David Daiches⟩ ⟨quotations are apt to break up a book . . . don't ~ them —J.E.Gloag⟩ **c** : to emphasize unduly : EXAGGERATE ⟨corruption is frequently *overdone* as a cause of national decay —*New Republic*⟩ **2** *archaic* : SURPASS, EXCEL **3 a** : to cook too long **b** : to feed (an animal) to excessive fatness **4** : OVERTAX, FATIGUE, EXHAUST ⟨~ one's strength⟩ ~ *vi* **1** : to do too much : go to extremes in doing ⟨his anxiety that she should not ~ —Ruth P. Randall⟩ **2** : OVERACT ⟨most of her mistakes came from ~*ing* —Claire Sterling & Max Ascoli⟩

**overdog** \ˈ=ˌ=\ *n* [3*over* + *dog* (after *underdog*)] : a member of a ruling or privileged class ⟨everybody in the play is stupid, both the ~*s* and the underdogs —Virgil Thomson⟩

**overdone** \ˌ=ˈ=\ *adj* [ME *overdoon*, fr. OE *oferdōn*, fr. past part. of *oferdōn* to overdo] **1** : done or carried to excess: as **a** : EXAGGERATED ⟨an absent and ~ smile —E.A.Poe⟩ ⟨a courtesy which was a little ~ —Robertson Davies⟩ **b** : cooked too much ⟨an ~ steak⟩ **2** : EXHAUSTED, FATIGUED ⟨looking a bit ~ —Dorothy Sayers⟩ ⟨you're just ~ —Agnes S. Turnbull⟩

**overdoor** \ˈ=ˌ=\ *n* [2*over* + *door*] : a picture or carved panel or other decorative member over a doorway or a doorframe

**overdosage** \ˌ=ˈ=\ *n* [2*overdose* + *-age*] **1** : the administration or taking of an excessive dose ⟨guard against ~ of this drug⟩ **2** : the condition of being overdosed ⟨the symptoms of acute ~ —Henry Borsook⟩

1**overdose** \ˈ=ˌ=\ *n* [3*over* + *dose*] : too great a dose : an excessive dose ⟨an ~ of sleeping pills⟩ ⟨an ~ of exposure to the sun —Morris Fishbein⟩ ⟨an ~ of sweetness and light —C. J.Rolo⟩

2**overdose** \"\ *vt* [1*over* + *dose*] : to dose to excess : give an overdose or too many doses to

**overdraft** \ˈ=ˌ=\ *n* [fr. *overdraw*, after E *draw: draft*] **1 a** : an act of overdrawing at a bank or the state of being overdrawn; *also* : the sum overdrawn ⟨an ~ results when a note discounted at a bank is not met when due⟩ **b** : the act, process, or an instance of drawing on or off too much ⟨a mounting ~ in the use of available sweet water —W.A.Ulman⟩ **2** [3*over* + *draft*] : a draft or current of air passing over a fire in a furnace

**overdrape** \ˈ=ˌ=\ *also* **overdrapery** \ˈ=ˌ=(ə)=\ *n* : one of a pair of draperies esp. of heavy fabric that are usu. hung over sheer curtains and are primarily for decoration

overdrapes

**overdraw** \ˌ=ˈ=\ *vb* [1*over* + *draw*] *vt* **1** : to draw checks upon (a bank account) in excess of the deposit balance of the drawer : make a draft upon beyond the proper or authorized amount ⟨*overdrew* his account⟩ **2** : to present or portray with exaggeration or overstatement ⟨has *overdrawn* the dangers —M.H. Swadesh⟩ ⟨have often *overdrawn* their villains —John Mason Brown⟩ ⟨purposely ~ the contrast —A.R.Oxenfeldt & Ernest Van den Haag⟩ **3** : to draw (a bow) beyond the arrow length for which it was designed ~ *vi* : to make an overdraft

**overdrawn** \ˌ=ˈ=\ *adj* **1 a** : drawn upon in excess of the deposit balance of the drawer at the bank ⟨an ~ account⟩ **b** : having made an overdraft : having an overdrawn account ⟨was ~ to quite a considerable extent —F.W.Crofts⟩ **2** : EXAGGERATED ⟨claim of having earned a graduate degree . . . appears ~ —Peter Wyden⟩ ⟨all this enthusiasm seems a little ~ —Gladys E. Brown⟩ ⟨particularly ~ comparisons —R.A.Hall b.1911⟩ ⟨like an ~ picture of an English gentleman —John Steinbeck⟩

1**overdress** \ˌ=ˈ=\ *vb* [1*over* + *dress*] *vt* : to dress or adorn to excess ~ *vi* : to dress oneself to excess

2**overdress** \ˈ=ˌ=\ *n* [3*over* + *dress*] : a dress worn over another; *specif* : one designed or draped to show an underdress

**overdrifted** \ˌ=ˈ=\ *adj* [1*over* + *drifted* (past part. of *drift*)] : covered with drifts (as of snow) ⟨steep, snowy, rutty, ~ roads —Stephen Graham⟩

1**overdrive** \ˌ=ˈ=\ *vt* [ME *overdriven*, fr. 1*over* + *driven* to drive] **1** : to drive too hard or far or beyond strength or a fixed limit ⟨*overdrove* the orchestra —*Current Biog.*⟩ ⟨skeletons of . . . beasts which had been *overdriven* by their anxious owners —Gordon Enders⟩ **2** : to drive (an automotive vehicle) esp. at night at such speed that one cannot stop or guide it safely within the limits of vision or available space

2**overdrive** \ˈ=ˌ=\ *n* [3*over* + *drive*] : an automotive transmission gear which transmits to the propeller shaft a speed greater than engine speed

**overdriven** \ˌ=ˈ=\ *adj* : driven or worked too hard : EXHAUSTED, OPPRESSED ⟨the tortured and ~ slave —Clive Bell⟩ ⟨I am ~ just now and am trying not to do anything —G.B. Shaw⟩

**overdue** \ˌ=ˈ=\ *adj* **1 a** : unpaid after the proper or assigned time of payment ⟨an ~ note⟩ **b** : delayed (as in arrival or presentation) beyond the proper or assigned time ⟨an ~ library book⟩ ⟨an ~ ship⟩ ⟨her gallant was . . . more than an hour ~ —Dorothy Barclay⟩ **c** : being something that fills a need of long standing, or that has been long awaited ⟨improvement is long ~ —Stuart Chase⟩ ⟨land reform which was long ~ —Richard Hunt⟩ ⟨the book is ~ —John Berryman⟩ ⟨got an ~ reward —*Time*⟩ **2** : exceeding its merits or what is appropriate : EXCESSIVE ⟨an ~ share of attention —Evelyn Whitehead⟩ ⟨if the tool is built with ~ sturdiness —*Amer. Machinist*⟩ **3** : more than ready or ripe ⟨colonies that are ~ for liberation —David Landman⟩ ⟨announcing that the country was ~ for democracy —*Time*⟩ **syn** see TARDY

**overdye** \ˌ=ˈ=\ *vt* **1** : to dye with excess of color **2** : to dye over with another color

**overeager** \ˌ=ˈ=\ *adj* : too eager ⟨~ for success⟩ ⟨~ in his pursuit of the girl⟩ — **overeagerly** *adv* — **overeagerness** *n* -ES

**overeat** \ˌ=ˈ=\ *vi* : to eat to excess or to the point of surfeit ~ *vt* : to indulge (oneself) in overeating ⟨nearly *overate* myself the other day —Norman Douglas⟩

**overeating disease** *n* : ENTEROTOXEMIA

**overed** *past of* OVER

**overedger** \ˈ=ˌ=\ *n* [prob. fr. *over edge* (fr. 2*over* + *edge* + *-er*] : SERGER

**overelaborate** \ˌ=ˌ=ˈ=ˌ=\ *vt* [1*over* + *elaborate*] : to elaborate too far or too much : elaborate beyond the point of need ⟨tended to ~ an intrinsically simple structure —W.A.Paton & A.C.Littleton⟩ — **overelaborately** \ˌ=ˌ=ˈ=(=)=\ *adv*

**overelaboration** \ˌ=ˌ=ˌ=ˈ=\ *n* [3*over* + *elaboration*] **1** : the act or an instance of overelaborating ⟨his taste ran to extreme ~ —*Atlantic*⟩ **2** : the condition of being overelaborated ⟨~ characterizes so much of present-day writing —E.S.McCartney⟩

**overembellish** \ˌ=ˌ=ˈ=\ *vt* : to embellish to excess

**overemotional** \ˌ=ˌ=ˈ=(=)=\ *adj* : abnormally or excessively emotional

**overemphasis** \ˌ=ˈ=ˌ=\ *n* : excessive emphasis

**overemphasize** \ˌ=ˈ=ˌ=\ *vt* : to give excessive emphasis to ⟨*overemphasizing* detail —*Amer. Guide Series: Pa.*⟩ ~ *vi* : to use too much emphasis ⟨I ~ and exaggerate —B.N.Cardozo⟩

**overemployment** \ˌ=ˌ=ˈ=\ *n* **1** : excessive employment or use ⟨in his case the ~ of the dash seems appropriate —*Jour. of Accountancy*⟩ **2** : a condition in which the demand for labor in a country or region exceeds the available supply ⟨~ caused by inadequacy of labor and other resources compared with all the work needing to be done —*Times Lit. Supp.*⟩

**overenthusiastic** \ˌ=ˌ=ˌ=ˈ=\ *adj* : unduly or extremely enthusiastic

**overesteem** \ˌ=ˌ=ˈ=\ *vt* : to esteem too highly

1**overestimate** \ˌ=ˈ=(ˌ)=\ *vt* [1*over* + *estimate*] : to estimate too highly : OVERVALUE — **overestimation** \ˌ=ˌ=ˈ=\ *n*

2**overestimate** \"\ *n* : an estimate that is too high

**overevaluation** \ˌ=ˌ=ˌ=ˈ=\ *n* : excessive evaluation

**overexcite** \ˌ=ˌ=ˈ=\ *vt* : to excite to an undue or excessive degree

**overexcitement** \ˌ=ˌ=ˈ=\ *n* : undue or excessive excitement

**overexert** \ˌ=ˌ=ˈ=\ *vt* : to exert too much ⟨don't ~ yourself⟩ ~ *vi* : to exert oneself to excess ⟨whenever he ~*ed* or was upset —William Humphrey⟩

**overexertion** \ˌ=ˌ=ˈ=\ *n* : excessive exertion

**overexpansion** \ˌ=ˌ=ˈ=\ *n* : excessive expansion

**overexpose** \ˌ=ˌ=ˈ=\ *vt* : to expose excessively; *specif* : to subject (a light-sensitive material) too long to the action of light or other radiation so that usu. lowered contrast in the developed image results

**overexposure** \ˌ=ˌ=ˈ=\ *n* : excessive exposure

**overextend** \ˌ=ˌ=ˈ=\ *vt* **1** : to extend or expand beyond a safe, proper, or reasonable point ⟨tends to ~ his claim —C.A. Madison⟩ ⟨reduce the peril of ~*ing* our economy —G.A.Sloan⟩ **2** : to spread (as a military force) so thinly or over so large an area as to weaken the total and endanger security ⟨~*ing* the German front lines —Max Werner⟩ **3** : to take upon (oneself) more liabilities, commitments, or risks than are safe ⟨~ themselves through additional land purchases —*Newsweek*⟩ ⟨any users of credit . . . may ~ themselves —C.W.Phelps⟩

**overextended** \ˌ=ˌ=ˈ=\ *adj* **1** : extended or expanded beyond a safe, proper, or reasonable point ⟨found it ~ and wordy —Philip Hamburger⟩ ⟨this elaborate, ~ vaudeville show —*Newsweek*⟩ **2** : spread too thinly or over too large an area for safety ⟨attacked and routed the ~ German divisions⟩ ⟨pulled back from positions of weakness where we were ~ —Walter Lippmann⟩ **3** : carrying or assuming liabilities, commitments, or risks beyond capacity or what is safe ⟨a speculator ~ in the market⟩ ⟨~ accounts⟩

**overextension** \ˌ=ˌ=ˈ=\ *n* **1** : the act or an instance of overextending **2** : the condition of being overextended

**overeye** *vt*, *obs* : OVERSEE

**overface** \ˌ=ˈ=\ *vt*, *dial chiefly Eng* : OUTFACE, OVERWHELM

**overfall** \ˈ=ˌ=\ *n* **1** : a turbulent surface of water caused by strong currents setting over submerged ridges or shoals or by winds opposing a current — usu. used in pl. **2** *obs* : CATARACT, WATERFALL **3** : a place provided for the overflow of surplus water (as from a canal or lock) **4** : a sudden increase of depth in the bottom of the sea or other large body of water

**overfastidious** \ˌ=(ˌ)=ˈ=\ *adj* : unduly or extremely fastidious

**overfed** \ˌ=ˈ=\ *adj* [1*over* + *fed* (past part. of *feed*)] : fed to excess ⟨shifting her ~ baby from one hip to the other —Evelyn Barkins⟩

1**overfeed** \ˌ=ˈ=\ *vb* [1*over* + *feed*] *vt* : to feed to excess ⟨~ a child⟩ ~ *vi* : to eat too much ⟨wanders off . . . and ~*s* —Allan Anderson⟩

2**overfeed** \ˈ=ˌ=\ *adj* [1*over* + *-feed* (fr. *feed*, v.)] : being fed or feeding from above ⟨an ~ stoker⟩ — opposed to *underfeed*

**overfertilization** \ˌ=ˌ=(ˌ)=ˈ=\ *n* : excessive fertilization

**overfill** \ˌ=ˈ=\ *vb* [ME *overfillen*, fr. OE *oferfyllan*, fr. *ofer*, adv., over + *fyllan* to fill] *vt* : to fill to excess or overflowing ~ *vi* : to become full to overflowing

**overfire** \ˌ=ˈ=\ *vt* : to apply heat treatment to (as a clay ware) beyond maturing ~ *vi* : to become subjected to excessive heat treatment ⟨clays that begin to ~ —Heinrich Ries⟩

**overfiring** *n* : excessive heat treatment of clay wares causing deformation, bloating, or other defects

**overfish** \ˌ=ˈ=\ *vt* : to fish to the detriment of a fishing ground or to the depletion of a kind of fish

**overfleshed** \ˌ=ˈflesht\ *adj* [1*over* + *-fleshed* (fr. *flesh*, n. + *-ed*)] : unduly or extremely fleshy : fattened beyond the point of optimum returns ⟨~ hogs⟩

**overflew** *past of* OVERFLY

**overflies** *pres 3d sing of* OVERFLY

**overflight** \ˈ=ˌ=\ *n* [fr. *overfly*, after E *fly: flight*] : a passage over an area in an airplane ⟨occasional Soviet refusals for ~*s* —*Internat'l Reference Service*⟩

**overfloat** *vt* **1** *obs* : OVERFLOW **2** \ˌ=ˈ=\ *archaic* : to float over

**overflood** \ˌ=ˈ=\ *vt* : INUNDATE

1**overflow** \ˌ=ˈ=\ *vb* [ME *overflowen*, fr. OE *oferflōwan*, fr. *ofer*, adv., over + *flōwan* to flow] *vt* **1** : to flow over : cover with or as if with water : INUNDATE ⟨the flooded river ~*ed* the adjacent fields⟩ **2** : to flow over the brim of ⟨a river ~*ing* its banks⟩ **3** : to cause to overflow ~ *vi* **1 a** : to run or flow over bounds ⟨every spring the river ~*s*⟩ **b** : to fill a space to capacity and spread beyond its limits ⟨the crowd ~*ed* into the street⟩ ⟨we can ~ in pleasant weather into my small garden —Eleanor Roosevelt⟩ **2 a** : to become filled to running over ⟨filled his glass till it ~*ed*⟩ **b** : SUPERABOUND ⟨their soil . . . ~*s* with wine and oil —H.T.Buckle⟩

2**overflow** \ˈ=ˌ=\ *n* **1** : a flowing over (as of water or other fluid) : INUNDATION **2 a** : something that flows over : SURPLUS, EXCESS ⟨territory into which her teeming human ~ can be siphoned —T.H.Fielding⟩ ⟨this year's ~ of applications —Cecile Starr⟩ **b** : the peripheral drift of excess population from a protected habitat to other suitable environments **3** : an outlet or a receptacle for surplus liquid **4** : OVERFLOW PIPE **5 a** : continuance of the sense or extension of a rhetorical unit from one line into the next : ENJAMBMENT **b** : continuance of rhythm from one line into the next so that a foot begun at the end of a line may be completed at the beginning of the next : SYNAPHEA

3**overflow** \"\ *adj* [2*overflow*] **1** : constituting an overflow ⟨~ population from central New York —*Amer. Guide Series: Pa.*⟩ ⟨~ patients lie on floors and corridors —Gertrude Samuels⟩ **2** : so large as to exceed capacity and overflow ⟨sang before ~ crowds —*Amer. Guide Series: La.*⟩ ⟨a program with an ~ attendance —W.F.Cunningham⟩

**overflow bug** *n* : a beetle (*Platynus maculicollis*) of the family Carabidae of the western U.S. that is sometimes locally so numerous as to be a nuisance

**overflower** \ˌ=ˈ=\ *vt* **1** : to cover over with flowers **2** : to put forth flowers beyond strength or well-being

1**overflowing** \ˌ=ˈ=\ *adj* [ME, alter. (influenced by *-inge*, *-ing*, n. suffix, -ing) of *overflowende*, fr. OE *oferflōwende*, fr. pres. part. of *oferflōwan* to overflow] **1 a** : flowing over the brim : filled too full ⟨raised to his lips the ~ cup⟩ **b** : SUPERABUNDANT ⟨an . . . expanding outlet for the ~ rural population —V.G.Childe⟩ **2** : EBULLIENT, EXUBERANT ⟨breathed with ~ life —E.K.Brown⟩ ⟨the same ~ vitality —Louis Bromfield⟩ — **over·flow·ing·ly** *adv* — **over·flow·ing·ness** *n*

2**overflowing** \"\ *n* [fr. gerund of 1*overflow*] **1** : a condition where overflow takes place ⟨full to ~⟩ **2 a** : something that flows over : EXCESS, SUPERFLUITY **b** : overflowing or exuberant feeling or thought : EBULLITION — usu. used in pl. ⟨the ~s of his full mind —T.B.Macaulay⟩

**overflow pipe** *n* : a pipe to carry off overflow (as from a cistern)

**overflow worm** *n* : FALL ARMYWORM

**overfly** \ˌ=ˌ=ˈ=\ *vt* [¹*over* + *fly*] **1 a** : to fly over; *esp* : to pass over in an aircraft ⟨will not tolerate that our borders be *overflown* —*Springfield (Mass.) Daily News*⟩ **b** : to fly beyond : OVERSHOOT ⟨~ a landing field⟩ **2** : to fly better, farther, or higher than **3** : to fly (as a falcon) too often or too long

¹**overfold** \ˌ=ˌ=ˈ=\ *vt* [ME *overfolden* to fold over, fr. ¹*over* + *folden* to fold] : to fold over; *specif* : to push over so as to form an overturned anticline

²**overfold** \ˈ=ˌ=ˌ=\ *n* [¹*overfold*; intended as trans. of G *überfaltung*] **1** : an overturned anticline **2** : a sigmoid fold comprising an overturned anticline and a syncline

**over frame** *adv* [²*over* + *frame*] : outside the frame — used as a direction in television writing to indicate that the source of a sound (as a speaker) is not seen on the screen

**overfreight** \ˈ=ˌ=ˌ=\ *n* **1** : an excessive load or freight **2** *usu* **over freight** \"\ : all or part of a shipment separated from its waybill and without adequate marks

**over·fulfill** \ˌōvə(r)+\ *vt* : to fulfill and more than fulfill ⟨should the local steel mill ~ its plan —Harry Schwartz⟩ — **over·fulfillment** \"+\ *n*

¹**overfull** \ˌ=ˌ=ˈ=\ *adj* [ME, fr. OE *oferfull*, fr. *ofer*, adv., over + *full*] : too full ⟨seems ~ of phrases —Clyde Eagleton⟩ — **overfullness** *n* -ES

²**overfull** \"\ *adv* : to excess ⟨having drunk ~ of the human race —*Time*⟩

**overfull employment** *n* : a state of employment in which employers' demand for labor exceeds the available supply

**overgaiter** \ˈ=ˌ=ˌ=\ *n* : GAITER

**overgang** \ˌ=ˌ=ˈ=\ *vt* [ME *overgangen*, fr. OE *ofergangan*, fr. *ofer*, adv., over + *gangan* to go — more at GANG] *chiefly Scot* : to go over; *specif* : OVERCOME

**overgarment** \ˈ=ˌ=ˌ=\ *n* [ME *over garment*, fr. ³*over* + *garment*] : an outer garment

**overgear** \ˈ=ˌ=ˌ=\ *n* : a gear train in which the ultimately driven shaft has greater angular speed than the original driving shaft

**overgenerous** \ˌ=ˌ=ˈ=(=)=\ *adj* : unduly or extremely generous

**overget** \ˌ=ˌ=ˈ=\ *vt* [ME *overgeten*, fr. ¹*over* + *geten* to get] **1** *dial chiefly Eng* **a** : REACH **b** : OVERTAKE, PASS **2** : to get beyond : get over : recover from

**overgild** \ˈ=ˌ=, ˌ=ˌ=ˈ=\ *vt* [ME *overgilden*, fr. OE *ofergyldan*, fr. *ofer*, adv., over + *gyldan* to gild] : to gild over : VARNISH

¹**overglaze** \ˈ=ˌ=, ˌ=ˌ=ˈ=\ *vt* [¹*over* + *glaze*, v.] : to glaze over : cover or coat with a glaze or polish : coat so as to conceal

²**overglaze** \ˌ=ˌ=ˈ=\ *adj* [²*over* + *glaze*, n.] : applied over the glaze after firing; *also* : suitable for so applying — used of some colors; compare UNDERGLAZE

³**overglaze** \"\ *n* [³*over* + *glaze*, n.] : a glaze (as on pottery ware) applied over another

**overgloom** \ˌ=ˌ=ˈ=\ *vt* : to make gloomy : OVERSHADOW

**overgo** \ˌ=ˌ=ˈ=\ *vt* [ME *overgon*, fr. OE *ofergān*, fr. *ofer*, adv., over + *gān* to go] **1** *dial chiefly Brit* : to cross over or through **2** : to get the better of : EXCEL, EXCEED; *specif*, *dial chiefly Eng* : OVERPOWER, OVERBEAR

**overgot** *past of* OVERGET

**overgotten** *past part of* OVERGET

**overgown** \ˈ=ˌ=\ *n* : an outer or upper gown

**overgrain** \ˌ=ˌ=ˈ=\ *vt* : to grain over (a grained surface) in painting so as to enrich or emphasize the effect

**over·grain·er** \"ə(r)\ *n* : a brush used for overgraining

**overgraze** \ˌ=ˌ=ˈ=\ *vt* : to graze to excess ⟨*overgrazed* pastures⟩

**overground** \ˈ=ˌ=ˌ=\ *adj* [²*over* + *ground*] : situated over or above ground ⟨operate injuriously to the ~ system —Alvin Johnson⟩

**overgrow** \ˌ=ˌ=ˈ=\ *vb* [ME *overgrowen*, fr. ¹*over* + *growen* to grow] *vt* **1 a** : to grow over : cover with growth or herbage ⟨cellar holes, *overgrown* by bushes —*Amer. Guide Series: Maine*⟩ **b** *archaic* : OVERCOME, OVERBURDEN **2** : to grow beyond or rise above : OUTGROW ⟨has long since *overgrown* the limitations of a coterie —R.U.Johnson⟩ ~ *vi* **1** : to grow beyond the normal or natural size : grow too large ⟨when a scar ~*s* into a keloid —Morris Fishbein⟩ **2** : to become grown over (as with weeds)

**overgrown** \ˌ=ˌ=ˈ=\ *adj* [ME *overgrowen*, fr. past part. of *overgrowen* to overgrow] **1** : covered with overgrowth **2** : abnormally, disproportionately, or excessively grown

**overgrowth** \ˈ=ˌ=ˌ=\ *n* [fr. *overgrow*, after E *grow*: *growth*] **1 a** : excessive growth or its result : superfluous abundance **b** : HYPERTROPHY, HYPERPLASIA **2** : something that has grown over a place or thing

**overhall** *n* [by alter.] *chiefly dial* : OVERALL

¹**overhand** \ˈ=ˌ=ˌ=\ *n* [ME, fr. ³*over* + *hand*, n.] **1** *chiefly dial* : the upper hand : ADVANTAGE **2** [²*overhand*] : an overhand stroke (as in tennis)

²**overhand** \"\ *adj* [³*over* + *hand*, n.] **1** : done by grasping with the palm of the hand downward or inward toward the body; *esp* : playing or played with the hand in this position ⟨an ~ stroke in tennis⟩ **2** : OVERARM

³**overhand** \"\ *adv* : in an overhand manner or style

⁴**overhand** \"\ *vt* [³*overhand*] : to sew (cloth) with short vertical stitches along an edge of a seam, buttonhole, or hem

**overhanded** \ˌ=ˌ=ˈ=\ *adv* [³*over* + *-handed* (fr. *hand*, n. + *-ed*)] : OVERHAND ⟨swung ~ with the cornstalk —J.H.Stuart⟩

**overhand knot** *n* : a small knot (as a stopper knot) often used as a part of other knots esp. as a means of preventing the end of a cord from fraying — called also *thumb knot*

overhand knot

**overhand loop knot** *n* : LOOP KNOT

**overhand stope** *n* : an excavation giving access to the under side of an ore body

¹**overhang** \ˌ=ˌ=ˈ=\ *vb* [¹*over* + *hang*] *vt* **1 a** : to jut, project, or be suspended over : hang over ⟨the wooden raft that *overhung* the iron hull —Fletcher Pratt⟩ **b** : to hang over threateningly : impend over ⟨the threat of death that *overhung* me —R.L.Stevenson⟩ **2** : to suspend (as a door) from above or from the top ~ *vi* : to project so as to be over something **syn** see BULGE

²**overhang** \ˈ=ˌ=\ *n* : something that overhangs: as **a** : the part of the bow or stern of a ship that projects over the water beyond the water line; *also* : the extent of the projection **b** : a projection of the roof or upper story of a building beyond the wall of the lower part : JETTY **c** : the forward pitch of a pile of lumber **d** : the part of a book cover extending beyond the page edges and forming squares — called also *overlap* **e** (1) : one half the difference in span of any two main supporting surfaces of an airplane, the overhang being positive when the upper of the two main supporting surfaces has the larger span (2) : the distance from the outer strut attachment to the tip of the wings (3) : the part of the balanced-control surface of an aircraft that extends ahead of the hinge

overhang b

**overhanging** \ˌ=ˌ=ˈ=\ *adj* **1** : JUTTING, PROJECTING ⟨crouching miserably under an ~ ledge —F.V.W.Mason⟩ **2** : hanging over threateningly

**overhappy** \ˌ=ˌ=ˈ=\ *adj* : too happy

**overhaste** \ˈ=ˌ=\ *n* [ME *overhast*, fr. ³*over* + *hast*, *haste* haste] : excessive haste

**overhasty** \ˌ=ˌ=ˈ=\ *adj* [ME, fr. ¹*over* + *hasty*] : too hasty : PRECIPITATE ⟨regarded as an ~ plan for reconversion —*Current Biog.*⟩

¹**over·haul** \ˌōvə(r)ˈhȯl\ *vb* [¹*over* + *haul*] *vt* **1 a** : to light (a ship's rope) along toward the block through which it is being hauled : pull (a ship's rope) through a block or lead so as to ease or slacken : CLEAR, DISENTANGLE **b** : to haul the parts of (a tackle) so as to separate the blocks **2 a** : to subject to strict examination with a view to correction or repair ⟨our systems of education are being constantly ~*ed* —*Saturday Rev.*⟩ ⟨the doctors ... ~*ed* him and found him pretty sound —C.P.Snow⟩ **b** : to repair (as by replacement of worn parts and readjustment) so as to restore to satisfactory working order ⟨~ an engine⟩ **c** : to clean up (a property) after a fire in order to make sure that the fire is extinguished and to prevent further damage (as by weather or falling debris) **3** : to gain upon in a chase : come up with : OVERTAKE ⟨~*ed* the transport very slowly —W.F.Jenkins⟩ ⟨~*ed* the U.S. in atomic research —*N.Y. Herald Tribune*⟩ ~ *vi* : to run or slack back when the pulling power is removed ⟨an ~*ing* tackle⟩

²**overhaul** \ˈ=ˌ=\ *n* **1** : OVERHAULING ⟨she had just finished ~ in the Navy Yard —Wirt Williams⟩ ⟨planning a major ~ of its highways —J.N.Robertson⟩ ⟨had an ~, and was treated for sinus trouble —Viola Meynell⟩ **2 a** : the distance for which payment is made for haulage of excavated material that is usu. the excess over a specified distance of free haulage **b** : the number of cubic yards moved through the overhaul distance multiplied by the overhaul distance in units of 100 feet

**over·haul·er** \ˌ=ˌ=ˈhȯlə(r)\ *n* : one that overhauls

**overhauling** \ˌ=ˌ=ˈ=\ *n* : the action of one that overhauls : an instance of such action ⟨our whole system of taxation needs ... ~ —D.D.Eisenhower⟩

¹**overhead** \ˌ=ˌ=ˈ=\ *adv* [²*over* + *head*, n.] **1** : above one's head: as **a** : in the sky : on high : ALOFT ⟨looking up at the stars ~⟩ ⟨~ the terns hovering close —E.A.Weeks⟩ **b** : in the story or on the floor above ⟨making a terrific racket ~⟩ **2** : so as to be covered head and all ⟨plunged ~ into the water⟩

²**overhead** \ˈ=ˌ=ˌ=\ *adj* **1 a** : operating or situated above or overhead ⟨gardens ... equipped with ~ irrigation —*Monsanto Mag.*⟩ **b** : passing over the head ⟨an ~ rein⟩ **c** : above the grade of a railway or highway ⟨an ~ crossing⟩ **d** : having the driving part above the part driven ⟨an ~ pulley shaft⟩ **2** : general, indirect, or undistributed as distinct from particular and direct ⟨~ charges⟩ ⟨~ expenses⟩

³**overhead** \ˈ=ˌ=\ *n* **1 a** : those general charges or expenses in a business which cannot be charged up as belonging exclusively to any particular part of the work or product (as rent, taxes, insurance, lighting, heating, accounting and other office expenses, and depreciation) **b** : a particular charge of such character ⟨there were too many ~*s* —F.D.Ommanney⟩ **2** : CEILING ⟨a big room with a low ~ —R.O.Bowen⟩; *esp* : the ceiling of a ship's compartment **3** *North & Midland* : a loft in a barn; *specif* : HAYMOW **4** : a stroke in a racket game made above head height : SMASH **5** : the effluent vapor from the top of a distillation column

**overhead fire** *n* : fire directed over the heads of friendly troops

**overhead man** *n* **1** : an electrician in a motion picture studio who plugs lighting, camera, sound, and telephone circuits into the power connection boxes located in the grid of the studio — called also *grid man* **2** : an operator of an electric bridge crane

**overhead railway** *n* : one track crossing another by an overhead bridge

**overhead valve** *n* : an internal-combustion engine valve operated from a camshaft running above the cylinder head

**overhear** \ˌ=ˌ=ˈ=\ *vt* : to hear (a speaker or his speech) without the speaker's knowledge or intention ⟨could not help ~*ing* the talk —A.W.Long⟩ ~ *vi* : to overhear something

¹**overheat** \ˌ=ˌ=ˈ=\ *vb* [ME *overheten*, fr. ¹*over* + *heten* to heat] *vt* **1** : to heat to excess; *specif* : to heat (a metal) to a temperature so high that the grain structure is coarsened to an undesirable but not irreparable degree **2** : to excite or agitate to excess or unduly ⟨~*ed* by nationalism —A.T.Bouscaren⟩ ~ *vi* : to become overheated

²**overheat** \"\ *n* : excessive heat or fervor

**overheated** *adj* **1** : heated beyond the safe or desirable point ⟨~ metal⟩ ⟨the child became ~⟩ **2** : marked by or arousing excessive passion, fervor, or excitement ⟨the perennially ~ Malthusian debate —*Economist*⟩ ⟨an occasional ~ adjective —Billy Rose⟩

**overheavy** \ˌ=ˌ=ˈ=\ *adj* : unduly or extremely heavy

**overhie** \ˌ=ˌ=ˈ=\ *vt* [ME *overhien*, fr. ¹*over* + *hien* to hasten — more at HIE] *archaic* : OVERTAKE

**overhook** \ˌ=ˌ=ˈ=\ *vt* : to pass an arm over so as to hook in wrestling

**overhung** *past of* OVERHANG

**overhung door** \ˈ=ˌ=-\ *n* : a sliding door suspended from the top (as upon rollers)

**overindulge** \ˌ=ˌ=ˈ=\ *vb* [¹*over* + *indulge*] : to indulge to excess

**overindulgence** \ˌ=ˌ=ˈ=\ *n* [³*over* + *indulgence*] : excessive indulgence ⟨~ in reading —H.G.Armstrong⟩

**overindulgent** \ˌ=ˌ=ˈ=\ *adj* [¹*over* + *indulgent*] : marked by overindulgence : too indulgent : indulging too much

**overinform** \ˌ=ˌ=ˈ=\ *vt* **1** : to actuate or animate excessively **2** : to furnish with abundant or excessive information

**overing** *pres part of* OVER

**over·insurance** \ˌōvə(r)+\ *n* [³*over* + *insurance*] **1** : insurance that exceeds in amount the actual cash value of the property insured **2** : insurance in a greater amount than the insured can afford

**over·insured** \"+\ *adj* [¹*over* + *insured* (past part. of *insure*)] **1** : insured for more than the real value **2** : insured in a greater amount than one can afford

**over·intricate** \"+\ *adj* [¹*over* + *intricate*] : unnecessarily or impracticably intricate ⟨an ~ scheme⟩

¹**overissue** \ˌ=ˌ=(ˌ)=\ *n* [³*over* + *issue*] **1** : an excessive issue : an issue (as of bonds) exceeding the limit of capital, credit, or authority **2** : printed matter remaining unsold or undistributed ⟨purchase ~ as wastepaper for pulping⟩

²**overissue** \"\ *vt* [¹*over* + *issue*] : to issue in excess

**over·ite** \ˈōvəˌrīt\ *n* -S [Edwin *Over b*1903 Am. mineral collector + E *-ite*] : a mineral $Ca_3Al_8(PO_4)_8(OH)_6.15H_2O$ consisting of hydrous basic phosphate of aluminum and calcium

**over·jet** \ˌ=ˈjet\ *n* [prob. fr. ³*over* + *-jet* (fr. *jet*, v., to jut)] : OVERBITE

**overjoy** \ˌ=ˌ=ˈ=\ *vt* : to fill with great joy : cause to rejoice ⟨~*ed* me when I read it —H.J.Laski⟩ ⟨the dealers it failed to ~ —J.M.Conly⟩

**overjump** \ˌ=ˌ=ˈ=\ *vt* **1** : to jump over **2** : to jump too far over

**overkeep** \ˌ=ˌ=ˈ=\ *vt* : to keep too strictly or too long

**overkind** \ˌ=ˌ=ˈ=\ *adj* [ME *overkinde*, fr. ¹*over* + *kinde* kind, natural — more at KIND] : excessively kind — **over·kind·ly** *adv* — **over·kind·ness** *n*

**overking** \ˈ=ˌ=\ *n* [ME, fr. ³*over* + *king*] : a king who has sovereignty over inferior kings or ruling princes

**overknee** \ˈ=ˌ=\ *adj* [²*over* + *knee*, n.] : extending above the knee ⟨~ boots⟩

**overlabor** \ˌ=ˌ=ˈ=\ *vt* : OVERWORK

**overlace** \ˌ=ˌ=ˈ=\ *vt* : to lace over : cover with a lacing ⟨*overlaced* with a fantasy of color and sculpture —H.B.Alexander⟩

**overlade** \ˌ=ˌ=ˈ=\ *vt* [ME *overladen*, fr. ¹*over* + *laden* to load — more at LADE] : to load with too great a cargo or burden : OVERLOAD ⟨*overladen* with detail and digression —H.S.Bennett⟩

**overlaid** *past of* OVERLAY

**overlain** *past part of* OVERLIE

¹**over·land** \ˈ=ˌland, -ˌlaa(ə)nd *also* ˌ=ˈ= *or* ˈ=ˌlənd\ *adv* [ME *overlond*, fr. ²*over* + *lond*, *land* land] : by, upon, or across land ⟨advantages of transport by river, instead of ~ —G.S.L.Clowes⟩

²**overland** \ˈ=ˌland, -ˌlaa(ə)nd *also* -lənd\ *adj* : going or accomplished over the land instead of by sea ⟨an ~ route⟩ ⟨~ emigrants⟩

³**overland** \ˈ=ˌ=\ *vt*, *Austral* : to drive (herds or flocks of livestock) overland esp. for considerable distances ~ *vi*, *Austral* : to make a journey overland esp. while driving livestock

⁴**overland** \ˈ=ˌ=\ *n* [prob. fr. ³*over* + *land*] : land formerly held in the severalty of England by any of several kinds of local tenure

**over·land·er** \ˈ=ˌlandə(r), -ˌlaan-\ *n* **1** : one that travels overland **2** *Austral* : one that drives livestock overland

¹**overlap** \ˌ=ˌ=ˈ=\ *vb* [¹*over* + *lap*] *vt* **1** : to extend over and cover a part of : lap over : OVERLIE ⟨the vertical siding has *overlapped* joints —*Amer. Guide Series: N.C.*⟩ ⟨if branches of a tree ~ the boundary of a neighbor —F.D.Smith & Barbara Wilcox⟩ **2** : to have something in common with : comprehend elements of : coincide in part with ⟨every personality ~*s* every other personality —*Encyc. Americana*⟩ ⟨the baroque period ~*s* the rococo⟩ ~ *vi* **1** : to lap over : occupy the same area in part ⟨the two towns ... now ~ —*Amer. Guide Series: Oregon*⟩ **2** : to have something in common : coincide in part ⟨the realm where philosophy and psychology ~ —L.W.Beck⟩ ⟨believe that aesthetics partly ~*s* with ethics —Peter Viereck⟩

²**overlap** \ˈ=ˌ=\ *n* **1 a** : the condition or relationship of things that overlap : an instance of such a condition or relationship ⟨found to have unexpected areas of ~ —*Times Lit. Supp.*⟩ ⟨this incongruous ~ of civilization and savagery —*Time*⟩ **b** : the extent to which or the area in which one thing overlaps another ⟨provide a good ~ between the jacket and trousers —H.G.Armstrong⟩ ⟨a large ~ between emotions and their understanding —S.J.Beck⟩ **c** : a part that overlaps **2** : OVERHANG d **3** : the position of two ships when one overtaking the other cannot without dropping astern pass on the other side from that on which she is approaching and when the ships cannot turn toward each other without the risk of fouling **4** : a geological unconformity in which each successively younger bed within the younger group of strata extends beyond the edge of the next older bed **5** : an area of deposited metal that is not fused to the parent metal in welding **6** : a section of railroad track controlled by one signal that extends into territory controlled by another signal

**overlap fault** *n* : a reversed fault

**overlap grip** *n* : a grip for holding a golf club in which the little finger of the right hand overlaps the left forefinger

**overlapping** \ˌ=ˌ=ˈ=\ *n* **1** : OVERLAP **2** *prosody* : ENJAMBMENT, SYNAPHEA — **over·lap·ping·ly** *adv*

**overlard** \ˌ=ˌ=ˈ=\ *vt* : to lard, line, or cover thickly ⟨a pride ~*ed* with fear —A.H.Raskin⟩

**overlarge** \ˌ=ˌ=ˈ=\ *adj* : too large

**overlaw** \ˈ=ˌ=\ *n* : a higher law ⟨some mystic ~ that it is bound to obey —O.W.Holmes †1935⟩

¹**overlay** \ˌ=ˌ=ˈ=\ *vt* [ME *overleyen*, fr. ¹*over* + *leyen* to lay] **1 a** : to lay or spread over or across : SUPERIMPOSE, COVER ⟨the whole subject ... is *overlaid* by stratum upon stratum of folklore —C.H.Andrewes⟩ ⟨*overlaid* with a thick veneer —Paul Pickrel⟩ **b** *printing* : to prepare an overlay for ⟨~ a cut⟩ **2 a** *obs* : to crush or overwhelm by massive force : OVERPOWER **b** : to smother (as an infant) by lying upon **c** *archaic* : to weigh down : OVERBURDEN, ENCUMBER **3** : to hide or obscure by or as if by superimposition

²**overlay** \ˈ=ˌ=\ *n* **1** *Scot* : NECKTIE, CRAVAT **2** : a covering either permanent or of a temporary and removable kind: as **a** : ornamental work formed by overlaying as with veneer **b** : an ornamental metal covering produced by inserting a decoration made of another metal **c** : a transparent cover on art work or a photograph; *esp* : such a cover carrying instructions to the engraver (as for color breaks or cropping) **d** : material (as paper patches) added to the packing on a printing press to make a stronger impression; *also* : the patched sheet itself — compare INTERLAY, UNDERLAY **e** : a decorative and contrasting design or article placed on top of a plain one ⟨an ~ of lace on a black collar⟩ **f** : a transparent sheet containing graphic matter (as map data) to be superimposed on another sheet (as a map or photograph) **3** : a betting situation in which the odds on a horse go up beyond those estimated by the track handicapper in the morning line

**overlayer** \ˈōvə(r)+ˌ\ *n* : one that overlays; *esp* : OVERLAY ⟨an ~ of whimsy and of sophistication —Frank Nugent⟩

**overleaf** \ˌ=ˌ=ˈ=\ *adv* [²*over* + *leaf*, n.] : on or to the other side of a leaf (as of a book) ⟨data ... tabulated ~ —A.L.Kroeber⟩

**overleap** \ˌ=ˌ=ˈ=\ *vt* [ME *overlepen*, fr. OE *oferhlēapan*, fr. *ofer*, adv., over + *hlēapan* to run, jump, leap] **1 a** : to leap over or across ⟨~*ing* the bars of caste —Douglas Bush⟩ **b** : OMIT, IGNORE ⟨perhaps ~*ed* logic —H.O.Taylor⟩ **2** : to cause (oneself) to leap beyond one's mark or aim : defeat (oneself) by leaping too far

**overlearn** \ˌ=ˌ=ˈ=\ *vt* : to continue to study or practice after reaching a criterion level of performance ⟨~*ed* techniques⟩

**overleather** *n* [ME *overlether*, fr. ³*over* + *lether* leather] *obs* : upper leather

¹**overleave** \ˌ=ˌ=ˈ=\ *adv* [²*over* + *leave*, n.] : after the period of leave granted ⟨that time they went back ... ~ —K.M.Dodson⟩

²**overleave** \"\ *adj* : absent beyond the period of leave granted ⟨might simply be ~ —T.O.Heggen⟩

**overleaven** *vt*, *obs* : to leaven too much; *also* : to cause to swell excessively

**overliberal** \ˌ=ˌ=ˈ=(=)=\ *adj* : too liberal — **overliberality** \ˌ=ˌ=ˌ=ˈ=\ *n* — **overliberally** \ˌ=ˌ=ˈ=(=)=\ *adv*

**overlie** \ˌ=ˌ=ˈ=\ *vt* [ME *overliggen*, *overlien*, fr. ¹*over* + *liggen*, *lien* to lie, recline] **1** : to lie over : lie or rest upon ⟨where warm water ~*s* colder waters —R.E.Coker⟩ ⟨the normal ... granitic layer that ~*s* it —A.E.Benfield⟩ **2** : to cause the death of by lying upon ⟨sows that ~ their piglets⟩ ⟨will join the tragedies of the *overlain* —*Times Lit. Supp.*⟩

¹**overlift** \ˌ=ˌ=ˈ=\ *vt* [¹*over* + *lift*] : to lift too high or too much

²**overlift** \ˈ=ˌ=\ *n* : a device to catch the bolt of a lock when one of the tumblers is overlifted

**overlight** \ˌ=ˌ=ˈ=\ *vt* : to subject to or provide with an excess of light ⟨an ~*ed* picture⟩ ⟨garish *overlit* rooms⟩

¹**overline** \ˌ=ˌ=ˈ=\ *vt* [¹*over* + *line*] : to draw a line or lines over or above

²**overline** \ˈ=ˌ=\ *n* [³*over* + *line*] **1** : a printed line usu. underlined and of a smaller size or different type face than the headline proper run above a headline and designed to introduce or identify the matter of the story or provoke to read on **2** : the title or explanatory matter above a picture or cartoon in a newspaper or periodical **3** : an insertion, correction, or alteration made above the printed or manuscript line it applies to — distinguished from *underline*

**overlive** \ˌ=ˌ=ˈ=\ *vb* [ME *overliven*, fr. OE *oferlibban*, fr. *ofer*, adv., over + *libban* to live] *vt*, *archaic* : OUTLIVE ~ *vi*, *archaic* : to continue to live : live too long

¹**overload** \ˌ=ˌ=ˈ=\ *vb* [¹*over* + *load*] *vt* : to load to excess : load with too great a burden ⟨~ a wagon⟩ ⟨~ a ship⟩ ⟨~ a circuit⟩ ~ *vi* : to assume or impose an excessive load ⟨tendency of most women travelers ... to ~ on beauty preparations —T.H.Fielding⟩

²**overload** \ˈ=ˌ=\ *n* : an excessive load : the excess beyond a proper load ⟨issue special permits for ~*s* —R.R.Ireland⟩

**overlock** \ˌ=ˌ=ˈ=\ *vt* **1** : to interlock or intertwine above **2** : to shoot (a bolt) beyond its first or normal locking **3** : to overcast by machine — compare SERGING

¹**overlong** \ˌ=ˌ=ˈ=\ *adj* [ME, fr. ¹*over* + *long*] : extremely long or too long ⟨thought some of the stories ~ —*Current Biog.*⟩ ⟨this ~ novel —Clifton Fadiman⟩

²**overlong** \"\ *adv* [ME *overlonge*, fr. ¹*over* + *longe* long] : for too long a time ⟨this period ... did not last ~ —J.T.Winterich⟩

¹**overlook** \ˌ=ˌ=ˈ=\ *vt* [ME *overloken*, fr. ¹*over* + *loken* to look] **1** : to look over or through : INSPECT, SURVEY, PERUSE ⟨took down a map and ~*ed* it —Eileen Duggan⟩ ⟨most good modern authors, which I have never even ~*ed* —Arnold Bennett⟩ **2 a** *obs* : to regard as inferior or low : SLIGHT **b** : to look down upon from a place that is over or above : look over or view from a higher position ⟨do not like living near water, and prefer not to be ~*ed* —G.W.B.Huntingford⟩ **c** : to rise above or afford a view of : OVERTOP ⟨a house ~*ing* the Pacific —*Current Biog.*⟩ ⟨deep-blue water, ~*ed* by seven volcanoes —Norman Zimmern⟩ ⟨a tower ~*ing* the city —*N.Y.Times*⟩ **3 a** : to look over and beyond so as to fail to see : miss or omit in looking : fail to notice ⟨which would otherwise be entirely ~*ed*, may be seen at night with a flashlight —*Boy Scout Handbook*⟩ ⟨whose sharpened senses ~ nothing —Richard Semon⟩ **b** : to fail to take due note of : pass over : IGNORE, DISREGARD ⟨hungry enough to ~ my scruples —Frank O'Leary⟩ ⟨the editor cannot ~ the problem —Bruce Westley⟩ **c** : to pass over without censure or punishment : EXCUSE ⟨decided to ~ the blank paper he turned in for Latin —*Current Biog.*⟩ ⟨minor misdemeanors may sometimes be ~*ed* —*Punch*⟩ **4** : to watch over : SUPERVISE, OVERSEE ⟨sent ... as her envoy to ~ the conduct of the Kalmucks —Thomas De Quincey⟩ **5** : to look on with the evil eye : bewitch by looking on ⟨a baby that has been ~*ed* will begin to pine away —F.G.Cassidy⟩ **syn** see NEGLECT

²**overlook** \ˈ=ˌ=\ *n* **1** : an act of overlooking; *specif* : OVERSIGHT ⟨a slight ~ on my part⟩ **2** : a place from which one may

look down upon a scene below ⟨plenty of ~s and trails — Thelma H. Bell⟩

**overlooker** \ˈ==ˌ==\ *n* [ME *overloker*, fr. *overloken* to overlook + *-er*] **:** one that overlooks: as **a :** a superintendent or overseer of workers **:** FOREMAN **b :** a worker that flips the ends of stacks of newly cut paper in order to discover and remove defective sheets

[1]**overlord** \ˈ=ˌ=\ *n* [ME, fr. [3]*over* + *lord*] **1 :** a lord that is lord over other lords or rulers **:** a lord paramount ⟨when a man died leaving children under age, the ~ took over his land —G.G.Coulton⟩ ⟨the church professed to be . . . ~ of all temporal sovereigns —W.H.Hamilton⟩ **2 :** an absolute or supreme ruler ⟨~s of the financial world —*Amer. Guide Series: Ind.*⟩ ⟨Asian resentment toward the traditional white ~ —L.S.Feuer⟩

[2]**overlord** \ˈ=ˌ=\ *vt* [[1]*over* + *lord*] **:** to lord it over **:** rule domineeringly **:** TYRANNIZE

**over·lord·ship** \ˈ==ˌship, ˌ==ˈ=\ *n* **:** the position, power, or authority of an overlord

**overloup** \ˌ=ˈ=\ *n* [[3]*over* + *loup*] *archaic Scot* **:** TRESPASS, TRANSGRESSION

**overlove** \ˌ=ˈ=\ *vt* **:** to love to excess

**overlusty** \ˌ=ˈ==\ *adj* **:** too lusty

[1]**overly** *adj* [ME, fr. [1]*over* + *-ly*, adj. suffix] **1** *obs* **:** CARELESS, SUPERFICIAL, NEGLIGENT **2** *archaic* **:** OVERBEARING, SUPERCILIOUS

[2]**over·ly** \ˈōvə(r)lē, -li\ *adv* [ME, fr. [1]*over* + *-ly*, adv. suffix] **1** *archaic* **:** SUPERFICIALLY, CARELESSLY **2 :** EXCESSIVELY, TOO ⟨~ anxious⟩ ⟨~ retiring⟩

**overlying** *pres part of* OVERLIE

[1]**over·man** *n, pl* **overmen** [ME, fr. [3]*over* + *man*, n.] **1** \ˈōvə(r)mən, -ˌman\ **:** a man in authority over others **:** CHIEF; *specif* **:** FOREMAN **2** \ˈō(ə)rˌman, ˈōvər-\ *Scots law* **:** an arbiter or umpire appointed to settle a dispute between arbiters **3** \ˈōvə(r)ˌman\ [trans. of G *übermensch*] **:** SUPERMAN

[2]**over·man** \ˌ=ˈman\ *vt* [[1]*over* + *man*, v.] **:** to have or get too many men for the needs of ⟨~ a ship⟩

**overmantel** \ˈ==ˌ==, ˌ==ˈ==\ *n* [[2]*over* + *mantel*] **:** an ornamental structure (as a painting or a bas-relief) above a mantelpiece

**overmast** \ˌ=ˈ=\ *vt* [[1]*over* + *mast*, v.] **:** to furnish (a ship) with too long or too heavy masts

**overmaster** \ˌ==ˈ==\ *vt* [ME *overmaistren*, fr. [1]*over* + *maistren* to master] **1 :** to establish mastery over **:** SUBDUE, VANQUISH ⟨the sensation ~*ed* me completely —Rudyard Kipling⟩ **2** *obs* **:** to be master over

**overmastering** \ˌ==ˈ=(=)=\ *adj* **:** having complete or decisive mastery **:** DOMINANT, OVERRIDING ⟨some ~ motive which he could not guess at —John Buchan⟩ ⟨choking down some ~ emotion —A. Conan Doyle⟩ — **over·mas·ter·ing·ly** *adv*

[1]**overmatch** \ˌ=ˈ=\ *vt* [ME *overmacchen*, fr. [1]*over* + *macchen* to match] **1 a :** to be more than equal to or a match for ⟨a bleakness that ~*ed* his boredom —Booth Tarkington⟩ **b :** VANQUISH, DEFEAT ⟨with the unobtrusive action of an ~*ed* man —Joseph Furphy⟩ ⟨occasionally victorious and usually ~*ed* gladiators —Bennett Cerf⟩ **2 :** to match (as a team, a player, a prizefighter) with a superior opponent ⟨does all right . . . until his owner ~*es* him —John McCarten⟩

[2]**overmatch** \ˈ==ˌ=\ *n* **1 :** one superior in power ⟨met his ~⟩ **2 :** a contest in which one of the opponents is overmatched

**overmatter** \ˈ==ˌ==\ *n* **:** overset type matter; *esp* **:** that portion of the overset that is not used

**overmature** \ˌ===ˈ=\ *adj* **:** more than matured **:** past the age or condition of maturity or of fitness characteristic of maturity — **overmaturity** \ˌ===ˈ===\ *n*

**overmeasure** \ˈ==ˌ==\ *n* **:** excessive measure **:** the excess beyond true or proper measure **:** SURPLUS

**overmodest** \ˌ=ˈ==\ *adj* **:** excessively modest

**overmodulation** \ˌ==ˌ==ˈ==\ *n* **:** defective modulation in which the modulating signal is made too strong

**over·most** \ˈō(ə)rˌmōst, ˈōvər-, -ˌmast\ *adj* [ME, fr. [3]*over* + *-most*] *chiefly Scot* **:** UPPERMOST, HIGHEST

**overmount** \ˌ=ˈ=\ *vb* [ME *overmounten*, fr. [1]*over* + *mounten* to mount] *vt, archaic* **:** to mount over **:** go higher than **:** rise above ~ *vi, obs* **:** to mount too high

**overmountain** \ˌ=ˈ==\ *adj* [[2]*over* + *mountain*, n.] **:** situated or residing over the mountains ⟨the ~ farmers —Broadus Mitchell⟩

[1]**overmuch** \ˌ=ˈ=\ *adj* [ME *overmuche*, fr. [1]*over* + *muche*, adj., much] **:** very great or excessive ⟨does not claim ~ merit —Clifford Leech⟩

[2]**overmuch** \"\ *n* [ME *overmuche*, fr. *overmuche*, adj.] **:** too great an amount **:** EXCESS

[3]**overmuch** \"\ *adv* [ME *overmuche*, fr. [1]*over* + *muche*, adv., much] **:** in too great a degree **:** too much ⟨do not bother ~ about notes —L.R.McColvin⟩

**over·much·ness** \ˌ=ˈ==\ *n* **:** the condition of being overmuch **:** EXCESS

**overname** \ˌ=ˈ=\ *vt* **:** to name over **:** name in a series

**overnet** \ˌ=ˈ=\ *vt* **:** to cover or to snare with a net ~ *vi* **:** to use nets to excess in fishing

**over·nice** \ˌōvə(r)+\ *adj* [ME, fr. [1]*over* + *nice*] **:** excessively nice or particular: **a :** too fastidious **b :** too scrupulous ⟨untroubled by an ~ conscience —V.L.Parrington⟩ — **overnicely** \"+\ *adv* — **overniceness** \"+\ *n* — **overnicety** \"+\ *n*

[1]**overnight** \ˌ=ˈ=\ *adv* [ME *over night*, fr. [2]*over* + *night*, n.] **1 a :** in the evening before ⟨trying to tell a good story he heard ~ —O.S.J.Gogarty⟩ **b :** in the interval between two days ⟨allowing the coarser particles to settle out . . . ~ —*Jour. of Infectious Diseases*⟩ **c :** during the night **:** till the following morning ⟨stayed with friends ~⟩ **2 :** with great or extreme speed or suddenness **:** very quickly or suddenly **:** all of a sudden ⟨sprang up ~ in answer to a labor need —*Amer. Guide Series: Maine*⟩ ⟨no such perfected technique is born ~ —L.H. Appleton⟩

[2]**overnight** \ˈ==ˌ=, ˌ==ˈ=\ *n* **:** the fore part of the night last past **:** the previous evening ⟨his emotional rapture of the ~ —George Meredith⟩

[3]**overnight** \ˌ=ˈ=\ *adj* **1 a :** of, relating to, or resulting from the previous evening **:** done or lasting during the night ⟨an ~ carouse⟩ ⟨~ laughter is a commodity that I . . . am always ready to buy —Robert Hatch⟩ **b :** being of the duration of one night ⟨an ~ stop⟩ **:** staying one night ⟨~ guests⟩ **2 :** happening or appearing overnight ⟨became an ~ sensation —*Amer. Guide Series: Ind.*⟩

[4]**overnight** \"\ *vi* **:** to stay overnight ⟨~*ed* at the official presidential residence —*Wilkes-Barre (Pa.) Record*⟩

**overnight bag** *or* **overnight case** *or* **over·night·er** \ˌ==ˈnīd·ə(r)\ *n* -s **:** a traveling bag of a size to carry clothing and personal articles for an overnight trip

**overnight race** *n* **:** a horse race for which entries close 72 hours (exclusive of Sundays) or less before the first race of the day on which the race is scheduled to be run

**overnumber** \ˌ=ˈ==\ *vt, archaic* **:** OUTNUMBER

**overoffice** *vt, obs* **:** to domineer over by virtue of office

**overoptimism** \ˌ==ˈ===\ *n* **:** excessive optimism

**overoptimist** \ˌ==ˈ===\ *n* **:** an excessively optimistic person

**overoptimistic** \ˌ==ˌ==ˈ==\ *adj* **:** marked by overoptimism

**over·organization** \ˌōvə(r)+\ *n* **:** the act of overorganizing or the state of being overorganized

**over·organize** \"+\ *vt* **:** to subject to unduly complex or elaborate organization ~ *vi* **:** to adopt an unduly complex or elaborate form of organization

**over·ornate** \ˌōvə(r)+\ *adj* **:** unduly or excessively ornate

[1]**overpack** \ˌ=ˈ=\ *vt* [[1]*over* + *pack*] **:** to pack in an overpack

[2]**overpack** \"\ *n* **:** a wooden or fiber box used over a domestic box for overseas shipments for greater strength and protection

**overpaint** \ˌ=ˈ=\ *vt* **1 :** to paint over **:** paint out **2 :** to color or describe too strongly ⟨heavily ~*ed* the depression of English learning —F.M.Stenton⟩

**over·part·ed** \ˌōvərˈpärd·əd\ *adj* [[1]*over* + *-parted* (fr. *part*, n. + *-ed*)] **:** charged with a part or role beyond one's ability

**overparticular** \ˌōvə(r)+\ *adj* **:** extremely or unduly particular

[1]**overpass** \ˌ=ˈ=\ *vb* [ME *overpassen*, fr. [1]*over* + *passen* to pass] *vt* **1 a :** to pass or get through **:** get to the end of ⟨when that six months were ~*ed* —*Ballad Book*⟩ **b :** to manage to get through **:** SURMOUNT **2 :** to pass beyond in quality, value, degree, or amount **:** SURPASS, EXCEED ⟨so completely had his moral passion ~*ed* his concern for poetry —D.S.Savage⟩ **3 a :** to pass across, over, or beyond **:** go to the other side of **:** CROSS ⟨the last American frontier had been ~*ed* —H.J.Laski⟩ **b :** to pass over or beyond the restrictions of **:** TRANSGRESS ⟨a limit to patience . . . and when that was ~*ed*, then my anger blazed out —W.H.Hudson †1922⟩ ⟨~ the bounds of propriety⟩ **4 a :** to pass over without comment or mention **b :** to pass over in favor of another ⟨colonels who have been ~*ed* for commands —Rudyard Kipling⟩ ~ *vi* **:** to pass over, by, away, or off

[2]**overpass** \ˈ=ˌ=\ *n* **1 :** a grade separation where clearance to traffic on the lower level is obtained by elevating the higher level (as with a bridge or viaduct) — compare UNDERPASS **2 :** the upper level of a grade separation — called also *overcrossing*

**overpast** \ˌ=ˈ=\ *adj* [fr. *overpast*, *overpassed*, past part. of [1]*overpass*] **:** ENDED, PAST, OVER ⟨all that was ~ —Mary Webb⟩ ⟨the danger was well ~ —Rafael Sabatini⟩

**overpay** \ˌ=ˈ=\ *vt* **:** to pay too much to or for **:** compensate or reward beyond what is due

**overpayment** \ˌ=ˈ==\ *n* **:** payment in excess of what is due; *also* **:** the amount of such excess

**overpeer** \ˌ=ˈ=\ *vt* **1** *archaic* **a :** to rise or tower above **b :** EXCEL **2 :** to peer over **:** look down on **:** OVERLOOK ⟨~ the cabin —Maristan Chapman⟩

**overpeopled** \ˌ=ˈ==\ *adj* **:** too densely peopled

**overperch** *vt, obs* **:** to pass over as if by perching upon

**overpersuade** \ˌ===ˈ=\ *vt* [[1]*over* + *persuade*] **:** to persuade to adopt one's side or view **:** bring over by persuasion ⟨*overpersuaded* her finally —*Manchester Guardian Weekly*⟩

**overpersuasion** \ˌ===ˈ==\ *n* [fr. *overpersuade*, after E *persuade: persuasion*] **:** the act of overpersuading ⟨drank two glasses by his ~ —Samuel Richardson⟩

**overpester** *vt, obs* **:** to encumber to excess

[1]**overpick** \ˈ==ˌ=\ *adj* [[3]*over* + *pick*, n. (throw of the shuttle)] *of a loom* **:** having the picking arm or shuttle-driving device over the shuttle boxes — compare UNDERPICK

[2]**overpick** \"\ *n* **:** an overpick loom

**overpicture** \ˌ=ˈ==\ *vt* **1 :** to surpass nature in the picture or representation of **2 :** to cover with pictures

**overpitch** \ˌ=ˈ=\ *vt* [[1]*over* + *pitch*] **:** to pitch (a bowled ball) too close to the wicket in cricket

**overpitched** \ˌ=ˈ=\ *adj* [[1]*over* + *pitched* (past part. of *pitch*)] **:** having a too great pitch or slope ⟨an ~ roof⟩

**overplacement** \ˌ=ˈ==\ *n* **:** SUPERPOSITION

**overplaid** \ˈ==ˌ=\ *n* [[3]*over* + *plaid*] **:** a textile design consisting of a plaid pattern superimposed on another plaid or on a textured ground (as of tweed or herringbone); *also* **:** a fabric with such a design

**overplant** \ˌ=ˈ=\ *vt* **:** to plant (a crop) in excess of market demand or of the allotted acreage under a crop control order ~ *vi* **:** to plant in excess of demand or of the allotted acreage

[1]**overplay** \ˌ=ˈ=\ *vb* [[1]*over* + *play*, v.] *vt* **1 a :** to exaggerate (as a part in a play or an artistic effect) ⟨~ a comic role⟩ ⟨~*ed* every crescendo⟩ **b :** to exaggerate the importance or value of **:** give undue emphasis or attention to **:** OVERSTRESS ⟨~ those features of human attention that are peripheral —*Psychological Rev.*⟩ ⟨tends to ~ the intellectual achievement —*Times Lit. Supp.*⟩ ⟨the most ~*ed* newspaper story of 1954 —*Time*⟩ ⟨the present text ~*s* its points of strength —A.R. Turquette⟩ **c :** OVERDO ⟨a theatrical cliché that's ~*ed* —Ethel Merman⟩ **2 :** to rely too much upon the strength of **:** seek to gain too much advantage from — usu. used in the phrase *overplay one's hand* ⟨~*ing* their hands and tending to be greedy —*Sunday Independent (Dublin)*⟩ **3 :** to strike a golf ball so that it is driven beyond (a putting green) ~ *vi* **:** to exaggerate a part or effect ⟨her tendency to ~ —R.A. Hague⟩

[2]**overplay** \ˈ==ˌ=\ *n* [in sense 1, fr. *over* + *play*, n. (after the verb phrase *play over*); in sense 2, fr. [1]*overplay*] **1 :** a replay of a hand in duplicate whist **2 :** exaggerated or undue emphasis or treatment **:** OVERSTRESS ⟨~ of highly sensational stories —F.L.Mott⟩

**overplot** \ˌ=ˈ=\ *vt* **:** to devise an unduly complex or elaborate plot for (as a novel)

**overplow** \ˌ=ˈ=\ *vt* **:** to plow, work, or exploit to excess ⟨Shakespearean commentary is a special and ~*ed* field —Henry Hewes⟩ ⟨grassy hills . . . were ~*ed* —Russell Lord⟩

**over·plus** \ˈōvə(r)ˌpləs\ *n* -ES [ME, part trans. of MF *surplus* — more at SURPLUS] **:** that which remains above a proper or fit supply or beyond a quantity proposed **:** SURPLUS ⟨a lack of leaders and an ~ of followers —*Brit. Birds in Colour*⟩ **syn** see EXCESS

[2]**overplus** *adv, obs* **:** in addition **:** beyond need

**overply** \ˌ=ˈ=\ *vt* **:** to ply to excess **:** OVEREXERT, OVERWORK

**overpoise** \ˌ=ˈ=\ *vt* [[1]*over* + obs. E *poise* to weigh, fr. ME *poisen* — more at POISE] *archaic* **:** OUTWEIGH

**overpole** \ˌ=ˈ=\ *vt* **:** to pole (a metal) too long

**overpopulate** \ˌ=ˈ===\ *vt* **:** to populate too densely **:** cause to have too great a population

**overpopulation** \ˌ==ˌ==ˈ==\ *n* **:** the condition of being overpopulated; *also* **:** an excess of population

**overpot** \ˌ=ˈ=\ *vt* **:** to plant in too large a pot

**overpotential** \ˌ===ˈ==\ *n* **:** OVERVOLTAGE

**overpower** \ˌ=ˈ==\ *vt* [[1]*over* + *-power* (fr. *power*, n.)] **1 :** to get the better of by superior force or power **:** SUBDUE, VANQUISH ⟨war ~*ed*, dragged out into the open —*Amer. Guide Series: Tenn.*⟩ ⟨by a margin of 15,000 votes . . . was ~*ed* by the winner —*Time*⟩ **2 :** to affect overwhelmingly by reason of great power or intensity ⟨when hunger ~*s* him —J.G. Frazer⟩ ⟨the odor ~*ed* him⟩ ⟨his instinct for heroics ~*ed* him —Gerald Beaumont⟩ **3 :** to supply with more power than is needed ⟨never ~ your boat —Peter Heaton⟩

**syn** OVERWHELM, WHELM, ENGULF, DELUGE, SWAMP: OVERPOWER applies to defeating or reducing to submission or ineffectiveness by vastly superior force ⟨a sentry *overpowered* by the attackers⟩ ⟨resistance *overpowered* in a few days⟩ ⟨*overpowered* by the show of wealth around him⟩ OVERWHELM may suggest submerging, overcoming, vanquishing, destroying, or overpowering in the manner of a breaking ocean wave ⟨Scotland was *overwhelmed* by the ice sheets of the great Ice Age —L.D.Stamp⟩ ⟨it was between the inner and outer shoal that disaster *overwhelmed* the lifeboat and her crew —G.G. Carter⟩ ⟨his hopeless endeavor to stem the rising flood of irrationalism and slave-spirit that were soon to *overwhelm* the great Roman world —Norman Douglas⟩ WHELM is a close synonym for OVERWHELM in its dire uses ⟨it seemed as though the entire town might go — as though the sea would *whelm* houses, vessels, and town together —Mary H. Vorse⟩ ⟨this report reached his periwigged Excellency about the time that his own city was being overwhelmed by earthquake; he had little time for ancient ruins when his own was *whelmed* with destruction —V.W. Von Hagen⟩ ENGULF suggests swallowing up as by rushing waters, or catching, burying, entangling, or covering hopelessly so that extrication is impossible ⟨Bonnet thought that periodically the world was *engulfed* by a major catastrophe, the last one being the Mosaic flood —S.F.Mason⟩ ⟨the doom of madness that had *engulfed* her aunt —Edith Sitwell⟩ DELUGE implies a concentrated massing, as of torrential rain, that overwhelms; it is usu. used figuratively ⟨the speaker was *deluged* with questions⟩ ⟨as Yellow Cabs drove up with strikebreakers they were *deluged* with rotten fruit from the trucks —R.M.Lovett⟩ SWAMP, originally in the passive suggesting entanglement or submersion in a swamp, now is close to DELUGE, although it may indicate more hopeless entangling or oppressing ⟨a sea broke over them, and would have *swamped* the *Otter*, had she not been the best of sea boats —Charles Kingsley⟩ ⟨the work rose about him like a tide. It *swamped* his days —Mary Austin⟩ ⟨the mind is *swamped* by the bewildering complexity of directions —R.W. Southern⟩

**overpowering** *adj* **:** exercising an irresistible influence **:** OVERWHELMING ⟨her ~ beauty struck his heart —George Meredith⟩ ⟨both men . . . were ~ personalities —Bernard Smith⟩ — **over·pow·er·ing·ly** *adv*

[1]**overpraise** \ˌ=ˈ=\ *vt* [ME *overpreisen*, fr. [1]*over* + *preisen* to praise] **:** to praise excessively

[2]**overpraise** \ˈ=ˌ=\ *n* **:** excessive praise

[1]**overpress** \ˌ=ˈ=\ *vt* [ME *overpressen*, fr. [1]*over* + *pressen* to press] **1** *obs* **:** AFFLICT, OPPRESS **2 :** to load with an excessive burden **:** OVERBURDEN ⟨all very tired and ~*ed* men —*Economist*⟩ **3 :** to press or insist upon unduly **:** drive or push (as a contention) too far ⟨does not ~ his case —P.R.Levin⟩

[2]**overpress** \ˈ=ˌ=\ *n* **:** OVERPRESSURE ⟨~ of work⟩

**overpressure** \ˈ=ˌ==\ *n* **:** excessive pressure

**overprice** \ˌ=ˈ=\ *vt* **:** to set too high a price on **:** charge too much for

[1]**overprint** \ˌ=ˈ=\ *vt* [[1]*over* + *print*] **1 a :** to print over (matter already printed) with something additional **:** SURPRINT **:** IMPRINT **b :** to print too many copies of **2** *photog* **a :** to print too long or with too great an intensity of light **b :** to print (one image) on another **3 a :** to place an overprint on (a stamp) **b :** to mark (a stamp) with a specified overprint ⟨a stamp ~*ed* Samoa⟩ **c :** to make (a specified mark) on a stamp as an overprint ⟨~ a date on a stamp⟩ **4 :** to type (typewriter characters) one over another to form a character not on the keys ⟨a star is formed by ~*ing* A and v⟩

[2]**overprint** \ˈ=ˌ=\ *n* **1 :** something added by overprinting ⟨road classification is shown by a red ~ —*U. S. Geol. Survey*⟩ **2 a :** a printed marking (as a letter, figure, name, date, inscription) added to a postage or revenue stamp before its sale as a postage or revenue item; *esp* **:** one that alters the original (as in denomination, locality, or use) or that commemorates a special event — compare SURCHARGE **b :** a stamp bearing an overprint

[3]**overprint** \"\ *adj* **:** used in overprinting ⟨~ ink⟩ ⟨~ varnish⟩

**overprivileged** \ˌ=ˈ=(=)=\ *adj* **:** privileged to excess; *specif* **:** endowed with too much of the world's goods

**overprize** \ˌ=ˈ=\ *vt* **1 :** to prize excessively **:** OVERVALUE **2** *obs* **:** to exceed in value

**overproduce** \ˌ===ˈ=\ *vt* **:** to produce beyond the demand or allotted amount

**overproduction** \ˌ===ˈ==\ *n* **:** excessive production **:** supply beyond the demand at remunerative prices

**overpronounce** \ˌ===ˈ=\ *vt* **:** to give an exaggerated, affected, or unnaturally accented pronunciation to (as in \ˈgůdē,nəf\ instead of \ˈgůdᵊn,əf\ for *good enough*) ~ *vi* **:** to overpronounce a word, phrase, or other speech element

**overpronunciation** \ˌ===ˌ==ˈ==\ *n* **:** the act or an instance of overpronouncing

**overproof** \ˌ=ˈ=\ *adj* [[2]*over* + *proof*, n.] **:** containing more alcohol than proof spirit

[1]**overproportion** \ˌ===ˈ==\ *vt* [[1]*over* + *proportion*] **:** to make of too great proportion **:** make disproportionately large

[2]**overproportion** \"\ *n* **:** proportion in excess of the norm

**overprotect** \ˌ===ˈ=\ *vt* **:** to protect or shield unduly or excessively ⟨~*ed* children⟩

**overprotection** \ˌ===ˈ==\ *n* **:** undue or excessive protection or shielding; *specif* **:** excessive restriction of a child's behavior allegedly in the interest of his health and welfare by an anxious, insecure, or domineering mother — compare MOMISM

**overprotective** \ˌ===ˈ==\ *adj* **:** unduly or excessively protective

**overprove** \ˌ=ˈ=\ *vt* **:** to provide more proof of than is needed

**overquick** \ˌ=ˈ=\ *adj* **:** too quick or ready — **over·quick·ly** *adv*

**over·rank** *R & -R* ˈōvə+, *R sometimes* -vər+ *esp for emphasis*\ *adj* **:** too rank or luxuriant in growth

[1]**overrate** \ˌ=ˈ=\ *vt* [[1]*over* + *rate*] **:** to rate, value, or estimate too highly ⟨inclined to say that you ~ morality —Havelock Ellis⟩

[2]**overrate** \ˈ=ˌ=\ *n* **:** an excessive rate; *also* **:** an extra rate

[1]**overreach** \ˌ=ˈ=\ *vb* [ME *overrechen*, fr. [1]*over* + *rechen* to reach] *vt* **1 :** to reach above or beyond **:** go beyond **:** OVERTOP ⟨regard anything as vulgar that ~*es* their own attempts —R. P.Warren⟩ **2 :** to reach or come up with **:** OVERTAKE **3 :** to defeat or thwart (oneself) by seeking to do or gain too much ⟨one promoter, ~*ing* himself, demanded an exorbitant price —*Amer. Guide Series: Pa.*⟩ ⟨owns a number of . . . properties but has never ~*ed* himself —W.L.Gresham⟩ or by being too crafty ⟨the red prowler's cunning ~*ed* itself —C.G.D.Roberts⟩ **4 :** to get the better of esp. by sharp, unfair, tricky, or deceitful means **:** OUTWIT ⟨never made any bargain without ~*ing* . . . the person with whom he dealt —Henry Fielding⟩ ~ *vi* **1** *of a horse* **:** to strike the toe of the hind foot against the heel or quarter of the forefoot **:** GRAB **2 a :** to reach or go too far **b :** to go to excess ⟨if at times the argument wears thin, it is because . . . he ~*es* —S.L.A.Marshall⟩ **b :** EXAGGERATE **syn** see CHEAT

[2]**overreach** \ˈ==ˌ=, ˌ==ˈ=\ *n* **1 :** the act of overreaching **2 a :** the act of striking the heel of the forefoot with the toe of the hind foot — used of a horse **b :** the injury so caused

**over·reach·er** \ˌ==ˈrēchə(r)\ *n* **:** one that overreaches

**overreaching** \ˌ==ˈ==\ *adj* **:** tending to overreach; *esp* **:** CHEATING ⟨are generally poor, greedy, and ~ —Tobias Smollett⟩ — **over·reach·ing·ly** *adv*

**overreact** \ˌ===ˈ=\ *vi* **:** to react excessively or too strongly ⟨~*s* to situations which do not entirely please him —A.C. Kinsey⟩

**overread** *vt* [ME *overreden*, fr. OE *oferrǣdan*, fr. *ofer*, adv., over + *rǣdan* to read] *obs* **:** to read over or through

**overreadiness** \ˌ==ˈ===\ *n* **:** the quality or state of being overready

**overready** \ˌ=ˈ==\ *adj* **:** extremely or unduly ready

**overreckon** \ˌ=ˈ==\ *vt* **1 :** OVERESTIMATE **2 :** to overcharge in a reckoning

**overred** \ˌ=ˈ=\ *vt, archaic* **:** to smear with red

**overrefine** \ˌ==ˈ=\ *vt* [[1]*over* + *refine*] **:** to refine to excess

**overrefinement** \ˌ==ˈ==\ *n* **:** excessive refinement

**overregulate** \ˌ=ˈ===\ *vt* **:** to subject to excessive regulation

**overregulation** \ˌ==ˌ==ˈ==\ *n* **:** excessive regulation

**overrepresent** \ˌ===ˈ=\ *vt* **:** to give excessive representation to ⟨~*s* the rural counties in the state⟩ — **overrepresentation** \ˌ===ˌ=(ˌ)=ˈ==\ *n*

[1]**override** \ˌ=ˈ=\ *vt* [ME *overriden*, fr. OE *oferrīdan*, fr. *ofer*, adv., over + *rīdan* to ride] **1 a :** to ride over or across ⟨where the beach is steep big waves break directly on it and ~ it —J.A.Steers⟩ ⟨prevent the ship from *overriding* her anchor —*Manual of Seamanship*⟩ **b :** to ride down **:** trample underfoot ⟨*overrode* the thin line of defenders⟩ **c :** to ride too close to (the hounds) in fox hunting **2** *obs* **:** to ride beyond **:** PASS, OUTRIDE **3 :** to ride (as a horse) too much or too hard **4 a :** to dominate or prevail over **:** VANQUISH, CONQUER ⟨panic *overrode* everything else —Marcia Davenport⟩ ⟨a verity of purpose which *overrode* common domestic trials —P.S.Klein⟩ **b :** to set aside **:** ANNUL, SUPERSEDE ⟨a rebellious congress *overrode* the president's veto⟩ ⟨the positive law may . . . ~ the law of justice —B.N.Cardozo⟩ ⟨the rights of the individual were being flagrantly *overridden* —C.L.Jones⟩ **5 :** to extend or pass over; *esp* **:** OVERLAP ⟨the lower end of the fractured bone *overrode* the upper⟩ **6 :** to pay a commission to (as a general agent or sales manager) on sales made by subordinates

[2]**override** \ˈ==ˌ=, ˌ==ˈ=\ *n* **1 :** a commission paid in addition to regular compensation; *esp* **:** a commission paid to managerial personnel on sales made by subordinates **2 :** an auxiliary control that may be temporarily applied by hand to supplant the operation of an otherwise automatic control

**over·rid·er** \ˌ=ˈrīdə(r)\ *n* [[1]*override* + *-er*] *Brit* **:** BUMPER GUARD

**overriding** *adj* [fr. pres. part. of [1]*override*] **1 :** DOMINEERING, ARROGANT ⟨in these fits he was the most ~ companion ever known —R.L.Stevenson⟩ **2 :** subordinating all others to itself **:** DOMINANT, PRINCIPAL, PRIMARY ⟨the ~ importance of imponderables in determining human conduct —John Russell b.1872⟩ ⟨a further and ~ reason —Harold Koontz & Cyril O'Donnell⟩ ⟨the ~ danger —*Newsweek*⟩ ⟨the ~ problems of business in the years to come —A.L.Nickerson⟩

**overright** \ˌ=ˈ=\ *prep* [[2]*over* + *right*, adv.] *dial chiefly Brit* **:** over against **:** OPPOSITE ⟨an acre of land ~ the river —Robert Gibbings⟩

**overrigid** \ˌ=ˈ==\ *adj* **:** excessively rigid or severe ⟨~ application of a theory⟩ — **overrigidly** \ˌ=ˈ===\ *adv*

**overripe** \ˌ=ˈ=\ *adj* **1 :** too ripe **:** advanced in development beyond the stage of maturity or ripeness ⟨~ fruit⟩ ⟨hide the flavor of ~ meat —Marjory S. Douglas⟩ **2 a :** advanced to or being a stage of development characterized by loss of vigor, creativity, or originality **:** DECADENT ⟨belonged to an ~ period of Greek art —Francis Steegmuller⟩ ⟨the relatively drab days of ~ Victorianism —I.J.Suloway⟩ ⟨languid ~ naturalism —Herbert Read⟩ **b :** marked by a fulsome, flabby, or cloying quality **:** lacking bite or vigor **:** FLAMBOYANT, ORNATE, SUGARY ⟨the sound is ~ —*Saturday Rev.*⟩ ⟨an early composition . . .

that is just a bit ~ and banal —Douglas Watt) (the atmosphere becomes sententious, the style turns ~ —C.J.Rolo)
**overroof** \ˌ==ˈ=\ *vt* : to roof over : ROOF
**overround** \ˌ==ˈ=\ *vt* : to round (as the lips, a vowel) more than usual
**1overruff** \ˌ==ˈ=\ *vb* [1*over* + *ruff*] : OVERTRUMP
**2overruff** \ˈ==ˌ=\ *n* : the act or an instance of overtrumping
**1overrule** \ˌ==ˈ=\ *vb* [1*over* + *rule*] *vt* **1** : to rule over : GOVERN (the guiding presence of the Holy Spirit to assist and ~ the teaching —A.J.Russell) (words plainly force and ~ the understanding —Francis Bacon) **2 a** : to prevail over : OVERCOME (tribal customs ~ everything —John Russell b.1872) (a force of attraction which is able to ~ the electrical force —G.W.Gray b.1886) **b** : to bring over by persuasion or other influence **3 a** : to decide or rule against esp. by virtue of superior authority (the chairman *overruled* the point of order) (*overruled* my father —Mary Austin) **b** : to set aside or reverse (as a previous decision or ruling) (the appellate court *overruled* the action of the trial judge) ~ *vi* **1** : to be supreme or superior in ruling or controlling (the same large mind that ~*s* —Henry Adams) **2** : to decide or determine by superior authority (all is as God ~*s* —Robert Browning)
**2overrule** \ˈ==ˌ=\ *n* : the rule of a superior power : SUPREMACY
**overruler** \ˌ==ˈ==\ *n* : one that overrules; *specif* : a supreme ruler
**1overruling** *adj* [fr. pres. part. of 1*overrule*] **1** : serving to overrule (an ~ opinion) **2** : OVERRIDING (the ~ end of government —J.P.deC.Day) — **over·rul·ing·ly** *adv*
**2overruling** *n* [fr. gerund of 1*overrule*] : the act of one that overrules : an instance of such an act
**1overrun** \ˌ==ˈ=\ *vb* [ME *overrinnen*, *overrennen*, fr. OE *oferyrnan*, fr. *ofer*, adv., over + *yrnan*, *iernan* to run] *vt* **1 a** (1) : to defeat utterly and occupy the positions of : OVERWHELM, OVERPOWER, CRUSH (one company of the 25th Division was ~ —*Time*) (2) : to invade and occupy or ravage (among the barbarous nations who *overran* the western provinces of the Roman Empire —Adam Smith) (had their own way in *overrunning* the seaboard —Paul Blanshard) **b** *obs* : to run over destructively or harmfully : run down **c** : to spread or swarm over : INFEST (the island was ~ by rats —*Current History*) (a crumbled ruin ~ by the jungle —James Reach) **2 a** : to run faster, further, or better than : pass in running : OUTRUN **b** (1) : to run, go, or extend beyond or past (the plane *overran* the runway) (2) : EXCEED (overran by so great a margin any possible gains —C.E.Black & E.C.Helmreich) (warned him not to ~ his time —*Punch*) **c** (1) : to readjust (as lines, columns, or pages) by shifting letters or words from one line into another or a line or lines from one column or page to another (2) : to print more copies of than were ordered; *also* : to print extra copies of (as a section of a magazine containing an article to be available separately) (3) : OVERSET **d** : to cause or permit (as an engine) to overrun **e** : to operate (as a lamp or a motor) at higher than normal or rated voltage, pressure, or power **3** : to flow over (the waves did little else than ~ the beach —J.A.Steers) ~ *vi* **1** : to run, pass, spread, or flow over or by something **2** : to go or extend beyond limits : be in excess: as **a** : to run too far (an engine operating a winch may ~) **b** : to run at a speed faster than that imparted by the normally driving element of a machine (when the machine stops . . . the bobbin tends to ~ —Albert Thompson & Sigfrid Bick)
**2overrun** \ˈ==ˌ=\ *n* **1** : the act or an instance of overrunning **2 a** (1) : the copies printed by overrunning (2) : a run in excess of the quantity of a product ordered by a customer **b** : the amount by which lumber actually sawed exceeds that estimated by log scale **c** : the volume increase of a product over the original volume that is accomplished by the incorporation of a worthless substance (as air whipped into a commercial ice cream mix, or water whipped into butter) (2½ gallons ~ in 5 gallons of ice cream) **3** : a cleared but unpaved area at the end of a runway offering extra landing roll to an airplane in an emergency
**overrunner** \ˌ==ˈ==\ *n* : one that overruns
**overrunning clutch** *n* **1** : a clutch used in a starter that transmits cranking effort but overruns freely when the engine tries to drive the starter **2** : a special clutch used in several mechanisms that permits a rotating member to turn freely under some conditions but not under others
**overs** *pres 3d sing of* OVER, *pl of* OVER
**oversail** \ˌ==ˈ=\ *vb* [1*over* + obs. E *sail* to project, sally, fr. MF *saillir* to sally, leap, dance — more at SALLY] *vt* : to lay (as bricks or stones) so that one projects beyond another upon which it rests; *also* : to cover by a roof or arch of such construction ~ *vi* : to project or jut out beyond the base
**oversanded** \ˌ==ˈ==\ *adj*, *of concrete* : containing more sand than is needed for normal use and working conditions
**oversanguine** \ˌ==ˈ==\ *adj* : too sanguine : too hopeful or optimistic
**oversaving** \ˌ==ˈ==\ *n* : a process of saving in excess of the amount capable of being absorbed by investment that is regarded by some economists as a major cause of depressions in the modern economy
**1overscore** \ˌ==ˈ=\ *vt* [1*over* + *score*] : to score over : obliterate by scoring
**2overscore** \ˈ==ˌ=\ *n* : a line drawn over a word, letter, or figure
**overscrupulous** \ˌ==ˈ===\ *adj* : unduly or excessively scrupulous
**1oversea** \ˈ==ˌ=, ˌ==ˈ=\ *adj* [2*over* + *sea*, n.] : OVERSEAS
**2oversea** \ˌ==ˈ=\ *adv* [2*over* + *sea*, n.] *chiefly Brit* : OVERSEAS
**overseal** \ˈ==ˌ=\ *n* : a secondary closure for bottles, drums, and other containers to prevent tampering and to protect the primary seal
**1overseam** \ˈ==ˌ=\ *n* [3*over* + *seam*, n.] : a seam with raw edges on the outside overcast with short close stitches that is used esp. for gloves
**2overseam** \ˈ==ˌ=\ *vt* [1*over* + *seam*, v.] : to seam by overcasting
**over·seam·er** \ˈ==ˌsēmə(r)\ *n* **1** : one that seams by overcasting **2** : SERGER
**1overseas** \ˌ==ˈ=\ *adv* [2*over* + *seas*, pl. of *sea*, n.] : beyond or across the sea : ABROAD (after serving ~ eight months —W.F. Brantley)
**2overseas** \ˈ==ˌ=, ˌ==ˈ=\ *adj* **1** : of or relating to movement, transport, or communication over the sea (some ~ trade in grain arose —Samuel Van Valkenburg & Ellsworth Huntington) (differed from all previous . . . Chinese ~ enterprise —C.P.Fitzgerald) (the importance of ~ broadcasting —*London Calling*) **2 a** : situated, originating in, or relating to lands beyond the sea (American ~ libraries —Malcolm Cowley) (~ markets) (culture was most often defined in terms of some ~ antecedent —Oscar Handlin) (the ~ Chinese) **b** : COLONIAL (changed the designation of France's colonial troops to ~ troops —*N.Y.Times*)
**3overseas** \ˈ==ˌ=\ *n pl but usu sing in constr* : the lands or regions overseas (the . . . route between the Great Lakes and ~ —H.M.Mayer) (visitors from ~)
**overseas cap** *n* : a woolen or cotton cap without visor or stiffening : GARRISON CAP
**oversee** \ˌ==ˈ=\ *vb* [ME *overseen*, fr. OE *oferseōn*, fr. *ofer*, adv., over + *seōn* to see] *vt* **1** : to look down upon : SURVEY, WATCH (from his second-floor window he ~*s* Parliament Hill —T.P.Whitney) **2** *dial* **a** : to fail to observe : NEGLECT, DISREGARD **b** : to deceive or delude (oneself) esp. so as to err or blunder **3 a** : to look over : INSPECT, EXAMINE **b** : SUPERINTEND, SUPERVISE (~ proofs) (~ workmen) **4** : to see clandestinely or accidentally (~*ing* . . . the intimate things of common life —John Grierson) ~ *vi* : to act as overseer : SUPERVISE
**over·seen** \ˌōvə(r)ˈsēn\ *adj* [ME *oversene*, *overseie*, fr. past part. of *overseen* to oversee, fail to observe] **1** *dial* : MISTAKEN, RASH **2** *dial* : INTOXICATED, TIPSY **3** *dial* : VERSED, LEARNED
**over·seer** \ˈ==ˌsi(ə)r, -ˌsiə *also* -ˌsē(ə)r *or* -ˌsēə *or* ˌ==ˈs-\ *n* [ME, person appointed to assist the executor of a will, fr. *overseen* to oversee + *-er*] : a person who oversees: as **a** : a person in charge of a piece of work or of workmen in their labor : SUPERINTENDENT, SUPERVISOR (an ~ of a mill) **b** : OVERSEER OF THE POOR **c** *obs* : EDITOR, CRITIC **d** : a person selected by a religious body to serve as a local or regional leader; *specif* : a Friend selected to manage the pastoral work of a congregation to which he belongs **e** : one of a number of elected or appointed officials forming a governing or supervisory board in a college or university usu. with final responsibility for the management of its affairs — compare TRUSTEE
**overseer of the poor** : a person who is appointed or elected to take care of or to assist the poor with money, supplies, or services furnished by public authority and whose duties are prescribed by local statutes
**over·seer·ship** \-ˌship\ *n* : the office or status of an overseer
**oversell** \ˌ==ˈ=\ *vt* **1** : to sell more than can be advantageously purchased (sometimes ~ their prospects, thereby laying the foundation for later defaults —H.E.Hoagland) **2** : to sell beyond means of delivery **3 a** : to make excessive claims for (doesn't pay to ~ an attraction —W.L.Gresham) (opinion research may be *oversold* —J.A.R.Pimlott) (should not seek to ~ psychiatry —Eugene Davidoff) **b** : to cause to have an exaggerated opinion of the value or importance of something (only to find that you have been slightly *oversold* —W.J. Reilly) (permitted the public to be *oversold* on the importance of increasing reading rate —G.D.Spache) ~ *vi* **1** : to oversell something or someone (great caution must be observed by public relations people not to overstate or ~ —L.A.Appley) **2** : to be excessively zealous or aggressive in selling something
**over·sensitive** \ˌōvə(r)+\ *adj* : unduly or extremely sensitive — **over·sensitiveness** \ˌōvə(r)+\ *n*
**oversentimentalize** \ˌ==ˌ==ˈ===\ *vt* : to treat with excessive sentimentalism : consider in an extremely sentimental manner
**1overset** \ˌ==ˈ=\ *vt* [ME *oversetten* to adorn with settings, overthrow, oppress, fr. 1*over* + *setten* to set] **1** : to adorn with settings (as of jewels) **2** *dial chiefly Brit* : to recover from (an illness) **3** : to disturb mentally or physically : affect so as to cause disorder of body or mind : UPSET (~ the delicate organization of the mind —Charles Dickens) **4** : to turn or tip over from an upright or proper position : OVERTURN (so quick he ~ his chair —Helen Eustis) **5** : to cause to fall or fail : SUBVERT (~ a tyranny —John Masefield) **6** : to set too much type matter for (~ a book) (~ an article); *also* : to set too wide (~ a line) ~ *vi* **1** : to turn or become turned over (the carriage ~) **2** : to become upset or disordered
**2overset** \ˈ==ˌ=\ *n* [ME, overthrow, fr. *oversetten*, v.] **1** : an upsetting or overturning (the ~ of a carriage) **2 a** : something that is overset (as type matter or a line of type) **b** : newspaper copy set in type for but not used in a particular edition
**oversew** \ˈ==ˌ=\ *vt* **1 a** : OVERHAND **b** : OVERCAST **2** : to sew (books) by machine simulating hand overcasting, the needles and thread passing diagonally through the book section near the binding edge
**oversexed** \ˌ==ˈ=\ *adj* : characterized by an inordinate degree of sexual drive or interest (a few ~ egomaniacs —Compton Mackenzie)
**overshade** \ˌ==ˈ=\ *vt* : to cover with shade : OVERSHADOW
**overshadow** \ˌ==ˈ(ˌ)=\ *vt* [ME *overschadewen*, fr. OE *ofersceadwian*, fr. *ofer*, adv., over + *sceadwian* to shadow] **1 a** : to cast a shadow or shade over : obscure with shadow (a valley ~*ed* by rugged mountains —*Amer. Guide Series: Tenn.*) **b** : to darken by some calamity or prospective calamity (our lives are ~*ed* now by the threat of impending doom —R.M. Hutchins) (~*ed* by nervous apprehension of a railroad strike —F.L.Paxson) **2 a** : to diminish the relative importance of : be more important than : tower over (threatened to ~ the state —C.L.Jones) (~*ed* his colleagues —D.J.Dallin) (the problem that ~*ed* all others —Vera M. Dean) **b** : OUTWEIGH, EXCEED (the good services of skunks . . . far ~ the harm they do —*Conservation in the U.S.*)
**1overshadowing** *n* [ME *overschadewing*, fr. gerund of *overschadewen*] : the act of one that overshadows : an instance of such an act
**2overshadowing** *adj* [fr. pres. part. of *overshadow*] : serving or tending to overshadow (the ~ event in the baseball world —*Collier's Yr. Bk.*) — **over·shad·ow·ing·ly** *adv*
**oversharp** \ˌ==ˈ=\ *adj* [ME *oversharpe*, fr. 1*over* + *sharpe*, *sharp* sharp] : too sharp (the ~ distinction between the rich and the poor —*Times Lit. Supp.*)
**overshifted** \ˌ==ˈ==\ *adj* : marked by an unusual or extreme shift (the unorthodox ~ defense of the opposing team)
**overshine** \ˌ==ˈ=\ *vt* **1** : to shine over or upon : ILLUMINE **2** : to excel in shining : OUTSHINE
**overship** \ˌ==ˈ=\ *vt* : to ship in excess of (if the restricted areas should ~ their quotas —*Barron's*) ~ *vi* : to ship in excess (tendency to . . . ~ during the months of May to October —*Experiment Station Record*)
**overshirt** \ˈ==ˌ=\ *n* : a shirt as distinguished from an undershirt
**1overshoe** *or* **overshoes** \ˌ==ˈ=\ *adv* [2*over* + *shoe*, n., or *shoes* (pl. of *shoe*, n.)] : beyond the depth to which the shoes cover the feet
**2overshoe** \ˈ==ˌ=\ *n* [3*over* + *shoe*, n.] : a shoe that is worn over another (as for extra warmth or for protection from wet); *esp* : GALOSH
**overshoot** \ˌ==ˈ=\ *vb* [ME *overshoten*, *oversheten*, fr. 1*over* + *shoten*, *sheten* to shoot] *vt* **1 a** : to pass swiftly beyond or ahead of : dart forward over, across, or by (woke to find I'd *overshot* my station —Julian Maclaren-Ross) **b** : to fly beyond (a designated point or area) while attempting to land an airplane **2 a** : to shoot over or beyond : miss by shooting too far or too high (~*ing* the target —S.L.Payne) **b** : EXCEED (~ a quota) **3** : to overreach (oneself) or cause (oneself) to go astray **4 a** : to shoot better than : excel in shooting **b** : to deplete of game by too much shooting **5 a** : to shoot down over (as water over a wheel) **b** : to pass swiftly over or above ~ *vi* **1** : to fly or shoot above or beyond the mark **2** : to swing or pass beyond the equilibrium point, often with resultant cycling — **overshoot the mark** **1** : to overstate a case : assert too much (whose enthusiasm for things Greek may sometimes have *overshot the mark* —Norman Douglas) **2** : to fall into error : go astray (the gossips *overshot the mark* —O.S.J.Gogarty)
**1overshot** \ˈ==ˌ=\ *adj* [fr. past part. of *overshoot*] **1** *obs* : wide of the mark : MISTAKEN, DECEIVED **2** : carried over on the upper side (an ~ hay stacker) (the ~ cylinder of a thresher) **3** : having the upper jaw extending beyond the lower (as the mouth or jaw of some dogs)
**2overshot** \"\ *n* **1** : a pattern or weave featuring filling floats which pass two or more warp yarns before reentering the fabric **2** : a fishing tool used to recover lost pipe in a drilled well
**overshot wheel** *n* : a vertical waterwheel the circumference of which is covered with cavities or buckets and is turned by water that shoots over the top filling the buckets on the farther side and acting chiefly by its weight

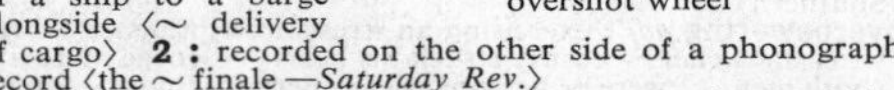

overshot wheel

**overshoulder** \ˌ==ˈ==\ *adv* [2*over* + *shoulder*, n.] : over the shoulder (laughing impudently ~ at him —Talbot Mundy)
**1overside** \ˈ==ˌ=, ˌ==ˈ=\ *adv* [2*over* + *side*, n.] **1** : over the side of a ship **2** : on the other side of a phonograph record
**2overside** \"\ *adj* **1** : done over the side of a ship to a barge alongside (~ delivery of cargo) **2** : recorded on the other side of a phonograph record (the ~ finale —*Saturday Rev.*)
**3overside** \ˈ==ˌ=\ *n* : the other side of a phonograph record (the ~ offers . . . an agreeable if unexciting example —Irving Kolodin)
**oversight** \ˈ==ˌ=\ *n* [ME, fr. *overseen* to oversee, after ME *seen* to see: *sight*] **1** : watchful care : general supervision : MANAGEMENT (you to whom ~ of the University is entrusted —N.M. Pusey) **2** : an act of overlooking or something overlooked : omission or error due to inadvertence (whether by ~ or intention —G.B.Shaw)
**oversigned** \ˈ==ˌ=\ *n* -s [1*over* + *signed* (fr. past part. of *sign*)] : the person whose name appears at the beginning of a report or other writing
**oversimplification** \ˌ==ˌ===ˈ==\ *n* [fr. *oversimplify*, after E *simplify*: *simplification*] **1** : the act or an instance of oversimplifying (such a definition . . . errs on the side of ~ —Ralph Linton) **2** : something that oversimplifies (this theory is an ~)
**oversimplify** \ˌ==ˈ===\ *vb* [1*over* + *simplify*] *vt* : to simplify to such an extent as to bring about distortion, misunderstanding, or error (seriously *oversimplifies* a complex . . . problem —W.H. Chamberlin) (*oversimplified* their heroes —John Mason Brown) ~ *vi* : to engage in undue or extreme simplification (would disagree with their books . . . because they overstate and ~ —F.M.Hechinger)
**1oversize** *vt* [1*over* + *-size* (fr. *size*, n. — glutinous material)] *obs* : to cover with or as if with size
**2oversize** \ˈ==ˌ=\ *n* [3*over* + *size*, n. (magnitude)] **1** : a size larger than the nominal or normal size (as of a book, shoe, tire) **2** : fragmental material (as mineral or ore) in pieces too large to pass a given screen or other selector
**3oversize** \ˌ==ˈ=\ *adj* : being of more than ordinary size (an ~ helping) (~ books) (~ pears)
**over·sized** \ˌ==ˈsīzd\ *adj* [2*oversize* + *-ed*] : OVERSIZE
**overskip** \ˌ==ˈ=\ *vt* [ME *overskippen*, fr. 1*over* + *skippen* to skip] : to skip or leap over : pass lightly over : OMIT
**overskirt** \ˈ==ˌ=\ *n* : a skirt worn over another skirt; *also* : an outer skirt draped up to show an underskirt
**1over·slaugh** \ˈōvə(r)ˌslȯ\ *vt* -ED/-ING/-S [D *overslaan* to pass over, omit, fr. MD *overslaen*, fr. *over* + *slaen* to strike; akin to OE *ofer*, adv. & prep., over and to OE *slēan* to strike, beat, slay — more at OVER, SLAY] **1** : to pass over or remit by overslaugh **2** : to pass over esp. for an appointment or promotion in favor of another : ignore the claims of **3** : HINDER, OBSTRUCT
**2overslaugh** \"\ *n* -s : exemption from a duty in the British armed forces because detailed on a superior duty
**oversleep** \ˌ==ˈ=\ *vb* [ME *oversleepen*, fr. 1*over* + *slepen* to sleep] *vi* : to sleep beyond the time for waking ~ *vt* : to allow (oneself) to sleep beyond the time for waking (*overslept* herself —Angela Thirkell)
**oversleeve** \ˈ==ˌ=\ *n* : a sleeve worn usu. hanging loosely over another sleeve
**1overslip** *vt* [ME *overslippen*, fr. 1*over* + *slippen* to slip] **1** *obs* : to slip or slide over : pass easily or carelessly beyond : OMIT, NEGLECT **2** *obs* : to slip away from, past, or by : ESCAPE
**2overslip** \ˈ==ˌ=\ *n* [3*over* + *slip*, n.] : a heavy-duty paper bag enclosing a filled shipping bag for added strength
**overslope** \ˈ==ˌ=\ *n* : an earmark on an animal made by a diagonal cut removing the upper corner of the ear — see EARMARK illustration
**overslung** \ˈ==ˌ=\ *adj* [1*over* + *slung* (past part. of *sling*)] : supported at a level above that of the wheel axles (an ~ automobile) — opposed to *underslung*
**overs·man** \ˈōvə(r)zmən\ *n*, *pl* **oversmen** [by alter. (prob. influenced by such words as *kinsman*)] : OVERMAN
**1oversnow** *vt* [1*over* + *snow*, v.] *obs* : to cover with or as if with snow
**2oversnow** \ˌ==ˈ=\ *adj* [2*over* + *snow*, n.] : used for transport or travel over snow (~ vehicles) (~ equipment)
**oversoar** \ˌ==ˈ=\ *vt*, *archaic* : to soar over
**oversoft** \ˌ==ˈ=\ *adj* : extremely soft
**oversold** \ˌ==ˈ=\ *adj* [fr. past part. of *oversell*] : characterized by prices held to be unjustifiably low as a result of heavy selling (~ stocks) (an ~ market) — compare OVERBOUGHT
**over-solicitous** \ˌōvə(r)+\ *adj* : excessively solicitous
**oversoul** \ˈ==ˌ=\ *n* : the absolute reality conceived as a spiritual being in which the ideal nature imperfectly manifested in human beings is perfectly realized and in which our finite and separate existences are grounded
**oversound** \ˌ==ˈ=\ *vi*, *of an organ pipe* : to sound a harmonic instead of the fundamental tone as a result of overblowing
**oversow** \ˌ==ˈ=\ *vt* **1** : to sow where something has already been sown **2 a** : to scatter seed over : SOW **b** : to sow too much
**overspan** \ˌ==ˈ=\ *vt* **1** : to reach or extend over (~ so many local variations —Ruth Benedict) **2** : to erect or throw a span over (as a space)
**overspeak** \ˌ==ˈ=\ *vt* **1** *obs* : EXAGGERATE **2** : to exceed or outdo in speaking
**over·specialization** \ˌōvə(r)+\ *n* : excessive specialization
**1overspeed** \ˈ==ˌ=\ *n* [3*over* + *speed*, n.] : speed greater than normal or rated speed (subjected to ~*s* —*Time*)
**2overspeed** \ˌ==ˈ=\ *vb* [1*over* + *speed*, v.] *vt* : to cause (as an engine) to run at an excessive speed ~ *vi* : to run at an excessive speed
**3overspeed** \ˈ==ˌ=\ *adj* [1*overspeed*] : operated or operating at greater than normal or rated speed
**overspend** \ˌ==ˈ=\ *vt* **1** : to spend or use to excess : wear out : EXHAUST (*overspent* his strength) **2 a** : to spend more than (*overspent* its income by $400 —*Time*) **b** : to permit (oneself) to spend beyond one's means (if we are not to ~ ourselves —Stafford Cripps) ~ *vi* : to spend beyond one's means (lived riotously and *overspent* recklessly —G.R.Batho)
**1overspill** \ˌ==ˈ=\ *vb* [1*over* + *spill*] : to spill over
**2overspill** \ˈ==ˌ=\ *n* **1 a** : the act or an instance of spilling over (prevent entirely an ~ from a very high surge —J.A.Steers) **b** : something that spills or flows over **2** : SURPLUS, EXCESS (to provide continued employment . . . we shipped that ~ abroad —Harold Wincott); *esp* : surplus population (when the ~ from the cities would go to the land —John Buchan)
**overspin** \ˈ==ˌ=\ *n* : TOP SPIN; *esp* : forward spin given by a bowler to a bowled ball in cricket
**overspray** \ˈ==ˌ=\ *n* : spray material that does not adhere in spray painting
**1overspread** \ˌ==ˈ=\ *vt* [ME *overspreden*, fr. OE *ofersprǣdan*, fr. *ofer*, adv., over + *sprǣdan* to spread] : to spread over or above : extend over (a paleness . . . ~ her face —S.M. Crothers)
**2overspread** \ˈ==ˌ=\ *n* : something spread over
**overspring** \ˌ==ˈ=\ *vt*, *archaic* : to spring over : leap over
**1oversquare** \ˈ==ˌ=\ *n* [3*over* + *square*, n.] : an earmark on an animal made by a rectangular cut removing the upper corner of the ear — see EARMARK illustration
**2oversquare** \ˌ==ˈ=\ *adj* [1*over* + *square*, adj.] : having a piston diameter greater than the length of stroke — used of a cylinder engine or pump
**overstaff** \ˌ==ˈ=\ *vt* : to staff to excess (lest the country be ~*ed* with lawyers —H.J.Carman)
**overstain** \ˌ==ˈ=\ *vt* : to stain to excess; *specif* : to stain (tissue sections) excessively esp. in order to demonstrate selected elements by controlled destaining
**overstand** \ˌ==ˈ=\ *vt* : to keep on a navigational course beyond (a mark)
**overstate** \ˌ==ˈ=\ *vt* : to state in too strong terms : EXAGGERATE
**overstatement** \ˌ==ˈ==\ *n* **1** : the act of overstating : EXAGGERATION **2** : an instance of overstatement : an exaggerated statement or account
**overstay** \ˌ==ˈ=\ *vt* **1** : to stay beyond the time or the limits of (~*ed* his leave) **2** : to carry a transaction in (a market) beyond the point at which the greatest profit would have been made by closing it (~*ed* his market)
**oversteepen** \ˌ==ˈ==\ *vt* : to make excessively steep (as by glacial erosion)
**oversteer** \ˈ==ˌ=\ *n* : the tendency of an automobile to steer into a sharper turn than the driver intends sometimes with a thrusting of the rear to the outside
**overstep** \ˌ==ˈ=\ *vt* [ME *oversteppen*, fr. OE *ofersteppan*, fr. *ofer*, adv., over + *steppan* to step] : to step over or beyond : TRANSGRESS (~ the bounds of propriety)
**1overstitch** \ˈ==ˌ=\ *n* [3*over* + *stitch*] : any of various stitches now usu. made on a sewing machine with one, two, or three threads for binding a raw edge on cloth or making an ornamental edge, finish, or hem
**2overstitch** \"\ *vt* : to edge, finish, or hem with an overstitch
**1overstock** \ˌ==ˈ=\ *vb* [1*over* + *stock*] *vt* **1** : to stock beyond requirements or facilities (~ a pasture) (~ merchandise) **2** : to leave (a cow) unmilked for too long a time ~ *vi* : to stock in excess of needs or facilities

**²overstock** \ˈ==ˌ=\ *n* **:** an excess of stock; *specif* **:** REMAINDER 4 ⟨publishers' ~ bought and sold —*Publishers' Weekly*⟩
**overstoping** \ˈ==ˌ==\ *n* **:** overhand stoping
**overstory** \ˈ==ˌ==\ *n* **:** the layer of foliage in a forest canopy; *also* **:** its trees
**¹overstrain** \ˌ==ˈ=\ *vb* [¹*over* + *strain*] *vt* **1 :** to subject to excessive strain **2 :** to load until the stress exceeds the elastic limit ~ *vi* **:** to subject oneself to excessive strain
**²overstrain** \ˈ==ˌ=, ˌ==ˈ=\ *n* **:** excessive mental or physical strain **:** a condition resulting from overstraining ⟨a serious bout of ~ and overwork —A.L.Rowse⟩
**overstream** \ˌ==ˈ=\ *vt* **:** to stream or flow over
**¹overstrength** \ˌ==ˈ=\ *adj* [²*over* + *strength*, n.] **:** having personnel in excess of that prescribed by a table of organization **:** being in excess of the personnel prescribed by a table of organization ⟨praying fervently some office or other would find some outfit or other ~ —James Jones⟩
**²overstrength** \ˈ==ˌ=, ˌ==ˈ=\ *n* **:** an excess of strength; *specif* **:** the excess of personnel over that prescribed by a table of organization
**¹overstress** \ˌ==ˈ=\ *vt* [¹*over* + *stress*] **1 :** to stress too much ⟨impossible to ~ the point —*New Republic*⟩ **2 :** to deform (a metal) permanently by a stress greater than the elastic limit
**²overstress** \ˈ==ˌ=, ˌ==ˈ=\ *n* **:** excessive stress
**overstretch** \ˌ==ˈ=\ *vt* [ME *overstretchen*, fr. ¹*over* + *stretchen*, *strecchen* to stretch] **1 :** to stretch to excess ⟨strategically ~*ed* around the world —Benjamin Welles⟩ **2 :** to stretch over or across
**overstrew** \ˌ==ˈ=\ *vt* **:** to strew or scatter over
**overstrict** \ˌ==ˈ=\ *adj* **:** excessively strict
**overstride** \ˌ==ˈ=\ *vt* [ME *overstriden*, fr. ¹*over* + *striden* to stride] **1 a :** to stride over, across, or beyond ⟨~ an obstruction⟩ **b :** BESTRIDE **2 :** to stride faster than or beyond ⟨*overstriding* his little orderly —L.M.Uris⟩
**¹overstrike** \ˌ==ˈ=\ *vt* [¹*over* + *strike*] **1 :** to impress (a finished coin) with the design of another coin **2 :** to impress (a specified coin design) onto a specified coin of another design ⟨~ an 1827 quarter on an 1806 quarter⟩
**²overstrike** \ˈ==ˌ=\ *n* **:** an overstruck coin
**overstring** \ˌ==ˈ=\ *vt* **:** to string (a bow) with too short a cord
**overstrung** \ˌ==ˈ=\ *adj* **1 :** too highly strung **:** too sensitive ⟨~ nerves⟩ **2** *archery* **:** HIGH-STRUNG
**¹overstudy** \ˌ==ˈ==\ *vb* [¹*over* + *study*] *vt* **:** to subject to overstudy ~ *vi* **:** to engage in overstudy
**²overstudy** \"\ *n* **:** excessive study
**overstuff** \ˌ==ˈ=\ *vt* **1 :** to stuff too full **2 :** to cover (as a chair, couch, sofa) completely and deeply with upholstery
**overstuffed** *adj* **1 a :** stuffed too full or to excess **:** padded or overbulky ⟨one of those ~ biographies that have recently become fashionable —Irving Howe⟩ **b :** too fat **:** CORPULENT ⟨the mother was an ~ . . . woman —Truman Capote⟩ **2 :** covered deeply and completely with upholstery ⟨~ furniture⟩
**oversubscribe** \ˌ===ˈ=\ *vt* [¹*over* + *subscribe*] **:** to subscribe for more of than is offered for sale ⟨~ an issue of bonds⟩
**oversubscription** \ˌ====ˈ==\ *n* [fr. *oversubscribe*, after E *subscribe: subscription*] **:** the act or an instance of oversubscribing ⟨~s became the rule —M.S.Kendrick⟩
**oversubtle** \ˌ==ˈ==\ *adj* **:** impracticably subtle
**oversubtlety** \ˌ==ˈ===\ *n* **:** excessive subtlety
**oversum** \ˌ==ˈ=\ *vt*, *archaic* **:** OVERRATE
**oversummer** \ˌ==ˈ==\ *vi* **:** to survive the summer ⟨urediospores may ~ at the high altitudes —*Experiment Station Record*⟩
**¹oversupply** \ˌ===ˈ=\ *n* [³*over* + *supply*, n.] **:** an excessive supply
**²oversupply** \"\ *vt* [¹*over* + *supply*, v.] **:** to supply in excess
**overswarm** \ˌ==ˈ=\ *vt* **:** to swarm over **:** OVERRUN ~ *vi* **:** to spread out
**oversway** \ˌ==ˈ=\ *vt* **1 a :** to bear sway over **:** rule over **:** DOMINATE, GOVERN ⟨~*ed* by expediency and self-interest —V.L. Parrington⟩ **b** *obs* **:** to have the upper hand over **:** prevail over **2 :** to induce to change over (as in a matter of opinion) **:** prevail upon **3** *obs* **:** to sway or swing over **:** cause to incline or overturn
**oversweep** \ˌ==ˈ=\ *vt* **:** to sweep over or across ⟨the main . . . beach was *overswept* —J.A.Steers⟩
**oversweet** \ˌ==ˈ=\ *adj* **:** too sweet **:** CLOYING ⟨~ religious sentiment —Stuart Preston⟩
**overswell** \ˌ==ˈ=\ *vt* **1 :** to cause to swell unduly or to excess **2 :** to swell so as to overflow or cover ~ *vi* **:** to rise above the usual level or boundary
**overt** \(ˈ)ō¦vər\|t, -ˈ¦vəl, -¦vəi\| *also* ˈō͟ˌvə(r)t\; *usu* \|d· +V\ *adj* [ME, fr. MF, past part. of *ovrir* to open, fr. (assumed) VL *operire*, alter. (influenced by L *cooperire* to cover) of L *aperire* — more at APERTURE, COVER] **:** open to view **:** not concealed **:** publicly observable **:** MANIFEST ⟨rules are maintained only by some form of coercion, ~ or covert —John Dewey⟩ ⟨~ behavior . . . is that which is manifest in motor activity —E.A. Hoebel⟩ ⟨an act of ~ hostility —Mabel R. Gillis⟩
**overt act** *n* **:** an outward act done in pursuance and manifestation of an intent or design that is not punishable in itself without such act: **a :** an act done in actual preparation for the illegal object and thereby sufficing for conviction **b** *under the treason clause of the U.S. Constitution* **:** an act of such nature as to sustain at least the finding that the accused gave aid and comfort to the enemy
**overtake** \ˌ==ˈ=\ *vb* [ME *overtaken*, fr. ¹*over* + *taken* to take] *vt* **1 a** (1) **:** to come or catch up with in pursuit or motion ⟨the next cart they *overtook* —F.V.W.Mason⟩ (2) **:** to catch up with in some course, rivalry, or task ⟨not for several months could the printers ~ the demand —I.M.Price⟩ ⟨already *overtaking* Britain in steel production —Giorgio de Santillana⟩ ⟨*overtaken* and easily passed by Berlin —*Times Lit. Supp.*⟩ (3) *chiefly Brit* **:** to accomplish within a prescribed time or under the pressure of other duties **b :** to catch up with and pass ⟨within four years it *overtook* all other American bands by leaps and bounds —Ann M. Lingg⟩; *specif*, *chiefly Brit* **:** to go by (another vehicle) ⟨got behind a lorry and could not ~ it for miles⟩ **2 :** to come upon or happen to suddenly or unexpectedly **:** SEIZE, INVOLVE ⟨*overtaken* by a sudden and vicious blizzard —Richard Thruelsen⟩ ⟨a strange adventure *overtook* him —*Brit. Bk. Centre*⟩ ⟨changes and contrasts that have *overtaken* England —S.P.B.Mais⟩ ⟨when calamities ~ the King —Donald Harrington⟩ **3 a** *chiefly Scot* **:** CAPTIVATE, ENSNARE ⟨who married, or rather was *overtaken* —R.M.Macandrew⟩ **b** *archaic* **:** INTOXICATE **4 :** to win a trick by playing a higher card than (one's partner's winning card) ~ *vi*, *chiefly Brit* **:** to pass another vehicle ⟨never attempt to ~ on the crest of a hill —Noreen Routledge⟩
**overtaking** *n*, *chiefly Brit* **:** an act of passing another vehicle ⟨no ~⟩
**overtalk** \ˌ==ˈ=\ *vi* **:** to talk too long or too much ⟨would not let him ~ at breakfast and miss the . . . bus —James Jones⟩ ~ *vt* **1 :** to overcome with talking **2 :** to talk too much about
**overtalkative** \ˌ==ˈ===\ *adj* **:** abnormally or excessively talkative — **overtalkativeness** *n*
**overtax** \ˌ==ˈ=\ *vt* **1 :** to tax too heavily or beyond what is due **2 :** to lay too heavy a burden or demand upon ⟨~ the weakened ability of the body —Morris Fishbein⟩ — **overtaxation** \ˌ==ˌ=ˈ==\ *n*
**overteem** \ˌ==ˈ=\ *vt*, *archaic* **:** to wear out or exhaust by breeding to excess ~ *vi* **:** to teem or breed to excess
**overtempt** \ˌ==ˈ=\ *vt* **:** to tempt to excess or beyond the power of resistance
**overtheatrical** \ˌ===ˈ===\ *adj* **:** unduly or excessively theatrical
**over-the-counter** \ˌ===ˈ==\ *adj* [*over the counter*] **1 a :** not traded on an organized securities exchange **:** traded in direct negotiations between buyers and sellers or their representatives **:** UNLISTED ⟨*over-the-counter* stocks⟩ **b :** not effected on an organized securities exchange ⟨*over-the-counter* transactions⟩ **2 :** capable of being sold legally without the prescription of a physician, dentist, or veterinarian ⟨*over-the-counter* drugs⟩
**over-the-road** \ˌ===ˈ=\ *adj* [fr. the phrase *over the road*] **:** used for, being, or relating to transportation between cities or states ⟨*over-the-road* common carriers⟩ ⟨*over-the-road* freight⟩ ⟨*over-the-road* trucks⟩
**¹overthrow** \ˌ==ˈ=\ *vb* [ME *overthrowen*, fr. ¹*over* + *throwen* to throw] *vt* **1 :** to throw over **:** knock or force over from an accustomed upright or level position **:** OVERTURN ⟨a dozen trees were *overthrown* by the storm⟩ **2 :** to cause the downfall of **:** bring low **:** DEFEAT, DESTROY, RUIN ⟨ancient mechanics were *overthrown* —S.F.Mason⟩ ⟨~ a government⟩ ⟨traditional beliefs which science may ~ —M.R.Cohen⟩ **3** *archaic* **:** DERANGE, DISORDER **4 :** to throw over or past ⟨the passer *overthrew* the receiver⟩; *specif* **:** to throw a baseball over or past (a base) thereby usu. being charged with an error ~ *vi* **:** to throw too far **syn** see CONQUER, OVERTURN
**²overthrow** \ˈ==ˌ=\ *n* **1 :** an act of overthrowing or the state of being overthrown **:** DEFEAT, RUIN ⟨its ~ was accomplished simultaneously —S.F.Mason⟩ ⟨the ~ of the monarchy⟩ **2 a :** a high throw made by a fielder in baseball that usu. results in his being charged with an error **b :** a return of the ball by a fielder in cricket that is missed by the wicketkeeper or fielder at the wicket; *also* **:** a run scored on such a missed ball
**over·throw·al** \ˌ==ˈthrōəl\ *n* -S **:** the act or an instance of overthrowing
**overthrower** \ˌ==ˈthrō(ə)r, -ōə\ *n* **:** one that overthrows
**overthrust** \ˈ==ˌ=\ *vt* [¹*over* + *thrust*] **:** to thrust over (as a rock mass)
**overthrust fault** *also* **overthrust** *n* **:** THRUST FAULT
**overthrusting** \ˈ==ˌ==\ *n* [³*over* + *thrusting*, gerund of *thrust*] **:** the process of producing an overthrust
**¹overthwart** \ˌ==ˈ=\ *adv* [ME *overthwart*, *overthwert*, fr. ¹*over* + *thwart*, *thwert*, adv., athwart — more at THWART] *archaic* **:** ACROSS, CROSSWISE, TRANSVERSELY
**²overthwart** \"\ *adj* [ME *overthwart*, *overthwert*, fr. *overthwart*, *overthwert*, adv.] **1** *archaic* **:** having a crosswise position **:** placed or situated across or over **:** TRANSVERSE **2** *archaic* **:** crossing in kind or disposition **:** ADVERSE, OPPOSING
**³overthwart** \"\ *prep* [ME *overthwart*, *overthwert*, fr. *overthwart*, *overthwert*, adv.] **1** *archaic* **:** from side to side of **:** ACROSS **2** *archaic* **:** on the opposite side of or opposite to
**⁴overthwart** \"\ *vt* [ME *overthwarten*, *overthwerten*, fr. *overthwart*, *overthwert*, adv.] *archaic* **:** to pass or lie athwart **:** CROSS, OBSTRUCT
**overtide** \ˈ==ˌ=\ *n* **:** a secondary tide of higher frequency than the principal tide to which it bears a relation analogous to that of a musical overtone to its fundamental
**overtilt** \ˌ==ˈ=\ *vt* **:** to tilt over **:** UPSET
**¹overtime** \ˈ==ˌ=\ *n*, *often attrib* [³*over* + *time*, n.] **1 :** time beyond or in excess of a set limit ⟨the game went into ~⟩ ⟨played two ~ periods to break the tie⟩; *esp* **:** working time in excess of a minimum total set for a given period ⟨got in a lot of ~ this week⟩ ⟨~ pay⟩ **2 :** an additional payment for overtime ⟨earned some ~ this month⟩
**²overtime** \"\ *adv* [²*over* + *time*, n.] **:** in excess of a set time limit ⟨the game went ~⟩ or of the regular working time ⟨is working ~ this week⟩ ⟨must work ~ to make our land once again attractive to new ideas —A.E.Stevenson b. 1900⟩
**³overtime** \ˌ==ˈ=\ *vt* [¹*over* + *time*, v.] **:** to exceed the proper limit in timing (as a photographic exposure)
**overt·ly** *pronunc at* OVERT +lē,li\ *adv* [ME, fr. *overt* + *-ly*] **:** PUBLICLY, OPENLY, MANIFESTLY ⟨~ aggressive behavior —J.H. Masserman⟩
**overtoil** \ˌ==ˈ=\ *vb* **:** OVERWORK
**¹overtone** \ˈ==ˌ=\ *n* [³*over* + *tone*, n.; trans. of G *oberton*] **1 :** one of the constituent higher tones or upper partials that, with the fundamental, comprise a musical tone **:** HARMONIC 1a **2 :** the color of the light reflected (as by a paint or varnish film) **3 :** a secondary or accompanying effect, quality, or meaning usu. of subtle or elusive character **:** IMPLICATION, SUGGESTION ⟨fairy tales with ~s . . . meant only for the sophisticated —John Lehmann⟩ ⟨the phrase carries a poetical ~ —*Times Lit. Supp.*⟩ ⟨a delicate . . . fantasy with profoundly philosophical ~s —John Martin⟩ ⟨an ~, an aftertaste, a flavor that lingers in the mind —Rumer Godden⟩
**²overtone** \"\ *vt* [¹*over* + *tone*, v.] **1 :** to dominate or drown (a subordinate or discordant tone) with a stronger tone **2 :** to color or produce color effects in by overshadowing the original tone
**¹overtop** \ˌ==ˈ=\ *vt* [¹*over* + *top*, v.] **1 :** to rise above the top of **:** exceed in height **:** tower above ⟨the unusual height of the surge . . . *overtopped* the wall —J.A.Steers⟩ **2 :** to be superior to in power, station, or importance **:** OVERRIDE ⟨where faith is *overtopped* by prelacy —Ellery Sedgwick⟩ ⟨where cattle raising ~s agriculture —*Amer. Guide Series: Va.*⟩ **3 :** to make of less importance or throw into the background by superior excellence **:** SURPASS, OBSCURE ⟨*overtopped* the rest, the giant of them all —H.O.Taylor⟩ **4 :** to cover, flow over, or cast shade over the top of
**²overtop** \ˌ==ˈ=\ *adv* [²*over* + *top*, n.] **:** over the top **:** OVERHEAD
**overtrade** \ˌ==ˈ=\ *vi* **:** to trade beyond one's capital **:** buy goods beyond the means of paying for or selling them ~ *vt* **:** to do business beyond (as one's capital)
**overtrain** \ˌ==ˈ=\ *vt* **:** to train to excess or beyond advantage **:** harm by too much training
**overtravel** \ˌ==ˈ==\ *n* **:** amplitude of motion of a machine part or tool beyond that necessary to complete its purpose
**overtrick** \ˈ==ˌ=\ *n* **:** a card trick won in excess of the number bid
**overtrip** *vt*, *obs* **:** to trip over nimbly
**overtrump** \ˌ==ˈ=\ *vt* **:** to trump with a higher trump card than the highest previously played to the same trick ~ *vi* **:** to play a higher trump card than the highest previously played to the same trick
**¹over·ture** *R* ˈōvər,chu̇(ə)r, \|,chər, \|,tu̇(ə)r, \|,tyu̇(ə)r, *by r-dissimilation* -vəl; *–R* -və,chu̇ə, -vəchə, -və,tu̇ə, -və-,tyu̇ə, +V " *or* -u̇(ə)r *or* -,chər\ *n* -S [ME, fr. MF, fr. (assumed) VL *opertura*, alter. (influenced by L *cooperire* to cover) of L *apertura* — more at APERTURE, COVER] **1 obs a :** APERTURE, HOLE, OPENING, RECESS **b :** DISCLOSURE, DISCOVERY, REVELATION **c :** an opening or opportunity for action **d :** OVERTURNING, OVERTHROW **2 a :** a formal or informal initiative looking to an agreement, action, or the establishment of a relationship **:** a first move **:** APPROACH, PROPOSAL ⟨making ~s to the authorities . . . for a free-trade agreement —*Amer. Guide Series: Maine*⟩ ⟨a very forward girl, who is not afraid to make ~s —C.B.Kelland⟩ ⟨received ~s from film directors here and abroad⟩ **b :** something that ushers in or introduces what follows **:** COMMENCEMENT, PRELUDE ⟨more often . . . the main thing at supper than it is an ~ to dinner —Jane Nickerson⟩ ⟨the ~ to a sense of panic —Marcia Davenport⟩ ⟨an ~ of speeches —*Time*⟩ **3 a :** a formal proposal or request in Scottish and English Presbyterian churches for legislation made to the highest court of the church **b :** the submission in American Presbyterian churches of a question of doctrine or polity by the highest court to the presbyteries for their judgment on it before formal determination by the court; *also* **:** the question thus submitted **4 a :** an orchestral composition introductory to an oratorio, opera, or other extended musical work consisting usu. of two or more contrasting sections of related material and in later developments esp. in the 19th century comprising a potpourri of melodies or themes of the ensuing work or a free prelude used to establish background or mood for the plot or opening scene **b :** an orchestral concert piece of similar construction or one written as a single movement in sonata form
**²overture** \", + *suffixal vowel* -u̇r *or* -,chər\ *vt* **:** to put forward as an overture **:** make or present an overture to
**¹overturn** \ˌ==ˈ=\ *vb* [ME *overturnen*, fr. ¹*over* + *turnen* to turn] *vt* **1 a :** to turn over **:** tilt or keel over from an upright, level, or proper position esp. with force **:** cause to fall over **:** UPSET ⟨a boat ~*ed* by waves⟩ ⟨~*ed* me in the dust —John Masters⟩ **b :** to tilt beyond a vertical position so that in one limb of an anticline the underside of a fold or of strata contains the younger beds **2 :** to cause the downfall or destruction of **:** bring to nothing **:** RUIN, INVALIDATE ⟨~*ing* the unity of religion —S.M.Crothers⟩ ⟨the degree to which accident could ~ the schemes of wise men —Oscar Handlin⟩ **3** *obs* **:** DERANGE, DISORDER ~ *vi* **1 :** to turn over **2 :** to produce an overturn
**syn** UPSET, OVERTHROW, SUBVERT, CAPSIZE: OVERTURN, as defined above, has less connotational power and wider range of meaning than others in this set, with which, however, in many uses it is interchangeable. UPSET lends itself to any use involving a tilting, knocking, or keeling over from an accustomed or proper position, and to any figurative use compatible with this notion. It is a simple and familiar word more likely than others in this set to be used in simple and familiar situations ⟨this littlest of carriages could make only a great sweep, and was in danger of *upsetting* at every corner —George Santayana⟩ ⟨wouldn't have believed they could be so *upset* by a hurt woodpecker —Willa Cather⟩ OVERTHROW suggests the same base idea as the preceding but implies more force and is likely to imply more conscious intent and to apply to matters of consequence and importance ⟨I got through about half the work on this scale. But my plans were *overthrown* —C.R. Darwin⟩ ⟨many laws which it would be vain to ask the court to *overthrow* could be shown, easily enough, to transgress . . . the Bill of Rights —O.W.Holmes †1935⟩ SUBVERT, originally a close synonym for the preceding in a literal sense, is now used mostly in reference to governmental systems, established religions, and institutional matters. It now appears more likely to imply insidious impairment than direct force ⟨would do their utmost to *subvert* all religion and all law —Edmund Burke⟩ ⟨and pressure groups will have demonstrated once again that the people's interest can be *subverted* by ruthless lobbyists —*New Republic*⟩ CAPSIZE is likely to involve the picture of a boat keeling over ⟨it may well have been the comedians who restored the theater's balance when the tragedians threatened to *capsize* it into absurdity —W.B.Adams⟩
**²overturn** \ˈ==ˌ=\ *n* **1 :** the act of overturning or the state of being overturned ⟨an ideological and political ~ —J.R.Wike & A.Z.Rubinstein⟩ **2 :** the sinking of surface water and rise of bottom water in a lake or sea that results from changes in density due to changes in temperature and that commonly occurs in spring and fall wherever lakes are icebound in winter
**over-under** \ˌ==ˈ==\ *n* -S **:** OVER-AND-UNDER
**¹overuse** \ˌ==ˈ=\ *vt* [¹*over* + *use*] **:** to use to excess
**²overuse** \ˌ==ˈ=\ *n* **:** excessive use
**¹overvalue** \ˌ==ˈ==\ *vt* [¹*over* + *value*] **:** to set too high a value on **:** OVERESTIMATE, OVERPRIZE
**²overvalue** \"\ *n* **:** an excessive value or estimate
**overveil** \ˌ==ˈ=\ *vt* **:** to veil over
**overventilation** \ˌ=====ˈ==\ *n* **:** excessively deep and rapid breathing; *also* **:** the physiological state resulting from such breathing
**¹overview** *vt* [¹*over* + *view*] *obs* **:** SURVEY, INSPECT
**²overview** \ˈ==ˌ=\ *n* **:** a general view **:** SURVEY ⟨the best ~ of contemporary psychology for the lay reader —*Key Reporter*⟩ ⟨give a broad ~ of the evidence —C.R.Rogers⟩ ⟨a quick ~ tempts one to make a few generalizations —F.L.Spain⟩
**overvoltage** \ˌ==ˈ==\ *n* **:** excess voltage; *specif* **:** the excess potential required for the discharge of an ion at an electrode over and above the equilibrium potential of the electrode
**overwalk** \ˌ==ˈ=\ *vt* **1** *archaic* **:** to walk over or upon **2 :** to exhaust or injure (oneself) by walking
**overwatch** \ˌ==ˈ=\ *vt* **1** *archaic* **:** to weary or exhaust by keeping awake **2 a** *obs* **:** to watch through or throughout (as the night) **b :** to watch over **3 :** to support by fire another element which is moving ⟨tanks ~*ing* an assault battalion⟩
**¹overwater** \ˌ==ˈ==\ *adv* [²*over* + *water*, n.] **:** over or across a body of water ⟨employed when flying ~ in the daytime —*Official Guide to the Army Air Forces*⟩
**²overwater** \"\ *adj* **:** situated or occurring over a body of water ⟨the ~ portion . . . had been spanned in four hours —Horace Sutton⟩ ⟨~ flights⟩ ⟨an ~ bridge⟩
**overwear** \ˌ==ˈ=\ *vt* **:** to use up or exhaust by wearing **:** wear out
**¹overweary** \ˌ==ˈ==\ *vt* [¹*over* + *weary*, v.] **:** to weary too much **:** tire out
**²overweary** \"\ *adj* [¹*over* + *weary*, adj.] **:** wearied to excess
**overweathered** *adj*, *obs* **:** WEATHERWORN
**over·ween** \ˌ==ˈwēn\ *vb* [ME *overwenen*, fr. ¹*over* + *wenen* to suppose, think, believe — more at WEEN] *vi*, *archaic* **:** to regard one's own thinking or conclusions too highly **:** become egotistic, arrogant, or rash in opinion ~ *vt*, *obs* **:** to hold in unwarranted esteem
**¹overweening** *n* [ME *overwening*, fr. gerund of *overwenen*] **1** *obs* **:** excessive self-importance, conceit, or arrogance **2** *archaic* **:** excessive esteem or estimation
**²overweening** *adj* [ME *overwening*, fr. pres. part. of *overwenen*] **1 :** unduly confident **:** ARROGANT, PRESUMPTUOUS, CONCEITED ⟨have no idea how ~ he would be —S.V.Benét⟩ ⟨revolt against an ~ aristocracy —*Encyc. Americana*⟩ **2 :** EXCESSIVE, EXAGGERATED, IMMODERATE, UNRESTRAINED ⟨his ~ ambition . . . has tripped him up —Woodrow Wyatt⟩ ⟨~ greed —H.H. Martin⟩ ⟨an ~ love of power —Helen Howe⟩ — **over·ween·ing·ness** \ˌ==ˈ===\ *n* -ES
**overweigh** \ˌ==ˈ=\ *vt* [ME *overweien*, fr. ¹*over* + *weien*, *weyen* to weigh] **1 :** to exceed in weight **:** OVERBALANCE ⟨sufficient to ~ the less abstract considerations —R.A.Solo⟩ **2 :** to weigh down **:** OPPRESS
**¹overweight** \ˈ==ˌ=, *in sense 2b usu* ˌ==ˈ=\ *n* [³*over* + *weight*, n.] **1 :** weight over and above what is required or allowed by law, demand, or custom **2 a :** superabundance of weight **:** PREPONDERANCE **b :** excessive or burdensome weight **3** [³*overweight*] **:** an individual of more than normal weight
**²overweight** \ˌ==ˈ=\ *vt* [¹*over* + *weight*, v.] **1 :** to give too much weight or consideration to ⟨said that historians ~ political aspects —A.L.Kroeber⟩ **2 :** to weight excessively ⟨sometimes ~s his paragraphs —*Horizon*⟩ **3 :** to exceed in weight **:** OVERBALANCE
**³overweight** \"\ *adj* [²*over* + *weight*, n.] **:** exceeding normal or proper weight ⟨an ~ individual⟩
**overwell** \ˌ==ˈ=\ *adv* [ME *overwel*, fr. ¹*over* + *wel* well] **:** too well
**overwelt** \ˌ==ˈ=\ *vb* [¹*over* + *welt*, v. (to roll)] *dial Eng* **:** OVERTURN
**over·whelm** \ˌ==ˈ(h)welm, -eu̇m\ *vt* [ME *overwhelmen*, fr. ¹*over* + *whelmen* to turn over — more at WHELM] **1 :** OVERTHROW, OVERTURN, UPSET **2 a :** to cover over completely (as by a great wave) **:** overflow and bury beneath **:** ENGULF, SUBMERGE ⟨all the rest has been ~*ed* by the desert —Alan Moorehead⟩ **b :** to overcome by great superiority of force or numbers **:** bring to ruin **:** DESTROY, OVERPOWER ⟨~*ed* by the air attack —Sir Winston Churchill⟩ **c :** to overpower in thought or feeling **:** subject to the grip of an overpowering emotion ⟨~*ed* by the death of his loving mother —John McCarten⟩ ⟨unbearable melancholy . . . threatened to ~ him —Christine Weston⟩ **3 :** to project over threateningly or dominatingly ⟨his . . . face, ~*ed* by a monstrous hooked blade of a nose —E.L.Wallant⟩ **syn** see OVERPOWER
**overwhelming** *adj* **:** tending or serving to overwhelm **:** OVERPOWERING ⟨an ~ happiness⟩ ⟨an ~ majority⟩ — **over·whelm·ing·ly** \ˌ==ˈ===\ *adv*
**over·whelm·ing·ness** \ˌ==ˈ===\ *n* -ES **:** the quality or state of being overwhelming
**overwin** \ˌ==ˈ=\ *vt* [ME *overwinnen*, fr. OE *oferwinnan*, fr. *ofer*, adv., over + *winnan* to struggle, fight — more at WIN] *archaic* **:** to win over **:** VANQUISH
**overwind** \ˌ==ˈwīnd\ *vt* **1 :** to wind (as a spring or rope) too tightly or too far **2 :** to wind (as a magnet in a series motor) so that magnetic saturation requires less than normal current
**overwing** *vt* [¹*over* + *-wing* (fr. *wing*, n.)] *obs* **:** OUTFLANK
**overwinter** \ˌ==ˈ==\ *vb* [¹*over* + *winter*, v.; prob. trans. of Norw *overvintre*] *vi* **:** to pass or last through the winter **:** WINTER ~ *vt* **:** to preserve through the winter
**overwise** \ˌ==ˈ=\ *adj* **:** too wise
**overwit** *vt*, *obs* **:** OUTWIT
**overwood** \ˈ==ˌ=\ *n* **:** OVERSTORY
**¹overword** \ˈ==ˌ=\ *n* [*over-* (fr. ¹*over* — again) + *word*, n.] **:** a word repeated or said over (as in a song) **:** BURDEN, REFRAIN
**²overword** \ˌ==ˈ=\ *vt* [¹*over* + *word*, v.] **:** to compose with an excess of words **:** write too wordily ⟨many of the poems seem to come out ~*ed* —John Ciardi⟩
**overwordy** \ˌ==ˈ==\ *adj* **:** too wordy
**¹overwork** \ˌ==ˈ=\ *vb* [¹*over* + *work*] *vt* **1 a :** to cause to work too hard or too long **:** work to the point of exhaustion ⟨apt to ~ themselves —Adam Smith⟩ **b :** to work upon the mind or feelings of to excess or so as to excite or confuse **2 :** to decorate all over ⟨~*ed* the body with black or red strands —W.G. Fischel⟩ **3 a :** to work too much on **:** OVERDO, OVERELABORATE ⟨~*ing* a design —*Jewelers' Circular - Keystone*⟩ **b :** to make excessive use of **:** employ too frequently ⟨an ~*ed* and sometimes misused term —Charles Ray⟩ ~ *vi* **:** to work too much or too long **:** OVERDO
**²overwork** \"\ *n* **:** excessively prolonged or severe work
**overworld** \ˈ==ˌ=\ *n* **1 :** the world of proper and respectable people ⟨the horizon line where underworld and ~ meet —Frank O'Leary⟩ **2 :** the spiritual or supernatural world ⟨the silent realm of the ~ —Sheldon Cheney⟩

**overworn** \¦==¦=\ *adj* **1 :** worn out **:** SPENT, EXHAUSTED **2 a :** OVERWORKED, STALE **b** *obs* **:** OBSOLETE

**1overwrap** \¦==¦=\ *vt* [[1]*over* + *wrap*] **:** to apply a wrapper over

**2overwrap** \'==,=\ *also* **overwrapper** \'==,==\ *n* [[2]*overwrap* fr. [1]*overwrap; overwrapper* fr. [1]*overwrap* + *-er*] **:** a flexible printed or transparent wrapper applied over a container (as a carton, case tray) or other a product

**overwrite** \¦==¦=\ *vt* **1 :** to write over the surface of **2 :** to write in too literary, diffuse, or labored style ⟨often ~s his speeches —Jack Gould⟩ ~ *vi* **:** to write too much

**over·wrought** \¦==¦rȯt, *usu* -ȯd·+V\ *adj* [fr. past part. of [1]*overwork*] **1 :** suffering from or revealing nervous strain **:** OVEREXCITED, AGITATED ⟨an unsteady ~ voice —Lester Atwell⟩ ⟨tell ~ businessmen to get a hobby —Doyle Smee & Kenneth Smith⟩ **2 :** elaborated to excess **:** OVERDONE ⟨the slightly ~ epigrammatic style —A.L.Guérard⟩

**1overyear** \¦==¦=\ *vt* [[2]*over* + *year*, n.] *archaic* **:** to keep over the year **:** SUPERANNUATE

**2overyear** \'==,=\ *adj* [[2]*over* + *year*, n.] **:** kept over one year for use in the next ⟨~ hay⟩

**overzealous** \¦==¦==\ *adj* **:** too zealous — **overzealously** \¦==¦===\ *adv* — **overzealousness** \,==¦===\ *n*

**ovhd** *abbr* overhead

**ovi-** — see OV-

**ovi·bos** \'ōvə,bäs, -bōs\ *n* [NL, fr. L *ovis* sheep + *bos* ox, cow — more at EWE, COW] **1** *cap* **:** a genus of arctic ruminant mammals (family Bovidae) that consists of the musk-ox **2** *pl* **ovibos :** MUSK OX

**ovi·capsule** \¦ōvə+\ *n* [ISV *ov-* + *capsule*] **:** an egg case **:** OOTHECA

**ovi·cell** \'ōvə+,-\ *n* [*ov-* + *cell*] **:** a dilatation of the zooecium in many bryozoans serving as a brood pouch — **ovi·cellular** \¦==+\ *adj*

**ovi·ci·dal** \¦ōvə¦sīdᵊl\ *adj* **:** capable of killing eggs **:** of, relating to, or being an ovicide

**ovi·cide** \'ōvə,sīd\ *n* -S [ISV *ov-* + *-cide*] **:** an agent that kills eggs; *esp* **:** an insecticide effective against the egg stage

**ovic·u·lar** \(')ō¦vikyələ(r)\ *adj* [NL *oviculum* egg (dim. of L *ovum* egg) + E *-ar* — more at EGG] **:** relating to or like an egg

**ovi·cyst** \'ōvə,sist\ *n* -S [*ov-* + *-cyst*] **:** the pouch in which the eggs develop in some tunicates — **ovi·cys·tic** \¦==¦sistik\ *adj*

**ovi·dae** \'ōvə,dē\ [NL, fr. *Ovis* + *-idae*] *syn of* CAPRIDAE

**ovid·i·an** \ä'vidēən, ō'v-\ *adj, usu cap* [*Ovid* (Publius Ovidius Naso) †A.D.17? Roman poet + E *-an*] **:** of, relating to, or characteristic of Ovid or his poetry which is noted for imaginative vividness and vivacity

**ovi·du·cal** \¦ōvə¦d(y)ükəl\ *adj* [*ov-* + L *ducere* to lead + E *-al* — more at TOW] **:** of or relating to an oviduct

**ovi·duct** \'ōvə,dəkt\ *n* [NL *oviductus*, fr. L *ov-* + NL *ductus* duct — more at DUCT] **:** a tube that serves exclusively or esp. for the passage of eggs from an ovary to the exterior of an animal or to some part communicating with the exterior whether directly continuous with the ovary or (as in most vertebrates) distinct from it, that receives the eggs only after their discharge into the body cavity, and that is often modified for secreting a shell or other covering for the eggs or has a part modified to form a uterus in which the eggs or embryos develop — **ovi·duc·tal** \¦ōvə¦dəktᵊl\ *adj*

**ovie·do** \¦ōvē¦ā(,)thō, -dō; ōv'yā(,)thō\ *adj, usu cap* [fr. *Oviedo*, city in northwest Spain] **:** of or from the city of Oviedo, Spain **:** of the kind or style prevalent in Oviedo

**1ovi·form** \'ōvə,fȯrm\ *adj* [*ov-* + *-form*] **:** shaped like an egg

**2oviform** \"\ *adj* [L *ovis* sheep + E *-form*] **:** resembling a sheep in shape

**ovi·genesis** \¦ōvə+\ *n* [*ov-* + *genesis*] **:** OOGENESIS

**ovigenetic** \"+\ *adj* [*ov-* + *-genetic*] **:** OOGENETIC

**ovi·ger** \'ōvəjər, -jə(ə)r\ *n* -S [prob. back-formation fr. *ovigerous*] **:** a leg modified for carrying the eggs in some pycnogonids

**ovig·er·ous** \(')ō¦vij(ə)rəs\ *adj* [*ov-* + *-gerous*] **:** bearing eggs or modified for the purpose of bearing them ⟨an ~ leg⟩

**ovi·jec·tor** \'ōvə,jektə(r)\ *var of* OVEJECTOR

**ovim·bun·du** \¦ōvəm'bün(,)dü\ *n, pl* **ovimbundu** *or* **ovimbundus** *usu cap* **:** MBUNDU 1

**ovi·na·tion** \¦ōvə'nāshən\ *n* -S [NL *ovinia* + E *-ation*] **:** introduction of sheep-pox virus locally into the body as formerly practiced to induce immunity or reduce the severity of the disease — compare INOCULATION a(1)

**1ovine** \'ō,vīn, -vēn\ *adj* [LL *ovinus*, fr. L *ovis* sheep + *-inus* -ine] **:** of, being, or relating to sheep

**2ovine** \"\ *n* -S **:** a sheep or a closely related animal

**ovine malaria** *n* **:** ICTEROHEMATURIA

**ovin·ia** \ō'vinēə\ *n* -S [NL, fr. LL *ovinus* + NL *-ia*] **:** SHEEP POX

**1ovip·a·ra** \ō'vipərə\ *n pl* [NL, fr. L, neut. pl. of *oviparus* oviparous] **:** oviparous animals

**2ovipara** \"\ *n, pl* **ovipa·rae** \-,rē\ [NL, fr. L, fem. of *oviparus* oviparous] **:** an egg-laying form of an aphid

**ovi·par·i·ty** \¦ōvə'parəd·ē\ *n* -ES [prob. fr. (assumed) NL *oviparitat-, oviparitas*, fr. L *oviparus* oviparous + *-itat-, -itas* -ity] **:** the quality or state of being oviparous

**ovip·a·rous** (')ō¦vipərəs\ *adj* [L *oviparus*, fr. *ov-* + *-parus* -parous] **:** producing eggs that develop and hatch outside the maternal body; *also* **:** involving the production of such eggs — compare OVOVIVIPAROUS, VIVIPAROUS — **ovip·a·rous·ly** \(')=¦====\ *adv* — **ovip·a·rous·ness** \=¦====\ *n* -ES

**ovi·pos·it** \'ōvə,päzət, ¦==¦=\ *vi* [*ov-* + *posit*] **:** to lay eggs — used esp. of insects; compare LARVIPOSIT — **ovi·po·si·tion** \,ōvəpə'zishən\ *n*

**ovi·pos·i·tor** \'ōvə,päzəd·ə(r), ,=='===\ *n* [*oviposit* + *-or*] **:** a specialized organ for depositing eggs in a position suitable for their development that is frequent in insects, consists of three pairs of unjointed styles at the end of the abdomen of the female, and forms a boring apparatus with which a hole (as in the ground or in a plant) is made where one or more eggs may be placed — see INSECT illustration

**ovis** \'ōvəs\ *n, cap* [NL, fr. L, sheep — more at EWE] **:** a genus of Bovidae consisting of the domestic sheep and the majority of the wild sheep most of whom are inhabitants of mountainous regions from western No. America to western Asia and have horns that curl from a lateral spiral — see ARGALI

**ovi·sac** \'ōvə,sak\ *n* -S [ISV *ov-* + *sac*] **1 :** an ootheca or other structure that serves to hold eggs (as the distal part of the oviduct of various amphibians) **2 :** GRAAFIAN FOLLICLE

**ovi·scapt** \'ōvə,skapt\ *n* -S [F *oviscapte*, fr. *ov-* + Gk *skaptein* to dig; akin to Gk *koptein* to smite, cut off — more at CAPON] **:** OVIPOSITOR

**ovism** \'ōvizəm\ *n* -S [ISV *ov-* + *-ism*] **:** an old theory that the egg contains the whole embryo of the future organism and the germs of all subsequent offspring — compare ANIMALCULISM

**ovi·spermary** \¦ōvə+\ *n* [*ov-* + *spermary*] **:** OVOTESTIS

**ovist** \'ōvəst\ *n* -S [ISV *ov-* + *-ist*] **:** one holding the theory of ovism

**ovis·tic** \(')ō¦vistik\ *adj* **:** of or relating to ovism or ovists

**ovo-** — see OV-

**ovo·cyte** \'ōvə,sīt\ *n* -S [ISV *ov-* + *-cyte*] **:** OOCYTE

**ovo·flavin** \¦ōvə+\ *n* [*ov-* + *flavin*] **:** RIBOFLAVIN

**ovo·genesis** \¦ōvə+\ *n* [NL, fr. L *ov-* + *genesis*] **:** OOGENESIS

**1ovoid** \'ō,vȯid\ *adj* [F *ovoïde*, fr. *ov-* + *-oïde* -oid] **:** shaped like an egg **:** OVATE ⟨an ~ apple⟩; *specif* **:** egg-shaped with the large end toward the point of attachment ⟨an ~ leaf⟩

**2ovoid** \"\ *n* -S **:** an ovoid body

**ovoi·dal** \(')ō¦vȯidᵊl\ *adj* [F *ovoïdal*, fr. *ovoïde* + *-al*] **:** OVOID

**ovo·lecithin** \¦(,)ōvō+\ *n* [*ov-* + *lecithin*] **1 :** lecithin from egg yolk **2 :** LECITHIN 2a

**ovo·lo** \'ōvə,lō, 'ōv-\ *n, pl* **ovo·li** \-,lē\ [It *ovolo, uovolo*, dim. of *ovo, uovo* egg, fr. L *ovum* — more at EGG] **:** a rounded convex molding that in Roman work is usu. a quarter circle in section, in Greek work is flatter, and in medieval architecture is not distinguishable from other convex moldings — compare BOLTEL, TORUS

ovolo

**ovo·mucin** \¦ōvə+\ *n* [*ov-* + *mucin*] **:** a mucin present in white of egg

**ovo·mucoid** \"+\ *n* [ISV *ov-* + *mucoid*] **:** a mucoid present in white of egg

**ovo·plasm** \'ōvə,plazəm\ *n* [ISV *ov-* + *-plasm*; orig. formed as G *ovoplasma*] **:** OOPLASM — **ovo·plas·mic** \¦ōvə¦plazmik\ *adj*

**ovo·testicular** \¦ō(,)vō+\ *adj* [fr. *ovotestis*, after E *testis: testicular*] **:** of or relating to an ovotestis

**ovo·testis** \¦ōvō+\ *n* [NL, fr. L *ov-* + *testis*] **:** a hermaphrodite gonad

**ovo·vitellin** \¦ō(,)vō+\ *n* [*ov-* + *vitellin*] **:** VITELLIN

**ovo·viviparity** \¦ō(,)vō+\ *n* [fr. *ovoviviparous*, after E *oviparous: oviparity* and E *viviparous: viviparity*] **:** the condition of being ovoviviparous

**ovo·viviparous** \"+\ *adj* [prob. fr. (assumed) NL *ovoviviparus*, fr. L *ov-* + *viviparus* viviparous] **:** producing eggs that develop within the maternal body and hatch within or immediately after extrusion from the parent (as in the case of many reptiles and elasmobranch fishes) — compare OVIPAROUS, VIVIPAROUS — **ovo·viviparously** \"+\ *adv* — **ovo·vivip·arousness** \"+\ *n*

**ovu·la** \'ōvyələ\ *n, cap* [NL, fr. L *ovum* egg + *-ula*] **:** a genus of marine snails related to and sometimes included in the Cypraeidae but now commonly made type of a separate family (Ovulidae)

**ovu·lar** \'ōvyələ(r), *in sense 1* " *or* -,vyül-\ *adj* [NL *ovularis*, fr. *ovulum* + L *-aris* -ar] **1 :** relating to or being an ovule **2 :** of or relating to ova

**ovu·lar·i·an** \¦ōvyə,la(a)rēən\ *adj* [perh. fr. NL *ovulum* ovule of a seed plant, small egg + E *-ary* + *-an*] **:** resembling an egg

**ovu·lary** \'ōvyə,lerē\ *n* -ES [*ovule* + *-ary*] **:** the lower part of a carpel in which the ovules are borne — compare OVARY

**1ovu·late** \'ōvyə,lāt; 'ōvyəlōt, -,vyülōt\ *adj* [prob. fr. (assumed) NL *ovulatus*, fr. NL *ovulum* + L *-atus* -ate] **:** bearing an ovule

**2ovu·late** \'ōvyə,lāt\ *vi* -ED/-ING/-S [*ovule* + *-ate*, v. suffix] **:** to produce ovules or discharge them from an ovary — **ovu·la·tion** \,ōvyə'lāshən\ *n* -S

**ovu·la·to·ry** \'ōvyələ,tōrē\ *adj* **:** of, relating to, or involving ovulation

**ovule** \'ō(,)vyül\ *n* -S [NL *ovulum* ovule of a seed plant, small egg, fr. L *ovum* egg + *-ulum*] **1 :** a rounded outgrowth of the ovary in seed plants that develops into a seed usu. only after fertilization and that consists of an embryo sac borne centrally within a nucellus, the latter surrounded by one or more integuments **2 :** a small egg **:** an egg in an early stage of growth

**ovu·lif·er·ous** \¦ōvyə¦lif(ə)rəs\ *adj* [*ovule* + *-iferous*] **:** bearing an ovule

**ovu·list** \'ōvyələst, -,vyül-\ *n* -S [ISV *ovule* + *-ist*; prob. orig. formed in G] **:** OVIST

**ovu·lum** \'ōvyələm\ *n, pl* **ovu·la** \-lə\ [NL] **:** OVULE

**ovum** \'ōvəm\ *n, pl* **ova** \-və\ [NL, fr. L, egg — more at EGG] **1 :** a female gamete **:** MACROGAMETE, EGG CELL: **a :** a mature egg that has undergone reduction, is ready for fertilization, and takes the form of a relatively large inactive gamete providing a comparatively great amount of reserve material and contributing most of the cytoplasm of the zygote — see OOSPHERE; compare CENTROLECITHAL, HOMOLECITHAL, MEGALECITHAL, MICROLECITHAL, OVARY, TELOLECITHAL **b :** an immature ovum (as an oocyte or oogonium) **c :** a fertilized ovum (as a zygote or embryo) — not used technically **2 :** an architectural ornament shaped like an egg

**ow** \'au̇, 'ü\ *interj* [ME] — used esp. to express sudden pain or surprise

**OW** *abbr* oil-in-water

**owa·la oil** \ō'wälə\ *n* [*owala* prob. fr. Mpongwe *owala, ovala, obala* owala tree] **:** a lubricant oil obtained from the seed of the owala tree

**owala tree** *n* **:** a tropical African tree (*Pentaclethra africana*) of the family Leguminosae having pods about two feet long and large flat seeds which yield owala oil

**owd** \'ōd, 'ōd, 'ad\ *dial var of* OLD

**1owe** \'ō\ *vb;* **owed** \'ōd\ *or archaic* **ought** \'ȯt\; **owed** *or archaic* **ought; owing; owes** [ME *owe, ogh & oweth, ogh* (1st & 3d pers. sing. pres. indic. respectively of *owen* to possess, own, owe, past *owede, oughte*), fr. OE *āh* (1st & 3d pers. sing. pres. indic. of *āgan* to possess, own, owe, past *āhte*); akin to OHG *eigun* (1st & 3d pers. pl. pres. indic.) possess, have, ON *ā* (1st & 3d pers. sing. pres. indic.) possess, have, am obliged (infin. *eiga*), Goth *aih* (1st & 3d pers. sing. pres. indic.) possess, have, Skt *īśe* he possesses, owns] *vt* **1 a** *archaic* **:** POSSESS, OWN **b** *dial Eng* **:** to claim as one's possession **c :** to have or bear (a specified feeling or relation) to someone or something ⟨~s his master a grudge⟩ **2 a** (1) **:** to be under an obligation to pay or repay in return for something received **:** be indebted in the sum of ⟨~s me five dollars⟩ (2) **:** to be under obligation to render (as duty or service) ⟨the homage which man ~s his Creator —M.W.Baldwin⟩ **b :** to have an obligation to on account of something done or received **:** be indebted to ⟨~s the grocer for supplies⟩ **3 :** to have or possess as something derived or bestowed **:** be indebted or obliged for ⟨*owed* his wealth to his father⟩ ⟨~s his fame chiefly to his professional activities —Dumas Malone⟩ ~ *vi* **1 :** to be in debt ⟨~s for his house⟩ **2** *obs* **:** to be under obligations to someone

**2owe** \'(y)ō\ *dial Eng var of* EWE

**ow·el·ty** \'ōəltē\ *n* -ES [MF *oelté* equality, fr. L *aequalitat-, aequalitas* — more at EQUALITY] **1 :** EQUALITY **2 a :** the amount paid or secured by one owner to another to equalize a partition of property in kind **b :** a payment made to achieve equality between those who exchange property

**owe·nia** \ō'(w)ēnēə\ *n, cap* [NL, fr. Sir Richard *Owen* †1892 Eng. anatomist and zoologist + NL *-ia*] **:** a small genus of tropical Australian trees (family Meliaceae) having pinnate leaves, small greenish panicled flowers, and edible acid drupaceous fruits — see NATIVE PLUM

**ow·en·ism** \'ōə,nizəm\ *n* -S *usu cap* [Robert *Owen* †1858 Welsh socialist and philanthropist + E *-ism*] **:** the political and social theories of Robert Owen who advocated a communistic reorganization of society and established an industrial community on the Clyde in Scotland and later in Indiana

**ow·en·ite** \-nīt\ *n* -S *usu cap* [Robert *Owen* + E *-ite*] **:** an adherent of the political and social theories of Robert Owen

**ow·er** \'ō(ə)r, 'ȯə\ *dial var of* OVER

**ow·er·ance** \'ō(ə)rən(t)s\ *n* -S [*ower* + *-ance*] *chiefly Scot* **:** MASTERY, CONTROL

**OWF** *abbr* optimum working frequency

**ow·ing** \'ōiŋ, 'ōēŋ\ *adj* [ME *owing, owinge*, fr. pres. part. of *owen* to possess, own, owe] **1** *archaic* **:** INDEBTED, BEHOLDEN **2 :** due to be paid or rendered **:** OWED ⟨sleep ~ to you because of some long vigil —Geoffrey Jefferson⟩ **3 :** ATTRIBUTABLE — used with *to* ⟨to whose . . . indulgence the errors of her daughters must be principally ~ —Jane Austen⟩

**owing to** *prep* **:** because of ⟨impassable by cars *owing to* soft sand —G.W.Murray⟩ ⟨was retired in the following July, *owing to* heart trouble —Allan Westcott⟩

**owk** \'ük\ *var of* OUK

**1owl** \'au̇l, *esp before pause or consonant* 'au̇əl\ *n* -S [ME *owle*, fr. OE *ūle*; akin to MD *ule* owl, OHG *uwila*, ON *ugla*] **1 :** any of numerous widely distributed birds of prey (order Strigiformes) distinguished by their large head and large more or less forwardly directed eyes, short hooked bill, strong talons with reversible outer toe, very soft fluffy usu. mottled plumage, and more or less nocturnal habits, as well as by many anatomical characters **2 :** a pigeon of a long-established breed from which the turbits and satinettes are supposed to be derived having a frill on the front of the neck and the bill very short with the upper mandible downwardly curved **3 :** a person suggestive of an owl in solemnity of appearance or manner, nocturnal mode of life, or other respect ⟨the ~s who . . . tell us that a dismal period of world history is no time for high musical spirits —Wilder Hobson⟩

**2owl** \"\ *vi* -ED/-ING/-S *chiefly dial* **:** to hoot or stare like an owl ⟨~ . . . with hoots that echo eerily down the valley —*Amer. Guide Series: Ark.*⟩

**3owl** \"\ *adj* **:** operating or open around or after midnight or all night ⟨the rattle of one of the ~ streetcars —Hamilton Basso⟩

**owl butterfly** *n* **:** a large So. American butterfly of the genus *Caligo*; *esp* **:** a butterfly (*C. eurylochus*) that has a large ocellated spot like an owl's eye on each hind wing

**1ow·ler** \'au̇lə(r)\ *n dial Eng var of* ALDER

**2owl·er** \'au̇lə(r)\ *n* -S [[1]*owl* + *-er*; prob. fr. the nocturnal habits of the owl] **:** a person or ship engaged in owling

**owl·ery** \'au̇lərē\ *n* -ES **:** an abode or a haunt of owls

**owl·et** \'au̇lət\ *n* -S [[1]*owl* + *-et*] **1 :** the European little owl or other small owl **2 :** a young owl

**owlet moth** *n* **:** a moth of the family Noctuidae

**owl-fly** \'=,=\ *n* **:** a neuropterous fly of the family Ascalaphidae

**owl·ing** \'au̇liŋ\ *n* -S [[1]*owl* + *-ing*; prob. fr. the nocturnal habits of the owl] **:** the act of smuggling wool or sheep out of England; *also* **:** the carrying on of contraband trade of any kind

**owl·ish** \'au̇lish, -lēsh\ *adj* **:** resembling, characteristic of, or suggestive of an owl ⟨the cigar-smoking man with an ~ look —*Newsweek*⟩ ⟨fluttering his eyelids in ~ bliss —Arline Thomas⟩ — **owl·ish·ly** \-ləshlē, -li\ *adv* — **owl·ish·ness** \-lishnəs -lēsh-\ *n* -ES

**owl-light** \'=,=\ *n* **:** DUSK ⟨the *owl-light* of the deep streets —F.M.Ford⟩

**owllike** \'=,=\ *adj* **:** like that of an owl ⟨an ancient and ~ demeanor —R.L.Stevenson⟩

**owl midge** *n* **:** a fly of the family Psychodidae

**owl monkey** *n* [so called fr. the large yellow eyes] **:** NIGHT APE

**owl moth** *n* **:** a Brazilian moth (*Erebus agrippina*) of the family Noctuidae that is the largest known moth and has a wingspread of 10 inches

**owl parrot** *n* **:** KAKAPO

**owl's clover** *or* **owlclover** \'=,==\ *n* **:** a California herb of the genus *Orthocarpus*

**owl swallow** *n* **:** a nightjar of the family Podargidae

**owly** \'au̇lē, -li\ *adj* **:** like an owl

**1own** \'ōn\ *adj* [ME *owen*, fr. OE *āgen*; akin to OHG *eigan* own, ON *eiginn*; derivative fr. the root of OE *āgan* to possess, own — more at OWE] **1 :** belonging to oneself or itself — usu. used following a possessive case or pronoun to emphasize or intensify the idea of property, peculiar interest, or exclusive ownership, and usu. with reflexive force ⟨my ~ father⟩ ⟨his ~ composition⟩ ⟨wants a room of her ~⟩ **2 —** used to specify an immediate or direct relationship ⟨an ~ brother⟩ ⟨an ~ cousin⟩ ⟨~ sister to the queen⟩ **3 —** used to indicate or intensify the idea of one's own self as agent or doer ⟨cooked his ~ meal⟩ ⟨acted as his ~ lawyer⟩ — **be one's own man :** to have command of oneself **:** not to be subject to another ⟨the college president must *be his own man* —Harold Taylor⟩ — **get one's own back :** to revenge oneself **:** get even ⟨they're out to *get their own back* —T.C.Worsley⟩ — **into one's own 1 :** into possession of that which rightfully belongs to one ⟨the despoiled heir at long last came *into his own*⟩ **2 :** into the prosperous or flourishing condition, status of leadership, or recognition to which one is entitled or of which one is capable ⟨Italian art poetry . . . now coming for the first time *into its own* —R.A.Hall b.1911⟩ ⟨recognizes that nationalism has finally come *into its own* in Asia —A.P.Ryan⟩ ⟨has begun, in a modest way, to come *into its own* —*Times Lit. Supp.*⟩ — **on one's own :** on one's own resources or initiative **:** independently of outer assistance or control **:** for or by oneself ⟨every ship was *on its own* —H.A.Chippendale⟩ ⟨gave the order . . . *on his own* —H.L.Ismay⟩

**2own** \"\ *vb* -ED/-ING/-S *vt* **1 :** to have or hold as property or appurtenance **:** have a rightful title to, whether legal or natural **:** POSSESS **2 a** (1) **:** to acknowledge as one's own ⟨~ a fault⟩ ⟨which the author had once ~*ed* as her habitat —C. W.Ferguson⟩ (2) *of a mother animal* **:** to acknowledge (offspring) as one's own by nursing and taking care of **b** *archaic* **:** to acknowledge as an acquaintance **:** give recognition to **c** *archaic* **:** to lay claim to **:** claim for one's own **3** *archaic* **:** to manifest one's approval or acceptance of **:** COUNTENANCE **4 a :** to acknowledge (someone or something) to be what is claimed **:** concede to be true or valid **:** ADMIT, RECOGNIZE ⟨~ a debt⟩ ⟨~*ed* him to be their master⟩ ⟨would not ~ his mistake⟩ **b :** to acknowledge the supremacy or authority of **:** yield obedience to **~** *vi* **:** ADMIT, CONFESS — used with *to* ⟨an old gentleman who ~*ed* to eighty-six years —Osbert Sitwell⟩ ⟨wouldn't ~ to knowin' me these days —Rex Ingamells⟩ **syn** see ACKNOWLEDGE, HAVE — **own the line** *chiefly Brit, of a hound* **:** to get the scent of a fox

**owned** \'ōnd\ *adj* **:** held as one's own possession — usu. used in combination ⟨state-*owned* railways⟩

**own·er** \'ōnə(r)\ *n* -S [ME *ownere*, fr. *ownen* to possess, take possession of (fr. OE *āgnian* take possession of, assign possession of) + *-ere* -er; akin to MD *eigenen, egenen* to take possession of, assign possession of, ON *eigna*; derivatives fr. the word represented by OE *āgen* own] **:** one that owns **:** one that has the legal or rightful title whether the possessor or not **:** PROPRIETOR — **at owner's risk** *adv* **:** on condition that the owner bear the risk (as of loss, damage or delay)

**own·er·less** \-ləs\ *adj* **:** having no owner ⟨~ land⟩

**owner's flag** *n* **:** PRIVATE SIGNAL

**own·er·ship** \-nə(r),ship\ *n* **:** the state, relation, or fact of being an owner **:** lawful claim or title **:** PROPERTY, PROPRIETORSHIP, DOMINIUM

**own·hood** \'ōn,hu̇d\ *n* [[1]*own* + *-hood*; trans. of G *eigenheit*] **:** the condition in which one holds oneself or one's own in isolation **:** reliance upon or desire for one's own way or will **:** EGOISM, SELFHOOD

**own·ness** \'ōnnəs\ *n* -ES **:** the quality or state of belonging to oneself

**own-root** \'=,=\ *or* **own-rooted** \'=¦==\ *adj, of a plant* **:** growing on its own roots rather than on roots obtained from a stock **:** developing from a seed, cutting, or layer rather than from grafting or budding ⟨*own-root* roses are frequently less vigorous than budded stock⟩ — compare SEEDLING-ROOTED

**own up** *vi* **:** to admit or confess frankly and fully ⟨if your ball broke the window . . . you *own up* —*Boy Scout Handbook*⟩

**owre** \(¦)ō(ə)r\ *chiefly Scot var of* OVER — often used in combination as a verbal prefix

**owse** *chiefly Scot var of* OX

**1owt** \'ōt\ *dial Eng var of* OUGHT

**2owt** \"\ *dial Eng var of* AUGHT

**owy·hee·ite** \ō'wīē,īt\ *n* -S [*Owyhee* county, southwestern Idaho, its locality + E *-ite*] **:** a mineral $Pb_5Ag_2Sb_6S_{15}$ consisting of a lead silver antimony sulfide occurring in metallic fibrous masses and needlelike crystals

**ox** \'äks\ *n, pl* **ox·en** \-ksən\ *also* **ox** *see sense 3* [ME, fr. OE *oxa*; akin to OHG *ohso* ox, ON *oxi*, Goth *auhsa*, W *ych* ox, Skt *ukṣan* ox, bull, *ukṣati* he sprinkles — more at HUMOR] **1 :** the domestic bovine (*Bos taurus*); *esp* **:** an adult castrated male used for a draft animal or for food ⟨pair of *oxen*⟩ ⟨span of *oxen*⟩ ⟨team of *oxen*⟩ ⟨yoke of *oxen*⟩ — compare BULL, BULLOCK, STEER **2 :** a member of *Bos* or a closely allied genus ⟨wild ~⟩ ⟨extinct *oxen*⟩ **3** *pl also* **oxes :** a person resembling an ox (as in placidity, stolidity, clumsiness, or strength) ⟨dumb ~⟩ ⟨big ~⟩

**1ox-** *or* **oxo-** *comb form* [F, fr. *oxygène* oxygen — more at OXYGEN] **1 :** containing oxygen — esp. in the names of various cyclic compounds ⟨*oxazole*⟩ **2** *usu* **oxo- :** containing oxygen in a carbonyl group specif. regarded as formed by replacement of two hydrogen atoms in a methylene group by oxygen — in names of ketones or compounds (as heterocyclic compounds) that are not true ketones because the carbonyl group is not attached to two carbon atoms ⟨*oxo*-acetic acid⟩ ⟨2-*oxo*-indoline⟩ ⟨oxindole⟩; distinguished from *oxy-*; compare KET-

**2ox-** *comb form* [by shortening] **:** OXAL- ⟨*ox*amide⟩

**oxa-** *or* **ox-** *comb form* [ISV, fr. [1]*ox-* + *-a-*] **:** containing oxygen in place of carbon or regarded as in place of carbon usu. in place of the methylene group $-CH_2-$ ⟨10*H*-9-*oxa*anthracene⟩ ⟨*oxa*zacycloheptane⟩ — compare AZA-, THIA-

**oxa·diazole** \¦äksə+\ *n* [[1]*ox-* + *diazole*] **:** any of four parent compounds $C_2H_2N_2O$ containing a five-membered ring composed of two carbon atoms, two nitrogen atoms, and one oxygen atom

**oxal-** *or* **oxalo-** *comb form* [F, fr. (*acide*) *oxalique* oxalic acid] **:** related to oxalic acid ⟨*oxal*amide⟩ ⟨*oxalo*succinic⟩

**ox·al·acetate** \¦äksəl+\ *or* **ox·a·lo·acetate** \¦äksə(,)lō, äk¦sa(-+\ *n* [ISV *oxalacetic* (in *oxalacetic acid*) + *-ate*] **:** a salt or ester of oxalacetic acid

**oxalacetic acid** \"+ . . . -\ *or* **oxaloacetic acid** \"+ . . . -\ *n* [*oxalacetic, oxaloacetic* ISV *oxal-* + *acetic*] **:** a crystalline acid $HOOCCOCH_2COOH$ formed by reversible oxidation of malic acid (as in the metabolism of fats and carbohydrates) and in reversible transamination reactions (as from aspartic acid) — compare CARBOXYLASE b

**ox·al·aldehyde** \¦äksəl+\ *n* [ISV *oxal-* + *aldehyde*] **:** GLYOXAL

**ox·al·amide** \,aksə'la,mīd, äk'salə,-, -məd\ *n* [ISV *oxal-* + *amide*; orig. formed in G] **:** OXAMIDE

**¹ox·a·late** \'äksə,lāt\ *n* -s [F, fr. *oxal-* (in *acide oxalique* oxalic acid) + *-ate*] **:** a salt or ester of oxalic acid
**²oxalate** \"\ *vt* -ED/-ING/-S **:** to treat with an oxalate; *specif* **:** to add an oxalate to (blood or plasma) to prevent coagulation
**ox·a·la·to-** \ˌäksəˈlād·(ˌ)ō\ *comb form* [¹*oxalate* + *-o-*] **:** oxalate — esp. in names of coordination complexes ⟨*oxalato*ferrate (III) ion $Fe(C_2O_4)_3{}^{3-}$⟩
**ox·aldehyde** \(ˈ)äks+\ *n* [²*ox-* + *aldehyde*] **:** GLYOXAL
**ox·al·ic acid** \(ˈ)äkˈsalik-, -lēk-\ *n* [*oxalic* fr. F *oxalique*, fr. L *oxalis* garden sorrel + F *-ique* -ic] **:** a poisonous strong dicarboxylic acid $(COOH)_2$ or $H_2C_2O_4$ that is usu. obtained as the hygroscopic crystalline dihydrate, that occurs in oxalis and other plants in the form of the acid potassium salt or the calcium salt, that is formed by the oxidation or fermentation of carbohydrates but is made industrially chiefly by heating sodium formate and finally acidifying, and that is used esp. as a neutralizing, acidifying, and bleaching agent (as in laundering and in the textile industry), as a cleaning and purifying agent, as a rust and scale remover, in the manufacture of dyes and other chemicals, and in chemical analysis
**ox·al·i·da·ce·ae** \(ˌ)äkˌsaləˈdāsēˌē\ *n pl, cap* [NL, fr. *Oxalid-, Oxalis*, type genus + *-aceae*] **:** a family of widely distributed herbs or rarely trees (order Geraniales) having compound leaves and regular pentamerous flowers with monadelphous stamens and five distinct styles — **ox·al·i·da·ceous** \(ˌ)äkˌsaləˈdāshəs\ *adj*
**ox·alis** \äkˈsaləs, ˈäksələs\ *n* [NL, fr. L, garden sorrel, fr. Gk, sorrel, fr. *oxys* sharp, keen — more at OXY-] **1** *cap* **:** a large genus (the type of the family Oxalidaceae) of acaulescent herbs mostly of warm or tropical regions having acid foliage, palmately or pinnately compound leaves, and white, pink, or purple flowers with 10 stamens — see OCA **2** -ES **:** any plant or flower of the genus *Oxalis*
**ox·alo·nitrile** \ˈäksə(ˌ)lō, äkˈsalə-+\ *n* [*oxal-* + *nitrile*] **:** CYANOGEN 2
**ox·alo·succinic acid** \"+ . . . -\ *n* [*oxal-* + *succinic*] **:** a tricarboxylic acid HOOCCOCH(COOH)$CH_2$COOH recognized as an intermediate stage in the metabolism of fats and carbohydrates
**ox·al·uria** \ˌäksəlˈyu̇rēə, -səˈlu̇rēə\ *n* -s [NL, fr. *oxal-* + *-uria*] **:** the presence of oxalic acid or oxalates in the urine esp. in excess
**ox·al·uric acid** \¦==¦=rik-\ *n* [ISV *oxal-* + *-uric*] **:** a crystalline acid $NH_2$CONHCOCOOH obtained in the form of salts by the action of alkalies on parabanic acid
**ox·a·lyl** \ˈäksəˌlil\ *n* -s [ISV *oxal-* + *-yl*] **:** the bivalent radical —COCO— of oxalic acid
**ox·a·lyl·urea** \¦äksəˌlilyu̇ˈrēə\ *n* [NL, fr. ISV *oxalyl* + NL *urea*] **:** PARABANIC ACID
**ox·amate** \ˈäksəˌmāt, äkˈsamət\ *n* -s [ISV *oxamic* (in *oxamic acid*) + *-ate*] **:** a salt or ester of oxamic acid
**ox·am·ic acid** \(ˈ)äk¦samik-\ *n* [*oxamic* fr. F *oxamique*, fr. *oxam-* (fr. *oxamide*) + *-ique* -ic] **:** a high-melting crystalline acid $NH_2$COCOOH intermediate between oxalic acid and oxamide **:** the monoamide of oxalic acid
**ox·amide** \äkˈsaməd; ˈäksəˌmīd, -ˌməd\ *n* [ISV ²*ox-* + *amide*; orig. formed in F] **:** a high-melting crystalline amide $(CONH_2)_2$ obtainable by treating ethyl oxalate with ammonia **:** the diamide of oxalic acid
**ox·amine dye** \ˈäksəˌmēn-, -ˌmən; äkˈsamən-\ *n, usu cap O* [ISV ¹*ox-* + *amine*] **:** any of several direct dyes — see DYE table I (under *Direct Red 53, Direct Violet 12, Direct Blue 3*)
**ox·am·mite** \ˈäksəˌmīt, äkˈsaˌm-\ *n* [*oxalate* + *ammonium* + *-ite*] **:** hydrous ammonium oxalate $(NH_4)_2C_2O_4.1H_2O$ occurring as a crystalline salt in guano
**ox·a·nil·ic acid** \¦äksə¦nilik-\ *n* [ISV ²*ox-* + *anilic*] **:** a crystalline acid $C_6H_5$NHCOCOOH obtained by heating oxalic acid with aniline; phenyl-oxamic acid
**ox·anilide** \(ˈ)aks+\ *n* [ISV ²*ox-* + *anilide*] **:** a crystalline amide $(CONHC_6H_5)_2$ obtainable by heating aniline oxalate and useful as a plasticizer; diphenyl-oxamide
**ox·a·zine** \ˈäksəˌzēn, -ˌzən\ *n* -s [ISV ¹*ox-* + *azine*] **:** any of several parent compounds $C_4H_5NO$ or their derivatives containing a ring composed of four carbon atoms, one oxygen atom, and one nitrogen atom; *esp* **:** OXAZINE DYE — see AZINE 1; compare MORPHOLINE
**oxazine dye** *n* **:** an azine dye containing at least one fused oxazine ring in which the oxygen atom and the nitrogen atom are in the para or 1,4-positions — compare PHENOXAZINE
**ox·a·zole** \ˈäksəˌzōl\ *n* [ISV ¹*ox-* + *azole*] **1 :** a parent compound $C_3H_3NO$ containing a ring composed of three carbon atoms, one oxygen atom, and one nitrogen atom with one carbon atom between the oxygen and nitrogen atoms — compare ISOXAZOLE **2 :** a derivative of oxazole
**ox·a·zol·i·dine** \ˌäksəˈzōləˌdēn, -zälˈ-\ *n* -s [ISV *oxazole* + *-idine*] **:** the tetrahydro derivative $C_3H_7NO$ of oxazole; *also* **:** a derivative of this compound of which some (as trimethadione) are used in the control of convulsions (as in the treatment of epilepsy)
**ox ball** *n* **:** a hair ball from an ox's stomach
**ox balm** *n* **:** HORSE BALM 1
**ox·ber·ry** \ˈäks- — *see* BERRY\ *n, dial Eng* **:** the fruit of the black bryony
**ox bile** *n* **:** OXGALL
**oxbird** \ˈ=ˌ=\ *n* **1 :** DUNLIN **2** *dial Eng* **:** the sanderling or other sandpiper **3 :** an African weaverbird (*Bubalornis albirostris*) **4 :** OXPECKER
**oxbiter** \ˈ=ˌ==\ *n* **1 :** COWBIRD **2 :** OXPECKER
**oxblood** \ˈ=ˌ=\ *or* **oxblood red** *n* **:** a moderate reddish brown that is yellower, stronger, and slightly darker than roan, stronger than mahogany, redder and stronger than rustic brown, and redder and deeper than russet tan — called also *beef's blood, coptic, Kazak, Malaga red, piccolopasso red, sang de boeuf*
**ox bot** *or* **ox botfly** *n* **:** WARBLE FLY
**¹oxbow** \ˈ=ˌ=\ *n* [ME *oxbowe*, fr. *ox* + *bowe* bow — more at OX, BOW] **1 :** a frame bent into the shape of the letter U and embracing an ox's neck as a kind of collar the upper ends of which pass through the bar of the yoke **2 a :** a river meander with extreme curvature such that only a neck of land is left between two parts of the stream **b :** OXBOW LAKE

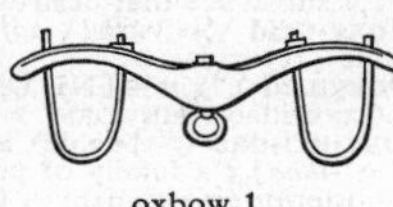

oxbow 1

**²oxbow** \ˈ=ˌ=\ *adj* **:** having a compound curve with concave center and convex ends — opposed to *serpentine*; used esp. of the front of a piece of cabinet furniture ⟨~ chest⟩
**oxbow lake** *n* **:** a crescent-shaped often ephemeral lake formed in the abandoned channel of a meander by the silting up of its ends after the stream has cut through the land within the meander at a narrow point
**oxbow stirrup** *n* **:** a large wooden stirrup resembling an oxbow in shape
**oxbrake** \ˈ=ˌ=\ *n* **:** a frame in which oxen are shod
**oxcart** \ˈ=ˌ=\ *n* **:** a cart drawn by oxen
**oxcheek** \ˈ=ˌ=\ *n* **:** an ox's cheek esp. when cut for meat
**oxea** \ˈäksēə, äkˈsēə\ *n, pl* **oxeas** \-ēəz\ *also* **oxe·ae** \-ēˌē\ [NL, fr. Gk *oxys* sharp — more at OXY-] **:** a needle-shaped sponge spicule sharp at both ends
**oxen** *pl of* OX
**²ox·en** \ˈäksən\ *n* -s [by alter. (influence of ¹*oxen*)] *dial* **:** OX
**oxen dance** *n* [trans. of Sw *oxdans*] **:** a comic Swedish male folk dance representing a mock duel
**ox·e·ote** \ˈäksēˌōt\ *also* **ox·e·ate** \-ēˌāt\ *adj* [*oxeote* fr. NL *oxea* + E *-ote* (as in *tylote*); *oxeate* fr. NL *oxea* + E *-ate*] **:** of, relating to, or forming an oxea; *also* **:** pointed and shaped like a rod
**ox·er** \ˈäksə(r)\ *n* -s [*ox* + *-er*] **:** a hedge with a guardrail running along one side at a distance of two or three feet and often a ditch along the other side to prevent cattle from passing through it — see DOUBLE OXER
**oxes** *pl of* OX
**oxeye** \ˈ=ˌ=\ *n* [ME, fr. *ox* + *eye*] **1 :** any of several composite plants having heads with both disk and ray flowers: as **a :** DAISY 1b **b :** FIELD CHAMOMILE **c :** a plant of the genus *Buphthalmum* **d :** a plant of the genus *Heliopsis* **e :** BLACK-EYED SUSAN **2 a** *dial Eng* **:** the dunlin or other small sandpiper **b** *dial Eng* **:** any of several titmice **c :** LEAST SANDPIPER **d :** BLACK-BELLIED PLOVER **3 :** a round or oval window **4 :** a small cloud that on the African coasts precedes a storm **5** *or* **oxeye herring :** TARPON 1b
**oxeye bean** *n* **:** the large orbicular brown seed of a tall tropical American woody vine (*Mucuna urens*) having flat bristly pods; *also* **:** the vine producing this seed
**ox-eyed** \ˈ=¦=\ *adj* [trans. of Gk *boōpis*] **:** having eyes like those of an ox ⟨*ox-eyed* Juno⟩ ⟨*ox-eyed* Hera⟩
**oxeye daisy** *also* **ox-eyed daisy** *n* **1 :** DAISY 1b **2 :** OXEYE 1d **3 :** BLACK-EYED SUSAN
**ox fence** *n* **:** OXER
**oxfly** \ˈ=ˌ=\ *n* **:** an ox warble fly or other fly troublesome to cattle
**¹ox·ford** \ˈäksfə(r)d\ *adj, usu cap* [fr. *Oxford*, city in central England] **1 :** of or from the city of Oxford, England **:** of the kind or style prevalent in Oxford **:** OXONIAN **2** [fr. *Oxford* University, Oxford, England] **:** of or relating to Oxford University **:** OXONIAN
**²oxford** \"\ *n* -s **1** *also* **oxford shoe** *sometimes cap O* **:** a low-cut usu. laced shoe coming to the instep or lower, often being of balmoral or blucher design, and usu. having three or more eyelets **2** *often cap* **:** OXFORD DOWN **3** *or* **oxford cloth** *sometimes cap O* **:** a soft durable shirting and general clothing fabric usu. of cotton but sometimes of spun rayon and made in plain weave or basket weaves having two fine warp yarns against one heavier filling yarn

oxford of balmoral design

**oxford bag** *n, usu cap O* **1 :** a bag resembling the Boston bag but larger **2 oxford bags** *pl* **:** trousers with very large baggy legs
**oxford blue** *n, often cap O* **:** a blackish purple that is bluer and darker than average eggplant and bluer and deeper than Burgundy (sense 2b)
**oxford chrome** *n, often cap O* **:** YELLOW OCHER
**oxford corner** *n, usu cap O* **:** a plain border rule projecting in each outward direction and making a square outside at each corner
**oxford dash** *n, often cap O* **:** DOUBLE DASH
**oxford down** *also* **oxfordshire down** *n* [fr. *Oxford* or *Oxfordshire*, county in central England where the breed originated] **1** *usu cap O&D* **:** a Down breed of large hornless sheep developed by crossing Cotswolds and Hampshire Downs **2** *usu cap O & often cap D* **:** a sheep of the Oxford Down breed
**oxford frame** *n, usu cap O* **:** a picture frame having sides that cross at the corners and project outward several inches
**oxford gray** *also* **oxford** *n* -s *often cap O* **:** a dark gray that is darker than pelican or Dover gray and lighter than fashion gray

Oxford frame

**oxford grouper** *n, usu cap O&G* **:** a member of the Oxford Group movement
**oxford group movement** *n, usu cap O&G* **:** a life-changing movement stressing personal and social regeneration founded in 1921 at Oxford, England, by Frank Buchman and replaced by moral re-armament in 1938 — called also *Buchmanism*
**¹ox·for·di·an** \(ˈ)äk¦sfȯrdēən\ *adj or n, usu cap* [*Oxford*, England + E *-ian*] **:** OXONIAN
**²oxfordian** \"\ *adj, usu cap* [Edward de Vere, Earl of *Oxford* †1604 Eng. courtier and lyric poet + E *-ian*] **:** of or relating to the 17th Earl of Oxford or to the doctrine that he was the author of the dramatic works usu. attributed to Shakespeare
**³oxfordian** \"\ *n* -s *usu cap* **:** a supporter of the doctrine that the 17th Earl of Oxford was the author of the dramatic works usu. attributed to Shakespeare
**oxford india paper** *n, usu cap O&I* **:** INDIA PAPER 2
**ox·ford·ism** \ˈäksfə(r)ˌdizəm\ *n* -s *usu cap* **1 :** an Oxonian habit or characteristic **2 :** TRACTARIANISM
**oxford movement** *n, usu cap O & sometimes cap M* **:** a High Church movement within the Church of England that was started at Oxford in 1833 and that attempted to revive pre-Reformation forms of piety in the interest of an Anglo-Catholicism
**oxford ocher** *n* **1** *usu cap 1st O* **:** a yellow ocher found near Oxford, England **2** *often cap 1st O* **:** YELLOW OCHER
**ox·ford·shire** \ˈäksfə(r)dˌshi(ə)r, -ˌshiə, -ˌshə(r)\ *or* **oxford** *adj, usu cap* [fr. *Oxfordshire* or *Oxford*, county in central England] **:** of or from the county of Oxford, England **:** of the kind or style prevalent in the county of Oxford
**oxford unit** *n, usu cap O* [fr. *Oxford* University, Oxford, England, where it was first adopted] **:** an international unit of penicillin equivalent to 0.606 micrograms of the crystalline compound
**oxford weed** *n, usu cap O* **:** KENILWORTH IVY
**oxgall** \ˈ=ˌ=\ *n* **1 :** the gall of the ox used esp. in medicine, painting, and the marbling of books **2 :** LIGHT CHROME YELLOW
**ox·gang** \ˈäksˌgaŋ\ *or* **ox·gate** \-ˌgāt\ *n* [*oxgang* fr. ME, fr. OE *oxan gang*, fr. *oxan*, gen. of *oxa* ox + *gang* way; *oxgate* fr. *ox* + *gate* (way); fr. its being measured by the work of one ox in a plowing team — more at OX, GANG] **:** BOVATE
**oxgoad** \ˈ=ˌ=\ *n* **:** a goad for driving oxen
**oxharrow** \ˈ=ˌ=(ˌ)=\ *n, archaic* **:** a large heavy harrow used esp. on clay land
**oxheart** \ˈ=ˌ=\ *n* **1 :** any of various large sweet cherries **2** *or* **oxheart cabbage :** any of various cabbages with oval or conical heads
**oxhide** \ˈ=ˌ=\ *n* [ME, fr. *ox* + *hide*] **1 :** the hide of an ox **2 :** leather made from the hide of an ox
**oxhorn** \ˈ=ˌ=\ *n* **1 :** the horn of an ox **2 :** a drinking cup made of an ox's horn
**ox·i·da·ble** \ˈäksədəbəl\ *adj* [F *oxidable, oxydable*, fr. *oxider, oxyder* to oxidize (fr. *oxide, oxyde*) + *-able* — more at OXIDE] **:** OXIDIZABLE
**ox·i·dant** \ˈäksədənt, -dᵊnt\ *n* -s [F *oxidant* (now *oxydant*), fr. pres. part. of *oxider* (now *oxyder*) to oxidize, fr. *oxide* (now *oxyde*) oxide] **:** OXIDIZING AGENT — compare REDUCTANT
**ox·i·dase** \ˈäksəˌdās, -āz\ *n* -s [ISV *oxid-* (fr. *oxidation*) + *-ase*] **:** any of various enzymes that catalyze oxidation and thus play an important role in biological oxidation-reduction processes; *esp* **:** a metal-containing enzyme (as cytochrome oxidase or tyrosinase) that differs in general from a dehydrogenase in its ability to react directly with molecular oxygen — compare OXIDOREDUCTASE, PEROXIDASE
**ox·i·da·sic** \¦==¦dāsik, -āzik\ *adj* **:** of, like, or relating to an oxidase
**ox·i·da·tion** \ˌäksəˈdāshən\ *n* -s [F *oxidation* (now *oxydation*), fr. *oxider* (now *oxyder*) to oxidize + *-ation*] **1 a :** the act or process of oxidizing ⟨anodic ~⟩ — compare COMBUSTION 1a, FERMENTATION 1b, RESPIRATION 2 **b :** the state or result of being oxidized **2 :** the stage in the firing of clayware in which the organic matter is burned away by the oxygen in the kiln atmosphere
**oxidation base** *or* **oxidation dye** *n* **:** any of a small class of dyes (as aniline black) that are formed by oxidation after application to furs or textiles — see DYE table I
**oxidation potential** *n* **:** the potential at which oxidation occurs at the anode in an electrochemical cell
**oxidation-reduction** *n* **:** a chemical reaction in which one or more electrons are transferred from one atom or molecule to another ⟨the hydrogen–hydrogen-ion system is an *oxidation-reduction* system⟩ — called also *redox*
**oxidation-reduction potential** *n* **:** the potential at which oxidation occurs at the anode and reduction at the cathode in an electrochemical cell; *esp* **:** the standard potential referred to the standard hydrogen electrode as zero — symbol *E°*; called also *redox potential*; compare ELECTROMOTIVE SERIES, REDUCTION POTENTIAL
**oxidation state** *or* **oxidation number** *n* **:** the degree of oxidation of an element or atom (as in a compound) that is usu. expressed as a positive or negative number representing the ionic charge or effective charge of the element or atom ⟨the usual *oxidation state* of hydrogen is +1 and of oxygen −2⟩ — compare VALENCE 1 a
**ox·i·da·tive** \ˈäksəˌdād·iv\ *adj* **:** relating to or characterized by oxidation ⟨~ rancidity⟩ **:** having oxidizing powers ⟨~ catalysts⟩ — **ox·i·da·tive·ly** \-d·əvlē\ *adv*
**ox·ide** *also* **ox·yde** \ˈäkˌsīd *also* -ˌsəd\ *n* -s [F *oxide* (now *oxyde*), fr. *ox-* (fr. *oxygène* oxygen) + *-ide* (fr. *acide* acid) — more at OXYGEN] **1 a :** a binary compound of oxygen with an element ⟨water is hydrogen ~⟩ ⟨~s of iron⟩ — compare OZONIDE, PEROXIDE, RUST 1a, SUPEROXIDE **b :** a compound of oxygen with one or more metallic elements ⟨many minerals (as spinels) are double or multiple ~s⟩ **2 :** a compound (as ethylene oxide) of oxygen with an organic radical **:** ETHER 3b ⟨diphenyl ~⟩ — **ox·id·ic** \(ˈ)äk¦sidik\ *adj*
**oxide blue** *n* **:** a strong greenish blue to blue
**oxide brown** *or* **oxide purple** *n* **:** a moderate reddish brown that is yellower and deeper than mahogany or roan, deeper than rustic brown, and yellower and duller than average brick (sense 5a) — called also *purple brown, purple oxide*
**oxide of iron :** IRON OXIDE
**oxide red** *n* **:** any of several colors (as Indian red, Venetian red, bole, iron-oxide red) resembling those of ferric oxide under various conditions — compare IRON-OXIDE RED, IRON RED
**oxide yellow** *n* **:** YELLOW OCHER
**ox·i·di·met·ric** \ˌäksədəˈme·trik, äk¦sidə-\ *adj* **:** of, relating to, or by means of oxidimetry
**ox·i·dim·e·try** \ˌäksəˈdimə·trē\ *n* -ES [ISV *oxid-* (fr. *oxidation*) + *-i-* + *-metry*] **:** quantitative determination in chemical analysis involving oxidation
**ox·i·diz·abil·i·ty** \ˌäksəˌdīzəˈbiləd·ē\ *n* **:** ability to be oxidized
**ox·i·diz·able** \ˈäksəˌdīzəbəl, ˌ==ˈ===\ *adj* **:** capable of being oxidized
**ox·i·di·za·tion** \ˌäksədəˈzāshən, -ˌdīˈz-\ *n* -s **:** OXIDATION
**ox·i·dize** \ˈäksəˌdīz\ *vb* -ED/-ING/-S [*oxide* + *-ize*] *vt* **1 a :** to combine with oxygen or with more oxygen ⟨~ copper to copper oxide⟩ **:** add oxygen chemically to (a substance) often by means of a series of reactions ⟨glucose is *oxidized* to carbon dioxide and water with the release of energy during the metabolism of carbohydrates⟩ — compare OXYGENATE **b :** to dehydrogenate esp. by the action of oxygen or other oxidizing agent ⟨~ an alcohol to an aldehyde⟩ **c :** to change (a compound) by increasing the proportion of the electronegative part ⟨~ copper (I) chloride to copper (II) chloride⟩ **:** change (an element or ion) from a lower to a higher oxidation state ⟨in electrolysis . . . ferrous ions are *oxidized* to ferric ions at the anode —Farrington Daniels & R.A.Alberty⟩ **:** remove one or more electrons from (an atom, ion, or molecule) ⟨~ metallic copper to ionic copper⟩ — opposed to *reduce* **2 :** to produce on (a metallic surface) a decorative film usu. of a compound (as a sulfide) ~ *vi* **:** to become oxidized; *specif* **:** RUST 1
**oxidized cellulose** *n* **:** an acid degradation product of cellulose that is usu. obtained by oxidizing cotton or gauze with nitrogen dioxide, that is a useful hemostatic (as in surgery), and that is absorbed by body fluids (as when used to pack wounds) — compare OXYCELLULOSE
**oxidized oil** *n* **:** an oil that has been treated with air or oxygen; *esp* **:** BLOWN OIL
**ox·i·diz·er** \-zə(r)\ *n* -s **:** one that oxidizes: as **a :** the oxidizing agent (as liquid oxygen) of a rocket propellant **b :** a worker who brushes a special chemical solution on a patterned surface of silver to darken it and make the design stand out after polishing
**oxidizing agent** *n* **:** a substance (as oxygen, nitric acid, carbon dioxide) that oxidizes by taking up electrons — called also *oxidant, oxidizer*; compare REDUCING AGENT
**oxidizing flame** *n* **:** a flame or the part of a flame having an excess of oxygen (as the outer cone of a gas flame)
**oxido-** *comb form* [ISV, fr. *oxide*] **1 :** oxide; *specif* **:** EPOXY- — in names of organic chemical compounds ⟨*oxido*ethane⟩ **2 :** oxidation ⟨*oxido*reduction⟩
**ox·i·do·reductase** \¦äksə(ˌ)dō+\ *n* [*oxido-* + *reductase*] **:** an enzyme that catalyzes oxidation-reduction reactions — compare DEHYDROGENASE, OXIDASE, PEROXIDASE, REDUCTASE
**ox·i·do·reduction** \"+\ *n* [ISV *oxido-* + *reduction*] **:** OXIDATION-REDUCTION
**ox·i·du·lat·ed** \äkˈsijəˌlād·əd\ *adj* [obs. F *oxidulé* (fr. *oxidule* oxide with lowest degree of oxidation, fr. F *oxide* + *-ule*) + E *-ate* + *-ed*] *archaic* **:** existing in a lower oxidation state ⟨~ iron $Fe_3O_4$⟩
**ox·i·mate** \ˈäksəˌmāt\ *vt* -ED/-ING/-S [*oxime* + *-ate*] **:** to convert into an oxime — **ox·i·ma·tion** \ˌäksəˈmāshən\ *n* -s
**ox·ime** \ˈakˌsēm, -ˌsəm\ *n* -s [ISV ¹*ox-* + *-ime* (fr. *imide*); orig. formed in G] **:** any of a class of compounds obtained chiefly by the action of hydroxylamine on aldehydes and ketones and characterized by the grouping >C=NOH in which the isonitroso group replaces the oxygen of the carbonyl group — compare BENZALDOXIME
**ox·im·e·ter** \äkˈsiməd·ə(r)\ *n* [¹*ox-* + *-i-* + *-meter*] **:** an instrument for measuring continuously the degree of oxygen saturation of the circulating blood — **ox·i·met·ric** \¦äksə¦me·trik\ *adj*
**ox·im·e·try** \äkˈsimə·trē\ *n* -ES [ISV ¹*ox-* + *-i-* + *-metry*] **:** the use of an oximeter
**oximino-** *also* **oximido-** *comb form* [ISV ¹*ox-* + *imin-* or *imid-*] **:** ISONITROSO-
**ox·in·dole** \ˈäksənˌdōl, äkˈsin-\ *n* [ISV ¹*ox-* + *indole*] **:** a crystalline compound $C_8H_7NO$ isomeric with indoxyl and obtainable by reduction of isatin; 2-oxo-indoline
**ox·ine** \ˈakˌsēn, -ˌsən\ *n* -s [¹*ox-* + *-ine*] **:** a crystalline phenolic base $HOC_9H_6N$ that is used in analysis to form insoluble chelated compounds with ions of metals (as iron, aluminum, titanium, bismuth, zinc) and esp. in the form of its yellow crystalline sulfate in medicine as an antiseptic; 8-hydroxyquinoline
**ox·i·rane** \ˈäksəˌrān\ *n* -s [¹*ox-* + *-ir-* (prob. alter. of *tri-*) + *-ane*] **:** ETHYLENE OXIDE
**ox kind** *n* **:** the group of animals comprising the Old World species (*Bos taurus*) and constituting the common bovine domesticated cattle
**oxlike** \ˈ=ˌ=\ *adj* **:** resembling, suggestive of, or having the characteristics of an ox
**ox·lip** \ˈäkˌslip\ *n* [OE *oxanslyppe*, fr. *oxan*, gen. of *oxa* ox + *slyppe, slypa* pulp, paste — more at OX, SLIP] **1 :** a hybrid primrose **2 :** a Eurasian primula (*Primula elatior*) differing from the cowslip chiefly in the flat corolla limb
**ox louse** *n* **:** any of several cattle lice (esp. *Haematopinus eurysternus* or *Linognathus vituli*)
**ox·man** \ˈäksmən\ *n, pl* **oxmen :** a man who tends or drives oxen
**oxo** \ˈäk(ˌ)sō\ *adj* [¹*ox-*] **:** containing oxygen ⟨inorganic ~ acids⟩; *esp* **:** containing oxygen in a carbonyl group ⟨2-*oxo* acids in the sugar series —C.D.Hurd⟩ — compare KETO, ¹OX-2
**¹oxo-** — see OX-
**²oxo-** *comb form* [¹*ox-*] **:** containing oxygen as a doubly coordinated group ⟨*dioxo*uranium(VI) $UO_2{}^{++}$⟩
**¹ox·o·nian** \äkˈsōnēən, -ōnyən\ *n* -s *cap* [ML *Oxonia* Oxford + E *-an*] **1 :** a native or resident of Oxford, England **2 :** a student or graduate of Oxford University
**²oxonian** \(ˈ)=¦=(=)=\ *adj, usu cap* **:** of, relating to, or characteristic of Oxford, England, or its university
**ox·on·ic acid** \(ˈ)äk¦sänik-\ *n* [ISV ¹*ox-* + *-onic* (prob. fr. *carbonic*); orig. formed in G] **:** ALLANTOXANIC ACID
**ox·o·ni·um** \äkˈsōnēəm\ *n* -s [NL, fr. ¹*ox-* + *-onium*] **1 :** the univalent cation $H_3O^+$ derived from oxygen and known esp. in the form of organic derivatives **:** the monohydrated hydrogen ion ⟨diethyl-*oxonium* chloride $[(C_2H_5)_2HO]^+Cl^-$⟩ — called also *hydronium*
**oxo·phen·ar·sine** \ˌaksəfə¦närˌsēn, -ˈärsən\ *n* [¹*ox-* + *phen-* + *arsine*] **:** an arsenical used in the form of its white powdery hydrochloride $HOC_6H_3(AsO)NH_2.HCl$ in the treatment of syphilis esp. as an adjuvant to penicillin and Vincent's angina
**oxo process** *or* **oxo reaction** *n* **1 :** a process for synthesizing aldehydes (as propionaldehyde) by the addition of carbon monoxide and hydrogen under pressure to olefins (as ethylene) in the presence of a usu. cobalt catalyst — compare HYDROFORMYLATION **2 :** a process for synthesizing alcohols

(as isooctyl alcohol) usu. by producing aldehydes from olefins and hydrogenating the aldehydes to alcohols — compare OXYL PROCESS

**ox·pecker** \ˈ=,=\ *n* : either of two small dull-colored African birds (*Buphagus africanus* and *Buphagoides erythrorhynchus*) that resemble and are closely related to starlings and feed on ticks which they pick from the backs of infested cattle and wild mammals

**ox ray** *n* : DEVILFISH 1

**oxshoe** \ˈ=,=\ *n* : a shoe for an ox often consisting of two pieces one for each side of the hoof

**ox·skin** \ˈäk(s),skin\ *n* : OXHIDE

**ox·tail** \ˈ=,=\ *n* [ME *ox taill*, fr. *ox* + *taill* tail — more at TAIL] : the tail of cattle; *esp* : the skinned tail used for soup

**oxteam** \ˈ=,=\ *n* : a team of oxen

**¹ox·ter** \ˈäkstə(r)\ *n* -s [OE *ōxta, ōcusta;* akin to OHG *uochsana* armpit, ON *ōstr* hollow of the neck, OE *ōxn* armpit, *eax* axis, axle — more at AXIS] **1** *chiefly Scot & Irish* **a** : the space between the inside upper arm and the body : ARMPIT **b** : the armhole of a garment **2** *chiefly Scot & Irish* : ARM

**²oxter** \"\ *vb* -ED/-ING/-S *vi, chiefly Scot* : to walk arm in arm ~ *vt* **1** *chiefly Scot* : to support at the elbow or by a part of the arm **2** *chiefly Scot* : to put or carry under the arm

**oxter plate** *n* : a molded plate used to continue the shell plates immediately above the propeller aperture of a ship

**oxtongue** \ˈ=,=\ *n* [ME *oxtonge, oxtunge*, fr. *ox* + *tonge, tunge* tongue — more at OX, TONGUE] : any of several plants that have rough tongue-shaped leaves: as **a** : BUGLOSS 1 **b** : BUGLOSS 3

**ox wagon** *n* : a heavy wagon drawn by oxen

**ox warble** *n* : the maggot of an ox warble fly

**ox warble fly** *n* : either of two warble flies (*Hypoderma lineata* and *H. bovis*)

**¹oxy** \ˈäksē\ *adj* [*ox* + *-y*] : of or relating to an ox

**²oxy** \"\ *adj* [*²oxy-*] **1** : containing oxygen — compare ²OXY- 1 **2** : HYDROXY

**¹oxy-** *comb form* [ME, fr. L, fr. Gk, fr. *oxys;* akin to Gk *achnē* chaff — more at EAR] **1** : sharp : keen : pointed : acute ⟨*oxy*aster⟩ ⟨*oxy*cephaly⟩ ⟨*oxy*dactyl⟩ ⟨*oxy*rhynchous⟩ **2** : quick ⟨*oxy*tocic⟩ **3** : acid ⟨*oxy*phytic⟩ ⟨*oxy*phile⟩

**²oxy-** *comb form* [F, fr. *oxygène* oxygen — more at OXYGEN] **1 a** : containing oxygen or additional oxygen ⟨*oxy*cellulose⟩ ⟨*oxy*hemoglobin⟩ **b** : containing oxygen in the form of an oxide ⟨*oxy*chloride⟩ **c** : containing an oxygen atom united to two different atoms — esp. in names of organic compounds; distinguished from *ket-*, ¹*ox-* 2; compare EPOXY- ⟨*oxy*diacetic acid $O(CH_2COOH)_2$⟩ **2** : HYDROXY- — not used systematically ⟨*oxy*naphthoic⟩ **3** : of oxygen and ⟨*oxy*hydrogen⟩

**oxy·acan·thine** \ˌäksēəˈkan,thēn, -an(t)thən\ *n* [ISV *oxyacanth-* (fr. NL *oxyacantha* — specific epithet of the hawthorn *Crataegus oxyacantha* —, fr. Gk *oxyakantha* sharp thorn, fr. *oxy-* ¹oxy- + *akantha* thorn) + *-ine;* prob. orig. formed as G *oxyakanthin* — more at ACANTH-] : a bitter crystalline alkaloid $C_{37}H_{40}N_2O_6$ obtained from barberry root

**oxy·acetylene** \ˌäksē+\ *adj* [ISV ²*oxy-* + *acetylene*] : of, relating to, or utilizing a mixture of oxygen and acetylene ⟨~ welding⟩

**oxyacetylene blowpipe** *or* **oxyacetylene torch** *n* : a welding

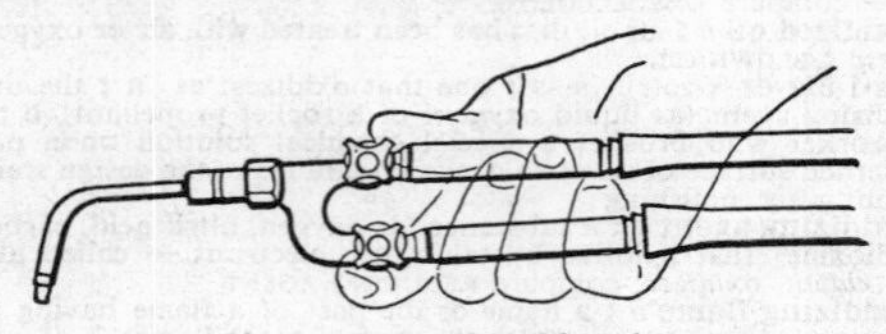

oxyacetylene blowpipe

blowpipe using oxygen and acetylene

**oxyacetylene cutting** *n* : OXYGEN-ACETYLENE CUTTING

**oxyacetylene welding** *n* : OXYGEN-ACETYLENE WELDING

**oxy·ae·na** \ˌäksēˈēnə\ *n, cap* [NL, fr. ¹*oxy-* + Gk *-aina*, fem. n. suffix] : a genus (the type of the family Oxyaenidae) of long-bodied short-legged plantigrade creodonts from the No. American Eocene

**oxy·as·ter** \ˈäksē,astə(r), ˌ==ˈ==\ *n* -s [NL, fr. ¹*oxy-* + *-aster*] : a stellate sponge spicule having acute rays

**ox·yb·e·lis** \äkˈsibələs\ *n, cap* [NL, fr. Gk *oxybelēs* sharp-pointed, fr. *oxy-* ¹oxy- + *-belēs* pointed, fr. *belos* arrow; akin to Gk *ballein* to throw — more at DEVIL] : a genus of slender chiefly arboreal back-fanged snakes (family Colubridae) having slender pointed snouts and being widely distributed in tropical America with one species occurring as far north as Arizona

**oxy·bi·o·sis** \ˌäksē,bīˈōsəs\ *n, pl* **oxybio·ses** \-ō,sēz\ [NL, fr. ²*oxy-* + *-biosis*] : AEROBIOSIS

**oxy·biotic** \ˌäksē+\ *adj* [²*oxy-* + *-biotic*] : AEROBIOTIC

**oxy·biotin** \ˌäksē+\ *n* [ISV ²*oxy-* + *biotin*] : a compound $C_{10}H_{16}N_2O_4$ that contains an oxygen atom in place of the sulfur atom in the biotin molecule and that is less active biologically than biotin

**oxy·blep·sia** \ˌäksəˈblepsēə, -ksēˈb-\ *n* -s [NL, fr. MGk, fr. Gk *oxy-* ¹oxy- + *blepsis* sight (fr. *blepein* to see) + *-ia* -y] : acuteness of sight

**oxy·calcium** \ˌäksē+\ *adj* [²*oxy-* + *calcium*] : of or relating to oxygen and calcium ⟨the ~ light or limelight⟩

**oxy·calorimeter** \ˌäksē+\ *n* [²*oxy-* + *calorimeter*] : a calorimeter in which the energy content of a substance is determined by the direct measurement of the oxygen consumed

**ox·y·ca·nus** \ˌäksəˈkānəs, -ksēˈk-\ *n, cap* [NL, fr. ¹*oxy-* + L *canus* white — more at HARE] : a genus of moths (family Hepialidae) whose larvae include the subterranean caterpillars of New Zealand

**oxy·cellulose** \ˌäksē+\ *n* [ISV ²*oxy-* + *cellulose*] : any of several substances formed by the oxidation of cellulose either naturally (as in wood fiber) or artificially (as in cotton bleached too much) — compare OXIDIZED CELLULOSE

**oxy·ce·phal·ic** \ˌäksəsəˈfalik, ˌäksēsə-\ *or* **oxy·ceph·a·lous** \-ˈsefələs\ *adj* : of, relating to, or exhibiting oxycephaly

**oxy·ceph·a·ly** \ˌ==ˈsefəlē\ *n* -ES [G *oxycephalie*, prob. fr. Gk *oxykephalos* sharp-headed (fr. *oxy-* ¹oxy + *-kephalos* headed, fr. *kephalē* head) + G *-ie* -y — more at CEPHALIC] : congenital deformity of the skull due to early synostosis of the parietal and occipital bones with compensating growth in the region of the anterior fontanel resulting in a pointed or pyramidal skull — called also *acrocephaly*

**oxy·chloride** \ˌäksē+\ *n* [ISV ²*oxy-* + *chloride*] : a compound of oxygen and chlorine with an element or radical : a basic chloride ⟨lead ~s such as $PbCl_2.PbO$ or $Pb_2OCl_2$⟩

**oxychloride cement** *n* : MAGNESIUM OXYCHLORIDE CEMENT

**oxy·chro·mat·ic** \ˌäksēkrōˈmad·ik\ *or* **oxy·chro·ma·tin·ic** \-,krōməˈtinik\ *adj* : of or relating to oxychromatin

**oxy·chromatin** \ˌäksē+\ *n* [ISV ²*oxy-* + *chromatin;* prob. orig. formed in G] : oxyphilic chromatin

**oxy·coc·cus** \ˌäksēˈkäkəs\ *n, cap* [NL, fr. ¹*oxy-* + *-coccus*] *in some classifications* : a small genus of trailing or prostrate shrubs consisting of the cranberries — see VACCINIUM

**oxy·cyanide** \ˌäksē+\ *n* [²*oxy-* + *cyanide*] : a compound of oxygen and cyanogen with an element or radical ⟨mercuric ~, $Hg_2O(CN)_2$⟩

**oxy·dac·tyl** \ˌäksəˈdakt°l, ˌäksē-\ *adj* [¹*oxy-* + *dactyl*] : having slender tapered digits

**oxyde** *var of* OXIDE

**oxy·di·act** \ˌäksəˈdī,akt, ˌäksē-\ *adj* [¹*oxy-* + *diact*] : having three axes but only two rays developed — used of a sponge spicule

**Oxy·di·a·mi·no·gen** \ äksē,dīəˈmēnəjən, -,jen\ *trademark* —used for a direct dye; see DYE table I (under *Direct Black 80*)

**oxy·fluoride** \ˌäksē+\ *n* [ISV ²*oxy-* + *fluoride*] : a compound of oxygen and fluorine with an element or radical

**oxy·gas** \ˌäksē,=\ *adj* [²*oxy-* + *gas*] : of or relating to a mixture of oxygen and fuel gas — compare OXYHYDROGEN

**ox·y·gen** \ˈäksəjən, -sēj-\ *n* -s [F *oxygène*, fr. *oxy-* ¹oxy- + *-gène* -gen] : a nonmetallic chiefly bivalent element that is normally a colorless odorless tasteless nonflammable diatomic gas slightly soluble in water, that is the most abundant of the elements on earth occurring uncombined in air to the extent of about 21 percent by volume and combined in water, in most common rocks and minerals (as oxides, silicates, carbonates), and in a great variety of organic compounds (as alcohols, acids, fats, carbohydrates, proteins), that has three naturally occurring nonradioactive isotopes of masses 16, 17, and 18 of relative abundance 2494:1:5, that is obtained industrially from liquid air by distilling off the nitrogen or from water by electrolysis or in the laboratory by decomposition by heat of various oxides, peroxides, or salts (as chlorates or permanganates), that combines with all other elements except those of the group of inert gases, and that is used chiefly in oxyacetylene and oxyhydrogen flames in welding and cutting metals, in making steel and in other metallurgical processes, in making glass, in medicine, aviation, and diving to aid respiration, and usu. in the form of air in many combustion and oxidation processes — symbol *O;* see LIQUID OXYGEN, OZONE; ELEMENT table

**oxygen-acetylene cutting** *n* : gas cutting with oxygen and acetylene

**oxygen-acetylene welding** *n* : gas welding with oxygen and acetylene

**oxygen acid** *n* : an acid (as chloric acid, sulfuric acid) containing oxygen — compare HETEROPOLY ACID, ISOPOLY ACID

**ox·y·gen·ate** \ˈäksəjə,nāt, -sēj-; äkˈsijə,-; *usu* -ād· +V\ *vt* -ED/-ING/-S [F *oxygéner* (fr. *oxygène* oxygen) + E *-ate*] : to impregnate or combine with oxygen : treat or supply with oxygen : saturate (as blood) with oxygen — compare AERATE, OXIDIZE 1 a — **ox·y·gen·a·tion** \ˌäksəjəˈnāshən, -sēj-; äk,sijəˈnāshən\ *n* -s

**oxygenated water** *n* **1** : water treated or supplied with gaseous oxygen **2** : HYDROGEN PEROXIDE

**ox·y·gen·a·tor** \-ād·ə(r), -ātə-\ *n* -s : one that oxygenates (as an apparatus for perfusing an organ or tissue)

**oxygen debt** *n* : the cumulative deficiency of oxygen that develops in the body during periods of intense activity and that must be made good when the bodily activity returns to a normal level

**ox·y·gen·er·a·tor** \ˌäksəˈjenə,rād·ə(r), -sēˈj-\ *n* -s [blend of *oxygen* and *generator*] : a machine for making oxygen

**oxygen-hydrogen welding** *n* : gas welding with oxygen and hydrogen at a temperature which is estimated at over 5000° F and which is sufficient to consume the diamond and easily fuse platinum

**ox·y·gen·ic** \ˌäksəˈjenik, -sēˈj-, -nēk\ *adj* : relating to, consisting of, containing, or resembling oxygen ⟨sheets of ~ paper . . . aid in maintaining color —C.E.Dobbins & R.W.Hoecker⟩ — **ox·y·gen·ic·i·ty** \ˌ==jəˈnisəd·ē\ *n* -ES

**ox·y·ge·ni·um** \ˌäksəˈjēnēəm\ *n* -s [NL, fr. ISV *oxygen* + NL *-ium*] : OXYGEN

**ox·y·gen·ize** \ˈäksəjə,nīz, -sēj-; äkˈsijə,-\ *vt* -ED/-ING/-S [*oxygen* + *-ize*] : OXIDIZE, OXYGENATE

**oxygen lance** *n* : an iron pipe that when supplied with oxygen through a hose burns and furnishes heat to cut thick metal

**oxygen mask** *n* : a mask covering esp. the mouth and nose and used in inhaling oxygen from a bottle, tank, or other source of supply

**ox·yg·e·nous** \(ˈ)äkˈsijənəs\ *adj* : OXYGENIC

**oxygen point** *n* : the normal boiling point of liquid oxygen which is −182.97°C and which is used as one of the fixed points of the international temperature scale

**oxygen ratio** *n* : ACIDITY COEFFICIENT

**oxygen tent** *n* : a canopy of usu. transparent material which is placed over a bedfast patient and within which a flow of oxygen can be maintained

**ox·yg·na·thous** \(ˈ)äkˈsignəthəs\ *adj* [¹*oxy-* + *-gnathous;* fr. the finely lined surface of the jaws] : having smooth or nearly smooth jaws ⟨~ land snails⟩ ⟨~ slugs⟩

**oxy·halide** \ˌäksē+\ *n* [²*oxy-* + *halide*] : a compound (as an oxychloride) of oxygen and a halogen with an element or radical : a basic halide

**oxy·hemocyanin** \"+\ *n* [²*oxy-* + *hemocyanin*] : a blue pigment formed by the combination of hemocyanin with oxygen in the ratio of one molecule of oxygen to two atoms of copper in the hemocyanin

**oxy·hemoglobin** \"+\ *n* [ISV ²*oxy-* + *hemoglobin*] : the bright red crystallizable pigment in the red blood cells chiefly of arterial blood that is formed in the lungs or gills by the combination of hemoglobin with oxygen in the ratio of one molecule of oxygen to each atom of iron in the hemoglobin without oxidation of the iron to the ferric state and that releases its oxygen to the tissues — symbol $HbO_2$

**oxy·hemo·graph** \ˌäksēˈhēmə,graf, -hem-, -rȧf\ *n* [²*oxy-* + *hem-* + *-graph*] : OXIMETER

**oxy·hexactine** \ˌäksē+\ *n* [¹*oxy-* + *hexactine*] : a hexactinal sponge spicule whose rays end in sharp points

**oxy·hexaster** \"+\ *n* [¹*oxy-* + *hexaster*] : a hexaster whose rays end in sharp points

**oxy·hydrogen** \"+\ *adj* [²*oxy-* + *hydrogen*] : of, relating to, or utilizing a mixture of oxygen and hydrogen

**oxyhydrogen blowpipe** *or* **oxyhydrogen torch** *n* : a welding blowpipe using oxygen and hydrogen

**oxyhydrogen light** *n* : a light produced by the incandescence of some substance (as lime) in the oxyhydrogen flame — compare LIMELIGHT 1

**ox·yl·o·phyte** \äkˈsilə,fīt\ *n* -s [²*oxy-* + *-lo-* (prob. fr. *halo-*) *-phyte*] : a plant that prefers or is restricted to an acid soil ⟨most heaths are obligatory ~s⟩ — **ox·yl·o·phyt·ic** \ˌ==ˈfid·ik\ *adj*

**oxyl process** \ˈäksəl-\ *n* [¹*ox-* + *-yl*] : a modified Fischer-Tropsch process for synthesizing alcohols from carbon monoxide and hydrogen under pressure in the presence of a usu. iron catalyst — compare OXO PROCESS 2

**oxy·luciferin** \ˌäksē+\ *n* [²*oxy-* + *luciferin*] : the product formed by the reversible oxidation of luciferin promoted by luciferase

**oxy·luminescence** \"+\ *n* [²*oxy-* + *luminescence*] : chemiluminescence caused by oxidation

**oxy·luminescent** \"+\ *adj* : marked by oxyluminescence

**ox·y·mel** \ˈäksə,mel, -sē,m-\ *n* -s [ME *oximel*, fr. L, fr. Gk *oxymeli*, fr. *oxy-* ¹oxy- + *meli* honey — more at MELLIFLUOUS] : a mixture of honey and dilute acetic acid used as an expectorant

**ox·y·mo·ron** \ˌäksəˈmōr,än, -sēˈm-\ *n, pl* **oxymo·ra** \-ōrə\ [Gk *oxymōron*, fr. neut. of *oxymōros* pointedly foolish, fr. *oxy-* ¹oxy- + *mōros* dull, foolish — more at MORON] : a combination for epigrammatic effect of contradictory or incongruous words (as *cruel kindness, laborious idleness*) — **ox·y·mo·ron·ic** \ˌ==məˈränik\ *adj*

**oxy·muriate** \ˌäksē+\ *n* [ISV ²*oxy-* + *muriate*] : a salt of oxymuriatic acid : CHLORIDE ⟨~ of tin⟩ : CHLORATE ⟨~ of potash⟩

**oxymuriate match** *or* **oxymuriated match** \ˌäksē+. . .-\ *n, archaic* : a match tipped with potassium chlorate

**oxy·muriatic** \ˌäksē+\ *adj* [ISV ²*oxy-* + *muriatic*] : relating to or consisting of oxidized hydrochloric acid ⟨chlorine was called ~ acid before it was known to be an element⟩

**oxy·myoglobin** \"+\ *n* [²*oxy-* + *myoglobin*] : a pigment formed by the combination of myoglobin with oxygen

**ox·yn** \ˈäksən\ *n* -s [²*oxy-* + *-in*] : a solid product (as linoxyn) formed when a drying oil is oxidized

**oxy·naphthoic acid** \ˌäksē+. . .-\ *n* [ISV ²*oxy-* + *naphthoic*] : HYDROXYNAPHTHOIC ACID — not used systematically

**oxy·neurine** \ˌäksē+\ *n* [ISV ²*oxy-* + *neurine;* prob. orig. formed in G] : BETAINE 1a

**oxy·nitrate** \"+\ *n* [²*oxy-* + *nitrate*] : a compound of oxygen and the nitrate group with an element or radical ⟨bismuth ~⟩ — compare SUBNITRATE

**ox·yn·tic** \(ˈ)äkˈsintik\ *adj* [Gk *oxynein* to sharpen, make acid (fr. *oxys* sharp, keen) + E connective *-t-* + *-ic* — more at OXY-] : secreting acid — used esp. of the parietal cells of the gastric glands

**oxy·opia** \ˌäksēˈōpēə\ *also* **oxy·opy** \ˈäksē,ōpē\ *n, pl* **oxyopias** *also* **oxyopies** [NL *oxyopia*, fr. ¹*oxy-* + *-opia*] : unusual acuteness of sight

**oxy·op·i·dae** \ˌäksēˈäpə,dē\ *n pl, cap* [NL, fr. *Oxyopes*, type genus (fr. Gk *oxyōpēs* sharp-eyed, fr. *oxy-* ¹oxy- + *-ōpēs* -eyed — fr. *ōps* eye —) + *-idae* — more at EYE] : a family of diurnal hunting spiders that have eight eyes and long legs and do not use webs to trap their prey

**oxy·petalous** \ˌäksē+\ *adj* [¹*oxy-* + *-petalous*] : having sharp-pointed petals

**¹oxy·phile** \ˈäksə,fīl, -sē,f-\ *or* **oxy·phil** \-,fil\ *or* **oxy·phil·ic** \ˌ==ˈfilik\ *or* **ox·yph·i·lous** \(ˈ)äkˈsifələs\ *adj* [¹*oxy-* + *-phile, -phil* or *-philic* or *-philous*] : ACIDOPHILIC

**²oxyphile** \"\ *adj* [ISV ²*oxy-* + *-phile*] : having such an affinity for oxygen that in a molten mass the greatest concentration of an element would be found in the oxide phase (as in the slag of a blast furnace) — compare CHALCOPHILE, SIDEROPHILE

**³oxyphile** \"\ *also* **oxyphil** \"\ *n* -s [ISV ¹*oxy-* + *-phile, -phil*] : ACIDOPHILE

**ox·yp·o·lis** \äkˈsipələs\ *n* [NL, fr. ¹*oxy-* + Gk *polis* city — more at POLICE] **1** *cap* : a genus of marsh herbs (family Umbelliferae) having clustered fusiform tuberous roots and leaves only once-pinnate or reduced to slender petioles like rushes — see COWBANE, WATER DROPWORT **2** -ES : any plant of the genus *Oxypolis*

**oxy·poly·gelatin** \ˌäksəˈpälə, -sēˈpälē +\ *n* [²*oxy-* + *poly-* (fr. *polymerization*) + *gelatin*] : gelatin modified by polymerization by means of glyoxal and oxidation with hydrogen peroxide for use as a plasma expander

**oxy·quinoline** \ˌäksē+\ *n* [ISV ²*oxy-* + *quinoline*] : HYDROXYQUINOLINE — not used systematically

**¹oxy·rhynch** \ˈäksə,riŋk, -sē,r-\ *n* -s [NL *Oxyrhyncha*] **1** : a crab having a pointed rostrum : one of the Oxyrhyncha **2** *also* **oxy·rhyn·chus** \ˌ==ˈriŋkəs\ *pl* **oxyrhyn·chi** \-,kī, -(,)kē\ [NL *oxyrhynchus* (specific epithet of *Mormyrus oxyrhynchus*), fr. Gk *oxyrrhynchos*, adj.] : a sacred fish (*Mormyrus oxyrhynchus*)

**²oxyrhynch** \"\ *adj* [Gk *oxyrrhynchos*, fr. *oxy-* ¹oxy- + *rhynchos* snout, beak — more at RHYNCH-] : sharp-snouted : sharp-billed

**oxy·rhyn·cha** \ˌ==ˈriŋkə\ *n pl, cap* [NL, fr. Gk *oxyrrhyncha*, neut. pl. of *oxyrrhynchos* sharp-snouted] : a large superfamily of Brachygnatha comprising crabs that have a distinct rostrum, a more or less triangular carapace, the orbits generally incomplete, nine pairs of gills, and the male genital apertures on the base of the last pairs of legs — compare SPIDER CRAB — **oxy·rhyn·chan** \ˌ==ˈ=kən\ *adj or n*

**oxy·rhyn·chous** \ˌ==ˈ=kəs\ *adj* [Gk *oxyrrhynchos*] **1** : OXYRHYNCH **2** : of or relating to the Oxyrhyncha

**oxy·spi·ru·ra** \ˌäksə,spīˈrürə, -ksē,sp-\ *n, cap* [NL, fr. ¹*oxy-* + *spir-* + *-ura*] : a genus of spiruroid nematode worms (family Thelaziidae) comprising the eye worms of domestic poultry and other birds

**oxy·sto·ma·ta** \-ˈstōməd·ə\ *n pl, cap* [NL, fr. ¹*oxy-* + *-stomata*] : a small superfamily or other division of crabs having the buccal area produced anteriorly and more or less acutely triangular and having almost no rostrum — **oxy·stoma·tous** \ˌ==ˈstäməd·əs, -tōm-\ *adj* — **oxy·stome** \ˈ==,stōm\ *adj or n*

**oxy·sulfide** \ˌäksē+\ *n* [ISV ²*oxy-* + *sulfide*] : a compound of oxygen and sulfur with an element or radical that may be regarded as a sulfide in which part of the sulfur is replaced by oxygen

**oxy·tetracycline** \"+\ *n* [²*oxy-* + *tetracycline*] : a yellow crystalline antibiotic $C_{22}H_{24}N_2O_9$ produced by a soil actinomycete (*Streptomyces rimosus*) and effective against numerous disease-causing microorganisms; hydroxy-tetracycline

**ox·y·to·cia** \ˌäksəˈtōsh(ē)ə, -ksēˈt-\ *n* -s [NL, fr. ¹*oxy-* + Gk *tokos* childbirth + *-ia* -y] : quick childbirth

**¹ox·y·to·cic** \ˌ==ˈtōsik\ *adj* [ISV ¹*oxy-* + *toc-* (fr. Gk *tokos* childbirth) + *-ic;* akin to Gk *teknon* child — more at THANE] : hastening parturition; *also* : inducing contraction of uterine smooth muscle ⟨an ~ principle of the neurohypophysis⟩

**²oxytocic** \"\ *n* -s : a substance that stimulates contraction of uterine smooth muscle or hastens childbirth

**ox·y·to·cin** \ˌ==ˈtōs°n\ *n* -s [ISV *oxytocic* + *-in*] : a polypeptide hormone $C_{43}H_{66}N_{12}O_{12}S_2$ that is secreted together with vasopressin by the posterior lobe of the pituitary, that is also obtained synthetically, and that stimulates esp. the contraction of uterine muscle and the ejection of milk — called also *alpha-hypophamine*

**¹ox·y·tone** \ˈäksə,tōn\ *n* [F *oxyton*, adj. & n., fr. Gk *oxytonos* having the acute accent, fr. *oxy-* ¹oxy- + *tonos* tone — more at TONE] : an oxytone word

**²oxytone** \"\ *adj* **1** : having or characterized by an acute accent on the last syllable of a Greek word **2** : having or characterized by heavy stress on the last syllable

**oxy·ton·ic** \ˌ==ˈtänik\ *or* **oxy·ton·i·cal** \-nəkəl\ *adj* : of or relating to an oxytone : OXYTONE

**ox·y·trich** \ˈäksə,trik\ *n* -s [NL *Oxytricha*] : a protozoan of the genus *Oxytricha*

**ox·yt·ri·cha** \äkˈsi·trəkə\ *n, cap* [NL, fr. ¹*oxy-* + *-tricha*] : a widely distributed genus (the type of the family Oxytrichidae) of flexible ellipsoidal hypotrichous ciliates with eight frontal, five ventral, and undeveloped caudal cirri — compare STYLONYCHIA — **ox·yt·ri·chid** \-rəkəd\ *adj or n*

**ox·yt·ro·pis** \äkˈsi·trəpəs\ *n, cap* [NL, fr. ¹*oxy-* + Gk *tropis* ship's keel; akin to Gk *trepein* to turn; fr. the pointed keel of the corolla — more at TROPE] : a large widely distributed genus of often shrubby herbs (family Leguminosae) having odd-pinnate leaves and racemose or spicate flowers each of which has a pealike corolla with a clawed petal — see LOCOWEED

**oxy·tylotate** \ˌäksē+\ *adj* [*oxytylote* + *-ate*] : resembling an oxytylote esp. in shape

**oxy·tylote** \"+\ *n* [¹*oxy-* + *tylote*] : a sponge spicule shaped like a common pin

**oxy·uri·a·sis** \ˌäksēyüˈrīəsəs\ *n, pl* **oxyuria·ses** \-ī,ə,sēz\ [NL, fr. *Oxyuris* + *-iasis*] : infestation with or disease caused by pinworms (family Oxyuridae) — see ENTEROBIASIS

**oxy·uric** \ˌ==ˈyürik\ *adj* [NL *Oxyuris* + E *-ic*] : of, relating to, or caused by pinworms of *Oxyuris* and related genera

**oxy·uri·cide** \ˌ==ˈyürə,sīd\ *n* -s [NL *Oxyuris* + E *-cide*] : a substance that destroys pinworms

**¹oxy·urid** \ˌ==ˈyürəd\ *adj* [NL *Oxyuridae*] : of or relating to the Oxyuridae

**²oxyurid** \"\ *n* -s [NL *Oxyuridae*] : a nematode of the family Oxyuridae : PINWORM

**oxy·uri·dae** \ˌ==ˈyürə,dē\ *n pl, cap* [NL, fr. *Oxyuris*, type genus + *-idae*] : a family of nematode worms that have a distinct posterior enlargement of the pharynx, a reduced bursa and no preanal suckers in the male, and meromyarian musculature and that are chiefly parasites of the vertebrate intestinal tract — see ENTEROBIUS, OXYURIS

**oxy·uris** \-rəs\ *n* [NL, fr. ¹*oxy-* + *-uris* (fr. Gk *oura* tail) — more at -UROUS] **1** *cap* : a genus (the type of the family Oxyuridae) of parasitic nematodes with a long slender tail and well-developed pharyngeal bulb **2** -ES : any worm of *Oxyuris* or a related genus (as *Enterobius*) : PINWORM

**oxy·uroid** \ˌ==ˈ=,rȯid\ *adj* [NL *Oxyuris* + E *-oid*] *of a nematode's pharynx* : having a bulbous posterior enlargement

**oxy·weld·ing** \ˈäksē,==\ *n* [by shortening] : OXYGEN-ACETYLENE WELDING

**oy** *or* **oye** \ˈȯi\ *n* -s [ME (Sc) *o*, of Celtic origin; akin to OIr *haue, aue* grandson — more at UNCLE] *Scot* : GRANDCHILD

**oy·a·pock** \ˈȯiə,päk\ *n* -s [fr. *Oyapock, Oyapok*, river between northern Brazil and French Guiana] : YAPOCK

**oy·er** \ˈȯiər\ *n* -s [ME, fr. AF, fr. OF *oir* to hear, fr. L *audire* — more at AUDIBLE] **1** : a criminal trial held under a commission of oyer and terminer **2 a** : the hearing of a document read in court; *specif* : the hearing of a deed or other instrument read in court by petition of a party to a suit **b** : a copy of the instrument given rather than read to the petitioning party

**oyer and ter·mi·ner** \ˌȯiərənˈtərmənər\ *n* [ME, fr. AF *oyer et terminer*, lit., to hear and determine] **1** : COMMISSION OF OYER AND TERMINER **2** : a high court of criminal jurisdiction in some U.S. states (as Delaware and Pennsylvania)

**¹oyez** \(ˈ)ōˈyā, -yes,-yez\ *v imper* [ME *oyes!*, fr. AF *oyez!* hear ye!, fr. OF *oiez, oyez*, imperative pl. of *oir* to hear] — used by criers of courts as a command to secure silence and attention before a proclamation

**²oyez** \"\ *n, pl* **oyesses** \-yesəz\ [ME *oyes*, fr. AF *oyez!* hear ye!] : a cry of oyez

**-o·yl** \ əwəl, ə(,)wil, ə,wēl\ *n comb form* -s [ISV *-o-* (as in *-oic*) + *-yl*] : acid radical — used in the system of nomenclature adopted by the International Union of Pure and Applied Chemistry in names of radicals derived from acids whose names end in *-oic* ⟨decano*yl*⟩ and also most other organic acids ⟨oleo*yl*⟩ ⟨phthalo*yl*⟩; compare -YL

**oy·let** *var of* OILLET

[1]**oys·ter** \ˈȯistə(r)\ *n* -s [ME *oistre*, fr. MF, fr. L *ostrea*, fr. Gk *ostreon*; akin to Gk *ostrakon* shell, *osteon* bone — more at OSSEOUS] **1 :** a marine bivalve mollusk (family Ostreidae) having a rough irregular shell closed by a single adductor muscle, the foot small or wanting, and no siphon, living free on the bottom or adhering to stones or other objects in shallow water along the seacoasts or in brackish water in the mouths of rivers, and feeding on minute plants and animals carried to them by the current — see CRASSOSTREA, OSTREA **2 :** any of various bivalve mollusks more or less resembling the true oyster; *esp* **:** a Bermuda mollusk (*Margaritophora radiata*) that is locally important for food — often used with a descriptive adjective ⟨pearl ~*s*⟩ ⟨reef ~⟩ ⟨rock ~⟩ **3 a :** something that is or can be readily attained or made to serve one's personal ends **:** something regarded as belonging to or due one because of one's actual or presumed qualities, abilities, or status ⟨had just married and the world looked like his ~ —*Think*⟩ ⟨the world is the salesman's ~ —D.W.Brogan⟩ ⟨as long as you dressed decently and used acceptable English, and as long as your name could be pronounced, the town was your ~ —Russell Thacher⟩ **b :** CUP OF TEA ⟨aviation is the college girl's ~ —*Mademoiselle*⟩ ⟨youth is conservative, and mild romanticism is its ~ —Virgil Thomson⟩ **4 :** a small mass of muscle contained in a concavity of the pelvic bone on each side of the back of a fowl and usu. regarded as a delicacy **5 :** an extremely taciturn or reserved person **6 :** a usu. sautéed croquette ⟨corn ~⟩ **7** *or* **oyster white a :** a light gray to white **b :** a pale yellow green that is paler and slightly yellower than oyster gray, paler than amber white, and paler and yellower than average Nile

[2]**oyster** \"\ *vi* **oystered; oystered; oystering** \-t(ə)riŋ\ **oysters :** to gather or dredge oysters

**oyster agaric** *n* **:** OYSTER MUSHROOM

**oys·ter·age** \-təriј\ *n* -s [*oyster* + *-age*] **:** OYSTER BED

**oyster bar** *n* **1** *South* **:** OYSTER BED **2 :** a restaurant that specializes in oysters prepared in various ways and served esp. at a counter

**oyster bay** *n* **:** a restaurant where oysters and other seafood are served

**oyster bay pine** *n, usu cap O&B* [fr. *Oyster Bay*, Tasmania, Australia] **:** either of two Australian cypress pines (*Callitris tasmanica* and *C. oblonga*)

**oyster bed** *n* **:** a place where oysters grow or are cultivated

**oysterbird** \ˈ==,=\ *n* **1 :** OYSTER CATCHER **2** *Southwest* **:** SANDERLING

**oyster catcher** *n* **:** any of various wading birds of the widely distributed genus *Haematopus* that are 16 to 20 inches long, have stout legs and a heavy wedge-shaped bill which are usu. pinkish or bright red, and in the common form of Europe, Asia, and northern Africa (*H. ostralegus ostralegus*) and that of the American Atlantic coast (*H. o. palliatus*) have plumage which is chiefly or entirely black and white — see BLACK OYSTER CATCHER

**oyster crab** *n* **:** a crab (*Pinnotheres ostreum*) that lives as a commensal in the gill cavity of the oyster — compare MUSSEL CRAB, PEA CRAB

**oyster cracker** *n* **:** a small salted cracker for serving with oyster stew and soups — compare PILOT BISCUIT

**oyster culture** *n* **:** the cultivation of oysters in prepared beds

**oyster–culturist** \ˈ==ˌ=(=)=\ *n* **:** one engaged in oyster culture

**oyster dredge** *n* **:** a dredge having a heavy iron frame with strong teeth along its lower lip and a bag of strong cord and used in taking oysters in deep water

**oyster drill** *n* **:** [5]DRILL 4

**oys·tered** \ˈȯistə(r)d\ *adj* **:** marked by oysterings ⟨~ veneer⟩

**oys·ter·er** \-tərə(r)\ *n* -s **1 :** a gatherer or seller of oysters **2 :** a boat used in oyster fishing

**oyster farm** *n* **:** a stretch of sea bottom devoted to oyster culture

**oyster–farm** \ˈ==,=\ *vi* **:** to culture or grow oysters

**oyster farmer** *n* **:** one who raises oysters as a crop

**oysterfish** \ˈ==,=\ *n* **1 :** TAUTOG **2** *also* **oyster–toad** \ˈ==,=\ **:** TOADFISH

**oyster fork** *n* **:** a long slender 3-tined fork used in eating shellfish

**oyster grass** *n* **1 :** KELP **2 :** SEA LETTUCE

**oyster gray** *n* **:** a pale yellow green that is yellower, stronger, and slightly lighter than smoke gray and yellower and paler than average Nile

**oystering** *n* -s **1 :** the act or business of taking oysters for the market or for food **2 a :** the matching (as on two side-by-side doors of a cabinet) of two oval-grained pieces of wood that are split from one piece **b :** a veneering (as on a table top) consisting of closely fitted pieces of attractively grained wood cut in diagonal section

**oyster knife** *n* **:** a knife for opening the shells of oysters

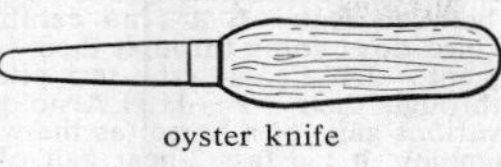
oyster knife

**oyster leech** *n* **:** a polyclad turbellarian worm (*Stylochus frontalis*) that is barred in brown and flesh and is a pest feeding on oysters along the coast of Florida

**oys·ter·ling** \ˈȯistə(r)liŋ\ *n* -s [*oyster* + *-ling*] **:** a young or small oyster

**oys·ter·man** \-mən\ *n, pl* **oystermen 1 :** a gatherer, opener, breeder, or seller of oysters **2 :** OYSTERER 2

**oyster mushroom** *or* **oyster fungus** *n* **:** an edible agaric (*Pleurotus ostreatus*) growing in shelving masses on dead wood; *also* **:** any of several related species of this genus

**oyster nut** *n* **:** a climbing plant (*Telfairia pedata*) that is indigenous to East Africa and has large edible nutlike seeds yielding an oil similar to olive oil

**oyster plant** *n* **1 :** SALSIFY **2 :** SEA LUNGWORT **3 :** a common West Indian herb (*Rhoeo discolor*) of the family Commelinaceae with purplish leaves and showy flower clusters

**oyster plover** *n* **:** OYSTER CATCHER

**oyster rake** *n* **:** a long-handled rake usu. with curved teeth for gathering oysters in water of moderate depth

**oysters** *pl of* OYSTER, *pres 3d sing of* OYSTER

**oysterseed** \ˈ==,=\ *n, pl* **oysterseed :** the spat of oysters

**oystershell** \ˈ==,=\ *n* **1 :** crushed or ground oyster shells often used as a mineral supplement in feeding poultry **2 :** OYSTERING 2b

**oystershell scale** *also* **oystershell bark louse** *n* **:** an abundant widely distributed scale insect (*Lepidosaphes ulmi*) that infests and greatly injures various trees and shrubs — see FIG SCALE

**oyster tongs** *n pl* **:** a pair of wooden tongs 12 to 20 feet long bearing opposing baskets shaped like rakes and used for gathering oysters

**oyster tree** *n* [so called fr. the fact that mollusks attach themselves to it] **:** MANGROVE 1

**oyster wench** *n, archaic* **:** a girl who sells oysters

**oyster white** *n* **:** OYSTER 7

**oysterwife** \ˈ==,=\ *n, pl* **oysterwives** *archaic* **:** OYSTERWOMAN

**oysterwoman** \ˈ==,==\ *n, pl* **oysterwomen :** a woman who sells oysters

**oysterwood** \ˈ==,=\ *n* **:** OYSTERING 2b

**oys·tery** \-st(ə)rē\ *adj* [*oyster* + *-y* (adj. suffix)] **:** somewhat resembling the color oyster

**oz** *abbr* **1** [It *onza*] ounce **2** ooze

**ozan·na** \ōˈzanə\ [NL] *syn of* HIPPOTRAGUS

**ozark** \ˈō,zärk, -zȧk\ *n, pl* **ozark** *or* **ozarks** *usu cap* [prob. alter. of *Aux Arcs*, early French post among the Quapaw in the area of Arkansas Post, Ark., fr. F *aux Arcs* at the Quapaw, prob. by shortening and alter. (influence of *arcs*, pl. of *arc* bow, fr. MF) fr. *aux Arkansas* — more at ARC] **:** an Indian of a division of the Quapaw

**ozark·er** \-kə(r)\ *n* -s *cap* [*Ozark* mountains + E *-er*] **:** OZARKIAN

[1]**ozark·ian** \(ˈ)ō¦zärkēən, -zȧk-\ *adj, usu cap* [*Ozark* mountains, tableland extending fr. Missouri across Arkansas into Oklahoma + E *-ian* (adj. suffix)] **:** of or relating to the inhabitants or region of the Ozark mountains

[2]**ozarkian** \"\ *n* -s *cap* [*Ozark* mountains + E *-ian* (n. suffix)] **:** a native or inhabitant of the Ozark mountains ⟨an *Ozarkian's* wealth is mostly dogs —*Chicago Tribune*⟩

**oze·na** *also* **ozae·na** *or* **ozoe·na** \ōˈzēnə\ *n* -s [L *ozaena*, fr. Gk *ozaina*, fr. *ozein* to smell — more at ODOR] **:** a chronic disease of the nose accompanied by a fetid discharge and marked by atrophic changes in the nasal structures

**ozo·brome process** \ˈōzə,brōm-\ *n* [*ozobrome* fr. ozone + *brom*ide] **:** an early form of the carbro process

**ozo·ke·rite** \,ōzəˈki,rīt; ōˈzōkə,r-, ōˈzäkə,r-\ *or* **ozo·ce·rite** \,ōzəˈsi,rīt; ōˈzōsə,r-, ōˈzäsə,r-\ *n* -s [G *ozokerit*, fr. *ozo-* (fr. Gk, bad smell, fr. *ozein* to smell) + *ker-* cer- + *-it* -ite] **:** a waxlike mineral that is a mixture of hydrocarbons, is colorless or white when pure but often greenish, yellowish, or brown, has in some varieties an unpleasant odor, and is used in making ceresin, candles, and impressions to be electrotyped — called also *ader wax, earth wax*

**ozon-** *or* **ozono-** *comb form* [ISV, fr. *ozone*] **:** ozone ⟨*ozon*ize⟩

**ozon·ate** \ˈō,zō,nāt, -,zə,n-\ *vt* -ED/-ING/-S [*ozon-* + *-ate*] **:** OZONIZE — **ozon·a·tion** \,=(,)=ˈnāshən\ *n* -s

**ozon·a·tor** \ˈ=(,)=,nād·ə(r)\ *n* -s [*ozon-* + *-ator*] **:** OZONIZER

**ozone** \ˈō,zōn\ *n* -s [G *ozon*, fr. Gk *ozōn*, pres. part. of *ozein* to smell — more at ODOR] **1 :** an allotropic triatomic form $O_3$ of oxygen that is normally a faintly blue irritating gas with a characteristic pungent odor but at −112° C condenses to a deep blue magnetic liquid, that occurs in minute amounts in air near the earth's surface and in larger amounts in the stratosphere as a product of the action of ultraviolet light of short wave lengths on ordinary oxygen, that is generated usu. in dilute form by a silent electric discharge in oxygen or air, that decomposes to oxygen (as when heated), that is a stronger oxidizing agent than oxygen, and that is used chiefly in disinfection and deodorization (as in water purification and air conditioning), in oxidation and bleaching (as in the treatment of industrial wastes), and in ozonolysis (as in the manufacture of azelaic acid from oleic acid) **2 :** pure and refreshing air ⟨the fresh crisp ~ of morning —Ashley Halsey⟩

**ozon·er** \-nə(r)\ *n* -s [*ozon-* + *-er*] *slang* **:** a drive-in theater

**ozonic** \(ˈ)ō¦zänik, -zōn-\ *adj* [*ozon-* + *-ic*] **:** relating to, like, or containing ozone ⟨the curious ~ smell of the plane —Noel Coward⟩

**ozon·ide** \ˈō,zō,nīd, -,zə,n-\ *n* -s [ISV *ozon-* + *-ide*; orig. formed as G *ozonid*] **:** any of a class of chemical compounds formed by the addition of ozone to the double or triple bond of an unsaturated organic compound; *esp* **:** such a compound formed from an olefinic compound, characterized by a peroxide-oxide grouping C-O-O-C-O forming a ring, by instability, and often by explosiveness in the pure state but not usu. in solution, and decomposed by water to yield aldehydes or ketones and hydrogen peroxide

**ozon·if·er·ous** \,ō,zō¦nif(ə)rəs, -,zə¦n-\ *adj* [*ozon-* + *-iferous*] **:** bearing or producing ozone

**ozo·ni·fi·ca·tion** \ō,zōnəfəˈkāshən\ *n* -s [fr. *ozonify*, after such pairs as E *identify*: *identification*] **:** OZONIZATION

**ozo·ni·fy** \ōˈzōnə,fī\ *vt* -ED/-ING/-ES [*ozon-* + *-ify*] **:** OZONIZE

**ozo·ni·um** \ōˈzōnēəm\ *n, cap* [NL, fr. Gk *ozos* branch + *-onium* (as in *cydonium*); akin to OE *ōst* knot, lump, OHG *ast* branch, Goth *asts*, Arm *ost* branch; prob. all derivative fr. the root of E *sit*; fr. the branching stems] **:** a form genus of fungi of the group Mycelia Sterilia

**ozon·iza·tion** \,ō,zōnəˈzāshən\ *n* -s **:** the process of ozonizing — compare OZONOLYSIS

**ozon·ize** \ˈō,zō,nīz, -,zə,n-\ *vb* -ED/-ING/-S *see -ize in Explan Notes* [ISV *ozon-* + *-ize*] *vt* **1 :** to convert (as oxygen) into ozone **2 :** to treat, impregnate, or combine with ozone ⟨*ozonized* air attacks most metals —R.E.Kirk & D.F.Othmer⟩ ~ *vi* **:** to become converted into ozone

**ozon·iz·er** \-zə(r)\ *n* -s [ISV *ozonize* + *-er*; orig. formed as F *ozoniseur*] **:** an apparatus for converting ordinary oxygen into ozone (as by passing a silent electric discharge through a current of oxygen or air)

**ozon·ol·y·sis** \,ō,zōˈnäləsəs, -,zəˈn-\ *n, pl* **ozonolyses** \-ə,sēz\ [*ozon-* + *-lysis*] **:** the cleavage of an unsaturated organic compound at the position of unsaturation by conversion to the ozonide followed by decomposition (as by hydrolysis)

**ozo·no·sphere** \ōˈzōnə,sfi(ə)r\ *n* [*ozon-* + *-sphere*] **:** an atmospheric layer at heights of approximately 20 to 30 miles characterized by high ozone content and relatively high temperature resulting from absorption of ultraviolet solar radiation

**ozon·ous** \ˈō,zōnəs\ *adj* **:** OZONIC

**ozo·sto·mia** \,ōzəˈstōmēə\ *n* -s [NL, fr. Gk *ozostomos* having bad breath (fr. *ozo-* bad smell — fr. *ozein* to smell — + *-stomos* -stomous) + NL *-ia* — more at ODOR] **:** foulness of breath

**ozo·type** \ˈōzə,tīp\ *n* [ISV *ozo-* (prob. fr. *ozone*) + *type*] **:** a modified carbon process in which transfer is obviated

**¹p** \ˈpē\ *n, pl* **p's** *or* **ps** \ˈpēz\ *often cap, often attrib* **1 a :** the 16th letter of the English alphabet **b :** an instance of this letter printed, written, or otherwise represented **c :** a speech counterpart of orthographic *p* (as *p* in *pill, spill, dip, apt,* or French *puis*) **2 :** a printer's type, a stamp, or some other instrument for reproducing the letter *p* **3 :** someone or something arbitrarily or conveniently designated *p* esp. as the 15th or when j is used for the 10th the 16th in order or class **4 :** something having the shape of the letter P

**²p** *abbr, often cap* **1** pacer **2** page **3** [L *papa*] pope **4** parallax **5** park **6** part **7** participle **8** [L *partim*] in part **9** past **10** paste **11** pastor **12** [L *pater*] father **13** patrol **14** pawn **15** pengö **16** penny **17** [L *per*] by **18** perch **19** [F *père*] father **20** perforation **21** perimeter **22** period **23** perishable **24** peseta **25** peso **26** pharmacopoeia **27** [It] piano **28** piaster **29** picot **30** pie **31** pint **32** pipe **33** pitch; pitcher **34** [L *pius*] holy **35** planed **36** plate **37** pleasant **38** point **39** polar **40** pole **41** population **42** [L *populus*] people **43** port **44** post **45** postage **46** posterior **47** power **48** predicate **49** present **50** president **51** pressure **52** priest **53** primary **54** prince **55** principal **56** [L *pro*] for **57** proconsul **58** prompter **59** pupil **60** purl **61** pursuit

**³p** *symbol* **1** *cap* phosphorus **2** *usu cap* parental; parental generation **3** proton **4 a** plaintext — used as a subscript ⟨$S_p$ means the letter S in plaintext or plain component⟩ **b** *usu cap* the numerical value of a plaintext letter when the plain component is serially numbered from 0 to 25 ⟨P+K=C is the Vigenère keying method⟩ **5** *usu cap* priestly code — used in biblical criticism to designate material and redactions belonging to a priestly commentary

**p-** \ˌparə *also* ˌperə\ *abbr* para-

**¹pa** \ˈpä, ˈpȯ, ˈpá, ˈpa, ˈpaa\ *n* -s [short for *papa*] **:** FATHER

**²pa** *or* **pah** \ˈpä\ *n* -s [Maori] **1 :** a fortified and stockaded Maori village usu. located on a hilltop — compare KAINGA **2 :** a Maori village

**pa** *abbr* **1** paper **2** piaster

**PA** \ˈpēˈā\ *n, pl* **PA's** *or* **PAs** \-āz\ [fr. *PA,* abbr. of *public address*] **:** the amplifier of a public-address system ⟨the *PA* of each ship had its own peculiar tone —K.M.Dodson⟩

**PA** *abbr* **1** *often not cap* participial adjective **2** particular average **3** passenger agent **4** *often not cap* per annum **5** post adjutant **6** power amplifier **7** power of attorney **8** prefect apostolic **9** *often not cap* press agent **10** press association **11** private account **12** prothonotary apostolic **13** public address **14** public administration; public assistance **15** purchasing agent

**Pa** *symbol* protactinium

**PABA** \ˈpabə\ *n* -s [*para-aminobenzoic acid*] **:** AMINOBENZOIC ACID a

**pa·blo** \ˈpä(ˌ)blō\ *n* -s [origin unknown] **:** a light brown to yellowish brown that is stronger than bran and lighter and stronger than aloma

**Pab·lum** \ˈpabləm\ *trademark* — used for a cereal for infants

**pab·u·lum** \ˈpabyələm\ *n* -s [L, food, fodder — more at FOOD] **1** *archaic* **:** fuel for fire **2 :** a material taken in by a living organism for use in its metabolism as a source of energy or growth **:** FOOD, NUTRIENT; *usu* **:** a more or less fluid medium containing dissolved or suspended nutritive elements in a state suitable for absorption (as through the roots of a plant or into a bacterial cell or a body organ) **3 a :** nourishment for the development of mind or character **:** intellectual sustenance ⟨no two generations need the same mental and emotional ~ —Bonamy Dobrée⟩ ⟨no idea, however freighted with ~ for the brain, is alien . . . to poetry —J.L.Lowes⟩; *esp* **:** a rudimentary or insipid piece of writing ⟨the kind of sentimental ~ which it offered its readers —*Publ's Mod. Lang. Assoc. of Amer.*⟩ **b :** source material for a discussion or document **:** GRIST ⟨never provided that flow of newspaper articles or of interviews which afford ~ to the contemporary biographer —*Times Lit. Supp.*⟩

**pac** *also* **pack** \ˈpak\ *n* -s [Delaware *paku*] **1 :** SHOEPAC **2 :** a laced heelless sheepskin or felt shoe worn inside a boot or overshoe in cold weather

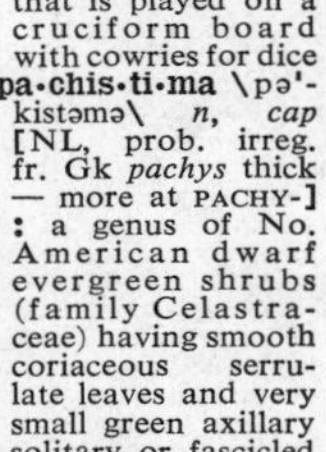

pac 2

**pa·ca** \ˈpäkə, ˈpakə\ *n* -s [Pg & Sp, fr. Tupi *páca*] **:** any of several large So. and Central American rodents of a genus (*Cuniculus*) that is closely related to *Dasyprocta; esp* **:** a common rodent (*C. paca*) of northern So. America having a brown coat spotted with white, a hide used locally for leather, and flesh highly esteemed as food — see FALSE PACA, MOUNTAIN PACA

**pa·ca·ra·na** \ˈpäkəˈränə\ *n* -s [Tupi *pacarana,* fr. *páca* paca + *rana* false] **:** FALSE PACA

**pacate** *adj* [L *pacatus,* past part. of *pacare* to pacify, fr. *pac-, pax* peace — more at PEACE] *obs* **:** TRANQUIL

**pa·cay** \pəˈkī\ *n* -s [Sp, fr. Quechua *pa'qay*] **:** a small arboreal guama of uncertain taxonomic identity that is sometimes cultivated in Peru, Ecuador, and Bolivia for ornament and for the white edible pulp of its large pods

**pa·ca·ya** \pəˈkīə\ *n* -s [AmerSp] **:** any of various Central American palms constituting the genus *Chamaedorea; esp* **:** one having low stems and edible spadices

**pac·chi·o·ni·an body** \ˌpakēˈōnēən-\ *or* **pacchionian corpuscle** *n, sometimes cap P* [Antonio *Pacchioni* †1726 Ital. anatomist + E *-an*] **:** a small whitish process that is one of the enlarged villi of the arachnoid membrane of the brain protruding into the superior sagittal sinus and into depressions in the neighboring bone

**¹pace** \ˈpās\ *n* -s [ME *pas,* fr. OF, fr. L *passus* step, pace, fr. *passus,* past part. of *pandere* to spread, unfold — more at FATHOM] **1 a :** rate of locomotion **:** rapidity with which distance is traversed ⟨led off at a good ~ so that they could cover as much ground as possible —Fred Majdalany⟩ ⟨the limousine moved at an easy ~ —John Hersey⟩ ⟨the river broadens, slackening its ~ as it spreads out —Ted Sumner⟩; *esp* **:** an established rate of locomotion ⟨the challenger made the ~ hot from the start —G.E.Odd⟩ **b :** rate of progress **:** rapidity of development ⟨the ~ of developments in science, agriculture, business, politics, international relations . . . is so swift —Lister Hill⟩; *specif* **:** a parallel rate of growth or development ⟨as the demand for livestock . . . grew, the development of shipping facilities kept ~ —*Amer. Guide Series: Minn.*⟩ **c** (1) **:** a rash or headlong course ⟨youth, sped by the ancient dream that seemed so new, . . . went the ~ with a high heart —C.E.Montague⟩ (2) **:** an example to be emulated ⟨one learns to go to church . . . because other members of the community set the ~ for this kind of activity —Edward Sapir⟩; *specif* **:** first place in a competition ⟨three strokes off the ~ —*Time*⟩ **d** (1) **:** rate of performance or delivery **:** TIMING, TEMPO ⟨see the story unwind . . . with an amiable ~ and plenty of time —Stark Young⟩ ⟨housewives, their routine quickened by the ~ of wartime living —*Monsanto Mag.*⟩ ⟨the ease and ~ of his turns and the precision of his beats place him in the line of the great Russian dancers —Caryl Brahms⟩; *specif* **:** SPEED ⟨his stories move at a breathless ~ —Henry Treece⟩ ⟨the ~ at which an audience can absorb ideas differs with the ideas —Henning Nelms⟩ ⟨the pitcher . . . whips the ball, varying ~, swerve and flight —*Dict. of Games*⟩ (2) **:** rhythmic animation **:** FLUENCY ⟨writes with color, with zest, and with ~ —Amy Loveman⟩ **e** (1) **:** the speed of a bowled ball or of bowling ⟨the bowler frequently changed ~⟩ (2) **:** the degree to which a cricket wicket affects the speed of a ball rebounding from it ⟨difference in ~ of matting and turf wickets⟩ **f :** a device in a loom to maintain even tension in pacing the take-up on the woven fabric **g :** ROUTINE ⟨the circus is change of ~ — beauty against our daily ugliness —John Steinbeck⟩ **2 a :** a manner of walking **:** TREAD ⟨walked slowly, with even, unhesitating ~ —Willa Cather⟩ **b** *obs* **:** a route of travel **:** COURSE ⟨we will direct our ~ downward now —James Howell⟩ **3 a :** a movement of the foot over a space to a new position in walking, running, or dancing **:** STEP ⟨took a ~ or two in the room —Guy McCrone⟩ **b** (1) **:** the space traversed by one step — used as an indefinite unit of measure ⟨cannot go five ~*s* without seeing some wretched object —*Irish Digest*⟩ (2) **:** any of various units of distance based on the length of a human step at a specified time (as for quick time 30 inches and for double time 36 inches) — see ROMAN PACE **4 a** (1) **:** a broad step or platform **:** a flat portion in a run of stairs (2) **:** a raised part of a floor (as around an altar) **b** *obs* **:** a narrow passageway **:** DEFILE ⟨making ~*s* through woods and thickets —Meredith Hanmer⟩ **c :** a passageway running the length of a church between seats **5 a :** an exhibition of skills or capacities ⟨bird dogs going through their ~*s* in the most alien environment —J.W.Cross⟩ ⟨the test pilots . . . put the new planes through their ~*s* —H.H.Arnold & I.C.Eaker⟩; *specif* **:** the various gaits of a horse (as the walk, trot, canter, gallop, and amble) **b :** a fast 2-beat gait of the horse and some other quadrupeds in which the legs move in lateral bipeds and support the animal alternately on the right and left pair of legs — compare TROT

**²pace** \"\ *vb* -ED/-ING/-S *vi* **1 a :** to go with slow or measured tread **:** WALK ⟨a stone platform where meditative persons might ~ to and fro —W.B.Yeats⟩ **b :** to move along **:** PROCEED ⟨they ~ through the obligations of their marriage with . . . cynicism —*Times Lit. Supp.*⟩ **2 :** to move with a lateral gait — usu. used of a horse or dog ⟨*pacing* . . . is characterized by its pistonlike drive with parallel sets of legs traveling together —F.A.Wrensch⟩ ~ *vt* **1 a :** to measure by pacing — often used with *off* ⟨~ off a 10-yard penalty⟩ ⟨had often wondered how far west his land extended, but had never taken the time to ~ it off —O.E.Rölvaag⟩ **b :** to cover at a walk ⟨was slowly *pacing* this narrow enclosure, in his accustomed walk —Sheridan Le Fanu⟩ **2** *archaic* **:** to execute by pacing ⟨~*s* a hornpipe among the eggs —Sir Walter Scott⟩ **3 a** *obs* **:** to train (a horse) to pace **b** *of a horse* **:** to cover (a course) by pacing ⟨*paced* the mile track in 1:55 flat —*Amer. Guide Series: Minn.*⟩ **4 a :** to set or regulate the pace of ⟨traffic, *paced* by clanging cable cars, climbs up and down at cautious speeds —G.W.Long⟩ ⟨advertising must be *paced* so that ads increase in size and frequency as Christmas gets closer —*Nat'l Furniture Rev.*⟩ ⟨must ~ himself, know what his physique will stand —Blair Moody⟩; *specif* **:** to run in advance of (a teammate) as a pacemaker in racing **b :** to let out or take up at regular intervals in weaving ⟨~ the warp⟩ ⟨~ the web⟩ **c** (1) **:** to go before **:** PRECEDE ⟨next in line, *paced* by the scoutmaster⟩ ⟨*paced* by tanks . . . infantrymen were storming a narrow gorge —*Time*⟩; *specif* **:** to draw away from (other competitors) in a race (2) **:** to set an example for **:** excel in accomplishment **:** LEAD ⟨food prices were *pacing* the upsurge —*Newsweek*⟩ ⟨oil advertisers *paced* all other classifications in space gains —*Wall Street Jour.*⟩; *specif* **:** to be high scorer of ⟨*paced* the team with three hits in the sixth game —Robert Shaplen⟩ **d :** to match the progress of **:** keep pace with ⟨schools of porpoises ~ the plodding ship —Tom Marvel⟩ ⟨the speed of the machine may be closely regulated to ~ the packing operation —*Modern Packaging*⟩ ⟨his own growth . . . *paced* that of his science —D.W. Atchley⟩ **5 :** to establish the tempo of **:** control the rhythm and flow of ⟨the dynamic director *paced* the show like a fast 440-yard relay —Henry Hewes⟩ ⟨*paced* the music with . . . sure and tasteful touch —Winthrop Sargeant⟩

**³pace** \"\ *n, usu cap* [ME (northern dial.) *pase, paas,* fr. MF *pasche,* fr. OF — more at PASCH] *dial chiefly Eng* **:** EASTER

**⁴pa·ce** \ˈpāsē\ *prep* [L, abl. of *pac-, pax* peace — more at PEACE] **:** with all due respect or courtesy to ⟨I do not, ~ . . . the correspondents, claim to have made any "discovery" —E.M. Almedingen⟩ ⟨~ the feminists, I believe my own sex is largely responsible for this . . . impertinent curiosity —Katharine F. Gerould⟩

**paceboard** \ˈ⸗,⸗\ *n* [¹*pace* + *board*] **:** the footboard of an altar

**paced** \ˈpāst\ *adj* **1 a :** having a specified speed or gait — usu. used in combination ⟨a fair-*paced* stroke . . . should have the desired effect —A.L.Goundrill⟩ **b :** having the pace set by a pacemaker ⟨a ~ mile⟩ **c :** ACCOMPLISHED ⟨one of the most thorough-*paced* scoundrels —Donn Byrne⟩ **2 :** having a controlled rhythm or tempo ⟨can't recall a better-*paced* performance —Douglas Watt⟩; *specif* **:** MEASURED ⟨in ~ tragic tones —Murray Schumach⟩

**pace egg** *n, often cap P* [³*pace*] *dial Eng* **:** EASTER EGG

**pacemaker** \ˈ⸗,⸗⸗\ *n* **1 a :** one that sets the pace for another — called also *pacesetter* **b :** one that takes the lead or sets an example ⟨ought to act as ~ of Europe unity —F.E.Hirsch⟩ **2 a :** a body part (as the sinoatrial node of the heart) that serves to establish and maintain a rhythmic activity **b :** an emergency device for stimulating the heart with an alternating current to steady the beat or to reestablish the rhythm of an arrested heart ⟨time it takes for the electrical impulse to travel from the ~ at the base of the heart —P.D.White⟩

**pacemaking** \ˈ⸗,⸗⸗\ *n* **:** the act or process of serving as a pacemaker

**pac·er** \ˈpāsə(r)\ *n* -s **1 a :** one that teaches pacing **b :** one that paces; *specif* **:** a horse with a lateral gait — compare TROTTER **2 :** PACEMAKER

**paces** *pl of* PACE, *pres 3d sing of* PACE

**pacesetter** \ˈ⸗,⸗⸗\ *n* **:** PACEMAKER 1

**pachalic** *var of* PASHALIC

**pacheneg** *usu cap, var of* PETCHENEG

**pa·chin·ko** \pəˈchiŋ(ˌ)kō\ *n* -s [Jap] **:** a Japanese gambling device resembling a pinball machine but with automatic payoff as in a gambling slot machine

**pa·chi·si** \pəˈchēzē\ *n* -s [Hindi *pacīsī,* fr. *pacīs* twenty-five, fr. Skt *pañca* five + *viṁśati* twenty; fr. twenty-five being the highest throw — more at FIVE, VICENARY] **:** an ancient board game resembling backgammon that is played on a cruciform board with cowries for dice

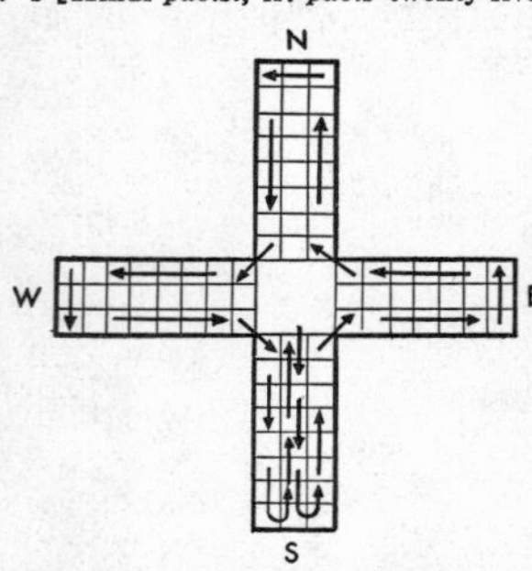


diagram of board for pachisi showing track of one player

**pa·chis·ti·ma** \pəˈkistəmə\ *n, cap* [NL, prob. irreg. fr. Gk *pachys* thick — more at PACHY-] **:** a genus of No. American dwarf evergreen shrubs (family Celastraceae) having smooth coriaceous serrulate leaves and very small green axillary solitary or fascicled flowers — see MOUNTAIN LOVER, OREGON BOX

**pach·no·lite** \ˈpaknəˌlīt\ *n* -s [G *pachnolit,* fr. Gk *pachnē* hoarfrost + G *-lit* -lite; akin to Gk *pēgnynai* to fasten together — more at PACT] **:** a mineral $NaCaAlF_6.H_2O$ consisting of a hydrous fluoride of sodium, calcium, and aluminum occurring in colorless to white monoclinic crystals (hardness 3, sp. gr. 3)

**pa·cho·mi·an** \pəˈkōmēən\ *adj, usu cap* [St. *Pachomius,* 4th cent. A.D. Egyptian monk + E *-an*] **:** of or relating to the cenobitic type of Eastern monasticism originated by St. Pachomius

**pachouli** *var of* PATCHOULI

**pa·chu·ca tank** \pəˈchükə-\ *n, usu cap P* [fr. *Pachuca,* Mexico, where it was first used] **:** a high narrow tank with a central cylinder for compressed air used in the agitation and settling of pulp during treatment by the cyanide process

**pa·chu·co** \pəˈchü(ˌ)kō\ *n* -s [MexSp, prob. fr. El *Paso,* Texas, city from which the pachucos and their families came to California] **:** a young usu. underprivileged Mexican-American of the Los Angeles area having a taste for flashy clothes and fast living, speaking a special jargon, usu. belonging to a neighborhood gang, and often identified by a small tattoo — compare CHOLO 3

**pachy-** *comb form* [NL, fr. Gk, fr. *pachys;* akin to ON *bingr* heap, Latvian *biezs* dense, thick, Av *bazah* high, deep, Skt *bahu* dense, much, many] **:** thick ⟨*Pachy*dermata⟩ ⟨*pachy*tene⟩ ⟨*pachy*meter⟩

**pachy·ceph·a·la** \ˌpakəˈsefələ\ *n pl, cap* [NL, fr. *pachy-* + Gk *kephalē* head] **:** a genus of chiefly arboreal and insectivorous birds (family Muscicapidae) that are intermediate in some respects between the typical flycatchers and the shrikes — see WHISTLER

**pachy·ce·pha·lia** \ˌpakəsəˈfālēə\ *or* **pachy·ceph·a·ly** \ˌpakəˈsefəlē\ *n, pl* **pachycephalias** *or* **pachycephalies** [*pachycephalia* fr. NL, fr. *pachy-* + *cephal-* + *-ia; pachycephaly* ISV *pachy-* + *cephal-* + *-y*] **:** thickness of skull or head

**pachy·derm** \ˈpakəˌdərm, -dəm, -dəim\ *n* -s [F *pachyderme,* fr. Gk *pachydermos* thick-skinned, fr. *pachy-* + *-dermos* -skinned (fr. *derma* skin) — more at DERM-] **:** one of the Pachydermata (as an elephant or rhinoceros)

**pachy·der·mal** \ˌ⸗⸗ˈdərməl\ *adj* **:** PACHYDERMATOUS

**pachy·der·ma·ta** \ˌ⸗⸗ˈdərmədˌə\ *n pl, cap* [NL, fr. *pachy-* + *-dermata*] **:** an artificial assemblage of nonruminant hoofed mammals usu. having a thick skin and including the elephants, hippopotamuses, rhinoceroses, tapirs, horses, pigs, and others

**pachy·der·ma·toid** \ˌ⸗⸗ˈdərməˌtȯid\ *adj* [NL *Pachydermata* + E *-oid*] **:** PACHYDERMOID

**pachy·der·ma·tous** \-mədəs\ *adj* [NL *Pachydermata* + E *-ous*] **1 :** of or relating to the pachyderms **2** [influenced in meaning by F *pachyderme* thick-skinned, fr. Gk *pachydermos*] **a :** THICK, THICKENED — used of skin ⟨the ~ hide that covered the soles of my bare feet —Ben Riker⟩ ⟨~ condition of the skin in elephantiasis⟩ **b :** CALLOUS, INSENSITIVE ⟨that condition of ~ resignation essential to a prolonged residence there —Louis Golding⟩ — **pachy·der·ma·tous·ly** *adv*

**pachy·der·mia** \ˌ⸗⸗ˈdərmēə\ *n* -s [NL, fr. *pachy-* + *-dermia*] **:** abnormal thickness of tissue (as of skin or of the laryngeal mucous membrane) — **pachy·der·mi·al** \ˌ⸗⸗ˈdərmēəl\ *adj*

**pachy·der·mic** \ˌ⸗⸗ˈdərmik\ *adj* **:** PACHYDERMATOUS

**pachy·der·moid** \-rˌmȯid\ *adj* [*pachyderm* + *-oid*] **:** resembling the pachyderms

**pachy·der·mous** \-rməs\ *adj* [Gk *pachydermos*] **1 :** PACHYDERMATOUS **2 :** having thick walls ⟨a moss with ~ cells⟩

**pachy·glossal** \ˈpakē+\ *or* **pachy·glossate** \"+\ *adj* [*pachy-* + *glossal* or *glossate*] **:** having a thick tongue — used of a lizard

**pachy·grapsus** \"+\ *n, cap* [NL, fr. *pachy-* + *Grapsus*] **:** a genus of common shore crabs (family Grapsidae) widely distributed along the western coast of No. America

**pa·chy·ma** \pəˈkīmə\ *n, cap* [NL, fr. Gk *pachys* thick — more at PACHY-] **:** a form genus of imperfect fungi based on sclerotial stages of members of the genus *Poria*

**pachy·meningitis** \ˌpakē+\ *n* [NL, fr. *pachy-* + *meningitis*] **:** inflammation of the dura mater

**pachy·meninx** \"+\ *n* [NL, fr. *pachy-* + *meninx*] **:** DURA MATER

**pa·chym·e·ter** \pəˈkimədˌə(r)\ *n* [ISV *pachy-* + *-meter*] **:** an instrument for measuring thickness (as of paper)

**pachy·ne·ma** \ˌpakəˈnēmə\ *n* -s [NL, fr. *pachy-* + *-nema*] **:** a postsynaptic meiotic chromosome — compare LEPTONEMA

**pachy·o·nych·ia** \ˌpakēōˈnikēə\ *n* -s [NL, fr. *pachy-* + *-onychia*] **:** extreme usu. congenital thickness of the nails

**pa·chyp·a·sa** \pəˈkipəsə\ *n, cap* [NL, prob. fr. *pachy-* + Gk *pas* all; akin to Skt *śaśvat* every, *śvayati* he swells — more at CAVE] **:** a genus of lasiocampid moths including a Syrian silkworm (*P. otus*) reared by the Greeks and Romans for its silk until the introduction of the Chinese silkworm in A.D. 550

**pachy·psylla** \ˌpakē+\ *n, cap* [NL, fr. *pachy-* + *Psylla*] **:** a genus of plant lice (family Psyllidae) containing several forms that produce galls on hackberry

**pachy·rhi·zus** \ˌpakəˈrīzəs\ *n, cap* [NL, fr. Gk *pachyrrhizos* having a thick root, fr. *pachy-* + *-rhizos* (fr. *rhiza* root) — more at ROOT] **:** a small genus of tropical herbaceous vines (family Leguminosae) with a tuberous root, trifoliate leaves, and white or purplish flowers — see YAM BEAN

**pachy·san·dra** \ˌpakəˈsandrə\ *n* [NL, fr. Gk *pachys* thick + NL *-andra* — more at PACHY-] **1** *cap* **:** a genus of evergreen woody herbs (family Buxaceae) having dentate leaves and often used as ground covers — see ALLEGHENY SPURGE, JAPANESE SPURGE **2** -s **:** any plant of the genus *Pachysandra*

**pachystima** *syn of* PACHISTIMA

**pachy·tene** \ˈpakəˌtēn\ *n* -s [ISV *pachy-* + *-tene;* orig. formed as F *pachytène*] **:** a stage of the meiotic prophase that immediately follows zygotene and is characterized by the splitting of the paired chromosomes into chromatids — compare DIPLOTENE, LEPTOTENE

**pa·chyt·y·lus** \pəˈkid·ᵊləs\ *n, cap* [NL, fr. *pachy-* + Gk *tylos* callus, knob — more at THOLE] **:** a genus of Acrididae that includes several destructive Old World migratory locusts

**pac·i·fi·able** \ˈpasəˌfīəbəl, ˌ⸗⸗ˈ⸗⸗⸗\ *adj* [*pacify* + *-able*] **:** capable of being pacified

**pa·cif·ic** \pəˈsifik, -fēk\ *adj* [MF *pacifique,* fr. L *pacificus,* fr. *pac-, pax* peace + *-i-* + *-ficus* -fic — more at PEACE] **1 a :** tending to lessen conflict and promote compromise **:** CONCILIATORY ⟨the effect of his ~ policy was that, in his time, no regular troops were needed —T.B.Macaulay⟩ **b :** rejecting the use of force as an instrument of policy **:** PEACEFUL ⟨make recommendations to the parties with a view to a ~ settlement of the dispute —*U.N. Charter*⟩ **2 a :** having a soothing appearance or effect **:** CALM, TRANQUIL ⟨cloud packs pass over it in soft, cumulus, ~ towers —Hugh MacLennan⟩ **b :** characterized by mildness of temper or disposition **:** disinclined to quarrel **:** PEACEABLE ⟨a naturally ~, sociable man —Glenway Wescott⟩ ⟨the polite and ~ . . . cultures of India and China —Lewis Mumford⟩ **3** *usu cap* [fr. *Pacific* ocean] **:** of or relating to the Pacific ocean ⟨*Pacific* barracuda⟩ ⟨ferrying . . . troops to *Pacific* battlefronts —Howell Walker⟩; *specif* **:** POLYNESIAN 3 ⟨the *Pacific* islands, east of Australia —L.F. de Beaufort⟩

**syn** PEACEABLE, PEACEFUL, PACIFIST, PACIFISTIC, IRENIC: PACIFIC is often used in reference to an individual or group enjoying peace and harboring no desire to arouse contention, strife, or war, more often to those exerting effort and influence to abate strife and attain to peace or to a state of tranquillity ⟨the *pacific* temper, which seeks to settle disputes on grounds of justice rather than by force —Bertrand Russell⟩ ⟨adoption of the resolutions came at a *pacific* final session of the convention after three days of fierce dissension —*N.Y. Times*⟩ PEACEABLE stresses enjoyment of peace as a way of life ⟨the primitive state of man, *peaceable,* contented, and sociable —William Bartram⟩ and may be used as the antonym of *forceful* or *warlike* ⟨they told us . . . that if *peaceable* means failed, they would seize little Jule —Herman Melville⟩ PEACEFUL suggests absence of strife or contention as well as of disturbing influences ⟨*peaceful* sisterhood, receive, and yield me sanctuary —Alfred Tennyson⟩ PACIFIST and PACIFISTIC concern peace only as contrasted with war; they refer to efforts to prevent or stop wars and to settle the issues involved by conference and compromise ⟨*pacifist* means have been variously termed "nonviolent coercion", "war without violence", "passive resistance" —M.Q.Sibley⟩ IRENIC concerns peace orig. in connection with religious controversy and may refer to attitudes or measures likely to allay dispute ⟨lived to see his synod adopt a very *irenic* attitude towards its former antagonists —J.M.Rohne⟩

**pa·cif·i·cal** \-fəkəl\ *adj* [ME, fr. LL *pacificalis,* fr. L *pacificus* + *-alis* -al] *archaic* **:** PACIFIC

**pa·cif·i·cal·ly** \-fək(ə)lē, -fēk-, -li\ *adv* **:** in a pacific manner **:** AMICABLY, PEACEABLY

**pacific athapaskan** *n, usu cap P&A* **1 :** a group of Athapaskan peoples occupying a discontinuous territory from southern British Columbia to northern California and including Chastacosta, Chetco, Chilula, Clatskanie, Hupa, Kato, Kwalhioqua, Lassik, Mattole, Whilkut, Sinkyone, Taltushtuntude, Tolowa, Tututni, Umpqua, Wailaki **2 :** a subdivision of the Athapaskan languages including the languages spoken by the Pacific Athapaskan peoples

**pac·i·fi·ca·tion** \ˌpasəfəˈkāshən\ *n* -s [MF, fr. L *pacification-, pacificatio,* fr. *pacificatus* (past part. of *pacificare* to pacify) + *-ion-, -io* -ion — more at PACIFY] **1 :** the act or process of achieving or restoring peace **:** elimination of disturbance **:** TRANQUILIZATION, SUBDUAL ⟨from the tumult of Hell, through the gradual ~ of Purgatory, to the perfect peace of Paradise —G.G.Coulton⟩ ⟨seven million Arabs and Berbers, whose ~ had been completed only eight years before —C.R. Codman) **2 :** a treaty of peace ⟨the *Pacification* of Ghent⟩

**pac·i·fi·ca·tor** \'===,kād·ə(r), -ātə- *also* pə'sifə,-\ *n* -s [L, fr. *pacificatus* + *-or*] **:** one that pacifies **:** ARBITRATOR, PEACEMAKER

**pa·cif·i·ca·tory** \pə'sifəkə,tōrē\ *adj* [L *pacificatorius,* fr. *pacificatus* + *-orius* -ory] **:** tending to promote peace **:** CONCILIATORY

**pacific blockade** *n* **:** a blockade by one country of the ports of another without recourse to war

**pacific bonito** *n, usu cap P* **:** a bonito that is prob. a northerly strain of the Chile bonito but is often treated as a distinct species (*Sarda lineolata*)

**pacific cedar** *or* **pacific arborvitae** *n, usu cap P* **:** RED CEDAR 2a

**pacific cod** *n, usu cap P* **:** ALASKA COD

**pacific cultus** *n, usu cap P* **:** LINGCOD

**pacific dogwood** *n, usu cap P* **:** a flowering dogwood (*Cornus nuttallii*)

**pacific godwit** *n, usu cap P* **:** a large godwit (*Limosa lapponica baueri*) distributed from eastern Siberia to Australia and New Zealand

**pacific gull** *n, usu cap P* **:** a large black-backed Australian gull (*Gabianus pacificus*) having a black band on the tail at maturity

**pacific halibut** *n, usu cap P* **:** a halibut (*Hippoglossus stenolepis*) of the northern Pacific ocean

**pacific hemlock** *n, usu cap P* **1 :** WESTERN HEMLOCK **2 :** the wood of the Pacific hemlock tree

**pacific herring** *n, usu cap P* **:** a herring (*Clupea pallasii*) of the northern Pacific ocean

**pacific iron** *n* **:** a metal band or fixture about the end of the yard of a sailing ship — see SAIL illustration

**pa·cif·i·cism** \pə'sifə,sizəm\ *n* -s [*pacific* + *-ism*] **:** PACIFISM

**pa·cif·i·cist** \-fəsəst\ *n* -s [*pacific* + *-ist*] **:** PACIFIST

**pacific kittiwake** *n, usu cap P* **:** a kittiwake (*Rissa tridactyla pollicaris*) of the northern Pacific ocean that is pure white with black feet, a pearl-gray mantle, and broadly black-tipped wings — compare ATLANTIC KITTIWAKE, RED-LEGGED KITTIWAKE

**pacific mackerel** *n, usu cap P* **:** a common and important food fish (*Pneumatophorus diego*) of the Pacific coast of No. America closely related to and greatly resembling the common mackerel of the Atlantic

**pacific madrone** *n, usu cap P* **:** MADRONA 1

**pacific maple** *n, usu cap P* **:** OREGON MAPLE

**pacific mite** *n, usu cap P* **:** a mite (*Eotetranychus pacificus*) that is a destructive pest of orchard crops and ornamentals along the Pacific coast of the U.S. and southern Canada

**pacific plum** *n, usu cap P* **:** SIERRA PLUM

**pacific rattlesnake** *n, usu cap P* **:** a common rattlesnake (*Crotalus viridis oreganus*) of the Pacific slope of No. America

**pacific red cedar** *n, usu cap P* **:** RED CEDAR 2a

**pacific sailfish** *n, usu cap P* **:** a sailfish (*Istiophorus greyi* or *I. orientalis*) of the Indian and tropical Pacific oceans that is larger and has a higher dorsal fin than the Atlantic sailfish

**pacific salmon** *n, usu cap P* **:** a salmon of the genus *Oncorhynchus* — compare BLUEBACK SALMON, DOG SALMON

**pacific sardine** *n, usu cap P* **:** an extremely abundant small clupeid fish (*Sardinops caerulea*) of the Pacific coast of No. America that is an important commercial fish used for canning and for production of fish meals and fish oils

**pacific silver fir** *n, usu cap P* **:** AMABILIS FIR

**pacific terrapin** *n, usu cap P* **:** an aquatic mud turtle (*Clemmys marmorata*) sold as terrapin in West Coast markets

**pacific time** *or* **pacific standard time** *n, usu cap P* **:** the time of the eighth time zone west of Greenwich based on the 120th meridian and used in the Pacific coastal region of Canada and the U.S. from the panhandle of Alaska southward — abbr. *PT, PST*

**pacific tree toad** *n, usu cap P* **:** a tree toad (*Hyla regilla*) widely distributed in western No. America

**pacific yellowtail** *n, usu cap P* **:** CALIFORNIA YELLOWTAIL

**pacific yew** *n, usu cap P* **:** a small or medium irregularly branched evergreen tree (*Taxus brevifolia*) of the Pacific coast yielding a fine hard close-grained wood — called also *California yew, western yew*

**pa·cif·id** \pə'sifəd\ *n* -s *usu cap* [*pacific* + *-id*] **:** an early American Indian of a physical type characterized by moderate stature, broad head usu. with low-vaulted cranium and flattened base, and a broad rugged face — compare CENTRALID, SYLVID

**pac·i·fi·er** \'pasə,fī(ə)r, -īə\ *n* -s **:** one that soothes or calms: as **a :** a usu. nipple-shaped device for babies to suck or bite upon **b :** SUGAR-TIT **c :** TRANQUILIZER

pacifier a

**pac·i·fism** \'pasə,fizəm\ *n* -s [F *pacifisme,* fr. *pacifique* pacific (fr. MF) + *-isme* -ism — more at PACIFIC] **1 :** opposition to war or violence as a means of settling disputes ⟨their ~ is rooted in their contemplative outlook, and in the fact that they do not desire to change whatever they see —Bertrand Russell⟩ ⟨the fundamental transformation from ~ to full war-mindedness that was necessary to meet the crisis —R. de R. de Sales⟩; *specif* **:** refusal to bear arms because of moral or religious principles ⟨Christian ~ . . . asserts that all warfare is categorically forbidden to followers of Our Lord —T.S.Eliot⟩ **2 :** an attitude or policy of nonresistance **:** PASSIVISM ⟨some assert that . . . ~ should be our aim, and a disarmed neutrality our policy —*Yale Rev.*⟩

**¹pac·i·fist** \-,fəst\ *n* -s [F *pacifiste,* fr. *pacifisme* + *-iste* -ist] **:** an adherent to pacifism ⟨~s . . . now found expression for their conviction that war in general is immoral and inexpedient —C.J.H.Hayes⟩; *specif* **:** CONSCIENTIOUS OBJECTOR

**²pacifist** \"\ *or* **pac·i·fis·tic** \¦==¦fistik\ *adj* **:** of, relating to, or characterized by pacifism ⟨distributing ~ literature⟩

**syn** see PACIFIC

**pac·i·fis·ti·cal·ly** \-tək(ə)lē\ *adv* **:** in a pacifistic manner ⟨the ~ inclined liberal —H.D.Lasswell⟩

**pac·i·fy** \'pasə,fī\ *vt* -ED/-ING/-ES [ME *pacifien,* fr. L *pacificare,* fr. *pac-, pax* peace + *-ificare* -ify — more at PEACE] **1 a :** to allay anger or agitation **:** PLACATE, SOOTHE ⟨bought the weeping child a lollipop to ~ her⟩ **b :** to make benign or amicable **:** APPEASE, PROPITIATE ⟨such concessions would ~ the Chinese Communist leaders —W.V.Shannon⟩ **2 a :** to restore to a tranquil state **:** QUIET, SETTLE ⟨throws the four of them . . . into a violent emotional upheaval not to be *pacified* until one of them dies —Charles Lee⟩ **b :** to reduce to a submissive state esp. by force of arms **:** SUBDUE ⟨U.S. Marines . . . went in as early as 1910 to ~ the country —*Time*⟩

**syn** APPEASE, PLACATE, MOLLIFY, PROPITIATE, CONCILIATE: PACIFY indicates a soothing or calming of anger, grievance, or agitation, or the quelling of insurrection esp. by force ⟨seeing his mounting rage, friends did all they could to *pacify* and restrain him⟩ ⟨second-grade troops, useful mainly to occupy parts of the country that have already been *pacified* —Brian Crozier⟩ APPEASE may indicate the quieting of agitation or insistent demand by the making of concessions ⟨open in manner, easy of access, a little quick of temper but readily *appeased* —John Buchan⟩ ⟨he is utterly and absolutely implacable; no prayers, no human sacrifices can ever for one moment *appease* his cold, malignant rage —L.P.Smith⟩ ⟨a frantic effort to *appease* mounting discontent at home —Paul Willen⟩ PLACATE is sometimes interchangeable with appease but may imply a more lasting assuagement of bitter feeling ⟨each and every new route projected was liable to drastic alteration to *placate* local opposition —O.S.Nock⟩ ⟨federal officials who try to *placate* witch-hunting Congressmen —*New Republic*⟩ MOLLIFY stresses softening or abatement of agitation, through mitigating circumstance ⟨*mollified* when they heard that the patio, with its famous cottonwood tree, will be left intact —Green Peyton⟩ PROPITIATE may refer to averting the anger or malevolence or winning the favor of a superior or of one possessing the power to injure greatly ⟨*propitiate* this far-shooting Apollo —George Grote⟩ ⟨Aunty Rosa, he argued, had the power to beat him with many stripes . . . it would be discreet in the future to *propitiate* Aunty Rosa —Rudyard Kipling⟩ ⟨the unlimited power of trustees to abuse their trust unless they are abjectly *propitiated* —H.G.Wells⟩ CONCILIATE may be used of situations in which an estrangement or desire is settled by arbitration or compromise ⟨policy of *conciliating* and amalgamating conquered nations —Agnes Repplier⟩ ⟨instinctively friendly and wholly free from inflammatory rhetoric, he did much to *conciliate* more stubborn Northern sentiment concerning the South —F.P.Gaines⟩

**pacing** *n* -s [fr. gerund of ²*pace*] **1 :** an act or instance of executing or controlling a pace ⟨the ~s for a few steps side by side through the crowds —R.M.Coates⟩ ⟨a masterpiece of crisp ~ and refined workmanship —Winthrop Sargeant⟩ ⟨there must be ~ in the introduction of new experiences —C.M.Louttit⟩ **2 :** harness racing for pacers ⟨Little Brown Jug, ~'s biggest race —Gerald Holland⟩

**pa·cin·i·an corpuscle** \pə'sinēən-\ *also* **pa·ci·ni's corpuscle** \pə'chēnēz-\ *n, sometimes cap P* [Filippo *Pacini* †1883 Ital. anatomist + E *-an* or *-'s* (gen. suffix)] **:** one of the oval bodies serving as terminal capsules of certain sensory nerve fibers esp. in the skin of the hands and feet

**¹pack** \'pak\ *n* -s *often attrib* [ME *pak, pack,* of LG origin; akin to MLG & MD *pak,* MFlem *pac*] **1 a** (1) **:** a compact bundle of goods or equipment arranged for convenience in carrying esp. on the back of an animal or man ⟨sat on the deck by the bulky aid ~s that the corpsmen had deposited —L.M.Uris⟩ ⟨parachute ~⟩ (2) **:** a knapsack or blanket roll for carrying personal effects ⟨have him roll a full field ~ . . . extra shoes helmet and all —James Jones⟩ (3) **:** a climb or hike with a pack on one's back **b :** a group or pile of related objects: as (1) **:** a shook of cask staves (2) **:** a bundle of sheet-metal plates for rolling simultaneously (3) **:** a number of separate photographic films packed so as to be inserted together into a camera and each attached to a paper tab that on being withdrawn moves the individual exposed film to the back of the lot (4) **:** a set of two or three color films or plates for simultaneous exposure — compare BIPACK, TRIPACK (5) **:** a stack of theatrical flats arranged in sequence **c** (1) **:** a number of individual components packaged as a unit usu. for marketing **:** PACKET ⟨~ of cigarettes⟩ ⟨a fiber drum ~ of dressed chickens —*Recommended Specifications for Poultry & Poultry Products*⟩ ⟨open a ~ of canned goods⟩ (2) **:** CONTAINER ⟨saw the little pilot chute whip out behind him, dragging the silk from the ~ —Howard Hunt⟩; *specif* **:** a package for a commercial product ⟨polyethylene makes ideal individual ~s for catsup, mustard, jelly —*Newsweek*⟩ (3) **:** a compact unitized assembly to perform a specific function (as a power pack to energize a radio set) (4) **:** a container shielded with lead or mercury for holding radium in large quantities esp. for therapeutic application **2 :** a group of people: as **a :** a set of persons with similar aims or background ⟨took her for granted as part of the family ~ —Anne D. Sedgwick⟩; *esp* **:** a hostile or destructive clique ⟨pursued . . . by a ~ of every able-bodied villager, armed with sticks and stones —T.H. White b.1906⟩ ⟨this heedless ~ of curiosity seekers were suffocating him —L.C.Douglas⟩ **b :** the forward line of a rugby team **c :** an organized troop (as of the Boy Scouts) ⟨a cub ~ may be started in any community where a group of interested parents obtain the sponsorship of a responsible institution —*Parents' Mag.*⟩ **3 a :** the contents of a pack **:** any of various units (as a 240-pound measure for wool, a linen yarn measure of 60,000 yards, 20 books of gold leaf) based on the amount in a standard pack **b :** a large amount or number **:** HEAP ⟨a . . . good fellow with ~s of courage —H. J.Laski⟩ ⟨a ~ of lies made up by a vindictive person —Rex Ingamells⟩ **c** (1) **:** a set of cards that is complete for the playing of a given game; *esp* **:** the full deck of 52 cards of 4 suits with all or part of which most card games are played (2) **:** any portion of a set of playing cards remaining undealt at any stage of a card game (3) **:** the discard pile in canasta and similar games (4) **:** a group of cards of special value in a card game because of their number or their high rank **:** a strong card hand **4 a :** an act or instance of packing ⟨field ~ of peaches by migrant workers⟩ ⟨the first experimental ~s were made in Denver in 1908 —M.A.Joslyn&L.A.Hohl⟩ **b :** a method of packing ⟨vacuum ~⟩ ⟨dry sugar ~s are in the proportion of three pounds of fruit to one of sugar —Anne Pierce⟩ **c :** the total amount (as of produce or fish) packed during a specified period ⟨the military requires . . . more than 9 percent of the national ~ of canned fruits and vegetables —R.B.Russell⟩ ⟨supplying the fish for a hundred thousand case ~ —N.C.McDonald⟩ **5 a** (1) **:** a group of domesticated animals trained to hunt or run together ⟨kept a ~ of tiny beagles —E.J.Oates⟩ ⟨led the ~ out of the starting gate —G.F. T.Ryall⟩ (2) **:** a group of usu. wild animals of the same kind congregating in herds, flocks, or schools ⟨baboons . . . ran in ~s of fifty or more —Alan Moorehead⟩ ⟨tunas roving the open sea in ~s —Rachel L. Carson⟩ ⟨prairie chickens congregating in winter ~s⟩; *specif* **:** a group of predatory animals hunting together ⟨wolf ~⟩ **b :** a group of vehicles traveling together ⟨made the freeway and flitted through the slower car ~s —*Motor Life*⟩; *esp* **:** an organized group of combat craft ⟨a submarine ~ that sank twelve ships in two hours —*Fortune*⟩ ⟨the ~ of jets . . . passed overhead on their way to the targets —B.J.Friedman⟩ **6 a :** a concentrated mass ⟨a great ~ of muscle shifting when his shoulder moved —Scott Fitzgerald⟩; *specif* **:** ICE PACK ⟨locked in the antarctic ice until the breakup of the ~ in the summer —Glen Jacobsen⟩ **b :** a supporting wall or pillar in a coal mine built of gob **7 a :** absorbent material saturated with water or other liquid for therapeutic application to the body or a body part — see COLD PACK, HOT PACK, ICE PACK **b :** a folded square or compress of gauze or other absorbent material used esp. to maintain a clear field in surgery, to plug cavities, to check bleeding by compression, or to apply medication **8 a :** MUDPACK **b :** an application or treatment of oils or creams for conditioning the scalp and hair **9 :** material used as packing

**²pack** \"\ *vb* -ED/-ING/-S [ME *pakken,* prob. fr. MD, fr. *pak* pack, n.] *vt* **1 a :** to stow in or as if in a container **:** make into a compact bundle ⟨~*ed* and unpacked all the gear in traveling —Weston La Barre⟩ ⟨a couple of staff sergeants were ~*ing* film into the combat cameras —Walter Peters⟩ ⟨put on his hat, ~*ed* up his family, and set off —*Atlantic*⟩ ⟨~s an extraordinary amount of information into a few pages —*Times Lit. Supp.*⟩ **b :** to fill completely **:** cram to capacity **:** STUFF, JAM ⟨~ a bag⟩ ⟨~ a stadium⟩ ⟨the whole horizon seemed ~*ed* with their white sails —Kenneth Roberts⟩ ⟨into twelve hours had been ~*ed* the events that well might have filled a lifetime —Rafael Sabatini⟩ ⟨a route . . . ~*ed* with scenes of mountain splendor —O.S.Nock⟩ **c :** to fill with packing: as (1) **:** to fill in (as in mine stopes or old workings) with waste rock to support the roof (2) **:** to fill (a fractionating column or tower) with loose pieces of solid material **d** *archaic* **:** to hoist and carry as much (sail) as possible — usu. used with *on* ⟨~*ed* on all sail —William Scoresby †1857⟩ **e :** to load with a pack ⟨~ a mule⟩ **f :** to put in a protective container **:** package or preserve for shipment or marketing ⟨vegetables usually reach Salinas by the truckload and there they are washed, trimmed, inspected and ~*ed* —*Monsanto Mag.*⟩ **2 a :** to crowd together **:** assemble in a compact group ⟨in the yard ~*ed* solid were the farmers, standing silently —Meridel Le Sueur⟩ ⟨in the past all the galaxies now so widely scattered were ~*ed* tightly together —George Gamow⟩ **b :** to increase the density of **:** COMPRESS ⟨~*ed* the lower soil so that capillarity could operate —W.P.Webb⟩ **3 a :** to cause or command to go **:** SEND ⟨saw her ~*ed* back to Holland when the Dutch exiled him —*Time*⟩ — usu. used with *off* ⟨the children are ~*ed* off to Sunday school —*Times Lit. Supp.*⟩ ⟨calmed him down and ~*ed* him off to bed —Clemence Dane⟩; *specif* **:** to dismiss unceremoniously ⟨could neither be tactfully paid off nor summarily ~*ed* off —S.H.Adams⟩ **b :** to bring or come to an end or halt **:** FINISH, STOP — used with *up* or *in* ⟨gossip . . . that he might soon ~ up his assignment and return to the United States —*Springfield (Mass.) Union*⟩ ⟨machine-gun bullets ~*ed* up the airplane's transmitter⟩ ⟨does not mean that . . . a supreme master in the saddle, will ~ in riding —*Irish Digest*⟩ **4 :** to gather into a tight formation **:** make a pack of ⟨hounds well ~*ed* as they close in on their quarry⟩; *specif* **:** to take one's place in (a rugby scrum) ⟨the coach came in and we ~*ed* a scrum for him —A.P.Gaskell⟩ **5 a :** to cover or surround with a pack ⟨~*ed* it away from the operative field with gauze packs —R.P.Parsons⟩; *specif* **:** to envelop (a patient) in a wet or dry sheet or blanket **b :** to caulk or fit by filling or surrounding with material that prevents passage (as of air, water, or steam) ⟨the valve stem is ~*ed* against exhaust pressure only —*Ingersoll-Rand General Catalogue*⟩ **6 a :** to carry or transport on foot ⟨~ a canoe over a portage⟩ ⟨two platoons . . . were ordered to ~ the ammunition to them on foot —*Infantry Jour.*⟩ ⟨~ a suitcase⟩ **b :** to convey usu. on the back of an animal ⟨would pay $20 a day each to be ~*ed* back into the . . . Gorge for trout —Frank Daugherty⟩ ⟨~*ed* guns and ammunition enough to make their horses swaybacked —F.B.Gipson⟩ **c :** to wear or carry as part of one's regular equipment ⟨~ a gun⟩ ⟨~ a union card⟩ ⟨clothes-conscious . . . although they stop somewhere short of ~*ing* a rolled-up umbrella —W.L.Worden⟩ **d :** to be supplied or equipped with **:** POSSESS ⟨the storm . . . ~*ing* winds of eighty to ninety miles —*N.Y. Times*⟩ ⟨these proven weapons . . . ~ nuclear warheads —R.C.Albrook⟩ ⟨few streets in America ~ more history to the square foot —Budd Schulberg⟩ **e** *slang* **:** to be capable of making (an impact) ⟨world's heavyweight champion . . . ~*ed* a wallop —*Springfield (Mass.) Union*⟩ ⟨a book that ~s a man-sized punch —C.J.Rolo⟩ ~ *vi* **1 a :** to go away **:** DEPART ⟨no one simply ~s off and leaves an obligation without first making some explanation —Dorothy Baker⟩; *specif* **:** to consider oneself summarily dismissed ⟨when he refused to work . . . he was calmly told by the youthful manager to ~ up —*Breeder's Gazette*⟩ **b :** to come to a halt **:** cease to function **:** QUIT, STOP — used with *up* or *in* ⟨the motors coughed and ~*ed* up —*Auckland (New Zealand) Weekly News*⟩ ⟨why don't you ~ in, before you kill yourself —Millard Lampell⟩ **2 a :** to stow goods and equipment (as clothes and personal belongings) in luggage or packs for transportation ⟨was given an overseas assignment and sent home to ~⟩ ⟨the company will probably ~ up and move south —*Time*⟩; *specif* **:** to package a product for shipment ⟨the final step in flour manufacture is ~*ing* —*Studies for Flour Salesmen*⟩ **b :** to become adapted for packing ⟨a knit dress ~s well⟩ ⟨air mattresses ~ away into a small space⟩ **c** *archaic* **:** to increase the speed of a ship by crowding on sail ⟨be ready to ~ after them, if they are gone to the bay —Horatio Nelson⟩ **d :** to become filled to capacity ⟨watch the big tarnished grange ~ to the rafters —William Du Bois⟩ **3 a :** to assemble in a group **:** CONGREGATE ⟨snow partridges are wont to ~ like grouse in the autumn —Douglas Carruthers⟩; *specif* **:** to run close together ⟨the dogs followed in fine order, ~*ing* and driving as they went —*Red Ranger*⟩ **b :** to crowd together ⟨excursionists . . . ~ into a bus —Richard Joseph⟩; *specif* **:** to form a rugby scrum ⟨forwards still mostly ~*ed* 3-2-3 —O.L. Owen⟩ **4 a :** to arrange a group of related objects in a compact mass ⟨one man handed up sandbags while the other ~*ed*⟩ **b :** to increase in density ⟨some broken ores tend to ~ in stopes, and must be blasted out —Robert Peele⟩ ⟨ice ~*ed* up against the cab glasses, and visibility was just about nil —O. S.Nock⟩ **5 a :** to carry or convey goods or equipment ⟨domesticated animals . . . used for ~*ing* —J.H.Steward⟩ **b :** to travel with one's baggage by horse or muleback ⟨telling about the summer he ~*ed* into the Big Horn mountains of Wyoming —Hamilton Basso⟩

**syn** CROWD, CRAM, STUFF, RAM, TAMP: PACK, orig. meaning to form into bundles for convenient handling esp. in transporting, implies also the orderly economical filling of a receptacle or a total often excessive or uncomfortable filling of anything ⟨*pack* a bag for an overnight trip⟩ ⟨*pack* a box until it splits open at the sides⟩ ⟨a play that *packs* the theater every night⟩ CROWD implies a great number of things out of proportion to the space available for them, sometimes suggesting pressing or serious inconvenience ⟨salmon *crowded* both streams —W.L. Worden⟩ ⟨various chapters of the book are *crowded* with references —Paolo Milano⟩ ⟨visitors *crowding* the vacation areas⟩ CRAM suggests more strongly the excessive packing to the point of bruising or squeezing, often implying a disorderly and forcible insertion of something into an inadequately large receptacle or area ⟨into a day that begins each morning at 7:30, Jim *crams* enough work to fill two —*Newsweek*⟩ ⟨the man whose shelves are *crammed* with horticultural books —A.J.P.Taylor⟩ ⟨a man doesn't try to *cram* his feet into his wife's shoes —Constance Foster⟩ STUFF implies a filling to the point of bulging or protrusion, often suggesting also the disorder of cramming ⟨*stuff* a pillow with feathers⟩ ⟨*stuff* a handful of bills into a wallet⟩ ⟨*stuffed* himself with cake⟩ RAM carries the idea of pounding, stamping, or pushing hard to force in ⟨*ram* a bullet into the rifle barrel⟩ ⟨pronging great slices of meat onto his fork and *ramming* them into his mouth —Bruce Marshall⟩ TAMP usu. implies a loose packing in (as of something granular) by the pressure of repeated light blows ⟨*tamping* the gravel back around the ties —Charlton Laird⟩ ⟨*tamp* tobacco in a pipe bowl⟩ ⟨the floors were of *tamped* earth —*Amer. Guide Series: Wash.*⟩

**³pack** \"\ *vb* -ED/-ING/-S [perh. alter. (influenced by ²*pack*) of ¹*pact*] *vi, obs* **:** to make a secret agreement **:** CONSPIRE ⟨go ~ with him, and give the mother gold —Shak.⟩ ~ *vt* **1** *obs* **a :** to let into a conspiracy **:** make an accomplice of ⟨that goldsmith there, were he not ~*ed* with her, could witness it —Shak.⟩ **b :** to arrange in secret **:** PLOT ⟨had it been a ~*ed* business, they would have been careful not to have differed in a title —Francis Bragge⟩ **2 a :** to influence the composition of (as a political agency) so as to bring about a desired result ⟨succeeded . . . in ~*ing* parliament with their adherents —*Publ's Mod. Lang. Assoc. of Amer.*⟩ ⟨could ~ the ballot with dummy candidates to split the vote —*New Republic*⟩ **b** *obs* **:** to manipulate (playing cards) fraudulently **:** STACK **3 :** to add a pack to — used chiefly of the price of an automobile or other item of durable goods ⟨those who sign contracts in blank are making it easy for the unethical dealer to ~ the account —*Facts About Buying Used Cars*⟩ — **pack cards** *archaic* **:** CONSPIRE ⟨she . . . has *packed cards* with Caesars and false played my glory —Shak.⟩

**⁴pack** \"\ *n* -s **1** *obs* **:** COMPACT, PLOT **2 :** an unjustified surcharge or markup added to a price by a dealer often in collusion with other dealers or with a finance company ⟨many a dealer admitted privately that he added a ~ . . . to allow more room for the discounts his customers expected —*Time*⟩

**⁵pack** \"\ *adj* [perh. fr. ³*pack*] *chiefly Scot* **:** very friendly **:** INTIMATE ⟨unco ~ and thick thegither —Robert Burns⟩

**⁶pack** *var of* PAC

**pack·abil·i·ty** \,pakə'biləd·ē\ *n* **:** the quality or state of being packable

**pack·able** \'pakəbəl\ *adj* **:** capable of being packed

**¹pack·age** \'pakij, -kēj\ *n* -s *often attrib* [prob. fr. D *pakkage,* fr. *pak* pack (fr. MD) + *-age* (after *bagage* baggage, fr. MD, fr. ME) — more at PACK, BAGGAGE] **1** [²*pack* + *-age*] *archaic* **:** the act or process of packing ⟨the privileges of the ~ of cloths and certain other outward-bound goods —Patrick Colquhoun⟩ **2 a :** a small or moderate-sized pack **:** BUNDLE, PARCEL ⟨carts, into which ~s were being shot from the warehouses —Virginia Woolf⟩ ⟨before any ~ or parcel is accepted for mailing the sender must . . . endorse the wrapper —*U. S. Official Postal Guide*⟩ **b :** a commodity in its container **:** a unit of a product uniformly processed, wrapped, or sealed for distribution ⟨~ of cigarettes⟩ ⟨handled 6.8 million ~s of fruits and vegetables —C.K.Baker⟩ ⟨the biggest seller was a ~ of four Chinese peel tub chairs —*Retailing Daily*⟩ **c :** a preassembled unit ready for installation or use ⟨with men responsible for the selection and installation of heating units, choice starts with the ~ itself —*Amer. Builder*⟩ ⟨a new self-contained machine gun ~ that is hooked on under the wings —*Science News Letter*⟩ **3 a :** a covering wrapper or container ⟨nature gave the banana a good ~ —*advt*⟩; *specif* **:** a protective unit for storing or shipping a commodity ⟨designing a ~ that attracts the eye of the customer and at the same time protects the merchandise —*Christian Science Monitor*⟩ **b :** any of the various forms (as cheeses, spools, pirns, tubes) in which yarn or thread is wound for processing and handling **4 :** something that resembles a package: as **a :** something organized into or constituting a compact unit ⟨Luxembourg is a diminutive ~ stretching for fifty-seven miles —*N.Y. Times*⟩ ⟨formless processes that are seldom easy to put in headline ~s —Joseph Alsop⟩ ⟨wry humor, pertinent reflection, and good . . . melodrama, all in one ~ —Phil Stong⟩ **b :** a combination of related elements to be accepted or rejected as a whole ⟨sell them a . . . complete ~ (lot, house, equipment and financing in a single transaction) —F.A.Gutheim⟩ ⟨a series of treaties and agreements forming a single ~ —S.B.Fay⟩ ⟨the purchaser is tendered a ~, consisting of a specified amount of common stock with each unit of the senior issue —R.U.Cooper⟩; *specif* : a complete show or series of shows ready for presentation and usu. bought by a sponsor or network for a lump sum ⟨purchasing the entire show as a live-talent or transcribed ~ —Roger Barton⟩ ⟨a quarter-hour TV ~ —R.L.Shayon⟩ ⟨swung through the Midwest (as part of a jazz concert ~) —*Time*⟩ **c** : a combination of benefits ⟨the consumer appeal of a dealer's credit plan depends . . . upon the size and composition of the ~ the consumer gets for what he pays —C.W. Phelps⟩; *esp* : contract benefits gained through collective bargaining ⟨a 10-cent hourly ~ — seven cents to go into a pension fund and three for health and welfare benefits —*Wall Street Jour.*⟩ **d** : a combination of necessaries (as food or tickets) and services usu. offered at a special rate ⟨the sports ~ includes accommodations in heated cabins, with or without bath and meals; two sessions at the ski school and unlimited use of the ski lifts —O.R.Geyer⟩ ⟨~ vacation⟩ **e** *slang* (1) : COMPOSITE ⟨only five feet tall but . . . a ~ of lovely curves —H.D.Osborne⟩ (2) : the police record of a criminal ⟨his ~ listed a prison record on a rape charge —Courtney McClendon⟩

**²package** \"\, *esp in pres part* -kəj\ *vt* -ED/-ING/-S **1** : to make into or as if into a package ⟨designers showed great ingenuity in constructing and *packaging* these houses —*Americana Annual*⟩ ⟨furnished as a *packaged*-type power unit ready to operate —*Air Tools*⟩ ⟨neatly ~*s* her findings —James Hilton⟩ ⟨his demands for Greece will probably be *packaged* with those for China and Turkey —*New Republic*⟩; *specif* : to produce as an entertainment package ⟨will ~ annually six half-hour TV shows by each writer —Henry Hewes⟩ **2** : to enclose in a package or protective covering ⟨there are two ways a designer can ~ this space —*New Yorker*⟩ ⟨the car ~*s* its riders like fragile merchandise —A.J.Despagni⟩ ⟨airplanes shipped overseas are now *packaged* with a spray of plastic solution —*Aero Products*⟩; *specif* : to put (a commodity) into a protective wrapper or container for shipment or storage ⟨cured hams . . . have been sent out frozen, canned, and otherwise *packaged* —*New Yorker*⟩ ⟨the company . . . will ~ about 50% of its beets and 50% of its turnips in these bags —Lee Geist⟩ ⟨besides aspirin . . . ~*s* saccharin, eye drops, rubbing alcohol —*Monsanto Mag.*⟩

**pack·age·able** \ˈpakijəbəl\ *adj* : capable of being made into a package

**package advertising** *n* : advertising placed on the package in which a commodity is sold

**package bees** *n pl* : bees packaged and sold by weight to constitute the nucleus of a hive

**package car** *n* : a railroad car for the shipment of goods in less-than-carload lots

**package conveyor** *n* : a mechanical device for moving packages from one area to another usu. on an endless belt

**package deal** *n* **1 a** : an offer or agreement to accept or pay a lump sum for a correlated group of goods or services ⟨a *package deal*, with all 30 to be leased for four years at a total fee reported somewhat in excess of $1,250,000 —*Wall Street Jour.*⟩ ⟨too often parents depend upon *package deals* in children's literature, or on the canned advice of book clubs —F.G.Jennings⟩; *specif* : a contract involving such an agreement achieved through collective bargaining ⟨union-management committees have reportedly worked out a *package deal*, with increased fringe benefits . . . but no flat wage increase —*Time*⟩ **b** : the goods or services supplied through such an agreement ⟨offers the franchise operator a complete *package deal*, including ground development, building construction —R.B.Andrews⟩ ⟨give the studio a *package deal* — story, star, and director all wrapped up —Bennett Cerf⟩ **2** : an offer or agreement making the acceptance of one proposal or candidate dependent upon the acceptance of another ⟨a *package deal* which tied neutralization to a multilateral agreement to share petroleum production —Fred Greene⟩ ⟨a *package deal* that would admit all applicants or none —*N. Y. Herald Tribune*⟩

**packaged fuel** *n* : fuel sold in bags or briquettes; *specif* : coal or coke briquettes wrapped in paper packages (as of 10 to 15 lb.)

**package freight** *n* : freight shipped in less-than-carload lots and billed by the piece

**package mortgage** *n* : a mortgage covering major items of equipment (as kitchen appliances) in addition to the house and lot

**package policy** *n* : an insurance policy combining coverages for a number of causes of loss or types of property

**package powerplant** *n* : a small portable steam-electric generating station

**pack·ag·er** \ˈpakijə(r), -kēj-\ *n* -s **1 a** : one that packages **b** : an operator of a machine that cuts several pieces of lumber to the same length at the same time **2** : an entrepreneur of complete shows for sale to sponsors or networks ⟨an impressively successful radio and television ~ —Gilbert Millstein⟩

**package store** *n* : a store licensed to sell alcoholic beverages that may not lawfully be drunk on the premises

**package tour** *also* **packaged tour** *n* : an all-expense tour ⟨*package tours* of the interior of Puerto Rico in five-passenger cars with a guide-driver —M.A.Santin⟩

**packaging** *n* -s [fr. gerund of ²*package*] **1** : an act or instance of packing ⟨industrial ~ is concerned with transit more than with trade —*Modern Packaging*⟩ ⟨the official lot-test number must . . . accompany the dyes through all subsequent ~*s* —*For Instance*⟩ ⟨a new ~ of the idea —*Newsweek*⟩ **2** : ¹PACKAGE 3a ⟨developing marketable products and their ~*s* —Ben Nash⟩

**pack basket** *n* : a basket with shoulder straps designed to be worn on the back

**packboard** \ˈ≈,≈\ *n* : a usu. canvas-covered light wood or metal frame with shoulder straps contoured so that only the canvas touches the wearer's back and used for carrying goods and equipment ⟨strapped the accordion to his ~ —Robert Lund⟩

**pack drill** *n* : a military punishment consisting of marching up and down a beat with full marching equipment

**packed** *adj* [fr. past part. of ²*pack*] **1 a** : CROWDED, STUFFED ⟨the characteristic ~ effects are apt to degenerate into cluttered obscurity —F.R.Leavis⟩ — often used in combination ⟨crowds his figures into narrow, closely *packed* groups —Roger Fry⟩ ⟨his vast and action-*packed* story —Arthur Knight⟩ **b** : COMPRESSED ⟨lay on the ~ sand —Hugh MacLennan⟩ — often used in combination ⟨ski boots squeak on the hard-*packed* snow —Corey Ford⟩ **2** : filled to capacity ⟨played to a ~ house⟩

pack basket

**packed jury** *n* : a jury brought together unfairly or corruptly thereby making it partial or venal

**packed out** *adj, Brit* : filled to capacity ⟨went first to the hotel at which I have frequently put up. *Packed out* —Elizabeth Boyd⟩

**¹pack·er** \ˈpakə(r)\ *n* -s [³*pack* + -*er*] *archaic* : CONSPIRATOR, MANIPULATOR

**²packer** \"\ *n* -s [²*pack* + -*er*] **1 a** : one that packages goods or equipment for shipment or storage ⟨works in the shipping department as a china ~⟩ ⟨cans arrive at the automatic ~ in a 4-bank conveyor —*Packaging*⟩; *specif* : a wholesale dealer ⟨tea ~⟩ **b** : one that is processed by a wholesale dealer; *specif* : a dressed hog split down the spine and head with the leaf fat removed **c** : a protective container; *esp* : a usu. wide-mouthed glass bottle **d** : one that loads or fills: as (1) : a specialist in loading pack animals ⟨the Missourian was an expert ~ —Theodore Roosevelt⟩ (2) : a worker who loads electrodes into a furnace for graphitizing (3) : a coal miner who fills worked-out rooms with waste material to prevent their collapse and builds rough pillars to support passageways and rooms where mining is being done (4) : a device for packing the space between the wall of an oil well and the pipe or between two strings of pipe in a well (5) : a workman who seals cracks and openings (as in a ship compartment) by packing with paper, canvas, or other caulking materials **2** : one that transports goods or equipment: as **a** : ¹BEARER 2a ⟨with eight native guides and ~*s* . . . our men began the march —Clifford Gessler⟩ **b** : one whose business is conveying goods on pack animals ⟨knowed more about pack mules than ary ~ in his outfit —Ross Santee⟩; *specif* : a peddler using horses or mules to carry his stock **c** *Austral* : a pack animal **3 a** : one that forms into a compact unit; *specif* : an attachment to a grain binder that forms the grain into sheaves before tying **b** : one that tamps; *esp* : an implement for firming or compacting a plowed and pulverized seedbed

**packer hide** *n* : a hide usu. of superior quality removed by skilled workmen at a recognized packinghouse in the U. S. or Canada where quantities of hides are uniformly cured and graded — compare COUNTRY HIDE

**packers' can** *n* : a tin-plated metal can used as a hermetic container for processed foods

**pack·ery** \ˈpak(ə)rē\ *n* -ES : PACKINGHOUSE

**¹pack·et** \ˈpakət, *usu* -əd.+V\ *n* -s *often attrib* [MF *pacquet*, fr. *pacquer* to pack (fr. *pakke* pack, fr. MD *pak*) + -*et* — more at PACK] **1 a** : a number of letters dispatched at one time ⟨the ~*s* kept coming from England, each sheet written to the rim —Virginia Woolf⟩ **b** : a small group or collection ⟨~ of rumors⟩ ⟨watched little ~*s* of twelve, fifteen, or eighteen tanks approach their positions —Russell Hill⟩ **c** : a small cluster or mass ⟨jumbled marl ~*s*, clay balls . . . and pebbles of Alpine origin —*Jour. of Geol.*⟩ ⟨a warm ~ of air rises quickly —*Meteorological Abstracts*⟩ **d** : a somewhat cubical cluster of organisms formed as a result of cell division in three planes **2** : a passenger boat carrying mail and cargo on a regular schedule; *specif* : PACKET BOAT **3 a** : a small bundle or parcel ⟨a vacuum bottle of coffee and a ~ of sandwiches —B.A.Williams⟩ ⟨immobility of the patient, film ~ and X-ray apparatus —Matthew Lozier⟩; *specif* : ¹PACK 1c(1) ⟨~ of cards⟩ **b** (1) : a small thin package (as an envelope or a flat bag) ⟨seed ~⟩ ⟨~*s*, each of which holds the right amount of powder to make a quart of reconstituted skim milk —*Marketing*⟩ (2) *Brit* : PAY ENVELOPE ⟨there wasn't one man in ten took his ~ home —John Morrison⟩ — usu. used with *pay* or *wage* ⟨full employment and full pay ~*s* —Sam Pollock⟩ ⟨counting of pounds, shillings, and pennies for a weekly wage ~ —H.O. Brayer⟩ **c** (1) *Brit* : SALARY, WAGE — usu. used with *pay* or *wage* ⟨the average Irishman is better off, in terms of what his wage ~ will buy —Kevin Devlin⟩ (2) : a considerable amount or number ⟨has faced a ~ of trouble since the end of the war —Margaret Stewart⟩ ⟨lost a ~ of votes up and down the country —Mollie Panter-Downes⟩ (3) : a sizable sum of money ⟨costing a ~, but worth it —Clemence Dane⟩ **d** : something that resembles a packet ⟨comes to us in verbal ~*s* —George Eiten⟩ **4** *slang Brit* : severe mental or physical distress; *esp* : the result of illness or of a beating

**²packet** \"\ *vt* -ED/-ING/-S : to make into or put up in a packet ⟨a ~*ed* roll mix —*Packet Foods*⟩

**packet boat** *also* **packet ship** *n* **1** : a boat (as orig. a fast sailing ship) chartered by a government to carry mail and dispatches ⟨letters . . . conveyed by government *packet boats* or by ordinary sailing ship —Samuel Graveson⟩ **2 a** : a river or coastal steamer usu. of shallow draft carrying mail, passengers, and cargo on a regular run ⟨took passage for Boston on the midweek *packet boat* —Kenneth Roberts⟩ **b** : a canalboat designed to carry passengers

**packfong** *var of* PAKTONG

**packhorse** \ˈ≈,≈\ *n* **1** : a horse used to carry loads (as of freight) on a packsaddle or in panniers on the back as distinguished from one used for riding or draft **2** *obs* : one that labors like a beast of burden : DRUDGE ⟨I was a ~ in his great affairs —Shak.⟩

**packhouse** \ˈ≈,≈\ *n* **1 a** : WAREHOUSE **b** : a building in which flue-cured tobacco is stored between the end of curing and its preparation for marketing **2** : an establishment for packing produce ⟨~ for processing citrus fruit⟩

**pack ice** *n* : sea ice formed into a chaotic mass by the crushing together of pans, floes, and brash

**pack·ing** \ˈpakiŋ, -kēŋ\ *n* -s [ME *pakking*, fr. gerund of *pakken* to pack — more at PACK] **1 a** : the act or process of preparing goods for shipment or storage ⟨planned the trip and had the car serviced but left the ~ to his wife⟩ ⟨~ . . . begins when these slabs of curd can be sliced into blocks —L.L. Van Slyke & W.V.Price⟩; *specif* : the wholesale processing of food for market ⟨the first American to give his whole time to the business of ~ —*Story of Meat*⟩ **b** : a method of inserting into a shipping container with appropriate protective covering, cushioning, or bracing ⟨typical compression ~: twelve one-quart bottles . . . each wrapped in cushioning material and separated by dividers within the shipping box —*Export Packing*⟩ **c** : the act or process of transporting or being transported on the backs of men or animals ⟨the camp is inaccessible by road and ~ is the only way to bring in supplies⟩ **d** : the therapeutic application of a pack ⟨hemorrhage . . . could not be controlled by suture or ~ —*Jour. Amer. Med. Assoc.*⟩ **e** : an act or instance of assembling in a compact group or mass ⟨~ of runners in a race⟩ **2 a** : a covering, stuffing, or holding apparatus used to protect, cushion, or brace goods packed for shipment or storage ⟨excelsior, paper wadding, partitions, chipboard boxes or other types of suitable interior ~ —*Export Packing*⟩ **b** (1) : a thin layer or ring of elastic material (as paper, rubber, asbestos, copper) inserted between the surfaces of a flange joint to make it impervious to leakage — compare GASKET (2) : the material in a stuffing box which prevents leakage (3) : a flexible ring surrounding a piston to maintain a tight fit (as inside a cylinder) (4) : material (as felt, wool, or rope) placed in the sawway of a circular saw to prevent vibration — compare HYDRAULIC PACKING, STEAM PACKING (5) : CAULKING **c** : a masonry filling (as mortar containing small stones) **d** : the material used beneath the drawsheet of a printing press **e** (1) : longitudinal timbers between the hull of a ship and the sliding ways of a launching cradle (2) : a liner between the frame and a raised strake of plating on a ship to make it watertight **f** : the arrangement of several structural members (as I bars or struts) on a single pin forming a truss joint **g** : the filling of a fractionating column consisting usu. of loose pieces of solid material (as glass beads or Raschig rings)

**packing box** *or* **packing case** *n* **1** : a shipping container; *esp* : a wooden crate for packaged or bulk goods **2** : STUFFING BOX

**packing fraction** *n* : a measure of the loss or gain of total mass in a group of nucleons when they are brought together to form an atomic nucleus : the ratio multiplied by 10,000 of the mass defect to the mass number

**packing gland** *n* : ²GLAND 1

**packinghouse** \ˈ≈≈,≈\ *or* **packing plant** *n* **1** : an establishment for the slaughtering, processing, and packing of livestock into meat, meat products, and by-products (as hides, soap, glue) **2** : an establishment for the processing and packing of foodstuffs ⟨an apple ~ —A.W.McKay & M.A.Abrahamsen⟩

**pack·ing·less** \ˈpakiŋləs\ *adj* : PACKLESS ⟨~ pump⟩

**packing nut** *n* : STUFFING NUT

**packing press** *or* **packing screw** *n* : a press for compressing or packing a substance into a smaller compass

**packing radius** *n* : half the distance of closest approach of atoms or ions in a crystal

**packing ring** *n* : PISTON RING

**pack·less** \ˈpakləs\ *adj* : using or requiring no packing ⟨~ valve⟩

**pack·man** \ˈpakmən\ *n, pl* **packmen** : PEDDLER ⟨on hot days a wandering ~ would . . . cool his dusty feet in the burn —Lavinia Derwent⟩

**packmaster** \ˈ≈,≈≈\ *n* : an officer in charge of a packtrain

**pack rat** *n* **1** : WOOD RAT; *esp* : a large bushy-tailed rodent (*Neotoma cinerea*) of the Rocky Mountain area having well-developed cheek pouches in which it carries food and the miscellaneous objects it has a tendency to hoard ⟨metal buttons and buckles . . . stored nearby by the *pack rats* —J.H. Cook⟩ — called also *trade rat* **2** : one that resembles a pack rat ⟨was a *pack rat* and saved everything he got his hands on —Charles Willard⟩

**pack road** *n* : a trail suitable for pack animals

**packs** *pl of* PACK, *pres 3d sing of* PACK

**packsack** \ˈ≈,≈\ *n* : a canvas or leather carrying case held on the back by shoulder straps and used to carry gear when traveling on foot

**packsaddle** \ˈ≈,≈≈\ *n* [ME *pakke sadil*, fr. *pakke*, *pak* pack + *sadil*, *sadle* saddle — more at PACK, SADDLE] : any of various saddles (as one with a high frame or a large mat-covered pad stuffed with hay or wool) designed to support loads on the backs of pack animals

**packstaff** \ˈ≈,≈\ *n, pl* **packstaves** *archaic* : a staff for supporting a peddler's pack : PIKESTAFF

packsack with tumpline

**packthread** \ˈ≈,≈\ *n* [ME *pakthrede*, fr. *pak* pack + *threde* thread — more at THREAD] : strong thread or small twine used for sewing or tying packs or parcels

**packtrain** \ˈ≈,≈\ *n* : a string of animals for transporting supplies and equipment ⟨a resting place for mule skinners guiding ~*s* across the twisting mountain trails to San Francisco —Hal Nielson⟩

**pack trip** *n* : a trip by horseback requiring one or more nights to be spent on the trail

**packwax** *var of* PAXWAX

**packway** \ˈ≈,≈\ *n, Brit* : PACK ROAD

**¹pa·co** \ˈpä(,)kō\ *n* -s [Sp, fr. Quechua] : ALPACA

**²paco** \"\ *n* -s [Sp, fr. Quechua, bay, reddish, prob. fr. *paco* alpaca] : an earthy looking ore consisting of a brown iron oxide with minute particles of native silver

**pa·cou·ry** \pəˈkürē\ *also* **pa·cou·ry·uva** \≈,≈rēˈyüvə\ *n, pl* **pacouries** *also* **pacouryuvas** [*pacoury* fr. Galibi; *pacouryuva* fr. Galibi *pacoury* + Tupi *ïuva*, *üba* tree] : BACURY

**pact** \ˈpakt\ *n* -s [ME, fr. MF, fr. L *pactum*, fr. neut. of *pactus*, past part. of *pacisci* to agree, contract; akin to OE *fōn* to take, seize, OHG & Goth *fāhan*, ON *fā* to take, seize, L *pangere* to fasten, Gk *pēgnynai* to fix, fasten together, Skt *pāśa* bond] **1** : ⁵COMPACT ⟨an unvoiced ~ between us to read him with . . . skepticism —H.V.Gregory⟩ ⟨the ~ also grants the broadcasting company exclusive rights —*Wall Street Jour.*⟩; *specif* : an international treaty ⟨~*s* made by mutual consent between states are the foundation of the law of nations —J.H.Hallowell⟩ **2** : PACTUM

**¹pac·tion** \ˈpakshən\ *n* -s [MF, fr. L *paction-*, *pactio*, fr. *pactus* (past part. of *pacisci* to agree, contract) + -*ion-*, -*io* -ion] **1** *chiefly Scot* : AGREEMENT, COMPACT, BARGAIN ⟨made ~ tween them twa —*Ballad Book*⟩ **2** : a short-term international convention terminating with the execution of a single act or performance — **pac·tion·al** \-shənᵊl, -shnəl\ *adj*

**²paction** \"\ *vi* -ED/-ING/-S *Scot* : to make a paction

**pactional rent** *n, Scots law* : penal rent or liquidated damages stipulated to be paid by a tenant for any breach of the conditions of a lease

**pac·to·li·an** \(ˈ)pak¦tōlēən\ *adj, usu cap* [*Pactolus*, river in Lydia, Asia Minor + E -*ian*] : of or relating to the Pactolus river or its gold-bearing sands : GOLDEN

**pac·tum** \ˈpäk,tům\ *also* **pac·tio** \-ktē,ō\ *n, pl* **pac·ta** \-ktə\ *also* **pac·ti·o·nes** \,päktēˈō,nās\ [L] *Roman law* : an informal agreement between two or more persons containing one or more promises and usu. legally unenforceable even when supported by a sufficient consideration except for certain pacta declared enforceable by praetorian edicts and imperial constitutions if arising out of a lawful cause or inducement

**pactum de con·sti·tu·en·da do·te** \-dākən,stid·əˈwendəˈdōtā\ *n* [LL] *Roman law* : an informal agreement to give a dowry

**pactum de con·sti·tu·to** \-,känstəˈtüd·(,)ō\ *n* [LL, pact of settlement] *Roman law* : a pactum vestitum whereby one promises to pay another's debt on a future day or to give security in consideration of the creditor's giving the debtor additional time

**pactum do·na·ti·o·nis** \-dō,näd·ēˈōnəs\ *n* [LL, donation pact] *Roman law* : a pactum legitimum without legal consideration to make a gratuitous donation enforceable against the donor and his heirs in favor of the prospective donee and his heirs

**pactum il·lic·i·tum** \-əˈlisə,tům\ *n, pl* **pacta illici·ta** \-səd·ə\ [L] *civil law* : an unlawful agreement or one contrary to public policy

**pactum le·git·i·mum** \-ləˈgid·ə,mům\ *n, pl* **pacta legiti·ma** \-,mə\ [L, lawful pact] *Roman law* : a pactum vestitum made enforceable by an imperial constitution

**pactum prae·to·ri·um** \-prīˈtōrē,ům\ *n, pl* **pacta praeto·ria** \-ēə\ [L, praetorian pact] *Roman law* : a pactum vestitum made enforceable by praetorian edict

**pactum ves·ti·tum** \-veˈstē,tům\ *n, pl* **pacta vesti·ta** \-ēd·ə\ [L, clothed pact] *Roman law* : an informal agreement made legally enforceable by an official act

**¹pad** \ˈpad, ˈpaa(ə)d\ *n* -s [origin unknown] **1 a** : a flat or shaped firm usu. resilient article that is usu. not very thick and that consists typically of dense or closely packed material (as rubber, felt, hair) often enclosed in a casing (as of cloth) and that is used like a mat or cushion to ease contact between two surfaces (as in preventing or lessening friction or pressure or jarring) or for personal comfort (as in sitting or reclining) or protection (as against the impact of blows) or that is used to fill out or expand or emphasize natural outlines or contours (as of the shoulders, hips) or to apparently increase natural size or height: as (1) : a piece of soft often stuffed material like a cushion placed on the back of an animal as a saddle or so as to prevent the animal's back from becoming chafed; *esp* : SADDLE BLANKET (2) : a piece of rubber or cloth shaped to fit a part of the body (as the shoulder) and used to improve the lines of the dressed figure (3) : a protective guard worn in some sports (as ice hockey) to shield parts of the body (as the knees or shins) against impact (4) : a protective cap for the knee of a horse (5) : a usu. square or rectangular piece of often folded typically absorbent material (as gauze) fixed in place over some part of the body as a dressing or other protective covering (6) : a piece of soft material fixed in place (as on the toes) so as to relieve pressure and prevent chafing (7) : a small firm cushion (as of sponge) used for sitting on (8) : a piece of material (as fiberboard) used to separate and protect articles packed for shipment or used as an insert at the top or bottom of a box to protect the contents (9) : a length of thick material often made up of layers used for covering a table top before laying the tablecloth and designed to protect the table top from heat and from marring or scratching (10) : a length of thick material laid over a mattress and under bed sheets to keep the mattress clean and to promote the comfort of one lying on the mattress (11) : a rectangular article resembling a very thin mattress that is laid out (as on a cot or couch) to promote the comfort of one lying on it **b** : a piece of moisture-retaining material typically set in a lidded metal box and saturated with ink for inking the surface of a rubber stamp **c** : a layer of material (as of crushed rock) designed esp. to serve as a cushioning or insulating medium **d** : a small leather cushion that lines the valves of wind instruments (as clarinets) and functions like a washer to prevent an unwanted escape of air **e** : a soft cushiony mass of something ⟨the hair falls in heavy ~*s* around the head —G.Monteil⟩ ⟨a gust of wind blew a snow ~ from the branches overhead —Morley Callaghan⟩ **2** : PALLET 2b **3** : BUNDLE, BUNCH; *esp* : a bundle of cigar wrapper leaves or of binder prepared to be sent to the cigar-making machines **4 a** (1) : the foot of an animal (as a fox, wolf, hare) ⟨discovered the mark of a fox's ~ in the mud —Adrian Bell⟩ (2) : one of the footprints made by an animal (3) : PULVILLUS **b** : a part of the body or of an appendage that resembles or is suggestive of a cushion : a thick fleshy resilient part: as (1) : the sole of the foot or underside of the toes of an animal (as a camel, dog) that is typically thickened so as to form a cushion (2) : the underside of the extremities of the fingers; *esp* : the ball of the thumb ⟨testing for smoothness with the ~ of her thumb —Elizabeth Bowen⟩ **5** : a floating leaf of a water plant (as a water lily) **6 a** : PADDING **b** : the dye liquor or other liquid used in padding fabrics

pad 1b

7 : a number of sheets of paper (as for writing or drawing) that are grouped together in a stack of varying thickness, that are fastened at one end (as by cementing the extreme edge of each sheet to a cloth strip) so that each sheet may be separately removed, and that are usu. backed by a paperboard stiffener placed below the last sheet : TABLET — called also *block* **8 a :** a piece of timber fitted on a beam of a ship to fill out the curve of a deck **b :** a flat plate fixed (as by welding) to a part of the structure of a ship so as to provide an attachment point (as for rigging) or so as to provide a seat to which another part may be fixed **9 a :** a local superimposed deposition of weld metal **b :** a thin adventitious projection that may appear on a casting or forging and that is usu. ground or chipped off **10 :** a nonadjustable attenuator **11 a :** a small area or expanse ⟨in a ~ of green lawn between two heathery steeps —John Buchan⟩ **b** (1) : a section of an airstrip or airway used for warming up the motors of a plane before takeoff (2) : the section of an airstrip or airway where a plane leaves the ground on takeoff or first touches the ground on landing (3) : an area in an airfield or heliport used as the takeoff or landing point of a helicopter **c :** LAUNCHING PAD **12** *slang* **a** (1) : APARTMENT (2) : ROOM (3) : BED **b :** HOVEL, JOINT, DEN **13** *slang* **:** money paid (as to racketeers) for immunity from molestation

²**pad** \"\ *vt* **padded; padded; padding; pads 1 a :** to line or cover or stuff or otherwise equip with or as if with material that serves to cushion or protect or fill out or heighten : furnish with a pad or padding ⟨*padded* the box with soft cloth⟩ ⟨his tone was fairly *padded* with caution —Owen Wister⟩ ⟨has a well-*padded* figure⟩ **b :** MUTE, MUFFLE ⟨there was an explosion of muffled coughing *padded* with the whirring of starters —W.W.Haines⟩ ⟨using the flush of water to ~ the sound of movement —Wallace Markfield⟩ **2 a** (1) : to expand or lengthen (as a book, magazine article, speech) by the insertion of additional material that is usu. essentially superfluous and often extraneous to the point of being irrelevant and that is usu. used merely to artificially bring the thing so expanded up to some desired size or length or that is used for some other usu. equivocal purpose (as to add impressiveness, suggest intellectual depth, mask an otherwise distasteful theme) : INFLATE — often used with *out* ⟨a collection of tourist's notes of the most obvious kind, *padded* out with generalizations that don't bear examining —Honor Tracy⟩ (2) : to add purely invented entries to (as an expense account) or fictitious often fraudulent details to (as a request for an allocation of money) ⟨*padded* expense accounts and postage and printing allowances —D.D.McKean⟩ (3) : to artificially or fraudulently increase the extent of (as a roster) with real or fictitious names ⟨accused of *padding* his office payroll⟩ ⟨the list of members . . . was heavily *padded* by the inclusion of persons without their knowledge and consent —*Observer*⟩ (4) : to artificially or fraudulently increase the numbers of (as an organization) with real or fictitious individuals ⟨*padded* the staff with a lot of unnecessary people⟩ (5) : to put fraudulent votes into (as a ballot box) **b :** to state as greater than the actual fact : OVERSTATE : magnify beyond truth : EXAGGERATE ⟨suspected she *padded* her age to work in a cabaret —Jobo Nakamura⟩ **c :** to increase in bulk by the addition of other material ⟨~ a soap⟩ **3 :** to impregnate with a liquid for a special purpose: as **a :** to impregnate (fabric) with dye liquor, mordant, or other liquid by squeezing between rolls **b :** to saturate (leather) with grease **4 :** to fasten (sheets of paper) at one end (as by cementing to a cloth strip) so as to form a pad

³**pad** \"\ *vb* **padded; padded; padding; pads** [perh. fr. MD *paden* to make a path, follow a path, fr. *pad, pat* path] *vt* **1 :** to go along (as a road) on foot ⟨*padding* the streets in search of a job⟩ **2** *dial chiefly Eng* **a :** to tread or trample down by foot travel **b :** to wear (a path) by walking ~ *vi* **1 a :** to go along on foot : get from one place to another by walking : tramp along : TRUDGE ⟨*padding* from one town to the next⟩ **b :** to move along in an easy unhurried way : walk in a leisurely nonchalant manner : AMBLE ⟨career men-about-town *padded* over to introduce themselves —J.A.Wechsler⟩ **2 a :** to move along usu. steadily with a soft almost noiseless step marked typically by a faint slapping sound or by a light muffled thud ⟨pilgrims hastening to prayers brushed by me, *padding* on brown bare feet —Abdul Ghafur⟩ ⟨~*s* in her stocking feet to the sofa —Clare B. Luce⟩ ⟨backwards and forwards we *padded* on the soft carpet —John Buchan⟩ ⟨turned and *padded* furtively away —C.G.D.Roberts⟩ ⟨might come *padding* on moccasined feet —J.W.Schaefer⟩ ⟨camels ~ along slowly, with their heads seemingly motionless at the end of their long, undulating necks —Christopher Rand⟩ **b :** to tap softly in such a way as to produce a light muffled sound ⟨he *padded* with his fingers on the tablecloth —Michael McLaverty⟩ — **pad the hoof** *slang chiefly Brit* **:** to travel on foot : tramp or trudge along or off or away

⁴**pad** \"\ *n* -s [MD or MLG *pad, pat* — more at PATH] **1 a** *dial chiefly Brit* (1) : PATH, TRAIL (2) : ROAD, ROUTE **b** *dial Eng* : CUSTOM, HABIT **2 :** a horse that moves along at an easy pace **3** *archaic* **:** ¹FOOTPAD

⁵**pad** \"\ *n* -s [alter. of ¹*ped*] *chiefly dial* **:** BASKET

⁶**pad** \"\ *n* -s [imit.] **:** a soft light muffled or faintly slapping sound ⟨hear only the ~ of a thousand felt soles on the pavement —James Cameron⟩

⁷**pad** \"\ *n* -s [prob. fr. obs. E, padlock, fr. ME] **1 a :** the socket of a brace into which the bit is inserted **b :** a tool handle into which tools of various sizes or kinds may be inserted **2 :** a chock or block to space and hold work for tooling

**pa·dauk** *or* **pa·douk** \pə'dau̇k\ *n* -s [native name in Burma] **1 :** any of several trees of the genus *Pterocarpus* that yield a reddish wood resembling mahogany: as **a :** AFRICAN PADAUK **b :** ANDAMAN PADAUK **c :** CARWOOD **d :** BURMA PADAUK **2 :** the wood of a padauk tree

**pa·daung** \pə'dau̇ŋ\ *n, pl* **padaung** *or* **padaungs** *usu cap* **:** KARENNI

**padcloth** \'=,=\ *n* **:** SADDLECLOTH

**pad·da** \'padə\ *n, cap* [NL, fr. Jav] **:** a genus of birds consisting of the Java sparrow

**padded** *adj* [fr. past part. of ²*pad*] **:** furnished with or as if with a pad or padding ⟨soundless caravans of camels, swaying with their ~ feet across the desert —L.P.Smith⟩ : CUSHIONY ⟨the ~, somber, luxurious hotel we had just left —Christopher Isherwood⟩

**padded soap** *n* **:** FILLED SOAP

¹**pad·der** \'padə(r), 'paad-\ *n* -s [⁴*pad* + *-er*] *archaic* **:** ¹FOOTPAD

²**padder** \"\ *n* -s [²*pad* + *-er*] **1 :** a person or a machine that pads: as **a** (1) : a worker that makes sheets of paper into pads (2) : a worker that places ordered tobacco leaves in boxes or on a conveyor for removal of stems (3) : a worker that sews padding material into garments (as coats) **b :** a dyeing machine consisting of rolls mounted over a trough for padding fabrics **2 :** a radio set circuit element (as a condenser) used to adjust the tuning of a circuit (as on the local oscillator of a superheterodyne receiver)

**paddier** *comparative of* PADDY

**paddies** *pl of* PADDY

**paddiest** *superlative of* PADDY

**padding** *n* -s [fr. gerund of ²*pad*] **:** material with which something is padded : WADDING, STUFFING

**padding stitch** *n* **1 :** a stitch used as a foundation for another stitch **2 :** a diagonal basting stitch for holding padding in place

¹**pad·dle** \'pad°l\ *n* -s [ME *padell*] **1** *dial Eng* **:** SPUD 2 **2 a :** a

paddle 2a

rather short light wooden pole with a broad fairly flat blade at one end or sometimes at both ends that is used for propelling and steering or stopping a canoe or other similar small light craft, that is not designed for use with an oarlock, and that is grasped and dipped vertically or nearly vertically into the water so that the blade can be pushed against and raised from the water or otherwise manipulated so as to propel or steer or stop **b :** something (as the flipper of a seal) used for propulsion through the water and suggestive of a paddle in appearance or function **c :** the arm or blade of a semaphore signal **3 :** an implement suggestive in shape of a paddle: as **a** (1) : a long metal implement used for stirring or mixing something (as molten ore materials in glass manufacture) (2) : a small light flat wooden implement used esp. for working butter **b :** an implement of moderate length used for beating clothes being washed by hand **c :** a flat rather heavy usu. wooden instrument used for administering physical punishment **4 a :** one of the broad boards at the circumference of a paddle wheel or waterwheel **b :** PADDLE WHEEL **5 a :** a small gate in a sluice or lock gate to let water in or out **b :** a sliding panel that regulates the quantity of grain running out of a hopper

²**paddle** \"\ *vb* **paddled; paddled; paddling** \-d(°)liŋ\ **paddles** *vi* **1 a** (1) : to go along the surface of water or through water by or as if by using a paddle ⟨*paddling* down the stream in a canoe⟩ (2) : to swim along easily or gently or with movements suggestive of one using a paddle **b :** to row a boat easily or gently ⟨were in no hurry so they just *paddled* along⟩ **2 :** to go along the surface of water by means of a paddle wheel ⟨watched the showboat *paddling* slowly toward the shore⟩ **3 :** to throw the feet to the side in running ~ *vt* **1 a :** to propel by or as if by a paddle ⟨*paddled* the little boat closer to shore⟩ **b :** to transport in a canoe or other similar light craft by using a paddle ⟨*paddled* us over to the other side of the river⟩ **2 a :** to beat or stir with a paddle or paddle wheel (as in washing, dyeing, puddling) **b :** to punish by or as if by beating with a paddle : THRASH, THWACK, SPANK ⟨her mother *paddled* her for not keeping quiet⟩ **3 :** to treat (hides or skins being processed for leather) in a vat equipped with a paddle wheel — **paddle one's own canoe :** to get along by one's own efforts ⟨told him that he could expect no more help and would have to *paddle his own canoe*⟩

³**paddle** \"\ *n* -s [²*paddle*] **:** the action of paddling ⟨returned to shore after a brief ~ on the lake⟩

⁴**paddle** \"\ *vb* **paddled; paddled; paddling; paddles** [origin unknown] *vi* **1 :** to move about or dabble (as in shallow water) making light splashes (as with the hands or feet) : wade about or play about splashing lightly and dabbling ⟨watched the children gleefully *paddling* in the rain puddles⟩ ⟨sat on the edge of the boat and *paddled* in the water with her feet⟩ **2** *archaic* **:** to keep touching something lightly with the fingers : toy with or pat or stroke something in an apparently idle or purposeless way ⟨let her keep *paddling* on with his hand —W.M.Thackeray⟩ **3 :** to walk with short often hesitant or somewhat unsteady steps like those of a child : TODDLE ⟨his little daughter *paddled* up to him and kissed him⟩ **4 :** to throw the feet to the side in running; *specif* **:** DISH 2 ~ *vt, dial Eng* **:** to tread upon : TRAMPLE

⁵**paddle** \"\ *n* -s [origin unknown] **:** LUMPFISH

**paddle ball** *n* **:** a game resembling squash racquets played in a four-wall handball court using a tennis ball and a wooden paddle

**paddle beam** *n* **:** one of two bracket-shaped beams projecting one before and one abaft the paddle wheel and helping to support the paddle box of a ship

**paddleboard** \'=,=\ *n* **:** a long narrow extremely buoyant board with rounded bow and pointed stern used esp. for surf-riding or propelled with arm strokes and used in rescuing swimmers

**paddle box** *n* **:** a structure enclosing the upper part of a paddle wheel of a ship

**paddlefish** \'=,=\ *n* **:** either of two freshwater relict fishes that are the only surviving members of the family Polyodontidae: **a :** an American fish (*Polyodon spathula*) found in the Mississippi river and its tributaries, having a long spatula-shaped snout, smooth skin, heterocercal tail, and long gill rakers, attaining a length of four feet or more, and having flesh which though coarse is used as food and roe that is made into caviar — called also *duckbill* **b :** a closely related Chinese fish (*Psephurus gladius*) having a narrower snout

**paddlefoot** \'=,=\ *n, pl* **paddlefeet 1** *slang* **:** INFANTRYMAN **2** *slang* **:** an air force personnel member that lacks distinctive rating and that is usu. occupied with ground duties

**pad·dler** \'pad(°)lə(r)\ *n* -s [²*paddle* + *-er*] **1 :** one that paddles **2 :** PADDLE STEAMER

**paddle shaft** *n* **:** a shaft carrying a paddle wheel

**paddle steamer** *n* **:** a steamer propelled by a paddle wheel

**paddle tennis** *n* **:** a game resembling tennis and played with a wooden paddle and sponge rubber ball over a low net on a court whose dimensions are one half those of a lawn tennis court

**paddle tumbler** *n* **:** a revolving drum fitted inside with paddles or round pins and used to keep a liquid in motion in tanning, dyeing, and other similar processes

**paddle–turn** \'=,=\ *n* **:** a ballroom step used in turning

**paddle wheel** *n* **1 :** a wheel used to propel a steamship and orig. having long paddles arranged about a hub or shaft end but later having floats or boards on its circumference and revolving in a vertical plane parallel to the ship's length **2 :** a wheel with paddles that is used in a vat and that revolves and keeps hides or skins in motion while they are soaking in the course of being processed for leather

**paddle–wheeler** \'=,==\ *n* **:** PADDLE STEAMER

**paddlewood** \'=,=\ *n* **:** the tough elastic wood of a tropical So. American tree (*Aspidosperma excelsa*) from whose fluted trunk paddles and rollers are made

¹**pad·dock** \'padək, -dēk\ *also* **pad·dow** \-də\ *n* -s [ME *paddok*, fr. *pad, pade* toad + *-ok* -ock; akin to ON *padda* toad, MLG *padde, pedde* toad, and perh. to OE *pæth* path — more at PATH] **1** *chiefly dial* **:** FROG **2** *chiefly dial* **:** TOAD

²**paddock** \"\ *n* -s [alter. of *parrock*] **1 a** *chiefly Brit* **:** a small area (as a field) often enclosed and typically adjoining or near a building (as a house or stable) and often used for a pasture **b** *Austral* **:** an often extensive area (as of grassland) usu. fenced in and often used as a pasture **2 a :** a turfed enclosure where horses are kept (as on a stud farm) **b :** an enclosure where racehorses are saddled and paraded before a race **3 :** a space or platform near the mouth of a shaft or excavation for temporary storage of ore or wash dirt

³**paddock** \"\ *vt* -ED/-ING/-S **1 a :** to put (an animal) into an enclosed area (as a field) **b :** to shut up in or as if in an enclosed area **2 :** to store (as ore) temporarily in a space or on a platform near the mouth of a mining shaft or excavation

**pad·dock·ride** *or* **pad·dock·rod** \'=,=\ *n* [¹*paddock* + *ride, rod*, alter. of E dial. *rud* toad spawn] *dial Brit* **:** frog or toad spawn

**paddock–stool** \'=,=\ *n, chiefly Scot* **:** TOADSTOOL

¹**pad·dy** *also* **padi** \'padē, -di\ *n, pl* **paddies** *also* **padis** [Malay *padi*] **1** *or* **paddy rice :** RICE; *esp* **:** threshed unmilled rice **2** *or* **paddy field :** a heavily irrigated or lightly flooded piece of land (as lowland) in which rice is grown : a wet field used for growing rice — called also *rice paddy*

²**paddy** \"\ *also* **paddybird** \'=,=\ *n* -ES **1 :** JAVA SPARROW **2 :** one of several small herons of the subcontinent of India **3 :** SHEATHBILL **4** [³*paddy*] **:** RUDDY DUCK

³**paddy** \"\ *n* -ES [fr. *Paddy*, common nickname among the Irish for the name *Patrick*] **1** *usu cap, slang* **:** IRISHMAN **2** *slang* **:** POLICEMAN, COP

⁴**paddy** \"\ *adj, usu* -ER/-EST [¹*pad* + *-y* (adj. suffix)] **:** resembling a pad (as in thickness, firm resiliency)

⁵**paddy** \"\ *n* -ES [¹*pad* + *-y* (dim. suffix)] **:** HAND; *esp* **:** a baby's or child's hand

**paddy blast** *n* **:** blast (sense 4b) of the rice plant

**pad dyeing** *n* **:** a process of dyeing fabrics by passing the fabrics between rollers that apply the dyestuff

**paddy's hurricane** *n, usu cap P* [³*paddy*] **:** a dead calm on the sea

**paddy's lucerne** *or* **paddy lucerne** *n* [³*paddy*] *Austral* **:** QUEENSLAND HEMP

**paddy wagon** *n* [prob. fr. ³*paddy*] **:** PATROL WAGON

¹**paddywhack** \'=,=\ *n* [³*paddy* + *whack*] **1** *often cap, slang* **:** IRISHMAN **2** *or* **paddy** *dial chiefly Eng* **:** a state of fuming rage : FURY, TEMPER ⟨don't be silly and get in a *paddy* about nothing —Compton Mackenzie⟩ **3 :** THRASHING, SPANKING, PADDLING **4 :** RUDDY DUCK

²**paddywhack** \"\ *vt* **:** THRASH, SPANK, PADDLE

**pad·e·melon** *also* **pad·dy·melon** \'padē,melən\ *n, pl* **pademelon** *also* **paddymelon** *or* **pademelons** [alter. (influence of *melon*) of earlier *paddymalla*, fr. native name in Australia] **:** any of several small usu. more or less reddish or chestnut brown wallabies with extensive distribution in Australia and New Guinea

**pad eye** *n* [¹*pad*] **:** a small usu. round opening that is in an edgewise projection of a plate welded or otherwise fixed to a part of a ship's structure and that is used like an eyebolt as a catch (as for hooks) or other point of attachment (as for rigging); *also* **:** a ring or similar projection forming part of and extending edgewise from a plate on a ship's structure and used in the same way

pad eyes

**padfoot** \'=,=\ *n, pl* **padfeet** [⁴*pad* + *foot*] **1** *dial Eng* **:** GOBLIN — compare BARGHEST, BOOGEYMAN **2** *dial Eng* **:** ¹FOOTPAD

**pad foot** *r* [¹*pad*] **:** CLUB FOOT

**padge** \'paj\ *also* **padge owl** *n* -s [alter. of *madge*] **:** BARN OWL

**pad hook** *n* **:** a fishhook having a flattened and enlarged shank instead of an eye

**pa·di·na** \pə'dīnə\ *n, cap* [NL] **:** a genus of fan-shaped somewhat leathery brown algae (family Dictyotaceae) that are found in warm seas

**pa·di·shah** \'pädə,shä\ *n* -s [Per *pādshāh*, fr. MPer *pātakhshah*, fr. OPer *pati* + *xshay-* to rule; akin to Av *xshayeti* he rules — more at CHECK] **1 :** a chief ruler : SOVEREIGN; *esp* **:** the shah of Iran **2 :** a powerful important personage : MOGUL ⟨a conference of movie ~*s*⟩

¹**pad·lock** \'pad,läk\ *n* [ME *padlok*, prob. fr. *pad* padlock + *lok* lock — more at LOCK] **:** a removable lock with a hinged or pivoted or sometimes sliding shackle that can be opened so as to pass through an eye (as of a staple, ring, link) and then closed so that the entire device hangs suspended and holds something (as a hasp) securely fastened

padlock

²**padlock** \"\ *vt* **1 :** to lock with or as if with a padlock : secure or fasten or keep closed or check with or as if with a padlock ⟨saw him ~ the rickety door behind us —Francis Stuart⟩ ⟨~*ed* the gate⟩ ⟨~*ing* their efforts to express themselves freely⟩ **2 :** to officially bar (as by an injunction, administrative order) entrance into or use of (as a hotel, theater, factory) as a means of enforcing a statute or of abating a nuisance ⟨~*ing* conspicuous restaurants and resorts where the laws have been contemptuously defied —*Rev. of Reviews*⟩

³**padlock** \"\ *n* [²*padlock*] **:** an official closing by padlocking ⟨the injunction is then carried through to final order and a ~ for one year is attempted —*U.S. Daily*⟩

**pad·nag** \'pad,nag\ *n* [⁴*pad* + *nag*] **:** ⁴PAD 2

**padouk** *var of* **padauk**

**pa·dre** \'pä(,)drā, 'pa̤(-\ *n* -s [Sp or It or Pg, fr. LL *pater* bishop, abbot, fr. L, father — more at FATHER] **1 a :** a Christian clergyman; *esp* **:** PRIEST **b :** a Christian monk usu. ordained to the priesthood — often used as a title or as a mode of address **2 :** a military chaplain

**pad roll** *n* **:** BLANKET ROLL 2

**pa·dro·ne** \pə'drōnā\ *n, pl* **padrones** \-āz\ *also* **padro·ni** \-nē\ [It, fr. L *patronus* — more at PATRON] **1 a :** PATRON, MASTER **b :** BOSS, CHIEF ⟨racketeering and shakedowns by the local ~*s* of the waterfront —*New Republic*⟩ **c :** INNKEEPER, LANDLORD **2 :** one that secures employment often under contract for immigrant usu. unskilled workers esp. of Italian extraction and that also acts as banker and commissary for them with the overall purpose of profit by exploitation

**pad room** *n* [so called fr. the fact that performing horses used to be padded and rigged in the same room] **:** a dressing room for circus performers

**pads** *pl of* PAD, *pres 3d sing of* PAD

**pad saw** *n* [⁷*pad*] **:** a small compass saw

**padstone** \'=,=\ *n* **:** a stone template fixed in a wall to support the end of a girder or roof truss

**pad·ua** \'pajəwə\ *adj, usu cap* [fr. *Padua*, Italy] **:** of or from the city of Padua, Italy **:** of the kind or style prevalent in Padua : PADUAN

**paduakan** *var of* PEDIWAK

¹**pad·u·an** \'pajəwən\ *adj, usu cap* [*Padua*, Italy + E *-an* (adj. suffix)] **:** of, relating to, or characteristic of the city of Padua, Italy

²**paduan** \"\ *n* -s *cap* [*Padua*, Italy + E *-an* (n. suffix)] **:** a native or inhabitant of Padua

**pad·u·a·soy** \'pajəwə,sȯi\ *n* -s [by folk etymology (influence of *Padua*, city in northeast Italy) fr. earlier *poudesoy*, fr. F *pou-de-soie*] **1 :** a rich heavy corded silk fabric for clothing and upholstery **2 :** a garment made of paduasoy

**pa·du·ca** *or* **pa·du·cah** \pə'd(y)ükə\ *n, pl* **paduca** *or* **paducas** *or* **paducah** *or* **paducahs** *usu cap* [F *Padouca*, of Siouan origin; prob. akin to Dakota *pa-hdŏ-ka* to pierce, bore] **:** an Amerind people of the southern Great Plains: as **a :** COMANCHE **b :** APACHE

**pa·dus** \'pādəs\ *n, cap* [NL, fr. Gk *pados*, a tree; prob. akin to Gk *pēdos*, a tree, *pidyein* to gush forth — more at FAT] *in some classifications* **:** a genus of shrubs and trees (family Rosaceae) of the north temperate zone that are now usu. included in the genus *Prunus* from which they are distinguished chiefly by racemose flowers

¹**pae·an** *also* **pe·an** \'pēən\ *n* -s [L *paean*, hymn of thanksgiving esp. addressed to Apollo, fr. Gk *paian, paiōn*, fr. *Paian, Paiōn*, epithet by which Apollo was invoked in the hymn] **1 :** a surging joyously exultant song or hymn (as of praise, tribute, thanksgiving, triumph) ⟨unite their voices in a great ~ to liberty —Edward Sackville-West & Desmond Shawe-Taylor⟩ **2 :** an exultant outburst ⟨a great cheer . . . rose in a wild ~ of frenzy —Donn Byrne⟩ **3 :** PAEON

²**paean** \"\ -ED/-ING/-S **:** to sing or otherwise express in or as if in a paean ⟨~*ed* the virtues of the poor and lowly —S.H. Adams⟩

**paed-** *or* **paedo-** *or* **ped-** *or* **pedo-** *also* **paid-** *or* **paido-** *comb form* [Gk *paid-, paido-*, fr. *paid-, pais* child, boy — more at FEW] **:** child ⟨*paedo*morphism⟩ ⟨*paedo*baptism⟩ ⟨*pedo*philia⟩ : offspring ⟨*paedo*genesis⟩

**paedagogy** *var of* PEDAGOGY

**paederasty** *var of* PEDERASTY

**paediatric** *var of* PEDIATRIC

**paedicatio** *var of* PEDICATIO

**paedobaptism** *var of* PEDOBAPTISM

**pae·dog·a·mous** \pē'dägəməs\ *adj* [*paed-* + *-gamous*] **:** of, relating to, or reproducing by paedogamy

**pae·dog·a·my** *also* **pe·dog·a·my** \-mē\ *n* -ES [ISV *paed-* + *-gamy*] **:** mutual fertilization of gametes ultimately derived from the same parent cell or gametangium

**pae·do·genesis** *also* **pe·do·genesis** \,pēdō+\ *n* [NL, fr. *paed-* + *genesis*] **:** reproduction by young or by larval animals : NEOTENY — compare PROGENESIS

**pae·do·ge·net·ic** \,==jə̇,ned·ik\ *or* **pae·do·gen·ic** \,==jenik\ *adj* [*paedogenesis* + *-etic* or *-ic*] **:** of, relating to, or characterized by paedogenesis

**pae·do·mor·phic** *also* **pedomorphic** \,==mȯrfik\ *adj* [*paedomorphosis, pedomorphosis* + E *-ic*] **1 :** of, relating to, or involving paedomorphosis or paedomorphism ⟨~ evolution⟩ **2** [*paed-* + *-morphic*] **:** resembling a child or something characteristic of a child ⟨a ~ outlook⟩

**pae·do·mor·phism** *or* **pe·do·mor·phism** \,==,fizəm\ *n* -s [*paed-* + *-morphism*] **1 :** retention in the adult of infantile or juvenile characters **2 :** PAEDOMORPHOSIS

**pae·do·mor·pho·sis** *also* **pe·do·mor·pho·sis** \,==mȯrfəsə̇s *sometimes* -,mȯr'fōs-\ *n, pl* **paedomorpho·ses** *also* **pedo·morpho·ses** \-,sēz\ [NL, fr. *paed-* + *-morphosis*] **:** phylogenetic change involving retention of juvenile characters by adult individuals and typically accompanied by increased capacity for further change and indicative of a potential for further evolution — compare FETALIZATION, GERONTOMORPHOSIS

**pae·do·mor·phy** \'==,mȯrfē\ *n* -ES [*paed-* + *-morphy*] **:** PAEDOMORPHISM

**paedophilia** *var of* PEDOPHILIA

**pae·do·tribe** \'pēdə,trīb\ *n* -s [Gk *paidotribēs*, fr. *paid-* +

-*tribēs* (fr. *tribein* to rub) — more at THROW] **:** a trainer in gymnastics often represented in ancient Greek art as supervising the exercises of young athletes

**¹pae·lig·ni·an** \pē'lignēən\ *n* -s *cap* [L *Paeligni*, a people of central Italy + E *-ian*] **:** a Sabellian dialect

**²paelignian** \"\ *adj, usu cap* **:** of or relating to Paelignian

**pa·el·la** \pä'elə\ *n* -s [Catal, lit., metal pot, frying pan, fr. MF *paelle*, fr. L *patella* small pan — more at PATELLA] **:** a saffron-flavored stew containing rice, chicken, seafood, and various vegetables

**pae·nu·la** \'pēnyələ\ *n, pl* **paenu·lae** \-,lē, -lī\ *or* **paenulas** [L, fr. Gk *phainolē* cloak] **1 :** a long sleeveless cloak of ancient Rome usu. having a hood and sometimes a front opening **2 :** an early form of chasuble

**paen·ungulata** \(')pēn+\ *n pl, cap* [NL, fr. L *paene* nearly, almost + NL *Ungulata;* so called fr. their position in the evolutionary scale] *in some classifications* **:** a major division of eutherian mammals comprising the extinct orders Pantodonta, Dinocerata, Pyrotheria, and Embrithopoda together with the surviving orders Proboscidea, Hyracoidea, and Sirenia

**¹paen·ungulate** \(')pēn+\ *adj* [NL *Paenungulata*] **:** of or relating to the Paenungulata

**²paenungulate** \"\ *n* -s **:** a mammal of the Paenungulata

**pae·on** \'pēən\ *n* -s [L *paeon*, fr. Gk *paiōn* fr. *paian, paiōn*, paean — more at PAEAN] **1 :** a metrical foot of four syllables with one of the syllables long and the other three short (as in classical prosody) or with one of the syllables stressed and the other three unstressed or lesser in stress (as in English prosody) and with the long or stressed syllable varying in position from first to second or third or fourth place — called also respectively (1) *first paeon* — symbol -◡◡◡ also óooo; (2) *second paeon* — symbol ◡-◡◡ also oóoo; (3) *third paeon* — symbol ◡◡-◡ also ooóo; (4) *fourth paeon* — symbol ◡◡◡- also oooó **2 :** a verse written in paeons

**pae·o·nia** \pē'ōnēə\ *n, cap* [NL, fr. L, peony, fr. Gk *paiōnia*, fr. *Paiōn* Paeon, physician of the gods, its reputed discoverer] **:** a genus of perennial herbs or subshrubs (family Ranunculaceae) that are native chiefly to Europe and Asia and have thickened or tuberous roots, divided leaves, flowers often double in cultivation, and fruit consisting of several many-seeded follicles — see PEONY

**pae·o·ni·a·ce·ae** \,==,'āsē,ē\ [NL, fr. *Paeonia*, type genus + *-aceae*] *syn of* RANUNCULACEAE

**¹pae·on·ic** \(')pē¦änik\ *adj* [LL *paeonicus*, fr. Gk *paiōnikos*, fr. *paiōn* paeon + *-ikos* -ic] **:** of, relating to, or having the meter of a paeon **:** HEMIOLIC

**²paeonic** \"\ *n* -s **:** PAEON

**pae·o·ny** *Brit var of* PEONY

**pae·pae** \'pī,pī\ *n* -s [Marquesan, Tahitian, Hawaiian, Samoan, & Tongan] **1 :** a usu. large stone platform (as of basalt) rising appreciably above ground level and used as the foundation for many native Polynesian houses or other buildings **2 :** a usu. extensive flagged pavement typically used in Polynesia in areas in front of some edifices (as temples)

**pa·ez** \pä'ez\ *n, pl* **paez** *or* **paezes** *usu cap* **1 a :** a Chibchan people of Colombia in the northwestern part of So. America **b :** a member of such people **2 :** the language of the Paez people

**¹pa·gan** \'pāgən\ *n* -s [ME, fr. LL *paganus*, fr. L, civilian, country dweller, fr. *paganus*, adj., of the country, fr. *pagus* country, village, district; akin to L *pangere* to fix, fasten, *pacisci* to agree, contract — more at PACT] **1 :** HEATHEN 1; *esp* **:** a follower of a polytheistic religion (as in ancient Rome) **2 :** one that has little or no religion and that is marked by a frank delight in and uninhibited seeking after sensual pleasures and material goods **:** an unrestrained irreligious hedonist and materialist ⟨is a ~ of the decadence . . . takes the world with exquisite nonchalance and prefers a well-ordered dinner to a dissertation on the immortality of the soul —T.L.Peacock⟩

**²pagan** \"\ *adj* **:** of, relating to, or having the characteristics of pagans **:** HEATHENISH ⟨~ customs⟩ ⟨represents the earthy, ~ acceptance of life in all its sensual vulgarity —R.M.Kain⟩ ⟨the ~ concept of death and oblivion as the natural end of life —Cyril Connolly⟩ — **pa·gan·ly** *adv*

**pagan cattle** *n* **:** half-wild dwarf cattle kept by natives of tropical western Africa

**pa·gan·dom** \'pāgəndəm\ *n* -s **:** the realm of pagans **:** the pagan world **:** HEATHENDOM

**paganic** *adj* [LL *paganicus* of a pagan, fr. *paganus* + L *-icus* -ic] *obs* **:** PAGAN

**pa·gan·ish** \'pāgənish\ *adj* **:** resembling or typical of a pagan **:** rather pagan ⟨a ~ way of life⟩ — **pa·gan·ish·ly** *adv*

**pa·gan·ism** \-,nizəm\ *n* -s [ME *paganysme*, fr. LL *paganismus*, fr. *paganus* pagan + L *-ismus* -ism] **1 a :** pagan beliefs or practices **:** HEATHENISM ⟨its conflict with modern ~ —C.J.C. Bergendoff⟩ ⟨the rites of ~⟩ ⟨powers which they had ascribed to the gods of ~ —K.S.Latourette⟩ **b :** a particular pagan religion ⟨ancient ~s were all polytheistic, with dozens of gods arranged in complex pantheons —John Bright b.1908⟩ **2 :** the quality or state of being a pagan (as in attitude or outlook) ⟨the natural, joyous ~ of the Greeks —Hunter Mead⟩

**pa·gan·i·ty** \pā'ganəd·ē\ *n* -ES [LL *paganitas*, fr. *paganus* + L *-itat-, -itas* -ity] *archaic* **:** PAGANISM 2

**pa·gan·ization** \,pāgənə'zāshən, -,nī'z-\ *n* -s **:** the action of paganizing or condition of being paganized ⟨were shocked by their sudden ~⟩

**pa·gan·ize** \'==,nīz\ *vb* -ED/-ING/-S *see -ize in Explan Notes* [*pagan* + *-ize*] *vt* **:** to make pagan **:** HEATHENIZE ⟨~s everything with which she comes in contact —*Commonweal*⟩ ⟨the new *paganized* way of life —R.A.Hall b.1911⟩ ⟨denounce such *paganizing* of the faith —G.E.Wright⟩ ~ *vi* [F or ML; F *paganiser*, fr. ML *paganizare*, fr. LL to be a pagan, fr. *paganus* + *-izare* -ize] **:** to become pagan or act in a pagan manner ⟨the *paganizing* Gnostics —W.F.Albright⟩ ⟨spent a riotous week *paganizing*⟩ — **pa·gan·iz·er** \-zə(r)\ *n* -s

**pa·gat·pat** \pə'gat,pat\ *n* -s [native name in the Philippines] **:** a tree (*Sonneratia apetala*) growing chiefly in mangrove swamps and producing a hard wood that ranges in color from reddish brown to black and is used extensively in construction work and furniture

**¹page** \'pāj\ *n* -s [ME, fr. OF, fr. It *paggio*, perh. fr. Gk *paidion* boy, dim. of *paid-*, *pais* child, boy — more at PAED-] **1 a** (1) **:** a youth being trained for the medieval rank of knight and attached for this purpose to the personal service of a knight — compare SQUIRE (2) **:** a youth employed as the personal attendant of some person of rank other than a knight esp. in the medieval period and typically holding this position so as to be trained in the usages of good society **b** — used usu. with some qualifying phrase as a title of one of several officers of a royal or princely household ⟨was chosen as a ~ of honor⟩ **c :** a young boy chosen to serve as an honorary attendant at some formal function (as a wedding) and typically acting as a trainbearer **2 a :** one that is employed in a usu. large establishment (as a club, hotel) to deliver messages, assist patrons or visitors esp. with their personal effects (as luggage), serve as a guide, or attend to other similar duties of a usu. routine nature and that is usu. dressed in livery or some similar distinctive formal uniform: as (1) *chiefly Brit* **:** BELLBOY 1 (2) **:** one employed to locate or summon individuals (as for the delivery of personal messages) usu. by walking about in the more frequented spots (as the lobby) while calling out the individual's name at regular intervals (3) **:** a theater attendant who hands out programs and does other small services for the patrons (4) **:** one that serves as a guide to visitors in a radio or television station and attends to miscellaneous light routine duties about the studio **b** (1) **:** an assistant in a library who does messenger duty or attends to other routine duties (as locating, shelving, lettering, and repairing books) (2) **:** a boy or man who does messenger duty and attends to other routine errands for Congress or some other legislative body **3 :** a track along which pallets carrying newly molded bricks are conveyed to the hack

**²page** \"\ *vt* -ED/-ING/-S **1 :** to wait on or attend or serve in the capacity of a page ⟨chose a new boy to ~ him⟩ **2 :** to try to locate or summon (as for the delivery of a personal message) by repeatedly calling out or relaying the name of ⟨asked the bellboy to ~ her brother⟩ ⟨said they would ~ him over the public-address system⟩

**³page** \"\ *n* -s [MF, fr. L *pagina;* akin to L *pangere* to fix, fasten — more at PACT] **1 a :** one of the leaves of a book, magazine, newspaper, piece of correspondence, or similar article ⟨tore one of the ~s⟩ ⟨decided to destroy the first ~ of the letter⟩ ⟨turned the ~s idly⟩ ⟨was told to leave one side of the ~ blank⟩ **b** (1) **:** a single side of one of these leaves ⟨found the item on ~ one of the newspaper⟩ ⟨asked the class to turn to the ~ with the picture on it⟩ (2) **:** a page (as in a newspaper) regularly carrying a particular feature ⟨the editorial ~⟩ or devoted to an area of special interest ⟨the amusement ~⟩ ⟨the sports ~s⟩ **c** (1) **:** the matter printed, written, drawn, or otherwise set down or reproduced on a page ⟨rapidly read through the first ten ~s⟩ ⟨could not understand a single ~⟩ (2) **:** the area bounded by the margins or edges of a page ⟨has written enough to fill about three ~s⟩ **d** (1) **:** the original setting (as of type) for a page that has been printed or is to be printed (2) **:** a plate or mold made from such a setting **2 a :** a written record **:** BOOK, WRITING ⟨the ~s of history⟩ **b :** something (as an event or sequence of events) contained in or suitable to be in a written record or report ⟨one of the brightest ~s in his life⟩ ⟨a ~ without parallel in our history⟩ **3 :** a section of a printed or written work ⟨these are among the author's best ~s⟩ ⟨the finale lacks the excitement that is proper to it, especially in the last ~s —Edward Sackville-West & Desmond Shawe-Taylor⟩ ⟨the finest ~s of the four symphonies —Edward Cushing⟩

**⁴page** \"\ *vb* -ED/-ING/-S *vt* **1 a** (1) **:** to number or otherwise mark for sequence the pages of (as a book) **:** PAGINATE — compare FOLIATE (2) **:** to check the page numbering of (as a book) so as to verify proper sequence **b :** to make up (as typeset or photocomposed matter) into pages — often used with *up* **2 :** to turn the pages of (as a book) esp. in a steady or a hasty or haphazard manner (as in reading rapidly or examining superficially) **:** riffle through **:** LEAF ⟨*paged* the book without interest⟩ ~ *vi* **:** to turn the pages of a book or magazine or similar article esp. in a steady or a hasty or haphazard manner — usu. used with *through* ⟨*paged* through the magazine impatiently⟩

**¹pag·eant** \'pajənt\ *n* -s [ME *pagyn, pagend, padgeant*, fr. ML *pagina* scene of a play, stage, fr. L *pagina* page] **1 a** (1) *obs* **:** a scene or act of a play (as a medieval mystery play) (2) *archaic* **:** PART, ROLE **b** *obs* **:** STAGE, PLATFORM; *specif* **:** a stage or platform used for the open-air performance of medieval mystery plays and often mounted on wheels so as to be capable of being moved from place to place **2 a :** a falsely impressive display that masks lack of substance and reality **:** a mere show **:** PRETENSE ⟨saw through the hollowness, the sham, the silliness of the empty ~ in which I had always played —Oscar Wilde⟩ **b :** an ostentatious often exhibitionistic display ⟨sympathize profoundly with a poetry that doesn't make a ~ of its bleeding heart —J.L.Lowes⟩ **3 a :** SHOW, SPECTACLE, EXHIBITION ⟨a beauty ~⟩ ⟨the variegated ~ of London life —Douglas Bush⟩; *esp* **:** an elaborate usu. open-air exhibition or spectacle that is marked typically by colorful often gorgeous costuming and scenery and often by vocal and instrumental music, that consists of a series of tableaux (as representations of important events in the history of a community) or of a loosely unified drama with spoken or sung parts or of an often resplendent parade or procession usu. with showy floats and with a loosely dramatic or commemorative theme, and that is usu. presented in celebration of an event or series of events or in honor of some personage or group or of a locality by amateur actors or other amateur performers recruited from or near the locality in which it is presented **b :** a steady continuous movement of things developing or passing by in or as if in a parade or procession ⟨this exciting ~ of events —J.H. Baker⟩ ⟨watch the ~ of the world go by —Ralph Hammond-Innes⟩ **4 :** PAGEANTRY 1 ⟨for ~ of language he has had no equal in English —W.R.Thayer⟩ ⟨lacked the Roman appetite for ~ —John Buchan⟩ ⟨full of stately dignity and somber ~ —Richard Harrison⟩

**²pageant** \"\ *adj, archaic* **:** of, relating to, or typical of pageants or pageantry ⟨the ~ pomp of such a servile throne —John Dryden⟩

**³pageant** \"\ *vt* -ED/-ING/-S *archaic* **:** to surround with pageantry

**pag·eant·eer** \¦pajən¦ti(ə)r, -iə\ *n* -s **1 :** an actor or other performer in a pageant **2 :** one that produces or directs a pageant

**pag·eant·ry** \'pajəntrē, -ri\ *n* -ES [*pageant* + *-ry*] **1 :** pageants and the presentation of pageants ⟨ritual *pageantries* of the British Crown —R.B.Pearsall⟩ **2 :** colorful, rich, or splendid display **:** grand spectacle **:** gorgeous show **3 :** mere show **:** empty display ⟨was tired of pomp and ~⟩

**page boy** *n* [¹*page*] **1 :** a boy or man serving as a page **2** *usu* **pageboy :** a woman's long often shoulder-length bob with the ends of the hair turned under so as to form a smooth roll

pageboy

**page cord** *n* [³*page*] **:** cord used to tie up pages of metal type matter

**page gauge** *n* **:** a device (as a strip of nicked metal or wood or marked paper) for measuring the vertical dimension of a page — compare LINE GAUGE

**page paper** *or* **page shoe** *n* **:** a strong stiff paper or card on which set and tied-up type is laid for storage

**page proof** *n* **:** a proof from type that has been made up into a page

**pag·er** \'pājə(r)\ *n* -s **1 :** one that pages; *specif* **:** an operator of a page-numbering machine **2 :** one that separates and cleans type after it has been taken from the mold

**pages** *pl of* PAGE, *pres 3d sing of* PAGE

**pag·et·oid** \'pajə,tȯid\ *adj* [*Paget's* disease + *-oid*] **:** belonging to or typical of Paget's disease ⟨~ symptoms⟩

**pag·et process** \'pajət-\ *n, usu cap 1st P* [origin unknown] **:** FINLAY PROCESS

**paget's disease** *n, usu cap P* [after Sir James *Paget* †1899 Eng. surgeon] **1 :** an eczematous inflammatory precancerous condition of the nipple and areola or rarely of other cutaneous areas **2 :** OSTEITIS DEFORMANS

**-pagi** *pl of* -PAGUS

**pag·i·nal** \'pajənəl\ *adj* [LL *paginalis*, fr. L *pagina* page + *-alis* -al — more at PAGE] **1 :** of, relating to, or referring to a page (as of a book) ⟨each subject in the index has a ~ reference to the section of the book where it is treated in full⟩ **2 :** consisting of pages; *esp* **:** consisting of one page after another ⟨a pirated edition that is a ~ reprint of the original⟩

**pag·i·nary** \-,nerē\ *adj* **:** PAGINAL

**pag·i·nate** \-,nāt, *usu* -ād·+V\ *vt* -ED/-ING/-S [L *pagina* + E *-ate*] **:** ⁴PAGE 1a(1)

**pag·i·na·tion** \,pajə'nāshən\ *n* -s [L *pagina* + E *-ation*] **1 :** the action of paging or the condition of being paged ⟨the alphabetical arrangement necessarily involved requires that a considerable number of galleys be available before final ~ —Wheeler Sammons⟩ **2 a :** the numbers or other figures or marks used to indicate the proper sequence of a set of pages (as of a book) **b** (1) **:** the number of numbered pages ⟨a catalog of new books that gives the ~ of each⟩ (2) **:** a statement of such number ⟨the book's title and author are listed but no ~ is given⟩

**paging** *n* -s [fr. gerund of ⁴*page*] **:** PAGINATION

**pa·gi·op·o·da** \,pājē'äpədə, ,paj-\ [NL, fr. Gk *pagios* solid, firm + NL *-poda;* akin to Gk *pēgnynai* to fix, fasten — more at PACT] *syn of* CRYPTOCERATA

**pa·gle** \'pāgəl\ *var of* PAIGLE

**pagne** \'pän'\ *n* -s [F, fr. Sp *paño* cloth, fr. L *pannus* — more at VANE] **:** a native costume worn esp. in Africa and consisting typically of a long rectangular often brightly colored or decorated piece of cloth that is wrapped tightly about the torso with the ends usu. falling free or that is used as a loincloth or undergarment

**pagod** \'pagəd, pə'gäd\ *n* -s [Pg *pagode* — more at PAGODA] **1** *archaic* **:** PAGODA **2 a :** an image of a Far Eastern deity **:** IDOL **b** *archaic* **:** ¹GOD 1,3,4

**pa·go·da** \pə'gōdə\ *n* -s [Pg *pagode* oriental idol, temple, fr. a Dravidian source, fr. Skt *bhagavatī*, epithet of Hindu goddesses, fem. of *bhagavat* blessed, possessing good fortune — more at BHAGAVAT] **1 a :** a Far Eastern structure resembling a tower of several stories that is often richly decorated and typically has projecting concavely curved roofs at the division of each story that terminate in sharp points turned upward but sometimes has a simple pyramidal outline and that is erected usu. as a temple or memorial or edifice built out of personal piety either in isolation or as an adjunct to other usu. sacred architecture **b :** a small often ornamental structure (as a summer-house) resembling or suggestive of a pagoda in outline **2 :** a gold or sometimes silver coin used in the subcontinent of India up to the second decade of the 19th century

pagoda 1a

**pagoda dogwood** *also* **pagoda cornel** *n* **:** a tall shrub (*Cornus alternifolia*) that has the branches arranged in horizontal tiers and flat clusters of white flowers followed by blue fruits

**pagoda tree** *n* **:** any of several trees of erect habit and conical form suggestive of a pagoda: as **a :** JAPANESE PAGODA TREE **b** *India* **:** BANYAN **c** (1) **:** a frangipani (*Plumeria acutifolia*) of India (2) **:** a frangipani (*Plumeria alba*) of the West Indies

**pag·o·dite** \'pagə,dīt, pə'gō,dīt\ *or* **pagoda stone** *n* -s [F *pagodite*, fr. *pagode* pagoda (fr. Pg) + *-ite;* so called from its use for carving miniature pagodas] **:** AGALMATOLITE

**pag·o·scope** \'pagə,skōp\ *n* [Gk *pagos* frost + E *-scope;* akin to Gk *pēgnynai* to fix, fasten together — more at PACT] **:** a device for showing at a glance whether the prevailing dew point is below freezing **:** HYGRODEIK

**pagri** *var of* PUGGAREE

**pa·grus** \'pāgrəs\ *n* [NL, fr. L, sea bream — more at PARGO] **1** *cap* **:** a genus of sea breams of the family Sparidae **2** -ES **:** PORGY 1a

**pa·gu·ma** \pə'gyümə\ *n, cap* [NL] **:** a genus of palm civets of southeastern Asia related to civets of the genus *Paradoxurus* but having the tail unmarked by rings

**pa·gu·ri·an** \pə'gyu̇rēən\ *n* -s [NL *Pagurus* + E *-ian*] **:** a hermit crab of the genus *Pagurus*

**pa·gu·ri·dae** \-rə,dē\ *n pl, cap* [NL, fr. *Pagurus*, type genus + *-idae*] **:** a cosmopolitan family of anomuran crustaceans that are related to the purse crabs and comprise the typical hermit crabs — compare PARAPAGURIDAE

**pa·gu·rus** \-rəs\ *n* [NL, fr. L, crab, fr. Gk *pagouros*, fr. *pagos* rock + *-uros* -urus; akin to Gk *pēgnynai* to fix, fasten — more at PACT] **1** *cap* **:** a large cosmopolitan genus (the type of the family Paguridae) of hermit crabs **2** -ES **:** KABURI

**-pa·gus** \pəgəs\ *n comb form, pl* **-pagi** [NL, fr. Gk *pagos* something fixed, rock, frost — more at PAGOSCOPE] **:** monster with a (specified) type of fixation ⟨cranio*pagus*⟩

**¹pah** *an energetically released p-sound, often followed by any of several vowel or consonant sounds; often read as* 'pä *or* 'pá\ *interj* — used typically to express disdain or contempt or disgust

**²pah** *var of* PA

**pa·ha** \pä'hä\ *n, pl* **paha** *or* **pahas** [Dakota *pahá* hill] **:** a hill or ridge of glacial origin with a capping of loess found esp. in the northeastern part of the state of Iowa

**pa·ha·ri** \pə'härē\ *n, pl* **pahari** *or* **paharis** *usu cap* [Hindi *pahārī* mountaineer, fr. *pahār* mountain] **1 a :** one of several chiefly hill peoples of the northeastern part of the subcontinent of India south and west of the Ganges river **b :** a member of one of these peoples **2 a :** a group of Indic languages or dialects used by the Pahari peoples **b :** any of the languages or dialects of this group

**pa·ha·ria** \pə'härēə\ *n, pl* **paharia** *or* **paharias** *usu cap* **:** PAHARI 1

**pa·hau·tea** \,pä,hau̇'tāə\ *n* -s [Maori] **:** a New Zealand cedar (*Libocedrus bidwillii*) with 4-sided ultimate branches

**pa·hi** \pə'hē\ *n* -s [Tahitian] **:** a large seagoing Polynesian canoe or ship often consisting of two connected hulls

**¹pah·la·vi** \'pälə(,)vē\ *also* **peh·le·vi** \'pele(,)vē\ *n* -s *cap* [Per *pahlawī*, fr. *Pahlav*, fr. MPer, alter. of OPer *Parthava-* Parthia] **1 :** the Iranian language of Sassanid Persia **2 :** a script used for writing Pahlavi

**²pahlavi** \"\ *or* **pahlevi** \"\ *n, pl* **pahlavi** *or* **pahlavis** *or* **pahlevi** *or* **pahlevis** [Per *pahlawī*, fr. Riza Shah *Pahlawi* (Pahlavi) †1944 Shah of Iran] **1 :** a gold coin of Iran first issued in 1927 with a value of 20 rials and in 1932 with a value of 100 rials **2 :** a unit of value based on the value of one pahlavi

**pah·mi** \'pämē\ *n, pl* **pahmi** *or* **pahmis** [origin unknown] **1 a :** BOBAC **b :** FERRET-BADGER **2 :** the fur of the bobac or of the ferret-badger

**pa·ho** \'pä,hō, -hü\ *also* **ba·ho** \'bä-\ *n* -s [Hopi *páaho*] **:** a Hopi Indian plumed prayer stick

**pa·ho·e·ho·e** \pə'hōē,hōē\ *n* -s [Hawaiian *pāhoehoe*] **:** cooled hard lava marked by a smooth often billowy shiny surface — contrasted with *aa*

**pa·houin** \(')pä¦wan\ *n, pl* **pahouin** *or* **pahouins** *usu cap* **:** ⁴FANG 1

**pa·hua** \pə'hüə\ *n, pl* **pahua** *or* **pahuas** [Marquesan] **:** GIANT CLAM

**pa·hu·tan** \pə'hü,tän\ *also* **pa·ho** \'pä(,)hō\ *n* -s [Tag *pahútan, páho*] **:** a Philippine mango (*Mangifera altissima*) with an edible fruit that is often pickled and a dark brown variegated wood used esp. in veneers and cabinetwork

**pai·che** \'pī(,)chā, -,chē\ *n* -s [AmerSp, prob. fr. AmerInd] **:** PIRARUCU

**paid** \'pād\ *adj* [fr. past part. of *pay*] **1 a :** receiving pay ⟨is a ~ official of the organization⟩ **b :** marked by the reception of pay esp. in an advance lump sum ⟨has a good job and a ~ vacation⟩ **2 :** that has been cashed ⟨a ~ check⟩ **3 :** that has been or will be paid for ⟨a ~ political announcement⟩

**paid-** *or* **paido-** — see PAED-

**pai·deia** \pī'dāə\ *n* -s [G, fr. Gk, education, culture, fr. *paideuein* to educate (fr. *paid-*, *pais* child) + *-ia* -y — more at FEW] **1 :** training of the physical and mental faculties in such a way as to produce a broad enlightened mature outlook harmoniously combined with maximum cultural development ⟨the long and noble tradition of ~, which made it impossible for a Greek or Roman to write a worthy book merely to record facts —Gilbert Highet⟩ **2 :** the ideal development envisioned or attained by paideia

**paid–in surplus** \'=¦=-\ *n* [fr. past part. of *pay in*] **:** surplus resulting from sale or exchange of capital stock at amounts in excess of par or stated value — compare CAPITAL SURPLUS

**paid-up** \'=¦=\ *adj* [fr. past part. of *pay up*] **:** that has satisfied an indicated or implied financial obligation ⟨facilities of the club are granted only to *paid-up* members⟩

**paid-up addition** *n* **:** addition to an existing insurance policy by using the annual dividend allotment to buy more insurance

**paige·ite** \'pā,jīt\ *n* -s [Sidney *Paige* *b*1880 Am. geologist + *-ite*] **:** a mineral $(Fe,Mg)FeBO_5$ consisting of borate of iron and magnesium in fibrous aggregates of coal-black crystals

**pai·gle** \'pāgəl\ *n* -s [origin unknown] *dial Eng* **:** one of several plants: as **a :** COWSLIP **b :** OXLIP

**pai–hua** \'bī'hwä\ *n* -s [Chin *pai² hua⁴*, lit., plain speech, fr. *pai²* white, plain + *hua⁴* speech] **:** a form of written Chinese based on modern colloquial — compare WEN-LI, WEN-YEN

**paik** \'pāk\ *vt* -ED/-ING/-S [origin unknown] *dial Brit* **:** to strike hard and repeatedly **:** PUMMEL

**¹pail** \'pāl, *esp before pause or consonant* -āəl\ *n* -s [ME *payle, paille* (infl. by MF *paelle* metal pot), prob. fr. OE *pægel* small measure, wine vessel, fr. ML *pagella* a measure, fr. L, small page, dim. of *pagina* page — more at PAELLA, PAGE] **1 a :** a typically cylindrical or nearly cylindrical vessel (as of metal or plastic) for catching, holding, or carrying liquids or solids and usu. having a bail handle or other handle and sometimes having a removable cover **:** BUCKET — often used in combination with a term suggesting the function ⟨milk ~⟩ ⟨lunch ~⟩ ⟨ice ~⟩ **b :** a usu. tapered or cylindrical shipping container (as of steel or fiber) used esp. for ice cream and other moist foods and having an average capacity of from one to twelve gallons **2 :** the quantity that a pail contains **:** PAILFUL

pail 1a

**²pail** \"\ *vt* -ED/-ING/-S *North* **:** MILK 1

**³pail** \"\ *vt* -ED/-ING/-S [origin unknown] *dial Eng* : BEAT, THRASH

**pail·ful** \ˈ=,fu̇l\ *n, pl* **pailfuls** *also* **pails·ful** \-l,fu̇lz, -lz,fu̇l\ : PAIL 2

**pail·lasse** \(ˈ)pī¦(y)as, ¦palē¦as, (ˈ)pal¦yas\ *n* -S [F, fr. *paille* straw, fr. L *palea* chaff, straw — more at PALLET] : PALLIASSE

**pail·las·son** \ˌpīəˈsōⁿ\ *n* -S [F, straw mat, fr. *paillasse*] : coarsely woven natural or synthetic straw used for hats

**paille finne** \(ˈ)pī¦fēn, -fin\ *n* [modif. of Amer F *paille fine,* lit., fine straw] : MAIDEN CANE

**pail·lette** *also* **pai·lette** \(ˈ)pī¦(y)et, (ˈ)pā¦yet, (ˈ)pa¦(y)et, pəˈlet\ *n* -S [F, fr. *paille* + *-ette*] **1 a :** one of usu. several or many small shiny objects (as spangles, sequins, beads, jewels) applied in small loosely designed clusters as a decorative trimming (as on women's clothing or accessories or on theatrical costumes) **b :** a trimming made of paillettes **2 :** a fabric (as of silk) so woven or treated as to give a shiny spangled effect

**pail·lett·ed** \-ed·əd\ *adj* : trimmed with paillettes ⟨~ gloves⟩

**pail·lon** \(ˈ)pī¦(y)ōⁿ, (ˈ)pā¦yōⁿ\ *n* -S [F, metallic foil, handful of straw, fr. *paille*] : a thin sheet of usu. fine metallic foil (as of silver or gold) used esp. in enameling and gilding and often overlaid with a translucent material so as to form a decorative feature

**pai·lou** *also* **pai·loo** \ˈpīˈlō\ *n, pl* **pai·lou** *or* **pai·lous** [Chin *p'ai²-lou²,* fr. *p'ai²* tablet + *lou²* tower] : a usu. elaborate Chinese commemorative archway erected in honor of someone highly esteemed (as for virtue) and consisting typically of four heavy square pillars topped with horizontal crossbeams and often buttressed with conventionalized lions and having an incised memorial tablet placed against or near the center crossbeam — compare TORAN, TORII

pai-lou

**¹pain** \ˈpān\ *n* -S [ME *peyne, paine,* fr. OF *peine,* fr. L *poena* penalty, punishment, fr. Gk *poinē* penalty, payment; akin to Gk *tinein* to pay, *tērein* to guard, *timē* price, value, honor, Skt *cayate* he punishes] **1 pains** *pl* : PUNISHMENTS — now used chiefly in the phrase *pains and penalties* ⟨passing acts of attainder and of *pains* and penalties —T.E.May⟩ ⟨there was the principle that civil courts may not add to the *pains* and penalties of crimes —B.N.Cardozo⟩ **2 a :** a state of physical or mental lack of well-being or physical or mental uneasiness that ranges from mild discomfort or dull distress to acute often unbearable agony, may be generalized or localized, and is the consequence of being injured or hurt physically or mentally or of some derangement of or lack of equilibrium in the physical or mental functions (as through disease), and that usu. produces a reaction of wanting to avoid, escape, or destroy the causative factor and its effects ⟨was in constant ~⟩ ⟨her ~, which had been merely a dull ache, was suddenly as keen as if a blade had been driven into her wound —Ellen Glasgow⟩ ⟨perhaps all physical existence is a weary ~ to man —T.E.Lawrence⟩ **b :** a sensation or feeling (as a sharp twinge, dull ache, generalized sense of physical or mental distress) or a complex of sensations or feelings that are produced by such a state or that are produced by some other factor either in isolation or in succession ⟨had no ~⟩ ⟨the ~ of a twisted ankle⟩ ⟨sharp ~s⟩ ⟨dreaded the ~ of separation from them⟩ ⟨his conduct in regard to them caused me the deepest ~ —W.M.Thackeray⟩ ⟨the ~ she had felt at those humiliating words —Morley Callaghan⟩ **c :** a sensation varying in quality from prick to ache that is commonly aroused by a stimulus which injures or nearly injures the skin or tissues, is usu. but not always unpleasant, and leads to avoiding reactions **3 pains** *pl* : the protracted series of involuntary contractions of the uterine musculature that constitute the major factor in parturient labor and that are often accompanied by considerable pain ⟨her ~s had begun⟩ **4 :** trouble, care, or effort taken for the accomplishment of something — usu. used in pl. but archaically often as sing. in construction ⟨has obviously taken great ~s to study the practical details —Nancie Matthews⟩ ⟨no ~s were spared in the workmanship —*Amer. Guide Series: N.Y. City*⟩ ⟨lavished their skill and ~s —Willa Cather⟩ ⟨for his ~s he incurred the enmity of the people —*Amer. Guide Series: La.*⟩ ⟨has been at ~s to avoid associating himself with this recommendation —Walter Goodman⟩ ⟨was at ~s to explain away his dangerous subject —Richard Mayne⟩ ⟨goes to ~s to impress —Lucy Crockett⟩ ⟨was at ~s to emphasize the nonpolitical character of the visit —H.J.Morgenthau⟩ ⟨takes that ~s about it —John Locke⟩ **5 a :** something that irks or annoys or that is otherwise troublesome : something provokingly displeasing ⟨she's a real ~⟩ **b :** a reaction of antipathy to something irksome or annoying or provokingly displeasing : a sensation or feeling of annoyance ⟨you give me a ~⟩

**syn** ACHE, PANG, THROE, TWINGE, STITCH: these nouns all indicate a bodily or mental sensation causing often acute discomfort or suffering. PAIN is the most comprehensive in that it may indicate bodily disturbance ranging from a localized discomfort to a general raging physical agony, although generally it implies a more or less acute sensation as from a cut, burn, or more severe injury ⟨a *pain* in the finger⟩ ⟨chest *pains*⟩ ⟨his face twisted with *pain*⟩ ⟨my craving to hear from her was at times a gnawing *pain* —Kenneth Roberts⟩ ACHE commonly implies a steady, usu. dull, generalized pain ⟨a head*ache*⟩ ⟨an *ache* in the back from bending over all day⟩ ⟨the dull *ache* of his disappointment —Agnes S. Turnbull⟩ PANG suggests a short sharp pain ⟨the *pangs* of toothache⟩ ⟨the *pangs* of grief⟩ THROE is a pain, usu. (and in the plural) intermittent, violent, and convulsive, characteristic of a process as that of labor in childbirth ⟨the *throes* of retching⟩ ⟨the *throes* of civil war —S.W.Chapman⟩ TWINGE is a momentary shooting or darting pain esp. causing muscular contraction ⟨*twinges* of pain in his back and shoulder —Walter O'Meara⟩ ⟨a *twinge* of pity⟩ ⟨a *twinge* of conscience⟩ STITCH suggests a brief sharp pain that runs through a part of the body (usu. the side) like a needle ⟨a *stitch* in the side forced him to drop out of the race⟩ **syn** see in addition EFFORT

— **on pain of** *or* **under pain of** *also* **upon pain of** *prep* : under penalty or punishment of — used with a following specifying word or phrase to indicate that the thing specified is invoked as a threat that will be fulfilled ⟨was told not to leave the country *on pain of* death⟩ ⟨forbidden to pronounce his or her own name, *on pain of* incurring some great evil —J.G.Frazer⟩ ⟨bringing pressure upon the commissioner . . . to appoint to office his favorites *under pain of* meeting his opposition in Congress —R.M.Lovett⟩ or archaically or obsoletely that the thing specified is something that will be forfeited ⟨that every one *upon pain of* life should return to their houses —James Howell⟩ or is a crime or offense with which one will be charged ⟨that every one should open his shop *under pain of* rebellion —James Howell⟩

**²pain** \"\ *vb* -ED/-ING/-S [ME *peynen,* fr. F *pener,* fr. *peine* pain] *vt* **1 a :** to cause to experience pain : inflict pain on : make suffer : cause distress to : HURT ⟨a nagging shoulder injury that ~*ed* him for four months —W.B.Furlong⟩ ⟨it ~*s* me to cast doubt on the competence of my friend —Alfred Burmeister⟩ **b :** to cause a feeling of annoyance in : IRK, PROVOKE ⟨don't ~ me by talking like that —Thomas Hardy⟩ ⟨it ~*s* him to have to go there⟩ **2** *archaic* : to put (oneself) to trouble or exertion for the accomplishment of something ⟨still ~ themselves to write Latin verses —J.R.Lowell⟩ ~ *vi* **1 a** *archaic* : to undergo pain : SUFFER ⟨the spirit that so is ~*ing* —*Calisto and Melebea*⟩ **b** *of the body or a bodily part* : to be in a condition that produces a sensation of pain : give or have a sensation of pain : be sore ⟨soaked her feet in hot water because they were ~*ing*⟩ ⟨could hardly think, his head ~*ed* so⟩ **2 :** to cause pain ⟨said that it ~*ed* when he moved his arm⟩

**pained** *adj* [fr. past part. of ²*pain*] **1 :** feeling pain : HURT ⟨was quite ~ when you refused her invitation⟩ **2 :** showing pain : indicative of pain ⟨the look of ~ attention on the faces of those boys —Robert Birley⟩ ⟨the clerk, lifting a ~ eyebrow, told me that I was in the wrong queue —H.V.Morton⟩ ⟨yawned with ~ boredom⟩

**pain·ful** \ˈpānfəl\ *adj, sometimes* **pain·ful·ler**; *sometimes* **pain·ful·lest** [ME *painefull, peynefull,* fr. *paine, peyne* pain + *-full, -ful*] **1 a :** marked by pain : full of pain : having or giving a sensation of pain : affected with pain ⟨a remedy for ~ feet⟩ ⟨a ~ wound⟩ ⟨the ~ awareness that they couldn't go home —Polly Adler⟩ **b :** ANNOYING, IRKSOME, VEXATIOUS ⟨works with ~ slowness⟩ ⟨is so shy that it's ~⟩ ⟨~ righteousness and piety —K.S.Davis⟩ ⟨a provinciality which is ~ —H.J.Laski⟩ **c :** disturbing to one's equilibrium : UPSETTING ⟨would be a ~ anachronism —A.L.Guérard⟩ **d :** extremely disagreeable : most unpleasant ⟨the ~ necessity of renouncing preconceived opinions —Charles Lyell⟩ ⟨received some ~ news⟩ **2 a :** marked by or entailing or requiring much effort or toilsome exertion ⟨a long ~ trip⟩ ⟨wrote the book with ~ care⟩; *esp* : stiff and labored ⟨was uncomfortable in this atmosphere of ~ hospitality⟩ **b :** beset with difficulties : TROUBLESOME ⟨~ problems of rehabilitation —Vera M. Dean⟩ ⟨groping one's ~ way through an imperfectly mastered idiom —A.L.Guérard⟩ **3** *archaic* **a :** done or accomplished or performed with great diligence and care ⟨their virtuous sermons and ~ preaching —Thomas Stapleton⟩ ⟨according to my most ~ discoveries —Ethan Allen⟩ **b :** working with great diligence and care ⟨laws of etymology, which ~ students have discovered —John Peile⟩ — **pain·ful·ly** \-fəlē, -li\ *adv* — **pain·ful·ness** \-lnəs\ *n* -ES

**pain-killer** \ˈ=,==\ *n* : something (as a drug) that relieves pain — **pain-killing** \ˈ=¦==\ *adj*

**pain·less** \ˈpānləs\ *adj* **1 :** not experiencing pain ⟨is a ~ baby suffering from indifference to injury —*Time*⟩ **2 :** not causing pain : not accompanied by pain : not painful ⟨~ surgery⟩ ⟨a completely ~ process —D.W.Mitchell⟩ ⟨a ~ solution to the problem⟩ ⟨a ~ transition⟩ — **pain·less·ly** *adv* — **pain·less·ness** *n* -ES

**pains** *pl of* PAIN, *pres 3d sing of* PAIN

**pain spot** *n* : one of many small localized areas of the skin that respond to stimulation (as by pricking or burning) by giving a sensation of pain

**painstaker** *n, obs* : one that takes pains

**¹pains·tak·ing** \ˈpānz,tākiŋ, -n,stā-\ *n* [*pains,* pl. of ¹*pain* + *taking,* gerund of *take*] : the action of taking pains : diligent care and effort ⟨greater ~ to achieve incidental verisimilitude and accuracy of detail —*Times Lit. Supp.*⟩

**²painstaking** \ˈ=¦==\ *adj* [*pains* + *taking,* pres. part. of *take*] : taking pains or marked by the taking of pains : expending or showing diligent care and effort ⟨a most ~ worker⟩ ⟨the results of scholarly, ~ investigation of historical sources —A.R. Newsome⟩ ⟨will go on painting, with scrupulous, ~ accuracy —D.I.Holman⟩ — **pains·tak·ing·ly** *adv* — **pains·tak·ing·ness** *n* -ES

**painsworthy** \ˈ=¦==\ *adj* : worth the expenditure of diligent care and effort ⟨a ~ task⟩

**¹paint** \ˈpānt\ *vb* -ED/-ING/-S [ME *peynten, painten,* fr. OF *peindre* (past part. *peint*), fr. L *pingere* to paint, embroider, tattoo; akin to OE *fāh* variegated, OHG *fēh,* ON *fā* to paint, Gk *poikilos* variegated, *pikros* pointed, sharp, bitter, Skt *pimśati* he cuts out, adorns] *vt* **1 a (1) :** to color all or part of (a surface) by or as if by applying a pigment ⟨~*ed* the whole house, inside and out⟩ : apply color to : add color to : coat or touch up with coloring matter ⟨Indians that had ~*ed* their faces with streaks of red and blue⟩; *esp* : to color (a surface) by applying and spreading (as with a brush, spray gun, roller) a liquid or paste composed of a mixture of a pigment and a vehicle (as oil or water) that dries opaque ⟨~*ed* the walls white⟩ **(2) :** to color with or as if with a cosmetic (as lipstick, rouge, fingernail polish) : apply a cosmetic or something like a cosmetic to ⟨wore blue and, as usual, ~*ed* her mouth —Margaret C. Harriman⟩ **b (1) :** to brush on or swab on or otherwise apply (a liquid) with a movement resembling or suggestive of that used in painting something ⟨~*ed* egg white over the surface of the cake⟩ **(2) :** to cover or treat or touch up (a localized area) with a liquid by brushing or swabbing or a similar movement ⟨~*ed* the wound with iodine⟩ ⟨savages ~*ing* their arms and legs with henna stain⟩ **2 a (1) :** to make or produce (as a picture, sketch, design) in lines and colors on a surface (as a canvas or wall) by brushing on or similarly applying pigments ⟨~*ed* a picture of his mother⟩ ⟨~*ed* abstract designs on the walls⟩ ⟨~*ed* big black letters on the sign⟩ **(2) :** to represent to the eye by the use of lines and colors applied in this way : depict or portray by such lines and colors ⟨was especially skillful at ~*ing* animals and birds⟩ ⟨~*ed* a vase of flowers against a dark background⟩ **(3) :** to depict or portray or delineate as having specified or implied characteristics ⟨is neither as black nor as white as he is ~*ed* —V.S. Pritchett⟩ ⟨~*s* them whiter than the evidence justifies —Oliver La Farge⟩ ⟨wished to ~ their candidate to the South as a free trader —Mary K. Hammond⟩ ⟨are not as unapproachable and unfriendly as a lot of propaganda has ~*ed* them to be —Werner Bamberger⟩ **b :** to decorate, adorn, or variegate by applying lines and colors in this way ⟨an ancient vase that had been ~*ed* with pastoral scenes⟩ **c :** to produce (as a picture, design, color) as if by painting ⟨the campfire ~*ed* queer pictures on the tree trunks and tinted the underbranches with a rosy glow —Myrtle R. White⟩ **3 :** to touch up, modify, or cover over by or as if by painting so as to hide defects or so as to deceptively heighten real or apparent attractiveness ⟨the town had been all ~*ed* up in preparation for the event⟩ ⟨difficult to be patient with those who ~ its defects —M.R. Cohen⟩ **4 :** to evoke a vivid mental picture or concept of esp. by a colorful or strikingly realistic description : delineate strikingly or colorfully ⟨~*ed* the picture of what would happen after war —F.L.Paxson⟩ ⟨scoured Europe in search of cheap labor, ~*ing* glowing pictures of the promised land across the sea —*Amer. Guide Series: Mass.*⟩ ⟨~*ed* this humanitarian effort so brilliantly —Farley Mowat⟩ ⟨~*s* in vivid words the fresh and free and high spirit of those who conceived the great enterprise —Edith Hamilton⟩ **5 a :** to force (a hearts player) to take a heart by playing it on a trick that must be taken **b :** to deal a face card to (a poker player who is drawing for a low hand) ~ *vi* **1 :** to paint things; *esp* : to practice the art of painting pictures or other representations or designs ⟨likes to ~ for relaxation⟩ **2 :** to use cosmetics for adding color ⟨is aging rapidly and now ~*s* heavily⟩ **3** *obs* : to become changed in facial color ⟨canst thou ~ pale so quickly —Thomas Middleton⟩ **4** *archaic* : to drink intoxicating liquor — **paint the lily** : to add something artificial or otherwise extraneous (as ornamentation) to something naturally beautiful or otherwise desirable in such a way as actually to lessen or hide or destroy the thing's original qualities — **paint the town red** *also* **paint the town** : to go out and celebrate riotously usu. by much drinking and general dissipation : CAROUSE

**²paint** \"\ *n* -S **1 a :** the action of painting ⟨the car needs a new ~ job⟩ **b :** something produced by painting ⟨portraits which are great pieces of ~ —David Low⟩ **2 :** MAKEUP; *esp* : a cosmetic (as lipstick or rouge) designed to add color **3 a (1) :** a mixture of a pigment and a suitable vehicle (as oil, water) that together form a liquid or paste that can be applied and spread (as with a brush, spray gun, roller) to a surface so as to form a thin closely adherent coating that dries opaque and imparts color to the surface and that is often designed to protect the surface (as against weathering) ⟨a can of ~⟩ ⟨a tube of ~⟩ **(2) :** the dry pigment used in making this mixture; *esp* : a usu. small cake of this dry pigment ⟨a box of ~*s*⟩ **b :** an applied coating of paint esp. when dry ⟨touched the ~ while it was still wet⟩ ⟨the ~ had already begun to chip off⟩ **4 :** a usu. antiseptic application (as of iodine) designed to be applied to a localized area (as of the skin) by painting **5** [short for *paint horse*] *chiefly West* : a horse or pony with irregular broad markings of white interspersed with some other solid color

**paint·abil·i·ty** \ˌpāntəˈbilədē\ *n* : the quality or state of being paintable

**paint·able** \ˈpāntəbəl\ *adj* : capable of being painted : lending itself well to being painted: as **a :** having arresting qualities (as of color, design, interest) that invite reproduction or interpretation through the art of painting ⟨a highly ~ landscape⟩ **b :** having a surface that takes paint well ⟨made of sturdy eminently ~ wood⟩

**paint·able·ness** *n* -ES : PAINTABILITY

**paint box** *n* : a box for paints; *specif* : a box that holds cakes of dry paint (as water colors) or usu. small containers (as jars, tubes) of liquid or semiliquid paint and that typically has one or more small pans for mixing and blending the paints

**paint bridge** *n* : BRIDGE 3m(2)

**paintbrush** \ˈ=,=\ *n* **1 :** a brush for applying paint **2 a :** ORANGE HAWKWEED **b :** MARSH PAINTED CUP **c :** SHRUBBY ST.-JOHN'S-WORT

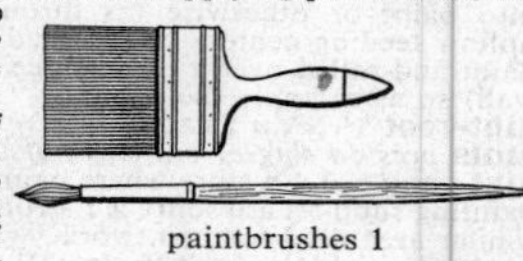
paintbrushes 1

**paint·ed** \ˈpāntəd\ *adj* [ME *peynted, painted,* fr. past part. of *peynten* to paint] **1 a :** produced through the medium of painting ⟨as idle as a ~ ship —S.T.Coleridge⟩ : done in colors that have been applied by painting on a surface ⟨treasured the ~ likeness of her son⟩ **b :** coated or touched up with paint or decorated with painted representations or designs ⟨scratched the ~ woodwork⟩ ⟨the ~ faces of the savages⟩; *esp* : heavily made up with cosmetics ⟨a region not quite used to ~ women⟩ **c :** marked by bright or contrasting colors ⟨the sunlit ~ meadow⟩ **2 :** lacking substance and vitality and correspondence with truth : HOLLOW, ARTIFICIAL, SHAM ⟨that ~ hope —Shak.⟩ ⟨enjoying ~ pleasures⟩

**painted bat** *n* [so called fr. its bright orange fur] : FOREST BAT

**painted beauty** *n* : an American butterfly (*Vanessa virginiensis*) with dark brown wings marked by large golden orange spots and several white spots

**painted bunting** *or* **painted finch** *n* **1 :** a brightly colored finch (*Passerina ciris*) of the southern part of the U.S. having in the male a deep blue head and neck and bright red rump and underparts with golden green wings and bluish purple tail and in the female green upper parts and yellowish underparts **2 :** SMITH'S LONGSPUR

**painted cup** *n* : INDIAN PAINTBRUSH 1

**painted daisy** *n* **1 :** PYRETHRUM 1b(2) **2 :** any of various annual garden chrysanthemums that are prob. largely derived from a Moroccan species (*Chrysanthemum carinatum*) and that have succulent leaves and solitary flower heads with ray flowers brilliantly banded in two or more colors

**painted duck** *n* **1 :** MANDARIN DUCK **2 :** HARLEQUIN DUCK

**painted enamel** *n* : LIMOGES ENAMEL

**painted goose** *n* : EMPEROR GOOSE

**painted grass** *n* : RIBBON GRASS

**painted horse** *or* **painted pony** *n* [trans. of AmerSp *pinto* — more at PINTO] : PAINT 5

**painted hyena** *n* : AFRICAN HUNTING DOG

**painted lady** *n* **1 :** a migratory butterfly (*Vanessa cardui*) with wings mottled in brown, orange, and white that has a brown or blackish yellow-striped caterpillar often destructive of crop plants **2 :** PYRETHRUM 1 b (2) **3 :** PAINTED TRILLIUM

**painted leaf** *n* : MEXICAN FIRE PLANT 1

**painted lobster** *n* : a large brilliantly marked spiny lobster (*Palinurus fasciatus*) of the Great Barrier reef off the northeastern coast of Queensland, Australia

**painted partridge** *n* : a francolin (*Francolinus pictus*) of the subcontinent of India

**painted pig** *n* : a reddish West African river hog (*Koiropotamus porcus*)

**painted quail** *n* **1 :** either of two small bright-plumaged quails: **a :** an African quail (*Coturnix adansonii*) — called also *blue quail* **b :** an Asiatic and Australasian quail (*C. chinensis*) — called also *blue-breasted quail* **2** *Austral* : a button quail (*Turnix varia*)

**painted sandgrouse** *n* : a sandgrouse (*Pterocles indicus*) of the subcontinent of India

**painted snipe** *n* : any of several highly colored limicoline birds of the genus *Rostratula* widely distributed in the southern hemisphere

**painted tongue** *n* : SALPIGLOSSIS 2

**painted trillium** *or* **painted wake-robin** *n* : a perennial herb (*Trillium undulatum*) of the northeastern part of No. America with three broad stalked leaves and a showy solitary flower with purple-streaked petals

**painted turtle** *also* **painted terrapin** *or* **painted tortoise** *n* : any of several common freshwater turtles of the genus *Chrysemys* that are found chiefly in the eastern part of the U.S. and that have a greenish black carapace with yellow bands bordering the shields, red markings on the marginal plates, and a yellow plastron

**¹paint·er** \ˈpāntə(r)\ *n* -S [ME *peynteur, painter,* fr. MF *peinteur, paintre,* fr. (assumed) VL *pinctor,* alter. (influenced by L *pingere*) of L *pictor,* fr. *pictus* (past part. of *pingere* to paint) + *-or* — more at PAINT] : one that paints: as **a :** an artist that paints (as pictures, designs) **b :** one who applies paint (as to buildings, ships, planes, or furniture) esp. as an occupation

**²painter** \"\ *n* -S [ME *paynter,* prob. fr. MF *pentoir, pendoir* clothesline, fr. *pendre* to hang (fr. L *pendēre*) + *-oir* -ory (fr. L *-orium*) — more at PENDANT] : ROPE, LINE; *specif* : a rope or other line attached to the bow of a boat (as a rowboat) and used for securing the boat (as to a pier) or for towing — **cut the painter** : to make a complete and definite break with something : sever all connection ⟨was *cutting the painter* so far as her past was concerned⟩

**³painter** \"\ *n* -S [alter. of *panther*] *chiefly South & Midland* : COUGAR

**paint·er·li·ness** \ˈpāntə(r)lēnəs, -lin-\ *n* -ES : the quality or state of being painterly

**paint·er·ly** \-lē, -li\ *adj* **1 :** of, relating to, or typical of a painter : ARTISTIC ⟨a ~ ability of no small order —*N.Y.Times*⟩ ⟨the ~ arts —Joseph Ehreth⟩ ⟨~ attitudes toward color —Matthew Lipman⟩ **2 a :** marked by or tending toward qualities of color or texture or other features that are present or created in a way distinctive of or esp. appropriate to the art of painting ⟨his work is spirited, ~, sensitive as to light and color and ambient surface pattern —Carlyle Burrows⟩ ⟨a free ~ style —Herbert Read⟩ **b :** marked by or tending toward an openness of form which is not linear and in which sharp outlines are wholly or nearly wholly lacking ⟨there was a ~ subtlety in the muted whites and grays —O.W.Larkin⟩

**painter's brush** *n* : INDIAN PAINTBRUSH 1

**painter's colic** *n* : LEAD COLIC

**painter's cream** *n* : a cream made of mastic, nut oil, lead acetate, and water and used to cover a partly finished painting so as to preserve its freshness until resumption of work

**painter's naphtha** *n* : a petroleum naphtha used as a thinner for paints

**paint frame** *n* : a large frame usu. suspended at the back of a stage and capable of being raised or lowered that is used for holding a stretched length of canvas on which an entire piece of stage scenery is to be painted

**paint horse** *or* **paint pony** *n* [trans. of AmerSp *pinto* — more at PINTO] : PAINT 5

**paintier** *comparative of* PAINTY

**paintiest** *superlative of* PAINTY

**paint·i·ness** \ˈpāntēnəs, -tin-\ *n* -ES : the quality or state of being painty

**painting** *n* -S [ME *painting, peintunge,* fr. gerund of *painten* to paint] **1 :** something produced through the process or art of painting : a product of painting: as **a :** decoration achieved by applying paint to a surface : PAINTWORK ⟨admired the ~ and gilding of his Excellency's carriages —T.B.Macaulay⟩ **b :** a picture or design or other work produced through the art of painting ⟨a ~ done in oils⟩ ⟨a water-color ~⟩ **2 :** the art or occupation of painting ⟨studied ~ for some years⟩

**painting knife** *n* : an artist's tool that consists of a very flexible tapered blade set in a handle and that is used like a small trowel for taking up and applying thick paints

**paint·less** \ˈpāntləs\ *adj* : devoid of paint ⟨of the same weathered color as the ~ church —William Faulkner⟩

**paint out** *vt* **1** *archaic* : to depict or portray or delineate by or as if by painting **2 :** to obliterate by covering over with paint

**paintpot** \ˈ=,=\ *n* **1 :** a receptacle (as a pot, pail, bucket) for holding paint **2** *usu* **paint pot** : an orifice in the earth (as in the vicinity of a volcano, geyser, hot spring) usu. marked by a protruding conical mud rim and containing a liquid mass of thin mud usu. agitated with hot vapors or gases and often vividly colored through chemical reaction induced by heat

**paint·ress** \ˈpān·trəs\ *n* -ES [F *peintresse,* fr. *peintre* painter + *-esse* -ess] : a female painter

**paint roller** *n* **:** a roller that consists typically of a rotating cylinder about two inches in diameter and six inches in length covered with an absorbent material and mounted on a handle so that the cylinder can be dipped into paint or otherwise (as through a hollow feeding center) be supplied with paint and rolled over a flat surface (as a wall) so as to apply the paint

paint roller

**paint-root** \ˈ=,=\ *n* **:** REDROOT 1

**paints** *pres 3d sing of* PAINT, *pl of* PAINT

**paint shop** *n* **1 :** a store where paint and painting supplies are sold **2 :** a room or similar area used for paintwork

**painture** *n* -s [ME *peynture,* fr. OF *peinture,* fr. (assumed) VL *pinctura,* alter. (influenced by L *pingere* to paint) of L *pictura* — more at PICTURE] *obs* **:** PAINTING

**paintwork** \ˈ=,=\ *n* **1 a :** the application of paint to a surface ⟨had not yet finished the ∼⟩ ⟨decorated with ∼⟩ **b :** the quality of work done in the application of paint to a surface ⟨fine ∼ was evident in every room⟩ **2 :** paint that has been applied to a surface ⟨was careful not to scratch the ∼⟩

**painty** \ˈpāntē, -ti\ *adj, usu* -ER/-EST **1 a :** of, relating to, or suggestive of paint ⟨a ∼ odor⟩ **b :** spattered or smeared with paint ⟨after doing the kitchen walls she found that her clothes were all ∼⟩ **2 :** marked by or suggestive of an excessive or often crudely obtrusive use of paint ⟨an unskillful ∼ portrait⟩ ⟨∼ stage scenery⟩

[1]**pair** \ˈpa(a)\|(ə)r, ˈpe\|, \|ə\ *n, pl* **pairs** *also* **pair** [ME *peire, paire,* fr. OF *paire,* fr. L *paria* equal things, fr. neut. pl. of *par* equal; prob. akin to Gk *pernanai* to sell, *pornē* harlot, *poreuein* to convey — more at FARE] **1 a** (1) **:** a set of two separate things designed to be used together that may correspond to each other to the extent of being identical (as in shape, size, color, material) ⟨a ∼ of candlesticks⟩ ⟨a ∼ of oars⟩ ⟨a ∼ of dice⟩ or nearly identical except for differences arising typically out of adaptation to use with or on the right and left sides or parts of something ⟨a ∼ of shoes⟩ ⟨a ∼ of socks⟩ ⟨a ∼ of stirrups⟩ ⟨a ∼ of bookends⟩ or with or on the upper or lower parts or levels of something ⟨had arranged a matching ∼ of shelves one above the other on the wall⟩ and that may sometimes have only a general correspondence (as in color, design) and otherwise differ markedly (as in shape) while designed to be used together and together forming a single integral unit ⟨a ∼ of pajamas⟩ (2) **:** a set of two corresponding bodily parts or members ⟨had a beautiful ∼ of eyes⟩ ⟨a ∼ of muscular hands⟩ **b :** something made up of two corresponding parts or pieces joined together at or near one end ⟨∼ of trousers⟩ ⟨∼ of scissors⟩ ⟨∼ of tweezers⟩ ⟨∼ of pliers⟩ or at some other point ⟨∼ of suspenders⟩ ⟨∼ of eyeglasses⟩ so as to form a single integral unit **2 a :** a set of two separate things that are identical or similar ⟨a ∼ of twins⟩ or that happen to be closely associated without necessarily being identical or similar ⟨the horse and rider made a fine ∼⟩ or that in some other way occur together or are brought together or are used together or are viewed as together forming a closely associated couple that is usu. but not necessarily made up of two things that are of the same kind or are identical or similar or that correspond in some other way **:** a group of two ⟨a ∼ of brothers⟩ ⟨noticed that some of the plants grew in ∼s⟩ ⟨a ∼ of champions⟩ ⟨picked up a ∼ of greeting cards⟩ ⟨minimal ∼s in phonemics⟩**:** as (1) **:** a mated couple of animals ⟨a ∼ of bears⟩ ⟨a ∼ of robins⟩ (2) **:** a couple in love; *esp* **:** an engaged or married couple ⟨were a devoted ∼⟩ ⟨congratulated the newly married ∼⟩ (3) **:** a combination of two playing cards of the same value or denomination ⟨held a ∼⟩ (4) **:** a couple of horses harnessed together side by side ⟨a carriage and ∼⟩ (5) **:** a couple of partners (as in a game, at a dance, in a business enterprise) ⟨a ∼ of bridge players⟩ ⟨enjoyed watching the waltzing ∼s⟩ ⟨are a shrewd ∼⟩ (6) **:** a couple of individuals that are members of opposite parties or hold opposed opinions in a deliberative body and that mutually agree not to vote on a specific issue during a time (as a period of absence of one or both) agreed on (7) **:** a couple of individuals that are being spoken of or otherwise considered ⟨you'll remember that ∼, I think⟩; *esp* **:** a couple of individuals that have something (as specific traits of character) in common ⟨were an honest ∼⟩ (8) **:** a combination of two kinematic parts applied to each other in such a way as mutually to constrain relative motion ⟨a cylinder and its piston are a sliding ∼⟩ (9) **:** a couple of postage stamps attached to each other (10) **:** a basketry plait made up of two rods woven alternately one over the other **b** (1) **:** PARTNERSHIP ⟨working in ∼s⟩; *esp* **:** a partnership of two players (as bridge players) or other contestants engaged in a game or other contest against another such partnership (2) **pairs** *pl* **:** a game, contest, or tournament engaged in by players or other contestants divided up into such partnerships ⟨succeeded in winning the ∼s⟩ **c :** an agreement not to vote made by the two members of a pair (sense 2a(6)) **d :** PAIR-OAR ⟨well-trained in sculls, ∼s and fours —*Sports Illustrated*⟩ **3** *chiefly dial* **:** an integral whole made up of a set or succession of more than two things (as parts, pieces, sections) that usu. closely resemble each other or belong together for completeness: as **a :** a series of small objects (as beads) strung together (as in a necklace or rosary) **:** STRING **b :** a musical instrument made up of several related parts ⟨a ∼ of beautiful old organs —W.M.Thackeray⟩ **c :** a graduated succession of steps **:** FLIGHT ⟨two ∼ of stairs —Henry Fielding⟩

[2]**pair** \ˈ"\ *vb* -ED/-ING/-S *vt* **1 a :** to make a pair of (as by bringing together, joining, matching, associating, mating) ⟨∼*ed* the two films in a double bill⟩ ⟨∼*ed* a couple of cards⟩ — often used with *off* or *up* ⟨∼*ed* off the animals⟩ **b** (1) **:** to cause to be a member of a pair — often used with *up* ⟨∼*ed* him up with an opponent about his equal⟩ (2) **:** to bring into a mutual agreement not to vote on a specific issue during a time agreed on ⟨missed a vote on an important issue . . . by being ∼*ed* —*Current Biog.*⟩ **2 :** to arrange in pairs **:** separate into pairs ⟨∼*ed* her guests into congenial couples⟩ — often used with *off* ⟨∼*ed* off the group into couples for the next dance⟩ ∼ *vi* **1 :** to form a matching or equal member of a pair — often used with *off* or *up* ⟨a shoe that doesn't ∼ up with the other⟩ **2 a** (1) **:** to become united or closely associated with another so as to form a pair (as by partnership, companionship, mating) — often used with *off* or *up* ⟨∼*ed* up with an old friend⟩ ⟨the season when most birds ∼ off⟩ (2) **:** to come to a mutual agreement with one of an opposite party or opinion not to vote on a specific issue during a time agreed on ⟨failed to appear, ∼, or announce his position —*N.Y.Times*⟩ **b :** to become grouped or separated into pairs — often used with *off* ⟨the happy crowd gradually ∼*ed* off⟩ **3 :** to achieve or show a combination of two playing cards of equal value or denomination ⟨on my fourth card I ∼*ed*⟩

[3]**pair** \ˈ"\ *vb* -ED/-ING/-S [ME *pairen,* short for *apairen, apeyren, ampayrien,* fr. OF *empeirier* — more at IMPAIR] *chiefly dial* **:** IMPAIR

[4]**pair** \ˈ"\ *n* -S [F *pair,* adj., even, equal, fr. L *par* equal] **:** the even numbers in roulette when a bet is made on them

**pair·age** \-rij, -rēj\ *n* -S **:** a quantity of pairs of shoes being manufactured or sold ⟨increased the monthly ∼ to reach a new high⟩

**pair·er** \-rə(r)\ *n* -S **:** one who pairs or matches like or related articles

**pair-horse** \ˈ=ˈ=\ *adj* **:** drawn by a pair of horses ⟨goes about in a *pair-horse* carriage in the evening —Arnold Bennett⟩

**pairing** *n* -S [fr. gerund of [2]*pair*] **1 a** (1) **:** the action of grouping (as players, other contestants) into pairs (2) **:** a listing of grouped pairs **b** (1) **:** the process of making basketry plaits consisting of two rods woven alternately one over the other (2) **:** a woven row made by this process **2 :** SYNAPSIS

**pairle** \ˈpa(a)r(ə)l, ˈper-\ *n* -S [F, prob. alter. of OF *paile* mantle, pall, fr. L *pallium* — more at PALL] **:** a heraldic ordinary in the form of a Y extending to the upper corners and the base of the field — called also *pall;* compare SHAKEFORK —

**in pairle** *adv* **1 :** in the direction and position of the three arms of a pairle ⟨tierced *in pairle* sable, gules, and azure⟩ **2 :** in such a way that of three heraldic bearings one is bendwise, one bendwise sinister, and one palewise so as to approach or join at a common center ⟨three shields arranged *in pairle* with the points meeting in the center of the escutcheon⟩

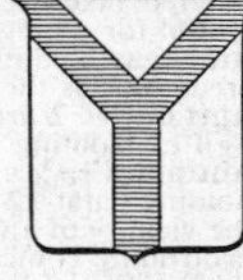
pairle

**pair-oar** \ˈ=,=\ *n* **:** a boat rowed by two rowers pulling one oar each and seated one abaft the other

**pair-oared** \ˈ=ˈ=\ *adj* **:** pulled or rigged as a pair-oar

**pair of colors 1** *chiefly Brit* **:** the national flag and regimental flag carried by a regiment **2 :** the position or commission of an ensign in the British army until the discontinuance of this rank in 1871

**pair of spectacles** *Brit* **:** a cricketer's score of nothing in each of his two innings in a single match

**pair production** *also* **pair formation** *or* **pair creation** *n* **:** the simultaneous and complete transformation of a quantum of radiant energy into an electron and a positron when the quantum interacts with the intense electric field near a nucleus

**pair royal** *n, pl* **pair royal** *or* **pairs royal** [[1]*pair* + *royal,* adj.] **:** three of a kind in the game of cribbage

**pairs** *pl of* PAIR, *pres 3d sing of* PAIR

**pairt** \ˈpärt\ *chiefly Scot var of* PART

**pair·trick** \ˈpär·trik\ *chiefly Scot var of* PARTRIDGE

**pai·sa** *also* **pais·sa** \ˈpīsə\ *n, pl* **pai·se** \-(,)sā\ *or* **paisas** *or* **paisa** [Hindi *paisā*] **1 a :** a monetary unit of India, Pakistan, Nepal, and Bhutan equal to 1/100 rupee; *also* **:** a coin representing one paisa — compare NAYA PAISA; see MONEY table **b :** PICE **2 a** (1) **:** an old copper coin of Afghanistan similar to the Indian pice (2) **:** a brass coin issued under Habibullah Khan (1901–19) **b :** an Afghan unit of value equivalent to that of one paisa

**pai·sa·no** \pīˈzä(,)nō, -ˈsä-\ *n* -S [Sp, fr. F *paysan* — more at PEASANT] **1** *Southwest* **a :** RUSTIC, PEASANT **b :** COMPATRIOT **c :** NATIVE; *esp* **:** an indigenous inhabitant of the state of California of mixed Spanish and Indian ancestry **2** *Southwest* **:** ROADRUNNER

[1]**pais·ley** \ˈpāzlē, -li\ *adj, often cap* [fr. *Paisley,* burgh of southwest Scotland] **1 :** made of soft wool or a similar material resembling cashmere and woven or printed with a colorful usu. elaborate design consisting typically of curved abstract figures ⟨a ∼ shawl⟩ **2 :** marked by or consisting of the designs, patterns, or figures typically used in paisley fabrics ⟨a ∼ print⟩ ⟨a ∼ pattern⟩

[2]**paisley** \ˈ"\ *n* -S *often cap* **1 :** a paisley fabric or design **2 :** an article (as a shawl, dress, trimming) made of a paisley fabric

**pai·ute** *also* **pi·ute** \ˈpī,(y)üt, =ˈ=\ *n, pl* **paiute** *or* **paiutes** *usu cap* **1 a :** a Shoshonean people of western Utah, northwestern Arizona, southeastern Nevada, and southeastern California — called also *Southern Paiute* **b :** a member of such people **2 :** the language of the Paiute people — compare NORTHERN PAIUTE

**paix·tle** \ˈpīchtlē\ *n* -S [MexSp, fr. Nahuatl *paixtli* hay] **:** a fiesta dance of Jalisco, Mexico, performed by men disguised in costumes of hay and representing sorcerers

**pa·ja·ma** \pəˈjämə, -ja-,-jà-\ *n* -S [Hindi *pāejāma, pājāma,* fr. Per *pā(e)* leg + *jāma* garment] **:** PAJAMAS

**pa·ja·maed** \-məd\ *adj* **:** wearing or fitted out with pajamas

**pajama party** *n* **:** SLUMBER PARTY

**pa·ja·mas** \-məz\ *n pl* [pl. of *pajama*] **1 :** loose lightweight trousers formerly much worn by both men and women in some countries of the Near East **2 :** a loosely fitting two-piece or sometimes one-piece lightweight suit in many styles and fabrics designed esp. for sleeping or lounging and consisting typically of trousers and a jacket or pullover top ⟨beach ∼⟩

**pa·ja·ro·el·lo** *or* **pajaroello tick** \,pähərəˈwe(,)lō-\ *also* **pa·ja·huel·lo** \,==ˈhwe(,)lō\ *n* -S [origin unknown] **:** a venomous tick (*Ornithodoros coriaceus*) that attacks man and other mammals and some birds and causes painful swellings

**paj·i·ta·nian** \,pajəˈtānēən, -nyən\ *adj, usu cap* [origin unknown] **:** of or relating to a Lower Paleolithic culture of Java characterized by choppers, chopping tools, and hand adzes made from cores with one side flat and the other rounded

**paj·on·ism** \ˈpajə,nizəm\ *n* -S *usu cap* [F *pajonisme,* fr. Claude *Pajon* †1685 French Protestant theologian + F *-isme* -ism] **:** a theological doctrine according to which the Holy Spirit does not act directly upon an individual but only indirectly (as by influencing intellectual judgments)

**pak-a-pu** \ˈpäkəˈpü\ *n* -S [Chin *pai*² *ko*¹ *p'iao*⁴ white pigeon ticket, fr. *pai*² white + *ko*¹ pigeon + *p'iao*⁴ ticket] **:** a Chinese lottery typically played with sheets of paper carrying columns of characters of which one group is a winning set that entitles the player choosing it to the stakes offered

**pa·ka·wan** \ˈpäkə,wän\ *n* -S *usu cap* **:** COAHUILTECAN

**pak·choi** \ˈbäkˈchȯi\ *n, pl* **pakchoi** *or* **pakchois** [Chin (Cantonese) *paāk ts'oi,* fr. *paāk* white + *ts'oi* vegetable] **:** CHINESE CABBAGE

**pa·ke·ha** \ˈpäkə,hä, -kē,ä; ˈpakēə\ *n, pl* **pakeha** *or* **pakehas** [Maori] *Austral & New Zeal* **:** one that is not of Maori ancestry; *esp* **:** a member of the white race

**pakh·pu·luk** \,päk(,)pùˈlük\ *n, pl* **pakhpuluk** *or* **pakhpuluks** *usu cap* **1 :** a people in the southern part of Kashmir in the subcontinent of India of Indo-Aryan and Turkish ancestry **2 :** a member of the Pakhpuluk people

**paki·stan** \ˈpakə,stan, -taa(ə)n *also* ,==ˈ=; ˈpäkēˈstän, ˈpäkēˈstän, -kəˈs-\ *adj, usu cap* [fr. *Pakistan,* republic in Indian subcontinent] **:** of or from Pakistan **:** of the kind or style prevalent in Pakistan **:** PAKISTANI

[1]**paki·stani** \,==ˈ=ē, -i\ *n, pl* **pakistanis** *or* **pakistani** *cap* [Hindustani *Pākistānī,* fr. *Pākistān* Pakistan] **:** a native or inhabitant of West Pakistan or East Pakistan in the northwestern or northeastern part of the Indian subcontinent

[2]**pakistani** \ˈ"\ *adj, usu cap* **:** PAKISTAN

**pa·kla·va** \ˈpäklə,vä, ,==ˈ=\ *n* -S [modif. of Turk *baklava*] **:** BAKLAVA

**pak·tong** \ˈpak,tȯŋ\ *also* **pack·fong** \-,fȯŋ\ *n* -S [Cantonese *paāk t'ūng,* fr. *paāk* white + *t'ūng* copper] **:** an alloy resembling nickel silver and consisting of nickel, zinc, and copper

[1]**pal** \ˈpal\ *n* -S [Romany (English) *phal* brother, friend, (Continental) *phral,* fr. Skt *bhrātṛ* brother — more at BROTHER] **:** PARTNER: as **a :** ACCOMPLICE **b :** a close friend or boon companion

[2]**pal** \ˈ"\ *vi* **palled; palled; palling; pals :** to be or become pals ⟨they *palled* around for years⟩ **:** keep company **:** act as pal to or behave as an intimate with someone

**pal** *abbr* paleontology

**PAL** *abbr* prisoner at large

**pala** *var of* PALLAH

[1]**pal·ace** \ˈpaləs\ *n* -S [ME *palais, paleis,* fr. OF, fr. L *palatium,* fr. *Palatium* Palatine Hill in Rome on which the residences of the emperors were built] **1 a :** the official residence of a sovereign **b** *chiefly Brit* **:** the official residence of an archbishop or bishop **2 a :** a large and stately house — used chiefly in translating from French and Italian **b :** a large public building (as for a legislature or superior court) **c :** a gaudy establishment fitted up as a place of public resort (as for amusement or refreshment) ⟨provincial movie ∼s —Lewis Mumford⟩ **3** *slang* **:** CABOOSE

[2]**palace** \ˈ"\ *adj* **1 :** of or relating to a palace ⟨∼ gardens⟩ **2 a :** close to or intimate with a sovereign **:** living at or frequenting the court ⟨∼ circles⟩ **b :** of, relating to, involving, or sponsored by the intimates of a sovereign or other chief executive ⟨a ∼ revolution⟩ ⟨∼ politics⟩ **3 :** showy and luxurious **:** DELUXE ⟨a ∼ hotel⟩

[3]**palace** \ˈ"\ *vt* -ED/-ING/-S **:** to place or house in or as if in a palace

[4]**palace** \ˈ"\ *n* -S [prob. fr. Corn *palas* to dig, fr. *pal* spade, fr. L *pala*] **:** an underground storehouse esp. popular in Cornwall for storing fish

**palace car** *n* **:** a luxuriously or superiorly fitted railway car (as a parlor car or sleeping car)

**pal·aced** \-sst\ *adj* **:** furnished with a palace **:** housed in a palace

**palace guard** *n* **1 :** a body of men stationed to protect a castle or its occupants **2 :** a king's, president's, or other chief executive's inner circle of intimates and advisers ⟨complained that a *palace guard* — made up of men never elected to serve — is running the government —*Springfield (Mass.) Union*⟩

**pal·ace·ward** \-wə(r)d\ *also* **pal·ace·wards** \-dz\ *adv* **:** toward a palace

**pal·a·din** \ˈpaləd°n, -dən\ *n* -S [F, fr. It *paladino,* fr. ML *palatinus* courtier, fr. L, palace official — more at PALATINE, n.] **1 :** a champion of a medieval prince **:** a legendary hero **2 :** a person of outstanding worth or quality who is firm in support of some cause or objective **:** PROTAGONIST

**palae-** — see PALE-

**palae·acanthocephala** \ˈpālē, ˈpalē+\ *n pl, cap* [NL, fr. *pale-* + *Acanthocephala*] **:** an order of Acanthocephala comprising parasites of fishes, birds, and mammals that have spines on the trunk and the proboscis hooks arranged in long rows

**palae·an·thro·pi·nae** \,==,an(t)thrəˈpī(,)nē\ *n pl, cap* [NL, fr. *pale-* + Gk *anthrōpos* human being + NL *-inae* — more at ANTHROP-] *syn of* PALEOANTHROPINAE

**palae·an·thro·pus** \,==ˈan(t)thrəpəs, -,anˈthrōpəs\ *syn of* PALAEOANTHROPUS

**palae·arctic** *or* **pale·arctic** \ˈ==+\ *adj, usu cap* [*pale-* + *arctic*] **:** of, relating to, or being a biogeographic region or subregion that includes Europe, Asia north of the Himalayas, northern Arabia, and Africa north of the Sahara **:** Old World Holarctic

**palae·asiatic** \ˈ==+\ *adj, usu cap* [*pale-* + *asiatic*] **:** PALEOASIATIC

**palae·echinoidea** \ˈ==+\ *n pl, cap* [NL, fr. *pale-* + *Echinoidea*] *in some classifications* **:** a division of extinct chiefly Paleozoic sea urchins having the test usu. composed of more than 20 meridional rows of plates that often overlap and jaws always present — compare EUECHINOIDEA — **palae·echinoidean** \ˈ==+\ *adj or n*

**palae·eu·dyp·tes** \,==yüˈdip(,)tēz\ *n, cap* [NL, fr. *pale-* + *Eudyptes,* genus of penguins, fr. *eu-* + Gk *dyptēs* diver, fr. *dyptein* to dive; akin to Gk *dyein* to enter, dive in — more at ADYTUM] **:** a genus of very large fossil penguins of the Eocene of New Zealand

**palae·ich·thy·es** \,==ˈikthē,ēz\ *n pl, cap* [NL, fr. *pale-* + Gk *ichthyes,* pl. of *ichthys* fish — more at ICHTHUS] *in some classifications* **:** a subclass of fishes consisting of the elasmobranchs, ganoids, dipnoans, and crossopterygians — **palae·ichthyic** \ˈ==+\ *adj*

**pa·lae·mon** \pəˈlē,män\ *n, cap* [NL, fr. L, name of a sea god, fr. Gk *Palaimōn*] **:** a large widely distributed genus (the type of the family Palaemonidae) of prawns with prominently toothed rostrum and three-jointed mandibular palp — **pa·lae·mo·nid** \-ˈmənəd\ *adj or n* — **pa·lae·mo·noid** \-,nȯid\ *adj*

**pa·lae·mo·ne·tes** \=,=məˈnē(,)tēz\ *n, cap* [NL, fr. *Palaemon*] **:** a genus of prawns related to and resembling those of the genus *Palaemon* but lacking the mandibular palp

**palaeo-** — see PALE-

**palaeo·an·throp·ic** \ˈpālēō,anˈthräpik, ˈpalē-, -pēk\ *also* **pale·anthropic** \ˈpālē, ˈpalē+\ *or* **paleo·anthropic** \ˈpālēō, ˈpalēō+\ *adj* [*pale-* + Gk *anthrōpos* human being + E *-ic* — more at ANTHROP-] **1 :** of or relating to hominids more primitive than those included in the species (*Homo sapiens*) that includes recent man — compare NEOANTHROPIC **2** [NL *Palaeoanthropus* + E *-ic*] **:** of, relating to, or belonging to the genus *Palaeoanthropus*

**palaeo·an·thro·pus** \,pālēōˈan(t)thrəpəs, ,palē-, -,anˈthrōpəs\ *n, cap* [NL, fr. *pale-* + *-anthropus*] *in some classifications* **:** a genus of hominids based on a single lower jaw found at Mauer near Heidelberg, Germany but now often extended to include the entire Neanderthaloid radiation and other primitive men of uncertain affinities (as Solo man and Rhodesian man)

**palaeo·ca·ri·da** \ˈ===kəˈrīdə, -ˈkarədə\ [NL, fr. *pale-* + Gk *karid-, karis* shrimp or prawn] *syn of* GIGANTOSTRACA

**palaeo·con·cha** \,===ˈkäŋkə\ *n pl, cap* [NL, fr. *pale-* + L *concha* conch] *in some classifications* **:** a division of Protobranchia comprising simple extinct bivalve mollusks with thin shells and a primitive hinge and sometimes including also a few recent marine bivalves

[1]**palaeo·cri·noid** \ˈ===ˈkrī,nȯid, -kri-,-\ *adj* [NL *Palaeocrinoidea*] **:** of or relating to the Palaeocrinoidea

[2]**palaeocrinoid** \ˈ"\ *n* -S **:** an animal or fossil of the order Palaeocrinoidea

**palaeo·crinoidea** \ˈ===+\ *n pl, cap* [NL, fr. *pale-* + *Crinoidea*] *in some classifications* **:** an order of Paleozoic stalked crinoids of supposedly primitive type having the actinal side of the calyx closed — compare NEOCRINOIDEA

**palaeo·dic·ty·op·tera** \,===,diktēˈäptərə\ *n pl, cap* [NL, fr. *pale-* + *dicty-* + *-ptera*] **:** an order of very primitive extinct insects known only from the Upper Carboniferous and Permian periods and characterized by homonomous segmentation of the thorax and abdomen and by a simple wing venation with a network of cross veins — **palaeo·dic·ty·op·ter·an** \ˈ===,==ˈ=tərən\ *adj or n* — **palaeo·dic·ty·op·ter·ous** \-rəs\ *adj*

**palaeo·dic·ty·op·ter·on** \-təˌrän\ *n, pl* **palaeodictyop·tera** \-tərə\ **:** an insect or fossil of the order Palaeodictyoptera

**palaeo·echinoidea** \ˈ===+\ *syn of* PALAEECHINOIDEA

**palaeo·ge·an** *or* **palaeo·ge·an** *also* **paleo·ge·an** \,pālēōˈjēən, ,pal-\ *adj, usu cap* [NL *Palaeogaea* eastern hemisphere, lit., old world (fr. *pale-* + *-gaea*) + E *-an*] **:** of, relating to, or being a biogeographic realm consisting of the entire eastern hemisphere

**palaeo·genesis** *also* **paleo·genesis** \ˈpālē, ˈpalē+\ *n* [NL, fr. *pale-* + L *genesis*] **:** PALINGENESIS c

**palaeo·ge·net·ic** \ˈ===jəˈned·ik\ *adj* [*pale-* + *genetic*] **:** exhibiting palingenesis **:** of, relating to, or characterized by the retention of ancestral larval characters into or in adulthood

**palae·og·na·thae** \,pālēˈägnə,thē, ,pal-\ *n pl, cap* [NL, fr. *pale-* + *-gnathae*] *in some esp former classifications* **:** a superorder of the subclass Neornithes comprising birds with a primitive reptilian type of palate that are now usu. included in Neognathae — **palae·og·nath·ic** \ˈ==əgˈnathik\ *or* **palae·og·na·thous** \ˈ==ˈägnəthəs\ *adj*

**palaeo·mastodon** \ˈpālēō, ˈpalēō+\ *n, cap* [NL, fr. *pale-* + *Mastodon*] **:** a genus of primitive proboscidean mammals of the Oligocene of Egypt that are characterized by a long skull, short tusks, a long lower jaw, 22 molars, and a body about half as large as that of the Indian elephant and are commonly regarded as ancestral to the mastodons

**palaeo·nemertea** \ˈ===+\ *n pl, cap* [NL, fr. *pale-* + *Nemertea*] **:** an order of nemertean worms (class Anopla) that have two layers of body-wall musculature, a proboscis without a stylet, and a brain that is not divided into lobes — **palaeo·nemertean** \ˈ===+\ *adj or n*

**palaeo·nemertine** \ˈ===+\ *adj or n* [NL *Palaeonemertinea*] **:** PALAEONEMERTEAN

**palaeo·nemertinea** \ˈ===+\ *or* **palaeonemertini** \ˈ===+\ [NL, fr. *pale-* + *Nemertinea* or *Nemertini*] *syn of* PALAEONEMERTEA

[1]**palaeo·nis·cid** \ˈ===ˈnisəd\ *adj* [NL *Palaeoniscidae*] **:** of or relating to the Palaeoniscidae

[2]**palaeoniscid** \ˈ"\ *n* -S **:** a fish or fossil of the family Palaeoniscidae

**palaeo·nis·ci·dae** \-===ˈnisə,dē\ *n pl, cap* [NL, fr. *Palaeoniscum,* type genus + *-idae*] **:** a family of extinct primitive ganoid fishes that lived from the Devonian to the Lias and have an elongate body covered usu. with rhombic plates, small pectoral and ventral fins, a single dorsal and anal fin, a heterocercal tail, a skull covered with bony plates, and jaws bearing small teeth

[1]**palaeo·nis·coid** \ˈ===ˈni,skȯid\ *adj* [NL *Palaeoniscum* + E *-oid*] **:** like or like that of the genus *Palaeoniscum*

[2]**palaeoniscoid** \ˈ"\ *n* -S **:** a palaeoniscoid fish or fossil

**palaeo·nis·cum** \,===ˈniskəm\ *n, cap* [NL, fr. *pale-* + Gk *oniskos,* a gadoid fish, dim. of *onos* ass — more at ASS] **:** the type genus of Palaeoniscidae

**palaeo·nis·cus** \-kəs\ *syn of* PALAEONISCUM

**palaeo·phile** \ˈpālēə,fīl, ˈpal-\ *also* **palae·oph·i·list** \,==ˈäfələst\ *n* -S [*pale-* + *-phile*] **:** one fond of or informed about what is ancient **:** ANTIQUARY

**pa·lae·o·phis** \pəˈlēəfəs\ *n, cap* [NL, fr. *pale-* + *-ophis*] **:** a genus of large extinct snakes from the Lower Eocene of England and France that are the earliest known members of the suborder Serpentes sharing many characters with and probably being ancestral to the recent pythons and boas

**palaeo·pi·the·cus** \,pālēōpəˈthēkəs, ,pal-, -ˈpithəkəs\ *n, cap* [NL, fr. *pale-* + *-pithecus*] **:** a genus of extinct Pliocene anthropoids from the Siwalik hills of India that is prob. rather closely related to the recent gorilla

**palae·op·tera** \,==ˈäptərə\ *n pl, cap* [NL, fr. *pale-* + *-ptera*] **:** a major division of Pterygota comprising winged insects that are unable to flex their wings over the abdomen and including the orders Odonata and Plectoptera — **palae·op·ter·ous** \¦==¦=t(ə)rəs\ *adj*

**palae·op·te·ryg·ii** \,===ˌäptə'rijēˌī\ *n pl, cap* [NL, fr. *pale-* + *-pterygii*] *in some classifications* **:** a subclass of Osteichthyes comprising the primitive orders Cladistia and Chondrostei

**palaeo·saur** *also* **paleo·saur** \'pālēə,só(ə)r, 'pal-\ *n* -s [NL *Palaeosaurus*] **:** a dinosaur of *Palaeosaurus* or a closely related genus

**palaeo·sau·rus** \,===ˈsȯrəs\ *n, cap* [NL, fr. *pale-* + *-saurus*] **:** a genus of carnivorous saurischian dinosaurs (suborder Theropoda) of the Upper Triassic of England that is related to *Allosaurus* and *Ceratosaurus*

**palaeo·simia** \¦palēō, ¦palēō+\ *n, cap* [NL, fr. *pale-* + L *simia* ape — more at SIMIAN] **:** a genus of Miocene fossil apes from the Siwalik hills of India that resemble and are prob. ancestral to the orangutan

**palaeo·spondylus** \¦===+\ *n, cap* [NL, fr. *pale-* + *-spondylus*] **:** a genus of extinct primitive vertebrates that are known from a single form (*P. gunni*) of the Devonian of Scotland that is usu. about one inch long with a large skull, branchial arches and jaws highly modified or possibly absent, a segmented vertebral column, and the caudal fin and limb girdles well-developed, and that is usu. placed among the Placodermi but sometimes considered a cyclostome — see CYCLIAE

**palae·os·tra·ca** \,palē'ästrəkə, ,pal- *also* -'ōs-\ *n pl, cap* [NL, fr. *pale-* + *-ostraca*] *in some classifications* **:** a class of arthropods comprising the king crabs, the eurypterids, and sometimes the trilobites — compare MEROSTOMATA — **palae·os·tra·can** \¦==¦==kən\ *adj or n*

**palaeo·then·ti·dae** \,===ˈthentə,dē\ [NL, fr. *Palaeothentes*, genus of marsupials + *-idae*] *syn of* CAENOLESTIDAE

**palaeo·there** *also* **paleo·there** \'pālēə,thi(ə)r, 'pal-\ *n* -s [NL *Palaeotheriidae*] **:** a mammal or fossil of the family Palaeotheriidae — **palaeo·the·ri·an** \¦===¦thirēən\ *adj*

**palaeo·the·ri·idae** \,==ōthə'rīə,dē\ *n pl, cap* [NL, fr. *Palaeotherium*, type genus (fr. *pale-* + *-therium*) + *-idae*] **:** a family of extinct perissodactyl mammals of the Eocene and Miocene of Europe and America that are related to the horses but in some respects resemble tapirs

**palaeo·the·ri·o·dont** \¦===¦thirēə,dänt\ *adj* [NL *Palaeotherium* + E *-odont*] **:** being or having lophodont teeth with the external tubercles longitudinal and the inner united with them by transverse oblique crests

**palaeo·trema·ta** \,===ˈtremədə, -rēm-\ *n pl, cap* [NL, fr. *pale-* + *-tremata*] **:** a small order of Brachiopoda comprising primitive inarticulate forms known from the Lower Cambrian through the Ordovician — **palaeo·tremate** \¦===¦=māt, -,māt\ *n* -s

**palaeo·tropical** *or* **paleo·tropical** \¦===+\ *adj, usu cap* [*pale-* + *tropical*] **:** of, relating to, or being a major biogeographic region that includes the Oriental and Ethiopian regions

**palaeo·typographist** \¦===+\ *n* -s [*palaeotypography* + *-ist*] **:** a student of palaeotypography

**palaeo·typography** \¦===+\ *n* -ES [*pale-* + *typography*] **:** ancient or early typography

**pa·laes·tra** *also* **pa·les·tra** \pə'lestrə, *chiefly Brit* -lēs-\ *or* **pa·lais·tra** \-līs-, -lās-\ *n, pl* **palaes·trae** \-e,strē\ *or* **palaes·tras** \-strəz\ *also* **pales·trae** \-e,strē\ *or* **pales·tras** \-strəz\ *or* **palais·trae** \-ī,strē, -ā,s-\ *also* **palais·tras** \-strəz\ [L *palaestra*, fr. Gk *palaistra*, fr. *palaiein* to wrestle; prob. akin to Gk *pallein* to brandish — more at POLEMIC] **1 a :** a place in ancient Greece or Rome for teaching and practicing wrestling and other sports **b :** a gymnasium or stadium **2 :** athletic exercise or practice; *esp* **:** WRESTLING — **pa·laes·tral** *also* **pa·les·tral** \-'lestrəl\ *adj*

**pa·lae·ti·o·log·i·cal** \pə¦lēdēə¦läjəkəl\ *adj* **:** of, relating to, or by means of palaetiology

**pa·lae·ti·ol·o·gy** *also* **pa·le·ti·ol·o·gy** \=,==ˈäləjē\ *n* -s [*pale-* + *etiology*] **:** explanation of past events (as in geology) by the laws of causation

**pal·a·fitte** \'palə,fit, -fēt, ,==ˈ=\ *n, pl* **palafittes** \-ts\ *also* **palafit·ti** \,==ˈfid-ē, -'fed-ē\ [F, fr. It *palafitta*, fr. *palo* stake, pile (fr. L *palus*) + *fitto* fixed, past part. of *figgere* to fix, fr. L *figere* to fix, fasten — more at POLE, DIKE] **:** an ancient dwelling built on piles over a lake; *specif* **:** a Neolithic lake dwelling in Switzerland or northern Italy

**pa·lag·o·nite** \pə'lagə,nīt\ *n* -s [G *palagonit*, fr. *Palagonia*, Sicily + G *-it* -ite] **:** basaltic glass that is more or less altered and devitrified and that occurs with volcanic ash in the form of a basaltic tuff — **pa·lag·o·nit·ic** \=¦==¦nid·ik\ *adj*

**pa·la·ic** \pə'lāik\ *n, cap* **:** an Anatolian language known from quotations in Hittite documents — see INDO-EUROPEAN LANGUAGES table

**pa·laih·ni·han** \pə'līnəhən\ *n, pl* **palaihnihan** *or* **palaihnihans** *usu cap* **1 a :** a Shasta people of northeastern California **b :** a member of such people **2 :** a subdivision of the Shastan language family comprising Achomawi and Atsugewi

**palaio-** — see PALE-

**pa·lais** \(')pa¦lā\ *n, pl* **palais** \-ā(z)\ *also* **pa·lais·es** \-āz\ [F, fr. L *palatium* — more at PALACE] **:** PALACE — used esp. of a French public building (as a courthouse) or official residence

**palais de danse** \-də'däⁿs\ *n, pl* **palais de danse** [F, lit., dance palace] **:** a public dance hall

**pa·la·ka** \pə'läkə\ *n* -s [Hawaiian, perh. fr. E *block*] **:** a long-sleeved Hawaiian shirt having a simple plaid or cross-striped pattern and usu. worn with the tail out

**pal·a·ma** \'paləmə\ *n, pl* **pala·mae** \-,mē, -,mī\ [NL, fr. Gk *palamē* palm — more at PALM] **:** the webbing on the feet of aquatic birds

**pal·a·mate** \-,mət, -,māt, *usu* -d·+V\ *adj* [NL *palama* + E *-ate*] **:** WEB-FOOTED

**pal·a·me·dea** \,palə'mēdēə\ [NL, fr. Gk *Palamēdēs*, Greek hero of the Trojan war] *syn of* ANHIMA

**pal·a·me·de·i·dae** \,==,mə'dēə,dē\ [NL, fr. *Palamedea* + *-idae*] *syn of* ANHIMIDAE

**palamino** *var of* PALOMINO

**pal·a·mite** \'palə,mīt\ *n* -s *usu cap* [Gregorius *Palamas* †1359 Greek mystic and chief apologist for the hesychasts + E *-ite*] **:** HESYCHAST

**pal·a·mit·ism** \'==,mīd-,izəm, -,mī,ti-\ *n* -s *usu cap* [*palamite* + *-ism*] **:** HESYCHASM

**pal·am·pore** \'paləm,pō(ə)r\ *also* **pal·am·poor** \-,pů(ə)r\ *n* -s [prob. fr. *Palanpur*, town in Rajputana, India] **:** a painted or printed cotton cloth used in India esp. for bedcovers, garments, and prayer rugs

**pal·an·der** \'paləndə(r)\ *n* -s [It *palandra*] **1 :** a flat-bottomed boat formerly used for horse transport **2** *obs* **:** FIRE SHIP

**pa·lan·ka** \pə'laŋkə\ *n* -s [Turk *palanka*, fr. It *palanca* fortified place, stake, prob. fr. L *palanga*, *phalanga* carrying pole, roller, fr. Gk *phalang-*, *phalanx* log, roller, phalanx — more at BALK] **:** a former Turkish palisaded camp

**pa·lan·quin** \¦palən¦kēn, -¦k(w)in; pə'laŋkwən, -ank-\ *also* **pal·an·keen** \¦palən¦kēn\ *n* -s [Pg *palanquim*, fr. Jav *pēlaṅki*, fr. Prakrit *pallaṅka*, fr. Skt *palyaṅka*, *paryaṅka*, fr. *pari* around + *añcati* he bends, curves; akin to Skt *aṅka* bend, hook — more at PER, ANGLE] **:** a conveyance that was formerly much used in eastern Asia esp. for the transport of one person, that consists of an enclosed litter usu. in the form of a box with wooden shutters, and that is borne on the shoulders of men by means of projecting poles

palanquin

**²palanquin** *also* **palankeen** \"\ *vi* -ED/-ING/-S **:** to travel in a palanquin

**pa·la·oa** \,pälə'ōə\ *n* -s [Hawaiian] **:** an Hawaiian pendant of whale's tooth ivory

**pa·la·pa·la** \,pälə'pälə\ *n* -s [Hawaiian] *Hawaii* **:** written matter **:** DOCUMENTS

**pa·la·pa·lai** \,päləpə'lī\ *n* -s [Hawaiian] **:** a large fern (*Microlepia hirta*) of the family Polypodiaceae that is widely distributed in tropical Asia and the Pacific islands

**pa·lap·ter·yx** \pə'laptə(,)riks\ [NL, fr. *pale-* + *Apteryx*] *syn of* DINORNIS

**pa·la·qui·um** \pə'läkwēəm\ *n, cap* [NL, fr. Tag *palak-palak*] **:** a large genus of East Indian trees (family Sapotaceae) with milky juice, leathery leaves, and hexamerous flowers

**pa·lar** \'pālə(r)\ *adj* [LL *palaris*, fr. L *palus* stake — more at POLE] **:** of, relating to, or resembling a stake ⟨a ~ line on a heraldic shield⟩

**pa·las** \pə'läsh\ *or* **palas tree** *also* **pu·las** \pə'l-\ *n* -ES [Hindi *palās*, fr. Skt *palāśa*] **:** DHAK

**pal·at·abil·i·ty** \,palәd·ə'bilәd-ē, -alətə'bilətē, -i\ *n* **:** the quality or state of being palatable

**palatability table** *n* **:** a tabular scheme for rating the palatability of range plants for grazing animals

**pa·lat·able** \'paləd·əbəl, -ətəb-\ *adj* ['*palate* + *-able*] **1 :** agreeable to the palate or taste **:** SAVORY **2 :** pleasing or agreeable to the mind **:** ACCEPTABLE

**syn** PALATABLE, APPETIZING, SAVORY, SAPID, SAPOROUS, TASTY, TOOTHSOME, FLAVORSOME, RELISHING signify, in common, agreeable or pleasant to the taste. PALATABLE usu. implies little more than merely acceptable, often applying to something one would not usu. expect to find pleasant to the taste ⟨the root, when properly cooked, was converted into a *palatable* and nutritious food —W.H.Prescott⟩ ⟨had eaten the raw fish prepared by the Indians of Otaheite, and found it *palatable* when dipped in a sauce of sea water —C.B.Nordhoff & J.N. Hall⟩ APPETIZING implies a whetting of the appetite in some way as by the smell and appearance of food ⟨the *appetizing* odor of roasting turkey⟩ ⟨*appetizing* ways of preparing hamburg⟩ SAVORY applies to foods that have agreeable odor as well as taste, usu. suggesting stimulating and well seasoned as opposed to bland dishes ⟨a *savory* stew⟩ ⟨deer steaks broiled and *savory* —Marjory S. Douglas⟩ ⟨*savory* fried oysters —*Amer. Guide Series: Conn.*⟩ SAPID and SAPOROUS are opposed to *insipid* and imply a marked taste or flavor, usu. keen or exhilarating ⟨roast beef is more *sapid* than roast veal⟩ ⟨a *saporous* onion stew⟩ TASTY implies marked taste and appetizing quality, often of something small and delectable ⟨good, solid, *tasty* food —Della Lutes⟩ ⟨haws, which can be made into a *tasty* jelly —*Amer. Guide Series: La.*⟩ ⟨the smelt — a *tasty* panfish —*Amer. Guide Series: Mich.*⟩ TOOTHSOME heightens the idea of agreeableness in taste and adds the idea of tenderness or daintiness ⟨one of the most *toothsome* chicken dinners you'll ever munch —Gelston Hardy⟩ ⟨venison. Sometimes it was tender and *toothsome*; at other times stringy and strong —Kenneth Roberts⟩ FLAVORSOME is interchangeable with SAVORY though it stresses more a richness of taste ⟨a preserve is made from the Japanese plum, but it is more *flavorsome* eaten raw —*Amer. Guide Series: La.*⟩ ⟨incredibly *flavorsome* wild mushrooms from the forests —Marcia Davenport⟩ RELISHING stresses gusto in enjoyment ⟨plain fare, *relishing* to a hungry boy⟩

**pal·at·able·ness** \-bəlnəs\ *n* -ES **:** PALATABILITY

**pal·at·ably** \-blē, -bli\ *adv* **:** so as to be palatable **:** PLEASINGLY

**¹pal·a·tal** \'paləd·ᵊl, -ət³l\ *adj* [F, fr. L *palatum* palate + F *-al* — more at PALATE] **1 :** of or relating to the palate **:** PALATINE **2 a :** formed with the front of the tongue behind the lowered tip near or touching the hard palate (as \k\ in German \ik\ *ich*, as \y\ in *yeast* or *yacht*, as \nʸ\ in French \änʸō\ *agneau*, as \lʸ\ in Italian \lʸē\ *gli*) — compare PALATALIZED, VELAR **b** (1) **:** formed with the blade of the tongue near the hard palate (as the sounds represented by *sh* in *she*, *si* in *vision*, *ch* in *chin*, *j* in *judge*) (2) *of a vowel* **:** FRONT

☞ Because some phoneticians make the hard palate alone their datum of reference, others the combined hard-soft palate, and because some make two subdivisions, others three, compounds of prefix and *palatal* are not consistently used, as indicated in the following rough chart, in which the solid line represents the hard palate, the dotted line the soft:

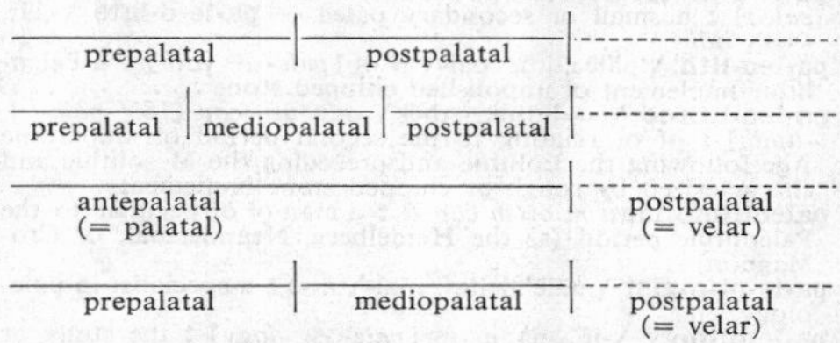

| prepalatal | postpalatal | ..... |
|---|---|---|

| prepalatal | mediopalatal | postpalatal | ..... |
|---|---|---|---|

| antepalatal (= palatal) | postpalatal (= velar) |
|---|---|

| prepalatal | mediopalatal | postpalatal (= velar) |
|---|---|---|

**c** *of a vowel in Russian* **:** SOFT 4c **3 :** of, relating to, or situated on the outside of the aperture of a univalve mollusk ⟨a ~ lip⟩ — **pal·a·tal·ly** \-ᵊlē, -ᵊli\ *adv*

**²palatal** \"\ *n* -s **1 :** PALATINE BONE **2 :** a palatal sound

**palatal index** *n* **:** the ratio of the length of the hard palate to its breadth multiplied by 100

**pal·a·tal·ism** \'paləd·ᵊl,izəm, -ət³l,i-\ *n* -s **:** palatal character

**pal·a·tal·i·ty** \,palə'taləd·ē\ *n* -ES **:** PALATALISM

**pal·a·tal·iza·tion** \,paləd·ᵊlə'zāshən, -lət³l-, -,lī'z-\ *n* -s **1 :** the quality or state of being palatalized **2 :** an act or instance of palatalizing an utterance

**pal·a·tal·ize** \'paləd·ᵊl,īz, -lət³l,-\ *vt* -ED/-ING/-S **1 :** to pronounce as or change into a palatal sound **2 :** to modify the utterance of (a nonpalatal sound) by simultaneously bringing the front of the tongue to or near the hard palate

**palatalized** *adj* [fr. past part. of *palatalize*] *of a vowel in Russian* **:** SOFT 4c

**palatal law** *n* **:** a statement in historical linguistics: Indo-European guttural consonants become palatals in Indo-Iranian when followed by the palatal vowel *i* or by an *a* which is equivalent to Greek and Latin *e* but remain gutturals when followed by the guttural vowel *u* or by an *a* which is equivalent to Greek and Latin *a* or *o*, thus establishing the *a*, *e*, and *o* found in the European languages as original Indo-European

**¹pal·ate** \'palət, *usu* -əd·+V\ *n* -s [ME, fr. L *palatum*, perh. of Etruscan origin] **1 :** the roof of the mouth consisting of the structures that separate the mouth from the nasal cavity — see HARD PALATE, SOFT PALATE **2 a :** mental relish **:** intellectual taste **b :** the seat of the sense of taste **3 :** a projection from the base of the lower lip into the throat of a personate corolla

**²palate** \"\ *vt* -ED/-ING/-S **:** to try with the palate **:** TASTE, RELISH

**palate bone** *n* **:** PALATINE BONE

**pal·ate·ful** \'==fəl\ *adj, of a beverage* **:** having body or substance — **pal·ate·ful·ness** *n* -ES

**pal·ate·less** \'==ləs\ *adj* **:** lacking in delicacy of taste

**pa·la·tial** \pə'lāshəl\ *adj* [L *palatium* palace + E *-al* — more at PALACE] **1 :** of, relating to, or being a palace ⟨a ~ residence⟩ **2 :** suitable for or used in a palace ⟨~ furnishings⟩ **3 :** MAGNIFICENT, LUXURIOUS ⟨a ~ yacht⟩ — **pa·la·tial·ly** \-shəlē, -li\ *adv* — **pa·la·tial·ness** \-lnəs\ *n* -ES

**pa·lat·ic** \pə'lad·ik\ *adj* **:** PALATAL

**pa·lat·i·nate** \pə'latᵊnət, -ᵊn,āt\ *usu* |d·+V\ *n* -s [²*palatine* + *-ate*] **1 :** the province or territory of a palatine or count palatine **:** COUNTY PALATINE **2** *cap* **:** a native or inhabitant of a state of the old German Empire that was under the jurisdiction of a count palatine of the Rhine and is now a part of Bavaria

**¹pal·a·tine** \'palə,tīn\ *adj* [L *palatinus*, fr. *palatium* palace] **1 a :** of or relating to a palace esp. of a caesar or an emperor of Germany **b :** being or suitable for a palace **:** PALATIAL **2** [F *palatin*, fr. L *palatinus*, n. — more at PALATINE, n.] **a :** possessing royal privileges **b :** of or relating to a count palatine or to a palatinate

**²palatine** \"\ *n* -s [L *palatinus*, fr. *palatinus*, adj.] **1 a :** an officer of an imperial palace: as (1) **:** MAYOR OF THE PALACE (2) **:** an imperial chamberlain or chief minister **b :** a medieval lord having sovereign power in an imperial or royal province or dependency **:** a vassal invested with royal privileges and rights within his domains **c :** a count palatine in England and Ireland **d :** the senior proprietor of a province in an American colony **2** *cap* **:** PALATINATE 2 **3** [F, after Elisabeth Charlotte of Bavaria †1722 Duchess of Orléans, and Princess *Palatine*] **:** a fur cape or stole covering the neck and shoulders

**³palatine** \"\ *adj* [F *palatin*, fr. (assumed) NL *palatinus*, fr. L *palatum* palate + *-inus* -ine] **:** of, relating to, or lying near the palate

**⁴palatine** \"\ *n* -s **:** a palatine part; *esp* **:** PALATINE BONE

**palatine artery** *n* [³*palatine*] **1 :** either of two arteries of each side of the face: **a :** an inferior artery that arises from the facial artery and supplies the soft palate, palatine glands, and tonsils **b :** a superior artery that arises from the internal maxillary and sends branches to the soft palate and one branch to the mucous membrane and glands of the hard palate and gums **2 :** any of the branches of the palatine arteries

**palatine bone** *n* **:** either of a pair of bones that are situated behind and between the maxillae and in front of the pterygoids and in man are of an extremely irregular form, each consisting of a horizontal plate which joins the bone of the opposite side and forms the back part of the hard palate and a vertical plate which is extended into three processes and helps to form the floor of the orbit, the outer wall of the nasal cavity, and several adjoining parts

**palatine canal** *n* **:** any of several small openings in the bony palate for the passage of vessels or nerves

**palatine gland** *n* **:** any of numerous small mucous glands in the palate opening into the mouth

**palatine nerve** *n* **:** one of the nerves arising from the sphenopalatine ganglion and supplying the roof of the mouth, parts of the nose, and adjoining parts

**palatine suture** *n* **:** either of two sutures in the hard palate: **a :** a transverse suture lying between the horizontal plates of the palate bones and the maxillary bones **b :** a median suture lying between the two maxillary bones in front and continued posteriorly between the palate bones

**palatine tonsil** *n* **:** TONSIL 1 a

**palating** *pres part of* PALATE

**pa·la·tion** \pə'lāshən\ *n* -s [NL, fr. L *palatum* palate + NL *-ion* (as in *acanthion*, *crotaphion*)] **:** the point where a line tangent to the maxillary tuberosities on the hard palate is bisected by the sagittal plane

**pal·a·ti·tis** \,palə'tīd·əs\ *n* -ES [NL, fr. L *palatum* + NL *-itis*] **:** inflammation of the palate

**palato-** *comb form* [L *palatum* palate] **1 :** palate **:** of the palate ⟨*palato*gram⟩ ⟨*palato*plegia⟩ **2 :** palatal and ⟨*palato*-dental⟩

**pal·a·to–alveolar** \¦paləd·ō+\ *adj* [*palato-* + *alveolar*] **:** being in the more alveolar of two positions between alveolar and palatal — compare ALVEOPALATAL

**pal·a·to·dental** \¦===+\ *adj* [*palato-* + *dental*] **:** relating to or involving both the palate and teeth

**pal·a·to·glos·sus** \,===ˈgläsəs, -lȯs-\ *n, pl* **palatoglos·si** \-,sī\ [NL, fr. *palato-* + *-glossus*, (fr. Gk *glōssa* tongue) — more at GLOSS (explanation)] **:** GLOSSOPALATINUS

**pal·a·to·gram** \'paləd·ə,gram\ *n* [ISV *palato-* + *-gram*] **:** the impression left on a dust-covered artificial palate by the tongue in the articulation of some sounds **:** a reproduction of such an impression

**pal·a·to·graphic** \¦paləd·ō+\ *adj* **:** of, relating to, or involving palatography

**pal·a·tog·ra·phy** \,palə'tägrəfē\ *n* -ES [*palato-* + *-graphy*] **:** the making or use of palatograms

**pal·a·to·maxillary** \¦paləd·ō +\ *adj* [*palato-* + *maxillary* adj.] **:** of, relating to, or involving the palate and maxilla

**pal·a·to·pha·ryn·ge·us** \,paləd·ōfə'rinjēəs, -,farən'jēəs\ *n* -ES [NL, fr. *palato-* + *pharyngeus* pharyngeal, fr. *pharyng-*, *pharynx*] **:** PHARYNGOPALATINUS

**pal·a·to·quadrate** \¦=== + \ *adj* [*palato-* + *quadrate*] **:** of, relating to, or replacing the palatine and quadrate bones; *esp* **:** constituting a series of bones or a continuous cartilaginous rod that forms part of the upper jaw or roof of the mouth of most vertebrates other than mammals

**pal·a·to·velar** \¦===+\ *adj* [*palato-* + *velar*] **1 :** of or relating to hard palate and velum **2 :** alternatively, simultaneously, or successively palatal and velar

**pa·la·tschin·ken** \,pälə'chiŋkən, ,pal-\ *n, pl* **palatschinken** [G, fr. Hung *palacsinta*, fr. Romanian *plăcintă* flat cake, fr. L *placenta* — more at PLACENTA] **:** a thin egg batter pancake stuffed with jam

**pa·lau** \pə'laů\ *also* **pe·lew** \pə'lü\ *n, usu cap* **:** the Austronesian language of the Palau islands

**pa·lau·an** \pə'laůən\ *n, pl* **palauan** *or* **palauans** *usu cap* [*Palau* islands + E *-an*] **:** a Micronesian native or inhabitant of the Palau islands

**pa·laung** \pə'laůŋ\ *n, pl* **palaung** *or* **palaungs** *usu cap* **1 a :** a people of the Shan States, Burma, comprising several tribes **b :** a member of such people **2 :** the Mon-Khmer language of the Palaung people

**palaung-wa** \=ˈ=ˈ=\ *n, pl* **palaung-wa** *usu cap* [*palaung* + *wa*] **:** a division of the Mon-Khmer language family

**¹pa·la·ver** \pə'lavə(r), -läv-\ *n* -s [Pg *palavra* word, speech, fr. LL *parabola* speech, parable — more at PARABLE] **1 a :** an often prolonged parley usu. between persons of different levels of culture or sophistication (as between a 19th century European trader and natives of the African west coast) **b :** CONFERENCE, DISCUSSION ⟨a ~ between union leaders⟩ **2 a :** CONVERSATION: as (1) **:** profuse, idle, or worthless talk **:** CHATTER (2) **:** talk intended to deceive **:** misleading or beguiling speech **b :** JARGON 2c, 3a **3 :** AFFAIR, BUSINESS ⟨that's your ~⟩

**²palaver** \"\ *vb* **palavered; palavered; palavering** \-v(ə)riŋ\ **palavers** *vi* **:** to use palaver: as **a :** to talk profusely or needlessly **b :** PARLEY **c :** to talk idly or beguilingly ~ *vt* **1 a :** to affect in a specified way by palavering ⟨he ~*ed* her into agreeing⟩ **b :** to alter the situation of by palavering ⟨~*ed* himself out of the mess⟩ **2 :** to use palaver to **:** CAJOLE, WHEEDLE ⟨alternately abused and ~*ed* his men⟩

**pa·la·ver·er** \-v(ə)rə(r)\ *n* -s [²*palaver* + *-er*] **:** one that palavers

**pa·la·ver·ous** \-v(ə)rəs\ *adj* [¹*palaver* + *-ous*] **:** full of or given to palaver **:** WORDY, VERBOSE

**pa·la·wan** \pə'läwən\ *n, pl* **palawan** *or* **palawans** *usu cap* [Native name in Palawan] **1 a :** a people of southern Palawan, Philippines **b :** a member of such people **2 :** the Austronesian language of the Palawan people

**pa·lay** \'pä,lī\ *n* -s [Tag, akin to Malay *padi*] **:** rice at any stage prior to husking — used esp. in the Philippines

**pa·lay·an** \pə'līən\ *n* -s [Tinggian *palayen*] **:** any of several Philippine oaks (genus *Quercus*)

**pa·laz·zo** \pə'lät(,)sō\ *n, pl* **palaz·zi** \-(,)sē\ [It, fr. L *palatium* — more at PALACE] **:** a palace or other large imposing residence — used esp. of a building in Italy

**pal·berry** \'pal- — *see* BERRY\ *n* [by folk etymology fr. *palbri*, native name in Australia] **:** BLUEBERRY 2a(1)

**pal·dao** \päl'dä(,)ō, -'daů\ *n* -s [Tag] **:** DAO

**¹pale** \'pāl, *esp before pause or consonant* -āəl\ *adj* -ER/-EST [ME, fr. MF, fr. L *pallidus*, fr. *pallēre* to be pale — more at FALLOW] **1 a :** deficient in color or in intensity or depth of color **:** dusky white **:** ASHEN, PALLID, WAN ⟨a ~ face⟩ **b :** having the countenance made pale esp. as a result of emotional or physical disorder ⟨she was ~ with rage⟩ **2 :** not bright or brilliant **:** of a faint luster **:** DIM ⟨a ~ sun shining through fog⟩ **3 :** deficient in intensity or strength **:** WEAK, FEEBLE, FAINT ⟨a ~ imitation of his mighty sire⟩ ⟨~ prose with the faint sweetness of stale lavender⟩ **4** *of a color* **:** deficient in chroma ⟨a ~ pink⟩ **:** deficient in vividness of hue or luster but of high brilliance — compare DULL

**²pale** \"\ *vb* -ED/-ING/-S [ME *palen*, fr. MF *palir*, fr. *pale*, adj.] *vi* **:** to turn pale **:** lose color or luster **:** BLANCH ⟨she *paled* at the sight⟩ ~ *vt* **:** to make pale **:** diminish the brightness of ⟨illness *paled* her cheek⟩

**³pale** \"\ *n* -s [¹*pale*] **:** PALENESS, PALLOR

**⁴pale** \"\ *vt* -ED/-ING/-S [ME *palen*, fr. MF *paler*, fr. *pal* pale (stake)] **1 :** to enclose, provide, or bar with a fence **:** encompass with or as if with pales **:** FENCE, ENCIRCLE **2** *obs* **:** to furnish with vertical stripes by way of adornment **:** STRIPE **3** *pres part* **paleing** [origin unknown] **:** SOLDER ⟨~ an embossed figure on the surface⟩

**⁵pale** \"\ *n* -s [ME, fr. MF *pal* stake, fr. L *palus* — more at POLE] **1 a** *archaic* **:** a palisade of stakes **:** an enclosing barrier **:** PALING **b** *obs* **:** a restraining boundary **:** DEFENSE **2 a :** a pointed stake driven into the ground in forming a palisade or fence **b :** a slat fastened to a nail at top and bottom for fencing **:** PICKET **3 a :** a space or field having bounds **:** an enclosed or limited region or place **:** ENCLOSURE **b :** a territory or district within certain bounds or under a particular jurisdiction **4 :** an area (as of conduct) or the limits (as of speech) within which one is privileged or protected esp. by custom (as from censure or retaliation) ⟨conduct that was beyond the ~⟩ **5 a** *obs* **:** a vertical stripe (as on a coat)

pale 5b

**b** : a perpendicular stripe in an escutcheon — **in pale** *adv* **1** : in a line in the direction of a pale — used of two or more heraldic charges **2** : PALEWISE 1 — **per pale** : divided in two by a vertical line down the middle — used of heraldic blazons
**⁶pale** \"\ *vt* [origin unknown] *dial Eng* : to beat (barley) to remove the awns
**⁷pale** \"\ *n* -s [NL *palea*] : the palea of a grass
**⁸pale** \"\ *n* -s [L *pala* spade, shovel — more at PALETTE] *Scot* : a cheese scoop
**⁹pale** \"\ *dial Eng var of* PEEL
**pale-** *or* **paleo-** *or* **palae-** *or* **palaeo-** *also* **palaio-** *comb form* [Gk *palai-*, *palaio-*, fr. *palaios* old, ancient, fr. *palai* long ago; akin to Gk *tēle* far, far off, Skt *carama* last, uttermost] **1 a** : remote in point of time ⟨*Paleocene*⟩ **b** : involving ancient forms or conditions ⟨*paleoclimate*⟩ **c** : of ancient origin : ancestral ⟨*Paleo-Eskimo*⟩ **d** : dealing with ancient or fossil forms ⟨*paleobotany*⟩ **2** : early : primitive : archaic ⟨*paleoanthropic*⟩ ⟨*palaeotypography*⟩ **3** : Old World ⟨*Paleotropical*⟩ **4** : of pre-Tertiary origin — in names of minerals ⟨*paleopicrite*⟩
**pa·lea** \ˈpālēə\ *n, pl* **pale·ae** \-lē,ē, -lē,ī\ [NL, fr. L, chaff — more at PALLET] **1 a** : one of the chaffy scales on the receptacle subtending the disk flowers in the heads of many composite plants (as sunflowers) **b** : the upper bract that with the lemma encloses the flower in grasses **c** : RAMENTUM **2** : one of the flattened enlarged setae that form the operculum of the tube of polychaete worms of *Sabellaria* and related genera — **pa·le·al** \-lēəl\ *adj*
**pa·le·a·ceous** \,pālēˈāshəs\ *adj* [NL *palea* + E *-aceous*] : covered with or resembling chaffy scales
**pa·le·ac·ri·ta** \,==ˈakrəd·ə\ *n, cap* [NL] : a genus of geometrid moths that contains the spring cankerworm
**paleanthropic** *var of* PALAEOANTHROPIC
**paleanthropus** *syn of* PALAEOANTHROPUS
**palearctic** *usu cap, var of* PALAEARCTIC
**pa·le·ate** \ˈpālēət, -ē,āt\ *adj* [NL *palea* + E *-ate*] : covered with chaffy scales ⟨a ~ rhizome⟩
**pale bark** *n* [¹*pale*] : cinchona bark from a tree (*Cinchona officinalis*) that contains an exceptionally high percentage of quinine
**pale brandy** *n* : brandy that has taken up a yellowish tint from the cask in which it is stored
**pale broomrape** *n* : YELLOW CANCERROOT
**pale·buck** \ˈpāl,bək\ *n* [prob. of Afrik origin] : ORIBI
**pale catechu** *n* : GAMBIER
**pale corydalis** *n* : an annual or biennial corydalis (*Corydalis sempervirens*) of northeastern No. America that has loose panicles of pink flowers with yellow tips
**pale crepe** *n* : almost white crepe rubber prepared by special treatment usu. with sodium bisulfite
**paled** \ˈpāld, -əld\ *adj* [ME, fr. ⁵*pale* + *-ed*] **1** *obs* : having vertical stripes : STRIPED **2** : enclosed with a fence or palisade ⟨a ~ garden⟩ **3** : made with pickets ⟨a ~ gate⟩
**pale dock** *n* : a tall erect perennial dock (*Rumex altissimus*) that has pale thick oblong-lanceolate leaves and is widely distributed in the better soils of most of No. America
**pale dry ginger ale** *n* : a pale-colored tart ginger ale suitable for mixing (as in a cocktail or highball)
**pa·le·echinoidea** \,pālē, ¦pālē+\ *or* **pa·lech·i·noi·dea** \pə-lekəˈnȯidēə\ *syn of* PALAEECHINOIDEA
**pa·le·encephalon** \,pālē, ¦pālē+\ *n* [NL, fr. *pale-* + *encephalon*] : the phylogenetically older part of the brain consisting of all parts except the cerebral cortex and closely related structures — compare NEENCEPHALON
**pa·le·ethnology** \¦==+\ *n* [ISV *pale-* + *ethnology*] : ethnology of early prehistoric man
**paleface** \ˈ=,=\ *n* : a white person : CAUCASIAN
**palegold** \ˈ=¦=\ *n* : a metallic powder made of a brass alloy and having the appearance of gold when used as a paint pigment
**pale goldfinch** *n* : a goldfinch (*Spinus tristis pallidus*) of the Rocky mountain area having the male less brilliantly yellow than that of the eastern goldfinches
**pale horse** *n, usu cap P&H* [fr. the *pale horse* ridden by Death in Rev 6:8] : DEATH — used with *the*
**pa·le·ichthyology** \,pālē, ¦pālē+\ *n* [*pale-* + *ichthyology*] : the study of fossil fishes
**pa·le·i·form** \ˈpālēə,fȯrm\ *adj* [L *palea* chaff + *-iform*] : CHAFFY, SCALY
**paleing** *pres part of* PALE
**pale laurel** *n* : SWAMP LAUREL 1
**paleleaf** \ˈ=¦=\ *or* **pale-leaved** \ˈ=¦=\ *adj* : having leaves of an exceptionally light green ⟨~ hickory⟩
**pale·ly** \ˈpāl(l)ē, -)ī\ *adv* : in a pale manner : with an effect of dimness or pallor : DIMLY, FAINTLY
**pale·man** \ˈ=mən\ *n, pl* **palemen** [⁵*pale* + *man*] : a dweller in a pale (as in the English pale in Ireland)
**pa·lem·bang** \ˈpäləm¦bäŋ\ *adj, usu cap* [fr. *Palembang*, Indonesia] : of or from the city of Palembang, Indonesia, in Sumatra : of the kind or style prevalent in Palembang
**pale·ness** *n* -ES [ME *palenesse*, fr. ¹*pale* + *-nesse* -ness] : the quality or state of being pale : PALLOR
**paleo-** — see PALE-
**pa·leo·agrostology** \,pālēō, ¦pālēō+\ *n* [*pale-* + *agrostology*] : a branch of paleobotany concerned with the study of fossil grasses
**paleo-american** \¦===+\ *or* **paleo-amerind** \"+\ *n, usu cap P&A* [*pale-* + *american* or *amerind*] : one of a hypothetical mixed Asian group migrant to No. America before the more typically Mongoloid Asians
**paleoanthropic** *var of* PALAEOANTHROPIC
**pa·leo·an·thro·pi·nae** \,===,an(t)thrəˈpī,nē\ *n pl, cap* [NL, fr. *pale-* + Gk *anthrōpos* + NL *-inae* — more at ANTHROP-] : an anthropological subdivision of Hominidae including Neanderthal man and related forms of the genus *Homo* but treated as if comparable to a subfamily — compare ARCHANTHROPINAE, NEOANTHROPINAE — **pa·leo·an·thro·pine** \¦===ˈan(t)thrə,pīn\ *adj or n*
**pa·leo·anthropologist** \¦===+\ *n* : a specialist in paleoanthropology
**pa·leo·anthropology** \¦===+\ *n* [*pale-* + *anthropology*] : a branch of anthropology dealing with fossil man
**paleoanthropus** *syn of* PALAEOANTHROPUS
**¹paleo-asiatic** \¦===+\ *n, usu cap P&A* [ISV *pale-* + *asiatic*] **1** : a member of a group of northeast Asian peoples including the Chukchi, Koryak, and Kamchadal of northeast Siberia and possibly also the Gilyaks of Sakhalin Island and the Ainu of northern Japan **2** *usu* **pa·leo·asiatic** \"\ *usu cap* : PALEOSIBERIAN
**²paleo-asiatic** \"\ *adj, usu cap P&A* : of or relating to the Paleo-Asiatics or to Paleosiberian languages
**pa·leo·biological** \¦===+\ *or* **pa·leo·biologic** \"+\ *adj* : of or relating to paleobiology
**pa·leo·biologist** \¦===+\ *n* : a specialist in paleobiology
**pa·leo·biology** \¦===+\ *n* [ISV *pale-* + *biology*] : a branch of paleontology that deals with fossils as organisms rather than as features of historical geology
**pa·leo·botanical** \¦===+\ *or* **pa·leo·botanic** \"+\ *adj* : of or relating to paleobotany — **pa·leo·botanically** \"+\ *adv*
**pa·leo·botanist** \¦===+\ *n* : a specialist in paleobotany
**pa·leo·botany** \¦===+\ *n* [ISV *pale-* + *botany*] : a branch of botany that deals with fossil plants
**pa·leo·cene** \ˈpālēə,sēn, ˈpal-\ *adj, usu cap* [ISV *pale-* + *-cene*; prob. orig. formed in G] : of or relating to a subdivision of the Tertiary — see GEOLOGIC TIME table
**pa·leo·cerebellar** \¦===+\ *adj* : of or relating to the paleocerebellum
**pa·leo·cerebellum** \¦===+\ *n* [NL, fr. *pale-* + *cerebellum*] : a phylogenetically old part of the cerebellum concerned with maintenance of normal postural relationships and made up chiefly of the anterior lobe of the vermis and of the pyramid — compare ARCHICEREBELLUM, NEOCEREBELLUM
**pa·leo·climatic** \¦===+\ *adj* [*pale-* + *climatic*] : of or relating to the climate of the earth in past ages
**pa·leo·climatological** \¦===+\ *adj* : of or relating to paleoclimatology
**pa·leo·climatology** \¦===+\ *n* [ISV *pale-* + *climatology*] : a branch of science dealing with the climate of past ages
**pa·leo·cortex** \¦===+\ *n* [NL, fr. *pale-* + *cortex*] : the olfactory cortex of the cerebrum
**pa·leo·crystallic** \¦===+\ *adj* [*pale-* + Gk *krystallos* ice + E *-ic* — more at CRUST] : PALEOCRYSTIC
**pa·leo·crys·tic** \¦===ˈkristik\ *adj* [*pale-* + Gk *krystallos* + E *-ic*] : being, relating to, or characterized by ice that has had prolonged existence ⟨~ sea⟩ ⟨~ ice is several years old; some of it may be dozens of years old —Vilhjalmur Stefansson⟩
**pa·leo·dendrology** \¦===+\ *n* [*pale-* + *dendrology*] : a branch of paleobotany that deals with fossil trees
**pa·leo·ecological** \¦===+\ *or* **pa·leo·ecologic** \"+\ *adj* : of or relating to paleoecology
**pa·leo·ecologist** \¦===+\ *n* : a specialist in paleoecology
**pa·leo·ecology** \¦===+\ *n* [*pale-* + *ecology*] : a branch of ecology concerned with the identification and interpretation of the relation of ancient plants and animals to their environment and with the characteristics of ancient environments
**pa·leo·encephalon** \¦===+\ *n* : PALEENCEPHALON
**pa·leo·entomological** \¦===+\ *adj* : of or relating to paleoentomology
**pa·leo·entomology** \¦===+\ *n* [*pale-* + *entomology*] : a branch of entomology that deals with fossil insects
**pa·leo·ethnic** \¦===+\ *adj* [*pale-* + Gk *ethnos* nation, people + E *-ic* — more at ETHNOS] : relating to the earliest human races
**pa·leo·ethnography** \¦===+\ *n* [*pale-* + *ethnography*] : the ethnography of paleolithic man
**paleogean** *usu cap, var of* PALAEOGAEAN
**¹pa·leo·gene** \ˈpālēə,jēn, ˈpal-\ *n, usu cap* [G *paläogen*, fr. *paläo-* pale- + *-gen* (fr. root of Gk *genesthai* to be born) — more at KIN] : the earlier part of the Tertiary including the Paleocene, Eocene, and Oligocene
**²paleogene** \"\ *adj, usu cap* : of or relating to the Paleogene
**paleogenesis** *var of* PALAEOGENESIS
**pa·leo·geographer** \,pālēō, ¦pālēō+\ *n* : a specialist in paleogeography
**pa·leo·geographic** \¦===+\ *also* **pa·leo·geographical** \"+\ *adj* : of or relating to paleogeography — **pa·leo·geographically** \"+\ *adv*
**pa·leo·geography** \¦===+\ *n* [ISV *pale-* + *geography*] : the geography of ancient times or of a particular former geological epoch
**pa·leo·geologic** \¦===+\ *adj* : of or relating to paleogeology
**pa·leo·geology** \¦===+\ *n* [*pale-* + *geology*] : a branch of geology concerned with the study of geologic features exposed at the surface during a past epoch or period but now buried beneath rocks formed in subsequent time
**pa·leo·geomorphology** \¦===+\ *n* [*pale-* + *geomorphology*] : a branch of geomorphology concerned with the study of ancient topographic features now either concealed beneath the surface or removed by erosion
**pa·le·og·ra·pher** \,pālēˈägrəfə(r), ,pal-\ *n* -s : a specialist in paleography
**pa·leo·graphic** \,pālēə¦grafik, ¦pal-, -fēk\ *also* **pa·leo·graph·i·cal** \-fəkəl, -fēk-\ *adj* : of or relating to paleography — **pa·leo·graph·i·cal·ly** \-fək(ə)lē, -fēk-, -li\ *adv*
**pa·le·og·ra·phy** \,pālēˈägrəfē, ,pal-, -fi\ *n* -ES [NL *palaeographia*, fr. Gk *palaio-* pale- + *-graphia* -graphy] **1 a** : an ancient manner of writing ⟨deciphering early Gaelic ~⟩ **b** : ancient writings **2** : the study of ancient modes of writing including inscriptions : the deciphering and identifying (as by origin or period) of ancient writings
**pa·leo·hydrology** \,pālēō, ¦pālēō+\ *n* [*pale-* + *hydrology*] : the study of ancient use and handling of water (as in irrigation or urban water supplies)
**pa·leo-indian** \¦===+\ *n, usu cap P&I* [*pale-* + *indian*] : PALEO-AMERICAN
**pa·le·o·la** \pəˈlēələ\ *n, pl* **paleo·lae** \-,lē, -lī\ [NL, dim. of *palea*] : a small or secondary palea — **pa·le·o·late** \-,lāt, -lət\ *adj*
**pa·leo·lith** \ˈpālēə,lith, ˈpal-\ *n* -s [*pale-* + *-lith*] : a Paleolithic implement of unpolished chipped stone
**pa·leo·lith·ic** \¦===¦lithik, -thēk\ *adj, usu cap* [ISV *pale-* + *-lithic*] : of or relating to the second period of the Stone Age following the Eolithic and preceding the Mesolithic and characterized by rough or chipped stone implements
**paleolithic man** *n, often cap P* : a man of or peculiar to the Paleolithic period (as the Heidelberg, Neanderthal, or Cro-Magnon)
**pa·le·ol·o·gist** \,pālēˈäləjəst, ,pal-\ *n* -s : a specialist in paleology
**pa·le·ol·o·gy** \-jē, -ji\ *n* -ES [*pale-* + *-logy*] : the study or knowledge of antiquities and esp. prehistoric antiquities
**pa·leo·mammalogy** \,pālēō, ¦pālēō+\ *n* [*pale-* + *mammalogy*] : paleontological mammalogy
**pa·le·on·tog·ra·phy** \,pālē,änˈtägrəfē, ,pal-, -ēən-ˈ-, -fi\ *n* -ES [F *paléontographie*, fr. *palé-* pale- + Gk *onta* existing things + F *-graphie* -graphy] : descriptive paleontology
**pa·le·on·to·log·i·cal** \¦==,äntə¦läjəkəl, -,ənt-, -jēk-\ *also* **pa·le·on·to·log·ic** \-jik, -jēk\ *adj* : of or relating to paleontology
**paleontologic geology** *n* : a branch of geology that deals with the succession and significance of past life
**pa·le·on·tol·o·gist** \,==,änˈtäləjəst, -,ənˈt-\ *n* -s : a specialist in paleontology
**pa·le·on·tol·o·gy** \-jē, -ji\ *n* -ES [F *paléontologie*, fr. *palé-* pale- + Gk *onta* existing things (fr. neut. pl. of *ont-*, *ōn*, pres. part of *einai* to be) + F *-logie* -logy — more at ONT-] **1 a** : science that deals with the life of past geological periods, is based on the study of fossil remains of plants and animals, and gives information esp. about the phylogeny and relationships of modern animals and plants and about the chronology of the history of the earth — compare PALEOBIOLOGY, PALEOBOTANY, PALEOCLIMATOLOGY, PALEOGEOGRAPHY, PALEOZOOLOGY **2 a** : a treatise on paleontology (as of a region or period) **b** : the materials of this science : FOSSILS **c** : the structural attributes of a fossil or extinct organism, type, or group
**pa·leo·pal·li·al** \¦==¦palēəl\ *adj* [NL *paleopallium* + E *-al*] : of, relating to, or mediated by the paleopallium
**pa·leo·pallium** \¦===+\ *n* [NL, fr. *pale-* + *pallium*] : a phylogenetically old part of the cerebral cortex that develops along the lateral aspect of the hemispheres and gives rise to the olfactory lobes in higher forms
**pa·leo·pathology** \,pālēō, ¦pālēō+\ *n* [ISV *pale-* + *pathology*] : a branch of pathology concerned with diseases of former times as evidenced esp. in fossil or other remains
**pa·leo·pedology** \¦===+\ *n* [*pale-* + *pedology*] : a branch of pedology that is concerned with the soils of past geological ages
**pa·leo·physiography** \¦===+\ *n* [*pale-* + *physiography*] : PALEOGEOMORPHOLOGY
**pa·leo·phyt·ic** \,pālēə¦fid·ik, ¦pal-\ *adj* [ISV *pale-* + *-phytic*] : PALEOBOTANICAL
**pa·leo·plain** \ˈ===+,-\ *n* [*pale-* + *plain*] : an ancient plain of degradation now more or less buried beneath deposits of later times
**pa·leo·psychic** \,pālēō, ¦pālēō+\ *adj* [*pale-* + *psychic*] : of, relating to, or involving remotely ancestral modes of thought and desire as if still operative in unconscious mentality
**pa·leo·psychology** \¦===+\ *n* [*paleopsychic* + *-logy*] : the study of paleopsychic phenomena
**pa·le·ornithology** \,pālē, ¦pālē+\ *n* [*pale-* + *ornithology*] : a branch of paleontology concerned with the study of fossil birds
**paleosaur** *var of* PALAEOSAUR
**¹pa·leo·siberian** \,pālēō, ¦pālēō+\ *adj, usu cap* [*pali-* + *siberian*] : PALEO-ASIATIC
**²paleosiberian** \"\ *n, usu cap* : a group of language families consisting of Luorawetlan, Yukaghir, Gilyak, and Yeniseian that are spoken by aboriginal peoples in northern and eastern Siberia, are not known to be related, but are conveniently treated together in contrast to the Altaic languages and Russian spoken in the same area
**pa·leo·striatal** \¦===+\ *adj* [NL *paleostriatum* + E *-al*] : of or relating to the paleostriatum
**pa·leo·striatum** \¦===+\ *n* [NL, fr. *pale-* + *striatum*] : the phylogenetically older part of the corpus striatum consisting of the globus pallidus
**pa·leo·technic** \¦===+\ *adj* [*pale-* + *technic*] **1** : belonging to or concerned with ancient art **2** : of, relating to, or constituting a period of industrial development marked by the predominance of hand tools and craft industries or by complex industries based on the use of coal and iron — compare NEOTECHNIC
**pa·leo·thalamus** \¦===+\ *n* [NL, fr. *pale-* + *thalamus*] : the phylogenetically older part of the thalamus
**paleothere** *var of* PALAEOTHERE
**pa·leo·thermal** \,pālēō, ¦pālēō+\ *or* **pa·leo·thermic** \"+\ *adj* [ISV *pale-* + *thermal* or *thermic*] : relating to or characteristic of warm climates of past geological time ⟨a ~ flora⟩
**paleotropical** *usu cap, var of* PALAEOTROPICAL
**pa·leo·volcanic** \¦===+\ *adj* [ISV *pale-* + *volcanic*] : of, relating to, or being igneous rocks erupted before the Tertiary
**¹pa·leo·zo·ic** \,pālēə¦zōik, ¦pal-, -ōēk\ *adj, usu cap* [*pale-* + *-zoic*] : of or relating to a grand division of geological history from the beginning of the Cambrian to the close of the Permian marked by the culmination of nearly all classes of invertebrates except the insects and in whose later epochs seed-bearing plants, amphibians, and reptiles first appeared — see GEOLOGIC TIME table ⟨many facts in *Paleozoic* stratigraphy —E.O.Ulrich⟩
**²paleozoic** \"\ *n* -s *usu cap* : the Paleozoic era or system of rocks
**pa·leo·zoological** \¦===+\ *adj* : of or relating to paleozoology
**pa·leo·zoologist** \¦===+\ *n* : a specialist in paleozoology
**pa·leo·zoology** \¦===+\ *n* [F *paléozoologie*, fr. *palé-* pale- + *zoologie* zoology] : a branch of paleontology that deals with ancient and fossil animals
**pale persicaria** *n* : a tall erect or decumbent annual persicaria (*Polygonum lapathifolium*) with somewhat glabrous leaves and slender spikes of pink to purplish flowers
**pale plantain** *n* : RUGEL'S PLANTAIN
**¹pal·er** \ˈpālə(r)\ *n* -s [⁴*pale* + *-er*] *archaic* : one in charge of palings
**²paler** *comparative of* PALE
**¹pa·ler·mi·tan** \pəˈlərmət°n, -ler-\ *adj, usu cap* [It *palermitano*, modif. (influenced by *Palermo* Palermo) of L *panormitanus*, fr. Gk *panormitēs* inhabitant of Palermo (fr. *Panormos* Palermo + *-itēs* -ite) + L *-anus* -an] : PALERMO
**²palermitan** \"\ *n* -s *cap* [It *palermitano*, fr. *palermitano*, adj.] : a native or resident of Palermo
**pa·ler·mo** \pəˈlər(,)mō, -ler-\ *adj, usu cap* [fr. *Palermo*, city in northern Sicily] : of or from the city of Palermo, Italy, in Sicily : of the kind or style prevalent in Palermo
**pale rose** *n* : CABBAGE ROSE
**pales** *pres 3d sing of* PALE, *pl of* PALE
**palest** *superlative of* PALE
**pal·es·tine man** \ˈpalə,stīn- *sometimes* -,stēn- *or* -,stən-\ *n, pl* **palestine men** *usu cap P* [fr. *Palestine*] : a member of a highly variable early Neanderthaloid population of southwestern Asia that are known chiefly from skulls and other skeletal remains from Palestinian caves, that typically exhibit strong intermixture of Neanderthal and neanthropic characters, and that may represent either transitional forms or hybrids — compare SKHUL MAN, TABUN MAN
**¹pal·es·tin·i·an** \¦palə¦stinēən, -inyən *sometimes* -tēn-\ *adj, usu cap* [*Palestine*, country of southwestern Asia + E *-ian*] : of or relating to Palestine
**²palestinian** \"\ *n* -s **1** *cap* : a native or inhabitant of Palestine : ISRAELI **2** *usu cap* : PALESTINE MAN
**palestra** *var of* PALAESTRA
**pa·les weevil** \ˈpā(,)lēz-\ *n* [NL *pales*, specific epithet of *Hylobius pales*] : a large brown weevil (*Hylobius pales*) that feeds on the bark of white pine and a few other pines frequently girdling and killing young trees
**pal·et** \(ˈ)pā¦let\ *n* -s [⁷*pale* + *-et*] : PALEA 1a, 1b
**paletiology** *var of* PALAETIOLOGY
**pal·e·tot** \ˈpalə,tō, -l(,)tō\ *n* -s [F, fr. MF *paletot*, *paltoke*, fr. ME *paltok* a kind of jacket] **1** : a man's loose outer coat **2** : a man's fitted overcoat; *also* : a woman's fitted jacket worn esp. in the 19th century over a costume with crinoline or bustle
**pale touch-me-not** *n* : a tall branching jewelweed (*Impatiens pallida*) with glaucous or blue-green foliage and usu. yellow flowers often with reddish brown spots
**pal·ette** \ˈpalət, *usu* -əd·+V\ *n* -s [F, fr. MF, small shovel, fr. *pale* spade, shovel (fr. L *pala*) + *-ette*; prob. akin to L *pangere* to fix, fasten, plant — more at PACT] **1 a** (1) : a thin oval or rectangular board or tablet in which is a thumbhole near one end for being held horizontally when in use and on which a painter lays and mixes pigments (2) : a surface (as a tabletop or a piece of glass or marble) similarly used **b** : the set or assortment of colors put on the palette (as for a particular picture) **c** (1) : a particular range, quality, or use of color ⟨his ~ predominated in muted tones⟩ (2) : a comparable range, quality, or use of available elements esp. in another art (as music) **2** *Brit* : a curved wooden implement used in transferring a pantile from the mold to the drying shelf

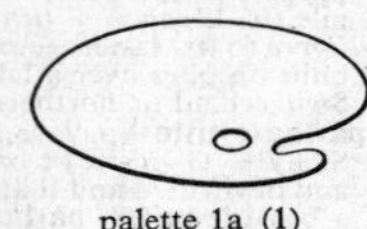
palette 1a (1)

**palette cup** *n* : a small metal cup for holding vehicle or diluent for paint and equipped with a flange for attachment to an artist's palette
**palette knife** *also* **pallet knife** *n* : a knife having a very flexible steel blade and no cutting edge that is used esp. by painters to mix colors or spread paint or by printers for distributing ink : SPATULA
**pale violet** *n* : a leafy-stemmed No. American violet (*Viola striata*) with large white or creamy flowers faintly marked with purple
**pale western cutworm** *n* : a cutworm that is the larva of a noctuid moth (*Agrotis orthogonia*) and that is a serious pest on grains in central U.S.
**pale·wise** \ˈpāl,wīz\ *also* **pale·ways** \-wāz\ *adv* [⁵*pale* + *-wise*, *-ways*] **1** *heraldry* : in the direction of a pale : VERTICALLY **2** *heraldry* : in pale
**pal·fre·nier** \,pȯlfrəˈni(ə)r\ *n* -s [MF *palefrenier*, fr. OProv *palafrenier*, fr. ML *palafrenarius*, alter. (influenced by L *frenum* bridle) of *palafridarius*, fr. *palafredus* + L *-arius* -ary — more at PALFREY] *archaic* : GROOM 2b
**pal·frey** \ˈpȯlfrē\ *n* -s [ME, fr. OF *palefrei*, fr. ML *palafredus*, fr. LL *paraveredus* post-horse for secondary roads, fr. Gk *para-* beside, subsidiary + L *veredus* post horse, fr. a Gaulish word akin to Welsh *gorwydd* horse, OIr *riadaim* I ride — more at PARA-, RIDE] *archaic* : a saddle horse other than a war= horse; *esp* : a light easy-gaited horse suitable for a lady
**palgrave** *var of* PALSGRAVE
**¹pa·li** \ˈpälē\ *n* -s *usu cap* [Skt *pāli* row, line, series, series of Buddhist sacred texts] : an Indic language found in the Buddhist canon and used today as the liturgical and scholarly language of Hinayana Buddhism
**²pali** *pl of* PALUS
**³pa·li** \ˈpälē\ *n* -s [Hawaiian] *Hawaii* : a steep slope : PRECIPICE
**⁴pali** \"\ *n* -s [Tamil *pālai*] : an Indian timber tree (*Palaquium ellipticum*) of the family Sapotaceae that yields a moderately hard, heavy, and durable reddish to reddish brown straight or wavy grained lumber which is used esp. for joinery, furniture, cooperage, and planking
**pali-** *comb form* [Gk *palin*, *pali* again, back; akin to Gk *polos* pivot, axis — more at POLE] : pathological state characterized by repetition of a (specified) act ⟨*palilalia*⟩ ⟨*palirrhea*⟩
**pali buddhism** *n, usu cap P&B* [¹*Pali*] : HINAYANA
**pal·i·cou·rea** \,paləˈkůrēə\ *n, cap* [NL] : a large genus of tropical American shrubs (family Rubiaceae) having white or yellow flowers with the tube of the corolla distended within and including several that are cultivated as ornamentals
**palier** *comparative of* PALY
**paliest** *superlative of* PALY
**pa·li·form** \ˈpālə,fȯrm\ *adj* [NL *palus* + E *-iform*] : resembling a palus ⟨the ~ lobes of the septa in corals⟩
**pal·i·kar** *also* **pal·i·car** \ˈpalə,kär\ *n* -s [NGk *palikari*, *pallēkari* youth, fr. LGk *pallikarion* page, dim. of *pallēx*, *pallēx* young man or woman] **1** : a Greek or Albanian soldier in the pay of the sultan of Turkey **2** : a soldier of the Greek militia in the war of independence (1821–28) against Turkey
**pa·li·la** \pəˈlēlə\ *n* -s [Hawaiian] : a Hawaiian honeycreeper (*Psittirostra bailleui*) that resembles a finch
**pali·la·lia** \,paləˈlālēə, -ālyə\ *n* -s [NL, fr. *pali-* + *-lalia*] : a speech defect marked by abnormal repetition of syllables, words, or phrases

**pa·lil·o·gy** *or* **pa·lil·lo·gy** \pəˈliləjē\ *n* -ES [LL *palilogia*, fr. Gk *palillogia*, recapitulation, fr. *palin* again, back + *-logia* — more at PALI-] **:** repetition of a word for emphasis (as in Is 38:19 "the living, the living, he shall praise thee")

**pal·im·bacchic** \ˌpaləm+\ *adj or n* [L *palimbacchius* + E *-ic*] **:** ANTIBACCHIC

**pal·im·bac·chius** \ˌpaləm, ˌpa,lim, pə¦lim+\ *n, pl* **palimbacchii** *or* **palimbacchiuses** [L, fr. Gk *palimbakcheios*, fr. *palin* back + *bakcheios* bacchius — more at BACCHIUS] **:** ANTIBACCHIUS

**¹pal·imp·sest** \ˈpaləm(p),sest\ *n* -S [L *palimpsestus*, fr. Gk *palimpsēstos* scraped again, fr. *palin* again, back + *-psēstos*, fr. *psēn* to rub, scrape, crumble; akin to Gk *psammos* sand — more at PALI-, SAND] **1** *obs* **:** writing material (as parchment or paper) so prepared that the writing can be erased and the material reused **2 a :** a parchment, tablet, or other portion of writing material that has been used twice or three times after the earlier writing has been erased **b :** a manuscript in which one or two earlier erased writings are found **3 :** a memorial brass having earlier engraving on the side opposite to that which is exposed

**²palimpsest** \ˈ"\ *adj* **1** *of a manuscript* **:** having besides its present writing one or two earlier erased writings **2** *of a memorial brass* **:** having earlier engraving on the side opposite to that exposed

**pal·imp·ses·tic** \¦==¦sestik\ *adj* **1 :** forming or appearing in a palimpsest **2 :** producing palimpsests

**pal·i·nal** \ˈpalənᵊl\ *adj* [Gk *palin* back + E *-al*] *of mastication* **:** effected by backward motion — compare ORTHAL, PROAL, PROPALINAL

**pal·in·drome** \ˈpalən,drōm\ *n* -S [Gk *palindromos* running back again, fr. *palin* back, again + *-dromos* -drome] **1 a :** a word, verse, or sentence (as "Able was I ere I saw Elba") that reads the same backward or forward **b :** WORD SQUARE **2 2 :** a number (as 18181) that expressed in arabic numerals has the same value when reversed

**pal·in·dro·mia** \ˌpalənˈdrōmēə\ *n* -S [NL, fr. Gk *palindromos* + NL *-ia*] **:** recurrence of a disease

**pal·in·dromic** \ˌpalən¦drämik, -rōm-\ *adj* [*palindrome* + *-ic*] **1 :** of, relating to, or constituting a palindrome ⟨a ~ sentence⟩ **2** [NL *palindromia* + E *-ic*] **:** RECURRENT ⟨~ rheumatism⟩ — **pal·in·dromi·cal·ly** \-mək(ə)lē\ *adv*

**¹pal·ing** \ˈpāliŋ, -lēŋ\ *pres part of* PALE

**²paling** \ˈ"\ *n* -S [ME, fr. gerund of *palen* to pale] **1 :** the act of building a fence or enclosing with pales **2 a :** a fence formed with pales or pickets **b :** wood for making pales **:** a stock of pales **3 :** a pale or picket for a fence

**pal·in·ge·ne·sia** \ˌpalənjəˈnēzh(ē)ə\ *n* -S [ML, fr. Gk, fr. *palin* again + *-genesia*] **:** PALINGENESIS

**pal·in·ge·ne·sian** \¦==¦=zhən\ *adj* [*palingenesia* + E *-an*] **:** relating to palingenesis

**pal·in·gen·e·sis** \ˌpalənˈjenəsəs\ *n* [Gk *palin* again + L *genesis* birth — more at GENESIS] **:** renewal by or as if by rebirth: as **a :** Christian baptism **b :** the doctrine of continued rebirths **:** METEMPSYCHOSIS **c** [G, fr. Gk *palin* + L *genesis*] **:** reproduction during development of characters or structures that have been maintained essentially unchanged throughout the phylogeny of a strain **:** RECAPITULATION — opposed to *cenogenesis*; compare RECAPITULATION THEORY **d :** the formation of new rocks by the re-fusion of former rocks deep within the earth

**pal·in·gen·e·sist** \-sə̇st\ *n* -S **:** a believer in palingenesis

**pal·in·gen·e·sy** \-nəsē\ *n* -ES [F *palingénésie*, fr. ML *palingenesia*] **:** PALINGENESIS

**pal·in·ge·net·ic** \ˌpalənjə̇¦ned·ik\ *adj* [*palingenesis* + *-etic*] **1 :** of or relating to palingenesis **2** *or* **pal·in·gen·ic** \¦palən¦jenik\ [*palingenic* fr. *palingenesis* + E *-ic*] **:** produced by or involved in geological or biological palingenesis — **pal·in·ge·net·i·cal·ly** \-jə̇ˈned·ək(ə)lē\ *adv*

**pal·in·ge·ni·idae** \ˌpalənjə̇ˈnīə,dē\ *n pl, cap* [NL, fr. *Palingenia*, type genus (fr. *palin-* + *-genia* -geny) + *-idae*] **:** a family of mayflies

**pal·in·gen·ist** \ˌpalənˈjenə̇st\ *n* -S [*palingenesis* + *-ist*] **:** PALINGENESIST

**paling fence** *n* **:** PICKET FENCE

**¹pal·in·ode** \ˈpalə,nōd\ *n* -S [Gk *palinōidia*, fr. *palin* back, again + *-ōidia* (fr. *aeidein* to sing) — more at PALI-, ODE] **1 :** an ode or song recanting or retracting something in a former one **2 :** RETRACTION; *esp* **:** a formal retraction

**²palinode** \ˈ"\ *vb* -ED/-ING/-S **:** RECANT, RETRACT

**pal·in·odi·al** \¦palə¦nōdēəl\ *adj* [*palinody* + *-al*] **:** of, relating to, or constituting a palinode

**pal·in·odic** \-ōdik, -äd-\ *adj* [Gk *palinōidikos*, fr. *palin* + *-ōid-* (fr. *aeidein*) + *-ikos* -ic — more at ODE] **:** of or relating to a form of symmetrical construction found in some ancient odes in which the fourth in a group of four strophes repeats the structure of the first and the third that of the second

**pal·in·odist** \ˈpalə,nōdə̇st, ˌ==ˈ==\ *n* -S **:** one who writes a palinode

**pal·in·ody** \ˈpalə,nōdē\ *n* -ES [MF *palinodie*, fr. Gk *palinōidia* — more at PALINODE] **:** PALINODE

**pal·in·spas·tic** \ˌpalənˈspastik\ *adj* [Gk *palin* back again + *spastikos* drawing — more at SPASTIC] **:** of or relating to the inferred original positions of landmasses prior to extensive diastrophic movements

**pal·in·trope** \ˈpalən,trōp\ *n* -S [Gk *palintropos* turning back, fr. *palin* again + *-tropos* -trope, adj. suffix] **:** the recurved posterior section of either valve of some brachiopod shells

**pal·i·nu·ra** \ˌpaləˈn(y)u̇rə\ *n pl, cap* [NL, fr. *Palinurus*] **:** a tribe of decapod crustaceans (suborder Reptantia) usu. having the rostrum and the inner lobes of the second maxillae and first maxillipeds reduced and including the Palinuridae, Scyllaridae, and a few related forms — **pal·i·nu·ran** \¦==¦=rən\ *adj or n*

**pal·i·nu·ri·dae** \ˌ==ˈ=rə,dē\ *n pl, cap* [NL, fr. *Palinurus*, type genus + *-idae*] **:** a family of decapod crustaceans (tribe Palinura) comprising the spiny lobsters — see PALINURUS; compare PANULIRUS

**pal·i·nu·rus** \-rəs\ *n, cap* [NL, fr. L, name of Aeneas's pilot, understood as fr. Gk *palin* back + *-ouros* -urus] **:** the type genus of Palinuridae comprising the European langouste and other Old World spiny lobsters — compare PANULIRUS

**palis** *pl of* PALI

**¹pal·i·sade** *also* **pal·li·sade** \ˌpaləˈsād, ˈ==,=\ *n* -S [F *palissade*, fr. OProv *palissada*, fr. *palissa*, fr. (assumed) VL *palicea*, fr. L *palus* stake — more at POLE] **1 a :** a fence of stakes; *esp* **:** a strong fence for defense **b :** a long strong stake pointed at the top and set in the ground vertically or obliquely with others in a close row as a means of defense **2 :** a line of bold cliffs; *esp* **:** one showing a columnar face weathered along vertical joints — usu. used in pl. **3 :** PALISADE PARENCHYMA

**²palisade** \ˈ"\ *vt* -ED/-ING/-S **:** to surround, furnish, enclose, or fortify with palisades

**palisade cell** *n* **:** a cell of palisade parenchyma

**palisade layer** *n* **1 :** the layer of palisade parenchyma in a leaf **2 :** a sclerenchymatous protective layer inside the epidermis of many hard seeds

**palisade parenchyma** *n* **:** a layer of columnar or cylindrical cells that are rich in chloroplasts, have small intercellular spaces, and are found typically just beneath the upper epidermis of foliage leaves — compare SPONGY PARENCHYMA

**palisade worm** *n* **:** any of several comparatively large blood-sucking nematode worms (genus *Strongylus*) that are parasitic in the large intestine of horses and have larvae which wander in the viscera and sometimes lodge in the intestinal blood vessels causing colic or more rarely a fatal aneurysm — called also *bloodworm, red worm*

**palisading** *n* -S [fr. gerund of ²*palisade*] **:** a row of palisades set in the ground esp. as a protective enclosure

**¹pal·i·sa·do** \ˌpaləˈsā(,)dō\ *n* -ES [Sp *palizada*, fr. OProv *palissada* — more at PALISADE] **:** PALISADE

**²palisado** \ˈ"\ *vt* -ED/-ING/-ES **:** PALISADE

**pal·i·san·der** *also* **pal·is·san·dre** *or* **pal·i·san·dre** \ˈpaləˌsandə(r), ˌ==ˈ==\ *n* -S [F *palissandre, palisandre*, prob. of AmerInd origin] **:** BRAZILIAN ROSEWOOD

**pal·ish** \ˈpālish, -lēsh\ *adj* [ME, fr. ¹*pale* + *-ish*] **:** rather pale

**pal·is·san·dre** \ˈpalə,sandə(r), ˌ==ˈ==\ *n* -S [F, palisander] **:** WALLFLOWER 4

**pa·lis·sy ware** \pəˈlisē-, ¦palə¦sē-\ *n, usu cap P* [after Bernard *Palissy* †1589 Fr. potter] **:** a 16th century French pottery decorated with colored glazes laid over embossments and usu. with figures (as of fishes or leaves) in high relief

**pal·i·u·rus** \ˌpalēˈyu̇rəs\ *n, cap* [NL, fr. L, Christ's-thorn, fr. Gk *paliouros*] **:** a small genus of thorny Eurasian shrubs (family Rhamnaceae) with cymose perfect flowers and dry woody winged fruit — see CHRIST'S-THORN

**pal·kee** *or* **pal·ki** \ˈpälkē\ *n* -S [Hindi *pālkī*, fr. Prakrit *pallaṅka* — more at PALANQUIN] *India* **:** PALANQUIN

**palkee gharry** \ˈ==,==\ *n* [Hindi *pālkī-gārī* fr. *pālkī* palkee + *gārī* gharry] **:** a gharry shaped somewhat like a palanquin

**¹pall** \ˈpȯl\ *n* -S [ME, fr. OE *pæll*, fr. L *pallium* pall, Greek mantle; akin to L *palla* women's mantle] **1** *archaic* **:** rich fine cloth used for the outer garments of persons of rank **2 a** *archaic* **:** an outer garment (as a cloak or mantle) esp. when of rich material **b :** PALLIUM 1b **3 a** (1) *archaic* **:** ALTAR CLOTH (2) **:** FRONTAL **2** (3) **:** a linen cloth for covering the chalice; *esp* **:** a square piece of cardboard covered with cloth that is usu. embroidered on the upper side **b** (1) **:** a fine cloth spread over or on something (as a canopy or counterpane); *esp* **:** a heavy cloth draped over a coffin, hearse, or tomb (2) **:** COFFIN; *esp* **:** one holding a body **c** *or* **pall·ing** \-liŋ\ **:** a canvas hatch cover on a ship **4 :** a thing that covers or conceals: as **a** *obs* **:** CLOAK 2c **b :** an overspreading element that produces an effect of gloom ⟨a ~ of smoke⟩ **5 a :** a conventionalized heraldic representation of the front half of an archiepiscopal pallium **b :** PAIRLE — **per pall** \¦pər¦=\ **:** divided in three parts by partition lines in the form of a Y **:** tierced in pairle

**²pall** \ˈ"\ *vt* -ED/-ING/-S **:** to cover with or as if with a pall **:** CLOAK, DRAPE

**³pall** \ˈ"\ *vb* -ED/-ING/-S [ME *pallen*, short for *apallen* to appall] *vi* **1 :** to lose strength **:** fail in vigor or effectiveness **2 a** *obs, of wine or beer* **:** to become flat **b :** to lose in interest or attraction ⟨these occupations ~*ed* —Virginia Woolf⟩ ⟨in the long run ugliness ~*s* almost as much as beauty —George Saintsbury⟩ — often used with *on* or *upon* ⟨smooth, rhetorical mind must have ~*ed* on one who liked sharp edges —John Buchan⟩ **3 :** to become tired of something at first pleasurable ⟨~ of too much music⟩ **~** *vt* **1** *obs* **:** to make faint or fainthearted **:** DAUNT, APPALL **2 a** *obs* **:** to cause (wine or beer) to become flat **b :** to cause (something pleasurable) to become insipid ⟨reason and reflection . . . ~ all his enjoyments —Francis Atterbury⟩ **3 :** to deprive (as a person or his senses) of pleasure in something usu. by cloying or satiating ⟨the choicest delicacies ~ the stomach in time⟩ **syn** see SATIATE

**⁴pall** [³*pall*] *n* -S *obs* **:** NAUSEA, QUALM

**⁵pall** *var of* PAWL

**¹pal·la** \ˈpalə\ *n, pl* **pal·lae** \-,lē\ *also* **pallas** [L] **1 :** a loose outer garment formed by wrapping or draping a large square of cloth and worn by women of ancient Rome — compare PALLIUM 1a **2 :** PALL 3a

palla 1

**²palla** *var of* PALLAH

**³pa·lla** \ˈpäyə\ *n* -S [Sp, fr. Quechua] **:** an Incan princess

**¹pal·la·di·an** \pəˈlādēən, (ˈ)pa¦l-\ *adj, often cap* [L *palladius*, of Pallas (fr. Gk *palladios*, fr. *Pallad-, Pallas* Pallas, goddess of wisdom) + E *-an*] **:** of or relating to wisdom or learning

**²pal·la·di·an** \pəˈlādēən\ *adj, usu cap* [Andrea *Palladio* †1580 Ital. architect + E *-an*] **:** of, relating to, or being a revived classic style in architecture based on the works of Andrea Palladio — see PALLADIAN WINDOW

**pal·la·di·an·ism** \-ädēə,nizəm\ *n* -S *usu cap* [²*palladian* + *-ism*] **:** the Palladian school or style of architecture

**palladian window** *n, usu cap P* [²*Palladian*] **:** an architectural unit consisting of a central window with an arched head and on each side a usu. narrower window with a square head

**pal·lad·ic** \pəˈladik, -lād-\ *adj* [NL *palladium* + E *-ic*] **:** of, relating to, or derived from palladium — used esp. of compounds in which this element is tetravalent; compare PALLADOUS

**pal·la·dif·er·ous** \¦palə¦dif(ə)rəs\ *adj* [NL *palladium* + E *-iferous*] **:** bearing palladium

**pal·la·di·nize** \ˈpalədə,nīz\ *vt* -ED/-ING/-S [irreg. (influenced by *platinize*) fr. NL *palladium* + E *-ize*] **:** to coat or treat (as charcoal or asbestos) with palladium

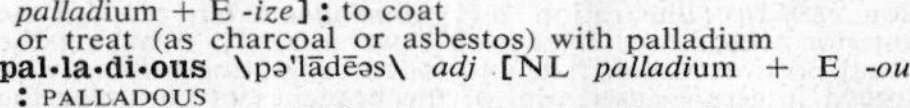

Palladian window

**pal·la·di·ous** \pəˈlādēəs\ *adj* [NL *palladium* + E *-ous*] **:** PALLADOUS

**pal·la·di·um** \pəˈlādēəm\ *n, pl* **palla·dia** \-ēə\ *also* **palladiums** [L, fr. Gk *palladion* statue of Pallas on the preservation of which was supposed to depend the safety of Troy, fr. *palladion*, neut. of *palladios* of Pallas, fr. *Pallad-, Pallas* Pallas] **:** something that affords effectual protection or security **:** SAFEGUARD ⟨trial by jury has been called the ~ of our civil rights⟩

**²palladium** \ˈ"\ *n* -S [NL, fr. *Pallad-, Pallas* Pallas, the asteroid + *-ium*] **:** a silver-white ductile malleable metallic element that is one of the platinum metals and resembles platinum, that does not tarnish at ordinary temperatures, that occurs usu. with platinum (as in nickel sulfide and gold ores), and that is used chiefly as a hydrogenation and dehydrogenation catalyst because of its ability to occlude large volumes of hydrogen and other gases, as ornamentation in the form of thin leaves esp. on book covers, as electrical contacts in telephone equipment, and in alloys (as with silver or ruthenium) for electrical apparatus and jewelry and in dentistry — symbol *Pd*; see ELEMENT table

**palladium process** *n* **:** a contact photographic printing process similar to the platinum process except that a palladium salt is used instead of a platinum salt for coating the paper

**pal·la·dize** \ˈpalə,dīz\ *vt* -ED/-ING/-S [NL *palladium* + E *-ize*] **:** PALLADINIZE

**pal·la·dous** \pəˈlādəs, ˈpaləd-\ *adj* [ISV *pallad-* (fr. NL *palladium*) + *-ous*] **:** of, relating to, or derived from palladium — used esp. of compounds in which this element is bivalent; compare PALLADIC

**pallae** *pl of* PALLA

**pal·lah** *also* **pal·la** *or* **pala** \ˈpalə\ *n* -S [Tswana *phala*] **:** IMPALA

**pal·lall** \paˈlal\ *n* -S [origin unknown] *chiefly Scot* **:** HOPSCOTCH

**pall·anesthesia** \ˌpal+\ *n* [NL, fr. Gk *pallein* to shake, brandish + NL *anesthesia* — more at POLEMIC] **:** loss of sensitivity to vibrational stimulus (as from a tuning fork)

**pal·lar** \ˈpalə(r)\ *n* -S *usu cap* **:** a member of a depressed caste of India

**pallas** *pl of* PALLA

**pal·las·ite** \ˈpalə,sīt\ *or* **pallas iron** *n* -S [Peter S. *Pallas* †1811 Ger. naturalist and traveler + E *-ite*] **:** a meteorite composed essentially of metallic iron and olivine

**pal·las's cat** \ˈpaləsəz-\ *or* **pallas cat** *n, usu cap P* [after Peter S. *Pallas*] **:** MANUL

**pallas's cormorant** *n, usu cap P* [after Peter S. *Pallas*] **:** a large small-winged cormorant (*Phalacrocorax perspicillatus*) of Bering Island that was exterminated by man

**pallas's sandgrouse** *n, usu cap P* [after Peter S. *Pallas*] **:** a Eurasiatic sandgrouse (*Syrrhaptes paradoxus*) that has long sharply-pointed tail feathers, wings without white markings, and a conspicuous black patch on the belly

**pallbearer** \ˈ=,==\ *n* **1** *archaic* **:** an attendant at a funeral who holds up a corner of the pall covering the coffin **2 a :** an attendant at a funeral who helps to carry the coffin **b :** a person who attends a funeral esp. as a representative of a fraternal order or other group and serves as a member of the immediate escort or honor guard of the coffin but does not actually assist in carrying it — called also *honorary pallbearer*

**palled** \ˈpȯld\ *adj* [¹*pall* + *-ed*] **:** covered with or wearing a pall

**pal·les·cent** \pəˈlesᵊnt, (ˈ)pa¦l-, (ˈ)pä¦l-\ *adj* [L *pallescent-, pallescens* pres. part. of *pallescere* to grow pale, incho. of *pallēre* to be pale — more at FALLOW] **:** growing or becoming pale **:** rather pale

**pall·es·the·sia** \ˌpaləsˈthēzh(ē)ə\ *n* [NL, fr. Gk *pallein* to shake + NL *esthesia* — more at POLEMIC] **:** awareness or perception of vibration esp. as transmitted through skin and bones

**¹pal·let** \ˈpalə̇t, *usu* -əd·+V\ *n* -S [ME *palet* headpiece, head, fr. MF, fr. *pal* stake, fr. L *palus* — more at POLE] *chiefly Scot* **:** HEAD, PATE

**²pallet** \ˈ"\ *n* -S [ME *paillet*, fr. (assumed) MF *paillet*, fr. *paille* straw, fr. L *palea* chaff, straw; akin to Skt *palāla* straw, *palāva* chaff, OSlav *plěva*, and prob. to L *pellis* skin — more at FELL] **1 :** a straw-filled tick or straw mattress **2 a** *or* **pallet bed :** a small, poor, or hard bed often without bedstead or springs ⟨monks retiring to their ~*s*⟩ **b :** a temporary or emergency bed usu. consisting of bedding spread on the ground or floor ⟨do stay, we can fix up a ~ in no time⟩

**³pallet** \ˈ"\ *n* -S [MF *palette*, lit., small shovel — more at PALETTE] **1 a :** a wooden instrument consisting of a flat blade or plate with a handle or handhold: as (1) **:** an implement used (as by potters) for forming, beating, or rounding clay work (2) **:** a plasterer's hawk (3) **:** PALETTE 1a(1) **b** (1) *obs* **:** a flat board, plate, or disk (as an oar blade) (2) **:** a flat piece of wood laid in a wall to furnish a means of securing more firmly woodwork that is to be fastened to the wall (3) **:** a board upon which a brick molded in a sanded mold is turned and conveyed from the mold **2 a :** a click or pawl driving or regulating a ratchet wheel **b :** any of various levers or surfaces in a timepiece that receives an impulse from the escape wheel and imparts motion to a balance or pendulum **c :** any of the disks or pistons in a chain pump **d :** a hinged valve on a pipe organ to admit or release compressed air: as (1) **:** a valve opened by a keyboard digital to admit the wind to a groove under the pipes (2) **:** a waste valve to release surplus air from the storage bellows **3 :** a flat brush used in manipulating gold leaves in gilding **4 a :** a usu. brass hand tool for impressing lines and patterns on the covers of books **b :** TYPEHOLDER **5 :** either of a pair of shelly plates borne on the siphon tubes of some bivalve mollusks **6 :** a portable platform of wood, metal, or other material designed for handling by a forklift truck or crane and used for storage or movement of materials and packages in warehouses, factories, or transport vehicles

**⁴pallet** \ˈ"\ *n* -S [⁵*pale* + *-et*] **:** a narrow heraldic pale

**pallet board** *n* [³*pallet*] **1 :** a brickmaker's pallet **2 :** PALLET 6

**pal·let·ing** \ˈpaləd·iŋ\ *n* -S [³*pallet* + *-ing*] **:** a light platform raised above the floor of the magazine of a ship to keep powder dry

**pal·let·iza·tion** \ˌpaləd·əˈzāshən, -d·ˌīˈz-\ *n* -S **:** the act or result of palletizing

**pal·let·ize** \ˈpaləd·ˌīz\ *vt* -ED/-ING/-S [³*pallet* + *-ize*] **1 :** to place on a pallet **:** transport or store by means of pallets **2 :** to alter (the materials-handling system of an organization) by the adoption of pallets and lift trucks

**pallet knife** *var of* PALETTE KNIFE

**pallet stone** *n* [³*pallet*] **:** a hard stone or jewel forming the rubbing face of the pallet of a timepiece and serving to diminish friction and wear

**pal·lette** \ˈpalə̇t\ *n* -S [alter. of *palette*] **:** one of the usu. rounded plates at the armpits of a suit of armor — see ARMOR illustration

**pallet truck** *n* [³*pallet*] **:** a lift truck for handling pallets

**palletwarmer** *n* **:** a heat-conducting tool upon which a watch pallet is placed to soften the shellac holding each pallet for readjustment

**pallholder** \ˈ=,==\ *n, archaic* **:** an attendant at a funeral that holds up a corner of the pall covering the coffin

**pal·li** \ˈpalē, ˈpälē\ *n* -S [Tamil *paḷḷi*] *India* **:** a member of a Sudra caste of field laborers

**pallia** *pl of* PALLIUM

**pal·li·al** \ˈpalēəl\ *adj* [NL *pallium* + E *-al*] **1 :** of or relating to the cerebral cortex **2 :** of, relating to, or produced by a mantle of a mollusk ⟨nacre is regarded as a ~ secretion⟩

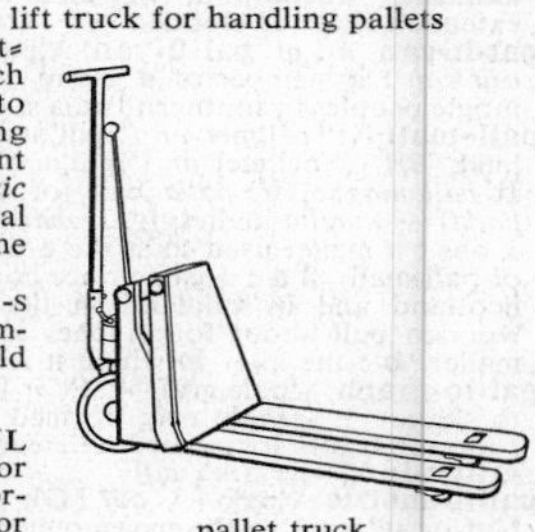

pallet truck

**pallial chamber** *n* **:** MANTLE CAVITY

**pallial line** *also* **pallial impression** *n* **:** a mark on the inner surface of a bivalve shell more or less parallel with the margin caused by the attachment of the mantle

**pallial nerve** *n* **:** either of a pair of dorsal nerves that innervate the mantle of a mollusk

**pallial sinus** *n* **1 :** an often conspicuous inward bend in the posterior part of the pallial line of a bivalve mollusk **2 :** any of the branching channels through which fluids circulate in the mantle of a brachiopod

**pal·liard** \ˈpalyə(r)d\ *n* -S [MF *paillard*, fr. *paille* straw; fr. his sleeping on straw — more at PALLET] *archaic* **:** a low or profligate rascal **:** BEGGAR, VAGABOND, LECHER

**pal·li·asse** \¦palē¦as, (ˈ)pal¦yas\ *n* -S [alter. of *paillasse*] **1 :** a usu. thin hard mattress made of a sack of strong fabric (as canvas) stuffed usu. with straw and used as a pallet or sometimes placed under another thicker and softer mattress **2 :** a supporting bed for masonry

**palliata** *n, pl* **palliatae** [L (*fabula*) *palliata*, lit., play costumed with the pallium, fr. fem. of *palliatus* wearing a pallium, fr. *pallium* + *-atus* -ate] **:** FABULA PALLIATA

**¹pal·li·ate** \ˈpalēə̇t, -ē,āt\ *adj* [L *palliatus*] **1 a :** covered with a mantle **b :** HIDDEN, DISGUISED **c :** MITIGATED, ALLEVIATED **2 :** having a pallium

**²pal·li·ate** \ˈpalē,āt, *usu* -ād·+V\ *vb* -ED/-ING/-S [LL *palliatus*, past part. of *palliare* to cloak, fr. L *pallium*] *vt* **1** *obs* **:** to cover with or as if with a mantle or cloak **:** CLOAK, SHELTER, HIDE, DISGUISE **2 :** to reduce the violence of (a disease) **:** cause to lessen or abate **:** ease without curing **3 :** to cover with excuses **:** conceal or disguise the enormity of by excuses and apologies **:** EXTENUATE, EXCUSE ⟨~ faults⟩ **4 :** to moderate the intensity of **:** LESSEN ⟨~ the boredom of our isolation⟩ **~** *vi, obs* **:** MODERATE, COMPROMISE

**syn** EXTENUATE, GLOZE, GLOSS, WHITEWASH, WHITEN: PALLIATE may stress disguising or concealing the badness or evil of and mitigating or alleviating their possible effects ⟨resort to coercive force and suppression of civil liberties are readily *palliated* in nominally democratic communities when the cry is raised that "law and order" are threatened —John Dewey⟩ ⟨writers of autobiographies, in so far as they are the chief factors in the action which they portray, *palliate*, embellish, or conceal —S.H.Adams⟩ EXTENUATE may imply intention of lessening seriousness or gravity by excuse, element consideration of circumstances, or palliation ⟨somewhat overpraised the virtues, and too much *extenuated* the faults —T.S.Eliot⟩ ⟨he did not *extenuate*, he rather emphasized, the criminality of Catiline and his confederates —J.A.Froude⟩ GLOZE may suggest aim to divert attention from the badness, evil, harshness, or unpleasantness of something unpleasant by specious irrelevance or dissembling ⟨the article of January 1878 endeavored to *gloze* over this point as unsuited to the exoteric public addressed —Justus Buchler⟩ ⟨our triangles do not have accurate straight lines for their sides nor exact points at their corners, but this is *glozed* over by saying that the sides are approximately straight and the corners approximately points —Bertrand Russell⟩ GLOSS, often a close synonym for GLOZE, may suggest a distracting of attention from the bad or difficult by artful omission or by explanation that belittles them ⟨when judges mask a change of substance, or *gloss* over its importance —B.N.Cardozo⟩ ⟨rough hard-driving men seeking to *gloss* over the harsh and ugly realities of their calling —Walter O'Meara⟩ WHITEWASH and WHITEN may be used of attempts to cover up, distract attention from, or exculpate by superficial investigation, perfunctory trial, or other rigged procedure ⟨if the police are out to *whitewash* the Mitchell family, I'll call in a bunch of reporters and tell them so —Mary R. Rinehart⟩ ⟨use some family influence to *whitewash* past acts of collusion against the government —James Kelly⟩

**pal·li·a·tion** \ˌpalēˈāshən\ *n* -s [MF, fr. ML *palliation-, palliatio* cloaking, concealing, fr. LL *palliatus* + L *-ion-, -io* -ion] **1** : the quality or state of being palliated **2** : an act of palliating

**¹pal·lia·tive** \ˈpalēˌād·iv, -lēəd·|, -lyəd·|, |ēv *also* |əv\ *adj* [F *palliatif*, fr. LL *palliatus* + F *-if* -ive] : serving to palliate ⟨~ drugs⟩ — **pal·li·a·tive·ly** \|əvlē, -li\ *adv*

**²palliative** \"\ *n* -s : something that palliates : a palliative agent or procedure

**pal·li·a·tor** \-lēˌād·ə(r), -ātə-\ *n* -s : one that palliates

**pal·li·a·to·ry** \-lēəˌtōrē, -lyə-, -tȯr-, -ri\ *adj* : PALLIATIVE, EXTENUATING ⟨~ circumstances⟩

**pal·lid** \ˈpaləd\ *adj* [L *pallidus* — more at PALE] : deficient in color: as **a** : lacking the normal amount of color : WAN — used esp. of the human countenance in illness ⟨a ~ liverish face⟩ **b** : lacking in brightness or intensity : PALE — used of a color or a colored object ⟨a ~ sky⟩ **c** : lacking sparkle or liveliness : DULL ⟨a ~ entertainment⟩ ⟨~ writings⟩ — **pallid·ly** *adv* — **pal·lid·ness** *n* -ES

**pal·li·dal** \ˈpaləd³l\ *adj* [NL (*globus*) *pallidus* + E *-al*] : of, relating to, or involving the globus pallidus ⟨a severe ~ lesion⟩

**pallid bat** *n* : a large light-colored insectivorous cave bat (*Antrozous pallidus*) of southwestern No. America — called also *desert bat*

**pallid cuckoo** *n* : a slender light-colored Australian cuckoo (*Cuculus pallidus*) with an irritatingly persistent and monotonous call — called also *brain-fever bird*

**pallidi-** *comb form* [L *pallidus*] : pale ⟨*pallidi*florous⟩ ⟨*pallidi*palpate⟩

**pal·lid·i·ty** \paˈlidəd·ē, pəˈl-\ *n* -ES [*pallid* + *-ity*] : PALLIDNESS, PALENESS

**pallido-** *comb form* [NL (*globus*) *pallidus* + *-o-*] **1** : globus pallidus ⟨*pallido*fugal⟩ **2** : pallidal and ⟨*pallido*hypothalamic⟩

**pal·li·dofu·gal** \ˌpalə(ˌ)dōˈfyügəl, -ləˈdäfyəg-\ *adj* [*pallido-* + *-fugal*] *of a nerve fiber or impulse* : passing out of the globus pallidus

**pallid wren-tit** *n* : a wren-tit of the interior valleys of southern California that constitutes a distinct subspecies (*Chamaea fasciata henshawi*) and is distinguished by pale grayish plumage

**¹palling** *pres part of* PALL *or of* PAL

**²palling** *var of* PALL

**pall·ing·ly** *adv* : so as to pall : TIRESOMELY

**pallio-** *comb form* [NL *pallium* + *-o-*] **1** : pallium : sheet ⟨*pallio*stratus⟩ **2** : pallial and ⟨*pallio*cardiac⟩

**pal·lion** \ˈpalyən\ *n* -s [origin unknown] : a small piece or pellet (as of solder)

**pallisade** *var of* PALISADE

**pal·li·sa·do** \ˌpaləˈsā(ˌ)dō-\ *adj* [alter. of *palisade*] : VALLARY

**pal·li·um** \ˈpalēəm\ *n, pl* **pal·lia** \-ēə\ *or* **palliums** [L — more at PALL] **1 a** : a cloak formed by draping a rectangular piece of cloth and worn by men of ancient Greece and Rome — compare PALLA 1 **b** : a circular band of white wool with pendants of the same material in front and back worn in the Latin rite by a pope and conferred by him on archbishops as a symbol of office **c** : ALTAR CLOTH, PALL **2** [NL, fr. L, cloak] **a** : the whole cerebral cortex covering the rest of the brain like a mantle **b** : the mantle of a mollusk, brachiopod, or bird **3** : an extended sheet of clouds

pallium 1b

**pal·li·yan** *n, pl* **pal·li·yan** \ˌpalē(y)ən\ *usu cap* : a member of a group of negroid jungle peoples in southern India speaking Dravidian languages

**pall-mall** \(ˈ)pelˈmel *or* (ˈ)palˈmal *or* (ˈ)pōlˈmōl *also* (ˈ)pälˈmäl, *Brit* (ˈ)pelˈmel *or* (ˈ)palˈmal\ *n* -s [MF *pallemaille*, fr. It *pallamaglio*, fr. *palla* ball (of Gmc origin; akin to OHG *balla*) + *maglio* mallet, fr. L *malleus* — more at BALL, MAUL] **1** *obs* : a mallet used to strike a ball esp. as used in the game of pall-mall **2 a** : a game once common in Italy, France, and Scotland and in England in the 17th century in which a wooden ball about four inches in diameter is driven with a mallet **b** : the alley in which it is played

**pal·lo·graph** \ˈpaləˌgraf, -rāf\ *n* [ISV *pallo-* (fr. Gk *pallein* to shake) + *-graph*; orig. formed in G — more at POLEMIC] : an apparatus for recording steamship vibrations — **pal·lo·graph·ic** \ˌ==ˈgrafik\ *adj*

**pal·lo·metric** \ˌpalə+\ *adj* [Gk *pallein* + E *-o-* + *metric*] : of or relating to the measurement of artificial vibrations of the earth's surface

**pal·lo·ne** \pəˈlōnē\ *n* -s [It, aug. of *palla* ball — more at PALL-MALL] : an Italian game somewhat like tennis played by striking a large leather ball with a cylindrical guard (as of wood, padded metal, or rubber) worn over hand and wrist

**pal·lor** \ˈpalə(r)\ *n* -s [L, fr. *pallēre* to be pale + *-or* — more at FALLOW] : deficiency of color : a wan or blanched appearance : PALENESS; *esp* : abnormal paleness of all or part of the human body

**pal·lot·tine** \ˈpaləˌtīn, -tēn\ *n* -s *usu cap* [It *pallottino*, fr. Vincenzo Maria *Pallotti* †1850 Ital. secular priest] : a member of a Roman Catholic religious society founded in 1835 to aid mission work esp. among immigrants

**palls** *pl of* PALL, *pres 3d sing of* PALL

**pallwise** \ˈ=ˌ=\ *adv* : in the manner of a pall

**pal·ly** \ˈpalē\ *adj* -ER/-EST [¹*pal* + *-y*] : sharing the relationship of pals : informally intimate

**¹palm** \ˈpälm, ˈpȧl *also* |lm; *archaic* ˈpam\ *n* -s [In sense 1, fr. ME *palme*, fr. OE *palm, palma, palme*; akin to OHG *palma* palm tree, ON *palmr*; all fr. a prehistoric NGmc-WGmc word borrowed fr. L *palma* palm of the hand, palm tree (fr. the resemblance of its leaves to an outstretched hand); in other senses, fr. ME *paume*, fr. MF, fr. L *palma*; akin to OE *folm* palm of the hand, OHG *folma*, Gk *palamē*, Skt *pāṇi* hand, OE *flōr* floor — more at FLOOR] **1 a** : a plant of the family Palmae — see BETEL PALM, CABBAGE PALM, COCONUT PALM, FAN PALM, FEATHER PALM, PIASSAVA, PALMETTO, PALMYRA, RATTAN, WAX PALM **b** (1) : a leaf of the palm borne or worn as a symbol of rejoicing or victory : PALM BRANCH (2) : a branch of any of various trees or shrubs (as hazel, willow, laurel, yew, larch) used esp. in religious observances as a substitute for symbolic palm; *also* : a tree or shrub yielding such palms **c** (1) : a symbol or token of superiority, success, or triumph (2) : the quality or state of being superior, successful, or triumphant **d** : an addition to a military or other honorary decoration in the form of a palm frond used esp. to indicate that the wearer has a second time merited the basic decoration **2 a** (1) : the somewhat concave part of the human hand between the bases of the fingers and the wrist upon which the fingers close when flexed (2) : the corresponding part of the forefoot of a lower mammal **b** : MERUS **3** : a flat expanded part esp. when at the end of a slenderer base or stalk: as **a** : the broad flattened part of an antler (as of a moose) **b** : the blade of an oar or paddle **c** : the end of a bar or pipe flattened to provide a surface for bolting or riveting to a support **d** (1) : the flat inner face of an anchor fluke — see ANCHOR illustration (2) : ²FLUKE 1 **e** : a flat surface on a shaft strut of a ship's hull or on the end of a deck stanchion **4** [L *palmus*, fr. *palma*] : any of various units of length based on the breadth of the hand and varying from around 3 to 4 inches or on the length of the hand from the wrist to the ends of the fingers and varying from around 7 to 10 inches **5** : something that covers the palm of the hand: as **a** : a piece of leather or heavy canvas fitted to the palm for protection when sewing heavy material (as harness leather or a sail) by hand and often equipped with a metal boss or slug for pushing the needle through the material **b** : the part of a glove that covers the palm ⟨a fabric glove with soft suede ~⟩ **6** [³*palm*] : an act of palming (as of cards, dice, or coins) ⟨did a skillful ~ of the extra card⟩

**²palm** \"\ *adj* **1** : of or relating to a palm (as the palm plant or the palm of the hand) ⟨~ leaves⟩ ⟨a firm ~ pressure⟩ **2** : derived from or made of palm ⟨~ fiber⟩

**³palm** \"\ *vt* -ED/-ING/-S **1** : to touch with the palm: as **a** : stroke with the palm or hand **b** : to shake hands with **c** : to allow (a basketball) to remain in contact with the hand while moving the hand and arm thus usu. committing a violation **2 a** : to conceal in or with the hand ⟨~ a card⟩ **b** : to abstract by picking up stealthily and concealing ⟨likely to ~ any small thing left lying around⟩ **3** : to impose by fraud — used with *on* or *upon* ⟨trash fit only to be ~*ed* on the unwary⟩; compare PALM OFF **4** : BRIBE, TIP

**⁴palm** *abbr* palmistry

**¹pal·ma** \ˈpälmə\ *n* -s [Sp, fr. L] **1 a** : ¹PALM 1a **b** : the leaves, fiber, or other part of a palm **2** : any of various plants (as screw pine and yucca) that resemble palms **3** : fiber from yucca; *esp* : a pale hard fiber from the leaves of a Mexican arborescent yucca (*Samuela carnerosana*)

**²palma** \"\ *adj, usu cap* [fr. *Palma* de Mallorca, port of Balearic islands] : of or from Palma de Mallorca, Spain : of the kind or style prevalent in Palma

**palma·ce·ae** \palˈmāsēˌē, päˈm-\ [NL, fr. L *palma* palm + NL *-aceae*] *syn of* PALMAE

**palma·ceous** \(ˈ)palˈmāshəs, (ˈ)päˈm-\ *adj* [NL *Palmaceae* + E *-ous*] : of or relating to a palm : being or resembling a palm

**pal·ma chris·ti** \ˌpalməˈkristē, -ˌstī\ *also* **palmcrist** *pronunc at* ¹PALM +ˌkrist\ *n, pl* **palmae christi** \-(ˌ)mē-, -ˌmī-\ *also* **palmcrists** *cap Christi* [ML *palma Christi*, lit., palm of Christ] : CASTOR-OIL PLANT

**palmad** \ˈpalˌmad, ˈpäˌm-\ *adv* [¹*palm* + *-ad*] : toward the palm

**palmae** \ˈpalˌmē, ˈpäˌm-, -mī\ *n pl, cap* [NL, pl. of L *palma* palm] : a family (coextensive with the order Palmales) of chiefly tropical trees, shrubs, and vines comprising the palms, having a usu. tall columnar trunk that lacks a cambium and is therefore incapable of true secondary growth and bears a crown of very large leaves with stout sheathing and often prickly petioles whose persistent bases often clothe the trunk, and producing small flowers in very large clusters each subtended by a spathe

**pal·ma istle** \ˈpälmə+\ *n* [AmerSp *palma ixtle*] : ISTLE

**palma·les** \palˈmā(ˌ)lēz, päˈm-\ *n pl, cap* [NL, fr. L *palma* palm + NL *-ales*] : a large order of chiefly tropical monocotyledonous plants that is coextensive with the family Palmae and in some classifications includes also the Cyclanthales

**palmar** \ˈpalmə(r), ˈpäm-\ *adj* [NL *palmaris*, fr. L *palma* palm + *-aris* -ar — more at PALM] : of, relating to, situated in, or involving the palm of the hand

**palmar arch** *n* : either of two loops of blood vessels in the palm of the hand: **a** : a deep arch that is formed by the continuation of the radial artery and a branch of the ulnar artery and supplies principally the deep muscles of the hand, thumb, and index finger **b** : a superficial arch that is the continuation of the ulnar artery which anastomoses with a branch derived from the radial artery, its branches mostly going to the fingers

**pal·ma re·al** \ˌpälməˈrāˈäl\ *n* [AmerSp, lit., royal palm] : any of several large palms esp. of the genus *Roystonea*

**palmar fascia** *n* : a very strong roughly triangular fascia that binds together and protects the structures of the palm of the hand

**palmar·i·an** \palˈmerēən, päˈm-\ *adj* [L *palmarius* of or deserving the palm + E *-an* — more at PALMARY] : bearing or worthy to bear the palm : PALMARY

**palmar·is** \palˈma(a)rəs, päˈm\ *n* -ES [NL, fr. *palmaris* palmar] : either of two muscles of the palm of the hand: **a** : a short transverse superficial muscle of the ulnar part of the palm **b** : a frequently absent superficial muscle that arises from the medial epicondyle of the humerus and is inserted into the palmar fascia and annular ligament

**palmar nerve** *n* : any of the branches of the ulnar and median nerves to the palm of the hand

**palma·ro·sa oil** \ˌpälməˈrōzə, ˈpäm-\ *n* [perh. fr. L *palma* palm + *rosa* rose] : a fragrant essential oil obtained from a rosha grass (*Cymbopogon martinii* var. *motia*) esp. of India and Java and used in soaps, cosmetics, and perfumes of the rose type and in the preparation of geraniol — called also *geranium oil*

**¹palma·ry** \ˈpalmərē, ˈpäm-\ *adj* [L *palmarius* of or deserving the palm, fr. *palma* palm + *-arius* -ary] : worthy of praise or notice : OUTSTANDING, SUPERIOR ⟨a ~ instance⟩ ⟨his ~ work⟩

**²palmary** \"\ *adj* [NL *palmaris* palmar] : PALMAR

**palmat-** *or* **palmati-** *comb form* [LL *palmatus* palmate] **1** : palmate ⟨*palmat*ic⟩ ⟨*palmati*form⟩ **2** : palmately ⟨*palmati*fid⟩

**palma·tae** \palˈmāˌtē, päˈm-, -mäˌtī\ *n pl, cap* [NL, fr. LL, fem. pl. of *palmatus*] *in former classifications* : a group consisting of the web-footed birds

**palmate** \ˈpalˌmāt, ˈpäˌm-\ *also* **palmat·ed** \-ād·əd\ *adj* [*palmate* fr. LL *palmatus*, fr. L, marked with the palm of a hand, fr. *palma* palm + *-atus* -ate, *palmated* fr. *palmate* + *-ed* — more at PALM] : having the shape of the hand : resembling a hand with the fingers spread: as **a** : having lobes radiating from a common point — used orig. only of 5-lobed leaves but now also of other lobed leaves, of leaf venation, and of other plant organs (as the tubers of some orchids); see LEAF illustration, VENATION illustration **b** (1) *of an aquatic bird* : having the anterior toes united by a web : WEBBED (2) : having the distal portion broad, flat, and lobed suggesting a hand with spread fingers — used esp. of the branches of corals or the antlers of a moose — **palmate·ly** *adv*

**palmated newt** *n* : a small European newt (*Triturus palmipes*) with webbed feet

**palmately cleft** *adj* : PALMATIFID

**palmat·i·fid** \palˈmad·əˌfid, päˈm-\ *adj* [ISV *palmat-* + *-fid*] : cleft in a palmate manner ⟨a ~ leaf⟩ — compare PINNATIFID

**palma·tine** \ˈpalməˌtēn, ˈpäm-\ *n* -s [NL *Jatrorrhiza palmata* plant producing calumba + E *-ine*] : an alkaloid $C_{21}H_{23}NO_5$ that occurs esp. in calumba and is related in structure to berberine

**palma·tion** \palˈmāshən, päˈm-\ *n* -s [³*palm* + *-ation*] **1** *obs* : an act of touching with the palm **2** [*palmate* + *-ion*] **a** : the quality or state of being palmate **b** : palmate lobation; *also* : a palmate part

**pal·ma·to·ria** \ˌpalməˈtōrēə\ *n* -s [NL, fr. L *palma* palm of the hand + *-atoria* -atory; fr. its being carried in the hand] : BUGIA

**palm ball** *n* : a change of pace pitch in baseball thrown from the palm of the hand with either two or three fingers

**palm beetle** *n* : a beetle that is destructive to palms; *esp* : PALM WEEVIL

**palm borer** *n* : any of several beetle larvae that live in palms; *esp* : that of a very large bostrychid beetle (*Dinapate wrighti*)

**palm branch** *n* : a palm leaf with its stalk used esp. as an emblem of victory or rejoicing

**palm butter** *n* : PALM OIL

**palm cabbage** *n* **1** : CABBAGE PALMETTO **2** : CABBAGE 2

**palm capital** *n* : an Egyptian capital resembling a spreading group of palm leaves

**palm civet** *also* **palm cat** *n* : any of various arboreal civets: as **a** : any of several black-spotted or black-striped yellowish gray or brownish gray civets of *Paradoxurus* or related genera that are widely distributed in southeastern Asia and the East Indies **b** : an African civet of the genus *Nandinia*

**palm cockatoo** *n* : GREAT BLACK COCKATOO

**palm crab** *n* : PURSE CRAB

**palmcrist** *var of* PALMA CHRISTI

**palm dove** *n* : any of various doves frequenting palms; *esp* : an Egyptian turtledove (*Streptopelia senegalensis aegyptiaca*)

palm capital

**¹palmed** \ˈpälmd, ˈpȧl *also* |lmd; *archaic* ˈpamd\ *adj* [ME *pawmed*, fr. *pawme*, *paume* palm + *-ed*] **1** : having a palm or palms esp. of a specified kind ⟨horny ~ hands⟩ **2** : PALMATE

**²palmed** \"\ *adj* [fr. past part. of ³*palm*] : held or hidden in the palm

**pal·mel·la** \palˈmelə\ *n, cap* [NL, fr. Gk *palmos* vibration, quivering (fr. *pallein* to shake) + NL *-ella* — more at POLEMIC] : a genus (the type of the family Palmellaceae) comprising terrestrial and freshwater green algae that form large masses of usu. immobile cells embedded in a gelatinous matrix and sometimes including forms generally held to be palmella stages of flagellated algae or plantlike flagellates

**pal·mel·la·ce·ae** \ˌpalməˈlāsēˌē\ *n pl, cap* [NL, fr. *Palmella*, type genus + *-aceae*] : a family of green algae (order Volvocales) — see PALMELLA — **pal·mel·la·ceous** \ˌpalməˈlāshəs\ *adj*

**pal·mel·lar** \(ˈ)palˈmelə(r)\ *adj* [*palmella* (*stage*) + *-ar*] : of or relating to a palmella stage : PALMELLOID

**palmella stage** *also* **palmella form** *n* [so called because orig. thought to be a member of the genus *Palmella*] : a colonial aggregate of immobile nonflagellated individuals occurring regularly in the life cycle or in response to increased firmness of medium of some flagellated green algae or plantlike flagellates (as members of the genera *Euglena* and *Chlamydomonas*)

**pal·mel·loid** \palˈmeˌlȯid\ *adj* [NL *Palmella* + E *-oid*] : resembling *Palmella*; *specif* : having a palmella stage in the life history ⟨~ algae⟩

**¹palm·er** \ˈpälmə(r), ˈpȧl *also* |lm-; *archaic* ˈpam-\ *n* -s [ME *palmere*, fr. MF *palmier, paumier*, fr. ML *palmarius*, fr. L *palmarius*, adj., of palms — more at PALMARY] **1** : a person wearing two crossed leaves of palm as a sign of his having made a pilgrimage to the Holy Land and its sacred places; *also* : a wandering religious votary **2 a** (1) : PALMERWORM (2) : PALMER FLY **b** : WOOD LOUSE 1

**²palmer** \"\ *n* -s [ME *palmer, pamere*, fr. MF *paumer*, fr. *paume* palm — more at PALM] : a ferule formerly used for punishing schoolboys with blows on the palm of the hand

**³palmer** \"\ *n* -s [³*palm* + *-er*] : one that palms something (as cards or dice) : PRESTIDIGITATOR

**palmer fly** *n* [¹*palmer*] : an angler's hackle fly in which the hackle extends along the entire body instead of radiating from the head only

**pal·me·rin** \ˈpalməˌrēn\ *n* -s *usu cap* [*Palmerin* de Oliva, hero of several 16th cent. Span. romances] *archaic* : a medieval knightly hero

**palmer moth** *n* : the adult of a palmerworm

**palmer oak** *n* [prob. fr. the name *Palmer*] : a large evergreen oak shrub (*Quercus palmeri*) of dry sunny areas of the southwestern U. S.

**palm·er·sto·ni·an** \ˌpä|mə(r)ˈstōnēən, ˌpȧl *also* |lm-\ *adj, usu cap* [Henry John Temple, 3d Viscount *Palmerston* †1865 Eng. prime minister + E *-ian*] : of, relating to, or in the manner of Lord Palmerston

**palmerworm** \ˈ==ˌ=\ *n* [¹*palmer* + *worm*] : a caterpillar that suddenly appears in great numbers devouring herbage; *esp* : one that is the larva of a No. American moth (*Dichomeris ligulella*) and that is destructive to fruit trees

**palm·ery** \ˈpä|mərē, ˈpȧl *also* |lm-\ *n* -ES [¹*palm* + *-ery*] : a place for growing palms; *also* : a collection of growing palms

**palm·es·the·sia** \ˌpalməsˈthēzh(ē)ə\ *n* -s [NL, fr. Gk *palmos* vibration + NL *esthesia* — more at PALMELLA] : PALLESTHESIA

**pal·mette** \(ˈ)palˈmet\ *n* -s [F, fr. *palme* palm (fr. L *palma*) + *-ette*] : a conventional ornament of very ancient origin consisting of radiating petals that spring from a base suggestive of a calyx and being closely related to the Egyptian lotus and Greek anthemion

**pal·met·to** \palˈmed·(ˌ)ō, -e(ˌ)tō\ *n, pl* **palmettos** *or* **palmettoes** [alter. (influenced by It *-etto* -ette) of ¹*palmito*] **1** : any of several usu. low-growing fan palms; *esp* : CABBAGE PALMETTO — see BLUE PALMETTO, SAW PALMETTO **2 a** : strips of the leaf blade of a palmetto used in weaving ⟨a ~ basket⟩ **b** : a hat woven of palmetto **3** *usu cap* : SOUTH CAROLINIAN — a nickname **4** : a tanning material obtained from the roots of the saw palmetto **5** *or* **palmetto green** : a grayish yellow green that is less strong and very slightly greener and darker than average sage green, greener and deeper than mermaid, and greener and darker than celadon

**palmetto weevil** *or* **palmetto billbug** *n* : a weevil (*Rhynchophorus cruentatus*) that breeds in cabbage palmetto and date palm in the southeastern U. S.

**palme·tum** \palˈmēd·əm, päˈm-\ *n* -s [L, palm grove, fr. *palma* palm + *-etum*] : PALMERY; *esp* : an area where palms are grown outdoors for botanical or ornamental purposes

**palm family** *n* : PALMAE

**palm fiber** *n* **1** : a fiber (as piassava) obtained from a palm **2** : the split leaves of a palm used for thatching, weaving, or rope making

**palm·ful** \ˈ=ˌfu̇l\ *n, pl* **palmfuls** *also* **palms·ful** \-mˌfu̇lz, -mzˌfu̇l\ : the quantity that would fill a human palm

**palm-grass** \ˈ=ˌ=\ *n* : a tall perennial Indian grass (*Setaria palmifolia*) that has large showy plicate blades and a long loose panicle and that is often cultivated as an ornamental in warm regions

**palm grease** *n* [¹*palm* (of the hand)] *slang* : money for bribing or tipping

**palm green** *n* [¹*palm* (tree)] : a variable color averaging a dark yellowish green that is yellower, less strong, and very slightly lighter than holly green (sense 1), lighter and stronger than deep chrome green, yellower and duller than golf green, and yellower and paler than average hunter green

**palm grub** *n* : PALM BORER

**palm honey** *n* : a sweet table syrup consisting of the sap of the coquito concentrated by boiling

**palm house** *n* : a greenhouse for growing palms

**palmi** *pl of* PALMUS

**palmi-** *comb form* [L, fr. *palma* palm] **1** : palm tree ⟨*palmi*colous⟩ ⟨*palmi*vorous⟩ **2 a** : palmat- ⟨*palmi*lobate⟩ ⟨*palmi*nerved⟩ **b** : with or on the palms ⟨*palmi*grade⟩

**palmier** *comparative of* PALMY

**pal·mie·rite** \ˌpalmēˈeˌrīt, palˈmi,r-\ *n* -s *often cap* [F *palmiérite*, fr. Luigi *Palmieri* †1896 Ital. meteorologist + F *-ite*] : a mineral $(K,Na)_2Pb(SO_4)_2$ that is a sulfate of lead, sodium, and potassium usu. with only a little sodium

**palmiest** *superlative of* PALMY

**pal·mi·fi·ca·tion** \ˌpäməfəˈkāshən, ˈpalm-\ *n* -s [*palmi-* + *caprification*] : artificial cross-pollination of the flowers of the date palm as practiced by the Babylonians by suspending clusters from the wild staminate trees among the pistillate blossoms of the cultivated trees

**pal·mi·lla** \pälˈmē(y)ə\ *n* -s [AmerSp, dim. of Sp *palma* palm — more at PALMITO] **1** : JIPIJAPA **2** *also* **pal·mi·llo** \-ē-(ˌ)(y)ō\ [*palmillo* AmerSp, dim. of Sp *palma*] : a soap plant (*Yucca elata*)

**palming** *pres part of* PALM

**¹palmi·ped** \ˈpalməˌped, ˈpäm-\ *adj* [L *palmiped-, palmipes*, fr. *palmi-* + *-ped-, -pes* -ped] : WEB-FOOTED

**²palmiped** \"\ *n* -s *archaic* : a web-footed bird

**palm·ist** \ˈpä|məst, ˈpȧl *also* |lm-\ *n* -s [prob. back-formation fr. *palmistry*] : one who practices palmistry ⟨current as truths among professional phrenologists and ~*s* —*Educational Rev.*⟩ — called also *palm reader*

**pal·miste** \(ˈ)palˈmēst\ *n* -s [AmerF, perh. modif. of Sp *palmito*] : any of several palms; *esp* : CABBAGE PALM 1b

**palm·is·ter** \ˈpä|məstə(r), ˈpȧl *also* |lm-\ *n* -s [prob. fr. *palmistry*, after such pairs as E *ministry: minister*] *archaic* : PALMIST

**palm·is·try** \-trē, -tri\ *n* -ES [ME *pawmestry*, prob. fr. *paume* palm + *maistrie* mastery — more at PALM, MASTERY] **1** : the

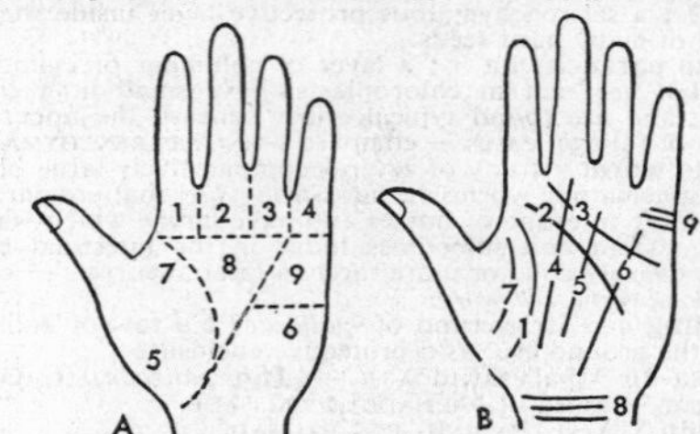


palmistry: diagrams showing Mounts, *A: 1* Jupiter, *2* Saturn, *3* Apollo, *4* Mercury, *5* Venus, *6* Luna, *7* Lower Mars, *8* Plain of Mars, *9* Upper Mars; lines, *B: 1* Life, *2* Head, *3* Heart, *4* Fate, *5* the Sun, *6* Mercury, *7* Mars, *8* rascettes, *9* lines of Affection

art or practice of reading a person's character or aptitudes and esp. his past and possible future from the general character and shape of his hands and fingers and the lines, Mounts, and marks on the palms — called also *chirognomy, chiromancy* **2 :** dexterity or trickery (as pocket picking) involving use of the hands

**palmi·tate** \'palmə,tāt, 'päm-\ *n* -s [ISV *palmit-* (fr. *palmitin*) + *-ate*] **:** a salt or ester of palmitic acid

**palmit·ic acid** \(')pal¦mid·ik-, (')pä¦m-\ *n* [ISV *palmit-* + *-ic;* orig. formed as F *palmitique*] **:** a waxy crystalline fatty acid $CH_3(CH_2)_{14}COOH$ that occurs both free and combined in the form of glycerides and other esters in palm oil, butter fat, tallow, and most other fats and fatty oils, and also in several essential oils and waxes and that is used chiefly in mixtures with stearic acid — called also *hexadecanoic acid*

**palmi·tin** \'palmətən, 'päm-\ *n* -s [F *palmitine,* prob. fr. *palmite* pith of the palm tree (fr. *palme* palm tree, fr. L *palma*) + *-ine* -in] **:** an ester of glycerol and palmitic acid; *esp* **:** TRIPALMITIN

**¹palmito** *n* -s [Sp, dim. of *palma* palm tree, fr. L — more at PALM] *obs* **:** PALMETTO

**²palmi·to** \pal'mēd·(,)ō, pä'm-\ *n* -s [AmerSp, fr. Sp *palmito* palmetto] **1 a :** CABBAGE 2 **b :** a palm whose terminal bud is used as food **2 :** any of several yuccas of Mexico and the southwestern U. S.

**pal·mit·ole·ic acid** \¦palmәd·ō¦lēik-, ¦päm-\ *n* [ISV *palmit-* (fr. *palmatin*) + *oleic* — more at PALMITIN] **:** a crystalline unsaturated fatty acid $C_6H_{13}CH{=}CH(CH_2)_7COOH$ occurring in the form of glycerides esp. in whale, seal, cod, and other marine animal oils and yielding palmitic acid on hydrogenation

**palm kernel** *or* **palm nut** *n* **:** the seed of any palm that yields palm-kernel oil

**palm-kernel oil** *n* **:** a white to yellowish edible fat that is obtained from palm kernels esp. of the African oil palm, that resembles coconut oil more than palm oil, and that is used chiefly in making soap and margarine

**palm leaf** *n* **1 :** the leaf of a palm; *esp* **:** the leaf of a fan palm used for palm fiber or thatching **2 a** *or* **palm-leaf hat :** a hat woven of palm fiber **b** *or* **palm-leaf fan :** a fan made of palm leaf **3** *or* **palm-leaf pattern :** a decorative motif that is common in oriental art and is possibly based on the palm leaf

**palmlike** \'=,=\ *adj* **:** resembling a palm esp. in habit of growth **:** like that of a palm ⟨~ leaves⟩

**palm lily** *n* **:** TI 1

**palm marten** *n* **:** PALM CIVET

**pal·mod·ic** \(')pal¦mädik\ *adj* [Gk *palmōdēs* throbbing (fr. *palmos* vibration, quivering + *-ōdēs* like) + E *-ic* — more at PALMELLA, -ODE] **:** relating to or resembling palmus **:** JERKY

**palm off** *vt* [³*palm*] **1 :** to dispose of usu. by trickery or guile in place of something expected or desired ⟨tried to *palm off* the worn-out farm as good bottomland⟩ **2 :** to deceive usu. by trickery or guile ⟨*palmed* his brother *off* with some story or other⟩ **3 :** to present (as oneself) in an untrue light ⟨*palmed* himself *off* as a millionaire sportsman⟩

**¹palm oil** *n* [¹*palm* (of the hand)] *slang* **:** money given as a bribe or tip

**²palm oil** *n* [¹*palm* (tree)] **:** a semisolid or solid red or yellowish brown edible fat obtained from the flesh of the fruit esp. of the African oil palm and used chiefly in making soap, candles, and lubricating greases and in coating iron or steel plates to be tinned

**pal·mo·spas·mus** \¦palmō¦spazməs\ *n* -ES [NL, fr. Gk *palmos* quivering + *spasmos* spasm — more at PALMELLA] **:** clonic spasm

**palm play** *n* **:** tennis as first played by striking the ball with the palm of the hand

**palm print** *n* **:** a print of the palm of the hand — compare FINGERPRINT

**palm reader** *n* **:** PALMIST

**palm rest** *n* **:** a device often fitted to the stock of a target rifle for supporting the rifle with the hand while firing

**palm rhinoceros beetle** *n* [¹*palm* (tree)] **:** a reddish brown rhinoceros beetle (*Oryctes rhinoceros*) of tropical Asia

**palms** *pl of* PALM, *pres 3d sing of* PALM

**palmsful** *pl of* PALMFUL

**palm squirrel** *n* **:** a small tree squirrel (*Funambulus palmarum*) of India that is gray with three broad white stripes down the back

**palm starch** *n* **:** SAGO 2

**palm stay** *n* [¹*palm* (flat part)] **:** a short boiler stay screwed through a surface into an angle piece riveted to another surface at right angles

**palm sugar** *n* [¹*palm* (tree)] **:** a usu. moist brown sugar (as jaggery) made from palm sap

**palm sunday** *n, usu cap P&S* [ME *palmesonday,* fr. OE *palmsunnandaeg,* fr. ¹*palm* + *sunnandaeg* Sunday] **:** the Sunday preceding Easter on which is commemorated Christ's triumphal entry into Jerusalem when the multitude strewed palm branches in his way

**palm swift** *n* **:** a swift of *Tachornis* or related genera: as **a :** a West Indian bird (*T. phoenicobia*) **b :** an African and Asiatic bird (*Cypsiurus parvus*)

**palm-tree cabbage** *n* **:** a kale with leafless stems 6 feet or more in height and a terminal cluster of very dark much-curled leaves

**pal·mu·la** \'palmyələ, 'päm-\ *n, pl* **palmu·lae** \-,lē, -,lī\ [NL, fr. L, palm of the hand, little palm, dim. of *palma* palm] **:** PULVILLUS

**pal·mus** \'palməs\ *n, pl* **pal·mi** \-,mī, -,mē\ [NL, fr. Gk *palmos* vibration, quivering — more at PALMELLA] **:** PALPITATION, TWITCHING, JERKINESS

**palm vaulting** *n* **:** a variation of Gothic rib vaulting in which many ribs of equal length form a palmlike pattern

**palm viper** *n* **:** any of numerous small arboreal pit vipers (genera *Bothrops* and *Trimeresurus*) of tropical America that are frequently green in color with prehensile tails which help them to move from tree to tree

**palm warbler** *n* **:** a widely distributed No. American warbler (*Dendroica palmarum*) occurring in a western subspecies (*D. p. palmarum*) chiefly of central Canada and the Mississippi valley that is distinguished by a chestnut crown when adult and yellowish underparts and a more easterly distributed subspecies (*D. p. hypochrysea*) in which the yellow is more marked

**palm·ward** \'=wə(r)d\ *adv* **:** toward the palm of the hand

**palm wax** *n* **:** a resinous wax obtained from a wax palm (*Ceroxylon andicolum*) and used in candles

**palm weevil** *n* **:** any of various weevils of the genus *Rhynchophorus* whose larvae bore in palm trees — compare GRUGRU 2

**palm wine** *n* **:** the fermented sap of any of various palms used as a beverage esp. in tropical countries

**palm wool** *n* **:** COIR

**palm worm** *n* **:** the larva of a palm weevil

**¹palmy** \'pälmē, 'päl, |mi *also* |lm-\ *adj* -ER/-EST **1 a :** abounding in or bearing palms ⟨a ~ strand⟩ **b :** resembling or derived from a palm ⟨rich ~ suds⟩ ⟨a slender ~ figure⟩ **2** [so called fr. the traditional use of the palm branch as an emblem of triumph] **:** outstanding among members of a class by reason of excellence or superiority **:** constituting an acme **:** notably flourishing or prosperous ⟨not likely to regain that ~ state⟩ ⟨knew her in her *palmier* days⟩

**²palmy** \'pämi\ *n* -ES [MF *palmée* blow with the palm, fr. ML *palmata,* fr. L *palma* palm] *Scot* **:** a blow on the palm of the hand as a punishment

**pal·my·ra** \pal'mīrə, *attrib* (')=¦==\ *n* -s [alter. (perh. influenced by *Palmyra,* ancient city of Syria) of earlier *palmeira,* fr. Pg, palm tree, fr. *palma,* fr. L] **1** *or* **palmyra palm :** a tall fan palm (*Borassus flabellifer*) that is native to Africa but widely cultivated in India and that yields a very hard moisture-resistant and insect-resistant wood, a sap rich in sugar and important as a source of palm wine and palm sugar, leaves used esp. for thatching and weaving, a coarse fiber similar to piassava, and large edible drupaceous fruits — see BASSINE **2** *or* **palmyra fiber :** BASSINE

**¹pal·my·rene** \'palmə,rēn, ,==¦=\ *adj, usu cap* [L *palmyrenus,* fr. *Palmyra* ancient city of Syria] **:** of or relating to the ancient city of Palmyra, Syria

**²palmyrene** \"\ *n* -s *cap* **1 :** a native or resident of Palmyra **2 :** the Aramaic dialect of ancient Palmyra

**pa·lo** \'pa(,)lō, 'pä(-\ *n* -s [AmerSp, stick, tree, fr. Sp, stick, timber, fr. L *palus* stake — more at POLE] *chiefly Southwest* **:** POLE, STICK — used in names of trees

**palo amarillo** *n* [MexSp, lit., yellow tree] **:** any of several tropical or western American trees or shrubs with yellowish bark or wood; *esp* **:** OREGON GRAPE

**palo blan·co** \-'blaŋ(,)kō\ *n* [MexSp, lit., white tree] **:** any of various tropical or western American trees or shrubs with whitish or pale wood or bark: as **a :** a western American hackberry (*Celtis reticulata*), having light-colored bark **b :** a tree (*Lysiloma candida*) of Lower California whose bark is used in tanning

**pa·lo·du·ro** \,palə'dú(,)rō, ,päl-\ *also* **pa·lo·du·ra** \-ùrə\ *n* -s [MexSp *palo duro,* lit., hard tree] **:** PALO BLANCO a

**paloe·an·thro·pus** \,pālē'an(t)thrəpəs, ,pal-, -,an'thrōp-\ *syn of* PALAEOANTHROPUS

**pa·lo·hier·ro** \,palō'ye(,)rō, ,päl-\ *or* **pa·lo de hier·ro** \-(,)lōdā'y-, -ōthā-\ *n* -s [MexSp, lit., iron tree] **:** any of several tropical or western American trees or shrubs with very hard strong tough wood; *esp* **:** DESERT IRONWOOD

**pa·lo·lo** \pə'lō(,)lō\ *or* **palolo worm** *also* **bo·lo·lo** \bə-\ *n* -s [Samoan & Tongan *palolo*] **:** a eunicid worm (*Eunice viridis*) that burrows in the coral reefs of various Pacific islands and swarms in vast numbers at the surface of the sea for breeding a little before the last quarter of the moon in October and November when they are gathered as highly esteemed food

**pa·lo·ma** \pə'lōmə\ *n* -s [prob. fr. AmerSp, fr. Sp, dove, pigeon, fr. L *palumba, palumbes;* akin to Gk *peleia* dove, pigeon, L *pallēre* to be pale — more at FALLOW] **1** *Southwest* **:** any of several sharks used as food **2** *often cap* **:** a brownish orange to light brown that is redder and lighter than sorrel and redder than caramel

**pa·lo ma·ria** \,pa(,)lōmə'rēə, ,pä(-\ *n* [PhilSp, lit., Mary tree] *Philippines* **:** POON

**pa·lom·bi·no** \,päləm'bē(,)nō, ,pal-\ *n* -s [It, lit., of or like a dove, fr. L *palumbinus,* fr. *palumba, palumbes* dove + *-inus* -ine — more at PALOMA] **:** a light gray Italian marble

**pal·o·meta** \,palə'med·ə\ *n* [Sp, dim. of *paloma* dove — more at PALOMA] **1** -s **:** any of several pompanos (as the longfin pompano and round pompano) **2 a** -s **:** any of various butterfishes (as the California pompano) of the family Stromateidae **b** *cap* **:** a genus of butterfishes that includes the California pompano

**pal·o·mi·no** *also* **pal·a·mi·no** \,palə'mē(,)nō, -ēnə\ *n* -s [AmerSp *palomino,* fr. Sp, of or like a dove, fr. L *palumbinus*] **:** a slender-legged short-coupled horse of a light tan or cream color with white markings on the face and legs and flaxen or white mane and tail from ancestry largely of Arabian stock

**pa·loo·ka** \pə'lükə\ *n* -s [origin unknown] **1 :** an inexperienced or incompetent boxer **2 :** a clumsy inept person **:** OAF

**pa·lo san·to** \,palō'san,tō, ,pälō'sän-\ *n* [AmerSp, lit., holy tree] **:** any of several So. American trees esteemed locally for medicinal or other special properties; *esp* **:** a tree (*Bulnesia sarmienti*) of the family Zygophyllaceae occurring in dry interior regions of Argentina and Paraguay and having a resinous heartwood used for incense — see GUAIAC WOOD

**pa·lo·sa·pis** \,palō'säpəs, ,päl-\ *n* -ES [Tag] **:** a tall tree (*Anisoptera thurifera*) of the family Dipterocarpaceae that is common in the Philippines and yields a resinous oil and valuable light-colored hard wood used in cabinetwork and paneling

**pa·louse** \pə'lüs\ *n, pl* **palouse** *or* **palouses** *usu cap* **1 a :** a Shahaptian people in the Palouse river valley, southeastern Washington and northwestern Idaho **b :** a member of the Palouse people **2 :** APPALOOSA

**pa·lous·er** \pə'lüzə(r)\ *n* -s [*Palouse* + *-er*] **:** an improvised light consisting of candle and a tin can

**pa·lo·verde** \,p|alō'vərdē, ¦p|alō¦vərd, |äl-\ *n* -s [MexSp, lit., green tree] **:** any of three thorny trees or shrubs (*Cercidium macrum, C. torreyanum,* and *C. microphyllum*) of the family Leguminosae that occur in dry parts of the southwestern U. S. and adjacent Mexico, have smooth light green bark, small transitory leaves, and racemes of bright yellow flowers, and are locally important as wildlife browse and bee pasture

**¹palp** \'palp, 'paùp\ *vt* -ED/-ING/-S [MF *palper,* fr. L *palpare* to stroke, caress, flatter — more at FEEL] **1 :** to experience a touch sensation from **:** TOUCH, FEEL, HANDLE **2** *obs* **:** to address in a manner designed to please or flatter **:** CAJOLE

**²palp** \"\ *n* -s [F *palpe,* fr. *palper* or fr. L *palpus* stroking, caress; akin to L *palpare*] **:** PALPUS: as **a :** one of two leaflike fleshy appendages on each side of the mouth of a lamellibranch mollusk **b :** a lobe-shaped sensory process of each side of the head of a chaetopod worm

**pal·pa·bil·i·ty** \,palpə'biləd·ē, -lətē, -i\ *n* -ES **1 :** the quality or state of being palpable **2 :** something palpable

**pal·pa·ble** \'palpəbəl\ *adj* [ME, fr. LL *palpabilis,* fr. L *palpare* to stroke, caress + *-abilis* -able — more at FEEL] **1 :** capable of being touched or felt **:** perceptible to the sense of touch **:** TANGIBLE ⟨a barely ~ dust⟩ ⟨an enlarged ~ spleen⟩ **2 :** easily perceptible by one or another of the senses other than touch **:** NOTICEABLE, PATENT **3 :** easily perceptible by the mind **:** PLAIN, DISTINCT, OBVIOUS, MANIFEST ⟨a ~ absurdity⟩ ⟨such ~ impostures⟩ **syn** see EVIDENT, PERCEPTIBLE

**pal·pa·ble·ness** *n* -ES **:** PALPABILITY 1

**pal·pa·bly** \-blē, -bli\ *adv* **:** in a palpable manner **:** so as to be palpable ⟨~ untrue⟩

**pal·pal** \'palpəl\ *adj* [NL *palpalis,* fr. *palpus* + L *-alis* -al] **:** of, relating to, or functioning as a palpus

**palpal organ** *n* **:** an accessory reproductive organ of a male spider developed on the terminal joint of each pedipalp and used to convey the sperms to the genital orifice of the female

**¹pal·pate** \'pal,pāt, *usu* -ād·+V\ *vb* -ED/-ING/-S [prob. back formation fr. *palpation*] *vt* **:** to examine by touch **:** explore by palpation ~ *vi* **:** to use the technique of palpation

**²palpate** \"\ *adj* [NL *palpatus,* fr. *palpus* + L *-atus* -ate] **:** having a palpus or palpi

**pal·pa·tion** \pal'pāshən\ *n* -s [L *palpation-, palpatio,* fr. *palpatus* (past. part. of *palpare* to stroke) + *-ion-, -io* -ion] **1 :** an act of touching or feeling **2 :** physical examination in medical diagnosis by pressure of the hand or fingers to the surface of the body esp. to determine the condition (as of size or consistency) of an underlying part or organ ⟨~ of the liver⟩ ⟨~ of cervical lymph glands⟩

**pal·pa·to·ry** \'palpə,tōrē\ *adj* [L *palpatus* (past part. of *palpare*) + E *-ory*] **:** of, involving, or used for palpation

**pal·pe·bra** \'palpəbrə, pal'pēb-, pal'peb-\ *n, pl* **pal·pe·brae** \'==,brē, -,brī; =¦=(,)brē\ [L; prob. akin to L *palpitare* to palpitate, *palpare* to stroke, caress — more at FEEL] **:** EYELID

**pal·pe·bral** \-brəl\ *adj* [LL *palpebralis,* fr. L *palpebra* + *-alis* -al] **:** of, relating to, or located on or near the eyelids

**palpebral disk** *n* **:** an often transparent complex scale that covers the eyelid of some lizards and is formed by fusion of several palpebral scales

**palpebral fissure** *n* **:** the space between the margins of the eyelids

**pal·pe·brate** \'palpə,brat; pal'pēbrət, -pebrət\ *adj* [NL *palpebratus,* fr. L *palpebra* + *-atus* -ate] **:** having eyelids

**palped** \'palpt, -aùpt\ *adj* [²*palp* + *-ed*] **:** PALPATE

**palpi** *pl of* PALPUS

**pal·pi·fer** \'palpəfər, -,fe(ə)r\ *n* -s [NL, fr. *palpus* + *-i-* + *-fer*] **1 :** a lobe of the maxilla of an insect on which the palpus is borne **2 :** PALPIGER — **pal·pif·er·ous** \(')pal-'pif(ə)rəs\ *adj*

**pal·pi·form** \'palpə,fórm\ *adj* [NL *palpus* + E *-iform*] **:** like a palpus

**pal·pi·ger** \'palpəjər, -,je(ə)r\ *n* -s [NL, fr. *palpus* + L *-i-* + *-ger* bearer (fr. *-ger* -gerous)] **:** the portion of the labium of an insect that bears the palpi — **pal·pig·er·ous** \(')pal¦pij(ə)rəs\ *adj*

**pal·pigra·di** \pal'pigrə,dī, -,dē; ,palpə'grā,dī\ [NL, fr. *palpus* + L *-i-* + *-gradi* (pl. of *-gradus* -grade)] *syn of* MICROTHELYPHONIDA

**pal·pi·tan·cy** \'palpəd·ənsē, -lpətən- *also* -t^ən-\ *n* -ES [*palpitant* + *-cy*] **:** the quality or state of being palpitant

**pal·pi·tant** \-nt\ *adj* [F or L; F fr. L *palpitant-, palpitans,* pres. part. of *palpitare* to palpitate] **1 :** TREMBLING, QUIVERING, THROBBING ⟨~ movements rather than violent eruptions —*Amer. Guide Series: Mich.*⟩ **2 :** inducing or likely to induce a palpitant condition ⟨a memorably harsh and ~ record of the nomadic men of the sea —Charles Lee⟩

**pal·pi·tate** \'palpə,tāt, *usu* -ād·+V\ *vb* -ED/-ING/-S [L *palpitatus,* past part. of *palpitare,* freq. of *palpare* to stroke, caress — more at FEEL] *vi* **:** to beat rapidly and strongly **:** THROB **:** bound with emotion or exertion **:** pulsate violently — used esp. of the heart when its pulsation is abnormally rapid ~ *vt* **:** to cause to palpitate **syn** see PULSATE

**pal·pi·tat·ing·ly** \'==,===, ,==¦===\ *adv* [*palpitating* (pres. part. of *palpitate*) + *-ly*] **:** so as to palpitate or cause palpitation

**pal·pi·ta·tion** \,palpə'tāshən\ *n* -s [L *palpitation-, palpitatio,* fr. *palpitatus* + *-ion-, -io* -ion] **:** a rapid pulsation **:** THROBBING, QUIVERING; *esp* **:** an abnormally rapid beating of the heart when excited by violent exertion, strong emotion, or disease

**palp·less** \'palpləs, 'paùp-\ *adj* [²*palp* + *-less*] **:** lacking palpi or palps

**pal·po·cil** \'palpə,sil\ *n* -s [ISV *palpo-* (fr. NL *palpus*) + *-cil* (fr. NL *cilium*); prob. orig. formed in G] **:** a fine filamentous tactile process (as of some hydroids) **:** TACTILE HAIR

**pal·pog·nath** \'palpəg,nath\ *n* -s [NL *palpus* + *-o-* + Gk *gnathos* jaw — more at -GNATHOUS] **:** either of the third pair of mouthparts of a centipede

**pal·pon** \'pal,pän\ *n* -s [prob. fr. ²*palp* + *siphon*] **:** a hollow dactylozooid of some siphonophores that resembles a tentacle

**palps** *pres 3d sing of* PALP, *pl of* PALP

**pal·pu·lus** \'palpyələs\ *n, pl* **palpu·li** \-,lī, -,lē\ [NL, dim. of *palpus*] **:** a small palpus; *specif* **:** one of the maxillary palpi of a butterfly or moth

**pal·pus** \'palpəs\ *n, pl* **pal·pi** \-l,pī, -l,pē\ [NL, fr. L, stroking, caress; akin to L *palpare* to stroke, caress — more at FEEL] **1 :** a segmented process attached to a mouthpart of an arthropod, usu. having a tactile or gustatory function, and occurring in insects usu. in pairs on the maxillae and on the labium **2 :** a process on any of various other invertebrates felt to resemble an insect's palpus — see PALP

**pals** *pl of* PAL, *pres 3d sing of* PAL

**pals·grave** \'pòlz,grāv\ *or* **pal·grave** \-l,g-\ *n* -s [D *paltsgrave;* akin to MHG *pfalzgrave;* both fr. a prehistoric D-G compound whose first element is represented by OHG *pfalanza* (fr. L *palatium* palace) and whose second element is represented by OHG *grāvo* count — more at PALACE, BURGRAVE] **:** COUNT PALATINE

**pals·gra·vine** \-lzgrə,vēn, ,==¦=\ *n* -s [D *paltsgravin,* fr. *paltsgrave* + *-in* -ine] **:** the wife or widow of a count palatine

**pal·ship** \'pal,ship\ *n* [¹*pal* + *-ship*] **:** the relation existing between pals **:** informal intimacy

**pal·sied** \'pòlzēd, -zid\ *adj* [¹*palsy* + *-ed*] **:** affected with palsy **:** PARALYZED, TOTTERING, SHAKY ⟨~ children⟩ ⟨hands weak and ~⟩

**pal·stave** *also* **pal·staff** \'pòl+,-\ *n* -s [Dan *paalstav,* fr. ON *pālstafr,* a heavy missile, prob. fr. *pāll* spade, hoe (fr. OE *pāl,* fr. L *pala*) + *stafr* staff — more at PALETTE, STAFF] **:** a usu. bronze celt designed for a split handle

**pal·ster** \'pòlztə(r), -l(t)st-\ *n* -s [MD] *archaic* **:** a pilgrim's staff

**¹pal·sy** \'pòlzē, -zi\ *n* -ES [ME *palsie, parlesie,* fr. MF *paralisie,* fr. L *paralysis* — more at PARALYSIS] **1 a :** PARALYSIS — used chiefly in combination ⟨shaking ~⟩ ⟨oculomotor ~⟩; compare BELL'S PALSY, CEREBRAL PALSY **b :** a condition that is characterized by uncontrollable tremor or quivering of the body or one or more of its parts ⟨the old man shook with the ~ so he could hardly hold his pipe⟩ — not used technically **2 a :** an enfeebling influence **:** something that causes weakness or uncertainty or impairs activity or effectiveness ⟨a creeping ~ has of late overtaken the liberal mind —*Saturday Rev.*⟩ ⟨the ~ of doubt and distraction hangs . . . upon my energies —Thomas De Quincey⟩ **b :** a weak, enfeebled, or uncertain condition often marked by lack of decisive or effective action ⟨enough to throw the entire diplomatic West into a ~ —*Reporter*⟩ **3 :** VIBRATION ⟨his whole body shook with the ~ of the motor —Kay Boyle⟩

**²palsy** \"\ *vb* -ED/-ING/-ES *vt* **:** to affect with or as if with palsy **:** deprive of action or energy **:** PARALYZE ~ *vi* **:** to become palsied **:** shake as if with the palsy

**palsy-walsy** \¦palzē¦walzē\ *adj* [redupl. of *palsy* pally, fr. *pals,* pl. of *pal* + *-y*] *slang* **:** having or giving the appearance of having a high degree of intimacy ⟨got very *palsy-walsy* with the boss all of a sudden⟩ ⟨his *palsy-walsy* attitude⟩

**pal·ta** \'pòltə, 'päl-\ *n* -s [AmerSp, fr. Quechua] **:** AVOCADO

**pal·ter** \'pòltə(r)\ *vi* **paltered; paltered; paltering** \-t(ə)riŋ\ **palters** [origin unknown] **1 :** to act insincerely or deceitfully **:** play false **:** use trickery **:** EQUIVOCATE **:** play fast and loose ⟨Romans, that have spoke the word, and will not ~ —Shak.⟩ **2 :** to haggle or chaffer in doing business **:** bargain or parley esp. with the intent of delay or compromise **syn** see LIE

**pal·ter·er** \'pòltərə(r)\ *n* -s **:** one that palters

**pal·ter·ly** \'pòltə(r)lē\ *adj* [alter. (influenced by *palter* & *-ly*) of *paltry*] *archaic* **:** PALTRY, SHABBY

**pal·tock** \'pal,täk\ *n* -s [ME *paltok*] **:** a man's doublet or tunic worn in the 14th and 15th centuries

**pal·tri·ly** \'pòl-trəlē, -əli\ *adv* **:** in a paltry manner **:** so as to be paltry

**pal·tri·ness** \-rēnəs, -rin-\ *n* -ES **:** the quality or state of being paltry

**¹paltry** *also* **paultry** *n* -ES [E dial. *palt, pelt* piece of coarse cloth, trash + E *-ry;* akin to MLG *palte* rag, Dan *pjalt,* Sw *palta*] *obs* **:** something useless or worthless **:** RUBBISH, TRASH

**²pal·try** *also* **paul·try** \'pòl-trē, -ri\ *adj* -ER/-EST **1 :** INFERIOR, TRASHY, WORTHLESS ⟨building ~ houses unfit for occupancy⟩ **2 :** MEAN, VILE, DESPICABLE ⟨a ~ trick⟩ **3 :** TRIVIAL, PETTY, SLIGHT ⟨a ~ excuse⟩ ⟨these ~ trials⟩ **syn** see PETTY

**¹pa·lu** \'pä(,)lü\ *n* -s [modif. of Hawaiian *walu* oilfish] **:** ESCOLAR

**²palu** \"\ *n* -s [of East Indian origin] **:** a hardwood tree (*Mimusops lexandra*) of India and Ceylon with astringent bark used for tanning and red to purplish brown timber resembling bulletwood

**pa·lu·dal** \pə'lüd^əl, 'palyəd^əl\ *adj* [L *palud-, palus* marsh + E *-al;* akin to Skt *palvala* pond and perh. to OE *full* — more at FULL] **:** of, relating to, or made up of marshes or fens **:** MARSHY ⟨~ plants⟩ ⟨a ~ environment⟩

**pa·lu·da·men·tum** \pə,lüdə'mentəm\ *or* **pa·lu·da·ment** \'=,==mənt\ *n, pl* **paludamen·ta** \=,==¦mentə\ *or* **paludaments** [L *paludamentum;* prob. akin to L *palla* palla] **:** a cloak worn by the rulers and chief military officers of ancient Rome

paludamentum

**paludi-** *comb form* [LL, fr. L *palud-, palus* marsh — more at PALUDAL] **:** marsh ⟨*paludicole*⟩

**pa·lu·di·cel·la** \pə,lüdə'selə\ *n, cap* [NL, fr. *paludi-* + *cella* cell] **:** a genus of ectoproctous bryozoans comprising a number of freshwater colonial forms that construct delicate branching tubes with club-shaped zooids and no statoblasts

**pal·u·dic·o·lae** \,palyə'dikə,lē, -ə,lī\ [NL, pl. of LL *paludicola* marsh dweller, fr. *paludi-* + L *-cola*] *syn of* GRUIFORMES

**pal·u·dic·o·lous** \,palyə¦dikələs\ *or* **pal·u·dic·o·line** \-ə,līn\ *adj* [LL *paludicola* + E *-ous* or *-ine*] **:** PALUSTRINE ⟨~ frogs⟩

**¹pal·u·di·na** \,palyə'dīnə, -dēnə\ [NL, fr. *paludi-* + *-ina*] *syn of* VIVIPARUS

**²paludina** \"\ *n* -s [NL *Paludina*] **:** a mollusk of the genus *Viviparus*

**pal·u·dism** \'palyə,dizəm\ *n* -s [ISV *paludi-* + *-ism*] **:** MALARIA

**palu·dous** \'palyədəs, pə'lüd-\ *adj* [L *paludosus* marshy, fr. *palud-, palus* marsh + *-osus* -ous — more at PALUDAL] **1 :** PALUSTRINE **2 :** of or relating to marshes or marshland

**Pal·u·drine** \'palyə,drēn, -,drən; pə'lüdrən\ *trademark* — used for derivatives of biguanide used as antimalarials

**pal·ule** \'pal(,)yül\ *or* **pal·u·lus** \-lyələs\ *n, pl* **pal·ules** \-yülz\ *or* **pal·u·li** \-yə,lī, -,lē\ [NL *palulus,* dim. of *palus*] **:** PALUS; *esp* **:** one not attached to a septum

**pa·lus** \'pāləs\ *n, pl* **pa·li** \-,lī\ [NL, fr. L, stake — more at

POLE] **:** any of several upright slender calcareous processes that surround the central part of the calyculus of some corals

**pa·lus·tral** \pə'ləstrəl\ *adj* [L *palustris* (fr. *palud-* *palus* marsh) + E *-al* — more at PALUDAL] **:** PALUDOUS

**pa·lus·trine** \pə'ləstrən\ *adj* [L *palustris* + E *-ine*] **:** living or thriving in a marshy environment ⟨~ plants⟩ **:** being or made up of marsh ⟨a ~ habitat⟩

[1]**paly** \'pālē\ *adj* [ME, fr. MF *palé*, fr. *pal* stake + *-é* -y — more at PALE (fence)] *heraldry* **:** divided into four or more equal parts by perpendicular lines and of two different tinctures disposed alternately

[2]**paly** \"\ *adj* -ER/-EST [*pale* + *-y*] **:** somewhat pale **:** WAN, PALLID

**paly-bendy** \ˌ=ˈ=ˌ=\ *adj, heraldry* **:** divided into lozenge-shaped figures by lines paly and bendy

**pal·y·gor·skite** \ˌpalə'gȯrˌskīt\ *n* -S [modif. of G *paligorskit*, fr. the locality in the Ural mountains near which it was found] **:** a hydrous basic silicate ($Mg_3$, $Al_2$)$Si_4O_{10}(OH)_2.H_2O$ of magnesium and aluminum that belongs to the family of the clay minerals

**pal·y·no·log·i·cal** \ˌpalənə'läjəkəl\ *adj* **:** of or relating to palynology **:** concerned with pollen or pollen grains ⟨~ studies⟩ — **pal·y·no·log·i·cal·ly** \-jək(ə)lē\ *adv*

**pal·y·nol·o·gy** \ˌpalə'näləjē\ *n* -ES [Gk *palynein* to strew, sprinkle (fr. *palē* fine meal, dust) + E *-o-* + *-logy* — more at POLLEN] **:** a branch of science concerned with the study of pollen and spores whether living or fossil

**pa·lys·tes** \pə'li(ˌ)stēz\ *n, cap* [NL] **:** a genus of hunting spiders (family Heteropodidae) that includes several large forms which prey on small fish, frogs, and lizards

[1]**pam** \'pam, 'paa(ə)m\ *n* -S [prob. short for Gk *pamphilos* beloved of all, fr. *pam-* + *philos* beloved] **1 :** the jack of clubs in loo played with 5-card hands **2 :** a game like napoleon in which the jack of clubs is the highest trump

pam 1

[2]**pam** \"\ *vb* **pammed; pammed; pamming; pams** [alter. of [8]*pan*] **:** PAN

**pam-** *comb form* [NL, fr. Gk, alter. of *pan-* — more at PAN-] **:** PAN-

**pam** *abbr* pamphlet

**PAM** *abbr* pulse-amplitude modulation

**pa·ma·ka·ni** \'pämə,kānē\ *n* -S [Hawaii *pā-makani(haole)*, fr. *pā-makani*, any of several native plants, lit., wind-blown, + *haole* foreign] **:** a tall tropical American perennial herb (*Eupatorium macrophyllum*) that is sometimes cultivated in the warm greenhouse for its showy corymbs of reddish lilac flower heads

**pam·a·quine** \'paməˌkwīn, -wēn,-ˌkwən\ *also* **pam·a·quin** \-ˌkwən\ *n* -S [*pentyl* + *amino* + *methoxyl* + connective *-a-* + *-quine, -quin* (fr. *quinoline*)] **:** a toxic antimalarial drug $C_{19}H_{29}N_3O$ derived from an amino-methoxy-quinoline; *also* **:** PAMAQUINE NAPHTHOATE

**pamaquine naphthoate** *n* **:** an insoluble salt $C_{42}H_{45}N_3O_7$ of pamaquine and a derivative of beta-naphthoic acid obtained as a yellow to orange-yellow powder

**pa·me** \'pämā\ *n, pl* **pame** *or* **pames** *usu cap* **1 a :** an Otomian people of San Luis Potosí and adjoining states, Mexico **b :** a member of such people **2 :** the language of the Pame people

**pa·ment** \'pāmənt\ *or* **pam·ment** \'pam-\ *n* -S [ME *pament*, alter. of *pavement*] **:** tile or brick used for paving a malthouse floor

**pa·mi·ri** \pə'mirē\ *n, pl* **pamiri** *or* **pamiris** *usu cap* **1 :** a moderately tall light-skinned people of the Pamirs **2 :** a member of the Pamiri people

**pam·li·co** \'pamləˌkō\ *n, pl* **pamlico** *or* **pamlicos** *usu cap* **1 a :** an Indian people of the Pamlico river valley, No. Carolina **b :** a member of such people **2 :** an Algonquian language of the Pamlico people

**pam·pa** \'pampə, 'paam-\ *n, pl* **pampas** \-əz, -əs\ [AmerSp, fr. Quechua & Aymara, plain] **1 :** an extensive generally grass-covered plain of So. America **:** PRAIRIE — compare CAMPO, MONTE **2 a** *usu cap* **:** an Indian of the pampas; *esp* **:** ARAUCANIAN **b :** PUELCHE

**pam·pan·gan** \päm'päŋgən\ *also* **pam·pan·ga** \-gə\ *or* **pam·pan·go** \-ŋ(ˌ)gō\ *n, pl* **pampangan** *or* **pampangans** *also* **pampanga** *or* **pampangas** *or* **pampango** *or* **pampangos** *usu cap* [*pampangan* modif. of Pampangan *Kapampangan*, fr. *pampang* river bank; *pampanga* prob. alter. of *Pampangan* (taken as adj.); *pampango* fr. Sp, modif. of Pampangan *Kapampangan*] **1 a :** a Christianized people of central Luzon, Philippines **b :** a member of such people **2 :** the Austronesian language of the Pampangan people

**pampano** *var of* POMPANO

**pampas cat** *n* [*pampas* fr. Sp, pl. of *pampa*] **:** a small wildcat (*Felis pajeros*) of Argentina and Patagonia that is yellowish gray with dark bands on the legs and tail and brownish stripes running obliquely from the back to the flanks

**pampas deer** *n* **:** a deer (*Blastoceros bezoarticus* or *Ozotoceras bezoarticus* syn. *B. campestris*) of southern So. America that is about the size of a roebuck with reddish brown above and white below and with small branched antlers

**pampas fox** *n* **:** any of several small mammals of So. America that resemble the fox

**pampas grass** *n* **:** a So. American grass (*Cortaderia selloana*) that is extensively cultivated as an ornamental, grows in thick tussocks with basal leaves, and sends up stalks 6 to 12 feet high crowned with ample silky white panicles

**pampas hare** *n* **:** MARA

**pam·pe·an** \'pampēən, =ˈ==\ *adj* [AmerSp *pampa* + E *-an*] **1 :** of or relating to the pampas of So. America **2** *usu cap* **a :** of or relating to the Indian inhabitants of the So. American pampas **b :** ARAUCANIAN

**pam·pel·moes** \'pampəlˌmüs\ *n* -ES [Afrik *pompelmoosje*, fr. *pampelmoose, pampelmoes* shaddock, fr. D *pompelmoes* — more at POMPELMOUS] **:** a large highly esteemed purplish or bluish butterfish (*Stromateus fiatola*) of the west coast of Africa and the Mediterranean

**pam·per** \'pampə(r), 'paam-\ *vt* **pampered; pampered; pampering** \-p(ə)riŋ\ **pampers** [ME *pamperen*, prob. of LG origin; akin to Flem *pamperen* to pamper; perh. akin to Sw dial. *pampen* to blow up, Lith *bamba* navel, Skt *bimba* ball, sphere; basic meaning: stuffing, inflating] **1** *archaic* **:** to feed luxuriously **:** GLUT **2 a :** to treat with extreme or excessive care and attention ⟨when cotton is in . . . their days are spent coddling and ~*ing* it —*Amer. Guide Series: Ark.*⟩ **b :** gratify or humor in one's tastes or desires ⟨the job has enabled him to ~ his wanderlust thoroughly —*New Yorker*⟩ ⟨a desire to ~ the . . . old man in his foibles —T.H.White b. 1915⟩ **syn** see INDULGE

**pam·pered·ly** *adv* **:** in a pampered manner

**pam·pered·ness** *n* -ES **:** the quality or state of being pampered

**pam·per·er** \'pampərə(r)\ *n* -S **:** one that pampers

**pam·pe·ro** \pam'perō\ *n* -S [AmerSp, lit., pampean, fr. *pampa* + *-ero* (n. suffix)] **:** a strong cold wind from the west or southwest that sweeps over the pampas of So. America from the Andes

**pam·phi·li·idae** \ˌpam(p)fə'līəˌdē\ *n pl, cap* [NL, fr. *Pamphilius*, type genus (perh. fr. Gk *pamphilos* beloved of all) + *-idae* — more at PAM] **:** a family of sawflies whose larvae are usu. gregarious and web together the leaves and twigs of trees on which they feed

**pamph·let** \'pam(p)flət, ÷ -mpl-, *usu* -əd·+V\ *n* -S *often attrib* [ME *pamflet*, fr. *Pamphilus* (*seu De Amore*) Pamphilus or About Love, popular Latin amatory poem of the 12th century + E *-let*] **1 a :** a brief treatment of a subject issued as a separate unbound publication ⟨scholarly monographs published as articles or ~s⟩ ⟨was first issued in ~ form⟩ ⟨under various names, the ~ . . . tells its readers what to believe, where to travel, what school or college to attend, what candidate to vote for, what cars to ride in and what merchandise to buy —F.F.Bond⟩ **b :** a controversial tract dealing with a religious or political question ⟨the best seller list also includes two books . . . which are fictionized journalistic ~s based upon timely situations —Louis Bromfield⟩ ⟨a ~ war⟩ **2 a :** a printed publication having a format with no binding and no cover or with a flush paper cover and often fastened with side or saddle stitches ⟨magazines and catalogs with ~ format⟩ — compare BOOK **b :** an unbound publication other than a periodical having fewer than a fixed number (as 50, 80, 100) of pages — used esp. in library science

**pam·phlet·ary** \-lə,terē\ *adj* **:** of, relating to, or of the character of a pamphlet

[1]**pam·phle·teer** \ˌ=ˈ=ti(ə)r, -iə\ *n* -S [*pamphlet* + *-eer*] **:** a writer of pamphlets attacking something or urging a cause ⟨interested in the politics of our time but . . . a novelist first, a creator of people and a storyteller, an artist rather than a ~ —Orville Prescott⟩

[2]**pamphleteer** \"\ *vi* -ED/-ING/-S **1 :** to write and publish pamphlets ⟨lecturing and ~*ing* in favor of free trade⟩ **2 :** to attempt to sway opinion on a matter of current interest (as by tracts or through literary works) **:** engage in partisan argument indirectly in writings ⟨that ~*ing* is . . . a valid aspect of theater —Brooks Atkinson⟩

**pam·phlet·ize** \'==ˌtīz\ *vb* -ED/-ING/-S [*pamphlet* + *-ize*] *vi* **:** to write pamphlets ~ *vt* **:** to write a pamphlet on

[1]**pam·phyl·i·an** \(ˈ)pam'filēən\ *adj, usu cap* [L *Pamphylius* (fr. *Pamphylia*) + E *-an*] **:** of or relating to the ancient region and sometime Roman province of Pamphylia in southern Asia Minor

[2]**pamphylian** \"\ *n* -S *cap* **:** a native or inhabitant of ancient Pamphylia

**pam·pin·i·form** \pam'pinəˌfȯrm\ *adj* [L *pampinus* tendril, vine-leaf (of non-IE origin) + E *-iform*; akin to the source of Gk *ampelos* vine] **:** convoluted and like a tendril — used of a venous plexus associated with the spermatic or ovarian veins

**pam·poo·tie** \pam'püd·ē\ *n* -S [perh. alter. of *papoosh*] **:** a shoe of untanned cowhide worn in the Aran islands, County Galway, Ireland

**pam·pre** \'pampə(r)\ *n* -S [F, fr. L *pampinus* tendril, vine-leaf] **:** an ornament of vine leaves and grapes

[1]**pam·pro·dactyl** \ˌpamprō+\ *or* **pam·pro·dactylous** \"+\ *adj* [*pam-* + *pro-* + *dactyl* or *dactylous*] **:** having the toes turned forward ⟨the ~ feet of the colies and some swifts⟩

[2]**pamprodactyl** \"\ *n* **:** a pamprodactyl animal

**pam·psychism** \(ˈ)pam+\ *n* [*pam-* + *psychism*] **:** PANPSYCHISM

**pams** *pl of* PAM, *pres 3d sing of* PAM

**pa·mun·key** \pə'məŋkē\ *n, pl* **pamunkey** *or* **pamunkeys** *usu cap* **1 :** an Algonquian people of Virginia formerly part of the Powhatan confederacy **2 :** a member of the Pamunkey people

[1]**pan** \'pan, 'paa(ə)n\ *n* -S [ME *panne*, fr. OE; akin to OFris *panne* pan, OHG *phanna*, ON *panna*; all fr. a prehistoric Gmc word borrowed fr. (assumed) VL *panna* pan, fr. L *patina*, fr. Gk *patanē*; akin to L *patēre* to be open — more at FATHOM] **1 a :** a metal, earthenware, or plastic container (as a warming pan, dustpan, dishpan) for domestic use that is usu. broad, shallow, and open **b :** any of various metal kitchen utensils of different shapes and sizes in which foods are cooked or baked ⟨baking ~⟩ ⟨cake ~⟩ — see FRYING PAN, LOAF PAN, SAUCEPAN, TUBE PAN **c :** any of various other receptacles usu. metal and typically broad, shallow, and open: as (1) *Brit* **:** BOWL 3c (2) **:** a vessel for evaporating a liquid (as salt brine, maple sap) (3) **:** the hollow part of the lock in old guns or pistols that receives the priming (4) **:** either of the receptacles for the weights or the bodies weighed in a pair of scales or a balance (5) **:** a round shallow metal container used in placer mining to separate gold or some other metal from waste (as gravel) by washing (6) **:** a sheet of metal used under the front end of a log while skidding it (7) **:** a metal or wood form used in constructing a poured concrete floor **2 a** *archaic* **:** CRANIUM **b** (1) **:** a natural basin or depression; *esp* **:** one containing standing water or mud and (as in southern Africa) in the dry season often drying up leaving a salt deposit (2) **:** an artificial basin (as for evaporating brine) **c :** a fragment typically about 200 feet in diameter of the flat relatively thin ice that forms in bays or fiords or along the shore and then becomes free and drifts about the sea — compare ICE FLOE **d :** the broad posterior part of the lower jawbone of a whale **e :** the round flat disk of metal on a steel trap on which an animal steps to spring the trap **3 :** HARDPAN 1 **4** *slang* **:** FACE **5 :** a harsh criticism — **on the pan** *adv* (*or adj*) **:** under criticism ⟨had him *on the pan* for coddling subversives⟩

[2]**pan** \"\ *vb* **panned; panned; panning; pans** *vi* **1 :** to wash earth, gravel, or other material in a pan in searching for gold or some other precious metal **2 :** to yield precious metal (as gold) in the process of panning ⟨gravel that *panned* well⟩ — usu. used with *out* ⟨dirt that ~s out 40 ounces of gold to a ton⟩ ~ *vt* **1 a** (1) **:** to wash (as dirt, gravel) in a pan for the purpose of separating heavy particles (as of gold) (2) **:** to separate (as gold) by panning **b :** to cook in a pan in a small quantity of fat or water **c :** to extract (salt) or reduce (maple sap) by evaporation in a pan **d :** to place (shaped bread dough) in pans **e :** to steam the leaves of (oolong tea) to stop fermentation **2 :** to attack with harsh criticism **:** criticize severely ⟨whether the critics would praise or ~ the new musical comedy⟩

[3]**pan** \"\ *n* -S [ME *panne*, fr. MF *pane*, fr. (assumed) VL *patina*, prob. fr. Gk *pathnē* manger, crib; akin to Gk *peisma* cable — more at BIND] *archaic* **:** PLATE 5a(1)

[4]**pan** \"\ *vb* **panned; panned; panning; pans** [origin unknown] *vi, chiefly Scot* **:** to join or fit together **:** AGREE ~ *vt* **:** to cause to fit together

[5]**pan** \'pän\ *n* -S [Hindi *pān*, fr. Skt *parna* wing, feather, leaf — more at FERN] **1 :** the leaf of the betel palm **2 :** a preparation of betel nut that is rolled in betel leaf with a little shell lime and is used esp. in India and the East Indies for chewing

[6]**pan** \'pan, 'paa(ə)n\ *n* -S [F, fr. MF, pane — more at PANE] **:** PANEL; *esp* **:** a structural panel (as of a wall or door) ⟨doors of double ~ construction⟩ ⟨a dormer ~⟩

[7]**pan** \"\ *n, cap* [NL, prob. fr. L *Pan*, ancient Greek god of woods and shepherds, fr. Gk] **:** a genus of anthropoid apes containing the chimpanzee

[8]**pan** \"\ *vb* **panned; panned; panning; pans** [short for *panoram*] *vi* **1 :** to rotate a motion-picture or television camera in any direction so as to keep an object in the picture or secure a panoramic effect ⟨never ~ if you can avoid it except to follow motion —K.A.Henderson⟩ **2** *of a camera* **:** to undergo such rotation ⟨the camera ~s to the main street of the village —J.P.Marquand⟩ ~ *vt* **:** to cause (a camera) to pan ⟨the camera is *panned* to follow the action as it moves from one location to another —A.L.Gaskill & D.A.Englander⟩

[9]**pan** \"\ *n* -S **:** the process of panning a motion-picture or television camera; *also* **:** a scene or sequence made by this process

[10]**pan** \"\ *adj* [by shortening] **:** PANCHROMATIC ⟨ortho film will give greater contrast than ~ film —Aaron Sussman⟩

[11]**pan** \"\ — an international radiotelephone signal word introducing an urgent message

[12]**pan** \"\ *n* -S ['*pan*] **:** a tractor-operated scraper that transports the material it collects

[13]**pan** \'păn\ *n* -S [by shortening] **:** PANGUINGUE

**pan-** *or* **pano-** *comb form* [Gk, fr. *pan*, neut. of *pas* all, every; akin to Skt *śaśvat* all, every, *śvayati* he swells — more at CAVE] **1 a :** all; completely ⟨*pan*cyclopedic⟩ ⟨*pano*phobia⟩ ⟨*pan*cultural⟩ ⟨*pan*sexualism⟩ ⟨*pan*genesis⟩ ⟨*pan*telegraph⟩ **b** *often cap* **:** all of a (specified) group — usu. joined to the second element with a hyphen ⟨*pan*-Hellenic⟩ ⟨*pan*-sectarian⟩ ⟨*Pan*=Asiatic⟩ ⟨*Pan*-Slavism⟩ **2 :** whole; general ⟨*pan*atrophy⟩ ⟨*pan*carditis⟩ ⟨*pan*hysterectomy⟩ ⟨*pan*esthesia⟩

**pan** *abbr* panorama

**pan·a·ce** \'panəsē\ *n* -S [L *panacea*] *archaic* **:** a fabulous herb said by the ancients to be a panacea

**pan·a·cea** \ˌpanə'sēə\ *n* -S [L, fr. Gk *panakeia*, fr. *panakēs* all-healing, panacea (fr. *pan-* + *-akēs* — fr. *akeisthai* to heal —) + *-ia* -y; akin to Gk *akos* remedy — more at AUTACOID] **:** a remedy for all ills or difficulties **:** a universal remedy **:** CURE-ALL ⟨all con men know that the ~ for all legal troubles is the fix —D.W.Maurer⟩

**pan·a·ce·an** \ˌ==ˈsēən\ *adj* **:** having the properties of a panacea

**pan·a·chage** \ˌpanə'shäzh\ *n* -S [F, lit., mixture (of colors), fr. *panacher* to variegate, plume (fr. *panache* mixture of colors, bouquet of plumes, tuft, fr. MF *pennache*) + *-age*] **:** a variation of the list system that permits the voter to redistribute names from several party lists into a list having names in an order of his own choice — compare CROSS-VOTING

[1]**pa·nache** \pə'nash, -näsh\ *n* -S [earlier *pennache*, fr. MF, fr. OIt *pennacchio*, fr. LL *pinnaculum* small wing — more at PINNACLE] **1 :** a tuft (as of feathers) used as a headdress or an ornament on a helmet **2 :** heroic flourish of manner **:** FLAMBOYANCE, SWAGGER, VERVE ⟨grew progressively more windy and histrionic without ever recapturing the vitality and ~ of the early period —*Times Lit. Supp.*⟩

[2]**pa·na·ché** \ˌpanə'shā\ *adj* [F, fr. past part. of *panacher* to variegate] **:** comprised of several foods ⟨beans — string beans, cooked navy beans, lima beans, flageolets, dressed in butter, cream sauce —J.D.Vehling⟩

panache 1

**pa·nached** \pə'nasht\ *adj* [F *panaché* (past part. of *panacher*) + E *-ed*] **:** variegated with stripes of color

**pan·a·chure** \ˌpanə'shu̇(ə)r\ *n* -S [F, fr. *panache* mixture of colors + *-ure*] **:** MOTTLING

**pa·na·da** \pə'nädə, -nādə\ *also* **pa·nade** \-näd, -nād\ *n* -S [Sp, fr. *pan* bread (fr. L *panis*) + *-ada* -ade (fr. LL *-ata*) — more at FOOD] **1 :** bread boiled to a pulp in milk, broth, or water **2 :** a paste made of flour or bread crumbs and water or stock and used as a base for sauce or for a binder for forcemeat or stuffing

**panage** *var of* PANNAGE

**pan·agglutinability** \ˌpan+\ *n* **:** a condition of red blood cells induced by products of some bacteria or viruses in which they are agglutinable by all human sera

**pan·agglutinable** \"+\ *adj* [*pan-* + *agglutinable*] *of a red blood cell* **:** agglutinable by all human sera in the presence of viruses or bacteria

**pan·agglutination** \"+\ *n* [*pan-* + *agglutination*] **:** agglutination of panagglutinable red blood cells

**pa·na·gia** \ˌpänə'yē(ˌ)ä\ *n* -S [LGk *Panagia* Virgin Mary, fr. fem. of Gk *panagios* all-holy, fr. *pan-* + *hagios* holy] **1** *usu cap* **:** a ceremony observed in monasteries of the Eastern Church at the first morning meal in honor of the Virgin Mary in which a loaf on a plate is elevated before being shared among participants **2 :** ENCOLPION

[1]**pan·a·ma** \'panəˌmä, -mȧ, -mȯ, ˌ==ˈ=\ *adj* [fr. *Panama*, republic in Central America] **1** *usu cap* **:** of or from the republic of Panama **:** of the kind or style prevalent in Panama **:** PANAMANIAN **2** *or* **panama city** *usu cap P&C* [fr. *Panama City*, Panama] **:** of or from Panama City, the capital of Panama **:** of the kind or style prevalent in Panama City

[2]**panama** \"\ *n* [AmSp, fr. *Panama*, Central America, prob. fr. Tupi *panamá* butterfly, migration of butterflies] **1** *also* **panama tree** -S *usu cap P* **:** a large handsome tree (*Sterculia apetala*) of tropical America having oily edible seeds **2** -S **a** *or* **panama hat** *often cap P* [so called fr. *Panama* being formerly its chief center of distribution] **:** a fine lightweight hat of natural-colored straw hand-plaited of narrow strips from the young leaves of the jipijapa; *also* **:** a machine-made imitation of this — compare TOQUILLA **b :** a straw made from jipijapa **3 a** *usu cap* **:** an American breed of sheep developed by crossing Lincoln rams on Rambouillet ewes **b** -S *often cap* **:** a sheep of this breed

**panama balata** *n, usu cap P* **:** gum from a bully tree (*Manilkara darienensis*)

**panama bark** *or* **panama wood** *n, usu cap P* **:** SOAPBARK

**panama disease** *n, usu cap P* [so called fr. its first occurrence in banana plantations of Panama] **:** a destructive vascular disease of the banana caused by a fungus (*Fusarium oxysporum cubense*) and characterized by wilting and yellowing of leaves and death of affected shoots

**panama hat plant** *or* **panama hat palm** *n, usu cap 1st P* **:** JIPIJAPA

**panama ipecac** *n, usu cap P* **:** CARTAGENA IPECAC

[1]**pan·a·ma·ni·an** \ˌpanə'mānēən\ *also* **pan·a·man** \ˌpanə'män\ *n* -S *cap* [*Panama*, republic in Central America + E *-anian* (as in *Lusitanian*) *or* *-an*] **:** a native or inhabitant of Panama

[2]**panamanian** \ˌ==ˈ===\ *also* **panaman** \ˌ==ˈ=\ *adj, usu cap* **:** of or relating to Panama or its inhabitants

**panama orange** *n, usu cap P* **:** CALAMONDIN

**panama redwood** *n, usu cap P* **:** the hard heavy red wood of a quira (*Platymiscium pinnatum*)

**pan-american** \ˌpan+\ *adj, usu cap P&A* **1 :** of or relating to the independent republics of No. and So. America ⟨*Pan*=*American* affairs⟩ **2 :** involving or participated in by the Pan-American nations ⟨*Pan-American* congress⟩ ⟨*Pan*=*American* games⟩

**pan-americanism** \"+\ *n, usu cap P&A* **:** a movement of the late 19th and 20th centuries favoring close cooperation (as mutual protection and the promotion of better commercial and cultural relations) among the Pan-American nations based upon a community of interests stemming largely from geographical proximity ⟨*Pan-Americanism* . . . has none of the spirit of empire in it —Woodrow Wilson⟩

**pan·a·mint** \'panəˌmint, -ˌmənt\ *n, pl* **panamint** *or* **panamints** *usu cap* **:** KOSO

**pan-arabism** \'pan+\ *n, usu cap P&A* **:** a 20th century movement having as its principal aim the political union of the Arab states

**pan·a·ri·ti·um** \ˌpanə'rishēəm\ *n, pl* **panari·tia** \-ēə\ [ME *panaricium*, fr. LL, alter. of L *paronychium* — more at PARONYCHIUM] **1 :** PARONYCHIA, [3]FELON 1 **2 :** FOOT ROT 2

**pan·arteritis** \(ˌ)pan+\ *n* [NL, fr. *pan-* + *arteritis*] **:** inflammation involving all coats of an artery

**pan·arthritis** \ˌpan+\ *n* [NL, fr. *pan-* + *arthritis*] **:** inflammation of all the structures of a joint

**pan·a·ry** \'panərē\ *adj* [F *panaire*, fr. L *panis* bread + F *-aire* -ary — more at FOOD] **:** of or relating to bread or breadmaking

**pan·a·tela** *also* **pan·a·tel·la** *or* **pan·e·tela** *or* **pan·e·tel·la** \ˌpanə'telə\ *n* -S [Sp *panatela*, fr. AmerSp, a long thin biscuit, bread pudding, fr. It *panatella*, fr. *panata* panada (fr. *pane* bread — fr. L *panis* — + *-ata* -ade) + *-ella* — more at FOOD] **:** a long slender cigar that has straight sides that are rounded off at the sealed end

**pan·ath·e·naea** \ˌpaˌnathə'nēə\ *n pl, usu cap* [NL, fr. Gk *panathēnaia*, fr. *pan-* + *Athēnaia*, fr. *Athēna*, fr. *Athēnē*, major Greek deity, goddess of war, fertility, arts, and wisdom] **:** the annual or quadrennial festivities of ancient Athens in honor of Athena celebrated in their greater form for several days during the third year of each olympiad and including a great procession in which the people marched to the acropolis bearing an embroidered peplos for their tutelary goddess and also athletic, musical, equestrian, and other contests — **pan·ath·e·nae·an** \ˌ=ˌ==ˈnēən\ *adj, usu cap*

**pan·ath·e·na·ic** \ˌ=ˌ==ˈnāik\ *adj, often cap* [L *panathenaicus*, fr. Gk *panathēnaikos*, fr. *panathēnaia* + *-ikos* -ic] **:** of, relating to, or connected with the Panathenaea **:** PANATHENAEAN ⟨the Parthenon frieze representing the ~ procession⟩ ⟨vases given as prizes in the ~ games⟩

**pan·automorphic** \(ˈ)pan+\ *adj* [*pan-* + *automorphic*] **:** PANIDIOMORPHIC

**pa·nax** \'paˌnaks\ *n* [NL, fr. L, a plant, panacea, fr. Gk *panak-*, *panax*, fr. *panakeia* — more at PANACEA] **1** *cap* **:** a genus of perennial herbs (family Araliaceae) of eastern No. America and Asia with aromatic tuberous roots, compound verticillate leaves, and a solitary umbel of flowers — see GINSENG **2** -ES **:** any plant of a genus (*Polyscias*) of trees and shrubs that is related to and sometimes esp. formerly included in *Panax*

**pa·nay·an** \pə'nīən\ *n* -S *usu cap* [*Panay*, one of the Visayan islands in the Philippines + E *-an*] **:** HILIGAYNON

**pan bolt** *n* **:** a bolt with the head shaped like an inverted pan

**pan-breaking** \'=ˌ==\ *n* **:** the loosening of hardpan or plow sole with a subsoiler, chisel, or similar deep-tillage implement

**panbroil** \'=ˌ=\ *vt* [[1]*pan* + *broil*] **:** to cook uncovered on a hot metal surface (as a frying pan) with little or no fat

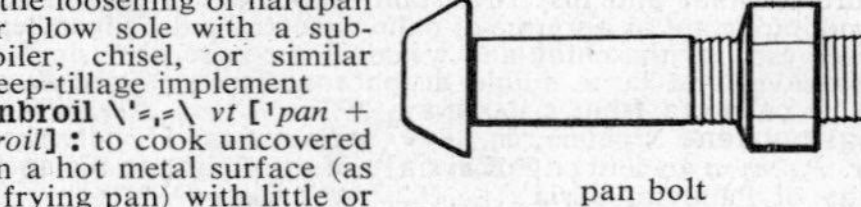

pan bolt

[1]**pan·cake** \'pa\|n,kāk, 'paa\| *sometimes* \|ŋ,-\ *n, often attrib* [ME,

fr. *panne* pan + *cake* — more at PAN] **1 a :** GRIDDLE CAKE ⟨~ mix⟩ **b :** a usu. very thin flat cake made of a batter enriched with eggs, milk, or cream, cooked on both sides in a pan or on a griddle and often rolled up with a sweet or savory filling and served in portions as a dessert or appetizer — compare CREPE SUZETTE **2 :** something thin and flat like a pancake; *specif* **:** a fabricated leather made of leather scraps glued together and pressed into sheets and often used in heels

**2pancake** \"\ *vi* **:** to make a pancake landing ⟨*pancaked* down to a forced landing —F.J.Taylor⟩ ⟨the plane struck . . . an apartment house and *pancaked* down in an orphanage baseball diamond —*N.Y.Times*⟩ ~ *vt* **1 :** to cause (an airplane) to make a pancake landing **2 :** FLATTEN ⟨found his hat had been *pancaked* under a suitcase⟩

**Pan–Cake** \"\ *trademark* — used for a cosmetic in semimoist cake form used in place of or as a foundation for face powder

**pancake bell** *n* **:** a bell rung in some English churches about noon on Shrove Tuesday sometimes regarded as a signal to stop work and prepare pancakes

**pancake coil** *n* **:** a coil having a flat spiral form

**pancake day** *or* **pancake tuesday** *n, usu cap P&D&T* [so called fr. the custom of having pancakes on that day] **:** SHROVE TUESDAY

**pancake engine** *n* **:** an engine arranged for compactness by stacking cylinders one above another horizontally or side by side (as for mounting in an airplane wing)

**pancake ice** *n* **:** thin new ice such as forms in the early fall in polar regions in pieces about one to six feet in diameter resembling pancakes

**pancake landing** *n* **:** a landing in which the airplane is leveled off higher than for a normal landing causing it to stall and drop in an approximately horizontal position with little forward motion

**pancake plant** *n* **:** DWARF MALLOW

**pancake turner** *n* **:** a record operator in a radio or television studio

**pan·carditis** \,pan+\ *n* [NL, fr. *pan-* + *carditis*] **:** general inflammation of the heart; *specif* **:** inflammation involving the pericardium, myocardium, and heart valves but not the whole endocardium

**pan·cha·ma** \'pənchəmə\ *n* -s [Skt *pañcama* fifth] **:** a member of the lowest caste group in India **:** HARIJAN, UNTOUCHABLE

**pan·chax** \'pan,chaks\ *n* -ES [NL *Panchax*, former generic name of the panchaxes] **:** any of numerous small brilliantly colored killifishes (genus *Aplocheilus*) of Africa and southeastern Asia that are often kept in the tropical aquarium

**pan·cha·yat** *also* **pan·cha·yet** *or* **pun·cha·yet** \(,)pən'chäyət, -chīət\ *n* -s [Hindi *pañcāyat*, fr. Skt *pañca* five — more at FIVE] **1 :** a village council in India: **a :** a former group of five influential older men acknowledged by the community as its governing body **b :** an elective council of about five members organized in the republic of India as an organ of village self-government **2 :** a Parsi council of six dasturs and ten mobeds regulating secular affairs

**pan·chen lama** \'pän,chen-\ *n, usu cap P&L* [panchen fr. Chin (Pek) *pan¹ ch'an²*] **:** the lama next in rank to the Dalai Lama

**pan·cheon** \'panchən\ *n* -s [prob. alter. (influenced by ¹*pan*) of *puncheon*] **:** a large flaring shallow earthen vessel formerly commonly used in rural England

**pan·chromatic** \,pan, ¦paan+(,)=¦==\ *adj* [ISV *pan-* + *chromatic*] **:** sensitive to light of all colors in the visible spectrum — used of a photographic emulsion, film, or plate

**pan·chro·ma·tize** \pan'krōmə,tīz\ *vt* [*panchromatic* + *-ize*] **:** to make panchromatic ⟨the emulsion must be *panchromatized* —J.S.Friedman⟩

**pan conveyor** *n* [¹*pan*] **:** a slow-moving chain conveyer in which a series of overlapping plates is attached to continuous chains

**pan·cosmic** \(')pan+\ *adj* [*pan-* + *cosmic*] **1 :** affecting or relating to the cosmos as a whole **2** [*pancosmism* + *-ic*] **:** of or relating to pancosmism ⟨pantheism in . . . its ~ or acosmic form —Aldous Huxley⟩

**pan·cos·mism** \pan'käz,mizəm\ *n* [*pan-* + Gk *kosmos* order, universe + *-ism*] **:** the theory that the material universe or cosmos in time and space is all that exists

**pan·cra·ti·ast** \pan'krāshē,ast\ *or* **pan·cra·tist** \'pankrəd·əst\ *n* -s [L *pancratiastes*, fr. Gk *pankratiastēs*, fr. *pankratiazein* to perform the exercises of the pancratium, fr. *pankration* pancratium] **:** a contestant or victor in a pancratium — **pan·cra·ti·as·tic** \,pan,krāshē¦astik\ *adj*

**pan·crat·ic** \(')pan¦krad·ik\ *adj* [L *pancratium* + E *-ic*] **1 :** of or relating to a pancratium **2** [*pan-* + *-cratic*] **:** marked by or giving mastery of all subjects or matters **3 :** having all or many degrees of power — used esp. of an adjustable eyepiece for a microscope

**pan·cra·ti·um** \pan'krāshēəm\ *n* [L, fr. Gk *pankration*, fr. *pankrates* all-powerful, fr. *pan-* + *kratos* strength, power — more at HARD] **1** *also* **pancration** -s **:** an ancient Greek athletic contest involving both boxing and wrestling **2** [NL, fr. Gk *pankration* sea-daffodil] **a** *cap* **:** a genus of Old World bulbous herbs (family Amaryllidaceae) having mostly pure white umbellate flowers with a funnel-shaped perianth and conspicuous crown — see SEA DAFFODIL **b** -s **:** any plant of the genus *Pancratium*

**pancre-** *or* **pancreo-** *comb form* [ISV, fr. NL *pancreas*] **:** PANCREAT- ⟨*pancre*ectomy⟩ ⟨*pancreo*zymin⟩

**pan·cre·as** \'paŋkrēəs, 'pank-, 'paank-\ *n* -ES [NL, fr. Gk *pankreas*, fr. *pan-* + *kreas* flesh, meat — more at RAW] **:** a large compound racemose gland that in man lies in front of the upper lumbar vertebrae and behind the stomach and is somewhat hammer-shaped and firmly attached anteriorly to the curve of the duodenum with which it communicates through one or more pancreatic ducts and that consists of (1) tubular acini secreting digestive ferments which pass to the intestine and function in the breakdown of proteins, fats, and carbohydrates; (2) modified acinar cells that form islets between the tubules and secrete the hormone insulin; and (3) a firm connective tissue capsule that extends supportive strands into the organ — see BEEF BREAD, ISLAND OF LANGERHANS; DIGESTION illustration

**pancreat-** *or* **pancreato-** *comb form* [NL, fr. Gk *pankreat-*, *pankreas*, fr. *pan-* + *kreas* flesh, meat — more at RAW] **:** a large and ⟨*pancreato*duodenectomy⟩ **2 :** pancreatic ⟨*pancreat*ism⟩

**pan·cre·a·tec·to·mize** \,paŋkrēə'tektə,mīz, ,pankr-\ *vt* -ED/-ING/-S [*pancreatectomy* + *-ize*] **:** to excise the pancreas of

**pan·cre·a·tec·to·my** \-ektəmē\ *n* -ES [*pancreat-* + *-ectomy*] **:** surgical excision of all or part of the pancreas

**pan·cre·at·ic** \¦paŋkrē¦ad·|ik, ¦pank-, ¦paank-, -at|, |ēk\ *adj* [prob. fr. (assumed) NL *pancreaticus*, fr. *pancreat-* + L *-icus* -ic] **:** of or relating to the pancreas

**pancreatic artery** *n* **:** any of the branches of the splenic artery that supply the pancreas

**pancreatic duct** *n* **:** a duct connecting the pancreas with the intestine; *specif* **:** DUCT OF WIRSUNG — distinguished from *duct of Santorini;* see DIGESTION illustration

**pancreatic fibrosis** *n* **:** MUCOVISCIDOSIS

**pancreatic juice** *n* **:** a clear alkaline pancreatic secretion that contains at least three different enzymes, trypsin, amylopsin, and lipase, or their precursors and that is poured into the duodenum where when mixed with bile and intestinal juices it furthers the digestion of foodstuffs already partly broken down by salivary and gastric enzymes

**pancreatico-** *comb form* [ISV, fr. *pancreatic*] **1 :** pancreatic ⟨*pancreatico*gastrostomy⟩ **2 :** pancreatic and ⟨*pancreatico*biliary⟩ ⟨*pancreatico*duodenal⟩

**pan·cre·a·tin** \'paŋkrēəd·ən, 'pank-\ *n* -s [ISV *pancreat-* + *-in*] **:** a mixture of enzymes from the pancreatic juice or a preparation containing such a mixture; *esp* **:** a cream-colored amorphous powder containing principally amylase, trypsin, and lipase obtained from the pancreas of the hog or ox and used chiefly in medicine as a digestant and in tanning as a bate

**pan·cre·a·tism** \-ēə,tizəm\ *n* -s [*pancreat-* + *-ism*] **:** pancreatic activity — used chiefly in combination ⟨dys*pancreatism*⟩

**pan·cre·a·ti·tis** \,paŋkrēə'tīd·əs, ,pank-\ *n, pl* **pancrea·titi·des** \-'tid·ə,dēz\ [NL, fr. *pancreat-* + *-itis*] **:** inflammation of the pancreas

**pan·cre·o·zy·min** \,paŋkrēō'zīmən, ,pank-\ *n* [ISV *pancreo-* + *zymin*] **:** a hormonal product of the duodenal mucosa that stimulates pancreatic enzyme production — compare SECRETIN

**pan·cytopenia** \(¦)pan+\ *n* [NL, fr. *pan-* + *cytopenia*] **:** APLASTIC ANEMIA — **pan·cytopenic** \"+\ *adj*

**pand** \'pand\ *n* -s [prob. modif. of MF *pente*, fr. *pendre* to hang — more at PENDANT] *archaic Scot* **:** a narrow drapery hung on a bedstead

**1pan·da** \'pandə, 'paan-\ *n* -s [F, fr. native name in Nepal] **1 :** a long-tailed Himalayan carnivore (*Ailurus fulgens*) that is related to and closely resembles the American raccoon, has long fur, and is basically rusty or chestnut in color with mottling and barring of black and with the muzzle, cheeks and ears conspicuously tufted with white — called also *bear cat, cat bear* **2 :** a large mammal (*Ailuropoda melanoleuca*) from Tibet that somewhat resembles a bear but is related to the raccoons though sometimes placed in a separate family and that is largely white above and black below with black patches about the eyes and black ears — called also *giant panda*

**2panda** \"\ *n* -s [NL, prob. by shortening & alter. fr. LL *pandura*, *pandurium* three-stringed lute — more at PANDURA] **:** a philodendron (*Philodendron panduriforme*) used as an ornamental and aquarium plant and having fiddle-shaped leaves

**3panda** \"\ *n* [NL, fr. native name in Gabon and So. Cameroons] **1** *cap* **:** a small West African genus (coextensive with the family Pandaceae and order Pandales) of dicotyledonous trees with drupaceous fruits that are rich in tannin and contain large seeds rich in edible oil **2** -s **a :** a small West African tree (*Panda oleosa*) **b :** the very hard heavy fine-grained brownish yellow to greenish wood of the panda

**pandaemonium** *var of* PANDEMONIUM

**pan·dal** \'pandᵊl\ *n* -s [Tamil-Malayalan *pantal*] **:** a shelter erected in India of upright poles supporting a roof that is usu. of bamboo matting; *esp* **:** a large open-sided temporary pavilion often used for large meetings

**pan·dal·i·dae** \pan'dalə,dē\ *n pl, cap* [NL, fr. *Pandalus*, type genus + *-idae*] **:** a family of deepwater prawns with elongated laterally compressed rostrum armed with spines and the first two pairs of legs slender

**pan·da·lus** \pan'dāləs\ *n, cap* [NL] **:** a genus of deepwater prawns that includes the common European edible prawn (*P. annulicornis*) and is the type of the family Pandalidae

**pan·dan** \'pandən\ *n* -s [NL *Pandanus*] **:** a plant of the family Pandanaceae; *esp* **:** TEXTILE SCREW PINE

**pan·da·na·ce·ae** \,pandə'nāsē,ē\ *n pl, cap* [NL, fr. *Pandanus*, type genus + *-aceae*] **:** a family of woody plants (order Pandanales) having rigid leaves and small dioecious flowers without a perianth — see FREYCINETIA, PANDANUS — **pan·da·na·ceous** \¦==¦nāshəs\ *adj*

**pan·da·na·les** \,==ˈnā(,)lēz\ *n pl, cap* [NL, fr. *Pandanus* + *-ales*] **:** an order of monocotyledonous plants including the families Typhaceae, Sparganiaceae, and Pandanaceae and distinguished by monoecious or dioecious flowers without a perianth that are borne in close spikes or heads and ovules with mealy or fleshy endosperm

**pan·da·nus** \pan'dānəs\ *n* [NL, fr. Malay *pandan*] **1** *cap* **:** a large genus (the type of the family Pandanaceae) of tropical trees that comprise the screw pines, are native chiefly to Malaysia and naturalized over a wide area, and have slender stems like those of palms, often immense prop roots, and branches with a terminal crown of sword-shaped leaves **2** -ES **a :** any plant of the genus *Pandanus* **b :** a fiber that is made from the leaf of the pandanus and is used for woven articles (as mats)

**pandar** *var of* PANDER

**pan·da·ram** \pən'därəm\ *n* -s [Tamil *paṇṭāram*] **1 :** a Hindu ascetic mendicant of the Sudra or sometimes a lower caste **2 :** a low-caste Hindu priest of southern India and Ceylon

**pan·darc·tos** \pan'därk,täs\ [NL, fr. ¹*panda* + Gk *arktos* bear — more at ARCTIC] *syn of* AILUROPODA

**pan·da·rus** \'pandərəs\ *n, cap* [NL, fr. L *Pandarus*, in Greek mythology leader of the Lycians in the Trojan war, fr. Gk *Pandaros*] **:** a genus of fish lice attacking the skin of marine fishes

**P and C** *abbr* put and call

**P and D** *abbr* pickup and delivery

**pan·de·an harmonica** \'pandēən-\ *n, usu cap P* [*pandean* irreg. fr. *Pan*, ancient Greek god of woods and shepherds + E *-an*] **:** a harmonica resembling a panpipe

**pandean pipes** *n pl, usu cap 1st P* **:** PANPIPE

**pan·dect** \'pan,dekt\ *n* -s [LL *Pandectes*, digest in fifty books of the Roman civil law compiled under the Emperor Justinian in the 6th century, fr. L *pandectes* book that contains everything, fr. Gk *pandektēs* all-receiving, all-containing, fr. *pan-* + *dektēs* receiver, fr. *dechesthai* to receive; akin to Gk *dokein* to seem good, seem, think — more at DECENT] **1 :** a complete code of the laws of a country or system of law **2 :** a treatise covering an entire subject **:** complete digest **3 :** a manuscript containing the whole Bible **syn** see COMPENDIUM

**pan·de·mia** \pan'dēmēə\ *n* -s [NL, fr. Gk *pandēmia* all the people, fr. *pandēmos* of or belonging to all the people + *-ia* -y] **:** PANDEMIC

**1pan·dem·ic** \(')pan¦demik\ *adj* [LL *pandemus* pandemic (fr. Gk *pandēmos* of or belonging to all the people, fr. *pan-* + *dēmos* deme, populace) + E *-ic* — more at DEM-] **1 a :** occurring over a wide geographic area and affecting an exceptionally high proportion of the population ⟨a ~ outbreak of malaria⟩ **b :** affecting the majority of people in a country or a number of countries ⟨~ alarm⟩ **2** *usu cap* [Gk *pandēmos Erōs* vulgar love (fr. *pandēmos* pandemic + *Erōs*, Greek god of love) + E *-ic* — more at EROS] **:** of or relating to common or sensual love **:** CARNAL **3 :** COSMOPOLITAN

**2pandemic** \"\ *n* -s **:** a pandemic outbreak of a disease **:** an epidemic of unusual extent and severity

**pan·de·mo·ni·ac** \,pandə¦mōnē,ak\ *also* **pan·de·mon·ic** \-mänik\ *or* **pan·de·mo·ni·a·cal** \,pandəmə'nīəkəl\ *adj* [*pandemonium* + *-ac* (after *demoniac*) or *-ic* (after *demonic*) or *-acal* (after *demoniacal*)] **1 :** of or relating to or resembling Pandemonium **:** INFERNAL **2 :** having the character of a pandemonium **:** RIOTOUS ⟨several hundred thousand hysterical . . . youths roaring ~ approval —J.A.Morris b. 1904⟩

**pan·de·mo·ni·um** \,pandə'mōnēəm, ,paand-\ *n* -s [NL, fr. *Pandaemonium*, capital of Hell in *Paradise Lost* (1667) epic poem by John Milton †1674 Eng. poet, fr. *pan-* + LL *daemonium* evil spirit, fr. Gk *daimonion*, fr. *daimōn* spirit, deity — more at DEMON] **1** *or* **pandaemonium a** *usu cap* **:** the abode of all the demons **:** the infernal regions **:** HELL ⟨a solemn council forthwith to be held at *Pandaemonium* —John Milton⟩ **b :** a center of vice **:** a wicked place **c :** a wildly lawless or riotous place or gathering **2 :** a state of wild uproar **:** tumultuous din ⟨the jubilation grew and grew to a positive ~ —Carolyn Hannay⟩ **syn** see DIN

**1pan·der** \'pandə(r), 'paan-\ *or* **pan·der·er** \-d(ə)rə(r)\ *also* **pan·dar** \-də(r)\ *n* -s [*pander* alter. (influenced by *-er*) of ME *Pandare*, character who procured for Troilus the love of Cressida in *Troilus and Criseyde* (1374) poem by Geoffrey Chaucer †1400 Eng. poet; *panderer* fr. ²*pander* + *-er*; *pandar* fr. ME *Pandare*] **1 a :** a go-between in love intrigues **b :** a man who solicits clients for a prostitute **:** PROCURER **2 :** someone who caters to and often exploits the weaknesses of others

**2pander** \"\ *vb* **pandered; pandered; pandering** \-d(ə)riŋ\ **panders** *vt* **:** to act as pander for **:** procure for ~ *vi* **:** to act as a pander ⟨~*ing* to the shortcomings of music students —A.E. Wier⟩; *esp* **:** to provide gratification for others' desires (as for sentimentality) ⟨those who ~ to the lower tastes of the young and ignorant —*Britain Today*⟩ ⟨institutions which ~*ed* to the factory workers . . . — a movie house, a quick-lunch wagon —Scott Fitzgerald⟩

**pan·der·ism** \-də,rizəm\ *n* -s [¹*pander* + *-ism*] **:** the practice of pandering

**pan·der·ly** \-də(r)lē\ *adj* **:** having the character of a pander

**P and I** *abbr* protection and indemnity

**pan·diagonal** \,pan+,=¦===\ *adj* [*pan-* + *diagonal*] **:** having the same sum along all possible diagonals ⟨~ magic squares⟩

**pan·diatonic** \(¦)pan+\ *adj* [*pan-* + *diatonic*] **:** marked by the use of the diatonic rather than the chromatic scale as the basic tonal material but without the classical harmonic restrictions ⟨~ style⟩

**pan·diatonicism** \"+\ *n* **:** the use of pandiatonic harmony

**pan·dic·u·la·tion** \pan,dikyə'lāshən\ *n* -s [F, fr. L *pandiculatus* (past part. of *pandiculari* to stretch oneself, fr. *pandere* to spread, unfold) + F *-ion* — more at FATHOM] **:** a stretching and stiffening esp. of the trunk and extremities (as when fatigued and drowsy or after waking from sleep)

**pan·di·on** \pan'dī,än\ *n, cap* [NL, fr. L, nightingale, fr. *Pandion*, a king of Athens in Greek mythology, fr. Gk *Pandiōn*] **:** a genus (coextensive with the family Pandionidae of the suborder Falcones) of fish-eating hawks comprising the ospreys

**pan·dit** \'pandət, 'pən-\ *n* -s [Hindi *paṇḍit*, fr. Skt *paṇḍita*] **1 :** a wise or learned man in India — often used before a name as an honorary title **2 :** a Brahman expert in Sanskrit and in the science, laws, and religion of the Hindus **:** SCHOLAR; *broadly* **:** TEACHER **3 :** a Hindu clerk or official in Kashmir

**pan·di·ta** \pän'dēd·ə\ *n* -s [Skt *paṇḍita* pandit] **:** a Moro priest

**P and L** *abbr* profit and loss

**1pan·do·ra** \pan'dōrə, paan-, -dȯrə\ *also* **pan·dore** \'pan-,dō(ə)r\ *n* -s [*pandora* fr. It *pandora*, *pandura*, fr. LL *pandura*, *pandurium* three-stringed lute; *pandore* fr. F, fr. LL *pandura*, *pandurium* — more at PANDURA] **1 :** BANDORE **2 :** PANDURA 2

**2pandora** \"\ *n* [NL, after *Pandora* (fr. L, fr. Gk *Pandōra*), the beautiful and gifted first woman of Greek mythology] **1** *cap* **:** a genus (the type of the family Pandoridae) of marine bivalve mollusks of the suborder Anatinacea with largely united siphons, thin equivalve shell, and tongue-shaped foot **2** -s **:** any mollusk of the genus *Pandora* or the family Pandoridae

**pandora moth** *n* [NL *pandora* (specific epithet of *Coloradia pandora*), fr. L *Pandora*] **:** a saturniid moth (*Coloradia pandora*) the larva of which is a defoliator of pines in western U. S.

**pandora's box** *n, usu cap P* [fr. *Pandora's box*, a box containing all the ills of mankind and given by Zeus to the mythological Pandora, who opened it against the command of Zeus] **:** something that produces many unforeseen difficulties **:** a prolific source of troubles

**pan·do·rea** \-rēə\ *n, cap* [NL, prob. fr. L *Pandora*, mythological first woman] **:** a genus of tropical Old World woody vines (family Bignoniaceae) having evergreen compound leaves and white or pink paniculate flowers — see BOWER PLANT, WONGA-WONGA

**pan·do·ri·na** \,pandə'rīnə\ *n, cap* [NL, prob. fr. *Pandora*, genus of mollusks + *-ina*] **:** a genus of plantlike flagellates closely related to *Volvox* that form a small spherical colony of sixteen cells enclosed in a delicate gelatinous envelope through which the flagella project

**pan·dour** \'pan,du̇(ə)r\ *n* -s [F *pandour*, *pandoure*, fr. Hung *pandur*, fr. Croatian, guard, constable, prob. fr. ML *banderius*, *bannerius* guardian of fields, summoner, fr. *bannum* proclamation, summons, ban, prob. of Gmc origin; akin to OHG *ban* command, prohibition, jurisdiction — more at BAN] **1 :** a member of a Croatian regiment in the Austrian army of the 18th century orig. organized as a local militia and having a reputation for cruelty and plundering **2 :** an armed servant or retainer of the nobility or member of a mounted constabulary in and near Croatia

**pan·dow·dy** \(')pan'dau̇dē, -au̇di\ *n* -ES [origin unknown] **:** a deep-dish apple dessert that is spiced, sweetened with sugar, molasses, or maple syrup and covered with a rich biscuit crust and baked and that is served warm with a sauce or cold with the crust cut into the apples — called also *apple pandowdy*

**pands** *pl of* PAND

**pan dul·ce** \'pän'dül(,)sā\ *n* [AmSp, sweet bread] **:** any of various sweet breads; *esp* **:** a raisin bun

**pan·du·ra** *also* **pan·dou·ra** \pan'd(y)u̇rə\ *n* -s [*pandura* fr. It *pandura*, *pandora*, fr. LL *pandura*, *pandurium* three-stringed lute, fr. Gk *pandoura*; *pandoura* fr. Gk] **1 :** BANDORE **2 :** an ancient long-necked small-bodied stringed instrument of the lute class **3 :** BANDURA

**pan·du·rate** \'pand(y)ərət, -ə,rāt\ *also* **pan·du·rat·ed** \-ə,rād·əd\ *adj* [*pandurate* prob. fr. (assumed) NL *panduratus*, fr. LL *pandura* + L *-atus* -ate; *pandurated* prob. fr. (assumed) NL *panduratus* + E *-ed*] **:** resembling a fiddle in outline — see LEAF illustration

**pan·du·ri·form** \pan'd(y)u̇rə,fȯrm\ *adj* [NL *panduriformis*, fr. LL *pandura* + L *-iformis* -iform] **:** PANDURATE

**pan·du·ri·na** \,pand(y)ə'rīnə\ *n* -s [NL, fr. LL *pandura* + L *-ina* (dim. suffix)] **:** a small lute with wire strings

**1pan·dy** \'pandi\ *n* -ES [prob. fr. L *pande* hold out, extend (the hand), imper. sing. of *pandere* to spread, unfold — more at FATHOM] *dial Brit* **:** a blow on the hand usu. with a cane or stick

**2pandy** \"\ *vt* -ED/-ING/-ES *dial Brit* **:** to strike (a person) a pandy

**3pan·dy** \'pandē\ *n* -ES *usu cap* [Bengali & Hindi *pā̃ṛe*, one of a subcaste of Brahmans, fr. Skt *paṇḍita* pandit; fr. their enlisting in the Bengal Army] **:** a mutineer in the Sepoy mutiny

**1pane** \'pān\ *n* -s [ME *pane*, *pan* piece of cloth, strip, section, pane, fr. MF *pan*, fr. L *pannus* cloth, rag, ribbon — more at VANE] **1 :** a piece, section, or side of something: as **a :** one of the compartments of a window or door consisting of one sheet of glass in a frame of wood, lead, or some other metal **b :** one of the sides of a nut or bolt head **2 a :** one of a series of sewn strips or panels often of different colors esp. characteristic of 16th century costumes and curtains **b :** a finished slit in a 16th century garment so slashed in order to show a lining of contrasting color or material — usu. used in pl. **3 a :** one of the sections into which an original plate-sized sheet of postage stamps is cut for distribution to post offices — called also *post-office pane* **b :** a block of stamps forming a page of a stamp booklet — called also *booklet pane*

**2pane** \"\ *n* -s [prob. by alter.] **:** PEEN

**3pane** \"\ *vt* -ED/-ING/-S **:** PEEN

**paned** \-nd\ *adj* **1 :** made of or with panes of cloth **2 :** provided with an often specified number or kind of panes ⟨a small-paned window⟩ ⟨a 6-paned nut⟩

**pan·e·gyr·ic** \,panə'jirik, -jīr-, -rēk\ *n* -s [L *panegyricus*, fr. *panegyricus*, adj., of the nature of a public assembly, festive, fr. Gk *panēgyrikos*, fr. *panēgyris* public festival, public assembly (fr. *pan-* + *agyris*, *agora* assembly) + *-ikos* -ic — more at AGORA] **:** a eulogistic oration or writing **:** a formal or elaborate eulogy or encomium **:** a laudatory discourse; *also* **:** formal or elaborate praise or eulogizing **:** LAUDATION

**pan·e·gyr·i·cal** \¦==¦jirəkəl, -jīr-, -rek-\ *or* **pan·e·gyr·ic** \¦==-=rik, -rēk\ *adj* [*panegyrical* fr. L *panegyricus* panegyric, n. + E *-al*; *panegyric* fr. L *panegyricus* festive] **:** like or constituting a panegyric **:** formally or elaborately eulogistic or encomiastic — **pan·e·gyr·i·cal·ly** \-rək(ə)lē, -rēk-, -li\ *adv*

**pa·neg·y·ris** \pə'nejərəs, -nēj-\ *or* **pa·neg·y·ry** \-rē\ *n* -ES [*panegyris* fr. Gk *panēgyris*; *panegyry* fr. Gk *panēgyris* + E *-y* (n. suffix)] **:** an ancient Greek public assembly; *esp* **:** a festival honoring a god

**pan·e·gyr·ist** \,panə'jirəst, -jīr-\ *n* -s [LL *panegyrista*, fr. Gk *panēgyristēs* participant in a public festival, fr. *panēgyrizein* to participate in a public festival, deliver a panegyric + *-istēs* -ist] **:** one who writes or delivers a panegyric **:** EULOGIST ⟨a ~ of country simplicity —John Buchan⟩

**pan·e·gy·rize** \'panəjə,rīz\ *vt* -ED/-ING/-S [Gk *panēgyrizein*, fr. *panēgyris* public festival + *-izein* -ize] **:** to praise highly **:** extol in public **:** write or deliver a panegyric on **:** EULOGIZE

**pa·ne·i·ty** \pə'nēəd·ē\ *n* -ES [L *panis* bread + E *-eity* (as in *corporeity*) — more at FOOD] **:** the quality or state of being bread ⟨the ~ of the eucharistic bread⟩

**1pan·el** \'panᵊl\ *n* -s *often attrib* [ME, fr. MF, prob. fr. (assumed) VL *pannellus*, alter. (influenced by L *-ellus* -el) of L *pannulus* small piece of cloth, fr. *pannus* cloth, rag, ribbon + *-ulus* -ule — more at VANE] **1** *obs* **:** ¹PANNEL **2 a** *obs* **:** a small piece of parchment **b** (1) **:** a schedule containing the names of persons summoned as jurors by a sheriff (2) **:** the whole group of persons so summoned from which the jury is selected (3) **:** JURY 1 **c :** the person or persons arraigned for trial **d :** a list or group of persons selected for some service (as research, investigation, arbitration) ⟨an advisory ~ of experts⟩ ⟨test results . . . accomplished by a ~ of tasters —*Biol.*

panels 3b

*Abstracts*⟩ **e** (1) **:** a list of physicians from among whom a patient may make a choice in accordance with various British health and insurance plans (2) **:** the patients cared for by a doctor under such a plan **f** (1) **:** a group of three or more people often skilled in various fields who conduct before an audience a discussion on a topic (as of political, economic, or social interest) in order to stimulate interest and to present different points of view rather than to arrive at a single solution or to establish the superiority of one viewpoint (2) *or* **panel discussion :** a discussion conducted by such a panel — compare DEBATE, SYMPOSIUM **g :** a group of three or more entertainers or guests engaged as players in a quiz game or guessing game conducted by a master of ceremonies on a radio or television program **h** (1) **:** a number of persons interviewed as a population sample on two or more occasions for the purposes of a survey (as to ascertain changes in attitude or situation during the interim) ⟨consumer ~⟩ ⟨listener ~⟩ ⟨labor force ~⟩ ⟨~ study⟩ (2) **:** a survey of attitudes, opinions, or objective data using such a panel ⟨a fact-finding ~⟩ **3** [prob. influenced in meaning by L *panis* door panel, table, fr. *panis* food — more at FOOD] **:** a separate or distinct part of a surface ⟨cuts steel sheets into exact sizes for fenders, hoods, and roof ~*s* —*Time*⟩ ⟨the transparent ~ of a window envelope⟩ ⟨the inscription engraved in the ~ of this Royal Medal —P.H.Pettiford⟩: as **a :** a fence section (as the part between two posts in a rail fence) **:** HURDLE **b** (1) **:** a thin usu. rectangular board set sunken in a frame (as in a door, wainscot, or chair back) (2) **:** a usu. sunken or raised section of a surface (as a wall or ceiling) set off by a molding or other margin sometimes of different material or color (3) **:** a flat usu. rectangular piece of construction material (as plywood, metal, concrete, plastic) made usu. in a standard size to form part of a surface (as a wall, ceiling, floor) ⟨quickly put up a wall of prefabricated plywood ~*s*⟩ **c** (1) **:** a compartment of some design in carpet bedding (2) **:** a level expanse of turf (as in a garden) **d** (1) **:** an area on a book cover enclosed by a tooled or stamped border (2) **:** an affixed or inserted label on a book cover on which tooling, stamping, or finishing may be done **e** (1) **:** a vertical section of fabric (as a gore in a skirt) usu. stitched by two or more sides into or onto a garment (2) **:** a length of fabric (as a curtain) allowed to hang freely from its upper edge (3) **:** one of the gores of a parachute canopy **f** (1) **:** BOX 9a, 9c (2) **:** a cartoon consisting of a single picture (3) **:** a space on a postage stamp set off by a border or a tinted ground and containing a value figure, inscription, separate unit of design, or insignia — called also *label, tablet* **g :** a flat-bottomed furrow with sloping or curved sides cut in ornamental glassware **h** (1) **:** any of several units of construction of a wing surface of an airplane (2) **:** any unit piece of fabric of which the envelope or outer cover of an aerostat is made (3) **:** the area in a rigid airship bounded by two adjacent longitudinals and two adjacent transverses **i** (1) **:** any of the flat faces of a box, carton, or case whether separate or in finished form ⟨the trademark printed on the front ~⟩ (2) **:** any flat, smooth, or unmarked area on a container ⟨a ~ on the jar lid for marking in the price⟩ **4 a :** a thin flat piece of wood on which a picture is painted usu. in tempera or oil and tempera combined; *also* **:** a painting on such a surface **b** *or* **panel photograph :** a long narrow photograph; *esp* **:** one about 4 inches by 8½ inches **c :** a picture painted or mounted on a section of wall **d :** a photograph mounted on a stiff backing for display **5 a** *obs* **:** a small portion of coal left uncut **b :** one of the divisions marked by pillars of extra size into which a mine is laid off in one system of extracting coal or ore **6 a :** one of the sections of a folding screen or triptych **b** (1) **:** a book forming part of a series (as a trilogy presenting a subject in historical sequence) (2) **:** a series of such works ⟨this book, the second of a projected ~ of four about the West —*Time*⟩ **7 a :** a section of a switchboard **b :** a flat insulating support for parts of an electrical device usu. with control handles arranged on one face **c :** a usu. vertical mount for controls or dials of instruments of measurement **8** [influenced in meaning by [1]*pane*] **:** a distinctively shaped or colored piece of cloth for display on the ground by troops as a means of signaling to airplanes or of marking front lines or friendly installations or vehicles **9 :** PANEL TRUCK — **in the panel** *or* **on the panel** *or* **upon the panel** *Scots law* **:** arraigned for trial **:** on trial

[2]**panel** \"\ *vt* **paneled** *or* **panelled; paneled** *or* **panelled; paneling** *or* **panelling; panels 1 :** to furnish or decorate with panels **2 :** to produce flat surfaces in (a container) by distortion or in manufacture

**pa·ne·la** \pə'nālə\ *n* -s [MexSp, dim. of Sp *pan* bread, fr. L *panis;* fr. the fact that it comes in round chunks that resemble rolls of bread — more at FOOD] **:** low-grade brown sugar

**panelboard** \'=,=\ *n* **1 :** a drawing board with an adjustable outside frame that is forced over paper so as to hold and strain it **2 :** a strong rigid paperboard used for paneling in automobile bodies and in building construction **3 :** an electrical panel containing switches and fuses or circuit breakers controlling branch circuits (as for lights or fan motors) that is enclosed in a metal cabinet and usu. placed in or against a wall — called also *distribution board*

**panel door** *n* **:** a door having panels framed by stiles and rails of greater thickness — compare FLUSH DOOR

**pan·el·er** \'panᵊlə(r)\ *n* -s **:** one that makes or fits (as the body of a vehicle) with panels

**pane·less** \'pānləs\ *adj* [[1]*pane* + *-less*] **:** having no pane **:** lacking panes ⟨windows left ~ by the explosion⟩

**panel game** *n* **:** theft in a panel house

**panel heating** *n* **:** space heating by means of wall, floor, baseboard, or ceiling panels with embedded electric conductors or hot-air or hot-water pipes — called also *radiant heating*

**panel house** *n* **:** a house of prostitution in which the rooms have secret entrances (as through sliding panels) to facilitate theft by accomplices of the inmates

**paneling** *n* -s [fr. gerund of [2]*panel*] **:** panels joined in a continuous surface; *esp* **:** a decorative covering for an interior wall or ceiling composed of wood panels and often framing

**pan·el·ist** \'panᵊləst\ *n* -s **1 :** a member of a discussion or advisory panel (as for debating a public issue before a forum or for investigating or mediating an industrial controversy) **2 :** a member of a radio or television panel participating in an entertainment program

**panel length** *n* **:** the distance between two adjacent joints on either the upper or the lower chord of a truss

**panel lighting** *n* **:** room illumination by means of metal panels electrically heated to emit fluorescence from phosphors embedded between the metal and a glass facing

**panel point** *n* **:** a point (as on one of the chord members) at which members of a truss intersect

**panel radiator** *n* **:** a heating radiator set into a wall panel or baseboard

**panel saw** *n* **:** a handsaw with fine teeth for cutting thin wood (as for panels)

**panel stamp** *n* **:** a metal plate with which engraved designs or pictorial decorations are mechanically impressed on the sides of leather book covers

**panel-stamped** \'=,=\ *adj, of a leather book cover* **:** stamped with engraved designs or pictorial decorations

**panel strip** *n* **1 :** a strip of molded wood or metal to cover a joint between two sheathing boards and form a panel **2 :** a strip between a stile and a panel to form a secondary or accessory panel

**panel thief** *n* **:** the person who performs the robbery in a panel house

**panel truck** *n* **:** a light motor truck approximately of passenger-car size with a fully enclosed body used principally for delivery

**panel wall** *n* **:** a nonbearing wall between columns or piers that is supported at each story — compare CURTAIN WALL

**pan·endoscope** \(')pan+\ *n* [*pan-* + *endoscope*] **:** a cystoscope fitted with an obliquely forward telescopic system that permits wide-angle viewing of the interior of the urinary bladder — **pan·endoscopic** \¦pan+\ *adj* — **pan·endoscopy** \¦pan+\ *n* -ES

**pan·en·the·ism** \pa'nen(t)thē,izəm\ *n* -s [G *panentheismus,* fr. *pan-* + Gk *en* in + G *theismus* theism (fr. Gk *theos* god + G *-ismus* -ism) — more at IN, THE-] **:** the doctrine that God includes the world as a part though not the whole of his being

**pan·en·the·ist** \-ēəst\ *n* **:** an adherent of panentheism

**pan·en·the·is·tic** \pa¦nen(t)thē¦istik\ *adj* [*panentheism* + *-istic*] **:** of or relating to panentheism

**panes** *pl of* PANE, *pres 3d sing of* PANE

**pan·es·thia** \pa'nesthēə\ *n, cap* [NL, fr. *pan-* + Gk *esthein* to eat + NL *-ia;* akin to Gk (Homeric) *edmenai* to eat; fr. the characteristic of biting off each other's wings — more at EAT] **:** a genus of subsocial burrowing cockroaches

**panetela** *or* **panetella** *var of* PANATELA

**pan·e·tière** \,panə'tye(ə)r\ *n* -s [F, fr. MF *panetiere* cupboard for keeping bread, fr. OF, bread sack, irreg. fr. *pan, pain* bread (fr. L *panis*) + *-iere* (fem. of *-ier* -er) — more at FOOD] **:** an ornate French-provincial bread box

**pan·et·to·ne** \,pänə'tōnē\ *n* -s [It, fr. *panetto* small loaf, fr. *pane* bread (fr. L *panis*) + *-etto* -et (fr. LL *-itus*)] **:** a usu. yeast-leavened holiday bread containing raisins and candied fruit peels

**pan-europe** \'pan+\ *or* **pan-eu·ro·pa** \'panyə'rōpə\ *n* -s *usu cap P&E* [*pan-europa* fr. G *pan-Europa,* fr. *pan-* + *Europa* Europe, continent extending west from Asia] **:** a primarily political union of the countries of Europe excluding Great Britain and the U. S. S. R. projected during the mid-20th century

**pan-european** \(¦)pan+\ *adj, usu cap P&E* **:** of, relating to, or involving all or most of the nations of Europe ⟨a *Pan-European* economic union⟩

**pan-fired** \'=,=\ *adj, of Japanese green tea* **:** steamed and then rolled in metal pans over the fire — compare BASKET-FIRED

[1]**panfish** \'=,=\ *n* [[1]*pan* + *fish;* fr. its being suitable for frying whole in a pan] **:** any of numerous small food fishes (as of the family Centrarchidae) usu. taken with hook and line and not available on the market — compare GAME FISH

[2]**panfish** \"\ *vi* **:** to angle for panfish

[3]**panfish** \"\ *n* [[1]*pan* + *fish;* fr. its shape] **:** KING CRAB

**pan·for·te** \pän'fórd·(,)ā\ *n* -s [It, fr. *pane* bread + *forte* strong, fr. L *fortis* — more at FORT] **:** a holiday bread that is hard in texture and is made with honey and nuts

**pan·fry** \'=,=\ *vt* **:** to fry (food) in a pan containing very little fat **:** SAUTÉ — distinguished from *deep fry*

**pan·ful** \'pan,fu̇l\ *n* -s **:** a quantity that fills a pan

[1]**pang** \'paŋ, 'paiŋ\ *n* -s [origin unknown] **1 :** a brief piercing spasm of pain ⟨the ~*s* of childbirth⟩ ⟨a hunger ~⟩ **2 :** a sudden sharp attack of mental pain **:** a feeling of piercing mental anguish ⟨a ~ of remorse⟩ ⟨felt a ~ of conscience⟩ ⟨the ~*s* of love⟩ **syn** see PAIN

[2]**pang** \"\ *vt* **:** to cause to have pangs **:** pain extremely **:** TORTURE, TORMENT

[3]**pang** \'paŋ\ *adj* [origin unknown] *Scot* **:** FULL, STUFFED

[4]**pang** \"\ *vt* -ED/-ING/-S *Scot* **:** to fill to capacity **:** CRAM, STUFF

[1]**pan·ga** \'päŋgə\ *n* -s [Afrik *panga, pangar,* prob. fr. Tag *panga* jawbone] **:** a small common sparid food fish (*Pterogymnus laniarus*) of southern Africa sometimes congregating in vast schools

[2]**panga** \"\ *n* -s [native name in East Africa] **:** a large broad-bladed knife used in Africa for heavy cutting (as of brush or bananas) and also as a weapon **:** MACHETE

**pan·ga·ne** \päŋ'gä(,)nā\ *n* -s [prob. fr. *Pangani,* river and town in Tanganyika Territory, East Africa] **1 :** an East African bowstring hemp (*Sansevieria kirkii*) **2 :** the strong leaf fiber of the pangane used for cordage

**pan·ga·si·nan** \päŋ,gäsē'nän\ *n, pl* **pangasinan** *or* **pangasinans** *usu cap* [Pangasinan *Pangasinán*] **1 a :** a Christianized people in central Luzon, Philippines **b :** a member of such people **2 :** the Austronesian language of the Pangasinan people

**pan·gen** \'panjən, -,jen\ *also* **pan·gene** \-,jēn\ *n* -s [G *pangen,* fr. *pan-* + *-gen*] **:** a hypothetical heredity-controlling particle of protoplasm — compare PANGENESIS

**pan·genesis** \(')pan+\ *n* [NL, fr. *pan-* + *genesis*] **:** a hypothetical mechanism of heredity in which the cells throw off pangens that circulate freely throughout the system, multiply by subdivision, and collect in the reproductive products or in buds so that the egg or bud contains pangens from all parts of the parent or parents — opposed to *blastogenesis*

**pan·ge·net·ic** \¦panjə¦ned·ik\ *adj* **:** of, relating to, or characterized by pangenesis — **pan·ge·net·i·cal·ly** \-d·ək(ə)lē\ *adv*

**pan·gen·ic** \(')pan¦jenik\ *adj* [NL *pangenesis* + E *-ic*] **:** PANGENETIC

[1]**pan-german** \'pan+\ *or* **pan-germanic** \¦pan+(,)=¦==\ *adj, usu cap P&G* **:** of, relating to, or favoring Pan-Germanism

[2]**pan-german** \"\ *or* **pan-germanist** \'pan+\ *n, usu cap P&G* **:** an advocate of Pan-Germanism

**pan-germanism** \'pan+\ *n* -s *usu cap P&G* [F *pangermanisme* (trans. of G *alldeutschtum*), fr. *pan-* + *germanisme* Germanism, fr. *Germanie* Germany (fr. L *Germania* land occupied by the Germanic peoples in western Europe in Roman times) + *-isme* -ism] **1 :** a chiefly 19th century movement having as its principal aim the political union of all Germans **2 :** a 20th century doctrine of German racial superiority and world domination by stages of imperial expansion

**pan·gi** \'pan,jī\ *n* -s [Bugi] **:** a Malayan tree (*Pangium edule*) having seeds that are edible after long boiling to remove their poisonous principle

**pan·gi·um** \'panjēəm\ *n, cap* [NL, fr. Bugi *pangi* + NL *-ium*] **:** a genus of Malayan trees (family Flacourtiaceae) having entire or 3-lobed leaves and axillary dioecious flowers with a scale at the base of each petal

**pang·less** \'paŋləs, 'paiŋ-\ *adj* **:** having or causing no pang — **pang·less·ly** *adv*

**pan·gli·ma** \päŋ'glēmə\ *n* -s [Malay *pĕnglima*] **:** a Malay noble of secondary rank **:** a petty raja

**pan·gloss·ian** \(')pan¦gläsēən\ *adj, usu cap* [*Pangloss,* optimistic tutor of Candide in the satire *Candide* (1759) by Voltaire †1778 Fr. writer (fr. F, fr. *pan-* + Gk *glōssa* tongue) + E *-an* + more at GLOSS] **:** marked by the view that all is for the best in this best of possible worlds ⟨~ economists . . . who had not so much predicted as seen the millenium —*Times Lit. Supp.*⟩

**pan·go·la grass** \pan'gōlə-\ *n* [*pangola* fr. native name in So. Africa] **:** a rapid-growing perennial grass (*Digitaria decumbens*) of southern Africa introduced into southern U. S. as a pasture grass

**pan·go·lin** \'paŋgələn, paŋ'gōl-\ *n* -s [Malay *pĕngguling,* fr. *guling* rolling over; fr. its characteristic of rolling itself into a ball] **:** any of several Asiatic and African edentate mammals of *Manis* or related genera of the order Pholidota having the body covered with large flattened reddish brown imbricated horny scales, feeding chiefly on ants, and somewhat resembling in habit and structure the American anteaters

**pan grave** *n* [[1]*pan*] **:** a shallow grave characteristic of an ancient people with Nubian associations included in the inhabitants of Egypt during the Middle Kingdom

**pan gravy** *n* [[1]*pan*] **:** gravy consisting of seasoned but not thickened juices extracted from meat in cooking and often a little water

**pangs** *pl of* PANG, *pres 3d sing of* PANG

**pan·guin·gue** \päŋ'gēŋgē\ *n* -s [Tag *pangguinggui*] **:** a card game which resembles rummy, which is played with several packs of cards shuffled together, and in which a player tries to meld his whole hand in groups or sequences and bonuses are paid for particular melds

**pang·we** \'päŋ(,)wā\ *n, pl* **pangwe** *or* **pangwes** *usu cap* [Fang *Mpangwe*] **:** [4]FANG

[1]**panhandle** \'=,==\ *n* [[1]*pan* + *handle* (n.)] **:** a comparatively narrow projection of a larger territory (as a state)

[2]**pan·han·dle** \'pan,handᵊl, 'paan,haan-\ *vb* **panhandled; panhandled; panhandling** \-d(ᵊ)liŋ\ **panhandles** [back-formation fr. *panhandler*] *vi* **:** to stop people on the street and ask for money often telling a hard-luck story **:** BEG ~ *vt* **1 :** to accost on the street and beg from **2 :** to get (as money) by panhandling

**pan·han·dler** \-d(ᵊ)lə(r)\ *n* [prob. fr. [1]*panhandle* + *-er;* fr. the extended forearm] **:** one that panhandles **:** an able-bodied street beggar

**pan·has** \'pän,häs\ *also* **pan·haus** \-hau̇s\ *or* **pann·haas** \-häs\ *or* **pann·haus** \-hau̇s\ *n* -ES [PaG *pannhas,* fr. *pann* pan (fr. MHG dial. *panne*) + *has* hare, rabbit, fr. MHG *hase;* akin to OHG *phanna* pan and to OHG *haso* hare — more at PAN, HARE] **:** SCRAPPLE

**panhead** \'=,=\ *n* **:** a head of a rivet or bolt shaped like an inverted cooking pan — **panheaded** \'=,==\ *adj*

panhead

**pan·hellenic** \¦pan+\ *adj, usu cap* [*pan-* + *hellenic*] **1 :** of or relating to all Greece **:** including or representing all Greece or all the Greeks **2 :** of or relating to the Greek-letter sororities or fraternities in American colleges and universities or to an association representing them

**pan-hispanism** \'pan+\ *n* -s *usu cap P&H* [AmerSp *pan-hispanismo,* fr. Sp *pan-* + *hispanismo* hispanism — more at HISPANISM] **:** a movement in So. and Central America emphasizing the cultural kinship of the Spanish-speaking peoples and opposing Pan-Americanism

**panhuman** \(')pan+\ *adj* [*pan-* + *human*] **:** of or relating to all humanity ⟨~ values⟩ ⟨a ~ culture⟩

**pan·hypopituitarism** \(¦)pan+\ *n* [*pan-* + *hypopituitarism*] **:** generalized secretory deficiency of the anterior lobe of the pituitary gland **:** SIMMONDS' DISEASE

**pan·hypopituitary** \"+\ *adj* **:** of or relating to panhypopituitarism

**pan·hysterectomy** \"+\ *n* [*pan-* + *hysterectomy*] **:** excision of the uterus and uterine cervix

[1]**pan·ic** \'panik, -nēk\ *n* -s [ME *panik,* fr. MF or L; MF *panic* Italian millet, fr. L *panicum,* fr. *panus* ear of millet, tuft, swelling, inflammation; akin to L *pantic-, pantex* paunch — more at PAUNCH] **1 :** PANIC GRASS **2 :** the edible grain of some panic grasses

[2]**panic** \"\ *adj* [F *panique,* fr. Gk *panikos,* fr. *Pan,* ancient Greek god of woods and shepherds who was regarded as the cause of the panic among the Persians at Marathon and of any sudden and groundless fear + *-ikos* -ic] **1 :** of, relating to, or resembling the mental or emotional state believed to be induced by the ancient Greek god Pan **:** WILD **:** extreme, sudden, and often groundless — used esp. of fear ⟨driven by a ~ fear that they would be massacred —Alan Moorehead⟩ ⟨no rational fear but a ~ terror —H.G.Wells⟩ **2 :** of, relating to, or coming from a panic ⟨a wave of ~ buying —Mary K. Hammond⟩ ⟨~ haste⟩ ⟨~ conditions⟩ **3 :** of or relating to the god Pan ⟨what old, earthy *Panic* rite came to extinction here —Aldous Huxley⟩ **4 :** being or belonging to hardware securing an exit door that opens readily outward when a bar or lever on the inside of the door is pushed ⟨~ bolts for theater exits⟩ ⟨~ bars for school doors⟩

[3]**panic** \"\ *n* -s [Gk *panikon,* fr. neut. of *panikos*] **1** *obs* **:** contagious emotion such as was supposed to be due to the ancient Greek god Pan **2 :** a sudden overpowering fright; *esp* **:** a sudden terror often inspired by a trifling cause or a misapprehension of danger and accompanied by unreasoning or frantic efforts to secure safety **3 :** a sudden widespread fright concerning financial affairs and resulting in a depression in values caused by violent measures for protection or for the sale of securities or other property — compare BUSINESS CYCLE **4** *slang* **:** something very funny **syn** see FEAR

[4]**panic** \"\ *vb* **panicked; panicked; panicking; panics** *vt* **1 :** to affect with panic ⟨a brutal murder . . . ~*s* the town —*Publishers' Weekly*⟩ **:** influence by arousing panic ⟨salesmen are attempting to ~ people into buying . . . by threatening a shortage —*Springfield (Mass.) Daily News*⟩ **2 :** to produce demonstrative appreciation on the part of ⟨~ an audience with a gag⟩ ~ *vi* **:** to be stricken with panic **:** lose one's head ⟨~*s* and attempts to flee from the fallout area —R.E.Lapp⟩

**pan·i·cal·ly** \-nək(ə)lē\ *adv* [obs. E *panical* of panic (fr. E [2]*panic* + *-al*) + E *-ly*] **:** in a manner suggesting panic ⟨his voice went up almost ~ at the end —R.M.Coates⟩

**panic button** *n* [so called fr. the control button or switch for emergency use in an airplane] **:** something setting off a precipitous emergency response

**panic grass** *n* [[1]*panic*] **:** a grass of the genus *Panicum* or of one of several closely related genera (as *Echinochloa*)

**pan·ick·i·ness** \-nəkēnəs\ *n* -ES **:** the quality or state of being panicky

**pan·icky** \'panəkē, -ki\ *adj, sometimes* -ER/-EST [[3]*panic* + *-y*] **1 :** characterized by or resulting from panic ⟨moments of ~ terror at the beginning of each attack —R.H.Newman⟩ **:** groundlessly or extremely fearful ⟨became ~ as the snow deepened —G.R.Stewart⟩ **2 :** inclined to panic ⟨~ sheep⟩

**pan·i·cle** \'panəkəl, -nēk-\ *n* -s [L *panicula* tuft, swelling, dim. of *panus* ear of millet, tuft, swelling] **1 :** a compound racemose inflorescence that is usu. a raceme in which the secondary branches are themselves racemose (as the inflorescence of yuccas) but sometimes merges into the cymose type (as in the horse chestnut) — called also *compound raceme;* see INFLORESCENCE illustration **2 :** any pyramidal loosely branched flower cluster — **pan·i·cled** \-ld\ *adj*

**panic party** *n* **:** an extra crew carried on a World War I mystery ship for the purpose of quitting it when attacked and thus leaving it apparently abandoned

**panic reaction** *also* **panic state** *n* **:** an acute overwhelming attack of fear or anxiety producing personality disorganization that may persist

**panic-stricken** \'==,==\ *or* **panic-struck** \'==,=\ *adj* **:** struck with panic **:** overcome by sudden fear ⟨keeping back the *panic-stricken* crowd —*Blue Bk.*⟩ ⟨a *panic-stricken* urge to hurry the educational process —V.M.Rogers⟩

**pa·nic·u·late** \pə'nikyələt, -yə,lāt\ *or* **pa·nic·u·lat·ed** \-yə,lād·əd\ *adj* [*paniculate* fr. NL *paniculatus,* fr. L *panicula* tuft + *-atus* -ate; *paniculated* fr. NL *paniculatus* + E *-ed*] **:** arranged or disposed in panicles **:** branching like a panicle — **pa·nic·u·late·ly** *adv*

**pan·i·cum** \'panəkəm\ *n, cap* [NL, fr. L, Italian millet — more at PANIC (grass)] **:** a large and widely distributed genus of grasses of very diverse habit having 1- to 2-flowered spikelets disposed in a close or open panicle — see MILLET 1a, GUINEA GRASS, PARA GRASS, WITCHGRASS

**pan·idiomorphic** \(¦)pan+\ *adj* [*pan-* + *idiomorphic*] **:** completely idiomorphic

**panier** *var of* PANNIER

**pa·ni·ne·an** \¦pänə¦nēən\ *adj, usu cap* [*Panini fl*350 B.C. Sanskrit grammarian + E *-an*] **1 :** of or being the grammatical system of the Sanskrit grammarian Panini **2** *of Sanskrit* **:** adhering rigidly to the rules

**paning** *pres 3d sing of* PANE

**pa·ni·ni** \pə'nēnē\ *n* -s [Hawaiian, fr. *pa* wall + *nini* fence] *Hawaii* **:** an arborescent prickly pear (*Opuntia megacantha*) introduced from California for its fruits

**pa·ni·o·lo** \,pänē'ō(,)lō\ *n* -s [Hawaiian, prob. fr. Sp *español* Spaniard, Spanish, fr. (assumed) VL *Hispaniolus,* fr. L *Hispania* Spain + *-olus* -ole] *Hawaii* **:** COWBOY

**pan·i·o·ni·an** \¦panē¦ōnēən\ *or* **pan·i·on·ic** \-¦änik\ *adj, usu cap* [L *panionium* + E *-an* or *-ic*] **:** of or relating to a Panionium

**pan·i·o·ni·um** \,==ˈōnēəm\ *n, pl* **panio·nia** \-ēə\ *usu cap* [NL, sing. of *panionia,* fr. Gk *paniōnia,* fr. *pan-* + *Iōnia* Ionia — more at IONIAN] **:** a gathering of all the Ionians held on Mycale at which Poseidon was worshiped and political matters were discussed

**pan·isc** *or* **pan·isk** \'panisk\ *n* -s [L *Paniscus,* fr. Gk *Paniskos,* dim. of *Pan,* Greek god of woods and shepherds] **:** a godling of the forest in Greek mythology that is half man and half goat and is commonly attendant on Pan

**pan-islam** \¦pan+\ *or* **pan-islamism** \"+\ *n* -s *usu cap P&I* [*pan-* + *islam* or *islamism*] **:** a political movement launched in Turkey at the end of the 19th century by Sultan Abdul-Hamid II for the purpose of combating the process of westernization and fostering the renascence and unification of Islam

**pan-islamic** \¦pan+\ *adj, usu cap P&I* [*pan-* + *Islamic*] **:** of, relating to, or favoring Pan-Islam ⟨ideal of *Pan-Islamic* union —Alford Carleton⟩

**pan-islamist** \"+\ *n, usu cap P&I* **:** an advocate of Pan-Islam

**pan·i·yan** \'panē,yan\ *n, pl* **paniyan** *or* **paniyans** *usu cap* **1 :** one of a number of pre-Dravidian peoples inhabiting the hills and jungles of central India **2 :** one of a Paniyan people

[1]**pan·ja·bi** \,pən'jäbē, -bi\ *n* -s *cap* [Hindi *pañjābī* — more at PUNJABI] **1 :** PUNJABI 1 **2 a :** an Indic language of Panjab that with Hindi is one of the official languages of East Panjab **b :** LAHNDA

**2panjabi** \"\ *adj, usu cap* : PUNJABI

**pan·jan·drum** \pan'jandrəm\ *n* -s [fr. Grand *Panjandrum*, burlesque title of an imaginary personage in some nonsense lines by Samuel Foote †1777 Eng. actor and playwright] : a powerful personage or pretentious official

**pank** \'paŋk\ *vi* -ED/-ING/-S [perh. alter. of *pant*] *dial Eng* : to breathe hard : PANT

**pan·leucopenia** *also* **pan·leukopenia** \(¦)pan+\ *n* [NL, fr. *pan-* + *leucopenia* or *leukopenia*] : an acute usu. fatal viral epizootic disease of cats characterized by fever, diarrhea and dehydration, and extensive destruction of white blood cells — called also *cat distemper*, *feline distemper*, *cat typhoid*

**pan·logical** \(')pan¦läjəkəl\ *adj* : of or relating to panlogism

**pan·lo·gism** \'panlə,jizəm\ *n* -s [G *panlogismus*, fr. *pan-* + Gk *logos* word, reason + G *-ismus* -ism (fr. L) — more at LEGEND] : the doctrine that the absolute or the absolute reality is of the nature of logos or reason; *esp* : Hegelian philosophy

**1pan·lo·gist** \-,jəst\ *or* **pan·lo·gis·tic** \¦==¦jistik\ *adj* [*panlogism* + *-ist* or *-istic*] : of or relating to panlogism

**2panlogist** \"\ *n* -s [*panlogism* + *-ist*] : an advocate of panlogism

**pan·man** \'panmən\ *n, pl* **panmen** [*1pan* + *man*] **1** : one who tends pans (as in evaporating, pulverizing, baking) **2** : a worker who loads cottonseed cakes into presses for extraction of oil **3** : an operator of a machine that whirls candy in a pan of syrup, wax coloring matter, or the like to give it a finishing coat or polish — called also *glazer*, *grosser*

**pan·mer·ism** \'panmə,rizəm\ *n* -s [ISV *panmeristic* + *-ism*] : a theory in biology: protoplasm is made up of panmeristic units whose adaptive responses are the ultimate cause of growth and evolutionary change

**pan·meristic** \¦pan+\ *adj* [ISV *pan-* + *meristic*] : of or involving a hypothetical perfectly adaptable ultimate protoplasmic unit ⟨~ growth⟩

**pan·mic·tic** \(')pan¦miktik\ *adj* [*pan-* + Gk *miktos* mixed (verbal of *mignynai* to mix) + E *-ic*] : of, relating to, or exhibiting panmixia

**pan·mix·ia** \pan'miksēə\ *also* **pan·mixy** *or* **pan·mix·ie** \'pan,miksē\ *or* **pan·mix·is** \pan'miksəs\ *n, pl* **panmixias** \-ēəz\ *also* **panmixies** \-ēz\ *or* **panmix·es** \-k,sēz\ *or* **panmixises** [*panmixia* fr. NL, fr. *pan-* + Gk *mixis* act of mingling (fr. *mignynai* to mix) + NL *-ia; panmixy* fr. NL *panmixia; panmixie* ISV, fr. NL, *panmixia; panmixis* fr. NL, fr. *pan-* + *-mixis* — more at MIX] : random or nonselective mating within a breeding population resulting ultimately in a high degree of uniformity if the population is strictly closed — opposed to *apomixy*

**pan·mne·sia** \pan'nēzh(ē)ə\ *n* -s [NL, fr. *pan-* + *-mnesia*] : the continuance in memory of all mental impression

**pan·myelopathy** \(¦)pan+\ *n* [*pan-* + *myelopathy*] : an abnormal condition of all the blood-forming elements of the bone marrow

**pan·myelophthisis** \"+\ *n* [NL, fr. *pan-* + *-myelophthisis*] : wasting or degeneration of the blood-forming elements of the bone marrow

**pan·nage** \'panij\ *or* **pan·age** *n* -s [ME *pannage*, fr. AF *pannage, pasnage*, fr. OF *paasnaige*, fr. ML *pasnagium, pannagium*, alter. of *pastionaticum* payment for pannage, fr. L *pastion-, pastio* feeding, grazing (fr. *pastus* — past part. of *pascere* to pasture, feed, graze — + *-ion-, -io* -ion) + *-aticum* -age — more at FOOD] **1 a** : the act of pasturing swine in a wood or forest (as in medieval England) **b** : the legal right or privilege of such pasturing **c** : the charge or payment made for this privilege **2** : food (as acorns, beechnuts) for swine in a forest

**panne** \'pan\ *n* -s [F, fr. OF *penne, panne* fur used for lining, fr. L *pinna* feather, wing, alter. of *penna* — more at PEN] **1** : a finish for velvet or satin produced by heat and roller pressure **2** *or* **panne velvet** : a silk or rayon velvet with a lustrous pile flattened in one direction **3** *or* **panne satin** : a heavy silk or rayon satin with a high luster and a waxy smoothness

**panned** *past of* PAN

**1pan·nel** \'panᵊl\ *n* -s [ME *panel* — more at PANEL] **1** : a pad or stuffed lining that serves to prevent galling by a saddle **2 a** : a usu. rude pad serving as a saddle **b** : a wooden saddle formerly used for a donkey

**2pannel** \"\ *n* -s [origin unknown] : the part of the alimentary canal of a hawk below the crop

**pan·ner** \'panə(r)\ *n* -s : one that pans or puts in a pan: as **a** : one who pans for gold **b** : a worker who places dough in pans for baking **c** : a worker who places sealed cans from a seamer or conveyor onto pans, racks, or trays — called also *racker*

**pan·ne·tier's green** \pan·'tyāz-\ *n, usu cap P* [prob. after Antoine C. *Pannetier* †1859 Fr. painter and chemist] : GUIGNET'S GREEN 1

**pannhaas** *or* **pannhaus** *var of* PANHAS

**pan·nic·u·li·tis** \pə,nikyə'līd·əs\ *n* -ES \-lid·ə,dēz\ [NL, fr. *panniculus* + *-itis*] : inflammation of the subcutaneous layer of abdominal fat

**pan·nic·u·lus** \pə'nikyələs\ *n, pl* **pannicu·li** \-yə,lī\ [NL, fr. L, small piece of cloth, dim. of *pannus* cloth — more at VANE] : a sheet or layer of tissue; *esp* : a layer of superficial fat-laden fascia

**panniculus car·no·sus** \-kär'nōsəs\ *n* [NL, fleshy panniculus] : a thin sheet of striated muscle lying within or just beneath the superficial fascia in many mammals and serving to produce local movement of the skin

**1pan·nier** *or* **pan·ier** \'panyə(r), -nēə-\ *n* -s [ME *panier*, fr. MF *panier, pannier*, fr. L *panarium, pannarium*, fr. *panis* bread — more at FOOD] **1 a** : a large basket (as for provisions); *esp* : a wicker basket often used in pairs and carried over the back of a beast of burden or on the shoulders of a person **b** : a pack consisting of two bags or cases for carriage by a pack animal or person **2** : CORBEIL 1 **3 a** : a covered basket holding surgical instruments and medicines for a military ambulance **b** : a conical basket with a pole passing through its axis that can be filled with stones and used as an anchor in bridge and pontoon laying **c** : a shield of basketry set in the ground and formerly used by archers **4 a** : one of a pair of hoops (as of steel or whalebone) formerly used to expand women's skirts at the sides **b** : an overskirt draped or looped at the sides for a similar effect

pannier 1 a

**2pannier** \"\ *n* -s [prob. short for *pannierman*] : a table¦waiter (as formerly at the Inner Temple, London)

**pan·niered** \-(r)d\ *adj* [fr. past part. of obs. E *pannier* to furnish with panniers, fr. E *1pannier*] : bearing or wearing panniers ⟨weary donkeys ~ with heavy baskets —Claudia Cassidy⟩ ⟨wide ~ hoop and pointed bodice —*Fashion Digest*⟩

**pan·nier·man** \-(r)mən\ *n, pl* **panniermen** [ME *panereman*, fr. *panere, panier* pannier (basket) + *man*] : an officer (as formerly at the Inns of Court) having various duties connected with the provision and serving of meals

**pan·ni·kin** \'panəkən\ *n* -s [*1pan* + *-kin* (after *cannikin*)] *Brit* : a small pan or cup often of tin : CANNIKIN ⟨got the ~*s* out and the tin plates —Mary S. Broome⟩

**pannikin boss** *n, Austral* : an overseer of a gang of laborers

**panning** *pres part of* PAN

**1pan·no·ni·an** \pə'nōnēən\ *adj, usu cap* [L *pannonius* Pannonian (fr. *Pannonia*) + E *-an*] : of or relating to Pannonia, a Roman province in what is now western Hungary, northern Yugoslavia, and eastern Austria, bounded north and east by the Danube

**2pannonian** \"\ *n* -s *cap* [L *Pannonia* + E *-an*] : a native or inhabitant of ancient Pannonia

**pan·non·ic** \pə'nänik\ *adj, usu cap* [L *pannonicus*, fr. *Pannonia*, Roman province + *-icus* -ic] : PANNONIAN

**pan·nose** \'pa,nōs\ *adj* [L *pannosus* ragged, raglike, fr. *pannus* cloth, rag + *-osus* -ose — more at VANE] : having the texture or appearance of felt or woolen cloth — **pan·nose·ly** *adv*

**pan·num** \'panəm\ *n* -s [NL] : the dried anthelmintic rootstock of various ferns of the genus *Dryopteris*

**pan·nus** \'panəs\ *n, pl* **pan·ni** \-a,nī\ [NL, prob. fr. L, cloth] **1** : a vascular tissue causing a superficial opacity of the cornea and occurring esp. in trachoma **2** : a sheet of inflammatory granulation tissue that spreads from the synovial membrane and invades the joint in rheumatoid arthritis ultimately leading to fibrous ankylosis

**pa·no** \'pä(,)nō\ *n, pl* **pano** *or* **panos** *usu cap* [AmerSp, a member of the Panoan peoples] **1 a** : an Indian people of the upper Amazon basin **b** : a member of such people **2** : PANOAN

**1pa·no·an** \'pänəwən\ *n* -s *usu cap* [AmerSp *Pano* + E *-an*] : a language family including languages spoken by the Panoan peoples

**2panoan** \"\ *adj, usu cap* : of, relating to, or constituting a group of peoples of western Brazil, Peru, and Bolivia or their language

**1pa·no·cha** \'pə'nōchə\ *n* -s [MexSp, dim. of Sp *pan* bread — more at PANELA] : a Mexican raw sugar

**2panocha** *or* **panoche** *var of* PENUCHE

**pan·o·is·tic** \¦panə¦wistik\ *adj* [*pan-* + *o-* (fr. Gk *ōion* egg) + *-istic* — more at EGG] : producing ova without nutritive cells — used of the ovaries of insects; compare POLYTROPHIC

**pa·no·lia deer** \pə'nōlēə-\ *n, usu cap P* [NL *Panolia* (genus name of *Panolia acuticornis*), perh. fr Gk *panōleia* all-destructive, fr. *panolēs*, fr. *pan-* + *ōlēs* destroyed, fr. *ollysthai* to destroy] : THAMIN

**pan·om·phe·an** *or* **pan·om·phae·an** \¦pa,näm¦fēən\ *also* **pan·om·pha·ic** \-fāik\ *or* **pan·om·phic** \(')pa¦näm(p)fik\ *adj* [L *Panomphaeus* Zeus (fr. Gk *Panomphaios*, fr. *panomphaios* all-divining, lit., author or sender of divine oracles, fr. *pan-* + *omphē* voice, oracle) + E *-an* or *-ic* — more at SING] **1** : giving forth all divination **2** : UNIVERSAL

**pan·o·pe·us** \,panə'pēəs\ *n, cap* [NL, fr. L *Panope*, a sea nymph, fr. Gk *Panopē*] : a genus of crabs (family Xanthidae) comprising the typical mud crabs

**pano·phobia** \¦panə+\ *n* [NL, fr. *pan-* + *phobia*] : a condition of vague nonspecific anxiety : generalized fear

**pan·ophthalmitis** \(¦)pan+\ *n* [NL, fr. *pan-* + *ophthalmitis*] : inflammation involving all the tissues of the eyeball

**pan·o·plied** \'panəplēd\ *adj* : dressed in or having a panoply ⟨no system of law springs into existence full-*panoplied* —P.C. Jessup⟩

**pan·o·ply** \-lē, -li\ *n* -ES [Gk *panoplia*, fr. *pan-* + *hopla* armor, arms (pl. of *hoplon* tool, implement) + *-ia* -y — more at HOPLITE] **1 a** : a full suit of armor (as of a hoplite or knight) **b** : ceremonial attire ⟨in the ~ of ostrich-feather head-dress, cape, gleaming spear, shield, sword, club, painted face and leg ornaments —G.W.B.Huntingford⟩ : DRESS UNIFORM **2** : something resembling armor in being a protective covering ⟨faces dim in a ~ of smoke —William Baucke⟩ ⟨tradition has become not a sword . . . but a ~ behind which to hide from the world —Max Lerner⟩ **3 a** : a magnificent or impressive array ⟨woods . . . in their full ~ of autumn foliage —S.P.B. Mais⟩ ⟨serving in the endless ~ of jobs for which it is uniquely qualified —*Aero Digest*⟩ : splendid display : POMP ⟨the military ~ of an empire on parade —*Newsweek*⟩ ⟨performed in a grand manner full of ~ and ringing sound —Herbert Weinstock⟩ **b** : a display of all appropriate appurtenances ⟨a colossal land speculation that assumed the full ~ of sovereignty —S.E.Morison & H.S.Commager⟩ ⟨windows . . . behind which the usual ~ of modern mechanical conveniences can brazenly flourish —Lewis Mumford⟩ **4** : a group of pieces of armor forming a collection of trophies, an emblem, or an ornament ⟨sports shirts of a fine lightweight wool printed with . . . *panoplies* of arms and medieval figures —*New Yorker*⟩

**pan·op·tic** \(')pa¦näptik\ *also* **pan·op·ti·cal** \-təkəl\ *adj* [Gk *panoptēs* all-seeing (fr. *pan-* + *optos* visible, verbal of *opsesthai* to be going to see) + *-ic* or *-ical* — more at OPTIC] **1** : comprising all in one view : all-seeing ⟨a ~ study of Soviet nationality —T.G.Winner⟩ **2** : permitting everything to be seen ⟨microscopic study of tissues treated with a ~ stain⟩

**pan·op·ti·con** \pa'näptə,kän\ *n* -s [*pan-* + Gk *optikon*, neut. of *optikos* optic — more at OPTIC] **1** : an optical instrument combining the telescope and microscope **2** : a prison so built radially that a guard at a central position can see all the prisoners

**pan·o·ram** \'panə,ram\ *vb* **panoramed** \-amd\ **panoramed** \"\ **panoraming** \-amiŋ\ **panorams** [by shortening fr. *panorama*] : 8PAN

**pan·o·rama** \,panə'ramə, -rämə, -råmə *sometimes* '==,==\ *n* -s [*pan-* + Gk *horama* sight, view, fr. *horan* to see — more at WARY] **1 a** : CYCLORAMA 1 **b** : a picture exhibited a part at a time by being unrolled before the spectator **c** : a building designed to contain and exhibit a panorama **2 a** (1) : an unobstructed or complete and comprehensive view of a region in every direction (2) : a photograph that includes a wide view of a scene or group of people made by a panoramic camera or by joining separate photographs (3) : the process or result of panning in making a motion picture **b** : a complete and comprehensive view or presentation of a subject matter ⟨a ~ of American history⟩ **c** : RANGE ⟨the entire vast ~ of problems which come under the heading of foreign policy —H.H.Lehman⟩ **3** : a scene that passes continuously before one : a mental picture of a series of images or events

**pan·o·ram·a·gram** \-mə,gram\ *n* [*panorama* + *-gram*] : a method of stereoscopic viewing in which the left-eye and right-eye photographs are divided into narrow juxtaposed strips and viewed through a superimposed ruled or lenticular screen in such a way that each of the observer's eyes is able to see only the correct picture

**pan·o·ram·ic** \¦==¦ramik, -mēk\ *adj* [*panorama* + *-ic*] : of, relating to, or resembling a panorama ⟨~ novels⟩ ⟨a lookout tower on a summit . . affords a ~ view —*Amer. Guide Series: Pa.*⟩ — **pan·o·ram·i·cal·ly** \-mək(ə)lē, -mēk-, -li\ *adv*

**panoramic camera** *n* : a camera for taking panoramic pictures by revolving a lens or by rotating the entire camera about a vertical axis so that the film is exposed through a narrow vertical slit

**panoramic perspective** *n* : perspective in which objects are represented on a concave cylindrical surface (as in a panorama)

**panoramic sight** *n* : a telescopic device for laying an artillery piece for direction that permits the gunner to sight in any direction without moving his head and has an azimuth scale permitting any setting from 0 to 6400 mils

**pan·o·ram·ist** \,=='raməst\ *n* -s [*panorama* + *-ist*] : one who paints panoramas

**pan·ornithic** \¦pan+ ,=¦==\ *adj* [*pan-* + *ornithic*] : affecting many birds of one kind at the same time — compare EPIDEMIC, EPIZOOTIC

**pa·nor·pa** \pə'nörpə\ *n, cap* [NL, fr. *pan-* + Gk *horpē, harpē* sickle — more at HARPES] : the type genus of the family Panorpidae

**pan·or·pa·tae** \,pa,nö(r)'pā,tē\ [NL, fr. *Panorpa* + *-atae*, fem. pl. of L *-atus* -ate] *syn of* MECOPTERA

**pa·nor·pi·dae** \pə'nö(r)pə,dē\ *n pl, cap* [NL, fr. *Panorpa*, type genus + *-idae*] : a cosmopolitan family of slender-winged insects (order Mecoptera) that have cylindrical bodies with the male genitalia enlarged into a swollen bulb and that include the typical scorpion flies

**pa·nor·pine** \pə'nör,pīn, -,pən\ *adj* : of or relating to the Panorpidae : resembling a scorpion fly

**pa·nor·poid** \-r,pöid\ *adj* [NL *Panorpa* + E *-oid*] : related to or resembling insects of the order Mecoptera

**pan out** *vi* [*2pan*] : to yield a result : turn out ⟨if things *pan out* as he expects⟩; *esp* : SUCCEED ⟨considered a genius if his experiments *panned out*⟩

**pan·pipe** \'pan,pīp\ *n, pl* **panpipes** *but sing or pl in constr* [*Pan*, the ancient Greek god of woods and shepherds who was regarded as its inventor + E *pipe*] : a primitive wind instrument that consists of a graduated series of short vertical flutes bound together with the mouth pieces in an even row and that is played in the manner of a harmonica — called also *mouth organ, syrinx*

panpipe

**pan·pla·na·tion** \,panplə'nāshən\ *n* [*pan-* + *planation*] : the process whereby panplanes are formed

**pan·plane** \'pan,plān\ *n* [*pan-* + *plane*] : a plain resulting from lateral erosion of neighboring streams so extensive that their floodplains coalesce

**pan·pneu·ma·tism** \pan'n(y)ümə,tizəm\ *n* [*pan-* + *pneumat-* + *-ism*] : a doctrine aiming to synthesize panlogism and panthelism by holding that the world or noumenal reality is both unconscious will and unconscious thought

**pan·psychic** \(')pan+\ *adj* [*panpsychism* + *-ic*] : of or relating to panpsychism

**pan·psychism** \"+\ *n* [*pan-* + *psychism*] : a theory that all nature is psychical or has a psychic aspect and that every physical happening participates in the mental — compare LEIBNIZIANISM, ORGANIC MECHANISM, WHITEHEADIAN

**pan·psychist** \"+\ *n* : an advocate of panpsychism ⟨the metaphysical materialist cannot admit as a real possibility any disembodied spirit, the ~ any absolutely insentient matter —W.P.Alston⟩ — **pan·psy·chis·tic** \¦pan,sī¦kistik\ *adj*

**pans** *pl of* PAN, *pres 3d sing of* PAN

**pan–satanism** \'pan+\ *n, usu cap P&S* [G *pansatanismus*, fr. *pan-* + *satanismus* satanism] : an orig. Gnostic doctrine that the world is the expression of the personality of Satan

**pansexual** \(')pan+\ *adj* : of, relating to, or of the character of pansexualism

**pan·sexualism** \"+\ *or* **pan·sexuality** \(¦)pan+\ *n* [*pansexualism* prob. fr. G *pansexualismus*, fr. *pan-* + *sexualismus* sexualism; *pansexuality* fr. *pan-* + *sexuality*] **1** : the suffusion of all experience and conduct with erotic feeling **2** : the view that all desire and interest are derived from the sex instinct

**pan·sexualist** \(')pan+\ *n* : an adherent to the theory of pansexualism

**pan·sexualize** \"+\ *vb* [*pansexualism* + *-ize*] *vt* : to interpret according to pansexualism ~ *vi* : to view all phenomena as manifestations, symbols, or derivatives of the sex instinct

**panshard** \'panshə(r)d\ *n* [*1pan* + *shard*] *dial Eng* : POTSHERD

**pan shovel** *n* [*1pan*] : a scoop excavator

**pan·sied** \'panzēd\ *adj* [*pansy* + *-ed*] : covered or adorned with pansies

**pan·si·fied** \-zə,fīd\ *adj* [*pansy* + *-ify* + *-ed*] : EFFEMINATE, SISSIFIED

**pan·sil** \'pan(t)səl\ *n* -s *usu cap* [Singhalese, fr. Pali *pañca sīlāni* five precepts, fr. Skt *pañca* five + *śīla* custom, moral conduct, moral precept — more at FIVE] : the rite in Hinayana Buddhism of undertaking ceremonially a set of five precepts of morality ⟨~ . . . is taken individually before a Buddhist shrine or collectively at the beginning of a Buddhist meeting of any kind —Christmas Humphreys⟩

**pan·sit** \'pän(t)sət\ *n* -s [Tag *pansit*] : a Chinese noodle dish of the Philippines

**pan–slav** \'pan+\ *adj, usu cap P&S* [back-formation fr. *pan-slavism*] : of, relating to, or favoring Pan-Slavism ⟨the history of Russian *Pan-Slav* imperialism —Kurt Glaser⟩

**pan–slavism** \"+\ *n, usu cap P&S* [G *panslavismus*, fr. *pan-* + *Slav* + *-ismus* -ism] : a political and cultural movement orig. emphasizing the cultural ties between the Slavic peoples but later associated chiefly with Russian expansionist policies

**pan·soph·ic** \(')pan¦säfik\ *or* **pan·soph·i·cal** \-fəkəl\ *adj* **1** : of or relating to pansophy **2** : OMNISCIENT — **pan·soph·i·cal·ly** \-fək(ə)lē\ *adv*

**pan·so·phism** \'pan(t)sə,fizəm\ *n* [Gk *pansophos* + E *-ism*] : universal wisdom or knowledge or pretension thereto

**pan·so·phist** \-,fəst\ *n* [Gk *pansophos* all-wise (fr. *pan-* + *sophos* wise) + E *-ist*] : one claiming or pretending to universal knowledge

**pan·so·phy** \-,fē\ *n* -ES [NL *pansophia*, fr. *pan-* + Gk *sophia* wisdom] **1** : universal wisdom or encyclopedic knowledge; *also* : a system of universal knowledge **2** : PANSOPHISM

**pan·sper·mia** \pan'spərmēə\ *also* **pan·sper·ma·tism** \-mə,tizəm\ *n* -s [*panspermia* fr. NL, fr. Gk, mixture of elements, fr. *pan-* + *sperm-* + *-ia* -y; *pan- spermatism* fr. *pan-* + *spermat-* + *-ism*] : a theory propounded in the 19th century in opposition to the theory of spontaneous generation and holding that reproductive bodies of living organisms exist throughout the universe and develop wherever the environment is favorable

**pan's pipes** *n pl, usu cap 1st P* [after *Pan*, ancient Greek god of woods and shepherds] : PANPIPE

**pan·sporoblast** \(')pan+\ *n* [*pan-* + *sporoblast*] : a typical cnidosporidian sporont containing two sporoblasts

**pan·strongylus** \"+\ *n, cap* [NL, fr. *pan-* + *Strongylus*] : a genus of triatomid bugs that contains the conenoses some of which transmit Chagas' disease

**pan supari** *n* : 5PAN 2

**pan·sy** \'panzē, 'paan-, -zi\ *n* -ES [MF *pensée*, lit., thought, fr. fem. of *pensé*, past part. of *penser* to think, fr. L *pensare* to weigh, ponder — more at PENSIVE] **1** : a garden plant (*Viola tricolor hortensis*), derived chiefly from the wild pansy of Europe by hybridizing the latter with other wild violets and having irregular 5-petaled flowers and lobed or incised leaves with large stipules **2** : a strong violet that is bluer and deeper than clematis and stronger and slightly darker than royal purple (sense 2) — called also *pensée* **3 a** : an effeminate youth **b** : a male homosexual

pansy

**pansy orchid** *n* : an orchid of the genus *Miltonia*

**pansy purple** *n* : a dark purplish red that is redder, lighter, and stronger than raisin, redgrape, or dahlia purple (sense 1), bluer, lighter, and stronger than Bokhara, and deeper and slightly bluer than Indian purple

**pansy violet** *n* **1** : a bird's-foot violet having the two upper petals very dark purple with the lower petals normally lilac-purple **2** : WILD PANSY **3** : a dark reddish purple that is bluer, lighter, and stronger than royal purple (sense 1) and redder, lighter, and stronger than average plum (sense 6a) — called also *Roman violet*

**1pant** \'pant, 'paa(ə)nt, 'paint\ *vb* -ED/-ING/-S [ME *panten*, fr. MF *pantiser, pantaisier*, fr. (assumed) VL *phantasiare* to have hallucinations, fr. Gk *phantasioun*, fr. *phantasia* appearance, image — more at FANCY] *vi* **1 a** : to breathe quickly, spasmodically, or in a labored manner (as from exertion, eagerness, or excitement) : respire with heaving of the chest **b** : to run panting ⟨~*ed* along beside the bicycle⟩ **c** : to move with or make a throbbing or puffing sound ⟨trains ~*ing* up the hill⟩ **2** : to long eagerly : desire earnestly : YEARN ⟨~*ed* for immortality, at least the immortality of being recorded —Clifton Fadiman⟩ **3** : PALPITATE, THROB, PULSATE **4** *of the sides of a ship* : to bulge in and out alternately due to the changes of pressure caused by pitching ~ *vt* : to utter with panting : GASP ⟨ran up and ~*ed* out his story⟩

**2pant** \"\ *n* -s **1 a** : one of a series of short and quick or spasmodic breaths (as after exertion) : a catching of the breath : GASP **b** : the visible physical movement of the chest accompanying such a breath **c** *obs* : a beat or palpitation of the heart **2** : the throbbing or puffing sound that accompanies each valve cycle of a steam engine

**3pant** *sing of* PANTS

**4pant** *adj* : of, relating to, or designed for use with pants ⟨~ legs⟩

**pant-** *or* **panto-** *also* **panta-** *comb form* [MF *panto-*, fr. L, fr. Gk *pant-, panto-*, fr. *pant-, pas* all, every — more at PAN-] : PAN- ⟨*panto*base⟩ ⟨*panta*graph⟩ ⟨*panto*phobia⟩ ⟨*panto*type⟩

**pant** *abbr* pantomime

**pan·tag·a·my** \pan·'tagəmē\ *n* -ES [*pant-* + *-gamy*] : marriage practiced in some communistic societies in which every man is regarded as the husband of every woman and vice versa

**pantagraph** *var of* PANTOGRAPH

**pan·ta·gru·el·i·an** \¦pantə,grü¦elēən\ *also* **pan·ta·gru·el·ic** \-lik\ *adj, usu cap* [*pantagruelian* fr. *Pantagruel*, coarsely humorous and gigantic son of Gargantua in the novel *Pantagruel* (1533) by François Rabelais †1553 Fr. satirist + E *-ian; pantagruelic* fr. F *pantagruelique*, fr. *Pantagruel* + F *-ique* -ic] : marked by coarse and extravagant satire — **pan·ta·gru·el·i·cal·ly** \-lək(ə)lē\ *adv, usu cap*

**pan·ta·gru·el·ism** \,pantə'grüə,lizəm, pan·'tagrüə,l-\ *n* -s *usu cap* [F *pantagruelisme*, fr. *Pantagruel* + F *-isme* -ism] : buffoonery or coarse humor with a satirical or serious purpose : CYNICAL HUMOR

**pan·ta·gru·el·ist** \-,ləst\ *n* -s *usu cap* [F *pantagrueliste*, fr. *Pantagruel* + F *-iste* -ist] : one who practices pantagruelism

**pan·ta·le·on** \pan·'talē,ăn\ *also* **pan·ta·lon** \'pantə,lăn\ *n* -s [G *pantalon, pantaleon,* fr. *Pantaleon* Hebenstreit †1750 Ger. musician, its inventor] **:** a large dulcimer invented about 1700 having from 100 to 250 gut and metal strings struck with wooden mallets

**pan·ta·lets** *or* **pan·ta·lettes** \,pant³l'ets, ,paan-\ *n pl* [*pantalet* fr. *pantaloon* + *-ets* (pl. of *-et*); *pantalettes* fr. *pantaloon* + *-ettes* (pl. of *-ette*)] **1 :** long drawers having an attached or detachable ruffle at the bottom of each leg usu. showing below the skirt and worn by women and children in the first half of the 19th century **2 :** women's drawers **:** BLOOMERS

pantalets 1

**pan·ta·loon** \,pant³l'ün, ,paan-\ *n* -s [MF *Pantalon* stage character wearing pantaloons, fr. OIt *Pantalone, Pantaleone,* fr. San *Pantaleone* 4th cent. A.D. physician and patron saint of physicians formerly often identified with Venice and Venetians] **1 a** *or* **pan·ta·lo·ne** \,päntə'lōnā\ *usu cap* **:** an orig. Venetian character in the commedia dell' arte that is usu. a lean old dotard with spectacles, slippers, and a tight-fitting combination of trousers and stockings **b :** a buffoon in pantomimes; *specif* **:** a vicious old dotard used as the butt of the clown **c** *obs* **:** a feeble or imbecile old man **:** an old dotard **2 a :** BREECHES; *specif* **:** wide breeches worn in England during Charles II's reign — usu. used in pl. **b :** TROUSERS; *specif* **:** close-fitting trousers usu. having straps passing under the insteps and worn esp. in the 19th century — usu. used in pl.

**pan·ta·loon·ery** \-n(ə)rē\ *n* -ES **:** the character or performance of a pantaloon **:** BUFFOONERY

**pan·tarch·ic** \(')pan·¦tärkik\ *adj* [Gk *pantarchia* + E *-ic*] **:** of or relating to a pantarchy **:** COSMOPOLITAN

**pan·tarchy** \'pan,tärkē\ *n* -ES [Gk *pantarchia,* fr. *pant-* + *-archia* -archy] **:** government (as of the world) by all the people

**pan·ta·stom·i·na** \,pantə'stämənə\ [NL, fr. *panta-* + *stoma* + *-ina*] *syn of* RHIZOMASTIGINA

**pan·tech·ni·con** \pan·'teknəkən, -nə,kän\ *n* [fr. *Pantechnicon,* 19th cent. bazaar in London orig. established for the sale of objects of art, fr. *pan-* + Gk *technikon,* neut. of *technikos* technical, artistic — more at TECHNICAL] **1** *Brit* **:** a large storage warehouse **2** *Brit* **:** ³VAN 1

**pan·telegraph** \(')pan+\ *n* [ISV *pan-* + *telegraph;* orig. formed as It *pantelegrafo*] **:** a facsimile telegraph using at both ends of the line two isochronously vibrating pendulums

**¹pan·ter** \'pantə(r)\ *or* **pan·ter·er** \-tərə(r)\ *n* -S [*panter* fr. ME *panter, paneter,* fr. OF *panetier,* irreg. fr. *pan, pain* bread (fr. L *panis*) + *-ier* -er; *panterer* fr. ME, fr. ¹*panter* + *-er* — more at FOOD] *archaic* **:** PANTLER

**²panter** *n* -S [ME, fr. MF *pantiere,* fr. L *panther,* fr. Gk *panthēros* supporting all animals, fr. *panthēra* fowler's catch, fr. *pan-* + *thēra* hunt (fr. *thēr* wild animal) — more at FIERCE] *obs* **:** a fowler's net or snare

**³pant·er** \'pantə(r)\ *n* -S [¹*pant* + *-er*] **:** one that pants; *specif* **:** a bovine animal exhibiting failure of the bodily heat-regulating mechanisms esp. as a sequel to foot-and-mouth disease

**pan·te·the·ine** \,pantə'thē,ēn, -thēən, pan-'teth-\ *n* -S [*pantethe-* (by shortening & alter. fr. *pantothenic* — in *pantothenic acid*) + *-ine*] **:** a growth factor $C_{11}H_{22}N_2O_4S$ that is essential for various microorganisms (as *Lactobacillus bulgaricus*) and that is a constituent of coenzyme A; the amide of pantothenic acid and beta-amino-ethyl mercaptan

**panth** \'păn(t)th\ *n* -S [Skt *patha* way path, course — more at FIND] *India* **:** a spiritual path or way **:** a religious faith **:** SECT

**pan·thay** \'pan(t)thā, -n,thā\ *n, pl* **panthay** *or* **panthays** *usu cap* **1 :** a Muslim people of Chinese and Turkic origin inhabiting the Burma-Chinese frontier region **2 :** a member of the Panthay people

**pan·the·ism** \'pan(t)thē,izəm, 'paan-\ *n* [F *panthéisme,* fr. E *pantheist* + F *-isme* -ism] **1 :** a doctrine that the universe conceived of as a whole is God **:** the doctrine that there is no God but the combined forces and laws that are manifested in the existing universe — compare ACOSMISM, THEISM **2 :** the worship of gods of different creeds, cults, or peoples indifferently; *also* **:** toleration of worship of all gods (as at certain periods in the Roman Empire)

**pan·the·ist** \-ēəst\ *n* [*pan-* + *theist*] **:** one who holds to pantheism

**pan·the·is·tic** \¦pan(t)thē¦istik, ¦paan-, -tēk\ *also* **pan·the·is·ti·cal** \-təkəl, -tēk-\ *adj* [*pantheist* + *-ic* or *-ical*] **:** of, relating to, or like pantheism **:** founded in or leading to pantheism — **pan·the·is·ti·cal·ly** \-tək(ə)lē, -tēk-, -li\ *adv*

**pan·the·lism** \'pan(t)thə,lizəm\ *n* -S [*pan-* + Gk *thelein* to will + *-ism*] **:** the doctrine that the ultimate reality of the universe is will; *specif* **:** the philosophy of Arthur Schopenhauer (1788–1860)

**pan·the·on** \'pan(t)thē,än, 'paan-, -ēən *sometimes* pan'thēən\ *n* -S [ME *Panteon,* temple at Rome built by the Roman statesman Agrippa †12 B.C. and rebuilt by the Roman emperor Hadrian †A.D.138, fr. L *Pantheon,* fr. Gk *pantheion* temple dedicated to all gods, fr. *pan-* + *theion,* neut. of *theios* of the gods, fr. *theos* god — more at THE-] **1 :** a temple dedicated to all the gods **2 :** a treatise on the pagan gods **3 :** a building serving as the burial place of or containing memorials to the famous dead of a nation **4 a :** the gods of a people; *esp* **:** the gods officially recognized as major or state deities **b :** the persons most highly esteemed by an individual or group ⟨the place which a contemporary writer will occupy in the ~ of letters —Anthony Powell⟩

**pan·ther** \'pan(t)thə(r), 'paan- *dial* -ntə-\ *n, pl* **panthers** *also* **panther** [ME *panter,* fr. OF *pantere,* fr. L *panthera,* fr. Gk *panthēr,* prob. of non-IE origin; prob. akin to the source of Skt *puṇḍarīka* tiger] **1 :** LEOPARD: as **a :** a leopard of a supposed exceptionally large fierce variety **b :** a leopard of the black color phase **2 :** COUGAR **3 :** JAGUAR

**panther cat** *n* **:** OCELOT

**panther cowrie** *n* **:** a spotted East Indian cowrie (*Cypraea pantherina*)

**pan·ther·ess** \-thərəs\ *n* -ES **:** a female panther

**pan·ther·ine** \-thə,rīn, -,rən\ *adj* [L *pantherinus,* fr. *panthera* panther + *-inus* -ine] **1 :** of or characteristic of a panther **2 :** resembling a panther (as in coloring, markings, or movement) **:** PANTHERISH ⟨a ~ snake⟩ ⟨moved with ~ grace⟩

**pan·ther·ish** \-thərish\ *adj* **:** resembling or suggestive of a panther ⟨a dark ~ man⟩ ⟨with ~ quickness he leaped for his gun —Zane Grey⟩ — **pan·ther·ish·ly** *adv*

**panther lily** *n* **:** LEOPARD LILY 1

**pant·ie** *or* **panty** \'pantē, 'paan-, 'pain-, -ti\ *n, pl* **panties** [*pants* + *-ie* or *-y*] **:** a woman's or child's undergarment covering the lower trunk and made with closed crotch and very short legs — usu. used in pl.

**pantie girdle** *or* **panty girdle** *n* **:** a woman's girdle with a sewed-in or detachable crotch made with or without garters and boning

**pantile** \'⸗,⸗\ *n* [¹*pan* + *tile*] **1 a :** a roofing tile whose cross section is a dissymmetrical ogee curve **b :** a longitudinally curved roofing tile laid alternately with convex covering tiles **2 :** a Dutch or Flemish flat paving tile **3 :** SEA BISCUIT, HARDTACK — **pantiled** \'⸗,⸗\ *adj*

pantiles 1 a

**pantiling** \'⸗,⸗\ *n* -S **:** pantile roofing

**pan·tine** \'pantən, -n,tin\ *n* -S [obs. F *pantine* (now *pantin*)] **:** a jointed pasteboard doll representing a well-known living person and carried about for amusement (as by members of the French court) in the 18th century

**pant·ing** \'pantiŋ\ *n* -S [³*pant* + *-ing*] **:** cloth used in making trousers **:** TROUSERING

**pant·ing·ly** *adv* **:** in a panting manner ⟨climbed slowly and ~⟩

**pant·i·soc·ra·cy** \,pantə'säkrəsē, -n,tī'-\ *n* -ES [*pant-* + *isocracy*] **:** a utopian community in which all rule equally

**pant·i·so·cra·tic** \¦pantəsō¦krad·ik, -n,tī¦-\ *or* **pant·i·so·crat·i·cal** \-d·əkəl\ *adj* **:** of, relating to, or favoring pantisocracy

**pant·i·soc·ra·tist** \,pantə'säkrəd·əst, -n,tī'-\ *n* -S **:** an advocate of pantisocracy

**pant·ler** \'pantlə(r)\ *n* -S [ME *pantelere,* alter. (influenced by *buteler, bottelar* butler) of *panter, paneter* panter — more at PANTER] *archaic* **:** a servant or officer in charge of the bread and the pantry in a great family

**pan·to** \'pan(,)tō\ *n* -S [by shortening] *Brit* **:** PANTOMIME 3c

**panto-** — see PANT-

**pan·to·chrome** \'pantə,krōm\ *or* **pan·to·chro·mic** \¦⸗⸗¦krōmik\ *adj* [*pantochrome* back-formation fr. *pantochromism; pantochromic* fr. *pantochromism* + *-ic*] **:** relating to or exhibiting pantochromism

**pan·to·chro·mism** \'⸗⸗,krō,mizəm\ *n* -S [*pant-* + *-chrome* + *-ism*] **:** the property possessed by some salts of occurring in any of several colors — compare CHROMOISOMERISM

**pan·toc·ra·tor** \pan·'täkrəd·ə(r)\ *n* -S *cap* [ML, fr. Gk *pantokratōr,* fr. *pant-* + *kratōr* ruler, fr. *kratein* to rule (fr. *kratos* strength) — more at HARD] **:** the omnipotent lord of the universe **:** almighty ruler — used esp. of Christ ⟨the typical Byzantine icon presents Jesus as the *Pantocrator* . . . on his heavenly throne —F.B.Artz⟩

**pan·to·don** \'pantə,dän\ *n* [NL, fr. *pant-* + *-odon*] **1** *cap* **:** a genus (the type of the family Pantodontidae) of freshwater isospondylous fishes of West Africa consisting of the butterfly fish (*Pantodon buchholzi*) **2** *also* **pan·to·dont** \-änt\ -S **:** BUTTERFLY FISH 1e

**pan·to·dont** \'pantə,dänt\ *n* -S [NL *Pantodonta*] **:** a mammal or fossil of the order Pantodonta

**pan·to·don·ta** \,⸗⸗'däntə\ *n pl, cap* [NL, fr. *pant-* + *-odonta*] **:** a small but widely distributed order of primitive ungulate mammals known from the Paleocene to the Oligocene of No. America, Europe, and Asia

**pan·tofle** *also* **pan·tou·fle** *or* **pan·to·fle** \'pantəfəl, pan-'täfəl, -'tüf-\ *n* -S [ME *pantufle,* fr. MF *pantoufle*] **1 :** a bedroom slipper **2 :** a chopine having front uppers only and a cork sole and used as an overshoe in the 16th century

**¹pan·to·graph** *also* **pan·ta·graph** \'pantə,graf, -răf\ *n* [F *pantographe,* fr. *pant-* + *-graphe* -graph] **1 a :** an instrument for copying (as a map or plan) on any predetermined scale consisting of four light rigid bars adjustably jointed in parallelogram form so that as one tracing point is moved over the outline to be copied the other makes the desired copy **b :** a linkwork of similar construction or a lazy-tongs device used as a reducing motion for an indicator, a parallel motion for a beam engine, or in a similar function **2 :** an electrical trolley carried by a collapsible and adjustable frame

pantograph 1a

**²pantograph** \"\ *vt* **:** to copy with a pantograph ~ *vi* **:** to function by the use of a pantograph

**pan·tog·ra·pher** \pan·'tägrəfə(r)\ *n* -S **:** one that pantographs; *specif* **:** a worker who engraves with a pantograph

**pan·to·graph·ic** \¦pantə¦grafik\ *adj* **:** of, relating to, or by means of a pantograph ⟨~ reductions⟩ — **pan·to·graph·i·cal·ly** \-fək(ə)lē\ *adv*

**pan·to·ic acid** \(')pan·¦tōik-\ *n* [*pant-* (fr. *pantothenic acid*) + *-oic*] **:** an unstable dihydroxy acid $HOCH_2C(CH_3)_2CH(OH)COOH$ that is usu. obtained in the form of salts or its crystalline gamma-lactone and that is a constituent of pantothenic acid and used in its synthesis

**pan·tol·o·gy** \pan·'täləjē\ *n* -ES [NL *pantologia,* fr. *pant-* + *-logia* -logy] **:** a systematic view of all knowledge

**pan·tom·e·ter** \pan·'tämәd·ә(r)\ *n* [F *pantomètre,* fr. *panto-* + *-mètre* -meter] **:** an instrument for measuring all angles (as in determining elevations, distances)

**¹pan·to·mime** \'pantə,mīm, 'paan- *also* -,mēm; ÷ -,mīn\ *n* [L *pantomimus,* fr. Gk *pantomimos* actor, mimic, fr. *pant-* + *mimos* mime — more at MIME] **1 a** *or* **pan·to·mi·mus** \,⸗⸗'mīməs\ *pl* **pantomi·mi** \-ī,mī\ **a :** a solo dancer of imperial Rome acting all the characters of a story (as of tragic love) usu. from myth or history by means of steps, postures, and gestures alone with the help of changes of mask and costume, a chorus singing the narrative usu. in Greek, an orchestra, and sometimes an assistant **b :** a performance featuring such a dancer — compare MIME 3 **2** *archaic* **:** PANTOMIMIST 1 **3 a :** an 18th century French or English ballet modeled on the Roman pantomime with subjects from classical mythology **b :** an 18th century English harlequinade orig. burlesquing the pantomime ballet, performed by dancing comedians, and serving as an interlude or afterpiece **c :** a British theatrical extravaganza of the Christmas season based on a story now usu. adapted from a traditional nursery tale, featuring topical songs, tableaux, dances, and similar entertainments in a blend of broad humor, fantasy, melodrama, sentimentality, and morality, and formerly incorporating a harlequinade introduced by a scene in which the persons of the tale are magically transformed into those of the harlequinade — called also *panto;* see DAME 5, PRINCIPAL BOY **4 :** a sequence of movements or actions not accompanied by speech or seen from beyond earshot ⟨her face enacting a vivid ~ of the criticisms passing in her mind —Thomas Hardy⟩ ⟨she strolled up to him . . . and I saw the ~ of the introduction —Mary Deasy⟩ **5 :** expressive bodily movement in drama or dance: **a :** expressive movements (as of the face, hands) of an actor; *esp* **:** silent acting **b :** movement in a ballet that develops a story and is more realistic and less conventionalized than dance movement **c :** expressive movements made by a ballet dancer except with the legs **6 a :** a dramatic performance using no dialogue **b :** a dance that enacts a story esp. by mimed action **:** a ballet mime **7 a :** the art of expressing the action of a story by simplified, exaggerated, and often conventionally symbolic gestures without words **b :** the genre of theatrical entertainment comprising pantomimes

**²pantomime** \"\ *vt* **:** to represent by pantomime ⟨the Butcher's Dance in which he would ~ the killing and carving of an animal —Phyllis Pearsall⟩ ⟨I *pantomimed* the fact that I'd come a long way —Sally Carrighar⟩ ~ *vi* **:** to engage in pantomime

**pan·to·mim·ic** \¦⸗⸗¦mimik, -mēk\ *or* **pan·to·mime** \'⸗⸗,mīm *also* -,mēm; ÷ -,mīn\ *adj* [*pantomimic* fr. L *pantomimicus,* fr. *pantomimus* pantomime + *-icus* -ic; *pantomime* fr. ¹*pantomime*] **1 :** having the characteristics of or constituting a pantomime ⟨a ~ entertainment⟩ ⟨a ~ dance⟩ **2 :** of or relating to a pantomime **3 :** resembling or suggestive of pantomime ⟨the ~ suddenness of the transformation⟩ **4** *dancing* **:** using realistic or symbolic gestures and body movements to suggest a narrative — **pan·to·mim·i·cal·ly** \-mək(ə)lē\ *adv*

**pan·to·mimist** \'⸗⸗,mīməst, -,mim-\ *n* -S **1 :** an actor of pantomimes or in pantomime **2 :** a composer of pantomimes

**pan·to·mo·rus** \,pantə'mōrəs\ *n, cap* [NL, fr. Gk *pantomōros* gluttonous, lit., all-sluggish, fr. *pant-* + *mōros* dull, sluggish, stupid — more at MORON] **:** a genus of weevils containing several (as the white-fringed beetle) that are important plant pests esp. in the southern U. S.

**pan·tonal** \(')pan+\ *adj* [*pan-* + *tonal*] **:** giving equal importance to each of the 12 semitones of the octave **:** DODECAPHONIC — **pan·to·nal·i·ty** \,pantō'naləd·ē\ *n*

**pan·to·nal·ism** \pan·'tōn³l,izəm\ *n* **:** the quality or state of being pantonal

**pan·toph·a·gous** \(')pan·'täfəgəs\ *adj* [*pant-* + *-phagous*] **:** eating or requiring a variety of foods — distinguished from *polyphagous*

**pan·toph·thal·mi·dae** \,pan,täf'thalmə,dē\ *n pl, cap* [NL, fr. *Pantophthalmus,* type genus (fr. *pant-* + *-ophthalmus*) + *-idae*] **:** a family of two-winged flies including large flies that are restricted to the American tropics and have larvae which bore in solid wood

**pan·top·o·da** \pan·'täpədə\ [NL, fr. *pant-* + *-poda*] *syn of* PYCNOGONIDA

**pan·to·then·ate** \,pantə'the,nāt, pan·'tăthə,-\ *n* -S [*pantothenic* acid + *-ate*] **:** a salt or ester of pantothenic acid

**pan·to·then·ic acid** \¦pantə¦thenik-\ *n* [*pantothenic* fr. Gk *pantothen* from every side (fr. *pant-, pas* all, every) + E *-ic* — more at PAN-] **:** a viscous oily acid $C_8H_{16}NO_5COOH$ that belongs to the vitamin B complex, occurs usu. combined (as in coenzyme A) in all living tissues esp. liver and elsewhere (as in royal jelly, yeast, and molasses), is made synthetically, and is essential for the growth of various animals and microorganisms; the amide of pantoic acid and beta-alanine

**pan·to·there** \'pantə,thi(ə)r\ *n* -S [NL *Pantotheria*] **:** a mammal or fossil of the order Pantotheria

**pan·to·the·ria** \,pantə'thirēə\ *n pl, cap* [NL, fr. *panto-* + *-theria*] **:** an order or other division of generalized mammals widespread during the Jurassic and commonly conceded to be ancestral to the marsupials and placental mammals — **pan·to·the·ri·an** \¦⸗⸗¦thirēən\ *adj or n*

**pantoufle** *var of* PANTOFLE

**pan·toum** \pan·'tüm\ *n* -S [F, fr. Malay *pantun*] **:** a series of quatrains rhyming *abab* in which the second rhyme of a quatrain recurs as the first in the succeeding quatrain, each quatrain introduces a new second rhyme (as *bcbc, cdcd*), and the initial rhyme of the series recurs as the second rhyme of the closing quatrain (*xaxa*)

**pan·to·yl** \'pantəwəl\ *n* -S [*pant-* (in *pantoic acid*) + *-yl*] **:** the acid radical $HOCH_2C(CH_3)_2CH(OH)CO$— of pantoic acid

**¹pan·tropic** \(')pan+\ *also* **pan·tropical** \"+\ *adj* [*pan-* + *tropic* or *tropical*] **:** occurring or distributed throughout the tropical regions of the earth ⟨~ plants and animals⟩

**²pantropic** \"\ *adj* [*pan-* + *-tropic*] **:** affecting various tissues without showing special affinity for one of them — used chiefly of viruses; compare DERMOTROPIC, NEUROTROPIC

**pan·try** \'pan·trē, 'paan-, -ri\ *n* -ES [ME *pantrie, panetrie,* fr. MF *paneterie,* fr. OF, fr. *panetier* pantler + *-erie* -ery — more at PANTER] **1 :** a room or closet adjacent to a kitchen or dining room used for storing provisions or glassware and china or for serving **2 :** a room (as in a hotel, ship, hospital) with refrigerating and other equipment for the preparation of cold foods (as salads, sandwiches, desserts) on order

**pan·try·man** \'⸗⸗mən\ *n, pl* **pantrymen :** a man in charge of or working in a pantry (as in a hotel, ship, hospital)

**pants** \'pants, 'paan-, 'pain-\ *n pl but sometimes sing in constr, often attrib* [short for *pantaloons,* pl. of *pantaloon*] **1** *also* **pant a** (1) **:** PANTALOON 2 (2) **:** TROUSERS, SLACKS **b** *chiefly Brit* **:** men's short underpants **c :** PANTIE **2 pant** *n sing* **:** half or one leg of a pair of pants **3 :** enclosures of streamline shape used to reduce the drag of airplane landing gear — **with one's pants down :** in an embarrassing position (as of being unprepared for an emergency) ⟨caught *with its pants down* by the surprise attack⟩

**pan·tun** *also* **pan·toun** \pan·'tün\ *n* -S [Malay *pantun*] **:** Indonesian verse consisting of four lines rhyming *abab* of which the first two present a figurative suggestion of what is more directly and clearly stated in the final lines

**pan-turanian** \¦pan+\ *adj, usu cap P&T* [*pan-* + *turanian*] **:** of, relating to, or being Pan-Turanianism ⟨opposition to Islam in the *Pan-Turanian* movement —*Mohammedan History*⟩

**pan-turanianism** \"+\ *also* **pan-turanism** \'pan+\ *n, usu cap P&T* [*pan-turanianism* fr. *pan-* + *turanian* + *-ism; pan-turanism* fr. *pan-* + *Turan,* ancient desert and steppe region of Central Asia north of Iran corresponding to the regions around the Jaxartes and Oxus in modern Uzbek and Kazakh Republics of the U. S. S. R. + E *-ism*] **:** a political and cultural movement of the early 20th century having as its principal aim the union of all peoples having a common Turkish heritage

**panty** *var of* PANTIE

**¹pantywaist** \'⸗⸗,⸗\ *n* [*panty* + *waist*] **1 :** a child's garment consisting of short pants buttoned to a waist **2 :** SISSY

**²pantywaist** \"\ *adj* **:** CHILDISH, INFANTILE **:** SISSIFIED ⟨the round robin of abuse which enlivened belles lettres before they went ~ in the twentieth century —Richard Hanser⟩

**pa·ñue·lo** \,pänyə'wā(,)lō\ *n* -S [Sp, dim. of *paño* cloth, fr. L *pannus* — more at VANE] **:** a square cloth folded triangularly and worn in the Philippines like a great ruffle or collar

**panulirus** *n, cap* [NL, anagram of *Palinurus*] **:** a genus of spiny lobsters comprising the American forms of the group — compare PALINURUS

**pa·nung** \'pä,nuŋ\ *n* -S [Thai *phā* cloth + *nŭŋ* one] **:** a Siamese garment for men and women consisting of a cloth about three yards long draped about the body somewhat in the manner of a loincloth

**pan·yan** \'pa,nyan\ *n, pl* **panyan** *or* **panyans** *usu cap* **:** a member of a Veddoid people in southern India

**¹pan·zer** \'panzə(r), 'paan, 'päntsə(r)\ *adj* [G, lit., coat of mail, armor, fr. MHG *panzier,* fr. OF *panciere,* fr. L *pantic-, pantex* paunch — more at PAUNCH] **:** of, consisting of, or carried out by a panzer division or similar German armored unit **:** ARMORED ⟨~ forces⟩ ⟨the importance of ~ thrusts⟩

**²panzer** \"\ *n* -S **:** a vehicle belonging to a panzer division; *esp* **:** TANK — usu. used in pl.

**panzer division** *n* [G *panzerdivision,* fr. ¹*panzer* + *division,* fr. F, fr. MF — more at DIVISION] **:** a mechanized unit of the German army (as in World War II) organized for rapid attack

**¹pan·zo·ot·ic** \¦panzō¦äd·ik\ *adj* [*pan-* + *zo-* + *-otic*] **:** affecting animals of many different species; *also* **:** epizootic over wide areas — compare PANDEMIC

**²panzootic** \"\ *n* -S **:** a panzootic disease

**pao·lo** \'pau̇(,)lō\ *n, pl* **pao·li** \-(,)lē\ [It, after Pope *Paolo* (Paul) III †1549] **:** a small papal silver coin worth $^1/_{10}$ scudo struck under Paul III

**paon** \'päⁿ\ *n* -S [F, fr. L *pavon-, pavo* peacock — more at PEACOCK] **:** PEACOCK 3

**pao·pao** \'pau̇,pau̇\ *n* -S [Samoan] **:** a small Samoan outrigger canoe

**pao·ting** \'bau̇'diŋ\ *adj, usu cap* [fr. *Paoting* (*Tsingyuan*), China] **:** of or from the city of Paoting, China **:** of the kind or style prevalent in Paoting

**¹pap** \'pap\ *n* -S [ME *pappe;* of imit. origin like Sw dial. & Norw dial. *pappe* pap, L *papilla* nipple, Lith *papas,* Skt *pippalakā*] **1** *chiefly dial* **:** NIPPLE, TEAT **2 :** something shaped like a nipple (as one of two or more hills) ⟨the *Paps* of Jura, Scotland⟩

**²pap** \"\ *n* -S [ME *pap, pape,* prob. fr. L (baby talk) *papa, pappa* food, father] **1 a :** a soft pulpy food (as of bread boiled or softened in milk or water) for infants or invalids **b :** any pulpy or semiliquid substance **:** MASH, PASTE **2 :** political patronage ⟨more concerned about giving honest, efficient, and enlightened government than they are about political ~ and boodle —D.E.Chamberlain⟩ **3 a :** simple discourse or esp. moralistic argument suitable for or felt to be suitable only for the minds of infants **b :** something (as reading matter) that serves only to entertain or is not otherwise intellectually stimulating ⟨persuade people to buy our papers with ~, else we cannot pay for the profound —J.S.C.Butz⟩ ⟨mystery novels and general escapist entertainment ~ —John Roeburt⟩

**³pap** \"\ *vt* **papped; papped; papping; paps :** to feed with pap

**⁴pap** \"\ *Scot & Irish var of* POP

**⁵pap** \"\ *n* -S [by shortening] *dial* **:** PAPA

**pap** *abbr* **1** paper **2** papyrus

**¹pa·pa** \'päpə, *in sense 2 "* or pə'pä\ *n* -S [LL (influenced in meaning by LGk *papas, pappas* priest, bishop, pope), fr. Gk (baby talk) *pappa* father, vocative of *papas, pappas*] **1** *usu cap, archaic* **:** the Roman pontiff, bishop of Rome and pope of the Roman Catholic Church **2** [LGk *papas, pappas* (taken as pl.) fr. Gk (baby talk), father] **:** a parish priest of the Eastern Orthodox Church

**²papa** \'päpə, 'pápə, *chiefly Brit* pə'pä\ *n* -S [F, fr. MF; of baby-talk origin like L *papa, pappa* food, father, Gk *papas, pappas* father, *pappos* grandfather] **1 :** FATHER ⟨a promise from ~ to supply more money —A.H.Raskin⟩ **2** *slang* **:** HUSBAND, LOVER

**³papa** *var of* PAPAW

**⁴pa·pa** \'päpə\ *n* -S [AmerSp, fr. Quechua] **:** POTATO

**⁵papa** \"\ *n* -S [Hawaiian, Tahitian, Marquesan, & Maori] **:** a bluish New Zealand clay like indurated pipe clay used for whitening fireplaces

**⁶papa** \"\ *n* -S [Skt *pāpa;* prob. akin to Skt *pāpman* harm, evil — more at PATIENT] *Jainism* **:** EVIL, SIN — compare PUNYA

**⁷papa** *usu cap* — a communications code word for the letter *p*

**pa·pa·bi·le** \pə'päbə,lā\ *adj* [It, fr. *papa* pope (fr. LL) + *-abile* -able] **:** PAPABLE

**pa·pa·ble** \'päpəbəl\ *adj* [MF, prob. fr. It *papabile*] **:** qualified for and considered likely to succeed to the papacy

**pa·pa·botte** *or* **pa·pa·bote** *also* **pa·pa·bot** \,päpə'bōt\ *n* -S [AmerF (Louisiana); prob. of imit. origin] *South* **:** UPLAND PLOVER

**pa·pa·cy** \'pāpəsē, -si\ *n* -ES [ME *papacie,* fr. ML *papatia,* fr. LL *papa* pope + *-atia* (as in LL *abbatia* abbacy) — more at ABBACY] **1 :** the office of pope **:** papal jurisdiction ⟨under control of the ~⟩ ⟨raised to the ~⟩ **2** : a succession of popes : a papal line ⟨the Avignon ~⟩ ⟨the Roman ~⟩ **3** : the period of time during which a pope is in office **4** *usu cap* : the system of government in the Roman Catholic Church of which the pope is the supreme head

**pa·pa·gal·lo** \ˌpäpəˈgī(ˌ)ō\ *n* -s [alter. (prob. influenced by Sp *gallo* cock, fr. L *gallus*) of Sp *papagayo*, lit., parrot; fr. the colored spines of the first dorsal fin that suggest a bird's comb — more at GALLUS] : a large brightly colored food fish (*Nematistius pectoralis*) related to the amberfishes and found from southern California to Peru — called also *roosterfish*

**pa·pa·ga·yo** \ˌpäpəˈgī(ˌ)ō\ *n* -s *often cap* [fr. Gulf of *Papagayo*, northwestern Costa Rica] : a violent often tornadic northerly wind occurring along the Pacific coast of Central America and esp. on the Gulf of Papagayo

**papa·go** \ˈpapəˌgō, ˈpäp-\ *n, pl* **papago** *or* **papagos** *usu cap* **1 a** : a Piman people of southwestern Arizona and northwestern Sonora, Mexico **b** : a member of such people **2** : the language of the Papago people

**papaia** *var of* PAPAYA

**pa·pa·in** \pəˈpāən, -ˈpīən\ *n* -s [ISV *papa-* (fr. *papaya*) + *-in*; orig. formed in G] : a crystallizable proteinase in the juice of the green fruit of the papaya obtained usu. as a brownish powder and used chiefly as a tenderizer for meat, in chillproofing beer, and in medicine as a digestant

**pa·pa·in·ase** \-əˌnās, -āz\ *n* -s [*papain* + *-ase*] : any of several proteinases (as papain, ficin, bromelin) that are found in plants, are activated by reducing agents (as cysteine, glutathione), and are inactivated by oxidizing agents (as hydrogen peroxide, iodine) toward which other proteinases are stable

**pa·pai·pe·ma** \pəˌpīˈpēmə\ *n, cap* [NL, prob. fr. Gk *papai*, exclamation of suffering + *pēma* suffering, calamity — more at PATIENT] : a genus of noctuid moths containing several that are pests on corn and other plants in parts of No. America

**pa·pal** \ˈpāpəl\ *adj* [ME, fr. MF, fr. ML *papalis*, fr. LL *papa* pope + L *-alis* -al] **1** : of or relating to a pope : proceeding from, ordered or uttered by, or subject to a pope ⟨~ edict⟩ **2** : of, supporting, adhering to, or relating to the Roman Catholic Church — **pa·pal·ly** \-pəlē, -li\ *adv*

**papal cross** *n* : a figure of a cross having a long upright shaft and three crossbars with the longest at or somewhat above its middle and the two other successively shorter crossbars above the longest one

**pa·pa·le** \pəˈpä(ˌ)lā\ *n* -s [Hawaiian] *Hawaii* : HAT

**papal infallibility** *n, Roman Catholicism* : the dogma decreed at the Vatican Council, July 18, 1870, that the pope cannot when speaking in his official character of supreme pontiff err in defining a doctrine of Christian faith or rule of morals

papal cross

**pa·pal·ism** \ˈpāpəˌlizəm\ *n* -s **1** : the papal system **2** : advocacy of papal supremacy

**¹pa·pal·ist** \-ˌləst\ *n* -s [F *papaliste*, fr. *papal* + *-iste* -ist] : an adherent of papalism

**²papalist** \"\ *or* **pa·pal·is·tic** \ˌ⸗⸗ˈlistik, -tēk\ *adj* [*papalism* + *-ist* or *-istic*] : of or relating to papalism

**pa·pal·i·ty** \pəˈpalədˌē, pāˈ-\ *n* -ES [ME *papalite*, fr. MF or ML; MF *papalité*, fr. ML *papalitas*, fr. LL *papa* pope + L *-itas* -ity — more at POPE] *archaic* : PAPACY

**pa·pal·ize** \ˈpāpəˌlīz\ *vt* -ED/-ING/-S [*papal* + *-ize*] : to make papal : imbue with papalism ⟨*papalized* sections of the medieval church⟩

**papal knight** *n* : one bearing a title of nobility conferred by the pope in his capacity as temporal sovereign

**pa·pa·loi** \ˌpäpəlˈwä\ *n* -s [Haitian Creole *papalwa*, fr. *papa* father + *lwa* loa] : a male voodoo priest esp. in Haiti — compare MAMALOI

**pa·pa·ni·co·laou test** \ˌpäpəˈnēkəˌlau̇, ˌpapəˈnikəˌlau̇-\ *n, usu cap P* [after George N. *Papanicolaou* b1883 Greco-American medical scientist] : a method for the early detection of cancer consisting of the application of a special staining technique to cells exfoliated from diseased tissue

**pa·par·chi·cal** \(ˈ)pāˈpärkəkəl\ *adj* : of or relating to a paparchy

**pa·par·chy** \ˈpāˌpärkē\ *n* -ES [LL *papa* pope + E *-archy*] : government by a pope

**papas** *pl of* PAPA

**papataci fever** *or* **papatasi fever** *var of* PAPPATACI FEVER

**pa·paver** \pəˈpavə(r), -ˈpāv-\ *n, cap* [NL, fr. L, poppy — more at POPPY] : a genus (the type of the family Papaveraceae) of chiefly bristly hairy herbs or occas. subshrubs with lobed or dissected leaves, long-peduncled often nodding usu. large and showy flowers, and a capsular fruit topped by a radiate disk and dehiscent by pores immediately below — see OPIUM POPPY

**pa·pav·er·a·ce·ae** \pəˌpavəˈrāsēˌē\ *n pl, cap* [NL, fr. *Papaver*, type genus + *-aceae*] : a family of herbs or shrubs (order Rhoeadales) having milky and often colored juice, regular flowers with caducous sepals and hypogynous stamens, and capsular fruit — compare CHELIDONIUM — **pa·pav·er·a·ceous** \⸗ˌ⸗⸗ˈrāshəs\ *adj*

**pa·pav·er·a·les** \⸗ˌ⸗⸗ˈrā(ˌ)lēz\ [NL, fr. *Papaver* + *-ales*] *syn of* RHOEADALES

**pa·pav·er·ine** \⸗ˈ⸗⸗ˌrīn, -ˌrən\ *n* -s [ISV *papaver-* (fr. NL *Papaver*) + *-ine*] : a crystalline alkaloid $C_{20}H_{21}NO_4$ derived from benzyl-isoquinoline that constitutes about one percent of opium, that is made synthetically from vanillin, and that usu. in the form of its hydrochloride is used chiefly as an antispasmodic because of its ability to relax smooth muscle (as in spasm of blood vessels due to blood clot)

**pa·paw** *or* **paw·paw** *n* -s [prob. modif. of Sp *papayo* papaya] **1** \pəˈpȯ, pȯˈpȯ\ : PAPAYA **2** \ˈpä(ˌ)pȯ, ˈpȯ(ˌ)pȯ\ *also* **pa·pa** \"\ **a** : any of several American shrubs or trees of the genus *Asimina*; *specif* : a No. American tree (*Asimina triloba*) with large obovate leaves, lurid purple flowers, and a large edible fruit **b** : the oblong yellowish sweet fruit of the No. American papaw

**papaw family** *n* : CARICACEAE

**pa·paya** *or* **pa·paia** \pəˈpī(y)ə, -ˈpäyə\ *n* -s [Sp, of AmerInd origin; akin to Otomac *papai*, Carib *ababai*] **1** : a tree (*Carica papaya*) native to tropical America and having long-petioled palmately 7-lobed leaves, clusters of dioecious yellow flowers, and large oblong yellow fruit that has a pulpy flesh and thick rind and is eaten raw, boiled as a vegetable, pickled, or preserved **2** : the fruit of the papaya tree — see CARPAINE

**pap·a·ya·ce·ae** \ˌpapəˈyāsēˌē, ˌpaˌpīˈāsēˌē\ [NL, fr. *papaya* (specific epithet of *Carica papaya*) + *-aceae*] *syn of* CARICACEAE

**pa·pay·o·tin** \pəˈpīəd·ən\ *n* -s [*papaya* + *-otin* (as in *picrotin*)] : PAPAIN

**papboat** \ˈ⸗ˌ⸗\ *n* [²*pap* + *boat*] **1** : a boat-shaped dish to hold pap for feeding infants or invalids **2** : a large spiral East Indian marine shell (*Turbinella rapa*)

papboat 1

**¹pape** \ˈpāp\ *Scot var of* POPE

**²pape** \ˈpap\ *n* -s [AmerF (Louisiana), fr. F, pope, fr. LL *papa* — more at POPE] : PAINTED BUNTING

**pa·pe·lon** \ˌpäpəˈlōn\ *n* -s [AmerSp *papelón*, fr. Sp, cardboard, aug. of *papel* paper, fr. Catal *paper*, fr. L *papyrus*; fr. its being hardened in cardboard molds — more at PAPER] : crude brown sugar produced esp. in northern So. America

**pap·e·lon·né** \ˌpapələˈnā\ *adj* [F, fr. OF *papeillone*, fr. *papeillon* butterfly, fr. L *papilion-, papilio* — more at PAVILION] *heraldry* : covered with rows of loops so placed as to suggest the appearance of overlapping scales

**¹pa·per** \ˈpāpə(r)\ *n* -s *often attrib* [ME *papir*, fr. MF *papier*, fr. L *papyrus* paper, papyrus, fr. Gk *papyros* papyrus] **1 a** (1) : a felted sheet of usu. vegetable but sometimes mineral or synthetic fibers laid down on a fine screen from a water suspension (2) : paper in sheets 6/1000 inch or thinner — compare BOARD **b** : a sheet or piece of paper **c** : a paper surface ⟨the mind can never resemble a blank ~ —J.H.Newman⟩ ⟨put pen to ~⟩ **d** : something resembling true paper in form and use or in composition: as (1) : PAPYRUS (2) : PAPIER-MÂCHÉ **2 a** : a piece of paper containing a written or printed statement (as of identity, authority, or ownership) : DOCUMENT, INSTRUMENT — usu. used in pl. whether applying to one or to more than one item ⟨naturalization ~*s*⟩ ⟨officer's ~*s*⟩ ⟨pedigree ~*s*⟩ ⟨were both forced to flee the country, separately and without ~*s* —*Current Biog.*⟩ ⟨this policy, including the endorsements and the attached ~*s* —*Mutual of Omaha*⟩ — compare SHIP'S PAPERS, WORKING PAPERS; FIRST PAPERS, SECOND PAPERS **b** : any piece of paper containing writing or print (as a letter or memorandum) — usu. used in pl. ⟨family ~*s*⟩ ⟨the state ~*s* of a president⟩ **c** : a literary composition esp. of brief, occasional, or fragmentary nature — usu. used in pl. ⟨his collected ~*s* — not all previously printed — are too short to be called essays —*Times Lit. Supp.*⟩ **3 a** : a piece of paper shaped to serve as a receptacle or wrapper (as for tacks) ⟨a ~ of peppermints in her pocket —Flora Thompson⟩ **b** : a card or paper folder to which articles (as needles) are attached ⟨the page he had marked with a ~ of matches —Frederick Buechner⟩ ⟨a ~ of pins⟩ **4 a** : NEWSPAPER ⟨daily ~⟩ ⟨his picture would be in the ~*s* —Mary Austin⟩ ⟨~ carrier⟩ ⟨~ route⟩ ⟨~ stand⟩ **b** : PUBLICATION; *esp* : one resembling a newspaper in format, content, or frequency of publication ⟨church ~⟩ ⟨school ~⟩ ⟨trade ~⟩ **5 a** : negotiable notes ⟨assets of the bank were shot through with bad ~ —W.A. White⟩ ⟨real-estate portfolios were choked with foreclosed ~ —*Fortune*⟩ ⟨long-term ~⟩ ⟨short-term ~⟩ — compare COMMERCIAL PAPER **b** : PAPER MONEY ⟨with a pocketful of ~ to grab rich mineral and timber lands —*Amer. Guide Series: Minn.*⟩ **6** : WALLPAPER ⟨pictorial ~*s* printed from wood blocks were imported —H.S.Morrison⟩ **7** : a piece of written schoolwork: **a** : a written examination — used of either the examiner's questions or the student's answers ⟨candidates may take . . . either (1) a ~ in Latin; or (2) a ~ in Greek —*Edinburgh Univ. Cal.*⟩ **b** : a written assignment done either as an exercise in composition or as a report on an assigned topic ⟨freshman English is a hard course to teach because of the many ~*s* coming in weekly⟩ ⟨our history ~ is due next week⟩ ⟨term ~⟩ — compare ESSAY, THESIS **8 a** : a composition of informational nature (as on a scientific or historical topic) for reading before a group ⟨do a ~ for our reading circle —Agnes S. Turnbull⟩; *also* : its presentation ⟨all of these ~*s* were extremely well attended and received —*Veterinary Record*⟩ **b** : a similar composition written for publication (as in a journal or in the form of a monograph) or circulation **9 a** : TICKETS ⟨the ~ at the box office is all sold —Barnaby Conrad⟩; *esp* : free passes **b** : persons admitted free (as to a theater performance) ⟨most of the first-night audience was ~⟩ ⟨saw at once that the house was filled with ~ —James Joyce⟩ **10** : CURLPAPER — usu. used in pl. **11** *slang* : marked playing cards **12** *slang* : bills, posters, or circulars distributed to advertise something (as an appearance of a traveling show) ⟨the circus fell a couple of days behind its ~⟩ **13** : PAPER WORK ⟨by ~ and red tape —Roy Lewis & Angus Maude⟩ — **off paper** *of a postage stamp* : removed from the cover on which it was used — **on paper** **1** : in writing or print ⟨the act of putting ideas *on paper* seems to distort our perspectives —E.S.McCartney⟩ ⟨get the agreement down *on paper*⟩ **2** : in theory as distinguished from fact, practice, accomplishment, or probable outcome ⟨the plan looks good *on paper*⟩ **3** : in the planning stage ⟨a project that is still *on paper*⟩ ⟨university, which had existed *on paper* for five years —*Amer. Guide Series: Wash.*⟩ **4** : figured at face value : NOMINALLY ⟨*on paper* he was worth nearly $1,000,000 —Gladwin Hill⟩ **5** *of a postage stamp* : remaining on the cover or on a piece of the cover on which it was used

**²paper** \"\ *vt* **papered; papered; papering** \-p(ə)riŋ\ **papers** **1** *archaic* : to put down on paper : make a memorandum of : describe in writing **2** : to fold or inclose in or attach to paper ⟨~ butterflies⟩ ⟨~ pins up⟩ **3** : to affix paper to : cover or line with paper; *esp* : to furnish with wallpaper ⟨~ a room⟩ **4** : SANDPAPER ⟨~ down until only sufficient color is left to lighten the wood —C.H.Hayward⟩ **5** : to supply with an audience augmented by giving out many free tickets ⟨~ a theater for an opening night⟩ **6** : to cover (an area) with advertising bills, posters, or circulars (as for a circus engagement or a boxing match) **7** *slang* : to pass or cover with worthless checks or counterfeit currency ⟨left after ~*ing* the country with bad checks —H.L.Davis⟩ ⟨can get ~*ed* like a circus billboard if you don't know the man you are doing black-market business with —David Dodge⟩ **8** : to gloss over, explain away, or patch up (major differences) so as to provide a semblance of amity or agreement — used esp. in the phrase *paper over the cracks* ⟨the meeting . . . has done little to ~ over the cracks between the member states —*Economist*⟩ ~ *vi* : to hang wallpaper ⟨passion for perpetual painting and ~*ing* —Mary H. Vorse⟩

**³paper** \"\ *adj* **1 a** : made wholly or almost wholly of paper, paperboard, or papier-mâché ⟨~ bag⟩ ⟨~ towel⟩ ⟨~ napkin⟩ ⟨~ mulch⟩ ⟨~ carton⟩ ⟨~ plate⟩ **b** : like paper (as in texture, strength, or thickness) : PAPERY **2 a** : carried on by the exchange of written or printed matter : consisting of written communications or printed matter ⟨~ friendships⟩ ⟨~ wars⟩ ⟨~ bullets⟩ **b** : involving or involved with paper work : CLERICAL, DESK ⟨those ~ procedures by which so much of the business of the Services is transacted —H.W.Dodds⟩ ⟨the fighting navy and the ~ navy —Frederic Wakeman⟩ ⟨the general was transferred to a ~ command⟩ **3 a** : authorized or decreed but not effectively enforced : planned but not put into execution : proffered but not fulfilled : NOMINAL ⟨~ blockade⟩ ⟨~ promises⟩ ⟨the ~ strength of an army⟩ ⟨a project still in the ~ stage⟩ **b** (1) : computed or computable as the result of hypothetical business transactions ⟨~ losses from selling the stocks too soon⟩ (2) : figured on paper without involving actual money or credit transfers ⟨~ surplus⟩ (3) : prospective but unrealized ⟨basing hopes for expansion on ~ profits⟩ **4** : composed largely of persons admitted by free passes ⟨~ audience⟩ ⟨~ house⟩ **5** : issued as paper currency ⟨~ mark⟩ ⟨~ peso⟩ **6** : PAPERBACK ⟨a ~ edition⟩ ⟨~ books⟩ **7** *of thin fabrics* : finished with a crisp smooth surface similar to that of paper ⟨~ taffeta⟩

**¹paperback** \ˈ⸗⸗ˌ⸗\ *n* : a paperback book — called also *paperbook, paperbound, paper-cover, soft-cover*

**²paperback** \ˌ⸗⸗ˈ⸗\ *also* **paperbacked** \ˌ⸗⸗ˈ⸗\ *adj* **1** *of a book* : made without rounding, backing, or rigid boards and usu. trimmed flush : PAPERBOUND, PAPER-COVER, SOFT-COVER ⟨~ mysteries⟩ ⟨~ reprints⟩ **2** : of or relating to paperback books ⟨~ storytelling⟩

**paper-bag bush** *n* [fr. the phrase *paper bag*] : a shrub (*Salazaria mexicana*) of the family Labiatae that occurs in the midwestern and southwestern U. S. and has numerous large inflated papery pods

**paper bail** *n* : ⁸BAIL 1f

**paperbark** \ˈ⸗⸗ˌ⸗\ *also* **paperbark tree** *n* [so called fr. the papery bark that peels off in sheets] : any of several Australian trees of the genera *Callistemon* and *Melaleuca*; *esp* : CAJEPUT

**paperbark maple** *n* : a tree (*Acer griseum*) that is native to China but widely used as an ornamental and that has flaky cinnamon-brown bark and 3-foliolate to 5-foliolate coarsely toothed leaves

**paper birch** *n* : an American birch (*Betula papyrifera*) with peeling white bark often worked into fancy articles (as baskets) — called also *canoe birch*; compare AMERICAN GRAY BIRCH; see TREE illustration

**paperboard** \ˈ⸗⸗ˌ⸗\ *n* : a composition board varying in thickness and rigidity according to the purpose for which it is to be used — compare BOARD 6a, CARDBOARD

**paper boards** *n pl* : a style of binding in which the usual board stiffening has a paper covering

**paper book** *n* **1** : a book prepared in English legal practice containing copies or abstracts of the pleadings and other papers exchanged between the parties and of the facts necessary to a complete understanding of a case **2** : a printed booklet containing a legal brief and the record and filed with an appellate court in connection with an appeal

**paperbook** \ˈ⸗⸗ˌ⸗\ *n* [³*paper* + *book*] : PAPERBACK

**paperbound** \ˈ⸗⸗ˌ⸗\ *adj or n* : PAPERBACK

**paper boy** *n* [by shortening] : NEWSBOY

**paper chase** *n* : the game of hare and hounds when paper is used as scent

**paper chromatography** *n* : chromatography with paper strips or sheets as the adsorbent through which the solution flows by gravity or is sucked up by capillarity — compare CAPILLARY ANALYSIS

**paper clip** *n* **1** : a device consisting of a length of wire bent into flat loops that can be separated by a slight pressure to clasp several sheets of paper together — see CLIP illustration **2** : a spring clamp designed as a clasp for papers

**paper coal** *n* : a variety of lignite splitting into papery layers

**paper-cover** \ˈ⸗⸗ˌ⸗⸗\ *adj or n* : PAPERBACK

**paper currency** *var of* PAPER MONEY

**paper curtain** *n* : an intangible barrier resulting from much red tape ⟨*paper curtain* of passport procedure —*Countryman*⟩

**paper cutter** *n* **1** : PAPER KNIFE **2** : a machine for cutting or trimming sheets of paper to required dimensions

**paper doll** *n* : a paper or cardboard representation of a person usu. in two dimensions for children to play with

**papered** *past of* PAPER

**pa·per·er** \ˈpāp(ə)rə(r)\ *n* -s **1** : one that lines with, wraps in, or fixes on paper **2** : PAPERHANGER

**paper finger** *n* : one of two movable clamps on some typewriters that are used in place of or in addition to the bail to hold paper firmly against the platen

paper cutter 2

**paperflower** \ˈ⸗⸗ˌ⸗\ *n* **1** : STRAWFLOWER **2** : BOUGAINVILLEA **3** : a rounded shrub (*Psilostrophe cooperi*) of the family Compositae native to the deserts of the western U.S. and having conspicuous flowers that turn straw-colored and papery with age

**paper folding** *n* : the art or process of folding squares of colored paper into representative shapes — see ORIGAMI

**paper foot** *n* : a foot (as of a dog) with very thin pads

**paper-footed** \ˈ⸗⸗ˈ⸗⸗\ *adj* : having paper feet ⟨a *paper-footed* dog⟩

**pa·per·ful** \ˈpāpə(r)ˌfu̇l\ *n, pl* **paperfuls** *also* **papersful** \-(r)ˌfu̇lz, -(r)zˌfu̇l\ : as much as will fill a paper ⟨a ~ of pins⟩

**pa·per·gram** \ˈpāpə(r)ˌgram\ *n* [³*paper* + chromato*gram*] : a chromatogram on paper

**paper guide** *n* : a movable attachment on the paper table of a typewriter that can be set at any point to serve as a left-edge guide for inserting paper

**paperhanger** \ˈ⸗⸗ˌ⸗⸗\ *n* **1** : one that hangs paper or fabric covering on interior walls : one that wallpapers **2** *slang* : one who passes worthless checks

**paperhanging** \ˈ⸗⸗ˌ⸗⸗\ *n* **1** *usu* **paper hangings** *pl, archaic* : WALLPAPER **2** : the occupation or work of hanging wallpaper

**paper hornet** *n* [so called fr. the papery nest it builds] : WHITE-FACED HORNET

**paper hunt** *n* : PAPER CHASE

**pa·per·i·ness** \ˈpāp(ə)rēnəs, -rin-\ *n* -ES [*papery* + *-ness*] : the condition of being papery ⟨the whole plant is of a dry ~, like the everlastings —M.B.Eldershaw⟩

**papering** *n* -s [fr. gerund of ²*paper*] **1** : PAPERHANGING 2 **2** : wallpaper esp. when covering a wall or ceiling

**paper joint** *n* : a joint by which built-up woodwork is secured to a faceplate for turning and which consists of a layer of paper glued to the faceplate and to the first course of the work

**paper knife** *n* **1** : a bladed often ornamental instrument (as of brass or ivory) for slitting envelopes or pages of uncut books **2** : the knife of a paper-cutting machine

**paperlike** \ˈ⸗⸗ˌ⸗\ *adj* : like or suggestive of paper (as in thickness, weight, or texture) ⟨~ walls⟩

**paper-mache** \ˌpāpə(r)məˈshā, -ˌmaˈ- *sometimes* -ˌmäˈ-\ *n or adj* [by alter.] : PAPIER-MÂCHÉ

**paper machine** *n* : a synchronized series of mechanical devices that rapidly and continuously transforms a dilute fibrous stock into a dry sheet of paper — see CYLINDER MACHINE, FOURDRINIER

**papermaker** \ˈ⸗⸗ˌ⸗⸗\ *n* : one that makes paper

**papermakers' alum** *n* : ALUMINUM SULFATE

**papermaking** \ˈ⸗⸗ˌ⸗⸗\ *n* : the making of paper

**paper match** *n* : a match having a stem made of paperboard : BOOK MATCH

**paper money** *n* **1** *or* **paper currency** : paper documents that circulate instead of metallic money: as **a** : paper forms issued for the purpose of circulation as money (as government notes and bank notes) **b** : paper instruments (as checks and negotiable drafts) that have the effect of replacing money in circulation **2** : JOSS PAPER

**papermouth** \ˈ⸗⸗ˌ⸗\ *n* [so called fr. the thin membrane of the mouth] : WHITE CRAPPIE

**paper mulberry** *n* [so called fr. the fact that its bark is used in papermaking in China and Japan] : an Asiatic tree (*Broussonetia papyrifera* of the family Moraceae) grown as a shade tree in Europe and America — see TAPA

**pa·pern** \ˈpāpə(r)n\ *adj* [¹*paper* + *-en*] *chiefly dial* : made of paper

**paper nautilus** *n* [so called fr. its delicate white shell] : a cephalopod of the genus *Argonauta*

**paper office** *n, obs* : an office where documents (as state or court papers) are kept or recorded

**paper patent** *n* : a patent for an invention never put into manufacture or commercial use

**paper plant** *or* **paper reed** *or* **paper rush** *n* : PAPYRUS

**paper pulp** *n* : PULP 1c

**paper rate** *n* : a railroad freight rate that is believed to be excessive or is otherwise not likely to promote a substantial or regular movement of the type of traffic to which it applies

**paper red A** *n* : an acid dye — see DYE table I (under *Acid Red 137*)

**paper release lever** *n* : a lever on the carriage of a typewriter that releases the pressure on the feed rolls so that paper may be straightened or removed

**papers** *pl of* PAPER, *pres 3d sing of* PAPER

**paper sailor** *n* : PAPER NAUTILUS

**paper shale** *n* [so called fr. its layers suggesting sheets of paper] : a very thinly laminated shale

**papershell** \ˈ⸗⸗ˌ⸗\ *adj* : PAPER-SHELLED ⟨~ pecan⟩ ⟨~ egg⟩

**paper-shelled** \ˈ⸗⸗ˌ⸗\ *adj* **1** : having a thin fragile shell ⟨*paper-shelled* almond⟩ **2** : recently shed ⟨*paper-shelled* crab⟩ ⟨*paper-shelled* lobster⟩

**paper standard** *n* : a monetary system based on inconvertible paper money as the standard

**paper stock** *n* **1** : any of various plants (as pine, poplar, or grass) from which paper is made **2** : fibrous material (as waste paper and boards) from which paper pulp may be made

**paper table** *n* : a tilted shelf at the back of the platen of a typewriter for supporting the paper

**paper-thin** \ˈ⸗⸗ˈ⸗\ *adj* : so thin as to suggest paper : very thin or narrow ⟨*paper-thin* slices of fat salt pork —Della Lutes⟩ ⟨*paper-thin* partitions of the office —*Bookman*⟩ ⟨won only *paper-thin* control of both houses —M.S.Forbes⟩

**paper tiger** *n* : one that is outwardly powerful or dangerous but inwardly weak or ineffectual ⟨claims that the alliance is only a *paper tiger*⟩

**paper title** *n* : a title to real property appearing on the face of a recorded instrument or of a conveyance or document — used chiefly of a title that is defective

**paper wasp** *n* : a wasp (as the yellow jacket and hornet) that makes a nest of papery material

**paperweight** \ˈ⸗⸗ˌ⸗\ *n* : an object designed to hold down loose papers by its weight

**paper white** *n* : a yellowish gray to white that resembles the white of good paper and is greener and paler than the colors sand or natural

**paper-white narcissus** *also* **paper-white** *n* : a polyanthus narcissus bearing clusters of small very fragrant pure white blossoms

**paper work** *n* : the writing or reviewing of papers (as records, reports, or examinations); *esp* : the procedures necessary in keeping administrative records ⟨the *paper work* involved in running a farm —Christopher Rand⟩ ⟨for meritorious *paper* *work* at the Navy Yard —Alva Johnston⟩ ⟨the predictable timing of his *paper work* —D.R.Morris⟩

**paperworker** \ˈ=,==\ *n* **:** PAPERMAKER

**paper worm** *n* **:** BOOKWORM 1

**pa·pery** \ˈpāp(ə)rē, -ri\ *adj* **:** like paper **:** of the thinness or consistency of paper ⟨a skirling of leaves, ~, ephemeral —Elizabeth Enright⟩ ⟨like ~ silk —*Women's Wear Daily*⟩ ⟨a ~ thirty-second of an inch —*Monsanto Mag.*⟩

**papery leaf spot** *n* **:** a blight and leaf spot of ginseng caused by a fungus (*Alternaria panax*)

**papes** *pl of* PAPE

**pa·pe·terie** \ˈpapə.trē, -ri\ *n* -s [F *papeterie* paper manufacture, stationery case (fr. *papet-* — irreg. fr. *papier* paper — + *-erie* -ery) + E *-s* — more at PAPER] **1 :** writing papers cut to size for use and boxed **2 :** stationery (as note paper, envelopes, and cards) boxed or otherwise packaged and sold as a unit — usu. used in pl.

**¹pa·phi·an** \ˈpāfēən\ *adj, usu cap* [L *paphius* Paphian (fr. Gk *paphios*, fr. *Paphos*, ancient city of Cyprus that was the center of worship of the Greek goddess of love Aphrodite) + E *-an*] **1 a :** of, relating to, or characteristic of Paphos **b :** of, relating to, or characteristic of the people of Paphos **2 :** relating esp. to illicit love **:** WANTON ⟨sail for some vague *Paphian* bourn —Robert Frost⟩

**²paphian** \ˈ"\ *n* -s **1** *cap* **:** a native or inhabitant of Paphos **2** *often cap* **:** PROSTITUTE

**¹paph·la·go·nian** \ˌpaflə¦gōnēən, -nyən\ *n* -s *cap* [L *Paphlagon* (fr. Gk *Paphlagōn*) + E *-ian*] **:** a native or inhabitant of Paphlagonia

**²paphlagonian** \ˈ"\ *adj, usu cap* [L *paphlagonius* Paphlagonian (fr. *Paphlagonia* ancient country in Asia Minor) + E *-an*] **1 :** of, relating to, or characteristic of Paphlagonia **2 :** of, relating to, or characteristic of the people of Paphlagonia

**pa·pia·men·to** \ˌpäpyəˈmen·(ˌ)tō\ *n* -s *usu cap* [Sp, fr. Papiamento *papia* talk (prob. fr. Pg *papear* to chatter, of imit. origin) + *-mento* -ment (fr. Sp, fr. L *-mentum*)] **:** a Spanish-based creole language of Curaçao

**pa·pier col·lé** \ˌpä,pyā,kȯˈlā\ *n, pl* **papiers collés** \-ā(z)\ [F, glued paper] **:** COLLAGE

**¹papier–mâché** *also* **pa·pier ma·che** *or* **papier–maché** \ˌpāpə(r)məˈshā, -ma'- *sometimes* ˌpäp,yā,mäˈshā\ *n* -s [F, lit., chewed paper] **:** a light and strong molding material of high plasticity made typically from wastepaper pulped with glue and other additives

**²papier–mâché** \¦==(ˌ)=¦=, ¦=,=¦=\ *adj* **1 :** formed of papier-mâché usu. with a lacquered or other decorative surface ⟨*papier-mâché* tray⟩ ⟨*papier-mâché* mask⟩ ⟨*papier-mâché* furniture⟩ **2 :** UNREAL, ARTIFICIAL, FALSE ⟨a real human being and not a *papier-mâché* hero —Leo Gershoy⟩ ⟨a *papier-mâché* crisis⟩ ⟨the *papier-mâché* facade of Allied harmony crumbled —J.P.O'Donnell⟩

**pa·pil·io** \pəˈpilē,ō, -il(ˌ)yō\ *n* [NL, fr. L, butterfly — more at PAVILION] **1** *cap* **:** a genus (the type of the family Papilionidae) of lepidopterous insects that as orig. formulated included all the butterflies but is now usu. restricted to the typical swallow-tailed butterflies and a few nearly related forms **2** -s **:** any butterfly of the genus *Papilio*

**pa·pil·i·o·na·ce·ae** \pə,pilēəˈnāsē,ē\ [NL, fr. L *papilion-, papilio* butterfly + NL *-aceae*] *syn of* LEGUMINOSAE

**pa·pil·i·o·na·ceous** \=¦===¦nāshəs\ *adj* [L *papilion-, papilio* + E *-aceous*] **1 :** resembling a butterfly; *specif* **:** irregular and suggestive of a butterfly in shape ⟨the corolla of many leguminous plants is ~⟩ **2** [NL *Papilionaceae* + E *-ous*] **:** of or relating to the family Leguminosae

**¹pa·pil·i·o·nid** \pəˈpilēənəd, -lyə-, -ˌnid\ *adj* [NL *Papilionidae*] **:** of or relating to the Papilionidae

**²papilionid** \ˈ"\ *n* -s [NL *Papilionidae*] **:** a butterfly of the family Papilionidae **:** SWALLOWTAIL

**pa·pil·i·on·i·dae** \pə,pilēˈänə,dē\ *n pl, cap* [NL, fr. *Papilion-, Papilio*, type genus + *-idae*] **:** a large family (superfamily Papilionoidea) of butterflies that have all three pairs of legs well developed in both sexes, larvae usu. with osmeteria, and pupae which are angular and typically attached by the anal end and a median loop of silk

**¹pa·pil·io·noid** \pəˈpilēə,nȯid, -lyə,-\ *adj* [NL *Papilionoidea*] **:** of or relating to the Papilionoidea

**²papilionoid** \ˈ"\ *n* -s [NL *Papilionoidea*] **:** a butterfly of the family Papilionoidea

**pa·pil·i·o·noi·dea** \=,=ēəˈnȯidēə\ *n pl, cap* [NL, fr. *Papilion-, Papilio* + *-oidea*] **:** a superfamily of Lepidoptera including all the typical butterflies — compare HESPERIOIDEA

**papill-** *or* **papillo-** *comb form* [F *papill-*, fr. L *papilla* nipple — more at PAP] **1 :** papilla ⟨*papilli*ferous⟩ ⟨*papilli*form⟩ **2 :** papillary ⟨*papill*edema⟩ ⟨*papill*oma⟩ ⟨*papillo*retinitis⟩ **3 :** papillomatous ⟨*papillo*carcinoma⟩ ⟨*papillo*sarcoma⟩

**pa·pil·la** \pəˈpilə\ *n, pl* **papil·lae** \-i,lē, -,lī\ [L] **1** *obs* **:** the nipple of the breast **2** [NL, fr. L, nipple] **:** a small projecting body part similar to a nipple in form: **a :** a vascular process of connective tissue extending into and nourishing the root of a hair, feather, or developing tooth **b :** one of the vascular protuberances of the dermal layer of the skin extending into the epidermal layer and often containing tactile corpuscles **c :** the apex of a Malpighian pyramid of the kidney **d :** one of the small protuberances on the upper surface of the tongue — see CIRCUMVALLATE PAPILLA, FILIFORM PAPILLA, FUNGIFORM PAPILLA

**papilla of va·ter** \-ˈfät·ə(r), -fāt-\ *usu cap V* [after Abraham *Vater* †1751, Ger. anatomist] **:** AMPULLA OF VATER

**pap·il·lar** \ˈpapələ(r), pəˈpil-\ *adj* [ISV *papill-* + *-ar*] **:** PAPILLARY

**pap·il·lary** \ˈpapə,lerē, pəˈpilərē, -ri\ *adj* [F *papillaire*, fr. *papille* nipple, papilla (fr. L *papilla* nipple) + *-aire* -ary] **:** of, relating to, or resembling a papilla **:** PAPILLOSE

**papillary carcinoma** *or* **papillary cancer** *n* **:** a carcinoma characterized by a papillary structure

**papillary layer** *n* **:** the superficial layer of the derma raised into papillae fitting in corresponding depressions on the inner surface of the epidermis

**papillary muscle** *n* **:** one of the small muscular columns attached at one end to the chordae tendineae and at the other to the wall of the ventricle and that maintain tension on the chordae as the ventricle contracts

**pap·il·late** \ˈpapə,lāt, pəˈpilət, *usu* -d+V\ *or* **pap·il·lat·ed** \ˈpapə,lād·əd\ *adj* [*papillate* fr. NL *papillatus*, fr. LL, shaped like a bud, fr. L *papilla* nipple, bud + *-atus* -ate; *papillated* fr. NL *papillatus* + E *-ed*] **1 :** covered with or bearing papillae **2 :** resembling a papilla

**pap·il·lec·to·my** \ˌpapəˈlektəmē, -mi\ *n* -ES [*papill-* + *-ectomy*] **:** the surgical removal of a papilla

**pap·il·ledema** *also* **pap·il·loedema** \ˌpapəl+\ *n* [NL, fr. *papill-* + *edema*] **:** CHOKED DISK

**pap·il·lif·er·ous** \ˌpapə¦lif(ə)rəs\ *adj* [NL *papillifer* (fr. *papill-* + L *-ifer*) + E *-ous*] **:** bearing papillae

**pa·pil·li·form** \pəˈpilə,fȯrm\ *adj* [prob. fr. (assumed) NL *papilliformis*, fr. *papill-* + L *-iformis*] **:** resembling a papilla

**pap·il·li·tis** \ˌpapəˈlīd·əs\ *n* -ES [NL, fr. *papill-* + *-itis*] **:** inflammation of a papilla: **a :** inflammation of the optic disk **b :** inflammation of a renal papilla

**pap·il·lo·ma** \ˌpapəˈlōmə\ *n, pl* **papillo·mas** \-məz\ *or* **papilloma·ta** \-məd·ə, -mətə\ [NL, fr. *papill-* + *-oma*] **1 :** a benign tumor (as a wart or condyloma) resulting from an overgrowth of epithelial tissue on papillae of vascularized connective tissue of skin and other organs that forms projections or ridges **2 :** an epithelial tumor caused by a virus — see PAPILLOMATOSIS

**pap·il·lo·ma·to·sis** \ˌ==,=mə'tōsəs\ *n, pl* **papillomato·ses** \-,sēz\ [NL, fr. *papillomat-, papilloma* + *-osis*] **1 :** a condition marked by the presence of numerous papillomas **2 :** a virus disease of various domestic and wild animals characterized by widespread development of warty tumors esp. on the skin or in the mouth ⟨~ of rabbits⟩

**pap·il·loma·tous** \ˌpapə¦lämədəs, -lōm-, -mətəs\ *adj* [NL *papillomat-, papilloma* + E *-ous*] **1 :** like or being a papilloma **2 :** marked by papillomas **:** having papillomas as a typical symptom

**pa·pil·lon** \¦päpē¦(y)ōⁿ\ *n* [F, lit., butterfly, fr. L *papilion-, papilio*; fr. the shape of its ears — more at PAVILION] **1** *usu cap* **:** a breed of small slender toy spaniels resembling long-haired Chihuahuas, having large usu. obliquely erect ears, and varying in color from brown to white with black spots **2** -s *often cap* **:** any dog of the Papillon breed

**pap·il·lose** \ˈpapə,lōs\ *adj* [prob. fr. (assumed) NL *papillosus*, fr. *papill-* + L *-osus* -ose] **:** PAPILLATE — **pap·il·los·i·ty** \ˌ==ˈläsəd·ē\ *n* -ES

**pap·il·lote** \ˈpapə,lōt\ *n* -s [F, fr. *papillon* butterfly] **1 :** CURLPAPER **2 :** a greased paper wrapper in which food is cooked and served

**pa·pil·lule** \pəˈpil(ˌ)yül\ *n* -s [NL *papillula*, fr. *papill-* + L *-ula* -ule] **:** a small papilla

**pa·pin·go** \ˈpäpən,gō\ *Scot var of* POPINJAY

**¹pa·pio** \ˈpāpē,ō\ *n, cap* [NL, fr. ML, baboon, prob. of baby-talk origin like L *papa, pappa* food, father — more at PAPA] **:** a genus consisting of the typical baboons

**²pa·pio** \ˈpä(ˌ)pyō\ *also* **pa·pio·pio** \ˈpäpyō,pyō\ *n, pl* **papio** *or* **papios** [Hawaiian] *Hawaii* **:** a young ulua

**pa·pi·on** \ˈpāpē,än\ *n* -s [ME *papioun*, fr. MF *papion*, fr. ML *papion-, papio*] **:** any of several baboons (esp. *Papio sphinx*) of West Africa

**¹pa·pish** \ˈpāpish, -pēsh\ *adj* [¹*pape* + *-ish*] *dial chiefly Brit* **:** PAPISTIC

**²papish** \ˈ"\ *n* -ES *often cap, dial chiefly Brit* **:** PAPIST

**pa·pism** \-,pizəm\ *n* -s [MF *papisme*, fr. *pape* pope (fr. LL *papa*) + *-isme* -ism — more at POPE] **:** authoritarian government by the Roman pope **:** ROMAN CATHOLICISM — usu. used disparagingly

**pa·pist** \-,pəst\ *n* -s *often cap* [MF or NL; MF *papiste*, fr. *pape* pope + *-iste* -ist; NL *papista*, fr. LL *papa* pope + L *-ista* -ist] **:** a Roman Catholic who is a partisan of the pope — usu. used disparagingly

**pa·pis·tic** \pəˈpistik, -tēk\ *or* **pa·pis·ti·cal** \-tәkəl, -tēk-\ *adj* [*papistic* prob. fr. MF *papistique*, fr. *papiste* + *-ique* -ic; *papistical* prob. fr. MF *papistique* + E *-al*] **:** of or relating to the Roman Catholic Church and its doctrines, ceremonies, or government — usu. used disparagingly — **pa·pis·ti·cal·ly** \-tək(ə)lē, -tēk-, -li\ *adv*

**pa·pist·ry** \ˈpāpəstrē, -tri\ *n* -ES [*papist* + *-ry*] **:** ROMAN CATHOLICISM — usu. used disparagingly

**pa·pize** \ˈpā,pīz\ *vb* -ED/-ING/-S [¹*papa* + *-ize*] *vt, archaic* **:** PAPALIZE ~ *vi* **1** *archaic* **:** to assume authority like a pope **2** *archaic* **:** to conform to the position of the pope or the papacy

**pa·poose** *also* **pap·poose** \paˈpüs, pəˈ-\ *n* -s [Narraganset *papoos* child, lit., very small, very young] **:** a young child of No. American Indian parents

**papoose board** *n* **:** CRADLEBOARD

**papooseroot** \=ˈ=,=\ *n* [*papoose* + *root*] **:** BLUE COHOSH

**pa·poosh** \pəˈpüsh, päˈ-\ *n* -ES [earlier *papouch*, fr. F, fr. Per *pāpūsh*] **:** BABOUCHE

**pa·pou·la** \pəˈpōlə\ *n* -s [Pg, poppy, kenaf, modif., of Ar dial. (Spain) *habapaura* poppy, modif. (influenced by Ar *ḥabba* grain, seed) of L *papaver* poppy — more at POPPY] **:** KENAF

**pap·pa·ta·ci fever** *also* **pa·pa·ta·ci fever** \ˌpäpə¦tächē-\ *or* **pa·pa·ta·si fever** \-täsē-\ *n* [It *pappataci* sand fly (*Phlebotomus papatasii*), lit., silent eater, fr. *pappare* to eat (fr. L *pappare, papare*, fr. *pappa, papa* food) + *-taci* (fr. *tacito* — past part. of *tacere* to be silent —, fr. L *tacitus*, past part. of *tacēre* to be silent) — more at PAPA, TACIT] **:** PHLEBOTOMUS FEVER

**pap·pea** \ˈpapēə\ *n, cap* [NL, fr. Karl W. L. *Pappe*, 19th cent. Ger. botanist] **:** a genus of southern African trees (family Sapindaceae) with regular flowers in panicled racemes and red sometimes edible fruit — see WILD PRUNE

**papped** *past of* PAP

**papping** *pres part of* PAP

**pap·pose** \ˈpa,pōs\ *also* **pap·pous** \-pəs\ *adj* [L *pappus* + E *-ose* or *-ous*] **:** furnished with a pappus **:** of the nature of a pappus

**pap·pus** \ˈpapəs\ *n, pl* **pap·pi** \-,pī\ [L, fr. Gk *pappos* grandfather, old man, pappus, down of the chin — more at PAPA] **1 a :** an appendage or tuft of appendages crowning the ovary or fruit in various seed plants (as composites), being adapted for dispersal of the fruit by wind or other agencies, and consisting of all or part of the perianth modified into bristles, scales, awns, or short teeth **b :** the group of bristles formed around the fruit by the calyx of members of the Dipsacaceae, Valerianaceae, and Calyceraceae **2** [NL, fr. Gk *pappos*] **:** DOWN; *esp* **:** the early growth of the beard

**¹pap·py** \ˈpapē, -pi\ *adj* -ER/-EST [²*pap* + *-y*] **:** consisting of pap **:** like pap **:** PULPY, SOFT, SUCCULENT ⟨like corn in a wet harvest — full, but ~, no good —D.H.Lawrence⟩

**²pappy** \ˈ"\ *n* -ES [²*papa* + *-y* (dim. suffix)] *chiefly South & Midland* **:** PAPA

**pa·preg** \ˈpā,preg\ *n* -s [*paper* + *impregnated*] **:** a material of high tensile strength composed of sheets of resin-impregnated paper bonded together by heat and pressure

**pa·pri·ka** \pəˈprēkə, paˈ-, pä'-, pā'- *sometimes* -ˈprikə *or* ˈpaprəkə *or* ˈpaprēkə *or* ˈpäp- *or* ˈpāp-\ *n* -s [Hung, fr. Serb, fr. *papar* pepper, fr. Gk *peperi* — more at PEPPER] **1 :** a condiment consisting of the dried finely ground pods of various cultivated sweet peppers (as the pimientos) — see HUNGARIAN PAPRIKA, KING'S PAPRIKA, SPANISH PAPRIKA **2 :** a sweet pepper that is used for or is suitable for making paprika **3 :** a strong reddish orange that is yellower and slightly darker than poppy, redder and deeper than fire red or scarlet vermilion, and redder and deeper than average coral red

**paps** *pl of* PAP, *pres 3d sing of* PAP

**pap·ua mace** \ˈpapyəwə-\ *n, usu cap P* [fr. *Papua* (New Guinea)] **:** MACASSAR MACE

**¹pap·u·an** \-wən\ *adj, usu cap* [*Papua* (New Guinea), island of the Malay Archipelago, Pacific ocean, and Territory of *Papua*, southeastern New Guinea (fr. Malay *pĕpuah* frizzled) + E *-an*] **1 a** (1) **:** of, relating to, or characteristic of the island of Papua (2) **:** of, relating to, or characteristic of the people of the island of Papua **b** (1) **:** of, relating to, or characteristic of the Territory of Papua (2) **:** of, relating to, or characteristic of the people of the Territory of Papua **2 :** of, relating to, or characteristic of the Negroid native peoples of New Guinea and adjacent areas of Melanesia **3 :** of, relating to, or characteristic of the Papuan languages **4 :** of, relating to, or being a subregion of the Australian biogeographic region that includes New Guinea and the Pacific islands to Wallace's line sometimes with the exception of Celebes

**²papuan** \ˈ"\ *n* -s *cap* [*Papua* and Territory of *Papua* + E *-an*] **1 a :** a native or inhabitant of the island of Papua **b :** a native or inhabitant of the Territory of Papua **2 :** a member of any of the negroid native peoples of New Guinea and adjacent areas of Melanesia; *specif* **:** a fuzzy-haired prominent-nosed nonpygmy Oceanic Negroid of New Guinea **3 :** the Papuan languages; *also* **:** any of this group of languages

**papuan languages** *n pl, usu cap P* **:** a heterogeneous group of languages spoken in New Guinea, New Britain, and the Solomon islands that do not belong to the Austronesian family and are not yet capable of classification

**papua nutmeg** *n, usu cap P* [fr. *Papua* (New Guinea)] **:** MACASSAR NUTMEG

**pap·u·la** \ˈpapyələ\ *n, pl* **papu·lae** \-,lē, -lī\ [in sense 1, fr. L; in other senses, fr. NL, fr. L, pimple] **1 :** PAPULE **2 :** a small papilla **3 :** a dermal branchia of an echinoderm

**pap·u·lar** \-lə(r)\ *adj* [L *papula* + E *-ar*] **:** consisting of or characterized by papules

**pap·u·lat·ed** \ˈpapyə,lād·əd\ *adj* [LL *papulatus* (past. part. of *papulare* to produce pimples, fr. L *papula* pimple) + E *-ed*] **:** covered with papules

**pap·u·la·tion** \ˌ==ˈlāshən\ *n* -s [LL *papulatus* + E *-ion*] **1 :** a stage in some eruptive conditions marked by the formation of papules **2 :** the formation of papules

**pap·ule** \ˈpap(ˌ)yül\ *n* -s [L *papula* pimple; akin to L *papilla* nipple — more at PAP] **:** a small solid usu. conical elevation of the skin caused by inflammation, accumulated secretion, or hypertrophy of tissue elements **:** PIMPLE

**pap·u·lif·er·ous** \ˌpapyə¦lif(ə)rəs\ *adj* [*papule* + *-iferous*] **:** having papules **:** PIMPLY

**papulo-** *comb form* [NL, fr. L *papula*] **1 :** papula ⟨*papulo*-pustular⟩ **2 :** papulous and ⟨*papulo*squamous⟩ ⟨*papulo*vesicular⟩

**pap·u·lo·necrotic** \¦papyəlō+\ *adj* [ISV *papulo-* + *necrotic*] **:** marked by the formation of papules that tend to break down and form open sores ⟨~ tuberculids⟩

**pap·u·lose** \ˈpapyə,lōs\ *adj* [NL *papulosus*, fr. L *papula* pimple + *-osus* -ose] **:** covered with papulae

**pap·u·lous** \-ləs\ *adj* [NL *papulosus*] **1 :** PAPULOSE **2 :** having papulae as a characteristic lesion ⟨a ~ eruption⟩

**pap·y·ra·ceous** \¦papə¦rāshəs\ *adj* [L *papyraceus* made of paper, fr. *papyrus* paper + *-aceus* -aceous] **:** resembling papyrus **:** PAPERY

**pap·y·rin** \ˈpapərən\ *or* **pap·y·rine** \-rən, -,rīn\ *n* -s [F *papyrin*, fr. L *papyrus* + F *-in*] **:** VEGETABLE PARCHMENT

**papyro-** *comb form* [Gk, fr. *papyros* papyrus] **1 :** papyrus ⟨*papyro*logy⟩ **2 :** paper ⟨*papyro*graph⟩

**pa·py·ro·logical** \pə¦pīrə,pə¦pirə+\ *adj* **:** of or relating to papyrology

**pap·y·rol·o·gist** \ˌpapəˈräləjəst\ *n* -s **:** a specialist in papyrology

**pap·y·rol·o·gy** \-jē, -ji\ *n* -ES [ISV *papyro-* + *-logy*] **:** the study of papyrus manuscripts

**pa·py·rus** \pəˈpīrəs, ÷ ˈpapər-, ÷ ˈpapēr-\ *n, pl* **papyrus·es** \-səz\ *or* **papy·ri** \=ˈ=(ˌ)rē, -,rī; ˈ==,rē, -,rī\ *often attrib* [ME *papirus*, fr. ML, fr. L *papyrus* — more at PAPER] **1 :** a tall sedge (*Cyperus papyrus*) of the Nile valley having a smooth triangular stem, a large compound umbel with drooping rays, and fiber that served many uses in historic times — called also *paper reed, paper rush* **2 a :** the pith of the papyrus plant **b :** a substance prepared from the pith of the papyrus plant by cutting it in longitudinal strips, arranging them crosswise in two or three layers, soaking them in water, and pressing them into a homogeneous surface and used by the ancient Egyptians, Greeks, and Romans as a writing material esp. between the 4th century B.C. and the 4th century A.D. **c :** a sheet or roll of this material **3 a :** a writing on papyrus **b :** a written scroll made of papyrus

**papyrus capital** *n* **:** an Egyptian capital resembling a bundle of papyrus buds

**papyrus column** *n* **:** an Egyptian column resembling a bundle of papyrus stalks

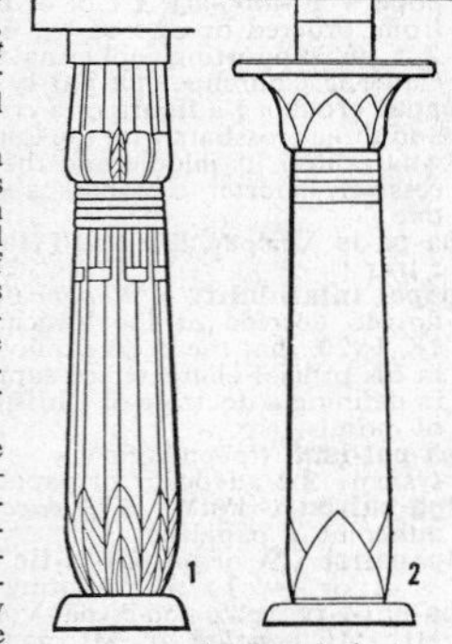

papyrus columns: *1* cluster bud, *2* flower

**paque·bot cover** \ˈpak(ə)-,bō(t)-\ *n* [*paquebot* fr. F, packet boat, fr. E *packet boat*] **:** a philatelic cover bearing a paquebot mail cancellation

**paquebot mail** *n* **:** mail to a U. S. address that originates on or is carried by a foreign ship outside of regular postal service and that on arrival of the ship in a U. S. port is transmitted by private messenger to the post office where it is canceled and forwarded through the regular mails

**¹par** \ˈpär, ˈpä(r\ *n* -s [L, one that is equal, fr. *par* equal — more at PAIR] **1 a :** the established value of the monetary unit of one country expressed in terms of the monetary unit of another country using the same metal as the standard of value and determined solely on the basis of the relative amounts of precious metal contained in the standard monetary units of the two countries — called also *mint par of exchange;* compare PURCHASING POWER PARITY **b** (1) **:** the nominal value of securities or certificates of value ⟨~ value for bonds in the U. S. is usually $1000⟩ ⟨a security is at ~ when the market price equals the ~ value⟩ — called also *face par, nominal par* (2) **:** the value or price at which securities or certificates of value are issued — compare NO-PAR **2 :** equality as to value, condition, or circumstances **:** common level — usu. used with *on* or *upon* ⟨had come out of the war on a ~ with the defeated nations —Osbert Sitwell⟩ ⟨his victories in statecraft and diplomacy were never on a ~ with his soaring ambitions —A.C.Cole⟩ ⟨I and my contemporary bards are by no means upon a ~ —William Cowper⟩ **3 a :** an amount that is taken as an average or mean **b :** a particular value or price taken as the par **c :** an accepted standard or normal level **:** AVERAGE, NORM ⟨novels below ~⟩ ⟨a portrait below ~⟩ ⟨bring a gauge reading up to ~⟩ ⟨keep one's appearance up to ~⟩; *specif* **:** such a level of physical condition or health ⟨not feeling up to ~⟩ **4 :** the score standard set for each hole of a golf course on the basis of the length of the hole allowing two putts for each green; *also* **:** a score equal to par **syn** see AVERAGE

**²par** \ˈ"\ *adj* **:** of or relating to par or a normal level **:** AVERAGE ⟨the acting is only ~ —Kappo Phelan⟩

**³par** \ˈ"\ *vt* **parred; parred; parring; pars 1 :** to put on a par **2 :** to make a golf score on (a hole) equal to par

**⁴par** \ˈ"\ *n* -s [by shortening] *Brit* **:** PARAGRAPH ⟨writing . . . fashionable ~s for the Belfast papers —Osbert Sitwell⟩

**par** *abbr* **1** paragraph **2** parallax **3** parallel **4** parenthesis **5** parish

**¹pa·ra** \ˈpärə\ *n* -s [Turk, fr. Per *pārah*, lit., piece] **1 a :** a Turkish monetary unit equal in modern Turkey to ¹⁄₄₀₀₀ of a lira **b :** a small orig. silver coin representing one para unit **2 a :** any one of several units of value formerly used in countries that at one time under the Turkish Empire (as in Serbia ¹⁄₁₀₀ dinar and in Montenegro ¹⁄₁₀₀ perper); *also* **:** one of the corresponding coins **b** [Serbo-Croatian, fr. Turk] **:** a Yugoslav unit of value equal to ¹⁄₁₀₀ of a dinar — see MONEY table

**²pará** \pəˈrä, *attributively as in "Para rubber" often* ˈpærə\ *adj, usu cap* [fr. *Pará* (Belém), Brazil] **:** BELÉM

**³para** \pəˈrä\ *n* -s *usu cap* **:** PARA RUBBER

**⁴para** \ˈparə, ˈpärə\ *n* -s [native name in India] **:** HOG DEER

**⁵para** \ˈparə\ *n, pl* **par·as** *or* **par·ae** \-,rē\ [*-para*] **:** a woman delivered of a specified number of children — used in combination with a term or figure to indicate the number ⟨a 36-year-old *para* 5⟩; compare GRAVIDA

**⁶para** \ˈ"\ *adj* [¹*para-*] **1 :** relating to, characterized by, or being two positions in the benzene ring that are separated by two carbon atoms — compare PARA- 2b **2 :** of, relating to, or being a diatomic molecule (as of hydrogen) in which the nuclei of the atoms are spinning in opposite directions — opposed to *ortho* ⟨ortho-*para* conversion⟩

**¹para-** *or* **par-** *prefix* [ME, fr. MF, fr. L, fr. Gk, fr. *para;* akin to Gk *pro* before, ahead — more at FOR] **1 a :** beside **:** alongside of ⟨*para*central⟩ ⟨*para*biosis⟩ ⟨*para*synapsis⟩ **b :** parallel ⟨*para*heliotropism⟩ **c :** parasitic ⟨*para*zoon⟩ **d :** associated in a subsidiary or accessory capacity ⟨*para*military⟩ **e :** closely resembling the true form **:** almost — esp. in names of diseases ⟨*para*typhoid⟩ **2 a :** isomeric with, polymeric with, or otherwise closely related to ⟨*par*aldehyde⟩ ⟨*para*casein⟩ ⟨*para*periodic acid⟩ — compare META- 4a **b** (1) **:** the relation of two opposite positions in the benzene ring that are separated by two carbon atoms (2) *para-, usu ital* **:** a derivative in which two substituting groups occupy such positions — abbr. *p-* ⟨*para*-xylene or *p*-xylene is 1,4-dimethyl-benzene⟩; compare META- 4b, ORTH- 3b **3 :** beyond **:** outside of ⟨*par*enteral⟩ **4 a :** faulty, irregular, or disordered condition **:** abnormal ⟨*par*alexia⟩ ⟨*para*noia⟩ ⟨*para*phrenia⟩ **b :** perversion ⟨*para*bulia⟩ ⟨*para*canthosis⟩ **c :** abortive ⟨*para*carpium⟩ ⟨*para*style⟩ **5 :** derived from an original sediment — in the name of a metamorphic rock ⟨*para*gneiss⟩; compare ORTH-

**²para-** *comb form* [*parachute*] **1 :** specially trained or equipped for descent by parachute from airplanes ⟨*para*bomb⟩ ⟨*para*marine⟩ ⟨*para*trooper⟩ **2 :** of, by, or in defense against armed parachutists ⟨*para*spotter⟩

**-pa·ra** \-pərə\ *n comb form, pl* **-paras** \-rəz\ *or* **-pa·rae** \-,rē, -,rī\ [L, fr. *parere* to bring forth, bear (young) — more at PARE] **1 :** woman that has been delivered of (a specified number of) children ⟨nulli*para*⟩ **2 :** female that produces (a specified kind or number of) eggs or gives birth to (a specified kind or number of) young ⟨gyno*para*⟩ ⟨multi*para*⟩

**para** *abbr* paragraph

**para–aminobenzoic acid** \¦parə+. . .-\ *n* [ISV ¹*para-* + *aminobenzoic*] **:** AMINOBENZOIC ACID a — written systematically with ital. *para-* or *p-*

**para–aminohippuric acid** \¦parə+. . .-\ *n* [¹*para-* + *amin-*

+ *hippuric*] **:** a crystalline acid $H_2NC_6H_4CONHCH_2COOH$ used chiefly in the form of its sodium salt in testing kidney function — written systematically with ital. *para-* or *p-*

**para-aminophenol** \ˌparə+\ *also* **par-aminophenol** \ˌpar+\ *n* [¹*para-* + *aminophenol*] **:** the para isomer of aminophenol — written systematically with ital. *para-* or *p-*

**para-aminosalicylic acid** \ˌparə+. . .-\ *n* [ISV ¹*para-* + *aminosalicylic*] **:** the para isomer of aminosalicylic acid — written systematically with ital. *para-* or *p-*

**para-analgesia** \ˌparə+\ *n* [NL, fr. ¹*para-* + *analgesia*] **:** analgesia of the lower part of the body

**para-anesthesia** \"+\ *n* [NL, fr. ¹*para-* + *anesthesia*] **:** anesthesia of both sides of the lower part of the body

**par·a·ban·ic acid** \ˌparəˌbanik-\ *n* [part trans. of G *parabansäure*, fr. *paraban-* (fr. Gk *parabainein* to pass over, fr. *para-* ¹para- + *bainein* to go) + *säure* acid — more at COME] **:** a crystalline nitrogenous cyclic diacid $C_3H_2N_2O_3$ made esp. by oxidation of uric acid; imidazole-trione — called also *oxalylurea*

**para·basal body** \ˌparə+. . .-\ *also* **parabasal** *n* [ISV ¹*para-* + *basal*] **:** a cytoplasmic body closely associated with the kinetoplast of certain flagellates

**par·a·ba·sic** \ˌparəˌbāsik\ *adj* [*parabasis* + *-ic*] **:** of or relating to parabasis

**pa·rab·a·sis** \pəˈrabəsəs\ *n, pl* **paraba·ses** \-əˌsēz\ [Gk, fr. *parabainein* to go aside, step forward, fr. *para-* ¹para- + *bainein* to walk, step, go — more at COME] **:** an important choral ode in the Old Greek comedy mainly in anapestic tetrameters delivered by the chorus at an intermission in the action while facing and moving toward the audience

**para·be·ma** \ˌparəˌbēmə\ *n, pl* **parabema·ta** \-məd·ə\ [NGk *parabēma*, fr. Gk *para-* ¹para- + LGk *bēma* bema — more at BEMA] **1 :** PROTHESIS **2 :** DIACONICON

**para-benzoquinone** \ˌparə+\ *n* [¹*para-* + *benzoquinone*] **:** QUINONE 1a — written systematically with ital. *para-* or *p-*

**para·bi·ont** \ˌparəˌbīˌänt\ *n* -s [ISV ¹*para-* + *-biont* (modif. of Gk *biount-, biōn*, pres. part. of *bioun* to live — more at -BIONT)] **:** either of the organisms joined in parabiosis

**para·biosis** \ˌparə+\ *n, pl* **parabioses** [NL, fr. ¹*para-* + *biosis*] **1 a :** reversible suspension of obvious vital activities (as by suitable drying of a rotifer) **b :** the temporary suppression of excitability in a nerve **2 :** the anatomical and physiological union of two organisms either natural (as in Siamese twins) or artificially produced **3 :** a condition in which members of two or more species live close to one another without conflict although maintaining separate colonies — used esp. of ants

**para·biotic** \"+\ *adj* **:** of, relating to, or marked by parabiosis ⟨~ twins⟩ — **para·biotically** \"+\ *adv*

**para·blast** \ˈparəˌblast\ *n* [¹*para-* + *-blast*] **1 :** the yolk of a meroblastic ovum **2 :** MESOBLAST; *esp* **:** the part of the mesoblast giving rise to vascular structures **3 :** blastomeres that give rise to extraembryonic membranes — **para·blas·tic** \ˌparəˌblastik\ *adj*

¹**par·a·ble** \ˈparəbəl *also* ˈper-\ *n* -s [ME, fr. MF *parable, parabole*, fr. LL *parabola*, fr. Gk *parabolē* juxtaposition, comparison, parable, superposition (in geometry), parabola, fr. *paraballein* to throw or set alongside, compare, superpose (in geometry), fr. *para-* ¹para- + *ballein* to throw — more at DEVIL] **:** COMPARISON, SIMILITUDE; *specif* **:** a usu. short fictitious story that illustrates a moral attitude or a religious principle ⟨relating the ~ of the prodigal son⟩ **syn** see ALLEGORY

²**parable** *adj* [L *parabilis*, fr. *parare* to get ready, prepare + *-abilis*, -able — more at PARE] *obs* **:** PROCURABLE

**para·blep·sia** \ˌparəˈblepsēə\ *also* **para·blep·sis** \-epsəs\ *or* **para·blep·sy** \-epsē\ *n, pl* **parablepsi·as** \-psēəz\ *or* **parablep·ses** \ˌ==ˈblep(ˌ)sēz\ *or* **parablep·sies** \ˈ==ˌblep sēz\ [NL *parablepsia* (fr. ¹*para-* + Gk *blepsis* sight — fr. *blepein* to see + *-sis* — + L *-ia* -y) & *parablepsis*, fr. ¹*para-* + Gk *blepsis*] **:** false or distorted vision

**pa·rab·o·la** \pəˈrabələ\ *n* -s [NL, fr. Gk *parabolē* — more at PARABLE] **1 :** a plane curve generated by a point so moving that its distance from a fixed point divided by its distance from a fixed line is equal to 1 **:** a conic section formed by the intersection of a cone with a plane parallel to an element of the cone **2 a :** a bowl-shaped microphone **b :** a bowl-shaped antenna to receive and transmit radio waves preferentially in one particular direction

parabola 1

**par·a·bo·la·nus** \ˌparəbōˈlānəs\ *n, pl* **parabola·ni** \-ä(ˌ)nē\ [LL *parabolanus, parabalanus*, prob. fr. (assumed) LGk *parabalaneus*, fr. Gk *para-* ¹para- + *balaneus* bathhouse servant, fr. *balaneion* bathhouse, hot bath — more at BAGNIO] **:** an official or a member of a brotherhood in the early church devoted to the care of the sick esp. in infectious or contagious cases

**par·a·bol·ic** \ˌparəˈbälik\ *or* **par·a·bol·i·cal** \-ləkəl\ *adj* [in sense 1, fr. LL *parabola* parable + L *-icus* -ic, -ical; in sense 2, fr. NL *parabola* + E *-ic* — more at PARABLE] **1 :** of the nature of or expressed by a parable or figure **:** ALLEGORICAL ⟨the ~ tradition of the Gospels —*Interpreter's Bible*⟩ ⟨an account in an ancient *parabolical* style of the spiritual life of the race —Helen Keller⟩ **2 :** of, having the form of, or relating to a parabola ⟨motion in a ~ curve⟩

**par·a·bol·i·cal·ly** \-lək(ə)lē\ *adv* **1 :** by way of parable **:** in a parabolic manner **2 :** in the form or manner of a parabola

**parabolic cylinder** *n* **:** a cylinder whose right section is a parabola

**parabolic geometry** *n* **:** EUCLIDEAN GEOMETRY

**parabolic reflector** *n* **1** *or* **parabolic mirror :** a concave mirror that has the form of a paraboloid of revolution so that rays emanating from the geometrical focus and reflected from the surface are all parallel to each other and to the axis of symmetry and rays from a distant source (as a star) are reflected to the focus and that is used in reflecting telescopes, searchlights, and headlights **2 :** a similar device for the directional reflection of microwaves and sound waves

**parabolic velocity** *n* **:** the speed at which a body at any point in a central gravitational field must move in order that its orbit be a parabola and which when the gravitational field is due to a spherical mass (as the earth) is equal to the velocity of escape

**pa·rab·o·lize** \pəˈrabəˌlīz\ *vt* -ED/-ING/-S [in sense 1, fr. LL *parabola* parable + E *-ize*; in sense 2, fr. NL *parabola* + E *-ize*] **1 :** to express in fables or explain as parables **2 :** to make (as a mirror for a telescope) parabolic or paraboloidal

**pa·rab·o·loid** \pəˈrabəˌlȯid\ *n* -s [NL *parabola* + E *-oid*] **:** a quadric surface for which sections parallel to two of the coordinate planes are parabolas and sections parallel to the third coordinate plane are ellipses, circles, or hyperbolas if proper orientation of the coordinate axes is assumed ⟨an elliptic ~ is dome-shaped⟩ — compare HYPERBOLIC PARABOLOID, PARABOLOID OF REVOLUTION

**pa·rab·o·loi·dal** \pəˌrabəˈlȯidᵊl\ *adj* **:** having the shape of, resembling, or relating to a paraboloid ⟨eight hyperbolic ~ domes . . . are used in pairs to form the roof of a textile factory —*Civil Engineering*⟩ ⟨1-meter focus off-axis ~ collimating mirror —*Jour. of Research*⟩

**paraboloid of revolution :** the surface generated by the rotation of a parabola about its axis ⟨it is a property of a *paraboloid of revolution* . . . that rays from an object at infinity are all imaged at the same point on the axis —F.W.Sears⟩

**para·bomb** \ˈparə+ˌ-\ *n* [²*para-* + *bomb*] **:** a bomb usu. with delayed-action fuze dropped from an airplane by parachute

**para·botulism** \ˌparə+\ *n* [¹*para-* + *botulism*] **:** FORAGE POISONING

**para·brake** \ˈparə+ˌ-\ *n* [²*para-* + *brake*] **:** a parachute used to assist braking an airplane

**para·bran·chia** \ˌparəˈbraŋkēə\ *n* -s [NL, fr. ¹*para-* + *-branchia*] **:** the osphradium of a mollusk when it is large and resembles a gill — **para·bran·chi·al** \ˌ==ˈ==kēəl\ *adj* — **para·bran·chi·ate** \-kēət, -kēˌāt\ *adj*

**para brown V** \-ˈvē, -ˈfīv\ *n, usu cap P&B* [⁶*para*] **:** a direct dye — see DYE table I (under *Direct Brown 151*)

**para·bu·lia** \ˌparəˈbyülēə\ *n* -s [NL, fr. ¹*para-* + *-bulia*] **:** abnormality or perversion of will power

**para·carmine** \ˌparə+\ *n* [¹*para-* + *carmine*] **:** a carmine microscopy stain containing calcium chloride and often aluminum chloride

**para·casein** \"+\ *n* [ISV ¹*para-* + *casein*] **:** CASEIN c

**par·a·cel·sian** \ˌparəˌsel(t)sēən, -lshən\ *adj, usu cap* [Philippus Aureolus *Paracelsus* (Theophrastus Bombastus von Hohenheim) †1541 Swiss alchemist and physician + E *-ian*] **:** of, relating to, or conforming to the practice or theories of Paracelsus according to whose teachings the activities of the human body are chemical, health depends on the proper chemical composition of the organs and fluids, and the object of chemistry is to prepare medicines ⟨certain *Paracelsian* medical and alchemical texts —W.A.Murray⟩

**para·cen·te·sis** \ˌparəˌsen·ˈtēsəs\ *n, pl* **paracente·ses** \-ē(ˌ)sēz\ [L, fr. Gk *parakentēsis*, fr. *parakentein* to pierce at the side (fr. *para-* ¹para- + *kentein* to prick) + *-sis* — more at CENTER] **:** a surgical puncture of a cavity of the body with a trocar, aspirator, or other instrument to draw off any effused fluid — called also *tapping*

**para·central** \ˌparə+\ *adj* [ISV ¹*para-* + *central*] **:** lying near a center or central part

¹**para·cen·tric** \ˌparəˈsen·trik\ *adj* [¹*para-* + *-centric*] **1 :** being a type of key and keyway used with pin-tumbler cylinder locks and having longitudinal ribs and grooves projecting beyond the center to hinder picking **2 :** being an inversion that occurs in a single arm of one chromosome and does not involve the chromomere — compare PERICENTRIC

²**paracentric** \"\ *n* -s **:** a paracentric key or keyway

**para·cerebellar** \ˌparə+\ *adj* [¹*para-* + *cerebellar*] **:** of or relating to the lateral part of the cerebellum

**par·acetaldehyde** \(ˌ)par+\ *n* [¹*para-* + *acetaldehyde*] **:** PARALDEHYDE

**par·a·chor** \ˈparəˌkō(ə)r\ *n* -s [¹*para-* + Gk *chōros* space; fr. its indicating volume — more at CHOR-] **:** an empirical constant for a liquid that relates the surface tension to the molecular volume and that may be used for a comparison of molecular volumes under conditions such that the liquids have the same surface tension and for determinations of partial structure of compounds by adding values obtained for constituent atoms and structural features — called also *molar parachor, molecular parachor*

¹**para·chordal** \"+\ *adj* [ISV ¹*para-* + *chordal*] **:** situated at the side of the notochord

²**parachordal** \"\ *n* -s **:** either of a pair of cartilaginous rods that develop on each side of the notochord beneath the posterior part of the embryonic brain and participate in formation of the basilar plate

**parachordal plate** *n* **:** BASILAR PLATE

**para·chromatin** \"+\ *n* [ISV ¹*para-* + *chromatin*] **:** any of various nonstaining or feebly staining nuclear elements that are a particular kind of protoplasm (as linin or spindle fibers) or are various artifacts

**para·chromophorous** \"+\ *adj* [¹*para-* + *chromophorous*] **:** excreting pigment that is insoluble in water and does not diffuse away from a cell wall or capsule — compare CHROMOPAROUS, CHROMOPHOROUS

**pa·rach·ro·nism** \pəˈrakrəˌnizəm, pəˈr-\ *n* -s [¹*para-* + *chron-* + *-ism*] **:** a chronological error; *esp* **:** one by which a date is set later than is correct — compare METACHRONISM

¹**para·chute** \ˈparəˌshüt *also* ˈper-; *usu* -üd·+V\ *n, often attrib* [F, fr. *para-* (as in *parasol*) + *chute* fall — more at PARASOL, CHUTE] **1 :** a folding umbrella-shaped device usu. made of light fabric for retarding the speed of a body attached to it by offering resistance to the air and used esp. for making a safe descent from an airplane, dropping equipment or supplies from an airplane, or slowing down an airplane upon landing **2 :** the patagium of a mammal or reptile **3 a :** a device or structure suggestive of a parachute in form, use, or operation (as to retard the descent of a cage in a mine or to protect the balance wheel of a watch from shock) **b :** the inverted cup acting as the holding part of a mushroom anchor **c :** the tuft of hairs enabling a dandelion seed to float in air **4 :** PARACHUTE SPINNAKER — **parachutic** *adj*

parachute 1: *1* shroud lines, *2* canopy, *3* pilot chute, *4* vent, *5* risers, *6* harness

²**parachute** \"\ *vb* -ED/-ING/-S *vt* **:** to convey by means of a parachute ~ *vi* **:** to descend by or as if by means of a parachute

**parachute rigger** *n* **:** a person who packs, inspects, and repairs parachutes; *specif* **:** an enlisted man in the U. S. Navy having such work as his major duties

**parachute spinnaker** *n* **:** an exceptionally large spinnaker used esp. on racing yachts

**para·chut·ist** \-üd·əst, -üt\ *also* **para·chut·er** \|ə(r)\ *n* -s **:** one that parachutes; *specif* **:** a soldier trained and equipped to parachute from an airplane

**par·a·clete** \ˈparəˌklēt\ *n* -s [ME *Paraclit*, fr. MF *Paraclet, Paraclet*, fr. LL *Paracletus, Paraclitus*, fr. Gk *Paraklētos*, lit., intercessor, comforter, fr. *parakalein* to summon, exhort, comfort, fr. *para-* ¹para- + *kalein* to call — more at LOW] **1** *cap* **:** HOLY SPIRIT **2 :** one called to aid or support **:** ADVOCATE

**para·colon** \ˌparə+\ *n, often attrib* [NL, fr. ¹*para-* + *colon*] **:** any of several bacteria closely related to the genus *Escherichia* but commonly regarded as forming a distinct genus (*Paracolobactrum*) that have been implicated as causative agents of a variety of human gastroenteritides

**par·a·col·pi·um** \ˌparəˈkälpēəm\ *n* [NL, fr. ¹*para-* + *colp-* + *-ium*] **:** the vascular and connective tissues alongside the vagina

**para·condyloid** \ˌparə+\ *adj* [¹*para-* + *condyloid*] **:** being a process of the occipital bone lying on the outer side of each condyle in the skull of some mammals

**para·cone** \ˈparə+ˌ-\ *n* [¹*para-* + *cone*] **:** the anterior of the three cusps of a primitive upper molar that in higher forms is the principal anterior and external cusp

**par·aconic acid** \ˌpar+. . .-\ *n* [ISV ¹*para-* + *aconic*] **:** a white crystalline lactonic acid $C_4H_5O_2COOH$ isomeric with itaconic, citraconic, and mesaconic acids; the beta-carboxy derivative of butyrolactone

**para·co·nid** \ˌparəˈkōnəd\ *n* -s [*paracone* + *-id*] **:** the cusp of a primitive lower molar that corresponds to the paracone of the upper molar and that in higher forms is the anterior and internal cusp

**para·co·nule** \-(ˌ)nyül\ *n* -s [*paracone* + *-ule*] **:** PROTOCONULE

**para·coquimbite** \ˌparə+\ *n* [F, fr. ¹*para-* + *coquimbite*] **:** a mineral $Fe_2(SO_4)_3 \cdot 9H_2O$ consisting of a hydrous ferric sulfate that is rhombohedral in crystallization and dimorphous with coquimbite

**para·coto bark** \ˌparə+. . .-\ *n* [¹*para-* + *coto bark*] **:** the dried bark of a Bolivian tree (*Ocotea pseudo-coto*) or of an undetermined tree of the family Lauraceae

**para-coumarone-indene resin** \ˌparə+\ *n* [¹*para-* + *coumarone-indene resin*] **:** COUMARONE-INDENE RESIN

**para·cresol** \ˌparə+\ *n* [ISV ¹*para-* + *cresol*] **:** the para isomer of cresol — written systematically with ital. *para-* or *p-*

**para·crystal** \"+\ *n* [¹*para-* + *crystal*] **:** a solid body with less than the three-dimensional order characteristic of a true crystal ⟨virus . . . in the form of needlelike ~s —C.A.Knight⟩ — compare PSEUDOCRYSTAL — **para·crystalline** \"+\ *adj*

**par·acu·sia** \ˌparəˈk(y)üzh(ē)ə\ *or* **par·acu·sis** \-üsəs\ *n, pl* **paracu·sias** \-üzh(ē)əz\ *or* **paracu·ses** \-üˌsēz\ [NL fr. ¹*para-* + *-acusia* or Gk *akousis* hearing — more at -ACUSIA] **:** a disorder in the sense of hearing — **par·acu·sic** \ˌ==ˈk(y)üzik, -üsik\ *adj or n*

**para·cyanogen** \ˌparə+\ *n* [ISV ¹*para-* + *cyanogen*] **:** a polymer of cyanogen obtained as a brown or black amorphous solid (as by heating cyanogen)

**para·cyesis** \"+\ *n, pl* **paracyeses** [NL, fr. ¹*para-* + *cyesis*] **:** EXTRAUTERINE PREGNANCY

**para·cystitis** \"+\ *n, pl* **paracystitides** [NL, fr. *paracystium* + *-itis*] **:** inflammation of the connective tissue about the bladder

**para·cys·ti·um** \ˌparəˈsistēəm\ *n, pl* **paracys·tia** \-ēə\ [NL, fr. ¹*para-* + *cyst-* + *-ium*] **:** the vascular and connective tissues alongside the bladder

¹**pa·rade** \pəˈrād, *in rapid speech* ˈpr-\ *n* -s [F, fr. MF, fr. *parer* to prepare, adorn + *-ade* — more at PARE] **1 a :** a pompous show **:** formal display **:** EXHIBITION ⟨make an important ~ of doing nothing —James Hilton⟩ ⟨could not be restrained from making rather an ostentatious ~ of his liberality —Charles Dickens⟩ ⟨wanted to find people as they always were, not on ~ —Margaret Biddle⟩ ⟨from early spring to late fall there is a constant ~ of gorgeous color —*Amer. Guide Series: Mass.*⟩ ⟨puts human flummery and pretentiousness on ~ in a crowded gallery of portraits —C.J. Rolo⟩ **b :** LISTING, RECITAL ⟨a radio program ~⟩ ⟨the book . . . is a pleasant ~ of the things he has enjoyed most —*Saturday Rev.*⟩ ⟨a ~ of popular songs⟩ **c** *Brit* **:** a style show or display of fashions by mannequins **2 a :** the ceremonial formation of a body of troops before its commanding or other high officer typically involving exercises in the manual of arms, a report on the numbers of the various units present or accounted for, and the publication of orders and ending with a review; *also* **:** any of various other ceremonial formations of a body of troops **b :** a place where troops assemble for regular formations or ceremonies **c :** troops that take part in a ceremonial formation **3 a :** an informal march or procession ⟨a ~ of witnesses testified⟩ ⟨a ~ of more outstanding singers than could possibly be cast in a single opera —Miles Kastendieck⟩ **b :** a formal public procession **:** the movement of any body of people or things marshaled in something like military order ⟨a ~ of firemen⟩ ⟨a circus ~⟩ ⟨a boat ~⟩ **c :** a showy array or succession ⟨a ~ of linament bottles along the chimneypiece —Elizabeth Bowen⟩ ⟨a ~ of long-distance pipelines —Gardiner Symonds⟩ ⟨slash pockets at the hips, from which a ~ of box pleats starts around the back —Lois Long⟩ ⟨discriminative sensing of the down-the-years ~ of American attitudes —C.L.Carmer⟩ **d :** a movement in favor of a particular policy or action ⟨joined the propaganda ~ —J.B.Reston⟩ ⟨join the UN ~ in accepting the Indian plan —Mark Feer⟩ **4 :** a place where people promenade **:** a public walk, square, or promenade **5 a :** those who parade **:** an assembly of promenaders **b :** an assembly of people ⟨there have been meets . . . at various places — annual ~s —R.E.Meyer⟩ **syn** see DISPLAY

²**parade** \"\ *vb* -ED/-ING/-S *vt* **1 :** to assemble (as troops) in formation **:** cause to maneuver or march ceremoniously **:** MARSHAL **2 :** to promenade (a place) ⟨veiled female had been *parading* the docks —T.B.Costain⟩ **3 :** to exhibit in a showy or ostentatious manner **:** SHOW OFF ⟨the ugly woman does not ~ herself vainly —*Irish Digest*⟩ ⟨lavish floats are *paraded* up and down the river —Green Peyton⟩ ⟨politicians . . . have *paraded* their artistic incapacity as a virtue —*Times Lit. Supp.*⟩ ⟨ladies and gentlemen . . . *paraded* their fine manners, wit, and charm —H.J.Muller⟩ ~ *vi* **1 a :** to march or take part in a procession ⟨this army of penguins would ~ along the beach —H.A.Chippendale⟩ ⟨mob of thousands recently *paraded* through Mustafa Kamal Square in Cairo —H.C. Atyeo⟩ ⟨freighters ~ in and out of the Capes —*Amer. Guide Series: Va.*⟩ **b :** to form a review **2 a :** to walk up and down ⟨~ beneath the balcony —Elizabeth Bowen⟩ ⟨down on the wharf the sentry *paraded* stiffly —K.M.Dodson⟩ **b :** to promenade esp. for showing off ⟨ladies wore black in the morning but in the afternoon *paraded* in dashing silk gowns —C.L. Jones⟩ **3 a :** SHOW OFF ⟨drove so well, so quietly, without making any disturbance, without *parading* to her —Jane Austen⟩ **b :** MASQUERADE ⟨myths which ~ as modern science —M.R.Cohen⟩ ⟨dogmatism *parading* as enlightenment —Eric Partridge⟩ **syn** see SHOW

³**pa·rade** \pəˈräd\ *n* -s [F, fr. *parer* to parry + *-ade* — more at PARRY] **:** PARRY

**para·dental** \ˌparə+\ *adj* [ISV ¹*para-* + *dental*] **:** adjacent to a tooth

**para·den·ti·tis** \ˌparəˌden·ˈtīd·əs\ *n* -ES [NL, fr. *paradentium* + *-itis*] **:** PERIODONTITIS

**para·den·tium** \ˌparəˈdentēəm, -nch(ē)əm\ *n, pl* **paraden·tia** \-tēə, -ch(ē)ə\ [NL *para-* + *dent-* + *-ium*] **:** the paradental tissues including the gums, the alveolar process, and the pericementum

**para·den·to·sis** \ˌparəˌden·ˈtōsəs\ *n, pl* **paradento·ses** \-ōˌsēz\ [NL, fr. *paradentium* + *-osis*] **:** PERIODONTOSIS

**pa·rad·er** \pəˈrād(ə)r\ *n* -s **:** one that parades

**parade rest** \=ˌ=ˈ=\ *n* **:** a formal position assumed by a soldier in ranks in which he remains silent and motionless with the left foot 12 inches to the left of the right foot and with the weight resting equally on both feet and when without arms clasps the hands behind the back with the palms to the rear and when with a rifle holds the rifle in the right hand with butt touching the ground and muzzle inclined forward and holds the left hand behind the back — used as a command to assume this position

parade rest

**para·dermal** \ˌparə+\ *adj* [¹*para-* + *dermal*] **:** lying parallel to the epidermis

**para·desmose** \"+\ *n* [¹*para-* + *desmose*] **:** a fibril connecting extranuclear division centers in mitosis (as in many flagellates) — compare CENTRODESMOSE

**para·diazine** \"+\ *n* [¹*para-* + *diazine*] **:** a compound containing a diazine ring with the two nitrogen atoms para to each other; *esp* **:** PYRAZINE

**para·dichlorobenzene** \"+\ *n* [ISV ¹*para-* + *dichlorobenzene*] **:** a white crystalline compound $C_6H_4Cl_2$ made by chlorinating benzene that sublimes easily and is used chiefly as a fumigant against clothes moths — called also *PDB, p-dichlorobenzene*; written systematically with ital. *para-* or *p-*

**par·a·did·dle** \ˌparəˌdidᵊl\ *n* -s [prob. of imit. origin] **:** a snare-drum stroke characterized by the left-handed and right-handed attack on successive principal beats

**para·did·y·mis** \ˌparəˈdidəməs\ *n, pl* **paradidymi·des** \-ˈdidəməˌdēz, -dəˈdimə-, -dīˈdimə-\ [NL, fr. ¹*para-* + *-didymis* (fr. Gk *didymos* twin, testicle) — more at DIDYM-] **:** irregular tubules found among the convolutions of the epididymis and considered to be a remnant of tubes of the mesonephros

**par·a·digm** \ˈparəˌdīm, -ˌdim *also* ˈper- *sometimes* -ˌdem *or* -ˌdəm\ *n, pl* **paradigms** \-mz\ *also* **paradig·ma·ta** \-dig-mədə, -mətə\ [LL *paradigma*, fr. Gk *paradeigma* pattern, model, example, fr. *paradeiknynai* to show side by side, compare, exhibit, fr. *para-* ¹para- + *deiknynai* to show — more at DICTION] **1 :** EXAMPLE, PATTERN ⟨mistaken the ~ for the theory —Margaret Mead⟩ ⟨a typical conditioned-response ~ —W.N.Kellogg⟩ ⟨regard science as the ~ of true knowledge —G.C.J.Midgley⟩ ⟨~s of musical perfection —H.G.Aiken⟩ **2 a :** an example of a conjugation or declension showing a word in all its inflectional forms **b :** a set of forms peculiar to a verb, noun, pronoun, or adjective **3 :** a narrative passage in the Gospels that illustrates a saying of Jesus and represents one of the literary patterns distinguished by form criticism ⟨the ~ . . . is represented in its purity by the healing of the paralytic —*Times Lit. Supp.*⟩ **syn** see MODEL

**par·a·dig·mat·ic** \ˌ==ˌdigˈmad·ik\ *also* **par·a·dig·mat·i·cal** \-d·əkəl\ *adj* [LL *paradigmaticos*, fr. Gk *paradeigmatikos* fr. *paradeigmat-, paradeigma* + *-ikos* -ic, -ical] **1 :** EXEMPLARY, TYPICAL ⟨situation is . . . felt to be not unique but modeled on, or ~ of old situations —*Psychiatry*⟩ ⟨~ analysis of concepts such as space and inertia —Otto Neurath⟩ ⟨a ~ significance for the religious situation of modern man —M.S. Friedman⟩ **2 a :** of or relating to a grammatical paradigm ⟨the ~ forms⟩ **b :** INFLECTIONAL — **par·a·dig·mat·i·cal·ly** \-d·ək(ə)lē\ *adv*

**paradigmatize** *vt* [Gk *paradeigmatizein*, fr. *paradeigmat-, paradeigma* + *-izein* -ize] *obs* **:** to set forth as a model

**para·diplomatic** \¦parə+\ *adj* [1*para-* + *diplomatic*] **:** concerned with or based on evidence apart from strict textual authority

**par·a·di·saea** \ˌparəˌdī'sēə, -'zēə, ˌ==' === *also* ˌper-\ *n, cap* [NL, irreg. fr. LL *paradisus* paradise] **:** the type genus of the family Paradisaeidae including various birds of paradise whose males are frequently predominantly brilliant metallic green

**par·a·di·sae·i·dae** \ˌ==ˌdī'sēəˌdē, -'zē-\ *n pl, cap* [NL, fr. *Paradisaea*, type genus + *-idae*] **:** a family of passerine birds comprising the birds of paradise and often also the bowerbirds

**par·a·di·sa·ic** \¦==ˌ=¦sāik, -¦zā-, -āek\ *or* **par·a·di·sa·i·cal** \-āəkəl\ *adj* [*paradise* + *-aic*, *-aical* (as in *pharisaic*, *pharisaical*)] **:** PARADISIACAL — **par·a·di·sa·i·cal·ly** \-āək(ə)lē, -li\ *adv*

**par·a·di·sal** \¦==¦dīsəl, -īzəl\ *adj* [*paradise* + *-al*] **:** PARADISIACAL ⟨a ~ state without work or struggle —*transl*⟩ ⟨vegetation was rich and ~ with flowers —Elinor Wylie⟩ ⟨together in that ~ place —Thomas Cole⟩

**par·a·dise** \'parəˌdīs *also* 'per- *or* -īz\ *n* -s [ME *paradis*, fr. OF, fr. LL *paradisus*, fr. Gk *paradeisos* enclosed park, garden, orchard, paradise, of Iranian origin; akin to Av *pairi-daēza-* enclosure, fr. *pairi* around + *daēza-* wall; akin to Gk *peri* around and to Gk *teichos* wall — more at PERI-, DOUGH] **1 a :** a place or state in which the souls of the righteous after death enjoy eternal bliss **:** HEAVEN **b :** an intermediate elysium for the souls of the righteous during the interval between death and final judgment **2 a :** a place of bliss **:** a region of supreme felicity or delight ⟨an earthly ~⟩ ⟨a ~ for children⟩; *esp* **:** a place characterized by favorable conditions, special opportunities, or the abundance of something ⟨a tourist's ~⟩ ⟨a gourmet's ~⟩ ⟨a vacation ~⟩ ⟨a ~ for ducks⟩ **b :** a state of happiness ⟨the lost ~ of childhood⟩ **3 a :** a pleasure garden; *esp* **:** an oriental park **b :** a preserve for foreign birds and animals **4 :** an open space in a monastery or next to a church (as in a cloister) or the open court before a basilica **5 :** the plumage (as the long tail feathers) of the male bird of paradise formerly used in millinery **6** *or* **paradise apple** *often cap P* **:** a small Asiatic wild apple (*Malus sylvestris paradisiaca*) used principally as a dwarfing rootstock and the source of several of the Malling rootstocks **7 :** PARADISE FISH

**par·a·dise·an** \¦==¦di¦sēən, -¦dī¦, ¦zē-\ *adj* [ML *paradiseus* paradisiacal (fr. L *paradisus*) + E *-an*] **:** relating to birds of paradise

**paradise bird** *n* **:** BIRD OF PARADISE 1

**paradise duck** *or* **paradise sheldrake** *n* **:** a highly colored New Zealand duck (*Tadorna variegata*) related to the sheldrake

**paradise finch** *n* **:** PAINTED BUNTING

**paradise fish** *n* **:** a brilliantly colored freshwater labyrinth fish (*Macropodus opercularis*) of eastern Asia with very large fins often kept in aquariums; *also* **:** a closely related fish (*M. chinensis*) having a rounded tail

**paradise flower** *n* **:** an arborescent cat's-claw (*Acacia greggii*) with fragrant creamy yellow flowers that is an important browse and wildlife feed in arid parts of the southwestern U.S. and adjacent Mexico

**paradise flycatcher** *n* **:** any of numerous Asiatic or African flycatchers belonging to the genus *Terpsiphone* in most of which the males have the central tail feathers greatly elongated

**paradise grackle** *or* **paradise pie** *n* **:** a beautiful long-tailed bird of paradise (*Astrapia nigra*) of New Guinea having dark velvety plumage with brilliant metallic tints

**paradise green** *n* **:** HIBERNIAN GREEN

**paradise grosbeak** *n* **:** CUTTHROAT 2

**paradise nut** *n* **:** SAPUCAIA NUT

**paradise plant** *n* **:** MEZEREON 1

**paradise tree** *n* **1 a :** a medium-sized to large-sized tree (*Simarouba glauca*) that occurs from southern Florida to the northern part of So. America and has odd-pinnate leaves and long terminal much branched panicles of small pale yellow flowers borne in early spring and followed by scarlet to dark purple fruits **b :** MARUPA **2 :** CHINABERRY 2

**paradise weaver** *or* **paradise whydah** *n* **:** a whydah (*Vidua paradiseae*) that is usu. marked with buff or brown and occurs in several distinct subspecies

**par·a·di·si·a·cal** \¦==də¦sīəkəl, -ˌdī¦-, -¦zī-\ *also* **par·a·dis·i·ac** \¦==¦disēˌak, -izē-\ *adj* [*paradisiacal* fr. LL *paradisiacus* (fr. *paradisus* paradise) + E *-al; paradisiac* fr. LL *paradisiacus*] **:** of, relating to, or resembling paradise ⟨an age of ~ happiness —H.A.Overstreet⟩ ⟨~ innocence⟩ ⟨conception of a ~ state of nature —W.A.Kaufmann⟩ — **par·a·di·si·a·cal·ly** \-ˌdə¦sīək(ə)lē, -ˌdī¦-, -¦zī-, -li\ *adv*

**par·a·dis·i·al** \¦==¦disēəl, -izē-\ *also* **par·a·dis·i·an** \-ēən\ *or* **par·a·dis·ic** \-sik,-zik\ *or* **par·a·dis·i·cal** \-səkəl, -zə-\ *adj* [*paradise* + *-ial* or *-ian* or *-ic* or *-ical*] **:** PARADISIACAL ⟨a ~ country⟩ ⟨a ~ people⟩ ⟨~ isles⟩

**pa·ra·do** \pə'rä(ˌ)dō, -rā(-\ *n* -s [modif. of F *parade* — more at PARADE] **1** *obs* **:** PARADE **2 :** a boastful swaggering air

**para·doctor** \'parə+ˌ-\ *n* [2*para-* + *doctor*] **:** a doctor who reaches isolated areas by parachute

**par·a·don·tal** \¦parə¦dänt'l\ *adj* [1*para-* + Gk *odont-* *odous* tooth + E *-al* — more at TOOTH] **:** PERIODONTAL 2 ⟨~ disease⟩

**par·a·don·to·sis** \ˌparəˌdän·'tōsəs\ *n, pl* **paradonto·ses** \-ōˌsēz\ [NL, fr. 1*para-* + Gk *odont-*, *odous* + NL *-osis*] **:** PERIODONTOSIS

**para·dos** \'parəˌdäs, -dōs,-dō\ *n, pl* **parados** \-dōz\ *or* **paradoses** \-däsəz,-dōsəz\ [F, fr. *para-* (as in *parasol*) + *dos* back, fr. L *dorsum* — more at PARASOL] **:** a bank of earth behind a fortification trench — compare PARAPET 1

1**par·a·dox** \'parəˌdäks *also* 'per-\ *n* -ES [L *paradoxum*, fr. Gk *paradoxon*, fr. neut. of *paradoxos* contrary to expectation, incredible, fr. *para-* 1para + *-doxos* (fr. *dokein* to think) — more at DECENT] **1 :** a tenet or proposition contrary to received opinion **2 a :** a statement or sentiment that is seemingly contradictory or opposed to common sense and yet perhaps true in fact ⟨present-day ~*es* like "mobilizing for peace" —E.R.May⟩ ⟨~ that the more terrible the prospect of thermonuclear war becomes, the less likely it is to happen —*Blackwood's*⟩ ⟨here is a noble ~: religion tries to satisfy man while its essential purpose is to make him dissatisfied —W.L.Sullivan⟩ **2 b** (1) **:** a statement that is actually self-contradictory and hence false even though its true character is not immediately apparent (2) **:** an argument that apparently derives self-contradictory conclusions by valid deduction from acceptable premises — see LIAR PARADOX, RUSSELL'S PARADOX **3 :** something (as a human being, phenomenon, state of affairs, or action) with seemingly contradictory qualities or phases ⟨she is an interesting ~, an infinitely shy person with an enormously intuitive gift for understanding people —*Current Biog.*⟩ ⟨the colonel . . . is a ~ — a well-known secret agent —John Kobler⟩ ⟨there is ~ in the fact that the artist has come into his own in an age which hates him —W.P.Clancy⟩ ⟨his lectures on mechanical ~*es* (such as man's lifting himself by his own bootstraps, rolling a barrel uphill by gravity) —C.W.Mitman⟩ ⟨the ~ of impoverished people in a rich land —*Univ. of Minn. Press Cat.*⟩

2**paradox** \"\ *vi* **:** to utter paradoxes

**par·a·dox·al** \¦==¦däksəl\ *adj* **:** PARADOXICAL — **par·a·dox·al·i·ty** \ˌ==ˌdäk'saləd·ē\ *n* -ES

**par·a·dox·er** \'==ˌdäksə(r)\ *n* -s **:** one that propounds paradoxes

**par·a·dox·i·al** \¦==¦däksēəl, -kshəl\ *or* **par·a·dox·ic** \-¦däksik, -sēk\ *adj* **:** PARADOXICAL

**par·a·dox·i·cal** \¦==¦däksəkəl, -sēk-\ *adj* **1 a :** of the nature of a paradox ⟨the ~ theory that ice ages occur as the sun gets hotter —R.W.Murray⟩ ⟨in the ~ heart of all of us is the perennial longing to be what we are not —J.L.Lowes⟩ ⟨however ~ it may look at first sight, idealism . . . is actually nearer to common sense than is materialism —C.H.Whiteley⟩ ⟨introvert with a strong and ~ sympathy for his fellowman —J.C.Cort⟩ **b :** inclined to paradoxes **2 :** not being the normal or usual kind ⟨~ embolism⟩ ⟨~ pulse⟩ — **par·a·dox·i·cal·i·ty** \ˌ==ˌ=='kaləd·ē, -ətē, -i\ *n* -ES — **par·a·dox·i·cal·ly** \¦==¦däksək(ə)lē, -sēk-, -li\ *adv* — **par·a·dox·i·cal·ness** \ˌ=='=səkəlnəs, -sēk-\ *n* -ES

**par·a·dox·i·des** \ˌ=='däksəˌdēz\ *n, cap* [NL, fr. L *paradoxum* paradox + *-ides*] **:** a genus of trilobites of the Middle Cambrian having from 17 to 20 free segments, a large cephalic shield, and a very small pygidium and sometimes reaching a length of about two feet

**par·a·dox·ist** \'==ˌdäksəst\ *n* -s **:** one who deals in paradoxes

**par·a·dox·ol·o·gist** \ˌ==ˌdäk'säləjəst\ *n* -s **:** one who uses or is skilled in the use of paradoxes; *specif* **:** one who stresses the use of paradoxes in theology

**par·a·dox·ol·o·gy** \-jē\ *n* -ES [Gk *paradoxologia*, fr. *paradoxon* paradox + *-logia* -logy — more at PARADOX] **:** the use of paradoxes

**par·a·dox·or·nis** \ˌparəˌdäk'sȯrnəs\ *n, cap* [NL, fr. L *paradoxus* contrary to expectation + NL *-ornis* — more at PARADOX] **:** a genus (the type of the family Paradoxornithidae) of Asiatic large-headed gregarious passerine birds including the typical crow tits

**par·a·dox·ure** \¦parə¦däkshə(r)\ *n* -s [NL *Paradoxurus*] **:** a palm civet of the genus *Paradoxurus*

1**par·a·dox·u·rine** \-shəˌrīn\ *adj* [NL *Paradoxurus* + E *-ine*] **:** of or relating to the genus *Paradoxurus*

2**paradoxurine** \"\ *n* -s **:** a palm civet of the genus *Paradoxurus*

**par·a·dox·urus** \ˌparəˌdäk'shu̇rəs\ *n, cap* [NL, fr. Gk *paradoxos* contrary to expectation + NL *-urus*] **:** a genus of carnivorous mammals (family Viverridae) comprising the typical palm civets

**par·a·doxy** \'==ˌdäksē\ *n* -ES [Gk *paradoxia*, fr. *paradoxos* + *-ia* -y — more at PARADOX] **:** the quality or state of being paradoxical

**para·dromic** \¦parə¦drämik, -rōm-\ *adj* [Gk *paradromos* paradromic (fr. *para-* 1para- + *-dromos* -dromous) + E *-ic*] **:** running side by side **:** following a parallel course

**para·dro·mism** \'parəˌdrōˌmizəm, pə'radrəˌmi-\ *n* -s [*paradromic* + *-ism*] **:** PARALLELISM

1**para·drop** \'parə+ˌ-\ *n* [2*para-* + *drop* (n.)] **:** AIRDROP

2**paradrop** \"\ *vt* [2*para-* + *drop* (v.)] **:** AIR-DROP

**parae** *pl of* PARA

**-parae** *pl of* -PARA

**pa·raene·sis** *also* **pa·rene·sis** \pə'rēnəsəs, -ren-\ *n, pl* **paraene·ses** *also* **parene·ses** \-nəˌsēz\ [LL *paraenesis*, fr. Gk *parainesis*, fr. *parainein* to advise (fr. *para-* 1para- + *ainein* to speak of, praise, advise, fr. *ainos* speech, fable) + *-sis*] **:** an exhortatory composition **:** ADVICE, COUNSEL — **par·ae·net·ic** *also* **par·e·net·ic** \¦parə¦ned·ik\ *adj* — **par·ae·net·i·cal** *also* **par·e·net·i·cal** \-d·əkəl\ *adj*

**paraesthesia** *var of* PARESTHESIA

1**par·af·fin** \'parəfən *also* 'per-\ *also* **par·af·fine** \" *also* -ˌfēn\ *n* -s [G *paraffin*, fr. L *parum* too little + *affinis* bordering on, related by marriage; akin to *paucus* few, little — more at FEW, AFFINITY] **1 a** *or* **paraffin wax :** a waxy crystalline substance that is white, translucent, odorless, and tasteless when pure, that is obtained esp. from distillates of wood, coal, or now usu. petroleum or shale oil, that is a complex mixture of hydrocarbons principally of the methane series, that is resistant to water and water vapor and is chemically inert, and that is used chiefly in coating and sealing, in making candles, in impregnating matches, in rubber compounding, in electrical insulation, and in pharmaceuticals and cosmetics — called also *hard paraffin;* compare CERESIN, MICROCRYSTALLINE WAX, SCALE WAX, SLACK WAX **b :** any of various mixtures of similar hydrocarbons including mixtures that are semisolid or oily ⟨soft ~⟩ — compare LIQUID PETROLATUM, PETROLATUM **2** *or* **paraffin hydrocarbon :** a hydrocarbon of the methane series **:** ALKANE **3** *chiefly Brit* **:** KEROSINE

2**paraffin** \"\ *vt* -ED/-ING/-S **:** to treat, coat, or saturate with paraffin **:** apply paraffin to

**paraffin-base** \¦===¦=\ *adj* **:** containing relatively large amounts of paraffin hydrocarbons **:** yielding paraffin wax on refining — used esp. of crude petroleum; compare ASPHALT-BASE, NAPHTHENE-BASE

**paraffin distillate** *n* **:** a petroleum fraction that is usu. obtained after most of the gas oil has distilled and that contains chiefly lubricating oils and paraffin wax

**par·af·fin·er** \'==ˌfənə(r) *also* -ˌfēn-\ *n* -s **:** a worker who pours or sprays melted paraffin into barrels to prevent leakage and contact of stored liquid with wood

**par·af·fin·ic** \¦==¦finik\ *adj* **:** of, relating to, or characterized by paraffin hydrocarbons or paraffin wax **:** PARAFFIN-BASE ⟨~ hydrocarbons⟩ ⟨~ crudes⟩ — **par·af·fin·ic·i·ty** \ˌ==ˌfə'nisəd·ē\ *n* -ES

**par·af·fin·ize** \'==ˌfəˌnīz\ *vt* -ED/-ING/-S [1*paraffin* + *-ize*] **:** PARAFFIN

**paraffin jelly** *n* **:** PETROLATUM a

**par·af·fin·oid** \'==ˌfəˌnȯid\ *adj* [1*paraffin* + *-oid*] **:** resembling or related to paraffin **:** belonging to the methane series

**paraffin oil** *n* **1 :** any of various hydrocarbon oils usu. obtained from petroleum: as **a :** a lubricating oil from paraffin distillate **b** *chiefly Brit* **:** KEROSINE **2 :** LIQUID PETROLATUM

**paraffin scale** *n* **:** SCALE WAX

**paraffin series** *n* **:** METHANE SERIES

**paraffin test** *n* **:** a test in which a paraffin cast of the hand of a person suspected of firing a gun is subjected to chemical analysis to determine the presence of powder particles

**para·flocculus** \¦parə+\ *n, pl* **paraflocculi** [NL, fr. 1*para-* + *flocculus*] **:** a lateral accessory part of the flocculus of the cerebellum

**para·follicular** \"+\ *adj* [1*para-* + *follicular*] **:** located in the vicinity of or surrounding a follicle ⟨~ cells of the canine thyroid⟩

**para·form** \'parəˌfȯrm\ *n* [by shortening] **:** PARAFORMALDEHYDE

**para·formaldehyde** \¦parə+\ *n* [ISV 1*para-* + *formaldehyde*] **:** a white solid that is a mixture of hydrated polymers of formaldehyde having the formula $(HCHO)_n.H_2O$ or $HO(CH_2O)_nH$ in which *n* varies from about 8 to 100, that is usu. made by evaporation of an aqueous solution of formaldehyde, that readily regenerates formaldehyde esp. on heating, and that is used as a source of formaldehyde **:** a mixture of polyoxymethylene glycols

**para·fos·sar·u·lus** \¦parəˌfä¦sar(y)ələs\ *n, cap* [NL, fr. 1*para-* + *Fossarulus* genus of snails, dim. of LL *fossarius* fossor — more at FOSSARIAN] **:** a genus of East Asian freshwater snails (family Bulimidae) including important intermediate hosts of the Chinese liver fluke

**para·foulbrood** \¦parə+\ *n* [1*para-* + *foulbrood*] **:** a bacterial disease of the honeybee

**para·foveal** \"+\ *adj* [1*para-* + *foveal*] **1 :** surrounding the fovea ⟨~ regions of the retina⟩ **2 :** dependent on parts of the retina external to the fovea ⟨~ vision⟩ ⟨~ threshold of reaction⟩

**para fuchsine** *n, often cap P&F* [6*para*] **:** the chloride of pararosaniline base — see DYE table I (under *Basic Red 9*)

**para·gam·ma·cism** \¦parə¦gaməˌsizəm\ *also* **para·gam·ma·cis·mus** \¦==ˌ==¦sizməs\ *n, pl* **paragammacisms** *also* **paragammacismuses** [NL *paragammacismus*, fr. 1*para-* + *gammacismus* gammacism — more at GAMMACISM] **:** inability to pronounce the sound of *g* and *k* or difficulty in pronouncing them

**para·ganglioma** \¦parə+\ *n* [NL, fr. 1*para-* + *ganglioma*] **:** a ganglioma derived from chromaffin cells

**para·ganglion** \"+\ *n* [ISV 1*para-* + *ganglion*] **:** one of numerous collections of chromaffin tissue associated with the collateral and chain ganglia of the sympathetic nerves and similar in structure to the medulla of the suprarenal glands — **para·ganglionic** \"+\ *adj*

**para·gas·ter** \'parəˌgastə(r), ˌ=='==\ *n* -s [1*para-* + *-gaster*] **:** a paragastric cavity

**para·gastric** *also* **para·gastral** \¦parə+\ *adj* [1*para-* + *gastric*, *gastral*] **1 :** situated near the stomach **2 :** being the cavity or one of the cavities of a sponge into which the radial canals open and which opens outwardly through the cloaca

**para·gastrula** \"+\ *n* [NL, fr. 1*para-* + *gastrula*] **:** the gastrula formed by the invagination of an amphiblastula (as in many sponges) — **para·gastrular** \"+\ *adj*

**parage** \'parij, pə'räzh\ *n* -s [ME, fr. OF *parage*, *perage*, fr. *par*, *per* equal (fr. L *par*) + *-age* — more at PAIR] **:** equality of condition, blood, or dignity; *specif* **:** equality between persons (as brothers) one of whom holds a part of a fee of the other, does homage to the lord paramount, and is responsible for the whole service of the fee

**para·genesis** \ˌparə+\ *n* [NL, fr. 1*para-* + *genesis*] **1 :** the formation of minerals in contact so as to affect one another's development **2 :** the order in which minerals occurring together in rocks and veins have developed together with the characteristic grouping or association of the minerals — **para·genetic** \¦parə+\ *adj*

**para·geosyncline** \¦parə+\ *n* [1*para-* + *geosyncline*] **:** a geosyncline within or adjacent to a craton and usu. less elongated, shallower, and less persistent than an orthogeosyncline

**par·agglutination** \¦par+\ *n* [ISV 1*para-* + *agglutination*] **:** CROSS AGGLUTINATION

**para·glossa** \"+\ *n, pl* **paraglossae** [NL, fr. *para-* + Gk *glōssa* tongue — more at GLOSS] **:** one of a pair of small appendages of the labium of various insects — **para·glossal** \"+\ *adj*

**para·glossate** \"+\ *adj* [NL *paraglossa* + E *-ate*] **:** having paraglossae

**para·glos·sia** \ˌparə'gläsēə, -lȯs-\ *n* -s [NL, fr. 1*para-* + *-glossia*] **:** inflammation of the tissues under or about the tongue

**para·glycogen** \¦parə+\ *n* [ISV 1*para-* + *glycogen*] **:** a carbohydrate storage product in protozoa that resembles glycogen of higher animals

**par·ag·nath** \'parəgˌnath\ *n* -s [ISV 1*para-* + Gk *gnathos* jaw — more at GNATH-] **1 :** one of a pair of foliose lobes of the metastoma lying behind the mandibles in most crustaceans **2 :** one of the paired lobes of the hypopharynx in various insects **3 :** one of the small horny toothlike jaws of various annelids

**pa·rag·na·thism** \pə'ragnəˌthizəm, pa'r-\ *n* -s [*paragnathous* + *-ism*] **:** the paragnathous condition

**pa·rag·na·thous** \pə'ragnəthəs, (')pa¦r-\ *adj* [1*para-* + *-gnathous*] **:** having both mandibles of equal length with the tips meeting — used esp. of a bird

**pa·rag·na·thus** \pə'ragnəthəs, pa'r-\ *n, pl* **paragna·tha** \-thə\ [NL, fr. 1*para-* + Gk *gnathos* jaw] **:** PARAGNATH

**para·gneiss** \¦parə+\ *n* [ISV 1*para-* + *gneiss*] **:** gneiss derived from a sedimentary rock

**par·a·go·ge** \'parəˌgōjē *sometimes* -gäjē *or* ˌ=='==\ *n* -s [LL, fr. Gk *paragōgē*, fr. *paragesthai* to be derived, be formed, passive of *paragein* to lead past, change (a letter slightly), fr. *par-* 1para- + *agein* to lead, drive — more at AGENT] **:** the addition of a sound or syllable to the end of a word either inorganically (as in *against*) or to give emphasis or modify the meaning (as in Hebrew)

**par·a·gog·ic** \¦==¦gäjik\ *also* **par·a·gog·i·cal** \-jəkəl\ *adj* **:** of, relating to, or constituting a paragoge ⟨a ~ vowel⟩ — **par·a·gog·i·cal·ly** \-jək(ə)lē\ *adv*

1**par·a·gon** \'parəˌgän *also* 'per- *or* -ˌgən\ *n* -s [MF, fr. OIt *paragone*, lit., touchstone, fr. *paragonare* to compare, test on a touchstone, fr. Gk *parakonan* to rub against, sharpen, fr. *par-* 1para- + *akonan* to sharpen, fr. *akonē* whetstone, fr. *akē* point — more at EDGE] **1 :** a model of excellence or perfection **:** PATTERN ⟨a ~ of beauty⟩ ⟨a ~ of eloquence⟩ ⟨a ~ of virtue⟩ ⟨these fictional ~*s*, whose unalloyed happiness depends upon the determination to grin and bear it —W.F.Hambly⟩ ⟨the handsome . . . factory, a ~ in its day —Lewis Mumford⟩ ⟨the French court . . . the ~ of all the lesser courts —Walter Lippmann⟩ **2 :** a match in rivalry or companionship **:** MATE **3** *obs* **:** EMULATION, RIVALRY, COMPETITION **4** *obs* **:** a clothing and upholstery fabric of the 17th and 18th centuries similar to camlet **5 a :** a perfect diamond of 100 carats or more **b :** a perfectly spherical pearl of exceptional size **6 :** a black marble **7 :** an old size of type of approximately 20 point and slightly larger than great primer

2**paragon** \"\ *vt* -ED/-ING/-S [MF *paragonner*, fr. *paragon*, n.] **1 :** to compare with **:** PARALLEL **2 :** to put in rivalry with, MATCH **3** *obs* **:** SURPASS ⟨a maid that ~*s* description —Shak.⟩

**par·a·gon·i·mi·a·sis** \ˌparəˌgänə'mīəsəs\ *n, pl* **paragonimiases** \-īəˌsēz\ [NL, fr. *Paragonimus* (genus name of *Paragonimus westermanii*) + *-iasis*] **:** infestation with or disease caused by a lung fluke (*Paragonimus westermanii*) that invades the lung where it produces chronic bronchitis with cough and reddish or brownish sputum and that occas. also enters other viscera or the brain

**par·a·gon·i·mus** \ˌparə'gänəməs\ *n, cap* [NL, fr. 1*para-* + Gk *gonimos* productive — more at GONIMOBLAST] **:** a genus of digenetic trematodes (family Troglotrematidae) comprising forms normally parasitic in the lungs of mammals including man — compare PARAGONIMIASIS

**pa·rag·o·nite** \pə'ragəˌnīt, 'parəg-\ *n* -s [G *paragonit*, fr. Gk *paragōn* (pres. part. of *paragein* to lead past, mislead) + G *-it* -ite — more at PARAGOGE] **:** a mica $NaAl_3Si_3O_{10}(OH)_2$ corresponding to muscovite but with sodium instead of potassium — **pa·rag·o·nit·ic** \=¦==¦nid·ik, ¦===-\ *adj*

**paragonize** *vt* -ED/-ING/-S [1*paragon* + *-ize*] *obs* **:** PARAGON

**para·gram** \'parəˌgram\ *n* [Gk (*skōmma*) *para gramma* (joke) by letter, fr. *para* beside, beyond, by + *gramma* letter — more at PARA-, GRAM] **:** a pun made by changing the letters of a word, esp. the initial letter — **para·gram·ma·tist** \ˌ==-'gramədəst\ *n* -s

1**par·a·graph** \'parəˌgraf, -graa(ə)f, -graif, -gráf *also* 'per-\ *n* [MF & ML; MF *paragraphe* section of writing, fr. ML *paragraphus* sign used to mark a new section of writing, fr. Gk *paragraphos* line used to mark change of persons in a dialogue, fr. *paragraphein* to write alongside, fr. *para-* 1para- + *graphein* to write — more at CARVE] **1 a :** a distinct section or subdivision of a written or printed composition that consists of from one to many sentences, forms a rhetorical unit (as by dealing with a particular point of the subject or by comprising the words of a distinct speaker), and is indicated by beginning on a new usu. indented line **b :** a usu. numbered article or section of a law or legal document **c :** a short composition consisting of a group of sentences dealing with a single topic **d :** a short article, item, or note in a newspaper or magazine that is complete in one typographical section **2 :** a character (as ¶) used to indicate the beginning of a paragraph (as in manuscripts and printer's proofs) and in printing as the sixth in series of the reference marks

2**paragraph** \"\ *vt* **1 :** to write paragraphs about **:** mention in a paragraph ⟨sneered at by all my acquaintance and ~*ed* in the newspapers —R.B.Sheridan⟩ **2 :** to divide into paragraphs ⟨the Revised Version is much better ~*ed* than the Authorized —J.T.Sunderland⟩ ~ *vi* **:** to write paragraphs; *specif* **:** to work as a paragrapher

**par·a·graph·er** \'==ˌ=ə(r)\ *n* -s **:** a writer of paragraphs esp. for the editorial page of a newspaper

**para·graph·ia** \ˌ=='grafēə\ *n* -s [NL, fr. 1*para-* + *-graphia*] **:** a condition in mental disorder or brain injury in which words or letters other than those intended are written

**par·a·graph·ic** \¦==¦grafik, -fēk\ *or* **para·graph·i·cal** \-fəkəl, -fēk-\ *adj* **:** of, relating to, or having the characteristics of a paragraph — **par·a·graph·i·cal·ly** \-fək(ə)lē, -fēk-, -li\ *adv*

**par·a·graph·ist** \'==ˌgrafəst, -raaf-,-raif-,-ráf-\ *n* -s **:** PARAGRAPHER

**para grass** *n, usu cap P* [fr. *Pará*, state and city in Brazil] **1 :** a perennial pasture and green forage grass (*Panicum purpurascens*) grown in tropical countries and esp. suited to soils too wet for other crops **2 :** piassava fiber

**par·a·guay** \'parəˌgwī, -wā *also* 'per-\ *adj, usu cap* [fr. *Paraguay*, country of So. America] **:** of or from Paraguay **:** of the kind or style prevalent in Paraguay **:** PARAGUAYAN

1**par·a·guay·an** \¦==¦gwīən, -¦gwāən\ *adj, usu cap* [Sp *paraguayano*, adj. & n., fr. *Paraguay*, country in So. America + Sp *-ano* -an] **:** of, relating to, or characteristic of Paraguay

2**paraguayan** \"\ *n* -s *cap* [Sp *paraguayano*] **:** a native or inhabitant of Paraguay

**paraguay bur** *n* **:** SHEEP BUR a

**paraguay tea** *n, usu cap P* **:** MATÉ

**para·hematin** \¦parə+\ *n* [1*para-* + *hematin*] **:** a combination of a ferriporphyrin with a nitrogen base (as pyridine) — compare HEMOCHROMOGEN 1

**para·hemophilia** \"+\ *n* [NL, fr. 1*para-* + *hemophilia*] **:** a tendency to bleed due to the absence of a clotting factor in the blood

**para·hepatic** \"+\ *adj* [1*para-* + *hepatic*] **:** adjacent to the liver

**para·hilgardite** \"+\ *n* [1*para-* + *hilgardite*] **:** a mineral $Ca_8(B_6O_{11})_3Cl_4.4H_2O$ consisting of a hydrous borate and chloride of calcium dimorphous with hilgardite

**para·hippus** \¦parə¦hipəs\ *n, cap* [NL, fr. 1*para-* + *-hippus*] **:** a genus of Miocene horses intermediate in structure between the genera *Miohippus* and *Merychippus* and having three digits on each foot

**para·hopeite** \ˌparə+\ *n* [¹*para-* + *hopeite*] **:** a mineral $Zn_3(PO_4)_2.4H_2O$ consisting of a hydrous zinc phosphate, being dimorphous with hopeite, and occurring in colorless tabular triclinic crystals (hardness 3.7, sp. gr. 3.3)

**para·hormone** *or* **para·hormonic** \"+\ *n* [*parahormone* fr. ¹*para-* + *hormone; parahormonic* fr. ¹*para-* + *hormone* + *-ic*] **:** a substance that functions as a hormone but is of relatively nonspecific nature (as carbon dioxide in its effect on the respiratory center in the brain)

**para-hydrogen** \ˌparə+\ *n* [¹*para-* + *hydrogen*] **:** molecular hydrogen in which the two hydrogen nuclei are spinning in opposite directions so that their contribution to the total angular momentum is zero — compare ORTHO-HYDROGEN

**para·hydroxybenzoic acid** \"+...-\ *n* [¹*para-* + *hydroxybenzoic*] **:** HYDROXYBENZOIC ACID a — written systematically with ital. *para-* or *p-*

**paraison** *var of* PARISON

**pa·rai·yan** \pəˈrī(y)ən\ *n* -s *usu cap* [Tamil *paraiyan* — more at PARIAH] **1 :** a member of the pariah caste **2 :** a Dravidian laboring class

**parakeet** *var of* PARRAKEET

**par·a·ke·lia** *also* **par·a·kee·lia** *or* **par·a·kil·ya** \ˌparəˈkēlyə\ *n* -s [native name in Australia] **:** a succulent herb (*Calandrinia balonensis*) that is an important livestock feed in drier parts of interior Australia

**para·keratosis** \ˌparə+\ *n* [NL, fr. ¹*para-* + *keratosis*] **:** an abnormality of the horny layer of the skin resulting in a disturbance in the process of keratinization — **para·keratotic** \"+\ *adj*

**para·ki·ne·sia** \ˌparəˌkīˈnēzh(ē)ə, -kə'-\ *or* **para·ki·ne·sis** \-ēsəs\ *n, pl* **parakine·sias** \-ēzh(ē)əz\ *or* **parakine·ses** \-ēˌsēz\ [NL, fr. ¹*para-* + *-kinesia* or Gk *kinēsis* motion — more at KINESIS] **:** disorder of motor function resulting in strange and abnormal movements — **para·ki·net·ic** \ˌ==(ˌ)==ˈned·ik\ *adj*

**pa·ral·a·brax** \pəˈraləˌbraks\ *n, cap* [NL, fr. ¹*para-* + Gk *labrax* bass] **:** a common genus of Pacific sea basses (family Serranidae) including the kelp bass of California

**para·lalia** \ˌparəˈlālēə, -ˈlal-\ *n* -s [NL, fr. ¹*para-* + *-lalia*] **:** a speech disorder marked by distortions of sounds or substitution of letters

**para·lambdacism** \ˌparə+\ *n* [¹*para-* + *lambdacism*] **:** inability to pronounce the sound of *l* or difficulty in pronouncing it with some other sound (as of *t, r,* or *w*) being usu. substituted — compare LAMBDACISM

**para·laurionite** \"+\ *n* [¹*para-* + *laurionite*] **:** a mineral PbCl(OH) consisting of a basic lead chloride dimorphous with laurionite (sp. gr. 6.1)

**par·aldehyde** \(ˈ)par+\ *n* [¹*para-* + *aldehyde*] **:** a colorless liquid of pleasant odor but disagreeable taste that is a cyclic trimer $C_6H_{12}O_3$ of acetaldehyde formed by adding a drop or two of sulfuric acid to acetaldehyde, that regenerates acetaldehyde on heating with dilute acids, and that is used chiefly as a source of acetaldehyde and as a hypnotic; trimethyl-trioxane — compare METALDEHYDE

**par·aldol** \"+\ *n* [ISV ¹*para-* + *aldol*] **:** a crystalline cyclic dimer $C_8H_{16}O_4$ of aldol that separates from aldol on standing

**para·lectotype** \ˌparə+\ *n* [¹*para-* + *lectotype*] **:** any of a type series remaining after the designation of the lectotype

**para·leip·sis** \ˌparəˈlīpsəs, -ˈlāp-\ *or* **para·lep·sis** \-lep-\ *or* **para·lip·sis** \-lip-\ *n, pl* **paraleip·ses** *or* **paralep·ses** *or* **paralip·ses** \-p(ˌ)sēz\ [LL & Gk; LL *paraleipsis, paralipsis,* fr. Gk *paraleipsis* neglect, omission, paraleipsis, fr. *paraleipein* to neglect, omit, leave untold (fr. *para-* ¹para- + *leipein* to leave) + *-sis* — more at LOAN] **:** a passing over with brief mention in order to emphasize rhetorically the suggestiveness of what is omitted (as in "I confine to this page the volume of his treacheries and debaucheries")

**para·lex·ia** \ˌparəˈleksēə\ *n* -s [NL, fr. ¹*para-* + *-lexia*] **:** a disturbance in reading ability marked by the transposition of words or syllables and usu. associated with brain injury — **para·lex·ic** \ˌ==ˈ=sik\ *adj*

**par·algesia** \ˌpar+\ *n* [NL, fr. ¹*para-* + *algesia*] **:** disordered or abnormal sensation — **par·algesic** \"+\ *adj*

**pa·ral·ic** \pəˈralik\ *adj* [ISV *paral-* (fr. Gk *paralia* seacoast, fr. *para-* ¹para- + *hal-, hals* salt, sea + *-ia* -y) + *-ic* — more at SALT] **:** of, relating to, or being interfingered marine and continental sediments

**pa·ral·ich·thys** \ˌparəˈlikthəs\ *n, cap* [NL, fr. Gk *paralia* + *ichthys* fish — more at ICHTHUS] **:** a widespread genus of flatfishes that includes the summer flounder, the California halibut, and other important food fishes and that is sometimes made type of a separate family but is usu. included in Bothidae

**para·limnetic** \ˌparə+\ *adj* [¹*para-* + *limnetic*] **:** of, relating to, or constituting a paralimnion

**para·limnion** \ˌparəˌlimnēˌän, -ēən\ *n* -s [NL, fr. ¹*para-* + *-limnion*] **:** the littoral portion of a lake extending from the margin to the deepest limit of rooted vegetation

**para·li·pom·e·na** \ˌparəlīˈpämənə, -ˌlī-\ *n pl* [LL, fr. Gk *paraleipomena*, lit., things left out, fr. neut. pl. of *paraleipomenos,* pres. pass. part. of *paraleipein* to omit — more at PARALEIPSIS] **:** things passed over but added as a supplement ⟨political writings as obvious ~ done merely to make money —H.J.Laski⟩

**par·al·lac·tic** \ˌparəˈlaktik\ *adj* [NL *parallacticus,* fr. Gk *parallaktikos,* fr. *parallaxis* parallax — more at PARALLAX] **:** of, relating to, or due to parallax

**parallactic angle** *n* **:** the spherical angle between the hour circle and the vertical circle passing through a celestial body

**parallactic equation** *n* **:** a minor inequality of the moon's orbital motion caused by the difference between the sun's perturbing action on the moon when at new and full and used in finding the sun's parallax

**parallactic libration of the moon :** diurnal libration of the moon caused by the observer's view over the upper limb of the moon when it is rising and setting

**parallactic motion** *n* **:** the part of the observed proper motion of a star that is caused by the motion of the observer with the solar system as a whole

**parallactic orbit** *n* **:** the orbit in which a star appears to move once round each year owing to the earth's orbital motion round the sun

**par·al·lax** \ˈparəˌlaks\ *n* -ES [MF *parallaxe,* fr. Gk *parallaxis* change, alternation, parallax, fr. *parallassein* to change, differ, fr. *para-* ¹para- + *allassein* to change, fr. *allos* other, different — more at ELSE] **1 :** the apparent displacement or the difference in apparent direction of an object as seen from two different points not on a straight line with the object ⟨our two eyes are as a rule only about 2½ inches apart; yet the small ~ caused by the slightly different angle of vision enables us to see three-dimensional, plastic images and to judge distances accurately —Erwin Raisz⟩ **2 a :** GEOCENTRIC PARALLAX **b :** HELIOCENTRIC PARALLAX **c :** STELLAR PARALLAX **d :** HORIZONTAL PARALLAX

**¹par·al·lel** \ˈparəˌlel *also* ˈper- *or* -rələl *sometimes* ˌ==ˈlel\ *adj* [L *parallelus,* fr. Gk *parallēlos,* fr. *para* beside + *allēlōn* of one another, fr. *allos . . . allos* one . . . the other — more at PARA-, ELSE] **1 :** extending in the same direction and everywhere equidistant **:** forming a line in the same direction but not meeting ⟨half a dozen ~ scars . . . ran from his forehead into the thickness of his hair —Eric Linklater⟩ ⟨~ rows of tall poplars —*Amer. Guide Series: Wash.*⟩ ⟨the ships steam on ~ courses as close together as feasible —W.D.Leggett⟩ ⟨a long, low house running ~ with the road —G.K.Chesterton⟩ ⟨a line ~ to the edge of a paper⟩ **2 a :** not meeting however far extended — used of lines in the same plane, of planes, or of a line and a plane **b :** everywhere equally distant ⟨concentric circles are ~⟩ ⟨concentric spheres are ~⟩ ⟨involutes of the same space curve are ~⟩ **3 a :** having parallel sides ⟨a ~ file⟩ ⟨a ~ gutter⟩ ⟨a ~ reamer⟩ **b :** being or relating to an electrical circuit having a number of conductors in parallel **4 a :** marked by likeness or correspondence esp. in time, direction, course, tendency, or development **:** similar, analogous, or interdependent in line followed **:** tending toward the same point or result ⟨~ strikes on the railroads, in the gas and electricity services —Percy Winner⟩ ⟨the standing committee systems in the two Houses are reasonably ~ —Harold Zink⟩ **b :** set side by side **:** capable of being matched **:** COMPANION **:** readily compared or contrasted ⟨the marriage rate turned upward . . . the birth rate entered upon a ~ climb —Oscar Handlin⟩ ⟨all sorts of pranks, ~ to the serious exploits performed by the heroes —R.A.Hall b.1911⟩ **c :** having identical syntactic elements in corresponding positions **d :** keeping at the same distance apart in musical pitch **:** having consecutive motion ⟨~ voice parts⟩ ⟨~ fifths⟩ — compare CONSECUTIVE INTERVALS **5 :** of or in accordance with philosophical parallelism **syn** see LIKE

**²parallel** \"\ *n* -s **1 a :** a parallel line, curve, or surface **b** (1) **:** one of the imaginary circles on the surface of the earth paralleling the equator and marking the latitude (2) **:** the corresponding line on a globe or map **c :** one of a series of long trenches that is approximately parallel to the face of fortification works attacked and that is constructed by a besieging force as a cover for troops **d :** a character ‖ used in printing as the fifth in series of the reference marks — often used in pl. **2 a :** something equal or similar in all essential details **:** COUNTERPART ⟨progress that is without ~ in the history of mankind —*Current Biog.*⟩ ⟨the situation of modern man . . . has no ~ in the past —Rudolf Allers⟩ ⟨conductor of such genius that he has no exact ~ in reality —Marcia Davenport⟩ ⟨implements from near the end of the old Stone Age find ~s among those of the Eskimo —A.L.Kroeber⟩ **b :** agreement in many or all essential details **:** RESEMBLANCE, SIMILARITY, ANALOGUE ⟨there are ~s in *Grettis Saga* . . . to encounters like this —W.P.Ker⟩ ⟨pre-Columbian cultural ~s found in the two hemispheres —R.W.Murray⟩ **3 :** a comparison to show resemblance **:** a tracing of similarity ⟨many interesting ~s are drawn with the historical plays of Shakespeare —*Times Lit. Supp.*⟩ **4 a :** parallel position or state of being physically parallel **:** PARALLELISM ⟨deviation of the two visual lines from ~ —H.G.Armstrong⟩ **b :** the arrangement of electrical devices (as incandescent lamps or the cells of a battery) in which all positive poles, electrodes, and terminals are joined to one conductor and all negative ones to another conductor so that each unit is in effect on a parallel branch ⟨several generators operated in ~⟩ — called also *multiple;* contrasted with *series* **5 a :** PARALLEL RULE **b :** a block or strip of metal made with two parallel sides and used esp. in machine-shop work (as for a gage block or for setting up work) **6 :** a raised platform that is parallel with the floor, that has a folding base, and that is used esp. for lights or cameras (as in the theater or in a television studio); *also* **:** the folding base **syn** see COMPARISON

**³parallel** \"\ *vb* -ED/-ING/-S *vt* **1 :** to set up as closely analogous or agreeing in essential qualities or characteristics **:** COMPARE ⟨he ~s the jollity of Christmas at Dingley Dell with the picture of country life in Attica —Lucien Price⟩ **2 a :** to show something equal or parallel to **:** MATCH ⟨~ that stage of national culture —Deems Taylor⟩ ⟨disablement behavior amongst birds may be ~ed in human life —E.A.Armstrong⟩ ⟨with a precipitancy only to be ~ed by her exit from this mortal scene —T.L.Peacock⟩ ⟨state of affairs is partially ~ed in contemporary medicine —A.L.Kroeber⟩ ⟨long head hair in some humans is ~ed by that of Angora cats —Weston LaBarre⟩ **b :** to be or form a parallel to **:** correspond to ⟨a piece of fiction ~ing a historical incident⟩ ⟨~ing this change in artistic practice is a change in the concurrent critical apologia —Bernard Smith⟩ ⟨program which roughly ~ed the private school —J.B.Conant⟩ ⟨the career of the principal character ~s the actual life story —Bennett Cerf⟩ **3** *obs* **:** to produce or adduce as a parallel ⟨my young remembrance cannot ~ a fellow to it —Shak.⟩ **4 :** to place so as to be parallel to or to conform in direction with something ⟨machines comb, ~, and blend the fibers —*Story of Twine in Agriculture*⟩ ⟨three rifles were ~ed on pegs —Stephen Crane⟩ **5 :** to extend, run, or move in a direction parallel to **:** correspond to or match in direction ⟨an airstrip ~ing the highway⟩ ⟨the route ~s the river⟩ ~ *vi* **:** to be parallel ⟨long and narrow farms, crowded by ~ing ridges —*Amer. Guide Series: Pa.*⟩

**⁴parallel** \"\ *adv* **:** in a parallel manner — often used with *with* or *to*

**parallel axiom** *n* **:** PARALLEL POSTULATE

**parallel bars** *n pl* **:** a pair of parallel wooden handrails adjustable in height and spacing, connected to metal uprights secured to a common base, and used for gymnastic exercises

parallel bars

**parallel christiania** *n, often cap C* **:** a stem christiania executed as close as possible to the fall line and at high speed so as to make the stem preparation indiscernible

**parallel cousin** *n* **:** one of two cousins who are the children of two brothers or two sisters — compare CROSS-COUSIN

**parallel dash** *n* **:** a graphic character ═══ sometimes used to mark page or column divisions in printed matter

**par·al·lel·epi·ped** \ˌparəˌleləˈpīpəd *also* -ˌleləˈpipəd *or* -ˌleˈlepəˌped *or* -ˌləˈlepəˌped\ *also* **par·al·lel·e·pip·e·don** \-ˌlelə'pipəˌdän, -ˌdᵊn\ *or* **par·al·lel·o·piped** \-ˌleləˈpīpəd *also* -ˈpip-\ *or* **par·al·lel·o·pip·e·don** \-ˌleləˈpipəˌdän, -ˌdᵊn\ *n* -s [Gk *parallēlepipedon,* fr. *parallēlos* parallel + *epipedon* plane surface, fr. neut. of *epipedos* level, flat, fr. *epi-* + *pedon* ground — more at PEDION] **:** a prism whose bases are parallelograms — **par·al·lel·e·pip·e·dal** \ˌparəˌleləˈpipədᵊl *also* -ˌleˌlepəˈpedᵊl *or* -ˌləˌlepəˈpedᵊl\ *or* **par·al·lel·o·pip·e·dal** \ˌparəˌleləˈpipədᵊl\ *adj*

parallelepiped

**parallel file** *n* **:** BLUNT FILE

**parallel forces** *n pl* **:** forces acting in parallel lines

**parallel induction** *n* **:** a hypothetical simultaneous modification of germ plasm and somatoplasm that is due to environmental factors and produces basically similar effects in germ and body cells so that offspring of a modified individual appear to inherit acquired somatic characters

**par·al·lel·ism** \ˈparəˌleˌlizəm, -rələˌli- *also* ˈper-\ *n* -s **1 :** the quality or state of being parallel ⟨a lack of ~ of the heads of the testing machine —*Proving Rings for Calibrating Testing Machines*⟩ **2 :** RESEMBLANCE, CORRESPONDENCE, SIMILARITY ⟨~ of interests⟩ ⟨~ in nomenclature between the kinship terms of affinity in English, French, and German —Edward Sapir⟩ ⟨~ between obesity and hypertension —H.M.Marvin⟩ **3 a :** similarity of construction of adjacent word groups equivalent, complementary, or antithetic in sense esp. for rhetorical effect or rhythm **b :** reiteration in similar phrases (as in Hebrew poetry) **4 :** a philosophical theory that mind and matter accompany one another but are not causally related: **a :** a theory that mind and matter are universally coordinate aspects of reality — compare DUALISM, INTERACTIONISM, OCCASIONALISM **b :** PSYCHOPHYSICAL PARALLELISM **5 :** the development or possession of similar new characters by two or more related organisms in response to similarity of environment — compare CONVERGENCE 3 **6 :** the independent development of similar elements or traits in several cultures from a common element — compare CONVERGENCE 4, DIFFUSION 1

**par·al·lel·ist** \-rəˌleləst *also* -rələlə-\ *n* -s **1 :** one who draws a parallel **2 :** an adherent of philosophical parallelism

**par·al·lel·is·tic** \ˌ==ˌleˈlistik, ˌ==ləˌli-\ *adj* **1 :** having the nature of or involving a parallelism **2 a :** of or relating to philosophical parallelism or parallelists **b :** resembling or leading to parallelism

**par·al·lel·iza·tion** \ˌ==ˌlelə'zāshən, ˌ|ī'z-, ˌ==ˌlə|\ *n* -s **:** the process of parallelizing or the state of being parallelized

**par·al·lel·ize** \ˈ==(ˌ)=ˌlīz\ *vt* -ED/-ING/-S [Gk *parallēlizein,* fr. *parallēlos* parallel + *-izein* -ize — more at PARALLEL] **1 :** to make parallel ⟨~ fibers⟩ **2 :** to place parallel to **:** bring into parallelism with

**par·al·lel·ly** \ˈ==ˌlel|lē, ˈ==ˌlə(l)|lē, |li\ *adv* **:** in a parallel manner

**parallel motion** *n* **1 :** a jointed link or other mechanism for reproducing motion parallel to itself; *also* **:** a straight-line motion **2 :** melodic progression of two voices moving in same direction by the same intervals

**parallel of altitude :** ALMUCANTAR 1

**parallel of declination :** one of the small circles of the celestial sphere that is parallel to the celestial equator

**parallel of latitude :** PARALLEL 1b

**par·al·lelo·gram** \ˌ==ˈleləˌgram, -raa(ə)m\ *n* [LL or Gk; LL *parallelogrammum,* fr. Gk *parallelogrammon,* fr. neut. of *parallelogrammos* bounded by parallel lines, fr. *parallēlos* parallel + *grammē* line, fr. *graphein* to write — more at PARALLEL, CARVE] **1 a :** a quadrilateral with opposite sides parallel — see RECTANGLE, RHOMBOID, RHOMBUS; AREA table **2 :** a four-bar mechanism jointed together in the form of a parallelogram with one link fixed

parallelograms

**parallelogram law** *n* **:** a law in physics: the resultant of two vector quantities represented in magnitude, direction, and sense by two adjacent sides of a parallelogram both of which are directed toward or away from their point of intersection is the diagonal of the parallelogram through that point

**par·al·lelo·gram·mat·ic** \ˌ==ˌleləgrəˈmad·ik\ *or* **par·al·lelo·gram·mat·i·cal** \-d·əkəl\ *adj* [*parallelogram* + *-atic* (as in *grammatic, grammatical*)] **:** of, relating to, or like a parallelogram

**par·al·lelo·gram·mic** \ˌ==ˌ==ˈgramik\ *or* **par·al·lelo·gram·mi·cal** \-məkəl\ *adj* **:** PARALLELOGRAMMATIC

**parallelogram of forces :** a parallelogram having two adjacent sides that represent two force vectors and an included diagonal that represents the vector sum

**par·al·lel·om·e·ter** \ˌ==ˌleˈlämәd·ə(r), ˌ==ˌləˈlä-\ *n* [*parallel* + *-o-* + *-meter*] **:** a device to test the parallelism of flat surfaces

**parallelopiped** *or* **parallelopipedon** *var of* PARALLELEPIPED

**parallel perspective** *n* **:** perspective in which the important edges and faces of objects are represented in the picture as either parallel or perpendicular to the picture plane — called also *one-point perspective*

**parallel postulate** *n* **:** a postulate in geometry: if a straight line incident on two straight lines make the sum of the angles within and on the same side less than two right angles the two straight lines being produced indefinitely meet one another on whichever side the two angles are less than the two right angles — called also *parallel axiom*

**parallel resonance** *n* **:** electrical antiresonance accomplished with a capacitance and an inductance in parallel

**parallel-resonant** \ˌ==(ˌ)=ˌ=(=)=\ *adj* **:** marked by parallel resonance

**parallel rule** *or* **parallel ruler** *n* **:** an instrument for drawing a line parallel to another or a series of parallel lines: as **a :** a flat rule running on a pair of rollers in one of its sides **b :** a pair of straightedges connected by two equal parallel links so that one straightedge can be moved only parallel to the other

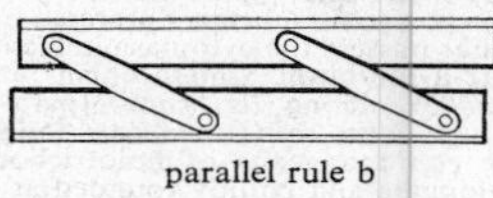

parallel rule b

**¹parallels** *n pl* [fr. pl. of ²*parallel*] **:** CONSECUTIVES

**²parallels** *pres 3d sing of* PARALLEL

**parallel sailing** *n* **:** spherical sailing in which the course is along a parallel and departure is the product of cosine latitude times the difference of longitude — opposed to *meridian sailing*

**parallel sphere** *n* **:** the celestial sphere seen from either the north or the south pole of the earth where all the celestial bodies seem to move in small circles parallel to the horizon

**parallel stance** *n* **:** SQUARE STANCE

**parallel standard** *n* **:** a monetary system in which both gold and silver are freely coined and are legal tender but in which their relative values are not fixed — compare BIMETALLISM

**parallel sulcus** *n* **:** a sulcus parallel to but some distance below the horizontal limb of the fissure of Sylvius

**parallel texture** *n, of rock* **:** a texture with tabular or prismatic crystals arranged more or less regularly in parallel positions

**parallel turn** *n* **:** TEMPO TURN

**parallel-veined** \ˌ==(ˌ)=ˌ=\ *adj, of a leaf* **:** having veins nearly or quite parallel to one another — compare NET-VEINED

**parallel vise** *n* **:** a vise with jaws so guided as to remain parallel

**parallel winding** *n* **:** LAP WINDING

**par·al·lely** *like* PARALLELLY\ *adv* **:** PARALLEL

**para·lo·gia** \ˌparəˈlōj(ē)ə\ *n* -s [NL, fr. ¹*para-* + *-logia*] **:** a reasoning disorder characterized by inappropriate responses to questioning and based on underlying autistic or dereistic processes (as in schizophrenia)

**para·log·i·cal** \ˌ==ˈläjəkəl\ *adj* [Gk *paralogos* unexpected, unreasonable + E *-ical*] **:** containing paralogism **:** ILLOGICAL

**pa·ral·o·gism** \pəˈraləˌjizəm\ *n* -s [MF *paralogisme,* fr. LL *paralogismus,* fr. Gk *paralogismos,* fr. *paralogos* unexpected, unreasonable (fr. *para-* ¹para- + *logos* word, reason, speech, account) + *-ismos* -ism — more at LEGEND] **1 :** a reasoning contrary to logical rules or formulas **:** FORMAL FALLACY **2 :** a fallacy of arguing from the empty concept of the ego to its substantiality and eternality

**pa·ral·o·gist** \-jəst\ *n* -s [*paralogism* + *-ist*] **:** one who uses reasoning that begs the question **:** one who uses a paralogism

**pa·ral·o·gis·tic** \=ˌ==ˈjistik\ *adj* **:** utilizing or having the nature of a paralogism **:** FALLACIOUS

**pa·ral·o·gize** \=ˈ==ˌjīz\ *vi* -ED/-ING/-S [ML *paralogizare,* fr. Gk *paralogizesthai,* fr. *paralogos* + *-izesthai,* middle & passive form of *-izein* -ize] **:** to reason falsely **:** to draw conclusions not warranted by the premises

**pa·ral·y·sis** \pəˈraləsəs\ *n, pl* **paraly·ses** \-əˌsēz\ [L, fr. Gk, fr. *paralyein* to loosen, disable (fr. *para-* ¹para- + *lyein* to unbind, release, paralyze) + *-sis* — more at LOSE] **1 a :** complete or partial loss of function involving the power of motion or of sensation in any part of the body **:** PALSY — see HEMIPLEGIA, PARAPLEGIA, PARESIS **b :** a disorder of the adult honeybee characterized by trembling **2 :** loss of the ability to move ⟨overcrowded office buildings add to the ~ of traffic —Lewis Mumford⟩ ⟨congestion is increased, sometimes almost to the point of ~, because of the increasing size and number of trucks —*Zoning for Truck-Loading Facilities*⟩ **3 :** a state of powerlessness or inactivity **:** IMPOTENCE ⟨with the ~ of industry will come the surrender of political authority —Louis Wasserman⟩ ⟨a sort of ~ seems to have affected the soldiers when they touched politics —R.C.K.Ensor⟩ ⟨the weakling . . . had succumbed to a ~ of fear —E.S.Miers⟩ ⟨enough idleness to threaten the nation's business . . . with complete ~ —Roger Burlingame⟩ ⟨recurrent depressions have brought ~ to as much as one third of our plants and machines —*U.S. Code*⟩

**paralysis ag·i·tans** \-ˈajəˌtanz\ *n* [NL, lit., shaking palsy] **:** a chronic progressive nervous disease occurring in advanced life and marked by tremor and weakness of resting muscles, rigidity, masklike facial expression, and a peculiar gait — called also *shaking palsy, Parkinson's disease*

**paralysis tick** *n* **:** a tick whose bite causes paralysis; *esp* **:** ROCKY MOUNTAIN WOOD TICK

**¹par·a·lyt·ic** \ˌparəˈlid·|ik, -lit|, |ēk *also* ˌper-\ *also* **par·a·lyt·i·cal** \|əkəl, |ēk-\ *adj* [*paralytic* fr. ME *peralitik,* fr. MF *paralitique,* fr. L *paralyticus,* fr. Gk *paralytikos,* fr. *paralytos* (verbal of *paralyein*) + *-ikos* -ic; *paralytical* fr. *paralytic* + *-al*] **1 :** affected with or accompanied by paralysis **2 :** of, relating to, or resembling paralysis **:** characteristic of paralysis

**²paralytic** \"\ *n* -s [ME *paralitik,* fr. MF *paralitique,* fr. *paralitique,* adj.] **1 :** a person affected with paralysis **2 :** a drug used to relieve skeletal muscle and prevent spasm esp. during surgery — compare RELAXANT

**par·a·lyt·i·cal·ly** \|ək(ə)lē, |ēk-, -li\ *adv* **:** in a paralytic manner

**paralytic dementia** *n* **:** SYPHILITIC PARESIS

**paralytic rabies** *n* **:** DUMB RABIES

**¹par·a·ly·zant** *also* **par·a·ly·sant** \ˈparəˌlīzᵊnt, pəˈraləzənt\ *adj* [ISV *paralyze, paralyse* + *-ant* (adj. suffix)] **:** causing paralysis

**²paralyzant** *also* **paralysant** \"\ *n* -s **:** an agent that causes paralysis

**par·a·ly·za·tion** \ˌparələˈzāshən, -ˌlīˈz-\ *n* -s **:** paralyzed state ⟨the ~ of the forces of law and order⟩; *also* **:** the act or process of paralyzing

**par·a·lyze** *also* **par·a·lyse** \ˈparəˌlīz *also* ˈper-\ *vt* -ED/-ING/-S [F *paralyser,* back-formation fr. *paralysie* paralysis, fr. L *paralysis* — more at PARALYSIS] **1 :** to affect with paralysis

**2 :** to deprive of strength or activity **:** make powerless **:** make ineffective ⟨a strike that ~s an industry⟩ ⟨the atomic bomb . . . can be used to ~ if not destroy a nation —W.O.Douglas⟩ ⟨grand jury could ~ government by indicting a number of important public officials for minor offenses —*N.Y. Times*⟩ ⟨a country economically bankrupt, politically *paralyzed* —W.D.Clark⟩ ⟨discriminating laws *paralyzed* our efforts to lend a helping hand —*Jour. of Internat'l Affairs*⟩ **3 :** UNNERVE ⟨the *paralyzing* thing is the uncertainty —Evelyn Whitehead⟩ ⟨pressure did not ~ the free world but, rather, forged its unity —A.E.Stevenson b.1900⟩ **4 :** STUN, STUPEFY, PETRIFY ⟨would ~ the empire with the news —Rudyard Kipling⟩ **5 :** to bring to an end **:** DESTROY, PREVENT ⟨the assertion that principles ~ action —M.R.Cohen⟩ ⟨deadlock *paralyzed* action —F.A.Ogg & Harold Zink⟩ ⟨moral passion . . . has ended by *paralyzing* his aesthetic appreciation —Edmund Wilson⟩ **syn** see DAZE

**par·a·lyzed·ly** \-z(ə)dlē\ *adv* **:** in a paralyzed manner

**par·a·lyz·er** \-zə(r)\ *n* -s **:** one that paralyzes

**par·a·lyz·ing·ly** *adv* **:** in a paralyzing manner

**para magenta** \ˌparə-\ *n, often cap P&M* [pararosaniline] **:** PARA FUCHSINE

**para·magnet** \ˈparə+,\ *n* [back-formation fr. *paramagnetic*] **:** a paramagnetic substance

**para·magnetic** \"+\ *adj* [ISV ¹*para-* + *magnetic*] **:** being or relating to a magnetizable substance that like aluminum and platinum has small but positive susceptibility varying but little with magnetizing force ⟨~ materials which are but slightly more magnetic than a vacuum, and are therefore attracted weakly by the poles of an electromagnet —R.M. Bozorth & R.A.Chegwidden⟩ — compare DIAMAGNETIC, FERROMAGNETIC

**para·magnetism** \"\ *n* [ISV ¹*para-* + *magnetism*] **:** the magnetism of a paramagnetic substance

**pa·ra·ma·ham·sa** \ˌpərəməˈham(p)sə\ *n* -s [Skt *paramahaṁsa*, fr. *parama* remotest, highest, best (superl. of *parā* away, off) + *haṁsa* swan, goose; akin to Skt *pra-* before, forward — more at FOR, GOOSE] **:** a sannyasi of the highest level of spiritual development in which union with ultimate reality is attained

**para·mastoid** \ˌparə+\ *adj* [¹*para-* + *mastoid*] **:** situated beside or adjacent to the mastoid process ⟨the ~ process⟩

**par·a·mat·ta** *or* **par·ra·mat·ta** \ˌparəˈmadə\ *n* -s [fr. *Parramatta*, Australia] **:** a fine lightweight dress fabric of silk and wool or cotton and wool

**par·a·me·cin** \ˌparəˈmēsᵊn\ *n* -s [NL *paramecium* + E *-in*] **:** a toxic substance secreted into the medium by paramecia that possess the cytoplasmic factor kappa

**par·a·me·cium** \-mēsh(ē)əm, -mēsē\ *n* [NL, fr. Gk *paramēkēs* oblong (fr. *para-* ¹para- + *mēkos* length) + NL *-ium*; akin to Gk *makros* long, tall — more at MEAGER] **1** *cap* **:** a genus of holotrichous ciliates having the body elongate and bluntly rounded at the anterior end and having an oblique funnel-shaped buccal groove on the oral surface with the mouth at the extremity **2** *pl* **parame·cia** \ə\ *or* **parameciums :** a protozoan of the genus *Paramecium*

**para·median** \ˌparə+\ *adj* [ISV ¹*para-* + *median*] **:** situated adjacent to the midline ⟨a ~ scar on the abdomen⟩

¹**para·medic** \ˈparə+,-\ *n* [²*para-* + *medic*] **:** a doctor who parachutes to areas where medical services are needed **:** PARADOCTOR

²**para·medic** *also* **para·medical** \ˌparə+\ *adj* **:** of or relating to a paramedic or paramedics ⟨a ~ team⟩

**para·medical** \ˌparə+\ *adj* [¹*para-* + *medical*] **:** concerned with supplementing the work of medical personnel **:** having a secondary relation to medicine ⟨technicians and pharmacists are ~ personnel⟩

**para·melaconite** \"+\ *n* [¹*para-* + *melaconite*] **:** a tetragonal mineral consisting of cupric and cuprous oxides and occurring in black pyramidal crystals

**para·me·nia** \ˌparəˈmēnēə\ *n* -s [NL, fr. ¹*para-* + *-menia* (fr. *men-* + *-ia*)] **:** disordered menstruation

**par·a·ment** \ˈparəmənt\ *n, pl* **paraments** \-ts\ *also* **para·men·ta** \ˌ==ˈmentə\ [ME, fr. ML *paramentum*, fr. *parare* to adorn (fr. L, to prepare, equip) + L *-mentum* -ment — more at PARE] **:** an ornamental ecclesiastical hanging or vestment — usu. used in pl. ⟨~s to adorn the altar⟩

**para·mer·al** \ˌparəˈmirəl\ *also* **para·mer·ic** \-merik, -mir-\ *adj* **:** of or relating to a paramere

**para·mere** \ˈparə,mi(ə)r\ *n* -s [ISV ¹*para-* + *-mere*] **1 :** the right or left half of a bilateral animal or of a somite **2 :** any of several paired structures of an insect and esp. of its ninth abdominal segment

**pa·ram·er·on** \pəˈramə,rän, -mərən\ *n, pl* **parameron** [NL, fr. ¹*para-* + *-meron* (fr. Gk *meros* part) — more at MERIT] **:** PARAMERE 2

**pa·ram·e·ter** \pəˈramədə(r)\ *n* -s [NL, fr. *para-* + *-meter* (fr. Gk *metron* measure) — more at MEASURE] **1 :** the relative intercept made by a plane on a crystallographic axis, the ratio of the intercepts determining the position of the plane **2 a :** an arbitrary constant characterizing by each of its particular values some particular member of a system (as of expressions, curves, surfaces, functions) ⟨a ~ is a quantity which may have various values each fixed within the limits of a stated case or discussion —T.F.Weldon⟩; *specif* **:** a quantity that describes a statistical population ⟨a clear distinction should always be drawn between ~s and estimates, i.e. between quantities which characterize the universe, and estimates of these quantities calculated from observations —*Statistical Methods in Research & Production*⟩ ⟨estimation of the values of the ~s which enter into the equation representing the chosen relation —Frank Yates⟩ **b :** an independent variable through functions of which other functions may be expressed ⟨four ~s are necessary to determine an event, namely the three which determine its position and the one which determines its time —P.W.Bridgman⟩

**para·metha·di·one** \ˌparə,methəˈdīˌōn\ *n* -s [¹*para-* + *trimethadione*] **:** a liquid compound $C_7H_{11}NO_3$ that is a derivative of trimethadione and is also used in the treatment of petit mal epilepsy

**para·me·tri·al** \ˌparəˈmētrēəl\ *or* **para·me·tric** \-trik\ *adj* [¹*para-* + *metrial* or *-metric* (fr. *metr-* + *-ic*)] **:** located near the uterus

**para·met·ric** \ˌparəˈme·trik\ *also* **pa·ram·e·tral** \pəˈramətrəl\ *adj* [*parameter* + *-ic* or *-al*] **:** of, relating to, or in terms of a parameter

**para·met·ri·cal·ly** \ˌparəˈmetrək(ə)lē\ *adv* **:** in a parametric manner

**para·me·tri·tis** \ˌparəməˈtrīdəs\ *n* -ES [NL, fr. *parametrium* + *-itis*] **:** inflammation of the parametrium

**para·me·tri·um** \ˌparəˈmētrēəm\ *n, pl* **parame·tria** \-trēə\ [NL, fr. ¹*para-* + *-metrium*] **:** connective tissue and fat adjacent to the uterus

**para·military** \ˌparə+\ *adj* [¹*para-* + *military*] **1 :** existing where there are no military services or existing alongside the military services and professedly nonmilitary but formed on an underlying military pattern as a potential auxiliary or diversionary military organization ⟨a ~ police force⟩ **2 :** of or relating to a paramilitary organization

**para·mim·ia** \ˌparəˈmimēə\ *n* -s [NL, fr. ¹*para-* + Gk *mimia, mimeia* mimicry, fr. *mimeisthai* to imitate, represent + *-ia* -y — more at MIME] *psychiatry* **:** a misuse of gestures in expressing thought that produces an appearance of inappropriateness of affect

**paraminophenol** *var of* PARA-AMINOPHENOL — used esp. in photography

**pa·ra·mi·ta** \pəˈrämətə\ *n* -s [Skt *pāramita*, fr. *pāramita*, adj., crossed, traversed, transcendent, fr. *pāra* bringing across + *ita* gone, past part. of *eti* he goes; akin to Skt *piparti* he brings over — more at FARE, ISSUE] **:** one of the perfect virtues (as morality, charity, patience, wisdom) that must be practiced by one who undertakes the path to Buddhahood

**para·mitome** \ˌparə+\ *n* [¹*para-* + *mitome*; orig. formed as G *paramitom*] **:** the ground substance of protoplasm as contrasted with mitome

**par·amne·sia** \ˌpaˌramˈnēzhə, ˌparəmˈnēzh(ē)ə, ˌparə-ˈnēzh(ē)ə\ *n* [NL, fr. ¹*para-* + *-mnesia*] **:** a disorder of memory: as **a :** a condition in which the proper meaning of words cannot be remembered **b :** the illusion of remembering scenes and events experienced for the first time

**pa·ra·mo** \ˈpärə,mō\ *n* -s [AmerSp *páramo*, fr. Sp, wasteland] **:** a high bleak plateau or district (as in the Andes); *specif* **:** alpine meadow of northern and western So. American uplands

**par·a·moe·cium** *syn of* PARAMECIUM

**para·morph** \ˈparə,mȯrf\ *n* [¹*para-* + *-morph*] **1 :** a pseudomorph having the same chemical composition as the original species **2 :** a variant biological form deviating from the mean of the species or other group to which it belongs **:** VARIETY — **para·mor·phic** \ˌ==ˈmȯrfik\ *or* **para·mor·phous** \-fəs\ *adj*

**para·morphine** \ˌparə+\ *n* [ISV ¹*para-* + *morphine*] **:** THEBAINE

**para·mor·phism** \ˌparəˈmȯr,fizəm\ *n* -s **:** the property of changing from one mineral species to another (as from aragonite to calcite) by a change in internal structure and physical characters but not in chemical composition

¹**par·a·mount** \ˈparə,maůnt *also* ˈper-; *substand New York City often* -mänt\ *adj* [AF *paramont*, fr. OF *par* by (fr. L *per* through, by) + *amont* above, fr. *a* to (fr. L *ad*) + *mont* mountain — more at FOR, AT, MOUNT] **1 :** having a higher or the highest rank or authority ⟨one of the ~ sheikhs in the desert —*Times Lit. Supp.*⟩ ⟨the ~ king of Yoruba land —J.G.Frazer⟩ ⟨the ~ patriarch of the group —Weston La Barre⟩ **2 :** superior to all others (as in power, position, or importance) **:** CHIEF, SUPREME, PREEMINENT ⟨the need of this people for water is ~ —M.J.Herskovits⟩ ⟨the new constitution should be . . . ~ over all other constitutions —F.A.Ogg & P.O.Ray⟩ ⟨Federal Government's claim of ~ right and dominion over the resources of the marginal sea —*U.S. Code*⟩ ⟨the reporter is the ~ performer —F.L.Mott⟩ ⟨the ~ problem of our time —Cecil Hobbs⟩ ⟨time is of ~ importance —F.D. Roosevelt⟩ **syn** see DOMINANT

²**paramount** \"\ *n* -s **:** a lord paramount **:** a supreme proprietor or ruler ⟨his cousin . . . the ~ of the tribe —T.E.Lawrence⟩

**par·a·mount·cy** \-n(t)sē, -si\ *n* -ES **:** the quality or state of being paramount

**par·a·mount·ly** \-ntlē, -li\ *adv* **:** in a paramount manner

**par·amour** \ˈparə,mů(ə)r, -mō(ə)r, -mȯ(ə)r, -ůə, -ōə, -ȯ(ə)\ *n* -s [ME, fr. *par amour* through love, by way of love, fr. OF] **:** one who loves or is loved illicitly **:** one taking the place without the legal rights of a husband or wife **:** MISTRESS — called also *lover*

**par·am·phis·tome** \ˌpaˈramˈfi,stōm, ˌparəm-\ *n* -s [NL *Paramphistomum*] **:** a worm of the genus *Paramphistomum* or the family Paramphistomidae

**par·am·phis·to·mum** \-stəməm\ *n, cap* [NL, fr. ¹*para-* + Gk *amphistomon*, neut. of *amphistomos* with a double mouth — more at AMPHISTOMOUS] **:** a genus (the type of the family Paramphistomidae) of conical digenetic trematodes with a large ventral sucker at the posterior end of the body

**par·am·y·lum** \(ˈ)paˈraməlom\ *also* **par·am·y·lon** \-lən, -,län\ *n* -s [NL, fr. ¹*para-* + L *amylum* starch or Gk *amylon* — more at AMYL-] **:** a reserve carbohydrate of various protozoa and algae that resembles starch

**para·my·oc·lo·nus mul·ti·plex** \ˌparə,mīˈäklənəˈsmәltə,-pleks\ *n* [NL, fr. *paramyoclonus* (fr. ¹*para-* + *myoclonus*) + *multiplex* multiple] **:** a nervous disease characterized by clonic spasms with tremor in corresponding muscles on the two sides

**para·myotonia** \ˌparə+\ *n* [NL, fr. ¹*para-* + *myotonia*] **:** an abnormal state characterized by tonic muscle spasm

**para·nagana** \"+\ *n* [¹*para-* + *nagana*] **:** GAMBIA FEVER

**par·anal** \(ˈ)par+\ *adj* [¹*para-* + *anal*] **:** adjacent to the anus ⟨~ glands⟩

**pa·ra·ná pine** \ˌparəˈnä-\ *n, usu cap 1st P* [fr. *Paraná*, river and state in Brazil] **1 :** a timber tree (*Araucaria brasiliana*) of southern Brazil and adjacent regions **2** *also* **parana pine** \" *or* **parana** -s **:** the rather soft yellowish to brown and often rose-streaked wood of paraná pine that is variable in weight and durability, is readily worked and polished, and is used largely in interior finish

**para·nasal** \ˌparə+\ *adj* [¹*para-* + *nasal*] **:** adjacent to the nasal cavities

**paranasal sinus** *n* **:** any of various sinuses (as the maxillary and frontal) in the bones of the face and head that are lined with mucous membrane derived from and continuous with the lining of the nasal cavity

**pa·ran·dja** *also* **pa·ran·ja** \pəˈranjə\ *n* -s [Uzbek] **:** a heavy black horsehair veil worn by women of central Asia

**par·an·drus** \pəˈrandrəs\ *n* -ES [NL, fr. ¹*para-* + Gk *-andrus* (fr. *andr-*, *anēr* man) — more at ANDR-] **:** a mythical stag able to change color like the chameleon

**par·a·nee** \ˌparəˈnē\ *n* -s [¹*paranoid* + *-ee*] **:** the object or victim of paranoid thinking **:** one on whom a paranoiac projects his delusions

**para·nephric** \ˌparə+\ *adj* [¹*para-* + *nephric*] **1 :** adjacent to the kidney **2 :** relating to or being an adrenal gland

**para·nephritis** \"+\ *n* [NL, fr. ¹*para-* + *nephritis*] **1 :** inflammation of the adrenal glands **2 :** inflammation of the connective tissue around the kidney

**para·neph·ros** \ˌparəˈnefrəs, -,fräs\ *n, pl* **paranephroi** [NL, fr. ¹*para-* + Gk *nephros* kidney — more at NEPHRITIS] **:** ADRENAL GLAND

**para·neu·rop·tera** \ˌparənyůˈräpt(ə)rə\ [NL, fr. ¹*para-* + *Neuroptera* order of insects, fr. *neur-* + *-ptera*] *syn of* ODONATA

**pa·rang** \pəˈräng\ *n* -s [Malay] **:** a short sword, cleaver, or machete common in Malaya, British Borneo, and Indonesia

**para·ni·tran·i·line red** \ˌparə,nīˈtranᵊlən- *sometimes* -ᵊl,īn-*or* -ᵊl,ēn-\ *n* **:** a para red dye produced on the fiber and used as a pigment — see DYE table I (under *Pigment Red 1*)

**para-nitro·an·i·line** \ˌparə,nī·trōˈanᵊlən *sometimes* -ᵊl,īn *or* -ᵊl,ēn\ *or* **para·ni·tran·i·line** \-ī·ˈtran-\ *n* [¹*para-* + *nitr-* + *aniline*] **:** NITROANILINE a

**par·a·noia** \ˌparəˈnȯi(y)ə *also* ˌper-\ *n* -s [NL, fr. Gk *paranoia* derangement, madness, fr. *paranoos, paranous* demented (fr. *para-* ¹para- + *noos, nous* mind) + *-ia* -y] **1 :** a rare chronic nondeteriorative psychosis characterized chiefly by systematized delusions of persecution or of grandeur that are commonly isolated from the mainstream of consciousness and that are usu. not associated with hallucinations **2 :** a tendency on the part of individuals or of groups toward suspiciousness and distrustfulness of others that is based not on objective reality but on a need to defend the ego against unconscious impulses, that uses projection as a mechanism of defense, and that often takes the form of a compensatory megalomania

¹**para·noi·ac** \ˌ==ˈnȯi,(y)ak, -ȯi·ik, -ȯiēk\ *also* **par·a·no·ic** \-nōik, -nȯēk\ *adj* [NL *paranoia* + E *-ac* (as in *maniac*) or *-ic*] **:** of or relating to paranoia **:** affected with or characteristic of paranoia

²**paranoiac** \"\ *also* **paranoic** \"\ *n* -s **:** a person who is affected with paranoia

¹**par·a·noid** \ˈ==,nȯid\ *also* **par·a·noi·dal** \ˌ==ˈnȯidᵊl\ *adj* [blend of NL *paranoia* & E *-oid, -oidal*] **1 :** resembling paranoia **2 :** characterized by suspiciousness, persecutory trends, or megalomania ⟨a ~ attitude⟩

²**paranoid** \"\ *n* -s **:** one afflicted with paranoia or paranoid schizophrenia

**paranoid schizophrenia** *n* **:** a psychosis resembling paranoia but commonly displaying hallucinations, autism, and dereistic thinking and often resulting in marked behavioral deterioration

**pa·ra·no·mia** \ˌparəˈnōmēə\ *n* -s [NL, irreg. fr. ¹*para-* + L *nomen* name + NL *-ia* — more at NAME] **:** an aphasia characterized by the incorrect naming of objects

**para·normal** \ˌparə+\ *adj* [¹*para-* + *normal*] **:** beyond the range of scientifically known or recognizable phenomena **:** RARE, UNUSUAL, SUPERNATURAL — **para·normality** \"+\ *n* — **paranormally** \"+\ *adv*

**para·notum** \"+\ *n, pl* **paranota** [NL, fr. ¹*para-* + *notum*] **:** one of the paired lateral lobes of the thoracic nota of insects

**par·anthelion** \ˌpar+\ *n, pl* **paranthelia** [NL, fr. ¹*para-* + *anthelion*] **:** a diffuse image of the sun appearing at the same altitude as the sun and 120 degrees distant on the parhelic circle and caused by reflection from atmospheric ice spicules

**par·an·thro·pus** \paˈran(t)thrəpəs, ˌpa,ranˈthrōp-\ *n* [NL, fr. ¹*para-* + *-anthropus*] **1** *cap* **:** a genus of australopithecine apes sometimes regarded as synonymous with *Australopithecus* — see KROMDRAAI APE-MAN, SWARTKRANZ APE-MAN **2** -ES **:** a member of the genus *Paranthropus*

**para·nuclear** \ˌparə+\ *adj* [¹*para-* + *nuclear*] **:** of or relating to a paranucleus

**para·nucleus** \"+\ *n, pl* **paranuclei** [NL, fr. ¹*para-* + *nucleus*] **1 :** an accessory or additional nucleus or body resembling a nucleus in a cell **2 :** one of the nuclei derived from polar bodies that function in the insect trophamnion

**para nut** *n, usu cap P* [fr. *Pará*, state and city in Brazil] **:** BRAZIL NUT

**para·nymph** \ˈparə+,-\ *n* [LL *paranymphus*, masc., & ML *paranympha*, fem., fr. Gk *paranymphos*, masc. & fem., fr. *para-* ¹para- + *nymphē* bride — more at NYMPH] **1 :** a friend who went with a bridegroom in a chariot to fetch home the bride in ancient Greece; *also* **:** the bridesmaid who conducted the bride to the bridegroom **2 a :** BEST MAN **b :** BRIDESMAID **c :** one who solicits or speaks for another **:** ADVOCATE

**par·an·zel·la net** *also* **paranzella trawl** \ˌparənˈzelə-\ *or* **pa·ran·ze trawl** \pəˈranzə-\ *n* [*paranzella* fr. It, small fishing boat, dim. of *paranza* trawler, fishing boat; *paranze* fr. It *paranza*] **:** a net dragged along the sea bottom between two boats used esp. in fishing for soles and flounders

**para·ox·on** \ˌparəˈäk,sän\ *n* -s [¹*para-* + *ox-* + *-on*] **:** a phosphate ester $(C_2H_5O)_2PO(OC_6H_4NO_2)$ that is formed from parathion in the body and that is a potent anticholinesterase; *O,O*-diethyl *O-para*-nitro-phenyl phosphate

**para·paguridae** \ˌparə+\ *n pl, cap* [NL, fr. ¹*para-* + *Paguridae*] **:** a family of crustaceans (suborder Macrura) comprising typical hermit crabs — compare PAGURIDAE

**para·paresis** \"+\ *n* [NL, fr. ¹*para-* + *paresis*] **:** partial paralysis affecting the lower limbs

**para·periodic acid** \"+ . . . -\ *n* [¹*para-* + *periodic*] **:** PERIODIC ACID a

**par·a·pet** \ˈparəpət, -rə,pe|, *also* ˈper-; *usu* |d.+V\ *n* -s [It *parapetto*, fr. *parare* to shield, guard (fr. L to prepare) + *petto* chest, fr. L *pectus* — more at PARE, PECTORAL] **1 :** a wall, rampart, or elevation of earth or stone to protect soldiers **:** BREASTWORK **:** a rampart raised upon or above the main wall in a permanent fortification **2 :** a low wall or similar barrier; *esp* **:** one to protect the edge of a platform, roof, bridge, or other structure

**par·a·pet·ed** \-rə,pe|d.əd, -ˌpə|, |təd\ *adj* **:** having a parapet

**par·a·pet·less** \-rəpətləs, -ˌpet-\ *adj* **:** not having a parapet

**paraph** \ˈparəf, pəˈraf\ *n* -s [MF *paraffe* paragraph, paraph, fr. L *paragraphus* paragraph — more at PARAGRAPH] **:** a flourish at the end of a signature sometimes used as a sort of rude safeguard against forgery ⟨a blot marred his ~ —V.C.Johnson⟩

**paraphase amplifier** \ˈparə,fāz-\ *n* [¹*para-* + *phase*] **:** an amplifier in which by means of a phase inverter the ordinary output of a single amplifier tube is given push-pull characteristics

**par·a·pha·sia** \ˌparəˈfāzh(ē)ə\ *n* [NL, fr. ¹*para-* + *-phasia*] **:** aphasia in which the patient uses wrong words or words in senseless combinations — **par·a·pha·sic** \ˌ==ˈfāzik\ *adj*

**para·phenylenediamine** \ˌparə+\ *n* [ISV ¹*para-* + *phenylenediamine*] **:** the para isomer of phenylenediamine — written systematically with ital. *para-*

**par·a·pher·na** \ˌparəˈfərnə\ *n pl* [LL, fr. Gk, fr. *para-* ¹para- + *phernē* dowry; akin to Gk *pherein* to carry — more at BEAR] *Roman & civil law* **:** the property of a woman that on her marriage is not made a part of her dower but remains her own and entirely free from the control of the husband

**par·a·pher·nal** \ˌ==ˈfərnᵊl\ *adj* [ML *paraphernalis*, fr. LL *parapherna* + L *-alis* -al] **:** being or relating to parapherna or paraphernalia

**par·a·pher·na·lia** *R* ˌparəfə(r)ˈnālyə, -lēə *also* ˌper-, *-R* -fəˈn-\ *n pl but sometimes sing in constr* [ML *paraphernalia* (*bona*), fr. *paraphernalia* (neut. pl. of *paraphernalis*) + L *bona* possessions] **1 :** the separate paraphernal real or personal property of a married woman that she can dispose of by will and sometimes according to common law during her life **2 :** personal belongings (as equipment or finery) ⟨bundled in the ~, down to scarves and woolly caps —Truman Capote⟩ ⟨toy soldiers, little chariot wheels, the entire ~ of a baby —Walter Pater⟩ **3 :** articles of equipment **:** FURNISHINGS, APPARATUS ⟨~ of art⟩ ⟨lighting ~⟩ ⟨~ of war⟩ ⟨ceremonial ~⟩ ⟨~ of a circus⟩ ⟨equestrian ~⟩ **4 :** APPURTENANCES ⟨disguising a naked fact in the ~ of philosophy —Ellen Glasgow⟩ ⟨freedom from the ~ of the modern university —*Rev. of Politics*⟩ ⟨his life . . . has been treated merely as part of the whole ~ of conspiracy and romance —Iris Origo⟩ ⟨the elaborate ~ of our democratic system of popular choice —A.E.Stevenson b.1900⟩ ⟨multitude of doctrinal disputes which are part of a lawyer's ~ —R.H.Jackson⟩ **syn** see EQUIPMENT

**para·phil·ia** \ˌparəˈfilēə\ *n* -s [NL, fr. ¹*para-* + *-philia*] **:** a preference for or addiction to unusual sexual practices — **para·phil·i·ac** \ˌ==ˈfilē,ak\ *adj or n*

**para·phimosis** \ˌparə+\ *n* [NL, fr. ¹*para-* + *phimosis*] **:** a condition in which the foreskin is retracted behind the glans penis and cannot be replaced

**para·pho·nia** \ˌparəˈfōnēə\ *n, pl* **paraphonias** \-ēəz\ *also* **paraphoni·ae** \-nē,ē\ [Gk *paraphōnia*, fr. *paraphōnos* sounding beside (fr. *para-* ¹para- + *phōnē* sound) + *-ia* -y — more at BAN] **1** *in Greek & medieval musical theory* **:** a consonance or joint melodic progression of fourths and fifths **2** *pl* **paraphonias** [NL, fr. ¹*para-* + *-phonia* -phony] **:** abnormal change of voice

**para·phon·ic** \ˌ==ˈfänik\ *adj* **:** of or relating to musical paraphonia — **para·phon·i·cal·ly** \-nək(ə)lē\ *adv*

**para·phras·able** \ˈparə,frāzəbəl *also* ˈper- *or* ˌ==ˈ===\ *adj* **:** capable of being paraphrased

¹**para·phrase** \ˈparə,frāz *also* ˈper-\ *n* -s [MF, fr. L *paraphrasis*, fr. Gk, fr. *paraphrazein* to paraphrase (fr. *para-* ¹para- + *phrazein* to point out, show, tell) + *-sis*] **1 a :** a restatement of a text, passage, or work giving the meaning in another form usu. for clearer and fuller exposition **:** a free rendering ⟨a ~ of eternal vigilance is the price of freedom —O.W.Holmes †1935⟩ ⟨plays which are not ~s from the Greek —John Buchan⟩ — opposed to *metaphrase* **b :** the use or process of paraphrasing in studying or teaching composition ⟨such subjects as précis, ~, punctuation —*English Language Teaching*⟩ ⟨~, which aims rather at recapturing the general impression of a foreign work —*Times Lit. Supp.*⟩ **2 :** a free or florid musical transcription ⟨a ~ of an ancient Gregorian *Dies Irae* —*Time*⟩ **3 :** an exemplification or an amplification of a theme, idea, or motive **4 :** any of the verses based on passages of Scripture and commonly printed along with the metrical version of the Psalms used in Scottish Presbyterian churches

²**paraphrase** \"\ *vb* -ED/-ING/-S [F *paraphraser*, fr. MF, fr. *paraphrase*, n.] *vt* **:** to express, interpret, or translate with latitude **:** give the meaning of (a work or passage) in other words **:** make a paraphrase of ⟨~s Descartes' famous sentence —Babette Deutsch⟩ ⟨*paraphrased* some of the telegrams —Sir Winston Churchill⟩ ⟨stories will have to be *paraphrased* by Mother —*My Baby*⟩ ⟨work of *paraphrasing* the obscure into the . . . comprehensible —S.E.Hyman⟩ **~** *vi* **1 :** to make a paraphrase **2** *archaic* **:** to comment or expand upon a topic

**para·phras·er** \-zə(r)\ *n* -s **:** one that paraphrases

**para·phra·sia** \ˌ==ˈfrāzh(ē)ə\ *n* -s [NL, fr. ¹*para-* + *-phrasia*] **:** speech defect characterized by incoherence in arrangement of words

**pa·raph·ra·sis** \pəˈrafrəsəs\ *n, pl* **paraphra·ses** \-ə,sēz\ [L] **:** PARAPHRASE

**para·phrast** \ˈparə,frast\ *n* -s [LL *paraphrastes*, fr. Gk *paraphrastēs*, fr. *paraphrazein* to paraphrase — more at PARAPHRASE] **:** PARAPHRASER

**para·phras·tic** \ˌ==ˈfrastik\ *also* **para·phras·ti·cal** \-təkəl\ *adj* [F *paraphrastique*, fr. MF, fr. Gk *paraphrastikos*, fr. (assumed) *paraphrastos* (verbal of *paraphrazein*) + *-ikos* -ic] **:** PARAPHRASING **:** having the nature of paraphrase **:** explaining or translating more clearly and amply an author's meaning — **para·phras·ti·cal·ly** \-tək(ə)lē\ *adv*

**para·phre·nia** \ˌparəˈfrēnēə\ *n* -s [NL, fr. ¹*para-* + *-phrenia*] **1 :** the group of paranoid disorders **2 :** any of the paranoid disorders usu. excluding paranoid schizophrenia — **para·phrenic** \ˌ==ˈfrenik *also* -rēn-\ *adj or n*

**paraphs** *pl of* PARAPH

**para·phyl·li·um** \ˌparəˈfilēəm\ *n, pl* **paraphyl·lia** \-ēə\ [NL, fr. ¹*para-* + *phyll-* + *-ium*] **:** one of the minute branched or stipuliform organs between the leaves of various mosses (as those of the genus *Thuidium*)

**pa·raph·y·sate** \pəˈrafəsət, -,sāt\ *adj* [NL *paraphysis* + E *-ate*] **:** bearing or marked by paraphyses

**pa·raph·y·se·al** \pəˈrafəˌsēəl, -ˈzē- *also* ˌparəˈfizēəl\ *or* **par·a·phys·i·al** \ˌparəˈfizēəl\ *adj* [NL *paraphysis* + E *-eal* (as in *laryngeal*) or *-ial*] **:** of or relating to a paraphysis

**para·physical** \ˌparə+\ *adj* [¹*para-* + *physical*] **:** resembling physical phenomena but without recognizable physical cause ⟨~ phenomena as levitation, telekinesis, materialization —Fred Sommers⟩

**pa·raph·y·sis** \pəˈrafəsəs\ *n, pl* **paraphy·ses** \-əˌsēz\ [NL, fr. ¹*para-* + Gk *physis* origin, growth, nature — more at PHYSICS] **1 :** one of the slender sterile filaments that are commonly borne among the sporogenous or gametogenous organs in many cryptogamic plants, that may be either unicellular or pluricellular or either simple or branched, and that are often septate **2 a :** a median evagination of the roof of the telencephalon anterior to the epiphysis of certain lower vertebrates **b :** one of several club-shaped chitinous projections near the edge of the pygidium of some scales

**pa·raph·y·soid** \pəˈrafəˌsȯid\ *n* -s [NL *paraphysis* + E *-oid*] **:** one of the hyphal threads that are between the asci of various fungi and that resemble paraphyses but lack free ends

**pará piassava** *n, usu cap 1st P* [fr. *Pará*, state and city in Brazil] **:** PIASSAVA 2

**para·pithe·cus** \ˌparəpəˈthēkəs, -ˈpithək-\ *n, cap* [NL, fr. ¹*para-* + *-pithecus*] **:** a genus of extremely primitive old-world monkeys from the Oligocene of Egypt that are commonly regarded as near the point of divergence of the Cercopithecidae and the higher anthropoid apes and are sometimes made type of a separate family

**para·plasm** \ˈparə+ˌ-\ *n* [ISV ¹*para-* + *-plasm*] **1 :** HYALOPLASM **2 :** the reserve and waste inclusions of protoplasm in a cell **3 :** ERGASTOPLASM

**para·ple·gia** \ˌparəˈplēj(ē)ə *also* ˌper-\ *n* -s [NL, fr. Gk *paraplēgiē* hemiplegia, fr. *para-* ¹para- + *-plēgiē*, *-plēgia* -plegia] **:** paralysis of the lower half of the body with involvement of both legs usu. due to disease of or injury to the spinal cord

**¹para·ple·gic** \ˌ⸗⸗ˈplējik, -jēk *sometimes* -lej-\ *adj* [Gk *paraplēgikos*, fr. *paraplēgiē* + *-ikos* -ic] **:** affected with paraplegia

**²paraplegic** \"\ *n* -s **:** an individual affected with paraplegia

**para·pod** \ˈparəˌpäd\ *n* -s [NL *parapodium*] **:** PARAPODIUM

**pa·po·di·al** \ˌ⸗⸗ˈpōdēəl\ *adj* [NL *parapodium* + E *-al*] **:** of or relating to a parapodium

**para·po·di·um** \ˌ⸗⸗ˈdēəm\ *n, pl* **parapo·dia** \-ēə\ [NL, fr. ¹*para-* + *podium*] **1 :** one of the short unsegmented processes borne one on each side of most of the body segments in many annelids and serving as locomotive organs and often also as tactile or branchial organs **2 :** a lateral expansion of either side of the foot usu. forming a broad swimming organ in gastropods (as the sea hares and pteropods)

**par·apophysis** \ˌpar+\ *n* [NL, fr. ¹*para* + *apophysis*] **:** one of the transverse processes that project from the centrum of each vertebra of many lower vertebrates — compare DIAPOPHYSIS

**para·prax·ia** \ˌparəˈpraksēə\ *or* **para·prax·is** \-səs\ *n, pl* **parapraxias** \-ksēəz\ *or* **parapraxes** \-kˌsēz\ [NL, fr. ¹*para-* + *-praxia* or Gk *praxis* action] **:** a faulty act (as a slip of the tongue or of memory) **:** BLUNDER, LAPSE

**para·proct** \ˈparəˌpräkt\ *n* -s [¹*para-* + Gk *prōktos* anus — more at PROCT-] **:** any of several differentiated lobes or sclerites adjacent to the anus of some insects

**para·proc·tium** \ˌ⸗⸗ˈpräktēəm, -ksh(ē)əm\ *n, pl* **paraproc·tia** \-ktēə, -ksh(ē)ə\ [NL, fr. ¹*para-* + *proct-* + *-ium*] **:** the connective tissue adjacent to the rectum

**pa·rap·si·da** \pəˈrapsədə\ *n pl, cap* [NL, fr. ¹*para-* + *-apsida* (fr. Gk *hapsid-*, *hapsis* arch, loop) — more at APSIS] *in some classifications* **:** a subclass of reptiles in which the skull has two dorsal temporal openings adjoining the parietals and which includes the ichthyosaurs and related extinct forms and sometimes the lizards and snakes — compare DIAPSIDA

**pa·rap·si·dal** \-dᵊl\ *adj* [NL *parapsid-*, *parapsis* + E *-al*] **:** of or relating to a parapsis

**parapsidal furrow** *n* **:** one of the longitudinal sutures that separates the parapsides from the median part of the mesonotum in hymenopterans

**pa·rap·sis** \pəˈrapsəs\ *n, pl* **parapsi·des** \-psəˌdēz\ [NL, fr. ¹*para-* + *apsis*] **:** one of the lateral pieces of the mesoscutum esp. in hymenopterans

**para·psychical** *also* **para·psychic** \ˌparə+\ *adj* [ISV ¹*para-* + *psychical, psychic*; orig. formed as F *parapsychique*] **:** PARAPSYCHOLOGICAL

**para·psychological** \"+\ *adj* **:** of or relating to parapsychology

**para·psychologist** \"+\ *n* **:** a specialist in parapsychology

**para·psychology** \"+\ *n* [ISV ¹*para-* + *psychology*] **:** a science concerned with the investigation esp. by experimental means of events that are apparently not accounted for by natural law and that are considered to be evidence of mental telepathy, clairvoyance, and psychokinesis

**pa·rap·ter·um** \pəˈraptərəm\ *also* **pa·rap·ter·on** \-təˌrän, -ˌrən\ *n, pl* **parap·tera** \-tərə\ *also* **parapterons** [NL, fr. *para-* + Gk *pteron* wing — more at FEATHER] **1 :** a small sclerite on the side of the mesothorax and metathorax of an insect **2 :** TEGULA 1a

**para·quadrate** \ˌparə+\ *n* [¹*para-* + *quadrate*] **:** SQUAMOSAL

**para–quinone** \ˌparə+\ *n* [¹*para-* + *quinone*] **1 :** QUINONE 1a **2 :** the para isomer of a quinone

**para·rammelsbergite** \"+\ *n* [¹*para-* + *rammelsbergite*] **:** a mineral $NiAs_2$ consisting of nickel arsenide dimorphous with rammelsbergite

**par·arc·ta·li·an** \ˌpaˌrärkˈtālēən\ *adj, usu cap* [NL, fr. *Pararctalia*, temperate marine realm of the northern hemisphere (fr. ¹*para-* + *Arctalia*, northern biogeographic realm) + E *-an* — more at ARCTALIAN] **:** of, relating to, or being the temperate marine biogeographic realm that is bounded by the isocrymes of 44 degrees and 68 degrees F and that includes northern seas from the northerly limit of reef-building corals to the southerly limit of floating ice

**para·rectus** \ˌparə+\ *adj* [NL, fr. ¹*para-* + *rectus*] **:** situated along the side of the rectus muscle ⟨a ~ incision⟩

**para red** \ˌparə+\ *n* [¹*para-*] **1 :** BLOOD RED **2** *also* **para red toner** *sometimes cap P&R* **:** any of a group of brilliant bluish or yellowish red azo dyes or pigments that have fair resistance to light but that may bleed in water and many organic solvents, that are made by coupling diazotized *para*-nitroaniline with beta-naphthol often mixed with a beta-naphthol-sulfonic acid for producing the darker shades of red, and that are used chiefly in paints and printing inks; *esp* **:** PARANITRANILINE RED — compare FIRE RED 2

**par·a·re·ka** \ˌparəˈrākə\ *n* -s [Maori] **:** POTATO FERN 1

**para·rescue** \ˌparə+\ *n* [²*para-* + *rescue*] **:** rescue of persons (as in a disaster area or an area having inadequate transportation facilities) by parachutists

**pará rhatany** *n, usu cap P* [fr. *Pará*, state and city in Brazil] **:** rhatany from a Brazilian shrub (*Krameria argentea*)

**para·rosaniline** \ˌparə+\ *n* [ISV ¹*para-* + *rosaniline*] **:** a white crystalline base $C(OH)(C_6H_4NH_2)_3$ that is the parent compound of many triphenylmethane dyes (as crystal violet or fuchsine); *also* **:** the red chloride of this base obtainable by oxidation of a mixture of aniline and the para isomer of toluidine and used chiefly in coloring paper, as a biological stain, and in the preparation of other dyes — see DYE table I (under *Basic Red 9*)

**para·rosolic acid** \"+ . . . -\ *n* [ISV ¹*para-* + *rosolic*] **:** AURIN

**par·ar·thria** \paˈrärthrēə, pəˈr-\ *n* -s [NL, fr. ¹*para-* + *arthr-* + *-ia*] **:** disorder of speech **:** difficult utterance

**para rubber** *n, usu cap P* [fr. *Pará*, state and city in Brazil] **1 :** native rubber obtained from So. American trees and usu. exported in dark-colored flat round cakes **2** *or* **para rubber tree :** a So. American euphorbiaceous tree (*Hevea braziliensis*) that is the chief source of Para rubber and is the rubber tree usu. cultivated in plantations

**paras** *pl of* PARA

**-paras** *pl of* -PARA

**para·sagittal** \ˌparə+\ *adj* [ISV ¹*para-* + *sagittal*] **:** situated alongside of or adjacent to a sagittal location or plane

**par·a·sang** \ˈparəˌsaŋ\ *n* -s [L *parasanga*, fr. Gk *parasangēs*, of Iranian origin; akin to Per *farsang* parasang] **:** any of various Persian units of distance; *esp* **:** an ancient unit equal to about four miles

**pará sarsaparilla** *n, usu cap P* [fr. *Pará*, state and city in Brazil] **:** a sarsaparilla obtained from a Brazilian plant of the genus *Smilax*

**pa·ras·ca·lops** \pəˈraskəˌläps\ *n, cap* [NL, fr. ¹*para-* + Gk *skalops* mole — more at HALF] **:** a genus of No. American insectivores comprising the brewer's moles

**par·ascaris** \(ˈ)par, pər+\ *n, cap* [NL, fr. ¹*para-* + *Ascaris*] **:** a genus of nematode worms (family Ascaridae) including the large roundworm of the horse (*P. equorum*)

**para·sce·ni·um** \ˌparəˈsēnēəm\ *n, pl* **parasce·nia** \-nēə\ [NL, fr. Gk *paraskēnion*, fr. *para-* ¹para- + *skēnē* stage — more at SCENE] **:** one of two projecting wings of the skene of an ancient Greek theater flanking and framing the proscenium

**par·a·sceve** \ˈparəˌsēv\ *n* -s [LL, fr. Gk *paraskeuē*, lit. preparation, fr. *paraskeuazein* to get ready, fr. *para-* ¹para- + *skeuazein* to prepare, fr. *skeuos* vessel, implement — more at SKEUOMORPH] **1** *archaic* **:** the day of preparation before the Jewish Sabbath or a feast of similar rank ⟨it was the ~ of the pasch —Jn 19:14 (DV)⟩ **2** *obs* **:** PREPARATION

**para·se·le·ne** \ˌparəsəˈlē(ˌ)nē\ *n, pl* **parasele·nae** \"\ [NL, fr. *para-* ¹para- + Gk *selēnē* moon — more at SELENIC] **:** a luminous appearance seen in connection with lunar halos — compare PARHELION — **para·se·len·ic** \-lenik\ *adj*

**para·sexuality** \ˌparə+\ *n* [¹*para-* + *sexuality*] **:** PARAPHILIA

**pa·ra·shah** \ˈpärəˌshä\ *n, pl* **para·shoth** *or* **para·shot** \ˌpärəˈshōt(h)\ *or* **parashi·oth** *or* **parashi·ot** \-ˌsheˈōt(h)\ *also* **par·shi·oth** \ˌpärsheˈōt(h)\ *or* **par·shi·ot** [Heb *pārāshāh*, lit., explanation, account] **1 :** one of the weekly portions or lessons that is read from the Pentateuch in the synagogue on the Jewish Sabbath **:** SIDRA — see HAFTARAH **2 :** one of the subsections of the weekly lesson read on Sabbaths, festivals, and on Mondays and Thursdays

**para·shoot** \ˈparə+ˌ-\ *vi* [²*para-* + *shoot*] **:** to attack a parachute invader by shooting

**para·shot** \"+ˌ-\ *n* [²*para-* + *shot*] **:** one trained in parashooting

**para·sigmatism** *also* **para·sigmatismus** \ˌparə+\ *n* [¹*para-* + *sigmatism* or *sigmatismus*] **:** inability to pronounce the sound of *s* with some other sound (as of *f*) being usu. substituted for it

**parasit-** *or* **parasito-** *also* **parasiti-** *comb form* [ISV, fr. ¹*parasite*] **:** parasite ⟨*parasit*emia⟩ ⟨*parasito*phobia⟩ ⟨*parasiti*cide⟩

**par·a·si·ta** \ˌparəˈsīd·ə\ *n pl, cap* [NL, fr. L *parasitus* parasite] *in former classifications* **:** any of several groups of externally parasitic invertebrate animals: as **a :** a group comprising parasitic insects and arachnids **b :** an order or other group coextensive with Anoplura or comprising Anoplura and Mallophaga **c :** ECTOZOA

**par·a·si·tal** \ˌ⸗⸗ˈsīd·ᵊl\ *adj* [*parasit-* + *-al*] **:** PARASITIC

**par·a·si·ta·ry** \ˌparəˈsīd·ərē\ *adj* [*parasit-* + *-ary*] **:** PARASITIC

**¹par·a·site** \ˈparəˌsīt *also* ˈper-, *usu* -īd·+V\ *n* -s [MF, fr. L *parasitus*, fr. Gk *parasitos*, fr. *para-* ¹para- + *sitos* grain, bread, food] **1 a :** one frequenting the tables of the rich or living at another's expense and earning welcome by flattery or diversion **b :** one of a class of assistants in ancient Greek religious rites who dine with the priests after a sacrifice **2 a :** an organism living in or on another living organism, obtaining from it part or all of its organic nutriment, and commonly exhibiting some degree of adaptive structural modification — compare AUTOPHYTE, SAPROPHYTE **b :** such an organism that causes some degree of real damage to its host — compare COMMENSAL, INQUILINE, SYMBIONT **3 :** something that resembles a biological parasite in dependence on something else for existence or support without making a useful or adequate return ⟨resourceful public enemies, ~*s* on the free⸗press privilege, who thrive on the profits derived from the exploitation of current pornographic materials —*U. S. House of Repr. Report*⟩ ⟨the great city is a ~ on the country —François Bondy⟩ ⟨foiled at one market, they move on to another . . . ~*s* on society, until justice catches up with them —*Irish Digest*⟩ ⟨the young girl is still left incapable of making a living; she can only vegetate as a ~ in her father's home —H.M.Parshley⟩ ⟨new friends who had faith in her ideas, as well as new ~*s* who hoped to profit by them —Havelock Ellis⟩ **4 :** a parasitic sound or letter **5 :** the less perfectly formed twin of a double monster — compare AUTOSITE

**syn** PARASITE, SYCOPHANT, FAVORITE, TOADY, LICKSPIT, LICKSPITTLE, BOOTLICK, BOOTLICKER, HANGER-ON, LEECH, SPONGE, and SPONGER all signify one that is supported or sustained or seeks support or sustenance, usu. physical but sometimes social or intellectual, from another without right or justification. PARASITE applies to one that as a matter of policy is supported more or less by another and gives nothing in return, extending commonly to anyone who clings to a person of wealth, power, or influence in order to derive personal advantage or who is useless and unnecessary to society ⟨the ones who evade the earth and live upon the others in some way they have devised. They are the *parasites*, and they are the despised —Pearl Buck⟩ ⟨a court society ridden with *parasites*⟩ ⟨as our present society disintegrates, this démodé figure will become clearer; the Bohemian, the outsider, the *parasite*, the rat — one of those figures which have at present no function either in a warring or peaceful world —E.M.Forster⟩ ⟨the poorer citizens were little more than *parasites*, fed with free state bread, amused by free state shows —John Buchan⟩ SYCOPHANT applies to one that clings to a person of wealth, power, or influence and wins or tries to win his favor by fawning, flattery, or adulation ⟨a man who rose in this world because he curried favor, a *sycophant* —Kenneth Roberts⟩ ⟨*sycophants* who kept him from wholesome contact with reality, who played upon his overweening conceit and confirmed him in his persecutional manias —H.A.Overstreet⟩ FAVORITE applies to a close associate or intimate of a king or noble who is unduly favored by him, esp. with power ⟨huge grants of land to court *favorites* —W.C.Ford⟩ ⟨reduced to the ranks every officer who had a good record and appointed scoundrelly *favorites* of his own in their places —Robert Graves⟩ ⟨Pharaoh, his family and his *favorites* —J.E.M.White⟩ TOADY, often interchangeable with SYCOPHANT, stresses more the servility and snobbery of the social climber ⟨he preens himself in the velvet coat, he spies out the land and sees that the Dowager is "the one"; he becomes the perfect *toady* —Stevie Smith⟩ ⟨this induced a sharp distaste for the flagrant political plunder, the obscene scramble for the loaves and fishes by the spoilsmen and their *toadies* —Sidney Warren⟩ LICKSPIT and LICKSPITTLE and BOOTLICK and BOOTLICKER are interchangeable in common speech with SYCOPHANT and TOADY, implying, however, even stronger contemptibleness ⟨characterized those who disagreed as *lickspittles* and toadies of official whiggery —Asahel Bush⟩ ⟨a *lickspittle* humility that went beyond flattery —Alan Moorehead⟩ ⟨*bootlicks* hanging around the mayor's office⟩ ⟨its principal characters were stupid and bemused commanders, or vicious *bootlickers* tainted with homosexuality —Horace Sutton⟩ HANGER-ON applies to anyone who is regarded, usu. contemptuously, as adhering to or depending unduly on another esp. for favors ⟨there were the *hangers-on* who might be called domestics by inheritance —T.R.Ybarra⟩ ⟨a *hanger-on* at Court, waiting for the preferment that somehow eluded him —*Times Lit. Supp.*⟩ ⟨those rather *hangers-on* than friends, whom he treated with the cynical contempt that they deserved —Robert Graves⟩ LEECH stresses the persistence of clinging to or bleeding another for one's own advantage ⟨hatred for the freeloader or deadbeat. Yet, as a student of humanity, he tolerated these *leeches* —H.E.Maule & M.H. Cane⟩ ⟨a *leech* living off his family and friends⟩ SPONGE or SPONGER stress a parasitic laziness, dependence, and indifference to the discomforts caused and usu. a certain pettiness and constant regard for opportunities to cadge ⟨a *sponge* who developed the habit of dropping in for a visit just before mealtimes⟩ ⟨a girl whose disappointment with the world has made her the prey of an unsuccessful crook and *sponger* —*Times Lit. Supp.*⟩

**²parasite** \"\ *vb* -ED/-ING/-S *vi* **:** to act as a parasite **~** *vt* **:** to cause to act as a parasite **:** PARASITIZE

**parasite drag** *or* **parasite resistance** *n* **:** the portion of the drag of an airplane that does not include the induced drag of the wings

**par·a·sit·emia** \ˌparəˌsīd·ˈēmēə, -īˈtēm-\ *n* -s [NL, fr. *parasit-* + *-emia*] **:** a condition in which parasites are present in the blood — used to distinguish presence of parasites from clinical state ⟨an afebrile ~ of malaria⟩

**parasites** *pl of* PARASITE, *pres 3d sing of* PARASITE

**parasiti-** — see PARASIT-

**¹par·a·sit·ic** \ˌparəˈsid·|ik, -sit|, |ēk *also* ˌper-\ *also* **par·a·sit·i·cal** \|əkəl, |ēk-\ *adj* [L *parasiticus*, fr. Gk *parasitikos*, fr. *parasitos* parasite + *-ikos* -ic, -ical — more at PARASITE] **1 a :** having the nature of a parasite **:** fawning for food or favors **:** SPONGING, SYCOPHANTIC ⟨one stable and independent nation . . . is worth a dozen ~ governments that fawn on the U.S. with simulated affection —M.W.Straight⟩ ⟨a ~ desire to thrive on the greatness of others —H.W.Haeusermann⟩ **b :** dependent but contributing or producing little or nothing ⟨a society in which a small class of wealthy people are ~ upon the labor of the masses —H.J.Laski⟩ ⟨criticism of literature and art is ~ and all but futile —Norman Foerster⟩ ⟨~ and unproductive occupations like those of stockbrokers, soldiers, philosophers, economists, and most middlemen —Louis Wasserman⟩ ⟨that religion is . . . intellectually ~ and not creative —M.R. Cohen⟩ **2** *usu* **parasitic a :** relating to or having the habit of a parasite **:** living on another organism **b :** caused by or resulting from the effects of parasites **c** *of a bird* **:** laying eggs in the nest of another **3 :** of, relating to, or constituting an inorganic sound or its orthographic counterpart developed next to another sound (as a liquid or a nasal) through euphony or to facilitate utterance ⟨the \ə\ in \ˈeləm\ for *elm* or in \ˈathəˌlēt\ for *athlete*, the \t\ in \ˈfents\ for *fence*, and the \b\ and *b* in \ˈnimbəl\ *nimble* from Middle English *nimel* are ~⟩ **4 a :** being or relating to undesirable component frequencies; *specif* **:** differing from the fundamental frequency that the equipment is designed to generate ⟨a ~ elective oscillation⟩ **b :** consisting of or caused by eddy currents in any conductor within reach of an alternating-current or rotating magnetic field ⟨~ loss in an induction motor⟩ **c :** being part of a radio antenna detached from the main conductor — **par·a·sit·i·cal·ly** \|ək(ə)lē, |ēk, -li\ *adv*

**²parasitic** \"\ *n* -s **:** a parasitic current or oscillation

**¹par·a·sit·i·ca** \ˌ⸗⸗ˈsid·əkə\ [NL, fr. L, neut. pl. of *parasiticus* parasitic] *syn of* ANOPLURA

**²parasitica** \"\ [NL, fr. L, neut. pl. of *parasiticus* parasitic] *syn of* TEREBRANTIA

**parasitic castration** *n* **:** inhibition of function or development of gonads by infestation of a host with parasites

**par·a·sit·i·ci·dal** \ˌ⸗⸗ˈsid·əˈsīdᵊl\ *also* **par·a·sit·i·cid·ic** \|idik\ *adj* **:** destructive to parasites ⟨~ action of a substance⟩

**par·a·sit·i·cide** \ˌ⸗⸗ˈsid·əˌsīd\ *n* -s [*parasit-* + *-cide*] **:** a parasiticidal agent

**parasitic jaeger** *n* **:** a jaeger (*Stercorarius parasiticus*) having moderately long, narrow, and pointed middle tail feathers

**parasitic wasp** *n* **:** any of numerous hymenopterous insects that are parasitic or parasitoid on other insects; *esp* **:** a member of the division Terebrantia

**¹par·a·sit·id** \ˌparəˈsīd·əd, -sid·-\ *adj* [NL *Parasitidae*] **:** of or relating to the Parasitidae

**²parasitid** \"\ *n* -s **:** any mite of the family Parasitidae

**par·a·sit·i·dae** \ˌ⸗⸗ˈsid·əˌdē\ *n pl, cap* [NL, fr. *Parasitus*, type genus (fr. L, parasite) + *-idae* — more at PARASITE] **:** a large family of parasitoid mites with rather short legs, hard body, no eyes, and retractile jaws

**par·a·sit·ism** \ˈ⸗⸗ˌsīd·ˌizəm, -ˌī,ti-\ *n* -s **1 :** the act or practice of a parasite **:** the parasitic state or condition ⟨the abolition of ~ and exploitation of man by man —Upton Sinclair⟩ ⟨countries that let themselves become dependent on the labor of other countries and settle down into a comfortable and ladylike ~ —G.B.Shaw⟩ ⟨economic ~ . . . willingness to live luxuriously at the expense of the poor —E.H.Faulkner⟩ **2 a :** a relationship in which an organism of one kind lives in, on, or in intimate association with an organism of another kind at the expense of which it obtains food and usu. other benefits (as shelter and transportation) causing some degree of overt damage but not usu. killing directly and immediately — compare COMMENSALISM, HELOTISM, PARASITOIDISM, PREDATISM, SYMBIOSIS **b :** a relationship that involves intimate association of organisms of two or more kinds including commensalism, symbiosis, parasitism, and parasitoidism — used esp. when it is not wished or possible to specify the precise relationship **3 :** PARASITOSIS

**par·a·sit·iza·tion** \ˌ⸗⸗ˌsīd·əˈzāshən, -ītə-\ *n* -s **:** the state of being parasitized

**par·a·si·tize** \ˈ⸗⸗ˌsəˌtīz, -ˌsīd·ˌīz, -ˌsīˌtīz\ *vt* -ED/-ING/-S [*parasit-* + *-ize*] **1 :** to infest or live on or with as a parasite **2 :** to lay eggs in the nest of (another kind of bird)

**parasito-** — see PARASIT-

**¹par·a·sitoid** \ˌ⸗⸗ˈsīd·ˌȯid, -īˌtȯid, ˈ⸗⸗səˌtȯid\ *adj* [*parasit-* + *-oid*] **1 :** resembling a parasite; *specif* **:** exhibiting or practicing parasitoidism **2 :** of or relating to the Parasitoidea

**²parasitoid** \"\ *n* -s **:** a parasitoid organism

**par·a·si·toi·dea** \ˌ⸗⸗ˌsīd·ˈȯidēə, -ˌsīˈtȯi-, -ˌsəˈtȯi-\ *n pl, cap* [NL, fr. *Parasitus*, genus of mites + *-oidea*] **:** a superfamily of mites that is characterized by a small simple hypostome and the absence of eyes and comprises numerous families including the economically and medically important Dermanyssidae

**par·a·sit·oid·ism** *pronunc at* ¹PARASITOID +ˌizəm\ *n* -s **:** a relation existing between various insect larvae and their hosts in which the larva feeds upon the living host tissues in an orderly sequence such that the host is not killed until the larval development is complete

**par·a·si·to·log·i·cal** \ˌ⸗⸗ˌsīd·əˈläjəkəl\ *adj* **:** of or relating to parasitology

**par·a·sitol·o·gist** \ˌ⸗⸗ˌsīd·ˈäləjəst, -ˌsīˈtä-, -ˌsəˈtä-\ *n* -s **:** a specialist in parasitology; *esp* **:** one that deals with the worm parasites of animals

**par·a·sitol·o·gy** \-jē\ *n* -ES [ISV *parasit-* + *-logy*] **:** a branch of biology that deals with parasites and the parasitic habit and that often is restricted to consideration of animal parasites

**par·a·sit·osis** \-ˌsīd·ˈōsəs, -ˌsīˈtō-, -ˌsəˈtō-\ *n, pl* **parasito·ses** \-ōˌsēz\ [NL, fr. *parasit-* + *-osis*] **:** infestation with or disease caused by parasites

**par·a·si·to·trop·ic** \ˌ⸗⸗ˌsīd·əˈträpik\ *adj* [ISV *parasit-* + *-tropic*] **:** having an affinity for parasites ⟨a ~ drug⟩

**para·ske·ni·on** \ˌparəˈskēnēˌän, |ˌän\ *n, pl* **paraske·nia** \|ə\ [Gk *paraskēnion* — more at PARASCENIUM] **:** PARASCENIUM

**¹par·a·sol** \ˈparəˌsȯl *also* ˈper- *or* -ˌsäl\ *n* -s [F, fr. MF, fr. OIt *parasole*, fr. *parare* to shield, guard (fr. L to prepare) + *sole* sun, fr. L *sol* — more at PARE, SOLAR] **1 :** a lightweight umbrella used as a sunshade esp. by women **2 :** a monoplane with parasol wings

**²parasol** \"\ *adj* **:** raised above a pilot's head to permit downward vision ⟨~ wings⟩

**parasol ant** *n* **:** an ant of the genus *Atta*

**par·a·soled** \-ld\ *adj* **:** carrying a parasol

**parasol mushroom** *n* **:** a mushroom of the genus *Lepiota*; *esp* **:** a long-stalked edible mushroom (*L. procera*) that appears in the fall in open woodlands and has white flesh, white gills, and white spores

**parasol pine** *n* **1 :** STONE PINE 2 **2** *also* **parasol fir :** UMBRELLA PINE 1

**para·specific** \ˌparə+\ *n* [¹*para-* + *specific*] **:** a drug or medicinal preparation having other than a specific curative action

**¹para·sphenoid** *also* **para·sphenoidal** \ˌparə+\ *adj* [¹*para-* + *sphenoid, sphenoidal*] **:** a bone situated in the base of the skull of many vertebrates and developed in the membrane underlying the basicranial axis

**²parasphenoid** \"\ *n* **:** a parasphenoid bone

**para·spinal** \ˌparə+\ *adj* [¹*para-* + *spinal*] **:** adjacent to the spinal column

**para·spore** \ˈparə+ˌ-\ *n* [¹*para-* + *spore*] **:** a spore produced by various red algae (as some members of the family Ceramiaceae) that in some cases acts as a tetraspore and in others germinates to produce a triploid generation

**par·a·stas** \ˈparəˌstas, pəˈrastəs\ *n, pl* **pa·ras·ta·des** \pəˈrastəˌdēz\ [Gk, fr. *paristanai* to place beside, fr. *para-* ¹para- + *histanai* to make stand — more at STAND] **:** ANTA; *esp* **:** one of the two large antas enclosing a pronaos in ancient Greek buildings

**para·sternal** \ˌparə+\ *adj* [¹*para-* + *sternal*] **:** adjacent to the sternum — **para·sternally** \"+\ *adv*

**para·sternum** \"+\ *n, pl* **parasternums** *or* **parasterna** [NL, fr. ¹*para-* + *sternum*] : a bony framework formed by the abdominal ribs in various reptiles
**pa·ras·ti·chy** \pəˈrastəkē\ *n* -ES [ISV ¹*para-* + Gk *stichos* row + ISV -*y* — more at STICH] : a hypothetical oblique or secondary spiral line joining leaves or scales where the internodes of the axis are short and the members crowded (as in a pine cone); *also* : the arrangement of leaves or scales along such lines — compare ORTHOSTICHY
**para·style** \ˈparəˌstīl\ *n* -S [ISV ¹*para-* + *style*] : a small cusp lying anterior to the paracone on the cingulum of a molar tooth
**par·a·su·chia** \ˌparəˈsükēə\ [NL, fr. ¹*para-* + Gk *souchos* crocodile + NL -*ia*] *syn of* PHYTOSAURIA
¹**para·sympathetic** \ˌ¦parə+\ *adj* [ISV ¹*para-* + *sympathetic*] **1** : of or relating to the parasympathetic nervous system ⟨~ fibers of the vascular wall⟩ **2** : acting on or originating in the parasympathetic nervous system ⟨~ drugs⟩ ⟨~ inhibition⟩
²**parasympathetic** \"\ *n* **1** : a parasympathetic nerve **2** : PARASYMPATHETIC NERVOUS SYSTEM ⟨stimulation of the ~ tends to increase smooth muscle tone⟩
**parasympathetic nervous system** *or* **parasympathetic system** *n* : the part of the autonomic nervous system that contains chiefly cholinergic fibers and tends to induce secretion, increase the tone and contractility of smooth muscle, and cause the dilatation of blood vessels and that consists of a cranial part made up of preganglionic fibers leaving and passing the midbrain by the oculomotor nerves and the hindbrain by the facial, glossopharyngeal, vagus, and accessory nerves and passing to the ciliary, sphenopalatine, submaxillary, and otic ganglia of the head or to ganglionated plexuses of the thorax and abdomen and post ganglionic fibers passing from these ganglia to end organs of the head and upper trunk and a sacral part made up of preganglionic fibers emerging and passing in the sacral nerves and passing to ganglionated plexuses of the lower trunk and postganglionic fibers passing from these chiefly to the viscera of the lower abdomen and the external genital organs — compare SYMPATHETIC NERVOUS SYSTEM
**para·sym·pa·thet·i·co·mimetic** \ˌparəˌsimpəˈthed·ə̇(ˌ)kō+\ *adj* [¹*parasympathetic* + -*o-* + *mimetic*] : PARASYMPATHOMIMETIC
**para·sympatholytic** \ˌ¦parə+\ *adj* [ISV ¹*para-* + *sympatholytic*] : tending to oppose the physiological results of parasympathetic nervous activity or of parasympathomimetic drugs — used chiefly of chemical substances and their effects; compare SYMPATHOLYTIC
**para·sym·pa·tho·mimetic** \ˌparəˌsimpə(ˌ)thō+\ *adj* [ISV ¹*para-* + *sympathomimetic*] : simulating parasympathetic nervous action in physiological effect — used of chemicals that stimulate secretion and increase smooth muscle activity or of their effects; compare PARASYMPATHOLYTIC, SYMPATHOMIMETIC
**para·synapsis** \ˌ¦parə+\ *n* [NL, fr. ¹*para-* + *synapsis*] : normal side-by-side union of chromosomes in synapsis in contrast to supposed end-to-end union that is now regarded as purely an observational artifact — compare TELOSYNAPSIS
**para·synaptic** \"+\ *adj* [¹*para-* + *synaptic*] : of, relating to, or marked by parasynapsis
**para·syndesis** \"+\ *n* [NL, fr. ¹*para-* + *syndesis*] : PARASYNAPSIS — **para·syndetic** \"+\ *adj* — **parasyndetically** \"+\ *adv*
**para·synthesis** \ˌparə+\ *n* [NL, fr. ¹*para-* + *synthesis*] : the formation of words esp. in the Romance languages by composition and derivation jointly : the process of word formation by adding a derivative ending and prefixing a particle (as in *denationalize*)
**para·synthetic** \ˌ¦parə+\ *adj* [¹*para-* + *synthetic*] : of, relating to, or resulting from parasynthesis
**para·syn·the·ton** \ˌparəˈsin(t)thəˌtän\ *n, pl* **parasynthe·ta** \-thəd·ə\ [NL, fr. Gk, neut. of *parasynthetos* formed from a compound, fr. *para-* ¹para- + *synthetos* put together, compounded — more at SYNTHETIC] : a word formed by parasynthesis
**para·syphilitic** \ˌ¦parə+\ *adj* [ISV ¹*para-* + *syphilitic*] *archaic* : due indirectly to syphilis — used chiefly of diseases of the nervous system formerly considered indirectly but now known to be directly due to syphilitic infection
**par·atacamite** \(ˌ)par+\ *n* [¹*para-* + *atacamite*] : a mineral that consists of a basic chloride of copper and is dimorphous with atacamite
**para·tac·tic** \ˌ¦parəˌtaktik\ *also* **para·tac·ti·cal** \-aktə̇kəl\ *adj* [fr. *parataxis*, after such pairs as LL *syntaxis* syntax: E *syntactic, syntactical*] : of, relating to, or exhibiting parataxis — **para·tac·ti·cal·ly** \-tə̇k(ə)lē\ *adv*
**para·tax·ic** \ˌ¦parəˌtaksik\ *adj* [NL *parataxis* + E -*ic*] : characterized by or relating to a mode of individual experience in which persons, events, and relationships are perceived as discrete phenomena, in which occurrences in the real world are seen as having no sequential or logical relationship, but in which all external stimuli have only idiosyncratic autistic significance — compare PROTOTAXIC
**para·tax·is** \ˌ==ˈtaksə̇s\ *n* [NL, fr. Gk, act of placing side by side, fr. *para-* ¹para- + -*taxis*] **1 a** : coordinate ranging of clauses, phrases, or words one after another without coordinating connectives (as in "he laughed; she cried") — opposed to *hypotaxis* **b** : the placing of a subordinate clause beside a main clause without a subordinating connective (as in "I believe it is true; there is a man wants to see you") **2** : the paratactic mode of experience
**para·tergite** \ˌ¦parə+\ *n* [¹*para-* + *tergite*] : the sclerotized lateral part of the dorsum of an insect
**para·tetranychus** \"+\ *n, cap* [NL, fr. ¹*para-* + *Tetranychus*] : a genus of red spiders that in some classifications includes the European red mite
**parathesis** *n, pl* **paratheses** [NL, fr. Gk, juxtaposition, fr. *paratithenai* to place beside, fr. *para-* ¹para- + *tithenai* to place — more at DO] *obs* : PARENTHESIS
**para·thi·on** \ˌparəˈthīˌän\ *n* -S [¹*para-* + *thio*phosphate + -*on*] : a liquid thiophosphate agricultural insecticide $(C_2H_5O)_2PS(OC_6H_4NO_2)$ of extreme toxicity to mammals as well as insects; *O,O*-diethyl *O*-para-nitro-phenyl thiophosphate
**Para–thor–mone** \ˌparəˈthȯrˌmōn\ *trademark* — used for an aqueous extract of the parathyroid glands of cattle used chiefly in preventing and treating tetanic convulsions
¹**para·thyroid** \ˌ¦parə+\ *n* [ISV ¹*para-* + *thyroid* (n.)] : PARATHYROID GLAND
²**para·thyroid** *also* **para·thyreoid** *or* **para·thyroidal** \ˌ¦parə+\ *adj* [ISV ¹*para-* + *thyroid* (adj.) or *thyreoid* or *thyroidal*] **1** : adjacent to a thyroid gland **2** : of, relating to, or produced by the parathyroid glands
**para·thyroidectomized** \ˌ¦parə+\ *adj* : having the parathyroid glands removed ⟨~ rats⟩
**para·thyroidectomy** \"+\ *n* [ISV ¹*parathyroid* + -*ectomy*] : excision of the parathyroid glands
**parathyroid gland** *n* : any of several usu. four small endocrine glands adjacent to or sometimes embedded in the thyroid gland that are composed of irregularly arranged secretory epithelial cells lying in a stroma rich in capillaries and producing a hormone that functions in maintaining normal calcium balance in the body — compare TETANY
**para·thy·ro·pri·val** \ˌparəˌthīrōˈprīvəl\ *also* **para·thy·ro·priv·ic** \-privik\ *adj* [¹*parathyroid* + -*prival* (fr. L *privus* single, deprived of + E -*al*) *or* -*privic* — more at PRIVATE] : of, relating to, or caused by functional deficiency of the parathyroid glands ⟨~ tetany⟩
**para·thy·ro·trop·ic** \-ˌ¦träpik\ *adj* [¹*parathyroid* + -*tropic*] : acting on or stimulating the parathyroid glands ⟨~ hormone⟩
**para·tomium** \ˌ¦parə+\ *n* [NL, fr. ¹*para-* + *tomium*] : the side of a bird's upper mandible between culmen and tomium
**pa·rat·o·my** \pəˈrad·əmē\ *n* -ES [¹*para-* + -*tomy*] : reproduction by fission along a special division zone following organization of the structures of a new individual from blastema tissue — compare ARCHITOMY
**para·tone brown ZUS** \ˌparəˌtōnˈbrau̇nˌzēˌyüˈes\ *n, usu cap P&B* [¹*para-* + *tone*] : an organic pigment — see DYE table I (under *Pigment Brown 2*)
**para·tonic** \ˌ¦parə+\ *adj* [ISV ¹*para-* + *tonic*; orig. formed as G *paratonisch*] : resulting from external stimuli ⟨~ plant growth⟩ — compare AUTONOMIC
**para·tracheal** \"+\ *adj* [¹*para-* + *tracheal*] : associated or contiguous with vessels or vascular tracheids ⟨~ parenchyma⟩ — compare APOTRACHEAL, METATRACHEAL, VASICENTRIC
**para·trichosis** \"+\ *n* [NL, fr. ¹*para-* + *trichosis*] : abnormal hair or hair growing in an abnormal place
**para·troop** \ˈparə+ˌ-\ *adj* [back-formation fr. *paratroops*] : of, relating to, or engaged in by paratroops ⟨~ boots⟩ ⟨~ landing⟩ ⟨~ action⟩
**para·trooper** \ˈparə+ˌ==\ *n* [²*para-* + *trooper*] **1** *also* **para·troop** [*paratroop* back-formation fr. *paratroops*] : a member of the paratroops **2** : a military person parachuting from an airplane
**para·trooping** \ˈparə+ˌ-\ *n* [²*para-* + *trooping*] : the action of a paratrooper
**para·troops** \ˈparə+ˌ-\ *n pl* [¹*para*chute + *troops*] : troops trained and equipped to parachute from an airplane
**para·troph·ic** \ˌ¦parə¦träfik\ *adj* **1** : of or relating to paratrophy **2** : deriving nourishment parasitically from other organisms ⟨~ pathogenic bacteria⟩
**pa·rat·ro·phy** \pəˈra·trəfē\ *n* -ES [NL *paratrophia*, fr. ¹*para-* + -*trophia* -trophy] : DYSTROPHY
**para·tuberculosis** \ˌ¦parə+\ *n, pl* **paratuberculoses** [NL, fr. ¹*para-* + *tuberculosis*] : JOHNE'S DISEASE — **para·tuberculous** \"+\ *adj*
**para·tungstate** \"+\ *n* [¹*para-* + *tungstate*] : a salt in which the ratio of a univalent metal or radical to tungsten may be either 10 to 12 [as in ammonium paratungstate $(NH_4)_{10}W_{12}O_{41}.11H_2O$] or 6 to 7
**para·tylenchus** \"+\ *n, cap* [NL, fr. ¹*para-* + *Tylenchus*] : a genus of soil nematodes (family Tylenchidae) that feeds on plant roots
**para·type** \ˈparə+ˌ-\ *n* [ISV ¹*para-* + *type*] **1** : a specimen of a type series other than the holotype — usu. used in zootaxy; compare ISOTYPE 1b(1) **2** : the environmental component of a phenotype — compare GENOTYPE 2
¹**para·typhoid** \ˌ¦parə+\ *adj* [ISV ¹*para-* + *typhoid*] **1** : resembling typhoid fever **2** : of, relating to, or involving paratyphoid or its causative organisms ⟨~ infection⟩
²**paratyphoid** \"\ *also* **paratyphoid fever** *n* : any of a great variety of infectious enteric diseases of man and animals more or less resembling typhoid fever and commonly contracted by eating food contaminated with bacteria of the genus *Salmonella*; *specif* : NECROTIC ENTERITIS — compare SALMONELLOSIS
**para·typic** *also* **para·typical** \ˌ¦parə+\ *adj* **1** : deviating from type : ATYPICAL **2** : of or relating to a paratype
**para·umbilical** \"+\ *adj* [ISV ¹*para-* + *umbilical*] : adjacent to the navel ⟨~ pain⟩
**para·urethral** \"\ *adj* [ISV ¹*para-* + *urethral*] : adjacent to the urethra ⟨~ glands that are the female homologue of the prostate⟩
**para·vaginal** \"+\ *adj* [ISV ¹*para-* + *vaginal*] : adjacent to the vagina or a vaginal part — **para·vaginally** \"+\ *adv*
**par·a·vail** \ˌ¦parəˌvā(ə)l\ *adj* [AF *paravale*, fr. OF *par aval* below, fr. *par* by + *aval* down, fr. *a* to + *val* valley — more at PARAMOUNT, VALE] *feudal law* : being below or at the bottom — used esp. of a tenant who holds of a tenant, esp. the lowest tenant of the fee in immediate possession
**para·vane** \ˈparə+ˌ-\ *n* [¹*para-* + *vane*] : a torpedo-shaped underwater protective device with sawlike teeth in its forward end towed from the bow of a ship in mined areas to sever the moorings of mines — called also *otter*
**para·vauxite** \ˌ¦parə+\ *n* [¹*para-* + *vauxite*] : a mineral $FeAl_2(PO_4)_2(OH)_2.8H_2O$ consisting of a hydrous basic aluminum phosphate having slightly more water than vauxite
**para·vent** \ˈparəˌvent\ *n* [F, fr. It *paravento*, fr. *parare* to shield, guard, ward off (fr. L, to prepare) + *vento* wind, fr. L *ventus* — more at PARE, WIND] : a screen from the wind
**para·vertebral** \ˌ¦parə+\ *adj* [ISV ¹*para-* + *vertebral*] : situated beside or adjacent to the vertebral column — **para·vertebrally** \"+\ *adv*
**para·vesical** \"+\ *adj* [¹*para-* + *vesical*] : adjacent to the urinary bladder — used chiefly of a peritoneal pouch or recess
**para·wollastonite** \"+\ *n* [¹*para-* + *wollastonite*] : a mineral $CaSiO_3$ consisting of calcium silicate dimorphous with wollastonite
**par·axial** \(ˈ)par+\ *adj* [ISV ¹*para-* + *axial*] **1** : located on each side of the cephalo-caudal axis of the body **2** : relating to or being the space in the immediate neighborhood of the optical axis of a lens or mirror ⟨~ rays⟩ — **par·axially** \"+\ *adv*
**par·axonia** \"+\ [NL, fr. ¹*para-* + *axonia*] *syn of* ARTIODACTYLA
**par·axonic** \ˌ¦par+\ *adj* [¹*para-* + *axonic*] : having the axis of the foot between the third and fourth digits ⟨a ~ artiodactyl⟩
**para·xylene** \ˌ¦parə+\ *n* [¹*para-* + *xylene*] : XYLENE 1b
**para·zoa** \ˌparəˈzōə\ *n pl, cap* [NL, fr. ¹*para-* + -*zoa*] : a group of invertebrate animals coextensive with Porifera and comprising multicellular forms that are essentially comparable to a gastrula in organization — compare METAZOA, PROTOZOA
**para·zo·ni·um** \ˌparəˈzōnēəm\ *n, pl* **parazo·nia** \-ēə\ [L, fr. Gk *parazōnion*, fr. *para-* ¹para- + -*zōnion* (fr. *zōnē* belt, girdle) — more at ZONE] **1** : a small sword or dagger of the ancient Greeks short enough to be worn in the girdle **2** : a short dagger of medieval times
**par·boil** \ˈpärˌ-\ *vt* [ME *parboilen* (influenced in meaning by *part*), fr. *parboilen* to boil thoroughly, fr. MF *parboillir, parbouillir*, fr. LL *perbullire*, fr. *per-* thoroughly (fr. *per* through) + *bullire* to bubble, boil — more at FOR, BOIL] **1** : to boil briefly as a preliminary or incomplete cooking procedure ⟨~*ed* it . . . then roasted it —Marjorie K. Rawlings⟩ **2** : OVERHEAT, SWEAT ⟨work out in the gym and then ~ themselves in steam cabinets⟩ — compare BLANCH, SCALD
**parboiled rice** *n* : rice that has been soaked, steamed, and dried before milling to improve the cooking quality, retain the water-soluble vitamins, and reduce the breakage in milling
¹**parbreak** *vb* [by folk etymology fr. older *parbrake*, fr. ME *parbraken*, fr. *par-* thoroughly (fr. OF, fr. L *per-*, fr. *per* through) + *braken* to vomit; akin to D *braken* to vomit, OE *brecan* to break — more at FOR, BREAK] *obs* : VOMIT
²**parbreak** *n, obs* : VOMIT
¹**par·buck·le** \ˈpärˌbəkəl\ *n* [alter. (influenced by *buckle*) of earlier *parbunkel*, of unknown origin] **1** : a purchase for hoisting or lowering a cylindrical object (as a cask) by making fast the middle of a long rope aloft and looping both ends around the object which rests in the loops and rolls in them as the ends are hauled up or paid out **2** : a double sling made of a single rope for slinging a cask, gun, or other object
²**parbuckle** \"\ *vt* : to hoist or lower by means of a parbuckle
¹**par·cel** \ˈpärsəl, ˈpȧs-, *dial except in sense 3* ˈpas- *or* ˈpaas-\ *n* -S [ME, fr. MF *parcelle, parcel*, fr. (assumed) VL *particella*, alter. of L *particula* small part — more at PARTICLE] **1 a** : a component part of a whole : DIVISION, FRAGMENT, PORTION ⟨nature in all her ~*s* and faculties fell apart —G.M.Hopkins⟩ — often used in the phrase *part and parcel* ⟨part and ~ of a larger tract⟩ **b** *obs* : a particular detail : ITEM ⟨I will die a hundred thousand deaths ere break the smallest ~ of this vow —Shak.⟩ **2 a** : a continuous tract or plot of land in one possession no part of which is separated from the rest by intervening land in other possession **b** : a tract or plot of land whose boundaries are readily ascertainable by natural or artificial monuments or markers **3** : a company, collection, or group of persons, animals, or things : LOT, PACK — often used as a generalized expression of disapproval ⟨shooing out a ~ of hens —Ida Treat⟩ ⟨a small ~ of cows and a few sheep —Elizabeth M. Roberts⟩ ⟨came to control a whole ~ of maritime companies —E.J.Kahn⟩ ⟨a ~ of giddy young kids —Mark Twain⟩ **4 a** : a wrapped bundle of one or more objects : PACKAGE ⟨the box was obviously a diamond ~ —Emily Hahn⟩ ⟨old ladies . . . rustling their luncheon ~*s* —Anthony Carson⟩ ⟨divide science into convenient pedagogic and administrative ~*s* —*Scientific American Reader*⟩ **b** : a unit of salable merchandise **5** : PARCELING 2 **syn** see PART
²**parcel** \"\ *adv* [ME, fr. *parcel*, n.] *archaic* : PARTLY
³**parcel** \"\ *vt* **parceled** *or* **parcelled**; **parceled** *or* **parcelled**; **parceling** *or* **parcelling** \-s(ə)liŋ\ **parcels** [¹*parcel*] **1** : to divide into parts or portions : DISTRIBUTE — often used with *out* ⟨small segments of the plantation were ~*ed* out to farmers —W.B.Furlong⟩ **2** : to make up into a parcel : BUNDLE, WRAP ⟨~ his purchase⟩ **3** : to cover (as a rope or a caulked seam) with strips of canvas **syn** see APPORTION
⁴**parcel** \"\ *adj* [¹*parcel*] : PART-TIME, PARTIAL
¹**parcel-gilt** \ˌ¦==¦=\ *adj* [ME, fr. ²*parcel* + *gilt*] : partly gilt (as on the inside only or so as to form ornamental figures)
²**parcel-gilt** \ˈ==ˌ=\ *n* : parcel-gilt ware
**parceling** *or* **parcelling** *n* -S **1** : an act of dividing and distributing in portions or parts or of wrapping into bundles **2 a** : the covering of a caulked seam with canvas and then tarring it **b** : long narrow slips of canvas usu. daubed with tar and wound about a rope like a bandage to exclude moisture usu. after the interstices between the strands have been wormed to make a smooth surface
**par·cel·la·tion** \ˌpärsəˈlāshən\ *n* -S : division into parcels ⟨endless land ~ and impoverishment —E.M.Kulischer⟩
**parcel post** *n* **1** : a mail service handling parcels **2** : packages handled by parcel post — compare FOURTH CLASS 2
**parcenary** *n* -ES [AF *parcenarie*, fr. OF *parçonerie*, fr. *parçon* division, distribution, portion (fr. L *partition-, partitio* partition) + -*erie* -ery — more at PARTITION] : COPARCENARY 1
**parcener** *n* -S [AF, fr. OF *parçonier*, fr. *parçon* + -*ier* -er] : COPARCENER
**par·center** \(ˈ)pär+\ *vt* [*par-* thoroughly (fr. F, fr. L *per-*, fr. *per* through) + *center* — more at FOR] : to align the centers of (optical lenses or diaphragms) along one axis — **parcentricity** \ˌ¦pär+\ *n* -ES
¹**parch** \ˈpärch, ˈpȧch\ *vb* -ED/-ING/-ES [ME *perchen, parchen*, perh. fr. ONF *perchier* to pierce, fr. (assumed) VL *pertusiare* — more at PIERCE] *vt* **1** : to toast under dry heat : burn or roast superficially : SCORCH ⟨~*ed* the kernels of sweet corn⟩ **2** : to dry to extremity : shrivel with heat ⟨cheekbones showed clearly under tightly drawn skin, which was tanned and ~*ed* —K.M.Dodson⟩ **3** : to dry or shrivel with cold ⟨busy restoring complexions that were ~*ed* by winter weather —*New Yorker*⟩ ~ *vi* : to lose moisture : become dry or scorched ⟨the skin . . . ~*es* and wrinkles early in life —Russell Lord⟩ **syn** see DRY
²**parch** \"\ *n* -ES : a drying out ⟨areas hit by the ~ of drought⟩
**parched** \-cht\ *adj* [ME *parchyd*, fr. past part. of *perchen, parchen*] : dried out : SCORCHED — **parched·ly** \-chə̇dlē, -chtlē\ *adv*
**parched·ness** \-chə̇dnə̇s, -ch(t)n-\ *n* -ES : the quality or state of being parched
**Par·chee·si** \pärˈchēzē, pȧˈch- *also* pə(r)ˈch-\ *trademark* — used for a board game adapted from pachisi
**parching** *adj* : DRYING, SCORCHING — **parch·ing·ly** *adv*
**parch·ment** \ˈpärchmənt, ˈpȧch-\ *n* -S [ME *perchement, parchement*, alter. (influenced by ML *pergamentum*, alter. of L *pergamena*) of *parchemin, perchemin*, fr. OF *parchemin*, alter. (influenced by *parche, parge*, a kind of leather, fr. L *Parthica -puellis-*, fr. *Parthica*, fem. of *Parthicus* Parthian + *puellis* leather) of *pargamin*, fr. ML *pergamina*, alter. of L *pergamena*, fr. Gk *pergamēnē*, fr. fem. of *Pergamēnos* of Pergamum, fr. *Perganon* (Pergamum), ancient city in Asia Minor (now Bergama, western Turkey)] **1 a** : the skin of a sheep, goat, or other animal esp. when prepared to receive writing **b** : any of various superior papers of well-beaten rag and wood pulp made to resemble parchment ⟨~ bond⟩ ⟨~ deed⟩ ⟨~ writing⟩ — see VEGETABLE PARCHMENT; compare VELLUM **c** : a document on parchment : a parchment manuscript ⟨here's a ~ with the seal of Caesar —*Shak.*⟩; *often* : an academic diploma **2** : the envelope of the coffee bean inside the pulp **3 a** : a variable color averaging a pale yellow green that is greener and paler than average Nile and yellower, lighter, and stronger than oyster gray **b** : a grayish yellow that is duller than chamois and redder and slightly less strong than old ivory
**parchment coffee** *n* : dried but unhulled coffee beans
**parch·ment·ed** \-məntəd, -ˌmen-\ *adj* : having a leathery surface
**parch·ment·ize** \-ˌmənt-ˌīz, -n-ˌtī-\ *vt* -ED/-ING/-S : to convert (as paper or other cellulosic material) into a substance resembling parchment esp. by treating with sulfuric acid
**parchment paper** *n* : VEGETABLE PARCHMENT
**parchment worm** *n* : a worm of the family Chaetopteridae
**parch·menty** \-məntē\ *adj* : of, relating to, or resembling parchment ⟨~ cheeks —William Fifield⟩
**par·ci·dentate** \ˌpärsə̇, -sē+\ *adj* [L *parci-* (fr. *parcus* sparing, fr. *parcere* to spare) + E *dentate* — more at PARSIMONY] : having few teeth
**parcimonious** *var of* PARSIMONIOUS
**par·ci·ty** \ˈpärsəd·ē\ *n* -ES [L *parcitas*, fr. *parcus* sparing, scanty + -*itas* -ity] : FRUGALITY, SCANTINESS
**par clearance** *n* : nationwide clearance of bank checks at face value conducted through the Federal Reserve system
¹**par·close** \ˈpärˌklōz\ *also* **per·close** \ˈpər-\ *n* [ME *parclose*, fr. MF, enclosure, end, fr. fem. of *parclos*, past part. of *parclore* to enclose, end, fr. *par-* thoroughly (fr. L *per-*, fr. *per* through) + *clore* to close — more at FOR, CLOSE] **1** *obs* : the end or conclusion of a sentence or discourse **2** : a screen or railing used esp. to separate a chapel from the main body of a church
²**par·close** \(ˈ)pär¦klōz\ *vt* [obs. F *parclos-*, stem of *parclore*] *archaic* : CONCLUDE, ENCLOSE
**par·cook** \(ˈ)pär+\ *vt* [*par-* (as in parboil) + *cook*] : PARBOIL
¹**pard** \ˈpärd\ *n* -S [ME *parde*, fr. OF, fr. L *pardus*, fr. Gk *pardalis, pardos*, of non-IE origin like Skt *pṛdāku* leopard, snake, Per *palang* leopard] *archaic* : LEOPARD
²**pard** \"\ *n* -S [short for *pardner*] *chiefly dial* : PARTNER, CHUM
**pardah** *var of* PURDAH
**pardal** *or* **pardale** *n* -S [L *pardalis* female leopard, fr. Gk *pardalis* leopard — more at PARD] *obs* : LEOPARD
**par·da·lote** \ˈpärdᵊlˌōt\ *n* -S [NL *Pardalotus* genus of birds including the diamond bird, fr. Gk *pardalōtos* spotted like a leopard, fr. *pardalis* leopard] : DIAMOND BIRD 1
**par·dao** \(ˈ)pär¦dau̇, pərˈd-\ *n* -S [Pg, fr. Skt *pratāpa* splendor, majesty, fr. *pra-* before, forward + *tapati* it heats; fr. the use of the word *pratāpa* as an epithet of kings on native coins — more at FOR, TEPID] : a half rupia coin of Portuguese India
**pard·ed** \ˈpärdə̇d\ *adj, archaic* : having spots like those of the leopard
**par·des·sus de vi·ole** \ˌ¦pärdə¦südəvēˈōl\ *n* [F, lit., above the viol] : a small viol higher in pitch than the treble viol
**par·dhan** \ˈpärˌdän\ *n, pl* **pardhan** *or* **pardhans** [Hindi *pardhān, pradhān*, fr. Skt *pradhāna* chief, fr. *pra-* before — more at FOR] : a bardic minstrel and ritual beggar of the Gond people
**par·die** *or* **per·die** *or* **par·di** *or* **par·dy** \(ˌ)pərˈdē, pärˈ-\ *interj* [ME *pardee*, fr. OF *par Dé* by God] *archaic* — a mild oath
**pard·ine** \ˈpärˌdīn, -ˌdēn\ *adj* [¹*pard* + -*ine*] : of, relating to, resembling, or spotted like a leopard
**pardine lynx** *n* [trans. of NL *Lynx pardina*] : SPOTTED LYNX
**pard·ner** \ˈpärdnər, ˈpȧdnə(r\ *n* -S [alter. of *partner*] *chiefly dial* : PARTNER, CHUM
**par·do** \(ˈ)pär¦dō, pərˈdō\ *n* -S [by alter.] : PARDAO
¹**par·don** \ˈpärdᵊn, ˈpȧd-\ *n* -S [ME *pardoun*, fr. OF *pardon*, fr. *pardonner* — more at ²PARDON] **1 a** : the excusing of an offense without exacting a penalty : remission of punishment **b** : divine forgiveness **2** *Roman Catholicism* **a** : INDULGENCE **b** : a festival at which an indulgence is granted **3 a** : a release by a sovereign or an officer having jurisdiction from the legal penalties or consequences of an offense or of a conviction **b** : an act of grace of the pardoning authority granted before or after conviction to one person by name or a number (as a class) of persons conditionally or absolutely or in any other form within the power of the pardoning authority — compare AMNESTY 2 **4** : an official warrant of remission of penalty **5 a** : excuse or forgiveness for a fault, offense, or discourtesy ⟨begged my ~ for his clumsiness⟩ — often used in polite apology or contradiction ⟨I beg your ~, but I think not⟩ **b** : excuse for failure to hear or understand ⟨beg ~⟩
**syn** AMNESTY, ABSOLUTION: PARDON in the sense here dealt with indicates a remission of punishment or penalty, entirely effective but without indicating exoneration from guilt ⟨a royal *pardon* later freed him from a death sentence —*Amer. Guide Series: Md.*⟩ ⟨decided that a parole wasn't enough — he wanted a full *pardon* —Green Peyton⟩ AMNESTY indicates a general remission of punishment, penalty, retribution, or disfavor to a whole group or class; it may imply a promise to forget ⟨a proclamation of universal *amnesty* . . . finally restored the civil rights of Jefferson Davis and a handful of others —A.D.Kirwan⟩ ⟨issued a general *amnesty* for all those who were imprisoned under the emergency decrees —C.E.

Black & E.C.Helmreich⟩ ABSOLUTION may indicate a formal acquittal in law or a definitive remission of punishment for sin in religion.

²**pardon** \"\ *vb* **pardoned; pardoned; pardoning** \-d(ᵊ)niŋ\ **pardons** [ME *pardonen*, fr. MF *pardoner*, *pardonner* to give, pardon, fr. LL *perdonare* to give with all one's heart, fr. L *per-*, intensive prefix (fr. *per* through) + *donare* to give — more at FOR, DONATION] *vt* **1 :** to absolve from the consequences of a fault or the punishment of crime **:** free from penalty **2 :** to remit the penalty of (an offense) **:** allow to pass without punishment **:** FORGIVE **3** *obs* **:** to refrain from exacting as a penalty ⟨I ~ thee thy life before thou ask it —Shak.⟩ **4 :** to make allowance for **:** TOLERATE — often used in courteous denial or apology ~ *vi* **:** to grant pardon or forgiveness **syn** see EXCUSE

**par·don·able** \-d(ᵊ)nəbəl\ *adj* [MF *pardonable*, *pardonnable*, fr. *pardoner*, *pardonner* + *-able* — more at PARDON] **:** admitting of being pardoned **:** EXCUSABLE ⟨her heart innocent of the most ~ guile —Joseph Conrad⟩ — **par·don·able·ness** \-nəs\ *n* -ES — **par·don·ably** \-blē,-bli\ *adv*

**par·don·er** \-d(ᵊ)nə(r)\ *n* -S [ME, fr. *pardonen* + *-er*] **1 :** a medieval preacher delegated to raise money for religious works by soliciting offerings and granting indulgences **2 :** one that pardons

**pards** *pl of* PARD

¹**pare** \'pa(a)|(ə)r, 'pe|, |ə\ *vt* -ED/-ING/-S [ME *paren*, fr. MF *parer* to prepare, trim, fr. L *parare* to prepare, procure; akin to OE *fearr* bull, ox, OHG *far*, *farro*, ON *farri* bull, L *parere* to give birth to, beget, produce, Gk *poris* calf, Skt *pṛthuka* head of cattle, calf, young of an animal, and perh. to OE *faran* to go, travel — more at FARE] **1 a :** to trim off excess, irregular, or surface parts of **:** shave off an outer edge or part of ⟨~ the horse's hoof⟩ **b :** to trim off an outside part (as the skin or rind) of ⟨~ apples for a pie⟩ — usu. used with *off* or *away* **c** *archaic* **:** to remove the turf from (a field) **:** clear a field of (turf) **2 :** to diminish the bulk of by or as if by paring **:** reduce gradually ⟨the navy poker players had *pared* the $70 I brought aboard to $14 —T.W.Lawson⟩ **3 :** to thin (leather, paper, and similar materials) with a knife (as in binding a book) **syn** see SKIN

²**pare** \"\ *chiefly dial var of* PAIR

¹**par·e·gor·ic** \¦parə¦gȯrik, -gäl, |rēk *also* ¦per-\ *also* **par·e·gor·i·cal** \|rəkəl, |rēk-\ *adj* [F *parégoreque*, fr. MF *paregorique*, fr. LL *paregoricus*, fr. Gk *parēgorikos*, fr. *parēgorein* to talk over, encourage, soothe (fr. *para-* ¹para- + *agora* assembly, marketplace) + *-ikos* -ic, -ical — more at AGORA] *archaic* **:** assuaging or soothing pain **:** MITIGATING

²**paregoric** \"\ *n* -S **1** *archaic* **:** a medicine that mitigates pain **:** ANODYNE **2 :** camphorated tincture of opium used to relieve pain

**pa·reia·saur** \pə'rīə,sȯ(ə)r\ *n* -S [NL *Pareiasaurus*] **:** a reptile of the family Pareiasauridae

**pa·reia·sau·ri·an** \pə¦rīə¦sȯrēən\ *adj* [NL *Pareiasaurus* + E *-ian*] **:** of or relating to pareiasaurs

**pa·reia·sau·ri·dae** \pə,rīə'sȯrə,dē\ *n pl, cap* [NL, fr. *Pareiasaurus*, type genus + *-idae*] **:** a widely distributed family of Permian terrestrial reptiles (order Cotylosauria) — see PAREIASAURUS

**pa·reia·sau·rus** \=,==ˈsȯrəs\ *n, cap* [NL, fr. Gk *pareia* cheek + NL *-saurus*] **:** the type genus of the family Pareiasauridae comprising heavily built reptiles from the Karroo formations of southern Africa

**pa·rei·ra** \pə'rerə, -rārə\ *n* -S [Pg *parreira* (*brava*), lit., wild vine, fr. *parreira* vine, vine on a trellis (fr. *parra* vine (leaf)) + *brava* wild] **1** *or* **pareira brava :** the root of a So. American vine (*Chondodendron tomentosum*) of the family Menispermaceae that is used as a diuretic, tonic, and aperient **2 :** any of several roots of related plants that are sometimes used like pareira — usu. used in combination; see FALSE PAREIRA, WHITE PAREIRA, YELLOW PAREIRA

**pa·re·ja** \pə'rā(,)hä\ *n* -S [Sp, lit., pair, fr. (assumed) VL *paricula*, dim. of L *par* pair, fr. *par* equal — more at PAIR] **:** a Spanish trawler using a dragnet that is often worked with the assistance of a second such trawler

**parel** *n* -S [ME *parail*, short for *apparail*, *appareil* — more at APPAREL] **1** *obs* **:** APPAREL, CLOTHING, ORNAMENT **2** *obs* **:** a preparation containing eggs and used to refine wine

**paremiographer** *var of* PAROEMIOGRAPHER

**pa·ren** \pə'ren\ *n* -S [by shortening] **:** PARENTHESIS 3

**pa·ren·chy·ma** \pə'reŋkəmə\ *also* **par·en·chym** \'parən,kim, pə'reŋkəm\ *or* **par·en·chyme** \'parən,kīm\ *n* -S [NL *parenchyma*, fr. Gk, visceral flesh, fr. *parenchein* to pour in beside, fr. *par-* ¹para- + *en-* ²en- + *chein* to pour; fr. the belief that the tissue of internal organs was poured in by the blood vessels of the organ — more at FOUND] **1 :** a tissue of higher plants consisting of thin-walled living cells that remain capable of cell division even when mature, that are agents of photosynthesis and storage, and that make up much of the substance of leaves and roots and the pulp of fruits as well as parts of stems and supporting structures **2 a :** the essential and distinctive tissue of an organ (as a gland) or an abnormal growth (as a tumor) as distinguished from its supportive framework **b :** the soft jellylike connective tissue containing stellate cells and fibers that fills the interstices between the internal organs in the flatworms and some other invertebrates **c :** the endoplasm of a protozoan

**pa·ren·chy·mal** \pə'reŋkəməl, ¦parən¦kīm-\ *or* **pa·ren·chy·mous** \-məs\ *adj* [NL *parenchyma* + E *-al* or *-ous*] **:** PARENCHYMATOUS

**par·en·chym·a·tous** \¦parən¦kimədəs\ *or* **pa·ren·chy·mat·ic** \pə¦reŋkə¦mad·ik\ *adj* [NL *parenchymat-*, *parenchyma* + E *-ous* or *-ic*] **:** of, relating to, made up of, or affecting parenchyma — **par·en·chym·a·tous·ly** *adv*

**par·en·chym·u·la** \,parən'kimyələ\ *n* -S [NL, dim. of *parenchyma*] **:** PLANULA

**parenesis** *var of* PARAENESIS

**pa·rens pa·tri·ae** \,pa(a)rənz'pā·trē,ē, -z'pa·t-; -z'pä·trē,ī\ *n* [L] **:** the father of the country constituted in law by the state (as in the U. S.) or by the sovereign (as in Great Britain) in the capacity of legal guardian of persons not sui juris and without natural guardians, of heir to persons without natural heirs, and of protector of all citizens or subjects unable to protect themselves ⟨the requirement of escheat to the *parens patriae* —*Harvard Law Rev.*⟩

¹**par·ent** \'pa(a)rənt, 'per-\ *n* -S *often attrib* [ME, fr. MF, fr. L *parent-*, *parens*, fr. pres. part. of *parere* to give birth to, beget, produce — more at PARE] **1 a :** one that begets or brings forth offspring **:** FATHER, MOTHER **b** *law* (1) **:** a lawful parent (2) **:** a person standing in loco parentis although not a natural parent (3) **:** ANCESTOR — compare PATRIA POTESTAS **2** *obs* **:** RELATIVE 3a **3 a :** an animal or plant regarded in relation to its offspring ⟨the genetic identity of a particular ~ tree —*Farmer's Weekly (So. Africa)*⟩ **b :** the material or source from which something is derived **:** AUTHOR, CAUSE, ORIGIN ⟨means of determining the rate of weathering of the ~ rock —J.P.Minard⟩ ⟨the outermost electrons can be detached from their ~ atoms —Leonard Engel⟩ ⟨while liberty was the ~ of eloquence, eloquence was the stay of liberty —Van Wyck Brooks⟩ **c :** a group (as a society, church, or business) from which another takes its rise and to which it sometimes remains subsidiary ⟨produces shoe linings for its ~ firm —*Amer. Guide Series: Ark.*⟩

²**parent** \"\ *vt* -ED/-ING/-S **1 :** to be or act as the parent of **:** ORIGINATE, PRODUCE **2 :** to provide with a parent or parents **:** trace the derivation of **:** show the real or assumed source of

**par·ent·age** \-tij, -tēj\ *n* -S [MF, fr. *parent* + *-age* — more at PARENT] **1** *archaic* **:** exercise of a parent's functions or prerogatives **2 :** descent from parents or ancestors **:** BIRTH, FAMILY, LINEAGE ⟨can you tell me anything of the ~ of the lady —Margaret Deland⟩ **3 :** derivation from a source **:** ORIGIN ⟨the ballads about them are of common ~ —G.B.Johnson⟩ ⟨it is sometimes difficult to sort out the ~ of a given idea —*Arctic*⟩ **4** *obs* **:** KINSHIP, KINDRED **5 :** the standing or position of a parent **:** PARENTHOOD

**pa·ren·tal** \pə'rentᵊl *sometimes* 'pa(a)rəntᵊl *or* 'perən-\ *adj* [L *parentalis*, fr. *parent-*, *parens* parent + *-alis* -al — more at PARENT] **1 :** of or relating to a parent **:** PATERNAL, MATERNAL ⟨participation in the tests now under way is only upon ~ request —*Monsanto Mag.*⟩ **2 a :** appropriate to, characteristic of, or resembling a parent ⟨maintained a nice balance between ~ authority and ~ affection⟩ ⟨the peculiar and indeed ~ relationship of the author to his work —Stanley Unwin⟩ **b :** of, relating to, or constituting a source or origin ⟨the progenitor of the gold, however, was some ~ magma —A.M. Bateman⟩

**parental generation** *n* **:** a generation made up of individuals of distinguishable genotypes that are crossed (as in experimental genetics) to produce hybrids — symbol *P*; compare FILIAL GENERATION

**par·en·ta·lia** \,pa(a)rən·'tālēə, ,per-\ *n pl, usu cap* [L, fr. neut. pl. of *parentalis* parental — more at PARENTAL] **:** the chief annual festival of the dead in ancient Rome from midday February 13 to February 21

**pa·ren·tal·ism** \pə'rentᵊl,izəm\ *n* -S **:** an attitude or the assumption of an attitude of superior authority **:** PATERNALISM

**pa·ren·tal·ly** \-tᵊlē, -li\ *adv* **:** in a parental manner

**parental school** *n* **:** a correctional school for truant children

**parentate** *vi* -ED/-ING/-S [L *parentatus*, past part. of *parentare* to make an offering or sacrifice to the spirits of the family dead, fr. *parent-*, *parens* parent — more at PARENT] *obs* **:** to perform funeral rites esp. for a parent or relative

**par·en·ta·tion** \,pa(a)rən·'tāshən, ,per-\ *n* -S [LL *parentation-*, *parentatio*, fr. L *parentatus* + *-ion-*, *-io* -ion] **1** *archaic* **:** the celebration of funeral rites for one's parents **2** *archaic* **:** any service memorializing the dead

**par·en·te·la** \,parən·'tēlə\ *n* -S [LL, fr. *parent-*, *parens* parent + *-ela* (as in *clientela* clientele) — more at CLIENTELE] *law* **:** the line of blood relatives **:** the kin of a person by descent

**par·en·tel·ic** \¦==¦telik\ *adj, law* **:** of, relating to, or tracing consanguinity through the parentela

¹**par·enteral** \pər+\ *adj* [ISV ¹*para-* + *enteral*] **1 :** not intestinal **:** situated or occurring outside the intestine **:** other than by way of the intestines ⟨~ digestion⟩ **2 :** injected or for injection subcutaneously, intramuscularly, or intravenously ⟨~ glucose⟩ ⟨~ saline⟩ — **par·enterally** \"+\ *adv*

²**parenteral** \"\ *n* -S **:** an agent (as a drug or solution) intended for parenteral administration

**pa·ren·the·sis** \pə'ren(t)thəsəs\ *n, pl* **parenthe·ses** \-ə,sēz\ [LL, fr. Gk, lit., action of inserting or interpolating, fr. *parentithenai* to insert, interpolate, fr. *para-* ¹para- + *entithenai* to put into, fr. *en-* ²en- + *tithenai* to place, set — more at DO] **1 a :** an amplifying or explanatory comment inserted in a passage to which it may be grammatically unrelated and from which it is usu. set off by punctuation (as curved lines, commas, or dashes) ⟨paused, at the end of this ~, to draw breath —Christopher Isherwood⟩ **b :** a remark or passage that constitutes a departure from the theme of a discourse **:** DIGRESSION **2 :** INTERLUDE, INTERVAL ⟨this sandy ~ —Thomas Wood †1950⟩ ⟨the fate of mankind is an irrelevancy, a ~ of no importance — C.I.Glicksberg⟩ **3 a :** one or both of the curved marks ( ) used in writing and printing to enclose a parenthetic expression **:** BRACKET 4c **b :** such a curve used as one of a pair to indicate which operands in a logical or mathematical expression are to be grouped and treated as a unit — compare BRACKET 4a

**pa·ren·the·size** \-,sīz\ *vb* -ED/-ING/-S [*parenthesis* + *-ize*] *vt* **1 :** to make a parenthesis of **:** interject as comment or digression **2 :** to insert a parenthesis in **:** scatter parentheses through ⟨*parenthesized* his address to the point of incoherence⟩ ~ *vi* **:** to say something in parenthesis

**par·en·thet·ic** \¦parən¦thed·|ik, -et|, |ēk\ *or* **par·en·thet·i·cal** \-əkəl, -ēk-\ *adj* [fr. *parenthesis*, after such pairs as E *antithesis*: *antithetic*, *antithetical*] **1 a :** of or relating to a parenthesis **:** expressed in or as if in a parenthesis **b :** enclosed in parentheses **2 :** containing parentheses **:** using or given to using parenthesis ⟨a ~ style⟩ — **par·en·thet·i·cal·ly** \-ək(ə)lē, -ēk-, -li\ *adv* — **par·en·thet·i·cal·ness** *n* -ES

**par·ent·hood** \'pa(a)rənt,hu̇d, 'per-\ *n* **:** the position, function, or standing of a parent

**pa·ren·ti·cide** \pə'rentə,sīd\ *n* -S [¹*parent* + *-i-* + *-cide*] **:** PARRICIDE

**parent-in-law** \'==ᵊn,=\ *n, pl* **parents-in-law :** the father or mother of one's spouse **:** FATHER-IN-LAW, MOTHER-IN-LAW

**par·ent·less** \'==ləs\ *adj* **:** having no parent ⟨a short wiry stalk of white heath grew, ~ and alone —Eve Langley⟩

**parent material** *n* **:** the disintegrated rock material usu. unconsolidated and unchanged or only slightly changed that underlies and generally gives rise to the true soil by the natural process of soil development — called also *source material*; compare HORIZON 2, SOLUM

**parent metal** *n* **:** BASE METAL 4

**parents** *pl of* PARENT, *pres 3d sing of* PARENT

**par·ent·ship** \'==,ship\ *n* **:** PARENTHOOD

**parent-teacher association** \'==ˈ==\ *n* **:** an organization of local groups of teachers and the parents of their pupils to work for the improvement of the schools and the benefit of the pupils — abbr. *PTA*

**par·e·oe·an** \,parē'ēən\ *n* -S *usu cap* [¹*para-* + Gk *ēōs* dawn + E *-ean* (as in *European*) — more at EAST] **:** a member of a Mongoloid people having black hair with scant face and body hair, yellowish brown skin, broad face, short flat nose, short stature, and the Mongolian eye fold — called also *Southern Mongol*

**par·epididymis** \(¦)par+\ *n* [NL, fr. ¹*para-* + *epididymis*] **:** PARADIDYMIS

**par·epigastric** \(¦)par+\ *adj* [ISV ¹*para-* + *epigastric*] **:** adjacent to the epigastric region

**par·er** \'pa(a)rə(r), 'per-\ *n* -S **:** one that pares: as **a :** a mechanical device for paring vegetables or fruits ⟨potato ~⟩ **b :** one who pares binding leather to proper thickness for use

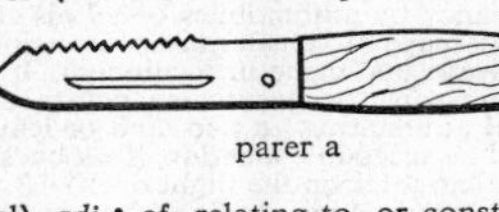

parer a

**par·er·gal** \(')pa¦rərgəl\ *adj* **:** of, relating to, or constituting a parergon **:** SUBORDINATE

**par·er·ga·sia** \¦par+\ *n* [NL, fr. ¹*para-* + *ergasia*] **:** schizophrenia regarded as a disorder of action

**pa·rer·gon** \pa'rər,gän\ *n, pl* **parer·ga** \-,gə\ [L, fr. Gk, fr. *par-* ¹para- + *ergon* work — more at WORK] **1 :** something subordinate or accessory; *esp* **:** an ornamental accessory or embellishment **2 :** a subordinate activity or work **:** work undertaken in addition to one's main employment ⟨a ~, pondered and written during . . . moments of leisure —J.D. Wilson⟩

**pares** *pres 3d sing of* PARE, *pl of* PARE

**pa·re·sis** \pə'rēsəs, 'parə-\ *n, pl* **pare·ses** \-,sēz\ [NL, fr. Gk, action of letting go or slackening, paralysis, neglect, fr. *parienai* to let fall at the side, let fall, fr. *par-* ¹para- + *hienai* to let go, send — more at JET] **1 :** slight or partial paralysis **2 :** GENERAL PARESIS

**pa·res·sí** \¦parə¦sē\ *n, pl* **paressí** *or* **paressís** *usu cap* [Pg, of AmerInd origin] **1 a :** a group of Arawakan peoples of central Brazil **b :** a member of any such people **2 :** the language of the Paressí peoples

**par·esthesia** *also* **par·aesthesia** \¦par+\ *n* [NL, fr. *para-* + *esthesia*, *aesthesia*] **:** a sensation of pricking, tingling, or creeping on the skin having no objective cause and usu. associated with injury or irritation of a sensory nerve or nerve root

**par·esthetic** *also* **par·aesthetic** \"+\ *adj* **:** of, relating to, or affected with paresthesia

¹**pa·ret·ic** \pə're|d·|ik, |t|, |ēk *sometimes* -rē|\ *adj* [fr. NL *paresis*, after such pairs as E *antithesis*: *antithetic*] **:** of, relating to, or affected with paresis — **pa·ret·i·cal·ly** \|ək(ə)lē, |ēk-, -li\ *adv*

²**paretic** \"\ *n* -S **:** an individual affected with paresis

**pa·re·to's law** \pə'rād·(,)ōz-\ *n, usu cap P* [after Vilfredo *Pareto* (Marchese di Parigi) †1923 Ital. economist and sociologist] **:** a statement in economics: the distribution of incomes in various countries and in various ages tends to be similar despite differences of governmental policy (as in taxation)

**pa·reu** \'pärā,ü\ *n* -S [Tahitian] **:** a wraparound skirt or loincloth worn throughout Polynesia and usu. made from a rectangular piece of printed cloth

**pa·reu·nia** \pə'rünēə\ *n* -S [NL, fr. Gk *pareunos* lying beside, bedfellow (fr. *par-* ¹para- + *eunē* bed) + NL *-ia*] **:** COITUS

**pa·re·ve** \¦pärə¦vā\ *or* **par·ve** \'pärvə\ *adj* [Yiddish *parev*] **:** made without milk, meat, or their derivatives

¹**par ex·cel·lence** \,pä,reksə'läⁿs, ,pä,(r)e-, -län(t)s, =ˈ==,=; *sometimes* =ˈ(r)eks(ə)lən(t)s\ *adv* [F, lit. by excellence] **:** PREEMINENTLY

²**par excellence** \"\ *adj* **:** being the best of its kind **:** being an epitome or embodiment ⟨bronze . . . was the metal *par excellence* of the more advanced nations —A.L.Kroeber⟩ ⟨the grassland *par excellence* that accounts for the legendary green of Erin —Samuel Van Valkenburg & Ellsworth Huntington⟩ ⟨the private secretary *par excellence* —John Gunther⟩

**par·fait** \pär'fā, pä'-, '=,=\ *n* -S [F, lit., something perfect, fr. *parfait* perfect, fr. L *perfectus* — more at PERFECT] **1 :** a flavored custard containing whipped cream and syrup frozen without stirring **2 :** a cold dessert consisting of alternating layers of fruit, syrup, ice cream, and whipped cream in a parfait glass

**parfait amour** *n* [F, lit., perfect love] **:** a violet-colored liqueur flavored principally with lemon, vanilla, cloves, and coriander

**parfait glass** *n* **:** a tall narrow glass with a short stem used for serving a parfait

parfait glass

**par·fit** \'pärfət, 'päf-\ *chiefly dial var of* PERFECT

**par·fleche** \'pär,flesh, =ˈ=\ *n* -S [CanF *parflèche*, fr. F *parer* to ward off, parry + *flèche* arrow — more at PARRY, FLÈCHE] **1 :** a rawhide (as of buffalo) soaked in lye to remove the hair and dried **2 :** an article (as a box, sack, or saddlebag) made of parfleche

**par·focal** \(')pär+\ *adj* [L *par* equal + E *focal* — more at PAIR] **:** having corresponding focal points all in the same plane **:** having sets of objectives or eyepieces so mounted that they may be interchanged without varying the focus of the instrument (as a microscope or telescope) with which they are used

**par·focalization** \(¦)=+\ *n* **:** a rendering parfocal

**par·focalize** \(')=+\ *vt* **:** to make parfocal

**par·ga·na** *or* **per·gun·nah** \pər'gənə, 'pərgə,nä\ *n* -S [Hindi *pargana*, fr. Per] **:** a group of towns in India constituting an administrative subdivision of the zillah

**par·gas·ite** \'pärgə,sīt\ *n* -S [G *pargasit*, fr. *Pargas*, town in Finland + G *-it* -ite] **:** a green or bluish green hornblende containing sodium

**parge** \'pärj\ *vt* -ED/-ING/-S [by shortening] **:** PARGET

**parge coat** *n* **:** PARGING

¹**par·get** \'pärjət\ *vt* **pargeted** *or* **pargetted; pargeted** *or* **pargetted; pargeting** *or* **pargetting; pargets** [ME *pargetten*, fr. MF *pargeter*, *parjeter* to throw on top of, fr. *par-*, intensive prefix (fr. L *per-*, fr. *per* through) + *geter*, *jeter* to throw — more at FOR, JET] **1 :** to coat with plaster; *esp* **:** to apply ornamental plasterwork to **2 :** to decorate with gilding or other ornamental surfacing **3** *archaic* **:** to cover with a fair outward appearance **:** WHITEWASH

²**parget** \"\ *n* -S [ME, fr. *pargetten*, v.] **1 a :** plaster, whitewash, or roughcast for coating a wall **b :** a plaster of cow's dung and lime for lining chimney flues **c :** ornamental pargeting on walls **2** *obs* **:** GYPSUM

**par·get·er** \-jəd·ə(r)\ *n* -S [¹*parget* + *-er*] *dial Eng* **:** PLASTERER

**par·get·ing** *or* **par·get·ting** *n* -S [ME, fr. gerund of *pargeten*, *pargetten* to parget — more at PARGET] **1 :** a decorative plasterwork in raised ornamental figures formerly used for interior and exterior decoration of houses **2 :** the interior plastering of flues intended to give a smooth surface and help the draft

**par·get·ry** \'pärjə·trē, -tri\ *n* -ES [²*parget* + *-ry*] **:** ornamental plaster or stucco relief work applied to a flat surface

**pargework** \'=,=\ *n* **:** PARGETRY

**parging** *n* -S [fr. gerund of *parge*] **:** a thin coat of mortar or plaster used to smooth or waterproof the surface of rough brick or stone walls or to line the inside of chimneys

**par·go** \'pär(,)gō\ *n* -S [Sp & Pg, fr. L *pagarus* sea bream, fr. Gk *phagros*, lit., whetstone; akin to Gk *phoxos* pointed, peaked, and perh. to Arm *bark* bitter, sharp-tasting] **1 :** any of various fishes of the family Sparidae; *esp* **:** the European porgy (*Pagrus pagrus*) **2 :** any of various snappers of the family Lutjanidae

**par·helic** \(')pär, (')pä+\ *or* **par·heliacal** \¦=+\ *adj* **:** of or relating to a parhelion

**parhelic circle** *or* **parhelic ring** *n* **:** a luminous circle or halo parallel to the horizon at the altitude of the sun

**par·helion** \"+\ *n, pl* **parhelia** [L *parelion*, fr. Gk *parēlion*, *parēlios*, fr. *par-* ¹para- + *hēlios* sun — more at SOLAR] **:** any one of several bright spots often tinged with color that often appear symmetrically distributed on the parhelic circle and are intensified parts of halos — called also *mock sun*, *sun dog*; compare PARASELENE

**par·homologous** \¦pär, ¦pä+\ *adj* [¹*para-* + *homologous*] **:** exhibiting parhomology

**par·homology** \"+\ *n* [ISV ¹*para-* + *homology*] **:** apparent or imitative homology esp. between metameres

**pari-** *comb form* [ME, fr. MF, fr. ML, fr. L *par* — more at PAIR] **:** equal **:** equally ⟨*paridigitate*⟩

**pa·ri·ah** \pə'rīə *sometimes* 'pa(a)rēə\ *n* -S [Tamil *paraiyan*, lit., drummer, fr. *parai* drum] **1 :** a member of a low caste of southern India and Burma that is below Sudra rank and has provided many farm laborers and domestic servants **2 :** a person despised or rejected by society **:** OUTCAST ⟨hundreds of thousands of lepers still exist throughout the world as social ~*s* —V.G.Heiser⟩ ⟨many virile minds dare not speak out for fear of . . . becoming political ~*s* —L.L.Rice⟩ ⟨a ~ to former friends, who were afraid to be seen with me —P.B.Williamson⟩

**pariah dog** *n* **:** a wild or domesticated native mongrel dog of No. Africa or southern Asia, varying greatly in conformation and important chiefly as a scavenger

**pa·ri·ah·dom** \-dəm\ *n* -S **:** the condition of a pariah ⟨they walked on together, and I dropped behind suddenly realizing my ~ —W.J.Locke⟩

**pa·ri·ah·ism** \-ə,izəm\ *n* -S **:** PARIAHDOM

**pariah kite** *n* **:** a scavenger kite (*Milvus migrans govinda*) of India

¹**par·i·an** \'pa(a)rēən, 'per-\ *adj, usu cap* [L *parius* Parian, fr. Gk *parios*, fr. *Paros*, one of the Cyclades islands in the Aegean sea) + E *-an*] **1 :** of or relating to the Cycladic island of Paros, noted for its beautiful marble extensively used for sculptures in ancient times **2 :** of, relating to, or being Parian ware

²**parian** \"\ *n* -S **:** PARIAN WARE ⟨his teeth . . . showed like ~ from his parted lips —Thomas Hardy⟩

**parian cement** *n, usu cap P* [(*plaster of*) *Paris* + E *-an*] **:** a hard-finish gypsum plaster to which borax has been added

**parian ware** *n, usu cap P* [¹*Parian*] **:** a relatively low-fired white to pale ivory ceramic body made of feldspar and china clay and used usu. for bisque statuary and ornamental items

**pa·ri·ca** \¦parə¦kä\ *n* -S [Pg *paricá*, fr. Tupi] **:** COHOBA

**pa·ri·dae** \'parə,dē\ *n, cap* [NL, fr. L *Parus*, type genus + *-idae*] **:** a large family of passerine birds (suborder Oscines) consisting of the titmice, verdins, and bushtits — compare SITTIDAE

**pa·ri·es** \'pa(a)rē,ēz\ *n, pl* **pari·e·tes** \pə'rīə,tēz\ [NL, fr. L, wall; akin to OSlav *podŭpora* prop, L *sparus*, *sparum* short spear — more at SPEAR] **1 :** the wall of a cavity or hollow organ — usu. used in pl. **2 :** the triangular middle part of each segment of the shell of a barnacle

¹**pa·ri·e·tal** \pə'rīəd·ᵊl\ *adj* [MF, fr. NL *pariet-*, *paries* + MF *-al*] **1 a :** of or relating to the walls of a part or cavity ⟨~ peritoneum⟩ — compare VISCERAL **b :** of, relating to, or located in the upper posterior part of the head; *specif* **:** relating to either of the pair of bones that form the cranial roof of this part of the skull **2** *of a plant part* **:** peripheral in location or orientation; *esp* **:** attached to the main wall rather than the axis or a cross wall of an ovary — used of an ovule or a placenta **3 :** of or relating to life within college walls or its order and regulation; *esp* **:** of or relating to the visitation regulations for members of the opposite sex in dormitories **4 :** of, relating to, or appearing on a wall ⟨upon the wall . . . some work of ~ art —G.B.Brown⟩

²**parietal** \"\ *n* -S **:** a parietal part (as a bone, scale, or plate)

**parietal angle** *n* **:** the angle formed by the intersection of lines from the auricular point to the bregma and to the lambda

**parietal bone** *n* **:** either of a pair of membrane bones of the roof of the skull between the frontals and occipitals that in

man are large and quadrilateral in outline, meet in the sagittal suture, and form much of the top and sides of the cranium
**parietal cell** *n* **:** any of the large oval acid-secreting cells of the gastric mucous membrane lying between the central cells and the basement membrane — compare CHIEF CELL
**pa·ri·e·ta·les** \pə,rīə'tā(,)lēz\ *n pl, cap* [NL, fr. LL *pariet-, paries* + *-ales*] **:** a large order of dicotyledonous plants with spirocyclic or cyclic flowers that have the ovary syncarpous and usu. parietal placentae
**parietal eye** *n* **:** PINEAL EYE
**parietal lobe** *n* **:** the middle division of each cerebral hemisphere situated behind the central sulcus, above the fissure of Sylvius, and in front of the parieto-occipital fissure
**pa·ri·e·tar·ia** \pə,rīə'ta(a)rēə\ *n, cap* [NL, fr. LL, pellitory-of-the-wall, fr. fem. of *parietarius* of a wall, fr. L *pariet-, paries* wall + *-arius* -ary — more at PARIES] **:** a small genus of widely distributed stingless herbs (family Urticaceae) with alternate entire leaves and small greenish flowers in the leaf axils — see PELLITORY 2
**parieto-** *comb form* [*parietal*] **:** parietal and ⟨*parieto*frontal⟩
**pa·ri·e·to-occipital fissure** \pə'rīəd·,ō+-\ *or* **parieto-occipital sulcus** *n* **:** a fissure near the posterior end of each cerebral hemisphere separating the parietal and occipital lobes
**pari-mutuel** \,parə'myüch(əw)əl, -chwəl\ *n, pl* **pari-mutuels** \-lz\ *also in sense 1* **par·is-mutuels** \,parə'm-\ [F *pari mutuel*, lit., mutual stake] **1 :** a system of betting (as on a horse race) in which those who bet on the winner share the total stakes minus a small percent for the management **2** *or* **pari-mutuel machine :** a machine for registering and indicating the number and nature of bets made (as on a horse race) in the pari-mutuel system of betting
**par·i·na·ri** \,parə'narē\ *n* -s [Galibi] **:** any of several trees of the genus *Parinarium; esp* **:** a tree (*P. rudolphi*) of the Amazonian rain forests that has extremely hard strong yellow wood which is rich in silica and is used in marine construction because of its resistance to borers
**par·i·nar·ic acid** \,parə'narik-\ *n* [ISV *parinar-* (fr. NL *Parinarium*) + *-ic*] **:** a crystalline highly unsaturated fatty acid $CH_3CH_2(CH{=}CH)_4(CH_2)_7COOH$ obtained esp. from seed fats of trees of the genus *Parinarium*
**par·i·nar·i·um** \,==ˈna(a)rēəm\ *n, cap* [NL, fr. Galibi *parinari*] **:** a large genus of tropical evergreen shrubs and trees (family Rosaceae) with showy white or pink flowers, drupaceous fruits some of which are edible, and in some larger forms valuable timber — see GINGERBREAD PLUM, PARINARI
**pa·rine** \'pā,rīn, -,rən\ *adj* [L *parus* titmouse + E *-ine*] **:** of, relating to, or resembling the titmice
**paring** *n* -s [ME, fr. gerund of *paren* to pare — more at PARE] **1 :** the cutting away of an edge or surface **2 :** something pared off ⟨potato ~s⟩ **3 parings** *pl* **:** BOXING 4
**paring chisel** *n* **:** a long-handled hand chisel having a short thin blade for paring wood surfaces — see CHISEL illustration
**paring gouge** *n* **:** a woodworker's gouge having a concave blade beveled inside to form the cutting edge
**paring iron** *n* **:** a knife used for paring a hoof
**paring knife** *n* **:** a small short-bladed knife for paring fruit and vegetables
**par·in·tin·tin** \,parən·,tin·'tin\ *n, pl* **parintintin** *or* **parintintins** *usu cap* [Pg, of AmerInd origin] **1 a :** a Tupian people of the southern part of the state of Amazonas, Brazil **b :** a member of such people **2 :** the language of the Parintintin people

paring knife

**pa·ri pas·su** \,parē'pa(,)sü, -ri'p-; ,pärē'pä(,)sü\ *adv (or adj)* [L, with equal step] **:** at an equal rate or pace **:** with identical and simultaneous progression ⟨the rate of development decreased *pari passu* with the density —*Ecology*⟩ ⟨the two made a *pari passu* advance⟩
**¹par·is** \'parəs *also* 'per-\ *adj, usu cap* [fr. *Paris*, France] **1 :** of or from Paris, the capital of France ⟨the *Paris* scene⟩ ⟨a *Paris* original⟩ **:** of the kind or style prevalent in Paris **:** PARISIAN **2** *of clothing* **:** made in Paris, France, or adapted from designs originating there ⟨girls in *Paris* frocks walked slowly back and forth —J.A.Michener⟩
**²paris** \"\ *n, cap* [NL, fr. ML or NL (*herba*) *paris* herb Paris — more at HERB PARIS] **:** a small genus of Eurasian herbs (family Liliaceae) not unlike *Trillium* in the whorled leaves and floral parts but having often tetramerous or pentamerous flowers — see HERB PARIS
**paris blue** *n* [¹*Paris*] **1** *usu cap P* **:** an iron-blue pigment similar to Prussian blue **2** *often cap P* **:** PRUSSIAN BLUE
**paris daisy** *n, usu cap P* **:** a marguerite (*Chrysanthemum frutescens*)
**paris garden** *n, usu cap P* [fr. *Paris Garden*, a 16th and 17th cent. bear garden in London, England] *obs* **:** a bear garden **:** a scene of uproar and confusion
**paris granite** *n, usu cap P* **:** SEMIPORCELAIN
**paris green** *n* **1** *usu cap P* **:** an insecticide and pigment prepared as a very poisonous bright green powder (as from arsenic trioxide and copper acetate) and consisting of copper acetoarsenite approximately $Cu(C_2H_3O_2)_2.3Cu(AsO_2)_2$ — called also *emerald green, Schweinfurt green* **2** *often cap P* **a :** a variable color averaging a brilliant yellowish green **b :** a moderate yellowish green that is greener, lighter, and stronger than tarragon, lighter and slightly stronger than malachite green, and yellower, lighter, and stronger than verdigris — called also *imperial green*
**¹par·ish** \'parish, -rēsh *also* 'per-\ *n* -ES [ME *paroche, parosshe, parisshe*, fr. MF *parroche, paroisse*, fr. LL *parochia*, fr. LGk *paroikia*, fr. *paroikos* Christian (fr. Gk, stranger, fr. *par-* ¹para- + *oikos* house) + *-ia* -y; fr. the early Christians' looking upon themselves as strangers on earth, their real home being heaven — more at VICINITY] **1 a :** the ecclesiastical unit of area committed to one pastor; *collectively* **:** the residents of such area or the members of one church **b** *Brit* **:** a subdivision of a county often coinciding with an original ecclesiastical parish and constituting the unit of local government **2 :** a portion of a diocese committed to the pastoral care of one clergyman **3 :** a local church community composed of the members or constituents of a Protestant church **4 :** SOCIETY 3b(2) **5 :** a civil division of the state of Louisiana corresponding to a county in other states **6 :** HOUSE 3d — see CURLING illustration
**²par·ish** \'parish\ *dial var of* PERISH
**parish court** *n* **:** a court established for each Louisiana parish and having a jurisdiction similar to that of a court of common pleas
**par·ish·en** \'parishən\ *n* -s [ME (northern dial.) *parichin, parishing*, prob. fr. *parisshe* parish + *-ing* — more at PARISH] *Scot* **:** PARISH
**parish house** *n* **1 :** an auxiliary building belonging to a church and used for its business, social, or extension activities **2 :** the residence of a clergyman (as a Roman Catholic priest)
**pa·rish·io·nal** \pə'rishənᵊl, -shnəl\ *adj* [*parishioner* + *-al*] *archaic* **:** PAROCHIAL
**pa·rish·io·ner** \-sh(ə)nə(r) *sometimes* -zh-\ *n* -s [ME *parisshoner*, prob. modif. of MF *parrochien, paroissien* parishioner (fr. *parroche, paroisse* parish + *-ien* -ian) + ME *-er* — more at PARISH] **:** a member or inhabitant of a parish
**parish lantern** *n, dial chiefly Eng* **:** MOON
**parish-pump** \'==,=\ *adj, chiefly Brit* **:** of local scope or purview **:** having a restricted outlook or limited interest **:** PAROCHIAL ⟨smacked less of a serious schism than of a *parish-pump* quarrel —*Times Lit. Supp.*⟩
**parish register** *n* **:** a register of the baptisms, marriages, and burials in a parish
**parish seat** *n* **:** a county seat in Louisiana
**¹pa·ri·sian** \pə'rizhən, -rēzh- *sometimes* pa'- *or* -rizēən\ *adj, usu cap* [F *parisien*, adj. & n., fr. *Paris*, France, + F *-ien* -ian] **1 a :** of, relating to, or characteristic of Paris, the capital of France **b :** of, relating to, or characteristic of the people of Paris **2 :** of, relating to, or characteristic of the standard French language
**²parisian** \"\ *n* -s *cap* [F *Parisien*] **1 :** a native or resident of Paris, France **2 a :** the French dialect of Paris **b :** the official and literary language of France based on this dialect **:** standard French
**pa·ri·sian·ism** \-,nizəm\ *n* -s *usu cap* [F *parisianisme*, fr. *parisien* + *-isme* -ism] **1 :** the traits of a Parisian ⟨his *Parisianism*, grafted upon an imperishable brogue, gave to his utterance a very curious charm —Max Beerbohm⟩ **2 :** a habit or mannerism (as of speech) observable esp. in Parisians
**pa·ri·si·enne** \pə,rēzē'en\ *n* -s *cap* [F, fem. of *Parisien*] **:** a Parisian woman or girl ⟨the 32-year-old *Parisienne* was stopped by . . . border guards —*Springfield (Mass.) Daily News*⟩
**par·is·ite** \'parə,sīt\ *n* -s [G *parisit*, fr. José *Paris* †1849 Colombian mineowner and philanthropist + G *-it* -ite] **:** a mineral $(Ce,La)_2Ca(CO_3)_3F_2$ consisting of a carbonate and fluoride of calcium, cerium, and lanthanum
**paris-mutuels** *pl of* PARI-MUTUEL
**par·i·sol·o·gy** \,parə'säləjē\ *n* -ES [Gk *parisos* almost equal, evenly balanced + *-logy*] **:** the use of equivocal or ambiguous words
**¹par·ison** \'parə,sän\ *n* -s [Gk, neut. of *parisos* almost equal, evenly balanced, fr. *par-* ¹para- + *isos* equal] **:** even balance between the members of a sentence — **par·ison·ic** \,==ˈsänik\ *adj*
**²par·i·son** \'parəsən\ *also* **par·ai·son** \", -rə,zän\ *n* -s [F *paraison*, fr. *parer* to prepare — more at PARE] **1 :** a gob of glass that has been partially shaped or molded into an object **2 :** a receptacle in a bottle-making machine from which the exact amount of metal for making a bottle is fed down
**par·i·so·sis** \,parə'sōsəs\ *n* -ES [Gk *parisōsis*, fr. *parisoun* to make equal (fr. *parisos* almost equal, equally balanced) + *-sis* — more at PARISON] **:** ¹PARISON
**paris red** *n* **1** *usu cap P* **:** an iron red used as a polishing agent and pigment **2 :** red lead used as a pigment **3** *often cap P* **:** FIRE RED 1
**par·isth·mi·on** \pa'rismēən, -ē,än\ *n* -s [Gk, fr. *par-* ¹para- + *isthmion* anything belonging to the neck or throat, fr. *isthmos* neck, narrow passage, neck of land — more at ISTHMUS] **:** TONSIL
**paris white** *n, usu cap P* **:** whiting esp. of good color and very fine particle size used as a pigment or filler
**paris yellow** *n* **1** *usu cap P* **:** any of various yellow pigments: as **a :** a chrome yellow pigment **b :** CASSEL YELLOW **2** *often cap P* **:** LIGHT CHROME YELLOW
**pari·syllabic** \,parə+\ *adj* [*pari-* + *syllabic*] *of a Greek or Latin noun* **:** having the same number of syllables in all inflections
**pa·riti** \pə'rīd·ē, -rid·ē\ *n, cap* [NL, fr. Malayalam *paritti, parutti* cotton plant, cotton tree] *in some classifications* **:** a small genus of tropical trees (family Malvaceae) with entire cordate leaves and yellow flowers now usu. included in the genus *Hibiscus*
**par·i·tor** \'parəd·ə(r)\ *n* -s [LL *paritor* servant, attendant, fr. L *paritus* (past part. of *parēre* to come forth, be visible, attend) + *-or* — more at APPEAR] *chiefly dial* **:** APPARITOR
**¹par·i·ty** \'parəd·ē, -ətē, -i *also* 'per-\ *n* -ES [L *paritas*, fr. *par* equal + *-itas* -ity — more at PAIR] **1 :** the quality or state of being equal **:** close equivalence or resemblance **:** equality of rank, nature, or value **:** LIKENESS ⟨~ must exist between authority and responsibility —Harold Koontz & Cyril O'Donnell⟩ **2 a :** equivalence of a commodity price expressed in one currency to its price expressed in another **b :** equality of purchasing power established by law between different kinds of money at a given ratio (as between gold and silver coins of a fixed weight and fineness) **3 :** an equivalence between farmers' current purchasing power and their purchasing power at a selected base period maintained by government support of agricultural commodity prices at a level fixed by law **:** a ratio between agricultural and nonagricultural prices at a specified past time ⟨~ is the price calculated to give the farmer a fair return in relation to the things he must buy —*N.Y.Times*⟩
**²parity** \"\ *n* -ES [*parous* + *-ity*] **:** parous condition **:** number of children previously borne ⟨the age and ~ of the mother may be a factor —*Jour. Amer. Med. Assoc.*⟩
**¹park** \'pärk, 'pák\ *n* -s [ME, fr. OF *parc* enclosure, enclosure for animals, park, fr. (assumed) VL *parricus* enclosure (whence ML *parricus*), perh. fr. L *pertica* pole, measuring rod, parcel of land measured off with such a rod — more at PERCH] **1 a** *Eng law* **:** an enclosed piece of ground stocked with beasts of the chase and held by royal prescription or grant — compare ²CHASE 3, FOREST 1 **b** *Brit* **:** a tract of land often including lawns, woodland, and pasture attached to a country house and used as a game preserve and for other purposes of recreation and manorial life **2 :** a tract of land maintained by a city or town as a place of beauty or of public recreation **3 :** a large area often of forested land reserved from settlement and maintained in its natural state for public use (as by campers or hunters) or as a wildlife refuge **4** *dial Eng* **:** HAYFIELD, PASTURE **5 a** (1) **:** a level valley between mountain ranges (2) *chiefly West* **:** an open area surrounded or partly surrounded by woodland and suitable for grazing or cultivation **b :** open grassland interrupted by clumps of trees, forbs, and shrubby vegetation **6 a :** a space occupied by military animals, vehicles, pontoons, or materials of any kind (as ammunition, ordnance stores, hospital stores, or provisions); *also* **:** the objects themselves ⟨a ~ of artillery⟩ **b :** PARKING LOT **7 :** an enclosed basin in which oysters are grown arranged so that the water may be renewed at high tide **:** CLAIRE **8 :** a large enclosed arena used for sports; *esp* **:** BALL PARK
**²park** \"\ *vb* -ED/-ING/-s *vt* **1 a :** to enclose in or as if in a park **b :** to make a park of **2 a** (1) **:** to bring to a stop and keep standing (as a motor vehicle) at the edge of a public way ⟨had never learned to ~ a car properly⟩ (2) **:** to leave temporarily on a public way or in an open space assigned or maintained for occupancy by automobiles ⟨~*ed* his car behind the building⟩ (3) **:** to leave (a vehicle) in an accessible place ⟨~*ed* his car in the garage and came in to dinner⟩ **b :** to set out (a railroad sleeping car) for occupancy before departure from or after arrival at a station **c :** to land or leave an airplane in an assigned or accessible location ⟨flew back to the carrier and ~*ed* the little fighter on the flight deck⟩ **3 a :** to set and leave in a particular place usu. to be picked up later ⟨~*ed* his bag at the club⟩ **b :** to deposit, settle, or establish esp. for a considerable time ⟨~*ed* himself in an easy chair⟩ ⟨the . . . anxiety that they might feel about ~*ing* the baby —J.M.Barzun⟩ **4 :** to assemble (as artillery, vehicles, or stores) in a military dump or park ~ *vi* **1 :** to park a vehicle ⟨after landing on the runway, private owners used to ~ at the far edge⟩ ⟨looked for a place to ~ long enough to run a few errands⟩ **2 :** to stop a vehicle in a secluded place to engage in lovemaking ⟨~*ed* with his girl in a local lovers' lane⟩
**par·ka** \'pärkə, 'pákə\ *n* -s [Aleut, skin, outer garment, fr. Russ, pelt from a reindeer, dog, or sheep, fr. Samoyed] **1 :** a hooded pullover garment reaching to the thighs or knees that is made usu. of fur and worn by Eskimos and others living in arctic regions **2 :** a garment shorter than the arctic parka but of similar style made of heavy windproof fabric for sports or military wear as either a jacket or a pullover
**park cattle** *n, usu cap P&C* **:** a breed or variety of white long-haired polled or horned cattle with dark points that is maintained in a semidomesticated state on a few English estates and is sometimes considered very close to the wild ancestors from which improved breeds have been derived
**parked** *adj* **:** laid out with greenery and decorative plantings ⟨~ terraces⟩
**park·er** \'pärkər, 'pákə(r\ *n* -s [ME, fr. *park* + *-er*] **1** *obs* **:** the keeper of a park **2** [²*park* + *-er*] **:** one that parks a vehicle ⟨facilities already filled by the all-day ~ —Richard Sheddon⟩

parka 2

**parker house roll** *n, usu cap P&H* [fr. *Parker House*, hotel in Boston, Mass., where the rolls were introduced] **:** a roll made by folding half of a flat circular piece of dough over the other half
**par·ke·ri·a·ce·ae** \(,)pärkirē'āsē,ē\ *n pl, cap* [NL, fr. *Parkeria*, type genus (fr. C. S. *Parker*, its 19th cent. discoverer) + *-aceae*] **:** a family of homosporous leptosporangiate ferns that is coextensive with the genus *Ceratopteris* and is sometimes included in Polypodiaceae
**par·ker·ite** \'pärkə,rīt, 'pák-\ *n* -s [Robert Lüling *Parker* *b*1893 Swiss mineralogist + E *-ite*] **:** a mineral $Ni_3(Bi,Pb)_2S_2$ consisting of a sulfide of nickel, bismuth, and lead
**parkes process** \'pärks, 'páks-\ *n, usu cap 1st P* [after Alexander *Parkes* †1890 Eng. chemist] **:** the principal process of desilverizing lead in which zinc is added to molten lead and the silver and gold are absorbed in an alloy of zinc, lead, and silver that rises to the top and is skimmed off
**park forest** *n* **:** a forest of trees isolated or in groups and interspersed with grass
**park green** *n* **:** a moderate yellow green that is greener and deeper than average moss green and yellower and deeper than average pea green or apple green (sense 1)
**park hack** *n* **:** a showy welltrained 3- or 5-gaited saddle horse well-suited for riding
**par·kia** \'pärkēə\ *n, cap* [NL, fr. Mungo *Park* †1806, Scottish African explorer and surgeon + NL *-ia*] **:** a genus of tropical Old World trees (family Leguminosae) with heads of red or yellow flowers followed by pods that commonly contain edible seeds and pulp — see NITTA TREE
**par·kin** \'pärkən\ *n* -s [origin unknown] **:** a cake orig. of oatmeal, butter, and molasses now leavened with baking powder and spiced with ginger and esp. popular in Scotland and the border country
**park·ing** \'pärkiŋ, 'pák-, -kēŋ\ *n* -s **1 a :** ground (as in a park) adorned with trees, lawn, or shrubbery **b** *chiefly North & West* **:** a strip of turf sometimes with trees along the side of a street — compare TREE BELT **2 a :** the leaving of a vehicle in an accessible location **b :** an area in which vehicles may be left ⟨ample ~ is available⟩
**parking brake** *n* **:** EMERGENCY BRAKE
**parking light** *n* **:** a small light on an automotive vehicle for use esp. in night parking along a public way
**parking lot** *n* **:** an outdoor lot for the parking of motor vehicles
**parking meter** *n* **:** a coin-operated timing device for regulating the parking of motor vehicles
**par·kin·so·nia** \,pärkən'sōnēə, ,pák-, -nyə\ *n, cap* [NL, fr. John *Parkinson* †1650 Eng. botanist + NL *-ia*] **:** a small genus of spiny shrubs or small trees (family Leguminosae) with minute pinnate early deciduous leaves and racemose yellow flowers with a valvate calyx — see JERUSALEM THORN
**par·kin·so·nian** \,==ˈsōnēən, -nyən\ *adj* [James *Parkinson* †1824 Eng. physician + E *-ian*] **1 :** of or like that of parkinsonism ⟨~ tremors⟩ **2 :** affected with parkinsonism
**par·kin·son·ism** \'pärkənsə,nizəm, 'pák-\ *n* -s *sometimes cap* [James *Parkinson* + E *-ism*] **1 :** PARALYSIS AGITANS **2 :** any chronic condition of the nervous system marked by muscle rigidity but without tremor of resting muscles
**par·kin·son's disease** \'pärkənsənz, 'pákənsənz-\ *n, usu cap P* [after James *Parkinson*] **:** PARALYSIS AGITANS
**parkinson's syndrome** *n, usu cap P* [after James *Parkinson*] **:** PARALYSIS AGITANS
**park·ish** \'pärkish, 'pák-, -kēsh\ *adj* **:** resembling a park
**parkland** \'=,=\ *n* **1 :** land with clumps of trees and shrubs in cultivated condition used as or felt to be suitable for use as a park **2 :** PARK 5b
**park·man crab** \'pärkmən, 'pákmən-\ *or* **parkman crab-apple** *n, usu cap P* [after Francis *Parkman* †1893 Amer. historian who cultivated it] **:** an ornamental tree (*Malus halliana parkmanii*) with double bright rose-colored flowers
**parks** *pl of* PARK, *pres 3d sing of* PARK
**parkway** \'=,=\ *n* **1 a :** a broad landscaped thoroughfare; *esp* **:** one from which trucks and other heavy vehicles are excluded **b :** a roadway in a park **:** a landscaped thoroughfare connecting parks **c :** an expressway located on a strip of land legally constituting a public park and therefore not open to heavy vehicles **2 :** a landscaped strip of land paralleling or running in the center of a thoroughfare **3** *North & Midland* **:** PARKING 1b
**parky** \'pärkē\ *adj* [¹*park* + *-y*] *dial Brit* **:** COLD
**parl** *abbr* parliament; parliamentary
**par·lance** \'pärlən(t)s, 'pál-\ *n* -s [MF, fr. OF, fr. *parler, parlier* to speak, talk + *-ance*] **1 :** an instance of speaking **:** SPEECH; *esp* **:** an instance of formal speaking (as a debate or parley) ⟨battle and not ~ should determine his right and title —John Speed⟩ **2 :** manner or mode of speech **:** DICTION, IDIOM, PHRASEOLOGY ⟨in educational ~, the new school is an activity school —W.H.Kilpatrick⟩ ⟨in movie ~ a junket is a special trip organized by a studio —*Saturday Rev.*⟩
**¹par·lan·do** \pär'län(,)dō\ *or* **par·lan·te** \-n·(,)tā\ *adj* [*parlando* fr. It, verbal of *parlare* to speak, talk, fr. ML *parabolare; parlante* fr. It, pres. part. of *parlare*] **:** delivered or performed in an unsustained style or manner suggestive of speech ⟨the vocal subtlety of the two big ~ solos —Marc Blitzstein⟩ — used as a direction in music
**²parlando** \"\ *n* -s **1 :** parlando style ⟨singing it in a poker-faced quick ~ —O.J.Gombosi⟩ — contrasted with *cantabile* **2 :** a piece or passage in parlando style
**par·la·to·ria** \,pärlə'tōrēə, -tȯr-\ *n* [NL, fr. Filippo *Parlatore* †1877 Ital. botanist + NL *-ia*] **1** *cap* **:** a genus of armored scales distinguished by the presence of very large second exuviae that are widespread in warm regions and include several economically important pests of cultivated plants **2** -s **:** a scale of the genus *Parlatoria*
**par·la·to·ry** \'==,tōrē, -tȯr-, -ri\ *n* -ES [ML *parlatorium*, fr. OF *parleor, parlour* parlor — more at PARLOR] **:** a reception room in a convent
**¹par·lay** \'pär,lā, 'pá,lā *also* -,lē *or* -,li\ *vt* -ED/-ING/-s [alter. of ²*paroli*] **1 :** to bet (as money) in a parlay **2 a :** to increase or otherwise transform into something of much greater value ⟨~ a few beat-up crates into a major airline —*Newsweek*⟩ ⟨~*ed* just four . . . $10 bills into a billion and a quarter dollar fortune —Robert Engler⟩ **b :** to utilize as a means to great gains or a desired objective ⟨100 ways to ~ a good idea and very little cash into a fortune —*advt*⟩ ⟨tried to ~ this Russophobia into a parliamentary career —*Newsweek*⟩
**²parlay** \"\ *n* -s **1 a :** a proposed series of two or more bets in which the bettor selects all contingencies in advance and irrevocably bets the original stake plus any winnings on each successive contingency **2 :** a risking of an original stake plus winnings or of an original investment plus earnings
**¹parle** \'pär(ə)l\ *vb* -ED/-ING/-s [ME *parlen*, fr. MF *parler* to speak, talk] *archaic* **:** PARLEY
**²parle** \"\ *n* -s *archaic* **:** PARLEY
**¹par·ley** \'pärlē, 'pál-, -li\ *vb* -ED/-ING/-s [MF *parler* to speak, talk, fr. ML *parabolare*, fr. LL *parabola* speech, parable — more at PARABLE] *vt* **1 :** UTTER; *esp* **:** SPEAK 3 ⟨that Yank can't half ~ the lingo —Richard Llewellyn⟩ **2** *archaic* **:** to grant a parley to **:** hold a conference or discussion with **:** ADDRESS ~ *vi* **:** to speak with another **:** CONFER ⟨the Russian delegations . . . refused to ~ with any Korean parties other than the Leftist —*Current Biog.*⟩; *specif* **:** to hold a parley with or as if with an enemy ⟨the . . . government was forced to ~ with the rebels —Richard Harrington⟩
**²parley** \"\ *n* -s **1 a :** a conference held usu. for the discussion of points in dispute ⟨the plan of the State Department to sponsor regional ~s for its missions throughout the world —*Current Biog.*⟩ ⟨other ~s were scheduled Thursday and Friday with the . . . electrical workers —*Retailing Daily*⟩ **b :** an oral and usu. informal conference with an enemy under a truce (as for the discussion of armistice terms or an exchange of prisoners) ⟨details of battle, ~, and further battle —G.B. Saul⟩ ⟨willingness to resume the cease-fire ~s —*Current Biog.*⟩ **2 :** mutual discourse **:** CONVERSATION, DISCUSSION ⟨without further ~ she proceeded in the direction indicated —Joseph Hergesheimer⟩ ⟨holding long and interesting ~ with these worthies —*Strand Mag.*⟩
**par·ley·er** \'pärlēər, 'pálēə(r\ *n* -s **:** one that parleys
**¹parley-voo** \,pärlē,vü\ *n* -s [F *parlez-vous* do you speak (in *parlez-vous français?* do you speak French?)] **1 :** the French language ⟨no words to spell, no sums to do . . . and no *parley-voo* —J.R.Lowell⟩ **2** *usu cap* **:** FRENCHMAN ⟨hardy British tars who had pity on a poor *Parley-voo* —W.S.Gilbert⟩
**²parley-voo** \"\ *vi* -ED/-ING/-s [F *parlez-vous*] **:** TALK; *esp* **:** to speak French or another language besides English ⟨nice to stop and *parley-voo* a second —Sinclair Lewis⟩
**par·lia·ment** \'pärləmənt, 'pál-, *chiefly non-British* -lyəm- *or sometimes* -lēəm-\ *n* -s *often attrib* [ME *parliament, parlement*, fr. OF *parlement*, fr. *parler, parlier* to speak, talk + *-ment*] **1 :** a formal conference for the discussion of public affairs; *specif* **:** a general or great council of state summoned by the

sovereign in early medieval England **2 a :** an assemblage of persons (as members of the nobility, clergy, and commons) called together by the British sovereign, sitting for a period of time and then being dissolved, and constituting the supreme legislative body in the United Kingdom ⟨provides for the election and meeting of a new ~ —T.E.May⟩ ⟨sat through three ~*s* —Christopher Hollis⟩ ⟨inspired . . . by the counsel of their elected ~*s* —Elizabeth II⟩ — compare CONGRESS 5 **b :** a similar assemblage in another political unit (as a nation or state) ⟨the third session of Ceylon's second ~ —*London Daily Telegraph*⟩ ⟨elected to Italy's first ~ —J.C.Adams & Paolo Barile⟩ **3 a :** the supreme legislative body of a usu. major political unit (as a nation or state) being a continuing institution comprising a series of individual parliaments ⟨the ~ of the United Kingdom is composed of the Sovereign, the House of Lords and the House of Commons —T.E.May⟩ ⟨reached the committee stage in the French ~ —*N.Y. Times*⟩ ⟨the imperial ~ is the supreme legislature for the whole of His Majesty's dominions —Martin Wight⟩ — compare CONGRESS 3 **b :** the British House of Commons ⟨confer office only upon members of ~ or peers —Ivor Jennings⟩ **4** [MF *parlement*, fr. OF] **:** one of several principal courts of justice existing in France before the revolution of 1789 **5 a :** an assembly representing a group or the members of an organization and usu. convened for the expression of opinion, enactment of policy, and the transaction of other business ⟨the Students' *Parliament* is the official undergraduate organization —*Univ. of Toronto Calendar*⟩ ⟨these general union meetings are . . . the ~*s* of any enterprise or plant —A.R.Williams⟩ **b :** a gathering resembling or held to resemble such a consultative assembly ⟨the rooks called one another to their evening ~ —Archibald Marshall⟩ **6 :** PARLIAMENT CAKE **7 :** FAN-TAN 2

**par·lia·men·tal** \\ˌ==ˈmentᵊl\\ *adj, archaic* **:** PARLIAMENTARY ⟨deriving their ~ authority only from the people —William Prynne⟩

**¹par·lia·men·tar·i·an** \\ˌpärləˌmen·ˈterēən, ˌpäl-, -lyə-, -ˌmən-, -ta(a)r-,-tär-\\ *n* -s [*parliament* + *-arian*] **1** *often cap* **:** an adherent of the parliament in opposition to the king during the English Civil War ⟨the civil wars forced both royalists and ~*s* into claims of supremacy —G.H.Sabine⟩ ⟨a ~ who had signed the English king's death warrant —R.C.Garvey⟩ — compare ¹CAVALIER 4, ROUNDHEAD, ROYALIST **2 :** an expert in the rules and usages of a parliament or other deliberative assembly; *specif* **:** an officer of a legislative body acting as adviser to the presiding officer on matters of procedure **3 :** a member of a parliament ⟨a small party . . . which has one ~ —R.C.Bone⟩

**²parliamentarian** \\"\\ *adj* **:** PARLIAMENTARY ⟨the ~ major was . . . embarrassed by this proposal —Sir Walter Scott⟩ ⟨a country with a ~ system of government⟩

**par·lia·men·tar·i·an·ism** \\-ēəˌnizəm\\ *n* -s **:** PARLIAMENTARISM

**par·lia·men·tar·i·ly** \\-ˈterəlē, -li\\ *adv* **:** in a parliamentary manner ⟨disliked proceeding ~ in this business —Horace Walpole⟩

**par·lia·men·ta·rism** \\ˌ==ˈmentəˌrizəm\\ *n* -s [¹*parliamentary* + *-ism*] **:** the parliamentary system of government **:** PARLIAMENTARY GOVERNMENT

**¹par·lia·men·ta·ry** \\ˌ==ˈmentərē, -n·trē, -ri\\ *adj* [*parliament* + *-ary*] **1 a :** of, relating to, or having the nature of a parliament ⟨~ reform⟩ ⟨~ body⟩ ⟨the organizations are largely forensic and ~ —*Amer. Guide Series: N. C.*⟩ **b :** enacted, done, or ratified by a parliament; *specif* **:** enacted, done, or ratified by the British parliament ⟨~ grant of money⟩ ⟨received a ~ title⟩ **c :** according to the procedures, customs, and usages of a parliament; *specif* **:** according to the procedures, customs, and usages of the British parliament ⟨proceed in a ~ way⟩ **d :** permitted or suitable to be permitted to be used in a parliament **:** CIVIL, COURTEOUS, POLITE ⟨two gentlemen politely and in strictly ~ language calling one another incompetent administrators —*Liverpool Daily Post*⟩ **e :** concerned with the business of a parliament ⟨~ correspondent of a newspaper⟩ **f :** taking place in or under the authority of a parliament ⟨proposed a ~ inquiry into the situation⟩ ⟨~ control of expenditures⟩ ⟨~ debate⟩ **2 :** of, belonging to, or adhering to the parliament as opposed to the king during the English Civil War ⟨rendered the ~ armies . . . victorious —David Hume †1776⟩ **3 :** of, relating to, or used on a parliamentary train **4 :** of, based upon, or having the characteristics of parliamentary government ⟨~ institutions in South Africa resemble . . . those in other dominions —Alexander Brady⟩ ⟨~ democracy⟩ ⟨~ socialism⟩ **5 :** of, relating to, or consisting of members of a parliament ⟨the sole object of ~ privilege is to protect the rights . . . of members —*Brit. Parliament*⟩ ⟨have the leader selected by the ~ caucus —*London Times*⟩ **6 :** of, according to, or based upon parliamentary law ⟨~ practice⟩ ⟨~ procedure⟩ ⟨~ inquiry . . . to obtain information from the presiding officer —Alice F. Sturgis⟩

**²parliamentary** \\"\\ *n* -ES **1 :** a member of the British parliament **2 :** PARLIAMENTARY TRAIN **3** [modif. of F *parlementaire*, fr. *parlement* negotiation, conference, parliament — more at PARLIAMENT] **:** one sent under a flag of truce to treat with an enemy

**parliamentary agent** *n* **:** a person professionally employed to represent and look after the interests of parties affected by private legislation of the British parliament

**parliamentary borough** *n* **:** a borough having the right to return a member to the British parliament **:** a borough forming a constituency

**parliamentary burgh** *n* **:** a parliamentary borough in Scotland

**parliamentary counsel** *n* **:** an official attached to the British treasury under whose direction government bills are drafted into the form required by law and custom for introduction into parliament

**parliamentary government** *n* **:** a system of government characterized by an interdependence of the executive and the legislature and usu. having under a titular chief of state the real executive power vested in a cabinet composed of members of the legislature who are individually and collectively responsible to the legislature **:** CABINET GOVERNMENT ⟨the heart of *parliamentary government* has come to be party responsibility —E.S.Griffith⟩ — compare PRESIDENTIAL GOVERNMENT

**parliamentary law** *n* **:** the body of rules and precedents used to govern the proceedings of deliberative assemblies and other organizations

**parliamentary party** *n* **:** the members of a legislative body belonging to a single political party and constituting an entity distinct from the party in the nation as a whole of which they are members

**parliamentary system** *n* **:** PARLIAMENTARY GOVERNMENT

**parliamentary train** *n* **:** a train required by a 19th century act of the British parliament to be run daily each way over the entire length of the system of a railway company, to stop at every station, and to provide minimum third-class conveniences at a rate of not over one penny a mile

**parliament cake** *n* **:** a thin ginger cookie

**¹par·lia·men·teer** \\ˌpärləˌmen·ˈti(ə)r, ˌpäl-, -lyə-, -ˌmən-, -iə\\ *n* -s [*parliament* + *-eer*] **:** PARLIAMENTARIAN 1

**²parliamenteer** \\"\\ *vi* -ED/-ING/-S **:** to take an active part in parliamentary affairs

**par·lia·men·ter** \\ˌpärlə'mentər\\ *n* -s *Scot* **:** a member of parliament

**parliament hinge** *n* **:** a hinge with so great a projection (as from a wall or frame) as to allow a door or shutter to swing back flat against the wall

**parliament house** *n* [ME *parlement-hous*, fr. *parlement* parliament + *hous* house] **:** the building in which a parliament sits

**parliament man** *n* **:** a member of a parliament; *esp* **:** a member of the British House of Commons

**parliament roll** *n* [ME *parlement rolle*, fr. *parlement* parliament + *rolle* roll] **:** one of a number of rolls of parchment inscribed by the chancery clerks with the records of the British parliament during the period from 1278 until the beginning of the use of journals by the two houses in 1509

**parling** *pres part of* PARLE

**¹par·lor** \\ˈpärlər, ˈpälə(r\\ *n* -s *see -or in Explan Notes* [ME *parlour*, fr. OF *parleor*, *parlour* parlor, reception room in a convent, fr. *parler* to speak, talk — more at PARLEY] **1 :** a room used primarily for conversation or the reception of guests: as **a :** an apartment in a monastery or nunnery where the monastics are permitted to meet and converse with each other or with visitors **b :** a room in a private dwelling kept chiefly for the reception of visitors rather than for family use and usu. better furnished than the other rooms in the dwelling — compare LIVING ROOM 1, SITTING ROOM **c :** a room in a large dwelling (as a mansion) or in a public building (as a city hall) used as a conference chamber or private reception room **d :** a room in a public building (as an inn, tavern, hotel, club) designed for conversation, rest, or semiprivacy **e :** one of a suite of rooms (as in a club or hotel) devoted to the general reception of members or guests ⟨the ~*s* of the hotels were lavishly furnished —D.D.Martin⟩ — usu. used in pl. ⟨the annual Christmas supper . . . will be held Monday night in the church ~*s* —*Hartford (Conn.) Courant*⟩ **2** *archaic* **:** DINING ROOM **3 :** something held to resemble an inner or special chamber ⟨the ~ of his heart —George Macdonald †1905⟩ **4 :** a business establishment usu. devoted to a specified service or to the sale of a specified item ⟨funeral ~⟩ ⟨beauty ~⟩ ⟨beer ~⟩ ⟨ice-cream ~⟩

**²parlor** \\"\\ *adj, see -or in Explan Notes* **1 :** used in or suitable for a parlor ⟨heard the ~ clock strike twelve —Helen Eustis⟩ ⟨~ trick⟩ ⟨a . . . young woman with a ~ voice —Douglas Watt⟩ ⟨~ furniture⟩ **2 a :** fostered or advocated in comfortable seclusion without consequent action or application to affairs ⟨~ bolshevism⟩ **b :** given to or characterized by fostering or advocating something (as a doctrine) in such a manner ⟨~ pink⟩ ⟨~ socialist⟩

**parlor boarder** *n* **1 :** a privileged pupil in an English boarding school living with the principal's family **2 :** a person esp. favored in a household

**parlor car** *n* **:** an extra-fare railroad passenger car for day travel equipped with individual revolving and reclining chairs and providing the services of an attendant — compare CHAIR CAR 1, COACH 1c, LOUNGE CAR, PALACE CAR, PULLMAN

**parlor game** *n* **:** a game suitable for playing indoors (as in a parlor)

**parlor grand** *n* **:** a grand piano intermediate in length between a concert grand and a baby grand

**parlor house** *n* **:** BROTHEL 2; *esp* **:** one having a well-furnished reception room

**parlormaid** \\ˈ==ˌ=\\ *n* **1 :** a maid in a private home whose chief duties are to attend to the parlor, the table, and the door **2 :** a maid in a hotel or restaurant who attends to rest rooms and offices — called also *matron*

**parlor match** *n* **:** a friction match containing little or no sulfur and igniting with less objectionable fumes than a sulfur match

**parlor palm** *n* **1 :** CAST-IRON PLANT **2 :** a small Mexican palm (*Collinia elegans*) with narrow pinnae and pale yellow flowers in panicles that is often used as a pot plant

**¹par·lous** \\ˈpärləs, ˈpäl-\\ *adj* [ME *parlous*, *perlous*, alter. of *perilous*] **1 a :** characterized by uncertainty **:** fraught with danger or risk **:** attended with peril **:** CRITICAL, DANGEROUS, HAZARDOUS ⟨the present ~ state of international relations —Denis Plimmer⟩ ⟨a ~ journey up a ladder —G.E.Fussell⟩ ⟨~ times⟩ **b :** involving risk **:** awkward to deal with ⟨a ~ bird to hit —H.C.Merivale⟩ **2** *obs* **:** shrewd or cunning usu. in a dangerous way — **par·lous·ly** *adv*

**²parlous** \\"\\ *adv* **:** to a very great extent **:** EXCEEDINGLY, EXCESSIVELY ⟨it was ~ boggy underfoot —*Strand Mag.*⟩ ⟨she is ~ handsome —J.G.Edgar⟩

**¹par·ma** \\ˈpärmə, ˈpämə\\ *n* -s [fr. *Parma*, city in northern Italy] **:** a low anticlinal fold; *esp* **:** one forming a barrier to the migration of marine faunas

**²parma** \\"\\ *adj, usu cap* **:** of or from the city of Parma, Italy **:** of the kind or style prevalent in Parma **:** PARMESAN

**par·ma·cety** \\ˌpärməˈsēd·ē, -sed·ē\\ *n* -ES [by alter.] *archaic* **:** SPERMACETI

**parma red** *n, often cap P* **:** BLOOD RED

**parma violet** *n* **1** *usu cap P* **:** a sweet violet widely cultivated for its pale lavender sweet-scented fully double flowers **2** *often cap P* **a :** a moderate violet that is bluer and lighter than damson, bluer and paler than Roman purple, and paler and slightly redder than prelate — called also *Parme, violet Parme* **b** *of textiles* **:** a strong violet that is redder and lighter than pansy, redder, lighter, and stronger than royal purple (sense 2), and lighter, stronger, and slightly redder than clematis

**par·ma·zo marble** \\ˈpärməˌzō-, pärˈmä(ˌ)zō-\\ *n* [*parmazo* perh. modif. of It *paonazzo, pavonazzo* pavonazzo — more at PAVONAZZO] **:** a marble of northern Italy having a coarse network of dark veins on a white or grayish ground

**parme** \\ˈpärm\\ *n* -s *often cap* [F *Parme* Parma, city in northern Italy] **:** PARMA VIOLET 2a

**par·me·lia** \\pärˈmēlēə, -lyə\\ *n, cap* [NL, prob. irreg. fr. L *parma* small shield] **:** a large genus (the type of the family Parmeliaceae) of chiefly alpine foliaceous lichens having cortex on both surfaces of a closely appressed thallus and including several that are important sources of purple and brown dyestuffs esp. in Scotland, Wales, and Scandinavia — see CROTTLE

**par·me·li·a·ceous** \\(ˌ)pärˌmēlēˈāshəs\\ *adj* [NL *Parmeliaceae* (fr. *Parmelia*, type genus + *-aceae*) + E *-ous*] **:** of or relating to the genus *Parmelia* or the family Parmeliaceae

**par·me·li·oid** \\(ˈ)pärˈmēlēˌȯid\\ *adj* [NL *Parmelia* + E *-oid*] **:** like or related to the genus *Parmelia*

**par·me·nid·e·an** \\ˌpärməˈnidēən\\ *adj, usu cap* [*Parmenides*, 5th cent. B.C. Greek philosopher + E *-an*] **:** of or relating to Parmenides or to his philosophy which emphasizes a conception of reality as absolute eternal in contrast to the Heraclitean conception of eternal change

**par·men·tier** \\pärmäⁿˈtyā\\ *also* **par·men·tière** \\-yer\\ *adj, usu cap* [F *parmentier* (fem. *parmentière*), fr. Antoine A. *Parmentier* †1813 Fr. horticulturist who popularized the cultivation of potatoes in France] **:** prepared or served with potatoes ⟨chopped beef *Parmentier*⟩

**par·men·ti·e·ra** \\ˌpärmənˈtirə\\ *n, cap* [NL, fr. Antoine A. *Parmentier*] **:** a small genus of tropical American trees (family Bignoniaceae) having trifoliolate leaves and rather large greenish flowers with a sheathing calyx — see CANDLE TREE

**¹par·me·san** \\ˈpärməˌzan, ˈpäm-, -ˌzän, -ˌzaa(ə)n, -ˌzän *sometimes* ˌ==ˈ=; ˈ==zən\\ *adj, usu cap* [MF, fr. OIt *parmigiano*] **:** of or relating to Parma, Italy

**²parmesan** \\"\\ *or* **parmesan cheese** *n* -s *usu cap P* **:** a very hard dry cheese with a sharp flavor that is cured for several years and used grated to season other foods (as spaghetti and sauces)

**par·mi·gia·na** \\ˌpärməˈjänə, ˌpäm-\\ *or* **par·mi·gia·no** \\-ä(ˌ)nō\\ *adj* [*parmigiana* fr. It, fem. of *parmigiano; parmigiano* fr. It, Parmesan, fr. OIt, fr. *Parma*] **:** seasoned with Parmesan cheese ⟨eggplant ~⟩

**par·mi·gia·no** \\-ä(ˌ)nō\\ *n* -s [It, fr. *parmigiano*, adj.] **:** PARMESAN

**par·mone** \\ˈpärˌmōn\\ *n* -s [F, fr. *parm-* (fr. *violette de Parme* Parma violet, fr. *Parme* Parma, city in northern Italy) + *-one*] **:** a terpenoid ketone $C_{13}H_{20}O$ found in oil from violet flowers

**par·nas** *or* **par·nass** \\pärˈnäs, ˈ=ˌ=\\ *n, pl* **par·nas·im** *or* **par·nass·im** \\ˌ=ˌnäˈsēm, -sim\\ [LHeb *parnās* manager] **:** the chief administrative officer of a Jewish congregation

**par·nas·sia** \\pärˈnasēə, -syə\\ *n* [NL, fr. L *Parnasus, Parnassus* Parnassus (fr. Gk *Parnasos, Parnassos*) + NL *-ia*] **1** *cap* **:** a genus of smooth bog herbs (family Saxifragaceae) native to arctic and temperate regions and having basal entire leaves and white flowers **2** -s **:** any plant of the genus *Parnassia*

**¹par·nas·sian** \\(ˈ)pärˈnasēən, (ˈ)päˈn-, -syən\\ *adj* [L *parnasius, parnassius* of or belonging to Parnassus (fr. Gk *parnasios*, fr. *Parnasos, Parnassos* Parnassus, mountain in central Greece sacred in ancient times to Apollo and the Muses) + E *-an*] **1** *usu cap* **:** of, relating to, or having the characteristics of poetry ⟨newspaper *Parnassian* columns invited the native muse —H.R.Warfel⟩ **2** *usu cap* [F *parnassien*, fr. *Parnasse* Parnassus (fr. L *Parnasus, Parnassus*, fr. Gk *Parnasos, Parnassos*) + *-ien* -an; fr. the publication in 1866 of an anthology of the work of the Parnassian poets entitled *Le Parnasse contemporain*] **:** of, having the characteristics of, or constituting a school of French poets of the second half of the 19th century emphasizing metrical form and making little use of emotion as poetic material ⟨the *Parnassian* movement⟩ ⟨*Parnassian* poets⟩ ⟨*Parnassian* style⟩ — compare ROMANTIC **3** [NL *Parnassius* + ISV *-an*, adj. suffix] **:** of or relating to the genus *Parnassius*

**²parnassian** \\"\\ *n* -s [¹*parnassian*] **1** *usu cap* **:** POET **2** *usu cap* [F *parnassien*, fr. *Parnasse* Parnassus + *-ien* -an] **:** a poet of the Parnassian school **3** [NL *Parnassius* + ISV *-an*, n. suffix] **:** a butterfly of *Parnassius* or a related genus

**par·nas·sian·ism** \\-ˌnizəm\\ *n* -s *usu cap* **:** the Parnassian style in poetry ⟨the cradle of both symbolism and *Parnassianism* —K.H.Cornell⟩

**par·nas·si·us** \\pärˈnasēəs\\ *n, cap* [NL, fr. L *parnasius, parnassius* of or belonging to Parnassus] **:** a genus of stout-bodied butterflies (family Papilionidae) having short antennae and almost transparent white or yellowish wings marked with black or red ocelli and occurring in the colder parts of the northern hemisphere

**par·nell·ite** \\pärˈneˌlīt *sometimes* ˈpärnᵊlˌīt\\ *adj, usu cap* [fr. Charles Stewart *Parnell* †1891 Irish nationalist leader + E *-ite*] **:** of, relating to, or being an adherent of Parnell esp. in his advocacy of home rule for Ireland during the latter part of the 19th century

**¹par·occipital** \\ˌpar+\\ *adj* [¹*para-* + *occipital*] **:** located at the side of the occipital bone or in the lateral aspect of the occipital region — used chiefly of a bony element or process

**²paroccipital** \\"\\ *n* -s **:** a paroccipital part

**pa·ro·cheth** *or* **pa·ro·chet** *or* **pa·ro·ket** \\pȧˈrōˌket(h)\\ *n* -s [Heb *pārokheth* curtain before the holy of holies] **:** a curtain of richly ornamented material hung before the holy ark in a synagogue as a reminder of the curtain used to screen the holy of holies in the tabernacle and the temple

**pa·ro·chial** \\pəˈrōkēəl, -kyəl\\ *adj* [ME *parochiell, parochiall*, fr. AF & MF; AF *parochiel* & MF *parochial*, fr. LL *parochialis*, fr. *parochia* parish + L *-alis* -al — more at PARISH] **1 a :** of or relating to a church parish ⟨subordinated the ~ clergy . . . to the authority of the Diocesan —R.C.Mortimer⟩ ⟨~ experience is not required in a bishop —R.G.G.Price⟩ ⟨a ~ church⟩ **b :** controlled by, supported by, or within the jurisdiction of a church parish ⟨construction of a ~ elementary school⟩ **2 :** of or relating to a parish as a unit of local government ⟨supplant the ~ authorities by the central ministry of health —G.B.Shaw⟩ ⟨excluded the able-bodied paupers from the ~ workhouse —G.E.Fussell⟩ **3 :** confined or restricted as if within the borders of a parish **:** limited in range or scope (as to a narrow area or region) **:** NARROW, PETTY, PROVINCIAL ⟨manifestations of national pride or other ~ bigotries —Reinhold Niebuhr⟩ ⟨little sympathy with ~ mentality . . . which would forbid philosophic inquiry —Judah Goldin⟩ ⟨by no means selfishly ~ in outlook —R.H.Pfeiffer⟩ **4 :** of, relating to, or being the charge of a bishop in the early Christian church

**parochial church council** *n* **:** a governing body of a parish of the Church of England consisting of the vicar, the churchwardens, and elected parishioners

**pa·ro·chial·ism** \\pəˈrōkēəˌlizəm, -kyə-,-\\ *n* -s **1 :** the quality or state of being parochial; *esp* **:** selfish pettiness or narrowness (as of interests, opinions, or views) ⟨the unconscious and invincible ~ of the specialists —A.L.Guérard⟩ ⟨a tendency to ~ in spite of increasing international contacts —*Brit. Book News*⟩ ⟨unity in an industry . . . hampered by ~ —C.G. Tickle⟩ **2 :** a system of management peculiar to parishes ⟨the fate of these children should no longer . . . rest on ~ or on charity —Marjory G. Allen⟩

**pa·ro·chi·al·i·ty** \\pəˌrōkēˈaləd·ē\\ *n* -ES **:** PAROCHIALISM

**pa·ro·chial·ize** \\pəˈrōkēəˌlīz, -kyə-\\ *vb* -ED/-ING/-S *vt* **:** to make parochial ~ *vi* **:** to work in a parish

**pa·ro·chial·ly** \\-əlē, -li\\ *adv* **1 :** in terms of a church parish **2 :** in a narrow or provincial way ⟨~ British in his political views —F.B.Millett⟩ ⟨a ~ partisan man —*N.Y.Times*⟩

**parochial school** *n* **:** a school maintained by a religious body usu. for elementary instruction

**par·och·in** *or* **par·och·ine** \\ˈparəkən\\ *n* -s [prob. back-formation fr. Sc *parochiner* parishioner, fr. ME (northern dial.) *parochoner, parochanar*, fr. ME *parochien, parochin* parishioner (fr. ML *parochianus*, fr. LL *parochia* parish + L *-anus* -an) + *-er*] *Scot* **:** PARISH

**par·o·di·a·ble** \\ˈparədēəbəl *also* ˈper-\\ *adj* **:** capable of being parodied

**pa·ro·di·al** \\pəˈrōdēəl\\ *adj* **:** PARODIC

**pa·rod·ic** \\pəˈrädik, -dēk\\ *also* **pa·rod·i·cal** \\-dəkəl, -dēk-\\ *adj* **:** having the character of parody

**par·o·dist** \\ˈparədəst *also* ˈper-\\ *n* -s [F *parodiste*, fr. *parodie* parody (fr. L *parodia*) + *-iste* -ist] **:** one that parodies; *esp* **:** a writer of literary parodies

**par·o·dis·tic** \\ˌparəˈdistik *also* ˌper-, -tēk\\ *adj* **:** of the nature of parody ⟨a ~ effect of singular irony —Ernst Feise⟩

**par·o·dize** \\ˈparəˌdīz\\ *vt* -ED/-ING/-S [L *parodia* parody + E *-ize*] **:** PARODY

**par·odon·tal** \\ˌparəˈdäntᵊl\\ *adj* [*par-* + *-odont* + *-al*] **:** PERIODONTAL 2

**paro·don·ti·tis** \\ˌparəˌdänˈtēd·əs\\ *n* [NL, fr. ¹*para-* + *odontitis*] **:** PERIODONTITIS

**par·o·dos** \\ˈparəˌdäs\\ *or* **par·o·dus** \\-ˌdəs\\ *n, pl* **paro·doi** \\-ˌdȯi\\ *or* **paro·di** \\-ˌdī\\ [Gk *parodos* entrance, passage, first choral passage in a drama, fr. *para* beside, beyond, past + *hodos* road, way, journey — more at PARA-, CEDE] **1 :** the first choral passage in an ancient Greek drama recited or sung as the chorus enters the orchestra — compare STASIMON **2 :** a passage in an ancient Greek theater between auditorium and skene by which spectators had access to the theater and actors might come and go during a play — see THEATER illustration

**¹par·o·dy** \\ˈparədē *also* ˈper- *or* -di\\ *n* -ES [L *parodia*, fr. Gk *parōidia*, fr. *para* beside + *-ōidia* (fr. *aeidein* to sing) — more at ODE] **1 a :** a writing in which the language and style of an author or work is closely imitated for comic effect or in ridicule often with certain peculiarities greatly heightened or exaggerated ⟨these plays . . . are *parodies* of eighteenth century French farce —Claudia Cassidy⟩ **b :** a literary style characterized by the reproduction of stylistic peculiarities of an author or work for comic effect or in ridicule ⟨the dialogue . . . lapses now and then into inadvertent ~ —Wolcott Gibbs⟩ — compare BURLESQUE 1 **2 :** a form or situation showing imitation that is faithful to a degree but that is weak, ridiculous, or distorted **:** a feeble or ridiculous imitation ⟨a straggling ~ of a military moustache —Fred Majdalany⟩ ⟨the . . . elite who live a ~ of 19th century French culture —Alastair Reid⟩ **3 a :** an imitation of a musical composition in which the original text or music has altered usu. in a comical manner **b :** PARODY MASS **syn** see CARICATURE

**²parody** \\"\\ *vt* -ED/-ING/-ES **1 :** to compose a parody on ⟨~ a poem⟩ ⟨~ a musical composition⟩ **2 :** to imitate in a way resembling or held to resemble a parody ⟨deliberately set out to ~ the . . . technique —Marshall Fishwick⟩ ⟨sounds that ~ rather than imitate the original —Louis Simpson⟩

**parody mass** *n* **:** a 16th century mass having the text of the mass added to musical material borrowed from an existing composition (as a motet or madrigal)

**pa·roe·mia** \\pəˈrēmēə\\ *n* -s [LL, fr. Gk *paroimia* proverb, maxim, incidental remark, fr. *para* beside + *oimos* way, path, path or strain of song; prob. akin to L *vis* strength, force — more at VIM] **:** a rhetorical proverb

**¹pa·roe·mi·ac** \\-mēˌak\\ *adj* [Gk *paroimiakos* proverbial, fr. *paroimia*] **:** of, relating to, or constituting a paroemiac

**²paroemiac** \\"\\ *n* -s [LL *paroemiacum*, fr. Gk *paroimiakon*, fr. neut. of *paroimiakos*] **:** an anapestic dimeter catalectic

**pa·roe·mi·og·ra·pher** *or* **pa·re·mi·og·ra·pher** \\pəˌ==ˈägrəfə(r)\\ *n* -s [NL *paroemiographus* (fr. *paroemio-* — fr. LL *paroemia* — + LL *-graphus* one that writes such material or in such a way) + E *-er* — more at -GRAPHER] **:** a writer of proverbs

**pa·roe·mi·og·ra·phy** \\-fē, -fi\\ *n* -ES [*paroemio-* (fr. LL *paroemia*) + *-graphy*] **:** the making of collections of proverbs

**pa·roe·mi·ol·o·gist** \\-ˈäləjəst\\ *n* -s [*paroemiology* + *-ist*] **:** a student of proverbs

**pa·roe·mi·ol·o·gy** \\jē, -ji\\ *n* -ES [*paroemio-* (fr. LL *paroemia*) + *-logy*] **:** the subject of proverbs

**par of exchange :** the value of the monetary unit of one country expressed in terms of the monetary unit of another country using a given standard of value (as purchasing power); *specif* **:** ¹PAR 1a

**pa·roi·cous** \pəˈrȯikəs\ *also* **pa·roe·cious** \pəˈrēshəs\ *adj* [¹*para-* + *-oicous, -oecious* (fr. Gk *oikos* house + E *-ous*) — more at VICINITY] **:** having archegonia and antheridia on the same branch with the antheridia usu. below and around the archegonia — compare AUTOICOUS, HETEROICOUS, MONOICOUS, POLYOICOUS, SYNOICOUS

**paroket** *var of* PAROCHETH

¹**pa·rol** \pəˈrōl, ˈparəl\ *n* -s [MF *parole* word, speech, fr. OF] **1 :** an oral declaration or statement **:** WORD OF MOUTH, UTTERANCE — used in the phrase *by parol* ⟨open to the defendant to prove by ~ —*Gottlieb v. Heyden Chemical Corp.*⟩ **2** *archaic* **:** the pleadings in a legal action formerly presented by word of mouth

²**parol** \"\ *adj* **1 :** executed or made by word of mouth or by a writing not under seal ⟨specific performance of an express ~ suit —J.W.Eggleston⟩ **2 :** given or expressed by word of mouth **:** oral as distinguished from documentary ⟨the defendant objected to the introduction of ~ evidence —*Jour. Amer. Med. Assoc.*⟩

**pa·rol·able** \pəˈrōləbəl\ *adj* **:** qualified for parole

**parol arrest** *n* **:** an arrest made in pursuance of a verbal order from a magistrate without written complaint or similar proceedings

**parol contract** *n* **1 :** a contract made orally or by a writing not under seal **:** contract not embodied in a judgment of record — called also *simple contract* **2 :** a contract partly or entirely oral and therefore unenforceable under the statute of frauds **:** contract orig. under seal but modified by an agreement not under seal

¹**pa·role** \pəˈrōl\ *n* -s [F, word of honor, word, speech, fr. OF, fr. LL *parabola* speech, parable — more at PARABLE] **1 :** WORD OF HONOR **:** plighted faith; *esp* **:** the promise of a prisoner of war upon his faith and honor to fulfill stated conditions (as to return to custody or not to bear arms against his captors) in consideration of special privileges, usu. release from captivity ⟨proposal that officers and men who gave their ~*s* not to take up arms against the United States be allowed to return to their homes —Virginius Dabney⟩ **2 :** the state or period of freedom resulting from a parole ⟨required to report during his ~⟩ ⟨a Federal prisoner . . . may be released on ~ after serving one third of such term —*U. S. Code*⟩ **3 :** a watchword given only to officers of the guard and of the day — distinguished from *countersign* **4 a :** a conditional and revocable release of a prisoner serving an indeterminate or unexpired sentence in a penal or correctional institution — compare PROBATION **b :** a release under similar conditions of one detained or kept in custody; *specif* **:** a release given a patient in a mental hospital enabling him to visit freely and unattended various designated areas on the hospital grounds or beyond its limits **5 :** the release of a defendant in a criminal case on his own recognizance or in the custody of his attorney during the period between indictment and trial **6 :** a linguistic act **:** linguistic behavior ⟨~ is from the linguist's point of view the simple raw material for scientific investigation —H.G.Lunt⟩ — contrasted with *langue*

²**parole** \"\ *vt* -ED/-ING/-S **:** to release on parole ⟨the . . . friend was *paroled* from the hospital in the custody of her sister —Ruth & Edward Brecher⟩ ⟨when a prisoner is *paroled* —C.V.Oje⟩

³**parole** \"\ *adj* **:** of or relating to parole or to persons on parole ⟨~ officer⟩ ⟨~ laws⟩ ⟨~ casework⟩

**pa·rol·ee** \pə,rōˈlē, pəˈrō(,)lē, ˌparəˈlē\ *n* -s **:** one released on parole ⟨a ~ is required to report . . . to a parole officer —*N.Y. Times*⟩

**par·olfactory** \ˌpar+\ *adj* [¹*para-* + *olfactory*] **:** of, relating to, or constituting an area and a sulcus of the cerebral cortex adjacent to the olfactory trigone

¹**par·o·li** \ˌparəˈlē, ˈ==(,)=\ *n* -ES [F, fr. It (Neapolitan dial.), pl. of *parolo*, fr. It (Neapolitan dial.) *paro* equal, fr. L *par* — more at PAIR] **:** a system of betting in which the bettor leaves staked money and its winnings as a further stake **:** PARLAY 1

²**paroli** \"\ *vi* -ED/-ING/-ES **:** to use the paroli in a series of bets

**par·o·mo·lo·gia** \ˌpa,rōməˈlōj(ē)ə\ *n* -s [Gk, fr. *para-* ¹para- + *homologia* agreement — more at HOMOLOGY] **:** a concession made in rhetoric to an adversary in order to strengthen one's own argument

**par·ono·masia** \ˌparənōˈmāzh(ē)ə, pə,ränəˈm-\ *n* -s [L, fr. Gk, fr. *paronomazein* to call with a slight change of name, fr. *para-* ¹para- + *onomazein* to call, name, fr. *onoma* name — more at NAME] **:** a play upon words in which the same word is used in different senses or words similar in sound are set in opposition so as to give antithetical force **:** PUN

**par·o·nych·ia** \ˌparəˈnikēə\ *n* [L, fr. Gk *parōnychia* whitlow, fr. *para-* ¹para- + *onych-, onyx* nail of the finger or toe + *-ia* — more at NAIL] **1** -s **:** inflammation of the tissues adjacent to the nail of a finger or toe usu. accompanied by infection and pus formation — compare FELON **2** *cap* [NL, fr. Gk *parōnychia*, a plant reputed to be a cure for whitlows, fr. *parōnychia* whitlow] **:** a genus of widely distributed herbs (family Caryophyllaceae) having scarious stipules and small flowers subtended by scarious bracts — see WHITLOWWORT

**par·o·nych·i·um** \-kēəm\ *n* [NL, fr. ¹*para-* + *onychium*] **:** a stiff filamentous appendage of the pulvillus of an insect's foot

**par·o·nym** \ˈparə,nim\ *n* -s [LL *paronymon*, fr. Gk *parōnymon*, neut. of *parōnymos*] **:** a paronymous word

**pa·ron·y·mous** \pəˈränəməs\ *adj* [Gk *parōnymos*, fr. *para-* ¹para- + *-ōnymos*, adj. comb. form (as in *homōnymos* having the same name) — more at HOMONYMOUS] **1 :** CONJUGATE 4 **2 a :** formed from a word in another language **b :** having a form similar to a cognate foreign word

**par·oophoron** \ˌpar+\ *n* [NL, fr. ¹*para-* + *oophoron*] **:** a group of rudimentary tubules in the broad ligament between the epoophoron and the uterus that constitutes a remnant of the lower part of the mesonephros in the female corresponding to the paradidymis of the male

**paroquet** *var of* PARRAKEET

**paroquet auklet** *n* **:** an auklet (*Cyclorrhynchus psittacula*) of the northern Pacific having the upper parts dark slate, the underparts white, and the bill orange red

**paroquet bur** *n* **1 a :** the bur of a Jamaica plant of the genus *Triumfetta* **b :** a plant that bears paroquet burs **2 :** a yellow-flowered annual weedy herb (*Sida rhombifolia*) of the southeastern U. S.

**par·o·rex·ia** \ˌparəˈreksēə\ *n* -s [NL, fr. ¹*para-* + *-orexia*] **:** an appetite for unusual foods — compare BULIMIA, PICA

**par·o·se·la** \ˌparəˈsēlə\ [NL, anagram of *Psoralea*] *syn of* DALEA

**pa·ro·tia** \pəˈrōsh(ē)ə, -ōd·ēə\ *n, cap* [NL, fr. L *parotis* tumor near the ear + NL *-ia*] **:** a genus of birds of paradise including several forms distinguished by the presence of three long spatulate feathers on each side of the head

**pa·rot·ic** \pəˈrōd·ik, -räl, |t|, |ēk, (ˈ)pa¦r-\ *adj* [NL *paroticus*, fr. L *para-* ¹para- + NL *oticus* otic, fr. Gk *ōtikos*] **:** adjacent to the ear

**parotic process** *n* **1 :** a process of opisthotic, exoccipital, and prootic elements in the skull of some reptiles **2 :** a process formed of pterotic and opisthotic elements articulating with the posttemporal in the skull of some fishes

¹**pa·rot·id** \pəˈräd·əd, -ätəd\ *adj* [NL *parotid-, parotis* parotid gland, fr. L, tumor near the ear, fr. Gk *parōtid-, parōtis*, fr. *para-* ¹para- + *ōtid-, ōtis* (fr. *ōt-, ous* ear) — more at EAR] **:** of, relating to, being, produced by, or located near the parotid gland

²**parotid** \"\ *n* -s [NL *parotid-, parotis*] **:** PAROTID GLAND

**parotid duct** *n* **:** STENO'S DUCT

**pa·rot·i·dec·to·my** \pə,räd·əˈdektəmē\ *n* -ES [ISV ²*parotid* + *-ectomy*] **:** surgical removal of the parotid gland

**parotid gland** *n* **:** either of a pair of salivary glands situated on the side of the face below and in front of the ear that in man are the largest salivary glands, are of pure serous type, and communicate with the mouth by Steno's duct

**pa·rot·i·di·tis** \pə,räd·əˈdīd·əs\ *n* -ES [NL, fr. *parotid-, parotis* + *-itis*] **:** PAROTITIS

**parotis** *n* -ES [NL *parotid-, parotis*] *obs* **:** PAROTID GLAND

**par·o·tit·ic** \ˌparəˈtid·ik\ *adj* [*parotitis* + *-ic*] **:** of, relating to, or having mumps

**par·o·ti·tis** \ˌ==ˈtīd·əs\ *n* -ES [NL, irreg. fr. *parotis* + *-itis*] **1 :** inflammation and swelling of one or both parotid glands or other salivary glands (as in mumps) **2 :** MUMPS — called also *epidemic parotitis*

**par·ous** \ˈparəs\ *adj* [*-parous*] **1 :** having produced offspring **2 :** PREGNANT

**-pa·rous** \pərəs\ *adj comb form* [L *-parus*, fr. *parere* to give birth to, beget, produce — more at PARE] **:** giving birth to **:** bearing **:** producing ⟨bi*parous*⟩ ⟨feti*parous*⟩ ⟨vivi*parous*⟩ ⟨ovi*parous*⟩

**par·ou·sia** \(ˈ)pa¦rüzēə, pəˈr-, -üsēə, -üzh(ē)ə, -üsh(ē)ə\ *n* [Gk, lit., presence, fr. *para-* ¹para- + *ousia* substance, being (after *pareinai* to be present, fr. *para-* ¹para- + *einai* to be) — more at OUSIA, IS] **1** *usu cap* **:** ADVENT 2b **2 :** the presence of a Platonic idea in something

**par·o·var·ian** \ˌparəˈva(a)rēən, -ver-, -vār-\ *adj* [*parovarium* + *-an*] **:** of or relating to a parovarium

**par·o·var·i·um** \ˌ==ˈ==əm\ *n* [NL, fr. L *para-* ¹para- + NL *ovarium*] **1 :** EPOOPHORON **2 :** one of the accessory glands of the female reproductive system of some insects

**par·ox·ysm** \ˈparək,sizəm\ *n* -s [F & ML; F *paroxysme*, fr. ML *paroxysmus*, fr. Gk *paroxysmos* paroxysm, irritation, fr. *paroxynein* to urge, stimulate, fr. *para-* ¹para- + *oxynein* to sharpen, provoke, fr. *oxys* sharp — more at OXY-] **1 a :** a sudden attack or spasm (as of a disease) ⟨convulsed . . . in the ~*s* of an epileptic seizure —Thomas Hardy⟩ **b :** a sudden recurrence of symptoms or an intensification of existing symptoms ⟨pain occurred in frequent ~*s* —*Therapeutic Notes*⟩ **2 a :** a sudden, violent, and uncontrollable action or occurrence of emotion ⟨threw himself at her feet in a ~ of grief —T. L.Peacock⟩ ⟨burst into a ~ of laughter —Harriet La Barre⟩ **b :** a similar action occurring in nature **:** a convulsion of physical forces (as an earthquake or the eruption of a volcano) ⟨the first great ~ of alpine orogeny —C.O.Dunbar⟩ ⟨horizontal compression induced by the main tectonic ~*s* of the mountain ranges —*Jour. of Geol.*⟩ **3 :** an extreme or climactic stage (as of a process, action, or series of developments) ⟨marks the ~ of subtropical conditions —Julia Gardner⟩ ⟨the very moment of fanatical ~ of the French Revolution —John Quincy Adams⟩ **4** *obs* **:** a violent and open disagreement or quarrel ⟨the disagreement did proceed so far as to produce a ~ —Cotton Mather⟩

**par·ox·ys·mal** \ˌ==¦sizməl\ *adj* **1 :** of, relating to, or of the nature of a paroxysm ⟨~ volcanic eruptions —Arthur Holmes⟩ ⟨~ seizure⟩ **2 :** marked or accompanied by paroxysms ⟨whooping cough . . . treated in the early ~ stage —*Therapeutic Notes*⟩ ⟨the ~ phase in the alpine type of orogeny —P.H.Kuenen & Albert Carozzi⟩

**paroxysmal dyspnea** *n* **:** CARDIAC ASTHMA

**paroxysmal tachycardia** *n* **:** tachycardia that begins and ends abruptly

**par·ox·ys·mic** \ˌparək¦sizmik, -mēk\ *adj* [ISV *paroxysm* + *-ic*] **:** PAROXYSMAL ⟨the tension . . . made their sleep too desperate and ~ to deserve being called rest —H.L.Davis⟩

**par·ox·ys·mist** \ˈ==,=məst\ *n* -s **:** CATASTROPHIST

¹**par·oxytone** \(ˈ)par+\ *adj* [NL *paroxytonus*, fr. Gk *paroxytonos*, fr. *para-* ¹para- + *oxytonos* oxytone] **1 :** having or characterized by an acute accent on the penult of a word in Greek **2 :** having or characterized by heavy stress on the penult

²**paroxytone** \"\ *n* [NL *paroxytonus*, fr. *paroxytonus*, adj.] **:** a word accented or stressed on the penult

**parpen** *var of* PERPEND

¹**par·quet** \(ˈ)pär¦kā\ *vt* **parqueted** \-ād\ **parqueted; parqueting** \-āiŋ\ **parquets** [F *parqueter*, fr. *parquet*, n.] **1 :** to furnish (as a room) with a floor of parquetry **2 :** to make (as a flooring) of parquetry

²**parquet** \"\ *n* -s [F, patterned flooring, branch of the government charged with the prosecution of crime as the representative of the public, (obs.) parquet of a theater or auditorium, fr. MF, small enclosure, judges' section of a courtroom, fr. *parc* enclosure, enclosure for animals, park + *-et* — more at PARK] **1 a :** a patterned flooring; *esp* **:** one made of parquetry ⟨the front hall where . . . rugs lay on the waxed ~ —Philip Wylie⟩ **b :** PARQUETRY ⟨a . . . very attractive floor is provided by ~ —W.P.Matthew⟩ **2 a :** the lower floor of a theater or auditorium; *specif* **:** the part extending from the area in front of the stage used by the orchestra to the parquet circle **b :** the forward part of such an area in a theater or auditorium **3 :** the branch of the administrative government in France and other countries having a legal system based on Roman law or the Napoleonic Code that is charged primarily with the prosecution of crime as the representative of the public rather than of the injured party

**par·que·tage** \ˈpärkəd·ij, ¦=kəˈtäzh\ *n* -s [F, fr. *parquet* + *-age*] **:** PARQUETRY

**parquet circle** *n* **:** the part of the lower floor of a theater at the rear of the parquet and beneath the galleries — called also *orchestra circle, parterre*

**par·que·try** \ˈpärkə·trē, ˈpȧk-, -ri\ *n* -ES [F *parqueterie*, fr. *parquet* + *-erie* -ery] **:** joinery or cabinetwork consisting of an inlay of geometric or other patterns usu. of different colors and used esp. for furniture and floors

parquetry

**par·quette** \(ˈ)pär¦ket, (ˈ)pȧ¦k-, *usu* -ed·+V\ *n* -s [by alter.] **:** PARQUET 2

**parr** \ˈpär, ˈpȧ(r\ *n, pl* **parr** *also* **parrs** [origin unknown] **1 :** a young salmon in the stage between alevin and smolt when it has parr marks on its sides and is actively feeding in fresh water **2 :** the young of any of several fishes other than salmon ⟨a trout ~⟩

**par·ra** \ˈparə\ [NL, fr. L, barn owl] *syn of* JACANA

**par·ra·keet** *or* **par·a·keet** \ˈparə,kēt *also* ˈper- *sometimes* ˌ==ˈ=, *usu* -ēd·+V\ *also* **par·o·quet** *or* **par·ro·quet** \-ket, *usu* -ed·+V\ *n* -s [MF & Sp; Sp *periquito*, fr. MF *perroquet, paroquet* parrot] **1 a :** any of numerous usu. rather small slender parrots with a long graduated tail — see CAROLINA PARRAKEET, GRASS PARRAKEET **b :** PUFFIN **2 :** PARROT GREEN

**parramatta** *var of* PARAMATTA

**parred** *past of* PAR

¹**par·rel** *or* **par·ral** \ˈparəl\ *n* -s [ME *perell*, alter. of *parail* apparel, equipment — more at PAREL] **:** a rope loop or sliding collar by which a yard or spar is held to a mast in such a way that it may be hoisted or lowered at pleasure — compare JACKSTAY

²**parrel** *or* **parral** \"\ *vb* -ED/-ING/-S **:** to fasten by means of a parrel

**parrel truck** *or* **parrel ball** *n* **:** a ball of hard wood with a hole in the middle that is strung on a parrel

**par·rhe·sia** \pəˈrēzh(ē)ə\ *n* -s [ML, fr. Gk *parrhēsia*, fr. *para-* ¹para- + *-rhēsia* (fr. *rhēsis* speech, speaking); akin to Gk *eirein* to say — more at WORD] **:** boldness or freedom of speech

**par·ri·ci·dal** \ˌparəˈsīdᵊl\ *adj* [L *parricidalis*, fr. *parricida* + *-alis* -al] **1 :** of, relating to, or having the nature of parricide **2 :** guilty of parricide

**par·ri·cide** \ˈ==,sīd\ *n* -s [in sense 1, fr. L *parricida, paricida* killer of a close relative, fr. *parri-, pari-* (akin to Gk *pēos* kinsman by marriage) + *-cida* -cide (killer); in sense 2, fr. L *parricidium* murder of a close relative, fr. *parri-, pari-* + *-cidium* -cide (killing)] **1 a** (1) **:** one that murders his father (2) **:** one that murders his mother or another close relative **b :** one that murders a person (as the ruler of his country) who stands in a relationship held to resemble that of a father **c :** one that commits the crime of treason against his country **2 :** the act of a parricide

**par·ri·cid·i·ous** \ˌ==¦sidēəs\ *adj* [*parricide* + *-ious*] *archaic* **:** PARRICIDAL

**par·ri·dae** \ˈparə,dē\ [NL, fr. *Parra* + *-idae*] *syn of* JACANIDAE

**par·ridge** \ˈparij, -rēj\ *chiefly Scot var of* PORRIDGE

**parring** *pres part of* PAR

**par·ritch** \ˈparich, -rēch\ *Scot var of* PORRIDGE

**parr mark** *n* **:** one of the dark traverse bands on the side of a young salmon

**par·rock** \ˈparək\ *n* -s [ME *parrok*, fr. OE *pearroc* fence, enclosure; akin to MD *parc, perc, parric* enclosure, OHG *pfarrih, pferrih*; all fr. a prehistoric WGmc word borrowed fr. (assumed) VL *parricus* enclosure (whence ML *parricus*) — more at PARK] *dial Brit* **:** a small field **:** PADDOCK

¹**par·rot** \ˈparət *also* ˈper-, *usu* -əd·+V\ *n* -s [prob. irreg. fr. MF *perroquet, paroquet*] **1 :** any of numerous zygodactyl birds (order Psittaciformes) widely distributed in tropical regions that have a distinctive stout curved cered hooked bill whose upper mandible is movably hinged to the skull, that are often crested and brightly variegated, and that are excellent mimics and often readily learn to simulate laughter and crying and to enunciate words and phrases; *esp* **:** an Old World parrot of the genus *Psittacus* having a rather stout form with a short square tail — see AFRICAN GRAY **2 :** a person who repeats the words and sometimes the actions of others mechanically and without understanding ⟨tends to become . . . the ~ of other men's thinking —R.W.Emerson⟩

²**parrot** \"\ *vb* -ED/-ING/-S *vi* **:** to chatter like a parrot ⟨the idiot clucked and ~*ed* to herself —Robinson Jeffers⟩; *esp* **:** repeat something mechanically in the manner of a trained parrot ⟨it is not praying but ~*ing* —John Trapp⟩ ~ *vt* **1 :** to repeat mechanically or by rote in the manner of a trained parrot **:** imitate the form of without understanding the sense or meaning involved ⟨~ obediently what the author expected them to say —John Woodburn⟩ ⟨any school boy . . . can ~ the explanation —D.M.Friedenberg⟩ ⟨a newspaper which ~*ed* to perfection the imperfections of the home press —Bruce Marshall⟩ **2 :** to teach to repeat in the mechanical manner of a parrot ⟨actors ~*ed* by the stage manager⟩

³**parrot** \"\ *adj* **1 :** of, resembling, or of the nature of a parrot ⟨~ tongue⟩ **2 :** of, characterized by, or resembling the mechanical imitation or repetition of the form of something (as a word) without meaning that characterizes a trained parrot ⟨blatant ignorance and assertive ~ knowledge —A.L. Guérard⟩

**parrot-back chair** \ˈ==,=-\ *n* **:** a chair having a splat so shaped that the openings on each side suggest two parrots facing each other

**parrotbill** \ˈ==,=\ *n* **1 :** CLIANTHUS 2 **2 a :** any of numerous thick-billed Asiatic songbirds of the genus *Paradoxornis* **b :** a bird of the genus *Pyrrhuloxia*

**parrot blue** *n* **:** a moderate bluish green to greenish blue that is lighter and stronger than gendarme and stronger than cyan blue

**parrot crossbill** *n* **:** a large European crossbill (*Loxia pityopsittacus*)

**parrot-cry** \ˈ==,=\ *n* **:** a cry (as a contention, complaint, or plea) made in stupid imitation or repeated mechanically without understanding ⟨the *parrot-cry* has gone up that these recommendations must be taken as a whole —*Contemporary Rev.*⟩

**parrot disease** *or* **parrot fever** *n* **:** PSITTACOSIS

**parrot finch** *n* **1 :** one of numerous brilliantly colored weaverbirds of the genus *Erythrura* found in tropical Asia and Australasia **2 :** CROSSBILL

**parrot fish** *n* **:** any of numerous marine percoid fish having the teeth in each jaw fused into a cutting plate or parrotlike beak: **a :** a fish of the family Scaridae **b :** any of various wrasses **c :** a fish of the family Oplegnathidae — called also *false parrot fish*

**parrot green** *n* **:** a strong yellow green that is yellower and duller than viridine yellow and duller and slightly yellower than love bird — called also *parrakeet, perruche, popinjay green, verd gay*

**par·rot·let** \ˈparətlət *also* ˈper-\ *n* -s **:** any of various very small short-tailed So. American parrots constituting the genus *Forpus*

**parrotlike** \ˈ==,=\ *adj* **:** resembling a parrot in physical appearance or characteristics ⟨a ~ beak⟩; *esp* **:** resembling the mechanical imitation or repetition of the form of something (as a word) without meaning that characterizes a trained parrot ⟨not reading at all but rather a mere ~ word-calling process —A.T.Weaver⟩

**parrot mouth** *or* **parrot jaw** *n* **:** a congenital anomaly of the mouth of a grazing animal in which the upper incisors project over the lower thus preventing apposition and interfering with normal prehension and mastication of food — **parrot-mouthed** \ˈ==¦=\ *adj*

**parrot's-beak** \ˈ==,=\ *or* **parrot's-bill** \ˈ==,=\ *or* **parrotbeak** \ˈ==,=\ *n, pl* **parrot's-beaks** *or* **parrot's-bills** *or* **parrotbeaks** [so called fr. its curved standard] **:** CLIANTHUS 2; *esp* **:** KAKA BEAK

**parrot's-feather** \ˈ==,==\ *or* **parrot feather** *n, pl* **parrot's-feathers** *or* **parrot feathers :** WATER MILFOIL; *esp* **:** a New World plant (*Myriophyllum brasiliense*) that has trailing stems, feathery pinnately dissected leaves, and minute flowers borne in the leaf axils, and that is often cultivated as an aquarium plant

**parrot tulip** *n* **:** any of various garden tulips usu. considered to constitute a distinct variety (*Tulipa gesneriana dracontia*) and characterized by ruffled laciniate and often variegated flowers

**parrot wrasse** *n* **:** PARROT FISH; *esp* **:** a parrot fish of the genus *Scarus*

**par·roty** \ˈparəd·ē *also* ˈper-\ *adj* **:** like or of the nature of a parrot

**parrs** *pl of* PARR

¹**par·ry** \ˈparē, -ri *also* ˈper-\ *vb* -ED/-ING/-ES [prob. fr. F *parez*, imper. of *parer* to parry, fr. MF, fr. OProv *parar*, fr. L *parare* to make ready, prepare — more at PARE] *vi* **1 :** to ward off a weapon or blow by means of a parry ⟨he *parried* in tierce and his blade continued along his opponent's sword —Frank Yerby⟩ **2 :** to evade or turn aside something by a similar defensive technique ⟨can ~ and thrust . . . without losing the thread of his argument —Stewart Cockburn⟩ ~ *vt* **1 :** to ward off or turn aside (as a thrust or blow) by means of a parry ⟨the knife had . . . *parried* the blow from the traitor's useless sword —W.H.G.Kingston⟩ **2 :** to turn aside or otherwise avert ⟨to ~ the encroachment of modifying forces, he made a virtue of his way of life —W.M.Kollmorgen⟩; *esp* **:** to avoid (as a question) by a skillful or adroit answer **:** EVADE ⟨*parried* every question with plain skill —*New Republic*⟩ **syn** see DODGE

²**parry** \"\ *n* -ES **1 :** a defensive action made (as with a blade or glove) to deflect a thrust or blow from an opponent **2 :** a defensive movement held to be similar to the parry ⟨skillful in the thrust and ~ of debate —Josiah Royce⟩

**parry pinyon** *or* **parry pine** *n, usu cap 1st P* [after Charles C. *Parry* †1890 Am. botanist] **:** a Mexican piñon (*Pinus cembroides parryana*) having the leaves in fours

**pars** *pl of* PAR, *pres 3d sing of* PAR

**parse** \ˈpärs, ˈpȧs, -ärz, -ȧz\ *vb* -ED/-ING/-S [L *pars* part (in *pars orationis* part of speech) — more at PART] *vt* **1 a :** to resolve (as a sentence) into component parts of speech and describe them grammatically **b :** to describe (as a word) grammatically by stating the part of speech and explaining the inflection and syntactical relationships **2 :** to examine in a minute way **:** analyze critically **:** ANATOMIZE 2, DISSECT 2 b ⟨~ problems and solutions —C.B.Marshall⟩ ⟨he excited no interest; he was merely something to ~ —Ben Riker⟩ ~ *vi* **1 :** to give a grammatical description of a word or a group of words ⟨learning to spell and ~⟩ **2 :** to admit of being parsed ⟨looked at first reading as if it wouldn't ~⟩

**par·sec** \ˈpär,sek, ˈpȧ,s-\ *n* -s [*parallax* + *second*] **:** a unit of measure for interstellar space equal to a distance having a heliocentric parallax of one second or to 206,265 times the radius of the earth's orbit or to 3.26 light-years or to 19.2 trillion miles

**pars·er** \ˈpärsər, ˈpȧsə(r, -ärzər, -ȧzə(r\ *n* -s **:** one that parses

**par·set·tens·ite** \pärˈsetᵊn,zīt\ *n* -s [G *parsettensit*, fr. *Parsettens*, mountain in Graubünden canton, Switzerland + G *-it* -ite] **:** a mineral $Mn_5Si_6O_{13}(OH)_8$ consisting of a hydrous manganese silicate forming cleavable copper-red masses

**par·se·val** \ˈpärzə,väl\ *n* -s *usu cap* [after August von *Parseval* †1942 Ger. engineer] **:** a nonrigid airship usu. having a car suspended beneath a gas envelope — compare ZEPPELIN

**par·shall flume** \ˈpärshəl\ *or* **parshall flume** *n* -s *usu cap P* [after Ralph L. *Parshall* b1881 Am. civil and hydraulic engineer] **:** a device for measuring flow in conduits by observing difference of head on opposite sides of a partial obstruction

**parshioth** *or* **parshiot** *pl of* PARASHAH

**par·si** *also* **par·see** \ˈpär,sē, ˈpȧ,sē, =ˈ=\ *n* -s *usu cap* [Per *pārsī*, fr. *Pārs* Persia, fr. OPer *Pārsa-*] **1 :** a Zoroastrian of India descended from Persian refugees fleeing Muhammadan persecution in the 7th century and settling principally at

Bombay — compare GABAR **2 :** the Iranian dialect of the Parsi religious literature
**par·si·ism** \-ˌizəm\ *or* **par·sism** \ˈ=ˌsizəm\ *or* **par·see·ism** \ˈ=ˌsēˌizəm, =ˈ==ˌ==\ *n* -s *usu cap* [*parsi* + *-ism*] **:** the religious teachings and customs of the Parsis — compare ZOROASTRIANISM
**par·sil** \ˈpärsᵊl, ˈpȧs-\ *dial Eng var of* PARSLEY
**par·si·mo·nious** *also* **par·ci·mo·nious** \ˌpärsəˈmōnēəs, ¦pȧs-, -nyəs\ *adj* [*parsimony* + *-ous*] **:** exhibiting or marked by parsimony: as **a :** excessively frugal **:** PENURIOUS, NIGGARDLY ⟨its ~ thrift, relieved by few generous impulses —V.L.Parrington⟩ ⟨a ~ person⟩ **b :** poor in quality or meager in quantity ⟨gleaned from . . . very ~ scraps of information —S.E. Hyman⟩ ⟨~ fare⟩ **c :** sparing in the use or display of something ⟨~ of editorial material —Allan Nevins⟩ ⟨~ in his use of American journals —D.C.Allen⟩ **syn** see STINGY
**par·si·mo·nious·ly** *adv* **:** in a parsimonious manner ⟨continued . . . to live most ~ in lodgings —Thomas De Quincey⟩
**par·si·mo·nious·ness** *n* -ES **:** the quality or state of being parsimonious
**par·si·mo·ny** \ˈ=səˌmōnē, -ni, *Brit usu & US sometimes* -sə̇mən-\ *n* -ES [ME *parcimony*, fr. L *parsimonia*, fr. *parsus* (past part. of *parcere* to spare); perh. akin to Gk *porkēs* hoop around the joint of a spearhead and its shaft, Arm *ors* fishnet] **1 a :** carefulness in the expenditure of money or resources **:** THRIFT ⟨not a single institution appropriate to an economy of ~ will remain unaltered in an economy of surplus —Lewis Mumford⟩ **b :** closeness in such expenditure; *specif* **:** reprehensively excessive frugality **:** NIGGARDLINESS, STINGINESS ⟨despised for their sordid ~ —G.E.Fussell⟩ **2 :** economy in the use of a specific means to an end: **a :** economy of assumption in reasoning or ascription of existence — used chiefly in the phrase *law of parsimony;* compare OCKHAM'S RAZOR **b :** animal or human economy (as of pain or effort) in seeking pleasure or gain
**pars in·ter·me·dia** \ˌpär,zintə(r)ˈmēdēə\ *n* [NL, lit., intermediate part] **:** a thin slip of tissue fused with the neurohypophysis and representing the remains of the posterior wall of Rathke's pouch
**pars le·gi·ti·ma** \-zləˈjidəmə\ *n* [NL, lit., legitimate part] **:** LEGITIM
**¹pars·ley** \ˈpär|slē, ˈpȧ|, |slī| *sometimes* |zl-\ *n* -s [ME *persely, persil,* fr. OE *petersilie* & OF *persil*, both fr. (assumed) VL *petrosilium*, alter. of L *petroselinum*, fr. Gk *petroselinon*, fr. *petros* stone + *selinon* celery] **:** an annual or biennial herb (*Petroselinum crispum*) of southern Europe that is widely cultivated for its finely dissected smooth or closely curled leaves which are extensively used as a culinary herb or garnish; *broadly* **:** any of various plants of the family Umbelliferae — usu. used with a qualifier; see FOOL'S PARSLEY, HAMBURG PARSLEY, HEMLOCK PARSLEY, STONE PARSLEY
**²parsley** \ˈ"\ *adj* **1 :** of, having the characteristics of, or resembling parsley ⟨~ bed⟩ ⟨~ frog⟩ **2 :** dressed or flavored with parsley ⟨~ butter⟩ ⟨~ potatoes⟩
**parsley camphor** *n* **:** APIOLE 1 a
**parsley family** *n* **:** UMBELLIFERAE
**parsley fern** *n* **:** any of several plants with finely cut foliage that suggests that of parsley: as **a :** a tansy (*Tanacetum vulgare*) **b** (1) **:** a lady fern (*Athyrium felix-femina*) (2) **:** a European rock brake (*Cryptogramma crispa*) that has a short creeping or ascending rhizome and densely tufted leaves of which the outer are sterile and the inner fertile and that grows chiefly on acid upland soils in cool regions (3) **:** ROCK FERN c
**parsley green** *n* **:** a moderate olive green that is lighter, stronger, and slightly yellower than cypress green and greener and stronger than holly green (sense 2) or Lincoln green
**parsley haw** *n* **:** a hawthorn (*Crataegus marshallii*) of the southern U. S. having pinnately lobed leaves
**parsley oil** *n* **:** a colorless or yellow viscid essential oil obtained from parsley seeds
**parsley piert** *n, pl* **parsley pierts** [prob. by folk etymology (influence of ¹*parsley* and of E dial. *piert*, alter. of E *pert*) fr. MF *perce-pierre*, fr. *percer* to pierce + *pierre* stone, fr. L *petra* rock, stone, fr. Gk — more at PIERCE] **1 :** a small European annual herb (*Alchemilla arvensis* or *Aphanes arvensis*) of the family Rosaceae having fan-shaped 3-parted leaves with the divisions 2-cleft to 4-cleft and axillary greenish flowers **2 :** a heath (*Erica aphanes*) of southern Africa **3 :** KNAWEL
**parsleyworm** \ˈ==ˌ=\ *n* **:** the caterpillar of the black swallowtail butterfly
**parsleywort** \ˈ==ˌ=\ *n* **:** a plant of the family Umbelliferae
**pars·lied** *or* **pars·leyed** \-lēd, -lid\ *adj* **:** dressed or seasoned with parsley ⟨~ onions⟩ ⟨~ potatoes⟩
**pars ner·vo·sa** \ˌpärznərˈvōsə\ *n* [NL, lit., nervous part] **:** NEUROHYPOPHYSIS
**pars·nip** \ˈpärsnəp, ˈpȧs-\ *n* -s [alter. of earlier *pasneppe*, fr. ME *pasnepe*, (influenced by ME *nepe* turnip) modif. of MF *pasnaie*, fr. L *pastinaca* parsnip, carrot, fr. *pastinum* 2-pronged dibble — more at NEEP] **1 :** a European biennial herb (*Pastinaca sativa*) with large pinnate leaves and yellow flowers that is naturalized as a weed in No. America **2 :** the long fusiform root of the parsnip that is somewhat poisonous in the wild state but made palatable and nutritious through cultivation and used for the table — usu. used in pl. **3 :** any of several related or similar plants — used with a qualifier; see COW PARSNIP, MEADOW PARSNIP, SEA PARSNIP, WILD PARSNIP
**parsnip swallowtail** *n* **:** BLACK SWALLOWTAIL
**parsnip webworm** *n* **:** the larva of the oecophorid moth (*Depressaria heracliana*) that feeds on parsnips
**par·son** \ˈpärsᵊn, ˈpȧs-\ *n* -s [ME *persone*, fr. OF, fr. ML *persona*, lit., person, fr. L — more at PERSON] **1 :** one that represents a parish in its ecclesiastical and corporate capacities; *esp* **:** the rector or incumbent of a parochial church charged with the pastoral care of the persons in the parish **2 :** CLERGYMAN 1; *esp* **:** one belonging to a Protestant denomination **3 :** an animal with a black coat or markings
**par·son·age** \-s(ᵊ)nij, -nēj\ *n* -s [ME *personage*, fr. MF *personage, personnage*, fr. OF, fr. *persone* + *-age*] **1 :** the benefice under English ecclesiastical law of the parson of a parish: **a :** a parish church and the income attached to it (as from rights, glebes, and tithes) **b :** a certain portion of lands, tithes, and offerings for the maintenance of the parson **2 a :** the house or the house and land provided by a parish or congregation for its pastor's use **b :** a clergyman's residence
**parson bird** *n* **:** TUI
**par·son·ess** \ˈpärsᵊnə̇s, ˈpȧs-\ *n* -ES **:** a parson's wife
**parson gull** *n, dial Eng* **:** GREAT BLACK-BACKED GULL
**par·son·ic** \(ˈ)pärˈsänik\ *also* **par·son·i·cal** \-nə̇kəl\ *adj* **:** of, resembling, or having the characteristics of a parson **:** CLERICAL 1 ⟨a secular as well as a ~ view of life —Edward Peacock⟩ ⟨his rejection of the *parsonical* career —W.J.Locke⟩
**parson-in-the-pulpit** \ˈ====ˈ=\ *n, pl* **parson-in-the-pulpits** *or* **parsons-in-the-pulpit :** CUCKOOPINT
**par·sons·ite** \ˈpärsᵊnˌzīt, ˈpȧs-\ *n* -s [F, fr. Arthur L. *Parsons* †1957 Canadian mineralogist + F *-ite*] **:** a mineral $Pb_2(UO_2)(PO_4)_2.2H_2O$ consisting of a hydrous lead uranyl phosphate found as a brownish powder in Katanga province, Congo
**parson's nose** *n* **:** POPE'S NOSE
**pars ra·ti·o·na·bi·lis** \ˌpärz,rad·ēəˈnäbələs, ¦pärs,r-\ *n* [NL] **:** REASONABLE PART
**¹part** \ˈpär|t, ˈpȧ|, *usu* |d·+V\ *n* -s [ME, fr. OF & OE, both fr. L *part-, pars;* akin to OIr *rann* part, Skt *pūrta* reward, L *parare* to prepare — more at PARE] **1 a** (1) **:** one of the equal or unequal portions into which something is or is regarded as divided **:** something less than a whole **:** a unit (as a number, quantity, or mass) held to constitute with one or more other units something larger **:** CONSTITUENT, FRACTION, FRAGMENT, MEMBER, PIECE ⟨the greater ~ of the highway . . . is full of sharp curves —*Amer. Guide Series: N.H.*⟩ ⟨the vast ~ of Englishmen who were conscious of a political change —Francis Hackett⟩ ⟨in the early ~ of the summer⟩ ⟨the road was passable only ~ of the year —Samuel Johnson⟩ (2) **:** an essential portion or integral element of something ⟨a Boer's wagon was as much a ~ of him as his bed —Stuart Cloete⟩ ⟨racial prejudice is very much a ~ of the country —B.M.Beck⟩ ⟨as if light and shadow were ~ of her being —Edith Sitwell⟩ **b :** an equal constituent portion **:** one of several or many like units into which something is divided or of which it is composed **:** a proportional division or ingredient ⟨mix the powder with three ~s of water⟩ ⟨the compound contained two ~s oxygen⟩ **c :** a constituent portion of something in mathematics: as (1) **:** ALIQUOT, SUBMULTIPLE (2) **:** a mathematical aggregate all of whose elements are also elements of another aggregate (3) **:** a line or other element of a geometrical figure **d :** a portion of a plant or animal body: as (1) **:** essential element **:** ORGAN, MEMBER ⟨the chief ~s of the digestive system are the esophagus, stomach, intestine, and associated glands⟩ (2) **:** an indefinite area or one lacking or not considered in respect to a natural boundary **:** SPOT, PLACE ⟨bathe the affected ~ with warm water⟩ (3) **:** the external genital and excretory organs — usu. used in pl.; called also *private parts, privy parts* **e** (1) **:** a formal or distinctive division of a literary work ⟨a story in four ~s⟩ (2) **:** one of a series of sections of a literary work sold separately and at intervals and designed eventually to be bound into one or more permanent volumes ⟨two volumes sold in ~s by subscription⟩ **f** (1) **:** a vocal or instrumental line or melody in concerted music or in harmony (2) **:** a particular voice or instrument in concerted music; *also* **:** the individual score for it ⟨the alto ~⟩ ⟨the viola ~⟩ **g :** a portion of a line in a ship's rigging ⟨standing ~s⟩ ⟨hauling ~s⟩ **h** (1) **:** a constituent member of a machine or other apparatus ⟨the . . . mechanics had the names for the ~s of the planes —Charlton Laird⟩ (2) **:** such a member existing separately apart from a machine ⟨a dealer in automobile ~s and accessories⟩ **2 :** something belonging to, assumed by, or falling to one (as in a division or apportionment) **:** SHARE ⟨wanted no ~ of the proposal⟩ ⟨bad men . . . claim as much ~ in God as his best servants —John Milton⟩ **3 :** one's share or allotted task in an action **:** DUTY, FUNCTION, OFFICE ⟨do its ~ in helping persons . . . interested in the field of research —*Bull. of Meharry Med. Coll.*⟩ ⟨it is the ~ of a poet to humor the imagination —Joseph Addison⟩ **4 :** one of the opposing sides in a relationship involving conflict or rivalry (as a contest, question, dispute, contract, or transaction) ⟨he that is not against us is on our ~ —Mk 9:40 (AV)⟩ ⟨make whole kingdoms take her brother's ~ —Edmund Waller⟩ **5 a** *archaic* **:** a side or direction in space ⟨on every ~ walled in —Thomas Hutchinson⟩ **b** *archaic* **:** HAND 3b ⟨on the other ~, I judged that I might lose nearly as much —R.L.Stevenson⟩ **6 a :** a portion of an unspecified territorial area (as of a country or the world) **:** DISTRICT, QUARTER, REGION ⟨go into . . . camp with the other fellows from our ~ —Alice F. Webb⟩ — usu. used in pl. ⟨taking off for ~s unknown —Meridel Le Sueur⟩ ⟨Australian soldiers in foreign ~s —William Power⟩ ⟨the oddest marker in these ~s —S.H. Holbrook⟩ **b** (1) **:** a portion of a specified territorial area ⟨lawyers came from all ~s of the state —*Amer. Guide Series: La.*⟩ ⟨no new state shall . . . be formed by the junction of two or more states or ~s of states —*U.S.Constitution*⟩ ⟨the central ~ of the eastern section of the state —*Amer. Guide Series: Oregon*⟩ (2) **parts** *pl, usu cap* **:** a territorial area forming one of the three major divisions of the county of Lincoln, England, and now constituting an administrative county ⟨the *Parts* of Holland⟩ ⟨the *Parts* of Kesteven⟩ ⟨the *Parts* of Lindsey⟩ **7 a :** a role or function assumed by a person in real life ⟨he will perform unto thee the ~ of a kinsman —Ruth 3:13 (AV)⟩ **b :** a function or course of action performed **:** a position undertaken ⟨objected to the government's ~ in the strike⟩ **8 a** (1) **:** the words and stage directions assigned to a particular actor in a dramatic production ⟨the actress learned her ~ well⟩ (2) **:** such words and directions set down in written form ⟨the director handed him the ~⟩ **b :** a particular character created by an actor in a dramatic production ⟨the ~ of Ophelia in *Hamlet*⟩ **c :** the role taken by an actor who creates such a character ⟨a speaking ~⟩ **9 a :** a constituent of character or capacity **:** a personal quality **:** a natural or acquired attribute (as an ability or talent) — usu. used in pl. ⟨a steady lad, of good brilliant ~s —Walter Besant⟩ ⟨a man of varied ~s, learning, and culture —Jossleyn Hennessy⟩ ⟨his natural ~s were respectable —V.L.Parrington⟩ **b parts** *pl* **:** such personal qualities of a superior kind (as high intellectual ability, cleverness, talent) ⟨he had ~s and his sisters . . . expected him to do great things —W.S.Maugham⟩ ⟨a man of ~s and of great culture —Geoffrey Boumphrey⟩ **10** *archaic* **:** a particle of matter **11 :** the line where the hair is parted ⟨the ~ in your hair is a bit crooked⟩ **12 :** a course of conduct ⟨I thought silence the better ~ —H.J.Laski⟩; *specif* **:** one required or suggested by a specified quality ⟨it would be the ~ of prudence . . . to moderate his behavior —G.F.Kennan⟩ ⟨it is the ~ of wisdom to compare different cases —John Dewey⟩

part 11

**syn** PART, PORTION, PIECE, DETAIL, MEMBER, DIVISION, SECTION, SEGMENT, SECTOR, FRACTION, FRAGMENT, and PARCEL agree in meaning something less than a whole that is considered apart or actually separated from it. PART is the most general and comprehensive, being interchangeable with any of the other terms ⟨a *part* of a machine⟩ ⟨the greater *part* of a square⟩ ⟨a *part* of a year⟩ ⟨a *part* of a statue⟩ PORTION, although it signifies a part, does not necessarily imply an integral or assembled part; it can also suggest an assigned or allotted part (see the synonymy at *fate*) ⟨a *portion* of a diary⟩ ⟨the greater *portion* of a life⟩ ⟨a considerable *portion* of the town was burned —*Amer. Guide Series: Minn.*⟩ ⟨a *portion* of the voting population⟩ PIECE usually applies to a separate or detached part of a whole, often so stressing the idea of independence that the sense of a whole is extremely weak or lacking ⟨a *piece* of pie⟩ ⟨a *piece* of hot pig iron⟩ ⟨a *piece* of furniture⟩ DETAIL applies to a part of a plan or design, esp. in a painting or other art work, often signifying a part or feature that is small but important ⟨the *details* of domestic life on a farm —Havelock Ellis⟩ ⟨the *details* of the landscape dissolved in shadows —*Amer. Guide Series: N.Y.City*⟩ ⟨the most interesting *detail* of the house plan was its ornamentation⟩ MEMBER applies to one of the units of which a body (as a human body, legislative body, club, or construction such as a chair) is composed, implying both association with and separability from the whole ⟨a *member* of a committee⟩ ⟨a loss of an arm or other *member* in an accident⟩ ⟨the design of compression *members* of bridge trusses —*U.S. Nat'l Bureau of Standards Annual Report*⟩ ⟨a mere shell covering the structural *members* —*Amer. Guide Series: N.Y.City*⟩ DIVISION and SECTION apply to a distinct often detached part formed by or as if by cutting, DIVISION often suggesting a larger part than SECTION ⟨the bureaus are subdivided into *divisions* —J.E.Pate⟩ ⟨the *division* of activities arranged by the museum —Ralph Linton⟩ ⟨the New York City Police Department is split into parts, the detective *division* and the uniformed *division* —Walter Arm⟩ ⟨in my *division* of the class were four friends⟩ ⟨a *section* of the country⟩ ⟨a *section* of a circle⟩ ⟨a *section* of a cake⟩ SEGMENT, often interchangeable with SECTION, is often preferred to SECTION in distinguishing a part separated by natural lines of cleavage or determined by the construction of the whole ⟨Berkeley's career in Virginia was divided into two *segments* by the English civil war —G.W.Johnson⟩ ⟨essential raw materials for a broad *segment* of American industry —*Crops in Peace & War*⟩ ⟨the *segments* of an orange⟩ In mathematical use SECTOR signifies any part of a circle bounded by an arc and two radii, and SECTOR in general use can be any section roughly corresponding to this or any section of a whole conceived of as divided like a statistical circle into statistical portions; or, by extension, it can mean any portion cut off or out ⟨we must consider the German problem as a whole and not in *sectors* —A.H.Vandenberg⟩ ⟨the expansion of military production will cut into the civilian *sector* of the economy —L.J.Walinsky⟩ ⟨each society divides its total membership into a series of categories and assigns different *sectors* of the total culture to each category —Ralph Linton⟩ ⟨the tiny *sector* of the puzzle which he has chosen for his own province, finding some new pieces that fit neatly into place and properly rearranging some old ones —R.D.Altick⟩ FRACTION usu. suggests a very small or negligible part of the whole ⟨only a *fraction* of the cost —*Dun's Rev.*⟩ ⟨told him the merest *fraction* of our experiences —Kenneth Roberts⟩ ⟨a reduction of immigration to a mere *fraction* of what it used to be —P.A.Sorokin⟩ FRAGMENT applies to a small part disconnected from the whole esp. by breaking, and often applies to a small piece of a whole remaining after the whole has been almost totally eaten, used, or worn away ⟨the *fragments* of a broken glass⟩ ⟨the artist takes up some *fragment* of that existence, transfigures it, shows it —Havelock Ellis⟩ ⟨they represent only a *fragment* of the dramatic literature that once existed —R.D.Altick⟩ ⟨a *fragment* of an ancient Greek vase⟩ PARCEL in this connection is now used chiefly in law to mean a piece of land or in such a fixed phrase as *part and parcel;* its general sense implies an undetached and undetachable connection with the whole of which it is a part ⟨a number of real estate *parcels* in the downtown area —*Current Biog.*⟩ ⟨Irian has always been part and *parcel* of Indonesia —Cecil Hobbs⟩ ⟨demanded increasing *parcels* of Indian territory —H.M.Hyman⟩ ⟨held a small *parcel* of stock —*Amer. Guide Series: Mich.*⟩
— **for one's part :** as far as the share or interest of the person specified is concerned ⟨*for my part*, I have no intention to dispute her free agency —Tobias Smollett⟩ ⟨*for their part*, the boys . . . gather wood —J.G.Frazer⟩ — **for the most part :** in most cases **:** in the main **:** with regard to the greatest portion ⟨the dunes were . . . *for the most part* protected by seawalls —J.A.Steers⟩ ⟨persons who *for the most part* have some special knowledge —Allan Nevins⟩ ⟨the mafic minerals are *for the most part* hornblende and biotite —*Amer. Jour. of Science*⟩ — **in good part** *adv* **:** without offense **:** FAVORABLY, GRACIOUSLY ⟨took his refusal *in good part* —Archie Binns⟩ ⟨accepted this criticism *in good part* —J.G.Cozzens⟩ — **in part** *adv* **:** with respect to a part rather than a whole **:** in some measure or degree **:** PARTLY ⟨taken his idea *in part* from a picture —Clara Morris⟩ ⟨built *in part* of beams and brick —Philip Brady⟩ — often used with a qualifier ⟨the procedure . . . is the result *in large part* of its long struggle —K.B.Smellie⟩ ⟨*in small part* . . . the ridge is entirely covered with bracken —C.B.Hitchcock⟩ — **of the part of** *obs* **:** on the side of ⟨what art thou? *of the part of* England —Shak.⟩ — **on the part of 1 :** on the side of **:** with regard to or so far as concerns the one specified ⟨the managers *on the part of* the House at the conference —*U.S.Code*⟩ ⟨vigilance *on our part* —Thomas De Quincey⟩ ⟨incentive for all-out effort *on the part of* every member —A.S.Igleheart⟩ **2 :** as experienced, performed, or shown by ⟨the thoughtfulness of this act *on the part of* these men —*Metronome*⟩
**²part** \ˈ"\ *vb* -ED/-ING/-S [ME *parten*, fr. OF *partir* to divide, go away, fr. L *partire, partiri* to divide, fr. *part-, pars* part — more at ¹PART] *vi* **1 a :** to separate from or take leave of someone — used with *from* ⟨this ring I gave him when he ~*ed* from me —Shak.⟩ or sometimes with *with* ⟨just after I had ~*ed* with him at his lodgings —Matthew Arnold⟩ **b :** to relinquish possession or control of something — used with *with* ⟨sell securities or . . . ~ with some liquid cash —R.B.Westerfield⟩ ⟨willing to ~ with his right to vote —E.H.Collis⟩ or sometimes with *from* ⟨his precious bag which he would by no means ~ from —George Eliot⟩ **2** *obs* **:** to have a part or share **:** PARTAKE ⟨they shall ~ alike —1 Sam 30:24 (AV)⟩ **3 a :** to become separated into distinct parts **:** come apart ⟨saw the curtains ~ . . . on the next act —Winifred Bambrick⟩ **b :** to quit each other's company **:** take leave of one another ⟨they ~*ed* at the door —Irving Bacheller⟩ **4 a :** to go away **:** set out **:** take one's leave **:** DEPART ⟨~*ed* hence to embark for Milan —Shak.⟩ **b :** DIE ⟨~*ed* ev'n just between twelve and one —Shak.⟩ **5 :** to become separated, freed, or detached from something ⟨strips of three-ply that had . . . ~*ed* from the glue —*Sydney (Australia) Bull.*⟩ **6 :** to become divided or broken (as into segments or pieces) ⟨the port cable suddenly ~*ed* —R.B.O'Brien⟩ **7 :** to cause separation, division, or distinction ⟨the lot causeth contentions to cease and ~*eth* between the mighty —Prov 18:18 (AV)⟩ ~ *vt* **1 a** (1) **:** to divide or separate into distinct parts (as by breaking, cutting, cleaving) ⟨thou shalt ~ it in pieces and pour oil thereon —Lev 2:6 (AV)⟩ (2) **:** to divide by assigning or making physical boundaries **b :** to separate (hair) into two portions on each side of a line of demarcation ⟨~*ed* her hair just right of the middle⟩ **c :** to break or suffer the breaking of (as a rope or anchor chain) ⟨the ship ~*ed* her hawser in the gale⟩ **2 a :** to divide into shares and distribute (as among a number of recipients) **:** ALLOT, APPORTION ⟨~*ed* my garments among them —Jn 19:24 (RSV)⟩ **b** *archaic* **:** to share with one or more other persons ⟨~*ed* his breakfast . . . with the child and her grandfather —Charles Dickens⟩ **3 a :** to remove from contact or contiguity **:** cause to go apart **:** DISUNITE, SEPARATE, SUNDER ⟨if aught but death ~ thee and me —Ruth 1:17 (AV)⟩ — often used with *from* ⟨had been ~*ed* from each other years before⟩ ⟨~ animals from a herd⟩ **b :** to keep separate **:** form a boundary or interval between **:** DIVIDE ⟨the narrow seas that ~ the French and English —Shak.⟩ **c :** to hold apart (as combatants) **:** stand between **:** intervene between ⟨~ them! They are incens'd —Shak.⟩ **d :** to separate by a process of extraction, elimination, or secretion ⟨~ gold from silver⟩ **4 :** to bring (as an association) to an end by separating the parties involved ⟨you are . . . come to ~ almost a fray —Shak.⟩ **5 a** *archaic* **:** to take leave of **:** depart from **:** LEAVE, QUIT ⟨since presently your souls must ~ your bodies —Shak.⟩ ⟨loth to ~ his country —Maria Edgeworth⟩ **b** *dial Brit* **:** to give up **:** RELINQUISH **6** *obs* **:** to take sides with **:** espouse the cause of ⟨who ~*ed* our disaffected people and stopped all prosecution of them —Robert Wodrow⟩ **syn** see SEPARATE — **part company 1 a :** to bring a companionship, association, or similar connection between two parties (as individuals, groups, or organizations) to an end ⟨a faint diverging path was reached, where they *parted company* —Thomas Hardy⟩ ⟨held the federal union together . . . when the states might easily have *parted company* —C.A. Herter⟩ **b :** to effect such a separation from someone or something — used with *with* ⟨*parted* legal *company* with his former boss . . . and has hired his own lawyer —Ted Princiotto⟩ **2 a :** to diverge from someone or something (as in opinion, policy, or common purpose) — used with *with* ⟨the Republican Senate leadership *parted company* with the President on this issue —Arthur Krock⟩ and sometimes with *from* ⟨here . . . *parts company* from most of the scholars —*Times Lit. Supp.*⟩ **b :** to diverge in such a way from each other ⟨on the tariff question the two philosophies *parted company*⟩
**³part** \ˈ"\ *adv* [¹*part*] **:** in a measure **:** PARTLY ⟨was at least ~ right⟩ ⟨the rains came down . . . , ~ spoiling the cochineal crop —Oliver La Farge⟩
**⁴part** \ˈ"\ *adj* [¹*part*] **:** PARTIAL ⟨this woman has lived only a ~ life —H.A.Overstreet⟩ ⟨a ~ truth⟩ ⟨~ payments⟩
**part** *abbr* **1** participating **2** participle; participial **3** particular **4** partner
**par·tage** \(ˈ)pärˈtäzh\ *n* -s [ME, fr. MF, portion, division, fr. OF, division, fr. *partir* to divide + *-age* — more at PART] **1 :** something resulting from a division **:** PART, PORTION, SHARE **2 :** the action of dividing or sharing **:** DIVISION, DISTRIBUTION ⟨a bishop made a ~ of money collected —Thomas Fuller⟩
**par·take** \pärˈtāk, pȧˈ-, pə(r)ˈ=\ *vb* **par·took** \-ˈtu̇k\ **par·tak·en** \-ˈtākən\ **partaking; partakes** [back-formation fr. *partaker*] *vi* **1 :** to take a part or share in something (as an action or condition) in common with others **:** PARTICIPATE ⟨~ in a common economic and political life —*Amer. Guide Series: N.Y.*⟩ — often used with *of* ⟨their inability to ~ of some of the activities —W.E.Ditmars⟩ **2 a :** to take or receive a portion of something (as food or drink) **:** take some of something — usu. used with *of* ⟨none shall ~ of the meat until the male has had his fill —J.J.Hayward⟩ ⟨invited . . . to ~ of our lowly fare —Charles Dickens⟩ **b :** to consume most or all of something (as a meal) **:** TAKE — usu. used with *of* ⟨her solitary meals she *partook* of in the apartment next the eating room —Emily Clark⟩ **3 :** to have some of the properties, qualities, or attributes of something — usu. used with *of* ⟨these dialects *partook* . . . of the common body of Indo-European vocabulary —Charlton Laird⟩ ⟨the . . . lakes *partook* of the nature of the open sea —*U.S.Code*⟩ ~ *vt* **1 :** to take a part in **:** SHARE ⟨adventurers who were willing to ~ his fortunes —A.W.Kinglake⟩ **2 :** to take some or all of (as food or drink) alone or in company with others ⟨they . . . reclined beside him and his frugal fare *partook* —Robert Southey⟩ **syn** see SHARE
**par·tak·er** \-kə(r)\ *n* [alter. of earlier *part taker*, fr. ME, fr. ¹*part* + *taker;* intended as trans. of L *particeps* participant] **1 :** one that partakes **:** PARTICIPANT, PARTNER, SHARER ⟨the sacrament . . . by which the Christian is made a ~ of the

anointing of the Christ —Donald Allghin⟩ 2 *obs* : one that takes the side of another : SUPPORTER ⟨the great displeasure . . . of King Henry and his ~s —Edward Hall⟩

**par·tan** \'pärt°n\ *n* -s [ME (Sc), of Celt origin; akin to ScGael *partan* crab] : a European crab (*Cancer pagurus*) often used as food

**part and parcel** *n* : an essential or constituent portion : an integral element ⟨courtesy and geniality are *part and parcel* of the north country makeup —S.P.B.Mais⟩ ⟨thousands of Aramaic words are now *part and parcel* of the language —William Chomsky⟩

**partan face** *n*, *Scot* : a person whose face wears a sour expression

**parted** *adj* [fr. past part. of ²*part*] 1 a *chiefly Scot* : ⁴PARTY 2 ⟨a shield ~ per pale —E.S.Holden⟩ b : divided into parts (as by a line or space) ⟨~ hair⟩ c : cleft so that the divisions reach nearly but not quite to the base — used chiefly in combination ⟨3-*parted* corolla⟩ ⟨5-*parted* calyx⟩ 2 *archaic* : departed from earthly life : DECEASED ⟨their ~ father's ghost —William Warner⟩ ⟨hymn the requiem to his ~ soul —Robert Southey⟩ 3 [¹*part* + *-ed*] *obs* : endowed with parts (as abilities or talents) ⟨a man well ~ —Ben Jonson⟩ 4 : being apart : SEPARATED ⟨~ lips⟩

**parted and fretted** *or* **parted and fretty** *adj* : having both arms divided into two separated narrow strips and the four strips interlacing in the form of a fret — used of a heraldic cross

**part·er** \'pär|d·ə(r), 'pȧ|, |tə-\ *n* -s [ME, one that divides, fr. *parten* to part, divide + *-er* — more at PART] : one that parts; *esp* : a worker that separates bundles or sheets

**par·terre** \(')pär;te(ə)r, (')pȧ;-, -eə\ *n* -s [F, fr. MF, fr. *par terre* on the ground, fr. *par* through, along (fr. L *per* through) + *terre* ground, earth, fr. L *terra* — more at FARE, TERRACE] 1 : a garden having an ornamental and diversified arrangement of beds or plots separated by paths; *esp* : one in which flowers are cultivated 2 : a level space including a building site 3 : the part of the floor of a theater behind the orchestra; *esp* : PARQUET CIRCLE

**par terre** \"\ *adv* (*or adj*) [F, lit., on the ground] *ballet* : along the ground : on the floor — opposed to *en l'air*

**par·terred** \-e(ə)rd, -eəd\ *adj* : laid out in parterres ⟨sundials rose among ~ flowers —H.T.Kane⟩

**parthen-** *or* **partheno-** *comb form* [Gk, maiden, virgin, fr. *parthenos*] : virgin : without fertilization ⟨*partheno*genesis⟩ ⟨*parthen*ote⟩

**par·then·i·ta** \pär'thenəd·ə\ *n*, *pl* **partheni·tae** \-nə,tē, -,tī\ [NL, fr. Gk *parthenos* maiden, virgin] : a juvenile trematode worm (as a miracidium, sporocyst, or redia) — compare ADOLESCARIA, MARITA

**par·the·ni·um** \pär'thēnēəm\ *n*, *cap* [NL, fr. Gk *parthenion* feverfew, fr. neut. of *parthenios* maidenly, fr. *parthenos* maiden, virgin] : a small genus of No. American woody herbs (family Compositae) having small heads of rayed flowers in a terminal panicle — see BASTARD FEVERFEW, GUAYULE

**par·the·no·car·pic** \,pärthənō;kärpik\ *also* **par·the·no·car·pi·cal** \-pəkəl\ *or* **par·the·no·car·pous** \-pəs\ *adj* [*parthenocarpic* ISV *parthenocarpy* + *-ic*; *parthenocarpical* fr. *parthenocarpy* + *-ical*; *parthenocarpous* fr. *parthen-* + *-carpous*] : exhibiting parthenocarpy — **par·the·no·car·pi·cal·ly** \-pək(ə)lē, -li\ *adv*

**par·the·no·car·py** \'≈≈≈,≈pē\ *n* -ES [ISV *parthen-* + *-carpy*; prob. orig. formed as G *parthenokarpie*] : the production of fruits without fertilization — compare STENOSPERMOCARPY

**par·the·no·cis·sus** \,≈≈≈'sisəs\ *n*, *cap* [NL, fr. *parthen-* + *Cissus*] : a genus of Asiatic and No. American woody vines (family Vitaceae) distinguished by disklike tips on the tendrils — see BOSTON IVY, VIRGINIA CREEPER

**par·the·no·genesis** \;≈≈≈+\ *n* [NL, fr. *parthen-* + L *genesis*] 1 : reproduction that involves development of a female or rarely of a male gamete without fertilization, that occurs commonly among lower plants and invertebrate animals but rarely as a natural process among seed plants and vertebrates although it may be induced by artificial mechanical or chemical stimulation of the eggs of some vertebrates and that in nature either constitutes the sole form of sexual reproduction or alternates with bisexual activities in a pattern adapted to the needs and peculiar life circumstances of the organism — distinguished from *asexual reproduction*; compare APOGAMY 2 : creation or production of something by a process held to resemble biological parthenogenesis ⟨atheism was supposed to have produced revolution by ~ —V.G.Kiernan⟩

**par·the·no·genetic** \;≈≈≈+\ *or* **par·the·no·gen·ic** \;≈≈≈;jenik\ *or* **par·the·no·gen·i·tive** \-;jenəd·iv, -ətiv\ *or* **par·the·nog·e·nous** \;≈≈'näjənəs\ *adj* [*parthenogenetic* fr. *parthenogenesis*, after E *genesis*: *genetic*; *parthenogenic*, *parthenogenous* fr. *parthenogeny* + *-ic* or *-ous*; *parthenogenitive* irreg. (influenced by E *-ive* and by L *genitus*, past part. of *gignere* to beget) fr. *parthenogenesis* — more at KIN] : of, characterized by, or capable of parthenogenesis : produced by parthenogenesis — **par·the·no·genetically** \;≈≈≈+\ *adv*

**par·the·nog·e·ny** \,≈≈'näjənē, -ni\ *n* -ES [*parthen-* + *-geny*] : PARTHENOGENESIS

**par·the·no·gonidium** \;≈≈nō+\ *n* [NL, fr. *parthen-* + *gonidium*] : an individual or gonidium (as in members of the genus *Volvox*) that can reproduce asexually

**par·the·nop·a·rous** \;≈≈'näpərəs\ *adj* [*parthen-* + *-parous*] : producing living young without fertilization ⟨~ aphids⟩

**par·then·o·pe** \pär'thenə(,)pē\ *n*, *cap* [NL, fr. L *Parthenope*, siren worshiped in Naples in ancient times, fr. Gk *Parthenopē*] : a large cosmopolitan genus (the type of the family Parthenopidae) of spider crabs with well-formed orbits and enlarged chelipeds

¹**par·then·o·pid** \-,pəd\ *adj* [NL *Parthenopidae*, fr. *Parthenope*, type genus + *-idae*] : of or relating to the Parthenopidae

²**parthenopid** \"\ *n* -s [NL *Parthenopidae*] : a spider crab of the family Parthenopidae

**par·the·nop·i·dae** \,pärthə'näpə,dē\ *n pl*, *cap* [NL, fr. *Parthenope*, type genus + *-idae*] : a widely distributed family of spider crabs with long heavy chelipeds

**par·the·no·spore** \'pärthənə+,-\ *n* [ISV *parthen-* + *spore*] : a spore produced parthenogenetically

**par·the·note** \'pärthə,nōt\ *n* -s [*parthen-* + *-ote* (as in *zygote*)] : an individual produced by parthenogenesis

¹**par·thi·an** \'pärthēən, 'pȧth-\ *n* -s *cap* [*Parthia* + E *-an*, n. suffix] 1 : a native or inhabitant of Parthia, an ancient country to the southeast of the Caspian sea 2 : an Iranian language or dialect of the Parthian people

²**parthian** \"\ *adj*, *usu cap* [*Parthia* + E *-an*, adj. suffix] 1 : of, relating to, or characteristic of ancient Parthia 2 : of, relating to, or characteristic of the people of ancient Parthia 3 : suggesting or held to suggest the mode of fighting on horseback with the bow as the only weapon employed by the Parthian people and characterized chiefly by the discharge of arrows while in real or feigned flight : delivered in or as if in flight or retreat : PARTING ⟨*Parthian* shot⟩

¹**par·ti** \(')pär;tē\ *n*, *pl* **partis** \-ē(z)\ [F, fr. MF, match, party, decision, fr. *parti*, past part. of *partir* to divide, go away — more at PART] 1 : ¹MATCH 4b ⟨the Englishman whom she naively assumes to be an excellent ~ —*Times Lit. Supp.*⟩ 2 : a good or desirable match ⟨you don't realize what a ~ he is —Mary Manning⟩

²**parti** \"\ *n* -s [F, fr. MF, match, party, decision] : the basic general scheme of an architectural design

¹**parti-** *also* **party-** *comb form* [obs. E *party*, adj., parti-colored, fr. ME *party*, *parti*, fr. MF *parti* striped, party per pale, fr. OF, fr. *parti*, past part. of *partir* to divide, go away] : various : variegated ⟨*parti*-striped⟩

²**parti-** *comb form* [L, fr. *part-*, *pars* — more at PART] : part ⟨*parti*-mortgage⟩

¹**par·tial** \'pärshəl, 'pȧsh-\ *adj* [ME *parcial*, fr. MF *partial* biased, incomplete, fr. ML *partialis*, fr. LL, incomplete, fr. L *part-*, *pars* part + *-ialis* -ial — more at PART] 1 : inclined to favor one party in a cause or one side of a question more than the other : BIASED, PREDISPOSED ⟨loss of the impartiality of the scientific spirit through affiliation with some partisan and ~ interest —John Dewey⟩ ⟨the ~ testimony of friends —H.D. Thoreau⟩ ⟨it is inconsistent with justice to be ~ —J.S.Mill⟩ 2 a (1) : having a predilection for a certain person or thing : favorably disposed toward someone or something : biased or prejudiced in one's favor (2) : inclined to favor a certain person or thing excessively : having an unreasonable fondness for something : foolishly fond ⟨the ~ father, loving one alone —F.W.Robertson⟩ b : having a liking for : fond of — used with *to* ⟨the horse is particularly ~ to salt —Henry Wynmalen⟩ ⟨a walk . . . was a marvelous idea for them ~ to it —Richard Llewellyn⟩ 3 : of, involving, or affecting a part rather than the whole of something : not total or entire : not general or universal : existing to a limited extent only : INCOMPLETE ⟨the ~ transfer of sovereignty . . . to a supranational authority —*Current Biog.*⟩ ⟨among ~ men, he stood for the complete man —Van Wyck Brooks⟩ ⟨provides only a ~ solution to the housing problem —D.D.Eisenhower⟩ ⟨~ paralysis⟩

²**partial** \"\ *n* -s 1 : one of the tones produced by the complex vibrations comprising a musical tone and extending in range from the fundamental upward through the entire overtone series — compare HARMONIC 1 2 : PARTIAL SCORE 3 : PARTIAL DENTURE

**partial adjunct** *n* : a grammatical adjunct that qualifies only a part of the following substantive (as *free* in *free churchman*)

**partial cleavage** *n* : embryonic cleavage in which the division into blastomeres involves only a part of the egg with the rest remaining undivided for a longer or shorter time

**partial correlation** *n* : the correlation between two statistical variables under the condition that all other relevant variables are fixed

**partial denture** *n* : a fixed or removable artificial replacement of one or more teeth in a dental arch

**partial derivative** *n* : the derivative of a function of several variables with respect to one of them and with the remaining variables treated as constants

**partial differential equation** *n* : a differential equation containing at least one partial derivative

**partial differentiation** *n* : the process of finding a partial derivative

**partial diphthong** *n* : a speech sound whose articulation resembles that of an ordinary diphthong in being a transition between two vowel positions but which differs in having a held beginning or ending — called also *imperfect diphthong*

**partial disability** *n* : a condition constituting less than total disability : incapacity preventing full performance of duties of an occupation as a result of accident or illness

**partial eclipse** *n* : an eclipse in which one celestial body is not completely obscured by the shadow or body of another

**partial fraction** *n* : one of the fractions into the sum of which a fraction may be decomposed

**par·tial·ism** \'pärshə,lizəm, 'pȧsh-\ *n* -s [¹*partial* + *-ism*] 1 : concentration of libidinal interest on one part of the body (as breasts or buttocks) 2 : a form of fetishism whose object is a part of the body rather than an inanimate symbol

**par·tial·ist** \-ləst\ *n* -s [MF *partialiste*, fr. *partial* biased + *-iste* -ist] 1 : one that is partial to one side (as of a controversy or question); *specif* : PARTISAN 2 [¹*partial* + *-ist*] : a believer in or advocate of theological particularism

**par·tial·i·ty** \,pärshē'aləd·ē, ,pȧsh-, -lətē, -i *also* ≈'shal-\ *n* -ES [ME *parcialite*, fr. MF *partialité*, fr. ML *partialitat-*, *partialitas*, fr. *partialis* + *-itat-*, *-itas* -ity] : the quality or state of being partial: a : the inclination to favor one side (as of a conflict or question) : BIAS ⟨difficult . . . to view his work without ~ —A.F.Fforde⟩ b : a predilection or fondness for one person or one thing rather than others : special taste or liking ⟨his ~ for his old comrades —*Atlantic*⟩ ⟨a huge . . . animal whose ~ for comparatively open country renders it an easy prey —James Stevenson-Hamilton⟩ **syn** see PREDILECTION

**par·tial·ize** \'pärshə,līz, 'pȧsh-\ *vb* -ED/-ING/-S [MF *partialiser*, fr. *partial* + *-iser* -ize] *vt* : to make partial : give bias to ⟨his hate will ~ his opinion —Owen Feltham⟩ ~ *vi* : to concern oneself with or give emphasis to a part rather than the whole of something

**partial lunar eclipse** *n* : an eclipse in which the moon is not completely immersed in the umbra of the earth's shadow

**par·tial·ly** \'pärsh(ə)lē, 'pȧsh-, -li\ *adv* [ME *parcially*, fr. *parcial* + *-ly*] 1 : to some extent : PARTLY ⟨a determined but only ~ successful attempt —*Amer. Guide Series: Minn.*⟩ ⟨the scarcity of suitable . . . material ~ explains the trend —*Publishers' Weekly*⟩ ⟨a sharp-featured face with a ~ bald head —Norman Mailer⟩ 2 a *obs* : with inclination or predilection toward one side rather than another b *archaic* : with affection or favor toward someone or something

**partial organ** *n* : a group of stops in a pipe organ controlled from one keyboard

**partial out** *vt* : to give (a variable) a fixed value while considering the relationship between two related variables

**partial rhyme** *n* : HALF RHYME

**partial score** *n* : PART-SCORE

**partial solar eclipse** *n* : an eclipse of the sun in which the moon does not completely hide the solar surface or photosphere so that some direct rays of sunlight reach the observer : all the part of a total solar eclipse outside of the path of totality

**partial stop** *n* : a stop in a pipe organ in which the pipes extend only through a portion of the keyboard — compare FOUNDATION STOP

**partial term** *n* : an undistributed term in logic

**partial tone** *n* : PARTIAL 1

**partial veil** *n* : a membrane of the young sporophore of various mushrooms that initially extends from the margin of the cap to the stem, is ruptured by growth, and is represented in the mature sporophore by an annulus about the stem and sometimes by a cortina on the margin of the cap — compare UNIVERSAL VEIL

**partial verdict** *n* 1 : a verdict finding the accused guilty of only part of what is charged 2 : a verdict covering only a part of the issues in dispute

**par·ti·bil·i·ty** \,pär|d·ə'biləd·ē, ,pȧ|, |tə-, -lətē, -i\ *n* -ES : the quality or state of being partible : DIVISIBILITY, SEPARABILITY ⟨ascribing ~ to God —S.T.Coleridge⟩

**par·ti·ble** \'≈≈bəl\ *adj* [LL *partibilis*, fr. L *partire*, *partiri* to divide + *-bilis* -able — more at PART] : capable of being separated or parted : admitting of partition : DIVISIBLE, SEPARABLE ⟨~ property⟩ ⟨a ~ inheritance⟩

**par·ti·cate** \'pärtə,kāt\ *n* -s [ML *particata*, *perticata*, fr. L *pertica* pole — more at PERCH] : an old Scotch unit of land area equal to about ¼ acre

**par·ti·ceps cri·mi·nis** \,pärd·ə,seps'krimənəs\ *n* [ML] : one who has a share in a crime : ACCOMPLICE

**par·tic·i·pa·ble** \pə(r)'tisəpəbəl, pär't-, pȧ't-\ *adj* [LL *participabilis*, fr. L *participare* + *-bilis* -able] : capable of being participated or shared ⟨the essence of God is . . . ~ by things without —John Norris †1711⟩

¹**par·tic·i·pant** \-pənt\ *adj* [L *participant-*, *participans*, pres. part. of *participare*] : having a share or part : PARTICIPATING

²**participant** \"\ *n* -s 1 : one that participates : one that takes part or shares in something with others ⟨an active ~ in social work —N.K.Burger⟩ ⟨a dance with the ~s in special costumes —*Amer. Guide Series: Nev.*⟩ ⟨these organs were not ~s in the visual response —F.A.Geldard⟩ 2 : a tone in an ecclesiastical mode lying between the mediant and either the dominant or the final

**participant observation** *n* : a research technique in anthropology and sociology characterized by the effort of an investigator to gain entrance into and social acceptance by a foreign culture or alien group so as better to attain a comprehensive understanding of the internal structure of the society

**participant observer** *n* : one that is engaged in participant observation

**par·tic·i·pate** \-,pāt, *usu* -ād.+V\ *vb* -ED/-ING/-S [L *participatus*, past part. of *participare*, fr. *particip-*, *particeps* participant, partaking, fr. *parti-* (fr. *part-*, *pars* part) + *-cip-*, *-ceps* (fr. *capere* to take) — more at PART, HEAVE] *vt* 1 : PARTAKE 1 ⟨I determined . . . to ~ my amorous flame with a genteel girl —James Boswell⟩ ⟨fit to ~ all rational delight —John Milton⟩ 2 *obs* : to impart a share of ⟨who often . . . ~s the profit of his sports with my son —Thomas Kyd⟩; *esp* : make known (as information) ⟨I have resolved . . . to write and ~ to you this opportunity —John Freind⟩ ~ *vi* 1 : to possess some of the properties, qualities, or attributes of something : possess something of the nature of a person or thing ⟨both members ~ of harmony —Samuel Johnson⟩ ⟨the individual man ~s in the ideal man —Frank Thilly⟩ 2 a : to take part in something (as an enterprise or activity) usu. in common with others ⟨three cabinet members from each country . . . would ~ in the Copenhagen meeting —L.B.Burbank⟩ ⟨the metal . . . did not ~ directly in the catalytic activity —Henry Tauber⟩ ⟨residents of this district often ~ in barn dances —*Amer. Guide Series: Conn.*⟩ b : to have a part or share in something ⟨your mother ~s in this ambition —Edith Wharton⟩ ⟨another term . . . which ~s in the impulse —R.M.Weaver⟩ ⟨convertible stock . . . ~s with the common stock, share by share alike, in additional dividends —*N. Y. Times*⟩ **syn** see SHARE

**participating** *adj* 1 : involving participation by more than one person or agency ⟨~ carrier⟩ ⟨~ sponsorship of a radio program⟩ — see PARTICIPATING MORTGAGE 2 : sharing in distributions: a : entitling the holder to a share in any distribution of surplus by the issuing insurance company ⟨~ policies⟩ ⟨~ insurance⟩ b : entitled to a share in additional distributions besides its regular fixed income ⟨~ preference shares⟩ — see PARTICIPATING BOND, PARTICIPATING STOCK

**participating bond** *n* : a bond that besides being entitled to interest at a fixed rate is further entitled to share in additional distributions on a specified basis with the common stock of the issuing company

**participating mortgage** *n* : a mortgage or sometimes a group of mortgages in which two or more persons have fractional equitable interests evidenced by certificates issued by the bank or other fiduciary having legal title to the mortgage and selling the fractional shares to investors or making the investment for the certificate holders

**participating stock** *n* : a preferred stock that besides being entitled to dividends at a fixed rate is further entitled to share in additional distributions on a specified basis with the common stock of the issuing company

**par·tic·i·pa·tion** \pə(r),tisə'pāshən, (,)pär,t-, (,)pȧ,t-\ *n* -s [ME *participacioun*, fr. LL *participation-*, *participatio*, fr. L *participatus* (past part. of *participare*) + *-ion-*, *-io* -ion] 1 : the action or state of participating: as a : the action or state of partaking of something (as a substance or quality) ⟨the common ~ of any pleasure —James Boswell⟩ — often used with *in* ⟨~ in the divine nature —K.S.Latourette⟩ ⟨the ~ in meanings and goods . . . effected by communication —John Dewey⟩ b (1) : association with others in a relationship (as a partnership) or an enterprise usu. on a formal basis with specified rights and obligations ⟨a loan made directly or in ~ with a bank⟩ (2) : PROFIT SHARING c (1) : the action or state of taking part with others in an activity ⟨~ in partisan politics —John Lodge⟩ ⟨active ~ in the field of international affairs —*Current Biog.*⟩ ⟨giving his readers a sense of personal ~ in these explorations —Rachel L. Carson⟩ (2) : social interaction in a group (as a family, club, community) esp. as carried on through attendance at and contributions to group activities ⟨measure the intensity of social ~ in a rural community⟩ 2 : the relation in Platonism of objects in the actual world to the transcendental universal forms or ideas constituting the essential nature of the universal objects, which are held to be only partial and imperfect embodiments of the ideas — compare IMITATION 3 : SHARE ⟨the theater . . . came in for a full ~ in the benefit —Tyrone Power †1841⟩ ⟨for a few dollars she buys a ~ in the creative act —*Harper's*⟩ 4 a : something in which shares are taken by more than one party — compare PARTICIPATING MORTGAGE, PARTICIPATION LOAN b : something that results in a share (as of a distribution) — compare PARTICIPATING 2

**participation loan** *n* : a large loan made by a bank or insurance company in which shares are taken by other banks or insurance companies

**par·tic·i·pa·tive** \≈'≈≈,pād·|iv, -āt|, |ēv *also* |əv\ *adj* : participating or capable of participating ⟨social science is by its nature . . . ~ in human affairs —W.H.Sheldon⟩

**par·tic·i·pa·tor** \-ād·ə(r), -ātə-\ *n* -s [LL *participator*, fr. L *participatus* (past part. of *participare*) + *-or*] : PARTICIPANT ⟨scenes in which she had been such an important ~ —J.D. Beresford⟩ ⟨an observer rather than a ~ —W.E.Collin⟩

**par·tic·i·pa·to·ry** \-,pə,tōrē, -ȯr-, -ri\ *adj* [*participate* + *-ory*] : characterized by or involving participation : PARTICIPATING; *esp* : providing the opportunity for individual participation ⟨~ democracy⟩

¹**par·ti·cip·i·al** \,pär|d·ə;sipēəl, ;pȧ|, |tə-\ *adj* [L *participialis*, fr. *participium* participle + *-alis* -al] : having the characteristics and use of a participle : formed with or from a participle — **par·ti·cip·i·al·ly** \-ēəlē, -li\ *adv*

²**participial** \"\ *n* -s *archaic* : a verbal derivative having the characteristics of a participle

**participial adjective** *n* : a participle (as *rolling* in *a rolling stone* or *written* in *the written word*) having an adjectival function

**par·ti·cip·ial·ize** \,līz\ *vt* -ED/-ING/-S : to make participial

¹**par·ti·ci·ple** \'pär|d·ə,sipəl, 'pȧ|, |tə- *also* -,səp-, *chiefly Brit* -tsəp-\ *n* -s [ME, fr. MF, modif. of L *participium* (trans. of Gk *metochē* participation, sharing, participle), fr. *particip-*, *particeps* participant, partaking] 1 : a word having the characteristics of both verb and adjective; *esp* : the English verbal adjective ending in *-ing* or in *-ed*, *-d*, *-t*, *-en*, or *-n* that has the function of an adjective and at the same time shows such verbal features as tense and voice and capacity to take an object — see PAST PARTICIPLE, PRESENT PARTICIPLE 2 *obs* : one that has the characteristics of two or more different classes ⟨certain ~s in nature which are almost ambiguous to which kind they should be referred —Francis Bacon⟩

²**participle** \"\ *adj* : PARTICIPIAL

**par·ti·cle** \'pär|d·əkəl, 'pȧ|, |tə-, -ēk-\ *n* -s [ME, fr. L *particula*, dim. of *part-*, *pars* part — more at PART] 1 *archaic* a : a small part, portion, or division of a whole b : a small portion (as a clause or article) of a composition or document 2 a : one of the minute subdivisions of matter (as a molecule, atom, electron, alpha particle) — see ELEMENTARY PARTICLE b : an ideal body that has finite mass but infinitesimal size 3 a : a very small portion of something material : minute quantity : tiny fragment ⟨her face was . . . beaded with small ~s of rain —Thomas Wolfe⟩ ⟨each ~ of the tape is magnetized to saturation —*Sound Recording & Reproduction*⟩ ⟨~s of sand⟩ b : a very small part of something having an immaterial nature : the smallest possible portion or amount of something ⟨there is not a ~ of truth in any of these statements —M.F.A.Montagu⟩ ⟨exertion of every ~ of strength she possessed —C.S.Forester⟩ ⟨a voice from which every ~ of emotion was painfully excluded —Thomas Hardy⟩ 4 a : a unit of speech serving almost as a loose affix, expressing some general aspect of meaning or some connective or limiting relation, and including the articles, most prepositions and conjunctions, and some interjections and adverbs b : an element that resembles a word but that is used only in composition : a derivational affix ⟨*un-* in *un*fair and *-ward* in back*ward* are ~s⟩ 5 a : a small-sized host distributed to a member of the laity in a communion service of the Roman Catholic Church b *Eastern Church* (1) : a portion taken from a loaf of oblation to be consecrated as the Lamb in a communion service (2) : one of the small pieces taken from prosphorae but not consecrated in memory of particular living or dead persons (3) : a small piece broken from the consecrated Lamb given to a member of the laity in a communion service

**particle accelerator** *n* : ACCELERATOR 1g

**particle velocity** *n* : the velocity with which the individual particles of a medium move when traversed by a wave — compare PHASE VELOCITY

¹**parti-color** \'pär|d·ē, 'pȧ|, |t|, |i+,-\ *adj* [¹*parti-* + *color*, n.] : variegated in color : PARTI-COLORED 1

²**parti-color** \"\ *n* [¹*parti-* + *color*, n.] : variegated color : MOTLEY ⟨the *parti-colors* of the atlas —*Spectator*⟩

**parti-colored** \'≈≈,≈≈\ *adj* [obs. E *party*, adj., parti-colored + E *colored*, adj. — more at PARTI-] 1 : marked by different colors or tints ⟨*parti-colored* iris⟩ ⟨*parti-colored* cows⟩ ⟨*parti-colored* beach balls⟩ 2 : characterized by variation or diversity : CHECKERED 2 ⟨their delights . . . *parti-colored* and spotted with mixture of sorrow —Samuel Ward⟩ **syn** see VARIEGATED

¹**par·tic·u·lar** \R pə(r)'tikyələr, -R pə'tikyələ(r; pär't-,pȧ't-, ÷ -k(ə)l-\ *adj* [ME *particuler*, fr. MF, fr. LL *particularis*, fr. L *particula* small part, particle + *-aris* -ar] 1 : of, relating to, or being a single definite person or thing as distinguished from some or all others — opposed to *general* ⟨preferred the general to the ~ approach —F.W.D.Deakin⟩ ⟨claims of the United States or any ~ state —*U. S. Constitution*⟩ ⟨how a ~ piece of land can be put to . . . use —*Wall Street Jour.*⟩ 2 *obs* : involv-

ing, affecting, or belonging to a part rather than the whole of something : partial in extent : not universal ⟨the three years drought . . . was but ~ and left people alive —Francis Bacon⟩ **3** : of, relating to, or concerned with the separate parts of a whole; *esp* : describing or setting forth the details of something : MINUTE, PRECISE ⟨a ~ account of the day's events⟩ **4 a** *archaic* : of, relating to, or concerning a single person, class, or thing : PERSONAL, PRIVATE ⟨these domestic and ~ broils are not the question —Shak.⟩ **b** *obs* : not occupying public office : PRIVATE **5 a** : distinctive among others of the same kind : out of the ordinary : markedly unusual : worthy of notice ⟨the . . . selection was the ~ gem of the evening —Douglas Watt⟩ ⟨an attack of ~ severity —*N. Y. Times*⟩ ⟨a rather ~ problem because of the immense size of the timbers —*London Calling*⟩ **b** *obs* : noteworthy as being peculiar, singular, or eccentric **6** : constituting a unit among a number : having a separate status : considered alone : INDIVIDUAL, SEPARATE ⟨each ~ hair to stand an end, like quills —Shak.⟩ ⟨provoked by ~ events in his life —T.S.Eliot⟩ **7 a** : having the character of a particular in logic ⟨all concrete individuals are ~ and all universal individuals are abstract —Nelson Goodman⟩ **b** : affirming or denying a predicate to some part of the subject — used of a proposition in logic; opposed to *universal* ⟨"some men are wise" is a ~ affirmative⟩ **8 a** *archaic* : markedly or esp. attentive to a person : familiar in manner or behavior ⟨never suffer this fellow to be ~ with you —Henry Fielding⟩ **b** : close or intimate in personal relationship ⟨my very ~ friend —Charles Dickens⟩ **9 a** : concerned with or attentive to details : CAREFUL, EXACT, PRECISE, SCRUPULOUS ⟨is very ~ about her housekeeping⟩ **b** : nice in taste : FASTIDIOUS **c** : EXACTING : hard to please : FINICKY, FUSSY ⟨these bacilli are not ~ in their habitats —Justina Hill⟩ ⟨never lost patience with even the most ~ customers⟩ **syn** see CIRCUMSTANTIAL, NICE, SINGLE, SPECIAL

²**particular** \"\ *n* -s **1** *archaic* : a separate part of a whole : a constituent element, section, or division of something ⟨let us divide the discourse into four ~*s* —Robert Johnson⟩ **2 a** : an individual fact, point, circumstance, or detail ⟨their dissimilarity in every ~ except shape and size —Scott Fitzgerald⟩ ⟨determined that history shall not repeat itself in that melancholy ~ —Dean Acheson⟩ **b** : a specific item of information : a factual detail (as of news, specifications, accounts) — usu. used in pl. ⟨everybody was stirred by the news and wanted to know the ~*s* —H.E.Scudder⟩ ⟨genealogical ~*s* and biographical details are given —*Brit. Book News*⟩; see BILL OF PARTICULARS **3 a** (1) : an individual specific separate thing, instance, or case as distinguished from a whole class ⟨a discussion that attempts to generalize from ~*s* —Harvey Breit⟩ ⟨from moral generalities to business ~*s* —G.B.Shaw⟩ (2) : an individual or a specific subclass in logic falling under some general concept or term : something that can be the subject of an atomic proposition **b** : a particular proposition in logic **4 a** *archaic* : an individual or personal case, business, or interest : special concern or condition ⟨return from the common cause to what concerns our ~ —William Warburton⟩ **b** *obs* : personal profit or advantage : private interest ⟨if the gentleman had kept all the allowance for his own ~ —Edward Nicholas⟩ **5 a** : an individual item or article ⟨a few letters and ~*s* in the possession of the present writer —Richard Garnett †1906⟩ **b** *obs* : an individual person; *esp* : one in private as distinguished from public life ⟨it is the greatest interest of ~*s* to advance the good of the community —Roger L'Estrange⟩ **6** : a statement setting forth the details of a matter ⟨a ~ of premises⟩ ⟨I send you the descriptive ~ —Frederick North⟩ **7** : something constituting a special distinguishing characteristic or feature (as of a place) — see LONDON PARTICULAR **syn** see ITEM — **in particular** *adv* **1** *obs* : one by one : in detail : INDIVIDUALLY ⟨now ye are the body of Christ, and members *in particular* —1 Cor 12:27 (AV)⟩ **2** : as one specific case distinguished from a group, general category, or all cases : in distinction from others : SPECIFICALLY ⟨her belief in the theatre in general and her new play *in particular* —Peter Forster⟩ ⟨the recovery of the Greek world, and of Plato *in particular* —M.R.Cohen⟩ ⟨the shops *in particular* allure the young man —S.P.B.Mais⟩

**particular average** *n* : a partial loss in marine insurance that must be borne by the interest or goods sustaining it without benefit of contribution from other interests — compare GENERAL AVERAGE

**particular baptist** *n, usu cap P&B* : a member of a British Baptist body of the 17th to 19th centuries holding Calvinistic doctrines — called also *Calvinistic Baptist;* compare GENERAL BAPTIST

**particular custom** *n* : a custom prevailing in a local area (as a county, city, town) and generally subject to a determination of its legal existence by a jury on proof rather than by the court — compare GENERAL CUSTOM

**particular estate** *n* : the smaller estate (as an estate for life, in tail, or for years) created from an inheritance as a precedent estate to a remainder

**particular integral** *n* : PARTICULAR SOLUTION

**par·tic·u·lar·ism** \-lə,rizəm\ *n* -s [F *particularisme,* fr. LL *particularis* particular + F *-isme* -ism] **1** : exclusive or special devotion to something particular (as an interest, subject, party, sect) ⟨bourgeois individualism . . . in France took the form of a family ~ —Malcolm Cowley⟩ ⟨an intense ~ that did not welcome outside influences —*Amer. Guide Series: Conn.*⟩ ⟨the forces of ~ are dominant and academic recognition is awarded the specialist —W.W.Stewart⟩ **2** : a theological doctrine that redemption through Christ is provided only for the elect **3** : a political theory or practice advocating a right and freedom for each politically conscious or organized group (as a minority group in a country of several groups or a state in a federation) to promote its own interests and esp. independence without regard to the interests of larger groups ⟨there is no nation . . . only ~ in nine small localities —Nathaniel Peffer⟩ ⟨that country will be hampered . . . by the existence of strong regional ~ —*Current History*⟩ — compare NATIONALISM, STATES' RIGHTS **4** : a tendency to explain complex social phenomena in terms of a single causative factor **5** : a logical system based on particulars

¹**par·tic·u·lar·ist** \-rəst\ *n* -s [F *particulariste,* fr. LL *particularis* particular + F *-iste* -ist] : an adherent of particularism

²**particularist** \"\ *adj* **1** : of, relating to, or having the characteristics of particularism ⟨~ . . . tendencies persisted and seriously complicated national political life —Renzo Sereno⟩ **2** : of, relating to, or being a society in which the family unit is individualized

**par·tic·u·lar·is·tic** \⸗¦⸗(⸗)lə¦ristik, -tēk\ *adj* **1** : of, characterized by, or adhering to particularism ⟨too ~ and too conscious of their historical divisions to unite politically —Robert Strausz-Hupé⟩ ⟨the ~ thesis that the isolation of farm life induces mental breakdown —Kimball Young⟩ ⟨the advancement of ~ and no doubt selfish purposes —Alan Barth⟩ ⟨~ . . . economic pressure groups —Walter Adams⟩ **2** : of, relating to, or characterizing a particularist society ⟨the ~ norms of the immigrants' groups —S.N.Eisenstadt⟩ ⟨~ relationships⟩ **3** : based on concrete spatially or temporally bounded particulars (as physical objects or phenomenal events) ⟨a ~ system⟩ **4** : based upon a particular situation or relationship rather than general principles ⟨a ~ response⟩ — opposed to *universalistic*

**par·tic·u·lar·i·ty** \⸗,⸗⸗ˈlarəd·ē, -rətē, -i\ *n* -ES [MF *particularité* minute detail, particular, fr. LL *particularitat-, particularitas* quality or state of being a part, fr. *particularis* particular + L *-tat-, -tas* -ty] **1** : something particular: as **a** : a special circumstance : a minute detail : PARTICULAR ⟨fixing exclusively on the *particularities* of the current situation —Will Herberg⟩ **b** : an individual characteristic : distinctive quality or feature : special attribute : PECULIARITY ⟨regional life with its *particularities* of outlook and idiom —Roger Manvell⟩ ⟨the *particularities* of French rural society —H.W.Ehrmann⟩ **c** *archaic* : an eccentric or odd distinction : a peculiar action or characteristic : SINGULARITY **2** : the quality or state of being particular: as **a** *archaic* : the fact or quality of being noteworthy : SPECIALITY **b** : the quality or fact of being particular as opposed to universal : quality of being or having a relation to one or some rather than all (as of a class or group) : INDIVIDUALITY ⟨the words . . . when written alone have of course no ~ —*Inland Printer*⟩ ⟨concrete human situations in their complexity and ~ —F.R.Leavis⟩ **c** : attentiveness to detail : precise carefulness (as of description, statement, investigation) ⟨the unimpaired ~ of the compilation —*Times Lit. Supp.*⟩ ⟨after the victim of a theft described with ~ the goods he was seeking —Wayne Morse⟩ ⟨the loving ~ of the essays —Douglas Bush⟩ **d** : preciseness in behavior or expression : FASTIDIOUSNESS **e** *archaic* : attentive or familiar behavior : INTIMACY ⟨this ~ with a young fellow is very indecent —Henry Fielding⟩

**par·tic·u·lar·ization** \⸗,⸗(⸗)lərə̇ˈzāshən, -,rīˈz-\ *n* -s [F *particularisation,* fr. MF, fr. *particulariser* + *-ation*] **1** : individualized description or treatment **2** : limitation or application to a particular case

**par·tic·u·lar·ize** \⸗ˈ⸗(⸗)lə,rīz\ *vb* -ED/-ING/-S [MF *particulariser* to give the particulars of, specify, fr. LL *particularis* particular + MF *-iser* -ize] *vt* **1** : to make particular rather than general : apply or limit to a particular case ⟨diocesan laws . . . may ~ or extend this general law in accordance with local needs —P.H.Furfey⟩ **2** : to give the particulars of : describe or state in detail : treat individually : name one by one : SPECIFY ⟨the supplemental answer . . . *particularized* the charges —A.C.Buchanan⟩ **3** : to place apart from others of the same class or group : INDIVIDUALIZE, SEPARATE ⟨woodland and similar landed appendages were common property but pasturage might be *particularized* —S.H.Cross⟩ ~ *vi* : to mention or attend to particulars : go into details (as in a narrative) ⟨even advanced American researchers in science and scholarship tend . . . to ~ excessively —Thomas Munro⟩

**par·tic·u·lar·ized** \-,rīzd\ *adj* : made particular: as **a** : directed toward a specific object rather than some or all objects ⟨critical ~ thinking as distinct from stereotyped slogan-thinking —David Bidney⟩ ⟨insurance companies were the next corporations on which ~ imposts were laid —M.S. Kendrick⟩ **b** : differentiated from others of the same category : INDIVIDUALIZED ⟨among the American Mongoloids, the Eskimo appear to be the most ~ subvariety —A.L.Kroeber⟩ **syn** see CIRCUMSTANTIAL

**particular lien** *n* : a lien upon specific property as security for the payment of a debt or the satisfaction of some other obligation arising out of a transaction or agreement involving that property — called also *specific lien;* compare COMMON-LAW LIEN, GENERAL LIEN

**par·tic·u·lar·ly** \-kyələ(r)lē, -kyəlē, ÷-k(ə)lə(r)lē, ÷-k(ə)lē, -li\ *adv* [ME *particulerly,* fr. *particuler* particular + *-ly*] **1** : in a particular manner: as **a** *archaic* : in the case of each one of a number : one by one : SEVERALLY, SINGLY **b** : in detail : in particulars : item by item : part by part ⟨appurtenances . . . more ~ described —*Act 5 George III*⟩ **c** : in the specific case of one person or thing as distinguished from others : in particular : INDIVIDUALLY, PERSONALLY, SPECIFICALLY ⟨the provision of such facilities, ~ in rural areas —D.D.Eisenhower⟩ ⟨trace major population movements . . . for the Pueblo groups ~, for other southwestern groups incidentally —E.K. Reed⟩ **d** : in a special or unusual degree : to an extent greater than in other cases or towards others : ESPECIALLY ⟨a poison ~ toxic to canines —*Monsanto Mag.*⟩ ⟨a ~ stormy . . . winter voyage —C.H.Grandgent⟩ ⟨the final effect, ~ with modern furniture, could . . . have been barnlike —Betty Pepis⟩ **e** *obs* : in a familiar or intimate way ⟨with whom he was very ~ acquainted —Henry Fielding⟩ **2** : in the manner of a particular (as a term, predication, or proposition) in logic

**particular partnership** *n* : a partnership formed for a single transaction or enterprise as distinguished from one organized for carrying on a general business

**particular solution** *n* : the solution of a differential equation obtained by assigning particular values to the arbitrary constants in the general solution

**particular synod** *n, often cap P&S* : a governing body above a classis and below a general synod in various Reformed Churches

**particular tenant** *n* : a tenant holding a particular estate

¹**par·tic·u·late** \-kyələt, -,lāt\ *adj* [L *particula* small part, particle + E *-ate* — more at PARTICLE] **1** : existing in the form of minute separate particles ⟨the transport of ~ matter by the atmosphere —Nelson Dingle⟩ ⟨the application of high-energy beams of . . . ~ radiation —*Nature*⟩ **2** : of or relating to distinct particles ⟨the ~ theory of heredity —Julian Huxley⟩ ⟨the radioactivity in fallout is largely in ~ form —Merril Eisenbud⟩

²**particulate** \"\ *n* -s : a particulate substance ⟨designed to indicate . . . the presence of airborne radioactive ~*s* —*Tracerlog*⟩ ⟨all cytoplasmic ~*s* remain constant in morphology during division —*Biol. Abstracts*⟩

**particulate inheritance** *n* : inheritance by the progeny of characters specif. transmitted by genes in the germ cells from one parent or the other or from both in accord with Mendel's laws — opposed to *blending inheritance;* compare QUANTITATIVE INHERITANCE

**par·ti·cule** \ˈpär|d·ə,kyül, ˈpä|, |tə-\ *n* -s [MF, fr. L *particula*] : PARTICLE — used esp. of *de* in French personal names

**par·tie car·rée** \,pär,tēkäˈrā, ,pärd·ē-\ *n* [F, party of two men and two women, fr. *partie* party + *carrée,* fem. of *carré* square] : a party of four persons ⟨as we were a *partie carrée,* you might have your rubber —A.Conan Doyle⟩

**partied** *past of* PARTY

**parties** *pl of* PARTY, *pres 3d sing of* PARTY

**par·tile** \ˈpär,tīl\ *adj* [LL *partilis* divisible, partial, fr. L *partire, partiri* to divide + *-ilis* -ile — more at PART] **1** *obs* : PARTIAL ⟨a ~ not a total eclipse —John Harvey⟩ **2** : exact to the same degree and minute or to the same degree — used of an astrological aspect

**par·ti·men** \ˈpärd·ə,men\ *n* -s [Prov, lit., division, fr. *parti* to divide (fr. L *partire, partiri*) + *-men* -ment (fr. L *-mentum*)] : a lyric poem of dispute composed by Provençal troubadours and characterized by a more limited range of debate than a tenson

**par·ti·men·to** \,pärd·əˈmen,tō\ *n, pl* **partimen·ti** \-,tē\ [It, lit., division, fr. *partire* to divide, go away (fr. L *partire, partiri* to divide) + *-mento* -ment (fr. L *-mentum*)] : a musical exercise in contrapuntal improvisation of the 17th and 18th centuries, generally played or written on a figured bass

**parti–mortgage certificate** *or* **parti–mortgage receipt** \ˈpär|d·ē, ˈpä|, |t|, |i + ,...\ *n* [*parti-mortgage* fr. ²*parti-* + *mortgage*] : a certificate of ownership of a fractional equitable interest in a participating mortgage

¹**parting** *n* -s [ME *partinge, parting,* fr. gerund of *parten* to part] **1** *archaic* : DEPARTURE ⟨nothing troubled me at my ~ from the island —Daniel Defoe⟩ **2 a** : the action of separating or dividing into parts : the state of being parted ⟨could feel the soft ~ of her lips —Hamilton Basso⟩ ⟨many failures which result in ~ of the drill pipe in the well bore —*Primer of Oil Well Drilling*⟩ **b** : separation of the constituents of alloys; *esp* : the separation of gold from silver (as in refining) **3 a** : mutual separation of two or more persons : the action of leaving one another : LEAVE-TAKING ⟨good night, good night! ~ is such sweet sorrow —Shak.⟩ **4** : a part or place where separation occurs: as **a** *chiefly Brit* : PART 11 ⟨wavy black hair, neatly brushed into a ~ —Christopher La Farge⟩ **b** : the joint where one section of a foundry mold meets another **5** : something that serves to separate two or more objects: **a** (1) : a thin depositional layer separating thick deposits (as shale in a coal seam) (2) : a geological joint or fissure **b** : the fine sand or other similar material used to prevent adhesions of the members of a foundry mold **6** : a process of making combs out of flat plates with little or no waste by cutting the combs two at a time so that the teeth of one comb are formed of the material in the interstices between the teeth of the other comb **7** : lamellar separation in a crystallized mineral due to a cause other than cleavage (as the presence of twinning lamellae) — **parting of the ways 1** : the place where a road divides into two or more roads leading in different directions **2 a** : a point of separation or divergence (as for persons traveling together) **b** : a point of decision : a place or time at which a choice must be made **c** : a critical point; *esp* : one at which events will shape the course of future developments

²**parting** *adj* [fr. pres. part. of ²*part*] **1** : being in the process of departing ⟨in the direction of the ~ figure —A.C.Benson⟩; *esp* : DYING 1a ⟨the curfew tolls the knell of ~ day —Thomas Gray⟩ ⟨fortify the ~ soul —J.M.Neale⟩ **2** : given, taken, or performed at parting : FAREWELL, FINAL ⟨he remembered his father's ~ advice —F.V.W.Mason⟩ ⟨added as a ~ shot⟩ **3** : serving to part : constituting a space or boundary between objects : DIVIDING, SEPARATING ⟨a ~ layer of pure flint —Charles Lyell⟩ **4** *archaic* : undergoing division : in the process of dividing : breaking up : BREAKING ⟨the ~ ship that instant is no more —William Falconer⟩ **5** : used in foundry work to prevent adhesion of parts of a mold to each other or of sand to molds ⟨~ compound⟩ ⟨~ dust⟩

**parting flask** *n* : a flask used for parting in assaying

**parting line** *n* : the line or plane along which sections of a foundry mold, die, or pattern separate

**parting pulley** *n* : SPLIT PULLEY

**parting stop** *n* : a piece of wood separating the top and bottom sashes in a double-hung window

**parting strip** *or* **parting slip** *n* : a thin piece used to separate two adjoining members in a sash window: **a** *or* **parting bead** : a thin strip of wood let into the pulley stile to keep the sashes apart **b** : a thin piece inserted in the window box to separate the weights

**parting tool** *n* **1** : a narrow-bladed tool used in turning or

parting tool 1

planing or for cutting a piece in two **2** : a tool used (as in lathe work) for cutting off pieces from the main body of stock being worked on

**par·ti pris** \,pär,tēˈprē\ *n, pl* **partis pris** \"\ [F] : a preconceived opinion : BIAS, PARTIALITY, PREJUDICE ⟨we can read without violent *parti pris* about the things of long ago —G.M. Trevelyan⟩ ⟨valuable workers, with no *parti pris* and a truly broad mind —*Times Lit. Supp.*⟩

¹**par·ti·san** *or* **par·ti·zan** \ˈpär|d·əzən, ˈpä|, |tə-, -əsən *sometimes* -,zaa *or* -aa(ə)n, *chiefly Brit* ,pätiˈzan\ *n* -s [MF *partisan,* fr. OIt *partigiano,* fr. *parte* part, party, faction, fr. L *part-, pars* part — more at PART] **1 a** : one that takes the part of another : an adherent to a party, faction, cause, or person ⟨neither by birth nor breeding . . . a ~ of the imperial cause —G.H.Sabine⟩ **b** : a strong or devoted supporter : a zealous advocate ⟨wrote frankly as a ~ of the liberals —W.A.White⟩ **c** : an adherent characterized by prejudiced, unreasoning, blind, or fanatical allegiance ⟨the chaotic, hysterical feelings of the . . . ~*s* of fascism —*Amer. Scholar*⟩ ⟨a doctrinaire and utopian ~ of democracy —R.A.Dahl⟩ **2 a** (1) : a member of a body of detached light troops engaged in making forays and harassing an enemy (2) : a leader or commander of such a body of light troops **b** : a member of a guerrilla band operating within enemy lines and engaged chiefly in demolition, incendiarism, sabotage, and diversionary attacks ⟨the ~*s* acted in . . . advance of regular army formations —C.P.Fitzgerald⟩ ⟨Polish ~*s* had blown up two trains —*Springfield (Mass.) Union*⟩ **3** [AmerF *partisan* leader of an Indian war party or hunting party, fr. F, member of a body of detached light troops, adherent to a party or person] : the leader of a band of No. American trappers

²**partisan** *or* **partizan** \"\ *adj* **1** : of, carried on by, or being military partisans ⟨captain of a ~ company of light dragoons —*Amer. Guide Series: Del.*⟩ ⟨~ fighters who . . . use every obscure trick of guerrilla warfare —*New Republic*⟩ ⟨~ warfare⟩ **2** : exhibiting, characterized by, or resulting from partisanship ⟨intensified ~ passions caused one noted duel —*Amer. Guide Series: Va.*⟩ ⟨the principle is that ~ politics stops at the water's edge —Arthur Krock⟩ ⟨criticism conceived in a purely fault-finding or ~ spirit —F.D.Roosevelt⟩ **3** : composed of, based upon, or controlled by a single political party or group ⟨change the Tariff Commission from a nonpartisan to a ~ body —*New Republic*⟩ ⟨giving the governor a greater degree of ~ control over the legislature —*Western Political Quarterly*⟩ — compare BIPARTISAN

³**partisan** *or* **partizan** \"\ *n* -s [MF *partisane,* fr. OIt *partigiana, partesana,* fem. of *partigiano*] : a military weapon of the 16th and 17th centuries having a long shaft and broad bladed head and resembling in part both a spear and a halberd

**par·ti·san·ism** \-,nizəm\ *n* -s : partisan spirit or conduct

**par·ti·san·ry** \-nrē, -ri\ *n* -ES : PARTISANSHIP

**par·ti·san·ship** *also* **par·ti·zan·ship** \ˈ⸗⸗⸗,ship\ *n* : the quality or state of being a partisan: as **a** : adherence to a single person or thing (as a cause, group, political party) **b** : a strong or sometimes blind and unreasoning adherence to a single cause or group : BIAS, ONE-SIDEDNESS, PREJUDICE ⟨choose between violent ~ and . . . cool detachment —J.F.Muehl⟩ ⟨seen . . . clearly and in due proportion, freed from the mists of prejudice and ~ —John Galsworthy⟩ **c** : conduct or attitudes resulting from or characterizing such adherence

**-par·tism** \,pär|,tizəm, ,pä|, *also* |d·,izəm\ *n comb form* -s [F *-partisme,* fr. *parti* political party (fr. MF, match, party, decision) + *-isme* — more at PARTI] : tendency toward or active operation of a (specified) number of political parties in a governmental system ⟨multi-*partism*⟩

**par·ti–striped** \ˈpär|d·ē, ˈpä|, |tē, -i+\ *adj* [¹*parti-* + *striped*] : having stripes of different colors

**par·ti·ta** \pärˈtēd·ə, päˈt-, -ētə\ *n* -s [It, fr. fem. of *partito,* past part. of *partire* to divide, go away, fr. L *partire, partiri* to divide — more at PART] **1** : a set of musical variations **2** : SUITE 2b(1)

**par·tite** \ˈpär,tīt, ˈpä| *also* |d·,īt, *usu* -īd·+V\ *adj* [L *partitus* divided, past part. of *partire, partiri* to divide] **1** : divided into a usu. specified number of parts or divisions ⟨the rule of four-*partite* military government —*New Republic*⟩ ⟨sex*partite* vaulting —T.F.Bumpus⟩ **2** : PARTED 1c ⟨a ~ leaf⟩

¹**par·ti·tion** \pärˈtishən, pə(r)ˈt-, päˈt-\ *n* -s *often attrib* [ME *particioun,* fr. MF *partition,* fr. L *partition-, partitio,* fr. *partitus* (past part. of *partire, partiri* to divide) + *-ion-, -io* -ion] **1 a** : the action of parting or the state of being parted : DISTRIBUTION, DIVISION, SEPARATION ⟨the exact ~ of power among kings, lords, and commons —T.B. Macaulay⟩ ⟨the ~ of the world into the animate and the inanimate —W.R.Inge⟩ ⟨the ~ of available living space among members of the same . . . species —W.H.Dowdeswell⟩ **b** : the severance voluntarily or by legal proceedings of common or undivided interests esp. in real estate : a division into severalty of property held jointly or in common or the sale of such property by a court and the division of the proceeds **c** (1) : the action of dividing an area forming a single governmental unit into two or more areas under separate authorities ⟨called for the ~ of that country into independent Jewish and Arab states —*Current Biog.*⟩ (2) : the condition or territorial and political organization resulting from such division ⟨the present ~ of Germany into eastern and western regions —*List of Books*⟩ ⟨conceived of a permanent ~ of the continent in terms of the natural boundaries —R.W.Van Alstyne⟩ **d** *logic* : analysis of a class into constituent subclasses **2 a** : something that divides or separates : something by which different things or distinct parts of the same thing are separated; *esp* : an interior wall dividing one part of a structure (as a house, room, or enclosure) from another ⟨a huge space subdivided by light, movable ~*s* —*Current Biog.*⟩ ⟨in banquet halls . . . folding ~*s* are very popular —*Sweet's Catalog Service*⟩ **b** : one of a set of paperboard sheets slotted and assembled in a case to form cells for holding and protecting goods or packages in shipment **3** : one of the parts into which a whole is divided (as a portion, section, or division) ⟨the fruit falls to the ground and splits into ~*s* —*Amer. Guide Series: La.*⟩ ⟨the temple was divided into two noble ~*s* —Frances Brooke⟩ **4** : PARTITUR

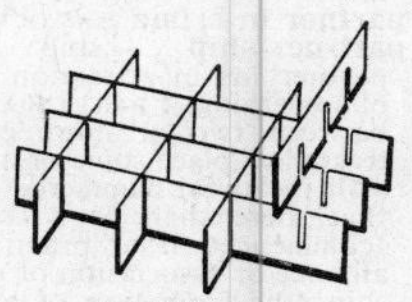

partitions 2b

²**partition** \"\ *vt* **partitioned; partitioned; partitioning** \-sh(ə)niŋ\ **partitions 1 a** : to divide into parts or shares; *specif* : divide (as an estate) into severalty **b** : to divide (as a country) into two or more territorial units having separate political status ⟨the foreign powers ~*ed* the whole country —Owen & Eleanor Lattimore⟩ ⟨the former German capital was ~*ed* among the . . . allies —*Saturday Rev.*⟩ **2** : to sepa-

rate or divide into distinct parts by a partition (as a wall) ⟨~ed the great hall into many cubicles⟩ — often used with *off* ⟨~ off a closet from the storage area⟩

**par·ti·tion·al** \-shənᵊl, -shnəl\ *adj, archaic* **:** of, relating to, or of the nature of a partition

**partition chromatography** *n* **:** a process for the separation of mixtures in columns or on filter paper based on partition of a solute between two solvents one of which is immobilized by the substance in the column or by the paper

**partition coefficient** *n* **:** DISTRIBUTION COEFFICIENT

**par·ti·tioned** \-shənd\ *adj* **:** furnished with or separated by partitions

**par·ti·tion·er** \-sh(ə)nə(r)\ *n* -S **:** one that partitions ⟨among the enemies and ~s of Czechoslovakia —*Times Lit. Supp.*⟩

**par·ti·tion·ing** \-sh(ə)niŋ, -nēŋ\ *n* -S [¹*partition* + *-ing*] **1 :** work (as in a building) consisting of partitions **2 :** material for partitions

**par·ti·tion·ist** \-sh(ə)nəst\ *n* -S **:** an advocate of political partition

¹**par·ti·tive** \'pärd·əd·iv, 'pä|, |tətiv\ *adj* [ML *partitivus* serving to indicate that of which a part is specified, fr. L *partitus* (past part. of *partire, partiri* to divide) + *-ivus* -ive] **1 :** serving to part or divide into parts **:** indicating or characterized by partition ⟨~ tendencies in education⟩ ⟨the tragedy of our present ~ social adaptation —W.E.Galt⟩ **2 a** (1) **:** of, relating to, or denoting a part ⟨a ~ construction⟩ (2) **:** serving to indicate that of which a part is specified ⟨a ~ genitive⟩ **b :** of, relating to, or constituting a grammatical case (as in Finnish) that denotes part of something

²**partitive** \"\ *n* -S **1 :** a word expressing partition or denoting a part **2 a :** the partitive case in a language **b :** a word in the partitive case

**par·ti·tive·ly** \-əvlē, -li\ *adv* **:** in a partitive way or sense

**par·ti·tur** \,pärd·ə¦tü(ə)r\ *or* **par·ti·tu·ra** \,==ˈtùrə\ *n* -S [*partitur* fr. G, fr. It *partitura*, fr. *partito* (past part. of *partire* to divide, go away, fr. L *partire, partiri* to divide) + *-ura* -ure (fr. L); *partitura* fr. It — more at PART] **:** a full musical score showing each part on a separate line or staff

**par·ti·ver·sal** \¦pärd·ə¦vərsəl\ *adj* [²*parti-* + *-versal* (as in *quaquaversal*)] *geol* **:** dipping in different directions approximately to the extent of half a circle (as at each end of an anticlinal axis) — contrasted with *quaquaversal*

**partizan** *var of* PARTISAN

**part leading** *n* **:** VOICE LEADING

¹**part·let** \'pärtlət, 'pät-, *usu* -əd·+V\ *n* -S [alter. of ME (Sc) *patelet*, fr. MF *patelette* band of cloth, dim. of *patte* paw — more at PATTEN] **:** a covering for the neck and shoulders worn chiefly by women in the 16th century and consisting of a separate fill-in for low necklines or of the decorative neckline of an undershirt made usu. of embroidered or pleated gauze or muslin and finished with a small ruff or frill

²**partlet** \"\ *n* -S [*Partlet*, proper name of a hen, fr. ME *Pertelote*, hen that is the favorite wife of Chanticleer (Chaunteclecr) in Chaucer's *Nun's Priest's Tale*] **:** HEN ⟨an ever resounding cackle from his complacent ~s —C.G.D.Roberts⟩

**part·ly** *adv* **:** with respect to a part rather than a whole **:** in some measure or degree **:** PARTIALLY ⟨an interpretation which, while not entirely convincing, is at least ~ true —E.O.Reischauer⟩ ⟨his disease was ~ magical and ~ natural —Robert Burton⟩

**part music** *n* **1 :** vocal music for several voices in independent parts usu. without accompaniment **2 :** concerted or harmonized music esp. of the vocal type

**partn** *abbr* partition

¹**part·ner** \'pär|tnər, 'pä|tnə(r, *chiefly in substand speech or as a term of address* |dn-\ *n* -S [ME *partener*, alter. (influenced by ¹*part*) of *parcener*, fr. AF, coparcener, partner — more at PARCENER] **1** *archaic* **:** one that shares in the possession or enjoyment of something with another **:** PARTAKER, SHARER ⟨entreated a gentleman . . . to admit me ~ of his bed —Fynes Moryson⟩ **2 a :** one that is associated in any action with another **:** ASSOCIATE, COLLEAGUE ⟨make us ~s in the deliberative process —B.N.Cardozo⟩ ⟨a steady military buildup with our ~s throughout the world —D.D.Eisenhower⟩ **b** (1) **:** either of a couple who dance together (2) **:** the lady on the right of a man or the man on the left of a lady in a square dance set — compare CORNER 7, CORNER LADY, OPPOSITE LADY, RIGHT-HAND LADY **c :** one of two or more persons who play together in a game against an opposing side **d :** either of two married persons **:** HUSBAND, WIFE **3 a :** one of two or more persons associated as joint principals in carrying on any business with a view to joint profit **:** a member of a partnership — compare GENERAL PARTNER, NOMINAL PARTNER, OSTENSIBLE PARTNER, SECRET PARTNER, SILENT PARTNER, SPECIAL PARTNER **b :** one held to resemble such a partner in having with others joint rights and responsibilities (as in an enterprise) ⟨can men of different races live as ~s —Elspeth Huxley⟩ **4 :** one of the heavy timbers forming a framework built around an opening in the deck of a ship to strengthen the deck (as for the support of a mast) — usu. used in pl.

²**partner** \"\ *vb* -ED/-ING/-S *vt* **1 :** to join or associate with another as a partner ⟨British seapower, ~ed with the French, beat them off —*Time*⟩ **2 :** to be or act as the partner of ⟨uncle has played alongside nephew and brother has ~ed brother —William Morrow⟩ ~ *vi* **:** to be or act as a partner ⟨him and me, we ~ed once —A.B.Mayse⟩ ⟨he still ~ed with Tom on the piers —R.O.Bowen⟩

**partner by estoppel :** NOMINAL PARTNER

**partner in commendam :** a partner in civil law whose liability to creditors of the partnership is restricted to the capital furnished or agreed to be furnished so long as he does not become active and who resembles a limited partner in common law

**partner in crime :** ASSOCIATE 1

**part·ner·ship** \'==,ship\ *n* **1 :** the fact or state of being a partner (as in an action or in the possession or enjoyment of something) **:** PARTICIPATION **2 a :** a legal relation existing between two or more competent persons who have contracted to place some or all of their money, effects, labor, and skill in lawful commerce or business with the understanding that there shall be a communion of profit between them ⟨commenced legal practice in ~ with his uncle⟩ **b :** an alliance or association of persons joined together in a partnership ⟨the formation of a ~ is a common-law right —*Jour. of Accountancy*⟩ **c :** the persons joined together in a partnership ⟨the ~ computes its net income . . . in a manner similar to that of an individual —J.K.Lasser⟩ **d :** the contract by which a partnership relation is created **3 :** a relationship resembling a legal partnership and usu. involving close cooperation between parties having specified and joint rights and responsibilities (as in a common enterprise) ⟨an effective working ~ between scientists and military men —Vannevar Bush⟩ ⟨~ in electric power projects between the states and the federal government⟩

**partnership life insurance** *n* **:** BUSINESS LIFE INSURANCE 1

**part of speech** [trans. of LL *pars orationis*, trans. of Gk *meros logou*] **1 :** a traditional class of words distinguished according to the kind of idea denoted and the function performed in a sentence **:** MAJOR FORM CLASS — compare ADJECTIVE, ADVERB, CONJUNCTION, INTERJECTION, NOUN, PREPOSITION, PRONOUN, VERB **2 :** a word belonging to a particular part of speech

**partook** *past of* PARTAKE

**part owner** *n* **:** one of several owners having no contractual agreement regarding their joint property (as tenants in common or sometimes joint tenants); *specif* **:** a co-owner of a ship

**par·trick** \'pär·trik\ *Scot var of* PARTRIDGE

¹**par·tridge** \'pär·trij, *chiefly dial & old-fash* 'pä·-\ *n* -S *see sense 1* [ME *partrich, partrik*, modif. of OF *perdris*, modif. of L *perdic-, perdix*, fr. Gk *perdik-, perdix*; perh. akin to Gk *perdesthai* to break wind; fr. the whirring sound of its wings as it takes flight — more at FART] **1** *or pl* **partridge a :** any of various typically medium-sized stout-bodied Old World gallinaceous game birds of *Perdix, Alectoris*, and related genera that have variegated but not gaudily colored plumage, short wings and tail, and rather short legs and neck — see GREEK PARTRIDGE, RED-LEGGED PARTRIDGE **b :** any of numerous gallinaceous birds that are more or less like the Old World partridges in size, habits, or value as game: (1) *chiefly NewEng* **:** RUFFED GROUSE (2) *chiefly South & Midland* **:** BOBWHITE (3) **:** any of several gamebirds belonging to the same subfamily as the bobwhite — usu. used with a qualifying term; see MOUNTAIN PARTRIDGE (4) **:** any of various Asiatic birds (as a bamboo partridge, snow partridge, or hill partridge) **c :** any of several tinamous **d** *Austral* **:** BUTTON QUAIL **2 :** PARTRIDGEWOOD **3 :** RAW UMBER 2

²**partridge** \"\ *adj, usu cap* **:** having a characteristic color pattern resembling that of a partridge — used esp. of poultry ⟨*Partridge* Wyandotte⟩ ⟨Plymouth Rock with *Partridge* plumage⟩

**partridgeberry** \'==·— *see* BERRY\ *n* **1 :** an American trailing plant (*Mitchella repens*) having roundish evergreen leaves and white fragrant flowers growing in pairs with the ovaries united **2 :** the persistent edible but insipid scarlet fruit of the partridgeberry — called also *checkerberry*

partridgeberry

**partridge bronzewing** *or* **partridge pigeon** *n* **:** an Australian bronzewing (*Geophaps scripta*) formerly abundant in dry inland parts of western Australia — called also *squatter*

**partridge dove** *n* **:** a Jamaican quail dove (*Oreopeleia montana*)

**partridge pea** *n* **:** SENSITIVE PEA

**partridge plant** *or* **partridge vine** *n* **:** WINTERGREEN 2a

**partridge shell** *n* **1 :** a large marine gastropod (*Dolium perdix*) **2 :** the varicolored shell of the partridge shell — compare TUN SHELL

**partridgewood** \'==,=\ *n* **1 a** (1) **:** the hard reddish mottled wood of a tree of the genus *Andira* (esp. *A. americana*) used esp. for walking sticks and cabinetwork — called also *acapu, pheasantwood* (2) **:** a tree yielding such wood **b :** the dark wood of any of several West Indian cabbage palms **c :** GRANADILLA WOOD 4 **d :** the light ornately marked gray wood of an Australian fan palm (*Livistona inermis*) **2 :** wood characteristically speckled as the result of attack by a fungus (*Stereum frustulosum*)

**parts** *pl of* PART, *pres 3d sing of* PART

**part-score** \'=¦=\ *n* **:** a trick score or contract in bridge that is less than enough for game — called also *partial score*

**parts maker** *n* **:** a manufacturer producing components for incorporation in assemblies made by another

**part-song** \'=,=\ *n* **1 :** a 15th century German song for several voice parts **2 :** a homophonic vocal composition usu. in four parts and often unaccompanied; *esp* **:** a choral work of the 19th century

**part time** *n* **:** an amount of time less than full time ⟨70 percent of the . . . pupils have been on *part time* —*Amer. Guide Series: N.J.*⟩

**part-time** *adj* [*part time*] **1 :** employed for or working less than the amount of time considered customary or standard ⟨*part-time* worker⟩ ⟨*part-time* student⟩ **2 :** involving or operating less than the amount of time considered customary or standard ⟨continuing their education on a *part-time* basis —L.L.Bethel⟩ ⟨*part-time* schools⟩ ⟨*part-time* jobs⟩

**part-timer** \'=¦==\ *n* **:** one that works or is employed on a part-time basis ⟨the lobstermen sometimes are *part-timers* who hold factory jobs ashore —Thomas Horgan⟩

**part title** *n* **:** DIVISIONAL TITLE

**par·tu·la** \'pärchələ\ *n* [NL] **1** *cap* **:** a genus of thin-shelled land and tree snails (suborder Stylommatophora) of the islands of the Pacific that are of great interest to collectors because of their very numerous and highly localized races and species **2** *pl* **partu·lae** \-ə,lē, -,lī\ **:** any snail of the genus *Partula*

**parturiency** *n* -ES [*parturient* + *-cy*] *obs* **:** the quality or state of being parturient ⟨~ with respect to politics and public counsels —George Berkeley⟩

¹**par·tu·ri·ent** \pär'tùrēənt, pä|, |·tyù-\ *adj* [L *parturient-, parturiens*, pres. part. of *parturire* to be in labor, desiderative of *parere* to give birth to, beget, produce — more at PARE] **1 a :** bringing forth or about to bring forth young **:** engaged in parturition ⟨a ~ heifer⟩ **b :** of or relating to parturition ⟨~ pangs⟩ **c :** typical of parturition ⟨the ~ uterus⟩ **2 :** being at the point of producing something (as an idea, discovery, or literary work)

²**parturient** \"\ *n* -S **:** a parturient individual

**parturient paresis** *or* **parturient apoplexy** *n* **:** MILK FEVER 2a

**par·tu·ri·fa·cient** \=¦rə¦fāshənt\ *adj* [L *parturire* to be in labor + E *-facient*] **:** inducing parturition

**par·tu·ri·tion** \,pärd·ə'rishən, ,pä|, |tə'-, |,tü'-, |chə'-, |,tyə'-, |·,tyü'-\ *n* -S [LL *parturition-, parturitio*, fr. *parturit-* (fr. L *parturire* to be in labor) + L *-ion-, -io* -ion] **:** the action or process of giving birth to offspring

**partway** \'=¦=\ *adv* **:** to a part of a distance **:** to some extent **:** PARTIALLY, PARTLY ⟨bony shelf . . . extends ~ toward the outer wall —F.A.Geldard⟩ ⟨an even ~ ideal state of human affairs —Charles Merz⟩ ⟨clawing with his feet and getting ~ up —Ernie Pyle⟩

**part writing** *n* **:** the writing of part music; *specif* **:** the art and science of counterpoint

¹**par·ty** \'pärd·ē, 'pä|, |tē, -i\ *n* -ES [ME *partie* part, portion, party, body of persons forming one side (as in a contest), fr. OF, fr. fem. of *parti*, past part. of *partir* to divide, go away — more at PART] **1** *obs* **:** a part of a whole **:** DIVISION, PORTION, SHARE **2 a :** one (as a person or group) constituting alone or with others one of the two sides in a proceeding ⟨the ~ of the first part and her husband . . . as ~ of the second part entered into a separation agreement —*Southeastern Reporter*⟩ ⟨the two *parties* to a marriage contract⟩ **b** (1) **:** one (as an individual, firm, or corporation) that constitutes the plaintiff or the defendant in a lawsuit **:** LITIGANT (2) **:** one directly disclosed by the record to be so involved in the prosecution or defense of a proceeding as to be bound by the decision or judgment therein (3) **:** one indirectly disclosed by the record as being directly interested in the subject matter of a suit or as having power to make a defense, control the proceedings, or appeal from the judgment **3 a :** a body of persons forming one side (as in a contest) **:** a group united in opinion or action as distinguished from or opposed to a similar or larger group (as the rest of a community or association) **:** a body of partisans or adherents ⟨a war . . . in which both *parties* exerted their utmost strength —William Robertson †1793⟩ **b** (1) **:** a group of persons organized for the purpose of directing the policies of a government esp. by providing the principal political personnel and usu. having as a basis for common action one or more factors (as principle, special interest, or tradition) upon which they have substantial agreement — compare FACTION 1, PRESSURE GROUP (2) **:** an organization constituted a political party under the laws of certain states (as New York) by polling a fixed number or percentage of the total votes cast at an election and thereby possessing the right to appear on the ballot at a succeeding election (3) **:** the political party constituting a principal focus of loyalty or the chief means of operating a governmental system ⟨we may deprecate some of the effects of ~ —Ernest Barker⟩ ⟨compelled . . . to modify his aversion to ~ —Kenneth Mackenzie⟩ **4** *archaic* **:** one of two or more sides (as in a contest, dispute, or contract) **:** CAUSE, INTEREST ⟨many feats of arms were there done on both *parties* —Richard Grafton⟩ **5 :** one (as a person or group) that takes part with others in an action or affair **:** one of several persons engaging or concerned in a transaction **:** PARTICIPANT ⟨should be a ~ in the educational council and participate freely in its deliberation —C.W.Hoff⟩ — usu. used with *to* ⟨Greece and Turkey were brought in as *parties* to the treaty —A.P.Ryan⟩ ⟨the candidate . . . was in no way a ~ to the transaction —S.H. Adams⟩ **6 a :** the individual in question or involved in the case at hand **:** the specific person to whom reference is made ⟨words . . . which generally make the *parties* affected melancholy —Robert Burton⟩ **b :** a particular individual **:** PERSON ⟨he is a shameless and determined old ~ —Winston Churchill⟩ ⟨a rich old ~ who . . . dies and leaves him a fortune —A.H. Weiler⟩ **7** [MF *parti* match, party, decision, fr. *parti*, past part. of *partir* to divide, go away] *obs* **:** a decision on one side or the other **:** RESOLUTION — used chiefly in the phrase *to take a party* ⟨I am not come to ask counsel . . . my ~ is taken —John Vanbrugh⟩ **8 :** a group usu. constituting a detachment from a larger body or company: as **a :** a small number of military personnel dispatched or detailed on special service or duty ⟨infantry . . . repulsed a landing ~ from the British fleet —*Amer. Guide Series: Md.*⟩ ⟨foraging ~⟩ ⟨firing ~⟩ **b :** a group of people working together on a common project or assignment ⟨the men were divided into *parties* of twelve, each ~ to build a hut —H.E.Scudder⟩ ⟨a working ~ on filing systems was . . . appointed —*Library Science Abstracts*⟩ **9** [F *parti* match, party, decision, fr. MF] *archaic* **:** ¹MATCH 4b ⟨try . . . to make him look upon either of your daughters as a desirable ~ for him —Charlotte Smith⟩ **10** [F *partie* social gathering for pleasure, part, portion, party, body of persons forming one side (as in a contest), fr. OF, part, portion, party, body of persons forming one side (as in a contest)] **a :** a social gathering or assembly of persons for entertainment, amusement, or pleasure ⟨asked to cocktail and dinner *parties* —Rose Thurburn⟩ ⟨impulse to gate-crash . . . a private ~ —*Encounter*⟩ ⟨dancing ~⟩ ⟨shooting ~⟩ **b :** something held to resemble (as in appearance or purpose) such a social gathering: as (1) **:** ¹BEE 3 ⟨donation ~⟩ ⟨lynching ~⟩ ⟨scalping ~⟩ (2) **:** a social gathering where the demonstration and sale of articles is the principal feature (3) **:** an occasion on which a specified person is predominant ⟨this is your ~. You're doing the talking —Erle Stanley Gardner⟩ **11** [F *partie* game (as of cards), part, portion, party, body of persons forming one side (as in a contest), fr. OF, part, portion, party, body of persons forming one side (as in a contest)] *archaic* **a :** a game of cards or backgammon **b :** a match in such a game **12 :** PARTISANSHIP ⟨the spirit of ~ which unhappily prevails amongst mankind —Joseph Butler⟩ **13 a :** a group of animals moving or otherwise gathered together ⟨a ~ of over forty hinds with calves . . . passed slowly —Richard Rhodes⟩ ⟨a lively bird seen . . . occasionally in small *parties* —Ernst Mayr⟩ **b :** a company or association of persons ⟨a ~ of visitors from the country —G.B.Shaw⟩; *specif* **:** one formed or gathered together for a particular purpose (as travel, amusement, or attendance at a function) ⟨join a ~ of thirteen American editors to visit Great Britain —Edward Bok⟩ ⟨snowshoeing *parties* . . . visit the snow-clad headland in winter —*Amer. Guide Series: Me.*⟩ **14 :** an act of sexual intercourse

²**party** \"\ *adj* **1 :** being a participating, interested, or otherwise involved party — used with *to* ⟨they refused to be ~ to any arrangement that coerced their employees —Mary K. Hammond⟩ ⟨individuals who are ~ to the relationship —A.J. Vidich⟩ **2 :** characterized by joint ownership or shared use ⟨the ~ fence that divided his backyard from that of his sisters —J.P.Bishop⟩ — see PARTY LINE 2, PARTY WALL **3 a** (1) **:** of, relating to, or associated with a political party ⟨leadership is inherent in ~ organization —C.J.Friedrich⟩ ⟨a conference of rural ~ secretaries —F.C.Barghoorn⟩ ⟨the ~ agent was . . . the sole official tie between the party and municipality —R.H.Wells⟩ (2) **:** in, toward, or favoring a political party ⟨a good ~ paper . . . never published fair news of the opposition —F.L.Mott⟩ ⟨~ membership⟩ ⟨~ loyalty⟩ ⟨~ discipline⟩ **b :** of, between, or based upon political parties ⟨the ~ system has become . . . an integral part of parliamentary democracy —*Brit. Parliament*⟩ ⟨~ alliances⟩ **4 :** suitable for a party or similar social gathering ⟨~ dress⟩ ⟨~ manners⟩ ⟨~ cake⟩ ⟨~ game⟩ **5 :** fond of or addicted to parties and high living ⟨~ boys . . . trying to recapture lost youth —F.J.Taylor⟩

³**party** \"\ *vb* -ED/-ING/-ES *vt* **1** *obs* **:** to side with **:** take the part of ⟨did assist and ~ them in all their enterprises —David Hume †1630?⟩ **2 :** to entertain at or by means of parties ⟨finds himself cocktailed, partied, and dined —Ray Josephs⟩ ~ *vi* **:** to attend, take part in, or hold parties and other social gatherings ⟨drinking . . . ~*ing*, or making love —J.W.Aldridge⟩ ⟨this season's . . . social slump on ~*ing* —Alice Dameron⟩

⁴**party** \"\ *adj* [MF *parti* striped, party per pale — more at PARTI-] **1 :** PARTY PER PALE 1 ⟨a silver leopard upon a field ~ gold and gules —W.H. St. John Hope⟩ **2** *heraldry* **:** divided into two or more parts having different tinctures or bearing different coats of arms ⟨arms with ~ fields —W.H. St. John Hope⟩; *esp* **:** divided into parts by a line or lines in the direction and position of one of the ordinaries — followed by a phrase beginning with *per* (as *per bend*) or an adverb in *-wise* or *-ways* (as *bendwise* or *bendways*) indicative of the direction and position of the partition; in modern blazon less usual than a phrase in *per* without preceding adj.

**party-** — see PARTI-

**party-column ballot** \¦==¦==-\ *n* **:** INDIANA BALLOT

**party emblem** *n* **:** a pictured device (as a gamecock, an eagle, a torch) placed at the head of the party column on a ballot to aid voters in identifying each party

**party girl** *n* **:** a woman employed to entertain men esp. at parties; *specif* **:** PROSTITUTE ⟨a *party girl* selling a night's pleasure —Luther Robbins⟩

**partygoer** \'==,==\ *n* **:** one that attends parties and similar social gatherings esp. regularly or frequently ⟨gay clothes . . . for the teen-age ~ —*New Yorker*⟩

**party government** *n* **:** the direction and control of the processes of government by a single political party usu. by provision of the principal political officials and operation of the formal governmental machinery ⟨in Europe the importance of *party government* has long been recognized —A.N.Holcombe⟩

**par·ty·ism** *pronunc at* PARTY +,izəm\ *n* -S **1 :** devotion to a political party **:** party spirit ⟨the ~ . . . by which the great issue was obscured —Goldwin Smith⟩ **2 :** a party system ⟨cliques and ~ were nonexistent —I.M.Price⟩ — often used in combination ⟨one-*partyism* is on the way out —*Birmingham (Ala.) News*⟩

**party jury** *n* [obs. E *party*, adj., parti-colored, having a mixed character + E *jury* — more at PARTI-] **:** a jury de medietate linguae

**party line** *n* **1 :** a line of demarcation held to distinguish a political party in policy or practice or to limit the action of all loyal party members — usu. used in pl. ⟨the house . . . organized quickly along straight *party lines* —W.V.Shannon⟩ ⟨elections . . . not fought on *party lines* —*Scotsman*⟩ ⟨cut across all *party lines* in . . . search for supporters —*Atlantic*⟩ **2** *or* **party wire :** a single telephone circuit connecting two or more subscribers with the exchange **3 :** the bounding line between the properties of two or more parties **4 a :** the complex of policies and attitudes followed or advocated by the Communist party — usu. used with *the* ⟨the *party line* changed from collaboration with the U.S. to antagonism —J.C.Cort⟩ ⟨Communists adhering to the *party line* shifted their stand —J.S.Roucek⟩ **b :** the complex of principles, policies, and attitudes advocated by or associated with an individual, group, or organization ⟨follows closely the official *party line* of organized medicine —H.B.Richardson⟩ ⟨the whole labor *party line* —D.C.Coyle⟩

**party-line** *adj* [*party line*] **:** characterized by or resulting from adherence to a party line (as of a political party) ⟨*party-line* doctrine⟩ ⟨*party-line* causes⟩

**party-liner** \¦==¦==\ *n* **:** one that adheres to a party line; *specif* **:** one that adheres to the Communist party line ⟨a directory of suspected Reds and *party-liners* —*Time*⟩ — compare FELLOW TRAVELER

**party man** *n* **:** a member or adherent of a political party; *esp* **:** one characterized in cases of conflicting interests by strong loyalty to the party as an institution and to its principles and policies

**party per pale** *adj* **1** *heraldry* **:** divided into two parts by a line down the middle ⟨three chevrons *party per pale* —A.R. Wagner⟩ **2** *archaic* **:** twofold in character **:** COMPOSITE, HALF-AND-HALF

**party politics** *n pl but usu sing in constr* **:** politics engaged in by, expressed through the medium of, or considered from the viewpoint of political parties as distinguished from other interests (as geographical sections or economic classes) ⟨a symbol of its unity over and above . . . *party politics* —A.L. Rowse⟩

**party question** *n* **:** a subject characterized by differences of opinion resulting from party allegiances rather than other factors

**party vote** *n* **:** a vote (as in a legislature) cast along party lines ⟨strict *party votes* occur . . . on the organization of the House and Senate —Dean Acheson⟩

**party wall** *n* **:** a wall which divides two adjoining properties usu. having half its thickness on each property and in which each of the owners of the adjoining properties has rights of enjoyment **:** a wall on or near the boundary line between adjoining owners and owned by them in common or in severalty or by one owner alone and providing mutual rights of support for the respective adjacent buildings or structures

**par·u·la** \ˈpar(y)ələ\ *n, cap* [NL, fr. L *parus* titmouse + *-ula*] **:** the type genus of Parulidae including the parula warblers

**parula blue** *n* **:** a grayish blue that is redder and paler than electric, greener and paler than copenhagen, and redder and lighter than Gobelin

**parula warbler** *n* **:** a small grayish blue American warbler (*Parula americana*) of eastern No. America having an olive-green patch on the back

**¹paru·lid** \ˈpar(y)ələd, pəˈrül-\ *adj* [NL *Parulidae*] **:** of or relating to the Parulidae

**²parulid** *n* -s **:** a bird of the family Parulidae **:** WOOD WARBLER

**pa·ru·li·dae** \pəˈrüləˌdē\ *n pl, cap* [NL, fr. *Parula*, type genus + *-idae*] **:** a family of small bright-colored passerine birds containing the American warblers — see WOOD WARBLER

**pa·ru·lis** \-ləs\ *n, pl* **paruli·des** \-ləˌdēz\ [NL *parulid-, parulis*, fr. Gk *paroulid-, paroulis*, fr. *para-* ¹para- + *-oulid-, -oulis* (fr. *oulon* gum); prob. akin to Gk *eilein* to wind, roll — more at VOLUBLE] **:** an abscess in the gum **:** GUMBOIL

**par·umbilical** \(ˈ)par+\ *adj* [ISV ¹*para-* + *umbilical*] **:** near the umbilicus; *specif* **:** being any of several small veins that connect the portal and epigastric veins

**pa·rure** \pəˈru̇(ə)r, -üə\ *n* -s [F, lit., adornment, fr. OF *pareure*, fr. *parer* to adorn, prepare + *-ure* — more at PARE] **:** a matched set of jewelry or other ornaments worn together ⟨a ~ of emeralds including a necklace, bracelets, earrings, and tiara⟩

**par·us** \ˈpa(a)rəs\ *n, cap* [NL, fr. L, titmouse] **:** the type genus of Paridae comprising various common titmice

**parv-** *or* **parvi-** *also* **parvo-** *comb form* [L *parv-, parvi-*, fr. *parvus*; akin to Gk *pauros* small, slight — more at FEW] **:** small ⟨*parv*animity⟩ ⟨*parvi*folious⟩ ⟨*Parvo*bacteriaceae⟩

**par·va** \ˈpärvə, ˈpȧvə\ *n* -s [NL, fr. L, fem. of *parvus* small] **:** a late larval stage of shrimps of the tribe Carides

**par value** *n* **:** ¹PAR 1b

**par·va·nim·i·ty** \ˌpärvəˈnimədē\ *n* -ES [*parv-* + *-animity* (as in *magnanimity*)] **:** the quality or state of having a little or ignoble mind **:** MEANNESS — opposed to *magnanimity*

**parve** *var of* PAREVE

**¹par·ve·nu** \ˈpärvəˌn(y)ü, ˈpȧv- *also* ˌ==ˈ=\ *n* -s [F, fr. *parvenu*, past part. of *parvenir* to arrive, fr. L *pervenire*, fr. *per* through + *venire* to come — more at FARE, COME] **:** one that has risen (as by the acquisition of wealth or power) above the station in life in which he was born; *esp* **:** one that is unaccustomed to his new station or that makes great pretensions because of his acquired wealth **:** UPSTART ⟨loudmouthed ~*s* who took care to obtain great publicity for their charitable works —Leslie Charteris⟩ ⟨the gentry may be the ~*s* of a few generations back —Roy Lewis & Angus Maude⟩

**²par·ve·nu** *or* **par·ve·nue** \"\ *adj* **:** newly risen to position esp. through the acquisition of wealth or power **:** like or having the characteristics of a parvenu ⟨the threatening power of the ~ middle class —Edmund Wilson⟩ ⟨that vulgar ~ house —Jean Stafford⟩ ⟨there was nothing ~ in the penniless lad —*Harper's*⟩

**parvenue** \"\ *n* -s [F, fr. *parvenue*, fem. of *parvenu*, past part. of *parvenir* to arrive] **:** a parvenu woman

**par·ve·nu·ism** \-üˌizəm\ *n* -s **:** parvenu nature or behavior ⟨there is an element of ~ about him —Emily Eden⟩

**par·vis** *also* **par·vise** \ˈpärvəs\ *n, pl* **parvises** [ME *parvys*, fr. MF *parvis, parevis* parvis, paradise, modif. of LL *paradisus* enclosed park, garden, paradise — more at PARADISE] **1 a :** a court or an enclosed space before a building (as a church or cathedral) often surrounded by a balustrade or parapet or with colonnades or porticos **b :** a single portico or colonnade before a church **:** a church porch **2** *obs* **:** a public and usu. academic conference or debate **3 :** a room over a church porch

**par·vi·tude** \ˈpärvəˌtüd, -vəˌtyüd\ *n* -s [*parv-* + *-tude*] **1** *obs* **:** an extremely small or minute thing **:** ATOM **2 :** the quality or state of being little **:** SMALLNESS ⟨differ in magnitude and ~ —Thomas Taylor⟩

**parvity** *n* -ES [L *parvitat-, parvitas*, fr. *parvus* small + *-itat-, -itas* -ity] *obs* **:** PARVITUDE 2

**par·vo·bacteriaceae** \ˌpärvō+\ [NL, fr. *parv-* + *Bacteriaceae*] *syn of* BRUCELLACEAE

**par·vule** \ˈpär(ˌ)vyül\ *n* -s [L *parvulus* very small, fr. *parvus* small] **:** a very small pill

**pa·ryph·o·drome** \pəˈrifəˌdrōm\ *adj* [*paryph-* (fr. Gk *paryphē* border woven along a robe, fr. *para-* ¹para- + *hyphē* web) + *-drome*; akin to Gk *hyphainein* to weave — more at WEAVE] **:** having a vein that closely follows the margin — used of a form of leaf venation

**pas** \ˈpä\ *n, pl* **pas** \ˈpä(z)\ [F, fr. L *passus* step, pace — more at PACE] **1 :** the right of precedence ⟨when she came in to any full assembly she would not yield the ~ to the best of them —John Arbuthnot⟩ **2 :** a dance step or combination of steps forming a pattern or figure

**PAS** *abbr* PARA-AMINOSALICYLIC ACID

**PA's** *or* **PAs** *pl of* PA

**pas·a·de·na** \ˌpasəˈdēnə\ *adj, usu cap* [fr. *Pasadena*, Calif.] **:** of or from the city of Pasadena, Calif. ⟨an annual *Pasadena* event⟩ **:** of the kind or style prevalent in Pasadena

**pa·sang** *also* **pa·san** \ˈpäzəŋ, -ən\ *n* -s [Per *pāzan* mountain goat, fr. MPer *pāchin*] **1 :** BEZOAR GOAT **2 :** ORYX

**pa·sang·gra·han** *or* **pas·san·gra·han** \ˌpäsəŋˈgräˌhän\ *n* -s [Indonesian *pasanggrahan*, fr. Jav] **:** an Indonesian guesthouse

**pa·sa·nia** \pəˈsānēə\ *or* **pa·sin·ia** \-sin-\ *n* -s [NL *Pasania*, genus of oaks, fr. Sundanese *pasang* oak] **:** the wood of a Formosan oak (*Quercus junghuhnii*) used for joinery and cabinetwork that resembles chestnut but has pronounced medullary rays

**pa·sar** \pəˈsär\ *n* -s [Malay, fr. Per *bāzār* bazaar] **:** an Indonesian public market

**pas·cal celery** \(ˈ)paˌskal- *also* (ˈ)paˌskäl- *or* ˈpaskəl-\ *n, often cap P* [perh. fr. the name *Pasqual*] **:** any of several cultivated celeries distinguished by long green firm stalks

**pas·cal's law** \(ˈ)paˌskalz-, ˈpaskəlz-\ *n, usu cap P* [after Blaise *Pascal* †1662 Fr. scientist and philosopher] **:** a statement in physics: the component of the pressure in a fluid in equilibrium that is due to forces externally applied is uniform throughout the body of fluid

**pascal's triangle** *n, usu cap P* [after Blaise *Pascal*] **:** a system of numbers triangularly arranged in rows consisting of the coefficients in the expansion of $(a + b)^n$ for $n = 0, 1, 2, 3,$ etc.

**pascal's vases** *n pl, usu cap P* [after Blaise *Pascal*] **:** a set of glass containers of various shapes that are used to demonstrate that gravity pressure at a given depth in a liquid is independent of the shape or size of the container

**pasch** \ˈpask, ˈpȧsk\ *also* **pas·cha** \-kə\ *n* -ES *usu cap* [*pasch* fr. ME *pasch, pasche* Passover, Easter, fr. OF *pasche, pasque*, fr. LL *pascha*, fr. LGk, fr. Gk, Passover, fr. Heb *pesaḥ*, fr. *pāsaḥ* to pass over; *pascha* fr. LL] **1 :** PASSOVER **2 :** EASTER

**¹pas·chal** \-kəl\ *n* -s *sometimes cap* [ME, fr. MF *pascal*, fr. *pascal* of Easter] **1 :** a paschal candle or candlestick **2 :** the paschal celebration or supper **3 :** PASCHAL LAMB

**²paschal** \"\ *adj, sometimes cap* [ME, fr. MF *pascal*, fr. LL *paschalis*, fr. *pascha* Passover, Easter + L *-alis* -al] **:** of or relating to Passover or Easter ⟨~ feast⟩

**paschal candle** *n, sometimes cap P* **:** a large white candle lighted in a church sanctuary on the evening before Easter and kept burning throughout the Easter season

**paschal lamb** *n, sometimes cap P* [ME] **1 :** a lamb slain and eaten at the Passover **2 :** LAMB OF GOD

**paschal letter** *n, sometimes cap P* **:** a letter sometimes having the character of a homily and written by patriarchs, archbishops, or bishops of the first six centuries to members of the clergy announcing the date of the next paschal or Easter celebration

**paschal moon** *n, sometimes cap P* [so called fr. its use in determining the date of Easter] **:** the lunar month whose 14th day falls on or next following March 21 according to ecclesiastical calendar rules employing the golden number and epact of the year

**paschal sacrifice** *n, sometimes cap P* **:** PASSOVER 2

**pa·schen-back effect** \ˈpäshənˈbäk-\ *n, usu cap P&B* [after Friedrich *Paschen* †1947 and Ernst *Back* b1881 Ger. physicists] **:** a limiting stage of the Zeeman effect which occurs as the magnetic field causing it is greatly increased and in which the extremely fine structure pattern after going through more or less complicated anomalous stages again approaches a normal triplet character

**paschen's law** *n, usu cap P* [after Friedrich *Paschen*] **:** a statement in electronics: the breakdown voltage between electrodes in a gas is a function of the product of the distance and the pressure so that if the distance is doubled the pressure must be halved

**pas·co·ite** \ˈpaskōˌīt\ *n* -s [Cerro de *Pasco*, mountain in central Peru + E *-ite*] **:** a mineral $Ca_2V_6O_{17}.11H_2O$ consisting of a hydrous calcium vanadate

**pas·co·la** \päˈskōlə\ *n* -s [MexSp, fr. Yaqui *pahko' ola*, lit., old man of the fiesta] **:** a masked fiesta dancer of the Cahita and Yaqui Indians who provides a ceremonial type of burlesquing and clowning through his ritual dances

**pas·cu·al** \ˈpaskyüəl\ *adj* [L *pascuum* pasture (fr. *pascere* to feed, pasture) + E *-al* — more at FOOD] **:** of, relating to, or growing in pastures

**pas d' ac·tion** \ˌpädakˈsyō\ *n, pl* **pas d' action** [F, lit., action step] **:** a pantomimic dance sequence representing a dramatic scene in a ballet

**pas-d'âne** \päˈdän\ *n, pl* **pas-d'âne** [F, lit., ass's step] **:** a ring-shaped guard on each side of the blade in rapiers of the 16th and 17th centuries

**pas de basque** \ˌpädə-\ *n, pl* **pas de basque** [F, lit., Basque step] **:** a dance step alternating from side to side in three counts that is characteristic of the Basque national dances

**pas de bourrée** \ˌpädə-\ *n, pl* **pas de bourrée** [F, lit., bourrée step] **:** a sideways ballet step in which one foot crosses behind or in front of the other

**pas de chat** \ˌpädəˈsha\ *n, pl* **pas de chat** [F, lit., cat's step] **:** a catlike forward leap in ballet

**pas de che·val** \-shəˈval\ *n, pl* **pas de cheval** [F, lit., horse's step] **:** a ballet step resembling the pawing of a horse

**pas de deux** \-ˈdə, -ˈdər, -ˈdü\ *n, pl* **pas de deux** [F, lit., step for two] **:** a dance or figure for two performers **:** DUET

**pas de trois** \-ˈtrwä\ *n, pl* **pas de trois** [F, lit., step for three] **:** a dance or figure for three performers **:** TRIO

**pa·se** \ˈpä(ˌ)sā\ *n* -s [Sp, fr. L, pass, feint, fr. *pase* let him pass, 3d sing. pres. subj. of *pasar* to pass, fr. (assumed) VL *passare* — more at PASS] **:** a movement of a cape by a matador in drawing a bull and taking his charge — compare NATURAL, VERONICA

**¹pa·se·ar** \ˌpäsāˈär\ *vi* -ED/-ING/-s [Sp, fr. *paseo* step — more at *paso*] *Southwest* **:** to take a walk

**²pasear** \"\ *n* -s *Southwest* **:** WALK, EXCURSION

**pa·seo** \pəˈsā(ˌ)ō\ *n* -s [Sp, fr. *pasear*] **1 a :** a leisurely stroll **:** PROMENADE ⟨at six in the evening Spanish towns are suddenly reborn: the women are out for the day's ~ —V.S.Pritchett⟩ **b :** EXCURSION ⟨while he was down on a little ~, a rich old don from below the Rio Grande happened to be visiting in the settlement also —J.F.Dobie⟩ **c :** a public walk or boulevard ⟨down its center extends a wide tree-bordered ~ —*Nat'l Geographic*⟩ **2** *or* **paseo de cuadrillas** \-dā-\ **:** a formal entrance march of bullfighters into an arena ⟨formed up for the ~ as soon as the bull had gone through —Ernest Hemingway⟩

**¹pash** \ˈpash\ *vb* -ED/-ING/-ES [ME *passhen*, prob. of imit. origin] *vt, dial chiefly Eng* **:** to throw or strike violently **:** SMASH ~ *vi, dial chiefly Eng* **:** to dash or break violently

**²pash** \"\ *n* -ES **1** *dial chiefly Eng* **:** a crushing or crashing blow **:** a heavy fall **2** *dial Eng* **a :** a heavy fall of rain or snow **b :** a soft or slushy mass

**³pash** \"\ *n* -ES [origin unknown] *dial Eng* **:** HEAD

**⁴pash** \"\ *n* -ES [by shortening & alter. fr. *passion*] *slang* **:** a schoolgirl infatuation **:** CRUSH ⟨like a fourteen-year-old with a ~, imitating the gym mistress —Nigel Balchin⟩

**pasha** \ˈpäshə, ˈpäshə, ˈpashə *sometimes* pəˈshä\ *also* **ba·shaw** \bəˈshȯ, baˈ-\ *n* -s *often cap* [Turk *paşa*] **:** a man of high rank or office; *esp* **:** a military commander or provincial governor in Turkey and No. Africa ⟨Mustapha Kemal *Pasha*⟩ ⟨Mohammed El Mokri, *Pasha* of Casablanca⟩ — a title illegal in Turkey since 1934 and abolished in Egypt in 1952

**pa·sha·dom** \ˈpäshədəm\ *n* -s **:** the rank, estate, or domain of pashas

**¹pa·sha·lic** *also* **pa·cha·lic** *or* **pa·sha·lik** \pəˈshälik\ *n* -s [Turk *paşalık* title or rank of pasha, fr. *paşa*] **:** the jurisdiction of a pasha or the territory governed by him

**²pashalic** \"\ *adj* [¹*pashalic*] **:** of or relating to a pasha

**pash·kov·ist** \ˈpäsh,kȯfəst\ *n* -s *usu cap* [V.A.*Pashkov* †1902 Russ. religious leader + E *-ist*] **:** a member of a Russian evangelical religious group founded in the 19th century

**pashm** \ˈpashəm\ *also* **pash·im** \-ˌshēm\ *or* **pash·mi·na** \ˌpəshˈmēnə\ *n* -s [*pashm, pashim* fr. Per *pashm* wool; *pashmina* fr. Per *pashmīn* woolen, fr. *pashm*] **:** the under fleece of upland goats of Kashmir and the Punjab that was formerly used locally for the production of rugs and shawls but is now largely exported

**pash·to** \ˈpəsh(ˌ)tō\ *or* **pash·tu** \-ˌtü\ *also* **push·tu** *or* **push·to** \ˈpəsh-\ *n* -s *cap* [Per *pashtu*, fr. Afghan] **:** the Iranian language of Pathan people and the chief vernacular of eastern Afghanistan, North-West Frontier Province of Pakistan, and northern Baluchistan

**pash·toon** *or* **pash·tun** \ˌpəshˈtün\ *n, pl* **pashtoon** *or* **pashtoons** *or* **pashtun** *or* **pashtuns** *usu cap* **1 :** a Moslem people of Afghanistan and the frontier region between Afghanistan and Pakistan **2 :** a member of the Pashtoon people

**pas·i·graph·ic** \ˌpasəˈgrafik\ *or* **pas·i·graph·i·cal** \-fəkəl\ *adj* **:** of or relating to pasigraphy

**pa·sig·ra·phy** \pəˈsigrəfē\ *n* -ES [Gk *pasi* for all (dat. pl. of *pant-, pas* all) + *-graphy* — more at PAN-] **:** any of various proposed international written languages using signs (as mathematical symbols) to represent ideas rather than words; *broadly* **:** an artificial international written language

**pa·si·llo** \pəˈsē(ˌ)(y)ō\ *n* -s [AmerSp, dim. of Sp *paso* step — more at *paso*] **:** a Latin-American dance for two in triple time

**pas·i·mol·o·gy** \ˌpasəˈmäləjē\ *n* -ES [prob. fr. Gk *pasi* for all + *sēma* sign + E *-o-* + *-logy* — more at PASIGRAPHY, SEMANTICS] **:** the study of gestures as a means of communication

**pa·sin** \ˈpäˌsēn\ *n* -s [Thai] **:** a loose straight skirt worn folded snugly about the body (as in Thailand) ⟨dressed like their mothers in ~*s* and white sleeveless blouses —Kathryn Grondahl⟩

**pasinia** *var of* PASANIA

**pas·mo** \ˈpaz(ˌ)mō\ *n* -s [AmerSp, fr. Sp, temporary paralysis, lockjaw, fr. L *spasmus* cramp, spasm — more at SPASM] **:** a widespread disease of flax that damages the fibers and reduces the yield of flaxseed and is caused by a fungus (*Mycosphaerella linorum*) which attacks stems, bolls, and leaves and forms characteristic circular brownish lesions on the cotyledons and lower leaves

**pa·so** \ˈpä(ˌ)sō\ *n* -s [Sp, lit., step, incident, fr. L *passus* step, pace — more at PACE] **:** ENTREMÉS

**paso do·ble** \-ˈdō(ˌ)blā\ *n* [Sp, lit., double step] **:** a Latin-American march step typically associated with bullfighting

**pas·pa·lum** \ˈpaspələm\ *n, cap* [NL, fr. Gk *paspalos* millet; prob. akin to Gk *palē* fine meal, dust — more at *pollen*] **1 :** a genus of mostly perennial grasses chiefly of warm regions having flat leaves and spikelets in several rows on second spikes — see DITCH MILLET, JOINT GRASS **2** -s **:** any grass of the genus *Paspalum*

**paspy** *var of* PASSEPIED

**pasque·flow·er** \ˈpask,flau̇(ə)r\ *n* [alter. (influenced by MF *pasque* Easter, fr. OF) of earlier *passeflower*, fr. MF *passefleur*, fr. *passer* to pass (fr. OF) + *fleur* flower, fr. L *flor-, flos* — more at PASCH, PASS, BLOW] **1 :** any of several low perennial herbs with palmately compound leaves and large usu. white or purple flowers borne in early spring that form a section of the genus *Anemone* — see AMERICAN PASQUEFLOWER, EUROPEAN PASQUEFLOWER, PULSATILLA **2 :** the blossom of a pasqueflower

**pas·quil** \ˈpaskwəl\ *n* -s [NL *pasquillus*, fr. It *pasquillo*, fr. *Pasquino*] **:** PASQUINADE

**pas·quin** \ˈpaskwən\ *n* -s [MF, fr. It *Pasquino*, name given to a statue in Rome on which anonymous lampoons were posted] **:** PASQUINADE ⟨~*s* and pamphlets rained against him —M.A.S.Hume⟩

**¹pas·quin·ade** \ˌpaskwəˈnād\ *n* -s [MF, fr. It *pasquinata*, fr. *Pasquino* + *-ata* -ade] **1 :** an anonymous lampoon posted in a public place **2 :** a lampoon or satire usu. having a political significance ⟨a writer of farce, burlesque and incisive ~ of political criticism —Bonamy Dobrée⟩

**²pasquinade** \"\ *vt* -ED/-ING/-s **:** LAMPOON, SATIRIZE ⟨been notoriously *pasquinaded* for his pains —E.A.Poe⟩

**¹pass** \ˈpas, ˈpaa(ə)s, ˈpais, ˈpȧs\ *vb* -ED/-ING/-ES [ME *passen*, fr. OF *passer*, fr. (assumed) VL *passare*, fr. L *passus* step — more at PACE] *vi* **1 a :** to move on **:** PROCEED ⟨from group to group the girls ~, laughing, prattling —Lafcadio Hearn⟩ **b :** to proceed to a specified place or destination ⟨the excess nitrogen ~*es* rapidly into the capillaries —H.G.Armstrong⟩ ⟨could ~ again into his neutral, godlike independence —R.W. Emerson⟩ ⟨all that lives must die, ~*ing* through nature, to eternity —Shak.⟩ **c :** to proceed along a specified route **:** take a particular course ⟨the blood ~*es* through the lungs —H.G.Armstrong⟩ ⟨~*es* between the rolling slopes —*Amer. Guide Series: Ark.*⟩ ⟨~*ed* freely along the great caravan routes —H.J.J.Winter⟩ **d :** to go on with a narrative or discussion ⟨we ~ down the centuries to Anselm —H.O.Taylor⟩ ⟨before I ~ to other matters —J.M.Wordie⟩ **2 a :** to go away from a place, object, or person **:** DEPART, LEAVE ⟨the fright ~*es* almost immediately —Fred Majdalany⟩ **b :** to depart from life **:** DIE ⟨every morning I pray God to let me ~ —Virginia Woolf⟩ ⟨when she ~*ed* there were editorials about her —*N.Y. Herald Tribune Bk. Rev.*⟩ — often used with *on* **3 a :** to go by or move past ⟨the wind ~*ed* again blowing up dust and rain —Greville Texidor⟩ ⟨the mail ~*ed* twice a week —John Burroughs⟩ ⟨the remark ~*ed* unnoticed —T.B.Costain⟩ **b :** to glide by **:** ELAPSE ⟨could not let this moment ~ without a few words of explanation —Gwyn Thomas⟩ ⟨poetical works conceived in the spirit of the ~*ing* time —Matthew Arnold⟩ **c :** to come to an end or finish **:** TERMINATE ⟨the strangeness of his life ~*ed*, and he began to feel what this city was —Pearl Buck⟩ ⟨aid . . . could not be given before the crisis had ~*ed* —C.L.Jones⟩ **d :** to move past another vehicle going in the same direction **:** OVERTAKE ⟨do not ~ on the right⟩ ⟨no ~*ing* permitted⟩ **4 a :** to go or make way through **:** secure a passage through ⟨guarded the door and permitted no one to ~⟩ ⟨better than ordinary glass, since they allowed the sun's actinic rays to ~ —*Amer. Guide Series: Mich.*⟩ **b :** to go uncensured or unchallenged **:** take place or come to view without hindrance or opposition ⟨if malice and vanity wear the coat of philanthropy, shall that ~ —R.W.Emerson⟩ ⟨such behavior cannot ~ in a schoolroom⟩ **c :** to go through a duct or the intestines **5 a :** to move or be transferred from one place to another ⟨from the college he ~*ed* to the novitiate of the order —*Amer. Guide Series: Md.*⟩ ⟨was first a stock clerk, ~*ed* from that to other service departments —*Current Biog.*⟩ **b :** to go from one quality, state, condition, or form to another ⟨a good player on a modern pianoforte can ~ at will . . . from an almost inaudible softness to a thundering loudness —R.V.Williams⟩ ⟨~ from relaxation and refreshment back to the routine of life's clamant duties —W.F.Hambly⟩ ⟨~*es* from a liquid to a gaseous state⟩ **c :** to go from one stage of development to another ⟨~ . . . imperceptibly from youth to age —D.H.Barber⟩ ⟨~*ed* . . . from a primitive, prehistoric stage . . . to the more advanced civilized state —David Bidney⟩ **d :** to go from one activity to another ⟨~*ed* from the study of physiology to the study of psychology —A.N.Whitehead⟩ **6** [AF *passer*, lit., to proceed, fr. OF] **a** *of a jury* (1) **:** to sit in inquest — used with *on* or *upon* (2) **:** to sit in adjudication — usu. used with *between* **b :** to become rendered, given, or done in legal procedure ⟨judgment ~*ed* for the defendant⟩ **c** (1) **:** to render a verdict or judgment **:** pass sentence **:** ADJUDICATE — usu. used with *on* or *upon* ⟨the court did not ~ on the constitutional question⟩ ⟨the jury found it difficult to ~ upon the case because of the conflicting testimony⟩ (2) **:** to give judgment **:** render an opinion or express a point of view — used with *on* or *upon* ⟨our concern here is not to ~ upon the merits of a particular controversy —R.M. Weaver⟩ **d** *of a juryman* **:** SERVE, SIT — used with *on* or *upon* **7 a :** to undergo conveyance or transfer (as by will, deed, or other instrument of conveyance) so as to become vested in another ⟨sold the house . . . the title ~*ed* this afternoon —J.C. Lincoln⟩ **b :** to go from the control or possession of one person, group, or country to that of another ⟨the throne ~*ed* to Darius the Great —W.K.Ferguson⟩ ⟨the institution ~*ed* from parish to state control —*Amer. Guide Series: La.*⟩ **8 a :** to take place **:** HAPPEN, OCCUR ⟨commenting freely on the transactions as they ~ —W.L.Sperry⟩ **b :** to take place as a mutual exchange or transaction (as speech, letters, or lovemaking) ⟨what hath ~*ed* between me and Ford's wife —Shak.⟩ ⟨words ~*ed* and then blows⟩ **c :** to come and go in consciousness **:** exist as ideas or sensations ⟨no one could tell what was ~*ing* within his mind⟩ ⟨visions of the future ~*ed* through his mind⟩ **9 a :** to secure the allowance or approval of a legislature or other body that has power to sanction or reject a bill or proposal ⟨the tax bill ~*ed* by a slim majority⟩ ⟨the proposal to change the date of the dance ~*ed* by unanimous vote of the class council⟩ **b :** to attain the required grade or level of achievement in an examination or course of study ⟨took the scholarship examination and ~*ed*⟩ ⟨did badly in the course and barely ~*ed*⟩ **c :** to go through an inspection or test successfully **:** achieve acceptance ⟨in a day when much that is careless and slipshod ~*es* in the name of realism —Sara H. Hay⟩ ⟨boatmen's skirts with blue stripes and a crew neck ~ nicely too —Horace Sutton⟩ **10 a :** to go from one person to another **:** be current **:** CIRCULATE ⟨bank notes ~ so long as nobody refuses them —William James⟩ **b :** to become falsely held, regarded, or identified — usu. used with *as* or *for* ⟨~ in society not for the person you are, but as a labeled dummy —Stuart Chase⟩ ⟨the doggerel verse that ~*ed* as poetry —*Amer. Guide Series: Minn.*⟩ ⟨~*ed* for being a very devoted couple —Mary Deasy⟩ **c :** to serve as a substitute — usu. used with *for* ⟨dreary lines of shell-like hovels that ~ for dwellings —*Amer. Guide Series: Va.*⟩ ⟨that awful jargon that ~*es* for English —John Hilton⟩ **d :** to identify oneself or accept identification as a white person though having some Negro ancestry ⟨the heroine who has been ~*ing* in the North, comes home to the South . . . to live among and learn to love her people —*Commentary*⟩ **11 a** *obs* **:** to make a pass in fencing ⟨you but dally, I pray you ~ with your best violence —Shak.⟩ **b :** to execute a pass (as in football, basketball, or hockey) ⟨the situation called for a kick but he decided to ~⟩ **12 a** (1) **:** to decline to bid, double, or redouble in a card game (as in bridge) (2) **:** to withdraw from the current poker pot **:** throw up one's hand (as in poker) (3) **:** to transfer a card to another player **b :** to make a winning cast or roll with dice ~ *vt* **1 a :** to go beyond in some degree, measure, or quality **:** SURPASS ⟨the reviews of a few dramatic critics ~ all others in the influence they have⟩ ⟨used to be the largest city in the state, but has now been ~*ed* by several others⟩ **b :** to advance or develop beyond ⟨had ~*ed* the barbaric stage when they invaded Chaldea —Edward Clodd⟩ **c :** to go beyond (a mark or limit) ⟨his drive to provide planetariums for the millions ~*ed* several important milestones —S.M.Spencer⟩ ⟨those who ~ 90 begin to think about reaching 100 —Morris Fishbein⟩ ⟨this information will never ~ my lips⟩ **d :** to go past **:** leave behind in running or racing **:** OUTSTRIP ⟨~*ed* the other runners in the homestretch⟩ **e :** to go beyond or transcend the range or limitations of **:** EXCEED ⟨so new to our experience that it ~*es* comprehension —*Saturday Rev.*⟩ **2 a :** to go by **:** proceed or extend beyond ⟨~*es* the school on his way to work⟩ ⟨an avenue that ~*es* several large churches —*Amer. Guide Series: Ark.*⟩ **b** (1) *obs* **:** NEGLECT, OMIT ⟨could not ~ admiring the great church —John Evelyn⟩ (2) **:** to omit a regularly scheduled declaration and payment of (a dividend) **c :** to leave out in an account or narration ⟨~ the trivial details and get to the heart of the story⟩ **3 a :** to go from one side to the other of **:** proceed across, over, or through **:** CROSS, TRAVERSE ⟨~ the straits and conquer the mountains —Walt Whitman⟩ ⟨nevermore did either ~ the gate —Alfred Tennyson⟩ **b :** to go or live through **:** have experience of **:** ENDURE, SUFFER, UNDERGO ⟨she loved me for the dangers I had ~*ed* —Shak.⟩ **c :** to cause or permit to elapse **:** abide the passage of **:** SPEND ⟨you may ~ half an hour pleasantly, even profitably, over an article of his —R.L. Stevenson⟩ ⟨~*ed* the summer at the beach⟩ ⟨~ his life in study⟩ **4 a :** to secure the approval or sanction of **:** gain the acceptance of ⟨the bill ~*ed* the senate⟩ **b :** to go through successfully or satisfactorily **:** attain the required standard in **:** satisfy the requirements of ⟨~*ed* the bar examination⟩ ⟨had ~*ed* a security check —*Time*⟩ **5 a** *obs* **:** to carry through to completion **:** EXECUTE, FINISH ⟨where he might hear his father ~ the deed —Ben Jonson⟩ **b** (1) **:** to cause or permit to proceed **:** cause or permit to win approval or legal or official sanction **:** CONFIRM, ENDORSE ⟨the legislature ~*ed* the bill⟩ ⟨the committee ~*ed* the nomination⟩ (2) **:** to approve as valid, correct, or proper **:** AUTHORIZE ⟨gave his work perfunctory attention and ~*ed* it without effort or interest —E.T.Bell⟩ ⟨always ~*ed* the final page proofs of the paper personally —*Times Lit. Supp.*⟩ **c :** to let go unnoticed **:** pass over **:** OVERLOOK ⟨his commander quietly ~*ed* his likes or dislikes —George Meredith⟩ **d :** to cause or allow to pass an examination or course of study ⟨the examiner ~*ed* him on his written test but failed him on his road test⟩ ⟨the professor ~*ed* most of his students⟩ **6 a :** PLEDGE ⟨had ~*ed* his word that he would repay the debt⟩ **b :** to transfer the right or property in **:** make over ⟨~ the title to an estate⟩ **7 a :** to place in circulation **:** give currency to ⟨~*ed* a counterfeit ten-dollar bill⟩ ⟨caught ~*ing* bad checks⟩ ⟨~*es* malicious gossip about her neighbors⟩ **b :** to transfer from one person to another **:** cause to go from hand to hand ⟨~ the jug⟩ ⟨please ~ the salt⟩ ⟨the problem of ~*ing* prosperity around —Elmer Davis⟩ ⟨signed the attendance sheet and ~*ed* it on⟩ **c :** to cause or make possible to go or proceed **:** transfer from one place to another **:** CONVEY, TRANSPORT ⟨waited till the soldiers and wounded were all ~*ed* over —Walt Whitman⟩ **d :** to cause to move in a particular manner or direction or over a specified place or area ⟨~*ed* his hand over his face⟩ ⟨~*ed* the cloth over the top of the desk⟩ **e** (1) **:** to take a turn with (a line) and make secure ⟨~ a line around a sail in furling⟩ (2) **:** to take a turn with (a rope or string) around something ⟨~*ed* a rope around the tree⟩ **f :** to transfer to another player on the same team ⟨~*ed* the ball to the left end⟩ ⟨~*ed* the puck to his teammate⟩ **g :** THROW ⟨they'd ~ a ball back and forth or play jackstones —Dorothy C. Fisher⟩ **8 a :** to pronounce judicially ⟨~*ed* sentence on the convicted man⟩ **b :** to give voice to **:** PRONOUNCE, UTTER ⟨~*ing* a word now and again with the man on the other side of the marble-topped table —Nevil Shute⟩ ⟨~*es* some practical remarks on the present standard locomotive designs —*Brit. Book News*⟩ **9 a :** to cause or permit to go past or through a barrier **:** cause or allow to gain entrance **b :** to cause to march or go by in order ⟨the general ~*ed* his troops in review⟩ ⟨~*es* rapidly in review the various forms of association between human beings —*Times Lit. Supp.*⟩ **10 :** to emit or discharge from the bowels or other part of the body **:** EVACUATE, VOID **11 a :** to permit (a batter in baseball) to reach first base by giving a base on balls **b :** to send a ball in a racket game to the side and out of reach of (an opponent) **12 a :** to decline to bid or bet on (one's hand) in a card game **b :** to transfer (a playing card) to another player **13 :** to take (a bull's charge) with a movement of a cape — **pass current :** to circulate freely **:** be accepted as genuine or valid ⟨now *pass current* as what was always known —F.R.Leavis⟩ — **pass in one's checks :** DIE — **pass muster 1 :** to pass an inspection or examination **:** be found satisfactory or valid ⟨these excuses will not *pass muster*⟩ **2 :** to pass a routine or casual inspection ⟨the variety of styles and tendencies that all *pass muster* under the name of modern music —Aaron Copland⟩ — **pass the buck :** to shift a responsibility to someone else ⟨inclined to *pass the buck* to some other futile body —Sir Winston Churchill⟩ — **pass the chair :** to complete a term as incumbent of a high office (as in a fraternal organization) — **pass the hat :** to take up a collection of money ⟨*passed the hat* to raise funds for the new youth center⟩ — **pass the time of day :** to exchange greetings or hold a friendly conversation

**²pass** \"\ *n* -ES [ME *pass, pas,* fr. OF *pas,* fr. L *passus* step — more at PACE] **1 :** an opening, road, channel, or other way that is the only means by which a barrier may be passed or access gained to a particular place: as **a** (1) *archaic* **:** ROAD, ROUTE (2) **:** a narrow place in a road or street **b** (1) **:** a break in a mountain range **:** an opening between two peaks usu. approached by a steep valley ⟨has the lowest altitude of the three main ~*es* across the Cascades —*Amer. Guide Series: Wash.*⟩ — compare COL, DEFILE, GAP, NOTCH (2) **:** a narrow road between a mountain and a sea ⟨the *Pass* of Thermopylae⟩ **c** (1) **:** a place or policy that controls the defense of a country ⟨believe that the government sold the ~ when it abandoned its ally⟩ (2) **:** a position that must be maintained usu. against odds ⟨our few repertory companies have held the ~ —*Report: (Canadian) Royal Commission on Nat'l Development*⟩ **d** (1) **:** a navigable channel in a delta ⟨attempts were made to increase the depth of the ~*es* by dredging with buckets —*Amer. Guide Series: La.*⟩ (2) **:** a narrow opening between two islands or through an obstruction (as a reef) **:** STRAIT ⟨when the engine that propelled us through the ~ had ceased its clatter, we lay, sails set, rocking in the swell —Ida Treat⟩ (3) **:** a stretch of open water in a marsh **e** (1) **:** a crossing over a river (2) **:** a passage for fish over a dam **2 :** a chute from one level of a mine to another **3 :** an aperture formed between two grooved rolls in a rolling mill through which a bar of metal is passed to be shaped **4 :** DUCK PASS **syn** see WAY

**³pass** \"\ *n* -ES [partly fr. ME *passe,* fr. MF, fr. *passer* to pass; partly fr. ¹*pass* — more at ¹PASS] **1 a :** the act or an instance of passing **:** PASSAGE ⟨charming the narrow seas to give you gentle ~ —Shak.⟩ **b** *archaic* **:** DEATH **2 :** ACCOMPLISHMENT, REALIZATION ⟨the boy's dream comes to ~ —R.W.Emerson⟩ ⟨plot and plan and bring to ~ —Robert Browning⟩ **3 :** a usu. difficult, dangerous, or unfortunate condition or state of affairs ⟨things had come to a pretty ~ when nobody would work for him any more⟩ ⟨a strange ~⟩ ⟨a terrible ~⟩ **4 a :** a written permission to move about freely in a particular area or place or to leave or enter its boundaries or limits ⟨under its provisions vagrancy was no more an offence, and . . . folk were free to move without ~*es* —C.W. de Kiewiet⟩ ⟨obtained a ~ to any port of the Low Countries —Margaret Toynbee⟩ **b :** a written leave of absence from a military post or station for a brief period ⟨if only all of life could be a three-day ~ —James Jones⟩ **c :** a written permission to enter an area or place closed to the general public (as an army post or defense establishment) **d :** a permit, ticket, or order allowing one free transportation (as on a railroad) or free admission (as to a theater) ⟨has a season ~ to the ball park⟩ — called also *free pass* **5 :** a thrust or lunge in fencing **6 a :** a transference of objects by sleight of hand or other deceptive means ⟨one of the most difficult ~*es* for the amateur magician to make⟩ **b :** a gesture or movement of the hands of a juggler or magician ⟨would make ~*es* over the picture, finally making the gesture of picking a grape off the canvas —Victoria Sackville-West⟩ **c :** a shifting of the position of the cards in card tricks ⟨it takes practice to learn to make the ~⟩ **d :** a moving of the hands over or along something **:** MANIPULATION ⟨a recalcitrant mechanism responded almost instantly to two or three ~*es* of his hands —Ben Riker⟩ **7** *archaic* **:** a witty or ingenious sally or stroke ⟨a curious ~ of wit —William Hazlitt⟩ **8 :** the passing of an examination or course of study; *also* **:** the mark or certification of such passing ⟨the examiners may award a ~ with distinction to any candidates who have attained a sufficiently high standard in all subjects —*Durham Univ. Cal.*⟩ ⟨a ~ mark⟩ ⟨a ~ grade⟩ **9 :** a single complete mechanical operation: as **a :** a single passage of a bar, rail, or sheet between the rolls of a rolling mill **b :** a single or multiple passage of the gases from the furnace across the tubes of a steam boiler **c :** a single progression along a joint in welding **d** (1) **:** a single passage of one or more cards through a punched-card machine (2) **:** a single sorting or arranging operation with hand-notched punched cards **10 a :** a transfer of a ball (as in football or basketball) or a puck (as in hockey) from one player to another player on the same team ⟨threw a long ~ into the corner⟩ ⟨threw a ~ the length of the court⟩ **b :** PASS STROKE **c :** a passing stroke in tennis **11 :** BASE ON BALLS **12 a :** a refusal to bid, bet, or draw an additional card in a card game **b :** an election not to bid, double, or redouble in bridge **c :** a transfer of a playing card to another player **13 :** a cast or combination of dice that wins the main bet **14 :** a single passage or movement of an airplane or other artificial flying object over a given area or place or in the direction of a given target ⟨made several low ~*es* over the field so the ground crew could inspect the wheel by searchlight —*Time*⟩ ⟨made seven ~*es* at that gun, each time dropping one bomb —Ira Wolfert⟩ ⟨the satellite will make its first ~ over the eastern half of the country at 4 a.m.⟩ **15 a :** EFFORT, TRY ⟨guessed wrong on the crime the first time they made a ~ at it —Erle Stanley Gardner⟩ ⟨told me in French, after a few unsuccessful ~*es* in other languages —A.J.Liebling⟩ **b :** a sexually inviting gesture or approach ⟨was always accusing her of making ~*es* at other men —*Time*⟩ ⟨a girl must be able to recognize a ~ —Bernard De Voto⟩ **16 :** PASE ⟨makes his ~*es* with a stylized, classical grace that catches crowds by the throat —John Stanton⟩ **syn** see JUNCTURE

**pass** *abbr* **1** passage **2** passenger **3** passim **4** passive

**pass·able** \ˈpasəbəl, ˈpaas-, ˈpais-, ˈpȧs-\ *adj* [ME, fr. MF, fr. *passer* to pass + *-able*] **1 a :** capable of being passed, crossed, or traveled on ⟨car owners who needed ~ roads —F.L.Paxson⟩ **b** *archaic* **:** capable of passing or going through **c :** capable of being freely circulated ⟨counterfeit money so good it was ~ in a bank⟩ **2 :** able to qualify or pass inspection **:** just good enough **:** TOLERABLE ⟨there are ~ maps and better summary notes on each territory —*Geog. Jour.*⟩ — **pass·able·ness** *n* -ES

**pass·ably** \-blē, -li\ *adv* [*passable* + *-ly*] **:** MODERATELY, TOLERABLY ⟨she was little more than ~ good-looking —Louis Auchincloss⟩

**pas·sa·ca·glia** \ˌpäsəˈkälyə, ˌpas-\ *also* **pas·sa·ca·glio** \-l(ˌ)yō\ *n* -S [modif. (influenced by It *passagaglia, passagallo,* fr. Sp *pasacalle,* a lively guitar tune) of F *passacaille,* fr. Sp *pasacalle,* fr. *pasar* to pass + *calle* street, fr. L *callis* path — more at PASE] **1 a :** an old Italian or Spanish dance tune **b :** an instrumental musical composition consisting of variations usu. on a ground bass in moderately slow triple time — compare CHACONNE **2 :** an old dance performed to a passacaglia

**pas·sa·caille** \ˌpäsəˈkī\ *or* **passe-caille** \ˈpäs-\ *n* -S [F] **:** PASSACAGLIA

**pas·sade** \pəˈsäd\ *n* -S [F, fr. It *passata,* fr. *passare* to pass (fr. — assumed — VL *passare*) + *-ata* -ade — more at PASS, vb.] **1 :** a turn or course of a horse backward or forward on the same spot **2 :** a passing love affair **:** FLIRTATION ⟨it describes a ~, a riffle on the surface of life —Anthony West⟩

**pas·sa·do** \pəˈsä(ˌ)dō\ *n, pl* **passados** *or* **passadoes** [modif. of F *passade* or It *passata* — more at PASSADE] **:** a thrust in fencing with one foot advanced

**¹pas·sage** \ˈpasij, -sēj, *in sense 3d* " *or* pəˈsäzh\ *n* -S [ME, fr. OF, fr. *passer* to pass + *-age*] **1 a :** the act or action of passing **:** movement or transference from one place or point to another, or through or across a space or element **:** TRANSIT ⟨made the ~ of their domain hazardous to settlers —*Amer. Guide Series: Texas*⟩ ⟨the ~ of the air from the lungs —*Encyc. Americana*⟩ ⟨the ~ of the Red sea —W.L.Sperry⟩ ⟨the ~ of an electric current through the wire⟩ **b** *obs* **:** DEATH ⟨when he is fit and seasoned for his ~ —Shak.⟩ **c** (1) **:** the process of passing **:** a transition from one mode of being, condition, or stage to another ⟨life enlightened is the ~ from irrational passion to reasoned attachment —J.P.Anton⟩ ⟨the indefinable ~ of a season —*Amer. Guide Series: Minn.*⟩ ⟨the ~ from barbarism to civilization —Edward Clodd⟩ (2) **:** a continuous movement or flow ⟨wounds, illnesses, sorrows were all weakened by the ~ of time —Stuart Cloete⟩ **d :** MIGRATION ⟨the black ducks were on ~ and we could see them coming in high from the north —V.C.Heilner⟩ **2 a :** a means of passing **:** a road, path, channel, or course through or by which something passes **:** a way of exit or entrance **:** PASS ⟨most of the streets were mere alleys, ~*s* between houses and groups of buildings —Edwin Benson⟩ ⟨breathing ~*s*⟩ **b :** a river crossing (as a ford or ferry) ⟨they took him, and slew him at the ~*s* of Jordan —Judg 12:6 (AV)⟩ **c :** a corridor or lobby giving access to the different rooms or parts of a building or apartment ⟨thinking how easy it would be to get lost in this hotel, in all these long ~*s* —Graham Greene⟩ **3 a** (1) **:** a specific act of traveling or passing from one place to another **:** a journey esp. by sea or air between two points ⟨the outward ~ was uneventful⟩ ⟨made a swift ~ between New York and Southampton⟩ ⟨the rocket satellite's ~*s* were coming so early that they would not show up in the bright sky of sunset —*N. Y. Times*⟩ (2) **:** a privilege of conveyance as a passenger **:** ACCOMMODATIONS ⟨was able to secure ~ on the next flight⟩ ⟨took ~ on a freighter⟩ **b :** an obsolete dice game for two played with three dice — compare PASSE-DIX **c :** the passing of a legislative measure or law **:** ENACTMENT ⟨government leaders bent upon securing ~ of their bills —F.A.Ogg & Harold Zink⟩ **d :** a slow lofty trot with a precise cadence that is often used in traversing **e :** a movement or an evacuation of the bowels **4 a :** the possibility or liberty of passing **:** a right or permission to pass ⟨attempted to force ~ through the town —C.A.Willoughby⟩ **b :** a toll formerly collected from passengers in England **5 a :** something that happens or is done **:** OCCURRENCE, ACT, TRANSACTION ⟨our American experience in psychological warfare from 1941 to 1945 was often chaotic and mad; and it had its wholly comic ~*s* —A.M.Schlesinger b.1917⟩ **b :** something that takes place between two persons mutually **:** a mutual act or transaction (as a negotiation, a quarrel, or lovemaking) ⟨this ~ of arms and wits amused the town —Robert Browning⟩ **6 a :** a usu. brief portion of a written work or speech that is quoted or referred to by itself as relevant to a point under discussion or as noteworthy for content or style ⟨one of the finest ~*s* in the novel⟩ ⟨betrays his inaccuracy in many ~*s*⟩ ⟨this ~ was greeted with laughter by the audience⟩ **b :** a phrase or short section of a musical composition; *esp* **:** a section demonstrating virtuosity in performance ⟨a scale ~⟩ ⟨the ~ in arpeggios⟩ **c :** a detail of a painting or other work of art ⟨find ~*s* to admire in his best canvases —J.T.Soby⟩ ⟨the picture contains several pretty ~*s* of color —Clive Bell⟩ **7 a :** the act or action of causing something to pass **b** (1) **:** incubation of a pathogen (as a virus) in a tissue culture, a developing egg, or a living organism to increase the amount of pathogen or to alter its characteristics (2) **:** an instance of such passage **syn** see WAY

**²pas·sage** \ˈpasij, -sēj, pəˈsäzh\ *vb* -ED/-ING/-S [F *passager,* alter. of *passéger,* fr. It *passeggiare,* fr. *passare* to pass, fr. (assumed) VL — more at PASS] *vi* **:** to move sideways in riding or being ridden ⟨the horse ~*s* gracefully⟩ ~ *vt* **:** to cause (a horse) to move sideways

**³pas·sage** \ˈpasij, -sēj\ *vb* -ED/-ING/-S [¹*passage*] *vi* **1 :** to engage in a passage of arms or wits **2 :** to go past or across (as in a voyage) **:** CROSS ⟨*passaged* to Europe last month⟩ ~ *vt* **:** to subject to passage ⟨the virus has been *passaged* in series seven times —*Jour. Amer. Med. Assoc.*⟩

**passage bed** *n* [¹*passage*] **:** a stratum that forms a transition between rocks of two geological systems

**passage bird** *n* **1 :** BIRD OF PASSAGE **2 :** PASSAGE HAWK

**passage boat** *n* **:** a passenger boat plying on regular schedule between two places

**passage cell** *n* **:** a thin-walled unsuberized cell found in the endodermis of vascular plants often opposite the protoxylem strands — called also *transfusion cell*

**passage grave** *n* **:** a subterranean burial chamber entered through a long passage resembling a tunnel

**passage hawk** *n* **:** a haggard hawk

**passageway** \ˈ==,=\ *n* **:** a way that allows passage to or from a place or between two points **:** CORRIDOR, PATH ⟨only one narrow ~ up the steep mountain —Burtt Evans⟩ ⟨outbuildings were connected to the main house by curved ~*s* —H.S.Morrison⟩

**passage winds** *n pl* **:** prevailing westerly winds that blow in the belt lying between the horse latitudes and the region of the pole in each hemisphere

**passage-work** \ˈ==,=\ *n* **:** a section or part of a musical composition characteristically unimportant thematically and generally consisting of repetitive notes or figures or scale or arpeggio passages

**pas·sag·gio** \pəˈsä(ˌ)jō\ *n* -S [It, lit., passage, fr. *passare* to pass (fr. — assumed — VL) + *-aggio* -age — more at PASS] **1 :** an improvised embellishment or flourish found esp. in 16th century music and usu. excluding plain scale passages or trills **2 :** MODULATION **3 :** PASSAGE-WORK

**¹pas·sa·lid** \ˈpasələd\ *adj* [NL *Passalidae*] **:** of or relating to the Passalidae

**²passalid** \"\ *n* -S **:** a beetle of the family Passalidae

**pas·sal·i·dae** \pəˈsaləˌdē\ *n pl, cap* [NL, fr. *Passalus,* type genus + *-idae*] **:** a family of rather large usu. black lamellicorn beetles chiefly of tropical countries that live and feed in decaying wood and are sometimes placed in the family Lucanidae — see BESS-BUG, PASSALUS

**pas·sa·lus** \ˈpasələs\ *n* [NL, fr. Gk *passalos* peg; akin to Gk *pēssein* to fix, fasten, *pēgnynai* to fix, fasten — more at PACT] **1** *cap* **:** the type genus of the family Passalidae **2** -ES **:** any beetle of *Passalus* or a related genus; *esp* **:** a flat shiny black gregarious bess-bug (*Popilius disjunctus*) of the southern U. S. — called also *horned passalus*

**pas·sa·ma·quod·dy** \ˌpasəməˈkwädē\ *n, pl* **passamaquoddy** *or* **passamaquoddies** *usu cap* **1 a :** an Indian people of Maine and New Brunswick, Canada **b :** a member of such people **2 :** a dialect of Malecite

**passament** *var of* PASSEMENT

**pas·sa·mez·zo** *or* **pas·se·mez·zo** \ˌpäsəˈmet(ˌ)sō, -ed(ˌ)zō, -e(ˌ)zō\ *n* -S [It *passamezzo, passo e mezzo,* fr. the phrase *passo e mezzo* step and a half] **:** an old orig. Italian dance in duple time resembling the pavan but about twice as fast; *also* **:** the music of this dance

**passangrahan** *var of* PASANGGRAHAN

**pas·sant** \ˈpasᵊnt\ *adj* [MF, fr. pres. part. of *passer* to pass] **1 :** walking with the further forepaw raised — used of a heraldic lion or other beast; compare COUNTERPASSANT **2** *archaic* **:** having general acceptance or use **:** CURRENT

**pas sauté** \ˌpäsōˈtā, -sōˈ-\ *n, pl* **pas sautés** \-ā(z)\ [F] **:** a jumping step in ballet

**pass away** *vb* [ME *passen away,* fr. *passen* to pass + *away*] *vi* **1 a :** to go out of existence **:** come to an end **:** PERISH, VANISH ⟨when those conditions have *passed away* and history returns to normal —W.P.Webb⟩ **b :** DIE ⟨died of a broken heart soon after his mother *passed away* —David Fairchild⟩ **2** *archaic* **:** DEPART ⟨saw the damsel *pass away* —Edmund Spenser⟩ **3 :** to slip by **:** ELAPSE ⟨the evening *passed away* very fairly —Henry Lapham⟩ ~ *vt* **1 :** to let slip by **:** SPEND ⟨*pass away* the winter⟩ **2** *archaic* **:** to give away **:** SURRENDER

**passback** \ˈ=,=\ *n* -S [¹*pass* + *back,* adv.] **:** SNAPBACK

**passband** \ˈ=,=\ *n* **:** the frequency band (as in a radio circuit or filter) that is transmitted with maximum efficiency and without intentional loss

**passbook** \ˈ=,=\ *n* **1 :** BANKBOOK **2 :** a customer's book in which a dealer enters articles bought on credit

**pass by** *vt* [ME *passen by,* fr. *passen* to pass + *by*] **:** to go past without stopping or noticing **:** DISREGARD, IGNORE ⟨the sort of writer present-day literary critics *pass by* —Oliver La Farge⟩ ⟨new methods have *passed* them *by* —George Farwell⟩

**pass course** *n* [³*pass*] **:** a general undergraduate course at British universities that is taken by all students who are not candidates for honors

**pass degree** *n* **:** a bachelor's degree without honors that is taken at a British university

**pass door** *n* **:** a door between the stage and the auditorium in a theater

**¹pas·sé** *or* **pas·sée** \(ˈ)paˈsā\ *adj* [F, fr. past part. of *passer* to pass] **1 :** past one's prime **:** no longer young **:** FADED ⟨a fine brain in a somewhat ~ body —*Amer. Mercury*⟩ ⟨a somewhat rakish but ~ miss —*Newsweek*⟩ **2 a :** no longer fashionable or in demand **:** OUTMODED ⟨the work which is spurned as ~ becomes a period piece —A.L.Guérard⟩ ⟨a broad, dark, tree-lined street of ~ frame houses —Lester Atwell⟩ **b :** not up-to-date **:** behind the times ⟨the clinician without an active experimental laboratory attached to his wards is apt to be called ~ —*Science*⟩

**²passé** \"\ *n* -S [F, fr. past part. of *passer*] **:** a ballet movement in which the leg passes from one position to another

**³passe** \ˈpäs\ *n* -S [F, fr. *passer*] **:** the high numbers in roulette when a bet is made on them

**passecaille** *var of* PASSACAILLE

**passed** *past of* PASS

**passed ball** *n* [fr. past part. of ¹*pass*] **:** a pitched ball not hit by the batter that passes the catcher when he should have stopped it and allows a base runner to advance a base ⟨one of his trick pitches shot by his catcher for a *passed ball* —John Drebinger⟩

**passe-dix** \päsˈdēs\ *n, pl* **passe-dixes** [F, fr. *passer* to pass + *dix* ten, fr. L *decem* — more at TEN] **:** a game played with three dice in which the caster who is the banker bets even money that the pips on his cast of the three dice will total 10 or more

**passed master** *n* [fr. past part. of ¹*pass* (to go through an inspection successfully)] **:** a person who has passed as a master **:** one who is proficient in a particular field or activity ⟨*passed masters* in the use of the cliché —E.H.Criswell⟩ — compare PAST MASTER

**passed pawn** *n* [fr. past part. of ¹*pass* (to go by)] **:** a chess pawn having no enemy pawn before it on its own or an adjacent file

**passe-garde** *or* **pass-guard** \ˈpas,gärd\ *n* -S [³*pass* (thrust) + *guard*] **:** a piece fastened on the left elbow in medieval tilting armor; *sometimes* **:** GARDE-COLLET

**pas·sel** \ˈpasəl\ *n* -S [alter. of *parcel*] **:** a large number **:** GROUP ⟨a ~ of towheaded kids —Shelby Foote⟩ ⟨a whole ~ of notables —*Time*⟩

**pas·se·meas·ure** \ˈpasē,mezhə(r)\ *n* [modif. (influenced by *measure*) of It *passo e mezzo* — more at PASSAMEZZO] **:** PASSAMEZZO

**¹passe·ment** \ˈpasmənt\ *also* **pas·sa·ment** \-səm-\ *n* -S [MF *passement,* fr. *passer* to pass + *-ment*] **:** an ornamental braid or decorative trimming resembling lace and made of gold, silver, or silk threads

**²passe·ment** \ˈpa,smənt\ *vt* -ED/-ING/-S **:** to trim or edge with passement

**passe·men·terie** \paˈsmen·trē\ *n* -S [F, fr. *passement* + *-erie* -ery] **:** a fancy edging or ornamental trimming made of braid, cord, gimp, beading, or metallic thread in various combinations and used on clothing and upholstery

**passemezzo** *var of* PASSAMEZZO

**pas·sen·ger** \ˈpasᵊnjə(r)\ *n* -S *often attrib* [ME *passyngere, passager,* fr. MF *passager,* fr. *passager, passagier,* adj., passing, fr. *passage* + *-ier* -ary] **1 :** one who passes by **:** TRAVELER, WAYFARER ⟨the roads are wide, well-kept, and full of ~*s* —Thomas Gray⟩ ⟨foot ~⟩ **2 a :** a traveler in a public conveyance (as a train, bus, airplane, or ship) ⟨carried more ~*s* last year than ever before⟩ **b :** one who is carried in a private conveyance (as an automobile) for compensation or expected benefit to the owner **c :** a rider in an automobile ⟨a six-passenger model⟩ **3 :** a member of a group (as an animal in a herd) that contributes little or nothing to the functioning or productivity of the group ⟨all ~*s* should be eliminated from dairy herds —*Farmer's Weekly (So. Africa)*⟩

**passenger car** *n* **1 :** a railroad car (as a coach, parlor car, dining car, or sleeping car) for carrying passengers **2 :** an automobile for carrying a limited number of passengers (as no more than nine)

**passenger liner** *n* **:** a liner used mainly to carry passengers

**passenger list** *n* **:** a list of the passengers on a ship that is submitted by the master to customs officials at ports visited

**passenger-mile** *n* **:** a statistical unit denoting one mile traveled by one passenger and used by agencies of public transportation (as railroads, bus lines, or airlines) in measuring the volume of passenger traffic

**passenger mileage** *n* **:** the total number of miles traveled by passengers on a given agency of public transportation during a given period

**passenger pigeon** *n* **:** an extinct No. American wild pigeon (*Ectopistes migratorius*) of irregularly migratory habits once very abundant esp. in the Mississippi valley and having a long graduated tail, bluish slate upper parts with iridescence on the neck, a vinaceous breast, and a white belly

**passenger-train car** *n* **:** a railroad car used in passenger-train service for carrying mail, baggage, or express

**¹passe-par·tout** \ˌpa|spə(r)ˈtü, ˌpä|, |ˌspär-, |ˌspȧ-\ *n, pl* **passe-partouts** \-ü(z)\ [F, fr. the phrase *passe partout* pass everywhere] **1 :** something that passes or enables one to pass everywhere **:** MASTER KEY **2 a :** a piece or plate usu. of cardboard or wood that has its central portion cut out for the reception of a picture **b** (1) **:** a method of framing in which a picture, a mat, a glass, and a back (as of cardboard) are held together by strips of paper or cloth pasted over the edges (2) **:** a picture framed in such manner **3 :** a strong paper gummed on one side and commonly used for binding lantern slides and mounting pictures

**²passe-partout** \"\ *vt* -ED/-ING/-S **:** to frame with a passe-partout

**passe-passe** \'pä'späs\ *n, pl* **passe-passes** \-s(əz)\ [F, fr. the phrase used by jugglers *passe, passe* pass, pass] **:** a skillful feat of juggling or manipulation ⟨moving divisions from north to south and south to north . . . the kind of *passe-passe* that is a . . . delight —A.J.Liebling⟩

**passe·pied** \pä'spyā\ *also* **pas·py** \'paspē\ *n, pl* **passepieds** \-ā(z)\ *also* **paspies** \-ēz\ [F *passe-pied,* fr. *passer* to pass + *pied* foot, fr. L *ped-, pes* — more at FOOT] **:** a lively 17th and 18th century dance of French peasant origin resembling the minuet and beginning on the last beat of the measure; *also* **:** the music for this dance typically found in suites

**¹pass·er** \'pasə(r), 'paas-, 'pais-, 'pás-\ *n* -S [ME, fr. *passen* to pass + *-er*] **:** one that passes or causes to pass

**²pas·ser** \'pasə(r)\ *n, cap* [NL, fr. L, sparrow] **:** a genus consisting of the house sparrow and its near relatives

**pass·er·by** \'==,=\ *n, pl* **passersby** [¹*passer* + *by*] **:** one who passes by usu. by chance ⟨the robbery had been planned for a day when there would be fewer than the usual number of *passersby* —*N.Y. Times*⟩

**passe·relle** \päs'rel\ *n* -S [F, fr. *passer* to pass] **:** FOOTBRIDGE

**¹pas·ser·es** \'pasə,rēz\ [NL, fr. pl. of L *passer* sparrow] *syn of* PASSERIFORMES

**²passeres** \"\ *n pl, cap* **:** a very large suborder of Passeriformes comprising the typical singing birds that have a specialized vocal apparatus with four or five pairs of diacromyodian syringeal muscles

**pas·ser·i·form** \'pasərə,fȯrm, pə'serə,-\ *adj* [NL *Passeriformes*] **:** of or relating to the Passeriformes **:** PASSERINE

**pas·ser·i·for·mes** \,pasərə'fȯr,mēz\ *n pl, cap* [NL, fr. L *passer* + NL *-iformes*] **:** the largest order of birds including more than 5000 species or more than half of all living birds, consisting chiefly of songbirds of perching habits that range in size from the smallest titmice to the ravens and birds of paradise, being usu. divided into the four suborders Eurylaimi, Tyranni, Menurae, and Passeres, and comprising birds that are altricial, lack the ambiens muscle, and have the vomer well developed and truncate anteriorly with its forked posterior end embracing the basisphenoid, three toes in front and one behind and none reversible, 10 primaries of which the first is often rudimentary, and usu. 12 rectrices

**pas·ser·i·na** \,pasə'rīnə\ *n, cap* [NL, fr. L *passer* sparrow + NL *-ina*] **:** a genus of small No. American bush-loving finches resembling the tanager that are in the male brightly colored in blue or red or variegated and that include the indigo, lazuli, and painted buntings

**¹pas·ser·ine** \'pasərən, -sə,rīn, -sə,rēn\ *adj* [L *passerinus* of sparrows, fr. *passer* + *-inus* -ine] **:** of or relating to the Passeres or Passeriformes

**²passerine** \"\ *n* -S **:** a passerine bird

**¹passes** *pl of* PASS *or of* PASSE, *pres 3d sing of* PASS

**²passés** *pl of* PASSÉ

**pas seul** \pä'sōl\ *n, pl* **pas seuls** \-l(z)\ [F, lit., solo step] **:** a solo performance of a dance or a dance figure

**pas·se·wa** \pə'sāwə\ *n* -S [Hindi *pasevā* sweat, fr. Skt *prasveda,* fr. *pra-* forth + *svedate* he sweats — more at FOR, SWEAT] **:** a viscous extract from the capsules of the poppy that is obtained after the seeds are removed, hardens on exposure, and is used in making coverings for opium cakes

**pass examination** *n* **:** an examination for a pass degree or in a pass course

**pass·gang** \'päs,gäŋ\ *n* -S [G, lit., stepping gait, fr. *pass* step (fr. L *passus*) + *gang* going, gait — more at PACE, GANG] **:** a method of cross-country ski running in which each pole is brought forward simultaneously with the ski on the same side and is thrust so as to produce a glide with the opposite ski

**passguard** *var of* PASSEGARDE

**pas·si·bil·i·ty** \,pasə'biləd·ē\ *n* -ES [LL *passibilitas,* fr. *passibilis* passible + *-itat-, -itas* -ity] **:** the quality or state of being passible **:** SENSIBILITY

**pas·si·ble** \'pasəbəl\ *adj* [ME, fr. MF, fr. ML *passibilis,* fr. L *passus* (past part. of *pati* to suffer) + *-ibilis* -ible — more at PATIENT] **:** capable of feeling or suffering **:** IMPRESSIONABLE ⟨the more nervous, emotional, excitable, and ~ sex —Rose Macaulay⟩

**pas·si·flo·ra** \,pasə'flōrə\ *n* [NL, fr. *passi-* (fr. L *passion-, passio* passion) + *-flora* (fr. L *flor-, flos* flower) — more at BLOW (bloom)] **1** *cap* **:** a genus (the type of the family Passifloraceae) of mainly tropical American and mostly tendril-bearing vines that have simple or lobed leaves and usu. very showy chiefly red, white, or purple flowers with a short calyx tube, four or five petals, a corona, and numerous stamens monadelphous at base and followed by fruits which are pulpy often edible berries — see GRANADILLA, MAYPOP, PASSIONFLOWER **2** -S **:** any plant of the genus *Passiflora*

**pas·si·flo·ra·ce·ae** \,pasəflə'rāsē,ē\ *n pl, cap* [NL, fr. *Passiflora,* type genus + *-aceae*] **:** a family of tropical woody tendril-climbing vines or erect herbs (order Parietales) mostly with showy flowers distinguished chiefly by a fringed corona borne on the throat of the calyx and with a fruit that is a berry or capsule — **pas·si·flo·ra·ceous** \;===;rāshəs\ *adj*

**pas·si·flo·ra·les** \,==='rā(,)lēz\ *n pl, cap* [NL, fr. *Passiflora* + *-ales*] *in some classifications* **:** an order of dicotyledonous herbs, tendril-bearing vines, shrubs, and trees that have alternate leaves, pentamerous flowers with a superior one-celled ovary, and a fruit which is a berry or capsule and that include plants now usu. placed in Parietales and Cucurbitales

**pas·sim** \'pasəm\ *adv* [L, fr. *passus* spread about, scattered, past part. of *pandere* to spread out, unfold — more at FATHOM] **:** here and there **:** THROUGHOUT — used esp. with the name of a book or writer to indicate that something (as a word, phrase, or idea) is to be found at many places in the same book or writer's work

**pas·sim·e·ter** \pə'siməd·ə(r)\ *n* [prob. fr. ¹*pass* + *-i-* + *-meter*] **:** a turnstile operated from inside a change booth that gives access to a public transportation area (as a subway platform)

**¹pass·ing** \'pasiŋ, 'paas-, 'pais-, 'pás-, -sēŋ\ *n* -S [ME, fr. gerund of *passen* to pass] **1 :** the act of one that passes or causes to pass ⟨the ~ of winter⟩ ⟨the ~ of a great man⟩ ⟨the ~ of a major bill⟩ ⟨the ~ of the million dollar mark⟩ ⟨forward ~⟩ **2 :** a means of passing or crossing **:** FORD **3 :** the act of identifying oneself or accepting identification as a white person — used of a person having some Negro ancestry — **in passing** *adv* **:** by the way **:** PARENTHETICALLY

**²passing** \"\ *adj* [ME, fr. pres. part. of *passen* to pass] **1 :** going by **:** moving past ⟨a ~ youngster called up to him —Judson Philips⟩ ⟨observe with bright-eyed interest the ~ show of the squalid tenement in which they live —*Time*⟩ **2 :** having a brief duration **:** quickly vanishing **:** FLEETING, TRANSITORY ⟨the ~ vogues of the best sellers of the day —J.L.Lowes⟩ ⟨~ interest⟩ ⟨~ sensations⟩ **3** *obs* **:** EXCEEDING, SURPASSING ⟨a ~ traitor, perjured and unjust —Shak.⟩ **4 :** marked by haste, inattention, or inadequacy **:** CURSORY, SUPERFICIAL ⟨a ~ glance⟩ ⟨a few ~ remarks⟩ ⟨has only a ~ acquaintance with the subject⟩ **5 a :** of, relating to, or used in or for the act or process of passing ⟨a ~ place⟩ ⟨a ~ track⟩ **b :** given on satisfactory completion of an examination or course of study ⟨a ~ grade⟩ **syn** see TRANSIENT

**³passing** \"\ *prep* [ME, fr. ²*passing*] *archaic* **:** BEYOND

**⁴passing** \"\ *adv* [ME, fr. ²*passing*] **:** to a surpassing degree **:** EXCEEDINGLY, EXTREMELY, VERY ⟨wildflowers or cacti that will prove ~ strange to your eastern eyes —Jack Goodman⟩ ⟨~ fair⟩

**passing bell** *n* [¹*passing*] **1 :** a bell tolled to announce a death or funeral service — called also *death bell* **2 :** something that announces or marks a death **:** KNELL ⟨a moment's thought is passion's *passing bell* —John Keats⟩

**passing duck** *n* [²*passing*] **:** KING EIDER

**passing hollow** *n* **:** CRESCENT 3d

**passing light** *n* [¹*passing*] **:** a strong red light to warn passing airplanes displayed usu. in the leading edge on an airplane flying after dark

**pass·ing·ly** *adv* [ME, fr. ²*passing* + *-ly*] **1 a :** TEMPORARILY ⟨were in Cambridge — ~ for a few days —Lucien Price⟩ **b :** in passing **:** CURSORILY ⟨he has only studied ~ and is in danger of failing the course⟩ **2** *archaic* **:** EXCEEDINGLY, SURPASSINGLY

**pass·ing·ness** *n* -ES [²*passing* + *-ness*] **:** the quality or state of being transitory

**passing note** *or* **passing tone** *n* [¹*passing*] **:** a note or tone foreign to the harmony and usu. unaccented that is interposed for melodic smoothness between essential notes or tones

**passing shot** *n* **:** a passing stroke in tennis

**passing spring** *n* **:** GOLD SPRING

**passing strake** *n* **:** a continuous strake between butts in the same vertical plane in a ship

**passing stroke** *n* **1 :** a pass stroke in croquet **2 :** a stroke in tennis aimed to drive the ball to one side of and beyond the reach of an opponent at or coming toward the net

**passing zone** *n* [¹*passing*] **:** a zone 20 yards long in which a baton must be passed to the next runner in a relay race

**¹pas·sion** \'pashən, 'paash-, 'paish-\ *n* -S [ME *passion, passiun,* fr. OF, fr. LL *passion-, passio,* lit., suffering, fr. L *passus* (past part. of *pati* to suffer) + *-ion-, -io* -ion; in senses 4 & 5 fr. ME, fr. MF, fr. LL *passion-, passio,* trans. of Gk *pathos* — more at PATIENT] **1** *often cap* **a** (1) **:** the sufferings of Jesus on the cross (2) **:** the sufferings of Jesus between the night of the Last Supper and his death including the agony in Gethsemane ⟨places the redeeming ~ of Christ at the heart of revelation —*Times Lit. Supp.*⟩ ⟨the last dark period culminating in the *Passion* —F.J.Rae⟩ **b :** one of the gospel narratives of the passion of Jesus read or sung as the Gospel for the Day on four different days in Holy Week **c :** a musical setting of such a narrative; *esp* **:** an oratorio with narrative, chorales, airs, and choruses based on such a narrative **d :** PASSION PLAY **2 a :** the sufferings of a martyr **:** MARTYRDOM **b :** a narrative of such sufferings **3 a** *obs* **:** SUFFERING ⟨give her what comforts the quality of her ~ shall require —Shak.⟩ **b** *archaic* **:** a bodily disorder causing suffering or distress **4 a :** the state of being subjected to or acted on by what is external or foreign to one's true nature; *esp* **:** a state of desire or emotion that represents the influence of what is external and opposes thought and reason as the true activity of the human mind — contrasted with *action* **b :** a capacity of being affected or acted upon by external agents or influences ⟨moldable and not moldable . . . and many other ~s of matter —Francis Bacon⟩ **5 a** (1) **:** EMOTION, FEELING ⟨give me that man that is not ~'s slave —Shak.⟩ ⟨his ruling ~ is greed⟩ (2) **passions** *pl* **:** the emotions as distinguished from reason ⟨a study of the ~s⟩ **b :** violent, intense, or overmastering emotion **:** depth or vehemence of feeling **:** a state of or capacity for emotional excitement ⟨blue eyes that blazed with ~ as he expounded his favorite theme —Honor Tracy⟩ ⟨with enough ~ to make a great poet —W.B.Yeats⟩ ⟨when the immediate ~s of the war recede into the background —C.E.Black & E.C.Helmreich⟩ **c :** an outbreak of anger or a display of bad temper ⟨she flew into a ~ and stabbed him —R.H.Davis⟩ ⟨the grave and stately lady was for once in her life in a towering ~ —William Black⟩ **d** *archaic* **:** a writing or speech marked by intense feeling ⟨here she comes, and her ~ ends the play —Shak.⟩ **e :** a fit of emotional agitation **:** a surrender to a particular feeling **:** an uncontrollable display of emotion ⟨jumped up in a ~ of alarm —Louis Auchincloss⟩ ⟨began to sob and weep like a little boy, in a perfect ~ of emotion —H.G.Wells⟩ **6 a :** ardent affection **:** LOVE ⟨one of the truest ~s that ever was inspired by woman was raised in this bosom by that lady —W.M.Thackeray⟩ **b :** a strong liking for or devotion to some activity, object, or concept **:** ENTHUSIASM ⟨became troubled with the ~ for reforming the world —T.L.Peacock⟩ ⟨a ~ for chess⟩ ⟨a ~ for glory⟩ **c :** sexual desire ⟨look with ruffian ~ in her face —John Keats⟩ **d :** an object of desire or interest **:** something that commands one's love or devotion ⟨she is his ~ of the moment⟩ ⟨fishing is his present ~⟩

**syn** FERVOR, ARDOR, ENTHUSIASM, ZEAL: PASSION applies to intense, overwhelming, or driving emotion, sometimes displayed with agitated vehemence, sometimes indicating intense erotic feeling ⟨with fanatical *passion* he attacked Calvinism and presented Methodism as teaching the only way of salvation —H.E.Starr⟩ ⟨an ungovernable childlike *passion* —W.B.Yeats⟩ ⟨launches into a frenzied oration with the *passion* of Savanarola —C.L.Sulzberger⟩ ⟨the purely physical urges of sex and its gratification can be summed up as *passion* —Lois Pemberton⟩ FERVOR may designate any strong steadily glowing lasting emotion ⟨preached emancipation as a revival in benevolence, with a *fervor* which mobs could not silence —G.H.Barnes⟩ ⟨the man who seizes on one deep-reaching idea, whether newly found or rediscovered, and with single-hearted *fervor* forces it upon the world —P.E.More⟩ ARDOR may differ in suggesting a more demonstrative and excited feeling not so long-lived, although the two words are sometimes interchangeable ⟨the raptures and *ardors* of sudden conversion to any cause —H.V.Gregory⟩ ⟨imperialism left slain behind, she embraced with *ardor* the fantastic ideal of the cleaning up of England —Rose Macaulay⟩ ENTHUSIASM may apply to intense interest or admiration for something, often a matter more objective, tangible, or mundane than those calling forth ardor ⟨whose proposed visit to the U.S. was then stirring *enthusiasm* among Louisiana-French people —*Amer. Guide Series: La.*⟩ ⟨waging the campaign of 1856 with *enthusiasm* —Carol L. Thompson⟩ ZEAL suggests enthusiastic devotion to a cause ⟨missionary *zeal*⟩ ⟨the *zeal* of the Inquisition to burn heretics —M.R.Cohen⟩ ⟨his health was further affected by his *zeal* in public affairs as well as his enthusiasm in study —Havelock Ellis⟩ **syn** see in addition DESIRE, DISTRESS, FEELING

**²passion** \"\ *vb* -ED/-ING/-S [ME *passionen,* fr. MF *passionner,* fr. *passion*] *vt* **:** to affect or fill with passion ⟨turtles ~ their voices cooingly —John Keats⟩ ~ *vi* **:** to display or become affected by passion ⟨beautiful garden where he had played and ~*ed* in varying moments of grief and glee —George Moore⟩

**¹pas·sion·al** \-shən°l, -shnəl\ *n* -S [ML *passionale,* fr. LL, neut. of *passionalis,* adj.] **:** a book that contains accounts of the sufferings of saints and martyrs to be read on their festivals

**²passional** \"\ *adj* [LL *passionalis,* fr. *passion-, passio* passion + L *-alis,* -al] **:** of or relating to passion or the passions **:** marked by, filled with, or exciting passion ⟨the emotional and ~ fervor of the evangelist —Adria Langley⟩

**pas·sion·ary** \'pashə,nerē\ *n* -ES [ML *passionarium,* fr. LL *passion-, passio* passion + L *-arium* -ary] **:** PASSIONAL

**¹pas·sion·ate** \'pash(ə)nət, 'paash-, 'paish, *usu* -əd·+V\ *adj* [ML *passionatus,* fr. LL *passion-, passio* + L *-atus,* -ate] **1 a :** easily aroused to anger **:** IRASCIBLE, QUICK-TEMPERED ⟨a ~ but not a vicious boy —H.E.Scudder⟩ **b :** filled with or marked by anger **:** ANGRY, ENRAGED ⟨was ~ in defense of her cub, and rage transformed her —G.D.Brown⟩ **2 a :** dominated by strong emotion **:** capable of or affected by intense feeling **:** ARDENT ⟨a ~ and stormy personality⟩ ⟨a ~ and unquestioned faith in the virtue of the cause he served —C.L.Becker⟩ **b :** expressing or communicating violent or intense feeling ⟨a ~ speech⟩ ⟨a ~ performance of the symphony⟩ ⟨a ~ bit of acting⟩ **c :** ENTHUSIASTIC, VEHEMENT ⟨the army was now ~ for an engagement —J.A.Froude⟩ ⟨has become a ~ housekeeper —Joseph Mitchell⟩ **d :** UNRESTRAINED ⟨broke down in a flood of ~ weeping —C.B.Nordhoff & J.N.Hall⟩ **3 :** swayed by or affected with sexual desire ⟨her beauty made an immediate appeal to his ~ temperament⟩ **4 a** *obs* **:** affected with grief **:** SAD, SORROWFUL **b** *chiefly dial* **:** COMPASSIONATE **syn** see IMPASSIONED

**²passionate** *vt* -ED/-ING/-S **1** *obs* **:** to fill with passion **2** *obs* **:** to express or portray with passion

**pas·sion·ate·ly** *adv* **:** in a passionate manner **:** with great feeling **:** ARDENTLY, ENTHUSIASTICALLY

**pas·sion·ate·ness** *n* -ES **:** the quality or state of being passionate

**pas·si·o·na·to** \,päsēə'nä(,)dō, ¦pas-, -syə¦-, ¦pashə¦-\ *adv (or adj)* [It, fr. ML *passionatus* passionate] **:** in a passionate manner **:** with passion **:** FERVENTLY — used as a direction in music

**passion cross** *n* **:** LATIN CROSS

**pas·sioned** \'pashənd, 'paash-, 'paish-\ *adj* [¹*passion* + *-ed*] **:** affected with or marked by passion **:** PASSIONATE

**pas·sionflower** \'==,=\ *n* [trans. of NL *flos passionis,* lit., flower of the Passion; fr. the fancied resemblance of parts of the flower to the instruments of Christ's crucifixion] **:** a plant of the genus *Passiflora*

**passionflower family** *n* **:** PASSIFLORACEAE

**passion fruit** *n* **:** an edible fruit of a passionflower

**pas·sion·ful** \'pashənfəl\ *adj* **:** full of or capable of passion **:** PASSIONATE — **pas·sion·ful·ness** *n* -ES

**passioning** *pres part of* PASSION

**pas·sion·ist** \'pashənəst\ *n* -S *usu cap* [It *passionista,* fr. *passione* passion (fr. LL *passion-, passio*) + It *-ista* -ist] **:** a member of a Roman Catholic religious order founded by St. Paul of the Cross in 1720 and devoted chiefly to missionary work

**pas·sion·less** \'pashənləs, 'paash-, 'paish-\ *adj* **1 :** devoid of passion **:** empty of feeling ⟨this ~ girl was like an icicle in the sunshine —Margaret Deland⟩ **2 :** CALM, DETACHED ⟨the same steady impersonal ~ observation of human nature —T.S.Eliot⟩ — **pas·sion·less·ly** *adv* — **pas·sion·less·ness** *n* -ES

**passion music** *n, usu cap P* **:** PASSION 1c

**passion play** *n* **1** *often cap 1st P* **:** a dramatic representation of the scenes connected with the passion of Jesus **2 :** a dramatic representation of the sufferings and death of an outstanding religious or spiritual leader

**passions** *pl of* PASSION, *pres 3d sing of* PASSION

**passion sunday** *n, usu cap P&S* [ME, trans. of ML *Dominica in Passione*] **:** the fifth Sunday in Lent or the second before Easter

**passiontide** \'==,=\ *n, usu cap* [¹*passion* + *tide* (time)] **:** the last two weeks of Lent

**passion vine** *n* **:** PASSIONFLOWER

**passion week** *n, usu cap P&W* [ME, trans. of ML *hebdomada Passionis*] **1 :** HOLY WEEK **2 :** the second week before Easter occurring between Passion Sunday and Palm Sunday

**pas·si·vate** \'pasə,vāt\ *vt* -ED/-ING/-S [¹*passive* + *-ate*] **:** to make passive or inactive — **pas·si·va·tion** \,==='vāshən\ *n* -S

**pas·si·va·tor** \'===,vād·ə(r)\ *n* -S [*passivate* + *-or*] **:** a substance (as a chromate) that passivates esp. by forming a protective film on a metal

**¹pas·sive** \'pasiv, 'paas-, 'pais-, -sēv *also* -səv\ *adj* [ME, fr. L *passivus,* fr. *passus* (past part. of *pati* to suffer, undergo) + *-ivus* -ive — more at PATIENT] **1 a :** not acting but acted upon **:** subject to or produced by an external agency **:** receptive to outside impressions or influences ⟨nature is neutral and ~ —W.P.Webb⟩ ⟨takes his color from his surroundings, a ~ agent of his environment —Van Wyck Brooks⟩ **b** (1) *of a verb form or voice* **:** asserting that the person or thing represented by the grammatical subject is subjected to or affected by the action represented by the verb ⟨*was hit* in "he was hit by the ball" and *was given* in "he was given a prize" are ~⟩ — compare ACTIVE (2) *of a grammatical construction* **:** containing a passive verb form **c :** lacking in energy or will **:** LETHARGIC ⟨its people are a ~, frustrated, and resigned lot —John Mason Brown⟩ ⟨a vague, ~ girl, content to remain at home and dream —Ruth Blodgett⟩ **d :** induced by an outside agency without either active participation or resistance of the individual affected ⟨neuromuscular reeducation through ~ exercise⟩ **2 a :** not active or operating **:** not moving **:** INERT, QUIESCENT ⟨the faint light from the street lamp outlined the ~ hump he made in the bedclothes —Dorothy Sayers⟩ ⟨engines ~ as great cats —Thomas Wolfe⟩ **b :** existing in a dormant state but capable of being used or brought into play **:** LATENT ⟨has a larger ~ vocabulary than he realizes⟩ **c :** of, relating to, or characterized by a state of chemical inactivity **:** not reacting readily **:** resistant to corrosion ⟨iron and nickel become ~ when treated with fuming nitric acid⟩ **3** *Scots law* **:** of, relating to, or subject to a liability **4 a :** receiving or enduring without resistance **:** PATIENT, SUBMISSIVE, UNRESISTING ⟨there is in her a ~ surrender to the powers of life —P.E. More⟩ ⟨no one has a right explicitly to make of another a mere ~ instrument of his will —G.L.Dickinson⟩ **b :** carried through or expressed by indirect means **:** existing without being active or open ⟨~ support⟩ **syn** see INACTIVE

**²passive** \"\ *n* -S [ME, fr. ¹*passive*] **1 a :** something (as a person, object, or quality) acted upon by something else — usu. used in pl. **b** *or* **passive bobbin :** HANGER 5 **2 a :** a passive verb **b :** the passive voice of a language or a form in it

**passive anaphylaxis** *n* **:** anaphylaxis in a normal animal sensitized to a specific substance by injection of serum from an animal sensitized to that substance by direct injection

**passive congestion** *n* **:** congestion caused by obstruction to the return flow of venous blood

**passive defense** *n* **:** a defense designed solely to resist in place or minimize the effects of an attack against a specified area, position, or front

**passive hyperemia** *n* **:** PASSIVE CONGESTION

**passive immunity** *n* **:** immunity acquired by transfer of antibodies from an actively immune individual

**pas·sive·ly** \-səvlē, -li\ *adv* **1 :** in a passive manner **2 :** in the passive voice **:** in a passive construction

**pas·sive·ness** \-sivnəs\ *n* -ES **:** the quality or state of being passive

**passive noun** *n* **:** a noun indicating the recipient of action ⟨*advisee* and *employee* are *passive nouns*⟩

**passive obedience** *n* **:** absolute obedience or submission of a subject to the authority of a ruler regarded by some political writers as mandatory even when the ruler is bad — compare DIVINE RIGHT

**passive resistance** *n* **:** resistance (as to a government or an occupying power) that does not resort to violence or active measures of opposition but depends mainly on techniques and acts of noncooperation

**passive resister** *n* **:** one who practices passive resistance

**passive transfer** *n* **:** a local transfer of skin sensitivity from an allergic to a normal person by injection of serum from the former used esp. for identifying specific allergens when a high degree of allergic sensitivity is suspected

**passive trust** *n* **:** a trust in which the trustee has no active duty other than to hold title for the benefit of the designated beneficiary — called also *dry trust*

**pas·siv·ism** \'pasə,vizəm, 'paas-, 'pais-\ *n* -S **:** a passive attitude, behavior, or way of life ⟨the ~ which has become so much a part of our American recreation —H.A.Block⟩

**pas·siv·ist** \-,vəst\ *n* -S **1 :** one given to passivism **2 :** PASSIVE RESISTER

**pas·siv·i·ty** \pa'sivəd·ē, -ətē, -i\ *n* -ES [¹*passive* + *-ity*] **1 a :** the quality or state of being acted upon from without **:** PASSIVENESS ⟨a certain obstinate patient ~, a certain lying back upon life —J.C.Powys⟩ ⟨his aggressive trends were efforts to compensate for his inherent ~ —Charles Anderson⟩ **b :** an instance of passiveness **:** something that is passive ⟨a vast activity of writers, a vast and hungry ~ of readers —Aldous Huxley⟩ **c** (1) **:** chemically inactive state **:** INACTIVITY — used esp. of a metal that has lost its normal chemical activity and is resistant to corrosion (2) **:** inactivity of an electrode due to polarization **2 :** an absence of activity, initiative, or decisiveness **:** INERTIA ⟨what amounts in modern battle to stupid ~ —Tom Wintringham⟩ **3 :** a submission to the will of another or to outside force **:** SUBMISSIVENESS ⟨has emerged from the ~ of defeat to seize and assert its independence —*Time*⟩ **4 :** the construction of the passive voice **:** the meaning expressed by the passive voice

**passkey** \'=,=\ *n* [¹*pass* + *key*] **1 :** MASTER KEY **2 :** LATCHKEY **3 :** SKELETON KEY

**pass·less** \'pasləs\ *adj* [¹*pass* + *-less*] **:** IMPASSABLE

**pass line** *n* [¹*pass*] **:** LINE 13a

**pass·man** \'pasman, -,maa(ə)n, -mən\ *n, pl* **passmen :** a student enrolled in a pass course at a British university ⟨they are not educated: they are only college *passmen* —G.B. Shaw⟩

**pass master** *n* [¹*pass*] **:** an officer under the old English poor laws having the duty of passing vagrant or nonresident paupers on to their own parishes or unions

**pass off** *vt* **1 :** to make public or offer for sale with intent to deceive **:** present fraudulently ⟨*passed* it *off* as a genuine antique⟩ ⟨*passed off* paste as jewels⟩ **2 :** to give a false identity or character to ⟨*passes* himself *off* as a learned man⟩ ~ *vi* **1 :** to disappear by degrees **:** go away gradually ⟨the numbness will *pass off* in a few hours⟩ **2 :** to last through to completion ⟨the rest of the evening *passed off* badly —Hamilton Basso⟩ ⟨his stay in France *passed off* smoothly —*Times Lit. Supp.*⟩

**pas·som·e·ter** \pa'sämәd·ә(r)\ *n* [L *passus* step + E *-o-* + *-meter* — more at PACE] **:** an instrument shaped like a watch that is used to count the number of a person's steps — compare PEDOMETER

**¹passout** \'ˌ,ˌ\ *or* **pass-out check** \'ˌ,ˌ-\ *n* -s [fr. the phrase *pass out*] **:** something (as a ticket) that permits one to pass out of or reenter a place (as a theater or ball park) to which admission has usu. been paid

**²passout** \"\ *n* -s [fr. the phrase *pass out*] **:** draw poker in which a player must either bet or drop out

**pass out** *vi* **1 a :** to lose consciousness ⟨was pretty well plastered, but he rarely got to the stage where he *passed out* —Myron Brinig⟩ ⟨three men *passed out* from heat exhaustion —F.J.Bell⟩ **b :** to go out of existence **:** DIE ⟨if it was going to *pass out*, I thought it ought to die as it had lived —Edmund Wilson⟩ **2** *Brit* **:** GRADUATE ⟨*passed out* when he was nineteen with a degree in chemistry —Nevil Shute⟩

**passover** \'ˌ,ˌˌ\ *n* -s [fr. the phrase *pass over*; fr. the exemption of the Israelites from the slaughter of the first-born in Egypt, Exod 12:23–27] **1** *usu cap* **:** an annual religious and spring festival of the Jews that commemorates the agricultural festival of the Jews that commemorates the liberation of the Hebrews from slavery in Egypt and that begins on the evening of the 14th day of the month of Nisan and by extension includes the 8 days following or (as orig. and among reform Jews and in modern Israel) the 7 days following — called also *Pesach* **2 :** the sacrifice at the feast of the Passover **:** PASCHAL LAMB ⟨Christ our ~ is sacrificed for us —1 Cor 5:7 (AV)⟩

**pass over** *vt* **1 :** to ignore in passing **:** deliberately fail to notice ⟨I will *pass over* this aspect of the book in silence⟩ **2 :** to pay no attention to the claims of **:** DISREGARD ⟨though he was next in line for the post, the committee *passed* him *over*⟩

**¹pass·port** \'pas,pō(ә)r|t, 'paas-, 'pais-, -pȯ(ә)r|, -ōә|, -ȯ(ә)|, *usu* |d·+V\ *n* [MF *passeport*, fr. *passer* to pass + *port* port, fr. L *portus* — more at FORD] **1 a :** a formal document issued by a competent officer (as a secretary of state) of a country to a citizen of the country and now usu. necessary for exit from and reentry into the country, that certifies to the identity and citizenship of the bearer, calls upon the officers of foreign governments to extend protection to him when needed, and allows him to travel within the borders of a foreign country when it has been endorsed with a visa by an authorized official of that country **b :** SEA LETTER **c :** a license issued by a state permitting a foreign citizen to pass or take goods through its territory **:** SAFE-CONDUCT **d :** a document of identification required by the laws of a country to be carried by persons residing or traveling within that country ⟨in Germany the labor ~s were compulsory only for persons under twenty-one —Manya Gordon⟩ **2 a :** a permission or authorization to go somewhere ⟨held that good works were a ~ to heaven —R.M.Lovett⟩ ⟨the composer managed to write a concerto . . . which proved to be his ~ to Paris —Howard Dietz⟩ **b :** something that introduces or guarantees admission or acceptance **:** VOUCHER **c :** something that secures admission or acceptance **:** a means of entry into some group, society, or condition of life ⟨may cultivate art as a culture, as a ~ to more exclusive circles of society —Herbert Read⟩ ⟨trained intellect was henceforth to be a young man's best ~ —G.M.Trevelyan⟩ ⟨a ~ to fame⟩

**²passport** \"\ *vt* -ED/-ING/-S **:** to provide with a passport

**pass·port·less** \-tlәs\ *adj* **:** having no passport

**pass shooting** *n* **:** the shooting of birds (as wild ducks) when they pass over a particular course

**pass stroke** *n* **:** a stroke in croqueting that sends the player's ball farther in the same direction than the other ball

**pass-through** \'ˌ,ˌ\ *n* -s [fr. the phrase *pass through*] **:** an opening in a wall between two rooms of a house or apartment (as between a kitchen and dining room) through which something (as dishes) may be passed

**passt-mir-nicht** \'päst,mi(ә)r'nikt\ *n* -s [G *passt mir nicht* does not suit me] **:** a player's right to reject the first card turned in the game of tournee and let the second card establish the trump suit

**pass up** *vt* **:** to let go by **:** DECLINE **:** DISREGARD **:** REJECT ⟨*passed up* an invitation to dinner⟩ ⟨*passed up* a chance for promotion⟩

**pas·sus** \'pasәs\ *n*, *pl* **passus** *or* **passuses** [ML, passage in a book or document, fr. L, step — more at PACE] **:** a division or part of a narrative or poem

**passwalk** \'ˌ,ˌ\ *n* [part trans. of G *passgang*] **:** PASSGANG

**passway** \'ˌ,ˌ\ *n* [¹*pass* + *way*] **:** a means of passage **:** PASS

**password** \'ˌ,ˌ\ *n* **1 a :** a word or phrase that must be spoken by a person before he is allowed to pass a barrier or guard **:** COUNTERSIGN **b :** something that enables one to pass or gain admission ⟨food in any form was the magic ~ to her heart —Evelyn Barkins⟩ **2 :** a secret word or formula used as a sign of greeting or recognition among members of a society or group **:** WATCHWORD ⟨has the usual grips and ~s —C.W.Ferguson⟩

**passymeasure** *n* [modif. (influenced by *measure*) of It *passo e mezzo* — more at PASSAMEZZO] *obs* **:** PASSAMEZZO

**¹past** \'past, 'paa(ә)st, 'paist, 'pȧst\ *adj* [ME *passed*, *past*, fr. past part. of *passen* to pass] **1 a :** gone by **:** AGO ⟨started working on this project ten years ~⟩ **b :** just gone by or elapsed **:** immediately preceding ⟨the oily swell of the ~ storm —Norman Douglas⟩ ⟨had been sitting in the darkness for nearly an hour —Lucien Price⟩ ⟨the ~ election⟩ ⟨the ~ few months⟩ **c** *archaic* **:** of the past month ⟨your letter of the 30th ~ —Earl of Chesterfield⟩ **2 :** belonging to a former time **:** having existed or taken place in a period before the present **:** BYGONE ⟨in explanation and defense of his own ~ acts —W.C.Ford⟩ ⟨lived in some ~ world, two or three hundred years ago —R.W.Emerson⟩ **3 :** of, relating to, or constituting a verb tense that in English is usu. formed by internal vowel change (as in *sang*) or by the addition of a suffix (as in *laughed*) and that is expressive of time gone by **4 :** having served as a specified officer in a society, order, or organization ⟨~ president⟩ ⟨~ commander⟩ ⟨~ medical director⟩

**²past** \"\ *prep* [ME *passed*, *past*, fr. past part. of *passen*] **1 a :** beyond the age for or of ⟨my father was just ~ his first vote —Ben Riker⟩ ⟨~ playing with dolls⟩ **b :** later than **:** AFTER ⟨it was now ~ sunset —Lucien Price⟩ ⟨~ the turn of the year —*Atlantic*⟩ ⟨a quarter ~ two⟩ **c :** older than ⟨is now ~ 60⟩ ⟨is just ~ four⟩ **2 a :** at the farther side of **:** BEYOND ⟨the entrance to the dining room is just ~ the elevators on your right —Hamilton Basso⟩ **b :** in a course going close to and then beyond ⟨women pushed ~ arguing men to reach the counter —Stuart Cloete⟩ ⟨the railroad runs ~ the house⟩ **c :** in a direction going close to and then beyond ⟨standing by the monument and gazing down the grassy aisle ~ the heaps of crumpled chimney stones —Frederick Nebel⟩ **3** *obs* **:** more than ⟨has not ~ three or four hairs on his chin —Shak.⟩ **4 a :** beyond the reach or influence of **:** out of the range, scope, or sphere of **:** incapable of ⟨has declined ~ all help —*Sat. Eve. Post*⟩ ⟨had a way with a horse that was ~ explaining —Gerald Beaumont⟩ ⟨a dilemma ~ solution —Jean Stafford⟩ **b :** beyond the capacity or power of ⟨wouldn't put it ~ him to play a trick like that⟩ **c :** beyond in degree or manner ⟨has gone far ~ other writers in his experiments with language⟩ — **past oneself** *dial Eng* **:** beside oneself

**³past** \"\ *n* -s [¹*past*] **1 a :** former time **:** time gone by ⟨men will turn to the ~ then, as we should now, chiefly to discover the ways of avoiding error —Harlow Shapley⟩ **b :** something that happened or was done in the past ⟨promised to atone for the ~⟩ **2 a :** the past tense of a language **b :** a verb form in the past tense **3 a :** a past life, history, or course of action ⟨for ancient families with chequered ~s he had a romantic reverence —John Buchan⟩ **b :** a past life or career that is unknown or deliberately kept secret; *esp* **:** a concealed episode or history of criminal or immoral behavior ⟨his ~ caught up with him when an old prison friend recognized him⟩ ⟨a woman with a ~⟩

**⁴past** \"\ *adv* [²*past*] **1 :** so as to reach and go by a point near at hand **:** BY ⟨every moment or so, the trains clank ~ —Hollis Alpert⟩ ⟨counted all eight porters coming ~ —D.L. Busk⟩ **2** *Scot & Irish* **:** ASIDE, AWAY ⟨lay them ~ to rust —William Carleton⟩

**pas·ta** \'pästә\ *n* -s [It, fr. LL, dough, paste — more at PASTE] **1 :** alimentary paste in processed form (as spaghetti, or macaroni) or in the form of fresh dough (as ravioli) **2 :** a dish of cooked pasta

**past absolute** *n* [³*past* + *absolute*, adj.] **:** PAST TENSE a

**pasta fi·la·ta cheese** \-fē'läd·ә-\ *n* [It *pasta filata*, lit., spun pasta] **:** a cheese characterized by plasticity of the curd while it is being worked and molded ⟨provolone and mozzarella are *pasta filata cheeses*⟩

**pas·tance** \'pastәn(t)s\ *n* -s [modif. of MF *passe-temps*, fr. *passer* to pass + *temps* time, fr. L *tempus* — more at TEMPORAL] *archaic* **:** PASTIME

**past continuous** *n* **:** PAST TENSE b

**past descriptive** *n* **:** PAST TENSE b

**past-due** \'ˌ,ˌ\ *adj* **:** OVERDUE

**¹paste** \'pāst\ *n* -s [ME, fr. MF, fr. LL *pasta* dough, paste, perh. fr. Gk *pastē* barley sauce, fr. fem. of *pastos* sprinkled, salted, fr. *passein* to sprinkle — more at QUASH] **1 a** (1) **:** a dough containing a large proportion of fat that is used for pastry crust (2) **:** a dough containing a moderate proportion of fat that is used for fancy rolls (as brioches) **b :** a confection made by evaporating fruit with sugar or by flavoring a gelatin, starch, or gum arabic preparation **c :** a soft or doughy mixture used as bait in fishing **d :** a smooth food product made by evaporation or grinding ⟨almond ~⟩ ⟨tomato ~⟩ ⟨sardine ~⟩ **e** [trans. of It *pasta*] **:** ALIMENTARY PASTE **2 :** a soft plastic mixture or composition: as **a** (1) **:** a preparation usu. of flour or starch and water used as a cement for uniting paper or other substances (as in bookbinding) (2) **:** a similar preparation used in calico printing as a vehicle for mordant or color **b :** a moistened clay mixture that is used in making pottery or porcelain — see HARD PASTE, SOFT PASTE **c :** an external medicament that has a stiffer consistency than an ointment but is less greasy because of its higher percentage of powdered ingredients **d :** a mixture of a pigment and a paint vehicle that requires the addition of more vehicle before it can be used **e :** a mixture of cement and water **:** the cement and water portion of mortar or concrete **3 :** MATERIAL, STUFF ⟨a man of a different ~ —Robert Browning⟩ **4 :** a brilliant glass of high lead content used for the manufacture of artificial gems; *also* **:** an imitation gem made of this material — called also *strass*

**²paste** \"\ *vb* -ED/-ING/-S *vt* **1 a :** to cause to adhere by or as if by means of paste **:** STICK ⟨a poster that had just been *pasted* on a pillar of the general post office —O.S.J.Gogarty⟩ ⟨a wry grin *pasted* onto his dirty face —William Chamberlain⟩ **b :** SPREAD ⟨gave him bread, and *pasted* the butter upon it very thickly —Louis Golding⟩ ⟨the lamps along the river *pasted* long oily golden tracks on the water —R.H.Newman⟩ **2 a :** to cover by or as if by pasting ⟨the ceiling is *pasted* with labels of liquor brands —*This Week in Chicago*⟩ **b :** to repair (a target) for reuse by pasting paper over bullet holes **3 :** to incorporate (as a color in dyeing) with a paste **:** apply paste to **4 :** to convert into a paste ⟨the dry powder is first *pasted* with cold water —*Encyc. of Chem. Technol.*⟩ ~ *vi* **:** to apply paste **:** paste something

**³paste** \"\ *n* -s [modif. of MF *passe*, part of a woman's hat that shades the face, fr. *passer* to pass] **:** a woman's ornamental headdress of the 16th century

**⁴paste** \"\ *vt* -ED/-ING/-S [alter. of *baste* (to beat)] **:** to strike hard at **:** deliver a blow or series of blows against ⟨*pasted* the enemy's greatest source of supply —*Newsweek*⟩ ⟨that time they *pasted* the command post —Fred Majdalany⟩

**⁵paste** \"\ *n* -s *slang* **:** a hard blow or punch ⟨a ~ in the jaw⟩

**¹pasteboard** \'ˌ,ˌ\ *n* [²*paste* + *board*] **1 :** paperboard made by pasting together two or more sheets or plies; *broadly* **:** paperboard esp. when comparatively thin and stiff **2 a :** VISITING CARD **b :** PLAYING CARD **c :** a railroad ticket or a ticket of admission (as to a theater or ball park) **3** [¹*paste* + *board*] **:** a board on which dough is rolled **:** BREADBOARD ⟨a snowy cloth with ~ and rolling pin upon it —Flora Thompson⟩ **4 :** a board on which a paperhanger or a paster lays the paper or work to be pasted

**²pasteboard** \"\ *adj* **1 :** made of pasteboard ⟨a ~ box⟩ **2 :** of inferior material, construction, or quality **:** FLIMSY, SHAM, UNSUBSTANTIAL ⟨the glittering but ~ life of the palace —F. Tennyson Jesse⟩ ⟨~ romanticism —V.S.Pritchett⟩

**pasted** *adj* [fr. past part. of ²*paste*] **:** fastened or covered with or as if with paste

**pastedown** \'ˌ,ˌ\ *n* -s **:** the outer leaf of an endpaper that is pasted down to the inside of the front or back cover of a book

**paste filler** *n* [¹*paste*] **:** a compound of silica and drying oil used as a filler for open grain wood (as oak)

**paste grain** *n* **:** a thin leather (as sheepskin) with an application of paste on the back to stiffen and strengthen it

**¹pas·tel** \(')pa'stel\ *n* -s [MF, fr. Prov, fr. LL *pastellus* woad, dim. of LL *pasta* paste; fr. the paste made of its twigs in producing the dye] **:** WOAD

**²pastel** \"\ *n* -s [F, fr. It *pastello* fr. LL *pastellus*] **1 :** a paste composed of a color ground and compounded with gum water and used for making crayons; *also* **:** a crayon made of such paste **2 a :** a drawing in pastel **b :** the process or art of drawing with pastels **3 :** a light, brief, and rather formless literary study or sketch **4 :** any of various pale or light colors ⟨its colors lost their infernal intensity, paled to harmless-looking but deadly ~s —*Time*⟩

**³pastel** \"\ *adj* **1 :** of or relating to a pastel **:** made with pastels ⟨a ~ drawing⟩ **2 :** pale and light in color **:** lacking in brilliance or intensity ⟨~ shades⟩ ⟨a ~ prettiness⟩ **3 :** resembling a pastel **:** lacking in body or vigor **:** DELICATE, LIGHT ⟨a ~ and dreamy world — rather thin and bloodless —J.F.Nims⟩ ⟨a tendency to suffuse with a ~ optimism even the dark moments —Leon Edel⟩

**pastel blue** *n* **1 :** a variable color averaging a pale blue that is redder than average powder blue and greener, lighter, and stronger than Sistine or average cadet gray **2** *of textiles* **:** a very pale blue that is redder and duller than baby blue (sense 1) and redder and deeper than cloud blue

**pastel gray** *n* **:** a grayish yellow that is paler and slightly redder than chamois and redder, lighter, and stronger than old ivory

**pastel green** *n* **:** a variable color averaging a light yellowish green that is paler than apple green (sense 2), greener and paler than pistachio green, and greener and duller than ocean green

**pas·tel·ist** *or* **pas·tel·list** \-lәst\ *n* -s **:** a maker of pastel drawings

**pastel orange** *n* **:** a moderate orange that is yellower and duller than honeydew, duller and slightly yellower than Persian orange, and redder and duller than mikado orange

**pastel pink** *n* **1 :** a moderate yellowish pink that is redder and lighter than coral pink, redder, lighter, and stronger than dusty pink, and redder and stronger than average peach **2** *of textiles* **:** a moderate pink that is yellower and less strong than arbutus pink and bluer and stronger than hydrangea pink

**pastel turquoise green** *n* **:** a light bluish green that is greener and paler than average turquoise green or average aqua green (sense 1) and bluer and lighter than robin's-egg blue (sense 2)

**pastel yellow** *n* **:** a variable color averaging a light greenish yellow that is redder and paler than sulphur yellow and redder, duller, and slightly less strong than Martius yellow

**paste mold** *n* [¹*paste*] **:** an iron mold lined with adherent carbon that is used wet to shape a circular glass object as it is blown

**paste paper** *n* **:** a patterned or textured paper made by applying brushes and hand tools to the surface of a paper that has been coated with thin colored paste and is still wet

**pastepot** *n* **:** a small container of paste that is ready to use (as by an editor)

**paste print** *n* **:** an impression made in glutinous ink or upon a thick paste from a white-line engraving or metal cut

**past·er** \'pāstә(r)\ *n* -s **1 :** one that pastes: as **a :** a worker who stretches leather for drying by pasting it smoothly on boards or plates **b :** a worker who arranges floor tiles into a form board according to a sketched design and pastes a sheet of paper to the top to preserve the pattern **c :** LUTER **d :** a machine that applies paste **2 :** a slip of paper with a gummed back that is intended to be pasted on or over something **:** STICKER

**pas·tern** \'pastә(r)n\ *n* -s [MF *pasturon*, fr. *pasture* pasture, tether attached to the foot of a horse at pasture, pastern — more at PASTURE] **:** a part of the foot of an equine that lies between the fetlock and the coffin joint; *broadly* **:** a corresponding part of the leg of other animals (as a dog) — see COW illustration

**pastern bone** *n* **:** either of two bones in the foot of an equine between the cannon bone and the coffin bone

**pastern joint** *n* **:** the joint between the great and small pastern bones

**pastes** *pl of* PASTE, *pres 3d sing of* PASTE

**paste-up** \'ˌ,ˌ\ *n* -s [²*paste*] **1 :** MECHANICAL **2 :** a literary work prepared for publication or production by the piecing together of material previously used ⟨this book is not a new work but a *paste-up* of old magazine articles⟩ **3 :** a picture made by pasting together parts of two or more photographs

**pas·teur effect** \pa'stәr-\ *n*, *usu cap P* [after Louis *Pasteur* †1895 Fr. chemist and bacteriologist] **:** the inhibiting effect of oxygen upon a fermentative process (as one carried on by facultative anaerobic organisms)

**pas·teu·rel·la** \,pastә'relә\ *n* [NL, fr. Louis *Pasteur* + NL *-ella*] **1** *cap* **:** a genus of bacteria (family Brucellaceae) that stain differentially at the poles of the cell and that include several important pathogens of man and domestic animals — see HEMORRHAGIC SEPTICEMIA, PLAGUE, TULAREMIA **2** *pl* **pasteurellas** *or* **pasturellae :** any bacterium of the genus *Pasteurella*

**pas·teu·rel·lo·sis** \,pastәrә'lōsәs\ *n*, *pl* **pasteurello·ses** \-ō,sēz\ [NL, fr. *Pasteurella* + *-osis*] **:** infection with or disease caused by bacteria of the genus *Pasteurella* — see HEMORRHAGIC SEPTICEMIA

**pas·teur·ian** \pa'stәrēәn\ *adj*, *usu cap* [Louis *Pasteur* + E *-ian*] **:** of, relating to, or deriving from Pasteur

**pas·teur·iza·tion** \,pas(h)chәrә'zāshәn, -stәr-, -,rī'-\ *n* -s [*pasteurize* + *-ation*] **1 :** a method devised by Pasteur to check fermentation (as in wine or milk) involving the partial sterilization of a substance (as a fluid) at a temperature and for a length of time that does not greatly change its chemical composition but does destroy many pathogenic organisms and other undesirable bacteria though spores and thermoduric organisms (as lactic acid bacteria) survive **2 :** the use of electricity, hot water, or steam to bring soil (as in a greenhouse bench) to a temperature of 180°F for a period of 30 minutes in order to kill nematodes, weed seeds, and various fungi and bacteria — compare STERILIZATION

**pas·teur·ize** \'pas(h)chә,rīz, -stә,-\ *vt* -ED/-ING/-S *see -ize in Explan Notes* [Louis *Pasteur* †1895 Fr. chemist and bacteriologist + E *-ize*] **:** to subject to pasteurization

**pas·teur·iz·er** \-zә(r)\ *n* -s **:** one that pasteurizes: as **a :** an apparatus for pasteurizing fluids **b :** a worker who does pasteurizing

**pasteur treatment** *n*, *usu cap P* [after Louis *Pasteur*] **:** a method devised by Pasteur of aborting rabies by stimulating production of antibodies during the long incubation period of the disease through successive inoculations with the virus in attenuated form gradually increasing in strength

**paste wash** *n* [¹*paste* + *wash*] **:** a very thin paste that is applied to the reverse side of leather to shrink and strengthen it, put on the backbone lining of a book to facilitate its removal before rebinding, and sponged on the surface of porous leather to improve the gold tooling

**paste-wash** \'ˌ,ˌ\ *vt* [*paste wash*] **:** to apply paste wash to

**¹past future** *adj* [¹*past* + *future*, adj.] **:** of, relating to, or constituting a verb tense that is traditionally formed in English with *would* or *should* and denotes an action or state as future from a past point of view (as *would write* in "he promised that he would write")

**²past future** *n* **1 :** the past future tense of a language **2 :** a verb form in the past future tense

**¹past future perfect** *adj* [¹*past* + *future perfect*, adj.] **:** of, relating to, or constituting a verb tense that is traditionally formed in English with *would have* or *should have* and denotes an action or state completed at a time formerly in prospect (as *would have finished* in "on Monday I saw that by Friday he would have finished")

**²past future perfect** *n* **1 :** the past future perfect tense of a language **2 :** a verb form in the past future perfect tense

**past historic** *n* [³*past* + *historic*] **:** PAST TENSE a

**pas·tic·cio** \pa'stē(,)chō, pä'-\ *n*, *pl* **pastic·ci** \-ēchē\ *or* **pasticcios** [It, pasty, hodgepodge, pastiche, fr. ML *pasticius* pasty, fr. LL *pasta* paste] **:** PASTICHE

**pas·tiche** \(')pa'stēsh, (')pä'-\ *n* -s [F, fr. It *pasticcio*] **1 :** a literary, artistic, or musical work that closely and usu. deliberately imitates the style of previous work ⟨an excellent ~ from European models —H.S.Canby⟩ ⟨will continue to write poetic ~s of Euripides and Shakespeare —T.S.Eliot⟩ ⟨any closer approach to their technique would lead us into ~ —C.D.Lewis⟩ **2 a :** a musical composition or piece of writing (as an opera or play) made up of selections from different works **:** POTPOURRI ⟨ending up not with a research paper but a ~, one paragraph drawn from one source, the next section lifted from another source —W.W.Bleifuss⟩ ⟨are rather biblical ~ than biblical material: they are full of biblical phrases and variations upon well-known themes —H.G.G.Herklots⟩ **b :** a usu. incongruous medley of different styles and materials **:** HODGEPODGE ⟨the poem is a ~ of images, tones, and styles —*Western Rev.*⟩ ⟨a ~ of the customs of the developers and of the natural backgrounds —Gilbert McAllister⟩

**pas·ti·cheur** \,pastē'shәr, ,päs-\ *n* -s [F, fr. *pasticher* to make pastiches (fr. *pastiche*) + *-eur* -or] **:** one who makes pastiches

**pastier** *comparative of* PASTY

**pastiest** *superlative of* PASTY

**pas·tille** \pa'stēl, -til\ *also* **pas·til** *or* **pas·tile** \'pastәl\ *n* -s [F *pastille*, fr. L *pastillus* small loaf, lozenge; akin to L *panis* bread — more at FOOD] **1 :** a small cone or mass made of a paste of gum, benzoin, cinnamon, and other aromatics and used for fumigating or scenting the air of a room **2 :** an aromatic or medicated lozenge **:** TROCHE **3 :** a paper tube filled with combustible material that on ignition causes a pinwheel or other fireworks to revolve

**pas·time** \'pa,stīm, 'paa,, 'pai,-, 'pȧ,-\ *n* -s [trans. of MF *passe-temps*] **1 :** something that amuses and serves to make time pass agreeably **:** DIVERSION, RECREATION ⟨would talk ominously for ~ —George Johnston⟩ ⟨indulged a taste for bookish ~ —*Times Lit. Supp.*⟩ **2 :** a specific form of amusement (as a game, hobby, or sport) ⟨gather around the plaza in ~s that bring the color of old Spain to the wilderness —*Amer. Guide Series: Oregon*⟩ ⟨the national ~⟩ ⟨defining public relations has been a favorite ~ —J.A.R.Pimlott⟩

**pas·ti·na·ca** \,pastә'nākә\ *n*, *cap* [NL, fr. L, parsnip, carrot — more at PARSNIP] **:** a genus of Eurasian mostly biennial herbs (family Umbelliferae) with pinnate leaves, compound umbels of yellow flowers, and very much flattened oval seeds — see PARSNIP

**past·i·ness** \'pāstēnәs\ *n* -ES **:** the quality or state of being pasty

**¹pasting** *n* -s [fr. gerund of ²*paste*] **1 pastings** *pl* **:** thin papers used for facing pasteboard **2 :** a tanning process for setting and drying leather by pasting the damp hide on boards or glass or metal plates **3** *or* **pasting-up** \'ˌ,ˌ'ˌ\ **:** occlusion of the anus of a young chick by pasty masses of feces adherent to the down usu. associated with diarrhea

**²pasting** *n* -s [fr. gerund of ⁴*paste*] **:** BEATING

**past·less·ness** \'pastlәsnәs\ *n* -ES **:** the quality or state of being without a past or a sense of the past

**past master** *n* [¹*past* + *master*] **1 :** one who has held the office of worshipful master in a lodge of Freemasons or of master in a guild, club, or other society **2** [alter. (influenced by ¹*past*) of *passed master*] **:** one who is expert in some art, subject, or activity **:** a thorough master **:** ADEPT ⟨a *past master* at exploiting differences among his opposition —W.G.Hardy⟩

**past mistress** *n* [*past* (as in *past master*) + *mistress*] **:** a woman who is proficient or thorough in some particular respect **:** ADEPT ⟨a *past mistress* of storytelling —*Newsweek*⟩

**past·ness** \'pas(t)nəs\ *n* -ES **1 :** the quality or state of being past ⟨involves a perception, not only of the ~ of the past, but of its presence —T.S.Eliot⟩ **2 :** the subjective quality of something that is remembered as contrasted with what is currently experienced or anticipated ⟨impressed . . . with the ~ of the old life —Iris Barry⟩

**pas·to** \'pä(,)stō\ *n, pl* **pasto** *or* **pastos** *usu cap* **1 a :** a group of Barbacoan peoples of the province of Carchi, Ecuador **b :** a member of any people of such group **2 :** the language of the Pasto people

**pas·to·pho·ri·um** \,pastə'fōrēəm\ *also* **pas·to·pho·ri·on** \-ē,än\ *n, pl* **pastopho·ria** \-ēə\ [LL, apartment of the bearer of the shrine, fr. Gk *pastophorion*, fr. *pastophoros* bearer of the shrine, fr. *pastos* shrine + *-phoros* -phore] **:** either of the two apartments at the sides of the bema that are found in contemporary Greek churches as well as in early Christian churches

**¹pas·tor** \'pastə(r), 'paas-, 'pais-, 'pås-\ *n* [ME *pastour*, fr. AF, fr. OF *pastur, pastor*, fr. L *pastor*, fr. *pastus* (past. part of *pascere* to pasture, feed, graze) + *-or* — more at FOOD] **1** -S *chiefly Southwest* **:** HERDSMAN **:** SHEPHERD **2** -S **a :** a spiritual overseer; *esp* **:** a clergyman serving a local church or parish ⟨the model of an eighteenth-century parish priest, scholar and squire and ~ of souls —Havelock Ellis⟩ **b :** one who gives protection or guidance to a group of people **3 a** *cap* [NL, fr. L] *in some classifications* **:** a genus of starlings that includes only the rose-colored starling and is now usu. incorporated in the genus *Sturnus* **b** -S **:** ROSE-COLORED STARLING **4** -S **:** MAN-OF-WAR FISH

**²pastor** \"\ *vt* -ED/-ING/-S **:** to serve as pastor to

**pas·tor·age** \-t(ə)rij\ *n* -S [¹*pastor* + *-age*] **:** PASTORATE

**¹pas·to·ral** \-rəl\ *n* -S **1 a** [LL *Cura Pastoralis*, title of St. Gregory's work on pastoral care] **:** a book or treatise on the duties of pastors **b** [²*pastoral*] **:** a letter of a pastor to his charge: as (1) **:** a letter addressed by a bishop to his diocese (2) **:** a letter of the House of Bishops of the Protestant Episcopal Church to be read in each parish **c** *usu cap* [by shortening] **:** PASTORAL EPISTLE — usu. used in pl. with *the* **2** [trans. of L *bucolicum*] **a :** a literary work (as a poem or play) dealing with the life of shepherds or rural life generally in a usu. artificial manner and frequently archaic style, typically drawing a conventional contrast between the innocence and serenity of the simple life and the misery and corruption of city and esp. court life, and often using the characters as vehicles for the expression of the author's moral, social, or literary views ⟨jaded and oversophisticated denizens of towns devote themselves to ~*s* —J.L.Lowes⟩ — compare IDYLL **b :** pastoral poetry or drama as a literary form or style ⟨the best actors in the world, either for tragedy, comedy, history, ~ —Shak.⟩ **c :** a pastoral or rural picture or scene **d :** PASTORALE **3** *or* **pastoral staff** [prob. fr. It *pastorale*, fr. LL *pastoralis* of a pastor, fr. L, of a shepherd] **:** CROSIER

**²pastoral** \"\ *adj* [ME, fr. L *pastoralis*, fr. *pastor* herdsman, shepherd + *-alis* -al] **1 a** (1) **:** of, relating to, or composed of shepherds or herdsmen ⟨a ~ people, seminomadic in their habits —J.M.Mogey⟩ ⟨~ simplicity⟩ (2) **:** devoted to or based upon the cultivation of sheep or cattle ⟨third-class ~ land, having a 10-in. rainfall and all held as sheep stations —T.A. Miles⟩ ⟨a ~ economy⟩ **b :** of or relating to the countryside as contrasted with the city **:** RURAL ⟨charming in its ~ setting amid these cultivated uplands —*Amer. Guide Series: Vt.*⟩ **c :** portraying or expressive of the life of shepherds or country people esp. in an idealized and conventionalized manner ⟨~ poetry⟩ ⟨~ drama⟩ ⟨a ~ symphony⟩ **d :** INNOCENT, IDYLLIC ⟨the ~ legends of America's golden age —August Heckscher⟩ ⟨waiting through a long, ~ afternoon —*Time*⟩ **2 a** (1) **:** of or relating to the spiritual care of a congregation or group of Christians ⟨~ duties⟩ ⟨a ~ letter⟩ (2) **:** of or relating to the pastor of a church ⟨observed that this represented a congregational and not a ~ reluctance to participate —*Episcopal Churchnews*⟩ **b :** of or relating to spiritual care or guidance esp. as carried on through visiting and counseling ⟨a missionary, or at least ~ activity on the part of the teacher —N.G. Fisher⟩ ⟨it was her custom to pay ~ calls at the residences of her pupils —Frances G. Patton⟩ — **pas·to·ral·ly** \-rəlē, -li\ *adv* — **pas·to·ral·ness** *n* -ES

**pas·to·rale** \,pastə'räl, -ral *sometimes* -'ālē\ *n* -S [It, fr. *pastorale* of herdsmen, fr. L *pastoralis*] **1 a :** an opera of the 16th or 17th centuries combining singing and dancing and having a pastoral plot **b :** an instrumental or vocal composition having a pastoral theme **2 :** PASTORAL 2a ⟨a ~, written in homely, muted prose, about life on a farm —*New Yorker*⟩

**pastoral epistle** *n* -S *usu cap P & sometimes cap E* **:** one of three New Testament letters including two addressed to Timothy and one to Titus and giving advice on matters of church government and discipline

**pas·to·ral·ism** \'past(ə)rə,lizəm, 'paas-, 'pais-, 'pås-\ *n* -S **1 :** the quality or style characteristic of pastoral writing **2 a :** HERDING **b :** social organization based upon herding as the primary economic activity

**pas·to·ral·ist** \-ləst\ *n* -S **1 :** a writer of pastorals **2 a :** a breeder and pasturer of sheep or cattle **b** *chiefly Austral* **:** a station holder who raises livestock and does little or no farming

**pas·to·ral·i·ty** \,pastə'raləd·ē\ *n* -ES **:** something pastoral **:** a pastoral object or quality

**pas·to·ral·iza·tion** \,pastərələ'zāshən\ *n* -S **:** the act or process of making pastoral; *specif* **:** the conversion of an industrial country into a pastoral one ⟨carrying industrial disarmament to the point of ~ —A.O.Wolfers⟩

**pas·to·ral·ize** \'past(ə)rə,līz\ *vt* -ED/-ING/-S *see -ize in Explan Notes* **1 :** to render pastoral or rural; *specif* **:** to convert to a pastoral economy or social organization ⟨his famous proposal to ~ the country —Robert Lekachman⟩ **2 :** to put into a pastoral or into the pastoral form

**pastoral prayer** *n* **:** the chief prayer of a church service typically including thanksgiving, supplication, and intercession

**pastoral theology** *n* **:** the study of the theological bases as well as the practical implications of the professional activities of religious workers

**pas·tor·ate** \'past(ə)rət, 'paas-, 'pais-, 'pås-, *usu* -əd·+V\ *n* -S [ML *pastoratus*, fr. LL *pastor* pastor (fr. L, shepherd) + L *-atus* -ate] **1 a :** the office, state, jurisdiction, or tenure of office of a pastor **b :** a body of pastors **2 :** PARSONAGE

**pastored** *past of* PASTOR

**pastoring** *pres 3d sing of* PASTOR

**pas·to·ri·um** \pa'stōrēəm, -tȯr-\ *n* -S [irreg. fr. ¹*pastor* + *-orium*] *chiefly South* **:** a Protestant parsonage

**pas·tor·less** \'pastə(r)ləs\ *adj* **:** having no pastor

**pas·tor·ly** \-lē\ *adj* **:** of, relating to, or appropriate to a pastor

**pastors** *pl of* PASTOR, *pres 3d sing of* PASTOR

**pas·tor·ship** \-(r),ship\ *n* [¹*pastor* + *-ship*] **:** PASTORATE 1

**pastos** *pl of* PASTO

**pas·tose** \(')pa'stōs\ *adj* [It *pastoso* doughy, soft, fr. *pasta* dough, paste (fr. LL) + *-oso* -ose — more at PASTE] **:** painted thickly **:** covered or filled with paint — **pas·tose·ly** *adv* — **pas·tos·i·ty** \pa'stäsəd·ē\ *n* -ES

**pas·tou·relle** *also* **pas·to·relle** \,pastə'rel\ *n* -S [F, young shepherdess, shepherdess's song, fem. dim. of OF *pastour* shepherd, fr. L *pastor* — more at PASTOR] **:** a conventional form of poetic pastoral composed in French during the late middle ages and Renaissance and consisting of a love debate between a knight and a shepherdess

**past participle** *n* **:** a participle that typically expresses completed action, that is traditionally one of the principal parts of the verb, and that is traditionally used in English in the formation of perfect tenses in the active voice and of all tenses in the passive voice and has a perfect active meaning when the verb sense is intransitive (as *arrived* in "the ship, arrived at last, signals for a tug") and usu. a passive meaning when the verb sense is transitive (as *buffeted* in "the ship, buffeted by waves, comes shoreward") and with participial auxiliaries may take a present passive form (as in *being written*), a perfect active form (as in *having written*), or a perfect passive form (as in *having been written*) — called also *perfect participle*

**¹past perfect** *adj* [¹*past* + *perfect*, adj.] **:** of, relating to, or constituting a verb tense that is traditionally formed in English with *had* and denotes an action or state as completed at or before a past time spoken of (as *had left* in "when he arrived I had left for the city")

**²past perfect** *n* **1 :** the past perfect tense of a language **2 :** a verb form in the past perfect tense

**pas·tra·mi** \pə'strämē, -mi\ *n* -S [Yiddish, fr. Romanian *pastramă*, fr. *păstra* to preserve, perh. fr. (assumed) VL *parsitare* to spare, fr. L *parsus*, past part. of *parcere* to spare — more at PARSIMONY] **:** a highly seasoned smoked beef prepared esp. from shoulder cuts

**pas·try** \'pāstrē, -ri\ *n* -ES *often attrib* [¹*paste* + *-ry*] **1 a :** sweet baked goods made with paste dough (as cakes, pies, or tarts) ⟨French ~⟩ ⟨Danish ~⟩ **b :** a piece of such baked goods ⟨had a ~ and a glass of milk⟩ **c :** PASTE 1a **2** *obs* **:** a place where pastry is made ⟨they call for dates and quinces in the ~ —Shak.⟩

**pastry bag** *n* **:** a funnel-shaped container for holding soft food mixtures (as mashed potatoes, icing, or whipped cream) from which the foods are forced through a pastry tube at the tip in making ornamental spreads or decorations

**pastry blender** *n* **:** a device consisting of a handle with wires fastened to each end so that they form a deep curve that is used in cutting fat into flour in pastry making

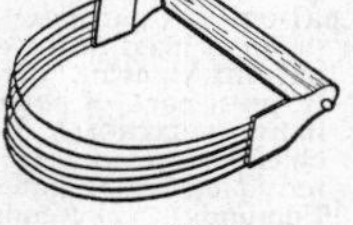

pastry blender

**pastrycook** \'==,=\ *n* **1 :** one who is employed (as by a hotel or restaurant) to make pastry **2 :** one who makes pastry for public sale

**pastry flour** *n* **:** a flour usu. manufactured from soft wheat low in gluten content and milled very fine that is esp. suitable for making pastry and cake

**pastry fork** *n* **:** a fork with four tines usu. including one with a cutting edge

**pastry tube** *n* **:** a usu. metal tip that is attached to the opening of a pastry bag and that is often shaped to form a specific pattern (as a star)

**pasts** *pl of* PAST

**past service** *n* [¹*past*] **:** the period of a worker's employment prior to the effective date of a pension plan for which credit is given in determining the amount of his pension

**past tense** *n* **:** a verb tense expressing action or state in or as if in the past: **a :** a verb tense expressive of time gone by (as *wrote* in "on arriving I wrote a letter") — called also *past absolute, past historic* **b :** a verb tense expressing action or state in progress or continuance or habitually done or customarily occurring at a past time (as *was writing* in "I was writing while he dictated" or *loved* in "their sons loved fishing") — called also *past continuous, past descriptive*

**pas·tur·able** \'pas(h)chərəbəl, 'paas-, 'pais-, 'pås-\ *adj* [partly fr. ¹*pasture* + *-able*, partly fr. ²*pasture* + *-able*] **:** fit for or affording pasture

**pas·tur·age** \-rij\ *n* -S [MF *pasturer* to pasture + *-age*] **1 a :** grazing land **:** HERBAGE, PASTURE ⟨its promise of fine ~ for sheep —*Amer. Guide Series: Oregon*⟩ **b :** a natural accumulation of food plants ⟨algal ~ of the sea⟩ ⟨bee ~⟩ **2 :** the act or process of pasturing **:** GRAZING ⟨two sample bills, one for irrigation districts, the other for cooperative ~ —Mari Sandoz⟩ **3** *Scots law* **:** the right of pasturing cattle or sheep on a common or another's land

**pas·tur·al** \-rəl\ *adj* [LL *pastura* pasture + E *-al*] **:** of or relating to pasture

**¹pas·ture** \-chə(r)\ *n* -S *often attrib* [ME, fr. MF, fr. LL *pastura*, fr. L *pastus* (past part. of *pascere* to pasture, feed, graze) + *-ura* -ure — more at FOOD] **1 a :** grass or other plants grown for the feeding of grazing animals **:** HERBAGE ⟨grows quickly and makes excellent ~ for cattle⟩ **b** *archaic* **:** FOOD, NOURISHMENT **2 a** (1) **:** land that is used for the grazing of animals or is suitable for such use ⟨makes me lie down in green ~*s* —Ps 23:2 (RSV)⟩ ⟨buffalo ~*s* on the prairie —R.L. Neuberger⟩ (2) **:** a lot used for grazing ⟨a small, fenced-in holding ~ —John Bird⟩ ⟨his lease was cut into two separate ~*s* —F.B.Gipson⟩ (3) **:** a large enclosed section of a cattle ranch **b :** FEEDING GROUND ⟨whales, like seals, feed in different ~*s* at different seasons —*Nat'l Geographic*⟩ **c :** a scene of activity ⟨people in more distant ~*s*, even in literature and science —Dallas Finn⟩ **d :** a place or state of retirement ⟨eased out and retired to ~ to make room for the younger man —James Jones⟩ **3 :** the feeding of livestock **:** GRAZING ⟨only about 19 percent is used for the ~ of animals —P.E.James⟩

**²pasture** \"\ *vb* -ED/-ING/-S [ME *pasturen*, fr. MF *pasturer*, fr. *pasture*, n.] *vi* **1 :** to feed on growing grass or herbage **:** GRAZE ⟨men and women holding cows on a rope in a field while the cows *pastured* —Arnold Bennett⟩ **2 :** to feed as if in a pasture ⟨the very early morning when the animals are *pasturing* on the seaweed —*Nautilus*⟩ ~ *vt* **1 :** FEED, NOURISH ⟨a sufficiently unwashed citizen may ~ more than ten thousand lice at one time —Gove Hambidge⟩ **2 a :** to cause or permit to feed on growing grass **:** put out to pasture ⟨*pastured* his cattle on the open range⟩ **b :** to supply growing grass as food for **:** let graze ⟨rich grassland that could ~ many cattle⟩ **3 a :** to eat down in grazing ⟨the field was *pastured* bare⟩ **b :** to put livestock to graze on **:** use as pasture ⟨a conflict between those who wanted to farm the land and those who wanted to ~ it⟩ ⟨some growers ~ young sweet clover as soon as the plants are large enough —D.C.McIntosh + D.M.Orr⟩ **syn** see FEED

**pasture bird** *n* **1 :** GOLDEN PLOVER **2 :** VESPER SPARROW

**pasture breeding** *n* **:** uncontrolled mating within a flock or herd — opposed to *hand breeding*

**pasture cockchafer** *or* **pasture scarab** *n* **:** any of several scarabaeid beetles esp. of the genus *Aphodius*

**pasture gooseberry** *n* **:** a wild gooseberry (*Ribes cynosbati*)

**pasture grub** *n* **:** the larva of a pasture cockchafer

**pastureland** \'==,=\ *n* **:** PASTURE 2a(1)

**pas·tur·er** \-chərə(r)\ *n* -S **:** one that pastures livestock

**pasture rose** *n* **:** a prickly shrub (*Rosa carolina*) of eastern No. America that has compound leaves, showy pink flowers, and globose sticky hairy fruit

**pasture thistle** *n* **:** an American thistle (*Cirsium pumilum*) that has large heads of purple flowers

**¹pas·ty** \'pastē, 'pās-, -ti\ *n* -ES [ME *pastee, paste, pastey*, fr. MF *pasté*, fr. *paste* dough — more at PASTE] **:** a pie consisting of a meat and vegetable mixture or fruit filling wholly surrounded with a crust made of a sheet of paste dough and often baked without a dish — see CORNISH PASTY; compare TURNOVER

**²pasty** \'pāstē, -ti\ *adj, usu* -ER/-EST [¹*paste* + *-y*] **1 :** resembling paste (as in color or consistency); *esp* **:** pallid and unhealthy in appearance ⟨his complexion was always ~, but for the last few nights it had been a chalky white —Agnes S. Turnbull⟩ **2 :** SICKLY ⟨the ~ little books that circulate from beneath the counter —Curtis Bok⟩

**pasty–faced** \'==;=\ *adj* [²*pasty*] **:** having a chalky unwholesome appearance suggestive of lack of exercise or fresh air ⟨the *pasty-faced* indoor cop leading me to jail —Gilbert Millstein⟩

**pa·sul** \pə'sül, 'pȯ,sůl\ *adj* [Heb *pāsūl* disqualified] **:** declared unfit for Jewish ceremonial use according to rabbinic law **:** DEFECTIVE

**pa system** *n, usu cap P&A* **:** PUBLIC-ADDRESS SYSTEM

**¹pat** \'pat, *usu* -ad·+V\ *n* -S [ME *patte*, prob. of imit. origin] **1 a :** a blow esp. with the hand or a flat or blunt instrument **b :** a light blow or tap given to shape or smooth ⟨a few final ~*s* around the newly planted flower⟩ **c :** a tap with the hand given in affection or approval ⟨with a quick reassuring ~ on her arm, their hostess left —Harriet La Barre⟩ **2 :** a light tapping sound esp. if rhythmical ⟨the ~ of bare feet⟩ **3 :** a small square of butter served as an individual portion or something resembling or suggesting it **:** DAB **4 :** a dropping of animal dung ⟨the most satisfactory control measure consists of scattering the cow ~*s* —Eric Hearle⟩ **5 :** an American Negro dance tune in time with which onlookers often pat their knees or thighs

**²pat** \"\ *vb* **patted; patted; patting; pats** *vt* **1 :** to hit with a flat or blunt implement **2 a :** to flatten, smooth, or put into place or shape with light strokes (as of the hand) ⟨women *patted* up tortillas by their stalls —G.A.Wagner⟩ **b :** to beat or slap lightly ⟨at 70 miles an hour, pontoons ~ the waves —Jim Wright⟩ **3 :** to stroke or tap gently with the hand to soothe, caress, or show approval ⟨had been *patted* on the head by . . . the city's founder —Alan Carmichael⟩ ~ *vi* **1 a :** to strike or beat gently ⟨snowflakes were *patting* against the windowpane —J.B.Clayton⟩ **b :** to tap lightly and quickly with the soles of the feet (as in dancing a jig) **2 :** to walk or run so as to make a light beating sound ⟨in summer she *patted* away to school —Hamlin Garland⟩ **3** *dial* **:** to keep time to dance music by patting the knee or thigh — **pat juba :** to perform the rhythmic accompaniment to a juba with hands or feet — **pat on the back :** APPLAUD, APPROVE, ENCOURAGE ⟨made speeches to him, *patted* him *on the back*, told him what a priceless fellow he was —H.A.Overstreet⟩

**³pat** \"\ *adv* **:** in a pat manner **:** APTLY, READILY, PROMPTLY

**⁴pat** \"\ *adj* **1 a :** exactly suited to the purpose or occasion **:** APT, OPPORTUNE ⟨this ~ tale got a big laugh —Dorothy Barclay⟩ **b :** too exactly suitable **:** CONTRIVED, FACILE, GLIB ⟨his characters flatten out, and his conclusions become annoyingly ~ —Nicolas Monjo⟩ **2 :** learned, mastered, or memorized exactly or with ready or fluent command ⟨didn't say that prayer over twice before he had it ~ —H.G.Wells⟩ **3 :** FIRM, UNYIELDING — usu. used in the phrase *to stand pat* ⟨a major issue on which it has stood ~ since the matter first arose —*Sydney (Australia) Bull.*⟩ **syn** see SEASONABLE

**⁵pat** \"\ *n* -S *usu cap* [fr. Pat, nickname for *Patrick*, a common Irish Christian name] **1 :** IRISHMAN **2** *Austral* **:** CHINESE

**pat** *abbr* **1** patent; patented **2** patrol **3** pattern

**PAT** *abbr* point after touchdown

**pa·ta·ca** \pə'täkə\ *n* -S [Pg] **1 :** the basic unit of monetary value in the Portuguese colonies of Macao and Timor **2 :** a coin of Macao representing one pataca

**pat–a–cake** \'==,=\ *n* [so called fr. the opening words of the rhyme] **:** a nursery play in which a child claps his hands to the words of a rhyme in imitation of another's actions

**pa·tache** \pə'tash, -tächə\ *n* -S [Sp, fr. OSp *pataxe*, prob. fr. Ar *baṭash* ship with two masts] **:** a tender to a fleet of sailing vessels

**pa·ta·gi·al** \pə'tājēəl\ *adj* [NL *patagium* + E *-al*] **:** of or relating to a patagium

**pa·ta·gi·ate** \-ēət, -ē,āt\ *adj* [NL *patagium* + E *-ate*] **1 :** having a patagium **2 :** PATAGIAL

**pa·ta·gi·um** \-ēəm, ,pad·ə'jīəm\ *n, pl* **pata·gia** \-ēə, -īə\ [NL, fr. L *patagium* gold edging or border on a woman's tunic] **1 :** a wing membrane: as **a :** the fold of skin connecting the forelimbs and hind limbs of certain arboreal animals (as flying squirrels and flying lizards) and serving to sustain them in making long leaps **b :** the fold of skin in front of the humeral and radio-ulnar parts of a bird's wing **2 a :** one of a pair of small processes on the back of the prothorax of most Lepidoptera **b :** TEGULA 1a

**¹pat·a·go·ni·an** \¦pad·ə¦gōnyən, -atə¦-, -nēən\ *adj, usu cap* [*Patagonia*, region in southern So. America belonging partly to Argentina and partly to Chile + E *-an*] **1 :** of, relating to, or characteristic of Patagonia **2 a :** of, relating to, or characteristic of the people of Patagonia **b** *obs* **:** GIGANTIC **3 :** CHILEAN 2

**²patagonian** \"\ *n* -S **1** *cap* **:** a native or inhabitant of Patagonia; *esp* **:** one of the aboriginal Indian stock — compare TEHUELCHE **2** *usu cap, obs* **:** someone or something that is very large **:** GIANT

**patagonian cavy** *or* **patagonian hare** *n, usu cap P* **:** MARA

**patamar** *var of* PATTAMAR

**pa·tan** \'pätən\ *adj, usu cap* [fr. *Patan*, Nepal] **:** of or from the city of Patan, Nepal **:** of the kind or style prevalent in Patan

**pa·ta·na** \pə'tänə\ *n* -S [Singhalese] **:** upland grassland of Ceylon that commonly succeeds forest and is maintained by burning

**pa·ta·ria** \pə'tarēə\ *n* -S *usu cap* [It, fr. *Pataria*, section of Milan] **:** the party of the Patarines (sense 2) or the movement instituted by them

**pat·a·rine** \'pad·ərən, -ə,rēn\ *or* **pat·a·rene** \-ə,rēn\ *n* -S *usu cap* [ML *Patarinus, Patarenus*, fr. *Pataria, Patarea*, poor section of Milan, Italy + L *-inus* -ine] **1 :** one of the Manichaean emigrants from Bulgaria who settled in the Pataria quarter of Milan **2 :** a member of a reform party at Milan in the 11th century formed to combat clerical concubinage and simony; *also* **:** one opposed to the marriage of priests **3 :** a Waldensian or one of various Cathari (as the Bogomils or Albigenses)

**pa·tas** \pə'tä\ *n, pl* **patas** \-ä(z)\ [F, fr. Wolof *pata*] **:** a reddish colored long-tailed monkey (*Erythrocebus patas*) of West Africa — called also *hussar monkey*

**pa·tash·te** \pə'tashtä\ *n* -S [AmerSp *pataxte, pataste*, fr. Maya] **1 :** a tropical American tree (*Theobroma bicolor*) resembling cacao and yielding a chocolate substitute **2 :** the cocoa obtained from the patashte tree — called also *tiger cocoa*

**pat·a·uá oil** \¦pad·ə¦wä-\ *n* [*patauá* fr. Pg, a Brazilian palm, fr. Tupi *batawá, patawá*] **:** a fatty oil similar to olive oil obtained from the fruit of a Brazilian palm (*Oenocarpus bataua*)

**pa·ta·vin·i·ty** \,pad·ə'vinəd·ē\ *n* -ES *usu cap* [L *patavinitas*, fr. *Patavium* (Padua), Italy, birthplace of the Roman historian Livy + L *-itas* -ity] **1 :** the dialectal characteristics of Padua as seen in the writings of Livy **2 :** the use of dialect

**pa·ta·yan** \¦päd·ə¦yän\ *adj, usu cap* [Walapai *pataya* ancient people + E *-an*] **:** of or belonging to a culture of western Arizona dating from about 700 to 1200 and characterized by crude brush and mud huts, clay pottery, and the cultivation of corn, beans, and cotton **:** YUMAN

**pat–ball** \'=,=\ *n* [²*pat* + *ball*] **1 :** ROUNDERS **2 :** slow or feeble cricket or lawn tennis

**¹patch** \'pach\ *n* -ES [ME *pacche*, perh. fr. MF *pece, piece, pieche* piece — more at PIECE] **1 :** a piece used to mend or cover a hole, rent, or breach or to reenforce or protect a weak spot ⟨wore a dirty . . . sweater with leather elbow ~*es* —W.B. Marsh⟩; *esp* **:** a piece of cloth used to repair or reinforce fabric that is torn or worn **2 :** a tiny decorative piece of black silk or court plaster worn on the face or neck esp. by women to hide a blemish or to heighten beauty by contrast **3 a :** a piece of adhesive plaster or other cover applied to a wound **b :** a shield (as of cloth) worn over an injured eye **4 a :** a small piece **:** BIT, SCRAP ⟨on all sides are small ~*es* of level ground, but nowhere is there a plain —Kenneth Roberts⟩ ⟨slept in ~*es*, cold and uncomfortable —A.P.Herbert⟩ ⟨the kind of book which in ~*es* has real interest —H.J.Laski⟩ **b :** a spot of color different from that around it ⟨a ~ of white is noticeable on his dog's head⟩ **c :** a small piece of ground distinct from that about it (as in appearance or in the vegetation it bears) ⟨cabbage ~⟩ ⟨~*es* of bare earth⟩ **d :** a constricted area of land occupied by mean or impoverished dwellings or farms **5 :** an ornament, badge, or tab of cloth sewed on a garment; *esp* **:** an emblem worn at the shoulder of a military uniform to show the unit to which a serviceman belongs ⟨wears the Third Army ~ —*Westinghouse Mag.*⟩ **6 a :** an irregular small mass of floating cakes of ice **b :** a herd of seals **7 a :** a piece of greased or moistened cloth formerly used as wadding for a rifle ball **b :** a small piece of cotton cloth used for cleaning the bore of small arms **c :** the hard metal covering over the lead core of jacketed bullets **8 :** a circumscribed region (as on the skin or in a section from an organ) differing esp. in color or composition from the tissue normal for that part **9 a :** OVERLAY 2d **b :** a replacement of part of a printing plate (as an electrotype) ⟨a 3-line ~⟩ **10 :** someone or something equal or comparable — usu. used in negative constructions ⟨what the advocates of economic nationalism had accomplished was not a ~ on what they planned —*Time*⟩ ⟨those headlines don't make a ~ against the ones on the front pages —*Newsweek*⟩ **11 :** a temporary connection in a communication system (as a telephone or broadcasting hookup) **12** *chiefly Brit* **:** PERIOD, SPELL ⟨it is not as though we now had large reserves to tide us over a difficult ~ —Donald MacDougall⟩ ⟨poetry is going through a bad ~ —Cyril Connolly⟩ **13 :** a circus lawyer **:** FIXER ⟨if the ~ says you can rip and tear, you can go the limit on anything —D.W.Maurer⟩

**²patch** \"\ *vt* -ED/-ING/-ES **1 :** to mend, cover, or fill up a hole, rent, or breach, or weak spot in **:** apply a patch to ⟨caulked her deck seams, slushed her rigging, and ~*ed* her sails —Kenneth Roberts⟩ ⟨was trying to get all the fences near the house ~*ed* —Ellen Glasgow⟩ **2 :** to provide with a patch or patches ⟨neat clearings ~*ing* the sides of the mountains —Slim Aarons⟩ ⟨went ~*ed* and darned and shamefaced through the village streets⟩ **3 a :** to make of patches, scraps, or fragments ⟨they possessed only suspicions . . . but out of these they succeeded in ~*ing* together a mosaic —Louis Bromfield⟩ **b :** to mend, repair, or put together esp. in hasty, insecure, or shabby fashion — usu. used with *up* ⟨was busy ~*ing* up that political disaster —J.P.O'Donnell⟩ ⟨relations between the two men had to be ~*ed* up repeatedly —Ishbel Ross⟩ ⟨sometimes offer a gift, with a view to ~*ing* up a quarrel —W.F.Hambly⟩ ⟨has been since diverted to ~ up the 118-year-old penal slum —Frank O'Leary⟩ **4 :** to apply as a patch ⟨~*ed* new cloth to the old coat until it seemed mere patchwork⟩ **5 :** to cover (a bullet) with a patch **syn** see MEND

**³patch** \"\ *n* -ES [perh. by folk etymology fr. It dial. (southern Italy) *paccio* fool] **1 :** a domestic fool or jester **2 :** CLOWN, DOLT, NINNY **3** *chiefly dial* **:** CROSSPATCH

**patch bolt** *n* **:** a bolt used in the repair of boilers and of ships with hulls of steel plate that has a countersunk head with a square knob which is twisted off when the bolt is screwed home

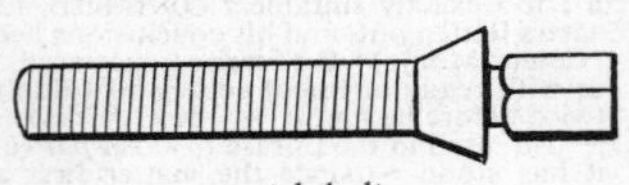
patch bolt

**patch box** *n* **1 :** a small shallow decorative box formerly used to contain the face patches fashionable in the 17th and 18th centuries **2 :** a recess in the stock of a muzzle-loading rifle for carrying patches, grease, and flints

**patch budding** *n* **:** plant budding in which a small rectangle of bark bearing a scion bud is fitted into a corresponding opening in the stock

**patch cord** *or* **patching cord** *n* **:** a wire with plugs at both ends that is used in communications patches

**patch·er** \ˈpachə(r)\ *n* -S **1 :** a worker who makes repairs to, reinforces, or decorates something by patching **2 :** CEMENTER 2e **3 :** a mine-car brakeman

**¹patch·ery** \-ch(ə)rē\ *n* -ES [²*patch* + *-ery*] **:** the act of patching **:** clumsy or hasty repairing or making **:** PATCHWORK ⟨a thin sample of poetic ~ —A.C.Swinburne⟩

**²patchery** *n* -ES [³*patch* + *-ery*] *obs* **:** ROGUERY, KNAVERY

**patchhead** \ˈ=,=\ *n* [¹*patch* + *head;* fr. the markings on its head] **:** SURF SCOTER

**patch·i·ly** \ˈpachəlē\ *adv* **:** in a patchy manner **:** in spots

**patch·i·ness** \-chēnəs\ *n* -ES **:** the quality or state of being patchy

**patch·ing** \-chiŋ\ *n* -S **1 :** ¹PATCH 7a **2 :** ¹PATCH 10 — usu. used with negative ⟨that boy's not a ~ to his big brother⟩

**patch·ou·li** *or* **patch·ou·ly** *also* **pach·ou·li** \ˈpachəlē, pəˈchülē\ *n, pl* **patchoulis** *or* **patchoulies** [Tamil *paccuḷi*] woolly patchouli] **1 :** an East Indian shrubby mint (*Pogostemon cablin*) that yields a fragrant essential oil **2 :** the perfume made from patchouli ⟨a pleasant perfume of summer flowers rather than a heavy odor of ~ —*Weekly Scotsman*⟩

**patchouli oil** *also* **patchouly oil** *n* **:** a fragrant brownish yellow to brown essential oil obtained from the leaves of the patchouli and used in perfumes and soaps

**patch pocket** *n* **:** a flat pocket applied to the outside of a garment

**patch–polled coot** \ˈpach,pōld-\ *n* [¹*patch* + *poll* (head) + *-ed;* fr. the markings on its head] **:** SURF SCOTER

**patch reef** *n* **:** a small flat table reef ⟨*patch reefs* . . . are by far the most numerous of the reefs around Australia —*Jour. of Geol.*⟩

**patch test** *n* **:** a test for determining hypersensitivity made by applying to the unbroken surface of the skin small pads soaked with the allergy-producing substance in question, susceptibility being indicated by the development of irritation at the point of application — compare SCRATCH TEST, SKIN TEST

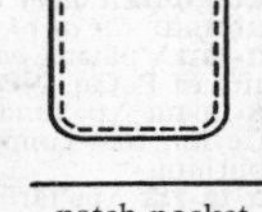
patch pocket

**patchwork** \ˈ=,=\ *n, often attrib* **1 a :** something composed of ill-assorted, miscellaneous, or incongruous parts **:** HODGEPODGE, JUMBLE ⟨a ~ of four languages laced with gestures and laughter —Claudia Cassidy⟩ ⟨had finished our ~ lunch —Gladys B. Stern⟩ ⟨a ~ report⟩ **b :** work performed in random or unsystematic fashion or confined to patching up ⟨desegregation has been a ~ in Kentucky —J.B.Martin⟩ ⟨argued . . . that economic reform by ~ is illogical and timid —F.L.Allen⟩ ⟨~ efforts⟩ **2 :** pieces of cloth of various colors and shapes sewed together usu. in a pattern to form a covering (as for a bed) ⟨a ~ quilt⟩ ⟨a counterpane of silk ~⟩ — **patchworked** \ˈ=,=\ *adj*

**¹patchy** \ˈpachē, -chi\ *adj* -ER/-EST [¹*patch* + *-y*] **1 :** marked by or diversified with patches **:** consisting of patches **:** resembling patchwork **:** SPOTTY ⟨~ sunlight shone on the coat of the bay stallion —Ernest Hemingway⟩ **2 :** appearing rough and uneven (as the coat of an animal)

**²patchy** \ˈpachi\ *adj* [³*patch* + *-y*] *dial Eng* **:** CROSS, TESTY

**patd** *abbr* patented

**¹pate** \ˈpāt, *usu* -ād.+V\ *n* -S [ME] **:** the head or part of the head of a person: **a :** the top or crown of the head **b :** the head as containing the brain **c :** BRAIN, BRAINS — used chiefly disparagingly ⟨the nunnish ~ bald as an ant's egg —William Sansom⟩

**²pate** \"\ *n* -S [perh. fr. ¹*pate;* fr. the white spot on the head] *dial Eng* **:** BADGER

**³pâ·té** \pä'tā\ *n* -S [F, fr. OF *pasté*, fr. *paste* paste, dough — more at PASTE] **1 :** a pie, patty, or pasty containing meat, fish, game, or poultry **2 :** a spread of finely mashed seasoned and spiced meat (as chicken or goose liver)

**⁴pâte** \ˈpät\ *n* -S [F, lit., paste, fr. OF *paste*] **1 :** the paste or plastic material for pottery or porcelain **2 :** PASTE 1a **3 :** pasty dough

**⁵paté** *or* **patée** *var of* PATTÉE

**pat·ed** \ˌpād.əd, ˈpātəd\ *adj* **:** having a pate of a specified kind — usu. used in combination ⟨addle*pated*⟩ ⟨feather*pated*⟩

**pâ·té de foie gras** \(ˌ)päˈtādəfˈwäˈgrä *also* (ˌ)paˈt- *sometimes* ˈpäd-ēd- *or* ˈpad-ēd-\ *n, pl* **pâ·tés de foie gras** \-ā(z)d-, -ē(z)d-\ [F, goose-liver pastry] **:** a paste of fat goose liver and truffles sometimes with added fat pork

**pat·e·fac·tion** \ˌpad-əˈfakshən\ *n* -S [L *patefaction-, patefactio,* fr. *patefactus* (past part. of *patefacere*) + *-ion-, -io* -ion] *archaic* **:** DISCLOSURE, MANIFESTATION, REVELATION

**patefy** *vt* -ED/-ING/-ES [modif. (influenced by E *-fy*) of L *patefacere,* fr. *patēre* to be open, be evident + *facere* to make, do — more at FATHOM, DO] *obs* **:** to make open or manifest **:** DECLARE, REVEAL

**pa·tel** \pəˈtel\ *n* -S [Hindi *paṭel* & Marathi *pāṭīl,* fr. Prakrit *paṭṭailla,* fr. Skt *paṭṭa* slab, tablet, copper plate for grants] **:** the headman of a village

**pa·tel·la** \pəˈtelə\ *n* [L, dim. of *patina* pan — more at PATEN] **1** *pl* **pa·tel·lae** \-e,lē, -,lī\ **:** a small dish, pan, or vase of ancient Rome **2** *pl* **patellae** *or* **patellas a :** a thick flat triangular movable bone that forms the anterior point of the knee and protects the front of the joint, increases the leverage of the quadriceps, and is usu. regarded as a sesamoid bone since it is developed in the tendon of the quadriceps and in structure is similar to other sesamoid bones **:** KNEECAP, KNEEPAN **b** [NL, fr. L] **:** the fourth segment in the pedipalpus or in the leg of an arachnid **3** *pl* **patellae** [NL, fr. L] **:** a rounded apothecium in a lichen that has a distinct marginal rim **4** [NL, fr. L] **a** *cap* **:** the type genus of the family Patellidae including the common European limpet (*P. vulgata*) **b** *pl* **patellas** *or* **patellae :** a limpet of the family Patellidae

**pa·tel·lar** \-lə(r)\ *adj* **:** of, relating to, or involving the patella

**patellar ligament** *n* **:** the part of the tendon of the quadriceps that extends from the patella to the tibia

**patellar reflex** *n* **:** KNEE JERK

**pa·tel·late** \-elət, -e,lāt\ *adj* [*patella* + *-ate*] **:** having a patella or patellula **:** PATELLIFORM

**patella ul·na·ris** \-,əlˈna(a)rəs\ *n, pl* **patella ulnarises** [NL, lit., elbow patella] **:** a sesamoid at the lower end of the humerus that takes the place of the olecranon process in some birds

**¹pa·tel·lid** \pəˈteləd\ *adj* [NL *Patellidae*] **:** of or relating to the Patellidae

**²patellid** \"\ *n* -S **:** a mollusk of the family Patellidae

**pa·tel·li·dae** \-lə,dē\ *n pl, cap* [NL, fr. *Patella,* type genus + *-idae*] **:** a family of gastropod mollusks (order Aspidobranchia) including numerous typical limpets — **pa·tel·li·dan** \-ləd³n\ *adj or n*

**pa·tel·li·form** \-lə,fȯrm\ *adj* [*patella* + *-iform*] **1 :** resembling a limpet **:** shaped like a limpet shell **2** *bot* **:** disk-shaped with a narrow rim

**pa·tel·line** \pəˈte,līn, ˈpad-³l,īn\ *adj* [*patella* + *-ine*] **1 :** PATELLIFORM **2** [NL *Patella* + E *-ine*] **:** of or relating to the Patellidae

**pa·tel·lo·femoral** \pəˈte(,)lō+\ *adj* [*patella* + *-o-* + *femoral*] **:** of or relating to the patella and femur

**pa·tel·loid** \pəˈte,lȯid\ *adj* [*patella* + *-oid*] **:** PATELLIFORM

**pa·tel·lu·la** \pəˈtelyələ\ *n, pl* **patellu·lae** \-yə,lē\ [NL, dim. of L *patella* — more at PATELLA] **:** a cuplike sucker on the tarsus of beetles of the family Dytiscidae

**pa·tel·lu·late** \-yələt, -yə,lāt\ *adj* [NL *patellula* + E *-ate*] **:** having patellulae

**pat·en** \ˈpat³n\ *n* -S [ME *pateyn, patin, paten,* fr. OF *patene,* fr. ML & L; ML *patina, patena* plate for the Eucharist, fr. L, shallow dish, fr. Gk *patanē;* akin to L *patēre* to be open — more at FATHOM] **1 :** a plate of precious metal used for the bread in the eucharistic service **2 :** PLATE **3 :** a thin metal disk or something resembling one

**pat·en·cy** \ˈpat³nsē, ˈpāt-, -si\ *n* -ES [¹*patent* + *-cy*] **1 :** the quality or state of being patent **:** OBVIOUSNESS **2 :** OPENNESS, UNOBSTRUCTEDNESS ⟨~ of a fistula⟩

**pat·en·er** \ˈpat³nə(r)\ *n* -S **:** an acolyte or priest bearing the paten at mass in the medieval church

**¹pat·ent** \ˈpat³nt, ˈpāt-\ *adj* [ME, fr. MF, fr. L *patent-, patens,* fr. pres. part. of *patēre* to be open, be exposed, be evident — more at FATHOM] **1 a :** open to public inspection — used chiefly in the phrase *letters patent;* opposed to *close* **b** (1) **:** conferred by letters patent ⟨the subject of a ~ privilege —L.H. Edmunds⟩ (2) **:** endowed with a right or privilege by letters patent (as some London theaters) (3) **:** appointed by letters patent **c** *law* **:** appropriated or protected by letters patent **:** secured by letters patent to the exclusive possession and control (as for manufacture) of some person or party **:** PATENTED ⟨~ foodstuffs have acquired an ever-increasing importance —Friedel Strauss⟩ **2 :** of, relating to, or concerned with the granting of patents esp. for inventions ⟨~ attorney⟩ ⟨~ award⟩ ⟨~ law⟩ **3 a :** marketed as a proprietary commodity **:** having patent or trademark protection ⟨a ~ can opener⟩ **b :** making exclusive or proprietary claims or pretensions **:** ostensibly original or superlative ⟨peddled his ~ notions in season and out⟩ **4 :** affording free passage **:** OPEN, UNOBSTRUCTED ⟨the nose ~ with no pathological discharge —*Jour. Amer. Med. Assoc.*⟩ **5** *biol* **:** PATULOUS, SPREADING **6** *archaic* **:** ACCESSIBLE, EXPOSED ⟨a circular temple, ~ to the sun —P.J.Bailey⟩ **7 :** open to view **:** readily visible or intelligible **:** EVIDENT, OBVIOUS ⟨the ~ dissolution of the comfortable scheme of scientific materialism —A.N.Whitehead⟩ ⟨blaze a new trail against ~ stupidity —W.H.Whyte⟩ **8** *archaic* **:** available for public use **syn** see EVIDENT

**²pat·ent** \ˈpat³nt, *chiefly Brit also* ˈpāt-\ *n* -S [ME *patente,* fr. AF, fr. MF (in *lettres patentes* letters patent), fem. of *patent,* adj.] **1 :** an official document; *esp* **:** one issued by a sovereign power conferring a right or privilege ⟨when a prince made a plebeian a noble . . . the ~ of nobility defined what arms he was to bear —T.B.Wigley⟩ **2 a** (1) *U. S. patent law* **:** a government grant of a monopoly right that gives to one who invents or discovers a new and useful process, machine, manufacture, or composition of matter or a new and useful improvement thereof the exclusive right for a specific term of 17 years with certain rights of extension to make, use, or sell his invention or discovery or to assign or license less than the full patent right and that when issued is prima facie evidence of its own validity but may be attacked in a federal court (2) *British patent law* **:** a grant by the sovereign that gives the true and first inventor or certain persons claiming under him the right to exclude for 16 years with certain rights of extension others from the manufacture or use of the inventor's commercially vendible, original, and useful article or method or process of manufacture or of control, improvement, or modification thereof or of any such new and useful method or process of testing such manufacture, control, improvement, or modification, that embraces any substance or material and any plant, machinery, or apparatus, and that is sometimes subject in the public interest to compulsory licenses or to revocation **b :** a monopoly or right granted according to U. S. patent law or British patent law or under similar statutes for the protection of inventions or discoveries that is protected against infringement by remedies provided by such law or statutes and by international conventions executed by the principal nations **:** letters patent for an invention **3 :** something likened to a patent **:** LICENSE, PRIVILEGE ⟨upstarts and outlaws of religion who were infringing its spiritual ~s —W.P. Webb⟩ ⟨give her ~ to offend —Shak.⟩ **4 a :** an instrument making a conveyance or grant of public lands **b :** the land or territory so conveyed ⟨gave these obstinate squatters their legal ~s —*Amer. Guide Series: Minn.*⟩ ⟨a ~ of 1500 acres —*Amer. Guide Series: N. Y. City*⟩ **5 a :** a patented article, device, or process ⟨one of the inventor's many ~s⟩ **b :** an exclusive property or claim **:** sole right of control ⟨the techniques of economic stability and expansion are no longer the ~ of one party —Raymond Aron⟩ ⟨has no ~ on that philosophy —Irving Kolodin⟩ **6 a :** PATENT LEATHER **b patents** *pl* **:** patent leather shoes **7 :** PATENT FLOUR

**³patent** \"\ *vt* -ED/-ING/-S **1 a :** to grant (someone) a privilege, right, or license by patent **b :** to grant a patent for ⟨~*ed* the device to its inventor⟩ **2 :** to obtain or secure by patent; *esp* **:** to secure by letters patent exclusive right to make, use, and vend (an invention) **3 :** to obtain or grant a patent right to (as land or minerals) **4 :** to heat (an iron-base alloy) above the critical temperature and then cool in air or molten lead at about 700° F.; *esp* **:** to produce a structure desired in wire to be cold-drawn

**pat·ent·abil·i·ty** \ˌpat³ntəˈbiləd-ē, -lətē, -i\ *n* **:** the quality or state of being patentable

**pat·ent·able** \ˈpat³ntəbəl\ *adj* **:** suitable for patenting **:** capable of being patented — **pat·ent·ably** \-blē, -li\ *adv*

**patent ambiguity** *n* **:** an ambiguity in a legal document arising from the words themselves — opposed to *latent ambiguity*

**patent base** *or* **patent block** *n* **:** a base usu. of metal and often in standard interchangeable units to which low-mounted or unmounted letterpress plates are secured in position for printing

**patent blue** *n, often cap P&B* **:** any of several acid triphenylmethane dyes — see DYE table I (under *Acid Blue 5*)

**patent–coated** \ˈ==ˌ==\ *adj, of paperboard* **:** vat-lined on one or both sides with an uncoated white liner

**pat·en·tee** \ˌpat³nˈtē\ *n* -S [ME, fr. *patente* patent + *-ee,* -e -ee — more at PATENT] **:** one to whom a grant is made or a privilege secured by patent

**patent flour** *n* **:** a high-grade wheat flour that is free from bran, embryo, and aleurone and that consists wholly of endosperm of sound wheat grains usu. with outer parts of the endosperm removed

**patent hammer** *or* **patent ax** *n* **:** BUSHHAMMER

**patent insides** *n pl* **:** readyprint that comes printed on the inside pages — compare BOILER PLATE, PATENT OUTSIDES

**pat·ent leather** \ˈpat³nt-, *Brit usu* ˈpāt³nt-\ *n* **1 :** a leather used for shoes, handbags, and belts that is given a hard smooth glossy surface by application of successive coats of daub and varnish with careful drying after each one — compare JAPANNED LEATHER **2 patent leathers** *pl* **:** a pair of patent leather shoes

**patent log** *n* **:** TAFFRAIL LOG

**pat·ent·ly** *adv* **:** in a patent manner **:** CLEARLY, OBVIOUSLY, PLAINLY ⟨walk a plane that is ~ air —Bernard DeVoto⟩ ⟨all of which is, ~, critical nonsense —Patrick Cruttwell⟩

**patent medicine** *n* **1 :** a packaged nonprescription drug or medicine of secret composition protected by a trademark and with the name of the medicine, directions for use, and name and business address of the manufacturer on the label or package **2 :** PROPRIETARY 6a

**patent note** *n* **:** SHAPE NOTE

**patent office** *n* **:** a government office for examining claims to patents and granting patents

**pat·en·tor** \ˈpat³ntə(r)\ *n* -S **1 :** one that grants a patent **2 :** PATENTEE

**patent outsides** *n pl* **:** readyprint that comes printed on the first and last pages — compare BOILER PLATE, PATENT INSIDES

**patent peg** *n* **:** a peg for a stringed instrument (as a banjo or guitar) having an internal friction device to prevent slipping

**patent plaster** *n* **:** CEMENT PLASTER

**patent pool** *n* **1 :** a pool or combination in which the agreements are enforced by centralized control of essential patent rights **2 :** an arrangement of cross-licensing in which several patent owners join together to make individually held patents available to all members of the group

**patent right** *n* **:** a right granted by letters patent; *esp* **:** the exclusive right to an invention and the control of its manufacture

**patent rolls** *n pl* **:** the parchment rolls in which British letters patent are recorded

**patents** *pl of* PATENT, *pres 3d sing of* PATENT

**patent slip** *n, chiefly Brit* **:** MARINE RAILWAY

**patent theater** *n* **:** a theater established or licensed by royal letters patent

**patent yellow** *n* **1 :** CASSEL YELLOW 1 **2 :** ORPIMENT 2

**pa·ter** \ˈpäd-ə(r), ˈpä|, ˈpā|, |tə(r)\ *n* -S [L, father — more at FATHER] **1** *often cap* [ME, by shortening] **:** PATERNOSTER **2 :** the socially acknowledged or legal father among some primitive peoples — compare GENITOR **3** *chiefly Brit* **:** FATHER

**pat·era** \ˈpad-ərə\ *n, pl* **pater·ae** \-ə,rē\ [L; akin to L *patēre* to lie open — more at FATHOM] **1 :** an earthenware or metal saucer used by the ancient Romans for drinking and libations at sacrifices **2 :** a round or oval disk or medallion bearing an ornamental design in bas-relief or intaglio and often used in decoration of buildings or furniture

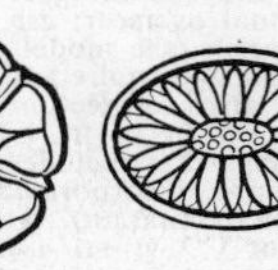
paterae

**pa·tera process** \pəˈtärə-\ *n, usu cap 1st P* [after Adolf von *Patera,* 19th cent. Ger. metallurgist] **:** extraction of silver from its ores by roasting with salt, leaching out the silver chloride with a solution of sodium thiosulfate, and precipitating the silver as sulfide by means of sodium sulfide

**patercove** *var of* PATRICO

**paterero** *var of* PEDRERO

**pa·ter·fa·mil·i·as** \ˌpa|d-ə(r)fəˈmilēəs, ˈpä|, ˈpā|, |tə(r), -ē,as\ *n* -ES *see sense 1* [L, fr. *pater* father + *familias,* old gen. of *familia* family — more at FATHER, FAMILY] **1** *pl* **pa·tres·fa·mil·i·as** \-ā(,)trēzf-; -ä-,träsf-, -ā-,-\ *Roman law* **a :** the head of a household **b :** someone who is his own master — compare PATRIA POTESTAS, SUI JURIS **2 :** the father of a family **:** the male head of a household ⟨was rapidly moving into the role of ~, for his own children numbered four —Jean Holloway⟩

**pat·er·i·form** \ˈpad-ərə,fȯrm\ *adj* [*patera* + *-iform*] **:** formed like a patera

**pat·er·is·sa** \ˌpad-əˈrisə\ *n* -S [NGk *pateritsa,* fr. MGk *pateriza,* perh. dim. of Gk *pater-, patēr* father — more at FATHER] *Eastern Church* **:** a crosier surmounted by a small cross from whose base issue two serpents

**pa·ter·nal** \pəˈtərn³l, -tōn-, -tәin-\ *adj* [LL *paternalis,* fr. *paternus* paternal (fr. *pater* father) + *-alis* -al — more at FATHER] **1 :** of or relating to a father **:** evincing a father's care or solicitude **:** FATHERLY ⟨his smile was almost ~ —Kenneth Roberts⟩ **2 :** belonging to or received or inherited from one's father ⟨passed his childhood on the ~ farm —*Current Biog.*⟩ **3 :** related (as an ancestor) through one's father ⟨~ grandfather⟩ — **pa·ter·nal·ly** \-³lē, -³li\ *adv*

**pa·ter·nal·ism** \-³l,izəm\ *n* -S **:** the care or control of subordinates (as by a government or employer) in a fatherly manner; *esp* **:** the principles or practices of a government that undertakes to supply needs or regulate conduct of the governed in matters affecting them as individuals as well as in their relations to the state and to each other

**¹pa·ter·nal·ist** \-³ləst\ *or* **pa·ter·nal·is·tic** \pəˌtərn³lˈistik, -tōn-, -tәin-, -stēk\ *adj* **:** of, relating to, or practicing paternalism — **pa·ter·nal·is·ti·cal·ly** \-stək(ə)lē, -stēk-, -li\ *adv*

**²paternalist** \"\ *n* -S **:** a practitioner of paternalism

**pat·er·nal·i·ty** \ˌpad-ə(r)ˈnaləd-ē\ *n* -S **:** the quality or state of being paternal **:** fatherly conduct or policy

**pa·ter·nal·ize** \pəˈtərn³l,īz\ *vt* -ED/-ING/-S **:** to treat paternalistically

**pa·ter·ni·ty** \pəˈtərnəd-ē, -tōn-, -tәin-, -nətē, -i\ *n* -ES [MF *paternité,* fr. LL *paternitat-, paternitas,* fr. L *paternus* paternal + *-itat-, -itas* -ity — more at PATERNAL] **1 :** the quality or state of being a father **:** FATHERHOOD ⟨the cares of ~⟩ **2 :** origin or descent from a father **:** male parentage ⟨provides for citizenship of the child born out of wedlock if ~ is established —William Samore⟩ **3 :** AUTHORSHIP, ORIGINATION ⟨the controversy which has attended the bipartisan policy has extended even to the question of its ~ —Norman Hill & Eugene Hangse⟩

**paternity test** *n* **:** a test to determine whether a given man could be father to a particular child made by comparison of the blood groups of the mother, child, and suspected man, a negative result proving that the man cannot be the father while a positive result shows only that it is biologically possible that he may be

**pa·ter·no·ite** \ˌpäd-ə(r)ˈnō,īt\ *n* -S [It, fr. Emanuele *Paternò* †1935 Ital. chemist + It *-ite*] **:** a mineral $MgB_8O_{13}.4H_2O$ consisting of a hydrous magnesium borate

**¹pa·ter·nos·ter** \ˈpa|d-ə(r),nästə(r), |tə- *also* ˈpä| *or* ˈpā| *or* -nȯs- *or* ˌ==ˈ==; ˈpä|,tərˈnō,stə(r), ,teəˈnō,steə(r *or* +V -ste(ə)r, -nä-,-\ *n* -S [ME, fr. ML, fr. L *pater noster* our father, the 1st 2 words of the Lord's Prayer] **1** *often cap* **:** a recital of the Lord's Prayer in any language esp. in Latin ⟨say ten ~*s*⟩ **2 a :** one of the large beads of a rosary on which the Lord's Prayer is said **b** *obs* (1) **:** a string with knots or beads for counting the repetitions of the Lord's Prayer (2) **:** ROSARY **3 :** something resembling a rosary: **a :** a beadwork ornament in architectural moldings **b** *or* **paternoster line :** a fishing line with a row of hooks and bead-shaped sinkers **4 :** a repetitious word formula muttered or repeated as a prayer or magical charm ⟨the mystic syllables, O-Mi-T'o Fo . . . the Buddhist ~⟩

**²paternoster** *pronunc before semicolon at* ¹PATERNOSTER\ *vi* -ED/-ING/-S **:** to fish with a paternoster

**paternoster lake** *n* **:** one of a series of lakes in a glaciated valley arranged like beads on a string

**paternoster while** *n* [ME] *archaic* **:** the time required to repeat a paternoster

**paters** *pl of* PATER

**pat·er·son** \ˈpad-ə(r)sən, -atə(r)-\ *adj, usu cap* [fr. *Paterson,* N. J.] **:** of or from the city of Paterson, N. J. ⟨*Paterson* silk mills⟩ **:** of the kind or style prevalent in Paterson

**pat·er·son's curse** \ˈpad-ə(r)sənz-\ *n, usu cap P* [after William *Paterson* †1810 Austral. administrator and botanist] **:** a perennial weed (*Echium plantagineum*) that is particularly troublesome on Australian rangeland

**pates** *pl of* PATE

**pa·te·si** \pəˈtāzē\ *n* -S [incorrect reading of Sumerian *ensi,* a title borne by the patesis] **:** a ruler of some of the Sumerian city-states who combined the religious and the secular chieftaincies **:** PRIEST-KING

**pâte–sur–pâte** \ˌpät,sərˈpät\ *n* [F, lit., paste on paste] **:** a low relief produced in ceramics or sculpture by applying slip in successive layers usu. with a brush

**pa·te·ti·co** \pəˈtad-ə,kō\ *adv (or adj)* [It, pathetic, fr. LL *patheticus* — more at PATHETIC] **:** with feeling **:** MOVINGLY — used as a direction in music

**¹path** \ˈpa|th, ˈpaa(ə)|, ˈpai|, ˈpá|\ *n, pl* **paths** \|t͟hz *also* |ths\ [ME, fr. OE *pæth, path;* akin to OFris *path,* MD & MLG *pad, pat,* OHG *pfad*] **1 :** a track made by the frequent or habitual use of men or animals **:** a trodden way ⟨a multiplicity of interesting ~s crossed the featureless land —E.E.Shipton⟩ **2 :** a track specially constructed for a particular use (as walking or horseback riding) ⟨a garden ~ of flagstones⟩ ⟨touring ~⟩ **3** *dial Brit* **:** a deep cut in a steep road **4 a :** the way or course traversed by something **:** ROUTE ⟨the ~ of a meteor⟩ ⟨a caravan's ~⟩ **b :** a way of life, conduct, or thought ⟨courage for the difficult ~ he must follow —H.M.Parshley⟩ ⟨families and friends put roadblocks on the ~ of romance —Bertha J. Lueck⟩ **c** *sometimes cap* **:** a course of religious duty **:** a prescription of religious obligation **:** a way or method of action prescribed for the devotees of a particular religion ⟨the Sufi ~⟩ **5** *math* **:** the continuous series of positions or configurations assumed in any motion or process of change by any moving or varying system **6 :** a line of communication over interconnecting neurones extending from one organ or center to another ⟨the optic ~ from the retina to the cerebral cortex⟩ **7 a :** the way or course traversed by light or electricity between two points **b :** the iron parts of a magnetic circuit

**2path** \"\ *vb* -ED/-ING/-S *vt, archaic* **:** go along (as a way or course) **:** TRAVEL, TREAD ~ *vi, obs* **:** MOVE, WALK ⟨for if thou ~, thy native semblance on —Shak.⟩

**path-** *or* **patho-** *comb form* [NL, fr. Gk, fr. *pathos* experience, emotion, passion, suffering — more at PATHOS] **1 :** pathological ⟨*patho*morphosis⟩ **2 :** pathological and ⟨*patho*histological⟩ **3 :** pathological state **:** disease ⟨*patho*gen⟩ ⟨*path*ergy⟩ **4 :** emotion ⟨*patho*meter⟩

**-path** \ˌpath, ˌpaa(ə)th, ˌpaith\ *n comb form* -S [in sense 1, fr. G, back-formation fr. *-pathie* -pathy; in sense 2, ISV, fr. Gk *-pathēs*, fr. *pathos*] **1 :** a practitioner of a (specified) system of medicine that emphasizes some one aspect of disease and its treatment ⟨allo*path*⟩ ⟨hydro*path*⟩ ⟨osteo*path*⟩ **2 :** one suffering from a (specified) kind of ailment ⟨psycho*path*⟩ ⟨neuro*path*⟩

**path** *abbr* pathological; pathology

**pa·than** \pə'tän, ˌpət'hän\ *n* -S *usu cap* [Hindi *Paṭhān*] **:** a member of an Iranian people who are the principal race of Afghanistan and colonies of whom are scattered throughout Pakistan and India — compare AFGHAN 1

**pat hand** *n* [4*pat*] **1 :** a hand in draw poker on which one stands pat **2 :** a dealt hand in draw poker (as a straight, flush, or full house) that usu. cannot be materially improved by drawing one or two cards

**pathbreaking** \'=ˌ==\ *adj* **:** making or pointing a new way **:** TRAILBLAZING ⟨~ scientific discoveries —Maurice Cranston & J.W.N.Watkins⟩

**path·e·mat·ic** \ˌpathəˈmad·ik\ *adj* [Gk *pathēmatikos*, fr. *pathēmat-* *pathēma* suffering, emotion (fr. *path-*, stem of *paschein* to experience, suffer) + *-ikos* -ic — more at PATHOS] *archaic* **:** EMOTIONAL — **path·e·mat·i·cal·ly** \-d·ək(ə)lē\ *adv*

**pa·thet·ic** \pə'thed·|ik, -et|, |ēk\ *also* **pa·thet·i·cal** \|əkəl, |ēk-\ *adj* [MF or LL; MF *pathetique*, fr. LL *patheticus*, fr. Gk *pathētikos* capable of feeling, sensitive, pathetic, fr. *pathētos* subject to suffering, liable to external influence (fr. *path-*, stem of *paschein* to experience, suffer) + *-ikos* -ic, -ical — more at PATHOS] **1** *obs* **a :** exciting or stirring emotion or passion **b :** marked by strong emotion **:** PASSIONATE **2 a :** evoking tenderness, pity, sympathy, or sorrow **:** AFFECTING, PITIABLE ⟨looked old and ~ —Ruth Park⟩ ⟨a ~ confusion between knowledge and guesswork —M.R.Cohen⟩ ⟨~ and misdirected efforts to be one's true self —Sara H. Hay⟩ **b :** marked by sorrow, suffering, or melancholy **:** SAD ⟨mingling playful with ~ thoughts —William Wordsworth⟩ ⟨you may be gentle and ~, or savage and cynical with perfect propriety —W.M.Thackeray⟩ ⟨the eloquent phrases I had arranged, ~ or indignant, seemed out of place —W.S. Maugham⟩ **3 :** of or relating to the superior oblique muscle or the trochlear nerve **syn** see MOVING

**pa·thet·i·cal·ly** \|ək(ə)lē, |ēk-, -li\ *adv* **:** in a pathetic manner

**pathetic fallacy** *n* **:** the ascription of human traits or feelings to inanimate nature (as in *cruel sea, pitiless storm, devouring flame*)

**pa·thet·ics** \|iks\ *n pl* **:** pathetic expression or conduct ⟨our wretched, shameful sentimentalities and ~ go on smouldering —Bernard DeVoto⟩

**pa·thet·i·cus** \pə'thed·əkəs\ *n, pl* **patheti·ci** \-d·əˌsī\ [NL, fr. LL, pathetic — more at PATHETIC] **:** TROCHLEAR NERVE

**pathfinder** \'=ˌ==\ *n* **1 :** one that discovers a way; *esp* **:** one that explores untraversed or unfrequented regions to mark out a new route **:** TRAILBLAZER ⟨a ~ of the air⟩ ⟨explore so many facets of human knowledge with so many scholars as ~*s* —Paul Fejos⟩ ⟨the average man of today is too gregarious to be a ~ —Hamlin Garland⟩ **2 :** an airplane that precedes the rest, locates the target, and marks it for the main force with flares, smoke bombs, or smoke rockets **3 :** a parachutist who drops into a target area to set up signals for guidance

**pathfinding** \'=ˌ==\ *n* **:** the action of a pathfinder

**-path·ia** \'pathēə\ *n comb form* -S [NL — more at -PATHY] **:** -PATHY 2 ⟨hyper*pathia*⟩ ⟨lympho*pathia*⟩

**1path·ic** \'pathik\ *n* -S [L *pathicus*, fr. (assumed) Gk *pathikos*, fr. Gk *path-* (stem of *paschein* to experience, have something happen to one, suffer) + *-ikos* -ic — more at PATHOS] **1 :** CATAMITE ⟨an elder boy whose ~ he was —W.B.Yeats⟩ **2 :** a passive party **:** SUBJECT, SUFFERER, VICTIM ⟨is at once the "healer" and the ~ who is to be healed —Julian Symons⟩

**2pathic** \"\ *adj* **1 :** PASSIVE ⟨the genius of the Orient is its discovery and practice of this sort of ~ or affective communion with nature-in-general —V.C.Aldrich⟩ **2 :** DISEASED, MORBID ⟨whether they are healthy or ~ —C.W.Morris⟩

**-path·ic** \ˈpathik, -thēk\ *adj comb form* [ISV *-pathy* + *-ic*] **1 :** feeling, suffering, or affected in a (specified) way ⟨tele*pathic*⟩ **2 :** affected by disease of a (specified) part or kind ⟨myo*pathic*⟩ **3 :** relating to therapy based on a (specified) unitary theory of disease or its treatment ⟨homeo*pathic*⟩

**-pathies** *pl of* -PATHY

**pathing** *pres part of* PATH

**path·less** \'pathləs\ *adj* **:** having no path **:** UNTROD, TRACKLESS ⟨~ woods⟩ — **path·less·ness** *n* -ES

**path·let** \-lət\ *n* -S **:** a little path

**path line** *n* **:** LINE OF FLOW

**pathmaster** \'=ˌ==\ *n* **:** one whose job it is to care for and maintain public paths and roads

**patho-** — see PATH-

**path·o·don·tia** \ˌpathə'dänch(ē)ə\ *n* -S [NL, fr. *path-* + *-odontia*] **:** a branch of dentistry concerned with diseases of the teeth

**path of emergence :** the direction of vibration of a particle at the earth's surface during an earthquake

**path·o·gen** \'pathəjən, -ˌjen\ *also* **path·o·gene** \-ˌjēn\ *n* -S [ISV *path-* + *-gen, -gene*] **:** a specific cause of disease (as a bacterium or virus) **syn** see MICROORGANISM

**patho·genesis** \ˈpathə+\ *n* [NL, fr. *path-* + L *genesis*] **:** the origination and development of a disease

**path·o·ge·net·ic** \ˈpathōjəˈned·ik\ *adj* [ISV *path-* + *-genetic*] **1 :** of or relating to pathogenesis **2 :** PATHOGENIC

**path·o·gen·ic** \ˈpathəˈjenik\ *adj* [ISV *path-* + *-genic*] **1 :** PATHOGENETIC ⟨a ~ process⟩ **2 :** causing or capable of causing disease ⟨~ microorganisms⟩ — **path·o·gen·i·cal·ly** \-nək(ə)lē\ *adv*

**path·o·ge·nic·i·ty** \ˌpathōjə'nisəd·ē\ *n* -ES **:** the quality or state of being pathogenic **:** degree of pathogenic capacity ⟨~ enhanced by mouse passage⟩

**pa·thog·e·ny** \pə'thäjənē, pa'-\ *n* -ES [*path-* + *-geny*] **:** PATHOGENESIS

**path·og·nom·ic** \ˈpathə(g)ˈnämik\ *also* **path·og·nom·i·cal** \-məkəl\ *adj* [contr. of *pathognomonic, pathognomonical*] **1 :** of or relating to pathognomy **2 :** PATHOGNOMONIC

**path·og·no·mon·ic** \ˈpathə(g)nəˈmänik\ *also* **path·og·no·mon·i·cal** \-nəkəl\ *adj* [Gk *pathognōmonikos* indicating a particular disease, fr. *patho-* path- + *gnōmonikos* fit to judge, fr. *gnōmon-*, *gnōmōn* one that knows or discerns, interpreter + *-ikos* -ic, -ical — more at GNOMON] **:** specially, distinctively, or decisively characteristic of a particular disease ⟨a ~ symptom⟩ — **path·og·no·mon·i·cal·ly** \-nək(ə)lē\ *adv*

**path·og·no·my** \pə'thägnəmē, pa'-\ *n* -ES [*path-* + *-gnomy*] **:** the study or recognition of emotions and passions through their outward signs or expressions

**path·o·log·i·cal** \ˈpathəˈläjəkəl, -jēk-\ *or* **path·o·log·ic** \-jik, -jēk\ *adj* [F *pathologique*, fr. MF, fr. Gk *pathologikos* of the study of the passions, fr. *pathologia* study of the passions + *-ikos* -ic, -ical — more at PATHOLOGY] **1 :** of, relating to, for the purposes of, or concerned with pathology ⟨~ laboratory⟩ ⟨~ garden⟩ ⟨a ~ anatomist⟩ **2 :** DISEASED **:** altered by disease ⟨~ tissue⟩ **3 :** caused by pathology ⟨~ changes⟩ **:** being manifestations of disease ⟨~ bodily processes⟩ **4** *Kantianism* **:** of or relating to passion (sense 4); *specif* **:** instinctually or sensuously determined **:** PASSIONAL **syn** see UNWHOLESOME

**pathological anatomy** *n* **:** a branch of anatomy concerned with structural changes accompanying disease

**pathological drinker** *n, psychiatry* **:** a person whose characteristic attempt to relieve emotional tension is by excessive consumption of intoxicating liquor

**pathological drunkenness** *or* **pathological intoxication** *n* **:** acute excitement with confusion and hallucinosis manifested over a short period of time after the drinking of alcohol and by some considered to be an allergic reaction to alcohol

**pathological illusion** *n* **:** HALLUCINATION 1

**pathological liar** *n* **:** a person who habitually tells lies so exaggerated or bizarre that they are suggestive of mental disorder

**path·o·log·i·cal·ly** \-jək(ə)lē, -jēk-, -li\ *adv* **:** in a pathological manner

**pathological signalment** *n* **:** description of a person's deformities and scars for purposes of identification by the Bertillon system

**pathologico-** *comb form* [ISV, fr. *pathological*] **:** pathological and ⟨*pathologico*anatomical⟩

**pa·thol·o·gist** \pə'thäləjəst, pa'-\ *n* -S **:** a specialist in pathology; *specif* **:** one who interprets and diagnoses the changes caused by disease in tissues — compare CLINICIAN

**pa·thol·o·gy** \-jē, -ji\ *n* -ES [NL *pathologia* & MF *pathologie*, fr. Gk *pathologia* study of the passions, fr. *patho-* path- + *-logia* -logy] **1 :** the study of abnormality; *esp* **:** the study of diseases, their essential nature, causes, and development, and the structural and functional changes produced by them **2 :** something abnormal: **a** (1) **:** the anatomic and physiologic deviations from the normal in the tissues of animals and plants that are manifested as disease ⟨the study of human ~⟩ (2) **:** the complex of signs, symptoms, and bodily changes that characterize a particular disease ⟨the ~ of pneumonia⟩ **b :** comparable abnormality of nonliving material ⟨the ~ of steel⟩ ⟨~ of wine⟩ **c :** deviation from propriety or from an assumed normal state of nonmaterial things ⟨the ~ of reaction⟩ ⟨social ~⟩ **3 :** a treatise on or compilation of abnormalities ⟨a new ~ of the eye⟩

**pa·thom·e·ter** \pə'thämәd·ə(r), pa'-\ *n* [*path-* + *-meter*] **:** a lie detector that measures electrical impulses of the body — compare POLYGRAPH

**patho·neurosis** \ˈpathō+\ *n* [NL, fr. *path-* + *neurosis*] **:** concentration of libido in a bodily organ esp. when the site of previous disease or trauma

**path·o·pho·bia** \ˌpathə'fōbēə\ *n* [NL, fr. *path-* + *phobia*] **:** morbid fear of disease **:** HYPOCHONDRIA

**patho·physiologic** \ˈpathō+\ *adj* **:** of or relating to pathophysiology

**patho·physiology** \"+\ *n* [*path-* + *physiology*] **:** the physiology of abnormal states; *specif* **:** the functional changes that accompany a particular syndrome or disease ⟨the ~ of diabetes⟩

**pa·thos** \'pāˌthäs *also* -thȯs *or* -thōs *sometimes* 'paˌ- *or* -ˌthəs\ *n* -ES [Gk, experience, emotion, passion, suffering, fr. *path-*, stem of *paschein* to experience, suffer; akin to OIr *cēssaim*, *cēssim* I suffer, Gk *penthos* grief, sorrow, Latvian *cìest* to endure, suffer] **1 a :** an element in experience or in artistic representation evoking pity or compassion ⟨~ she has, the nearest to tragedy the comedian can come —W.B.Yeats⟩ **b :** an emotion of sympathetic pity ⟨felt a stab of ~ —Rex Ingamells⟩ **2 :** the transient or accidental factor in an event or experience as distinguished from that based on personal character — compare ETHOS 2 a (2)

**pa·tho·sis** \pə'thōsəs, pa'-\ *n, pl* **patho·ses** \-ōˌsēz\ [NL, fr. *path-* + *-sis*] **:** a diseased state **:** an abnormal condition ⟨dental ~⟩

**path-reversal principle** \'=='==-\ *n* **:** a statement in optics: if light traverses a given course it can traverse the same course in the opposite direction and hence it follows that any object point and its real image are interchangeable

**paths** *pl of* PATH, *pres 3d sing of* PATH

**pathway** \'=ˌ=\ *n* **1 :** a way that is or serves as a path **:** a beaten track **:** COURSE, FOOTPATH ⟨trail drivers forced the ~ for permanent settlement —*Amer. Guide Series: Texas*⟩ ⟨the ~ of the river . . . may sometimes be beset with difficulties —R.E.Janssen⟩ ⟨the ~*s* of pure and applied science are under continuous survey —*Americana Annual*⟩ **2 :** PATH 6 **3 :** the sequence of enzyme-catalyzed reactions by which any energy-yielding substrate is catabolized by protoplasm

**pathy** \'pathē\ *n* -ES [*-pathy*] **:** a system of treating disease — usu. used disparagingly

**-pa·thy** \pəthē, -thi\ *n comb form* -ES [L *-pathia*, fr. Gk *-patheia*, fr. *path-*, stem of *paschein* to experience, suffer — more at PATHOS] **1 :** feeling **:** suffering ⟨a*pathy*⟩ ⟨tele*pathy*⟩ **2 :** disease of a (specified) part or kind ⟨idio*pathy*⟩ ⟨myo*pathy*⟩ **3 :** therapy or system of therapy based on a (specified) unitary theory of disease or its treatment ⟨homeo*pathy*⟩

**1pat·i·ble** \'pad·əbəl\ *n* -S [L *patibulum* fork-shaped yoke for the punishment of criminals, fork-shaped gibbet, fr. *patēre* to be open, stretch out + *-ibulum*, suffix used to denote instrumentality — more at FATHOM] **:** the transom of a cross

**2patible** \"\ *adj* [L *patibilis*, fr. *pati* to bear, undergo + *-ibilis* -ible — more at PATIENT] *archaic* **:** capable of suffering or of being acted on

**pa·tib·u·lary** \pə'tibyəˌlerē\ *adj* [ML *patibulum* gallows (fr. L, fork-shaped yoke for punishing criminals, fork-shaped gibbet) + E *-ary* — more at PATIBLE] *archaic* **:** of, relating to, or suggesting the gallows or hanging

**1pa·tience** \'pāshən(t)s\ *n* -S [ME *pacience*, fr. OF *patience*, *pacience*, fr. L *patientia*, fr. *patient-*, *patiens*, (pres. part. of *pati* to suffer) + *-ia* -y — more at PATIENT] **1 a :** the capacity or habit of enduring evil, adversity, or pain with fortitude ⟨~, like charity, is long-suffering and kind. It is, moreover, the most practical of the virtues —Irwin Edman⟩ ⟨~ as well as courage — if there be any difference between them — is a necessary mark of the liberal mind —John Dewey⟩ **b :** forbearance under stress, provocation, or indignity **:** toleration or magnanimity for the faults or affronts of others **:** courageous endurance ⟨he conducted himself with ~ and tact, endeavoring to enforce the laws and to check any revolutionary moves —W.E.Stevens⟩ **c :** calm self-possession in confronting obstacles or delays **:** STEADFASTNESS ⟨~ is the capacity to endure all that is necessary in attaining a desired end . . . ~ never forsakes the ultimate goal —Margaret Kennedy⟩ **2** *obs* **:** PERMISSION, LEAVE **3** *also* **patience dock :** a coarse European dock (*Rumex patientia*) formerly used like spinach **4** *chiefly Brit* **:** SOLITAIRE 3a

**syn** PATIENCE, LONG-SUFFERING, LONG-SUFFERANCE, LONGANIMITY, FORBEARANCE, and RESIGNATION can all signify a power of enduring without complaint what is disagreeable. PATIENCE stresses composure under suffering as in awaiting an unduly delayed outcome or in performing an exacting task ⟨endured with smiling *patience* —Lafcadio Hearn⟩ ⟨by his *patience* in reading manuscript and proofs —E.A.Armstrong⟩ ⟨twigs, which he carried to his room and later with great *patience* wove into the form of a basket —Sherwood Anderson⟩ ⟨the calm and infinite *patience* of those who have no ambition —G.S.Gale⟩ LONG-SUFFERING (or LONG-SUFFERANCE) and LONGANIMITY imply extraordinary patience under provocation or trial; LONG-SUFFERING sometimes suggests undue meekness or submissiveness; LONGANIMITY more often designates the virtue rather than the capacity of enduring ⟨the earliest heroines in English literature were *long-suffering* creatures. They were subjected to constant masculine persecution —F.A.Swinnerton⟩ ⟨the *long-sufferance* of the army is almost exhausted —George Washington⟩ ⟨the attitude of the officials towards him was one, at first of amused tolerance, then of bored *longanimity*, and finally . . . of irritation —George Antonius⟩ FORBEARANCE adds to LONG-SUFFERING the implication of restraint in expression of feelings or in exaction of penalties, connoting a tolerance of what merits censure ⟨her *forbearance* with her incorrigible husband —Willa Cather⟩ ⟨he dwelt on his *forbearance*, on the concessions which he had offered —J.A.Froude⟩ ⟨show great *forbearance* in the face of insult⟩ RESIGNATION implies submission to or acceptance of suffering, often connoting stoicism or fatalism ⟨most readers either positively enjoy the snobbery columns of their newspapers, or else accept them with *resignation*, as part of the established order of things —Aldous Huxley⟩ ⟨we need *resignation* to learn to live in a world that is not formed just for our comfort —M.R.Cohen⟩ ⟨notable for their endurance, capacity for suffering and *resignation* —W.C.Huntington⟩

**2patience** \"\ *vb* -ED/-ING/-S *vi, archaic* **:** to have or practice patience ~ *vt, obs* **:** to make patient

**patience plant** *n* **:** BALSAM 4

**pa·tien·cy** \-nsē\ *n* -ES [L *patientia* — more at PATIENCE] *archaic* **:** the quality or state of being patient or passive

**1pa·tient** \'pāshənt\ *adj, sometimes* -ER/-EST [ME *pacient*, fr. MF *patient*, *pacient*, fr. L *patient-*, *patiens*, fr. pres. part. of *pati* to suffer; akin to L *paene* almost, *penuria* want, need, Gk *pēma* suffering, calamity, Skt *pāpman* want, need] **1 :** bearing pains or trials calmly or uncomplainingly **:** exhibiting power to endure hardship or physical or mental distress ⟨love is ~ and kind . . . love bears all things —1 Cor 13:4–7 (RSV)⟩ **2 :** manifesting forbearance under provocation or strain **:** lenient to the shortcomings or offenses of others **:** LONG-SUFFERING ⟨is an orator of great power and persuasiveness; and the most reasonable and ~ negotiator —T.S.Steele⟩ ⟨a ~ teacher⟩ **3 :** exhibiting deliberation or restraint **:** calm in expectation **:** not hasty or impetuous ⟨he had been marvelously ~ and discreet, and he had been miraculously bold —John Buchan⟩ ⟨that means a lot of ~ discussion and consultation —Hugh Gaitskell⟩ **4 :** steadfast despite opposition, difficulty, or adversity **:** UNDAUNTED ⟨the flint miner extracted his stone, and by ~ effort shaped it to his needs —Lewis Mumford⟩ **5 :** able or willing to bear **:** ENDURING — used with *of* ⟨~ of misrepresentations —*Current Biog.*⟩ **6 :** SUSCEPTIBLE, ADMITTING — used with *of* ⟨this passage seems to be ~ of only one interpretation —C.T.Onions⟩ **7** *archaic* **:** acted upon rather than acting **:** PASSIVE — opposed to *agent* — **pa·tient·ly** *adv* — **pa·tient·ness** *n* -ES

**2patient** \"\ *n* -S [ME *pacient*, fr. MF *pacient*, *patient*, fr. *pacient*, *patient*, adj.] **1** *archaic* **:** one that suffers, endures, or is victimized **2 a** (1) **:** a sick individual esp. when awaiting or under the care and treatment of a physician or surgeon ⟨the hospital is equipped to handle 500 ~*s*⟩ (2) **:** a client for medical service (as of a physician or dentist) ⟨a good practice with a large number of ~*s*⟩ **b** (1) **:** the recipient of any of various personal services (as cosmetic care) **:** CUSTOMER, PATRON ⟨found the beauty shop filled with ~*s*⟩ (2) **:** a hypnotist's subject **3 :** one that is subjected to action or external force — opposed to *agent* ⟨are agents as well as ~*s* and observers in the world —C.H.Whiteley⟩

**3patient** *vt* -ED/-ING/-S [1*patient*] *obs* **:** to make patient **:** COMPOSE, CALM

**pa·tient·less** \-tləs\ *adj* **:** having no patients

**patimokkha** *var of* PRATIMOKSHA

**pat·i·na** \'pad·ənə, -atə-, -atᵊnə, pə'tēnə\ *n, pl* **patinas** *or* **pati·nae** \-ˌnē, -ᵊnˌē\ [in sense 1, fr. ML, fr. L, shallow dish; in other senses, NL, fr. L — more at PATEN] **1 :** a eucharistic paten **2 :** a usu. green film that is formed naturally on copper and bronze by long exposure esp. to a moist atmosphere or artificially (as by treatment with acids), that is a basic salt (as a carbonate) of copper protecting the metal from further oxidation, and that is often valued aesthetically for its color **3 :** a surface appearance (as a coloring or mellowing) of something grown beautiful esp. with age or use ⟨~ is to sterling what character is to a fine face —Sarah T. Lee⟩ **4 :** a finish or coloration derived from association, habit, or established character **:** the look acquired from long custom or settled use ⟨a ~ of laughter wrinkles around his eyes —H.W.Baldwin⟩ ⟨those old moments have acquired a ~ of value —J.J.Godwin⟩ ⟨takes on for a time the ~ of the international set —*Newsweek*⟩ ⟨it is only I who have coated them with the ~ of my own childhood happiness —Helen Howe⟩

**pat·i·naed** \-nəd, -ᵊnəd\ *adj* **:** having a patina ⟨a leather snap purse ~ like old silver —William Faulkner⟩

**patina green** *n* **:** a light to moderate yellowish green

**pat·i·nate** \'pad·əˌnāt\ *vb* -ED/-ING/-S *vt* **:** to coat with a patina **:** cast a patina on ⟨had taken time and pains to ~ them with good manners —Jean Stafford⟩ ~ *vi* **:** to become coated with a patina

**pat·i·na·tion** \ˌ=='nāshən\ *n* -S **1 :** the quality or state of being patinated **2 :** the act or process of patinating

**1pa·tine** \pə'tēn\ *n* -S [F, fr. ML & NL *patina* — more at PATINA] **1 :** PATEN **2 :** PATINA ⟨time has bestowed a ~ of oxidation on these vessels —Dorothy Adlow⟩ ⟨a slight ~ of the ruddiness of youth —Glenway Wescott⟩

**2patine** \"\ *vt* -ED/-ING/-S **:** PATINATE

**pa·tined** \-nd\ *adj* [1*patine* + *-ed*] **:** having a patina

**pat·i·nize** \'pad·əˌnīz\ *vt* -ED/-ING/-S [*patina* + *-ize*] **:** PATINATE

**pat·i·nous** \-ˌnəs\ *adj* [*patina* + *-ous*] **:** coated with or having a patina

**pat·io** \'pa|d·ēˌō, 'pä|, 'pá|, |tēˌō\ *n* -S [Sp, fr. OSp, untilled land, building lot, courtyard enclosed by columns, prob. fr. OProv *patu*, *pati* rented land, rented pasture, pasture, perh. fr. L *pactum* agreement, contract — more at PACT] **1 a :** the court or courtyard of a house or other building; *esp* **:** an inner court open to the sky **b :** a recreation area adjoining a dwelling, often paved, and adapted esp. to outdoor dining **2 :** a paved yard or floor where ores are cleaned and sorted or reduced

**pat·i·oed** \-ōd\ *adj* **:** having a patio

**patio process** *n* **:** an amalgamation process of reducing silver ore in which ore crushed to pulp is spread on the patio and mixed with salt, copper sulfate, and mercury by spading the mass and driving horses or mules through it

**pa·tis·se·rie** \pə'tisərē\ *n* -S [F *pâtisserie*, fr. MF *pastiserie* pastry (collectively), fr. (assumed) OF *pastis* cake (fr. — assumed — VL *pasticium*, fr. LL *pasta* dough, paste) + OF *-erie* -ery — more at PASTE] **1 :** a shop that sells French pastry **2 :** dessert pastry; *esp* **:** FRENCH PASTRY

**patlid** *var of* POTLID

**patly** *adv* [4*pat* + *-ly*] **:** in a pat manner **:** APTLY, SUITABLY ⟨the too ~ remembered conversations, and all the other fakeries that have become standard in the "as told to" books —Gilbert Seldes⟩

**patmkg** *abbr* patternmaking

**pat·na** \'pətnə, 'pat-\ *adj, usu cap* [fr. *Patna*, India] **:** of or from the city of Patna, India **:** of the kind or style prevalent in Patna

**patna rice** *n, usu cap P* **:** a rice that originated in the Ganges valley of India and is distinguished by an elongated firm grain of excellent culinary quality which holds its shape well on boiling and is used esp. in commercial soups

**pat·ness** *n* -ES [4*pat* + *-ness*] **:** the quality or state of being pat **:** APTNESS, OPPORTUNENESS, SUITABILITY

**pa·to·co** \pə'tō(ˌ)kō\ *n, pl* **patoco** *or* **patocos** *usu cap* **1 :** an Indian people with a language belonging to the Coche language family **2 :** the language of the Patoco people

**pa·tois** \'pa·ˌtwä, 'pä·-, 'pá·-\ *n, pl* **patois** \-wäz\ [F, fr. OF, peasant speech, prob. fr. *pate*, *patte* paw + *-ois* (as in *françois* French) — more at PATTEN] **1 a :** a dialect other than the standard or literary dialect ⟨the polyglot ~ of a Balkan borderland —*Amer. Guide Series: Minn.*⟩ **b :** illiterate or provincial speech **2 :** the characteristic special language of an occupational or social group or of the followers of a sport or other interest **:** CANT, JARGON ⟨the deportment and language of the gangsters and their "molls" was aped . . . by the "swells", and the ~ of prison yard and call house became the lingua franca of society —Polly Adler⟩ **syn** see DIALECT

**1pa·to·la** \pə'tōlə\ *n* -S [Gujarati *paṭolũ*, fr. Skt *paṭola*] **1 :** a silk cloth of India **2 :** a wedding sari woven in Gujarat, India, in chiné technique

**2patola** \"\ *n* -S [Tag] *Philippines* **:** a dishcloth gourd (*Luffa acutangula*) that is eaten green or cooked

**pa·to·lli** \pə'tōl(y)ē\ *n* -S [Sp, fr. Nahuatl] **:** an Aztec board game similar to pachisi

**pa·tonce** \pə'tän(t)s\ *adj* [prob. modif. of MF *potencé* having arms like a crutch, fr. *potence* crutch — more at POTENCE] *of a heraldic cross* **:** having the arms concave and expanding toward 3-pointed ends similar to but less recurved than those of a cross fleury — usu. used postpositively; compare FLEURY, PATY; see CROSS illustration

**patr-** *or* **patri-** *or* **patro-** *comb form* [*patr-* partly fr. L, fr. *patr-*, *pater;* partly fr. Gk, fr. *patr-*, *patēr; patri-* fr. ME, fr. MF, fr. L, fr. *patr-*, *pater; patro-*, NL, fr. Gk, fr. *patr-*, *patēr* — more at FATHER] **:** father ⟨*patri*kin⟩ ⟨*patri*lineal⟩ ⟨*patri*stic⟩ ⟨*patro*clinal⟩ ⟨*patro*genesis⟩ ⟨*patro*nomatology⟩

**patresfamilias** *pl of* PATERFAMILIAS

**pa·tria** \'pā·trēə\ *n* -S [NL, fr. L, native country — more at EXPATRIATE] *biol* **:** natural habitat

**1pa·tri·al** \'pā·trēəl\ *adj* [ML *patrialis*, fr. L *patria* + *-alis* -al] **1 :** of or relating to one's fatherland **2** *of a word* **:** derived from the name of a country or place and used to denote a native or inhabitant of it

²**patrial** \"\ *n* -s **:** a patrial word

**pa·tria po·tes·tas** \ˌpä·trēəpōˈteˌstäs\ *n* [L, power of a father] **:** the power of the head of a Roman family over his wife, children, agnatic descendants, slaves, and freedmen including orig. the right to punish by death and always embracing complete control over the limited personal and private rights and duties of all members of the family — compare PATERFAMILIAS

**pa·tri·arch** \ˈpā·trēˌärk, -ˌäk\ *n* -s [ME *patriark*, fr. OF *patriarche*, fr. LL *patriarcha*, fr. Gk *patriarchēs*, fr. *patria* lineage, descent, clan, family (fr. *patr-*, *patēr* father) + *-archēs* -arch — more at FATHER] **1 a :** one of the Scriptural fathers of the human race or of the Hebrew people; *specif* **:** one of a group comprising Abraham, Isaac, Jacob, and the twelve sons of Jacob **b :** a man regarded as father or founder (as of a race, science, religion, or class of men) ⟨became one of the great cattlemen of the West, and sheepmen of a later day referred to him as the ~ of their industry —H.J.Peterson⟩ **c** (1) **:** the oldest member or representative of a group ⟨a bullfrog, the ~ of the swamp, blew suddenly on his mighty tuba, "jug-o-rum" —*Springfield (Mass.) Union*⟩ ⟨the cypress of the eastern river courses, growing to heights of 150 feet or more, is the ~ of native trees, going back to the time of the dinosaur —*Amer. Guide Series: Texas*⟩ (2) **:** a venerable old man **:** ELDER, VETERAN ⟨was a whiskered ~, spry for his age —Frank Sullivan⟩ ⟨consultations with the party ~*s* —W.S. White⟩ **2 a** (1) **:** any of the bishops of the ancient or Eastern Orthodox sees of Constantinople, Alexandria, Antioch, and Jerusalem or the ancient and Western see of Rome with authority over other bishops (2) **:** the spiritual head of any of various Eastern churches either autocephalous (as the Russian Orthodox Church) or no longer in communion with the ecumenical patriarch of Constantinople and the Eastern Orthodox Church (as the Syrian or Coptic churches) **b :** an ecclesiastical dignitary next in rank to the pope: (1) **:** a Roman Catholic bishop with purely titular or with metropolitan jurisdiction (2) **:** the active ecclesiastical head of a Uniate body **3 :** the head or president of the Sanhedrin in Palestine; *sometimes* **:** the head of the Jewish college at Babylon **4 :** one of the Melchizedek priesthood in the Mormon church empowered to perform the ordinances of the church and to invoke and pronounce blessings within a stake or other prescribed jurisdiction **5 :** a dark reddish purple that is bluer and stronger than amaranth, auricula purple, or raisin purple

**pa·tri·ar·chal** \ˌ=ˈärkəl, -ˈäk-\ *adj* [LL *patriarchalis*, fr. *patriarcha* patriarch + *-alis* -al] **1 :** of or relating to a patriarch or patriarchs **:** governed by or subject to patriarchs **:** of the nature or rank of a patriarch ⟨political independence was . . . at times preceded by the throwing off of the ~ yoke —K.S.Latourette⟩ **2 :** resembling or suggesting a patriarch **:** ANCIENT, VENERABLE ⟨the long bearded moss festoons the branches . . . a young yellow birch has a venerable, ~ look, and seems ill at ease under such premature honors —John Burroughs⟩ — **pa·tri·ar·chal·ly** \-kəlē\ *adv*

**patriarchal cross** *n* **:** a chiefly heraldic cross denoting a cardinal's or archbishop's rank and having two crossbars of which the lower is the longer and intersects the upright above or at its center — called also *archiepiscopal cross;* see CROSS OF LORRAINE 2

**pa·tri·ar·chal·ism** \ˌ=ˈärkəˌlizəm\ *n* -s **1 :** government by a patriarch **2 :** a patriarchal social organization

**pa·tri·arch·ate** \ˈ=ˌärkət, -ˌkāt\ *n* -s [ML *patriarchatus*, fr. LL *patriarcha* patriarch + L *-atus* -ate — more at PATRIARCH] **1 a :** the office, dignity, jurisdiction, province, or see of a patriarch **b :** the residence or business office of a patriarch **2 :** PATRIARCHY 2

**pa·tri·ar·chic** \ˌ=ˈärkik, -ˈäk-, -kēk\ *or* **pa·tri·ar·chi·cal** \-kəkəl, -kēk-\ *adj* [LL *patriarchicus*, fr. Gk *patriarchikos*, fr. *patriarchēs* patriarch + *-ikos* -ic, -ical — more at PATRIARCH] **:** PATRIARCHAL

**pa·tri·arch·ism** \ˈ=ˌär,kizəm\ *n* -s **:** patriarchal organization in society or church

**pa·tri·arch·ist** \-kəst\ *n* -s **:** a supporter of a patriarch or of patriarchy

**pa·tri·archy** \ˈ=ˌärkē, -ˌäk-, -ki\ *n* -ES [LGk *patriarchia*, fr. Gk *patriarchēs* patriarch + *-ia* -y] **1** *obs* **:** PATRIARCHATE 1 **2 a :** social organization marked by the supremacy of the father in the clan or family in both domestic and religious functions, the legal dependence of wife or wives and children, and the reckoning of descent and inheritance in the male line **b :** a society so organized — compare MATRIARCHY

**pat·ri·centric** \ˌpa·trə *sometimes* ˌpā- +\ *adj* [*patr-* + *-centric*] **:** gravitating toward or centered upon the father — compare MATRICENTRIC

**patrices** *pl of* PATRIX

¹**pa·tri·cian** \pəˈtrishən\ *n* -s [ME *patricion*, fr. MF *patricien*, fr. L *patricius* (fr. *patres* fathers, senators, pl. of *pater* father) + MF *-en* -an — more at FATHER] **1 :** a member of one of the original citizen families of ancient Rome to whom until about 350 B.C. such offices as those of senator, consul, and pontifex were restricted **2 a :** a member of a noble class created by Constantine and continued by succeeding emperors at Byzantium **b :** an official orig. of this class appointed supreme magistrate of the provinces of Italy and Africa by the Byzantine emperor **c :** a Holy Roman emperor assuming the title of patrician or granted it by the pope **3 a :** a hereditary noble of a medieval Italian city republic **b :** a member of an order of citizens eligible for the senate or council in the German free cities and towns **4 a :** a person of high birth **:** ARISTOCRAT, NOBLEMAN **b :** a person of breeding and cultivation **:** GENTLEMAN ⟨as cultivated a ~ as ever found himself leading the proletariat to Utopia —E.P.Snow⟩

²**patrician** \"\ *adj* [F *patricien*, fr. MF, fr. *patricien*, n.] **1 :** of or relating to the patricians of ancient Rome ⟨the ~ families had the start in the race. Great names and great possessions came to them by inheritance —J.A.Froude⟩ **2 :** of or relating to the patricians of the medieval Italian city republics or the German free cities **3 :** of, relating to, or characteristic of gentle or noble birth or of breeding and cultivation ⟨in the South, ~ landholders and merchants tried to set up a political monopoly —Allan Nevins & H.S.Commager⟩ — **pa·tri·cian·ly** *adv*

**pa·tri·cian·ism** \-shəˌnizəm\ *n* -s **:** the quality or state of being patrician

**pa·tri·ci·ate** \-shēət, -ēˌāt\ *n* -s [L *patriciatus*, fr. *patricius* patrician + *-atus* -ate — more at PATRICIAN] **1 :** the position or dignity of a patrician **:** NOBILITY **2 :** the term of office of a patrician **3 :** a patrician class **:** ARISTOCRACY

**pat·ri·cid·al** \ˌpa·trəˈsīdᵊl *sometimes* ˌpā-\ *adj* **:** of or relating to patricide **:** PARRICIDAL

**pat·ri·cide** \ˈ=ˌsīd\ *n* -s [in sense 1, fr. L *patricida*, fr. *patri-* patr- + *-cida* -cide (killer); in sense 2, fr. LL *patricidium*, fr. L *patri-* + *-cidium* -cide (killing)] **1 :** one that murders his own father **2 :** the murder of one's own father

**pa·trick** \ˈpa·trik\ *chiefly Scot var of* PARTRIDGE

**pat·ri·clan** \ˈpa·trəˌklan, ˈpā-\ *n* [*patr-* + *clan*] **:** a patrilineal clan — contrasted with *matriclan*

**patriclinous** *var of* PATROCLINOUS

**pat·ri·co** \ˈpa·trəˌkō\ *n* -ES [perh. fr. ML *pater* priest (fr. L, father) + obs. E *co* boy, prob. short for *cove* (man) — more at FATHER] *archaic* **:** HEDGE-PRIEST

**pat·ridge sight** \ˈpa·trij-\ *n* [after E. E. *Patridge*, 19th cent. Am. sportsman, its inventor] **:** a gunsight consisting of a square post front sight and a rectangular notch rear sight; *sometimes* **:** the square post front sight only

**pat·ri·kin** \ˈpa·trəˌkin, ˈpā-\ *n* [*patr-* + *kin*] **:** paternal relatives

**pat·ri·lateral** \ˌpa·trə, ˌpā·trə+\ *adj* [*patr-* + *lateral*] **:** on the father's side **:** PATERNAL — contrasted with *matrilateral*

**pat·ri·line** \ˈpa·trəˌlīn, ˈpā-\ *n* [*patr-* + *line*] **:** an aggregate of patrilineages

**pat·ri·lineage** \ˌpa·trə, ˌpā·trə+\ *n* [*patr-* + *lineage*] **:** lineage based on or tracing descent through the paternal line — contrasted with *matrilineage*

**pat·ri·lineal** \"+\ *adj* [*patr-* + *lineal*] **:** tracing descent through the father and his ancestry **:** organized on the basis of male descent and inheritance ⟨a ~ society⟩ — contrasted with *matrilineal*

**pat·ri·linear** \"+\ *adj* [*patr-* + *linear*] **:** PATRILINEAL

**pat·ri·li·ny** \ˈpa·trəˌlīnē, ˈpā-\ *n* -ES [*patrilineal* + *-y*] **:** the practice of tracing descent through the father's line — contrasted with *matriliny*

**pat·ri·local** \ˌpa·trə, ˌpā·trə+\ *adj* [*patr-* + *local*] **:** located at or centered around the residence of the husband's family or tribe ⟨a ~ marriage⟩ — contrasted with *matrilocal;* compare AVUNCULOCAL, NEOLOCAL

**pat·ri·locality** \"+\ *n* [*patr-* + *locality*] **:** residence of a couple esp. of the newly married with the husband's family or tribe — contrasted with *matrilocality*

**pat·ri·mo·ni·al** \ˌpa·trəˈmōnēəl, -nyəl\ *adj* [MF, fr. LL *patrimonialis*, fr. L *patrimonium* patrimony + *-alis* -al] **:** of, relating to, or constituting a patrimony **:** inherited from ancestors **:** HEREDITARY ⟨a ~ estate⟩ — **pat·ri·mo·ni·al·ly** \-əlē, -li\ *adv*

**pat·ri·mo·ny** \ˈ==ˌmōnē, -ni\ *n* -ES [ME *patrimoine*, *patrimonie*, fr. MF, fr. L *patrimonium*, fr. *patr-*, *pater* father — more at FATHER] **1 a :** an estate inherited from one's father or other ancestor ⟨financially that decision cost him a great share of his ~ —R.J.B.Sellar⟩ **b :** anything derived from one's father or ancestors **:** HERITAGE **c :** an inheritance from the past ⟨man may soon use up his ~ of oil, and after that his inheritance of coal —Leonard Engel⟩ ⟨a most important part of the intellectual ~ of Italy —R.A.Hall b. 1911⟩ **2 a :** an estate or property held by ancient right **b :** an ancient right **c :** an ancient estate or endowment (as of a church)

**pat·rin** \ˈpa·trən\ *or* **pat·ter·an** \ˈpad·ərən\ *n* -s [Romany *patrin*, lit., leaf, fr. Skt *patra* wing, feather, leaf; akin to Skt *patati* he flies — more at FEATHER] **:** a handful of leaves or grass thrown down at intervals by gypsies to indicate their course

**pat·ri·o·fe·lis** \ˌpa·trēōˈfēləs\ *n, cap* [NL, fr. L *patrius* of a father + *-o-* + *felis* cat — more at EXPATRIATE] **:** a genus of creodont mammals (family Oxyaenidae) of the Eocene of Wyoming having a skull as large as that of a lion and teeth like those of a cat

**pa·tri·ot** \ˈpā·trēət, -ēˌät, *usu Brit* ˈpa-; *usu* -d.+V\ *n* -s *often attrib* [MF *patriote*, fr. LL *patriota*, fr. Gk *patriōtēs*, fr. *patrios* of one's father, of or characteristic of one's forefathers, fr. *patr-*, *patēr* father — more at FATHER] **1** *obs* **:** a fellow countryman **:** COMPATRIOT **2 a :** a person who loves his country and defends and promotes its interests; *esp* **:** a soldier who fights for love of country **b :** an enthusiast for a cause other than national ⟨the South's cotton ~*s* —*Time*⟩ **3** *obs* **:** LOVER, AMATEUR **4 a** *usu cap* **:** an English parliamentary faction opposed to Sir Robert Walpole esp. from 1732–1742 **b :** one who advocates or promotes the independence of his native soil or people from the country or union of countries of which it is a part (as a colony) ⟨immortalized by the illustrious appellation of the ~ army —George Washington⟩ ⟨a band of fiery ~*s* —D.G.Haring⟩ **c :** PATRIOTEER ⟨the most bloodthirsty ~*s* in the safest swivel chairs —Walter Lippmann⟩ **5 a :** one who remains loyal to his country when it is occupied by an enemy **b :** a member of a resistance group

¹**pa·tri·o·teer** \ˌpā·trēəˈti(ə)r\ *n* -s [*patriot* + *-eer*] **:** one who makes an ostentatious show of patriotism from venal or degraded motives **:** an insincere, misguided, or spurious patriot **:** FLAG-WAVER ⟨they are quick to detect the phony and they can distinguish a patriot from a ~ —Dorothy Thompson⟩ ⟨catchword ~*s* —S.V.Benét⟩ ⟨~*s*, roaring nationalists and reformers with apparently simple devices for making the world better and safer —Stanley Walker⟩

²**patrioteer** \"\ *vi* -ED/-ING/-s **:** to behave as a patrioteer

¹**pa·tri·ot·ic** \ˌpā·trēˈäd·ik, -ät|, |ēk, *sometimes & Brit usu* ˌpa-\ *also* **pa·tri·ot·i·cal** \|əkəl, |ēk-\ *adj* [¹*patriot* + *-ic*, *-ical*] **:** inspired by patriotism **:** befitting or characteristic of a patriot **:** actuated by love of one's country **:** devoted to one's country ⟨a ~ statesman⟩ ⟨stirring ~ exercises —*Springfield (Mass.) Union*⟩ — **pa·tri·ot·i·cal·ly** \|ək(ə)lē, |ēk-, -li\ *adv*

²**patriotic** \"\ *n* -s **:** PATRIOTIC COVER

**patriotic cover** *n* **:** a mailable envelope bearing a patriotic legend, picture, or design and manufactured privately for use in wartime

**pa·tri·ot·ics** \ˌpā·trēˈäd·iks\ *n pl* **:** patriotic writings, speeches, or activities **:** a display of patriotism

**pa·tri·ot·ism** \ˈpā·trēəˌtizəm *also* -eəd.ˌi- *chiefly Brit* ˈpa-\ *n* -s **:** love for or devotion to country **:** the virtues and actions of a patriot ⟨the passionate language of ~ —J.A.Froude⟩

**patriots' day** *n, usu cap P&D* **:** April 19 commemorating the anniversary of the battles of Lexington and Concord in 1775 and observed as a legal holiday in Maine and Massachusetts

**pat·ri·pas·si·an** \ˌpa·trəˈpasēən, ˌpā-\ *n* -s *often cap* [LL *patripassianus*, fr. L *patri-* patr- + *passus* (past part. of *pati* to bear, undergo, suffer) + *-ianus* -ian — more at PATIENT] **:** one who defends or advocates Patripassianism

**pat·ri·pas·si·an·ism** \-sēəˌnizəm\ *n* -s *usu cap* **:** the doctrine that in the sufferings of Jesus Christ God the Father also suffered — compare SABELLIANISM

**pat·ri·pas·si·an·ist** \-ˌnəst\ *n* -s **:** PATRIPASSIAN

**pat·ri·potestal** \ˌpa·trə, ˌpā·trə+\ *adj* [*patr-* + *potestal*] **:** marked by the authority of the father or of a council of the father's relatives — contrasted with *matripotestal*

**pa·tris·tic** \pəˈtristik, -stēk\ *or* **pa·tris·ti·cal** \-stəkəl, -stēk-\ *adj* [ISV *patr-* + *-istic*, *-istical*] **1 :** of or relating to the philosophical and theological writings of the early church fathers ⟨the revival of ~ studies in the U.S. —*Times Lit. Supp.*⟩ **2 :** of or relating to the basic early writings of any cult or system ⟨the ~ texts of Soviet Marxism —Daniel Lerner⟩ ⟨Pahlavi ~ literature —A.V.W.Jackson⟩ ⟨the ~ literature of America —D.C.Mearns⟩

**patristic greek** *n, usu cap P&G* **:** Greek as written by the Greek fathers of the Christian church

**pa·tris·ti·cism** \-stəˌsizəm\ *n* -s **:** a system based on patristics **:** the theology or mode of thought of the church fathers

**patristic latin** *n, usu cap P&L* **:** Latin as written by the Western church fathers

**patristic philosophy** *n* **:** the philosophy developed by the fathers of the Christian church divided with reference to the Nicene Council in A.D. 325 into the ante-Nicene period during which it took the form of defenses of the Christian faith and the post-Nicene period up to St. Augustine with whom it culminates

**pa·tris·tics** \-ristiks\ *n pl but sing in constr* **:** PATROLOGY

**pa·trix** \ˈpā·triks\ *n, pl* **pa·tri·ces** \-rəˌsēz\ [NL, fr. L *patr-*, *pater* father + E *-ix* (as in *matrix*) — more at FATHER] **:** a pattern or die used in typefounding to form a matrix **:** PUNCH 1a(7)

**patrizate** *vi* -ED/-ING/-s [L *patrizatus*, *patrissatus*, past part. of *patrizare*, *patrissare*, fr. *patr-* + *-issare*, *-izare* -ize] *obs* **:** to imitate one's father or forebears

**patro-** — see PATR-

**pa·troc·i·nate** \pəˈträsəˌnāt\ *vt* -ED/-ING/-s [L *patrocinatus*, past part. of *patrocinari*, fr. *patrocinium* protection, defense, fr. *patronus* protector, defender — more at PATRON] *archaic* **:** DEFEND, PATRONIZE, SUPPORT — **pa·troc·i·na·tion** \ˌ=ˌ=ˈ=nāshən\ *n* -s

**pat·ro·cli·nal** \ˌpa·trəˈklīnᵊl\ *or* **pat·ro·clin·ic** \-linik\ *also* **pat·ri·cli·nal** \-līnᵊl\ *or* **pat·ri·clin·ic** \-linik\ *adj* [*patr-* + *-clinal*, *-clinic*] **:** PATROCLINOUS

**pat·ro·cli·nous** *also* **pat·ri·cli·nous** \-līnəs\ *adj* [*patr-* + *-clinous*] **:** derived or inherited from the father or paternal line — compare MATROCLINOUS — **pat·ro·cli·ny** *also* **pat·ri·cli·ny** \ˈ==ˌklīnē\ *n* -ES

**pat·ro·genesis** \ˌpa·trə +\ *n* [NL, fr. *patr-* + L *genesis*] **:** ANDROGENESIS

¹**pa·trol** \pəˈtrōl, *dial* ˈpad·əˌrōl\ *n* -s [F *patrouille*, fr. *patrouiller*] **1 a :** the action of going the rounds along a chain of sentinels or outguards to ensure greater security from attack or to check disorder **b :** the guard or men who go the rounds **c :** a detachment of two or more men employed for reconnaissance, security, or combat **d :** a unit (as of police cars, ships, or airplanes) assigned to any of various patrol duties **2 a :** the perambulation of a district or beat to watch or guard it **b :** the men assigned to this duty ⟨coast ~⟩ ⟨fire ~⟩ **3 a :** a watchful guardianship ⟨lawyers do have peculiar responsibilities for maintaining a vigilant ~ of the domestic scene against infractions of these fundamental constitutional rights —W.O.Douglas⟩ **b :** a routine of regular observation ⟨has discovered three supernovae in extragalactic nebulae in his . . . camera ~ —*American Yr. Bk.*⟩ **4 a :** a subdivision of a boy scout troop made up of two or more boys **b :** a subdivision of a girl scout troop usu. composed of from six to eight girls

²**patrol** \"\ *vb* **patrolled; patrolled; patrolling; patrols** [F *patrouiller*, fr. MF *patouiller*, *patrouiller* to paw or tramp around in the mud, fr. *patte*, *pate* paw, hoof + *-ouiller*, v. suffix — more at PATTEN] *vi* **1 :** to cover the beat of a military, police, or other guard on foot or in a vehicle **2 :** to carry out any of various military, naval, or air patrol missions ⟨carrier-based aircraft *patrolled* above —*Newsweek*⟩ ~ *vt* **:** to carry out a patrol of **:** make routine observations of for purposes of defense or protection ⟨put into service *patrolling* the north Atlantic coast —H.A.Chippendale⟩

**patrol judge** *n* **:** a horse racing official responsible for detecting fouls committed by the jockeys

**pa·trol·ler** \-lə(r)\ *n* -s **:** one that patrols **:** a member of a patrol

**pa·trol·man** \-lmən\ *n, pl* **patrolmen 1 a :** a policeman on patrol duty **b :** a rank-and-file policeman **:** one without supervisory rank or authority **2 :** an inspector of electric power lines **3 :** a fire guard patrolling a section (as of a forest)

**pat·ro·log·ic** \ˌpa·trəˈläjik\ *or* **pat·ro·log·i·cal** \-jəkəl\ *adj* **:** of or relating to patrology

**pa·trol·o·gist** \pəˈträləjəst\ *n* -s **:** a specialist in patrology

**pa·trol·o·gy** \-jē\ *n* -ES [NL *patrologia*, fr. *patr-* + *-logia* -logy] **1 :** a branch of historical theology treating of the teachings of the fathers of the Christian church — called also *patristics* **2 :** a collection of the writings of the church fathers

**patrol wagon** *n* **:** an enclosed police wagon or motor truck used to carry prisoners — called also *Black Maria*, *paddy wagon*

patrol wagon

**patrolwoman** \ˈ=ˌ=ˌ=\ *n, pl* **patrolwomen :** a woman member of a police force without officer's rank

¹**pa·tron** \ˈpā·trən\ *n* -s [ME *patroun*, fr. MF *patrun*, *patron*, fr. ML & L; ML *patronus* patron of a benefice, patron saint, master, pattern, fr. L, defender, protector, advocate, fr. *patr-*, *pater* father — more at FATHER] **1 a :** a person chosen, named, or honored as a special guardian, protector, or supporter **b :** PATRON SAINT **c :** a wealthy or influential supporter of an artist or writer ⟨a ~ of scholars, a grand seigneur —R.W.Southern⟩ **d :** a social or financial sponsor of an entertainment or other function (as for charity) ⟨included among the ~*s* of the Junior League dance⟩ **2 a :** one who gives of his means or uses his influence to help or benefit an individual, an institution, or a cause **:** BENEFACTOR ⟨philanthropist and ~ of arts —*N.Y.Times*⟩ ⟨widely known as an explorer and a ~ of exploration —W.J.Ghent⟩ **b** *obs* **:** the declared champion of a theory, teaching, or position ⟨a ~ of anarchy —John Locke⟩ **3 :** a steady or regular client: as **a :** an habitual customer of a merchant **b :** a regular client of a physician **c :** a parent or guardian of a child in a private school **d :** one who uses the services of a library and esp. of a public library **4 :** the master or steersman of a galley or of a river boat or coasting ship **5** *obs* **:** an owner of slaves or captives **6** *archaic* **:** a case for pistol cartridges **7 :** the conductor or master of an atelier for the study of architectural design **8 :** the holder of the right of presentation to an English ecclesiastical benefice **:** the owner of the advowson **9 :** a Roman patrician under whose protection a client places himself **10** *Roman law* **:** a master who frees his slave but retains some rights over him — compare OBSEQUIUM **11** \paˈtrōⁿ\ **:** the proprietor of an establishment (as an inn) — compare PATRONNE **12 :** the chief male officer in some fraternal lodges having both men and women members — compare MATRON

²**patron** \"\ *vt* -ED/-ING/-s [prob. fr. F *patronner*, fr. MF, fr. *patron*] *archaic* **:** to serve as patron of **:** PATRONIZE

¹**patron·age** \ˈpa·trənij, ˈpā-\ *n* -s [ME, fr. MF, fr. *patron* + *-age*] **1 :** the right of presentation to an ecclesiastical benefice orig. carrying with it the obligation to protect the rights of the church within the parish **:** ADVOWSON **2 a :** the support or influence of a patron; *esp* **:** a benefactor's provision (as for an artist or institution) ⟨the ~ of science by and through universities is its most proper form —J.R.Oppenheimer⟩ **b** *archaic* **:** DEFENSE, PROTECTION **c** *obs* **:** ADVOCACY **3 :** the tutelary care or guardianship of a deity or saint **4 :** kindness done with an air of superiority **:** condescending favor ⟨accept ~? . . . Never —Marguerite Steen⟩ **5 :** the trade of customers ⟨though it was not yet noon, there was a considerable ~ —C.B.Kelland⟩ **6 :** the right to appoint to government jobs **:** control of political appointments ⟨oust his enemies from office and use the ~ to support his policies —H.K.Beale⟩

²**patronage** *vt* -ED/-ING/-s **:** to act as patron of **:** MAINTAIN, DEFEND

**pa·tron·al** \ˈpā·trənᵊl, ˈpa-, pəˈtrōnᵊl\ *adj* [F or LL; F, fr. LL *patronalis*, fr. L *patronus* patron + *-alis* -al — more at PATRON] **:** of or relating to a patron or patron saint

**pa·tron·ate** \ˈpā·trənət, ˈpa-, -əˌnāt\ *n* -s [LL *patronatus*, fr. *patronus* patron + *-atus* -ate — more at PATRON] **:** the right, duty, position, jurisdiction, or possession of a patron **:** PATRONAGE

**pa·tron·ess** \ˈpā·trənəs\ *n* -ES [ME *patronesse*, fr. *patron*, *patroun* patron + *-esse* -ess — more at PATRON] **:** a female patron: as **a :** a female patron saint **b :** a woman sponsor of a social or charitable affair **c :** a woman who provides for or promotes the interests of a protégé

**pat·ro·nite** \ˈpa·trəˌnīt\ *n* -s [Antenor Rizo-*Patrona*, 20th cent. Peruvian mineralogist + E *-ite*] **:** a black mixture of vanadium minerals found at Minasragra, Peru, and there mined as an ore of vanadium

**pa·tron·iza·tion** \ˌpā·trənəˈzāshən *also* ˌpa-\ *n* -s **:** the act of patronizing

**pa·tron·ize** \ˈpā·trəˌnīz *also* ˈpa-\ *vt* -ED/-ING/-s *see -ize in Explan Notes* [MF or ML; MF *patroniser*, fr. ML *patronizare*, fr. L & ML *patronus* patron + L *-izare* -ize — more at PATRON] **1 :** to act as patron of **:** FAVOR, PROTECT, SUPPORT ⟨he did feel real gratitude to the woman who had *patronized* his early ambition —Hilaire Belloc⟩ **2** *obs* **:** DEFEND **3** *obs* **:** to lay responsibility for **:** FATHER — used with *upon* **4 :** to adopt an air of superiority and condescension toward **:** treat haughtily or superciliously ⟨breaks through established formulas to please the judicious without *patronizing* the larger public —*Saturday Rev.*⟩ **5 :** to trade or deal with habitually **:** be a customer or client of **:** USE, FREQUENT ⟨a restaurant . . . *patronized* by democratic folk —P.B.Kyne⟩ ⟨ranchmen ~ stores strung out over a large space —*Amer. Guide Series: Texas*⟩ ⟨we both *patronized* the city library —W.A.White⟩ ⟨introductory astronomy is often a popular undergraduate course, although not as heavily *patronized* as other sciences —F.D.Miller⟩

**pa·tron·iz·er** \-zə(r)\ *n* -s *archaic* **:** one that patronizes

**pa·tron·iz·ing** \-ziŋ, -zēŋ\ *adj* **:** CONDESCENDING ⟨her tone was . . . insufferably ~ —P.I.Wellman⟩ — **pa·tron·iz·ing·ly** *adv*

**pa·tron·less** \ˈpā·trənləs\ *adj, archaic* **:** having no patron

**pa·tronne** \paˈtrȯn, -ˈtrən\ *n* -s [F, fr. MF, fem. of *patron* — more at PATRON] **1 :** a female patron saint **2 :** the proprietress of an establishment (as an inn)

**patrons** *pl of* PATRON, *pres 3d sing of* PATRON

**patron saint** *n* **1 :** a saint to whose protection and intercession a person, a society, a church, or a place is dedicated — compare TITULAR **2 :** an original leader or prime exemplar ⟨a $100-a-plate . . . dinner honoring the party's *patron saints* —*Springfield (Mass.) Union*⟩

¹**pat·ro·nym·ic** \ˌpa·trəˈnimik, -mēk\ *n* -s [LL *patronymicum*, fr. neut. of *patronymicus* of a patronymic, fr. Gk *patronymikos*, fr. *patronymia* patronymic (fr. *patr-* + *-onyma* name + *-ia* -y) + *-ikos* -ic] **1 :** a name derived from that of the father or a paternal ancestor usu. by the addition of a prefix or suffix (as in *MacDonald*, son of Donald, or *Ivanovich*, son of Ivan) — contrasted with *matronymic;* compare TEKNONYMY **2 :** a patrilineal surname or family name

²**patronymic** \ˌ=ˈ=\ *also* **pat·ro·nym·i·cal** \-məkəl\ *adj*

[*patronymic* fr. LL *patronymicus; patronymical* fr. LL *patronymicus* + E *-al*] : of, relating to, or constituting a patronymic — **pat·ro·nym·i·cal·ly** \-mək(ə)lē\ *adv*

**pa·troon** \pə'trün\ *n* -s [in sense 1, fr. F *patron* & Sp *patrón*, lit., master, fr. ML *patronus;* in sense 2, fr. D, fr. F *patron* patron, master — more at PATRON] **1** *archaic* : the captain or officer commanding a ship **2** : the proprietor of one of the tracts of land with manorial privileges granted to members of the Dutch West India Company under the old Dutch governments of New York and New Jersey

**pa·troon·ship** \-n,ship\ *n* : the rank or estate of a patroon

**pats** *pl of* PAT, *pres 3d sing of* PAT

**¹pat·sy** \'patsē, -si\ *n* -ES [perh. fr. It *pazzo* fool, lunatic] **1** : a butt of ridicule : ODDBALL ⟨knew this ~ was a disastrous mistake socially —Elizabeth Janeway⟩ **2 a** : a person on whom blame is foisted : FALL GUY ⟨not going to be the ~ for that gang of his —S.H.Adams⟩ **b** : one readily deceived or victimized : EASY MARK, SUCKER ⟨a perfect ~ for his enthusiasms —George Sklar⟩

**²patsy** \"\ *n, pl* **patsys** *usu cap* [fr. *Patsy*, nickname for *Patricia*] : any of several awards that are given annually by humane organizations to animals that perform in motion pictures

**patt** *abbr* pattern

**pat·ta·mar** *or* **pat·a·mar** \'pad·ə,mär\ *n* -s [Pg *patamar*, fr. Malayalam *pattamāri*] **1** *obs* : COURIER, MESSENGER **2** : a ship used in the coasting trade of Bombay and Ceylon having lateen sails, a keel hollowing upward in the middle, and long overhangs

**patted** *past of* PAT

**pat·tée** *also* **pa·té** *or* **pa·tée** \pə'tā\ *adj* [MF *paté, patté* (masc.) & *patee, pattee* (fem.), fr. *pate, patte* paw + *-é, -ee* -ate] *of a cross* : FORMÉE

**pat·ten** \'pat³n\ *n* -s [ME *paten, patin, pateyn*, fr. MF *patin*, fr. *pate, patte* paw, hoof, fr. (assumed) VL *patta*, of imit. origin] **1** : a clog, sandal, or overshoe often with a wooden sole or metal device to elevate the foot and increase the wearer's height or aid in walking in mud — compare CHOPINE, GETA, PLATFORM, SABOT **2** *Brit* : a round wooden plate fastened to the hind feet of horses to prevent their sinking into soft or boggy land that is being plowed or cultivated **3** : an ice skate of an early variety **4** *archaic* : an architectural base, stand, support, foot, bottom plate, or sill

**pat·ten·er** \'patənə(r)\ *n* -s *dial Eng* : SKATER

**¹pat·ter** \'pad·ə(r), -atə-\ *vb* -ED/-ING/-S [ME *patren, patern*, fr. *paternoster*] *vt* **1** : to say or repeat in a rapid or mechanical manner : MUTTER ⟨~ the jargon of two different tribes —F.L.Lucas⟩ **2** : to speak glibly ⟨they're college-reared and can ~ languages —John Buchan⟩ ~ *vi* **1** : to recite paternosters or other prayers rapidly, mechanically, or perfunctorily ⟨I'd be ~*ing* away with my tongue, in church, like all the rest —Lord Dunsany⟩ **2** : to talk glibly and volubly usu. without close attention to sense : chatter gibberish, jargon, or cant ⟨~*ed*, all smiles, through a soft-voiced colorless recital of events —Lester Atwell⟩ **3** : to speak or sing the rapid-fire words of a theatrical patter speech or song **4** : to issue (as words) in staccato fashion ⟨a poem lightly ~*ing* into his ear —Amy Lowell⟩ ⟨jokes . . . ~*ed* regularly from variety comedians —Anthony Glyn⟩

**²patter** \"\ *n* -s **1** : a cant or specialized lingo ⟨the sociologist's sometimes useful ~ —Dwight MacDonald⟩ ⟨the ~ of science —Ellen Glasgow⟩ ⟨ad-libbing a sales ~ —*Fortune*⟩ ⟨the silly pseudosophisticated ~ of the most unpleasant smart people —J.C.Powys⟩: as **a** : the jargon of thieves or other criminals **b** : the spiel of a street hawker or of a circus barker **2** : empty chattering talk : GABBLE ⟨the incessant ~ of the argument —F.R.Leavis⟩ ⟨nothing's too petty for her to make controversial ~ of —Rex Ingamells⟩ ⟨table talk couched in cliché and ~ —H.R.Warfel⟩ **3 a** : the rapid-fire talk of a comedian or the talk with which any of various performers accompanies his routine **b** : the words of a comic or musical comedy song or of a rapidly spoken usu. humorous monologue introduced into such a song **c** : metrical lines often of nonsense interpolated by a western square dance caller to fill in between commands to the dancers

**³patter** \"\ *vb* -ED/-ING/-S [freq. of ²*pat*] *vi* **1** : to strike, pat, or tap rapidly usu. so as to make quick light sounds ⟨on the shingled roof the rain was ~*ing* like a multitude of tiny feet —Ellen Glasgow⟩ **2** : to run with short quick light-sounding steps ⟨~*ed* softly down the stairs —Marcia Davenport⟩ ~ *vt* : to cause to patter

**⁴patter** \"\ *n* -s : a quick succession of slight sounds or pats ⟨the ~ of rain⟩ ⟨the ~ of little feet⟩

**patteran** *var of* PATRIN

**pat·ter·er** \'pad·ərə(r)\ *n* -s [¹*patter* + *-er*] : one that patters; *esp* : one that talks patter

**¹pat·tern** *R* 'pad·ərn, -atə-, -*R* -d·ən, -tən, -t³n; *R* & -*R chiefly substand* -d·ərən *or* -tərən\ *n* -s [ME *patron*, fr. MF, fr. ML *patronus* — more at PATRON] **1** : a fully realized form, original, or model accepted or proposed for imitation : something regarded as a normative example to be copied : ARCHETYPE, EXEMPLAR ⟨has been acting like a practically model ~ for a constructive opposition —*New Yorker*⟩ **2** : something designed or used as a model for making things : OUTLINE, PLAN ⟨a dressmaker's ~⟩ **3 a** *obs* : a foundry matrix **b** : a model usu. made of varnished or painted wood or of metal for making a mold into which molten metal is poured to form a casting **4 a** : a representative instance : a typical example **b** : a specimen offered as a sample of the whole **5** : an artistic or mechanical design or form: as **a** : the shape or style of a manufactured article ⟨bought a silver service of open stock ~⟩ **b** : a design or figure used in decoration ⟨the simple dignity of ~ of a New England colonial doorframe⟩ ⟨the geometrical ~ of a rug⟩ **c** : form or style in literary or musical composition : coherent structure or design ⟨the whole book forms a rich and subtle but highly organized ~ —F.R.Leavis⟩ **d** : the composition or plan of a work of graphic or plastic art **e** : architectural design or style **f** : the tracing made by skate blades by a figure or dance step executed on ice **6** : a natural or chance configuration (as of markings or of events) ⟨frost ~*s*⟩ **7 a** : a patron saint's day in Ireland **b** : the festivity connected with such a day **c** : a dance on any holiday **8** : a specimen of a proposed coin or coin design; *esp* : one that has not been authorized for regular issue **9** : a length of fabric sufficient for an article (as a dress) **10 a** : the distribution of the shot from a shotgun or the bullets from an exploded shrapnel on a target perpendicular to the plane of fire **b** : a diagram showing such distribution **c** : the grouping made on a target by rifle or handgun bullets and regarded as a test of marksmanship or of the qualities of the gun **11** : a reliable sample of traits, acts, or other observable features characterizing an individual ⟨behavior ~⟩ ⟨personality ~⟩ — compare PROFILE **12** : the approaches, turns, and altitudes prescribed for an airplane that is coming in for a landing **13** : an established mode of behavior or cluster of mental attitudes, beliefs, and values held in common by the members of a group **14** : the largest unit of classification in the midwestern system for American archaeology constituting a group of phases having several distinguishing and fundamental features in common — compare ASPECT, COMPONENT, FOCUS **15** : the manner in which smaller units of language are grouped or groupable into larger units (as sounds into sound classes or into words) ⟨the ~ voiceless stop/voiced stop/nasal seen in the bilabials \p\, \b\, \m\ is paralleled in the alveolars \t\, \d\, \n\ and in the velars \k\, \g\, \ŋ\⟩ **16** : a standard diagram transmitted for testing television circuits **syn** see MODEL

**²pattern** \"\ *vb* -ED/-ING/-S *vt* **1** *obs* : to serve as a pattern for : FORESHADOW **2** : to make, fashion, or design according to a pattern ⟨the . . . chantey was ~*ed* on a salt-water model —*Amer. Guide Series: Mich.*⟩ **3** *chiefly dial Eng* **a** : MATCH, PARALLEL **b** : to use as a pattern or model : IMITATE **4** : to furnish, adorn, or mark with a pattern or design ⟨scarlet, violet, and purple togas ~ the mass of black and brown —Amy Lowell⟩ ~ *vi* **1** : to form patterns ⟨the dancer is always ~*ing* in space, as well as in time —Ruth A. Radir⟩ **2** *of a firearm* : to make a pattern on a target with shot or bullets **3** : to constitute or fit into a language pattern

**pattern bargaining** *n* : bargaining by a labor union for a number of work contracts based on the example of one that it considers desirable

**pattern bombing** *n* : AREA BOMBING

**pattern card** *n* : any of the perforated cards used in jacquard weaving

**pattern chain** *n* : any of various devices on looms or knitting machines that resemble chains and control the working of the figures or designs in the material by bringing into action or taking out of action various shuttles and harnesses in weaving or various needles and stitches in knitting

**pat·terned** \-nd\ *adj* : arranged in or formed into patterns

**pat·tern·ing** \-niŋ, -nēŋ\ *n* -s **1** : decoration, composition, or configuration according to a pattern ⟨the sober ~ of his cravat —Osbert Sitwell⟩ **2 a** : personal conduct illustrating a sociocultural pattern **b** : the characteristic form of a sociocultural custom or institution

**pat·tern·ize** \-,nīz\ *vt* -ED/-ING/-S : to make conform to, reduce to, or arrange in a pattern

**pat·tern·less** \-nləs\ *adj* **1** *obs* : MATCHLESS, PEERLESS **2** : wanting pattern

**patternmaker** \'==,==\ *n* : one that makes patterns (as for founding, woodworking, sewing, or weaving)

**patternmaker's saw** *n* : a short thin-bladed handsaw with extra sharp teeth and raised handle used for fine work in cabinetmaking and patternmaking

**patternmaking** \'==,==\ *n*: the process of making wood patterns or models for foundry use

patternmaker's saw

**pattern mold** *n* : a mold having depressions or protuberances forming patterns on the interior surface into which a parison of glass is forced or blown — **pattern-molded** \'==;==\ *adj* — **pattern molder** *n*

**pattern plate** *n* : ¹CASTER 1b

**patterns** *pl of* PATTERN, *pres 3d sing of* PATTERN

**patternwood** \'==,=\ *n* **1** : an African tree (*Alstonia congensis*) having light soft even-textured straight-grained wood **2** : the wood of the patternwood tree used esp. for box making

**pattern-word** \'==,=\ *n, cryptology* : a plaintext idiomorph

**pat·terny** \-nē\ *adj* : conspicuously patterned

**patters** *pres 3d sing of* PATTER, *pl of* PATTER

**patter song** *n* [²*patter*] : a song (as in musical comedy or comic opera) in which patter is used for humorous effect

**patting** *pres part of* PAT

**pat·tin·son process** \'pat³nsən-\ *n, usu cap 1st P* [after Hugh Lee *Pattinson* †1858 Eng. metallurgist] : a process for desilverizing and purifying lead

**patton's spruce** *or* **patton's hemlock** \'pat³nz-\ *n, usu cap P* [fr. the name *Patton*] : MOUNTAIN HEMLOCK

**pat·tu** *also* **pat·too** *or* **put·too** \'pə(,)tü\ *n* -s [Hindi *paṭṭū*, fr. Skt *paṭṭa* cloth — more at PUTTEE] **1** : a homespun woolen fabric resembling tweed that is woven usu. of goat hair in northern India **2** : a blanket or wrap of pattu

**pat·ty** *also* **pat·tie** \'pad·ē, -at|, |i\ *n, pl* **patties** [F *pâté* — more at PÂTÉ] **1** : a little pie or pasty **2 a** : a small flat cake of chopped food (as ground meat) **b** : a small flat candy ⟨peppermint ~⟩ **3** : PATTY SHELL

**patty-cake** \'==,=\ *n* [by alter.] : PAT-A-CAKE

**pattypan** \'==,=\ *n* **1** : a pan for baking patties : MUFFIN PAN **2** *or* **pattypan squash** : CYMLING

**patty shell** *n* : a shell of puff paste made to hold a creamed meat, fish, or vegetable filling

**pa·tu** \'pä(,)tü\ *or* **pa·tu-pa·tu** \-ü'pä(,)tü\ *n* -s [Maori] : a short two-edged Maori weapon of stone, wood, or bone resembling a club and tapering in thickness but expanding in width from the butt and designed to give a crushing rather than cutting blow

**pat·u·lin** \'pachələn\ *n* -s [ISV *patul-* (fr. NL *patulum* — specific epithet of *Penicillium patulum* — fr. L, neut. of *patulus*) + *-in*] : CLAVACIN

**pat·u·lous** \'pachələs\ *adj* [L *patulus*, fr. *patēre* to be open — more at FATHOM] **1** : spread widely apart : wide open : DISTENDED ⟨a wound with ~ margins⟩ **2** : spreading widely from a center : loosely or diffusely expanded or spread out ⟨an old apple with ~ branches⟩ — **pat·u·lous·ly** *adv* — **pat·u·lous·ness** *n* -ES

**pat·u·ron** \'pachə,rän\ *n* -s [F, fr. Gk *patein* to tread, trample on + NL *-uron* (fr. Gk *oura* tail); akin to Gk *patos* path — more at FIND, -UROUS] : the basal segment of the arachnid chelicera

**¹pa·tux·ent** \pə'təksənt\ *n, pl* **patuxent** *or* **patuxents** *usu cap* **1** : an extinct Algonquian Indian people formerly dwelling in Calvert county, Maryland **2** : one of the Patuxent people

**²patuxent** \"\ *adj, usu cap* [¹*Patuxent*] : of or relating to a subdivision of the Comanchean — see GEOLOGIC TIME table

**pat·wa·ri** *or* **put·wa·ri** \(,)pət'wärē\ *n* -s [Hindi *paṭwārī*, fr. Skt *paṭṭa* land grant + Eastern Hindi *-wārī*, agent suffix] : a village registrar or accountant in India

**pat·win** \'pat,win\ *n, pl* **patwin** *or* **patwins** *usu cap* **1 a** : an Indian people of the Sacramento valley, Calif. **b** : a member of such people **2** : a Copehan language of the Patwin people

**paty** \'pad·ē\ *adj* [MF *paté, patté* (masc.) & *patee, pattee* (fem.) — more at PATTEE] *of a heraldic cross* : having the ends of the arms splayed or spread out — compare FLEURY, FORMÉE, MOLINE, PATONCE

**pau** \'paù\ *adj* [Hawaiian] : COMPLETED, CONSUMED, FINISHED

**pa'u** \'pä,ü\ *n* -s [Hawaiian] : an Hawaiian sarong formerly made of tapa and now of cotton or silk and worn by women for dancing, horseback riding in parades, and ceremonies

**paua** \'paùə\ *n* -s [Maori] : an abalone of New Zealand

**pau bra·sil** *also* **pau bra·zil** \,paùbrə'zil\ *n* [Pg *pau Brasil*, lit., Brazil wood] : a variety of brazilwood (*Caesalpinia echinata*)

**pauci-** *comb form* [L, fr. *paucus* little] : few ⟨*pauci*foliate⟩ ⟨*pauci*disperse⟩

**pau·cil·o·quy** \pò'siləkwē\ *n* -ES [L *pauciloquium* fr. *pauci-* + *-loquium* (fr. *loqui* to speak)] *archaic* : brevity in speech

**pau·ci·spiral** \'pòsē+\ *adj* [*pauci-* + *spiral*] : spiral with few turns

**pau·ci·ty** \'pòsəd·ē, -ətē, -i\ *n* -ES [ME *paucite*, fr. MF or L; MF *paucité*, fr. L *paucitat-, paucitas*, fr. *paucus* little + *-itat-, -itas* -ity — more at FEW] **1** : a small number : FEWNESS ⟨the chorus suffered slightly from a ~ of male voices —Douglas Watt⟩ ⟨make up in quality for their ~ of numbers —R.B. Morris⟩ **2** : smallness of quantity : DEARTH, INSUFFICIENCY, SCARCITY ⟨the simplicity that never was ~ —C.D.Lewis⟩ ⟨the ~ of help accorded to me —Rudyard Kipling⟩ ⟨a language now almost unknown because of the extreme ~ of its remains —G.B.Saul⟩

**paughty** \'pòti, 'päk-\ *adj* [origin unknown] *chiefly Scot* : HAUGHTY, HIGHFALUTIN

**pauk·pan** \'pòk,pan\ *n* -s [Burmese] **1** : the bast fiber of the sola **2** : SOLA

**¹paul** *var of* PAWL

**²paul** \'pòl\ *n* -s [It *paolo*] : PAOLO

**paul-bun·nell antibody** \'pòl'bən³l-\ *n, usu cap P&B* [after John R. *Paul* b1893 and Walls W. *Bunnell* b1902 Am. physicians] : HETEROPHIL ANTIBODY

**paul-bunnell reaction** *or* **paul-bunnell test** *n, usu cap P&B* [after John R. *Paul* & W. W. *Bunnell*, 20th cent. Am. physicians] : a test for heterophil antibody used in the diagnosis of infectious mononucleosis

**paul bun·yan** \'pòl'bənyən\ *n, usu cap P&B* [after *Paul Bunyan*, legendary American lumberjack who was capable of amazing feats of lumbering] : a person often of great size who performs unusual often prodigious feats of strength or endurance ⟨a milder *Paul Bunyan* of the coal mines, steel mills, and construction jobs —*N. Y. Herald Tribune Bk. Rev.*⟩

**paul·dron** \'pòldrən\ *or* **poul·dron** \'pōl-\ *n* -s [ME *polrond*, modif. of MF *espauleron*, fr. *espaule* shoulder, fr. OF — more at EPAULET] : a piece of armor covering the shoulder where the body piece and arm piece join — compare EPAULET 1b

**paul·i·an·ist** \'pòlēənəst\ *n* -s *usu cap* [obs. E *paulian* Paulianist (fr. *Paul* of Samosata *fl.* A.D.260 bishop of Antioch + E *-ian*) + E *-ist*] : a follower of the dynamic Monarchian Paul of Samosata who denied a distinction of persons in God and maintained that Christ was a mere man raised above other men by the indwelling Logos

**pau·li·cian** \pò'lishən\ *n* -s *usu cap* [ML *Pauliciani* pl., fr. MGk *Paulikianoi*] : a member of a dualistic Christian sect originating in Armenia in the 7th century, influencing the rise of the Bogomils, becoming nearly extinct in the 12th century, and characterized by the belief that matter is evil and that the creator of the material universe is an evil demiurge to be distinguished from the heavenly God who created and rules souls, by denial of the Incarnation, and by rejection of the Old Testament, the cross, and all images — see THONDRAKI

**pau·li exclusion principle** \'pòlē-\ *also* **pauli principle** *n, usu cap 1st P* [after Wolfgang *Pauli* b1900 Swiss physicist] : a principle in physics: no two electrons in an atom or molecule can exist simultaneously in states defined by the same set of quantum numbers — called also *exclusion principle*

**pau·lin** \'pòlən\ *n* -s [by shortening] : TARPAULIN ⟨waterproof material for ~*s* and ponchos —Howell Walker⟩

**paul·ine** \'pò,līn, -lēn\ *adj, usu cap* [ML *paulinus*, fr. LL *Paulus* Paul †*ab* A.D. 67 Christian saint who was apostle to the Gentiles and author of several epistles in the New Testament + L *-inus* -ine] : of, relating to, or characteristic of the apostle Paul or his writings : conforming to Paul's teachings

**pauline privilege** *n, usu cap 1st P* [so called fr. its being based on Paul's doctrine in 1 Cor 7:12–17] : the option available to a previously unbaptized person who becomes a Roman Catholic after marriage to another unbaptized person of dissolving the marriage through legal action undertaken with the consent of ecclesiastical authority if the other person refuses to become a Catholic and impedes the convert's practice of religion

**¹pau·lin·i·an** \pò'linēən\ *adj, usu cap* [L *paulinus* of or pertaining to Paul (fr. *Paulus* Paul) + E *-an*] : PAULINE

**²paulinian** \"\ *n* -s *usu cap* : PAULINIST

**paul·in·ism** \'pòlə,nizəm\ *n* -s *usu cap* [*pauline* + *-ism*] : the theological principles taught by or ascribed to the apostle Paul; *esp* : Paul's teaching of emancipation from the Jewish law, the indwelling spirit of Christ, and justification by faith

**paul·in·ist** \-,nəst\ *n* -s *usu cap* [*pauline* + *-ist*] : a follower of the apostle Paul or of his teachings

**paul·in·ize** \-lə,nīz\ *vb* -ED/-ING/-S *often cap* [*pauline* + *-ize*] *vi* : to follow the teachings of the apostle Paul ~ *vt* : to indoctrinate with Paulinism

**paul·ism** \'pò,lizəm\ *n* -s *usu cap* [*Paul* of Tarsus †A.D.67? Christian apostle and saint + E *-ism*] : PAULINISM

**paul·ist** \-ləst\ *n* -s *usu cap* [St. *Paul* + E *-ist*] *Roman Catholicism* : a member of the Congregation of the Missionary Priests of St. Paul the Apostle

**pau·lis·ta** \paù'lēstə\ *n* -s *cap* [Pg *Paulista*, fr. São *Paulo*, state and city in Brazil + Pg *-ista* -ist (fr. L)] **1** : a Brazilian descended from the first Portuguese colonists and from Indian women **2** : a native or inhabitant of the city of São Paulo, Brazil

**paul jones** \'pòl'jōnz\ *n, usu cap P&J* [prob. after John *Paul Jones* †1792 Am. naval officer and hero of the American Revolution] : a method of changing partners during a dance whereby at a signal the dancers form a circle and execute a grand right and left until at another signal each man resumes the original dance taking as his new partner the lady who is opposite him

**paul·lin·ia** \pò'linēə\ *n* [NL, fr. Simon *Paulli* †1680 Dan. botanist + L *-inus* -ine + NL *-ia*] **1** *cap* : a genus of chiefly tropical American woody vines (family Sapindaceae) with compound leaves, irregular flowers, and pyriform capsules — see GUARANA, SUPPLEJACK **2** -s : any vine of the genus *Paullinia*

**pau·lo·post** \'pòlə,pōst\ *adj* [L *paulo post* a little after] : somewhat later; *specif* : relating to changes taking place in an igneous rock just after its consolidation

**pau·lo·spore** \'pòlə,spō(ə)r\ *n* [Gk *paula* rest + E *spore* — more at PAUSE] : a specialized growth or development serving as a resting stage in the life of a fungus

**pau·low·nia** \pò'lōnēə\ *n* [NL, fr. Anna *Paulovna* †1865 Russ. princess and queen of William II of the Netherlands + NL *-ia*] **1** *cap* : a small genus of medium-sized deciduous Chinese trees (family Scrophulariaceae) with large opposite trilobate or entire leaves and terminal panicles of whitish to deep violet-purple flowers **2** -s : any tree of the genus *Paulownia*; *esp* : a tree (*P. tomentosa*) that is widely cultivated in mild regions for its showy panicles of fragrant violet flowers — see KIRI

**paul pry** \'pòl'prī\ *n, pl* **paul prys** *usu cap both Ps* [after *Paul Pry* meddlesome hero of the comedy *Paul Pry* (1853) by John Poole †1872 Eng. playwright] : an excessively inquisitive person ⟨we don't want any *Paul Prys* in this country at present —John Buchan⟩

**pauls** *pl of* PAUL

**paultry** *var of* PALTRY

**paul ve·ro·ne·se green** \'pòl,varə'nāsā-\ *n, often cap P&V* [after *Paul Veronese* †1588 Ital. painter] : EMERALD 2a

**paum** \'pàm\ *dial Brit var of* PALM

**pa'u·mo·tu·an** \,päü'mōtüən\ *n* -s *usu cap* [*Paumotu* (Tuamotu), archipelago in the south Pacific ocean + E *-an*] : TUAMOTUAN

**¹paunch** \'pònch, 'pänch, 'pánch\ *n* -ES [ME *paunche*, fr. MF *pance, panche*, fr. L *pantic-, pantex;* perh. akin to OSlav *pǫčiti* (*sę*) to inflate] **1 a** : the belly and its contents **b** : POTBELLY ⟨a comfortable ~ swelled out beneath the buttons of his dinner jacket —Hamilton Basso⟩ **2 a** : RUMEN **b** *chiefly dial* : TRIPE — usu. used in pl. **3 a** : PAUNCH MAT **b** : a thin shield of wood on a mast that permits the lower yards to slide easily over the hoops

**²paunch** \"\ *vt* -ED/-ING/-ES **1** : to wound in the stomach ⟨with a log batter his skull or ~ him with a stake —Shak.⟩ **2** *obs* : to stuff the stomach of with food and drink **3** : to open the paunch of : EVISCERATE ⟨rabbits must not be ~*ed* out of doors in hot weather —F.D.Smith & Barbara Wilcox⟩

**paunch·i·ness** \-chēnəs\ *n* -ES : the quality or state of being paunchy ⟨in cattle it depends upon the condition, ~, type, and quality —F.B.Hadley⟩

**paunch mat** *n* : a thick mat of strands of rope that prevents the yard or rigging from chafing

**paunchy** \-chē, -chi\ *adj* -ER/-EST [*paunch* + *-y*] : having a paunch : POTBELLIED

**paup** \'pòp\ *vi* -ED/-ING/-S [prob. of Scand origin; akin to ON *paufa* to walk slowly, walk stealthily; akin to OE *potian* to push, butt, goad — more at PUT] *dial Eng* : to walk about aimlessly

**¹pau·per** \'pòpə(r)\ *n* -s *often attrib* [L, poor — more at POOR] **1** : a person destitute of means except such as are derived from charity; *specif* : one who receives aid from public poor funds ⟨buried in a ~'s grave⟩ ⟨found his name on the town ~ list⟩ ⟨~ support⟩ **2** : a very poor person **3** : one allowed to sue in forma pauperis ⟨~ costs⟩

**²pauper** \"\ *vt* -ED/-ING/-S : PAUPERIZE

**pau·per·age** \-pərij\ *n* -s [¹*pauper* + *-age*] : the condition of being a pauper

**pau·per·ism** \-pə,rizəm\ *n* -s : the quality or state of being a pauper

**pau·per·it·ic** \',pòpə'rid·ik\ *adj* [*pauper* + *-itic*] : appearing to be checked in growth by poor environment : STUNTED

**pau·per·iza·tion** \,pòpərə'zāshən\ *n* -s [*pauperize* + *-ation*] : the act or process of being pauperized : the state of pauperism ⟨the social restrictions and economic ~ . . . reached a point requiring urgent means of correction —*Collier's Yr. Bk.*⟩

**pau·per·ize** \'pòpə,rīz\ *vt* -ED/-ING/-S [¹*pauper* + *-ize*] : to make a pauper of : reduce to abject poverty : imbue with the spirit of a pauper : BEGGAR, IMPOVERISH ⟨those ragged days when he was only a shaver and his old man was a *pauperized* greenhorn —J.T.Farrell⟩

**pau·ra·que** \paù'räkā\ *n* -s [MexSp] : CUIEJO

**pau·ro·me·tab·o·la** \,pòrōmə'tabələ\ *n pl, cap* [NL, fr. Gk *pauros* small, slight + NL *metabola*, fr. neut. pl. of Gk *metabolos* changeable — more at FEW, METABOLA] *in some classifications* : a group comprising all insects that are paurometabolous

**pau·ro·me·tab·o·lism** \-bə,lizəm\ *also* **pau·ro·me·tab·o·ly** \-bəlē\ *n* [Gk *pauros* + *metabolism* or *metaboly*] : heterometabolism in which the nymph is fundamentally similar to the adult; *broadly* : HETEROMETABOLISM — compare HEMIMETABOLISM — **pau·ro·me·tab·o·lous** \¦==¦tabələs\ *adj*

¹**pau·ro·pod** \'pȯrə,päd\ *or* **pau·rop·o·dous** \pȯ'räpədəs\ *adj* [*pauropod* fr. NL *Pauropoda*; *pauropodous* fr. NL *Pauropoda* + E *-ous*] : of or relating to the Pauropoda

²**pauropod** \"\ *n* -s [NL *Pauropoda*] : any arthropod of the class Pauropoda

**pau·rop·o·da** \pȯ'räpədə\ *n pl, cap* [NL, fr. Gk *pauros* small, slight + NL *-poda*] : an obscure class of minute progoneate arthropods with branched antennae, 8 to 10 pairs of legs, and no trachea

**pau·ro·pod·i·dae** \,pȯrə'pädə,dē\ *n pl, cap* [NL, fr. *Pauropoda* + *-idae*] : the largest family of the Pauropoda

**pau·ro·pus** \'pȯrəpəs\ *n, cap* [NL, fr. Gk *pauros* + NL *-pus*] : a genus of arthropods that is the type of the family Pauropodidae

**pau ro·xo** \¦paủ'rō(,)shō\ *n, pl* **pau roxos** [Pg, lit., purple wood] **1** : a purpleheart (esp. *Peltogyne densiflora*) yielding valuable timber **2** : the wood of pau roxo

**pa'us** *pl of* PA'U

**paus·al** \'pȯzəl\ *adj* **1** : of, relating to, or occurring at a pause (as at the end of a clause or sentence) **2** : of, relating to, or constituting the form taken by a word or vowel before a pause (as in Hebrew)

**pau san·to** \¦paủ'san(,)tō\ *n* [Pg, lit., holy wood] : a Brazilian tree (*Kielmeyera coriacea*) of the family Guttiferae having bark that is similar to cork and used for insulation

**pau·sa·tion** \pȯ'zāshən\ *n* -s [LL *pausation-, pausatio*, fr. *pausatus* (past. part. of *pausare* to halt, pause, fr. L *pausa* pause) + *-ion-, -io* -ion] : the act of pausing : PAUSE

¹**pause** \'pȯz\ *n* -s [ME *pause*, fr. L *pausa*, fr. Gk *pausis*, fr. *pauein* to stop + *-sis*; akin to Gk *paula* rest and perh. to OSlav *pustŭ* waste, desert] **1** : a temporary stop : intermission of movement or speech : brief cessation : RESPITE ⟨there is often value in a ~ followed by a fresh start —Leslie Rees⟩ ⟨came to a ~, frowning in concentration —T.S.Stribling⟩ **2 a** : a break in a verse **b** : a brief suspension of the voice to indicate the limits and relations of sentences and their parts ⟨have opened up a new dimension of grammar by listening to its intonations, stresses, and ~s —Richard Braddock⟩ **3** : temporary inaction often caused by doubt or uncertainty ⟨had my moments of anxious ~ —W.A.White⟩ **4 a** : ¹REST 5 **b** : FERMATA 2 **c** : a break or paragraph in writing **d** : a pausal stop or intermission in speaking (as in Hebrew) **e** : the form taken by a word or vowel when occurring before a pausal stop (as in Hebrew) **5** : a reason for pausing ⟨a thought that should give tremendous ~ —Alistair Cooke⟩

²**pause** \"\ *vb* -ED/-ING/-S [prob. fr. LL *pausare* to stop, rest, fr. L *pausa* pause] *vi* **1 a** : to cease for a time : refrain from acting or speaking for a brief interval : stop temporarily ⟨people seemed to ~, listening for a message —Sylvia Berkman⟩ **b** : to become silent : wait silently ⟨I ~ for a reply —Shak.⟩ **2** : to hold for a time : LINGER — used with *on* or *upon* ⟨the singer *paused* on the high note⟩ ⟨*paused* upon the threshold to survey the room⟩ **3** : to stop to consider before proceeding : HESITATE ⟨one ought also to ~ and ponder seriously —Lionel Whitby⟩ ⟨*paused* thoughtfully for perhaps two seconds before she consented —G.B.Shaw⟩ **4** : to delay before going on : REMAIN, STAY, TARRY ⟨here hikers ~ to rest —*Amer. Guide Series: Conn.*⟩ ⟨the expedition had to ~ while barges were built —R.A.Billington⟩ ~ *vt* : to cause to cease or rest ⟨bad times before . . . had but *paused* him in his climb —Adrian Bell⟩

³**pause** \"\ *vt* -ED/-ING/-S [origin unknown] *dial Eng* : KICK

**pause·less** \-zləs\ *adj* : having no pauses : CEASELESS, CONTINUOUS ⟨swung up and veered and kept a ~ speed —William Alfred⟩

**pause·less·ly** *adv* : without pause : CEASELESSLY

**paus·er** \-zə(r)\ *n* -s : one that pauses or holds back

**pau·ser·na** \paủ'sernə\ *n, pl* **pauserna** *or* **pausernas** *usu cap* [Pg *Pau Cerne*, fr. *pau cerne* heartwood; fr. the Pauserna living on the upper Guaporé river where heartwood is abundant] **1** : a division of the Chiriguano people **2** : a member of the Pauserna people

**paus·ing·ly** *adv* : with hesitation

¹**paus·sid** \'pȯsəd\ *adj* [NL *Paussidae*] : of or relating to the Paussidae

²**paussid** \"\ *n* -s [NL *Paussidae*] : any beetle of the family Paussidae

**paus·si·dae** \-sə,dē\ *n pl, cap* [NL, fr. *Paussus*, type genus + *-idae*] : a family of small beetles closely related to the Carabidae that live exclusively in ants' nests and have very thick antennae with the joints fused to form a large club

**paut** \'pȯt\ *vi* -ED/-ING/-S [origin unknown] **1** *chiefly Scot* **a** : to paw the ground : STAMP **b** : FINGER, POKE **2** *chiefly Scot* : to walk about slowly

**pav·age** \'pāvij\ *n* -s [AF, fr. OF *paver* to pave + *-age*] **1 a** : a tax levied to pay for the paving of highways **b** : the right to impose such a tax **2** : the act of laying a pavement

**pavais** *var of* PAVIS

**pa·vane** \pə'vän, -van\ *also* **pav·an** *or* **pav·in** \'pavən\ *n* -s [MF *pavane*, fr. OSp *pavana*, fr. OIt, prob. alter. of *padovana*, fem. of *padovano* of Padua, city in northeastern Italy, fr. *Padova* Padua + *-ano* -an (fr. L *-anus*)] **1** : a stately court dance by couples in ceremonial costume introduced from southern Europe into England in the 16th century **2 a** : music for the pavane **b** : music having the duple and slow stately rhythm of the pavane

¹**pave** \'pāv\ *vt* -ED/-ING/-S [ME *paven*, fr. MF *paver*, fr. L *pavire* to strike, stamp; akin to OE *fȳran* to castrate, OHG *arfūrian* to castrate, L *putare* to prune, esteem, consider, think, Gk *paiein* to strike, Lith *pjauti* to cut, reap, slaughter] **1 a** : to lay or cover with stone, brick, asphalt, concrete, or other material making a firm, level, or convenient surface for travel : floor with brick, stone, or other solid material ⟨the street . . . is *paved* with timeworn cobblestones —Dana Burnet⟩ **b** : to overlie or cover like a pavement ⟨tables inlaid with baskets of many-colored fruit; sideboards *paved* with green marble —Virginia Woolf⟩ **2** : to cover firmly and solidly as if with paving material ⟨the path of reform was to be *paved* with parliamentary action —Louis Wasserman⟩ ⟨hell is *paved* with good intentions —Samuel Johnson⟩ **3** : to serve as or provide material for a covering or pavement of ⟨bricks that ~ the cloister⟩ ⟨tons of wire sieves, rolls of sheet lead . . . were used to ~ muddy streets in the rainy season —Julian Dana⟩ — **pave the way** : to prepare a smooth easy way : facilitate the means — usu. used with *to* or *for* ⟨alchemy . . . *paved the way* for the modern science of chemistry —*Encyc. Americana*⟩ ⟨the . . . treaty *paved the way* to still closer forms of joint action —Maurice Duverger⟩ ⟨favorable reception by the press *paved the way* for appearance of other verses —G.F.Whicher⟩

²**pa·vé** \pə'vā, 'pa(,)vā\ *n* -s [F, fr. past part. of *paver* to pave] : a paved public road or street : PAVEMENT ⟨found stretches of ~ where the horses' hooves struck sparks —Alan Sullivan⟩

³**pave** \'pāv\ *n* -s [F *pavé*] : PAVEMENT ⟨a lantern hung, casting a dim radiance . . . upon the step and ~ below —John Bennett⟩

**paved** \-vd\ *adj* [ME, fr. past part. of *paven* to pave] **1** : covered with a pavement ⟨the ~ crest of the central road —Thomas De Quincey⟩ **2** *or* **pa·vé** \pə'vā, 'pa(,)vā\ *also* **pa·véed** \-ād\ [*pavé* fr. ²*pavé*; *pavéed* fr. ²*pavé* + *-ed*] *of jewels* : set as close together as possible to conceal a metal base ⟨a frosty, half-opened rose, realistically contrived of ~ diamonds —*New Yorker*⟩

**pave·ment** \'pāvmənt, *in rapid speech sometimes* -ābm-\ *n* -s [ME, fr. OF, fr. L *pavimentum*, fr. *pavire* to strike, stamp + *-mentum* -ment] **1 a** : a paved surface: as **(1)** : the artificially covered surface of a public thoroughfare ⟨stopped his car just off the ~⟩ **(2)** *chiefly Brit* : SIDEWALK ⟨there were crowds on the ~s and roads everywhere —G.W.Talbot⟩ **(3)** : a decorative interior floor of tiles or colored bricks ⟨the tessellated ~ of the hall —G.B.Shaw⟩ **(4)** : a factory floor paved with wood blocks, bricks, or concrete **b** : the material with which something is paved ⟨concrete makes excellent ~⟩ **2** : something that suggests a pavement (as in flatness, hardness, and extent of surface or in the formation and compact arrangement of its units) ⟨a *pavement*-toothed shark⟩ ⟨~ cells⟩ — see DESERT PAVEMENT

**pave·men·tal** \pāv'mentᵊl\ *adj* : of or relating to a pavement

**pavement ant** *n* : a yellowish ant (*Tetramorium caespitum*) that builds its nests in yards and gardens and often infests houses

**pavement artist** *n* : SIDEWALK ARTIST

**pave·ment·ed** \'pāvməntəd\ *adj* : PAVED ⟨a beautifully ~ staircase⟩

**pavement epithelium** *n* : an epithelium made up of a single layer of flat cells

**pavement light** *n* : a window in a pavement for admitting light into a cellar or storage space beneath

**pav·er** \'pāvə(r)\ *n* -s [ME, fr. *paven* to pave + *-er*] **1** : one that lays or sets paving **2** : a paving stone, brick, or block **3** : a traveling concrete mixer to which unmixed batches are brought and which deposits the mixture directly in place in the pavement **4** : the bed stone of a grinding mill

**pavestone** \'=,=\ *n* [¹*pave* + *stone*] : PAVING STONE

**pa·vet·ta** \pə'vedə\ *n, cap* [NL, fr. Sinhalese *pāwaṭṭā*] : a genus of tropical Old World shrubs (family Rubiaceae) having white corymbose flowers with long-exserted styles and being chiefly of interest for the nitrogen-fixing bacteria found in structures resembling warts on the leaves of various species

**pa·via** \'pāvēə\ *n, cap* [NL, fr. Petrus *Pavius* (Latinized form of Peter Paaw) †1617 Du. botanist + NL *-ia*] *in some classifications* : a genus of trees that is now usu. included in the genus *Aesculus* and comprises buckeyes with smooth capsules and four-petaled flowers

**pav·id** \'pavəd\ *adj* [L *pavidus*, fr. *pavēre* to be frightened, to fear; akin to L *pavire* to strike, stamp — more at PAVE] : showing fear : TIMID ⟨he was infinitely ~ and stingy —Antonio Barolini⟩ — **pav·id·ly** *adv*

**pa·vie** \'pāvi\ *n* -s [prob. alter. of ³*paw*] *Scot* : a quick or deft motion : a neat trick

¹**pa·vil·ion** \pə'vilyən\ *n* -s [ME *pavilon*, fr. OF *paveillon*, fr. L *papilion-, papilio* butterfly; akin to OE *fifalde* butterfly, OHG *fifaltra*, ON *fifrildi* butterfly, Lith *petelìške* flighty, *piepala* quail; fr. its spreading out like a butterfly's wings] **1 a** : a large often sumptuous tent ⟨amongst them rose the white ~s of the Turkish irregular cavalry —A.H.Layard⟩ **b** : something resembling a canopy or tent ⟨tree ferns spread their delicate ~s —Blanche E. Baughan⟩ **2 a** : a part of a building usu. having some distinguishing feature and projecting from the rest ⟨rang the bell of the little ~ and was taken into the tiny hall and then into the small dining room —Gertrude Stein⟩ ⟨the country house . . . accented by two-story terminal ~s at the ends —H.S.Morrison⟩ **b** : one of several detached or semidetached units into which a building (as a hospital) is sometimes divided ⟨became supervisor of the dependents' ~ —*Current Biog.*⟩ **3 a** : a light sometimes ornamental structure in a garden, park, or place of recreation that is used for entertainment or shelter ⟨picnicked in ~s —Green Peyton⟩ ⟨the band ~ . . . is the scene of summer concerts —*Amer. Guide Series: Minn.*⟩ ⟨there was a ~, a dance hall up on the highway —Morley Callaghan⟩ **b** : a temporary structure erected at an exposition by an individual exhibitor ⟨the national ~s . . . are the actual property of the nations which display their wares in them —David Sylvester⟩ **4** : the lower faceted part of a brilliant between the girdle and the culet — compare BEZEL; see BRILLIANT illustration **5 a** : PINNA 2b **b** : INFUNDIBULUM f **6** *chiefly Brit* : a permanent structure erected for the use of players and often spectators on a cricket ground

²**pavilion** \"\ *vt* -ED/-ING/-S [ME *pavilionen*, fr. *pavilion*, n.] : to furnish or cover with : put, enclose, or shelter in or as if in a pavilion ⟨~*ed* in splendor and girded with praise —Robert Grant †1838⟩

**pavilion roof** *n* : a roof hipped equally on all sides

**pa·vil·lon** \¦pävē¦yō\ⁿ *n* -s [F, lit., pavilion, fr. OF *paveillon*] : the bell of a wind instrument

**pavillon chi·nois** \-,shēn'wä\ *n* [F, lit., Chinese pavillon] : a showy jingling device that consists of small bells hung from a crescent-shaped crosspiece on a pole or from a hat-shaped canopy surmounting the pole — called also *Chinese crescent, Chinese pavilion, jingling Johnny, Turkish crescent*

pavillon chinois

**pavin** *var of* PAVANE

**pav·ing** \'pāviŋ\ *n* -s [ME, fr. gerund of *paven* to pave] : PAVEMENT ⟨hear him coming quiet as anything over the ~s —Kay Boyle⟩

**paving brick** *n* : a vitrified clay brick slightly larger than building brick and used in the construction of pavement surfaces

**paving mixer** *n* : PAVER 3

**paving roller** *n* : ROAD ROLLER

**paving stone** *n* [ME] : a dressed stone used for the wearing surface of a stone-block pavement

**paving tile** *n* [ME] : a glazed decorated tile used for floors, sidewalks, courtyards, and sometimes for walls

**pav·ior** *or* **pav·iour** *or* **pav·ier** \'pāvyə(r)\ *n* -s [ME *pavier*, fr. *paven* to pave + *-ier* -er — more at PAVE] **1** : PAVER 1 **2** : an implement for ramming down paving stones **3** : a material or a piece of material (as a brick or slab) used for paving **4** : a hard building brick

**pa·vi·o·tso** \,pävē'ōt(,)sō\ *n* -s *usu cap* : NORTHERN PAIUTE

**pav·is** *or* **pav·ise** *also* **pav·ais** \'pavəs\ *n, pl* **pavises** [ME *pavis*, *pavise*, fr. MF *pavais*, fr. OIt *pavese*, prob. fr. *pavese* of Pavia, city in northeast Italy where pavises were made, fr. *Pavia* + *-ese*] : a large shield covering the whole body used esp. in siege operations to protect crossbowmen and sometimes carried by a pavisor before a knight or archer

**pavisade** *n* -s [F *pavesade*, fr. It *pavesata*, fr. *pavese* pavis + *-ata* -ade (fr. L *-ata*)] : a continuous defensive screen (as of pavises) joined in a line

**pav·i·sor** *or* **pav·i·ser** \'pavəsə(r)\ *n* -s : a page, varlet, or soldier assigned to carry a pavis in front of a knight or archer

**pav·lov·i·an** \pav'lōfēən, -lȯ¦, ¦vē-, '=¦===, pav'lōvē-\ *adj*, *usu cap* [Ivan P. *Pavlov* †1936 Russ. physiologist + E *-ian*] : of or relating to the Russian physiologist Ivan Pavlov or to his work and experiments

**pav·lov pouch** \'pav,lȯ¦f-, -lä¦, ¦v-\ *n*, *usu cap 1st P* [after Ivan P. *Pavlov* †1936] : an isolated portion of the stomach separated by surgical operation from the main part, open to the exterior, and used for study of gastric secretion

**pa·vo** \'pä(,)vō, 'pā(-\ *n, cap* [NL, fr. L, peacock] : a genus of gallinaceous birds (family Phasianidae) consisting of the peacocks

**pa·vo·naz·zo**\,pävə'nät(,)sō\ *or* **pa·vo·naz·zet·to** \,pävənət'sed·(,)ō\ *n* -s [*pavonazzo* fr. It, fr. *pavonazzo* peacock-colored, purplish, fr. L *pavonaceus* like a peacock's tail, variegated, fr. *pavon-, pavo* peacock + *-aceus* -aceous; *pavonazzetto* fr. It, fr. *pavonazzo* + *-etto* -et (fr. LL *-itus* & *-ita*)] **1** : a marble with veins usu. of red, violet, or purple found in ancient Roman buildings and thought to be Phrygian **2** : a contemporary marble resembling pavonazzo

**pa·vo·nia** \pə'vōnēə\ *n* [NL, fr. José *Pavon* †1844 Span. botanist + NL *-ia*] **1** *cap* : a genus of tropical hairy shrubs or herbs (family Malvaceae) having flowers with an epicalyx of four to eight bracts and aristate carpels **2** -s : any plant of the genus *Pavonia*

**pa·vo·ni·an** \pə'vōnēən\ *adj* [L *pavon-, pavo* peacock + E *-an*] : PAVONINE

**pav·o·nine** \'pavə,nīn, -,nən\ *adj* [L *pavoninus*, fr. *pavon-, pavo* peacock + *-inus* -ine] **1 a** : of, relating to, or resembling the peacock **b** : colored like a peacock's tail or neck : IRIDESCENT **2** : of the color peacock

**pav·o·nite** \'pavə,nīt\ *n* -s [L *pavon-, pavo* peacock (intended as Latin rendering of Martin A. *Peacock* †1950 Canadian mineralogist) + E *-ite*] : a mineral $AgBi_3S_5$ consisting of a sulfide of silver and bismuth

¹**paw** \'pȯ\ *n* -s [ME, fr. MF *poue*] **1** : the foot of a quadruped (as the lion, dog, or cat) having claws; *broadly* : the foot of an animal **b** : fur taken from the legs and flanks of an animal and sewn together for garments ⟨a coat of mink ~⟩ **2** : a human hand: as **a** : a large clumsy hand ⟨selected a cigaret with a vast ~ —Ellery Queen⟩ **b** : a child's small often grubby hand ⟨go and wash those ~s before dinner⟩ **3** *archaic* : something done by hand (as handwriting) **4** : the foreleg of an animal depicted in heraldry as couped or erased near the middle joint — distinguished from *gamb*

²**paw** \"\ *vb* -ED/-ING/-S *vt* **1** : to stroke with the hand : feel or touch clumsily, indelicately, or rudely ⟨he ~*ed* his ear with a doubtful air —Arthur Morrison⟩ ⟨an important man could find more to do than ~ a lady's knees —Kenneth Roberts⟩ **2** : to touch or strike at with a paw : CLAW ⟨barely escaped being ~*ed* by the lion⟩ **3** : to scrape or beat with or as if with a hoof ⟨long lines of pack mules ~*ed* the dust of the street —*Amer. Guide Series: Oregon*⟩ ⟨the curb where his charger was ~*ing* the gutter —Winston Churchill⟩ **4** : to handle clumsily or roughly esp. while looking or examining ⟨he ~*ed* the stones hurriedly, searching —Liam O'Flaherty⟩ ⟨don't care to have the critics ~ the book at all —Mark Twain⟩ **5** : to flail at or grab for wildly ⟨his right hand ~*ed* the steel side ineffectually —R.O.Bowen⟩ **6** : to struggle to progress ⟨the troops ~*ed* forward gingerly a few hundred yards at a time —Norman Mailer⟩ ⟨walked, stumbled, groped, and ~*ed* our way through the fields —Herbert Passin⟩ ~ *vi* **1** : to beat or scrape with a hoof ⟨horses . . . begin tossing their heads and ~*ing* and neighing —S.E.Morison⟩ ⟨~*ed* vaguely with his foot for the brass rail —Dorothy Sayers⟩ **2** : to touch or strike with a paw ⟨the kitten ~*ed* at the mouse⟩ ⟨the dog ~*ed* at the back door begging to come in⟩ **3** : to feel or touch clumsily or rudely with the hand ⟨his hand ~*ed* about his skull —Liam O'Flaherty⟩ **4** : to search esp. by handling carelessly or roughly ⟨went back into the woodshed and ~*ed* around for a heavy block of wood —Raymond Chandler⟩ ⟨~*ed* through the bottom of the trunk⟩ **5** : to flail or grab wildly with the hand ⟨sprang to the door and ~*ed* at the bolt —William Faulkner⟩ ⟨were all on their feet . . . their hands ~*ing* at their daggers —T.B.Costain⟩

³**paw** \"\ *n* -s [prob. alter. of obs. E (northern dial.) *pawk* trick] *Scot* : a quick or deft movement : TRICK

⁴**paw** \"\ *or* **paw–paw** \'pȯ,pȯ\ *adj* [*paw* prob. alter. of ¹*pah*; *paw-paw* redupl. of *paw*] **1** : childishly improper : NAUGHTY **2** : INDECENT, OBSCENE

**paw foot** *n* : a decorative foot used on a piece of furniture that is usu. in the form of a lion's paw often showing large claws clasping a ball

**pawk·ery** \'pȯkəri\ *n* -ES [obs. E (northern dial.) *pawk* trick + E *-ery*] *Scot* : SLYNESS, TRICKINESS

**pawk·i·ly** \'pȯkəli\ *adv* : in a pawky manner

**pawk·i·ness** \-kinəs\ *n* -ES : the quality or state of being pawky

**pawky** \'pȯki\ *adj* [obs. E (northern dial.) *pawk* trick + E *-y*] **1** *chiefly Brit* : artfully shrewd : CANNY ⟨that favorite of fiction, the ~ rich old lady who incessantly scores off her parasitical descendants —*Punch*⟩ **2** *chiefly Scot* **a** : LIVELY, UNINHIBITED **b** : BOLD, FORWARD ⟨a rude and ~ child⟩ **3** *chiefly Scot* : overly fastidious : SQUEAMISH

¹**pawl** *also* **pall** *or* **paul** \'pȯl\ *n* -s [perh. modif. of D *pal* pawl] **1** : a pivoted tongue or sliding bolt on one part of a machine that is adapted to fall into notches or interdental spaces on another part (as a ratchet wheel) so as to permit motion in one direction and prevent it in the reverse (as in a capstan or windlass) : CATCH, DETENT — see RATCHET WHEEL illustration **2** : a part of a poise of a weighing scale shaped to fit into the notches of a beam bar for the definite positioning of the poise

²**pawl** \"\ *vt* -ED/-ING/-S : to check (as a capstan) by a pawl

³**pawl** \"\ *n* -s [Hindi *pāl* sail, small tent] : a small double-poled tent with steep sloping sides used in India

**pawl bitt** *also* **pawl post** *n* : a heavy post set abaft a windlass to receive the strain of pawls which are attached to it

**pawl head** *n* : the part of a capstan usu. the circular base to which the pawls are attached

**pawl rim** *n* : a stationary ring about the base of a capstan with notches for the pawls to catch in

¹**pawn** \'pȯn, 'pän\ *n* -s [ME *paun*, modif. (prob. influenced by MFlem *paen* pawn, fr. MF *pan*) of MF *pan*, prob. fr. *pan* piece of cloth, pane; fr. the practice of holding a garment as security — more at PANE] **1 a** : something delivered to or deposited with another as security for a loan **b** : a person left as a hostage ⟨he must leave behind for ~s, his mother, wife, and son —John Dryden⟩ **2** : the state of being pledged ⟨the hock shop continued to take into ~ things to charm —John McNulty⟩ **3 a** : something used as a pledge : EARNEST, GUARANTY ⟨the new school is the ~ given by the community to its children⟩ **b** : GAGE 2 **4** : the act of pawning **5** : a slave held as security for debt **syn** see PLEDGE

²**pawn** \"\ *vt* -ED/-ING/-S : to give or deposit in pledge or as security for the payment of a loan, a debt, or for the performance of some action : put in pawn : PLEDGE, STAKE, WAGER ⟨in the end he had to ~ that coat —Vicki Baum⟩ ⟨~ my victories, all my honors to you —Shak.⟩ ⟨he now ~*ed* his royal word —T.B.Macaulay⟩ ⟨exploited their own shame, ~*ing* their dignity for profit —Lillian Smith⟩

³**pawn** \"\ *n* -s [ME *pown, poune*, fr. MF *poon*, fr. ML *pedon-, pedo* foot soldier, fr. LL, one who has broad feet, fr. L *ped-, pes* foot — more at FOOT] **1 a** : one of the chessmen of least value having the power to move only one square forward at a time or at option two on its first move and to capture an enemy only on either of the two squares diagonally forward **b** : a counter in Polish checkers **2** : one that can be used often to his own disadvantage to further the purposes of another ⟨have become ~s in the hands of those who thrive on agitation and unrest —Elijah Adlow⟩ ⟨innocent-eyed but willing ~ of the family —Leo Gershoy⟩

pawn 1 a

⁴**pawn** \"\ *n* -s [ME *poune*, fr. MF *poun, paon*, fr. L *pavon-, pavo* peacock] *archaic* : PEACOCK

⁵**pawn** \"\ *n* -s [prob. fr. MD *paen* hall, vestibule, fr. MF *pan* pane — more at PANE] : a gallery or covered passage esp. in a bazaar

**pawn·age** \-nij\ *n* -s [²*pawn* + *-age*] : an act of pawning

**pawnbroker** \'=,==\ *n* [¹*pawn* + *broker*] : one that loans money on the security of personal property pledged in his keeping

**pawn·bro·ker·age** \'=,brōk(ə)rij\ *n* : PAWNBROKING

**pawn·bro·ker·ing** \-riŋ\ *n* -s : PAWNBROKING

**pawn·bro·kery** \-rē\ *n* **1** : PAWNSHOP **2** : PAWNBROKING

¹**pawnbroking** \'=,==\ *adj* [¹*pawn* + *broking*] : conducting the business of pawnbroking

²**pawnbroking** \"\ *n* : the business of lending money on the security of pawned articles

¹**pawn·ee** \(')pȯ¦nē, (')pä¦-\ *n* -s [¹*pawn* + *-ee*] : one to whom a pledge is given as security : one who takes something in pawn : PLEDGEE

²**paw·nee** \"\ *n, pl* **pawnee** *or* **pawnees** **1** *usu cap* **a (1)** : a Caddo confederacy of the Platte and Republican river valleys in Nebraska and Kansas **(2)** : a member of such a confederacy **b** : the language of the Pawnee people **2** : ALMOND 6a

³**paw·nee** \"\ *n* -s [Hindi *pānī*, fr. Skt *pānīya* drink, fr. *pāti, pibati* he drinks — more at POTABLE] *India* : WATER ⟨brandy-*pawnee*⟩

**pawn·er** \'pȯnə(r), 'pän-\ *or* **pawn·or** \", (')=¦nȯ(ə)r, -ȯ(ə)\ *n* -s [¹*pawn* + *-er* or *-or*] : one who pawns or pledges something as security

**pawn roller** *n* : an irresistible advance of pawns in a middle game of chess

**pawns** *pl of* PAWN, *pres 3d sing of* PAWN

**pawnshop** \'=,=\ *n* [¹*pawn* + *shop*] : a pawnbroker's shop

**pawn ticket** *n* : a pawnbroker's receipt for a pledge

**paw–paw** *var of* PAW

**paw·paw** *var of* PAPAW

**paws** *pl of* PAW, *pres 3d sing of* PAW

¹**pax** \'paks, 'päks\ *n* -ES [ME, fr. ML, fr. L, peace — more at PEACE] **1** : a tablet or board decorated with a figure or symbol of Christ, the Virgin Mary, or a saint and customarily in medieval times kissed before the communion by the priest and then by the people **2 a** : KISS OF PEACE **b** : a liturgical greeting passed along from the celebrant of the mass shortly before the communion to the other officers of the mass and members of the liturgical choir **3** *usu cap* : a period of international history characterized by an absence of major wars

and a general stability of international affairs usu. resulting from the predominance of a specified political authority ⟨during the *Pax Britannica* of the nineteenth century a vast empire of trade was built up —E.H.Jacoby⟩ ⟨*Pax Romana*⟩ **4** [L, interj., finished! enough! fr. Gk, adv., very well, enough; akin to Gk *pēgnynai* to fix, fasten together — more at PACT] *Brit* — used as a cry for quarter to end a schoolboy fight

**²pax** \ˈpaks\ *n* -ES [by alter.] **:** POX

**pax·il·la** \pakˈsilə\ *n, pl* **paxil·lae** \-i,lē\ [NL, fr. L *paxillus* peg, dim. of *palus* stake — more at POLE] **:** a spine like a pillar with a flattened summit bearing minute spinules or granules in various starfishes — **pax·il·lar** \-lə(r)\ *adj* — **pax·il·late** \-lət, -,lāt\ *adj* — **pax·il·lif·er·ous** \ˌpaksəˈlif(ə)rəs\ *adj* — **pax·il·li·form** \pakˈsilə,fȯrm\ *adj*

**pax·il·lo·sa** \ˌpaksəˈlōsə\ *n pl, cap* [NL, fr. neut. pl. of (assumed) NL *paxillosus*, fr. NL *paxilla* + L *-osus* -ose] *in some esp. former classifications* **:** an order that comprises starfishes with dorsal paxillae and is sometimes regarded as a suborder of Phanerozonia

**pax·il·lose** \ˈpaksə,lōs\ *adj* [L *paxillus* + E *-ose*] **1 :** resembling a little stake **2** [NL *paxilla* + E *-ose*] **:** bearing paxillae **:** PAXILLATE

**pax·il·lus** \ˈpaksələs\ *n* [NL, fr. L, peg] **1** *cap* **:** a genus of rusty-spored mushrooms (family Agaricaceae) having a fleshy thallus with no annulus and decurrent gills separating easily from the cap **2** *pl* **paxil·li** \-sə,lī\ *or* **paxilluses :** any fungus of the genus *Paxillus*; *esp* **:** an edible mushroom (*P. involutus*)

**pa·xi·u·ba** \ˌpäshēˈübə\ *or* **paxiuba palm** *n* -S [*paxiuba* fr. Pg, fr. Tupi] **:** a Brazilian pinnate-leaved palm (*Iriartea exorrhiza*) with remarkable prop roots from which the trunk rises as if on stilts

**pax·wax** \ˈpak,swaks\ *or* **paxy·waxy** \ˈpaksē,waksē\ *n* -ES [ME *paxwax*, alter. of *faxwax*, prob. fr. *fax* hair of the head (fr. OE *feax*) + *wax* growth, fr. *waxen* to grow — more at PECTINATE, WAX] *chiefly dial* **:** the nuchal ligament of a quadruped

**¹pay** \ˈpā\ *vb* **paid** *also in sense 8* **payed** \ˈpād\ **paid; paying; pays** [ME *payen*, fr. OF *paier*, fr. L *pacare* to pacify, fr. *pac-, pax* peace — more at PEACE] *vt* **1** *obs* **:** PACIFY, APPEASE, GRATIFY **2 a :** to satisfy (someone) for services rendered or property delivered **:** discharge an obligation to **:** make due return to ⟨factory hands are *paid* by the hour⟩ ⟨*paid* all his creditors⟩ **b :** to engage for money **:** HIRE ⟨you couldn't ~ me to do that⟩ ⟨have to ~ someone to mow the lawn⟩ **3 a :** to give in return for goods or service ⟨~ high wages⟩ ⟨*paid* a stiff price for the house⟩ ⟨~ interest on borrowed money⟩ **b :** to discharge indebtedness for **:** SETTLE ⟨~ a bill⟩ ⟨~ a tax⟩ ⟨~ a debt⟩ ⟨~ a bet⟩ ⟨~ rent for the house⟩ **c :** to assume the charge of ⟨~ expenses⟩ ⟨*paid* his son's tuition⟩ ⟨~ the freight⟩ **d :** to make any agreed disposal or transfer of (money) ⟨*paid* a few dollars weekly into his savings account⟩ ⟨counting all the contributions actually *paid* in to date⟩ ⟨obliged to ~ out his entire wages every Saturday⟩ ⟨*paid* over a large sum to the lawyer⟩ **4 :** to give or forfeit in expiation or retribution ⟨if he has broken the law he must ~ the penalty⟩ ⟨permanent injury is a high price to ~ for a moment's carelessness⟩ **5 a :** to make compensation for **:** make up for **:** RECOMPENSE ⟨his trouble was well *paid* in the end⟩ **b :** to make retaliation for — usu. used with *back* ⟨*paid* him back blow for blow⟩ **c :** to requite (someone) according to what is deserved **:** get even with — usu. used with *back* ⟨~ back a social obligation⟩ ⟨how can I ~ you back for all your kindness⟩ ⟨cheated me but I'll find some way to ~ him back⟩ **d** *archaic* **:** THRASH, PUNISH **6 :** to give, offer, or make freely or as fitting ⟨~ attention to business⟩ ⟨*paid* no heed to repeated warnings⟩ ⟨~ a visit to the capital⟩ ⟨~*ing* lip service to democratic ideals⟩ ⟨has come to ~ his respects to you⟩ **7 a :** to return value or profit to ⟨it *paid* the store to stay open evenings⟩ **b :** to bring in as a return ⟨the investment *paid* five percent⟩ **8 :** to slacken (as a rope) and allow to run out ⟨wires are *paid* out and their eyes are slipped over the ship's bitts —N.D.Ford & W.J.Redgrave⟩ ⟨*payed* out the line to lower him to the ledge⟩ **~** *vi* **1 :** to give a recompense **:** make payment **:** discharge a debt or obligation ⟨owing doesn't mean ~*ing*, as any butcher or baker or candlestick maker can tell you —Margaret Deland⟩ **2 :** to make suitable return for expense or trouble **:** be worth the effort or pains **:** be profitable ⟨it ~*s* to be careful⟩ ⟨his job ~*s* very little⟩ ⟨justly emphatic against the delusion that persecution never ~*s* —G.G.Coulton⟩ **3 :** to be amiss or afoot — used chiefly in *what's to pay, something is to pay*

**syn** COMPENSATE, REMUNERATE, SATISFY, REIMBURSE, INDEMNIFY, RECOMPENSE, REPAY: PAY is a general term, usu. lacking particular connotation but sometimes bluntly stressing the purchase of services ⟨*pay* a machinist high wages⟩ ⟨*pay* a person to whom one has lost a bet⟩ In situations involving retaliation or retribution it may connote the bitter or dire ⟨didn't want anything except an opportunity to make somebody *pay* for the injustices, the inhumanities that my father had suffered —Kenneth Roberts⟩ COMPENSATE may indicate the giving of some return felt to be roughly equivalent in value to a service or favor; the extending of some balancing or countering consideration ⟨*compensate* one for his additional trouble⟩ ⟨an epoch in which the immense costs of a war could never be *compensated* by any economic gains that came from it —Max Lerner⟩ ⟨the loss will be far more than *compensated* by the growing tourist business —*Amer. Guide Series: Nev.*⟩ REMUNERATE, generally more formal than PAY, is applicable to rewards generous, not contracted for, or unexpected ⟨the king *remunerated* his retainers with large grants⟩ SATISFY implies payment asked, required, stipulated ⟨the Swedish government bought the shares of the Dutch investors in the New Sweden Company and *satisfied* all Dutch claims —*Amer. Guide Series: Del.*⟩ REIMBURSE applies to the return of an exact equivalent for an expenditure ⟨county charges are admitted, the state *reimbursing* the county in the amount of 75¢ a day for each person; patients financially able to pay are charged $3 a day —*Amer. Guide Series: Mich.*⟩ INDEMNIFY applies to compensations for loss, damage, or injury ⟨the insurance company *indemnified* him for his losses⟩ RECOMPENSE suggests fit return, either in compensation, amends, friendly or loyal repayment, or reward ⟨*recompensed* for unusual services⟩ ⟨from this heritage her writing derives a graciousness and urbanity that *recompense* one, to a degree, for the essential superficiality of her observation and insight —F.B.Millett⟩ REPAY always implies the notion of a return, a paying back, answering, countering, or reprisal ⟨every last one of them eager to *repay* with interest a few of the things that had been done to them —Kenneth Roberts⟩ ⟨the doctor is *repaid* all he wants simply by the interest of your case —Graham Greene⟩ ⟨the region would *repay* investigation —Douglas Carruthers⟩

— **pay as you go 1 :** to pay bills when due **2 :** to limit expenditures to actual income **3 :** to pay taxes on income as it is received — compare WITHHOLDING TAX — **pay for 1 :** to conclude the purchase of by delivering the price ⟨bought and *paid for* the house out of their savings⟩ **2 :** to yield or forfeit an equivalent value for **:** atone for ⟨in life as in business things had to be *paid for* —Louis Bromfield⟩ **3 :** to bear the cost of ⟨willing to *pay for* his son's education⟩ ⟨some improvements *pay for* themselves in increased economy of operation⟩ — **pay home :** to pay back or retaliate in full measure — **pay one's way** *or* **pay one's own way 1 :** to pay expenses as they are incurred **2 :** to yield an income at least equal to operating expenses — **pay the piper 1 :** to bear the cost of something ⟨artists will be chosen . . . supported by the state . . . the people will *pay the piper* and call the tune —Clive Bell⟩ **2 :** to suffer the consequences of or penalty for an act — **pay the shot :** to pay the bill **:** stand the expense — **pay through the nose :** to pay exorbitantly or dearly

**²pay** \ˈ"\ *n* -S [ME *pay, paye*, fr. MF *paie*, fr. *paier* to pay] **1** *obs* **:** SATISFACTION, LIKING **2 a :** the act or fact of paying or being paid ⟨no ~, no work⟩ ⟨demanded ~ for overtime work⟩ ⟨long interval between ~*s* . . . to prevent frequent drunkenness among the men —*Times Lit. Supp.*⟩ **b :** the status of being paid by an employer **:** EMPLOY ⟨time when England had not a single battalion in constant ~ —T.B.Macaulay⟩ ⟨suspected of being in the ~ of a foreign power⟩ **3** *archaic* **:** something given in return by way of reward or retaliation ⟨when her lips were ready for his ~ —Shak.⟩ **4 a :** WAGES, SALARY, REMUNERATION ⟨equal ~ for equal work⟩ ⟨stayed just long enough to collect his ~⟩; *esp* **:** money regularly allotted to a member of the armed forces **b :** money paid in addition to basic wages or salary ⟨travel ~⟩ ⟨flying ~⟩ ⟨severance ~⟩ **5 :** a person viewed as to reliability or promptitude in paying debts or bills ⟨business people say the best ~ are Japanese, Filipinos, and Chinese —Joseph Driscoll⟩ **6 a :** earth, rock, or sand that yields metal (esp. gold) in profitable amounts **b :** a zone or stratum (as of sand) that yields oil **syn** see WAGE

**³pay** \ˈ"\ *adj* **1 :** containing or leading to something precious or valuable (as gold, oil) ⟨~ ore⟩ ⟨~ rock⟩ **2 :** equipped with a coin slot for receiving a fee for use ⟨~ telephone⟩ ⟨~ toilet⟩ **3 :** concerned with or used for payment ⟨~ clerk⟩ ⟨~ office⟩ **4 :** requiring payment ⟨~ hospital⟩ ⟨~ TV⟩

**⁴pay** \ˈ"\ *vt* **payed** *also* **paid; payed** *also* **paid; paying; pays** [obs. F *peier*, fr. OF, fr. L *picare*, fr. *pic-, pix* pitch — more at PITCH] **:** to smear or coat (as a spar, caulked seam) with hot tar or pitch or any waterproof composition

**paya** \ˈpī(y)ə\ *n, pl* **paya** *or* **payas** *usu cap* **1 a :** an Indian people of northern Honduras **b :** a member of such people **2 :** the language of the Paya

**pay·abil·i·ty** \ˌpāəˈbiləd-ē\ *n* **:** the quality or state of being payable

**pay·able** \ˈpāəbəl\ *adj* [ME *paiable*, fr. MF, fr. OF, fr. *paier* to pay + *-able* — more at PAY] **1 a :** requiring to be paid ⟨bills ~⟩ **:** capable of being paid ⟨~ prices⟩ **:** DUE ⟨the interest is ~ in advance⟩ **b** *of a note, bill, or check* **:** specifying payment to a particular payee ⟨~ to John Doe⟩ ⟨~ to cash⟩, at a specified time or occasion ⟨~ on demand⟩, or in a specified manner ⟨~ in monthly installments⟩ **2 :** capable of being profitably worked ⟨~ vein of ore⟩ **:** PROFITABLE, PAYING ⟨~ enterprise⟩ ⟨~ crop of fruit⟩

**pay·able·ness** *n* -ES **:** the quality or state of being payable

**pay·ably** \-blē\ *adv* **:** PROFITABLY

**pay·a·guá** \ˌpī(y)əˈgwä\ *n, pl* **payaguá** *or* **payaguás** *usu cap* **1 a :** an extinct Guaicuruan people of the Paraguay river valley including the Agaz **b :** a member of such people **2 :** the language of the Payaguá

**payan** \ˈpī(y)ən\ *n* -S *usu cap* [*Paya* + E *-an*] **:** a language family of uncertain relationships comprising the Paya language

**payback** \ˈ=,=\ *n* -S [fr. *pay back*, v.] **:** return of an amount in profits secured as the result of a capital expenditure such as to offset the expenditure

**paybook** \ˈ=,=\ *n* **:** an individual pay record of a member of the armed forces

**paybox** \ˈ=,=\ *n, Brit* **:** a cashier's or ticket seller's booth

**paycheck** \ˈ=,=\ *n* **1 :** a check in payment of wages or salary ⟨with his first ~ a month off —*Newsweek*⟩ **2 :** WAGES, SALARY ⟨meager, if rising, ~*s* —*Time*⟩

**payday** \ˈ=,=\ *n* **1 :** the day on which wages or salary is regularly paid **2 :** SETTLEMENT DAY

**pay dirt** *n* **1 :** earth or ore that yields a profit to a miner **2 :** any useful or remunerative discovery or attained object ⟨after hours of questioning the police struck *pay dirt*⟩ ⟨the *pay dirt* for the fact-seeking reader is there —*Amer. Antiquity*⟩ **3 :** the end zone of a football field

**PAYE** *abbr* **1** pay as you earn **2** pay as you enter

**payed** *past of* PAY

**pay·ee** \(ˈ)pāˈē\ *n* -S [²*pay* + *-ee*] **:** the person to whom money is to be or has been paid **:** the person named in a bill of exchange, note, or check as the one to whom the amount is promised or directed to be paid

**pa·ye·na** \pāˈyēnə\ *n, cap* [NL, after Anselme *Payen* †1871 Fr. chemist and botanical writer] **:** a genus of Malayan trees (family Sapotaceae) of medium to very large size having fascicled flowers growing at or near the leaf axils, bearing fruit with one or two endospermous seeds, and yielding gutta-percha

**pay envelope** *n* **:** an envelope containing one's wages; *often* **:** WAGES, SALARY, STIPEND ⟨hard times affect *pay envelopes*⟩

**pay·er** \ˈpāər\ *also* **pay·or** \ˈ", (ˈ)pā;ˈȯ(ə)r\ *n* -S [*payer* fr. ME, fr. *payen* to pay + *-er*; *payor* fr. ¹*pay* + *-or* — more at PAY] **:** one that pays: as **a :** the person by whom a bill or note has been or should be paid **b :** a person (as a parent) who agrees to pay the premium on a juvenile policy

**payetan** *var of* PAYYETAN

**pay in** *vt* **:** to deposit in an account **~** *vi* **:** to make a deposit into an account

**paying** *n* -S [fr. gerund of ⁴*pay*] **:** waterproof material used to pay seams or rigging

**paying guest** *n* **:** one that pays for board and lodging esp. in a private house; *often* **:** BOARDER

**paying–in book** \ˈ==ˈ=-\ *n, Brit* **:** BANKBOOK

**paying–in slip** *n, Brit* **:** DEPOSIT SLIP

**paying load** *n* **:** PAYLOAD 2

**payload** \ˈ=,=\ *n* **1 :** the financial burden of the regular payrolls (as in a factory or business) **2 :** the revenue-producing or useful load that a vehicle of transport can carry **:** net load; *also* **:** the explosive charge carried in the warhead of a missile

**paymaster** \ˈ=,==\ *n* [²*pay* + *master*] **:** an officer or agent of a government, a corporation, or an employer whose duty it is to pay salaries or wages and keep account of them

**paymaster general** *n, pl* **paymasters general 1 :** a military officer in command of the pay department of an army or navy **2 a :** a government officer in Great Britain formerly making all civil and military payments on the authority of the treasury **b :** a British officer of state whose official duties are nominal but who is often made a member of the cabinet and entrusted with special functions

**pay·ment** \ˈpāmənt\ *n* -S [ME *payment, payement*, fr. MF *paiement*, fr. OF, fr. *paier* to pay + *-ment* — more at PAY] **1 :** the act of paying or giving compensation **:** the discharge of a debt or an obligation ⟨prompt ~ of debts⟩ ⟨~ of a fine⟩ **2 :** something that is paid **:** something given to discharge a debt or obligation or to fulfill a promise **:** PAY, RETURN, REQUITAL ⟨amortize a debt with monthly ~*s*⟩ ⟨accepted a judgeship as ~ for loyal service to the party⟩ **3** *archaic* **:** PUNISHMENT, CHASTISEMENT

**payment bill** *n* **:** a bill of exchange under which the drawee can obtain the documents of title only by paying the bill — compare ACCEPTANCE 4

**payment by intervention :** INTERVENTION 2 a

**payment for honor :** payment of a protested bill or draft by someone other than the primary debtor made with the purpose of saving the credit of such debtor

**payne's gray** \ˈpānz-\ *n, often cap P* [after William *Payne* fl 1800 Eng. artist, its inventor] **:** a grayish to dark grayish blue

**pay·nim** \ˈpānəm\ *n* -S [ME *painim*, fr. OF *paienime*, fr. LL *paganismus* heathendom, fr. *paganus* heathen (fr. L, country dweller) + L *-ismus* -ism — more at PAGAN] **1** *archaic* **:** PAGANDOM **2** *archaic* **:** PAGAN, INFIDEL ⟨clasped like a missal where swart ~*s* pray —John Keats⟩; *esp* **:** MUHAMMADAN

**pay·nim·ry** *or* **pay·nim·rie** \-mrē\ *n* -ES [ME *paynimery, paynimrie*, fr. *painim* + *-ery* or *-rie* -ry] *archaic* **:** PAGANDOM

**pay off** *vt* **1 a :** to give (an employee) all due wages; *esp* **:** to pay in full and discharge (a crew of hands or workmen) **b :** to pay (a debt or a creditor) in full ⟨expects to *pay* all his debts *off* shortly⟩ **c :** BRIBE **2 :** to inflict retribution on **:** get back at **:** settle a grudge with ⟨wanted to *pay* him *off* for stealing his girl⟩ **3 :** to turn the head of (a ship) to leeward **4 :** to allow (a thread, rope) to run off a spool or drum **:** UNWIND **~** *vi* **1** *of a ship* **:** to swing to leeward **2 a :** to yield returns either of profit or loss ⟨the investment *paid off* handsomely⟩ **b :** to reach successful realization ⟨the years of patience and persistence had at last *paid off*⟩ ⟨boldness is the only course that will *pay off* —E.B.George⟩

**¹payoff** \ˈ=,=\ *n* -S [fr. *pay off*, v.] **1 :** the act or occasion of paying employees' wages or gambling winnings or distributing profits, booty, or bribe money **2 a :** PROFIT, REWARD **b :** RETRIBUTION **3 :** the climax of an incident or enterprise; *specif* **:** the denouement of a narrative ⟨now listen to the ~⟩ **4 :** a decisive fact or factor resolving a situation or bringing about a definitive conclusion ⟨the opinion of the tax court on taxability is the ~⟩

**²payoff** \ˈ"\ *adj* **:** yielding results in the final test **:** REWARDING, DECISIVE ⟨gave him the ~ shot —Chester Roth⟩ ⟨maneuvering for a ~ play⟩ ⟨wound up for the ~ pitch⟩

**pay·o·la** \pāˈōlə\ *n* -S [prob. alter. (influenced by *-ola*, as in *Victrola*) of ¹*payoff*] **1 :** an undercover or indirect payment for a commercial favor (as to a disc jockey for plugging a song) **2 :** the practice of engaging in payolas

**payor** *var of* PAYER

**payote** *var of* PEYOTE

**pay out** *vt* **:** to get even with **:** get revenge on ⟨the women did not dare *pay* her *out* for snubbing them —Sherwood Anderson⟩

**payout** \ˈ=,=\ *n* -S [fr. the phrase *pay out*] **:** the act of paying out **:** EXPENDITURE, DISBURSEMENT ⟨federal ~ for military aircraft —C.J.V.Murphy⟩ ⟨bookmakers had a heavy ~ on the winner —*Sydney (Australia) Bull.*⟩

**pay packet** *n, Brit* **:** PAY ENVELOPE

**payr** *abbr* paymaster

**payroll** \ˈ=,=\ *n* [²*pay* + *roll*] **1 :** a paymaster's or employer's list of those entitled to receive compensation at a given time and of the amounts due to each ⟨make out a ~⟩ **2 :** the sum necessary for distribution to those on a payroll; *also* **:** the money to be distributed ⟨increase the weekly ~⟩ — **on the payroll** *adv (or adj)* **:** in the service or employ of someone

**pay–roll·er** \ˈ=,rōlə(r)\ *n* **:** one receiving pay or periodical stipends; *esp* **:** a state or federal employee

**payroll tax** *n* **:** a government or state tax levied on employers as a percentage of wages and salaries paid to employees — compare WITHHOLDING TAX

**pays** *pres 3d sing of* PAY, *pl of* PAY

**pay·sage** \ˈpāsij, ˌpāēˈzäzh\ *n* -S [F, fr. MF, fr. *pays* country (fr. OF *pais*, fr. LL *pagensis* inhabitant of a district, fr. L *pagus* district) + *-age* — more at PAGAN] **:** LANDSCAPE

**pay·sa·gist** \ˈpāsəjəst\ *or* **pay·sa·giste** \ˌpāēzäˈzhēst\ *n* -S [F *paysagiste*, fr. *paysage* + *-iste* -ist] **:** a landscape artist

**pay·sanne** \(ˈ)pāˈzan\ *adj* [F, fr. *paysanne*, n., fem. of *paysan* rustic, peasant, fr. MF *paisant* — more at PEASANT] **:** prepared (as with diced root vegetables) in country or simple style ⟨~ sauce⟩ ⟨potatoes ~⟩

**pay school** *n* **:** a school charging tuition **:** PRIVATE SCHOOL

**pay sheet** *n, Brit* **:** PAYROLL

**pay station** *n* **:** a public telephone usu. equipped with a slot-machine device for payment of toll

pay station

**pay streak** *n* **:** a stratum of mineral deposit capable of yielding profitable amounts of oil or ore

**payt** *abbr* payment

**pay up** *vb* [ME *payen up*, fr. *payen* to pay + *up* — more at PAY] *vt* **:** to pay in full **:** bring (as debts, dues) up to date by paying **~** *vi* **:** to pay what is due or what is demanded ⟨the threat of court action was enough to make him *pay up*⟩

**pay·ye·tan** *or* **pay·e·tan** \ˌpīəˈtän\ *n, pl* **payyeta·nim** *or* **payeta·nim** \ˌpīətäˈnēm\ [LHeb *payyĕṭān*, fr. *piyyūṭ* poem — more at PIYYUT] **:** an author of liturgical poems forming part of the Jewish liturgy on special Sabbaths and festivals — compare PIYYUT — **pay·ye·tan·ic** *or* **pay·e·tan·ic** \ˌ=;=ˈtänik\ *adj*

**pa·zend** \ˈpä,zend\ *also* **pa·zand** \-zand\ *n* -S *cap* **:** the language of the transcriptions of Pahlavi texts into the script used for Avestan with substitution of Persian words for the Semitic words in the original; *also* **:** such transcriptions

**PB** *abbr* **1** passbook **2** passed ball **3** patrol boat **4** patrol bomber **5** permanent bunkers **6** phonetically balanced **7** piebald **8** pocket book **9** prayer book **10** privately bonded

**Pb** *symbol* [L *plumbum*] lead

**PBA** *abbr* permanent budget account

**PBM** *abbr* permanent bench mark

**PBX** \ˌpē(,)bēˈeks\ *n* -S [*private branch exchange*] **:** a private telephone switchboard

**pc** *abbr* piece

**PC** *abbr* **1** past commander **2** *often not cap* percent **3** percentage **4** perpetual curate **5** *often not cap* petty cash **6** pitch circle **7** *often not cap* police constable **8** postcard **9** [L *post cibum*] after meals **10** post commander **11** price current **12** privy council; privy councillor **13** purified concentrate

**PCB** *abbr* petty cashbook

**pce** *abbr* piece

**PCE** *abbr, often not cap* pyrometric cone equivalent

**p–celtic** \ˈ=;=\ *n, cap P&C* **:** those Celtic languages comprising the Gaulish and Brythonic in which the Indo-European labiovelar *qu* has become *p* — compare Q-CELTIC

**pchs** *abbr* purchase

**pcl** *abbr* parcel

**PCM** *abbr* pulse-code modulation

**PCO** *abbr* pest control operator

**pcpn** *abbr* precipitation

**pcs** *abbr* preconscious

**PCS** *abbr* **1** permanent change of station **2** principal clerk of session

**pct** *abbr* percent

**pd** *abbr* **1** paid **2** passed **3** pond **4** pound

**PD** *abbr* **1** [L *per diem*] by the day **2** pitch diameter **3** point detonating **4** police department **5** port dues **6** port of debarkation **7** position doubtful **8** postage due **9** postal district **10** postdated **11** potential difference **12** prism diopter **13** property damage **14** public domain

**Pd** *symbol* palladium

**PDB** *abbr or n* -S paradichlorobenzene

**PDF** *abbr* point detonating fuse

**pdg** *abbr* paradigm

**PDI** *abbr* pilot direction indicator

**pdl** *abbr* poundal

**PDQ** *adv, often not cap* [abbr. of *pretty damned quick*] **:** at once **:** IMMEDIATELY

**pdr** *abbr* **1** pounder **2** powder

**¹pe** *or* **phe** \ˈpā\ *n* -S [Heb *pē*] **1 :** the 17th letter of the Hebrew alphabet — symbol פ; see ALPHABET table **2 :** the letter of the Phoenician or of any of various other Semitic alphabets corresponding to Hebrew pe

**²pe** \ˈpē\ *var of* PEE

**-pe-** *comb form* [piperidine] **:** complete hydrogenation — in names of cyclic bases ⟨*lupetidine*⟩ ⟨*pipecoline*⟩

**PE** \(ˈ)pēˈē\ *abbr or n* -S **:** a petroleum engineer

**PE** *abbr* **1** *often not cap* photoelectric **2** pinion end **3** port of embarkation **4** post exchange **5** presiding elder **6** *often not cap* printer's error **7** probable error **8** professional engineer **9** pulley end

**¹pea** \ˈpē\ *n, pl* **peas** *also* **pease** \-ēz\ *often attrib* [back-formation fr. *pease* (taken as a plural), fr. ME *pese*, fr. OE *pise, peose*, fr. L *pisa*, pl. of *pisum*, fr. Gk *pisos, pison*] **1 a :** a variable annual leguminous vine (*Pisum sativum*) that is of uncertain natural origin and has been cultivated prob. since prehistoric times for its rounded smooth or wrinkled edible seeds which are rich in protein and are borne severally in dehiscent pods — called also *garden pea*; see FIELD PEA **b :** the seed of the pea widely used in its green immature stage as a cooked vegetable or stored in the mature dry stage (as for use in porridges or soups) ⟨a crab-and-*pea* bisque⟩ — usu. used in pl. ⟨steak and fresh buttered ~*s*⟩ **c peas** *pl* **:** the immature pods of the pea with their included seeds ⟨bought a bushel of new ~*s*⟩ **2 a :** any of various leguminous plants related to the pea or felt to resemble it in seed, flower, or use — usu. used with a qualifying term; see BEACH PEA, BLACK-EYED PEA, CHICK-PEA, COWPEA, SWEET PEA **b :** the seed of such a plant **3 :** something resembling a pea usu. in size, shape, or formation: **a :** a small piece or fragment (as of coal, gravel, iron pyrites) **b :** the small object that is hidden in the game of thimblerig

**²pea** *also* **pee** \ˈ"\ *n* -S [by shortening] **:** PEAK 6c

**pea aphid** *n* **:** a widely distributed aphid (*Acyrthosiphon pisum*) that is a serious pest on legumes (as alfalfa, pea, clover, vetch)

**pea bean** *n* **:** any of various kidney beans that are cultivated chiefly for their small white seeds which are used dried (as for baking)

**pea beetle** *n* **:** PEA WEEVIL

**pea·ber·ry** \ˈpē— *see* BERRY\ *n* **:** a coffeeberry with a single round seed resembling a pea

**peabird** \ˈ=,=\ *n* **1** *dial Eng* **:** WRYNECK **2 :** BALTIMORE ORIOLE

**pea·body** \'pē,bädē, -bədē\ *n, sometimes cap* [fr. the name *Peabody*] **:** a fast ballroom dance in open position

**peabody bird** \"-\ *n, usu cap P* [prob. imit.] **:** WHITE-THROATED SPARROW

**pea bug** *n* **:** PEA WEEVIL

[1]**peace** \'pēs\ *n* -s *often attrib* [ME *pes, pees, pais,* fr. OF *pes, pais,* fr. L *pac-, pax* peace; akin to L *pacisci* to agree, contract — more at PACT] **1 a :** freedom from civil clamor and confusion **:** a state of public quiet ⟨~ and order were finally restored in the town⟩ **b :** a state of security or order within a community provided for by law, custom, or public opinion — often used with *the* ⟨a breach of the ~⟩ **2 :** a mental or spiritual condition marked by freedom from disquieting or oppressive thoughts or emotions **:** calmness of mind and heart **:** serenity of spirit ⟨the bitter, restless struggling of the last months gave way to ~ —Rose Macaulay⟩ ⟨I have been in perfect ~ and contentment; I never have had one doubt —J.H.Newman⟩ ⟨a ~ of mind because you could no longer be surprised —Stuart Cloete⟩ ⟨farewell and ~ be with you⟩ — compare PEACE OF GOD **3 a :** a tranquil state of freedom from outside disturbance and harassment ⟨decided to accept a year-round post . . . and have ~ to write —*Newsweek*⟩ ⟨now remembered sharply the ~ and quiet of the place —Sherwood Anderson⟩ **b :** eternal repose ⟨may he rest in ~⟩ **4 :** harmony in human or personal relations **:** mutual concord and esteem ⟨he knew that there would never be ~ again while they lived —Graham Greene⟩ **5 a** (1) **:** a state of mutual concord between governments **:** absence of hostilities or war ⟨he had given the world ~, and the world now turned to him for security —John Buchan⟩ (2) **:** the period of such freedom from war ⟨a ~ of 50 years⟩ **b :** a pact or agreement to end hostilities or to come together in amity between those who have been at war or in a state of enmity or dissension **:** a formal reconciliation between contending parties; *esp* **:** a peace treaty ⟨signed ~ in the spring of 1918 —C.E.Black & E.C.Helmreich⟩ ⟨offered the possibility of a negotiated ~ —*N.Y.Times*⟩ **6 :** absence of activity and noise **:** deep stillness **:** QUIETNESS ⟨the ~ of the woods⟩ ⟨the ~ of sky and mountain⟩ **7 :** one that makes, gives, or maintains tranquillity ⟨God is our only ~⟩ — **at peace** *adv* **:** in a state of concord or tranquillity ⟨the problem was settled and his mind was *at peace*⟩ ⟨help man live *at peace* with his unconscious —*Time*⟩

[2]**peace** \"\ *vi* -ED/-ING/-S [ME *peesen,* fr. *pes, pees, pais* peace (n.)] **:** to become quiet or still **:** be, become, or keep silent ⟨when the thunder would not ~ at my bidding —Shak.⟩ — often used interjectionally

**peace·abil·i·ty** \,pēsə'bilәd·ē, -lətē, -i\ *n* **:** PEACEABLENESS ⟨snore himself to ~ —P.A.Rollins⟩

**peace·able** \'pēsəbəl\ *adj* [ME *pesible, pesable, paisible,* fr. MF *pesible, paisible,* fr. *pes, pais* peace + *-ible* — more at PEACE] **1 a :** disposed to peace **:** having an amicable disposition disinclined to strife **:** not contentious or quarrelsome ⟨the quiet, humble, modest and ~ person —William Cowper⟩ ⟨his tongue was not always ~ —W.R.Inge⟩ **b :** lacking noisiness or restlessness **:** quietly behaved **:** CALM ⟨was pleased to see how ~ the horse had become⟩ **2 :** marked by freedom from war, strife, hostilities, or disorder ⟨in the most ~ and orderly manner, without the smallest sign of tumult or sedition in the city —J.G.Frazer⟩ ⟨the company . . . in ~ times makes chiefly freight cars —E.D.Kennedy⟩ **syn** see PACIFIC

**peace·able·ness** *n* -ES [ME *pesiblenesse,* fr. *pesible, pesable, paisible* peaceable + *-nesse* -ness] **:** the quality or state of being peaceable

**peace·ably** \-blē, -bli\ *adv* [ME *pesibly, paisibly,* fr. *pesible, paisible* + *-y*] **1 :** in a peaceable and friendly manner **:** without contention or strife ⟨possible for more than one religion to survive comparatively ~ in the same state —Alfred Cobban⟩ **2 :** without subjection to annoyance or confusion **:** in peace **:** QUIETLY ⟨disturb him not; let him pass ~ —Shak.⟩

**peace belt** *n* **:** a wampum belt used to symbolize peace among No. American Indians

**peacebreaker** \'⸗,⸗⸗\ *n* **:** a violator of peace or of the peace **:** a perpetrator of strife ⟨international obligations to repress ~*s* —*Contemporary Rev.*⟩

**peacebreaking** \'⸗,⸗⸗\ *n* **:** the action of violating peace **:** the commission of a breach of the peace

**peace democrat** *n, usu cap P&D* **:** a Democrat in the northern states advocating peaceful measures as opposed to prosecution of the Civil War; *esp* **:** COPPERHEAD 2a

**peace dollar** *n* **:** a silver dollar of the U.S. struck from 1921 to 1928 and in 1934 and 1935

**peace·ful** \'pēsfəl\ *adj, sometimes* **peacefuller**; *sometimes* **peacefullest** [ME *paisful, pesful,* fr. *pais, pes, pees* peace + *-ful* — more at PEACE] **1 :** PEACEABLE 1 ⟨the ~ comportment of the seals had quieted my alarm —Jack London⟩ ⟨the modest man becomes bold . . . or the impetuous prudent and ~ —W.M.Thackeray⟩ **2 :** marked by, conducive to, or enjoying peace, quiet, or calm **:** untroubled by conflict, agitation, or commotion ⟨the feeling . . . that we as neighbors could settle any disputes in ~ fashion —F.D.Roosevelt⟩ ⟨rocky promontories shelter ~ bays —Samuel Van Valkenburg & Ellsworth Huntington⟩ **3 :** of or relating to a state or time of peace ⟨a bomb material as well as a ~ fuel —Oliver Townsend⟩ **4 :** devoid of violence or force **:** without recourse to warlike methods ⟨all the political groups . . . employed ~ tactics —*Collier's Yr. Bk.*⟩ ⟨~ procedures . . . mediation, investigation and conciliation —*Current History*⟩ **syn** see CALM, PACIFIC

**peace·ful·ly** \-fəlē, -li\ *adv* **:** in a peaceful manner ⟨cattle which ~ browse —Tom Marvel⟩ ⟨a ~ inclined and responsible government —Vera M. Dean⟩

**peace·ful·ness** \-fəlnəs\ *n* -ES **:** the quality or state of being peaceful ⟨the ~ and neighborliness of the parish is proverbial —*Amer. Guide Series: La.*⟩

**peace-keeper** \'⸗,⸗⸗\ *n* **:** a maintainer of peace or of the peace **:** a pacific country or person

**peace·less** \'pēsləs\ *adj* **:** having no peace — **peace·less·ness** *n* -ES

**peacemaker** \'⸗,⸗⸗\ *n* [ME *peace maker,* fr. *pease, pes, pees, pais* peace + *maker*] **:** one that makes or seeks to make peace esp. by reconciling parties or persons at variance

[1]**peacemaking** \'⸗,⸗⸗\ *n* **:** the action of bringing about peace

[2]**peacemaking** \"\ *adj* **:** bringing about peace or done in an effort to bring about peace

**peacemonger** \'⸗,⸗⸗\ *n* **:** PEACEMAKER; *esp* **:** one making or seeking peace unrealistically or at the expense of honor — usu. used disparagingly

**peacemongering** \'⸗,⸗(⸗)⸗\ *adj* **:** PEACEMAKING — usu. used disparagingly

**peace offensive** *n* **:** a campaign designed to serve the interests of a nation by the expression of wishes to end a war or of intentions to resolve conflicts peacefully and thus cause hostile or unfriendly nations to relax their efforts or become less vigilant

**peace offering** *n* **1 :** an ancient Hebrew votive, freewill, or thank offering **2 :** a gift or service to procure peace or reconciliation

**peace officer** *n* **:** a civil officer (as a sheriff, constable, policeman) whose duty it is to preserve the public peace

**peace of god** **1** *cap G* **:** the peace of heart which is the gift of God **2** *usu cap P & cap G* **:** an exemption from attack in feudal warfare urged by the church beginning in the latter part of the 9th century for all consecrated persons and places and later for all who claimed the protection of the church (as pilgrims, the poor) — compare TRUCE OF GOD

**peace pipe** *n* **:** CALUMET

**peaces** *pl of* PEACE, *pres 3d sing of* PEACE

**peacetime** \'⸗,⸗\ *n, often attrib* **:** a time when a nation is not at war ⟨as anxious to save lives in ~ as . . . in wartime —*Tomorrow*⟩

[1]**peach** \'pēch\ *n* -ES [ME *peche,* fr. MF (the fruit) fr. LL *persica,* fr. L *persicum,* fr. neut. of *Persicus* Persian] **1 a :** a low spreading freely branching tree (*Prunus persica*) that is native to China but cosmopolitan in cultivation in temperate areas and often found as an escape and that has drooping lanceolate leaves, sessile usu. pink flowers borne on the naked twigs in early spring, and a fruit which is a drupe with a single seed enclosed in a hard endocarp, a pulpy white or yellow mesocarp, and a thin firm downy epicarp — compare CHERRY 1a, PLUM **b :** the sweet juicy edible fruit of the peach which is widely used as a fresh or cooked fruit, in preserves, or dried **2 :** the quandong of Australia **3 :** any of various trees or shrubs or their edible fruits resembling the peach **4 :** a variable color averaging a moderate yellowish pink that is yellower, less strong, and slightly darker than peach pink, yellower and paler than coral pink, and yellower, lighter, and stronger than dusty pink **5 :** peach brandy **6 :** one likened to a peach in sweetness, beauty, or excellence **:** something particularly good in its class ⟨is a ~ to work with —*Atlantic*⟩ ⟨should be a ~ of a game —*Holiday*⟩ ⟨she's got a studio with a ~ of an English girl —A.H.Gibbs⟩

[2]**peach** \"\ *vb* -ED/-ING/-ES [ME *pechen,* short for *apechen* to appeach — more at APPEACH] *vt* **:** to inform against **:** BETRAY ⟨the woman was about to play false, and to ~ the rest —George Borrow⟩ ~ *vi* **:** to turn informer **:** BLAB, TATTLE ⟨the vilest of all sins — is to ~ to the headmaster —F.M.Ford⟩

**pea chaparral** *n* **:** CHAPARRAL PEA

**peach aphid** *n* **:** an aphid destructive to the peach — see BLACK PEACH APHID, GREEN PEACH APHID

**peach bark beetle** *n* **:** a scolytid beetle (*Phloeotribus liminaris*) the larvae of which feed on the inner bark of cherry and other stone-fruit trees

**peach-bark borer** *n* **:** PEACH TREE BORER

**peach bell** *n* **:** a perennial European bellflower (*Campanula persicifolia*) with racemose white or blue flowers — usu. used in pl.

**peach bisque** *n* **:** a light reddish brown that is redder and slightly deeper than copper tan and darker than monkey skin

**peach blight** *n* **1 :** a brown rot of stone fruits characterized by blighting of the twigs, leaves, or flowers **2 :** CALIFORNIA BLIGHT

**peach blister** *n* **:** LEAF CURL a

**peach bloom** *n* **1 :** a moderate yellowish pink that is yellower and paler than coral pink, less strong and slightly redder and darker than peach pink, and redder, less strong, and slightly darker than average peach — called also *rose morn* **2 :** a reduced copper glaze that is used esp. on Chinese porcelain and is mottled pinkish red often streaked with russet and green

**peachblossom** \'⸗,⸗⸗\ *n* **1** *also* **peachblossom pink** *or* **peachblossom red :** a moderate to strong pink that is yellower and lighter than hermosa pink or nymph pink **2** *of textiles* **:** a deep pink to moderate purplish red that is bluer and stronger than rambler rose

**peachblossom ore** *n* **:** ERYTHRITE 2

**peachblow** \'⸗,⸗\ *n* **1 :** a pale orange yellow that is slightly redder, lighter, and stronger than sunset and redder and stronger than freestone — called also *fakir* **2 :** PEACH BLOOM 2 **3 :** *or* **peachblow glass :** a late 19th century opaque and often satinized art glass of graduated color which shades from red or rose to yellow or pale blue or white

**peach borer** *n* **1 :** PEACH TREE BORER **2 :** the larva of a large beetle (*Dicerca divaricata*) of the family Buprestidae which bores esp. in the peach, cherry, and maple

**peach canker** *n* **:** a disease of peaches characterized by production of cankers (as those caused by fungi of the genera *Valsa* and *Sclerotinia*) — compare BROWN ROT 1a

**peach curl** *n* **:** LEAF CURL a

**peach·er·i·no** \,pēchə'rē(,)nō\ *n* -S [prob. irreg. fr. [1]*peach* + It *-ino,* dim. suffix] *slang* **:** PEACH 6

**peach family** *n* **:** ROSACEAE

**peachick** \'⸗,⸗\ *n* **:** the chick of the peafowl

**peachier** *comparative of* PEACHY

**peachiest** *superlative of* PEACHY

**peach-kernel oil** *n* **:** either of two oils obtained from peach kernels that are very similar in properties and uses to the true almond oils: **a :** a colorless or straw-colored nondrying fatty oil obtained by expression — called also *persic oil* **b :** a colorless to yellow aromatic toxic essential oil obtained by steam distillation — called also *bitter almond oil*

**peach leaf curl** *n* **:** LEAF CURL a

**peachleaf willow** \'⸗,⸗-\ *or* **peach-leaved willow** \'⸗,⸗-\ *n* **:** a willow (*Salix amygdaloides*) of the western U. S. with leaves like those of the peach or almond — called also *almond-leaved willow*

**peach lecanium** *n* **:** TERRAPIN SCALE

**peach melba** *n, sometimes cap M* [trans. of F *pêche Melba*] **:** PÊCHE MELBA

**peach mildew** *n* **:** a powdery mildew of peaches caused by a fungus (*Sphaerotheca pannosa*)

**peach moth** *n* **:** a moth having larvae that attack the peach; *esp* **:** ORIENTAL PEACH MOTH

**peach oak** *n* **1 :** WILLOW OAK **2 :** TANBARK OAK a

**peach palm** *n* **1 :** a So. American pinnate-leaved palm (*Bactris gasipaes*) with thorny stems and edible fruit **2 :** a spiny So. American palm (*Guilielma utilis*) that is prized for its hard wood and edible fruit

**peach pink** *n* **:** a moderate yellowish pink that is yellower and lighter than coral pink, yellower, lighter, and stronger than dusty pink, and redder, stronger, and slightly lighter than average peach

**peach red** *n* **:** a strong yellowish pink that is redder and darker than salmon pink, redder and deeper than melon, and yellower than madder scarlet

**peach rosette** *n* **:** a very destructive virus disease attacking peach, plum, and almond trees and characterized by the growth of dense rosettes of dwarfed leaves at the ends of the branches and by the failure to bear fruit

**peach rust** *n* **:** a fungous disease of stone fruits caused by rust fungi of the genus *Tranzschelia* (as *T. discolor* and *T. pruni-spinosae*) and attacking the peach, plum, apricot, and cherry

**peach scab** *n* **:** a fungous disease of the peach and related plants (as cherry and plum) caused by a scab (*Cladosporium carpophilum*) producing freckles on the fruit and small brown spots on the leaves and twigs — called also *cherry scab, plum scab*

**peach scale** *n* **:** any of several scales infesting peach trees: as **a :** a large dark-colored hemispherical scale (*Lecanium persicae*) **b :** a flatter and lighter-colored scale (*Pseudaulacaspis pentagona*)

**peach silver mite** *n* **:** an eriophyid mite (*Aculus cornutus*) that is a pest on peach trees

**peach tan** *n* **:** a light reddish brown that is lighter, stronger, and slightly redder than copper tan and yellower, lighter, and stronger than monkey skin or peach bisque

**peach tip moth** *n* **:** an olethreutid moth (*Carpocapsa molesta*) having a larva that damages twigs and fruit of cherry, peach, and some other fruit trees

**peach tree bark beetle** *n* **:** PEACH BARK BEETLE

**peach tree borer** *n* **:** any of several moth larvae that are destructive to peach trees, boring in the wood usu. near ground level; *esp* **:** a white brown-headed grub that is the larva of a blue-black orange-marked clearwing moth (*Sanninoidea exitiosa*) and that attacks peach and other stone fruit trees in much of eastern No. America — see LESSER PEACH TREE BORER, WESTERN PEACH BORER

**peach twig borer** *n* **:** the larva of a small gelechiid moth (*Anarsia lineatella*) that bores into the smaller twigs of the peach and other fruit trees

**peach wart** *n* **:** a virus disease of the peach characterized by leathery or hard outgrowths of fruit tissue that at first are bleached and later tan or reddish, that appear esp. near the style end where they frequently form patterns like rings or are clustered, and that may exhibit russeting

**peach weevil** *n* **:** a large curculio (*Ithycerus noveboracensis*) that attacks the buds and twigs of the peach and oak

**peachwood** \'⸗,⸗\ *n* **:** a brazilwood (*Caesalpinia echinata*)

**peachy** \'pēchē, -chi\ *adj, sometimes* -ER/-EST **1 :** resembling a peach ⟨~ cheeks and slender figure —Edmund Wilson⟩ **2 :** unusually fine **:** DANDY ⟨airedales were ~ dogs —J.T. Farrell⟩ ⟨thinks things are pretty ~ as they are —J.R.Newman⟩

**peach yellows** *n pl but usu sing in constr* **:** a destructive virus disease of the peach producing yellowing or browning and curling up of the leaves, dwarfing of the branches, the growth of willowlike sterile shoots, dwarfing and premature ripening of fruit, and in a few years death

**pea coal** *n* **:** anthracite coal of a small size — see ANTHRACITE table

**pea coat** *n* [*pea* (as in *pea jacket*) + *coat*] **:** PEA JACKET

[1]**pea·cock** \'pē,⸗\ *n* [ME *pecok, pocok,* fr. *pe-* (fr. OE *pēa* peafowl) & *po-* (fr. OE *pāwa* peafowl) + *cok* cock; akin to Fris *pau* peafowl, OS *pāo,* OHG *pfāwo,* ON *pāi;* all fr. a prehistoric WGmc-NGmc word borrowed fr. L *pavon-, pavo* peacock, prob. of imit. origin like Gk *taōs* peacock — more at COCK] **1** *pl also* **peacock :** a male peafowl distinguished by a crest of upright plumules and by greatly elongated loosely webbed upper tail coverts that are mostly tipped with ocellate spots and are erected and spread at will in a fan shimmering with iridescent color; *broadly* **:** PEAFOWL — see INDIAN PEACOCK, JAPANNED PEACOCK, JAVAN PEACOCK **2 :** one making a proud or arrogant display of himself ⟨the poodles were the ~*s* of the local dog show⟩; *esp* **:** a vainglorious person ⟨would take the young ~ down a peg —Marguerite Steen⟩ **3** *or* **peacock blue :** a variable color averaging a moderate greenish blue that is greener and deeper than Brittany or average colonial blue and deeper and slightly greener than larkspur — called also *paon* **4 :** PEACOCK BUTTERFLY

[2]**peacock** \"\ *vb* -ED/-ING/-S *vt* **1 :** to cause to be like a peacock (as in vainglorious display) ⟨he may have ~*ed* it a bit, he supposed he did —William Humphrey⟩ ⟨attempted to ~ his way through the world —C.S.Bluemel⟩ **2** *slang Austral* **:** to pick out or buy the choicest pieces of (land) esp. by the use of dummies ~ *vi* **:** to make a vainglorious display (as in gait, dress, speech) **:** POSE, STRUT ⟨all the girls . . . were ~*ing* in their bustles —Flora Thompson⟩ ⟨my father ~*ing* about on the lawn —Osbert Sitwell⟩

**peacock bittern** *or* **peacock heron** *n* **:** SUN-GREBE

**peacock blue** *n* **:** any of several bright blue pigments; *esp* **:** a clear fugitive lake made from Azure Blue AEG and used chiefly in printing inks — see DYE table I (under *Pigment Blue 24*); compare PEACOCK 3

**peacock butterfly** *n* **:** any of several butterflies having ocellate spots on the wings: as **a :** a widespread European butterfly (*Nymphalis io*) **b :** BUCKEYE 4

**peacock coal** *n* **:** coal (as anthracite) with iridescent films on broken surfaces

**pea·cock·ery** \'⸗,⸗ərē\ *n* **:** the dress or mannerism of a fop **:** ostentatious display ⟨his vanity is extreme but . . . he has no ~ —John Gunther⟩ ⟨designs ranged from elaborate ~ to sexy sheaths of black sequins —*Time*⟩

**peacock flounder** *n* **:** a large West Indian flounder (*Platophrys lunatus*) that is dark olive covered with bright blue spots

**peacock flower** *n* **1 :** ROYAL POINCIANA **2 :** PRIDE OF BARBADOS

**peacock green** *n* **:** a moderate yellowish green that is greener and stronger than tarragon, deeper than malachite green, and deeper and slightly yellower than verdigris

**peacock iris** *n* **:** an ornamental South African herb (*Moraea pavonia*) having orange-red flowers with a black spot at the base of each perianth segment

**pea·cock·ish** \'⸗,⸗ish\ *adj* **:** resembling a peacock **:** FLAMBOYANT, OSTENTATIOUS — **pea·cock·ish·ly** *adv* — **pea·cock·ish·ness** *n* -ES

**peacock moth** *n* **:** EMPEROR MOTH

**peacock ore** *n* **:** a mineral consisting of an iridescent variety of copper ore: as **a :** BORNITE **b :** CHALCOPYRITE

**peacock pheasant** *n* **:** any of several showy Asiatic pheasants of the genus *Polyplectron* having in the male two or three spurs on the leg, erectile tail coverts, and brilliantly ocellated plumage

**peacock's-tail** \'⸗,⸗,⸗\ *n, pl* **peacock's-tails :** a widely distributed tropical alga (*Padina pavonia*) with fan-shaped fronds

**pea·cocky** \'pē,käkē\ *adj* -ER/-EST **1 :** PEACOCKISH ⟨a decidedly ~ horse in the ring⟩ **2 :** exhibiting a showy air

**pea comb** *n* **:** a comb of a gallinaceous bird (as a Brahma fowl) consisting of three low weakly serrated and usu. partly fused crests side by side of which the middle one is the highest — see COMB illustration

**pea crab** *n* **:** a minute commensal crab of the family Pinnotheridae living in bivalve mollusks; *esp* **:** a European crab (*Pinnotheres pisum*) found in mussels and cockles and regarded as a great delicacy — compare OYSTER CRAB

**pea dove** *n* **:** the zenaida dove of Jamaica

**pea family** *n* **:** LEGUMINOSAE

**pea finch** *n, Brit* **:** CHAFFINCH

**pea flower** *n* **1 :** the flower of the pea **2 :** any flower of the papilionaceous type

**peafowl** \'pē,⸗\ *n* [*pea-* (as in *peacock*) + *fowl*] **:** a very large terrestrial pheasant (genus *Pavo*) of southeastern Asia and the East Indies that occurs chiefly in the open woodland and at the margins of cultivated areas and is often reared as an ornamental fowl — see PEACOCK, PEAHEN

**peag** *also* **peage** \'pēg\ *or* **peak** \-ēk\ *n* -S [Narraganset *wampompeag* — more at WAMPUM] **:** WAMPUM

**pea-gall** \'⸗,⸗\ *n* **:** a small gall on rosaceous plants caused by gall wasps of the genus *Rhodites*

**pe·age** \'pāij\ *n* -S [ME *payage,* fr. MF *paiage,* fr. ML *pedaticum, pedagium,* fr. L *ped-, pes* foot + *-aticum* -age or ML *-agium* (alter. of L *-aticum*) — more at FOOT] *archaic* **:** toll for passage

**pea·goose** \'pē,⸗\ *or* **peak·goose** \'pēk,⸗\ *n* [obs. E *peke* simpleton + *goose*] *obs* **:** a poor simpleton **:** NINNY

**pea green** *n* **:** a variable color averaging a moderate yellow-green that is greener, lighter, and stronger than average moss green, greener and lighter than mosstone, and lighter and slightly stronger than spinach green

**pea grit** *n* **:** PISOLITE

**peahen** \'pē,⸗\ *n* [ME *pehenne, pohenne,* fr. *pe-* (fr. OE *pēa* peafowl) & *po-* (fr. OE *pāwa* peafowl) + *henne* hen — more at PEACOCK, HEN] **:** a female peafowl

**pea huller** *n* **:** VINER 1

**pe·ai** \pē'ī\ *or* **pe·ai·man** \-īmən\ *n, pl* **peais** *or* **peaimen** [*peai* fr. Galibi *piaye; peaiman* fr. *peai* + *man*] **:** a medicine man of the Indian peoples of northeastern So. America

**pea jacket** \'pē,⸗⸗\ *n* [by folk etymology fr. D *pijjekker,* fr. *pij,* a kind of coarse cloth, a coat made of this material (fr. MD *pie*) + *jekker* jacket] **:** a heavy woolen double-breasted jacket that is straight-hanging and hip-length and is worn chiefly by seamen — called also *pea coat*

pea jacket

[1]**peak** \'pēk\ *vi* -ED/-ING/-S [origin unknown] **1** *obs* **:** to go about quietly or dejectedly **:** be spiritless ⟨I, a dull and muddy-mettled rascal ~ . . . and can say nothing —Shak.⟩ **2 :** to acquire sharpness of figure or features **:** grow thin **:** look wan or sickly ⟨the new baby was due next month, and its mother inclined to ~ —Margery Sharp⟩ **3 :** to dwindle away **:** FADE, PETER — often used with *out* ⟨before long the game began to ~ —T.A.G.Hungerford⟩ ⟨the little business they had started finally ~*ed* out⟩

[2]**peak** \"\ *n* -S [prob. alter. (perh. influenced by *beak*) of [1] and [3]*pike*] **1 :** a pointed or projecting part of a garment: as **a** *obs* **:** the pointed front of a woman's headdress **b :** the visor of a cap or hat **:** BILL ⟨by way of salutation, jerked the ~ of his cap —George Seddon⟩ **2 :** a jut of land **:** PROMONTORY **3 a :** sharp or pointed end **:** a projecting point ⟨the ~*s* of the roof —Fiske Kimball⟩ **4** *obs* **:** a pointed beard **5 a** (1) **:** the top of a hill or mountain **:** one of the crests of a mountain or mountain range **:** SUMMIT ⟨where pines . . . look out towards ~*s* that tower in the distance —Laurence Binyon⟩ ⟨the fog hung . . . heavily on the ~ of the hill —H.D.Skidmore⟩ (2) **:** a whole hill or mountain esp. when isolated **b :** something resembling a mountain peak ⟨the clouds are piled . . . in frothy white ~*s* —Claudia Cassidy⟩ ⟨beat steadily . . . until the frosting will form ~*s* when the beater is lifted —Marjorie M. Heseltine & Ula M. Dow⟩ **6 a** (1) **:** the upper aftermost corner of a fore-and-aft sail esp. when extended by a gaff (2) **:** the upper end of the gaff **b** (1) **:** AFTERPEAK (2) **:** FOREPEAK **c :** the bill of an anchor **7 a :** the very top **:** PINNACLE **:** the highest level or greatest degree (as of efficiency or excellence) **:** ULTIMATE ⟨his vocal control was at its ~ when he did the recording —Paul Hume⟩ ⟨the illusion of setting and atmosphere was carried to its ~ —W.P.Eaton⟩ ⟨none of them attained the highest ~*s* of the Greek genius —G.A.L.Sarton⟩ **b :** a high point in a course of development esp. as represented or capable of representation on a graph ⟨the community prospered . . . reaching its ~ of prosperity and population about 1840 —*Amer. Guide Series: Maine*⟩ ⟨regularize employment and reduce ~*s* and

valleys —*N.Y.Times*⟩ ⟨here for the ~ of the season —A.L. Himbert⟩ **c :** the highest point to which prices rise in a given period **8 :** a point formed by the hair on the forehead — called also *widow's peak* **9 :** the maximum value of a periodically varying quantity during a cycle (as of voltage or current): as **a :** the strongest part of an electronic communications signal **b :** the maximum signal recorded on a volume indicator in a broadcasting studio **10 :** the most sonorous part of a syllable (as a vowel or a syllabic consonant)

**³peak** \"\ *vb* -ED/-ING/-S *vi* **1 :** to rise or extend to a peak or point **:** form or appear as a peak ⟨beat egg whites until they ~ —D.L.Bolinger⟩ **2 :** to reach a maximum (as of capacity, value, or activity) ⟨a firm whose business ~*s* from July to December —*N.Y.Times*⟩ ~ *vt* **1 :** to cause to come to a peak or point ⟨pursed her pretty lips and ~*ed* her eyebrows — Marcia Davenport⟩ **2 :** to bring to a maximum ⟨stores ~ spring stocks too late —*Women's Wear Daily*⟩ **3 :** to adjust (as an electronic communication circuit) so as to cause a signal to have a maximum or a higher value

**⁴peak** \"\ *adj* **:** reaching the maximum of capacity, value, or activity ⟨the factories of all countries going at ~ productivity —*Current Biog.*⟩ ⟨the street at ~ hours is congested with traffic —*Amer. Guide Series: La.*⟩

**⁵peak** \"\ *vt* -ED/-ING/-S [*apeak*] **1 :** to set nearer the perpendicular (as a gaff or yard) **2** *of a whale* **:** to raise (as tail or flukes) straight up in the air in diving vertically ⟨the interesting motion known as ~*ing* flukes —R.L.Cook⟩ **3 :** to tilt up to a perpendicular or nearly perpendicular position; *esp* **:** to hold (oars) with blades well raised

**⁶peak** \"\ *dial var of* PIQUE

**⁷peak** *var of* PEAG

**peak arch** *n* **:** a pointed or Gothic arch

**peak crest** *n* **:** a pointed crest on the head (as of various pigeons) — distinguished from *shell crest*

**¹peaked** \'pēkt, -kəd, *dial* 'pikəd\ *adj* [ME *peked*, alter. of *piked* — more at PIKED] **:** having a peak **:** rising to or ending in a peak **:** POINTED ⟨pointed to the ~ ceiling —Erle Stanley Gardner⟩ ⟨the ~ hills of the islands —William Black⟩

**²peak·ed** \'pēkəd, *dial* 'pikəd\ *adj* [fr. past part. of ¹*peak*] **:** looking pale and wan **:** SICKLY, THIN ⟨the boy looked sallow and ~, slept uneasily —Aldous Huxley⟩ ⟨they were smiling, but . . . both looked a little ~ —Ellery Queen⟩

**peaked·ness** \'pēk(t)nəs, -kədn-\ *n* -ES **:** the quality or state of being peaked; *specif* **:** the degree to which conditions that constitute a peak in a frequency curve are present

**peaked roof** *n* **:** a roof of two or more slopes rising to a ridge

**peak·er** \'pēkə(r)\ *n* -S **1 :** a load of logs narrowing toward the top **2 :** the top log of a load

**peak-fresh** \'ˌ=ˈ=\ *adj* **:** having reached but not passed the optimum stage of maturity for use — used of fruits and vegetables

**peakgoose** *var of* PEAGOOSE

**peaking** *adj* [fr. gerund of ¹*peak*] **1** *dial Eng* **:** MEAN, SNEAKING **2** *dial Eng* **:** ²PEAKED

**peak load** *n* **:** the maximum load carried during a given period (as by a railroad, telegraph line, power plant, pumping station) ⟨the person who uses the highways only on such days as . . . Labor Day makes a marginal contribution to the *peak load* — W.H.Anderson⟩

**peaks** *pres 3d sing of* PEAK, *pl of* PEAK

**peak voltmeter** *n* **:** an instrument for measuring the maximum voltage during an alternating current cycle — called also *crest voltmeter*

**¹peaky** \'pēkē\ *adj* -ER/-EST [²*peak* + -*y*] **1 :** having a peak or peaks **:** marked by peaks ⟨crossed the ~ ridge⟩ **2 :** POINTED, SHARP ⟨a ~ face⟩

**²peaky** \"\ *adj* -ER/-EST [²*peaked* + -*y*] **:** PEAKED, SICKLY ⟨he was a small boy, nine at most, and ~ —Margery Allingham⟩

**³peaky** \"\ *var of* PECKY

**¹peal** \'pēl, *esp before pause or consonant* -ēəl\ *n* -S [ME *pele* appeal, summons to church by bell-ringing, short for *appel, apel, apele* appeal — more at APPEAL] **1 a :** the loud ringing of bells ⟨the ~ of victory won —*Bull. of Bates Coll.*⟩ **b** (1) **:** a complete set of changes on a given number of bells; *esp* **:** the series on seven bells usu. with the tenor struck at the end of each change ⟨each tower ~ took three hours —*Christian Science Monitor*⟩ — compare TOUCH 12 (2) **:** a shorter performance than a full peal **c :** a set of bells tuned to the tones of the major scale for change ringing ⟨the original bells . . . will be melted down and recast into another ~ —Sylvia Gray⟩ **2 :** a loud sound or succession of sounds ⟨send him into ~*s* of laughter —H.A.Overstreet⟩ ⟨heavy ~*s* of thunder —W.J.Humphreys⟩ ⟨the loud ~ of the doorbell —Agnes S. Turnbull⟩ — **in peal** *adv* **:** in rhythmic and melodic order in change ringing

**²peal** \"\ *vb* -ED/-ING/-S *vi* **:** to utter or give out peals **:** RESOUND ⟨silvery laughter ~*ed* against the ceiling —Frank Yerby⟩ ⟨the bells in the parish churches . . . began ~*ing* —*Saturday Rev.*⟩ ~ *vt* **1** *obs* **:** to assail or din (as the ear) with sound ⟨nor was his ear less ~*ed* with noises loud and ruinous —John Milton⟩ **2 :** to utter or give forth loudly **:** sound forth in a peal **:** noise abroad ⟨~*ed* his ideas through all the neighborhood⟩ ⟨~*ed* a high C on the trumpet⟩

**³peal** \"\ *vb* -ED/-ING/-S [ME *pelen*, short for *apelen, appelen* to appeal — more at APPEAL] *dial Eng* **:** APPEAL

**⁴peal** \"\ *n* -S [origin unknown] *Brit* **:** GRILSE

**pea leaf miner** *n* **:** a leaf miner that is the larva of an agromyzid fly (*Liriomyza bryoniae*) and that tunnels in celery, spinach, and similar plants esp. in California

**peale's falcon** \'pē(ə)lz-\ *n, usu cap P* [after Titian R. *Peale* †1885 Am. naturalist] **:** a medium-sized hawk of western No. America that constitutes a dark variety (*Falco peregrinus pealei*) of the duck hawk — compare PEREGRINE FALCON

**pealike** \'ˌ=ˌ=\ *adj* **1 :** resembling a garden pea esp. in size, firmness, and shape ⟨a palpable ~ mass under the skin⟩ **2 a :** resembling a plant of the genus *Lathyrus* or that of such a plant ⟨a ~ pod⟩ ⟨~ vines⟩ **b** *of a flower* **:** showy and papilionaceous

**peal ringing** *n* [¹*peal*] **:** CHANGE RINGING

**peameal** \'ˌ=ˌ=\ *n* **:** meal made from ground dried peas and used to coat cured meats ⟨~ bacon⟩

**pea mildew** *n* **1 :** either of two fungous diseases attacking peas: **a :** one caused by a powdery mildew (*Eripiphe polygoni*) **b :** one caused by a downy mildew (*Peronospora viciae*) **2 :** a fungus causing pea mildew

**pea moth** *n* **:** a small dark moth (*Laspeyresia nigricana*) of the family Olethreutidae whose larva feeds in pea pods destroying the seeds and that is native to Europe but is now a major pest in No. American commercial plantings

**¹pean** *var of* PAEAN

**²pean** \'pēn\ *n* -S [MF *pene*, lit., feather, fr. L *penna* — more at PEN] **:** a heraldic fur consisting of ermine spots of gold on a black field

**³pean** \"\ *adj* **:** of the heraldic fur pean

**⁴pean** *var of* PEEN

**¹pea·nut** \'pē(ˌ)nət, *usu* -əd·+V\ *n* [¹*pea* + *nut*] **1 a :** a low branching annual herb (*Arachis hypogaea*) that has slightly hairy stems, bijugate leaves, and showy yellow flowers initially sessile but with a hypanthium which elongates and bends into the soil where the ovary ripens into a reticulated usu. constricted indehiscent pod containing one to three edible seeds and that is prob. native to Brazil but is cultivated in most tropical and many mild temperate regions for its oily seeds and as forage **b :** the seed of the peanut either enclosed in its papery husk and outer pod or freed from these — see PEANUT BUTTER, PEANUT OIL **2 :** FLAX 3 **3 :** an insignificant, petty, or tiny person ⟨shows a lot of strength for such a ~⟩ — often used disparagingly **4 peanuts** *pl* **a :** something small, inconsequential, or of little value ⟨the rush of westward traffic was ~*s* to what the roads will be handling late this summer —*Time*⟩ ⟨total volume of business . . . is so small that I used to call it ~*s* —W.M.Mason⟩ **b :** a very petty sum of money usu. in comparison to the total amount involved ⟨compared to present prices . . . I was getting ~*s* —John Lardner⟩ ⟨persuading big names to appear for ~*s* in his productions —Al Hine⟩

**²peanut** \"\ *adj* **:** characterized by smallness or insignificance **:** MEAN, PETTY ⟨~ politicians —*New Republic*⟩ ⟨no time for congress to be dawdling over ~ legislation —*Newsweek*⟩ ⟨I haven't got all day for this ~ case — Douglass Welch⟩

**peanut butter** *n* **:** a paste made by grinding roasted, skinned, and degermed peanuts

**peanut cactus** *n* **:** a cactus (*Chamaecereus silvestrii*) of So. America that forms clumps of cylindrical joints resembling a peanut in shape and is used as an ornamental

**peanut gallery** *n* **:** the upper balcony of a theater

**peanut oil** *n* **:** a colorless to yellow nondrying fatty oil obtained from peanuts and used chiefly as a salad oil, in margarine, in soap, and as a vehicle in pharmaceutical preparations and cosmetics — called also *arachis oil*

**peanut shaker** *n* **:** an implement attached to a tractor for freeing the vines from soil as peanuts are dug

**peanut tube** *n* **:** a small vacuum tube

**peanut worm** *n* **:** SIPUNCULID

**pea ore** *n* **:** limonite occurring in round grains about the size of a pea

**peapod** \'ˌ=ˌ=\ *n* **:** a clinker-built open double-ended boat used for fishing in Maine

**¹pear** \'pa(a)(ə)r, 'pe\|, \|a\ *n* -S [ME *pere*, fr. OE *pere, peru*, fr. L *pirum*, of non-IE origin; akin to the source of Gk *apios* pear tree, *apion* pear] **1 :** the fleshy oblong pome fruit of a tree of the genus *Pyrus* (esp. *P. communis*) that is generally larger at the apical end and has grit cells throughout the flesh — compare APPLE **2 :** a tree that bears pears

**²pear** \'pi(ə)r, -iə\ *vi* -ED/-ING/-S [ME *peren*, short for *aperen, apperen* — more at APPEAR] *now dial* **:** APPEAR

**pear bark beetle** *n* **:** a small beetle (*Scolytus rugulosus*) whose larva bores under the bark of the pear and other fruit trees (as the peach, plum, apple)

**pear blight** *n* **1 :** FIRE BLIGHT **2 a** *also* **pear blight beetle :** a minute beetle (*Anisandrus pyri*) whose larvae bore in the twigs of pear and other hardwood trees **b :** a mealybug (*Pseudococcus adonidum*)

**pear blister mite** *n* **:** PEAR LEAF BLISTER MITE

**pear borer** *n* **1 :** the larva of a small clearwing moth (*Thamnosphecia pyri*) that is similar to the peach-tree borer but smaller and that bores beneath the bark of the pear **2 :** the larva of a beetle (*Chrysobothris femorata*) of the family Buprestidae that attacks apple, pear, oak, and maple trees **3 :** the larva of a related European beetle (*Agrilus sinuatus*) that bores under the bark making zigzag galleries

**pearce·ite** \'pir,sīt\ *n* -S [Richard *Pearce* †1927 Eng. metallurgist + E -*ite*] **:** a mineral $Ag_{16}As_2S_{11}$ consisting of a monoclinic silver and arsenic sulfide

**pear drop** *n* **:** a drop (as a jewel or a candy) that is shaped like a pear

**pear-drop** \'ˌ=ˌ=\ *adj* [*pear drop*] **:** having the shape of a pear — used of handles on furniture and also of supports for small arches employed in place of pillars in the 18th century

**pear fruit chafer** *n* **:** BUMBLE FLOWER BEETLE

**pear haw** *or* **pear hawthorn** *n* **:** any of several American hawthorns (as *Crataegus tomentosa*) with somewhat pyriform fruit

**pea rifle** *n, chiefly dial* **:** a muzzle-loading rifle having a thick barrel and firing a ball about the size of a pea

**¹pearl** \'pərl, *esp before pause or consonant* 'pər·əl; 'pəl, 'pəil\ *n* -S [ME *perle*, fr. MF, fr. (assumed) VL *pernula*, dim. of L *perna* haunch, ham, sea mussel attached to the ocean floor by a peduncle shaped like a ham; akin to OE *fyrsn*, *fiersn* heel, OS *fersna*, OHG *fersana*, Goth *fairzna* heel, Gk *pternē* heel, hip, Skt *pārṣṇi* heel] **1 a** (1) **:** a dense concretion that is formed in various mollusks by deposition of thin concentric layers of nacre about a foreign particle within or beneath the mantle and is free from or attached to the shell, that occurs in various forms but is typically more or less round, that exhibits various colors but is usu. white or light-colored, and that has various degrees of luster — see CULTURED PEARL (2) **:** SIMULATED PEARL **b pearls** *pl* **:** a necklace of pearls **2 :** MOTHER-OF-PEARL **3 :** one that is very choice or precious **:** the finest or noblest of its kind **:** a supreme rarity ⟨enunciated this ~ of wisdom —J.C.Snaith⟩ ⟨learned from him one tale which is a ~ of price —H.J.Laski⟩ **4 :** something resembling a pearl intrinsically or physically: as **a** *dial Eng* **:** a whitish film on the eye **:** CATARACT **b :** a small round globule (as a teardrop or dewdrop) ⟨~*s* of dew glistened on the grass⟩ **c :** one of the tubercles forming the burr on an antler — usu. used in pl. **d :** white shining teeth ⟨a red lip, with two rows of ~ beneath —Lord Byron⟩ **e :** one of several small white or silver balls on a coronet **f :** a small piece, fragment, or size esp. of coal or of molten metal cooled by being dropped in water **g :** a small white circle on a colored ground (as on a postage stamp) **h :** ¹PERLE **i :** one of a succession of beads or small bosses used ornamentally (as on the edge of a piece of furniture) **5 :** an old size of type (approximately 5 point) between diamond and agate **6 a :** SHELL TINT **b** *or* **pearl blue** *or* **pearl white :** a nearly neutral slightly bluish medium gray that is lighter than battleship gray — called also *granite blue, moonbeam* **7 :** TALL OAT GRASS **8** *dial Eng* **:** TERN **9 :** one of the rounded concentric masses of squamous epithelial cells characteristic of certain tumors

**²pearl** \"\ *vb* -ED/-ING/-S [ME *perlen*, fr. *perle*, n.] *vt* **1 :** to set or adorn with pearls or with mother-of-pearl **2 :** to sprinkle or bead with pearly drops ⟨sweat ~*ed* his forehead —William DuBois⟩ ⟨morning dew ~*ed* the garden⟩ **3 :** to form esp. by machine into small round grains ⟨~ barley⟩ **4 :** to give a pearly color, luster, or radiance to ⟨his mind was still ~*ed* with . . . roseate ideals —Francis Hackett⟩ ~ *vi* **1 :** to form drops or beads like pearls ⟨rain ~*ed* down the window⟩ **2 :** to fish or search for pearls ⟨tried gold mining, ~*ing*, and fur trapping —*Current Biog.*⟩ **3** *of hot syrup* **:** to form small or large bubbles in boiling usu. at 220° F or a long thread without breaking when dropped from a spoon

**³pearl** \"\ *adj* [¹*pearl*] **1 :** of, relating to, or resembling pearl **:** made of or adorned with pearls or mother-of-pearl **:** having the color or luster of pearl **:** PEARLY **2 :** having grains or particles of medium size — compare PEARL BARLEY, PEARL HOMINY, PEARL TAPIOCA

**⁴pearl** \"\ *n* -S [alter. of *purl*] **1** *Brit* **:** one of a series of tiny loops forming a decorative edging usu. on ribbon or lace **:** PICOT **2 :** ¹PURL 5

**⁵pearl** \"\ *vt* -ED/-ING/-S *Brit* **:** to finish (an edge) with picot

**pearl ash** *n* **:** POTASSIUM CARBONATE a; *esp* **:** an impure product obtained by partial purification of potash from wood ashes

**pearl barley** *n* **:** barley ground into small round pellets

**pearl blush** *n* **:** a brownish pink to light grayish brown — called also *rosetan*

**pearlbush** \'ˌ=ˌ=\ *n* **:** a Chinese ornamental shrub (*Exochorda racemosa*) with lanceolate leaves and racemes of white flowers

**pearl-coated** \'ˌ=ˈ=ˌ=\ *adj* **:** coated to resemble a pearl usu. in whiteness or smoothness — used esp. of pills

**pearl cotton** *n* **:** a mercerized cotton yarn for needlework (as embroidery)

**pearl crescent** *n* **:** a nymphalid butterfly (*Phyciodes tharos*) common in eastern No. America

**pearl danio** *n* **:** a small lustrous cyprinid fish (*Brachydanio albolineatus*) that is often kept in the tropical aquarium

**pearl disease** *n* **:** tuberculosis of serous membranes (as the pleura or peritoneum) with lesions in small rounded grayish elevations and appearing chiefly in cattle — called also *pearly disease*

**pear leaf blister mite** *n* **:** an eriophyid mite (*Eriophyes pyri*) that attacks the young leaves of pear trees — called also *pear blister mite*

**pearled** \-ld\ *adj* [ME *perled*, fr. past part. of *perlen* to pearl — more at PEARL] **1 :** set or adorned with pearls or mother-of-pearl ⟨the fancy vest, the ~ revolver —A.B.Guthrie⟩ **2 :** formed into, covered, or filled with drops ⟨the gossamer . . . ~ with the morning dew —Sir Walter Scott⟩ ⟨a ~ sea-mist —William Sansom⟩ ⟨~ with women's tears —J.G.Neihardt⟩ **3 :** formed into grains like pearls **4 :** resembling a pearl in color or luster **:** PEARLY ⟨the ~ splendor of the moonlit scene⟩

**pearl edge** *n* [⁴*pearl*] **:** a very narrow edging or ribbon with tiny loops on one or both sides

**pearl·er** \-lə(r)\ *n* -S **1 a :** a person that dives for pearls **b :** one that employs pearl divers **c :** a boat used in pearl fishing **2 :** BARLEY PEARLER **3 :** a worker that uses a special tool on a vertical lathe to decorate watch pillar plates with an interlocking ring design

**pearl·es·cent** \ˌpər'les°nt\ *adj* [¹*pearl* + -*escent*] **:** having the appearance of mother-of-pearl ⟨our swanlike necks should be swathed in ~ beads and other glitter —Lois Long⟩

**pearl essence** *n* **1 :** a translucent substance containing guanine and constituting the silvery coloring matter of the scales of various fish (as the bleak or herring) that is used in making artificial pearls and also lacquers and plastics — compare ESSENCE D'ORIENT **2 :** a synthetic translucent substance (as crystallized mercuric chloride)

**pearl·et** \ˌpər¦let, 'pərlət\ *n* -S [¹*pearl* + -*let*] **:** a small pearl

**pearl eye** *n* **1 :** PEARLY EYE **2 :** a bird's eye (as of a pigeon) suggestive of a pearl — **pearl-eyed** *adj*

**pearlfish** \'ˌ=ˌ=\ *n* **1** [so called fr. its inhabiting the mantle cavity of the pearl oyster] **:** a fish of the family Carapidae and esp. of the genus *Carapus* **2 :** PEARLSIDES **3 :** any of various cyprinoid and clupeoid fishes having scales which yield pearl essence

**pearl glue** *n* **:** glue in the form of beads or pellets

**pearl grain** *n* **:** CARAT GRAIN

**pearl gray** *n* **1 :** a yellowish gray to light gray **2 :** a variable color averaging a pale blue that is redder and paler than Sistine or average powder blue and redder and lighter than baby blue (sense 2)

**¹pearl harbor** \ˌ=ˈ=ˌ=\ *n, usu cap P&H* [fr. *Pearl Harbor*, Oahu, Hawaii, Am. naval station attacked without warning by the Japanese on Dec. 7, 1941] **:** a sneak attack usu. with devastating effect ⟨remove the possibility of atomic *Pearl Harbors* —Bertrand Russell⟩

**²pearl harbor** \"\ *vt, usu cap P&H* [¹*Pearl Harbor*] **:** to attack suddenly without warning and usu. with devastating effect ⟨got to thinking of the danger of being *Pearl Harbored* —*Time*⟩

**pearl hominy** *n* **:** hominy milled to pellets of medium size

**pearlies** *pl of* PEARLY

**pearl·i·ness** \'pərlēnəs, 'pəl-, 'pəil-, -lin-\ *n* -ES **:** the quality or state of being pearly ⟨that faint blue haze . . . that almost imagined ~ against the distant hills —S.E.White⟩

**pearl·ing** *or* **pearl·in** \'pərlən, -liŋ\ *n* -S [⁴*pearl* + -*ing* or -*in* (alter. of -*ing*)] **1** *chiefly Scot* **:** a lace of silk or thread **2 pearlings** *pl, chiefly Scot* **a :** trimmings made of pearling **b :** clothes trimmed with pearling **c :** PEARLS 1b

**pearl·ite** \'pər,līt\ *n* -S [F *perlite*, fr. *perle* pearl + -*ite* — more at PEARL] **1 :** the lamellar mixture of ferrite and cementite in the microstructure of slowly cooled iron-carbon-base alloys occurring normally as a principal constituent of both steel and cast iron **2 :** PERLITE — **pearl·it·ic** \ˌ=ˈlid·ik\ *adj*

**pearl·ized** \'pər,līzd\ *adj* **:** having the appearance of mother-of-pearl ⟨a tiara of ~ orange blossoms —*Springfield (Mass.) Daily News*⟩ ⟨hats . . . of white ~ straw with straight brims — *New Yorker*⟩

**pearl kite** *n* **:** WHITE-TAILED KITE

**pearl lamp** *n* **:** an electric lamp having the inside of the glass frosted

**pearl millet** *n* **1 :** a tall cereal grass (*Pennisetum glaucum*) that is prob. of East Indian origin, is grown in Africa and Asia for its seeds and in the U.S. chiefly for forage, and has long broad leaves and dense round spikes like those of the cattail — called also *bulrush millet, cattail millet* **2 :** COMMON SORGHUM

**pearl moss** *n* **:** CARRAGEEN

**pearl mussel** *n* **:** a freshwater mussel producing pearls or mother-of-pearl

**pearl onion** *n* **:** a very small onion resembling a pearl in size and used pickled in appetizers and as a garnish

**pearl opal** *n* **:** CACHOLONG

**pear louse** *n* **:** PEAR PSYLLA

**pearl oyster** *n* **:** any of several large marine bivalve mollusks of the genera *Avicula* and *Pinctada* (esp. *P. margaritifera*) that often produce pearls, differ from the ordinary oyster in having a byssus, and are found chiefly in the East Indies (as at Ceylon), in the Persian gulf, on the northern coasts of Australia, and on the Pacific coast of America

**pearl perch** *n* **:** EPAULET FISH

**pearl pink** *n* **:** a variable color averaging a pale yellowish pink

**pearl plant** *n* **1 :** GROMWELL **2 :** CORN GROMWELL

**pearls** *pl of* PEARL, *pres 3d sing of* PEARL

**pearl shell** *n* **:** a nacreous or pearl-bearing shell **:** PEARL OYSTER

**pearl shell·er** \'ˌ=ˌshelə(r)\ *n* **:** a fisher for pearl shells

**pearlsides** \'ˌ=ˌ=\ *n, pl* **pearlsides :** a small silvery isospondylous fish (*Maurolicus pennanti*) with several rows of luminous organs like pearls on the head and body that is widely distributed in the North Atlantic

**pearl sinter** *n* **:** geyserite of pearly luster

**pearlspar** *n* **:** a dolomite with a pearly luster

**pearlstone** \'ˌ=ˌ=\ *n* **:** PERLITE

**pearl tapioca** *n* **:** tapioca formed during processing into pellets that retain their shape in cooking but swell

**pearl-twist** \'ˌ=ˌ=\ *n* **:** an orchid of the genus *Speranthes* — usu. used in pl.

**pearl ware** *n* **:** an improved white variant of queensware introduced by Josiah Wedgwood in 1779

**pearl white** *n* **1 :** any of several white or pearly white substances: as **a :** bismuth subnitrate esp. when used in cosmetics or ceramics **b :** bismuth oxychloride esp. when used as a pigment or in cosmetics **c :** a nacreous preparation (as of mother-of-pearl or pearl essence) used in imitating pearls **2 :** PEARL 6b

**pearlwort** *also* **pearlweed** \'ˌ=ˌ=\ *n* **:** a plant of the genus *Sagina* resembling chickweed

**¹pearly** \'pərlē, 'pəl-, -pəil-, -li\ *adj* -ER/-EST [ME *peerly*, fr. *perle* pearl + -*y* — more at PEARL] **1 :** having the appearance of a pearl or of mother-of-pearl (as in luster, shape, texture) ⟨a ~ complexion that was the envy of her companions⟩ **2 :** containing a pearl or mother-of-pearl ⟨~ oyster⟩ **3 :** adorned or set with pearls or mother-of-pearl ⟨loved her ~ Juliet cap⟩ **4 :** highly precious **:** rare and beautiful ⟨in the delicate etching with which he makes the daughter shine with a kind of ~ virginity —Marjory S. Douglas⟩ **5 :** having the color of pearl ⟨his teeth of a ~ whiteness —Mary W. Shelley⟩ **6 :** having a pear-shaped tone ⟨crooning ~ high notes —*Time*⟩

**²pearly** \"\ *adv* **:** in a way suggesting a pearl (as in luster, color, texture) ⟨~ white satin⟩

**³pearly** \"\ *n* -ES *Brit* **1 :** clothing heavily ornamented or sometimes nearly covered with pearl buttons and worn by costermongers on special occasions **2 :** COSTERMONGER

**pearly disease** *n* **:** PEARL DISEASE

**pearly everlasting** *n* **:** an American everlasting (*Anaphalis margaritacea*) having floccose-woolly herbage and small corymbose heads with pearly white scarious involucres

**pearly eye** *n* **1 :** any of several satyrid butterflies of the genus *Lethe* (esp. *L. portlandia*) **2 :** ocular lymphocytomatosis of poultry — called also *pearl eye*

**pearly gate** *n* **:** one of the 12 gates of heaven — usu. used in pl. and in allusion to Rev 21:21

**pearly nautilus** *n* **:** NAUTILUS 1a

**pearly tumor** *n* **:** CHOLESTEATOMA

**pear midge** *n* **:** a minute gall midge (*Contarinia pyrivora*) which lays its eggs in the flower buds of the pear and whose larvae destroy the developing fruits

**pear molding** *n* **:** KEEL MOLDING

**pearmonger** *n, obs* **:** a pear seller ⟨you are as pert as a ~ this morning —Jonathan Swift⟩

**pear oil** *n* **:** either of two esters: **a :** ISOAMYL ACETATE **b :** AMYL ACETATE a

**pear psylla** *also* **pear tree psylla** *n* **:** a yellowish or greenish jumping plant louse (*Psylla pyricola*) that is often destructive to the pear — called also *pear louse*

**pears** *pl of* PEAR, *pres 3d sing of* PEAR

**pear sawfly** *n* **:** PEAR SLUG

**pear scab** *n* **:** a disease of the pear caused by a fungus (*Venturia pyrina*) that is similar to apple scab but produces lesions more frequently on the twigs

**pear scale** *n* **:** any of several scales which infest pear trees

**pear-shaped** \'ˌ=ˌ=\ *adj* **1 :** having an oval shape markedly tapering at one end **2** *of a vocal tone* **:** free from harshness, thinness, or nasality **:** FULL, MELLOW, ROUNDED

**pear shell** *n* **:** FIGSHELL 1

**pear slug** *n* **:** a sluglike caterpillar that is the larva of a sawfly (*Caliroa cerasi*), that feeds on the foliage of the pear and cherry trees, and that has a wide distribution in both New and Old Worlds

**pearsonian coefficient of correlation** \(')pir¦sōnēən-\ *usu cap P* [*pearsonian* fr. Karl *Pearson* †1936 Eng. scientist + E -*an*] **:** CORRELATION COEFFICIENT

**peart** \'pi(ə)r|t, -iə|, *usu* |d.+V\ *adj, sometimes* -ER/-EST [alter. of *pert*] *chiefly South and Midland* : LIVELY, CHIPPER ⟨sleep well and wake up ~ —Ellen Glasgow⟩ — **peart·ly** *adv*

**peart·en** \|tᵊn\ *vb* -ED/-ING/-S *vt, chiefly dial* : to make peart or cheerful — usu. used with *up* ~ *vi, chiefly dial* : to become peart or cheerful — usu. used with *up* ⟨when he ~*ed* up, we all took fresh heart —H.E.Giles⟩

**pear thrips** *n* : a destructive thrips (*Taeniothrips inconsequens*) native to Europe that attacks the buds and young fruits of prune, cherry, pear, and almond trees

**pear tomato** *n* : a tomato with pear-shaped fruit that is usu. considered to constitute a distinct variety (*Lycopersicon esculentum pyriforme*)

**pearwood** \'≈,≈\ *n* : the wood of any pear; *esp* : the wood of a white pear (*Pterocelastrus rostratus*)

**peas** *pl of* PEA

**¹peas·ant** \'pezᵊnt\ *n* -S [ME *paissaunt*, fr. MF *paisant*, fr. OF *paisant*, fr. *pais* country — more at PAYSAGE] **1** : one of a chiefly European class that tills the soil as small free landowners or hired laborers ⟨burgesses, ~*s* . . . have borne arms indistinguishable from those of the nobility —D.L.Galbreath⟩ **2** *obs* : a rascally person : SCAMP ⟨thou shalt know I will predominate over the ~ —Shak.⟩ **3** : a rather uneducated uncouth person in the low income group ⟨nobody gave a thought to the rest of us ~*s* —Bernard Taper⟩ ⟨she was a complete ~ when she came here —Margery Allingham⟩

**²peasant** \"\ *adj* **1 a** : of or relating to peasants : having the status of a peasant ⟨the conservative ~ ideas of . . . immigrants —Oscar Handlin⟩ ⟨most . . . were ~ stock whose descendants today hold important positions —*Amer. Guide Series: Minn.*⟩ **b** : based upon and characterized by a simple agricultural economy ⟨Asian ~ societies⟩ **2** : of or resembling the designs in the clothing of peasants ⟨a very pretty girl in a ~ blouse —Calvin Tompkins⟩ **3** : relating to native culture or art : produced by native craftsmen ⟨lacking . . . any marked tradition of decorative ~ art —Charles Marriott⟩ ⟨~ wares were often so cheap —W.E.Cox⟩

**peasant blue** *n* : a grayish blue that is redder and darker than electric, greener and deeper than copenhagen or old china, and redder and deeper than Gobelin

**peas·ant·ize** \-ᵊnt,īz\ *vt* -ED/-ING/-S : to make peasants of : cause to resemble peasants ⟨you cannot ~ a common people who have been educated in their vocations —*Rev. of Reviews*⟩

**peasantlike** \'≈≈,≈\ *adj* : of, relating to, or characteristic of a peasant

**peasantly** *adj, obs* : of, relating to, or characteristic of a peasant ⟨their ~ throats —Sir Walter Scott⟩

**peasant proprietor** *n* : a peasant who owns the soil he cultivates

**peas·ant·ry** \'pezᵊntrē, -ri\ *n* -ES **1** : PEASANTS : a body of peasants ⟨the ~ of this unhappy country have never been much more than slaves —Darrell Berrigan⟩ ⟨the rich ~ of that region rose —F.M.Stenton⟩ **2** : the state, position, or rank of a peasant : the quality or behavior of a peasant ⟨as a gentleman, you could have never descended to such ~ of language —Samuel Butler †1680⟩

**peas·anty** \-ᵊntē, -ti\ *adj* : having or suggesting a peasant manner or style ⟨the ~ English countryside of the Georgian short story —Naomi Lewis⟩ ⟨a small crowd . . . garishly dressed in ~ clothes —Ann Bridge⟩

**¹pease** \'pēz\ *n, pl* **peases** [ME *pese* — more at PEA] *chiefly Brit* : PEA — archaic except in attrib. use

**²pease** \"\ *pl of* PEA

**peasecod** *or* **peascod** \'≈,≈\ *n* [ME *pesecod*, fr. *pese* pea + *cod* — more at PEA, COD (husk)] **1** : a pea pod **2** : the stuffed or quilted front of a 16th century doublet extending to a point below the waistline

**pease crow** *n, dial Eng* : TERN

**peas·en** *also* **peas·on** \'pēzᵊn\ *dial chiefly Brit pl of* PEASE

**pease porridge** *n* [¹*pease*] : PEA SOUP

**pease pudding** *n* [¹*pease*] : a pudding made of cooked and strained split peas and eggs boiled in a cloth or mold

**peaseweep** *or* **peasweep** *var of* PEESWEEP

**pea·sey hut** \'pēzē-\ *n* [*peasey* alter. of *pisé*] : a construction of rammed earth

**pea-shoot** \'≈,≈\ *vb* [back-formation fr. *peashooter*] *vt* : to shoot peas at ⟨*pea-shooting* pigeons from an attic window⟩ ~ *vi* : to shoot with a peashooter

**peashooter** \'≈,≈≈\ *n* [¹*pea* + *shooter*] **1** : a toy blowgun for shooting peas **2** *slang* : a small caliber pistol ⟨a burglar carrying a little ~ like that —William Norsworthy⟩

**pea shrub** *n* : PEA TREE

**pea soup** *n* **1** : a thick soup made of dried green or yellow peas usu. pureed **2** *or* **pea-souper** : a heavy dull yellow fog ⟨a wall of the thickest *pea soup* I had ever seen —H.A.Chippendale⟩

**pea-soupy** \'≈¦≈≈\ *adj* [*pea soup* + *-y*] : resembling pea soup ⟨the *pea-soupy* January evening —Robert Benton⟩

**peas porridge** *n* [alter. of *pease porridge*] : PEA SOUP

**peas pudding** *n* [by alter.] : PEASE PUDDING

**pea-stick** \'≈,≈\ *n* : a long stake or branch upon which garden peas are trained ⟨cutting down the green young branches for *pea-sticks* —Georgianna Bruce⟩

**peastone** \'≈,≈\ *n* : PISOLITE

**¹peat** \'pēt, *usu* -ēd+V\ *n* -S *often attrib* [ME *pete*, fr. ML *peta*, perh. of Celt origin; akin to W *peth* thing — more at PIECE] **1** : a piece of turf cut for use as fuel ⟨in a moment he had the ~*s* in the grate blazing —Elizabeth Goudge⟩ **2** : a mass of partially carbonized vegetable tissue formed by partial decomposition in water of various plants and esp. of mosses of the genus *Sphagnum*, widely found in many parts of the world, varying in consistency from a turf to a slime, and used as a fertilizer, as stable litter, as a fuel, and for making charcoal

**²peat** \"\ *n* -S [origin unknown] : a bold gay woman ⟨a pretty ~ —Shak.⟩ ⟨you were always a proud, undaunted ~ of a lass —Henrietta Keddie⟩

**peat bank** *n* : a place from which peat is cut

**peat bog** *or* **peat moor** *n* : a bog containing peat : an accumulation of peat

**peat coal** *n* **1** : a natural product intermediate between peat and lignite **2** : an artificial fuel made by carbonizing peat

**peat·ery** \'pēd·ərē\ *n* -ES **1** : PEAT BANK **2** : PEAT BOG

**peat fiber** *n* : finely chopped roots and rootstocks of various wild ferns used for potting orchids

**peat gas** *n* : gas made by carbonizing peat

**peat hag** *n* : ground from which peat has been cut

**peat machine** *n* : a machine for grinding and briquetting peat

**peat·man** \'pētmən\ *n, pl* **peatmen** : a digger or seller of peat

**peat moss** *n* **1** : any moss from which peat has formed or may form; *specif* : SPHAGNUM **2** *chiefly Brit* : PEAT BOG

**pea tree** *n* : any of several plants of the family Leguminosae; *esp* : an Asiatic tree of the genus *Caragana* (as Chinese pea tree)

**peat-reek** \'≈,≈\ *n* **1** : the smoke of burning peat ⟨when I get a sniff of wood smoke it makes me sick with longing for *peat-reek* —John Buchan⟩ **2 a** : the peculiar flavor of whiskey distilled over peat as fuel **b** : whiskey made in this manner

**peat scours** *n pl* : acute copper-deficiency disease of New Zealand sheep and cattle marked by severe persistent diarrhea and occurring esp. in animals pastured on peaty land

**peat soil** *n* : a soil consisting largely of peat and consequently rich in humus and of acid reaction

**peat spade** *n* : a spade with an L-shaped blade for cutting out peat in blocks

**peatwood** *or* **peatweed** \'≈,≈\ *n* : SWAMP LOOSESTRIFE

**peaty** \'pēd·ē\ *adj* -ER/-EST : of, resembling, or containing peat

**peau d'ange** \(')pō¦dāⁿzh\ *n* [F, lit., angel skin] **1** : a dull waxy smooth finish usu. used for crepes, satins, and lace **2** : a fabric with a finish of peau d'ange

**peau de soie** \¦pōdə¦swä\ *n* [F, lit., skin of silk] : a silk or rayon dress fabric with a smooth satiny texture and a fine ribbed or grained surface

**pea·vey** *or* **pea·vy** *or* **pe·vey** *or* **pe·vy** \'pēvē\ *n, pl* **peaveys** *or* **peavies** *or* **peevies** *or* **pevies** [prob. fr. the name *Peavey*] : a stout lever used in lumbering that is like a cant hook but has the end armed with a strong sharp spike

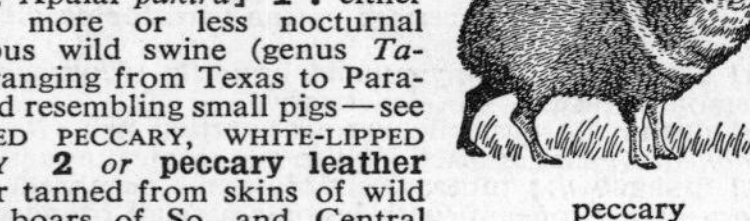

peavey

**peavine** \'≈,≈\ *n* : any of various usu. twining American herbaceous leguminous plants: as **a** : the vine of the common edible pea or of the cowpea esp. when stripped of pods and used for hay **b** : AMERICAN VETCH **c** : a locoweed (*Astragalus emoryanus*) of the Big Bend area of Texas

**peavine clover** *n* : ZIGZAG CLOVER

**pea weevil** *n* **1** : a small weevil (*Bruchus pisorum*) that destroys peas by eating out the interior **2** : a European weevil (*Sitones lineatus*) that feeds on the leaves of peas

**peba** \'pebə\ *n* -S [Pg, fr. Tupi *tatupeba*, fr. *tatu* armadillo + *peba* flat] : a small armadillo (*Dasypus novemcinctus*) having nine movable bands of scutes and ranging from Texas to Paraguay

**¹peb·ble** \'pebəl\ *n* -S [ME *pibbil, puble, pobble*, fr. OE *papolstān*, fr. *papol-* stone (prob. of imit. origin) + *stān* stone] **1 a** : a small usu. round stone esp. when worn and rounded by the action of water **b** : one of the pieces in a mass of material obtained in a form resembling pebbles ⟨lime ~*s*⟩ **2 a** : transparent and colorless quartz : ROCK CRYSTAL ⟨Brazilian ~⟩ **b** : a rough gem sometimes found in a stream ⟨delighted to find a small ~ of agate⟩ **3** : PEBBLEWARE **4 a** *also* **pebble leather** (1) : leather that has been pebbled (2) : the surface on the leather produced by pebbling **b** : an irregular, crinkled, or grainy surface on a fabric produced by fancy weaves or finishing processes **c** : a formation of tiny protuberances produced on the surface of a curling rink by sprinkling water on the ice **5** : FLAX 3

**²pebble** \"\ *vt* **pebbled; pebbled; pebbling** \-b(ə)liŋ\ **pebbles 1** : to pelt with or as if with pebbles ⟨teased the dog by *pebbling* it with acorns⟩ **2** : to pave or cover with pebbles or something resembling pebbles ⟨cookies . . . fat ones with white sugar *pebbling* the surface — Warren Eyster⟩ **3** : to grain (as leather or paper) so as to produce a rough and irregularly indented surface **4** : to produce pebble on (a curling rink)

**pebble cast** *n* : a cast or casting of pebbles esp. from the sea

**peb·bled** \-bəld\ *adj* [¹*pebble* + *-ed*] : containing, covered, or strewn with pebbles or something resembling pebbles ⟨areas of sandstone . . . as well as ~ plains —W.G.East⟩

**pebble dash** *n* : ROCK DASH

**pebble gravel** *n* : gravel with pebbles between 4 and 64 millimeters in diameter

**pebble mill** *n* : a rotating cylinder in which usu. hard rounded stones or flint pebbles grind ceramic materials to extreme fineness

**pebble powder** *n* : gunpowder or black powder pressed and cut into large cubical grains so as to make it slow-burning

**peb·bler** \-b(ə)lə(r)\ *n* -S **1** : one who pebbles leather by hand or by machine **2** : one who pebbles a curling rink

**pebblestone** \'≈≈,≈\ *n* [ME *pibbil ston, publestone*, fr. OE *papolstān* — more at PEBBLE] : PEBBLE 1

**pebbleware** \'≈≈,≈\ *n* : a variety of Wedgwood ware having a mottled surface produced by mingling colored pastes in the body of the pottery

**peb·bly** \-b(ə)lē, -li\ *adj, sometimes* -ER/-EST : containing or resembling pebbles : PEBBLED ⟨chuckled over its ~ bed or plunged down in little waterfalls —Margaret Deland⟩ ⟨done in ~ navy wool —Lois Long⟩

**pé·brine** \(')pā¦brēn\ *n* -S [F, fr. Prov *pebrino*, fr. *pebre* pepper, fr. L *piper* — more at PEPPER] : a contagious disease of the silkworm and other caterpillars produced by a microsporidian protozoan (*Nosema bombycis*) — **peb·ri·nous** \'pebrənəs\ *adj*

**PEC** *abbr, often not cap* photoelectric cell

**pe·can** \pə'kän, -'kan,-'kaa(ə)n,-'kän, (')pē¦k-; *sometimes* 'pēkən\ *n* -S [fr. earlier *paccan*, of Algonquian origin; akin to Ojibwa *pagân* any hard-shelled nut, Abnaki *pagann*, Cree *pakan*] **1** : a hickory (*Carya illinoensis*) of the south central U.S. having roughish bark and hard but brittle wood, sometimes attaining great size, and producing an edible nut **2** : the wood of the pecan tree **3** : the smooth oblong thin-shell nut of the pecan tree

**pecan brown** *n* : GOLDEN CHESTNUT

**pecan carpenter worm** *n* : a worm that is the larva of a cossid moth (*Cossula magnifica*) and that bores in the twigs, branches, and trunk of pecan, oak, and hickory

**pecan nut casebearer** *n* : a grub that is the larva of a moth (*Acrobasis caryae*) and that feeds on various hickories and walnuts

**pecan scab** *n* : a disease of the pecan caused by a fungus (*Cladosporium effusum*) and characterized by the smoky superficial growth of the fungus on leaves, twigs, and nuts

**pecan weevil** *n* : a weevil (*Curculio caryae*) that attacks hickory and pecan nuts esp. in the southern U.S.

**pec·a·ri** \'pekə,rē\ [NL, fr. F *pécari* peccary, of Cariban origin like E *peccary* — more at PECCARY] *syn of* TAYASSU

**pec·ca·bil·i·ty** \,pekə'biləd·ē, -lətē, -i\ *n* : the quality or state of being peccable : capability of sinning ⟨the common ~ of mankind —Henry More⟩

**pec·ca·ble** \'pekəbəl\ *adj* [MF, fr. L *peccare* to sin + MF *-able* — more at PECCANT] : liable or prone to sin : susceptible to temptation ⟨a frail and ~ mortal —Sir Walter Scott⟩

**pec·ca·dil·lo** \,pekə'di(,)lō\ *n, pl* **peccadilloes** *or* **peccadillos** [Sp *pecadillo*, dim. of *pecado* sin, fr. L *peccatum*, fr. neut. of *peccatus*, past part. of *peccare* to sin] : a slight offense : a petty fault ⟨lapses and ~*es* —Herbert Askwith⟩ ⟨the sexual ~*es* of a bygone time —Edmund Fuller⟩

**peccan** *or* **peccane** *archaic var of* PECAN

**pec·can·cy** \'pekənsē, -nsi\ *n* -ES [LL *peccantia*, fr. L *peccant-*, *peccans* (pres. part. of *peccare*) + *-ia* *-y*] **1** : the quality or state of being peccant ⟨horrible exultation at the universal ~ of husbands —George Meredith⟩ **2** : OFFENSE, FAULT ⟨his trivial *peccancies* —Carl Van Vechten⟩

**pec·cant** \'pekənt\ *adj* [L *peccant-*, *peccans*, pres. part. of *peccare* to stumble, commit a fault, sin, prob. fr. (assumed) L *peccus* having an injured foot, stumbling, fr. L *ped-*, *pes* foot — more at FOOT] **1** : guilty of a moral offense : SINNING, CORRUPT ⟨~ humanity —*Saturday Rev.*⟩ ⟨imposing severe . . . discipline in public on ~ parishioners —*Times Lit. Supp.*⟩ ⟨~ corporations —*Times Lit. Supp.*⟩ **2** : violating a principle or rule (as of taste or propriety) : FAULTY ⟨intervene to save the ~ poet —George Saintsbury⟩ **3** : DISEASED, UNWHOLESOME ⟨by the lopping of a ~ member the body is saved from decay —John Austin⟩ ⟨capable of sloughing off its ~ parts —K.L. Bates⟩

**pec·ca·ry** *also* **pec·a·ri** *or* **pec·a·ry** \'pekərē\ *n, pl* **peccaries** *also* **pecaris** *or* **pecaries** [of Cariban origin; akin to Chayma *paquera* peccary, Apalai *pakirâ*] **1** : either of two more or less nocturnal gregarious wild swine (genus *Tayassu*) ranging from Texas to Paraguay and resembling small pigs — see COLLARED PECCARY, WHITE-LIPPED PECCARY **2** *or* **peccary leather** : leather tanned from skins of wild peccary boars of So. and Central America and used chiefly for gloves

peccary

**pec·ca·vi** \pe'kä(,)vē *sometimes* -kā,vī\ *n* -S [L, I have sinned] : a humble acknowledgment of sin or error : CONFESSION ⟨chanting their ~*s* —*Saturday Rev.*⟩

**pech** *var of* PEGH

**pech·an** \'pekən\ *n* -S [origin unknown] *dial Scot* : STOMACH, GULLET

**pechay** *n* -S [Sp, fr. Tag *petsay*, fr. Chin *pe²ts'ai⁴*] : CHINESE CABBAGE

**pêche mel·ba** \'pēch'melbə, 'pesh-,'pash-\ *n, pl* **pêches melba** \,pēchəz'm-, 'pesh'm-, 'pāsh'm-\ *usu cap M* [F, lit., Melba peach] : half a peach filled with cream set on a bed of vanilla ice cream and covered with raspberry sauce

**pecheneg** *usu cap, var of* PETCHENEG

**¹peck** \'pek\ *n* -S [ME *pek*, fr. OF] **1 a** : either of two units of dry capacity equal to ¼ bushel: (1) : a U.S. unit equivalent to 537.605 cubic inches (2) : a British unit equivalent to 554.84 cubic inches — see MEASURE table **b** : the quantity measured by a peck **c** : a container used as a peck measure **2** : a large quantity or number ⟨a ~ of trouble⟩ ⟨a ~ of dirt⟩ ⟨a ~ of uncertainties and doubts —John Milton⟩

**²peck** \"\ *vb* -ED/-ING/-S [ME *pecken*, alter. of *piken* to pierce — more at PICK] *vt* **1 a** : to strike, pierce, or make holes in (as wood) with or as if with quick movements of the beak ⟨~*ed* the tree all morning⟩ **b** : to kiss in a quick perfunctory fashion ⟨she ~*ed* his forehead —John Galsworthy⟩ **2** : to pick up (as food) with the beak ⟨give the hens a feed of whole grain . . . to ~ and peck over —Emily Holt⟩ — often used with *up* ⟨watching hens . . . ~ up the pulps from the sand —Lillian Smith⟩ **3 a** : to make or produce by repeated strokes of the beak or of a pointed tool ⟨the group of elk were ~*ed* out . . . on a rocky monolith —W.D.Hartley⟩ ⟨figures . . . ~*ed* into the rock —F.H.H.Roberts⟩ **b** : to shape (stone) by striking or abrading with a hammerstone ⟨stone was . . . ~*ed* and ground into cylindrical pestles —A.C.Spaulding⟩ ~ *vi* **1 a** : to strike, pierce, or pick up something with repeated small blows or movements with or as if with a beak — often used with *at* ⟨a hen that ~*s* all day⟩ ⟨~*ed* at the hard ground with a pickaxe⟩ **b** : to deliver a series of petty and repeated blows — usu. used with *at* ⟨left hand ~*ed* . . . at the old fighter's eyes —Donn Byrne⟩ ⟨there wasn't any use just ~*ing* at them —J.P.Marquand⟩ **c** : CARP, SCOLD, NAG — usu. used with *at* ⟨my wife keeps *peckin'* at me —H.L.Davis⟩ **d** : to strike the keys esp. of a typewriter or piano with quick downward thrusts of the fingers — usu. used with *at* ⟨started ~*ing* at the keys —Eleanor Bayer⟩ ⟨~*ing* away at the yellowed keys —Frank Brookhouser⟩ **2 a** : EAT ⟨wants to know if you'll ~ with us —Richard Dehan⟩ **b** : to bite daintily : NIBBLE — usu. used with *at* ⟨~*ed*, without enthusiasm, at a lamb chop —P.B.Kyne⟩

**³peck** \"\ *n* -S **1** : FOOD, GRUB 3 **2** : an impression or hole made by pecking **3 a** : an act of pecking : a quick sharp stroke (as with the beak of a bird or a pointed instrument) **b** : a kiss like a bird's peck ⟨leaned down to give her a brief ~ on the cheek —Louis Auchincloss⟩ **4** : PECKINESS

**⁴peck** \"\ *vb* -ED/-ING/-S [alter. of *pick* (to pitch)] *vt, chiefly dial* : PITCH, FLING, JERK ~ *vi, of a horse* : to stumble as a result of landing on the toe after taking a jump ⟨~*ed* badly, but recovered and won by a head —Adrian Bell⟩

**⁵peck** *dial var of* PICK

**peck·ed** \'pekəd, -kət\ *adj* [by alter.] *chiefly dial* : PEAKED

**peck·er** \'pekə(r)\ *n* -S [²*peck* + *-er*] **1** : one that pecks: as **a** : an instrument for pecking (as a pick) **b** : WOODPECKER **c** : a bird's bill **2 a** : NOSE **b** *chiefly Brit* : COURAGE, SPIRITS — used chiefly in the phrase *keep one's pecker up* ⟨one thing . . . helped to *keep the pecker up* during the journey —P.G. Wodehouse⟩ **3** : PENIS — often considered vulgar

**peck·er·wood** \'pekə(r),wu̇d\ *n* [inversion of *woodpecker*] **1** *South* : WOODPECKER **2** *South & Midland* : CRACKER 5a **3** : PECKERWOOD MILL

**peckerwood mill** *or* **peckerwood sawmill** *n, chiefly South* : a small usu. portable sawmill characterized by slipshod equipment and operation

**peck horn** *n* [prob. fr. the name *Peck*] : MELLOPHONE

**peck·i·ness** \'pekēnəs, -kin-\ *n* -ES [*pecky* + *-ness*] : any of several diseases of the heartwood of trees caused by polypores and related fungi and characterized by lens-shaped or finger-shaped pockets of decay running with the grain — called also *dry rot, pocket dry rot*; compare PIN ROT

**peck·ish** \-kish,-kēsh\ *adj* [²*peck* + *-ish*] **1** *chiefly dial* : ready to eat : having a keen appetite : HUNGRY ⟨pork pies and what all, case they come over a bit ~ —Richard Llewellyn⟩ ⟨their swim had made them ~ —*Harper's*⟩ **2** : inclined to peck : NAGGING, IRRITABLE ⟨the old woman, in constant pain, was spiteful and ~ —Jean Stafford⟩

**¹peck·le** \'pekəl\ *n* -S [alter. of *speckle*, n.] *dial Brit* : SPOT, SPECK

**²peckle** \"\ *vt* -ED/-ING/-S [by alter.] *dial Brit* : SPECKLE

**peckled** *adj* [by alter.] *chiefly dial* : SPECKLED

**peck order** *also* **pecking order** *n* [trans. of G *hackordnung*] **1** : the basic pattern of social organization within a flock of poultry in which each bird is permitted to peck another lower in the scale without fear of retaliation and is expected to submit to pecking by one of higher rank and in which separate peck orders usu. exist for each sex with all the males normally dominating all the females — compare HOOK ORDER **2** : a hierarchy of social dominance, prestige, or authority ⟨got to the top of the *pecking order* in their own town —Margaret Mead⟩ ⟨the *peck order* in women's clubs, faculty groups, families, or churches —W.C.Allee⟩

**pecks** *pl of* PECK, *pres 3d sing of* PECK

**peck·sniff·ery** \'pek,snifərē\ *or* **peck·sniff·ian·ism** \pek'snifēə,nizəm\ *n, pl* **pecksniffferies** *or* **pecksniffianisms** *often cap* [*pecksniffery* fr. Seth *Pecksniff*, character in *Martin Chuzzlewit* (1843–44) by Charles Dickens †1870 Eng. novelist + E *-ery*; *pecksniffianism* fr. *pecksniffian* + *-ism*] : the quality or state of being pecksniffian ⟨the national ~ —H.L.Mencken⟩

**peck·sniff·ian** \(')pek¦snifēən\ *adj, often cap* [Seth *Pecksniff* + E *-ian*] : marked by unctuous hypocrisy : selfish and corrupt behind a display of seeming benevolence : SANCTIMONIOUS, HOLIER-THAN-THOU ⟨~ cant⟩ ⟨legislation designed to correct injustice and to translate ~ phrases into living realities —*Nation*⟩ ⟨a censorship that is . . . ~ suppression —*Springfield (Mass.) Union*⟩

**pecky** \'pekē\ *also* **peaky** \'pēkē\ *adj* -ER/-EST [³*peck* + *-y*] **1** : marked by peckiness — used esp. of lumber; see PECKY CYPRESS **2** : containing discolored and shriveled grains ⟨~ rice⟩

**pecky cypress** *n* : cypress lumber affected by peckiness that is very durable in damp ground and is much used in greenhouse benches and in ornamental work (as paneling)

**pecky dry rot** *n* : PECKINESS

**pe·cop·ter·is** \pə'käptərəs\ *n, cap* [NL, fr. Gk *pekein* to comb + NL *-pteris* — more at FEE] : a genus of Carboniferous fossil ferns characterized by a regular arrangement of the leaflets resembling a comb

**pe·cop·ter·oid** \-,rȯid\ *adj* [NL *Pecopteris* + E *-oid*] : like or related to the genus *Pecopteris*

**pec·o·ra** \'pekərə\ *n pl, cap* [NL, fr. L, cattle, pl. of *pecor-*, *pecus* cattle, herd; akin to L *pecu* cattle, *pecud-*, *pecus* head of cattle, Gk *pekos* fleece — more at FEE] : a division of Artiodactyla equivalent to the suborder Ruminantia with the chevrotains and their extinct related forms excluded

**pec·o·ri·no** \,pekə'rē(,)nō, *attrib* ¦≈≈¦≈≈\ *or* **pecorino cheese** *n, pl* **pecorinos** *also* **pecori·ni** \,≈≈'≈(,)nē\ *often cap P* [It, fr. *pecorino* of ewes, fr. *pecora* ewe, sheep (fr. L *pecora* cattle) + *-ino* -ine] : romano cheese made of ewe's milk

**pe·cos** \'pākəs\ *n, pl* **pecos** *usu cap* **1** : a Tanoan people formerly occupying a pueblo in New Mexico **2** : a member of the Pecos people

**pec·tase** \'pek,tās, -āz\ *n* -S [ISV *pect-* (fr. *pectin*) + *-ase*; prob. orig. formed in F] : PECTINESTERASE

**pec·tate** \-āt\ *n* -S [ISV *pect-* (fr. *pectic*) + *-ate*; prob. orig. formed in F] : a salt or ester of a pectic acid

**pec·ten** \'pektən\ *n* [NL *pectin-*, *pecten*, fr. L, comb, pubic hair, pubic bone, scallop — more at PECTINATE] **1** *pl* **pectens** \-tənz\ *also* **pecti·nes** \-tə,nēz\ : any of various animal body parts resembling a comb in structure: as **a** : a vascular pigmented membrane in the eyes of nearly all birds and many reptiles that has parallel plications suggesting the teeth of a comb and that projects into the vitreous humor of the eye from the point of entrance of the optic nerve **b** *archaic* : PUBIS **c** : one of a pair of appendages of a scorpion that are located on the underside of the body behind the legs and are thought to be sensory organs **d** : an arrangement of bristles on the respiratory tube of a mosquito larva resembling a comb **e** : a series of modified bristles forming a part of the stridulating organ of some spiders **2 a** *cap* : a genus (the type of the family Pectinidae) of marine bivalve mollusks including the common market scallops — see BAY SCALLOP, SEA SCALLOP **b** -S : any mollusk of this genus; *broadly* : a mollusk of the suborder Pectinacea

**pec·tic** \'pektik\ *adj* [F *pectique*, fr. Gk *pēktikos* coagulating, fr. *pēktos* coagulated (fr. *pēgnynai* to fix, coagulate) + *-ikos* -ic — more at PACT] : of, relating to, or derived from pectin

**pectic acid** *n* [F *acide pectique*] : any of the pectic substances composed mostly of colloidal polymeric galacturonic acids and essentially free from methyl ester groups

**pectic substance** *n* : any of a group of complex colloidal carbohydrate derivatives of plant origin containing a large proportion of units derived from galacturonic acid and subdivided into protopectins, pectins, pectinic acids, and pectic acids

**pec·tin** \'pektən\ n -s [F *pectine*, fr. *pectique* pectic + *-ine* -in] **1 :** any of the group of colorless amorphous methylated pectic substances occurring in plant tissues or obtained by restricted treatment of protopectin (as with protopectinase or acids) that are found in or obtained esp. from fruits or succulent vegetables, that yield viscous solutions with water and when combined with acid and sugar in proper concentration yield a gel constituting the basis of fruit jellies, and that on hydrolysis yield pectic acids and methanol; *esp* **:** a pectinic acid containing at least 7 to 8 percent methyl ester groups expressed as methoxyl **2 :** a product containing mostly pectin obtained as a powder or syrup (as by extraction with acid of citrus peels, dried apple pomace, or dried sugar beet slices) and used chiefly in making jelly and other foods, in pharmaceutical products, and in cosmetics

**pectin-** or **pectini-** *comb form* [NL *pectin-*, *pecten* pecten] **:** comb **:** comb ⟨*pectin*oid⟩ ⟨*pectini*form⟩ ⟨*Pectini*branchia⟩

**pec·ti·na·cea** \,pektə'nāshēə\ n pl, *cap* [NL, fr. *Pectin-*, *Pecten*, type genus + *-acea*] **:** a suborder of Filibranchia comprising active bivalve mollusks that have a fan-shaped shell and no siphons including the typical pectens and related forms — **pec·ti·na·cean** \,pektə'nāsh(ē)ən\ n -s

**pec·ti·na·ceous** \¦pektə¦nāshəs\ adj **1** [*pectin* + *-aceous*] **:** of, relating to, or containing pectin **2** [NL *Pectinacea* + E *-ous*] **:** of or relating to the Pectinacea

**pec·ti·nal** \'pektənəl\ adj [LL *pectinalis*, fr. L *pectin-*, *pecten* comb, pubic bone + *-alis* -al — more at PECTINATE] **1 :** PECTINEAL **2** *obs* **:** of, relating to, or resembling a comb

**pec·tin·ase** \'pektə,nās, -āz\ n -s [ISV *pectin* + *-ase*] **:** an enzyme or complex of enzymes that catalyzes the hydrolysis of pectic substances; *esp* **:** the polygalacturonase that is active toward pectic acid

**¹pec·ti·nate** \'pektə,nāt\ *also* **pec·ti·nat·ed** \-ād·əd\ adj [L *pectinatus*, fr. *pectin-*, *pecten* comb + *-atus* -ate; akin to L *pectere* to comb, Gk *kten-*, *kteis* comb, Skt *pakṣman* eyelashes, OE *feax* head of hair — more at FEE] **:** shaped like a comb **:** having narrow parallel projections, teeth, or divisions suggestive of the teeth of a comb ⟨a ~ leaf⟩ ⟨a ~ antenna⟩ — see ANTENNA illustration — **pec·ti·nate·ly** adv

**²pectinate** \"\ n -s [*pectinic* acid + *-ate*] **:** a salt or ester of a pectinic acid

**pectinate claw** n **:** a claw found in some birds that has a serrate edge and is believed to be used in cleaning the feathers

**pec·ti·na·tel·la** \,pektə,nā'telə, -,nət-\ n, *cap* [NL, fr. L *pectinatus* pectinate + *-ella*] **:** a common genus of freshwater colonial bryozoans forming large lobate gelatinous colonies with circular or subquadrangular statoblasts having a single row of marginal hooks

**pec·ti·na·tion** \,pektə'nāshən\ n -s [*pectinate* + *-ion*] **1 :** the quality or state of being pectinate **2 :** a pectinate part or structure

**pec·tin·e·al** \(')pek¦tinēəl\ adj [NL *pectineus* + E *-al*] **:** of, relating to, or located near the pubic bone

**pectineal line** n **:** ILIOPECTINEAL LINE

**pec·tin·esterase** \¦pektən+\ n [*pectin* + *esterase*] **:** an enzyme that catalyzes the hydrolysis of pectins into pectic acids and methanol and that occurs esp. in higher plants — called also *pectase*

**pec·tin·e·us** \pek'tinēəs\ n, pl **pectin·ei** \-ē,ī, -ē,ē\ [NL, fr. *pectineus* of the pubic bone, fr. *pectin-*, *pecten* pecten + L *-eus* -eous] **:** a flat quadrangular muscle of the upper front and inner aspect of the thigh that arises mostly from the iliopectineal line of the pubis and is inserted between the lesser trochanter and a marked posterior ridge on the femur

**pec·tini·bran·chia** \,pektənə'braŋkēə, pek,tin-\ n pl, *cap* [NL, fr. *pectin-* + *-branchia*] **:** a large order of Gastropoda (subclass Streptoneura) comprising univalve mollusks that have a single kidney, have typically a single ctenidium which resembles a comb and is usu. attached to the mantle throughout its length, and have a heart with only one auricle

**pec·tini·bran·chi·a·ta** \-,braŋkē'ād·ə, -'äd·ə\ [NL, fr. *pectin-* + *branchia* + *-ata*] *syn of* PECTINIBRANCHIA

**¹pec·tini·bran·chi·ate** \¦==¦braŋkēət, =¦==-, -ē,āt\ *also* **pec·tini·bran·chi·an** \-ēən\ adj [NL *Pectinibranchia* + E *-ate* or *-ian*] **:** of, relating to, or resembling the Pectinibranchia **:** having gills that resemble combs

**²pectinibranchiate** \"\ *also* **pectinibranchian** \"\ n -s **:** a mollusk of the order Pectinibranchia

**pec·tin·ic acid** \(')pek¦tinik-\ n [*pectin* + *-ic*] **:** any of the colloidal polysaccharides of acidic nature that are obtained by partial hydrolysis of protopectins and are intermediate in methyl ester content between pectic acids and the usual pectin

**¹pec·ti·nid** \'pektənəd\ adj [NL *Pectinidae*] **:** of or relating to the Pectinidae

**²pectinid** \"\ n -s **:** a mollusk of the family Pectinidae **:** SCALLOP

**pec·tin·i·dae** \pek'tinə,dē\ n pl, *cap* [NL, fr. *Pectin-*, *Pecten*, type genus + *-idae*] **:** a family of bivalve mollusks having a single adductor muscle, comprising the pectens, and belonging to and formerly being coextensive with the suborder Pectinacea

**pec·tini·form** \pek'tinə,fórm, 'pektən-\ adj [L *pectin-*, *pecten* comb + E *-iform* — more at PECTINATE] **1 :** PECTINATE **2** [*pectin-* + *-form*] **:** resembling a scallop shell

**pectiniform septum** n **:** a fibrous septum between the corpora cavernosa

**pec·ti·nite** \'pektə,nīt\ n -s [*pectin-* + *-ite*] **:** a fossil scallop shell

**pec·tin·o·gen** \pek'tinəjən, -,jen\ n -s [*pectin* + *-o-* + *-gen*] **:** PROTOPECTIN

**pec·ti·no·lyt·ic** \¦pektənō¦lid·ik\ adj [*pectin* + hydro*lytic*] **:** producing hydrolysis of pectins

**pec·ti·noph·o·ra** \,pektə'näf(ə)rə\ n, *cap* [NL, fr. *pectin-* + *-o-* + *-phora*] **:** a genus of gelechiid moths containing the pink bollworm

**pec·tin·ous** \'pektənəs\ adj [*pectin* + *-ous*] **:** of, relating to, or containing pectin

**pec·tiz·able** \'pek,tīzəbəl\ adj **:** capable of being pectized

**pec·ti·za·tion** \,pektə'zāshən\ n -s **:** the act or process of pectizing

**pec·tize** \'pek,tīz\ vb -ED/-ING/-S [Gk *pēktos* coagulated + E *-ize* — more at PECTIC] *vt* **:** to change from a sol to a gel — compare PEPTIZE ~ *vi* **:** to undergo a change from a sol to a gel

**pec·to·cellulose** \¦pek(,)tō+\ n [*pectic* + *-o-* + *cellulose*] **:** any of several protopectins formerly regarded as combinations of pectic substances and celluloses

**pec·to·lite** \'pektə,līt\ n -s [G *pektolith*, fr. Gk *pēktos* compacted (fr. *pēgnynai* to fix, fasten) + G *-lith* -lite — more at PACT] **:** a whitish or grayish monoclinic mineral $NaCa_2Si_3O_8(OH)$ consisting of a basic sodium calcium silicate occurring in crystal aggregates or fibrous masses (hardness 5, sp. gr. 2.68–2.78)

**pec·to·lyt·ic** \¦pektə¦lid·ik\ adj [*pectic* + hydro*lytic*] **:** producing hydrolysis of pectic substances

**¹pec·to·ral** \'pekt(ə)rəl\ n -s [ME, fr. MF, fr. L *pectorale* breastplate, fr. neut. of *pectoralis* of the breast] **1 :** something worn on the breast for protection or ornament: as **a :** a breastplate or cloth worn as an ecclesiastical vestment **b :** a breastplate worn as armor **c :** PECTORAL CROSS **d** *obs* **:** ²HOUSING **2** [²*pectoral*] **:** a pectoral part or organ: as **a :** PECTORAL FIN **b :** PECTORAL MUSCLE **c :** a pectoral scale, plate, or shield

**²pectoral** \"\ adj [MF, or L; MF, fr. L *pectoralis*, fr. *pector-*, *pectus* breast + *-alis* -al; akin to Toch A *päśśäṃ* (dual) the two breasts, and perh. to OIr *hucht* breast, Skt *pakṣas* side, wing] **1 :** of, relating to, situated or occurring in or on, or worn on the chest ⟨~ arch⟩ ⟨the ~ plates of a turtle's plastron⟩ **2 :** relating to or good for diseases of the respiratory tract ⟨a ~ syrup⟩ **3 :** coming from the breast or heart as the seat of emotion or spiritual inspiration **:** SUBJECTIVE, FERVENT ⟨wildly implausible tale . . . conforms to every ~ rule of historical fiction without ever quite spinning an illusion —James Kelly⟩ ⟨the genre of the ~ historical romance —*New Yorker*⟩

**pectoral cross** n **:** a cross worn on the breast by various ecclesiastics as a mark of office

**pectoral fin** n **:** either of the fins of a fish that correspond to the forelimbs of a quadruped — see FISH illustration

**pectoral girdle** *also* **pectoral arch** n **:** the bony or cartilaginous arch supporting the forelimbs of a vertebrate that corresponds to the pelvic girdle of the hind limbs but is usu. not attached to the spinal column and that consists primitively of a single cartilage on each side which in higher forms becomes ossified, divided into the scapula above and the precoracoid and coracoid below, and complicated by the addition or substitution of one or more membrane bones and which in man is highly modified with the scapula alone of the original elements well developed, the coracoid being represented only by a process, and the precoracoid being replaced by the clavicle that connects the scapula with the sternum and is the only bony connection of the arm bones with the rest of the skeleton

**pec·to·ra·lis** \,pektə'raləs, -räl-, -rāl-\ or **pectoralis muscle** n, pl **pectora·les** \-(,)lēz\ [NL, fr. L *pectoralis* pectoral] **:** one of the muscles that connect the ventral walls of the chest with the bones of the upper arm and shoulder, in man being two in number on each side: (1) a larger that arises from the clavicle, the sternum, the cartilages of most or all of the ribs, and from the aponeurosis of the external oblique muscle, and is inserted by a strong, flat tendon into the posterior bicipital ridge of the humerus and (2) a smaller that lies beneath the larger, arises from the third, fourth, and fifth ribs, and is inserted by a flat tendon into the coracoid process of the scapula — called also respectively (1) *pectoralis major*, (2) *pectoralis minor*

**pectoral limb** n **:** either member of the anterior of the two pairs of limbs characteristic of a vertebrate (as an arm, forelimb, wing, or pectoral fin)

**pectoral ridge** n **:** a ridge on the upper ventral part of the humerus

**pectoral sandpiper** n **:** a rather small sandpiper (*Erolia melanotos*) with a thickly streaked breast that breeds in Arctic America and migrates through most of No. and So. America — called also *grass snipe*, *jacksnipe*

**pec·to·ril·o·quy** \,pektə'riləkwē\ n -ES [F *pectoriloquie*, fr. L *pector-*, *pectus* breast + *-loquium* speaking (fr. *loqui* to speak) — more at PECTORAL] **:** the sound of words heard through the chest wall and usu. indicating a cavity or consolidation of lung tissue — compare BRONCHOPHONY

**pec·tose** \'pek,tōs, -ōz\ n -s [ISV *pect-* (fr. *pectic*) + *-ose*] **:** PROTOPECTIN

**pec·tous** \'pektəs\ adj [*pectic* or *pectin* + *-ous*] **1 :** of, relating to, or consisting of protopectin or pectin **2 :** resembling a jelly esp. in consistency

**pec·tun·cu·late** \(')pek¦təŋkyələt, -,lāt\ adj [L *pectunculus* small scallop (dim. of *pectin-*, *pecten* comb, scallop) + E *-ate* — more at PECTINATE] **:** minutely pectinate

**pec·tus** \'pektəs\ n, pl **pec·to·ra** \-tərə\ [NL, fr. L, breast — more at PECTORAL] **1 :** the breast of a bird **2 :** the lower surface of the thorax or of the prothorax of an insect

**pecul** *var of* PICUL

**¹peculate** n -s [L *peculatus*, fr. past part. of *peculari* to embezzle] *obs* **:** PECULATION

**²pec·u·late** \'pekyə,lāt\ vb -ED/-ING/-S [L *peculatus*, past part. of *peculari* to embezzle, fr. *peculium* private property — more at PECULIAR] *vt* **:** to steal or appropriate wrongfully to one's own use (as public money entrusted to one's care) **:** EMBEZZLE ⟨a large sum *peculated* from the treasury⟩ ~ *vi* **:** to engage in the wrongful appropriation of money committed to one's charge ⟨the . . . chef began to ~ —Arnold Bennett⟩

**pec·u·la·tion** \,pekyə'lāshən\ n -s [LL *peculation-*, *peculatio*, fr. L *peculatus* + *-ion-*, *-io* -ion] **:** the act or practice of peculating **:** EMBEZZLEMENT ⟨the ~ of state revenue —Owen Lattimore⟩

**pec·u·la·tor** \'pekyə,lād·ə(r)\ n -s [L, fr. *peculatus* + *-or*] **:** one who peculates **:** EMBEZZLER

**¹pe·cu·liar** \pə'kyülyə(r), pē'k-\ adj [ME *peculier*, fr. L *peculiaris* of private property, owned privately, special, extraordinary, fr. *peculium* private property, peculium (fr. *pecu* cattle) + *-aris* -ar; akin to L *pecus* cattle — more at FEE] **1 a :** belonging exclusively or esp. to a person or group ⟨a ~ garb of their own⟩ ⟨a mystic belief in a ~ soil —M.R.Cohen⟩ **b** *obs* **:** owned or used privately rather than publicly or in common ⟨~ fields are turn'd to common roads —William Davenant⟩ ⟨groping for trouts in a ~ river —Shak.⟩ **2 a** *archaic* **:** SEPARATE, INDEPENDENT **b :** of or relating to an ecclesiastical jurisdiction not subject in English canon law to the ordinary of the diocese ⟨the *Peculiar* Jurisdiction of the Dean of Sarum —H.W.Jones⟩ **3 :** tending to be characteristic of one only **:** DISTINCTIVE ⟨the ~ character of the Government of the U.S. —R.B.Taney⟩ ⟨the ~ responsibility of the junior college —L.L.Medsker⟩ — often used postpositively with *to* ⟨a drowsy fervor . . . quite ~ to her —Thomas Hardy⟩ ⟨problems . . . ~ to particular segments of the engineering profession —H.A. Wagner⟩ **4 a :** different from the usual or normal **:** SINGULAR, SPECIAL, PARTICULAR ⟨a matter of ~ interest⟩ ⟨this truth comes to us with ~ shock —R.B.Heilman⟩ ⟨a man still feels it a ~ insult to be taunted with cowardice by a woman —Virginia Woolf⟩ **b :** STRANGE, CURIOUS ⟨a ~ situation⟩ ⟨said in a ~ tone —Guy Fowler⟩ ⟨feel a bit ~ —Richard Joseph⟩ **c :** ECCENTRIC, QUEER ⟨her ~ behavior⟩ ⟨all great writers have been . . . ~ —*Time*⟩ **syn** see CHARACTERISTIC, STRANGE

**²peculiar** \"\ n -s **1 :** something (as an office or place) exempt from ordinary jurisdiction **:** INDEPENDENT: as **a :** a church or parish exempt from the jurisdiction of the ordinary in whose territory it lies ⟨the Deanery . . . one of the three *Peculiars* in the Province —*Manchester Guardian Weekly*⟩ — compare ROYAL PECULIAR **b :** a piece of land, precinct, or district in the New England colonies not in any town and not constituting a town **2 :** something peculiarly one's own: as **a** *obs* **:** an exclusive quality **:** PECULIARITY **b** *obs* **:** a private or special interest **c :** an exclusive property or privilege **:** PREROGATIVE **3** *usu cap* **:** one of a religious group called the Peculiar People

**peculiar institution** n **:** Negro slavery — used formerly of slavery as an institution peculiar to the South

**pe·cu·liar·ism** \-yə,rizəm\ n -s **1** *sometimes cap* **:** the teachings or practices of Peculiars **2 :** the cult of peculiarity ⟨library ~⟩

**pe·cu·liar·i·ty** \=,kyül'yarəd·ē, -lē'a-, -rətē, -i *also* -yer- or -ē'er-\ n -ES [LL *peculiaritat-*, *peculiaritas*, fr. L *peculiaris* peculiar + *-itat-*, *-itas* -ity] **1 :** the quality or state of being peculiar **:** DISTINCTIVENESS ⟨that sweet ~ of manner . . . so much a part of herself —Jane Austen⟩ **2 :** partiality in interest or affection ⟨his regard for her seemed to have lost all its ~ —Fanny Burney⟩ **3 :** something peculiar in a person or thing **:** a distinguishing characteristic **:** a distinctive feature ⟨the intrusion of his personal *peculiarities* —Matthew Arnold⟩ ⟨all her shoes had this ~ —Ruth Park⟩ **4 :** ODDITY, QUIRK ⟨for all their tribal *peculiarities* . . . a happy people —Patrick Smith⟩

**pe·cu·liar·ize** \=¦kyülyə,rīz\ vt -ED/-ING/-S **1** *obs* **:** to assign or appropriate as exclusive **2 :** to make peculiar or distinctive **:** INDIVIDUALIZE

**pe·cu·liar·ly** adv **:** in a peculiar manner: as **a :** UNIQUELY, EXCLUSIVELY ⟨a ~ French phenomenon —D.W.Brogan⟩ ⟨dowered with some . . . combination of gifts — his own —W.F. Hambly⟩ **b :** CHARACTERISTICALLY, DISTINCTIVELY ⟨bar associations . . . ~ fitted to protect the individual —W.O. Douglas⟩ ⟨the ~ metaphysical problems . . . involved —J.E. Smith⟩ **c :** PARTICULARLY, UNUSUALLY ⟨under ~ tragic circumstances —Allen Johnson⟩ ⟨a ~ indecent form of rudeness —W.L.Alden⟩ **d :** ODDLY, STRANGELY ⟨taught ordinary subjects ~ —Richard McLaughlin⟩ ⟨~, the key to the room was under the bed —E.D.Radin⟩

**peculiar motion** n **:** the actual motion of a star after its observed proper motion and radial velocity are corrected for the effect of the sun's motion

**peculiar people** n pl [ME *peculier people*, fr. *peculier* peculiar] **1 :** God's own chosen people — used by various Christians to emphasize their nonconformity to the world **2** *cap both Ps* **:** an Evangelical Christian organization founded in England in the 19th century that holds to essentially fundamentalist doctrines and practices divine healing to the extent of refusing medical aid

**pe·cu·li·um** \=¦k(y)ülēəm\ n, pl **pecu·lia** \-ēə\ [L — more at PECULIAR] **1 :** the property held by a person (as a wife, child, slave) under the potestas, manus, or mancipium of another as his own private property either by the permission of the paterfamilias or master or by the rules of law but becoming with certain exceptions the property of the paterfamilias or master at his pleasure — compare BONA ADVENTITIA **2 :** a fund or property held by one as his own exclusive possession or for his own private use (as the salary of a Roman soldier or the separate personal property of a wife in Scotland)

**peculium ad·ven·ti·ci·um** \-,ad,ven'tikēəm, -,ven-, -tishē-\ n [LL] **:** BONA ADVENTITIA

**pe·cu·niar·i·ly** \pə¦kyünē¦erəlē, pē'k-, -ün¦ye-, -li\ adv **:** in a pecuniary manner **:** with respect to money ⟨~ profitable —*Times Lit. Supp.*⟩

**pe·cu·niary** \pə'kyünē,erē, pē'k-, -ri *also* -nyər-\ adj [L *pecuniarius*, fr. *pecunia* money + *-arius* -ary — more at FEE] **1 :** taking the form of or consisting of money ⟨the chief . . . entitled to certain regular gifts, ~ or in kind —*Notes & Queries on Anthropology*⟩ ⟨a system of ~ mulcts —J.M. Kemble⟩ **2 :** of or relating to money **:** MONETARY ⟨~ gain⟩ ⟨~ needs⟩ ⟨the ~ aims and class animosities of capitalist production —Lewis Mumford⟩ ⟨the medieval cathedrals were not built with any ~ motive —Bertrand Russell⟩

**pecuniary unit** n **:** MONETARY UNIT

**¹ped** \'ped\ n -s [ME *pedde*] *dial chiefly Eng* **:** a covered basket **:** HAMPER

**²ped** \"\ n -s [Gk *pedon* ground, earth — more at PEDION] **:** a natural soil aggregate — compare CLOD

**¹ped-** or **pedi-** or **pedo-** *comb form* [*ped-*, *pedi-* fr. L, fr. *ped-*, *pes* foot; *pedo-* fr. *ped-* + *-o-* — more at FOOT] **1 :** foot **:** feet ⟨*pedi*form⟩ ⟨*pedi*gerous⟩ ⟨*pedi*cure⟩ **2 :** a creature or object (specified) having feet or footlike projections ⟨*Pedi*astrum⟩ ⟨*ped*rail⟩ **3 :** something (specified) involving the feet ⟨*pedo*motor⟩

**²ped-** or **pedo-** *comb form* [Gk *pedon* ground, earth — more at PEDION] **:** soil ⟨*pedo*genesis⟩ ⟨*pedo*geography⟩

**³ped-** — see PAED-

**¹-ped** \,ped\ or **-pede** \,pēd\ adj *comb form* [L *-ped-*, *-pes*, *-pedus*, fr. *ped-*, *pes* foot — more at FOOT] **:** having (such or so many) feet ⟨pinni*ped*⟩ ⟨tali*ped*⟩ ⟨quadru*ped*⟩

**²-ped** \"\ or **-pede** \"\ n *comb form* -s [L *-ped-*, *-pes*, *-peda*, fr. *ped-*, *pes* foot] **:** a creature having (such or so many) feet ⟨soli*ped*⟩ ⟨centi*pede*⟩

**ped** *abbr* **1** pedal **2** pedestal **3** pedestrian

**ped·age** \'pedij\ n -s [ME, fr. ML *pedagium* — more at PEAGE] *archaic* **:** toll for passage

**ped·a·gese** or **ped·a·guese** \¦pedə¦gēz, -gēs\ n -s [*pedagogue* + *-ese*] **:** gobbledygook in the speeches or writings of educationists ⟨reads like a Fourth-of-July oration in ~ —R.M. Hutchins⟩ ⟨turgid ~ —H.M.Kallen⟩ ⟨convert ~ into lucid and workmanlike English —*Amer. Scholar*⟩

**ped·a·gog·ic** \¦pedə¦gäjik, -gōj, -gäg|, |ēk *sometimes* -gōg-\ or **ped·a·gog·i·cal** \|ə̇kəl, |ēk-\ *also* **paed·a·gog·ic** \¦pedə-\ adj [*pedagogic* fr. Gk *paidagōgikos*, fr. *paidagōgos* pedagogue + *-ikos* -ic; *pedagogical* fr. Gk *paidagōgikos* + E *-al*] **1 :** of, relating to, or befitting a pedagogue or teacher ⟨~ zeal⟩ ⟨the ~ mind⟩ ⟨tends to give a ~ tone to his discourse that makes me shrink from it —O.W.Holmes †1935⟩ **2 :** of or relating to teaching or pedagogy **:** EDUCATIONAL ⟨~ innovations⟩ ⟨the material selected . . . must have regard to our own ~ techniques —C.F.Strong⟩ ⟨contemporary . . . ~ thinking —Alfred Kähler & Ernest Hamburger⟩ — **ped·a·gog·ically** \|ə̇k(ə)lē, |ēk-, -li\ adv

**ped·a·gog·ics** \|iks, |ēks\ n pl *but sing in constr* [*pedagogy* + *-ics*] **:** the science or art of teaching **:** PEDAGOGY ⟨~ is the most revolutionary of all sciences —Alice Balint⟩ ⟨an ultramodern school of ~ —Rudolf Hirschberg⟩

**ped·a·gog·ist** \'==,gäjəst, -gōj-, ,==¦==\ n -s [perh. fr. F *pédagogiste*, fr. *pédagogie* pedagogy + *-iste* -ist] **:** a specialist in pedagogy

**ped·a·gogue** *also* **ped·a·gog** or **paed·a·gogue** \'==,gäg *sometimes* -gōg\ n -s [ME *pedagoge*, fr. MF *pedagoge*, *pedagogue*, fr. L *paedagogus*, fr. Gk *paidagōgos*, fr. *paid-* paed- + *agōgos* leader, escort, fr. *agein* to lead, drive — more at AGENT] **1 :** a teacher of children or youth **:** SCHOOLMASTER ⟨the opinion of . . . experienced ~s —Virgil Thomson⟩ ⟨a fine ~ —A.J.Liebling⟩ ⟨the mere ~ —W.S.Deffenbaugh⟩ ⟨a wooden and perfunctory ~ —John Dewey⟩ **2 a :** one (as a slave) having charge of a boy chiefly on the way to and from school in classical antiquity **b :** a youth's tutor and often traveling companion esp. in the Renaissance

**ped·a·gogy** *also* **paed·a·gogy** \'==,gäjē, -gōj, -gäg|, |i *sometimes* -gōg|\ n -ES [MF *pedagogie*, fr. Gk *paidagōgia* training, fr. *paidagōgos* + *-ia* -y] **1 :** INSTRUCTION ⟨knowledge . . . not as ~ but as gossip in the market place —A.W.Griswold⟩ **2 :** the art, science, or profession of teaching; *esp* **:** the study that deals with principles and methods in formal education **:** EDUCATION 4 ⟨convinced . . . that ~ should be recognized as one of the major "disciplines" —J.L.Childs⟩ **3** [prob. fr. L *paedogogium*, fr. Gk *paidagōgeion*, fr. *paidagōgos* pedagogue] **:** a place of instruction in medieval times **:** SCHOOL

**¹ped·al** \'ped°l\ n -s [MF *pedale*, fr. It, organ pedal, tree trunk, plant stem, fr. L *pedalis* of the foot] **1 :** a lever acted on by the foot in the playing of musical instruments: as **a** (1) **:** any of the keys of an organ keyboard played upon with the feet; *broadly* **:** PEDAL KEYBOARD (2) **:** a foot lever for drawing or shutting off one or more organ stops, for opening or shutting the swell box, or for coupling two keyboards **b :** one of the foot levers functioning as stops on a harpsichord **c** (1) **:** any of the levers used to alter the quality of or to sustain the tone of a piano (2) **:** any of the keys of a pedalier **d :** one of the seven foot levers by which the strings of a harp are stopped to raise their pitch either one or two half steps — see HARP illustration **e :** a foot lever or treadle used to pump the bellows of a reed organ **f** (1) **:** a foot lever used to change the pitch of a kettledrum quickly (2) **:** a foot lever used to beat a bass drum in a jazz orchestra **2 :** PEDAL POINT **3 :** a foot lever or treadle by which a part is activated in a mechanism (as a bicycle, loom, or sewing machine) — see BICYCLE illustration, HYDRAULIC BRAKE illustration **4** [It. *pedale*] or **pedal straw a :** the light straw from the lower portion of wheat stalks **b :** a plait made of this straw and used esp. for millinery

**²ped·al** \", 'pēd°l\ adj [L *pedalis*, fr. *ped-*, *pes* foot + *-alis* -al — more at FOOT] **1 :** of or relating to the foot **2 :** of, relating to, or involving a pedal

**³ped·al** \'ped°l\ vb **pedaled** *also* **pedalled**; **pedaled** *also* **pedalled**; **pedaling** *also* **pedalling**; **pedals** [¹*pedal*] *vi* **1 :** to use or work a pedal (as of an organ, piano, or bicycle) ⟨complimenting a pianist upon the accuracy of his . . . ~*ing* —Dudley Fitts⟩ **2 :** to ride a bicycle **:** CYCLE 2 ⟨~*ed* off . . . to summon a mason —Ida Treat⟩ ~ *vt* **:** to work the pedals of ⟨~*ing* a bicyle⟩ ⟨~*s* the garbage can —Herbert Gold⟩

**pedal board** or **pedal clavier** n [¹*pedal*] **:** a pedal keyboard esp. of a pipe organ

**pedal boat** n **:** a boat propelled like a bicycle by pedaling — see SWAN BOAT

**pedal bone** n [²*pedal*] **:** COFFIN BONE

**pedal clarinet** n **:** CONTRABASS CLARINET

**pedal coupler** n [¹*pedal*] **:** a coupling mechanism in the pipe organ to make a manual stop sound when the pedals are played

**pedal disk** n [²*pedal*] **:** the broad base by which most sea anemones attach themselves to the substrate

**pe·dal·fer** \pə'dalfə(r)\ n -s [²*ped-* + *al*umen + L *fer*rum iron — more at FARRIER] **:** a soil that lacks a hardened layer of accumulated carbonates — compare PEDOCAL — **ped·al·fer·ic** \¦pe,dal¦ferik\ adj

**pedal ganglion** n [²*pedal*] **:** either of a pair of ganglia in most mollusks that supply nerves to the muscles of the foot and that correspond to the subesophageal ganglia of many other invertebrates but are often far removed from the esophagus and joined to the central ganglia by long nerves

**pedal gland** n **:** any of the unicellular or syncytial glands that occur in the foot of many rotifers and secrete an adhesive substance

**pe·da·li·a·ce·ae** \pə,dālē'āsē,ē\ n pl, *cap* [NL, fr. *Pedalium*, type genus + *-aceae*] **:** a family of annual or perennial hairy tropical herbs (order Polemoniales) with opposite leaves and zygomorphic flowers having bilabiate corollas and 4-loculate ovaries with two carpels — **pe·da·li·a·ceous** \=¦==¦āshəs\ adj

**ped·a·lier** \,ped°l'i(ə)r, -iə\ n -s [F *pedalier*, fr. *pédale* fr. MF *pedale* — more at PEDAL, n.] **1 a :** the pedal keyboard of an organ **b :** one attached to a harpsichord or piano **2 :** an independent pedal keyboard for practice

**ped·al·ine** \'ped°l,ēn, ,==¦=\ n -s [*pedal* + *-ine*] **:** a strawy material that has usu. a hemp or cotton core covered with a cellulose mixture or cellophane and that is made into a braid and used for millinery and ribbon

**pe·dal·i·ter** \pə'dalәd·ә(r)\ *adv* [NL, fr. L *pedalis* of the foot + *-ter*, adv. suffix] **:** on the pedal keyboard — used as a direction in organ music; compare MANUALITER

**pe·da·li·um** \pə'dālēəm, -lyəm\ *n, cap* [NL, fr. Gk *pēdalion* rudder, fr. *pēdon* oar blade; akin to Gk *pod-, pous* foot — more at FOOT] **:** a genus (the type of the family Pedaliaceae) of smooth annual musky Indian or tropical African herbs having dentate leaves, axillary yellow flowers, and mucilaginous seeds

**pedal key** *n* [¹*pedal*] **:** any of the keys of the pedal keyboard of an organ

**pedal keyboard** *n* **:** a keyboard of pedals (as in a pipe organ)

**pedal-note** \'==,=\ *n* **1 :** PEDAL POINT **2 :** a tone produced by depressing a pedal; *also* **:** its notation **3 :** one of the lowest tones sounded by a brass wind instrument being an octave below the normal usable range, and representing the fundamental of the harmonic series

**pedal organ** *n* **:** the portion of a pipe organ that is controlled from the pedal keyboard

**pedal piano** *n* **:** a piano with a pedal keyboard attached

**pedal point** *n* **1 :** a single tone usu. the tonic or dominant that is normally sustained in the bass and sounds against changing harmonies in the other parts — called also *organ point;* compare DRONE BASS **2 :** the phrase or passage in which a pedal point occurs

**pedal pushers** *n pl* **:** women's and girls' calf-length trousers for sportswear

**ped·ant** \'ped°nt\ *n* -s [MF *pedant*, fr. It *pedante*, perh. fr. L *paedagogant-, paedagogans*, pres. part. of *paedagogare* to instruct, fr. *paedagogus* pedagogue] **1** *obs* **a :** a household tutor **b :** a male schoolteacher ⟨like a ~ that keeps a school in the church —Shak.⟩ **2 a :** one who parades his learning esp. book learning ⟨a pompous ~ —T.B.Macaulay⟩ ⟨the polysyllabic obscurantist style of the . . . ~ —Marvin Lowenthal⟩ **b :** one who is uninspired, unimaginative, or narrowly academic or who unduly emphasizes minutiae in the presentation or use of knowledge ⟨some dusty college of ~*s*, their noses buried in . . . bibliographical data —Herbert Read⟩ ⟨a scholar, yet surely no ~ —Oliver Goldsmith⟩ **c :** a formalist or precisionist in teaching ⟨the great musicians of the past were not ~*s* —Irving Babbitt⟩

**pe·dan·tic** \pə'dantik, -daan-, -tēk\ *adj* [*pedant* + *-ic*] **:** marked by pedantry: as **a :** ostentatiously learned ⟨the ~ style, the profuse classical quotations —J.R.Green⟩ **b :** narrowly academic ⟨the intellectual life that remained came to be ~ . . . rather than humane and broad —J.T.Adams⟩ **c :** UNIMAGINATIVE, PEDESTRIAN ⟨dull ~ minds —Lewis Mumford⟩ **d :** excessively meticulous ⟨a ~ speaker —G.A.Kennedy⟩ **e :** FORMALISTIC ⟨the living Bach as opposed to the dry and ~ Bach —A.E.Wier⟩ — **pe·dan·ti·cal·ly** \-tək(ə)lē, -tēk-, -li\ *adv*

**pe·dan·ti·cal** \-təkəl, -tēk-\ *adj, archaic* **:** PEDANTIC

**pe·dan·ti·cism** \-tə,sizəm\ *or* **ped·ant·ism** \'ped°n-,tizəm\ *n* -s [*pedanticism* fr. *pedantic* + *-ism*; *pedantism* fr. *pedant* + *-ism*] **:** PEDANTRY

**ped·an·toc·ra·cy** \,ped°n-'täkrəsē\ *n* -ES [F *pédantocratie*, fr. *pédant* pedant (fr. MF *pedant*) + *-o-* + *-cratie* -cracy] **:** a government of pedants

**pe·dan·to·crat** \pə'dantə,krat\ *n* -s [*pedant* + *-o-* + *-crat*] **:** one who rules according to a pedantic system — **pe·dan·to·crat·ic** \-¦==¦krad·ik\ *adj*

**ped·ant·ry** \'ped°ntrē, -ri\ *n* -ES [F or It; F *pédanterie*, fr. It *pedanteria*, fr. *pedante* pedant + *-eria* -ry] **1 :** pedantic presentation or application of knowledge or learning esp. by a teacher or scholar ⟨the book . . . is a demonstration of scholarship without ~ —W.S.Woytinsky⟩ ⟨to correct popular speech according to formal canons is sheer ~ —A.L.Guérard⟩ **2 :** an instance of pedantry ⟨methods of study may involve . . . specialized *pedantries* —G.W.Sherburn⟩

**pe·da·ta** \pə'dād·ə, -ād·ə\ *n pl, cap* [NL, fr. L, neut. pl. of *pedatus* footed] *in some classifications* **:** a division of Holothurioidea comprising forms that have tube feet either in longitudinal rows or scattered over the surface of the body and including the orders Aspidochirota and Dendrochirota or broadly all holothurians except the Apoda

**ped·ate** \'pe,dāt, -,dət, *usu* -d·+V\ *adj* [L *pedatus* footed, fr. *ped-, pes* foot + *-atus* -ate — more at FOOT] **1 a :** having a foot **b :** having tube feet ⟨many holothurians are ~⟩ **2** [NL *Pedata*] **:** of or relating to the Pedata **3 :** palmate with the lateral lobes cleft into two or more segments ⟨~ leaves⟩ — see LEAF illustration — **ped·ate·ly** *adv*

**pedati-** *comb form* [L *pedatus*] **:** pedate ⟨*pedati*form⟩ **:** pedately ⟨*pedati*sect⟩

**ped·der** \'pedə(r)\ *n* -s [ME *peddere*, prob. fr. *pedde* covered basket + *-ere* -er] *dial chiefly Brit* **:** PEDDLER, HAWKER

**ped·dle** \'ped°l\ *vb* **peddled; peddled; ped·dling** \-d(°)liŋ\ **peddles** [back-formation fr. *peddler*] *vi* **1 :** to travel about with wares for sale **:** pursue the occupation of a peddler ⟨~ without a license⟩ ⟨have been *peddling* on the corner for . . . weeks —John O'Hara⟩ **2 :** to be busy with trifles **:** PIDDLE ⟨no science *peddling* with the names of things —J.R.Lowell⟩ ~ *vt* **1 :** to sell or offer for sale from place to place **:** HAWK ⟨*peddled* fish from a pushcart —Phil Stong⟩ ⟨tried to ~ their wares to smart shops —Martha McDowell⟩ ⟨*peddled* his unwanted manuscripts —*Amer. Guide Series: N.Y. City*⟩ **2 :** to deal out or seek to disseminate (as ideas or opinions) **:** RETAIL, CIRCULATE ⟨*peddling* personal advice —G.F.Kennan⟩ ⟨*peddling* secondhand truths and undigested truisms to popular audiences —William Phillips b.1907⟩

**ped·dler** *or* **ped·lar** *or* **ped·ler** \'ped(°)lə(r)\ *n* -s [ME *pedlere*, prob. alter. of *peddere* peddler] **1 :** one that peddles: as **a :** one that offers merchandise (as fruit or vegetables) for sale along the street or from door to door usu. carrying his goods in a pushcart, wagon, or truck as distinguished from a canvasser who takes orders for future delivery — called also *arab, hawker, huckster, vendor* ⟨an itinerant ~ crying his wares⟩ **b :** one that retails or offers for sale something intangible (as an idea or personal asset) ⟨a ~ of dreams⟩ ⟨~*s* of race hatred⟩ ⟨influence ~*s*⟩ **2 :** the larva of various leaf beetles of the genus *Cassida* and related forms **3 :** a local or way freight train

**peddler car** *n* **:** a freight car carrying less-than-carload shipments from one consignor over a specified route with deliveries direct to consignees

**peddler truck** *n* **:** a truck carrying less-than-truckload shipments from one consignor over a specified route with deliveries direct to consignees

**ped·dlery** *or* **ped·lary** \'pedlərē, -ri\ *n* -ES [*peddler* + *-y*] **1 :** peddlers' merchandise **2 :** the trade of a peddler

**ped·dling** \'ped(°)liŋ, -lēŋ\ *adj* [alter. of *piddling*] **:** PETTY, PIDDLING ⟨a ~ and pettifogging view of morality —George Saintsbury⟩ — **ped·dling·ly** *adv*

**-pede** — see -PED

**pede cloth** \'pēd-\ *n* [L *ped-, pes* foot — more at FOOT] **:** an altar carpet

¹**pedee** *n* -s [origin unknown] *obs* **:** a serving boy **:** FOOTBOY

²**pe·dee** \'pē,dē\ *n, pl* **pedee** *or* **pedees** *usu cap* **1 a :** a Siouan people of the Pee Dee river valley in So. Carolina **2 :** a member of the Pedee people

**ped·er·ast** *also* **paed·er·ast** \'pedə,rast, 'pēd-\ *n* -s [Gk *paiderastēs*, lit., lover of boys, fr. *paid-* paed- + *erastēs* lover, fr. *erasthai* to love] **:** one that practices pederasty — **ped·er·as·tic** \¦==¦rastik, -tēk\ *adj* — **ped·er·as·ti·cal·ly** \-tək(ə)lē, -tēk-, -li\ *adv*

**ped·er·as·ty** *also* **paed·er·as·ty** \'==,rastē, -ti\ *n* -ES [Gk *paiderastia* love of boys, fr. *paiderastēs* + *-ia* -y] **:** anal intercourse esp. with a boy as the passive partner

**pederero** *var of* PEDRERO

**pe·der·sen device** \'pedə(r)sən-\ *n, usu cap P* [after J. D. *Pedersen*, 20th cent. Amer. inventor] **:** a device consisting of a special bolt and magazine for converting a slightly modified version of the bolt action Springfield rifle into a semiautomatic firearm

**pedes** *pl of* PES

**pe·de·sis** \pə'dēsəs\ *n, pl* **pede·ses** \-,sēz\ [NL, fr. Gk *pēdēsis* leaping, fr. *pēdan* to leap; akin to L *ped-, pes* foot — more at FOOT] **:** BROWNIAN MOVEMENT

¹**ped·es·tal** \'pedəst°l\ *n* -s *often attrib* [MF *piedestal*, fr. OIt *piedestallo*, fr. *pie di stallo* foot of a stall] **1 a :** the support or foot of a late classic or neoclassic column consisting of base, dado, and surbase moldings **b :** the base of an upright structure (as a statue, vase, lamp, harp) ⟨a ~ worthy of a storyteller's statue —Van Wyck Brooks⟩ **c :** a supporting part (as of a table or kneehole desk) **d :** PIVOT STAND **e :** a cone or column of ice that supports or has supported a boulder or block of rock **:** PEDESTAL ROCK **2 a :** the supporting base or foundation of something intangible ⟨pedigree was the ~ of the British constitution —Wilfrid Lawson⟩ **b :** an elevated plane **:** position of esteem ⟨places him . . . on a ~ —E.V.Buckholder⟩ ⟨shown off his ~ . . . as the members of his family group saw him —Dorothy C. Fisher⟩ **3 a :** a guide in the frame or truck of a car or locomotive that slides against the sides of the journal box and holds it in place as the body rides on the springs **b** *Brit* **:** an axle guard of a railroad car **4 a :** a separate bearing or pillow block; *also* **:** a housing for a bearing or pillow block **b :** a metal support that carries one end of a bridge truss or girder and transmits the load it receives to the top of a pier or abutment **5 :** the strength of the television signal on which the synchronizing signal is superimposed corresponding to black or slightly blacker than black in the picture

²**pedestal** \"\ *vt* **pedestaled** *or* **pedestalled; pedestaled** *or* **pedestalled; pedestaling** *or* **pedestalling; pedestals 1 :** to place on or furnish with a pedestal ⟨the pride of the . . . collection stands *pedestalled* in an alcove —Aldous Huxley⟩ **2 :** to elevate in position **:** EXALT ⟨desired not to be . . . *pedestalled*, but to sink into the crowd —John Buchan⟩

**pedestal box** *n* **:** JOURNAL BOX

**pedestal desk** *n* **:** a usu. kneehole desk with the top supported by one or two pedestals containing cupboards or drawers

**pedestal mount** *n* **:** a gun mount having its pivot stand in the general form of a truncated cone

**pedestal pile** *n* **:** a concrete pile that is cast in place with a bulb-shaped enlargement at its lower end

**pedestal ring** *n* **:** the element or part of a packing gland that applies pressure to the packing **:** a stepped ring

**pedestal rock** *n* **:** a residual or erosional rock mass balanced upon a relatively slender neck or pedestal

**pedestal table** *n* **:** a table having a central supporting column or pillar

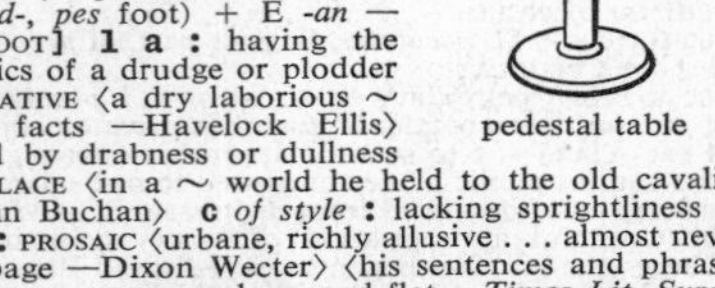

pedestal table

**pedestrial** *adj* [L *pedestr-, pedester, pedestris* going on foot + E *-al*] *obs* **:** PEDESTRIAN 2

¹**pe·des·tri·an** \pə'destrēən\ *adj* [L *pedestr-, pedester, pedestris* going on foot, prosaic (fr. *pedes* one going on foot, fr. *ped-, pes* foot) + E *-an* — more at FOOT] **1 a :** having the characteristics of a drudge or plodder **:** UNIMAGINATIVE ⟨a dry laborious ~ student of facts —Havelock Ellis⟩ **b :** marked by drabness or dullness **:** COMMONPLACE ⟨in a ~ world he held to the old cavalier grace —John Buchan⟩ **c** *of style* **:** lacking sprightliness or inspiration **:** PROSAIC ⟨urbane, richly allusive . . . almost never pens a ~ page —Dixon Wecter⟩ ⟨his sentences and phrases are too often ~, commonplace, and flat —*Times Lit. Supp.*⟩ **2 a :** going on foot ⟨a dog will scurry before and behind his ~ master —George Santayana⟩ **b :** performed on foot ⟨a ~ journey⟩ ⟨~ races⟩ **c :** of or relating to walking ⟨complained about the ~ distances —Lewis Mumford⟩

²**pedestrian** \"\ *n* -s **:** a person who travels on foot **:** WALKER: as **a :** one who walks for pleasure, sport, or exercise **:** HIKER ⟨an indefatigable ~⟩ ⟨he liked company on a walk . . . and most of his guests were not ~*s* —R.M.Lovett⟩ **b :** one walking as distinguished from one travelling by car or cycle ⟨signalled traffic to halt to allow ~*s* to cross the street⟩

**pe·des·tri·an·ate** \-,nāt\ *or* **pe·des·tri·nate** \-trə,nāt\ *vi* -ED/-ING/-S **:** PEDESTRIANIZE

**pedestrian island** *n* **:** a space between roadways where pedestrians can await a break in vehicular traffic

**pe·des·tri·an·ism** \pə'destrēə,nizəm\ *n* -s **1 a :** the practice of walking ⟨a feat of ~⟩ **b :** addiction to walking for exercise or recreation **2 :** the quality or state of being pedestrian **:** BANALITY ⟨the latest mass medium to bewitch the multitude with canned ~ —Jack Gould⟩ — used esp. of literary style ⟨a ~ which may defeat the heaven-sent chance to deal fully and splendidly with a mighty subject —Oliver La Farge⟩

**pe·des·tri·an·ize** \-,nīz\ *vi* -ED/-ING/-S **:** to do some walking **:** go afoot

**pe·de·tes** \pə'dēd·(,)ēz\ *n, cap* [NL, fr. Gk *pēdētēs* leaper, fr. *pēdan* to leap — more at PEDESIS] **:** a genus (the type and sole recent representative of the family Pedetidae) of rodents that consists of the jumping hare

¹**pe·det·id** \-'dedəd\ *adj* [NL *Pedetidae*] **:** of or relating to the genus *Pedetes* or the family Pedetidae

²**pedetid** \"\ *n* -s **:** a rodent of the genus *Pedetes* or the family Pedetidae

**pede window** \'pēd-\ *n* [L *ped-, pes* foot — more at FOOT] **:** a window placed at the foot of a cross (as in the west end of a cruciform church)

¹**pedi-** — see ¹PED-

²**pedi-** *or* **pedio-** *comb form* [Gk, fr. *pedion* — more at PEDION] **:** flat surface **:** plain ⟨*Pedioecetes*⟩ **:** sole of the foot ⟨*pedialgia*⟩ ⟨*Pediococcus*⟩

**pedia** *pl of* PEDION

**ped·i·al** \'pedēəl, 'pēd-\ *adj* [NL *pedion* + E *-al*] **:** of or relating to a pedion **:** ASYMMETRIC d

**ped·i·as·trum** \,pedē'astrəm, ,pēd-\ *n, cap* [NL, fr. ²*pedi-* + Gk *astron* star — more at STAR] **:** a genus of free-floating green algae (family Hydrodictyaceae) that have flat platelike colonies of two or more polygonal cells with the marginal cells usu. differing in shape and having usu. two projections of the cell wall

**pe·di·at·ric** *also* **pae·di·at·ric** \,pēdē¦a·trik, ¦ped-, -rēk\ *adj* [*paed-* + *-iatric*] **:** of or relating to the care and medical treatment of children ⟨an effective ~ service⟩ **:** belonging to or concerned with pediatrics

**pe·di·a·tri·cian** \,pēdēə'trishən, ,ped-\ *also* **pe·di·at·rist** \,==¦a·trəst, pə'dīə·trəst\ *n* -s [*pediatrician* fr. *pediatric* + *-ian*; *pediatrist* fr. *paed-* + *-iatrist*] **:** a specialist in pediatrics

**pe·di·at·rics** *also* **pae·di·at·rics** \,pēdē'a·triks, ped-\ *n pl but sing or pl in constr* [*paed-* + *-iatrics*] **:** a branch of medicine that deals with the child, its development, care, and diseases

**ped·i·cab** \'pedə, 'pedē+ ,-\ *n* [¹*ped-* + *cab*] **:** a light 3-wheeled pedaled or sometimes motorized vehicle used esp. in the Orient for transporting passengers for hire ⟨boys who used to pull rickshaws now pedal . . . ~*s* —G.W.Long⟩

**ped·i·ca·tio** *also* **paed·i·ca·tio** \,pedə'kāshē,ō, -kād·ē-\ *n* -s [NL *paedication-, paedicatio*, fr. L *paedicatus* (past part. of *paedicare* to engage in pederasty, fr. Gk *paidika* boy favorite, fr. neut. pl. of *paidikos* of boys, fr. *paid-, pais* boy + *-ikos* -ic) + *-ion-, -io* -ion — more at PAED-] **:** anal intercourse

**ped·i·cel** \'pedə,sel\ *n* -s [NL *pedicellus*, dim. of L *pediculus* little foot, footstalk — more at PEDICLE] **1 a :** a slender plant stalk; *esp* **:** one that supports a fruiting or spore-bearing organ ⟨the ~ of a sporangium⟩ **b (1) :** one of the ultimate single flower-bearing divisions of a common peduncle **(2) :** a peduncle esp. if slender or delicate that bears a single flower — see FLOWER illustration **2 a :** a small or short stalk or stem in an animal body **:** a narrow basal part by which a larger part or body is attached (as the outgrowth of the frontal bone that supports the antler of a deer or the pedicle of a vertebra) **:** PEDUNCLE, FOOTSTALK **b :** a small foot or footlike organ (as a tube foot of an echinoderm) **c :** the second joint of the antenna of an insect between the scope and funicle **d :** the nodiform basal segment of the abdomen of an ant **e :** the narrow anterior portion of the abdomen of a spider that links abdomen and cephalothorax

**ped·i·celed** *or* **ped·i·celled** \-,seld\ *adj* **:** PEDICELLATE

**ped·i·cel·lar·ia** \,pedəsə'la(a)rēə\ *n, pl* **pedicellar·i·ae** \-rē,ē\ [NL, fr. *pedicellus* pedicel + *-aria*] **:** any of various peculiar minute organs resembling forceps that are borne in large numbers on the external integument of sea urchins and starfish and also often on the spines of the latter and that have as their probable function keeping the body clear of small parasites and other foreign objects — compare FORCIPULATE

**ped·i·cel·late** \¦==¦selət, -,lāt, *usu* -d·+V\ *also* **ped·i·cel·lat·ed** \-,lād·əd\ *adj* [NL *pedicellus* pedicel + E *-ate*] **:** having or attached by a pedicel

**ped·i·cel·li·form** \¦==¦selə,fȯrm\ *adj* [NL *pedicellus* + E *-iform*] **:** having the form of a pedicel

**ped·i·cel·li·na** \,==sə'līnə\ *n, cap* [NL, fr. *pedicellus* + *-ina*] **:** a genus (the type of the family Pedicillinidae) of colonial bryozoans in which the zooids have a bell-shaped body on a slender pedicel

**ped·i·cel·lin·i·dae** \,==sə'linə,dē\ *n pl, cap* [NL, fr. *Pedicellina*, type genus + *-idae*] **:** a family of small noncalcareous usu. solitary and hermaphroditic bryozoans

**ped·i·cle** \'pedəkəl\ *n* -s [L *pediculus* little foot, footstalk, dim. of *ped-, pes* foot — more at FOOT] **:** PEDICEL: as **a :** the basal part of each side of the neural arch of a vertebra connecting the laminae with the centrum **b :** the narrow basal part by which various organs (as a kidney or spleen) are continuous with other body structures **c :** the narrow base of a tumor **d :** the part of a skin or tissue graft left attached to the original site during preliminary stages of union

**ped·i·cled** \-kəld\ *adj* [*pedicle* + *-ed*] **:** having or having the form of a pedicle

**pe·dic·u·lar** \pə'dikyələ(r)\ *adj* [L *pedicularis*, fr. *pediculus* louse, dim. of *pedis* louse; perh. akin to L *pedere* to break wind — more at PETARD] **:** of or relating to lice **:** PEDICULOUS, LOUSY

**pe·dic·u·lar·is** \pə,dikyə'la(a)rəs\ *n, cap* [NL, fr. L (*herba*) *pedicularis* lousewort] **:** a large genus of hemiparasitic herbs (family Scrophulareaceae) found in temperate or alpine regions that have pinnate or pinnatifid leaves and variously colored bilabiate flowers in terminal spikes — see LOUSEWORT

¹**pe·dic·u·late** \=¦==,lət, -,lāt, *usu* -d·+V\ *adj* [NL *pediculatus*, fr. L *pediculus* footstalk + *-atus* -ate — more at PEDICLE] **1 :** PEDICELLATE **2** [NL *Pediculati*] **:** of or relating to the Pediculati

²**pediculate** \"\ *n* -s [NL *Pediculati*] **:** a fish of the order Pediculati

**pe·dic·u·lat·ed** \=¦==¦lād·əd\ *adj* [L *pediculus* footstalk + E *-ate* + *-ed*] **:** PEDICELLATE, PEDUNCULATE

**pe·dic·u·la·ti** \=,==¦'lād·,ī\ *n pl, cap* [NL, fr. pl. of *pediculatus* pediculate] **:** an order of highly specialized marine teleost fishes including the anglers and batfishes that have the ventral fins on the throat and the pectoral fins at the end of a process suggesting a wrist or arm and consisting of the elongated and modified hypercoracoid and hypocoracoid and that have the anterior portion of the dorsal fin modified into a movable structure which stands out from the protectively colored body as a lure attracting prey within reach of the very large mouth

**ped·i·cule** \'pedə,kyül\ *n* -s [F *pédicule*, fr. L *pediculus* footstalk] **:** PEDICEL

**pe·dic·u·li·ci·dal** \pə¦dikyələ¦sīd°l\ *adj* **:** of, relating to, or being a pediculicide

**pe·dic·u·li·cide** \=¦===,sīd\ *n* -s [L *pediculus* louse + E *-i-* + *-cide* — more at PEDICULAR] **:** an agent for destroying lice

¹**pe·dic·u·lid** \=¦==ləd, -,lid\ *adj* [NL *Pediculidae*] **:** of or relating to the Pediculidae

²**pediculid** \"\ *n* -s **:** a louse of the family Pediculidae

**pe·dic·u·li·dae** \,pedə'kyülə,dē\ *n pl, cap* [NL, fr. *Pediculus*, type genus + *-idae*] **:** a family of true lice (order Anoplura) including the human lice and related forms

**pe·dic·u·li·na** \pə,dikyə'līnə\ *n pl, cap* [NL, fr. *Pediculus* + *-ina*] *in some classifications* **:** a group of lice: as **a :** a group coextensive with Anoplura **b :** a group coextensive with Pediculidae

**pe·dic·u·line** \=¦==,līn, -,lən\ *adj* [NL *Pediculina*] **:** of, relating to, or resembling the Pediculina

**pe·dic·u·loid** \-,lȯid\ *adj* [NL *Pediculus* + E *-oid*] **:** resembling or related to the common lice

**pe·dic·u·loi·des** \=,==¦lȯi(,)dēz\ *n, cap* [NL, fr. L *pediculus* louse + *-oides*] *syn of* PYEMOTES

**pe·dic·u·lo·sis** \-'lōsəs\ *n, pl* **pediculo·ses** \-ō,sēz\ [NL, fr. L *pediculus* louse + *-osis* — more at PEDICULAR] **:** infestation with lice esp. of the genus *Pediculus*

**pe·dic·u·lous** \=¦==ləs\ *adj* [L *pediculosus*, fr. *pediculus* louse + *-osus* -ous — more at PEDICULAR] **:** infested with lice **:** LOUSY

**pe·dic·u·lus** \"\ *n* [NL, fr. L, louse] **1** *cap* **:** the type genus of Pediculidae including common lice infesting man **2** *pl* **pedicu·li** \-,lī\ *or* **pediculus :** any louse of the genus *Pediculus*

**ped·i·cure** \'pedə,kyù(ə)r, 'pedē,-, -ùə\ *n* [F *pédicure*, fr. *péd-* ped- + L *curare* to take care of, fr. *cura* care — more at CURE] **1 :** CHIROPODIST **2 a :** care of the feet, toes, and nails **b :** a single treatment of these parts ⟨she had a ~ today⟩

**ped·i·form** \'==,fȯrm\ *adj* [F *pédiforme*, fr. *péd-* ped- + *-iforme* -iform] **:** resembling a foot — used chiefly of segmental appendages of insects and other arthropods that are not characteristically of this form ⟨~ antennae⟩

**pe·dig·er·ous** \pə'dijərəs\ *adj* [¹*ped-* + *-gerous*] **:** having feet **:** FOOTED ⟨the three ~ segments of the adult insect⟩

¹**ped·i·gree** \'pedə,grē\ *n* -s [ME *pedegru*, fr. MF *pie de grue* crane's foot; fr. the shape made by the lines of a genealogical chart] **1 :** a register (as a table or chart) recording a line of ancestors **:** a genealogical tree **:** STEMMA ⟨drawing up a family ~⟩ **2 a :** an ancestral line **:** LINEAGE, DESCENT ⟨the dowager scrutinized his ~ and background⟩ **b (1) :** the origin and the history (as of the developmental stages or the successive states or owners) of something ⟨the ~ of a document⟩ ⟨~*s* of ideas or influences —*Times Lit. Supp.*⟩ ⟨the ~ of the house we lived in —Mary A. Allen⟩ **(2) :** the sequence of owners of a work of art (as a painting) ⟨the condition of the pictures . . . their ~, the subjects represented —*Times Lit. Supp.*⟩ **(3) :** the history of a collector's coin or stamp including facts about its original issuance, its rarity, and the sales in which it has changed hands **3 a :** distinguished ancestry ⟨actions spoke louder than ~*s* in the trenches —Dixon Wecter⟩ **b :** recorded purity of breed (as of horses or plant strains) ⟨vouch for a horse's ~⟩ **4 :** a long line of succession (as of persons holding an office or continuing a tradition) ⟨the whole ~ of club presidents⟩ **syn** see ANCESTRY

²**pedigree** \"\ *adj* **:** having a pedigree **:** PUREBRED ⟨a ~ cocker spaniel⟩ ⟨a four-year-old ~ Guernsey bull —*Veterinary Record*⟩

³**pedigree** \"\ *vt* **pedigreed; pedigreed; pedigreeing; pedigrees :** to breed or propagate so that descent is known and can be recorded **:** provide with a pedigree

**pedigree theory** *n* **:** FAMILY-TREE THEORY

**ped·i·lan·thus** \,pedə'lan(t)thəs\ *n, cap* [NL, fr. Gk *pedilon* sandal + NL *-anthus*; akin to L *ped-, pes* foot — more at FOOT] **:** a genus of tropical American shrubby plants (family Euphorbiaceae) resembling cactus and differing from members of the genus *Euphorbia* chiefly in having an irregular involucre with a short spur on the upper side containing the glands

**pe·dim·a·na** \pə'dimənə; pedə'manə, -ānə\ *n pl* [NL, fr. ¹*ped-* + *-mana*, fr. L *manus* hand — more at MANUAL] **1** *cap, in former classifications* **:** a division of Marsupialia equivalent to Didelphidae **2 :** QUADRUMANA

**ped·i·mane** \'pedə,mān\ *n* -s [NL *Pedimana*] **:** a mammal of the group Pedimana — **pe·dim·a·nous** \pə'dimənəs\ *adj*

**ped·i·ment** \'pedəmənt\ *n* -s [alter. of obs. E *periment*, prob. alter. of E *pyramid*] **1 a :** the triangular space forming the gable of a 2-pitched roof in classic architecture **b :** a similar form used as a decoration (as over porticoes, doors, windows) **c :** a rounded or broken frontal having a similar position and use **2 :** a part in decorative art resembling or suggestive of an architectural pediment in form and position **3** [perh. fr. It *pedamento* flooring, fr. L *pedamentum* vine prop, fr. *pedare* to supply with feet (fr. *ped-, pes* foot) + *-mentum* -ment — more at FOOT] **:** BASE 1a, PAVEMENT **4 :** a broad gently sloping bedrock surface with low relief that is situated at the foot of a much steeper mountain slope in an arid or semiarid region, is usu. covered with a thin veneer of alluvial gravel and sand, and is an erosional surface in contrast to a depositional piedmont plain

pediments 1

**ped·i·men·tal** \¦==¦ment³l\ *adj* **:** of, relating to, or resembling a pediment

**ped·i·men·ta·tion** \ˌpedəmən'tāshən, -(ˌ)men-\ *n* -s **:** the action or process that produces a geological pediment; *also* **:** the formation resulting from such an action or process

**ped·i·ment·ed** \'==ˌmentəd\ *adj* [*pediment* + *-ed*] **:** having or resembling a pediment ⟨a ~ gable was used —H.S.Morrison⟩

**pedio-** — see ²PEDI-

**pe·di·o·coc·cus** \ˌpedēō'käkəs\ *n* [NL, fr. ²*pedi-* + *-coccus*] **1** *cap, in some classifications* **:** a genus of micrococci (family Micrococcaceae) that grow in beer and wort producing clouding and acid **2** *pl* **pediococ·ci** \-'käˌkē, -ä(ˌ)kē, -äkˌsē, -äk(ˌ)sē\ **:** any member of the genus *Pediococcus*

**pe·di·oe·ce·tes** \ˌ==ē'sēd·(ˌ)ēz\ *n, cap* [NL, fr. ²*pedi-* + Gk *oikētēs* dweller, fr. *oikein* to dwell, fr. *oikos* house — more at VICINITY] **:** a genus of birds (family Tetraonidae) consisting of the sharp-tailed grouse

**ped·i·on** \'pedēən, 'pēd-\ *n, pl* **ped·ia** \-dēə\ [NL, fr. Gk, plain, flat surface, fr. *pedon* ground; akin to L *oppido* thoroughly, ON *fet* step, Skt *pada* step, track, L *ped-, pes* foot — more at FOOT] **:** a form of crystal having only a single face and belonging to the rare asymmetric class of the triclinic system

**pe·di·o·no·mus** \ˌpedē'änəməs\ *n, cap* [NL, fr. Gk *pediono-mos* plain-dweller, fr. *pedi-* + *-nomos* (fr. *nemein* to inhabit, pasture) — more at NIMBLE] **:** a monotypic genus of Australian birds (family Turnicidae) consisting of the plain wanderer and closely related to the button quails

**ped·i·palp** \'pedəˌpalp, 'pedē-\ *n* -s [NL *pedipalpus*] **1 :** PEDIPALPUS **2** [NL *Pedipalpida*] **:** an arachnid of the order Pedipalpida

**ped·i·pal·pal** \¦==¦palpəl\ *adj* [*pedipalp* + *-al*] **:** of or relating to a pedipalpus

**ped·i·pal·pate** \-ˌpāt, -ˌpət\ *adj* [NL *pedipalpus* + E *-ate*] **:** having pedipalpi

**ped·i·pal·pi** \ˌ==¦==ˌpī\ [NL *pedipalpus*] *syn of* PEDIPALPIDA

¹**ped·i·pal·pid** \ˌ==¦==pəd\ *adj* [NL *Pedipalpida*] **:** of or relating to the Pedipalpida

²**pedipalpid** \"\ *n* -s **:** an arachnid of the order Pedipalpida

**ped·i·pal·pi·da** \ˌ==ˌ'==pədə\ *n pl, cap* [NL, fr. *pedipalpus* + *-ida*] **:** an order of Arachnida limited to warm or tropical regions that includes the whip scorpions and other moderate-sized arachnids having an unsegmented cephalothorax and a segmented flattened abdomen, small often retractile 2-segmented chelicerae, large usu. chelate pedipalps, and a slender many-jointed first pair of legs

**ped·i·pal·pous** \¦==¦palpəs\ *adj* [NL *Pedipalpida* + E *-ous*] **:** of, relating to, or resembling the Pedipalpida

**ped·i·pal·pus** \ˌ==='==pəs\ *n, pl* **pedipal·pi** \-ˌpī\ [NL, fr. ¹*ped-* + *palpus*] **:** one of the second pair of appendages of an arachnid that lie on each side of the mouth and are variously developed in the different orders, that in spiders are small and resemble legs, in the scorpions are the largest appendages and end in pincers, and in the solpugids are long and resemble the four pairs of walking legs

**ped·i·plain** *or* **ped·i·plane** \'pedəˌ+-\ *n* [*pediment* + *plain*] **:** an extensive geological pediment or a plain resulting from the coalescence of two or more pediments

**ped·i·pla·na·tion** \ˌ==(ˌ)plā'nāshən\ *n* -s [*pediplane* + *-ation*] **:** pedimentation on a regional scale

**ped·i·wak** \'pedəˌwak\ *also* **pa·duak·an** \pə'dwakən\ *n* -s [native name in Celebes] **:** a decked sailing boat of northern Celebes in the Malay archipelago

**pedlar** *or* **pedler** *var of* PEDDLER

¹**pedo-** — see PED-

²**pedo-** — see PAED-

**pe·do·baptism** *also* **pae·do·baptism** \¦pēdō+\ *n* [*paed-* + *baptism*] **:** infant baptism

**pe·do·baptist** \"+\ *n* **:** one who advocates or practices infant baptism

**ped·o·cal** \'pedəˌkal\ *n* -s [²*ped-* + L *calc-, calx* lime — more at CHALK] **:** a soil that includes a definite hardened layer of accumulated carbonates — compare PEDALFER

**pe·do·don·tia** \ˌpēdō'dänch(ē)ə\ *n* -s [NL, fr. *paed-* + *-odontia*] **:** PEDODONTICS

**pe·do·don·tic** \¦==¦däntik\ *adj* [NL *pedodontia* + E *-ic*] **:** of or relating to pedodontics ⟨~ procedures⟩

**pe·do·don·tics** \ˌ=='=tiks\ *n pl but sing or pl in constr* **:** a branch of dentistry that is concerned with the dental care of children

**pe·do·don·tist** \ˌ=='däntəst, '==ˌ==\ *n* -s [NL *pedodontia* + E *-ist*] **:** a specialist in pedodontics

**pedogamy** *var of* PAEDOGAMY

¹**pedogenesis** *var of* PAEDOGENESIS

²**ped·o·genesis** \¦pedō+\ *n* [NL, fr. ²*ped-* + L *genesis*] **:** the formation and development of soil

**ped·o·gen·ic** \¦==¦jenik\ *adj* [²*ped-* + *-genic*] **:** of, relating to, or involved in soil formation ⟨~ agents⟩ ⟨~ processes⟩

**ped·o·geography** \¦==+\ *n* [²*ped-* + *geography*] **:** the geography of soils

**pedo·log·ic** \¦pedō¦läjik, *in sense 2* ¦pēd-\ *or* **pedo·log·i·cal** \-jəkəl\ *adj* **1 :** of or relating to soil science **2 :** of or relating to child study

¹**pe·dol·o·gist** \pə'däləjəst\ *n* -s [¹*pedology* + *-ist*] **:** a specialist in child study

²**pedologist** \"\ *n* -s [²*pedology* + *-ist*] **:** a soil scientist

¹**pe·dol·o·gy** \-jē, -ji\ *n* -ES [*paed-* + *-logy*] **:** the science and study of the life and development of children

²**pedology** \"\ *n* -ES [ISV ²*ped-* + *-logy*; prob. orig. formed as Russ *pedologiya*] **:** a science that treats of soils — called also *soil science*

**pe·dom·e·ter** \pə'däməd·ə(r), -mətə-\ *n* [F *pédomètre*, fr. *péd-* ped- + *-mètre* -meter] **:** an instrument usu. in watch form that records the distance a walker covers by responding to his body motion at each step — compare PASSOMETER

**pedo·met·ri·cal** \¦pedə¦me·trəkəl\ *also* **pedo·met·ric** \-¦me·trik\ *adj* **:** of, relating to, or functioning as a pedometer — **pedo·met·ri·cal·ly** \-trək(ə)lē, -li\ *adv*

**pe·dom·e·tri·cian** \pəˌdämə'trishən\ *n* -s [*pedometer* + *-ician*] **:** a pedometer maker

**pedo·motive** \'pedə, ¦pēdə+\ *adj* [¹*ped-* + *motive*] **:** moved by foot power (as of a velocipede)

**pedo·motor** \¦==+\ *n* [¹*ped-* + *motor*] **1 :** a machine (as a bicycle) driven by foot power **2 :** a device (as a treadle) for applying foot power

**pe·do·phil·ia** *or* **pae·do·phil·ia** \ˌpēdə'filēə\ *n* -s [NL, fr. *paed-* + *-philia*] **:** paraphilia in which children are the preferred sexual object — **pe·do·phil·i·ac** \¦==¦filēˌak\ *or* **pe·do·phil·ic** \-'filik\ *adj*

**pedo·sphere** \'pedə+ˌ-\ *n* [²*ped-* + *sphere*] **:** a part of the earth's surface that contains the soil layer

**ped·rail** \'ped+ˌ-\ *n* [¹*ped-* + *rail*] **1 :** a tractor wheel with circular feet fastened about its periphery so that they come successively in contact with the road **2 :** a vehicle (as a traction engine) having pedrails

**pe·dre·ro** \pə'drə(ə)(ˌ)rō\ *also* **pa·te·re·ro** \ˌpäd·ə're(ə)-(ˌ)rō\ *or* **pe·de·re·ro** \ˌpädə'r-\ *n* -s [Sp *pedrero*, fr. ML *petraria*, fr. L, fem. of *petrarius* of stones, fr. *petra* stone (fr. Gk, rock, stone) + *-arius* -ary] **:** a piece of chambered ordnance used for throwing chiefly stones and scraps of iron

**pe·dro** \'pē(ˌ)drō\ *n* -s [Sp *Pedro* Peter] **1 :** the five of trumps in card games of the all fours family **2 :** a card game (as cinch) of the all fours family

**pedro sancho** *n* **:** SANCHO PEDRO

**pe·dro xi·me·nez** \¦pā(ˌ)drōhē'mā(ˌ)nās\ *n, usu cap P&X* [Sp *pedroximenes, pedrojimenez*, perh. fr. the name *Pedro Ximenes* or *Pedro Jimenez*] **:** a rich usu. sweet sherry from Pajarete near Arcos in Spain sometimes used for blending with and flavoring other wine

**peds** *pl of* PED

**-peds** *pl of* -PED

**ped·ule** \'pe(ˌ)dyül\ *n* -s [LL *pedulis*, fr. L, of the foot, fr. *ped-, pes* foot — more at FOOT] **:** a long socklike boot made of leather or cloth and worn esp. by ancient and early medieval Gauls

**pe·dun·cle** \'pēˌdəŋkəl, =ˈ==\ *n* -s [NL *pedunculus*, dim. of L *ped-, pes*] **1 a :** a stalk that bears a flower or a flower cluster — see PEDICEL 1b **b :** the stalk supporting the fructification in some thallophytes **2 :** a narrow part by which some larger part or the whole body of an organism is attached (as the footstalk of a brachiopod or the petiole joining the abdomen of an ant or wasp to the thorax) **:** STEM, STALK, PEDICEL, PEDICLE — see BARNACLE illustration **3 :** a band of white matter joining different parts of the brain ⟨the ~s of the pineal body pass from its base to the pillars of the fornix⟩ — see CEREBELLAR PEDUNCLE, CEREBRAL PEDUNCLE **4 :** a narrow stalk by which a tumor or polyp is attached to an organ

**pe·dun·cled** \-kəld\ *adj* [*peduncle* + *-ed*] **:** pedunculate or as if pedunculate

**pe·dun·cu·lar** \(')pē¦dəŋkyələ(r)\ *adj* [NL *pedunculus* + E *-ar*] **:** of or relating to a peduncle

**pe·dun·cu·late** \-lət, -lāt, *usu* -d.+V\ *or* **pe·dun·cu·lat·ed** \-ˌlād·əd\ *adj* [NL *pedunculus* + E *-ate* or *-ate* + *-ed*] **:** having a peduncle **:** growing on or from a peduncle ⟨a ~ flower⟩; *esp* **:** being attached by a peduncle ⟨a ~ tumor⟩

**pedunculate barnacle** *n* **:** a barnacle (as the goose barnacle) attached to the substrate by the base of a fleshy foot or stalk — compare SESSILE BARNACLE

**pedunculate body** *n* **:** a group of association neurones or their fibers in the insect forebrain

**pedunculate oak** *n* **:** ENGLISH OAK

**pe·dun·cu·la·tion** \(ˌ)pēˌdəŋkyə'lāshən\ *n* -s [*pedunculate* + *-ion*] **:** the quality or state of being pedunculate

**pe·dun·cu·lus** \=ˈ==ləs\ *n, pl* **pedunculi** \-ˌlī\ [NL — more at PEDUNCLE] **:** PEDUNCLE

¹**pee** *also* **pe** \'pē\ *n* -s **:** the letter *p*

²**pee** \'pē\ *vi* **peed; peed; peeing; pees** [euphemism fr. the initial letter of *piss*] **:** URINATE — not often in polite use

³**pee** \"\ *n* -s **1 :** URINE — not often in polite use **2 :** an act of urination — often used with *take;* not often in polite use

⁴**pee** *var of* PEA

**pee·bles·shire** \'pēbəl(z)ˌshi(ə)r, -lzh,-, -ˌshiə, -ˌshə(r)\ *or* **pee·bles** \'pēbəlz\ *adj, usu cap* [fr. *Peeblesshire, Peebles*, county in southeast Scotland] **:** of or from the county of Peebles, Scotland **:** of the kind or style prevalent in Peebles

**pee-gee hydrangea** \'pē¦jē-\ *n* [*peegee* prob. fr. the initial letters of NL *paniculata* (specific epithet of *Hydrangea paniculata grandiflora*), fem. of *paniculatus* paniculate, and NL *grandiflora* (varietal epithet of *Hydrangea paniculata grandiflora*), fem. of *grandiflorus* large-flowered, fr. L *grandis* large, great + LL *-florus* -florous — more at PANICULATE, GRAND] **:** a shrub (*Hydrangea paniculata grandiflora*) having large panicles of white flowers that turn pink as the flowers mature

¹**peek** \'pēk\ *vi* -ED/-ING/-S [ME *piken*] **1 :** to look slyly or furtively **:** peer through a crack or hole or from a place of concealment **:** PEEP ⟨~*ing* around the corner of the chair is a little girl —H.E.Salisbury⟩ — often used with *in* or *out* ⟨~*ed* in through a window —J.M.Flagler⟩ ⟨~ out at us from behind the curtains —Winifred Bambrick⟩ **2 :** to take a brief look **:** GLANCE — usu. used with *at* ⟨~*ed* at his flashlight —Herbert Gold⟩

²**peek** \"\ *n* -s **1 :** a surreptitious look **:** PEEP ⟨an investigatory ~ through the side window —S.H.Adams⟩ ⟨newest ~ into the royal boudoir —*Saturday Rev.*⟩ **2 :** a brief look **:** GLANCE, GLIMPSE ⟨exclusive ~ at new products —*Modern Industry*⟩ ⟨a ~ inside the laboratory gives you some idea . . . of the future —*Dun's Rev.*⟩

¹**peek·a·boo** \'pēkəˌbü\ *n* [¹*peek* + connective *-a-* + *boo*, interj.] **:** a game for amusing a baby in which one repeatedly hides his face or body and pops back into view exclaiming "Peekaboo!"

²**peekaboo** \¦==¦=\ *adj* **1 :** trimmed with eyelet embroidery ⟨a ~ blouse⟩ **2 :** made of sheer or transparent fabric ⟨dons a ~ negligee —S.J.Perelman⟩

¹**peel** \'pēl, *esp before pause or consonant* -ēəl\ *n* -s [ME *pele*, fr. OE *pyle* — more at PILLOW] *dial Eng* **:** PILLOW

²**peel** \"\ *vb* -ED/-ING/-S [ME *pelen* to rob, peel, fr. MF *peler* to peel, remove the hair from, fr. L *pilare* to remove the hair from, make bald, fr. *pilus* hair — more at PILE] *vt* **1** *obs* **:** ²PILL **1 2 a :** to strip off the outer layer of **:** PARE, DECORTICATE ⟨~ an apple⟩ ⟨~*ing* potatoes⟩ ⟨machine automatically ~*s* . . . shrimp —*Time*⟩ **b :** to remove (the outer layer or covering) by stripping, tearing off, or rolling back — usu. used with *off* or *from* ⟨~*ing* off the skin of a banana⟩ ⟨~*ing* the white bark from his . . . trees —E.W.Smith⟩ ⟨stamps should never be ~*ed* from the paper —H.M.Ellis⟩ ⟨~*ed* the . . . shirt off over his head —Kay Boyle⟩ ⟨the canvas coverings were ~*ed* back —R.F.Mirvish⟩ **c :** to remove part of the bran from (the grains of wheat or rice) by abrasion **3 :** to cause (a ball other than one's own) to pass through a wicket in croquet ⟨~*ed* his partner's ball through the last wicket⟩ ~ *vi* **1 a :** to become detached **:** come off **:** scale off **:** DESQUAMATE ⟨sunburned skin ~*s*⟩ ⟨the paint was ~*ing* off⟩ ⟨the . . . roof from which shingles were ~*ing* off —Ellen Glasgow⟩ **b :** to lose the outer layer of skin ⟨his face is ~*ing*⟩ **2 :** to take off one's clothes ⟨it got hotter . . . you had to ~ to get relief —L.M.Uris⟩ **syn** see SKIN

³**peel** \"\ *n* -s **1 a :** the skin or rind of a fruit ⟨letting the ~*s* drop on the floor —Truman Capote⟩ **b :** such rind candied ⟨orange ~⟩ **2 :** a thin layer of organic material embedded in a film of collodion and stripped from the surface of an object (as a plant fossil) for microscopic study

⁴**peel** \"\ *also* **peel tower** *n* -s [ME *pel, pele* castle, stockade, stake, fr. AF *pel, pele* stockade & MF *pel* stake, fr. L *palus* stake — more at POLE] **:** a medieval small massive fortified tower along the Scottish-English border having a usu. vaulted ground floor for confining and protecting cattle and a floor above for the family dwelling place reached by outside movable stairs or a ladder

⁵**peel** \"\ *n* -s [ME *pele* shovel, oven peel, fr. MF, shovel, fr. L *pala* spade, oven peel; prob. akin to L *pangere* to fix, fasten, plant — more at PACT] **1 a :** SHOVEL **b** *dial Eng* **:** a fire shovel **2 :** a usu. long-handled spade-shaped instrument used chiefly by bakers (as for getting loaves and pies into and out of an oven) **3 :** a T-shaped implement formerly in use by printers and papermakers for hanging up sheets of paper to dry

⁶**peel** *dial var of* PEAL

⁷**peel** \'pēl, *esp before pause or consonant* -ēəl\ *vt* -ED/-ING/-S [origin unknown] *Scot* **:** to equal **:** MATCH

⁸**peel** \"\ *n* -s **1** *chiefly Scot* **:** EQUAL, MATCH **2 peels** *pl, chiefly Scot* **:** an even game in curling **:** tie score ⟨it was ~*s* at 8 to 8 in the tenth head —*Time*⟩

⁹**peel** \"\ *Scot var of* POOL

¹⁰**peel** \"\ *chiefly dial var of* PAIL

**peeled** *adj* [ME (Sc) *peilit*, fr. past part. of *pelen* to peel] **:** BALD, TONSURED ⟨my ~ head and . . . white whiskers —Mark Twain⟩ ⟨~ priest —Shak.⟩

¹**peel·er** \'pēlə(r)\ *n* -s [ME *peler* pillager, plunderer, fr. *pelen* to rob, peel + *-er* — more at PEEL] **1 :** one that peels **:** PARER, STRIPPER: as **a :** one whose work it is to peel a specified thing ⟨potato ~ in a restaurant⟩ **b :** a worker who peels bark from felled trees or logs — called also *rosser, spudder* **c :** an instrument or machine that performs an operation of peeling, paring, or stripping ⟨the swivel-blade ~ . . . for fruit and vegetable paring —*Tools for Food Preparation & Dishwashing*⟩ ⟨electric paint ~⟩ **d :** STRIPTEASER **2 :** a crab that has begun to shed its shell **3 :** a log of softwood (as Douglas fir) having a diameter of 24 or more inches and suitable for cutting into veneer that is peeled cylindrically from the log by a lathe **4 a :** long-staple cotton orig. from the Delta region of northwestern Mississippi **b :** yarn spun from such cotton **5 :** an energetic industrious person **:** HUSTLER ⟨a real ~ for work —Esther Forbes⟩ **6 :** a cowhand who specializes in breaking horses

²**peeler** \"\ *n* -s [origin unknown] *dial Eng* **:** an iron bar used to make holes in the ground esp. for hop poles

³**peeler** \"\ *n* -s [Sir Robert *Peel* †1850 Eng. statesman who instituted the Irish constabulary + E *-er*] *Brit* **:** POLICE OFFICER; *specif* **:** a policeman of the lowest rank ⟨an officious ~ arrested him as a vagabond —W.B.Yeats⟩

**peelgarlic** *var of* PILGARLIC

**peel·ing** \'pēliŋ, -ēəŋ\ *n* -s **1 :** a peeled-off piece or strip (as of skin or rind) **:** PEEL **2** *archaic* **:** a thin dress material **3 :** a defect in a ceramic glaze or enamel caused by high contraction

**peel·ite** \'pēˌlīt\ *n* -s *usu cap* [Sir Robert *Peel* + E *-ite*] **:** one of a group of 19th century British Tories supporting Peel in the repeal of the Corn Laws and later maintaining a position between the protectionist Tories and the Liberals until eventually merging with the Liberals

**peel off** *vi* **1 :** to veer away in a wingover to the outside of a flight formation esp. from the bottom of an echelon for a steep dive or for a landing **2 :** to veer away from ships in convoy (as for an attack upon a submarine)

**peels** *pl of* PEEL, *pres 3d sing of* PEEL

¹**peen** *also* **pean** \'pēn\ *vt* -ED/-ING/-S [prob. of Scand origin; akin to Norw *penne* to hammer out thin, fr. *penn*, n., peen] **1 :** to draw, bend or flatten (as metal or leather) by hammering with a peen **2 :** to work the surface of (metal) by a stream of shot ⟨great improvement has been brought about in the service life of springs by shot ~*ing* —D.K.Bullens⟩

²**peen** *or* **pein** *also* **pean** \'pēn\ *n* -s [prob. of Scand origin; akin to Norw *penn* peen, Sw *pen*] **:** the hemispherical, wedge-shaped, or otherwise formed end of the head of a hammer opposite the face, used for bending, indenting, or cutting the material being struck — compare BALL PEEN, CROSS PEEN

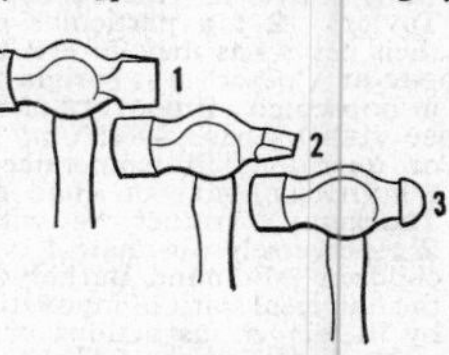

peens: *1* straight peen; *2* cross peen; *3* ball peen

**peenge** \'pēnzh, -nj\ *vi* -ED/-ING/-S [prob. imit.] *chiefly Scot* **:** to complain **:** GRUMBLE

**peening rammer** *n* **:** PEGGING RAMMER

**peen-to** \'pēnˌtō\ *n* -s [Chin (Pek) *pien³ t'ao²*, fr. *pien³* flat + *t'ao²* peach] **:** any of several peaches with a flattened shape; *esp* **:** a peach of Chinese origin grown in the southern U.S.

**pee·oy** \pē'ōi\ *n* -s [prob. imit.] *Scot* **:** a cone of damp gunpowder used for fireworks

¹**peep** \'pēp\ *vi* -ED/-ING/-S [ME *pepen*, of imit. origin] **1 :** to utter a feeble shrill sound as of a bird hatching or newly hatched **:** CHEEP, CHIRP ⟨a brood of chickens ~*ed* in a coop —*Harper's*⟩ **2 :** to speak with a small weak voice **:** utter the slightest sound ⟨every time he ~*s*, she jumps to see what's the matter —Benjamin Spock⟩

²**peep** \"\ *n* -s [ME *pepe*, fr. *pepen* to peep, chirp] **1 :** a feeble shrill sound (as by a young chicken or mouse) **:** CHEEP, CHIRP, SQUEAK **2 :** a slight utterance esp. of complaint or protest ⟨don't let me hear another ~ out of you⟩ **3 a :** any of several small sandpipers: as (1) **:** LEAST SANDPIPER (2) **:** SEMIPALMATED SANDPIPER **b** *Brit* **:** MEADOW PIPIT

³**peep** \"\ *vb* -ED/-ING/-S [ME *pepen*, perh. alter. of *piken* to peek] *vi* **1 a :** to peer through or as if through a crevice ⟨~*ing* . . . out from chinks and knotholes —George Orwell⟩ **b :** to look cautiously or slyly **:** PEEK, SPY ⟨~ behind the scenes⟩ ⟨would never . . . ~ under her bed —Oliver Goldsmith⟩ **2 :** to begin to emerge from or as if from concealment **:** become partly evident **:** show slightly — usu. used with *through, out,* or *from* ⟨crocuses ~*ing* through the grass⟩ ⟨the ancient belief . . . keeps ~*ing* out in unexpected quarters —C.W.Cunnington⟩ ⟨his brown curls ~*ed* from the edges of his cap —Marcia Davenport⟩ ~ *vt* **:** to put forth or cause to protrude slightly (as the head of one peeping) — usu. used with *out* ⟨not a dangerous action can ~ out his head —Shak.⟩

⁴**peep** \"\ *n* -s **1 :** the first glimpse or faint appearance ⟨at the ~ of dawn⟩ **2 a :** a slight or brief look **:** GLANCE ⟨take a quick ~ at the past —*London Calling*⟩ **b :** a furtive look through or as if through a crevice or from or into a hiding place **:** PEEK ⟨a ~ at the neighbors through the blinds⟩ **3 :** PEEP SIGHT **4 :** PEEKABOO

⁵**peep** *n* -s [obs. E *peep* one of the dots used on dice and dominoes to indicate numerical value, of unknown origin] *obs* **:** STEP, DEGREE

⁶**peep** \'pēp\ *n* -s [by alter.] **:** JEEP

**peep-bo** \'=ˌbō\ *n* -s [³*peep* + *boo*, interj.] **:** PEEKABOO

¹**peep·er** \'pēpə(r)\ *n* -s [¹*peep* + *-er*] **1 :** one (as a young chicken or pigeon) that peeps or chirps **2 :** any of various frogs (esp. of the family Hylidae) that make peeping sounds; *specif* **:** SPRING PEEPER ⟨the sound of ~*s* in springtime pools —*Sat. Eve. Post*⟩

²**peeper** \"\ *n* -s [³*peep* + *-er*] **1 :** one that peeps; *specif* **:** PEEPING TOM, VOYEUR **2 :** EYE — usu. used in pl. ⟨let his ~*s* roll over towards our table —Ring Lardner⟩

**peep frog** *n* **:** ¹PEEPER 2

**peep hawk** *n, Irish* **:** KESTREL

**peephole** \'=ˌ=\ *n* **:** a hole or crevice (as in a furnace, oven, or door) through which one may peep ⟨a ~ was uncovered, an eye peered at me, the door was opened —Joseph Wechsberg⟩

**peeping tom** *n* -s *often cap P&T* [after *Peeping Tom*, legendary 11th cent. tailor of Coventry supposed to have been struck blind for peeping at Lady Godiva as she rode naked through the town in order to win relief for its inhabitants from burdensome taxation] **:** a pruriently prying person **:** VOYEUR, PEEPER ⟨*peeping toms* . . . who spy on spooning couples —Morris Ploscowe⟩

**peep show** *n* **:** a small show or object exhibited that is viewed through an orifice or a magnifying glass ⟨a carnival with *peep shows* and flea acts —Stanley Walker⟩ ⟨sexual exhibitions reminiscent of the modern . . . *peep show* —Ralph Linton⟩

**peep sight** *n* **:** a rear sight having an adjustable metal piece pierced with a small hole to peep through in aiming

**peepul** *also* **peepal** *var of* PIPAL

**peepy** \'pēpē, -pi\ *adj* -ER/-EST [³*peep* + *-y*] *dial Eng* **:** SLEEPY ⟨the potboy, very tousled and ~ —Ngaio Marsh⟩

¹**peer** \'pi(ə)r, -iə\ *n* -s [ME *per, pere, peere*, fr. OF *per*, fr. *per*, adj., equal, fr. L *par* — more at PAIR] **1 a :** one that is of the same or equal standing (as in law, rank, quality, age, ability) with another **:** EQUAL ⟨scholars of the first rank welcomed him as their ~ —B.W.Bond⟩ ⟨an electrode material without ~ —B.W.Gamson⟩ ⟨boys and girls in their teens . . . form groups of their ~*s* —Martha M. Eliot⟩ **b :** a fellow citizen ⟨a jury of his ~*s*⟩ **2** *archaic* **:** COMPANION, FELLOW **3 a :** a member of one of the five ranks of the British peerage (as a duke, marquess, earl, viscount, or baron) **b :** a man of high rank or position in any country or organization that recognizes different orders **:** NOBLE ⟨high capital of Satan and his ~*s* —John Milton⟩

²**peer** \"\ *vt* -ED/-ING/-S [ME *peeren, peren*, fr. *peer, peere*, n.] *archaic* **:** to equal in rank **:** be the peer of **:** RIVAL, MATCH

³**peer** \"\ *adj* [¹*peer*] **:** belonging to the same group in society esp. when membership is determined by age, grade, or status ⟨a ~ group of adolescents⟩ ⟨school children oriented to ~ culture values, rather than adult ones⟩

⁴**peer** *obs var of* PIER

⁵**peer** \'pi(ə)r, -iə\ *vi* -ED/-ING/-S [perh. by shortening & alter. fr. *appear*] **1 :** to look intently or curiously **:** STARE ⟨the natives . . . were ~*ing* from behind trees —Francis Birtles⟩ ⟨~*ing* impudently into your face —L.C.Douglas⟩; *esp* **:** to look searchingly at something difficult to discern ⟨~*ing* into the distance⟩ ⟨drove . . . and began to ~ at the signs on street corners —Raymond Chandler⟩ **2 :** to come slightly into view **:** emerge partly **:** peep out ⟨when daffodils begin to ~ —Shak.⟩ ⟨a vast white cloud, through which the sun ~*ed* —Francis Kingdon-Ward⟩ **3** *archaic* **:** APPEAR ⟨darkly a project ~*s* upon his mind —John Home⟩ **syn** see GAZE

⁶**peer** \'pēr\ *Scot var of* POOR

**peer·age** \'pirij, -rēj\ *n* -s [ME *perage*, fr. *per, peer, peere* peer + *-age*] **1 :** the body of peers **:** NOBILITY ⟨Charlemagne with all his ~ —John Milton⟩ **2 :** the rank or dignity of a peer ⟨the prime minister submitted the industrialist's name for a ~⟩ **3 :** a book containing a list of the peers with their genealogy, history, and titles ⟨his name is in the ~⟩

**peer·ess** \-rəs\ *n* -ES **1 :** the wife or widow of a peer **2 :** a woman who holds in her own right the rank of a peer

¹**peer·ie** *or* **peery** \'pirē\ *n, pl* **peeries** [perh. irreg. fr. ¹*pear* + *-ie*; fr. its shape] *chiefly Scot* **:** PEG TOP 1

²**peerie** \"\ *adj* [origin unknown] *Scot* **:** SMALL ⟨a ~ lad⟩

**peer·ing·ly** *adv* [*peering* (pres. part. of ⁵*peer*) + *-ly*] **:** in a peering manner

**peer·less** \'pi(ə)rləs, 'piəl-\ *adj* [ME *pereles*, fr. *pere, peer, peere* peer + *-les* -less] **:** MATCHLESS, INCOMPARABLE ⟨a ~ among women —H.O.Taylor⟩ ⟨his ~ readings —Margaret Rutherford⟩ — **peer·less·ly** *adv* — **peer·less·ness** *n* -ES

**peert** \'pi(ə)r|t, -iə|, *usu* |d.+V\ *var of* PEART

**peery** \'pirē, -ri\ *adj* -ER/-EST [⁵*peer* + *-y*] **:** INQUISITIVE, SUSPICIOUS ⟨~ envious eyes —Bruce Marshall⟩

**pees** *pl of* PEE, *pres 3d sing of* PEE

**pees·weep** *or* **peese·weep** \'pēzˌwēp\ *also* **pee·weep** \'pē-

,wēp\ *n* -s [imit.] **1** *dial Brit* : LAPWING **2** *dial Brit* : GREENFINCH

**peet·weet** \'pē,twēt, *usu* -wēd·+V\ *n* -s [imit.] : SPOTTED SANDPIPER

**¹peeve** \'pēv\ *vt* -ED/-ING/-S [back-formation fr. *peevish*] : to make peevish or resentful : ANNOY ⟨don't believe you'll ever be able to ~ that boy —H.L.Wilson⟩ ⟨was very *peeved* about being left out —C.B.Palmer b. 1910⟩ **syn** see IRRITATE

**²peeve** \"\ *n* -s **1** : a peevish mood : a feeling of resentment ⟨in a ~ over it⟩ ⟨the atmosphere . . . charged with ~ —R.L. Taylor⟩ **2** : a particular grievance : GRUDGE ⟨grumbling their pet ~s as they go —R.L.Smith⟩

**peev·er** \'pēvə(r)\ *n* -s [origin unknown] **1** *Scot* : a stone used in hopscotch **2 peevers** *pl* : HOPSCOTCH

**pee·vish** \'pēvish, -vēsh\ *adj* [ME *pevish* spiteful] **1** : morose or querulous in temperament or mood : hard to please : IRRITABLE, FRETFUL ⟨had never known her so ~ —W.M. Thackeray⟩ ⟨rather ~ with waiting —Edmund Wilson⟩ **2** : perversely obstinate : CONTRARY ⟨the forwardness of ~ children —Edmund Burke⟩ ⟨a frequently ~ struggle against the universal spirit of innovation —Daniel Aaron⟩ **3** : marked by ill temper (as actions or words) ⟨with a ~ gesture she slapped over the rest of the notes —A.J.Cronin⟩ ⟨her accent was ~ —Jane Austen⟩ ⟨that ~ sort of criticism —*Times Lit. Supp.*⟩ **syn** see IRRITABLE

**pee·vish·ly** \-vəshlē, -vēsh-, -li\ *adv* : in a peevish manner ⟨everybody ordered him around, he complained to himself ~ —John Dos Passos⟩

**pee·vish·ness** \-vishnəs, -vēsh-\ *n* -ES [ME *pevyshnesse* spitefulness, fr. *pevysh, pevish* spiteful + *-nesse* -ness] : the quality or state of being peevish : PETULANCE ⟨mumbled with childish ~ —Richard Blaker⟩

**peevit** *var of* PEWIT

**peevy** *var of* PEAVEY

**¹pee·wee** *or* **pe·wee** \'pē,wē\ *n* -s [imit.] **1 a** *usu* **pewee** : any of various small olivaceous flycatchers; *esp* : WOOD PEWEE **b** *Scot* : LAPWING **c** *Austral* : MAGPIE LARK **2** : something diminutive or tiny: as **a** : a small child **b** : an abnormally small animal : RUNT **c** *dial* : a small marble usu. of poor quality **d** : an egg of the smallest size **e** : a low-topped cowboy boot

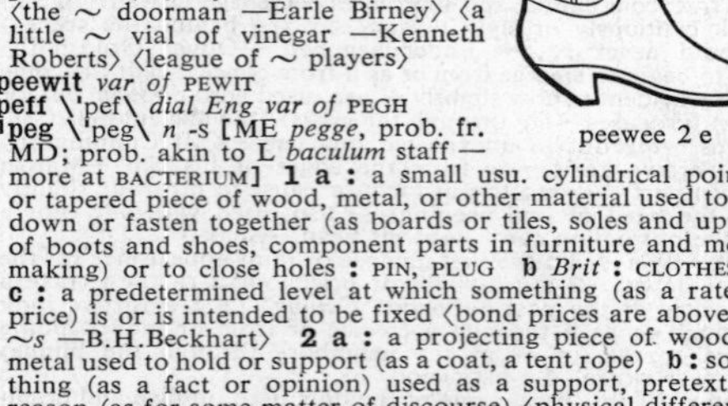

peewee 2 e

**²peewee** \"\ *adj* : DIMINUTIVE, TINY ⟨the ~ doorman —Earle Birney⟩ ⟨a little ~ vial of vinegar —Kenneth Roberts⟩ ⟨league of ~ players⟩

**peewit** *var of* PEWIT

**peff** \'pef\ *dial Eng var of* PEGH

**¹peg** \'peg\ *n* -s [ME *pegge*, prob. fr. MD; prob. akin to L *baculum* staff — more at BACTERIUM] **1 a** : a small usu. cylindrical pointed or tapered piece of wood, metal, or other material used to pin down or fasten together (as boards or tiles, soles and uppers of boots and shoes, component parts in furniture and model making) or to close holes : PIN, PLUG **b** *Brit* : CLOTHESPIN **c** : a predetermined level at which something (as a rate or price) is or is intended to be fixed ⟨bond prices are above the ~s —B.H.Beckhart⟩ **2 a** : a projecting piece of wood or metal used to hold or support (as a coat, a tent rope) **b** : something (as a fact or opinion) used as a support, pretext, or reason (as for some matter of discourse) ⟨physical differences are merely the ~s upon which culturally generated hostilities are made to hang —M.F.A.Montagu⟩ ⟨the ~ for these comments is the . . . strike and its aftermath —*Janata*⟩ **c** : a usu. tapered piece of wood or metal driven into the ground (as to mark a boundary or limit or to stake out a claim) **d** : STUMP 7a **e** : a cylinder or pin fitting into a hole on a pegboard **3 a** (1) : one of the wooden or metal pins of a stringed musical instrument that are turned to regulate the pitch of the strings : TUNING PEG ⟨a skillful musician . . . can let down his strings a ~ lower —Joseph Hall⟩ — see VIOLIN illustration (2) : END PIN 2 **b** : a downward step or degree (as in estimation) ⟨set him down a ~⟩ ⟨our pride in our achievements comes down a ~ —*Times Lit. Supp.*⟩ **4** : a pointed prong or claw for catching or tearing — see HUSKING PEG, TURTLE PEG **5** *Brit* **a** : a pin set as a mark in a drinking vessel **b** : the amount of drink marked by the level of such a peg **c** : DRINK — usu. used of alcoholic beverages ⟨poured himself out a stiff ~ —Dorothy Sayers⟩ **6 a** : something felt to resemble a peg (as a foot, leg, tooth, kernel of corn) **b** : a wooden leg **c** : the elongated hypanthium of the peanut flower that bends over and forms the subterranean stem on which the pod is borne **7** : PEG TOP **8** [²*peg*] : THROW; *esp* : one made in baseball by a fielder or a baseman ⟨scooped up hot grounders with one hand . . . and made lightning ~s to first —Edwin Corle⟩

**²peg** \"\ *vb* **pegged; pegged; pegging; pegs** *vt* **1 a** : to put a peg into : pin, attach, fasten together, plug, or block with a peg ⟨~ a notice to a post⟩ ⟨~ shoes⟩ ⟨~ seedlings⟩ ⟨a wooden plank . . . *pegged* to the ground —J.G.Frazer⟩ ⟨articles should be *pegged* to a workboard —F.J.Christopher⟩ **b** *Brit* : to pin or hang (laundry) on a clothesline — usu. used with *up* ⟨in the garden *pegging* up the clothes⟩ **c** : to keep in place : pin down : RESTRICT — usu. used with *down* ⟨set on *pegging* him safely down —Clemence Dane⟩ **d** : to fix or hold (as prices, wages, rate of exchange) at a constant or predetermined point or level ⟨*pegging* the price of grapefruit —*New Republic*⟩ ⟨the ruble was *pegged* at four to the dollar —Horace Sutton⟩ **e** : to place in a definite category : nail down : IDENTIFY ⟨had you *pegged* for one of these ladies with fainting spells —Wallace Stegner⟩ ⟨*pegging* it as the cause of vast future unemployment —D.S.Harder⟩ **f** : to give (something) support, reason, or relevance by attaching it to or making it depend on something else ⟨~ your sales talk to some recent happening⟩ ⟨broadcasts . . . *pegged* to themes that reflect a continuing propaganda compaign —H.R.Lieberman⟩ **2** *obs* : HAMMER **3** : to strike or pierce (as a turtle, lobster, shellfish) with a thrown peg **4** : to score (a specified number of points) in cribbage esp. by advancing a peg on the board **5** : to mark (as a boundary) by pegs — usu. used with *out* ⟨~ out a certain patch for the hose —*Gadgets Annual*⟩; *specif* : to mark out (a miner's claim or an agricultural selection) at the four corners by pegs bearing the claimant's name ⟨had got in first . . . had *pegged* out a claim —Eleanor Dark⟩ **6** *of a hunting dog* : POINT **7 a** : to throw (as a baseball) esp. low and fast ⟨the shortstop *pegged* the ball to the first baseman⟩ ⟨*pegged* stones at the trains —Rosemary V. Donatelli⟩ **b** : to retire (a batter or base runner) in baseball by a throw to a base or to home plate ⟨*pegged* the runner at third⟩ — often used with *out* ⟨*pegged* the runner out⟩ ~ *vi* **1** : to throw, cast, or let fly with a missile (as a peg) or ball; *specif* : to cast a fly in fishing **2** : to work steadily and diligently : PLOD, PLUG — usu. used with *away, at, on* ⟨*pegging* away at his writing —Brooks Atkinson⟩ ⟨find it terribly hard to ~ at things —*Atlantic*⟩ **3** : to move along vigorously or hastily : HUSTLE ⟨*pegging* down the stairs —Elizabeth Bowen⟩ **4** : to make a score (as in cribbage) esp. when the score is recorded on a pegboard

**³peg** \"\ *or* **pegged** \'pegd\ *adj* : PEG-TOP ⟨had on a black coat and black ~ pants —Thurston Scott⟩

**PEG** *abbr* prior endorsement guaranteed

**pe·ga** \'pāgə\ *or* **peg·a·dor** \,pegə'dō(ə)r, -ō(ə)\ *n* -s [*pega* fr. Sp, lit., act of sticking, fr. *pegar* to stick, paste, cling, fr. L *picare* to daub with pitch, fr. *pic-, pix* pitch; *pegador* fr. Sp, fr. *pegar* — more at PITCH] : REMORA

**peg and eye** *n* : LOOP HINGE

**peg-and-socket** \'⸗⸗'⸗⸗\ *adj* : of, relating to, or constituting the method of jointing of the scales in ganoid fishes by which processes suggestive of pegs on the anterior end of a scale fit into corresponding depressions in the posterior end of the one in front of it

**peg·a·num** \'pegənəm\ *n, cap* [NL, fr. Gk *pēganon* rue; prob. akin to Gk *pēgnynai* to fix, fasten together — more at PACT] : a widely distributed genus of herbs (family Zygophyllaceae) having alternate leaves and large white solitary flowers with 12 to 15 stamens — see AFRICAN RUE

**peg·a·se·an** \,pegə'sēən, pə'gāsēən\ *also* **pe·ga·si·an** \pə'gāsēən\ *adj, usu cap* [*pegasean* fr. L *pegaseus* pegasean (fr. *Pegasus*, mythological winged horse + *-eus* -eous) + E *-an*; *pegasian* alter. of *pegasean*] **1** : of, relating to, or resembling the mythological winged horse Pegasus; *esp* : SWIFT **2** : of or relating to poetic inspiration : highly imaginative : POETIC

**peg·a·sid** \'pegəsəd, -,sid\ *n* -s [NL *Pegasidae*] : a fish of the family Pegasidae

**pe·gas·i·dae** \pə'gasə,dē\ *n pl, cap* [NL, fr. *Pegasus*, type genus + *-idae*] : a small family (order Hypostomides) of marine fishes — see PEGASUS 2

**peg·a·soid** \'pegə,sȯid\ *adj* [NL *Pegasus* + E *-oid*] : like or related to the Pegasidae

**peg·a·sus** \'pegəsəs\ *n* [L *Pegasus*, mythological winged horse fabled to have created by a blow of his hoof the fountain Hippocrene that was supposed to be a source of poetic inspiration, fr. Gk *Pēgasos*] **1** *pl* **pegasi** \-ə,sī\ *or* **pegasuses** *often cap* **a** : a fabulous winged horse ⟨many interesting figures of . . . griffins, *pegasi* —G.W.Eve⟩; *esp* : the winged steed thought of as bearing a poet in his flights of fancy **b** : poetic inspiration ⟨each spurs his jaded *Pegasus* apace —Lord Byron⟩ **2** [NL, fr. L *Pegasus*, mythological winged horse] **a** *cap* : a genus (the type and best known genus of the family Pegasidae) of small chiefly tropical Indo-Pacific marine fishes having a long snout, a small toothless mouth, a body wholly covered with bony plates, pelvic fins of only two rays, and pectoral fins spread horizontally like a pair of wings **b** -ES : any fish of the genus *Pegasus* : SEA MOTH

**pegboard** \'⸗,⸗\ *n* **1** : a small usu. about 6 in. x 6 in. board perforated with a pattern of holes into which pegs are stuck in playing certain games (as solitaire) **2** : an educational toy consisting of a board with holes into which a child hammers or thrusts pegs

pegboard 2

**pegbox** \'⸗,⸗\ *n* : the open part of the head in a stringed musical instrument in which pegs are set

**peg float** *also* **peg cutter** *n* : a short knife set at an angle across the end of a shaft that is inserted into finished pegged shoes to cut off the protruding peg ends

**pegged** *adj* [fr. past part. of ²*peg*] **1** : maintained at or near a predetermined level, rate, or price ⟨~ rate of exchange⟩ ⟨buying at the present ~ prices⟩ **2** : PEG-TOPPED ⟨sharply ~ pants with deep pleats —Irving Shulman⟩

**pegged boot** *also* **peg boot** *n* : a boot having soles fastened on by wooden pegs

**pegged shoe** *also* **peg shoe** *n* : a shoe having soles fastened on by wooden pegs

**pegged splint** *n* : a splint or exostosis on the back of the cannon bone of a quadruped that lies beneath the flexor tendons and frequently interferes with their movement causing lameness

**pegging** *pres part of* PEG

**pegging rammer** *n* : a rammer used in a foundry for soft open sand courses that consists of an oblong piece of iron varying usu. from a quarter of an inch to an inch in thickness which is secured to the end of a piece of tubing or bar iron

cross section of a pegged shoe: *1* lining, *2* upper, *3* insole, *4* outsole, *5* lasting tack, *6* peg

**peg graft** *n* : a side graft in which a scion of leafless dormant wood with wedge-shaped base is driven into an opening cut in the stock and sealed with wax or other material

**¹peg·gy** \'pegē, -gi\ *n* -ES [fr. *Peggy*, nickname fr. the name *Margaret*] *dial Eng* : any of several small birds: as **a** : WHITETHROAT **b** : BLACKCAP **c** : CHIFFCHAFF **d** : WILLOW WREN

**²peggy** \"\ *adj* [by alter.] : PECKY 1

**¹pegh** \'pef, 'pek\ *vi* -ED/-ING/-S [ME (northern dial.) *pechen*, prob. of imit. origin] *dial chiefly Scot* : to breathe hard after bodily exercise : PANT

**²pegh** \"\ *n* -s *dial chiefly Scot* : a breath taken with difficulty : PANT

**peg in the ring** : a game of spinning a peg top within the bounds of a marked-out circle

**¹peg leg** *n* [¹*peg* + *leg*] **1** : an artificial leg; *esp* : one fitted to the bent knee **2** : a person wearing such a leg ⟨tale . . . concerns a choleric British ex-soldier and *peg leg* —Anthony West⟩

**²peg leg** *vi* : to strike bottom only intermittently or on alternate strokes — used of a cable tool in drilling

**pegma** *also* **pegme** *n* -s [L *pegmat-, pegma*, fr. Gk *pēgmat-, pēgma* framework, stage or scaffold in theaters, fr. *pēgnynai* to fix, fasten together — more at PACT] **1** *obs* : a movable theatrical structure used esp. in pageants **2** *obs* : an inscription on a pegma

**peg·man** \'⸗mən\ *n, pl* **pegmen** : a man who attends to a peg (as one blocking a power hammer)

**peg·ma·tite** \'pegmə,tīt\ *n* -s [F, fr. Gk *pēgmat-, pēgma* something fastened together, framework + F *-ite*] **1** : GRAPHIC GRANITE **2 a** : a natural igneous rock formation consisting of a variety of granite that occurs in dikes or veins and is usu. characterized by extremely coarse texture caused by crystallization from an exceptionally fluid magma rich in mineralizers containing rare elements that frequently form unusual minerals (as tourmaline spodumene, beryl) **b** : a similar formation in a rock other than granite ⟨syenite ~⟩ ⟨diorite ~⟩

**peg·ma·tit·ic** \,⸗⸗'tid·ik\ *adj* [ISV *pegmatite* + *-ic*] : having a texture like that of pegmatite

**peg·ma·tit·ization** \,⸗⸗,tīd·ə'zāshən, -d·,ī'z-\ *n* -s [*pegmatite* + *-ization*] : the formation of pegmatite from other rocks

**peg·ma·tize** \'⸗⸗,tīz\ *vt* -ED/-ING/-S [*pegmatite* + *-ize*] : to convert into pegmatite

**¹peg·ma·toid** \-,tȯid\ *adj* [*pegmatite* + *-oid*] : PEGMATITIC

**²pegmatoid** \"\ *n* -s **1** : a pegmatite containing a feldspathoid as an essential constituent **2** : a coarse-grained pegmatite of normal habit as distinguished from graphic granite

**peg·mat·o·phyre** \peg'madə,fī(ə)r\ *n* -s [*pegmatite* + *-o-* + *-phyre*] : a granite porphyry with micropegmatitic groundmass

**peg organ** *n* : an insect sense organ that is basically an innervated hair

**peg out** *vt* **1** : to put out of the game in croquet by making (a rover ball) hit the stake **2** : to toss out or allow to run out (as a line) : pay out ~ *vi* **1 a** : to end one's play by pegging out one's ball in croquet **b** : to score the winning point in a cribbage game **2 a** : to give out : FAIL **b** : DIE ⟨you only pretend to care because you thought I was going to *peg out* —Miles Franklin⟩

**pegs** *pl of* PEG, *pres 3d sing of* PEG

**peg shoe** *var of* PEGGED SHOE

**peg switch** *n* : PLUG SWITCH

**peg tankard** *n* : a tankard with a vertical row of pegs set at equal distances on the inner surface to mark the quantity of drink permitted each person at the passing of the cup

**peg tooth** *n* **1** : a sawtooth shaped like a peg **2** : a cylindrical or conical gear-wheel tooth projecting axially or radially from the rim of the wheel

**peg-tooth harrow** *n* : a harrow consisting of a set of horizontal transverse wooden or iron bars fitted with wooden or iron teeth

**peg top** *n* **1** : a pear-shaped wooden top that ends in a sharp metal peg and that is made to spin by the unwinding of a string wound round its center **2** : a game played with peg tops **3 peg tops** *pl* : peg-top trousers

**peg-top** \'⸗;⸗\ *or* **peg-topped** \'⸗;⸗\ *adj* [*peg-top* fr. *peg top*; *peg-topped* fr. *peg top* + *-ed*] : wide at the top and narrow at the bottom — used esp. of trousers, skirts, and pockets with pleated or draped fullness at the top

**¹pe·gu·an** \pe'güən\ *adj, usu cap* [*Pegu*, town, district, division, and river in south central Burma + E *-an*] : of, relating to, or characteristic of Pegu, Burma

**²peguan** \"\ *n* -s *cap* : a native or resident of Pegu, Burma : MON

**pe·gu catechu** \pe'gü-\ *n, usu cap P* : CATECHU 1 a

**pegwood** \'⸗,⸗\ *n* **1** : a spindle tree (*Euonymus europaeus*) **2** : wood used in splints whittled to a point for cleaning out pivot holes in watchmaking

**pehlevi** *cap, var of* PAHLAVI

**peh-tsai** *var of* PE-TSAI

**peign·oir** *R* pān'wä(r), '⸗,⸗ *also* -wȯ(ə)r; *-R* -wä(r *also* -wȯ(ə)(r\ *n* -s [F, peignoir, garment worn over the shoulders while combing the hair, fr. MF, garment worn over the shoulders while combing the hair, fr. *peigner* to comb the hair, fr. L *pectinare* to comb, fr. *pectin-, pecten* comb — more at PECTINATE] : a woman's loose negligee or dressing gown

**pein** *var of* PEEN

**pei·ping** \'pā'piŋ, 'bā'-\ *adj, usu cap* [*Peiping* (name used by the Nationalist government of China) (fr. Chin — Pek — *Pe⁴ p'ing²*, fr. *pe⁴* north + *p'ing²* peace), *Peking* (name used up to 1928 by the imperial and republican governments of China and since 1949 by the Communist government) (fr. Chin — Pek — *Pe⁴ ching¹*, fr. *pe⁴* north + *ching¹* capital), city in northeast China that was the capital up to 1928 and has been the capital of the Communist government of China since 1949] : PEKING

**pei·ram·e·ter** \pī'ramәd·ә(r), -ətə-\ *n* [Gk *peira* trial, attempt + E *-meter*; akin to Gk *peiran* to attempt — more at FEAR] : a dynamometer of the kind used to indicate the power necessary to haul a truck or carriage over a road or track

**pei·ras·tic** \(')pī;rastik, -tēk\ *also* **pei·ras·ti·cal** \-təkəl, -tēk-\ *adj* [Gk *peirastikos*, fr. *peiran* to attempt] : fitted for trial : EXPERIMENTAL, TENTATIVE — **pei·ras·ti·cal·ly** \-tək(ə)lē, -tēk-, -li\ *adv*

**peirc·e·an** \'pərsēən *also* 'pirs-\ *adj, usu cap* [Charles S. *Peirce* †1914 Am. physicist, mathematician, and logician + E *-an*] : of, relating to, or resembling Charles Sanders Peirce or his philosophical teachings (as pragmatism, metaphysical realism) — compare FIRSTNESS, SECONDNESS, THIRDNESS

**pei·res·kia** \pə'reskēə, pē'-\ *n, cap* [NL, fr. Nicolas-Claude Fabri de *Peiresc* †1637 Fr. antiquarian and naturalist + NL *-ia*] : a genus of shrubby spinose tropical American plants (family Cactaceae) having slender branches, broad flat leaves, and large pyramidal flowers — see BARBADOS GOOSEBERRY

**¹peise** \'pāz, 'pēz\ *n* -s [ME *peis*, fr. ONF, fr. L *pensum* — more at POISE] **1** *dial Brit* : WEIGHT **2** *dial Brit* : BALANCE, POISE

**²peise** \"\ *vb* -ED/-ING/-S [ME *peisen*, fr. ONF *peser* (3d pers. sing. pres. indic. *peise*), fr. L *pensare* to weigh (something) — more at PENSIVE] *vi* **1** *dial Brit* : to have weight : WEIGH **2** *dial Brit* : to bear down with weight ~ *vt* **1** *dial Brit* : to estimate the weight of : weigh (as in the hand) **2** *dial Brit* : to exert weight or force upon : open or lift by force

**peishwa** *var of* PESHWA

**pei·xe rei** *or* **pei·xe-rei** *or* **pei·xe·rey** \,pāshə'rā\ *n* -s [Pg *peixe-rei* silversides, fr. *peixe* fish (fr. L *piscis*) + *rei* king, fr. L *reg-, rex* — more at FISH, ROYAL] : any of several silversides (as the jacksmelt of California)

**pej·er·rey** \,pāhə'rā\ *n, pl* **pejerre·yes** \-(,)yās\ *or* **pejerreys** [Sp, silversides, fr. Sp dial. *peje* fish (fr. L *piscis*) + Sp *rey* king, fr. L *reg-, rex*] : any of various silversides of the So. American coasts; *esp* : any of several relatively large silversides that resemble mackerel and are important as food

**pej·i·ba·ye** \,pāhē'bāyə\ *also* **pe·ji·ba·ve** \-və\ *n* -s [AmerSp *pejibaye, pijibay*, perh. fr. Arawak] : PEACH PALM

**pe·jo·rate** \'pejə,rāt, 'pēj-, *usu* -ād·+V\ *vt* -ED/-ING/-S [LL *pejoratus*, past part. of *pejorare* to become worse, make worse] : to make worse : DEPRECIATE

**pe·jo·ra·tion** \,⸗⸗'rāshən\ *n* -s [ML *pejoration-, pejoratio*, fr. LL *pejoratus* (past part. of *pejorare* to become worse, make worse) + L *-ion-, -io* -ion] : a change for the worse : DEPRECIATION; *specif* : an historical process by which the semantic and connotative status of a word tends to decline — compare MELIORATION

**¹pe·jo·ra·tive** \pə'jȯrəd·iv; 'pej(ə)rəd-, -jə,rād-, 'pēj-\ *adj* [prob. fr. (assumed) NL *pejorativus*, fr. LL *pejoratus* (past part. of *pejorare* to become worse, make worse, fr. L *pejor* worse) + L *-ivus* -ive; akin to L *pessimus* worst, Skt *padyate* he falls, goes, L *ped-, pes* foot — more at FOOT] : having a tendency to make or become worse : DEPRECIATORY, DISPARAGING ⟨resort to ~ epithets as their argument —M.R. Cohen⟩ ⟨the ~ sense given the word "scholasticism" by the Renaissance —Frank Thilly⟩ — often used of words whose basic meaning is depreciated either by a suffix or by semantic application or association ⟨the ~ "poetaster" for a mere versifier⟩ ⟨we use the neutral word "paranormal" in preference to "abnormal" which is faintly ~ —A.G.N.Flew⟩ — **pe·jo·ra·tive·ly** \-əvlē, -li\ *adv*

**²pejorative** \"\ *n* -s : a pejorative word

**pek·an** \'pekən\ *n* -s [CanF *pékan, pécan*, of Algonquian origin; akin to Abnaki *pékané*] : FISHER 2

**peke** \'pēk\ *n* -s *often cap* [by shortening & alter.] : PEKINGESE 2

**peke-faced** \'⸗;⸗\ *adj* : having a short wrinkled muzzle like that of a Pekingese dog — used esp. of a long-haired show cat

**¹pe·kin** \'pē'kin\ *n* -s [F *pékin*, fr. *Pékin* Peking, city in northeast China, fr. Chin (Pek) *Pe⁴ ching¹*] *often cap* : a clothing fabric orig. of silk that is usu. characterized by wide vertical stripes in contrasting colors or weaves

**²pekin** \"\ *n, usu cap* [*Peking, Pekin*, city in northeast China] **1** : a breed of large active creamy white ducks of Chinese origin that is the breed chiefly used for commercial meat duck production in the U. S. **2** -s : a duck of the Pekin breed

**¹pe·king** \'pē'kiŋ\ *also* **pe·kin** \-'kin\ *adj, usu cap* [*peking* fr. *Peking* (name used up to 1928 by the imperial and republican governments of China and since 1949 by the Communist government), city in northeast China that was the capital up to 1928 and has been the capital of the Communist government of China since 1949, fr. Chin (Pek) *Pe⁴ ching¹*, fr. *pe⁴* north + *ching¹* capital; *pekin* fr. *Pekin* Peking, fr. F *Pékin*, fr. Chin (Pek) *Pe⁴ ching¹*] : of or from the city of Peking, China : of the kind or style prevalent in Peking

**²peking** \"\ *or* **peking duck** *n, usu cap P* : PEKIN

**peking blue** *n, often cap P* : a dark blue that is greener, lighter, and stronger than Japan blue or Majolica blue and stronger and slightly greener than Flemish blue

**peking cotoneaster** *n, often cap P* : a deciduous spreading shrub (*Cotoneaster acutifolia*) that is native to China but is used elsewhere as an ornamental esp. for hedges and that has the young branchlets pubescent, the leaves dull green above and pale and more pubescent below, and the flowers pink and in 2- to 5-flowered clusters

**¹pe·king·ese** \,pēkiŋ¦ēz,-kə¦nēz, -ēs\ *or* **pe·kin·ese** \,pēkə¦nēz, -ēs\ *n, pl* **pekingese** *or* **pekinese** [*Peking, Pekin*, city in northeast China + E *-ese*, n. suffix] **1** *cap* **a** : a native or resident of Peking **b** : the Chinese dialect of Peking **2 a** *usu cap* : a breed of very small dogs originating in China over 2000 years ago that have a flat face, a broad skull flat between the ears, bowed forelegs, a deep stop, prominent eyes, and a long soft coat with profuse coarser mane and thick undercoat, that are of all colors (as red, fawn, black, and parti-color) with the lighter-colored dogs often having a black mask, and that may weigh up to 14 pounds **b** *often cap* : a dog of the Pekingese breed

**²pekingese** \"\ *or* **pekinese** \"\ *adj, usu cap* [*Peking, Pekin*, city in northeast China + E *-ese*, adj. suffix] : of, from, relating to, or characteristic of Peking, China

**peking man** *also* **pekin man** *n, usu cap P* : an extinct man that is known from fragmentary skulls and parts of skeletons found in Pleistocene cave deposits at Choukoutien, China, that is more advanced in some details than Java man but nearer to him than to other fossil hominids or to recent man, and that though orig. set apart as a distinct species (*Sinanthropus pekinensis*) is now often made congeneric with Java man in a species (*Pithecanthropus pekinensis*) or even congeneric with recent man in a species (*Homo erectus*)

**peking nightingale** *n, usu cap P* : JAPANESE NIGHTINGALE

**pe·koe** \'pē,kō *also chiefly Brit* 'pe,-\ *n* -s *sometimes cap* [Chin (Amoy) *pek-ho*, fr. *pek* white + *ho* down] **1** : a tea made from the first three leaves on the spray **2** : any tea of India or Ceylon made from leaves of approximately the same size obtained by screening fired tea

**pel-** or **pelo-** *comb form* [ISV, fr. Gk *pēl-, pēlo-,* fr. *pēlos;* perh. akin to L *pallēre* to be pale — more at FALLOW] **:** clay **:** mud ⟨*pelite*⟩ ⟨*Pelomyxa*⟩

**pe·la** \ˈpālə\ *n* -S [Chin (Pek) *pe² la⁴*, fr. *pe²* white + *la⁴* wax] **1 :** CHINESE WAX **2 :** a scale (*Ericerus pela*) that secretes Chinese wax

**pe·la·do** \pāˈlä(ˌ)dō\ *n* -S [AmerSp, fr. *pelado*, adj., penniless, fr. Sp, bare, bald, fr. past part. of *pelar* to cut (the hair), pluck, skin, fr. L *pilare* to make bald, fr. *pilus* hair — more at PILE] *Southwest* **:** a Mexican peon — usu. used disparagingly

**pelag-** or **pelago-** *comb form* [L *pelag-*, fr. Gk *pelag-, pelago-,* fr. *pelagos* — more at FLAKE] **:** sea ⟨*pelagial*⟩

**pel·age** \ˈpelij, -lēj\ *n* -S [F, fr. MF, fr. *poil* hair (fr. L *pilus*) + *-age*] **:** the hairy covering of a mammal ⟨color variation of the . . . hare's ~ —R.E.Trippensee⟩

**pe·la·gi·al** \pəˈlājēəl\ *adj* [*pelag-* + *-ial*] **:** PELAGIC

**¹pe·la·gian** \-j(ē)ən\ *n* -S *usu cap* [LL *pelagianus*, adj. & n., fr. *Pelagius* †A.D.420? Brit. monk and theologian + L *-anus* -an] **:** an advocate of or believer in Pelagianism

**²pelagian** \"\ *adj, usu cap* [LL *pelagianus*] **:** of or relating to Pelagius or Pelagianism

**³pelagian** \"\ *adj* [*pelag-* + *-an*] **:** PELAGIC

**⁴pelagian** \"\ *n* -S **:** a pelagic animal

**pe·la·gian·ism** \-əˌnizəm\ *n* -S *usu cap* [¹*Pelagian* + *-ism*] **:** the teachings of Pelagius condemned as heretical in A.D.431 and marked by the denial of original sin, the assertion that each individual has freedom of the will to choose not to sin, and the avowal that each person's freedom of the will includes the unassisted initiating power to move toward salvation and to appropriate the divine grace necessary thereto

**pe·la·gian·ize** \-ˌnīz\ *vb* -ED/-ING/-S *often cap* [¹*Pelagian* + *-ize*] *vi* **:** to become Pelagian ~ *vt* **:** to make Pelagian — **pe·la·gian·iz·er** \-zə(r)\ *n* -S *often cap*

**pe·lag·ic** \pəˈlajik, -jēk\ *adj* [L *pelagicus*, fr. Gk *pelagikos*, fr. *pelagos* sea + *-ikos* -ic] **1 :** of, relating to, or living in the open sea **:** OCEANIC **2 :** of, relating to, or constituting a biogeographic realm consisting of the open sea and esp. those portions beyond the outer border of the littoral zone which are above the abyssal zone and to which light penetrates — compare BATHYPELAGIC, NERITIC

**pelagic deposits** *n pl* **:** sedimentary deposits in the abyssal parts of the ocean composed largely of the remains of pelagic organisms, volcanic dust, and meteoritic particles

**pelagic sealing** *n* **:** the act or occupation of killing, capturing, or pursuing fur seals in the ocean as distinguished from killing them at their breeding places on land

**pel·a·go·thu·ria** \ˌpeləgōˈthu̇rēə\ *n, cap* [NL, fr. *pelag-* + *-thuria* (as in *Holothuria*)] **:** a genus (the type of the family Pelagothuriidae) of free-swimming pelagic holothurians totally lacking skeletal plates

**pel·a·myd** \ˈpeləməd, -ˌmid\ *n* -S [L *pelamyd-, pelamys*, fr. Gk *pēlamyd-, pēlamys*] **:** a young tuna

**pe·lar·gi** \pəˈlärˌjī\ *n pl, cap* [NL, fr. Gk *pelargoi*, pl. of *pelargos* stork, prob. fr. *pela-* (akin to Gk *polios* gray) + *argos* white — more at FALLOW, ARGENT] *in some classifications* **:** a group of birds coextensive with or including the Ciconiidae

**pe·lar·gic** \-jik\ *adj* [Gk *pelargikos*, fr. *pelargos* stork + *-ikos* -ic] **:** of or relating to the stork

**pe·lar·go·morph** \pəˈlärgəˌmȯrf\ *n* -S [NL *Pelargomorphae*] **:** a bird of the division Pelargomorphae — **pe·lar·go·mor·phic** \=ˌ==ˈmȯrfik\ *adj*

**pe·lar·go·mor·phae** \=ˌ==ˈmȯr(ˌ)fē\ *n pl, cap* [NL, fr. *pelargo-* (fr. Gk *pelargos* stork) + *-morphae*] *in some esp former classifications* **:** a major division of birds comprising the storks, herons, and ibises or these together with the remainder of the Ciconiiformes, the Anseriformes, and Falconiformes

**pel·ar·gon·aldehyde** \ˌpeˌlärˌgän+\ *n* [ISV *pelargonic* + *aldehyde*] **:** a liquid aliphatic aldehyde $CH_3(CH_2)_7CHO$ that occurs in many essential oils (as of orrisroot, cinnamon, or lemongrass) and is used in perfumes and flavors; nonanal

**pel·ar·go·nate** \peˈlärgəˌnāt\ *n* -S [ISV *pelargonic* + *-ate*] **:** a salt or ester of pelargonic acid

**pel·ar·gon·ic acid** \ˌpeˌlärˈgänik, -gōnik-\ *n* [*pelargonic* ISV *pelargon-* (fr. NL *Pelargonium*) + *-ic*] **:** an oily fatty acid $CH_3(CH_2)_7COOH$ found esp. in fusel oil and rancid fats, obtained in the form of esters esp. from the leaves of pelargoniums and related plants, and usu. made synthetically along with azelaic acid by oxidation of oleic acid — called also *nonanoic acid*

**pel·ar·gon·i·din** \ˌ=ˌ=ˈgänədən\ *n* -S [ISV *pelargonic* + *-idin*] **:** an anthocyanidin pigment obtained in the form of its red-brown crystalline chloride $C_{15}H_{11}ClO_5$ by hydrolysis of pelargonin and also made synthetically

**pel·ar·go·nin** \ˌ=ˌ=ˈgōnən\ *n* -S [ISV *pelargonic* + *-in*] **:** an anthocyanin that is extracted from the dried petals of red pelargoniums or blue cornflowers or various dahlias in the form of its red crystalline chloride $C_{27}H_{31}ClO_{15}$, that changes to the blue sodium salt $C_{27}H_{29}O_{15}Na$ if made alkaline, and that is a diglucoside of pelargonidin

**pel·ar·go·ni·um** \ˌpeˌlärˈgōnēəm, -ˌla(r)ˈg-\ *n* [NL, fr. *pelargo-* (fr. Gk *pelargos* stork) + *-nium* (as in *Geranium*); fr. the resemblance of the capsules to the bill of a stork] **1** *cap* **:** a large genus of southern African herbs (family Geraniaceae) with showy flowers of various shades of red or white distinguished by the spurred calyx and irregular corolla — compare GERANIUM **2** -S **:** any plant of the genus *Pelargonium; esp* **:** one that is cultivated

**pelargonium oil** *n* **:** GERANIUM OIL 1

**pelas** *pl of* PELA

**pe·las·gi** \pəˈlazˌjī\ *n pl, usu cap* [L, fr. Gk *Pelasgoi*] **:** PELASGIANS

**¹pe·las·gi·an** \-jēən, -gē-\ *n* -S *usu cap* [Gk *pelasgios*, adj., Pelasgian (fr. *Pelasgoi*) + E *-an*, n. suffix] **1 :** one of an ancient people or group of peoples mentioned by classical writers as earlier inhabitants of Greece and the eastern islands of the Mediterranean — compare MINOAN, MYCENAEAN, PHILISTINE **2 :** a putative Indo-European language of the Pelasgians

**²pelasgian** \"\ *adj, usu cap* [Gk *pelasgios*, adj., Pelasgian + E *-an*, adj. suffix] **1 :** of, relating to, or characteristic of the Pelasgians **2 :** of, relating to, or characteristic of the Pelasgian language

**pe·las·gic** \-jik, -gik\ *adj, usu cap* [Gk *pelasgikos*, fr. *Pelasgoi* + *-ikos* -ic] **:** PELASGIAN

**pe·le·an** \pəˈlēən, -ˈlā-\ *adj* [Mount *Pelée*, volcano in Martinique + E *-an*] **:** of, relating to, or resembling volcanic eruptions characterized by violent expulsion of clouds or blasts of incandescent volcanic ash

**pel·e·can·i·dae** \ˌpeləˈkanəˌdē\ *n pl, cap* [NL, fr. *Pelecanus*, type genus + *-idae*] **:** a family formerly held to be nearly coextensive with Pelecaniformes but now restricted to the pelicans and constituting with the boobies, cormorants, and snakebirds a suborder of Pelecaniformes

**pel·e·can·i·for·mes** \ˌ=ˌ==ˈfȯrˌmēz\ *n pl, cap* [NL, fr. *Pelecanus* + *-iformes*] **:** an order of swimming birds having all four toes united by a broad web and including the pelicans, gannets, cormorants, tropic birds, snakebirds, and frigate birds

**pel·e·ca·noi·des** \ˌ==ˌkəˈnȯi(ˌ)dēz\ *n, cap* [NL, fr. LL *pelecanus* pelican + L *-oides* -oid] **:** a genus (the type of the family Pelecanoididae) comprising the diving petrels

**pel·e·ca·nus** \ˌ==ˈkānəs\ *n, cap* [NL, fr. LL, pelican — more at PELICAN] **:** a genus of aquatic birds (family Pelecanidae) comprising the pelicans

**pel·e·cin·i·dae** \ˌ==ˈsinəˌdē\ *n pl, cap* [NL, fr. *Pelecinus*, type genus (fr. Gk *pelekinos*, *pelekan* pelican) + *-idae* — more at PELICAN] **:** a New World family of large parasitic wasps

**pe·lec·y·pod** \pəˈlesəˌpäd\ *adj or n* [NL *Pelecypoda*] **:** LAMELLIBRANCH

**pel·e·cyp·o·da** \ˌpeləˈsipədə\ [NL, fr. Gk *pelekys* ax, battle-ax + NL *-poda*] *syn of* LAMELLIBRANCHIA

**pel·e·cyp·o·dous** \ˌ==ˈsipədəs\ *adj* [NL *Pelecypoda* + E *-ous*] **:** LAMELLIBRANCHIATE

**pe·le·lith** \pəˈlēˌlith\ *n* -S [Mount *Pelée*, volcano in Martinique + E *-lith*] **:** a plug or spine of vesicular or pumiceous lava thrust upward in the throat of a volcano

**pêle-mêle** \ˈpelˈmel\ *archaic var of* PELL-MELL

**pel·er·ine** \ˈpeləˌrēn, ˈ==ˌ=, ˈ==ˌrən\ *n* -S [obs. F, neckerchief, fr. F *pèlerine*, fem. of *pèlerin* pilgrim, fr. LL *pelegrinus* — more at PILGRIM] **:** a woman's narrow cape of fabric or fur usu. with long ends hanging down in front

**pe·le's hair** \ˌpālāz-, ˌpēlēz-\ *n, usu cap P* [trans. of Hawaiian *lauoho-o-Pele*, fr. *Pele*, Hawaiian volcano goddess] **:** glass threads or fibers blown by the wind from frothy lava, the tips of lava jets, or drops of liquid lava thrown into the air that often collect in thick masses resembling tow

**pele's tears** *n pl, usu cap P* [after Pele, Hawaiian volcano goddess] **1 :** small drops of volcanic glass **2** *Hawaii* **:** a clear chalcedony or opal in cabochon cut

**pel·e·thite** \ˈpeləˌthīt, ˈpēl-\ *n* -S *usu cap* [Heb *pĕlēthī* Pelethite + E *-ite*] **:** a member of a group of ancient Philistines forming part of the bodyguard of David, King of Israel

**pelew** *cap, var of* PALAU

**pelf** \ˈpelf\ *n* -S [ME, fr. MF *pelfre* booty] **1 a** *archaic* **:** PROPERTY, BELONGINGS ⟨providing them weapon and other like ~ —Thomas Tusser⟩ **b :** MONEY, RICHES, WEALTH ⟨let him disenslave himself from the ~ of the world —Robert South⟩ ⟨looked on him as an asset to earn us ~ or glory —John Galsworthy⟩ **2** *chiefly Brit* **a :** TRASH, REFUSE **b** *dial chiefly Brit* **:** COMPOST **3** *dial Brit* **:** GOOD-FOR-NOTHING

**pel·ham** \ˈpeləm\ *n* -S *usu cap* [prob. fr. the name *Pelham*] **:** a horse's bit with a bar mouthpiece and double rings commonly used in riding bridles and designed to combine the function of curb and snaffle — see BIT illustration

**pel·i·can** \ˈpelәkən, -lēk-\ *n* -S [ME *pelican, pellican*, fr. OE *pellican*, fr. LL *pelicanus, pelecanus*, fr. Gk *pelekan;* akin to Gk *pelekys* ax, battle-ax, prob. of non-IE origin; akin to the source of Skt *paraśu* ax] **1 :** any of various large totipalmate birds of the genus *Pelecanus* with a very large bill and distensible gular pouch in which fish are caught and with very long wings — see BROWN PELICAN, CALIFORNIA BROWN PELICAN, SPECTACLED PELICAN, WHITE PELICAN; BILL illustration **2 :** a representation of a pelican in heraldry or art **3 :** a retort or still with curved tubes leading from the head to the body for continuous condensation and redistillation **4 :** a dark gray that is lighter than fashion gray, Oxford gray, or Dover gray — called also *charcoal gray, dove, light gunmetal, pigeon's-neck* **5 :** a device that consists of a pocket attached to a long wooden handle and that is used for sampling a stream of falling grain in an elevator or on a loading ship

**pelican fish** or **pelican eel** *n* **:** a deep-sea fish (*Eurypharynx pelecanoides*) of the order Lyomeri that is black in color and has a head very long in proportion to the trunk, an enormous mouth, and a body ending in a tapering tail

**pelican flower** *n* **:** any of several tropical vines of the genus *Aristolochia* (esp. *A. grandiflora*) the shape of whose flowers suggests a pelican

**pelican hook** *n* **:** a hinged hook held closed by a ring and used (as on boat gripes and cargo gear) to provide instantaneous release

**pel·i·can·ry** \-rē, -ri\ *n* -ES [*pelican* + *-ry*] **:** a breeding place of pelicans

**pelican's-foot** \ˈ===ˌ=\ *n, pl* **pelican's-foots 1 :** a European marine gastropod (*Aporrhais pespelicani*) having fingerlike processes at the edge of the shell **2 :** the shell of the pelican's-foot

**pel·id·no·ta** \ˌpeləd'nōd·ə\ *n* [NL, fr. Gk *pelidnos, pelitnos* livid; akin to Gk *polios* gray — more at FALLOW] **1** *cap* **:** a genus of American scarabaeoid beetles related to the goldsmith beetles **2** -S **:** any beetle of the genus *Pelidnota* — see SPOTTED PELIDNOTA

1

2

pelican hook: *1* open, *2* closed

**pel·i·got's blue** \ˈpeləˌgōz-\ *n, often cap P* [prob. after Eugène Melchior *Péligot* †1890 Fr. chemist] **:** BREMEN BLUE

**pel·i·ke** \ˈpelәkē\ *n* -S [Gk *pelikē* wooden bowl, pitcher — more at PELVIS] **:** an ancient Greek amphora with a wide mouth, little or no neck, and the body set plump on the base

**pe·lisse** \pəˈlēs, peˈ-\ *n* -S [F, fr. LL *pellicia* cloak, fr. fem. of *pellicius* made of skin, fr. L *pellis* skin — more at FELL] **1 a :** a long cloak or coat made of fur or lined or trimmed with fur **b :** a woman's loose lightweight cloak with wide collar and fur trimming

**pe·lite** \ˈpeˌlīt\ *n* -S [ISV *pel-* + *-ite*] **:** a rock composed of fine particles of clay or mud — compare PSAMMITE, PSEPHITE — **pe·lit·ic** \pəˈlid·ik\ *adj*

**¹pell** \ˈpel\ *vb* -ED/-ING/-S [ME *pellen*] *vi, dial chiefly Eng* **:** HASTEN, HURRY ~ *vt, obs* **:** BEAT, PELT

**²pell** \"\ *n* -S [ME *pel* skin, roll of parchment, fr. MF, fr. L *pellis* skin] **:** a roll of parchment; *specif* **:** one formerly used in the English Exchequer to record receipts and expenditures ⟨appointed . . . his second brother clerk of the ~s —G.O. Trevelyan⟩

**pel·laea** \pəˈlēə, peˈ-\ *n, cap* [NL, fr. LGk *pellaia*, fem. of *pellaios* dark-colored; fr. the dark leaves; akin to Gk *polios* gray — more at FALLOW] **:** a genus of mostly small rock-loving ferns (family Polypodiaceae) having pinnate or pinnatifid often evergreen fronds and intramarginal sori with the indusium formed by the reflexed margins of the fertile segments

**pel·la·gra** \pəˈlagrə, -lāg-\ *n* -S [It, fr. *pelle* skin (fr. L *pellis*) + *-agra* (as in *podagra*, fr. L)] **:** a disease marked by dermatitis, inflammation of mucous membranes, gastrointestinal disorders, and central nervous symptoms and associated with a diet deficient in niacin and protein — compare KWASHIORKOR

**pel·la·gra·gen·ic** \=ˌ==ˈjenik\ *adj* **:** producing pellagra

**pellagra-preventive factor** *n* **:** either of the two members of the vitamin B complex nicotinic acid or nicotinamide — called also *PP factor*

**pel·lagric** \=ˈ=grik\ *adj* [*pellagra* + *-ic*] **:** of, relating to, or causing pellagra

**pel·lagrin** \-grən\ *n* -S [irreg. fr. *pellagra*] **:** a person having pellagra

**pel·lagroid** \-ˌgrȯid\ *adj* [ISV *pellagra* + *-oid*] **:** resembling pellagra

**pel·lagrous** \-grəs\ *adj* [NL *pellagrosus*, fr. *pellagra* (fr. It) + L *-osus* -ose] **:** of, relating to, or affected with pellagra ⟨~ insanity⟩ ⟨~ symptoms⟩ ⟨~ patients⟩

**¹pel·let** \ˈpelət, *usu* -əd·+V\ *n* -S *often attrib* [ME *pelet, pelote*, fr. MF *pelote*, fr. (assumed) VL *pilota*, dim. of L *pila* ball — more at PILL] **1 a :** a usu. small round or spherical body **:** a little ball **b :** a small cylindrical chunk of compressed feeding stuffs used for livestock, poultry, or pets to avoid waste and to increase the attractiveness of the food **c :** a small cylindrical or ovoid compressed mass (as of a hormone) for implantation in muscular tissues **d :** a wad or bolus of indigestible material (as bones and other resistant remains of prey) regurgitated by a carnivorous bird **e :** a small firm mass of dung (as that dropped by a mouse or rabbit) **2 a :** a usu. stone ball used as a missile (as in a mangonel) during later medieval times **b :** CANNONBALL **c :** a ball for firearms **:** BULLET **d** (1) **:** one of a charge of small shot ⟨~s of buckshot⟩ (2) **:** a piece of small shot fired singly (as from a BB gun) ⟨~ gun⟩ **e :** an imitation bullet (as of cork, paper, wax) for use in a popgun **3** *heraldry* **:** a roundel sable **:** OGRESS, GUNSTONE **4 a :** a circular boss in decorative work **b :** BEAD 4g

**²pellet** \"\ *vt* -ED/-ING/-S **1 a :** to form into pellets **b :** to coat (seeds) with soluble adhesive material mixed with plant foods and protective substances to facilitate planting and promote growth **2 :** to strike with pellets **:** throw pellets at

**pel·let·er** \ˈpeləd·ə(r)\ *n* -S **:** one that pellets

**pel·le·tier·ine** \ˌpeləˈtiˌrēn, -ˌrən\ *n* -S [ISV *pelletier-* (fr. Pierre Joseph *Pelletier* †1842 Fr. chemist) + *-ine*] **1 :** a liquid alkaloid $C_8H_{15}NO$ derived from piperidine and found in the bark of the pomegranate **2 :** a mixture of alkaloids from the bark of the pomegranate used esp. in the form of the tannate against tapeworm

**pel·let·i·za·tion** \ˌpeləd·əˈzāshən, -d·ˌīˈz-\ *n* -S **:** the process of pelletizing

**pel·let·ize** \ˈpeləd·ˌīz\ *vt* -ED/-ING/-S **:** to make into pellets ⟨~ foodstuffs for animals and fowl⟩ ⟨~ ore⟩

**pel·let·iz·er** \-zə(r)\ *n* -S **:** one that pelletizes; *specif* **:** an operator of a machine for compressing plastics powder into pellets from which plastic objects are molded

**pel·lett clover** \ˈpelət-\ *n* [after Frank C. *Pellett* †1951 Am. apiculturist] **:** KURA CLOVER

**pel·let·té** or **pel·let·tée** \ˌpeləd·ˈā, -əˈtā; ˈpeləd·ē, -i\ or **pel·lety** \ˈpeləd·ē, -i\ *adj* [¹*pellet* + *-y*] **:** charged with heraldic pellets

**-pellic** \ˈpelik, -lēk\ *adj comb form* [Gk *pella* wooden bowl + E *-ic* — more at PELVIS] **:** having (such) a pelvis ⟨dolicho*pellic*⟩

**pel·li·cle** \ˈpelәkəl, -lēk-\ *n* -S [MF *pellicule*, fr. ML *pellicula*, fr. L, small skin, dim. of *pellis* skin — more at FELL] **1 a :** a thin skin or membrane **b :** a semipermeable membrane; *esp* **:** PLASMA MEMBRANE **2 :** a film on a liquid; *specif* **:** a bacterial growth in the form of a sheet on the surface of a liquid medium **3 :** a semitransparent partially reflecting thin membrane used in cameras for color photography to divide a light beam and form two optical images of a single subject

**pel·lic·u·la** \pəˈlikyələ\ *n* -S [ML] **:** PELLICLE

**pel·lic·u·lar** \-lə(r)\ *adj* [prob. fr. (assumed) NL *pellicularis*, fr. ML *pellicula* + L *-aris* -ar] **:** of, relating to, or having the characteristics of a pellicle **:** MEMBRANOUS, FILMY

**pel·lic·u·lar·ia** \=ˌ==ˈla(a)rēə\ *n, cap* [NL, fr. ML *pellicula* + NL *-aria*] **:** a genus of fungi (family Thelephoraceae) having the hymenium in the form of a crust

**pellicularia disease** *n* **:** a disease of coffee and some other tropical plants caused by a fungus (*Pellicularia koleroga*) and producing leaf spots and effects similar to those of thread blight

**pellicular water** *n* **:** ground water suspended above the water table in films that adhere to the surface of solid particles or the walls of cavities

**pel·lic·u·late** \-lət, -ˌlāt\ *adj* [prob. fr. (assumed) NL *pelliculatus*, fr. ML *pellicula* + L *-atus* -ate] **:** characterized by or covered with a pellicle **:** PELLICULAR

**pel·li·cule** \ˈpeləˌkyül\ *n* -S [ME, fr. ML *pellicula*] **:** PELLICLE

**pelling** *pres part of* PELL

**pel·li·to·ry** \ˈpeləˌtōrē, -tȯr-, -ri\ *n* -ES [alter. of earlier *peletyr*, fr. ME *peletre*, modif. of MF *piretre*, fr. L *pyrethrum* — more at PYRETHRUM] **1 a** or **pellitory-of-spain** \ˈ==ˌ===ˈ=\ *usu cap S* **:** a southern European plant (*Anacyclus pyrethrum*) resembling yarrow **b :** the root of this plant formerly used as a sialagogue and as a constituent of dentifrice **2** or **pellitory-of-the-wall** \ˈ==ˌ====ˈ=\ [alter. of earlier *paritory*, fr. ME *paritorie*, modif. of MF *paritaire*, fr. LL *parietaria* — more at PARIETARIA] **:** any plant of the genus *Parietaria* (as *P. officinalis, P. pennsylvanica*) **3 :** any of various plants resembling the southern European pellitory: as **a :** FEVERFEW **b :** a yarrow (*Achillea millefolium*) **c :** MASTERWORT a

**pellitory bark** *n* **:** PRICKLY ASH 1a

**¹pell-mell** \ˈpelˈmel\ *adv* [MF *pelemele*, fr. OF *pesle mesle*, prob. redupl. of *mesle*, imper. sing. of *mesler* to mix, mingle — more at MEDDLE] **1 :** in mingled confusion or disorder ⟨the infantry followed *pell-mell* —W.H.Prescott⟩ ⟨piles of volumes that were heaped *pell-mell* around him —Christopher Morley⟩ **2 :** without distinction or discrimination **:** INDISCRIMINATELY ⟨so that you will not simply read everything *pell-mell* and without judgment —N.N.Glatzer⟩ **3 :** in or as if in confused haste **:** HEADLONG ⟨hesitated to barge ahead *pell-mell* as he had done in previous years —Clay Blair⟩

**²pell-mell** \"\ *adj* **:** marked by confusion, disorder, or haste **:** HELTER-SKELTER ⟨the *pell-mell* rush of magnitudinous events —Marian E. Wagner⟩ ⟨a shelf that contained a *pell-mell* assortment of French novels —Nicolas Nabokov⟩

**³pell-mell** \"\ *n* -S **1 :** an indiscriminate medley ⟨five setters . . . came down the drive in a *pell-mell* of welcome —James Reynolds⟩ **2 :** CONFUSION, DISORDER ⟨the *pell-mell* of life's disorganized and casual happenings —J.C.Powys⟩

**⁴pell-mell** \"\ *vb* -ED/-ING/-S *vt* **:** to mix up in an indiscriminate manner ⟨they *pell-mell* the dead with the living all in one kirk —William Birnie⟩ ~ *vi* **:** to hurry in a confused or disorderly manner **:** RUSH ⟨they all *pell-melled* out of that river —Esther Forbes⟩

**pel·lock** \ˈpelək\ *n* -S [ME (Sc) *pelok*] *Scot* **:** PORPOISE

**pello·te** \pəˈlōd·ə, pəˈyō-\ *n* -S [modif. of MexSp *peyote* — more at PEYOTE] **:** PEYOTE

**pel·lo·tine** \ˈpeləˌtēn, -ətᵊn, -ətən, -əd·ən\ *also* **pel·lo·tin** \-ətᵊn, -ətən, -əd·ən\ *n* -S [ISV *pellote* + *-ine*] **:** a crystalline narcotic alkaloid $C_{13}H_{19}NO_3$ derived from isoquinoline and obtained from mescal and other cacti of the genus *Lophophora*

**pells** *pres 3d sing of* PELL, *pl of* PELL

**pel·lu·cid** \pəˈlüsəd, pelˈyü-\ *adj* [L *pellucidus*, fr. *per* through + *lucidus* lucid — more at FARE, LUCID] **1 :** admitting maximum passage of light without diffusion or distortion **:** permitting one to see through to a remarkable degree **:** TRANSLUCENT, TRANSPARENT ⟨water in a white glass beaker, clear, ~, without shadow —W.J.Turner⟩ **2 :** pleasing in appearance: **a :** pure in color and pleasing as genuine or appropriate ⟨the fresh green blade of corn is . . . so ~, so clear —Richard Jefferies⟩ **b :** reflecting light evenly from all surfaces **:** SHINING, IRIDESCENT ⟨~ as a pearl —Robert Browning⟩ **3 :** extremely easy to understand **:** readily intelligible or comprehensible **:** completely lacking in ambiguity or turgidity ⟨apposite quotations from the classics . . . grace the ~ flow of his English —V.L.Parrington⟩ ⟨the chiseled ~ beauty of many an image . . . lends distinction to the best work of the new school —J.L. Lowes⟩ ⟨the firm, round ~ handwriting which was so great a contrast to his wife's temperamental scrawl —Margaret Cole⟩ **syn** see CLEAR

**pel·lu·cid·i·ty** \ˌpelyəˈsidəd·ē, -ətē, -i\ *n* -ES [L *pelluciditat-, pelluciditas*, fr. *pellucidus* + *-itat-, -itas* -ity] **:** the quality or state of being pellucid

**pel·lu·cid·ly** *adv* **:** in a pellucid manner

**pel·lu·cid·ness** *n* -ES **:** PELLUCIDITY

**pel·man·ism** \ˈpelməˌnizəm\ *n* -S *usu cap* [*Pelman* Institute, institution for training of the mind founded in London 1898 + E *-ism*] **1 :** a system of training held to develop the mind **2 :** CONCENTRATION 5

**pel·mat·o·gram** \pelˈmad·əˌgram, -raa(ə)m\ *n* -S [*pelmato-* (fr. Gk *pelmat-, pelma* sole of the foot) + *-gram*] **:** an impression of the sole of the foot

**pel·ma·to·zoa** \ˌpelməd·əˈzōə\ *n pl, cap* [NL, fr. *pelmato-* (fr. Gk *pelmat-, pelma* sole of the foot) + *-zoa*] **:** a subphylum or other division of Echinodermata comprising the crinoids, cystoids, blastoids, and edrioasteroids — compare ELEUTHEROZOA — **pel·ma·to·zo·an** \ˌ===ˈzōən\ *adj or n* — **pel·ma·to·zo·ic** \-zōik\ *adj*

**pel·met** \ˈpelmət, *usu* -əd·+V\ *n* -S [prob. modif. of F *palmette* — more at PALMETTE] **:** a short valance or small cornice for concealing curtain fixtures

**-pel·mous** \ˈpelməs\ *adj comb form* [Gk *pelma* sole of the foot + E *-ous* — more at FELL] **:** having (such) a sole ⟨hetero*pelmous*⟩

**pelo-** — see PEL-

**pel·o·bat·id** \ˌpelōˈbad·əd, ˌpēl-\ *n* -S [NL *Pelobatidae*] **:** an amphibian of the family Pelobatidae

**pel·o·bat·i·dae** \-bad·əˌdē\ *n pl, cap* [NL, fr. *Pelobates*, type genus (fr. *pel-* + *-bates*) + *-idae*] **:** a large widely distributed family of anomocoelous amphibians including the spadefoot toads

**pel·o·bat·oid** \ˌ==ˈbad·ˌȯid\ *adj* [NL *Pelobates* + E *-oid*] **:** related to or resembling the Pelobatidae

**pe·loc·o·ris** \pəˈläkərəs\ *n, cap* [NL, fr. *pel-* + *-coris* (fr. Gk *koris* bedbug) — more at COREIDAE] **:** a No. American genus of nepid bugs

**pe·lod·y·tes** \pəˈlädəd·(ˌ)ēz\ *n, cap* [NL, fr. *pel-* + *-dytes*] **:** a genus of Eurasian frogs (family Pelobatidae) distinguished from the spadefoot toads by their slender build and unmodified tarsus — **pel·o·dyt·id** \ˌpelōˈdid·əd\ *n* -S — **pel·o·dyt·oid** \ˌ==ˈdiˌtȯid\ *adj*

**pel·oid** \ˈpeˌlȯid\ *n* -S [ISV *pel-* + *-oid*] **:** mud prepared and used for therapeutic purposes ⟨remedies . . . at spas include natural mineral waters, ~s, and climate —W.S.McClellan⟩

**pel·ok** \ˈpelək\ *also* **pel·og** \-ləg\ *n* -S [Jav] **:** a Javanese pentatonic scale approximately equal to the tones G♯, A, C♯, D, E, G♯

**pel·o·me·du·si·dae** \ˌpelōməˈd(y)üsəˌdē\ *n pl, cap* [NL, fr. *Pelomedusa*, type genus (fr. *pel-* + L *Medusa*, one of the three Gorgons) + *-idae* — more at MEDUSA] **:** a family of freshwater pleurodiran tortoises of Africa, Madagascar, and So. America

**pel·o·myxa** \-ˈmiksə\ *n, cap* [NL, fr. *pel-* + *-myxa*] **:** a genus of large sluggish multinucleate freshwater amoebas (family Amoebidae) with the cytoplasm obscured by metabolic and other inclusions

**pel·o·pae·us** \ˌpeləˈpēəs\ [NL, modif. of LGk *pēlopoios* potter, fr. Gk *pēlos* clay, mud + *-poios* (fr. *poiein* to make) — more at PEL-, POET] *syn of* SCELIPHRON

[1]**pel·o·pon·ne·sian** \ˌpeləpəˈnēzhən, -shən\ *adj, usu cap* [L *peloponnesius* Peloponnesian (fr. Gk *peloponnēsios*, fr. *Peloponnēsos* Peloponnesus, peninsula forming southern part of the mainland of Greece) + E *-an*] **1 :** of or relating to the southern peninsula of Greece **2 :** of or relating to the people of the southern peninsula of Greece

[2]**peloponnesian** \"\ *n* -s *cap* **:** a native or inhabitant of the southern peninsula of Greece

**pe·lo·ria** \pəˈlōrēə, -lȯr-\ *n* -s [NL, fr. Gk *pelōros* monstrous (fr. *pelōr* portent, monster) + NL *-ia;* akin to Gk *terat-, teras* portent, monster — more at TERAT-] **:** an abnormal often hereditary regularity of structure occurring in normally irregular flowers — see IRREGULAR PELORIA, REGULAR PELORIA

**pe·lor·ic** \-ōrik, -är-\ *or* **pe·lo·ri·an** \-ōrēən, -ȯr-\ *or* **pe·lo·ri·ate** \-ēət, -ēˌāt\ *adj* [*peloric* fr. NL *peloricus*, fr. *peloria* + L *-icus* -ic; *pelorian* fr. *peloria* + *-an; peloriate* prob. fr. (assumed) NL *peloriatus*, fr. NL *peloria* + L *-atus* -ate] *of a flower* **:** having peloria **:** abnormally regular or symmetrical

**pel·o·ri·za·tion** \ˌpelərəˈzāshən, -ˌrīˈz-\ *n* -s [ISV *pelorize* + *-ation*] **:** the process of pelorizing

**pel·o·rize** \ˈpeləˌrīz\ *vt* -ED/-ING/-S [ISV *peloria* + *-ize*] **:** to affect with peloria

**pe·lo·rus** \pəˈlōrəs, -lȯr-\ *n* -ES [origin unknown] **:** a navigational instrument resembling a mariner's compass without magnetic needles and having two sight vanes by which bearings are taken

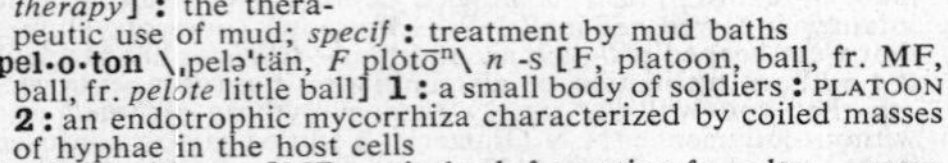
portable pelorus

**pe·lo·ta** \pəˈlōd·ə\ *n* -s [Sp, ball, ball game, fr. OF *pelote* little ball — more at PELLET] **1 :** any of various Basque, Spanish, or Spanish-American games played in a court with a ball and a wickerwork racket; *specif* **:** JAI ALAI **2 :** the ball used in pelota

**pelo·therapy** \ˌpelō, ˈpelō+\ *n* [*pel-* + *therapy*] **:** the therapeutic use of mud; *specif* **:** treatment by mud baths

**pel·o·ton** \ˌpeləˈtän, *F* plȯtō<sup></sup>\ *n* -s [F, platoon, ball, fr. MF, ball, fr. *pelote* little ball] **1 :** a small body of soldiers **:** PLATOON **2 :** an endotrophic mycorrhiza characterized by coiled masses of hyphae in the host cells

[1]**pelt** \ˈpelt\ *n* -s [ME, perh. back-formation fr. *peltry* — more at PELTRY] **1 a :** a usu. undressed skin with its hair, wool, or fur **b :** a skin (as of a sheep or goat) stripped of hair or wool for tanning **2 :** the human skin **3 :** the dead body of a hawk's quarry

[2]**pelt** \"\ *vb* -ED/-ING/-S *vt* **:** to remove the skin or pelt from (an animal) ~ *vi* **:** to remove the skin or pelt from animals

[3]**pelt** \"\ *vb* -ED/-ING/-S [ME *pelten*] *vt* **1 a :** to strike with a succession of blows or missiles ⟨the chidden billow seems to ~ the clouds —Shak.⟩ ⟨boys . . . ~*ed* the girls with green apples —Sherwood Anderson⟩ **b :** to assail repeatedly and usu. forcefully with words **:** BESET ⟨~*ing* him with ridicule and vilification —Walter O'Meara⟩ ⟨the crowd ~*ed* him with questions while he slid from his saddle —*Everybody's Mag.*⟩ **2 :** to drive by means of a succession of blows or missiles ⟨lads . . . ~*ing* through the gloaming their sheep and goats —Sir Richard Burton⟩ **3 :** to throw a succession or stream of (as missiles) ⟨the rout followed and ~*ed* stones —Anthony Wood⟩ **4 :** to fall upon or dash against with a succession of vigorous impacts ⟨~*ed* the sides of houses like hailstones —R.A.Billington⟩ ~ *vi* **1 a :** to deliver a succession of strokes or blows ⟨the smith . . . ~*ing* away at his hot iron —James Hogg⟩ **b** *obs* **:** to utter a succession of angry words **2 :** to throw a succession of missiles ⟨filled their pockets full of pebblestones and . . . so fast at one another's pate —Shak.⟩ **3 :** to fall or dash with a succession of vigorous impacts **:** beat incessantly ⟨listening to the rain ~ and rattle on the tin roof —Marcia Davenport⟩ **4 :** to move rapidly and vigorously **:** HURRY ⟨riding low . . . as hard as the mare could ~ —H.L.Davis⟩ ⟨imagine the whole crowd ~*ing* to the telephones —C.W.Morton⟩

[4]**pelt** \"\ *n* -s **1 :** a blow with or as if with something thrown **:** WHACK ⟨gave him . . . a good ~ on the head with his crutch —Tobias Smollett⟩ **2** *dial chiefly Eng* **:** a fit of rage **3 :** a rapid vigorous pace **:** SPEED ⟨the tug going by, full ~, down the river —Joseph Conrad⟩ **4 :** a persistent falling or beating (as of rain) **:** a pelting storm ⟨the swish and ~ of the rain were heard in pauses —D.C.Murray⟩

**pel·ta** \ˈpeltə\ *n, pl* **pel·tae** \-ˌtē, -ˌtī\ [L, small shield, fr. Gk *peltē*; perh. akin to L *pellis* skin — more at FELL] **1 :** a small light shield used by the ancient Greeks and Romans **2** [NL, fr. L] **:** a body of unknown function found in association with the blepharoplast of a flagellate

**pel·tan·dra** \pelˈtandrə\ *n, cap* [NL, fr. L *pelta* + NL *-andra*] **:** a genus of aquatic or marsh herbs (family Araceae) of the eastern U.S. having large hastate or sagittate leaves and elongated spathes

**pel·tast** \ˈpelˌtast\ *n* -s [Gk *peltastēs*, fr. *peltē* pelta] **:** a soldier of ancient Greece armed with a pelta

**pel·tate** \ˈpelˌtāt\ *adj* [prob. fr. (assumed) NL *peltatus*, fr. L *pelta* + *-atus* -ate] **:** SCUTIFORM; *specif* **:** having the stem or support attached to the lower surface instead of at the base or margin ⟨a ~ leaf⟩ — see LEAF illustration — **pel·tate·ly** *adv*

[1]**pelt·er** \ˈpeltə(r)\ *vb* -ED/-ING/-S [freq. of [3]*pelt*] **:** PELT

[2]**pelter** \"\ *n* -s [[3]*pelt* + *-er*] **1 :** one that pelts **2 :** an old slow horse **3 :** SKEET

[3]**pelter** \"\ *n* -s [[2]*pelt* + *-er*] **1 :** one that pelts small animals **2 :** an animal raised for pelting

**pel·ter·er** \-tərə(r)\ *n* -s [[1]*pelt* + *-erer* (as in *fruiterer*)] **:** a dealer in pelts or peltry

**pel·tier effect** \ˈpelˌtyā-\ *n, usu cap P* [after Jean C. A. *Peltier* †1845 Fr. physicist who discovered it] **:** the production or absorption of heat at the junction of two metals on the passage of a current

**pel·ti·form** \ˈpeltəˌfȯrm\ *adj* [NL *peltiformis*, fr. *pelti-* (fr. L *pelta*) + L *-formis* -form] **:** PELTATE

**pel·tig·era** \pelˈtijərə\ *n, cap* [NL, fr. *pelti-* (fr. *pelta*) + *-gera* (fr. L, fem. of *-ger*, fr. *gerere* to bear, wage, cherish) — more at CAST] **:** a large genus (the type of the family Peltigeraceae) of foliaceous lichens with shield-shaped or tooth-shaped apothecia

**pel·tig·er·ous** \(ˈ)=ˈtijərəs\ *adj* [*pelti-* (fr. NL *pelta*) + *-gerous*] **:** bearing a pelta or peltate part ⟨a ~ lichen⟩

[1]**pelt·ing** \ˈpeltiŋ, -tēŋ\ *adj* [prob. fr. E dial. *palt, pelt* piece of coarse cloth, trash + E *-ing* — more at PALTRY] *archaic* **:** PALTRY, INSIGNIFICANT ⟨flourishing cities . . . dwindled into ~ villages —R.C.Trench⟩

[2]**pelting** \"\ *adj* [fr. pres. part. of [3]*pelt*] *chiefly dial* **:** RAGING, FURIOUS

**pel·to·gas·ter** \ˌpeltōˈgastə(r)\ *n, cap* [NL, fr. *pelto-* (fr. L *pelta*) + *-gaster*] **:** a genus of parasitic cirripedes order Rhizocephala

**pel·ton wheel** \ˈpeltᵊn *also* -tən-\ *n, usu cap P* [after Lester Allen *Pelton* †1908 Am. engineer who invented it] **:** an impulse turbine or waterwheel consisting of a row of double cup-shaped buckets arranged around the rim of a wheel and actuated by one or more jets of water playing into the cups at high velocity

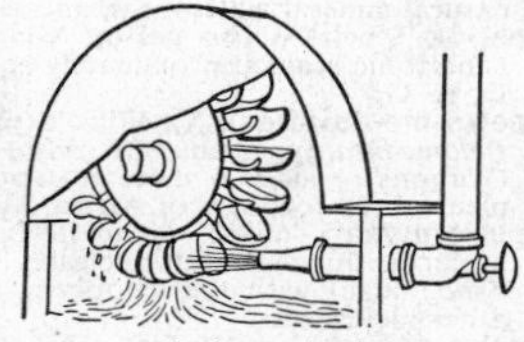
Pelton wheel

**pel·try** \ˈpel·trē, -ri\ *n* -ES [ME, fr. AF *pelterie*, fr. OF *peleterie*, fr. *peleter*, *peletier* furrier (prob. fr. assumed OF *pelet* small skin — fr. OF *pel* skin, fr. L *pellis* + OF *-et* — + OF *-er, -ier* -er) + *-ie* -y — more at FELL] **:** PELTS, SKINS, FURS; *esp* **:** raw undressed skins

**pelts** *pl of* PELT, *pres 3d sing of* PELT

**pelt wool** *n* **1 :** a short skin wool from the pelt of a sheep that has been killed within about three months after shearing **2 :** wool that has been removed from the pelt of a dead sheep

**pe·lu** \ˈpāˌlü\ *n* -s [Sp *pelú*, fr. Araucanian *pùlu*] **:** KOWHAI

**pe·lu·do** \pəˈlü(ˌ)dō\ *n* -s [AmerSp, fr. Sp, hairy, fr. *pelo* hair, fr. L *pilus* — more at PILE] **1 :** an Argentine armadillo (*Euphractus sexcinctus*) having six movable bands and hairy underparts **2 :** any of several armadillos similar to and congeneric with the peludo

**pe·lure paper** \pəˈlu̇(ə)r, pelˈyu̇(ə)r, -üə-\ *n* [*pelure* fr. F, lit., peel, fr. OF *peleure*, fr. *peler* to peel, remove the hair from (fr. L *pilare* to remove the hair from, make bald, fr. *pilus* hair) + *-ure*] **:** a crisp hard thin paper sometimes used for postage stamps

**pe·lu·si·os** \pəˈlüsēˌäs\ *n, cap* [NL, irreg. fr. Gk *pēlos* clay, mud — more at PEL-] **:** a genus of African and Malagasy freshwater turtles of the family Pelomedusidae

**pelv-** *or* **pelvi-** *or* **pelvo-** *comb form* [ISV, fr. NL *pelvis* — more at PELVIS] **1 :** pelvis ⟨*pelvic*⟩ ⟨*pelviscope*⟩ **2 :** pelvic and ⟨*pelvisacral*⟩ ⟨*pelvorenal*⟩

**pelves** *pl of* PELVIS

**pel·ve·tia** \(ˈ)pelˈvēsh(ē)ə\ *n, cap* [NL, fr. *Pelvet*, 19th cent. Fr. naturalist and physician + NL *-ia*] **:** a genus of rockweeds (family Fucaceae) having a cylindrical branched thallus — see CHANNELED WRACK

[1]**pel·vic** \ˈpelvik, -vēk\ *adj* [*pelv-* + *-ic*] **:** of, relating to, or located in or near the pelvis ⟨~ arteries⟩ ⟨deep ~ pain⟩

[2]**pelvic** \"\ *n* -s **:** a pelvic part (as a bone or fin)

**pelvic brim** *n* **:** the bony ridge that marks the boundary between the upper and lower parts of the cavity of the pelvis

**pelvic cavity** *n* **:** PELVIS 2

**pelvic colon** *n* **:** the sigmoid flexure of the colon

**pelvic diaphragm** *or* **pelvic floor** *n* **:** the muscular floor of the pelvis

**pelvic fascia** *n* **:** the fascia lining the cavity of the pelvis

**pelvic fin** *n* **:** one of the paired fins of a fish homologous with the hind limbs of a quadruped — called also *ventral fin;* see FISH illustration

**pelvic girdle** *also* **pelvic arch** *n* **:** a bony or cartilaginous arch that supports the hind limbs of a vertebrate, that corresponds to the pectoral girdle of the forelimbs but is usu. more rigid and firmly attached to the vertebral column, and that consists primitively of a single cartilage which is replaced in higher forms by paired innominate bones articulating solidly with the sacrum dorsally and with one another at the pubic symphysis

**pelvic index** *n* **:** the ratio of the transverse to the dorsoventral diameter of the brim of the pelvis opening multiplied by 100

**pelvic limb** *n* **:** either member of the posterior of the two pairs of limbs characteristic of vertebrates **:** a leg, hind limb, or pelvic fin

**pelvic outlet** *n* **:** the irregular bony opening bounded by the lower border of pelvis and closed by muscle and other soft tissues through which the terminal parts of the excretory, reproductive, and digestive systems pass to communicate with the surface of the body

**pelvic plexus** *n* **:** the inferior hypogastric plexus

**pel·vi·form** \ˈpelvəˌfȯrm\ *adj* [ISV *pelv-* + *-form*] **:** having the shape of a basin

**pel·vi·graph** \-ˌgraf\ *n* [ISV *pelv-* + *-graph*] **:** a recording pelvimeter

**pel·vim·e·ter** \pelˈvimәd·ə(r)\ *n* [ISV *pelv-* + *-meter*] **:** an instrument for measuring the dimensions of the pelvis

**pel·vim·e·try** \-ə·trē, -tri\ *n* -ES [ISV *pelv-* + *-metry*] **:** measurement of the pelvis (as by a pelvimeter or by X-ray examination)

**pel·vis** \ˈpelvəs\ *n, pl* **pelvis·es** \-vəsəz\ *or* **pel·ves** \-ˌvēz\ [NL, fr. L, basin; akin to OE & ON *full* cup, Gk *pella* wooden bowl] **1 a :** a basin-shaped structure in the skeleton of many vertebrates that is formed by the pelvic girdle together with the sacrum and often various coccygeal and caudal vertebrae and that in man is composed of the two innominate bones bounding it on each side and in front while the sacrum and coccyx complete it behind — see BAT illustration **b :** the bones of the pelvic girdle viewed as a structural unit in vertebrates in which these bones are not arranged in a basin-shaped structure **c :** the enlarged basipterygial bones that in teleost fishes replace the pelvic bones and support the pelvic fins **2 :** the cavity of the bony pelvis comprising in man a broad upper and a more contracted lower part — called also respectively *false pelvis* and *true pelvis* **3 :** the main cavity of the kidney into which the nephrons discharge urine

**pel·vi·sacral** \ˌpelvē+\ *adj* [*pelv-* + *sacral*] **:** of or relating to the pelvis and the sacrum

**pel·vi·scope** \ˈpelvəˌskōp\ *n* [*pelv-* + *-scope*] **:** an instrument that is equipped with lighting and optical systems and that permits direct and oblique visualization of the pelvis through the vagina — compare CULDOSCOPE

**pelvo-** — see PELV-

**pel·vo·renal** \ˌpelvō+\ *adj* [*pelv-* + *renal*] **:** of, relating to, or involving the pelvis of the kidney

**pel·y·co·saur** \ˈpeləkōˌsȯ(ə)r\ *n* -s [NL *Pelycosauria*] **:** one of the Pelycosauria

**pel·y·co·sau·ria** \ˌ===ˈsȯrēə\ *n pl, cap* [NL, fr. *pelyco-* (fr. Gk *pelyk-, pelyx* wooden bowl) + *-sauria*] **:** an order of primitive Permian reptiles (subclass Synapsida) that resemble mammals and often have extreme development of the dorsal vertebral processes — compare DIMETRODON, EDAPHOSAURUS — **pel·y·co·sau·ri·an** \ˌ===ˈsȯrēən\ *adj or n*

**pem·bi·na** \pemˈbēnə, ˈpembənə\ *n* -s [CanF *pimbina*, perh. modif. of Cree *nipiminān*, lit., berry growing by the water] **:** CRANBERRY TREE

**pem·broke** \ˈpemˌbru̇k, -rōk\ *n* -s *usu cap* [fr. *Pembroke*, Wales, where it was orig. bred] **:** a Welsh corgi of a variety that is characterized by pointed erect ears, straight legs, and short tail

**pem·broke·shire** \-kˌshi(ə)r, -ˌshiə, -ˌshə(r)\ *or* **pembroke** *adj, usu cap* [fr. *Pembrokeshire* or *Pembroke*, county in Wales] **:** of or from the county of Pembroke, Wales **:** of the kind or style prevalent in Pembroke

**pembroke table** *also* **pembroke** *n* -s *usu cap P* [prob. fr. *Pembroke*, English family of noblemen] **:** a small often profusely ornamented four-legged table originating in the Georgian period and having a drawer and on each side a narrow leaf supported by a swinging bracket

Pembroke table

**pem·mi·can** *also* **pem·i·can** \ˈpemәkәn\ *n* -s [Cree *pimikān*, fr. *pimii* grease, fat] **1 a :** a concentrated food used by No. American Indians consisting essentially of lean buffalo meat or venison cut in thin slices, dried in the sun, pounded fine, mixed with melted fat, and packed in sacks of hide **b :** a similar preparation (as of dried beef, flour, molasses, suet) used for emergency rations (as by explorers) **2 :** information or thought condensed into little compass

**pem·phi·goid** \ˈpem(p)fəˌgȯid\ *adj* [NL *pemphigus* + E *-oid*] **:** resembling pemphigus

[1]**pem·phi·gus** \-gəs, pemˈfīgəs\ *n, pl* **pemphiguses** \-səz\ *or* **pemphi·gi** \-fəˌjī, -ˌīˌjī\ [NL, fr. Gk *pemphig-, pemphix* breath, drop, storm, pustule; akin to Gk *pomphos* blister, *bembix* buzzing insect, top, whirlpool, cyclone — more at BEMBIX] **:** a disease of unknown cause characterized by the formation of successive crops of large blisters on apparently normal skin and mucous membranes often in association with sensations of itching or burning and with constitutional symptoms

[2]**pemphigus** \"\ *n, cap* [NL, fr. Gk *pemphig-, pemphix*] **:** a genus of gall-making aphids (family Eriosomatidae) with both primary hosts (as trees and woody shrubs) and secondary hosts (as roots of sugar beets and lettuce)

**pem·phre·don·i·dae** \ˌpem(p)frəˈdänəˌdē\ *n pl, cap* [NL, fr. *Pemphredon*, type genus (fr. Gk *pemphrēdōn*, a wasp) + *-idae;* akin to Skt *bambhara* bee] **:** a family of small wasps that provision their nests with aphids and other small homopterous insects

[1]**pen** \ˈpen\ *n* -s [ME, fr. OE *penn*] **1 a :** a small enclosure for animals; *also* **:** the animals in one such enclosure ⟨erected a ~ for the calves⟩ or enough to fill one ⟨stole a whole ~ of sheep⟩ **b :** a specified number of animals entered in an exhibition as a unit ⟨a ~ of one cock and four hens⟩ **c :** a number of animals regarded as a suitable breeding unit whether kept together or not ⟨start with a ~ of one buck and 10 does⟩ **2 :** a device to dam the water in a stream **:** DAM **3 :** any small place of confinement or storage: as **a :** BULLPEN 1 **b :** PLAYPEN **4** *Jamaica* **:** a farm where livestock is bred and raised **5 a :** a berthing area for small ships or boats formed by enclosing piers or jetties **b :** a dock or slip for reconditioning submarines that is protected against aerial bombs by a superstructure of thick concrete **6 :** a hollow square crib of pulpwood stacked for storage

[2]**pen** \"\ *vt* **penned; penned; penning; pens** [ME *pennen*, fr. OE *-pennian*, fr. *penn* pen] **1 :** to shut in or as if in a pen **:** place in an enclosure to prevent straying **:** confine in a restricted location ⟨~*s* the sheep in the barnyard⟩ ⟨a convalescent child *penned* up in a house⟩ ⟨the individual's being so bafflingly *penned* within himself —W.M.Frohock⟩ **2 :** to exhibit (as rabbits, poultry) in pens **:** arrange a show of penned animals **syn** see ENCLOSE

[3]**pen** \"\ *n* -s *often attrib* [ME *penne*, fr. MF, feather, wing, pen, fr. L *pinna*, alter. of *penna* feather, wing; akin to Gk *pteron* wing, feather — more at FEATHER] **1** *archaic* **a :** FEATHER **b pens** *pl* **:** PINIONS, WINGS **c :** QUILL 2a(1) **2 :** an implement for writing or drawing with ink or a similar fluid: **a :** QUILL 3a **b :** a small thin convex metal device tapering to a split point and fitting into a holder for writing and drawing with ink or a similar fluid — called also *nib;* see STUB **c :** a penholder (as of wood) containing a pen **d :** any of various similar implements (as a fountain pen, ball-point pen, ruling pen) **3 a :** a writing instrument regarded as a means of expression (as of thoughts, feelings) ⟨lived by his ~⟩ ⟨verses from her ~ had been published in the . . . newspapers —H.E.Starr⟩ ⟨enlisted the ~*s* of the best writers —F.H.Chase⟩ ⟨such a scene as no ~ can describe —*Irish Digest*⟩ **b :** a manner of style of writing ⟨his vivid ~ gave a truthful picture of the Southern capital —J.S.Wilson b. 1880⟩ **c :** WRITER **4 :** PINFEATHER **5 :** the internal horny feather-shaped shell of a squid — called also *gladius*

[4]**pen** \"\ *vt* **penned; penned; penning; pens** [ME *pennen*, fr. *penne* pen] **:** WRITE: **a :** to record in writing in proper form ⟨a minute was *penned* that the Corporation might pay . . . the cost —*Crompton & Royton Chronicle*⟩ **b :** to compose and commit to paper ⟨~ a letter⟩ ⟨the best novel he ever *penned*⟩ **c :** to write with a pen ⟨Salesman A ~*s* angular letters —H.O. Teltscher⟩

[5]**pen** \"\ *n* -s [origin unknown] **:** a female swan — compare [3]COB 2

[6]**pen** \"\ *n* -s [by shortening] *slang* **:** PENITENTIARY

[1]**pen-** — see PENE-

[2]**pen-** — see PENTA-

**pen** *abbr* **1** penetration **2** peninsula **3** penitent

**pe·naea** \pəˈnēə\ *n* [NL, fr. Pierre *Pena* 16th cent. Fr. botanist] **1** *cap* **:** a genus (the type of the family Penaeaceae) of southern African shrubs with small sessile leaves and spicate yellowish or reddish flowers **2** -s **:** any plant of the genus *Penaea*

**pen·ae·a·ce·ae** \ˌpenēˈāsēˌē\ *n pl, cap* [NL, fr. *Penaea*, type genus + *-aceae*] **:** a family of small heathlike evergreen shrubs (order Myrtales) with solitary red, apetalous flowers with 4-valvate calyx lobes and 4 stamens — **pen·ae·a·ceous** \ˌ==ˈāshəs\ *adj*

**penaeid** *var of* PENEID

**pe·nae·us** \pəˈnēəs\ *syn of* PENEUS

[1]**pe·nal** \ˈpēnᵊl\ *adj* [ME, fr. MF, fr. L *poenalis*, fr. *poena* penalty, punishment + *-alis* -al — more at PAIN] **1 :** designed to impose punishment **:** prescribing, enacting, or threatening punishment **:** PUNITIVE ⟨the ~ clause⟩ **2 :** liable or subject to punishment or a penalty **:** incurring punishment ⟨a ~ offense⟩ **3 :** inflicted as or constituting punishment or penalty or used as a means of punishment ⟨marks for any infraction of the rules . . . were worked off in ~ study —A.W.Long⟩ **4 a :** forfeitable or payable as a penalty **b :** involving or imposing a pecuniary penalty — see PENAL SUM **5 :** of or relating to punishment, penalty, penal laws, or penal servitude ⟨~ reform⟩ **6 :** used as a place of confinement and punishment ⟨a ~ colony⟩ ⟨a ~ farm⟩ **7 :** inflicting a penalty **:** severely disadvantageous ⟨terms decidedly ~ to those who . . . put their money into steel —*Economist*⟩

[2]**penal** \"\ *adj* [*penis* + *-al*] **:** PENIAL

**penal action** *or* **penal suit** *n* **:** an action under a penal statute

**penal code** *n* **:** a code of laws concerning crimes and offenses and their punishment

**pe·nal·i·ty** \pēˈnaləd·ē\ *n* -ES [ML *poenalitas*, fr. L *poenalis* penal + *-itas* -ity] **:** liability to punishment

**pe·nal·iz·able** \ˈpēnᵊlˌīzəbəl, ˈpen-, ===ˈ==\ *adj* **:** capable of or subject to being penalized

**pe·nal·iza·tion** \ˌpēnᵊlәˈzāshәn, ˌpen-, -ᵊlˌī-\ *n* -s **1 :** the act of penalizing **2 :** the state of being penalized

**pe·nal·ize** \ˈpēnᵊlˌīz, ˈpen-\ *vt* -ED/-ING/-S *see -ize in Explan Notes* [[1]*penal* + *-ize*] **1 :** to inflict a penalty on ⟨~ unlicensed drivers⟩ ⟨~ the team 10 yards for unnecessary roughness⟩ **:** put at a serious disadvantage ⟨following his initial triumph he was bound to be *penalized* by his own achievement —John Mason Brown⟩ **2 :** to make (an action) legally punishable

**penal law** *n* **1 a :** a law imposing a penalty (as of fine, imprisonment, loss of civil rights) on persons who do or forbear a certain act or acts **b :** the body of such laws **:** CRIMINAL LAW **2 :** PENAL STATUTE 2

**pe·nal·ly** \ˈpēnᵊlē\ *adv* **:** in a penal manner

**penal servitude** *n* **:** imprisonment with hard labor in a prison orig. in lieu of transportation

**penal statute** *n* **1 :** PENAL LAW 1 a **2 :** a statute that provides for the use of the state or a private person wronged a forfeiture or penalty and not compensatory damages against the wrongdoer committing an offense against the state by violating the provisions of the statute and that is distinguished from a statute awarding a civil remedy for compensatory damages against a wrongdoer in favor of the person wronged

**penal sum** *n* **1 :** a sum of money payable under a statute as a forfeiture for wrongdoing by the wrongdoer to the person wronged **2 :** a sum of money or penalty agreed upon in a bond or in a contract to be paid to one party in case there is a breach of the condition of the bond or in case the other fails to perform his contract in some respect specified

**penal theory** *n* **:** a development of the satisfaction theory of the atonement introduced by the Protestant reformers and prevalent in Lutheran and Reformed orthodoxy that holds that Christ reconciled man to God by participating in human life to the extent of taking on himself without corruption the status of sinner and bearing in his soul the penal torment and desolation

[1]**pen·al·ty** \ˈpenᵊltē, -ti\ *n* -ES [modif. (influenced by *-ty*) of ML *poenalitas*, fr. L *poenalis* penal + *-itas* -ity] **1 a :** the suffering in person, rights, or property which is annexed by law or judicial decision to the commission of a crime or public offense **:** punishment for crime or offense **:** penal retribution ⟨where a life sentence is the extreme ~⟩ ⟨trespassing forbidden under ~ of imprisonment⟩; *specif* **:** a fine or mulct imposed as such a punishment **b :** a sum of money made recoverable in a civil action by the state or an informer for the less serious offenses not mala in se — compare FINE **2 :** the suffering or the sum to be forfeited to which a person subjects himself by covenant or agreement in case of nonfulfillment of stipulations and which is if imposed in good faith as liquidated damages in general recoverable and enforceable in equity **:** FORFEITURE, FINE **3 :** disadvantage, loss, or hardship due to some action (as transgression or error) **4 :** a disadvantage (as loss of yardage, time, or possession of the ball) imposed for violation of the rules of a contest **5 a** *usu pl* **:** points scored in bridge by a side that defeats the opposing contract **b :** ROYALTY 6

[2]**penalty** \"\ *adj* **1 a** *of government free mail* **:** imprinted with the penalty clause ⟨a ~ envelope⟩ ⟨~ labels⟩ ⟨~ mail⟩ **b :** of or relating to the use of penalty mail ⟨the ~ privilege⟩

**2 :** involving or received in compensation for hardship ⟨~ taxation⟩ ⟨~ cargo⟩ ⟨~ overtime⟩ ⟨~ pay⟩ ⟨a ~ throw⟩ **3 a :** imposed as a penalty ⟨~ time⟩ ⟨a ~ charge⟩ **b :** used in determining or carrying out a penalty ⟨crossed the ~ line⟩ ⟨~ spot⟩ **4 :** being or containing a clause specifying a penalty for violation of an agreement or regulation ⟨a ~ bond⟩ ⟨contained certain ~ provisions⟩

**penalty area** *n* **:** an area 44 yards wide and 18 yards deep in front of each goal on a soccer field within which an infringement of given rules by a defending player causes a penalty kick to be awarded to the opposing team

**penalty box** *n* **1 :** a box adjoining an ice-hockey rink for seating penalized players, timekeepers, and scorers **2 :** a desk to which a lacrosse player reports when suspended from the game

**penalty bully** *n* **:** a penalty in field hockey that is awarded when a member of the defending team fouls inside the striking circle and thus prevents a goal and that consists of a bully five yards in front of the goal between the offending player and any member of the attacking team

**penalty card** *n, bridge* **:** a card that has been illegally exposed and must be left faceup on the table and played at the first legal opportunity

**penalty clause** *also* **penalty indicia** *n* **:** the statement printed on the cover of a piece of government free mail giving notice of the penalty for private use to avoid payment of postage — compare FRANK *vt* 1

**penalty corner** *n* **:** a hit awarded an attacking player in field hockey from any point on the goal line not less than 10 yards from the nearest goalpost when the defending team fouls in its own striking circle — called also *short corner*

**penalty double** *n* **:** a double made for the purpose of increasing a bridge score if the opponents' contract is defeated

**penalty goal** *n* **1 :** a goal in rugby or soccer that results from a penalty kick and counts three points **2 :** a goal in field hockey resulting from a penalty bully **3 :** an automatic goal in ice hockey awarded an attacking team if an opponent throws his stick at the puck in his own defense zone

**penalty kick** *n* **1 :** a free kick allowed in rugby because of some violation of the rules by the opponents **2 :** a free kick allowed in soccer for certain infringements of the rules within the penalty area and made from a mark 12 yards in front of the center of the goal with all players of both sides except the player making the kick and the opposing goalkeeper barred from the penalty area

**penalty pass** *n, bridge* **:** a pass of a double that one's partner intended to be taken out

**penalty shot** *n* **1 :** a shot at the goal in ice hockey awarded a team for certain violations by the opposing defense **2 :** a free throw in basketball

**penalty stroke** *n* **:** a stroke in golf added to the score of a side under certain rules (as when a ball has been lost or hit out of bounds or is deemed unplayable)

**¹pen·ance** \'penən(t)s\ *n* -s [ME *penaunce*, fr. OF *penance*, fr. ML *paenitentia* penitence — more at PENITENCE] **1 a :** an act of self-abasement, mortification, or devotion either voluntarily performed to show sorrow or repentance for sin or imposed as a punishment for sin by a church official ⟨required to do ~⟩ **b :** a sacrament in the Roman Catholic and Eastern Churches consisting in repentance or contrition for sin, confession to a priest, satisfaction as imposed by the confessor, and absolution **2 :** sorrow or contrition for sin **:** REPENTANCE, PENITENCE **3 :** consequent or compensating hardship or suffering **4** *obs* **a :** punishment or sufferings after death (as in Hades or purgatory) in expiation of sin **b :** PUNISHMENT; *specif* **:** PEINE FORTE ET DURE **5 :** PAIN, SORROW, DISTRESS

**²penance** \"\ *vt* -ED/-ING/-S **:** to impose penance on

**¹pen-and-ink** \ˌ≈≈'≈\ *adj* [fr. the phrase *pen and ink*] **:** executed with pen and ink ⟨a *pen-and-ink* sketch⟩

**²pen-and-ink** \"\ *n, pl* **pen-and-inks :** a pen-and-ink drawing

**penang** *var of* PINANG

**pe·nang-lawyer** \pə'naŋ-\ *n* [*penang* fr. *Penang*, Federation of Malaya] **1 :** a walking stick having usu. a bulbous head and made of the stem of an East Asiatic palm (*Licuala acutifida*) **2 :** the palm from which a penang-lawyer is made

**pen·annular** \(ˈ)pen+\ *adj* [¹*pen-* + *annular*] **:** having the form of a ring with a small break in the circumference ⟨~ silver brooch used to fasten . . . the Highlander's dress —Ian Finlay⟩

**pe·na·tes** \pə'nād·(ˌ)ēz, -näd-\ *n pl* [L — more at PENETRATE] **1 :** the Roman gods of the household and primarily of the storeroom worshiped in close connection with Vesta, goddess of the hearth, and with the lares and household genius **2 :** treasured household furnishings

**pen-cancel** \'pen'kan(t)səl\ *vt* [back-formation fr. *pen cancellation*] **:** to cancel (a stamp) by hand with a pen

**pen cancellation** *n* **:** a stamp cancellation made by hand with a pen (as on a revenue stamp or on a postage stamp) prior to the general use of the handstamp and canceling machine

**pence** \'pen(t)s\ *pl of* PENNY

**pen·cel** *or* **pen·cil** *also* **pen·sil** \'pen(t)səl\ *n* -s [ME *pencel*, *pensil*, modif. of OF *penoncel* — more at PENNONCEL] **:** PENNONCEL

**pence·less** \'pen(t)sləs\ *adj* **:** having no pence **:** PENNILESS

**pench·ant** \'penchənt *sometimes* (ˈ)päⁿ'shäⁿ\ *n* -s [F, fr. pres. part. of *pencher* to incline, bend, fr. (assumed) VL *pendicare*, fr. L *pendere* to weigh — more at PENDANT] **:** a strong leaning or attraction **:** strong and continued inclination; *broadly* **:** LIKING ⟨a ~ for sharp criticism that often offended⟩; decided taste ⟨a ~ for art⟩ **syn** see LEANING

**pen·ché** \(ˈ)päⁿ'shā\ *adj* [F, leaning, stooped, fr. past part. of *pencher* to incline, bend] *ballet* **:** LEANING, FLEXED

**¹pen·cil** \'pen(t)səl\ *n* -s *often attrib* [ME *pensel*, *pencel*, fr. MF *pincel*, fr. (assumed) VL *penicellus*, fr. L *penicillus* brush, pencil, lit., little tail, dim. of *penis* tail, penis — more at PENIS] **1 :** a brush of hair or bristles used to lay on colors; *esp* **:** a small brush for fine art work **2 :** the individual style or technique of an artist or descriptive writer **3 :** a tufted growth (as of hair or feathers) **4 a :** an implement for writing, drawing, or marking made of or containing a slender rod or strip of a solid marking substance: (1) **:** a stick of marking substance (as chalk, slate) often encased in paper — see GREASE PENCIL (2) **:** a wooden rod containing a core of marking substance exposed at one end by sharpening and often having an eraser on the other end ⟨corrected with a red ~⟩ ⟨a ~ sketch⟩ — see LEAD PENCIL (3) **:** a mechanical device consisting of a cylinder of metal or plastic containing a lead projected by means of a screw **b :** a small medicated or cosmetic roll or stick for local applications ⟨a menthol ~⟩ **c :** a writing or marking device resembling a pencil that uses another means of marking ⟨etched by a hot electric ~⟩ **5 a :** an aggregate of rays of light or other radiation esp. when diverging from or converging to a point **b :** the lines passing through a given point and lying on a plane **6 :** something long and thin like a pencil ⟨the flashlight sent a long, white ~ of illumination stabbing through the darkness —Erle Stanley Gardner⟩ **7 :** PENCIL DIAMOND **8 :** graphite used as the marking substance in pencils ⟨written in ~ rather than in ink⟩ ⟨a page half typewritten and half ~⟩

**²pencil** \"\ *vb* **penciled** *or* **pencilled; penciled** *or* **pencilled; penciling** *or* **pencilling** \-s(ə)liŋ\ **pencils** *vt* **1 a :** to paint, draw, shade, write, or mark with or as if with a pencil ⟨a typewritten manuscript with corrections ~*ed* in⟩ **:** SKETCH ⟨~ in a cartoon with rapid strokes⟩ **b :** to make a tentative plan of **:** write (as an assignment) subject to change ⟨had been ~*ed* in for the lead —Budd Schulberg⟩ **2 :** to treat (as a wound) by means of a medicated pencil ~ *vi* **:** to take the shape of a pencil **:** form into pencils ⟨rays of light ~*ing* through the darkness⟩ ⟨the pale smoke from the cottage chimneys ~ up —William Sansom⟩

**³pencil** *var of* PENCEL

**pencil and pearl** *n* **:** BEAD AND REEL

**pencil beam** *n* **:** a sharp-focus radar beam nearly round in its axis used to pick up an intruder located by a search radar beam and give it better definition on the radar screen

**pencil cedar** *n* **1 a :** any of several junipers with wood suitable for or used for making pencils: as (1) **:** RED CEDAR 1 a (2) **:** EAST AFRICAN CEDAR (3) **:** a rather small densely pyramidal tree (*Juniperus bermudiana*) that is grown in warm regions as an ornamental **b :** INCENSE CEDAR **2** *Austral* **a :** RED BEAN **b :** SHE-PINE 1 **3 :** the wood of a pencil cedar

**pencil compass** *n* **:** a compass with a pencil on one leg for use in drawing

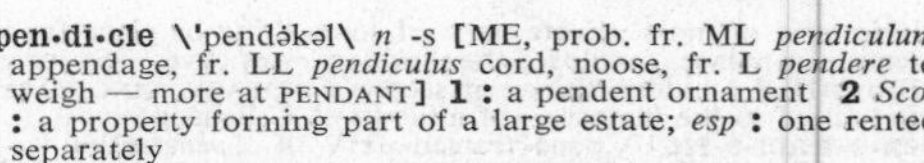

pencil compass

**pencil diamond** *n* **:** a chip diamond set in a wooden handle for cutting glass

**penciled** *adj* [fr. past part. of ²*pencil*] **:** marked with narrow usu. transverse or concentric lines — used of a feather esp. of a domestic fowl; compare ¹BARRED

**pencil fish** *n* **:** a small slender So. American topminnow (*Poecilobrycon auratus*) that is sometimes kept in the tropical aquarium and is golden brown with gold, brown, and black stripes running the length of the body and a red spot on the anal fin

**pencil flower** *n* **:** a plant of the genus *Stylosanthes*

**penciling** *n* -s [fr. gerund of ²*pencil*] **1 :** the work of the pencil or brush or a product of this ⟨delicate ~ in a picture⟩ **2 :** the narrow linear markings of penciled feathers **3 :** lines of white or other color drawn along a mortar joint in a brick wall

**pen·cil·ler** \'pen(t)s(ə)lə(r)\ *n* -s **1 :** one that pencils **2 :** one that makes or removes pencil marks **3** *Brit* **:** BOOKMAKER

**pencillike** \'≈≈ˌ≈\ *adj* **:** having the shape of a pointed rod **:** STYLOID

**pencil orchid** *n* **:** an Australian orchid (*Dendrobium teretifolium*) with terete fleshy leaves

**pencil pusher** *n* **:** a person (as a writer, clerk, or bookkeeper) whose work involves writing **:** INKSLINGER

**pencil rod** *n* **:** a round steel rod with a diameter of ¼ inch

**pencils** *pl of* PENCIL, *pres 3d sing of* PENCIL

**pencil sharpener** *n* **:** a device for sharpening the point of a lead pencil by pressure against a rotating blade or cutting edges

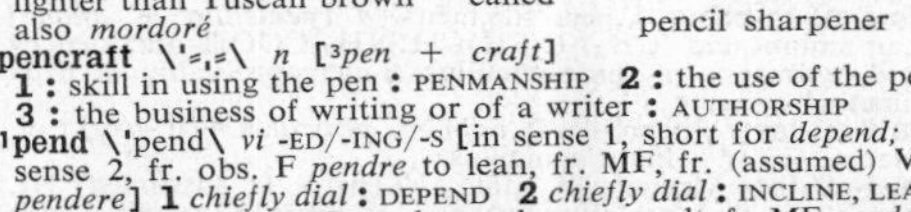

pencil sharpener

**pencil stone** *n* **:** a compact pyrophyllite used for making slate pencils

**pencil stripe** *n* **:** a textile design of fine warp stripes in white or pastel against a dark ground; *also* **:** a fabric with such a design

**pencilwood** \'≈≈ˌ≈\ *n* **:** a moderate brown to reddish brown that is lighter than Tuscan brown — called also *mordoré*

**pencraft** \'≈ˌ≈\ *n* [³*pen* + *craft*] **1 :** skill in using the pen **:** PENMANSHIP **2 :** the use of the pen **3 :** the business of writing or of a writer **:** AUTHORSHIP

**¹pend** \'pend\ *vi* -ED/-ING/-S [in sense 1, short for *depend;* in sense 2, fr. obs. F *pendre* to lean, fr. MF, fr. (assumed) VL *pendere*] **1** *chiefly dial* **:** DEPEND **2** *chiefly dial* **:** INCLINE, LEAN

**²pend** \"\ *n* -s [obs. E *pend* to arch over, vault, fr. ME *penden*, prob. fr. MF *pendre* to overhang, hang] **1** *Scot* **:** ARCH, ARCHWAY **2** *Scot* **:** a covered passage

**³pend** \"\ *n* -s [prob. fr. obs. E *pend* to pen, confine, fr. ME *penden*, prob. alter. of *pennen* to pen — more at PEN] *dial Eng* **:** PRESSURE, EMERGENCY

**pen·da** \'pendə\ *n* -s [native name in Australia] **:** an Australian timber tree (*Xanthostemon oppositifolium*) of the family Myrtaceae with exceptionally heavy hard wood

**¹pen·dant** *also* **pen·dent** \'pendənt, *in sense 4* 'penənt\ *n* -s [ME *pendaunt*, fr. MF *pendant*, fr. pres. part. of *pendre* to hang, fr. (assumed) VL *pendere*, fr. L *pendēre*; akin to L *pendere* to weigh, estimate, pay, *pondus* weight, pound, *pendēre* to hang, OSlav *pędĭ* span, *spǫdyti* to span, Gk *span* to pull, draw — more at SPAN] **1 :** something suspended **:** a hanging object: as **a :** an ornament that is attached by its upper edge and allowed to hang free ⟨a jeweled ~ on a chain⟩ ⟨ear ~*s*⟩ ⟨a crystal chandelier with 40 ~*s*⟩ **b :** an electrical fixture (as a droplight or cord switch) suspended from the ceiling **2 a :** the often decoratively carved terminal of a vertical member of a structure projecting below another member attached to it: as (1) **:** a boss formed on the base of a keystone extended below the junction of ribs in late Gothic vaulting (2) **:** the sculptured lower end of a newel post at the angle of a stair (3) **:** the end of a vertical timber projecting below the overhanging second floor of an early American colonial house — called also *drop, pendill* **b :** a carved or molded often bas-relief ornament (as a representation of fruit or flowers) attached to a ceiling or wall in a hanging position **3** *naut* **a :** a short rope or wire rope hanging from a spar and having at its free end a block or spliced thimble — called also *pennant* **b :** a length of rope or wire rope with eyes, blocks, or hooks spliced in the ends — often used with a qualifier specifying position or purpose ⟨a centerboard ~⟩ ⟨a mooring ~⟩ — see SHIP illustration **4 :** PENNANT 2 a — used chiefly by the British navy **5 :** the part of a pocket watch from which the chain is suspended; *specif* **:** the shank on the watch stem to which the bow attaches **6 a :** something (as a picture) forming a match, companion piece, or counterpart to another **b :** something forming a supplement (as to a book) ⟨publishes the present book frankly as a ~ to his earlier one —Lionel Stevenson⟩ **syn** see FLAG

**²pendant** *var of* PENDENT

**pendant post** *n* **:** a part of the framing of an open-timbered roof that consists of a post set against the wall, resting on a corbel or other solid support, and supporting the ends of a collar beam or any other part of the roof

**pendant-set** \ˌ≈≈'≈\ *adj, of a watch* **:** set by pulling out the stem

**pendant switch** *n* **:** CORD SWITCH

**pendant tackle** *n* **:** a tackle attached to a pendant (as on a masthead) for hoisting, tautening, or staying purposes

**pendant-winding** \ˌ≈≈'≈≈\ *adj* **:** STEM-WINDING

**pend d'o·reille** \ˌpändə'rā\ *n, pl* **pend d'oreille** *or* **pend d'oreilles** *or* **pends d'oreille** \-ā(z)\ *usu cap P&O* [modif. of F *pendant d'oreille* earring; prob. fr. the fact that members of the tribe used to wear large shell earrings] **:** KALISPEL

**pen·de·loque** \ˌpäⁿdə'lōk\ *n* -s [F, blend of obs. F *pendeler* to dangle (dim. of F *pendre* to hang) and F *breloque* charm, breloque] **1 :** a diamond or other gemstone cut in the form of a pear-shaped brilliant with a table — compare BRIOLETTE; see CUT illustration **2 :** a usu. pear-shaped glass pendant used for ornamenting a lamp or chandelier

**pen·den·cy** \'pendənsē, -si\ *n* -ES [¹*pendent* + *-cy*] **:** the state of being pending ⟨during the ~ of a suit at law⟩ ⟨during the ~ of the war⟩

**¹pen·dent** *or* **pen·dant** \'pendənt\ *adj* [ME *pendaunt* — more at PENDANT] **1 a :** supported from above **:** SUSPENDED ⟨vines bearing ~ bunches of grapes⟩ ⟨a plant with a ~ blossom⟩ ⟨icicles ~ from the eaves⟩ **b** *archaic* **:** hanging without visible support **:** FLOATING ⟨blown . . . round about the ~ world —Shak.⟩ **2 :** sloping steeply down ⟨a ~ hillside⟩ **3 :** jutting or leaning over **:** OVERHANGING ⟨a ~ cliff⟩ **4 :** remaining undetermined **:** PENDING ⟨a claim still ~⟩ **5 :** marked by incomplete grammatical construction

**²pendent** *var of* PENDANT

**pen·den·te lite** \pen'dentē'lītē\ *adv* [NL] **:** during the suit **:** while litigation continues ⟨the granting of an injunction *pendente lite* —Benjamin Werne⟩

**¹pen·den·tive** \pen'dentiv, -tēv *also* -təv\ *n* -s [F *pendentif*, fr. L *pendent-*, *pendens* (pres. part. of *pendēre* to hang) + F *-if* -ive] **1 :** one of the triangular spherical sections of vaulting that spring from the corners of a rectangular ground plan and serve to allow the room enclosing it to be covered by a cupola of rounded or polygonal plan **2 :** any supporting member at the corner of a square or polygonal plan for making transition to a circular or octagonal plan — compare SQUINCH **3 :** the part of a groined vault that springs from a single pier or corbel

pendentives 1 supporting a dome

**²pendentive** \(ˈ)≈'≈≈\ *adj* **1 :** of, relating to, or having pendentives **2 :** formed like a pendentive

**pen·dent·ly** *adv* **:** in a pendent manner

**pen·di·cle** \'pendəkəl\ *n* -s [ME, prob. fr. ML *pendiculum* appendage, fr. LL *pendiculus* cord, noose, fr. L *pendere* to weigh — more at PENDANT] **1 :** a pendent ornament **2** *Scot* **:** a property forming part of a large estate; *esp* **:** one rented separately

**pen·dill** \'pendᵊl\ *n* -s [earlier *pendle* overhanging part, pendant, prob. modif. of MF *pendisel*, dim. of *pendre* to hang — more at PENDANT] **:** PENDANT 2 a (3)

**¹pending** *pres part of* PEND

**²pend·ing** \'pendiŋ, -dēŋ\ *prep* [F *pendant* (fr. pres. part. of *pendre* to hang, suspend, after L *pendente*, abl. of *pendent-*, *pendens*, pres. part.) + E *-ing*] **1 :** through the period of continuance or indeterminacy of **:** DURING ⟨their opportunity to develop trade ~ the laborious and fruitless negotiations —Theodore Hsi-En Chen⟩ **2 :** until the occurrence or completion of **:** while awaiting ⟨military rule . . . prevailed ~ the adoption of a new constitution —*Amer. Guide Series: N.C.*⟩ ⟨four withholding a vote ~ further information —*Jour. of Accountancy*⟩

**³pending** \"\ *adj* [F *pendant* + E *-ing*] **1 :** not yet decided **:** in continuance **:** in suspense ⟨the drafting of opinions and decisions on cases ~ before the Commission —*Current Biog.*⟩ ⟨that on all important ~ problems he be given . . . also minority views —Dorothy Fosdick⟩ **2 :** IMPENDING, IMMINENT ⟨the war scare in Europe, with the ~ strife between communism and fascism —Leon Halden⟩

**pen·dle** \'pendᵊl\ *n* -s [F *pendille*, fr. *pendiller* to hang, fr. MF, fr. *pendre*] *chiefly dial* **:** a pendent object (as an earring or a pendulum)

**pen·drag·on** \pen'dragən\ *n* -s [ME, fr. W, fr. *pen* chief + *dragon* leader, fr. L *dracon-*, *draco* dragon; fr. the figure of a dragon on the leader's standard — more at DRAGON] *often cap* **:** a chief leader among the ancient British chiefs (as in time of war) **:** head of all the chiefs **:** KING

**pends** *pres 3d sing of* PEND, *pl of* PEND

**pen·du·lant** *or* **pen·du·lent** \'penjələnt, -nd(y)əl-\ *adj* [L *pendulus* hanging, pendent (fr. *pendere* to weigh) + E *-ant* or *-ent*] **:** PENDULOUS

**pen·du·lar** \-lə(r)\ *adj* [F *pendulaire*, fr. *pendule* pendulum (fr. L *pendulus*) + *-aire* -ar] **:** being or resembling the movement of a pendulum **:** swinging or undulating back and forth ⟨public opinion has moved in violent ~ swings between optimism and pessimism —*New Republic*⟩ ⟨~ vibrations produce the sine wave —C.S.Myers⟩ ⟨the ~ movements of the isolated rat intestine —Gilles Papineau-Couture⟩

**pen·du·late** \-ˌlāt\ *vi* -ED/-ING/-S [NL *pendulum* + E *-ate*] **1 :** to swing as a pendulum **2 :** FLUCTUATE, UNDULATE **syn** see SWING

**pen·du·la·tion** \ˌ≈≈'lāshən\ *n* -s [NL *pendulum* + E *-ation*] **:** a pendular movement **:** OSCILLATION

**pen·dule** \'penˌjül\ *n* -s [F, fr. L *pendulus* hanging, pendent] **:** a timepiece having a pendulum; *specif* **:** an ornate French chamber clock of the late 18th century sometimes with escutcheons, shields, masts, and historical or mythical figures

**pen·du·lette** \ˌpenjə'let\ *n* -s [F, fr. *pendule* + *-ette*] **:** a small table clock with short fast-moving pendulum

**¹pen·du·line** \'penjələn, -ˌlīn\ *adj* [NL *pendulinus* (specific epithet of *Anthoscopus pendulinus*, genus of titmice), fr. L *pendulus* hanging, pendent + *-inus* -ine] **:** constructing hanging nests

**²penduline** \"\ *n* -s [NL *Pendulinus*, a genus of titmice (Aegithalos) in former classifications, fr. L *pendulus* + *-inus* -ine] **:** a penduline bird

**penduline titmouse** *n* **:** a titmouse (*Remiz pendulinus*) of southern Europe that builds an ovoid nest suspended in the twigs of a bush or tree

**pen·du·los·i·ty** \ˌpenjə'läsəd·ē\ *n* -ES **:** the quality or state of being pendulous

**pen·du·lous** \'penjələs, -nd(y)əl-\ *adj* [L *pendulus*, fr. *pendere* to weigh — more at PENDANT] **1 a :** so suspended or projecting so as to overhang **b** *archaic* **:** poised without visible support **2 a :** suspended so as to swing freely ⟨branches hung with ~ vines⟩ **b :** inclined or hanging downward **:** DROOPING ⟨a ~ ovule on the upper part of a carpel⟩ ⟨a corpulent old man with flabby, ~ jowls⟩ **3 :** WAVERING, VACILLATING ⟨a state of ~ uncertainty⟩ — **pen·du·lous·ly** *adv* — **pen·du·lous·ness** *n* -ES

**pendulous crop** *n* **:** a greatly dilated crop occurring esp. in strains of the turkey as a permanent deformity following initial distention by heavy liquid intake during hot weather — called also *drop crop*

**pen·du·lum** \-ləm\ *n* -s *often attrib* [NL, fr. L, neut. of *pendulus* hanging, pendent] **1 a :** a body suspended from a fixed point so as to swing freely to and fro under the action of gravity and commonly used to regulate the movements of clockwork and other machinery **b :** a suspended body that vibrates not by swinging but by rotating, with alternate twisting and untwisting (as the balance wheel of a watch) — called also *torsion pendulum* **2 :** something that alternates between opposites ⟨the ~ of public opinion⟩ **3 :** a technique used in mountain climbing to accomplish a difficult traverse by swinging across on a rope

**pendulum gun** *n* [so called fr. its motion when fired] **:** a mechanism for obtaining certain ballistic data for given shotshell loadings that consists of a tube fitted with a breech and a firing mechanism and moving freely on its four supporting wires and that by means of attached and coordinated instruments determines velocity, time required for shot charge to pass through barrel, chamber pressure, energy of recoil, and shot pattern

**pendulum level** *n* **:** PLUMB LEVEL

**pendulum press** *n* **:** a small foot-operated punch press with a swinging treadle

**pendulum saw** *n* **:** a circular saw arranged to swing in a vertical arc for crosscut work

**pendulum watch** *n* **:** a late 18th century watch with a mock pendulum attached to a concealed balance wheel and showing through a curved slit in the dial

**pene-** *also* **pen-** *prefix* [L *paene-*, *pene-*, fr. *paene*, *pene* almost — more at PATIENT] **:** almost ⟨*peneplain*⟩ ⟨*penacute*⟩

**pe·ne·contemporaneous** \ˌpēnē+\ *adj* [*pene-* + *contemporaneous*] **:** of, relating to, or being a geological phenomenon originating or effectuated during or soon after the formation of the rocks in which it is displayed ⟨a ~ mineral⟩ ⟨~ structures⟩ — **pe·ne·con·tem·po·ra·ne·ous·ly** *adv*

**¹pe·ne·id** *also* **pe·nae·id** \pə'nēəd\ *adj* [NL *Peneidae*] **:** of or relating to the Peneidae

**²peneid** *also* **penaeid** \"\ *n* -s **:** a prawn of the family Peneidae

**pe·ne·idae** \-ēəˌdē\ *n pl, cap* [NL, fr. *Peneus*, type genus + *-idae*] **:** a family of chiefly warm water and tropical prawns — see PENEUS

**pe·ne·ides** \-ˌdēz\ *n pl, cap* [NL, fr. *Peneus* + *-ides*] **:** a tribe (tribe Peneides) including several edible prawns of decapod crustaceans (suborder Natantia) comprising shrimps and prawns in which the lateral plates of the second abdominal segment do not overlap those of the first segment

**pe·nel·o·pe** \pə'neləpē\ *n, cap* [NL, fr. L *Penelope*, faithful wife of Ulysses in Greek legend, fr. Gk *Pēnelopē*] **:** a genus of guans

**pe·nel·o·pine** \-lə,pīn, -ˌpən\ *adj* [NL *Penelope* + E *-ine*] **:** of or relating to the genus *Penelope*

**¹pe·ne·plain** *also* **pe·ne·plane** \ˈpēnē, ˈpēnə+\ *n* [*pene-* + *plain* or *plane*] **:** an erosion surface of considerable area and slight relief — called also *endrumpf;* compare BASELEVEL PLAIN

**²peneplain** *or* **peneplane** \"\ *vt* -ED/-ING/-S **:** to erode to a peneplain

**pe·ne·pla·na·tion** \ˌpēnəplə'nāshən\ *n* **:** the process of peneplaining a land surface **:** erosion to a peneplain

**penes** *pl of* PENIS

**pe·ne·seismic** \ˌpēnē+\ *adj* [ISV *pene-* + *seismic*] **:** being or relating to a region rarely affected by earthquakes

**pen·e·tra·bil·i·ty** \ˌpenətrə'biləd·ē, -lətē, -i\ *n* [F *pénétrabilité*, fr. *pénétrable* penetrable (fr. L *penetrabilis*) + *-ité* -ity] **:** the quality or state of being penetrable

**pen·e·tra·ble** \'penətrəbəl\ *adj* [L *penetrabilis*, fr. *penetrare* to penetrate + *-abilis* -able] **:** capable of being penetrated — **pen·e·tra·ble·ness** *n* -ES — **pen·e·tra·bly** \-blē, -li\ *adv*

**pen·e·trale** \ˌpenə'trālē\ *or* **pen·e·tral** \'penətrəl\ *n* -s [L, fr. *penetralis* inner, interior, fr. *penetrare* to penetrate + *-alis* -al] **:** an innermost part

**pen·e·tra·lia** \ˌpenə'trālēə\ *n pl* [L, pl. of *penetrale*] **1 :** the innermost or most private parts of some thing or place ⟨as a temple or palace⟩ ⟨explored the shuddery ~ of caves —Spencer Brown⟩ **2 :** hidden things or secrets **:** PRIVACY, SANCTUARY ⟨admitted to the inmost ~ of affairs —A.C.Benson⟩

**pen·e·tram·e·ter** \ˌpenəˈtramədə(r)\ *n* [*penetration* + *-meter*] **:** a device for measuring the penetrating power of X rays or other radiation by comparing transmission through different absorbers — called also *penetrometer*

**pen·e·trance** \ˈpenətrən(t)s\ *n* -s [ISV *penetrant* + *-ance*] **:** the relative ability of a gene to produce its specific effect in any degree whatever in the organism of which it is a part sometimes measured as the percentage of individuals that detectably manifest the effect in a group in which the gene is present — compare EXPRESSIVITY

**¹pen·e·trant** \-rənt\ *adj* [MF or L; MF *penetrant*, fr. L *penetrant-*, *penetrans*, pres. part. of *penetrare* to penetrate] **:** that penetrates **:** PENETRATING ⟨a ~ wind⟩ ⟨a ~ fumigant⟩

**²penetrant** \"\ *n* -s **:** one that penetrates or is capable of penetrating: as **a :** a large barbed nematocyst designed to pierce the body of the prey and inject a paralyzing substance **b :** a penetrating agent **:** a surface-active agent having high penetrating power — compare WETTING AGENT

**pen·e·trate** \ˈpenəˌtrāt, *usu* -ād·+V\ *vb* -ED/-ING/-S [L *penetratus*, past part. of *penetrare* to penetrate; akin to L *penitus* inward, inwardly, *penes* with, in the possession of, *penus* food provisions, innermost part of a house, *Penates* household gods, Lith *peneti* to nourish, fatten and perh. to Goth *fenea* pearl barley] *vt* **1 a :** to pass into or through: (1) **:** to extend into the interior of ⟨this route . . . ~*s* the leading resort and lake areas —*Amer. Guide Series: Minn.*⟩ (2) **:** to enter or go through by overcoming resistance ⟨nails . . . of sufficient length to pass through the insulation and ~ the roof boards at least ¾ of an inch —P.D.Close⟩ ⟨it required a long time for an idea to ~ the heads of this stubborn people —V.G.Heiser⟩ **:** PIERCE ⟨the salt rain driven by the wind ~*s* the thickest coat —Richard Jefferies⟩ ⟨a smooth voice that *penetrated* the mighty vibrations of the falls —C.G.D.Roberts⟩ ⟨the doctor's words of encouragement finally *penetrated* my despair —Herbert King⟩ (3) **:** to gain entrance to ⟨an apartment I now *penetrated* for the first time —Osbert Lancaster⟩ ⟨youngsters under 21 who, 10 years ago, could never have *penetrated* the underworld circles where they now circulate freely —D.W.Maurer & V.H. Vogel⟩ **b :** to see into or through ⟨their keen eyes can ~ the water to a depth of . . . forty feet —L.K.Porritt⟩ **c :** to insert the penis into the vagina of in copulation **2 a :** to pierce into with the mind **:** discover the inner contents or meaning of ⟨a scientific secret which will eventually be *penetrated* by other countries —Vera M. Dean⟩ **:** perceive or recognize the precise nature of ⟨~ his disguise and expose his true identity⟩ **:** UNDERSTAND, FATHOM ⟨the seer who ~*s* the underlying principles of men and things —C.H.Grandgent⟩ **b :** to affect profoundly through the senses or feelings **:** touch with feeling **:** move deeply ⟨men may still be *penetrated* with awe by the divine righteousness —R.W.Dale⟩ **3 a :** to diffuse through **:** PERMEATE ⟨the cold began to ~ his bones —E.K.Gann⟩ ⟨corruption *penetrated* . . . the country's mercantile class —T.E. Ennis⟩ **:** INFILTRATE ⟨the Communist plan to ~ political parties and unions⟩ **b :** to cause to be diffused (as with a feeling) **:** IMBUE, STEEP ⟨choose a fitting action, ~ yourself with the feeling of its situations —Matthew Arnold⟩ ~ *vi* **1 a** (1) **:** to pass, extend, pierce, or diffuse into or through something ⟨fishes . . . which enter tidal rivers and ~ almost to fresh water —J.L.B.Smith⟩ ⟨fjords . . . ~ more than 300 kilometers inland —Valter Schytt⟩ ⟨an acid that ~*s* into the tissues⟩ ⟨time for the news to ~ to all the distant country places —Mary Austin⟩ (2) **:** to get (as by force or resolution) past an obstacle or boundary ⟨*penetrated* . . . beyond the Rhine, the Alps, and the Pyrenees —Alfred Cobban⟩ ⟨circumnavigated the southern ice region . . . , *penetrating* beyond lat. 67 S. —*Encyc. Americana*⟩ (3) **:** to gain admittance (as to an exclusive group) ⟨women who ~ to the upper levels of the bureaucracy⟩ ⟨secret Communist agents had *penetrated* into high government circles —T.R. Fyvel⟩ **b :** to pierce something with the eye or mind **:** see or enable to see into or through something hidden or obscure ⟨strained his eyes to ~ beyond the thick cloud of dust⟩ ⟨a telescope that ~*s* to the remote parts of the universe⟩ ⟨insight that ~*s* to the very heart of some . . . problem —W.F.Hambly⟩ **2 :** to affect deeply the senses or feelings ⟨the suggestion might ~ deeply enough . . . to make her a good deal more wary —H.A.Overstreet⟩ **syn** see ENTER, PERMEATE

**penetrating** *adj* **1 :** having the power of entering, piercing, or pervading **:** PENETRATIVE ⟨a ~ oil⟩ ⟨a ~ shriek⟩ ⟨a ~ odor⟩ **2 :** quick to discover **:** ACUTE, DISCERNING ⟨a ~ mind⟩ — **pen·e·trat·ing·ly** *adv* — **pen·e·trat·ing·ness** *n* -ES

**pen·e·tra·tion** \ˌpenəˈtrāshən\ *n* -s [L *penetration-*, *penetratio*, fr. *penetratus* (past part. of *penetrare*) + *-ion-*, *-io* -ion] **1 :** the act or process of penetrating ⟨Indian groups . . . angered by the constant ~*s* of whites into their new territories —P.W.Gates⟩ ⟨the ~ of the theater by scholarship and taste —R.W.Speaight⟩: as **a :** the act (as of a foreign diplomatic or commercial body) of entering a country so continued or repeated that actual establishment of influence is accomplished **b :** an attack that drives a wedge into or through the enemy's front ⟨when the situation does not favor an envelopment, the main attack is directed toward a ~ —C.E.Welsh⟩ **c :** flight in air warfare over enemy territory and through enemy air defenses to attack ground targets ⟨a shallow ~ mission⟩ ⟨~ tactics⟩ ⟨a ~ fighter⟩ **2 a :** the depth to which something penetrates; *specif* **:** the depth to which a projectile sinks into any substance at which it is fired **b :** the power or ability to penetrate or its manifestation **:** PENETRATIVENESS ⟨used a lighter oil for its superior ~⟩ ⟨the human eye aided by telescopes and microscopes of ever greater ~⟩; *specif* **:** the ability to discern acutely the inner nature or meaning of something or the resulting perceptive quality of expression (as in a written work) ⟨a writer who analyzes the underlying causes with great ~⟩ ⟨good little novels, full of Gallic irony and ~ —*Time*⟩ **c :** depth of field (as of a microscope) **d :** the extent to which a commercial product or agency is familiar or sells in a market ⟨the manufacturer's view of the dealer's performance is based on ~ of the market —Hartley Howe⟩ **3 :** the intersection of a minor architectural form and a major one ⟨the ~ of a minor vault with a main vault⟩ **4 :** the penetrability of a bituminous material expressed as the distance that a standard needle vertically penetrates a sample of the material under known conditions of loading, time, and temperature

**penetration gland** *n* **:** one of the anterior glands of some cercarias that actively invade the skin of the definitive host and are believed to produce a histolytic secretion

**penetration path** *n* **:** the course taken by the sperm in entering the egg — compare COPULATION PATH

**penetration twin** *n* **:** a twin crystal in which the two parts are joined along a complex surface so that they appear to penetrate through one another — see TWIN illustration

**pen·e·tra·tive** \ˈpenəˌtrād·iv, -trəl, |t|, |ēv *also* |əv\ *adj* [ME, fr. MF or ML; MF *penetratif*, fr. ML *penetrativus*, fr. L *penetratus*, past part. + *-ivus* -ive] **1 :** tending to penetrate **:** of a penetrating quality **:** PIERCING ⟨applying a toxic ~ spray to the bark surface —F.C.Craighead b. 1890 & J.M.Miller⟩ **2 :** ACUTE ⟨stimulate in the reader intuitive faculties more ~ than formal reasoning —C.E.Montague⟩ ⟨frequent ~ observations —J.C.Ireson⟩ **3 :** IMPRESSIVE ⟨~ lecturers . . . sent the hearer home with an idea, or a fact, or an enthusiasm firmly and usefully planted —H.S.Canby⟩ — **pen·e·tra·tive·ly** \|əvlē, -li\ *adv* — **pen·e·tra·tive·ness** \|ivnəs\ *n* -ES

**pen·e·tra·tiv·i·ty** \ˌpenəˌtrāˈtivəd·ē\ *n* -ES **:** the quality or state of being penetrative **:** PENETRATIVENESS

**pen·e·tra·tor** \ˈpenəˌtrād·ə(r)\ *n* -s [LL, fr. L *penetratus* (past part. of *penetrare* to penetrate) + *-or* — more at PENETRATE] **:** one that penetrates

**pen·e·trom·e·ter** \ˌpenəˈträmədə(r)\ *n* [ISV *penetro-* (fr. L *penetrare* + *-o-*) + *-meter*] **:** an instrument for determining penetrability or ability to penetrate: as **a :** an instrument for measuring the consistency of semisolids (as pitch, grease) from the depth to which a needle penetrates under given conditions **b :** PENETRAMETER

**pe·ne·us** \pəˈnēəs\ *n, cap* [NL, prob. fr. L *Peneus*, river in northwestern Peloponnesus, Greece, fr. Gk *Pēneios*] **:** a genus (the type of the family Peneidae) of edible prawns with well-developed rostrum and exopodites on all but the last pair of legs

**pen feather** [³*pen*] *n* **:** a quill feather

**pen·field·ite** \ˈpenˌfēlˌdīt\ *n* -s [Samuel L. *Penfield* †1905 Am. mineralogist + E *-ite*] **:** a mineral $Pb_2(OH)Cl_3$ consisting of a basic lead chloride and occurring in white hexagonal prisms

**penfold** *var of* PINFOLD

**pen-friend** \ˈ=,=\ *n* **:** PEN PAL

**peng·hu·lu** \peŋˈü(ˌ)lü\ *n* -s [Malay *pĕnghulu*, fr. *hulu* head, top] **:** a district or village headman in Indonesia, Malaya, or British Borneo

**pen·gö** \ˈpenˌgə̄\ *n, pl* **pengö** *or* **pengös** [Hung *pengő*, lit., sounding, fr. *pengeni* to sound, jingle] **1 :** the basic monetary unit of Hungary from 1925 to 1946 **2 :** a coin representing one pengö unit

**pen·guin** \ˈpengwən, -eng-\ *n* -s [perh. fr. W *pen gwyn* white head, fr. *pen* head + *gwyn* white; perh. fr. a white promontory on an island near Newfoundland where great auks were found in large numbers in the 16th century — more at ARPENT, FINNOCK] **1** *archaic* **:** GREAT AUK **2 :** any of various short-legged flightless aquatic birds of the southern hemisphere that constitute the family Spheniscidae, are most numerous about the Antarctic continent, the Falkland islands, and New Zealand, stand erect on land but walk clumsily, are covered with short, stiff, scalelike feathers many of which are simple shafts without barbs, have wings resembling flippers, bearing only rudimentary scalelike quills, being used for swimming and incapable of flexure but moved with a rotary motion by specially developed muscles, and feed chiefly on crustaceans, mollusks, and fish — see EMPEROR PENGUIN, JACKASS PENGUIN, KING PENGUIN, ROCK HOPPER

**penguin duck** *n* **:** INDIAN RUNNER

**pen·guin·ery** *also* **pen·guin·ry** \-ən(ə)rē\ *n* -ES **:** a breeding place of penguins

**pengun** \ˈ=,=\ *n* [³*pen* + *gun*; fr. its being orig. made from quills] *Scot* **:** POPGUN

**penholder** \ˈ=,==\ *n* **1 :** a holder or handle for a pen **2 :** a rack for holding pens

**-pe·nia** \ˈpēnēə\ *n comb form* -s [NL, fr. Gk *penia* poverty, lack] **:** deficiency of ⟨erythro*penia*⟩ ⟨thrombo*penia*⟩ ⟨eosino*penia*⟩

penholder 2

**pe·ni·al** \ˈpēnēəl\ *adj* [F *pénial*, fr. *pénis* penis, fr. L *penis* — more at PENIS] **1 :** PENILE **2 :** functioning as a penis ⟨~ setae⟩

**pen·i·cil·la·mine** \ˌpenəˈsiləˌmēn\ *n* [*penicill*in + *amine*] **:** an amino acid $(CH_3)_2C(SH)CH(NH_2)COOH$ obtained by acid hydrolysis of the penicillins; β-mercapto-valine or β,β-dimethyl-cysteine

**pen·i·cil·lary** \ˌpenəˈsilərē\ *adj* [NL *penicillus* + E *-ary*] **:** of, relating to, or being a penicillus

**pen·i·cil·late** \ˌpenəˈsilət, -ˌlāt\ *adj* [prob. fr. (assumed) NL *penicillatus*, fr. L *penicillus* brush + *-atus* -ate] **:** furnished with a tuft of fine hairs **:** ending in a tuft of hairs like a camel's-hair brush **:** PENICILLIFORM ⟨a grass with ~ stigmas⟩ ⟨the ~ ear of the squirrel⟩ — **pen·i·cil·late·ly** *adv* — **pen·i·cil·la·tion** \ˌpenəsəˈlāshən\ *n* -s

**pen·i·cil·lat·ed** \ˈ==ˌsiˌlād·əd\ *adj* **:** PENICILLATE

**pen·i·cil·lic acid** \ˈ==ˈsilik-\ *n* [NL *Penicillium* + E *-ic*] **:** a crystalline antibiotic unsaturated keto acid $CH_2{=}C(CH_3)$-$COC(OCH_3){=}CHCOOH$ or the tautomeric hydroxy lactone produced by several molds of the genera *Penicillium* and *Aspergillus*

**pen·i·cil·li·form** \ˈ==ˈsiləˌfȯrm\ *adj* [prob. fr. (assumed) NL *penicilliformis*, fr. L *penicillus* brush + *-iformis* -iform] **:** PENICILLATE

**pen·i·cil·lin** \ˌpenəˈsilən\ *n* -s [*penicill-* (fr. NL *Penicillium*) + *-in*] **1 :** a mixture of antibiotic relatively nontoxic acids produced esp. by molds of the genus *Penicillium* (as *P. notatum* or *P. chrysogenum*) and having a powerful bacteriostatic effect against various bacteria (as staphylococci, gonococci, pneumococci, hemolytic streptococci, or some meningococci) **2 :** any of numerous often hygroscopic and unstable amido acids that have the general formula $RCONH(C_7H_9NOS)COOH$ and contain fused thiazolidine and beta-lactam rings in their structures and that are components of the penicillin mixture or are produced biosynthetically by the use of different strains of molds or different media or are synthesized chemically: as **a** *or* **penicillin F** *also* **penicillin I :** the first penicillin $C_5H_9$-$CONH(C_7H_9NOS)COOH$ isolated in Britain; 2-pentenyl-penicillin **b** *or* **penicillin G** *also* **penicillin II :** the penicillin $C_6H_5CH_2CONH(C_7H_9NOS)COOH$ that constitutes the principal or sole component of most commercial preparations and is used chiefly in the form of stable salts (as the crystalline sodium salt or the crystalline procaine salt) — called also benzylpenicillin **c** *or* **penicillin V :** a crystalline nonhygroscopic acid $C_6H_5OCH_2CONH(C_7H_9NOS)COOH$ that is produced biosynthetically and synthetically and that is similar to penicillin G in antibacterial action but is better absorbed by the gastrointestinal tract — called also *phenoxymethylpenicillin* **3 :** a salt or ester of a penicillin acid or a mixture of such salts or esters

**pen·i·cil·lin·ase** \-əˌnās\ *n* -s [*penicillin* + *-ase*] **:** an enzyme that inactivates the penicillins by hydrolyzing them and that is found esp. in bacteria

**pen·i·cil·lin·ic acid** \ˈpenəsəˈlinik-\ *n* [*penicillin* + *-ic*] **:** PENICILLIN 2

**pen·i·cil·li·o·sis** \ˌpenəˌsilēˈōsəs\ *n, pl* **penicillio·ses** \-ōˌsēz\ [NL, fr. *Penicillium* + *-osis*] **:** infection with or disease caused by molds of the genus *Penicillium*

**pen·i·cil·li·um** \ˌpenəˈsilēəm\ *n* [NL, fr. L *penicillus* brush + NL *-ium*] **1** *cap* **:** a genus of fungi (family Moniliaceae) comprising the blue molds found chiefly on moist nonliving organic matter (as decaying fruit), characterized by the erect branching conidiophores ending in tufts of club-shaped cells from which conidia are formed in chains, and including molds useful in economic fermentation — compare CAMEMBERT CHEESE, PENICILLIN **2** *pl* **penicil·lia** \-ēə\ **:** any mold of the genus *Penicillium*

**pen·i·cil·lo·ic acid** \ˌpenəsəˈlōik-\ *n* [*penicillin* + *-oic*] **:** an amido dicarboxylic acid that has the general formula $RCONH$-$(C_6H_{10}NS)(COOH)_2$ and is obtained from a penicillin by hydrolytic opening of the lactam ring (as by mild treatment with alkali or by the action of a penicillinase)

**pen·i·cil·lus** \ˌpenəˈsiləs\ *n, pl* **penicil·li** \-iˌlī\ [NL, fr. L, brush, pencil — more at PENCIL] **1 :** one of the small straight arteries of the red pulp of the spleen **2 :** the branching penicillate conidiophore in fungi of *Penicillium* or similar genera

**pe·ni·el mission** \pəˈnīəl-, ˈpenēəl-\ *n, usu cap P&M* [*peniel* prob. fr. Heb *Pĕniel*, *Pĕnuel*, lit., face of God, place on the Jabbok river in Jordan where Jacob wrestled with a stranger and received a blessing (Gen 32: 30 AV)] **:** one of a number of religious groups centering in California that carry on a program of mass evangelism on city streets

**pe·ni·form** \ˈpēnəˌfȯrm\ *adj* [*penis* + *-form*] **:** resembling a penis ⟨~ setae⟩

**¹penile** *n* -s [*pene-* + obs. *ile* isle, fr. ME — more at ISLE] *obs* **:** PENINSULA

**²pe·nile** \ˈpēˌnīl, -ēnᵊl\ *adj* [*penis* + *-ile* (adj. suffix)] **:** of, relating to, by means of, or affecting the penis

**pe·nil·lion** \pəˈnilyən\ *n pl* [W, pl. of *penill* verse] **:** orig. improvised but now usu. traditional Welsh verses and melody sung (as in an eisteddfod) in counterpoint to a familiar tune played on the harp

**pe·nin·su·la** \pəˈnin(t)s(ə)lə, -inchələ, -inshələ *sometimes* -insyələ\ *n* -s [L *paeninsula*, fr. *paene-* pene- + *insula* island — more at ISLE] **1 a :** a portion of land nearly surrounded by water and connected with a larger body by an isthmus — distinguished from *mainland* **b :** a piece of land jutting out into the water whether with or without a well-defined isthmus ⟨the Italian ~⟩ **2 :** something that juts out in the manner of a peninsula ⟨the ~ of land at the angle of the two roads⟩ ⟨a cooking ~ projecting from one wall and dividing the working and eating areas⟩

**peninsula pine** *n* **:** JEFFREY PINE

**¹pe·nin·su·lar** \-lə(r)\ *adj* [L *paeninsula* + E *-ar*] **1 :** of, belonging to, forming, or like a peninsula ⟨the many beaches of the ~ region⟩ **2** *often cap* **:** of, relating to, or characteristic of the Iberian peninsula ⟨the Spanish Civil War . . . worked out with a peculiar ~ glory and despair —*Newsweek*⟩

**²peninsular** \"\ *n* -s **:** an inhabitant of a peninsula

**pe·nin·su·lar·i·ty** \pəˌnin(t)səˈlarəd·ē\ *n* -ES **1 :** the state of being a peninsula **2 :** adherence to local ideas and customs (as due to peninsular isolation) **:** PROVINCIALISM

**pe·nin·su·late** \pəˈnin(t)səˌlāt\ *vt* -ED/-ING/-S [L *paeninsula* + E *-ate*] **:** to form into a peninsula

**pe·nis** \ˈpēnəs\ *n, pl* **pe·nes** \-ēˌnēz\ *or* **penises** [L, penis, tail; akin to Gk *peos*, *posthē* penis, Skt *pasas* penis, OE *fæsl* fetus, offspring, OHG *faselt* penis, *fasel* fetus, offspring, ON *fösull*] **1 :** the copulatory organ of the male of a higher vertebrate animal that in mammals usu. provides also the channel by which urine leaves the body and is typically a cylindrical organ made up of a broad root by which it is suspended from the pubic arch, an elongated cylindrical body consisting chiefly of a pair of large lateral corpora cavernosa and a smaller ventromedial corpus cavernosum containing the urethra, and a terminal glans enclosing the ends of the corpora cavernosa, covered by mucous membrane, and sheathed by a foreskin continuous with the skin covering the body of the organ **2 :** any of various male copulatory organs that are not homologous with the vertebrate penis (as the aedeagus of an insect or the copulatory setae of some worms)

**penis bone** *n* **:** BACULUM

**penis envy** *n* **:** the unverbalized longing of a girl or woman to be a boy or man

**pen·i·ston** *also* **pen·i·stone** \ˈpenəstən\ *n* -s *often cap* [fr. *Penistone*, town in Yorkshire, England, where it was first made] **:** a coarse woolen cloth used for clothing from the 16th into the 19th century

**pen·i·tence** \ˈpenəd·ən(t)s, -ətən- *also* -ətᵊn-\ *n* -s [ME, fr. OF, fr. ML *poenitentia*, alter. (influenced by L *poena* penalty, pain) of L *paenitentia* regret, fr. *paenitent-*, *paenitens* (pres. part. of *paenitēre* to be sorry, cause to be sorry) + *-ia* -y; akin to L *paene* almost — more at PAIN, PATIENT] **1 :** PENANCE **2 :** the quality or state of being penitent **:** sorrow for sins or faults ⟨forgiveness following true ~⟩

**syn** REPENTANCE, CONTRITION, ATTRITION, REMORSE, COMPUNCTION: PENITENCE describes the state of mind of one who acknowledges and deeply regrets his wrongs and is determined to amend ⟨that no sin is beyond forgiveness if it is followed by true *penitence* —K.S.Latourette⟩ REPENTANCE emphasizes the change of mind of one who not only regrets specific faults or errors but has abandoned his former way of life and is following a new standard ⟨for godly grief produces a *repentance* that leads to salvation —2 Cor 7: 10 (RSV)⟩ ⟨without *repentance* . . . man is too much his own god to feel the need of . . . knowing the true God —Reinhold Niebuhr⟩ CONTRITION stresses a sense of unworthiness; in general use it implies penitence that is manifest in signs of pain or grief ⟨you must — whether you feel it or not — present an appearance of *contrition* —George Meredith⟩; in theological use, CONTRITION implies sorrow arising out of love of God and one's failure to respond to his graces; in this sense, it is contrasted with ATTRITION, which means sorrow over one's sin due to a lower motive, such as fear of punishment ⟨most Christian churches hold that *attrition* is imperfect contrition and is not sufficient for salvation⟩; ATTRITION, in this sense, is limited to theological use. All these terms imply an authority, religious or secular, to which one submits; this implication is absent from REMORSE and COMPUNCTION, both of which denote a painful sting of conscience, without necessarily connoting humility or hope of forgiveness; but REMORSE emphasizes mental anguish and often intense suffering for consequences which cannot be escaped, not necessarily accompanied by any resolve to reform ⟨*remorse* that makes one walk on thorns —Oscar Wilde⟩ ⟨chronic *remorse*, as all the moralists are agreed, is a most undesirable sentiment —Aldous Huxley⟩ COMPUNCTION, the least powerful of these terms, usu. suggests a momentary reaction, not only for something done, but also for something being done or about to be done ⟨would not hurt a gnat unless his party . . . told him to do so, and then only with *compunction* —Sir Winston Churchill⟩

**pen·i·ten·cy** \-nsē\ *n* -ES [ME *penitencie*, fr. ML *poenitentia*] **:** PENITENCE 2

**¹pen·i·tent** \-nt\ *adj* [ME, fr. MF, fr. L *paenitent-*, *paenitens*, pres. part. of *paenitēre* to be sorry, cause to be sorry] **:** feeling or expressing pain or sorrow for sins or offenses **:** sincerely affected by a sense of guilt and resolved on amendment of life ⟨saw him lose his temper . . . for a second and he was ~ about it for a day or two —W.A.White⟩ ⟨wrote a ~ letter apologizing for her hasty words⟩

**²penitent** \"\ *n* -s [ME, fr. *penitent* (adj.)] **1 :** a person who repents of sin **:** one sorrowful because of his transgressions **2 :** a person under church censure but admitted to penance esp. under the direction of a confessor **3** *often cap* **:** a member of one of many confraternities of lay persons bound to penitential exercises and works of charity very numerous from the 13th to the 16th centuries and often named from their garb ⟨blue ~*s*⟩ ⟨white ~*s*⟩

**pen·i·ten·te** \ˌpenəˈtentā, -tē\ *n, pl* **penitentes** \-ās, -ēz\ *usu cap* [AmerSp, lit., penitent, sing. of *Penitentes* Penitents, short for *Los Hermanos Penitentes* The Penitent Brothers, religious society that originated in Mexico] **:** a member of a religious society of Flagellants in Spanish-American communities of the southwestern U.S. (as New Mexico) who practice self-whipping and other forms of penitential torture particularly during Holy Week

**penitent-form** \ˈ=,==,=\ *n* **:** the bench at which salvation seekers kneel at a Salvation Army meeting

**¹pen·i·ten·tial** \ˌpenəˈtenchəl\ *adj* [ML *poenitentialis*, fr. *poenitentia* penitence + L *-alis* -al] **:** of or relating to penitence or penance **:** expressing penitence **:** of the nature of penance ⟨~ tears⟩ ⟨the Day of Atonement which is the great ~ day of the Hebrew calendar —Nathaniel Micklem⟩ ⟨collections of the penances which he had appointed . . . came to influence the whole ~ system of the West —F.M.Stenton⟩ — **pen·i·ten·tial·ly** \-chəlē, -li\ *adv*

**²penitential** \"\ *n* -s [in sense 1, fr. ML *poenitentiale*, fr. *poenitentialis* penitential, adj.; in other senses, fr. *penitential*, adj.] **1 :** a manual of ecclesiastical rules for the imposition of penances suitable to different sins **2 :** PENITENT **3 penitentials** *pl* **:** penitential garb; *also* **:** garments of black

**penitential psalm** *n* **:** one of a group of seven liturgical psalms including psalms 6, 32, 38, 51, 102, 130, 143 in the RSV or 6, 31, 37, 50, 101, 129, 142 in the DV

**¹pen·i·ten·tia·ry** \ˌpenəˈtench(ə)rē, -ri *sometimes* -chēˌer-\ *n* -ES [ME *penitenciary*, fr. ML *poenitentiarius*, fr. *poenitentia* penitence + L *-arius* -ary — more at PENITENCE] **1 a :** an officer in some Roman Catholic dioceses vested with power from the bishop to absolve in cases reserved to him **b** [ML *poenitentiaria*, fem. of *poenitentiarius*] **:** a tribunal of the Roman curia dealing with cases concerning the private spiritual good of individuals esp. in relation to the sacrament of penance, presided over by a cardinal priest, granting absolutions, dispensations, commutations, ratifications of impediments, and condonations, regulating the use and granting of indulgences, and deciding questions of conscience referred to the Holy See **2** *obs* **a :** a place for penitents **b :** PENITENT **3 :** a place of refuge for reformation of prostitutes in 19th century England **4 :** a public institution in which offenders against the law are confined for detention or for punishment, discipline, and reformation and in which they are generally compelled to labor; *specif* **:** a state or federal prison in the U.S. — compare HOUSE OF CORRECTION, REFORMATORY

**²penitentiary** \ˈ==ˈ=(=)=, ˈ=ˈ==,==\ *adj* [ML *poenitentiarius*] **1 a :** of or relating to penance **:** prescribing or doing penance **b :** of or expressing penitence **2 a :** used for punishment, discipline, and reformation **b :** making one liable to a term in a penitentiary ⟨a ~ offense⟩ **c :** of, relating to, or confined in a penitentiary ⟨improve ~ conditions⟩ ⟨~ inmates⟩

**pen·i·tent·ly** *adv* **:** in a penitent manner ⟨returned ~ to beg their pardon⟩

**penk** *dial Eng var of* ⁴PINK 1

**penkeeper** \ˈ=,==\ *n* [¹*pen* + *keeper*] **:** a person engaged in breeding and raising livestock in Jamaica **:** RANCHER

**pen-keeping** \ˈ=,==\ *n* **:** stock raising in Jamaica

**penknife** \ˈ=,=\ *n* [ME *peneknif*, fr. *penne* quill, feather + *knif* knife — more at PEN, KNIFE] **1 :** a small knife used for

making and mending quill pens **2 :** a small pocketknife usu. with only one blade
**penlight** \'⸗,⸗\ *or* **pen·lite** \'⸗,līt\ *n* [*penlight* fr. ³*pen* + *light* (as in *flashlight*); *penlite* alter. of *penlight*] **:** a small flashlight resembling a fountain pen in size or shape
**pen·lop** \'penləp\ *n* -s *often cap* [native name in Bhutan] **:** the feudal ruler of one of the provinces of Bhutan **:** CHIEF, GOVERNOR
**pen machine** *n* [³*pen*] **:** a machine for ruling with pens
¹**pen·man** \'penmən\ *n, pl* **penmen** [³*pen* + *man*] **1 a :** a person who writes or copies (as documents) for another **:** CLERK, SCRIBE **b :** a person with a specified quality or kind of handwriting ⟨a poor ∼⟩ ⟨a swift ∼⟩ ⟨a good shorthand ∼⟩ **c :** one who is expert in penmanship — called also *calligrapher* **2 :** AUTHOR
²**penman** \"\ *n, pl* **penmen** [¹*pen* + *man*] **:** a stockyard worker who drives hogs to and from weighing pens and tattoos identification marks on them
**pen·man·ship** \'penmən,ship\ *n* [¹*penman* + -*ship*] **1 :** the art or practice of writing with the pen ⟨skills in ∼, spelling, and sentence structure —*Education Digest*⟩ **2 :** the action of writing with a pen ⟨shading . . . involves no extra ∼ —*Pitman Shorthand*⟩ **3 :** quality or style of handwriting **:** writing of an often specified kind or quality ⟨drills to improve your ∼⟩ ⟨written in his best ∼⟩ ⟨deciphers the awful ∼ of the captain —Elbridge Colby⟩
**pen-mate** \'⸗,⸗\ *vt* [¹*pen*] **:** to breed (poultry) as a pen consisting of one male with a selected group of females — compare FLOCK-MATE, STUD-MATE
**pen·na** \'penə\ *n, pl* **pen·nae** \-e,nē\ [L, feather, wing — more at PEN] **:** a normal contour feather as distinguished esp. from down or plume feathers
**pen·na·ceous** \pə'nāshəs\ *adj* [NL *pennaceus*, fr. L *penna* + -*aceus* -aceous] **:** of, being, or resembling a penna
**pen·na·cook** \'penə,ku̇k\ *n, pl* **pennacook** *or* **pennacooks** *usu cap* [of Algonquian origin; akin to Abnaki *pinâkuk* downhill] **1 :** a confederacy of Algonquian peoples of southwestern Maine, northeastern Massachusetts, and New Hampshire **2 :** a member of the Pennacook confederacy
**pen·na·les** \pə'na(,)lēz\ *n pl, cap* [NL, fr. L *penna* feather + NL -*ales*] **:** an order of diatoms having a raphe or pseudoraphe and ornamentation of the valves always bilaterally arranged in relation to a line rather than to a point — compare CENTRALES
**pen name** *n* **:** an author's pseudonym **:** NOM DE PLUME ⟨writes both under his own name and under a *pen name*⟩
**pen·nant** \'penənt\ *n* -s [alter. (influenced by *pennon*) of ¹*pendant*] **1 :** PENDANT 3 **2 a :** any of various nautical flags tapering usu. to a point or swallowtail and used for identification or signaling: as (1) **:** LONG PENNANT (2) **:** BROAD PENNANT (3) *Brit* **:** a long tapering flag cut off at the outward end by a line parallel to the staff and used esp. as a signal flag (4) **pennants** *pl* **:** a visual call sign of a British naval vessel consisting of an alphabetical flag above two or more numbered pennants (5) **:** a signal flag longer in the fly than in the hoist and tapering to a point ⟨flags and ∼s used for international signals⟩ **b :** a flag or banner that tapers toward the fly ⟨a new filling station decorated with lines of fluttering ∼s⟩; *esp* **:** one that tapers to a point **3 :** a flag emblematic of championship (as in a league of professional baseball clubs) ⟨the team that won the ∼⟩ — called also *flag* **4 :** ⁵FLAG 3a **5 :** PENNON 1a
**syn** see FLAG
**pennant fish** *n* [so called fr. the appearance of the fins] **:** THREADFISH 1
**pen·nant·ite** \'penənt·,īt\ *n* -s [Thomas *Pennant* †1798 Welsh naturalist + E -*ite*] **:** a mineral $Mn_9Al_6Si_5O_{20}(OH)_{16}$ of the chlorite group consisting of basic silicate of manganese and aluminum isomorphous with thuringite
**pennant's marten** \'penənts-\ *n, usu cap P* [after Thomas *Pennant* †1798] **:** FISHER 2
**pennant-winged nightjar** \'⸗⸗,⸗-\ *n* **:** either of two African nightjars: **a :** a bird (*Macrodipteryx longipennis*) that has second primary in the male with a very long almost naked shaft and a broad racketlike web at the tip **b :** a bird (*Semeiophorus vexillarius*) that has the second to fifth primaries more or less lengthened and the ninth extremely so although the shaft is not bare for any portion of its length
**pen·nar·ia** \pə'na(a)rēə\ *n, cap* [NL, perh. fr. L *penna* feather, wing + NL -*aria*] **:** a genus (the type of the family Pennaridae) comprising gymnoblastic hydroids in which the hydranth has a basal whorl of ten to twelve tentacles with a number of short knobbed tentacles on the hypostome
**pen·na·tae** \pə'nā,tē\ *n pl, cap* [NL, fr. L *penna* feather + NL -*atae* (fem. pl. of L -*atus* -ate)] *in some classifications* **:** a group equivalent to the order Pennales
**pen·nate** \'pe,nāt\ *also* **pen·nat·ed** \-ād·əd\ *adj* [*pennate* fr. L *pennatus* winged, fr. *penna* feather, wing + -*atus* -ate; *pennated* fr. L *pennatus* + E -*ed* — more at PEN] **1 :** PINNATE **2 :** WINGED, FEATHERED **3 :** having the shape of a wing **4** [*penna-* (fr. NL *Pennales*) + -*ate*] **:** of or resembling the Pennales
**pen·nat·u·la** \pə'nachələ\ *n* [NL, fr. LL, fem. of *pennatulus* winged, fr. L *pennatus* winged + -*ulus* -ule] **1** *cap* **:** a common genus (the type of the family Pennatulidae) of sea pens **2** *pl* **pennatu·lae** \-chə,lē\ *or* **pennatulas :** SEA PEN — **pen·nat·u·lid** \-ləd\ *adj or n*
**pen·nat·u·la·cea** \pə,nachə'lāshēə\ *n pl, cap* [NL, fr. *Pennatula* + -*acea*] **:** an order of Alcyonaria including the sea pens, sea pansies, and related forms that develop a colony which usu. resembles a feather, leaf, or club, is often more or less bilaterally symmetrical with the polyps arranged along the distal part of a central axis or on lateral branches and has the basal end of the axis destitute of polyps and embedded in the mud of the sea bottom — **pen·nat·u·la·cean** \⸗¦⸗⸗'lāshən\ *adj or n* — **pen·nat·u·la·ceous** \-shəs\ *adj*
¹**pen·nat·u·lar·i·an** \⸗¦⸗⸗¦la(a)rēən\ *adj* [NL *Pennatularia*, former family of sea pens (fr. *Pennatula* + -*aria*) + E -*an*] **:** of or relating to the Pennatulacea
²**pennatularian** \"\ *n* -s **:** a member of the Pennatulacea
**pen·na·tu·li·da** \,penə'tüləda, -ə'tyü-\ *n* [NL, fr. *Pennatula* + -*ida*] *syn of* PENNATULACEA
**pen·nat·u·loid** \pə'nachə,lȯid\ *adj* [NL *Pennatula* + E -*oid*] **:** of, relating to, or resembling the Pennatulacea
**penned** *past of* PEN
**pen·neech** *also* **pen·neeck** \pə'nēk\ *n* -s [origin unknown] **:** an old game that is played with hands of seven cards and that has a card turned up before each trick in order to determine trumps
¹**pen·ner** \'penər\ *n* -s [ME, fr. *penne* pen + -*er* — more at PEN] *chiefly Scot* **:** a case worn at the waist for holding pens
²**pen·ner** \'penə(r)\ *n* -s [⁴*pen* + -*er*] **:** one that pens a document **:** WRITER
³**penner** \"\ *n* -s [²*pen* + -*er*] **:** one that pens animals or attends to their pens
**pen·ni** \'penē\ *n, pl* **pen·nia** \-ēə\ *or* **pennis** [Finn, prob. fr. G *pfennig* penny (fr. OHG *pfenning*) — more at PENNY] **1 :** a unit of value of Finland equal to ¹⁄₁₀₀ markka — see MONEY table **2 :** a coin representing one penni unit
**penni-** *also* **penno-** *comb form* [L *penni-*, fr. *penna* feather, wing — more at PEN] **1 :** feather ⟨*pennoplume*⟩ ⟨*penniform*⟩ **2 :** pinnately ⟨*penninerved*⟩ ⟨*penniveined*⟩
**pen·nied** \'penēd\ *adj* **:** having pennies
**pennies** *pl of* PENNY
**pen·ni·less** \'penᵊləs, -nēl-\ *adj* [ME *peniles*, fr. *peni* penny + -*les* -less] **:** destitute of money **:** extremely poor ⟨in one day the rich man . . . saw himself ∼, landless, a bankrupt among creditors —J.G.Lockhart⟩ **syn** see POOR
**pen·ni·less·ly** *adv* **:** in a penniless condition
**pen·ni·less·ness** *n* -ES **:** the quality or state of being penniless
**penning** *pres part of* PEN
**pen·ni·nite** \'penə,nīt\ *also* **pen·nine** \'penən, -,nīn\ *n* -s [*penninite* fr. G *pennin* (fr. *Pennine* Alps) + E -*ite*; *pennine* fr. G *pennin*] **:** a mineral approximately $(Mg,Fe,Al)_6(Si,Al)_4O_{11}(OH)_8$ of the chlorite group consisting of a basic aluminosilicate of magnesium, iron, and aluminum, that is monoclinic and is commonly emerald or olive green (hardness 2–2.5, sp. gr. 2.6–2.85)
**pen·ni·se·tum** \,penə'sēd·əm\ *n, cap* [NL, fr. *penni-* + L *seta* bristle — more at SINEW] **:** a large genus of Old World grasses having a bristly involucre surrounding the jointed pedicels of the spikelet — see FOUNTAIN GRASS, PEARL MILLET

**pen·non** *also* **pen·on** \'penən\ *n* -s [ME, fr. MF *penon*, aug. of *penne* feather, wing — more at PEN] **1 a :** a long usu. triangular or swallow-tailed streamer typically attached to the head of a lance: as (1) **:** one borne as the ensign of a knight bachelor in the middle ages (2) **:** one borne as the ensign of a modern regiment of lancers **b :** PENNANT 2a **2 :** a flag of any shape **:** BANNER **3 :** WING, PINION **4 :** a retractor muscle of the septa of a zooantharian — called also *muscle pennon*
**syn** see FLAG
**pen·non·cel** *or* **pen·on·cel** *also* **pen·non·celle** \'penən,sel\ *n* -s [ME *penoncelle*, *penouncell*, fr. MF *penoncel*, dim. of *penon* pennon] **1 :** a small narrow flag or streamer borne by a man-at-arms in late medieval or Renaissance times; *esp* **:** such a flag borne at the head of a lance **2 :** a flag borne by a ship in the later middle ages and similar in shape to but smaller than a long pennant
**pen·no·pluma** \,penə'plümə\ *or* **pen·no·plume** \'⸗⸗,plüm\ *n* [*pennopluma* fr. NL, fr. *penno-* + L *pluma* down; *pennoplume* fr. *penno-* + *plume* — more at FLEECE] **:** SEMIPLUME
**pen·north** \'penə(r)th\ *n* -s [by contr.] **:** PENNYWORTH
**penn·syl·va·nia** \¦pen(t)səl¦vānyə, -ānēə\ *adj, usu cap* [fr. *Pennsylvania*, middle Atlantic state of the U.S., fr. NL, fr. Sir William *Penn* †1670 Eng. naval commander and father of William Penn †1718 founder of the colony of Pennsylvania + NL -*sylvania* (fr. L *silva*, *sylva* wood, forest)] **:** of or from the state of Pennsylvania ⟨*Pennsylvania* coal⟩ **:** of the kind or style prevalent in Pennsylvania **:** PENNSYLVANIAN
**pennsylvania dutch** *n, usu cap P&D* **1 pennsylvania dutch** *pl* **:** people living mostly in eastern Pennsylvania whose characteristic cultural traditions go back to the German migrations of the 18th century **2** *or* **pennsylvania german** *usu cap P&G* **:** a dialect of High German spoken in parts of Pennsylvania and Maryland by descendants of 17th and 18th century immigrants from southwest Germany and Switzerland **3 :** the architectural and decorative style associated with the Pennsylvania Dutch
**pennsylvania dutchman** *n, usu cap P&D* **:** a member of the Pennsylvania Dutch
¹**penn·syl·va·nian** \-nyən, -nēən\ *adj, usu cap* [*Pennsylvania*, state of the U.S. + E -*an*] **1 :** of, relating to, or characteristic of Pennsylvania or Pennsylvanians **2 a :** of or relating to the Paleozoic period between the Mississippian and Permian **b :** of or relating to the system formed during this period which contains most of the coal of the U.S. east of the Great Plains — see GEOLOGIC TIME table
²**pennsylvanian** \"\ *n* -s **1** *cap* **:** a native or resident of the state of Pennsylvania **2** *usu cap* **:** the Pennsylvanian period or system
**pennsylvania system** *n, usu cap P* **:** a system of prison discipline introduced in Pennsylvania in the late 18th century and characterized by solitary confinement of prisoners convicted of serious offenses
**pennsylvania truss** *n, usu cap P* **:** a truss developed from the Pratt truss esp. for bridges with long spans and having subdivided panels, curved top chords for through trusses, and curved bottom chords for deck spans
**pen·ny** \'penē, -ni\ *n, pl* **pennies** \-ēz, -iz\ *or* **pence** \'pen(t)s\ *often attrib* [ME *penny*, *peny*, fr. OE *penig*, *penning*; akin to OHG *pfenning*, *pfenting* coin, penny, ON *penningr*] **1 a :** a British monetary unit equal to ¹⁄₂₄₀ pound or ¹⁄₁₂ shilling — see MONEY table **b :** a British coin representing one penny, orig. made of silver but after the 18th century except for the silver maundy money made of copper or of bronze **2 :** any of various coins of small denomination or the monetary units they represent: as **a** (1) **:** a Roman denarius ⟨three measures of barley for a ∼ —Rev 6:6 (AV)⟩ ⟨they brought unto him a ∼ —Mt 22:19 (AV)⟩ (2) *pl pennies* **:** a Roman quadrans **:** FARTHING ⟨are not two sparrows sold for a ∼ —Mt 10:29 (RSV)⟩ **b** *pl pennies* **:** a cent of the U.S. or Canada ⟨∼ candy⟩ **3 a** *archaic* **:** the part of an amount of money indicated by a specified ordinal ⟨interest was reduced from the twentieth to the fiftieth ∼ or from five to two percent —Adam Smith⟩ **b :** the sum exacted by a specified tax or customary payment ⟨earnest ∼⟩ — often used in combination ⟨ale*penny*⟩ ⟨fish*penny*⟩ **4 :** a trivial amount **:** the least bit ⟨never a ∼ the worse⟩ **5 :** a piece or sum of money ⟨make an honest ∼⟩ ⟨saved every ∼ he earned⟩ **6** *pl pennies* **:** a token or good-luck piece worth or resembling a cent or a penny — **pennies from heaven :** something had without effort or payment **:** an unexpected benefit
**pen·ny-a-lin·er** \'penēə'līnə(r)\ *n* [fr. *penny-a-line*, adj. (fr. the phrase *a penny a line*) + -*er*] **:** a hack writer or journalist
**penny ante** *n* **1 :** poker played for very low stakes (as pennies) **2 :** any dealings on a small scale or with picayune sums involved
**penny arcade** *n* **:** an amusement center where each device for entertainment may be operated for a penny
**penny bank** *n* **1 :** a savings bank setting no minimum limit on a deposit **2 :** a small, often slotted, box or safe designed to receive deposits of pennies
**pennycress** \'⸗⸗,⸗\ *n* [prob. alter. (influenced by *cress*) of *penny grass*] **:** a plant of the genus *Thlaspi*; *esp* **:** a Eurasian herb (*T. arvense*) having round flat pods — called also *fanweed*, *field pennycress*, *French weed*, *penny grass*
**penny dreadful** *n, pl* **penny dreadfuls 1 :** a novel of violent adventure or crime esp. popular in late Victorian England and costing orig. one penny — compare DIME NOVEL, SHILLING SHOCKER **2 :** a story or periodical characterized by sensationalism and violence
**penny-farthing** \'⸗⸗'⸗⸗\ *n, Brit* **:** a bicycle with a large front wheel and a small rear wheel common from about 1870 to 1890
**pennyflower** \'⸗⸗,⸗⸗\ *n* [so called fr. its round flat pods] **:** HONESTY 3
**penny gaff** *n, Brit* **:** ⁵GAFF
**penny grass** *n* [ME *penygres*, fr. *peny* penny + *gres*, *gras* grass; fr. the round flat pods — more at PENNY, GRASS] **:** PENNYCRESS
**pennyland** \'⸗⸗,⸗\ *n* **:** a small piece of land in Orkney and Shetland once taxed about a penny a year
**penny mountain** *n* **:** WILD THYME
**pen·ny-pinch** \'penē,pinch\ *vt* [back-formation fr. *penny pincher*] **:** to give out money to in a niggardly manner ⟨takes a sinister but fascinating kind of joy in . . . *penny-pinching* his own family —James Yaffe⟩ **:** deprive of funds by petty economy ⟨*penny-pinched* himself out of . . . millions of dollars —S.N.Behrman⟩
**penny pincher** *n* **:** a niggardly or parsimonious person
**penny-pinching** \¦⸗⸗¦⸗⸗\ *adj* **:** given to or marked by mean and petty economy and miserliness ⟨*penny-pinching* cuts in appropriations crippling the project⟩ **syn** see STINGY
**penny-plain** \¦⸗⸗¦⸗\ *adj, Brit* **:** having no decorative or pretentious features ⟨can have it *penny-plain* and no nonsense —Rose Macaulay⟩
**penny post** *n* **1 a :** a postal system carrying a letter for a penny: (1) **:** a system established in London about 1680 (2) **:** the former system of Great Britain established in 1840 (3) **:** a local mail service in colonial America carrying letters from post office to addressee **b :** a mail carrier in such a system **2 :** a common American marsh pennywort (*Hydrocotyle americana*)
**pen·ny·prick** \'penē,prik\ *n* [ME *penyprike*, fr. *peny* penny + *prike* prick — more at PENNY, PRICK] *archaic* **:** an old game of throwing at a penny
**penny rent** *n* **:** a nominal rent
**pen·ny·roy·al** \¦penē¦rȯi(y)əl, -nə'-, -ȯil, *dial* ¦penə¦rīl\ *n* [prob. by folk etymology (influence of *pennywort* and *royal*) fr. MF *poullieul*, *poliol*, modif. of L *puleium*, *pulegium* fleabane, fleawort, pennyroyal] **1 :** a European perennial mint (*Mentha pulegium*) with small pungently aromatic leaves **2 :** a plant of the genus *Hedeoma*; *esp* **:** an erect hairy branching American herb (*H. pulegioides*) that yields an essential oil and is sometimes used in folk medicine as an emmenagogue and diaphoretic — called also *American pennyroyal*; see PENNYROYAL OIL **3 :** any of several western No. American aromatic herbs of the genus *Monardella*; *esp* **:** an herb (*M. villosa*) of California
**pennyroyal oil** *n* **:** either of two yellowish essential oils obtained from pennyroyal: **a :** the oil obtained from European pennyroyal that has an odor like mint and is used chiefly in soaps **b :** the aromatic oil from an American pennyroyal (*Hedeoma pulegioides*) — called also *hedeoma oil*

**pennysiller** \'⸗⸗,⸗⸗\ *n* -s [*penny* + *siller*] *Scot* **:** MONEY, CASH
**penny stock** *n* **:** stock selling under one dollar a share and quoted in cents
**pennystone** \'⸗⸗,⸗\ *n* [ME *penystan*, fr. *peny* penny + *stan* stone — more at STONE] *Scot* **:** a flat circular stone used as a quoit
**pennystones** \'⸗⸗,⸗\ *n pl but usu sing in constr*, *Scot* **:** a game resembling quoits
**penny wedding** *n* **:** a wedding paid for by money collected from the guests and formerly common in Scotland
**pennyweight** \'⸗⸗,⸗\ *n* [ME *penyweight*, fr. *peny* penny + *weight* — more at WEIGHT] **:** a unit of troy weight equal to 24 grains or ¹⁄₂₀ troy ounce — see MEASURE table
**pen·ny·weight·er** \'penē,wād·ə(r)\ *n* -s [fr. obs. E *pennyweight* jewelry (fr. E *pennyweight*, weight unit) + E -*er*] **:** a thief that steals jewelry by substituting a fake for a valuable piece
**penny whistle** *n* **1 :** a small fipple flute — called also *tin whistle* **2 :** a simple toy whistle
**pen·ny·win·kle** \'penē,wiŋkəl\ *n* [by alter.] *dial* **:** PERIWINKLE
**penny-wise** \¦⸗⸗¦⸗\ *adj* **:** wise or prudent only in small matters **:** excessively sparing in expenditure — used chiefly in *penny-wise and pound-foolish*
**pennywort** \'⸗⸗,⸗\ *n* [ME *penywort*, fr. *peny* penny + *wort* — more at PENNY, WORT] **:** any of several round-leaved plants: as **a :** NAVELWORT **b :** any of various umbelliferous plants of the genera *Hydrocotyle* and *Centella* — called also *marsh pennywort* **c :** KENILWORTH IVY **d :** a leafless perennial (*Obolaria virginica*) of the family Gentianaceae with white or purplish flowers
**pennyworth** \'⸗⸗,⸗\ *n, pl* **pennyworth** *or* **pennyworths** [ME *penyworth*, fr. OE *penigwurth*, fr. *penig* penny + *wurth* worth — more at PENNY, WORTH] **1 :** the amount that a penny buys **:** a penny's worth ⟨sold fruit . . . by the ∼ —*Commonweal*⟩ ⟨two ∼ of bread⟩ ⟨more ∼s of birdseed — Richard Llewellyn⟩ **2 :** value for money expended **:** BUY, BARGAIN ⟨seemed a ∼ at that price⟩ ⟨a good ∼⟩ **3 :** a small quantity **:** MODICUM
**pe·nob·scot** \pə'näbzkət, -bsk-, -bz,kät, -b,skät\ *n, pl* **penobscot** *or* **penobscots** *usu cap* **1 a :** an Indian people of the Penobscot river valley and Penobscot Bay region **b :** a member of such people **2 :** a dialect of Abnaki
**penoche** *var of* PENUCHE
**pe·no·correctional** \¦pēnō+\ *adj* [*penology* + *correctional*] **:** combining correctional treatment with penal confinement ⟨an institution offering a ∼ program⟩
**pe·no·log·i·cal** \¦pēnᵊl¦äjəkəl\ *adj* **:** of or relating to penology ⟨∼ methods⟩
**pe·nol·o·gist** \pē'näləjəst, pə'-\ *n* -s **:** a specialist in penology
**pe·nol·o·gy** \-jē, -ji\ *n* -ES [*peno-* (fr. Gk *poinо-*, fr. *poinē* penalty) + -*logy* — more at PAIN] **:** the study of punishment for crime; *specif* **:** a branch of criminology dealing with prison management and the treatment of offenders esp. with regard to their rehabilitation
**penon** *var of* PENNON
**penoncel** *var of* PENNONCEL
**pe·nor·con** \pə'nȯrkən\ *n* -s [NL] **:** an obsolete 17th century cittern
**pen pal** *n* [³*pen*] **:** a person with whom one carries on a friendly correspondence usu. without ever meeting
**pen palsy** *or* **pen paralysis** *n* **:** WRITERS' CRAMP
**pen picture** *or* **pen portrait** *n* **1 :** a picture drawn with a pen **2 :** a written description **:** SKETCH
**pen pot** *n* [¹*pen*] **:** a fisherman's pot for keeping crabs or lobsters
**pen-pusher** \'⸗,⸗⸗\ *n* **:** PENMAN; *esp* **:** a clerical worker
**pen·rose·ite** \'pen,rō,zīt\ *n* -s [Richard A. F. *Penrose* †1931 Am. geologist + E -*ite*] **:** a mineral $(Ni,Cu,Pb)Se_2$ structurally like pyrite consisting of a selenide of lead, copper, and nickel and occurring in lead gray radiating columnar masses (hardness 3, sp. gr. 6.9)
**pens** *pl of* PEN, *pres 3d sing of* PEN
**pen·sa·co·la** \,pen(t)sə'kōlə\ *n, pl* **pensacola** *or* **pensacolas** *usu cap* [modif. of Choctaw *panshiokla*, fr. *panshi* hair + *okla* people] **1 :** a Muskogian people near Pensacola Bay, Fla. **2 :** a member of the Pensacola people
**pensacola snapper** *n, usu cap P* [fr. *Pensacola* Bay, inlet of Gulf of Mexico] **:** GRAY SNAPPER
**penscript** \'⸗,⸗\ *n* **:** matter written with a pen
**pen·sée** \päⁿ'sā\ *n* -s [in sense 1, fr. F, fr. *Pensées* (1670), literary work by Blaise Pascal †1662 Fr. scientist and philosopher; in sense 2, fr. F, fr. MF — more at PANSY] **1 :** a thought expressed in literary form ⟨not a system of ethics at all but simply a collection of maxims and ∼s —J.C.Ransom⟩ **2 :** PANSY 2
**pen shell** *n* **:** a bivalve mollusk of the family Pinnidae having the shell resembling a quill pen in outline — compare PINNA
**pensil** *var of* PENCEL
**pen·sile** \'pen(t)səl\ *adj* [L *pensilis*, fr. *pensus* (past part. of *pendĕre* to hang) + -*ilis* -ile — more at PENDANT] **1 a :** suspended from above **:** HANGING, PENDENT **b :** set or poised on a declivity **:** OVERHANGING **2 :** having or building a hanging nest
¹**pen·sion** \'penchən, *in sense 3* (')päⁿs¦yōⁿ *or* ¦päⁿsē¦ōⁿ\ *n* -s *often attrib* [ME *pensioun*, fr. MF & ML; MF *pension*, fr. ML *pension-*, *pensio*, fr. L, payment, fr. *pensus* (past part. of *pendere* to weigh, estimate, pay) + -*ion-*, -*io* -ion — more at PENDANT] **1 a :** a fixed sum of money charged annually upon the revenues of a benefice by an ecclesiastical superior and paid to a cleric for any just cause (as the work of the church, reward for services, support of a former incumbent) **b** *obs* **:** a payment required of a person or group; *specif* **:** the dues payable by a member of a society (as a guild or Inn of Court) — often used in pl. **2 :** a fixed sum paid regularly to a person: **a** *archaic* **:** one paid to an employee for current services **:** WAGE **b :** one paid for secret service or for a claim upon assistance when needed **c :** a gratuity granted (as by a government) as a favor or reward or as a subsidy to a person of recognized merit in art, literature, or science **d** (1) **:** one paid under given conditions to a person following his retirement from service (as due to age or disability) or to the surviving dependents of a person entitled to such a pension (2) **:** the portion of an employee's retirement income provided by the employer's contributions under a contributory plan — compare ANNUITY **3 a** (1) **:** payment for board and room ⟨strolled to the inn where he paid his ∼ —Robert Hichens⟩ (2) **:** accommodations at a European hotel or boardinghouse **:** ROOM AND BOARD ⟨charges $3 a day for . . . full ∼ or $2.50 for half-pension, breakfast and one meal —Horace Sutton⟩ **b** *also* **pen·si·o·ne** \,pen(t)sē'ōnē\ [*pensione* fr. It, pension, fr. OIt, fr. MF] **:** a boardinghouse in continental Europe or Latin America
²**pen·sion** \'penchən, *in vi sense* (')päⁿs¦yōⁿ *or* ¦päⁿsē¦ōⁿ\ *vb* -ED/-ING/-s *vi* **:** to receive board and lodging at a fixed rate ⟨the small country house where we ∼*ed* —W.J.Cory⟩ ∼ *vt* **:** to grant or pay a pension to **:** dismiss or retire from service with a pension ⟨the present nizam . . . is ∼*ed* by the new State Government and has withdrawn from politics —*Jewelers' Circular*⟩ — often followed by *off* ⟨finally ∼*ed* off his faithful old servant⟩
**pen·sion·able** \'penchənəbəl\ *adj* **1 :** qualified to receive a pension ⟨a ∼ employee⟩ **2 :** that qualifies a person to receive a pension ⟨the post is ∼ after three years' probation —*Nature*⟩ ⟨∼ disabilities⟩ ⟨a ∼ age⟩ **3** *chiefly Brit* **:** connected with or affecting a pension ⟨for ∼ purposes⟩ ⟨a ∼ salary⟩ — **pen·sion·ably** \-blē\ *adv*
**pen·si·o·na·do** \,pen(t)sēə'nä(,)dō\ *n* -s [PhilSp, fr. Sp, pensioned, fr. past part. of *pensionar* to pension, fr. *pensión* pension, fr. L *pension-*, *pensio* payment] **:** a Philippine student whose expenses are paid by the government while he studies abroad
¹**pen·sion·ary** \'penchə,nerē, -ri\ *n* -ES [MF & ML; MF *pensionnaire*, fr. ML *pensionarius*, fr. *pension-*, *pensio* pension + -*arius* -ary] **1 :** PENSIONER; *esp* **:** HIRELING ⟨those who predicted ill success for France in the cafes were suspected of being *pensionaries* . . . of the . . . English chargé d'affaires —Evelyn G. Cruickshanks⟩ **2** [trans. of MD *pensionarijs*, *pensionaris*] **:** an official of the province of Holland or one of its cities

during the 17th and 18th centuries giving legal counsel, representing the city or province in the provincial or general legislature, and in the case of the provincial pensionary presiding over the provincial legislature

[2]**pensionary** \"\ *adj* [ML *pensionarius*] **1 :** receiving a pension : serving as a pensionary **2 :** consisting of a pension

**pen·sion·er** \'pench(ə)nə(r)\ *n* -s [ME, fr. MF *pensionnier*, fr. ML *pensionarius* pensionary] **1 :** a former officer in the Inns of Court responsible for collecting and recording pensions **2 :** a student at Cambridge University who pays for his own board, room, and tuition instead of being dependent on a foundation — compare COMMONER **3 :** a person who receives a pension ⟨payments to ~s of the Spanish-American War⟩ : one subsisting on a pension ⟨the diet of our low-income families, ~s, unemployed and the institutionalized —C.C. Mitchell⟩ **4** *obs* **a :** GENTLEMAN-AT-ARMS **b :** a member of a bodyguard : RETAINER **5** [modif. (influenced by *pensioner* in earlier senses) of D *pensionaris*, fr. MD *pensionarijs*, *pensionaris*, fr. ML *pensionarius* pensionary] *archaic* : [1]PENSIONARY 2 **6** [F *pensionnaire*, fr. MF] : a boarder in a pension or institution (as a continental school)

**pen·sion·less** \'penchənləs\ *adj* : having no pension

**pen·sion·naire** \,päⁿ,syȯ'na(a)(ə)r\ *n* -s [MF] **1 :** PENSIONER; *esp* : BOARDER **2 :** one of a junior class of actors appointed annually at the Comédie Française — compare SOCIÉTAIRE

**pen·sion·nat** \-'nä\ *n* -s [F, fr. *pension*, fr. MF — more at PENSION] : a European boarding school

**pension plan** *n* : systematic provision by an employer for definitely determinable periodic incomes to employees upon retirement with or without funding; *specif* : one financed exclusively by the employer — compare RETIREMENT PLAN

**pensions** *pl of* PENSION, *pres 3d sing of* PENSION

**pension trust** *n* : a trust established to provide financial administration of a pension or retirement fund

**pen·sive** \'pen(t)siv, -sēv *also* -səv\ *adj* [ME *pensif*, fr. MF, fr. *penser* to think (fr. L *pensare* to weigh, ponder, consider, fr. *pensus*, past part. of *pendere* to weigh, estimate, pay) + *-if* -ive — more at PENDANT] **1 :** absorbed or engrossed in or given to sober thoughtfulness; *esp* : musingly or dreamily occupied with grave, mildly regretful, or melancholy meditations often with contriving or anxiety for the future ⟨as she gazed at the view . . . she would grow ~ —Owen Wister⟩ ⟨a ~ mood⟩ **2 :** expressing or suggesting thoughtfulness with sadness ⟨her face had the ~ mournfulness of a seraph in an old sad painting —Herman Wouk⟩ **3 :** conducive or favorable to or fostering serious thoughtfulness or melancholy — **pen·sive·ly** \-səvlē, -li\ *adv* — **pen·sive·ness** \-sivnəs, -sēv- *also* -səv-\ *n* -ES

**pen sketch** *n* **1 :** a sketch made with a pen **2 :** a literary sketch

**pen-stabling** \'=,=(=)=\ *n* : stabling (as of dairy cattle) in a loafing barn — compare LOOSE-HOUSING SYSTEM

**pen staff** *n*, *dial* : PENHOLDER

[1]**pen·ste·mon** \pen'stēmən, 'pen(t)stəm-\ *n*, *cap* [NL, fr. *penta-* + Gk *stēmōn* warp, thread — more at STAMEN] : a genus of chiefly American herbs or rarely shrubs (family Scrophulariaceae) having opposite or verticillate leaves and showy blue, purple, red, yellow, or white flowers, four perfect stamens, and one sterile stamen

[2]**penstemon** *var of* PENTSTEMON

**pen·ster** \'penztə(r), -n(t)st-\ *n* -s [[3]*pen* + *-ster*] : WRITER; *esp* : a hack writer

**penstick** \'=,=\ *n* [[3]*pen* + *stick*] : PENHOLDER

**penstock** \'=,=\ *n* [[1]*pen* + *stock*] **1 :** a sluice gate, or valve for restraining, deviating, or otherwise regulating a flow (as of water or sewage) **2 :** PENTROUGH **3 :** a closed conduit or pipe for conducting water to a waterwheel

**pen·sum** \'pen(t)səm\ *n* -s [NL, fr. L, duty, charge, something weighed out, fr. neut. of *pensus*, past part. of *pendere* to weigh, estimate, pay] : a task assigned in school often as a punishment

**pen·sy** \'pen(t)sē\ *adj* [ME *pensie*, *pensey*, prob. fr. MF *pensif* pensive] **1** *dial* : PENSIVE, THOUGHTFUL **2** *dial Eng* : SQUEAMISH **3** *chiefly Scot* : SELF-IMPORTANT, CONCEITED

[1]**pent** \'pent\ *adj* [prob. fr. past part. of obs. E *pend* to pen, confine, fr. ME *penden* — more at PEND] : shut up : PENNED, CONFINED — often used with *up* or *in* ⟨slow-moving vehicles can turn aside to allow *pent-up* traffic . . . in the rear to proceed onward —*N.Y. Times*⟩ ⟨she listened until her ~ breath tore itself from her lungs —John Faulkner⟩ ⟨famous Quarter . . . ~ in a sliver of space, seven blocks long, three wide —*Saturday Rev.*⟩

[2]**pent** *n* -s *obs* : a place containing pent-up water : RESERVOIR

[3]**pent** \'pent\ *n* -s [by shortening] : PENTHOUSE 1

**penta-** *or* **pent-** *or* **pen-** *comb form* [ME *pent-*, fr. Gk *pent-*, *penta-*, fr. *pente* — more at FIVE] **1 :** five ⟨*penta*cyclic⟩ ⟨*penta*hedron⟩ ⟨*penta*lobate⟩ ⟨*pen*tode⟩ **2 :** containing five atoms, groups, or equivalents ⟨*penta*hydrate⟩ ⟨*pent*amine⟩ ⟨*penta*acetate⟩ ⟨*pen*thiophene⟩

**pen·ta·basic** \¦pentə+\ *adj* [*penta-* + *basic*] **1 :** having five hydrogen atoms capable of replacement by basic atoms or radicals — used of acids **2 :** containing five atoms of a univalent metal or their equivalent — used of salts

**pen·ta·carbonyl** \"+\ *n* [*penta-* + *carbonyl*] a compound containing five carbonyl groups esp. combined with a metal

**pen·ta·chloride** \"+\ *n* [*penta-* + *chloride*] : a chloride containing five atoms of chlorine in the molecule

**pen·ta·chlo·ro·phe·nate** \,pentə,klōrə'fē,nāt\ *n* [*pentachlorophenol* + *-ate*] : a salt of pentachlorophenol — not used systematically

**pen·ta·chlorophenol** \¦pentə+\ *n* [*penta-* + *chlorophenol*] : a crystalline compound $C_6Cl_5OH$ made by reaction of hexachlorobenzene with sodium hydroxide or of chlorine with phenol and used chiefly as a wood preservative, fungicide, and disinfectant usu. in solution in hydrocarbon oils or in a water solution of its sodium salt

**pen·ta·chord** \'pentə,kȯrd\ *n* [Gk *pentachordon*, fr. neut. of *pentachordos* five-stringed, fr. *penta-* + *-chordos* stringed (fr. *chordē* string) — more at CORD] **1 :** an ancient musical instrument with five strings **2 :** a diatonic system of five tones

**pent·acid** \(')pent+\ *adj* [*penta-* + *acid*] **1 :** able to react with five molecules of a monobasic acid (as to form a salt) — used esp. of bases **2 :** containing five hydrogen atoms replaceable by basic atoms or radicals — used esp. of acids

**pen·ta·cle** \'pentəkəl\ *n* -s [OIt *pentacol*, *pentacolo*, fr. (assumed) ML *pentaculum*, prob. fr. L *penta-* + (fr. Gk) *-culum* -cle] **1 :** a 5-pointed star having points formed by extension of the sides of a usu. regular pentagon, producible by one continuous line, and used as a magical or talismanic symbol — called also *pentagram*, *pentalpha*, *pentangle* **2 :** any of several occult symbols resembling the true pentacle (as in being producible by a continuous line); *esp* : HEXAGRAM

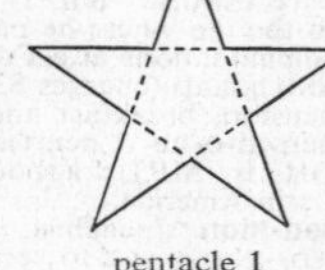

pentacle 1

**pen·ta·con·tane** \,pentə'kän,tān\ *n* -s [Gk *pentēkonta* fifty + E *-ane* — more at PENTECOST] : a paraffin hydrocarbon $C_{50}H_{102}$; *esp* : the normal hydrocarbon $CH_3(CH_2)_{48}CH_3$

**pen·ta·co·sane** \-'kō,sān\ *n* -s [ISV *penta-* + *eicosane*] : a paraffin hydrocarbon $C_{25}H_{52}$; *esp* : the crystalline normal hydrocarbon $CH_3(CH_2)_{23}CH_3$

**pen·tac·ri·nite** \pen'takrə,nīt\ *n* -s [NL *Pentacrinus* + E *-ite*] **1 :** a fossil of the genus *Pentacrinus* **2 :** a Jurassic crinoid with star-shaped columnals

**pen·tac·ri·noid** \-,nȯid\ *n* -s [NL *Pentacrinus* + E *-oid*] : a larval form of some crinoids (as members of the genus *Antedon*) resembling crinoids of the genus *Pentacrinus*

**pen·tac·ri·nus** \-nəs\ *n*, *cap* [NL, fr. *penta-* (fr. Gk) + *-crinus*] : a genus (the type of the family Pentacrinidae) comprising large stalked Jurassic crinoids having a small bowl-shaped calyx, strong numerously branched and pinnulate arms, and a pentangular stalk

**pen·tact** \'pen,takt\ *adj* [*penta-* + *-act*] : having five rays

**pen·tac·tu·la** \pen'takchələ\ *n* -s [NL, fr. *penta-* + *-act-* (fr. Gk *aktis* ray) + *-ula* — more at ACTIN-] : a late larval echinoderm having five tentacles

**pen·ta·cyclic** \¦pentə+\ *adj* [*penta-* + *cyclic*] : containing five usu. fused rings in the molecular structure

**pen·tad** \'pen,tad\ *n* -s [Gk *pentad-*, *pentas*, fr. *pente* five — more at FIVE] **1 a :** a group of five **b :** a period of five days **2 :** a pentavalent element, atom, or radical

**pen·ta·dac·tyl** \¦pentə¦daktəl\ *also* **pen·ta·dac·ty·late** \-ktəlāt, -ktə,lāt\ *adj* [*pentadactyl* fr. L *pentadactylus*, fr. Gk *pentadaktylos*, fr. *penta-* + *daktylos* finger; *pentadactylate* fr. *pentadactyl* + *-ate*] : having five digits to the hand or foot or five fingerlike parts

**pen·ta·dac·tyl·ism** \,==='daktə,lizəm\ *n* -s : the condition of being pentadactyl

**pentadeca-** *or* **pentadec-** *comb form* [L Gk *pentedeka-*, fr. Gk *pentekaideka*, lit., five and ten, fr. *penta-* + *kai* and + *deka* ten — more at TEN] : fifteen ⟨*pentadeca*hydrate⟩

**pen·ta·dec·a·gon** \,pentə'dekə,gän\ *n* -s [*pentadeca-* + *-gon*] : a polygon of 15 sides

**pen·ta·deca·hydrate** \¦pentə¦dekə+\ *n* [*pentadeca-* + *hydrate*] : a chemical compound with 15 molecules of water

**pen·ta·dec·ane** \¦pentə¦de,kān\ *n* -s [ISV *pentadeca-* + *-ane*] : any of numerous paraffin hydrocarbons $C_{15}H_{32}$ one of which has been obtained from petroleum; *esp* : the oily liquid normal hydrocarbon $CH_3(CH_2)_{13}CH_3$

**pen·ta·decyl** \¦pentə+\ *n* [*penta-* + *decyl*] : an alkyl radical, $C_{15}H_{31}$ derived from a pentadecane; *esp* : the normal radical $CH_3(CH_2)_{13}CH_2$—

**pen·ta·del·phous** \¦pentə¦delfəs\ *adj* [*penta-* + *-adelphous*] : having the stamens in five sets or clusters with the filaments in each cluster more or less united

**pen·ta·diene** \¦pentə+\ *n* [*penta-* + *-diene*] : any of several straight-chain liquid diolefins $C_5H_8$; *esp* : PIPERYLENE — compare CYCLOPENTADIENE

**pen·ta·erythritol** \"+\ *n* [*penta-* + *erythritol*] **1 :** a crystalline tetrahydroxy alcohol $C(CH_2OH)_4$ derived from neopentane that is made by reaction of formaldehyde and acetaldehyde in the presence of an alkaline condensing agent (as a slurry of calcium hydroxide) and that is used chiefly in making alkyd resins and other synthetic resins, synthetic drying oils, and explosives **2 :** a polyhydroxy ether alcohol formed by condensation usu. of two or three molecules of pentaerythritol in the synthesis of pentaerythritol

**pentaerythritol tetranitrate** *n* : a crystalline ester $C(CH_2ONO_2)_4$ made by nitrating pentaerythritol and used as a powerful high explosive and in the treatment of angina pectoris — called also *penthrite*, *pentrite*, *PETN*

[1]**pen·ta·gon** \'pentə,gän, -tē,- *sometimes* -təgən *or* -tēg-\ *n* -s [LL *pentagonum*, fr. Gk *pentagōnon*, fr. neut. of *pentagōnos* five-angled, fr. *penta-* + *-gōnos* (fr. *gōnia* angle) — more at -GON] : a polygon having five sides — see AREA table

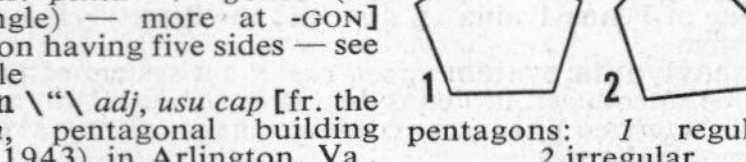

pentagons: *1* regular, *2* irregular

[2]**pentagon** \"\ *adj*, *usu cap* [fr. the *Pentagon*, pentagonal building (erected 1943) in Arlington, Va., that is the headquarters of the U. S. Dept. of Defense and other government offices] : of or relating to the Pentagon building esp. as symbolizing the U. S. military, naval, and air force leadership concentrated there

**pen·tag·o·nal** \(')pen¦tagənᵊl, -taig-\ *adj* [MF, fr. ML *pentagonalis*, fr. LL *pentagonum* + *-alis* -al] **1 :** having five angles and five sides : five-sided : divided into pentagons ⟨a ~ dodecahedron⟩ **2 :** having a pentagon as section or base ⟨a ~ column⟩ ⟨a ~ pyramid⟩ **3 :** relating or belonging to a pentagonal system — **pen·tag·o·nal·ly** \-ᵊlē -ᵊli\ *adv*

**pentagon crab** *n* [so called fr. its shape] : a small dully colored angular parthenopid crab (*Heterocrypta granulata*) living at moderate depths along the eastern coast of No. America

**pen·ta·gon·ese** \,pentə,gä¦nēz, -tē,-, -nēs\ *n* -s *usu cap* [*Pentagon*, headquarters of the U. S. Dept. of Defense + E *-ese*] : a style of writing characteristic of the Pentagon bureaucracy

**pen·tag·o·noid** \(')pen¦tagə,nȯid\ *adj* [[1]*pentagon* + *-oid*] **1 :** somewhat pentagonal **2** *of a skull* : resembling a pentagon as viewed from the inferior aspect

**pen·ta·gram** \'pentə,gram\ *n* [Gk *pentagrammon*, fr. *penta-* + *-grammon* (akin to Gk *gramma* letter) — more at GRAM] : PENTACLE 1

**pen·ta·graph** \'pentə,graf, -răf\ *n* [*penta-* + *-graph*] : a cluster of five successive letters — **pen·ta·graph·ic** \¦==¦grafik\ *adj* — **pen·ta·graph·i·cal·ly** \-fək(ə)lē\ *adv*

**pen·ta·grid** \'pentə,grid\ *adj* [*penta-* + *grid*] : having five grids ⟨a ~ converter⟩

**pen·ta·gyn·ia** \,pentə'jinēə\ *n pl*, *cap* [NL, fr. *penta-* + *-gynia*] *in former classifications* : a group of plants comprising those having flowers with five styles or pistils

**pen·ta·he·dral** \¦pentə¦hēdrəl\ *adj* [NL *pentahedron* + E *-al*] : having five faces

**pen·ta·he·dron** \,==+'hē-drən\ *n* -s [NL, fr. *penta-* + *-hedron*] : a solid bounded by five faces

**pen·ta·hydrate** \¦pentə+\ *n* [*penta-* + *hydrate*] : a chemical compound with five molecules of water — **pen·ta·hydrated** \"+\ *adj*

**pen·ta·hy·dric** \¦pentə¦hīdrik\ *adj* [*penta-* + *-hydric*] : PENTAHYDROXY — used esp. of alcohols and phenols

**pen·ta·hy·drite** \,pentə'hī,drīt\ *n* -s [*penta-* + *hydr-* + *-ite*] : a mineral $MgSO_4.5H_2O$ consisting of hydrous sulfate of magnesium isostructural with chalcanthite and containing less water than epsomite

**pen·ta·hy·droxy** \,pentə,hī'dräksē\ *adj* [*pentahydroxy-*] : containing five hydroxyl groups in the molecule

**pentahydroxy-** *comb form* [*penta-* + *hydroxy-*] : containing five hydroxyl groups — in names of chemical compounds

**pentail** \'=,=\ *n* [[3]*pen* + *tail*] **1** *also* **pen-tailed tree shrew** \'=,=-\ : a tree shrew (genus *Ptilocercus*) of Malaysia and adjacent islands that is dark brown above and white below and has a naked tail bilaterally fringed with long stiff hairs on its distal third **2** *also* **pen-tailed phalanger** : a small New Guinea phalanger (genus *Distoechurus*) related to the mouse opossums but distinguished by a tail fringed with long hairs **3** [by alter.] : PINTAIL 1

**pen·tal·o·gy** \pen'taləjē\ *n* -ES [*penta-* + *-logy* (as in *trilogy*)] : a series of five closely related published works

**pen·ta·lo·nia** \,pentə'lōnēə\ *n*, *cap* [NL] : a genus of aphids containing forms which transmit bunchy top disease to some bananas

**pen·tal·pha** \pen'talfə\ *n* [Gk, fr. *penta-* + *alpha*; fr. its presenting the form of an A on each of its five corners — more at ALPHA] : PENTACLE 1

**pen·ta·mer** \'pentəmə(r)\ *n* -s [*penta-* + *-mer*] : a polymer formed from five molecules of a monomer

**pen·tam·e·ra** \pen'tamərə\ *n pl*, *cap* [NL, fr. *penta-* + Gk *meros* part — more at MERIT] : an artificial division of beetles including those normally having five-jointed tarsi and embracing about half of all the known beetles — **pen·tam·er·an** \-rən\ *n* -s

**pen·tam·er·al** \(')=¦==rəl\ *adj* [*penta-* + *mer-* + *-al*] : PENTAMEROUS

**pen·tam·er·id** \pen'tamərəd\ *n* -s [NL *Pentameridae*, family of brachiopods, fr. *Pentamerus*, type genus + *-idae*] : a brachiopod of *Pentamerus* or related genera

**pen·tam·er·ism** \pen'tamə,rizəm\ *n* -s : the state of being pentamerous

**pen·tam·er·ous** \(')pen¦tamərəs\ *adj* [NL *pentamerus*, fr. *penta-* (fr. Gk) + *-merus* -merous] : divided into or consisting of five parts : arranged in five sets of parts; *specif* : having each floral whorl consisting of five or a multiple of five members — often written *5-merous*

**pen·tam·er·us** \pen'tamərəs\ *n*, *cap* [NL, fr. *penta-* (fr. Gk) + *-merus* -merous] : a genus (the type of the family Pentameridae) comprising Paleozoic brachiopods of the order Protremata abundant in the Silurian and having the shell rostrate and oval or somewhat pentagonal with its cavity divided by two internal vertical ridges and a spondylium in each valve

[1]**pen·tam·e·ter** \(')pen¦tamədə(r)\ *also* **pen·ta·met·ric** \¦pentə¦me·trik\ *adj* [*pentameter* fr. MF *pentametre*, fr. Gk *pentametros*, fr. *penta-* + *-metros* (fr. *metron* measure, meter); *pentametric* fr. *pentameter*, n. + *-ic* — more at MEASURE] : having five metrical feet

[2]**pentameter** \"\ *n* [L, fr. Gk *pentametros*] : a line of five metrical feet: *as* **a :** ELEGIAC PENTAMETER **b :** HEROIC VERSE 3

**pen·ta·methine** \¦pentə+\ *n* [*penta-* + *methine*] : DICARBOCYANINE

**pen·ta·methyl** \¦pentə+\ *adj* [*penta-* + *methyl*] : containing five methyl groups in the molecule

**pen·ta·methylene** \"+\ *n* [ISV *penta-* + *methylene*] **1 :** CYCLOPENTANE **2 :** the bivalent radical $-CH_2CH_2CH_2CH_2CH_2-$ derived from normal pentane by removal of one hydrogen atom from each end carbon atom

**pen·ta·methylene·diamine** \"+\ *n* [*pentamethylene* + *diamine*] : CADAVERINE

**pen·tam·e·trist** \pen'tamə·trəst\ *n* : a writer of pentameters

**pent·am·i·dine** \pen'tamə,dēn, -dən\ *n* [*penta-* + *amidine*] : a diamidine used chiefly in the form of its bitter crystalline isethionate salt $C_{23}H_{36}N_4O_{10}S_2$ in the treatment of early stages of African sleeping sickness

**pent·am·mine** \pen'ta,mēn, -mən, 'pentə,mēn\ *n* [*penta-* + *ammine*] : an ammine containing five molecules of ammonia

**pen·tan·dria** \pen'tandrēə\ *n pl*, *cap* [NL, fr. *penta-* (fr. Gk) + *-andria*] *in former classifications* : a class comprising all plants having five stamens

**pen·tan·drous** \(')pen¦tandrəs\ *adj* [NL *pentandrus*, fr. *penta-* + *-andrus* -androus] *of a flower* : having five stamens

**pen·tane** \'pen,tān\ *n* -s [ISV *penta-* + *-ane*] : any of three isomeric paraffin hydrocarbons $C_5H_{12}$ found in petroleum and natural gas: **a :** the volatile flammable liquid normal hydrocarbon $CH_3CH_2CH_2CH_2CH_3$ used chiefly in gasoline, in organic synthesis, and as a solvent — called also *n-pentane*, *normal pentane* **b :** ISOPENTANE **c :** NEOPENTANE

**pen·tane·dione** \,pen,tān'dī,ōn\ *n* -s [*pentane* + *-dione*] : a diketone derived from normal pentane; *esp* : ACETYLACETONE

**pentane lamp** *n* : a lamp having an Argand burner that burns pentane vapor and formerly being used as a photometric standard developing about ten candles

**pen·tan·gle** \'pen,taŋgəl\ *n* [*penta-* + *angle*] : PENTACLE 1

**pen·tan·gu·lar** \(')pen¦taŋgyələ(r)\ *adj* [*penta-* + *angular*] : having five angles : PENTAGONAL

**pen·ta·no·ic acid** \¦pentə¦nōik-\ *n* [*pentane* + *-oic*] : VALERIC ACID a — used in the system of nomenclature adopted by the International Union of Pure and Applied Chemistry

**pen·ta·nol** \'pentə,nȯl, -nōl\ *n* -s [*pentane* + *-ol*] : any of three pentyl alcohols derived from normal pentane; *esp* : PENTYL ALCOHOL a

**pen·ta·none** \'pentə,nōn\ *n* -s [*pentane* + *-one*] : either of two isomeric flammable liquid ketones derived from normal pentane: **a :** the unsymmetrical compound $CH_3CH_2CH_2COCH_3$ — called also *methyl propyl ketone*, *2-pentanone* **b :** the symmetrical compound $(C_2H_5)_2CO$ obtainable from propionic acid — called also *diethyl ketone*, *3-pentanone*, *propione*

**pen·ta·phyl·a·ca·ce·ae** \,pentə,filə'kāsē,ē\ *n pl*, *cap* [NL, fr. *Pentaphylac-*, *Pentaphylax*, type genus + *-aceae*] : a family of plants (order Sapindales) coextensive with the genus *Pentaphylax*

**pen·taph·y·lax** \pen'tafə,laks\ *n*, *cap* [NL, fr. *penta-* + Gk *phylax* guard] : a genus of Chinese and Malayan shrubs comprising the family Pentaphylacaceae and having alternate leathery leaves and racemose pentamerous flowers

[1]**pen·ta·ploid** \'pentə,plȯid\ *also* **pen·ta·ploi·dic** \¦==¦plȯidik\ *adj* [*pentaploid* fr. *penta-* + *-ploid*; *pentaploidic* fr. [2]*pentaploid* + *-ic*] : fivefold in appearance or arrangement : having or being a chromosome number that is five times the basic number — **pen·ta·ploi·dy** \'==,plȯidē\ *n* -ES

[2]**pentaploid** \"\ *n* -s **1 :** a pentaploid chromosome number **2 :** something (as an individual or generation) characterized by the pentaploid chromosome number

**pen·tap·o·dy** \pen'tapədē\ *n* -ES [*penta-* + *-pody* (as in *dipody*)] : a metrical unit or verse consisting of five feet

**pen·tap·o·lis** \pen'tapələs\ *n* -ES [LL, a district of five towns on the Dead Sea, fr. Gk, group of five cities, fr. *penta-* + *polis* city — more at POLICE] : a union, confederacy, or group of five cities

**pen·ta·pol·i·tan** \¦pentə¦pälətᵊn\ *adj* [LL *pentapolitanus*, fr. *pentapolis*, after such pairs as LL *metropolis*: *metropolitanus* metropolitan] : of or relating to a pentapolis

**pen·ta·prism** \'pentə+,-\ *n* [*penta-* + *prism*] : a pentagonal prism having one angle 90° and the others 112° 30′, producing a constant deviation of 90° for any wavelength, and used as a reflector in range finders

**pen·ta·quine** *also* **pen·ta·quin** \'pentə,kwēn, -,kwən\ *n* -s [*penta-* + *quinoline*] : a liquid basic antimalarial $C_{18}H_{27}N_3O$ that is an amino-methoxy-quinoline derivative and is used chiefly in the form of its pale yellow crystalline phosphate

[1]**pen·tarch** \'pen,tärk\ *n* -s [*pent-* + *-arch*] : one of five joint rulers

[2]**pentarch** \"\ *adj* [ISV *pent-* + *-arch*] : having five protoxylem groups

**pen·tarchy** \-kē\ *n* -ES [Gk *pentarchia*, fr. *penta-* + *-archia* -archy] **1 :** a government by five persons : five joint rulers **2 :** a union of five powers

**pen·tas** \'pentəs\ *n* [NL, irreg. fr. Gk *pente* five — more at FIVE] **1** *cap* : a genus of chiefly African herbs or subshrubs (family Rubiaceae) that are grown as ornamentals esp. in mild regions or in greenhouses and have opposite leaves, tubular flowers with a hairy throat, and capsular fruit **2** *pl* **pentas** : any plant of the genus *Pentas*

**pen·ta·stich** \'pentə,stik\ *n* -s [LGk *pentastichos* of five verses, fr. Gk *penta-* + *stichos* verse, line — more at STICH] : a unit, stanza, or poem consisting of five lines

**pen·tas·ti·chous** \(')pen¦tastəkəs\ *adj* [NL *pentastichus*, fr. *penta-* (fr. Gk) + *-stichus* -stichous] : arranged in five orthostichies in such a manner that each leaf diverges from the preceding by an angle equal to two fifths of the circumference of the stem so that the sixth leaf stands above the first ⟨~ arrangement of leaves⟩ — **pen·tas·ti·chy** \=¦=kē\ *n* -ES

**pen·ta·stome** \'pentə,stōm\ *or* **pen·tas·to·mid** \pen·'tastəməd\ *or* **pen·tas·to·moid** \-ə,mȯid\ *n* -s [NL *pentastome* ISV, fr. NL *Pentastomum*; *pentastomid* ISV, fr. NL *Pentastomidae*, family of tongue worms, fr. *Pentastomum* + *-idae*; *pentastomoid* fr. NL *Pentastomum* + E *-oid*] : TONGUE WORM

**pen·ta·stom·i·da** \,pentə'stämədə\ [NL, fr. *Pentastomum* + *-ida*] *syn of* LINGUATULIDA

**pen·tas·to·mum** \pen'tastəməm\ *n*, *cap* [NL, fr. neut. of *pentastomus* having five stomata, fr. *penta-* + *-stomus* -stomous] : a genus of tongue worms that are chiefly parasitic in carnivorous mammals

**pen·ta·style** \'pentə,stīl\ *adj* [*penta-* + *-style*] : marked by columniation with five columns across the front — compare DISTYLE

**pen·ta·sty·los** \,==¦stī,läs\ *n* -ES [NL, fr. *penta-* + *-stylos* -style] : a pentastyle building

**pen·ta·sulfide** \¦pentə+\ *n* [*penta-* + *sulfide*] : a sulfide containing five atoms of sulfur in the molecule

**pen·ta·syllabic** \"+\ *adj* [LL *pentasyllabus* (fr. Gk *pentasyllabos*, fr. *penta-* + *syllabē* syllable) + E *-ic* — more at SYLLABLE] : having five syllables

**pen·ta·syllable** \"+\ *n* [*penta-* + *syllable*] : a word of five syllables

**pen·ta·teu·chal** \¦pentə¦tükəl, -ə¦tyü-\ *adj*, *usu cap* [*Pentateuch*, the first five books of the Old Testament (fr. LL *Pentateuchus*, fr. Gk *Pentateuchos*, fr. *penta-* + *teuchos* tool, implement, roll of writing material) + E *-al*; akin to Gk *teuchein* to make, build — more at DOUGHTY] : of or relating to the first five books of the Old Testament

**pen·ta·thionic acid** \¦pentə+¦==-\ *n* [ISV *penta-* + *thionic*] : the thionic acid $H_2S_5O_6$ containing five atoms of sulfur in the molecule

**pen·tath·lete** \pen·'tath,lēt\ *n* [LGk *pentathlētēs*, fr. Gk *pentathlein* to practice the pentathlon, fr. *pentathlon*, *pentaethlon*] : an athlete participating in a pentathlon

**pen·tath·lon** \pen·'tathlən, -th,län\ *n* -s [Gk *pentathlon*, *pentaethlon*, fr. *penta-* + *athlon*, *aethlon* prize, contest — more at ATHLETE] **1 :** an ancient Greek athletic contest in which each contestant participates in five different events (as leaping, foot racing, wrestling, throwing the discus, and throwing the spear) **2 :** an athletic contest involving participation by each contestant in five different events (as formerly in the Olympic games a running broad jump, a javelin throw, a 200-meter flat race, a discus throw, and a 1500-meter flat race) **3 :** a contest in the modern Olympic games involving participation by each contestant in horseback riding, shooting, fencing, swimming, and running — see MODERN PENTATHLON

**pen·ta·tom·ic** \ˌpentəˈtämik\ *adj* [ISV *penta-* + *atomic*] **1 :** consisting of five atoms **2 :** having five replaceable atoms or radicals

**¹pen·ta·tom·id** \ˌpentəˈtäməd\ *adj* [NL *Pentatomidae*] **:** of or relating to the Pentatomidae

**²pentatomid** \"\ *n* -s [NL *Pentatomidae*] **:** a bug of the family Pentatomidae

**pen·ta·tom·i·dae** \ˌ==ˈtäməˌdē\ *n pl, cap* [NL, fr. *Pentatoma*, type genus (fr. *penta-* + *-toma*) + *-idae*] **:** a large and widely distributed family of terrestrial bugs (order Hemiptera) usu. flattened and angular in form and often brilliantly colored that live mainly on the juices of plants and fruits though some are important predators of caterpillars and other insect pests — compare HARLEQUIN BUG

**pen·ta·tone** \ˈpentəˌtōn\ *n* [*penta-* + *tone*] **:** PENTATONIC SCALE

**pen·ta·tonic** \ˌpentə+\ *adj* [*penta-* + *tonic*] **1 :** consisting of five musical tones **2 :** relating to a pentatonic scale — **pen·ta·ton·i·cism** \ˌpentəˈtänəˌsizəm\ *n* -s

**pentatonic scale** *n* **:** a musical scale of five tones in which the octave is reached at the sixth tone; *specif* **:** a scale in which the tones are arranged like a major scale with its fourth and seventh tones omitted

pentatonic scale

**pen·ta·triacontane** \ˌpentə+\ *n* [ISV *penta-* + *triacontane*] **:** a paraffin hydrocarbon $C_{35}H_{72}$; *esp* **:** the normal hydrocarbon $CH_3(CH_2)_{33}CH_3$

**pen·ta·trichomonas** \"+\ *n, cap* [NL, fr. *penta-* (fr. Gk) + *Trichomonas*] **:** a genus of flagellates related to *Trichomonas* but possessing five anterior flagella and often regarded as indistinguishable from or a subgenus of *Trichomonas*

**pen·ta·valent** \ˌpentə+\ *adj* [*penta-* + *valent*] **:** having a valence of five **:** QUINQUEVALENT

**pen·te·con·ter** \ˌpentəˈkäntə(r)\ *n* -s [Gk *pentēkonteros*, fr. *pentēkonta* fifty] **:** an early Hellenic galley characterized by decks fore and aft and carrying fifty rowers

**pen·te·cost** \ˈpentəˌkȯst, -tē,-, -ˌkäst\ *n* -s *usu cap* [ME *Pentecost*, fr. OE *Pentecosten*, fr. LL *Pentecoste*, fr. Gk *pentēkostē* fiftieth day, Pentecost, fr. *pentēkostos* fiftieth, fr. *pentēkonta* fifty, fr. *penta-* + *-konta* (akin to L *-ginti* in *viginti* twenty) — more at VICENARY] **1 :** SHABUOTH **2 :** a Christian church festival on the 7th Sunday after Easter commemorating the descent of the Holy Spirit on the apostles — called also *Whitsunday*

**¹pen·te·cos·tal** \ˌ==ˈkȯstᵊl, -käs-\ *n* -s *usu cap* [NL *pentecostalia* (pl.), fr. LL, neut. pl. of *pentecostalis*, adj.] **1** *obs* **:** an offering given in the Church of England by parishioners to the parish priest or by a subordinate church to the cathedral church at the celebration of Pentecost **2** *also* **pen·te·cos·tal·ist** \-stələst\ **:** a member of a Pentecostal religious body

**²pentecostal** \ˌ==ˈ==\ *adj, usu cap* [LL *pentecostalis*, fr. *Pentecoste* Pentecost + *-alis* -al] **1 :** of, relating to, or resembling Pentecost or the descent of the Holy Spirit described in Acts 2 **2 :** of, relating to, or being one of various Christian religious bodies that employ revivalistic methods typically including the generating of great emotionalism within the congregation, that stress the individual attainment of holiness, perfection, and a regenerative experience comparable to the Pentecostal experience of the first Christian disciples, that particularly seek the gift of tongues and observe such other practices as foot washing, divine healing, and spirit baptism, and that are generally fundamentalist in outlook

**pen·te·cos·tal·ism** \ˌ==ˈstəˌlizəm\ *n* -s *sometimes cap* **:** the doctrines and practices of Pentecostal religious bodies; *esp* **:** religious excitement or emotionalism accompanied by ecstatic utterances interpreted as the gift of tongues

**pen·te·cos·ta·ri·on** \ˌ==ˌkȯˈsta(a)rēˌän, -kä,-\ *n* -s [LGk *pentēkostarion*, fr. *pentēkostē* Pentecost] **:** a liturgical book in the Eastern Church containing offices for the period from Easter Sunday to the first Sunday after Pentecost

**pen·te·cos·tys** \ˌpentəˈkästəs\ *n, pl* **pentecosty·es** \-ästēˌēz\ [Gk *pentēkostys* body of fifty, fr. *pentēkostos* fiftieth] **:** a troop of 50 soldiers in the Spartan army

**pen·tel·ic** \(ˈ)penˈtelik\ *adj, usu cap* [L *pentelicus*, fr. Gk *pentelikos*, fr. *Pentelē*, area near Athens, Greece + *-ikos* -ic] **:** of or from Mount Pentelicus, Greece ⟨*Pentelic* marble⟩

**pen·tene** \ˈpenˌtēn\ *n* -s [ISV *penta-* + *-ene*] **:** either of the two normal amylenes obtained from gasoline: **a :** the alpha or 1-isomer $CH_3CH_2CH_2CH{=}CH_2$ — called also *alpha-n-amylene, 1-pentene* **b :** the beta or 2-isomer $CH_3CH_2CH{=}CHCH_3$ — called also *beta-n-amylene, 2-pentene*

**pen·te·nyl** \ˈpentəˌnil\ *n* -s [*pentene* + *-yl*] **:** any of four univalent radicals $C_5H_9$ derived from the pentenes by removal of one hydrogen atom

**pen·the·mim·er** \ˌpen(t)thəˈmimə(r)\ *n* -s [LL *penthemimeres*, *penthemimeris*, fr. Gk *penthēmimerēs*, fr. *penta-* + *hēmimerēs* halved, fr. *hēmi-* hemi- + *meros* part — more at MERIT] **:** a group of five half feet in Greek and Latin prosody **:** a catalectic colon of two and a half feet — **pen·the·mim·er·al** \ˌ==ˈmimərəl\ *adj*

**penthemimeral caesura** *n* **:** a caesura in classical verse occurring after the fifth half foot

**pen·thes·tes** \penˈtheˌstēz\ [NL, prob. fr. Gk *penthein* to mourn (akin to Gk *penthos* grief, sorrow) + *-esthēs* clothing; fr. its including the black-capped variety — more at PATHOS, WEAR] *syn of* PARUS

**pen·tho·rum** \ˈpen(t)thərəm\ *n, cap* [NL, fr. *penta-* (fr. Gk) + *-horum* (fr. Gk *horos* boundary, limit)] **:** a genus of herbs (family Crassulaceae) with thin leaves and greenish pentamerous flowers — see DITCH STONECROP

**¹pent·house** \ˈpentˌhau̇s\ *n* [by folk etymology (influence of MF *pente* slope — fr. *pendant* — and E *house*) fr. ME *pentis*, fr. MF *appentis*, prob. fr. ML *appenticium*, *appendicium* appendage, fr. L *appendic-, appendix* appendage, supplement, fr. *appendere* to append — more at PENDANT, APPEND] **1 a :** a shed or roof attached to and sloping from a wall or building (as to shelter a passage, door, window) **b :** a smaller structure joined to a building **:** ANNEX **2 a :** a structure built on the roof of a building to cover a stairway, elevator shaft, water tank, or ventilating or other equipment — called also *bulkhead* **b :** a dwelling built on a roof **c :** a corridor with a sloping roof surrounding a court-tennis court on three sides

**²penthouse** \"\ *vt* **:** to furnish with or as if with or to make like a penthouse

**pen·thrite** \ˈpenˌthrīt\ *n* -s [*pentaerythritol tetranitrate*] **:** PENTAERYTHRITOL TETRANITRATE

**pen·tice** \ˈpentəs\ *archaic var of* PENTHOUSE

**pen·ti·men·to** \ˌpentəˈmen(ˌ)tō\ *n, pl* **pentimen·ti** \-(ˌ)tē\ [It, repentance, correction, fr. *pentire* to repent (fr. L *paenitere*) + *-mento* -ment — more at PENITENCE] **:** a reappearance in a painting of a design which has been painted over

**pent·it** \ˈpentət\ *adj* [prob. alter. (influenced by ¹*pent*) of obs. E *pended*, past. part. of *pend* to pen, confine, fr. ME *penden* — more at PEND] **1** *chiefly Scot* **:** PENT, CONFINED **2** *chiefly Scot* **:** COMFORTABLE, SNUG

**pen·ti·tol** \ˈpentəˌtōl, -tōl\ *n* -s [*penta-* + *-itol*] **:** any of the pentahydroxy alcohols $HOCH_2(CHOH)_3CH_2OH$ obtainable by reducing the corresponding pentoses

**pent·land·ite** \ˈpentlənˌdīt\ *n* -s [F *pentlandite*, fr. Joseph B. *Pentland* †1873 Irish traveler & scientist + F *-ite*] **:** a mineral $(Fe,Ni)_9S_8$ consisting of an isometric nickel iron sulfide that is found in pale bronze-yellow masses and that is the principal ore of nickel (hardness 3.5–4, sp. gr. 4.60)

**pentlatch** *usu cap, var of* PUNTLATSH

**pen·to·barbital** \ˌpentō+\ *n* [*penta-* + *-o-* + *barbital*] **:** a granular barbiturate $C_{11}H_{18}N_2O_3$ used chiefly in the form of its sodium or calcium salt as a sedative, hypnotic, and antispasmodic; 5-ethyl-5-(1-methyl-butyl)barbituric acid

**pen·tode** \ˈpenˌtōd\ *n* -s [ISV *penta-* + *-ode*] **:** a vacuum tube with five electrodes including a cathode, an anode, a control grid, and two additional grids or other electrodes

**pen·to·lite** \ˈpentəˌlīt\ *n* -s [*penta-* + *-ol* + *-ite*] **:** a high-explosive mixture of pentaerythritol tetranitrate and trinitrotoluene

**pen·tom·ic** \(ˈ)penˈtämik\ *adj* [*penta-* + atomic] **1** *of an army division* **:** made up of five battle groups **2 :** organized into pentomic divisions ⟨a ~ army⟩

**pen·to·san** \ˈpentəˌsan\ *n* -s [ISV *pentose* + *-an*] **:** any of a class of polysaccharides (as xylan or araban) that yield only pentoses on hydrolysis and that are widely distributed in plants (as in corncobs, oat hulls, wood, straw, mesquite gum, gum arabic) — compare FURFURAL, HEMICELLULOSE

**pen·tose** \ˈpenˌtōs *also* -ōz\ *n* -s [ISV *penta-* + *-ose*] **:** any of a class of monosaccharides $C_5H_{10}O_5$ (as xylose or ribulose) containing five carbon atoms in the molecule that are obtained esp. from pentosans, nucleic acids, or nucleosides by hydrolysis or from hexoses by degradation — compare DEOXYPENTOSE, METHYLPENTOSE

**pentose nucleic acid** *n* **:** any of various nucleic acids yielding a pentose on hydrolysis; *esp* **:** RIBONUCLEIC ACID

**pen·to·side** \-təˌsīd\ *n* -s [ISV *pentose* + *-ide*] **:** a glycoside that yields a pentose on hydrolysis

**pen·tos·uria** \ˌpentəˈs(h)u̇rēə, -təsˈyu̇-\ *n* -s [NL, fr. ISV *pentose* + NL *-uria*] **:** the excretion of pentoses in the urine; *specif* **:** a rare hereditary anomaly characterized by regular excretion of pentoses

**Pen·to·thal** \ˈpentəˌthȯl\ *trademark* — used for thiopental

**pent·oxide** \(ˈ)pent+\ *n* [ISV *penta-* + *oxide*] **:** an oxide containing five atoms of oxygen in the molecule

**pen·tre·mi·tes** \ˌpentrəˈmīˌtēz\ *n, cap* [NL, fr. *penta-* (fr. Gk) + Gk *trēma* hole + NL *-ites* — more at THROW] **:** a genus (the type of the family Pentremitidae) comprising Mississippian blastoid echinoderms having an ovate or pyriform calyx with five ambulacral areas suggestive of petals

**¹pen·tre·mit·id** \ˌ==ˈmidəd\ *adj* [NL *Pentremitidae*, family of echinoderms, fr. *Pentremites*, type genus + *-idae*] **:** of or relating to the genus *Pentremites* or the family Pentremitidae

**²pentremitid** \"\ *n* -s [NL *Pentremitidae*] **:** an echinoderm or fossil of the genus *Pentremites* or the family Pentremitidae

**pen·trite** \ˈpenˌtrīt\ *n* -s [*pentaerythritol tetranitrate*] **:** PENTAERYTHRITOL TETRANITRATE

**pent road** *n* [¹*pent*] *NewEng* **:** a public road that may be barred or enclosed by gates or bars esp. at its terminal points

**pent roof** *n* [*pent* short for *penthouse*] **:** a roof sloping one way only — called also *shed roof*

**pentrough** \ˈ=,=\ *n* [¹*pen* + *trough*] **:** an open usu. planked or boarded trough or tank from which water falls onto a waterwheel

**pen·tryl** \ˈpenˌtrəl\ *n* -s [*penta-* + *-ryl* (as in *tetryl*)] **:** an explosive $C_8H_6(NO_2)_4ONO_2$ that is derived from nitramide, picric acid, and ethyl nitrate and that is somewhat more sensitive than tetryl and much more sensitive than picric acid or trinitrotoluene

**pents** *pl of* PENT

**pent·ste·mon** *or* **pen·ste·mon** \pen(t)ˈstēmən, ˈpen(t)stəm-\ *n* -s [*pentstemon* fr. NL, alter. (influenced by *penta-*) of *penstemon*; *penstemon* fr. NL — more at PENSTEMON] **:** a plant or flower of the genus *Penstemon*

**pen·tu·lose** \ˈpenchəˌlōs\ *n* -s [*penta-* + *-ulose* (as in *ribulose*)] **:** a ketose $C_5H_{10}O_5$ (as ribulose or xylulose) containing five carbon atoms in the molecule

**pen·tyl** \ˈpentᵊl\ *n* -s [ISV *penta-* + *-yl*] **:** any of eight isomeric alkyl radicals $C_5H_{11}$ derived from the three pentanes by removal of one hydrogen atom: as **a :** the normal radical $CH_3(CH_2)_3CH_2$— — called also *amyl, n-amyl, n-pentyl* **b :** ISOPENTYL **c :** NEOPENTYL

**pentyl alcohol** *n* **:** any of eight isomeric liquid alcohols $C_5H_{11}OH$ used chiefly as solvents and in making esters: as **a :** the normal primary alcohol $CH_3(CH_2)_3CH_2OH$ that in vapor form is irritating to the eyes and respiratory tract and that is used in organic synthesis; 1-pentanol — called also *amyl alcohol, n-amyl alcohol, n-pentyl alcohol* **b :** ISOPENTYL ALCOHOL **c :** ACTIVE AMYL ALCOHOL **d :** TERTIARY AMYL ALCOHOL

**pen·tyl·ene** \-təˌlēn\ *n* -s [*pentyl* + *-ene*] **:** AMYLENE

**pen·tyl·ene·tet·ra·zol** \ˌpentəˌlēnˈteˌtrəˌzōl, -zōl\ *n* -s [*pentamethylene-tetrazole*] **:** a white crystalline drug $C_6H_{10}N_4$ used as a respiratory and circulatory stimulant and for producing a state of convulsion in treating certain mental disorders; pentamethylene-tetrazole

**pen·tyli·dene** \penˈtiləˌdēn\ *n* -s [*pentyl-* + *-idene*] **:** the bivalent radical $CH_3CH_2CH_2CH_2CH$< derived from normal pentane by removal of two hydrogen atoms from an end carbon atom — called also *amylidene*

**pen·tyne** \ˈpenˌtīn\ *n* -s [*penta-* + *-yne*] **:** either of two normal isomeric hydrocarbons $C_5H_8$ of the acetylene series

**pentz·ia** \ˈpentsēə\ *n, cap* [NL, fr. Charles J. *Pentz*, 18th cent. Swedish student + NL *-ia*] **:** a small genus of southern African hoary shrubs (family Compositae) having small wedge-shaped leaves, yellow flowers in small heads, and achenes crowned with a cleft and cuplike pappus

**pe·nu·che** \pəˈnüchē\ *also* **pa·no·cha** \-nōchə\ *or* **pa·no·che** \-chē\ *or* **pe·nu·chi** \-nüchē\ *or* **pi·no·che** *or* **pi·no·chi** *or* **pe·no·che** \-nōchē\ *n* -s [MexSp *panocha* raw sugar — more at PANOCHA] **:** fudge made usu. of brown sugar, butter, cream or milk, and nuts

**penuchle** *var of* PINOCHLE

**pe·nult** \ˈpēˌnəlt\ *also* **pe·nul·ti·mate** \pəˈnəltəmət\ *or* **pe·nul·ti·ma** \-məˌ\ *n* -s [*penult* fr. *penult*, adj.; *penultimate* fr. *penultimate*, adj.; *penultima* fr. L *paenultima* penult, fr. fem. of *paenultimus, penultimus*] **:** the next to the last member of a series; *esp* **:** the next to the last syllable of a word

**penultimate** *also* **penult** *adj* [*penultimate* fr. *pene-* + *ultimate*; *penult* fr. L *paenultimus, penultimus*, fr. *paene-, pene-* pene- + *ultimus* last — more at ULTIMATE] **1 :** next to the last ⟨the ~ chapter of a book⟩ ⟨the ~ phase of a war⟩ **2 :** of or relating to a penult ⟨a ~ accent⟩ — **pe·nul·ti·mate·ly** *adv*

**pe·num·bra** \pəˈnəmbrə\ *n, pl* **penumbrae** \-mˌbrē, -rī\ *or* **penumbras** [NL, fr. L *pene-* + *umbra* shadow — more at UMBRAGE] **1 :** a shadow cast (as in an eclipse) where the light is partly but not wholly cut off by the intervening body **:** a space of partial illumination between the perfect shadow on all sides and the full light **2 :** the shaded region surrounding the dark central portion of a sunspot **3 a :** a surrounding or adjoining region in which something exists in a lesser degree **:** a marginal area **:** FRINGE ⟨the ~ of consciousness⟩ ⟨Thracian existed in a sort of cultural ~ on the border line of the civilized world —Jaan Puhvel⟩ ⟨the seventeenth century lay in the ~ of the middle ages —Edward Eggleston⟩ ⟨the few sure findings remain surrounded by a much larger ~ of uncertainties —A.L. Kroeber⟩ **b :** a surrounding atmosphere (as of obscurity, emotion, meaning) **:** AURA, NIMBUS ⟨love . . . has been stripped of its mystical ~ —J.W.Krutch⟩ ⟨symbols carrying with them vital ~s of meaning —M.R.Cohen⟩ **c :** an area containing things of obscure classification **:** an uncertain middle ground between fields of thought or activity **:** BORDERLAND, NO-MAN'S-LAND ⟨orthodoxy and heterodoxy have too large a ~ of doubt —*New Republic*⟩ **4 :** a part of a picture where shade gradually blends with light — **pe·num·bral** \-rəl\ *adj*

**penumbral lunar eclipse** *n* **:** an eclipse of the moon caused when the moon passes through the penumbra of the earth's shadow but not into the umbra

**pe·nu·ri·ous** \pəˈn(y)u̇rēəs\ *adj* [ML *penuriosus*, fr. L *penuria* want, need + *-osus* -ose] **1 :** marked by or suffering from penury ⟨actually saved money in these ~ times —R.V.Mills⟩ **2 :** given to or marked by extreme stinting frugality ⟨as keen on the penny as a ~ weaver —G.D.Brown⟩ **syn** see STINGY

**pe·nu·ri·ous·ly** *adv* **:** in a penurious manner ⟨incurred a few modest liabilities, and then lived ~ till next term — Samuel Butler †1902⟩

**pe·nu·ri·ous·ness** *n* -ES **:** the quality or state of being penurious

**pen·ury** \ˈpenyərē, -ri\ *n* -ES [ME, fr. L *penuria* want, need — more at PATIENT] **1 a :** extreme poverty **:** PRIVATION **b :** absence of resources **:** SCANTINESS **2 :** PENURIOUSNESS

**pe·nu·tian** \pəˈnüdēən\ *n* -s *usu cap* [Wintun & Maidu *pen* two + Miwok & Costanoan *uti* two + E *-an*] **1 :** a language stock of California comprising the Copehan, Costanoan, Mariposan, Moquelumnan, and Pujunan families **2 :** a language phylum comprising the Penutian stock plus Chinookan, Kalapooian, Kusan, Shahaptian, and Takilman centering in Oregon and Tsimshian of British Columbia to which some add other families extending into Central America

**penwoman** \ˈ=,=\ *n, pl* **penwomen** [³*pen* + *woman*] **:** a female writer **:** AUTHORESS

**penwrite** \ˈ=,=\ *vt* [³*pen* + *write* (as in *typewrite*)] **:** to write with a pen ⟨puts both penwritten and typewritten signatures on his letters⟩

**pen·za** \ˈpenzə\ *adj, usu cap* [fr. *Penza*, U.S.S.R.] **:** of or from the city of Penza, U.S.S.R. **:** of the kind or style prevalent in Penza

**pe·on** \ˈpēˌän, ˈpēən, *in sense 2c usu* pāˈōn\ *n, pl* **peons** \-nz\ *or* **peo·nes** \-ōˌnās\ *see numbered senses* [Pg *peão* & F *pion*, fr. ML *pedon-, pedo* foot soldier — more at PAWN] **1 :** any of several Indian or Ceylonese workers: **a :** FOOT SOLDIER **b :** CONSTABLE **c :** an office attendant or messenger **2 :** a member of the usu. landless laboring class in Spanish America: as **a :** an agricultural worker or miner of native Indian or mixed blood forced to serve virtually in bondage to creditors **b :** an unskilled laborer **c** *pl usu peones* **:** a bullfighter's attendant **3** *pl peons* **a :** a person held in a state of compulsory servitude to a master (as in the southwestern states formerly part of Mexico) for the working out of an indebtedness **b :** a convict laborer in parts of the southeastern U.S. **4** *pl peons* **:** a person occupying a position of subordination or drudgery esp. through stupidity or lack of initiative

**pe·on·age** \ˈpēənij\ *n* -s **1 :** the condition of a peon **2 a :** the use of peon labor; *esp* **:** the use of laborers bound in servitude because of debt or a penal sentence **b :** the system of convict labor by which convicts are leased to contractors in parts of the southeastern U.S. **3 a :** compulsory or involuntary servitude in working out indebtedness to a master **b :** a scheme effecting coercion for such servitude

**pe·o·ni·din** \pēˈänədən\ *n* -s [*peon-* (in *peonin*) + *-id* + *-in*] **:** an anthocyanidin obtained by hydrolysis of peonin usu. in the form of its reddish brown chloride $C_{16}H_{13}ClO_6$ **:** a monomethyl ether of cyanidin

**pe·o·nin** \ˈpēənən\ *n* -s [*peony* + *-in*] **:** an anthocyanin pigment that is the coloring matter esp. of violet red peonies and is usu. obtained in the form of its reddish violet crystalline chloride $C_{28}H_{33}ClO_{16}$

**pe·on·ism** \ˈpēəˌnizəm\ *n* -s *archaic* **:** PEONAGE 2a

**pe·on·ize** \-ˌnīz\ *vt* -ED/-ING/-S **:** to reduce to the status of a peon ⟨*peonized* farm labor —*Atlantic*⟩

**pe·o·ny** \ˈpēənē, -ni, *dial* pēˈōn- *or* ˈpī(ə)n- *or* ˈpēn-\ *n* -ES [ME *piony, pione, pioine*, fr. OE & OF; OE *peonie* & OF *peone, pioine*, fr. L *paeonia*, fr. Gk *paiōnia*] **1 :** an herbaceous or shrubby plant of the genus *Paeonia* including numerous chiefly hybrid plants that are widely cultivated for their showy single or double red, pink, or white flowers — see TREE PEONY **2 :** a dark red that is less strong and slightly yellower and darker than cranberry and bluer, lighter, and stronger than average garnet or average wine — called also *Burmese ruby*

**peony-flowered** \ˈ===ˌ==\ *or* **peony-flowering** \ˈ===ˌ===\ *adj* **:** having a flower resembling that of a peony ⟨a *peony-flowering* camellia⟩

**peony-flowered dahlia** *also* **peony dahlia** *n* **:** any of numerous showy cultivated dahlias having open-centered flowers with not more than four rows of functional ray flowers and with smaller curled or twisted ray flowers around the disk

**peony red** *n* **:** a dark to deep red — compare PEONY

**¹peo·ple** \ˈpēpəl\ *n, pl* **people** *or* **peoples** *see numbered senses* [ME *peple, poeple*, fr. OF *pueple*, fr. L *populus* — more at POPULAR] **1** *people pl* **a :** human beings not individually known or considered as individuals ⟨~ say⟩ ⟨tell ~ about his luck⟩ **b** (1) **:** human beings who form a segment of humanity usu. sharing a common characteristic ⟨stupid ~⟩ ⟨met all sorts of ~ on the trip⟩ ⟨~ who live in glass houses⟩ (2) **:** human beings distributively as individuals or constituting a numerable group ⟨we saw many ~ on our walk⟩ ⟨shelter for thousands of ~⟩ **c :** human beings as distinguished from the lower animals ⟨diseases that ~ catch from their pets⟩ ⟨it is hard to avoid thinking of some dogs as ~⟩ ⟨we heard cows lowing but saw no ~⟩ **2 a** *people pl* **:** human beings making up a group or assembly **:** persons linked by a common factor: as (1) **:** the members of a geographically distinct community ⟨the ~ of the next town⟩ (2) **:** persons who share in common a point of origin or residence ⟨city ~⟩ ⟨mountain ~⟩ (3) **:** members of a racial or national group or of a common ancestry ⟨Chinese ~⟩ ⟨the Slavic ~ in the U.S.⟩ ⟨Negro ~⟩ (4) **:** the members of a caste, class, or other isolable or identifiable group ⟨illiterate ~ of the community⟩ (5) **:** persons sharing a common occupation or interest ⟨academic ~⟩ (6) **:** the members of an organization (as a society or congregation) ⟨the ~ of the new synagogue⟩ **b** *pl peoples, obs* **:** a concourse of persons **:** THRONG, MULTITUDE **3** *people pl* **a :** human beings that constitute an organized body subordinate to a superior: as (1) **:** the subjects of a ruler ⟨a king's duty to his ~⟩ (2) **:** a body of retainers, servants, or followers ⟨the family and the ~ of the household⟩ (3) **:** the crew of a ship as distinguished from the officers **b :** the members of a family or kinship **:** ANCESTORS ⟨his ~ have been farmers for generations⟩ ⟨her ~ are all dead⟩ **4** *people pl* **a :** the mass of a community as distinguished from a special class: as (1) **:** the common crowd **:** COMMONALTY, POPULACE ⟨disputes between the ~ and the nobles⟩ (2) **:** LAITY 2 ⟨the priest shall say to the ~⟩ **b :** plain-mannered persons of unassuming and friendly nature **:** FOLKS ⟨real ~, kind and unpretentious⟩ **c** *usu cap* **:** the common people of a country as distinguished from a privileged minority — used esp. by Communists to distinguish Communists or those under Communist control from other people ⟨if one compares the situation in the *People's* Democracies . . . with that in the capitalist countries —Hilary Minc⟩ ⟨in other Communist states . . . justice is administered by *People's* Courts —N.D.Palmer⟩ ⟨the Bulgarian *People's* Republic was proclaimed by the national assembly —*Statesman's Yr. Bk.*⟩ **5** *pl peoples* **a :** a body of persons that are united by a common culture, tradition, or sense of kinship though not necessarily by consanguinity or by racial or political ties and that typically have common language, institutions, and beliefs ⟨many European nations are populated by several distinct ~s⟩ ⟨primitive ~s⟩ ⟨each ~ builds a culture adapted to its peculiar needs⟩ **b :** a body of persons constituting a politically organized or consanguineous group (as a tribe, nation, or race) ⟨the ~s of Europe⟩ ⟨the Caucasian ~ gradually populated Europe and much of northern Africa⟩ ⟨the military genius of the German ~⟩ **6 a :** lower animals usu. of a specified kind or situation ⟨squirrels, mice, and other mischievous little ~s of field and forest⟩ ⟨the clever bee ~⟩ **b :** supernatural beings that are thought of as similar to humans in many respects ⟨the little ~⟩ ⟨kobolds, trolls, and such ~s are not to be trusted⟩ **7 :** the body of enfranchised citizens of a state **:** ELECTORATE; *broadly* **:** the body of persons in whom is vested the sovereignty of a nation or who are capable of expressing their general wish — usu. used with *the* and pl. in constr. **8** *slang* **:** a human being **syn** see RACE

**²people** \"\ *vb* **peopled; peopled; peopling** \-p(ə)liŋ\ **peoples** [MF *peupler*, fr. OF, fr. *peuple*, n.] *vt* **1 :** to supply, stock, or fill with or as if with people ⟨settlers were *peopling* the new lands⟩ *also* **:** to represent or picture as full of inhabitants **2 :** to be the inhabitants of **:** dwell in **:** INHABIT ⟨dreams that ~ idle hours⟩ ⟨a winter sky *peopled* with stars⟩ ~ *vi* **:** to become inhabited ⟨the drier lands *peopled* slowly⟩

**peopled** *adj* **:** POPULATED

**peopledom** *n* -s **1** *obs* **:** an ancient Grecian community or province **2** *obs* **:** a democratic rule

**peo·ple·hood** \ˈpēpəlˌhu̇d\ *n* **:** the quality or state of constituting a people; *also* **:** awareness of the underlying unity that makes the individual a part of a people ⟨tried to weld the groups together on a broad basis of ~ rather than theological doctrine —*Time*⟩

**peo·ple·ize** \-pəˌlīz\ *vt* -ED/-ING/-S **:** POPULARIZE

**people-king** \ˈ==ˌ=\ *n* [trans. of F *peuple-roi*, trans. of L *populus rex*] **:** a people as sovereign

**peo·ple·less** \ˈpēpəlləs\ *adj* **:** void of people **:** UNPOPULATED

**people of god** *usu cap P&G* **:** members of a Russian Christian sect developed in reaction to the extreme ritualism of the official church probably during the 17th century and characterized by disbelief in inspiration of written scriptures and absence of any formal ritual

**people of the book** *usu cap P&B* **:** KITABIS

**peo·pler** \-p(ə)lə(r)\ *n* -s **:** one that peoples **:** SETTLER, INHABITANT

**peoples** *pl of* PEOPLE, *pres 3d sing of* PEOPLE

**people's bank** *n* **:** any of various chiefly European cooperative financial institutions (as a credit union)

**people's party** *n* **:** a political party representing or claiming to represent the great majority of the inhabitants of a territorial unit (as a nation) as opposed to a particular class or group ⟨attempted to transform themselves from a class party into a *people's party*⟩ ⟨the Austrian *People's Party* . . . represents farmers, industrialists, and merchants, as well as some labor and many white-collar workers —Hans Kohn⟩

**peo·plet** \ˈpēplət\ *n* -s [*people* + *-et*] **:** a people small in numbers or very local in distribution

**peopling** *n* -s [fr. gerund of ²*people*] **:** POPULATING, SETTLING

**peo·plish** \ˈpēp(ə)lish\ *adj* [ME, fr. ¹*people* + *-ish*] **:** POPULAR 4

**¹pe·o·ria** \pēˈōrēə, -ˈȯr-\ *n, pl* **peoria** *or* **peorias** *usu cap* [F, fr. Peoria *Piwarea*] **1 a :** an Indian people of Illinois and Iowa associated with the Illinois confederacy **b :** a member of such people **2 :** a dialect of Illinois

**²peoria** \"\ *also* **pe·o·ri·an** \-ən\ *adj, usu cap* [*peoria* fr. *Peoria*, Ill.; *peorian* fr. *Peoria*, Ill. + E *-an*] **:** of or from the city of Peoria, Ill. ⟨a *Peoria* industry⟩ **:** of the kind or style prevalent in Peoria

**¹pep** \ˈpep\ *n* -s [short for ¹*pepper*] **:** brisk energy or initiative usu. accompanied by high spirits **:** animated activity **:** LIVELINESS, DASH, GO ⟨a progressive tiredness and malaise, a loss of ~, an inability to work effectively —H.C.Hopps⟩

**²pep** \"\ *vt* **pepped; pepped; pepping; peps :** to inject pep into **:** quicken or stimulate to greater alertness or brightness — usu. used with *up*

**pep·er·ek** \ˈpeperək\ *n* -s [fr. native name in Indonesia] **:** SAPSAP

**pep·er·o·mia** \ˌpepəˈrōmēə\ *n* [NL, fr. Gk *peperi* pepper + *homoios* like, same + NL *-ia* — more at SAME] **1** *cap* **:** a very large genus of tropical fleshy often epiphytic climbing herbs (family Piperaceae) having flowers with two stamens and confluent anther cells and being often cultivated for their showy variegated leaves **2** -s **:** any plant of *Peperomia* or a closely related genus

**peperoni** *var of* PEPPERONI

**pep·ful** \ˈpepfəl\ *adj* [¹*pep* + *-ful*] **:** PEPPY, VIGOROUS

**pe·pi·no** \pəˈpē(ˌ)nō\ *n* -s [AmerSp, fr. Sp, cucumber, fr. L *pepon-, pepo*, a melon] **:** a bushy somewhat woody perennial plant of temperate uplands of Peru that is sometimes cultivated for its ovoid purple-marked edible yellow fruits which have a juicy aromatic yellow pulp

**pep·lis** \ˈpepləs\ *n, cap* [NL, fr. L, a plant, fr. Gk, wild purslane] **:** a genus of chiefly aquatic herbs (family Lythraceae) that have opposite leaves and minute solitary greenish flowers in the axils and are sometimes used as aerators in the balanced aquarium — see WATER PURSLANE

**pep·los** *also* **pep·lus** \ˈpepləs\ *n* -ES [L *peplus*, fr. Gk *peplos*; prob. akin to L *pellis* skin — more at FELL] **:** a garment worn by women of ancient Greece consisting of a rectangular cloth folded and draped on the upper body and clasped usu. with a brooch at the shoulder — compare HIMATION

**pep·losed** \-st\ *adj* **:** having or clothed with a peplos

**pep·lum** \ˈpepləm\ *n, pl* **peplums** \-mz\ *also* **pep·la** \-lə\ [L, fr. Gk *peplos*] **1** *obs* **:** PEPLOS **2 :** a short skirtlike section usu. attached to the waistline of a blouse, jacket, dress, and made usu. with a flared, pleated, or ruffled design — **pep·lumed** \-md\ *adj*

peplum 2

**pe·po** \ˈpē(ˌ)pō\ *n* -s [L, a melon — more at PUMPKIN] **1 :** an indehiscent fleshy 1-celled or falsely 3-celled many-seeded berry usu. with a hard rind (as a pumpkin, squash, melon, and cucumber) that is the characteristic fruit of the family Cucurbitaceae — see FRUIT illustration **2 :** the dried ripe seed of the cultivated pumpkin used as an anthelmintic and a source of oil

**¹pep·per** \ˈpepə(r)\ *n* -s *often attrib* [ME *peper*, fr. OE *pipor*; akin to OHG *pfeffar* pepper, ON *piparr*; all fr. a prehistoric Gmc word borrowed fr. L *piper* pepper, fr. Gk *peperi*, prob. fr. Skt *pippali* long pepper] **1 a :** a pungent product obtained from the fruit of an East Indian plant (*Piper nigrum*), used as a condiment and sometimes as a carminative or stimulant, and prepared in a form (1) consisting of the entire dried berry or (2) consisting of the dried seeds divested of all membranes and pulp with both forms being usu. ground into powder before use — called also (1) *black pepper*, (2) *white pepper* **b :** any of several somewhat similar products obtained from other plants of the genus *Piper* — often used with a qualifying term; see LONG PEPPER **c :** any of various pungent condiments obtained from plants other than those of the genus *Piper* — used with a qualifying term ⟨paprika is sometimes known as Hungarian ~⟩; see CAYENNE PEPPER **2 :** a plant of the genus *Piper*; *esp* **:** a woody vine (*Piper nigrum*) with ovate leaves and spicate flowers that is native to the oriental tropics but widely cultivated in tropical regions for its red berries from which pepper is prepared **3 a :** a plant of the genus *Capsicum* (esp. *C. frutescens*) **b :** the many-seeded berry enclosed in a thickened integument like an indehiscent pod that is the fruit of any of these plants, varies greatly in shape and size in different varieties, is usu. red or yellow when ripe, and includes numerous cultivated forms used in the preparation of condiments and relishes and as vegetables — see BIRD PEPPER, CHERRY PEPPER, CONE PEPPER, LONG PEPPER; HOT PEPPER, SWEET PEPPER **4 :** any of numerous plants other than members of the genera *Piper* and *Capsicum* that have pungent or aromatic qualities — usu. used with a qualifying term ⟨African ~⟩ **5 :** PEPPERBOX 1 **6** *or* **pepper trash :** finely broken leaf present as an impurity in raw cotton **7 :** PEPPER GAME

**²pepper** \"\ *vb* **peppered; peppered; peppering** \-p(ə)riŋ\ **peppers** *vt* **1 a :** to sprinkle or season with pepper ⟨~ a stew⟩ **b :** to sprinkle as if with pepper **:** cover with small dots, marks, or injuries ⟨~*ed* with freckles⟩ ⟨the bees ~*ed* him with stings⟩ **c :** to shower with or as if with shot or other missiles ⟨~ the boys with bird shot⟩ ⟨~*ing* them with questions⟩ **2 :** to make (as writing) spicy or provocative **3 a :** to thrash or beat thoroughly with or as if with rapid repeated blows ⟨~*ed* his opponent with short lefts⟩ **b** *obs* **:** to conquer or ruin by or as if by beating **4** *archaic* **:** to infect with a venereal disease **:** POX **5 :** to sprinkle as pepper is sprinkled **:** strew in or as if in grains ⟨~*ing* classical quotations right and left⟩ ⟨the wind ~*ed* stinging sleet into our faces⟩ ~ *vi* **1 a :** to shower in small particles and usu. briskly ⟨the rain came ~*ing* down⟩ ⟨shot ~*ed* among the leaves⟩ **b** *archaic* **:** to shower flattery or fulsome praise **2 :** to apply pepper esp. as a seasoning ⟨don't ~ so heavily⟩

**¹pepper-and-salt** \ˌ==ˈ=\ *n* **1 :** a suiting or other fabric woven with flecks of dark and light (as black and white or dark gray and light gray) **2 :** a pepper-and-salt color **3** [so called fr. the effect of dark stamens against white petals] **:** HARBINGER-OF-SPRING

**²pepper-and-salt** \"\ *adj* **:** having black and white or dark and light color intermingled in small flecks giving an irregular gray or grayed effect

**pepper-and-salt cat** *n* [so called fr. its color] **:** a small active diurnal grizzled gray mongoose (*Mungos pulverulentus*) of southern Africa

**pepper-and-salt moth** *n* [so called fr. the sprinkling of dark brown or black on its dull white wings] **:** a geometrid moth (*Biston cognataria*) having a larva that feeds on various deciduous plants (as willow, apple, and black currant)

**pepperbox** \ˈ==ˌ=\ *n* **1 :** a small box or bottle with a perforated top used for sprinkling ground pepper on food **2 :** something resembling a pepperbox in shape or contents: as **a :** a small cylindrical tower or turret **b :** a temperamental person **:** SPITFIRE **c :** a pistol developed in the late 18th century having five or six barrels revolving upon a central axis and fired individually by a single striker **d :** a prepared military position (as of concrete) sheltering a machine gun and its crew

pepperbox 2 c

**pepperbush** *n* **:** SWEET PEPPERBUSH

**pepper caster** *n* **:** a caster or bottle for pepper **:** PEPPERBOX

**¹pep·per·corn** \ˈpepərˌkȯrn, -pəˌkȯ(ə)n\ *n* [ME *pepercorn*, fr. OE *piporcorn*, fr. *pipor* pepper + *corn* — more at CORN] **1 :** a dried berry of the black pepper **2 :** a trifling return by way of acknowledgment — compare PEPPERCORN RENT

**²peppercorn** \"\ *adj* **1 :** consisting of a peppercorn **:** TRIVIAL **2** *of hair* **:** woolly and closely spiraled into twisted clumps or knots ⟨the ~ hair of the Hottentots⟩

**peppercorn rent** *n* **1 :** a rent formerly often stipulated in deeds and consisting in supplying a certain amount (as a pound) of black peppercorns at stated intervals **2 :** a merely nominal rent in kind operating to keep alive a title

**pepper cress** *n* **:** PEPPERGRASS

**pepper dulse** *n, chiefly Scot* **:** a pungent edible red alga (*Laurencia pinnatifida*) with fine feathery fronds

**peppered moth** *n* **:** a European geometrid moth (*Biston betularia*) having white wings with small black specks

**pep·per·er** \ˈpep(ə)rə(r)\ *n* -s [¹*pepper* + *-er*] *archaic* **:** a dealer in pepper **:** GROCER

**pepper family** *n* **:** PIPERACEAE

**pep·per game** \ˈpepə(r)-\ *n* [*pepper* fr. ²*pep* + *-er*] **:** a group warm-up usu. preceding a baseball or softball game consisting of short quick throws bunted in return by a single batter

**peppergrass** \ˈ==ˌ=\ *n* [¹*pepper* + *grass*; fr. the pungent flavor] **1 :** a cress of the genus *Lepidium*; *esp* **:** GARDEN CRESS **2 :** SHEPHERD'S PURSE

**peppergrass beetle** *n* **:** a beetle (*Galeruca browni*) of the family Galerucidae that feeds on turnips and other plants in western U. S. and Canada

**pepper green** *n* **:** a strong green that is very slightly bluer than mintleaf (sense 1) and yellower and less strong than primitive green

**pep·per·idge** \ˈpep(ə)rij\ *also* **pip·per·idge** *or* **pip·er·idge** \ˈpip-\ *n* -s [origin unknown] **1 :** BLACK GUM 1 a **2** *dial Eng* **:** COMMON BARBERRY

**pep·per·i·ly** \ˈpepərəlē\ *adv* **:** in a peppery manner

**pep·per·i·ness** \-rēnəs\ *n* -ES **:** the quality or state of being peppery

**peppering** *pres part of* PEPPER

**pep·per·ish** \ˈpep(ə)rish\ *adj* **:** somewhat peppery — **pep·per·ish·ly** *adv*

**pepper maggot** *n* **:** a maggot that is the larva of a trypetid fly (*Zonosternata electa*) and that infests pepper plants in various parts of the U. S.

**pepper mill** *n* **:** a hand mill for grinding peppercorns

**pep·per·mint** \ˈpepə(r)ˌmint, -pˌm-, -ˌmənt, -pᵊmˌi-, -pᵊmə-\ *n* [¹*pepper* + *mint*] **1 a :** a pungent and aromatic mint (*Mentha piperita*) with dark green lanceolate leaves and whorls of small pink flowers in spikes **b :** any of several related mints (as *M. arvensis*) **2 a :** PEPPERMINT OIL **b :** PEPPERMINT SPIRIT **c :** a preparation consisting of the dried leaf and flowering top of peppermint **3 :** candy flavored with peppermint **4** *Austral* **a :** PEPPERMINT GUM **b :** WILLOW MYRTLE

**peppermint camphor** *n* **:** MENTHOL

**peppermint gum** *n* **:** any of various Australian eucalypts with aromatic leaves (as *Eucalyptus piperita, E. amygdalina, E. microcorys*, and *E. stuartiana*)

**peppermint oil** *n* **:** either of two essential oils obtained from mints: **a :** an oil that has a strong peppermint odor and produces a cooling sensation in the mouth, is obtained from peppermint, and is used chiefly as a flavoring agent and as a carminative **b :** JAPANESE MINT OIL

**peppermint spirit** *n* **:** an alcoholic solution of peppermint oil that is green if made from the leaves of peppermint

**peppernut** \ˈ==ˌ=\ *n* [by trans.] **:** PFEFFERNUSS

**pepper oil** *n* **:** a volatile oil that has an odor like that of pepper but no pungency, is obtained from the fruit usu. of black pepper, and is used chiefly in flavoring

**pep·per·o·ni** *also* **pep·er·o·ni** \ˌpepəˈrōnē\ *n* -s [It *peperoni* chilies, pl. of *peperone* chili, aug. of *pepe* pepper, fr. L *piper* — more at PEPPER] **:** a highly seasoned beef and pork sausage

**pepper plant** *n* **1 :** a plant yielding pepper **2 :** any of several pungent plants: as **a :** SHEPHERD'S PURSE **b :** an Australian plant (*Alpinia caerulea*) with a pungent edible rootstock **c :** a widely distributed smartweed (*Polygonum hydropiper*)

**pepper pot** *n* **1 :** PEPPERBOX **2 a :** a stew of vegetables, meat or fish, cassareep, and other condiments common in the West Indies **b :** a thick soup of tripe, meat, dumplings, and vegetables highly seasoned esp. with crushed peppercorns — called also *Philadelphia pepper pot*

**pepper red** *n* **:** a moderate red that is yellower and paler than cerise, Harvard crimson (sense 1), or Turkey red and yellower and less strong than claret (sense 3a) or average strawberry (sense 2a) — called also *bronze red*

**pepperroot** \ˈ==ˌ=\ *n* [so called fr. its pungent flavor] **:** TOOTHWORT 2

**peppers** *pl of* PEPPER, *pres 3d sing of* PEPPER

**pepper sauce** *n* **:** vinegar in which small hot peppers are steeped and which is used as a condiment at table

**pepper trash** *n* **:** PEPPER 6

**pepper tree** *n* **1 :** a Peruvian evergreen tree (*Schinus molle*) with broad rounded head, graceful pinnate leaves, and panicles of greenish flowers succeeded by small red drupes **2** *also* **pepper shrub :** a small often shrubby New Zealand tree (*Wintera colorata*) with foliage conspicuously blotched with red and yellow and small blackish fruits

**pepper turnip** *n* **:** JACK-IN-THE-PULPIT

**pepper vine** *n* **1 :** PEPPER PLANT 1 **2 :** a woody vine (*Ampelopsis arborea*) of the southern U. S. with bipinnate leaves and pungent black berries

**pepperweed** \ˈ==ˌ=\ *n* **1 :** a plant of the genus *Peperomia* **2 :** PEPPERGRASS

**pepper weevil** *n* **:** a small black weevil (*Anthonomus eugenii*) that is a serious pest on pepper plants in warmer parts of the New World

**pepperwood** \ˈ==ˌ=\ *n* **1 :** HERCULES'-CLUB 1 a **2 :** CALIFORNIA LAUREL

**pepperwort** \ˈ==ˌ=\ *n* **1 :** PEPPERGRASS 1 **2 a :** a water fern of the family Marsileaceae 1 **b :** TOOTHWORT 2

**pep·pery** \ˈpep(ə)rē, -ri\ *adj* **1 :** of or relating to pepper **:** having the qualities of pepper **:** HOT, PUNGENT, PIQUANT **2 :** easily moved to anger or irascibility **:** HOT-TEMPERED, TOUCHY; *also* **:** SPIRITED, PASSIONATE **3 :** FIERY, STINGING ⟨a ~ satire⟩

**pep pill** *n* [¹*pep*] **:** any of various stimulant drugs (as amphetamine) dispensed in pill or tablet form

**pep·pin** \ˈpepən\ *dial var of* PIPPIN

**pep·pi·ness** \ˈpepēnəs, -pin-\ *n* -ES **:** the quality or state of being peppy

**pepping** *pres part of* PEP

**pep·py** \ˈpepē, -pi\ *adj* -ER/-EST **:** full of pep **:** KEEN, ALERT, LIVELY ⟨the members responded to the ~ and interesting program —*Nat'l Miller*⟩

**pep rally** *n* **:** a mass meeting (as of students before an athletic contest) usu. featuring songs, cheers, and inspiring talks

**peps** *pl of* PEP, *pres 3d sing of* PEP

**-pep·sia** \ˈpepshə, -psēə\ *n comb form* -s [L, fr. Gk, fr. *pepsis* digestion] **:** digestion ⟨brady*pepsia*⟩

**pep·si·gogue** \ˈpepsəˌgäg *also* -gȯg\ *adj* [*pepsin* + *-agogue*] **:** inducing the secretion of pepsin

**pep·sin** \ˈpepsən\ *n* -s [G, fr. Gk *pepsis* digestion (fr. *peptein*, *pessein* to cook, digest) + G *-in*] **1 :** a crystallizable proteinase that in an acid medium digests most proteins to polypeptides (as by dissolving coagulated egg albumin or causing casein to precipitate from skim milk), that is secreted by glands in the mucous membrane of the stomach of higher animals, and that in combination with dilute hydrochloric acid is the chief active principle of gastric juice **2 :** a preparation containing pepsin obtained as a powder or scales from the stomach esp. of the hog and used chiefly as a digestant, in making peptones, and in digesting gelatin for the recovery of silver from photographic film

**pep·sin·if·er·ous** \ˌpepsəˈnif(ə)rəs\ *adj* [*pepsin* + *-iferous*] **:** producing or yielding pepsin

**pepsino-** *comb form* [ISV, fr. *pepsin*] **:** pepsin ⟨*pepsino*genic⟩

**pep·sin·o·gen** \pepˈsinəjən, -ˌjen\ *n* -s [ISV *pepsino-* + *-gen*] **:** a crystallizable zymogen occurring in the form of granules in the peptic cells of the gastric glands and readily converted into pepsin in a slightly acid medium

**pep·sis** \ˈpepsəs\ *n, cap* [NL, fr. Gk, digestion] **:** a genus of large spider-hunting wasps (family Pompilidae) comprising the tarantula hawks

**pep·si·ten·sin** \ˌpepsəˈten(t)sən\ *n* -s [*pepsin* + *-tensin* (as in *hypertensin*)] **:** a vasoconstrictor pressor polypeptide similar to hypertensin formed by the action of pepsin on hypertensinogen

**-pep·sy** \ˈpepsē, -si\ *n comb form* -ES [L *-pepsia*] **:** -PEPSIA

**pept-** *or* **pepto-** *comb form* [ISV, fr. *peptone*] **:** peptone ⟨*pept*ide⟩ ⟨*pepto*genic⟩

**pep talk** *n* [¹*pep*] **:** a usu. brief, high-pressure, and emotional utterance designed to influence or encourage an audience (as to some outstanding effort or sacrifice)

**peptalk** \ˈ=ˌ=\ *vi* **:** to give a pep talk ~ *vt* **:** to influence with a pep talk

**pep·tic** \ˈpeptik, -tēk\ *adj* [L *pepticus*, fr. Gk *peptikos*, fr. *peptos* cooked (fr. *peptein, pessein* to cook, digest) + *-ikos* -ic — more at COOK] **1 :** relating to digestion **:** promoting or aiding digestion **:** DIGESTIVE ⟨~ sauces⟩ **2 :** able to digest **3 :** of, relating to, or resembling pepsin ⟨a ~ secretion⟩ **:** containing pepsin or a substance of similar properties ⟨the ~ glands⟩ **:** involving or like that produced by pepsin ⟨~ digestion⟩ **4 :** connected with or to some degree caused by the action of digestive juices — see PEPTIC ULCER

**peptic gland** *n* **:** a cardiac gland of the stomach

**pep·tics** \-ks\ *n pl* **:** the digestive organs

**peptic ulcer** *n* **:** an ulcer in the wall of the stomach or duodenum resulting from the digestive action of the gastric juice on the mucous membrane when the latter is rendered susceptible to its action (as by psychosomatic or local factors)

**pep·ti·dase** \ˈpeptəˌdās\ *n* -s [ISV *peptide* + *-ase*] **:** any of a group of enzymes that hydrolyze simple peptides or their derivatives containing free amino or carboxyl groups **:** EXOPEPTIDASE — distinguished from *proteinase*

**pep·tide** \ˈpepˌtīd\ *n* -s [ISV *pept-* + *-ide*; prob. orig. formed as G *peptid*] **:** any of a class of amides that are derived from two or more amino acids by combination of the amino group of one acid with the carboxyl group of another, that yield these acids on hydrolysis, that are classified according to the number of component amino acids, and that are obtained by partial hydrolysis of proteins or by synthesis (as from alpha-amino acids or their derivatives) — compare DIPEPTIDE, POLYPEPTIDE

**peptide bond** *or* **peptide linkage** *n* **:** the bond between carbon and nitrogen in the amide group —CO—NH— that unites the amino acid residues in a peptide

**pep·tiz·able** \ˌpep¦tīzəbəl\ *adj* **:** capable of being peptized

**pep·ti·za·tion** \ˌpeptəˈzāshən\ *n* -s **:** the process of peptizing

**pep·tize** \ˈpepˌtīz\ *vt* -ED/-ING/-S [prob. fr. Gk *peptein* to cook, digest + E *-ize*] **:** to bring into colloidal solution **:** convert into a sol — **pep·tiz·er** \-zə(r)\ *n* -s

**pepton-** *comb form* [ISV, fr. *peptone*] **:** PEPT- ⟨*pepton*uria⟩ ⟨*pepton*ize⟩

**pep·to·nate** \ˈpeptəˌnāt\ *n* -s [ISV *pepton-* + *-ate*] **:** a combination of pepsin with a metallic salt

**pep·tone** \ˈpepˌtōn\ *n* -s [G *pepton*, fr. Gk, neut. of *peptos* cooked] **1 :** any of various protein derivatives that are formed by the partial hydrolysis of proteins (as by enzymes of the gastric and pancreatic juices or by acids or alkalies), that are not coagulated by heat, and that are soluble in water but unlike proteoses are not precipitated from solution by saturation with ammonium sulfate **2 :** a complex water-soluble product containing proteoses as well as peptones that is obtained by digesting protein (as meat) with an enzyme (as pepsin or trypsin) and is used chiefly in nutrient media in bacteriology

**pep·to·nephridium** \ˌpeptō+\ *n* [NL, fr. *pept-* + *nephridium*] **:** a nephridium that opens into the alimentary canal and is regarded as having a digestive function

**pep·to·niz·ation** \ˌpeptənəˈzāshən\ *n* -s [ISV *peptonize* + *-ation*] **:** the process of peptonizing **:** PROTEOLYSIS

**pep·to·nize** \ˈpeptəˌnīz\ *vt* -ED/-ING/-S [*pepton-* + *-ize*] **1 :** to convert into peptone **:** digest or dissolve by a proteolytic enzyme **2 :** to combine with peptone ⟨*peptonized* iron⟩

**pep·to·noid** \ˈpeptəˌnȯid\ *n* -s [ISV *pepton-* + *-oid*] **:** a substance resembling peptone

**pepys·i·an** \ˈpēpsēən\ *adj, usu cap* [Samuel *Pepys* †1703 Eng. official in navy office and diarist + E *-ian*] **:** of or relating to Samuel Pepys or his diary

**pe·quot** \ˈpēˌkwät\ *n, pl* **pequot** *or* **pequots** *usu cap* [prob. modif. of Narraganset *paquatanog* destroyers] **1 a :** an Indian people of southeastern Connecticut **b :** a member of such people **2 :** an Algonquian language of the Pequot people

**¹per** *R* ˌpər, ¦pər, +V ¦pər-; *-R* ˌpə(r, ¦pə, +V ¦pər- *or* ¦pə *also* ¦pər\ *prep* [L, through, by means of, for the sake of, for each — more at FOR] **1 :** by the means or agency of **:** by way of **:** THROUGH ⟨~ bearer⟩ ⟨wealth . . . of a nation could increase only ~ medium of an expanded consumption —*Economica*⟩ ⟨enter through the mouth lining and ~ the bloodstream to the stomach —*Sydney (Australia) Bull.*⟩ **2 :** with respect to every member of a specified group or series **:** for each ⟨miles ~ hour⟩ ⟨income ~ person⟩ ⟨greater number of trout ~ cubic foot than any other Vermont stream —H.E.McDaniel⟩ ⟨capital investment abroad ~ dollar stimulates no more production or development than . . . consumption expenditure at home —T.J.Kreps⟩ **3 :** as indicated by **:** as directed or stated in **:** according to ⟨~ list price⟩ ⟨employers paid their quota . . . ~ the number of employees working for them —C.P.Curtis⟩ ⟨mats are moistened as ~ his specifications —G.A.Kubler⟩ ⟨calling in his coach as ~ family arrangement —*Times Lit. Supp.*⟩ **4 :** in the direction of — used in heraldry to indicate division of the field or a charge into parts by a line or lines having the direction and unless otherwise specified the customary position of one of the ordinaries ⟨~ fess⟩ ⟨~ saltire⟩ ⟨~ pale or and sable is borne by the English family of Serle —John Woodward⟩

**²per** \ˈ=\ *adv* **1** *slang* **a :** for each of an implied unit (as of time) ⟨swung crazily down the road at sixty-five ~ —Glenn Scott⟩ **b :** APIECE ⟨back numbers two-fifty ~ —Susan Glaspell⟩ **2** *slang* **:** in the usual manner **:** CUSTOMARILY ⟨she was by herself, as ~, reading —Richard Llewellyn⟩

**³per** \ˈpər(ˌ), ˈpe(ə)r\ *adj* [*per-*] **1 :** containing a chemical element in its highest or relatively high oxidation state **2 :** PEROXY — not used systematically

**per-** *prefix* [in sense 1, fr. L, throughout, thoroughly, completely, deviating from (also, used as verbal prefix with the meanings "through", "throughout", "thoroughly", "detrimentally", and to denote completion or perfection or intensification), fr. *per* through, by; in sense 2, fr. *per* through, by — more at FOR] **1 a :** throughout ⟨*per*dominant⟩ **b** (1) **:** containing the largest possible or a relatively large proportion of a (specified) chemical element esp. as a result of exhaustive substitution for hydrogen or of exhaustive addition in an organic compound or group ⟨*per*chloroethylene⟩ ⟨*per*hydronaphthalene $C_{10}H_{18}$⟩ — compare PEROXIDE 1, PROT- 2a (2) **:** containing an element in its highest or a high oxidation state ⟨*per*chloric acid⟩ (3) **:** PEROXY- — not used systematically ⟨*per*sulfate⟩ ⟨*per*benzoic acid⟩ **2- :** through ⟨*per*radius⟩ **:** by means of ⟨*per*lingual⟩ ⟨*per*rectal⟩

**per** *abbr* **1** perdendosi **2** perennial **3** period **4** person

**pera·car·i·da** \ˌperəˈkarədə\ *n pl, cap* [NL, fr. Gk *pēra* pouch, bag + NL *-carida* (fr. L *carid-, caris*, a kind of sea crab) — more at -CARIS] **:** a division of Malacostraca including among others the amphipods and isopods all having the first thoracic segment fused with the head, the thoracic legs flexed between the fifth and sixth segments, and the young developed in a brood pouch from which they escape at a late stage

**per ac·ci·dens** \ˌpəˈraksəˌdenz, ˌpərˈa-, peˈra-\ *adv* [LL] **1 :** by chance or extraneous circumstance **:** ACCIDENTALLY ⟨he is not learned, except *per accidens* —Walter Moberly⟩ **2 :** in accidental or nonessential character

**per·acetic acid** \¦pər-, ¦per+...-\ *n* [ISV *per-* + *acetic*] **:** a corrosive toxic strongly oxidizing unstable pungent liquid acid $CH_3COOOH$ made usu. by oxidation of acetaldehyde or by reaction of hydrogen peroxide with acetic acid or acetic anhydride and used chiefly in a solution in acetic acid or an inert solvent in bleaching, in organic synthesis, and as a fungicide and disinfectant — called also *peroxyacetic acid;* not used systematically

**peracid** *n* [ISV *per-* + *acid*] **1 :** an acid (as perchloric acid or permanganic acid) derived from the highest oxidation state of an element **2 :** PEROXY ACID

**per·act** \pə'rakt\ *vt* -ED/-ING/-S [L *peractus*, past part. of *peragere*, fr. *per-*, prefix denoting completion or perfection + *agere* to drive, act, do — more at PER-, AGENT] *archaic* **:** PERFORM, ACCOMPLISH

**per·acute** \ˌpər, ˈpər+\ *adj* [L *peracutus*, fr. *per-* + *acutus* acute — more at ACUTE] *of disease* **:** very acute and violent ⟨anthrax occurs in four forms: ~, acute, subacute and chronic —G.W.Stamm⟩

**¹per·adventure** \ˌpər·, ˈpər+\ *adv* [ME *per aventure*, fr. OF *per aventure, par aventure*, fr. *per, par* by (fr. L *per* through, by) + *aventure* chance — more at FOR, ADVENTURE] *archaic* **:** PERHAPS, POSSIBLY ⟨~ I will with you to the court —Shak.⟩ ⟨it may ~ be thought there was never such a time —Thomas Hobbes⟩

**²peradventure** \"\ *n* **1 :** a possibility of error or uncertainty **:** DOUBT, CHANCE ⟨the foregoing facts establish beyond ~ the conclusion —E.H.Wilkins⟩ ⟨put federal credit beyond ~ of a doubt —B.M.Baruch⟩ **2 :** an opinion based on guesswork **:** SURMISE ⟨beyond the reach of ~ —H.J.Laski⟩

**peraeon** *var of* PEREION

**peraeopod** *var of* PEREIOPOD

**per aes et li·bram** \ˌpeˌrīˌsetˈlēˌbrām\ [L] **:** with bronze and balance — used to designate the formal ceremony by which mancipatory contracts were made in ancient Rome

**peragration** *n* -S [L *peragration-, peragratio* action of wandering or traversing, fr. *peragratus* (past part. of *peragrare* to wander, traverse, fr. the phrase *per agros* through fields, fr. *per* through + *agros*, acc. pl. of *agr-, ager* field) + *-ion-, -io* -ion — more at FOR, ACRE] *obs* **:** an act of traversing; *specif* **:** a sidereal revolution of the moon

**per·alkaline** \ˌpər·, (ˈ)pər+\ *adj* [*per-* + *alkaline*] **:** having a molecular proportion of alumina less than that of soda and potash combined — used of an igneous rock

**per·aluminous** \ˌpər·, ˈpər+\ *adj* [*per-* + *aluminous*] **:** having a molecular proportion of alumina greater than that of soda and potash combined — used of an igneous rock

**per·am·bu·lant** \pəˈrambyələnt, -ˈraam-\ *adj* [L *perambulant-, perambulans*, pres. part. of *perambulare*] **:** PERAMBULATORY

**per·am·bu·late** \-ˌlāt, *usu* -ād·+V\ *vb* -ED/-ING/-S [L *perambulatus*, past part. of *perambulare*, fr. *per-* through + *ambulare* to walk — more at PER-, AMBLE] *vt* **1 a :** to travel over or through esp. on foot **:** TRAVERSE ⟨~ the park or . . . bask and loiter and gossip on its benches —Virginia Woolf⟩ **b :** to push in a perambulator ⟨mothers, with toddlers and *perambulated* infants in tow —*Time*⟩ **2 :** to make an official inspection of (a boundary) on foot ⟨according to tradition, selectmen . . . are required by law to ~ the bounds every five years —*Springfield (Mass.) Daily News*⟩ **~** *vi* **1 a :** to cover ground at a leisurely pace **:** STROLL, PROMENADE ⟨when woman was a *perambulating* clothes closet —H.A.Overstreet⟩ **b :** to follow a meandering course **:** RAMBLE ⟨the road, winding about in the *perambulating* style of all mountain roads —N.H.Fulbright⟩ **2 :** to walk a boundary for purposes of inspection

**per·am·bu·la·tion** \ˌ=ˌ==ˈlāshən, ˌpər·ˌa- *also* pəˌra-\ *n* -S [ME *perambulacion*, fr. ML *perambulation-, perambulatio*, fr. L *perambulatus* (past part. of *perambulare*) + *-ion-, -io* -ion] **1 a :** an act of walking about **:** a tour on foot **:** STROLL ⟨his ~ to the river for his midday bath is a progress in the grand manner —Alan Moorehead⟩ **b :** an official act or ceremony of walking around an area (as a town, parish, forest) to assert and record its boundaries and thereby maintain the rights of possession **c :** an act of traveling through and inspecting an area ⟨spent his whole reign . . . in a ~ or survey of the Roman Empire —Francis Bacon⟩ **2 :** a written account of a perambulation **3 :** the boundary or extent of an area as determined by walking its perimeter ⟨enlarged the ~*s* of what they had —Edmund Hickeringill⟩ **4** *obs* **:** a comprehensive account **:** SURVEY ⟨a . . . ~ of learning —Francis Bacon⟩

**per·am·bu·la·tor** \=ˈ==ˌlād·ə(r), -ātə-\ *n* -S [ML, fr. L *perambulatus* (past part. of *perambulare*) + *-or*] **1 a** *archaic* **:** an inveterate rambler **:** TRAVELER **b :** one that inspects a boundary on foot **2 :** ODOMETER 2 **3** *chiefly Brit* **:** BABY CARRIAGE

**per·am·bu·la·to·ry** \=ˈ==ləˌtōrē, -tȯr-, -ri\ *adj* [*perambulate* + *-ory*] **1 :** inclined to move about **:** ITINERANT **2 :** of, relating to, or characterized by perambulation

**pera·mel·i·dae** \ˌperəˈmeləˌdē\ *n pl, cap* [NL, fr. *Perameles*, type genus (fr. Gk *pēra* pouch, bag + L *meles* marten, badger) + *-idae*] **:** a family of marsupials consisting of the bandicoots

**pe·ra·mi·um** \pəˈrāmēəm\ *n, cap* [NL, fr. L *pera* bag, pouch (fr. Gk *pēra*) + NL *-amium* (origin unknown)] *in some classifications* **:** a small genus of No. American orchids comprising a few rattlesnake plantains more commonly included in *Goodyera*

**per·a·na·kan** \ˌperəˈnäkən\ *n -s often cap* [Jav] **:** an old established Chinese immigrant of West Java

**per an·num** \pəˈranəm\ *adv* [L] **:** in or for each year **:** ANNUALLY

**pe·ra·tes** \pəˈrāˌtēz\ *n, pl* **pera·tae** \-ˌtē\ *or* **perates** *usu cap* [LL *Peratae*, pl., fr. LGk *Peratai*, fr. pl. of Gk *peratēs* one that crosses over, fr. *peran* to cross over, pass through — more at FARE] **:** a member of a Gnostic school venerating the serpent as a powerful being intermediary between God the Father and unformed matter

**per·bend** \ˈpərbənd\ *n* -S [by alter.] **:** PERPEND

**per·borate** \ˌpər, (ˈ)pər+\ *n* [ISV *per-* + *borate*] **1 :** a salt containing the anion $BO_3^-$ formed by the action of hydrogen peroxide on a borate — called also *true perborate* **2 :** a salt (as sodium perborate) that is a compound of a borate with hydrogen peroxide

**per·bromide** \"+\ *n* [*per-* + *bromide*] **:** a bromide containing a relatively high proportion of bromine

**Per·bu·nan** \ˌpərˈb(y)ünən, (ˈ)pərˈb-\ *trademark* — used for a nitrile rubber

**perc** *abbr* percussion

**per·ca** \ˈpərkə\ *n, cap* [NL, fr. L *perca* perch — more at PERCH] **:** the type genus of Percidae formerly including numerous perches and related fishes but now restricted to the typical perches — see YELLOW PERCH

**per·cale** \pə(r)ˈkā(ə)l, ˈpərˌkā-, ˈpəˌkā-, ˈpəiˌkā-, *esp in the southern US* ˌpə(r)ˈkal\ *n -s often attrib* [Per *pargālah*] **:** a firm smooth cotton cloth closely woven in plain weave and variously finished for clothing, sheeting, and industrial uses

**per·ca·line** \ˌpərkəˈlēn\ *n* -S [F, fr. *percale* (fr. Per *pargālah*) + *-ine*] **:** a lightweight cotton fabric made in plain weave, given various finishes (as glazing, moiré), and used esp. for clothing and linings; *esp* **:** a glossy fabric usu. of one color used for bookbindings

**per cap·i·ta** \pə(r)ˈkapəd·ə, ˌpərˈk-, pəˈk-, -pətə\ *adv (or adj)* [L by heads] **1 :** per unit of population **:** by or for each person ⟨the heaviest debt *per capita* and in proportion to wealth in the union —D.Y.Thomas⟩ ⟨*per capita* consumption⟩ ⟨*per capita* tax⟩ **2 :** equally to each individual — used of the sharing of an inheritance; compare PER STIRPES

**per cap·ut** \-pət\ *adv (or adj)* [L, by the head] **:** PER CAPITA

**per·carbonate** \ˌpər, (ˈ)pər+\ *n* [*per-* + *carbonate*] **:** a salt or ester of a percarbonic acid — called also *peroxycarbonate*

**per·carbonic acid** \ˌpər, ˈpər+. . .-\ *n* [*per-* + *carbonic*] **:** any of three peroxy acids derived from carbonic acid and known only in the form of their salts and esters; *esp* **:** the peroxy-di-carbonic acid $H_2C_2O_6$ — called also *peroxycarbonic acid;* not used systematically

**per·ceant** \ˈpərsᵊnt\ *adj* [ME *persaunt*, fr. MF *perçant*, pres. part. of *percer* to pierce — more at PIERCE] *archaic* **:** PENETRATING, PIERCING ⟨~ was his spright —Edmund Spenser⟩

**per·ceiv·able** \pə(r)ˈsēvəbəl\ *adj* [ME *perceyvable*, fr. *perceyven, perceiven* to perceive + *-able*] **:** PERCEPTIBLE, INTELLIGIBLE — **per·ceiv·ably** \-blē, -bli\ *adv*

**per·ceiv·ance** \-vən(t)s\ *n* -S *dial* **:** PERCEPTION, NOTICE

**per·ceive** \pə(r)ˈsēv\ *vt* -ED/-ING/-S [ME *perceiven*, fr. OF *perceivre, percevoir*, fr. L *percipere* to take possession of, obtain, receive, perceive, fr. *per-*, prefix denoting completion or perfection + *-cipere* (fr. *capere* to seize, take) — more at PER-, HEAVE] **1 a :** to become conscious of **:** DISCERN, REALIZE ⟨the reasoning process which ~*s* divergence among authorities —H.O.Taylor⟩ ⟨*perceiving* the uselessness of further resistance, surrendered —Marquis James⟩ **b :** to recognize or identify esp. as a basis for or as verified by action ⟨goes beyond simple observation and begins to ~ things like causal principle —R.M.Weaver⟩ **2 :** to become aware of through the senses **:** NOTE, OBSERVE ⟨~ roughness and smoothness —R.S.Woodworth⟩ ⟨the length of the interval determines whether the delayed sound is *perceived* as completely merged with the first —R.D.Darrell⟩; *esp* **:** to look at ⟨people have become so used to the sight of ruins that they hardly ~ them any more —Norbert Mühlen⟩ **3** *obs* **:** GET, RECEIVE ⟨I could ~ nothing at all from her; no, not so much as a ducat for delivering your letter —Shak.⟩ **syn** see SEE

**per·ceiv·er** \-və(r)\ *n* -S **:** one that perceives

**perceiving** *adj* [ME, fr. gerund of *perceiven* to perceive] **:** OBSERVANT, DISCERNING

**¹per·cent** \pə(r)ˈsent\ *adv* [fr. *per cent.*, abbr. for *per centum*, fr. L] **:** in the hundred **:** of each hundred ⟨a rate of . . . 1 shilling 3 pence ~ —W.D.Winter⟩ ⟨cannot recover if he is even one ~ responsible for the accident —S.H.Hofstadter⟩ ⟨agreed with her suggestions a hundred ~ —Sally Benson⟩

**²percent** \"\ *n, pl* **percent** *or* **percents 1 a :** one part in a hundred **:** HUNDREDTH ⟨while they are laboring with tenths of a ~, the rest of us are letting tens of ~*s* slip through our fingers —S.L.Payne⟩ ⟨come upon stars which can not have spent more than a few ~ of their hydrogen —G.W.Gray b. 1886⟩ provided forty ~ of Europe's requirements —Harold Butler⟩ — symbol % **b :** PERCENTAGE ⟨a large ~ of the hotel's income . . . stems from convention visitors —G.T.Hellman⟩ ⟨manufacturing and mercantile rates are both ~*s* of the fire insurance rate —Robert Riegel & J.S.Miller⟩ **2** *percents pl, Brit* **:** securities bearing a specified rate of interest ⟨invested in three ~*s*⟩

**³percent** \"\ *adj* **1 :** reckoned on the basis of a whole divided into one hundred parts ⟨a five ~ increase⟩ ⟨harvested 50 ~ more wheat because of timely rains⟩ ⟨another 100 ~ result —*Manchester Guardian Weekly*⟩ **2 :** paying interest at a specified percent ⟨a 3½ ~ government bond⟩

**per·cent·age** \pə(r)ˈsentij, -tēj\ *n -s often attrib* [¹*percent* + *-age*] **1 :** a part of a whole expressed in hundredths **:** rate in percent ⟨the higher the income, the larger is the ~ saved —George Soule⟩ ⟨the ~ of production as compared with . . . earlier years —S.B.Fay⟩ **2 a :** a share of winnings or profits **:** COMMISSION, CUT ⟨saw one of my troupe of clients . . . brought me thick slices of ~ —Christopher Morley⟩ **b :** ADVANTAGE, PROFIT ⟨no ~ in going around looking like an old sack of laundry —Wallace Stegner⟩ ⟨there must be some ~ in this for the kid —J.A.MacEwen⟩ **3 :** an indeterminate part or number **:** PROPORTION ⟨an infinitesimal ~ of the agricultural population —Sumner Welles⟩ ⟨a high ~ of textbook publishers are themselves former school teachers —*Textbooks in Education*⟩ **4 a :** a likelihood based on cumulative statistics **:** PROBABILITY ⟨more use is made of the ~ today, such as playing the hitter where he hits the ball most of the time —Ted Williams⟩ **b :** the mathematical odds in favor of success ⟨chooses his career, his connections, his mistresses . . . solely on the ~*s* —Isaac Rosenfeld⟩; *specif* **:** the degree by which a gambler's expectancy of winning exceeds that of his opponent — compare VIGORISH

**percentage bridge** *n* **:** contract bridge employing a fifth suit as a percentage suit

**percentage composition** *n* **:** composition expressed by percentages of constituents

**percentage error** *n* **:** RELATIVE ERROR

**percentage lease** *n* **:** a lease of business property at a base rental plus a specified percent of receipts from the business

**percentage shop** *n* **:** a shop in which by agreement between union and management a specified percentage of the work force must be union members

**percentage tare** *n* **:** tare computed as a percentage of the gross weight

**per·cent·age·wise** \=ˈ==ˌwīz\ *adv* [*percentage* + *-wise*] **:** in terms of percentage ⟨this college ranked second in the nation ~ in the production of scientists —W.K.Hicks⟩

**per·cent·ile** \=ˈsenˌtīl, -ntᵊl, -ntᵊl\ *n -s often attrib* [prob. fr. ¹*percent* + *-ile* (as in *quartile*, n. — quartile aspect — and *sextile*, n.)] **:** the value of the statistical variable that marks the boundary between any two consecutive intervals in a distribution of 100 intervals each containing one percent of the total population — called also *centile*

**per cen·tum** \pə(r)ˈsentəm\ *n* [L] **:** PERCENT

**per·cept** \ˈpərˌsept\ *n* -S [back-formation fr. *perception*] **1** *archaic* **:** an object perceived **2 :** the meaningful impression of an object obtained by use of the senses **:** SENSE-DATUM

**percepta** *pl of* PERCEPTUM

**per·cep·ti·bil·i·ty** \pə(r)ˌseptəˈbiləd·ē, -lətē, -i\ *n* -ES **:** capability of being perceived

**per·cep·ti·ble** \pə(r)ˈseptəbəl\ *adj* [LL *perceptibilis*, fr. L *perceptus* (past part. of *percipere* to perceive) + *-ibilis* -ible — more at PERCEIVE] **1** *archaic* **:** able to perceive **:** PERCEPTIVE, SENSITIVE ⟨the soul . . . becomes more ~ of happiness or misery —Thomas Green⟩ **2 :** capable of being perceived **:** DISCERNIBLE, RECOGNIZABLE ⟨rotating . . . discs, driven at speeds sufficiently high to eliminate all ~ flicker —F.A. Geldard⟩ ⟨something strange was in the air, ~ to a little boy but utterly beyond his understanding —H.G.Wells⟩ ⟨a ~ trend . . . away from dairying —E.C.Higbee⟩

**syn** SENSIBLE, PALPABLE, TANGIBLE, APPRECIABLE, PONDERABLE: PERCEPTIBLE applies to that which may be discerned by the senses even to the smallest extent ⟨out of the stillness, little scarcely *perceptible* noises began to emphasize themselves —Mark Twain⟩ ⟨the traces left by ages of slaughter and pillage were still distinctly *perceptible* —T.B.Macaulay⟩ or recognized by the intellect ⟨greeted the idea with a *perceptible* lack of enthusiasm⟩ SENSIBLE in its earlier senses applies to what is discerned by the senses as opposed to the intellect ⟨our true ideas of *sensible* things do indeed copy them —William James⟩ ⟨the distinction between some elements of subject matter as rational and others as *sensible* —John Dewey⟩ PALPABLE applies to that which has physical substance ⟨touch beauty as though it were a *palpable* thing —W.S.Maugham⟩ or is obvious or unmistakable ⟨carry, besides their *palpable* meaning, another which is veiled and more spiritual —H.O.Taylor⟩ TANGIBLE stresses tactile quality or utilitarian value ⟨free negative electricity, released from dense matter, disconnected from atoms, and finer and subtler substance than any which is *tangible* —K.K.Darrow⟩ ⟨a summer job at a national park offers many *tangible* advantages, such as fresh air and scenery⟩ ⟨a cloud, a pillar of fire, a *tangible* physical something —Jack London⟩ APPRECIABLE refers to that which is distinctly discernible esp. by the senses, or definitely measurable ⟨the temperature of even a single day plays an *appreciable* and measurable part in determining the general health of the community —Ellsworth Huntington⟩ ⟨an *appreciable* pause fell . . . a pause that must have lasted fully a minute —Jack London⟩ PONDERABLE suggests esp. what is bulky, massive, or of weighty importance ⟨energy, at any rate kinetic energy, resists motion in the same way as *ponderable* masses —Albert Einstein & Leopold Infeld⟩ ⟨*ponderable* and powerful reasons peculiarly his own for feeling as he did —Hervey Allen⟩

**per·cep·ti·bly** \-blē, -bli\ *adv* **:** in a perceptible manner **:** to a perceptible extent **:** VISIBLY, DISCERNIBLY

**per·cep·tion** \pə(r)ˈsepshən\ *n* -S [L *perception-, perceptio* act of taking possession, obtaining, receiving, perceiving, fr. *perceptus* (past part. of *percipere* to take possession of, obtain, receive, perceive) + *-ion-, -io* -ion — more at PERCEIVE] **1 :** the receipt or collection of profits, rents, or crops — used chiefly in civil law ⟨the lessee had the benefit of . . . the ~ of the profits for the whole term —C.G.Addison⟩ **2** *obs* **:** power of apprehension ⟨matter hath no life nor ~, and is not conscious of its own existence —Richard Bentley †1742⟩ **3 a :** a result of perceiving **:** OBSERVATION, DISCERNMENT ⟨it is a film bristling with sharp ~*s* but lacking in coherence —Arthur Knight⟩ **b :** a mental image **:** CONCEPT ⟨lyric ~*s* of friendship, of love and lust —Edward Hubler⟩ ⟨endeavor to correct their ~ of what is beautiful by the opinions of other people —A.C. Benson⟩ **4 a :** awareness of the elements of environment through physical sensation **:** reaction to sensory stimulus ⟨color ~⟩ ⟨depth ~⟩ ⟨since smell is a chemical sense, a contact is necessary for ~ —R.N.Shreve⟩ ⟨some sensation of ~ of the extremity after amputation is felt by 98% of patients —*Orthopedics & Traumatic Surgery*⟩ **b :** physical sensation as interpreted in the light of experience **:** the integration of sensory impressions of events in the external world by a conscious organism esp. as a function of nonconscious expectations derived from past experience and serving as a basis for or as verified by further meaningful motivated action **5 a :** direct or intuitive recognition **:** intelligent discernment **:** APPRECIATION, INSIGHT ⟨a clear ~ of the uncertain boundary which exists between the liberties freely permitted to the press and the area in which there are bound to be limitations —F.L. Mott⟩ ⟨renewed ~ into the heart of human activity —H.V. Gregory⟩ **b :** a capacity for comprehension **:** intellectual grasp ⟨persecutors were ordinary, reasonably well-intentioned people lacking in keen ~ —C.H.Sykes⟩

**per·cep·tion·ism** \-shəˌnizəm\ *n* -S **:** the theory that all knowledge is relative to sense perception

**per·cep·tion·ist** \-ˌnəst\ *n* -S **:** an advocate or adherent of perceptionism

**per·cep·tive** \pə(r)ˈseptiv, -tēv\ *adj* [*perception* + *-ive*] **1 :** responsive to sensory stimulus **:** SHARP, DISCERNING ⟨a ~ eye⟩ ⟨the children developed a taste that was as ~ as her own —S.N.Behrman⟩ **2 a :** capable of or exhibiting keen perception **:** OBSERVANT, KNOWING ⟨here the moralist . . . has overcome the artist who can be so ~ —M.D.Geismar⟩ ⟨a wise and ~ scholar who knows how to relate the past to the present —L.C.Eiseley⟩ **b :** characterized by sympathetic understanding or insight **:** SENSITIVE, PENETRATING ⟨effective music and . . . ~ staging —*Time*⟩ ⟨one of the most ~ essays by one of our poets about another —F.O.Matthiessen⟩ ⟨an eloquent and warmly ~ exploration . . . of intimate human relationships —John Nerber⟩ — **per·cep·tive·ly** \-tə̇vlē, -li\ *adv*

**per·cep·tive·ness** \-tivnə̇s, -tēv-\ *n* -ES **:** the quality or state of being perceptive

**per·cep·tiv·i·ty** \pə(r)ˌsepˈtivəd·ē, ˌpərˌs-, ˌpəˌs-, ˌpəiˌs-, -vətē, -i\ *n* -ES **:** PERCEPTIVENESS

**per·cep·tu·al** \pə(r)ˈsepch(əw)əl, -psh-\ *adj* [L *perceptus* (past part. of *percipere* to perceive) + E *-al* — more at PERCEIVE] **:** of or relating to sensory stimulus as opposed to abstract concept ⟨the greater part of our knowledge may in fact be ~; we learn about . . . our total environment principally through the senses —C.W.Shumaker⟩; *specif* **:** of, relating to, or characterized by physical sensation as conditioned by experience ⟨personal preference is always an element of ~ response to a work of art⟩ ⟨the ~ pattern . . . selects, rejects, and distorts sense stimuli in such a way as to maintain its own integrity —J.W.Woodard⟩ — compare IDEATIONAL

**per·cep·tu·al·ly** \-əlē, -əli\ *adv* **:** in a perceptual manner

**per·cep·tum** \pə(r)ˈseptəm\ *n, pl* **percep·ta** \-tə\ [NL, fr. L, neut. of *perceptus*, past part. of *percipere*] **:** PERCEPT

**perc·es·o·ces** \(ˈ)pərˈkesəˌsēz, -ˈse-\ *n pl, cap* [NL, fr. L *perca* perch + *esoces*, pl. of *esox* pike — more at PERCH, ESOX] *in some classifications* **:** a suborder of Percomorphi or sometimes a separate order including the gray mullets (Mugilidae), the barracudas, the silversides, and other related fishes — **perc·es·o·cine** \-esəˌsīn\ *adj or n*

**¹perch** \ˈpərch, -ə̄-,-əi-\ *n* -ES [ME *perche*, fr. OF, fr. L *pertica* pole, staff, measuring stick; prob. akin to Gk *porthos* young branch, shoot, Arm *ort'* vine, grapevine] **1 a** *obs* **:** a wooden prop or pole **b (1) :** a frame of uprights with a horizontal bar for holding cloth at full width during inspection **(2) :** a textile machine with a similar frame **c :** a pole used esp. to mark a buoy, shoal, or rock ⟨the end of the channel . . . where two iron ~*es* stood —J.O.Hannay⟩ **d :** the main shaft connecting the front and rear axles of a coach or other vehicle **:** REACH **e :** a long pole used by an acrobat for climbing and balancing feats ⟨his celebrated headstand atop a swaying forty-foot ~ —R.L.Taylor⟩ **2 :** a bar or peg on which something is hung ⟨spotlights . . . hung from ~*es* in a forest of pipes above the stage —Winthrop Sargeant⟩; *specif* **:** a horizontal pole to which a skin is attached while being scraped with a moon knife in the hand softening of leather **3 a :** a roost for a bird **b :** something that resembles a roost: as (1) **:** a small usu. elevated seat for a liveryman on a coach or carriage (2) **:** a short nonretractable trapeze on an airship **c :** a resting place or vantage point **:** SEAT, STATION ⟨our favorite ~ . . . was the roof of the wheelhouse —J.W. Brown⟩ ⟨from my ~ in an attic window —Jan Valtin⟩ **d :** a secure or prominent position **:** EMINENCE ⟨his new ~ as president of one of the most important concert managements in the country —Helen Howe⟩ **e :** a pad on the axle of an automotive vehicle on which the spring is mounted — called also *spring chair* **4 a** *chiefly Brit* **:** ¹ROD 3 **b :** any of various units of measure (as 24¾ cubic feet representing a pile 1 rod long by 1 foot by 1½ feet, or 16½ cubic feet, or 25 cubic feet) for stonework

**²perch** \"\ *vb* -ED/-ING/-ES [ME *perchen*, fr. MF *percher*, fr. *perche*, n. — more at ¹PERCH] *vt* **1 :** to place on or as if on a perch, a height, or other precarious spot **:** SET, STATION ⟨~ a pullet at three months⟩ ⟨~ a hat on his head⟩ ⟨red brick buildings with carved white sandstone demons ~*ed* on their entrance gates —Faubion Bowers⟩ ⟨a cottage . . . ~*ed* on a wild sea cliff —Van Wyck Brooks⟩ ⟨islands ~*ed* on the edge of Europe —Jacquetta & Christopher Hawkes⟩ ⟨~*ed* himself on the table, his hands gripping the edges of it —Rafael Sabatini⟩ **2 :** to examine (cloth from the loom) for imperfections by placing on a perch **~** *vi* **1 :** to come to rest often uneasily or precariously on or as if on a perch **:** settle oneself **:** ALIGHT, SIT ⟨flew off to ~ on their eyries —C.G.D.Roberts⟩ ⟨the pianist ~*es* on a small suitcase to make his chair high enough —Claudia Cassidy⟩ ⟨~ happily on a hillside and watch the sea —M.P.O'Connor⟩ **2 :** to occupy a usu. precipitous location ⟨tall apartment buildings ~ on the top of rocky cliffs —*Amer. Guide Series: N.Y. City*⟩

**³perch** \"\ *n, pl* **perch** *or* **perches** [ME *perche*, fr. MF, fr. L *perca*, fr. Gk *perkē*; akin to OE *forn* trout, OHG *forhana* trout, *faro* colored, Sw *färna* whiting, L *porcus*, a spiny fish, Gk *perknos* dusky, dark, Skt *pṛśni* speckled, and perh. to Gk *prēthein* to blow up — more at FROTH] **1 a :** a rather small European freshwater spiny-finned fish (*Perca fluviatilis*) **b :** a closely related fish (*P. flavescens*) of the eastern and central U.S. inhabiting lakes and streams and well known as a sport and food fish — see YELLOW PERCH **2 a :** any of numerous marine or freshwater teleost fishes more or less resembling the European perch and mostly belonging to Percidae, Centrarchidae, Serranidae, and related families — usu. used in combination; compare BLACK PERCH, WHITE PERCH **b** *West* **:** SURF FISH

**percha** *n* -S [by shortening] **:** GUTTA-PERCHA

**per·chance** \ˌpə(r)+\ *adv* [ME *perchaunce, parchaunce*, fr. MF *par chance, par chance*, fr. *per, par* by (fr. L *per* by, through) + *chance* — more at FOR, CHANCE] **:** PERHAPS, POSSIBLY ⟨~ he is not drowned —Shak.⟩ ⟨if ~ what they know of you is not to their liking —H.J.Johnson⟩ ⟨come to obtain vacation travel data or ~ to brush up on their geography —H.H.Baetjer⟩

**perched** *adj* [fr. past part. of ²*perch*] **:** seated on or as if on a perch ⟨~ on the seat of a bright red peddler's wagon —Lucy M. Montgomery⟩

**perched block** *or* **perched rock** *n* **:** a perched boulder esp. when notably angular

**perched boulder** *n* **:** a boulder transported and deposited by a glacier in a conspicuous and relatively unstable position — compare BALANCED ROCK

**perched water** *or* **perched groundwater** *n* **:** groundwater occurring in a saturated zone separated from the main body of groundwater by unsaturated rock

**perched water table** *n* **:** the upper surface of a body of perched groundwater

**perch·er** \ˈpərchə(r), ˈpə̄ch-, ˈpəich-\ *n* -S [²*perch* + *-er*] **:** one that perches: as **a :** a bird having feet adapted for perching **b :** a textile worker who inspects cloth **c :** a tannery worker who softens hides — called also *staker*

**per·che·ron** \ˈpərchəˌrän, -rsh-\ *n -s usu cap* [F, fr. *Perche*, region in northern France] **1 :** a breed of powerful rugged usu. dapple-gray or black draft horses originating in the Perche region of France but now much used in America and other countries **2 :** a horse of the Percheron breed

**perching** *adj* [fr. pres. part. of ²*perch*] **1 :** coming to rest usu. on an elevated perch (as a twig or bough) — used of a wild bird **2** : old enough to roost on a perch — used of poultry ⟨the small flock is often better started with ~ pullets⟩

**perchlor-** *or* **perchloro-** *comb form* [ISV *per-* + *chlor-*] : containing a relatively large amount of chlorine esp. in place of hydrogen ⟨*perchlor*oethylene⟩ ⟨*perchloro*methyl $CCl_3$⟩

**per·chlorate** \ˌpər, (ˈ)per+\ *n* [ISV *per-* + *chlorate*] : a salt or ester of perchloric acid — compare AMMONIUM PERCHLORATE, LITHIUM PERCHLORATE

**per·chloric acid** \"+ . . . -\ *n* [*per-* + *chloric*] : a fuming liquid strong acid $HClO_4$ that is the highest oxygen acid of chlorine, that is a powerful oxidizing agent when heated, is corrosive, and is explosive in contact with combustible material, that is usu. made by treating a perchlorate (as sodium perchlorate) with acid, and that is used chiefly in chemical analysis, in electroplating, and as a catalyst

**per·chloride** \ˌpər, (ˈ)per+\ *n* [ISV *per-* + *chloride*] : a chloride containing a relatively high proportion of chlorine

**per·chlorinate** \ˌpər, ˌper+\ *vt* [*per-* + *chlorinate*] : to combine with the maximum amount of chlorine esp. in place of hydrogen

**per·chlorination** \ˌpər, ˌper+\ *n* : the process of perchlorinating

**per·chlo·ro·ethane** \ˌpər,klōrō, ˌper-+\ *n* [ISV *perchlor-* + *ethane*] : HEXACHLOROETHANE

**per·chlo·ro·ethylene** \"+\ *also* **per·chlor·ethylene** \ˌpər-,klōr, ˌper-+\ *n* [*perchlor-* + *ethylene*] : TETRACHLOROETHYLENE

**per·chlo·ryl** \ˌpərˈklōrəl, per-\ *n* [*perchlor-* + *-yl*] : the univalent ion $ClO_3^+$ or radical $ClO_3$ of perchloric acid

**perch pole** *n* : [1]PERCH 1e

**per·chromate** \ˌpər, (ˈ)per+\ *n* [ISV *perchromic* (in *perchromic acid*) + *-ate*] : a salt of a perchromic acid formed by the action of hydrogen peroxide on a chromate — called also *peroxychromate*

**per·chromic acid** \"+. . .-\ *n* [ISV *per-* + *chromic*] : any of several peroxy compounds of chromium known esp. in the form of salts — called also *peroxychromic acid;* not used systematically

[1]**per·cid** \ˈpərsəd\ *adj* [NL *Percidae*] : of or relating to the Percidae

[2]**percid** \"\ *n* -s : a fish of the family Percidae

**per·ci·dae** \-səˌdē\ *n pl, cap* [NL, fr. *Perca*, type genus + *-idae*] : a family of vigorous active percoid fishes that is now usu. restricted to freshwater forms of the northern hemisphere including the true perches, pike perches, and a few related forms (as the zingel) but that formerly also included the sand darters or was sometimes made nearly coextensive with Percoidea — see PERCA

[1]**per·ci·form** \-sə,fȯrm\ *adj* [NL *Perciformes*] **1** : resembling a perch **2** : of or relating to the Perciformes or Percoidea

[2]**perciform** \"\ *n* -s : a perciform fish

**per·ci·for·mes** \ˌ==ˈfȯr(ˌ)mēz\ *n pl, cap* [NL, fr. L *perca* perch + NL *-iformes* — more at PERCH] *in some classifications* : a group of fishes nearly or exactly equivalent to Percoidea

**per·ci·pi** \ˈpərkəˌpī, ˈpərsəˌpī, -əˌpē\ *n* -s [L, to be perceived, pres. pass. inf. of *percipere* to perceive — more at PERCEIVE] : the condition of being perceived — see ESSE EST PERCIPI

**per·cip·i·ence** \pə(r)ˈsipēən(t)s\ *n* -s : capacity to perceive : perceptive quality : PERCEPTION ⟨a mood of exaltation which combined intense ~ with intense benevolence —John Connell⟩ ⟨their informal style, ~ and urbane charm endear them to every generation —*Brit. Book News*⟩

**per·cip·i·en·cy** \-nsē,-nsi\ *n* -ES : PERCIPIENCE

[1]**per·cip·i·ent** \-nt\ *n* -s [L *percipient-, percipiens*, pres. part. of *percipere* to perceive — more at PERCEIVE] **1** : one that perceives **2** : a person on whose mind a telepathic impulse or message is held to fall — compare AGENT 2b

[2]**percipient** \"\ *adj* [L *percipient-, percipiens*, pres. part. of *percipere*] : capable of or characterized by perception : DISCERNING ⟨~ critic⟩ ⟨five ~, satirical and compassionate tales —Anne Fremantle⟩

**perclose** *var of* PARCLOSE

**perc·no·some** \ˈpərknəˌsōm\ *n* -s [Gk *perknos* dusky, dark + E *-some* — more at PERCH] : a small body occurring in the androcyte of a fern

[1]**per·coid** \ˈpərˌkȯid\ *or* **per·coi·de·an** \(ˌ)pərˈkȯidēən\ *adj* [*percoid* fr. NL *Percoidea; percoidean* fr. NL *Percoidea* + E *-an*] : of or relating to the Percoidea

[2]**percoid** \"\ *or* **percoidean** \"\ *n* -s : a fish of the suborder Percoidea

**per·coi·dea** \(ˌ)pərˈkȯidēə\ *n pl, cap* [NL, fr. *Perca* + *-oidea*] : a suborder of Percomorphi of uncertain limits that includes Percidae, Centrarchidae, Serranidae, Sparidae, and numerous other families and constitutes even in its least extensive application one of the largest natural groups of fishes

[1]**per·co·late** \ˈpərkəˌlāt, ˈpə̄k-,ˈpəik-, *chiefly in substand speech* -kyə-; *usu* -ād·+V\ *vb* -ED/-ING/-S [L *percolatus*, past part. of *percolare*, fr. *per-* through + *colare* to filter, strain, sieve — more at PER-, COLANDER] *vt* **1 a** : to cause (a liquid) to pass through a permeable substance : FILTER, STRAIN **b** (1) : to cause a liquid to pass through (as coffee) in order to extract the essence (2) : to prepare (coffee) by percolation **c** : to ooze or drain slowly through (a porous medium) **2** : to be diffused through : PENETRATE ⟨events . . . *percolated* the censorships and reached the cables —F.L.Paxson⟩ ~ *vi* **1** : to ooze or trickle through a permeable substance : SEEP ⟨rainwaters . . . ~ between the loose sands and gravels that fill the buried valley —R.E.Janssen⟩ **2 a** : to undergo percolation ⟨waited for the coffee to ~ —Willa Cather⟩ **b** : to be or become lively or effervescent : show animation ⟨once his voice is *percolating* to his satisfaction —Joseph Wechsberg⟩ ⟨keep college football spirit *percolating* —F.J.Taylor⟩ **3** : to become diffused : spread gradually ⟨allow the sunlight to ~ into our rooms —Norman Douglas⟩ ⟨soldiers and political police had already *percolated* into Bulgaria —Sir Winston Churchill⟩

[2]**per·co·late** \"; -lət, *usu* -əd·+V\ *n* -s : a product of percolation ⟨no increase in nitrite in the soil ~ —*Biol. Abstracts*⟩

**percolating filter** *n* : TRICKLING FILTER

**per·co·la·tion** \ˌ==ˈlāshən\ *n* -s [L *percolation-, percolatio*, fr. *percolatus* + *-ion-, -io* -ion] **1 a** : the slow passage of a liquid through a filtering medium : LEACHING, SEEPAGE ⟨~ of water downward through the soil —Russell Lord⟩ **b** : a method of extraction or purification by means of filtration ⟨decolorization of lubricating oils by ~⟩ **c** : the process of brewing coffee by causing hot water to pass through it in a percolator **d** : the process of extracting the soluble constituents of a powdered drug by passage of a liquid through it **2** : diffusion by gradual spreading or penetration ⟨a gradual ~ of Scandinavian motives into sculpture —O. Elfrida Saunders⟩ ⟨the ~ downward through the whole middle class of the sense of freedom —Roy Lewis & Angus Maude⟩

**per·co·la·tive** \ˈ==ˌlād·iv\ *adj* [[1]*percolate* + *-ive*] : of, relating to, or permitting percolation : POROUS

**per·co·la·tor** \-ˌlād·ə(r), -ātə-\ *n* -s [*percolate* + *-or*] : one that percolates: as **a** : a coffeepot in which boiling water rising through a tube is repeatedly deflected downward through a perforated basket containing ground coffee beans to extract their essence **b** : an apparatus for the extraction of a drug with a liquid solvent by downward displacement

[1]**per·co·morph** \ˈpərkəˌmȯrf\ *adj* [NL *Percomorphi*] : of or relating to the Percomorphi

[2]**percomorph** \"\ *n* -s : a fish of the order Percomorphi

**per·co·mor·phi** \ˌ==ˈmȯrˌfī\ *n pl, cap* [NL, fr. L *perca* perch + NL *-o-* + *-morphi* (fr. Gk *morphē* form) — more at PERCH, FORM] : the largest order of teleost fishes comprising typically small or moderate-sized more or less streamlined or fusiform fishes with the ventral fin possessing not more than one spine and five rays and the first dorsal fin always spinose, being divided into a number of suborders, and including the perches, basses, gobies, mackerels, blennies, and numerous related forms — **per·co·mor·phous** \ˌ==ˈ==fəs\ *adj*

**percomorph liver oil** *n* : a fatty oil obtained from the fresh livers of percomorph fishes and administered to infants as a source of vitamins A and D

**per·con·ta·tion** \ˌpər,känˈtāshən\ *n* -s [L *percontation-, percontatio*, fr. *percontatus* (past part. of *percontari* to inquire, lit., to sound with a punting pole, fr. *per* through, by means of, + *contus* pole, punting pole, fr. Gk *kontos*) + *-ion-, -io* -ion; akin to Gk *kentein* to prick — more at FOR, CENTER] *archaic* : an act or process of questioning : INQUIRY

**per con·tra** \(ˌ)pərˈkän·trə, per-, -kȯn·(ˌ)trä, -kōn·(ˌ)trä\ *adv* [L] **1 a** : on the contrary ⟨*per contra* I don't ask you to forget but to remember —J.H.Wheelwright⟩ **b** : on the other hand : by way of contrast ⟨the female is generally drab . . . the male, *per contra*, brilliant —Julian Huxley⟩ **2** : as an offset — compare [3]CONTRA 2

[1]**per·cop·sid** \(ˌ)pərˈkäpsəd\ *adj* [NL *Percopsidae*] : of or relating to the Percopsidae

[2]**percopsid** \"\ *n* -s : a fish of the family Percopsidae

**per·cop·sis** \-psəs\ *n, cap* [NL, fr. L *perca* perch + NL *-opsis* — more at PERCH] : a small genus (the type of the family Percopsidae) of trout-perches much resembling young walleyed pikes and in many respects intermediate between typical isospondyls and the percoids — compare PIRATE PERCH

**per cu·ri·am** \perˈkúrēˌäm\ *adv* (*or adj*) [ML, lit., by the court] : summarily or immediately and usu. by unanimous action of the court

**per curiam decision** *or* **per curiam opinion** *n* : a very brief usu. unanimous opinion or decision of a court rendered without elaborate discussion of the principles or reasons therefor — compare MEMORANDUM DECISION

**per·current** \ˌpər, (ˈ)per+\ *adj* [L *percurrent-, percurrens*, pres. part. of *percurrere* to run through, fr. *per-* through + *currere* to run, hasten — more at PER-, CURRENT] : extending from the base to the apex — used of the midrib of a leaf

**per·cuss** \pə(r)ˈkəs\ *vb* -ED/-ING/-ES [L *percussus*, past part. of *percutere*] *vt* : to strike on or against : RAP; *esp* : to tap (a body part) repeatedly to elicit evidence (as sounds) of use in medical diagnosis ⟨a healthy tooth ~*ed* with a metal instrument . . . gives a metallic sound —K.H.Thoma⟩ ~ *vi* : TAP; *esp* : to percuss a body part ⟨~*ing* with the ends of our fingers over the lungs —Robert Chawner⟩

[1]**per·cus·sion** \pə(r)ˈkəshən\ *n* -s [L *percussion-, percussio*, fr. *percussus* (past part. of *percutere* to beat, strike, fr. *per-*, intensifying prefix + *-cutere*, fr. *quatere* to shake, strike, beat) + *-ion-, -io* -ion — more at PER, QUASH] **1** : a forcible impact : BLOW, STROKE: as **a** : an act or process of striking together ⟨use flint and steel in making fire by ~⟩ **b** (1) : the beating or striking of a musical instrument ⟨a drum is played by ~⟩ (2) : the sounding of a dissonant tone or chord — compare RESOLUTION 1d **c** : the setting off of an explosive charge by forcible contact; *specif* : the striking of a gun hammer on fulminating powder **d** (1) : the act of tapping or striking the surface of a body part (as chest or abdomen) to learn the condition of the parts beneath by the resultant sound — compare AUSCULTATION (2) : massage consisting of the striking of a body part with light rapid blows : TAPOTEMENT **2** : a sharp auditory impact : vibratory shock ⟨a long, quasi-narrative poem . . . which has ~, if not much distinction as poetry —*New Yorker*⟩ **3** : the edge of the palm below the fourth finger — used chiefly by palmists **4 a** : the section of a band or orchestra consisting of percussion instruments ⟨enough strings to balance the brass and ~ —Virgil Thomson⟩ **b** : percussion instruments ⟨big orchestras, with their brasses, woodwinds, and ~ —Joseph Wechsberg⟩ **syn** see IMPACT

[2]**percussion** \"\ *adj* **1 a** : of, relating to, or produced by percussion ⟨classification of the ~ note into resonant, dull, and tympanitic —*Medical Physics*⟩ **b** : actuated or operating by percussion ⟨~ rifle⟩; *specif* : PNEUMATIC ⟨a ~ drill for drilling holes in rock⟩ **2** : of or relating to percussion instruments ⟨members of the ~ choir are the tympani, the bass drum, the snare drum, the cymbals —Henry Melnik⟩

**per·cus·sion·al** \-shənᵊl,-shnəl\ *adj* : PERCUSSION

**percussion cap** *n* : [1]CAP 8a

**percussion drilling** *n* : ROPE DRILLING

**percussion figure** *n* : the figure formed by cracks started in a cleavage plate of a crystal by a blow from a dull-pointed instrument

**percussion flaking** *n* : the shaping of a stone implement by striking or chipping off flakes with another stone or a piece of wood, bone, or antler — compare PRESSURE FLAKING

**percussion fuse** *n* : [1]FUSE 2

**percussion instrument** *n* : a musical instrument (as a piano) on which the tone is produced by striking; *specif* : an instrument (as kettledrum, bass drum, triangle, bells) belonging to the choir of band and orchestral percussion instruments as distinguished from the string or wind choirs and having both definite and indefinite pitch

**per·cus·sion·ist** \-sh(ə)nəst\ *n* -s : one skilled in the playing of percussion instruments

**percussion lock** *n* : the lock of a gun fired by percussion — compare FLINTLOCK

**percussion mark** *n* : a crescentic scar on a pebble (as of chert or quartzite) caused by impact

**percussion stop** *n* **1** : a draw-knob in the reed organ by which a mechanism is made to strike a reed as it is sounded to give promptness and force to its tone **2** : a pipe-organ stop (as the xylophone) whose tone is produced by striking

**percussion table** *n* : an inclined table suspended on springs and used as an apparatus for sorting particles of ore according to specific gravity by running the ore in a thin sheet of water over the table and jarring it to effect separation

**percussion wave** *n* : a shock wave esp. from a blow or an explosion

**per·cus·sive** \-ˈkəsiv, -sēv *also* -səv\ *adj* [*percussion* + *-ive*] **1 a** (1) : characterized by percussion or featuring percussion instruments ⟨the occurrence . . . of inexplicable noises, usually ~ — thuds, taps, drumbeats, raps —A.G.N.Flew⟩ ⟨~, furious, this wind sweeps down the mountain —Barbara Howes⟩ ⟨~ rhythms⟩ (2) *dancing* : staccato and vigorous with suddenly checked impulse ⟨a solemn minuet . . . interrupted by tropical drumbeats and ~ primitive movement —*Dance Observer*⟩ **b** : having powerful impact : STRIKING, SHOCKING ⟨the stark dramatic power of the scenes is ~ and stabbing —William Goyen⟩ **2** : PERCUSSION ⟨~ drill⟩ — **per·cus·sive·ly** \-səvlē, -li\ *adv*

**per·cus·sive·ness** \-sivnəs, -sēv- *also* -səv-\ *n* -ES : the quality or state of being percussive ⟨to his harpsichord style he carries over a pianistic ~ —*Saturday Rev.*⟩

**percussive welding** *or* **percussion welding** *n* : resistance welding in which a hammer blow is applied simultaneously with or immediately following a sudden discharge of current across the contact area of the parts to be united

**per·cus·sor** \-sə(r)\ *n* -s [NL, fr. L, one that strikes or beats, fr. *percussus* (past part. of *percutere* to strike, beat) + *-or* — more at PERCUSSION] : PLEXOR

**per·cutaneous** \ˌpər, ˌper+\ *adj* [*per-* + *cutaneous*] : effected or performed through the skin ⟨~ absorption⟩ — **per·cutaneously** \"+\ *adv*

**per·cy·lite** \ˈpərsēˌlīt, -səˌl-\ *n* -s [John *Percy* †1889 Eng. metallurgist + E *-lite*] : a mineral $PbCuCl_2(OH)_2$(?) consisting of a rare basic chloride of lead and copper

**per·den·do** \pə(r)ˈden(ˌ)dō\ *adj* (*or adv*) [It (verbal of *perdere* to lose), fr. L *perdendum*, gerund of *perdere* to destroy, lose — more at PERDITION] : PERDENDOSI

**per·den·do·si** \-ˌdōˌsē\ *adj* (*or adv*) [It, lit., losing itself] : dying away — used as a direction in music

**per·di·cine** \ˈpərdəˌsīn\ *adj* [NL *Perdic-, Perdix* + E *-ine*] : of or relating to the genus *Perdix*

**perdie** *var of* PARDIE

[1]**per di·em** \ˌpə(r)ˈdēəm, ˌpərˈ-, pə̄ˈ- *sometimes* -dīəm\ *adv* [L] : by the day : for each day ⟨computed the total of man-hours saved *per diem* —C.D.Lewis⟩

[2]**per diem** \", ˈ=ˌ==\ *adj* **1** : based on use or service by the day : DAILY ⟨*per diem* allowance⟩ ⟨a large firm can establish hourly or *per diem* rates for various levels of performance —R.E. Witschey⟩ ⟨the fee is charged on a *per diem* basis —Jules Backman⟩ ⟨when *per diem* costs are high, fast turnarounds become increasingly important —Daniel Marx⟩ **2** : paid by the day ⟨a *per diem* assignment⟩ ⟨Hawaii uses a *per diem* referee —*Comparison of State Unemployment Insurance Laws*⟩

[3]**per diem** \(ˌ)=ˈ==\ *n, pl* **per diems** **1** : a daily allowance ⟨given a fixed *per diem* for each day he was away from . . . his home base —Linda Braidwood⟩ — compare CAR MILEAGE 2 **2** : a daily fee ⟨a detective works day and night for a measly *per diem* —Erle Stanley Gardner⟩ **3** : the daily rental paid by one railroad for the use of cars of another

**per·di·tion** \pə(r)ˈdishən, ˌpərˈ-, pə̄-, pəi-\ *n* -s [ME *perdicioun*, fr. LL *perdition-, perditio*, fr. L *perditus* (past part. of *perdere* to destroy, squander, lose, fr. *per-* destructively, detrimentally + *-dere*, fr. *dare* to give) + *-ion-, -io* -ion — more at PER-, DATE] **1 a** *archaic* : utter destruction : complete ruin ⟨certain tidings . . . importing the mere ~ of the Turkish fleet —Shak.⟩ **b** *obs* : LOSS, DIMINUTION ⟨not so much ~ as an hair betid to any creature in the vessel —Shak.⟩ **c** *obs* : something that causes loss or destruction ⟨revelings, carnivals and balls which are the ~ of precious hours —Jeremy Taylor⟩ **2 a** : utter loss of the soul or of final happiness in a future state : eternal damnation ⟨reserved unto fire against the day of judgment and ~ of ungodly men —2 Pet 3: 7 (AV)⟩ **b** : the place of eternal damnation : HELL ⟨send a soul straight to ~, dying frank an atheist —Robert Browning⟩

**per·dix** \ˈpərdiks\ *n, cap* [NL, fr. L, partridge — more at PARTRIDGE] : a once extensive genus of birds (family Phasianidae) now limited to the European partridge and near related forms

**per·dominant** \ˌpər, (ˈ)per+\ *n* [*per-* + *dominant*] : a plant widely distributed in a climax and usu. a dominant in at least some of the constituent associations

[1]**per·du** *or* **per·due** \(ˌ)pərˈd(y)ü, per-\ *adj* [MF *perdu* (masc.) & *perdue* (fem.), fr. past part. of *perdre* to lose, fr. L *perdere* to destroy, lose — more at PERDITION] **1 a** *obs* (1) : keeping covert watch in a hazardous military outpost or ambush ⟨so many . . . desire to enter upon breaches, lie sentinel ~, give the first onset —Robert Burton⟩ (2) : being in a desperate plight **b** : remaining out of sight : CONCEALED ⟨seek shelter in a cavern, stay there ~ for three days —Thomas Carlyle⟩ **2** : withdrawn from the public eye : OBSCURED, UNNOTICED ⟨the evidence has been lying ~ . . . in the preface —I.A.Shapiro⟩ ⟨suffered from . . . lack of appreciation, remaining ~ in Italy —*Publ's Mod. Lang. Assoc. of Amer.*⟩

[2]**perdu** *or* **perdue** \"\ *n* -s **1** *obs* **a** : a soldier assigned to extremely hazardous duty **b** : FORLORN HOPE 1 **2** *obs* : one that guards or reconnoiters : WATCH, SPY

**per·du·el·lion** \ˌpərd(y)üˈelyən\ *n* -s [L *perduellion-, perduellio*, fr. *perduellis* enemy, fr. *per* by + OL *duellum* war — more at DUEL] *Roman law* : TREASON, SUBVERSION

**per·durability** \(ˌ)pər+, *archaic* ˌpərjərəˈbiləd·ē\ *n* : the quality or state of being perdurable : PERSISTENCE, PERMANENCE

**per·durable** \(ˌ)pər+, *archaic* ˈpərjərəbəl\ *adj* [ME, fr. OF *perdurable, pardurable*, fr. LL *perdurabilis*, fr. L *perdurare* to endure, last long + *-abilis* -able — more at PERDURE] **1** : very durable : lasting a very long time or indefinitely ⟨the ~ granite of the ancient Appalachian spine of the eastern continent —Marjory S. Douglas⟩ ⟨our literature is going to be our most ~ claim on man's remembrance —A.T.Quiller-Couch⟩ **2** : ETERNAL — **per·du·ra·bly** \-blē\ *adv*

**per·durableness** \(ˌ)pər+, *archaic* ˈpərjərəbəlnəs\ *n* -ES *archaic* : PERDURABILITY

**per·dur·ance** \(ˌ)pərˈd(y)ùrən(t)s\ *n* -s [*perdure* + *-ance*] : PERMANENCE, PERSISTENCE

**per·dur·ant** \-nt\ *adj* [L *perdurant-, perdurans*, pres. part. of *perdurare* to endure, last — more at PERDURE] : PERDURABLE

**per·duration** \ˌpər+\ *n* [LL *perduration-, perduratio*, fr. L *perduratus* (past part. of *perdurare*) + *-ion-, -io* -ion] *archaic* : PERDURANCE

**per·dure** \(ˌ)pərˈd(y)ù(ə)r\ *vi* -ED/-ING/-S [ME *perduren*, fr. L *perdurare*, fr. *per-*, intensifying prefix + *durare* to endure, last — more at PER-, DURE] : to continue to exist : LAST

**perduring** *adj* [fr. pres. part. of *perdure*] : long lasting : PERSISTENT — **per·dur·ing·ly** *adv*

**perea** *var of* APEREA

**père da·vid's deer** \ˌperdəˈvēdz-, (ˈ)perˈdāvədz-\ *n, usu cap P & 1st D* [after *Père* Armand *David* †1900 French Catholic missionary and naturalist] : a large grayish deer (*Elaphurus davidianus*) having long slender antlers and prob. originating in northern China but known only from domesticated herds

**per·e·gri·na** \ˌperəˈgrēnə\ *n* -s [AmerSp, fr. Sp, woman pilgrim, fr. ML, fem. of *peregrinus* male pilgrim — more at PILGRIM] : a Cuban shrub (*Adenoropium hastatum*) of the family Euphorbiaceae having showy cymes of scarlet or rose-colored flowers

[1]**per·e·gri·nate** \ˈperəgrəˌnāt, *usu* -ād·+V\ *vb* -ED/-ING/-S [L *peregrinatus*, past part. of *peregrinari* to travel in foreign lands, fr. *peregrinus* foreigner — more at PILGRIM] *vi* : to travel on foot : WALK, TOUR ⟨a land bridge . . . which enabled prehistoric man to ~ from North Africa —Hendrik de Leeuw⟩ ⟨a callboy *peregrinating* backstage —R.L.Shayon⟩ ~ *vt* : to walk over : TRAVERSE ⟨*peregrinate* the country for seasonal jobs —John Buchan⟩

[2]**peregrinate** \"\ *adj* [L *peregrinatus*, past part of *peregrinari*] : having the air of one who has traveled or lived abroad : FOREIGN ⟨too affected, too odd, as it were, too ~ —Shak.⟩

**per·e·gri·na·tion** \ˌ===ˈnāshən\ *n* -s [MF or L; MF, fr. L *peregrination-, peregrinatio*, fr. *peregrinatus* (past. part. of *peregrinari*) + *-ion-, -io* -ion] **1 a** : an act of traveling or traversing ⟨stopped a moment in his ~ of the room —J.C.Snaith⟩; *esp* : foreign travel **b** : an excursion esp. on foot or to a foreign country : JOURNEY, TRAVEL — usu. used in pl. ⟨his anthropological ~*s* took him into the hylean Amazon⟩ ⟨desire to promote national sentiment through the ~*s* of the Supreme Court justices maintained the circuit riding system —Felix Frankfurter⟩ ⟨built great boats for his posthumous ~*s* —J.D. Hillaby⟩ **c** *obs* (1) : a stay in a foreign country : SOJOURN, EXILE (2) : the period of man's life on earth ⟨pray that God would pour down upon us graces for our ~ here —John Donne⟩ **2** : a widely ranging discourse or treatment ⟨an unevenly rambling intellectual ~ —Jacob Hammer⟩

**per·e·gri·na·tor** \ˈ===ˌnād·ə(r)\ *n* -s [L, fr. *peregrinatus* + *-or*] *archaic* : TRAVELER, WANDERER

[1]**per·e·grine** \ˈ==grən, -ˌgrēn, -ˌgrīn\ *adj* [in sense 1, fr. L *peregrinus;* in other senses, fr. ML *peregrinus*, fr. L — more at PILGRIM] **1** *archaic* : of or from a foreign country : ALIEN, IMPORTED **2** *archaic* : engaged in or traveling on a pilgrimage ⟨~ Christians going to visit the Holy Sepulchre —Matthew Carter⟩ **3 a** : having a tendency to wander : ROVING ⟨believes the profession of ~ typist has a happy future —*Saturday Rev.*⟩ **b** *also* **per·e·grin·ic** \ˌperəˈgrinik\ [*peregrinic* fr. ML *peregrinus* + E *-ic*] : widely distributed : found in many parts of the world ⟨*Allolobophora* is a markedly ~ genus of earthworms⟩

[2]**peregrine** \"\ *n* -s [in sense 1, fr. ML *peregrinus*, fr. L, stranger; in sense 2, fr. L *peregrinus;* in sense 3, fr. (*falcon*) *peregrine* — more at PILGRIM] **1** *obs* : TRAVELER, PILGRIM **2** : a sojourner in a foreign country; *specif* : an alien resident of ancient Rome **3** : PEREGRINE FALCON

**peregrine falcon** *n* [ME *faucon peregrin*, trans. of ML *falco peregrinus*] : a swift falcon (*Falco peregrinus*) much used in falconry that is of almost cosmopolitan distribution and has adult plumage which is dark bluish ash on the back, nearly black on the head and cheeks, white beneath, and barred with black below the throat — compare DUCK HAWK 1, PEALE'S FALCON

**per·e·grin·ism** \-ˌgrəˌnizəm, -ˌgrē,n-\ *n* -s : tendency to wander

**per·e·grin·i·ty** \ˌ==ˈgrinəd·ē\ *n* -ES [MF or L; MF *peregrinité*, fr. L *peregrinitat-, peregrinitas*, fr. *peregrinus* foreign + *-itat-, -itas* -ity — more at PILGRIM] : the quality or state of being peregrine

**pe·rei·on** \pəˈrīˌän, -rā, -rē\ *also* **pe·rae·on** \-rē,än\ *n, pl* **pe·reia** \-ə\ [NL, fr. Gk *peraiōn*, pres. part. of *peraioun* to transport, carry over, fr. *peraios* situated beyond, fr. *pera* beyond; fr. the walking appendages; akin to Skt *para* further, ulterior, Gk *peran* to pass through — more at FARE] : the thorax or the 7 metameres typically constituting the thorax of a decapod crustacean

**pe·reio·pod** \-īəˌpäd, -āə-,-ēə-\ *n* -s [NL *pereion* + E *-pod*] : an appendage of the pereion : THORACIC LIMB

**pe·rei·ra bark** \pəˈrerə-, -ˈrārə-\ *or* **pereira** *n* -s [after Jonathan *Pereira* †1853 Eng. pharmacologist.] **1** : a Brazilian tree (*Geissospermum vellosii*) of the family Apocynaceae **2** : the bark of the pereira tree used in Brazil as a tonic and febrifuge

**perempt** *vt* [L *peremptus*, past part. of *perimere* — more at PEREMPTORY] *obs* : QUASH

**pe·remp·tion** \pəˈrem(p)shən\ *n* -s [LL *peremption-, peremptio*, fr. L *peremptus* + *-ion-, -io* -ion] : the act or process of quashing

**pe·remp·tive** \-m(p)tiv\ *adj* : of, relating to, or marked by peremption

**pe·remp·to·ri·ly** \pəˈrem(p)t(ə)rəlē, -li *sometimes* pəˈrem(p)-ˌtōr- *or* ˌperəm(p)ˌtōr- *or* -tȯr-\ *adv* : in a peremptory manner : HAUGHTILY, IMPERATIVELY

**pe·remp·to·ri·ness** \pronunc at ¹PEREMPTORY +nəs\ n -ES : the quality or state of being peremptory

**¹pe·remp·to·ry** \pə'remp(t)(ə)rē, -ri sometimes 'perəm(p)-,tōr- or 'perəm(p),tȯr-; substand prē'em-\ adj [LL & L; LL *peremptorius* final, decisive, fr. L, destructive, fr. *peremptus* (past part. of *perimere* to take away entirely, destroy, kill, fr. *per-* detrimentally, destructively + *-imere*, fr. *emere* to buy, obtain, acquire) + *-orius* -ory — more at PER-, REDEEM] **1 a :** putting an end to or precluding a right of action, debate, or delay **b** *obs* : admitting no contradiction : ABSOLUTE, FINAL ⟨a mathematician's conclusions ought to be ~ and grounded in . . . infallible evidence —Edward Reynolds⟩ **2 a :** expressive of urgency or command : IMPERATIVE ⟨knew only a few words of practical, ~ Greek —Glenway Wescott⟩ ⟨the brassy, ~ shout of the ship's siren —R.B.Robertson⟩ **b** *archaic* : of an indispensable nature : ESSENTIAL ⟨find this law of one to one ~ for conversation —R.W.Emerson⟩ **3 a** (1) : marked by self-assurance : CONFIDENT, POSITIVE ⟨is a man of conviction . . . and requires no excessive prodding to let fly a ~ speech —*New Yorker*⟩ (2) : DOGMATIC ⟨has clear and ~ ideas about right and wrong —W.C.Brownell⟩ **b** (1) : marked by determination : DECISIVE, RESOLUTE ⟨the ~ use of force, if needed —*Time*⟩ (2) : OBSTINATE ⟨~ lack of interest in commercial affairs —Brooks Atkinson⟩ **4 :** of an arrogant or imperious nature : HAUGHTY, DICTATORIAL ⟨ordered around in the most ~ terms —Frank Oliver⟩ ⟨asserting their ~ claim to a grander knowledge —J.D.Adams⟩ **syn** see MASTERFUL

**²peremptory** \"\ adv, *archaic* : PEREMPTORILY

**³peremptory** \"\ n -ES *obs* : a case, circumstance, document, or command that cannot be ignored ⟨two or three afternoons he allotted every week to hear *peremptories* —John Hacket⟩ ⟨went up with my father's ~ . . . to my sister —Samuel Richardson⟩

**peremptory challenge** n : a challenge (as of a juror) made as of right without assigning any cause

**peremptory exception** *or* **peremptory plea** n : a legal exception or plea attacking the cause of action or defense on its merits

**peremptory instruction** n : an instruction charging a jury that if they agree to the truth of certain stated facts they must find for a designated party

**peremptory mandamus** n : a final and absolute mandamus to enforce the court's judgment

**peren·nate** \'perə,nāt, pə're,n-\ vi -ED/-ING/-S [L *perennatus*, past part. of *perennare*, fr. *perennis* perennial] : to live over from season to season : be perennial : PERSIST ⟨a *perennating* rhizome from which flowering shoots arise annually —Clarence Sterling⟩ — **peren·na·tion** \,perə'nāshən, ,pe,re'n-, pə,re'n-\ n -S

**¹pe·ren·nial** \pə'renēəl, -nyəl\ adj [L *perennis* perennial (fr. *per-* throughout + *-ennis*, fr. *annus* year) + E *-al* — more at PER-, ANNUAL] **1 a** *obs* : EVERGREEN ⟨where round the scene ~ laurels bloom —William Falconer⟩ **b :** present at all seasons of the year ⟨~ stream⟩ ⟨the ~ snow fields are of such great depth that glacial ice forms —W.W.Atwood †1949⟩ **2 a :** continuing or lasting for several years — used specif. of a plant (as delphinium) that dies back seasonally and produces new growth from a perennating part; compare ANNUAL, BIENNIAL **b :** existing for more than one season ⟨~ insect⟩ ⟨~ colony of bees⟩ **3 a :** lasting indefinitely : impervious to change : PERMANENT, ENDURING ⟨the ~, elemental processes of nature —J.L.Lowes⟩ ⟨the family and the church have proved ~ in the experience of man —*Political Science Quarterly*⟩ ⟨the ~ value of this comparative study —*Digest of Neurology & Psychiatry*⟩ **b :** continuing without interruption : invariably present : CONSTANT, PERPETUAL ⟨a ~ twinkle in his eye —F.W.Crofts⟩ ⟨the ~ conflict among the services over the question of defense organization —*Atlantic*⟩ ⟨a ~ problem of the land, erosion —Leslie Rees⟩ ⟨the ~ quest for certainty —D.A.Wells⟩ : unfailingly popular ⟨as ~ as *Uncle Tom's Cabin* —*New Republic*⟩ **c :** regularly repeated : RECURRENT ⟨has begun to locate the ~ problems of man in the ordinary affairs of the men of his own time —Vincent Buckley⟩ ⟨~ efforts . . . to stipulate the requirements demanded of their discipline —R.C.Hinkle⟩ **syn** see CONTINUAL

**²perennial** \"\ n -S **1 :** a plant (as a tree or shrub, or an herb renewing the top growth seasonally) that lives for an indefinite number of years — compare ANNUAL, BIENNIAL **2 a :** a permanent fixture or continuing question ⟨hardy ~ among independent producers —Budd Schulberg⟩ ⟨that vexatious ~ of Southern politics, the status of the Negro —W.G.Carleton⟩; *specif* : a stock item ⟨a hardy ~ in the book trade —A.L. Guérard⟩ **b :** a recurrent topic or item ⟨certain to become fiery ~*s* on the assembly agenda —W.R.Frye⟩ ⟨infantile paralysis, that hardy summer ~ on magazine covers —Edith M. Stern⟩

**perennial canker** n : a canker that lives over from one season to the next; *specif* : a serious disease of apples caused by a fungus (*Gloeosporium perennans*) and characterized by cankers on the trunk and limbs

**perennial european sow thistle** n, *usu cap E* : a perennial sow thistle (*Sonchus arvensis*) that is native to Europe but widely naturalized as a weed, spreads by creeping underground rhizomes, and has clasping spiny leaves and heads of yellow flowers on long peduncles — called also *field sow thistle*

**pe·ren·nial·ly** \-əlē, -əli\ adv : in a perennial manner : REPEATEDLY, PERPETUALLY

**perennial pea** n : EVERLASTING PEA

**perennial peppercress** n : a European peppergrass (*Lepidium latifolium*) introduced into No. America and esp. troublesome as a weed in the southwestern U.S. having extensive rhizomes and leaves distinctly tapered to the base

**perennial peppergrass** n : HOARY CRESS

**perennial philosophy** n : the philosophical tradition of the world's great thinkers from Plato, Aristotle, and Aquinas to their modern successors dealing with problems of ultimate reality (as the nature of being) and sometimes emphasizing mysticism — opposed to *skepticism;* compare RATIONALISM

**perennial phlox** n : any of various garden phlox derived chiefly from a No. American species (*Phlox paniculata*) and having erect stems 2 to 4 feet high, leaves 3 to 5 inches long and all opposite, and flowers that are distinctly stalked — compare ANNUAL PHLOX

**perennial ragweed** n : WESTERN RAGWEED

**perennial ryegrass** n : a European perennial grass (*Lolium perenne*) with erect culms and spikelets borne in a zigzag spike that is widely cultivated for pasture and hay and as a lawn grass — called also *English ryegrass;* compare ITALIAN RYEGRASS

**perennial teeth** n pl : teeth (as those of rodents) that grow continuously at the root as they are worn away at the crown

**pe·ren·ni·branch** \pə'renə,braŋk\ n or adj [NL *Perennibranchia* (syn. of *Perennibranchiata*), fr. L *perennis* perennial + NL *-branchia* — more at PERENNIAL] : PERENNIBRANCHIATE

**pe·ren·ni·bran·chi·a·ta** \=,==,braŋkē'ād·ə, -'ād·ə\ n pl, *cap* [NL, fr. L *perennis* perennial + NL *branchi-* + *-ata*] *in former classifications* : a division of Caudata comprising amphibians (as salamanders of the genus *Necturus*) that retain their gills through life — compare CADUCIBRANCHIATA

**¹pe·ren·ni·bran·chi·ate** \=;==;kēət\ adj [NL *Perennibranchiata*] : having permanent gills : of or relating to the Perennibranchiata

**²perennibranchiate** \"\ n -S : an amphibian of the division Perennibranchiata

**pe·ren·ni·chor·da·ta** \=,==,kȯ(r)'dād·ə, -'dād·ə\ [NL, fr. L *perennis* + NL *chord-* + *-ata*] *syn of* LARVACEA

**pe·res·kia** \pə'reskēə\ [NL, irreg. fr. N.C. de Fabre de *Peiresc* †1637 French scientist and author + NL *-ia*] *syn of* PEIRESKIA

**pere·zone** \'perə,zōn\ n [L *peresus* (past part. of *peredere* to eat up, consume, waste away, fr. *per-*, prefix denoting completion + *edere* to eat) + E *zone* — more at EAT] : the zone of deposition along low coastal lands lying chiefly between low tide and land undergoing active erosion and including lagoons and brackish-water bays with the accumulated sediments being usu. nonfossiliferous but sometimes containing terrestrial or brackish water forms

**perf** abbr **1** perfect **2** perforate; perforated; perforation **3** performance; performed; performer

**¹per·fect** \'pərfikt, 'pə̄f-,'pəif-, -fēkt\ adj, *sometimes* -ER/-EST [alter. (influenced by L *perfectus*) of ME *perfit, parfit*, fr. OFr *parfit*, fr. L *perfectus* perfect, fr. past part. of *perficere* to carry out, complete, perfect, fr. *per-*, prefix denoting completion or perfection + *-ficere* (fr. *facere* to do, make) — more at PER-, DO] **1 :** accomplished in knowledge or performance : EXPERT, PROFICIENT ⟨men more ~ in the use of arms —Shak.⟩ — used chiefly in the phrase *practice makes perfect* **2 a :** entirely without fault or defect : meeting supreme standards of excellence : FLAWLESS ⟨a ~ technique⟩ ⟨a ~ gem⟩ ⟨a ~ crime⟩ ⟨must be ~ as your heavenly Father is perfect —Mt 5:48 (RSV)⟩ ⟨a starched shirtfront . . . if it is not ~ is nothing —Robert Lynd⟩ **b :** satisfying all requirements: as (1) : having precision of form or identity of relationship : ACCURATE, EXACT ⟨~ circle⟩ ⟨only the stronger and more ~ parts of his music reach me —John Burroughs⟩ ⟨its cleavage is in ~ parallel with the base —*Encyc. Americana*⟩ (2) : corresponding to an archetype : having all the proper characteristics : IDEAL ⟨a ~ gentleman⟩ ⟨the ~ Christmas gift⟩ ⟨~ money should be . . . endowed with unchanging purchasing power —Ludwig Von Mises⟩ ⟨we, the people of the United States, in order to form a more ~ union —*U.S. Constitution*⟩ (3) : conforming in every particular to an abstract concept ⟨a gas thermometer containing a ~ gas . . . would give readings directly on Kelvin's thermodynamic scale of temperature —L.C.Jackson⟩ (4) : faithfully reproducing the original ⟨a ~ likeness⟩ ⟨record engineers . . . finally succeeded in giving us music that was acoustically ~ —E.T.Canby⟩; *specif* : LETTER-PERFECT (5) : free from any valid legal objection : valid and effective in law ⟨a ~ title⟩ **3 a :** free from admixture or limitation : PURE, TOTAL ⟨the dim trees below me were in ~ stillness —John Galsworthy⟩ **b :** lacking in no essential detail : fully developed : COMPLETE, WHOLE ⟨have a ~ baby⟩ ⟨the memory of that night remained intact and ~ —Elinor Wylie⟩ ⟨complete justification of belief does not depend on . . . ~ knowledge —W.F.Hambly⟩ **c** *obs* : possessing all one's mental faculties : SANE ⟨I fear I am not in my ~ mind —Shak.⟩ **d :** being without qualification : ABSOLUTE, UNEQUIVOCAL ⟨God possesses ~ power —Charles Hartshorne⟩ ⟨has a ~ right to use this division —James Jeans⟩ ⟨treats him like a ~ stranger⟩ ⟨looks like a ~ angel in her organdy pinafore⟩ **e :** of an extreme kind : UNMITIGATED ⟨a ~ little snob —Eugene Walter⟩ ⟨a ~ tirade of abuse —S.H.Holbrook⟩ ⟨the dog had been in a ~ frenzy, trying to get out —Erle Stanley Gardner⟩ **4** *obs* : fully grown or legally competent : MATURE ⟨sons at ~ age —Shak.⟩ **5** [LL *perfectus*, fr. L] : of, relating to, or constituting a form of the verb or verbal that expresses an action or state completed at the time of speaking or at a time spoken of — compare FUTURE PERFECT, PAST PERFECT, PRESENT PERFECT **6** *obs* **a :** CERTAIN, SURE ⟨thou art ~ then, our ship hath touched upon . . . Bohemia —Shak.⟩ **b :** SATISFIED, CONTENT ⟨then comes my fit again: I had else been ~ —Shak.⟩ **7 a** *of an interval* : belonging to the consonances (as unison, fourth, fifth, and octave) that retain their character when inverted and when raised or lowered by a half step become augmented or diminished — compare MAJOR **b** (1) : of or relating to a note (as a large) in mensural notation equaling three rather than two of the next lower denomination (as a long) (2) *of a rhythmic mode* : being in triple time **8 a :** having its distinctive characters fully developed : TYPICAL ⟨a ~ lesion⟩ ⟨a ~ jellyfish⟩ **b :** sexually mature and fully differentiated — used esp. of an insect in the imago stage ⟨the click beetle (the ~ stage of the wireworm) —*Farming*⟩ **c :** MONOCLINOUS

**²per·fect** \pə(r)'fekt *sometimes* 'pərfikt *or* 'pə̄f- *or* 'pəif-\ vt -ED/-ING/-S [alter. (influenced by L *perfectus*) of ME *perfiten, parfiten*, fr. *perfit, parfit*, adj.] **1 :** to bring to a state of supreme excellence : rid of faults or drawbacks : IMPROVE, REFINE ⟨art must be selective; nature must be ~*ed* —G.C. Sellery⟩ ⟨rhetoric . . . seeks to ~ men by showing them better versions of themselves —R.M.Weaver⟩ ⟨laboratory methods for examining foods had been still further ~*ed* —V.G. Heiser⟩ **2 a :** to plan or carry out to the last detail : bring to a successful conclusion : FINISH ⟨arrangements we're ~*ing* to keep newspaper reporters from bothering you —Erle Stanley Gardner⟩ ⟨youthful learners who desired to . . . ~ their education —H.O.Taylor⟩ **b :** to complete or put in final form in conformity with law ⟨to defeat the federal priority a lien . . . must be both specific and ~*ed* —*Harvard Law Rev.*⟩ **c :** to print the second side of (a sheet already printed on one side) : back up **3 :** to instruct or inform fully ⟨the object of this society is . . . to ~ its members practically and scientifically —G.B.Cummings⟩ **syn** see UNFOLD

**³perfect** \like ¹PERFECT\ adv [alter. (influenced by L *perfectus*) of ME *perfit, parfit*, fr. *perfit, parfit*, adj.] *chiefly dial* : PERFECTLY

**⁴perfect** \like ¹PERFECT\ n -S [¹*perfect*] **1 :** one that is perfect ⟨the ~*s* go into one bag and the rejects into another —*Listener*⟩ **2 a :** the perfect tense of a language **b :** a verb form in the perfect tense

**per·fect·abil·i·ty** \like PERFECTIBILITY\ n [by alter.] : PERFECTIBILITY

**per·fect·able** \like PERFECTIBLE\ adj [by alter.] : PERFECTIBLE

**perfect binder** n : a machine for producing perfect-bound books and pamphlets

**perfect binding** n : a bookbinding in which single leaves are held together with a backbone adhesive

**perfect-bound** \;=;=\ adj : produced by perfect binding ⟨*perfect-bound* books⟩

**perfect cadence** n : a cadence consisting of a dominant to tonic harmony with the root of the tonic appearing in both the bass and the soprano — called also *full cadence;* compare IMPERFECT CADENCE; see CADENCE illustration

**perfect cocktail** n : a cocktail consisting of equal parts of French vermouth, Italian vermouth, and gin shaken with ice and strained before serving

**perfect competition** n : COMPETITION 4b

**perfect correlation** n : correlation for which the Pearsonian coefficient or its equivalent for multiple correlation is 1

**perfected** adj [fr. past part. of ²*perfect*] : brought to a state of perfection : COMPLETED, REFINED — **per·fect·ed·ly** adv

**perfect engine** n : IDEAL ENGINE

**¹per·fect·er** \pronunc at ¹PERFECT + ə(r)\ *comparative of* PERFECT

**²per·fect·er** \pronunc at ²PERFECT + ə(r)\ n -S **1 :** one that perfects **2 :** PERFECTING PRESS

**perfectest** *superlative of* PERFECT

**perfect flower** n : a monoclinous flower

**perfect form** n : PERFECT STAGE

**perfect fungus** n : a fungus known to produce sexual spores (as zygospores, ascospores, basidiospores)

**perfect game** n : a no-hit no-run baseball game in which no batter reaches first base ⟨a pitcher has to be . . . doubly fortunate to pitch a *perfect game* —Vic Wall⟩

**perfect gas** n : IDEAL GAS

**per·fec·ti** \pə(r)'fek,tī, -,tē\ n pl [ML, fr. L, pl. of *perfectus* perfect — more at PERFECT] : members of the most extreme and ascetic class constituting the elite of various religious sects (as the Cathari or the Manichaeans)

**per·fect·ibil·ian** \(,)pər,fektə'bilēən, ,pərfik-, -lyən\ n -S [*perfectibility* + *-an*] : PERFECTIONIST

**per·fect·ibil·ism** \pər'fektəbə,lizəm, 'pərfik-\ n -S [*perfectibility* + *-ism*] : PERFECTIONISM

**per·fect·ibil·ist** \pər'fektəbələst\ n -S [*perfectibility* + *-ist*] **1 :** a believer in perfectibility : PERFECTIONIST **2 perfectibilists** *pl, usu cap* : ILLUMINATI 1b **3** *usu cap* : ALUMBRADO

**per·fect·ibil·i·tar·i·an** \pər,fektə,bilə'terēən, ,pərfik-\ n -S [*perfectibility* + *-arian*] : PERFECTIONIST 1

**per·fect·ibil·i·ty** \pər,fektə'biləd·ē *sometimes* ,pərfik-\ n -ES [F *perfectibilité*, fr. *perfectible* + *-ité* -ity] **1 a :** a capacity for progress or improvement esp. in the attainment of moral excellence ⟨believed in rationalism, progress, and the infinite ~ of the human race —J.G.Colton⟩ **b :** PERFECTIONISM 1 ⟨the New England mind turned from ~ . . . to intellectual progress —H.S.Canby⟩ **c :** a belief advanced by Lessing that religion is rooted in humanitarian morality rather than dogmatic creed and is therefore subject to improvement **2 :** PERFECTION ⟨ever the craftsman seeking ~ in . . . art —*Saturday Rev.*⟩

**per·fect·ible** \pər'fektəbəl *sometimes* 'pərfik-\ adj [F, fr. ML *perfectibilis*, fr. L *perfectus* perfect + *-ibilis* -ible — more at PERFECT] : capable of being improved or attaining to perfection ⟨if men are not perfect, they are at least indefinitely ~ —M.R.Cohen⟩

**perfect induction** n : ENUMERATIVE INDUCTION

**perfecting** n -S [fr. gerund of ²*perfect*] : an act or instance of completion or refinement ⟨man seems not to be evolving at all . . . except in minor ~*s* of his vertical posture —Weston La Barre⟩

**perfecting press** n : a press that prints paper on both sides at the same time

**¹per·fec·tion** \pə(r)'fekshən\ n -S [ME *perfeccioun*, fr. OF *perfection*, fr. L *perfection-, perfectio*, fr. *perfectus* (past part. of *perficere* to complete, perfect) + *-ion-, -io* -ion — more at ¹PERFECT] **1 a** *obs* : the quality or state of being finished : COMPLETION, WHOLENESS **b :** the condition of having reached full development : MATURITY, RIPENESS ⟨Greek civilization, as it slowly flowered to ~ —Agnes Repplier⟩ **c :** an exemplification of supreme moral or physical excellence ⟨her figure was ~ —Max Peacock⟩ **2 a :** freedom from fault or defect : correspondence with or approximation to an ideal concept : FLAWLESSNESS ⟨the diminutive ~ and wonder of leaf, berry, sand whorl —E.B.Garside⟩ ⟨collection . . . noteworthy for its ~ of preparation and mounting —*City Library Bull. Springfield (Mass.)*⟩ ⟨postulated a progressive evolution in human history toward . . . ~ —Allen Johnson⟩; *specif* : SAINTLINESS ⟨the grand aim of the Buddhist is to attain a ~ like Buddha's —A.M.Fairbairn⟩ **b :** an unsurpassable degree of accuracy or excellence : CULMINATION ⟨difficult to find solitude to such ~ upon earth nowadays —Richard Semon⟩ **3 :** the act or process of freeing from faults or drawbacks : IMPROVEMENT, REFINEMENT ⟨worked toward the ~ of the fountain pen⟩ ⟨charity will be the foremost virtue in the active ~ of a Christian —D.J.Unger⟩ **4 a :** skillful execution : complete mastery of technique : PROFICIENCY, VIRTUOSITY ⟨~ is what we strive for constantly in the ballet —Moira Shearer⟩ ⟨ancient rock drawings of amazing ~ and complexity —*Geog. Jour.*⟩ **b** *archaic* : a trait or skill acquired by education or practice : ACCOMPLISHMENT ⟨I am not master of any of those ~*s* —John Dryden⟩ **5 :** triple time in mensural notation **syn** see EXCELLENCE

**²perfection** \"\ vt -ED/-ING/-S : PERFECT

**per·fec·tion·ate** \-shə,nāt\ vt -ED/-ING/-S [¹*perfection* + *-ate*] *archaic* : PERFECT

**per·fec·tion·ism** \-shə,nizəm\ n -S **1 :** a belief in perfectibility: as **a :** the ethical doctrine that self-realization or the perfection of moral character constitutes man's highest good **b :** the theological doctrine that a state of freedom from sin is attainable or has been attained in the earthly life **c** *usu cap* : the utopian principles governing the 19th century Christian communist community at Oneida, N.Y. **2 :** a disposition to regard anything short of perfection as unacceptable ⟨~ no less than isolationism . . . may obstruct the paths to international peace —F.D.Roosevelt⟩

**¹per·fec·tion·ist** \-sh(ə)nəst\ n -S [¹*perfection* + *-ist*] **1 :** an adherent of perfectionism: as **a :** one who believes in the ethical or spiritual perfectibility of mankind ⟨a Puritan ~ —*Saturday Rev.*⟩ **b** *usu cap* : a member of the original Oneida Community practicing perfectionism **c :** one who claims to have attained moral perfection or sinlessness **2 :** one that demands or works to achieve perfection ⟨they are ~*s* and will either have the best or nothing at all —Nancy Mitford⟩ ⟨a ~, he rehearsed one scene . . . 50 times —*Time*⟩

**²perfectionist** \"\ *also* **per·fec·tion·is·tic** \pə(r);feksha'nistik, -tēk\ adj : of, relating to, or characterized by perfection or perfectionism

**per·fec·tion·ize** \=ˈ=shə,nīz\ vt -ED/-ING/-S [¹*perfection* + *-ize*] *archaic* : PERFECT

**perfection loop knot** n : a knot used by anglers to tie a fixed loop in a leader or spinning line

**per·fec·tion·ment** \-shənmənt\ n -S [²*perfection* + *-ment*] : the act or process of bringing to perfection : IMPROVEMENT, REFINEMENT

**per·fect·ist** \pər'fektəst, 'pərfik-\ n -S [¹*perfect* + *-ist*] **1 :** one of the perfecti **2 :** PERFECTIONIST

**¹per·fec·tive** \pər'fektiv, 'pərfik-\ adj [ML *perfectivus*, fr. L *perfectus* (past part. of *perficere* to complete, perfect) + *-ivus* -ive — more at PERFECT] **1** *archaic* **a :** tending to make perfect **b :** being in the process of improvement : becoming better **2 :** expressing action as complete or as implying the notion of completion, conclusion, or result — used of a form or aspect of the verb; opposed to *imperfective* — **perfectively** adv — **perfectiveness** n -ES — **perfectivity** n -ES

**²perfective** \"\ n -S **1 :** the perfective aspect of a language **2 :** a verb form in the perfective aspect

**per·fec·tiv·iza·tion** \pər,fektəvə'zāshən, -,vī'z-\ n -S : the act or process of perfectivizing

**per·fec·tiv·ize** \=ˈ==,vīz\ vt -ED/-ING/-S [¹*perfective* + *-ize*] : to make perfective

**per·fect·ly** \'pərfik(t)lē, 'pə̄f-,'pəif-, -fēk-, -li\ adv [alter. (influenced by L *perfectus* perfect) of ME *perfitly, parfitly*, fr. *perfit, parfit* perfect + *-ly* — more at PERFECT] **1 a :** to the fullest extent : COMPLETELY, THOROUGHLY ⟨a ~ deliberate measure —Ralph Linton⟩ ⟨a ~ straight face⟩ ⟨poems . . . ~ suited to an occasion —J.D.Hart⟩ **b :** to a precise degree : ACCURATELY ⟨breadboard, which is ~ round —*New Yorker*⟩ ⟨~ predictable electronic reactions —Robert Bendiner⟩ **c :** to an adequate extent : QUITE ⟨most parents . . . manage to raise ~ good children —B.M.Beck⟩ **d** *dial* : EXACTLY ⟨~ as if she were back on her own porch —Maristan Chapman⟩ **2 :** in a flawless manner : FAULTLESSLY, IDEALLY ⟨attractive churches, ~ kept parks, playgrounds —*Amer. Guide Series: Minn.*⟩ ⟨sang ~ —Virgil Thomson⟩

**per·fect·ness** \-k(t)nəs\ n -ES [alter. (influenced by L *perfectus*) of ME *perfitnesse, parfitnesse*, fr. *perfit, parfit* + *-nesse* -ness] : PERFECTION; *esp* : moral excellence

**perfect number** n : an integer (as 6) the sum of whose divisors including 1 but excluding itself is equal to itself ⟨28, which = 1 + 2 + 4 + 7 + 14, is a *perfect number*⟩ — compare IMPERFECT NUMBER

**per·fec·to** \pə(r)'fek(,)tō\ n -S [Sp, perfect, fr. L *perfectus* — more at PERFECT] : a cigar that is thick in the middle and tapers almost to a point at each end

**per·fec·tor** \pər'fektə(r), 'pərfik-\ n -S [L, fr. *perfectus* (past part. of *perficere* to complete, perfect) + *-or* — more at PERFECT] **1 :** one that perfects **2** *or* **perfector press** : PERFECTING PRESS

**perfect participle** n : PAST PARTICIPLE

**perfect radiator** n : an ideal black body absorbing all the radiation falling upon it and therefore constituting the best possible radiator

**perfect ream** n : PRINTER'S REAM

**perfects** *pres 3d sing of* PERFECT, *pl of* PERFECT

**perfect square** n : a number or expression that is the square of a number or expression of the class under consideration; *esp* : an integral rational term that is the square of an integral rational term ⟨9 is a *perfect square* because it is the square of 3⟩ or a trinomial that is the square of a binomial ⟨$a^2 + 2ab + b^2$ is the *perfect square* of $a + b$⟩

**perfect stage** n : the stage in the life cycle of a fungus at which sexual spores are produced — compare PERFECT FUNGUS

**per·fec·tum** \pə(r)'fektəm\ n -S [NL, fr. neut. of L *perfectus* perfect — more at PERFECT] : an aspectual category of tenses in Latin that includes all which indicate that action or state is completed in contrast with those tenses which indicate that action or state is in progress — compare INFECTUM

**perfect usufruct** n : a usufruct whose subject matter is not destroyed by its normal use and enjoyment though it may be subject to depreciation or gradual deterioration

**perfect year** n : a common year of 355 days or a leap year of 385 days in the Jewish calendar — see YEAR table

**per·fer·vid** \,pər, (')per+\ adj [NL *perfervidus*, fr. L *per-* thoroughly + *fervidus* fervid — more at PER-, FERVID] : extremely or excessively fervent : ZEALOUS, IMPASSIONED ⟨the ~ beliefs of religious converts —Edward Glover⟩ ⟨a ~ patriot —R.A.Austen-Leigh⟩ ⟨~ adolescent sexuality —John Farrelly⟩ ⟨~ screams from the press about freedom of the press —J.W. Albig⟩ **syn** see IMPASSIONED

**per·fi·cient** \pə(r)'fishənt\ adj [L *perficient-, perficiens*, pres. part. of *perficere* to complete, perfect — more at PERFECT] *archaic* : having decisive influence or authority : EFFECTIVE

**per·fid·i·ous** \pə(r)ˈfidēəs\ *adj* [L *perfidiosus*, fr. *perfidia* perfidy + *-osus* -ous — more at PERFIDY] **:** of, relating to, or characterized by perfidy **:** DECEITFUL, TREACHEROUS ⟨that common but most ~ refuge of men of letters . . . the profession of teaching —Matthew Arnold⟩ **syn** see FAITHLESS

**per·fid·i·ous·ly** *adv* **:** in a perfidious manner ⟨~ playing one side against the other⟩

**per·fid·i·ous·ness** *n* -ES **:** PERFIDY

**per·fi·dy** \ˈpərfədē, ˈpə̄f-, ˈpəif-, -di\ *n* -ES [L *perfidia*, fr. *perfidus* faithless, dishonest (fr. *per-* deviating from + *fides* faith) + *-ia* -y] **1 :** the quality or state of being dishonest or disloyal **:** DECEIT, TREACHERY ⟨such obvious liars that their ~ palled after it ceased to be amusing —W.A.White⟩ ⟨the name of Judas has become a byword of covetousness and ~ —Samuel Cox⟩ **2 :** an act or instance of deception or betrayal ⟨tirades of a slighted lover against the beloved object's *perfidies* —C.E. Montague⟩

**per·filo·graph** \(ˌ)pərˈfīləˌgraf, -fil-, -ˌrȧf\ *n* [L *per filum* by means of a cord (fr. *per* by means of, through + *filum* cord, thread) + E *-o-* + *-graph* — more at FOR, FILE] **:** an instrument for recording undulations in the bottom of a river or harbor channel

**perf·ins** \ˈpərˌfinz\ *n pl* [*perf*orated *in*itial*s*] **:** PERFORATED INITIALS

**per·fit** \ˈpərfət, ˈpärfət, (ˌ)pərˈfēt\ *dial var of* PERFECT

**per·flate** \pə(r)ˈflāt\ *vt* -ED/-ING/-S [L *perflatus*, past part. of *perflare*, fr. *per-* + *flare* to blow — more at BLOW] *archaic* **:** VENTILATE 3

**perflatile** *adj* [L *perflatilis*, fr. *perflatus* + *-ilis* -ile] *obs* **:** open to the wind

**per·fla·tion** \pə(r)ˈflāshən\ *n* -S [LL *perflation-*, *perflatio*, fr. L *perflatus* + *-ion-*, *-io* -ion] **:** VENTILATION

**per·flu·ent** \(ˌ)pərˈflüənt, ˈpərˌflüə-, ˈpərfləwə-\ *adj* [L *perfluent-*, *perfluens*, pres. part. of *perfluere* to flow through, fr. *per-* + *fluere* to flow — more at FLUENT] *archaic* **:** flowing through **:** FLOWING

**perfluor-** *or* **perfluoro-** *comb form* [ISV *per-* + *fluor-*] **:** containing a relatively large amount of fluorine esp. in place of hydrogen ⟨*perfluoro*octane $C_8F_{18}$⟩

**per·fluorinate** \ˌpər, (ˈ)per+\ *vt* [*per-* + *fluorinate*] **:** to combine with the maximum amount of fluorine esp. in place of hydrogen

**per·foliate** \ˌpər, (ˈ)per+\ *adj* [NL *perfoliata*, an herb having leaves pierced by the stem, fr. L *per* through + *foliata*, fem. of *foliatus* foliate — more at FOR, FOLIATE] **1 :** having the basal part naturally united around the stem — used of a leaf (as of many honeysuckles) apparently perforated by the stem or petiole **2 :** having the terminal joints expanded into flattened plates and encircling the stalk which connects them — used of the antenna of an insect (as a lamellicorn beetle) — **per·folia·tion** \ˌpər, ˌper+\ *n*

**per·fo·ra·ble** \ˈpərf(ə)rəbəl, ˈpə̄f-,ˈpəif-\ *adj* [*perforate* + *-able*] **:** capable of being perforated

**per·fo·ra·ta** \ˌ=ˈrād·ə, -rad·ə\ *n pl, cap* [NL, fr. L, neut. pl. of *perforatus* — more at PERFORATE] **1 :** a division of corals including those (as members of the genus *Porites*) whose skeleton has a porous texture — opposed to *Aporosa* **2 :** a division of Foraminifera including those having shells with small perforations for the protrusion of pseudopodia

**¹per·fo·rate** \ˈpərfəˌrāt, ˈpə̄f-,ˈpəif-, *usu* -ād.+V\ *vb* -ED/-ING/-S [L *perforatus*, past part. of *perforare* to bore through, fr. *per-* + *forare* to bore — more at BORE] *vt* **1 a :** to make a hole through **:** PIERCE, PUNCTURE ⟨~ a jar top to give a captured butterfly air⟩ ⟨tarpaulins liberally *perforated* by small V-shaped rents —I.T.Sanderson⟩ ⟨~ a stamp in making a cut cancellation⟩ ⟨an ulcer ~*s* the duodenal wall⟩; *specif* **:** to make a line of holes or small incisions in (as a sheet of stamps or coupons) to facilitate separation **b :** to make a hole or opening in **:** PIT, INDENT ⟨gopher holes ~ the range⟩ ⟨scenic fjords ~ the coastline⟩ **c :** to enter or extend through ⟨divisions of the eighth nerve . . . again ~ the dura mater through smaller openings —G.V.Ellis⟩ **2 :** to make (a hole or design) by boring or piercing ⟨tools for *perforating* thousands of different patterns —*Industrial Equipment News*⟩ ~ *vi* **1 :** to penetrate a surface ⟨occasionally an ulcer ~*s* . . . just when it seems to be well under control —Frank Forty⟩ **2 :** to pierce the casing of an oil well at a desired depth to allow the oil to seep in

**syn** PERFORATE, PUNCTURE, PUNCH, PRICK, BORE, and DRILL mean, in common, to pierce so as to leave a hole. PERFORATE, though it can mean to pierce, now applies chiefly to the making, usu. by machine, of a series of small holes in a line or pattern for ornamentation, identification, or ease of separation ⟨boat stones, resembling canoes and sometimes *perforated* to be worn as pendants —*Amer. Guide Series: N.J.*⟩ ⟨a monogram *perforated* on each title page⟩ ⟨a set of pins that *perforates* an entire sheet at one operation —Al Burns⟩ PUNCTURE implies the passing of a sharp pointed instrument into or through a tissue, substance, or material, often carrying also the added connotation of deflation ⟨the dark green blind that was *punctured* here and there, admitting starlike bits of light —Jean Stafford⟩ ⟨today we have holes that *puncture* the earth's shell as much as three miles —*Lamp*⟩ ⟨*puncture* a balloon or a tire⟩ PUNCH is often interchangeable with PERFORATE esp. when a mechanical device is used ⟨a bullet an inch and a half in diameter was formerly big enough to *punch* holes in a tank —G.R.Harrison⟩ ⟨an army captain had invented a system of dot-and-dash symbols which could be *punched* out on thick paper and read by touch at night —*Time*⟩ ⟨cement mixer . . . crashed through a buried septic tank early yesterday afternoon, *punching* a large crater in the earth —*Springfield (Mass.) Union*⟩ ⟨a machine for *punching* cards for automatic computing machines⟩ PRICK implies a piercing with a sharp fine point to make a small hole or inflict a superficial wound ⟨*prick* a finger with a needle⟩ ⟨urged the laggards along by *pricking* them with the point of his bayonet⟩ ⟨seedlings were *pricking* through the soil —Anne Dorrance⟩ BORE suggests excavation or the use of a rotating cutting tool, as an auger or broach; in figurative use, as distinguished from DRILL, BORE suggests a slow continuous penetrating by force ⟨three tunnels were *bored* —Tom Marvel⟩ ⟨holes *bored* in the beach by small reddish crabs —J.G.Frazer⟩ ⟨*bore* one's way patiently through a dense crowd of spectators⟩ DRILL commonly implies the use of a pointed or sharp rotating tool for boring holes in hard substances; in figurative use, as distinguished from BORE, DRILL suggests a forced penetration through repetitive persistence ⟨*drill* a hole through a plank⟩ ⟨*drill* a sheet of metal in several places⟩ ⟨it is firmly *drilled* into the minds of ministers by their officials that only in red tape can security be found in war —E.H.Collis⟩

**²per·fo·rate** \-f(ə)rə̇t, -fəˌrāt, *usu* |d.+V\ *adj* [L *perforatus*, past part. of *perforare*] **1 :** PERFORATED **2 a :** having a permanently open umbilicus at the origin of the whorls **:** UMBILICATE — used of a spiral shell; compare IMPERFORATE **b :** of or relating to the Perforata

**perforated** *adj* **:** having a hole or series of holes **:** PIERCED, PUNCTURED ⟨~ eardrum⟩ ⟨~ answer sheet for correcting tests⟩ ⟨cream cheese, made of clabber drained in ~ molds —*Amer. Guide Series: La.*⟩ ⟨~ cancellation⟩; *specif* **:** having a (specified) number of perforations in 20 millimeters ⟨the stamps are ~ 13 —Yoshitsugu Mishima & Helen K. Zirkle⟩

**perforated ax** *n* **:** a prehistoric stone ax head pierced by a hole for the insertion of a handle

**perforated initials** *n pl* **1 :** a set of initials (as a business monogram) or other design pierced into a postage stamp as a means of identification or as a safeguard against theft **2 :** stamps having perforated initials

**perforated space** *also* **perforate space** *n* **:** any of three small areas on the lower surface of the brain that are perforated by many small openings for blood vessels and that are situated two anteriorly at the commencement of the fissure of Sylvius and one posteriorly between the mammillary bodies in front and the cerebral peduncles laterally

**perforating** *n* -S [fr. gerund of ¹*perforate*] **:** PERFORATION

**perforating rule** *n* **:** a notched steel or brass printer's rule a little more than type high used for making perforations

**per·fo·ra·tion** \ˌpərfəˈrāshən, ˌpə̄f-, ˌpəif-\ *n* -S [NL, fr. L *perforatus* + NL *-orium* — more at PERFORATE] **1 :** the act or process of perforating ⟨a machine for the ~ of a sheet of stamps at one stroke⟩; *specif* **:** the penetration of a body part through accident or disease ⟨spontaneous ~ of the sigmoid colon in the presence of diverticulosis —*Jour. Amer. Med. Assoc.*⟩ **2 a** (1) **:** a hole or pattern made by piercing or boring ⟨~*s* on the edge of the film engage sprockets in the projector⟩ ⟨mark all ~*s* which indicate seams, darts . . . and buttonhole locations —*Needlecraft for the Home*⟩ ⟨overprints gave way to ~*s* —Gordon Ward⟩; *specif* **:** a series or one of a series of holes made in a shoe upper for ornament or ventilation (2) **:** a series of small incisions to facilitate tearing along a predetermined line **b** (1) **:** one of the series of holes made between rows of postage stamps in a sheet — compare PIN PERFORATION, ROULETTE (2) **:** one of the teeth on the edge of a detached stamp resulting from tearing along the series of holes (3) *or* **perforation number :** a philatelic classification based on the number of perforations along the edge of a stamp per 20 millimeters **c :** a rupture in a body part caused by accident or disease **d :** a natural opening in an organ or body part ⟨small ~*s* opening at the bottom of the sulci —Ferdinand Canu & R.S.Bassler⟩

**perforation gauge** *n* **:** a calibrated strip of cardboard, celluloid, or metal for determining the perforation number of a stamp

**perforation tooth** *n* **:** TOOTH 3e

**per·fo·ra·tor** \ˈ==ˌrād·ə(r), -ātə-\ *n* -S **:** one that perforates: as **a :** a prehistoric stone or bone implement for drilling or boring holes **b :** a mechanical device for punching holes or designs through or into a flat surface ⟨check ~⟩ ⟨hand ~ that punches up to 12 sheets without tearing⟩ ⟨railroads use ~*s* for dating tickets —*Office Appliance Manual*⟩; *specif* **:** a telegraphic apparatus that perforates a continuous tape according to code (as for use in a tape transmitter) **c :** an operator of a machine that makes perforations (as in paper or leather) **d :** a device resembling a gun for puncturing an oil well casing at the oil stratum

**per·fo·ra·to·ri·um** \ˌpərf(ə)rəˈtōrēəm\ *n, pl* **perforato·ria** \-ēə\ [NL, fr. L *perforator* + *-ium*] **:** ACROSOME

**per·force** \ˌpə(r)+\ *adv* [ME *par force*, fr. MF, fr. *par* by (fr. L *per* through, by) + *force* — more at FOR, FORCE] **1** *obs* **:** by physical coercion **:** FORCIBLY ⟨he rushed into my house and took ~ my ring away —Shak.⟩ **2 :** by force of circumstances or of necessity **:** WILLY-NILLY ⟨steppe folk must . . . dwell ~ in skin tents or in subterranean shelters —V.G.Childe⟩ ⟨antistatism and the distrust of governmental power has been ~ swept away in a world in which only the cohesive civilization can survive —Max Lerner⟩

**per·form** *R* pə(r)ˈfȯ(ə)rm, *-R* pəˈfȯ(ə)m\ *vb* -ED/-ING/-S [ME *parformen, performen*, fr. AF *parformer, performer*, alter. (influenced by OF *forme, fourme* form) of OF *parfournir, perfournir*, fr. *par-, per-* thoroughly (fr. L *per-*) + *fournir* to complete, carry out, accomplish — more at FORM, PER-, FURNISH] *vt* **1 a :** to adhere to the terms of **:** treat as an obligation **:** IMPLEMENT, FULFILL ⟨~ a contract⟩ ⟨when she promised a thing she was . . . scrupulous in ~*ing* it —Jane Austen⟩ **b** *obs* **:** to effect as an agent **:** ACTUATE, ENACT ⟨hast thou, spirit, ~*ed* to point the tempest that I bade thee —Shak.⟩ **c :** to bring to a finished state **:** COMPLETE ⟨passenger miles ~*ed* by Class I railways —*Yrbk. of Railroad Information*⟩ ⟨a student who . . . fails to ~ satisfactorily the work of his course —*Univ. of Toronto Cal.*⟩ **2 a :** to carry out or bring about **:** ACCOMPLISH, EXECUTE ⟨~ a function⟩ ⟨~ calculations with astronomical speed —Stuart Chase⟩ ⟨figurines which once ~*ed* amusing antics actuated by power from a waterwheel —*Amer. Guide Series: Conn.*⟩ ⟨imaginative editing can ~ miracles in creating interest —F.L.Mott⟩ ⟨dissections were ~*ed* on monkeys —Benjamin Farrington⟩ **b :** to make available or do in line of duty **:** PROVIDE ⟨the university ~*s* more than 50 distinct services to the state —*Amer. Guide Series: Mich.*⟩ ⟨services ~*ed* by New Zealand forces in Korea —*Americana Annual*⟩ **3** *archaic* **:** to construct or give aesthetic form to **:** DESIGN ⟨a ship . . . may be as well ~*ed* as such large buildings —William Sutherland⟩ **4 a :** to do in a formal manner or according to prescribed ritual ⟨~ a marriage ceremony⟩ ⟨dramatic satisfaction . . . in a High Mass well ~*ed* —T.S.Eliot⟩ **b :** to give a rendition of **:** PRESENT, PLAY ⟨~*ed* a hula . . . to entertain the passengers —Horace Sutton⟩ ⟨guest conductors ~*ed* certain new scores on tolerance —Virgil Thomson⟩ ⟨two of his plays had been ~*ed* by the dramatic club —Gilbert Millstein⟩ ~ *vi* **1 :** to carry out an action or pattern of behavior **:** fulfill a threat or promise **:** ACT, FUNCTION ⟨not only promised but ~*ed* —V.L.Albjerg⟩ ⟨about one third of one's time must be spent in sleep if one is to ~ effectively —Webb Garrison⟩ ⟨the car ~*ed* beautifully except on a short incline —M.M.Musselman⟩ **2 :** to give a performance **:** put on a show **:** PLAY ⟨~ under a circus tent⟩ ⟨experience as a composer helps him understand the problems of ~*ing* —*Time*⟩

**syn** EXECUTE, DISCHARGE, ACCOMPLISH, ACHIEVE, EFFECT, FULFILL: PERFORM usu. implies an act for which a process or pattern of movement has already been established, esp. one calling for skill or precision, or for the assignment or assumption of responsibility ⟨*perform* a dance⟩ ⟨*perform* drill work in rhythm⟩ ⟨*perform* a miracle⟩ ⟨*perform* an experiment⟩ ⟨*perform* one's duties⟩ ⟨they examine patients and *perform* simple forms of treatment under supervision —*Bull. of Meharry Med. Coll.*⟩ ⟨*perform* such courtesies as writing letters of thanks to those who assisted —W.T.Gruhn⟩ ⟨there were certain important functions which it was expected to *perform* —W.B.Graves⟩ EXECUTE, similar to PERFORM, stresses more the completion, esp. the skillful completion, of the process or pattern of movement ⟨*execute* a dance step⟩ ⟨*execute* maneuvers⟩ ⟨*execute* a difficult task⟩ ⟨the escape was planned meticulously and *executed* boldly —Edmond Taylor⟩ ⟨*executed* a precise and calculated campaign —V.L.Albjerg⟩ DISCHARGE is generally used of the execution, esp. in full, of duties or obligations ⟨*discharge* a debt to society⟩ ⟨*discharge* a monetary obligation⟩ ⟨before setting sail he *discharged* all arrears of business and heard last-minute petitions and appeals —P.J.Phelan⟩ ACCOMPLISH emphasizes the idea of successful, often triumphant, completion of an act or attainment of an objective, esp. one involving some difficulty ⟨society enabled them to *accomplish* difficult enterprises —H.M.Parshley⟩ ⟨this project was so vast and so quickly *accomplished* that it has no parallel —Lou Stoumen⟩ ⟨elementary education . . . has tried to *accomplish* something when it should merely have tried to begin something —George Sampson⟩ ⟨help a man to *accomplish* his destiny —W.J.Locke⟩ ACHIEVE emphasizes the notion of a difficult end gained or of honor acquired in the process ⟨*achieve* distinction⟩ ⟨*achieved* a long-hoped-for dream —*Americana Annual*⟩ ⟨the heights he has since *achieved* —Alec Bishop⟩ EFFECT, like ACHIEVE, emphasizes the notion of a difficult end gained but focuses the mind more on the force of the effective agent ⟨were imprisoned until Aug. 6, when friends *effected* their release —*Amer. Guide Series: Del.*⟩ ⟨a chance to *effect* a compromise —*Amer. Guide Series: N. C.*⟩ ⟨done more than perhaps any other modern critic to *effect* a revaluation of English literature —Edmund Wilson⟩ FULFILL implies a full realization of what exists potentially, or hitherto in conception, or in the nature or sense of responsibility of the agent ⟨*fulfill* a promise⟩ ⟨*fulfilled* his last duty —C.S.Forester⟩ ⟨*fulfill* human hopes —A.E.Stevenson b.1900⟩ ⟨*fulfill* the whole purpose of language —A.L.Guérard⟩

**per·form·able** \-məbəl\ *adj* **:** capable of being performed

**per for·mam do·ni** \ˌperˌfȯrˌmämˈdōˌnē\ *adv* [L, through the form of a gift] **:** in accordance with the terms of the gift — used of the disposition of an estate as designated by the donor rather than by operation of the law

**per·form·ance** *R* pə(r)ˈfȯrmən(t)s, *-R* pəˈfȯ(ə)m-\ *n* -S **1 a :** the act or process of carrying out something **:** the execution of an action ⟨a repetitive act the ~ of which is facilitated by repetition —D.W.Maurer & V.H.Vogel⟩ ⟨satisfactory ~ on achievement tests —S.C.Brownstein & Mitchel Weiner⟩ **b :** something accomplished or carried out **:** ACCOMPLISHMENT, FEAT ⟨could entertain in his own house — a difficult if not impossible ~ in the present dearth of domestic help —E.H.Collis⟩ **c :** a literary or artistic composition **:** WORK ⟨for a new writer this novel would be rated a brilliant ~ —E.C.Wagenknecht⟩ **2 :** the fulfillment of a claim, promise, or request **:** IMPLEMENTATION ⟨contracts whose ~ would violate the act are unenforceable —*Harvard Law Rev.*⟩ **3 a :** the action of representing a character in a dramatic work ⟨congratulated him on his daughter's ~ in the play⟩ **b :** a public presentation or exhibition ⟨his current collection of sculpture and paintings . . . is a truly handsome ~ —R.M.Coates⟩ ⟨the play ran for 285 ~*s*⟩ ⟨the orchestra gave a benefit ~⟩ ⟨the first ~ of a new symphony⟩ **c :** something resembling a dramatic representation ⟨get the child to a place where you both can get over the effects of such a ~ —H.R.Litchfield & L.H.Dembo⟩ ⟨looking to see if anyone caught them going through such a silly ~ —G.E. & Nettie MacGinitie⟩ **4 a :** the ability to perform **:** capacity to achieve a desired result **:** EFFICIENCY ⟨senescence represents a marked decline in function and ~ —George Lawton⟩ ⟨a good power-weight ratio not only improves ~ but lowers fuel consumption —Grenville Manton⟩ **b :** the factors (as speed, rate of climb, ceiling) influencing such capacity in an airplane **c :** the acceleration, power, and speed of an automobile **5 :** the manner of reacting to various stimuli **:** BEHAVIOR ⟨variation in the ~ of the skin structures⟩ ⟨the ~ of the stock market⟩; *specif* **:** the rate of sale of a product ⟨the bookseller enters the Christmas and spring selling seasons . . . with hundreds of unknown books whose ~ he must watch —*Canadian Forum*⟩

**performance bond** *n* **:** a surety bond guaranteeing faithful performance of a contract — compare CONTRACT BOND

**performance test** *n* **:** a test of capacity to achieve a desired result; *esp* **:** an intelligence test (as by a form board, maze, or picture completion) requiring little use of language

**per·form·ato·ry** \-məˌtōrē, -tȯr-, -ri\ *adj* [*perform* + *-atory*] **:** of, relating to, or based on performance ⟨"I'll do it" is a ~ utterance⟩

**per·form·er** \-mə(r)\ *n* -S **:** one that performs ⟨~ of a contract⟩ ⟨the common stock . . . has not been a vigorous ~ —*Brookmire Investment Reports*⟩; *specif* **:** ENTERTAINER ⟨the ~*s* would have kept on with unabated zest as long as any audience remained —V.G.Heiser⟩

**performing** *adj* **1 :** of, relating to, or capable of giving a performance ⟨~ rights of a lyric —*Westminster Gazette*⟩ ⟨~ seals⟩ **2 :** of, relating to, or constituting an art (as drama) that involves public performance ⟨project an image of the U.S. through displays, films, publications, fine arts, and the ~ arts —Virginia Krepela⟩

**perfricate** *vt* -ED/-ING/-S [L *perfricatus*, past part. of *perfricare*, fr. *per-* throughout, thoroughly + *fricare* to rub — more at PER-, FRICTION] *obs* **:** to rub thoroughly

**per·fri·ca·tion** \ˌpərfrəˈkāshən, ˌper-\ *n* -S [LL *perfrication-*, *perfricatio*, fr. L *perfricatus* + *-ion-*, *-io* -ion] *archaic* **:** thorough rubbing

**per·fum·ato·ry** \(ˌ)pərˈfyüməˌtōrē\ *adj* [¹*perfume* + *-atory*] *obs* **:** of or relating to perfumes

**¹per·fume** \ˈpərˌfyüm, ˈpə̄ˌf-, ˈpəiˌf-, ˌpə(r)ˈf-, ˌpərˈf-, pə̄ˈf-, pəiˈf-\ *n* [MF *parfum, perfum*, prob. fr. OProv *perfum*, fr. *perfumar* to perfume, fr. *per-* thoroughly (fr. L) + *fumar* to smoke, expose to fumes, fr. L *fumare* to smoke — more at PER-, FUME] **1 a** *obs* **:** the fumes generated by burning (as to fumigate a room or to fill it with an agreeable odor) **b :** the scent of something usu. sweet-smelling ⟨~ of violets⟩ ⟨a house fragrant with the ~ of freshly baked cookies —June Platt⟩ ⟨~ of the stockyards —Francis Hackett⟩ **c :** a distinctive atmosphere or pleasurable quality **:** AURA ⟨the literary ~ . . . in the grand salons of the nineteenth century —Frederic Morton⟩ **2 :** a substance that emits a pleasant odor; *esp* **:** a fluid preparation (as one containing essences of flowers, synthetics, and a fixative) used for scenting **syn** see FRAGRANCE

**²per·fume** \(ˌ)=ˈ=, ˈ=ˌ=\ *vb* -ED/-ING/-S [MF *parfumer, perfumer*, prob. fr. OProv *perfumar*] *vt* **1 a** *obs* **:** FUMIGATE **b :** to fill or impregnate with the pleasantly odorous fumes of a burning substance **2 a :** to fill or impregnate with an odor (as of flowers) **:** SCENT ⟨the heavy odor of the frangipani . . . ~*s* the air —Tom Marvel⟩ **b :** to pervade with an aura ⟨subtly to ~ an art nominally concerned with the aspects of earth and sky —Laurence Binyon⟩ ~ *vi* **:** to emit a sweet odor

**per·fumed** \ˈ=ˌ=, (ˌ)=ˈ=\ *adj* **1 a :** filled or impregnated with perfume **:** SCENTED ⟨~ boudoir⟩ ⟨~ stationery⟩ ⟨breathing the . . . ~ air of June —A.W.Long⟩ **b :** having a natural fragrance ⟨thick drops of their ~ gums oozed through the . . . branches —Edith Sitwell⟩ **2 :** gracious or refined often to excess **:** DELICATE, SACCHARINE ⟨rapid, rather ~ playing —E.T.Canby⟩ ⟨elegant, ~, lyric, but largely . . . unconvincing works —P.H. Lang⟩

**perfumed cherry** *n* **:** MAHALEB

**per·fume·less** \ˈ=ˌ=ləs, (ˌ)=ˈ=-\ *adj* **:** lacking perfume

**per·fum·er** *R* ˌpə(r)ˈfyümər, ˈpərˌf-, ˌpərˈf-; *-R* ˌpəˈfyümə(r, ˈpə̄ˌf-, ˈpəiˌf-, pə̄ˈf-, pəiˈf-\ *n* -S [¹*perfume* + *-er*] **1 a :** one that makes or sells perfumes **b :** a specialist in blending new perfumes **2** [²*perfume* + *-er*] *obs* **:** one who is hired to fumigate or scent a room

**per·fum·ery** \-m(ə)rē, -ri\ *n* -ES [¹*perfume* + *-ery*] **1 a :** the art or process of making perfume **b :** the products made by a perfumer **2 :** a perfume establishment

**per·fumy** *pronunc at* ¹PERFUME +ē *or* i\ *adj* [¹*perfume* + *-y*] **:** SCENTED, FRAGRANT

**per·func·to·ri·ly** \pə(r)ˈfəŋ(k)t(ə)rəlē, -li\ *adv* **:** in a perfunctory manner **:** CARELESSLY, APATHETICALLY

**per·func·to·ri·ness** \-t(ə)rēnəs, -rin-\ *n* -ES **:** the quality or state of being perfunctory **:** CARELESSNESS, INDIFFERENCE

**per·func·to·ri·ous** \ˌpərˌfəŋ(k)ˈtōrēəs\ *adj* [LL *perfunctorius*] *archaic* **:** PERFUNCTORY — **per·func·to·ri·ous·ly** *adv, archaic*

**per·func·to·ry** \pə(r)ˈfəŋ(k)t(ə)rē, -ri\ *adj* [LL *perfunctorius*, fr. L *perfunctus* (past part. of *perfungi* to accomplish, perform, get through with, fr. *per-*, prefix denoting completion + *fungi* to perform) + *-orius* -ory — more at PER-, FUNCTION] **1 :** characterized by routine or superficiality **:** done merely as a duty **:** CURSORY, MECHANICAL ⟨gave a ~ smile and became again immersed in the folder —Ethel Wilson⟩ ⟨a speech more lifeless and ~ than most of its mechanical type —S.H.Adams⟩ ⟨the subject of eternal life is a ~ addendum to the last chapter —Walter Lowrie⟩ **2 :** lacking in interest or enthusiasm **:** APATHETIC, INDIFFERENT ⟨a wooden and ~ pedagogue —John Dewey⟩

**per·fus·ate** \(ˌ)pərˈfyüˌzāt, -zə̇t\ *n* -S [*perfuse* + *-ate*] **:** a fluid (as a solution pumped through the heart) that is perfused

**per·fuse** \-üz\ *vt* -ED/-ING/-S [L *perfusus*, past part. of *perfundere* to pour over, fr. *per-* through, throughout + *fundere* to pour — more at PER-, FOUND] **1 :** SUFFUSE ⟨rubbing of ice over the skin . . . permitted the cold skin to be *perfused* by blood from which heat was extracted —*Yr. Bk. of Physical Medicine & Rehabilitation*⟩ **2 :** to cause to flow or spread **:** DIFFUSE; *specif* **:** to force a fluid through (an organ or tissue) esp. by way of the blood vessels ⟨~ a liver with salt solution⟩

**per·fu·sion** \-üzhən\ *n* [L *perfusion-*, *perfusio* act of pouring over, fr. *perfusus* + *-ion-*, *-io* -ion] **:** an act or instance of perfusing: as **a :** baptism by affusion **b :** the pumping of a fluid through an organ or tissue ⟨believes that intermittent injection . . . is better and safer than continuous ~ —*Yr. Bk. of Urology*⟩

**per·ga·mene** \ˈpərgəˌmēn, ˌ==ˈ=\ *adj, usu cap* [L *Pergamenus*, fr. Gk *Pergamēnos*, fr. *Pergamos* (Pergamum), ancient city in Asia Minor] **:** of or relating to the ancient city of Pergamum

**per·ga·me·ne·ous** \ˌpərgəˈmēnēəs\ *adj* [L *pergamena* parchment + E *-eous* — more at PARCHMENT] **:** resembling parchment

**per·gel·i·sol** \pərˈjeləˌsȯl, -säl\ *n* -S [*per*manent + L *gelare* to freeze + E *-i-* + L *solum* ground — more at COLD, SOIL] **:** permanently or perennially frozen ground **:** PERMAFROST

**per·go·la** \ˈpərgələ, ÷ (ˌ)pərˈgōlə\ *n* -S [It, fr. L *pergula* projecting roof, vine arbor] **1 a :** an openwork arch or covering for a walk or passageway over which climbing plants are trained **:** ARBOR, TRELLIS **b :** a usu. vine-covered openwork shelter in a garden **:** BOWER **c :** a small usu. circular structure consisting of a roof supported by columns ⟨policemen in Panama have . . . pillared ~*s* from which to direct traffic —Flora Lewis⟩ **2 :** a structure usu. consisting of parallel colonnades supporting an open roof of girders and cross rafters ⟨at the end of the ~ are the industrial exhibits —*Architectural Rev.*⟩

pergola 1a

**pergunnah** *var of* PARGANA

**per·halide** \ˌpər, (ˈ)per+\ *n* [*per-* + *halide*] **:** a halide containing a relatively high proportion of halogen

**per·halogen** \"+\ *adj* [*per-* + *halogen*] **:** containing a relatively high proportion of halogen

¹**per·haps** \pə(r)ˈhaps, pəˈra-, ˈpra- *also chiefly –R* ˈpa- *sometimes –R* pəˈa-\ *adv* [*per* + *haps*, pl. of *hap* (chance)] **:** possibly but not certainly **:** MAYBE ⟨drove on . . . for ~ fifty yards —William Faulkner⟩ ⟨~ this is true, but it is certainly debatable —R.H.Walker⟩ ⟨here ~ I ought to say —James Gray⟩

²**perhaps** \"\ *n* -ES **1 :** something open to doubt or conjecture **:** SPECULATION, SUPPOSITION ⟨make ourselves uncomfortable to any extent with ~*es* —John Ruskin⟩ **2** *usu cap* **:** the postulate of a life after death ⟨a belief in the great *Perhaps* —Thornton Wilder⟩

**perhydr-** *or* **perhydro-** *comb form* [ISV *per-* + *hydr-*] **:** combined with the maximum amount of hydrogen ⟨*perhydro*anthracene $C_{14}H_{24}$⟩

**per·hydrogenate** \ˌpər, (ˈ)per+\ *vt* [*per-* + *hydrogenate*] **:** to hydrogenate to the fullest extent — **per·hydrogenation** \"+\ *n*

**per·hydrogenize** \"+\ *vt* [*per-* + *hydrogenize*] **:** PERHYDROGENATE

**pe·ri** \ˈpirē\ *n* -S [Per *perī* fairy, genius, fr. MPer *parīk*, modif. of Av *pairikā* seducing sorceress, witch; akin to L *paelex* concubine, Gk *pallax* boy, girl, *pallakis* concubine] **1** *Persian folklore* **:** a male or female supernatural being like an elf or fairy but formed of fire, descended from fallen angels and excluded from paradise until penance is accomplished, and orig. regarded as evil but later as benevolent and beautiful — compare HOURI **2 :** a beautiful and graceful girl or woman

**peri-** *prefix* [L, fr. Gk, fr. *peri*; akin to Gk *peran* to pass through — more at FARE] **1 :** all around **:** about **:** round ⟨*Peri*arctic⟩ ⟨*peri*center⟩ ⟨*peri*cyclone⟩ ⟨*peri*scope⟩ **2 :** near ⟨*peri*helion⟩ **3 a :** enclosing or surrounding ⟨*peri*neurium⟩ ⟨*peri*proct⟩ ⟨*peri*sinuous⟩ **b :** tissue surrounding (a specified part) — in terms in *-itis* ⟨*peri*arthritis⟩ **4** *usu ital* **:** having substituents in or relating to positions 1 and 8 in two fused 6-membered rings (as in naphthalene)

**peri** *abbr* perigee

**peri acid** \ˈperē+\ *n* [*peri* fr. *peri-*] **:** a crystalline naphthylaminesulfonic acid $H_2NC_{10}H_6SO_3H$ used as a dye intermediate; 8-amino-1-naphthalenesulfonic acid

**peri·aci·nal** \ˌperēˈasənᵊl, -ēəˈsīn-\ *also* **peri·acinous** \ˌperē+\ *adj* [*periacinal* fr. *peri-* + NL *acinus* + E *-al*; *periacinous* fr. *peri-* + *acinous*] **:** located about or surrounding an acinus

**peri·ac·tus** \ˌperēˈaktəs\ *n, pl* **periac·ti** \-ˌtī, -ˌtē\ [NL, fr. Gk *periaktos* — more at PERIAKTOS] **:** PERIAKTOS

**per·i·a·gua** \ˌperē; "*-agua*" *as in* PIRAGUA\ *archaic var of* PIRAGUA

**peri·ak·tos** \ˌperēˈaktəs\ *n, pl* **periak·toi** \-ˌtȯi\ [Gk, fr. *periaktos* revolving, fr. *periagein* to lead around, turn around, fr. *peri-* + *agein* to lead, drive — more at AGENT] **:** a 3-sided revolving apparatus painted with scenery and used at each side of the stage in ancient Greek theaters

**peri·anal** \ˌperē+\ *adj* [ISV *peri-* + *anal*] **:** located about or surrounding the anus

**peri·anth** \ˈperēˌan(t)th\ *n* -S [NL *perianthium*, fr. *peri-* + *anth-* + *-ium*] **1 :** the external envelope of a flower **:** floral leaves esp. when not differentiated into calyx and corolla — see FLOWER illustration **2 :** the protective envelope that surrounds the archegonium or group of archegonia of various mosses

**peri·aortal** *or* **peri·aortic** \ˌperē+\ *adj* [*peri-* + *aortal* or *aortic*] **:** about or surrounding the aorta

**peri·apical** \"+\ *adj* [*peri-* + *apical*] **:** about or surrounding the apex of the root of a tooth — **peri·apically** \"+\ *adv*

**per·i·apt** \ˈperēˌapt\ *n* -S [MF or Gk; MF *periapte*, fr. Gk *periapton*, fr. neut. of *periaptos* hung around (one), fr. *periaptein* to fasten around (oneself), fr. *peri-* + *haptein* to fasten — more at APSIS] **:** a charm worn esp. as a protection against disease or mischief **:** AMULET

**peri·arctic** \ˌperē+\ *adj, usu cap* [*peri-* + *arctic*] **:** HOLARCTIC

**peri·ar·ter·i·tis no·do·sa** \ˌperēˌärdəˈrīd·əsnōˈdōsə\ *n* [NL, fr. *periarteritis* (fr. *peri-* + *arteritis*) + L *nodosa*, fem. of *nodosus* knotty, nodose — more at NODOSE] **:** an acute inflammatory disease that involves all layers of the arterial wall and is characterized by degeneration, necrosis, exudation, and the formation of inflammatory nodules along the outer layer

**peri·arthritis** \ˌperē+\ *n* [NL, fr. *peri-* + *arthritis*] **:** inflammation of the structures (as the muscles, tendons, and bursa of the shoulder) around a joint

**peri·articular** \"+\ *adj* [ISV *peri-* + *articular*] **:** about or surrounding a joint

**peri·as·tron** \ˌperēˈastrən, -ˌsträn\ *n, pl* **perias·tra** \-strə\ [NL, fr. *peri-* + Gk *astron* star — more at STAR] **:** the point in the orbit of a star or other celestial body where it is nearest to the primary star with reference to which it is revolving ⟨the ~ of a comet⟩ — compare APASTRON

**per·i·au·ger** \ˌperēˌȯgə(r)\ *archaic var of* PIRAGUA

**peri·blast** \ˈperəˌblast\ *n* [ISV *peri-* + *-blast*] **1 :** the nucleated cytoplasmic layer surrounding the blastodisc of an egg undergoing discoidal cleavage **2 a :** CYTOPLASM **b :** PERIPLASM — **peri·blas·tic** \ˌ≈≈ˈblastik\ *adj*

**peri·blastula** \ˌperə+\ *n* [NL, fr. *peri-* + *blastula*] **:** a blastula resulting from superficial segmentation of a centrolecithal egg

**peri·blem** \ˈperəˌblem\ *n* -S [G, fr. Gk *periblēma* garment, fortification, fr. *periballein* to throw around, encompass, put on, fr. *peri-* + *ballein* to throw — more at DEVIL] *according to the histogen theory* **:** a primary meristem that gives rise to the cortex and is located between plerome and dermatogen **:** the cortical region of the root tip

**pe·rib·o·los** \pəˈribələs, -ˌläs\ *or* **pe·rib·o·lus** \-ləs\ *n, pl* **peribo·loi** \-ˌlȯi\ *or* **peribo·li** \-ˌlī, -ˌlē\ [LL & Gk; LL *peribolus*, fr. Gk *peribolos*, fr. *peribolos*, adj., encompassing, fr. *periballein* to throw around, encompass] **:** an enclosed court esp. about a temple of classical times; *also* **:** the wall of such a court

**peri·branchial cavity** \ˌperə+ . . . -\ *n* [*peri-* + *branchial*] **:** ATRIUM 4

**peri·cambium** \ˌperə+\ *n* [NL, fr. *peri-* + *cambium*] **:** PERICYCLE

**peri·capillary** \"+\ *adj* [*peri-* + *capillary*] **:** lying or occurring in the vicinity of the capillaries of a part or organ ⟨~ infiltration⟩

**pericardi-** *or* **pericardio-** *or* **pericardo-** *comb form* [NL *pericardium*] **1 :** pericardium ⟨*pericardi*ectomy⟩ ⟨*pericardio*symphysis⟩ ⟨*pericardo*tomy⟩ **2 :** pericardial and ⟨*pericardio*phrenic⟩ ⟨*pericardio*pleural⟩

**peri·cardial** *also* **peri·cardiac** \ˌperə+\ *adj* [NL *pericardium* + E *-al* or *-ac* (as in *cardiac*)] **:** of, relating to, or affecting the pericardium **:** situated around the heart

**pericardial cavity** *n* **1 :** the fluid-filled space between the two layers of the vertebrate pericardium **2 :** PERICARDIUM 2

**pericardial cell** *n* **:** one of many cells along the sides of the insect heart usu. occurring in strands

**pericardial fluid** *n* **:** the serous fluid that fills the pericardial cavity and protects the heart from friction

**pericardial septum** *n* **:** a membrane separating the pericardium of an insect from the main body cavity and formed in part by the alary muscles

**pericardial sinus** *or* **pericardial space** *n* **:** PERICARDIUM 2

**peri·car·dit·ic** \ˌperəˌkärˈdid·ik\ *adj* [NL *pericarditis* + E *-ic*] **:** of or relating to pericarditis

**peri·car·di·tis** \ˌperəˌkärˈdīd·əs\ *n, pl* **pericar·dit·i·des** \-ˈrˈdid·əˌdēz\ [NL, fr. *pericardi-* + *-itis*] **:** inflammation of the pericardium

**peri·car·di·um** \ˌperəˈkärdēəm\ *n, pl* **pericar·dia** \-ēə\ [NL, fr. Gk *perikardion*, neut. of *perikardios* around the heart, fr. *peri-* + *kardia* heart — more at HEART] **1 :** the conical sac of serous membrane that encloses the heart and the roots of the great blood vessels of vertebrates and consists of an outer fibrous coat that loosely invests the heart and is prolonged on the outer surface of the great vessels except the inferior vena cava and a double inner serous coat of which one layer is closely adherent to the heart while the other lines the inner surface of the outer coat, the intervening space being filled with pericardial fluid **2 :** a cavity or space that contains the heart of an invertebrate and in arthropods is a part of the hemocoele and contains blood which passes directly from it into the heart through the ostia in the walls of the latter

**peri·carp** \ˈperəˌkärp\ *n* -S [NL *pericarpium*, fr. Gk *perikarpion* pod, husk, fr. *peri-* + *-karpion* -carp] **:** the ripened and variously modified walls of a plant ovary that are thin and foliaceous or membranous (as in the legume and most capsules), fleshy (as in berries), or hard and bony (as in nuts) and are more or less homogeneous or consist of up to three distinct layers — see EPICARP, MESOCARP, ENDOCARP illustration — **peri·car·pi·al** \ˌ≈≈ˈkärpēəl\ *or* **peri·car·pic** \-pik\ *adj*

**peri·car·pi·um** \ˌperəˈkärpēəm\ *n, pl* **pericar·pia** \-ēə\ [NL] **:** PERICARP

**peri·car·poi·dal** \ˌperəˌkärˈpȯidᵊl\ *adj* [*pericarp* + *-oid* + *-al*] **:** resembling a pericarp

**pericaryon** *var of* PERIKARYON

**peri·cellular** \ˌperə+\ *adj* [*peri-* + *cellular*] **:** PERICYTIAL 1

**peri·ce·ment·al** \ˌperəsəˈmentᵊl\ *adj* [NL *pericementum* + E *-al*] **1 :** around the cement layer of a tooth **2 :** of, relating to, or involving the pericementum

**peri·ce·men·ti·tis** \ˌperəˌsēˌmenˈtīd·əs\ *n* -ES [NL, fr. *pericementum* + *-itis*] **:** PERIODONTITIS

**peri·cementum** \ˌperə+\ *n* [NL, fr. *peri-* + *cementum*] **:** the connective-tissue membrane covering the cement layer of a tooth

**peri·center** \ˈperə+,-ˌ≈≈ˈ≈≈\ *n* [*peri-* + *center*] **:** the point in the orbit of a revolving body nearest the center of gravity about which the body moves — compare PERIGEE, PERIHELION

**peri·central cell** \ˌperə+ . . . -\ *n* [*peri-* + *central*] **:** any of various cells surrounding the central cells of the thallus in many red algae (as of the genus *Polysiphonia*) and in some cases acting as the apical cells of laterals or in others producing an outer cortical layer or branches

**peri·cen·tric** \ˌperəˈsen·trik\ *adj* [NL *pericentricus*, fr. *peri-* + ML *-centricus* -centric] **:** of, relating to, or involving the centromere of a chromosome ⟨~ inversion⟩ — compare PARACENTRIC

**peri·chaete** *or* **peri·chete** \ˈperəˌkēt\ *n* -S [NL *perichaetium*] **:** PERICHAETIUM

**peri·chae·ti·al** \ˌ≈≈ˈkēd·ēəl\ *adj* [NL *perichaetium* + E *-al*] **:** of or relating to the perichaetium

**peri·chae·tine** \ˌ≈≈ˈkēˌtīn\ *adj* [NL *Perichaeta*, genus of earthworms (fr. *peri-* + *-chaeta*) + E *-ine*] **:** having numerous setae arranged about each segment in a ring usu. interrupted dorsally and ventrally and in a distribution characteristic of a common genus (*Perichaeta*) of earthworms — compare LUMBRICINE

**peri·chae·ti·um** \ˌ≈≈ˈkēd·ēəm\ *n, pl* **perichae·tia** \-d·ēə\ [NL, fr. *peri-* + Gk *chaitē* flowing hair, mane, foliage + NL *-ium* — more at CHAETA] **:** an enveloping sheath in a bryophyte; *esp* **:** a cluster of modified leaves surrounding the sex organs or later the seta of mosses

**peri·chon·dral** \ˌperəˈkändrəl\ *adj* [*peri-* + *chondr-* + *-al*] **:** occurring about or surrounding cartilage — used chiefly of bone and bone formation occurring peripherally beneath the perichondrium of a cartilage; compare ENDOCHONDRAL

**peri·chon·dri·al** \-drēəl\ *also* **peri·chon·dral** \-drəl\ *adj* [NL *perichondrium* + E *-al*] **:** of or relating to the perichondrium

**peri·chon·dri·um** \ˌperəˈkändrēəm\ *n, pl* **perichon·dria** \-ēə\ [NL, fr. *peri-* + *chondr-* + *-ium*] **:** the membrane of fibrous connective tissue investing a cartilage except at joints

**peri·chord** \ˈperəˌkȯrd\ *n* -S [*peri-* + *notochord*] **:** the sheath of the notochord — **peri·chord·al** \ˌ≈≈ˈkȯrdᵊl\ *adj*

**peri·cho·re·sis** \ˌperəkəˈrēsəs\ *n, pl* **perichore·ses** \-ēˌsēz\ [Gk *perichōrēsis* rotation, fr. *perichōrein* to go around, rotate (fr. *peri-* + *chōrein* to make room, give way) + *-sis* — more at ANCHORITE] **:** a doctrine of the reciprocal inherence of the human and divine natures of Christ in each other; *also* **:** CIRCUMINCESSION

**peri·clase** \ˈperəˌklās, -āz\ *or* **peri·cla·site** \ˌperəˈklāˌsīt, pəˈriklə|, |ˌzīt\ *n* -S [*periclase* fr. G *periklas*, modif. of It *periclasia*, fr. Gk *periklasis* act of twisting or breaking around (fr. *periklan* to twist around, break around — fr. *peri-* + *klan* to break — + *-sis*) + *-ia* -y (fr. L); *periclasite* fr. *periclase* + *-ite* — more at HALT (lame)] **:** native magnesia MgO in granular forms or isometric crystals (hardness 6, sp. gr. 3.67–3.90)

**Per·i·cle·an** \ˌperəˈklēən\ *adj, usu cap* [*Pericles* †429 B.C. Athenian statesman + E *-an*] **:** of or relating to Pericles or his age when Athens was at its highest material and intellectual state

**peri·cli·nal** \ˌperəˈklīnᵊl\ *adj* [Gk *periklinēs* sloping on all sides (fr. *peri-* + *-klinēs*, fr. *klinein* to lean, slope) + E *-al* — more at LEAN] **1 :** parallel to the surface or circumference of an organ — compare ANTICLINAL **2 :** QUAQUAVERSAL **3** *of a plant chimera* **:** having tissue of one kind completely surrounded by another kind — compare SECTORIAL — **peri·cli·nal·ly** \-ᵊlē\ *adv*

**peri·cline** \ˈperəˌklīn\ *n* -S [Gk *periklinēs*, adj., sloping on all sides] **1 :** a variety of albite occurring in white opaque crystals elongated in the direction of the macro-axis and often twinned with this axis as twinning axis **2 :** one of the layers making up a periclinal chimera **3 :** a periclinal cell wall

**peri·clin·i·um** \ˌperəˈklinēəm\ *n, pl* **periclin·ia** \-ēə\ [NL, fr. *peri-* + *clin-* + *-ium*] **:** the involucre of a composite plant

**pe·ric·li·tate** \pəˈrikləˌtāt\ *vb* -ED/-ING/-S [L *periclitatus*, past part. of *periclitari*, fr. *periclum*, *periculum* danger, trial — more at PERIL] *vt* **:** to expose or put in a perilous situation **:** IMPERIL ~ *vi* **:** to be in a perilous situation — **pe·ric·li·ta·tion** \pəˌrikləˈtāshən\ *n* -S

**pe·ri·cón** \ˌperəˈkōn\ *n, pl* **peri·co·nes** \-kō(ˌ)nās\ [AmerSp, prob. fr. Sp, large fan, aug. of *perico* parrakeet, large fan, dim. of the name *Pero*, alter. of *Pedro* (Peter)] **:** a group circle dance of the Uruguayan and Argentine pampas with shouting and rugged movements expressive of the gaucho

**pe·ric·o·pal** \pəˈrikəpəl\ *or* **peri·cop·ic** \ˌperəˈkäpik\ *adj* **:** of, relating to, or constituting a pericope

**pe·ric·o·pe** \pəˈrikə(ˌ)pē\ *n, pl* **pericopes** \-ēz\ *also* **perico·pae** \-(ˌ)pē, -ˌpī\ [LL, section of a book, fr. Gk *perikopē* act of cutting around, section, fr. *peri-* + *kopē* action of cutting; akin to Gk *koptein* to smite, cut off — more at CAPON] **1 :** a selection or extract from a book; *esp* **:** a selection from the Bible appointed to be read in church or used as a text for a sermon **2** [Gk *perikopē* section (as in the phrase *kata perikopēn anomoiomerē* of unlike parts as far as the section is concerned — used to describe such a group of strophes)] *Greek & Latin prosody* **:** a group of strophes in choral lyric each of which has a different structure corresponding to another such group in which each will have similarly differentiated structures

**peri·coronal** \ˌperə+\ *adj* [*peri-* + *coronal*] **:** occurring about or surrounding the crown of a tooth ⟨~ infection⟩

**peri·coronitis** \"+\ *n, pl* **pericoronitides** [NL, fr. *peri-* + *coronitis*] **:** inflammation of the gum about the crown of an unerupted tooth

**peri·crane** \ˈperəˌkrān\ *n* -S [MF, fr. NL *pericraneum*, *pericranium*] *archaic* **:** PERICRANIUM

**peri·cranial** \ˌperə+\ *adj* [NL *pericranium* + E *-al*] **1 :** surrounding the head **2 :** of or relating to the pericranium

**peri·cranium** \"+\ *n, pl* **pericrania** [NL, fr. Gk *perikranion*, neut. of *perikranios* around the skull, fr. *peri-* + *kranion* skull — more at CRANIUM] **1 :** the external periosteum of the skull **2** *archaic* **:** the head or brain esp. as the seat of thought

**Per·i·cu** \ˈperəˌkü\ *n, pl* **Pericu** *or* **Pericus** *usu cap* [Sp *pericú*, of AmerInd origin] **1 a :** an Indian people of southern Lower California, Mexico **b :** a member of such people **2 :** the language of the Pericu people

**pe·ric·u·lous** \pəˈrikyələs\ *adj* [L *periculosus*, fr. *periculum* danger + *-osus* -ous] **:** PERILOUS

**peri·cycle** \ˈperə+\ *n* [F *péricycle*, fr. Gk *perikyklos*, adj., spherical, extending all around, fr. *peri-* + *kyklos* circle, wheel — more at WHEEL] **:** a layer of parenchymatous or sclerenchymatous cells from one to a few cells thick and in some cases discontinuous that sheathes the stele esp. of the root of most vascular plants and in roots is associated with the formation of vascular cambium, phellogen, and lateral roots — called also *pericambium*

**peri·cyclic** \ˌperə+\ *adj* **:** relating to, consisting of, or located adjacent to or in the pericycle ⟨~ cell⟩ ⟨~ fiber⟩

**peri·cyclone** \ˌperə+\ *n* [*peri-* + *cyclone*] **:** the boundary line or ring of slightly rising pressure that usu. precedes and partly surrounds a cyclonic storm area — **peri·cyclonic** \"+\ *adj*

**peri·cyst** \ˈperəˌsist\ *n* [*peri-* + *cyst*] **:** the enclosing wall of fibrous tissue laid down by the host about various parasites (as a hydatid)

**peri·cys·tic** \ˌperəˈsistik\ *adj* [in sense 1, fr. *peri-* + *cystic*; in sense 2, fr. NL *pericystium* + E *-ic*] **1 :** occurring about or surrounding a cyst or bladder **2 :** of, relating to, or being a pericystium

**peri·cys·ti·um** \ˌperəˈsistēəm\ *n, pl* **pericys·tia** \-ēə\ [NL, fr. *peri-* + *cyst-* + *-ium*] **:** the vascular and connective tissues surrounding a cyst or bladder

**peri·cyte** \ˈperəˌsīt\ *n* -S [ISV *peri-* + *-cyte*] **:** an adventitious cell of the connective tissue about capillaries or other small blood vessels that is variously regarded as a macrophage or a contractile element

**peri·cy·tial** \ˌperəˈsīd·ēəl, -sish(ē)əl, -sid·ēəl\ *adj* [in sense 1, fr. *peri-* + *cyt-* + *-ial*; in sense 2 fr. *pericyte* + *-ial*] **1 :** situated around or enveloping a cell **2 :** of, relating to, or being a pericyte

**peri·dental** \ˌperə+\ *adj* [*peri-* + *dental*] **:** PERIODONTAL

**peri·den·ti·tis** \ˌperəˌdenˈtīd·əs\ *n* -ES [NL, fr. *peridentium* + *-itis*] **:** PERIODONTITIS

**peri·den·ti·um** \ˌperəˈdenchēəm, -ntēəm\ *n, pl* **periden·tia** \-ēə\ [NL, fr. *peri-* + *dent-* + *-ium*] **:** PERIODONTIUM

**peri·derm** \ˈperəˌdərm\ *n* -S [NL *peridermis*, fr. *peri-* + *-dermis*] **1 :** a protective layer of secondary tissue that develops first in the epidermis or subepidermal layers of many stems, roots, and other plant organs, is usu. continuous and followed by similar but only partial deeper-lying layers, and in full development consists of an initiating layer, an inner parenchymatous layer, and an outer cork layer — compare PHELLEM, PHELLODERM, PHELLOGEN **2 :** the perisarc of a hydroid **3 :** the outer layer of the epidermis of the skin esp. of an embryo — **peri·der·mal** \ˌ≈≈ˈdərməl\ *or* **peri·der·mic** \-mik\ *adj*

**peri·der·mi·um** \ˌ≈≈ˈdərmēəm\ *n, cap* [NL, fr. *peri-* + *derm-* + *-ium*] **:** a form genus of rust fungi having only the pycnial and aecial stages, characterized by the irregularly split or torn peridium, and formerly including many fungi that have since the discovery of their telial stages been placed in various other genera (as *Cronartium* and *Coleosporium*)

**peri·desm** \ˈperəˌdezəm\ *n* -S [ISV *peri-* + *-desm* (fr. Gk *desmē* bundle, fr. *dein* to bind — more at DIADEM] **:** the conjunctive tissue about a vascular bundle in astelic stems — **peri·des·mic** \ˌ≈≈ˈdezmik\ *adj*

**pe·rid·i·al** \pəˈridēəl\ *adj* [NL *peridium* + E *-al*] **:** of or relating to a peridium

**peri·diastole** \ˌperə+\ *n* [*peri-* + *diastole*] **:** the interval between the systole and the diastole of the heart

**peri·did·y·mis** \ˌperəˈdidəməs\ *n, pl* **perididymi·des** \-ˈdidəməˌdēz, -ˌdəˈdiməˌ-, -dīˈdimə-\ [NL, fr. *peri-* + *-didymis* (as in *epididymis*)] **:** the tunica albuginea of the testicle

**pe·rid·i·i·form** \pəˈridēəˌfȯrm\ *adj* [NL *peridium* + E *-iform*] **:** of the form of a peridium

**peri·din·i·a·ce·ae** \ˌperəˌdinēˈāsēˌē\ *n, pl, cap* [NL, fr. *Peridinium*, type genus + *-aceae*] **:** a family of unicellular algae (order Peridiniales) that was formerly nearly coextensive with the zoological family Peridiniidae but is now often restricted to *Peridinium* and a few closely related marine forms — **peri·din·i·a·ceous** \ˌ≈≈ˌ≈≈ˈāshəs\ *adj*

**peri·din·i·a·les** \ˌ≈≈ˌ≈≈ˈā(ˌ)lēz\ *n, pl, cap* [NL, fr. *Peridinium* + *-ales*] **:** an order of algae (class Dinophyceae) that is coextensive with or somewhat more inclusive than the zoological family Peridiniidae

¹**peri·din·i·an** \ˌ≈≈ˈdinēən\ *or* **peri·din·i·al** \-inēəl\ *adj* [NL *Peridinium* + E *-an* or *-al*] **:** of or relating to the Peridiniidae

²**peridinian** \"\ *n* -S **:** a dinoflagellate of the family Peridiniidae; *broadly* **:** DINOFLAGELLATE

**peri·di·ni·idae** \ˌperədəˈnīəˌdē\ *n pl, cap* [NL, fr. *Peridinium*, type genus + *-idae*] **:** a family of marine and freshwater dinoflagellates that have a thick test composed of plates and well-marked flagellar grooves — compare CERATIUM, GONYAULAX, PERIDINIACEAE

**peri·din·i·um** \ˌperəˈdinēəm\ *n* [NL, fr. Gk *peridinēs* whirled around (fr. *peridinein* to whirl around, fr. *peri-* + *dinein* to whirl, rotate) + NL *-ium*; akin to Gk *dinos* rotation, whirling — more at DINO-] **1** *cap* **:** the type genus of Peridiniidae comprising marine and freshwater dinoflagellates that are typically subspherical to ovoid in outline and that sometimes have the test prolonged into short horns — compare CERATIUM **2** *pl* **peridiniums** \-ēəmz\ *or* **peridinia** \-ēə\ **:** any flagellate of the genus *Peridinium*

**pe·rid·i·ole** \pəˈridēˌōl\ *n* -S [NL *peridiolum*, dim. of *peridium*] **:** any of the lenticular bodies situated either free or attached within the peridium of fungi of the family Nidulariaceae and containing the spores

**pe·rid·i·o·lum** \ˌ≈≈ˈēələm\ *n, pl* **peridio·la** \-lə\ [NL] **:** PERIDIOLE

**pe·rid·i·um** \pəˈridēəm\ *n, pl* **perid·ia** \-ēə\ *also* **peridiums** [NL, fr. Gk *pēridion* small leather bag, dim. of *pēra* leather bag, wallet] **:** the outer envelope of the sporophore of many fungi: as **a :** the tough often two-layered cortical investment of the gleba of a gasteromycete **b :** the layer of sterile hyphae that surrounds an aecium of a rust fungus

**per·i·dot** \ˈperəˌdō, -dät\ *n* -S [F *péridot*, fr. OF *peritot*] **1** *also* **per·i·dote** \-dōt\ **:** a deep yellowish green transparent variety of olivine used as a gem **2 :** WOODBINE GREEN

**per·i·dot·ic** \ˌperəˈdäd·ik\ *adj* [F *péridotique*, fr. *péridot* + *-ique* -ic] **:** of or relating to peridot

**pe·rid·o·tite** \pəˈridəˌtīt\ *n* -S [F *péridotite*, fr. *péridot* + *-ite*] **:** any of a group of granitoid igneous rocks composed of olivine and usu. other ferromagnesian minerals but with little or no feldspar and usu. occurring in dikes or small intrusive bodies — **pe·rid·o·tit·ic** \≈ˌ≈≈ˈtid·ik\ *adj*

**peri·dural** \ˌperə+\ *adj* [*peri-* + *dural*] **:** occurring or applied about the dura mater — used chiefly of anesthesia in which the anesthetic agent is injected along the spinal column so as to act on spinal nerves as they emerge from the dura

**peri·eg·e·sis** \ˌperēˈejəsəs\ *n, pl* **periege·ses** \-ēˌsēz\ [LL, fr. Gk *periēgēsis* act of leading or showing around, geographical description, fr. *periēgeisthai* to show around, describe, fr. *peri-* + *hēgeisthai* to lead — more at SEEK] **:** a description of a region ⟨a ~ of the Italian peninsula⟩

**peri·enteric** \ˌperē+\ *adj* [in sense 1, fr. *peri-* + *enteric*; in sense 2, fr. NL *peri enteron* + E *-ic*] **1 :** around the intestine **2 :** of or relating to the perienteron

**peri·enteron** \ˌperē+\ *n* [NL, fr. *peri-* + *enteron*] **:** the space between the inner and outer gastrular walls of an embryo **:** the primitive body cavity — distinguished from *archenteron*

**peri·focal** \ˌperə+\ *adj* [ISV *peri-* + *focal*] **:** occurring about or surrounding a focus ⟨~ proliferation of fibroblasts⟩

**peri·follicular** \"+\ *adj* [*peri-* + *follicular*] **:** occurring about or surrounding a follicle

**peri·ge·an** \ˌperəˈjēən\ *also* **peri·ge·al** \-ēəl\ *adj* [*perigee* + *-an* or *-al*] **:** of or relating to perigee

**perigean tide** *n* **:** any of the spring tides that occur soon after the moon passes her perigee

**peri·gee** \ˈperə(ˌ)jē, -əji\ *n* -S [MF & NL; MF, fr. NL *perigaeum*, *perigeum*, fr. Gk *perigeion*, fr. neut. of *perigeios* near the earth, fr. *peri-* + *-geios* (fr. *gē* earth)] **:** the point in the orbit of a satellite (as the moon or an artificial body) of the earth that is nearest to the center of the earth — opposed to *apogee*; compare APSIS, PERICENTER, PERIHELION

**peri·glacial** \ˌperə+\ *adj* [ISV *peri-* + *glacial*] **:** of or relating to the area marginal to a frozen or ice-covered region (as an ice sheet or glacier) esp. with respect to its climate or the influence of its climate upon geological processes ⟨~ topography⟩ ⟨~ weathering⟩ ⟨~ wind action —*Jour. of Geol.*⟩

**peri·gloea** \ˌperəˈglēə\ *n* [NL, fr. *peri-* + *gloea*] **:** the gelatinous covering of a diatom

**peri·glottis** \ˌperə+\ *n* [Gk *periglōttis*, fr. *peri-* + *glōttis* glottis — more at GLOTTIS] **:** the mucous membrane covering the tongue

**peri·gon** \ˈperəˌgän\ *n* -S [*peri-* + *-gon*] **:** an angle obtained by rotating a half line in the same plane once around the point from which it extends

**peri·gone** \-gōn\ *n* -S [F & NL; F *périgone*, fr. NL *perigonium*] **:** PERIGONIUM

**peri·go·ni·al** \¦==¦gōnēəl\ *or* **peri·go·nal** \¦==¦gōnᵊl, pə'rigən-\ *adj* [NL *perigon*ium + E *-ial* or *-al*] **:** of or relating to a perigonium

**peri·go·ni·um** \,perə'gōnēəm\ *n, pl* **perigo·nia** \-ēə\ [NL, fr. *peri-* + *gon-* + *-ium*] **1 :** a perianth esp. of a liverwort — compare PERICHAETIUM **2 :** a sac surrounding the generative bodies in the gonophore of a hydroid

**per·i·gor·di·an** \¦perə¦gȯ(r)dēən\ *adj, usu cap* [*Périgord*, region in southwestern France + E *-ian*] **:** of or belonging to a Paleolithic culture epoch of western Europe including the Châterperronian and Gravettian phases and characterized by narrow pointed flint knife blades and the art of Lascaux Cave

**peri·gyn·i·al** \¦perə¦jinēəl, -¦gi-\ *adj* [NL *perigyni*um + E *-al*] **:** of or relating to the perigynium

**peri·gyn·i·um** \,=='=nēəm\ *n, pl* **perigyn·ia** \-ēə\ [NL, fr. *peri-* + *-gynium* (fr. Gk *gynē* woman, wife, pistil + NL *-ium*) — more at QUEEN] **1 :** a fleshy cup or tube that surrounds the archegonium of various bryophytes (as of the liverwort group) and that is formed either from the stem apex or from the thallus **2 :** the saclike bract that subtends the pistillate flower of sedges of the genus *Carex* and that in fruit becomes a flask-shaped envelope investing the achene

**pe·rig·y·nous** \pə'rijənəs\ *adj* [NL *perigynus*, fr. *peri-* + *-gynus* -gynous] **1 :** borne on a ring or cup of the receptacle surrounding a pistil ⟨~ petals⟩ ⟨~ stamens⟩ **2 :** having stamens and petals borne on a ring or cup of the receptacle surrounding a pistil and usu. adnate to the calyx although appearing to be situated upon it — compare EPIGYNOUS

**pe·rig·y·ny** \-nē\ *n* -ES [*peri-* + *-gyny*] **:** the quality or state of being perigynous

**peri·he·li·al** \¦perə¦hēlēəl\ *adj* [NL *perihelion* + E *-al*] **:** of or relating to perihelion

**peri·he·lion** \¦perə¦hēlyən, -lēən\ *n* -S [NL *perihelium*, *perihelion*, fr. *peri-* + *-helium*, *-helion* (fr. Gk *hēlios* sun) — more at SOLAR] **:** periastron in the solar system **:** the point in the path of a planet, comet, meteor, artificial planetoid, passing star, or other celestial body that is nearest to the sun — opposed to *aphelion*; compare APSIS, PERICENTER, PERIGEE; see APHELION illustration

**peri·hepatitis** \¦perə+\ *n* [NL, fr. *peri-* + *hepatitis*] **:** inflammation of the peritoneal capsule of the liver

**peri·jove** \'perə,jōv\ *n* -S [F *périjove*, fr. *péri-* peri- (fr. Gk *peri-*) + *Jove* (Jupiter), 5th planet from the sun] **:** the point in the orbit of a satellite of Jupiter nearest the planet's center — compare APOJOVE

**peri·kar·y·al** \¦perə¦karēəl\ *adj* [NL *perikary*on + E *-al*] **:** of or relating to a perikaryon

**peri·karyon** \¦perə+\ *also* **pericaryon** \"\ *n, pl* **perikarya** [NL, fr. *peri-* + Gk *karyon* nut, kernel — more at CAREEN] **:** the cytoplasmic body of a nerve cell

**[1]per·il** \'perəl *sometimes* -(,)ril\ *n* -S [ME, fr. OF, fr. L *periculum*, *periclum* trial, attempt, danger — more at FEAR] **1 :** the situation or state of being in imminent or fearful danger **:** exposure (as of one's person, property, health, or morals) to the risk of being injured, destroyed, or lost **:** a position of jeopardy ⟨in constant ~ of death⟩ ⟨a time of moral ~⟩ **2 a :** something that imperils **:** a source of danger or possible cause of loss **:** RISK ⟨to lessen the ~*s* of the streets⟩ ⟨the ~*s* of a turgid rhetoric —Van Wyck Brooks⟩ ⟨a ~ is marine if it threatens a waterborne vessel —H.L.Haehl⟩ **b :** conduct subjecting one to possible civil or criminal liabilities **3** *archaic* **:** risk of incurring a penalty or of suffering unhappy consequences in saying or doing something that is prohibited — used as an imprecation ⟨by my soul's ~⟩ ⟨that I speak the truth, my ~ be my proof —Lord Byron⟩ **syn** see DANGER — **at one's peril :** being responsible for any harmful or destructive consequences ⟨a new order in party politics, which party leaders will disregard *at their peril* —A.N.Holcombe⟩ ⟨a person who uses fire is bound to keep it under control *at his peril* —F.D.Smith & Barbara Wilcox⟩

**[2]peril** \"\ *vt* **periled** *also* **perilled; periled** *also* **perilled; periling** *also* **perilling; perils :** to expose to danger **:** HAZARD, RISK ⟨and ~*ed* his life daily to find out what would happen if you pulled a Mountain Battery mule's tail—Rudyard Kipling⟩

**peri·lampidae** \,perə'lampə,dē\ *n pl, cap* [NL, fr. *Perilampus*, type genus (fr. Gk *perilampein* to shine around, fr. *peri-* + *lampein* to give light, shine) + *-idae* — more at LAMP] **:** a small family of Hymenoptera comprising insects that are mostly secondary parasites on other insects (as of the orders Diptera and Hymenoptera)

**pe·ril·la** \pə'rilə\ *n, cap* [NL, perh. dim. of *pera* leather bag, wallet, fr. Gk *pēra*] **:** a genus of Asiatic mints having four didynamous stamens, a bilabiate fruiting calyx, and rugose nutlets — see BEEFSTEAK PLANT

**per·ill·aldehyde** \¦perəl+\ *n* [*perilla* (*oil*) + *aldehyde*] **:** a liquid compound $C_3H_5C_6H_8CHO$ found esp. in the essential oil of an Asiatic mint (*Perilla frutescens* var. *nankinensis*) and yielding an *anti*-oxime that is about 2000 times sweeter than sucrose; 4-isopropenyl-3,4,5,6-tetrahydro-benzaldehyde

**perilla oil** *n* **:** a light yellow drying oil obtained from the seeds of mints of the genus *Perilla* and used chiefly in varnish, printing ink, and linoleum and in the Orient as an edible oil

**perilla purple** *n* **:** a dark purplish red that is paler and slightly bluer than pansy purple, redder and paler than raisin, and bluer and paler than Bokhara

**per·il·less** \'perəlləs *sometimes* -(,)rill-\ *adj* **:** free from peril

**per·il·ous** \'perələs *sometimes* -eril-\ *adj* [ME, fr. OF *perilleus*, fr. L *periculosus*, fr. *periculum* danger + *-osus* -ous — more at FEAR] **1 :** full of, attended with, or involving peril **:** beset by perils **:** HAZARDOUS ⟨perpetual struggle for the preservation of a ~ and precarious existence —T.L.Peacock⟩ ⟨feel that ~ fascination which haunts the brow of precipices —Nathaniel Hawthorne⟩ ⟨if crossing the parkway was ~ for them on weekends, it was risky at all times —E.J.Kahn⟩ **2 :** capable of inflicting harm or injury **:** DREADFUL ⟨foam of ~ seas —John Keats⟩ ⟨a ~ stone cliff high above the river —*Amer. Guide Series: Pa.*⟩ **3 :** subject to the possibility of destruction, damage, loss, or grave change at any moment ⟨never lose a sense of the whimsical and ~ charm of daily life —L.P. Smith⟩ ⟨old man who trots along under a ~ tower of painted straw chairs —Gertrude Diamant⟩ **syn** see DANGEROUS

**per·il·ous·ly** *adv* [ME, fr. *perilous* + *-ly*] **:** in a manner or to a degree involving peril ⟨~ close to defeat⟩

**per·il·ous·ness** *n* -ES **:** the quality or state of being perilous

**peril point** *n* **:** the rate in tariff legislation at or below which imports of a commodity reach a volume that endangers business or employment

**perils of the sea :** perils resulting from dangers peculiar to sea navigation **:** MARINE PERILS; *specif* **:** perils to a ship or her cargo causing damage to or loss of ship or cargo in the course of navigation on the high seas or navigable waters that in admiralty law is not attributable to latent defects in ship or cargo, to an unseaworthy ship, or to unskillful seamanship

**perils of war :** the war hazards specif. assumed under a policy of insurance

**peri·lymph** \'perə+,-\ *n* [ISV *peri-* + *lymph*] **:** the fluid between the membranous and bony labyrinths of the ear — compare ENDOLYMPH

**peri·lymphatic** \¦perə+\ *adj* [*perilymph* + *-atic* (as in *lymphatic*)] **:** relating to or containing perilymph

**perimedullary zone** \¦perə+...-\ *n* [ISV *peri-* + *medullary*] **:** MEDULLARY SHEATH

**pe·rim·e·ter** \pə'rimәd·ә(r)\ *n* -S *often attrib* [F *périmètre*, fr. L *perimetros*, fr. Gk, fr. *peri-* + *metron* measure — more at MEASURE] **1 a** (1) **:** the boundary of a closed plane figure ⟨the ~ of a circle⟩ (2) **:** the measure of the boundary of a closed plane figure; *specif* **:** the sum of the lengths of the line segments forming a polygon **b :** a line or strip bounding or protecting an area ⟨small cities on the ~ of the reservation —Zdenek Salzmann⟩ ⟨digging in behind a barbed-wire ~ with antitank guns —Barrett McGurn⟩ ⟨the ~ of a shopping district⟩ **c :** outer limits ⟨criticism which attempts to bring to literature insights found outside its ~ —C.W.Shumaker⟩ ⟨the ~ of possible excursions was reduced —André Maurois⟩ ⟨House of Representatives report described the ~ of the legislation —*U. S. Code*⟩ **2 a :** an instrument for examining the discriminative powers of different parts of the retina often consisting of an adjustable semicircular arm with a fixation point for the eye and variable stations for the visual stimuli **b :** a similar instrument used in studying auditory space perception — **peri·met·ric** \¦perə¦me·trik\ *or* **peri·met·ri·cal** \-·trəkəl\ *adj* — **peri·met·ri·cal·ly** \-·trək(ə)lē\ *adv* — **pe·rim·e·try** \pə'rimə·trē\ *n* -ES

**peri·me·tri·um** \,perə'mē·trēəm\ *n, pl* **perime·tria** \-·trēə\ [NL, fr. *peri-* + *-metrium*] **:** the peritoneum covering the fundus and ventral and dorsal aspects of the uterus

**peri·morph** \'perə,mȯrf\ *n* [ISV *peri-* + *-morph*] **:** a crystal of one species enclosing one of another species

**per im·pos·si·bi·le** \¦pe,rimpə'sibə,lā, ¦pər·,impə'sibə(,)lē\ *adv* [L, lit., through the impossible] **:** as is impossible ⟨if, *per impossibile*, stones could reason⟩

**peri·my·si·al** \¦perə¦miz(h)ēəl\ *adj* [NL *perimysi*um + E *-al*] **:** of, belonging to, or being perimysium

**peri·my·si·um** \,=='miz(h)ēəm\ *n, pl* **perimy·sia** \-ēə\ [NL, irreg. fr. *peri-* + Gk *mys* mouse, muscle + NL *-ium* — more at MOUSE] **:** the connective-tissue sheath that surrounds a muscle and sends partitions inward which form sheaths for the bundles of muscle fibers; *often* **:** the portion sheathing the bundles — distinguished from *epimysium*

**peri·natal** \¦perə+\ *adj* [ISV *peri-* + *natal*] **:** occurring at about the time of birth ⟨~ mortality⟩

**per·ine** \'pe,rēn, -rīn\ *n* -S [prob. fr. G, fr. NL *perinium*] **:** PERINIUM

**per·i·ne·al** \¦perə¦nēəl\ *adj* [NL *perine*um + E *-al*] **:** of or relating to the perineum

**perineo-** *comb form* [NL *perineum*] **1 :** perineum ⟨*perineo*cele⟩ ⟨*perineo*plasty⟩ ⟨*perineo*tomy⟩ **2 :** perineum and ⟨*perineo*vaginal⟩

**per·i·ne·or·rha·phy** \,perənē'ȯrəfē\ *n* -ES [ISV *perineo-* + *-rrhaphy*] **:** suture of the perineum usu. to repair a laceration occurring during labor

**peri·nephric** \¦perə+\ *adj* [NL *perinephr*ium + E *-ic*] **1 :** of or relating to the perinephrium **2 :** occurring about or surrounding the kidney

**peri·nephritic** \"+\ *adj* [ISV *perinephrit-* (fr. NL *perinephritis*) + *-ic*] **:** PERINEPHRIC; *also* **:** of or affected with perinephritis

**peri·nephritis** \"+\ *n* [NL, fr. *perinephrium* + *-itis*] **:** inflammation of the perinephric tissue

**peri·neph·ri·um** \,perə'nefrēəm\ *n, pl* **perineph·ria** \-ēə\ [NL, fr. Gk *perinephros* fat about the kidneys (fr. *peri-* + *nephros* kidney) + NL *-ium* — more at NEPHRITIS] **:** the capsule of connective and fatty tissue about the kidney

**per·i·ne·um** *also* **per·i·nae·um** \,perə'nēəm\ *n, pl* **peri·nea** \-ēə\ [NL, fr. LL *perinaion*, *perineon*, fr. Gk *perinaion*, *perineos*, fr. *peri-* + *-inaion*, *-ineos* (fr. *inan*, *inein* to empty out, defecate) — more at IRE] **:** an area of tissue marking externally the approximate boundary of the outlet of the pelvis and as usu. demarked giving passage to the urinogenital ducts and the rectum; *sometimes* **:** the area between the anus and the posterior part of the external genitalia esp. in the female

**peri·neural** \¦perə+\ *adj* [ISV *peri-* + *neural*] **:** occurring about or surrounding nervous tissue or nerves

**peri·neu·ri·al** \¦perə¦nyu̇rēəl\ *adj* [NL *perineuri*um + E *-al*] **1 :** of or relating to perineurium **2 :** PERINEURAL

**peri·neu·ri·um** \,perə'nyu̇rēəm\ *n, pl* **perineu·ria** \-ēə\ [NL, fr. *peri-* + *neur-* + *-ium*] **:** the connective-tissue sheath that surrounds a bundle of nerve fibers

**pe·rin·i·um** \pə'rinēəm\ *n, pl* **perin·ia** \-ēə\ [NL, fr. *peri-* + [3]*in-* + *-ium*] **:** the sculptured outer coat of a pollen grain

**peri·ocular** \¦perē+\ *adj* [*peri-* + *ocular*] **:** surrounding the eyeball but within the orbit ⟨~ space⟩

**[1]pe·ri·od** \'pirēəd, 'pēr-\ *n* -S [ME *pariode*, fr. MF *periode*, fr. ML, L, & Gk; ML *periodus* period of time, punctuation mark, fr. L & Gk; L, rhetorical period, fr. Gk *periodos* way around, circuit, period of time, rhetorical period, fr. *peri-* + *hodos* way, journey — more at CEDE] **1 a** *obs* **:** customary or ordained length of existence **:** LIFETIME ⟨make plants more lasting than their ordinary ~ —Francis Bacon⟩ **b :** the half-life of a radioactive element **2 a :** an utterance from one full stop to another **:** SENTENCE; *esp* **:** a well-proportioned sentence of several clauses ⟨rounded ~*s*⟩ ⟨stately ~*s*⟩ **b :** PERIODIC SENTENCE **c :** a musical structure or melodic section usu. of eight or sixteen measures and of two or more contrasting or complementary phrases and ending with a cadence **3 a :** the full pause with which the utterance of a sentence closes **b :** a point of time marking a termination of a course or an action **:** END, STOP, CESSATION ⟨progress . . . towards the perfection of nature without arriving at a ~ in it —S.F.Mason⟩ ⟨worries, together with . . . disease put a ~ to his honorable life —C.G.Bowers⟩ **4 a** *obs* **:** final outcome **:** CONSUMMATION **b** *obs* **:** the goal of an action or a journey **c** *obs* **:** a particular point in a progress **:** MOMENT, OCCASION **d** *obs* **:** the highest point **:** CULMINATION **e :** PERORATION ⟨to hear the admiral's ~ to the piece —Lee Rogow⟩ **5 a :** a point . used to mark the end of a declarative sentence, the end of an abbreviation (as *Eng.*, *Mr.*), or the end of a paragraph heading or outline heading — often used interjectionally at the end of a statement to indicate and emphasize that the statement is finished and complete without further qualification or discussion ⟨private profit by public servants at the expense of the general welfare is corrupt, ~ —Estes Kefauver⟩ ⟨conclusion that we fought the war to win, ~ —H.W.Baldwin⟩ ⟨not just unlucky in love, but unlucky, ~⟩ **b :** a division of time in a rhythmic series **:** a temporal unit of measure; *specif* **:** a rhythmical unit in Greek verse composed of a series of two or more cola **6 :** the completion of a cycle, a series of events, or a single action **:** CONCLUSION ⟨certain cheeses . . . serve as a brilliant ~ for a gay, well-ordered meal —*This Week Mag.*⟩ **7 a :** a portion of time determined by some recurring phenomenon **:** a division of time in which something is completed and ready to commence and go on in the same order ⟨~ of the earth's orbit⟩ ⟨~ of a flashing beacon⟩ **b :** the interval of time required for a cyclic motion or phenomenon to complete a cycle and begin to repeat itself ⟨the ~ of a pendulum⟩ ⟨~ of an alternating current⟩ being equal to one divided by the frequency **c :** a single cyclic occurrence of menstruation — called also *menstrual period* **8 a :** a chronological division (as of a life, a development) **:** STAGE ⟨~ of infancy⟩ ⟨~ of preparation and training⟩ ⟨~ of incubation of a disease⟩ **b :** an extent of time that is an epoch or era in the history of civilization ⟨the Reformation ~⟩ ⟨art in the Victorian ~⟩ ⟨furniture of the Empire ~⟩ **c :** a time often of indefinite length but of distinctive or specified character **:** SPELL ⟨~ of laziness⟩ ⟨~*s* of anxiety⟩ ⟨a ~ of wet weather⟩ ⟨~*s* of rising prices⟩ **d :** a division of geologic time longer than an epoch and included in an era **e :** a stage of culture having a definable place in time and space; *specif* **:** the length of time a pottery style is maintained in a certain area **9 :** the number of units in the recurring interval of a periodic function **10 :** a sequence of elements of increasing atomic numbers as represented usu. in horizontal rows in the periodic table from one inert gas to the next and that may be short (as from helium through fluorine or from neon through chlorine) or long (as from argon through bromine) **11 a :** one of the divisions of the academic day **:** the time appointed for a recitation or lecture or for study, physical training, luncheon, assembly, or other activity **:** a class hour **b :** one of the portions usu. of equal duration into which the playing time of a game (as hockey, polo) is divided

**syn** EPOCH, ERA, AGE, AEON: PERIOD, the most general of these terms, can designate any extent of time ⟨a *period* of a few seconds⟩ ⟨the *period* of five thousand years prior to recorded history⟩ EPOCH often designates the beginning of a period, esp. a striking or remarkable beginning ⟨this is an *epoch* . . . the end and the beginning of an age —H.G.Wells⟩, but more often designates a period set off by some significant or striking quality, event, or series of related events ⟨an *epoch* in the annals of printing —*Encyc. Americana*⟩ ⟨the Renaissance *epoch* —G.C.Sellery⟩ ERA, often interchangeable with EPOCH in its more frequent meaning, is a period, usu. of history, marked by some new or characterizable order of things ⟨the Victorian *era*⟩ ⟨the Christian *era*⟩ ⟨an *era* of singular crisis and upheaval —J.W.Aldridge⟩ AGE, usu. interchangeable with but possibly more definite than ERA, is used frequently of a period dominated by a central figure or clearly marked feature ⟨the atomic *age*⟩ ⟨the *age* of Shakespeare⟩ ⟨the *age* of Reason⟩ AEON is an immeasurable or indefinitely long period ⟨Mars is a planet which has rusted away, its oxygen having been used up *aeons* ago —J.G.Vaeth⟩ ⟨the hour of waiting seemed an *aeon* to the impatient child⟩

Antecedent Phrase — Consequent Phrase

1st Section — 2nd Section — 3rd Section — 4th Section

period 2c

**[2]period** \"\ *adj* **1 :** relating or belonging to an historical period **:** deriving from or fashioned after the style prevalent in a particular period ⟨~ furniture⟩ ⟨~ costume⟩ **2 :** representing realistically a particular historical period; *esp* **:** depending largely on evocation of a period for effect ⟨~ play⟩ ⟨~ novel⟩ ⟨an amusing ~ study of manners —*Time*⟩ ⟨~ film⟩

**per·iodate** \¦pər, (')per+\ *n* -S [ISV *periodic* (*acid*) + *-ate*] **:** a salt of a periodic acid

**pe·ri·od·ic** \¦==¦ädik, -dēk\ *adj* [F *périodique*, fr. L *periodicus*, fr. Gk *periodikos*, fr. *periodos* period + *-ikos* -ic — more at PERIOD] **1 a :** characterized by periods **:** occurring at regular intervals ⟨~ phases of the moon⟩ ⟨~ elections of public officers⟩ **b :** occurring repeatedly from time to time **:** RECURRENT, INTERMITTENT ⟨~ epidemics⟩ ⟨~ drinking sprees⟩ **:** FREQUENT ⟨one of Bermuda's ~ power failures —*Time*⟩ **2 :** consisting of a series of stages or processes that is regularly repeated **:** CYCLIC ⟨~ vibration⟩ **3 :** of or relating to a period ⟨house was pleasant and comfortable, they were too sophisticated to be ~ —*Scribner's*⟩ **4 a :** of or relating to a form of construction found in some Greek odes in which the second and third in a group of four strophes are alike in structure and the first and fourth differ from these and from each other **b :** expressed in or characterized by periodic sentences ⟨~ style⟩

**per·iod·ic acid** \¦pər·|,ī¦ädik-, ¦per|\ *n* [ISV *per-* + *iodic*] **:** any of a series of strongly oxidizing acids that are the highest oxygen acids of iodine and may be regarded as derived from a hypothetical iodine heptoxide $I_2O_7$ by union with varying amounts of water: as **a :** a hygroscopic crystalline acid $H_5IO_6$ obtainable by electrolytic oxidation of iodic acid — called also *orthoperiodic acid*, *paraperiodic acid* **b :** an unstable acid $HIO_4$ that forms stable salts and is obtained as a white residue by dehydration of orthoperiodic acid by heat — called also *metaperiodic acid*

**[1]pe·ri·od·i·cal** \¦pirē¦ädəkəl, ¦pēr-, -dēk-\ *adj* [L *periodic*us + E *-al*] **1 :** PERIODIC 1 ⟨when the bookmobile pulls in for its ~ call —*Saturday Rev.*⟩ **2 a :** published with a fixed interval usu. longer than a day between the issues or numbers ⟨newspapers and ~ publications⟩ ⟨keeping up with the ~ literature on the arts⟩ **b :** published in, characteristic of, or connected with a periodical ⟨~ fiction⟩ ⟨~ staff⟩ ⟨~ book reviews⟩ ⟨~ room in a library⟩

**[2]periodical** \"\ *n* -S **:** a magazine or other publication of which the issues appear at stated or regular intervals — usu. used of a publication appearing more frequently than annually but infrequently used of a newspaper

**periodical cicada** *n* **:** SEVENTEEN-YEAR LOCUST

**pe·ri·od·i·cal·ly** \¦pirē¦ädək(ə)lē, -dēk-, -li\ *adv* **1 :** at regular intervals of time **2 :** from time to time **:** RECURRENTLY, FREQUENTLY

## PERIODIC TABLE

This is a common long form of the table. Roman numerals and letters heading the vertical columns indicate the groups (there are differences of opinion regarding the letter designations, those given here being probably the most generally used). The horizontal rows represent the periods, with two series removed from the two very long periods and represented below the main table. Atomic numbers are given above the symbols for the elements, and atomic weights or (in square brackets) mass numbers of the isotopes of longest known half-life are given below the symbols. Compare ELEMENT table

| IA | IIA | IIIB | IVB | VB | VIB | VIIB | VIII | VIII | VIII | IB | IIB | IIIA | IVA | VA | VIA | VIIA | Zero |
|---|---|---|---|---|---|---|---|---|---|---|---|---|---|---|---|---|---|
| 1 H 1.008 | | | | | | | | | | | | | | | | 1 H 1.008 | 2 He 4.003 |
| 3 Li 6.940 | 4 Be 9.013 | | | | | | | | | | | 5 B 10.82 | 6 C 12.011 | 7 N 14.008 | 8 O 16.000 | 9 F 19.00 | 10 Ne 20.183 |
| 11 Na 22.991 | 12 Mg 24.32 | | | | | | | | | | | 13 Al 26.98 | 14 Si 28.09 | 15 P 30.975 | 16 S 32.066 | 17 Cl 35.457 | 18 Ar 39.944 |
| 19 K 39.100 | 20 Ca 40.08 | 21 Sc 44.96 | 22 Ti 47.90 | 23 V 50.95 | 24 Cr 52.01 | 25 Mn 54.94 | 26 Fe 55.85 | 27 Co 58.94 | 28 Ni 58.71 | 29 Cu 63.54 | 30 Zn 65.38 | 31 Ga 69.72 | 32 Ge 72.60 | 33 As 74.91 | 34 Se 78.96 | 35 Br 79.916 | 36 Kr 83.80 |
| 37 Rb 85.48 | 38 Sr 87.63 | 39 Y 88.92 | 40 Zr 91.22 | 41 Nb 92.91 | 42 Mo 95.95 | 43 Tc [99] | 44 Ru 101.1 | 45 Rh 102.91 | 46 Pd 106.4 | 47 Ag 107.88 | 48 Cd 112.41 | 49 In 114.82 | 50 Sn 118.70 | 51 Sb 121.76 | 52 Te 127.61 | 53 I 126.91 | 54 Xe 131.30 |
| 55 Cs 132.91 | 56 Ba 137.36 | 57 *La 138.92 | 72 Hf 178.50 | 73 Ta 180.95 | 74 W 183.86 | 75 Re 186.22 | 76 Os 190.2 | 77 Ir 192.2 | 78 Pt 195.09 | 79 Au 197.0 | 80 Hg 200.61 | 81 Tl 204.39 | 82 Pb 207.21 | 83 Bi 209.00 | 84 Po 210 | 85 At [210] | 86 Rn 222 |
| 87 Fr [223] | 88 Ra 226.05 | 89 #Ac 227 | | | | | | | | | | | | | | | |

| | | | | | | | | | | | | | | |
|---|---|---|---|---|---|---|---|---|---|---|---|---|---|---|
| *LANTHANIDE SERIES | 58 Ce 140.13 | 59 Pr 140.92 | 60 Nd 144.27 | 61 Pm [145] | 62 Sm 150.35 | 63 Eu 152.0 | 64 Gd 157.26 | 65 Tb 158.93 | 66 Dy 162.51 | 67 Ho 164.94 | 68 Er 167.27 | 69 Tm 168.94 | 70 Yb 173.04 | 71 Lu 174.99 |
| #ACTINIDE SERIES | 90 Th 232.05 | 91 Pa 231 | 92 U 238.07 | 93 Np [237] | 94 Pu [244] | 95 Am [243] | 96 Cm [248] | 97 Bk [247] | 98 Cf [251] | 99 Es [254] | 100 Fm [253] | 101 Md [256] | 102 No [253] | |

**pe·ri·od·i·cal·ness** \\,==ˈädəkəlnəs, -dēk-\\ *n* -ES : PERIODICITY
**periodical year** *n* : ANOMALISTIC YEAR
**periodic comet** *n* : a comet that moves about the sun in a closed orbit
**periodic current** *n* **1** : an electric current whose strength or direction varies periodically **2** : a current caused by the tide-producing forces of moon and sun
**periodic curve** *n* : a curve formed by the continued repetition of some part of itself : the graph of a periodic function
**periodic decimal** *n* : REPEATING DECIMAL
**periodic function** *n* : a function any value of which recurs at regular intervals
**pe·ri·o·dic·i·ty** \\,pirēəˈdisəd·ē, ,pēr-, -sətē, -i\\ *n* -ES [F *périodicité*, fr. L *periodicus* + F *-ité* -ity] : the quality, state, or fact of being regularly recurrent: as **a** : the tendency of a plant to exhibit rhythmical changes in such vital functions as nyctitropic movements, root pressure, flowering, and fruiting **b** : the position of an element in the periodic table **c** : electrical frequency
**periodic key** *n* : a cryptographic keying sequence consisting of a repeated series
**periodic kiln** *n* : a kiln operated in periods or cycles of loading, firing, cooling, and drawing ware
**periodic law** *n* **1** : a law in chemistry according to Mendeléeff: the physical and chemical properties of the elements are periodic functions of their atomic weights **2** : a law in chemistry: the physical and chemical properties of the elements are dependent on the structure of the atom and are for the most part periodic functions of the atomic numbers
**periodic motion** *n* : a recurrent motion in which the intervals of time required to complete each cycle are equal
**periodic ophthalmia** *n* : ophthalmia that recurs at approximately regular intervals; *specif* : moon blindness of the horse
**periodic sentence** *n* : a usu. complex sentence in which the principal clause comes last or which has no subordinate or trailing elements following full grammatical statement of the essential idea (as in "yesterday while I was walking down the street, I saw him") — compare LOOSE SENTENCE
**periodic table** *n* : an arrangement of chemical elements based on the periodic law and proposed in various forms that are usu. either short with only short periods (as in Mendeléeff's original table) or long with long as well as short periods (as in most modern tables) *(see previous page for table)*
**per·iodide** \\ˈpər-, (ˈ)per+\\ *n* [*per-* + *iodide*] : an iodide containing a relatively high proportion of iodine ⟨potassium ~ $KI_3$⟩
**pe·ri·od·iza·tion** \\,pirēədəˈzāshən, ,pēr-, -,dīˈz-\\ *n* -S : division of history in periods ⟨the easy ~ of history into ancient, medieval, and modern —Herbert Weisinger⟩ ⟨a ~ of the material which permits the author to convey a sense of continuity —K.W.Kapp⟩
**period key** *n* : the set of cryptographic key details which are kept unchanged during an agreed time — compare SPECIFIC KEY
**period–luminosity law** *n* : a law in astronomy: the period of light variation of a Cepheid variable is in direct relation with its absolute magnitude whereby intrinsically fainter stars have the shorter periods
**period of reverberation** : REVERBERATION TIME
**pe·ri·od·o·gram** \\,pirēˈädə,gram, ˈpirēədə-\\ *n* [ISV ¹*period* + *-o-* + *-gram*] : a curve exhibiting graphically the periodicity of any natural or physical phenomenon
**pe·ri·od·o·graph** \\-raf, -räf\\ *n* [ISV ¹*period* + *-o-* + *-graph*] : HARMONIC ANALYZER
**peri·odon·tal** \\ˌperēōˈdäntᵊl\\ *adj* [*peri-* + *odont-* + *-al*] **1** : investing or surrounding a tooth : PERICEMENTAL **2** : of or affecting periodontal tissues or regions ⟨~ infection⟩
**periodontal disease** *n* : PERIODONTOSIS
**periodontal membrane** *n* : PERICEMENTUM
**peri·odon·tia** \\,perēōˈdänch(ē)ə\\ *n* -S [NL, fr. *periodontium* + *-ia*] : PERIODONTICS — **peri·odon·tic** \\ˌ==ˈdäntik\\ *adj*
**peri·odon·tics** \\,==ˈdantiks\\ *n pl but sing or pl in constr* [NL *periodontium* + E *-ics*] : a branch of dentistry that is concerned with diseases of the supporting structures of the teeth
**peri·odon·tist** \\-ntəst\\ *n* -S [*periodontics* + *-ist*] : a specialist in periodontics
**peri·odon·ti·tis** \\-(,)ō,dän·ˈtīd·əs\\ *n* -ES [NL, fr. *periodontium* + *-itis*] : inflammation of the pericementum
**peri·odon·ti·um** \\-ˌōˈdänch(ē)əm\\ *n, pl* **periodon·tia** \\-)ə\\ [NL, fr. *peri-* + *-odont-* + *-ium*] : the periodontal tissue; *specif* : PERICEMENTUM
**peri·odon·to·cla·sia** \\-ˌō,däntəˈklāzh(ē)ə\\ *n* -S [NL, fr. *periodontium* + *-o-* + *-clasia*] : inflammatory and degenerative disease of the periodontal tissues characterized by resorption of alveolar bone with consequent loosening of the teeth and often with shrinking of the gums
**peri·odon·tol·o·gy** \\-(,)ō,dän·ˈtäləjē\\ *n* -ES [NL *periodontium* + E *-o-* + *-logy*] : PERIODONTICS
**peri·odon·to·sis** \\-(,)ō,dän·ˈtōsəs\\ *n, pl* **periodonto·ses** \\-tō,sēz\\ [NL, fr. *periodontium* + *-osis*] : disease involving the supporting structures of the teeth (as the gums and periodontal membranes)
**pe·ri·od·o·scope** \\,pirēˈädə,skōp\\ *n* [¹*period* + *-o-* + *-scope*] : a table or dial for calculating the probable date of parturition
**period piece** *n* : a piece (as of fiction, art, furniture, music) whose special or chief value lies in its characterization or evocation of an historical period
**periods** *pl of* PERIOD
**peri·oe·ci** \\,perēˈē,sī\\ *n pl* [NL, fr. Gk *perioikoi*, lit., neighbors, fr. pl. of *perioikos* neighboring, fr. *peri-* + *oikos* dwelling, house — more at VICINITY] **1** : those who live on the same parallel of latitude but on opposite meridians so that it is noon in one place when it is midnight in the other — compare ANTOECI **2** *usu cap* : free citizens without political rights constituting the subject class of ancient Sparta who carried on the trade and industry of the country and served in the armed forces — compare HELOT 1, SPARTIATE — **peri·oe·cic** \\ˌ==ˈēsik\\ *or* **peri·oe·cid** \\-səd\\ *adj*
**peri·oe·cian** \\,perēˈēshən\\ *n* -S [NL *perioeci* + E *-an*] : one of the perioeci
**perioecus** *sing of* PERIOECI
**per·i·ogue** \\ˈperē,ōg\\ *archaic var of* PIROGUE
**peri·onych·ia** \\,perēōˈnikēə\\ *n* -S [NL, fr. *perionychium* + *-ia*] : inflammation of the perionychium
**peri·onych·i·um** \\-kēəm\\ *n, pl* **perionych·ia** \\-ēə\\ [NL, fr. *peri-* + *onych-* + *-ium*] : the tissue bordering the root and sides of a fingernail or toenail
**peri·on·yx** \\,perēˈäniks\\ *n* [NL, fr. *peri-* + Gk *onyx* fingernail, claw — more at NAIL] : the persistent layer of stratum corneum at the base of a fingernail or toenail
**peri·ople** \\ˈperē,ōpəl, ,==ˈ==\\ *n* -S [F *périople*, fr. *péri-* peri- + Gk *hoplē* hoof] : the thin waxy outer layer of a hoof — **peri·op·lic** \\ˌperēˈäplik\\ *adj*
**peri·optic** \\ˌperē+\\ *adj* [*peri-* + *optic*] : situated about or surrounding the eyeball
**peri·optometry** \\"+\\ *n* [*peri-* + *optometry*] : the measurement of the limits of the visual field
**peri·orbital** \\"+\\ *adj* [*peri-* + *orbital*] : situated about, surrounding, or lining the orbit of the eye; *also* : constituting or belonging to a structure having a periorbital location
**peri·orchitis** \\"+\\ *n* [NL, fr. *peri-* + Gk *orchis* testicle + *-itis* — more at ORCHIS] : inflammation of the tissue around the testis
**peri·orificial** \\"+\\ *adj* [*peri-* + *orificial*] : situated about or surrounding an opening
**peri·ost** \\ˈperē,äst\\ *n* -S [NL *periosteum*] : PERIOSTEUM
**periost-** *or* **perioste-** *or* **periosteo-** *comb form* [NL *periosteum*] **1** : periosteum ⟨*periosteo*myelitis⟩ ⟨*periost*eoma⟩ ⟨*periost*itis⟩ **2** : periosteal and ⟨*periosteo*alveolar⟩
**peri·os·te·al** \\ˌperēˈästēəl\\ *adj* [*periost-* + *-al*] **1** : situated around bone or produced external to existing bone **2** : of, relating to, or involving the periosteum
**peri·os·te·o·ma** \\,perē,ästēˈōmə\\ *n, pl* **periosteomas** \\-məz\\ *or* **periosteoma·ta** \\-məd·ə\\ [NL, fr. *periost-* + *-oma*] : a tumor on the outer surface of a bone
**peri·os·te·um** \\,perēˈästēəm\\ *n, pl* **perios·tea** \\-ēə\\ [NL, fr. LL *periosteon*, fr. Gk, neut. of *periosteos* around the bones, fr. *peri-* + *osteon* bone — more at OSSEOUS] **1** : the membrane of connective tissue that closely invests all bones except at the articular surfaces and is made up of an outer fibrous layer that furnishes attachment for muscles and an inner layer that furnishes osteoblasts and contains blood vessels by which the bone is nourished **2** : the vascular areolar tissue lining the marrow cavity of a bone — called also *internal periosteum*
**peri·os·tit·ic** \\ˌperēˌäˈstid·ik\\ *adj* [NL *periostitis* + E *-ic*] : of or relating to periostitis
**peri·os·ti·tis** \\,perē,äˈstīd·əs\\ *n* -ES [NL, fr. *periost-* + *-itis*] : inflammation of the periosteum
**peri·os·tra·cal** \\ˌperēˈästrəkəl\\ *adj* [NL *periostracum* + E *-al*] : of, relating to, or being the periostracum
**peri·os·tra·cum** \\,perēˈästrəkəm\\ *n, pl* **periostra·ca** \\-kə\\ [NL, fr. *peri-* + Gk *ostrakon* shell — more at OYSTER] : a chitinous layer covering the exterior of the shell in many mollusks, being usu. well developed in freshwater forms, and serving to protect the shell from corrosion
¹**peri·otic** \\ˌperē+\\ *adj* [*peri-* + *-otic*] : situated around the ear; *specif* : being, relating to, or composed of the typically three bony elements that surround the internal ear and form or help to form its capsule
²**periotic** \\"\\ *n* -S : one of the periotic bones or cartilages that in man form the petrous and mastoid portions of the temporal bone on each side
¹**peri·pa·tet·ic** \\,perəpəˈted·|ik, -et|, |ēk\\ *n* -S [ME *perypatetik*, fr. L *peripateticus*, fr. *peripateticus*, adj.] **1** *usu cap* : a follower of the philosophy of Aristotle : ARISTOTELIAN **2** : PEDESTRIAN, ITINERANT **3 peripatetics** *pl* : movements or journeyings hither and thither ⟨the kind of mixed bag of travelogues and ~*s* to which publishers accustomed us —Maurice Richardson⟩
²**peripatetic** \\ˌ===ˈ==\\ *adj* **1** [MF & L; MF *peripatetique*, fr. L *peripateticus*, fr. Gk *peripatētikos*, irreg. fr. *peripatos* place for walking, covered walk in the Lyceum where Aristotle taught — more at PERIPATUS] *usu cap* : of or relating to the philosophy of Aristotle or of his followers : ARISTOTELIAN **2** [Gk *peripatētikos*, fr. *peripatein* to walk around, fr. *peri-* + *patein* to walk; akin to Gk *patos* path — more at FIND] : of or relating to walking or moving from place to place : performed or performing while moving about : ITINERANT ⟨~ habits⟩ ⟨~ teaching⟩ ⟨a ~ fruit stand which he pushed about on a cart —W.D. Howells⟩ ⟨his camera is never aimlessly ~ —Arthur Knight⟩ ⟨~ candidates⟩
**peri·pa·tet·i·cal·ly** \\ˌ===ˈted·|ək(ə)lē, -et|, |ēk-, -li\\ *adv* : in the manner of a peripatetic; *esp* : while walking ⟨wakefully, soberly, and ~ conscious of the world outside him —Thomas Wolfe⟩ ⟨philosophized ~ in its orientally luxuriant gardens —Mary Lindsay⟩
**peri·pa·tet·i·cism** \\|ə,sizəm\\ *n* -S **1** *usu cap* : the doctrines or philosophy of the Peripatetics **2** : peripatetic exercise : the habit of being peripatetic ⟨interrupted his slovenly ~ long enough to remark —*Amer. Mercury*⟩
**peri·pa·tid·ea** \\,perəpəˈtidēə\\ [NL, fr. *Peripatus* + *-idea*] *syn of* ONYCHOPHORA
**pe·rip·a·toid** \\pəˈripə,tȯid\\ *adj* [NL *Peripatus* + E *-oid*] **1** : of or relating to the genus *Peripatus* **2** : resembling a peripatus
**pe·rip·a·top·sis** \\pə,ripəˈtäpsəs\\ *n* [NL, fr. *Peripatus* + *-opsis*] **1** *cap* : a genus (the type of the family Peripatopsidae) of chiefly palaeotropical onychophorans — compare PERIPATUS **2** *pl* **peripatop·ses** \\-äp,sēz\\ : an arthropod of the genus *Peripatopsis*
**pe·rip·a·tus** \\pəˈripəd·əs\\ *n* [NL, fr. Gk *peripatos* act of walking, place for walking, fr. *peri-* + *patos* path — more at FIND] **1** *cap* : a genus (the type of the family Peripatidae) comprising chiefly neotropical onychophorans or in former classifications made coextensive with the class Onychophora — compare PERIPATOPSIS **2** -ES : any arthropod of the genus *Peripatus*; *broadly* : ONYCHOPHORAN
**peri·pe·teia** \\,perəpəˈtē(y)ə, -tīə\\ *also* **peri·pe·tia** \\-tīə\\ *n* -S [Gk *peripeteia*, fr. (assumed) Gk *peripetos* (verbal of Gk *peripiptein* to fall around, fall into, change suddenly, fr. *peri-* + *piptein* to fall) + Gk *-eia* -y — more at FEATHER] : a sudden or unexpected reversal of circumstances or situation in a literary work ⟨a thrilling nick-of-time ~ —F.R.Leavis⟩; *also* : a similar change in actual affairs ⟨participating in the major intellectual ~ of the past eighty years —Hugh Kenner⟩
**pe·rip·e·ty** \\pəˈripəd·ē, ˈperəp-\\ *n* -ES [F *péripétie*, fr. Gk *peripeteia*] : PERIPETEIA ⟨simply that ~ in either direction is a law of dramatic interest —W.H.Auden⟩
**peri·pha·ci·tis** \\,perəfəˈsīd·əs\\ *n* -ES [NL, fr. *peri-* + *phac-* + *-itis*] : inflammation of the capsule around the crystalline lens of the eye
**peri·pharyngeal** \\ˌperə+\\ *adj* [*peri-* + *pharyngeal*] : surrounding the pharynx; *specif* : being or relating to two bands of cilia encircling the inside of the pharynx of an ascidian at the oral end
**peripher-** *or* **periphero-** *comb form* [*periphery*] **1** : periphery ⟨*peripher*ad⟩ : peripheral ⟨*periphero*neural⟩ **2** : peripheral and ⟨*periphero*central⟩
**pe·riph·er·ad** \\pəˈrifə,rad\\ *adv* [*peripher-* + *-ad*] : toward the periphery ⟨the region of the rete ~ —L.B.Arey⟩
**pe·riph·er·al** \\pəˈrif(ə)rəl\\ *also* **peri·pher·ic** \\ˌperəˈferik, pəˈrifər-\\ *adj* [*peripher-* + *-al* or *-ic*] **1** : of, relating to, or forming a periphery : originating in a periphery : MARGINAL ⟨rotary boiler . . . was run at various speeds up to a ~ speed of 830 ft./sec. —G.G.Smith⟩ ⟨~ parking space⟩ ⟨~ wars⟩ ⟨rather ~ criticisms of a fine book —Paul Pickrel⟩ ⟨security programs which are ~ to the main business of democratic living —Sidney Hook⟩ ⟨such retarded cultures are often spoken of as ~ whether their situation be on the edges or in the interiors of land masses —A.L.Kroeber⟩ **2** : located away from a center or central portion : EXTERNAL; *esp* : located at or near the surface of the body ⟨~ nerve endings⟩ **3** : of, relating to, or involving the surface of the body ⟨~ vascular disorders⟩ **4** : of or relating to the peripheral field ⟨~ acuity⟩ ⟨~ vision⟩
**peripheral field** *n* : the outer part of the field of vision; *specif* : the part that lies more than 30 degrees from the line of sight
**pe·riph·er·al·ism** \\-rə,lizəm\\ *n* -S : emphasis on sensory motor processes rather than cognitive or other central processes as determinants of behavior
**pe·riph·er·al·ly** \\-rəlē, -li\\ *also* **peri·pher·i·cal·ly** \\-rək(ə)lē, -li\\ *adv* : in a peripheral position or relationship : at, near, or from a periphery : in a peripheral role or function : MARGINALLY
**peripheral neuritis** *n* : inflammation of one or more peripheral nerves
**peripheral vascular disease** *n* : vascular disease involving peripheral blood vessels (as thromboangiitis obliterans)
**pe·riph·ery** \\pəˈrif(ə)rē, -ri\\ *n* -ES [MF *peripherie*, fr. LL *peripheria*, fr. Gk *periphereia*, fr. *peripherēs* moving around (fr. *peripherein* to carry around, turn around, fr. *peri-* + *pherein* to carry) + *-eia* -y — more at BEAR] **1** : the perimeter of a circle, ellipse, or other closed curvilinear figure; *also* : the perimeter of a polygonal figure **2** : the external boundary or surface of any body ⟨the ~ of an orange⟩ ⟨the ~ of a tire⟩ **3 a** : the outward bounds of something as distinguished from its internal regions or center : encompassing limits : CONFINES ⟨the drift toward the ~ of the great metropolitan districts —Oscar Handlin⟩ ⟨the ~ of the retina —F.A. Geldard⟩ ⟨the fixed stars at the ~ of the universe were stationary —S.F.Mason⟩ ⟨an exploration of the ~ of logic —M.R.Cohen⟩ **b** : surrounding space : an area lying beyond the strict limits of a thing ⟨around each of these states was a ~ of mixed populations that made exact boundaries on racial lines hopeless —Herbert Hoover⟩ **4** : the regions (as the sense organs, the muscles, and the viscera) in which nerves terminate
**peri·phlebitis** \\ˌperə+\\ *n* [NL, fr. *peri-* + *phlebitis*] : inflammation of the outer coat of a vein or of tissues around a vein
¹**peri·phrase** \\ˈperə,frāz\\ *n* [MF, fr. L *periphrasis*] : PERIPHRASIS
²**periphrase** \\"\\ *vb* [F *périphraser*, fr. MF *periphraser*, fr. *periphrase*] *vt* : to express by periphrasis ~ *vi* : to use periphrasis
**pe·riph·ra·sis** \\pəˈrifrəsəs\\ *n, pl* **periphra·ses** \\-ə,sēz\\ [L, fr. Gk, fr. *periphrazein* to express periphrastically (fr. *peri-* + *phrazein* to point out, show, declare) + *-sis*] **1** : the use of a longer phrasing (as in naming by descriptive epithet, introduction of abstract general terms) in place of a possible shorter and plainer form of expression : the use of a negative, passive, or inverted construction in place of a positive, active, or normal construction : a roundabout or indirect way of speaking : CIRCUMLOCUTION **2** : an instance of periphrasis ⟨"the answer is in the negative" is a ~ for "no" —*Time*⟩
**peri·phras·tic** \\ˌperəˈfrastik, -raas-, -tēk\\ *adj* [Gk *periphrastikos*, fr. (assumed) Gk *periphrastos* (verbal of Gk *periphrazein*) + Gk *-ikos* -ic] **1** : of, relating to, or characterized by periphrasis : CIRCUMLOCUTORY **2** : formed by the use of function words or auxiliaries instead of by inflection ⟨*more fair* is a ~ comparative⟩ ⟨*of man* is a ~ phrase⟩ ⟨*does go* is a ~ verb⟩ — **peri·phras·ti·cal·ly** \\-tək(ə)lē, -tēk, -li\\ *adv*
**pe·riph·y·sis** \\pəˈrifəsəs\\ *n, pl* **periphy·ses** \\-ə,sēz\\ [NL, fr. Gk, overgrowth, fr. *periphyein* to grow around, grow over (fr. *peri-* + *phyein* to grow, bring forth) + *-sis* — more at BE] : one of the sterile filaments that line the ostiole of many perithecia and other fruiting structures — compare PARAPHYSIS
**peri·phyt·ic** \\ˌperəˈfid·ik\\ *adj* [NL *periphyton* + E *-ic*] : of, relating to, or forming part of the periphyton ⟨~ organisms⟩
**pe·riph·y·ton** \\pəˈrifə,tän\\ *n* [NL, fr. *peri-* + Gk *phyton* plant — more at PHYT-] : organisms that live attached to underwater surfaces ⟨rotifers that browse on bacteria and other ~⟩
**peri·pla·ne·ta** \\,perəpləˈnēd·ə\\ *n, cap* [NL, fr. *peri-* + Gk *planētēs* wanderer — more at PLANET] : a genus of large cockroaches including the American cockroach (*P. americana*) and the Australian cockroach (*P. australasiae*) which are two common cosmopolitan species
**peri·plasm** \\ˈperə+,-\\ *n* -S [ISV *peri-* + *-plasm*] : a peripheral layer of protoplasm (as of a yolk-filled egg or an oogonium) — compare OOPLASM
**peri·plasmodium** \\ˌperə+\\ *n* [NL, fr. *peri-* + *plasmodium*] : a multinucleate mass of protoplasm in various anthers that surrounds the sporocytes and pollen grains and is formed by fusion of tapetal cells following breakdown of their walls
**peri·plast** \\ˈperə,plast\\ *n* -S [*peri-* + *-plast*] **1** : STROMA 1a **2 a** : CYTOPLASM **b** : PERIPLASM **c** : a cell membrane — **peri·plas·tic** \\ˌ==ˈplastik\\ *adj*
**pe·rip·lo·ca** \\pəˈripləkə\\ *n, cap* [NL, fr. Gk *periplokē* action of twining round, interlacing, fr. *peri-* + *plokē* action of twisting or turning, fr. the stem of *plekein* to plait, twine — more at PLY] : a genus of woody vines (family Asclepiadaceae) found in warm regions of the Old World and having opposite entire leaves, cymose flowers with a rotate corolla, and cylindrical follicles — see SILK VINE
**peri·plus** \\ˈperə(,)pləs, -rə,plüs\\ *n, pl* **peri·pli** \\-,plī, -,plē\\ [L & Gk; L, circumnavigation, fr. Gk *periplous* circumnavigation, account of a coasting voyage, fr. *periplein* to sail around, fr. *peri-* + *plein* to sail — more at FLOW] **1** : a voyage or a trip around something (as an island or a coast) : CIRCUIT, CIRCUMNAVIGATION **2** : an account of a circumnavigation
**per·ip·neus·tic** \\ˌperəpˈn(y)üstik\\ *adj* [ISV *peri-* + Gk *pneustikos* of breathing, fr. *pneust-* (fr. *pnein* to breathe) + *-ikos* -ic — more at SNEEZE] : having spiracles in a row on each side of the body ⟨~ insects⟩
**peri·portal** \\ˌperə+\\ *adj* [*peri-* + *portal*] : situated about or surrounding a portal vein
**peri·printer** \\ˈperə+,-\\ *n* [*peri-* + *printer*] : a grooved inking roller that is used to force plastic ink through a stencil in a special method of printing solid tangible braille points on paper
**peri·proct** \\ˈperə,präkt\\ *n* -S [ISV *peri-* + Gk *prōktos* anus — more at PROCT-] : the well-defined area surrounding the anus of various invertebrates (as a sea urchin) — **peri·proc·tal** \\ˌ==ˈpräktᵊl\\ *or* **peri·proc·tic** \\-ktik\\ *or* **peri·proc·tous** \\-ktəs\\ *adj*
**pe·rip·ter·al** \\pəˈript(ə)rəl\\ *adj* [L *peripteros* peristylar (fr. Gk, flying around, peristylar, fr. *peri-* + *pteron* feather, wing, row of columns) + E *-al* — more at FEATHER] **1** : having a row of columns on all sides : PERISTYLAR — see COLUMNIATION illustration **2** : relating to or characterized by the motions of the air surrounding a moving body
**pe·rip·ter·os** \\-tə,räs\\ *n, pl* **peripter·oi** \\-,rȯi\\ [NL, fr. L, adj., peristylar] : a peripteral building
**pe·rip·tery** \\pəˈript(ə)rē\\ *n* -ES [L & Gk *peripteros* + E *-y*] **1** : PERIPTEROS **2** : the region surrounding a moving body (as the wing of a bird or a gliding airplane) within which cyclic or vortical motions of the air occur
**peri·py·lea** \\,perə,pīˈlēə\\ *n pl, cap* [NL, fr. *peri-* + *-pylea* (fr. Gk *pylē* gate) — more at PYLON] : a suborder of Radiolaria comprising mostly spherical protozoans without skeletons or with simple spicules and with the central capsule uniformly perforated
**pe·rique** \\pəˈrēk\\ *n* -S [LaF *périque*, prob. fr. *Périque*, nickname of Pierre Chenet, Am. pioneer tobacco grower who introduced it] **1** : a strong-flavored tobacco with tough and gummy fiber raised in St. James parish, Louisiana, cured in its own juices, and used chiefly in smoking mixtures **2** : OTTER 4
**peris** *pl of* PERI
**peri·sarc** \\ˈperə,särk\\ *n* -S [ISV *peri-* + *-sarc*] : the outer usu. chitinous integument of a hydroid — **peri·sar·cal** \\ˌ==ˈsärkəl\\ *or* **peri·sar·cous** \\-rkəs\\ *adj*
**pe·ris·cho·ech·i·noi·da** \\pə,ris(,)kō,ekəˈnȯidə\\ *n pl, cap* [NL *perischo-* (fr. Gk *perischesis* surrounding, fr. *periechein*, *perischein* to surround — fr. *peri-* + *echein*, *schein* to have, hold — + *-sis*) + *echin-* + *-oida* — more at SCHEME] : a large order of regular Paleozoic Echinoidea
¹**pe·ris·cian** \\pəˈrisēən, -ish(ē)ən\\ *adj* [NL *periscii* + E *-an*] : of or relating to the periscii
²**periscian** \\"\\ *n* -S : one of the periscii
**pe·ris·cii** \\pəˈrisē,ī, -ishē,ī\\ *n pl* [NL, fr. Gk *periskioi*, pl. of *periskios* throwing a shadow all around, fr. *peri-* + *skia* shadow — more at SCENE] : those who live within a polar circle and whose shadows during some summer days will therefore move entirely round and fall toward every point of the compass
**peri·scope** \\ˈperə,skōp\\ *n* [ISV *peri-* + *-scope*] : an optical instrument by which an observer (as on a submerged submarine or in work with highly radioactive materials) looks through or as if through an eyepiece into a mirror or totally reflecting prism attached at an angle of 45 degrees to one end of a tube containing a system of lenses and obtains an otherwise obstructed field of view from another mirror or prism correspondingly attached to the other end of the tube

diagram of a periscope

**peri·scop·ic** \\ˌperəˈskäpik, -äpēk\\ *adj* [Gk *periskopein* to look around (fr. *peri-* + *skopein* to look, view) + E *-ic* — more at SPY] **1** : viewing all around or on all sides : giving a distinct image of objects viewed obliquely as well as those in a direct line — used esp. of various compound lenses for the microscope or camera and of spectacles having meniscus lenses with the concave surface toward the eye **2** : of, relating to, by means of, or resembling a periscope
¹**per·ish** \\ˈperish, -rēsh, *esp in pres part* -rəsh\\ *vb* -ED/-ING/-ES [ME *perissen*, *perisshen*, fr. OF *periss-*, stem of *perir*, fr. L *perire* to pass away, be destroyed, perish, fr. *per-* detrimentally, destructively + *ire* to go — more at PER-, ISSUE] *vi* **1** : to become destroyed or ruined : come to an esp. violent or untimely end : pass away completely (as by disintegration) : DIE ⟨~*ed* by the tomahawk —*Amer. Guide Series: N.H.*⟩ ⟨many elephants were known to have ~*ed* of their wounds —Stuart Cloete⟩ ⟨their skeletons have ~*ed* —Ruth Benedict⟩ ⟨recollection of a past already long since ~*ed* —Philip Sherrard⟩ ⟨that the great human energy which manifests itself in free thought will not ~ —M.R.Cohen⟩ — formerly often used in imprecations but now so used chiefly with *thought* ⟨guard

against your mistakes or your attempts ⟨~ the thought⟩ to cheat —C.B.Davis⟩ **2 :** to suffer spiritual or moral death **:** become spiritually lost ⟨~ in one's sins⟩ ⟨nations ~*ing* for want of religious teachers⟩ **3** *chiefly dial* **:** to deteriorate or decay to the point of being unserviceable or useless **:** SPOIL ⟨window frames . . . cannot be left bare of paint indefinitely without the woodwork ~*ing* —*Country Life*⟩ ⟨belts should then be carefully examined for any signs of ~*ing* —*Fire Service Drill Bk.*⟩ ~ *vt* **1** *chiefly dial* **:** to cause to die, be lost, spoiled, hurt, or ruined **:** DESTROY ⟨the boots I get nowadays wholly ~ my feet —Adrian Bell⟩ ⟨this process has a tendency to ~ the straw —Beryl Fegan⟩ **2** *chiefly Scot* **:** to cause to vanish **:** SQUANDER, WASTE

**²perish** \"\ *n* -ES *Austral* **:** a state of privation in the bush — **do a perish** *Austral* **:** to come near to dying esp. from hunger, thirst, or exposure

**per·ish·abil·i·ty** \ˌperəshəˈbilədˌē, -rēsh-, -lətē, -i\ *n* -ES **:** the quality or condition of being perishable

**¹per·ish·able** \ˈperəshəbəl, -rēsh-\ *adj* [¹*perish* + *-able*] **1 :** liable to perish **:** subject to destruction, death, decay, or deterioration **:** not durable ⟨human life on this minute and ~ planet is but a mock episode —L.P.Smith⟩; *esp* **:** subject to quick deterioration or spoilage except under proper conditions (as of temperature or moisture content) ⟨~ foods such as butter and fruit⟩ **2 :** that cannot be conserved indefinitely **:** highly consumable ⟨no art is so ~ as music —P.H.Lang⟩ ⟨jazz is ~, ephemeral, elusive —Whitney Balliett⟩ ⟨news is one of the ~ products that can lose much or all of its value by delays —*Modern Industry*⟩ ⟨estimates for ~ tools and tool grinding —R.E.Cross⟩ ⟨skills are highly ~ . . . unless practice keeps pace with technological improvements —*Newsweek*⟩

**²perishable** \"\ *n* -S **:** something subject to death, destruction, or esp. rapid decay or deterioration — usu. used in pl. (as of foodstuffs) ⟨~*s* such as dairy products, meats, and fruits⟩

**per·ish·able·ness** *n* -ES **:** PERISHABILITY

**per·ish·ably** \-blē, -bli\ *adv* **:** in a perishable manner or degree

**perished** *adj* [fr. past part. of ¹*perish*] **1** *chiefly dial* **a :** injuriously affected esp. by exposure or age **b :** feeling the effects of exposure or deprivation of necessities ⟨blowing on their ~ fingers —Lawrence Durrell⟩ **2 :** deadened or weakened by exposure (as to weather or heat) ⟨~ staple⟩ ⟨~ cotton⟩

**per·ish·er** \-rishə(r), -rēsh-\ *n* -S [¹*perish* + *-er*] *Austral* **:** BOUNDER, CHAP, FELLOW — **do a perisher** *Austral* **:** do a perish

**perishing** *adj* [ME *perissing, perisshing*, fr. pres. part. of *perissen, perisshen* to perish — more at PERISH] **1 :** that perishes **:** that causes extreme discomfort, pain, or hardship; *specif* **:** FREEZING ⟨~ cold⟩ **2 :** CONFOUNDED ⟨the ~ old blighter wouldn't have it —Margery Allingham⟩ ⟨a ~ amateur —J.M. Barzun⟩ ⟨a ~, jerky little town —James Reynolds⟩

**per·ish·ing·ly** *adv* **:** in a manner or to a degree causing extreme discomfort or hardship **:** BITTERLY, EXTREMELY, VERY ⟨~ humid in the fall —Alan Moorehead⟩ ⟨a half-a-gale of ~ cold wind —Llewellyn Howland⟩ ⟨promises all kinds of miracles in his person — and delivers ~ few of them —Weston La Barre⟩

**per·ish·less** \-rishləs, -rēsh-\ *adj* [¹*perish* + *-less*] **:** IMPERISHABLE

**per·ish·ment** \-shmənt\ *n* -S **:** the act of perishing; *also* **:** something that perishes (another thing)

**peri·sin·u·ous** \ˌperəˈsinyəwəs\ *adj* [*peri-* + *sinus* + *-ous*] **:** surrounding a venous sinus (as of the brain)

**peri·som·al** \ˌperəˈsōməl\ *or* **peri·so·mi·al** \-ˈsōmēəl\ *or* **peri·so·mat·ic** \-sōˈmad·ik\ *adj* [*perisomal, perisomial* fr. *perisome* + *-al* or *-ial*; *perisomatic* fr. NL *perisomat-, perisoma* + E *-ic*] **:** of, relating to, or being a perisome

**peri·some** \ˈperəˌsōm\ *also* **peri·so·ma** \ˌ==ˈsōmə\ *n* -S [NL *perisoma*, fr. *peri-* + *-soma*] **:** the body wall of an invertebrate; *esp* **:** the body wall of an echinoderm

**peri·sperm** \ˈperəˌspərm\ *n* [F *périsperme*, fr. *péri-* peri- + *-sperme* -sperm] **1 :** nutritive tissue of a seed derived from the nucellus and deposited external to the embryo sac — distinguished from *endosperm* **2 :** nutritive tissue of a seed that includes both endosperm and perisperm — not used technically — **peri·sperm·al** \ˌ==ˈspərməl\ *or* **peri·sper·mic** \-mik\ *adj*

**peri·sphinc·tes** \ˌperəˈsfiŋ(k)(ˌ)tēz\ *n, cap* [NL, fr. *peri-* + *-sphinctes* (fr. Gk *sphinktos* tightly bound, fr. *sphingein* to bind fast) — more at SPHINCTER] **:** a genus (the type of the family Perisphinctidae) comprising discoidal ammonites having bifurcating ribs not interrupted on the ventral side and being characteristic of the Upper Jurassic — **peri·sphinc·toid** \ˌ==ˈsfiŋ(k)ˌtȯid\ *adj*

**peri·spome·non** \ˌperəˈspōmənən, -pōm-, -məˌnän\ *n, pl* **perispomena** [Gk *perispōmenon* neut. of *perispōmenos*, pres. passive part. of *perispan* to pronounce with a circumflex accent, draw off from around, fr. *peri-* + *span* to draw — more at SPAN] **:** a word having the circumflex accent on the last syllable

**peri·spore** \ˈperə+ˌ-\ *n* [F *périspore*, fr. NL *perisporum*, fr. *peri-* + *-sporum* -spore (fr. Gk *spora* seed) — more at SPORE] **:** the covering of a spore — compare EPISPORE

**peri·spo·ri·a·ce·ae** \ˌperəˌspōrēˈāsēˌē\ *n pl, cap* [NL, fr. *Perisporium*, type genus (fr. *peri-* + *-sporium*) + *-aceae*] **1** *in some classifications* **:** a family of fungi placed in the order Perisporiales and characterized by dark-colored mycelium **2** *in some classifications* **:** a family coextensive with or including Erysiphaceae — **peri·spo·ri·a·ceous** \ˌ==ˌ==ˈāshəs\ *adj*

**peri·spo·ri·a·les** \-ˈā(ˌ)lēz\ *n pl, cap* [NL, fr. *Perisporium* + *-ales*] *in some classifications* **:** an order of parasitic or saprophytic fungi nearly coextensive with the order Erysiphales

**pe·ris·sad** \pəˈrisəd, -iˌsad\ *n* -S [Gk *perissos* beyond the regular number or size, superfluous, excessive, uneven (fr. *peri* around, beyond) + E *-ad*] **1** *obs* **:** an element or radical of odd valence **2 :** an element of odd atomic number — contrasted with *artiad*

**¹pe·ris·so·dac·tyl** \pəˈrisəˌdaktᵊl\ *also* **pe·ris·so·dac·tyle** \", -ˌtīl\ *adj* [NL *Perissodactyla*] **:** having the toes in odd numbers or unevenly disposed in relation to the axis of the foot **:** relating to Perissodactyla

**²perissodactyl** \"\ *n* -S **:** one of the Perissodactyla

**pe·ris·so·dac·ty·la** \=ˌ==ˈdaktələ\ *n pl, cap* [NL, fr. MGk *perissodaktyla*, neut. pl. of *perissodaktylos* having more than the usual number of fingers or toes, fr. Gk *perissos* beyond the regular number or size, extraordinary, excessive, uneven (fr. *peri* around, beyond) + *daktylos* finger, toe — more at PERI-] **:** an order of nonruminant ungulate mammals including the horse, tapir, rhinoceros, and related forms and usu. having an odd number of toes, lophodont teeth with the posterior premolars resembling true molars, and 23 dorsolumbar vertebrae — compare ARTIODACTYLA

**pe·ris·so·dac·ty·late** \=ˌ==ˈ==lət\ *or* **pe·ris·so·dac·tyl·ic** \=ˌ==ˈ==ˌ==\ *or* **pe·ris·so·dac·ty·lous** \=ˌ==ˈ===\ *adj* [NL *Perissodactyla* + E *-ate* or *-ic* or *-ous*] **:** PERISSODACTYL

**pe·ris·so·dac·ty·lism** \=ˌ==ˈ===ˌlizəm\ *n* -S **:** the condition of being perissodactyl

**per·is·sol·o·gy** \ˌperəˈsäləjē\ *n* -ES [LL *perissologia*, fr. Gk, fr. *perissologos* speaking too much (fr. *perissos* + *logos* speech) + *-ia* -y — more at LEGEND] *archaic* **:** superfluity of words **:** PLEONASM

**pe·ris·ta·lith** \pəˈristəˌlith\ *n* -S [Gk *peristatos* standing around (fr. *periistanai* to stand around, fr. *peri-* + *histanai* to stand) + E *-lith* — more at STAND] **:** a ring of upright stones around a mound or dolmen **:** STONE CIRCLE

**peri·stal·sis** \ˌperəˈstȯlsəs, -tal-\ *n, pl* **peristal·ses** \-lˌsēz\ [NL, fr. *peristalticus* peristaltic (fr. Gk *peristaltikos*), after such pairs as LL *antitheticus: antithesis*] **:** successive waves of involuntary contraction passing along the walls of the intestine or other hollow muscular structure and forcing the contents onward — compare SEGMENTATION

**peri·stal·tic** \ˌ==ˈ==tik\ *adj* [Gk *peristaltikos*, fr. (assumed) Gk *peristaltos* (verbal of Gk *peristellein* to wrap around, fr. *peri-* + *stellein* to set, place, send) + Gk *-ikos* -ic — more at STALL] **:** of, relating to, resulting from, or being peristalsis

**peri·stal·ti·cal·ly** \-tək(ə)lē\ *adv* **:** in a peristaltic manner **:** with peristaltic action

**peri·stal·toid** \ˌ==ˈ==ˌtȯid\ *adj* [*peristaltic* + *-oid*] **:** resembling peristalsis

**peri·stele** \ˈperəˌstēlē, ˌ==ˈ==; ˈperəˌstēl\ *n* [*peri-* + Gk *stēlē* block of stone, slab — more at STELA] **:** a stone in a peristalith

**pe·ris·te·rite** \pəˈristəˌrīt\ *n* -S [Gk *peristera* dove, pigeon + E *-ite*] **:** a gem variety of albite resembling moonstone and showing internal reflections of blue, green, and yellow

**pe·ris·te·ro·mor·phae** \pəˌristərōˈmȯr(ˌ)fē, -ˌfī\ *n pl, cap* [NL, fr. *peristero-* (fr. Gk *peristera* dove, pigeon) + *-morphae*] *in former classifications* **:** a superfamily of birds consisting of the pigeons — **pe·ris·te·ro·mor·phic** \=ˈ===ˈ==fik\ *adj*

**pe·ris·te·ron·ic** \=ˌ==ˈränik\ *adj* [Gk *peristera* dove, pigeon + E *-onic* (as in *demonic*)] **:** of or relating to pigeons

**pe·ris·te·ro·pod** \pəˈristərōˌpäd\ *or* **pe·ris·te·ro·pode** \-ˌpōd\ *n* -S [NL *Peristeropodes*] **:** a bird of the group Peristeropodes

**pe·ris·te·rop·o·des** \=ˌ==ˈräpəˌdēz\ *n pl, cap* [NL, fr. *peristero-* (fr. Gk *peristera* dove, pigeon) + *-podes* (fr. Gk *pod-, pous* foot) — more at FOOT] *in former classifications* **:** a group of birds comprising the curassows and megapodes and having feet with the hind toe inserted low down (as in pigeons) — **pe·ris·te·rop·o·dous** \=ˌ==ˈ==dəs\ *adj*

**peri·stethi·um** \ˌperəˈstēthēəm, -steth-\ *n, pl* **peri·stethia** \-thēə\ [NL, fr. *peri-* + *steth-* + *-ium*] **:** the mesosternum of an insect

**peri·stom·al** \ˌperəˈstōməl\ *or* **peri·sto·mat·ic** \-ˌstōˈmadik\ *adj* [*peristomal* fr. *peristome* + *-al*; *peristomatic* fr. NL *peristomat-, peristoma* + E *-ic*] **:** PERISTOMIAL

**peri·stome** \ˈperəˌstōm\ *n* -S [NL *peristoma*, fr. *peri-* + *-stoma*] **1 :** the fringe of teeth surrounding the orifice of a moss capsule **2 :** the region around the mouth in various invertebrates: as **a :** the lip of a spiral shell **b :** the membranous area around an echinoderm's mouth **c :** the margin of the mouth opening of an insect formed by the skeleton of the head **d :** the area surrounding the mouth or cytostome of a protozoan

**peri·sto·mi·al** \ˌperəˈstōmēəl\ *adj* **:** of or relating to the peristome

**peri·sto·mice** \ˌperəˈstōməs, pəˈristəm-\ *n* -S [*peristome* + *orifice*] **:** the opening of a chamber of a bryozoan colony

**peri·sto·mi·um** \ˌperəˈstōmēəm\ *n, pl* **peristo·mia** \-ēə\ [NL, fr. *peri-* + *stom-* + *-ium*] **:** PERISTOME; *esp* **:** the foremost true segment of an annelid worm usu. bearing the mouth

**peri·sty·lar** \ˌperəˈstīlə(r)\ *adj* [*peri-* + *-stylar*] **:** marked by columniation consisting of a row of free columns completely encircling the structure or an area of the structure — compare PSEUDOPERIPTERAL

**peri·style** \ˈperəˌstīl\ *n* [F *péristyle*, fr. L *peristylum*, fr. Gk *peristylon, peristylos*, fr. neut. & masc. respectively of *peristylos*, adj., surrounded by a colonnade, fr. *peri-* + *stylos* pillar — more at STEER] **1 :** a colonnade surrounding a building or court; *specif* **:** a range of roof-supporting columns together with their entablature on all sides of a building (as the cella of a temple) or an inner court **2 :** an open space enclosed by a colonnade (as the larger and inner court of a Roman dwelling) — compare ATRIUM

**peri·styl·i·um** \ˌperəˈstilēəm, -til-\ *n, pl* **peri·stylia** \-ēə\ [L, fr. Gk *peristylion*, dim. of *peristylon*] **:** PERISTYLE

**peri·sty·los** \ˌperəˈstīləs, -ˌläs\ *n, pl* **peristy·loi** \-ˌlȯi\ [Gk] **:** a building with a peristyle

**per·it** \ˈperət\ *n* -S [origin unknown] **:** a former moneyers' unit of weight equal to $\frac{1}{20}$ droit or $\frac{1}{9600}$ grain

**pe·rite** \pəˈrīt\ *adj* [L *peritus*; akin to L *periculum* danger — more at FEAR] *archaic* **:** SKILLED

**peri·tec·tic** \ˌperəˈtektik\ *adj* [*peri-* + Gk *tēktikos* able to dissolve, fr. *tēktos* molten, capable of being dissolved (fr. *tēkein* to melt) + *-ikos* -ic — more at THAW] **:** taking place between the solid phases and the still unsolidified portions of the liquid melt

**peri·ten·din·e·um** \ˌperəˌtenˈdinēəm\ *n, pl* **peritendin·ea** \-ēə\ [NL, fr. *peri-* + ML *tendin-, tendo* tendon + L *-eum*, neut. of *-eus* -eous — more at TENDON] **:** the connective tissue sheath of a tendon

**peri·ten·on** \ˌperəˈtenən, pəˈritᵊnˌän\ *n* -S [NL, fr. *peri-* + LL *tenon* tendon, fr. Gk *tenōn* — more at TENDON] **:** PERITENDINEUM

**peri·the·cial** \ˌperəˈthēsh(ē)əl, -thēsēəl\ *adj* [NL *perithecium* + E *-al*] **:** of, relating to, or being a perithecium ⟨~ wall⟩

**peri·the·ci·um** \ˌperəˈthēs(h)ēəm\ *n, pl* **perithe·cia** \-(ē)ə\ [NL, fr. *peri-* + *-thecium*] **:** a spherical, cylindrical, or flask-shaped hollow fruiting body in various ascomycetous fungi that contains the asci, usu. opens by a terminal pore, and sometimes includes the cleistothecium — compare APOTHECIUM

**peri·the·li·al** \ˌperəˈthēlēəl\ *adj* [NL *perithelium* + E *-al*] **:** of, relating to, or made up of perithelium

**peri·the·li·o·ma** \-ˌthēlēˈōmə\ *n, pl* **peritheliomas** \-məz\ *or* **perithelioma·ta** \-məd·ə\ [NL, fr. *perithelium* + *-oma*] **:** a sarcomatous tumor originating from adventitious connective tissue around a blood vessel or from the surrounding lymphatics

**peri·the·li·um** \ˌperəˈthēlēəm\ *n, pl* **perithe·lia** \-lēə\ [NL, fr. *peri-* + *-thelium* (as in *epithelium*)] **:** a layer of connective tissue surrounding a small vessel (as a capillary)

**periton-** *or* **peritone-** *or* **peritoneo-** *comb form* [LL *peritoneum*] **1 :** peritoneum ⟨*peritone*algia⟩ ⟨*peritoneo*plasty⟩ ⟨*periton*itis⟩ **2 :** peritoneal and ⟨*peritoneo*muscular⟩ ⟨*peritoneo*pericardial⟩

**peri·to·ne·al** *also* **peri·to·nae·al** \ˌperətəˈnēəl, -rətᵊnˈē-, -rəd·əˈnē-\ *adj* [LL *peritoneum, peritonaeum* + E *-al*] **:** of, relating to, or affecting the peritoneum — **peri·to·ne·al·ly** *also* **peri·to·nae·al·ly** \-ēəlē\ *adv*

**peri·to·ne·al·ize** \-ēəˌlīz\ *vt* -ED/-ING/-S **:** to cover (a surgical surface) with peritoneum

**peri·to·neo·scope** \ˌperətəˈnēəˌskōp\ *n* [*periton-* + *-scope*] **:** a tubular instrument with an optical and lighting system used to examine the abdominal and pelvic cavities through an opening in the abdominal wall — **peri·to·neo·scop·ic** \ˌ===ˈ==ˈskäpik\ *adj*

**peri·to·ne·os·co·pist** \-ˌnēˈäskəpəst\ *n* -S **:** a specialist in peritoneoscopy

**peri·to·ne·os·co·py** \-ᵊpē\ *n* -ES [*periton-* + *-scopy*] **:** the study of the abdominal and pelvic cavities by means of the peritoneoscope

**peri·to·ne·um** *also* **peri·to·nae·um** \ˌperətəˈnēəm, -rətᵊnˈē-, -rəd·əˈnē-\ *n, pl* **peritoneums** *or* **perito·nea** *also* **perito·naea** \-ēə\ [LL, fr. Gk *peritonaion*, neut. of *peritonaios*, stretched across, fr. *peritonos* stretched over, fr. *peri-* + *-tonos* (fr. *teinein* to stretch) — more at THIN] **1 :** the smooth transparent serous membrane that lines the cavity of the abdomen of a mammal, is reflected inward over the abdominal and pelvic viscera, and consists of (1) an outer layer closely adherent to the walls of the abdomen except in some places along the back where it extends forward to form (2) an inner layer that folds to invest the viscera — called also (1) *parietal peritoneum*, (2) *visceral peritoneum*; compare MESENTERY **2 :** PLEUROPERITONEUM **3 :** the membranous lining of the body cavity of certain invertebrates

**peri·to·nit·ic** \ˌ===ˈnid·ik, ˌ===ˈid-\ *adj* [NL *peritonitis* + E *-ic*] **:** of, relating to, or belonging to peritonitis ⟨~ symptoms⟩

**peri·to·ni·tis** \ˌperətəˈnīd·əs, -rətᵊnˈī-, -rəd·əˈnī-, -ītəs\ *n* -ES [NL, fr. *periton-* + *-itis*] **:** inflammation of the peritoneum

**peri·tonsillar abscess** \ˌperə+ . . -\ *n* [ISV *peri-* + *tonsillar*] **:** an abscess in the connective tissue around a tonsil usu. resulting from acute infection of a tonsil and extension of pus through the tonsil capsule into the surrounding tissue and being accompanied by fever, pain, and swelling — called also *quinsy*

**peri·tre·ma** \ˌperəˈtrēmə\ *n* -S [NL] **:** PERITREME

**peri·tre·mal** \ˌ==ˈ==məl\ *adj* **:** being or functioning as a peritreme

**peri·trema·tous** \-ˈtreməd·əs, -rēm-\ *adj* [NL *peritremat-, peritrema* + E *-ous*] **:** of or relating to a peritreme

**peri·treme** \ˈperəˌtrēm\ *n* -S [NL *peritrema*, fr. *peri-* + *-trema*] **1 :** a rounded plate that surrounds the spiracles in some insects **2 :** the edge of the aperture of a shell

**peri·trich** \ˈperəˌtrik\ *n* -S [NL *Peritricha*] **:** a ciliate of the order Peritricha

**pe·rit·ri·cha** \pəˈri·trəkə\ *n pl, cap* [NL, fr. *peri-* + *-tricha* (fr. Gk *trich-, thrix* hair) — more at TRICHINA] **:** an order of Ciliophora comprising euciliate protozoans with an enlarged disklike ciliated anterior end leading to the cytostome via a counterclockwise adoral zone and with reduced body ciliation and often being attached to the substrate by a contractile stalk

**pe·rit·ri·chate** \-kət, -ˌkāt\ *adj* [*peri-* + *trich-* + *-ate*] **:** PERITRICHOUS 1

**peri·trich·ic** \ˌperəˈtrikik\ *adj* [*peri-* + *trich-* + *-ic*] **:** PERITRICHOUS

**peri·trich·i·da** \ˌ==ˈ==kədə\ [NL, fr. *peri-* + *trich-* + *-ida*] *syn of* PERITRICHA

**pe·rit·ri·chous** \pəˈri·trəkəs\ *adj* [*peri-* + *-trichous*] **1 :** having flagella uniformly distributed over the body — used chiefly of bacteria **2 :** having a spiral line of modified cilia around the oral disc — used of various protozoa — **pe·rit·ri·chous·ly** *adv*

**peri·troch** \ˈperəˌträk\ *n* -S [*peri-* + *-troch*] **1 :** an embryo or larva surrounded by a band of cilia **2 :** a band of cilia — **pe·rit·ro·chal** \pəˈri·trəkəl\ *adj*

**peri·troph·ic membrane** \ˌperəˈträfik-\ *n* [ISV *peri-* + *-trophic*] **:** a tubular chitinous sheath inside the midgut of many insects that is continuously secreted at the anterior end of the midgut

**perits** *pl of* PERIT

**peri·typhl·ic** \ˌperəˈtiflik\ *adj* [*peri-* + *typhl-* + *-ic*] **:** surrounding the cecum

**peri·typhlitis** \ˌperə+\ *n* -ES [NL, fr. *peri-* + *typhl-* + *-itis*] **:** inflammation of the connective tissue about the cecum and appendix **:** APPENDICITIS

**peri·umbilical** \ˌperē+\ *adj* [*peri-* + *umbilical*] **:** situated about or in the neighborhood of the navel

**peri-urban** \"+\ *adj* [*peri-* + *urban*] **:** of or relating to an area immediately surrounding a city or town ⟨154,000 urban and *peri-urban* houses were required —Leo Marquard⟩ ⟨occupying land in urban or *peri-urban* areas —*African Abstracts*⟩ ⟨undaunted *peri-urban* hyenas —Isabel Talbot⟩

**peri·vacuolar layer** \"+ . . .-\ *n* [*peri-* + *vacuolar*] *bot* **:** TONOPLAST

**peri·vascular** \ˌperə+\ *adj* [ISV *peri-* + *vascular*] **:** situated about or surrounding a blood vessel **:** occurring in the neighborhood of a blood vessel

**peri·visceral** \ˌperē+\ *adj* [*peri-* + *visceral*] **:** situated about, surrounding, or enclosing the viscera

**peri·vitelline space** \"+ . . .-\ *n* [*peri-* + *vitelline*] **:** the fluid-filled space between fertilization membrane and ovum after the entry of a sperm into the egg

**¹peri·wig** \ˈperəˌwig, -rēˌ-\ *n* [alter. of earlier *perwyke*, modif. of MF *perruque* — more at PERUKE] **:** PERUKE

**²periwig** \"\ *vt* **:** to dress or supply with or as if with a periwig

**peri·wig·pat·ed** \ˌ==ˌ=ˈpād·əd\ *adj* **:** PERIWIGGED

**¹peri·win·kle** \ˈperəˌwiŋkəl, -rēˌ-\ *n* -S [alter= (prob. influenced by ²*periwinkle*) of ME *pervenke, pervinke, perwynke*, fr. OE *perfince, perwince*, fr. L *pervinca, pervica*, (*vinca*) *pervinca*, perh. fr. *per* through + *-vinca, -vica* (fr. *vincire* to bind) — more at FOR, VETCH] **1 :** any of several plants of the genus *Vinca*: as **a :** a trailing evergreen herb (*V. minor*) with solitary blue or white flowers often cultivated and frequently escaping — called also *myrtle* **b :** a trailing foliage plant (*V. major*) often variegated and used for window boxes — called also *large periwinkle* **c :** a commonly cultivated woody herb (*V. rosea*) of the Old World tropics having opposite entire leaves and large white, pinkish, or rosy flowers often with a red eye — called also *Cape periwinkle, Madagascar periwinkle, red periwinkle* **2** *or* **periwinkle blue :** a variable color averaging a light purplish blue that is redder and deeper than lupine or zenith

**²periwinkle** \"\ *n* -S [fr. (assumed) ME, alter. (influenced by ME *pervenke, perwynke*) of (assumed) ME *pinewinkle* (whence E dial. *pennywinkle*), fr. OE *pinewincle*, fr. L *pina*, a mussel (fr. Gk *pinē, pina*) + OE *-wincle* (akin to Dan *vinkel* snail shell); akin to OE *wincel* corner, OFris *winkel*, OHG *winkil* corner, OE *wincian* to wink — more at WINK] **:** any of various gastropod mollusks: as **a :** any of numerous edible shallow-water or littoral marine snails (genus *Littorina*) having the shell thick, solid, and conical without an umbilicus and the foot longitudinally divided; *also* **:** the shell of such a mollusk **b :** any of various other marine snails or their shells similar or related to those of *Littorina* (as various American members of *Thais* or in Australia some of the Trochidae) **c :** any of several No. American freshwater snails

**³periwinkle** \"\ *vi* -ED/-ING/-S **:** to gather periwinkles ⟨go *periwinkling* on the beach⟩

**peri·win·kler** \-k(ə)lə(r)\ *n* -S **:** one who gathers or sells periwinkles

**peri·zo·ni·um** \ˌperəˈzōnēəm\ *n, pl* **perizo·nia** \-ēə\ [NL, fr. *peri-* + Gk *zōnē* girdle + NL *-ium* — more at ZONE] **:** the thin membrane that invests the young auxospore in diatoms

**periz·zite** \ˈperəˌzīt, pəˈriˌz-\ *n* -S *usu cap* [Heb *pĕrizzī* Perizzite + E *-ite*] **:** a member of an ancient people of Palestine before its conquest by the Israelites

**per·jink** \pərˈjiŋk\ *adj* [origin unknown] *Scot* **:** PRECISE, NEAT

**per·jure** \ˈpərjər, ˈpəjə(r), ˈpəijə(r)\ *vb* **perjured; perjured; perjuring** \-j(ə)riŋ\ **perjures** [MF *parjurer, perjurer*, fr. L *perjurare*, fr. *per-* detrimentally + *jurare* to swear — more at PER-, JURY] *vi, archaic* **:** to violate one's oath, vow, or sworn promise **:** take an oath with the intention of breaking it **:** commit perjury ⟨resolved to abjure and ~, as occasion might serve —Edward Gibbon⟩ ~ *vt* **1** *obs* **:** to cause to commit perjury ⟨want will ~ the ne'er touched vestal —Shak.⟩ **2 :** to make a perjurer of (oneself) esp. by telling what is false when sworn or swearing to tell the truth **:** to be involved in or proved guilty of perjury or falsely swearing ⟨claimed that the witness *perjured* himself⟩ ⟨thanked her, with as much enthusiasm as he could muster without actually *perjuring* himself —Archibald Marshall⟩

**perjured** *adj* **1 :** guilty of perjury **:** FORSWORN ⟨O ~ woman! thou dost stone my heart —Shak.⟩ **2 :** marked by perjury **:** PERJURIOUS ⟨a conviction manifestly based on ~ testimony —O.K.Fraenkel⟩

**per·jur·er** \-j(ə)rə(r)\ *n* -S **:** a person guilty of perjury ⟨a self-confessed ~⟩

**per·ju·ri·ous** \pə(r)ˈju̇rēəs, ˈpər\j-, (ˈ)pə\j-, (ˈ)pəi\j-, -jür-\ *adj* [L *perjuriosus* fr. *perjurium* perjury + *-osus* -ous] **:** marked by perjury ⟨~ divorce court testimony⟩ — **per·ju·ri·ous·ly** *adv* — **per·ju·ri·ous·ness** *n* -ES

**per·jur·ous** \ˈpərj(ə)rəs\ *adj* [L *perjurus*, fr. *perjurare*] **:** PERJURIOUS

**per·ju·ry** \ˈpərj(ə)rē, ˈpəj-, ˈpəij-, -ri\ *n* -ES [ME *perjurie, parjurie*, fr. AF *parjurie*, fr. L *perjurium*, fr. *perjurus*] **1 :** the voluntary violation of an oath or vow either by swearing to what is untrue or by omission to do what has been promised under oath **:** false swearing; *specif* **:** a willfully false statement of fact material to the issue made by a witness under oath in a competent judicial proceeding or under statute law so made on affirmation and in some jurisdictions any case including one that is extrajudicial of willful false statement made under an oath authorized to be administered by law ⟨convicted of ~⟩ ⟨subornation of ~⟩ **2 :** an instance of false swearing or willful breach of oath ⟨at lovers' *perjuries*, they say, Jove laughs —Shak.⟩ ⟨brazen it out . . . in the box by absurd and silly *perjuries* —Oscar Wilde⟩

**¹perk** \ˈpərk, ˈpək, ˈpəik\ *vb* -ED/-ING/-S [ME *perken*, perh. fr. ONF *perquer* to perch, fr. *perque* perch, fr. L *pertica* pole — more at PERCH] *vi* **1 a :** to thrust up the head, stretch out the neck, or carry the body in a bold, self-assertive, or insolent manner ⟨a file of geese ~*ing* down the roadway —Ellen Glasgow⟩ **b :** to stick up or out jauntily ⟨a . . . sand-colored handkerchief with monogram in brown ~*ed* from his breast pocket —Adria Langley⟩ **2 :** to wear or assume an air of superiority or condescension **:** become presumptuous **:** exalt oneself ⟨~*ing* over her neighbors⟩ **3 :** to gain or assume an appearance of vigor, animation, or cheerfulness esp. after a period of weakness or depression — usu. used with *up* ⟨had ~*ed up* considerably . . . the morale had plainly stiffened —P.G.Wodehouse⟩ ~ *vt* **1 :** to make smart, trim, or spruce in appearance **:** make brisk or acute **:** FRESHEN ⟨~ the taste and lift the spirit —Irving Kolodin⟩ — often used with *up* ⟨~ up their jaded zest in life —Dorothy C. Fisher⟩ ⟨denims are ~*ed up* with . . . embroidery —*Woman's Wear Daily*⟩ ⟨a giveaway . . . helps ~ up sales —*Sales Management*⟩ **2 :** to lift or thrust quickly, assertively, or impudently ⟨~*s* his tail up and challenges the world —Richard Jefferies⟩

**²perk** \"\ *adj* [prob. fr. ¹*perk*] **:** proud or jaunty in bearing **:** SELF-CONFIDENT, BRISK ⟨~ as a peacock⟩

**³perk** \"\ *n* -S [ME *perke*, fr. ONF *perque* — more at ¹PERK] *n, dial* **:** PERCH

**⁴perk** \"\ *vb* -ED/-ING/-S **:** PERCH

**5perk** \"\ n -s [by shortening & alter.] *chiefly Brit* : PERQUISITE — usu. used in pl. ⟨as pay and ~s go, it's a good job —Ian Scott⟩

**6perk** \"\ vi -ED/-ING/-s [by shortening & alter.] : PERCOLATE ⟨smelled and heard the coffee ~ing —Vance Packard⟩

**perk·i·ly** \-kəlē, -li\ *adv* : in a perky manner : IMPUDENTLY, SAUCILY ⟨stuck ~, like a bustle on a woman's skirt —Kenneth Roberts⟩

**perk·i·ness** \-kēnəs, -kin-\ *n* -ES : the quality or state of being perky : JAUNTINESS ⟨kept his . . . ~ of spirit —Richard Church⟩ ⟨his ~ and his occasional irascibility have marked him out as an average man —*London Daily Mail*⟩

**perking** *adj* [fr. pres. part. of 1*perk*] : PERKY

**per·kin reaction** *also* **perkin synthesis** \'pərkən-\ *n, usu cap P* [after Sir William Henry *Perkin* †1907 Eng. chemist] : a reaction for making an unsaturated aromatic acid (as cinnamic acid) by heating an aromatic aldehyde with an acid anhydride (as acetic anhydride) in the presence of a base (as sodium acetate or potassium carbonate)

**per·kin·si·el·la** \,pərkənzē'elə, (,)pər,kin-\ *n, cap* [NL, fr. Robert C.L.*Perkins* †1955 Brit. entomologist + NL *-i-* + *-ella*] : a genus of leafhoppers that includes some which are vectors of Fiji disease of sugarcane in Fiji and Samoa

**per·kin's purple** *or* **perkin's violet** \'pərkənz-\ *n, often cap 1st P* [after Sir W. H. *Perkin*] : MAUVE 2

**perky** \'pərkē, 'pək-, 'pəik-, -ki\ *adj* -ER/-EST [1*perk* + *-y*] **1** : briskly self-assured : COCKY ⟨the common barnyard rooster . . . every step ~ —*Atlantic*⟩ ⟨a short, ~ woman with . . . the agile, inquisitive appearance of a monkey —Edwin O'Connor⟩ **2** : JAUNTY, SPRIGHTLY, CHIPPER ⟨from ~ jeeps to leviathan trailer trucks —*Amer. Fabrics*⟩ ⟨a ~ . . . waltz —*New Yorker*⟩ ⟨always in good health, always ~ —*Listener*⟩ **3** : standing up, away, or out from a garment to which it is attached ⟨caps are . . . of velvet with a ~ little fence of trimming around the edges —Lois Long⟩

**per·la** \'pərlə\ *n, cap* [NL, fr. ML, pearl, fr. OF *perle* — more at PEARL] : a genus (the type of the family Perlidae) of stone flies

**per·la·ceous** \,pər'lāshəs\ *adj* [ML *perla* pearl + E *-aceous*] : resembling pearl : PEARLY

**per·lar·ia** \,pər'la(a)rēə\ [NL, fr. *Perla* + *-aria*] *syn of* PLECOPTERA

**1per·la·tive** \pər'lād·iv, 'pərləd-·\ *adj* [L *perlatus* (suppletive past part. of *perferre* to carry through, convey; *perlatus* fr. *per-* through + *latus*, suppletive past part. of *ferre* to carry) + E *-ive* — more at PER-, BEAR, TOLERATE] : of, relating to, or constituting a grammatical case that signifies the means of transportation

**2perlative** \"\ *n* -s : the perlative case of a language or a form in the perlative case

**1perle** *like* PEARL\ *n* -s [F, lit., pearl — more at PEARL] **1** : a soft gelatin capsule for enclosing volatile or unpleasant tasting liquids intended to be swallowed **2** : a fragile glass ampul that contains a liquid (as amyl nitrite) and that is intended to be crushed and the vapor inhaled

**2perle** \"\ *n* -s [alter. of *purl*] : PICOT

**per·lèche** \(')per¦lesh\ *n* -s [F, fr. F dial. *perlicher* to lick one's lips, fr. *per-* thoroughly (fr. L) + *licher* to lick, of Gmc origin; akin to OS *likkon* to lick — more at LICK] : a superficial inflammatory condition of the angles of the mouth often with fissuring that is caused esp. by infection, avitaminosis

**perle cotton** *n* [by alter. (influenced by F *perle*)] : PEARL COTTON

**1per·lid** \'pərləd\ *adj* [NL *Perlidae*] : of or relating to the Perlidae

**2perlid** \"\ *n* -s : a stone fly of the family Perlidae

**per·li·dae** \-lə,dē\ *n pl, cap* [NL, fr. *Perla*, type genus + *-idae*] : a large family of stone flies

**per·lingual** \,pər, (')pər+\ *adj* [ISV 1*per-* + *lingual*] : through or by way of the tongue ⟨~ administration of a drug⟩ ⟨~ medication⟩ — **per·lingually** \"+\ *adv*

**per·lite** \'pər,līt\ *n* -s [F, fr. *perle* pearl + *-ite* — more at PEARL] : volcanic glass that has a concentric shelly structure, appears as if composed of concretions, is usu. grayish and sometimes spherulitic, and when expanded by heat forms insulating material and a lightweight aggregate used esp. in concrete and plaster

**per·lit·ic** \,pər¦lid·ik\ *adj* [ISV *perlite* + *-ic*] : of, relating to, or having a texture like perlite

**per·loir** \,pərl¦wär\ *n* -s [F, fr. *perler* to make in the shape of pearls, fr. *perle*] : a steel punch of half-bead form used esp. for modeling balls on metal and for cutting foil to be inserted in enamel

**Per·lon** \'pər,län\ *trademark* — used for either of two synthetic polyamide fibers similar to nylon

**per·lus·trate** \(,)pər'lə,strāt\ *vt* -ED/-ING/-s [L *perlustratus*, past part. of *perlustrare*, fr. *per-* through + *lustrare* to traverse, survey, lustrate, brighten — more at PER-, LUSTRATE] : to go through and examine thoroughly : SURVEY ⟨~ a building⟩

**per·lus·tra·tion** \,pər,lə'strāshən\ *n* -s : the act or process of perlustrating

**1perm** \'p(y)e(ə)rm\ *adj, usu cap* [*Perm*, city near the Ural mountains, U.S.S.R.] : of or from the city of Perm, U.S.S.R. : of the kind or style prevalent in Perm

**2perm** \'pərm\ *n* -s [by shortening] : PERMANENT WAVE

**perm** *abbr* permanent

**per·ma·frost** \'pərmə+,-\ *n* [*permanent* + *frost*] : a permanently frozen layer of soil, subsoil, or other deposit sometimes including the bedrock and occurring at variable depth below the earth's surface in arctic or subarctic regions : PERGELISOL

**Perm·al·loy** \'pərmə,lȯi\ *trademark* — used for an easily magnetized and demagnetized alloy composed of about 80 percent nickel and 20 percent iron

**per·ma·nence** \'pərmənən|(t)s, 'pəm-, 'pəim- *also* -mnən|\ *n* -s [ME, fr. MF, fr. ML *permanentia*, fr. L *permanent-*, *permanens* + *-ia* -y] **1** : the quality or state of being permanent : DURABILITY ⟨a pioneer town . . . that has not yet acquired an air of ~ —Ivor Jones⟩ ⟨the ~ of his achievement —Hilaire Belloc⟩ ⟨the degree of ~ of different ruling inks —*Ruling Inks & Dyes*⟩ **2** : two adjacent like signs in a series of positive and negative signs in mathematics — opposed to *variation* ⟨in the series of coefficients of the polynomial $3x^3-x^2-8x+7$ there is one ~⟩

**per·ma·nen·cy** \|sē, |si\ *n* -ES [ML *permanentia*] **1** : the quality or state of being permanent : DURATION, FIXEDNESS ⟨old homes and churches have about them an air of . . . ~ —L.O. Warner⟩ **2** : one that is permanent ⟨the visit developed into a ~ —Humphrey Bullock⟩ ⟨the *permanencies* of the human heart —Clifton Fadiman⟩

**1per·ma·nent** \|t\ *adj* [ME, fr. MF, fr. L *permanent-*, *permanens*, pres. part. of *permanēre* to endure, remain, fr. *per-* through, throughout + *manēre* to remain — more at PER-, MANSION] : continuing or enduring (as in the same state, status, place) without fundamental or marked change : not subject to fluctuation or alteration : fixed or intended to be fixed : LASTING, STABLE ⟨literature of ~, not ephemeral, value⟩ ⟨likely to cause ~ injury⟩ ⟨the paintings in the ~ collection⟩ ⟨elected ~ chairman of the convention⟩ — **per·ma·nent·ness** *n* -ES

**2permanent** *n* -s **1** : one that is permanent; *specif* : something (as a quality, element, entity) conceived of as abiding or eternal ⟨the ~s of existence —D.W.Gotshalk⟩ **2** : PERMANENT WAVE ⟨an unbecoming ~ —Ruth Domino⟩

**permanent alimony** *n* : alimony decreed after a hearing on the merits of a divorce, separate support, or separation case — compare ALIMONY PENDENTE LITE

**permanent assets** *n pl* : CAPITAL ASSETS

**permanent axis** *n* : the axis about which a free rigid body can rotate in equilibrium being in general the axis of greatest moment of inertia through the center of mass — compare PRINCIPAL AXIS

**permanent blue** *n* : FRENCH BLUE

**permanent bordeaux FRR** \-,e,fä'rär\ *n, usu cap P&B* : an organic pigment — see DYE table I (under *Pigment Red 12*)

**permanent capital** *n* : capital that does not require replacement but is in continuous existence

**permanent carmine FB** \-,ef'bē\ *n, usu cap P&C* : an organic pigment — see DYE table I (under *Pigment Red 5*)

**permanent fast yellow NCG** \,en,sē'jē\ *n, usu cap P&F&Y* : an organic pigment — see DYE table I (under *Pigment Yellow 16*)

**permanent gas** *n* **1** : a gas (as hydrogen, nitrogen, carbon monoxide) believed to be incapable of liquefaction **2** : a substance that remains gaseous under normal conditions; *esp* : one whose critical temperature is far below room temperature — compare VAPOR

**permanent green** *n* : TERRE VERTE 2

**permanent hardness** *n* : the part of the total hardness of water that persists after boiling — distinguished from *temporary hardness*

**per·ma·nent·ly** *adv* [ME, fr. *permanent* + *-ly*] : in a permanent manner

**permanent magnet** *n* : a magnet that retains its magnetism after removal of the magnetizing force — see MAGNETO illustration

**permanent magnetism** *n* : magnetism that remains after the exciting force has been removed : stable residual magnetism

**permanent mold** *n* : a metal mold into which liquid metal is poured by gravity for the production of many successive castings of the same shape

**permanent oil** *n* : NONDRYING OIL

**permanent pasture** *also* **permanent meadow** *n* : natural or seeded grassland that remains unplowed for many years

**permanent red** *n* **1** : BLOOD RED **2** *often cap P&R* : any of several organic pigments — see DYE table I (under *Pigment Orange 5* and *Pigment Red 2, 7, 10, 48*)

**permanent red R** \-'är\ *n, usu cap P&R* : FIRE RED 2 — see DYE table I (under *Pigment Red 4*)

**permanent set** *n* : the amount by which a material stressed beyond its elastic limit fails to return to its original size or shape when the load is removed

**permanent strain** *n* : a strain that develops within a body upon rapid or nonuniform solidification and that may be removed by careful annealing

**permanent tissue** *n* : a tissue that has completed its growth and differentiation and is generally incapable of meristematic activity — compare MERISTEM

**permanent tooth** *n* : one of the second set of teeth of a mammal that follow the milk teeth, typically persist into old age, and in man are 32 in number including 4 incisors, 2 canines, and 10 premolars and molars in each jaw

**permanent violet** *n* : MANGANESE VIOLET

**permanent wave** *n* : a long-lasting hair wave produced by winding hair on curlers and applying chemicals or chemicals and heat — compare COLD WAVE

**permanent way** *n, Brit* : the roadway of a railroad

**permanent white** *n* : a durable white pigment that does not darken on exposure: as **a** : BLANC FIXE **b** : ZINC WHITE **c** : TITANIUM WHITE

**permanent wilting** *n* : wilting from which a plant will recover only upon addition of moisture to the soil

**permanent yellow** *n* : YELLOW OCHER 2

**per·manganate** \,pər, (')per+\ *n* -s [ISV *permanganic* + *-ate*] : a salt of permanganic acid; *esp* : POTASSIUM PERMANGANATE

**per·manganic acid** \,pər, ¦per+. . .\ *n* [ISV *per-* + *manganic*] : an unstable strong acid $HMnO_4$ known only in purple-colored strongly oxidizing aqueous solutions (as those prepared by dissolving manganese heptoxide in water) and in the form of purple salts

**permanganic anhydride** *n* : MANGANESE HEPTOXIDE

**per·man·sive** \pə(r)'man(t)siv\ *adj* [L *permansus* (past part. of *permanēre* to endure, remain) + E *-ive* — more at PERMANENT] : of, relating to, or constituting an aspect of the verb (as in Akkadian) denoting that the action is a continuous procedure

**per·ma red** \,pərmə-\ *n* [*permanent red*] : BLOOD RED

**per·ma·tron** \'pərmə,trän\ *n* -s [*permanent* + *-tron*] : a vacuum tube in which the electron flow is controlled by a magnetic field

**per·me·abil·i·ty** \,pərmēə'biləd·ē, ,pəm-, ,pəim-, -lətē, -i\ *n* **1** : the quality or state of being permeable ⟨the ~ of protective films⟩ ⟨the ~ of a membrane⟩ ⟨the water vapor ~ of leather is inherently high —*Technical News Bull.*⟩ **2** : the property of a porous material that is measured by the rate by volume at which a fluid of unit viscosity passes through unit cross section of the material under unit pressure gradient; *specif* : a measure of the ease of fluid flow through rocks — compare DARCY, DARCY'S LAW **3** : the measure of the rate of diffusion of gas through intact balloon fabric usu. expressed in liters per square meter of fabric per 24 hours under standard conditions **4** : the property of a magnetizable substance that determines the degree in which it modifies the magnetic flux in the region occupied by it in a magnetic field; *specif* : the ratio of the induction to the magnetizing force in the substance

**per·me·able** \'==əbəl\ *adj* [LL *permeabilis*, fr. L *permeare* to permeate + *-abilis* -able — more at PERMEATE] : capable of being permeated : PASSABLE, PENETRABLE, PERVIOUS ⟨class lines are moderately ~ in a democratic society —Abram Kardiner⟩ — used esp. of a substance that allows the passage of fluids ⟨a ~ membrane⟩ ⟨white limestone . . . extremely ~ to water —*Jour. of Geol.*⟩ — **per·me·able·ness** *n* -ES — **per·me·ably** \-blē, -bli\ *adv*

**per·meam·e·ter** \'pərmēə,mēd·ər, ,pərmē'aməd·-\ *n* [*permeability* + *-meter*] **1** : an instrument for measuring magnetic permeability — compare PERMEABILITY 4 **2** : an apparatus for measuring porous permeability — compare PERMEABILITY 2

**per·me·ance** \'pərmēən(t)s, 'pəm-, 'pəim-\ *n* -s [fr. *permeant*, after such pairs as E *abundant*: *abundance*] **1** : PERMEATION **2** : the reciprocal of magnetic reluctance

**1per·me·ant** \-nt\ *adj* [L *permeant-*, *permeans*, pres. part. of *permeare* to pass through, permeate — more at PERMEATE] : PERMEATING

**2permeant** \"\ *n* -s : an animal influent that ranges widely within the ecological community of which it is a part

**per·me·ate** \-ē,āt, *usu* -ād·+V\ *vb* -ED/-ING/-s [L *permeatus*, past part. of *permeare*, fr. *per-* through + *meare* to go, pass; akin to MW *mynet* to go, OSlav *minǫti* to go past, pass] *vi* : to diffuse through or penetrate something ⟨liquid *permeating* through the porous substance⟩ ~ *vt* **1** : to spread or diffuse through ⟨the air is *permeated* by the pungent scent of tobacco —*Amer. Guide Series: N.C.*⟩ ⟨an atmosphere of distrust . . . has been allowed to ~ the government —Vannevar Bush⟩ **2** : to pass through the pores or interstices of : penetrate and pass through without causing rupture or displacement — used esp. of a fluid that passes through substances of loose texture ⟨water ~s sand⟩

**syn** PERMEATE, PERVADE, PENETRATE, IMPENETRATE, INTERPENETRATE, IMPREGNATE, and SATURATE can mean, in common, to pass or cause to pass through every part of a thing, literally or figuratively. PERMEATE implies diffusion through the total or all the pores or interstices of a substance or entity ⟨a green dye *permeating* a garment⟩ ⟨a pleasant smell which *permeated* the shop from morning till night —Ben Riker⟩ ⟨the entire Divine Comedy is *permeated* with the spirit of courtly love —R.A. Hall b.1911⟩ ⟨how deeply the sense of beauty had *permeated* the whole nation —Laurence Binyon⟩ ⟨their tribes gradually became *permeated* with a good deal of Chinese culture —Owen & Eleanor Lattimore⟩ PERVADE, close to PERMEATE, stresses a spreading diffusion throughout every part of a whole ⟨I want kindness and tolerance to *pervade* the earth —F.A.Swinnerton⟩ ⟨an eerie silence *pervades* the place —Lewis Mumford⟩ ⟨the artistry of this first chapter . . . *pervades* and illumines the entire novel —G.H.Genzmer⟩ ⟨the influence of Descartes *pervades* economics even today —Phoebe T. Danière⟩ PENETRATE in this context implies the entrance of something that goes deep and transmits its characteristic or efficient force throughout ⟨a commanding significance, which *penetrates* the whole, informing and ordering everything —F.R.Leavis⟩ ⟨the whole poem is *penetrated* with religion —G.G.Coulton⟩ ⟨the remains of the aristocratic society . . . are *penetrated* not only with an aristocratic but with a political spirit —Walter Bagehot⟩ IMPENETRATE is an intensive of PENETRATE, often throwing more stress on the idea of diffusion than of entrance ⟨some coloring substance with which the liquid was *impenetrated*⟩ INTERPENETRATE, an intensive of PENETRATE, can also apply to the mutual penetration of two substances or entities ⟨it overlaps and *interpenetrates* every other major field of human enterprise —Thomas Munro⟩ ⟨the way in which the Bible — and the *Book of Common Prayer* — have *interpenetrated* English life —Douglas Bush⟩ ⟨the air and the earth *interpenetrated* in the warm gusts of spring; the soil was full of sunlight, and the sunlight full of red dust —Willa Cather⟩ ⟨the organization of the sonnet often demands that the discourse and the moral should *interpenetrate* —Iain Fletcher⟩ IMPREGNATE can strongly imply a causative power and stress a strong influence or effect on a thing or diffusion of something within it to the point of pervasion of all parts of the whole ⟨the water is *impregnated* with magnesia —Aldous Huxley⟩ ⟨the air is *impregnated* with a sort of frigid clamminess —E.A.Robinson⟩ ⟨from his environment the boy had been thoroughly *impregnated* with what was to become the prevailing American doctrine —Harriot B. Barbour⟩ SATURATE in this context implies impregnation, usu. by something obvious or overabundant, to the point where nothing more may be taken up or absorbed ⟨the air is warm, thick, sticky, and . . . *saturated* with vegetable odours —E.J.Banfield⟩ ⟨the air is *saturated* with golden light —Gertrude Diamant⟩ ⟨grew up in an atmosphere *saturated* by the strictest Puritan dogma and doctrine —David Fairchild⟩ ⟨verse that is *saturated* with emotion —J.L.Lowes⟩ ⟨the lugubrious vigilance that *saturates* the whole document —J.V. Kelleher⟩

**per·me·ation** \,==='āshən\ *n* -s **1** : the quality or state of being permeated : PERVASION ⟨the ~ of this theme . . . in all the areas of communication —J.D.Adams⟩ **2 a** : the act or process of permeating : PENETRATION ⟨the sands are so compacted . . . there is no more space for ~ —*Oil*⟩ ⟨assisted in the ~ of principles of mental hygiene in all agencies —*U.S. Dept. of Labor Bull.*⟩ **b** : IMPREGNATION 2a

**per·me·ative** \'==,ād·|iv, -,ātl, |ēv *also* |əv\ *adj* : PERMEATING ⟨armed with ~ irony . . . he punctures affectations —James Kelly⟩

**permed** \'pərmd\ *adj, chiefly Brit* [1*perm* + *-ed*] : having a permanent wave ⟨an exquisitely ~ . . . blonde with delicate features —Phelim Brady⟩

**per men·sem** \(,)pər'men(t)səm, per-, -n,sem\ *adv* [L] : by the month : MONTHLY ⟨salary . . . *per mensem* —*Scotsman*⟩ ⟨the number of men transported . . . *per mensem* —*Times Hist. of the War*⟩

**per·miak** *or* **per·myak** \'pərmē,ak, 'per-, -m,yak\ *n* -s *usu cap* [Russ *Permyak*, fr. *Perm'* (Perm), region in eastern Russia] : a member of a Russian-Finnish people northeast of Perm in the U.S.S.R. that are part of the Komi or Zyrians — called also *Permian*

**1per·mi·an** \'pərmēən\ *adj, usu cap* [*Perm*, region in eastern Russia (fr. Russ *Perm'*) + E *-ian*] : of or relating to the last major division of the Paleozoic marked by extensive glaciation in India, So. Africa, So. America, and Australia, by decline of the amphibians and increase of primitive reptiles, and by rocks consisting largely of red sandstone and shale — see GEOLOGIC TIME table

**2permian** \"\ *n* -s *usu cap* **1** : the Permian period or system of rocks **2 a** : PERMIAK **b** : the Finno-Ugric languages of the Permiaks, Votyaks, and Zyrians

**per mill** *also* **per mille** *or* **per mil** \(,)pər'mil\ *adv* [*mill*, *mille*, *mil* fr. L *mille* thousand — more at MILE] : by the thousand : per thousand

**per·mil·lage** \(,)pər'milij\ *n* -s [*per mill* + *-age*] : rate or proportion per thousand

**per·mis·si·bil·i·ty** \pə(r),misə'biləd·ē, -lətē, -i\ *n* -ES : the quality or state of being permissible ⟨a greater emotional ~, a greater readiness to welcome tears or laughter —Irving Howe & Eliezer Greenberg⟩

**1per·mis·si·ble** \pə(r)'misəbəl\ *adj* [ME, fr. ML *permissibilis*, fr. L *permissus* (past part. of *permittere* to permit) + *-ibilis* -ible — more at PERMIT] **1** : that may be permitted : ALLOWABLE, ADMISSIBLE ⟨~ error⟩ ⟨~ dose⟩ ⟨maximum ~ exposure to radiation⟩ ⟨always ~ in a crisis but now a regular practice —John Buchan⟩ **2 a** *of an explosive* : permitted by law to be owned, purchased, or sold **b** : approved by the Federal Bureau of Mines for use in gassy coal mines — **per·mis·si·ble·ness** *n* -ES

**2permissible** \"\ *n* -s : a permissible explosive ⟨sales of ~s and other high explosives —*U.S.Daily*⟩

**per·mis·si·bly** \-blē, -bli\ *adv* : in a permissible manner

**per·mis·sion** \pə(r)'mishən\ *n* -s [ME, fr. MF, fr. L *permission-*, *permissio*, fr. *permissus* (past part. of *permittere* to permit) + *-ion-*, *-io* -ion — more at PERMIT] : the act of permitting : formal consent : AUTHORIZATION ⟨by the gracious ~ of the party in power —J.B.Priestley⟩ ⟨had asked her ~ —Willa Cather⟩ ⟨obtain written ~s from the holders of the copyrights —*Publisher to Author*⟩

**per·mis·sive** \pə(r)'misiv, -sēv *also* -səv\ *adj* [F *permissif*, fr. MF, fr. L *permissus* (past part. of *permittere* to permit) + MF *-if* -ive] **1** *archaic* : granted on sufferance : TOLERATED ⟨with what ~ glory since his fall —John Milton⟩ **2** : granting permission : allowing freedom (as of choice, development, behavior) : TOLERANT, INDULGENT ⟨a ~ environment⟩ ⟨the ~ tendencies of the age —C.A.Tonsor⟩ ⟨a cordial ~ pat —Marjorie Brace⟩ ⟨~ parents⟩ **3** : allowing discretion : OPTIONAL ⟨a ~ standard⟩ — used often of legislation enacted by a higher body to be put into effect or not at the option of local authorities ⟨direct primary legislation is largely ~ rather than prescriptive —V.O.Key⟩ — **per·mis·sive·ly** \-səvlē, -li\ *adv* — **per·mis·sive·ness** \-sēvnəs, -siv-\ *n* -ES

**permissive blocking** *n* : BLOCK SYSTEM

**permissive waste** *n* : waste arising from a tenant's neglect to repair, take reasonable care of, or keep in proper order or condition an estate or freehold

**1per·mit** \pə(r)'mit, *usu* -id·+V\ *vb* **permitted**; **permitted**; **permitting**; **permits** [L *permittere* to let through, allow, permit, fr. *per-* through + *mittere* to let go, send — more at PER-, SMITE] *vt* **1** : to consent to expressly or formally : grant leave for or the privilege of : ALLOW, TOLERATE ⟨~ smoking⟩ ⟨~ an appeal⟩ ⟨~ access to records⟩ **2** : to give (a person) leave : AUTHORIZE ⟨obliged to ~ others to use his patent —Tris Coffin⟩ ⟨one must ~ oneself . . . a certain margin of misstatement —B.N.Cardozo⟩ ⟨~ me to offer my congratulations⟩ **3** *archaic* : to give over : COMMIT ⟨to the gods ~ the event of things —Joseph Addison⟩ **4** : to make possible ⟨building has been divided . . . to ~ an unobstructed view —*Amer. Guide Series: Conn.*⟩ ~ *vi* **1** : to give an opportunity ⟨if time *permitted* I could go on —H.G.Doyle⟩ ⟨made himself as comfortable as the hard rock *permitted* —Fred Majdalany⟩ **2** : ADMIT — usu. used with *of* ⟨the distance . . . was too great to ~ of frequent social intercourse —Martha T. Stephenson⟩

**syn** see LET

**2per·mit** \'pər,mit, 'pə̄,m-, 'pəi,m-, ,pə(r)'m-, *usu* -id·+V\ *n* -s **1** : a written warrant or license granted by one having authority ⟨a building ~⟩ ⟨a work ~⟩ ⟨a fishing ~⟩ **2** : PERMISSION, ALLOWANCE ⟨had their ~ to proceed⟩ **3** *or* **permit indicia** : postal indicia giving notice that postage has been paid under a special permit (as for bulk mailing)

**3permit** \"\ *n* -s [by folk etymology fr. Sp *palometa* — more at PALOMETA] **1** : a large up to three feet long blue and silver pompano (*Trachinotus goodei*) found esp. off the West Indies and Florida — called also *great pompano* **2** : ROUND POMPANO

**permit bond** *n* : a surety bond required by law as a condition precedent to the enjoyment of some privilege granted by governmental permit

**permit card** *n* : a card issued by a union to a nonmember allowing him to work on a temporary basis on a union job

**per·mit·tance** \pə(r)'mit^ən(t)s\ *n* -s [1*permit* + *-ance*] : PERMISSION

**permitted** *adj* : ALLOWED

**permitted explosive** *n, Brit* : a permissible explosive

**per·mit·tee** \,pərmə'tē, pər'mid·(,)ē\ *n* -s : one to whom a permission or permit is given ⟨the ~ should begin drilling operations within six months —W.F.Cloud⟩

**per·mit·tiv·i·ty** \,pərmə'tivəd·ē\ *n* -ES [1*permit* + *-ive* + *-ity*] : DIELECTRIC CONSTANT

**permix** *vt* [back-formation fr. obs. *permixt* mixed thoroughly, fr. ME, fr. L *permixtus*, past part. of *permiscēre* to mix thoroughly, fr. *per-* thoroughly + *miscēre* to mix — more at PER-, MIX] *obs* : to mix thoroughly

**permo-** *comb form, usu cap* [ISV, fr. 1*Permian*] : Permian and — esp. in the names of geologic strata ⟨*Permocarboniferous*⟩ ⟨*Permopennsylvanian*⟩ ⟨*Permotriassic*⟩

**per·mono·sulfuric acid** \,pər,mänō, -mō+ . . . -\ *n* [*per-* + *mon-* + *sulfuric*] : an unstable crystalline strong monobasic acid $H_2SO_5$ obtained by acid hydrolysis of persulfates or by the action of hydrogen peroxide on chlorosulfonic acid or sulfuric acid — called also *Caro's acid, peroxymonosulfuric acid*

**perm·selective** \ˌpərm+\ *adj* [*permeable* + *selective*] **:** of, relating to, or being a semipermeable membrane that is also an ion exchanger

**per·mu·tate** \ˈpərmyəˌtāt, (ˌ)pərˈmyüˌtāt\ *vt* -ED/-ING/-S [L *permutatus*, past part. of *permutare* to change thoroughly, exchange — more at PERMUTE] **:** CHANGE, INTERCHANGE; *esp* **:** to arrange in a different order

**per·mu·ta·tion** \ˌpərmyəˈtāshən, ˌpēm-, ˌpəim-, -myüˈt-\ *n* -S [ME *permutacioun*, fr. MF *permutation*, fr. L *permutation-, permutatio*, fr. *permutatus* + *-ion-, -io* -ion] **1 :** exchange of one thing for another as distinguished from a sale for money **:** BARTER **2 :** a thorough change (as in character or condition) **:** TRANSMUTATION, TRANSFORMATION ⟨the ~s . . . taking place in the physical world —Henry Miller⟩ **3 a :** the act or process of changing the lineal order of a set of objects arranged in a group **b :** an arrangement of a given number of objects ⟨~s of the three items *a, b,* and *c: abc, acb, bac* . . . —A.K.Kurtz & H.A.Edgerton⟩ — compare COMBINATION 1b(3) — **per·mu·ta·tion·al** \ˌ==ˈtāshənᵊl, -shnəl\ *adj*

**permutation lock** *n* **:** a lock having tumblers that may be changed to require different keys or setting combinations

**permutation table** *n* **:** a synoptic chart governing the construction of the code groups of a particular code and serving to facilitate correction of garbles

**per·mu·ta·tor** \ˈ==ˌtād·ə(r)\ *n* -S **:** a rotary converter with stationary commutator and rotating brushes that has the exciting field induced by the alternating current in a short-circuited magnetic core instead of produced by an external magnet

**per·mute** \pə(r)ˈmyüt\ *vt* -ED/-ING/-S [ME *permuten* (also, to exchange), fr. MF or L; MF *permuter*, fr. L *permutare*, fr. *per-* thoroughly + *mutare* to change — more at PER-, MUTABLE] **1** *obs* **:** to change thoroughly **:** TRANSFORM **2 :** to change the order or arrangement of; *esp* **:** to arrange (objects in a series) in all the possible ways in which they can be arranged

**permyak** *usu cap, var of* PERMIAK

**¹pern** *chiefly Brit var of* PIRN 1

**²pern** \ˈpərn\ *n* -S [NL *Pernis*] **:** HONEY BUZZARD

**per·nam·bu·co** \ˌpərnamˈb(y)ü(ˌ)kō, ¦pernam¦bü-\ *adj, usu cap* [fr. *Pernambuco* (Recife), Brazil] **:** RECIFE

**pernambuco cotton** *n, usu cap P* **:** KIDNEY COTTON

**pernambuco jaborandi** *n, usu cap P* **:** JABORANDI 1a

**pernambuco rubber** *n, usu cap P* **:** MANGABEIRA RUBBER

**pernambuco wood** *n, usu cap P* **:** a brazilwood from a leguminous tree (*Caesalpinia echinata*)

**per·nan·cy** \ˈpərnənsē\ *n* -ES [AF *pernance* (alter. of OF *prenance*, fr. *prendre* to take — fr. L *prehendere* to seize, grasp — + *-ance*) + E *-y* — more at GET] **:** a taking or receiving of something (as profits or rents or tithes in kind)

**per·net·tia** \pə(r)ˈned·ēə\ [NL, fr. Antoine J. *Pernetty* †1796 Fr. traveler and naturalist + NL *-ia*] *syn of* PERNETTYA

**per·net·tya** \"\ *n, cap* [NL, after A.J.*Pernetty*] **:** a genus of chiefly American evergreen shrubs (family Ericaceae) having small serrate leaves and usu. solitary axillary flowers

**¹per·ni·cious** \pə(r)ˈnishəs\ *adj* [MF *pernicieus*, fr. L *perniciosus*, fr. *pernicies* ruin, destruction (fr. *per* through + *-nicies*, fr. *nec-, nex* violent death) + *-osus* -ous — more at FOR, NOXIOUS] **1 :** highly injurious or destructive **:** tending to a fatal issue **:** DEADLY ⟨a ~ influence⟩ ⟨~ habits⟩ ⟨~ nonsense⟩ ⟨a ~ practice⟩ ⟨~ disease⟩ ⟨emphasis on fixed order frequently results in ~ restraints against growing and vital movement —M.R.Cohen⟩ ⟨no excuse for allowing our children to be taught a morality which we ourselves believe to be ~ —Bertrand Russell⟩ **2** *archaic* **:** intending or doing evil **:** WICKED, VILLAINOUS ⟨two ~ daughters —Shak.⟩

**syn** BANEFUL, NOXIOUS, DELETERIOUS, DETRIMENTAL: PERNICIOUS describes that which harms exceedingly or irreparably by evil or insidious corrupting or enervating ⟨*pernicious* social institutions which stifle the nobler impulses and encourage the baser —V.L.Parrington⟩ ⟨addiction, on the other hand, carries with it a certain stigma which is not unjustified; it suggests the connotation of a *pernicious* or harmful repetitive act which gets out of the control of the individual —D.W.Maurer & V.H.Vogel⟩ BANEFUL may describe anything malevolent or malignant that is likely to kill, poison, or destroy ⟨the *baneful* influence of this narrow construction on all the operations of the government —John Marshall⟩ ⟨seen to be the outward projections of *baneful* subconscious elements and add up to a fearful indictment of the man —*Times Lit. Supp.*⟩ NOXIOUS may refer to what is at once harmful and unwholesome, corrupting, or noisome ⟨the primitive plumbing of the 1870s, by conveying *noxious* odors into the rooms, was often a threat to the family health —A.M.Schlesinger b.1888⟩ ⟨when the educator shall have been educated, the air cleared of *noxious* fallacies, and a sound and virile conception of learning restored —C.H.Grandgent⟩ DELETERIOUS describes whatever has a harmful effect, often in some concealed or unguessed way ⟨it was obvious that lime juice adulterated with five percent sulphuric acid, jellies with formaldehyde, peas with copper, cheap flavoring extracts with wood alcohol, and coloring matter with arsenic or mercury were highly *deleterious* to health —V.G.Heiser⟩ ⟨heroin and other *deleterious* drugs —H.L.Ickes⟩ DETRIMENTAL is a general adjective for anything that harms ⟨neutralizing or eliminating those influences in military aviation which are *detrimental* to the efficiency, health, or life of flying personnel —H.G.Armstrong⟩ ⟨the wheat is cleaned and scrubbed and the fine hairs, *detrimental* to color and quality, removed —*Amer. Guide Series: Minn.*⟩

**²pernicious** \"\ *adj* [L *pernic-, pernix* swift (fr. *perna* haunch, ham) + E *-ious* — more at PEARL] *archaic* **:** QUICK, SWIFT

**pernicious anemia** *n* **1 :** a severe hyperchromic anemia characterized by a progressive decrease in number and increase in size of the red blood cells and by pallor, weakness, and gastrointestinal and nervous disturbances resulting from absence from the gastric juice of hydrochloric acid and the intrinsic factor necessary for the intestinal absorption of vitamin $B_{12}$ **2 :** INFECTIOUS ANEMIA

**per·ni·cious·ly** *adv* **:** in a pernicious manner

**pernicious malaria** *n* **:** FALCIPARUM MALARIA

**per·ni·cious·ness** *n* -ES **:** the quality or state of being pernicious

**pernicious scale** *n* **:** SAN JOSE SCALE

**per·nick·e·ti·ness** \pə(r)ˈnikəd·ēnəs, -kət|, |in-\ *n* -ES **:** the quality or state of being pernickety **:** FINICALITY, FASTIDIOUSNESS ⟨~ and refinement, resulting in a sterile preciosity —Michael Williams⟩

**per·nick·e·ty** \|ē, |i\ *adj* [perh. alter. of *particular*] **1 :** having extremely exacting standards **:** FINICAL, FUSSY, METICULOUS ⟨dons who can be . . . obstinate and ~ —R.F.Harrod⟩ **2 :** requiring great precision **:** TICKLISH ⟨his ~, very nasty job —Paul de Kruif⟩ **syn** see NICE

**per·nine** \ˈpərˌnīn\ *adj* [NL *Pernis* + E *-ine*] **:** of or relating to the genus *Pernis*

**per·nio** \ˈpərnēˌō\ *n, pl* **perni·o·nes** \ˌ==ˈō(ˌ)nēz\ [L, fr. *perna* haunch, ham + *-io* -ion — more at PEARL] **:** CHILBLAIN

**per·ni·o·sis** \ˌpərnēˈōsəs\ *n, pl* **pernio·ses** \-ōˌsēz\ [NL, fr. L *pernio* + NL *-osis*] **:** a skin abnormality resulting from cold

**per·nis** \ˈpərnəs\ *n, cap* [NL, modif. of Gk *pternis*, a hawk] **:** a genus of hawks (family Falconidae) consisting of the honey buzzards

**per·nitric acid** \ˌpər+. . .-\ *n* [ISV *per-* + *nitric*] **:** an explosive acid $HNO_4$ held to be obtained as a liquid or in the form of salts (as by oxidation of nitrogen pentoxide with anhydrous hydrogen peroxide) — called also *peroxynitric acid;* not used systematically

**per·noc·tate** \(ˌ)pərˈnäkˌtāt\ *vi* -ED/-ING/-S [L *pernoctatus*, past part. of *pernoctare*, fr. *per-* through + *noct-, nox* night — more at PER-, NIGHT] **:** to stay up or out all night; *esp* **:** to pass the night in vigil or prayer ⟨I *pernoctated* with the . . . students once —J.C.Ransom⟩

**per·noc·ta·tion** \ˌpərnäkˈtāshən\ *n* -S [LL *pernoctation-, pernoctatio*, fr. L *pernoctatus* + *-ion-, -io* -ion] **:** the act of pernoctating; *esp* **:** an all-night vigil

**Per·nod** \(ˈ)perˈnō\ *trademark* — used for an aromatic French liqueur that is used as an aperitif and has a flavor somewhat like that of anisette

**per·nor** \ˈpərnər, -ˌnō(ə)r\ *n* -S [ME *pernour*, fr. AF, alter. of OF *preneor, preneur* taker, fr. *prendre* to take + *-eor, -eur* -or — more at PERNANCY] **:** a taker or receiver esp. of income (as from rents) or profits

**per·not furnace** \(ˈ)perˈnō-\ *n, usu cap P* [after Charles *Pernot*, its inventor] **:** a reverberatory furnace with a circular revolving hearth used in making steel

**perns** *pl of* PERN

**per·nyi moth** \ˈpərnēˌī-, ˈpernēˌē-\ *n* [NL *pernyi* (specific epithet of *Antheraea pernyi*), after Paul H. *Perny* †1907 French missionary and Chinese scholar] **:** a Chinese silk-producing moth (*Antheraea pernyi*)

**pernyi silkworm** *n* **:** a caterpillar that is the larva of the pernyi moth, feeds on oak leaves, and produces pongee silk

**pe·ro·ba** \pəˈrōbə\ *n* -S [Pg, fr. Tupi *iperoba, peroba*] **:** any of several important Brazilian timber trees: as **a** *or* **peroba rosa :** a tree (*Aspidosperma polyneuron*) with very hard rose-yellow wood common in the state of São Paulo **b :** a tree (*Paratecoma peroba*) of the family Apocynaceae with yellowish brown wood found along the coast of So. America — called also *ipé peroba*

**perofskite** *var of* PEROVSKITE

**pe·rog·na·thus** \pəˈrägnəthəs\ *n, cap* [NL, fr. Gk *pēro-* (fr. *pēra* pouch, wallet) + *-gnathus*] **:** a genus of sciuromorph rodents (family Heteromyidae) consisting of the pocket mice

**pero·medusae** \ˌperō+\ *n pl, cap* [NL, fr. Gk *pēro-* (fr. *pēra* pouch) + *medusae*, pl. of *medusa*] *in some classifications* **:** a division of Scyphozoa that is characterized by the presence of four interradial tentaculocysts and is approximately equal to the order Coronatae

**¹peromedusan** \"+\ *adj* [NL *Peromedusae* + E *-an*] **:** of or relating to the Peromedusae

**²peromedusan** \"\ *n* -S **:** a coelenterate of the division Peromedusae

**pe·rom·e·la** \pəˈrämələ\ [NL, fr. Gk *pēromelēs* with maimed limbs, fr. *pēros* maimed + *melos* limb; akin to Gk *pēma* suffering, calamity — more at PATIENT, MELODY] *syn of* AISTOPODA

**pero·mys·cus** \ˌperəˈmiskəs\ *n, cap* [NL, fr. Gk *pēros* maimed + *myskos* small mouse, dim. of *mys* mouse — more at MOUSE] **:** a genus of rodents (family Cricetidae) comprising the white-footed mice of No. America

**pero·nate** \pəˈrōnət, ˈperəˌnāt\ *adj* [L *peronatus* having boots of untanned leather, fr. *peron-, pero* hide boot (prob. fr. *pera* leather sack, pouch, fr. Gk *pēra*) + *-atus* -ate] **:** having a mealy or woolly covering resembling a boot or stocking — used of the stipe of a mushroom

**per·o·ne·al** \ˌperəˈnēəl\ *adj* [NL *peroneus* peroneal, fr. *perone* fibula (fr. Gk *peronē* pin, fibula) + E *-al;* akin to Gk *peran* to pass through — more at FARE] **1 :** of or relating to the fibula **2 :** near the fibula; *esp* **:** being a body part so located **3 :** of, relating to, or involving a peroneal part ⟨~ spasm⟩

**peroneal artery** *n* **:** a deeply seated artery running along the back part of the fibular side of the leg to the heel, arising from the posterior tibial, and giving off or dividing near the ankle into an anterior and posterior branch

**peroneal atrophy** *n* **:** wasting of the muscles of the calf

**peroneal nerve** *n* **:** the smaller of the popliteal nerves passing obliquely outward and downward from the popliteal space and to the neck of the fibula where it divides into deep and superficial branches that supply certain muscles and skin areas of the leg and foot

**peroneo-** *comb form* [*peroneal*] **:** peroneal and ⟨*peroneo*calcaneal⟩

**per·o·ne·us** \ˌperəˈnēəs\ *n, pl* **pero·nei** \-ēˌī\ [NL, fr. *perone*] **:** any of several muscles (as the peroneus longus) of the lower leg that arise from the fibula and are inserted on one of the metatarsal bones of the foot — more at PERONEAL

**pe·ro·ni·al** \pəˈrōnēəl\ *adj* [NL *peronium* + E *-al*] **:** of or relating to a peronium

**pero·nism** \pəˈrōˌnizəm *sometimes* ˈperəˌn-\ *or* **pe·ro·nis·mo** \ˌperəˈniz(ˌ)mō, -ˈnēz-\ *n* -S *usu cap* [Sp *peronismo*, fr. Juan Domingo *Perón b ab*1896 Argentine politician + Sp *-ismo* -ism] **:** the political, economic, and social principles and policies associated with Perón and his regime and usu. regarded as fascist ⟨a . . . factual indictment of the aims and methods of *Peronism* —*Times Lit. Supp.*⟩

**¹pero·nist** \pəˈrōnəst *sometimes* ˈperən-\ *or* **pe·ro·nis·ta** \ˌperəˈnistə, -ˈnēs-\ *n* -S *usu cap* [Sp *peronista*, fr. J. D. *Perón* + Sp *-ista* -ist] **:** a follower of Perón **:** an adherent of Peronism

**²peronist** \"\ *or* **peronista** \"\ *adj, usu cap* [Sp *peronista*, fr. *peronista*, n.] **:** of, relating to, or having the characteristics of Peronism or Peronists ⟨free the economy from strangling *Peronist* controls —*Time*⟩ ⟨efforts to build a *Peronista* bloc in South America —*New Republic*⟩

**pe·ro·ni·um** \pəˈrōnēəm\ *n, pl* **pero·nia** \-ēə\ [NL, fr. Gk *peronion*, small pin, dim. of *peronē* pin, fibula — more at PERONEAL] **:** a tract of modified epithelium between the margin of the umbrella and the base of a tentacle in some Hydromedusae

**perono-** *comb form, cap* [NL, fr. *perone* fibula — more at PERONEAL] **:** pin **:** fibula ⟨*Perono*spora⟩ — in the names of taxa

**per·o·nos·po·ra** \ˌperəˈnäspərə\ *n, cap* [NL, fr. *perono-* + *-spora*] **:** a genus (the type of the family Peronosporaceae) of destructive downy mildews having the sporangiophores dichotomously branched and with pointed tips — see ONION MILDEW, TOBACCO BLUE MOLD

**per·o·no·spo·ra·ce·ae** \ˌperənōspəˈrāsēˌē\ *n pl, cap* [NL, *Peronospora*, type genus + *-aceae*] **:** a family of parasitic fungi (order Peronosporales) in which the conidiophores form outside the epidermis of the host and develop conidia or sporangia singly or in clusters but never in chains — see DOWNY MILDEW — **per·o·no·spo·ra·ceous** \ˌ=====ˈrāshəs\ *adj*

**per·o·nos·po·ra·les** \ˌperəˌnäspəˈrā(ˌ)lēz\ *n pl, cap* [NL, fr. *Peronospora* + *-ales*] **:** an order comprising chiefly parasitic lower fungi (subclass Oomycetes) that have equally biflagellate zoospores and conidia which either germinate directly or act as sporangia and contain the families Albuginaceae, Peronosporaceae, and Pythiaceae

**pe·rop·o·dous** \pəˈräpədəs\ *adj* [Gk *pēros* maimed + E *-podous* — more at PEROMELA] **:** having rudimentary hind limbs — used of a snake (as a boa, python)

**peropus** *n* -ES [origin unknown] *obs* **:** a 17th century fabric resembling paragon

**per·oral** \ˌpər, (ˈ)per+\ *adj* [ISV *per-* + *oral*] **:** occurring through or by way of the mouth ⟨~ administration of a drug⟩ ⟨~ infection⟩ — **per·orally** \"+\ *adv*

**per·orate** \ˈperəˌrāt, |ōˌr- *also* ¦pər·| *sometimes* ¦pər|; *usu* -ād.+V\ *vb* [L *peroratus*, past part. of *perorare*, fr. *per-*, prefix used to denote completion + *orare* to speak — more at ORATION] *vi* **1 :** to deliver an oration esp. in a grandiloquent style **:** speak at length **2 :** to make a peroration **:** conclude or sum up a speech ~ *vt* **:** to utter in a declamatory manner

**per·ora·tion** \-ˈrāshən\ *n* -S [ME *peroracyon*, fr. L *peroration-, peroratio*, fr. *peroratus* + *-ion-, -io* -ion] **1 :** the concluding part of a composition or discourse (as an oration) **:** a final usu. formal summing up of the argument (as in a speech) ⟨concludes, in a moving ~ —Alice S. Morris⟩ ⟨framing . . . the ~ of his powerful maiden speech —Harold Nicolson⟩ **2 :** a flowery highly rhetorical speech ⟨what means this passionate discourse? this ~ with such circumstance —Shak.⟩ — **per·ora·tion·al** \-shənᵊl, -shnəl\ *adj*

**per·ora·tive** \ˈ==ˌrād·iv\ *adj* **:** of, relating to, or suitable for a peroration ⟨~ examples —John Caffrey⟩

**per os** \peˈrōs, ˌpərˈōs, ˌpər-ˈäs\ *adv* [L] **:** by way of the mouth

**pe·ro·sis** \pəˈrōsəs\ *n, pl* **pero·ses** \-ōˌsēz\ [NL, fr. Gk *pēros* maimed + NL *-osis* — more at PEROMELA] **:** a disorder of chicks, turkey poults, and young swans characterized by enlargement of the hock, twisted metatarsi, and slipped tendons and largely eliminable by additions of choline to the diet

**pe·rot·ic** \pəˈräd·ik\ *adj* [fr. NL *perosis*, after such pairs as NL *narcosis*: E *narcotic*] **:** of or relating to perosis

**pe·rov·skite** \pəˈrävzˌkīt, -äfˌsk-\ *or* **pe·rof·skite** \-äf-\ *n* -S [G *perowskit*, fr. Count L. A. *Perovski* †1856 Russian statesman + G *-it* -ite] **:** a mineral $CaTiO_3$ consisting of calcium titanate, sometimes having also cerium and other rare-earth metals, and occurring in yellow, brown, or grayish black crystals of cubic habit or in reniform masses (hardness 5.5, sp. gr. 4.02–4.04)

**per·ox·i·dase** \pəˈräksəˌdās, -āz\ *n* -S [ISV *peroxide* + *-ase*] **:** an enzyme occurring esp. in plants, milk, and leukocytes and consisting of a protein complex with hematin groups that catalyzes the oxidation of various substances (as diphenols or aromatic amines) by peroxides — compare CATALASE

**per·ox·i·date** \pəˈräksəˌdāt\ *vb* [¹*peroxide* + *-ate*] **:** PEROXIDIZE

**peroxidatic** \pəˌräksəˈdad·ik\ *adj* [fr. *peroxidase*, after such pairs as E *catalase*: *catalatic*] **:** of or relating to peroxidase

**per·ox·i·da·tion** \=ˌ==ˈdāshən\ *n* **:** the process of peroxidizing

**¹per·ox·ide** \pəˈräkˌsīd\ *n* [ISV *per-* + *oxide*] **1 :** an oxide containing a relatively high proportion of oxygen — not used systematically **2 a :** a compound (as sodium peroxide or benzoyl peroxide) characterized by the bivalent group or anion -O-O- consisting of two oxygen atoms united to each other and yielding a solution of hydrogen peroxide when treated with acid — compare SUPEROXIDE **b :** HYDROGEN PEROXIDE

**²peroxide** \"\ *vt* -ED/-ING/-S **:** to treat with a peroxide; *esp* **:** to bleach (hair) with hydrogen peroxide

**peroxide blonde** *n* **:** a woman with bleached hair ⟨doting on a *peroxide blonde* . . . a brazen gold digger —Ngaio Marsh⟩

**per·ox·i·dize** \pəˈräksəˌdīz\ *vb* [¹*peroxide* + *-ize*] *vt* **:** to oxidize to the utmost or so as to form a peroxide ~ *vi* **:** to become oxidized to the utmost or so as to form a peroxide

**peroxo-** *comb form* [ISV *per-* + *ox-*] **:** PEROXY- — in names of coordination complexes ⟨hex-oxo-*peroxo*-disulfate $S_2O_8^{=}$⟩

**per·oxy** \pəˈräksē\ *adj* [*peroxy-*] **:** containing the group -O-O-

**peroxy-** *comb form* [ISV *per-* + *oxy-*] **:** containing the group -O-O- characteristic of a peroxide ⟨*peroxy*disulfate⟩ ⟨*peroxy*benzoic acid⟩

**per·oxy·acetic acid** \pəˌräksē+. . .-\ *n* [*peroxy-* + *acetic*] **:** PERACETIC ACID

**peroxy acid** *n* **:** an acid (as persulfuric acid) containing the peroxide group

**per·oxy·carbonate** \pəˌräksē+\ *n* [*peroxy-* + *carbonate*] **:** PERCARBONATE

**per·oxy·carbonic acid** \"+. . .-\ *n* [*peroxy-* + *carbonic*] **:** PERCARBONIC ACID

**per·oxy·chromate** \pəˌräksē+\ *n* [*peroxy-* + *chromate*] **:** PERCHROMATE

**per·oxy·chromic acid** \"+. . .-\ *n* [*peroxy-* + *chromic*] **:** PERCHROMIC ACID

**per·oxy·disulfate** \pəˌräksē+\ *n* [*peroxy-* + *disulfate*] **:** a persulfate of the acid $H_2S_2O_8$

**per·oxy·disulfuric acid** \"+. . .-\ *n* [*peroxy-* + *disulfuric*] **:** PERSULFURIC ACID a

**per·oxygen** \(ˈ)pər+\ *adj* [*per-* + *oxygen*] **:** PEROXY

**per·oxy·mono·sulfuric acid** \pəˌräksēˌmänō, -mōnō+. . .-\ *n* [*peroxy-* + *mon-* + *sulfuric*] **:** PERMONOSULFURIC ACID

**per·oxy·nitric acid** \pəˌräksē+. . .-\ *n* [*peroxy-* + *nitric*] **:** PERNITRIC ACID

**peroxy salt** *n* **:** a salt (as ammonium persulfate) of a peroxy acid

**per·oxy·sulfate** \pəˌräksē+\ *n* [*peroxy-* + *sulfate*] **:** PERSULFATE 2

**per·oxy·sulfuric acid** \"+. . .-\ *n* [*peroxy-* + *sulfuric*] **:** PERSULFURIC ACID

**perp** *abbr* **1** perpendicular **2** perpetual

**per pais** *or* **per pays** \ˌpərˈpā\ *adv* [AF] **:** by the country **:** by a jury or by matter triable by a jury ⟨trials *per pais*⟩

**per pa·res** \perˈpäˌrās, ˌpərˈpa(ə)rēz\ *adv* [L] **:** by one's peers

**¹per·pend** \pə(r)ˈpend\ *vb* -ED/-ING/-S [L *perpendere*, fr. *per-* thoroughly + *pendere* to weigh — more at PER-, PENDANT] *vt* **:** to weigh carefully in the mind **:** reflect on **:** PONDER ⟨~ my words —Sir Walter Scott⟩ ⟨found himself . . . ~*ing* it as an experiment in realism —Leonard Merrick⟩ ~ *vi* **:** to be attentive **:** REFLECT, CONSIDER ⟨~, my princess, and give ear —Shak.⟩ ⟨~, and do not compel me to use violence —Benjamin Jowett⟩

**²per·pend** \ˈpərpənd\ *or* **per·pent** \-nt\ *or* **par·pen** \ˈpärpən\ *n* -S [ME *perpend, perpoynt*, fr. MF *perpain, parpain*] **1 :** a brick or large stone reaching through a wall so as to appear on both sides of it and acting as a binder **2 :** PERPEND WALL

**¹per·pen·dic·u·lar** \ˌpər|pənˈdikyələr, ¦pə|. . .lə(r, ¦pəi|. . .lə(r, |pᵊm|d-\ *adj* [alter. (influenced by L *perpendicularis*, of ME *perpendiculer*, fr. MF, fr. L *perpendicularis*, fr. *perpendiculum* plumb line (fr. *per-* through + *pendēre* to hang + *-iculum*, suffix denoting an instrument) + *-aris* -ar — more at PER-, PENDANT] **1 a :** standing at right angles to the plane of the horizon **:** pointing to the zenith **:** exactly vertical or upright ⟨measure the ~ height⟩ **b :** being or set at right angles to a given line or plane ⟨the lines are ~ to each other⟩ ⟨an almost ~ rise in share prices —*U.S. News & World Report*⟩ **2** *obs* **:** leading directly to **:** IMMEDIATE ⟨~ cause⟩ **3 :** extremely steep **:** PRECIPITOUS ⟨a lofty ~ cliff —E.V.Lucas⟩ **4** *of a person* **a :** erect in bearing ⟨a ~ retired colonel⟩ **b :** standing up ⟨a bus . . . its platform weighed down with ~ men —Bruce Marshall⟩ **5 :** of, relating to, or in a medieval English Gothic style of architecture in which vertical lines predominate **6 :** relating to, uniting, or consisting of individuals of dissimilar type or on different levels ⟨~, in the sense of providing a strand that will run through both high school and college, uniting different ages —*General Education in a Free Society*⟩ **syn** see VERTICAL

**²perpendicular** \"\ *n* -S **1 a :** a line at right angles to another line or plane **b :** a line through a vertex at right angles to the opposite side or face in a triangle or tetrahedron **2 :** an instrument for indicating the vertical line from any point **3 a :** a line at right angles to the plane of the horizon **:** a vertical line or direction **b :** a vertical plane **c :** an extremely steep or precipitous face (as of a mountain)

**per·pen·dic·u·lar·i·ty** \ˌ==ˌ==ˈlarəd·ē, -rətē, -i *also* -ˈler-\ *n* -ES [ML *perpendicularitas*, fr. L *perpendicularis* + *-itas* -ity] **:** the quality or state of being perpendicular

**perpendicularly** *adv* **:** in a perpendicular manner

**perpendicular separation** *n* **:** the distance between the two dislocated parts of an orig. continuous surface (as the top of a stratum) measured normal to the plane — called also *stratigraphic separation*

**perpend wall** *n* [²*perpend*] **:** a wall built of perpends **:** a thin wall

**per·pen·sion** \pə(r)ˈpenchən\ *n* -S [LL *perpension-, perpensio*, fr. L *perpensus* (past part. of *perpendere* to perpend) + *-ion, -io* -ion — more at PERPEND] **:** careful weighing in the mind **:** REFLECTION, CONSIDERATION ⟨give me the results of your ~s —R.L.Stevenson⟩

**per·per** \ˈperpə(r)\ *n, pl* **perpers** \-(r)z\ *or* **per·pera** \-ərə\ [Serbo-Croatian] **:** the basic unit of monetary value of Montenegro from 1908 to 1919 equivalent to the Austrian krone

**per·pe·trate** \ˈpərpəˌtrāt, ˈpəp-, ˈpəip-, *usu* -ād.+V\ *vt* -ED/-ING/-S [L *perpetratus*, past part. of *perpetrare*, fr. *per-*, prefix denoting completion + *-petrare* (fr. *patrare* to carry out, accomplish — prob. orig. "to perform a ritual" — fr. *patr-, pater* father, religious leader) — more at PER-, FATHER] **1 a :** to be guilty of (as a crime, an offense) **:** COMMIT ⟨*perpetrated* the . . . massacre —*Amer. Guide Series: Pa.*⟩ ⟨the horrors . . . their former rulers had *perpetrated* —F.E.Hirsch⟩ ⟨that the press . . . should ~ this calumny —Stephen Spender⟩ **b :** to carry through (a deception) ⟨had *perpetrated* a delightful fraud —L.P.Smith⟩ ⟨~*s* a successful practical joke —J.A. Morris b. 1904⟩ — often used with *on* or *upon* ⟨a huge hoax *perpetrated* on a band of solemn votaries —C.H.Grandgent⟩ **2 :** to produce, perform, or execute badly or in a manner held to be execrable or shocking ⟨~ such an ungainly sentence⟩ ⟨~ a pun⟩ ⟨the simpering family groups *perpetrated* on canvas —Dixon Wecter⟩

**per·pe·tra·tion** \ˌ==ˈtrāshən\ *n* -S [ME *perpetracionne*, fr. LL *perpetration-, perpetratio*, fr. L *perpetratus* + *-ion-, -io* -ion] **1 :** the act or process of perpetrating **:** COMMISSION ⟨the ~ of a series of thefts⟩ ⟨the effective ~ of sabotage —J.J.McCarthy⟩ **2 :** something perpetrated **:** an evil or offensive act ⟨savage ~s —J.H.Newman⟩

**per·pe·tra·tor** \ˈ==ˌtrād·ə(r), -ātə-\ *n* -S [LL, fr. L *perpetratus* + *-or*] **:** one that perpetrates esp. an offense or crime ⟨war is a crime, for which its instigators and ~s can be tried —Vera M. Dean⟩

**¹per·pet·u·al** \pə(r)ˈpech(əw)əl, -chwəl\ *adj* [ME *perpetuel*, fr. MF, fr. L *perpetualis*, fr. *perpetuus* continuous, perpetual (fr. *perpet-, perpes*, fr. *per* through, by means of + *-pet-, -pes*, fr. *petere* to go to or toward, seek) + *-alis* -al — more at FOR, FEATHER] **1 a :** continuing forever **:** EVERLASTING, ETERNAL, UNCEASING ⟨~ torment after death —H.O.Taylor⟩ ⟨dedicated to a life of ~ virginity —J.G.Frazer⟩ ⟨the song of the minstrel moved through a ~ Maytime —J.R.Green⟩ **b** (1) **:** granted to be valid for all time ⟨was awarded a ~ right-of-way⟩ ⟨granted a ~ charter by the national government —C.W. Ferguson⟩ (2) **:** holding (as an office) for life or for an unlimited time ⟨~ curate⟩ ⟨~ president of a club⟩ ⟨elected ~ fellow —A.G.Chester⟩ **2 :** occurring continually **:** indefinitely long-continued **:** not intermittent **:** CONSTANT ⟨a ~ source of amusement —Havelock Ellis⟩ ⟨the ~ struggle to maintain standards in a democracy —F.N.Robinson⟩ ⟨~ quarreling between one parish and the next —Dorothy Sayers⟩ **3 a :** PERENNIAL 2a **b :** blooming more or less continuously throughout the season **:** REMONTANT ⟨a hybrid ~ rose⟩ **syn** see CONTINUAL

**²perpetual** \"\ *adv* [ME *perpetuel*, fr. *perpetuel*, adj.] *archaic* **:** PERPETUALLY

**³perpetual** \"\ *n* -s [¹*perpetual*] **1 :** PERENNIAL 1 **2 :** a hybrid perpetual rose

**perpetual adoration** *n* **:** unceasing adoration of the consecrated Host as practised in the convents of several Roman Catholic orders of that name

**perpetual calendar** *n* **1 :** a table for finding the day of the week for any one of a wide range of dates

PERPETUAL CALENDAR (1753–2000)

| DAY OF THE MONTH | | | | | Jan. Oct. | Apr. July *Jan.* * | Sept. Dec. | June | Feb. Mar. Nov. | Aug. *Feb.* * | May | DAY OF WEEK |
|---|---|---|---|---|---|---|---|---|---|---|---|---|
| 1 | 8 | 15 | 22 | 29 | a | b | c | d | e | f | g | Mon. |
| 2 | 9 | 16 | 23 | 30 | g | a | b | c | d | e | f | Tues. |
| 3 | 10 | 17 | 24 | 31 | f | g | a | b | c | d | e | Wed. |
| 4 | 11 | 18 | 25 | | e | f | g | a | b | c | d | Thurs. |
| 5 | 12 | 19 | 26 | | d | e | f | g | a | b | c | Fri. |
| 6 | 13 | 20 | 27 | | c | d | e | f | g | a | b | Sat. |
| 7 | 14 | 21 | 28 | | b | c | d | e | f | g | a | Sun. |
| | | | | | 1753 | 1754 | 1755 | 1761 | *1756* | 1757 | 1758 | |
| | | | | | 1759 | 1765 | *1760* | 1767 | 1762 | 1763 | 1769 | |
| | | | | | *1764* | 1771 | 1766 | *1772* | 1773 | *1768* | 1775 | |
| | | | | | 1770 | *1776* | 1777 | 1778 | 1779 | 1774 | *1780* | |
| | | | | | 1781 | 1782 | 1783 | 1789 | *1784* | 1785 | 1786 | |
| | | | | | 1787 | 1793 | *1788* | 1795 | 1790 | 1791 | 1797 | |
| | | | | | *1792* | 1799 | 1794 | 1801 | 1802 | *1796* | 1809 | |
| | | | | | 1798 | 1805 | 1800 | 1807 | 1813 | 1803 | 1815 | |
| | | | | | *1804* | 1811 | 1806 | *1812* | 1819 | *1808* | *1820* | |
| | | | | | 1810 | *1816* | 1817 | 1818 | *1824* | 1814 | 1826 | |
| | | | | | 1821 | 1822 | 1823 | 1829 | 1830 | 1825 | 1837 | |
| | | | | | 1827 | 1833 | *1828* | 1835 | 1841 | 1831 | 1843 | |
| | | | | | *1832* | 1839 | 1834 | *1840* | 1847 | *1836* | *1848* | |
| | | | | | 1838 | *1844* | 1845 | 1846 | *1852* | 1842 | 1854 | |
| | | | | | 1849 | 1850 | 1851 | 1857 | 1858 | 1853 | 1865 | |
| | | | | | 1855 | 1861 | *1856* | 1863 | 1869 | 1859 | 1871 | |
| | | | | | *1860* | 1867 | 1862 | *1868* | 1875 | *1864* | *1876* | |
| | | | | | 1866 | *1872* | 1873 | 1874 | *1880* | 1870 | 1882 | |
| | | | | | 1877 | 1878 | 1879 | 1885 | 1886 | 1881 | 1893 | |
| | | | | | 1883 | 1889 | *1884* | 1891 | 1897 | 1887 | 1899 | |
| | | | | | *1888* | 1895 | 1890 | *1896* | 1909 | *1892* | 1905 | |
| | | | | | 1894 | 1901 | 1902 | 1903 | 1915 | 1898 | 1911 | |
| | | | | | 1900 | 1907 | 1913 | *1908* | *1920* | *1904* | *1916* | |
| | | | | | 1906 | *1912* | 1919 | 1914 | 1926 | 1910 | 1922 | |
| | | | | | 1917 | 1918 | *1924* | 1925 | 1937 | 1921 | 1933 | |
| | | | | | 1923 | 1929 | 1930 | 1931 | 1943 | 1927 | 1939 | |
| | | | | | *1928* | 1935 | 1941 | *1936* | *1948* | *1932* | *1944* | |
| | | | | | 1934 | *1940* | 1947 | 1942 | 1954 | 1938 | 1950 | |
| | | | | | 1945 | 1946 | *1952* | 1953 | 1965 | 1949 | 1961 | |
| | | | | | 1951 | 1957 | 1958 | 1959 | 1971 | 1955 | 1967 | |
| | | | | | *1956* | 1963 | 1969 | *1964* | *1976* | *1960* | *1972* | |
| | | | | | 1962 | *1968* | 1975 | 1970 | 1982 | 1966 | 1978 | |
| | | | | | 1973 | 1974 | *1980* | 1981 | 1993 | 1977 | 1989 | |
| | | | | | 1979 | 1985 | 1986 | 1987 | 1999 | 1983 | 1995 | |
| | | | | | *1984* | 1991 | 1997 | *1992* | | *1988* | *2000* | |
| | | | | | 1990 | *1996* | | 1998 | | 1994 | | |

*For dates occurring in Jan. or Feb. of a leap year (indicated by italics), use *italic* names of months, above.

To find the day of the week corresponding to any date, find the small letter directly under the name of the month and opposite the number of the day of the month; then find the column containing the number of the year and follow up to where that same letter appears at the top of the year column; then, following out to the right, find the day of the week. Thus, to find the day on which March 18, 1930, fell, from the date and month columns find the letter *b* in the fifth letter column, then finding the year 1930 in the third year column follow up to the letter *b* above it and then to the right to the day, Tuesday.

**2 :** a mechanical calendar for keeping track of current dates over a period of many years **3 :** a calendar in which the years are uniform in the correspondence of days and dates (as in the proposed World Calendar of equal quarter-years and uniform months)

perpetual calendar 2

**perpetual canon** *n* **:** CIRCULAR CANON 1

**perpetual check** *n* **:** an endless succession of checks to which the opponent's king in chess may sometimes be subjected to force a draw; *also* **:** a situation involving such an attack

**perpetual day** *n* **:** the period of nearly six months alternately at the earth's north and south poles when the sun does not set — compare PERPETUAL NIGHT

**perpetual inventory** *n* **:** a book record of inventory kept continuously up to date by detailed entries for all incoming and outgoing items — compare BOOK INVENTORY

**per·pet·u·al·ism** \-ə,lizəm\ *n* -s **:** a doctrine of the everlastingness or perpetuation of something (as a system, creed, natural state)

**per·pet·u·al·ist** \-ələst\ *n* -s **:** an advocate of perpetualism; *specif* **:** one advocating the perpetuation of Negro slavery in the U.S. — **per·pet·u·al·is·tic** \=ˌ=(ˌ)=ˈlistik\ *adj*

**per·pet·u·al·i·ty** \pə(r),pechəˈwaləd·ē\ *n* -ES [L *perpetualitas*, fr. *perpetualis* perpetual + *-itas* -ity — more at PERPETUAL] **:** PERPETUITY

**perpetual lease** *n* **:** a lease renewable forever at the lessee's option

**per·pet·u·al·ly** \pə(r)ˈpechəlē, -ch(ə)wəlē, -li\ *adv* [ME *perpetuelly*, fr. *perpetuel* perpetual + *-ly*] **1 :** EVERLASTINGLY, FOREVER ⟨an annuity for life or ~⟩ ⟨rays . . . streaming ~ from the sun —Stuart Chase⟩ **2 :** CONSTANTLY, INCESSANTLY ⟨claims people were ~ making on him —Mary Deasy⟩

**perpetual motion** *n* **1 :** the motion of an ideal mechanism that could continue to operate indefinitely without drawing upon an external source of energy **2** *obs* **:** PERPETUAL MOTION MACHINE

**perpetual motion machine** *n* **:** a device inherently impossible under the law of conservation of energy that can continue to do work indefinitely without drawing energy from external sources

**per·pet·u·al·ness** *n* -ES **:** the quality or state of being perpetual

**perpetual night** *n* **:** the period of nearly six months alternately at the earth's north and south poles when the sun does not rise — compare PERPETUAL DAY

**perpetuals** *pl of* PERPETUAL

**perpetual succession** *n* **1 :** the capacity of a corporation to have continuous enjoyment of its property so long as it is legally in existence **2 :** the perpetual existence of a corporation

**perpetual trust** *n* **:** a trust estate bearing no specific limitation as to its duration — compare PERPETUITY 3b

**per·pet·u·a·na** \pə(r),pechəˈwänə\ *n* -s [L *perpetuus* continuous, perpetual + *-ana*, fem. of *-anus* -an] **:** a durable usu. wool or worsted fabric made in England from the late 16th through the 18th centuries

**per·pet·u·ate** \pə(r)ˈpechə,wāt, *usu* -ād.+V\ *vt* -ED/-ING/-S [L *perpetuatus*, past part. of *perpetuare*, fr. *perpetuus* perpetual — more at PERPETUAL] **:** to make perpetual **:** preserve from extinction **:** cause to last indefinitely ⟨~ the species⟩ ⟨~ his memory⟩ ⟨*perpetuating* a defunct tradition —Herbert Read⟩ ⟨~ their absolute control —W.E.McManus⟩

**per·pet·u·a·tion** \=ˌ=ˈwāshən\ *n* -s [ME *perpetuacioun*, fr. ML *perpetuation-*, *perpetuatio*, fr. L *perpetuatus* + *-ion-*, *-io* -ion] **:** the act or process of perpetuating **:** PRESERVATION ⟨~ of the culture —A.L.Kroeber⟩ ⟨the ~ of social inequalities —George Sampson⟩

**per·pet·u·a·tor** \=ˈ==,wād·ə(r), -ātə-\ *n* -s **:** one that perpetuates

**per·pe·tu·i·ty** \,pərpəˈtüəd·ē, -pə̄], ,pə̄], ,pə·ˈtyü-, -üətē, -i\ *n* -ES [ME *perpetuite*, fr. MF *perpetuité*, fr. L *perpetuitat-*, *perpetuitas*, fr. *perpetuus* continuous, perpetual + *-itat-*, *-itas* -ity — more at PERPETUAL] **1 :** endless time **:** ETERNITY ⟨so lost to ~ —John Milton⟩ ⟨his companions are playing for ~ —Sacheverell Sitwell⟩ **2 :** the quality or state of being perpetual ⟨a path to ~ of fame —Lord Byron⟩ — often used with *in* ⟨bequeathed them to the nation in ~ —S.P.B.Mais⟩ **3 a :** duration without limitations as to time **b :** the condition of an estate limited so that it will not take effect or vest within the period fixed by law or so limited as to be or have a possibility of being inalienable either perpetually or beyond the bounds fixed by law **c :** an estate so limited — see RULE AGAINST PERPETUITIES **4 a :** a perpetual annuity **b :** the number of years in which simple interest equals the principal **c :** the number of years' purchase to be given for an annuity to continue forever

**per·pet·u·um mo·bi·le** \pə(r)ˈpechəwəmˈmōbə,lē,-,lā\ *n* [NL, lit., perpetual moving (thing)] **1 :** perpetual motion **2 :** a musical composition having the same rapid motion from beginning to end — called also *moto perpetuo*

**per·plex** \pə(r)ˈpleks\ *vt* -ED/-ING/-ES [obs. E *perplex*, adj., perplexed, involved, fr. L *perplexus*, fr. *per-* thoroughly + *plexus* involved, fr. past part. of *plectere* to plait, braid, interweave — more at PER-, PLY] **1 :** to disturb mentally esp. so as to make impossible clear or decisive thinking on the matter at hand **:** fill with doubt, uncertainty, or confusion **:** BEWILDER, NONPLUS ⟨~*ed* by many cares⟩ ⟨such contradictions ~ the historian⟩ ⟨questions that have ~*ed* men since time began —C.F.Strubbe⟩ **2 a :** to make intricate, involved, or difficult to understand **:** COMPLICATE, CONFUSE ⟨no attempts at wit obscure or ~ his matter —Earl of Chesterfield⟩ **b :** INTERWEAVE, ENTANGLE ⟨brambles . . . ~*ed* and interwoven with one another —Joseph Addison⟩ **3** *obs* **:** PLAGUE, VEX, TORMENT **syn** see PUZZLE

**per·plexed** \-kst\ *adj* [L *perplexus* + E *-ed*] **1 a** *archaic* **:** emotionally disturbed by the intricacy or difficulty of a situation **:** ANXIOUS, TROUBLED, DISTRAUGHT ⟨undaunted . . . though wearied and ~ —William Cowper⟩ **b :** filled with doubt or uncertainty **:** PUZZLED, BEWILDERED ⟨the ~ person who . . . no longer trusts the sources of information —E.C.Lindeman⟩ **2 :** full of difficulty **:** COMPLICATED ⟨~ language⟩ ⟨this ~ age of the world —Bliss Perry⟩ **3 :** ENTANGLED ⟨~ with thorn —Alexander Pope⟩

**per·plexed·ly** \-ksədlē, -kstlē, -li\ *adv* **:** in a perplexed manner

**per·plexed·ness** \-ksədnəs, -ks(t)n-\ *n* -ES *archaic* **:** PERPLEXITY

**per·plex·ful** \-ksfəl\ *adj* [*perplex* + *-ful*] **:** full of perplexity **:** PERPLEXING

**perplexing** *adj* **:** that causes perplexity **:** PUZZLING, BEWILDERING ⟨the situation was most ~ —J.A.Froude⟩ ⟨~ problems . . . had led to the violations of law —T.W.Arnold⟩ — **per·plex·ing·ly** *adv*

**per·plex·i·ty** \pə(r)ˈpleksəd·ē, -sətē, -i\ *n* -ES [ME *perplexite*, fr. OF *perplexité*, fr. LL *perplexitat-*, *perplexitas*, fr. L *perplexus* + *-itat-*, *-itas* -ity] **1 :** an agitated or confused mental condition caused by a disturbing or puzzling situation or state of affairs **:** BEWILDERMENT ⟨the look of ~ on his face⟩ ⟨in bitter ~ she kneeled down and prayed —D.H.Lawrence⟩ **2 :** something that perplexes ⟨beset with *perplexities*⟩ **3 :** ENTANGLEMENT ⟨the dense ~ of vines⟩

**per pri·mam** \perˈprē,mäm, ,pər-, -ēməm\ *adv* [NL *per primam* (*intentionem*)] **:** by first intention ⟨a wound that heals *per primam* usually leaves little scarring⟩

**per pro·cu·ra·ti·o·nem** \,per,präkə,räd·ēˈō,nem\ *also* **per procuration** \,pər+\ *adv* [L *per procurationem*] **:** by agency **:** by the authority of an agent **:** by proxy

**per·qui·site** \ˈpərkwəzət, ˈpə̄k-, ˈpəik-, *usu* -əd.+V\ *n* -s [ME, fr. ML *perquisitum*, fr. neut. of *perquisitus*, past part. of *perquirere* to obtain, acquire, fr. L, to ask about diligently, to make diligent search for, fr. *per-* thoroughly + *-quirere* (fr. *quaerere* to seek, gain, obtain, ask) — more at PER-] **1** *obs* **:** CONQUEST 5 **2 a :** casual income or profits (as from heriots, escheats, reliefs) accruing to the lord of a feudal manor **b :** a privilege, gain, or profit incidental to an employment in addition to regular salary or wages; *esp* **:** one expected or promised ⟨the ~*s* of the college president include a home and car⟩ ⟨the easy profits of a navy purser's ~*s* —*Times Lit. Supp.*⟩ **3 :** GRATUITY, TIP; *esp* **:** one expected or claimed by custom for a service ⟨a servant's wages and ~*s*⟩ **4 :** something held or claimed as an exclusive right or possession ⟨concepts . . . not the ~*s* of any particular groups —Gilbert Ryle⟩ **syn** see RIGHT

**per·qui·si·tion** \,pərkwəˈzishən\ *n* -s [F, fr. LL *perquisition-*, *perquisitio*, fr. L *perquisitus* + *-ion-*, *-io* -ion] **:** a thorough search; *specif* **:** a search by warrant

**per·quis·i·tor** \(,)pərˈkwizəd·ə(r)\ *n* -s [ML & L; ML, one that obtains or acquires, fr. L, one that searches diligently, fr. *perquisitus* + *-or*] **1 :** the original owner or first purchaser of an estate **2 :** one who makes a perquisition

**per·ra·di·al** \,pər, (ˈ)per+\ *adj* [NL *perradius* + E *-al*] **:** of, relating to, or involving a perradius — **per·ra·di·al·ly** \"+\ *adv*

**per·ra·di·us** \"+\ *n* [NL, fr. *per-* + *radius*] **:** any one of the usu. four primary radii of a medusa that pass through radial canals

**per·rec·tal** \"+\ *adj* [*per-* + *rectal*] **:** entering through or by way of the rectum ⟨~ feeding⟩ — **per·rec·tal·ly** \"+\ *adv*

**per·rhe·nate** \(,)pər, ,pə, pe+\ *n* -s [*perrhenic* + *-ate*] **:** a salt of perrhenic acid; *esp* **:** a salt of metaperrhenic acid

**per·rhe·nic acid** \,pər, ,pə, (ˈ)per+. . .-\ *n* [*per-* + NL *rhenium* + E *-ic*] **:** either of two acids formed by the oxidation of rhenium or rhenium compounds of lower valence states and known only in solution or in the form of salts: **a :** the monobasic acid $HReO_4$ analogous to permanganic acid that forms colorless stable salts — called also *metaperrhenic acid* **b :** the tribasic acid $H_3ReO_5$ that forms yellow salts turning red when heated and hydrolyzed in water to salts of metaperrhenic acid — called also *mesoperrhenic acid*

**per·ri·er** \ˈperēə(r)\ *n* -s [ME *perrerer*, fr. MF *perrier*, fr. *pierre* stone, rock (fr. L *petra*) + *-ier* -er — more at PETROUS] **1 :** a medieval engine for throwing stones **2 :** a short mortar formerly used on ships for throwing stones and light shot **:** PEDRERO

**per·rine lemon** \pəˈrīn-\ *n* [after Henry *Perrine* †1840 Am. physician and naturalist] **:** a hybrid produced by crossing the lime and the lemon

**per·rin·ist** \ˈperənəst\ *n* -s *usu cap* [F *Perriniste*, fr. Ami *Perrin*, 16th cent. Swiss political leader + F *-iste* -ist] **:** LIBERTINE 2a

**per·ron** \ˈperən, pəˈrōⁿ\ *n* -s [F, fr. OF, large block of stone, aug. of *perre*, *pierre* stone, rock — more at PERRIER] **1 :** an outdoor stairway leading up to an entrance to a large building (as a church or a mansion) **2 :** a platform at the top of a perron

**per·ruche** \pəˈrüsh\ *n* -s [F, lit., a kind of parrot, alter. of *perroquet* parrot] **:** PARROT GREEN

**perruque** *var of* PERUKE

**perruquier** *var of* PERUKIER

**per·ry** \ˈperē\ *n* -ES [ME *pereye*, *peirrie*, *perre*, fr. MF *peré*, fr. (assumed) VL *piratum*, fr. L *pirum* pear + *-atum* -ate — more at PEAR] *chiefly Brit* **:** the expressed juice of pears often made alcoholic by fermentation and sometimes effervescent by carbonation or by fermentation in a closed container

**pers** *abbr* **1** person; personal; personally **2** personnel

**per·sae** \ˈpər,sē, ˈper,sī\ *n pl*, *usu cap* [L, fr. Gk *Persai*, pl. of *Persēs* Persian] **:** PERSIAN 5

**per·salt** \ˈpər, ˈper+,-\ *n* [*per* + *salt*] **1 a :** a salt containing a relatively large proportion of the acidic element or group ⟨ferric salts are *persalts* of iron⟩ **b :** a salt of a peroxy acid (as sodium perchlorate) of a per acid **2 :** PEROXY SALT

**per sal·tum** \(ˈ)pərˈsóltəm, (ˈ)perˈsäl-\ *adv* (*or adj*) [L] **:** by a leap, spring, or bound **:** at a single bound; *specif* **:** without intermediate stages ⟨*per saltum* evolution⟩

**per·scru·ta·tion** \,pər,skrüˈtāshən\ *n* -s [F, fr. MF, fr. L *perscrutation-*, *perscrutatio*, fr. *perscrutatus* (past part. of *perscrutari* to examine thoroughly, fr. *per-* thoroughly + *scrutari* to search, examine) + *-ion-*, *-io* -ion — more at SCRUTINY] **:** a thorough examination **:** careful investigation

**perse** \ˈpərs\ *adj* [ME *pers*, fr. MF, fr. ML *persus*, prob. fr. L *Persa* Persian] **1** *obs* **:** light or pale blue and grayish **2 :** dark grayish blue resembling indigo

**per se** \ˌpərˈsā, ˌpəˈsā *also* ˌpə(r)ˈsā *or* (ˈ)pe(ə)rˈsā *or* (ˈ)peəˈsā *or* ˌpərˈsē *or* (ˈ)pəˈsē *or* ˌpə(r)ˈsē\ *adv* [L] **:** by, of, or in itself or oneself or themselves **:** as such **:** INDEPENDENTLY, INTRINSICALLY ⟨a lover of language *per se* —W.T.Scott⟩ ⟨not a scientist *per se* and so he had none of the inhibitions of the scientist —W.L.Howard⟩ ⟨his manufactory of fireworks was *per se* a public nuisance —*McDade vs. City of Chester (Pa.)*⟩ ⟨the mathematician is not interested in the truth, *per se*, of his postulates —Harry Lass⟩ ⟨money is evil *per se* and must be apologized for —Dwight Macdonald⟩ ⟨natural environment cannot *per se* cause forms of culture —A.L.Kroeber⟩ ⟨egoistic or altruistic dispositions . . . are *per se* neither rational nor irrational —W.M.Sibley⟩

**per·sea** \ˈpərsēə\ *n* [NL, fr. L, a tree growing in Egypt and Persia, fr. Gk] **1** *cap* **:** a large genus of chiefly tropical trees and shrubs (family Lauraceae) having thick alternate leaves, small panicled flowers with nine stamens, and a fleshy one-seeded fruit and in some kinds yielding superior cabinet woods — see AVOCADO **2** -s **:** any tree or fruit of the genus *Persea*

**per second per second** *adv* **:** per second every second — used of a rate of acceleration over an indefinite period ⟨the value of the acceleration of gravity is . . . about 32 feet *per second per second* —N.H.Black & H.N.Davis⟩

**per·se·cute** \ˈpərsə,kyüt, ˈpə̄s-,ˈpəis-, -sē,k-, *usu* -üd.+V\ *vt* -ED/-ING/-S [MF *persecuter*, back-formation fr. *persecuteur* persecutor — more at PERSECUTOR] **1** *obs* **a :** to follow with the intent of killing, capturing, or harming **:** hunt down **:** PURSUE **b :** to follow up with vigor or to the end **2 :** to harass in a manner to injure, grieve, or afflict usu. because of some difference of outlook or opinion **:** set upon with cruelty or malignity **:** OPPRESS; *specif* **:** to cause to suffer or put to death because of belief (as in a religion) **3** *chiefly dial* **:** to prosecute at law **4 :** to afflict, harass, or annoy with persistent or urgent approaches (as attacks, pleas, importunities) **:** PESTER, VEX **syn** see WRONG

**per·se·cut·ee** \ˌ==,kyüˈtē, -üˈtē\ *n* -s **:** a victim of persecution

**per·se·cut·ing·ly** *adv* **:** in a persecuting manner **:** so as to constitute persecution ⟨flies buzzed ~ about our faces⟩

**per·se·cu·tion** \ˌ==ˈkyüshən\ *n* -s [ME *persecucioun*, fr. MF *persecution*, fr. LL *persecution-*, *persecutio*, fr. L, action of pursuing, fr. *persecutus* (past part. of *persequi* to continue to follow, pursue, fr. *per-*, prefix denoting completion or perfection + *sequi* to follow) + *-ion-*, *-io* -ion — more at PER-, SUE] **1 a :** the act or practice of persecuting: as (1) **:** the infliction of sufferings, harm, or death on those who differ (as in origin, religion, or social outlook) in a way regarded as offensive or meriting extirpation (2) *obs* **:** a carrying out (as of an aim or course of action) **:** PROSECUTION **b :** a campaign having for its object the subjugation or extirpation of the adherents of a religion or way of life ⟨pogroms and ~*s* in imperial Russia⟩ **2 :** the condition of being persecuted, harassed, or annoyed ⟨live through ~ and exile⟩

**per·se·cu·tion·al** \ˌ==ˈkyüshənᵊl, -shnəl\ *adj* **:** of or relating to persecution ⟨a ~ mania⟩

**persecution complex** *n* **:** the feeling of being persecuted esp. without basis in reality

**per·se·cu·tive** \ˈ==,kyüd·iv\ *adj* **:** marked by or tending toward persecution ⟨~ views⟩

**per·se·cu·tor** \-üd·ə(r), -ütə-\ *n* -s [MF *persecuteur*, fr. LL *persecutor*, fr. *persecutus* (past part. of *persequi* to persecute, fr. L, to continue to follow, pursue) + L *-or* — more at PERSECUTION] **:** one that persecutes

**per·se·cu·to·ry** \ˈ==kyə,tōrē, ˈ==,kyüd·ərē, pə(r)ˈsekyə,tōrē\ *adj* [*persecute* + *-ory*] **:** of or relating to persecution **:** PERSECUTIVE

**per·se·cu·tress** \ˈpərsə,kyü·trəs, ˈpə̄s-,ˈpəis-\ *n* -ES [*persecutor* + *-ess*] **:** a female persecutor

**per·se·cu·trix** \ˌ==ˈkyü·triks\ *n*, *pl* **persecutri·ces** \ˌ==ˈkyü·trə,sēz, -kyü·ˈtrī(,)sēz\ [LL, fr. L *persecutor*] **:** PERSECUTRESS

**per·se·id** \ˈpərsēəd\ *n* -s *usu cap* [*Perseus*, a constellation (fr. L, fr. Gk *Perseus*, a hero of ancient Greek mythology) + E *-id*] **:** one of a group of meteors appearing annually about August 11

**per·se·i·tol** \ˈpərsēə,tól, ,pər-, -tōl\ *n* -s [ISV *perse-* (fr. NL *Persea*, genus name of *Persea gratissima*) + *-itol*] **:** a crystalline polyhydric alcohol $CH_2OH(CHOH)_5CH_2OH$ found in the fruit and leaves of avocados

**per·se·i·ty** \(,)pərˈsāəd·ē, -sēə-\ *n* -ES [ML *perseitas*, fr. L *per se* + *-itas* -ity] **:** the quality or state of being per se **:** self-inclusive or self-sufficient being

**per·se·pol·i·tan** \ˌpərsəˈpälətᵊn\ *adj*, *usu cap* [fr. *Persepolis*, ancient capital of Persia situated about 30 miles northeast of present-day Shiraz, Iran, after such pairs as E *metropolis*: *metropolitan*] **:** of or relating to the ancient city of Persepolis

**per·se·quent** \ˈpərsəkwənt\ *adj* [L *persequent-*, *persequens*, pres. part. of *persequi* to pursue — more at PERSECUTION] **:** PURSUING

**per·se·ulose** \ˈpərsēyə,lōs, ,pərˈsē-\ *n* -s [ISV *perseitol* + *-ulose*] **:** the heptulose sugar $C_7H_{14}O_7$ obtained by bacterial oxidation of perseitol

**per·se·ver·ance** \,pərsəˈvirən(t)s, ,pə̄s-, ,pəis-, *archaic* pə(r)ˈsevər-\ *n* -s [ME *perseveraunce*, fr. MF *perseverance*, fr. L *perseverantia*, fr. *perseverant-*, *perseverans* (pres. part. of *perseverare* to persevere) + *-ia* -y — more at PERSEVERE] **1 :** the action or fact or an instance of persevering **:** continued or steadfast pursuit or prosecution of an undertaking or aim ⟨owing to an obstinate ~ in error —Edmund Burke⟩ **2 :** the condition or power of persevering **:** persistence in the pursuit of objectives or prosecution of any project **:** STEADFASTNESS ⟨the king-becoming graces as justice, verity . . . ~ —Shak.⟩ **3 :** continuance in a state of religious or spiritual grace until it is succeeded by a state of glory ⟨final ~⟩ ⟨the ~ of the saints⟩

**per·se·ver·ant** \-nt\ *adj* [ME *perseveraunt*, fr. MF *perseverant*, fr. L *perseverant-*, *perseverans*, pres. part. of *perseverare*] **:** able or willing to persevere **:** ENDURING ⟨with hope ~ —Coventry Patmore⟩

**per·sev·er·ate** \pə(r)ˈsevə,rāt\ *vi* -ED/-ING/-S [L *perseveratus*, past part. of *perseverare* to persevere] **1 :** to manifest the phenomenon of perseveration ⟨the *perseverating* tendency in stutterers in sensorimotor tasks —*Quarterly Jour. of Speech*⟩ **2 :** to repeat or recur persistently ⟨the tune ~*s* in my mind⟩ **3 :** to go back over previously covered ground ⟨a careful scholar who ~*s* unhesitatingly to reevaluate and incorporate new data⟩

**per·sev·er·a·tion** \=ˌ==ˈrāshən\ *n* -s [L *perseveration-*, *perseveratio* perseverance, fr. *perseveratus* + *-ion-*, *-io* -ion] **:** continuation of something (as an activity or pursuit) usu. to an exceptional degree or beyond a desired point: as **a :** continual repetition of a mental act usu. evidenced by speech or by some other form of overt behavior esp. as a mechanism of defense **b :** spontaneous and persistent recurrence of something (as an idea, mental image, tune, or word)

**per·sev·er·a·tive** \=ˈ==,rād·iv\ *adj* **:** characterized by perseveration

**per·se·vere** \ˌpərsəˈvi(ə)r, ˌpə̄s-, ˌpəis-, -iə, *archaic* pə(r)ˈsevə(r)\ *vb* -ED/-ING/-S [ME *perseveren*, fr. MF *perseverer*, fr. L *perseverare*, fr. *per-*, intensive prefix + *-severare* (fr. *severus* serious, severe) — more at PER-, SEVERE] *vi* **1 :** to persist in a state of life, in the pursuit of an end, or esp. in an enterprise undertaken in spite of counter influences, opposition, or discouragement **:** pursue steadily any project or course begun **2 a** *archaic* **:** to continue either actively or passively **:** REMAIN, ABIDE **b :** to continue in a state of religious or spiritual grace **3 :** to be persistent (as in arguing) **:** INSIST ~ *vt* **:** to give continued existence or assistance to **:** make steadfast

**syn** PERSIST: PERSEVERE and PERSIST are often interchangeable in indicating continuing in the face of difficulty, opposition, and discouragement ⟨I do not intend to take that cowardly course, but, on the contrary, to stand to my post and *persevere* in accordance with my duty as I see it —Sir Winston Churchill⟩ ⟨this is the poetry within history, this is what causes mankind to *persist* beyond every defeat —Jean S. Untermeyer⟩ ⟨*persisted* long after I was willing to abandon the search and to try to get some sleep —Mary R. Rinehart⟩ PERSIST may be more likely than PERSEVERE to imply stubborn obstinacy in an ill-advised course or to lead to a regrettable outcome ⟨the eyes become tired if they *persist* in the work —Morris Fishbein⟩ ⟨it is hard to see how they can have *persisted* so long in inflicting useless misery —Bertrand Russell⟩ ⟨old savage customs have been allowed to *persevere* too long in many parts of the continent —C.L.Sulzberger⟩

**per·se·ver·er** \-ərə(r)\ *n* -s : one that perseveres : a persistent person

**persevering** *adj* : of or characterized by perseverance : PERSISTENT — **per·se·ver·ing·ly** *adv*

**persh** *abbr* perishable

**per·sia** \ˈpərzhə, ˈpə̄|, ˈpəi| *sometimes* |shə\ *adj, usu cap* [fr. *Persia* (Iran), country in southwestern Asia] : IRAN

**¹per·sian** \|zhən *sometimes* |shən\ *n* -s [ME *Persien*, fr. MF, adj. & n., fr. *Persie* Persia (fr. L *Persia*, fr. Gk *Persis* + L -*ia* -y) + MF -*ien* -ian] **1** *cap* : one of the people of Persia: as **a** : one of the ancient Iranian Caucasians who under Cyrus and his successors became the dominant Asiatic race **b** : a member of one of the peoples forming the modern Iranian nationality **2** *cap* **a** : any of several Iranian languages dominant in Persia at different periods — compare AVESTAN, MIDDLE PERSIAN, OLD PERSIAN, PAHLAVI **b** : the modern language of Iran and western Afghanistan that is used also in Pakistan and by Indian Muslims as a literary language **3** *usu cap* : a thin soft plain or printed silk in plain weave formerly used esp. for linings (as of women's clothing) **4 persians** *or* **persian blinds** *pl, usu cap P* : PERSIENNES **5** *usu cap* : a male figure replacing a column in the Persian style — usu. used in pl.; compare ATLAS 4 **6** *or* **persian leather** *usu cap P* : leather from India-tanned hair sheepskins **7** *usu cap* **a** : PERSIAN CAT **b** : PERSIAN LAMB **c** : BLACKHEAD PERSIAN

**²persian** \"\ *adj, usu cap* [ME *percynne*, fr. MF *persien*] **1** : of or relating to Persia, the Persians, or their language **2** : relating to or consisting of Persian lamb **3** : constituting an order and a style of ancient art in which architectural columns are replaced by male figures in oriental costume or are adorned by such figures

**per·si·ana** \ˌpərz(h)ēˈanə, -rs(h)ē-, -ˈänə\ *n* -s [by alter.] : PERSIENNE 1

**persian ammoniac** *n, usu cap P* : AMMONIAC 1

**persian apple** *n, usu cap P* : CITRON 1a, 1b

**persian berry** *n, usu cap P* : any of several buckthorn berries from southern Europe, Asia Minor, and Iran that are used esp. in textile dyeing — compare AVIGNON BERRY

**persian blue** *n, often cap P* **1** : a pale blue that is redder and lighter than average powder blue and redder and paler than Sistine **2** : REGIMENTAL 2

**persian buttercup** *n, usu cap P* : TURBAN BUTTERCUP

**persian cat** *n, usu cap P* : a cobby round-headed domestic cat with long and silky fur that is the long-haired cat of shows and fanciers

**persian clover** *n, usu cap P* : a winter annual Asiatic clover (*Trifolium resupinatum*) sometimes used as a pasture and fodder crop in regions of mild winter

**persian daisy** *n, usu cap P* : a perennial chrysanthemum (*Chrysanthemum roseum*) with solitary flower heads borne on long peduncles and flesh-colored to rosy-red ray flowers

**persian date** *n, usu cap P* : any of several rather large light-skinned soft-fleshed dates grown in southwestern Asia

**persian deer** *n, usu cap P* **1** : a fallow deer (*Dama dama mesopotamiae*) of western Asia **2** : MARAL

**persian earth** *n, often cap P* : INDIAN RED 2b

**persian gazelle** *n, usu cap P* : a gazelle (*Gazella gutturosa*) of central Asia

**persian green** *n, often cap P* : a dark grayish green that is bluer, lighter, and stronger than average ivy and yellower and lighter than hemlock green — called also *sea moss*

**persian gulf oxide** *n, usu cap P & G* [fr. the *Persian Gulf*, arm of the Arabian sea between Arabia and Iran] : INDIAN RED 1a

**persian insect powder** *n, usu cap 1st P* : pyrethrum derived from an Asiatic pyrethrum

**persian iris** *n, usu cap P* : a bulbous iris (*Iris persica*) that is native to Asia Minor and is cultivated for its pale lilac-colored flowers with small often minute deflexed falls

**per·sian·ized** \ˈpərzhəˌnīzd *sometimes* -rsh-\ *adj, usu cap* : rendered Persian in orientation or culture

**persian lamb** *n, usu cap P* **1** : the young of the karakul sheep esp. of Bokhara and other parts of central Asia that furnishes skins used in furriery — compare BROADTAIL **2** : a pelt obtained from karakul lambs older than those yielding broadtail and characterized by very silky tightly curled fur — compare ASTRAKHAN 1, BOKHARA

**persian lawn** *n, usu cap P* : a very fine usu. white cotton fabric of plain weave that resembles a sheer linen

**persian lilac** *n* **1** *usu cap P* **a** : CHINABERRY 2 **b** : a showy Asiatic shrub (*Syringa persica*) cultivated for its terminal panicles of fragrant lilac-colored flowers **2** *often cap P* : a dark purplish pink that is redder than clover pink and bluer and stronger than rhodonite pink

**persian lime** *n, usu cap P* : a vigorously growing lime that has a large oval to elliptical light yellow or slightly orange acid fruit, is possibly of hybrid origin, and was introduced into the southern U.S. from Tahiti — called also *Tahiti orange*

**persian lynx** *n, usu cap P* : CARACAL

**persian melon** *n* **1** *usu cap P* : a large globular muskmelon having a netted unribbed grayish outer surface and orange-colored flesh that is considered superior for freezing **2** *often cap P* : a grayish reddish orange that is redder and lighter than Etruscan red or hyacinth red and redder and paler than light persimmon

**persian morocco** *n, usu cap P&M* **1** : a fine leather made orig. from Persian goatskin and later from skins of various hair sheep and used chiefly in bookbinding **2** : an imitation leather resembling Persian Morocco

**persian nightingale** *n, usu cap P* : BULBUL 1a

**persian orange** *n, often cap P* : a moderate orange that is yellower, stronger, and slightly darker than honeydew, redder and lighter than ocher brown, and redder and deeper than average apricot

**persian red** *n* **1** *usu cap P* **a** : INDIAN RED 1a **b** : CHROME RED 1 **2** *often cap P* **a** : INDIAN RED 2b **b** : vermilion or a color resembling it

**persian rose** *n, often cap P* : a vivid purplish red that is bluer and lighter than rubellite and bluer and paler than Indiana

**persian rug** *or* **persian carpet** *n, usu cap P* : an Oriental rug made in Persia

**persians** *pl of* PERSIAN

**persian stonecrop** *n, often cap P* : a somewhat woody Asiatic stonecress (*Aethionema grandiflorum*) that is sometimes cultivated for its racemes of showy rose-colored flowers

**persian tick** *n, usu cap P* : CHICKEN TICK

**persian violet** *n, often cap P* : CYCLAMEN 2a

**persian walnut** *n, usu cap P* : ENGLISH WALNUT

**persian wheat** *n, usu cap P* : a hardy productive Eurasian wheat with short stems and heavy heads regarded as a variety of the common wheat or as a distinct species (*Triticum persicum*)

**persian wheel** *n, usu cap P* : an undershot waterwheel adapted for raising water and occurring in several varieties all fitted with radial floats

**per·sic** \ˈpərsik, -rzik\ *adj, usu cap* [L *Persicus*, fr. *Persia* + -*icus* -ic — more at PERSIAN] : of or relating to Persia or the Persian language

**per·si·car·ia** \ˌpərsəˈka(a)rēə\ *n* [ML, fr. L *persicum* peach + -*aria* -ary — more at PEACH] **1** -s : a plant of the genus *Polygonum* that has flowers in spicate racemes (as the lady's thumb or water pepper) **2** *cap* [NL, fr. L] *in some classifications* : a genus of herbs (family Polygonaceae) having flowers in spicate racemes and being now usu. included in the genus *Polygonum*

**per·si·cary** \ˈpərsəˌkerē\ *n* -ES [ME *persicarie*, fr. ML *persicaria*] : PERSICARIA 1

**per·si·co** *also* **per·si·cot** \ˈpərsəˌkō\ *n* -s [F *persicot*, fr. L *persicum* peach — more at PEACH] : a liqueur made from brandy or rectified spirit flavored with peach or apricot kernels, parsley, bitter almonds, and cloves

**per·sic oil** \ˈpərsik-, -rzik-\ *n* [*persic* fr. NL *persica* (specific epithet of *Prunus persica*), fr. L, fem. of *Persicus* Persian, fr. Gk *Persikos* fr. *Persis* Persia + -*ikos* -ic] : either of two fatty oils: **a** : APRICOT-KERNEL OIL **a b** : PEACH-KERNEL OIL **a**

**per·si·enne** \ˌpərzēˈen, -rsē-\ *n* -s [F, fr. fem. of adj. *persien* Persian — more at PERSIAN] **1** : painted or printed cotton or silk orig. made in Persia and later imitated in Europe **2 a** : an exterior window shutter having adjustable horizontal slats or louvers fixed at an angle so as to admit light but exclude sun and rain — usu. used in pl. **b** : VENETIAN BLIND — usu. used in pl.

**per·si·flage** \ˈpərsəˌfläzh, ˈper-, ˌ==ˈ=\ *n* -s [F, fr. *persifler* to banter (fr. *per-*, intensive prefix — fr. Latin — + *siffler* to whistle, hiss, boo) + -*age* — more at SIFFLE] : frivolous bantering talk : a frivolous and somewhat derisive manner of treating a subject : light raillery

**per·si·flate** \ˈ==ˌflāt\ *vi* -ED/-ING/-S [*persiflage* + -*ate*] : to indulge in persiflage

**per·si·fleur** \ˈ==ˌflər(·), ˌ==ˈ=\ *n* -s [F, fr. *persifler* + -*eur* -or] : a person who indulges in persiflage : one given to frivolous banter esp. about matters usu. given serious consideration ⟨this indolent sceptic; this ~ who . . . posed as a martyr of remorse because he had driven his mistress out of his house —J.C. Powys⟩

**per·silicic** \ˌpər, ˈper+\ *adj* [*per-* + *silicic*] *of a rock* : containing much silica : ACID — distinguished from SUBSILICIC

**per·sil·lade** \ˌpersēˈyäd, -səˈyäd\ *adj* [F, fr. *persil* parsley + -*ade* — more at PARSLEY] : dressed with or containing parsley ⟨~ potatoes⟩

**per·sim·mon** \pə(r)ˈsimən\ *n* -s [of Algonquian origin; akin to Cree *pasiminan* dried fruit, Del *pasimĕnan*] **1** : a tree or shrub of the genus *Diospyros*: as **a** : a medium-sized tree (*D. virginiana*) of the southern and eastern U.S. with hard fine-grained wood, oblong leaves, and greenish yellow or greenish white bell-shaped flowers followed by a pale orange to reddish orange several-seeded berry that is edible when fully ripe but usu. extremely astringent when unripe **b** : JAPANESE PERSIMMON **2** : the fruit of a persimmon **3 a** : a variable color averaging a moderate reddish orange that is yellower and duller than crab apple or flamingo **b** : a strong brown that is redder and deeper than average russet and redder and duller than rust

**per·sis** \ˈpərsəs\ *also* **per·sio** \-rsēˌō\ *n, pl* **persises** *also* **persios** [G] : archil in a dry paste form : CUDBEAR

**per·sist** \pə(r)ˈsist *also* -ˈzi-\ *vb* -ED/-ING/-S [MF *persister*, fr. L *persistere*, fr. *per-*, intensive prefix + *sistere* to stand firm; akin to L *stare* to stand — more at PER-, STAND] *vi* **1** : to go on resolutely or stubbornly despite opposition, importunity, or warning : continue firmly or obstinately ⟨~ in a bad habit⟩ **2** *obs* : to remain unchanged or fixed in a usu. specified character, condition, or position : continue to be ⟨but for thee, I had ~*ed* happy —John Milton⟩ **3** : to be insistent in the repetition or pressing of an utterance (as a question, an excuse, or an opinion) **4** : to continue to exist or endure (as beyond a normal period or after the removal of a cause) : recur constantly ⟨characteristics that ~ through generations⟩ ⟨a melody that ~*s* in the mind⟩ ~ *vt* : to repeat or press (an utterance) insistently : continue saying : URGE **syn** see CONTINUE, PERSEVERE

**per·sist·ence** \-tən(t)s\ *n* -s [MF, fr. *persister* + -*ence*] **1** : the action or fact of persisting : determined or stubborn continuance (as in a course of action) in spite of opposition ⟨their ~ in pressing the invitation⟩ ⟨annoyed by the salesman's ~⟩ **2** : the quality or state of being persistent: as **a** : continued existence ⟨the ~ of a fever⟩ **b** : power or capacity of continuing in a course in the face of difficulties : PERSEVERANCE ⟨developing ~ in children⟩ **c** : continuance of an effect after its cause is removed ⟨~ of smoke in the air⟩ ⟨~ of sounds⟩; *esp* : AFTERIMAGE — see PERSISTENCE OF VISION

**persistence of vision** : a visual phenomenon that is responsible for the apparent continuity of rapidly presented discrete images (as in motion pictures or television) consisting essentially of a brief retinal persistence of one image so that it is overlapped by the next and the whole is centrally interpreted as continuous — compare FUSION 2d(2)

**per·sist·en·cy** \-nsē, -nsi\ *n* -ES [MF *persistence* + E -*y*] : the quality or state of being persistent: as **a** : the continuance of an insurance policy in full force until death of the insured or completion of the term of the policy **b** : capacity (as of an animal) for long-continued production of a valuable product ⟨a cow milking heavily but lacking ~⟩

**per·sist·ent** \-nt\ *adj* [L *persistent-*, *persistens*, pres. part. of *persistere* to persist — more at PERSIST] **1 a** : continuing in a course of action without regard to opposition or previous failure : tenacious of position or purpose : inclined to persist ⟨~ in good works⟩ ⟨this ~ suitor⟩ ⟨a ~ effort⟩ **b** : continuing to exist in spite of interference or treatment ⟨a ~ cancer⟩ : tending to recur ⟨a ~ cough⟩ **2** : existing for a long or longer than usual time or continuously : ENDURING, LINGERING ⟨a ~ odor of boiling cabbage⟩: as **a** (1) *of a plant corolla* : retained beyond the period of anthesis — opposed to *caducous* (2) *of a leaf* : clinging all winter even though withered ⟨some oaks and beeches have ~ leaves⟩ — opposed to *deciduous*; compare HALF-EVERGREEN **b** : continuing without change in function or structure — used chiefly of animal structures that are characteristic of some ancestral type or of a larval or young stage ⟨~ gills⟩; opposed to *deciduous* **c** *of a chemical warfare agent* : effective in the open for an appreciable time (as at least 2 to 10 minutes) : volatilizing relatively slowly ⟨mustard gas is a ~ gas⟩ — **per·sist·ent·ly** *adv*

**per·sist·er** \-tə(r)\ *n* -s : one that persists

**persisting** *adj* : inclined to persist : tenacious of purpose : PERSISTENT, ENDURING — **per·sist·ing·ly** *adv*

**per·sis·tive** \-tiv\ *adj* : tending to persist : PERSISTENT

**per·snick·e·ti·ness** \pə(r)ˈsnikəd·|ēnəs, -kət|, |in-\ *n* -ES : the quality or state of being persnickety

**per·snick·e·ty** *also* **per·snick·i·ty** \|ē, |i\ *adj* [alter. of *pernickety*] **1 a** : excessively meticulous : FINICAL, FUSSY ⟨approached native food and drink pretty much like a ~ peacetime tourist —Ernie Pyle⟩ **b** : having the characteristics of a snob ⟨have no manners, . . . they're stuck up, uppity, ~ —Carl Withers⟩ **2** : indicative of or requiring great precision, delicacy, or punctiliousness

**per·son** \ˈpərsᵊn, ˈpə̄s-,ˈpəis-\ *n* -s [ME *persone, person, persoun*, fr. OF *persone, persoune*, fr. L *persona* mask (esp. one worn by an actor), actor, role, character, person, prob. fr. Etruscan *phersu* mask] **1 a** : an individual human being ⟨a very interesting ~⟩ ⟨any ~ present⟩ **b** *archaic* : PERSONAGE 3 **c** : a human being as distinguished from an animal or thing ⟨only ~*s* can inherit under a will⟩ **d** : an inferior human being ⟨people in our position could scarcely know a ~ in trade socially⟩ ⟨the young ~ I mentioned in my letter⟩ **2** *archaic* : a character or part in or as if in a play : a particular manifestation of individual character whether real or fictional : GUISE, SEMBLANCE **3** *sometimes cap* **a** : one of the three modes of being in the Godhead as understood by Trinitarians : HYPOSTASIS **b** : the unitary personality of Christ that unites the divine and human natures **4 a** (1) *archaic* : bodily appearance ⟨had a goodly ~⟩ (2) : an individual having a specified kind of bodily appearance ⟨a fairer ~ lost not heaven —John Milton⟩ **b** : the body of a human being as distinguished from the mind ⟨pure in mind and ~⟩ **c** : the body of a human being as presented to public view usu. with its appropriate coverings and clothing ⟨an unlawful search of the ~⟩ **5 a** : the individual personality of a human being : SELF ⟨a very touchy ~⟩ ⟨in his proper ~⟩ **b** : bodily presence — usu. used in the phrase *in person* ⟨a well-known comedian appearing in ~⟩ **6** : a human being, a body of persons, or a corporation, partnership, or other legal entity that is recognized by law as the subject of rights and duties — see JURISTIC PERSON **7** : any one of the three relations underlying discourse that are distinguished by certain pronouns and in many languages by inflected forms of the verb — see FIRST PERSON, SECOND PERSON, THIRD PERSON **8 a** : a being characterized by conscious apprehension, rationality, and a moral sense **b** : a being possessing or forming the subject of personality **9** : a living individual unit; *specif* : a single zooid in a compound animal (as a colonial hydrozoan or coral) — **in the person of 1** : in the character of **2** : in the place of : acting for

**per·sona** \pə(r)ˈsōnə, ˌpər's-, pə̄'s-, pəi's- *sometimes* -sänə\ *n, pl* **personae** *see sense 2* \-(ˌ)nē, -ˌnī\ [L — more at PERSON] **1** *personae pl* : the characters of a fictional presentation (as a novel or play) ⟨comic *personae*⟩ **2** *pl* **personas** \-nəz\ : the social front, facade, or mark an individual assumes to depict to the world at large the role in life that he is playing — often contrasted with *anima* in the analytic psychology of C. G. Jung; compare EGO 3 **3** [ML, fr. L] : a parson or rector of a parish **4** [LL, fr. L] : JURISTIC PERSON **5** : PERSON 9

**per·son·abil·i·ty** \ˌpərs(ᵊ)nəˈbiləd·ē, ˌpə̄s-, ˌpəis-, -lətē, -i\ *n* : the quality or state of being personable

**per·son·able** \ˈpərs(ᵊ)nəbəl, ˈpə̄s-,ˈpəis-\ *adj* [ME, fr. *persone* + -*able*] **1** : pleasing in person : well-favored esp. in body or person : COMELY, SHAPELY, ATTRACTIVE **2** : having the legal status of a person with a right to maintain pleas in court and to take anything granted; *also* : SUI JURIS — **per·son·able·ness** *n* -ES

**per·son·age** \-s(ᵊ)nij, -nēj\ *n* -s [ME, fr. MF *personnage*, fr. *persone, personne* person + -*age* — more at PERSON] **1 a** *archaic* : the physical form or appearance of a person : form, bearing, and stature of one's body **b** *obs* : a person of specified bodily form or makeup **2 a** *obs* : a representation of a human being **b** : the human figure as an element in design (as for a tapestry) **3** : a person of rank, note, or distinction : an eminent man or woman; *esp* : one distinguished for presence and personal power ⟨fast becoming a ~⟩ **4** *obs* : one's self, personality, or personal identity : one's character or status as an individual **5** : a dramatic, fictional, or historical character; *also* : a character as assumed or represented : IMPERSONATION **6** : a human individual : a person not meriting specific identification

**person aggrieved** *n, pl* **persons aggrieved** : a person sufficiently harmed by a legal judgment, decree, or order to have standing to prosecute an appellate remedy

**persona grata** \see PERSONA NON GRATA\ *n, pl* **personae gratae** *or* **persona grata** [L] : an acceptable person ⟨informed the . . . ambassador that these two officers were no longer *persona grata* —*Christian Science Monitor*⟩ — compare PERSONA NON GRATA

**persona gra·tis·si·ma** \=ˌ==grəˈtisəmə\ *n, pl* **personae gratissi·mae** \-(ˌ)mē, -ˌmī\ [L] : a highly favored person

**¹per·son·al** \ˈpərs(ᵊ)nəl, ˈpə̄s-,ˈpəis-\ *adj* [ME, fr. MF *personnel, personel, personal*, fr. LL *personalis*, fr. L *persona* person + -*alis* -al — more at PERSON] **1** : of or relating to a particular person : affecting one individual or each of many individuals : peculiar or proper to private concerns : not public or general ⟨~ allegiance⟩ ⟨~ baggage⟩ ⟨~ correspondence⟩ **2 a** : done in person without the intervention of another : direct from one person to another ⟨a ~ inquiry⟩; *also* : originating in or proceeding from a single person ⟨a ~ ultimatum⟩ ⟨~ government⟩ **b** *obs* : engaged or present in person **c** : carried on between individuals directly ⟨a ~ interview⟩ **3** : relating to the person or body : BODILY ⟨~ appearance⟩ ⟨~ liberty⟩ **4 a** : relating to an individual, his character, conduct, motives, or private affairs esp. in an invidious and offensive manner ⟨~ reflections⟩; *also* : relating to oneself ⟨~ vanity⟩ **b** : making or given to making personal reflection ⟨very ~ in his comments⟩ **5 a** : relating to or characteristic of human beings as distinct from things **b** : rational and self-conscious ⟨a ~ God⟩ **6** : exclusively for a given individual ⟨a ~ letter⟩ **7** *substand* : PERSONABLE 1 **8** : of, relating to, or constituting personal property ⟨a ~ estate⟩ ⟨~ interests⟩ — compare REAL 1a **9 a** : denoting grammatical person ⟨a ~ suffix⟩ **b** *of a verb* : inflected for all three persons — compare IMPERSONAL

**²personal** \"\ *n* -s : something of which the relation to a human individual is a basic attribute: as **a personals** *pl, archaic* : personal property : CHATTELS **b** (1) : a personal remark (2) : a short newspaper item giving information about the social or other activities of a local person, family, or group (3) : a short personal or private communication printed in a special column of the classified ads section of a newspaper or periodical — compare AGONY COLUMN **c** *archaic* : PERSONNEL **d** : PERSONAL PRONOUN **e** : a personal foul in a sports contest

**³personal** \"\ *adv, substand* : PERSONALLY

**personal account** *n* : DRAWING ACCOUNT

**personal action** *n* **1** : an action under a civil law system for the enforcement of an obligation which therefore must be brought against the person obligated **2** : an action under the common law not brought for the recovery of or involving rights in lands, tenements, or hereditaments : an action brought to enforce or recover a debt or personal duty or damages in lieu of it or damages for an injury to person or property or for the specific recovery of or enforcement of a lien upon goods or chattels — compare REAL ACTION

**personal covenant** *n* : a legal covenant that does not run with the property but is binding upon the covenantor and his personal representatives — compare REAL COVENANT

**personal effects** *n pl* : effects of a personal character: as **a** : property esp. appertaining to one's person and having a close relationship thereto — used in legal contexts (as wills, tariff laws) **b** : such property as is usu. or normally carried by a traveler for his use and comfort — used esp. in connection with insurance **c** : personal property other than that employed in business — used esp. in a residuary clause of a will

**personal equation** *n* **1** : a constant or systematic deviation from an assumed correct observational result depending on personal qualities of the observer: **a** : ABSOLUTE PERSONAL EQUATION **b** : RELATIVE PERSONAL EQUATION **2** : variation of judgment or method occasioned by individual bias or limitation or temperamental qualities of individuals ⟨eliminating the *personal equation* in historical writing⟩

**personal estate** *n* : all of a person's property not coming under the denomination of real estate including corporeal tangibles and incorporeal intangibles, movables, chattels, choses in action, or rights : PERSONAL PROPERTY

**personal finance company** *n* : a company primarily or solely engaged in making loans of 300 dollars or less to private individuals

**personal flag** *n* : a flag indicative of the command rank of an officer (as in the U.S. Navy) and flown by a ship or station to which he is attached and present — compare DISTINGUISHING FLAG, FLAG OFFICER

**personal foul** *n* : a foul in a game (as basketball or lacrosse) involving usu. personal contact with or deliberate roughing of an opponent

**personal freedom** *n* : freedom of the person in going and coming, equality before the courts, security of private property, freedom of opinion and its expression, and freedom of conscience subject to the rights of others and of the public — compare PERSONAL LIBERTY

**personal holding company** *n* : a corporation more than one half of whose stock is owned by not more than five persons and more than 80 percent of whose income is from investments

**per·so·na·lia** \ˌpərsᵊnˈālyə, -lēə\ *n pl* [NL, fr. LL, neut. pl. of *personalis* personal — more at PERSONAL] **1** : biographical or personal anecdotes or notes **2** : personal belongings or concerns

**personal idealism** *or* **personalistic idealism** *n* : PERSONALISM 2a

**personal identity** *n* : the persistent and continuous unity of the individual person normally attested by continuity of memory with present consciousness

**personal income** *n* : the current income received by persons from all sources excluding transfers among persons — used esp. in national income accounting

**personal injury** *n* **1** : an injury affecting one's physical and mental person as contrasted with one causing damage to one's property **2** : an injury giving rise to a personal action at law

**personal insurance** *n* **1** : insurance of human life values against the risks of death, injury, illness or against expenses incidental to the latter **2** : insurance purchased for personal or family protection purposes as contrasted with insurance of business property or interests

**per·son·al·ism** \ˈpərs(ᵊ)nəˌlizəm\ *n* -s **1** : personal quality or state : individuality of character or influence : INDIVIDUALISM **2** : a doctrine, theory, or school of thought emphasizing the significance, uniqueness, and inviolability of personality: as **a** : the philosophical theory developed in America principally by Borden P. Bowne and George H. Howison but foreshadowed in Walt Whitman and Bronson Alcott holding that ultimate reality consists of a plurality of spiritual beings or independent persons ⟨~ is a modern title used particularly to indicate a break, not only with absolutisms of every kind and with fundamental monisms, but also to distinguish its system from those personal idealisms and theisms which retain a hidden Absolute treated as a person —R.T.Flewelling⟩ **b** : a theory that psychology is properly concerned with the person or self

**¹per·son·al·ist** \-ləst\ *n* -s [¹*personal* + -*ist*] **1** : a writer of personalia **2** : an advocate of personalism

**²personalist** \"\ *adj* : concerned with or oriented toward personalism ⟨a ~ theme⟩

**per·son·al·is·tic** \¦=(=)=¦listik\ *adj* **1 :** PERSONAL, INDIVIDUAL **2 :** of or relating to personalism **:** PERSONALIST

**personalistic psychology** *n* **:** organismic psychology that emphasizes the self or the individual personality

**per·son·al·i·ty** \ˌpərsᵊn'aləd·ē, ˌpə̄s-, ˌpəis-, -lətē, -i\ *n* -ES [ME *personalite*, fr. LL *personalitas*, fr. *personalis* personal + L *-itas* -ity — more at PERSONAL] **1 a :** the quality or state of being a person and not an abstraction, thing, or lower being **:** the fact of being an individual person **:** personal existence or entity **:** capacity for the choices, experiences, and liabilities of an individual person ⟨questions which must be answered by man not as part of nature but as a ~ —Christian Gauss⟩ ⟨the proper moral relation between the individual and society, or . . . between ~ and community —J.A.Hobson⟩ **b :** the distinctive quality or state of a spiritual entity ⟨the three *Personalities* of the Trinity⟩ **2 :** the qualities of a person that constitute or fix his legal status or general legal capacity **3 :** a personal being **:** a single individual **4 a :** the condition or fact of relating to a particular person; *specif* **:** the condition of referring directly to or being aimed at an individual esp. disparagingly or hostilely **b :** an utterance that refers to the person, conduct, or other aspect of some individual usu. disparagingly or offensively **:** personal remark — usu. used in pl. ⟨indulgence in *personalities*⟩ **5 a :** the complex of characteristics that distinguishes a particular individual or individualizes or characterizes him in his relationships with others ⟨the organization flourished under her administration, for she had a winning ~ and a capacity for hard work —Marie A. Kasten⟩ ⟨a pious and good man, but an utterly negligible ~ —Compton Mackenzie⟩ **b :** a comparable complex characteristic of a group or nation ⟨southeast Asia had now attained a diplomatic ~ of its own —Virginia M. Thompson & Richard Adloff⟩ **c :** the total of distinctive traits and characteristics ⟨the ~ of the English countryside —S.W.Wooldridge⟩ **d** (1) **:** the totality of an individual's emergent tendencies to act or behave esp. self-consciously or to act on, interact with, perceive, react to, or otherwise meaningfully influence or experience his environment (2) **:** the organization of the individual's distinguishing character traits, attitudes, or habits — compare EGO, SELF **6 a :** distinction or excellence of personal and social traits **:** the social characteristic of commanding notice, admiration, respect, or influence through personal characteristics ⟨a superior in charm, in experience, in knowledge of the world and in force of ~ —Arnold Bennett⟩ **b :** a person having such quality; *also* **:** a person of importance, prominence, renown, or notoriety ⟨an able speaker, a strong and positive character, and a gentle and lovable ~ —F.T.Persons⟩ **syn** see DISPOSITION

**personality disorder** *n* **:** a psychopathological condition or group of conditions in which an individual's entire life pattern is considered deviant or nonadaptive although he shows neither neurotic symptoms nor psychotic disorganization

**personality test** *n* **:** any of several tests consisting of standardized tasks designed to determine various aspects of the personality type or the emotional status of the person examined

**per·son·al·iza·tion** \ˌpərs(ᵊ)nələ'zāshən, ˌpə̄s-, ˌpəis-, -ˌlī'z-\ *n* -S **1 :** the quality or state of being personalized ⟨the ~ of natural forces in myth and religion⟩ **2 :** the act or process of personalizing ⟨~ of propaganda⟩

**per·son·al·ize** \'=(=)=ˌlīz\ *vt* -ED/-ING/-S *see -ize in Explan Notes* [¹*personal* + *-ize*] **1 :** to ascribe personality to **:** invest or endow with human qualities **:** ANTHROPOMORPHIZE ⟨death *personalized* as a man with a scythe⟩ **2 :** to realize or embody in one's personality **:** TYPIFY ⟨~ the genius of his age⟩ ⟨a man who *personalized* an ideal of our childhood⟩ **3 :** to make personal or individual: as **a :** to take (as a remark) personally **b :** to mark so as to identify as the property of a particular person ⟨*personalized* luggage⟩ **c :** to direct or adjust to the individual ⟨*personalizing* sales techniques⟩

**personal law** *n* **:** law that applies to a particular person or class of persons only wherever situated — distinguished from *territorial law*

**personal liberty** *n* **:** the freedom of the individual to do as he pleases limited only by the authority of politically organized society to regulate his action to secure the public health, safety, or morals or of other recognized social interests

**per·son·al·ly** \-s(ᵊ)nəlē, -li\ *adv* [ME, fr. *personal* + *-ly*] **:** so as to be personal **:** in a personal manner; *often* **:** as oneself **:** on or for one's own part ⟨~ I don't want to go⟩

**personal name** *n* **:** a name (as the praenomen or the forename) by which an individual is intimately known or designated and which may be displaced or supplemented by a surname, a cognomen, or a royal name

**per·son·al·ness** *n* -ES **:** the quality or state of being personal; *esp* **:** appeal to the individual ⟨the ~ of this message⟩

**personal pronoun** *n* **:** a pronoun (as *I*, *you*, *they*) expressing a distinction of person

**personal property** *n* **:** estate or property other than real property consisting in general of things temporary or movable including intangible property **:** property recoverable by a personal action **:** CHATTELS

**personal representative** *n* **:** a person (as an executor or administrator for a deceased person, heir, or next of kin for an ancestor, a devisee or legatee for a testator, a receiver for an absent or insolvent person or a guardian or conservator or committee for an incompetent) who stands in the place of another or who represents his legal interests

**personal rights** *n pl* **:** rights (as of personal security, personal liberty, and private property) appertaining to the person

**personals** *pl of* PERSONAL

**personal service** *n* **1 :** service of a legal process by delivering it or a copy thereof to the defendant or by statute to an agent of the defendant authorized to receive service in the case in issue **2 :** economic service involving the either intellectual or manual personal labor of the server rather than a salable product of his skill ⟨physicians, architects, and garbage collectors equally sell *personal service*⟩

**personal servitude** *n* **:** a servitude (as use, usufruct, or habitation) due to a particular person for his lifetime under civil law as distinguished from praedial or real servitudes due to a tract of land

**personal shopper** *n* **:** a person (as a store employee) who assists shoppers to choose their purchases or who personally selects merchandise to fill telephone or written orders

**personal staff** *n* **:** the military aides of a general officer or flag officer — distinguished from *general staff* and *special staff*

**personal standard** *n* **:** a flag (as the royal banner of Great Britain) that is the emblem of a particular person (as a sovereign)

**personal tithe** *n* **:** a tithe arising entirely from the personal industry of man (as fish caught in the sea) — compare MIXED TITHE, PRAEDIAL TITHE

**personal treaty** *n* **:** a treaty that relates only to the persons of the contracting parties — compare REAL TREATY

**personal trust** *n* **:** a trust in which the beneficiary is an individual or individuals — opposed to *corporate trust*

**per·son·al·ty** \-s(ə)nəltē, -ti\ *n* -ES [AF *personalte*, fr. LL *personalitat-*, *personalitas* personality — more at PERSONALITY] **:** PERSONAL PROPERTY

**personal union** *n* **:** a union of two states consituted by their becoming subject to the same personal ruler without loss of independent sovereignty

**per·sona non gra·ta** \pə(r)ˌsōnəˌnän'gra|d·ə, -grä|, -grȧ|, |tə *also* -ˌnōn'g- *or* -grā| *sometimes* -sän-\ *n*, *pl* **per·sonae non gratae** \-(ˌ)nē . . . |d·(ˌ)ē, |(ˌ)tē; -ˌnī . . . |d ˌt, |ˌtī\ *or* **persona non grata** [L] **:** an unacceptable person; *specif* **:** a diplomatic official who is personally not acceptable to the government of the foreign country to which he is accredited

**personas** *pl of* PERSONA

**¹per·son·ate** \'pərsᵊnət, -ᵊnˌāt\ *adj* [L *personatus* masked, counterfeited, fr. *persona* mask + *-atus* -ate — more at PERSON] **1 a** *archaic* **:** PERSONATED, FEIGNED, COUNTERFEIT **b :** MASKED, DISGUISED; *esp* **:** having a form differing from the typical adult form ⟨a ~ larva⟩ **c** *of a bilabiate corolla* **:** having the throat nearly closed by a palate; *also* **:** having such a corolla ⟨a ~ flower⟩ **2** *obs* **:** having personality or personal existence **:** embodied in a person

**²per·son·ate** \'pərsᵊnˌāt, 'pə̄s-,'pəis-, *usu* -ād·+V\ *vb* -ED/-ING/-S [*person* + *-ate*] *vt* **1 :** to impersonate or represent as an actor, pretender, or masquerader **:** act the part of **:** pretend or represent oneself to be ⟨I do not ~ the stage-play emperor to entrap applause —John Keats⟩ **2 :** PERSONALIZE: as **a :** to invest with personality or with personal characteristics **:** represent as a person ⟨in fable, hymn, or song, so *personating* their gods ridiculous, and themselves past shame —John Milton⟩ **b :** to serve as a representative, embodiment, or symbol of **:** TYPIFY **3 :** to give the appearance of possessing (as a quality, emotion) **:** FEIGN **4 a :** to give an imitation of (as a person's manner or speech) **:** MIMIC **b :** to pretend without authority to be **:** create a wrongful appearance of being (someone other than oneself whether fictitious or real) **:** assume without authority and with criminal or fraudulent intent (some character or capacity) ⟨~ an officer of the law⟩ **~** *vi* **:** to play or assume a character

**per·son·ate·ly** *adv* **:** in a personate manner or arrangement **:** so as to be personate

**personating** *n* -S **:** the act of one that personates **:** IMPERSONATION

**per·son·a·tion** \ˌ=='āshən\ *n* -S **1 :** IMPERSONATION **2 :** PERSONIFICATION, EMBODIMENT

**per·son·ative** \'==ˌād·iv\ *adj* **:** of or relating to personation; *esp* **:** employing dramatic representation

**per·son·ator** \-ˌād·ə(r)\ *n* -S **:** one that personates

**per·son·eity** \ˌ=='ēəd·ē\ *n* -ES [*person* + *-eity* (as in *corporeity*)] **1 :** PERSONALITY 1b **2** *archaic* **:** ANIMISM **3 :** PERSONAGE 3

**per·son·i·fi·able** \pə(r)'sänəˌfīəbəl, =ˌ=='===\ *adj* **:** capable of being personified

**per·son·i·fi·ca·tion** \pə(r)ˌsänəfə'kāshən\ *n* -S [fr. *personify*, after such pairs as E *amplify: amplification*] **:** an act of personifying or something that personifies: as **a :** attribution of personal qualities (as of form, character) **:** representation of a thing or abstraction as a person or by the human form **b :** rhetorical representation of an inanimate object or abstract idea as a personality or as endowed with personal attributes **:** PROSOPOPOEIA; *also* **:** an instance of this ⟨"the floods clap their hands" is a ~⟩ **c :** a divinity or imaginary being thought of as representing a thing or abstraction ⟨Aeolus is the ~ of wind⟩ **d :** EMBODIMENT, INCARNATION ⟨be the ~ of pride⟩ **e :** a dramatic or literary representation of a character ⟨a series of excellent readings and ~*s*⟩

**per·son·i·fi·ca·tive** \='===ˌkād·iv\ *adj* [*personification* + *-ive*] **:** tending or serving to personify ⟨a ~ principle in primitive social organizations⟩

**per·son·i·fi·ca·tor** \-ād·ə(r)\ *n* -S [*personification* + *-or*] **:** PERSONIFIER

**per·son·i·fi·er** \pə(r)'sänəˌfī(ə)r, -īə\ *n* -S **:** one that personifies

**per·son·i·fy** \pə(r)'sänəˌfī\ *vb* -ED/-ING/-ES [F *personnifier*, fr. *personne* person + *-ifier* -ify — more at PERSON] *vt* **1 :** to conceive of or represent as a person or as having human qualities or powers **:** impute personality to ⟨~ justice as a blindfolded woman⟩ **2 :** to be the embodiment or personification of **:** INCARNATE ⟨*personifies* the law⟩ ⟨courage *personified*⟩ **~** *vi* **:** to employ personification **:** make personifications

**per·son·ize** \'pərsᵊnˌīz\ *vt* -ED/-ING/-S [*person* + *-ize*] **:** PERSONIFY 1

**per·son·nel** \¦pərsᵊn¦el, ¦pə̄s-, ¦pəis-\ *n*, *pl* **personnel** *or* **personnels** *often attrib* [F, modif. (influenced by *personnel*, adj., personal) of G *personal*, alter. of *personale*, fr. LL, neut. of *personalis* personal — more at PERSONAL] **1 a :** a body of persons employed in some service (as the army or navy, a factory, office, airplane) — distinguished from *matériel* **b** *personnel pl* **:** persons of a particular (as professional or occupational) group ⟨military ~⟩ ⟨missionary ~⟩ ⟨34,000 ~ in the expanded operation⟩ ⟨the changing ~ of the theater⟩ **2 a :** a body of employees that is a factor in business administration esp. with respect to efficiency, selection, training, service, and health **b :** the division of an organization concerned primarily with the selection, placement, and training of employees and with the formulation of policies, procedures, and relations with employees or their representatives

**personnel administration** *or* **personnel management** *n* **:** the phase of management concerned with the engagement and effective utilization of manpower to obtain optimum efficiency of human resources

**personnel carrier** *n* **:** a usu. armored motor vehicle for transporting military personnel and their equipment

**person of color** **1 :** NEGRO **2 :** a person of partially Negro ancestry

**person of incidence :** a person against whom a legal right may be enforced by another or upon whom a correlative duty falls

**person of inherence :** a person having a legal right enforceable against another

**person–to–person** \¦===¦==\ *adv* (*or adj*) **:** from one person to another ⟨the inoculum was transferred *person-to-person*⟩ ⟨made a *person-to-person* call⟩

**persp** *abbr* perspective

**per·spec·tiv·al** \pə(r)'spektivəl\ *adj* **:** exhibiting or concerned with perspective **:** marked by the use of perspective

**¹per·spec·tive** \pə(r)'spektiv, -tēv *also* -təv\ *n* -S [ME; in sense 1, fr. ML *perspectiva*, fr. fem. of *perspectivus* of sight, optical, fr. L *perspectus* (past part. of *perspicere* to look through, look at, examine, fr. *per-* through + *-spicere*, fr. *specere* to look) + *-ivus* -ive; in sense 2, fr. ML *perspectivum*, fr. neut. of *perspectivus* — more at PER-, SPY] **1** *or* **perspectives** *pl*, *obs* **:** OPTICS **2 :** an optical glass: as **a :** a telescope that shows objects in the right position **b :** any of various optical devices for producing a fantastic effect or optical illusion

**²perspective** \"\ *adj* [ME, fr. ML *perspectivus*] **1** *obs* **:** of or relating to vision **:** OPTICAL **2 a** *obs*, *of an optical glass* **:** aiding the vision **:** used for seeing, viewing, or looking **b :** seen in mental perspective — **per·spec·tive·ly** \-təvlē, -tēv-, -li\ *adv*

**³perspective** \"\ *n* -S [MF, prob. modif. (influenced by *perspective* optics, fr. ML *perspectiva*) of OIt *prospettiva*, fr. *prospetto* view, prospect (fr. L *prospectus*) + *-iva* n. suffix (fr. L, fr. fem. of *-ivus* -ive) — more at ¹PERSPECTIVE, PROSPECT] **1 a :** the technique of representing on a plane or curved surface the space relationships of natural objects as they appear to the eye **b :** the technique of adjusting the apparent sources of sounds (as on a radio program) into a natural-seeming and integrated whole **c :** a picture or figure that looks distorted except when viewed from some particular point **2 a :** the interrelation in which parts of a subject are mentally viewed **:** the aspect of an object of thought from a particular standpoint **:** CONFIGURATION ⟨thrown into a fresh ~⟩ ⟨time and experience, which alter all ~*s* —Henry Adams⟩ **b :** capacity to view things in their true relations or relative importance ⟨some folks cannot see the wood for the trees, while others have ~⟩ **3 a** (1) **:** a visible scene; *esp* **:** one giving a distinctive impression of distance **:** VISTA (2) **:** a mental view or prospect **b :** a picture in linear perspective; *specif* **:** a scenic picture giving an effect of extension of the vista (as on a stage) **4 :** the appearance to the eye of objects in respect to their relative distance and positions **5 :** HOMOLOGY 4 ⟨two geometric configurations in ~⟩ ⟨center of ~⟩ **6 a :** a perceptible appearance **b :** appearance of a thing at a given place and time conceived (as by Bertrand Russell) as something actually existing at that place and time even when no perceiver is present and as being a constituent of the object whose appearance it is — **in perspective** **1 :** as viewed in the mind **:** in prospect **:** ANTICIPATED **2 a :** represented according to the principles of perspective **b :** viewed with a proper pattern of relationships as to value, importance, or other basic quality ⟨keeping the temporary advantage strictly *in perspective*⟩

**perspective formula** *n* **:** a structural formula representing three dimensions and used primarily to distinguish among optical isomers — compare PROJECTION FORMULA

COOH / C / $CH_2OH$ / H / $NH_2$ — **D–serine**

COOH / C / $CH_2OH$ / $H_2N$ / H — **L–serine**

perspective formula

**per·spec·tive·less** \-tivləs, -tēv- *also* -təv-\ *adj* **:** lacking perspective

**perspective transformation** *n* **:** the collineation set up in a plane by projecting on it the points of another plane from two different centers of projection

**per·spec·tiv·ic** \¦pərspek¦tivik\ *or* **per·spec·tiv·is·tic** \pər¦spektə¦vistik\ *adj* **:** of, relating to, or concerned with perspectivism

**per·spec·tiv·ism** \pə(r)'spektəˌvizəm\ *n* -S [ISV ³*perspective* + *-ism*; orig. formed as G *perspektivismus*] **1 :** a concept in philosophy: the world forms a complex of interacting interpretive processes in which every entity views every entity and event from an orientation peculiar to itself **2 :** consciousness of or the process of using different points of view (as in literary criticism or artistic representation)

**¹per·spec·tiv·ist** \-ˌvəst\ *n* -S [³*perspective* + *-ist*] **:** an advocate or user of perspectivism

**²perspectivist** \"\ *adj* **:** of, relating to, or based on perspectivism ⟨~ theories⟩ ⟨a ~ outlook⟩

**per·spec·tiv·i·ty** \ˌpərˌspek'tivəd·ē\ *n* -ES [ISV ³*perspective* + *-ity*] **:** the correspondence between the points, lines, or planes of two geometric configurations in perspective

**per·spec·to·graph** \pə(r)'spektəˌgraf, -räf\ *n* [L *perspectus* (past part. of *perspicere* to look through) + E *-o* + *-graph* — more at PERSPECTIVE] **:** an instrument used as an aid to drawing in perspective by fixing in the picture the positions of some of the points or outlines of the objects to be represented

**per·spec·tom·e·ter** \ˌpərˌspek'tämәd·ər\ *n* [L *perspectus* (past part. of *perspicere*) + E *-o-* + *-meter*] **:** PERSPECTOGRAPH

**Per·spex** \'pərˌspeks\ *trademark* — used for an acrylic plastic consisting essentially of polymerized methyl methacrylate

**per·spi·ca·cious** \¦pərspə¦kāshəs, ¦pə̄s-, ¦pəis-\ *adj* [L *perspicac-*, *perspicax* clear-sighted, (fr. *perspicere* to see through) + E *-ious* — more at PERSPECTIVE] **1** *archaic* **:** CLEAR-SIGHTED, QUICK-SIGHTED, SHARP-SIGHTED **2 :** of acute mental vision or discernment **:** KEEN **3** *substand* **:** PERSPICUOUS **syn** see SHREWD

**per·spi·ca·cious·ly** *adv* **:** in a perspicacious way **:** with perspicacity

**per·spi·ca·cious·ness** *n* -ES **:** PERSPICACITY

**per·spi·cac·i·ty** \ˌ=='kasəd·ē, -sətē, -i\ *n* -ES [LL *perspicacitas*, fr. L *perspicac-*, *perspicax* perspicacious + *-itas* -ity — more at PERSPICACIOUS] **:** the quality or state of being perspicacious; *esp* **:** acuteness of discernment

**perspicil** *n* -S [NL *perspicillum*, fr. L *perspicere* to look through + *-illum*, suffix denoting an instrument — more at PERSPECTIVE] *obs* **:** an optical glass (as a telescope)

**per·spi·cu·ity** \ˌpərspə'kyüəd·ē, ˌpə̄s-, ˌpəis-, -üətē, -i\ *n* -ES [L *perspicuitas*, fr. *perspicuus* perspicuous + *-itas* -ity] **1** *obs* **:** TRANSPARENCY, TRANSLUCENCY **2 :** the quality or state of being clear to the understanding **:** lucidity in expression or development of ideas **3** *obs* **:** the quality or state of being distinctly visible **4 :** PERSPICACITY

**per·spic·u·ous** \pə(r)'spikyəwəs\ *adj* [L *perspicuus*, fr. *perspicere* to look through — more at PERSPECTIVE] **1** *obs* **:** capable of being seen through **:** not opaque **:** TRANSPARENT, TRANSLUCENT **2 :** capable of being clearly and readily understood **:** plain to the understanding ⟨~ in meaning⟩: as **a :** clear in presentation and expression of thought and free from obscurity or ambiguity ⟨a ~ argument⟩ **b :** speaking or writing clearly **:** precise and intelligible in utterance ⟨try to be ~⟩ **3** *archaic* **:** easily seen **:** distinctly visible **:** CONSPICUOUS, MANIFEST **4 :** PERSPICACIOUS **syn** see CLEAR

**per·spic·u·ous·ly** *adv* **:** in a perspicuous manner **:** with perspicuity

**per·spic·u·ous·ness** *n* -ES **:** PERSPICUITY

**per·spir·able** \pə(r)'spīrəbəl\ *adj* [F, fr. MF, fr. *perspirer* to perspire + *-able* — more at PERSPIRE] **1 :** capable of perspiring or being perspired **2** *obs* **:** permitting circulation of air or wind **:** DRAFTY, BREEZY, AIRY

**per·spi·rate** \'pərspəˌrāt\ *vi* -ED/-ING/-S [back-formation fr. *perspiration*] *archaic* **:** PERSPIRE

**per·spi·ra·tion** \ˌpərspə'rāshən, ˌpə̄s-, ˌpəis-, *substand* ˌpres-\ *n* -S [F, fr. MF, fr. *perspirer* to perspire + *-ation* — more at PERSPIRE] **1 :** the act or process of perspiring **2 :** a saline fluid that is secreted by the sweat glands, that consists chiefly of water containing sodium chloride and other salts, nitrogenous substances (as urea), carbon dioxide, and other solutes, and that serves both as a means of excretion and as a body temperature regulator through the cooling effect of its evaporation **:** SWEAT **3 :** vigorous effort such as might be expected to cause sweating ⟨more is usually accomplished by ~ than by inspiration⟩

**per·spira·tive** \pər'spīrəd·iv, 'pərspəˌrād·-\ *adj* [*perspiration* + *-ive*] **:** causing perspiration

**per·spir·a·to·ry** \pə(r)'spīrəˌtōrē\ *adj* [*perspiration* + *-ory*] **:** of, relating to, secreting, or inducing perspiration ⟨~ glands⟩

**per·spire** \pə(r)'spī(ə)r, -īə\ *vb* -ED/-ING/-S [F *perspirer*, fr. MF, fr. *per-* through (fr. L) + *-spirer* (fr. L *spirare* to blow, breathe) — more at PER-, SPIRIT] *vi* **1 :** to pass off by evaporation or exhalation esp. through the pores of a substance ⟨beads of moisture *perspiring* through the porous walls of a clay water jug⟩ **2 :** to emit matter through the skin; *specif* **:** to secrete and emit perspiration **3 :** to expend effort (as in thought) to such a degree as might be expected to cause sweating **~** *vt* **1 :** to emit, exhale, or evacuate through pores ⟨firs . . . ~ a fine balsam of turpentine —Tobias Smollett⟩ **2 :** to emit (a substance) as or in perspiration ⟨whooped and drank and *perspired* beer —Christopher Isherwood⟩

**perspired** *adj* **:** covered with perspiration **:** SWEATY

**perspiring** *adj* **1 :** that perspires esp. as a result of effort; *also* **:** laboring diligently ⟨this aspiring and ~ young man⟩ **2 :** likely to cause sweating **:** hot and sticky ⟨a ~ atmosphere⟩ ⟨~ weather⟩

**per·spir·ing·ly** *adv* **:** in a perspiring manner

**per·spiry** \pə(r)'spīrē\ *adj* **:** SWEATY ⟨put on his coat for a ~ luncheon talk —*Newsweek*⟩

**per stir·pes** \per'stirˌpās, ˌpər'stər(ˌ)pēz\ *adv* (*or adj*) [L] **:** by familial stocks **:** as representatives of the branches of the descendants of a person — used of a mode of reckoning the rights or liabilities of descendants in which the children of any one descendant have or take only the share that their parent would have taken if living — compare PER CAPITA

**per·stringe** \pə(r)'strinj\ *vt* -ED/-ING/-S [L *perstringere* to bind up, graze, touch upon, censure, fr. *per-*, intensive prefix + *stringere* to draw tight, bind, touch upon — more at PER-, STRAIN] **1 :** to find fault with **:** CENSURE, CRITICIZE **2** *obs* **:** to dull the vision of **3** *archaic* **:** to touch upon lightly or in passing

**per·suad·abil·i·ty** \pə(r)ˌswādə'biləd·ē, -lətē, -i\ *n* **:** the quality or state of being persuadable

**per·suad·able** \pə(r)'swādəbəl\ *adj* [*persuade* + *-able*] **1 a :** capable of persuading **b :** subject to being persuaded **2** *obs* **:** commendable to the judgment — **per·suad·able·ness** \-nəs\ *n* -ES — **per·suad·ably** \-blē,-bli\ *adv*

**per·suade** \pə(r)'swād\ *vb* -ED/-ING/-S [L *persuadēre*, fr. *per-*, prefix denoting completion + *suadēre* to advise, urge — more at PER-, SUASION] *vt* **1 :** to induce by argument, entreaty, or expostulation into some mental position (as a determination, decision, conclusion, belief) **:** win over by an appeal to one's reason and feelings (as into doing or believing something) **:** bring (oneself or another) to belief, certainty, or conviction **:** argue into an opinion or procedure ⟨he ~*s* his friend to study law⟩ ⟨*persuaded* us that we were wrong⟩ ⟨~ yourself that you cannot fail⟩ **2 :** to use persuasion upon **:** plead with **:** URGE ⟨even now at my elbow, *persuading* me not to kill the duke —Shak.⟩ **3 :** to demonstrate or prove (something) to be true, credible, essential, commendable, or worthy (as of belief, adoption, practice) **:** bring about by argument and persuasion the doing, practicing, or believing of ⟨hadst thou thy wits, and didst ~ revenge —Shak.⟩ **4 :** to obtain or get with difficulty (as by coaxing) ⟨finally *persuaded* an answer out of him⟩ **~** *vi* **1 :** to use or to prevail by persuasion **:** plead movingly or successfully — sometimes formerly used with *with* **2 :** to become persuaded ⟨he ~*s* easily⟩ **syn** see INDUCE

**per·suad·er** \-də(r)\ *n* -S **1 :** one that persuades **2 :** something (as a gun or whip) used in compelling

**per·suad·ing·ly** *adv* **:** in a persuading manner **:** so as to persuade ⟨spoke ~ and at length⟩

**per·sua·si·bil·i·ty** \pə(r)ˌswāzə'biləd·ē, -āsə-, -lətē, -i\ *n* -ES **:** PERSUADABILITY

**per·sua·si·ble** \-ˈ-zəbəl, -səb-\ *adj* [MF, fr. L *persuasibilis* persuasive, fr. *persuasus* + *-ibilis* -ible] **:** PERSUADABLE

**per·sua·sion** \pə(r)ˈswāzhən\ *n* -s [ME *persuasioun*, fr. MF or L; MF *persuasion*, fr. L *persuasion-, persuasio*, fr. *persuasus* (past part. of *persuadēre* to persuade) + *-ion-, -io* -ion — more at PERSUADE] **1 a :** an act or the action of influencing the mind by arguments or reasons offered or by anything that moves the mind or passions or inclines the will to a determination **b :** something that serves to persuade **:** a persuading argument **:** INDUCEMENT ⟨if none of these ~s move you⟩ **c :** ability to persuade **:** PERSUASIVENESS ⟨there is an inherent ~ in some voices⟩ **2 :** the condition of having the mind influenced (as to decision, acceptance, or belief) from without **:** the quality or state of being persuaded **3 :** something of which one is persuaded: as **a :** a notion or opinion receiving full credence **:** a view held with complete assurance ⟨holding the ~ that they could not fail⟩; *esp* **:** a system of religious or other beliefs ⟨the several Protestant ~s⟩ **b :** a group, faction, sect, or party that adheres to a particular system of beliefs or ideas or promotes a particular view, theory, or cause ⟨composers of all different ~s —Arthur Berger⟩ ⟨the Tory ~⟩ **4 :** KIND, SORT, DESCRIPTION ⟨persons of the male ~⟩ **5 :** an act of persuading by force; *also* **:** compulsive force **6 :** a method of treating the neuroses consisting essentially in rational conversation and reeducation **syn** see OPINION, RELIGION

**¹per·sua·sive** \-āsiv, \ēv *also* -āz\ *or* \əv\ *adj* [MF *persuasif*, fr. ML *persuasivus*, fr. L *persuasus* (past part. of *persuadēre* to persuade) + *-ivus* -ive — more at PERSUADE] **:** tending to persuade **:** having the power of persuading ⟨~ eloquence⟩ ⟨a most ~ speaker⟩ — **per·sua·sive·ly** \əvlē, \ēv-, -li\ *adv* — **per·sua·sive·ness** \ivnəs, \ēv- *also* \əv-\ *n* -ES

**²persuasive** \"\ *n* -s **:** something that persuades or is intended to persuade **:** INDUCEMENT, INCENTIVE ⟨bribes and other ~s⟩

**persuasive definition** *n* **:** a definition that seeks to influence the attitude of the hearer to something by redefining its name ⟨that jazz is really classical music free of artificial constraints is a typical *persuasive definition*⟩

**per·sua·so·ry** \pə(r)ˈswāzərē, -āsə-\ *adj* [ML *persuasorius*, fr. L *persuasus* + *-orius* -ory] *archaic* **:** PERSUASIVE

**per·sulfate** \ˌpər, (ˈ)per+\ *n* [ISV *per-* + *sulfate*] **1 :** a sulfate in which the metal has a relatively high valence ⟨~ of iron $Fe_2(SO_4)_3$⟩ **2 :** a salt of persulfuric acid; *esp* **:** a salt (as potassium persulfate) of the acid $H_2S_2O_8$

**per·sulfuric acid** \ˌpər, ˌper+ . . . -\ *n* [ISV *per-* + *sulfuric;* prob. orig. formed as F *persulphurique*] **:** either of two peroxy acids of sulfur: **a :** a crystalline strongly oxidizing acid $H_2S_2O_8$ obtained usu. by electrolysis of sulfuric acid and used chiefly in making hydrogen peroxide and in the form of salts — called also *peroxydisulfuric acid;* not used systematically **b :** PERMONOSULFURIC ACID

**¹pert** \ˈpərt, ˈpə̄t, ˈpəit, *usu* \d.+V\ *adj, usu* -ER/-EST [ME, modif. of OF *apert* — more at APERT] **1** *obs* **:** CLEVER, SHARP ⟨the ~*est* operations of wit —John Milton⟩ **2 a :** marked by a saucy freedom and forwardness **:** flippantly cocky and self-assertive **:** IMPUDENT, IMPERTINENT ⟨children were ~, disobedient, irreverent at home —Dixon Wecter⟩; *esp* **:** mischievously or heedlessly aggressive and rather disrespectful ⟨was amused by the boy's ~ answer⟩ ⟨with a ~ toss of her head —W.M.Thackeray⟩ ⟨~ little girls in short frocks —Siegfried Sassoon⟩ **b :** marked by a smart crisp jauntiness **:** trim and chic ⟨the ~ little hat —F. Tennyson Jesse⟩ ⟨bought a ~ little business suit for herself⟩ ⟨stories about ~ young career girls and junior executives —J.D.Adams⟩ **c :** piquantly stimulating ⟨is a ~ notion and one to fascinate the attention —G.J.Nathan⟩ ⟨a ~ turn in the end of a sentence —O.W. Holmes †1935⟩ **3 a** (1) **:** full of good spirits and vitality **:** chipper and frisky **:** full of pep ⟨felt ~ and relaxed after their long vacation⟩ (2) **:** LIVELY, BRISK, SPRY ⟨were moving along at a ~ pace⟩ **b :** brightly vivacious **:** PERKY ⟨was as rosy and ~ as a schoolgirl —Vera Caspary⟩ ⟨finds fun in ~, informal chatter —Flora Lewis⟩

**²pert** \"\ *adv* [ME, fr. *pert*, adj.] **:** PERTLY

**pert** *abbr* pertaining

**per·tain** \pə(r)ˈtān\ *vi* -ED/-ING/-S [ME *parteinen, partenen, perteinen, pertenen*, fr. MF *partenir*, fr. (assumed) VL *partenēre*, alter. of L *pertinēre* to reach to, belong, fr. *per-*, intensive prefix + *-tinēre* (fr. *tenēre* to hold) — more at PER-, THIN] **1 a** (1) **:** to belong to something as a part or member or accessory or product ⟨those who ~*ed* to the Christian tradition —J.D.Conway⟩ (2) **:** to belong to something as an attribute or adjunct or attendant feature or function ⟨the destruction and havoc ~*ing* to war⟩ ⟨a job that ~s to one man alone⟩ (3) **:** to belong to something as a care or concern or duty ⟨responsibilities that ~ to fatherhood⟩ (4) **:** to belong to something by inherent character, right, assignment, or established association ⟨privileges that ~*ed* only to the wealthier class⟩ **b :** to be appropriate to something **:** be right or proper or suitable ⟨trades ~*ing* to military activities —*Amer. Guide Series: Minn.*⟩ **:** be pertinent ⟨the criteria for their appointments will be different from those that ~ elsewhere in the faculty —J.B.Conant⟩ **2 :** to have some connection with or relation to something **:** have reference **:** RELATE ⟨in matters ~*ing* to man and his environment —*Current Biog.*⟩ ⟨his intention to translate some historical documents ~*ing* to Christopher Columbus —Saxe Commins⟩ ⟨the enormous stress which women lay on everything ~*ing* to clothes —P.M. Gregory⟩

**perth** \ˈpərth\ *adj, usu cap* **1** [fr. *Perth*, burgh and county in Scotland] **a :** of or from the burgh of Perth, Scotland **:** of the kind or style prevalent in Perth **b :** PERTHSHIRE **2** [fr. *Perth*, Western Australia] **:** of or from Perth, the capital of Western Australia **:** of the kind or style prevalent in Perth

**perth·ite** \ˈpər,thīt\ *n* -s [*Perth*, Ontario, Canada + E *-ite*] **:** a feldspar rock consisting of orthoclase or microcline in which is interlaminated albite — **per·thit·ic** \ˌpərˈthid·ik\ *adj* — **per·thit·i·cal·ly** \-d·ək(ə)lē\ *adv*

**per·tho·phyte** \ˈpərthə,fīt\ *n* -s [Gk *perthein* to destroy + E *-o-* + *-phyte;* akin to L *ferire* to strike — more at BORE] **:** a plant (as a fungus) that lives on dead or decaying tissue forming part of a living plant — compare SAPROPHYTE

**perth·shire** \ˈpərth,shi(ə)r, -ˌshər\ *adj, usu cap* [fr. *Perthshire*, Scotland] **:** of or from the county of Perth, Scotland **:** of the kind or style prevalent in Perth

**per·ti·na·cious** \ˌpərtᵊnˈāshəs, ˌpə̄t-, ˌpəit-\ *adj* [L *pertinac-, pertinax* (fr. *per-* thoroughly, completely + *-tinac-, -tinax*, fr. *tenac-, tenax* tenacious) + E *-ious* — more at PER-, TENACIOUS] **1 :** marked by an unyieldingly persistent fixedness (as of opinion, purpose, action) that is often annoyingly perverse in fact or in appearance **:** stubbornly inflexible ⟨a ~ opponent⟩ ⟨~ opinions⟩ **2 :** hard to get rid of **:** doggedly tenacious: as **a :** that resolutely or obstinately continues to last **:** not easily dislodged or dismissed or brought to an end ⟨many years of ~ advertising —Berton Roueché⟩ ⟨the theater . . . is a ~ institution, always confounding the prophets who announce from time to time that it is about to die —John Brophy⟩ ⟨~ curiosity⟩ **b :** that resolutely or obstinately persists in asking or demanding **:** refusing to be put off or denied **:** IMPORTUNATE ⟨a ~ beggar⟩ ⟨~ creditors⟩ **c :** stubbornly unshakable ⟨when the danger was so obvious that all but the most ~ optimists or partisans were silent —D.W.Brogan⟩ **d :** that resists treatment ⟨a ~ fever⟩ **syn** see OBSTINATE

**per·ti·na·cious·ly** *adv* **:** in a pertinacious manner **:** with pertinacity

**per·ti·na·cious·ness** *n* -ES **:** PERTINACITY

**per·ti·nac·i·ty** \ˌ-ˈ-ˈasəd·ē, -ˈaas-, -sətē, -i\ *n* -ES [MF *pertinacité*, fr. LL *pertinacitas*, fr. L *pertinac-, pertinax* pertenacious + MF *-ité* -ity — more at PERTINACIOUS] **:** the quality or state of being pertinacious

**pertinacy** *n* -ES [ME *pertinacie*, fr. L *pertinacia*, fr. *pertinac-, pertinax* pertinacious + *-ia* -y] *obs* **:** PERTINACITY

**per·ti·nence** \ˈpərt(ᵊ)nən(t)s, ˈpə̄t, ˈpəit *also* \d·ənə- *or* \tənə-\ *n* -s [ME, fr. MF, fr. *pertinent*] **:** PERTINENCY

**per·ti·nen·cy** \-ənsē, -si\ *n* -ES [MF *pertinence* + E *-y*] **:** the quality or state of being pertinent **:** RELEVANCE ⟨the ~ of the evidence —Sidney Hyman⟩

**¹per·ti·nent** \-ənt\ *adj* [ME, fr. MF, fr. L *pertinent-, pertinens*, pres. part. of *pertinēre* to reach, belong — more at PERTAIN] **:** that has some connection or relation with something (as a matter under discussion) **:** that is to the point **:** that is relevant or applicable ⟨the message of the book is as ~ today as at the time it was written —*Forth*⟩ ⟨had some ~ comments —Cormac Philip⟩ ⟨a ~ question⟩ ⟨~ facts⟩ ⟨~ information⟩ ⟨data ~ to such federal aid —*Collier's Yr. Bk.*⟩ **syn** see RELEVANT

**²pertinent** \"\ *n* -s [ME, fr. ML *pertinentia*, fr. L, pl. of *pertinent-, pertinens*] *chiefly Scots law* **:** APPURTENANCE; *specif* **:** something belonging to an estate and passing with ownership of the estate to any new owner ⟨the dignity . . . was territorial and a part and ~ of the lands —F.J.Grant⟩ — usu. used in pl. ⟨conveying the land with parts and ~s⟩

**per·ti·nen·tia** \ˌpərtᵊnˈenchēə\ *n pl* [ML] *civil & Scots law* **:** appurtenances belonging to real or personal property and passing with ownership of the property to any new owner

**per·ti·nent·ly** *adv* **:** in a pertinent way **:** with pertinency

**pert·ly** *adv* [ME, fr. *pert* + *-ly*] **:** in a pert manner **:** with pertness

**pert·ness** *n* -ES **:** the quality or state of being pert

**per tout et non per my** \pə(r)ˈtüä,nänpə(r)ˈmē\ [AF] **:** by the whole and not by a share, moiety, or divisible part — used esp. in property law with reference to concurrent ownership by two or more persons

**per·turb** \pərˈtərb; pəˈtə̄b, -təib\ *vt* -ED/-ING/-S [ME *perturben*, fr. MF *perturber*, fr. L *perturbare*, fr. *per-*, intensive prefix + *turbare* to throw into disorder, disturb, make turbid — more at PER-, TURBID] **1 :** to disturb considerably in mind **:** make quite uneasy **:** cause to be upset or worried or alarmed **:** DISQUIET, UNSETTLE ⟨was ~*ed* by the news⟩ ⟨had not expected this development and it rather ~*ed* him⟩ **2 :** to put into considerable disorder or confusion **:** throw out of kilter **:** DERANGE ⟨~*ing* good social order with their lies and propaganda⟩ **3 a :** to cause (a planet or other celestial body) to deviate from a theoretically regular orbital motion usu. as a result of interposed or otherwise extraordinary gravitational pull **b :** to disturb or interfere with or modify the usual or expected motion or course or arrangement of (as atoms) ⟨interaction between a hydrogen atom ~*ed* by a passing ion —*Physical Rev.*⟩ **4 :** to subject to tonal perturbation **syn** see DISCOMPOSE

**¹per·tur·bate** \ˈpərd·ər,bāt\ *vt* -ED/-ING/-S [L *perturbatus*, past part. of *perturbare*] *archaic* **:** PERTURB

**²perturbate** \"\ *adj* [L *perturbatus*, past part.] *archaic* **:** PERTURBED

**per·tur·ba·tion** \ˌpərd·ərˈbāshən, ˌpərtər'-, ˌpər,tər'-; ˌpə̄d·ə'-, ˌpə̄tə'-, ˌpə̄,tə̄'-, ˌpəi,təi'-\ *n* -s [ME *perturbacioun*, fr. MF *perturbation*, fr. L *perturbation-, perturbatio*, fr. *perturbatus* + *-ion-, -io* -ion] **1 :** the action of perturbing or condition of being perturbed **:** COMMOTION ⟨the ~s of the period of revolution —Ernest Barker⟩; *esp* **:** mental or emotional disturbance or agitation ⟨was in great ~ of mind⟩ **2 :** irregular variation in or alteration of or deviation from what is usual or expected (as in the orbital motion of a celestial body affected by extraordinary gravitational pull) **3 :** alternation of tone conditioned by phonetic environment — **per·tur·ba·tion·al** \ˌ-ˈ-ˈbāshənᵊl, -shnəl\ *adj*

**per·tur·ba·tive** \ˈpərd·ər,bād·iv, ˌpərˈtərbəd·-\ *adj* [LL *perturbativus*, fr. L *perturbatus* (past part. of *perturbare* to perturb) + *-ivus* -ive — more at PERTURB] *archaic* **:** tending to perturb **:** PERTURBING

**per·tur·ba·tor** \ˈpərd·ər,bād·ə(r)\ *n* -s [LL, fr. L *perturbatus* + *-or*] *archaic* **:** one that perturbs

**per·turbed** *pronunc at* PERTURB + d\ *adj* **:** DISTURBED, AGITATED, UPSET ⟨was . . . so ~ as to forget the convention of the usual greetings —Joseph Conrad⟩ — **per·turbed·ly** \-bədlē, -bdlē\ *adv*

**perturbing** *adj* **:** DISTURBING, UPSETTING ⟨a revelation that was most ~⟩ — **per·turb·ing·ly** *adv*

**per·tu·sar·ia** \ˌpərd·əˈsa(a)rēə\ *n, cap* [NL, fr. L *pertusus* (past part. of *pertundere* to bore through) + NL *-aria* — more at PIERCE] **:** a large widely distributed genus (the type of the family Pertusariaceae) of crustose lichens that have the fruiting bodies in structures resembling knobs and that are one of the sources of litmus and archil — compare ROCCELLA

**per·tus·sal** \pə(r)ˈtəsəl\ *adj* [NL *pertussis* + E *-al*] **:** of or relating to whooping cough

**per·tus·sis** \-səs\ *n* [NL, irreg. fr. L *per-* thoroughly + *tussis* cough] **:** WHOOPING COUGH

**pe·ru** \pəˈrü *sometimes* piˈ- *or* pēˈ- *or* pāˈ- *or* peˈ-\ *adj, usu cap* [fr. *Peru*, country in So. America] **:** of or from Peru **:** of the kind or style prevalent in Peru **:** PERUVIAN

**peru balsam** *n, usu cap P* **:** BALSAM OF PERU

**¹pe·ru·gian** \pəˈrüj(ē)ən, pāˈ-\ *adj, usu cap* [*Perugia*, city in Umbria, Italy + E *-an*] **:** of or relating to Perugia, Italy

**²perugian** \"\ *n* -s *cap* **:** a native or inhabitant of Perugia

**pe·ru·gi·nesque** \pə,(ˌ)rüjəˈnesk, ˌpe(-, pā,rü-, pe,rü-, pə,rü-\ *adj, usu cap* [F *péruginesque*, fr. *Perugino* (Pietro Vannucci) †1523 Ital. painter + F *-esque*] **:** resembling or suggestive of the paintings of the early Renaissance Italian artist Perugino

**pe·ruke** *also* **pe·ruque** *or* **per·ruque** \pəˈrük\ *n* -s [MF *perruque*, fr. OIt *parrucca, perrucca* head of hair, wig] **:** WIG; *specif* **:** one of several wigs popularly worn in the period extending from the 17th century to the early 19th century

**pe·ruk·er** \pəˈrükə(r)\ *or* **per·u·kier** *or* **per·ru·quier** \pəˈrükēə(r); ˌperəˈki(ə)r, -rəkˈyā\ *n* -s [F *perruquier*, fr. *perruque* + *-ier* -er] **:** WIGMAKER

**pe·ru·lar·ia** \ˌper(y)əˈla(a)rēə\ *n, cap* [NL, fr. *perula* scale of a leaf bud (fr. L, small wallet, dim. of *pera* wallet, fr. Gk *pēra*) + NL *-aria*] **:** a genus of leafy-stemmed greenish flowered terrestrial orchids with fibrous roots and a bracted spicate inflorescence

**pe·rus·able** \pəˈrüzəbəl\ *adj* **:** that may be perused

**pe·rus·al** \-zəl\ *n* -s [*peruse* + *-al*] **:** the action of perusing ⟨had not finished his ~ of the evening papers⟩ ⟨a magazine article that deserves careful ~⟩

**peru saltpeter** *n, usu cap P* **:** CHILE SALTPETER

**pe·ruse** \pəˈrüz\ *vb* -ED/-ING/-S [ME *perusen*, prob. fr. L *per-* completely, thoroughly + ME *usen* to use — more at PER-, USE] *vt* **1 :** to examine or consider or survey with some attention and typically for the purpose of discovering or noting one or more specific points **:** look at or look through fairly attentively **:** go through **:** STUDY ⟨applicants should ~ the lists carefully —*Official Register of Harvard Univ.*⟩ ⟨as we ~ the course of history of civilized man —Sumner Welles⟩ ⟨people who began by beholding him ended by *perusing* him —Thomas Hardy⟩ ⟨*perused* the terms of the contract⟩ **2 :** READ ⟨evenings spent in *perusing* the world's masterpieces —L.P.Smith⟩ ⟨*perusing* the newspaper⟩; *specif* **:** to read through or read over with some attention and typically for the purpose of discovering or noting one or more specific points ⟨thought something more might be learned by carefully *perusing* the letter she had written⟩ ⟨*perused* the book in the hope of getting needed material for further research⟩ ~ *vi* **1 :** to spend time in perusal **:** peruse something ⟨have tried to ~ and learn all my life —Thomas Hardy⟩ ⟨sat there *perusing* until he was ready to speak⟩ **2** *chiefly dial* **:** to proceed somewhere and take a look around ⟨let's go ~ down that draw —C.T.Jackson⟩ — **peruser** *n* -s

**¹pe·ru·vi·an** \pəˈrüvēən\ *adj, usu cap* [NL *Peruvia* Peru (fr. Sp *Perú*) + E *-an*] **1 :** of, relating to, or characteristic of Peru in So. America **2 :** of, relating to, or characteristic of the people of Peru

**²peruvian** \"\ *n* -s *cap* **:** a native or inhabitant of Peru

**peruvian balsam** *n, usu cap P* **:** BALSAM OF PERU

**peruvian bark** *n, usu cap P* **:** CINCHONA 3

**peruvian coca** *n, usu cap P* **:** COCA 2b

**peruvian cotton** *n, usu cap P* **:** a cotton with long rough hairy fibers that is derived from a Peruvian plant (*Gossypium peruvianum*)

**peruvian cypress** *n, usu cap P* **:** MING TREE

**peruvian daffodil** *n, usu cap P* **:** any of several Peruvian herbs of the genus *Hymenocallis*

**peruvian lily** *n, usu cap P* **:** an Andean herb (*Alstroemeria pelegrina*) that resembles a lily and has showy pinkish purple unspotted flowers and that is used as an ornamental

**peruvian mastic tree** *n, usu cap P* **:** PEPPER TREE 1

**peruvian nutmeg** *n, usu cap P* **:** the aromatic fruit of a So. American tree (*Laurelia aromatica*) of the family Monimiaceae

**peruvian rhatany** *n, usu cap P* **:** a rhatany obtained from an American shrub (*Krameria triandra*) and used as an astringent — called also *knotty rhatany*

**peruvian saltpeter** *n, usu cap P* **:** CHILE SALTPETER

**peruvian yellow** *n, often cap P* **:** a moderate reddish orange that is stronger than burnt ocher and yellower, darker, and slightly less strong than crab apple

**per·vade** \pə(r)ˈvād\ *vb* -ED/-ING/-S [L *pervadere*, fr. *per-* through + *vadere* to go — more at PER-, WADE] *vt* **1** *archaic* **:** to move along through **:** TRAVERSE ⟨*pervaded* Westminster Hall and looked into most of the courts —A.K.H.Boyd⟩ **2 :** to become diffused throughout every part of **:** spread throughout **:** PERMEATE ⟨that heavy, still, musty odor that ~s all railroad waiting rooms —Thomas Whiteside⟩ ⟨an air of Sunday boredom ~s the streets —S.J.Roche⟩ ⟨the lassitude that ~s most of our prisons —Frank O'Leary⟩ ~ *vi* **:** to become diffused throughout every part of something ⟨it is pleasant to live in a locality where this spirit ~s —*Railway Gazette*⟩ **syn** see PERMEATE

**pervading** *adj* **:** prevalent or dominant by reason of having become widely diffused or diffused through every part of something ⟨reflects the crisis in the world and its ~ sense of insecurity —Walter Moberly⟩ — **per·vad·ing·ly** *adv*

**per·valvar axis** \ˌpər, (ˈ)per+...-\ *n* [*per-* + *valvar*] **:** the longitudinal axis of the frustule of a diatom

**per·vap·o·rate** \(ˌ)pərˈvapə,rāt\ *vt* -ED/-ING/-S [*per-* + *evaporate*] **:** to subject to pervaporation

**per·vap·o·ra·tion** \(ˌ)pər,vapəˈrāshən\ *n* -s **:** the concentration of a colloidal solution whose colloid will not pass through a semipermeable membrane by placing the solution in a bag made of the membrane material and blowing warm air against the surface of the bag

**per·va·sion** \pə(r)ˈvāzhən\ *n* -s [LL *pervasion-, pervasio*, fr. L *pervasus* (past part. of *pervadere* to pervade) + *-ion-, -io* -ion — more at PERVADE] **:** the action of pervading or condition of being pervaded **:** PERMEATION

**per·va·sive** \pə(r)ˈvāsiv, \ēv *also* \əv *sometimes* -āz\ *adj* [L *pervasus* + E *-ive*] **:** that pervades or tends to pervade esp. in such a way as to be or become prevalent or dominant **:** PERVADING ⟨a ~ odor that clings stubbornly to clothes —M.M. Gassman⟩ ⟨the ~ dampness of the stone-flagged floor —Elinor Wylie⟩ ⟨an age in which large-scale catastrophe and ~ anxiety have overshadowed the triumphs of individual men —C.J.Rolo⟩ — **per·va·sive·ly** \əvlē, \ēv-, -li\ *adv* — **per·va·sive·ness** \ivnəs, \ēv- *also* \əv-\ *n* -ES

**per·venche** \ˈpər,vänch, -ˌvinch\ *n* -s [F, lit., periwinkle (plant), fr. L *pervinca* — more at PERIWINKLE] **:** a grayish purplish blue that is duller than average delft, bluer, lighter, and stronger than regimental, and lighter and stronger than average navy blue

**per ver·ba de prae·sen·ti** \ˌperˈverbə,dā,prīˈsentē\ *adv* [L] **:** by words of the present tense

**per·verse** \pərˈvərs, pəˈvə̄s, pəˈvəis, ˈpər,v-, ˈpə̄,v-, ˈpəi,v-\ *adj* [ME *pervers*, fr. L *perversus*, fr. past part. of *pervertere* to turn the wrong way, destroy, corrupt, pervert — more at PERVERT] **1 a :** turned away from what is right or good **:** CORRUPT, WICKED ⟨the only righteous in a world ~ —John Milton⟩ **b :** contrary to accepted standards or practice **:** INCORRECT, IMPROPER ⟨felt it ~ that a bondman's son should be made a bishop —G.G.Coulton⟩ **c** *of a verdict* **:** contrary to the evidence or the direction of the judge on a point of law **2 a :** stubborn, obstinate, and persistent by temperament and disposition in opposing what is right, reasonable, correct, or accepted **:** WRONGHEADED ⟨a dual nature, one half positive, and passionate to yearning, one half negative, satirical, and really ~ —H.S.Canby⟩ ⟨certain matters of fact which not even the most ~ of . . . clerks could disguise —F.M.Stenton⟩ **b :** arising from or indicative of stubbornness or obstinacy ⟨will gain nothing by keeping it except a possible ~ satisfaction in doing so —Hervey Allen⟩ **3** *obs* **:** ADVERSE, UNFAVORABLE **4 :** marked by peevishness or petulance **:** CRANKY ⟨if thou thinkest I am too quickly won, I'll frown and be ~ —Shak.⟩ **5 a :** relating to, characterized by, or resulting from a perverted disposition or inclination ⟨the last ~ whim which has taken possession of the debauchee —J.W.Krutch⟩ **b :** suffering from a perversion **syn** see CONTRARY

**per·verse·ly** *adv* **:** in a perverse manner **:** with perverseness

**per·verse·ness** *n* -ES **:** PERVERSITY

**per·ver·sion** \pərˈvərzhən, pəˈvə̄, pəˈvəi\ *also* \shən\ *n* -s [ME, fr. L *perversion-, perversio*, fr. *perversus* (past part. of *pervertere* to pervert) + *-ion-, -io* -ion — more at PERVERT] **1 a :** the action of perverting **b :** the condition of being perverted **2 :** a perverted form of something; *esp* **:** some form of sex gratification (as fellatio, exhibitionism) preferred to heterosexual coitus and habitually sought after as the primary or only form of sex gratification desired

**per·ver·si·ty** \səd·ē, -ətē, -i\ *n* -ES [L *perversitas*, fr. *perversus* perverse + *-itas* -ity — more at PERVERSE] **1 :** the quality or state of being perverse ⟨some sort of ~ in our souls —D.H. Lawrence⟩ **2 :** an instance of perversity ⟨in spite of a hundred *perversities* —C.E.Montague⟩ ⟨one of the ironic *perversities* that often attend the course of affairs —John Dewey⟩

**per·ver·sive** \s|iv, \ēv *also* \z| *or* \əv\ *adj* [L *perversus* (past part. of *pervertere* to pervert) + E *-ive* — more at PERVERT] **:** that perverts or tends to pervert **:** marked by perversion ⟨illegitimate sex drives, ~ behavior —Ben Karpman⟩

**¹per·vert** \pərˈvərt, pəˈvə̄t, pəˈvəit, ˈpər,v-, ˈpə̄,v-, ˈpəi,v-, *usu* \d.+V\ *vt* -ED/-ING/-S [ME *perverten*, fr. MF *pervertir*, fr. L *pervertere* to turn the wrong way, destroy, corrupt, pervert, fr. *per-*, prefix denoting deviation + *vertere* to turn — more at PER-, WORTH] **1 a** (1) **:** to cause to turn aside or away from what is viewed as good or true or morally right **:** lead astray **:** CORRUPT ⟨was accused of ~*ing* youth⟩; *esp* **:** to make a moral pervert of (2) **:** to cause to turn aside or away from what is generally done or generally accepted **:** divert into what is wrong or incorrect or not normal or usual **:** MISDIRECT ⟨~*ed* the course of justice⟩ ⟨were deliberately ~*ing* to their ends essentially the same techniques —*New Republic*⟩ **b** (1) **:** to make use of usu. willfully in a wrong or improper way **:** divert to a wrong end or purpose **:** MISUSE ⟨the idea is one that may easily deteriorate or be ~*ed* —Lionel Trilling⟩ (2) **:** to twist the meaning or sense of usu. willfully **:** MISINTERPRET, MISCONSTRUE, MISAPPLY ⟨~s some evidence and omits the rest —Norman Douglas⟩ **2 :** to effect a symmetric exchange between the right and left parts of ⟨an object as viewed in a plane mirror is ~*ed* from its actual appearance⟩ **syn** see DEBASE

**²per·vert** \ˈpər,vərt, ˈpə̄,və̄t, ˈpəi,vəi\ *sometimes* pə(r)ˈv-; *usu* \d.+V\ *n* -s **:** one that has been perverted or that manifests or is given to some form of perversion esp. sexual

**perverted** *adj* **1 :** that has been perverted **:** TWISTED, CORRUPT, VICIOUS ⟨a custom as ~ as any ever recorded⟩ **2 :** marked by perversion esp. sexual ⟨a still more ~ form of behavior⟩ — **per·vert·ed·ly** *adv* — **per·vert·ed·ness** *n* -ES

**per·vert·er** *pronunc at* ¹PERVERT + ə(r)\ *n* -s **:** one that perverts

**per·vert·i·ble** \-d·əbəl, -təb-\ *adj* [F, fr. MF, fr. *pervertir* to pervert + *-ible* — more at PERVERT] **:** capable of being perverted ⟨incompetent and therefore easily ~ —James Bryce⟩

**per·vi·ca·cious** \ˌpərvəˈkāshəs\ *adj* [L *pervicac-, pervicax* pervicacious (fr. *per-* thoroughly + *-vicac-, vicax*, fr. the stem of *vincere* to prevail, win a point, conquer) + E *-ious* — more at PER-, VICTOR] **:** very obstinate **:** WILLFUL, REFRACTORY — **per·vi·ca·cious·ly** *adv*

**per·vi·ca·cious·ness** *n* -ES **:** the quality or state of being pervicacious **:** great obstinacy or willfulness

**per·vi·cac·i·ty** \ˌpərvəˈkasəd·ē\ *n* -ES [ML *pervicacitas*, fr. L *pervicac-, pervicax* + *-itas* -ity] **:** PERVICACIOUSNESS

**pervicacy** *n* -ES [L *pervicacia*, fr. *pervicac-, pervicax* + *-ia* -y] *obs* **:** PERVICACIOUSNESS

**per·vi·ous** \ˈpərvēəs, ˈpə̄v-, ˈpəiv-\ *adj* [L *pervius*, fr. *per* through + *-vius* (fr. *via* way, road) — more at FOR, VIA] **1 a** *archaic* **:** lying open to the understanding **:** INTELLIGIBLE **b :** being of such a kind as to permit access to something indicated ⟨~ to reason and the logic of facts —*Scotsman*⟩ **2 a :** being of a substance that can be penetrated or permeated ⟨a ~ rock⟩ ⟨~ soil⟩ or that allows passage through ⟨a metal especially ~ to heat⟩ **:** not impervious **b** *archaic* **:** that is passable (as by a traveler) **c :** PERFORATE 2a **3** *archaic* **:** PERVADING — **per·vi·ous·ness** *n* -ES

**per·wits·ky** \pərˈwitskē\ *n* -ES [prob. modif. of Russ *perevyazka*] **1 :** a tiger weasel (*Vormela peregusna*) of eastern Europe and northern Asia that is mottled reddish and white above and black below **2 :** the fur of the perwitsky

**per·y·lene** \ˈperə,lēn\ *n* -s [*peri-di-naphthylene*] **:** a yellow crystalline aromatic hydrocarbon $C_{20}H_{12}$ that is constituted of two naphthalene residues joined to each other through the peri-positions, that is found in small amounts in coal tar and that can be made from naphthalene by the action of aluminum chloride

**pes** \'pēz\ *n, pl* **pe·des** \'pē(,)dēz, 'pe,-\ [NL *ped-, pes*, fr. L, foot — more at FOOT] **1 :** the distal segment of the hind limb of a vertebrate including the tarsus and foot **2 :** a part resembling a foot: as **a :** the diverging branches of the facial nerve in and near the parotid gland **b :** the enlarged lower extremity of the hippocampus major **c :** the crusta of either of the cerebral peduncles **3** [ML *ped-, pes*, fr. L, foot] **a :** a neume indicating an ascending motion **b :** the tenor in medieval choral music **c :** the ground bass of a canon

**pes** *abbr* peseta

**pe·sach** *or* **pe·sah** \'pā,säk\ *n* -s *usu cap* [Heb *Pesaḥ*] **:** PASSOVER

**pe·sade** \pə'säd, -zäd, -zād\ *n* -s [F, alter. (influenced by *peser* to weigh, fr. L *pensare*) of obs. F *posade*, fr. MF, fr. OIt *posata*, fr. *posare* to put, rest, pause, fr. LL *pausare* to stop, rest, fr. L *pausa* pause — more at PAUSE, PENSIVE] **:** a dressage maneuver in which a horse is made to raise his forequarters while keeping his hind feet on the ground without advancing

**pe·san·te** \pā'sän·(,)tā\ *adv (or adj)* [It, heavy, fr. pres. part. of *pesare* to weigh, fr. L *pensare* to weigh (something) — more at PENSIVE] **:** in a heavy manner — used as a direction in music

**pes·cha·ni·ki** \pes'chänəkē\ *also* **pes·cha·nik** \pes'chänik\ *n* -s [Russ *peschanik* sandstone, fr. *pesok* sand; prob. akin to Skt *pāṁsu* sand] **:** the fur of a suslik (*Citellus fulvus*)

**pes·cod** \'pes,käd\ *dial Eng var of* PEASECOD

**pe·se·ta** \pə'sād·ə, pe'-, -sed·ə\ *n* -s [Sp, dim. of *peso*] **1 a :** an old Spanish silver coin worth ¼ of the piece of eight **b :** a corresponding unit of value **2 a :** the basic monetary unit of Spain since 1868 — see MONEY table **b :** a coin or note representing this unit

**pe·sha·war** \pə'shäwər, -shau̇(ə)r\ *adj, usu cap* [fr. *Peshawar*, city in northwest Pakistan] **:** of or from the city of Peshawar, Pakistan **:** of the kind or style prevalent in Peshawar

**pesh·wa** *or* **peish·wa** \'pāshwə\ *n* -s [Hindi & Marathi *peśvā*, fr. Per *peshwā* leader, guide, fr. *pesh* before] **:** the chief minister of a Maratha prince

**pes·ki·ly** \'peskəlē, -li\ *adv* **:** in a pesky manner

**pes·ki·ness** \-kēnəs, -kin-\ *n* -ES **:** the quality or state of being pesky

[1]**pes·ky** \'peskē, -ki\ *adj* -ER/-EST [prob. irreg. fr. *pest* + *-y*] **:** giving rise to annoyance or vexation **:** TROUBLESOME ⟨how to dress the wall behind the range is a ~ decorating problem —Marion Mayer⟩ ⟨tired after that ~ train —Jean Stafford⟩

[2]**pesky** \"\ *adv* **:** EXTREMELY, VERY — used as an intensive ⟨those who are so ~ mean as to destroy library books —*Star of Hope*⟩

**pe·so** \'pā(,)sō, 'pe(-\ *n* -s [Sp, lit., weight, fr. L *pensum* — more at POISE] **1 a :** a former unit of value in Spain and Spanish America equal to 8 reales **:** the Spanish dollar **b :** a coin (as a gold ½ escudo) equal in value to one peso **2 a :** the basic monetary unit in Argentina, Colombia, Cuba, Dominican Republic, Mexico, Uruguay, and formerly Chile **b :** a coin or note representing one of these units (as in Argentina) — see MONEY table **3 a :** the basic monetary unit in the Republic of the Philippines **b :** a coin or note representing this unit — see MONEY table

**pes·sa·ry** \'pesərē, -ri\ *n* -ES [ME *pessarie*, fr. LL *pessarium*, fr. *pessum, pessus* pessary (fr. Gk *pessos* pessary, oval stone for playing checkers or backgammon) + L *-arium* -ary] **1 :** a vaginal suppository **2 :** an instrument or device to be introduced into and worn in the vagina to support the uterus, remedy a malposition, or prevent conception

**pes·si·mal** \'pesəməl\ *adj* [*pessimum* + *-al*] **:** of, relating to, or constituting a pessimum **:** WORST ⟨a ~ environment⟩

**pes·si·mism** \'pesə,mizəm, 'pez-\ *n* -s [F *pessimisme*, fr. L *pessimus* + F *-isme* -ism — more at PEJORATIVE] **1 :** the worst possible or conceivable state ⟨an age when public criticism is . . . at the very point of ~ —Robert Southey⟩ **2 :** an inclination to put the least favorable construction on actions and happenings, to emphasize adverse aspects, conditions, and possibilities, or to anticipate the worst possible outcome ⟨the ~ with which some of us view the prospect of establishing . . . brotherhood among the human race —Elmer Davis⟩ **3 a :** the philosophical doctrine or opinion that reality is essentially evil, completely evil, or as evil as it conceivably can be **b :** the philosophical doctrine that the evils of life overbalance the happiness it affords and that life is preponderantly evil — compare OPTIMISM

**pes·si·mist** \-məst\ *n* -s *often attrib* [F *pessimiste*, fr. *pessimisme*, after such pairs as F *déisme* deism: *déiste* deist] **:** one given to pessimism; *esp* **:** an adherent of philosophical pessimism — compare OPTIMIST

**pes·si·mis·tic** \¦==¦mistik, -tēk\ *also* **pes·si·mis·ti·cal** \-təkəl, -tēk-\ *adj* **:** of, relating to, or characterized by pessimism **:** marked by disbelief, distrust, or a lack of confidence, hope, or joy **:** GLOOMY, DESPAIRING **syn** see CYNICAL

**pes·si·mis·ti·cal·ly** \-tək(ə)lē, -tēk-, -li\ *adv* **:** in a pessimistic manner

**pes·si·mum** \'pesəməm\ *n* -s [L, neut. of *pessimus* worst] **:** the least favorable environmental condition under which an organism can survive

**pes·su·lar** \'pes(y)ələ(r)\ *adj* [*pessulus* + *-ar*] **:** of, relating to, or resembling the pessulus

**pes·su·lus** \-ləs\ *n, pl* **pessu·li** \-,lī\ [L, bolt, modif. of Gk *passalos* peg, stake; akin to Gk *pēgnynai* to fix, fasten together — more at PACT] **:** a bony or cartilaginous bar crossing the lower end of the windpipe of a bird dorsoventrally at its division into bronchi

**pest** \'pest\ *n* -s *often attrib* [MF *peste*, fr. L *pestis*] **1 :** an epidemic disease associated with high mortality; *specif* **:** PLAGUE **2 :** something resembling a pest esp. in destructiveness or noxiousness; *esp* **:** a plant or animal detrimental to man or to his interests **3 :** one that pesters or annoys **:** NUISANCE ⟨gave the greatest encouragement to those ~s of society, mercenary informers —Edmund Burke⟩

**pes·ta·loz·zian** \¦pestə¦lätsēən, -syən\ *adj, usu cap* [Johann H. *Pestalozzi* †1827 Swiss educational reformer + E *-an*] **:** of, relating to, or constituting a system of education in which the sense perceptions are first trained and the other faculties are then developed in what is held to be natural order

[1]**pes·ter** \'pestə(r)\ *vt* **pestered; pestered; pestering** \-st(ə)riŋ\ **pesters** [modif. of MF *empestrer* to hobble (an animal), impede, embarrass, fr. (assumed) VL *impastoriare* to hobble (an animal), fr. L *in-* ²in- + (assumed) VL *pastoria*, n., hobble, fr. L, fem. of *pastorius* of or belonging to a herdsman, fr. L *pastor* herdsman, shepherd + *-ius* -ious — more at PASTOR] **1** *obs* **a :** OBSTRUCT, IMPEDE ⟨seeing him ~*ed* in a narrow passage —Henry Holcroft⟩ **b :** ENCUMBER, OVERBURDEN ⟨shall not ~ my account . . . with descriptions of places —Daniel Defoe⟩ **c :** to crowd together ⟨men . . . confined and ~*ed* in this pinfold —John Milton⟩ **2** [influenced in meaning by *pest*] *archaic* **:** INFEST ⟨is rich and fertile but ~*ed* with green adders —Jedidiah Morse⟩ **3** [influenced in meaning by *pest*] **:** to harass with petty and repeated irritations **:** ANNOY, BOTHER, VEX ⟨~*ed* him . . . so that he could not keep his mind on reading —Jean Stafford⟩ ⟨would ~ people with irritating questions —Elsa Maxwell⟩ **syn** see WORRY

[2]**pester** \"\ *n* -s **:** one that obstructs, encumbers, or annoys

**pes·ter·er** \-t(ə)rə(r)\ *n* -s **:** one that pesters

**pes·ter·ing·ly** *adv* **:** in a pestering manner

**pes·ter·ment** \-tə(r)mənt\ *n* -s *dial chiefly Brit* **:** ANNOYANCE

**pes·ter·ous** \-t(ə)rəs\ *adj* **:** inclined to pester **:** TROUBLESOME

**pest·ful** \'pestfəl\ *adj* **:** PESTIFEROUS

**pesthole** \'=,=\ *n* **:** a place subject or liable to epidemic disease

**pesthouse** \'=,=\ *n* **:** a shelter or hospital for those infected with a pestilential or contagious disease

**pes·ti·ci·dal** \¦pestə¦sīdᵊl\ *adj* **:** of, relating to, or constituting a pesticide

**pes·ti·cide** \'==,sīd\ *n* -s [*pest* + *-i-* + *-cide*] **:** an agent (as a chemical) used to destroy a pest **:** ECONOMIC POISON

**pes·tif·er·ous** \(')pe¦stif(ə)rəs\ *adj* [ME, fr. L *pestifer, pestiferus* pestilential, noxious, fr. *pestis* plague + *-fer, -ferus* (fr. *ferre* to bear, carry) — more at BEAR] **1 :** dangerous to society **:** PERNICIOUS, EVIL ⟨one of the most ~ forms of calumny —Gilbert Burnet⟩ **2 a :** carrying or propagating infection **:** destructive of health **:** PESTILENTIAL ⟨~ vermin⟩ **b :** infected with a pestilential disease ⟨poor ~ creatures begging alms —John Evelyn⟩ **3 :** causing annoyance, irritation, or vexation **:** TROUBLESOME ⟨a ~, high-principled, gimlet-eyed old gentleman —*Today*⟩ — **pes·tif·er·ous·ly** *adv* — **pes·tif·er·ous·ness** *n* -ES

**pes·ti·lence** \'pestələn(t)s\ *n* -s [ME, fr. MF, fr. L *pestilentia*, fr. *pestilent-, pestilens* + *-ia* -y] **1 :** a contagious or infectious epidemic disease that is virulent and devastating; *specif* **:** BUBONIC PLAGUE **2 :** something that is destructive or pernicious ⟨I'll pour this ~ into his ear —Shak.⟩

**pes·ti·lent** \-lənt\ *adj* [ME, fr. L *pestilent-, pestilens*, fr. *pestis* plague] **1 :** destructive of life **:** FATAL, DEADLY ⟨a ~ land where people died like flies —Maurice Carr⟩ **2 :** injuring or endangering society **:** PERNICIOUS ⟨grew impatient with such ~ heresies —V.L.Parrington⟩ **3 :** giving rise to annoyance **:** VEXING, IRRITATING ⟨~ outsiders . . . assailing the reputation of the neighborhood —Arthur Morrison⟩ **4 :** INFECTIOUS, CONTAGIOUS ⟨an antidote to a ~ disease —E.M.Lustgarten⟩ — **pes·ti·lent·ly** *adv*

**pes·ti·len·tial** \¦pestə¦lenchəl\ *adj* [ME *pestilencial*, fr. ML *pestilentialis*, fr. L *pestilentia* pestilence + *-alis* -al] **1 a :** causing or tending to cause pestilence **:** DEADLY ⟨a ~ malignancy in the air —Jonathan Swift⟩ **b :** of, relating to, or having the characteristics of a pestilence ⟨~ diseases⟩ **2 :** morally harmful or injurious **:** PERNICIOUS ⟨blow up the blind rage of the populace with a continued blast of ~ libels —Edmund Burke⟩ **3 :** giving rise to vexation or annoyance **:** IRRITATING ⟨the ~ nuisances who write for autographs —W.S.Gilbert⟩ — **pes·ti·len·tial·ly** \-chəlē, -li\ *adv*

**pestilentious** *adj* [MF or LL; MF *pestilencieux*, fr. LL *pestilentiosus*, fr. L *pestilentia* + *-osus* -ose] *obs* **:** PESTILENTIAL

**pes·tis** \'pestəs\ *n* -ES [L] **:** PLAGUE

[1]**pes·tle** \'pesəl *also* -stᵊl\ *n* -s [ME *pestel*, fr. MF, fr. L *pistillum*; akin to MLG *vīsel* pestle, L *pilum* pestle, javelin, *pinsere* to pound, crush, Gk *ptissein* to crush, Skt *pinaṣṭi* he pounds, crushes] **1 a :** a usu. club-shaped implement for pounding or grinding substances esp. in a mortar **b :** any of various devices for pounding, stamping, or pressing **2** *dial chiefly Eng* **:** the leg or a part of the leg of an animal used for food

[2]**pestle** \"\ *vb* **pestled; pestled; pestling** \-s(ə)liŋ *also* -st(ᵊ)l-\ **pestles** [ME *pestelen*, fr. MF *pesteler*, fr. OF, fr. *pestel*, n.] *vt* **:** to beat, pound, or pulverize with or as if with a pestle ~ *vi* **:** to work with a pestle **:** use a pestle

**pes·to** \'pe(,)stō\ *n* -s [It, fr. *pesto*, adj., pounded, fr. *pestare* to pound, fr. LL *pistare*, freq. of L *pinsere* to pound, crush] **:** a green spaghetti sauce made of green herbs, garlic, and olive oil

**pes·tol·o·gy** \pe'stäləjē, -ji\ *n* -ES [*pest* + *-o-* + *-logy*] **:** a branch of science dealing esp. with insect pests

**pest pear** *n* **:** an American prickly pear (*Opuntia inermis*) introduced into Australia where it is a troublesome weed

**pests** *pl of* PEST

[1]**pet** \'pet, *usu* -ed·+V\ *n* -s [perh. back-formation fr. obs. E *petty* small, fr. ME *pety* — more at PETTY] **1 a :** a domesticated animal kept for pleasure rather than utility **b** *dial Brit* **:** a pet lamb **2 a :** a pampered and usu. spoiled child **b :** a person who is treated with unusual kindness or consideration **:** DARLING ⟨the spoilt ~ of America's idle rich —Bernard Smith⟩ ⟨teacher's ~⟩ **3 :** something having marked popularity **:** current favorite ⟨enormous buttons put together like cuff links are another . . . ~ —Lois Long⟩ **4** *South & Midland* **:** BOIL, SORE

[2]**pet** \"\ *adj* **1 a :** kept or treated as a pet ⟨~ dogs⟩ **b :** treated with unusual kindness or consideration **:** CHERISHED, INDULGED ⟨~ students⟩ **2 :** expressing fondness or endearment ⟨a ~ name⟩ **3 :** FAVORITE ⟨~ theories⟩ ⟨~ stories⟩

[3]**pet** \"\ *vb* **petted; petted; petting; pets** *vt* **1 a :** to make a pet of **:** treat as a pet ⟨died . . . in the newest and largest of hospitals *petted* by all her nurses —Randall Jarrell⟩ **b :** to stroke in a gentle or loving manner **:** CARESS ⟨*petted* the seat with his fingers as though that would mend it —John Steinbeck⟩ **c :** to treat with unusual kindness and consideration **:** PAMPER, INDULGE ⟨that a man whom he had *petted* and favored . . . should go back on him was more than he could endure —John Buchan⟩ **2 :** to embrace and kiss (a member of the opposite sex) in sexual play **:** NECK ~ *vi* **:** to engage in embracing, caressing, and kissing a member of the opposite sex ⟨a girl is . . . more popular with boys if she ~*s* —Valeria H. Parker⟩

[4]**pet** \"\ *n* -s [origin unknown] **1 :** OFFENSE, UMBRAGE ⟨take the ~ in a case of failure and go off in disgust —R.H.Elliot⟩ **2 :** a fit of peevishness, sulkiness, or anger ⟨resigned in a ~, went off to improve his mind by travel —*Time*⟩

[5]**pet** \"\ *vi* **petted; petted; petting; pets :** to take offense **:** SULK

**pet** *abbr* **1** petrolatum **2** petroleum

**pe·ta** \'päd·ə\ *n* -s [Pali, fr. Skt *preta* — more at PRETA] **:** PRETA

[1]**pet·al** \'ped·ᵊl, 'petᵊl\ *n* -s [NL *petalum*, fr. Gk *petalon* leaf; akin to Gk *petannynai* to spread out — more at FATHOM] **1 :** one of the usu. leaf-shaped members that comprise the corolla of a flower — compare SEPAL **2 :** the expanded part of a petaloid ambulacrum in an irregular sea urchin of the order Exocycloida

[2]**petal** \"\ *vb* **petaled** *or* **petalled; petaled** *or* **petalled; petaling** *or* **petalling; petals** *vi* **:** to put forth petals ~ *vt* **:** to cover with or as if with petals

**-pe·tal** \-pəd·ᵊl, -pətᵊl, *esp Brit also* ¦pēt-\ *adj comb form* [NL *-petus* -petal (fr. L *petere* to go toward, seek) + E *-al* — more at FEATHER] **:** going toward **:** seeking ⟨acro*petal*⟩

**petala** *pl of* PETALON

**-pet·a·lae** \'ped·ᵊl,ē\ *n pl comb form* [NL, fr. fem. pl. of *-petalus* -petalous] **:** ones having (such or so many) petals — in names of botanical groups ⟨*Choripetalae*⟩

**pet·al·age** \'ped·ᵊlij, 'petᵊl-, -lēj\ *n* -s **:** the petals of a flower

**pet·aled** *or* **pet·alled** \¦ped·ᵊld, -etᵊld\ *adj* **1 :** having petals — often used in combination ⟨crimson-*petaled*⟩ **2 :** resembling a petal esp. in shape

**petal fall spray** *n* **:** CALYX SPRAY

**pe·ta·lia** \pə'tālēə\ [NL, fr. *petalum* petal + *-ia*] *syn of* NYCTERIS

**pet·al·ine** \'ped·ᵊl,īn, -,ən\ *adj* [NL *petalinus*, fr. *petalum* petal + L *-inus* -ine] **:** relating to, attached to, or resembling a petal

**pet·al·ism** \-l,izəm\ *n* -s [Gk *petalismos* banishment by voting with olive leaves, fr. *petalon* leaf + *-ismos* -ism] **:** an ancient Syracusan method of banishing for five years a citizen suspected of having dangerous influence or ambition — compare OSTRACISM

**pet·al·ite** \-,īt\ *n* -s [G *petalit*, fr. Gk *petalon* leaf + G *-it* -ite] **:** a usu. white mineral $LiAl(Si_2O_5)_2$ consisting of a lithium aluminum silicate occurring in foliated cleavable masses or in monoclinic crystals (hardness 6–6.5, sp. gr. 2.39–2.46)

**pet·al·less** \'ped·ᵊl(l)əs, -etᵊl-\ *adj* **:** having no petals

**petallike** \'=,=\ *adj* **:** resembling a petal

**pet·a·loc·er·ous** \¦ped·ᵊl¦äsərəs\ *adj* [NL *Petalocera* (syn. of *Lamellicornia*) (fr. *petalo-* — fr. Gk *petalon* leaf — + *-cera*) + E *-ous*] **:** having the joints of the antennae lamellate or leafshaped

**pet·al·odont** \'ped·ᵊlə,dänt\ *n* -s [NL *Petalodontidae*] **:** an elasmobranch of the family Petalodontidae

**pet·al·o·don·ti·dae** \,===¦däntə,dē\ *n pl, cap* [NL, fr. *Petalodont-, Petalodus*, type genus + *-idae*] **:** a family of Carboniferous and Permian elasmobranchs (subclass Holocephali) related to the rays and having peculiar flattened petaloid teeth and greatly enlarged pectoral fins — see PETALODUS

**pet·a·lo·dus** \,==¦ōdəs\ *n, cap* [NL *Petalodont-, Petalodus*, fr. *petal-* (fr. Gk *petalon* leaf) + *-odont-, -odus* -odus] **:** the type genus of the family Petalodontidae known only from fossil teeth

**pet·a·lo·dy** \'==,ōdē\ *n* -ES [ISV *petal* + *-ody*] **:** the metamorphosis of various floral organs (as stamens) into petals

**pet·al·oid** \'==,ȯid\ *adj* [prob. fr. (assumed) NL *petaloides*, fr. NL *petalum* petal + L *-oides* -oid] **1 :** resembling a flower petal in form, appearance, or texture **2 :** consisting of petaloid elements ⟨a ~ perianth⟩

**petaloid ambulacrum** *n* **:** an ambulacrum in which the apical portion is expanded to form an area petaloid in outline on the aboral surface of the test (as in most irregular sea urchins)

**pet·a·lon** \'ped·ᵊl,än\ *n, pl* **peta·la** \-ᵊlə\ [Gk, petalon, leaf, leaf of metal — more at PETAL] **:** a plate of gold fastened to the front of the Jewish high priest's miter

**pet·a·lo·ste·mon** \,ped·ᵊlō'stē,män\ *n, cap* [NL, fr. *petalo-* (fr. Gk *petalon* leaf) + Gk *stēmōn* warp, thread — more at STAMEN] **:** a genus of perennial glandular herbs (family Leguminosae) of the central and western U. S. and Mexico having pinnately compound leaves and pink, purple, or white pealike flowers in close heads or spikes and exhibiting a superficial resemblance to clover — see PRAIRIE CLOVER

**pet·al·ous** \'ped·ᵊləs, -etᵊl-\ *adj* [*-petalous*] **:** having petals **:** PETALED

**-pet·al·ous** \¦===\ *adj comb form* [NL *-petalus*, fr. *petalum* petal — more at PETAL] **:** having (such or so many) petals ⟨apo*petalous*⟩

**petal pink** *n* **:** a light yellowish pink that is redder and paler than light apricot and lighter than opera pink

**petals** *pl of* PETAL, *pres 3d sing of* PETAL

**petar** *obs var of* PETARD

**pe·tard** \pə'tärd, -tȧd\ *n* -s [MF, fr. *peter* to break wind (fr. *pet* expulsion of intestinal gas, fr. L *peditum*, fr. neut. of *peditus*, past part. of *pedere* to break wind) + *-ard*; akin to Gk *bdein* to break wind silently, Russ *bzdet'*] **1 :** a metal or wood case containing an explosive for use in breaking down a door or gate or in breaching a wall **2 :** a firework that explodes with a loud report

**pet·ar·dier** \¦ped·ər¦di(ə)r\ *n* -s [F *pétardier*, fr. *pétard* petard (fr. MF *petard*) + *-ier*] **:** a soldier who manages a petard

**pe·ta·ry** \'ped·ərē\ *n* -ES [ML *petaria*, fr. *peta* peat + L *-aria* -ary — more at PEAT] **:** PEATERY

**pe·ta·si·tes** \,ped·ə'sīd·(,)ēz\ *n, cap* [NL, fr. Gk *petasitēs*, *petasitēs* butterbur, fr. *petasos* broad-brimmed hat; prob. fr. the shape of the leaves; akin to Gk *petannynai* to spread out — more at FATHOM] **:** a genus of herbs (family Compositae) that are native to temperate and subarctic regions, have thick rootstocks, large basal leaves, and radiate white or purplish flowers, and possess medicinal properties similar to those of the true coltsfoot — see BUTTERBUR

**pe·tas·ma** \pə'tazmə\ *n* -s [NL, fr. Gk, something spread out; akin to Gk *petannynai* to spread out] **:** a membranous modified endopodite of the first abdominal appendage in a male decapod crustacean

**pet·a·sos** *or* **pet·a·sus** \'ped·əsəs\ *n* -ES [L & Gk; L *petasus*, fr. Gk *petasos*] **:** a broad-brimmed low-crowned hat worn by ancient Greeks and Romans; *esp* **:** the winged hat of Hermes or Mercury as represented in art

**pe·ta·te** \pə'täd·ē\ *n* -s [Sp, fr. Nahuatl *petlatl*] **:** a mat or matting made of dried palm leaves or grass

**pe·tau·rine** \pə'tó,rīn, -,rən\ *adj* [NL *Petaurina* group of mammals in some classifications consisting of the flying phalangers, fr. *Petaurus* + *-ina*] **:** of, relating to, or resembling a flying phalanger

**pe·tau·rist** \-,rəst\ *n* -s [NL *Petaurista* (syn. of *Petaurus*), fr. L *petaurista* ropedancer] **:** FLYING PHALANGER

**pet·au·ris·ta** \,ped·ó'ristə\ *n, cap* [NL, fr. L *petaurista* ropedancer, fr. *petaurum* stage or springboard used by ropedancers (modif. of Gk *peteuron* platform, roost) + *-ista* -ist; akin to Gk *petesthai* to fly — more at FEATHER] **:** a genus of large Asiatic flying squirrels some of which may reach a length of 18 inches excluding the long bushy tail

**pet·au·ris·ti·dae** \-tə,dē\ *n pl, cap* [NL, fr. *Petaurista* + *-idae*] *in some classifications* **:** a family of rodents comprising the flying squirrels but now usu. regarded as constituting a subfamily of Sciuridae

**pet·au·roi·des** \-'rȯi,dēz\ [NL, fr. *Petaurus* + L *-oides* -oid] *syn of* SCHOINOBATES

**pe·tau·rus** \pə'tórəs\ *n, cap* [NL, alter. of L *petaurista* ropedancer] **:** a genus of flying phalangers

**pet bank** *n* **:** any of a group of state banks selected as depositories of federal funds removed from the U. S. Bank during the first Jacksonian administration

**pe·tchary** \pə'cha(a)rē\ *n* -ES [imit.] **:** GRAY KINGBIRD

**petch·e·neg** *or* **pech·e·neg** \'pechə,neg\ *also* **pach·e·neg** \'pach-\ *n* -s *usu cap* [Russ *Pecheneg*] **:** a member of a Turkish people invading the South Russian, Danubian, and Moldavian steppes during the early middle ages

**pet cock** *n* **:** a small cock, faucet, or valve set in a water pipe or pump to let air out, at the end of a steam cylinder or in a radiator or water jacket to drain it, or at the end of an internal-combustion-engine cylinder to release compression — called also *draw cock*

**pet day** *n, chiefly Scot* **:** an unseasonably fine or pleasant day

**pete** \'pēt, *usu* -ēd·+V\ *n* -s [short for ¹*peter*] *slang* **:** SAFE 1b

[1]**pe·te·ca** \pə'tēkə\ *n* -s [modif. of It *petecchia*] **:** a disease of the lemon characterized by deep pitting of the surface of the rind

[2]**peteca** \"\ *n* -s [Pg] **1 :** a large feathered shuttlecock with a rubber or leather base **2 :** a net game in which a peteca is batted with the palm of the hand

**pe·te·chia** \pə'tēkēə, -tek-\ *n, pl* **petechi·ae** \-kē,ē\ [NL, fr. It *petecchia*, perh. fr. (assumed) VL *peticula*, short for (assumed) VL *impeticula*, fr. L *impetic-, impetix* impetigo (alter. of *impetigo*) + *-ula* — more at IMPETIGO] **:** one of the minute hemorrhages or purpuric spots that appear on the skin or mucous and serous membranes or within an organ esp. in some infectious diseases (as typhus or typhoid) — compare ECCHYMOSIS

**pe·te·chi·al** \-kēəl\ *adj* [NL *petechialis*, fr. *petechia* + L *-alis* -al] **:** giving rise to petechiae ⟨~ hemorrhage⟩ **:** marked by petechiae ⟨a ~ rash⟩ **:** relating to petechiae or petechiation ⟨a ~ index⟩

**petechial fever** *also* **petechial typhus** *n* **:** purpura hemorrhagica of the horse

**pe·te·chi·ate** \-kēət, -ē,āt\ *or* **pe·te·chi·at·ed** \-ē,ād·əd\ *adj* [*petechiate* fr. *petechia* + *-ate*; *petechiated* fr. *petechiate* + *-ed*] **:** marked by petechiae ⟨a severely ~ heart⟩

**pe·te·chi·a·tion** \=,==¦āshən\ *n* -s **:** the state of being petechiate

**pete·man** \'pētmən\ *n, pl* **petemen** *slang* **:** SAFECRACKER

[1]**pe·ter** \'pēd·ə(r), -ētə-\ *n* -s [fr. the name *Peter*] **1** *slang* **a :** SAFE 1b **b :** a prison cell **2 :** PENIS — often considered vulgar

[2]**peter** \"\ *vi* **petered; petered; petering** \-əriŋ *also* -ē·triŋ\ **peters** [origin unknown] **1 a :** to diminish gradually and cease **:** run out and disappear **:** give out ⟨when the rain had ~*ed* to a misty drizzle —Hugh Fosburgh⟩ — usu. used with *out* ⟨the stream ~*s* out between the rocks⟩ ⟨when the rich copper deposits ~*ed* out —Harold Griffin⟩ **b :** to come to an end ⟨broad daylight song ~*s* to diminuendo —Lee Anderson⟩ — usu. used with *out* ⟨that all the old American families are ~*ing* out —*N. Y. Times Mag.*⟩ **2 :** to become exhausted ⟨after a long desert journey the oxen became much ~*ed* —*Overland Monthly*⟩ — usu. used with *out* ⟨I am plumb ~*ed* out⟩

[3]**peter** \"\ *n* -s [fr. *blue peter*] **:** a signal given by a whist player to his partner to play trumps

[4]**peter** \"\ *vi* **petered; petered; petering** \-əriŋ *also* -ē·triŋ\ **:** to signal to a whist partner to play trumps

[5]**peter** \"\ *usu cap* [fr. the name *Peter*] — a communications code word for the letter *p*

**peter boat** *n, often cap P* [prob. fr. *peterman* + *boat*] **:** a small double-ended half-decked fishing boat used on some English rivers

**pe·ter·bor·ough** *also* **pe·ter·boro** \'pēd·ə(r),bərə\ *n* -s *usu cap* [*Peterborough*, city in southeast Ontario, Canada] **:** a birch-bark or all-wood canoe

**peter funk** \'==,fəŋk\ *n, usu cap P&F* [fr. the name *Peter Funk* (not necessarily in reference to any real person)] **1 :** SHILLER **2 :** BY-BIDDER

**peter·man** \'==mən\ *n, pl* **petermen** [ME, fr. St. *Peter* †A.D.67? disciple of Jesus + ME *man*; fr. the fact that St. Peter was a fisherman (Mt. 4:18)] **1 :** FISHERMAN **2** [¹*peter* + *man*] *slang* **:** SAFECRACKER

**peter pan** \'==¦pan, -aa(ə)n\ *n, usu cap both Ps* [after *Peter Pan*, boy hero of the play *Peter Pan, or the Boy who wouldn't grow up* (1904), by Sir James M. Barrie †1937 Scot. novelist & dramatist] **1 :** a person who retains in mature years the naturalness, simplicity of spirit, and charm associated with childhood ⟨we could all remain perpetual children, clean, happy, epicene *Peter Pans* —Dwight Macdonald⟩ ⟨you're married to a

peter pan 2

*Peter Pan* who absolutely will refuse to escape from the comfortable irresponsible stage of childhood —Dorothy Dix⟩ **2 :** a small flat close-fitting collar usu. with rounded ends meeting in front used on women's and children's clothing

**peter's cress** *n* [*Peter's* (gen. of the name *Peter*) + E *cress*] **:** SAMPHIRE 1

**pe·ter·sen coil** \ˈpēd·ə(r)sən-\ *n, usu cap P* [prob. after Waldemar *Petersen* *b*1880 Ger. electrical engineer] **:** a ground-fault neutralizer for high-voltage power circuits

**peter's fish** *n, usu cap P* **:** SAINT PETER'S FISH

**pe·ter·sham** \ˈpēd·ə(r),sham, -,shəm\ *n* -s [after Charles Stanhope, Lord *Petersham* †1851 Eng. colonel] **1 a :** a rough nubby woolen cloth used chiefly for men's coats **b :** a coat made of such material **2 :** a heavy corded ribbon used for belts and hatbands

**peter's pence** *n pl but usu sing in constr, usu cap 1st P* [ME *Peteres pens*, pl. of *Peteres peny* (trans. of ML *denarius Sancti Petri*), fr. *Peteres* (gen. of *Peter* St. Peter †A.D.67? disciple of Jesus) + ME *peny* penny; fr. the Roman Catholic tradition that St. Peter founded the papal see] **1 :** an annual tax or tribute of a penny formerly paid by each householder in England to the papal see **2 a :** a voluntary annual contribution made by Roman Catholics to the pope **b :** the collection in a Roman Catholic Church at which such contributions are made

**petes** *pl of* PETE

**pether** *var of* PEDDER

**peth·i·dine** \ˈpethə,dēn, -,dən\ *n* -s [perh. blend of *piperidine* and *ethyl*] **:** meperidine or its hydrochloride

**pé·til·lant** *or* **pe·til·lant** \pātē(y)äⁿ\ *adj* [F *pétillant*, pres. part. of *pétiller* to effervesce with a crackling sound, fr. MF *petiller* to crackle, fr. *peter* to break wind — more at PETARD] *of wine* **:** mildly and slowly effervescing

**pet·i·o·lar** \ˈped·ē,ōlə(r), ,══ˈ══\ *adj* [NL *petiolaris*, fr. *petiolus* petiole + L *-aris* -ar] **:** of, relating to, or proceeding from a petiole **:** growing or supported upon a petiole ⟨a ~ tendril⟩ ⟨a ~ gland⟩

**pet·i·o·lary** \ˈ══,ə,lerē\ *adj* [*petiole* + *-ary*] **:** PETIOLAR

**pet·i·o·la·ta** \,═══ˈläd·ə, -ād·ə\ [NL, fr. *petiolus* petiole + *-ata*] *syn of* CLISTOGASTRA

**pet·i·o·late** \ˈ═══,lāt, *usu* -ād·+V\ *also* **pet·i·o·lat·ed** \-ād·əd\ *adj* [*petiolate* fr. NL *petiolatus*, fr. *petiolus* + L *-atus* -ate; *petiolated* fr. *petiolate* + *-ed*] **:** having a stalk or petiole

**pet·i·ole** \ˈ══,ōl\ *n* -s [NL *petiolus*, fr. L, small foot, fruitstalk, spelling in some MSS of *peciolus*, irreg. fr. *pediculus* small foot, fruitstalk, dim. of *ped-*, *pes* foot — more at FOOT] **1 :** a slender stem that supports the blade of a foliage leaf and that is usu. cylindrical but sometimes flattened or even winged — called also *leafstalk* **2 :** a part resembling the stalk of a plant **:** PEDUNCLE; *specif* **:** the slender abdominal segment joining the rest of the abdomen to the thorax in an insect

**pet·i·oled** \-ld\ *adj* **:** PETIOLATE

**pet·i·o·li·ven·tres** \,ped·ē,ōlə'ven,trēz\ [NL, fr. *petioli-* (fr. *petiolus*) + *-ventres* (fr. L *venter* belly) — more at VENTER] *syn of* CLISTOGASTRA

**pet·i·ol·u·lar** \,ped·ē¦älyələ(r)\ *adj* [prob. fr. (assumed) NL *petiolularis*, fr. NL *petiolulus* petiolule + L *-aris* -ar] **:** of or relating to a petiolule

**pet·i·ol·u·late** \-,lāt, -lət, *usu* -d·+V\ *adj* [prob. fr. (assumed) NL *petiolulatus*, fr. NL *petiolulus* petiolule + L *-atus* -ate] **:** having a petiolule

**pet·i·o·lule** \ˈ══ə,lül, -əl,yül; ══ˈäl,yül\ *n* -s [NL *petiolulus*, fr. *petiolus* petiole + *-ulus*] **:** a stalk of a leaflet or other segment of a compound leaf

**petit** \ˈped·|ē, ˈpet|, |i, |ət; pəˈtēt\ *adj* [ME, fr. MF, fr. OF] **1** *archaic* **:** SMALL ⟨a really handsome man ... with ... an erect though somewhat ~ figure —Hugh Miller †1856⟩ **2** *obs* **:** INSIGNIFICANT, TRIFLING ⟨he hated every thing ~ —W.H. Dilworth⟩ **3** *archaic* **:** SECONDARY, SUBORDINATE ⟨tried all ~ cases relating to the inhabitants —*Genealogical Mag.*⟩

**pe·tit battement** \pəˈtē-\ *n* [F, lit., small battement] **:** a battement with the free foot lifted slightly usu. without taking the toes from the floor

**pe·tit bourgeois** \"-\ *n* [F, lit., small bourgeois] **:** a member of the petite bourgeoisie

**pet·it ca·pe** \ˈped·|ē, ˈpet|, |iˈkā(,)pē, -ˈkä(,)pā\ *n* [AF (part trans. of ML *cape parvum*), fr. *petit* small + *cape* any of several writs including the grand cape and the petit cape — more at GRAND CAPE] **:** a writ formerly used in English real actions for the recovery of land

**¹pe·tite** \pəˈtēt, *usu* -ēd·+V\ *adj* [F, fem. of *petit*] **:** small and trim of figure **:** LITTLE — usu. used of a woman ⟨a bit incongruous that such a ~ woman should write such huge tomes —Vardis Fisher⟩ **syn** see SMALL

**²petite** \"\ *n* -s **:** a clothing size for short women

**petite bourgeoisie** *n* [F, lit., small bourgeoisie] **:** the least affluent or influential class of the bourgeoisie **:** lower middle class

**petite marmite** *n* [F, lit., small kettle] **1 :** a soup of brown stock made with a few large pieces of vegetable, fowl, or beef and served in a marmite with slices of French bread **2 :** MARMITE 1b

**pe·tite·ness** *n* -ES **:** the quality or state of being petite

**petite no·blesse** \-nōˈbles\ *n* [F, lit., small nobility] **:** the lesser nobility of France; *esp* **:** rural landowners of noble ancestry

**pe·tites perceptions** *n pl* \pə¦tēt-\ [F, lit., small perceptions] **:** vague or unconscious perceptions

**pe·tit four** \pə,tēˈfō(ə)r, -fȯ(ə)r, ˌped·ē¦═ *sometimes* -fü(ə)r\ *n, pl* **petits fours** *or* **petit fours** \-ō(ə)rz, -ȯ(ə)rz, -ü(ə)r(z)\ [F, lit., small oven] **:** a small cake cut in a fancy shape from pound or sponge cake, decoratively frosted, and ornamented with sugar flowers or crystallized fruit

**pet·it·grain** \ˈped·ē,grān\ *n* [F *petit grain* unripe bitter orange, fr. *petit* small + *grain* seed] **:** PETITGRAIN OIL

**petitgrain oil** *n* **:** a fragrant yellowish essential oil obtained from the leaves and twigs of the sour orange and other trees of the genus *Citrus* and used chiefly in perfumes, soaps, and cosmetics

**¹pe·ti·tion** \pəˈtishən\ *n* -s [ME *peticioun*, fr. MF *petition*, fr. L *petition-*, *petitio*, fr. *petitus* (past part. of *petere* to go to or toward, seek, request) + *-ion-*, *-io* -ion — more at FEATHER] **1 a :** an earnest request **:** ENTREATY, SUPPLICATION ⟨listens with a vinegar aspect to your ~ for shelter —C.E.Montague⟩ **b** (1) **:** a solemn prayer to God ⟨our ~ in the litany against sudden death —John Ruskin⟩ (2) **:** a single clause in such a prayer **2 a :** a formal written request addressed to an official person or organized body: (1) **:** a bill in the form of a request by which Parliament formerly presented measures for the king's granting (2) **:** a formal written request addressed to a sovereign or political superior for a particular grace or right (3) **:** a formal written request addressed to a magistrate or court praying for preliminary, incidental, or final specific relief and setting forth the facts or reasons therefor (4) **:** a formal statement of a cause of action that is addressed to a court or magistrate and is based on a statute or on an extraordinary remedy for which common-law declarations cannot be invoked or is founded on equity, probate, or ecclesiastical jurisdiction (5) *civil law* **:** COMPLAINT **b :** a document embodying a formal written request **3 :** the act or action of formally asking or humbly requesting ⟨an ancient right guaranteed by the early state constitutions ... is that of ~ —Harvey Walker⟩ **4 :** something asked or requested ⟨I make thee promise, ... thou receivest thy full ~ —Shak.⟩ **syn** see PRAYER

**²petition** \"\ *vb* **petitioned; petitioned; petitioning** \-sh(ə)niŋ\ **petitions** *vt* **1 :** to make a request to **:** ENTREAT; *esp* **:** to make a formal written request to ⟨the right of the people ... to ~ the government for a redress of grievances —*U.S.Constitution*⟩ **2 :** to make a request for **:** SOLICIT ⟨all that I hope, ~, or expect —George Crabbe †1832⟩ ~ *vi* **:** to make a request; *esp* **:** to make a formal written request ⟨she neither ~ed for her right nor claimed it —George Meredith⟩

**pe·ti·tion·al** \-shən³l, -shnəl\ *adj* **:** of, relating to, or having the characteristics of a petition ⟨~ prayer⟩

**pe·ti·tion·ary** \-shə,nerē, -ri\ *adj* **1 :** of, relating to, or containing a petition ⟨the ~ procedure ... had a certain impermanent quality of indecisiveness —J.G.Edwards⟩ **2** *archaic* **:** SUPPLIANT ⟨say no to a poor ~ rogue —Charles Lamb⟩

**pe·ti·tion·ee** \═¦══ˈnē\ *n* -s **:** a person cited to answer or defend against a petition

**pe·ti·tion·er** \-sh(ə)nə(r)\ *n* -s [ME *peticioner*, fr. *peticion*, *peticioun* petition + *-er*] **1 :** one that petitions **2** *usu cap* **:** one of those signing petitions to Charles II in 1679 for an assembling of Parliament — compare ABHORRER

**petition for intervention :** a petition in which a person seeks to be permitted to intervene in a lawsuit involving other parties so that his own rights and interests may be protected by a judgment or decree binding all

**petition in bankruptcy :** a written application by a debtor for the benefit of the Bankruptcy Act or by creditors to have a debtor adjudicated a bankrupt

**petition in error :** an application for a hearing to reverse action in a lower court that is a statutory substitute in some jurisdictions for the common-law writ of error — compare APPEAL

**petition of right** [ME] **:** a legal petition formerly used to obtain redress (as possession or restitution of property) from the British Crown for breach of contract or to remedy manifest injustice

**pe·ti·tio prin·ci·pii** \pə¦tid·ē,ō,prin'kipē,ē, pə¦tishē,ō,prin'sipē,ī, pā¦tētsē,ō,prin'chēpē,ē\ *n* [ML, lit., postulation of the beginning] **:** a logical fallacy in which a premise is assumed to be true without warrant or in which what is to be proved is implicitly taken for granted

**pet·it juror** \ˈped·|ē, ˈpet|, |i-\ *n* [fr. *petit jury*, after E *jury: juror*] **:** one that serves on a petit jury

**petit jury** *n* [ME, lit., small jury] **:** a jury of twelve men or in some jurisdictions twelve men and women that is guaranteed by constitutional rights and that is impaneled to try and decide finally upon the facts at issue in causes for trial in a court — compare GRAND JURY

**petit larceny** \"-\ *n* **:** PETTY LARCENY

**petit-maître** \pətēmātrᵊ, -ā·tr, -ā·trə, -āt\ *n, pl* **petits-maîtres** *or* **petit-maîtres** \"\ [F, lit., small master] **:** DANDY, FOP ⟨the most finished gentleman in every sense of the word ... without an atom of frippery or a shade of the *petit-maître* —W.G.Hammond⟩

**petit mal** \pə¦tē¦mäl, -mal,-mȧl\ *n* [F, lit., small illness] **:** epilepsy due to an inborn usu. inherited dysrhythmia of the electrical pulsations of the brain and characterized by attacks of mild convulsive seizures with transient clouding of consciousness without amnesia and with or without slight movements of the head, eyes, or extremities — compare GRAND MAL

**petit-nègre** \pə,tēˈnegrə, -g(rᵊ)\ *n, usu cap P&N* [F *petit nègre*, lit., small Negro] **:** a French-based Creole language of West Africa

**pet·i·to·ry** \ˈped·ə,tōrē\ *adj* [L *petitorius*, fr. *petitus* (past part. of *petere* to go to or toward, seek, request) + *-orius* -ory — more at FEATHER] **1** *archaic* **:** PETITIONARY, SUPPLICATORY **2 a :** of or relating to an admiralty or civil law action or suit in rem as distinguished from one in personam **b :** of or relating to a civil law action to adjudge title to and ownership of real estate as distinguished from one to try merely the right of possession **c :** of or relating to a suit in Scots law in which the plaintiff claims ownership of property or damages or money due from the defendant **3 :** of or relating to a petitio principii

**petitory action** *n* **1** *civil & admiralty law* **:** an action in rem to establish a right or title in or ownership of specific property — compare POSSESSORY ACTION **2** *Scots law* **:** an action in which property, money, or damages are demanded from the defendant

**pet·it point** \ˈped·|ē, ˈpet|, |i-\ *n* [F, lit., small point] **1 :** canvas work made with small tent stitches each of which crosses one vertical and one horizontal thread — compare GROS POINT **2 :** TENT STITCH

**pe·tits che·vaux** \pə¦tēshəˈvō\ *n pl but sing in constr* [F, lit., small horses] **:** a gambling machine on which eight toy horses are spun on a circular track and bets are made on which horse will reach the finish line first

**pet·it sergeanty** \ˈped·|ē, ˈpet|, |i-\ *n* [AF *petit serjeanty*, lit., small sergeanty] **:** the rendering of an implement of war (as a bow, sword, lance) annually to the king in accordance with English feudal law **2 :** the right to or the duty of petit sergeanty

**petits fours** *pl of* PETIT FOUR

**pe·tits pois** \pə,tēpˈwä\ *n pl* [F, small peas] **:** very small green peas

**pet·it treason** \ˈped·|ē, ˈpet|, |i-\ *n* [alter. (influenced by *petit*) of *petty treason*] *Eng law* **:** the crime committed by a servant in killing his master, by a wife in killing her husband, or by an ecclesiastic in killing his superior

**pet·i·ve·ria** \,ped·əˈvirēə\ *n, cap* [NL, fr. James *Petiver* †1718 Eng. botanist and entomologist + NL *-ia*] **:** a genus of tropical American garlic-scented herbs (family Phytolaccaceae) with small greenish spicate flowers

**petn** *abbr* petition

**PETN** *n* -s [*pentaerythritol tetranitrate*] **:** PENTAERYTHRITOL TETRANITRATE

**pe·to** \ˈpād·(,)ō\ *n* -s [AmerSp, fr. Sp, breastplate, fr. It *petto* breast, breastplate, fr. L *pectus* breast — more at PECTORAL] **:** ³WAHOO

**petr-** *or* **petri-** *or* **petro-** *comb form* [MF *petr-*, *petri-* & L *petr-* & NL *petro-*, fr. Gk *petr-*, *petro-*, fr. *petros* stone & *petra* rock] **1 a :** stone **:** rock ⟨*petrescent*⟩ ⟨*Petricola*⟩ ⟨*petrogenesis*⟩ **b :** petroleum ⟨*petroporphyrins*⟩ **2 :** of or relating to the petrous portion of the temporal bone and ⟨*petrohyoid*⟩

**pe·tra·le sole** \pəˈträlē-\ *n* [*petrale* perh. fr. It dial., a flatfish] **:** a large brown brill (*Eopsetta jordani*) of the Pacific coast of No. America that is an important market flatfish highly esteemed as food — called also *English sole*

**¹pe·trar·chan** \(ˈ)pē¦trärkən, (ˈ)pe-, -rȧk- *sometimes* (ˈ)pā-\ *also* **pe·trar·chi·an** \-kēən\ *adj, usu cap* [*Petrarch* (Francesco *Petrarca*) †1374 Ital. poet + E *-an*] **:** of, relating to, or having the characteristics of Petrarch **:** imitative of the style of Petrarch

**²petrarchan** \"\ *n* -s *usu cap* **:** PETRARCHIST

**petrarchan sonnet** *n, usu cap P* **:** a sonnet composed of an octave rhyming *abba abba* and a sestet with two or three rhymes (as *cdc dcd* or *cde cde*) — called also *Italian sonnet*; compare ENGLISH SONNET

**pe·trar·chi·an·ism** \-kēə,nizəm\ *or* **pe·trarch·ism** \ˈ═,═-,kizəm\ *n* -s *usu cap* **:** the poetic style characteristic or imitative of Petrarch

**pe·trarch·ist** \ˈ═,═kəst\ *n* -s *usu cap* **:** a poet writing in a manner characteristic or imitative of Petrarch; *specif* **:** one of the poets of the English Renaissance whose sonnets reflect the influence of Petrarch in their conceits, play upon words, and involved structure

**pe·trarch·ize** \-,kīz\ *vi* -ED/-ING/-S *usu cap* [MF *petrarchiser*, fr. Francesco *Petrarca* + MF *-iser* -ize] **:** to write in a manner characteristic or imitative of Petrarch

**pet·ra·ry** \ˈpe·trərē\ *n* -ES [ML *petraria* — more at PEDRERO] **:** PEDRERO

**pe·trea** \ˈpē·trēə\ *n, cap* [NL, fr. Robert James, Baron *Petre* †1743 Eng. patron of botany] **:** a genus of tropical American woody vines (family Verbenaceae) having large blue or purple flowers in long racemes with the colored sepals enlarging in fruiting — see PURPLE WREATH

**pe·trel** \ˈpe·trəl *sometimes* ˈpē-\ *n* -s [alter. of earlier *pitteral*, perh. irreg. fr. St. *Peter* †A.D.67? disciple of Jesus; fr. the gospel account of St. Peter's walking on the sea (Mt 14:29)] **1 :** any of numerous sea birds constituting the families Procellariidae and Hydrobatidae; *esp* **:** any of various small to medium-sized long-winged birds that fly far from land, feed on small surface-swimming creatures and refuse from ships, breed in burrows and crevices in rocks and cliffs usu. on islands, and have a plumage chiefly dark but sometimes with white areas near the rump — see DIVING PETREL, GIANT PETREL, MOTHER CAREY'S CHICKEN, STORM PETREL **2 :** STORM PETREL

**pe·tres·cent** \pəˈtresᵊnt\ *adj* [*petr-* + *-escent*] *archaic* **:** having the quality of petrifying **:** causing petrifaction

**petri-** — see PETR-

**pe·tric·o·la** \pəˈtrikələ\ *n, cap* [NL, fr. *petr-* + *-cola*] **:** a genus (the type of the family Petricolidae) of bivalve mollusks living in holes that they excavate in rocks, clay, or mud and having an oval shell slightly gaping behind, a large mantle, and a small foot

**pet·ri·col·i·dae** \,pe·trəˈkälə,dē\ *n pl, cap* [NL, fr. *Petricola*, type genus + *-idae*] **:** a family of bivalve mollusks (suborder Veneracea) having an elongated shell with which they burrow in soft rock or clay

**pe·tric·o·lous** \-ləs\ *adj* [*petr-* + *-colous*] **:** living in rocks

**pe·tri dish** \ˈpē|trē- *sometimes* ˈpā| *or* ˈpe|\ *or* **petri plate** *n, often cap 1st P* [after Julius R. *Petri* †1921 Ger. bacteriologist] **:** a small shallow dish of thin glass with a loosely fitting overlapping cover used esp. for plate cultures in bacteriology

petri dish

**pet·ri·fac·tion** \,pe·trəˈfakshən\ *n* -s [fr. *petrify*, after such pairs as E *satisfy: satisfaction*] **1 :** the process of petrifying; *specif* **:** the conversion of organic matter into stone or a substance of stony hardness through the infiltration of water containing dissolved mineral matter (as calcium, carbonate, silica) that replaces the organic material particle by particle with the original structure sometimes retained — compare CAST **2 :** something that is petrified; *specif* **:** an organic body infiltrated with mineral matter and preserving more or less clearly its original form or structure — compare FOSSIL **3 :** the quality or state of being petrified ⟨a ~ ... of the artist's soul —G.E.Woodberry⟩

**pet·ri·fac·tive** \¦══¦faktiv\ *adj* [fr. *petrify*, after such pairs as E *putrefy: putrefactive*] **:** having the quality of converting organic matter into stone **:** PETRIFYING

**pe·trif·ic** \pəˈtrifik\ *adj* [ML *petrificus*, fr. L *petra* rock, stone + *-ficus* -fic] **:** PETRIFACTIVE

**pet·ri·fi·ca·tion** \,pe·trəfəˈkāshən\ *n* -s [F *pétrification*, fr. MF *petrification*, fr. *petr-* + *-fication*] **:** PETRIFACTION

**pet·ri·fi·er** \ˈ══,fī(ə)r\ *n* -s **:** one that petrifies

**pet·ri·fy** \ˈ══,fī\ *vb* -ED/-ING/-ES [MF *petrifier*, fr. *petr-* + *-fier* -fy] *vt* **1 :** to convert into stone; *specif* **:** to convert (organic matter) into stone or a substance of stony hardness through the infiltration of water containing dissolved mineral matter **2 :** to make hard, rigid, or inert like or as if like stone: **a :** to make lifeless or inactive **:** DEADEN ⟨slogans are apt to ~ a man's thinking —*Saturday Rev.*⟩ ⟨his independence had not *petrified* his sympathies —*Times Lit. Supp.*⟩ **b :** to confound with fear, amazement, or awe **:** PARALYZE, STUPEFY ⟨the original purpose of the aboriginal objects was to ~ uninitiated members of the tribe —T.H.Robsjohn-Gibbings⟩ ⟨is *petrified* of talking in public —Alan Frank⟩ ~ *vi* **1 :** to become stone or a substance of stony hardness **2 :** to become hard, rigid, or inert like or as if like stone ⟨principles and rules ... have *petrified* with the accumulated weight of precedent on precedent —B.N.Cardozo⟩ ⟨her face had *petrified* into the fearsome pioneer resolution of unremitting housewifery —Nigel Dennis⟩ **syn** see DAZE

**pe·trine** \ˈpē,trīn, -,trən\ *adj, usu cap* [LL *Petrus* St. Peter †A.D.67? disciple of Jesus (fr. Gk *Petros*) + E *-ine*] **:** of, relating to, or having the characteristics of the apostle Peter, his teachings, or the doctrines associated with his name ⟨the *Petrine* tradition⟩

**pe·trin·ism** \ˈpē·trə,nizəm\ *n* -s *usu cap* **:** the theological principles taught by or ascribed to the apostle Peter

**pe·trin·ist** \-,nəst\ *n* -s *usu cap* **:** a follower of the apostle Peter **:** an adherent of Petrinism

**pe·tris·sage** \¦pā·trə¦säzh\ *n* -s [F *pétrissage*, lit., kneading, fr. *pétriss-* (stem of *pétrir* to knead, fr. ML *pistrire*, fr. L *pistrix* female baker, fem. of *pistor* baker, miller) + *-age*; akin to L *pinsere* to pound, crush — more at PESTLE] **:** massage in which the muscles are kneaded

**pe·tro·bia** \pəˈtrōbēə\ *n, cap* [NL, perh. fr. *petr-* + *-bia*] **:** a genus of mites containing the brown wheat mite

**pet·ro·bru·sian** \¦pe·trō¦brüzhən, -shən\ *n* -s *usu cap* [ML *petrobrusianus*, fr. *Petrus Brusius* Pierre de Bruys †*ab*1126 Fr. religious reformer who founded the sect of the Petrobrusians + L *-anus* -an] **:** a member of a 12th-century French sect rejecting infant baptism, the mass, prayers for the dead, and the veneration of the cross and opposing the construction of churches

**pet·ro·chel·i·don** \,pe·trōˈkelə,dän\ *n, cap* [NL, fr. *petr-* + Gk *chelidōn* swallow — more at CELANDINE] **:** a genus of swallows consisting of the American cliff swallows

**¹pe·tro·chemical** \¦pe·trō+\ *adj* [*petr-* + *chemical*, adj.] **1 :** of or relating to the chemistry of rocks ⟨a thorough ~ study of certain weathering profiles —F.J.Pettijohn⟩ **2 a :** of or relating to the production of petrochemicals ⟨the ~ industry⟩ **b :** produced as a petrochemical ⟨~ acetone⟩

**²petrochemical** \"\ *n* [*petr-* + *chemical*, n.] **:** a chemical isolated from petroleum or natural gas or a derivative produced from such a substance by chemical reaction — used chiefly commercially ⟨chemicals derived from petroleum and natural gas, such as ammonia, carbon black, and thousands of organic chemicals, are classified as ~s —*Chemical & Engineering News*⟩

**pe·tro·chemistry** \"+\ *n* [*petr-* + *chemistry*] **1 :** the chemistry of rocks **2 :** the chemistry of petroleum; *esp* **:** a branch of chemistry dealing with the production of petrochemicals

**pet·ro·cole** *or* **pet·ri·cole** \ˈpe·trə,kōl\ *n* -s [*petr-* + *-cole* (fr. NL *-cola*)] **:** an organism that inhabits or prefers rocky terrain

**pet·ro·fabric** \¦pe·trō+\ *adj* [*petr-* + *fabric*, n.] **:** of or relating to the analysis of rock fabric in contrast to rock composition

**petrofabric diagram** *n* **:** a diagram showing spatial distribution of fabric features of a rock (as crystal axes, twin planes, or fracture surfaces)

**pet·ro·fabrics** \¦══+\ *n pl but sing in constr* **:** the investigation of rock fabric with particular emphasis on the microscopic features

**pe·trog·a·le** \pəˈträgə,lē\ *n* [NL, fr. *petr-* + Gk *galē* weasel, ferret — more at GALEA] **1** *cap* **:** a genus of marsupial mammals consisting of the rock wallabies **2** -s **:** ROCK WALLABY

**pet·ro·genesis** \¦pe·trō+\ *n* [NL, fr. *petr-* + L *genesis*] **:** the origin of rocks

**pet·ro·genetic** \¦══+\ *adj* [fr. *petrogenesis*, after E *genesis: genetic*] **:** PETROGENIC

**pet·ro·genic** \¦══¦jenik\ *adj* [*petr-* + *-genic*] **:** of or relating to the origin or formation of rocks and esp. of igneous rocks

**pe·trog·e·ny** \pəˈträjənē, -ni\ *n* -ES [*petr-* + *-geny*] **:** the science of the origin of rocks

**pet·ro·glyph** \ˈpe·trə,glif\ *n* -s [F *pétroglyphe*, fr. *pétr-* petr- + *-glyphe* (as in *hiéroglyphe* hieroglyph)] **:** a carving or inscription on a rock — compare PICTOGRAPH

**pet·ro·glyph·ic** \¦══¦glifik\ *adj* [*petroglyph* + *-ic*] **:** of or relating to a petroglyph or to petroglyphy

**pe·trog·ly·phy** \pəˈträgləfē, -fi\ *n* -ES [*petroglyph* + *-y*] **:** the art or operation of carving figures or inscriptions on rock or stone

**pe·tro·graph** \ˈpe·trə,graf\ *n* [*petr-* + *-graph*] **:** PETROGLYPH

**pe·trog·ra·pher** \pəˈträgrəfə(r)\ *n* -s [*petrography* + *-er*] **:** a specialist in petrography

**pet·ro·graph·ic** \,pe·trə¦grafik, -fēk\ *or* **pet·ro·graph·i·cal** \-fəkəl, -fēk-\ *adj* [*petrographic* prob. fr. (assumed) NL *petrographicus*, fr. NL *petrographia* petrography + L *-icus* -ic; *petrographical* fr. *petrographic* + E *-ical*] **:** of or relating to petrography — **pet·ro·graph·i·cal·ly** \-fək(ə)lē, -fēk-, -li\ *adv*

**petrographic province** *n* **:** a region in which the various igneous rocks are so related as to indicate origin from a common magma

**pe·trog·ra·phy** \pəˈträgrəfē, -fi\ *n* -ES [NL *petrographia*, fr. *petr-* + L *-graphia* -graphy] **:** the description and systematic classification of rocks usu. based on microscopic study — compare PETROLOGY

**pet·ro·hyoid** \¦petrō+\ *adj* [*petr-* + *hyoid*] **:** connecting the petrous region of the skull and the hyoid

**pe·troi·ca** \pəˈtrōikə, -rōēkə\ *n, cap* [NL] **:** a genus of flycatchers (family Muscicapidae) of Australia and the Pacific islands that are usu. dark above with pale underparts and pink to scarlet breasts

**pet·rol** \ˈpe·trəl, -,träl\ *n* -s [MF *petrole*, fr. ML *petroleum*] **1** *archaic* **:** PETROLEUM **2** [F *pétrole* petroleum (in the term *essence de pétrole* gasoline), fr. MF *petrole*] *Brit* **:** petroleum motor fuel **:** GASOLINE

**pet·ro·lage** \ˈpe·trəlij\ *n* -s [ISV *petrol* + *-age*] **:** the treatment of stagnant water with petroleum so as to exterminate mosquitoes

**pet·ro·la·tum** \,pe·trəˈlād·əm, -lȧd-\ *n* -s [NL, fr. ML *petroleum* + NL *-atum* -ate] **:** a neutral unctuous substance that is practically odorless and tasteless and is insoluble in water, that is obtained from petroleum and differs chemically from paraffin wax in containing unsaturated hydrocarbons or naphthenes as well as hydrocarbons of the methane series, and that is produced in several forms: as **a :** a yellowish to light amber semisolid mass obtained in various ways (as by purifying the residue from the distillation of petroleum or by dewaxing heavy lubricating oils) and used chiefly as a base for ointments and cosmetics, as a protective dressing (as for burns), and in lubricating greases — called also *petroleum jelly, yellow petrolatum, yellow soft paraffin;* compare MICROCRYSTALLINE WAX, MINERAL JELLY **b :** a white or faintly yellowish mass obtained by decolorizing yellow petrolatum and used similarly to it — called also *white petrolatum, white petroleum jelly, white soft paraffin* **c :** LIQUID PETROLATUM

**pet·ro·lene** \ˈpe·trə,lēn, ˌ==ˈ=\ *n* -s [G *petrolen,* irreg. fr. *petroleum,* fr. ML] **:** the part of asphalt soluble in paraffin naphtha or hexane and free from asphaltenes and carbenes

**pe·tro·le·ous** \pəˈtrōlēəs\ *adj* [*petroleum* + *-ous*] **:** containing petroleum

**pe·tro·le·um** \pəˈtrōlēəm, -lyəm\ *n* -s *often attrib* [ML, fr L *petr-* + *oleum* oil — more at OIL] **1 :** an oily flammable bituminous liquid that in the crude state often has a very disagreeable odor and may vary from almost colorless to black but is usu. of a dark brown or greenish hue and sometimes fluorescent, that occurs in many places in the upper strata of the earth either in seepages or in reservoir formations from which it is obtained by drilling and pumping if necessary, that is essentially a complex mixture of hydrocarbons of different types with small amounts of other substances (as oxygen compounds, sulfur compounds, nitrogen compounds, resinous and asphaltic components, and metallic compounds), that is sometimes classed as paraffin-base, asphalt-base or naphthene-base, or mixed-base, and that is subjected to various refining processes (as fractional distillation, cracking, catalytic re-forming, hydroforming, alkylation, polymerization) for producing useful products (as gasoline, naphtha, kerosine, fuel oils, lubricants, waxes, asphalt, coke, and chemicals) — called also *mineral oil, rock oil* **2 :** any of various substances (as natural gas or shale oil) similar in composition to petroleum

**petroleum asphalt** *n* **:** ARTIFICIAL ASPHALT

**petroleum benzin** *n* **:** a flammable petroleum distillate boiling between 35° and 80°C, containing largely pentanes, hexanes, and heptanes, and used chiefly as a solvent esp. in pharmacy

**petroleum coke** *n* **:** a solid nonvolatile residue which is obtained as the final still product in the distillation of crude petroleum and whose purity makes it desirable for metallurgical processes, for carbon electrodes, and as a fuel

**petroleum engine** *n* **:** GASOLINE ENGINE

**petroleum ether** *n* **:** a volatile flammable petroleum distillate (as ligroin or petroleum benzin)

**petroleum fly** *n* **:** an ephydrid fly (*Psilopa petrolei*) that breeds in pools of waste petroleum

**petroleum gas oil** *n* **:** GAS OIL

**petroleum geologist** *n* **:** a specialist in petroleum geology

**petroleum geology** *n* **:** a branch of economic geology that deals with the origin, occurrence, and exploitation of oil and gas

**petroleum grease** *n* **:** a grease made from a petroleum product (as still bottoms)

**petroleum hexane** *n* **:** a mixture of hexanes that occurs in petroleum and is separated therefrom by distillation in the range 50° to 70°C and that is used as a solvent — compare LIGROIN

**petroleum jelly** *n* **:** PETROLATUM a, b

**petroleum naphtha** *n* **:** NAPHTHA 3a

**petroleum pentane** *n* **:** a mixture essentially of pentane and isopentane that occurs in petroleum and is separated therefrom by distillation below 50°C and that is used as a low-boiling solvent

**petroleum spirit** *n* **:** a flammable petroleum distillate that boils lower than kerosine and is suitable for use as a solvent and thinner esp. for paints and varnishes — usu. used in pl.; compare NAPHTHA 3

**petroleum sulfonate** *n* **:** any of various sulfonic acid derivatives of petroleum (as mahogany acids or green acids)

**petroleum wax** *n* **:** a wax obtained from petroleum — compare CERESIN, MICROCRYSTALLINE WAX, PARAFFIN 1

**pe·trol·ic** \pəˈträlik\ *adj* [*petroleum* + *-ic*] **1 :** of or relating to petroleum or gasoline **2 :** of or relating to gasoline engines or motor cars

**pet·ro·lif·er·ous** \ˌpe·trəˈlif(ə)rəs\ *adj* [ISV *petroleum* + *-i-* + *-ferous*] **:** containing or producing petroleum

**pet·ro·lif·ic** \ˌ==ˈlifik\ *adj* [*petroleum* + *-i-* + *-fic*] **:** PETROLIFEROUS

**pet·ro·lith·ic** \ˌ==ˈlithik\ *adj* [*petr-* + *lithic*] **1 :** of, relating to, or constituting a road surface consolidated to a rocklike firmness **2 :** of, relating to, or constituting the tampers and other apparatus used to harden a road surface

**pet·ro·li·za·tion** \ˌ==ˌləˈzāshən, -ˌlīˈz-\ *n* -s **:** the act or process of petrolizing

**pet·ro·lize** \ˈpe·trə,līz\ *vt* -ED/-ING/-S [*petroleum* + *-ize*] **1 :** to ignite by means of petroleum **2 :** to treat or impregnate with petroleum or a petroleum product **3 :** to cover the surface of (as water) with petroleum for mosquito control

**pet·ro·log·ic** \ˌpe·trəˈläjik, -jēk\ *or* **pet·ro·log·i·cal** \-jəkəl, -jēk-\ *adj* [*petrology* + *-ic* or *-ical*] **:** of or relating to petrology — **pet·ro·log·i·cal·ly** \-jək(ə)lē, -jēk-, -li\ *adv*

**pe·trol·o·gist** \pəˈträləjəst\ *n* -s [*petrology* + *-ist*] **:** a geologist who specializes in petrology

**pe·trol·o·gy** \-jē, -ji\ *n* -ES [ISV *petr-* + *-logy*] **1 :** a science that deals with the origin, history, occurrence, structure, chemical composition, and classification of rocks — compare PETROGRAPHY **2 :** the materials of petrology ⟨the ~ of New England⟩ **3 :** a treatise on petrology

**petrols** *pl of* PETROL

**pet·ro·my·zon** \ˌpe·trōˈmī,zän\ *n* [NL *Petromyzont-, Petromyzon,* fr. *petr-* + *-myzont-, -myzon* -myzon] **1** *cap* **:** a genus (the type of the family Petromyzontidae) of cyclostomes comprising the typical lampreys **2** -s **:** any cyclostome of the genus *Petromyzon*

**pet·ro·my·zon·i·dae** \ˌ==ˌmīˈzänə,dē\ *syn of* PETROMYZONTIDAE

**pet·ro·my·zont** \ˌ==ˈmī,zänt\ *n* -s [NL *Petromyzontidae*] **:** a cyclostome of the family Petromyzontidae **:** LAMPREY

**pet·ro·my·zon·tes** \ˌ==mīˈzän·,tēz\ [NL, pl. of *Petromyzont-, Petromyzon*] *syn of* HYPEROARTIA

**pet·ro·my·zon·ti·dae** \-mīˈzäntə,dē\ *n pl, cap* [NL, fr. *Petromyzont-, Petromyzon,* type genus + *-idae*] **:** a family of cyclostomes (order Hyperoartia) comprising elongated animals that resemble eels or hagfishes, have no barbels and seven pairs of circular gill openings, and feed on the blood of fishes which they obtain by rasping the flesh with their toothed circular mouth — see PETROMYZON; compare LAMPREY — **pet·ro·my·zon·toid** \ˌ==ˈzän·,tȯid\ *adj or n*

**pet·ro·nel** \ˈpe·trənəl\ *n* -s [perh. modif. of MF *petrinal,* alter. of *poitrinal,* fr. *poitrinal,* adj., of the chest, fr. *poitrine* chest, breast (fr. assumed VL *pectorina,* fr. fem. of assumed VL *pectorinus,* adj., of the breast, fr. L *pector-, pectus* breast + *-inus* -ine) + *-al* — more at PECTORAL] **:** a portable firearm resembling a carbine of large caliber and fired with the butt resting against the chest

**pet·ro·nel·la** \ˌ==ˈnelə\ *n* -s [perh. fr. the feminine name *Petronella*] **:** a Scottish country-dance of the 19th century

**pe·tro·nian** \pəˈtrōnēən, -nyən\ *adj, usu cap* [Gaius *Petronius,* 1st cent. A.D. Rom. director of entertainments at Nero's court + E *-an*] **:** of, relating to, or reminiscent of Petronius or his writings

**pe·troph·i·lous** \pəˈträfələs\ *adj* [ISV *petr-* + *-philous*] **:** attached to or living on rock — used esp. of algae and crustaceans

**pe·tro·sa** \pəˈtrōsə\ *n, pl* **petro·sae** \-ō,sē, -,sī\ [NL, fr. L, fem. of *petrosus* rocky] **:** the petrous part of the temporal bone

**pe·tro·sal** \-səl\ *adj* [NL *petrosa* + E *-al*] **:** PETROUS, HARD, STONY; *specif* **:** of, relating to, or situated in the region of the petrous portion of the temporal bone or capsule of the internal ear

**petrosal bone** *also* **petrosal** *n* -s **1 :** a bone corresponding to the petrous portion of the temporal bone of man **2 :** a bone forming more or less of the capsule of the internal ear and composed of one or more periotic bones

**petrosal ganglion** *n* **:** the lower and larger of two sensory ganglia on the glossopharyngeal nerve

**petrosal nerve** *n* **:** any of several small nerves passing through foramina in the petrous portion of the temporal bone

**petrosal sinus** *n* **:** any of four venous sinuses at the base of the brain: **a :** a small superior sinus on each side that connects the cavernous and lateral sinuses of the same side **b :** a larger inferior sinus on each side that extends from the end of the cavernous sinus into the jugular foramen and there joins the lateral sinus to form the corresponding jugular vein

**pet·ro·se·li·num** \ˌpe·trōsəˈlīnəm\ *n, cap* [NL, fr. L, parsley — more at PARSLEY] **:** a small genus of European glabrous herbs (family Umbelliferae) having slender stems, bracts that are not reflexed, and oval fruits — see PARSLEY

**pet·ro·sphere** \ˈpe·trə,-\ *n* [*petr-* + *sphere*] **:** LITHOSPHERE

**pet·ro·stearin** *or* **pet·ro·stearine** \ˌpe·trō+\ *n* [*petr-* + *stearin*] **:** MINERAL WAX, OZOKERITE

**pet·ro·tympanic** \ˌ==+\ *adj* [*petr-* + *tympanic*] **:** of or relating to the petrous and tympanic portions of the temporal bone

**petrotympanic fissure** *n* **:** a narrow transverse slit dividing the mandibular fossa of the temporal bone — called also *Glaserian fissure*

**pet·rous** \ˈpe·trəs, ˈpē-\ *adj* [MF *petreux,* fr. L *petrosus* rocky, fr. *petra* rock (fr. Gk) + *-osus* -ose] **:** resembling stone esp. in hardness **:** ROCKY; *specif* **:** of, relating to, or constituting the exceptionally hard and dense portion of the temporal bone of man that contains the internal auditory organs, corresponds chiefly to the periotic bones of many vertebrates, and is a pyramidal process wedged in at the base of the skull between the sphenoid and occipital bones with its lower half exposed on the surface of the skull and pierced by the external auditory meatus

**petrous ganglion** *n* **:** PETROSAL GANGLION

**pe·trox·o·lin** \pəˈträksələn\ *n* -s [*petroleum* + Gk *oxys* sharp, acid + E *-ol* + *-in* — more at OXY-] **:** a mixture of liquid petrolatum and ammonia soap medicated and perfumed for use by inunction

**pets** *pl of* PET, *pres 3d sing of* PET

**pe-tsai** *or* **peh-tsai** \ˈbātˈsī\ *n* -s [Chin (Pek) *pe² ts'ai⁴,* fr. *pe²* white + *ts'ai⁴* vegetable, greens] **:** CHINESE CABBAGE

**pet·ta·ble** \ˈped·əbəl, ˈpetə-\ *adj* [³*pet* + *-able*] **:** capable of, fit for, or worthy of being petted

**pet·tah** \ˈped·ə\ *n* -s [Tamil *pēṭṭai,* Malayalam *pēṭṭa,* & Kanarese *pēṭe*] **:** a village or suburb outside a fort in India or Ceylon

**pet·ted** \ˈped·əd, ˈpetəd\ *adj* [⁴*pet* + *-ed*] **:** marked by peevishness, sulkiness, or anger ⟨poverty brought on a ~ mood and a sore temper —William Wordsworth⟩ — **pet·ted·ly** *adv* — **pet·ted·ness** *n* -ES

**pet·ter** \ˈped·ə(r), -etə-\ *n* -s [³*pet* + *-er*] **:** one that pets

**pet·ti·au·ger** \ˌped·ēˈōgə(r)\ *n* -s [by alter.] **:** PIRAGUA

**pet·ti·chaps** \ˈped·ē,-\ *n pl but sing or pl in constr* [perh. fr. obs. E *petty* small (fr. ME *pety*) + E *chaps,* pl. of *chap* (jaw)] **:** any of several European warblers: as **a :** CHIFFCHAFF **b :** GARDEN WARBLER

¹**pet·ti·coat** \ˈped·ē|,kōt, ˈpet|, |ə|, *usu* -ōd·+V\ *n* [ME *petycote,* lit., small coat, fr. *pety* small + *cote* coat — more at PETTY] **1 :** a skirt worn by women, girls, or young children: as **a :** an outer skirt usu. constituting part of a dress formerly worn by women and small children **b :** a fancy skirt made to show below a draped-up overskirt **c :** a skirt on its own waistband that is usu. a little shorter than outer clothing, is often made with a ruffled, pleated, or lace edge, and is worn by women and girls as underwear **d** *archaic* **:** the skirt of a woman's riding habit **2 a :** a garment characteristic or typical of women — often used in the phrase *in petticoats* **b :** WOMAN ⟨a little nervous lest ~s in a government office might demoralize the male staff —Langston Day⟩ **3 :** the skirt of a garment worn by men or boys: as **a :** KILT **b :** FUSTANELLA **4 a :** the space outside the white ring of an archery target **b :** a hit in such a space **5 :** something resembling a petticoat: as **a :** a gathered or pleated skirt of cloth concealing the lower part of a table, bed, or chair **b :** the flaring base of a lamp or tankard **c :** a sheeting hung about a yacht before launching to hide its outline **d** (1) **:** any of the sleeves or cups forming part of a petticoat insulator (2) **:** PETTICOAT INSULATOR **e :** PETTICOAT PIPE

petticoat 1c

²**petticoat** \"\ *adj* **:** of, relating to, or exercised by women **:** FEMALE ⟨~ rule⟩ ⟨~ government⟩ ⟨~ influence⟩

**petticoat breeches** *n pl* **:** elaborate breeches with legs resembling skirts worn by Englishmen in the late 17th century

**pet·ti·coat·ed** \ˈ==,kōd·əd\ *adj* **:** wearing or furnished with a petticoat ⟨the ~ girls⟩ ⟨a ~ table⟩

**petticoat insulator** *n* **:** an insulator made in the form of superposed inverted cups and used for high insulation

**petticoat·less** \ˈ==,=ləs\ *adj* **:** having or wearing no petticoat

**petticoat pipe** *n* **:** a short flaring pipe around the blast nozzle in the smokebox of a steam locomotive to equalize the draft

**petticoat tails** *n pl but sing or pl in constr, chiefly Scot* **:** a small cake

**petticoat trousers** *n pl* **:** trousers with very wide legs that resemble skirts

**petties** *pl of* PETTY

**pet·ti·fog** \ˈped·ē,fäg, -etē-, -,fȯg\ *vb* **pettifogged; pettifogged; pettifogging; pettifogs** [back-formation fr. *pettifogger*] *vi* **1 :** to engage in legal chicanery **2 :** to quibble over insignificant details **:** CAVIL, BICKER ~ *vt* **:** to plead (as a case) with legal chicanery

**pet·ti·fog·ger** \-gə(r)\ *n* -s [prob. fr. *petty* + obs. E *fogger* pettifogger, perh. irreg. fr. *Fugger,* 15th & 16th cent. Ger. family of financiers and merchants] **1 :** a lawyer whose methods are petty, underhanded, or disreputable **:** SHYSTER ⟨a gentleman of the law — there was nothing of the ~ about him —George Borrow⟩ **2 :** one given to quibbling over insignificant details ⟨a ringing indictment of all the proud and cautious ~s who could agree only on what could not be done —*Time*⟩

**pet·ti·fog·gery** \-g(ə)rē, -ri\ *n* -ES **:** the practice of a pettifogger **:** CHICANERY ⟨are apt to fall victims to . . . ~ on a huge scale —Howard Cosell⟩

**pet·ti·fog·ging** *adj* **1 :** having the characteristics of a pettifogger **:** marked by pettifoggery ⟨this curious combination of the masterfulness of the man of action with the ~ lawyer's mind —G.G.Coulton⟩ **2 :** having little or no significance or importance **:** PETTY, TRIVIAL ⟨all the complex ~ little quirks of doctrine —A.J.Cronin⟩

**pet·ti·ly** \ˈped·ᵊlē, -et|, |əlē, -li\ *adv* **:** in a petty manner

**pet·ti·ness** \|ēnəs, |in-\ *n* -ES **1 :** the quality or state of being petty ⟨seeking . . . freedom from the ~ he found everywhere —Peggy Bennett⟩ **2 :** something petty **:** TRIVIALITY ⟨life was made up of innumerable little ~es —Sherwood Anderson⟩

**petting** *pres part of* PET

**pet·tish** \ˈped·|ish, -et|, |ēsh\ *adj* [prob. fr. ⁴*pet* + *-ish*] **:** marked by ill temper **:** FRETFUL, PEEVISH **syn** see IRRITABLE

**pet·tish·ly** \-əshlē, -ēsh-, -li\ *adv* **:** in a pettish manner

**pet·tish·ness** \-ishnəs, -ēsh-\ *n* -ES **:** the quality or state of being pettish

**pet·ti·skirt** \ˈped·ē,-\ *n* [*petticoat* + *skirt*] **:** PETTICOAT 1c

**pet·ti·toes** \ˈ==,tōz\ *n pl* [pl. (influenced in meaning by *toes,* pl. of *toe*) of obs. E *pettytoe* offal, fr. MF *petite oye,* fr. *petite* (fem. of *petit* small) + *oye* goose, fr. LL *auca* — more at OCARINA] **1 :** the feet of a pig used as food **2 :** TOES, FEET ⟨a child's ~⟩

**pet·tle** \ˈpetᵊl\ *vb* [³*pet* + *-le*] *vt, chiefly Scot* **:** FONDLE, CARESS ~ *vi* **1** *chiefly Scot* **:** NESTLE, CUDDLE **2** *chiefly Scot* **:** TRIFLE, POTTER

¹**pet·ty** \ˈped·|ē, -et|, |i\ *adj* -ER/-EST [ME *pety* small, minor, alter. of *petit*] **1 :** having secondary rank or importance **:** MINOR, SUBORDINATE ⟨the mountainous character of Greece explains its division into a crowd of ~ states —Edward Clodd⟩ ⟨a primarily agrarian society of ~ producers —R.H.Hilton⟩ **2 :** having little or no importance or significance **:** FUTILE ⟨defend with our lives the ~ principles which divide us —Henry Miller⟩ ⟨the ~ cares and vexations that absorb life's energies —M.R.Cohen⟩ **3 a :** marked by narrow interests and sympathies **:** SMALL-MINDED ⟨thought that little colleges are woefully circumscribed and ~ places —A.C.Benson⟩ ⟨suffering . . . makes men ~ and vindictive —W.S.Maugham⟩ **b :** reflecting small-mindedness or meanness **:** unnecessarily harsh or severe ⟨revealed to us the ~ cruelty of men, not the large injustice of the gods —Virginia Woolf⟩

**syn** PETTY, PUNY, TRIVIAL, TRIFLING, PALTRY, MEASLY, PICAYUNISH, and PICAYUNE can mean little or insignificant, esp. contemptibly so. PETTY applies to what is very small or unimportant and often contemptible by comparison to other things of its kind ⟨giants beside whom we seem *petty* —Sinclair Lewis⟩ ⟨the universe of our fathers shrinks to a *petty* compass, not much larger than the snug little state of Connecticut —V.L. Parrington⟩ ⟨*petty* courts⟩ ⟨fruit dealers, chestnut roasters, cigar venders, and other people, whose *petty* and wandering traffic is transacted in the open air —Nathaniel Hawthorne⟩ ⟨the contrast between a dying way of life which is spacious and noble and a new way which is *petty* and crude —E.K.Brown⟩ ⟨the *petty,* quibbling type of lawyer —Kenneth Roberts⟩ PUNY applies to what is small or slight enough to seem feeble or ineffectual ⟨a man of *puny* frame⟩ ⟨the streams, often *puny* and insignificant during dry weather, become raging torrents during a storm —C.L.White & G.T.Renner⟩ ⟨he was a *puny* eater —Lenard Kaufman⟩ ⟨his *puny* accomplishments and his many failures —F.G.Slaughter⟩ TRIVIAL applies to what is petty and commonplace, esp. not worth any special notice, extending to apply to persons or activities marked by concern for mainly trivial matters ⟨philosophy is at once the most sublime and the most *trivial* of human pursuits —William James⟩ ⟨had seemed to him *trivial* and of no import —Oscar Wilde⟩ ⟨the incessant hurry and *trivial* activity of daily life —C.W.Eliot⟩ ⟨light, *trivial* conversation over tea⟩ TRIFLING applies to what is so small or unimportant as to have little if any value or significance ⟨their estimate of her very *trifling* merits: and their wonder that their brothers could find any charms in her —W. M.Thackeray⟩ ⟨a considerable sum was paid to Egmont and a *trifling* one to the Prince —J.L.Motley⟩ ⟨most accidents are of *trifling* extent, and involve nothing more than the loss of time —*Amer. Guide Series: N. Y. City*⟩ PALTRY applies to what is ridiculously or contemptibly small esp. by comparison with what it should be ⟨how unsubstantial then appear our hopes and dreams, our little ambitions, our *paltry* joys —A.C.Benson⟩ ⟨*paltry* personal details prevail over world problems and cosmic questions —O.W.Holmes †1935⟩ ⟨a little equipment costing a *paltry* amount —F.T.Williams⟩ MEASLY applies to what is contemptibly small or petty ⟨snatch at a little *measly* advantage and miss the big one —Sherwood Anderson⟩ ⟨a *measly* portion of pie⟩ ⟨a *measly* stingy individual⟩ PICAYUNISH and PICAYUNE usu. apply to the petty and insignificant, or to what is paltry in outlook or interests ⟨a lifetime of *picayunish* drudgery in the company of louts —H.L.Davis⟩ ⟨weed out dishonest or *picayunish* government employees⟩ ⟨a narrow, *picayune* mind —Felix Lazarus⟩ ⟨the obvious futility, the *picayune,* question-begging character, of such ethical analyses —Asher Moore⟩

²**petty** \"\ *n* -ES **1** *archaic* **:** a boy in a lower form of an English school **:** a small schoolboy **2** *dial Eng* **:** PRIVY

**petty average** *n* **:** AVERAGE 2b

**petty bag** *or* **petty-bag office** *n* [*petty bag* fr. obs. E *petty* small (fr. ME *pety*) + E *bag;* fr. the fact that the record of each case was kept in a small bag] **:** a former office of the common-law side of the English Chancery Court having jurisdiction in suits for and against solicitors and officers of the court, in proceedings by extents on statutes, recognizance, scire facias, certiorari, and in other cases closely affecting the interests of the subject

**petty bourgeois** *or* **petty bourgeoisie** *n* [*petty bourgeois* alter. (influenced by ¹*petty*) of *petit bourgeois; petty bourgeoisie* alter. (influenced by ¹*petty*) of *petite bourgeoisie*] **:** PETIT BOURGEOIS

**petty cash** *n* **1 :** money expended or received in small items or amounts **2 :** a cash fund kept on hand for the payment of minor items

**petty constable** *n* **:** an officer of a British parish or township formerly appointed to act as keeper of the peace and to perform various minor administrative duties

**pettygod** *n, obs* **:** a minor deity **:** DEMIGOD

**petty jury** *n* [by alter. (influenced by ¹*petty*)] **:** PETIT JURY

**petty larceny** *n* [alter. (influenced by ¹*petty*) of *petit larceny*] **1** *common law* **:** larceny of property having a value of less than a shilling **2** *statutory law* **:** larceny of property having a value ranging in the U.S. from $10 to $200 — compare GRAND LARCENY

**petty morel** *n* **1 :** BLACK NIGHTSHADE **2 :** SPIKENARD 2a

**petty offense** *n* **1 :** a minor offense for which one may be tried at common law without a jury or for which there is no constitutional right to trial by jury **2 :** MISDEMEANOR; *esp* **:** one that may not be the subject of an indictment

**petty officer** *n* **:** a person belonging to one of three classes of lowest rating among noncommissioned naval officers ⟨a *petty officer* second class rates just below one of the first class and above one of the third class⟩

**petty sergeanty** *n* [by alter. (influenced by ¹*petty*)] **:** PETIT SERGEANTY

**petty sessions** *n pl* **:** the sessions of magistrates or justices that require no jury and that are held in exercise of summary jurisdiction and similar minor matters

**petty spurge** *n* **:** an Old World devil's milk (*Euphorbia peplus*) that is an introduced weed in the eastern U.S.

**petty treason** *n* [ME, fr. *petty, pety* small, minor + *treason, tresoun* treason — more at PETTY] **:** PETIT TREASON

**petty whin** *n* **1 :** NEEDLE FURZE **2 :** RESTHARROW

**pet·u·lance** \ˈpechələn(t)s\ *n* -s [F *pétulance,* fr. L *petulantia* impudence, fr. *petulant-, petulans* impudent + *-ia* -y] **1 :** the quality or state of being petulant: **a** *archaic* **:** wantonness or insolence in speech or behavior **:** RUDENESS ⟨the ~ with which obscure scribblers . . . treat men of the most respectable character —James Boswell⟩ **b :** temporary or capricious ill humor **:** PEEVISHNESS ⟨the ~ and crankiness of an old man who has been at the head of affairs all his life —Robert Graves⟩ **2 :** a petulant expression ⟨his dexterous ~s making the air all like needles round you —Thomas Carlyle⟩

**pet·u·lan·cy** \-nsē, -si\ *n* -ES [L *petulantia* impudence] *archaic* **:** PETULANCE

¹**pet·u·lant** \-lənt\ *adj* [L or MF; MF *petulant* impudent, fr. L *petulant-, petulans;* akin to L *petere* to go to or toward, seek — more at FEATHER] **1** *archaic* **a :** wanton or immodest in speech or behavior ⟨corrupted . . . amongst lascivious and ~ men and women —Thomas Tryon⟩ **b :** insolent or rude in speech or behavior ⟨as fair a mark as factious animosity and ~ wit could desire —T.B.Macaulay⟩ **2** [influenced in meaning by ⁴*pet*] **:** characterized by temporary or capricious ill humor **:** PEEVISH ⟨grew moody and ~ and would not eat —Pearl Buck⟩ ⟨developed a ~ and fussy disposition —E.L. Pearson⟩ **syn** see IRRITABLE

²**petulant** \"\ *n* -s **:** a person who is petulant

**pet·u·lant·ly** *adv* **:** in a petulant manner

**pe·tun** \pəˈtün\ *n* -s [MF *petun, petum*] *archaic* **:** TOBACCO

**pe·tune** \pəˈtün, pəˈtyün\ *vt* -ED/-ING/-S [perh. fr. obs. F *petuner* to smoke tobacco, fr. obs. F *petun* tobacco, fr. MF *petun, petum*] **:** to heighten the flavor and aroma of (tobacco) by dipping in or spraying with a thick infusion of tobacco stems of the best quality or a liquid of other materials

**pe·tu·nia** \pəˈtünyə, pəˈtyü-, -nēə\ *n* [NL, fr. obs. F *petun* tobacco (fr. MF *petun, petum,* fr. Tupi *petyn, petyma*) + NL *-ia*] **1 a** *cap* **:** a genus of branching and often straggling annual or perennial So. American herbs (family Solanaceae) that have viscid and pubescent stems and foliage, bear abundant flowers with funnel-form or salver-shaped flowers, and are widely cultivated as ornamentals **b** -s **:** any plant of the genus *Petunia* **2** -s **:** a dark purple that is bluer, lighter, and stronger than average prune, bluer and stronger than plum (sense 6b) and bluer and duller than mulberry (sense 2a)

petunia 1b

**petunia violet** *n* **:** a deep purple that is redder and slightly lighter than hyacinth violet, redder and lighter than pontiff, paler than dahlia purple (sense 2), and bluer, lighter, and stronger than imperial purple (sense 2)

**pe·tun·tse** *also* **pe·tun·se** *or* **pe·tun·tze** \pə'tùntsə, bī-'dəndzə\ *n* -s [Chin (Pek) *pe*[2] *tun*[1] *tzŭ*[3], fr. *pe*[2] white + *tun*[1] *tzŭ*[3] mound of earth, fr. *tun*[1] mound, heap + *tzŭ*[3] son, child] **:** CHINA STONE

**pet·wood** \'pe‚twu̇d\ *also* **pet·wun wood** \-‚twən-\ *n* [Burmese *phetwūn*] **:** TRINCOMALI WOOD

**petz·ite** \'pet‚sīt\ *n* -s [G *petzit*, fr. W.K.*Pecz* †1873 Hung. geologist who analyzed it + G *-it* -ite] **:** a mineral $Ag_3AuTe_2$ consisting of a silver gold telluride that is steel gray to iron black (hardness 2.5–3, sp. gr. 8.7–9.0)

**petz·val lens** \'pets‚väl-\ *n, usu cap P* [after Joseph *Petzval* †1891 Austrian mathematician and opticist] **:** a two-element highly achromatized camera objective having low transmission loss

**peu·ced·a·num** \pyə'sedᵊnəm\ *n, cap* [NL, fr. L, sulphurweed, fr. Gk *peukedanon*, prob. fr. neut. of *peukedanos* sharp, piercing — more at PUNGENT] **:** a genus of Old World tall branching herbs (family Umbelliferae) characterized by a conical stylopodium and solitary oil tubes

**peul** *or* **peuhl** \'p(y)ül\ *n* -s *usu cap* **:** FULANI

**peu·mus** \'pyüməs\ *n, cap* [NL, fr. Sp *peumo* boldo, fr. Mapuche *peumo*] **:** a genus of Chilean evergreen shrubs (family Monimiaceae) with elliptic or ovate revolute coriaceous leaves

**pevy** *var of* PEAVEY

[1]**pew** \'pyü\ *n* -s *often attrib* [ME *pue, pewe, puwe*, fr. MF *puie* balcony, fr. L *podia*, pl. of *podium* balcony, fr. Gk *podion* small foot, base, dim. of *pod-, pous* foot — more at FOOT] **1 a :** a compartment in the auditorium of a church providing seats for several persons: (1) **:** a compartment esp. in an old English church raised on a footpace, separated by partitions, furnished with a long seat or when square with seats facing each other, and designed for the use of a family (2) **:** one of the benches with backs and sometimes doors fixed in rows in a church **b :** the persons occupying such pews **:** CONGREGATION **2** *obs* **:** station in life **:** allotted place or position **3 a** *obs* **:** a raised place for a speaker in a church; *esp* **:** a preacher's stall or desk **b** *archaic* **:** a raised seat or bench for a person (as a judge) sitting in an official capacity

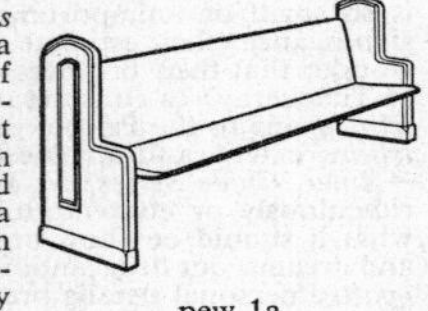

pew 1a

[2]**pew** \"\ *vt* -ED/-ING/-S [ME *puyen*, fr. *pue, pewe, puwe*, n.] **1 :** to furnish with pews ⟨they ~ their churches and sometimes lock them —E.A.Freeman⟩ **2 :** to enclose in or as if in a pew ⟨men who were as willingly ~*ed* in the parish church as their sheep were in night folds —*Examiner*⟩

[3]**pew** *\a sound made by blowing or whistling through rounded lips, often with the tongue moving from the front to the back of the mouth in the process; often read as* 'pyü\ *interj* [origin unknown] — used to express contempt or disgust (as at an odor)

[4]**pew** \'pyü\ *n* -s *Scot* **:** a thin stream of air or smoke

[5]**pew** \"\ *n* -s [F *pieu* stake, fr. L *palus* — more at POLE] **:** a long-handled hooked prong for pitching fish (as on a cannery wharf)

**pew·age** \'pyüij, -ēj\ *n* -s **1 :** the amount paid for the use of a pew in a church **2 :** the pews in a church

**pew chair** *n* **:** a seat hinged against the end of a pew to afford accommodation when needed in the aisle

**pew·dom** \'pyüdəm\ *n* -s **:** the system or prevalence of pews in churches

**pewee** *var of* PEEWEE

**pew·ful** \'pyü‚fu̇l\ *n, pl* **pewfuls** \-ü‚fu̇lz\ *or* **pews·ful** \-üz‚fu̇l\ [[1]*pew* + *-ful*] **:** as many as a pew will hold

**pewholder** \'≈‚≈≈\ *n* **:** a renter or owner of a church pew

**pewing** *n* -s [fr. gerund of [2]*pew*] **:** PEWAGE 2

**pe·wit** *or* **pee·wit** \'pē‚wit, -ē‚wit, 'pyüət *usu* -d·+V\ *also* **pee·vit** \'pēvət, -‚vit\ *n* -s [imit.] **1 :** LAPWING **2** *also* **pewit gull :** LAUGHING GULL **1 3 :** PEEWEE 1a

**pew·less** \'pyüləs\ *adj* **:** having no pews

**pew rent** *n* **:** the rent for a pew or for sittings in a church

**pews** *pl of* PEW, *pres 3d sing of* PEW

**pew·ter** \'pyüd·ə(r), -ütə-\ *n* -s *often attrib* [ME *pewtre*, fr. MF *peutre, peautre*; akin to OProv *peltre* pewter, It *peltro*] **1 :** any of various alloys having tin as their principal component: as **a :** a dull alloy with lead used formerly for domestic utensils **b :** a bright alloy hardened with antimony and copper and used esp. for artware — compare BRITANNIA METAL **2 :** utensils or vessels made of pewter: as **a :** a pewter tankard or mug **b** *Brit* **:** a prize cup **3 :** MONEY **4 a :** a grayish blue that is redder and paler than electric or Gobelin, paler than copenhagen, and paler and slightly greener than old china **b :** a nearly neutral slightly bluish dark gray that is darker than mole

**pew·ter·er** \-ərə(r)\ *n* -s [ME *peautrer, peuterer*, fr. MF *peautrier*, fr. *peutre, peautre* pewter + *-ier* -er] **:** one that makes pewter utensils or vessels

**pewter mill** *n* **:** a lapidary's wheel used for stones of the hardness of amethyst or agate

**-pexy** \‚peksē, -si\ *n comb form* -ES [NL *-pexia*, fr. Gk *-pēxia* solidity, fr. *pēxis* solidity, freezing, putting together (fr. *pēgnynai* to fix, fasten together) + *-ia* -y — more at PACT] **:** fixation **:** making fast ⟨colloido*pexy*⟩ ⟨gastro*pexy*⟩

**pey·e·ri·an gland** \(')pī¦irēən-\ *n, usu cap P* [*peyerian* fr. Johann K. *Peyer* †1712 Swiss physician and anatomist + E *-an*] **:** PEYER'S PATCH

**pey·er's patch** \'pī(ə)rz-\ *also* **peyer's gland** *n, usu cap 1st P* **:** any of numerous large oval patches of closely aggregated lymph follicles in the walls of the small intestines esp. in the ileum that partially or entirely disappear in advanced life and in typhoid fever become the seat of ulcers which may perforate the intestines

**pe·yo·te** \pā'(y)ōd·ē\ *also* **pe·yotl** \-d·ᵊl\ *or* **pa·yo·te** \-d·ē\ *n* -s [MexSp *peyote*, fr. Nahuatl *peyotl*] **1 :** any of several cacti (genus *Lophophora*) of the southwestern U.S. and northern Mexico; *esp* **:** MESCAL **2 :** a stimulant drug derived from mescal buttons and used in religious ceremonials by some Indian peoples

**peyote cult** *n, often cap P* **1 :** an American Indian religious society or form of worship centering around the sacramental use of peyote **2 :** PEYOTISM

**peyote dance** *n* **:** an ecstatic fertility dance of the Huichol and Tarahumara Indians of northern Mexico with visions induced by eating the mescal button

**pe·yo·tism** \pā'yōd‚izəm\ *n* -s **:** an intertribal American Indian religion adapting Christian elements to traditional tribal beliefs and practices and distinguished by the sacramental use of peyote

**pe·yo·tist** \-d·əst\ *n* -s **:** an adherent of peyotism **:** a member of a peyote cult

**pey·ro·nie's disease** \¦pārə¦nēz-\ *n, usu cap P* [prob. after François Gigot de La *Peyronie* †1747 Fr. surgeon] **:** the formation of fibrous plaques in one or both corpora cavernosa of the penis resulting in distortion or deflection of the erect organ

**pey·tral** *or* **pey·trel** \'pā·trəl\ *n* -s [ME *peytrel*, fr. MF *peitral, poitral* — more at POITREL] **:** POITREL

**pe·zi·za** \pə'zīzə\ *n, cap* [NL, alter. of L *pezica* puffball, modif. of Gk *pezis*; perh. akin to L *pedere* to break wind — more at PETARD] **:** the type genus of Pezizaceae comprising cup fungi with sessile usu. dull tan or brown apothecia that lack external hairs or bristles — see PLECTANIA

**pez·i·za·ce·ae** \‚pezə'zāsē‚ē\ *n pl, cap* [NL, fr. *Peziza*, type genus + *-aceae*] **:** a large and widely distributed family of fungi (order Pezizales) comprising many typical cup fungi — see PEZIZA

**pe·zi·zae·form** *also* **pe·zi·zi·form** \pə'zīzə‚fȯrm\ *adj* [*pezizaeform* irreg. fr. NL *Peziza* + E *-form*; *peziziform* fr. NL *Peziza* + E *-iform*] **:** having the shape of a fungus of the genus *Peziza* **:** cup-shaped

**pez·i·za·les** \‚pezə'zā(‚)lēz\ *n pl, cap* [NL, fr. *Peziza* + *-ales*] **:** an order of epigeal mostly saprophytic fungi (subclass Euascomycetes) having asci borne in a hymenium that is usu. exposed before maturity and on or in a fleshy or horny apothecium often colored and typically shaped like a cup, saucer, or disc — see HELVELLACEAE, PEZIZACEAE

**pe·zi·zoid** \pə'zī‚zȯid, 'pezə‚z-\ *adj* [ISV *peziz-* (fr. NL *Peziza*) + *-oid*] **:** resembling a fungus of the genus *Peziza* **:** cup-shaped

**pez·o·graph** \'pezə‚graf\ *n* [perh. fr. Gk *pezis* puffball + E *-o-* + *-graph*] **:** any of various small pits suggestive of the imprints of finger tips that are common on meteorites

**pez·o·phaps** \-‚faps\ *n, cap* [NL, fr. Gk *pezos* walking, on foot + *phaps* wild pigeon; akin to L *ped-, pes* foot — more at FOOT] **:** a genus of birds (family Rhaphidae) constituted by the extinct solitaire

**pf** *abbr* **1** perfect **2** pfennig **3** preferred

**pF** *symbol* — used when *p* denotes logarithm and *F* indicates free energy to express logarithmically the water-holding energy of soil that is usu. measured by the height in centimeters of a column of water which produces a tension of equal force ⟨a tension of 40 centimeters equals ~ 1.6⟩

**PF** *abbr* **1** *often not cap* pianoforte **2** *often not cap* picofarad **3** *often not cap* [It *più forte*] a little louder **4** *often not cap* power factor **5** procurator fiscal **6** pro forma

**pfc** \¦pē¦ef¦sē\ *abbr or n* -s *often cap P* private first class

**pfce** *abbr* performance

**pfd** *abbr* preferred

**pfef·fer·ku·chen** \'fefə(r)‚kükən, *G* '(p)fefər‚küẋən\ *n* [G, fr. *pfeffer* pepper (fr. OHG *pfeffar*) + *kuchen* cake, fr. OHG *kuocho* — more at PEPPER, CAKE] **:** GINGERBREAD

**pfef·fer·nuss** \'fefə(r)‚nüs, -nu̇s, *G* '(p)fefər‚nu̇s\ *n, pl* **pfeffernüs·se** \-nüsə, -nu̇sə, *G* -nʏsə\ [G, fr. *pfeffer* + *nuss* nut, fr. OHG *nuz* — more at NUT] **:** a small hard highly spiced cookie made traditionally for the Christmas holidays

**pfeif·fer·el·la** \‚fīfə'relə\ [NL, fr. Richard F. J. *Pfeiffer* †1945? Ger. bacteriologist + NL *-ella*] *syn of* ACTINOBACILLUS

**pfeif·fer's bacillus** \'fīfə(r)z-\ *also* **pfeiffer's influenza bacillus** *n, usu cap P* [after Richard F. J. *Pfeiffer*] **:** a minute bacillus (*Hemophilus influenzae*) associated with acute respiratory infections and meningitis — compare KOCH-WEEKS BACILLUS

**pfen·nig** \'fenig, -ik, *often (by persistence of the nasality of the* n) -iŋ; *G* '(p)fenik\ *n, pl* **pfennigs** \-igz, -iks, -iŋz\ *or* **pfennige** \-nigə, -niyə\ [G, fr. OHG *pfenning* — more at PENNY] **1** *in Germany before 1871* **:** any of several units of value or their corresponding coins (as, in Bavaria, ¼ kreuzer; in Lübeck, ½ schilling) **2** *in Germany after 1871* **:** a unit of value equal to ¹⁄₁₀₀ mark; *also* **:** a coin representing this value — see MONEY table

**pfg** *abbr* pfennig

**PFI** *abbr* physical fitness index

**pfit·zer's juniper** \'fitsə(r)z-\ *or* **pfitzer juniper** *n, usu cap P* [after Ernst *Pfitzer* †1906 Ger. botanist] **:** a low-growing evergreen shrub (*Juniperus chinensis pfitzeriana*) that has spreading chiefly horizontal branches and gray green foliage and is extensively used in landscaping

**pflei·der·er** \'flīdərə(r)\ *or* **pflei·der·ing machine** \-dəriŋ-\ *n* -s [perh. fr. the name *Pfleiderer*] **:** a machine for shredding cellulose sheets to bits in rayon manufacturing

**pfte** *abbr* pianoforte

**pfx** *abbr* prefix

**pg** *abbr* page

**PG** *abbr* **1** Paris granite **2** paying guest **3** postgraduate **4** proving ground **5** public gaol

**PGA** \¦pē¦jē¦ā\ *n* -s [*pteroylglutamic acid*] **:** FOLIC ACID 1

**pgn** *abbr* pigeon

**PGR** *abbr* psychogalvanic reaction or response

**PGT** *abbr, often not cap* per gross ton

**ph** *abbr* **1** phase **2** phone **3** pharmacopoeia **4** phosphor **5** phot

**pH** *symbol* the negative logarithm of the effective hydrogen-ion concentration or hydrogen-ion activity in gram equivalents per liter determined in various ways (as by means of a hydrogen electrode or a glass electrode) and used for convenience in expressing both acidity and alkalinity usu. on a scale of 0 to 14 on which 7 represents the value for pure water at 25°C or neutrality, values less than 7 represent increasing hydrogen-ion concentration and increasing acidity (as 3.1 for vinegar, 2.3 for lemon juice, and 1.04 for tenth-normal hydrochloric acid), and values greater than 7 represent decreasing hydrogen-ion concentration and increasing alkalinity (as 8.2 for one percent sodium bicarbonate solution, 10.7 for one percent sodium carbonate solution, 13 for tenth-normal sodium hydroxide) ⟨instead of saying that the concentration of hydrogen ion in pure water is $1.00 \times 10^{-7}$, it is customary to say that the ~ of pure water is 7 —Linus Pauling⟩ ⟨soils may vary in ~ from about 3.5 to 9, but the general range most favorable for ordinary crops is from 6.0 to 7.5 —E.G.Davies⟩ — compare PK, RH

**PH** *abbr* public health

**Ph** *symbol* phenyl

**phac-** *or* **phaco-** *or* **phak-** *or* **phako-** *comb form* [Gk *phak-, phako-*, fr. *phakos* lentil, object shaped like a lentil, mole, wart] **1 :** lentil **:** thing shaped like a lentil ⟨*Phaco*choerus⟩ ⟨*phaco*lith⟩ ⟨*Phac*ops⟩ **2 a :** lens ⟨*phaco*meter⟩ **b** *usu phak-or phako-* **:** crystalline lens of the eye ⟨*phak*oma⟩

**pha·ce·lia** \fə'sēlēə\ *n* [NL, fr. Gk *phakelos* bundle, faggot + NL *-ia*] **1** *cap* **:** a genus of American herbs (family Hydrophyllaceae) with usu. pinnatifid or dissected leaves and blue, purple, or white flowers in scorpioid cymes — see CALIFORNIA BLUEBELL **2** -s **:** any plant of the genus *Phacelia*

**pha·cel·la** \fə'selə\ *also* **phacel·lus** \-ləs\ *n, pl* **phacel·lae** \-‚lē, -‚lī\ *also* **phacel·li** \-‚lī\ [NL, fr. Gk *phakellos*, MS var. of *phakelos* bundle, faggot] **:** one of the rows of filaments usu. bearing nematocysts on the inner surface of the gastric cavity of some scyphozoan jellyfishes

**pha·cid·i·a·ce·ae** \fə‚sidē'āsē‚ē\ *n pl, cap* [NL, fr. *Phacidium*, type genus (fr. Gk *phakos* lentil + NL *-idium*) + *-aceae*] **:** a family of fungi (order Phacidiales) having a thin hypothecium and ascocarps that are embedded in the host tissue or in a stroma

**pha·cid·i·a·les** \-'ā(‚)lēz\ *n pl, cap* [NL, fr. *Phacidium* genus of fungi + *-ales*] **:** an order of fungi (subclass Euascomycetes) having the hymenium covered by a membrane until the ascospores mature following which the membrane breaks up into stellate or irregular fragments

**phac·o·choere** *or* **phac·o·chere** \'fakə‚ki(ə)r\ *n* -s [NL *Phacochoerus*] **:** WARTHOG

**phac·o·choe·rus** \‚≈≈'kirəs, -kēr-\ *n, cap* [NL, fr. *phac-* + *-choerus*] **:** a genus of mammals that comprises the warthogs and was formerly made the type of a separate family but is now placed in the family Suidae near the genus *Sus*

**phac·o·lith** \'≈≈‚lith\ *n* -s [*phac-* + *-lith*] **:** a lens-shaped mass of igneous rock intruded in folded sedimentary beds with which it is approximately concordant and having its greatest thickness along the axes of synclines or anticlines — **phac·o·lith·ic** \¦≈≈¦lithik\ *adj*

**pha·com·e·ter** \fə'kämәd·ə(r)\ *n* [ISV *phac-* + *-meter*] **:** an instrument for measuring the focal power of lenses

**pha·cops** \'fā‚käps\ *n, cap* [NL, fr. *phac-* + *-ops*] **:** a genus (the type of the family Phacopidae) comprising Silurian and Devonian trilobites with a large rounded glabella and a large pygidium

**phae·dra·nas·sa** \‚fēdrə'nasə\ *n, cap* [NL, fr. Gk *phaidros* bright + *anassa* queen] **:** a small genus of chiefly Andean bulbous herbs (family Amaryllidaceae) with tall hollow scapes bearing umbels of showy drooping usu. red or rose green-marked flowers — see QUEEN LILY

**phae·ism** \'fē‚izəm\ *n* -s [Gk *phaios* dusky, gray + E *-ism*; akin to Gk *phaidros* bright, Lith *giedras* bright, clear, Latvian *gàiss* air, weather] **:** incomplete melanism in a butterfly

**phaen-** *or* **phaeno-** — see PHEN-

**phaeo-** *or* **pheo-** *comb form* [Gk *phaio-*, fr. *phaios* dusky, gray] **:** dun-colored ⟨*phaeo*derm⟩ ⟨*Phaeo*phyceae⟩ — often in names of compounds related to chlorophyll ⟨*pheo*phytin⟩

**phae·och·rous** \fē'äkrəs\ *adj* [*phaeo-* + *-chrous*, irreg. fr. Gk *-chroos, -chrous* -colored — more at -CHROOUS] **:** DUSKY

**phaeo·derm** \'fēə‚dərm\ *n* -s [*phaeo-* + Gk *derma* skin — more at DERM-] **:** a person with a grayish brown skin

**phaeo·melanin** \¦fēō+\ *n* [*phaeo-* + *melanin*] **:** a reddish or yellowish brown animal pigment related to melanin and common in animals of arid areas

**phaeo·phy·ce·ae** \‚≈≈'fīsē‚ē, -fis-\ *n pl, cap* [NL, fr. *phaeo-* + *-phyceae*] *in some classifications* **:** a class comprising the brown algae and being coextensive with the division Phaeophyta — **phaeo·phy·cean** \¦≈≈¦fishən\ *adj or n* — **phaeo·phy·ceous** \-shəs\ *adj*

**phae·oph·y·ta** \fē'äfəd·ə\ *n pl, cap* [NL, fr. *phaeo-* + *-phyta*] **:** a division or other category of algae that have the chlorophyll masked by brown pigments, are mostly marine, diverse in form, often of gigantic size, and anchored by holdfasts to the substrate, and are usu. divided among the classes Isogeneratae, Heterogeneratae, and Cyclosporeae — see BROWN ALGA

**phaeophytin** *var of* PHEOPHYTIN

**phae·o·plast** \'fēə‚plast\ *n* -s [ISV *phaeo-* + *-plast*] **:** one of the brownish chromatophores occurring in the brown algae — compare RHODOPLAST

**phaeoporphyrin** *var of* PHEOPORPHYRIN

**phaeo·spo·ra·les** \‚fēōspə'rā(‚)lēz\ *n pl, cap* [NL, fr. *phaeo-* + *spora* spore + *-ales*] *in some classifications* **:** an order of brown algae orig. equivalent to Phaeosporeae but later excluding the Laminariales

**phaeo·spore** \'fēə‚spō(ə)r\ *n* [*phaeo-* + *spore*] **:** a spore (as a zoospore) containing phaeoplasts

**phaeo·spo·re·ae** \‚fēō'spōrē‚ē\ *n pl, cap* [NL, fr. *phaeo-* + *spora* spore + *-eae*] *in some classifications* **:** an order or other group of brown algae characterized by the production of asexual swarm spores and usu. comprising all the Phaeophyceae except the Dictyotales and Fucales — compare CYCLOSPOREAE — **phaeo·spor·ous** \¦≈≈¦spōrəs, (')fē¦äspərəs\ *adj*

**phaeo·tham·ni·on** \‚fēō'thamnē‚än\ *n, cap* [NL, fr. *phaeo-* + Gk *thamnion* little bush, dim. of *thamnos* bush — more at THAMN-] **:** a genus (the type of the family Phaeothamniaceae) of rare yellow green algae growing upon other algae and having a definite central axis and ascending lateral filaments made up of cylindrical to subovoid cells

**pha·ë·thon** \'fāəthən, -‚thän\ *n, cap* [NL, fr. L, name of son of Helios] **:** a genus (the type of the family Phaëthontidae) of tropical sea birds of the order Pelecaniformes — see TROPIC BIRD — **pha·ë·thon·ic** \¦≈≈¦thänik\ *or* **pha·ë·thon·tic** \-ntik\ *adj*

**pha·e·ton** \'fāətᵊn *also* -ät-\ *n* -s [L *Phaethon*, son of Helios who attempted to drive the chariot of the sun with the result of setting the earth on fire, fr. Gk *Phaethōn*] **1** *archaic, usu cap* **a :** one who drives a chariot or coach esp. at a reckless or dangerous speed **b :** one that would or may set the world on fire **2 :** any of various light four-wheeled horse-drawn vehicles usu. having no sidepieces in front of the seats **3 :** TOURING CAR

**phag-** *or* **phago-** *comb form* [Gk, fr. *phagein* to eat — more at BAKSHEESH] **1 :** eating **:** feeding ⟨*phag*edena⟩ ⟨*phago*mania⟩ **2 :** phagocyte ⟨*phago*lysis⟩

**-pha·ga** \fəgə\ *n comb form, pl* **-phaga** \"\ [NL, fr. Gk *phagein*] **:** eater **:** eaters — in taxonomic names in zoology ⟨Entomo*phaga*⟩ ⟨Litho*phaga*⟩ ⟨Xylo*phaga*⟩ ⟨Glosso*phaga*⟩

**phage** \'fāj *sometimes* 'fäzh *or* 'fȧzh\ *n* -s [by shortening] **:** BACTERIOPHAGE

**-phage** \‚fāj *sometimes* ‚fäzh *or* ‚fȧzh\ *also* **-phag** \‚fag, -aa(ə)g, -aig\ *n comb form* -s [Gk *-phagos*, fr. *phagein*] **1 :** one that eats ⟨ostreo*phage*⟩ ⟨xylo*phage*⟩ **2 :** cell (as a phagocyte) that devours cells ⟨bacterio*phage*⟩

**phag·e·de·na** *also* **phag·e·dae·na** \‚fajə'dēnə\ *n* -s [L, fr. Gk *phagedaina*, fr. *phagein* to eat — more at BAKSHEESH] **:** rapidly spreading destructive ulceration of soft tissue

**phag·e·den·ic** *also* **phag·e·daen·ic** \¦≈≈¦denik, -dēn-\ *adj* **1** *of a lesion* **:** being or marked by phagedena **2 :** of, like, or resembling phagedena ⟨the ~ form of chancroid⟩

**phage type** *n* **:** the phages to which a particular bacterium is susceptible

**phage-typing** *n* **:** determination of the phage type of a bacterium

**-pha·gia** \'fāj(ē)ə\ *n comb form* -s [NL, fr. Gk — more at -PHAGY] **1 :** -PHAGY ⟨hemo*phagia*⟩ **2 :** desire for food ⟨hyper*phagia*⟩

**pha·gin·e·ae** \fə'jinē‚ē\ *n pl, cap* [NL, fr. *phag-* + *-ineae*] *in some classifications* **:** a suborder of Virales comprising the bacteriophages

**phago·cyt·able** \¦fagə¦sīd·əbəl\ *adj* [*phagocytosis* + *-able*] **:** susceptible to phagocytosis

**phago·cy·ta·ry** \¦≈≈¦sīd·ərē\ *adj* [ISV *phagocyte* + *-ary*] **:** functioning or supposed to function as a phagocyte

[1]**phago·cyte** \'fagə‚sīt\ *n* -s [ISV *phag-* + *-cyte*] **:** any cell that characteristically engulfs foreign material, is typically a leukocyte or reticuloendothelial cell and often amoeboid, and functions in the body to remove and consume debris and foreign bodies (as degenerating tissue or bacteria) — compare ATHROCYTE

[2]**phagocyte** \"\ *vt* -ED/-ING/-S **:** PHAGOCYTIZE

**phago·cyt·ic** \¦≈≈¦sid·ik\ *adj* **:** having the ability to phagocytize **:** capable of functioning as phagocytes

**phagocytic index** *n* **:** a measure of phagocytic activity determined by counting the number of bacteria ingested per phagocyte during a limited period of incubation of a suspension of bacteria and phagocytes in serum

**phago·cyt·ize** \'≈≈‚sīd‚īz, -‚sə‚tīz\ *vt* -ED/-ING/-S **:** to consume by phagocytosis

**phago·cy·tose** \≈≈‚sī‚tōs, -ōz\ *also* **phago·cy·toze** \-ōz\ *vt* -ED/-ING/-S [back-formation fr. *phagocytosis*] **:** PHAGOCYTIZE

**phago·cy·to·sis** \‚fagə‚sī'tōsəs\ *n, pl* **phagocyto·ses** \-ō‚sēz\ [NL, fr. ISV *phagocyte* + NL *-osis*] **:** the process of ingestion and usu. of isolation or destruction of particulate material by cells that in vertebrates is a characteristic function of various leukocytes and reticuloendothelial cells and serves as an important bodily defense mechanism against infection by microorganisms and against occlusion of mucous surfaces or tissues by foreign particles and tissue debris

**phago·cy·tot·ic** \¦≈≈≈¦täd·ik\ *adj* **:** of or relating to phagocytosis

**phago·dynamometer** \¦≈≈+\ *n* [*phag-* + *dynamometer*] **:** an instrument for measuring the force that may be exerted by the jaws in bringing the teeth together (as in chewing)

**pha·gol·y·sis** \fə'gäləsəs\ *n, pl* **phagoly·ses** \-ə‚sēz\ [NL, fr. *phag-* + *-lysis*] **:** destruction of phagocytes

**phago·lyt·ic** \¦fagə¦lid·ik\ *adj* **:** of or relating to phagolysis

**-pha·gous** \fəgəs\ *adj comb form* [Gk *-phagos*, fr. *phagein* to eat — more at BAKSHEESH] **:** feeding esp. on a (specified) kind of food ⟨anthropo*phagous*⟩ ⟨creo*phagous*⟩ ⟨cyto*phagous*⟩ ⟨sapro*phagous*⟩

**pha·gun** \'pägün, 'fä-\ *n* -s *usu cap* [Hindi *phāgun*, fr. Skt *phālguna*] **:** a month of the Hindu year — see MONTH table

**-pha·gus** \fəgəs\ *n comb form* [NL, fr. Gk *-phagos*] **:** eater **:** one that eats an indicated thing or in an indicated way — in generic names of animals ⟨Melo*phagus*⟩

**-pha·gy** \fəjē, -ji\ *n comb form* -ES [Gk *-phagia*, fr. *phagein* to eat + *-ia* -y — more at BAKSHEESH] **:** eating of a (specified) type or substance — esp. in biological and medical terms ⟨anthropo*phagy*⟩ ⟨bio*phagy*⟩ ⟨cyto*phagy*⟩ ⟨geo*phagy*⟩

**phai·no·pep·la** \‚fānə'peplə, ‚fīn-\ *n* [NL, fr. Gk *phaeinos* shining + *peplos* robe; akin to Gk *phaos, phōs* light — more at FANCY, PEPLOS] **1** *cap* **:** a monotypic genus of passerine birds of Mexico and southwestern U.S. of which the male is uniform glossy blue-black with a white spot on each primary and the female is brownish **2** -s **:** any bird of the genus *Phainopepla*

**phai·us** \'fīəs\ *n, cap* [NL, fr. Gk *phaios* dusky — more at PHAEISM] **:** a genus of Asiatic orchids that are locally naturalized in tropical America and are sometimes cultivated for their large plicate leaves and showy racemose flowers

**pha·jus** \'fājəs\ [NL, fr. Gk *phaios*] *syn of* PHAIUS

**phak-** *or* **phako-** — see PHAC-

**phal·a·cro·cor·a·cine** \¦falək¦rō¦kȯrə‚sīn, -‚sən\ *adj* [NL *Phalacrocorac-, Phalacrocorax* + E *-ine*] **:** of or relating to the genus *Phalacrocorax*

**phal·a·cro·co·rax** \-'krōkə‚raks\ *n, cap* [NL, fr. L, coot, cormorant, fr. Gk *phalakros* bald + *korak-, korax* raven — more at RAVEN] **:** a genus consisting of the cormorants and constituting a family of the order Pelecaniformes

**phal·a·cro·sis** \ˌfalə'krōsə̇s\ *n, pl* **phalacro·ses** \-ˌsēz\ [NL, fr. Gk *phalakrōsis*, fr. *phalakros* bald (fr. *phalos* white + *akron* top) + *-ōsis* -osis; akin to Gk *phalios* having a white spot, and to Gk *akmē* point — more at BALD, EDGE] **:** BALDNESS, ALOPECIA

**pha·lae·ce·an** \ˌfalə'sēən\ *n* -S *usu cap* [Gk *phalaikeion* phalaecean (fr. *Phalaikos* Phalaecus, Greek poet) + E *-an*] **:** a hendecasyllabic verse in Greek and Latin prosody that is a glyconic with three additional syllables forming a single bacchius or an iambic dipody catalectic **:** a logaoedic verse of five feet the first of which is indeterminate, the second a dactyl, and the last three trochees

**pha·laen·i·dae** \fə'lenəˌdē\ [NL, fr. *Phalaena*, genus of moths (fr. Gk *phalaina*, *phallaina* whale, moth) + *-idae* — more at BALAENA] *syn of* NOCTUIDAE

**phal·ae·nop·sid** \ˌfalə'näpsəd, -ˌsid\ *n* -S [NL, fr. *Phalaenopsis*] **:** an orchid of the genus *Phalaenopsis*

**phal·ae·nop·sis** \-ˌsə̇s\ *n, cap* [NL, fr. Gk *phalaina* moth + *-opsis*] **:** a genus of ornamental epiphytic orchids that are natives of India and the Malay archipelago and have fleshy leaves with persistent sheathing bases and large flowers of various colors with broad lateral petals — see BUTTERFLY PLANT 2, MOTH ORCHID

**pha·lange** \'fāˌlanj, fə'l-, -aa(ə)nj\ *n* -S [F, fr. NL *phalang-*, *phalanx* — more at PHALANX] **1 :** PHALANX 2 **2 :** one of the segments of an insect's tarsus

**pha·lan·ge·al** \fə'lanj(ē)əl, fā'-\ *adj* [L *phalang-*, *phalanx* + E *-al*] **1 :** of or relating to a phalanx **2** [NL *phalang-*, *phalanx* + E *-al*] **:** of or relating to the phalanges

**phalangeal bone** *n* **:** PHALANX 2

**pha·lan·ger** \fə'lanjə(r), fā'-\ *n* [NL, fr. *phalang-*, *phalanx* — more at PHALANX] **1** -S **:** any of various marsupial mammals of the family Phalangeridae ranging in size from a mouse to a large cat, having soft thick fur and a long and usu. prehensile tail, and being chiefly nocturnal, arboreal, and frugivorous or insectivorous — see FLYING PHALANGER **2** *cap* **:** a genus (the type of the family Phalangeridae) comprising the cuscuses

**phal·an·ger·i·dae** \ˌfalən'jerəˌdē\ *n pl, cap* [NL, fr. *Phalanger*, type genus + *-idae*] **:** a family of marsupial mammals (suborder Diprotodontia) consisting of the phalangers, the flying phalangers, the koala, and related forms

**phalanges** *pl of* PHALANX

**phal·an·gette** \ˌfalən'jet\ *n* -S [F, fr. *phalange* phalanx (fr. NL *phalang-*, *phalanx*) + *-ette*] **:** a distal phalanx of a finger or toe

**-pha·lan·gia** \fə'lanj(ē)ə, fā'-\ *n comb form* -S [NL, fr. *phalang-*, *phalanx* + *-ia*] **:** condition of the phalanges ⟨brachy*phalangia*⟩

**pha·lan·gi·an** \fə'lanj(ē)ən, fā'-\ *adj or n* [NL *Phalangium* + E *-an*] **:** PHALANGID

**¹pha·lan·gid** \-jə̇d, -jid\ *adj* [NL *Phalangida*] **:** of or relating to the Phalangida

**²phalangid** \"\ *n* -S **:** an arachnid of the order Phalangida

**pha·lan·gi·da** \-jədə\ *n pl, cap* [NL, fr. *Phalangium* + *-ida*] **:** a cosmopolitan order of Arachnida comprising the harvestmen

**pha·lan·gi·dan** \-jədən, -dᵊn\ *or* **phal·an·gid·e·an** \ˌfalən'jidēən\ *adj* [*phalangidan* fr. NL *Phalangida* + E *-an*; *phalangidean* fr. NL *Phalangidea* + E *-an*] **:** ¹PHALANGID

**phal·an·gid·ea** \ˌfalən'jidēə\ [NL, fr. *Phalangium* + *-idea*] *syn of* PHALANGIDA

**phal·an·gid·e·an** \-dēən\ *n* -S [NL *Phalangidea* + E *-an*] **:** ²PHALANGID

**pha·lan·gi·des** \fə'lanjəˌdēz, fā'-\ [NL, fr. *Phalangium*] *syn of* PHALANGIDA

**pha·lan·gi·form** \-jəˌfȯrm\ *adj* [ISV *phalangi-* (fr. NL *phalang-*, *phalanx*) + *-iform*] **:** resembling a phalanx ⟨a ~ bone⟩

**pha·lan·gi·gra·da** \⸗ˌ⸗⸗'grādə\ [NL, fr. neut. pl. of *phalangigradus* phalangigrade] *syn of* TYLOPODA

**pha·lan·gi·grade** \fə'lanjəˌgrād, fā'-\ *adj* [NL *phalangigradus*, fr. *phalang-*, *phalanx* phalanx + *-gradus* -grade] **:** walking on the phalanges

**pha·lan·gist** \fə'lanjə̇st, fā'-\ *n* -S [by alter.] **:** FALANGIST

**phal·an·gis·ta** \ˌfalən'jistə\ [NL, fr. *phalang-*, *phalanx* + *-ista* -ist] *syn of* PHALANGER

**phal·an·gis·ti·dae** \-təˌdē\ [NL *Phalangista* + *-idae*] *syn of* PHALANGERIDAE

**phal·an·gi·ta** \-'jēdə\ [NL *Phalangium*] *syn of* PHALANGIDA

**phal·an·gite** \'falənˌjīt\ *n* -S [Gk *phalangitēs*, fr. *phalang-*, *phalanx* phalanx + *-itēs* -ite] **:** a soldier of a phalanx

**pha·lan·gi·um** \fə'lanjēəm, fā'-\ *n* [NL, fr. Gk *phalangion*, a spider, fr. *phalang-*, *phalanx* phalanx] **1** *pl* **phalan·gia** \-jēə\ *obs* **:** a venomous spider **2** *cap* **:** a genus (the type of the family Phalangiidae) of harvestmen

**¹phal·an·ste·ri·an** \ˌfalən'stirēən\ *adj* [F *phalanstérien*, fr. *phalanstère* phalanstery + *-ien* -ian] **:** of or relating to a phalanstery, to phalansterianism, or to a system of phalansteries

**²phalansterian** \"\ *n* -S **1 :** a member of a phalanstery **2 :** one who favors the system of phalansteries proposed by Fourier **:** FOURIERIST

**phal·an·ste·ri·an·ism** \-ˌnizəm\ *n* -S **:** FOURIERISM

**phal·an·stery** \'falənˌsterē, -ri\ *n* -ES [F *phalanstère* dwelling of a Fourierite community, fr. *phalange* phalanx (fr. L *phalang-*, *phalanx*) + *monastère* monastery (fr. LL *monasterium*) — more at PHALANX, MONASTERY] **1 a :** an association or community organized on the plan of Fourier **b :** the dwelling or buildings of such an association — compare FOURIERISM **2 a :** a group or association of persons who live together more or less cooperatively **b :** the dwelling of such a group

**¹pha·lanx** \'fāˌlaŋks, 'fa,-, -aiŋks\ *n, pl* **phalanx·es** \-ksə̇z\ *or* **pha·lan·ges** \fə'lanˌjēz, fā'-\ *see numbered senses* [L *phalang-*, *phalanx* line of battle, fr. Gk, log, line of battle, bone of the finger or toe — more at BALK] **1 a :** a body of heavily armed infantry in ancient Greece formed in close deep ranks and files with joined shields and long lances ⟨the Macedonian ~, formed by Philip, was first 8 ranks, later from 12 to 16 ranks, deep⟩ **b :** any of various compact orders of battle like the Greek phalanx (as the parallelogrammatic one of the ancient Gauls and Germans); *broadly* **:** a body of troops in close array **2** [NL, fr. Gk] *pl* **phalanges :** one of the digital bones of the hand or foot beyond the metacarpus or metatarsus of a vertebrate that in man are three to each finger and toe with the exception of the thumb and great toe which have but two each, in many other vertebrates vary slightly in numbers, and are greatly increased in some aquatic forms with paddle-shaped limbs **3** *pl usu* **phalanxes a :** a group or body in close formation **:** a massed arrangement of persons, animals, or things ⟨a ~ of umbrellas —Betty W. Powers⟩ **b :** an organized or closely united body of persons (as for aggressive or defensive action) ⟨police locked and barred all but one door, and formed a solid ~ in front of it —Green Peyton⟩ ⟨a solid ~ of orthodoxy against which the revolutionaries shatter themselves —Sheldon Cheney⟩ **4 :** chess pawns of one player placed side by side **5 :** a rarely used taxonomic category to which various ranks have been assigned **6** [trans. of F *phalange*] **:** a Fourierist community **:** PHALANSTERY

**²phalanx** \"\ *vt* -ED/-ING/-ES **:** to form into a phalanx ⟨back of him the graduating class was ~*ed* —J.T.Farrell⟩ ⟨whose homes are in the ~*ed* apartment buildings and hotels nearby —*Amer. Guide Series: N.Y. City*⟩

**phal·a·ris** \'falərə̇s\ *n, cap* [NL, fr. L, canary-grass, fr. *phalaros* having a white spot; akin to Gk *phalios* having a white spot — more at BALD] **:** a genus of American and European grasses with broad leaves and a dense head or spike of flowers — see CANARY GRASS 1, RIBBON GRASS

**phal·a·rope** \'faləˌrōp\ *n* -S [F, fr. NL *phalaropus*, fr. Gk *phalaris* coot (fr. *phalaros* having a white spot) + NL *-o-* + *-pus*] **:** a bird of the family Phalaropodidae — see NORTHERN PHALAROPE, RED PHALAROPE, WILSON'S PHALAROPE

**phal·a·ro·pod·i·dae** \ˌfalərō'pädəˌdē\ *n pl, cap* [NL, fr. *Phalaropod-*, *Phalaropus* type genus, fr. *phalaropus* phalarope] **:** a family of small shorebirds that resemble sandpipers but have lobate toes and are good swimmers, breed in the arctic, winter in the tropics, and often occur in large flocks far out at sea, and are distinguished by having the female perform the courtship and the dully colored male the incubation

**phal·era** \'falərə\ *n, pl* **phaler·ae** \-əˌrē, -ˌrī\ [L, fr. Gk *phalara*, pl.; akin to Gk *phalos* horn of a helmet and prob. to Skt *hvarate* he bends, *hruṇāti* he gets lost — more at FAIL] **:** a metal boss or disk (as of bronze or silver) worn in ancient times on the heads or breasts of horses or sometimes by men as signs of military rank; *also* **:** a cameo worn as an ornament

**phal·gun** \'pälˌgün, 'fä-\ *n, usu cap* [Skt *phālguna*] **:** PHAGUN

**phall-** *or* **phallo-** *comb form* [Gk *phallos* — more at BLOW] **:** penis ⟨*phall*algia⟩ ⟨*phallo*plasty⟩ ⟨*phallo*rrhagia⟩

**phal·la·ce·ae** \fə'lāsēˌē\ *n pl, cap* [NL, fr. *Phallus* type genus + *-aceae*] **:** a family of fungi (order Phallales) comprising the true stinkhorns and distinguished from Clathraceae by having the gleba external to the tubular receptacle — see PHALLUS — **phal·la·ceous** \-shəs\ *adj*

**phal·la·les** \fə'lā(ˌ)lēz\ *n pl, cap* [NL, fr. *Phallus* + *-ales*] **:** an order of fungi (subclass Homobasidiomycetes) comprising the stinkhorns and related forms whose hymenium is on an elongated or enlarged receptacle that is slimy and fetid at maturity — see CLATHRACEAE, PHALLACEAE

**phal·lic** \'falik, -lēk\ *adj* [Gk *phallikos*, fr. *phallos* phallus + *-ikos* -ic] **1 :** of or relating to phallicism ⟨~ cult⟩ ⟨~ fertility symbol⟩ **2 :** of, relating to, or being a phallus ⟨~ eroticism⟩ **3 :** resembling or symbolizing a phallus ⟨~ tree trunks⟩ **:** PHALLOID

**phal·li·cism** \-ləˌsizəm\ *n* -S [*phallic* + *-ism*] **:** the worship of or reverence for the generative principle in nature as symbolized esp. by the phallus

**phal·lism** \'faˌlizəm\ *n* -S [ISV *phall-* + *-ism*] **:** PHALLICISM

**phal·lo·base** \'faləˌbās\ *n* [*phall-* + *base*] **:** the proximal part of the phallic organ

**¹phal·loid** \'faˌlȯid\ *adj* [ISV *phall-* + *-oid*] **:** resembling a penis; *specif* **:** relating to or resembling fungi of the genus *Phallus* or the family Phallaceae

**²phalloid** \"\ *n* -S [NL *Phallus* + E *-oid*] **:** a fungus of the genus *Phallus* or the family Phallaceae

**phal·loi·dine** \fa'lȯidᵊn, 'faˌlȯiˌdīn\ *also* **phal·loi·din** \fa'lȯidᵊn\ *n* -S [NL *phalloides* (specific epithet of the death cup *Amanita phalloides*) (fr. *phall-* + *-oides* -oid) + E *-ine* or *-in*] **:** a very toxic crystalline peptide $C_{35}H_{46}N_8O_{10}S.H_2O$ obtained from the death cup mushroom

**phal·lo·mere** \'faləˌmi(ə)r\ *n* -S [*phall-* + *-mere*] **:** any of various lobes formed at the sides of the gonopore of many insects and commonly fusing to form the phallus

**phal·lo·some** \-ˌsōm\ *n* -S [*phall-* + *-some*] **:** a chitinized tube enclosing the penis of some mosquitoes and other insects

**phal·lo·steth·i·dae** \ˌfalō'stethəˌdē\ *n pl, cap* [NL, fr. *Phallostethus*, type genus (fr. *phall-* + Gk *stēthos* breast) + *-idae*] **:** a family of small freshwater and brackish-water fishes of southeastern Asia and the Philippines that are of very uncertain systematic position and are sometimes isolated in a suborder of Percomorphi and regarded as related to the Atherinidae or are made a separate order and held to have affinities chiefly with the Microcyprini

**phal·lus** \'faləs\ *n* [L, fr. Gk *phallos* penis, representation of the penis — more at BLOW] **1** *pl* **phal·li** \-aˌlī\ *or* **phalluses :** a symbol or representation of the male organ of generation — compare LINGAM, YONI **2** *pl* **phalli** *or* **phalluses** [NL, fr. Gk *phallos*] **a** (1) **:** a vertebrate intromittent organ **:** PENIS, CLITORIS (2) **:** an embryonic or primitive organ homologous with a penis or clitoris **b :** any of various structures of a male invertebrate that play a specific part in copulation; *esp* **:** a median intromittent organ of the ninth abdominal segment of a male insect **3** [NL, fr. Gk *phallos* penis] *cap* **:** a genus of fungi (family Phallaceae) with the pileus hanging free around the stem — see DICTYOPHORA, STINKHORN

**phal·lu·sia** \fə'l(y)üzh(ē)ə\ *n, cap* [NL, irreg. fr. Gk *phallos* + NL *-ia*] *in some classifications* **:** a genus of simple ascidians — see ASCIDIA

**pha·nar·i·ot** *or* **fa·nar·i·ot** \fə'na(a)rēət, -ēˌät\ *n* -S *usu cap* [NGk *phanariōtēs*, lit., inhabitant of the Fanar, fr. *Phanari* Fanar, chief Greek quarter in Constantinople under the Turks + Gk *-ōtēs* -ote] **:** one of the Greeks of Constantinople who became powerful in clerical and other offices under Turkish patronage

**phanatron** *var of* PHANOTRON

**-phane** \ˌfān\ *n comb form* -S [Gk *-phanēs* appearing, shining, fr. *phainein* to show — more at FANCY] **:** substance having a (specified) form, quality, or appearance ⟨cymo*phane*⟩ ⟨glauco*phane*⟩ ⟨hydro*phane*⟩

**phaner-** *or* **phanero-** *comb form* [Gk, fr. *phaneros*, fr. *phainein* to show] **:** visible **:** manifest **:** open ⟨*phanero*cryst⟩ ⟨*phanero*gam⟩

**phan·er·ite** \'fanəˌrīt\ *n* -S [ISV *phaner-* + *-ite*] **:** a rock having grains that are large enough to be seen with the unaided eye

**phan·er·it·ic** \ˌ⸗⸗'ridˌik\ *adj* **:** of, relating to, or characteristic of phanerite

**phan·er·o·car·pae** \ˌfanərō'kärˌpē\ [NL, fr. *phaner-* + Gk *karpos* fruit — more at HARVEST] *syn of* ACRASPEDA

**phan·er·o·ceph·a·la** \ˌ⸗⸗⸗'sefələ\ *n pl, cap* [NL, fr. *phaner-* + *-cephala*] *in some classifications* **:** a division of Polychaeta distinguished by the well-developed prostomium corresponding to Errantia together with many Sedentaria — **phan·er·o·ceph·a·lous** \ˌ⸗⸗⸗'sefələs\ *adj*

**phan·er·o·co·don·ic** \ˌ⸗⸗⸗kō'dänik\ *adj* [*phaner-* + Gk *kōdōn* bell + E *-ic*] **:** developing an umbrella and becoming detached — used of the sexual zooids of hydroids; compare ADELOCODONIC

**phan·er·o·cryst** \'⸗⸗⸗ˌkrist\ *n* -S [*phaner-* + *crystal*] **:** a crystal visible megascopically

**phan·er·o·crystalline** \ˌ⸗⸗⸗+\ *adj* [ISV *phaner-* + *crystalline*] **:** megascopically crystalline — compare CRYPTOCRYSTALLINE

**phan·er·o·gam** \'⸗⸗⸗ˌgam\ *n* -S [F *phanérogame*, fr. NL *Phanerogamia*] **:** a seed plant or flowering plant **:** SPERMATOPHYTE — compare CRYPTOGAM

**phan·er·o·gam·ia** \ˌ⸗⸗⸗'gamēə, -gām-\ *n, cap* [NL, fr. *phaner-* + *-gamia* (fr. Gk *-gamia* -gamy)] *in some esp former classifications* **:** a division of plants comprising all the seed plants — compare CRYPTOGAMIA — **phan·er·o·gam·i·an** \ˌ⸗⸗⸗'gamēən, -gām-\ *or* **phan·er·o·gam·ic** \-'gamik\ *or* **phan·er·og·a·mous** \ˌ⸗⸗'rägəməs\ *adj* — **phan·er·og·a·my** \ˌ⸗⸗'rägəmē\ *n* -ES

**phan·er·o·gen·ic** \ˌfanərō'jenik\ *also* **phan·er·o·genetic** \ˌ⸗⸗⸗+\ *adj* [*phanerogenic* fr. *phaner-* + *-genic*; *phanerogenetic* fr. *phaner-* + *genetic*] **:** of known origin — opposed to *cryptogenic*

**phan·er·o·glos·sa** \ˌ⸗⸗⸗'gläsə, -lȯsə\ *n pl, cap* [NL, fr. *phaner-* + *-glossa*] *in former classifications* **:** a division of Amphibia comprising frogs and toads with tongues and being equivalent to Lingusta and Costata of other classifications — **phan·er·o·glos·sal** \ˌ⸗⸗⸗'gläsəl, -lȯs-\ *adj* — **phan·er·o·glos·sate** \ˌ⸗⸗⸗+\ *adj or n*

**phan·er·o·mania** \ˌ⸗⸗⸗+\ *n* [NL, fr. *phaner-* + L *mania*] **:** a persistent or obsessive picking at some superficial body growth (as in habitual nail-biting)

**phan·er·o·phyte** \'⸗⸗⸗ˌfīt\ *n* -S [ISV *phaner-* + *-phyte*] **:** a perennial plant that bears its overwintering buds well above the surface of the ground — compare CHAMAEPHYTE, GEOPHYTE

**phan·er·os·co·py** \ˌfanə'räskəpē\ *n* -ES [*phaner-* + *-scopy*] **:** the formal analysis of appearances apart from the questions of to whom they appear and of their material content that discovers broad classes of appearances, describes their features, proves that a short list of classes is exhaustive, and enumerates the principal subdivisions of the categories

**phan·er·o·sis** \ˌfanə'rōsə̇s\ *n, pl* **phanero·ses** \-ōˌsēz\ [NL, fr. *phaner-* + *-osis*] **:** the attaining of visibility — used chiefly of intercellular lipoids that become visible fatty droplets as the cells degenerate

**phan·er·o·zo·ic** \ˌfanərō'zōik\ *adj* [*phaner-* + *-zoic*] **1 :** living unconcealed esp. in daylight — compare CRYPTOBIOTIC **2 :** PHANEROZOITIC **3** *of a geologic eon* **:** of or relating to the Paleozoic, Mesozoic, and Cenozoic eras taken together — compare CRYPTOZOIC 2

**phan·er·o·zo·ite** \ˌ⸗⸗⸗'zōˌīt\ *n* -S [*phaner-* + *-zoite* (as in *sporozoite*)] **:** an exoerythrocytic malaria parasite found late in the course of an infection

**phan·er·o·zo·it·ic** \ˌ⸗⸗⸗ˌzō'id·ik\ *adj* **:** of, relating to, or being a phanerozoite ⟨~ stage⟩

**phan·er·o·zo·nate** \ˌ⸗⸗⸗'zōˌnāt\ *adj* [NL *Phanerozonia* + E *-ate*] **:** of or relating to the Phanerozonia

**phan·er·o·zo·nia** \ˌ⸗⸗⸗'zōnēə\ *n pl, cap* [NL, fr. *phaner-* + Gk *zōnē* girdle + NL *-ia* — more at ZONE] **:** an order of starfishes distinguished by large marginal plates

**phano** \'fa(ˌ)nō\ *n* -S [alter. of *fanon*] **:** FANON

**phan·o·tron** *also* **phan·a·tron** \'fanəˌträn\ *n* -S [perh. fr. Gk *phano-* showing (fr. *phainein* to show) + E *-tron* — more at FANCY] **:** a low-pressure diode filled with mercury vapor or an inert gas and used as a rectifier for radio transmitters and industrial direct current power

**phan·si·gar** \'pän(t)səˌgär, 'fä-\ *n* -S [Hindi *phāsīgār*, fr. *phāsī* snare, noose + Per *-gār* doer, doing] **:** an East Indian robber and assassin **:** THUG

**phan·ta·si·ast** \fan'tāzēˌast, -ə̇st\ *n* -S *usu cap* [LGk *phantasiastēs*, fr. Gk *phantasia* appearance, image, imagination + *-astēs* -ast; fr. the belief that Christ's body was only a phantom — more at FANCY] **:** JULIANIST — **phan·ta·si·as·tic** \⸗ˌ⸗⸗'astik\ *adj, usu cap*

**phan·tasm** *or* **fan·tasm** \'fanˌtazəm\ *n* -S [ME *fantasme*, fr. OF, fr. L *phantasma*, fr. Gk, fr. *phantazein* to present to the mind — more at FANCY] **1 :** a product of phantasy: as **a :** delusive appearance **:** ILLUSION, DECEPTION ⟨a fleeting ~, born and gone, intangible as a flash of lightning —Heinrich Zimmer⟩ **b :** GHOST, SPECTER, SPIRIT ⟨~*s* of the dark⟩ **c :** a figment of the imagination, fancy, or disordered mind **:** an imaginative conception **:** FANTASY, DREAM, DELUSION ⟨twilight ~*s*, and deep noonday thought —P.B.Shelley⟩ ⟨husband who is "an utter coward" about the ~*s* of his own imagination —Scott Fitzgerald⟩ ⟨now first the cloud of ~*s* cleared away: he beheld his real life —George Meredith⟩ **2 :** a mental image or representation of a real object **:** a sensuous idea or impression — compare SPECIES 2b ⟨all of the sensible qualities are but ~*s* of the observer, not properties of the object —Douglas Bush⟩ **3 a** *obs* **:** one that counterfeits the real or true **b :** a deceptive or illusory appearance of a thing **:** SHADOW, ADUMBRATION ⟨follow ~*s* of truth⟩ ⟨grasping at every ~ of hope⟩ **4 :** an apparition of a living or dead person in a place where his body is known not to be **syn** see FANCY

**phan·tas·ma** \fan'tazmə\ *n, pl* **phantas·mas** \-məz\ *or* **phantas·ma·ta** \-mədˌə\ [L] **:** PHANTASM 1 ⟨the ice runs surrealistically riot in a ~ of frozen sculpture —Glen Jacobsen⟩

**phan·tas·ma·go·ria** \(ˌ)⸗ˌ⸗⸗mə'gōrēə, -gȯr-\ *also* **phan·tas·ma·go·ry** \⸗'⸗⸗ˌgōrē, -gȯr-, -ri\ *n, pl* **phantasmagorias** *also* **phantasmagories** [modif. of F *phantasmagorie* production of images appearing to be phantoms, fr. *phantasme* phantasm (fr. L *phantasma*) + *-agorie* (prob. fr. Gk *ageirein* to assemble, collect) — more at GREGARIOUS] **1 a** (1) **:** an optical effect by which figures on a screen appear to dwindle into the distance or to rush toward the observer with enormous increase of size (2) **:** any of various similar optical effects **b :** an apparatus for producing the effect of phantasmagoria consisting of a magic lantern arranged to be moved toward and from a screen and having an automatic device for keeping the correct focus **2 a :** a constantly shifting, complex succession of things seen or imagined (as in a dream or fever state) ⟨a simple view of the ~ of life —C.E.Norton⟩ ⟨supernatural visions which reveal past, present, and future under the guise of a ~ of symbolic persons and animals, divine and diabolical beings, celestial and infernal phenomena —Edmund Wilson⟩ **b :** a scene that constantly changes or fluctuates ⟨lowlands under the hills became an undulating ~ as mirages flickered endlessly —Farley Mowat⟩ ⟨streets were a nightmarish *phantasmagory* —Van Wyck Brooks⟩

**phan·tas·ma·gor·ic** \⸗ˌ⸗⸗'gȯrik, -gär-\ *also* **phan·tas·ma·gor·i·cal** \-rə̇kəl\ *adj* **:** of, relating to, or like a phantasmagoria ⟨the ~ armorial trophies which rattled as I strode —E.A. Poe⟩ ⟨a great concourse of ~ shadows —J.C.Powys⟩

**phan·tas·mal** \(')fan'tazməl\ *adj* **:** of, relating to, or like a phantasm **:** transitory as a phantasm **:** ILLUSIVE, SPECTRAL, UNREAL ⟨his fear of the last few hours looked thin and ~ in the presence of so much light —Walter Gilkyson⟩ ⟨coastline of frozen ~ peaks —Marguerite Young⟩ ⟨the moon's ~ fire —Walter de la Mare⟩ — **phan·tas·mal·i·ty** \ˌ⸗ˌ⸗'malədˌē, -ətē, -i\ *n* -ES — **phan·tas·mal·ly** \(')⸗'⸗məlē, -li\ *adv*

**phan·tas·mic** \(')⸗'⸗mik, -mēk\ *adj* **:** PHANTASMAL ⟨seemed, for all his bulk, ~ —D.C.Loughlin⟩ ⟨farewell, your lost ~ truth —John Erskine †1951⟩

**phantasy** *var of* FANTASY **syn** see FANCY

**¹phan·tom** *also* **fan·tom** \'fantəm, 'faan-\ *n* -S [ME *fantosme*, *fantome*, *fantom* fr. MF *fantosme*, fr. L *phantasma* — more at PHANTASM] **1** *obs* **:** mere appearance or seeming **:** ILLUSION **2 a :** something (as a specter or an optical illusion) that is apparent to the sight or other sense but has no actual or substantial existence **:** APPARITION, FIGMENT ⟨is not all that I see a lie — a deceitful ~ —George Borrow⟩ **b :** something elusive or visionary **:** WILL-O'-THE-WISP ⟨the glittering ~*s* of wealth and fashion, the whole pageantry of the metropolis, were dissolved by the suicide —M.D.Geismar⟩ **c :** an object of continual dread or abhorrence **:** BOGEY, BUGBEAR ⟨the ~ of a Holy War has been exorcised —A.L.Guérard⟩ ⟨the ~*s* of disease and want⟩ **3 :** one that is something in appearance but not in reality **:** a mere show **:** SHADOW ⟨only a ~ of a king⟩ ⟨maintain but the ~ of authority⟩ **4 :** a representation or shadowing forth of something abstract, ideal, or incorporeal ⟨she was a ~ of delight —William Wordsworth⟩ **5 a :** a manikin or a model of the body or one of its parts **b :** a body of material resembling a body part in mass, composition, and dimensions and used to measure absorption of radiations **6 :** PHANTOM CIRCUIT **7 :** GHOST 14 **8 :** a halftone or drawing having certain details shown as though transparent or translucent so as to indicate various esp. internal parts of a machine in their working position

**²phantom** \"\ *adj* [ME *fantom*, fr. *fantom*, n.] **1 :** being a phantom **:** of the nature of or suggesting a phantom ⟨headless blacksmiths, ~ black dogs, haunted houses —*Amer. Guide Series: Md.*⟩ ⟨a ~ ship⟩ **a :** ILLUSORY ⟨~ pain⟩ ⟨~ pregnancy⟩ ⟨amputee's illusion of a ~ organ —*Psychological Abstracts*⟩ ⟨conjuring up ~ dangers of feudal aristocracy —V.L.Parrington⟩ — compare PHANTOM LIMB **b :** operating or placed so as to seem or to be invisible **:** UNEMBODIED, ELUSIVE ⟨proved again that they are a ~ army —W.O.Douglas⟩ ⟨his ~ crew miles away on the ground —*Time*⟩ ⟨~ voices⟩ **c :** FICTITIOUS, DUMMY ⟨~ voters⟩ ⟨a ~ regime⟩ **2 :** of or relating to a phantom circuit ⟨~ wire⟩ **3 :** showing certain details as though transparent or translucent so as to indicate various esp. internal parts of a machine in their working position ⟨~ drawing⟩ ⟨~ halftone⟩ ⟨~ view⟩ — compare EXPLODED

**phantom circuit** *n* **:** the equivalent of an additional circuit or wire that in reality does not exist obtained by certain arrangements of real circuits (as in some telephone and multiplex telegraph systems)

**phantom crane fly** *n* **:** a fly of the family Ptychopteridae

**phantom freight** *n* **:** a transportation charge included in the delivered price of a commodity (as an automobile) that is in excess of the charge for service actually performed

**phan·tom·ist** \-məst\ *n* -S *usu cap* [*phantom* + *-ist*] **:** JULIANIST

**phantom larva** *n* **:** the colorless transparent aquatic larva of any of the small flies of the family Chaoboridae

**phantomlike** \'⸗⸗ˌ⸗\ *adv (or adj)* **:** like a phantom (as in appearance or elusiveness) ⟨swans which glided ~ across the pond —*Current History*⟩ ⟨escaped ~ from jail —*Springfield (Mass.) Daily News*⟩

**phantom limb** *n* **:** an often painful sensation of the presence of a limb that has been amputated

**phantom orchid** *or* **phantom orchis** *n* **:** a saprophytic white orchid (*Cephalanthera austinae*) of the western U.S.

**phantom tumor** *n* **:** a swelling (as of the abdomen) suggesting a tumor and occurring in hysterical persons

**phan·to·scope** \'fantəˌskōp\ *n* [Gk *phantos* visible (fr. *phainein* to show) + E *-scope* — more at FANCY] **:** a kaleidoscope into which small objects may be introduced to vary the design

**-pha·ny** \fənē, -ni\ *n comb form* -ES [LGk *-phania*, *-phaneia*, fr. Gk *phainein* to show — more at FANCY] **:** appearance **:** manifestation ⟨pneumato*phany*⟩ ⟨Satano*phany*⟩

**phar** *abbr* **1** pharmaceutical; pharmacist; pharmacy **2** pharmacopeia

**phar·aoh** \'fe(ˌ)rō, 'fa(a)l, 'fā| *sometimes* |ˌrēˌō\ *n* -S *often cap* [LL *Pharaon-*, *Pharao*, fr. Gk *Pharaō*, fr. Heb *par'ōh*, fr. Egypt *pr-'*] **1 a :** a ruler of ancient Egypt **b :** TYRANT ⟨they tell me he's a regular *Pharaoh* —John Cheever⟩ ⟨that tough old *Pharaoh* of a captain —*Theatre Arts*⟩ **2** [trans. of F *pharaon* or It *faraone*] *archaic* : FARO

**pharaoh ant** *or* **pharaoh's ant** *n, often cap P* : a little red ant (*Monomorium pharaonis*) that is a common household pest

**pharaoh's chicken** *or* **pharaoh's hen** *n, usu cap P* : EGYPTIAN VULTURE

**pharaoh's fig** *n, usu cap P* : SYCAMORE 1

**pharaoh's mouse** *or* **pharaoh's rat** *n, usu cap P* : the common ichneumon of Egypt and adjacent regions

**pharaoh's serpent** *or* **pharaoh's serpents** *or* **pharaoh's serpents' eggs** *n, usu cap P* : a firework consisting of pelleted mercury thiocyanate that on burning expands greatly to yield a porous serpentine ash

**phar·a·on·ic** \ˌferāˈänik, ˈfa(a)r-, ˈfār-, -rēˈ-\ *adj, usu cap* [F *pharaonique*, fr. *pharaon* pharaoh, fr. LL *Pharaon-, Pharao*] : of, relating to, or characteristic of a pharaoh or the pharaohs

**phare** \ˈfa(a)(ə)r, ˈfe(ə)r\ *n* -s [F, fr. L *pharus*, fr. Gk *pharos* — more at PHAROS] : PHAROS ⟨afternoons I walk to the ~ —Archibald MacLeish⟩ ⟨a lightship, or some ~ —William Beebe⟩

**pha·re·o·dus** \fəˈrēədəs\ *n, cap* [NL, prob. fr. Gk *pharepharos* cloth, mantle + NL *-odus* — more at BRAT] : a genus of fossil fishes (family Osteoglossidae) widely distributed in Eocene formations

[1]**phar·e·trone** \ˈfarəˌtrōn\ *adj* [NL *Pharetrones*] : of or relating to the Pharetrones

[2]**pharetrone** \"\ *n* -s : a sponge of the group Pharetrones

**phar·e·tro·nes** \ˌ==ˈtrō(ˌ)nēz\ *n pl, cap* [NL, fr. L *pharetra* quiver, fr. Gk, fr. *pherein* to bear + *-tra*, suffix denoting instrument — more at BEAR] : a group of sponges (class Calcispongiae) that are thick-walled and have the spicules united in a rigid network — **phar·e·tro·nid** \ˌ==ˈ=nəd\ *adj*

[1]**phar·i·an** \ˈfa(a)rēən\ *adj, usu cap* [L *pharius* (fr. Gk *pharios*, fr. *Pharos* Egyptian island) + E *-an*] **1** : of or relating to the peninsula or ancient island of Pharos **2** *archaic* : EGYPTIAN 1

[2]**pharian** \"\ *n* -s *cap, archaic* : EGYPTIAN 1

**phar·i·sa·ic** \ˌfarəˈsāik, -āēk *also* ˌfer-\ *adj* [LL *pharisaicus*, fr. LGk *pharisaikos*, fr. Gk *pharisaios* Pharisee + *-ikos* -ic] **1** *usu cap* : of or relating to the Pharisees **2** *sometimes cap* : PHARISAICAL ⟨the ~ voice of a society wholly absorbed in barricading itself against the unpleasant —Edith Wharton⟩

**phar·i·sa·i·cal** \-āəkəl, -ēk-\ *adj, sometimes cap* [LL *pharisaicus* + E *-al*] : resembling the Pharisees esp. in strictness of doctrine and in rigid observance of forms and ceremonies : making an outward show of piety and morality but lacking the inward spirit : censorious of others' morals or practices : FORMAL, SANCTIMONIOUS, SELF-RIGHTEOUS, HYPOCRITICAL ⟨censure of any sort is apt to sound ~, I suppose —P.A.Hope-Wallace⟩ ⟨in this process of reeducation we should be ~ if we did not include ourselves —Llewellyn Woodward⟩ — **phar·i·sa·i·cal·ly** \-ək(ə)lē, -ēk-, -li\ *adv* — **phar·i·sa·i·cal·ness** \-əkəlnəs, -ēk-\ *n* -ES

**phar·i·sa·ism** \ˈ==ˌsāˌizəm\ *n* -s [NL *pharisaismus*, fr. Gk *pharisaios* Pharisee + L *-ismus* -ism] **1** *usu cap* : the doctrines or practices of the Pharisees ⟨the path of withdrawal, separation, and dedication, which is the path of *Pharasaism* —Maurice Samuel⟩ **2** *often cap* : pharisaical character, spirit, or attitude : SELF-RIGHTEOUSNESS, SANCTIMONIOUSNESS, HYPOCRISY ⟨~, stupidity, and despotism reign not in merchants' houses and prisons alone —J.T.Farrell⟩

**phar·i·se·an** \ˌ==ˈsēən\ *adj, usu cap* [LL *pharisaeus* Pharisee + E *-an*] : PHARISAIC 1

**phar·i·see** \ˈfarəˌsē *also* ˈfer- *or* -ˌsē *or* -si\ *n* -s [ME *pharise*, fr. OE *farise*, fr. LL *pharisaeus*, fr. Gk *pharisaios*, fr. Aram *pĕrīshayyā*, pl. of *pĕrīsh*, lit., separated; akin to Heb *pārūsh* separated, distinct] **1** *usu cap* : a member of a school or party among the ancient Jews who were noted for strict and formal observance of rites and ceremonies of the written law and for insistence on the validity of the traditions of the elders, who differed from the Sadducees in traditionalism and in their teachings concerning the immortality of the soul, the resurrection of the body, future retribution, and a coming Messiah, and whose interpretation provided the standard of observance and belief for the great majority of Jews from the 1st century A.D. **2** *often cap* : a pharisaical person

**phar·i·see·ism** \ˈ==(ˌ)=ˌizəm\ *n* -s *usu cap* [*pharisee* + *-ism*] : PHARISAISM

**phar·ma·cal** \ˈfärməkəl, ˈfam-, -mēk-\ *adj* [Gk *pharmakon* drug + E *-al* — more at PHARMACY] : PHARMACEUTICAL

**phar·ma·ceu·tic** \ˌ=məˈsüd·ik, -ütˌ, ēk\ *adj or n* [LL *pharmaceuticus*, fr. Gk *pharmakeutikos*, fr. (assumed) *pharmakeutos* (verbal of *pharmakeuein* to administer drugs, fr. *pharmakon* drug) + *-ikos* -ic] : PHARMACEUTICAL

[1]**phar·ma·ceu·ti·cal** \ˌəkəl, ēk-\ *adj* [LL *pharmaceuticus* + E *-al*] : of or relating to pharmacy or pharmacists — **phar·ma·ceu·ti·cal·ly** \-ək(ə)lē, -ēk-, -li\ *adv*

[2]**pharmaceutical** \"\ *n* -s : a pharmaceutical preparation : medicinal drug

**pharmaceutical chemist** *n* **1** *Brit* : DRUGGIST **2** : one engaged in research in medicinal chemicals or in the production thereof

**phar·ma·ceu·tics** \ˌ==ˈsüd·iks, -ütiks, -ēks\ *n pl but sing in constr* [*pharmaceutic* + *-s*] : the science of preparing, using, or dispensing medicines : PHARMACY

**phar·ma·ceu·tist** \ˌ==ˈsüd·əst, -ütə-\ *n* -s [*pharmaceutic* + *-ist*] : PHARMACIST

**pharmacies** *pl of* PHARMACY

**phar·ma·cist** \ˈfärməsəst, ˈfam-\ *n* -s [*pharmacy* + *-ist*] : one skilled in pharmacy : one engaged in the practice of pharmacy — compare APOTHECARY, DRUGGIST

**phar·ma·co-** *in pronunciations below*, ˈ====ˈfärmə(ˌ)kō *or* ˈfamə(ˌ)kō *or* -ˌkə\ *comb form* [Gk *pharmako-*, fr. *pharmakon* — more at PHARMACY] : medicine : drug ⟨*pharmaco*mania⟩ ⟨*pharmaco*phobia⟩ ⟨*pharmaco*therapy⟩

**phar·ma·co·dynamic** \ˌ====+\ *adj* [*pharmacodynamics*] : of, relating to, or used in pharmacodynamics ⟨responses of the autonomic nervous system to various ~ substances —*Psychosomatic Medicine*⟩ — **phar·ma·co·dynamically** \"+\ *adv*

**phar·ma·co·dynamics** \"+\ *n pl but sing in constr* [*pharmaco-* + Gk *dynamis* power (fr. *dynasthai* to be able) + E *-ics*] : a branch of pharmacology dealing with the reactions between drugs and living structures; *specif* : the experimental study of the action and fate of drugs in the animal organism ⟨the ~ of magnesium sulfate⟩ ⟨the ~ of streptomycin in man⟩

**phar·ma·cog·no·sist** \ˌfärməˈkägnəsəst, ˌfam-\ *n* -s [*pharmacognosy* + *-ist*] : a specialist in pharmacognosy

**phar·ma·cog·nos·tic** \ˌ==(ˌ)kägˈnästik, -tēk\ *adj* [ISV *pharmaco-* + *-gnostic*] : of or relating to pharmacognosy

**phar·ma·cog·no·sy** \ˌ==ˈkägnəsē, -si\ *also* **phar·ma·cog·no·sia** \-ˌkägˈnōzh(ē)ə\ *n, pl* **pharmacognosies** *also* **pharmacognosias** [*pharmacognosy*, ISV *pharmaco-* + *-gnosy*; *pharmacognosia*, NL, fr. *pharmaco-* + *-gnosia*] : a science dealing with the composition, production, use, and history of drugs of plant and animal origin — compare PHARMACOLOGY

**phar·mac·o·lite** \färˈmakəˌlīt, faˈm-; ˈ=məkə-\ *n* -s [G *pharmakolith*, fr. *pharmako-* pharmaco- + *-lith* -lite] : a monoclinic mineral $CaH(AsO_4).2H_2O$ that is a hydrous acid calcium arsenate occurring in silky fibers of a white or grayish color (hardness 2–2.5, sp. gr. 2.64–2.73)

**phar·ma·co·logical** \ˌ=== *at* PHARMACO- +\ *or* **phar·ma·co·logic** \"+\ *adj* : of, relating to, or determined by pharmacology ⟨~ action⟩ ⟨~ methods⟩ — **phar·ma·co·logically** \"+\ *adv*

**phar·ma·col·o·gist** \ˌfärməˈkäləjəst, ˌfam-\ *n* -s : a specialist in pharmacology

**phar·ma·col·o·gy** \-jē, -ji\ *also* **phar·ma·co·logia** \ˌ=== *at* PHARMACO- + ˈlōj(ē)ə\ *n, pl* **pharmacologies** *also* **pharmacologias** [*pharmacology* fr. *pharmaco-* + *-logy*; *pharmacologia* NL, fr. *pharmaco-* + *-logia*] **1** : the science of drugs including materia medica, toxicology, and therapeutics; *specif* : PHARMACODYNAMICS **2** : the materials of the science of pharmacology : the properties and reactions of drugs esp. with relation to their therapeutic value

**phar·ma·con** \ˈfärməˌkän, ˈfam-\ *n* -s [NL, fr. Gk — more at PHARMACY] : MEDICINE, DRUG, POISON

**pharmaco-oryctology** \ˌ=== *at* PHARMACO- + \ *n* [*pharmaco-* + *oryctology*] : the science of mineral drugs

**phar·ma·co·pe·dia** \ˌfärməkəˈpēdēə, ˌfam-\ *n* -s [NL, fr. *pharmaco-* + Gk *paideia* education — more at ENCYCLOPEDIA] : information concerning drugs and medicinal preparations

**phar·ma·co·pe·dic** \ˌ===ˈpēdik, -dēk\ *adj* : of or relating to pharmacopedia or to pharmacopedics

**phar·ma·co·pe·dics** \ˌ===ˈdiks, -dēks\ *n pl but sing in constr* [NL *pharmacopedia* + E *-ics*] : the scientific study of drugs and medicinal preparations

**phar·ma·co·poe·ia** *also* **phar·ma·co·peia** \-ˈpē(y)ə\ *n* -s [NL, fr. LGk *pharmakopoiia* preparation of drugs, fr. Gk *pharmakopoios* preparing drugs (fr. *pharmako-* pharmaco- + *-poios* making, fr. *poiein* to make) + *-ia* -y — more at POET] **1** : a book containing a selected list of drugs, chemicals, and medicinal preparations with descriptions of them, tests for their identity, purity, and strength, and formulas for making the preparations; *esp* : one issued by official authority and recognized as a standard **2** : a collection or stock of drugs

**phar·ma·co·poe·ial** \ˌ===ˈpē(y)əl\ *adj* : of or relating to a pharmacopoeia : according to the pharmacopoeia

**phar·ma·co·poe·ist** \ˌ===ˈpēəst\ *n* -s : a compiler of a pharmacopoeia

**phar·ma·cop·o·list** \ˌfärməˈkäpələst, ˌfam-\ *n* -s [L *pharmacopola* seller of drugs (fr. Gk *pharmakopōlēs*, fr. *pharmako-* pharmaco- + *-pōlēs* seller, fr. *pōlein* to sell) + E *-ist* — more at MONOPOLY] *archaic* : one who sells drugs : APOTHECARY

**phar·ma·co·siderite** \ˌ=== *at* PHARMACO- +\ *n* [G *pharmakosiderit*, fr. *pharmako-* pharmaco- + *siderit* siderite] : a mineral $Fe_3(AsO_4)_2(OH)_3.5H_2O$ consisting of a hydrous basic iron arsenate commonly occurring in green or yellowish green cubic crystals (hardness 2.5, sp. gr. 2.9–3)

**phar·ma·co·therapeutic** \"+\ *or* **phar·ma·co·therapeutical** \"+\ *adj* [*pharmaco-* + *therapeutic*] : relating to the use or value of drugs in the treatment of disease

**phar·ma·co·therapeutics** \"+\ *n pl but sing or pl in constr* [*pharmaco-* + *therapeutics*] : the therapeutic aspect of pharmacology

**phar·ma·co·therapy** \"+\ *n* [ISV *pharmaco-* + *therapy*] : the treatment of disease with drugs

**phar·ma·cy** \ˈfärməsē, ˈfam-, -si\ *n* -ES [ME *fermacie*, fr. MF *farmacie*, fr. LL *pharmacia*, fr. Gk *pharmakeia*, fr. *pharmakon* drug, medicine, poison, magic potion, charm; akin to Lith *burti* to practice divination or magic] **1** : the administering of drugs : treatment by drugs **2** : the art or practice of preparing, preserving, compounding, and dispensing drugs, of discovering new drugs through research, and of synthesizing organic compounds of therapeutic value **3** : a place where medicines are compounded or dispensed ⟨a hospital ~⟩; *broadly* : DRUGSTORE 1 — compare DISPENSARY **4** : PHARMACOPOEIA 2 ⟨never traveled without a complete family ~ —Edith Wharton⟩

**phar·ma·kos** \ˈfärməˌkäs\ *n, pl* **pharma·koi** \-ˌkȯi\ [Gk, prob. irreg. fr. *pharmakon* medicine, charm + *-ikos* -ic] : a person often already condemned to death sacrificed in ancient Greece as a means of purification or atonement for a city or community

**phar·mic** \ˈfärmik, ˈfam-, -mēk\ *adj* [*pharmacy* + *-ic*] : relating to drugs or pharmacy

**pharo fig** \ˈfa(a)(ˌ)rō, ˈfe, fā|-\ *n, usu cap P* [alter. of *pharaoh's fig*] : SYCAMORE 1

**phar·o·mach·rus** \ˌfarəˈmakrəs\ *n, cap* [NL, fr. Gk *pharos* cloth, mantle + *makros* long — more at BRAT, MEAGER] : a genus of trogons consisting of the quetzal and related birds

**pha·ros** \ˈfaˌräs, ˈfa(a)r-\ *n* -ES [Gk, fr. *Pharos*, island in the bay of Alexandria, Egypt, famous for its lighthouse] **1** : a lighthouse or beacon to guide seamen **2 a** : a conspicuous light; *specif* : a ship's lantern **b** : CANDELABRUM

**pharyng-** *or* **pharyngo-** *comb form* [Gk, fr. *pharyng-, pharynx*] **1** : pharynx ⟨*pharyng*algia⟩ ⟨*pharyng*itis⟩ **2** : pharyngeal and ⟨*pharyngo*nasal⟩

**pha·ryn·gal** \fəˈriŋgəl\ *adj or n* [NL *pharyng-, pharynx* + E *-al*] : PHARYNGEAL

[1]**pha·ryn·ge·al** \fəˈrinj(ē)əl, ˌfarənˈjēəl\ *adj* [NL *pharyngeus* pharyngeal (fr. *pharyng-, pharynx* pharynx) + E *-al*] **1** : relating to or found in the region of the pharynx **2** *of a sound* : formed with the base of the tongue near the back of the pharynx and with the pharynx walls strongly constricted

[2]**pharyngeal** \"\ *n* -s **1** : a pharyngeal part (as a bone) **2** : a pharyngeal sound

**pharyngeal aponeurosis** *n* : the middle or fibrous coat of the walls of the pharynx

**pharyngeal arch** *n* : BRANCHIAL ARCH

**pharyngeal basket** *n* : a circle of trichites that reinforces and stiffens the gullet of various predaceous ciliates

**pharyngeal bone** *n* : one of the bones of the pharynx of a fish — compare HYPOPHARYNGEAL, PHARYNGOBRANCHIAL

**pharyngeal bursa** *n* : a crypt in the pharyngeal tonsil thought to represent the communication that exists during fetal life between the pharynx and the hypophysis

**pharyngeal cleft** *or* **pharyngeal slit** *n* : VISCERAL CLEFT

**pharyngeal gland** *n* : a gland in the pharynx of an insect; *esp* : one of those that produce royal jelly in the honeybee

**pha·ryn·gal·iza·tion** \fəˌrinj(ē)ələˈzāshən, ˌfarənˌjēə-, -ˌlīˈz-\ *also* **pha·ryn·gal·iza·tion** \fəˌriŋgələˈzāshən, -ˌlīˈz-\ *n* -s : the action of pharyngealizing or the state of being pharyngealized

**pha·ryn·ge·al·ize** \fəˈrinj(ē)əˌlīz, ˌfarənˈjēə-\ *also* **pha·ryn·gal·ize** \fəˈriŋgəˌlīz\ *vb* -ED/-ING/-S [[1]*pharyngeal, pharyngal* + *-ize*] *vt* : to produce (a sound) by strong constriction of the pharynx ~ *vi* : to acquire or to be regularly accompanied by strong constriction of the pharynx

**pharyngeal membrane** *n* : STOMODAEUM

**pharyngeal plexus** *n* **1** : a plexus formed by branches of the glossopharyngeal, vagus, and sympathetic nerves supplying the muscles and mucous membrane of the pharynx and adjoining parts **2** : either of a pair of small venous plexuses at the side of and behind the pharynx

**pharyngeal pouch** *n* : any of a series of outpocketings of ectoderm on either side of the pharynx that meet the corresponding visceral furrows and give rise to the visceral clefts of the vertebrate embryo

**pharyngeal tonsil** *n* : a mass of lymphoid tissue at the back of the pharynx between the eustachian tubes that is usu. best developed in young children, is commonly atrophied in the adult, and is markedly subject to hypertrophy and adenoid formation esp. in children

**pharyngeal tooth** *n* : one of the teeth developed on the pharyngeal bones and esp. on the hypopharyngeals in many fishes

**pharynges** *pl of* PHARYNX

**phar·yn·gis·mus** \ˌfarənˈjizməs\ *n, pl* **pharyngis·mi** \-ˌmī\ [NL, fr. *pharyng-* + L *-ismus* -ism] : spasm of the pharynx

**phar·yn·gi·tis** \ˌfarənˈjīd·əs, -ītəs *also* ˌfer-\ *n, pl* **pharyn·git·i·des** \-ˈjid·əˌdēz, -itə-\ [NL, fr. *pharyng-* + *-itis*] : inflammation of the pharynx

**pha·ryn·gob·del·lae** \fəˌriŋˌgäbˈde(ˌ)lē\ [NL, fr. *pharyng-* + *-bdellae* (fr. Gk *bdella* leech)] *syn of* PHARYNGOBDELLIDA

**pha·ryn·go·bdel·li·da** \-ˈdeləd·ə\ *n pl, cap* [NL, fr. *pharyng-* + *bdell-* + *-ida*] : an order or other division of Hirudinea sometimes regarded as a subdivision of Gnathobdellida and comprising leeches lacking both proboscis and jaws

[1]**pha·ryn·go·branchial** \fəˈriŋ(ˌ)gō+\ *adj* [NL, fr. *pharyng-* + *-branchii* (fr. L *branchia* gill) — more at BRANCHIA] : of or relating to the pharynx and the gills; *specif* : of, relating to, or constituting the dorsal bony elements in the branchial arches of fishes that in teleosts form four pairs two or more of which may be provided with teeth opposed to those of the hypopharyngeals

[2]**pharyngobranchial** \"\ *n* -s : a pharyngobranchial element; *esp* : one of the pharyngobranchial bones of a teleost fish — called also *superior pharyngeal, upper pharyngeal*

**pha·ryn·go·branchii** \ˌ=ˈ=(ˌ)=+\ [NL, fr. *pharyng-* + *branchia*] *syn of* LEPTOCARDII

**pha·ryn·go·glos·sus** \=ˌ=(ˌ)=ˈgläsəs, -lȯs-\ *n, pl* **pharyngo·glos·si** \-ˌsī\ [NL, fr. *pharyng-* + *-glossus* (fr. Gk *glōssa* tongue) — more at GLOSS] : a part of the superior constrictor muscle of the pharynx inserting in the base of the tongue

[1]**pha·ryn·gog·nath** \fəˈriŋgəgˌnath\ *adj* [NL *Pharyngognathi*] : of or relating to the Pharyngognathi

[2]**pharyngognath** \"\ *n* -s : a fish of the order Pharyngognathi

**phar·yn·gog·na·thi** \ˌfarənˈgägnəˌthī\ *n pl, cap* [NL, fr. *pharyng-* + *-gnathi* (fr. Gk *gnathos* jaw) — more at -GNATHOUS] *in some classifications* : an order or other division of teleost fishes comprising forms (as scaroid and labroid fishes and formerly cichlid and embiotocid fishes) in which the lower pharyngeal bones are united and which are now usu. placed in Percoidea — **phar·yn·gog·na·thous** \ˌ==ˈ=nəthəs\ *adj*

**pha·ryn·go·log·i·cal** \fəˌriŋgəˈläjəkəl\ *adj* : of or relating to pharyngology

**phar·yn·gol·o·gy** \ˌfarənˈgäləjē, -ji *also* ˌfer-\ *n* -ES [*pharyng-* + *-logy*] : a branch of medical science treating of the pharynx and its diseases

**pha·ryn·go·palatine arch** \fəˈriŋ(ˌ)gō + -\ *n* [NL *pharyngopalatinus*] : either of the posterior pillars of the fauces; *also* : the arch formed by both

**pha·ryn·go·pal·a·ti·nus** \fəˌriŋgōˌpaləˈtīnəs\ *n, pl* **pharyngopalati·ni** \-ˌīˌnī\ [NL, fr. *pharyng-* + *palatinus* palatine] : one of the longitudinal muscles of the pharynx arising from the soft palate and inserting into the thyroid cartilage

**pha·ryn·go·scope** \fəˈriŋgəˌskōp\ *n* [F, fr. *pharyng-* + *-scope*] : an instrument for inspecting the pharynx

**phar·ynx** \ˈfariŋ(k)s, -rēŋ- *also* ˈfer-, *substand* ˈfärniks *or* ˈfän- *or* -nēks\ *n, pl* **pha·ryn·ges** \fəˈrin(ˌ)jēz\ *also* **pharynxes** [NL *pharyng-, pharynx*, fr. Gk, throat, pharynx; akin to ON *barki* throat, windpipe, L *frumen* larynx, throat, Gk *pharanx* gully, chasm, L *forare* to bore — more at BORE] **1 a** : the part of the alimentary canal between the cavity of the mouth and the esophagus that is in man a conical musculomembranous tube about four and a half inches long, continuous above with the mouth and nasal passages, communicating through the eustachian tubes with the ears, and extending downward past the opening into the larynx to the lower border of the cricoid cartilage where it is continuous with the esophagus **b** : the corresponding part of the alimentary canal in which the gills of water-breathing vertebrates are lodged **2** : a differentiated part of the alimentary canal in many invertebrates that is commonly thickened and muscular or in some worms eversible and toothed or adapted as a suctorial organ

**phas·al** \ˈfāzəl\ *adj* [[2]*phase* + *-al*] : PHASIC

**phas·cog·a·le** \faˈskägə(ˌ)lē\ *n, cap* [NL, irreg. fr. Gk *phaskōlos* pouch + *galē* weasel — more at GALEA] : a genus of small ratlike chiefly arboreal polyprotodont marsupials comprising the broad-footed pouched mice of Australia

**phas·co·larc·tos** \ˌfaskōˈlärktəs\ *n, cap* [NL, fr. Gk *phaskōlos* pouch + *arktos* bear — more at ARCTIC] : a genus comprising the koala and formerly regarded as the type of a distinct family but now usu. referred to the Phalangeridae

**phas·co·lom·i·dae** \ˌfaskəˈlämәˌdē\ *n pl, cap* [NL, fr. *Phascolomis*, type genus + *-idae*] : a family of stockily built partially fossorial Australian marsupials that comprise the wombats and related extinct forms and have strong five-toed forefeet with digging claws and a very short tail

**phas·co·lo·mis** \-ˈlōməs\ *n, cap* [NL, irreg. fr. Gk *phaskōlos* pouch + NL *-mys*] : a genus (the type of the family Phascolomidae) comprising the common Australian wombats

**phas·co·lo·my·i·dae** \ˌfaskələˈmīəˌdē\ [NL, fr. *Phascolomys* + *-idae*] *syn of* PHASCOLOMIDAE

**phas·co·lo·mys** \ˌ==ˈlōməs\ [NL, fr. Gk *phaskōlos* pouch + NL *-mys*] *syn of* PHASCOLOMIS

**phas·col·o·nus** \faˈskälənəs\ *n, cap* [NL, fr. Gk *phaskōlos* + *onos* ass — more at ASS] : a genus of Pleistocene Australian diprotodont marsupials related to the wombats and as large as tapirs

**phas·co·lo·so·ma** \faˌskäləˈsōmə\ *n, cap* [NL, fr. Gk *phaskōlos* + NL *-soma*] : a cosmopolitan genus of sipunculid worms

**phas·cum** \ˈfaskəm\ *n, cap* [NL, fr. Gk *phaskon* tuft of moss] : a small genus of terrestrial cleistocarpous mosses having costate leaves covering subglobose or ovate-oblong capsules and included in the Tortulaceae or made type of a separate family

[1]**phase** \ˈfāz\ *n* -s *usu cap* [LL, fr. Gk *phasech, phasek*, fr. Heb *pesaḥ* — more at PASCH] : PASSOVER — so translated in the Douay Version of the Bible

[2]**phase** \"\ *n* -s [NL *phasis*, fr. Gk, appearance of a star, phase of the moon, fr. *phainein* to show — more at FANCY] **1** *astron* : a particular appearance or state in a regularly recurring cycle of changes with respect to quantity of illumination or form of illuminated disk (as of a planet, the moon) **2 a** : a stage or interval in a development or cycle : a subdivision or an activity or operation on the basis of time, place, or accomplishment ⟨the assembly ~ of production —*advt*⟩ ⟨the way children develop and the different ~*s* they go through —Dorothy Barclay⟩ ⟨the final ~ of a war⟩ ⟨addition of a left-turn ~ to the . . . intersection traffic light —*Amarillo (Texas) Sunday News-Globe*⟩ **b** : an aspect or part (as of a situation or activity) being subjected to consideration ⟨the moral ~ of the problem —John Dewey⟩ ⟨engaged in several ~*s* of transportation in the course of his career —*Current Biog.*⟩ ⟨monographs which take up special ~*s* of life within the localities —C.L.Jones⟩ **3** : the point or stage in a period in uniform circular motion, simple harmonic motion, or the periodic changes of any magnitude varying according to a simple harmonic law (as sound vibrations, alternating currents, or electric oscillations) to which the rotation, oscillation, or variation has advanced considered in its relation to a standard position or assumed instant of starting and expressed in angular measure with one cycle or period being 360 degrees **4 a** : a homogeneous, physically distinct, and mechanically separable portion of matter that is present in a nonhomogeneous physical-chemical system and that may be either a single compound or a mixture — compare STATE 2a ⟨water exists in the solid ~ as ice, in the liquid as water, and in the gaseous as water vapor or steam⟩ **b** : a part of a soil unit or type varying slightly from the normal in the characteristics used in its classification **5** : an individual or subgroup distinguishably different in appearance or behavior from the norm of the group to which it belongs ⟨the gregaria ~ of a grasshopper⟩; *also* : the distinguishing peculiarity ⟨the silver ~ of the red fox⟩ ⟨an avirulent ~ of *Brucella abortus*⟩ — compare COLOR PHASE **6** : a unit of classification in the Midwestern system for American archaeology constituting a group of aspects having in common a significant number of those features determinative of type — see PATTERN; compare COMPONENT, FOCUS

**syn** ASPECT, SIDE, FACET, ANGLE: PHASE may apply to a manifestation of change or to a stage in growth or development ⟨the *phases* of the moon⟩ ⟨the red fox shows various color *phases*⟩ ⟨another war, he explained recently, would be likely to start with an opening *phase* of unparalleled intensity —A.P. Ryan⟩ ⟨felt that one *phase* of his poetic development was completed —Douglas Cleverdon⟩ ASPECT may also suggest an appearance showing a change or stage, sometimes a minor or superficial one; it is frequently used to indicate changes in the observer's point of view or specific compartmenting of his notions ⟨the lower part of the basin of the Tweed takes on a kindly *aspect* of ploughed land, grass fields —L.D.Stamp⟩ ⟨from a certain *aspect* it is acceptable for the artist to ignore his public —Huntington Hartford⟩ ⟨only the military side of European defense will be considered, leaving the economic *aspects* for a later article —S.B.Fay⟩ SIDE in this sense may be interchangeable with PHASE and ASPECT but is likely to suggest more forcefully the existence of an opposed or tangential point of view ⟨I have shown you only one *side*, or rather one phase, of her —Edith Wharton⟩ ⟨asked to be allowed to tell his own *side* of the story⟩ ⟨the history as a whole is deficient on the economic *side* —Allen Johnson⟩ FACET implies a multiplicity of other faces or sides comparable to the one singled out for attention ⟨the *facets* of a cut diamond⟩ ⟨his talk revealed every *facet* of his glittering, bizarre personality, his wit, his scholarship, his quick, penetrating intellect, his delight in the use of decorative, high-sounding words, his love of the ornate and picturesque —Alvin Redman⟩ ⟨conferences of the chief departmental officers of the railways are regularly held, including accounts, advertising, engineering, traffic, stores — in fact every conceivable *facet* of railway operation —O.S.Nock⟩ ANGLE may suggest concentration on one restricted specific viewpoint ⟨much safer from the technical *angle*, but terrible for the actors —Denis Johnston⟩ ⟨views these developments from a fresh *angle* —Dumas Malone⟩

— **in phase** *adv* **1** : in or of the same phase : of magnitudes whose maximum values are simultaneous ⟨this voltage must be *in phase* with the primary antenna voltage —*Proceedings of the Institute of Radio Engineers*⟩ **2** : in a synchronized or correlated manner ⟨sure that at least one propeller was moving *in* and out of *phase* —E.K.Gann⟩ — **out of phase** *adv* **1** : in or of different phases : of magnitudes whose maximum values are not simultaneous **2** : in an unsynchronized manner : not in step-by-step correspondence : not in correlation ⟨windshield wipers were *out of phase* —Ralph Robin⟩ ⟨the cultural evolution of man has got *out of phase*, and armaments have developed faster than inhibitions —Marston Bates⟩ ⟨occasionally the Latin and the English are *out of phase* on the opposing pages —*Times Lit. Supp.*⟩

**[3]phase** \"\ *vt* -ED/-ING/-S **1** : to adjust so as to be in phase ⟨the *phasing* of the recorder to the incoming signals —M.G. Artzt⟩ **2 a** : to conduct or carry out by esp. planned phases ⟨a *phased* advance, with coordination between units —*Time*⟩ ⟨fundamental approach in the *phased* march toward "socialized agriculture" —H.R.Lieberman⟩ ⟨drastic plan for *phased* disarmament in all weapons —M.W.Straight⟩ **b** : to schedule (as operations) or contract for (as goods or services) to be performed or supplied as required ⟨guiding industry to ~ its development programs —Barbara Ward⟩ ⟨could talk their language — production *phasing*, subcontracting —*Time*⟩ ⟨construction power was *phased* along with combat power —J.L.Collins⟩ **3** : to introduce (as into a system, plan, or operation) in stages ⟨the new weapons and methods will be *phased* into the system —*Sydney (Australia) Bull.*⟩ ⟨~ . . . the establishment of a neutral zone —H.W.Baldwin⟩ — often used with *in* ⟨~ in reinforcements in accordance with tactical plans⟩ ⟨new-model autos are now being *phased in*⟩

**[4]phase** *var of* FAZE

**phase advancer** *n* [[2]*phase*] : a synchronous or asynchronous machine for supplying leading reactive volt amperes to the system to which it is connected

**phase angle** *n* **1** : the angle between the earth and the sun as seen from a planet **2** : an angle expressing phase or phase difference

**phase-contrast** \ˈ=ˌ=ˌ=\ *adj* : of or employing the phase microscope ⟨*phase-contrast* microscopy⟩

**phase converter** *n* : a machine for converting an alternating current into an alternating current of a different number of phases and the same frequency

**phase diagram** *n* : a diagram composed of equilibrium curves between different phases of the same substance ⟨the *phase diagram* of the gold-uranium system —*Jour. of Research*⟩

**phase distortion** *n* : change of wave form of a composite wave due to change of relative phase of its component harmonics

**phase inverter** *n* : a communications circuit in which the phase of a signal is reversed

**phase·less** \ˈfāzləs\ *adj* : having no phases

**phase line** *n* : a line (as a terrain feature extending across the zone of action) used to control and coordinate a military advance or withdrawal ⟨the regimental commander may prescribe any *phase lines* —*Infantry Jour.*⟩ ⟨reach a *phase line* one mile inland by 1600 hours —Irwin Shaw⟩ — abbr. *PL*

**phasemeter** \ˈ=ˌ==\ *n* [*phase* + *-meter*] : a device for measuring the difference in phase of two alternating currents or electromotive forces

**phase microscope** *also* **phase-contrast microscope** *or* **phase-difference microscope** *n* : a microscope that translates differences in phase of the light transmitted through or reflected by the object into differences of intensity in the image and thus provides contrast among parts and with the background

**phase modulation** *n* : modulation of the phase of a radio carrier wave by voice or other signal

**pha·se·my bean** \ˈfāsəmē-\ *also* **phasemy** *n* -ES [irreg. blend of *phas-* and *semi-* in NL *Phaseolus semierectus*, binomial designation of a species of bean] : an erect tropical American herb (*Phaseolus lathyroides*) sometimes cultivated in warm regions for forage or green manure

**pha·se·o·lin** \fəˈsēələn\ *n* -S [NL *Phaseolus* + ISV *-in*] : a crystalline globulin found esp. in the kidney bean

**pha·seo·lu·na·tin** \ˌfāzē(ˌ)ōlüˈnātᵊn\ *n* -S [ISV *phaseolunat-* (fr. NL *Phaseolus lunatus*, binomial designation of a species of bean) + *-in*] : LINAMARIN

**pha·se·o·lus** \fəˈsēələs\ *n, cap* [NL, fr. L, dim. of *phaselus*, a bean, fr. Gk *phasēlos*] : a genus of herbs (family Leguminosae) which are widely distributed throughout warm regions, which include most of the true American beans, and whose flowers are in axillary racemes or panicles with the corolla having a spirally twisted keel — see BEAN 1b, LIMA BEAN, MUNG BEAN, SIEVA BEAN

**phase out** *vt* **1** : to eliminate as a phase of an operation or system **2** : to discontinue the practice, production, or use of by phases **3** : to complete (as an operation or activity) by planned phases ⟨*phase out* an advertising campaign⟩ ~ *vi* **1** : to stop production or operation by phases (as by discontinuing the manufacture of component parts exceeding the quantity required for the assembling of items scheduled for completion) ⟨the company has *phased out* of the truck manufacturing business⟩ **2** : to pass from one phase into another ⟨groups have *phased out* into a new command⟩

**phase plate** *n* : a transparent plate of doubly refracting material that changes the relative phase of the components of polarized light

**phas·er** \ˈfāzə(r)\ *n* -S : one that phases

**phase rule** *n* : a law in physical chemistry: the number of degrees of freedom of a system in equilibrium is equal to the number of components minus the number of phases plus the constant two (as in the system ice –liquid water– water vapor consisting of the one chemical component water and its three physical phases there are no degrees of freedom and the system can exist at only one temperature and pressure)

**phases** *pl of* PHASE, *pres 3d sing of* PHASE

**phase shift** *n* : change of phase of an oscillation or a wave train

**phase space** *n* : an ideal often multidimensional space of which the coordinate dimensions represent the variables required to specify the phase or state of a system or substance — see COORDINATE SPACE

**phase splitter** *n* : a device by which a single-phase current is split into two or more currents differing in phase and which is used in starting a single-phase induction motor

**phase transformer** *n* : PHASING TRANSFORMER

**phase velocity** *n* : the velocity of a wave motion as determined by the product of the wavelength and frequency — called also *wave velocity*; compare GROUP VELOCITY, PARTICLE VELOCITY

**phase-wound** \ˈ=ˌ=\ *adj, of an induction motor* : having the secondary wound — compare SQUIRREL CAGE

**phas·go·nu·rid** \ˌfazgəˈn(y)u̇rəd\ *adj or n* [NL *Phasgonuridae*] : TETTIGONIID

**phas·go·nu·ri·dae** \ˌ==ˈn(y)u̇rəˌdē\ [NL, fr. *Phasgonura*, type genus, fr. Gk *phasganon* sword + NL *-ura*] *syn of* TETTIGONIIDAE

**-pha·sia** \ˈfāzh(ē)ə\ *also* **-pha·sy** \ˌfəsē, -si\ *n comb form, pl* **-phasias** *also* **-phasies** [*-phasia*, NL, fr. Gk, speech, fr. *phasis* utterance, statement, fr. *phanai* to say, speak; *-phasy* fr. NL *-phasia* — more at BAN] : speech disorder (of a specified type esp. relating to the symbolic use of language) ⟨dys*phasia*⟩ ⟨tachy*phasia*⟩ — compare -LALIA, -PHEMIA, -PHONY 2

**pha·si·a·nel·la** \ˌfāzēəˈnelə, -āsē-\ *n, cap* [NL, fr. L *phasianus* pheasant + *-ella* — more at PHASIANUS] : a genus (the type of the family Phasianellidae) of marine rhipidoglossate snails having intricately patterned porcelaneous shells

**pha·si·an·ic** \ˌ==ˈanik\ *adj* [NL *Phasianus* + E *-ic*] : of or relating to the genus *Phasianus*

**pha·si·an·id** \ˌ==ˈanəd, -ˈān-\ *n* -S [NL *Phasianidae*] : a bird of the family Phasianidae

**pha·si·an·i·dae** \-ˈanəˌdē\ *n pl, cap* [NL *Phasianus*, type genus + *-idae*] : a large family of gallinaceous birds including the Asiatic pheasants, domestic fowls, jungle fowls, argus pheasants, Old World partridges, often also the turkeys and guinea fowls, and sometimes the grouse — see COTURNIX

**pha·si·a·noid** \ˌ== əˌnȯid\ *adj* [NL *Phasianus* + E *-oid*] : resembling or related to the genus *Phasianus*

**pha·si·a·nus** \ˌ==ˈānəs\ *n, cap* [NL, fr. L, pheasant — more at PHEASANT] : a genus (the type of the family Phasianidae) containing the typical pheasants

**pha·sic** \ˈfāzik, -zēk\ *adj* [ISV [2]*phase* + *-ic*] : of, relating to, or of the nature of a phase : having phases : functioning by phases ⟨~ alternation of excitability and inexcitability —*Encyc. Britannica*⟩

**phasing** *pres part of* PHASE

**phasing current** *n* [fr. pres. part. of [3]*phase*] : the momentary current between two alternating-current generators when juxtaposed in parallel and not agreeing exactly in phase or period

**phasing transformer** *also* **phase transformer** *n* : a transformer whose purpose is to produce a secondary current differing in phase from the primary current

**pha·sis** \ˈfāsəs\ *n, pl* **pha·ses** \-ˌsēz\ [NL — more at PHASE] : PHASE ⟨direct our survey chiefly to that religious ~ of the matter —Thomas Carlyle⟩

**pha·si·tron** \ˈfāzəˌträn\ *n* -S [[2]*phase* + *-i-* + *-tron*] : a vacuum tube used for frequency modulation of a signal and having a cathode, deflector electrodes, two anodes, and an external inductor

**phasm** \ˈfazəm\ *n, pl* **phasms** \-zəmz\ *or* **phas·ma·ta** \-zmədˑə\ [Gk *phasmat-, phasma*, fr. *phainein* to show — more at FANCY] **1** *archaic* : an extraordinary appearance (as of light) : METEOR **2** *archaic* : APPARITION, PHANTOM

**phas·ma** \ˈfazmə\ *n, cap* [NL *Phasmat-, Phasma* fr. Gk, apparition] : the type genus of Phasmatidae

**phas·ma·tid** \ˈfazmədˑəd, -mətəd\ *n* -S [NL *Phasmatida*] : [2]PHASMID

**phas·mat·i·da** \fazˈmadˑədə\ *or* **phas·ma·toi·dea** \ˌfazməˈtȯidēə\ *or* **phas·mi·da** \ˈfazmədə\ [*Phasmatida, Phasmida*, NL, fr. *Phasmat-, Phasma* + *-ida*; *Phasmatoidea*, NL, fr. *Phasmat-, Phasma* + *-oidea*] *syn of* PHASMATODEA

**phas·mat·i·dae** \fazˈmadˑəˌdē\ *n pl, cap* [NL, fr. *Phasmat-, Phasma*, type genus + *-idae*] : a family of cursorial insects (suborder Phasmatodea) with long antennae and the abdomen simple and cylindrical or expanded laterally through part of its length

**phas·ma·to·dea** \ˌfazməˈtōdēə\ *n pl, cap* [NL, fr. *Phasmat-, Phasma* + *-odea*] : a suborder of Orthoptera often considered a separate order, comprising large, cylindrical or sometimes flattened, chiefly tropical insects with long strong legs, strictly phytophagous habits, and very slight metamorphosis and including the stick insects and leaf insects

**[1]phas·mid** \ˈfazməd\ *adj* [NL *Phasmida*] : of or relating to the Phasmatodea

**[2]phasmid** \"\ *n* -S : an insect of the suborder Phasmatodea (as a leaf insect or a stick insect)

**[3]phasmid** \"\ *n* -S [origin unknown] : either of the paired lateral postanal organs characteristic of most parasitic nematodes and usu. regarded as chemoreceptors — see PHASMIDIA — **phas·mid·i·al** \(ˈ)fazˈmidēəl\ *adj*

**phas·mi·dae** \ˈfazməˌdē\ [NL, fr. *Phasma*, type genus + *-idae*] *syn of* PHASMATIDAE

**phas·mid·ia** \fazˈmidēə\ *n pl, cap* [NL, fr. ISV *phasmid* + NL *-ia*] *in many classifications* : a subclass of Nematoda comprising worms having phasmids, simple amphids like pores, usu. deirids, and sensory organs that are typically papillose or, rarely, setose — compare APHASMIDIA — **phas·mid·i·an** \-dēən\ *n* -S

**phaso-** *comb form* [[2]*phase*] : phase ⟨*phaso*geneous⟩

**pha·so·ge·neous** \ˌfāzōˈjēnyəs, -nēəs\ *adj* [*phaso-* + chrono*geneous*] : appearing synchronously with a particular phase of development ⟨a ~ engram and its ecphoria⟩ — compare CHRONOGENEOUS

**pha·sor** \ˈfāzə(r) *also* -ˌzȯ(ə)r *or* -ˌō(ə)r\ *n* -S [[2]*phase* + *vector*] : a vector (as one representing an alternating current or voltage) whose vectorial angle represents a phase or phase difference

**-phasy** — see -PHASIA

**[1]phat** *or* **fat** \ˈfat, *usu* -ad.+V\ *adj* [alter. of *fat*] *of copy or type matter* : susceptible of easy and rapid setting (as because of plentiful white space or the existence of standing type) — contrasted with *lean*

**[2]phat** *or* **fat** \"\ *n* -S : phat matter

**[3]phat** *or* **fat** \"\ *vt* **phatted** *or* **fatted; phatted** *or* **fatted; phatting** *or* **fatting; phats** *or* **fats** : to keep (type) standing in hope of a further order

**phat·ic** \ˈfadˑik, -atik, -ēk\ *adj* [Gk *phatos* spoken (fr. *phanai* to speak, say) + E *-ic* — more at BAN] : employing or involving speech for the purpose of revealing or sharing feelings or establishing an atmosphere of sociability rather than for communicating ideas ⟨greetings, bromides, ~ communion —I.A. Richards⟩ ⟨indulged in a little ~ communion and were about to part —M.J.Maloney⟩ ⟨transition from the symbolic level to the ~ —Arthur Minton⟩ — **phat·i·cal·ly** \-ək(ə)lē, -ēk-, -li\ *adv*

**PhD** \ˌpēˌāchˈdē\ *abbr or n* -S [L *philosophiae doctor*] : a doctor of philosophy

**phe** *var of* PE

**pheas·ant** \ˈfezᵊnt\ *n, pl* **pheasant** *or* **pheasants** [ME *fesaunt*, fr. AF, fr. OF *fesan*, fr. L *phasianus*, fr. Gk *phasianos*, fr. *phasianos* of the Phasis river, fr. *Phasis*, river in Colchis] **1** : any of numerous large, often long-tailed, and brilliantly colored Old World gallinaceous birds that constitute *Phasianus* and related genera of the family Phasianidae, are most abundant in Asia and the adjacent islands, and include many forms raised in semidomestication as ornamentals and one widely distributed species (*P. colchicum*) which has been naturalized in many parts of the world — see ARGUS 2, BLOOD PHEASANT, GOLDEN PHEASANT, KALIJ, LADY AMHERST'S PHEASANT, MONAL, MONGOLIAN PHEASANT, RING-NECKED PHEASANT, SILVER PHEASANT, TRAGOPAN **2** : any of various birds having real or fancied resemblance to a pheasant: as **a** *South & Midland* : RUFFED GROUSE **b** *Austral* : LEIPOA **c** *Austral* : LYREBIRD **d** *Brit* : MAGPIE **e** : any of various guans **f** : a francolin (as *Francolinus capensis* or *Pternistis afer*) of southern Africa **3** *pl* **pheasants** : a moderate orange to light brown

**pheasant cuckoo** *n* : COUCAL

**pheasant duck** *n* **1** : a pintail (*Anas acuta*) **2** : MERGANSER

**pheasant finch** *n* : a small African waxbill (*Estrilda astrild*)

**pheas·ant·ry** \ˈfezᵊntrē, -ri\ *n* -ES [*pheasant* + *-ry*] : a place for keeping and rearing pheasants

**pheasant's-eye** \ˈ==ˌ=\ *n, pl* **pheasant's-eyes** **1** : a plant of the genus *Adonis*; *esp* : a Eurasian herb (*A. annua*) often cultivated for its deep red dark-centered flowers **2** : PHEASANT'S-EYE PINK **3** : POET'S NARCISSUS

**pheasant's-eye pink** *n* : a ring-marked cottage pink

**pheasant shell** *n* : a tropical gastropod mollusk of the family Phasianellidae or its smooth shell having a moderately high spire and an intricate pattern suggesting the plumage of a pheasant

**pheasant-tailed jacana** *n* \ˈ==ˌ=-\ : a jacana (*Hydrophasianus chirurgus*) of India and the East Indies having no frontal plate and the four middle tail feathers much elongated — called also *Indian jacana*

**pheasant-tailed widgeon** *n* : a pintail duck (*Anas acuta*)

**pheasantwood** \ˈ==ˌ=\ *n* : PARTRIDGEWOOD 1a

**phebe** *var of* PHOEBE

**phe·gop·ter·is** \fəˈgäptərəs\ [NL, fr. Gk *phēgos* oak + *pteris* fern — more at BEECH, PTERIS] *syn of* DRYOPTERIS

**phei·do·le** \ˈfīˈdōlē\ *n, cap* [NL, fr. Gk *pheidōlē*, fem. of *pheidōlos* thrifty, fr. *pheidesthai* to spare, be sparing; prob. akin to Skt *bhedati* he splits — more at BITE] : a large and widely distributed genus of seed-storing ants having highly polymorphic workers

**phel·lan·dral** \fəˈlanˌdral, -drəl\ *n* -S [fr. NL *phellandrium* (specific epithet of *Oenanthe phellandrium*) + ISV *-al*] : a liquid aldehyde $C_3H_7C_6H_8CHO$ that is related to alpha-phellandrene and is found esp. in eucalyptus oils and water-fennel oil

**phel·lan·drene** \-ˌdrēn\ *n* -S [NL *phellandrium* + ISV *-ene*] : either of two isomeric aromatic oily liquid terpene hydrocarbons $C_{10}H_{16}$ occurring in many essential oils: **a** : the terpene $C_3H_7C_6H_6CH_3$ occurring in the dextrorotatory form esp. in bitter fennel oil and ginger-grass oil and in the levorotatory form esp. in eucalyptus oils (as from *Eucalyptus phellandra*); 1,5-*para*-menthadiene — called also *alpha-phellandrene* **b** : the terpene $C_3H_7C_6H_7{=}CH_2$ occurring in the dextrorotatory form esp. in water-fennel oil and in the levorotatory form esp. in turpentine; 1(7),2-*para*-menthadiene — called also *beta-phellandrene*

**phel·lem** \ˈfeləm, -ˌlem\ *n* -S [*phello-* + *-em* (as in *phloem*)] : a layer of usu. suberized cells produced outwardly by a phellogen — called also *cork*; compare PHELLODERM

**phello-** *comb form* [Gk, cork, fr. *phellos*; prob. akin to Gk *phloos* bark — more at PHLOEM] : cork : bark ⟨*phello*derm⟩ ⟨*phello*gen⟩

**phel·lo·den·dron** \ˌfeləˈdendrən\ *n, cap* [NL, fr. *phello-* + *-dendron*] : a genus of aromatic deciduous trees (family Rutaceae) of eastern Asia that have handsome compound leaves turning yellow in autumn, dioecious yellowish green flowers, and black persistent drupes — see CORK TREE

**phel·lo·derm** \ˈfeləˌdərm\ *n* -S [ISV *phello-* + *-derm*] : a layer of parenchyma produced inwardly by a phellogen — compare PHELLEM — **phel·lo·der·mal** \ˌ==ˈdərməl\ *adj*

**phel·lo·gen** \ˈfeləjən, -ˌjen\ *n* -S [ISV *phello-* + *-gen*] : a secondary meristem that initiates phellem and phelloderm in the periderm — called also *cork cambium* — **phel·lo·gen·et·ic** \ˌ==jəˈnedˑik\ *adj* — **phel·lo·gen·ic** \ˌ==ˈjenik\ *adj*

**phel·lon·ic acid** \fəˈlänik-, feˈl-\ *n* [*phellonic* ISV *phellon-* (fr. Gk *phellos* cork) + *-ic*] : a crystalline hydroxy acid $HOCH_2(CH_2)_{20}COOH$ that is isolated esp. from cork by alkaline cleavage and extraction : 22-hydroxy-behenic acid — see SUBERIN

**phe·lo·ni·on** \fəˈlōnēən\ *n* -S [LGk *phelōnion, phailonion*, alter. of *phainolion*, fr. L *paenula* cloak — more at PAENULA] : a priest's vestment of the Eastern Orthodox Church that is similar to a western chasuble

**-phe·mia** \ˈfēmēə\ *n comb form* -S [NL, fr. Gk *-phēmia* speech, fr. *-phēmos* speaking (fr. *phēmē* speech, fr. *phanai* to speak, say) + *-ia* -y — more at BAN] : speech disorder (of a specified type esp. relating to the articulation or fluency of speech sounds) ⟨a*phemia*⟩ ⟨brachy*phemia*⟩ — compare -LALIA, -PHASIA, -PHONY 2

**phen-** *or* **pheno-** *comb form* [Gk *phain-, phaino-*, fr. *phainein* to show — more at FANCY] **1** *also* **phaen-** *or* **phaeno-** **a** : showing ⟨*pheno*cryst⟩ **b** : PHANER- ⟨*phaeno*gam⟩ **2** [*phene*] **a** : related to benzene ⟨*phen*ol⟩ : containing phenyl ⟨*phen*ethyl⟩ ⟨*pheno*barbital⟩; *esp* : containing two benzene rings ⟨*phen*azine⟩ ⟨*pheno*thiazine⟩ **b** : phenol (sense 1) ⟨*phen*oxide⟩

**phena·caine** *or* **pheno·cain** \ˈfēnəˌkān, ˈfen-\ *n* -S [*phenacaine* prob. fr. *phenetidine* + *acet-* + *-caine*; *phenocain* prob. irreg. fr. *phen-* + *-caine*] : a crystalline base $C_{18}H_{22}N_2O_2$ or its hydrochloride used chiefly for producing local anesthesia in the eye

**phen·acetin** \(ˈ)fēn, fən+\ *n* [ISV *phen-* + *acetin*] : ACETOPHENETIDIN

**phen·aceturic acid** \(ˌ)fēn, (ˌ)fen+ . . . -\ *n* [ISV *phen-* + *acetyl* + *hippuric*] : a crystalline amido acid $C_6H_5CH_2CONHCH_2COOH$ found in the urine of the horse and sometimes in that of man and also made synthetically; *N*-(phenylacetyl)-glycine

**phe·nac·odus** \fəˈnakədəs\ *n, cap* [NL, fr. Gk *phenak-, phenax* deceiver + NL *-odus*] : a genus (type of the family Phenacodontidae) of condylarths of the Eocene of Europe and America

**phe·nac·o·mys** \fəˈnakəˌmis\ *n, cap* [NL, fr. Gk *phenak-, phenax* + NL *-mys*] : a genus of chiefly arboreal No. American voles — see LEMMING MOUSE 2, RED TREE MOUSE

**phen·a·cyl** \ˈfenəˌsil, -sēl\ *n* -S [ISV *phen-* + *acetyl*] : the univalent radical $C_6H_5COCH_2$– derived from acetophenone

**phenacyl chloride** *n* : CHLOROACETOPHENONE

**phenagle** *var of* FINAGLE

**phen·a·kis·to·scope** \ˌfenəˈkistəˌskōp\ *n* [modif. of F *phénakisticope*, fr. Gk *phenakistēs* deceiver (fr. *phenakizein* to deceive, fr. *phenak-, phenax* deceiver + *-izein* -ize) + F *-scope*] : an optical toy resembling the zoetrope in principle and use and in one form consisting of a disk with the figures arranged about the center and having near the edge radial slits through which the figures are viewed by means of a mirror

**phen·a·kite** \ˈfenəˌkīt\ *or* **phen·a·cite** \-ˌsīt\ *n* -S [Sw *phenakit*, fr. Gk *phenak-, phenax* deceiver + Sw *-it* -ite; fr. its being easily mistaken for quartz] : a colorless, wine-yellow, rose-red, or brown glassy mineral that is a beryllium silicate $Be_2SiO_4$, occurs in rhombohedral crystals, and is sometimes used as a gem (hardness 7.5–8, sp. gr. 2.97–3.00)

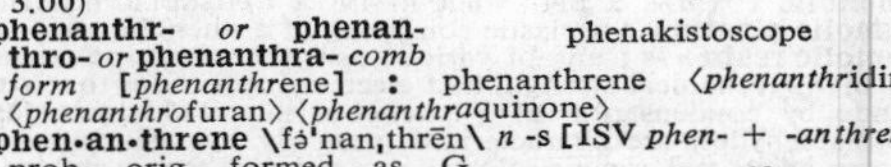

phenakistoscope

**phenanthr-** *or* **phenanthro-** *or* **phenanthra-** *comb form* [*phenanthrene*] : phenanthrene ⟨*phenanthr*idine⟩ ⟨*phenanthro*furan⟩ ⟨*phenanthra*quinone⟩

**phen·an·threne** \fəˈnanˌthrēn\ *n* -S [ISV *phen-* + *-anthrene*; prob. orig. formed as G *phenanthren*] : a crystalline tricyclic aromatic hydrocarbon $C_{14}H_{10}$ that is isomeric with anthracene, that is obtained chiefly from the anthracene oil fraction of coal tar and is also made synthetically, and that provides the ring system in whole or in part for many complex naturally occurring compounds (as resin acids, morphine, codeine, steroids) — compare STRUCTURAL FORMULA

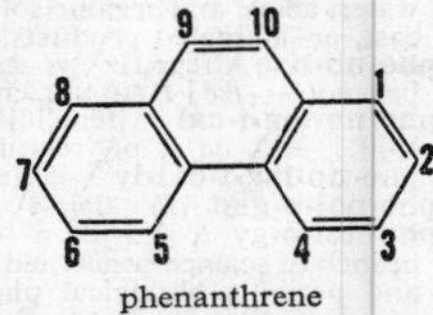


phenanthrene

**phen·an·thri·dine** \fəˈnan(t)thrəˌdēn, -dən\ *n* -S [ISV *phenanthr-* + *pyridine*; prob. orig. formed in G] : a crystalline base $C_{13}H_9N$ isomeric with acridine; 5-aza-phenanthrene

**phe·nan·thri·din·i·um** \fəˌnan(t)thrəˈdinēəm\ *n* -S [NL, fr. ISV *phenanthridine* + *-ium*] : the ion $[C_{13}H_9NH]^+$ derived from phenanthridine and occurring in substituted form in quaternary salts used as trypanocides

**phe·nan·thri·done** \fəˈnan(t)thrəˌdōn\ *n* -S [ISV *phenanthridine* + *-one*] : a crystalline lactam $C_{13}H_9NO$ obtainable from phenanthridine by oxidation

**phe·nan·thro·line** \fəˈnan(t)thrəˌlēn, -ˌlən\ *n* -S [ISV *phenanthr-* + *quinoline*] : any of three crystalline nitrogen bases $C_{12}H_8N_2$ related to phenanthrene and derivable from *ortho-*, *meta-*, and *para*-phenylenediamine; di-aza-phenanthrene; *esp* : the ortho or 1,10-isomer that forms a red coordination complex with ferrous ions useful as an oxidation-reduction indicator (as with potassium permanganate as oxidizing agent) because it becomes faint blue in the oxidized form

**phe·nan·thryl** \fəˈnan(t)thrəl\ *n* -S [*phenanthr-* + *-yl*] : a univalent radical $C_{14}H_9$ derived from phenanthrene

**phen·ar·sa·zine chloride** \fəˈnärsəˌzēn-\ [*phen-* + *arsenic* + *azine*] : ADAMSITE

**phe·nate** \ˈfēˌnāt, ˈfe-\ *n* -S [ISV *phen-* + *-ate*] : PHENOXIDE

**phen·azine** \ˈfenəˌzēn, -zən\ *n* [ISV *phen-* + *azine*] : a yellowish crystalline tricyclic nitrogen base $C_6H_4N_2C_6H_4$ that is the parent compound of many azine dyes (as the safranines) and a few antibiotics (as pyocyanin); 9,10-di-aza-anthracene

**phen·a·zone** \ˈfenəˌzōn\ *n* -S [ISV *phen-* + *az-* + *-one*] : ANTIPYRINE

**phene** \ˈfēn\ *n* -S [F *phène*, fr. Gk *phainein* to show; from its occurrence in illuminating gas — more at FANCY] : BENZENE — used esp. in names of derivatives; compare PHEN-

**phen·ethyl** \(ˈ)fen+\ *n* [*phen-* + *ethyl*] : the phenylethyl radical $C_6H_5CH_2CH_2$–

**phenethyl alcohol** *n* : PHENYLETHYL ALCOHOL

**phe·net·i·dine** \fəˈnedˑəˌdēn, -dən\ *n* -S [ISV *phenetole* + *-idine*] : any of three isomeric liquid basic amino derivatives $C_6H_4(NH_2)OC_2H_5$ of phenetole of which the ortho and para isomers are used in the manufacture of dyes and pharmaceuticals

**phen·e·tole** \ˈfenəˌtōl, -ˌtäl\ *n* -S [ISV *phen-* + *-et-* + *-ole*] : an aromatic liquid $C_6H_5OC_2H_5$ that is the ethyl ether of phenol

**phen·gite** \ˈfenˌjīt\ *n* -S [G *phengit*, fr. L *phengites*, fr. Gk, fr. *phengos* light, moonlight + *-itēs* -ite] **1** : a transparent or translucent stone prob. selenite or crystallized gypsum used by the ancients for windows **2 :** a variety of muscovite with substitution of aluminum for magnesium and silicon — **phen·gitic** \(ˈ)fen¦jid·ik\ *adj*

**phe·nic acid** \ˈfēnik, ˈfenik-\ *n* [F *acide phénique*, fr. *phén-* phen- + *-ique* -ic] **:** PHENOL — not used systematically

**phenician** *usu cap, var of* PHOENICIAN

**phenicochroite** *var of* PHOENICOCHROITE

**pheni·cop·ter** \¦fenə¦käptə(r), ˈfēn-, -nē¦k-\ *n* -s [MF *phoenicoptere*, fr. L *phoenicopterus*, fr. Gk *phoinikopteros*, lit., red-feathered, fr. *phoinik-, phoinix* red, purple, crimson + *-pteros* -feathered (fr. *pteron* feather, wing) — more at PHOENICIAN, FEATHER] **:** FLAMINGO

**phen·mi·azine** \ˌfen,mī+\ *n* -s [G *phenmiazin*] **:** QUINAZOLINE

**pheno-** — see PHEN-

**phe·no·barbital** \¦fē(ˌ)nō+\ *n* [*phen-* + *barbital*] **:** a crystalline barbiturate $C_{12}H_{12}N_2O_3$ that is used as a hypnotic and sedative esp. in grand mal epilepsy; 5-ethyl-5-phenyl-barbituric acid

**pheno·barbitone** \"+\ *n* [*phen-* + *barbitone*] *Brit* **:** PHENOBARBITAL

**phenocain** *var of* PHENACAINE

**pheno·clast** \ˈfēnə,klast, ˈfen-\ *n* -s [*phen-* + *-clast*] **:** a large fragment in sediment composed of various sizes of material

**pheno·coll** \-,käl\ *n* -s [ISV *phen-* + glycocoll] **:** a crystalline base $C_{10}H_{14}N_2O_2$ used in the form of a salt (as the hydrochloride) as an antipyretic and analgesic

**phe·no·contour** \¦fēnə+\ *n* [*phenotype* + *contour*] **:** a line that shows the geographic distribution of a particular phenotype

**phe·no·cop·ic** \¦==¦käpik\ *adj* [*phenocopy* + *-ic*] **:** of or relating to a phenocopy

**phe·no·copy** \"+\ *n* [*phenotype* + *copy*] **:** a phenotypic variation due to modifying environmental influences that mimics the expression of a genotype other than its own

**phe·no·critical period** \"+-\ *n* [*phenotype* + *critical*] **:** a period in the development of an organism when a particular gene effect can be most readily modified by environmental factors

**pheno·cryst** \ˈfēnə,krist, ˈfen-\ *n* -s [F *phénocryste*, fr. *phéno-* phen- + *-cryste* (fr. *crystal*)] **:** one of the prominent embedded crystals of a porphyry — **pheno·crys·tic** \¦==¦kristik\ *adj*

**phe·no·genesis** \¦fēnə+\ *n* [NL, fr. *phenotype* + *genesis*] **:** DEVELOPMENT; *specif* **:** differentiation of the phenotype

**phe·no·genetic** \¦==+\ *adj* **:** of or pertaining to phenogenetics or to phenogenesis — **pheno·genetically** \"+\ *adv*

**phe·no·genetics** \"+\ *n pl but sing in constr* [*phenotype* + *genetics*] **:** developmental genetics **:** the part of genetics that deals with the mechanisms of development and the differentiation of the concrete qualities controlled by the genes

**phe·nol** \ˈfē,nōl, -,nōl, -,näl, fēˈnōl\ *n* -s [ISV *phen-* + *-ol*] **1 :** a soluble crystalline acidic compound $C_6H_5OH$ that turns pinkish on exposure to light and air and has a characteristic odor, that is present in coal tar and wood tar, occurs in urine esp. of herbivorous animals, and is synthesized by various methods (as from sodium benzenesulfonate by alkaline fusion, from chlorobenzene by hydrolysis, or from cumene by oxidation to cumene hydroperoxide and treatment with sulfuric acid) that is a powerful caustic poison and in dilute solution is a useful disinfectant and that is used otherwise chiefly in making resins and plastics, dyes, pharmaceuticals (as aspirin), and other products (as *picric acid* 2,4-D) and as a solvent for refining lubricating oils; hydroxy-benzene — called also *carbolic acid* **2 :** any of a class of acidic compounds (as the cresols or resorcinol) analogous to phenol in constitution and regarded as hydroxyl derivatives of aromatic hydrocarbons in which one or more hydroxyl groups are attached directly to the aromatic ring — see NAPHTHOL 2, TAR ACID; compare ALCOHOL 4

**phe·no·lase** \ˈfēnə,lās, -lāz\ *n* -s [*phenol* + *-ase*] **:** PHENOL OXIDASE

**¹phe·no·late** \-,lāt, -,lət, *usu* -d·+V\ *n* -s [ISV *phenol* + *-ate*, n. suffix] **:** PHENOXIDE

**²phe·no·late** \-,lāt, *usu* -ād·+V\ *vt* -ED/-ING/-S [*phenol* + *-ate*, vb. suffix] **:** to treat, mix, or impregnate with phenol

**phenol coefficient** *n* **:** a number relating the germicidal efficiency of a compound to phenol regarded as having an arbitrarily assigned value of 1 toward specified bacteria (as typhoid bacteria) under specified conditions ⟨if disinfectant X has a *phenol coefficient* of 2 that means that . . . X is twice as strong as phenol —H.C.Wood †1920 & Arthur Osol⟩

**phenol-formaldehyde** \¦=,=¦==,=\ *n* **:** a condensation product, resin, or plastic made from phenol itself or another phenol and formaldehyde

**¹phe·no·lic** \fēˈnōlik, fəˈn-, -nāl-, -lēk\ *adj* [ISV *phenol* + *-ic*] **1 a :** of, relating to, or having the characteristics of phenol or a phenol **b :** containing or derived from phenol or a phenol **2 :** of, relating to, or containing phenolic resin

**²phenolic** \"\ *n* -s **1 :** PHENOLIC RESIN **2 :** PHENOLIC PLASTIC

**phenolic plastic** *n* **:** a plastic consisting of a phenolic resin

**phenolic resin** *n* -s **:** any of various usu. thermosetting resins of high mechanical strength and electrical resistance that are made by condensation of a phenol with an aldehyde (as formaldehyde), are characterized generally by resistance to water, acids, and organic solvents, and are used esp. in molded, cast, or laminated products, as adhesives, or in coatings

**phe·no·lize** \ˈfēnə,līz\ *vt* -ED/-ING/-S *see -ize in Explan Notes* [*phenol* + *-ize*] **:** PHENOLATE

**phe·no·log·i·cal** \¦fēnə¦läjəkəl, -jēk-\ *also* **phe·no·log·ic** \-jik, -jēk\ *adj* **:** of, relating to, or involving phenology — **phe·no·log·i·cal·ly** \-jək(ə)lē, -jēk-, -li\ *adv*

**phe·nol·o·gist** \fəˈnäləjəst\ *n* -s **:** a specialist in phenology

**phe·nol·o·gy** \-jē, -ji\ *n* -ES [*phenomena* + *-logy*] **1 :** a branch of science concerned with the relations between climate and periodic biological phenomena (as the migrations and breeding of birds or the flowering and fruiting of plants) ⟨a student of ~⟩ **2 :** the relation between climate and periodic biological phenomena (as of a kind of organism) ⟨studies in nest ~⟩ ⟨the ~ of Tasmanian lichens⟩

**phenol oxidase** *n* **:** any of various copper-containing enzymes (as one from potatoes) that promote the oxidation of phenols — called also *phenolase*; compare POLYPHENOL OXIDASE

**phe·nol·phthalein** \¦=,=+\ *n* [ISV *phenol* + *phthalein*] **:** a white or yellowish white crystalline compound $C_{20}H_{14}O_4$ formed by condensation of phthalic anhydride and phenol and used in medicine as a laxative and in analysis as an indicator because its solution is brilliant red in alkalies and is decolorized by weak acids — compare PHTHALEIN

**phenol red** *n* **:** PHENOLSULFONEPHTHALEIN

**phe·nol·sulfonate** \¦=,=+\ *n* [ISV *phenolsulfonic* (in *phenolsulfonic acid*) + *-ate*] **:** a salt or ester of a phenolsulfonic acid

**phenolsulfonephthalein** *or* **phenolsulfonphthalein** \¦=,=-¦=,=¦=(=)=\ *n* [ISV *phenol* + *sulfonephthalein* or *sulfonphthalein*] **:** a red crystalline compound $C_{19}H_{14}O_5S$ formed by condensation of the anhydride of *ortho*-sulfobenzoic acid and phenol and used chiefly as a test of kidney function and as an acid-base indicator — called also *phenol red*

**phe·nol·sulfonic acid** \¦=,=+-\ *n* [*phenolsulfonic* ISV *phenol* + *sulfonic*] **:** a sulfonic acid derived from phenol; *esp* **:** a crystalline monosulfonic acid $HOC_6H_4SO_3H$ (as the para isomer) used chiefly as an intermediate for dyes and pharmaceuticals

**phe·nom** \fəˈnäm\ *n* -s [by shortening] **:** PHENOMENON; *esp* **:** a person of phenomenal ability or promise ⟨a prep ~ whom major-league scouts are battling to sign —Robert Cromie⟩

**¹phe·nom·e·nal** \fəˈnämən°l\ *adj* [*phenomenon* + *-al*] **:** relating to or being a phenomenon or phenomena: as **a :** known through the senses and immediate experience rather than through thought or intuition **:** SENSIBLE ⟨the ~ world⟩ **b :** concerned with phenomena rather than with hypotheses ⟨~ science⟩ **c :** EXTRAORDINARY, REMARKABLE ⟨his influence over juries was ~ —H.W.H.Knott⟩ ⟨crop yields are ~ —*Americana Annual*⟩ ⟨claimed for himself one talent: a ~ memory for places —James Stern⟩ ⟨a ~ sandstorm —W.B.Fisher⟩ ⟨book enjoyed a ~ sale⟩ **syn** see MATERIAL

**²phenomenal** \"\ *n* -s **:** that which is known through observation; *also* **:** PHENOMENA

**phe·nom·e·nal·ism** \-n°l,izəm\ *n* -s [¹*phenomenal* + *-ism*] **1 :** a theory that limits positive or scientific knowledge to phenomena only **2 :** a theory that we know only phenomena and that there is no existence except the phenomenal **3 :** a theory that any statements containing names of things or physical objects can be expressed in terms of statements containing the names of sense-data to the exclusion of names of physical objects

**¹phe·nom·e·nal·ist** \-,ləst\ *n* -s **:** an advocate or proponent of phenomenalism

**²phenomenalist** \"\ *adj* **:** of or relating to phenomenalism or phenomenalists

**phe·nom·e·nal·is·tic** \=¦===¦istik, -tēk\ *adj* **:** of or relating to phenomena or phenomenalism ⟨a ~ system . . . is one that takes some perceptible physical individuals as its basic units —Nelson Goodman⟩ — **phe·nom·e·nal·is·ti·cal·ly** \-tək(ə)lē, -tēk-, -li\ *adv*

**phe·nom·e·nal·i·ty** \=,==ˈnaləd·ē\ *n* -ES **:** the quality or state of being phenomenal

**phe·nom·e·nal·ize** \=ˈ==n°l,īz\ *vt* -ED/-ING/-S *see -ize in Explan Notes* [¹*phenomenal* + *-ize*] **1 :** to treat or view as phenomenal **2 :** to interpret phenomenalistically

**phe·nom·e·nal·ly** \-n°lē, -li\ *adv* [¹*phenomenal* + *-ly*] **1 :** in relation to phenomena ⟨view that man is normally free although ~ determined —*Times Lit. Supp.*⟩ **2 :** EXTRAORDINARILY, REMARKABLY ⟨~ successful classes —*N. Y. Times Bk. Rev.*⟩ ⟨a ~ dull and tasteless comedy —Wolcott Gibbs⟩

**phen·o·men·ic** \¦fenə¦menik\ *adj* [*phenomenon* + *-ic*] **:** PHENOMENAL 1 ⟨such reality was for them not ~ —Giorgio de Santillana⟩

**phe·nom·e·nism** \fəˈnämə,nizəm\ *n* -s [*phenomenon* + *-ism*] **:** PHENOMENALISM

**phe·nom·e·nist** \-,nəst\ *n* -s **:** PHENOMENALIST

**phe·nom·e·nis·tic** \¦=¦==¦nistik\ *adj* **:** PHENOMENALISTIC

**phe·nom·e·nize** \=ˈ==,nīz\ *vt* -ED/-ING/-S *see -ize in Explan Notes* [*phenomenon* + *-ize*] **:** PHENOMENALIZE

**phe·nom·e·no·logical** \fə¦nämənə+\ *also* **phe·nom·e·no·logic** \"+\ *adj* **1 :** of, relating to, or advocating phenomenology **2 :** of or relating to phenomena — **phe·nom·e·no·logically** \"+\ *adv*

**phe·nom·e·nol·o·gist** \=,==ˈnäləjəst\ *n* -s **:** an advocate of phenomenology

**phe·nom·e·nol·o·gy** \-jē, -ji\ *n* -ES [*phenomenon* + *-logy*] **1 :** a branch of a science dealing with the description and classification of phenomena **2** [G *phänomenologie*, fr. *phänomenon* phenomenon (fr. LL *phaenomenon*) + *logie* -logy] **a** *Kantianism* **:** a division of metaphysics that treats of motion and rest as predicables of things **b** *Hegelianism* **:** a doctrine of the growth of science or knowledge **:** the progress of mind from the lowest to the highest stages **c :** PHANEROSCOPY **d** *Husserlian philos* **:** a discipline endeavoring to lay foundations for all sciences by describing the formal structures of phenomena or of both actual and possible material essences that are given through a suspension of the natural attitude in pure acts of intuition — compare EPOCHE

**phe·nom·e·non** \fəˈnämə,nän, -,nən\ *n, pl* **phenome·na** \-,nä, -nə\ *or* **phenomenons** *see numbered senses* [LL *phaenomenon*, fr. Gk *phainomenon*, fr. neut. of pres. pass. part. of *phainein* to show — more at FANCY] **1** *pl phenomena* **:** an observable fact or event **:** an item of experience or reality ⟨studied capitalism, not mankind, and reduced economics to the *phenomena* of price —H.J.Muller⟩ ⟨from the moment of its birth surrealism was an international ~ —Herbert Read⟩ **2** *pl phenomena* **a :** a fact or event in the changing and perceptible forms as distinguished from the permanent essences of things: as (1) **:** a mutable, caused, or developing aspect of things as contrasted with their fixed and substantial natures (2) **:** a perceptible aspect or appearance of things as contrasted with their true or ideal being (3) **:** an object of sense perception as distinguished from an ultimate reality (4) [G *phänomenon, phänomen*, fr. LL *phaenomenon*] *Kantianism* **:** an object of experience in space and time as distinguished from a thing-in-itself (5) **:** a sense impression or sense-datum as distinguished from a thing ⟨*phenomena*, not only physical things, have spatial and temporal aspects —Nelson Goodman⟩ **b :** a fact or event of scientific interest susceptible of scientific description and explanation — in common usage retaining the implication of change or mode of being esp. illustrating the operation of some general law **3 a :** a rare fact or event **:** a fact or event of special or unique significance ⟨authorities explained the fiery light as an optical ~ —Fred Zimmer⟩ **b** *pl usu phenomenons* **:** an exceptional, unusual, or abnormal thing or occurrence ⟨the annual is . . . something of a publishing ~: selling for $3.95, it has a circulation of 40,000 —Harvey Breit⟩ **c** *pl phenomenons* **:** an extraordinary or remarkable person esp. in ability **:** PRODIGY ⟨a ~ at tennis⟩ **syn** see WONDER

**phe·nom·ic** \fəˈnämik, -mēk\ *adj* [prob. fr. *phenomenon* + *-ic*] **:** PHENOTYPIC

**phenoms** *pl of* PHENOM

**-phe·none** \fəˈnōn, ˈfē,nōn\ *n comb form* -s [*phen-* + *-one*] **:** aromatic ketone containing a phenyl or substituted phenyl group attached to a (specified) acyl group ⟨aceto*phenone*⟩ ⟨benzo*phenone*⟩ ⟨resaceto*phenone*⟩

**phe·no·plast** \ˈfēnə,plast\ *n* -s [ISV *phen-* + *-plast*] **:** PHENOLIC RESIN — **phe·no·plas·tic** \¦==¦plastik\ *adj*

**phe·no·quinone** \¦fēnō+\ *n* [ISV *phen-* + *quinone*] **:** a deep red crystalline complex $C_6H_4O_2.2C_6H_5OH$ formed by the union of phenol with quinone

**phe·no·safranine** \¦==+\ *n* [ISV *phen-* + *safranine*] **:** a simple red safranine dye made by oxidation of a 1:2 mixture of *para*-phenylenediamine and aniline and used chiefly as a desensitizer in photography

**phe·no·sper·my** \ˈfēnə,spərmē\ *n* -ES [¹*phen-* + *-spermy*] **:** the production with or without pollination of empty or abortive seeds

**phe·no·thiazine** \¦fēnō+\ *n* [ISV *phen-* + *thiazine*] **:** a greenish yellow crystalline compound $C_{12}H_9NS$ that is formed by heating diphenylamine with sulfur, that is an anthelmintic and insecticide, and that is used chiefly in veterinary practice to rid farm animals of internal parasites — called also *thiodiphenylamine*; compare STRUCTURAL FORMULA

H
N
S
phenothiazine

**phe·no·type** \ˈfēnə,tīp, ˈfen-\ *n* [G *phänotypus*, fr. *phäno-* phen- + *typus* type, character, fr. L — more at TYPE] **1 a :** the detectable expression of the interaction of genotype and environment **b :** the visible characters of an organism **2 :** a group of organisms sharing a particular phenotype — compare GENOTYPE

**phe·no·typ·ic** \¦==¦tipik\ *or* **phe·no·typ·i·cal** \-pəkəl\ *adj* [G *phänotypisch*, fr. *phänotypus* + *-isch* -ic, -ical] **:** of, relating to, or constituting a phenotype ⟨~ pigmentation combinations —*Science*⟩ — **phe·no·typ·i·cal·ly** \-pək(ə)lē\ *adv*

**phen·ox·azine** \(ˈ)fēn, (ˈ)fen+\ *n* [ISV *phen-* + *oxazine*] **:** a crystalline compound $C_{12}H_9NO$ that is analogous in structure to phenothiazine with oxygen in place of sulfur and that is the parent of oxazine dyes (as gallocyanine)

**phen·oxide** \fən+\ *n* [*phen-* + *oxide*] **1 :** a salt of phenol in its capacity as a weak acid ⟨sodium ~ $C_6H_5ONa$⟩ **2 :** a salt of any phenol

**phe·noxy** \fəˈnäksē\ *adj* [*phenoxy-*] **:** containing the radical $C_6H_5O$-

**phenoxy-** *comb form* [*phen-* + *oxy-*] **:** containing the univalent radical $C_6H_5(-)$ composed of phenyl united with oxygen — in names of chemical compounds ⟨*phenoxy*acetic acid $C_6H_5OCH_2COOH$⟩

**phe·noxy·methylpenicillin** \fə¦näksē+\ *n* [*phenoxy-* + *methyl* + *penicillin*] **:** PENICILLIN 2c

**phenyl** \ˈfen°l, ˈfēn-\ *n* -s [ISV *phen-* + *-yl*; orig. formed as F *phényle*] **:** a univalent radical $C_6H_5$ derived from benzene by removal of one hydrogen atom — compare BIPHENYL

**phenyl·acetaldehyde** \¦==+\ *n* [ISV *phenylacetic* + *aldehyde*] **:** a liquid compound $C_6H_5CH_2CHO$ of hyacinth odor used in perfumes

**phenyl·acetamide** \¦==+\ *n* [ISV *phenyl* + *acetamide*] **:** ACETANILIDE

**phenyl·acetic acid** \¦==+-\ *n* [*phenylacetic* ISV *phenyl* + *acetic*] **:** a crystalline acid $C_6H_5CH_2COOH$ obtained usu. by hydrolyzing benzyl cyanide and used chiefly in the manufacture of penicillin and in the form of esters with odor like honey in perfumes (as for soap); alpha-toluic acid

**phenyl·alanine** \¦==+\ *n* [ISV *phenyl* + *alanine*] **:** a crystalline alpha-amino acid $C_6H_5CH_2CH(NH_2)COOH$ that is obtained in its levorotatory L form by the hydrolysis of proteins (as lactalbumin), that is essential in the nutrition of man and lower animals, and that is converted in the normal body to tyrosine; α-amino-beta-phenyl-propionic acid — compare PHENYLKETONURIA, PHENYLPYRUVIC ACID

**¹phenyl·ate** \ˈfen°l,āt, ˈfēn-, -n°lət, *usu* -d·+V\ *n* -s [ISV *phenyl* + *-ate*, n. suffix] **:** PHENOXIDE 1

**²phenyl·ate** \-n°l,āt, *usu* -ād·+V\ *vt* -ED/-ING/-S [*phenyl* + *-ate*, v. suffix] **:** to introduce the phenyl group into (a compound) — **phenyl·a·tion** \,==ˈāshən\ *n* -s

**phenyl·bu·ta·zone** \,==ˈbyüd·ə,zōn\ *n* -s [*phenyl* + *but-* + *pyrazolone*] **:** a white or light yellow powder $C_{19}H_{20}N_2O_2$ derived from pyrazolone and used for its analgesic and antipyretic effects

**phenyl·carbamate** \¦==+\ *n* [*phenylcarbamic* + *-ate*] **:** CARBANILATE

**phenyl·carbamic acid** \¦==+-\ *n* [ISV *phenyl* + *carbamic*] **:** CARBANILIC ACID

**phenyl chloride** *n* **:** CHLOROBENZENE

**phenyl cyanide** *n* **:** BENZONITRILE

**phenyl·ene** \ˈfen°l,ēn, ˈfēn-\ *n* -s [ISV *phenyl* + *-ene*] **:** any of three bivalent radicals $-C_6H_4-$ derived from benzene by removal of two hydrogen atoms from the ortho, meta, or para positions

**phenyl·ene·diamine** \¦==,=+\ *n* [ISV *phenylene* + *diamine*] **:** any of three toxic isomeric crystalline compounds $C_6H_4(NH_2)_2$ that are ortho, meta, and para diamino derivatives of benzene of which the ortho and para isomers are used as photographic developers and the meta and para isomers in dye manufacture

**phenyl·eph·rine** \,==ˈe,frēn, -,frən\ *n* -s [*phenyl* + epinephrine] **:** a basic compound $C_9H_{13}NO_2$ related chemically to epinephrine and ephedrine and used in the form of the hydrochloride as a vasoconstrictor to the nasal mucosa, a mydriatic in ophthalmology, and by injection to raise the blood pressure

**phenyl ether** *n* **1 :** a low-melting crystalline compound $(C_6H_5)_2O$ of geranium odor used chiefly in perfumes (as for soaps) and in a mixture with biphenyl as a heat-transfer medium — called also *diphenyl ether, diphenyl oxide* **2 :** an ether in which one of the radicals united to oxygen is phenyl

**phenyl·ethyl** \¦==+\ *n* [ISV *phenyl* + *ethyl*] **:** either of two univalent radicals derived from ethylbenzene by removal of one hydrogen atom from the side chain; *esp* **:** the beta or 2-derivative $C_6H_5CH_2CH_2-$

**phenylethyl alcohol** *n* **:** a fragrant liquid alcohol $C_6H_5CH_2CH_2OH$ that is found in rose oil and neroli oil but is usu. made synthetically and that is used chiefly in perfumes of the rose type — called also *beta-phenylethyl alcohol, phenethyl alcohol, 2-phenylethyl alcohol*

**phenyl·ethylene** \¦==+\ *n* [ISV *phenyl* + *ethylene*] **:** STYRENE

**phenyl·glycine** \¦==+\ *n* [ISV *phenyl* + *glycine*] **:** a phenyl derivative of glycine; *esp* **:** the crystalline synthetic acid $C_6H_5NHCH_2COOH$ containing a phenyl group attached to nitrogen and used in the manufacture of indigoid dyes

**phenylglyoxylic acid** \¦==+-\ *n* [ISV *phenyl* + *glyoxylic*] **:** a crystalline keto acid $C_6H_5COCOOH$ obtained esp. by oxidizing styrene or mandelic acid; benzoyl-formic acid

**phenyl·hydrazide** \¦==+\ *n* [ISV *phenyl* + *hydrazide*] **:** a hydrazide $RCONHNHC_6H_5$ formed from phenylhydrazine by reaction usu. with an ester, acid chloride, or acid anhydride

**phenyl·hydrazine** \¦==+\ *n* [ISV *phenyl* + *hydrazine*; orig. formed as G *phenylhydrazin*] **:** a toxic liquid nitrogen base $C_6H_5NHNH_2$ that is made by reduction of benzenediazonium chloride and that reacts with aldehydes, ketones, acids, and related compounds to form hydrazides, hydrazones, and osazones useful in the identification of such compounds esp. as sugars

**phenyl·hydrazone** \¦==+\ *n* [ISV *phenyl* + *hydrazone*] **:** a hydrazone derived from phenylhydrazine

**phe·nyl·ic** \fəˈnilik\ *adj* [ISV *phenyl* + *-ic*] **:** relating to, derived from, or containing phenyl

**phenyl iodide** *n* **:** IODOBENZENE

**phenyl isocyanate** *n* **:** a colorless liquid ester $C_6H_5NCO$ of acrid odor made usu. by the action of phosgene on aniline and used in identifying alcohols and amines by the formation of phenylurethans and phenyl-ureas respectively

**phenyl·ketonuria** \¦==+\ *n* [NL, fr. *phenyl* + *ketonuria*] **:** a rare genetic anomaly in man marked by inability to oxidize phenylpyruvic acid and by severe mental deficiency — called also *phenylpyruvic amentia, phenylpyruvic oligophrenia*

**phenyl·ke·to·nu·ric** \,==,kēd·ə¦n(y)ùrik\ *n* -s **:** one affected with phenylketonuria

**phenyl mercaptan** *n* **:** THIOPHENOL 1

**phenyl·mercuric acetate** \¦==+-\ *n* [*phenyl* + *mercuric*] **:** a crystalline salt $C_6H_5HgOOCCH_3$ made by reaction of benzene with mercuric acetate in alcoholic solution and used chiefly as a fungicide and herbicide

**phenylmercuric nitrate** *n* [*phenyl* + *mercuric*] **:** a crystalline basic salt approximately $C_6H_5HgNO_3.C_6H_5HgOH$ used chiefly as a fungicide and external antiseptic

**phenyl methyl ketone** *n* **:** ACETOPHENONE

**phenyl·osazone** \¦==+\ *n* [*phenyl* + *osazone*] **:** an osazone (as glucose phenylosazone) derived from phenylhydrazine that is usu. yellow and crystalline and that is useful esp. in the study of carbohydrates

**phenyl·propanolamine** \¦==+\ *n* [*phenyl* + *propanol* + *amine*] **:** NOREPHEDRINE

**phenyl·pyruvic acid** \¦==+-\ *n* [*phenyl* + *pyruvic*] **:** a crystalline keto acid $C_6H_5CH_2COCOOH$ found in the urine as a metabolic product of phenylalanine esp. in phenylketonuria

**phenylpyruvic amentia** *or* **phenylpyruvic oligophrenia** *n* **:** PHENYLKETONURIA

**phenyl salicylate** *n* **:** a crystalline ester $HOC_6H_4COOC_6H_5$ used chiefly as a stabilizer for cellulosic plastics and vinyl plastics and as an ingredient of suntan preparations because of its ability to absorb ultraviolet light and also esp. formerly as an internal antiseptic

**phenyl·thiocarbamide** \¦==+\ *n* [*phenyl* + *thiocarbamide*] **:** PHENYLTHIOUREA

**phenyl·thiourea** \¦==+\ *n* [NL, fr. *phenyl* + *thiourea*] **:** a crystalline compound $C_6H_5NHCSNH_2$ that is made from aniline, carbon disulfide, and ammonia and is tasteless to many persons and extremely bitter to others — called also *phenylthiocarbamide*

**phenyl·urethan** \¦==+\ *or* **phenyl·urethane** \¦==+\ *n* [ISV *phenyl* + *urethan*] **1 :** an aromatic crystalline ester $C_6H_5NHCOOC_2H_5$ made usu. by addition of ethyl alcohol to phenyl isocyanate **2 :** any ester of carbanilic acid

**phe·nyt·o·in** \fəˈnid·əwən\ *n* -s [di*phenyl*hydan*toin*] **:** DIPHENYLHYDANTOIN

**pheo-** — see PHAEO-

**pheo·chrome** \ˈfēə,krōm\ *adj* [ISV *phaeo-* + *-chrome*] **:** CHROMAFFIN

**pheo·chro·mo·blast** \¦fēō+\ *also* **pheo·chro·mo·cy·to·blast** \,fēō,krōmōˈsīd·ə,blast\ *n* [*pheochromoblast* fr. *pheochrome* + *-o-* + *-blast*; *pheochromocytoblast* fr. *pheochromocyte* + *-o-* + *-blast*] **:** an embryonic cell destined to give rise to chromaffin tissue esp. of the adrenal medulla

**pheo·chromocyte** \¦fēō+\ *n* [ISV *phaeochrome* + *-o-* + *-cyte*] **:** a chromaffin cell

**pheo·chro·mo·cy·to·ma** \,==,krōmōsīˈtōmə\ *n, pl* **pheochromocytomas** \-məz\ *or* **pheochromocytoma·ta** \-məd·ə\ [NL, fr. ISV *phaeochromocyte* + NL *-oma*] **:** a tumor derived from chromaffin cells and usu. associated with paroxysmal or sustained hypertension

**phe·on** \ˈfē,än\ *n* -s [ME *feon*] **1 :** a conventional heraldic representation of the head of a javelin, dart, or arrow point downward with two long barbs engrailed on the inner edge **2 :** a head of an arrow borne as a heraldic charge

pheon

**pheo·phor·bide** \,fēəˈfȯr,bēd, -,bəd\ *n* -s [ISV *phaeo-* + *phorb-* (fr. Gk *phorbē* pasture, fodder) + *-ide*; akin to Gk *pherbein* to feed and prob. to OE *byrgan* to taste, eat, ON *bergja*] **:** a blue-black crystalline acid obtained from chlorophyll or pheophytin by treatment with hydrochloric acid

**pheo·phy·tin** *or* **phaeo·phy·tin** \,fēəˈfīd·ən\ *n* [ISV *pheo*phorbide + *phytyl* + *-in*] **:** a bluish black waxy pigment that is olive-brown in solution, that is obtained from chlorophyll by mild treatment with acid (as oxalic acid), and that differs from chlorophyll structurally only by the replacement of the magnesium atom in the molecule by two hydrogen atoms; the phytyl ester of pheophorbide

**pheo·porphyrin** *or* **phaeo·porphyrin** \¦fēō+\ *n* [*pheophorbide* + *porphyrin*] : a crystalline isomer of pheophorbide that is obtained from pheophorbide by treatment with hydriodic acid and that is not of typical porphyrin structure but is a substituted dehydro-phorbin

**-pher** \fə(r)\ *n comb form* -s [Gk *pherein* to carry — more at BEAR] : one that carries ⟨chrono*pher*⟩ ⟨tel*pher*⟩

**pher·e·crat·ic** \¦ferə¦krad·ik\ *also* **pher·e·cra·te·an** \-krād·ēən\ *or* **pher·e·cra·tian** \-āshən\ *n* -s *sometimes cap* [*pherecratic* fr. *Pherecrates*, 5th cent. B.C. Greek poet (fr. Gk *Pherekratēs*) + E -*ic*; *pherecratean* alter. of *pherecratian*, fr. LL *pherecratius* of Pherecrates (fr. Gk *pherekrateios*, fr. *Pherekratēs*) + E -*an*] **1** : a classical verse or rhythmic system of the form –◡◡–◡–⏓ — called also *aristophanic, first pherecratic* **2** : a classical verse or rhythmic system of the form ⏓⏓–◡◡–⏓ — called also *second pherecratic*

**phew** *voiceless whistling breath emitted through rounded lips & usu followed by a voiceless* (y)ü *or* ue *sound; often read as* 'fyü\ *interj* [imit. of a whistling sound] — used to express discomfort caused usu. by heat or humidity; compare PHOO

**phi** \'fī\ *n* -s [MGk, fr. Gk *phei*] : the 21st letter of the Greek alphabet — symbol Φ or φ; see ALPHABET table

**phi** *abbr* philosophy

**phi·al** \'fī(ə)l\ *n* -s [ME *fiole*, fr. MF, fr. OProv *fiola*, fr. L *phiala*, fr. Gk *phialē*] : a container for liquids; *esp* : a small glass bottle for medicines : VIAL

**phi·a·le** \'fīəlē\ *n, pl* **phi·a·lae** \-ə,lē\ [Gk *phialē*] **1** : a shallow Greek bowl resembling a Roman patera usu. made with a boss in the center and used in ancient times for drinking or pouring libations **2** : a fountain or laver in a church (as at the entrance)

**phi·a·lide** \'fīə,līd\ *n* -s [F, fr. Gk *phialidion*, dim. of *phialē* bowl] : STERIGMA; *esp* : one that is flask-shaped or constricted just below the apex and in some forms is the end cell of the phialophore

**phi·a·lid·i·um** \,fīə'lidēəm\ *n, cap* [NL, prob. fr. Gk *phialidion*] : a widely distributed genus of hydrozoan medusae

**phi·a·loph·o·ra** \,fīə'läf(ə)rə\ *n, cap* [NL, fr. Gk *phialē* + NL -*phora*] : a form genus of imperfect fungi (family Dematiaceae) which are characterized esp. by spores borne on phialides and some forms of which are important in mycotic infections of man (as chromoblastomycosis)

**phi·a·lo·pore** \'fīəlō,pō(ə)r\ *n* [Gk *phialo-* (fr. *phialē* bowl) + E -*pore*] : the aperture through which the hollow asexual daughter colony of a volvox inverts itself

**phi be·ta kap·pa** \'fī¦bād·ə'kapə, ¦tə'- *sometimes* -bē¦\ *n, usu cap P&B&K* [so called fr. the initials of the society's Greek motto, *philosophia biou kybernētēs* philosophy the guide of life] : a person winning high scholastic distinction usu. in course in an American college or university and being elected to membership in a national honor society founded in 1776 — called also *Phi Bete*

**phi bete** \'fī'bāt\ *n, usu cap P&B* [by shortening & alter.] : PHI BETA KAPPA

**phid·i·an** \'fidēən\ *adj, usu cap* [*Phidias*, 5th cent. B.C. Greek sculptor + E -*an*] : of, relating to, or characteristic of the Greek sculptor Phidias or his school

**phil** *abbr* **1** philharmonic **2** philological; philologist; philology **3** philosopher; philosophical; philosophy

**phil-** *or* **philo-** *comb form* [ME, fr. OF, fr. L, fr. Gk, fr. *philein* to love, fr. *philos* beloved, dear, loving — more at -PHILOUS] : loving : having an affinity for ⟨*phil*ydraceous⟩ ⟨*philo*-Celticism⟩ ⟨*philo*graph⟩

**¹-phil** \,fil\ *or* **-phile** \,fīl\ *n comb form* -s [F -*phile*, fr. Gk -*philos*, fr. *philos* beloved, dear, loving] : one that loves : lover : one having a fondness or affinity for or a strong attraction to ⟨acido*phil*⟩ ⟨hemo*phile*⟩ ⟨biblio*phile*⟩ ⟨Anglo*phile*⟩

**²-phil** \"\ *or* **-phile** \"\ *adj comb form* [NL -*philus*, fr. L, fr. Gk *philos* beloved, dear, loving] : loving : having a fondness or affinity for ⟨hemo*phile*⟩ ⟨Franco*phil*⟩ ⟨negro*phile*⟩ ⟨organo*phile*⟩

**-phi·la** \fələ\ *n comb form, pl* **-phila** [NL, fr. L, fem. sing. and neut. pl. of -*philus*] : one or ones attracted to or living or growing by preference in — in names of biological taxa ⟨*Ammophila*⟩ ⟨*Anthophila*⟩

**philabeg** *var of* FILLEBEG

**phil·a·del·phia** \¦filə¦delfyə, -fēə\ *adj, usu cap* [fr. *Philadelphia*, Pa.] : of or from the city of Philadelphia, Pa. ⟨*Philadelphia* department stores⟩ : of the kind or style prevalent in Philadelphia : PHILADELPHIAN

**philadelphia chair** *n, usu cap P* : WINDSOR CHAIR

**philadelphia chippendale** *n, usu cap P&C* : a style of 18th century furniture made in Philadelphia and characterized by rich ornamental carving

**philadelphia fleabane** *n, usu cap P* : SKEVISH

**philadelphia ice cream** *n, usu cap P* : ice cream made from flavored cream without eggs or other thickening

**philadelphia lawyer** *n, usu cap P* : an exceptionally competent lawyer ⟨language that . . . cannot be correctly and definitely interpreted even by a *Philadelphia lawyer* —*Jour. of Accountancy*⟩; *esp* : a shrewd lawyer versed in the intricacies of legal phraseology and adept at exploiting legal technicalities ⟨involves . . . a murder syndicate, blackmail, and enough complicated talk to require the services of a dozen *Philadelphia lawyers* —Charles Lee⟩

**¹phil·a·del·phian** \-fyən, -fēən\ *adj, usu cap* [Gk *philadelphia* brotherly love (fr. *philadelphos* brotherly — fr. *phil-* + *adelphos* brother — + -*ia* -y) + E -*an*] **1** : of or relating to the Philadelphian Society of Boehmenists **2** [*Philadelphia*, Pa. + E -*an*] : PHILADELPHIA

**²philadelphian** \"\ *n* -s [Gk *philadelphia* brotherly love + E -*an*] **1** *usu cap* : a member of the Philadelphian Society founded in London in 1670 as a sect of Boehmenism **2** *cap* [*Philadelphia*, Pa. + E -*an*] : a native or resident of Philadelphia, Pa.

**philadelphia pepper pot** *n, usu cap 1st P* : PEPPER POT 2 b

**philadelphia vireo** *n, usu cap P* : a vireo (*Vireo philadelphicus*) of eastern No. America with a grayish green back and yellowish underparts

**phil·a·del·phus** \,filə'delfəs\ *n* [NL, fr. Gk *philadelphos* brotherly] **1** *cap* : a genus of ornamental shrubs (family Saxifragaceae) of wide distribution in temperate regions that are distinguished by the numerous stamens and the inferior ovary — see MOCK ORANGE **2** -ES : any plant of the genus *Philadelphus*

**phil·a·mot** \'filə,mät\ *n* -s [obs. *fieulamort*, adj., of the color of faded leaf, fr. F *feuille morte* philamot] : FEUILLE MORTE

**¹phi·lan·der** \fə'landə(r), -laan-\ *n* [Gk *philandros* loving men, fr. *phil-* + *andr-*, *anēr* man — more at ANDR-] **1** -s **a** : PHILANDERER **b** : FLIRTATION **2** [alter. of *filander*] **a** -s : any of several medium-sized woolly opossums of So. and Central America **b** *cap* : a genus of marsupials including the woolly opossums

**²philander** \"\ *vi* **philandered; philandered; philandering** \-d(ə)riŋ\ **philanders** : to make love frivolously or in a trifling or fickle way : DALLY, FLIRT ⟨belles and beaux ~*ed* in the big hotels —Van Wyck Brooks⟩ ⟨his penchant for ~*ing* with pretty stenographers finally drove his wife to sue for divorce⟩

**phi·lan·der·er** \-d(ə)rə(r)\ *n* -s [²*philander* + -*er*] : one that plays at courtship : a fickle lover : FLIRT ⟨"like all ~*s* you're afraid you've never been in love," she said sharply —Louis Auchincloss⟩

**¹phi·lan·thid** \fə'lan(t)thəd\ *n* -s [NL *Philanthidae*] : a wasp of the family Philanthidae

**²philanthid** \"\ *adj* [NL *Philanthidae*] : of or relating to the Philanthidae

**phi·lan·thi·dae** \-thə,dē\ *n pl, cap* [NL, fr. *Philanthus*, type genus + -*idae*] : a family of digger wasps that are usu. black with conspicuous yellow markings

**phil·an·thrope** \'filən,thrōp\ *n* -s [F, fr. Gk *philanthrōpos* loving mankind] *archaic* : PHILANTHROPIST

**phil·an·throp·ic** \¦≈≈¦thräpik, -pēk\ *also* **phil·an·throp·i·cal** \-pəkəl, -pēk-\ *adj* [*philanthropic* fr. F *philanthropique*, fr. Gk *philanthrōpos* + F -*ique* -ic; *philanthropical* fr. *philanthropy* + -*ical*] **1** : of, relating to, or characterized by philanthropy : BENEVOLENT, HUMANITARIAN ⟨~ sympathy for the cause of the slave —V.L.Parrington⟩ ⟨found time to devote to church, civic, and ~ affairs —Marian Silveus⟩ **2** : dispensing or receiving aid from funds set aside for humanitarian purposes : ELEEMOSYNARY ⟨~ foundation⟩ ⟨the need for books at nearby hospitals and ~ homes —*Wonderful World of Books*⟩ — **phil·an·throp·i·cal·ly** \-pək(ə)lē, -pēk-, -li\ *adv*

**phi·lan·thro·pism** \fə'lan(t)thrə,pizəm, -laan-\ *n* -s [*philanthropy* + -*ism*] : PHILANTHROPY

**phi·lan·thro·pist** \-,pəst\ *n* -s [*philanthropy* + -*ist*] : one characterized by or practicing philanthropy : ALTRUIST, HUMANITARIAN — **phi·lan·thro·pis·tic** \-¦≈≈¦pistik\ *adj*

**phi·lan·thro·py** \fə'lan(t)thrəpē, -laan-, -pi\ *n* -ES [LL *philanthropia*, fr. Gk *philanthrōpia*, fr. *philanthrōpos* loving mankind (fr. *phil-* + *anthrōpos* man) + -*ia* -y — more at ANTHROP-] **1** : goodwill toward one's fellowmen esp. as expressed through active efforts to promote human welfare : HUMANITARIANISM ⟨~ . . . is civic, social, and amply beneficial —J.A.Franquiz⟩ — contrasted with *misanthropy* **2 a** : an act or instance of deliberative generosity : a contribution made in a spirit of humanitarianism ⟨among his *philanthropies* were full tuition scholarships for deserving students⟩ **b** (1) : an organization distributing funds for humanitarian purposes ⟨funds for the new rehabilitation center came from two of the big *philanthropies*⟩ (2) : an institution or agency supported by such contributions ⟨community chest funds are distributed among various *philanthropies*⟩

**phi·lan·thus** \fə'lan(t)thəs\ *n, cap* [NL, fr. *phil-* + -*anthus*] : a genus of digger wasps that is the type of the family Philanthidae

**phil·an·tom·ba** \,filən'tämbə\ *n* -s [origin unknown] : a West African duiker (*Cephalophus maxwelli*)

**phil·a·tel·ic** \¦filə¦telik, -lēk\ *adj* [*philately* + -*ic*] **1** : of or relating to philately ⟨~ data⟩ ⟨~ organizations⟩ ⟨~ accessories⟩ **2** : of interest or value to philatelists ⟨~ features of a stamp⟩ — **phil·a·tel·i·cal·ly** \-lək(ə)lē, -lēk-, -(ə)li\ *adv*

**philatelic mail** *n* : mail whose primary purpose is the acquisition of special stamps or postal markings

**phi·lat·e·list** \fə'lad·ᵊləst, ¦tᵊl- *also* -lā\ *n* -s [F *philatéliste*, fr. *philatélie* + -*iste* -ist] : a specialist in philately : one that collects or studies stamps ⟨the primary motive which actuates collectors (as opposed to ~*s*) is cash value —A.E.Hopkins⟩

**phi·lat·e·ly** \-ᵊlē, -ᵊli\ *n* -ES [F *philatélie*, fr. *phil-* + Gk *ateleia* tax exemption, immunity, fr. *atelēs* free from tax or tribute, immune from public duties (fr. *a-* ²a- + *telos* tax) + -*ia* -y; akin to Gk *telein* to pay, *tlēnai* to bear; fr. the fact that the postage stamp exempted the recipient from paying the mailing charge or tax — more at TOLERATE] **1** : the collection and study of postage stamps and of postal stationery that has passed through the mail : stamp collecting ⟨it is with adhesive postage stamps that ~ is primarily concerned —R.H.P.Curle⟩ **2** : stamp collectors : PHILATELISTS ⟨surprised and delighted ~ by his early announcement of . . . commemorative stamps —K.B.Stiles⟩

**-phile** — see -PHIL

**phil·e·nor butterfly** \fə'lēnə(r)-\ *n* [NL *philenor* (specific epithet of *Papilio philenor*, species of swallowtails) fr. Gk *philēnōr* conjugal] : PIPE-VINE SWALLOWTAIL

**phil·e·pit·ta** \,filə'pid·ə\ *n, cap* [NL] : a genus of Madagascan birds related to the pittas but constituting a distinct family

**phil·e·tai·rus** \,filə'tīrəs\ *n, cap* [NL, fr. *phil-* + Gk *hetairos* companion] : a monotypic genus of passerine birds consisting of the sociable weaverbird of southern Africa

**¹phil·har·mon·ic** \¦filə(r)¦mänik, -il,här¦-, -i,lär¦-, -il,hä¦-, -i,lä¦-, -nēk *sometimes* -ilhə(r)¦-\ *n* [F *philharmonique*, fr. It *filarmonico*, adj., fr. *fil-* phil- + *armonico* harmonic, fr. L *harmonicus* — more at HARMONIC] **1** *archaic* : a lover of music **2** *often cap* : a musical concert or musical organization (as a society or orchestra) ⟨served as guest conductor for the ~⟩

**²philharmonic** \"\ *adj* [F *philharmonique*, fr. It *filarmonico*] **1** *archaic* : of or relating to a lover of music ⟨the most ~ ear is at times deeply affected by a simple air —*New Monthly Mag.*⟩ **2** : of or relating to a musical organization, esp. a symphony orchestra ⟨a ~ pace is slower than the pace set by a . . . pit band —Ethel Merman⟩

**philharmonic pitch** *n* : a tuning standard of English origin of approximately 450 vibrations per second for A above middle C — contrasted with *new philharmonic pitch*

**¹phil·hel·lene** \(')fil¦he,lēn\ *adj* [Gk *philellēn*, fr. *phil-* + *Hellēn* Hellene] : venerating Greece or the Greeks ⟨more ~ than the Greeks themselves —J.H.Moulton⟩

**²philhellene** \"\ *n, often cap* : an admirer or supporter of Greece or of the Greeks ⟨an almost fanatical ~, fluent in both ancient and modern Greek —Alistair MacLean⟩

**phil·hel·len·ic** \¦filhe¦lenik\ *adj* **1** : PHILHELLENE **2** : supporting the Greek struggle for independence from Ottoman domination ⟨~ dispositions of the satrap —George Grote⟩

**phil·hel·len·ism** \fil'helə,nizəm\ *n* : veneration of Greece or the Greeks ⟨literary ~ from Shakespeare to Byron —Terence Spencer⟩

**phil·hel·len·ist** \-,nəst\ *n* [Gk *philellēn* + E -*ist*] : PHILHELLENE

**phil·ia** \'filēə\ *n* -s [NL, fr. Gk, friendship, fr. *philos* loving, friendly + -*ia* -y — more at -PHILOUS] : love of friends or of one's fellowman : social sympathy — compare AGAPE, EROS

**-philia** \"\ *n comb form* -s [NL, fr. Gk *philia*, fr. *philos* loving — more at -PHILOUS] **1** : tendency toward ⟨chromato*philia*⟩ ⟨spasmo*philia*⟩ **2** : abnormal appetite or liking for ⟨alcoholo*philia*⟩ ⟨copro*philia*⟩

**phil·i·a·ter** \,filē,ad·ə(r), ,≈≈'≈≈\ *n* -s [Gk *philiatros*, fr. *phil-* + *iatēr* healer, doctor] : one interested in medical science

**philibeg** *var of* FILLEBEG

**-phil·ic** \¦filik, -lēk\ *adj comb form* [*phil-* + -*ic*] : having an affinity for : loving : attracted by : adapted to : ⟨electro*philic*⟩ ⟨helio*philic*⟩ ⟨lyo*philic*⟩ — opposed to -*phobic*

**-philies** *pl of* -PHILY

**phi·li·ne** \fə'līnē\ *n* -s [NL] : a bubble shell of the family Philinidae

**phi·lin·i·dae** \fə'linə,dē\ *n pl, cap* [NL, fr. *Philine* + -*idae*] : a small but widely distributed family of marine bubble shells with the shell wholly concealed in the mantle

**phil·ip** \'filəp\ *n* -s [fr. the name *Philip*; prob. fr. the name resembling the sound of their chirps] **1** *dial Eng* : HEDGE SPARROW **2** *dial Eng* : HOUSE SPARROW

**philippan** *adj, usu cap* [*Philippi*, town in ancient Macedonia, Greece + E -*an*] *obs* : used at Philippi ⟨while I wore his sword ~ —Shak.⟩

**¹phi·lip·pi·an** \fə'lipēən\ *adj, usu cap* [*Philippi* + E -*an*] : of, relating to, or characteristic of Philippi, a city of ancient Macedonia

**²philippian** \"\ *n* -s *cap* [*Philippi* + E -*an*] : a native or inhabitant of Philippi

**¹phi·lip·pic** \fə'lipik, -pēk\ *n* -s [MF *philippique*, fr. LL & Gk; LL (*orationes*) *philippicae*, speeches of the Greek orator Demosthenes †322 B.C. against Philip II †336 B.C. king of Macedon and speeches of the Roman orator Cicero †43 B.C. against Mark Anthony †30 B.C. Roman orator, triumvir, and soldier, fr. L, fem. pl. of *philippicus* of Philip, fr. Gk *philippikos* of or against Philip; Gk *philippikoi* (*logoi*), speeches of Demosthenes against Philip II, fr. masc. pl. of *philippikos* of Philip, fr. *Philippos* Philip + -*ikos* -ic] : a discourse or declamation full of acrimonious invective : TIRADE ⟨a ~ so withering that it roused a lethargic Senate —S.H.Adams⟩

**²philippic** *adj, obs* : characterized by acrimony : ABUSIVE

**philippina** *or* **philippine** *var of* PHILOPENA

**phil·ip·pine** \'filə,pēn, ,≈≈'≈\ *adj, usu cap* [fr. the *Philippine* islands, north Malay archipelago, southeast Asia] : of or from the Philippines : of the kind or style prevalent in the Philippines : FILIPINO

**philippine cedar** *n, usu cap P* : a Philippine timber tree (*Toona calantas* syn *Cedrela toona*) with red or pale red hard fragrant wood used esp. for cigar boxes and interior finish — called also *kalantas*

**philippine fowl disease** *n, usu cap P* : NEWCASTLE DISEASE

**philippine mahogany** *n, usu cap P* **1** : any of several Philippine timber trees with wood resembling that of the true mahogany: as **a** : PHILIPPINE CEDAR **b** : NARRA **c** : LUMBAYAO **d** : RED LAUAN **e** : TANGUILE **f** : ALMON **2** : the wood of a Philippine mahogany; *esp* : BAGTIKAN

**phil·ip·pism** \'filə,pizəm\ *n* -s *cap* [F *philippisme*, fr. *Philipp* Melanchthon (Schwarzert) †1560 Ger. scholar and religious reformer + F -*isme* -ism] : the doctrines of the Lutheran theologian Philipp Melanchthon or his followers marked by a conciliatory policy toward both the Calvinists and the Roman Catholic Church

**phil·ip·pist** \-,pəst\ *n* -s *usu cap* [F *philippiste*, fr. *Philipp* Melanchthon †1560 + F -*iste* -ist] : an adherent to or supporter of Philippism — **phil·ip·pis·tic** \¦≈≈¦pistik\ *adj, usu cap*

**phil·ip·pize** \'filə,pīz\ *vi* -ED/-ING/-S *often cap* [Gk *Philippizein* to be on Philip's side, fr. *Philippos* Philip (of Macedon) + -*izein* -ize] : to speak in support of a cause under the influence of a bribe

**phi·lip·pus** \fə'lipəs\ *n, pl* **philip·pi** \-i,pī\ [L] **1** : a gold stater of Philip II of Macedon **2** : any of several gold or silver 15th or 16th century coins of France, Spain, and Burgundy issued by rulers named Philip

**phil·ip·stad·ite** \'filəp,stä,dīt\ *n* -s [*Philipstad*, Sweden, its locality + E -*ite*] : a mineral approximately $Ca_2(Fe, Mg)_5(Si, Al)_8O_{22}(OH)_2$ consisting of silicate of calcium, iron, magnesium, and aluminum and belonging to the amphibole group

**phi·lis·tia** \fə'listēə\ *n pl, often cap* [NL, fr. LL *Philistaea*, ancient country in southwestern Palestine that was the land of the Philistines] : cultural Philistines as a class : the Philistine world ⟨the perennial tendency of ~ to suspect what it does not understand —Mary McCarthy⟩ ⟨fierce . . . refusal to compromise with ~ which she shared with writers to whom she was in no other way allied —*New Republic*⟩

**¹phil·is·tine** \'filə,stēn, fə'listən, fə'li,stēn *sometimes* 'filə,stīn *or* -stən\ *n* -s [ME, fr. LL *Philistinus*, fr. Gk *Philistinos*, fr. Heb *Pĕlishtī*] **1** *cap* : a native or inhabitant of ancient Philistia in the coastal regions of southwest Palestine **2** *usu cap*, *archaic* : someone (as a bailiff, a critic) regarded as a natural or traditional enemy because belonging to a despised class **3** [trans. of G *Philister*] *often cap* **a** : a crass prosaic often priggish individual guided by material rather than intellectual values : ⁴BABBITT, BOURGEOIS ⟨it is only the *Philistine* who seeks to estimate a personality by the vulgar test of production —Oscar Wilde⟩ ⟨the *Philistine* wants to talk about morals, not to understand what is morally wrong —J.T.Farrell⟩ **b** (1) : one deficient in originality or aesthetic sensitivity ⟨the *Philistine's* sturdy preference for reproduction of the familiar —John Dewey⟩ ⟨irresponsible ~*s* will bring about the disfigurement of Trinity's front greens and the walled banks of the Liffey —*Dublin Sunday Independent*⟩ (2) : one uninformed in a special area of knowledge : IGNORAMUS, OUTSIDER ⟨a course . . . designed to bring ~*s* to like literature —L.A.King⟩ ⟨the history . . . makes fascinating reading even for philatelic *Philistines* —Mollie Panter-Downes⟩

**²philistine** \"\ *adj* **1** *usu cap* : of or relating to the people of ancient Philistia **2** *often cap* : of, relating to, or characteristic of a Babbitt : BOURGEOIS, MATERIALISTIC ⟨a slightly missionary flavor as of one bringing the gospel of culture to a *Philistine* world —*Yale Rev.*⟩ — compare BIEDERMEIER **3** *often cap* **a** : oblivious to aesthetics : INSENSITIVE ⟨the old familiar theme of the misunderstood genius at war with ~ society —Henry Miller⟩ **b** : displaying or marked by indifference or lack of specialized knowledge : UNINFORMED ⟨my attitude toward the ballet, which is *Philistine* and ignorant —John Woodburn⟩

**phil·is·tin·ic** \¦filə¦stinik\ *also* **phil·is·tin·ish** *pronunc at* PHILISTINE + ish\ *adj, often cap* [¹*philistine* + -*ic* or -*ish*] : PHILISTINE

**phil·is·tin·ism** *pronunc at* PHILISTINE +,izəm\ *n* -s *often cap* : the attitudes, beliefs, and conduct characteristic of the modern philistine : MATERIALISM, BARBARISM ⟨his protest against the ~ of bourgeois values, emphasizes that art should be appreciated for its own sake —Bernard Smith⟩ ⟨what he called the cant of the great middle part of the English nation, what we call its *Philistinism* —Matthew Arnold⟩

**phil·li·lew** \'filə,lü\ *n* -s [prob. imit.] *Irish* : OUTCRY, UPROAR

**phil·lips code** \'filəps-\ *n, cap P* [after Walter P. *Phillips* †1920 Am. telegrapher and journalist] : a code of abbreviations formerly used for telegraphic messages and esp. for press dispatches

**phil·lips·ite** \'filəp,sīt\ *n* -s [William *Phillips* †1828 Eng. mineralogist and geologist + E -*ite*] : a white or reddish mineral approximately $(K_2,Na_2,Ca)Al_2Si_4O_{12}.4\frac{1}{2}H_2O$ consisting of a hydrous silicate of potassium, calcium, and aluminum, belonging to the zeolite family, and commonly occurring in complex often cruciform crystals (hardness 4–4.5, sp. gr. 2.2)

**Phillips Screws** *trademark* — used for screws having a special head with a cross slot for use with a special screwdriver

**phil·ly** \'filē, -li\ *adj, usu cap* [fr. *Philly*, nickname for *Philadelphia*, Pa.] *slang* : of or relating to the city of Philadelphia, Pa. ⟨*Philly* sportswriters⟩

**phil·lyr·ea** \fə'lirēə\ *n, cap* [NL, fr. Gk *philyrea* mock privet] : a genus of evergreen shrubs (family Oleaceae) of the Mediterranean region with small greenish white flowers and fruit resembling olives

**philo-** — see PHIL-

**phil·o·bib·list** \,filə'bibləst, -'bīb-\ *n* -s [Gk *philobiblos* (fr. *phil-* + *biblos* book) + E -*ist* — more at BIBLE] : a lover of books : BIBLIOPHILE

**philo-celticism** \¦fi(,)lō+\ *n, cap C* : a fondness for Celtic expressions or idioms ⟨dismissed his entire essay as another example of crackpot *philo-Celticism* —J.V.Kelleher⟩

**phil·o·den·dron** \,filə'dendrən\ *n* [NL, fr. Gk, neut. of *philodendros* loving trees, fr. *phil-* + *dendron* tree — more at DENDR-] **1** *cap* : a genus of tropical American climbing aroids with prominent sheathing leafstalks, fleshy spathes of various colors, and flowers in a dense spadix **2** *pl* **philodendrons** \-nz\ *or* **philoden·dra** \-rə\ **a** : any plant of the genus *Philodendron* grown commonly as a house plant often in water alone **b** : any of various other aroid plants (as the ceriman) that are cultivated for their showy foliage

**phil·o·di·na** \,filə'dīnə\ *n, cap* [NL, fr. *phil-* + Gk *dinos* rotation, whirling] : a genus (the type of the family Philodinidae of the order Bdelloidea) comprising rotifers with a corona made up of two nearly circular disks on short stalks

**phi·log·e·ny** \fə'läjənē\ *n* -ES [by alter. (influence of *phil-*)] : PHYLOGENY

**phil·o·graph** \'filə,graf, -răf\ *n* [*phil-* + -*graph*] : an apparatus with a transparent plane (as of glass or celluloid) on which to trace a facsimile of a view or object seen through an adjustable eyepiece — **phil·o·graph·ic** \¦≈≈¦grafik\ *adj*

**phi·log·y·nous** \fə'läjənəs\ *adj* [*philogyny* + -*ous*] : fond of women

**phi·log·y·ny** \-nē\ *n* -ES [Gk *philogynia*, fr. *phil-* + *gyn-* + -*ia* -y] : fondness for women

**phi·lo·he·la** \fə'lōhēlə\ *n, cap* [NL, fr. *phil-* + Gk *helē* sun's heat, fr. *hēlios* sun — more at SOLAR] : a genus of birds (family Scolopacidae) consisting of the American woodcock

**phi·lol·o·gas·ter** \fə'lälə,gastə(r), ≈,≈≈'≈≈\ *n* -s [*philologist* + -*aster*] : an incompetent philologist : dabbler in philology — **phi·lol·o·gas·try** \-trē\ *n* -ES

**phi·lol·o·ger** \fə'läləjə(r)\ *n* -s [MF *philologie* philology + E -*er*] : PHILOLOGIST ⟨primarily a ~ and only secondarily a prosodist —T.S.Omond⟩

**phil·o·lo·gi·an** \,filə'lōjēən\ *n* -s [L *philologia* philology + E -*an*] : PHILOLOGIST 2

**phil·o·log·i·cal** \¦filə¦läjəkəl, -jēk-\ *also* **phil·o·log·ic** \-jik, -jēk\ *adj* [*philological* fr. L *philologia* philology + E -*ical*; *philologic* fr. F *philologique*, fr. MF *philologie* philology + -*ique* -ic] : of, relating to, or dealing with philology ⟨~ studies⟩ ⟨a ~ society⟩ ⟨a date based chiefly on ~ evidence⟩ — **phil·o·log·i·cal·ly** \-jək(ə)lē, -jēk-, -li\ *adv*

**phi·lol·o·gist** \fə'läləjəst\ *n* -s **1** : one that loves learning or literature : a learned or literary man : a scholar esp. of classical antiquity **2** : LINGUIST 2; *esp* : one that concerns himself with human speech as the vehicle of literature and as a field of study that sheds light on cultural history

**phi·lol·o·gize** \≈'≈≈,jīz\ *vb* -ED/-ING/-S [*philology* + -*ize*] *vt* : to render by philological investigation ~ *vi* : to study or make investigations in philology

**phil·o·logue** *or* **phil·o·log** \'filə,lȯg *also* -,läg\ *n* -s [MF, fr. L *philologus* lover of learning, fr. Gk *philologos* lover of words and learning, fr. *phil-* + *logos* word, reason, speech — more at LEGEND] : PHILOLOGIST

**phi·lol·o·gy** \fə'läləjē, -ji\ *n* -ES [F *philologie*, fr. MF, fr. L *philologia* love of talk, speech, or argument, fr. Gk, love of argument, learning, and literature, fr. *philologos* love of words and learning + *-ia* -y] **1 :** study of literature that includes or may include grammar, criticism, literary history, language history, systems of writing, and anything else that is relevant to literature or to language as used in literature **:** literary or classical learning **2 a :** LINGUISTICS; *esp* **:** historical and comparative linguistics **b :** the study of human speech esp. as the vehicle of literature and as a field of study that sheds light on cultural history

**phi·lom·a·chus** \fə'läməkəs\ *n, cap* [NL, fr. Gk *philomachos* loving fighting, warlike, fr. *phil-* + *machē* battle, fight (fr. *machesthai* to battle, fight)] **:** a genus of shorebirds (family Scolopacidae) consisting of the ruff

**phil·o·math** \'filə,math\ *n* -S [Gk *philomathēs*, fr. *phil-* + *-mathēs* (fr. *mathein*, *manthanein* to learn) — more at MATHEMATICAL] **:** a lover of learning **:** SCHOLAR; *esp* **:** a student of mathematics — **phil·o·math·e·an** \¦==¦mathēən\ *adj*

**phil·o·math·ic** \¦==¦mathik\ *or* **phil·o·math·i·cal** \-thəkəl\ *adj* **:** of or relating to a philomath or to love of learning

**phil·o·mel** \'filə,mel\ *n* -S *usu cap* [ME *philomene*, fr. ML *philomena*, modif. of L *philomela*, fr. *Philomela*, Athenian princess in Greek mythology who was changed into a nightingale, fr. Gk *Philomēla*] **:** NIGHTINGALE ⟨clear was the song from *Philomel's* far bower —John Keats⟩

**philomela** \,filə'mēlə\ *n* -S [L, nightingale] **1** *usu cap* **:** PHILOMEL **2 a :** a large-scale solo Doppelflöte organ stop **b :** a high-pitched small-scale pipe-organ stop of sweet tone

**phi·lo·ni·an** \fə'lōnēən, (')fī¦l-\ *or* **phi·lon·ic** \-länik\ *adj, usu cap* [LL *philonianus*, fr. *philon-*, *Philo* Judaeus *fl* late 1st century B.C. and early 1st century A.D. Hellenistic Jewish philosopher + L *-ianus* -ian] **:** of or relating to the Alexandrian Jewish philosopher Philo Judaeus or based on his system of philosophy consisting of a combination of Judaism and Platonism and being a precursor of Neoplatonism

**phi·lo·nism** \'fīlə,nizəm\ *n* -S *usu cap* [LL *philon-*, *Philo* + E *-ism*] **:** the Philonian philosophy

**phi·lo·nist** \-,nəst\ *n* -S *usu cap* [LL *philon-*, *Philo* + E *-ist*] **:** a supporter of Philonism

**phi·lo·ni·um** \fə'lōnēəm\ *n* -S [LL, after L *Philon-*, *Philo*, 1st cent. A.D. Greek physician] **:** an ancient remedy for colic containing opium, saffron, euphorbium, henbane, spikenard, and honey

**phi·lon·o·tis** \fə'länətəs, fī'l-\ *n, cap* [NL, fr. *phil-* + Gk *notis* moisture; akin to Gk *noteros* damp — more at NOURISH] **:** a genus of acrocarpous mosses (order Eubryales) that is related to *Bartramia* and includes the fountain mosses

**phil·o·pe·na** *or* **phil·ip·pi·na** \,filə'pēnə\ *or* **phil·ip·pine** \-ēn\ *n* -S [modif. (influenced by Gk *philos* loving and L *poena* penalty) of G *vielliebchen*, lit., much loved; perh. fr. the idea that the gift was a penalty of friendship or love — more at PAIN] **1 :** a game in which a man and woman who have shared the twin kernels of a nut each try to claim a gift from the other as a forfeit at their next meeting by fulfilling certain conditions (as by being the first to exclaim "philopena") — called also *fillipeen* **2 a :** a nut with two kernels **b :** a gift given as a forfeit

**phil·o·po·tam·i·dae** \,filəpə'tamə,dē\ *n pl, cap* [NL, fr. *Philopotamus*, type genus (fr. *phil-* + Gk *potamos* river, stream) + *-idae*] **:** a small but widely distributed family of caddis flies

**phil·o·pro·ge·ne·i·ty** \,filō,prōjə'nēəd·ē\ *n* -ES [*phil-* + *progeny* + *-ity*] **:** PHILOPROGENITIVENESS

**philo·progenitive** \¦fi(,)lō+\ *adj* [*phil-* + *progenitive*] **1 :** tending to produce offspring **:** PROLIFIC ⟨younger writers . . . have been more ~, and some of them will end by having four or five children —Malcolm Cowley⟩ **2 :** of, relating to, or characterized by love of offspring ⟨the ~ drive is less powerful in men than in women —*Jour. Amer. Med. Assoc.*⟩

**philoprogenitiveness** *n* -ES **:** love of offspring

**¹phi·lop·ter·id** \fə'läptərəd\ *adj* [NL *Philopteridae*] **:** of or relating to the Philopteridae

**²philopterid** \"\ *n* -S [NL *Philopteridae*] **:** a louse of the family Philopteridae

**phil·op·ter·i·dae** \,fi,läp'terə,dē\ *n pl, cap* [NL, fr. *Philopterus*, type genus (fr. *phil-* + *-pterus*) + *-idae*] **:** a family of bird lice (order Mallophaga) having the tarsi fitted with two claws for clinging to the feathers of their host

**philo·samia** \¦filə+\ *n, cap* [NL, fr. *phil-* + *Samia*] **:** a genus of large silk-spinning saturniid moths

**phi·los·o·phas·ter** \fə¦läsə¦fastə(r)\ *n* -S [LL, fr. L *philosophus* philosopher + *-aster*] **:** a pretender or dabbler in philosophy

**phi·los·o·phas·ter·ing** \-t(ə)riŋ\ *adj* **:** acting the philosopher **:** philosophizing in a shallow or pretentious manner

**phi·los·o·phas·try** \-trē\ *n* -ES [*philosophaster* + *-y*] **:** spurious or pretended philosophy

**philosophate** *vi* -ED/-ING/-S [L *philosophatus*, past part. of *philosophari* to philosophize, fr. *philosophus* philosopher] *obs* **:** PHILOSOPHIZE

**phil·o·sophe** *also* **phil·o·soph** \'filə,säf, ,==¦zäf\ *n* -S [F *philosophe*, fr. MF] **1 :** PHILOSOPHER; *esp* **:** one of the popular quasi-philosophers of the 18th century French Enlightenment **2 :** PHILOSOPHASTER

**phi·los·o·pheme** \fə'läsə,fēm\ *n* -S [LL *philosophema*, fr. Gk *philosophēma*, fr. *philosophein* to love or pursue knowledge, fr. *philosophos* lover of wisdom] **:** a philosophical formulation or principle **:** PROPOSITION

**phi·los·o·pher** \fə'läs(ə)fə(r) *sometimes* -äzəf-\ *n* -S [ME *philosopher*, *philosophre*, modif. (influenced by *-er*) of MF *philosophe*, fr. L *philosophus*, fr. Gk *philosophos*, fr. *phil-* + *-sophos* (fr. *sophia* wisdom, fr. *sophos* wise + *-ia* -y)] **1 a :** one who seeks wisdom or enlightenment **:** reflective thinker **:** SCHOLAR, INVESTIGATOR ⟨the ~, traditionally, is thought of as a person whose chief interest is in attempting to discover the innermost essence of reality —Theodore Brameld⟩ **b :** a specialist in the synthesis of knowledge ⟨a ~ . . . must attempt to give us a comprehensive account of human values and a plausible theory of human destiny —Eliseo Vivas⟩ — compare PHILOSOPHY 2d **c :** a student of philosophy **2** *obs* **:** one versed in an occult science; *specif* **:** ALCHEMIST **3 a :** one whose life is governed by reason **:** a person whose philosophical perspective enables him to meet trouble with equanimity **:** RATIONALIST ⟨to a ~ there is some compensation for blindness in the increased acuity of the other senses⟩ **b :** the expounder of a theory in a particular area of experience ⟨he is no ~ of freedom, but he is certainly a fighter for freedom —C.P. Romulo⟩ **c :** PHILOSOPHIZER ⟨Bowery Thespian and ~ —*Amer. Guide Series: N.Y. City*⟩

**philosophers' egg** *n* **1 a :** the first matter of the philosophers' stone composed of salt, sulfur, and mercury **b :** GRIPE'S EGG **2 :** a medicine made of saffron and the yolk of an egg and once considered a cure for plague and poison

**philosopher's game** *or* **philosopher's table** *also* **philosophy**

BLACK

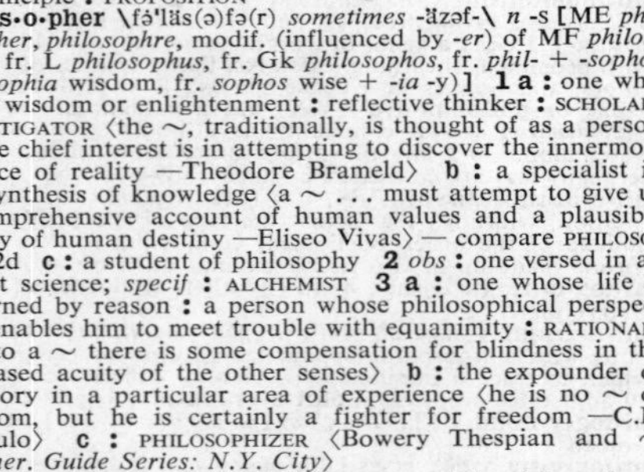

WHITE

board for philosopher's game with men arranged as at beginning of a game

**game** *n* **:** an old form of chess or checkers played on a double board each side having 24 numbered men cut into circles, triangles, and squares

**philosophers' oil** *n* **:** a remedy described in old pharmacopoeias and consisting of linseed oil and powdered brick

**philosophers' stone** *also* **philosopher's stone** *n* [ME *philosophres stoon*, prob. trans. of ML *lapis philosophorum*] **1 :** an imaginary stone, substance, or chemical preparation believed to have the power of transmuting the baser metals into gold, much sought for by alchemists, and by some identified with elixir **2 :** a principle or concept capable of achieving the spiritual regeneration of man ⟨exuded confidence that Turkey possessed the political *philosopher's stone* in its policies of modernization —William Clark⟩

**philosopher's wool** *n, archaic* **:** FLOWERS OF ZINC

**phil·o·so·phia pe·ren·nis** \,filə'sōfēəpə'renəs\ *n, sometimes cap both P's* [NL, lit., perennial philosophy] **:** a group of universal philosophical problems, principles, and ideas (as concepts of God, freedom, and immortality) that perennially constitutes the primary subject matter of philosophical thought **:** the foundations of Roman Catholic Christian principles esp. as philosophically formulated by St. Thomas Aquinas and Neothomists ⟨some *Philosophia Perennis* which would be agreed on in advance as a sort of intellectual base of operations —H.D.Aiken⟩

**philosophia pri·ma** \-'prēmə, -'prīmə\ *n* [L] **:** FIRST PHILOSOPHY

**phil·o·soph·ic** \¦filə¦säfik, -fēk *also* -¦zä-\ *adj* [L *philosophicus*, fr. Gk *philosophikos*, fr. *philosophos* philosopher + *-ikos* -ic] **1 a :** of or relating to philosophers or philosophy ⟨the very ~ dogma that God is everywhere —George Santayana⟩ ⟨a considerable knowledge of ~ terminology —Paul Woodring⟩ **b :** based on philosophy ⟨a doctrine of ~ anarchism —Benjamin Farrington⟩ **2 :** imbued with or characterized by the attitude of a philosopher ⟨that breadth of outlook which distinguishes the ~ mind —*Manchester Guardian Weekly*⟩ ⟨papers of a more ~ temper —G.N.Shuster⟩; *specif* **:** meeting trouble with level-headed detachment **:** TEMPERATE ⟨this ~, long term attitude towards life —B.K.Sandwell⟩ **3** *of a hand* **:** long and angular with bony fingers having developed joints and long nails usu. held by palmists to indicate a studious and analytical nature and a love of mystery in all things — **phil·o·soph·i·cal·ly** \-fək(ə)lē, -fēk-, -li\ *adv*

**phil·o·soph·i·cal** \-fəkəl, -fēk-\ *adj* [L *philosophicus* + E *-al*] **1** *archaic* **:** characterized by learning or the spirit of inquiry **:** SCHOLARLY ⟨a ~ chemist would probably make a very unprofitable business of farming —Humphry Davy⟩ **2** *archaic* **:** of or relating to the physical sciences ⟨a manufacturer of ~ instruments⟩ **3 :** PHILOSOPHIC ⟨no ~ system is ever final, for life itself is never final —*Time*⟩ ⟨a ~ resignation toward disaster —Harrison Smith⟩

**philosophical existentialism** *n* **:** EXISTENTIALISM a

**philosophical grammar** *n* **:** GENERAL GRAMMAR

**philosophical induction** *n* **:** BACONIAN INDUCTION

**phil·o·soph·i·cal·ness** *n* -ES [*philosophical* + *-ness*] **:** the quality or state of being philosophic

**philosophical pitch** *n* **:** a theoretical tuning standard of 427 vibrations per second for A above middle C used for convenience in scientific calculations

**philosophical radical** *n, usu cap P&R* **:** one of a group of early 19th century English liberals characterized chiefly by a belief in Benthamite utilitarianism and advocating legal, economic, and social reforms including free trade and reform of Parliament and the judiciary

**philosophical radicalism** *n, usu cap P&R* **:** the doctrines of the Philosophical Radicals

**phi·los·o·phism** \fə'läsə,fizəm\ *n* -S [F *philosophisme*, fr. MF, fr. OF *philosophie* philosophy + *-isme* -ism] **1 :** spurious philosophic argument **:** SOPHISTRY **2 :** SOPHISM

**phi·los·o·phist** \-,fəst\ *n* -S [F *philosophiste*, fr. *philosophie* + *-iste* -ist] *archaic* **:** SOPHIST, PHILOSOPHIZER — **phi·los·o·phis·ti·cal** \¦=¦==¦fistəkəl\ *adj*

**phi·los·o·phize** \fə'läsə,fīz *sometimes* -äzə,-\ *vb* -ED/-ING/-S [*philosophy* + *-ize*] *vi* **1 :** to reason as or as if a philosopher **:** seek a rational basis for fact and experience **:** REFLECT, THEORIZE ⟨one can draw conclusions about behavior; about instinct one can only ~ —Abram Kardiner⟩ **2 :** to expound a philosophy often superficially ⟨songs that ~, like "Love Thy Neighbor" and "Count Your Blessings" —Mitch Miller⟩ ~ *vt* **:** to consider from or bring into conformity with a philosophic point of view ⟨the course should be history, but history *philosophized*, a history of ideas as well as of events —W.C. DeVane⟩ ⟨tried to ~ himself out of his sense of social maladjustment —H.S.Canby⟩

**phi·los·o·phiz·er** \-īzə(r)\ *n* -S **:** one that philosophizes; *esp* **:** one that expounds a superficial philosophy

**philosophizing** *n* -S [fr. gerund of *philosophize*] **:** an inquiry into the essence and value of some aspect of life ⟨Plato's ~s on art —*Publishers' Weekly*⟩; *specif* **:** MORALIZING ⟨in explaining why she had to be in at 11, the girl's mother chose a middle course between admonition and ~⟩

**phi·los·o·phy** \fə'läs(ə)fē, -fi *sometimes* -äzəf-\ *n* -ES [ME *philosophie*, fr. OF, fr. L *philosophia*, fr. Gk, fr. *phil-* + *sophia* wisdom, fr. *sophos* wise + *-ia* -y] **1 a :** a love or pursuit of wisdom **:** a search for the underlying causes and principles of reality **:** INVESTIGATION, INQUIRY ⟨~ is a natural function of the human mind —Stuart Hampshire⟩ — see FIRST PHILOSOPHY **b :** a quest for truth through logical reasoning rather than factual observation ⟨every advance in knowledge robs ~ of some problems which formerly it had —Bertrand Russell⟩ **c :** a critical examination of the grounds for fundamental beliefs and an analysis of the basic concepts employed in the expression of such beliefs ⟨the job of ~ is the study and statement of the logic, informal and formal, of the employment of expressions —V.C.Aldrich⟩ **d :** a synthesis of learning ⟨it is the primary aim of ~ to unify completely . . . all departments of rational thought —Henry Sidgwick⟩ **2 a** *archaic* **:** the study of natural phenomena **:** PHYSICAL SCIENCE — see SECOND PHILOSOPHY **b :** the study of the principles of human nature and conduct **:** ETHICS **c :** a science that comprises all learning exclusive only of technical precepts and practical arts **d :** the coordinate disciplines of sciences and liberal arts exclusive only of medicine, law, and theology ⟨the ~ of the medieval universities⟩ ⟨the academic degree doctor of ~⟩ ⟨an English bachelor of ~⟩ **e :** a science that comprises logic, ethics, aesthetics, metaphysics, and epistemology **3 a :** a system of motivating beliefs, concepts, and principles ⟨the ~ of a culture determines the general pattern of its . . . institutions —David Bidney⟩ ⟨three *philosophies* contending for dominance in contemporary politics —*Times Lit. Supp.*⟩ ⟨the changing ~ of the courts with regard to many questions —Margaret Nicholson⟩ ⟨set the . . . ~ and the basic course of the museum —Roger Angell⟩ **b :** a basic theory concerning a particular subject, process, or sphere of activity ⟨design ~ in chemical plants —D.E.Pierce⟩ — usu. used with *of* ⟨~ of religion⟩ ⟨~ of education⟩ ⟨the whole ~ of the bill is to ignore the realities —*New Republic*⟩ ⟨a chance to prove my ~ of flying the mail —C.A.Lindbergh b.1902⟩ ⟨automation is a completely new ~ of production —John Diebold⟩ **4 a :** the sum of an individual's ideas and convictions **:** personal attitude ⟨lived by the plain ~ . . . do your best, be loyal to your friends, never forget your enemies —*Time*⟩ ⟨every writer has not one but two *philosophies* — his more or less conscious artistic credo and . . . his often unconscious vision of life and scheme of values —Max Lerner & Edwin Mims⟩ **b :** calmness of temper and judgment befitting a philosopher **:** mental serenity or equanimity ⟨this is the place that calls out all a composer's self-control; it's a moment for ~ —Aaron Copland⟩

**philosophy of organism :** a theory advanced by A. N. Whitehead that the ultimate entities of nature though governed by mechanical principles are not inert but are enduring structures of activity and that the nature of each reflects its organic relations with the larger structures of nature into which it enters — called also *organic mechanism*

**philosophy of the garden** *usu cap G* [so called fr. the fact that Epicurus taught in a garden in Athens] **:** EPICUREANISM 1a

**phi·lo·tria** \fə'lō·trēə\ [NL, irreg. fr. Gk *phyllon* leaf + *tria* three — more at BLADE, THREE] *syn of* ELODEA

**-phi·lous** \f(ə)ləs\ *adj comb form* [Gk *philos* beloved, dear, loving; prob. akin to OE *bile-* simple, innocent, OHG *bil-*, *bila-* good-natured, friendly, MIr *bil* good] **:** loving **:** having an affinity for ⟨dendrophilous⟩ ⟨lithophilous⟩ ⟨acidophilous⟩

**-phils** *pl of* -PHIL

**¹phil·ter** *or* **phil·tre** \'filtə(r)\ *n* -S [MF *philtre*, fr. L *philtrum*, fr. Gk *philtron*, fr. *philein* to love, fr. *philos* loving] **1 :** a potion, drug, or charm supposedly having the power to excite sexual passion esp. toward a particular person — called also *love-philter*, *love-potion* **2 :** a potion credited with magical power

**²philter** *or* **philtre** \"\ *vt* -ED/-ING/-S *archaic* **:** to bewitch by the use of a philter **:** EXCITE, FASCINATE

**phil·trum** \'fil·trəm\ *n, pl* **phil·tra** \-rə\ [NL, fr. Gk *philtron* philter, charm, dimple in the upper lip] **:** the vertical groove on the median line of the upper lip

**-phi·lus** \f(ə)ləs\ *n comb form* [NL, fr. L, loving, fr. Gk *philos*] **:** creature attracted to (such) a food or habitat — in generic names ⟨Campephilus⟩ ⟨Spermophilus⟩

**-phi·ly** \f(ə)lē, -li\ *n comb form* -ES [NL *-philia*] **1 :** fondness for ⟨toxophily⟩ **2 :** affinity for ⟨hydrophily⟩ ⟨photophily⟩ ⟨zoophily⟩ — chiefly in biological and chemical terms

**phil·y·dra·ce·ae** \,filə'drāsē,ē\ *n pl, cap* [NL, fr. *Philydrum*, type genus (fr. *phil-* + Gk *hydōr* water) + *-aceae* — more at WATER] **:** a family of Asiatic and Australian perennial herbs (order Xyridales) with sheathing narrow leaves and spicate flowers resembling orchids — **phil·y·dra·ceous** \¦=¦=drāshəs\ *adj*

**phi·mosed** \'fī,mōzd, -ōst\ *adj* [NL *phimosis* + E *-ed*] **:** affected with phimosis

**phi·mo·sis** \fī'mōsəs, fə'-\ *n, pl* **phimo·ses** \-ō,sēz\ [NL, fr. Gk *phimōsis* muzzling, stopping up of an orifice, contraction of the prepuce, fr. *phimos* muzzle] **:** tightness or constriction of the orifice of the prepuce arising either congenitally or from inflammation, congestion, or other postnatal causes and making it impossible to bare the glans

**phi·mot·ic** \(')fī¦mäd·ik, fə¦m-\ *adj* **:** of, relating to, or marked by phimosis

**phi·o·mia** \fī'ōmēə\ *n, cap* [NL, fr. Copt *ph-iom* the sea, the lake (fr. Egypt *ym* sea, fr. a Canaanite word akin to Heb *yām*) + NL *-ia*; fr. its discovery in the Faiyum, lake province of Egypt] **:** a genus of long-jawed mastodons (family Gomphotheriidae) found in the Oligocene of Egypt

**phi phenomenon** *n, sometimes cap 1st P* **:** the apparent motion of lines, pictures, or other objects shown in a rapid succession of different positions without any actual motion being presented to the eye

**phis** *pl of* PHI

**phi tong luang** \'fē'tŭŋlü'äŋ\ *n, pl* **phi tong luang** *or* **phi tong luangs** *usu cap P&T&L* **1 :** a nomadic food-gathering people of southeast Asia believed to be the most primitive discovered in that area and showing signs of early extinction **2 :** a member of the Phi Tong Luang people

**phiz** \'fiz\ *n* -ES [by shortening & alter. fr. *physiognomy*] **:** FACE ⟨he'd never dare show his ~ again —S.H.Adams⟩

**phleb-** *or* **phlebo-** *comb form* [ME *fleb-*, fr. MF, fr. LL *phleb-*, fr. Gk, fr. *phleb-*, *phleps* blood vessel, vein; akin to Gk *phlyein*, *phlyzein* to boil over — more at FLUID] **:** vein ⟨*phleb*itis⟩ ⟨*phlebo*gram⟩

**phle·bit·ic** \flə'bid·ik, flē'-, fle'-\ *adj* [NL *phlebitis* + E *-ic*] **:** of or relating to phlebitis

**phle·bi·tis** \-bīd·əs, -bītəs\ *n, pl* **phle·bit·i·des** \-bid·ə,dēz, -bitə,-\ [NL, fr. *phleb-* + *-itis*] **:** inflammation of a vein

**phlebo·clysis** \¦flebō+\ *n* [NL, fr. *phleb-* + *clysis*] **:** administration of a large volume of fluid intravenously

**phle·bo·di·um** \flə'bōdēəm\ *n, cap* [NL, fr. Gk *phlebōdēs* full of veins, with large veins, veinlike (fr. *phleb-* + *-ōdēs* -ode) + NL *-ium*] **:** a genus of mostly epiphytic tropical ferns (family Polypodiaceae) having the areolae of the fronds each with two or more free veinlets bearing sori — see SERPENT FERN

**phleb·oe·de·sis** \,flebē'dēsəs\ *n* -ES [NL, fr. *phleb-* + Gk *oidēsis* swelling] **:** the condition of having the terminal parts of the vascular system so expanded as to largely obliterate the coelom which is replaced by a hemocoel (as in arthropods and mollusks)

**phleb·o·gram** \'flebə,gram\ *n* [ISV *phleb-* + *-gram*] **:** a figure of a vein or a record of its movements (as by roentgenography following injection of a radiopaque substance)

**phleb·o·graph·ic** \¦==¦grafik\ *adj* [ISV *phlebography* + *-ic*] **:** of or relating to phlebography

**phle·bog·ra·phy** \flə'bägrəfē\ *n* -ES [ISV *phleb-* + *-graphy*] **:** the art of making phlebograms

**phleb·oid** \'fle,bȯid\ *also* **phle·boi·dal** \flə'bȯidᵊl\ *adj* [*phleb-* + *-oid*] **:** having the properties of or characterized by veins

**phleb·o·lith** \'flebə,lith\ *n* -S [ISV *phleb-* + *-lith*] **:** a calculus in a vein usu. resulting from the calcification of an old thrombus

**phlebo·sclerosis** \¦flebō+\ *n* [NL, fr. *phleb-* + *sclerosis*] **:** sclerosis of the wall of a vein esp. of its inner coats

**phlebo·sclerotic** \"+\ *adj* **:** of, relating to, or affected by phlebosclerosis

**phlebo·thrombosis** \"+\ *n* [NL, fr. *phleb-* + *thrombosis*] **:** venous thrombosis accompanied by little or no inflammation — compare THROMBOPHLEBITIS

**phleb·o·tom·ic** \¦flebə¦tämik\ *also* **phleb·o·tom·i·cal** \-məkəl\ *adj* [*phlebotomic* fr. F *phlébotomique*, fr. MF *phlebotomie* phlebotomy + *-ique* -ic; *phlebotomical* fr. *phlebotomy* + *-ical*] **1 :** of or relating to phlebotomy **2 :** BLOODSUCKING—used of insects—**phleb·o·tom·i·cal·ly** \-mək(ə)lē\ *adv*

**phle·bot·o·mist** \flə'bäd·əməst, flē'-, fle'-, -ätəm-\ *n* -S [*phlebotomy* + *-ist*] **:** one that practices phlebotomy

**phle·bot·o·mize** \-ə,mīz\ *vb* -ED/-ING/-S [MF *phlebotomiser*, fr. ML *flebotomizare*, fr. LL *phlebotomia*, *flebotomia* phlebotomy + *-izare* -ize] *vt* **:** to draw blood from **:** BLEED ~ *vi* **1 :** to practice phlebotomy **2 :** to submit to phlebotomy **:** undergo bleeding

**phle·bot·o·mus** \flə'bäd·əməs\ *n* [NL, fr. LL, lancet, fleam — more at FLEAM] **1** *cap* **:** a genus of small delicate bloodsucking sand flies (family Psychodidae) including one (*P. papatasii*) that is the carrier of phlebotomus fever and others suspected of carrying other human diseases **2** *pl* **phleboto·mi** \-d·ə,mī\ *also* **phlebotomuses :** a fly of the genus *Phlebotomus*

**phlebotomus fever** *n* **:** a virus disease of brief duration characterized by fever, headache, pain in the eyes, malaise, and leukopenia and transmitted by the bite of a sand fly (*Phlebotomus papatasii*) — called also *sand-fly fever*

**phle·bot·o·my** \flə'bäd·əmē, flē'-, fle'-, -ätə-, mi\ *n* -ES [ME *fleobotomie*, fr. MF *flebotomie*, fr. LL *phlebotomia*, *flebotomia*, fr. Gk *phlebotomia*, fr. *phleb-* + *-tomia* (fr. *temnein* to cut) — more at TOME] **:** the letting of blood in the treatment of disease **:** VENESECTION

**phleg·e·thon·tal** \¦flegə¦thäntᵊl, -ejə¦-\ *or* **phleg·e·thon·tic** \-tik\ *adj, usu cap* [L *phlegethontis* phlegethontal (fr. *Phlegethon*, principal river of Hades that ran with fire instead of water, fr. Gk *Phlegethōn*, fr. *phlegethein* to blaze, fr. *phlegein* to burn) + E *-al* or *-ic*] *archaic* **:** of, relating to, or resembling a river of fire **:** BURNING

**phlegm** \'flem\ *n* -S [ME *fleem*, *fleume*, fr. MF *fleume*, fr. LL *phlegma*, *flegma*, fr. Gk *phlegma* flame, inflammation, phlegm, fr. *phlegein* to burn — more at BLACK] **1 :** the one of the four humors of early physiology that was supposed to be cold and moist and to cause sluggishness **2 :** MUCUS; *usu* **:** viscid mucus secreted in abnormal quantity in the respiratory passages and discharged through the mouth **3** *archaic* **:** a watery distillation that in early chemistry is one of the five principles of bodies **:** WATER, MOISTURE **4 :** temperament or conduct supposedly associated with abundance of the humor phlegm: **a :** dull or apathetic coldness or indifference **b :** intrepid coolness or calm fortitude ⟨a lofty ~, a detachment in the midst of action, a capacity for watching in silence and commanding without excitement —Edmund Wilson⟩ **syn** see EQUANIMITY

**phleg·ma** \'flegmə\ *n* -S [LL, phlegm] **:** a watery distilled liquor as distinguished by distillers from a spirituous liquor

**phleg·ma·sia** \fleg'māzh(ē)ə, -āzēə\ *n, pl* **phlegmasiae** \-āz(h)ē,ē\ [Gk, fr. *phlegma*] **:** INFLAMMATION

**phlegmasia al·ba do·lens** \-'albə'dō,lenz\ *n* [NL, lit., painful white inflammation] **:** MILK LEG

**¹phleg·mat·ic** \(')fleg¦mad·ik, -at|, |ēk\ *or* **phleg·mat·i·cal** \|əkəl, |ēk-\ *adj* [*phlegmatic* fr. ME *flaumatike*, fr. MF *flaumatique*, *phlegme*, fr. LL *phlegmaticus*, fr. Gk *phlegmatikos*, fr. *phlegmat-*, *phlegma* flame + *-ikos* -ic; *phlegmatical* fr. ²*phlegmatic* + *-al*] **1 a :** like or consisting of the humor phlegm ⟨~ matter⟩ **:** abounding in or producing phlegm ⟨a ~ constitution⟩ **b** *obs* **:** MUCOID, VISCOUS, WATERY **2 :** having or showing the character or temperament formerly associated with a predominance of the humor phlegm : marked by sluggishness and stolidity : CALM, COMPOSED, UNDEMONSTRATIVE ⟨as ~ in the way of a man who accepts all things, and accepts them in the spirit of cool bravery —Bram Stoker⟩ **syn** see IMPASSIVE

**²phlegmatic** \"\ *n* -s : a person of phlegmatic constitution or temperament

**phleg·mat·i·cal·ly** \|ə̇k(ə)lē, |ēk-, -li\ *adv* [*phlegmatical* + *-ly*] : in a phlegmatic manner

**phleg·ma·tous** \ˈflegmədəs\ *adj* [Gk *phlegmat-, phlegma* + E *-ous*] : PHLEGMATIC

**phleg·mon** \ˈfleg,män\ *n* -s [ME *flegmone*, fr. L *phlegmone, phlegmon*, fr. Gk *phlegmonē* inflammation, boil, fr. *phlegein* to burn — more at PHLEGM] : purulent inflammation and infiltration of connective tissue — compare ABSCESS

**phleg·mon·ic** \(ˈ)fleg¦mänik\ *adj* [ML *phlegmonicus*, fr. Gk *phlegmonikos*, fr. *phlegmon* + *-ikos* -ic] : PHLEGMONOUS

**phleg·mon·ous** \ˈflegmənəs\ *adj* [F *phlegmoneux*, fr. *phlegmon* (fr. L *phlegmone, phlegmon*) + *-eux* -ous] : of, relating to, or constituting a phlegmon : accompanied by or characterized by phlegmons — **phleg·mon·ous·ly** *adv*

**phlegmy** \ˈflemē\ *adj* -ER/-EST [*phlegm* + *-y* (adj. suffix)] : of, constituting, characterized by, or due to phlegm ⟨a ~ cough⟩ : PHLEGMATIC; *sometimes* : WATERY

**phlep·si·us** \ˈflepsēəs\ *n*, *cap* [NL, fr. Gk *phleps* blood vessel, vein — more at PHLEB-] : a large and widely distributed genus of leafhoppers

**phle·um** \ˈflēəm\ *n*, *cap* [NL, prob. fr. Gk *phleōs* wool-tufted reed] : a genus of grasses that are natives of temperate regions and have dense oblong or terete spike and long mucronate empty glumes — see TIMOTHY

**phlob·a·phene** \ˈfläbə,fēn\ *n* -s [ISV *phlobaph-* (fr. Gk *phloos, phloios* bark + *baphē* dye — fr. *baptein* to dip, dye —) + *-ene* — more at BAPTIZE] **1** : a reddish brown complex substance found in oak bark and also formed by heating quercitannin with dilute acids **2** : any of several substances that are similar to phlobaphene and are obtained esp. from barks or from condensed tannins

**phloba·tannin** \¦fläbə+\ *n* [*phlobaphene* + *tannin*] : a tannin that with hot dilute acids yields a phlobaphene

**phlo·em** \ˈflō,em\ *n* -s [G, fr. Gk *phloios, phloos* bark; akin to Gk *phallos* penis — more at BLOW] : a complex tissue in the vascular system of higher plants consisting mainly of sieve tubes and companion cells and usu. also of fibers and parenchyma cells and functioning chiefly in translocation but also in support and storage — called also *bast, sieve tissue*

**phloem fiber** *n* : a fiber found in or associated with the phloem that is often commercially useful (as in flax) because of its great tensile strength and pliability and that differs from the xylem fiber in that its pits are usu. small and simple — called also *bast fiber*

**phloem necrosis** *n* : any pathological state in a plant characterized by brown discoloration and disintegration of the phloem: as **a** : a phase of potato leaf roll in which such changes occur **b** : a virus disease of tea **c** : a fatal virus disease of the American elm widespread in the U.S. characterized by yellowish often black-flecked discoloration and degeneration of the phloem and resulting in death of the root system through lack of food followed by wilting, yellowing, and loss of leaves

**phloem parenchyma** *n* : the nonspecialized vertically arranged parenchyma of the phloem — called also *bast parenchyma*; compare WOOD PARENCHYMA

**phloem ray** *n* : a vascular ray or part of a vascular ray that is located in phloem — called also *bast ray*; compare XYLEM RAY

**phloe·o·thrip·i·dae** \,flēō'thripə,dē\ *n pl*, *cap* [NL, fr. *Phloeothrips*, type genus (fr. Gk *phloios, phloos* bark + *thrips*) + *-idae*] : a widely distributed family of thrips many of which are serious pests on a great variety of plants

**phlo·gis·tian** \flō'jis(h)chən\ *n* -s [NL *phlogiston* + E *-an*] : PHLOGISTONIST

**phlo·gis·tic** \flō'jistik, -tēk\ *adj* [in sense 1, prob. fr. (assumed) NL *phlogisticus*, fr. *phlogiston* + L *-icus* -ic; in sense 2, fr. Gk *phlogistos* inflammable + E *-ic*] **1** *archaic* : of or relating to phlogiston or the phlogiston theory **2** : of or relating to inflammations and fevers : INFLAMMATORY **3** *archaic* **a** : BURNING, FIERY **b** : IMPASSIONED, HEATED

**phlo·gis·ti·cate** \-tə,kāt\ *vt* -ED/-ING/-s [*phlogistic* + *-ate*] : to combine phlogiston with ⟨highly *phlogisticated* substances⟩ — **phlo·gis·ti·ca·tion** \⸗,⸗⸗'kāshən\ *n* -s

**phlogisticated air** *n* **1** *archaic* : air exhausted of oxygen by burning a combustible (as charcoal or phosphorus) in it and therefore composed chiefly of nitrogen **2** *archaic* : hydrogen regarded as inflammable air

**phlo·gis·ton** \flō'jistən\ *n* -s [NL, fr. Gk, neut. of *phlogistos* burnt, inflammable, fr. *phlogizein* to set on fire, fr. *phlog-, phlox* flame, fr. *phlegein* to burn — more at BLACK] : the hypothetical principle of fire or inflammability regarded by the early chemists as a material substance ⟨metals were supposed to be prepared from their calxes by the union of the latter with ~ —M.C.Sneed & J.L.Maynard⟩ ⟨what manner of substance or principle could ~ be that when it was added to another material the total mass or weight diminished? —J.B.Conant⟩

**phlo·gis·ton·ism** \-ə,nizəm\ *n* -s : the phlogiston theory or the system of chemistry built upon it

**phlo·gis·ton·ist** \-,nəst\ *n* -s : an adherent of the phlogiston theory

**phlogiston theory** *n* : a theory in 18th century chemistry disproved by Lavoisier: every combustible substance is a compound of phlogiston and the phenomena of combustion are due to the liberation of phlogiston with the other constituent left as a residue ⟨the *phlogiston theory* thus provided a general explanation of the chemical processes of oxidation and reduction: oxidation was taken to be the liberation of phlogiston, and reduction combination with phlogiston —Linus Pauling⟩

**phlog·o·ge·net·ic** \¦flägōjə¦ned·ik\ *adj* [Gk *phlog-, phlox* flame + *-genetic*] : PHLOGOGENIC

**phlog·o·gen·ic** \¦flägə¦jenik\ *also* **phlo·gog·e·nous** \flō'gäjənəs\ *adj* [Gk *phlog-, phlox* flame + E *-genic* or *-genous*] : producing inflammation

**phlog·o·pite** \ˈflägə,pīt\ *n* -s [G *phlogopit*, fr. Gk *phlogōpos* fiery-looking, flaming red (fr. *phlog-, phlox* flame + *ōps* eye) + G *-it* -ite — more at EYE] : a usu. yellowish brown to brownish red or copper form of mica that is typically a silicate of potassium, magnesium, and aluminum with some fluorine or hydroxyl and that is grouped with biotite

**phlog·o·pi·ti·za·tion** \,⸗⸗,pīd·ə'zāshən\ *n* -s [*phlogopite* + *-ization*] : the development of phlogopite in a solid rock

**phlo·ic** \ˈflōik\ *adj* [*phloem* + *-ic*] : relating to, consisting of, or located in the phloem

**phlo·i·on·ic acid** \¦flōē¦änik-\ *n* [*phloionic* fr. Gk *phloios* bark + E *-onic*] : a crystalline hydroxy acid [$-CH(OH)-(CH_2)_7COOH]_2$ that is among the acidic products formed by alkaline hydrolysis of cork; 9,10-dihydroxy-octadecanedioic acid — see SUBERIN

**phlo·mis** \ˈflōməs\ *n* [NL, fr. L *phlomis, phlomos* mullein, fr. Gk] **1** *cap* : a genus of Old World mints having rugose often woolly leaves and whorls of white, yellow, or purple flowers with bilabiate corolla **2** -ES : a plant of the genus *Phlomis*

**phlor-** or **phloro-** *comb form* [F, fr. ISV *phlorizin*] **1** : related to phlorizin ⟨*phlor*etin⟩ ⟨*phloro*glucin⟩ **2** : related to phloroglucinol ⟨*phloro*-acetophenone $CH_3COC_6H_4(OH)_3$⟩

**phlor·e·tin** \ˈflōrəd·ən, ˈflär-, flə'rēd·ən\ *n* -s [F *phlorétine*, fr. *phlor-* (in *phlorizin*) + Gk *rhētinē* resin] : a crystalline phenolic ketone $C_{15}H_{14}O_5$ derived from phloroglucinol and phenol and obtained esp. by hydrolysis of phlorizin

**phlor·i·zin** \ˈflōrəzən, ˈflär-, flə'rīzᵊn\ *or* **phlo·rhi·zin** *or* **phlo·rid·zin** \flə'ridzən\ *also* **phlor·rhi·zin** \ˈflōrəzən, ˈflär-, flə'rīzᵊn\ *n* -s [ISV *phlo-* (fr. Gk *phloios, phloos* bark) + *-riz-* or *-rhiz-* or *-ridz-* or *-rrhiz-* (fr. Gk *rhiza* root) + *-in*; perh. orig. formed as F *phlorizine* — more at ROOT] : a bitter crystalline glucoside $C_{21}H_{24}O_{10}$ that is extracted from root bark or bark esp. of the apple, pear, cherry, or plum, that on hydrolysis yields glucose and phloretin, and that produces glycosuria if injected hypodermically and is used chiefly in producing experimental diabetes in animals

**phlor·i·zin·ize** \ˈflōrəzə,nīz, ˈflär-, flə'rīzᵊn,īz\ *also* **phlo·rhi·zin·ize** *or* **phlo·rid·zin·ize** \flə'ridzə,nīz\ *vt* -ED/-ING/-s : to administer phlorizin to

**phlor·o·glu·cin** \¦flōrə¦glüsᵊn, ¦flär-\ *n* -s [ISV *phlor-* + *gluc-* + *-in*] : PHLOROGLUCINOL

**phlor·o·glu·cin·ol** \-sᵊn,ōl, -,ōl\ *n* -s [*phloroglucin* + *-ol*] : a sweet crystalline phenol $C_6H_3(OH)_3$ that occurs in combined form in glycosides (as phlorizin), in resins, and in tannins, that is usu. made from trinitrotoluene by a series of steps, and that is used chiefly as a developer in black-and-white reproduction; 1,3,5-trihydroxy-benzene

**phlox** \ˈfläks\ *n* [NL, fr. L, a flower, fr. Gk, wallflower, flame, fr. *phlegein* to burn — more at BLACK] **1** *cap* : a genus of American herbs (family Polemoniaceae) having red, purple, white, or variegated flowers, the corolla salver-shaped with the stamens on its tube, and a 3-valved capsular fruit — see ANNUAL PHLOX, MOSS PINK **2** *pl* **phlox** *or* **phloxes** : any plant of the genus *Phlox* **3** -ES : a dark purplish red that is bluer and less strong than pansy purple and bluer, lighter, and stronger than raisin, Bokhara, dahlia purple (sense 1), or redgrape

**phlox family** *n* : POLEMONIACEAE

**phlox·ine** \ˈfläk,sēn, -,sən\ *n* -s *often cap* [Gk *phlox* flame + E *-ine*] : either of two acid dyes or their sodium salts that are chloro derivatives of eosine and are used chiefly as biological stains and organic pigments: **a** *or* **phloxine B** : the dichloro derivative **b** : the tetrachloro derivative — see DYE table I (under *Acid Red 92, Solvent Red 48*)

**phlox pink** *n* : a pale purple that is redder and paler than average lavender, redder and darker than wistaria (sense 2a), and redder and stronger than flossflower blue

**phlox purple** *n* : a strong reddish purple that is bluer, lighter, and stronger than average fuchsia purple and redder and paler than purple orchid

**phlyc·te·na** *or* **phlyc·tae·na** \flik'tēnə\ *n*, *pl* **phlycte·nae** *or* **phlyctae·nae** \-ē,nē\ [NL, fr. Gk *phlyktaina* blister, fr. *phlyein, phlyzein* to boil over — more at FLUID] : PHLYCTENULE

**phlyc·te·noid** \-ē,nȯid\ *adj* [NL *phlyctena* + E *-oid*] : resembling a phlyctenule

**phlyc·ten·u·la** *or* **phlyc·taen·u·la** \-'tenyələ, -tēn-\ *n*, *pl* **phlyctenu·lae** *or* **phlyctaenu·lae** \-yə,lē\ [NL, fr. *phlyctena, phlyctaena* + *-ula* (fr. *-ulus*)] : PHLYCTENULE

**phlyc·ten·u·lar** \-'tenyələ(r)\ *adj* [NL *phlyctenula* + E *-ar*] : marked by or associated with phlyctenules ⟨~ conjunctivitis⟩

**phlyc·ten·ule** \-n,yül\ *n* -s [NL *phlyctenula*] : a small vesicle or pustule; *esp* : one on the conjunctiva or cornea of the eye

**pho** *abbr* photographer

**phob-** *or* **phobo-** *comb form* [LL, fr. Gk, fr. *phobos*] : fear : avoidance ⟨*phob*ism⟩ ⟨*phobo*phobia⟩ ⟨*phobo*taxis⟩

**-phobe** \,fōb\ *n comb form* -s [Gk *-phobos* -fearing, fr. *phobos* fear, flight] : one having a (specified) phobia ⟨Anglo*phobe*⟩ ⟨chromo*phobe*⟩ ⟨helio*phobe*⟩ ⟨photo*phobe*⟩

**pho·bia** \ˈfōbēə\ *n* -s [NL, fr. LL *-phobia* fear of something, fr. Gk, fr. *phobos* fear, flight + *-ia* -y; akin to Gk *phebesthai* to flee, be frightened, Lith *bėgti* to run, flee] : an exaggerated and often disabling fear usu. inexplicable to the subject, having occas. a logical but usu. an illogical or symbolic object, and serving to protect the ego against anxiety arising from unexpressed aggressive impulses — compare COMPULSION, OBSESSION

**pho·bi·ac** \-ē,ak\ *n* -s [*phobia* + *-ac* (as in *maniac*)] : one that exhibits a phobia

**¹pho·bic** \ˈfōbik, -bēk *also* ˈfäb-\ *adj* [NL *phobia* + E *-ic*] **1** : of, relating to, characterized by, or arising from phobia **2** *of a taxis* : based on withdrawal from an unpleasant rather than movement toward a pleasing stimulus

**²phobic** \"\ *n* -s : PHOBIAC

**-pho·bic** \¦fōbik, -bēk *also* ¦fäb-\ *or* **-pho·bous** \fəbəs\ *adj comb form* [*-phobic* fr. F *-phobique*, fr. LL *-phobicus*, fr. Gk *-phobikos*, fr. *-phobos* fearing + *-ikos* -ic; *-phobous* fr. LL *-phobus*, fr. Gk *-phobos*] **1** : exhibiting a phobia: having an aversion for ⟨Anglo*phobic*⟩ ⟨calci*phobous*⟩ ⟨helio*phobous*⟩ **2** *chem* : lacking or relating to lack of strong affinity for (such) a substance — opposed to *-philic*

**phobic reaction** *n* : a psychoneurosis in which the principal symptom is a phobia

**pho·bism** \ˈfō,bizəm *also* ˈfä,-\ *n* -s [*phobia* + *-ism*] : the state of one affected by a phobia

**pho·bo·tac·tic** \¦fōbə¦taktik\ *adj* [*phob-* + *-tactic*] : of or relating to phobotaxis : involving random trial and error

**pho·bo·tax·is** \,⸗⸗'taksə̇s\ *n* [NL, fr. *phob-* + *-taxis*] : a random avoiding reaction in response to a distasteful stimulus

**pho·by cat** \ˈfōbē-\ *n* [*phoby* by shortening and alter. fr. *hydrophobia*; fr. the belief that its bite causes hydrophobia] *West* : LITTLE SPOTTED SKUNK

**pho·ca** \ˈfōkə\ *n*, *cap* [NL, fr. L, seal, fr. Gk *phōkē*] : a genus of seals formerly nearly coextensive with the family Phocidae but now restricted to the harbor seal and a few closely related forms

**pho·ca·cean** \fō'kāshən\ *or* **pho·ca·ceous** \-shəs\ *adj* [NL *Phoca* + E *-acean* or *-aceous*] : PHOCINE

**¹pho·cae·an** \fō'sēən\ *adj*, *usu cap* [L *Phocaea* (fr. Gk *Phōkaia*) + E *-an*] **1** : of, relating to, or characteristic of the ancient Ionian city of Phocaea in Asia Minor **2** : of, relating to, or characteristic of the people of Phocaea

**²phocaean** \"\ *n* -s *cap* : a native or inhabitant of Phocaea

**pho·cae·na** \fō'sēnə\ *n*, *cap* [NL, fr. Gk *phōkaina* porpoise] : a widely distributed genus of porpoises that includes the harbor porpoise and other common porpoises

**¹pho·cae·nid** \-nəd\ *adj* [NL *Phocaenidae*] : of or relating to porpoises

**²phocaenid** \"\ *n* -s [NL *Phocaenidae*] : PORPOISE

**pho·cae·ni·dae** \-nə,dē\ *n pl*, *cap* [NL, fr. *Phocaena*, type genus + *-idae*] *in some classifications* : a small family of toothed whales that comprises the porpoises and is now usu. included in Delphinidae

**pho·cal** \ˈfōkəl\ *adj* [NL *Phoca* + E *-al*] : PHOCINE

**¹pho·cian** \ˈfōshən\ *adj*, *usu cap* [L *Phocis* (fr. Gk *Phōkis*) + E *-an*] **1** : of, relating to, or characteristic of the ancient Greek state of Phocis between Boeotia and Locris **2** : of, relating to, or characteristic of the people of Phocis

**²phocian** \"\ *n* -s *cap* : a native or inhabitant of Phocis

**¹pho·cid** \ˈfōsə̇d\ *adj* [NL *Phocidae*] : of or relating to the Phocidae

**²phocid** \"\ *n* -s [NL *Phocidae*] : a seal of the family Phocidae

**pho·ci·dae** \-sə,dē\ *n pl*, *cap* [NL, fr. *Phoca*, type genus + *-idae*] : a family of mammals (suborder Pinnipedia) comprising the hair seals and lacking external ears — **pho·ci·form** \-sə,fȯrm\ *adj* — **pho·coid** \ˈfō,kȯid\ *adj or n*

**pho·cine** \ˈfō,sīn, -,sən\ *adj* [NL *Phoca* + E *-ine*] : of, relating to, or resembling seals

**pho·coe·na** \fō'sēnə\ [NL] *syn of* PHOCAENA

**pho·co·me·lia** *also* **pho·ko·me·lia** \,fōkə'mēlēə\ *n* -s [NL, fr. Gk *phōkē* seal + NL *-melia*] : the condition of having the limbs extremely shortened so that feet or hands arise close to the trunk (as in creeper fowls) — **pho·co·me·lic** \¦⸗⸗¦mēlik\ *adj*

**pho·com·e·lus** \fō'kämələs\ *n* -ES [NL, fr. Gk *phōkē* seal + NL *-melus*] : an individual affected with phocomelia

**¹phoe·be** \ˈfēbē, -bi\ *or* **phoebe bird** *also* **phe·be** \"\ *n* -s [alter. (influenced by the name *Phoebe*) of *pewee*] : any of several American flycatchers of the genus *Sayornis*; *esp* : a flycatcher (*S. phoebe*) of the eastern U.S. that has a slight crest, is plain grayish brown above and yellowish white below, and often places its nest built of mud and grass about old buildings

**²phoebe** \"\ *n* -s *usu cap* [prob. fr. the name *Phoebe*] *slang* : a throw of five in the game of craps

**phoe·be·an** \ˈfēbēən, ⸗'⸗⸗\ *adj*, *usu cap* [L *phoebeus* Phoebean (fr. Gk *phoibeios*, fr. *Phoibos* Phoebus, Greco-Roman god of the sun and of poetry) + E *-an*] : of, relating to, or characteristic of Phoebus Apollo

**phoebe lamp** *n*, *usu cap P* [prob. fr. the name *Phoebe*] : a shallow early American fat-burning or grease-burning lamp of metal, pottery, or stone with a spout to hold the wick and often a cup attached to catch drippings — compare BETTY LAMP

Phoebe lamp

**¹phoe·ni·cian** *also* **phe·ni·cian** \fə'nishən, fē'-, fə'nēshən\ *n* -s *cap* [ME *phenicien*, fr. L *phoenicius* fr. *Phoenice* Phoenicia, fr. Gk *Phoinikē*, fr. *phoinik-, phoinix* Phoenician, phoenix, date palm, purple, crimson) + ME *-ien* -ian; akin to Gk *phoinos* bloodred, *phonos* murder and perh. to Gk *theinein* to strike — more at DEFEND] **1** : a native or inhabitant of ancient Phoenicia **2** : the Semitic language of ancient Phoenicia differing only dialectically from Hebrew

**²phoenician** *also* **phe·ni·cian** \"\ *adj*, *usu cap* **1 a** : of, relating to, or characteristic of the ancient land of Phoenicia on the coast of Syria **b** : of, relating to, or characteristic of the people of Phoenicia **2** : of, relating to, or characteristic of the Phoenician language

**³phoe·ni·cian** \fē'nishən\ *n* -s *cap* [*Phoenix*, Ariz. + E *-an*] : a native or resident of Phoenix, Ariz.

**phoenician alphabet** *n*, *usu cap P* **1** : an extinct northern Semitic alphabet used by the Phoenicians of Syria and their Carthaginian colonists from the 13th century B.C. and the immediate ancestor of the Greek alphabet **2** : the ancestor of the alphabets used by the Phoenicians and other contemporary Semitic inhabitants of western Syria that is held to be the earliest system of alphabetic writing **3** : the oldest Hebrew alphabet as distinguished from the square Hebrew or Aramaic alphabet

**phoe·ni·cite** \ˈfēnə,sīt, ˈfen-\ *n* -s [G *phönikit*, contr. of *phönikochroit*] : PHOENICOCHROITE

**phoe·ni·coch·ro·ite** *or* **phe·ni·coch·ro·ite** \,fēnə'kākrə,wīt\ *n* -s [G *phönikochroit*, fr. Gk *phoinik-*, phoinix purple, crimson + *-chroia* + G *-it* -ite] : a mineral $Pb_3(CrO_4)_2O$(?) consisting of a basic lead chromate in red crystals and masses

**phoenicopter** *var of* PHENICOPTER

**phoe·ni·cop·teri** \,fēnə'käptə,rī\ *n pl*, *cap* [NL, fr. pl. of *Phoenicopterus*] : a small suborder of Ciconiiformes comprising the flamingos and related extinct birds

**phoe·ni·cop·ter·i·dae** \,fēnə,käp'terə,dē\ *n pl*, *cap* [NL, fr. *Phoenicopterus*, type genus + *-idae*] : a family of large showy wading birds that comprises the flamingos, usu. constitutes a suborder of the order Ciconiiformes, but was formerly considered to form a distinct order — **phoe·ni·cop·ter·oid** \¦⸗⸗¦käptə,rȯid\ *adj or n* — **phoe·ni·cop·ter·ous** \-tərəs\ *adj*

**phoe·ni·cop·ter·i·for·mes** \,⸗⸗,käptərə'fȯr,mēz\ *n pl*, *cap* [NL, fr. *Phoenicopterus* + *-iformes*] *in some esp. former classifications* : an order of wading birds coextensive with the family Phoenicopteridae

**phoe·ni·cop·ter·us** \,⸗⸗'käptərəs\ *n*, *cap* [NL, fr. L, flamingo — more at PHENICOPTER] : a genus (the type of the family Phoenicopteridae) comprising the European flamingos and some New World forms including the one (*P. ruber*) that ranges into the southern U.S.

**phoe·nic·u·lus** \fē'nikyələs\ *n*, *cap* [NL, fr. *phoenic-, phoenix* (fr. L *phoenix*) + *-ulus*] : an African genus (coextensive with the family Phoeniculidae of the suborder Coracii) comprising the wood hoopoes and having a long decurved bill, a long wedge-shaped tail, and no crest

**¹phoe·nix** \ˈfēniks, -nēks\ *n* -ES [ME *fenix*, fr. OE, fr. L *phoenix*, fr. Gk *phoinix* phoenix, Phoenician, date palm, purple, crimson — more at PHOENICIAN] **1** : a legendary bird represented by the ancient Egyptians as living five or six centuries in the Arabian desert, being consumed in fire by its own act, and rising in youthful freshness from its own ashes and often regarded as an emblem of immortality or of the resurrection **2** : a person or thing likened to the phoenix: as **a** : a paragon of excellence or beauty ⟨concerned at seeing the ~ of modern culture throw herself away on a man unworthy of her —G.B.Shaw⟩ **b** : one that experiences a restoration, renewal, or seeming rebirth after ruin or destruction ⟨natural law is the ~ of legal speculation; however often it is criticized to extinction, it rises again, an old spirit in a new and vigorous body —Glenn Negley⟩ **3** : a representation of the phoenix (as in heraldry) **4** : FENG HUANG

**²phoenix** \"\ *n*, *cap* [NL, fr. Gk *phoinix* date palm] : a large genus of pinnate-leaved palms distributed throughout tropical Asia and Africa and having dioecious flowers and an ovary with three carpels only one of which matures — see ¹DATE

**³phoenix** \"\ *adj*, *usu cap* [fr. *Phoenix*, Ariz.] : of or from Phoenix, the capital of Arizona ⟨a *Phoenix* motel⟩ : of the kind or style prevalent in Phoenix

**phoenix brown** *n*, *often cap P&B* : a basic dye — see DYE table I (under *Basic Brown 2*)

**phoenix fowl** *n* : JAPANESE FOWL

**phoe·nix·i·ty** \fē'niksəd·ē\ *n* -ES [¹*phoenix* + *-ity*] : the quality or state of being a phoenix; *esp* : UNIQUENESS ⟨she —poor girl!—cannot appreciate even her own ~ —G.B.Shaw⟩

**phoenix tree** *n* : CHINESE PARASOL TREE

**phokomelia** *var of* PHOCOMELIA

**¹pho·lad** \ˈfō,lad\ *n* -s [Gk *phōlad-, phōlas* stone-boring mollusk] : a mollusk of the family Pholadidae : PIDDOCK — **pho·la·di·an** \fō'lādēən\ *adj or n*

**²pholad** \"\ *adj* : of, relating to, or due to a pholad

**pho·la·da·cea** \,fōlə'dāshēə\ *n pl*, *cap* [NL, fr. *Pholad-, Pholas* + *-acea*] *in some classifications* : a suborder of Eulamellibranchia comprising the piddocks and shipworms

**¹pho·la·did** \ˈfōlədəd\ *adj* [NL *Pholadidae*] : of or relating to the Pholadidae

**²pholadid** \"\ *n* -s [NL *Pholadidae*] : a mollusk of the family Pholadidae

**pho·lad·i·dae** \fō'ladə,dē\ *n pl*, *cap* [NL, fr. *Pholad-, Pholas*, type genus + *-idae*] : a family of bivalve mollusks (order Eulamellibranchia) comprising the piddocks and related borers — **pho·la·doid** \ˈfōlə,dȯid\ *adj*

**pho·las** \ˈfōləs\ *n* [NL, fr. Gk *phōlas* stone-boring mollusk, lit., lying in a hole; akin to Gk *phylē* tribe, clan — more at PHYSIC] **1** *cap* : a large genus of bivalve usu. marine mollusks (family Pholadidae) with an elongate-oval rough shell having no hinge ligament, gaping at the end, and having two accessory valves to protect the dorsal margin that with the foot serves as a rasp to bore in wood and stone **2** *pl* **phola·des** \-lə,dēz\ : any mollusk of the genus *Pholas* or of the family Pholadidae : PIDDOCK

**¹phol·cid** \ˈfälsəd\ *adj* [NL *Pholcidae*] : of or relating to the Pholcidae

**²pholcid** \"\ *n* -s [NL *Pholcidae*] : a spider of the family Pholcidae

**phol·ci·dae** \-sə,dē\ *n pl*, *cap* [NL, fr. *Pholcus*, type genus + *-idae*] : a family of spiders having very long slender legs and weaving irregular webs in which they rest with the back downward — **phol·coid** \ˈfäl,kȯid\ *adj or n*

**phol·cus** \ˈfälkəs\ *n*, *cap* [NL, fr. Gk *pholkos* bowlegged] : a genus of spiders that is the type of the family Pholcidae

**pholid-** *or* **pholido-** *comb form* [NL, fr. Gk, fr. *pholid-, pholis* scale of a reptile; akin to Gk *phloos* bark — more at PHLOEM] : scale ⟨*pholid*osis⟩ ⟨*pholido*lite⟩

**phol·i·do·sis** \,fälə'dōsə̇s\ *n*, *pl* **pholido·ses** \-ō,sēz\ [NL, fr. *pholid-* + *-osis*] : LEPIDOSIS 2

**phol·i·do·ta** \,fälə'dōd·ə\ *n pl*, *cap* [NL, fr. Gk *pholidōtos* covered with scales, fr. *pholid-, pholis*] : an order of toothless scaly eutherian mammals comprising the pangolins that in many respects resemble true edentates and were formerly included in Edentata

**phol·i·o·ta** \,fälē'ōd·ə\ *n*, *cap* [NL, fr. Gk *pholis* scale of a reptile + *ōt-, ous* ear — more at EAR] : a genus of brown-spored agarics of Europe and No. America having an annulus and growing on open ground or decaying wood

**-pho·lis** \fələs\ *n comb form* [NL, fr. Gk *pholis* scale of a reptile] : organism having a (specified) kind of scale — in generic names ⟨Cono*pholis*⟩

**pho·ma** \ˈfōmə\ *n*, *cap* [NL, fr. Gk *phōis* blister] : a large form genus of imperfect fungi (family Sphaeropsidaceae) typically stem-inhabiting but some causing destructive rots of fruits or roots and having nonseptate hyaline ovate to elongate pycnospores in pycnidia — compare PHOMOPSIS

**pho·mop·sis** \fō'mäpsə̇s\ *n*, *cap* [NL, fr. *Phoma* + *-opsis*] : a form genus of imperfect fungi (family Sphaeropsidaceae) producing pycnospores and also filiform scolecospores

**phon** \ˈfän\ *n* -s [ISV, fr. Gk *phōnē* sound, voice] : the unit of loudness level on a scale beginning at zero for the faintest audible sound and corresponding to the decibel scale of sound intensity with the number of phons of a given sound being

equal to the decibels of a pure 1000-cycle tone judged by the listener to be equally loud
**phon-** or **phono-** *comb form* [L, fr. Gk *phōn-*, *phōno-*, fr. *phōnē* — more at BAN] : sound : voice : speech : tone ⟨*phonal*⟩ ⟨*phonograph*⟩ ⟨*phonology*⟩
**phon** *abbr* **1** phonetics **2** phonology
**pho·nal** \ˈfōnᵊl\ *adj* [*phon-* + *-al*] : of, relating to, or producing speech sounds
**pho·nas·the·nia** \ˌfōnəsˈthēnēə\ *n* [NL, fr. *phon-* + *asthenia*] : weakness or hoarseness of voice
**pho·nate** \ˈfōˌnāt\ *vi* -ED/-ING/-S [*phon-* + *-ate*] : to produce speech sounds : use the voice
**pho·na·tion** \fōˈnāshən\ *n* -S [ISV *phon-* + *-ation*] : the act or process of producing speech sounds
**pho·na·to·ry** \ˈfōnəˌtōrē\ *adj* : of or relating to phonation
**phon·au·to·graph** \fōˈnȯd·əˌgraf, -rȧf\ *n* [*phon-* + *aut-* + *-graph*] : an instrument by which a sound can be made to produce a visible record of itself — **phon·au·to·graph·ic** \ˌ=ˌ==ˈgrafik\ *adj* — **phon·au·to·graph·i·cal·ly** \-fək(ə)lē\ *adv*
[1]**phone** \ˈfōn\ *n* -S [short for *telephone*] : EARPHONE, TELEPHONE, TELEPHONE RECEIVER
[2]**phone** \"\ *vb* -ED/-ING/-S : TELEPHONE ⟨if I didn't ~ the office, she would close up at 5 p.m. —Christopher Morley⟩
[3]**phone** \"\ *n* -S [Gk *phōnē* sound, voice] **1** : ALLOPHONE **2** : a speech sound considered as a physical event without regard to how it fits into the structure of a language — compare PHONEME
**-phone** \ˌfōn\ *n comb form* -S [LL *-phona*, fr. LGk *-phōna*, fr. Gk, neut. pl. of *-phōnos* -sounding, fr. *phōnein* to sound] : sound : voice — in names of musical instruments and sound-transmitting devices ⟨saxo*phone*⟩ ⟨ear*phone*⟩ ⟨radio*phone*⟩
**pho·ne·mal** \fəˈnēməl\ *adj* [*phoneme* + *-al*] : PHONEMIC
**pho·ne·mat·ic** \ˌfōnəˈmad·ik\ *adj* [ISV *phonemat-* (fr. Gk *phōnēmat-*, *phōnēma* sound) + *-ic*] : PHONEMIC; *esp* : of or relating to segmental phonemes
**pho·ne·mat·ics** \ˌ==ˈmad·iks\ *n pl but sing in constr* [Gk *phōnēmat-*, *phōnēma* sound + E *-ics*] : PHONEMICS; *esp* : segmental phonemics
**pho·neme** \ˈfōˌnēm\ *n* -S [F *phonème*, fr. Gk *phōnēma* sound, fr. *phōnein* to sound] **1** : the smallest unit of speech that distinguishes one utterance from another in all of the variations that it displays in the speech of a single person or particular dialect as the result of modifying influences (as neighboring sounds and stress) ⟨the *p* of English *pin* and the *f* of English *fin* are two different ~s⟩ — compare ALLOPHONE, PHONE **2** [G *phonem*, fr. Gk *phōnēma* sound] : an auditory hallucination of voices and spoken words
**pho·ne·mic** \fōˈnēmik, fəˈ-, -mēk\ *adj* **1** : of, relating to, or having the characteristics of a phoneme ⟨~ analysis⟩ **2 a** *of speech sounds* : constituting members of different phonemes ⟨Welsh *l* and *ll* are ~⟩ **b** : DISTINCTIVE 3 ⟨must regard length . . . as being significant or ~ —A.L.James⟩ — **pho·ne·mi·cal·ly** \-mək(ə)lē, -mēk-, -li\ *adv*
**phonemic change** *n* : a phonological development that causes an alteration in the distribution of phoneme constituents of a language
**pho·ne·mi·cist** \fōˈnēməsəst\ *n* -S : a specialist in phonemics
**pho·ne·mic·i·ty** \ˌfōnəˈmisəd·ē\ *n* -ES : the quality or state of being phonemic
**pho·ne·mi·ci·za·tion** \fōˌnēməsəˈzāshən\ *n* -S [*phonemicize* + *-ation*] : analysis into phonemes
**pho·ne·mi·cize** \fōˈnēməˌsīz\ *vt* -ED/-ING/-S : to analyze into or reduce to phonemes : represent by or convert into phonemic symbols : treat as a phoneme : make (a phonetic distinction) phonemic rather than allophonic
**phonemicness** *n* -ES : the quality or state of being phonemic
**pho·ne·mics** \fōˈnēmiks, -mēks\ *n pl but sing in constr* [*phoneme* + *-ics*] **1** : a branch of linguistic analysis that consists of the study of phonemes and often includes a study of their allophones **2 a** : the structure of a language in terms of phonemes **b** : a statement of such structure in terms of phonemes
**pho·nen·do·scope** \fōˈnendəˌskōp\ *n* [ISV *phon-* + *end-* + *-scope*; prob. orig. formed as It *fonendoscopio*] : a stethoscope for intensifying auscultatory sounds
**pho·nes·theme** \fōˈnesˌthēm\ *n* -S [blend of *phoneme* and *esthetic*] : the common feature of sound occurring in a group of symbolic words
[1]**pho·net·ic** \fōˈned·|ik, fəˈ-, -et|, |ēk\ *adj* [NL *phoneticus*, fr. Gk *phōnētikos*, fr. *phōnētos* to be spoken (fr. *phōnein* to sound, speak, fr. *phōnē* sound, voice) + *-ikos* -ic — more at BAN] **1 a** : of or relating to spoken language or speech sounds ⟨~ developments in English since Chaucer's time⟩ ⟨~ differences between ancient and modern Greek⟩ **b** : of or relating to the science of phonetics ⟨~ texts⟩ ⟨~ laboratory apparatus⟩ **2** : representing the sounds and other phenomena (as stress, pitch) of speech ⟨~ symbols⟩: **a** : constituting an alteration of the ordinary orthographic spelling that better represents its value in the spoken language, that employs only characters of the regular alphabet, and that is used in a context of conventionally spelled orthographies ⟨*thru* and *nite* are fairly common ~ spellings⟩ **b** : constituting those characters in some ancient writings (as Egyptian) that represent speech sounds as distinguished from such as are ideographic or pictorial **c** : representing speech sounds by means of symbols that have one value only ⟨in this ~ system *g* always has the value of *g* in *go*, never of *g* in *gem*⟩ **d** : employing for speech sounds more than the minimum number of symbols necessary to represent the significant differences in a speaker's speech ⟨the minutely ~ transcriptions of this linguistic atlas⟩ — contrasted with *phonemic*
[2]**phonetic** \"\ *n* -S : a Chinese character used with a radical to form a new character whose pronunciation it suggests
**pho·net·i·cal** \|əkəl\ *adj* [[1]*phonetic* + *-al*] : PHONETIC
**pho·net·i·cal·ly** \|ək(ə)lē\ *adv* : in a phonetic manner : in a phonetic sense or from a phonetic point of view ⟨words spelled ~⟩ ⟨~ similar⟩
**phonetic alphabet** *n* **1** : a set of symbols used for phonetic transcription **2** : any of various systems of identifying letters of the alphabet by means of code words in voice communication (as radio) ⟨*Alfa* and *Bravo* represent *a* and *b* in one *phonetic alphabet*⟩
**phonetic change** *n* : a phonological development in a language that affects one or more allophones of a phoneme but causes no alteration in the phoneme constituents
**pho·ne·ti·cian** \ˌfōnəˈtishən *sometimes* ˌfän-\ *n* -S : a specialist in phonetics
**pho·net·i·cism** \fōˈned·əˌsizəm\ *n* -S **1** : the quality or state of being phonetic **2** : phonetic representation
**pho·net·i·cist** \-səst\ *n* -S **1** : PHONETIST 2 **2** : PHONETICIAN
**pho·net·i·ci·za·tion** \fōˌned·əsəˈzāshən\ *n* -S : phonetic representation
**pho·net·i·cize** \fōˈned·əˌsīz\ *vt* -ED/-ING/-S : to make phonetic : spell phonetically
**phonetic law** *n* : a formula deduced from observed uniformity in the development under given conditions of a sound or combination of sounds within a linguistic area at or during a given time
**pho·net·ics** \fōˈned·|iks, fəˈ-, -et|, |ēks\ *n pl but sing in constr* **1 a** : the study and systematic classification of the sounds made in spoken utterance as they are produced by the organs of speech and as they register on the ear and on instruments **b** : the practical application of this science to the understanding and speaking of languages **2** : the system of speech sounds of a language or group of languages ⟨reads Portuguese with some ease but finds its ~ difficult⟩ **3** : a written representation other than conventional spelling ⟨*thru* is pretty fair ~⟩
**pho·ne·tism** \ˈfōnəˌtizəm\ *n* -S [[1]*phonetic* + *-ism*] : alteration of orthography for better agreement with pronunciation
**pho·ne·tist** \-nəd·əst, -nətəst\ *n* -S [[1]*phonetic* + *-ist*] **1** : PHONETICIAN **2** : one who advocates or uses phonetic spelling
**Phone·vi·sion** \ˈfōnˌvizhən\ *trademark* — used for a system of television transmission over telephone lines designed to make possible the distribution of television programs for paying subscribers
**phoney** *var of* PHONY
**phongyi** *var of* PONGYI
**-phonia** — see -PHONY
**pho·ni·at·ric** \ˌfōnēˈa·trik\ *adj* [*phon-* + *-iatric*] : of or relating to the treatment of speech defects
**phon·ic** \ˈfänik, -nēk *sometimes* ˈfōn-\ *adj* [*phon-* + *-ic*] **1** : of, relating to, or producing sound : ACOUSTIC **2 a** : of or relating to the sounds of speech : PHONETIC **b** : of or relating to phonics — **phon·i·cal·ly** \-nək(ə)lē\ *adv*
**phon·ics** \-ks\ *n pl but sing in constr* [*phon-* + *-ics*] **1** : the science of sound : ACOUSTICS **2** : a method of teaching beginners to read and pronounce words by learning the phonetic value of letters and letter groups
**phonic wheel** *n* : either of two wheels one of which is at the receiving and the other at the transmitting station that rotate synchronously in some synchronous multiplex telegraph systems
**phonied** *past of* PHONY
**phonier** *comparative of* PHONY
**phonies** *pl of* PHONY, *pres 3d sing of* PHONY
**-phonies** *pl of* -PHONY
**phoniest** *superlative of* PHONY
**pho·ni·ly** \ˈfōnᵊlē\ *adv* : in a phony manner : SPURIOUSLY ⟨~ flamboyant amours and impossible deeds of derring-do —C.J.Rolo⟩
**pho·ni·ness** *also* **pho·ny·ness** \-nēnəs\ *n* -ES : the quality or state of being phony : FALSITY, SPURIOUSNESS ⟨describes vicious, idle, and deliriously acquisitive sides of American life — the eccentric cruelties, the lack of standards, the scintillating ~ —Alfred Kazin⟩
**pho·nism** \ˈfōˌnizəm\ *n* -S [*phon-* + *-ism*] : a synesthetic auditory sensation
**phono** *abbr* phonograph
**phono-** — see PHON-
**pho·no·camp·tic** \ˌfōnəˈkam(p)tik\ *adj* [*phon-* + *campt-* (fr. Gk *kamptein* to bend) + *-ic*; akin to Gk *kampē* bend — more at CAMP] *archaic* : reflecting sound
**pho·no·cardiogram** \ˌfōnō+\ *n* [ISV *phon-* + *cardiogram*] : a graphic record of heart sounds made by means of a microphone, amplifier, and galvanometer
**pho·no·cardiography** \"+\ *n* [*phon-* + *cardiography*] : the graphic recording of the sounds of the heart by phonocardiogram
**pho·no·deik** \ˈfōnəˌdīk\ *n* -S [*phon-* + *-deik* (fr. Gk *deiknynai* to show) — more at DICTION] : an instrument for making photographic records of sound waves in air by means of a tiny mirror that is oscillated in a rotary manner by sound waves agitating a glass diaphragm and that by its reflections of a ray of light traces corresponding paths on a moving film
**pho·no·gen·ic** \ˌfōnəˈjenik\ *adj* [ISV *phon-* + *-genic*] : adapted to or suitable for successful production or reproduction of sound ⟨some scores are more ~ than others —*Saturday Rev.*⟩ ⟨their wonderfully ~ hall —J.M.Conly⟩
**pho·no·gram** \ˈfōnəˌgram\ *n* [ISV *phon-* + *-gram*] **1** : a character or symbol used to represent a word, syllable, or phoneme — compare IDEOGRAM **2** : a succession of orthographic letters that occurs with the same phonetic value in several or many words (as the *ight* of *bright*, *fight*, *flight*, *light*) ⟨~s are used in teaching phonics⟩ **3** : a compound character in Chinese writing consisting of a radical and a phonetic — **pho·no·gram·mic** *or* **pho·no·gram·ic** \ˌ==ˈgramik\ *adj* — **pho·no·gram·mi·cal·ly** *or* **pho·no·gram·i·cal·ly** \-mək(ə)lē\ *adv*
**pho·no·graph** \ˈfōnəˌgraf, -raa(ə)f, -raif, -rȧf\ *n* [*phon-* + *-graph*] : an instrument for reproducing sounds by means of the vibration of a stylus or needle following a spiral groove on a revolving circular disc or cylinder
**pho·nog·ra·pher** \fəˈnägrəfə(r), fōˈ-\ *n* -S [*phonography* + *-er*] : a specialist in phonography
**pho·no·graph·ic** \ˌfōnəˈgrafik, -fēk\ *adj* [in sense 1, fr. *phonography* + *-ic*; in sense 2, fr. *phonograph* + *-ic*] **1** : of or relating to phonography **2** : of, relating to, or resembling the phonograph ⟨a witness of almost ~ fidelity —*Atlantic*⟩ — **pho·no·graph·i·cal·ly** \-fək(ə)lē, -fēk-, -li\ *adv*
**pho·nog·ra·phy** \fəˈnägrəfē, fōˈ-\ *n* -ES [*phon-* + *-graphy*] **1** : spelling based on pronunciation **2** : a system of shorthand writing based on sound
**pho·no·lite** \ˈfōnəˌlīt\ *n* -S [F, fr. G *phonolith*, fr. *phon-* + *-lith*; fr. the fact that a slab of the fresh compact rock gives a ringing sound when struck] : a gray or green volcanic rock consisting essentially of orthoclase and nepheline — called also *clinkstone* — **pho·no·lit·ic** \ˌ==ˈlid·ik\ *adj*
**pho·no·log·i·cal** \ˌfōnᵊlˈäjəkəl, -jēk-\ *also* **pho·no·log·ic** \-jik, -jēk\ *adj* : of or relating to phonology — **pho·no·log·i·cal·ly** \-jək(ə)lē, -jek-, -li\ *adv*
**pho·nol·o·gist** \fəˈnäləjəst, fōˈ-\ *n* -S : a specialist in phonology
**pho·nol·o·gi·za·tion** \fəˌnäləjəˈzāshən\ *n* -S : the act or process of phonologizing or the state of being phonologized
**pho·nol·o·gize** \fəˈnäləˌjīz\ *vt* -ED/-ING/-S [*phonology* + *-ize*] : to transform (an allophonic distinction) into a phonemic distinction
**pho·nol·o·gy** \fəˈnäləjē, fəˈ-, -ji\ *n* -ES [*phon-* + *-logy*] **1** : the science of speech sounds including esp. the history and theory of sound changes in a single language or in two or more related languages considered together for comparative purposes **2** : the phonetics and the segmental and suprasegmental phonemics of a language at a particular time
**pho·no·ma·nia** \ˌfōnəˈmānēə\ *n* [NL, fr. *phono-* (fr. Gk *phonos* murder) + *mania* — more at PHOENICIAN] : homicidal mania
**pho·nom·e·ter** \fəˈnämәd·ə(r)\ *n* [prob. fr. F *phonomètre*, fr. *phon-* + *-mètre* -meter] : an instrument for measuring the intensity of sound or the frequency of its vibration
**pho·no·met·ric** \ˌfōnəˈme·trik\ *adj* [F *phonométrique*, fr. *phonomètre* + *-ique* -ic] : of, relating to, or measured by a phonometer
**pho·nom·e·try** \fəˈnämə·trē\ *n* -ES [F *phonométrie*, fr. *phonomètre* + *-ie* -y] : the measurement of sounds by a phonometer
**pho·no·mo·tor** \ˌfōnəˈmōd·ə(r)\ *n* [*phon-* + *motor*] : an instrument in which the motion produced by the vibrations of a sounding body is communicated to a small wheel
**pho·non** \ˈfōˌnän\ *n* -S [*phon-* + *-on*] : one of the quanta into which compression-wave energy is assumed to be divided and which like photons are supposed to have individual identity and mean free path — compare SECOND SOUND
**pho·nop·a·thy** \fəˈnäpəthē\ *n* -ES [*phon-* + *-pathy*] : a disorder of phonation
**pho·no·phile** \ˈfōnəˌfīl\ *n* -S [*phon-* + *-phil*] : a collector or connoisseur of phonograph records
**pho·no·pho·bia** \ˌfōnəˈfōbēə\ *n* [NL, fr. *phon-* + *phobia*] : pathological fear of sound, voice, or speaking aloud
**pho·no·phore** \ˈfōnəˌfō(ə)r\ *n* -S [ISV *phon-* + *-phore*] **1 a** : a device that enables telephone messages to be sent over a telegraph line simultaneously with the use of ordinary currents operating code instruments **b** : a system using this apparatus **2** : a device to enable the deaf to hear by conducting vibrations from the speaker's larynx to the hearer's teeth — **pho·no·phor·ic** \ˌ==ˈfórik\ *adj*
**pho·noph·o·rous** \fəˈnäf(ə)rəs\ *adj* : capable of transmitting sound waves
**pho·no·photogram** \ˌfōnō+\ *n* [*phon-* + *photogram*] : a record made by phonophotography
**pho·no·photograph** \"+\ *n* [*phon-* + *photograph*] : PHONOPHOTOGRAM
**pho·no·photography** \"+\ *n* [*phon-* + *photography*] : the art or process of recording sound-vibration curves photographically (as by means of the phonodeik)
**pho·no·pro·jec·to·scope** \ˌfōnōprəˈjektəˌskōp\ *n* [*phon-* + *project* + connective *-o-* + *-scope*] : an instrument for projecting sound-vibration curves directly on a screen without first recording them photographically
**pho·no·reception** \ˌfōnō+\ *n* [*phon-* + *reception*] : the perception of vibratory motion of relatively high frequency; *specif* : HEARING
**pho·no·receptor** \"+\ *n* [*phon-* + *receptor*] : an animal organ for phonoreception; *esp* : OTOCYST
**pho·no·scope** \ˈfōnəˌskōp\ *n* [*phon-* + *-scope*] : an instrument for observing or exhibiting motions or properties of sounding bodies; *esp* : a device for testing the quality of musical strings
**pho·no·telemeter** \ˌfōnō+\ *n* [*phon-* + *telemeter*] : a device for estimating the distance of firearms in action by measuring the interval between the flash and the arrival of the sound from the discharge
**Pho·no·vi·sion** \ˈfōnəˌvizhən\ *trademark* — used for a Phonevision system
**pho·nus bo·lo·nus** \ˈfōnəsbəˈlōnəs\ *n* [alter. of *phony baloney*] **1** : pretentious falsity : PIFFLE, TRIPE ⟨all the stylish humbug he is fond of calling *phonus bolonus* —*N.Y.Times*⟩ **2** : CHICANERY, SKULDUGGERY, TRICKERY ⟨it was owing to some *phonus bolonus* on his part that the conflagration had been unleashed —P.G.Wodehouse⟩
[1]**pho·ny** *or* **pho·ney** \ˈfōnē, -ni\ *adj* **phonier; phoniest** [origin unknown] : marked by empty pretension : FALSE, SPURIOUS ⟨a perpetually ~ front of good fellowship is assumed —V.A.Young⟩ **syn** see COUNTERFEIT
[2]**phony** *or* **phoney** \"\ *n, pl* **phonies** *or* **phoneys** : one that is fraudulent or spurious : FAKE, SHAM ⟨this political issue — absenteeism — is a ~ if there ever was one —T.R.Ybarra⟩ ⟨he who writes or composes without the true inner fire . . . will always be a ~ —H.W.Van Loon⟩
[3]**phony** *or* **phoney** \"\ *vt* **phonied** *or* **phoneyed; phonied** *or* **phoneyed; phonying** *or* **phoneying; phonies** *or* **phoneys** : COUNTERFEIT, FAKE ⟨no one could ~ a list like that —Frances Lindley⟩
**-pho·ny** \fənē, -ni\ *also* **-pho·nia** \ˈfōnēə\ *n comb form, pl* **-phonies** *also* **-phonias** [ME *-phonie*, fr. OF, fr. L *-phonia*, fr. Gk *-phōnia*, fr. *-phōnos* -sounding (fr. *phōnein* to sound) + *-ia* -y — more at PHONETIC] **1** : sound ⟨acro*phony*⟩ ⟨caco*phony*⟩ **2** *usu* **-phonia** : speech disorder (of a specified type esp. relating to phonation) ⟨dys*phonia*⟩ ⟨bary*phony*⟩ — compare -LALIA, -PHASIA, -PHEMIA
**phony disease** *also* **phony peach** *n* [*phony* alter. (influenced by [1]*phony*) of [1]*pony*; fr. the dwarfing effect of the disease] : a serious virus disease of the peach that causes dwarfing, abnormally dark green leaves, and a light crop of small but highly colored fruit, makes the trees stop bearing after a few years, and is of lesser importance on almond, apricot, nectarine, and plum
**phonyness** *var of* PHONINESS
**phoo** \ˈfü\ *interj* — used to express contempt, repudiation, or astonishment; compare PHEW
**phoo·ey** \ˈfüē, -üi\ *interj* [*phoo* + *-y*] — used to express repudiation or disgust ⟨but an American garden suburb ~ —Sinclair Lewis⟩ ⟨~ on this fellow —John & Ward Hawkins⟩
**phooka** *var of* POOKA
**pho·ra** \ˈfōrə\ *n, cap* [NL, fr. Gk *phōr* thief; akin to L *fur* thief — more at FURTIVE] : a genus of small flies that is the type of the family Phoridae
[1]**-pho·ra** \f(ə)rə\ *n comb form, pl* **-phora** [NL, fr. fem. sing. & neut. pl. of *-phorus*] : organism bearing a (specified) structure ⟨Clado*phora*⟩ : organisms bearing a (specified) structure ⟨Cteno*phora*⟩
[2]**-phora** *pl of* -PHORUM
**pho·ra·den·dron** \ˌfōrəˈdendrən\ *n, cap* [NL, fr. Gk *phōr* thief + *dendron* tree; fr. the parasitic habit — more at DENDR-] : a genus of American hemiparasitic plants (family Loranthaceae) having erect and vertically 2-celled anthers — see MISTLETOE 2a
**-pho·rae** \fəˌrē\ *n pl comb form* [NL, fr. fem. pl. of *-phorus*] : organisms carrying a (specified) structure ⟨Disco*phorae*⟩ ⟨Physo*phorae*⟩
**phor·bide** \ˈfórˌbīd\ *n* -S [*phorbin* + *-ide*] : PHORBIN 2
**phor·bin** \-rbən\ *n* -S [ISV *phorb-* (GK *phorbē* pasture, fodder) + *-in* — more at PHEOPHORBIDE] **1** : a magnesium-free compound $C_{22}H_{18}N_4$ that is the parent of chlorophyll in that it contains the unsubstituted ring structure of chlorophyll consisting of one carbocyclic ring in addition to the porphin ring system **2** : any of several magnesium-free derivatives of chlorophyll (as pheophytin) that contain its characteristic ring structure — compare CHLORIN
**-phore** *or* **-phor** \ˌfō(ə)r, ˌfó(ə)r, -ōə, -ó(ə)\ *n comb form* -S [NL *-phorus*, fr. Gk *-phoros*, fr. *pherein* to carry — more at BEAR] : carrier ⟨chromo*phore*⟩ ⟨cteno*phore*⟩ ⟨gameto*phore*⟩ ⟨lumino*phor*⟩ ⟨sema*phore*⟩
**pho·re·sis** \fəˈrēsəs\ *also* **pho·re·sia** \-ēzēə\ *n, pl* **phoreses** *also* **phoresias** [*phoresis* fr. NL, fr. Gk *phorēsis* being carried; *phoresia* fr. NL] : PHORESY
**-pho·re·sis** \fəˈrēsəs, fōˈ-\ *n comb form, pl* **-phore·ses** \-ēˌsēz\ [NL, fr. Gk *phorēsis* being carried] : transmission ⟨electro*phoresis*⟩ ⟨ionto*phoresis*⟩
**phor·e·sy** \ˈfórəsē\ *n* -ES [NL *phoresia*, fr. Gk *phorēsis* being carried (fr. *phorein* to carry along, wear, freq. of *pherein* to carry) + L *-ia* -y] : the nonparasitic association of one kind of animal (as a larval insect) with another in order to obtain transportation
**pho·ret·ic** \fəˈred·ik\ *adj* [fr. *phoresy*, after such pairs as E *heresy*: *heretic*] : of, relating to, or exhibiting phoresy
**pho·ria** \ˈfōrēə\ *n* -S [NL, fr. *-phoria*] : any of various tendencies of the lines of vision to deviate from the normal
**-pho·ria** \ˈfōr-, ˈfór-\ *n comb form* -S [NL, fr. Gk, act of carrying, fr. *-phoros* -phorous + *-ia* -y] : bearing : state : tendency ⟨eu*phoria*⟩ ⟨idea*phoria*⟩ ⟨hetero*phoria*⟩
**-phor·ic** \ˈfórik, ˈfär-, -rēk\ *adj comb form* [*-phore* + *-ic*] : having (such) a bearing or tendency ⟨eccoproti*cophoric*⟩
[1]**phor·id** \ˈfōrəd, ˈfór-\ *adj* [NL *Phoridae*] : of or relating to the Phoridae
[2]**phorid** \"\ *n* -S [NL *Phoridae*] : a fly of the family Phoridae
**phor·i·dae** \ˈfōrəˌdē\ *n pl, cap* [NL, fr. *Phora*, type genus + *-idae*] : a family of small two-winged flies of hunchbacked appearance with short apparently one-jointed antennae and without crossveins in the wing
**phor·mia** \ˈfórmēə\ *n, cap* [NL, prob. irreg. fr. Gk *phōr* thief — more at PHORA] : a genus of calliphorid flies some of which are parasitic as larvae on sheep
**phor·minx** \ˈfórˌmiŋks\ *n, pl* **phormin·ges** \fȯ(r)ˈminˌjēz\ [Gk, lyre] : CITHARA 1
**phor·mi·um** \ˈfó(r)mēəm\ *n* [NL, fr. Gk *phormion*, a plant, small mat, dim. of *phormos* mat, basket for carrying corn, fr. *pherein* to carry] **1** *cap* : a genus of herbs (family Liliaceae) with rigid sword-shaped leaves and red or yellow flowers on a leafless scape — see NEW ZEALAND FLAX **2** -S : a hard fiber from New Zealand flax used for bagging and cordage
**phoro-** *comb form* [NL, fr. ML, fr. Gk, fr. *phorein* to carry along, freq. of *pherein* to carry — more at BEAR] : carrying on : having motion : direction ⟨*phoro*zooid⟩ ⟨*phoro*nomy⟩ ⟨*phoro*metry⟩
**pho·rom·e·ter** \fəˈrämәd·ə(r)\ *n* [*phoro-* + *-meter*] : any of various instruments for measuring the strength, deviation, and direction of the extrinsic muscles of the eyes and for inducing exercise to correct defects in their functioning
**phor·o·met·ric** \ˌfórəˈme·trik\ *adj* : of or relating to phorometry
**pho·rom·e·try** \fəˈrämə·trē\ *n* -ES [*phoro-* + *-metry*] : the science or practice of testing and correcting the action of the extrinsic muscles of the eyes in order to cure strabismus and to produce stereoscopic vision
**pho·rone** \ˈfōˌrōn\ *n* -S [ISV cam*phor* + *-one*] : a yellowish green unsaturated open-chain ketone $[(CH_3)_2C{=}CH]_2CO$ that is isomeric with camphorone and isophorone, is obtained by condensation of acetone, and is used chiefly as a solvent
[1]**pho·ro·nid** \fəˈrōnəd\ *adj* [NL *Phoronidea*] : of or relating to the Phoronidea
[2]**phoronid** \"\ *n* -S [NL *Phoronidea*] : one of the Phoronidea
**pho·ron·i·da** \-ˈränədə\ [NL, fr. *Phoronis* + *-ida*] *syn of* PHORONIDEA
**pho·ro·nid·ea** \ˌfōrəˈnidēə\ *n pl, cap* [NL, fr. *Phoronis* + *-idea*] : a group (coextensive with the genus *Phoronis*) of marine animals of uncertain systematic position that has at various times been associated with the Molluscoidea, the Gephyrea, or the Hemichordata or treated as a separate phylum
**pho·ro·nis** \fəˈrōnəs\ *n, cap* [NL, prob. fr. L *Phoronis* (Io, mythical priestess of Argos who was loved by Zeus)] : a genus of small marine tubicolous unsegmented wormlike animals that have the mouth, anal opening, and nephridial apertures at one end of the body close together and surrounded by a horseshoe-shaped lophophore bearing numerous tentacles, a closed system of blood vessels containing red blood, and free-swimming larvae which pass through a complex metamorphosis — see ACTINOTROCHA, PHORONIDEA

**pho·ron·o·my** \fə'ränəmē\ *n* -ES [NL *phoronomia*, fr. Gk *phoro-* (fr. *phorein* to carry along) + NL *-nomia* (fr. Gk, fr. *nomos* law) — more at NIMBLE] **:** a Kantian theory of motion deducible from a priori conceptions — compare KINEMATICS

**Pho·rop·tor** \fə'räptə(r)\ *trademark* — used for an instrument used to determine the corrective eyeglass lenses needed by an individual

**phor·o·rhac·i·dae** \,fȯrə'rasə,dē\ *n pl, cap* [NL, fr. *Phororhacos*, type genus + *-idae*] **:** a family of gigantic flightless birds of the order Gruiformes from the Miocene of Patagonia

**pho·ro·rha·cos** \fə'rȯrə,käs\ *n, cap* [NL, fr. Gk *phōr* thief + *rhakos* rag — more at *phora*] **:** a genus of prehistoric birds that is the type of the family Phororhacidae

**-pho·rous** \f(ə)rəs\ *adj comb form* [Gk *-phoros*, fr. *pherein* to carry — more at BEAR] **:** carrying **:** -FEROUS ⟨ascophorous⟩ ⟨phyllophorous⟩ ⟨androphorous⟩

**phoro·zooid** \ˌfōrə+\ *n* [*phoro-* + *zooid*] **:** a zooid of the sexual generation of some free-swimming tunicates which though it becomes free-swimming does not mature sexually

**-pho·rum** \f(ə)rəm\ *n comb form, pl* **-pho·ra** \-rə\ [NL, fr. Gk *-phoron*, neut. of *-phoros* -phorous] **:** -PHORE ⟨hymenophorum⟩

**-pho·rus** \f(ə)rəs\ *n comb form* [NL, fr. Gk *-phoros* -phorous] **:** carrier — in generic names in zoology ⟨Istiophorus⟩

**phos-** *comb form* [Gk *phōs-*, fr. *phōs* — more at FANCY] **:** light ⟨phosacid⟩ ⟨phosnitric⟩

**phose** \'fōz, -ōs\ *n* -S [Gk *phōs* light] **:** a subjective visual sensation (as of light or color)

**phos·gene** \'fäz,jēn\ *n* -S [*phos-* + *-gene*; fr. its being orig. obtained by exposing equal volumes of chlorine and carbon monoxide to the sun's rays] **:** a colorless gaseous compound $COCl_2$ of unpleasant sour odor that condenses to a liquid at the temperature of ice, is usu. made from carbon monoxide and chlorine in the presence of a catalyst, causes severe and often fatal edema of the lungs some hours after inhalation (as used as a poison gas in World War I), and is now used chiefly as an intermediate (as in the manufacture of organic isocyanates, polyurethanes, and carbonic esters) — called also *carbon oxychloride, carbonyl chloride*

**phos·gen·ic** \(')fäz¦jenik\ *adj* [*phos-* + *-genic*] **:** PHOTOGENIC

**phos·gen·ite** \'fäzjə,nīt, -jə,n-\ *n* -S [G *phosgenit*, fr. *phosgen* phosgene + *-it* -ite] **:** a mineral $Pb_2Cl_2CO_3$ consisting of lead chloroformate occurring in tetragonal crystals of a white, yellow, or grayish color and adamantine luster (hardness 3, sp. gr. 6.0–6.3)

**phosph-** *or* **phospho-** *comb form* [F, fr. *phosphorique* phosphoric (in *acide phosphorique* phosphoric acid) — more at PHOSPHORIC] **1 :** phosphoric acid **:** phosphate ⟨*phosph*ergot⟩ ⟨*phospho*arginine⟩ **2 :** phosphorus ⟨*phospho*ferrite⟩

**phos·pha·gen** \'fäsfəjən, -,jen\ *n* -S [ISV *phosphate* + *-gen* (as in *glycogen*)] **:** any of several organic phosphate compounds (as phosphocreatine or phosphoarginine) occurring esp. in muscle and releasing energy on hydrolysis of the phosphate

**phos·pham·ic acid** \(')fäs¦famik-\ *n* [*phosphamic* fr. *phosph-* + *amidogen* + *-ic*] **:** AMIDOPHOSPHORIC ACID

**phos·pha·tase** \'fäsfə,tās, -āz\ *n* -S [ISV *phosphate* + *-ase*] **:** any of a large group of widely occurring enzymes that accelerate the hydrolysis and synthesis of organic esters of phosphoric acid and the transfer of phosphate groups to other compounds and that are active (1) in alkaline media in many instances (as the phosphomonoesterases from blood plasma, milk, intestinal mucosa, or bone) and (2) in acid media in other instances (as the phosphomonoesterase from the prostate gland) — called respectively (1) *alkaline phosphatase*, (2) *acid phosphatase;* compare PYROPHOSPHATASE ⟨~s play an important role in bone formation, muscle metabolism, lactation, and alcoholic fermentation —Henry Tauber⟩

**phosphatase test** *n* **:** a test for the efficiency of pasteurization of milk and other dairy products based on a determination of the activity of the phosphatase that is present in raw milk and is inactivated by proper pasteurization

**¹phos·phate** \'fä,sfāt, *usu* -ād.+V\ *n* -S [F, fr. *phosphorique* phosphoric (in *acide phosphorique* phosphoric acid) + *-ate*] **1 a :** a salt of a phosphoric acid classified often as primary, secondary, or tertiary according to the number of hydrogen atoms replaced in the acid; *esp* **:** ORTHOPHOSPHATE — called also *inorganic phosphate;* see CALCIUM PHOSPHATE, SODIUM PHOSPHATE **b :** an ester of a phosphoric acid that often plays an important role in metabolism — called also *organic phosphate* — compare ADENOSINE DIPHOSPHATE, ADENOSINE TRIPHOSPHATE, ADENYLIC ACID, GLUCOSE PHOSPHATE, NUCLEIC ACID, PHOSPHOGLYCERIC ACID **c :** an organic compound of phosphoric acid in which the acid unit is bound to nitrogen (as in phosphocreatine) or to a carboxyl group (as in acetyl phosphate) in such a manner that useful energy is released on hydrolysis during metabolism — called also *organic phosphate* **2 :** an effervescent drink of carbonated water with a small amount of phosphoric acid or of an acid phosphate of potassium, magnesium, sodium, or calcium or a mixture of them flavored with fruit syrup ⟨orange ~⟩ **3 :** a phosphatic material used for fertilizers — see SUPERPHOSPHATE

**²phosphate** \"\ *vt* -ED/-ING/-S **:** to treat with phosphoric acid or a phosphate (as in coating iron)

**phosphated flour** *n* **:** flour made from soft wheat to which monocalcium phosphate is added to improve the baking qualities

**phos·pha·te·mia** \,fäsfə'tēmēə, -,sfād·'ēm-\ *n* -S [NL, fr. *phosphate* + *-emia*] **:** the occurrence of phosphate in the blood esp. in excessive amounts

**phosphate rock** *n* **:** a rock that consists of calcium phosphate largely in the form of apatite or carbonate-apatite usu. together with calcium carbonate and other minerals, that is useful in fertilizers and is a source of phosphorus compounds, and that occurs in large beds in the southeastern U. S. and in extensive deposits in Arkansas and the northwestern U. S. — compare SUPERPHOSPHATE

**phos·phat·ic** \(')fä¦sfad·ik, -fād-\ *adj* [¹*phosphate* + *-ic*] **:** of, relating to, or containing phosphoric acid or phosphates

**phosphatic slag** *n* **:** BASIC SLAG

**phos·pha·tide** \'fäsfə,tīd\ *n* -S [ISV *phosphate* + *-ide*] **:** any of a class of complex phosphoric ester lipides (as the lecithins, cephalins, sphingomyelins, lipositol) that are found in all living cells in association with depot fats esp. in active tissues (as nerve tissue) and that on hydrolysis yield phosphoric acid, fatty acids, a polyhydric alcohol (as glycerol or inositol), and usu. a nitrogen base (as choline or ethanolamine) — called also *phospholipide* — **phos·pha·tid·ic** \¦fäsfə¦tidik\ *adj*

**phosphatidic acid** *n* [*phosphatidic* fr. *phosphatide* + *-ic*] **:** any of several acids $(RCOO)_2C_3H_5OPO_3H_2$ that are formed from phosphatides by partial hydrolysis (as by removal of the nitrogen base), that are glycerides of glycerophosphoric acids, and that yield on hydrolysis two fatty-acid molecules RCOOH and one molecule each of glycerol and phosphoric acid

**phos·phati·dyl** \¦fäsfə¦tīdᵊl, fä'sfad·əd-\ *n* -S [*phosphatidic acid* + *-yl*] **:** any of several univalent radicals $(RCOO)_2C_3H_5$-$OPO(OH)$— derived from the phosphatidic acids ⟨*phosphatidyl*-serine is one of the cephalins⟩

**phos·pha·tion** \fä'sfāshən\ *n* -S [*phosphate* + *-ion*] **:** PHOSPHATIZATION

**phos·pha·ti·za·tion** \,fäsfəd·ə'zāshən, -sfə,tī'z-, -,sfād·ə'z-\ *n* -S **:** the process of phosphatizing

**phos·pha·tize** \'fäsfə,tīz\ *vt* -ED/-ING/-S [ISV *phosphate* + *-ize*] **1 :** to convert to a phosphate or phosphates **2 :** PHOSPHATE

**phosphato-** *comb form* [fr. *phosphate*] **:** containing the phosphate group $PO_4$ — esp. in names of coordination complexes ⟨*phosphato*-ferrates(III)⟩

**phos·pha·tu·ria** \,fäsfə'tu̇rēə, -sfə'tyu̇-\ *n* -S [NL, fr. ISV ¹*phosphate* + NL *-uria*] **:** the excretion of phosphates in urine esp. in excessive amounts — **phos·pha·tu·ric** \¦==¦rik\ *adj*

**phosphazo-** *comb form* [*phosph-* + *az-*] **:** containing the bivalent unsaturated group —P=N— consisting of phosphorus and nitrogen

**phos·phene** \'fä,sfēn\ *n* -S [ISV *phos-* + *-phene* (fr. Gk *phainein* to show) — more at FANCY] **:** a luminous impression due to excitation of the retina of the eye by some cause other than the impingement of rays of light (as by pressure on the eyeball when the lids are closed) — compare AFTERIMAGE

**phos·phide** \'fä,sfīd, -,sfəd\ *n* -S [ISV *phosph-* + *-ide*] **:** a binary compound of phosphorus usu. with a more electropositive element or radical

**phos·phi·nate** \'fäsfə,nāt\ *n* -S [*phosphinic* acid + *-ate*] **:** a salt or ester of a phosphinic acid

**phos·phine** \'fä,sfēn, -,sfən\ *n* -S [ISV *phosph-* + *-ine*] **1 :** a colorless very poisonous gaseous compound $PH_3$ that may ignite spontaneously when mixed with air or oxygen, that is a weaker base than ammonia but forms phosphonium salts with strong acids, and that is made in various ways (as by decomposing metallic phosphides with water) **2 :** any of a class of organic compounds derived from phosphine that are analogous to amines but are much weaker bases **3 :** an orange-yellow basic dye consisting essentially of a nitrate of chrysaniline — see DYE TABLE I (under *Basic Orange 15*)

**phosphine oxide** *n* **:** any of a series of oxides having the general formula $R_3PO$ that are obtained by oxidation of trisubstituted phosphines

**phos·phin·ic acid** \(')fä¦sfinik-\ *n* [*phosphinic* ISV *phosphine* + *-ic*] **:** any of a series of monobasic organic acids RR'PO-(OH) [as diphenyl-phosphinic acid $(C_6H_5)_2PO(OH)$] obtainable from disubstituted phosphines by oxidation — compare PHOSPHONIC ACID

**phos·phite** \'fä,sfīt\ *n* -S [F, fr. *phosph-* + *-ite*] **:** a salt or ester of phosphorous acid

**phospho-** — see PHOSPH-

**phos·pho·ami·no·lipide** *or* **phos·pho·ami·no·lipid** \¦fä-(,)sfōə,mēnō, -sfō,amə(,)nō+\ *n* [*phosph-* + *amino* + *lipide*] **:** a phosphatide containing a nitrogen base

**phos·pho·arginine** \¦fä(,)sfō+\ *n* [*phosph-* + *arginine*] **:** a compound $C_6H_{13}N_4O_2PO_3H_2$ of arginine and phosphoric acid that functions in various invertebrates (as crustaceans) in a way similar to that of phosphocreatine in vertebrates

**phos·pho·creatine** \"+\ *n* [ISV *phosph-* + *creatine*] **:** a compound $C_4H_8N_3O_2PO_3H_2$ of creatine and phosphoric acid occurring esp. in the muscles of vertebrates where its enzymatic hydrolysis releases phosphate and available energy for the work of muscular contraction — called also *creatine phosphate;* see ADENOSINE DIPHOSPHATE

**phos·pho·di·es·ter·ase** \,fä(,)sfō,dī'estə,rās, -'dī,e-, -āz\ *n* [*phosph-* + *diester* + *-ase*] **:** a phosphatase (as from snake venom) that acts on diesters (as some nucleotides) to hydrolyze only one of the two ester groups — compare PHOSPHOMONOESTERASE

**phos·pho·enol·pyruvic acid** \,fäs,fōə,nōl, ,fäsfō,ē,nōl, -nōl+\ *n* [*phosph-* + *enol* + *pyruvic*] **:** PHOSPHOPYRUVIC ACID

**phos·pho·ferrite** \,fäsfō+\ *n* [*phosph-* + *ferrous* + *-ite*] **:** a mineral $(Fe,Mn)_3(PO_4)_2.3H_2O$ consisting of a manganese ferrous hydrous phosphate and occurring in white or greenish crystalline masses (hardness 4–5, sp. gr. 3.2)

**phos·pho·glu·co·mutase** \,fäsfō,glükō+\ *n* [*phosph-* + *glucose* + *mutase*] **:** an enzyme found in all plant and animal cells and obtained crystalline from rabbit-muscle extracts that catalyzes esp. the acylal-ester interconversion of glucose phosphates

**phos·pho·glycerate** \,fäsfō+\ *n* [ISV *phosphoglycer-* (in *phosphoglyceric acid*) + *-ate*] **:** a salt or ester of a phosphoglyceric acid

**phos·pho·glyceric acid** \¦fä(,)sfō+...-\ *n* [*phosphoglyceric* ISV *phosph-* + *glyceric*] **:** either of two isomeric mono-phosphates $HOOCC_2H_3(OH)OPO_3H_2$ of glyceric acid formed as intermediates in photosynthesis and in carbohydrate metabolism

**phos·pho·glycerol** \,fäsfō+\ *n* [*phosph-* + *glycerol*] **:** GLYCEROPHOSPHORIC ACID

**phos·pho·lipase** \¦fäsfō+\ *n* [*phosph-* + *lipase*] **:** LECITHINASE

**phos·pho·lipide** *or* **phos·pho·lipid** \"+\ *n* [*phosph-* + *lipide*] **:** PHOSPHATIDE

**phos·pho·lipin** \"+\ *n* [*phosph-* + *lipin*] **:** PHOSPHATIDE

**phos·pho·molybdate** \¦fä(,)sfō+\ *n* [ISV *phosphomolybd-* (in *phosphomolybdic acid*) + *-ate*] **:** a salt of a phosphomolybdic acid — called also *molybdophosphate*

**phos·pho·molybdic acid** \"+...-\ *n* [ISV *phosph-* + *molybdic*] **:** any of several heteropoly acids obtainable from solutions of phosphoric acid and molybdic acid and used chiefly as precipitants (as for alkaloids and for basic dyes for organic pigments); *esp* **:** the yellow crystalline acid $H_3PMo_{12}O_{40}.xH_2O$ containing twelve atoms of molybdenum in the molecule — called also *molybdophosphoric acid*

**phos·pho·mono·es·ter·ase** \,fä(,)sfō,mänō'estə,rās, -'mänōe-, -mōnō-, -āz\ *n* [*phosph-* + *monoester* + *-ase*] **:** a phosphatase that acts on monoesters (as a beta-glycerophosphate or glucose phosphate)

**phos·pho·nate** \'fäsfə,nāt\ *n* -S [*phosphonic* acid + *-ate*] **:** a salt or ester of a phosphonic acid

**phos·phon·ic acid** \(')fä¦sfänik-\ *n* [*phosphonic* alter. (influenced by *-onic*) of *phosphinic*] **:** any of a series of dibasic organic acids $RPO(OH)_2$ [as phenyl-phosphonic acid $C_6H_5$-$PO(OH)_2$] obtainable from monosubstituted phosphines by oxidation — compare PHOSPHINIC ACID

**phos·pho·nitrile** \¦fäsfō+\ *n* [*phosph-* + *nitrile*] **:** a bivalent ion $PN^{++}$ or radical PN consisting of phosphorus and nitrogen and known in the form of polymeric compounds esp. halides [as phosphonitrile chloride $(PNCl_2)_n$] — **phos·pho·nitrilic** \"+\ *adj*

**phos·pho·ni·um** \fä'sfōnēəm\ *n* -S [NL, fr. *phosph-* + *-onium*] **:** a univalent ion $PH_4^+$ or radical $PH_4$ analogous to ammonium that is derived from phosphine and is known esp. in the form of salts (as phosphonium iodide $PH_4I$) and organic derivatives [as tetraphenyl-phosphonium iodide $(C_6H_5)_4PI$] — compare QUATERNARY AMMONIUM COMPOUND

**phos·pho·phyllite** \,fäsfō+\ *n* [*phosph-* + *phyllite*] **:** a mineral $Zn_2(FeMn)(PO_4)_2.4H_2O$ consisting of a hydrous phosphate of zinc, ferrous iron, and manganese and forming colorless or pale blue monoclinic crystals with perfect micaceous cleavage (hardness 3–4, sp. gr. 3.1)

**phos·pho·protein** \¦fä(,)sfō+\ *n* [*phosph-* + *protein*] **:** any of a class of proteins containing combined phosphoric acid (as casein or phosvitin)

**phos·pho·pyruvic acid** \"+...-\ *n* [*phosph-* + *pyruvic*] **:** the phosphate $CH_2{=}C(OPO_3H_2)COOH$ of the enol form of pyruvic acid formed as an intermediate in carbohydrate metabolism (as from phosphoglyceric acid by reversible dehydration) — called also *phosphoenolpyruvic acid*

**phos·phor** \'fäsfər, -,sfō(ə)r\ *n* -S [F *phosphore*, fr. NL *phosphorus* — more at PHOSPHORUS] **1 :** anything that exhibits phosphorescence ⟨her eyes . . . flashed ~ and sharp sparks —John Keats⟩ **2** *also* **phos·phore** \-,sfō(ə)r\ **:** any of various phosphorescent or fluorescent materials (as zinc sulfide activated with silver or copper or zinc silicate activated with manganese) that may occur as minerals (as wurtzite or willemite) but are now usu. produced synthetically and are used chiefly in fluorescent lamps, in cathode-ray tubes (as for television and radar), in instruments for detecting various radiations, and in luminous paints and inks

**phosphor-** *or* **phosphoro-** *comb form* [NL *phosphorus*] **:** phosphorus ⟨*phosphor*ate⟩ **:** phosphoric acid ⟨*phosphor*amidic acid⟩ ⟨*phosphoro*thioic acid⟩

**phos·phor·amidic acid** \¦fäsfər+...-\ *n* [*phosphor-* + *amidic*] **:** AMIDOPHOSPHORIC ACID

**phos·pho·rate** \'fäsfə,rāt\ *vt* -ED/-ING/-S [*phosphor-* + *-ate*] **1 :** to impregnate or combine with phosphorus or a compound of phosphorus **2 :** to make phosphorescent **:** cause to phosphoresce

**phosphorated oil** *n* **:** a one percent solution of phosphorus in almond oil formerly used as a nerve stimulant and tonic

**phosphor bronze** *n* **:** a bronze of great hardness, elasticity, and toughness whose superiority is due to the introduction of a small amount of phosphorus

**phosphor copper** *n* **:** a crude alloy of copper and phosphorus used to deoxidize copper and to make phosphor bronze

**phos·pho·re·al** *also* **phos·pho·ri·al** \(')fä¦sfōrēəl\ *adj* [prob. fr. (assumed) NL *phosphoreus* phosphorous (fr. NL *phosphorus*) + E *-al* or *-ial*] **:** of, relating to, or having the characteristics of phosphorus

**phos·pho·resce** \¦fäsfə¦res\ *vi* -ED/-ING/-S [prob. back-formation fr. *phosphorescent*] **:** to exhibit phosphorescence **:** glow esp. in the dark

**phos·pho·res·cence** \,fäsfə'resᵊn(t)s\ *n* -S [*phosphorescent* + *-ence*] **1 :** luminescence that is perceptible with characteristic rate of decay after the exciting cause ceases to act — compare FLUORESCENCE **2 :** an enduring luminescence (as the chemiluminescence of phosphorus and many forms of bioluminescence)

**phos·pho·res·cent** \¦==¦resᵊnt\ *adj* [*phosphor* + *-escent*] **:** exhibiting or characterized by phosphorescence ⟨the ~ glow of decaying wood —Nathaniel Hawthorne⟩ — **phos·pho·res·cent·ly** *adv*

**phos·pho·ret·ed** *or* **phos·pho·ret·ted** \'fäsfə,red·əd\ *adj* [alter. of *phosphureted*] **:** impregnated or combined with phosphorus ⟨~ hydrogen⟩

**phosphori** *pl of* PHOSPHORUS

**phos·phor·ic** \(')fä¦sfȯrik, -sfär-, -rēk; 'fäsfərik\ *adj* [F *phosphorique*, fr. *phosphore* phosphor (fr. NL *phosphorus*) + *-ique* -ic — more at PHOSPHORUS] **1 :** PHOSPHORESCENT **2 :** of, relating to, or resembling phosphorus — used esp. of compounds in which this element has a valence higher than in phosphorous compounds

**phosphoric acid** *n* [F *acide phosphorique*] **1 a :** a syrupy or deliquescent crystalline tribasic acid $H_3PO_4$ that is obtained by hydration of phosphorus pentoxide or by decomposition of phosphates (as phosphate rock) by leaching with sulfuric acid, that is converted to pyrophosphoric acid when heated above 150°C and to metaphosphoric acid when heated until dense white fumes appear, and that is used chiefly in making fertilizers and other phosphates, in rust-proofing metals, in sugar refining, and as a flavoring agent in soft drinks — called also *orthophosphoric acid* **b :** any of several other hydrated forms of phosphorus pentoxide (as metaphosphoric acid or pyrophosphoric acid) **2 :** phosphorus pentoxide in combined form as determined by analysis esp. in soils and fertilizers

**phosphoric anhydride** *n* **:** PHOSPHORUS PENTOXIDE

**phosphoric oxide** *n* **:** PHOSPHORUS PENTOXIDE

**phos·pho·rif·er·ous** \¦fäsfə¦rif(ə)rəs\ *adj* [*phosphor-* + *-iferous*] **:** bearing or yielding phosphorus

**phos·pho·rism** \'fäsfə,rizəm\ *n* -S [ISV *phosphor-* + *-ism*] **:** a poisoning by phosphorus esp. when chronic

**phos·pho·rite** \'fäsfə,rīt\ *n* -S [*phosphor-* + *-ite*] **1 :** a fibrous concretionary apatite **2 :** PHOSPHATE ROCK — **phos·pho·rit·ic** \¦==¦rid·ik\ *adj*

**phos·pho·rize** \'fäsfə,rīz\ *vt* -ED/-ING/-S [F *phosphoriser*, fr. *phosphore* phosphor + *-iser* -ize] **:** PHOSPHORATE

**phosphoro-** — see PHOSPHOR-

**phos·pho·ro·clas·tic** \¦fäsfərō¦klastik\ *adj* [*phosphor-* + *-clastic*] **:** of, relating to, or inducing a reaction in which a phosphate is involved in the splitting of a compound (as pyruvic acid)

**phos·pho·ro·fluoridic acid** *n* \¦fäsfə(,)rō+...-\ [*phosphor-* + *fluoride* + *-ic*] **:** the fluorophosphoric acid $H_2PO_3F$

**phos·phor·o·gen** \fä'sfȯrəjən, -,jen\ *n* -S [ISV *phosphor-* + *-gen*; perh. orig. formed as F *phosphorogène*] **:** a substance or group that produces or helps to produce phosphorescence or luminescence

**phos·pho·ro·gen·ic** \¦fäsfərō¦jenik\ *adj* [ISV *phosphor-* + *-genic*] **:** generating phosphorescence

**phos·phoro·graph** \fä'sfȯrə,graf, -räf\ *n* [*phosphor-* + *-graph*] **:** a photographic impression made by laying a phosphorescent body directly upon the photographic film in order to detect phosphorescence too feeble to be observed visually — **phos·pho·ro·graph·ic** \¦fäsfərə¦grafik\ *adj* — **phos·pho·rog·ra·phy** \,fäsfə'rägrəfē\ *n* -ES

**phos·pho·rol·y·sis** \,fäsfə'räləsəs\ *n* [NL, fr. *phosphor-* + *-lysis*] **:** a reversible reaction analogous to hydrolysis in which phosphoric acid functions in a manner similar to that of water with the formation of a phosphate; *esp* **:** the reaction of a glycoside (as sucrose, starch, or glycogen) with phosphate in the presence of a phosphorylase to yield a phosphate of a monosaccharide (as glucose) — compare PHOSPHORYLATION — **phos·pho·ro·lyt·ic** \¦fäsfərō¦lid·ik\ *adj*

**phos·phoro·scope** \fä'sfȯrə,skōp\ *n* [ISV *phosphor-* + *-scope;* orig. formed in F] **:** an apparatus for observing phosphorescence and esp. for studying its rate of decay

**phos·pho·ro·thio·ic acid** \¦fäsfə(,)rō,thī¦ōik-\ *n* [*phosphorothioic* fr. *phosphor-* + *-thioic*] **:** the thiophosphoric acid $H_3PO_3S$

**phos·pho·rous** \'fäsf(ə)rəs\ *adj* [prob. fr. (assumed) NL *phosphoreus*, fr. *phosphorus*] **1 :** PHOSPHORESCENT ⟨the overlapping waves shiny and ~ —R.V.Cassill⟩ **2 :** of, resembling, or containing phosphorus — used of compounds in which this element has a valence lower than in phosphoric compounds

**phosphorous acid** *n* **:** a deliquescent crystalline usu. dibasic acid $H_3PO_3$ made esp. by hydrolysis of phosphorus trichloride and used chiefly as a reducing agent and in making phosphites

**phosphorous anhydride** *n* **:** PHOSPHORUS TRIOXIDE

**phos·phor·roesslerite** \¦fäsfə(r)+\ *n* -S [G *phosphorrösslerit*, fr. *phosphor-* + *rösslerit* roesslerite] **:** a mineral $MgH(PO_4).7H_2O$ consisting of an acid hydrous phosphate of magnesium

**phosphors** *pl of* PHOSPHOR

**phos·pho·rus** \'fäsf(ə)rəs\ *n, pl* **phospho·ri** \-sfə,rī, -,rē\ [NL, fr. Gk *phōsphoros* light-bearing, fr. *phōs-* phos- + *-phoros* -phorous] **1 :** a phosphorescent substance or body; *esp* **:** one that shines or glows in the dark **2 :** a nonmetallic multivalent element of the nitrogen family that occurs widely in combined form esp. as inorganic phosphates in minerals (as the apatites), soils, natural waters, bones, and teeth and as organic phosphates in all living cells and that exists in several allotropic forms including (1) a low-melting distillable corrosive poisonous white or yellowish soft waxy crystallizable solid which glows faintly in air and ignites readily in warm moist air giving off dense white smoke, which is manufactured usu. from phosphate rock, sand, and coke in an electric furnace, and which is used chiefly in making phosphorus pentoxide, phosphoric acid, phosphates, and other phosphorus compounds, in incendiaries and screening smokes, and in roach and rat poisons, (2) a violet to red nonpoisonous less reactive powder obtained by heating white phosphorus with a catalyst (as iodine) at temperatures usu. around 250°C and used chiefly in the abrasive surfaces on which safety matches are to be scratched and in pyrotechnics, and (3) a black electrically conducting solid resembling graphite and obtained by heating white phosphorus to high temperatures under high pressure — symbol *P;* see ELEMENT table

**phosphorus chloride** *n* **:** a chloride of phosphorus: as **a :** PHOSPHORUS TRICHLORIDE **b :** PHOSPHORUS PENTACHLORIDE

**phosphorus hep·ta·sulfide** \-¦heptə+\ *n* [*heptasulfide* fr. *hepta-* + *sulfide*] **:** a yellow crystalline compound $P_4S_7$ made by heating a mixture of phosphorus and sulfur in a ratio of about 4 to 7 equivalents, regarded formerly as a trisulfide, and used chiefly in the synthesis of organic sulfur compounds (as thiophene); tetra-phosphorus heptasulfide

**phosphorus oxide** *n* **:** an oxide of phosphorus: as **a :** PHOSPHORUS TRIOXIDE **b :** PHOSPHORUS PENTOXIDE

**phosphorus oxychloride** *n* **:** a volatile fuming liquid compound $POCl_3$ made usu. by oxidation of phosphorus trichloride or by reaction of phosphorus pentachloride with phosphorus pentoxide and used chiefly in making phosphoric esters (as tricresyl phosphate) — called also *phosphoryl chloride*

**phosphorus pentachloride** *n* **:** a fuming irritating white or yellowish crystalline compound $PCl_5$ made by reaction of phosphorus or phosphorus trichloride with chlorine and used much like phosphorus trichloride

**phosphorus pentasulfide** *n* **:** a light-yellow hygroscopic crystalline compound $P_2S_5$ or $P_4S_{10}$ used chiefly in making organic sulfur compounds, flotation reagents, and additives for lubricating oils; di-phosphorus pentasulfide

**phosphorus pentoxide** *n* **:** a compound known in various polymeric forms $(P_2O_5)_x$ (as the dimer $P_4O_{10}$ in the vapor and one crystalline modification) that is obtained usu. by burning phosphorus in an excess of dry air and occurs as a white powder that reacts vigorously and sometimes explosively with water to form phosphoric acids irritating to the skin and mucous membranes, and is used chiefly as a drying agent, as a condensing agent in organic synthesis, and in making phosphoric acids and derivatives; di-phosphorus pentoxide — called also *phosphoric anhydride*

**phosphorus sesquisulfide** *n* **:** a flammable yellow crystalline compound $P_4S_3$ used chiefly in the manufacture of matches; tetra-phosphorus trisulfide — not used systematically

**phosphorus sulfide** *n* **:** any of several compounds of phosphorus and sulfur obtained by heating these elements: as **a :** PHOSPHORUS SESQUISULFIDE **b :** PHOSPHORUS PENTASULFIDE

**phosphorus 32** \\-,thərd-ē'tü\\ *n* **:** a heavy radioactive isotope of phosphorus having a mass number of 32 and a half-life of 14.3 days that is produced in nuclear reactors and used chiefly in tracer studies (as in biology and in chemical analysis) and in medical diagnosis (as in location of tumors) and therapy (as of polycythemia vera) — symbol $P^{32}$ or $^{32}P$; called also *radiophosphorus*

**phosphorus trichloride** *n* **:** a volatile fuming liquid compound $PCl_3$ made usu. by reaction of phosphorus with chlorine and used chiefly in chlorinating organic compounds and in making organic phosphorus compounds

**phosphorus trioxide** *n* **:** a deliquescent volatile crystalline compound $P_4O_6$ that is made by burning phosphorus in a limited supply of air or oxygen, that reacts with cold water to form phosphorous acid, and that decomposes with hot water; tetra-phosphorus hexoxide — called also *phosphorous anhydride*

**phos·pho·ryl** \\'fäsfərəl\\ *n* -s [ISV *phosphor-* + *-yl*] **:** the usu. trivalent radical PO consisting of phosphorus and oxygen

**phos·pho·ryl·ase** \\-rə,lās, -āz\\ *n* -s [*phosphoryl* + *-ase*] **:** any of a group of enzymes that catalyze phosphorolysis and act through the formation of organic phosphates (as glucose phosphate in the breakdown and synthesis of glycogen and other carbohydrates) and that occur widely in animal and plant tissues — compare KINASE 2; TRANSPHOSPHORYLASE

**phos·pho·ryl·ate** \\-āt\\ *vt* -ED/-ING/-S [*phosphoryl* + *-ate*] **:** to convert (an organic compound) into an organic phosphate

**phos·pho·ryl·ation** \\,===ˈlāshən\\ *n* -s [*phosphoryl* + *-ation*] **:** the process of phosphorylating either by reaction with inorganic phosphate or by transfer of phosphate from another organic phosphate; *esp* **:** the enzymatic conversion of carbohydrates into their phosphoric esters in metabolic processes (as of glucose to glucose 6-phosphate by adenosine triphosphate and the enzyme hexokinase) ⟨it was shown that oxidative ~ was the link between fermentation and respiration on the one hand, and life on the other —V.R.Potter⟩ — compare PHOSPHOROLYSIS, TRANSPHOSPHORYLATION

**phos·pho·ryl·ative** \\'===,lād·iv\\ *adj* [*phosphorylate* + *-ive*] **:** of, relating to, or characterized by phosphorylation

**phosphoryl chloride** *n* **:** PHOSPHORUS OXYCHLORIDE

**phos·pho·silicate** \\¦fä(,)sfō+\\ *n* [*phosph-* + *silicate*] **:** a combined phosphate and silicate

**phos·pho·tungstate** \\"+\\ *n* [*phosphotungstic* + *-ate*] **:** a salt of a phosphotungstic acid — called also *tungstophosphate*

**phos·pho·tungstic acid** \\"+. . .-\\ *n* [*phosph-* + *tungstic*] **:** any of several heteropoly acids obtainable from solutions of phosphoric acid and tungstic acid and used chiefly as precipitants (as for alkaloids and for basic dyes for pigments) and in analytical reagents; *esp* **:** the greenish yellow crystalline acid $H_3PW_{12}O_{40}.xH_2O$ containing twelve atoms of tungsten in the molecule — called also *tungstophosphoric acid*

**phos·phu·ran·yl·ite** \\,fäsfyə'ranᵊl,īt\\ *n* -s [*phosph-* + *uranyl* + *-ite*] **:** a mineral $(UO_2)_3(PO_4)_2 6H_2O$ consisting of a hydrous uranyl phosphate and occurring as a deep lemon-yellow powdery substance that exhibits phosphorescence upon exposure to radium emanations

**phos·phu·ret·ed** *or* **phos·phu·ret·ted** \\'fäsfyə,red·əd\\ *adj* [obs. E *phosphuret* something combined with phosphorus (modif. — influenced by F *phosphure* something combined with phosphorus — of NL *phosphoretum* phosphuret, fr. *phosphorus*) + E *-ed*] **:** PHOSPHORETED

**phos·sy jaw** \\'fäsē-\\ *n* [*phossy* fr. *phos* (short for NL *phosphorus*) + *-y*] **:** a jawbone destroyed by chronic phosphorus poisoning

**phos·vi·tin** \\'fäs,vītᵊn, -svətən\\ *n* -s [*phos-* (fr. *phosphoprotein*) + *vit-* + *-in*] **:** a phosphoprotein obtained from egg yolk

**phot** \\'fōt, 'fät\\ *n* -s [ISV, fr. Gk *phōt-, phōs* light] **:** the cgs unit of illumination equal to one lumen per square centimeter and therefore to 10,000 luxes or about 929 footcandles

**phot** *abbr* photograph; photographer; photographic; photography

**phot-** *or* **photo-** *comb form* [Gk, fr. *phōt-, phōs* light — more at FANCY] **1 :** light ⟨*phot*eolic⟩ ⟨*phot*on⟩ ⟨*photo*graphy⟩ ⟨*photo*period⟩ **2 :** photograph **:** photographic ⟨*photo*finish⟩ ⟨*photo*album⟩ ⟨*photo*film⟩ **3 :** photoelectric ⟨*photo*cell⟩ ⟨*photo*current⟩ **4 :** photon ⟨*photo*meson⟩ ⟨*photo*disintegration⟩ **5 :** photochemical ⟨*photo*chlorination⟩ ⟨*photo*product⟩

**phot·eol·ic** \\¦fōd·ē¦älik\\ *adj* [*phot-* + *-eol-* (fr. Gk *aiolos* quick-moving) + *-ic;* prob. akin to Skt *āyus* life — more at AYE] **:** NYCTITROPIC

**pho·tian** \\'fōsh(ē)ən\\ *adj, usu cap* [*Photius* †A.D. 891 Patriarch of Constantinople + E *-an*] **:** of or relating to the patriarch Photius noted for precipitating an early schism between the Eastern and Western churches by challenging the claim of the Roman see to supremacy and charging the Latin churches with heretical innovations (as the credal phrase "and the son")

**pho·tic** \\'fōd·ik\\ *adj* [*phot-* + *-ic*] **1 a :** of, relating to, or caused by light **b :** of or relating to the reaction to or the production of light by living organisms **2 a :** penetrated by light esp. of the sun ⟨~ layers⟩ **b :** of, relating to, or constituting the part of the oceanic waters of the seas that light is able to penetrate — compare ABYSSAL

**photic region** *or* **photic zone** *n* **:** the uppermost layer of the sea or other body of water receiving sufficient light from the sun to affect living organisms esp. by permitting the occurrence of photosynthesis

**pho·tics** \\-ks\\ *n pl but usu sing in constr* [*photic* + *-s*] **:** a science that deals with light — compare OPTICS

**pho·tin·ia** \\fō'tinēə\\ *n, cap* [NL, fr. Gk *phōteinos* shining, bright (fr. *phōt-, phōs* light) + NL *-ia*] **:** a genus of small trees and shrubs (family Rosaceae) of eastern Asia including the toyon and other plants that have shining green leaves, showy white paniculate or corymbose flower clusters, and red fruits and that are widely cultivated as ornamentals — compare HETEROMELES

**pho·tism** \\'fōd·,izəm\\ *n* -s [ISV, fr. Gk *phōtismos* illumination, light, fr. *phōtizein* to shine, give light (fr. *phōt-, phōs* light) + *-ismos* -ism] **:** a synesthetic visual sensation

**¹pho·to** \\'fōd·(,)ō, 'fō(,)tō\\ *n* -s [by shortening] **:** PHOTOGRAPH

**²photo** \\"\\ *vb* -ED/-ING/-S [by shortening] **:** PHOTOGRAPH

**³photo** \\"\\ *adj* [*phot-*] **:** PHOTOGRAPHIC

**pho·to·activate** \\¦fōd·(,)ō+\\ *vt* [*phot-* + *activate*] **:** to activate (a substance) by means of radiant energy (as light) **:** subject (a reaction) to photocatalysis

**pho·to·activation** \\"+\\ *n* [*photoactive* + *-ation*] **:** the process of photoactivating — opposed to *photoinactivation*

**pho·to·active** \\"+\\ *adj* [*phot-* + *active*] **:** physically or chemically responsive to radiant energy and esp. to light: as **a :** susceptible to photoelectric stimulation **b :** photochemically sensitive — **pho·to·activity** \\"+\\ *n*

**pho·to·allergy** \\"+\\ *n* [*phot-* + *allergy*] **:** an allergic sensitivity to light

**pho·to·aquatint** \\"+\\ *n* [*phot-* + *aquatint*] **:** an aquatint made by a photomechanical process resembling photogravure

**pho·to·autotrophic** \\"+\\ *adj* [*phot-* + *autotrophic*] **:** autotrophic and obtaining energy from light ⟨green plants and various photosynthetic bacteria are ~⟩ — compare CHEMOAUTOTROPHIC

**pho·to·biography** \\"+\\ *n* [*phot-* + *biography*] **:** a history of a person's life in photographs

**pho·to·biologic** *or* **pho·to·biological** \\"+\\ *adj* [*phot-* + *biologic* or *biological*] **:** of or relating to photobiology

**pho·to·biology** \\"+\\ *n* [ISV *phot-* + *biology*] **:** a branch of biology that deals with the effects on living beings of light and other forms of radiant energy

**pho·to·biotic** \\"+\\ *adj* [*phot-* + *biotic*] **:** requiring light in order to live or thrive ⟨~ cells⟩

**pho·to·catalysis** \\¦fōd·(,)ō+\\ *n* [NL, fr. *phot-* + *catalysis*] **:** the acceleration of a chemical reaction by radiant energy (as light) acting either directly or by exciting a substance that in turn catalyzes the main reaction — opposed to *photoinactivation*

**pho·to·catalyst** \\"+\\ *n* [*phot-* + *catalyst*] **:** a substance that catalyzes the main reaction in photocatalysis

**pho·to·catalytic** \\"+\\ *adj* **:** of or relating to photocatalysis

**pho·to·catalyze** \\"+\\ *vt* [NL *photocatalysis* + E *-ize*] **:** to subject to photocatalysis

**pho·to·cathode** \\"+\\ *n* [ISV *phot-* + *cathode*] **:** a cathode (as in a photoelectric cell) that emits electrons when exposed to light or other radiation

**pho·to·cell** \\'fōd·ō,sel\\ *n* [ISV *phot-* + *cell*] **:** PHOTOELECTRIC CELL

**pho·to·ceramics** \\¦fōd·(,)ō+\\ *n pl but usu sing in constr* [*phot-* + *ceramics*] **:** the art or process of decorating pottery with photographically prepared designs

**Pho·to·charger** \\'fōd·(,)ō+,-\\ *trademark* — used for a camera that uses rolls of paper negative for making a record of library books being borrowed

**pho·to·chemical** \\"+\\ *adj* [*phot-* + *chemical*] **1 :** of, relating to, or produced by the chemical action of radiant energy and esp. of light **2 :** relating to photochemistry — **pho·to·chemically** \\"+\\ *adv*

**pho·to·chemigraphy** \\"+\\ *n* [ISV *phot-* + *chemigraphy*] **1 :** the process of making zinc etchings from line drawings by the aid of chemistry and photography **2 :** any of various photomechanical engraving processes

**pho·to·chemist** \\"+\\ *n* [*phot-* + *chemist*] **:** a specialist in photochemistry

**pho·to·chemistry** \\"+\\ *n* [*phot-* + *chemistry*] **1 :** a branch of chemistry that deals with the effect of radiant energy (as light) in producing chemical changes (as in photography) — compare RADIATION CHEMISTRY **2 a :** the photochemical properties of a substance ⟨~ of gases⟩ **b :** photochemical processes ⟨the ~ of vision⟩

**pho·to·chlorination** \\"+\\ *n* [*phot-* + *chlorination*] **:** photochemical chlorination

**pho·to·chrome** \\'fōd·ə,krōm\\ *n* [ISV *phot-* + *-chrome*] **:** a photograph in colors

**pho·to·chromoscope** \\¦fōd·(,)ō+\\ *n* [ISV *phot-* + *chromoscope*] **:** a device for combining three color-separation positives optically according to the additive principle and viewing them as a color photograph

**pho·to·chro·my** \\'fōd·ə,krōmē\\ *n* -ES [ISV *phot-* + *-chromy*] **:** a formerly used process of color photography in which a silver chloride emulsion layer assumes approximately the color of the exposing light

**pho·to·chronograph** \\¦fōd·(,)ō+\\ *n* [ISV *phot-* + *chronograph;* perh. orig. formed in F] **1 :** CHRONOPHOTOGRAPH; *also* **:** an apparatus for taking chronophotographs **2 :** an instrument for the photographic recording of star transits **3 :** an instrument for recording minute intervals of time photographically

**pho·to·chronography** \\"+\\ *n* **1 :** the art of recording or measuring intervals of time by the photochronograph **2 :** CHRONOPHOTOGRAPHY

**photocinesis** *var of* PHOTOKINESIS

**pho·to·compose** \\¦fōd·(,)ō+\\ *vt* [*phot-* + *compose*] **:** to compose (reading matter) by means of characters photographed on a film that when developed serves as a basis for making (as by photoengraving or photo-offset) a usu. letterpress or planographic printing surface — **pho·to·composition** \\"+\\ *n*

**pho·to·conductance** \\"+\\ *n* [*phot-* + *conductance*] **:** PHOTOCONDUCTIVITY

**pho·to·conducting** \\"+\\ *adj* [*phot-* + *conducting*] **:** PHOTOCONDUCTIVE

**pho·to·conduction** \\"+\\ *n* [*phot-* + *conduction*] **:** variation of current in a circuit due to the photoconductivity of some part of it under varying illumination

**pho·to·conductive** \\"+\\ *adj* [*phot-* + *conductive*] **:** of, having, or relating to photoconductivity

**photoconductive cell** *n* **:** a photoelectric cell utilizing photoconductivity (as in a layer of selenium) so that an increase in illumination causes a decrease in electrical resistance and permits the flow of a greater electrical current

**pho·to·conductivity** \\"+\\ *n* [*phot-* + *conductivity*] **:** electrical conductivity of a substance (as selenium) as affected by exposure to light or other radiation ⟨the increase in conductivity induced by light is termed ~ —T.H.James & G.C.Higgins⟩

**pho·to·conductor** \\"+\\ *n* [*phot-* + *conductor*] **:** a photoconductive substance

**pho·to·copier** \\"+\\ *n* [¹*photocopy* + *-er*] **:** one that makes photocopies

**¹pho·to·copy** \\'fōd·ō+,-\\ *n* [ISV *phot-* + *copy*] **:** a negative or positive photographic reproduction of graphic matter (as a drawing or printing)

**²photocopy** \\"\\ *vt* **:** to make a photocopy of **~** *vi* **:** to make a photocopy

**pho·to·current** \\¦fōd·(,)ō+\\ *n* [short for *photoelectric current*] **:** a stream of electrons produced by photoelectric or photovoltaic effects

**pho·to·decomposition** \\"+\\ *n* [*phot-* + *decomposition*] **:** chemical decomposition by means of radiant energy (as light) **:** PHOTOLYSIS

**pho·to·degradation** \\"+\\ *n* [*phot-* + *degradation*] **:** chemical degradation by means of radiant energy (as light)

**pho·to·disintegration** \\"+\\ *n* [*phot-* + *disintegration*] **:** a disintegration of the nucleus of an atom produced by absorption of radiant energy — compare ELECTRODISINTEGRATION

**pho·to·dissociation** \\"+\\ *n* [*phot-* + *dissociation*] **:** a dissociation (as of a chemical compound) produced by the absorption of radiant energy (as light)

**pho·to·drama** \\'fōd·ō+,-\\ *n* [*phot-* + *drama*] **:** MOTION PICTURE; *esp* **:** one based upon a tragic, melodramatic, or otherwise serious plot and characterized by sustained action and exciting incident

**¹pho·to·duplicate** \\¦fōd·(,)ō+\\ *vb* [*phot-* + *duplicate*] **:** PHOTOCOPY

**²pho·to·duplicate** \\"+\\ *n* **:** PHOTOCOPY

**pho·to·duplication** \\"+\\ *n* [*phot-* + *duplication*] **1 :** the process of making photocopies **2 :** PHOTOCOPY

**pho·to·dynamic** \\"+\\ *adj* [ISV *phot-* + *dynamic*] **:** of, relating to, or having the property of intensifying or inducing a toxic reaction to light and esp. sunlight in living systems — used of a chemical (as a fluorescent dye or a hemoglobin derivative) or of its action or effect ⟨a ~ pigment⟩ ⟨~ action in fagopyrism⟩ ⟨~ disorders in sheep⟩ — **pho·to·dynamically** \\"+\\ *adv*

**photoed** *past of* PHOTO

**pho·to·effect** \\"+\\ *n* [ISV *phot-* + *effect*] **1 :** PHOTOELECTRIC EFFECT **2 :** the effect of high-energy radiation (as gamma rays) on an atomic nucleus; *esp* **:** PHOTODISINTEGRATION

**pho·to·elastic** \\"+\\ *adj* [*phot-* + *elastic*] **:** of, relating to, or exhibiting photoelasticity — **pho·to·elastically** \\"+\\ *adv*

**pho·to·elasticity** \\"+\\ *n* [ISV *phot-* + *elasticity*] **:** the property exhibited by transparent isotropic solids of becoming doubly refracting when subjected to either tensile or compressive stress making possible a detailed study of the stress distribution from the patterns observed when the solid is examined in a polariscope ⟨~ (used by scientists to determine which parts of industrial structures and machinery will bear the greatest stresses and strains) —*Wall Street Jour.*⟩

**pho·to·electric** \\¦fōd·(,)ō+\\ *adj* [ISV *phot-* + *electric*] **:** relating to or utilizing any of various electrical effects due to the interaction of light or other radiation with matter — compare PHOTOCONDUCTIVE, PHOTOEMISSIVE, PHOTOVOLTAIC — **pho·to·electrically** \\"+\\ *adv*

**photoelectric cell** *n* **:** a photoelectric device: as **a :** PHOTOTUBE **b :** PHOTOCONDUCTIVE CELL **c :** PHOTOVOLTAIC CELL

**photoelectric current** *n* **:** PHOTOCURRENT

**photoelectric effect** *n* **:** the effect of light falling upon metal surfaces and causing them to give out electrons, to generate an electromotive force, or to undergo a change in resistance

**photoelectric emission** *n* **:** PHOTOEMISSION

**pho·to·electricity** \\"+\\ *n* [ISV *photoelectric* + *-ity*] **1 :** electricity produced by the action of light **2 :** a branch of physics that deals with the electrical effects of light

**photoelectric threshold** *n* **:** the least quantum energy or the lowest frequency that will enable incident radiation to release photoelectrons from a surface

**photoelectric tube** *n* **:** PHOTOTUBE

**pho·to·electron** \\"+\\ *n* [ISV *phot-* + *electron*] **:** an electron released in photoemission (as in a phototube)

**pho·to·element** \\"+\\ *n* [ISV *phot-* + *element*] **:** PHOTOVOLTAIC CELL

**pho·to·emission** \\"+\\ *n* [*phot-* + *emission*] **:** the release of electrons from a metal (as cesium) by means of energy supplied by incidence of light or other radiation — compare FIELD EMISSION

**pho·to·emissive** \\"+\\ *adj* [*phot-* + *emissive*] **:** emitting or capable of emitting electrons when exposed to light or other radiation of suitable wavelength

**photoemissive cell** *n* **:** PHOTOTUBE

**pho·to·engrave** \\¦fōd·(,)ō+\\ *vt* [back-formation fr. *photoengraving*] **:** to make a photoengraving of

**pho·to·engraver** \\"+\\ *n* [*photoengrave* + *-er*] **:** one that makes photoengraved plates; *also* **:** a worker who performs one or more of the operations of photoengraving

**pho·to·engraving** \\"+\\ *n* [*phot-* + *engraving*] **1 :** a photomechanical process for making linecuts and halftone cuts by photographing an image on a metal plate and then etching **2 a :** a plate made by photoengraving **b :** a print made from such a plate

**pho·to·etch** \\"+\\ *vt* [*phot-* + *etch*] **:** PHOTOENGRAVE

**pho·to·etching** \\"+\\ *n* [fr. gerund of *photoetch*] **:** PHOTOENGRAVING

**photo finish** *n* **1 :** a finish in which racing contestants are so close that a photograph of them as they cross the finish line has to be examined to determine the winner **2 :** a close contest (as in an election) ⟨newsmen who covered the campaign . . . foresaw a *photo finish* —*Newsweek*⟩

**pho·to·finisher** \\"+\\ *n* [*phot-* + *finisher*] **:** one that engages in photofinishing

**pho·to·finishing** \\"+\\ *n* [*phot-* + *finishing*] **:** the commercial development and printing of films exposed usu. by amateur photographers

**pho·to·fission** \\"+\\ *n* [*phot-* + *fission*] **:** nuclear fission produced by the absorption of radiant energy (as gamma rays)

**pho·to·flash** \\'fōd·ō+,-\\ *or* **photoflash lamp** *also* **photoflash bulb** *n* [*phot-* + *flash*] **:** an electrically operated flash lamp; *esp* **:** FLASHBULB

**photoflash bomb** *n* **:** FLASH BOMB

**pho·to·flood** \\"+,-\\ *or* **photoflood lamp** *also* **photoflood bulb** *n* [*phot-* + *flood*] **:** an electric lamp using excess voltage to give intense sustained illumination for taking photographs

**pho·to·flu·o·ro·gram** \\¦fōd·(,)ō¦flü(ə)rə,gram, -lōr-, -lȯr-\\ *n* [*phot-* + *fluor-* + *-gram*] **:** a photograph made by photofluorography

**pho·to·fluorographic** \\¦fōd·(,)ō+\\ *adj* [*photofluorography* + *-ic*] **:** of, used in, or relating to photofluorography

**pho·to·fluorography** \\"+\\ *n* [*phot-* + *fluorography*] **:** the photography of the image produced on a fluorescent screen by X rays — called also *photoradiography, photoroentgenography*

**pho·to·fluorometer** \\"+\\ *n* [*phot-* + *fluorometer*] **:** a photoelectric fluorometer — **pho·to·fluorometric** \\"+\\ *adj* — **pho·to·fluorometrically** \\"+\\ *adv*

**pho·to·fluoroscopy** \\"+\\ *n* [*phot-* + *fluoroscopy*] **:** PHOTOFLUOROGRAPHY

**pho·tog** \\fə'täg, fō'-\\ *n* -s [by shortening] **1 :** PHOTOGRAPH **2 :** PHOTOGRAPHER **3 :** PHOTOGRAPHY

**pho·to·galvanic** \\¦fōd·(,)ō+\\ *adj* [*phot-* + *galvanic*] **:** PHOTOVOLTAIC

**pho·to·gelatin process** \\"+. . .-\\ *n* [*phot-* + *gelatin*] **:** COLLOTYPE 1

**pho·to·gene** \\'fōd·ə,jēn\\ *n* -s [ISV *phot-* + *-gene;* prob. orig. formed in F] **:** an afterimage or retinal impression

**pho·to·genic** \\¦fōd·ə¦jenik, -ōtə-, -jēn-, -nēk\\ *adj* [*phot-* + *-genic*] **1 a :** produced or precipitated by light ⟨~ epilepsy⟩ ⟨~ dermatitis⟩ **b :** marked by a tendency to darken on exposure to sunlight ⟨the ~ property of a pigment⟩ **2 :** PHOTOGRAPHIC **3 :** producing or generating light **:** PHOSPHORESCENT ⟨~ bacteria⟩ ⟨~ organs of a firefly⟩ **4 :** eminently suitable for being photographed esp. from the aesthetic point of view ⟨~ hands⟩ — **pho·to·geni·cal·ly** \\-nək(ə)lē, -nēk-, -li\\ *adv*

**pho·to·geologic** *also* **pho·to·geological** \\¦fōd·(,)ō+\\ *adj* [*photogeology* + *-ic* or *-ical*] **:** of or relating to photogeology

**pho·to·geology** \\"+\\ *n* [*phot-* + *geology*] **:** the geologic interpretation of aerial photographs; *esp* **:** the identification of geologic structures by studying such photographs

**pho·to·gram** \\'fōd·ə,gram\\ *n* [ISV *phot-* + *-gram*] **1 :** a photograph usu. of a pictorial nature **2 :** a shadowlike picture made by placing opaque, translucent, or transparent objects between light-sensitive paper and a light source and developing the latent photographic image

**pho·to·gram·met·ric** \\¦==,gra¦me·trik\\ *also* **pho·to·gram·met·ri·cal** \\-trəkəl\\ *adj* [*photogrammetric* ISV *photogrammetry* + *-ic; photogrammetrical* fr. *photogrammetry* + *-ical*] **:** of, made by, or relating to photogrammetry ⟨~ methods⟩ — **pho·to·gram·met·ri·cal·ly** \\-ək(ə)lē\\ *adv*

**pho·to·gram·me·trist** \\,=='gramə·trəst\\ *n* -s [*photogrammetry* + *-ist*] **:** a specialist in photogrammetry

**pho·to·gram·me·try** \\-trē\\ *n* -ES [ISV *photogram* + *-metry;* orig. formed as G *photogrammetrie*] **:** a science of making reliable measurements by the use of usu. aerial photographs in surveying and mapmaking

**¹pho·to·graph** \\'fōd·ə,graf, -ōtə-, -raa(ə)f, -raif, -räf\\ *n* [*phot-* + *-graph*] **1 :** a picture, image, or likeness obtained by photography **2 :** a portrayal, description, or mental picture or image characterized by great truth of representation or minute detail in reproduction

**²photograph** \\"\\ *vb* -ED/-ING/-S *vt* **1 :** to take a photograph of **2 :** to depict vividly in words ⟨verse ~*ed* the human ruins —*Time*⟩ ⟨editorial . . . ~*s* the upper layer of my mind —W.A. White⟩ **3 :** to impress on the mind ⟨a man may see your signal, ~ it in his mind's eye —H.A.Calahan⟩ **~** *vi* **1 :** to practice photography **:** take photographs **2 :** to undergo being photographed

**pho·to·graph·able** \\-əbəl, ,==¦===\\ *adj* **1 :** capable of being photographed **2 :** PHOTOGENIC 4

**pho·tog·ra·pher** \\fə'tägrəfə(r), fō'-, *in rapid speech often* -gəf- *by r-dissimilation*\\ *n* -s **:** one who practices or is skilled in photography; *esp* **:** one who makes a business of taking photographs

**pho·to·graph·ic** \\¦fōd·ə¦grafik, -ōtə-, -fēk\\ *adj* **1 :** of or relating to photography **:** obtained by or used in photography **2 :** representing nature and human beings with the exactness, fidelity, and minuteness of a photograph **:** concerned only with accurate presentation of external objective details ⟨~ paintings⟩ ⟨~ realism in literature⟩ **3 :** capable of retaining vivid impressions ⟨a ~ mind⟩ ⟨a few detectives have ~ memories which enable them to carry a whole rogues' gallery right under their hats—D.W.Maurer⟩ — **pho·to·graph·i·cal·ly** \\-fək(ə)lē, -fēk-, -li\\ *adv*

**photographic magnitude** *n* **:** the magnitude of a celestial body as determined by observations with an ordinary blue-sensitive photographic plate

**photographic paper** *n* **:** light-sensitive photographic printing paper

**pho·tog·ra·phist** \\fə'tägrəfəst, fō'-\\ *n* -s **:** PHOTOGRAPHER

**pho·tog·ra·phy** \\-rəfē, -fi\\ *n* -ES [*phot-* + *-graphy*] **1 :** an art or process of producing a negative or positive image directly or indirectly on a sensitized surface by the action of light or other form of radiant energy **2 :** extremely faithful, minutely detailed, or mechanically accurate reproduction or representation

**¹pho·to·gra·vure** \\¦fōd·əgrə¦vyu̇(ə)r, -ōtə-, -grā¦v-, -u̇ə\\ *n* [F, fr. *phot-* + *gravure*] **1 :** any of several printing processes in which an intaglio usu. copper printing plate is prepared by photographing an image through a screen onto the sensitized surface that after development is etched **2 :** a print produced by photogravure

**²photogravure** \\"\\ *vt* **:** to reproduce by photogravure

**photogs** *pl of* PHOTOG

**pho·to·halide** \\¦fōd·(,)ō+\\ *n* [*phot-* + *halide*] **:** any of a series of variously colored products formed by the action of radiant energy on silver halide or obtained by the introduction of colloidal silver into silver halide during its preparation

**pho·to·heliograph** \\"+\\ *n* [*phot-* + *heliograph*] **:** a telescope adapted for photographing the sun

**pho·to·impose** \\"+\\ *vt* [*phot-* + *impose*] **:** to arrange (matter from which a printing surface is to be made by a photographic process) in final form

**pho·to·inactivation** \\"+\\ *n* [*phot-* + *inactivation*] **1 :** the retardation or prevention of a chemical reaction by radiant energy (as light) — opposed to *photocatalysis* **2 :** the inactivation of a substance by radiant energy (as light) — opposed to *photoactivation*

**pho·to·induction** \\"+\\ *n* [*phot-* + *induction*] **:** the action of light on an organism (as when the length of day affects the flowering of a plant) — **pho·to·inductive** \\"+\\ *adj*

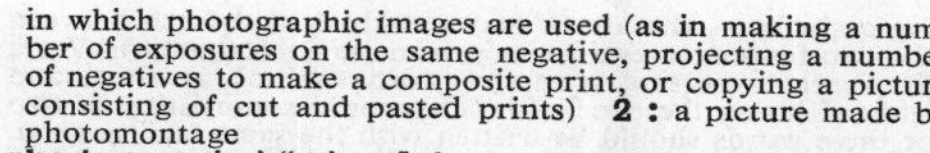

**photoing** *pres part of* PHOTO

**pho·to·intaglio** \ˌfōd·(ˌ)ō+\ *n* [*phot-* + *intaglio*] **:** an intaglio printing surface produced photographically

**photo interpretation** *n* **:** a science of identifying and describing objects in photographs (as for military or topographic significance)

**photo interpreter** *n* **:** a specialist in photo interpretation

**photo–ionization** \ˌfōd·(ˌ)ō+\ *n* **:** ionization by the action (as in the ionosphere) of radiant energy (as light)

**pho·to·ist** \ˈfōd·əwəst\ *n* -s [[1]*photo* + *-ist*] **:** PHOTOGRAPHER

**pho·to·journalism** \ˌfōd·(ˌ)ō+\ *n* [*phot-* + *journalism*] **:** journalism in which written copy is subordinate to pictorial usu. photographic presentation of news stories or in which a high proportion of such pictorial presentation is used

**pho·to·journalist** \"+\ *n* [*photojournal*ism + *-ist*] **:** a news photographer whose work is photojournalism or whose photographs serve or are extremely suitable to photojournalism

**pho·to·kinesis** *or* **pho·to·cinesis** \"+\ *n* [NL, fr. *phot-* + *-kinesis*] **:** motion or activity induced by light ⟨∼ (locomotion in a variable direction with respect to the light source) is seen in lampreys, hagfishes, and blinded catfish —Norman Millott⟩ — **pho·to·kinetic** \"+\ *adj*

**pho·to·kymograph** \"+\ *n* [*phot-* + *kymograph*] **:** a kymograph in which the record is made photographically — **pho·to·kymographic** \"+\ *adj*

**pho·to·labile** \"+\ *adj* [*phot-* + *labile*] **:** susceptible of change under the influence of radiant energy and esp. of light **:** unstable in the presence of light — opposed to *photostable*

**pho·to·lability** \"+\ *n* **:** the quality or state of being photolabile

**pho·to·lettering** \"+\ *n* [*phot-* + *lettering*] **:** lettering produced photomechanically from alphabets on film made from original drawings or existing type designs

[1]**pho·to·lith** \ˈfōd·əˌlith\ *adj* [by shortening] **:** PHOTOLITHOGRAPHIC

[2]**photolith** \"+\ *vt* -ED/-ING/-S [by shortening] **:** PHOTOLITHOGRAPH

[1]**pho·to·litho** \ˌfōd·əˈli(ˌ)thō\ *adj* [by shortening] **:** PHOTOLITHOGRAPHIC

[2]**photolitho** \"\ *n* [by shortening] **:** PHOTOLITHOGRAPH

[1]**pho·to·lithograph** \ˌfōd·(ˌ)ō+\ *n* [*phot-* + *lithograph*] **:** a print made by photolithography

[2]**photolithograph** \"\ *vt* **:** to make a photolithograph of

**pho·to·lithographer** \ˌfōd·(ˌ)ō+\ *n* **:** a specialist in photolithography

**pho·to·lithographic** \"+\ *adj* [ISV *photolithograph* + *-ic*] **:** of, made by, or used in photolithography

**pho·to·lithography** \"+\ *n* [ISV *phot-* + *lithography*] **:** lithography in which photographically prepared plates are used — compare PHOTO-OFFSET

[1]**pho·to·lithoprint** \"+\ *n* [*phot-* + *lithoprint*] **:** PHOTOLITHOGRAPH

[2]**photolithoprint** \"\ *vt* **:** PHOTOLITHOGRAPH

**pho·to·lofting** \ˌfōd·(ˌ)ō+\ *n* [*phot-* + *lofting*] **:** the production of full-scale templates or patterns of large objects by the use of a photographic process

**pho·to·luminescence** \"+\ *n* [ISV *phot-* + *luminescence*] **:** luminescence in which the excitation is produced by visible or invisible light — **pho·to·luminescent** \"+\ *adj*

**pho·tol·y·sis** \fōˈtäləsəs\ *n, pl* **photoly·ses** \-ləˌsēz\ [NL, fr. *phot-* + *-lysis*] **:** chemical decomposition or dissociation by the action of radiant energy (as light)

**pho·to·lyt·ic** \ˌfōd·ᵊlˈid·ik\ *adj* [*phot-* + *-lytic*] **:** of, relating to, or formed by photolysis — **pho·to·lyt·i·cal·ly** \-d·ək(ə)lē\ *adv*

**pho·to·lyze** \ˈfōd·ᵊlˌīz\ *vt* -ED/-ING/-S [NL *photoly*sis + E *-ize*] **:** to subject to photolysis

**pho·to·ma** \fəˈtōmə, fōˈ-\ *n, pl* **photoma·ta** \-məd·ə\ [NL, fr. *phot-* + *-oma*] **:** a rudimentary subjective visual sensation (as of sparks or flashes of light or color)

**pho·to·macrograph** \ˌfōd·(ˌ)ō+\ *n* [*phot-* + *macrograph*] **1 :** a photograph in which the object is either unmagnified or slightly magnified up to a limit of magnification often of about 10 diameters **:** a macrograph made by photography **2 :** a photomicrograph of very low magnification

**pho·to·macrographic** \"+\ *adj* [*photomacrograph* + *-ic*] **:** of or relating to photomacrography

**pho·to·macrography** \"+\ *n* [*phot-* + *macrography*] **:** the making of photomacrographs

**pho·to·magnetic** \"+\ *adj* [ISV *phot-* + *magnetic*] **1 :** of or relating to the direct effect of light upon the magnetic properties of substances **2 :** of or relating to interactions between the magnetic component of electromagnetic radiation (as gamma rays) and the magnetic dipole moments of nuclear particles

[1]**pho·to·map** \ˈfōd·ōˌmap\ *n* [*phot-* + *map*] **:** a photograph or series of matched photographs taken vertically from an airplane upon which a grid and data pertinent to maps (as scale and place names) have been added

[2]**photomap** \"\ *vt* **:** to make a photomap of ∼ *vi* **:** to make a photomap

**pho·to·mechanical** \ˌfōd·(ˌ)ō+\ *adj* [ISV *phot-* + *mechanical*] **:** relating to or being any process of printing mechanically from a photographically prepared surface — **pho·to·mechan·ically** \"+\ *adv*

**pho·to·mechanics** \"+\ *n pl but usu sing in constr* [*photomechan*ical + *-ics*] **:** the technique of photomechanical methods

**pho·to·meson** \"+\ *n* [*phot-* + *meson*] **:** a meson ejected from an atomic nucleus as a result of the incidence of a gamma ray or other high energy photon

**pho·to·meteor** \"+\ *n* [ISV *phot-* + *meteor*] **:** a temporary luminous phenomenon (as lightning, a rainbow, a halo) in the sky

[1]**pho·tom·e·ter** \fōˈtämәd·ə(r)\ *n* [NL *photometrum*, fr. *phot-* + *-metrum* -meter] **:** an instrument for measuring luminous intensity, luminous flux, illumination, or brightness by comparison of two unequal lights from different sources usu. by reducing the illumination of one (as by varying the distance of the source or using a polarizing device) until the two lights appear equal, the amount of adjustment serving as the basis of comparison and the equality of illumination being judged by various means

[2]**photometer** \"\ *vt* **:** to examine with a photometer

**pho·to·met·ric** \ˌfōd·əˈme·trik\ *also* **pho·to·metrical** \-rəkəl\ *adj* [*photometric* ISV *photometer* + *-ic; photometrical* fr. *photometer* + *-ical*] **:** of or relating to photometry or the photometer — **pho·to·met·ri·cal·ly** \-rək(ə)lē\ *adv*

**pho·tom·e·try** \fōˈtämə·trē\ *n* -ES [NL *photometria*, fr. *phot-* + *-metria* -metry] **:** a branch of science that deals with measuring the intensity of light; *also* **:** the practice of using a photometer

**pho·to·microgram** \ˌfōd·(ˌ)ō+\ *n* [*phot-* + *microgram*] **:** PHOTOMICROGRAPH

[1]**pho·to·micrograph** \"+\ *n* [*phot-* + *micr-* + *-graph*] **:** a photograph of a magnified image of a small object **:** a micrograph made by photography — compare MICROPHOTOGRAPH, PHOTOMACROGRAPH

[2]**photomicrograph** \"\ *vt* **:** to make a photomicrograph of

**pho·to·micrographer** \ˌfōd·(ˌ)ō+\ *n* **:** one who makes photomicrographs

**pho·to·micrographic** *also* **pho·to·micrographical** \"+\ *adj* [*photomicrographic* ISV *photomicrograph* + *-ic; photomicrographical* fr. *photomicrograph* + *-ical*] **:** of or relating to photomicrography — **pho·to·micrographically** \"+\ *adv*

**pho·to·micrography** \"+\ *n* [ISV *photomicrograph* + *-y*] **:** the making of photomicrographs

**pho·to·microscope** \ˌfōd·(ˌ)ō+\ *n* [*phot-* + *microscope*] **:** a combined microscope, camera, and suitable light source

**pho·to·microscopy** \"+\ *n* [*phot-* + *microscopy*] **:** PHOTOMICROGRAPHY

photomicroscope

**pho·to·montage** \"+\ *n* [ISV *phot-* + *montage*] **1 :** montage in which photographic images are used (as in making a number of exposures on the same negative, projecting a number of negatives to make a composite print, or copying a picture consisting of cut and pasted prints) **2 :** a picture made by photomontage

**pho·to·mosaic** \"+\ *n* [*phot-* + *mosaic*] **:** a photographic mosaic; *esp* **:** one composed of aerial photographs

**pho·to·multiplier** \"+\ *also* **pho·tomultiplier tube** *n* [*phot-* + *multiplier*] **:** an electron multiplier in which the first stage consists of photoelectric emission from a suitable cathode — called also *multiplier phototube*

**pho·to·mural** \"+\ *n* [*phot-* + *mural*] **:** an enlarged photograph usu. several yards long used on walls esp. as decoration

**pho·ton** \ˈfōˌtän\ *n* -s [*phot-* + *-on*] **1 :** a quantum of radiant energy (as light or X rays) **2 :** a unit of intensity of light at the retina equal to the illumination received per square millimeter of a pupillary area from a surface having a brightness of one candle per square meter — called also *troland*

**pho·to·nas·tic** \ˌfōd·ōˈnastik\ *adj* [*photonasty* + *-ic*] **:** of relating to, or caused by photonasty — **pho·to·nas·ti·cal·ly** \-tək(ə)lē\ *adv*

**pho·to·nas·ty** \ˈ==ˌnastē\ *n* -ES [ISV *phot-* + *-nasty;* prob. orig. formed as G *photonastie*] **:** a nastic movement that is associated with changes in light intensity

**pho·to·negative** \ˌfōd·(ˌ)ō+\ *adj* [*phot-* + *negative*] **:** exhibiting negative phototropism or phototaxis

**pho·to·neutron** \"+\ *n* [*phot-* + *neutron*] **:** a neutron released as a result of photodisintegration

**pho·ton·ic** \(ˈ)fōˈtänik\ *adj* [ISV *photon* + *-ic*] **:** of or relating to a photon ⟨∼ nature of the incoming rays —R.A.Millikan⟩

**pho·ton·o·sus** \fōˈtänəsəs\ *n, pl* **photono·si** \-nəˌsī\ [NL, fr. *phot-* + Gk *nosos* disease] **:** an abnormality (as snow blindness) caused by exposure to light

**pho·to·nuclear** \ˌfōd·(ˌ)ō+\ *adj* [ISV *phot-* + *nuclear*] **:** relating to or caused by the incidence of radiant energy (as X rays or gamma rays) upon atomic nuclei ⟨∼ reaction⟩

**photo–offset** \"+\ *n* **:** offset using a photographically prepared planographic printing plate — compare PHOTOLITHOGRAPHY

**pho·to·oxidation** \"+\ *n* [*phot-* + *oxidation*] **:** oxidation under the influence of radiant energy (as light) **:** photochemical oxidation ⟨∼ of polyethylene, nylon and cellulose esters . . . causes crazing, cracking, embrittlement —B.S.Biggs⟩ — **pho·to·oxidative** \"+\ *adj*

**pho·to·oxidize** \"+\ *vb* [*photooxid*ation + *-ize*] *vi* **:** to undergo photooxidation ∼ *vt* **:** to subject to photooxidation

**pho·to·path·ic** \ˌfōd·əˈpathik\ *adj* [*photopathy* + *-ic*] **:** of or relating to photopathy

**pho·top·a·thy** \fōˈtäpəthē\ *n* -ES [*phot-* + *-pathy*] **1 :** pronounced and usu. negative phototaxis or phototropism **2 :** any diseased condition caused by light esp. through overexposure

**pho·to·period** \ˌfōd·(ˌ)ō+\ *n* [*phot-* + *period*] **:** the relative lengths of alternating periods of lightness and darkness as they affect the growth and maturity of an organism (as in the effect upon the flowering of plants and the breeding of animals) — compare THERMOPERIOD — **pho·to·periodic** *or* **pho·to·periodical** \"+\ *adj* — **pho·to·periodically** \"+\ *adv*

**pho·to·pe·ri·od·ism** \ˌfōd·(ˌ)ōˈpirēəˌdizəm\ *also* **pho·to·periodicity** \ˌfōd·(ˌ)ō+\ *n, pl* **photoperiodisms** *also* **photoperiodicities** [*photoperiodism* ISV *phot-* + *period* + *-ism; photoperiodicity* fr. *photoperiodic* (fr. *phot-* + *periodic*) + *-ity*] **:** capacity to respond to the photoperiod

**pho·to·phil·ic** \ˌfōd·ōˈfilik\ *also* **pho·toph·i·lous** \(ˈ)fōˈtäfələs\ *or* **pho·to·phile** \ˈfōd·ōˌfīl\ *adj* [*photophilic* fr. *phot-* + *-philic; photophilous* ISV *phot-* + *-philous; photophile* fr. *phot-* + *-phile*] **:** thriving in full light **:** requiring abundant light for complete and normal development **:** light-loving ⟨∼ grasses⟩ — **pho·toph·i·ly** \(ˈ)fōˈtäfəlē, -li\ *n* -ES

**pho·to·phobe** \ˈfōd·əˌfōb\ *n* -s [*phot-* + *-phobe*] **:** an organ or organism that thrives best in the dark or turns away from light

**pho·to·pho·bia** \ˌ==ˈfōbēə\ *n* [NL, fr. *photo-* + *phobia*] **:** intolerance to light; *esp* **:** painful sensitiveness to strong light

**pho·to·phobic** \ˌ==ˈfōbik *also* -ˈfäb-\ *also* **pho·to·phobe** \ˈ==ˌfōb\ *adj* [*photophobic* fr. NL *photophobicus*, fr. *phot-* + *-phobicus* -phobic; *photophobe* fr. *phot-* + *-phobe*] **1 a :** shunning or avoiding light **:** exhibiting negative phototropism ⟨the bedbug and other ∼ insects⟩ **b :** growing best under reduced illumination **2 :** of or relating to photophobia

**pho·to·phone** \ˈ==ˌfōn\ *n* [*phot-* + *-phone*] **:** a device whereby a sound signal (as a voice) is transmitted by causing it to modulate a beam of visible or infrared light which is received by a photoelectric cell, amplified, and reconverted into sound

**pho·to·phore** \-ˌfō(ə)r\ *n* -s [ISV *phot-* + *-phore;* prob. orig. formed in F] **:** a light-emitting organ; *specif* **:** one of the luminous spots on various marine mostly deep-sea fishes

**pho·to·pho·re·sis** \ˌfōd·əfəˈrēsəs\ *n, pl* **photophore·ses** \-ēˌsēz\ [NL, fr. *phot-* + *-phoresis*] **:** movement of small particles (as dust particles) under the influence of radiant energy (as light) that is considered positive when the movement is away from the source of energy and negative when toward it — compare MAGNETOPHOTOPHORESIS — **pho·to·pho·ret·ic** \ˌ===ˈred·ik\ *adj*

**pho·to·phosphorescence** \ˌfōd·(ˌ)ō+\ *n* [*phot-* + *phosphorescence*] **:** phosphorescence excited by visible or invisible light — **pho·to·phosphorescent** \"+\ *adj*

**pho·toph·y·gous** \(ˈ)fōˈtäfəgəs\ *adj* [*phot-* + Gk *phygē* flight (fr. *pheugein* to flee) + E *-ous* — more at FUGITIVE] **:** preferring or thriving in shade ⟨a ∼ plant⟩

**pho·to·pia** \fōˈtōpēə\ *n* -s [NL, fr. *phot-* + *-opia*] **:** vision in bright light with light-adapted eyes believed to be mediated by the cones of the retina — opposed to *scotopia* — **pho·topic** \(ˈ)fōˈtōpik, -täpik\ *adj*

**pho·to·play** \ˈfōd·əˌ -d·ō+ˌ-\ *n* [*phot-* + *play*] **:** a motion picture of a story or play

**pho·to·polymerization** \ˌfōd·(ˌ)ō+\ *n* [*phot-* + *polymerization*] **:** polymerization under the influence of radiant energy (as light) **:** photochemical polymerization

**pho·to·positive** \"+\ *adj* [*phot-* + *positive*] **:** exhibiting positive phototropism or phototaxis

**pho·to·print** \ˈfōd·ō+ˌ-\ *n* [*phot-* + *print*] **:** an image formed on paper or other sensitive material by photographic means **:** a photographic print

**pho·to·printing** \+ˌ-\ *n* [*photoprint* + *-ing*] **:** the making of photoprints

**pho·to·product** \+ˌ-\ *n* [*phot-* + *product*] **:** a product of a photochemical reaction

**pho·to·production** \ˌfōd·ō+\ *n* [*phot-* + *production*] **:** the production of mesons as a result of the action of high energy photons on atomic nuclei

**pho·to·proton** \"+\ *n* [*phot-* + *proton*] **:** a proton ejected from an atomic nucleus as a result of photodisintegration

**phot·optometer** \ˌfōd·+\ *n* [*phot-* + *optometer*] **:** an instrument for studying visual impressions

**pho·to·radio** \ˌfōd·(ˌ)ō+\ *n* [*phot-* + *radio*] **:** the process of transmitting photographs or pictures by radio

**pho·to·radiogram** \"+\ *n* [fr. *Photoradiogram*, a trademark] **:** a picture or image reproduced at a distance by radio transmission

**pho·to·radiograph** \"+\ *n* [*phot-* + *radiograph*] **:** PHOTOFLUOROGRAM

**pho·to·radiographic** \"+\ *adj* [*photoradiography* + *-ic*] **:** PHOTOFLUOROGRAPHIC

**pho·to·radiography** \"+\ *n* [*phot-* + *radiography*] **:** PHOTOFLUOROGRAPHY

**pho·to·reaction** \"+\ *n* [ISV *phot-* + *reaction*] **:** a chemical reaction brought about by radiant energy (as light) **:** a photochemical reaction

**pho·to·reception** \"+\ *n* [*phot-* + *reception*] **:** perception of waves in the range of visible light; *specif* **:** VISION — **pho·to·receptive** \"+\ *adj*

**pho·to·receptor** \"+\ *n* [*phot-* + *receptor*] **:** a receptor for light stimuli

**pho·to·reconnaissance** \"+\ *n* [*phot-* + *reconnaissance*] **:** reconnaissance in which aerial photographs are taken

**pho·to·record** \ˈfōd·ō+ˌ-\ *n* [*phot-* + *record*] **:** a photographic record

**pho·to·recorder** \ˌfōd·(ˌ)ō+\ *n* **:** an apparatus (as a camera) for making photorecords

**pho·to·recording** \"+\ *n* **:** the making of photorecords

**pho·to·reduction** \"+\ *n* [*phot-* + *reduction*] **:** chemical reduction under the influence of radiant energy (as light) **:** photochemical reduction

**pho·to·report** \"+\ *n* [*phot-* + *report*] **:** a sequence of photographs (as of an event or phenomenon) combined with a minimum of text in such a way that the words and pictures supplement each other

**pho·to·reproduction** \"+\ *n* [*phot-* + *reproduction*] **:** the process of reproducing (as pictures or printed matter) by photographic means; *also* **:** a photographic reproduction

**pho·to·resistance** \"+\ *n* [*phot-* + *resistance*] **:** PHOTOCONDUCTIVITY

**pho·to·resistive** \"+\ *adj* [*phot-* + *resistive*] **:** of, having, or relating to photoconductivity

**pho·to·roentgen** *or* **pho·to·roentgenographic** \ˌfōd·(ˌ)ō+\ *adj* [*photoroentgen* fr. *phot-* + *roentgen; photoroentgenographic* fr. *photoroentgenography* + *-ic*] **:** PHOTOFLUOROGRAPHIC

**pho·to·roentgenogram** \"+\ *n* [*phot-* + *roentgenogram*] **:** PHOTOFLUOROGRAM

**pho·to·roentgenography** \"+\ *n* [*phot-* + *roentgenography*] **:** PHOTOFLUOROGRAPHY

**photos** *pl of* PHOTO, *pres 3d sing of* PHOTO

**pho·to·scope** \ˈfōd·əˌskōp\ *n* [ISV *phot-* + *-scope*] **:** a photofluorographic screen and camera

**pho·to·sculpture** \ˈfōd·ō+ˌ-\ *n* [F, fr. *phot-* + *sculpture*] **:** a method of sculpture whereby one or more cameras are used to produce photographs that are processed and combined in one of various ways to make either a bas-relief or a solid sculpture

**pho·to·sensitive** \ˌfōd·(ˌ)ō+\ *adj* [*phot-* + *sensitive*] **:** sensitive chemically, electrically, or otherwise to the action of radiant energy (as light) — **pho·to·sensitivity** \"+\ *n*

**pho·to·sensitization** \"+\ *n* [*phot-* + *sensitization*] **1 :** the process of photosensitizing **2 :** the condition of a cell, tissue, or organism acted upon by a substance (as a dyestuff) that renders it sensitive to a particular region of the spectrum to which it was previously insensitive **3 :** the development in light-colored skin of an abnormal capacity to react to sunlight typically by edematous swelling and dermatitis that in grazing animals results from ingestion of toxic substances (as porphyrins) that cause the body to absorb ultraviolet rays to an excessive degree where these are not screened out by skin pigments — compare BIGHEAD, FAGOPYRISM, HYPERICISM **4 :** a chemical change through the agency of a substance excited by the absorption of radiant energy (as light)

**pho·to·sensitize** \"+\ *vt* [*phot-* + *sensitize*] **1 :** to make photosensitive by means of chemical or optical sensitizers **2 :** to induce (as a chemical reaction) by means of an intermediary substance that absorbs radiant energy (as light) ⟨hydrogenation of ethylene *photosensitized* by mercury vapor —*Industrial & Engineering Chemistry*⟩

**pho·to·sensitizer** \"+\ *n* **:** a substance (as a dye) capable of sensitizing a material (as photographic film or paper) to rays to which it is not normally sensitive

**pho·to·sensory** \"+\ *adj* [*phot-* + *sensory*] **:** relating to the perception of light in animals

**pho·to·set** \ˈfōd·ō+ˌ-\ *vt* [*phot-* + *set*] **:** PHOTOCOMPOSE

**pho·to·shock** \"+ˌ-\ *n* [*phot-* + *shock*] **:** a method of treating psychosis by exposing the patient to a flashing light while he is under the influence of a sensitizing drug

**pho·to·sphere** \"+ˌ-\ *n* [*phot-* + *sphere*] **1 :** a sphere of light or glory **2 :** the luminous surface of the sun or a star beneath which it is completely opaque to the visible region of the spectrum — **pho·to·spheric** \ˌfōd·ō+\ *adj*

**pho·to·stability** \ˌfōd·(ˌ)ō+\ *n* **:** the property of being photostable

**pho·to·stable** \"+\ *adj* [*phot-* + *stable*] **:** resistant to change under the influence of radiant energy and esp. of light — opposed to *photolabile*

**pho·to·stage** \ˈfōd·ō+ˌ-\ *n* [*phot-* + *stage*] **:** a phase of plant development during which light exerts a dominant effect

**pho·to·stat** \ˈfōd·əˌstat, -ōd·ōˌs-, *usu* -ad·+V\ *vb* **photostated; photostated; photostating; photostats** [*Photostat*] *vt* **:** to make a Photostat copy of ∼ *vi* **:** to photostat graphic matter

**Photostat** \"\ *trademark* **1** — used for a device for making a photographic copy of graphic matter directly upon the surface of prepared paper with the image in correct position **2 :** a copy made by a Photostat machine

**pho·to·stationary** \ˌfōd·(ˌ)ō+\ *adj* [*phot-* + *stationary*] **:** of, relating to, or being a stationary state in which the rate of photochemical dissociation of reactants is equaled by the rate of recombination

**pho·to·stereograph** \"+\ *n* [*phot-* + *stereograph*] **:** a double photograph mounted for use with a stereoscope — **pho·to·stereographic** \"+\ *adj*

**pho·to·syn·thate** \ˌfōd·ōˈsinˌthāt\ *n* -s [NL *photosynthesis* + E *-ate*] **:** a product of photosynthesis

**pho·to·synthesis** \ˌfōd·ō+\ *n* [NL, fr. *phot-* + *synthesis*] **:** synthesis of chemical compounds with the aid of light sometimes including the near infrared or near ultraviolet; *esp* **:** the formation of carbohydrates from carbon dioxide and a source of hydrogen (as water) in chlorophyll-containing cells (as of green plants) exposed to light involving a photochemical release of oxygen through the decomposition of water followed by various enzymatic synthetic reactions that usu. do not require the presence of light

**pho·to·synthesize** \ˌfōd·ō+\ *vi* [*photosynthes*is + *-ize*] **:** to engage in photosynthesis

**pho·to·synthetic** \ˌfōd·ō+\ *adj* **:** using, relating to, or formed by photosynthesis ⟨the direct or indirect source of free energy for all living organisms is the sunlight utilized by ∼ organisms —S.L.Miller & H.C.Urey⟩ — **pho·to·synthetically** \"+\ *adv*

**photosynthetic ratio** *also* **photosynthetic quotient** *n* **:** the ratio of the volume of oxygen given off to the volume of carbon dioxide absorbed by a plant during photosynthesis, this ratio being theoretically near 1 when the primary product of photosynthesis is a simple carbohydrate

**pho·to·tac·tic** \ˌfōd·əˈtaktik\ *adj* [ISV *phot-* + *-tactic*] **:** of, relating to, or exhibiting phototaxis

**pho·to·taxis** \"+\ *also* **pho·to·taxy** \ˈfōd·əˌtaksē\ *n, pl* **phototax·es** \-ˈtakˌsēz\ *or* **phototax·ies** \-ˌtakˌsēz\ [NL, fr. *phot-* + *-taxis*] **:** a taxis in which light is the directive factor (as in the movement of an infusorian toward the lighted side of a vessel); *also* **:** the orientation of various chloroplasts to light

**pho·to·telegraph** \ˌfōd·(ˌ)ō+\ *n* [ISV *phot-* + *telegraph*] **:** a picture received by phototelegraphy; *also* **:** the apparatus used for transmitting such a picture — **pho·to·telegraphic** \"+\ *adj*

**pho·to·telegraphy** \"+\ *n* [ISV *phot-* + *telegraphy*] **1 :** telegraphy by means of light (as by the heliograph) **2 :** the transmission of photographs or pictures by telegraphy

**pho·to·theodolite** \"+\ *n* [ISV *phot-* + *theodolite*] **:** an instrument consisting of a theodolite mounted on a camera which can take at each of several stations of known position and elevation (as determined by transit survey) a series of photographs used in terrestrial photogrammetry

**pho·to·therapeutics** \"+\ *n pl but sing or pl in constr* [*phot-* + *therapeutics*] **:** PHOTOTHERAPY

**pho·to·therapy** \"+\ *n* [ISV *phot-* + *therapy*] **:** the application of light for therapeutic purposes

**pho·to·thermal** *also* **pho·to·thermic** \"+\ *adj* [*phot-* + *thermal* or *thermic*] **:** of or relating to both light and heat

**pho·to·timer** \ˈfōd·ō+ˌ-\ *n* [*phot-* + *timer*] **1 :** a photoelectric device that automatically controls photographic exposures (as to X rays or light) **2 :** an electrically operated camera for photographing the finish of a race and the record of the elapsed time from start to finish

**pho·tot·o·nus** \fōˈtätᵊnəs\ *n* [NL, fr. *phot-* + *tonus*] **:** tonic condition (as of musculature) resulting from exposure to particular conditions of lighting ⟨∼ in plants usu. results in curvature towards a source of light⟩

**pho·to·topography** \ˌfōd·(ˌ)ō+\ *n* [ISV *phot-* + *topography*] **:** PHOTOGRAMMETRY

**pho·to·transistor** \"+\ *n* [*phot-* + *transistor*] **:** a transistor that acts as a photoconductive cell

**pho·to·trope** \ˈfōd·əˌtrōp\ *n* [*phot-* + *-trope*] **1 :** a phototropic organism or organ **2 :** a substance that changes color when exposed to radiant energy (as light)

**pho·to·troph·ic** \ˌfōd·əˈträfik\ *adj* [*phot-* + *-trophic*]

**:** capable of utilizing carbon dioxide in the presence of light as a source of metabolic carbon ⟨a ~ organism⟩
**pho·to·trop·ic** \-äpik\ *adj* [ISV *phototrope* + *-ic*] **:** of, relating to, or capable of undergoing phototropism ⟨study . . . was confined to ~ dyes —*Chem. & Engineering News*⟩
**pho·tot·ro·pism** \fō'tä·trə,pizəm\ *n* [ISV *phot-* + *-tropism*] **1 :** a tropism in which light is the orienting stimulus (as in the turning toward a light of a plant shoot or a tube worm and in the creeping away from a light of a blowfly larva) — compare HELIOTROPISM **2 :** the reversible change in color of a substance produced by the formation of an isomeric modification when exposed to radiant energy (as light)
**pho·tot·ro·py** \-,pē\ *n* -ES [ISV *phot-* + *-tropy*] **:** PHOTOTROPISM 2
**pho·to·tube** \'fōd·ō+,-\ *n* [*phot-* + *tube*] **:** an electron tube having a photoemissive cathode whose released electrons are drawn to the anode by reason of its positive potential
**pho·to·typesetting** \¦fōd·(,)ō+\ *n* [*phot-* + *typesetting*] **:** PHOTOCOMPOSITION; *esp* **:** photocomposition done on a keyboard composing machine
**pho·to·typographic** *or* **pho·to·typographical** \"+\ *adj* [*phototypographic* ISV *phot-* + *typographic; phototypographical* fr. *phototypography* + *-ical*] **:** producing matter used in phototypography ⟨a ~ composing machine⟩
**pho·to·typography** \"+\ *n* -ES [ISV *phot-* + *typography*] **:** a photomechanical process producing matter resembling that done by typographical printing
**pho·to·visual** \"+\ *adj* [*phot-* + *visual*] **:** having the same focal length for actinic rays and for the brightest of the visual rays — used of an achromatic lense
**photovisual magnitude** *n* **:** the magnitude of a celestial body that is determined by observations with a photographic plate and filter combination giving nearly the same yellow-green sensitivity as the human eye and that is nearly equal to the visual magnitude
**pho·to·voltage** \"+\ *n* [*phot-* + *voltage*] **:** electromotive force developed by a photosensitive device as a result of the incidence of radiant energy
**pho·to·voltaic** \"+\ *adj* [ISV *phot-* + *voltaic*] **:** of, utilizing, or relating to the generation of an electromotive force when radiant energy (as light) falls on the boundary between certain dissimilar substances in close contact (as cuprous oxide and copper or an electrode and an electrolyte) ⟨produced the ~ effect in the sample under investigation —Kurt Lehovec⟩
**photovoltaic cell** *n* **:** a cell having a photovoltaic element mounted for exposure to light and provided with terminals for connection with a sensitive current meter
[1]**pho·to·zincograph** \"+\ *n* [*phot-* + *zincograph*] **:** a print made by photozincography
[2]**photozincograph** \"\ *vt* -ED/-ING/-S **:** to produce by photozincography
**pho·to·zincography** \¦fōd·(,)ō+\ *n* [ISV *phot-* + *zincography*] **:** zincography using photographically prepared plates
**pho·to·zin·co·typy** \"+¦ziŋkə,tīpē\ *n* -ES [ISV *phot-* + *zinco-* + *-typy*] **:** PHOTOZINCOGRAPHY
**Pho·tron·ic** \(')fō¦tränik\ *trademark* — used for a photoelectric cell in which the action of light upon the contact between two dissimilar metals causes generation of an electromotive force
**phous·dar** \'faùz·,där\ *archaic var of* FAUJDAR
**PHP** *abbr* **1** packing-house products **2** pump horsepower
**phr** *abbr* **1** phrase **2** phraseology
**phrag·ma** \'fragmə\ *n, pl* **phragma·ta** \-məd·ə, -mətə\ *also* **phragmas** [NL, fr. Gk *phragma* fence, fr. *phrassein, phrattein* to enclose, fence in — more at FARCE] **1 :** a septum or partial diaphragm; *esp* **:** an infolded part or inwardly extending process of the walls of the thorax of an insect or other arthropod **2 :** a false dissepiment in a plant ovary
**phrag·mid·i·um** \frag'midēəm\ *n, cap* [NL, fr. Gk *phragma* fence + NL *-idium*] **:** a genus of rust fungi of the family Pucciniaceae having teliospores of more than three cells lineally arranged — see ROSE RUST
**phrag·mi·tes** \frag'mīd·(,)ēz\ *n, cap* [NL, fr. Gk *phragmitēs* growing in hedges, fr. *phragma* fence, hedge + *-itēs* -ite] **:** a genus of widely distributed reedlike grasses with tall stems and large showy panicles resembling plumes — see DITCH REED
**phrag·mo·cone** *also* **phrag·ma·cone** \'fragmə,kōn\ *n* -S [*phragmocone* ISV *phragmo-* (fr. Gk *phragmos* fence, fencing in, fr. *phrassein, phrattein* to enclose, fence in) + *cone; phragmacone* ISV *phragma-* (fr. Gk *phragma* fence) + *cone*] **:** the thin conical chambered internal shell of a belemnite that is either straight or curved, is produced in front into a very thin process resembling a blade or leaf, and fits behind into a deep cavity in the anterior end of the guard — **phrag·mo·con·ic** \¦==¦känik\ *adj*
**phrag·mo·cyt·ta·rous** \¦fragmō¦sid·ərəs\ *adj* [*phragmo-* (fr. Gk *phragmos* fence, fencing in) + Gk *kyttaros* cell of a honeycomb; akin to Gk *kytos* hollow vessel — more at HIDE] **:** of, relating to, or being a type of nest of social wasps (family Vespidae) in which the layers of brood comb are attached by the periphery to the envelope — compare POECILOCYTTAROUS
**phrag·moid** \'frag,mòid\ *adj* [Gk *phragma* fence + E *-oid*] *bot* **:** septate at right angles to the long axis ⟨the ~ conidia of various fungi⟩
**phrag·moph·o·ra** \frag'mäf(ə)rə\ *n pl, cap* [NL, fr. *phragmo-* (fr. Gk *phragmos* fence) + *-phora*] *in some classifications* **:** a suborder of Decapoda comprising the fossil belemnites and the surviving genus *Spirula*
**phrag·mo·plast** \'fragmə,plast\ *n* -S [ISV *phragmo-* (fr. Gk *phragmos* fence) + *-plast*] **:** the enlarged barrel-shaped spindle characteristic of the later stages of plant mitosis within which the cell plate forms
**phrag·mo·sis** \frag'mōsəs\ *n* -ES [NL, fr. Gk *phragmos* fence, fencing in + NL *-osis*] **:** a method of closing the burrow or nest by means of some specially adapted part of the body (as the flattened head in some ants)
**phrag·mo·some** \'fragmə,sōm\ *n* -S [*phragmo-* (fr. Gk *phragmos* fence) + *-some*] **:** a differentiated cytoplasmic diaphragm that develops from the strands of parietal cytoplasm during cell division in plant cells and forms a medium in which the phragmoplast and cell plate develop
**phrag·mo·spore** \'==+,-\ *n* [*phragmo-* (fr. Gk *phragmos* fence) + *spore*] **:** a plant spore having two or more septa — **phrag·mo·spor·ous** \¦==¦spōrəs, (')frag¦mäspərəs\ *adj*
**phras·able** *or* **phrase·able** \'frāzəbəl\ *adj* **:** capable of being phrased
**phras·al** \'frāzəl\ *adj* **:** of, relating to, or consisting of a phrase ⟨~ felicity⟩ ⟨the danger of ~ hypnosis —J.M.Mitchell⟩ ⟨~ rhythm —J.L.Lowes⟩ ⟨a ~ modifier⟩ — **phras·al·ly** \-zəlē, -li\ *adv*
[1]**phrase** \'frāz\ *n* -S [L *phrasis*, fr. Gk, fr. *phrazein* to point out, show, explain] **1 :** a characteristic manner of style or expression **:** a mode or form of speech **:** DICTION, PHRASEOLOGY ⟨writes in a stilted, self-conscious ~⟩ ⟨a welcome occasional crack of American ~ —Sean O'Faolain⟩ ⟨half past one — three bells in the sea ~ —R.L.Stevenson⟩ **2 a :** a brief expression; *esp* **:** one that is pithy, felicitous, or memorable **:** CATCHWORD ⟨sum the matter up in a ~⟩ ⟨good at turning a ~⟩ ⟨a fine ~⟩ ⟨a hackneyed ~⟩ **b :** WORD ⟨denounced . . . as socialistic, a ~ they evidently never get tired of —A.E.Stevenson b.1900⟩ ⟨"accommodated" . . . a good ~ —Shak.⟩ **3** *also* **phraise** \"\ *chiefly Scot* **a :** smooth unmeaning talk **:** FLATTERY **b :** FUSS, COMMOTION ⟨an honest lad . . . though he made little ~ about it —Sir Walter Scott⟩ **4 :** a short musical thought that is typically two to four measures long and that closes with a cadence ⟨a cymbal crash followed immediately by a low ~ in the bassoon —*Saturday Rev.*⟩ **5 :** a group of two or more words that form a sense unit expressing a thought either fragmentarily without a complete predication (as in *Good for you!*) or with a weakened form of predication (as in *God willing*) or as a sentence element not containing a predication but having the force of a single part of speech (as in *could have been found*) and that bear to one another either the modifying relation (as in *faithful dog*) or the coordinate or multiple relation (as in *dogs and cats*) or the composite relation (as in *might have been found*) — often used with a qualifying grammatical term indicating structure ⟨participial ~⟩ ⟨infinitive ~⟩ ⟨prepositional ~⟩ ⟨verb ~⟩ or syntactical relation ⟨adverbial ~⟩ ⟨appositive ~⟩ ⟨noun ~⟩ ⟨verbal ~⟩ **6 :** a continuous series of attacks and parries in fencing ⟨during a single ~, the attack may pass back and forth between the two fencers several times —Jeanette Schlottmann⟩ **7 :** a frequently occurring group of words written in shorthand without lifting the pencil ⟨the common ~*s* consisting of two or three words should be written with the same facility as an ordinary word form —J.R.Gregg⟩ **8 :** a series of dance movements comprising a section of a pattern ⟨learning to move in terms of ~*s* rather than in steps⟩
[2]**phrase** \"\ *vb* -ED/-ING/-S *vt* **1 a :** to express in words **:** formulate in appropriate or telling terms **:** WORD, PUT ⟨unable to ~ his idea⟩ ⟨a thought . . . imperishably *phrased* —J.L.Lowes⟩ ⟨a poor but proud family, as he ~*s* it⟩ **b :** to designate by a descriptive word or phrase **:** TERM, STYLE ⟨these suns — for so they ~ 'em —Shak.⟩ **2** *also* **phraise** \"\ *Scot* **:** FLATTER **3 :** to divide (a musical composition) into melodic phrases ⟨the job before her, that of *phrasing* and rephrasing a fugue of Bach's —Osbert Sitwell⟩ **4 :** to write (a frequently occurring group of words) in shorthand without lifting the pencil ⟨have the student insert hyphens in the text between words which the teacher desires to have *phrased* —E.H.Eldridge⟩ ~ *vi* **:** to group notes or tones into a musical phrase **:** perform music so as to show its melodic phrasing ⟨they sang with ease and confidence . . . and *phrased* with the subtlety of master musicians —*Time*⟩
**phrase book** *n* **:** a book containing idiomatic expressions of a foreign language and their translation
**phrasemaker** \'=,==\ *n* **1 :** one that coins telling phrases ⟨was a born ~ —G.W.Johnson⟩ ⟨a humorist, a wit, a vivid ~, a superb paradoxer —*Outlook*⟩ **2 :** one given to making fine-sounding but often hollow and meaningless phrases ⟨shame the demagogue ~ and the smart heckler into discomfited silence —*World's Work*⟩ — compare PHRASEMONGER
**phrasemaking** \'=,==\ *n* **:** the art or practice of making vivid striking phrases ⟨lavishes his own power of ~ alike on king, abbot . . . and mendicants —*Irish Statesman*⟩
**phrase·man** \'frāzmən\ *n, pl* **phrasemen :** PHRASEMONGER
**phrasemonger** \'=,==\ *n* **:** one habitually using fine-sounding but often empty phrases usu. not of his own invention — called also *phraseman;* compare PHRASEMAKER 2
**phra·se·o·gram** \'frāzēə,gram, -aa(ə)m\ *n* [*phraseo-* (as in *phraseology*) + *-gram*] **:** a symbol for a phrase **:** a conventional combination of signs or letters representing a phrase in certain shorthand systems **:** PHRASE ⟨described the . . . pleasure he experienced on seeing the first ~ in a letter —*Pitman's Phonographic Phrase Bk.*⟩
**phra·se·o·graph** \-,graf, -răf\ *n* [*phraseo-* (as in *phraseology*) + *-graph*] **:** PHRASEOGRAM — **phra·se·o·graph·ic** \¦===¦grafik\ *adj*
**phra·se·og·ra·phy** \,frāzē'ägrəfē, -fi\ *n* -ES [*phraseo-* (as in *phraseology*) + *-graphy*] **:** representation of word phrases by phraseograms
**phra·se·o·log·i·cal** \¦frāzēə¦läjəkəl, -jēk-\ *adj* **1 a :** expressed in formal often sententious phrases ⟨her father professed an elaborate ~ love for her —William Black⟩ **b :** marked by the frequently insincere use of such phrases ⟨would be only a ~ liberal and a practicing conservative —Roscoe Drummond⟩ **2 :** of or relating to phraseology ⟨~ annotations —C.J. Ellicott⟩; *esp* **:** of or relating to the phraseology characteristic of a language, a writer, or a work ⟨a ~ peculiarity of these tracts —H.G.Graham⟩ — **phra·se·o·log·i·cal·ly** \-jək(ə)lē, -jēk-, -li\ *adv*
**phra·se·ol·o·gist** \,==='äləjəst\ *n* -S **:** PHRASEMAKER, PHRASEMONGER
**phrase·ol·o·gy** \,frāzē'äləjē, -ji *also* frā'zä-\ *n* -ES [NL *phraseologia*, fr. *phraseo-* (fr. L *phrasis* phrase) + L *-logia* -logy] **1 :** a manner of organization of words into phrases and of phrases into longer elements of expression **:** idiomatic or peculiar phrasing **:** STYLE ⟨meetings . . . characterized by religious singing, biblical ~, and prayer —*Current Biog.*⟩ **2 :** choice of words **:** VOCABULARY ⟨called a flapper in the ~ of the twenties⟩
**phras·er** \'frāzə(r)\ *n* -S **:** PHRASEMAKER, PHRASEMONGER
**phrasey** *also* **phrasy** \'frāzē, -zi\ *adj* **:** marked by an excessive use of phrases ⟨~ fellow —John Galsworthy⟩
**-phra·sia** \'frāzh(ē)ə, -zēə\ *n comb form* -S [NL, fr. L *phrasis* diction + NL *-ia* — more at PHRASE] **:** speech disorder (of a specified type) ⟨embolo*phrasia*⟩
**phrasing** *n* -S [fr. gerund of [2]*phrase*] **1 :** style of expression **:** PHRASEOLOGY, WORDING ⟨the great artists of that age knew that without ~ dramatic verse was a dead thing —Lytton Strachey⟩ ⟨the exquisite ~ in which we feel that every word is in its place —Edmund Wilson⟩ **2 :** the act, method, or result of grouping notes so as to form distinct musical phrases ⟨critics were wondering at the sureness of his ~ and rhythmic pulse —*Time*⟩
**phra·tor** \'frād·ə(r), -ātə- *also* -,tò(ə)r *or* -ò(ə)\ *n* -S [Gk *phratōr;* akin to Gk *phratēr* member of the same clan] **:** a member of a phratry ⟨at important funerals the ~*s* of the dead person mourned while the other phratry conducted the ceremonies —E.R.Embree⟩
**phra·tric** \'frā·trik\ *or* **phra·tral** \-trəl\ *adj* [*phratric* fr. Gk *phratrikos*, fr. *phratra, phratria* phratry + *-ikos* -ic; *phratral* fr. *phratry* + *-al*] **:** of or relating to a phratry ⟨~ exogamy⟩
**phra·try** \'frā·trē, -ri\ *n* -ES [Gk *phratria*, fr. *phratēr* member of the same clan, member of a phratry — more at BROTHER] **1** *also* **phra·tria** \'frā·trēə\ -S **:** a kinship group forming a subdivision of a Greek phyle and serving to give religious recognition to the citizenship of its members ⟨no deme coincided with a *phratria* or with any subdivision of a *phratria* —*Athenaeum*⟩ — compare CLAN, DEME **2 :** a social tribal subdivision; *specif* **:** an exogamous group typically comprising several totemic clans ⟨the ~ overruled its clans in many ways —Diamond Jenness⟩
**phre·at·ic** \frē'ad·ik\ *adj* [Gk *phreat-, phrear* well + E *-ic* — more at BOURN] **:** of or relating to a well — used of underground waters reachable or probably reachable by drilling wells ⟨survival . . . in deep ~ waters —*Biol. Abstracts*⟩
**phre·at·o·phyte** \frē'ad·ə,fīt\ *n* -S [Gk *phreat-, phrear* well + E *-o-* + *-phyte*] **:** a deep-rooted plant that obtains its water from the water table or the layer of soil just above it — **phre·at·o·phyt·ic** \(')=¦==¦fid·ik\ *adj*
**phren** \'fren, 'frēn\ *n, pl* **phre·nes** \'frē(,)nēz\ [NL, fr. Gk *phren-, phrēn* diaphragm, mind] **:** DIAPHRAGM 1
**phren-** *or* **phreni-** *or* **phreno-** *comb form* [L *phren-*, fr. Gk *phren-, phreno-*, fr. *phren-, phrēn* diaphragm, mind — more at FRENETIC] **1 :** mind ⟨*phreno*logy⟩ **2 a :** diaphragm ⟨*phren*ic⟩ **b :** diaphragmatic and ⟨*phreno*cardiac⟩ **3 :** phrenic nerve ⟨*phreni*clasia⟩
**phren·em·phrax·is** \,fre,nem'fraksəs\ *n, pl* **phrenemphrax·es** \-k,sēz\ [NL, fr. *phren-* + Gk *emphraxis* stoppage, fr. *emphrassein, emphrattein* to stop up, block, fr. *em-* [2]*en-* + *phrassein, phrattein* to enclose, fence in — more at FARCE] **:** crushing of the phrenic nerve for therapeutic reasons
**phre·net·ic** \frə'ned·ik, -etik\ *also* **phre·net·i·cal** \-əkəl\ *adj* [L *phreneticus* — more at FRENETIC] **:** FRENETIC
[2]**phrenetic** \"\ *n* -S *archaic* **:** one who is phrenetic **:** MADMAN
**-phrenia** \'frēnēə *sometimes* -ren-\ *n comb form* -S [NL, fr. Gk *phren-, phrēn* diaphragm, mind + NL *-ia*] **:** disordered condition of mental functions ⟨hebe*phrenia*⟩
**phrenic** \'frenik, -rēn-\ *adj* [NL *phrenicus*, fr. *phren-* + L *-icus* -ic] **1 :** of or relating to the diaphragm **:** DIAPHRAGMATIC **2 :** of or relating to the mind **:** MENTAL
**phrenic artery** *n* **:** any of the arteries supplying the diaphragm and consisting of a superior pair that arise from the thoracic aorta and are distributed over the upper surface of the diaphragm and an inferior pair from the abdominal aorta that pass to the under surface
**phren·i·cec·to·my** \,frenə'sektəmē, -mi\ *n* -ES [ISV *phrenic* + *-ectomy*] **:** surgical removal of part of a phrenic nerve to secure collapse of a diseased lung — compare PHRENICOTOMY
**phren·i·cla·sia** \-'klāzh(ē)ə\ *or* **phren·i·cla·sis** \,==='klāsəs; frə'nikləsəs, fre'-\ *n, pl* **phreniclasi·as** \-əz\ *or* **phreniclases** \-,sēz\ [NL, fr. *phreni-* + *-clasia* or *-clasis*] **:** PHRENEMPHRAXIS
**phrenic nerve** *n* **:** a nerve of each side of the body arising chiefly from the fourth cervical nerve, passing down through the thorax to the diaphragm, and giving branches to the pericardium and pleura but distributed mostly over the lower surface of the diaphragm
**phren·i·cot·o·my** \,frenə'käd·əmē, -mi\ *n* -ES [ISV *phrenic* + *-o-* + *-tomy*] **:** surgical division of a phrenic nerve to secure collapse of a diseased lung — compare PHRENICECTOMY
**phrenic vein** *n* **:** any of the veins accompanying the phrenic arteries
**phren·o·cardiac** \¦frenō+\ *adj* [*phren-* + *cardiac*] **:** of, relating to, or constituting the region between the heart and the diaphragm
**phren·o·log·i·cal** \¦fren°l¦äjəkəl, -jēk-\ *also* **phren·o·log·ic** \-jik, -ēk\ *adj* [*phrenology* + *-ical* or *-ic*] **:** of or relating to phrenology — **phren·o·log·i·cal·ly** \-jək(ə)lē, -jēk-, -li\ *adv*
**phre·nol·o·gist** \frə'näləjəst, fre'-\ *n* -S [*phrenology* + *-ist*] **:** one versed in phrenology
**phre·nol·o·gy** \-jē, -ji\ *n* -ES [*phren-* + *-logy*] **:** the study of the conformation of the skull as indicative of mental faculties and traits of character esp. according to the hypothesis of F. J. Gall (1758–1828); *also* **:** the system of faculties and their localization based on this hypothesis
**phren·o·sin** \'frenəsən\ *n* -S [ISV *phren-* + *-ose* + *-in*] **:** a crystalline cerebroside that yields cerebronic acid on hydrolysis
**phren·o·sin·ic acid** \¦==¦sinik-\ *n* [*phrenosinic* ISV *phrenosin* + *-ic*] **:** CEREBRONIC ACID
**phrensy** *var of* FRENZY
**phren·zy** \'frenzē, -zi\ *archaic var of* FRENZY
**phron·i·ma** \'frānəmə\ *n, cap* [NL, fr. Gk *phronimos* sane, sensible; prob. akin to Gk *phren-, phrēn* diaphragm, mind — more at FRENETIC] **:** a genus (the type of the family Phronimidae) of pelagic amphipod crustaceans having one known member (*P. sedentaria*) that lives in a barrel-shaped case made from the swimming bell of a siphonophore or the test of a tunicate
**phron·tis·tery** \'frāntə,sterē\ *n* -ES [Gk *phrontistērion*, fr. *phrontistēs* philosopher, deep thinker, person with intellectual pretensions, fr. *phrontizein* to reflect, take thought, fr. *phrontid-, phrontis* reflection, thought; akin to Gk *phren-, phrēn* diaphragm, mind] **:** a place for thinking or study
**phry·ga·nea** \frī'ganēə\ *n, cap* [NL, fr. Gk *phryganon* dry stick; akin to Gk *phrygein* to roast — more at FRY] **:** a genus (the type of the family Phryganeidae) of caddis flies
[1]**phryg·a·ne·id** \¦frigə¦nēəd\ *adj* [NL *Phryganeidae*] **:** of or relating to the Phryganeidae
[2]**phryganeid** \"\ *n* -S [NL *Phryganeidae*] **:** a caddis fly of the family Phryganeidae
**phryg·a·ne·i·dae** \,=='nēə,dē\ *n pl, cap* [NL, fr. *Phryganea*, type genus + *-idae*] **:** a family of caddis flies containing rather large insects whose larvae live in still water and construct portable cases of very regular form
**phry·ga·ne·oid** \frī'ganē,òid\ *adj* [NL *Phryganea* + E *-oid*] **:** resembling or related to the Phryganeidae
[1]**phryg·i·an** \'frijēən\ *adj, usu cap* [L *phrygianus*, fr. *Phrygia*, ancient country in west central Asia Minor + L *-anus* -an] **1 :** of, relating to, or characteristic of the ancient country of Phrygia **2 :** of, relating to, or characteristic of the Phrygians
[2]**phrygian** \"\ *n* -S **1** *cap* **:** a native or inhabitant of ancient Phrygia **2** *cap* **:** the language of the Phrygians that is generally assumed to be Indo-European but of uncertain position within the family **3** *usu cap* **:** MONTANIST
**phrygian cap** *n, usu cap P* **:** a close-fitting cap represented in Greek art as conical and identified in modern art with the liberty cap — compare BONNET ROUGE
**phrygian marble** *n, usu cap P* **:** a marble from Phrygia noted in antiquity — see PAVONAZZO
**phrygian mode** *n, usu cap P* **1 :** one of seven diatonic octave species in ancient Greek music consisting of two disjunct tetrachords represented on the white keys of the piano by a descending diatonic scale from D to D — see GREEK MODE illustration **2 :** an authentic ecclesiastical mode consisting of a pentachord and an upper conjunct tetrachord represented on the white keys of the piano by an ascending diatonic scale from E to E — see MODE illustration

Phrygian cap

**phrygian stone** *n, usu cap P* **:** a stone used by the ancients in dyeing and believed to have been a sort of pumice
**phrygian tetrachord** *n, usu cap P* **:** a descending tetrachord in Greek music consisting of a whole step and a half step followed by a whole step
**phry·ma** \'frīmə\ *n, cap* [NL] **:** a genus of plants constituting the family Phrymaceae and having opposite leaves and small purplish spicate flowers reflexed in fruit — see LOPSEED
**phry·ma·ce·ae** \frī'māsē,ē\ *n pl, cap* [NL, fr. *Phryma*, type genus + *-aceae*] **:** a family of plants (order Polemoniales) coextensive with the genus *Phryma*
**phryn·i·dae** \'frinə,dē\ *n pl, cap* [NL, fr. *Phrynus*, genus of whip scorpions (fr. Gk *phrynos, phrynē* toad) + *-idae*] *syn of* TARANTULIDAE
**phry·nin** \'frīnən\ *n* -S [Gk *phrynos, phrynē* toad + E *-in*] **:** a poisonous substance secreted from the glands of various toads that resembles digitalin in its physiologic action — compare BUFOTOXIN
**phry·no·der·ma** \,frīnə'dərmə\ *n* -S [NL, fr. *phryno-* (fr. Gk *phrynos, phrynē* toad) + *-derma*] **:** a rough dry skin eruption marked by keratosis and usu. associated with vitamin A deficiency
**phry·no·so·ma** \-'sōmə\ *n, cap* [NL, fr. *phryno-* (fr. Gk *phrynos, phrynē* toad) + *-soma* — more at BROWN] **:** a genus comprising the horned toads
**phthal-** *or* **phthalo-** *comb form* [ISV, fr. *phthalic* (in *phthalic acid*)] **:** phthalic acid **:** related to phthalic acid ⟨*phthal*amic acid⟩ ⟨*phthalo*nitrile⟩
**phtha·lam·ic acid** \thə'lamik-\ *n* [ISV *phthal-* + *amide* + *-ic*] **:** a crystalline compound $HOOCC_6H_4CONH_2$ formed by reaction of phthalic anhydride and ammonia; the half amide of phthalic acid
**phthal·anilic acid** \¦thal+-\ *n* [ISV *phthal-* + *anilic*] **:** a crystalline amido acid $HOOCC_6H_4CONHC_6H_5$ prepared by reaction of phthalic anhydride and aniline
[1]**phthal·ate** \'tha,lāt\ *n* -S [ISV *phthal-* + *-ate*, n. suffix] **:** a salt or ester of phthalic acid
[2]**phthalate** \"\ *vt* -ED/-ING/-S [*phthal-* + *-ate*, v. suffix] **:** to treat with or combine with phthalic acid or phthalic anhydride
**phthal·azine** \(')thal+\ *n* [ISV *phthal-* + *azine*] **:** a crystalline base $C_8H_6N_2$ that is the azine of the dialdehyde related to phthalic acid; 2,3-di-aza-naphthalene — compare HYDRALAZINE, LUMINOL
**phthalein** \'thalēən, -āl-, -,lēn\ *also* **phthalein dye** *n* -S [ISV *phthal-* + *-ein*] **:** any of a group of xanthene dyes (as phenolphthalein, fluorescein, rhodamine) that are intensely colored in alkaline solution and are obtained by condensation of phenols with phthalic anhydride
**phthalic acid** \'thalik-, 'thālik-\ *n* [*phthalic* ISV, short for *naphthalic* (in *naphthalic acid*)] **:** any of three isomeric dicarboxylic acids $C_6H_4(COOH)_2$ obtained by oxidation of various benzene derivatives: **a :** a crystalline acid made usu. by hydration of phthalic anhydride that regenerates the anhydride on heating and is used chiefly in making esters, benzoic acid, dyes, and intermediates; *ortho*-benzene-dicarboxylic acid **b :** ISOPHTHALIC ACID **c :** TEREPHTHALIC ACID
**phthalic anhydride** *n* **:** a crystalline cyclic acid anhydride $C_6H_4(CO)_2O$ made usu. by hot vapor-phase oxidation of naphthalene or *ortho*-xylene over a vanadium pentoxide catalyst and used chiefly in making alkyd resins and other polyester resins, phthalate esters for use as plasticizers and solvents, dyes, and intermediates
**phthalide** \'tha,līd, 'thā-, -ləd\ *n* -S [ISV *phthal-* + *-ide*] **:** a crystalline lactone $C_8H_6O_2$ made usu. by reduction of phthalic anhydride
**phthal·imide** \(')thal+\ *n* [ISV *phthal-* + *imide*] **:** a crystalline weakly acidic cyclic compound $C_6H_4(CO)_2NH$ made usu. by action of ammonia on phthalic anhydride and used chiefly in the synthesis of amines and amino acids, anthranilic acid, and formerly of indigo
**phthal·in** \'thalən\ *n* -S [ISV *phthal-* + *-in*] **:** any of a group of colorless compounds obtained by reduction of the phthaleins into which they are easily reconverted by oxidation; *esp* **:** the compound $C_{20}H_{16}O_4$ from phenolphthalein
**phthal·o·cyanine** \¦thalō+\ *n* [ISV *phthal-* + *cyanine*] **1** *or* **phthalocyanine blue G :** a bright greenish blue crystalline compound $C_{32}H_{18}N_8$ related to porphin — called also *metal-free phthalocyanine;* see DYE TABLE I (under *Pigment Blue 16*) **2 :** any of various derivatives of phthalocyanine that in the case of the metal derivatives are brilliant fast blue

to green dyes or pigments made usu. by heating phthalonitrile with a metal (as copper powder) or metallic salt

**phthalocyanine blue** *or* **phthalocyanine blue B** *n* **:** a blue pigment used chiefly in printing ink esp. for outdoor use, in roofing shingles, and in paint for automobiles; the copper derivative of phthalocyanine — see DYE table I (under *Pigment Blue 15*)

**phthalocyanine green** *or* **phthalocyanine green G** *n* **:** a green pigment that is made by passing chlorine into a melt containing the copper derivative of phthalocyanine and aluminum chloride until it is almost completely chlorinated and that is used similarly to phthalocyanine blue — see DYE table I (under *Pigment Green 7*)

**phthal·o·gen brilliant blue IF3G** \ˈthaləjən-\ *n, usu cap P & both Bs* [*phthalogen* fr. *phthal-* + *-gen*] **:** an ingrain dye — see DYE table I (under *Ingrain Blue 2*)

**phthal·o·nitrile** \ˌthalō+\ *n* [ISV *phthal-* + *nitrile*] **:** a crystalline compound $C_6H_4(CN)_2$ made usu. by heating phthalic anhydride and ammonia under dehydrating conditions and used chiefly in making phthalocyanines

**phthal·o·yl** \ˈthalə,wil\ *n* -s [*phthal-* + *-oyl*] **:** the bivalent radical $C_6H_4(CO—)_2$ of phthalic acid

**phthal·yl·sulfathiazole** \ˌtha,lil, -,lēl+\ *n* [*phthal-* + *-yl* + *sulfathiazole*] **:** a crystalline compound $C_{17}H_{13}N_3O_5S_2$ derived from phthalamic acid and sulfathiazole and used in the treatment of intestinal infections

**phthar·tol·a·trae** \thärˈtälə,trē\ *n pl, usu cap* [NL, fr. LGk *phthartolatrai*, pl. of *phthartolatrēs* worshiper of the corruptible, fr. Gk *phthartos* destructible + *-latrēs* -later — more at APHTHARTODOCETAE] **:** SEVERIANS — compare APHTHARTODOCETAE

**phthi·o·col** \ˈthīə,kōl, -kōl\ *n* -s [prob. fr. *phthisis* + connective *-o-* + *-ol*] **:** a yellow crystalline quinone $C_{11}H_8O_3$ with vitamin K activity that is isolated from the human tubercle bacillus and also made synthetically; 2-hydroxy-3-methyl-1,-4-naphthoquinone

**phthi·o·ic acid** \thīˈōik-\ *n* [*phthioic* fr. *phthisis* + *-oic*] **:** a branched-chain optically active fatty acid or mixture of such acids isolated from the human tubercle bacillus that causes the formation of tubercular lesions on injection into animals

**phthir·a·car·i·dae** \,thirəˈkarə,dē\ *n pl, cap* [NL, fr. *Phthiracarus*, type genus (fr. Gk *phtheir* louse + NL *Acarus*) + *-idae*] **:** a family of oribatid mites

**phthi·ri·a·sis** \thīˈrīəsəs\ *n, pl* **phthiria·ses** \-,sēz\ [L, pediculosis, fr. Gk *phtheiriasis*, fr. *phtheir* louse + *-iasis*; akin to Gk *phtheirein* to destroy, corrupt, defile, Skt *kṣarati* it flows, perishes] **:** PEDICULOSIS; *esp* **:** infestation with crab lice **:** pubic pediculosis

**phthir·i·us** \ˈthirēəs\ *n, cap* [NL, fr. Gk *phtheir* louse] **:** a genus (the type of the family Phthiriidae) containing the crab louse

**phthi·roph·a·gous** \thīˈräfəgəs\ *adj* [prob. fr. (assumed) NL *phthirophagus*, fr. Gk *phtheir* louse + NL *-o-* + *-phagus* -phagous] **:** eating lice

**phthi·rus** \ˈthīrəs\ *syn of* PHTHIRIUS

**¹phthisic** \ˈtiz|ik, |ēk *also* ˈthis| *or* ˈtis|\ *n* -s [alter. (influenced by *phthisis*) of earlier *ptisique*, *ptisicke*, fr. ME *ptisike*, alter. (influenced by L *phthisicus*, adj., phthisic) of *tisike*, fr. MF *tisique*, fr. OF, fr. *tisique*, adj.] **1 a :** pulmonary tuberculosis **b :** a tubercular person **2** *obs* **:** any of various throat or lung conditions (as asthma)

**²phthisic** \"\ *or* **phthisi·cal** \|əkəl, |ēk-\ *adj* [*phthisic* alter. (influenced by *phthisis*) of earlier *ptisicke*, alter. (influenced by L *phthisicus*) of ME *tisike*, fr. MF *tisique*, fr. OF, fr. L *phthisicus*, fr. Gk *phthisikos*, fr. *phthisis* + *-ikos* -ic; *phthisical* alter. (influenced by *phthisis*) of earlier *ptisicall*, alter. (influenced by L *phthisicus*) of earlier *tizicall*, *tysicall*, fr. (assumed) obs. E *tisike*, adj., phthisic (fr. ME) + E *-al*] **1 :** TUBERCULAR, TUBERCULOUS **2 :** ENFEEBLED, WEAK, DEBILITATED

**phthis·icky** \ˈtizəkē, -zēk-, -ki\ *adj* [¹*phthisic* + *-y*] **:** PHTHISIC, ASTHMATIC, WHEEZY

**phthisio-** *comb form* [ISV, fr. *phthisis*] **:** phthisis ⟨*phthisio*therapy⟩

**phthis·io·genesis** \ˌtizēō, ˌtizēə+\ *n* [NL, fr. *phthisio-* + L *genesis*] **:** the development of pulmonary tuberculosis

**phthis·io·genic** \ˌ==+ˈjenik\ *adj* [*phthisio-* + *-genic*] **:** of or relating to phthisiogenesis

**phthis·i·ol·o·gist** \ˌ==ˈäləjəst\ *n* -s **:** a physician who specializes in phthisiology

**phthis·i·ol·o·gy** \-jē\ *n* -ES [ISV *phthisio-* + *-logy*] **:** the care, treatment, and study of tuberculosis

**phthis·io·therapy** \ˌtizēō, ˌtizēə+\ *n* [ISV *phthisio-* + *therapy*] **:** the treatment of pulmonary tuberculosis

**phthi·sis** \ˈthīsəs, ˈtī-\ *n, pl* **phthi·ses** \-(,)sēz\ [L, fr. Gk; akin to Gk *phthiein*, *phthinein* to decay, wane, Skt *kṣiṇāti*, *kṣiṇoti* he destroys, and prob. to L *sitis* thirst] **:** a progressively wasting or consumptive disease; *usu* **:** pulmonary tuberculosis **:** CONSUMPTION

**phthisis bul·bi** \-ˈbəl,bī\ *n* [NL] **:** wasting and shrinkage of the eyeball following destructive diseases of the eye (as panophthalmitis)

**phthor** \ˈthō(ə)r, -ō(ə)\ *n* -s [F *phthore*, fr. Gk *phthora*] *archaic* **:** FLUORINE

**-phtho·ra** \fthərə\ *n comb form* [NL, fr. Gk *phthora* destruction, death, fr. *phtheirein* to destroy — more at PHTHIRIASIS] **:** destroyer — in generic names of fungi ⟨*Entomophthora*⟩

**phu·goid** \ˈfyü,gòid\ *adj* [irreg. fr. Gk *phygē* act of fleeing, avoidance, flight + E *-oid*; akin to Gk *pheugein* to run away, flee — more at FUGITIVE] **:** of, relating to, or representing variations in the longitudinal motion or course of the center of mass of an airplane in flight

**phugoid chart** *n* **:** a chart showing a complete series of phugoid curves corresponding to different starting conditions

**phugoid curve** *also* **phugoid** *n* -s **:** a curve showing the motion of the center of mass of an airplane during a phugoid oscillation

**phugoid oscillation** *n* **:** a long-period oscillation in the longitudinal motion of an airplane

**phugoid theory** *n* **:** the theory dealing with the longitudinal stability and the form and equations of the flight path of a glider

**phul·ka·ri** \ˈpül,kärē\ *n* -ES [Hindi *phulkārī*, lit., flowered] **1 :** a flower pattern embroidery made in India **2 :** a cloth embroidered with phulkari; *esp* **:** a Punjabi peasant's chador

**phul·wa butter** \ˈfülwə-\ *also* **phul·wa·ra butter** \fülˈwärə-\ *n* [Beng *phulwāra* Himalayan butter tree] **:** INDIAN BUTTER

**phut** \ft, ˈfət\ *n* -s [imit.] **:** a dull sound of impact (as of a bullet or distant shell) **:** a light thud ⟨~ of a tennis ball against a racket —H.V.Morton⟩ — often used interjectionally to express a feeling of hopelessness ⟨otherwise — ~ —S.H.Adams⟩

**phu·teng** *or* **pu·teng** \ˈpü,teŋ\ *n, pl* **phuteng** *or* **phutengs** *or* **puteng** *or* **putengs** *usu cap* **1 :** a mountain people of Laos occupying the intermediate slopes between the plains and the higher mountain lands of the Miao people **2 :** a member of the Phuteng people

**phyc-** *or* **phyco-** *comb form* [ISV, fr. Gk *phyk-*, *phyko-* seaweed, fr. *phykos* — more at FUCUS] **:** seaweed **:** algae ⟨*phyc*itol⟩ ⟨*phyco*chrome⟩

**-phyce·ae** \ˈfīsē,ē, ˈfis-\ *n pl comb form* [NL, fr. Gk *phykos* seaweed] **:** seaweed **:** algae — in names of major groups of algae ⟨Chloro*phyceae*⟩ ⟨Myxo*phyceae*⟩

**phy·ci·o·des** \fiˈsīə,dēz\ *n, cap* [NL, prob. fr. Gk *phykion* seaweed, rouge (fr. *phykos* seaweed) + NL *-odes*] **:** a large genus of small butterflies (family Nymphalidae) that are usu. fulvous with black markings

**¹phyc·i·tid** \ˈfisəd·əd\ *adj* [NL *Phycitidae*] **:** of or relating to the Phycitidae

**²phycitid** \"\ *n* -s [NL *Phycitidae*] **:** a moth of the family Phycitidae

**phy·cit·i·dae** \fīˈsid·ə,dē\ *n pl, cap* [NL, fr. *Phycita*, type genus (perh. fr. Gk *phykos* seaweed, rouge) + *-idae*] **:** a family of small moths that are related to and sometimes placed among the Pyralidae, include the Mediterranean flour moth and other pests having larvae which feed in stored cereals, and are usu. mottled gray and brown with long narrow fore wings

**phy·co·bilin** \ˌfīkōˈbīlən, -bil-\ *n* -s [*phyc-* + *bil-* (fr. L *bilis* bile) + *-in* — more at BILE] **:** any of a class of pigments that occur in the cells of algae, are active in photosynthesis, and are proteins combined with pyrrole derivatives related to the bile pigments — compare PHYCOCYANIN, PHYCOERYTHRIN

**phy·co·chro·ma·ce·ae** \,fīkōkrōˈmāsē,ē\ [NL, fr. ISV *phycochrome* + NL *-aceae*] *syn of* MYXOPHYCEAE

**phy·co·chrome** *also* **phy·co·chrom** \ˈfīkə,krōm\ *n* -s [ISV *phyc-* + *-chrome*] **1 :** a mixture of chlorophyll and phycocyanin that is the characteristic coloring matter of blue-green algae **2 :** BLUE-GREEN ALGA

**phy·co·chro·mo·phyce·ae** \,fīkō,krōməˈfīsē,ē, -fisē,ē\ [NL, fr. ISV *phycochrome* + NL *-o-* + *-phyceae*] *syn of* MYXOPHYCEAE

**phy·co·colloid** \ˌ==+\ *n* [*phyc-* + *colloid*] **:** any of several polysaccharide hydrocolloids from brown or red seaweeds

**phy·co·cyanin** \ˌfīkō+\ *or* **phy·co·cy·an** \ˌ==ˈsī,an, -ən\ *n* -s [*phycocyanin* ISV *phycocyan* + *-in*; *phycocyan* ISV *phyc-* + *-cyan*] **:** any of the bluish green protein pigments in the cells of blue-green algae

**phy·co·cyanogen** \ˌ==+\ *n* -s [*phyc-* + *cyan-* + *-gen*] **:** PHYCOCYANIN

**phy·co·drom·i·dae** \,fīkōˈdrämə,dē\ [NL, fr. *Phycodroma*, genus of Diptera (fr. *phyc-* + *-droma*, fr. fem. of *-dromus* -dromous) + *-idae*] *syn of* COELOPIDAE

**phy·co·er·y·thrin** \ˌ==ˈerəthrən, -əˈrith-\ *n* -s [ISV *phyc-* + *erythr-* + *-in*] **:** any of the red protein pigments in the cells of red algae

**phy·co·log·i·cal** \ˌfīkəˈläjəkəl\ *adj* **:** ALGOLOGICAL

**phy·col·o·gist** \fīˈkäləjəst\ *n* -s [ISV *phycology* + *-ist*] **:** ALGOLOGIST

**phy·col·o·gy** \-jē, -ji\ *n* -ES [ISV *phyc-* + *-logy*] **:** ALGOLOGY

**phy·co·my·ces** \,fīkōˈmī,sēz\ *n, cap* [NL, fr. *phyc-* + *-myces*] **:** a genus of fungi (family Mucoraceae) forming a metallic mycelium with large, simple, stiffly erect, and often very tall sporangiophores

**phy·co·my·ce·tae** \,==mīˈsēd·ē\ *or* **phycomyce·te·ae** \-ēd·ē,ē\ *syn of* PHYCOMYCETES

**phy·co·my·cete** \ˌ==ˈmī,sēt, ˌ==ˌ=ˈ=\ *n* -s [NL *Phycomycetes*] **:** a fungus of the class Phycomycetes

**phy·co·my·ce·tes** \,==mīˈsēd·(,)ēz\ *n pl, cap* [NL, fr. *phyc-* + *-mycetes*] **:** a large class of fungi having a plant body that ranges from an undifferentiated mass of protoplasm to a well-developed and much-branched coenocytic mycelium in which septations commonly occur in age or where reproductive structures develop and having reproduction that is mainly asexual by the formation of conidia or sporangia but includes every form of transition from this method through simple conjugation to sexual reproduction by the union of egg and sperm in the higher forms — see OOMYCETES, ZYGOMYCETES — **phy·co·my·ce·tous** \ˌ==,=ˈsēd·əs\ *adj*

**phy·co·phae·in** *or* **phy·co·phe·in** \ˌ==ˈfēən\ *n* -s [ISV *phyc-* + *-phaein*, *-phein* (fr. Gk *phaios* dusky + ISV *-in*)] **:** a brown pigment in the cells of brown algae (as the kelps) now believed to be no more than a postmortem oxidation product of fucosan

**phy·co·xanthin** \ˌ==+\ *n* -s [ISV *phyc-* + *xanth-* + *-in*] **:** DIATOMIN

**phyl-** *or* **phylo-** *comb form* [L *phyl-*, fr. Gk *phyl-*, *phylo-*, fr. *phylē* tribe, clan, phyle & *phylon* tribe, race; both akin to Gk *phyein* to bring forth — more at BE] **1 :** tribe **:** race ⟨*phylo*graphy⟩ **2 :** phylum ⟨*phylo*geny⟩ ⟨*phyl*ar⟩

**phy·la** *pl of* PHYLUM

**phyl·a·co·bi·o·sis** \,filəkō,bīˈōsəs\ *n, pl* **phylacobioses** [NL, fr. *phylaco-* (fr. Gk *phylak-*, *phylax* guard) + *-biosis*] **:** a mixobiosis in which ants of a particular species live in a termite nest and appear to replace functionally the nasute or soldier caste of the termite — **phyl·a·co·bi·ot·ic** \ˌ===,bīˈäd·ik -,bē-\ *adj*

**phy·lac·ter·ied** \fəˈlakt(ə)rēd, -rid\ *adj* **:** wearing or furnished with a phylactery

**phy·lac·tery** \-t(ə)rē, -ri\ *n* -ES [alter. (influenced by LL *phylacterium*) of earlier *philatery*, fr. ME *philaterie*, fr. ML *philaterium*, alter. of LL *phylacterium*, fr. Gk *phylaktērion* phylactery, amulet, safeguard, fr. *phylak-*, *phylax* guard] **1 :** either of two small square leather boxes with leather straps attached that contain parchment slips inscribed in Hebrew with the four scriptural passages Deuteronomy 6: 4–9 and 11: 13–21 and Exodus 13: 1–10 and 11–16 and that are worn fastened in a prescribed manner one on the left arm and one on the forehead by orthodox and conservative Jewish males during morning weekday prayers as reminders of their obligation to keep the Law **2 :** a case or chest enclosing a holy relic **3** [by confusion of the phylacteries (sense 1) mentioned in Mt 23: 5 with the zizith mentioned in Num 15: 38–39] **:** a distinctive fringe or border **4 :** something worn as a charm or preservative against danger or disease **:** AMULET **5 a :** an inscribed scroll that in medieval art is made to appear as if held or coming from the mouth to show what is being said; *broadly* **:** RECORD **b :** an infula of a miter

**phy·lac·tic** \fəˈlaktik\ *adj* [ISV, fr. Gk *phylaktikos* preservative, fr. *phylassein* to guard, preserve, fr. *phylak-*, *phylax* guard] **:** of or relating to defense **:** COUNTERACTIVE ⟨~ power against infection⟩ — compare PROPHYLACTIC

**phy·lac·to·carp** \fəˈlaktə,kärp\ *n* -s [Gk *phylaktos* (verbal of *phylassein* to guard, preserve) + E *-carp*] **:** a branch of a plumularian hydroid modified to protect the gonothecae — **phy·lac·to·car·pal** \ˌ=ˌ==ˈkärpəl\ *adj*

**phy·lac·to·le·ma** *or* **phy·lac·to·le·ma** \=,==ˈlēmə\ *or* **phy·lac·to·le·ma·ta** \-məd·ə\ *syn of* PHYLACTOLAEMATA

**phy·lac·to·lae·ma·ta** \-məd·ə\ *n pl, cap* [NL, fr. *phylacto-* (fr. Gk *phylaktos*, verbal of *phylassein* to guard, preserve) + *-laem-* (fr. Gk *laimos* throat, gullet) + *-ata* — more at GYMNOLAEMATA] **:** a class or other division of Bryozoa comprising freshwater forms having the tentacles arranged on a horseshoe-shaped lophophore and the mouth covered by an epistome — compare GYMNOLAEMATA — **phy·lac·to·lae·ma·tous** \ˌ=ˌ==ˈ=məd·əs\ *adj*

**phy·lad** \ˈfī,lad\ *n* -s [*phyl-* + *-ad*, n. suffix] **:** a small group of closely related species presumably of common origin

**phy·lar** \ˈfīlə(r)\ *adj* [*phyl-* + *-ar*] **:** of or relating to a phylum

**phy·larch** \ˈfī,lärk\ *n* -s [L *phylarchus*, fr. Gk *phylarchos*, fr. *phylē* + *archos* ruler — more at ARCHI-] **1 a :** the chief ruler of an ancient Grecian phyle **b :** the commander of the cavalry furnished by each ancient Athenian tribe **2 :** the magistrate or head of a recognized tribal division of any of the Asiatic provinces of the Roman empire — **phy·lar·chic** \(ˈ)fīˈlärkik\ *or* **phy·lar·chi·cal** \-kəkəl\ *adj*

**phy·le** \ˈfīlē\ *n, pl* **phy·lae** \-,lē\ [Gk *phylē* — more at PHYL-] **1 :** the largest political subdivision among the ancient Athenians and a principal division of the army — see DEME 1, PHRATRY 1 **2 :** any of the four orders into which the population of Egypt was divided during the Old and Middle Kingdoms

**phyl·ephe·bic** \ˌfil+\ *adj* [*phyl-* + *ephebic*] **:** being or relating to the phase of maximum vigor of a race

**phy·le·sis** \fīˈlēsəs\ *n, pl* **phyle·ses** \-,sēz\ *also* **phylesises** [NL, fr. *phyl-* + *-esis*] **:** the course of evolutionary or phylogenetic development (as of a natural group of organisms)

**phy·let·ic** \fīˈled·ik\ *adj* [ISV, fr. NL *phylesis*, after such pairs as LL *antithesis*: *antitheticus* antithetical] **:** of or relating to a line of descent or to phylesis **:** PHYLOGENETIC, RACIAL — **phy·let·i·cal·ly** \-ək(ə)lē\ *adv*

**phy·le·tism** \ˈfīləd·,izəm\ *n* -s [NGk *phyletismos*, fr. Gk *phyletēs* fellow tribesman (fr. *phylē* tribe, clan, phyle) + *-ismos* -ism] **:** nationalism applied to ecclesiastical affairs; *specif* **:** a doctrine that a nationality should be served by its own independent ecclesiastical administration even on the territory of another church

**phy·lic** \ˈfīlik\ *adj* [*phyl-* + *-ic*] **1 :** of or relating to a Grecian phyle **2 :** being or viewed as a member of a group ⟨man as a ~ organism⟩

**phyll-** *or* **phyllo-** *comb form* [NL *phyllo-*, fr. Gk *phyll-*, *phyllo-*, fr. *phyllon* — more at BLOW] **1 :** leaf ⟨*phyllo*morphous⟩ **2 :** part or thing resembling a leaf ⟨*phyll*idium⟩ **3 :** chlorophyll ⟨*phyll*in⟩

**-phyll** \ˌfil\ *n comb form* -s [F *-phylle*, fr. Gk *phyllon* leaf] **1 :** coloring matter occurring in plants ⟨chloro*phyll*⟩ **2** [NL *-phyllum*, fr. Gk *phyllon* leaf] **:** leaf ⟨micro*phyll*⟩

**-phylla** *pl of* -PHYLLUM

**phyl·lac·o·ra** \fəˈlakərə\ *n, cap* [NL, fr. *phyll-* + *-acora* (fr. Gk *achōr* dandruff, scurf)] **:** a genus of fungi (order Dothideales) that have the perithecia embedded in flattened black stromata and that include economically important parasites of grasses — see TAR SPOT 2

**phyl·lac·tin·ia** \ˌfi,lakˈtinēə\ *n, cap* [NL, fr. *phyll-* + *actin-* ray + *-ia* — more at ACTIN-] **:** a genus of powdery mildews having perithecia with several asci and rigid pointed appendages swollen at the base and occurring on the leaves of various trees and shrubs

**phyl·lade** \ˈfi,lād\ *n* -s [irreg. fr. *phyll-*] **:** CATAPHYLL; *specif* **:** one of the reduced leaves in a quillwort

**phyl·lan·thus** \fəˈlan(t)thəs\ *n, cap* [NL, fr. *phyll-* + *-anthus*] **:** a very large genus of tropical plants (family Euphorbiaceae) with alternate leaves and small monoecious flowers succeeded by polycarpellary capsules

**phyl·la·ry** \ˈfilərē, -ri\ *n* -ES [NL *phyllarium*, fr. Gk *phyllarion* small leaf, dim. of *phyllon* leaf] **:** one of the involucral bracts subtending the flower head of a composite plant

**phyl·li·dae** \ˈfilə,dē\ *n pl, cap* [NL, fr. *Phyllium*, type genus + *-idae*] **:** a family of insects (order Orthoptera) that includes the leaf insects

**phyl·lid·i·um** \fəˈlidēəm\ *n, pl* **phyllid·ia** \-ēə\ [NL, fr. *phyll-* + *-idium*] **:** any of two or four complex muscular usu. leaf-shaped or cuplike outgrowths from the lateral wall of the scolex of some tapeworms

**phyl·li·form** \ˈfilə,fȯrm\ *adj* [*phyll-* + *-iform*] **:** having the shape of a leaf

**phyl·lin** \ˈfilən\ *n* -s [*phyll-* + *-in*] **:** a complex magnesium derivative of a porphyrin or a phorbin ⟨the ~ formed from etioporphyrin⟩

**phyl·line** \ˈfi,lēn, -lən\ *adj* [*phyll-* + *-ine*] **:** LEAFLIKE

**phyl·lite** \ˈfi,līt\ *n* -s [*phyll-* + *-ite*] **:** a foliated rock that is intermediate in composition and fabric between slate and schist — **phyl·lit·ic** \fəˈlid·ik\ *adj*

**phyl·li·tis** \fəˈlīd·əs\ *n, cap* [NL, fr. Gk *phyllitis* hart's-tongue, fr. *phyllon* leaf] **:** a small genus of ferns (family Polypodiaceae) with large oblong or strap-shaped fronds and linear elongated sori contiguous in pairs that give the appearance of a double indusium — see HART'S-TONGUE 1

**phyl·li·um** \ˈfilēəm\ *n, cap* [NL, fr. *phyll-* + *-ium*] **:** a genus of Asiatic leaf insects

**phyl·lo·both·ri·oi·dea** \,filō,bäthrēˈȯidēə\ [NL, fr. *phyll-* + *bothri-* + *-oidea*] *syn of* TETRAPHYLLIDEA

**phyl·lo·bran·chia** \ˌ==ˈbraŋkēə\ *n* [NL, fr. *phyll-* + *-branchia*] **:** a crustacean gill composed of lamellae — **phyl·lo·bran·chi·al** \ˌ==ˈbraŋkēəl\ *or* **phyl·lo·bran·chi·ate** \-ēət, -ē,āt\ *adj*

**phyl·lo·caline** \ˈfilō+\ *n* [*phyll-* + *caline*] **:** a hormone or hormonoid substance distinct from auxin that is held to play a role in the development of mesophyll parts of a leaf

**¹phyl·lo·car·id** \ˌfilōˈkarəd\ *adj* [NL *Phyllocarida*] **:** of or relating to the Phyllocarida

**²phyllocarid** \"\ *n* -s [NL *Phyllocarida*] **:** a crustacean of the group Phyllocarida

**phyl·lo·car·i·da** \ˌ==ˈkarədə\ *n pl, cap* [NL, fr. *phyll-* + *-carida* (fr. Gk *karid-*, *karis* shrimp, prawn); perh. akin to Gk *kara* head — more at CEREBRAL] **:** a group of Malacostraca comprising forms with the head and thorax enclosed in a chitinous or calcareous bivalve carapace and including Nebaliidae and related extinct families — **phyl·lo·car·i·dan** \-ədən\ *adj or n*

**phyl·loc·er·as** \fəˈläsərəs\ *n, cap* [NL *Phyllocerat-*, *Phylloceras*, fr. *phyll-* + *-cerat-*, *-ceras* -ceras] **:** a genus (the type of the family Phylloceratidae) comprising smooth involute compressed ammonites with complex sutures that occur first in the Triassic and are believed to have been ancestral to most Jurassic and Cretaceous ammonites

**phyl·lo·cer·a·tid** \ˌfilōˈserəd·əd, -ətəd\ *n* -s [NL *Phylloceratidae*, family of ammonites, fr. *Phyllocerat-*, *Phylloceras*, type genus + *-idae*] **:** an ammonite of the genus *Phylloceras* or family Phylloceratidae

**phyl·lo·clade** \ˈfilə,klād\ *also* **phyl·lo·clad** \-,klad\ *n* -s [NL *phyllocladium*] **:** a flattened stem or branch (as a joint of a cactus or a cladophyll) that functions as a leaf — compare PHYLLODE

**phyl·lo·cla·di·oid** \ˌ==ˈklādē,ȯid\ *adj* [NL *phyllocladium* + E *-oid*] **:** being or resembling a phylloclade ⟨a ~ stem⟩

**phyl·lo·cla·di·um** \ˌ==ˈ=dēəm\ *n, pl* **phyllocla·dia** \-dēə\ [NL, fr. *phyll-* + *clad-* + *-ium*] **:** PHYLLOCLADE

**phyl·loc·la·dous** \fəˈläklədəs\ *adj* [*phylloclade* + *-ous*] **:** having phylloclades

**phyl·lo·cop·tes** \,filəˈkäp,tēz\ *n, cap* [NL, fr. *phyll-* + *-coptes* (fr. Gk *koptein* to cut off) — more at CAPON] **:** a genus of eriophyid mites containing several that attack various economically important plants

**phyl·lo·cop·tru·ta** \ˌ==,käpˈtrüd·ə\ *n, cap* [NL, fr. *phyll-* + *-coptruta* (prob. fr. Gk *koptein* to cut off)] **:** a genus of eriophyid mites that includes the citrus rust mite

**phyl·lo·cyst** \ˈfilə,sist\ *n* -s [*phyll-* + *-cyst*] **:** the cavity of a hydrophyllium — **phyl·lo·cys·tic** \ˌ==ˈsistik\ *adj*

**phyl·lode** \ˈfi,lōd\ *n* -s [NL *phyllodium*, fr. Gk *phyllōdēs* like leaves (fr. *phyllon* leaf) + NL *-ium*] **1 :** a flat expanded petiole that replaces the blade of a foliage leaf, fulfills the same functions, and is analogous to but not homologous with a cladophyll — compare PHYLLOCLADE **2 :** the expanded and more or less depressed oral end of an ambulacrum in some sea urchins — **phyl·lo·di·al** \fəˈlōdēəl\ *adj*

**phyl·lo·din·e·ous** \ˌfiləˈdinēəs\ *or* **phyl·lod·i·nous** \fəˈlädˈnəs\ *adj* [*phyllodineous* prob. fr. (assumed) NL *phyllodineus*, irreg. fr. NL *phyllodium* phyllode + L *-eus* -eous; *phyllodinous* alter. of *phyllodineous*] **:** relating to or having phyllodes

**phyl·lo·di·um** \fəˈlōdēəm\ *n, pl* **phyllo·dia** \-dēə\ [NL] **:** PHYLLODE 1

**phyl·lod·o·ce** \fəˈlädə,sē\ *n, cap* [NL, fr. L *Phyllodoce*, one of the Nereids] **1 :** a small genus of arctic and alpine shrubs (family Ericaceae) with linear evergreen leaves and nodding umbellate flowers having an ovoid pink, blue, or purple corolla — see MOUNTAIN HEATH **2 :** a genus of polychaete worms that is the type of the family Phyllodocidae

**phyl·lo·doc·i·dae** \,filəˈdäsə,dē\ *n pl, cap* [NL, fr. *Phyllodoce*, type genus + *-idae*] **:** a cosmopolitan family of elongated active polychaete worms with broad leaflike cirri, several prostomial tentacles, and one or two pairs of eyes

**phyl·lo·dro·mi·idae** \,filōdrəˈmīə,dē\ *n pl, cap* [NL, fr. *Phyllodromia*, type genus (fr. *phyll-* + *drom-* + *-ia*) + *-idae*] **:** a family of cockroaches that includes the croton bug

**phyl·lo·dy** \ˈfilədē, -di\ *n* -ES [ISV *phyll-* + *-ody*] **:** metamorphosis of a specialized plant organ (as a flower petal) into a foliage leaf (as by the action of a virus)

**phyl·lo·er·y·thrin** \ˌfilōˈerəthrən, -əˈrith-\ *n* -s [ISV *phyll-* + *erythr-* + *-in*] **:** a rose-red photosensitizing porphyrin pigment formed as a degradation product of chlorophyll in the digestive tract of herbivorous animals and normally excreted esp. in the bile but absorbed by the blood in pathological conditions (as geeldikkop)

**phyl·lo·genetic** \ˌfilō+\ *adj* [*phyll-* + *-genetic*] **:** relating to or concerned with the development of leaves

**¹phyl·loid** \ˈfi,lȯid\ *also* **phyl·loi·dal** \fəˈlȯidᵊl\ *adj* [*phylloid* fr. NL *phylloides*, fr. *phyll-* + L *-oides* -oid; *phylloidal* fr. *phylloid* + *-al*] **:** resembling a leaf **:** FOLIACEOUS

**²phylloid** \"\ *n* -s **:** a plant part functioning as or of similar origin to a leaf; *esp* **:** a leaf or leaflike structure organogenetically derived by fusion of a system of orig. dichotomizing telomes — used in connection with the telome theory

**phyl·lo·man·cy** \ˈfilə,man(t)sē, -si\ *n* -ES [MGk *phyllomanteia*, fr. Gk *phyll-* + *manteia* divination — more at -MANCY] **:** divination by means of leaves

**phyl·lo·mania** \ˌ==+\ *n* [NL, fr. *phyll-* + LL *mania*] **:** an abnormal or excessive production of leaves — **phyl·lo·ma·ni·ac** \ˌ==+\ *adj*

**phyl·lome** \ˈfi,lōm\ *n* -s [ISV *phyll-* + *-ome*] **:** a plant part that is a leaf or is phylogenetically derived from a leaf **:** a foliar organ (as a leaf, petal, or phylloid) — **phyl·lom·ic** \fəˈlämik, -lōm-\ *adj*

**phyl·lo·morph** \ˈfilə,mȯrf\ *n* [*phyll-* + *-morph*] **:** a detail in art resembling a leaf — **phyl·lo·mor·phic** \ˌ==ˈmȯrfik\ *adj*

**phyl·lo·mor·pho·sis** \ˌ==ˈmȯrfəsəs *sometimes* -,mȯrˈfōs-\ *n* [NL, fr. *phyll-* + *-morphosis*] **1 :** succession and variation of leaves during different seasons **2 :** PHYLLODY

**phyl·lo·mor·phous** \ˌ==ˈmȯrfəs\ *adj* [*phyll-* + *-morphous*] **:** resembling a leaf in appearance ⟨a ~ insect⟩

**phyl·lo·mor·phy** \ˈ==,mȯrfē\ *n* -ES [ISV *phyll-* + *-morphy*] **:** PHYLLODY

**phyl·lo·nite** \ˈfilə,nīt\ *n* -s [*phyllite* + *mylonite*] **:** a phyllite of cataclastic origin

**phyl·loph·a·ga** \fə'läfəgə\ *n, cap* [NL, fr. *phyll-* + *-phaga*] **:** a large genus of beetles (family Scarabaeidae) including the common june beetles of the northern U. S. — **phyl·loph·a·gan** \-gən\ *adj*

**phyl·lo·phag·ic** \ˌfilə¦fājik\ *adj* [*phyll-* + *phag-* + *-ic*] *of a green plant* **:** deriving nutritive material from foliar activities

**phyl·loph·a·gous** \fə'läfəgəs\ *adj* [prob. fr. (assumed) NL *phyllophagus*, fr. NL *phyll-* + *-phagus* -phagous] **:** feeding on leaves

**phyl·lo·phore** \'filə,fō(ə)r\ *n* -s [*phyll-* + *-phore*] **:** a leaf-bearing axis; *specif* **:** the apex of a palm stem

**phyl·loph·o·rous** \fə'läf(ə)rəs\ *adj* [Gk *phyllophoros*, fr. *phyll-* + *-phoros* -phorous] **:** producing leaves **:** leaf-bearing ⟨~ plants⟩

**phyl·lo·pod** \'filə,päd\ *also* **phyl·lop·o·dan** \fə'läpədən\ *n* -s [*phyllopod* fr. NL *Phyllopoda; phyllopodan* fr. NL *Phyllopoda* + E *-an*, n. suffix] **:** a phyllopodous crustacean

**phyl·lop·o·da** \fə'läpədə\ *n pl, cap* [NL, fr. *phyll-* + *-poda*] *in some esp former classifications* **:** a group comprising entomostracan crustaceans with leaflike swimming appendages that serve as gills, mandibles without palpi, and reduced maxillae: as **a :** BRANCHIOPODA 1 **b :** an order or suborder coextensive with the combined orders Anostraca, Notostraca, and Conchostraca

**phyl·lo·pod·ic** \¦filə¦pädik\ *adj* [*phyll-* + *pod-* + *-ic*] **:** having a leafy base ⟨a ~ culm⟩

**phyl·lo·po·di·um** \ˌ==ˈpōdēəm\ *n, pl* **phyllopo·dia** \-dēə\ [NL, fr. *phyll-* + *-podium*] **1 :** a primordial leaf or leaf axis **:** a leaf in the undifferentiated state — compare EPIPODIUM **2 a** *chiefly Brit* **:** the basal portion of a mature leaf which is sometimes inconspicuous or absent or modified into a sheath (as in grasses) **b :** a stem or axis made up of the expanded and fused bases of leaves

**phyl·lop·o·dous** \fə'läpədəs\ *or* **phyl·lo·pod** \'filə,päd\ *also* **phyl·lop·o·dan** \fə'läpədən\ *adj* [*phyllopodous* fr. NL *Phyllopoda* + E *-ous; phyllopod* fr. NL *Phyllopoda; phyllopodan* fr. NL *Phyllopoda* + E *-an*, adj. suffix] **:** of or relating to the Phyllopoda

**phyl·lo·porphyrin** \¦filō+\ *n* [ISV *phyll-* + *porphyrin*; prob. orig. formed in G] **:** a dark red crystalline porphyrin $C_{20}H_6N_4(CH_3)_5(C_2H_5)_2CH_2CH_2COOH$ with a violet luster obtained by degradation of chlorophyll or pheophytin

**phyl·lop·ter·yx** \fə'läptə(ˌ)riks\ *n, cap* [NL, fr. *phyll-* + *-pteryx*] **:** a genus of syngnathid fishes comprising several Australian sea dragons

**phyl·lo·pyrrole** \¦filō+\ *n* [ISV *phyll-* + *pyrrole*] **:** a crystalline homologue $C_9H_{15}N$ of pyrrole formed during reduction of hemin, chlorophyll, or phylloporphyrin with hydriodic acid; 2,3,5-trimethyl-4-ethyl-pyrrole

**phyl·lo·quinone** \¦==+\ *n* [ISV *phyll-* + *quinone*] **:** VITAMIN K 1a

**phyl·lo·rhine** \'filə,rīn, -,rən\ *adj* [NL *Phyllorhina* (syn. of *Hipposideros*), fr. *phyll-* + *-rhina*] **1 :** LEAF-NOSED **2 :** of or relating to leaf-nosed bats or to the genera they belong to

**phyl·los·co·pus** \fə'läskəpəs\ *n, cap* [NL, fr. *phyll-* + *-scopus*] **:** a genus of Old World warblers including the chiffchaff and the willow warbler

**phyl·lo·silicate** \¦filō+\ *n* [*phyll-* + *silicate*] **:** a mineral of a class of polymeric silicates in which the silicon-oxygen tetrahedral groups are linked by sharing three of every four oxygen atoms so as to form sheets of indefinite extent, in which the ratio of silicon to oxygen is 2:5, and in which some silicon atoms may be replaced by aluminum (as in mica, chlorite, kaolinite) — called also *sheet-silicate;* compare CYCLOSILICATE, INOSILICATE, NESOSILICATE, SOROSILICATE, TECTOSILICATE

**phyl·lo·siphon** \"+\ *n, cap* [NL, fr. *phyll-* + Gk *siphōn* siphon, tube] **:** a genus (the type of the family Phyllosiphonaceae of the order Siphonales) of filamentous green algae that live as intracellular parasites of plants of the family Araceae (as the jack-in-the-pulpit) and cause yellowing and discoloration of the leaves and stems

**phyl·lo·siphonic** \"+\ *adj* [*phyll-* + *siphonic*] *of a pteropsid plant* **:** possessing leaf gaps ⟨ferns, gymnosperms, and angiosperms are ~⟩

**phyl·lo·so·ma** \ˌfilə'sōmə\ *n* [NL, fr. *phyll-* + *-soma*] **:** a flat transparent long-legged larva that is typical of various spiny lobsters and was formerly supposed to constitute a distinct genus

**phyl·lo·spon·dy·li** \ˌfilō'spändə,lī\ *n pl, cap* [NL, fr. *phyll-* + *-spondyli*] *in some esp former classifications* **:** an order of extinct amphibians with phyllospondylous vertebrae that are now usu. regarded as larval labyrinthodonts — compare BRANCHIOSAURUS

**phyl·lo·spon·dy·lous** \¦===ˌ==ləs\ *adj* [NL *Phyllospondyli* + E *-ous*] **:** being or having vertebrae with a hypocentrum but no pleurocentra, the neural arch extending down to enclose the notochord and form transverse processes to support the ribs — used esp. of a larval labyrinthodont amphibian

**phyl·los·ta·chys** \fə'lästəkəs\ *n, cap* [NL, fr. *phyll-* + Gk *stachys* spike of grain — more at STING] **:** a genus of Chinese and Japanese bamboo grasses having slender cylindrical culms used esp. for walking sticks and bamboo furniture

**phyl·lo·stic·ta** \ˌfilə'stiktə\ *n, cap* [NL, fr. *phyll-* + *-sticta* (fr. Gk *stiktos* tattooed, spotted, fr. *stizein* to tattoo) — more at STICK] **:** a very large form genus of imperfect fungi (family Sphaeropsidaceae) that are characterized by hyaline ovate to elongate nonseptate pycniospores produced typically in leaf spots within dark globose leathery or carbonaceous pycnidia and that include forms causing leaf blights of economically important plants — see BLOTCH 2a

**phyl·lo·stic·ta·ce·ae** \ˌ==(ˌ)=ˈtāsēˌē\ [NL, fr. *Phyllosticta* + *-aceae*] *syn of* SPHAEROPSIDACEAE

**phyl·lo·stic·ta·les** \ˌ==ˌ=ˈtā(ˌ)lēz\ [NL, fr. *Phyllosticta* + *-ales*] *syn of* SPHAEROPSIDALES

**phyl·los·to·ma** \fə'lästəmə\ [NL *Phyllostomat-, Phyllostoma*, fr. *phyll-* + *-stomat-, -stoma* -stoma] *syn of* PHYLLOSTOMUS

**phyl·lo·stom·a·tid** \ˌfilə'stäməd·əd\ *adj* [NL *Phyllostomatidae*] **:** of or relating to the Phyllostomatidae

**phyl·lo·sto·mat·i·dae** \ˌfilōstō'mad·əˌdē\ *n pl, cap* [NL, irreg. fr. *Phyllostomus*, type genus + *-idae*] **:** a large family of leaf-nosed bats that range from the southern U. S. to Paraguay and are distinguished from the Old World horseshoe bats by the well-developed tragus — see SPEARNOSE BAT

**phyl·lo·stoma·tous** \¦==ˈstäməd·əs, -stōm-\ *adj* [NL *Phyllostomat-, Phyllostoma* + E *-ous*] **1 :** LEAF-NOSED **2 :** belonging to the Phyllostomatidae

**phyl·lo·stome** \'filə,stōm\ *n* -s [NL *Phyllostomus*] **:** a bat of the family Phyllostomatidae; *broadly* **:** LEAF-NOSED BAT

**phyl·los·to·mid** \fə'lästəməd, -,mid\ *n* -s [NL *Phyllostomidae*] **:** a bat of the family Phyllostomatidae

**phyl·lo·stom·i·dae** \ˌfilə'stäməˌdē\ [NL, fr. *Phyllostomus* + *-idae*] *syn of* PHYLLOSTOMATIDAE

**phyl·los·to·mine** \fə'lästə,mīn, -ˌmən\ *adj* [NL *Phyllostomus* + E *-ine*] **:** LEAF-NOSED

**phyl·los·to·mous** \-məs\ *adj* [NL *Phyllostomus* + E *-ous*] **:** PHYLLOSTOMATOUS

**phyl·los·to·mus** \-məs\ *n, cap* [NL, fr. *phyll-* + *-stomus*] **:** the type genus of Phyllostomatidae — see JAVELIN BAT

**phyl·lo·tac·tic** \¦filō¦taktik\ *or* **phyl·lo·tac·ti·cal** \-təkəl\ *adj* [*phyllotactic* fr. *phyll-* + *-tactic; phyllotactical* fr. *phyllotactic* + *-al*] **:** of or relating to phyllotaxy

**phyl·lo·tax·ic** \-¦taksik\ *adj* [*phyllotaxy* + *-ic*] **:** PHYLLOTACTIC

**phyl·lo·taxy** \'filə¦taksē, -si\ *or* **phyl·lo·tax·is** \-ksəs\ *n, pl* **phyllotax·ies** \-sēz, -siz\ *or* **phyllotax·es** \-ˌsēz\ [NL *phyllotaxis*, fr. *phyll-* + *-taxis*] **1 :** the arrangement of leaves on a stem and in relation to one another ⟨decussate ~⟩ ⟨alternate ~⟩ — compare GENETIC SPIRAL, ORTHOSTICHY, PARASTICHY **2 :** the study of phyllotaxy and of the laws that govern it

**phyl·lo·tre·ta** \ˌfilə'trēd·ə\ *n, cap* [NL, fr. *phyll-* + *-treta* (fr. Gk *trētos* perforated, fr. *tetrainein* to perforate, pierce) — more at THROW] **:** a genus of chrysomelid beetles that includes flea beetles which are serious pests on garden plants and which transmit a mosaic disease to cabbage and other plants of the genus *Brassica*

**-phyl·lous** \¦filəs\ *adj comb form* [NL *-phyllus*, fr. Gk *-phyllos*, fr. *phyllon* leaf — more at BLOW] **1 :** having (such or so many) leaves, leaflets, or leaflike parts ⟨isophyllous⟩ ⟨oligophyllous⟩ ⟨macrophyllous⟩ **2 :** being in (such) a position in relation to a leaf ⟨epiphyllous⟩

**phyl·lox·era** \ˌfiˌläk'sirə, -ˌlək-; fə'läksərə\ *n* [NL, fr. *phyll-* + *-xera* (fr. Gk *xēros* dry) — more at SERENE] **1** *cap* **:** the type genus of Phylloxeridae comprising plant lice that differ from the aphids in wing structure, in being continuously oviparous, in lacking honey tubes, and in their extreme polymorphism and that are very destructive to many plants (as grapes) **2** -s **:** any plant louse of the genus *Phylloxera* or family Phylloxeridae — **phyl·lox·er·an** \fə'läksərən\ *adj or n* — **phyl·lox·er·ic** \¦fiˌläk¦serik\ *adj*

**phyl·lox·er·i·dae** \ˌfiˌläk'serəˌdē\ *n pl, cap* [NL, fr. *Phylloxera*, type genus + *-idae*] **:** a small family of destructive plant lice in which the wings when present are laid flat upon the abdomen when at rest — see PHYLLOXERA

**phyl·lo·zooid** \¦filō+\ *n* [*phyll-* + *zooid*] **:** HYDROPHYLLIUM

**-phylls** *pl of* -PHYLL

**-phyl·lum** \'filəm\ *n comb form* [NL, fr. Gk *phyllon* leaf] **1 :** one having (such) leaves or leaflike parts — in generic names of animals ⟨Cyathophyllum⟩ and esp. plants ⟨Brachyphyllum⟩ ⟨Podophyllum⟩ **2** *pl* **-phyl·la** \-lə\ **:** leaf ⟨mesophyllum⟩ **3 :** fossil resembling a plant of a (specified) group — in generic names ⟨Sapindophyllum⟩

**phylo-** — see PHYL-

**phy·lo·genesis** \¦fīlō+\ *n* [NL, fr. *phyl-* + L *genesis*] **:** PHYLOGENY 2

**phy·lo·ge·net·ic** \¦fīlōjə¦ned·ik\ *adj* [ISV, fr. NL *phylogenesis*, after such pairs as LL *antithesis: antitheticus* antithetical] **1 :** of or relating to phylogeny ⟨~ studies⟩ **2 :** based on natural evolutionary relationships ⟨a ~ system of classification⟩ **3 :** acquired in the course of phylogenetic development **:** RACIAL ⟨a ~ trait⟩ ⟨the hypothetical ~ drive and the actual social behavior —I.Atkin⟩ — **phy·lo·ge·net·i·cal·ly** \-ək(ə)lē\ *adv*

**phy·lo·genetics** \¦fīlō+\ *n pl but sing or pl in constr* **:** a branch of science that deals with phylogeny

**phy·lo·gen·ic** \¦fīlə¦jenik\ *adj* [ISV *phylogeny* + *-ic*] **:** PHYLOGENETIC

**phy·log·e·nist** \fī'läjənəst\ *n* -s **:** a specialist in phylogeny

**phy·log·e·ny** \-nē, -ni\ *n* -ES [ISV *phyl-* + *-geny*] **1 :** the racial history of a specified kind of organism **2 :** the evolution of a race or genetically related group of organisms (as a species, family, or order) as distinguished from the development of the individual organism — compare ONTOGENY **3 :** the history or course of the development of an immaterial thing (as a word or custom) ⟨we cannot hope ~ will explain the morphology of philosophies —W.P.Kent⟩

**phy·lon** \'fīˌlän\ *n, pl* **phy·la** \-ˌlə\ [NL, fr. Gk, tribe, race] **:** a genetically related group **:** TRIBE, RACE

**phy·lum** \'fīləm\ *n, pl* **phy·la** \-lə\ [NL, fr. Gk *phylon* tribe, race — more at PHYL-] **1 a :** a direct line of descent within a group presumably from a single point of origin ⟨the various evolutionary *phyla* of plants⟩ **b :** a group that constitutes or has the unity of such a phylum ⟨whole *phyla* of resentments —W.H.Auden⟩ ⟨a family of birds containing three *phyla* of subfamilial rank⟩ **2 :** a major taxonomic unit comprising organisms sharing a fundamental pattern of organization and presumably a common descent: **a :** one of the usu. primary divisions of the animal kingdom ⟨the ~ Arthropoda⟩ ⟨the ~ Chordata⟩ — called also *branch* **b** (1) **:** DIVISION (2) **:** any of several major categories of plants; *esp* **:** CLASS **3 :** a group of languages related more remotely than those of a family or stock

**phy·ma** \'fīmə\ *n, pl* **phymas** \-məz\ *or* **phyma·ta** \-məd·ə, -mətə\ [L *phymat-, phyma*, fr. Gk, swelling, tumor, fr. *phyein* to bring forth, grow — more at BE] **:** an external nodule or swelling **:** a skin tumor — **phy·matic** \(ˈ)fī¦mad·ik, -atik, -ēk\ *adj*

**phy·ma·ta** \'fīməd·ə, -mətə\ *n, cap* [NL, fr. L *phymat-, phyma*] **:** the type genus of the family Phymatidae

**[1]phy·mat·id** \fī'mad·əd\ *adj* [NL *Phymatidae*] **:** of or relating to the Phymatidae

**[2]phymatid** \"\ *n* -s [NL *Phymatidae*] **:** a bug of the family Phymatidae **:** AMBUSH BUG

**phy·mat·i·dae** \fī'mad·əˌdē\ *n pl, cap* [NL, fr. *Phymata*, type genus + *-idae*] **:** a family of short stocky carnivorous bugs that have strong thick forelegs, live chiefly in or about flowers, and feed on other insects — see AMBUSH BUG

**phy·ma·to·des** \ˌfīmə'tō(ˌ)dēz\ *n, cap* [NL, fr. L *phymat-, phyma* + NL *-odes*] **:** a genus of tropical ferns (family Polypodiaceae) in general resembling members of *Polypodium* but having fronds with many areolae, irregularly anastomosing veins, and free veinlets

**phy·ma·to·rhy·sin** \ˌfīmə'tōrəsən\ *n* -s [*phymato-* (fr. L *phymat-, phyma*) + *-rhysin* (fr. Gk *rhysis* flow — fr. *rhein* to flow — + E *-in*) — more at STREAM] **:** a melanin pigment found in certain melanotic tumors in man and in the urine of persons affected with them

**phy·ma·to·sis** \ˌfīmə'tōsəs\ *n, pl* **phymato·ses** \-ōˌsēz\ [NL, fr. L *phymat-, phyma* + NL *-osis*] **:** skin disease marked by phymas

**phy·ma·tot·ri·chum** \ˌfīmə'tä·trəkəm\ *n* [NL, fr. *phymato-* (fr. L *phymat-, phyma*) + *-trichum* (fr. Gk *trich-, thrix* hair) — more at TRICHINA] **1** *cap* **:** a genus of imperfect fungi (order Moniliales) including a species (*P. omnivorum*) that causes cotton root rot and similar rots of various other plants **2** -s **:** any fungus of the genus *Phymatotrichum*

**phy·mo·sis** \fī'mōsəs, fə'-\ *n, pl* **phymo·ses** \-ōˌsēz\ [NL, modif. of Gk *phimōsis* stopping up of an orifice — more at PHIMOSIS] **:** PHIMOSIS

**-phyre** \ˌfī(ə)r, ˌfīə\ *n comb form* -s [F *-phyre*, fr. *porphyre* porphyry, fr. ML *porphyrium* — more at PORPHYRY] **:** porphyritic rock ⟨aphanophyre⟩

**-phyric** \¦firik, -īrik, -rēk\ *adj comb form* [ISV *-phyre* + *-ic*] **:** porphyritic ⟨aphyric⟩

**phys** *abbr* **1** physical **2** physician **3** physicist; physics **4** physiological

**phys-** *or* **physo-** *comb form* [NL, fr. Gk *physa* bellows] **1 a :** marked by the presence of gas ⟨physocele⟩ **b :** swollen **:** bladdery ⟨Physocephalus⟩ ⟨Physopsis⟩ **2 :** air bladder ⟨Physostomi⟩

**phy·sa** \'fīsə\ *n* [NL, fr. Gk *physa* bellows — more at PUSTULE] **1 a** *cap* **:** a widely distributed genus (the type of the family Physidae) of freshwater air-breathing snails, having a sinistral, ovate, usu. rather short-spired shell and slender nonretractile tentacles with the eyes at their bases **b** -s **:** any snail of the genus *Physa* **2** *pl* **phy·sae** \-ˌsē, -ˌsī\ *also* **physas :** the lower often retractile part of the body of some anthozoans

**phy·sa·lia** \fī'sālēə, -lyə\ *n* [NL, modif. of Gk *physallis* bladder, bubble; akin to Gk *physa* bellows] **1** *cap* **:** a genus (the type of the family Physaliidae) of large oceanic siphonophores including the Portuguese man-of-war **2** -s **:** any member of the genus *Physalia* — **phy·sa·lian** \-ən\ *adj or n*

**physa·lis** \'fīsələs, 'fis-; fī'saləs\ *n* [NL, modif. of LGk *physallis* Chinese lantern plant, fr. Gk, bladder, bubble] **1** *cap* **:** a large genus of low-growing chiefly American annual or perennial herbs (family Solanaceae) that have an angled campanulate corolla and an inflated and sometimes brightly colored calyx enclosing a fruit which is a greenish or yellow 2-celled globular berry and that include several plants which are cultivated for their edible fruit or their showy calyxes — see CAPE GOOSEBERRY, CHINESE LANTERN PLANT, GROUND-CHERRY, STRAWBERRY TOMATO **2** -ES **:** any plant of the genus *Physalis*

**physa·lop·tera** \ˌfīsə'läptərə, ˌfis-\ *n, cap* [NL, fr. *physalo-* (irreg. fr. Gk *physallis* bladder, bubble) + *-ptera*] **:** a large genus (the type of the family Physalopteridae) of spiruroid nematode worms parasitic in the digestive tract of various vertebrates including man

**physa·lop·ter·oid** \¦==¦=təˌrȯid\ *adj* [NL *Physaloptera* + E *-oid*] *of a nematode worm* **:** resembling worms of the genus *Physaloptera*

**physa·los·po·ra** \ˌ==ˈläspərə\ *n, cap* [NL, fr. *physalo-* (irreg. fr. Gk *physalles* bladder, bubble) + *-spora*] **:** a genus of fungi (family Mycosphaerellaceae) with hyaline ovoid to oblong nonseptate ascospores including some species that were formerly placed in the form genus *Sphaeropsis* — see BLACK ROT

**phy·sap·o·da** \fī'sapədə\ [NL, fr. Gk *physa* bellows + NL *-poda*] *syn of* THYSANOPTERA

**phy·sar·ia** \fī'sa(a)rēə\ *n, cap* [NL, fr. *phys-* + *-aria*] **:** a small genus of herbs (family Cruciferae) of western No. America having racemose yellow flowers and inflated pods — see BLADDERPOD

**physa·rum** \'fīsərəm, 'fis-\ *n, cap* [NL, modif. of Gk *physarion* small bellows, dim. of *physa*] **:** a large genus of slime molds (subclass Myxogastres) that have violet to brownish spores and a sporangium covered with fine granules of lime

**phy·scia** \'fish(ē)ə, -isēə\ *n, cap* [NL, fr. Gk *physkē* large intestine, sausage + NL *-ia;* akin to Gk *physa* bellows] **:** a genus (the type of the family Physciaceae) of usu. foliaceous grayish ascolichens with brown 2-celled ascospores and a distinct cortical tissue of short closely united and interwoven filaments — **phy·sci·oid** \-ēˌȯid\ *adj*

**phys·co·mit·ri·um** \ˌfiskō'mi·trēəm\ *n, cap* [NL, fr. *physco-* (fr. Gk *physkē* large intestine, sausage) + *mitr-* (fr. L *mitra* headband, turban) + *-ium* — more at MITER] **:** a genus of mostly minute mud-inhabiting mosses (family Funariaceae) having globose to pyriform erect capsules with no peristome — see URN MOSS

**phy·se·ter** \fī'sēd·ə(r)\ *n, cap* [NL, fr. L, sperm whale, fr. Gk *physētēr* bellows, blowhole of a whale, sperm whale; akin to Gk *physa* bellows] **:** the type genus of the family Physeteridae comprising the sperm whales

**[1]phy·se·ter·id** \-d·ərəd\ *adj* [NL *Physeteridae*] **:** of or relating to the Physeteridae

**[2]physeterid** \"\ *n* -s [NL *Physeteridae*] **:** a whale of the family Physeteridae

**phys·e·ter·i·dae** \ˌfisə'terəˌdē\ *n pl, cap* [NL, fr. *Physeter*, type genus + *-idae*] **:** a family of whales that includes the sperm whales, pygmy sperm whale, various related extinct forms, and formerly also the beaked whales — compare PHYSETEROIDEA

**phy·se·ter·oid** \fī'sēd·əˌrȯid\ *n* -s [NL *Physeteroidea*] **:** a member of the superfamily Physeteroidea **:** BEAKED WHALE, SPERM WHALE

**phys·e·ter·oi·dea** \ˌfisəd·ə'rȯidēə\ *n pl, cap* [NL, fr. *Physeter* + *-oidea*] **:** a superfamily of toothed whales comprising the beaked whales and the sperm whales

**phys·harmonica** \¦fis+\ *n* [G *physharmonika*, fr. Gk *physa* bellows + L *harmonica*, fem. of *harmonicus* musical — more at HARMONIC] **:** a small reed organ that is a precursor of the harmonium

**phys·har·mon·i·ka** \"\ *n* -s [G, lit., physharmonica] **:** a set of harmonium reeds incorporated into a pipe organ

**physi-** *or* **physio-** *comb form* [L *physio-*, fr. Gk *physi-*, *physio-*, fr. *physis* nature] **1 a :** nature **:** natural **:** belonging to or concerned with the natural order ⟨physitheism⟩ **b :** of, relating to, or concerned with the body esp. as distinct from the mind ⟨physiogenic⟩ **2 :** physical ⟨physiotherapy⟩ **:** physical and ⟨physiopsychic⟩ **3 :** physiological ⟨physiopsychology⟩ **:** physiological and ⟨physiopathologic⟩

**phys·i·an·thro·py** \ˌfizē'an(t)thrəpē\ *n* -ES [*physi-* + *anthrop-* + *-y*] **:** the study of the constitution of man and his diseases and their remedies

**phys·i·at·rics** \ˌfizē'a·triks, -rēks\ *n pl but sing or pl in constr* [ISV *phys-* (fr. Gk *physis* nature) + *-iatrics*] **1** *also* **phys·i·at·ric** \¦==ˈa·trik, -rēk\ **:** a system of medicine based on utilization of the healing powers of nature **2 a :** PHYSICAL MEDICINE **b :** PHYSICAL THERAPY

**phys·i·at·rist** \ˌ==ˈa·trəst, '==ˌ==\ *n* -s [*physiatrics* + *-ist*] **:** a physician who specializes in physical medicine

**[1]physic** *var of* PHYSICS

**[2]phys·ic** \'fizik, -zēk, *chiefly in pres part* -zək\ *vt* **physicked; physicked; physicking; physics** *or* **physicks** [ME *phisiken*, fr. *phisik, fisike* medical science — more at PHYSICS] **1 :** to treat with medicine **:** administer medicine to; *esp* **:** PURGE **2 :** RELIEVE, HEAL, CURE

**[3]physic** \"\ *adj* [in sense 1, fr. ME *fisike*, fr. ML *physicus*, fr. L, natural, of, or relating to natural philosophy, fr. Gk *physikos;* in other senses, fr. L *physicus* — more at PHYSICS] **1** *obs* **:** MEDICAL, MEDICINAL **2** *archaic* **:** NATURAL, PHYSICAL **3 :** of or relating to natural philosophy

**[1]phys·i·cal** \'fizəkəl, -zēk-\ *adj* [ME *phisycal*, fr. ML *physicalis* medicinal, physical, fr. L *physica* study of nature + *-alis* -al — more at PHYSICS] **1 a** *archaic* **:** of or relating to medicine or the practice of medicine **b** (1) *obs* **:** curing or alleviating ill health **:** beneficial to health (2) *archaic* **:** used in medicine **c** *obs* **:** needing or having medical treatment **:** ILL **d** *archaic* **:** practicing medicine **2 a :** of or belonging to all created existences in nature **:** relating to or in accordance with the laws of nature **b :** of or relating to natural or material things as opposed to things mental, moral, spiritual, or imaginary **:** MATERIAL, NATURAL ⟨labor, in the ~ world, is . . . employed in putting objects in motion —J.S.Mill⟩ **3 a :** of, relating to, concerned with, or devoted to natural science **b :** of or relating to physics **:** characterized or produced by the forces and operations of physics **:** employed in the processes of physics ⟨~ changes⟩ ⟨~ laws⟩ ⟨~ forces⟩ **4 a :** of or relating to the body ⟨~ strength⟩ — often opposed to *mental* **b :** concerned or preoccupied with the body and its needs **:** CARNAL, LUSTY ⟨a purely ~ person⟩ **syn** see BODILY, MATERIAL

**[2]physical** \"\ *n* -s **:** PHYSICAL EXAMINATION

**physical anthropologist** *n* **:** an anthropologist specializing in physical anthropology

**physical anthropology** *n* **:** a branch of anthropology primarily concerned with the comparative study of human evolution, variation, and classification esp. through measurement and observation — distinguished from *cultural anthropology*

**physical astronomy** *n* **:** CELESTIAL MECHANICS

**physical chemistry** *n* **:** a branch of science applying physical methods and theory to the study of chemical systems

**physical culture** *n* **:** the systematic care and development of the physique

**physical culturist** *n* **:** an exponent or practicer of physical culture

**physical double star** *also* **physical double** *n* **:** BINARY STAR — compare OPTICAL DOUBLE STAR

**physical education** *n* **:** education in methods designed to promote the development and care of the body and usu. involving instruction in hygiene and systematic exercises and in various sports and games

**physical environment** *n* **:** the part of the human environment that includes purely physical factors (as soil, climate, water supply)

**physical examination** *n* **:** an examination of the bodily functions and condition of an individual: as **a :** an examination to determine the fitness of an individual for a particular purpose (as military service, participation in a strenuous sport, driving a locomotive) **b :** an examination by a physician under direction from a judge or court of the body and sometimes the mental state of a party to an action usu. before trial and chiefly in actions for damages for personal injury but also in some divorce proceedings and in some criminal causes

**physical geography** *n* **:** a branch of geography that deals with the exterior physical features and changes of the earth in land, sea, and air

**physical geology** *n* **:** a branch of geology made up of structural geology and dynamic geology

**physical inventory** *n* **:** an actual count of all stock or equipment or both of a manufacturing or mercantile concern — distinguished from *book inventory*

**phys·i·cal·ism** \'fizəkəˌlizəm, -zēk-\ *n* -s [G *physikalismus*, fr. ML *physicalis* physical + G *-ismus* -ism] **:** a thesis that the descriptive terms of scientific language are reducible to terms which refer to spatiotemporal things or events or to their properties

**phys·i·cal·ist** \-ˌləst\ *n* -s [[1]*physical* + *-ist*] **1 :** one who holds human thoughts and acts to be determined by physical laws **2 :** an advocate of physicalism

**phys·i·cal·is·tic** \¦===ˈlistik, -tēk\ *also* **phys·i·cal·ist** *adj* **1 :** of or relating to the physical **2 a :** constituting, marked by, or based on physicalism **b :** advocated by physicalists — **phys·i·cal·is·ti·cal·ly** \-tək(ə)lē, -tēk-, -li\ *adv*

**phys·i·cal·i·ty** \ˌfizə'kalədˌē, -zēk-, -latē, -i\ *n* -ES **:** intensely physical orientation **:** predominance of the physical usu. at the expense of the mental, spiritual, or social **:** preoccupation with the body ⟨alert attitudes and nervous silhouettes of the beasts have an intense ~ —*New Republic*⟩ ⟨a vigorous earthy man with strong appetites and great ~⟩

**physical jerks** *n pl, Brit* : CALISTHENICS

**physical language** or **physicalistic language** *n* : the language of physics : a language that employs in addition to the terms of a thing-language those needed for quantitative descriptions

**physical libration** *n* : the oscillation of the moon's body with respect to the earth caused by gravitational stresses on the former's unsymmetrical shape

**phys·i·cal·ly** \'fizək(ə)lē, -zēk-, -li\ *adv* **1 a** : in a physical manner : in accord with physical laws ⟨~ impossible to go⟩ **b** : in respect to the body ⟨~ adapted to cold⟩ **2** *archaic* : as a natural or intrinsic quality : ESSENTIALLY, FUNDAMENTALLY

**physical medicine** *n* : a branch of medicine that deals with the diagnosis and treatment of disease and disability by physical means (as radiation, heat, cold, electricity) — compare PHYSICAL THERAPY

**physical metallurgy** *n* : a branch of metallurgy that deals with the physical properties and structure of metals and alloys

**physical mixture** *n* : a mixture in which the constituent substances are not chemically combined though they may be so intimately mingled (as by solution or diffusion) as to be impossible to separate by simple mechanical means

**phys·i·cal·ness** \'fizəkəlnəs, -zēk-\ *n* -ES : the quality or state of being physical

**physical oceanography** *n* : a branch of oceanography that deals with the physical and chemical properties of ocean water and the topography and composition of the ocean bottom

**physical optics** *n pl but usu sing in constr* : a branch of optics that deals with the description and explanation of all optical phenomena in terms of physical theories (as undulatory theory, electromagnetic phenomena, or quantum mechanics)

**physical pendulum** *n* : a rigid body so mounted on a horizontal axis through its center of suspension that when the body is displaced it vibrates freely about its position of equilibrium — distinguished from *simple pendulum*

**physical poetry** *n* : poetry (as imagist poetry) that is primarily concerned with the projection of a descriptive image of material things

**physical property** *n* : a property (as color, hardness, boiling point) of matter not involving in its manifestation a chemical change

**physical punishment** *n* : CORPORAL PUNISHMENT

**physicals** *pl of* PHYSICAL

**physical science** *n* : the natural sciences (as mineralogy, astronomy, meteorology, geology) that deal primarily with nonliving materials — compare BIOLOGY

**physical sign** *n* : an indication of bodily condition that can be directly perceived (as by sight or hearing) by an examining physician — compare SIGN 7d(1)

**physical therapist** *n* : one skilled in the methods of physical therapy and qualified to use these methods in the treatment of disease or disability usu. under the supervision of a physician

**physical therapy** *n* : the treatment of disease by physical and mechanical means (as massage, regulated exercise, water, light, heat, electricity) — compare PHYSICAL MEDICINE

**physical valuation** *n* : the use of reproduction cost of physical property as a basis for calculating the investment on which stockholders in railroads or public-utility companies are entitled to a reasonable return

**physical value** *n* : the cost of reproduction of physical property less depreciation and other allowances as of a given date

**physic garden** *n* : a botanical garden devoted to the cultivation and display of medicinal plants

**phy·si·cian** \fə'zishən\ *n* -S [ME *fisicien*, fr. OF, fr. *phisike*, *fisique* medical science — more at PHYSICS] **1** : a person skilled in the art of healing : one duly authorized to treat disease : a doctor of medicine — often distinguished from *surgeon* **2** : one who restores (as a troubled spirit or the body politic) : one exerting a remedial or salutary influence ⟨a ~ of the soul⟩ ⟨nature as a ~⟩ **3** *obs* : NATURAL PHILOSOPHER, PHYSICIST

**phy·si·cian·er** \-sh(ə)nə(r)\ *n* -S *archaic* : PHYSICIAN 1

**phy·si·cian·less** \-shənləs\ *adj* : lacking a physician : having no physician in attendance

**phy·si·cian·ly** *adj* : suitable to or typical of a physician ⟨a ~ attitude⟩

**phy·si·cian·ship** \-ˌship\ *n* : the condition or position of a physician; *esp* : a particular appointment as physician ⟨appointed to the municipal ~⟩

**phys·i·cism** \'fizəˌsizəm\ *n* -S : a physical view or explanation of the universe : a materialistic doctrine or theory

**phys·i·cist** \'fizəsəst, *in rapid speech* -zsəst\ *n* -S **1 a** : a specialist in physics **b** *archaic* : a person skilled in one or more branches of natural science **2** : a believer in physicism : MATERIALIST; *esp* : HYLOZOIST

**phys·ick** \'fizik, -zēk\ *archaic var of* PHYSIC

**physicked** *past of* PHYSIC

**physicking** *pres part of* PHYSIC

**physicks** *pres 3d sing of* PHYSIC

**phys·icky** \'fizəkē, -ki\ *adj* [[1]*physic* + *-y*] : like physic in a specified way : resulting from physic ⟨~ cramps⟩

**physic nut** *n* **1** : the seed of a small tropical American tree (*Jatropha curcas*) containing a strongly purgative oil that is poisonous if taken in large quantities **2** : the tree that bears the physic nut and yields a purple dye and a tanning extract

**physic–nut oil** *n* : CURCAS OIL

**physico-** *comb form* [NL, fr. L *physicus* natural, of or relating to natural philosophy, fr. Gk *physikos* — more at PHYSICS] **1** : natural : based on the study of nature ⟨*physico*theology⟩ **2** : physical ⟨*physico*optics⟩ : physical and ⟨*physico*mental⟩ **3** : combined with physics ⟨*physico*chemistry⟩ : relating to physics and ⟨*physico*mathematical⟩

**phys·i·co·chemical** \ˌfizə(ˌ)kō, -zē(-+\ *adj* [alter. of earlier *physicochymical*, fr. NL *physicochymicus* physicochemical (fr. *physico-* + *-chymicus* — fr. *chimicus*, n., alchemist) + E -al — more at CHEMIC] **1** : physical and chemical ⟨~ properties⟩ **2** : relating to physical chemistry ⟨~ experiments⟩ — **phys·i·co·chemically** \"+\ *adv*

**phys·i·co·geographical** \"+\ *adj* : of or relating to physical geography

**phys·i·co·morph** \'==(ˌ)=ˌmȯrf\ *n* [*physico-* + *-morph*] : a detail in art resembling something in inanimate nature

**phys·i·co·mor·phism** \ˌ==(ˌ)='mȯrˌfizəm\ *n* -S [*physico-* + *-morphism*] : a representation or conceptualization of nonphysical things (as deity or spiritual realities) in terms of physical categories

**phys·i·co·theological** \ˌfizə(ˌ)kō, -zē(-+\ *adj* **1** : of, relating to, or based on physicotheology ⟨~ argument⟩ **2** : TELEOLOGICAL ⟨the ~ argument for the existence of God⟩

**phys·i·co·theology** \"+\ *n* : theology illustrated or enforced by evidences of purpose in nature

**physic root** *n* : CULVER'S ROOT

[1]**phys·ics** \'fiziks, -zēks\ *n pl but usu sing in constr* [*physics* pl. of *physic* (intended as trans. of L *physica*, neut. pl., natural science, fr. Gk *physika*, fr. neut. pl. of *physikos* natural); *physic* fr. ME *phisik*, *fisike* medical science, natural science, fr. OF *phisike*, *fisique*, fr. L *physica*, fem. sing., study of nature, fr. Gk *physikē*, fr. fem. of *physikos* natural, fr. *physis* nature + *-ikos* -ic; akin to Gk *phylē* tribe, clan, *phyein* to bring forth — more at BE] **1 physic** *n sing* **a** : the art or practice of healing diseases : the science of therapeutics : the practice or profession of medicine; *also*, *archaic* : medical science : the theory of diseases and their treatment **b** *obs* : medical treatment; *also* : a health-giving or curative practice or regimen **c** (1) : a remedy for disease : a medicinal agent or preparation; *esp* : a medicine (as a laxative) that purges (2) *obs* : a mental, moral, or spiritual medicine **syn** see REMEDY **2** *also* **physic** *archaic* : NATURAL SCIENCE **3 a** : a science that deals with matter and energy and their interactions in the fields of mechanics, acoustics, optics, heat, electricity, magnetism, radiation, atomic structure, and nuclear phenomena **b** : a particular system or branch of physics ⟨classical ~⟩ ⟨nuclear ~⟩ **4** : a treatise or manual of physics ⟨left his ~ on the bench⟩ **5 a** : physical processes and phenomena (as of a particular system) ⟨~ of the living cell⟩ **b** : the physical properties and composition of something ⟨the ~ of different soils⟩ ⟨the study of marine ~⟩

[2]**physics** *pres 3d sing of* PHYSIC

[1]**physid** \'fisəd, 'fīs-\ *adj* [NL *Physidae*] : of or relating to the Physidae

[2]**physid** \"\ *n* -S [NL *Physidae*] : a snail of the family Physidae

**physi·dae** \'fisəˌdē, 'fīs-\ *n pl, cap* [NL, fr. *Physa*, type genus + *-idae*] : a family of freshwater pulmonate snails (suborder Basommatophora) including *Physa* and related genera

**phy·sig·na·thus** \fə'zignəthəs\ *n, cap* [NL, fr. *physi-* + *-gnathus*] : a genus of lizards closely related to *Draco* — see WATER DRAGON

**physio-** — see PHYSI-

**phys·i·o·chemical** \ˌfizēə+\ *adj* [*physi-* + *chemical*] : of or relating to physiological chemistry — **phys·i·o·chemically** \"+\ *adv*

**phys·i·oc·ra·cy** \ˌfizē'äkrəsē, -si\ *n* -ES [F *physiocratie*, fr. *physi-* + *-cratie* -cracy] **1** : government according to supposed natural order **2** : a physiocratic doctrine or system

**phys·i·o·crat** \'fizēəˌkrat\ *n* -S [F *physiocrate*, fr. *physi-* + *-crate* -crat] : a follower of a French physician and economist François Quesnay who in the 18th century founded a system of political and economic doctrines based on the supremacy of natural order and emphasizing the powers of nature as the source of public wealth and national prosperity and the only proper source of public revenue and the necessity for governing so as not to interfere with the natural laws which affect the relations and processes of society and industry — **phys·i·o·crat·ic** \ˌ===ˌkrad·ik, -atik\ *adj*

**phys·i·oc·ra·tism** \ˌ=='äkrəˌtizəm\ *n* -S [*physiocrat* + *-ism*] : PHYSIOCRACY 2

**phys·io·gen·ic** \ˌfizēəˌjenik\ *adj* [ISV *physi-* + *-genic*] **1** : of bodily origin : SOMATOGENIC — often opposed to *psychogenic* **2** *of a plant disease* : due to environmental or physiological abnormalities rather than parasites

**phys·i·ognom·ic** \ˌfizēə(g)ˌ'nämik, -mēk\ *also* **phys·i·ognom·i·cal** \-məkəl, -mēk-\ *adj* [*physiognomic* fr. LL *physiognomicus*, fr. LL *physiognomia* physiognomy + L *-icus* -ic; *physiognomical* fr. LL *physiognomicus* + E *-al*] **1 a** : of, relating to, pertaining to, or characteristic of physiognomy or the physiognomy **b** : relating to or depending upon anthropometric landmarks that are present on the living or the cadaver but not on the skeleton — compare MORPHOLOGICAL **2** : according with the theories of physiognomy ⟨~ laws⟩; *also* : skilled in or treating of physiognomy ⟨~ treatises⟩ — **phys·i·ognom·i·cal·ly** \-mək(ə)lē, -mēk-, -li\ *adv*

**phys·i·ognom·ics** \ˌ==='=miks, -mēks\ *n pl but usu sing in constr* : PHYSIOGNOMY 1

**phys·i·ogno·mist** \ˌfizē'ä(g)nəməst\ *n* -S [*physiognomy* + *-ist*] : one skilled in physiognomy; *esp* : one who professes to tell character through physiognomy

**phys·i·ogno·mize** \ˌ=='=nəˌmīz\ *vt* -ED/-ING/-S [*physiognomy* + *-ize*] : to observe and study the physiognomy of : deduce the character or qualities of from the physiognomy

**phys·i·ogno·mon·ic** \ˌ==ˌ=nəˌmänik\ *also* **phys·i·ogno·mon·i·cal** \-nəkəl\ *adj* [*physiognomonic* fr. Gk *physiognōmonikos*, fr. *physiognōmonia* physiognomy + *-ikos* -ic; *physiognomonical* fr. Gk *physiognōmonikos* + E *-al*] : PHYSIOGNOMIC

**phys·i·ogno·my** \ˌfizē'ä(g)nəmē, -mi\ *n* -ES [alter. (influenced by LL *physiognomia*) of earlier *phisnami*, fr. ME *fysnamye*, *phisnomye*, *phisonomie*, fr. MF *phisonomie*, fr. LL *physiognomia*, fr. Gk *physiognōmia*, alter. of *physiognōmonia*, fr. *physi-* + *gnōmon-*, *gnōmōn* interpreter, discerner + *-ia* -y — more at GNOMON] **1 a** : the technique or art of discovering temperament and character from outward appearance (as from facial features) **b** : divination by means of facial features : fortune-telling or a fortune told by one reading a face **2 a** : the facial features that show the qualities of mind or character by peculiarities of configuration or cast or characteristic expression ⟨a stern ~ indicative of great pride⟩; *broadly* : characteristic facial appearance or type (as of a race or group) ⟨a Grecian ~⟩ ⟨slender aristocratic ~⟩ **b** *obs* : a representation of a human face **3** : external aspect : characteristic or peculiar contour; *also* : inner character or quality as revealed outwardly ⟨the ~ of a mountain⟩ ⟨~ of a political party⟩ **syn** see FACE

**phys·i·og·o·ny** \ˌfizē'ägənē, -ni\ *n* -ES [*physi-* + *-gony*] : a theory of natural origins

**phys·i·og·ra·pher** \ˌ=='ägrəfə(r)\ *n* -S [*physiography* + *-er*] : a specialist in physiography

**phys·io·graph·ic** \ˌfizēəˌgrafik, -fēk\ *also* **phys·io·graph·i·cal** \-fəkəl, -fēk-\ *adj* [prob. fr. (assumed) NL *physiographia* physiography + E *-ic* or *-ical*] : of, relating to, or employing the methods of physiography ⟨~ studies⟩ ⟨~ features⟩ — **phys·io·graph·i·cal·ly** \-fək(ə)lē, -fēk-, -li\ *adv*

**physiographic climax** *n* : an ecological climax that develops in association with a particular physiographic situation and persists only while the physiographic component remains stable — compare EDAPHIC CLIMAX

**physiographic geology** *n* : a branch of geology that deals with topography

**physiographic province** *n* : a region having a particular pattern of relief features or land forms that differs significantly from that of adjacent regions

**phys·i·og·ra·phy** \ˌfizē'ägrəfē, -fi\ *n* -ES [prob. fr. (assumed) NL *physiographia*, fr. NL *physi-* + L *-graphia* -graphy] **1** : a description of nature or natural phenomena in general : phenomenal as distinguished from theoretical or etiological natural science — sometimes used of the descriptive part of a particular science **2 a** : PHYSICAL GEOGRAPHY **b** : the description and genetic interpretation of the relief features of the earth's surface : GEOMORPHOLOGY

**phys·i·ol·a·ter** \ˌfizē'äləd·ə(r)\ *n* -S [fr. *physiolatry*, after such pairs as E *idolatry: idolater*] : a nature worshiper

**phys·i·ol·a·trous** \ˌ==ˌälə·trəs\ *adj* [fr. *physiolatry*, after such pairs as E *idolatry: idolatrous*] **1** : of or relating to nature worship **2** : constituting physiolatry ⟨~ behavior⟩

**phys·i·ol·a·try** \ˌ=='älə·trē, -ri\ *n* -ES [*physi-* + *-latry*] : nature worship

**phys·i·ol·o·ger** \-ləjə(r)\ *n* -S [*physiology* + *-er*] **1** *archaic* : NATURAL PHILOSOPHER **2** *archaic* : a student of vital phenomena : PHYSIOLOGIST

**phys·i·o·log·i·cal** \ˌfizēəˌläjəkəl, -jēk-\ *or* **phys·i·o·log·ic** \-jik, -jēk\ *adj* [*physiological* fr. LL *physiologicus* physiological (fr. Gk *physiologikos* relating to natural science, fr. *physiologia* natural science + *-ikos* -ic) + E *-al; physiologic* fr. LL *physiologicus*] **1** : of or relating to physiology **2** : characteristic of or appropriate to an organism's healthy or normal functioning — contrasted with *pathological* **3** : differing in reactions or functional properties rather than in morphological features ⟨a ~ strain of a bacterium⟩ — see PHYSIOLOGIC RACE **4** : of, relating to, associated with, or caused by disorganization of functions or of metabolism — used in plant pathology and sometimes opposed to *infectious* ⟨a ~ rather than an infective disorder⟩ ⟨a ~ destruction of tissue⟩ — **phys·i·o·log·i·cal·ly** \-jək(ə)lē, -jēk-, -li\ *adv*

**physiological assay** *or* **physiological standardization** *n* : BIOASSAY

**physiological chemistry** *n* : a branch of science dealing with the chemical aspects of physiological and biological systems : BIOCHEMISTRY

**physiological psychology** *n* : a branch of psychology that deals with the effects of normal and pathological physiological processes on mental life

**physiological saline** *or* **physiological saline solution** *or* **physiological salt solution** *n* : a solution of a salt or salts that is essentially isotonic with tissue fluids or blood; *esp* : an approximately 0.9 percent solution of sodium chloride — compare RINGER'S SOLUTION

**physiological spray** *n* : a spray applied primarily to the foliage of plants to supply nutrient elements

**physiological zero** *n* : a temperature that is felt by the skin as neither warm nor cold and that under ordinary conditions usu. falls at about 85° to 90° F

**physiologic race** *also* **physiologic form** *n* : a biotype or group of biotypes within a taxonomic group distinguished by some physiological peculiarity (as host preference, chemical dependence, or pathogenicity) — used esp. of economically important fungi, insects, or bacteria

**physiologic specialization** *n* : the presence or development of physiologic races within a taxonomic group

**phys·i·ol·o·gist** \ˌfizē'äləjəst\ *n* -S [*physiology* + *-ist*] : a specialist in physiology

**phys·i·ol·o·gize** \-ˌjīz\ *vb* -ED/-ING/-S [*physiology* + *-ize*] *vi* **1** *archaic* : to enquire into or theorize on natural phenomena **2** : to formulate theories or explanations in accord with physiology ~ *vt, archaic* : to explain (as a phenomenon) in terms of natural laws

**phys·i·ol·o·giz·er** \-zə(r)\ *n* -S : one that physiologizes

**phys·i·ol·o·goi** \ˌfizē'äləˌgȯi\ *n pl* [Gk, pl. of *physiologos*, fr. *physi-* + *logos* word, speech — more at LEGEND] : the ancient Greek nature philosophers

**phys·i·o·logue** \'fizēəˌlȯg *also* -läg\ *n* -S [LL *physiologus*, fr. Gk *physiologos*] : a natural philosopher : PHYSIOLOGIZER

**phys·i·ol·o·gy** \ˌfizē'älə·jē, -ji\ *n* -ES [L *physiologia*, fr. Gk, fr. *physi-* + *-logia* -logy] **1** *obs* **a** : NATURAL SCIENCE, NATURAL PHILOSOPHY 1 **b** : a particular theory or view of nature **2** : a branch of biology dealing with the processes, activities, and phenomena incidental to and characteristic of life or of living organisms : the study of the functions and activities of living matter (as of organs, tissues, or cells) as such and of the physical and chemical phenomena involved — distinguished from *anatomy;* compare PSYCHOLOGY **3** : the organic processes and phenomena of an organism or any of its parts or of a particular bodily process ⟨the ~ of the jellyfish⟩ ⟨~ of the thyroid gland⟩ ⟨~ of a rust fungus⟩ ⟨the ~ of digestion⟩ **4** : a treatise on physiology

**phys·i·om·e·try** \ˌ=='äm·ə·trē, -ri\ *n* -ES [*physi-* + *-metry*] : the measurement of bodily functions esp. as a feature of anthropometric studies — compare PSYCHOMETRICS

**phys·io·neurosis** \ˌfizēō+\ *n* [NL, fr. *physi-* + *neurosis*] : the somatic component of a psychosomatic ailment

**phys·i·on·o·trace** \ˌfizē'änə·ˌtrās\ *n* -S [F, fr. *physiono-* (fr. *physionomie* facial features, fr. MF *phisonomie*, *physionomie* facial features, physiognomy) + *-trace* (fr. *tracer* to trace, draw) — more at PHYSIOGNOMY, TRACE] : a device used in the late 18th and early 19th centuries to trace the profile of a sitter with chalk or white crayon on a red paper, the image being then completed in black or white crayon

**phys·io·pathologic** \ˌfizēō+\ *also* **phys·io·pathological** \"+\ *adj* [*physi-* + *pathologic*, *pathological*] **1** : of or relating to both physiology and pathology **2** : involving pathological alteration of bodily function — **phys·io·pathology** \"+\ *n*

**phys·io·philosophy** \"+\ *n* [*physi-* + *philosophy;* intended as trans. of G *naturphilosophie*] : a system of natural philosophy expounded by Lorenz Oken (1779–1851) and designed to set forth a natural system of universal relations

**phys·io·plastic** \"+\ *adj* [*physi-* + *plastic*] : following or being in accord with nature ⟨a ~ representation⟩

**phys·io·psychic** \"+\ *adj* [*physi-* + *psychic*] : of, relating to, or involving the physical and the psychical or their interrelations

**phys·io·psychological** \"+\ *adj* : of or relating to physiological psychology

**phys·io·psychology** \"+\ *n* [*physi-* + *psychology*] : PHYSIOLOGICAL PSYCHOLOGY

**phys·io·sociological** \"+\ *adj* [*physi-* + *sociological*] : of or relating to both physiology and sociology

**phys·i·os·o·phy** \ˌfizē'äsəfē\ *n* -ES [*physi-* + *-sophy*] : wisdom about nature

**phys·io·therapeutic** \ˌfizēō+\ *adj* [*physi-* + *therapeutic*] : of or relating to physical therapy

**phys·io·therapeutics** \"+\ *n pl but usu sing in constr* [*physi-* + *therapeutics*] : PHYSICAL THERAPY

**phys·io·therapist** \"+\ *n* [*physiotherapy* + *-ist*] : PHYSICAL THERAPIST

**phys·io·therapy** \"+\ *n* [NL *physiotherapia*, fr. *physi-* + *therapia* therapy] : PHYSICAL THERAPY

**phy·sique** \fə'zēk\ *n* -S [F, fr. *physique*, adj., physical, bodily, fr. L *physicus* natural, fr. Gk *physikos* — more at PHYSIC] **1** : bodily makeup or type : the structure, constitution, appearance, or strength of the human body ⟨a muscular ~⟩ ⟨a race of slender ~ and notable alertness⟩ **2** : physical form or construction (as of a geographic area) ⟨the ~ of the Alps is such as to make access from the north . . . easier than movement northwards from Italy —W.G.East⟩

**syn** BUILD, CONSTITUTION, HABIT: PHYSIQUE designates the total bodily or physical construction or qualities of an individual ⟨tall of stature, slender in *physique* —H.W.H.Knott⟩ ⟨his five-foot-nine-inch *physique* —*Current Biog.*⟩ BUILD, usu. interchangeable with PHYSIQUE, often stresses the geometrically determinable qualities of the physique ⟨a man of rather square *build*⟩ ⟨leisure and heredity gave me a husky *build*⟩ CONSTITUTION is the overall makeup of an individual comprising both mental and physical qualities ⟨extremely high-spirited, my greatest advantage was that my *constitution* did not allow me to be depressed —Osbert Sitwell⟩ ⟨a frail *constitution* necessitated his living in the South —H.E.Starr⟩ ⟨wealthy by inheritance but saving by *constitution* —Ellen Glasgow⟩ HABIT, usu. occurring with a qualifier, is generally confined to characteristic mental or moral quality, makeup, or disposition ⟨the country is where he has gone to indulge a contemplative *habit* —L.J.Halle⟩ ⟨an educated person . . . was one who possessed a certain intellectual *habit* —H.A.Overstreet⟩ ⟨a girl of frivolous *habit*⟩

**phy·siqued** \-kt\ *adj* : having a specified physique

**phy·sis** \'fīsəs\ *n, pl* **phy·ses** \-īˌsēz\ [Gk, nature — more at PHYSIC] : the source of growth or change inherent in or construed as nature : something that grows or becomes

**phys·i·theism** \ˌfizə+\ *n* [*physi-* + *theism*] **1** : ascription of physical form to deity **2** : veneration of the physical powers of nature

**phys·i·urgic** \ˌfizēˌərjik\ *adj* [*physi-* + *-urgic* (as in *theurgic*)] : effected or brought about by natural as distinguished from divine or human influences

**physo-** — see PHYS-

**phy·so·car·pous** \ˌfīsəˌkärpəs\ *adj* [*phys-* + *-carpous*] : having bladdery fruit

**phy·so·car·pus** \ˌ=='=pəs\ *n, cap* [NL, fr. *phys-* + *-carpus*] : a genus of chiefly No. American shrubs (family Rosaceae) with palmately lobed leaves and corymbose white flowers — see NINEBARK

**phy·so·ceph·a·lus** \ˌ=='sefələs\ *n, cap* [NL, fr. *phys-* + *-cephalus*] : a genus of nematode worms (family Thelaziidae) including a common parasite (*P. sexalatus*) of the stomach and small intestine of swine

[1]**phy·so·clist** \'fīsəˌklist\ *n* -S [NL *Physoclisti*] : a teleost fish lacking a duct between the air bladder and the alimentary canal

[2]**physoclist** \"\ *also* **phy·so·clis·tous** \ˌ==ˌklistəs\ *or* **phy·so·clis·tic** \-tik\ *adj* [*physoclist* fr. NL *Physoclisti; physoclistous*, *physoclistic* fr. NL *Physoclisti* + E *-ous* or *-ic*] **1** : of or relating to a physoclist or to the Physoclisti **2** : lacking a duct between the air bladder and alimentary canal

**phy·so·clis·ti** \ˌ=='kliˌstī\ *n pl, cap* [NL, fr. *phys-* + *-clisti* (fr. Gk *kleistos* closed) — more at CLEIST-] *in some classifications* : an order of fishes comprising the physoclists — compare PHYSOSTOMI

**phy·sode** \'fīˌsōd\ *n* -S [G, fr. Gk *physōdēs* full of wind, fr. *physa* bellows — more at PUSTULE] : any of various vesicular intracellular inclusions of brown algae that are of uncertain constitution and function

**phy·so·der·ma** \ˌfīsə'dərmə\ *n, cap* [NL, fr. *phys-* + *-derma*] : a genus of parasitic fungi (order Chytridiales) that have an intracellular thallus of fine fibrils and usu. extracellular sporangia — see BROWN SPOT

**physoderma disease** *n* : BROWN SPOT

**phy·so·gas·tric** \ˌfīsəˌgastrik\ *adj* [*physogastry* + *-ic*] *of an insect* : having the abdomen greatly distended

**phy·so·gas·try** \'==ˌgastrē\ *also* **phy·so·gas·trism** \ˌ=='gaˌstrizəm\ *n, pl* **physogastries** *also* **physogastrisms** [*physogastry* ISV *phys-* + *gastr-* + *-y; physogastrism* fr. *phys-* + *gastr-* + *-ism*] : the condition (as of some termitophiles) of having the abdomen greatly distended — compare STENOGASTRY

**phy·so·nec·tae** \ˌ=='nekˌtē, -ˌtī\ *n pl, cap* [NL, fr. *phys-* + *-nectae*] : a group of siphonophores having a float and usu. a series of swimming bells — **phy·so·nec·tous** \ˌ==ˌnektəs\ *adj*

**phy·soph·o·rae** \fī'säfəˌrē\ [NL, fr. *phys-* + *-phorae*] *syn of* PHYSOPHORIDA

**phy·so·phore** \'fīsəˌfō(ə)r\ *n* -S [NL *Physophorae*] : a siphonophore of the suborder Physophorida

**phy·so·phor·i·da** \ˌ=='fȯrədə\ *n pl, cap* [NL, fr. *Physophora*, included genus (fr. *phys-* + *-phora*) + *-ida*] : a suborder of siphonophores characterized by possession of a pneumatophore

**phy·so·pod** \ˈfīsə,päd\ *or* **phy·sop·o·dan** \(ˈ)fīˈsäpədən\ *adj or n* [*physopod* fr. NL *Physopoda*; *physopodan* fr. NL *Physopoda* + E *-an*] : THYSANOPTERAN, THRIPID

**phy·sop·o·da** \fīˈsäpədə\ [NL, fr. *phys-* + *-poda*] *syn of* THYSANOPTERA

**phy·sop·sis** \fīˈsäpsəs\ *n, cap* [NL, fr. *phys-* + *-opsis*] : a genus of Old World freshwater pulmonate snails (family Bulinidae) including important intermediate hosts of the schistosome (*Schistosoma haematobium*) and other trematodes of medical or veterinary significance

**phy·so·ste·gia** \,fīsəˈstējēə\ *n* [NL, fr. *phys-* + Gk *stegē* roof + NL *-ia*; akin to Gk *stegein* to cover, shelter — more at THATCH] **1** *cap* : a genus of No. American perennial herbs (family Labiatae) having sessile linear to oblong leaves and showy white, rose, or lavender flowers with an inflated 5-toothed calyx — see FALSE DRAGONHEAD **2** -s : any plant of the genus *Physostegia*

**phy·so·stigma** \ˌ≈≈+\ *n* [NL, fr. *phys-* + L *stigma* mark — more at STIGMA] **1** *cap* : a genus of African woody vines (family Leguminosae) whose fruit is the Calabar bean **2** -s : CALABAR BEAN

**phy·so·stig·mine** \,≈≈ˈstig,mēn, -,mən\ *n* -s [ISV *physostigm-* (fr. NL *Physostigma*) + *-ine*; orig. formed as G *physostigmin*] : a crystalline tasteless tricyclic alkaloid $C_{15}H_{21}N_3O_2$ that is the chief alkaloid of the Calabar bean and is used in medicine esp. in the form of its salicylate as a myotic; eseroline methylcarbamate — called also *eserine*

[1]**phy·so·stome** \ˈfīsə,stōm\ *n* -s [NL *Physostomi*] : a teleost fish having a duct between the air bladder and the alimentary canal; *broadly* : one of the Physostomi

[2]**physostome** \"\ *adj* [NL *Physostomi*] : PHYSOSTOMOUS

**phy·sos·to·mi** \fīˈsästə,mī\ *n pl, cap* [NL, fr. *phys-* + *-stomi*] *in some classifications* : an order of teleost fishes comprising those in which the air bladder when present is joined with the esophagus by an open duct and the ventral fins when present are abdominal, including the salmons, herrings, carps, catfishes, and others, and being more or less nearly equivalent to Isospondyli — compare MALACOPTERYGII, PHYSOCLISTI

**phy·sos·to·mous** \(ˈ)≈ˈ≈≈məs\ *also* **phy·so·stoma·tous** \,fīsōˈstämədəs, -stōm-\ *adj* [*physostomous* fr. NL *Physostomi* + E *-ous*; *physostomatous* fr. *phys-* + *-stomatous*] **1** : of or relating to a physostome or the Physostomi : ISOSPONDYLOUS **2** : having a duct between the air bladder and alimentary canal

**phyt-** *or* **phyto-** *comb form* [NL, fr. Gk, fr. *phyton*; akin to Gk *phyein* to bring forth — more at BE] : plant ⟨*phyto*bacteriology⟩ ⟨*phyt*osis⟩

**-phy·ta** \fəd·ə, fətə\ *n pl comb form* [NL, fr. Gk *phyta*, pl. of *phyton*] : plants — in names of taxa ⟨Bryo*phyta*⟩ ⟨Cormo*phyta*⟩

**phyt·albumose** \(ˈ)fīd·+\ *n* [*phyt-* + *albumose*] : a vegetable albumose

**phy·tase** \ˈfī,tās, -āz\ *n* -s [ISV *phytin* + *-ase*] : an esterase present in grains, alfalfa, molds, and kidneys that accelerates the hydrolysis of phytin or phytic acid into inositol and phosphoric acid

**phy·tate** \ˈfī,tāt\ *n* -s [ISV *phytin* + *-ate*] : a salt or ester of phytic acid

**-phyte** \,fīt, *usu* -īd·+V\ *n comb form* -s [ISV, fr. Gk *phyton* plant] **1** : plant having a (specified) characteristic or habitat ⟨xero*phyte*⟩ ⟨micro*phyte*⟩ **2** : pathological growth ⟨osteo*phyte*⟩

**phy·tel·e·phas** \fīˈtelə,fas\ *n, cap* [NL, fr. *phyt-* + Gk *elephas* elephant, ivory — more at ELEPHANT] : a small genus of So. American pinnate-leaved palms having simple drooping flower spikes with many stamens and syncarpous fruit — see IVORY NUT

**phyter·al** \ˈfīd·ərəl, ˈfid-\ *n* -s [*phyt-* + *-eral* (as in *mineral*)] : recognizable plant forms and fossils in coal as distinguished from the organic coal substance

**phythrpst** *abbr* physiotherapist

**-phyt·ic** \ˈfid·|ik, -it|, |ēk\ *adj comb form* [ISV *-phyte* + *-ic*] : like a plant ⟨holo*phytic*⟩

**phytic acid** \ˈfīd·|ik-, ˈfi|, |t|, |ēk-\ *n* [*phytic* fr. *Phytin* + *-ic*] : an acid $C_6H_6(OPO_3H_2)_6$ obtained on acidification of Phytin salt that yields inositol and phosphoric acid on hydrolysis; inositol hexa-phosphoric acid ester

**Phy·tin** \ˈfīt°n\ *trademark* — used for a calcium magnesium salt of phytic acid that occurs as a reserve material esp. in seeds or tubers and is obtained usu. by processing corn steepwater and that is used chiefly as a source of inositol

**phy·tiv·o·rous** \fīˈtiv(ə)rəs\ *adj* [*phyt-* + *-i-* + *-vorous*] : PHYTOPHAGOUS

**phy·to·bacteriology** \ˌfīd·(,)ō, ˌfī(,)tō+\ *n* [*phyt-* + *bacteriology*] : a branch of bacteriology that deals with organisms associated with or pathogenic for plants

**phy·to·bezoar** \ˌ≈≈+\ *n* [ISV *phyt-* + *bezoar*] : a bezoar composed chiefly of undigested compacted vegetable fiber

**phy·to·biology** \"+\ *n* [ISV *phyt-* + *biology*] : plant ecology

**phy·to·cecidium** \"+\ *n* [NL, fr. *phyt-* + *cecidium*] : a gall caused by the presence of a plant (as a parasitic bacterium or fungus) — compare CROWN GALL

**phy·to·chlore** \ˈfīd·ə,klō(ə)r\ *n* -s [*phyt-* + Gk *chlōros* greenish yellow — more at YELLOW] *archaic* : CHLOROPHYLL

**phy·to·ci·dal** \ˌfīd·əˈsīd°l\ *adj* [*phyt-* + *-cide* + *-al*] : killing or tending to kill plants

**phy·to·cide** \ˈ≈≈,sīd\ *n* -s [*phyt-* + *-cide*] : a substance (as a herbicide) used to kill unwanted plants

**phy·to·climatology** \ˌ≈≈+\ *n* [ISV *phyt-* + *climatology*] : the bioclimatology of plants

**phy·to·coe·no·sis** \,fīd·(,)ōsēˈnōsəs\ *n, pl* **phytocoeno·ses** \-,sēz\ [NL, fr. *phyt-* + *coen-* + *-osis*] : the whole body of plants occupying a particular habitat

**phy·to·concretion** \ˌ≈≈+\ *n* [*phyt-* + *concretion*] : PHYTOBEZOAR

**phy·to·flagellata** \ˌfīd·ə+\ [NL, fr. *phyt-* + *Flagellata*] *syn of* PHYTOMASTIGINA

**phy·to·flagellate** \ˌ≈≈+\ *n* [NL *Phytoflagellata*] : PLANTLIKE FLAGELLATE

**phy·to·flu·ene** \,≈≈ˈflü,ēn\ *n* -s [prob. fr. *phyt-* + *flu-* (fr. *fluorescent*) + *-ene*] : a polyene hydrocarbon $C_{40}H_{64}$ occurring with carotenoids in plants

**phy·tog·a·my** \fīˈtägəmē\ *n* -ES [ISV *phyt-* + *-gamy*] : CROSS-FERTILIZATION

**phy·to·genesis** \ˌfīd·ə+\ *n* [NL, fr. *phyt-* + L *genesis*] : the origin and developmental history of plants

**phy·to·genetical** \"+\ *also* **phy·to·genetic** \"+\ *adj* [fr. *phytogenesis*, after E *genesis*: *genetic*, *genetical*] : of or relating to phytogenesis or to the phylogeny of plants — **phy·to·genetically** \"+\ *adv*

**phy·to·gen·ic** \ˌ≈≈ˈjenik\ *adj* [*phyt-* + *-genic*] : of plant origin ⟨a ~ skin lesion⟩; *esp* : of, relating to, or constituting an organic deposit directly attributable to the presence of plants ⟨~ rocks⟩

**phy·tog·e·ny** \fīˈtäjənē\ *n* -ES [*phyt-* + *-geny*] : PHYTOGENESIS

**phy·to·geographer** \ˌfīd·(,)ō+\ *n* [*phytogeography* + *-er*] : a specialist in phytogeography

**phy·to·geographical** \"+\ *or* **phy·to·geographic** \"+\ *adj* [*phytogeographical* fr. *phytogeography* + *-ical*; *phytogeographic* ISV *phytogeography* + *-ic*] : of or relating to phytogeography — **phy·to·geographically** \"+\ *adv*

**phy·to·geography** \"+\ *n* [ISV *phyt-* + *geography*] : the biogeography of plants

**phy·to·globulin** \"+\ *n* [ISV *phyt-* + *globulin*] : a plant globulin

**phy·to·graph** \ˈfīd·ə,graf, -ráf\ *n* [*phyt-* + *-graph*] : a diagram expressing measurements of various plant characteristics by means of lines crossing each other

**phy·tog·ra·phy** \fīˈtägrəfē, -fi\ *n* -ES [NL *phytographia*, fr. *phyt-* + L *-graphia* -graphy] : descriptive botany sometimes including plant taxonomy

**phy·to·hormone** \ˌfīd·(,)ō, ˌfī(,)tō+\ *n* [ISV *phyt-* + *hormone*] : PLANT HORMONE

**phy·toid** \ˈfī,tȯid\ *adj* [ISV *phyt-* + *-oid*] : resembling a plant

**phy·tol** \ˈfī,tōl, -ȯl\ *n* -s [ISV *phyt-* + *-ol*] : an oily aliphatic diterpenoid primary alcohol $C_{20}H_{39}OH$ obtained by hydrolysis of chlorophyll (as by means of chlorophyllase), also made synthetically, and used in synthesizing vitamin E and vitamin $K_1$

**phy·to·lac·ca** \ˌfīd·əˈlakə\ *n, cap* [NL, fr. *phyt-* + *lacca* lac — more at LACCA] : a genus (the type of the family Phytolaccaceae) of mostly tropical perennial herbs or occasionally trees having a 5- to 15-celled berry — see POKEWEED, UMBRA TREE

**phy·to·lac·ca·ce·ae** \ˌ≈≈laˈkāsē,ē\ *n pl, cap* [NL, fr. *Phytolacca*, type genus + *-aceae*] : a family of chiefly tropical herbs, shrubs, and trees (order Caryophyllales) with racemose flowers and fruit of many carpels — **phy·to·lac·ca·ceous** \ˌ≈≈≈ˈkāshəs\ *adj*

**phy·tol·a·try** \fīˈtälətrē\ *n* -ES [*phyt-* + *-latry*] : worship of plants

**phy·to·lite** \ˈfīd·ə,līt\ *or* **phy·to·lith** \-,lith\ *n* -s [*phyt-* + *-lite* or *-lith*] : a plant fossil

**phy·to·log·ic** \ˌfīd·əˈläjik, -jēk\ *or* **phy·to·log·i·cal** \-jəkəl, -jēk-\ *adj* [*phytologic* ISV *phytology* + *-ic*; *phytological* fr. *phytology* + *-ical*] : BOTANICAL

**phy·to·log·i·cal·ly** \-jək(ə)lē, -jēk-\ *adv* : BOTANICALLY

**phy·tol·o·gist** \fīˈtäləjəst\ *n* -s [*phytology* + *-ist*] : BOTANIST

**phy·tol·o·gy** \-jē, -ji\ *n* -ES [NL *phytologia*, fr. *phyt-* + L *-logia* -logy] : BOTANY

**phy·to·mas·tig·i·da** \ˌfīd·ō,masˈstijədə\ *or* **phy·to·mas·ti·go·da** \-,mastəˈgōdə\ *or* **phy·to·mas·ti·go·ta** \-ōd·ə\ *syn of* PHYTOMASTIGINA

**phy·to·mas·ti·gi·na** \-,mastəˈjīnə\ *n pl, cap* [NL, fr. *phyt-* + *mastig-* + *-ina*] : a subclass of Mastigophora comprising the plantlike flagellates that are often regarded as unicellular algae, have chromatophores which contain chlorophyll, usu. secrete a covering of cellulose, and have a pigmented eyespot — compare ZOOMASTIGINA

**phy·to·mer** \ˈfīd·əmə(r)\ *n, pl* **phytomers** \-mə(r)z\ *also* **phy·tom·era** \fīˈtämərə\ [NL *phytomeron*, fr. *phyt-* + *-meron* (fr. Gk *meros* part) — more at MERIT] : one of the individual structural units that in serial arrangement make up the body of a plant ⟨a bud-bearing node is a typical ~⟩

**phy·tom·e·ter** \fīˈtäməd·ə(r), -mətə-\ *n* [*phyt-* + *-meter*] : a plant or group of plants grown usu. under controlled conditions and used as a measure of the physiological responses to various environmental factors

**phy·to·met·ric** \ˌfīd·əˈme·trik\ *adj* : of or relating to phytometry

**phy·tom·e·try** \fīˈtämə·trē, -ri\ *n* -ES [*phyt-* + *-metry*] : the measurement of the physiological responses of a plant or group of plants to various environmental factors

[1]**phy·tom·o·nad** \fīˈtämə,nad\ *adj* [NL *Phytomonadina*] : of or relating to the Phytomonadina

[2]**phytomonad** \"\ *n* -s [NL *Phytomonadina*] : a flagellate of the order Phytomonadina

**phy·to·mon·a·di·na** \ˌfīd·(,)ō,mänəˈdīnə\ *n pl, cap* [NL, fr. *Phytomonad-*, *Phytomonas* (genus of flagellates) + *-ina*] : an order of small green plantlike flagellates (subclass Phytomastigina) comprising solitary forms (as *Polytoma uvella*) and complex colonial forms (as members of the genus *Volvox*) — compare VOLVOCALES

**phy·tom·o·nas** \fīˈtämənəs, -,nas\ *n, cap* [NL, fr. *phyt-* + *-monas*] **1** : a genus of flagellates (family Trypanosomatidae) that are morphologically similar to members of the genus *Leptomonas* but alternate between a hemipterous insect and a latex plant as hosts **2** [NL, fr. *phyt-* + *-monas*] *in some esp former classifications* : a large genus of plant-pathogenic bacteria (family Pseudomonadaceae) the members of which are now usu. divided between the genera *Pseudomonas* and *Xanthomonas*

**phy·to·morph** \ˈfīd·ə,mȯrf\ *n* [*phyt-* + *-morph*] : a conventionalized representation of a plant — used esp. of primitive art

**phy·to·mor·phic** \ˌ≈≈ˈmȯrfik\ *adj* [ISV *phyt-* + *-morphic*] : having or represented with the attributes of a plant ⟨~ bryozoans⟩

**phy·to·myx·i·nae** \ˌfīd·(,)ō,mikˈsī,nē\ *n pl, cap* [NL, fr. *phyt-* + *myx-* + *-inae*] *in some classifications* : a class of fungi coextensive with the order Plasmodiophorales

**phy·to·my·za** \ˌfīd·əˈmīzə\ *n, cap* [NL, fr. *phyt-* + *-myza*] : a genus of two-winged flies having larvae that are leaf miners in corn, sugarcane, and related plants

**phy·ton** \ˈfī,tän\ *n* -s [NL, fr. Gk, plant — more at PHYT-] **1** : a structural unit of a plant consisting of a leaf and its associated portion of stem : PHYTOMER **2** : the smallest part of a stem, root, or leaf that when severed may grow into a new plant : a potential cutting — **phy·ton·ic** \(ˈ)fīˈtänik\ *adj*

**phy·to·na·di·one** \ˌfīd·ōnəˈdī,ōn\ *n* -s [*phyto-* (fr. *phytyl*) + *na-* (fr. *napthoquinone*) + *-dione*] : VITAMIN K 1a — used in the U. S. Pharmacopoeia

**phy·to·parasite** \ˌfīd·(,)ō+\ *n* [*phyt-* + *parasite*] : a parasitic plant

**phy·to·pathogen** \ˌ≈≈+\ *n* [*phyt-* + *pathogen*] : an organism parasitic on a plant host — **phy·to·pathogenic** \ˌ≈≈+\ *adj* — **phy·to·pathogenicity** \ˌ≈≈+\ *n*

**phy·to·pathologic** \ˌ≈≈+\ *or* **phy·to·pathological** \ˌ≈≈+\ *adj* [*phytopathologic* ISV *phytopathology* + *-ic*; *phytopathological* fr. *phytopathology* + *-ical*] : of or relating to plant pathology

**phy·to·pathologist** \ˌ≈≈+\ *n* [ISV *phytopathology* + *-ist*] : a plant pathologist

**phy·to·pathology** \ˌ≈≈+\ *n* [ISV *phyt-* + *pathology*] **1** : PLANT PATHOLOGY **2** : an abnormal condition caused by parasitic plants

[1]**phy·toph·a·ga** \fīˈtäfəgə\ *n pl, cap* [NL, fr. *phyt-* + *-phaga*] : any of several groups of vegetable-feeding animals: as **a** : a very large division of Coleoptera comprising beetles that have all the tarsi apparently 4-jointed, the head not rostrate, the labrum exposed, and the palpi never wholly occluded in the mouth and including the families Bruchidae, Chrysomelidae, and Cerambycidae or being made coextensive with Chrysomelidae **b** : a division of Hymenoptera comprising forms (as the sawflies) with larvae that feed on plants **c** : a group of Edentata including the sloths

[2]**phytophaga** \"\ *n, cap* [NL, fr. *phyt-* + *-phaga*] : a genus of gall midges

**phy·toph·a·gan** \-gən\ *also* **phy·to·phage** \ˈfīd·ə,fāj\ *n* -s [*phytophagan* fr. NL [1]*Phytophaga* + E *-an*; *phytophage* fr. NL [1]*Phytophaga*] : a phytophagous animal; *esp* : one of the Phytophaga

**phy·to·phag·ic** \ˌfīd·əˈfajik\ *adj* [*phyt-* + *-phagic* (fr. *-phagy* + *-ic*)] : PHYTOPHAGOUS 1

**phy·to·pha·gin·e·ae** \ˌ≈≈fəˈjinē,ē\ *n pl, cap* [NL, fr. *phyt-* + *phag-* + *-ineae*] *in some classifications* : a suborder of Virales comprising plant-parasitic viruses

**phy·toph·a·gous** \fīˈtäfəgəs\ *adj* [*phyt-* + *-phagous*] **1** : feeding on plants — used esp. of a lower animal (as an insect); distinguished from *herbivorous* and *vegetarian* **2** [NL [1]*Phytophaga* + E *-ous*] : of or relating to the Phytophaga

**phy·toph·a·gy** \-jē\ *n* -ES [*phytophagous* + *-y*] : the condition of being phytophagous

**phy·to·pharmacology** \ˌfīd·(,)ō+\ *n* [*phyt-* + *pharmacology*] : the study of the influences of drugs on the physiological processes of plants

**phy·toph·i·lous** \fīˈtäfələs\ *adj* [*phyt-* + *-philous*] : fond of plants : living or feeding on plants — **phy·toph·i·ly** \-əlē\ *n* -ES

**phy·toph·tho·ra** \fīˈtäfthərə\ *n* [NL, fr. *phyt-* + *-phthora*] **1** *cap* : a genus of destructive parasitic fungi (family Pythiaceae) having conidia that usu. act as sporangia esp. under moist cool conditions and sporangiophores that are simple or branched — see LATE BLIGHT, PYTHIACYSTIS **2** -s **a** : any fungus of the genus *Phytophthora* **b** : a disease (as late blight) caused by such a fungus

**phy·to·plankter** \ˌfīd·ə+\ *n* [*phyt-* + *plankter*] : a planktonic plant ⟨diatoms and other ~s⟩

**phy·to·plankton** \ˌ≈≈+\ *n* [ISV *phyt-* + *plankton*] : plankton consisting of plant life — **phy·to·planktonic** \ˌ≈≈+\ *adj*

**phy·to·plasm** \ˈfīd·ə,plazəm\ *n* -s [ISV *phyt-* + *-plasm*] : plant protoplasm

[1]**phy·top·tid** \fīˈtäptəd\ *adj* [NL *Phytoptidae*] : of or relating to the Phytoptidae

[2]**phytoptid** \"\ *n* -s [NL *Phytoptidae*] : a mite of the family Phytoptidae

**phy·top·ti·dae** \-təˌdē\ *n pl, cap* [NL, fr. *Phytoptus*, type genus + *-idae*] : a family of minute plant-parasitic mites that includes various destructive bud mites and blister mites and is often treated as a subfamily of Eriophyidae

**phy·top·tus** \-təs\ *n, cap* [NL, fr. *phyt-* + *-ptus* (fr. Gk *ptoia* terror, flight); akin to Gk *petesthai* to fly — more at FEATHER] : the type genus of Phytoptidae

**phy·to·saur** \ˈfīd·ə,sȯ(ə)r\ *n* -s [NL *Phytosauria*] : a reptile of the suborder Phytosauria

**phy·to·sau·ria** \ˌ≈≈ˈsȯrēə\ *n pl, cap* [NL, fr. *phyt-* + *-sauria*] : a suborder of Thecodontia comprising Triassic reptiles similar to long-snouted crocodiles but having narial openings far back on the head — **phy·to·sau·ri·an** \ˌ≈≈ˈsȯrēən\ *adj or n*

**phy·to·serology** \ˌfīd·ō+\ *n* [*phyt-* + *serology*] : a branch of serology that deals with plants and plant products esp. in respect to identification, determination of relationships, and study of plant viruses

**phy·to·sis** \fīˈtōsəs\ *n, pl* **phyto·ses** \-ō,sēz\ [NL, fr. *phyt-* + *-osis*] : an infection with or a disease caused by parasitic plants

**phy·to·sociological** \ˌfīd·(,)ō+\ *also* **phy·to·sociologic** \ˌ≈≈+\ *adj* : of or relating to phytosociology : pertinent to or involved in floral interrelations ⟨~ factors⟩ — **phy·to·sociologically** \ˌ≈≈+\ *adv*

**phy·to·sociologist** \ˌ≈≈+\ *n* : a specialist in phytosociology

**phy·to·sociology** \ˌ≈≈+\ *n* [*phyt-* + *sociology*] : a branch of ecology that deals with the interrelations among the flora of particular areas and esp. with plant communities

**phy·tos·te·rol** \fīˈtästə,rōl, -rōl\ *n* [ISV *phyt-* + *-sterol* (as in *cholesterol*)] : any of a group of sterols (as ergosterol, sitosterol, stigmasterol) derived from plants

**phy·to·succivorous** \ˌfīd·(,)ō+\ *adj* [*phyt-* + *succivorous*] : feeding on the sap of plants — used esp. of an insect

**phy·to·therapy** \ˌfīd·ō+\ *n* [ISV *phyt-* + *therapy*] **1** : the use of vegetable drugs in medicine **2** : the treatment of disease or parasitism in the individual plant

**phy·to·tom·i·dae** \ˌfīd·əˈtämə,dē\ *n pl, cap* [NL, fr. *Phytotoma*, type genus (fr. *phyt-* + Gk *tomē* action of cutting, fr. *temnein* to cut) + *-idae* — more at TOME] : a family of So. American passerine birds that resemble finches but have serrated bills with which they nip off the young shoots and buds of plants

**phy·tot·o·my** \fīˈtäd·əmē\ *n* -ES [ISV *phyt-* + *-tomy*] : the anatomy of plants

**phy·to·toxic** \ˌfīd·ə+\ *adj* [*phyt-* + *toxic*] **1** : of or relating to a phytotoxin **2** : poisonous to plants — **phy·to·toxicity** \ˌ≈≈+\ *n*

**phy·to·toxin** \ˌ≈≈+\ *n* [ISV *phyt-* + *toxin*] : a toxin (as ricin) produced by a plant

**phy·to·zo·on** \ˌfīd·əˈzō,än\ *n, pl* **phyto·zoa** \-ōə\ [NL, fr. *phyt-* + *-zoon*] : ZOOPHYTE

**phy·tyl** \ˈfīd·°l\ *n* -s [*phytol* + *-yl*] : the univalent radical $C_{20}H_{39}$ derived from phytol

[1]**pi** \ˈpī\ *n* -s [MGk, fr. Gk *pei*, of Sem origin; akin to Heb *pē*] **1** : the 16th letter of the Greek alphabet — symbol Π or π; see ALPHABET table **2 a** : the symbol π denoting the ratio of the circumference of a circle to its diameter **b** : the ratio itself : a transcendental number having a value to eight decimal places of 3.14159265

[2]**pi** *also* **pie** \"\ *n, pl* **pies** [origin unknown] **1 a** : type or type matter that is spilled, mixed, or incorrectly distributed ⟨when . . . a disaster occurs and the type falls or collapses, the resulting disordered heap is the famous printer's ~ —Seán Jennett⟩ **b** : the condition of pi ⟨a great deal of what he has set up is often thrown into ~ —John Southward⟩ **2** : a pi character or matrix **syn** see CONFUSION

[3]**pi** \"\ *adj* **1** : not intended to appear in final printing because improperly set or containing a temporary instruction to the printer — used of a line of type or print **2** : not carried in a keyboard-controlled channel and therefore insertable only by hand — used of a typesetting-machine matrix

[4]**pi** *also* **pie** \"\ *vb* **pied**; **pied**; **piing** *or* **pieing**; **pies** *vt* : to spill or throw (type or type matter) into disorder ⟨~ a case⟩ ⟨~ a form⟩ ⟨~ a galley⟩ ~ *vi* : to become pied ⟨some display matter ~es easily⟩

[5]**pi** \"\ *adv* [[3]*pi*] : as a pi character ⟨border matrices always run ~ but can have special combinations cut to run in magazine —*Intertype Faces*⟩

[6]**pi** \"\ *adj* [short for *pious*] *Brit* : MORALIZING, PREACHY, GOODY-GOODY

**pi** *abbr* piaster

**PI** *abbr* **1** paper insulated **2** photo interpreter; photo interpretation

[1]**pia** \ˈpīə\ *n* -s [by shortening] : PIA MATER

[2]**pia** \ˈpēə\ *n* -s [Hawaiian] : a perennial herb (*Tacca pinnatifida*) of East India, Australasia, and Polynesia cultivated for its large starch-yielding root — see OTAHEITE ARROWROOT

**pia-arach·noid** \ˈ≈≈ˌ≈ˈ≈\ *or* **pi·a·rach·noid** \,pīəˈrak,nȯid\ *n* [[1]*pia*] : the pia mater and the arachnoid regarded as a single membrane investing the brain and spinal cord — **pia-arachnoidal** \ˌ≈≈≈ˌ≈≈\ *adj*

**pia·ce·vo·le** \pyäˈchävə,lā\ *adv* (*or adj*) [It, fr. LL *placibilis* fr. L *placēre* to please + *-ibilis* -ible — more at PLEASE] : PLEASANTLY, AGREEABLY — used as a direction in music

**pi·a·cle** \ˈpīəkəl\ *n* -s [L *piaculum*, fr. *piare* to appease, atone for — more at PIOUS] **1** *archaic* : a sacrificial offering : PIACULUM **2** *archaic* : OFFENSE, SIN, CRIME

**pi·ac·u·lar** \(ˈ)pīˈakyələ(r)\ *adj* [L *piacularis*, fr. *piaculum* + *-aris* -ar] **1** : SACRIFICIAL, EXPIATORY ⟨required to make a ~ offering for their sins⟩ **2** : requiring expiation : SINFUL, HEINOUS ⟨~ offense⟩ — **pi·ac·u·lar·ly** *adv* — **pi·ac·u·lar·ness** *n* -ES

**pi·ac·u·lum** \pīˈakyələm\ *n, pl* **piacu·la** \-lə\ [L] : a sacrificial rite by which communion is reestablished between a god and worshiper : an expiatory offering

**pia family** *n* [[2]*pia*] : TACCACEAE

[1]**piaffe** \ˈpyaf\ *vi* **piaffed**; **piaffed**; **piaffing**; **piaffes** [F *piaffer*, lit., to strut] *of a horse* : to execute a piaffe

[2]**piaffe** \"\ *n* -s : a dressage movement consisting of a collected trot executed in place

**piaffer** *vi* -ED/-ING/-S [F] *obs* : PIAFFE

**pi·al** \ˈpī(ə)l\ *adj* [[1]*pia* + *-al*] : of or relating to the pia mater ⟨a ~ artery⟩

**pia ma·ter** \ˈpīəˈmād·ə(r), -ātə-\ *n* [ME, fr. ML, fr. L, tender mother] : the delicate and highly vascular membrane of connective tissue investing the brain and spinal cord, lying internal to the arachnoid and dura mater, dipping down between the convolutions of the brain, and sending an ingrowth into the anterior fissure of the cord

**pia-ma·tral** \ˌpīəˈmā·trəl\ *adj* [*pia mater* + *-al*] : of or relating to the pia mater : PIAL

**pi·an** \pēˈan, ˈpyän\ *n* -s [F, fr. Tupi & Guarani] : YAWS

**pi·a·nette** \,pēəˈnet\ *n* -s [[3]*piano* + *-ette*] : PIANINO

**pian·gen·do** \(ˈ)pyänˈjen(,)dō\ *adv* (*or adj*) [It, fr. L *plangendum*, gerund of *plangere* to lament — more at PLAINT] : PLAINTIVELY — used as a direction in music

**pi·a·ni·no** \,pēəˈnē(,)nō\ *n* -s [It, dim. of *piano*] : a small upright piano

**pi·a·nism** \ˈpēə,nizəm, pēˈa,-\ *n* -s [[3]*piano* + *-ism*] **1** : the art or technique of piano playing **2** : the composition or adaptation of music for performance on the piano

[1]**pi·a·nis·si·mo** \,pēəˈnisə,mō\ *adv* (*or adj*) [It, fr. *piano* softly + *-issimo*, suffix denoting a high degree of (fr. L *-issimus*, superl. suffix)] : very softly — used as a direction in music; abbr. *pp*, *ppp*

[2]**pianissimo** \"\ *n, pl* **pianissi·mi** \-sə(,)mē\ *or* **pianissimos** : a passage played, sung, or spoken very softly ⟨whispering *pianissimi*⟩

**pi·an·ist** \pēˈanəst, ˈpēən-\ *n* -s [F *pianiste*, fr. It *pianista*, fr. *piano* + *-ista* -ist] : one who plays the piano; *esp* : a skilled or professional performer on the piano

**pi·a·niste** \,pēəˈnēst\ *n* -s [F] : PIANIST; *often* : a female pianist

**pi·a·nis·tic** \ˌpēəˈnistik\ *adj* [[3]*piano* + *-istic*] **1** : relating to or characteristic of the piano **2** [*pianist* + *-ic*] : skilled in or adapted to piano playing — **pi·a·nis·ti·cal·ly** \-tək(ə)lē\ *adv*

**pi·a·nis·tics** \ˌ≈≈ˈnistiks\ *n pl but sometimes sing in constr* : the art or practice of performing on the piano; *esp* : display of virtuosity in piano playing

**pianist's cramp** *n* : painful spasm of the muscles of the forearm caused by excessive piano playing

**pi·an·ka·shaw** *or* **pi·an·ke·shaw** \pīˈaŋkə,shȯ\ *n, pl* **piankashaw** *or* **piankashaws** *or* **piankeshaw** *or* **piankeshaws** *usu cap* **1** : an Indian people of southwestern Indiana associated with the Miami **2 :** a member of the Piankashaw people

**pi·an·net** *or* **pi·a·net** \'pīə,net\ *n* -S [prob. fr. ¹*pie* + *Annet*, fr. *Ann*, feminine name + *-et*] : MAGPIE 1a

¹**pi·a·no** \pē'ä(,)nō, -'ā(-\ *adv* (*or adj*) [It, fr. LL *planus* smooth, graceful] : SOFTLY, QUIETLY — used as a direction in music; opposed to *forte;* abbr. *p*

²**piano** \"\ *n* -S : a softly performed passage or tone (as in a voice or instrument)

³**pi·ano** \pē'a(,)nō, -,nə *sometimes* -'ä(-\ *n* -S [It, short for *pianoforte*, fr. *piano e forte* soft and strong, fr. *piano* soft (fr. LL *planus* smooth, graceful, fr. L, even, level, flat) + *e* and (fr. L *et*) + *forte* strong (fr. L *fortis*); fr. its being chiefly distinguished from the spinet in that its tones could be made softer or stronger — more at FLOOR, FORT] **1 :** a stringed percussion instrument structurally derived from the dulcimer but historically from the clavichord and harpsichord and having steel wire strings stretched over a sounding board that sound when struck by felt-covered hammers operated from a keyboard and pedals that alter or modify the quantity and quality of sound produced — called also *pianoforte;* see GRAND PIANO, UPRIGHT PIANO **2 :** a machine operated by a keyboard for perforating the cards for a jacquard apparatus

**piano accordion** *n* **:** an accordion with a keyboard for the right hand resembling and corresponding to the middle register of a piano keyboard

piano accordion

**piano as·sai** \-ə'sī\ *adv* (*or adj*) [It] **:** very softly — used as a direction in music

**pi·ano·forte** \pē'anə,fōr|d·(ē), |t(ē), -fȯr|, -fōə|, -fȯ(ə)|, ═,══:═; *in the 4-syllable pronunc,* |d· *does not occur before consonants other than* ᵊl\ *n* -S [It] **:** PIANO 1

**pi·an·o·fort·ist** \pē'anə,fōrd·əst\ *n* -S **:** PIANIST

**pi·an·o·graph** \pē'anə,graf, -rȧf\ *n* [³*piano* + *-graph*] **:** a melograph applied to a piano

**piano hinge** *n* **:** a hinge having a thin pin joint and extending along the full length of the turning part — called also *continuous hinge*

**pi·a·no·la** \,pēə'nōlə\ *n* -S [*Pianola*] **1 :** a deal or hand (as in contract) that offers no difficulty in the play **2 :** something easy to perform or accomplish **:** CINCH

**Pianola** \"\ *trademark* — used for an automatic piano player

**piano legs** *n pl* **:** fat or disproportionately thick legs ⟨some were bowlegged and some were knock-kneed, some had pipestems and some *piano legs* —Esther Forbes⟩

**pi·an·o·logue** \pē'anᵊl,ȯg *also* -,äg\ *n* -S [³*piano* + *-logue*] **:** a comic monologue accompanied by piano playing

**pia·no no·bi·le** \'pyä(,)nō'nōbē,lā\ *n* [It] **:** the principal story of a house

**piano organ** *n* **:** a mechanical piano built like a barrel organ and operated like a hand organ **:** STREET PIANO

**piano player** *n* **1 :** PIANIST **2 :** a mechanism for reproducing the playing of piano music usu. housed in a portable cabinet and consisting of an electropneumatic apparatus for turning a perforated roll representing the composition to be played and for actuating a series of levers which operate the piano keys

**piano quartet** *n* **:** a musical composition written for piano, violin, viola, and cello; *also* **:** the performers for such a composition

**piano score** *n* **:** a musical score having the separate instrumental parts condensed upon two staffs

**piano–violin** \═'═(,)═,══'══\ *n* **:** a sostinente pianoforte producing tones resembling those of the violin

**piano wire** *n* [so called fr. its being used for the strings of pianos] **:** steel wire of high tensile strength and evenness of thickness containing 0.75 to 0.85 percent carbon

**pi·a·po·co** *n, pl* **piapoco** *or* **piapocos** *usu cap* **1 a :** an Arawakan people of the lower Guaviar river in Colombia, So. America **b :** a member of such people **2 :** the language of the Piapoco people

**piarachnoid** *var of* PIA-ARACHNOID

**pi·a·rist** \'pīərəst\ *n* -S *usu cap* [prob. fr. (assumed) NL *piarista*, fr. *piarum* (in the phrase *patres scholarum piarum* fathers of the religious schools) + *-ista* -ist] **:** a member of a religious teaching institute founded at Rome early in the 17th century by St. Joseph of Calasanza

**pias** *pl of* PIA

**pias** *abbr* piaster

**pi·as·sa·va** *also* **pi·as·sa·ba** *or* **pi·a·sa·va** *or* **pi·a·sa·ba** \,pēə'sävə, -äbə\ *n* -S [Pg *piassaba*, fr. Tupi *piaçaba*] **1 a :** a coarse brown fiber that invests the bases of the leaf sheaths of a Brazilian palm and is used in making ropes, mats, and brushes; *also* **:** the palm (*Attalea funifera*) that bears this fiber and yields the coquilla nut **2 :** a fiber from a Brazilian palm (*Leopoldinia piassaba*) common along the Amazon river; *also* **:** the tree yielding this fiber **3 :** the stiff coarse bast fiber of an African palm (*Raphia vinifera*) **4 :** coarse fiber derived from any of several palms (as tucum, gomuti, and hemp palm)

**piast** \'pyäst\ *n* -S *usu cap* [after *Piast*, legendary peasant who was believed to be the founder of the first dynasty of Polish rulers] **1 :** a member of the first dynasty of Polish rulers that ended with the death of Casimir III in 1370 **2 a :** a member of the native Polish nobility **b :** a man of purely Polish descent

**pi·as·ter** *or* **pi·as·tre** \pē'astə(r)\ *n* -S [F *piastre*, fr. It *piastra* thin metal plate, coin, fr. OIt, fr. L *emplastra*, *emplastrum* plaster — more at PLASTER] **1 a :** a Spanish dollar **:** PIECE OF EIGHT — see MONEY table **b :** a coin or note representing one piaster **2 a** (1) **:** any of several monetary units of some Middle Eastern countries (as Turkey, Egypt, Syria, or Libya) equal to ¹⁄₁₀₀ pound — see MONEY table (2) **:** a former Saudi Arabian unit equal to ¹⁄₂₂ rial **b :** a coin representing one of these units **3 a :** a monetary unit of Cyprus equal to ¹⁄₉ shilling or ¹⁄₁₈₀ pound sterling **b :** a coin representing this unit **4 :** the basic monetary unit of French Indochina until 1954 and of the Republic of Vietnam from 1955

**pi·at** \'pī,at\ *n* -S [projector infantry antitank] **:** a short-range antitank gun used in the British and Canadian armies weighing 33 pounds and firing a 2.75-pound projectile that explodes on impact with force sufficient to penetrate four inches of tempered armor plate

**piat·ti** \'pyäd·ē\ *n pl* [It, fr. pl. of *piatto* plate, fr. *piatto* level, flat, fr. (assumed) VL *plattus* — more at PLATE] **:** CYMBALS

**pi·az·za** \pē'azə, *in sense 1 usu* -atsə\ *n, pl* **piazzas** \-əz\ *or* **piaz·ze** \-t(,)sā\ [It, fr. L *platea* street, courtyard — more at PLACE] **1** *pl* **piazze :** an open square in an Italian or other European town **:** a town square or open market **2 a :** an arcaded and roofed gallery that often surrounds an open court; *also* **:** a portico or single colonnade before a building **b** *chiefly North & Midland* **:** VERANDA, PORCH **syn** see BALCONY

**pi·az·zaed** \-əd\ *adj* **:** furnished with a piazza ⟨long-*piazzaed* summer hotel⟩

**pib·ble** \'pibəl\ *dial var of* PEBBLE

**pib·gorn** \'pib,gȯrn\ *also* **pib·corn** \-,kȯrn\ *n* -S [W, fr. *pib* pipe + *corn* horn] **:** an obsolete Welsh single-reed woodwind instrument similar to the hornpipe

pibgorn

**pi·blok·to** *or* **pi·block·to** \pə'bläk(,)tō\ *n* -S [Esk *piblokto*] **:** a hysteria among Eskimos characterized by excitement and sometimes by mania, usu. followed by depression, and occurring chiefly in winter and usu. to women

**pi·broch** *or* **piob·aireachd** \'pē,bräk\ *n* -S [ScGael *piobaireachd* pipe-music, fr. *piobair* piper, fr. *pìob* pipe] **:** elaborate variations for the Scottish Highland bagpipe on a traditional theme

¹**pic** \'pēk\ *n* -S [F, prob. fr. Sp *pico*, fr. *picar* to prick, pierce, prob. fr. (assumed) VL *piccare* — more at PIKE (weapon)] **:** PEAK 5a

²**pic** \"\ *n* -S [F, fr. MF *picq*, fr. *piquer* to prick — more at PIKE] **:** ³PIQUE

³**pic** *var of* PIK

⁴**pic** \'pik\ *n, pl* **pics** *or* **pix** \-ks\ [short for *picture*] **1 :** PHOTOGRAPH ⟨these ~*s* tell the story —*Springfield (Mass.) Republican*⟩ **2 :** MOTION PICTURE

⁵**pic** \"\ *n* -S [Sp *pica*, fr. *picar* to prick] **1 :** the picador's lance **2** [by shortening] **:** PICADOR

⁶**pic** \"\ *vt* **pic·ed** \-kt\ **pic·ed; pic·ing** \-kiŋ\ **pics** \-ks\ **:** to prod or thrust at (a bull) with a pic

¹**pi·ca** \'pīkə\ *n* -S [prob. fr. ML, collection of church rules, prob. fr. L, magpie; perh. fr. its use in printing the service book and its resemblance to the colors of the bird] **1 :** an old size of type between small pica and english **2 a :** a size of type equivalent to 12 point **b :** a unit equal to 12 point or about ⅙ inch used in measuring composing materials, line and cut widths, and type-page dimensions — compare EM, LINE 9c, POINT SYSTEM **3 :** a size of typewriter type with 10 characters to the linear inch and six lines to the vertical inch

²**pica** \"\ *n* [NL, fr. L, magpie — more at ¹PIE] **1** *cap* **:** the genus containing the magpies **2** -S [prob. fr. the fact that the magpie is omnivorous] **:** a craving for and eating of unnatural substances (as chalk, ashes, or bones) that occurs in nutritional deficiency states (as aphosphorosis) in man or animals or in hysteric or insane conditions in man **:** GEOPHAGY — called also *depraved appetite;* compare LICKING DISEASE, WOOL EATING

**pi·ca·cho** \pə'kä(,)chō\ *n* -S [Sp, fr. *pico* peak + *-acho* (fr. L *-aceus* -aceous)] **:** a large pointed isolated hill

**pic·a·dor** \'pikə,dȯ(ə)r, -ō(ə)\ *n, pl* **picadors** \-rz, -(ə)z\ *or* **picado·res** \,══'dō,rēz, -dō,-, -rās\ [Sp, fr. *picado* (past part. of *picar* to prick, pierce) + *-or*] **:** a mounted member of the bullfighting cuadrilla who prods the bull with a lance in order to weaken the neck and shoulder muscles — compare TORERO

**pic·a·du·ra** \,pikə'dürə\ *n* -S [Sp, fr. *picado* (past part. of *picar*) + *-ura* -ure (fr. L)] **:** cut tobacco for cigarettes

**pi·cae** \'pī,sē\ *n pl, cap* [NL, fr. L *pica* magpie] *in former classifications* **:** an order of birds including most of the recent order Coraciiformes together with the parrots, cuckoos, and various passerine birds

**pic·ail·lon** \,pikəl'yōn\ *n* -S [F — more at PICAYUNE] **:** PICAYUNE 1

**picaninny** *var of* PICKANINNY

¹**pic·ard** \'pikərd, -i,kärd\ *n* -S *cap* [F, fr. MF, fr. *Picardie* Picardy, province of northern France] **1 :** a native or inhabitant of Picardy in northern France **2 :** the French dialect of Picardy

²**picard** \"\ *adj, usu cap* [F, fr. *Picardie*] **:** of, relating to, or coming from Picardy

³**picard** \"\ *n* -S *usu cap* [ML *Picardus*, fr. *picardus* inhabitant or native of Picardy, fr. MF *picard;* fr. the fact that the group was founded by Picards who were accused of heresy and driven out of France] **:** one of a religious group active in Bohemia around the 15th century

**pic·ar·dy third** \'pikə(r)dē-\ *n, sometimes cap P* [trans. of F *tierce de Picardie;* fr. its being chiefly practiced in the church music of Picardy] **:** the major third as introduced into the final chord of a musical composition written in a minor key

**pic·a·rel** \,pikə'rel\ *n* -S [F] **:** a small European marine fish (*Spicara smaris*) of the family Maenidae

¹**pic·a·resque** \'pikə'resk *sometimes* 'pēk-\ *adj* [Sp *picaresco*, fr. *picaro* rogue + *-esco* -esque] **:** of, relating to, or characteristic of rogues or rascals; *specif* **:** relating to or being a type of prose fiction of Spanish origin in modern literature in which the principal character is a rogue or vagabond and the narrative is a series of incidents or episodes connected chronologically but with little or no motivation or complication of plot ⟨~ novel⟩ ⟨~ career⟩ ⟨waifs of the ~ tradition —Asher Brunes⟩

²**picaresque** \"\ *n* -S **:** someone or something that is picaresque ⟨forming a kind of children's ~ of loosely connected episodes —Irving Howe⟩

**pi·car·i·ae** \pə'ka(a)rē,ē\ *n pl, cap* [NL, irreg. fr. L *picus* woodpecker — more at PIE] *in former classifications* **:** an order of birds nearly equivalent to the Coraciiformes but often including the parrots and cuckoos

**pi·car·i·an** \-rēən\ *adj* [NL *Picariae* + E *-an*] **:** of or relating to the Picariae

**pi·carii** \-rē,ī\ *n pl, cap* [NL, prob. alter. of *Picariae*] *in former classifications* **:** a group of birds practically equivalent to the Picariae together with the Clamatores

**pic·a·ro** \'pikə,rō\ *n* -S [Sp *picaro*] **:** ROGUE, TRAMP, VAGABOND, BOHEMIAN

¹**pic·a·roon** *or* **pick·a·roon** \'pikə'rün\ *n* -S [Sp *picarón*, aug. of *picaro*] **1 :** PICARO **2 :** PIRATE, CORSAIR — used of a man or a ship

²**picaroon** \"\ -ED/-ING/-S *vi* **:** to act as a pirate or brigand watching or searching for a prize or victim

**picas** *pl of* PICA

¹**pic·a·yune** \,pikē'yün, -kə'-\ *n* -S [F *picaillon* old copper coin of Piedmont, halfpenny, fr. Prov *picaioun*, fr. *picaio* money, fr. *pica* to strike, prick, sound, jingle (fr. — assumed — VL *piccare* to prick, pierce) + *-aio* -al (fr. L *-alia*) — more at PIKE (weapon)] **1 a :** a Spanish half real piece formerly current in Louisiana and other southern states **b :** HALF DIME **2 :** something of very small or of the least value ⟨not worth a ~⟩

²**picayune** \'══'═\ *adj* **1 :** of little value **:** PALTRY, MEASLY ⟨not more than two or three countries are carrying on any sort of forest research, and these programs are ~ —William Vogt⟩ ⟨compared to the total number of people employed, such cutbacks were still ~ —*Time*⟩ **2 :** concerned with trifling matters **:** petty, narrow, or small-minded in point of view ⟨within the limits of a short review it would seem ~ to be critical —W.F.Stolper⟩ **syn** see PETTY

**pic·a·yun·ish** \-nish, nēsh\ *adj* [¹*picayune* + *-ish*] **:** PICAYUNE ⟨a lifetime of ~ drudgery in the company of louts —H.L. Davis⟩ **syn** see PETTY

**pic·ca·dil·ly** \'pikə'dilē\ *n* -ES [F *picadilles*, pl. of *picadille* pickadil — more at PICKADIL] **1 :** PICKADIL **2 :** a high wing collar worn by men in the late 19th century

**piccage** *var of* PICKAGE

**pic·ca·lil·li** \'pikə'lilē\ *n* -S [earlier *piccalillo*, prob. alter. (perh. influenced by Sp *picadillo* hash) of ¹*pickle*] **:** a relish of chopped vegetables and pungent spices

**pic·ca·nin** \'pikə,nin\ *n* -S [Afrik, short for *piccaninny*, fr. E — more at PICKANINNY] *southern Africa* **:** PICKANINNY

**pic·ca·nin·ny** \'pikə,ninī\ *Brit var of* PICKANINNY

¹**pic·co·lo** \'pikə,lō\ *n* -S [It, lit., small, prob. fr. It dial. *picca* little] **1 :** a small shrill flute pitched an octave higher than the ordinary flute **2 :** a two-foot labial pipe-organ stop with a high piercing tone **3 :** an apprentice waiter in a European restaurant **:** BUSBOY **4** *South* **:** JUKEBOX

piccolo 1

²**piccolo** \"\ *adj* [It] *of a musical instrument* **:** smaller than ordinary size ⟨~ banjo⟩ ⟨~ cornet⟩ ⟨~ piano⟩

**pic·co·lo·ist** \-lōəst\ *n* -S **:** a piccolo player

**pic·co·lo·pas·so red** \'pikəlō'pä(,)sō-\ *n* [*piccolopasso* fr. It *piccolo* small + *passo* raisin wine] **:** OXBLOOD

**piccotah** *var of* PICOTAH

**pice** \'pīs\ *n, pl* **pice** [Hindi *paisā*] **1 a :** a unit of value of India equal before 1955 to ¼ of an anna or ¹⁄₆₄ rupee **b :** PAISA 1 **2 :** a bronze or copper coin representing one pice

**pi·cea** \'pisēə, 'pīs-\ *n, cap* [NL, fr. L, pitch pine, fr. *pic-*, *pix* pitch] **:** a genus of temperate and arctic evergreen trees (family Pinaceae) having acicular leaves that are keeled on both surfaces and borne individually on persistent peg-shaped bases and cones that become pendulous and have reflexed scales — see SPRUCE

**pic·e·in** \'pisēən, 'pīs-\ *n* -S [NL *Picea* (genus name of the Norway spruce *Picea abies*) + ISV *-in*] **:** a bitter crystalline glucoside $C_{14}H_{18}O_7$ obtained esp. from the needles of the Norway spruce and from the barks of willows

¹**pi·cene** \'pī,sēn\ *adj, usu cap* [L *picenus* of Picenum, fr. *Picenum*, ancient Roman province in eastern central Italy] **:** PICENIAN

²**picene** \"\ *n* -S *cap* **:** a native or inhabitant of ancient Picenum

³**picene** \"\ *n* -S [ISV *pic-* (fr. L *pic-*, *pix* pitch) + *-ene*] **:** a fluorescent crystalline hydrocarbon $C_{22}H_{14}$ obtained from the pitchy residue of petroleum or lignite tar; benzo-chrysene

¹**pi·ce·ni·an** \(')pī'sēnēən\ *adj, usu cap* [L *picenus* Picenian + E *-an*] **:** of or relating to Picenum, the Picenes, or their language — compare SABELLIAN

²**picenian** \"\ *n* -S *cap* **1 :** PICENE **2 :** the Italic language of the Picenian people

**pic·e·ous** \'pisēəs, 'pīs-\ *adj* [L *piceus* fr. *pic-*, *pix* pitch + *-eus* -eous — more at PITCH] **:** of, relating to, or resembling pitch **:** PITCHY; *esp* **:** glossy brownish black in color

¹**pi·chi** \'pēchē\ *n* -S [AmerSp *pichi*, *piche*, fr. Araucan *pichi*, *pichin* small thing] **:** a small armadillo (*Zaedyus pichiy* syn. *Z. minutus*) of southern So. America

²**pichi** \"\ *n* -S [AmerSp *pichi*, *piche*, fr. Araucan *pichi*, *pichin*] **:** a Peruvian shrub (*Fabiana imbricata*) the herbage of which yields a tonic and diuretic

**pich·i·ci·a·go** \,pichēsē'|ä(,)gō, |ā(-\ *also* **pich·i·cha·go** \-chē'ch|\ *n* -S [perh. fr. Allentiac] **:** a small burrowing So. American armadillo (*Chlamyphorus truncatus*) armored with many bands of plates that are laterally replaced by thick hair; *also* **:** a larger but very similar form that constitutes a separate genus (*Burmeisteria*)

**pich·u·rim** \'pishərəm\ *or* **pichurim bean** *n* -S [Pg *pichurim*, fr. Tupi *pechurim*] **:** one of the thick strongly aromatic cotyledons of a tropical American tree (*Nectandra pichurim*) used as a substitute for nutmegs and as a flavoring agent and stimulant tonic

**pi·ci** \'pī,sī\ *n pl, cap* [NL, fr. L, pl. of *picus* woodpecker — more at ¹PIE] **:** a group of birds formerly coextensive with or more extensive than the order Piciformes but now usu. made a suborder of Piciformes comprising the woodpeckers and piculets

**pic·i·dae** \'pisə,dē, 'pīs-\ *n pl, cap* [NL, fr. *Picus*, type genus + *-idae*] **:** a family of birds (suborder Pici) comprising the woodpeckers, the piculets, and the wrynecks

**pic·i·form** \'pisə,fȯrm, 'pīs-\ *adj* [prob. fr. (assumed) NL *piciformis*, fr. L *picus* woodpecker + *-iformis* -iform] **1 :** like a woodpecker **2** [NL *Piciformes*] **:** of or relating to the Piciformes

**pic·i·for·mes** \,══'fȯr,mēz\ *n pl, cap* [NL, fr. *Picus* + *-iformes*] **:** an order of nonpasserine birds formerly restricted to the woodpeckers but now usu. including also the jacamars, puffbirds, barbets, honey guides, and toucans

**pi·cine** \'pī,sīn, -,sən\ *adj* [L *picus* woodpecker + E *-ine*] **:** of or relating to woodpeckers **:** PICIFORM

¹**pick** \'pik\ *vb* -ED/-ING/-S [ME *piken*, partly fr. MF *piquer* to prick, pick, pluck, strike & partly fr. (assumed) OE *pician* to prick (whence OE *pīcung* pricking); akin to MD *picken*, *pecken* to prick, hoe, pick, ON *pikka* to peck, hack — more at PIKE (weapon)] *vt* **1 :** to pierce, penetrate, or break up with a pointed instrument ⟨~*ing* the hard clay⟩ ⟨~ the surface of a millstone⟩ **2 :** to remove covering or adhering matter from bit by bit ⟨~*ed* the bones clean⟩; *specif* **:** to remove feathers from ⟨~ a goose⟩ **3 a :** to separate and remove with the fingers or fingertips **:** PLUCK ⟨~*ing* flowers for the table⟩ **b :** to take lightly, neatly, or selectively **:** CULL ⟨~*ing* only the ripest berries⟩ **c :** to gather one by one or bit by bit ⟨~ apples⟩ ⟨~ rags⟩ **d :** to take needed sorts from (standing type) ⟨if you ~ this form chalk the chase⟩ **4 :** to select from among a group **:** CHOOSE, NAME ⟨attempts to ~ an exact synonym —Johnson O'Connor⟩ ⟨tried to ~ the shortest route⟩ ⟨~*ed* his way cautiously through the swamp⟩ ⟨~*ed* a winner in the next race⟩ **5 :** to take the contents of (as a pocket) by stealth ⟨suspected of ~*ing* pockets⟩ ⟨skilled at ~*ing* the brains of his associates⟩ **6 :** to seek and find occasion for **:** provoke deliberately ⟨~ a quarrel⟩ **7 a :** to dig into or pull lightly at with fingertips or fingernails or a pointed instrument ⟨~*ing* his teeth with a knife⟩ ⟨~*ed* the shoestring until it came untied⟩ **b :** to pluck (the strings of a stringed musical instrument) with a plectrum or with the fingers to cause vibrations; *also* **:** to play music on (a stringed instrument) ⟨reputed to ~ a mighty mean guitar —G.S.Perry⟩ **c :** to loosen or pull apart with a sharp point ⟨~ wool⟩ ⟨~ oakum⟩ **8 :** to turn (a lock) with a wire or a pointed tool instead of the key esp. with intent to steal **9 a** *of a bird* (1) **:** to strike with the bill ⟨cruelly ~*ed* by the stronger chicks⟩ (2) **:** to take up (food) with the bill **b :** to eat sparingly or mincingly **10 :** to cause (bits of the surface of paper) to stick to type and be pulled off — used of ink **11 :** to finish (an edge of cloth) with a line of fine running stitches parallel to the edge ⟨pocket flaps ~*ed* by hand⟩ ~ *vi* **1 :** to use or work with a pick or pickax **2 :** to gather something from a plant **:** HARVEST ⟨the ~*ing* season⟩ ⟨fruit ripe for ~*ing*⟩ **3 :** PILFER, FILCH — used chiefly in the phrase *picking and stealing* **4 a** *of a bird* **:** to strike or take things up with the bill ⟨chickens ~*ing* about the yard⟩ **b :** to eat sparingly or mincingly **:** eat with little appetite ⟨~*ing* listlessly at his dinner⟩ **5 :** to lose bits of the surface by adhesion to the inked form during printing — used of paper — **pick a hole in :** to find or reveal a flaw in (as an argument) or blemish in (as a reputation) — **pick and choose :** to select with care and deliberation or with notable fastidiousness ⟨*picking and choosing*, dillying and dallying; not a man to have straightforward love for a woman —Virginia Woolf⟩ — **pick at 1 :** to try to pull or seize with the fingertips ⟨*picking at the* bedclothes⟩ **2 :** to find fault with continually **:** pick on **:** NAG, PESTER — **pick on 1 :** to pick at **:** HARASS, NAG, TEASE ⟨felt that he was *picked on* because he was better than the others —Robertson Davies⟩ **2** *or* **pick upon :** to single out for special attention **:** choose for a particular purpose or reason ⟨they had *picked on* a poor camping site⟩

²**pick** \"\ *n* -S **1 :** a blow or stroke with a pointed instrument **2 a :** the act of choosing or selecting **:** right or privilege of selection **:** CHOICE ⟨had the ~ of several jobs⟩ ⟨here are several brands, take your ~⟩ **b :** something that is or would be chosen first **:** the best or choicest part or member ⟨the ~ of the herd⟩ ⟨the ~ of the rebel forces⟩ **3** *dial* **a :** the taking of a bit of food **:** PECK **b :** a scanty meal **c :** a little bit **:** SCRAP **4 :** the portion or quantity of a crop gathered at one time **:** PICKING ⟨biggest berry ~ in several years⟩ ⟨the first ~ of peaches⟩ **5 :** something that is picked in with a point or pointed pencil **6 a :** a particle (as of hardened ink, dirt, or paper) embedded in the hollow of a letter and causing a spot on a printed sheet; *also* **:** the spot so caused **b :** a burr on the face of a plate or cut or of newly cast type **c :** the tendency of paper to pick **7 :** a maneuver (as in basketball) for cutting off a player from the play **:** SCREEN

³**pick** \"\ *adj* [²*pick*] **:** PICKED, BEST ⟨handed out the new guns to the ~ rifle shots of his crew —F.B.Gipson⟩

⁴**pick** \"\ *vb* -ED/-ING/-S [ME *pykken*, alter. of *picchen* pitch, v.] *vt* **1** *obs* **:** to set up or fix in place (as a tent) **2 a** *chiefly dial* **:** to throw or thrust with effort **:** HURL ⟨high as I could ~ my lance —Shak.⟩ **b :** PITCH ⟨time to ~ the hay⟩ **3** *dial* **:** to give birth to prematurely **4 :** to throw (a shuttle) across the loom ~ *vi* **1** *dial Eng* **:** to fall or topple forward **2 :** to throw the shuttle across the loom

⁵**pick** \"\ *n* -S **1** *dial Eng* **a :** the act of pitching or throwing **:** CAST **b :** something that is thrown **2 a :** a throw of the shuttle — used esp. in calculating the speed of a loom ⟨so many ~*s* per minute⟩ **b :** one filling thread — used esp. in describing the fineness of a fabric ⟨so many ~*s* to an inch⟩

⁶**pick** \"\ *n* -S [ME *pik*, prob. alter. of ¹*pike*] **1** *obs* **a :** PIKE **b :** a sharp point **:** SPIKE **2 a :** a heavy iron or steel tool pointed at one or both ends and often curved, wielded by means of a wooden handle inserted in an eye between the ends, and used by quarrymen, roadmakers, miners, and stonecutters **3** *dial Brit* **:** any of various pointed or pronged implements: as **a :** PITCHFORK **b :** GAFF **4 :** a sharp-pointed instrument for picking: as **a :** TOOTHPICK **b :** PICKLOCK **c :** PLECTRUM 1 **5** *dial Eng* **:** a diamond in playing cards **6 :** one of the points on the forepart of a figure skate blade

⁷**pick** \"\ *dial var of* PIQUE

**pickaback** *also* **pickback** *or* **pickapack** *var of* PIGGYBACK

**pickaback plant** \'═══,═-\ *also* **piggyback plant** \'═══,═-\ *n* **:** a glandular pubescent perennial herb (*Tolmiea menziesii*) of the family Saxifragaceae that is native to western No. America, has young plants borne at the junction of leaf blade and petiole, and is used as a foliage plant — called also *youth-on-age*

**pick·able** \ˈpikəbəl\ *adj* [¹*pick* + *-able*] **:** able or suitable to be picked — **pick·able·ness** *n* -ES

**pick·a·dil** \ˈpikə,dil\ *or* **pick·a·dil·ly** \ˌ==ˈdilē\ *n, pl* **picka·dils** *or* **pickadillies** [F *picadille*, prob. fr. Sp *picado* pierced, cut (fr. past part. of *picar* to prick, pierce) + F *-ille*, dim. suffix — more at PIC] **1 :** a decorative trimming of cutwork that is scalloped, tabbed, or pointed and used as an edging on doublets, collars, and other garments of the late 16th and early 17th centuries **2 :** a ruff or standing collar trimmed with cutwork **3 :** a stiff support for a ruff or standing collar

**pick·age** *or* **pic·cage** \ˈpikij\ *n* -S [ME *pikage*, fr. *piken* to pick + *-age*] **:** a toll paid at fairs for leave to break ground for booths

**pick-and-pick** \ˌ==ˈ=\ *adj* [⁵*pick*] **:** capable of weaving a succession of different filling yarns into a fabric ⟨*pick-and-pick* loom⟩; *also* **:** woven with such yarns

**pick-and-shovel** \ˌ==ˈ==\ *adj* **:** done with or as if with a pick and shovel **:** LABORIOUS, DRUDGING ⟨*pick-and-shovel* routine⟩

**pick·a·nin·ny** *or* **pic·a·nin·ny** \ˈpikə,ninē, -ni\ *n* -ES [prob. modif. of Pg *pequenino* very little, fr. *pequeno* little, small + *-ino*, dim. suffix] **1 a :** a Negro child **b** *Africa* **:** a child of any of various native peoples (as Kaffirs or Zulus) **c** *Australia* **:** a child of one of the aboriginal peoples **2 :** OTTER 4

¹**pickaroon** *var of* PICAROON

²**pick·a·roon** \ˌpikəˈrün\ *n* -S [prob. fr. obs. F *piqueron* spur, prickle, fr. F *piquer* to prick, fr. MF — more at PIKE] **:** a piked pole with a hook used by lumbermen in river driving and by tracklayers in aligning railroad ties — called also *hookaroon*

pickaroons

**pickaternie** *var of* PICTARNIE

**pick·a·way anise** \ˈpikə,wā-\ *n* [*pickaway* perh. fr. *Pickaway* county, Ohio] **:** HOP TREE

¹**pick·ax** *or* **pick·axe** \ˈpi,kaks\ *n* [alter. (influenced by *ax, axe*) of ME *pikois, pikeis* pickax, fr. OF *picois*, fr. *pic* pick, fr. L *picus* woodpecker — more at PIE] **:** ⁶PICK 2

²**pickax** *or* **pickaxe** \"\ *vt* **:** to break up or dig with a pickax ~ *vi* **:** to work with a pickax

**pickax sheldrake** *n* **:** HOODED MERGANSER

**pickax team** *n* **:** UNICORN 4

**pick-can** \ˈ=,=\ *n* [¹*pick*] **:** a metal container holding water in which the stems of flowers are placed as they are cut

**pick clock** *or* **pick counter** *n* [⁵*pick*] **:** a device installed on a loom to determine the number of picks woven and thus the length of cut and amount of weaver's pay at a rate per thousand picks

**pick dressing** *n* [²*pick*] **:** a facing in cut stonework made by a pointed tool that leaves the surface in little pits

¹**picked** \ˈpikt\ *adj* [ME *piked*, fr. past part. of *piken* to pick — more at PICK] **1 a** *obs* **:** ADORNED, TRIM **b** *obs* **:** DAINTY, FASTIDIOUS **2 :** selected as being the best obtainable or best for the purpose ⟨a ~ crew⟩ ⟨a raiding party of ~ men⟩

²**pick·ed** \ˈpikəd, -kt\ *adj* [ME, fr. ⁶*pick* + *-ed*] *chiefly dial* **:** POINTED, PEAKED

**picked dogfish** *n* **1 :** SPINY DOGFISH **2 :** a sand shark (*Carcharias littoralis*)

**pickedevant** *n* -S [earlier *pique de vant*, prob. fr. F *pique* point, tip (fr. *piquer* to prick, puncture) + E *de vent*, modif. of F *devant* in front — more at DEVANT] *obs* **:** VANDYKE BEARD

**pickeer** *vi* -ED/-ING/-S [prob. modif. of F *picorer* to maraud, lit., to steal sheep, fr. MF, alter. (influenced by *piquer* to pick, prick) of *pecore* sheep, fr. OIt *pecora*, fr. L, neut. pl. of *pecor-, pecus* cattle — more at PIKE, FEE] **1** *obs* **:** to engage in piracy **:** PRIVATEER, MARAUD **2 a** *obs* **:** to skirmish in advance of an army **b** *obs* **:** SCOUT, RECONNOITER

**pickeerer** *n* -S *obs* **:** SKIRMISHER

**pick·el** \ˈpikəl\ *n* -S [prob. alter. of *pikel*] **:** ICE AX

**pick·el·hau·be** \ˈpikəl,hau̇bə\ *n, pl* **pickelhau·ben** \-bən\ *or* **pickelhaubes** [G, alter. (influenced by *pickel* pickax) of MHG *beckelhūbe, beckenhūbe*, fr. *becken* basin (fr. OHG *beckīn*, fr. LL *bacchinon*) + *hūbe* cap (fr. OHG *hūba*); akin to OE *hȳf* hive — more at BASIN, HIVE] **:** a spiked helmet worn by German soldiers

¹**pick·er** \ˈpikə(r)\ *n* -S [¹*pick* + *-er*] **1 :** one that picks: as **a :** one that uses a pickax **b :** one that picks the fruit of agricultural crops **c :** a worker who selects material or articles suitable to a given purpose or one who picks out foreign matter **d :** one that operates a picking machine **2 :** any of various tools or devices: as **a :** a tool for clearing out small openings **b :** a machine for picking fibrous materials to pieces so as to loosen and separate the fiber; *specif* **:** a machine that precedes the card in textile manufacturing **c** *or* **picking machine :** a mechanical device consisting essentially of a revolving drum with numerous rubber fingers for the removal of feathers from table poultry

²**picker** \"\ *n* -S [⁴*pick* + *-er*] **:** the hard leather piece of a picker stick that hits the shuttle in a loom

**pick·er·el** \ˈpik(ə)rəl\ *n, pl* **pickerel** *or* **pickerels** [ME *pikerel*, dim. of *pik, pike* pike (fish) — more at PIKE] **1 a** *dial chiefly Brit* **:** a young or small pike **b :** any of several comparatively small fishes of the genus *Esox* — usu. used with a qualifying term; see CHAIN PICKEREL, GRASS PICKEREL, REDFIN PICKEREL **2 :** WALLEYE 4

**pickerel frog** *n* **:** a meadow frog (*Rana palustris*) of eastern No. America very similar to the leopard frog but distinguished by squarish dark spots on the back

**pickerelweed** \ˈ=(=)=,=\ *n* **1 :** a plant of the genus *Pontederia*; *esp* **:** an American aquatic herb (*P. cordata*) growing in shallow water of streams and ponds and having spikes of blue flowers and cordate or sagittate leaves **2 :** any of various still-water species of the genus *Potamogeton*

**pickerelweed family** *n* **:** PONTEDERIACEAE

**pick·er·ing** \ˈpik(ə)riŋ\ *n* -S [alter. (prob. influenced by *herring*) of *pickerel*] **1 :** PICKEREL **2 :** SAUGER

**pick·er·ing governor** \ˈpik(ə)riŋ-\ *n, usu cap P* [after Thomas R. *Pickering* Am. engineer] **:** a governor in which the revolving balls act against curved flat springs

**pick·er·ing·ite** \ˈpik(ə)riŋ,īt\ *n* -S [John *Pickering* †1846 Am. scientist + E *-ite*] **:** a mineral $MgAl_2(SO_4)_4.22H_2O$ composed of a hydrous magnesium aluminum sulfate occurring in white to faintly colored fibrous masses

**pickering's tree frog** *n, usu cap P* [after Charles *Pickering* †1878 Am. naturalist] **:** SPRING PEEPER

**picker stick** *n* [²*picker*] **:** a lever that transmits the crank action of a loom motion into the thrust which drives the shuttle across the loom

**picker-up** \ˌ==ˈ=\ *n, pl* **pickers-up :** one who picks up (as bits of information or articles to be transported or cleared away); *specif* **:** one who picks up a fleece from the shearer and tosses it on the sorting table

**pick·ery** \ˈpik(ə)rī\ *n* -ES [¹*pick* + *-ery*] *Scots law* **:** petty theft

¹**pick·et** *also* **pi·quet** \ˈpikət, *usu* -əd.+V\ *n* -S [F *piquet*, fr. MF, fr. *piquer* to prick, pierce + *-et* — more at PIKE] **1 :** a pointed or sharpened stake, post, peg, or pale: as **a :** a pale used in making fences **b :** a stake used in constructing revetments, obstacles, and fences **c :** PICKET PIN 1 **d :** a peg for a tent rope **e :** RANGE POLE **f :** a stake on which in a former mode of military punishment the offender was forced to stand with one foot; *also* **:** this punishment **2 a :** a detached body of soldiers serving to guard an army from surprise and to oppose reconnoitering parties of the enemy — called also *outlying picket* **b :** a detachment kept ready in camp for such duty — called also *inlying picket* **c :** a detail to bring in those who have overstayed leave **d :** SENTINEL **e :** the duty of serving as a picket **f :** PICKET SHIP **3 :** a person posted by a labor organization at an approach to the place of work affected by a strike to ascertain the workmen going and coming and to persuade or otherwise influence them to quit working there; *also* **:** one posted similarly in a demonstration as a protest against a policy of government **4 :** an elongated bullet of cylindroconical form

²**picket** \"\ *vb* -ED/-ING/-S *vt* **1 :** to enclose, fasten, fence, or fortify with pickets **:** PALISADE **2 a :** to guard (as a camp or road) by an outlying picket **b :** to post as a picket **3 :** TETHER **4 a :** to post pickets at (a place of employment) **b :** to walk or stand in front of as a picket ~ *vi* **:** to take up the station and duties of a military or labor picket **:** do or go on picket duty

³**picket** \"\ *n* -S [origin unknown] **:** TERN

**picketboat** \ˈ==,=\ *n* [¹*picket* + *boat*] **:** a craft used (as by the Coast Guard) for harbor patrol

**pick·et·er** \ˈpikəd.ə(r), -ətə-\ *n* -S **:** PICKET 3

**picket fence** *n* **:** a fence made of pickets

**picket line** *n* **1 :** a position held by a line of pickets **2 :** a rope to which horses or mules are secured by halter shanks esp. while being groomed **3 :** a line of workers picketing a place of employment

**picket pin** *n* **1 :** a short stake driven into the ground for tethering a horse **2** *West* **:** any of several species of small ground squirrels of the genus *Citellus* which when sitting erect and motionless resemble a stake at a short distance

**picket ship** *n* **:** a ship or airplane stationed outside a formation of ships or a geographical area as a scout or warning unit

picket fence

**pick·fork** \ˈpik,fȯrk\ *n* [ME *pikfork* — more at PITCHFORK] *dial Eng* **:** PITCHFORK

**pick glass** *n* [⁵*pick*] **:** a magnifying glass for comparing and counting yarns in fabrics

**pick hammer** *n* **:** a pick with one end sharp and the other blunt

**pickier** *comparative of* PICKY

**pickiest** *superlative of* PICKY

**pick in** *vt* [¹*pick*] **:** to work (as a shadow) into a painting with a pointed tool

**picking** *n* -S [fr. gerund of ¹*pick*] **1 pickings** *pl* **:** something that is picked or picked up: as **a :** gleanable or eatable fragments esp. from refuse **:** SCRAPS ⟨the dogs have scanty ~*s* in that house⟩ **b :** share of spoils **c :** yield or return for effort expended ⟨the U-boats . . . shifted to fields where the ~*s* were easier —J.P.Baxter⟩ **2 :** a soft brick or one not fully burned

pick hammer

**picking machine** *n* **:** PICKER 2c

**pick key** *n* [¹*pick*] **:** SKELETON KEY

¹**pick·le** \ˈpikəl\ *n* -S [ME *pekille*, prob. fr. MD *pekel, peekel*; perh. akin to MD *picken, pecken* to prick, pick — more at PICK] **1 a :** a salt-and-water solution for preserving or corning fish or meat **:** BRINE **b :** plain or spiced vinegar for preserving vegetables, fruit, fish, eggs, oysters **c :** a bath usu. of sulfuric acid and salt for treating skins after bating in chrome tanning **d :** a bath of dilute sulfuric or nitric acid used to cleanse or brighten the surface of castings or other articles of metal **e :** a solution of caustic soda or other antiseptic used for cleaning wort or beer pipes **f :** any of various solutions (as of alcohol or formaldehyde) in which organic substances are soaked for preservation **2 a :** an unpleasant or difficult situation or condition **:** PLIGHT, PREDICAMENT, TROUBLE **b** *chiefly Brit* **:** a state of disorder **:** MESS ⟨small boy who had . . . left a bathroom in a ~ —C.S.Lewis⟩ **3 a :** an article of food (as a cucumber) that has been preserved in brine or in vinegar ⟨sour as a ~⟩ **b** *dial* **:** a fresh cucumber **4 a** *Brit* **:** a mischievous or troublesome person **b :** a person with a forbidding face or unsociable disposition — **in pickle :** in reserve or use on occasion **:** saved up **:** in readiness ⟨there's a rod *in pickle* for bad boys like you⟩ **syn** see PREDICAMENT

²**pickle** \"\ *vt* **pickled; pickled; pickling** \-k(ə)liŋ\ **pickles 1 a :** to steep in a solution of salt or vinegar for preservation ⟨~ herring⟩ ⟨~ fruit in syrup and vinegar⟩ **b :** to soak in a chemical solution in order to cleanse ⟨~ steel castings⟩ or condition ⟨*pickled* leather⟩ ⟨*pickled* seeds to induce sprouting⟩ **c :** to steep or soak (as seed) in a fungicide for the control of seed-borne diseases **d :** to hold (cut flowers) under refrigeration for an extended period of time with or without the use of a material in order to lengthen the life **2 a :** to give an antique appearance to — used of copies or imitations of paintings by the old masters **b :** to give a light finish to (as a piece of furniture) by bleaching or painting and wiping ⟨paneled in *pickled* pine⟩ **3 :** to rub salt or salt and vinegar on (a wound made by flogging)

³**pickle** \"\ *vb* [ME *pikelen*, fr. *piken* to pick + *-len* -le] **1** *chiefly Scot* **:** to pick a little at a time **:** eat sparingly or mincingly **2** *chiefly Scot* **:** TRIFLE, DAWDLE **3** *chiefly Scot* **:** PILFER

⁴**pickle** \"\ *n* -S [perh. fr. ³*pickle*] **1 :** GRAIN, KERNEL **2** *dial* **:** a small quantity or amount — usu. with no preposition following ⟨get my ~ meal —Sir Walter Scott⟩

**pickle-cured** \ˌ==ˈ=\ *adj* **:** preserved in pickle

**pickled** *adj* [fr. past part. of ²*pickle*] **1 :** preserved in or cured with pickle **2** *slang* **:** DRUNK ⟨seldom gets thoroughly ~ before dinner —*New Yorker*⟩

**pickled brood** *or* **pickle brood** *n* [prob. so called fr. the fact that the dead brood develops a sour smell] **:** a disease of honeybees caused by a fungus (*Aspergillus pollinis*)

**pickle grass** *or* **pickle plant** *n* **:** GLASSWORT 1

**pickle-herring** \ˈ==,==\ *n* [obs. D *pekel-haerinck* (now *pekelharing*), fr. D *pekel* pickle + obs. D *haerinck* herring (fr. MD *harinc, herinc*) — more at HERRING] **1 :** a pickled herring **2** [D *pekelharing*, fr. G *pickelhering*, fr. *Pickelhering*, droll comic character of the 17th cent. German stage] **:** BUFFOON

**pick·le·man** \ˈpikəlmən\ *n, pl* **picklemen 1 :** one who makes or deals in pickles **2 :** one who prepares pickling solution

**pick·ler** \ˈpik(ə)lə(r)\ *n* -S **1 :** a vegetable (as a cucumber or onion) of a suitable size or quality for pickling **2 :** one that prepares or uses pickling solution for the preservation of food or hides or the cleaning of metal

**pickleweed** \ˈ==,=\ *n* [¹*pickle* + *weed*] **1 :** IODINE BUSH **2 :** GLASSWORT 1

**pickleworm** \ˈ==,=\ *n* [¹*pickle* + *worm*] **:** the larva of a brown-and-yellow moth (*Diaphania nitidales*) of the family Pyralididae that attacks the vines of cucurbits in No. and So. America

**pickling cabbage** *n* **:** any of various cabbages (as the red-leafed cabbage) that are esp. suitable for pickling

**pickling cucumber** *n* **:** any of various cucumbers grown primarily for pickling and characterized by the production of large crops of uniform rather small fruits with few spines

¹**picklock** \ˈ=,=\ *n* [¹*pick* + *lock*] **:** one that picks a lock: as **a :** a tool for picking locks **b :** BURGLAR, THIEF

²**picklock** \"\ *adj* **:** resembling or relating to a picklock

**pick·man** \ˈpikmən\ *n, pl* **pickmen 1 :** a laborer who uses a pick or pickax **2 :** one in charge of picks (as in a mine)

**pick-mattock** \ˈ=ˈ==\ *n* **:** a digging tool with a head having a point at one end and a transverse blade at the other

**pickmaw** \ˈ=,=\ *n* [¹*pick* + *maw*] *dial Eng* **:** BLACK-HEADED GULL

**pick-me-up** \ˈ===,=\ *n* -S [fr. *pick (me) up*, v.] **1 :** something that stimulates or restores **:** TONIC, BRACER **2 :** KITTIWAKE

**pick·nick** *var of* PICNIC

**pick off** *vt* **1 :** to remove by plucking ⟨*picked* the dog hairs *off* his coat⟩ **2 a :** to shoot or bring down singly or selectively ⟨*picked off* his pursuers as they emerged from the pass⟩ ⟨wolves trailed the herd to *pick off* stragglers⟩ ⟨had time to reload and *pick off* first one single, then the other —W.G. Means⟩ **b :** to catch (a base runner) off base with a quick throw by either the pitcher or the catcher that often results in a put-out

¹**pick-off** \ˈ=,=\ *n* -S [*pick off*] **1 :** a baseball play in which a base runner is caught off base by a quick throw from the catcher or pitcher **2 :** electrical means for automatic correction of flight stability by means of impulses from a gyro

²**pick-off** \"\ *adj* [*pick off*] **:** REMOVABLE ⟨*pick-off* gears for changing speeds of a lathe⟩

**pick out** *vt* [ME *piken out*, fr. *piken* to pick + *out* — more at PICK] **1 a :** to take out or remove by picking **:** peck out **b :** to play the notes of (a melody) by ear or one by one **2 a :** SELECT, CHOOSE ⟨bright students are *picked out* at the age of 10 or 11 and brought along on scholarships —Douglas Bush⟩ **b :** to make out or distinguish with the senses or the understanding ⟨many famous summits can be *picked out* on a clear day —O.S.Nock⟩ **3 a :** to relieve (a plain surface) or accentuate (a pattern or outline) with lines or flecks of color **b :** to cause to stand out clearly **:** make distinct or emphatic ⟨help to *pick out* morals which have already been hinted —G.N.Flew⟩ ⟨in snow-white gaucho costume, *picked out* by the spotlights —Winifred Bambrick⟩

**pickout** \ˈ=,=\ *n* -S [*pick out*] **:** cannibalistic attack of young fowls on the extruded tissues of individuals in the flock afflicted with prolapse of the cloaca or oviducts

**pick over** *vt* [¹*pick*] **:** to examine (a collection of objects or mass of material) in order to select the best or remove unwanted bits ⟨*pick over* a junkpile⟩ ⟨*picked* the berries *over* for stems and leaves⟩

**pickover** \ˈ==,=\ *n* -S [*pick over*] *archaic* **:** FLOAT 10

**pickpocket** \ˈ=,==\ *n* **1 :** one who steals money or valuables that someone is carrying in his pockets or on his person **2 :** SHEPHERD'S PURSE

**pickpole** \ˈ=,=\ *n* [⁶*pick* + *pole*] **:** PIKE POLE

**pickproof** \ˈ=ˈ=\ *adj* [¹*pick* + *proof*] **:** designed to prevent picking ⟨~ lock⟩

**pick·purse** \ˈpik,pərs\ *n* [ME *pikepurs, pikepors*, fr. *piken* to pick + *purs, pors* purse — more at PURSE] **1** *archaic* **:** PICKPOCKET **2 :** SHEPHERD'S PURSE

**picks** *pres 3d sing of* PICK, *pl of* PICK

**pick sack** *or* **picker sack** *n* **:** a deep cloth bag suspended from the shoulder with a wide band and dragged between cotton rows to receive the cotton picked by hand

¹**pick's disease** \ˈpiks-\ *n, usu cap P* [after Arnold *Pick* †1924 Czech psychiatrist] **:** a condition marked by progressive impairment of intellect and judgment and transitory aphasia, caused by progressive atrophic changes of the cerebral cortex, and found chiefly in elderly women

²**pick's disease** *n, usu cap P* [after Friedel *Pick* †1926 Ger. physician] **:** pericarditis with adherent pericardium resulting in circulatory disturbances with edema and ascites

**picks·man** \ˈpiksmən\ *n, pl* **picksmen** [*picks* (poss. of ⁶*pick*) + *man*] **:** a workman who uses a pickax

**pick·some** \ˈpiksəm\ *adj* [¹*pick* + *-some*] **:** PARTICULAR, FASTIDIOUS, CHOOSY

**pickthank** \ˈ=,=\ *n* [fr. the phrase *pick a thank* "to seek someone's favor"] *archaic* **:** one who tries to curry favor by flattery, sycophancy, or talebearing ⟨smiling ~*s* and base newsmongers —Shak.⟩

**pickthatch** *n* [contr. of obs. E *picked-hatch*, fr. E ²*picked* + ¹*hatch*; fr. the fact that the entrance would usu. be guarded by iron pikes] *obs* **:** BROTHEL

**pick tongs** *n pl* [⁶*pick*] **:** tongs for handling hot metal

¹**picktooth** \ˈ=,=\ *n* [¹*pick* + *tooth*] **:** TOOTHPICK

²**picktooth** \"\ *adj* **:** LEISURELY, INDOLENT

**pick tree** *n* [⁶*pick*] **:** HERCULES'-CLUB 3

**pick up** *vb* [ME *piken up*, fr. *piken* to pick + *up* — more at PICK] *vt* **1 a :** to take up or lift from the ground or a low surface ⟨*picking up* sticks for firewood⟩ **:** lift or recover something dropped or fallen ⟨bent to *pick up* his hat⟩ ⟨tripped and fell, *picked* himself *up* and ran on⟩ **b :** to take or accept with the purpose of paying ⟨offered to *pick up* the bill for all expenses of the trip⟩ **c :** to do over (a dropped stitch) **d :** to start (a knitting or crochet stitch) by inserting the needle into a loop of a finished stitch **2 a :** to take (passengers or freight) into a vehicle or ship **b :** to rescue from the water ⟨*picked up* by a passing freighter⟩ **3 a** (1) **:** to get by bits **:** acquire or gain as occasions offer **:** acquire casually ⟨*picked up* a few dollars doing odd jobs⟩ (2) **:** to learn informally ⟨*pick up* a trade⟩ ⟨where do you *pick up* such expressions⟩ **b :** to gather in or up one by one ⟨time to *pick up* tools and go home⟩ **c :** to tidy up **:** put in order ⟨this room must be *picked up* before the company comes⟩ **4 a :** to happen upon or catch sight of ⟨*picked up* the harbor lights⟩ **b :** to bring within the range of vision or audition (as by a telescope or radio) **:** discover or receive (as a radio wave or signal) by ear **5 a :** to enter informally into conversation or companionship with ⟨had a brief affair with a girl he *picked up* in a bar⟩ **b :** to find or come upon and take into custody ⟨*picked up* by the police for questioning⟩ **6 a :** to come to and follow ⟨*picked up* the trail of the fugitives⟩ **b :** to respond promptly to (an acting cue) ⟨if he *picks up* his cue and speaks promptly he will kill the laugh —Henning Nelms⟩ **c :** to move in conjunction with in an athletic contest: as (1) **:** to move into position to guard (an opponent) (2) **:** to move so as to gain the protection of (a teammate) **7 :** PILFER ⟨didn't bother to *pick up* any other valuables —*N.Y.Times*⟩ **8 :** to prepare (a meal) from materials at hand or already cooked **9 a :** to pick up **:** revive the spirits of ⟨a bite of something might *pick* you *up* as well as me —Ellen Glasgow⟩ **b :** to increase the speed or tempo of ⟨urging the band to *pick it up*⟩ **10 :** to resume (a narrative, an activity, or a relation) after a break ⟨narrative switches back . . . to *pick up* its major characters —Richard Sullivan⟩ **11 :** LIFT 12 ~ *vi* **1 :** to recover speed, vigor, or activity (as after a check or setback) ⟨business began to *pick up* towards summer⟩ **:** IMPROVE **2 :** to gain speed **:** ACCELERATE ⟨to see how fast they can *pick up* from a standing start —*Lamp*⟩ **3 :** to strike up an acquaintance **:** enter informally on a relationship ⟨the danger of *picking up* with anyone who happens to come along —Erle Stanley Gardner⟩ **4 :** to gather up or pack up one's belongings ⟨many other Georgians had *picked up* and gone to Texas —Laura Krey⟩

¹**pickup** \ˈ=,=\ *n* -S [*pick up*] **1 :** the act or process of picking up: as **a :** the taking aboard of passengers, freight, or mail by a carrier **b :** the taking on of a railway car by a train or of a barge by a tow **c :** revival of activity (as after a business slump) **:** IMPROVEMENT **d :** ACCELERATION **e :** ARREST **f :** the act of making a chance acquaintance **g :** the fielding or hitting of a ball just after it strikes the ground; *specif* **:** HALF VOLLEY **2 a :** translation of mechanical movements into electrical impulses in the reproduction of sound **b :** the reception of sound in a radio transmitting apparatus for conversion into electrical energy **c :** the conversion of the image of a scene into electrical energy in the transmitting apparatus **3 a :** a dance step consisting of a hop with a pullback **b :** a progressive accumulation of the other couples by the leading couple in square dancing **4 :** something that is picked up: as **a :** an article (as a golf ball) found by chance **b :** an article or consignment taken up for shipment by a carrier **c :** a railway car, barge, trailer added to a train, tow, or tractor **d :** type matter saved for reuse with new copy **e** (1) **:** a sum or balance brought forward on accounts or records esp. in machine bookkeeping (2) **:** the receipts collected from a single cash register or the total collected for a certain period **f :** material to be broadcast or telecast that originates outside the studio or station ⟨the program was a live ~ from the theater⟩ **g :** an unaccented note or group of notes preceding the strong beat of the measure and beginning a musical phrase or composition **:** ANACRUSIS **5 :** someone who is picked up: as **a :** HITCHHIKER **b :** a chance and usu. temporary companion or acquaintance ⟨may pass the disease along to ~, prostitute, or wife —H.V.Tooker⟩ **6 :** something that picks up or is used for picking up: as **a :** ³BRUSH 3a **b :** a device (as a microphone or a thermocouple) that serves as a transducer between the source of vibrations (as of sound or heat) to be detected or measured and the part of the system that translates the collected signals into observable form; *esp* **:** a device for converting record groove undulations into corresponding electrical voltages which may be amplified in an electrical phonograph **c :** the electrical system or arrangements for connecting to a broadcasting station or studio a radio or television program produced outside the studio **d :** the apparatus used for picking up images and sound for television transmission ⟨the field ~ included four cameras⟩ **e :** an attachment to a harvester used for picking up grain or hay left in windrows by a swather for curing **7** *or* **pickup truck :** a light truck having an open body with low sides and tailboard mounted usu. on a passenger car chassis

pickup 7

**²pickup** \"\ *adj* **1 :** picking up or used in picking up ⟨~ station⟩ ⟨~ tongs⟩ **2 :** utilizing the available or convenient without prior planning ⟨a ~ ballgame⟩ ⟨leftovers enough for a ~ meal⟩

**pickup arm** *n* **:** TONE ARM

**pick-up baler** \'ˌ=ˌ=-\ *n* **:** a hay baler that gathers hay from a windrow and compresses it into bales

**pickup cartridge** *n* **:** a usu. removable portion of a phonograph pickup containing the stylus and the mechanism for converting stylus motion into an electrical voltage

**pickup current** *or* **pickup voltage** *n* **:** the current or voltage at which a magnetic contactor starts to close under normal operating temperature

**pick-up man** *n* **:** a mounted attendant in a rodeo who lifts a bucking horse rider from his mount when the time limit has expired

**pickup service** *n* **:** the collection of small shipments from a customer's door by trucks acting for railroads, truck lines, or airlines

**pickup tube** *n* **:** CAMERA TUBE

**pick·wick·i·an** \(')pik¦wikēən\ *adj, usu cap* [Samuel *Pickwick*, benevolent and simple-minded character in the novel *Pickwick Papers* (1836–37) by Charles Dickens †1870 Eng. novelist + E *-an*] **1 :** marked by simplicity and generosity of character or by an appearance and manner suggesting these qualities ⟨struck one as an almost *Pickwickian* old gentleman —Louis Auchincloss⟩ ⟨welcomed by a *Pickwickian* headmaster, a jolly, rotund man —Norris Houghton⟩ **2** [so called fr. the peculiar sense given to common words by Mr. Blotton and Mr. Pickwick, characters in the novel *Pickwick Papers*] **:** intended or taken in a sense other than the obvious or literal one **:** specially or whimsically limited or distorted in intended meaning ⟨injustice . . . is merely a *Pickwickian* expression for what human beings do not like —*Nation*⟩ ⟨evidently England is starving to death, if at all, only in a strictly *Pickwickian* sense —*Economist*⟩

**picky** \'pikē, -ki\ *adj* -ER/-EST [¹*pick* + *-y*] **:** overly fastidious **:** FUSSY, CHOOSY, FINNICKY ⟨a ~ eater⟩ ⟨a tedious day of ~ objections to the agriculture appropriations bill —*Time*⟩

**¹pic·nic** *also* **pick·nick** \'pik,nik\ *n* -S *often attrib* [G or F; G *picknick*, fr. F *pique-nique*, prob. redupl. (influenced by obs. F *nique* trifle, of imit. origin) of *piquer* to pick, peck, prick — more at PIKE] **1 a :** a social entertainment at which each person contributes food to a common table **b :** an excursion or outing with food usu. provided by members of the group and eaten in the open **2 a :** a pleasant or amusing experience **:** a time free of ordinary cares and responsibilities ⟨I don't expect being married to be a ~ like you seem to —Josephine Pinckney⟩ **b :** an easy task or feat ⟨as the fight started . . . any thoughts . . . that this was to be a ~ for him were dissipated —*Ring*⟩ **3 a :** a standard size of container for canned food **b :** a standard size of cheddar cheese **4** *or* **picnic ham** *or* **picnic shoulder :** a shoulder of pork with much of the butt removed commonly smoked and often boned — see PORK illustration

**²picnic** \"\ *vb* **picnicked; picnicked; picnicking; picnics** *vt* **:** to entertain with a picnic ~ *vi* **:** to go on or hold a picnic **:** eat in picnic fashion — **pic·nick·er** \-kə(r)\ *n* -S

**pic·nicky** \-kē\ *adj* [¹*picnic* + *-y*] **:** relating to or characteristic of picnics

**picnometer** *var of* PYCNOMETER

**pico-** *comb form* [ISV, fr. Sp *pico* odd number, small quantity, peak — more at PIC] **:** one trillionth ($10^{-12}$) part of — in units of the metric system ⟨*pico*farad⟩ ⟨*pico*gram⟩

**pi·coid** \'pī,kȯid\ *adj* [*pic-* (fr. NL *Picidae*) + *-oid*] **:** resembling or related to the Picidae

**picol** *var of* PICUL

**pic·o·line** \'pikə,lēn, -ˌlən\ *n* -S [ISV *pic-* (fr. L *pic-*, *pix* pitch) + *-ol* + *-ine* — more at PITCH] **:** any of the three liquid pyridine bases $CH_3C_5H_4N$ that are monomethyl derivatives of pyridine, are found in coal tar, ammonia liquor, and bone oil, and are used chiefly as solvents and in organic synthesis: **a :** the flammable alpha derivative that has an odor resembling that of pyridine — called also *2-picoline* **b :** the beta derivative that has a sweetish odor and is used in making nicotinic acid — called also *3-picoline* **c :** the gamma derivative used in making isonicotinic acid — called also *4-picoline*

**pic·o·lin·ic acid** \¦==¦linik-\ *n* **:** a crystalline acid $C_5H_4N(COOH)$ obtained by oxidation of 2-picoline; 2-pyridinecarboxylic acid

**pi·co·pi·co·gram** \'pīkō'pīkō,gram\ *n* [*pico-* + *pico-* + *-gram*] **:** a unit of mass equal to $10^{-24}$ gram — abbr *ppg*

**picory** *n* -ES [MF *picoree*, fr. *picorer* to maraud + *-ee* -y — more at PICKEER] *obs* **:** PILLAGE, FORAGING

**¹pi·cot** \'pē(,)kō\ *n* -S *often attrib* [F, lit., small point, fr. MF, fr. *pic* peak, point, prick, fr. *piquer* to prick] **1 :** one of a series of small ornamental loops forming an edging on ribbon or lace **2 :** an edge finish made by cutting through the center of a line of machine hemstitching or folding on a line of open stitches in hosiery **3 :** one of the small loops used for tatting and lace patterns

**²picot** \"\ *vt* -ED/-ING/-S **:** to finish with a picot

**pi·co·tah** *or* **pi·cot·tah** *or* **pic·co·tah** \pə'kōd·ə, -kädə\ *n* -S [Pg *picota*, lit., post, pillory, fr. *pico* point, peak, fr. *picar* to prick, pierce, fr. (assumed) VL *piccare* — more at PIKE] **:** a counterpoised sweep used in India for raising water from wells

**pic·o·tee** \,pikə'tē\ *n* -S [modif. of F *picoté* furnished with points, fr. past part. of *picoter* to mark with points or pricks, fr. *picot* small point, prick; fr. a variety of carnation that had a white ground marked with specks of color] **:** a flower (as carnation, tulip, rose) having one basic color with a margin of another color ⟨~ pattern⟩ ⟨~ edging⟩

**pic·o·tite** \'pikə,tīt\ *n* -S [F *picotite*, fr. *Picot*, Baron de la Peyrouse †1818 Fr. botanist + F *-ite*] **:** a dark brown variety of spinel containing chromium and iron

**¹picquet** *var of* PIQUET

**²pic·quet** \'pikət\ *chiefly Brit var of* PICKET

**pic·quet·er** \'pikəd·ə(r)\ *n* -S [F *piquet* (*de fleurs*) spray of flowers, spade, post, pointed object (fr. *piquer* to prick + *-et*) + E *-er* — more at PIKE] **:** one who bunches artificial flowers

**picr-** *or* **picro-** *comb form* [F, fr. Gk, fr. *pikros* bitter — more at PAINT] **1 :** bitter ⟨*Picr*amnia⟩ ⟨*Picro*dendron⟩ **2 :** picric acid ⟨*picr*yl⟩ ⟨*picro*carmine⟩ **3 :** containing magnesium ⟨*picro*merite⟩

**pic·ram·ic acid** \(')pi¦kramik-\ *n* [*picramic* ISV *picr-* + *amic* (acid)] **:** a red crystalline acid $C_6H_2(NO_2)_2(NH_2)OH$ obtained by reducing picric acid and used chiefly in making azo dyes

**pic·ram·ide** \pi'kra,mīd, 'pikrə,-, -ˌməd\ *n* [*picr-* + *amide*] **:** a yellow crystalline compound $C_6H_2(NO_2)_3NH_2$ made from picryl chloride and ammonia; 2,4,6-trinitro-aniline

**pic·ram·nia** \pik'ramnēə\ *n, cap* [NL, irreg. fr. *picr-* + Gk *thamnos* shrub + NL *-ia* — more at THAMN-] **:** a genus of tropical American shrubs or trees (family Simaroubaceae) with alternate pinnate leaves, small dioecious flowers, and baccate fruit — see BITTERBUSH

**pic·ras·min** \pik'razmən\ *n* -S [NL *Picrasma* (genus name of the bitterwood *Picrasma excelsum* — fr. Gk *pikrasmos* bitterness, fr. *pikros* bitter) + ISV *-in*] **:** a bitter crystalline principle $C_{22}H_{28}O_6$ occurring in Jamaica quassia

**pic·rate** \'pi,krāt\ *n* -S [ISV *picr-* + *-ate*] **1 :** a salt or ester of picric acid **2 :** a molecular complex formed by addition of picric acid to another compound (as a bicyclic or polycyclic aromatic hydrocarbon)

**pic·ric acid** \'pikrik-, -rēk-\ *n* [*picric* ISV *picr-* + *-ic*] **:** a bitter toxic explosive yellow crystalline strong acid $C_6H_2(NO_2)_3OH$ made usu. by nitration of phenolsulfonic acids or chlorobenzene and used chiefly in high explosives, as a dye or biological stain, as an antiseptic, and as a precipitant for organic bases and polycyclic hydrocarbons; 2,4,6-trinitrophenol

**-pic·rin** \'pikrən\ *n suffix* -S [ISV *-picr-* (fr. Gk *pikros* bitter) + *-in*] **1 :** bitterness ⟨gentio*picrin*⟩ **2 :** relation to picric acid ⟨chloro*picrin*⟩

**pic·ris** \'pikrəs\ *n, cap* [NL, fr. L, bitter lettuce, a salad, fr. Gk *pikris* oxtongue, fr. *pikros* bitter] **:** a genus of weedy herbs (family Compositae) chiefly of the Old World having leafy stems, large yellow ray flowers, and linear achenes

**pic·rite** \'pi,krīt\ *n* -S [F, fr. *picr-* + *-ite*] **1 :** a variety of olivine-diabase without feldspar **2 :** a variety of often porphyritic periodotite composed of either augite or hornblende and olivine

**pic·ro·carmine** \¦pikrō+\ *n* [ISV *picr-* + *carmine*] **:** a stain for tissue sections made by mixing solutions of carmine and picric acid

**pic·ro·chromite** \"+\ *n* [*picr-* + *chromite*] **:** MAGNESIOCHROMITE

**pic·ro·crocin** \¦pikrō+\ *n* [*picr-* + *crocin*] **:** a bitter crystalline terpene-glucoside $C_{16}H_{26}O_7$ from saffron (sense 2)

**pic·ro·den·dra·ce·ae** \,pikrōden'drāsē,ē\ *n pl, cap* [NL, fr. *Picrodendron*, type genus + *-aceae*] *in some classifications* **:** a family of plants coextensive with the genus *Picrodendron*

**pic·ro·den·dron** \,pikrō'dendrən\ *n, cap* [NL, fr. *picr-* + *-dendron*] **:** a small genus of West Indian trees and shrubs (family Simaroubaceae) with bitter wood, 3-foliolate leaves, and dioecious flowers — see JAMAICA WALNUT

**pic·ro·lite** \'pikrə,līt\ *n* -S [G *pikrolith*, fr. *picr-* + *-lith* -lite] **:** a dark green, gray, or brown fibrous variety of serpentine

**pic·ro·lon·ic acid** \¦pikrə¦länik-\ *n* [*picrolonic* fr. *picr-* + *-olon-* (in *pyrazolone*) + *-ic*] **:** a yellow crystalline acidic compound $C_{10}H_8N_4O_5$ made by nitration of methyl-phenylpyrazolone that yields yellow solutions with alkalies and is used as a precipitant for organic bases (as alkaloids)

**pic·rom·er·ite** \pi'krämə,rīt\ *n* -S [ISV *picr-* + *mer-* + *-ite*; orig. formed in It] **:** a mineral $K_2Mg(SO_4)_2.6H_2O$ consisting of a hydrous magnesium potassium sulfate and occurring as a white or colorless incrustation

**pic·ro·pharmacolite** \¦pikrō+\ *n* -S [G *pikropharmakolith*, fr. *pikr-* picr- + *pharmakolith* pharmacolite — more at PHARMACOLITE] **:** a mineral $(Ca,Mg)_3(AsO_4)_2.6H_2O$ composed of a hydrous arsenate of calcium and magnesium

**pic·ro·podophyllin** \"+\ *n* [ISV *picr-* + *podophyllin*] **:** a bitter crystalline compound obtained from podophyllin

**pic·ro·rhi·za** \,pikrə'rīzə\ *n* -S [NL, fr. *picr-* + *-rhiza*] **:** the dried rhizome of a Himalayan herb (*Picrorhiza kurrooa*) of the family Scrophulariaceae that is used in India as a bitter tonic and antiperiodic

**pic·ro·tin** \'pikrəd·ən\ *n* -S [ISV *picrotoxin* + *-in*] **:** a nonpoisonous bitter crystalline compound $C_{15}H_{18}O_7$ obtained from picrotoxin

**pic·ro·tox·in** \,pikrə'täksən\ *n* [ISV *picr-* + *tox-* + *-in*; orig. formed as F *picrotoxine*] **:** a poisonous bitter crystalline principle $C_{30}H_{34}O_{13}$ found esp. in cocculus indicus that is an equimolecular compound of picrotoxinin and picrotin and is a stimulant and convulsant drug administered intravenously as an antidote for poisoning by overdoses of barbiturates

**pic·ro·tox·in·in** \-sənən\ *n* -S [*picrotoxin* + *-in*] **:** a poisonous bitter crystalline compound $C_{15}H_{16}O_6$ obtained from picrotoxin

**pic·ry** \'pikrē\ *n* -ES [perh. fr. *picr-* + *-y*] **:** POISON IVY

**pic·ryl** \'pikrəl\ *n* -S [ISV *picr-* + *-yl*] **:** the univalent radical $C_6H_2(NO_2)_3-$ derived from picric acid by removal of the hydroxyl group; 2,4,6-trinitro-phenyl

**pics** *pl of* PIC

**pict** \'pikt\ *n* -S *usu cap* [ME *Pictes*, pl., Picts, fr. LL *Picti*] **:** one of a possibly non-Celtic people older than the Gaelic and Brythonic peoples who once occupied Great Britain, were in many places displaced by the Britons, carried on continual border wars with the Romans, and about the 9th century became finally amalgamated with the Scots

**pict** *abbr* pictorial

**pic·tar·nie** \'pik,tärni\ *also* **pick·a·ter·nie** \'pikə,tərni\ *n* -S [origin unknown] **1** *chiefly Scot* **:** BLACK-HEADED GULL **2** *chiefly Scot* **:** COMMON TERN

**pic·ta·vi** \pik'tā,vī\ *n pl, usu cap* [LL] **:** PICTONES

**¹pict·ish** \'piktish, -tēsh\ *adj, usu cap* [*Pict* + *-ish*] **:** of or relating to the Picts **:** resembling a Pict

**²pictish** \"\ *n* -ES *usu cap* **:** the language of the Picts that is known only from a few proper names, glosses, and inscriptions

**picto-** *comb form* [L *pictus* (past part. of *pingere* to paint) + E *-o-* — more at PAINT] **:** picture ⟨*picto*graph⟩

**pic·to·gram** \'piktə,gram\ *n* [ISV *picto-* + *-gram*] **:** PICTOGRAPH

**pic·to·graph** \-raf, -raa(ə)f, -raif, -råf\ *n* [*picto-* + *-graph*] **1 :** an ancient or prehistoric drawing or painting on a rock wall (as of a cave, cliff) — compare PETROGLYPH **2 a :** a pictorial representation of some object used to symbolize that object in pictography or in writing that includes elements of pictography **b :** a record in such symbols **3 :** one of the symbols belonging to any graphic system the characters of which are to a considerable extent pictorial in appearance regardless of whether the symbols serve a pictographic, ideographic, or phonetic function **4 :** a diagram representing statistical data by pictorial forms which can be varied in color, size, or number to indicate change

**pic·to·graph·ic** \¦==¦grafik\ *adj* [ISV *picto-* + *-graphic*] **1 :** consisting of or characterized by use of pictographs ⟨a ~ script⟩ ⟨the ~ stage in the development of writing⟩ **2 :** being a pictograph ⟨a ~ character⟩ **3 :** displaying the characteristics of a pictograph ⟨a character in its primitive ~ form⟩

**pic·to·graph·i·cal·ly** \-fək(ə)lē\ *adv* **:** by means of or in the manner of pictographs

**pic·tog·ra·phy** \pik'tägrəfē\ *n* -ES [ISV *picto-* + *-graphy*] **:** use of pictographs **:** PICTURE WRITING 1 a

**pic·to·nes** \'piktə,nēz\ *n pl, usu cap* [L] **:** an ancient people of western Gaul

**¹pic·to·ri·al** \(')pik¦tōrēəl, -tȯr-\ *adj* [LL *pictorius* pictorial (fr. L *pictor* painter + *-ius* -ious) + E *-al* — more at PICTURESQUE] **1 :** of or relating to a painter, a painting, or the painting or drawing of pictures ⟨~ perspective⟩ ⟨~ invention⟩ **2 a :** consisting of pictures **:** being in the form of a picture or pictograph ⟨~ records⟩ **b :** illustrated by or adorned with pictures ⟨~ weekly⟩ **c :** PICTOGRAPHIC **3 :** having the qualities of a picture **:** suggesting or conveying visual images ⟨~ imagination⟩ ⟨~ poetry⟩ — **pic·to·ri·al·ly** \-əlē, -li\ *adv* — **pic·to·ri·al·ness** *n* -ES

**²pictorial** \"\ *n* -S **1 :** a periodical employing a high proportion of pictorial matter **2 :** a postage stamp having a picture as the central feature of its design

**pic·to·ri·al·ism** \pik'tōrēə,lizəm\ *n* -S **:** the use or creation of pictures or visual images ⟨development from his original level of illustration into full ~ —Virgil Barker⟩

**pic·to·ri·al·ist** \-ˌləst\ *n* -S **:** one who produces a picture esp. by photography for its own sake or as an end in itself ⟨interesting both to the ~ and the professional is the article on architectural photography —*Photography Yr. Bk.*⟩

**pic·to·ri·al·iza·tion** \pik,tōrēələ'zāshən\ *n* -S [*pictorialize* + *-ation*] **:** the act or process of representing by a picture or illustrating with pictures ⟨detailed ~ of the . . . coronation —*Newsweek*⟩

**pic·to·ri·al·ize** \pik'tōrēə,līz\ *vt* -ED/-ING/-S [¹*pictorial* + *-ize*] **:** to make pictorial **:** represent in or as if in a picture ⟨each of the stories . . . recreated . . . with a *pictorialized* concept by the finest . . . artists —*adv*⟩

**pic·tor·ic** \(')pik¦tȯrik\ *adj* [LL *pictorius* + E *-ic*] **:** PICTORIAL — **pic·tor·i·cal·ly** \-rək(ə)lē\ *adv*

**pic·tou disease** \'pik(,)tü-\ *n, usu cap P* [fr. *Pictou*, Nova Scotia] **:** WINTON DISEASE

**picts** *pl of* PICT

**picts' house** *n, usu cap P* [so called fr. being attributed to the Picts] **:** one of the prehistoric dwellings in Scotland consisting of subterranean chambers with convergent stone walls

**pic·tun** \'pik,tün\ *n* -S [Maya, fr. *pic* 8000 + *tun* year of 360 days] **:** a period of 400 katuns or 8000 tuns in the Maya calendar — compare BAKTUN

**pic·tur·abil·i·ty** \,pikchərə'bilәd·ē\ *n* **:** the quality or state of being picturable

**pic·tur·able** \'pikchərəbəl\ *adj* **:** capable of or suited for being represented by a picture or visual image ⟨~ objects of everyday experience⟩ — **pic·tur·able·ness** *n* -ES — **pic·tur·ably** \-blē\ *adv*

**pic·tur·al** \'pikchərəl\ *adj* [L *pictura* + E *-al*] **:** PICTORIAL

**¹pic·ture** \'pikchə(r), -ksh-\ *n* -S *often attrib* [ME, fr. L *pictura*, fr. *pictus* (past part. of *pingere* to paint) + *-ura* -ure — more at PAINT] **1** *obs* **a :** the act, process, or art of painting **:** representation by painting **b :** pictorial representations **2 a :** a representation (as of a person, landscape, building) on canvas, paper, or other surface produced by painting, drawing, engraving, or photography ⟨old ~s of the family⟩ ⟨~s of the wedding⟩; *esp* **:** such representation as a work of art ⟨walls hung with ~s⟩ ⟨~ dealer⟩ **b** *obs* **:** STATUE, MODEL **3 :** a description so vivid or graphic as to suggest a mental image or give an accurate idea of the thing described ⟨he hath drawn my ~ in his letter —Shak.⟩ ⟨language, our most faithful and indispensable ~ of human experience —Susanne K. Langer⟩ ⟨horn and trumpet become parts of a musical ~⟩ **4 a :** something that by its likeness vividly suggests some other thing **:** COPY ⟨the boy is the ~ of his father⟩ **b :** a concrete embodiment of an abstraction **:** ILLUSTRATION, SYMBOL ⟨she was the very ~ of grief⟩ ⟨the ~ of health⟩ **5 a :** a transitory visible image or reproduction due to the working of physical laws or made by utilizing such laws (as with a lens) ⟨adjusting the television set for a brighter ~⟩ **b :** MOTION PICTURE ⟨a Western ~⟩ **c pictures** *pl, chiefly Brit* **:** MOVIES ⟨have a few drinks with their friends, and a grill, and then perhaps the ~*s* —Nevil Shute⟩ **6 :** a mental image ⟨shocks of corn were dotted about in her mind ~*s* —Elizabeth M. Roberts⟩ **7 :** a picturesque person or thing ⟨the ship was really a ~ with all her sails unfurled⟩ **8 :** TABLEAU 1 ⟨created a world with his words, and his fine image is never lost because of unnecessary stage ~*s* —Virginia B. Slaughter⟩ **9 a :** a scene or a set of facts or circumstances immediately present to the attention **:** a field of observation ⟨in all matters artistic, personal taste enters into the ~ —John Gutman⟩ **b :** verbal or graphic presentation of a problem or situation ⟨drew an alarming ~ of the economic future⟩ **c :** PATTERN, CONFIGURATION ⟨need more details to understand the full ~⟩ **d :** SITUATION ⟨in the spring the employment ~ will change⟩

**²picture** \"\ *vt* **pictured; pictured; picturing** \-chəriŋ, -sh(ə)r-\ **pictures** [ME *picturen*, fr. ¹*picture*] **1 a :** to paint or draw a representation, image, or visual conception of **:** form a likeness of on a surface **:** DEPICT ⟨*pictured* holding a banner aloft⟩ **b :** to show a picture of ⟨the room they finished for him is *pictured* on this page —Kathryn Larson⟩ **c :** to present (as a narrative) in pictures or provide with pictures **:** ILLUSTRATE ⟨printing, airing, and *picturing* the news —F.L. Mott⟩ **2 :** to represent (something abstract or imperceptible) in visible or symbolic form **:** PORTRAY ⟨illustrated his letters as he did, *picturing* what he couldn't put so well into words —J.K.Hutchens⟩ **3 :** to describe graphically **:** describe vividly in words ⟨likes to ~ the triumph of well-born Nordics over the Canadian wilderness —Malcolm Cowley⟩ **4 :** to form a mental image or definite impression of **:** IMAGINE ⟨the children . . . were *picturing* a beautiful, sad face, and the figure of a noble lady moving among her soldiers —Grace Kinnicut⟩ **5 :** to photograph for showing as a motion picture
**syn** see REPRESENT

**picture book** *n* **:** a book that consists wholly or chiefly of pictures

**picture bride** *n* **:** a bride in a picture marriage

**picture card** *n* **1 :** FACE CARD **2 :** PICTURE POSTCARD

**pic·ture·dom** \-(r)dəm\ *n* -S [¹*picture* + *-dom*] **:** FILMDOM

**pic·ture·drome** \'pikchə,drōm\ *n* -S [¹*picture* + *-drome*] *Brit* **:** a movie theater

**pictured-wing fly** \'==ˌ=-\ *n* **:** a member of the dipterous family Otitidae

**picture element** *n* **:** the smallest subdivision into which a television picture is divided in scanning

**picture frequency** *n* **:** the number of complete images sent or received per second in television transmission

**picture gallery** *n* **:** a large room for the exhibition of pictures; *also* **:** a collection of pictures

**pic·ture-go·er** \'pikchə,gōə(r\ *n, Brit* **:** one who goes regularly or frequently to see motion pictures

**picture hat** *n* **:** a woman's dressy broad-brimmed hat usu. for afternoon wear

**picture house** *or* **picture palace** *n, chiefly Brit* **:** a motion-picture theater

**pic·ture·less** \'pikchə(r)ləs\ *adj* **:** being without pictures

**picturelike** \'==ˌ=\ *adj* **:** PICTURESQUE

**picture marriage** *n* **:** a marriage (as between persons living in different countries) contracted after acquaintance only by an exchange of photographs; *specif* **:** such a marriage effected by a ceremony in the absence of the groom for the purpose of entitling the bride to enter the country of the groom's residence

**picture mirror** *n* **:** a mirror having a picture painted on the back of a glass framed with and immediately above the looking glass

**picture molding** *or* **picture mold** *n* **:** a narrow molding fastened to the walls of a room near the ceiling to support pictures hung by hooks

**picture ore** *n* **:** ore in which gold or silver can be seen before processing

**picture paper** *n, chiefly Brit* **:** an illustrated newspaper

**picture plane** *n* **:** the surface of a picture drawn in linear perspective regarded as a transparent plane perpendicular to the lines of sight on which the points of objects in the scene may be considered as projected by straight lines drawn from these points to the eye

**picture postcard** *n* **:** a postcard bearing a picture typically of a scene or place of interest

**picture puzzle** *n* **:** JIGSAW PUZZLE

**pic·tur·er** \'pikchərə(r)\ *n* -S **:** one that makes pictures **:** PAINTER

**picture rail** *n* **:** PICTURE MOLDING

**pictures** *pl of* PICTURE, *pres 3d sing of* PICTURE

**picture show** *n* **1 :** an exhibition of paintings **2 :** MOTION PICTURE

**picture signal** *n* **:** the electrical signal derived from the television camera — called also *video signal*

**¹pic·tur·esque** \¦pikchə¦resk, -ksh-\ *adj* [modif. (influenced by ¹*picture*) of F & It; F *pittoresque*, fr. It *pittoresco*, fr. *pittore* painter (fr. L *pictor*, fr. *pictus* — past part. of *pingere* to paint — + *-or*) + *-esco* -esque — more at PAINT] **1 a :** like a picture **:** resembling or suggesting a painted scene **:** suitable as a subject for painting ⟨~ village⟩ ⟨~ fishing fleet⟩ ⟨discovered grouped in ~ attitudes about the stage —W.S. Gilbert⟩ **b :** charmingly or pleasingly irregular or casual in appearance **:** creating informal patterns of shape, light, and color ⟨~ style of architecture⟩ ⟨venerable family mansion in a highly ~ state of semidilapidation —T.L.Peacock⟩ **c :** unusual, primitive, or markedly characteristic in appearance **:** QUAINT ⟨modern touches without sacrificing its ~ French colonial charm —Mary R. Johnson⟩ ⟨pioneering conditions that are ~ to look back upon but were rather trying to live through —Marquis James⟩ **2 :** characterized by an interest in what is picturesque ⟨easy for a ~ historian to lay side by side the most glaring contrasts —Virginia Woolf⟩ **3 :** evoking mental images **:** VIVID ⟨~ epithets⟩ ⟨gave a ~ account of his adventure⟩ — **pic·tur·esque·ly** *adv* — **pic·tur·esque·ness** *n* -ES

**²picturesque** \"\ *n* -S **:** picturesque quality **:** PICTURESQUENESS; *esp* **:** esthetic quality that evokes the atmosphere of another age, environment, or mode of existence — used with *the* ⟨the novelist of contemporary manners needs to be saturated with a sense of the ~ in modern things —Arnold Bennett⟩

**picture tube** *n* **:** KINESCOPE 1

**picture window** *n* **:** an outsize window (as in a living room) placed to frame or as if to frame a desirable exterior view and often between two narrower windows

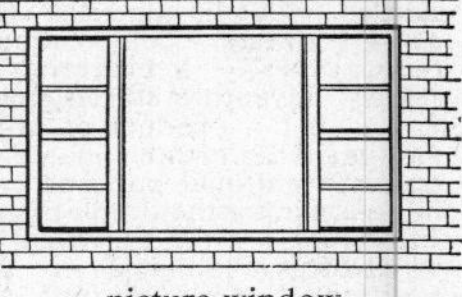
picture window

**picture writing** *n* **1 a :** the act or art of recording events or expressing messages by pictures representing actions or facts **b :** the record or message so represented **2 :** a graphic system of symbols that are to a considerable extent pictorial in appearance regardless of whether they serve pictographic, ideographic, or phonetic functions

**pic·tur·iza·tion** \,pikchərə'zāshən\ *n* -S [*picturize* + *-ation*] **:** the act or fact of presenting in pictures

**pic·tur·ize** \'pikchə,rīz\ *vt* -ED/-ING/-S *see -ize in Explan Notes* [¹*picture* + *-ize*] **:** to make a picture of **:** present in pictures; *esp* **:** to make into a motion picture

**pic·u·cule** \'pikyə,kyül\ *n* -s [F, prob. fr. *pic* woodpecker (fr. L *picus*) + L *cuculus* cuckoo — more at CUCKOO] : WOODHEWER 1
**pi·cu·da** \pə̇'küdə\ *n* -s [AmerSp, fr. Sp, fem. of *picudo* beaked, pointed, sharp, fr. *pico* beak, modif. of L *beccus* beak, fr. Gaulish] : GREAT BARRACUDA
**pic·u·dil·la** \,pikyə'dilə\ *n* -s [AmerSp, dim. of *picuda*] : a small West Indian and tropical Atlantic barracuda (*Sphyraena picudilla*)
**pi·cu·do** \pə̇'kü(,)dō\ *n* -s [AmerSp, fr. Sp, sharp] : BOLL WEEVIL
**pic·ul** *or* **pic·ol** *also* **pik·ol** \'pikəl\ *or* **pec·ul** \'pek-\ *n* -s [Malay *pikul* to carry a heavy load (i.e. as much as an ordinary man can lift)] : any of various units of weight used in China and southeast Asia; *esp* : a Chinese unit equal to 133.33 pounds
**pic·u·let** \'pikyələ̇t\ *also* **pic·ule** \'pi,kyül\ *n* -s [*piculet* fr. L *picus* woodpecker + E *-let; picule* fr. L *picus* + E *-ule*] : any of numerous small woodpeckers that form a distinct subfamily of Picidae, have the tail feathers soft and rounded, and are widely distributed in So. America, Africa, and the East Indies
**pi·cun·che** \pə̇'künchē\ *n, pl* **picunche** *or* **picunches** *usu cap* **1 a :** an Araucanian people of central Chile **b :** a member of such people **2 :** the language of the Picunche people
**pi·cu·ris** \'pikərə̇s\ *n, pl* **picuris** *or* **picurises** *usu cap* **1 a :** a Tanoan people occupying a pueblo in New Mexico **b :** a member of such people **2 :** the language of the Picuris people
**pi·cus** \'pīkəs\ *n, cap* [NL, fr. L, woodpecker — more at PIE] : a genus formerly including all woodpeckers but now usu. restricted to the green woodpecker (*P. viridis*) of Europe and western Asia and its related forms
**pi·dan** \pē'dän\ *n* -s [Chin (Pek) *p'i[2]tan[4]*, lit., covered eggs] : duck eggs preserved in a brine to which lime, ashes, and an infusion of tea are added and after several months coated with rice hulls
**pid·dle** \'pidᵊl\ *vi* **piddled; piddled; piddling** \-d(ᵊ)liŋ\ **piddles** [origin unknown] **1 :** to deal or work in trifling or petty ways : act idly or inefficiently : waste time : TRIFLE, PUTTER, DAWDLE **2 :** to pick at one's food **3 :** URINATE — not often in polite use
**pid·dler** \-d(ᵊ)lə(r)\ *n* -s : one that piddles : TRIFLER, PUTTERER
**pid·dling** *adj* : TRIFLING, TRIVIAL, PALTRY ⟨~ profits⟩ ⟨wore my patience . . . with her endless and ~ detail —U.P.Hass⟩
**pid·dock** \'pidək\ *n* -s [origin unknown] : a bivalve mollusk of the genus *Pholas* or family Pholadidae characterized by boring holes in wood, clay, peat, and rocks
**pi·ded** \'pīdə̇d\ *adj* [by alter.] *dial* : PIED
**pid·gin** *also* **pi·geon** \'pijə̇n\ *n* -s [*Pidgin English*] **1 :** a form of speech that usu. has a simplified grammar and a limited often mixed vocabulary and is used principally for intergroup communication: as **a :** BÊCHE-DE-MER 2 **b :** WEST AFRICAN PIDGIN **c :** PIDGIN ENGLISH **2 :** PIGEON 5
**pidgin english** *n, usu cap P&E* [*pidgin* fr. Pidgin English, business modif. of E *business*] : an English-based pidgin orig. used in Chinese ports
**pid·gin·iza·tion** \,pijə̇nə̇'zāshən\ *n* -s : the process of pidginizing
**pid·gin·ize** \'pijə̇,nīz\ *vt* -ED/-ING/-S [*pidgin* + *-ize*] : to cause (a language) to develop pidgin : adapt to pidgin ⟨a *pidginized* variety of English —R.A.Hall b.1911⟩
**pi–dog** *var of* PYE-DOG
**pid·yon ha·ben** \,pidyənhə'ben\ *n, pl* **pidyon habens** *or* **pidyon habonin** [LHeb *pidyōn habēn*, lit., redemption of the son] : a traditional Jewish ceremonial rite observed on the 30th day after the birth of a first-born male child of one not a Cohen or a Levite in which the father symbolically relieves the child of ritual responsibilities by redeeming him from a Cohen for a certain sum
[1]**pie** \'pī\ *n* -s [ME, fr. OF, fr. L *pica;* akin to L *picus* woodpecker, OHG *speh, speht,* ON *spætr* and perh. to Skt *pika* cuckoo] **1 a :** MAGPIE 1 **b** *dial chiefly Brit* : MAGPIE 2 **2 a** *obs* : a cunning or wily person **b** *archaic* : a voluble, talkative, or impudent person **3 :** a pied or parti-colored animal
[2]**pie** \"\ *n* -s [ME, perh. fr. [1]*pie*] **1 a :** a food usu. consisting of meat or fruit baked in or under dough esp. in a dish or pan lined with pastry or topped with pastry or both ⟨deep-dish ~⟩ ⟨apple ~⟩ **b :** a layer of cake split in half horizontally and spread with a custard, cream, or jam filling — see BOSTON CREAM PIE, WASHINGTON PIE **2 :** something resembling a pie ⟨mud ~⟩ **3 :** a heap or pile: as **a** *dial Eng* : a pile of potatoes or other root crop stored in a pit and covered with straw **b** *dial Eng* : a manure pile **4 :** something easy or much desired ⟨caught him, and the rest was ~ —G.F.T.Ryall⟩ ⟨we can get four million dollars, easy as ~ —Nancy Rutledge⟩ ⟨if there is going to be any ~, they want to be in —*New Republic*⟩ **5 a :** AFFAIR, BUSINESS, UNDERTAKING ⟨she wanted her finger . . . in every possible social ~ —Mary Deasy⟩ **b :** a whole regarded as divisible into shares ⟨industry is getting its share of the prosperity ~ —A.H.Raskin⟩
[3]**pie** \"\ *or* **pye** \"\ *n* -s [ME, prob. fr. [1]*pie*] **1 :** a table or collection of ecclesiastical rules used in England before the Reformation to ascertain the proper service or office for the day **2** *obs* : an alphabetical index or catalog (as of court records)
[4]**pie** \"\ *var of* PI
[5]**pie** \"\ *n* -s [Hindi *pāī*, fr. Skt *pādikā* quarter, fr. *pāda* foot, leg, quarter — more at FOOT] **1 :** a former monetary unit of India and Pakistan equal to 1/192 rupee **2 :** a coin representing one pie unit
[1]**piebald** \'=,=\ *adj* [[1]*pie* + *bald*] **1 :** marked by or with usu. two different colors: **a :** spotted or blotched with black and white **b :** SKEWBALD **2 :** composed of incongruous parts : HETEROGENEOUS, MIXED, MOTLEY ⟨this ~ jargon —Sir Walter Scott⟩ **syn** see VARIEGATED
[2]**piebald** \"\ *n* -s **1 :** a piebald animal (as a horse) **2 :** a person or animal of mixed blood or qualities
**pie·bald·ly** \-ȯl(d)lē\ *adv* : in a piebald manner
**pie·bald·ness** \-ȯl(d)nə̇s\ *n* -ES : the quality or state of being piebald
**pie–bed** \'=,=\ *n* [by shortening] : APPLE-PIE BED
[1]**piece** \'pēs\ *n* -s [ME *pece, piece,* fr. OF, fr. (assumed) VL *pettia*, fr. (assumed) Gaulish; akin to Bret *pez* piece, W *peth* part, thing, OIr *cuit* part] **1 :** a part of a whole : FRAGMENT, PORTION ⟨the besieging forces would try to mine under a ~ of wall —Tom Wintringham⟩ **2 a** *obs* : MAN — usu. used disparagingly **b :** GIRL, WOMAN, BAGGAGE **3 :** an object or individual regarded as a unit of a kind or class : EXAMPLE ⟨handsome teak tables copied . . . from antique ~s —*New Yorker*⟩ ⟨each ~ of ripe fruit . . . has to be picked by hand —*Sat. Eve. Post*⟩: as **a :** a person exemplifying a particular quality ⟨thy mother was a ~ of virtue —Shak.⟩ **b :** a period of time esp. if brief ⟨sat thinking for a ~⟩ **c :** an interval of space regarded as part of a longer distance ⟨had gone a fair ~ of the way —A.J.Liebling⟩ **d :** an individual instance or specimen ⟨a ~ of impudence⟩ ⟨a ~ of news⟩ **4 a :** a length varying from 40 to 120 yards of cloth suitable for processing and esp. for dyeing and finishing **b** *archaic* : a standard or customary quantity or length of merchandise (as wallpaper, wine) made up for sale or use **c :** a pair, block, strip, or sheet of stamps or a single stamp considered as a single unit for sale as philatelic material **5 :** a product of creative work: as **a :** a literary composition ⟨a collection of mostly out-of-the-way ~s — a biography, a fictional biography, horror stories, adventure stories, and long short stories —*Saturday Rev.*⟩ **b :** a product of graphic or plastic art : PAINTING, PICTURE, SCULPTURE ⟨images of the Buddha are made to certain conventional patterns and there is often great difficulty in determining the origin of any ~ on stylistic grounds —C.P. Fitzgerald⟩ **c :** a theatrical production : DRAMA, PLAY ⟨the series of psychological ~s —Leslie Rees⟩ **d :** a musical composition ⟨has played four American ~s in a row —Virgil Thomson⟩ **e :** a passage to be recited : DECLAMATION ⟨spoke his ~ at the school graduation⟩ **6 :** a projectile weapon (as a rifle, revolver, or artillery big gun) ⟨ceased to debate the question of his ~ being loaded —Stephen Crane⟩ **7 a :** a coin of a specified metal ⟨gold ~⟩ ⟨~ of silver⟩ or denomination ⟨shilling ~⟩ ⟨10-cent ~⟩ **b** *obs* : any of several 17th and early 18th century English gold coins (as the unite, sovereign, or guinea) **c :** TOKEN, COUNTER ⟨good-luck ~⟩ **8** *chiefly dial* : a light simple lunch esp. when not eaten as a regular meal ⟨a ~ in our pockets, so that mealtimes didn't matter —Margaret Aitken⟩ **9** *obs* : a fortified city or other stronghold **10 :** a strip of leather inserted in a panel or affixed between bands on the backbone of a book and lettered **11 :** FLOOR 10 **12 a :** a man used in playing a board game; *specif* : any of the 16 chessmen of superior rank as distinguished from the pawns — see BISHOP, KING, KNIGHT, QUEEN, ROOK **b** *slang* : PLAYING CARD ⟨a ~ of trump⟩ **13 :** LOG 1a **14 :** a chunk of whole blubber **15 pieces** *pl* : portions picked out of the skirtings as suitable to be included with better grade wools **16** *archaic* : an inferior crystallized sugar obtained as one of the products of a now obsolete manufacturing process **17 :** OPINION, VIEWPOINT, MIND ⟨you have to know your ~ to get by them —H.J.Laski⟩ ⟨just about every accredited Republican spokesman has said his ~ —R.H.Rovere⟩ **18 a :** an act of copulation — usu. considered vulgar **b :** a partner in sexual intercourse — usu. considered vulgar **19 :** something composed of a specified material ⟨fur ~⟩ ⟨floral ~⟩ **20 :** part ownership of an enterprise or property ⟨had a ~ of a nearby automobile dealership⟩ **syn** see PART — **by the piece** *adv* : at a piecework rate ⟨paid *by the piece*⟩ — **of a piece :** of uniform kind or quality : CONSISTENT — sometimes used with *with* ⟨his performance under stress was *of a piece* with his honorable record⟩ — **on piece :** on a piece of cover — used of an adhesive stamp — **piece of one's mind :** TONGUE-LASHING ⟨was giving his jockey a *piece of his mind* —*Irish Digest*⟩ — **to pieces** *adv* **1 :** THOROUGHLY, COMPLETELY ⟨love you *to pieces*⟩ — often used with *all* **2 a :** into fragments : to bits : APART ⟨an elaborate toy fell *to pieces*⟩ — often used with *all* **b :** out of control : out of command — often used with *all* ⟨went *all to pieces* when the news came⟩
[2]**piece** \"\ *vb* -ED/-ING/-S [ME *pecen*, fr. *pece* piece, n.] *vt* **1 :** to repair, renew, or complete by adding pieces : PATCH ⟨*pieced* from scrap a locomotive —A.F.Harlow⟩ ⟨*pieced* out a set of china⟩ **2 :** to join into a whole : unite the parts of : combine out of pieces ⟨had been *piecing* a quilt all afternoon⟩ — often used with *together* ⟨his new book . . . has been *pieced* together from talks —Merle Miller⟩ **3 a :** FOOT 8 ⟨~ an arrow⟩ **b :** to splice (a stele) with other wood **c :** to splice (new wood) in a bow where a defect has been cut out ~ *vi* **1** *obs* : to come or fit together : coalesce from parts : AGREE, ASSEMBLE **2** *chiefly dial* : to eat between meals : nibble at snacks ⟨there he was, *piecing* on the ham —Eudora Welty⟩ **3 :** to join broken threads, slivers, or rovings in spinning or other textile manufacturing operations — **piece up :** to raise the temperature of mash in brewing by putting hot water into the mash tun under the false bottom
**piece accent** *n* : an accent cast by itself on a separate type body ⟨*piece accents* are available for the diacritics ˊ ˆ ¨ ˜ ³⟩ — called also *floating accent, loose accent*
**piece bag** *n* : a bag of cloth scraps suitable for quilting or for patches ⟨silk and ribbon from her *piece bag* —Amy Lowell⟩
**piece broker** *n, archaic* : a dealer in cloth remnants
**piece by piece** *adv* : bit by bit
**pièce de ré·sis·tance** \pē,esdərə̇'zē'stäⁿ(t)s, -(,)rā'z-, -zi's-, -äⁿs *sometimes* ,pēsd- *or* -_rə̇'zistən(t)s *or* -_rē'zistən(t)s\ *n, pl* **pièces de résistance** \"\ [F, lit., piece of resistance] **1 :** the chief dish of a meal ⟨the official *pièce de résistance*, labeled fried chicken on toast, proved after careful examination to be sea gull —*Textile World*⟩ **2 :** the showpiece of a collection : the outstanding item of a group : the prize piece or main exhibit ⟨the *pièce de résistance* — a Christmas mummers' play —Angelica Gibbs⟩ ⟨the *pièce de résistance* appears in a luxurious black antelope coat —*Women's Wear Daily*⟩
**piece–dye** \'=,=\ *vt* : to dye after weaving or knitting — distinguished from *yarn-dye*
**piece fraction** *n* : a fraction set in type on two separate type bodies (as 17/32 by juxtaposing 17/ and /32) — called also *built-up fraction, split fraction*
**piece goods** *n pl* : cloth fabrics that are sold from the bolt at retail in lengths specified by the customer — called also *yard goods*
**piece mark** *n* : ASSEMBLY MARK
[1]**piece·meal** \'pē'smē(ə)l\ *adv* [ME *pece-mele*, fr. *pece* piece + *-mele* -meal] **1 :** one piece at a time : by degrees : little by little : GRADUALLY ⟨has achieved the real substance of independence gradually and ~ —H.R.Lieberman⟩ **2 :** in pieces or fragments : APART ⟨the beasts will tear thee ~ —Alfred Tennyson⟩
[2]**piecemeal** \"\ *n* : FRAGMENT — usu. used with *by* ⟨we know . . . by ~ and accumulation —J.H.Newman⟩
[3]**piecemeal** \"\ *adj* : done, made, or accomplished piece by piece or in a fragmentary way : GRADUAL ⟨engaged in ~ attacks upon discrimination —*Collier's Yr. Bk.*⟩
[4]**piecemeal** \"\ *vt* : to divide piecemeal : separate into pieces
**piece mold** *n* : a sculptor's mold (as of plaster of paris) that can be removed from the cast in pieces
**piec·en** \'pēsᵊn\ *vt* -ED/-ING/-S [[1]*piece* + *-en*] *dial Eng* : to piece together : SPLICE
**piece of eight :** an old Spanish peso of eight reals
**piece of perspective 1** *obs* : a picture painted so as to appear distorted or confused except when viewed from a single viewpoint **2** *obs* : PEEP SHOW
**piece of water :** LAKE, POND
**piece price** *n* : PIECE RATE
**piece price system** *n* : a convict labor system in which a private contractor furnishes the raw materials and pays the government a stipulated price for the work done on each piece or article produced
**piec·er** \'pēsə(r)\ *n* -s **1 :** one that pieces : PATCHER **2 :** one that joins or collects pieces; *esp* : a textile worker who pieces threads
**piece rate** *n* : the price per unit of production paid to a pieceworker
**piece–root grafting** *n* : propagation in which the root of a seedling is cut into two or more parts and each is used as a stock
**pieces** *pl of* PIECE, *pres 3d sing of* PIECE
**piecework** \'=,=\ *n* : work done by the piece and paid for at a standard rate for each unit produced — compare TIMEWORK
**piece·work·er** \"ə(r)\ *n* [*piecework* + *-er*] : a worker engaged on piecework
**pie chart** *n* [[2]*pie*] : a circle divided by several radii into sectors showing by their relative areas the relative magnitudes of quantities or the relative frequencies of items of a frequency distribution

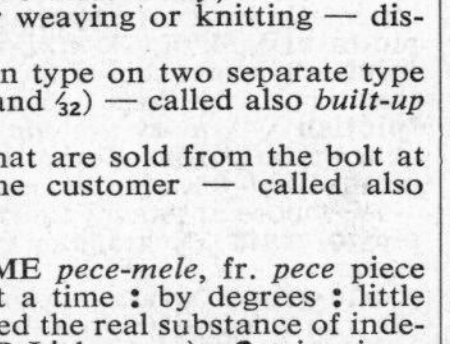

transportation 4% | operating 12% | savings 10% | food 32% | self improvement 6% | clothes 12% | shelter 24%

pie chart

**piecing** *n* -s [ME *pecing*, fr. gerund of *pecen* to piece] **1 :** the uniting of pieces : MENDING, PATCHING **2 :** an arrow footing or any piece of wood set in an arrow or bow
**pie–counter** \'=,==\ *n* [[2]*pie*] : political patronage or spoils esp. when regarded as venal or corrupt ⟨has been kept away from the *pie-counter* for these four long years —*Los Angeles (Calif.) Times*⟩
**piecrust** \'=,=\ *n* **1 :** paste for pies **2 :** the pastry shell of a pie
**piecrust table** *n* : a tip-top table of the Chippendale style and period with raised and decoratively carved edge

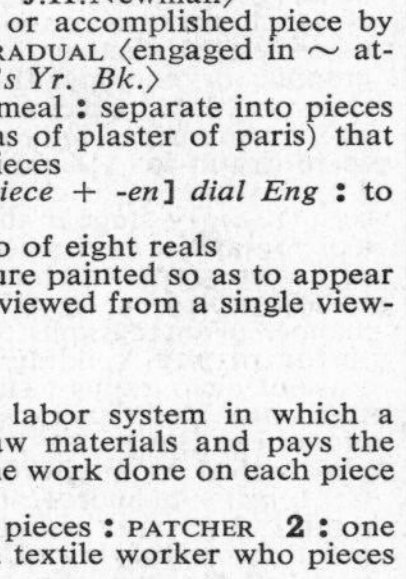

piecrust table

[1]**pied** \'pīd\ *adj* [ME, fr. [1]*pie* + *-ed*] : of two or more colors in blotches (as black and white) : PARTI-COLORED, PIEBALD, VARIEGATED ⟨a ~ coat⟩; *also* : wearing or having a parti-colored coat ⟨a ~ horse⟩ **syn** see VARIEGATED
[2]**pied** *past of* PI *or of* PIE
**pied antelope** *n* [[1]*pied*] : BONTEBOK
**pied–à–terre** \pē'ād·ə'te(ə)r, ,pyā-\ *n, pl* **pieds–à–terre** \-ād·ə-\ [F, lit., foot to the ground] : a temporary or second lodging (as a city apartment maintained by a country dweller)
**pied–billed grebe** \'=,=-\ *n* [[1]*pied*] : a medium-sized No. American grebe (*Podilymbus podiceps*) that is largely dark grayish brown above and whitish below and has a whitish bill encircled by a black band — called also *dabchick, hell-diver*
**pied brant** *n* : WHITE-FRONTED GOOSE
**pied dishwasher** *n* : PIED WAGTAIL
**pied duck** *n* : LABRADOR DUCK
**pied·ed** \'pīdə̇d\ *adj* [[1]*pied* + *-ed*] *dial* : PIED
**pied finch** *n* **1 :** CHAFFINCH **2** *dial Eng* : a snow bunting in immature plumage
**pied flycatcher** *n* : a common European flycatcher (*Muscicapa hypoleuca*) having the male black and white
**pied·fort** *or* **pie·fort** \pē'ā'fȯ(ə)r, (')pyā-\ *n* -s [F *pied-fort*, fr. *pied* foot (fr. L *ped-, pes*) + *fort* strong, fr. L *fortis* — more at FOOT, FORT] : a coin struck on an unusually thick flan (as some pattern pieces and multiple coins of France, Bohemia, and the Low Countries)
**pied goose** *n* [[1]*pied*] **1 :** WHITE-FRONTED GOOSE **2 :** MAGPIE GOOSE
**piedish** \'=,=\ *n* [[2]*pie* + *dish*] *Brit* : a pie plate or deep baking dish
**pied lemming** *n* [[1]*pied*] : any of various No. American lemmings (genus *Dicrostonyx*) that have some claws much enlarged and a white winter coat — compare COLLARED LEMMING
[1]**pied·mont** \'pēd,mänt\ *adj* [fr. *Piedmont*, region of northwest Italy] : lying or formed at the base of mountains
[2]**piedmont** \"\ *n* -s : a piedmont district, plain, or glacier
[1]**pied·mon·tese** \'pēdmən·'tēz, -ēs\ *n, pl* **piedmontese** *cap* [*Piedmont*, region in northwest Italy + E *-ese*] : a native or inhabitant of Piedmont, Italy
[2]**piedmontese** \"\ *adj, usu cap* **1 :** of, relating to, or characteristic of Piedmont, Italy **2 :** of, relating to, or characteristic of people of Piedmont
**piedmont glacier** *n* : a glacier formed by convergence of the ends of valley glaciers at the base of mountains
**pied·mont·ite** \'pēd,mänt·,īt\ *n* -s [modif. of G *piemontit*, fr. It *Piemonte* Piedmont + G *-it* -ite] : a reddish brown or black mineral allied to epidote and containing manganese
**pied·ness** *n* -ES : the quality or state of being pied : VARIEGATION
**pie–dog** *var of* PYE-DOG
**pied pip·er** \'pīd'pīpə(r)\ *n, usu cap both Ps* [fr. the *Pied Piper of Hamelin*, title and hero of poem (1842) by Robert Browning †1889 Eng. poet] : one that offers strong but delusive enticement : a leader who makes irresponsible promises
**pie·dra** \pē'ādrə, 'pyā-\ *n* -s [AmSp, fr. Sp, stone, fr. L *petra* rock, stone, fr. Gk] : a fungus disease of the hair marked by the formation of small stony nodules along the hair shafts
**pied starling** *n* [[1]*pied*] : a large crested gray-and-white starling (*Fregilupus varius*) of Réunion Island now extinct
**pied stilt** *n* : WHITE-HEADED STILT
**pied wagtail** *n* : a water wagtail (*Motacilla alba yarrellii*) having chiefly black-and-white plumage that is the commonest wagtail in the British Isles
**pied widgeon** *n* **1 :** GARGANEY **2 :** GOOSANDER
**pied–winged coot** \'=,wiŋd-\ *n* : VELVET SCOTER
**pied–winged curlew** *n* : WILLET
**pied woodpecker** *n* : GREAT SPOTTED WOODPECKER
**piedy** \'pīdē\ *adj* [[1]*pied* + *-y*] *chiefly Midland* : PIED
**pie–eyed** \'='=\ *adj* [[2]*pie*] : INTOXICATED ⟨can a grown man get *pie-eyed* on beer —Maxwell Anderson⟩
**pie–faced** \'='=\ *adj* : having a round, smooth, or blank face ⟨a pair of *pie-faced* louts —A.J.Liebling⟩
**piefort** *var of* PIEDFORT
**pie·gan** \pē'gan\ *n, pl* **piegan** *or* **piegans** *usu cap* **1 a :** an Indian people of the Blackfoot confederacy **b :** a member of the Piegan people **2 :** the language of the Piegan people
**pieing** *pres part of* PIE
**pie in the sky** [fr. *You'll get pie in the sky when you die*, line in *The Preacher and the Slave* (*ab*1906), song by Joe Hill] : a prospect or promise of deferred happiness or prosperity ⟨good, solid, efficient government is more palatable than *pie in the sky* —Gordon Harrison⟩
**pie·man** \'pīmən\ *n, pl* **piemen 1 :** a baker or cook who specializes in making pies **2 :** a pie vendor
**piemarker** \'=,==\ *n* [so called fr. the use of its pods for stamping pie crust] : an Indian mallow (*Abutilon theophrasti*)
**pien** *or* **piend** \'pēn(d)\ *n* -s [perh. alter. of *peen*] : ARRIS
**pien check** *n* : a rabbet cut out of a pien (as in the upper of two consecutive stone steps) as a partial means of support
**pien niu** \pē,ennē'(y)ü\ *n* [prob. fr. Chin *pien[1]* frontier + *niu[2]* ox, cow] : a hybrid between Chinese domestic cattle and the yak
**pieplant** \'=,=\ *n, chiefly dial* : RHUBARB
**pie plate** *n* : a metal, ceramic, or glass plate for baking pies
**pie·pou·dre** *or* **pie·pow·der** \'pī,pau̇də(r)\ *n* -s [ME *pipoudre* itinerant trader — more at COURT OF PIEPOUDRE] : TRAVELER, WAYFARER; *esp* : an itinerant merchant — see COURT OF PIEPOUDRE; compare DUSTYFOOT
**pieprint** \'=,=\ *n* [so called fr. the use of its pods for stamping pie crust] : an Indian mallow (*Abutilon theophrasti*)
**pier** \'pi(ə)r, -iə\ *n* -s [ME *pere, per,* fr. OE *per*, fr. ML *pera*] **1 :** an intermediate support for the adjacent ends of two bridge spans — distinguished from *abutment* **2 a :** a breakwater, groin, or mole extending into navigable water for use as a landing place or promenade or to protect or form a harbor **b :** a structure built out into the water on piles for use as a landing place or pleasure resort **c** *obs* : HAVEN **3 :** a vertical structural support: as **a :** the wall between two windows, doors, or other openings **b :** PILLAR, PILASTER; *esp* : one that carries a major load (as at a church crossing) **c :** a pillar, post, or other vertical member that supports the end of an arch or lintel : DOORPOST, GATEPOST, BUTTRESS **d :** an auxiliary mass of masonry used to stiffen a wall **e :** a vertical layer of ashlars in a rubble wall **4 :** a structural mount (as of a large telescope) usu. of stonework, concrete, or steel **syn** see WHARF
**pier·age** \'pirij\ *n* -s [*pier* + *-age*] : WHARFAGE
**pier arch** *n* : an arch supported by piers; *esp* : a side arch of the nave of a basilican church
**pier buttress** *n* : the pier that receives the thrust of a flying buttress
[1]**pierce** \'pi(ə)rs, -iəs\ *vb* -ED/-ING/-S [ME *percen*, fr. OF *percer, percier,* perh. fr. (assumed) VL *pertusiare*, fr. L *pertusus*, past part. of *pertundere* to pierce, fr. *per* through + *tundere* to beat, pound — more at FOR, STUTTER] *vt* **1 a :** to run into or through as a pointed instrument or weapon does : make a thrust into or through : STAB ⟨the needle *pierced* an ear lobe⟩ ⟨argued that the meaty edges of steak neither should be gashed or *pierced* with a fork —Jane Nickerson⟩ ⟨*pierced* his side with a spear⟩ ⟨the rigid, eternal obelisk *piercing* the mist like a sword —Louis Bromfield⟩ **b :** to penetrate sharply or painfully ⟨the cold *pierced* him to the bone⟩ ⟨tight-lipped whistles *pierced* the din —Darrell Berrigan⟩ ⟨bullets *pierced* his flesh⟩ **2 :** to make a hole in or through : BORE, PERFORATE, TUNNEL ⟨cylinders *pierced* by three or more . . . longitudinal perforations —*Encyc. Americana*⟩ ⟨the marble walls are *pierced* with four doors —*Amer. Guide Series: N.J.*⟩ ⟨the railway tunnel . . . ~s the rolling uplands —Guy McCrone⟩ **3 :** to force or make a way into or through : break into or through ⟨wanted to get swiftly through the field of fire and ~ and overthrow the enemy lines —Tom Wintringham⟩ ⟨the market . . . has already made new lows for the year and the question in the minds of technical followers is whether it will ~ the lows of last October —C.N.Stabler⟩ **4 :** to penetrate with the eye or mind : see through : COMPREHEND, DISCERN ⟨stood hidden in the doorway of an old empty house, *piercing* the darkness with wild eyes —Liam O'Flaherty⟩ ⟨a Shakespeare, *piercing* and developing the springs of passion —T.L.Peacock⟩ ⟨the curious and indiscreet who might wish to ~ the mystery that is taking place in the temple —J.G.Frazer⟩ **5 :** to penetrate so as to move or touch the emotions of : affect poignantly ⟨the remembrance of all that made life dear *pierced* me to the core —W.H.Hudson †1922⟩ ~ *vi* : to make a way into or through something as a pointed instrument does : break through : ENTER, PENETRATE ⟨tried to ~ into the enigma of her conduct for some sort of meaning⟩ **syn** see ENTER
[2]**pierce** \"\ *n* -s **1 :** PIERCING, STAB **2 :** a pierced hole : PERFORATION
**pierce·able** \-səbəl\ *adj* : capable of being pierced : PENETRABLE

**pierced** *adj* [ME *perced*, fr. past part. of *percen* to pierce] **1 :** having holes; *esp* **:** perforated so as to form an ornamental design **:** decorated with perforations ⟨beautiful creations in ~ brass —*New Yorker*⟩ ⟨porcelain with lattice-*pierced* borders⟩ **2** *heraldry* **:** perforated (as a cross) with the tincture of the field showing through the hole **3 :** having the earlobe punctured for an earring ⟨~ ears⟩

**pierced dollar** *n* **:** HOLEY DOLLAR

**pierced nose** *n, pl* **pierced nose** *or* **pierced noses** *usu cap P&N* [trans. of F *Nez Percé*] **:** NEZ PERCÉ

**pierc·er** \-sə(r)\ *n* -s [ME *percer, persour*, fr. AF *perceour, persour*, fr. OF *percer* to pierce + AF *-our, -eour* -er — more at PIERCE] **:** one that pierces: as **a** *archaic* **:** a keen eye **b :** an instrument (as an auger, gimlet, or stiletto) for boring or making holes **c :** a worker that pierces by hand or machine **d :** the ovipositor or the sting of an insect

**pierce's disease** \ˈpir|səz-, -iə|\ *n, usu cap P* [after Newton B. *Pierce* †1917 Am. plant pathologist] **:** a virus disease of grapes marked by delay in leafing out and interveinal mottling and spotting followed by scalding and blighting of the leaves, premature defoliation, early ripening and withering of the fruit, reduced growth, and eventual death of the vines — called also *Anaheim disease, California vine disease;* see ALFALFA DWARF

**¹piercing** *n* -s [ME *percing*, from gerund of *percen* to pierce] **:** the act or process of perforating or the perforations made by it; *esp* **:** openwork design (as in metalwork)

**²piercing** *adj* [ME *percing*, fr. pres. part. of *percen* to pierce] **:** PENETRATING: as **a :** LOUD, SHRILL ⟨~ cries⟩ **b :** seeing clear or deep **:** DISCERNING, PERCEPTIVE, SHREWD ⟨an alert and enthusiastic face, with clear, ~ eyes and tender mouth —Walter Hough⟩ **c :** penetratingly cold **:** BITING ⟨a bitter ~ winter wind⟩ **d :** CUTTING, INCISIVE, KEEN ⟨~ sarcasm⟩ ⟨a ~ conviction⟩ ⟨looked through her with ~ wisdom —Zane Grey⟩ — **pierc·ing·ly** *adv* — **pierc·ing·ness** *n* -ES

**piercing punch** *n* **:** a metal-perforating punch that is often part of a stamping die

**pier dam** *n* **:** a pier built from shore to deepen a channel or to divert logs — called also *wing dam*

**pier glass** *n* **:** a large high mirror; *esp* **:** one designed to occupy the wall space between windows — see PIER TABLE illustration

**pierhead** \ˈ=,=\ *n* **:** the outer end of a wharf

**pierhead line** *n* **:** a line beyond which no structure may extend out into navigable waters

**pi·eri·an** \(ˈ)pī¦irēən, -īˈer-\ *adj, usu cap* [L *pierius* Pierian (fr. Gk *Pieria*, region of ancient Macedonia) + E *-an*] **1 :** of or relating to the region of Pieria in ancient Macedonia or to the Muses as early worshiped there **2 :** of or relating to learning or poetry

**¹pi·er·id** \ˈpīərəd, (ˈ)pī¦erəd\ *adj* [NL *Pieridae*] **:** of or relating to the Pieridae

**²pierid** \"\ *n* -s **:** a butterfly of the family Pieridae

**pi·er·i·dae** \pīˈerə,dē\ *n pl, cap* [NL, fr. *Pieris*, type genus + *-idae*] **:** a very large and almost cosmopolitan family of butterflies formerly regarded as a subfamily of Papilionidae that comprises the cabbage butterflies, sulphur butterflies, and others having three pairs of well-developed legs in both sexes and being usu. of medium size and white or yellow color with dark markings esp. on the edges of the wings

**¹pi·er·ine** \ˈpīə,rīn, (ˈ)pī¦erən\ *adj* [NL *Pieris* + E *-ine*] **:** of or relating to the genus *Pieris*

**²pierine** \"\ *n* -s **:** a member of the genus *Pieris*

**pi·er·is** \ˈpīərəs\ *n cap* [NL, fr. Gk, Pierian Muse fr. *Pieria* — more at PIERIAN] **1 :** a small genus of American and Asiatic evergreen shrubs (family Ericaceae) having white flowers in bracted racemes and a cylindrical or urn-shaped corolla — see JAPANESE ANDROMEDA, MOUNTAIN FETTERBUSH **2 :** the type genus of Pieridae containing the common cabbage butterflies

**pier·less** \ˈpi(ə)rləs, -iəl-\ *adj* **:** having no pier

**pierre** \ˈpi(ə)r, -iə\ *adj, usu cap* [fr. *Pierre*, capital of So. Dakota] **:** of or from Pierre, the capital of So. Dakota ⟨a *Pierre* merchant⟩ **:** of the kind or style prevalent in Pierre

**pierre-perdue** \pe¦er,per¦d(y)ü\ *n* -s [F *pierre perdue*, lit., lost stone] **:** blocks of stone or concrete heaped loosely in the water to make a foundation (as for a seawall)

**pier·rette** \¦pēə¦ret, (ˈ)pi¦r-\ *n* -s *often cap* [F, fem. dim. of *Pierre* Peter] **:** a female pierrot

**pier·rot** \ˈpēə,rō, ˈpi,rō\ *n* -s *often cap* [F, dim. of *Pierre* Peter] **1 a :** a standard comic character of old French pantomime usu. with whitened face and loose white clothes **b :** BUFFOON, CLOWN, MINSTREL **2 :** a masked carnival reveler dressed as a pierrot

**pier·ro·tage** \pe¦erə¦täzh\ *n* -s [F, collection of small stones, fr. (assumed) *pierrot* (dim. of *pierre* stone, fr. L *petra*) + *-age*] **:** a stone and mortar filler used between framing members in southern colonial architecture

**pier·rot·ic** \¦pēə¦rō(d·)ik, -räd·ik, (ˈ)pi¦r-\ *adj* [*pierrot* + *-ic*] **:** of, relating to, or resembling a pierrot or the pierrot tradition in pantomime and clowning

**piers** *pl of* PIER

**pier table** *n* **:** a table to be placed against a wall between two windows and usu. under a pier glass

pier table under a pier glass

**pies** *pl of* PI *or of* PIE, *pres 3d sing of* PI *or of* PIE

**pi·es·ma** \pēˈezmə, pīˈez-\ *n, cap* [NL, fr. Gk, pressed mass, pulp, fr. *piezein* to squeeze, press — more at PIEZO-] **:** a genus of tingid bugs including several that transmit virus diseases of sugar beets

**pi·et** \ˈpīət\ *n* -s [alter. of ME *piot*, dim. of ¹*pie*] *archaic* **:** MAGPIE 1

**pie·tà** \¦pēā¦tä\ *n* -s *often cap* [It, lit., pity, fr. L *pietat-, pietas* piety, pity — more at PIETY] **:** a representation in painting or sculpture of the Virgin Mary mourning over the dead body of Christ often held on her knees

**pi·etism** \ˈpīə,tizəm\ *n* -s [G *pietismus*, fr. *pietist* + *-ismus* -ism] **1** *usu cap* **:** a 17th century religious movement originating in Germany that emphasized the need for a revitalized evangelical Christianity over against an excessive formalism and intellectualism, and stressed informal devotional meetings, Bible study, and personal religious experience **2 a :** emphasis on devotional experience and practices **b :** affectation of devotion **:** RELIGIOSITY

**pi·etist** \ˈpīəd·əst, -ətə-\ *n* -s [G, fr. L *pietat-, pietas* piety + G *-ist*] **1** *usu cap* **:** an adherent of Pietism **2 a :** a devoutly religious person **b :** an affectedly or excessively religious person

**pi·etis·tic** \¦pīə¦tistik\ *or* **pi·etis·ti·cal** \-stəkəl\ *adj* [*pietist* + *-ic, -ical*] **1 :** of or relating to Pietism **2 a :** of or relating to religious devotion or devout persons **b :** affectedly or excessively religious **syn** see DEVOUT

**pi·etis·ti·cal·ly** \-stək(ə)lē\ *adv* **:** in a pietistic manner

**pieto·so** \,pēəˈtō(,)sō, pyäˈt-, -)zō\ *adv (or adj)* [It, fr. ML *pietosus*, fr. L *pietas* + *-osus* -ous] **:** with pity or sympathy **:** COMPASSIONATELY — used as a direction in music

**pi·e·ty** \ˈpīəd·ē, -ətē, -i\ *n* -ES [F *pieté* piety, pity, fr. L *pietat-, pietas*, fr. *pius* dutiful, kindly — more at PIOUS] **1 :** the quality or state of being pious: as **a :** fidelity to natural obligations **:** devoted loyalty to parents, family, or race **b :** dutifulness in religion **:** habitual reverence for God or accepted deities **:** zeal in religious service or worship **:** DEVOUTNESS ⟨a man noted for his ~ and devotion to the Church —R.P.Casey⟩ **c :** religious simplicity and devotion **:** PIETISM ⟨was sympathetic to the ~ of the revivalists —J.C.Brauer⟩ **2 :** an act inspired by piety **:** an instance of devotion ⟨the *pieties* of a simple life justly and charitably lived⟩ **3 :** the moral or spiritual resources of an individual or a group ⟨has achieved the broadest, most harmonious synthesis of living writers, but only after a drastic cross-examination of his deepest *pieties* —H.J. Muller⟩ **4 :** a conventional belief or standard **:** ORTHODOXY, SANCTION ⟨massed social *pieties* . . . were invested in the established economic order —David Riesman⟩ **syn** see FIDELITY

**pie wagon** *n* [²*pie*] **:** PATROL WAGON

**pie wool** *n* [¹*pie*] *Austral* **:** inferior wool obtained from scraps and pieces of sheepskin sweated in heaps to loosen the fibers from the skin

**pi·ezo** \pēˈā(,)zō, pēˈāt(,)sō, pīˈē(,)zō\ *adj* [by shortening] **:** PIEZOELECTRIC

**piezo-** *comb form* [Gk *piezein* to squeeze, press; akin to Skt *pīdayati* to squeeze, press; both fr. an IE compound whose first constituent is akin to Gk *epi* on and whose second constituent is akin to Gk *hezesthai* to sit — more at EPI-, SIT] **:** pressure ⟨*piezometer*⟩

**pi·ezo·chemistry** \pē¦āzō, pē¦ātsō, pī¦ēzō+\ *n* [ISV *piezo-* + *chemistry*] **:** a science dealing with the effect of pressure on chemical phenomena

**piezo crystal** *n* **:** a piezoelectric crystal used in an oscillating electric circuit

**pi·ezo·crystallization** \=¦=(,)=+\ *n* [ISV *piezo-* + *crystallization*] **:** crystallization under pressure caused by orogenic forces

**pi·ezo·electric** \"+\ *adj* [ISV *piezo-* + *electric*] **:** of, relating to, or marked by piezoelectricity — **pi·ezo·electrically** \"+\ *adv*

**pi·ezo·electricity** \"+\ *n* [ISV *piezo-* + *electricity*] **:** electricity or electric polarity due to pressure esp. in a crystalline substance (as quartz or Rochelle salt)

**piezoelectric oscillator** *n* **:** a vacuum-tube circuit that contains a plate of piezoelectric material and is used as a generator of electric oscillations of a particular frequency

**pi·ezo·luminescence** \"+\ *n* [*piezo-* + *luminescence*] **:** TRIBOLUMINESCENCE

**pi·ezom·e·ter** \,pēəˈzämәd·ə(r), ,pīə-\ *n* [*piezo-* + *-meter*] **1 :** an instrument for measuring pressure; *specif* **:** a gage joined to a main for indicating the pressure of liquid or gas inside **2 :** an apparatus for determining the compressibility of materials; *specif* **:** a vessel for measuring the change in volume of a solid, liquid, or gas when subjected to hydrostatic pressure

**pi·ezo·met·ric** \pē¦āzō¦me·trik, pē¦ātsō-, pī¦ēzō-\ *adj* [*piezometry* & *piezometer* + *-ic*] **:** of or relating to pressure or the piezometer

**piezometric surface** *n* **:** the imaginary surface to which groundwater rises under hydrostatic pressure in wells or springs

**pi·ezom·e·try** \,pēəˈzämə·trē, ,pīə-\ *n* -ES [ISV *piezo-* + *-metry*] **:** the measurement of hydrostatic pressure affecting the occurrence and movement of groundwater

**piezo resonator** *n* **:** PIEZOELECTRIC OSCILLATOR

**piff·er** \ˈpifə(r)\ *n* -s *usu cap* [*P*unjab *I*rregular *F*rontier *F*orce + *-er*] **:** a member of the Punjab Irregular Frontier Force or of a successor regiment

**pif·fe·ro** *or* **pif·e·ro** *also* **pif·fa·ro** \ˈpifə,rō\ *n* -s [It *piffero, piffaro*, fr. MHG *pfîfer* piper, fr. *pfîfe* pipe, fife (fr. OHG *pfīfa*) + *-er* — more at PIPE] **1 :** one of various old Italian wind instruments used by shepherds (as the bagpipe or oboe) **2 :** FIFE

**¹pif·fle** \ˈpifəl\ *vi* -ED/-ING/-s [perh. blend of *piddle* and *trifle*] **:** to talk or act in a trivial, inept, or ineffective way **:** TRIFLE, TWADDLE

**²piffle** \"\ *n* -s **:** trivial nonsense or ineptitude **:** empty babble ⟨has written ~ —Geoffrey Grigson⟩

**pif·fler** \ˈpif(ə)lə(r)\ *n* -s **:** one that piffles

**pif·fling** \-f(ə)liŋ\ *adj* [fr. pres. part. of ¹*piffle*] **:** TRIVIAL ⟨brushed aside this ~ bit of legalistic hairsplitting —Ernest Cuneo⟩

**pif paf** \ˈpif,paf, ˈpef,päf\ *n* -s [Pg] **:** a card game played like rummy and bet on like poker

**¹pig** \ˈpig\ *n* -s *often attrib* [ME *pigge*] **1 :** a young swine of either sex that has not reached sexual maturity; *broadly* **:** a wild or domestic swine — see HOG 1a **2 a :** pig's flesh as food **:** BACON, HAM, PORK **b :** the dressed carcass of a young swine weighing less than 130 pounds **c :** PIGSKIN **3 :** one thought to resemble or suggest a pig in habits or behavior (as in dirtiness, greediness, selfishness) ⟨profit by such a lesson and not make such a gorging ~ of himself —F.S.Anthony⟩ ⟨feel a ~ for having allowed a fortnight to go by without a letter —H.J.Laski⟩ **4 :** an animal likened to the pig (as a guinea pig or bushpig) — usu. used in combination or with a qualifying word **5** [so called fr. the resemblance of the arrangement of the molds in the pig bed to suckling pigs] **a :** a crude casting of metal (as iron or lead) convenient for storage, transportation, or melting; *esp* **:** one of standard size and shape for marketing run directly from the smelting furnace — compare INGOT **b :** a mold or channel in the pig bed **c :** PIG IRON, PIG LEAD **6 a :** a small iron or steel car pulled by a cable on a narrow-gage track and used for handling a railway freight car on an incline too steep for a locomotive **b** *slang* **:** a railroad locomotive **7 :** a flask having two or more tubulures to which smaller flasks may be attached and used esp. to collect fractions during fractional distillation **8 :** a brush, swab, or scraper pushed or pulled through a pipe or duct to clean it **9 :** a simple card game in which as cards are passed one at a time from player to player the first player to hold four of a kind lays his hand on the table and puts a finger against his nose and the last to notice and do likewise becomes the pig **10** *slang* **:** an immoral woman — **in pig :** PREGNANT — used of a sow

**²pig** \"\ *vb* **pigged; pigged; pigging; pigs** *vi* **1 :** to bring forth in the manner of pigs **:** FARROW **2 :** to huddle, lie together, or live in a way attributed to pigs ⟨a rare collection of human animals . . . *pigging* together in mean huts —V.L. Parrington⟩ ~ *vt* **1 :** LITTER **2 :** to crowd like pigs ⟨they love fighting and they get more chance when they're all *pigged* in together —J.N.Hall⟩ — **pig it 1** *chiefly Brit* **:** to live in a way attributed to pigs **2** *chiefly Brit* **:** to exist in very poor circumstances or under considerable hardship ⟨had a whole house . . . and did not have to *pig it* in one room —Flora Thompson⟩

**³pig** \"\ *n* -s [ME *pygg*] *chiefly Scot* **a :** an earthenware vessel **b :** CROCK

**pig-a-back** *var of* PIGGYBACK

**pig bed** *n* **1 :** PIGSTY **2 :** a bed of sand in which iron is cast into pigs

**pigboat** \ˈ=,=\ *n* [¹*pig* + *boat;* fr. the resemblance of submarines nosed against a tender to suckling pigs] *slang* **:** SUBMARINE ⟨the boys . . . who'd been in ~s —Frederic Wakeman⟩

**pig deer** *n* **:** BABIRUSA

**¹pi·geon** \ˈpijən\ *n* -s [ME *pejon, pijon, pigeon*, fr. MF *pijon* young bird, pigeon, fr. LL *pipion-, pipio* young bird, fr. L *pipire* to chirp; akin to L *pipare* — more at PIPE] **1 :** a bird of the widely distributed family Columbidae (order Columbiformes) having a stout body with rather short legs, a bill horny at the tip but with a soft cere at the base, and smooth and compact plumage; *esp* **:** a member of one of the many domesticated varieties derived from the rock pigeon (*Columba livia*) of the coasts of Europe — see BILL illustration **2 :** a young girl ⟨he was taking out a very pretty ~⟩ **3 :** one who is an easy mark **:** DUPE **4 :** CLAY PIGEON **5** [alter. of *pidgin*] **:** an object of special concern **:** accepted business or interest ⟨she's not our ~ unless she's an accessory —Ngaio Marsh⟩ ⟨tennis was not his ~⟩ **6 :** the final card received in a deal of stud poker when it makes the hand a winner **7 :** a pari-mutuel ticket that is counterfeit or has been canceled **8 :** a dark purplish gray that is redder and paler than slate, redder, lighter, and stronger than charcoal, and redder and lighter than taupe gray

**²pigeon** \"\ *adj* **:** of or characteristic of pigeons **:** made of or for pigeons ⟨~ roost⟩ ⟨~ pie⟩

**³pigeon** \"\ *vt* -ED/-ING/-s **:** to fleece esp. by tricks in gambling **:** make a pigeon of **:** GULL ⟨sit down with him in private to cards and ~ him —W.M.Thackeray⟩

**⁴pigeon** *var of* PIDGIN

**pigeonberry** \ˈ== — *see* BERRY\ *n* **1 a :** POKEWEED **b :** the berry of the pokeweed **2 :** JUNEBERRY **3 :** a dogwood (*Cornus alternifolia*) **4 :** any of several No. American buckthorns (as cascara buckthorn or California coffee) **5 :** PARTRIDGEBERRY **6** *West Indies* **:** GOLDEN DEWDROP **7** *Austral* **:** either of two timber trees (*Litsea ferruginea* and *L. dealbata*) **8 :** BRISTLY SARSAPARILLA

**pigeon blood** *or* **pigeon's blood** *n* **:** a dark red that is yellower and duller than cranberry, yellower, lighter, and stronger than average garnet, and yellower and stronger than average wine — called also *Spanish wine*

**pigeon breast** *n* **:** a deformity of the chest that is marked by sharp projection of the sternum and that occurs esp. in rickets — opposed to *funnel chest* — **pigeon-breasted** \¦==¦=\ *adj*

**pigeon cherry** *n* **:** PIN CHERRY

**pi·geon·dom** \ˈ==,dəm\ *n* -s [¹*pigeon* + *-dom*] **:** the world of pigeons or of pigeon fanciers ⟨prominently associated with pigeons and ~ ever since it became a hobby —*Amer. Pigeon Jour.*⟩

**pigeon-dropper** \ˈ==,==\ *n* **:** one who practices pigeon-dropping

**pigeon-dropping** \ˈ==,==\ *n* **:** a confidence game

**pi·geon·eer** \¦pijə¦ni(ə)r\ *n* -s [¹*pigeon* + *-eer*] **1 :** a person who cares for and manages pigeons; *esp* **:** one in military service who has charge of the breeding, training, housing, and care of homing pigeons **2 :** one who kills or captures unwanted pigeons

**pigeon fly** *n* **:** a hippoboscid fly (*Pseudolynchia canariensis*) that is an ectoparasite of pigeons esp. in the southern U.S. and a vector of pigeon malaria

**pigeon flying** *n* **:** the sport of racing homing pigeons

**pigeonfoot** \ˈ==,=\ *n, pl* **pigeonfoots :** DOVE'S-FOOT

**pi·geon·gram** \ˈ==,gram\ *n* [¹*pigeon* + *-gram*] **:** a message carried by a pigeon

**pigeon grape** *n* **:** SUMMER GRAPE

**pigeon grass** *n* **1 :** YELLOW FOXTAIL **2 :** GREEN FOXTAIL **3 :** BUR BRISTLEGRASS **4 :** CRABGRASS 1a

**pigeon guillemot** *n* **:** a guillemot (*Cepphus columba*) of the north Pacific

**pigeon hawk** *n* **:** any of several small hawks: as **a :** a small American falcon (*Falco columbarius*) related to the European merlin **b :** SHARPSHINNED HAWK

**pigeonhearted** \ˈ=¦=\ *adj* **:** marked by timidity **:** CHICKENHEARTED ⟨don't talk sniveling and ~ like you —Conrad Richter⟩

**¹pigeonhole** \ˈ==,=\ *n* [¹*pigeon* + *hole*] **1 a :** a hole or small recess for pigeons to nest **b :** an excessively small room **:** CUBBYHOLE ⟨hated the little ~ where she had to work⟩ **2 a :** one of a series of holes usu. in a wall or door for the passage of pigeons **b :** one of a set of holes for passage (as of gases in a furnace arch) **3 pigeonholes** *pl, obs* **:** ¹STOCK 4 **4 :** excessive space between printed words **5 :** a seat in the upper gallery of a theater or in the top row of the gallery **6 :** a small open compartment usu. in a desk, case, or cabinet esp. for keeping letters or documents **7 :** a storing place in the mind for a classified item or topic **8 :** a place in a rigidly conventional pattern **:** a neat category ⟨they label or ticket our public men too patly, putting them into ~s —*Kiplinger Washington Letter*⟩

**²pigeonhole** \"\ *vt* -ED/-ING/-s **1 :** to provide with or divide into pigeonholes ⟨the cabinet was conveniently *pigeonholed* for the tiny glass figures she collected⟩ **2 a :** to place in or as if in the pigeonhole of a desk ⟨accepted the papers and *pigeonholed* them in his desk —C.G.Norris⟩ **b :** to put away as if in a place readily accessible or for future reference **:** to lay aside indefinitely **:** SHELVE ⟨find some polite formula for *pigeonholing* the whole idea —Denis Healey⟩ ⟨any new projects and plans . . . will inevitably be *pigeonholed* to await better times —Grenville Manton⟩ **3 :** to assign to a proper class or category **:** arrange according to a logical scheme **:** analyze and classify **:** LABEL ⟨life was neatly *pigeonholed* into compartments —Alan Moorehead⟩ ⟨attempted to ~ the new knowledge in the light of his experience⟩

**³pigeonhole** \"\ *adj* [¹*pigeonhole*] **:** based on a rigid system of classification ⟨~ theories of art —John Dewey⟩ ⟨combat the static thinking that derives from ~ diagnosis —E.A. Strecker⟩

**pigeon horntail** *or* **pigeon tremex** *n* **:** a large American horntail (*Tremex columba*) having a burrowing larva that is preyed upon by a large ichneumon fly (*Thallesa lunator*)

**pigeon house** *n* **:** DOVECOTE 1

**pigeoning** *pres part of* PIGEON

**pi·geon·ite** \ˈpijə,nīt\ *n* -s [*Pigeon* Point, northeast Minn. + E *-ite*] **:** a monoclinic mineral $(Mg,Fe,Ca)_2Si_2O_6$ consisting of pyroxene with rather low calcium, little or no aluminum or ferric iron, and less ferrous iron than magnesium

**pigeon-livered** \¦==¦==\ *adj* [¹*pigeon* + *livered*] **:** GENTLE, MILD ⟨it cannot be but I am *pigeon-livered* and lack gall to make oppression bitter —Shak.⟩

**pigeon louse** *n* **:** any of several philopterid bird lice that are parasitic on wild and domestic pigeons

**pigeon louse fly** *n* **:** PIGEON FLY

**pigeon pea** *n* **1 :** a tropical woody herb (*Cajanus cajan*) with trifoliate leaves, showy yellow flowers, and flattish pods much cultivated esp. in the tropics **2 :** the small highly nutritious seed of the pigeon pea

**pigeon plover** *n* **:** BLACK-BELLIED PLOVER

**pigeon plum** *n* **1 a :** the edible drupaceous fruit of any of several tropical American plants of the genus *Coccoloba* (esp. *C. laurifolia*) **b :** the edible fruit of an African tree (*Chrysobalanus ellipticus*) **2 :** a tree that bears pigeon plums

**pigeon post** *n* **1 :** a postal or private communications system using pigeons as carriers **2 :** letters or messages carried by pigeons **:** mail carried by pigeons

**pigeon pox** *n* **:** a virus disease of pigeons which is closely related to fowl pox and the virus of which is often used to produce a vaccine against fowl pox that is safer though less lastingly effective than that prepared with fowl pox virus

**pi·geon·ry** \ˈpijənrē\ *n* -ES [¹*pigeon* + *-ry*] **:** DOVECOTE ⟨picturesque villages with their *pigeonries* —H.H.Johnston⟩

**pigeons** *pl of* PIGEON, *pres 3d sing of* PIGEON

**pigeon's blood** *var of* PIGEON BLOOD

**pigeon's-foot** \ˈ==,=\ *n, pl* **pigeon's-foots :** DOVE'S-FOOT

**pigeon's-grass** \ˈ==,=\ *n, pl* **pigeon's-grasses** [so called fr. its attractiveness to pigeons] **:** a common vervain (*Verbena officinalis*)

**pigeon's milk** *or* **pigeon milk** *n* **:** a milky fluid with solid particles resembling cheese that is produced by the breaking down and discharge of the cells lining the crop and regurgitated by pigeons for their young

**pigeon's-neck** \ˈ==,=\ *n, pl* **pigeon's-necks :** PELICAN 4

**pigeontail** \ˈ==,=\ *n* **:** PINTAIL 1

**pigeon tick** *n* **:** an argasid tick (*Argas reflexus*) that is an ectoparasite on various birds and mammals

**pigeon-toe** \¦==¦=\ *vb* [back-formation fr. *pigeon-toed*] *vi* **:** to walk with toes turned in ⟨will go *pigeon-toeing* off —J.A. Phillips⟩ ~ *vt* **:** to go along with toes turned in ⟨*pigeon-toed* his way into the new editor's presence —Eugene Field⟩

**pigeon-toed** \¦==¦=\ *adj* [¹*pigeon* + *toed*] **:** having the toes turned in ⟨a *pigeon-toed* boy⟩

**pigeon tree** *n* **:** HERCULES'-CLUB 3

**pigeonweed** \ˈ==,=\ *n* **:** CORN GROMWELL

**pigeon-wheat** \ˈ==,=\ *also* **pigeon-wheat moss** *n* **:** a moss of the genus *Polytrichum* in which the capsules resemble small grains of wheat

**¹pigeonwing** \ˈ==,=\ *n* **1 a :** a wing of a pigeon **b :** a wing resembling that of a pigeon **2 a :** a fancy dance step executed by jumping and striking the legs together ⟨performing capers . . . and ~s around each other —H.L.Davis⟩ **b :** a fancy figure in skating **3 :** a style of dressing men's side hair in waves or curls resembling pigeon's wings **4 :** a brown dappled with purple that comes between dark brown and light blue in the table of colors in tempering of hardened steel

**²pigeonwing** \"\ *vt* **:** to move by doing pigeonwings ⟨~*ed* himself across the floor⟩ ~ *vi* **:** to dance a pigeonwing ⟨~*ed* in the middle of the dance floor⟩

**pigeonwood** \ˈ==,=\ *n* **:** any of various tropical trees with marked or mottled wood: as **a :** BLOLLY **b :** BUSTIC **c :** a West Indian tree (*Diospyros tetrasperma*) **d :** ZEBRAWOOD 1b **e :** ZEBRAWOOD 1a **f :** a tree of the genus *Coccoloba*

**pigeon woodpecker** *n* **:** FLICKER

**pig-eyed** \ˈ=,=\ *adj* **:** having small deep-set eyes

**pigface** \ˈ=,=\ *n* [¹*pig* + *face*] *Austral* **:** the fruit of the beach apple

**pigfish** \ˈ=,=\ *n* [so called fr. the grunting sound it makes when taken from the water] **:** any of various fishes: as **a :** any of several salt-water grunts; *esp* **:** a food fish (*Orthopristis*

*chrysopterus*) of the U.S. from Long Island southward **b :** PINFISH a **c** *Austral* **:** any of several wrasses (esp. of the genera *Diastodon* and *Verreo*) of the family Labridae
**pigfoot** \ˈ=,=\ *n, pl* **pigfoots :** a mottled reddish brown marine fish (*Scorpaena porcus*) of southern Europe; *also* **:** a fish of a related species
**pig-footed bandicoot** \ˈ=,==-\ *n* **:** a large-eared herbivorous bandicoot (*Chaeropus ecaudatus* syn. *C. castanotis*) formerly abundant in much of Australia, with two functional toes resembling hooves on each foot
**pigged** *past of* PIG
**1pig·gery** \ˈpig(ə)rē, -ri\ *n* -ES [1*pig* + *-ery*] **1 a :** a pig breeding or rearing establishment **b :** PIGSTY **2 :** PIGS
**2piggery** \"\ *n* -ES [3*pig* + *-ery*] *Scot* **:** CROCKERY
**pig·gin** \ˈpigən\ *n* -S [origin unknown] **1 a** *chiefly dial* **:** a wooden vessel shaped approximately like a pail and often having one stave extended upward for use as a handle **b :** a dish shaped like a piggin, often made of glass or silver, and used usu. for butter or sugar **2 a** *dial Eng* **:** a one-handled wooden drinking vessel **b** *chiefly Midland* **:** a milking pail

piggin 1a

**pigging** *pres part of* PIG
**pig·gin' string** \ˈpigən-\ *n* [origin unknown] *West* **:** a small rope used by cowhands for tying cattle by the feet
**pig·gish** \ˈpigish, -gēsh\ *adj* **:** of, relating to, or resembling those characteristics thought to be typical of a pig **:** DIRTY, GREEDY, MEAN, STUBBORN ⟨a somewhat ~ material happiness —Paul de Kruif⟩ ⟨~ obstinacy —Louis Bromfield⟩ ⟨his sharp ~ eyes and . . . piercing voice —Vincent Sheean⟩ — **pig·gish·ly** *adv*
**1pig·gy** \ˈpigē, -gi\ *n* -ES [1*pig* + *-y*, dim. suffix] **:** a little pig
**2piggy** \"\ *adj* -ER/-EST [1*pig* + *-y*, adj. suffix] **1 :** having qualities felt to resemble those attributed to a pig ⟨plump, with round ~ cheeks —L.K.Liang⟩ **2** *of a sow* **:** appearing to be in pig
**1pig·gy·back** *or* **pick·a·back** *also* **pig-a-back** \ˈpig|ē,bak, |i,b- *sometimes* -ik| *or* |ə,b-\ *adv* [alter. of earlier *a pick pack, a pickback*, of unknown origin] **1 :** up on the back and shoulders ⟨had her child with her . . . astraddle on her hip, or ~ —John Bennett⟩ ⟨shows a flood victim being carried from his home ~ —*Altoona (Pa.) Mirror*⟩ **2 :** on a railroad flatcar ⟨the trailer rode ~ from coast to coast⟩
**2piggyback** *or* **pickaback** *also* **pig-a-back** \"\ *n* **1 :** the act of carrying piggyback **:** the state of being carried piggyback ⟨beg daddy for a ~ —*Parents' Mag.*⟩ **2 :** the process of loading, transporting, and unloading truck trailers on railroad flatcars or cars of special design ⟨estimate the cost of shipping by ~⟩
**3piggyback** *or* **pickaback** *also* **pig-a-back** \"\ *adj* **1 :** marked by being up on the shoulders and back ⟨a child needs hugging, tussling, and ~ rides —Benjamin Spock⟩ **2 :** of or relating to the hauling of truck trailers on railroad flatcars ⟨~ service⟩ ⟨~ cars⟩
**4piggyback** \"\ *vt* **1 :** to carry up on the shoulders and back ⟨swum with them and ~*ed* them and attended them —R.P. Smith⟩ ⟨~*ing* a crippled classmate to school for a whole year —*Saturday Rev.*⟩ **2 :** to haul (as a truck trailer) by railroad car ~ *vi* **:** to haul truck trailers usu. loaded with commodities on railroad cars ⟨the railroad has been ~*ing* for quite a number of years⟩
**piggyback plant** *var of* PICKABACK PLANT
**piggy bank** *n* [1*piggy*] **:** a bank often in the shape of a pig and usu. used by children for saving small coins
**pigheaded** \ˈ=;==\ *adj* [1*pig* + *headed*] **:** stupidly perverse **:** STUBBORN, WILLFUL **:** refusing to yield **syn** see OBSTINATE
**pig·head·ed·ness** \(ˈ)=ˈ==nəs\ *n* -ES **:** the quality or state of being pigheaded ⟨thanks to their ~ —Kenneth Roberts⟩
**pig hickory** *n* **:** PIGNUT 2
**pight** [ME *pihte*, past of *pichen* to pitch] *archaic past of* PITCH
**pigh·tle** *or* **pigh·tel** \ˈpīd·ᵊl\ *n* -S [origin unknown] *dial* **:** a small field or enclosure usu. near or surrounding a building (as a house, barn, shed); *specif* **:** BARNYARD

piggy bank

**pig in a poke :** something offered in such a way that the one to whom it is offered does not know exactly what the thing is nor what its real value is ⟨was too shrewd ever to buy a *pig in a poke*⟩
**pig iron** *n* [1*pig*] **:** crude iron that is the direct product of the blast furnace and that is either refined to produce steel, wrought iron, or ingot iron or is remelted and cast into special shapes — compare CAST IRON
**pig islander** \ˈ=ˈ===\ *n, usu cap P&I* [so called from the introduction of pigs into New Zealand by Captain Cook] *Austral* **:** NEW ZEALANDER
**pig latin** *n, often cap L* **:** a jargon that is made by systematic mutilation of English (as *amscray the ointjay* for *scram the joint*)
**pig lead** *n* **:** lead cast in pigs
**pig·let** \ˈpiglət\ *n* -S [1*pig* + *-let*] **:** a small usu. young hog
**piglike** \ˈ=,=\ *adj* [1*pig* + *-like*] **:** resembling a pig
**pig lily** *n* **:** CALLA LILY
**pig·ling** \ˈpigliŋ\ *n* -S [1*pig* + *-ling*] **:** PIGLET
**pig louse** *n* **:** HOG LOUSE
**pigmaker** \ˈ=,==\ *n* [1*pig* + *maker*] **:** a manufacturer of pig iron
**pig·man** \ˈpigmən\ *n, pl* **pigmen :** one who takes care of pigs
**pig meat** *n* [1*pig* + *meat*] *Brit* **:** PORK
**1pig·ment** \ˈpigmənt\ *n* -S [L *pigmentum* pigment, paint, fr. *pingere* to paint + *-mentum* -ment — more at PAINT] **1 a :** a natural or synthetic inorganic or organic substance that imparts a color including black or white to other materials; *esp* **:** a powder or easily powdered substance mixed with a liquid in which it is relatively insoluble and used in making paints, enamels, and other coating materials, inks, plastics, and rubber and also for imparting opacity and other desirable properties as well as color **b :** a compounding ingredient (as a filler or reinforcing agent) used in the manufacture of rubber or plastics — compare 1DYE 2 **2 a :** any of various coloring matters in animals and plants; *esp* **:** solid or opaque coloring matter in a cell or tissue **b :** any of various related colorless substances (as various respiratory enzymes)
**2pig·ment** \-mənt, -,ment — *see* 2-MENT\ *vb* -ED/-ING/-S *vt* **:** to color or imbue with or as if with pigment ⟨wished to ~ the photograph⟩ ~ *vi* **:** to acquire pigment **:** become colored or imbued ⟨those who ~*ed* well gave about the same values as those who did not ~ well —*Experiment Station Record*⟩
**pig·men·tal** \(ˈ)pig¦ment³l\ *adj* [1*pigment* + *-al*] **:** PIGMENTARY — **pig·men·tal·ly** \-³lē\ *adv*
**pig·men·tary** \ˈpigmən,terē\ *adj* [L *pigmentarius*, fr. *pigmentum* + *-arius* -ary] **:** of, relating to, or producing or containing pigment **:** furnished with or characterized by pigment
**pig·men·ta·tion** \,pigmən·ˈtāshən, -,men-\ *n* -S [LL *pigmentatus* painted, colored (fr. L *pigmentum* + *-atus* -ate) + E *-ion*] **:** coloration with, compounding with, or deposition of pigment; *esp* **:** an excessive deposition of pigment in body tissues
**pigment black B** *n, usu cap P & 1st B* **:** an organic pigment — see DYE table I (under *Pigment Black 1*)
**pigment blue WNL** *n, usu cap P&B* **:** an organic pigment — see DYE table I (under *Pigment Blue 25*)
**pigment bordeaux N** *n, usu cap P&B* **:** an organic pigment — see DYE table I (under *Pigment Red 40*)
**pigment cell** *n* **:** a cell containing a deposition of coloring matter — compare CHROMATOPHORE 1
**pig·ment·ed** \-,mentəd, -,mən-\ *adj* [1*pigment* + *-ed*] **:** dulled by adding a pigment to the spinning solution — used esp. of rayon yarn
**pigment finish** *n* **:** leather finished with coating containing pigment or other opaque substance
**pigment green B** *n, usu cap P&G* **:** an organic pigment — see DYE table I (under *Pigment Green 8*)
**pig·ment·ize** \ˈpigmənt·,īz, -n·,tīz\ *vt* -ED/-ING/-S [1*pigment* + *-ize*] **:** PIGMENT
**pigmento-** *comb form* [L *pigmentum* — more at PIGMENT] **:** pigment ⟨*pigmento*genic⟩
**pig·men·to·phage** \pigˈmentə,fāj\ *n* [ISV *pigmento-* + *-phage*; prob. orig. formed in F] **:** a cell that ingests pigment
**pigment orange R** *n, usu cap P&O* **:** an organic pigment — see DYE table I (under *Pigment Red 22*)
**pigment process** *n* **:** a photographic printing process in which the image consists of a black or colored pigment distributed in a colloidal medium (as gelatin)
**pigment purple A** *n, usu cap both Ps* **:** a solvent dye — see DYE table I (under *Solvent Red 1*)
**pigment scarlet 3B** *n, usu cap P&S* **:** an organic pigment — see DYE table I (under *Pigment Red 60*)
**pigment volume** *n* **:** the space occupied by pigment in paint or ink expressed as a percent of the total nonvolatile volume
**pig metal** *n* **:** metal cast in pigs
**pigmy** *var of* PYGMY
**pigmy blue** *n* **:** any of the several small butterflies of the lycaenid genus *Brephidium*
**pigmy deer** *n* **:** KEY DEER
**pi·gnet index** \(ˈ)pēn¦yā-\ *n, usu cap P* [after M. C. J. Pignet *b*1871 Fr. physician] **:** a measure of the type of body-build obtained by subtracting the sum of the weight in kilograms and the chest circumference in centimeters from the stature in centimeters
**pi·gno·lia** \pēnˈyōlēə\ *or* **pi·gno·li** \-lē\ *n* -S [It *pignolo*, fr. (assumed) VL *pineolus*, dim. of L *pineus* of the pine, fr. *pinus* pine] **:** the edible seed of the nut pine
**pi·gnon** \ˈpēn,yän\ *n* -S [F, fr. (assumed) VL *pineon-*, *pineo*, fr. L *pineus* of the pine] **1 :** the nutlike seed of any of several pines (as the European stone pine) **2 :** PHYSIC NUT
**1pig·no·rate** \ˈpignərət\ *adj* [L *pigneratus*, *pignoratus*, past part. of *pignerare*, *pignorare* to pledge — more at PIGNORATION] **1 :** given or taken in pledge **:** PLEDGED **2 :** of or relating to something pledged or to a contract of pignus **:** PIGNORATITIOUS
**2pig·no·rate** \-,rāt\ *vt* -ED/-ING/-S [L *pigneratus*, *pignoratus*] **1 :** to give over (as a pledge) **:** PAWN **2 :** to take in pawn
**pig·no·ra·tion** \,pignəˈrāshən\ *n* -S [LL *pigneration-*, *pigneratio*, *pignoration-*, *pignoratio*, fr. L *pigneratus*, *pignoratus* (past part. of *pignerare*, *pignorare* to pledge, fr. *pigner-*, *pignor-*, *pignus* pledge, stake) + *-ion-*, *-io* -ion] **1 :** the act of pledging or pawning **2 :** a civil-law process answering in general to common-law distraint
**pig·no·ra·ti·tious** \ˌpignəraˈtishəs\ *adj* [LL *pigneraticius*, *pignoraticius*, fr. L *pigneratus*, *pignoratus* + *-icius* -itious] **:** of or relating to pignoration
**pig·no·ra·tive** \ˈpignə,rād·iv\ *adj* [F *pignoratif*, fr. L *pigneratus*, *pignoratus* + F *-if* -ive] **1 :** giving in pledge **2 :** PIGNORATITIOUS
**pig·nus** \ˈpignəs\ *n, pl* **pigno·ra** \-nərə\ [L *pigner-*, *pignor-*, *pignus* pledge, stake] *Roman & civil law* **:** a pledge or pawn arising where a creditor has power of sale and takes possession for security
**pignus ju·di·ci·a·le** \-,yü,dikēˈä(,)lā, -,jü,dishēˈālē\ *or* **pignus prae·to·ri·um** \-,prīˈtōrēəm, -,prē-\ *n* [*pignus judiciale* fr. NL, lit., judge's pledge; *pignus praetorium* fr. LL, lit., praetor's pledge] **:** the right or lien that a judgment creditor has in the property of the judgment debtor
**pignus le·ga·le** \-,lāˈgä(,)lā, -ləˈgālē\ *n* [L] **:** a pledge or lien arising by operation of law (as in case of a landlord)
**pignut** \ˈ=,=\ *n* [1*pig* + *nut*] **1 :** EARTHNUT **2 a :** any of several bitter-flavored hickory nuts **b** *also* **pignut hickory :** a hickory (as *Carya glabra*, *C. ovalis*, or *C. cordiformis*) bearing pignuts **3 :** JOJOBA
**pigpen** \ˈ=,=\ *n* **1 :** PIGSTY **2 :** a place that is dirty or littered up
**pig potato** *n* **1 :** GROUNDNUT 2a **2 :** COWBANE b **3 :** a small or inferior potato suitable for pig feed
**pig rat** *n* **:** BANDICOOT 1
**pigs** *pl of* PIG, *pres 3d sing of* PIG
**pigs and whistles** *n pl* [3*pig*] *Scot* **:** RUIN ⟨poor girl, gone to *pigs and whistles*⟩
**pig's-face** \ˈ=,=\ *n, pl* **pig's-faces** [1*pig*] **:** PIGFACE
**pigs' feet** *n pl* **:** the feet of swine used as an article of food esp. after boiling and pickling
**pigs in blankets :** oysters, chicken livers, or other choice morsels wrapped in thin slices of bacon, fastened with skewers, and broiled or sautéed
**pigs in clover** [1*pig*] **:** a game played by tilting a small box containing holes and marbles so that every marble will roll into a hole
**1pigskin** \ˈ=,=\ *n* **1 a :** the skin of a swine or leather made of it used typically in bookbindings, saddles, shoes, and wallets **b :** leather for gloves made chiefly from skins of capybaras and peccaries **2 a :** a jockey's saddle **b :** FOOTBALL 2a
**2pigskin** *adj* **:** having dimpled depressions like pigskin — used of the skin over a malignant tumor esp. of the breast
**pigs·ney** \ˈpigznē\ *n* -S [ME *piggesnye*, lit., pig's eye, fr. *pigges* (gen. of *pigge* pig) + *nye* eye, alter. (resulting from incorrect division of *an ye, an eye*) of *ye, eye* eye] **1 :** DARLING, SWEETHEART **2 :** a little eye
**pigstick** \ˈ=,=\ *vi* [back-formation fr. *pigsticking* action of hunting the wild boar with a spear, fr. *pig* + *sticking*, fr. gerund of *stick*] **:** to hunt the wild boar on horseback with a spear
**pigsticker** \ˈ=,==\ *n* [1*pig* + *sticker*] **:** 1STICKER 1a(1)
**pigsty** \ˈ=,=\ *n* [1*pig* + *sty*] **1 :** an enclosure with covered shed or area for pigs **2 :** a dirty dwelling or room thought to resemble a pigsty ⟨you would end up in some dark ~ over a smelly stable —T.B.Costain⟩ **3 :** a timber crib often filled with rock used to support a roof in a mine working
**pigsty daisy** *n* **:** MAYWEED 1
**pig's-wash** \ˈ=,=\ *n, pl* **pig's-washes** [1*pig*] **:** SWILL 1a
**pigtail** \ˈ=,=\ *n* [so called from its resemblance to the tail of a pig] **1 :** tobacco in small twisted ropes or rolls **2 :** a tight braid of hair — compare QUEUE 1 **3 :** a device used in logging that is usu. driven into a stump for supporting a rope or wire **4 :** a cleavers (*Galium aparine*) **5 :** a short flexible band or lead of stranded or braided copper wire used for electrical connections **6 :** a spirally twisted wire or ceramic used as a guide in yarn manufacturing
**pig-tailed** \ˈ=,tāld\ *adj* [1*pig* + *tailed*] **1 :** having a tail like a pig's **2** [*pigtail* + *-ed*] **:** having or wearing a pigtail ⟨a *pig-tailed* little girl⟩
**pig-tailed ape** *or* **pig-tailed macaque** *or* **pig-tailed monkey** *n* **:** a macaque (*Macaca nemestrina*) of the Malay peninsula and the East Indies with a short slender tail which is held in the shape of a letter S when the animal is excited
**pig-tailed langur** *n* **:** a large dark snub-nosed langur (*Simias concolor*) of Sumatra distinguished by a very short nearly naked tail
**pig tin** *n* [1*pig*] **:** tin cast in pigs
**pig typhoid** *or* **pig typhus** *n* **:** NECROTIC ENTERITIS
**pigwash** \ˈ=,=\ *n* [1*pig* + *wash*] **:** SWILL 1a
**pigweed** \ˈ=,=\ *n* [1*pig* + *weed*] **:** any of various strongly growing weedy plants: as **a :** any of several plants of the genus *Amaranthus* (as *A. retroflexus* and *A. hybridus*) that are sometimes used as potherbs, have edible seeds for which they have been cultivated locally, and produce pollen that is an important hay fever allergen **b :** GOOSEFOOT 1; *esp* **:** LAMB'S-QUARTERS 1 **c** *Austral* **:** a purslane (*Portulaca oleracea*)
**pigweed family** *n* **:** CHENOPODIACEAE
**pig·wid·geon** *also* **pig·wid·gin** \ˈpig,wijən\ *n* [origin unknown] **:** an insignificant or simple person
**piing** *pres part of* PI
**pi-jaw** \ˈ=,=\ *n* [6*pi* + *jaw*] *Brit* **:** pious or moralizing talk or cant ⟨millions of hours under schoolroom discipline, reading the Bible, listening to *pi-jaws* —Aldous Huxley⟩
**pik** *also* **pic** *or* **pike** \ˈpik, ˈpēk\ *n* -S [F *pic*, fr. Gk *pēchys* forearm, cubit — more at BOUGH] **:** any of various units of length used in Mediterranean countries (as Greece, Turkey, Egypt, Algeria) equal to between 18 and 30 inches
**pi·ka** \ˈpīkə, ˈpēkə\ *n* -S [Tungusic *piika*] **:** any of various small lagomorph mammals of the family Ochotonidae inhabiting rocky parts of high mountains in Asia and western No. America that are closely related to the rabbits, but have small ears, the tail rudimentary, and the hind legs relatively short — called also *mouse hare*; see LITTLE CHIEF HARE
**pi·ka·ke** \ˈpēkə,kā\ *n* -S [Hawaiian *pikake*] **:** ARABIAN JASMINE
**1pike** \ˈpīk\ *n* -S [ME, fr. OE *pīc*, prob. of Celt origin; akin to ScGael *pic* pickax, Bret *pik*, IrGael *pice* pitchfork, W *pig* point, beak] **1** *dial chiefly Eng* **:** PICK 2 **2 :** PIKESTAFF 1 **3 :** a sharp point, pointed tip, or spike (as in the center of a buckler) **:** the tip of a spear **4 :** the long pointed toe of a shoe worn in the 14th and 15th centuries **:** POULAINE **5** *dial Eng* **:** one of various sharp-pointed tools or implements (as a pitchfork) ⟨the windrows are loaded on a wagon by hand with a ~ —F.D.Smith & Barbara Wilcox⟩
**2pike** \"\ *vi* -ED/-ING/-S [ME *pyken* to pike (oneself), perh. fr. 1*pike* pikestaff] **1 :** to leave abruptly **:** take off **:** DEPART ⟨get lonely and sore, and ~ out —Sinclair Lewis⟩ **2 :** to make one's way — used with *along* ⟨should he begin in a small way and ~ along —Theodore Dreiser⟩
**3pike** \"\ *n* -S [ME, perh. of Scandinavian origin; akin to Norw dial. *pik* pointed mountain] **1** *dial Eng* **:** a mountain or hill having a peaked summit — used esp in place names **2 :** a pile of hay or grain having a pointed top **3** [Sp *pico*, fr. *picar* to prick, pierce, fr. (assumed) VL *piccare* — more at 6PIKE] *archaic* **:** 2PEAK
**4pike** \"\ *n, pl* **pike** *or* **pikes** [ME, fr. 1*pike*, fr. the shape of its head] **1 a :** an elongate long-snouted voracious teleost fish (*Esox lucius*) that reaches a length of four feet, is valued for food and sport, and is widely distributed in cooler parts of the northern hemisphere — called also *northern pike* **b :** a fish of the family Esocidae: as (1) **:** MUSKELLUNGE (2) **:** PICKEREL **2 :** any of various fishes of families other than Esocidae that are felt to resemble the pike in appearance or habits: as **a :** SNOOK **b :** BARRACUDA 1 **c :** WALLEYE 4 **d :** SAUGER **e :** SQUAWFISH
**5pike** \"\ *chiefly dial var of* PICK
**6pike** \"\ *n* -S [MF *pique*, fr. *piquer* to prick, pierce, nettle, pique, fr. (assumed) VL *piccare*, fr. (assumed) *piccus* woodpecker, fr. L *picus* — more at PIE] **1 :** a weapon consisting of a long wooden shaft with a pointed steel head sometimes having a hook or pick on the side and used by the foot soldier until superseded by the bayonet **2** *obs* **:** PIKEMAN **3 :** the sharp-tipped staff on which a flag is carried ⟨carried on a ~ 9 feet, 10 inches long including the spear tip —W.F.Harris⟩
**7pike** \"\ *vt* -ED/-ING/-S **1 :** to pierce, kill, or wound with or as if with a pike **2 :** to thrust with or as if with a pike
**8pike** *var of* PIK
**9pike** \ˈpīk\ *n* -S [short for *turnpike*] **1 a** (1) **:** a guarded entrance for the collection of tolls for the use of a road (2) **:** a toll paid for the use of a road **b** (1) **:** a usu. publicly maintained road for direct travel from one place to another ⟨water transportation was outmoded by railroads and good ~*s* —*Amer. Guide Series: Tenn.*⟩ (2) **:** TURNPIKE 3 ⟨ridden the ~*s* enough to know the price of dozing off at the wheel —P.W. Kearney⟩ **2 :** a railroad or model railroad line or system ⟨railroading on . . . backwoods ~*s* —F.P.Donovan⟩
**10pike** \"\ *n* -S [fr. *Pike* county, Missouri, whence they were first believed to have come to California] *West* **:** a migratory farmer — usu. used disparagingly
**11pike** \"\ *n* -S **:** a body position used in diving and gymnastics in which the hips are bent, the knees are straight, the head is pressed forward, and the hands touch the toes or clasp the legs behind and just above the knees — compare JACKKNIFE, TUCK
**piked** \ˈpīkəd, -kt\ *adj* [ME, fr. 1*pike* + *-ed*] **:** having a pike, sharp point, or spine **:** PEAKED, POINTED
**piked dogfish** *n* **:** SPINY DOGFISH
**piked whale** *n* **:** a small north Atlantic finback whale (*Balaenoptera acutorostrata*) having a prominent dorsal fin
**pikel** \ˈpīkəl, ˈpik-\ *n* -S [prob. fr. 1*pike* + *-el* (as in *shovel*)] *dial chiefly Eng* **:** PITCHFORK
**1pike·let** \ˈpīklət\ *n* -S [by shortening and alter. fr. earlier *bara-picklet*, fr. W *bara pyglyd* pitchy bread] **:** a small round thick pancake baked on a griddle and traditionally served on Christmas day in Great Britain **:** CRUMPET
**2pikelet** \"\ *n* -S [4*pike* + *-let*] **:** a small usu. young pike
**pikelike** \ˈ=,=\ *adj* [4*pike* + *like*] **:** resembling a pike
**1pike·man** \ˈpīkmən\ *n, pl* **pikemen** [6*pike* + *man*] **:** a soldier armed with a pike
**2pikeman** \"\ *n, pl* **pikemen** [1*pike* + *man*] **:** PICKMAN
**3pikeman** \"\ *n, pl* **pikemen** [9*pike* + *man*] **:** a keeper of a turnpike gate or entrance
**pike perch** *n* [4*pike*] **:** any of various perches of the family Percidae that are felt to resemble pikes: as **a :** any of several large vigorous sport fishes of the Old World genus *Lucioperca* **b :** a fish of the genus *Stizostedion* (as a sauger or a walleye)
**pike pole** *n* [1*pike*] **1 :** a pole usu. 12 to 20 feet long with a pike in one end used in directing floating logs or to hold utility poles upright while they are being raised or removed **2 :** a fire hook having a head with a sharp point at the tip
**1pik·er** \ˈpīkə(r)\ *n* -S [9*pike* + *-er*] **:** TRAMP, VAGRANT
**2pik·er** \"\ *n* -S [*Pike* county, Missouri (thought to be the original home of many shiftless farmers who migrated to California) + E *-er*] **1** *usu cap* **:** MISSOURIAN — used as a nickname **2** *slang* **:** one who gambles or speculates with small amounts of money **3 :** one who does things in a small way **:** a niggard in money or effort **:** TIGHTWAD
**3piker** \"\ *n* -S [1*pike* + *-er*] **:** a user of a pike
**pikes** *pl of* PIKE, *pres 3d sing of* PIKE
**pikestaff** \ˈ=,=\ *n* [ME, fr. 1*pike* + *staff*] **1 :** a staff or walking stick with a spike at the end to guard the user from slipping **2** [6*pike* + *staff*] **:** 6PIKE 3
**pike whale** *n* [1*pike*] **:** PIKED WHALE
**pi·ki** \ˈpēkē\ *n* -S [Hopi] **:** maize bread baked in thin sheets by the Indians of the southwestern U. S.
**pik·ing** \ˈpīkiŋ\ *n* -S [4*pike*] **:** fishing for pike
**pi·kle** \ˈpīkəl\ *var of* PIGHTLE
**pikol** *var of* PICUL
**piks** *pl of* PIK
**pil** *abbr* **1** [L *pilula*] pill **2** pilot
**1pil-** *or* **pili-** *or* **pilo-** *comb form* [L *pilus* — more at PILE] **:** hair ⟨*pil*osis⟩ ⟨*pili*fer⟩ ⟨*pilo*cystic⟩
**2pil-** *or* **pilo-** *comb form* [Gk, fr. *pilos* — more at PILE (hair)] **:** felt ⟨*Pilo*carpus⟩
**1pila** *pl of* PILUM
**2pi·la** \ˈpīlə\ *n, cap* [NL, fr. L *pila* ball — more at PILE (hair)] **:** the type genus of the family Pilidae comprising apple snails with dextral shells
**3pi·la** \ˈpēlə\ *n* -S [AmSp, fr. Sp, basin, font, fr. L, pillar] **:** a communal fountain
**pi·laf** *or* **pi·laff** *or* **pi·lau** *also* **pi·lav** *or* **pi·law** \pəˈläf, pē'-, -laf, -laa(ə)f, -läf, -laù, -lò, -lō, ˈpē,l-, ˈpi,l-, *in southern U S often* ˈpə(,)lü *or* ˈpə(,)lü *or* -lō\ *n* -S [Per & Turk *pilāu*, *palāu*] **:** rice usu. combined with meat and vegetables, fried in oil, steamed in stock, and seasoned with any of numerous herbs (as saffron or curry) ⟨chicken ~⟩ ⟨Turkish ~⟩
**pi·la·gá** \,pēləˈgä\ *n, pl* **pilagá** *or* **pilagás** *usu cap* **1 a :** a Guaicuruan people of the Gran Chaco, Argentina **b :** a member of such people **2 :** the language of the Pilagá people
**pi·lar** \ˈpīlə(r)\ *adj* [NL *pilaris*, fr. L *pilus* hair + *-aris* -ar — more at PILE] **:** of or relating to the hair or a hair **:** HAIRY
**pi·la·ry** \-ərē\ *adj* [1*pil-* + *-ary*] **:** PILAR
**pi·las·ter** \pəˈlastə(r), -laas-\ *n* -S [MF *pilastre*, fr. It *pilastro*, prob. modif. (influenced by L *pila* pillar & *-aster*, suffix denoting partial resemblance) of L *parastata*, fr. Gk *parastatēs*, lit., one that stands beside, fr. *paristanai* to stand beside, fr. *para* beside + *histanai* to stand — more at PARA-, STAND] **1 :** an upright architectural member that is rectangular in plan and is structurally a pier but architecturally treated as a column, that with capital, shaft, and base usu. projects one third of its width or less from the wall, and that may be load-bearing or merely applied as surface decoration **2 :** a member in furniture resembling the architectural pilaster but always purely decorative and often elaborately carved **3 :** an elongated hardened ridge; *esp* **:** a longitudinal bony ridge on the back of the femur

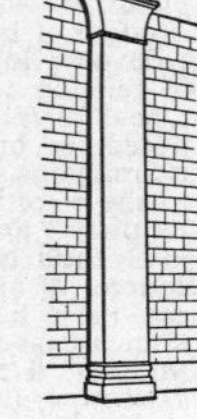
pilaster 1

**pi·las·tered** \-(r)d\ *adj* [*pilaster* + *-ed*] **:** having or borne on pilasters

**pilasterlike** \ˈ==,=\ *adj* **:** resembling a pilaster
**pilaster mass** *n* **:** a pier projecting from but usu. built with a wall and differing from the anta and parastas in that it does not form the termination of the projecting wall but usu. stiffens it (as between two windows)
**pilaster strip** *n* **:** a pilaster mass of slight projection or of slender proportions
**pil·as·trade** \ˌpilə¦strād\ *n* -s [It *pilastrata*, fr. *pilastro* — more at PILASTER] **:** a row or series of pilasters — **pil·as·trad·ed** \-dəd\ *adj*
**pi·las·tric** \pəˈlastrik\ *adj* [*pilaster* + *-ic*] **:** characterized by or like pilasters
**pi·lau** *also* **pilav** *or* **pilaw** *var of* PILAF
**pilch** \ˈpilch\ *n* -ES [ME *pilche*, fr. OE *pylce, pylece*, fr. ML *pellicea*, fem. of LL *pelliceus, pellicius* made of skin, fr. L *pellis* skin — more at FELL] **1 :** an outer garment made orig. of skin or fur and later of leather or wool **2 a** *obs* **:** a saddle cover **b :** a light child's saddle **3 :** an infant's wrapper covering the diaper
**pil·chard** \ˈpilchə(r)d\ *n* -s [origin unknown] **1 :** a clupeid fish (*Sardinia pilchardus* or *Sardinella pilchardus*) that resembles the herring, occurs in great schools along the coasts of Europe, attains a length of 8 or 10 inches, and that is extensively used for food — see SARDINE **2 :** any of several fishes (family Clupeidae) related to the European pilchard: as **a :** CALIFORNIA SARDINE **b :** a sardine (*Sardinops sagax* or *Arengus sagax*) of the west coast of So. America and the coast of southern Africa that may be identical with the California sardine **c :** an Australian sardine (*Sardinops neopilchardus*)
**pilchard oil** *n* **:** a pale yellow drying oil obtained from pilchards (as *Sardinops caerulea*) — compare SARDINE OIL
**¹pil·cher** \ˈpilchə(r)\ *archaic var of* PILCHARD
**²pilch·er** \ˈ"\ *n* -s [alter. of *pilch*] **:** SCABBARD ⟨will you pluck your sword out of his ~ by the ears —Shak.⟩
**³pilcher** *n* -s [perh. fr. *pilch* + *-er*] *obs* **:** a contemptible person
**pil·crow** \ˈpil,krō\ *n* -s [prob. alter. of ME *pylcrafte*, modif. of LL *paragraphus* — more at PARAGRAPH] **:** a paragraph mark ¶
**¹pile** \ˈpīl, *esp before pause or consonant* -īəl\ *n* -s [ME, dart, pointed shaft, stake, fr. OE *pīl*; akin to OHG *pfīl* dart, arrow, stake; both fr. a prehistoric WGmc word borrowed fr. L *pilum* heavy javelin, pestle — more at PESTLE] **1 :** a long slender member usu. of timber, steel, or reinforced concrete driven into the ground to carry a vertical load, to resist a lateral force, or to resist water or earth pressure — see BATTER PILE, BEARING PILE, SHEET PILE **2 :** a wedge-shaped heraldic charge usu. placed palewise with the broad end up **3 :** a pointed blade of grass **4 a :** a target-shooting arrowhead without cutting edges that is usu. cylindrical or conoidal in shape and either pointed or blunt — called also *point, tip* **b** [L *pilum*] **:** an ancient Roman foot soldier's heavy javelin

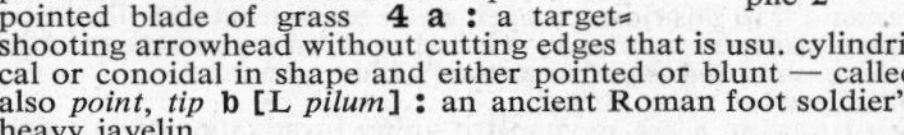
pile 2

**²pile** \ˈ"\ *vt* -ED/-ING/-S [ME *pilen*, fr. ¹*pile*] **:** to drive piles into **:** fill, support, or strengthen with piles
**³pile** \ˈ"\ *adj* [¹*pile*] **:** relating to or used as a pile **:** formed of or supported on piles ⟨a ~ road⟩
**⁴pile** *n* -s [ME] *obs* **:** a small fortified tower; *esp* **:** PEEL
**⁵pile** \ˈpīl, *esp before pause or consonant* -īəl\ *n* -s [ME, fr. MF, fr. L *pila* pillar, pier, mole of stone] **1** *obs* **:** a pier of a bridge **2 a :** a quantity of things heaped together or laid one on top of the other ⟨a ~ of dishes⟩ ⟨a small ~ of clothes on a chair —Arnold Bennett⟩ ⟨a ~ of wood by the fireplace⟩: as (1) *obs* **:** a series of weights fitting together and forming a solid figure usu. a cone (2) **:** a heap usu. of wood for burning a corpse or a sacrifice **:** PYRE (3) **:** a stack of arms (4) **:** FAGOT 3 **b :** any great number or large quantity **:** HEAP, LOT ⟨had had a ~ of troubles in his lifetime⟩ ⟨anyone who wants to teach has to take ~s of their education courses —W.L.Miller⟩ ⟨~s of good things to eat, fish, meat, fowls, vegetables —Stringfellow Barr⟩ **3 a :** the lower die of an old English apparatus for striking coins by hand with a hammer — compare TRUSSELL **b :** the reverse of a coin **4 :** a large often imposing building or group of buildings ⟨a Gothic ~⟩ ⟨contrast between the vast ~ of the cathedral and the pigmy men in the street —H.J. Laski⟩ ⟨a great ~ of houses, inhabited by a great number of people —Charles Dickens⟩ **5 a :** a great amount of money **:** FORTUNE ⟨one went to the city . . . made one's ~ and married —Van Wyck Brooks⟩ **b :** all the money or chips a player has available for play in a particular game or at a particular juncture in a game **6 a :** a vertical series of alternate disks of two dissimilar metals (as copper and zinc) with disks of cloth or paper moistened with an electrolyte between them for producing a current of electricity — called also *voltaic pile, Volta's pile* **b :** a battery made up of cells similarly constructed ⟨a dry ~⟩ **7 :** REACTOR
**⁶pile** \ˈ"\ *vb* -ED/-ING/-S [ME *pilen*, fr. ⁵*pile*] *vt* **1 a :** to lay or place in or as if in a pile **:** put or throw on top of a heap **:** STACK — often used with *on* or *up* ⟨sand dunes *piled* up by the winds —Samuel Van Valkenburg & Ellsworth Huntington⟩ ⟨her black hair cut in a straight fringe . . . and *piled* up on top of her head —Edith Sitwell⟩ **b :** to place (as weapons) so as to be easily available ⟨outside the station we *piled* arms and waited —John Sommerfield⟩ **c :** to form a fagot of (lengths of iron) **2 :** to heap in abundance **:** LOAD ⟨*piled* . . . the salad on her plate —Hamilton Basso⟩ **3 a :** to add to esp. for an intensified effect **:** INCREASE ⟨I do think he *piled* the agony up a little too high in that last scene —Frederick Marryat⟩ **b :** to build or gather together **:** AMASS — usu. used with *up* ⟨*piled* up a wealth of information on the American Indian —Ruth Underhill⟩ ⟨forebears were early settlers . . . and quickly *piled* up fortunes —*Amer. Guide Series: Md.*⟩ ⟨hunting down and *piling* up quantities of knowledge —E.M.Burns⟩ **~** *vi* **1 :** to form a pile **:** ACCUMULATE — usu. used with *up* ⟨found the yield of this crop *piling* up on its hands —C.L. Jones⟩ ⟨office work which had *piled* up for months —D.A. Howarth⟩ **2 a :** to move or press forward in or as if in a mass **:** CROWD ⟨pushing one another . . . they *piled* out of the restaurant —Morley Callaghan⟩ ⟨our whole party *piled* into one . . . compartment —O.S.Nock⟩ **b :** to get in, off, or out ⟨he *piled* quickly into bed⟩ **3 :** to thicken and accumulate (as ink on printing plates, rollers, or blankets or paint on a brush) instead of transferring or spreading properly
**⁷pile** \ˈ"\ *n* -s [ME, fr. L *pila* ball — more at ⁸PILE] **1 :** a single hemorrhoid **2 piles** *pl* **:** HEMORRHOIDS; *also* **:** the condition of one affected with hemorrhoids ⟨is suffering terribly from ~s⟩
**⁸pile** \ˈ"\ *n* -s [ME, fr. L *pilus* hair; akin to L *pilleus, pilleum, pileus* felt cap, Gk *pilos* felt, felt cap, ball, L *pila* ball] **1 a :** HAIR; *esp* **:** a growth of short fine hair like fur **:** DOWN **b :** a thick undercoat (as of certain dogs) **c :** a velvety surface of fine hairs on various insects; *collectively* **:** the hairs making up such a surface **2 :** a mass of raised loops or tufts covering all or part of a fabric or carpet that is formed by extra warp or weft yarns during the weaving and that produces a soft even compact furry or velvety surface **3 :** a quality possessed by bread when the crumb is silky in appearance and texture **4 a :** yellowish red coloration on wingbows, neck, saddle, back, and flight feathers of various white domestic fowls that is a disqualification in standard breeds but characteristic of some game types **b :** a bird colored in this manner
**¹pi·lea** \ˈpīlēə, ˈpil-\ *n, cap* [NL, fr. L *pileus, pilleus* felt cap; fr. the shape of a section of the perianth] **:** a genus of chiefly tropical smooth stingless herbs (family Urticaceae) with opposite leaves and greenish axillary flowers
**²pilea** *pl of* PILEUM
**pi·le·a·ta** \ˌpīlē¦ād·ə, ¦pil-\ *adj* [NL, fr. L, fem. of *pileatus, pilleatus*] *of an organ pipe* **:** STOPPED
**pi·le·ate** \ˈpīlēət, ˈpil-, -ē,āt\ *or* **pi·le·at·ed** \-ē,ād·əd\ *adj* [L *pilleatus, pileatus*, fr. *pilleus, pileus* felt cap + *-atus* -ate — more at PILE (hair)] **:** having a pileus; *specif* **:** having a crest covering the pileum
**pileated woodpecker** *n* **:** a No. American woodpecker (*Dryocopus pileatus*) that is black with a red crest and white on the wings and sides of the neck and that inhabits dense forests
**pile bent** *n* [¹*pile*] **:** the part of a trestle that carries the adjacent ends of timber stringers or concrete slabs and consists of a row of timber or concrete bearing piles and a timber or concrete cap
**pile bridge** *n* **:** a bridge supported by pile bents
**pile cap** *n* **1 :** a member passing over and connecting the heads of a row of piles **2 :** a block used to protect the head of a pile and to hold it in the leads while being driven in the ground
**¹piled** \ˈpīld, *esp before pause or consonant* -īəld\ *adj* [ME, fr. ⁸*pile* + *-ed*] **1 :** having pile **:** covered with hair or down **2 :** having a pile ⟨~ textiles⟩ ⟨~ bread⟩
**²piled** \ˈ"\ *adj* [fr. past part. of ⁶*pile*] **:** heaped in or into a pile or piles
**³piled** \ˈ"\ *adj* [¹*pile* + *-ed*] **:** built on piles
**pile drawer** *n* [¹*pile*] **:** a machine for withdrawing piles
**pile driver** *n* **1** *or* **pile engine :** a machine for driving down piles usu. consisting of a high frame with appliances for raising and dropping a pile hammer or for supporting and guiding a steam or air hammer **2 :** an operator of a pile driver
**pile dweller** *n* **:** LAKE DWELLER
**pile dwelling** *or* **pile house** *n* **:** LAKE DWELLING
**pile hammer** *n* **:** the heavy weight of the pile driver whose impact forces a pile into the earth
**pi·le·i·form** \pīˈlēə,fȯrm, ˈpīl-, ˈpil-\ *adj* [NL *pileiformis*, fr. *pileus* + *-iformis* -iform] **:** having the form of a pileus
**pile·less** \ˈpīlləs\ *adj* **:** having no pile ⟨~ carpet⟩
**pi·le·o·lat·ed warbler** \ˈpīlēə,lād·əd-\ *n* [*pileolated* capped, fr. L *pilleolus, pileolus* small cap (dim. of *pilleus, pileus* felt cap) + E *-ate* + *-ed* — more at PILE (hair)] **:** a northwestern warbler that is a variety (*Wilsonia pusilla pileolata*) of Wilson's warbler distinguished by a brighter olive green on the upper parts and a deeper yellow beneath
**pi·le·o·lus** \pīˈlēələs\ *n, pl* **pileo·li** \-ə,lī\ [NL, dim. of *pileus*] *biol* **:** a small pileus
**pi·le·ous** \ˈpīlēəs, ˈpil-\ *adj* [¹*pil-* + *-eous*] **:** HAIRY, PILOSE
**pile perch** *n* [¹*pile*] **1 :** a common surf fish (*Rhacochilus vacca*) dusky with a silvery luster above fading to silver below that is common along sandy shores of the Pacific coast of No. America and is a leading market fish of the area **2 :** RUBBERLIP PERCH
**pile plank** *n* **:** a thick plank used as a pile in sheetpiling
**pil·er** \ˈpīlə(r)\ *n* -s [⁶*pile* + *-er*] **:** one that piles or heaps up; *esp* **:** one whose work is piling materials or products for storage, transportation, or processing
**piles** *pl of* PILE, *pres 3d sing of* PILE
**pile saw** *n* [¹*pile*] **:** a saw for cutting piles under water
**pile start** *n* **:** a pintail (*Anas acuta*)
**pi·le·um** \ˈpīlēəm, ˈpil-\ *n, pl* **pi·lea** \-ēə\ [NL, fr. L *pilleum, pileum* felt cap, fr. *pilleus, pileus*] **:** the top of the head of a bird from the bill to the nape
**pile up** *vi* [⁶*pile*] **1 :** to get into a tangle or confused mass ⟨angry horn blasts from cars that had *piled up* in the intersection⟩ **2 :** to run aground **:** become stranded ⟨that difficult coast where the wrecks still *piled up* —Marjory S. Douglas⟩ ⟨*piled up* on a reef just off a lovely island —*Time*⟩ **3 a :** to become involved in a pileup of vehicles; *broadly* **:** to wreck one's car **:** crack up **b :** to crash an airplane
**pileup** \ˈ=,=\ *n* -s [⁶*pile* + *up*] **:** a collision involving usu. several objects and causing damage or injury ⟨was instantly killed in an automobile ~ —*Springfield (Mass.) Union*⟩
**pi·le·us** \ˈpīlēəs, ˈpil-\ *n, pl* **pi·lei** \-ē,ī\ [NL, fr. L *pilleus, pileus* felt cap — more at PILE (hair)] **1 :** an umbrella-shaped upper cap of many fungi (as the mushrooms and other basidiomycetes) **2** [L *pilleus, pileus*] **a :** a pointed or close-fitting cap worn by ancient Romans **b :** a cap worn by some ecclesiastics **3 :** the umbrella of a jellyfish **4 :** a cloud resembling a cap that sometimes appears above and partially obscures the bulging top of a cumulus cloud
**pilework** \ˈ=,=\ *n* [¹*pile* + *work*] **1 :** work consisting of piles **2 :** a structure of piles (as in lake dwellings)
**pileworm** \ˈ=,=\ *n* [¹*pile* + *worm*] **:** SHIPWORM
**pilewort** \ˈ=,=\ *n* [⁷*pile* + *wort*; fr. its use in treating piles] **1 :** LESSER CELANDINE **2 :** a coarse hairy erect but much branched perennial figwort (*Scrophularia marilandica*) of the eastern and central U.S. that was formerly believed useful in the treatment of scrofula **3 :** a very variable fireweed (*Erechtites hieracifolia*) chiefly of damp woodlands of eastern No. America that has heads of straw-colored tubular flowers **4 :** PRINCE'S-FEATHER 1
**piley** \ˈpīlē\ *adj* [⁸*pile* + *-y*] **:** having pile; *esp* **:** having a strong development of pile
**¹pil·fer** \ˈpilfə(r)\ *n* -s [ME *pilfre*, fr. MF *pelfre*] *archaic* **:** something that is pilfered; *also* **:** the act of pilfering **:** PILFERAGE
**²pilfer** \ˈ"\ *vb* **pilfered; pilfered; pilfering** \-f(ə)riŋ\ **pilfers** [MF *pelfrer*, fr. *pelfre* booty] *vi* **:** PLUNDER, ROB; *esp* **:** to steal little by little or by taking articles of small value **:** commit or practice petty theft ⟨~*ed* from his fellow students —*Times Lit. Supp.*⟩ **~** *vt* **1 :** to steal in small quantities **:** FILCH ⟨~*ed* his roommate's stamps and writing paper⟩ **2 :** to take (as ideas or thoughts) and use as one's own **:** CRIB ⟨able to ~ all the new ideas of industrial construction —Emil Lengyel⟩ **syn** see STEAL
**pil·fer·age** \-f(ə)rij\ *n* -s [²*pilfer* + *-age*] **1 a :** the act of pilfering **b :** something that is pilfered **2** *insurance law* **:** the theft of insured property by one not in possession
**pilferage hazard** *n* **:** the risk of loss to cargo when specifically covered by marine insurance through theft committed by the ship's crew, stevedores, or others having access to the insured subject matter
**pil·fer·er** \-f(ə)rə(r)\ *n* -s **:** one that pilfers **:** a petty thief
**pil·fery** \-rē\ *n* -ES [prob. alter. of earlier *pelfery* booty, fr. (assumed) ONF *pelferie*, fr. the source of MF *pelfre* booty] **:** petty theft
**pil·gar·lic** \pil'gärlik\ *also* **peel·gar·lic** \pēl'-\ *n* -s [*pilgarlic* fr. *pilled garlic*, fr. ²*pill; peelgarlic*, alter. (influenced by ²*peel*) of *pilgarlic*] **1 a :** a bald head **b :** a bald-headed man **2 :** a man looked upon with humorous contempt or mock pity **:** a poor creature
**¹pil·grim** \ˈpilgrəm\ *n* -s *except sense 6a* [ME, fr. OF *peligrin*, fr. LL *pelegrinus*, alter. of L *peregrinus* foreigner, fr. *peregre* abroad, fr. *pereger* being abroad, fr. *per* through + *agr-, ager* land, field — more at FARE, ACRE] **1 a :** one who journeys esp. in alien lands **:** TRAVELER, WAYFARER **b :** a person who passes through life as if in exile from a heavenly homeland or in search of it or of some high goal (as truth) **2 :** one who travels to visit a shrine or holy place as a devotee ⟨realizes the ideal of every devout ~ and journeys to the Holy Land —R.M.French⟩ **3 a** *usu cap* **:** one of the Pilgrim Fathers **b :** a first settler ⟨trace their line back to the original . . . ~s —*Amer. Guide Series: Md.*⟩ **4 :** a recent immigrant or settler **:** one that is new or strange in a locality **5 :** FASHION GRAY **6 a** *usu cap* **:** an American breed of rather small domestic geese distinguished by having the male white and the female gray **b** *sometimes cap* **:** a bird of this breed
**²pilgrim** \ˈ"\ *vi* -ED/-ING/-S **:** to be or act as a pilgrim **:** PILGRIMAGE ⟨they had ~*ed* for that peace —R.O.Bowen⟩
**¹pil·grim·age** \ˈpilgrəmij\ *n* -s [ME *pelrimage, pilgrimage*, fr. OF *pelerinage*, fr. *pelerin, peligrin* pilgrim + *-age*] **1 a :** a journey of a pilgrim; *esp* **:** one to a shrine or a sacred place ⟨Arabs make ~s to worship at his tomb —Robert Hichens⟩ **b :** the act of making such a journey ⟨~ had . . . been adopted by the church as a form of canonical penance —M.W.Baldwin⟩ **2 :** a trip taken to visit a place of historic or sentimental interest or to participate in a specific event or for a definite purpose ⟨American writers, artists and composers have made ~s to France —G.W.Chapman⟩ ⟨every spring the rhododendron inspires . . . ~s —*Amer. Guide Series: Wash.*⟩ **3 :** the course of life on earth ⟨prosperity . . . came to him during his earthly ~ —V.L.Parrington⟩ **b :** a particular part of the life course of an individual ⟨my ~ from prep school to University —Osbert Lancaster⟩ **4 :** a search for mental and spiritual values ⟨the pursuit of knowledge was no mere intellectual search, but a ~ —H.O.Taylor⟩
**²pilgrimage** \ˈ"\ *vi* -ED/-ING/-S **:** to go on or as if on a pilgrimage ⟨all . . . had *pilgrimaged* to the capital —Walter Goodman⟩
**pilgrimage festival** *n* **:** any of three great festivals in the Jewish calendar orig. celebrated in part by a pilgrimage to Jerusalem — compare PASSOVER, SHABUOTH, SUKKOTH
**pilgrim bottle** *also* **pilgrim's bottle** *n* **:** a flat usu. circular bottle with a small spout and with rings to hold a cord for slinging it over the shoulder
**pilgrim brown** *n* **:** a grayish brown to dark grayish brown — called also *friar, mandalay*
**pil·grim·er** \-rəmə(r)\ *n* -s [²*pilgrim* + *-er*] **:** PILGRIM
**pil·grim·ess** \-məs\ *n* -ES [¹*pilgrim* + *-ess*] **:** a female pilgrim
**pilgrim father** *n, usu cap P&F* **:** one of the English colonists who under the dominant religious motivation of a minority of Separatists from the Church of England sailed to America in 1620 aboard the *Mayflower* and founded the first permanent settlement in New England
**pil·grim·ize** \-rə,mīz\ *vb* -ED/-ING/-S *vi* **:** to go or act as a pilgrim **~** *vt* **:** to make a pilgrim of
**pilgrim psalm** *n, usu cap both Ps* **:** SONG OF ASCENTS
**pilgrim scallop** *or* **pilgrim's scallop shell** *also* **pilgrim's shell** *n* **:** a scallop shell or something resembling it worn as a pilgrim sign
**pilgrim sign** *n* **:** a symbol or badge (as palm leaves, a catherine wheel, a Canterbury bell) carried by a pilgrim to indicate the shrine he sought or had visited and believed to preserve him against molestation
**¹pili** *pl of* PILUS
**²pi·li** \pēˈlē\ *or* **pili nut** *n* -s [Tag *pili*] **1 :** the nut of any of various trees of the genus *Canarium*; *esp* **:** the edible nut of a Philippine tree (*Canarium ovatum*) **2 :** JAVA ALMOND
**³pi·li** \ˈpēlē\ *or* **pili grass** *n* -s [Hawaiian, lit., to adhere, cling] *Hawaii* **:** TANGLEHEAD
**pili-** — see PIL-
**pi·li·bezoar** \ˌpīlə+\ *n* [¹*pil-* + *bezoar*] **:** HAIR BALL
**pil·i·dae** \ˈpilə,dē\ *n pl, cap* [NL, fr. *Pila*, type genus + *-idae*] **:** a family of oviparous freshwater snails having the respiratory cavity modified to permit breathing in either air or water — see APPLE SNAIL, PILA
**pi·lid·i·um** \pīˈlidēəm\ *n, pl* **pilid·ia** \-ēə\ [NL, fr. Gk *pilidion*, dim. of *pilos* felt cap — more at PILE (hair)] **:** the free-swimming hat-shaped larva of various nemertean worms in whose interior the young worm develops
**pilier** *comparative of* PILY
**piliest** *superlative of* PILY
**pil·i·fer** \ˈpiləfə(r)\ *n* -s [NL, fr. ¹*pil-* + *-fer*] **:** a lateral hairy process of the labrum in Lepidoptera formerly regarded as the vestige of the mandible
**pi·lif·er·ous** \(ˈ)pī¦lif(ə)rəs\ *adj* [¹*pil-* + *-ferous*] **:** bearing or producing hairs — compare PILOSE
**pi·li·gan** \ˈpēlē,gän\ *n* -s [NL *Piligena*, genus of Lycopodiaceae, fr. ²*pil-* + *-gena* -gen] **:** a club moss (*Lycopodium saururus*) of Brazil and Argentina with cathartic properties
**pili gum** *n* [²*pili*] **:** BREA 1 a (2)
**pi·li·kia** \ˌpēlēˈkēə\ *n* -s [Hawaiian] *Hawaii* **:** TROUBLE
**pi·line** \ˈpī,līn, -lən\ *adj* [¹*pil-* + *-ine*] **:** HAIRY
**piling** *n* -s [ME, fr. gerund of ²*pile*] **1 :** pile driving **:** the formation (as of a foundation) with piles **2 :** a structure of piles **:** PILEWORK; *collectively* **:** PILES **3 :** logs suitable for or ready to be made into piles
**piling strip** *n* **:** a narrow piece of lumber used to separate the courses in a pile
**¹pill** \ˈpil\ *n* -s [earlier *pille*, fr. (assumed) ME, fr. OE *pyll*, alter. of *pull* pool, creek, prob. of OW origin] **1** *dial Eng* **:** POOL **2** *dial Eng* **:** a running stream **:** CREEK
**²pill** \ˈ"\ *vb* -ED/-ING/-S [ME *pilen, pillen*, partly fr. OE *pilian* to peel (prob. fr. L *pilare* to depilate, fr. *pilus* hair), partly fr. MF *piller* to plunder — more at PILE, PILLAGE] *vi, dial chiefly Eng* **:** PEEL **:** come off esp. in flakes or scales **~** *vt* **1 a** *archaic* **:** to subject to depredation or extortion **:** DESPOIL, ROB ⟨the commons hath he ~*ed* with grievous taxes and quite lost their hearts —Shak.⟩ **b** *obs* **:** to seize by violence **:** EXTORT ⟨hear me, you wrangling pirates, that fall out in sharing that which you have ~*ed* from me —Shak.⟩ **2** *dial* **:** to peel or strip off (as bark) ⟨took him rods of green poplar . . . and ~*ed* white streaks in them —Gen 30:37 (AV)⟩ **3** *obs* **:** to deprive of hair **:** remove hair from
**³pill** \ˈ"\ *n* -s [ME *pile*, fr. *pilen* to pill] *dial* **:** the peel or rind of fruit **:** the shell or skin of fruits and bulbous roots **:** the bark of a tree
**⁴pill** \ˈ"\ *n* -s [L *pilula*, lit., little ball, dim. of *pila* ball — more at PILE (hair)] **1 :** a medicine in the form of a little ball or small rounded mass that may be coated or uncoated and is to be swallowed whole — compare TABLET **2 :** something offensive, repugnant, or unpleasant that must be accepted or endured ⟨the loss of the promotion was a bitter ~ to swallow⟩ **3 :** something resembling a pill usu. in size or shape: as **a :** PELLET 1a ⟨kneading his bread into little white ~s —Robin Maugham⟩ **b** (1) **:** CANNONBALL (2) **:** a musket ball ⟨thirty thousand muskets flung their ~s like hail —Lord Byron⟩ **c** *slang* (1) **:** BASEBALL (2) **:** GOLF BALL **d :** a small ball of textile fibers often formed by the balling of nap when subject to friction **e :** a compressed mass of a plastic material for use in a mold **:** PREFORM **4 :** a disagreeable or tiresome person ⟨she was considered in some circles a vast ~ —Alma Stone⟩ **5 a** *slang* **:** CIGARETTE **b :** a portion of opium prepared for smoking
**⁵pill** \ˈ"\ *vb* -ED/-ING/-S *vt* **1 :** to dose with pills **2 :** BLACKBALL **3 :** to make or form into or as if into pills **~** *vi* **:** to form balls ⟨sweaters made of wool yarns may have a tendency to ~ —*Chicago Daily Drovers Jour.*⟩
**¹pil·lage** \ˈpilij, -lēj\ *n* -s [ME, fr. MF, fr. *piller* to plunder (fr. *peille* rag, fr. L *pilleum* felt cap) + *-age* — more at PILL (hair)] **1 a :** the act of stripping of money and goods esp. during war **:** SACK ⟨the painting may have been ruined in a ~ or massacre —Willa Cather⟩ ⟨plan for the ~ and enslavement of the earth —Calvin Coolidge⟩ **b :** the unlawful taking of property **:** ROBBERY **2** *archaic* **:** something taken as booty **:** SPOIL ⟨robbed all the country there about and brought the ~ home —Edmund Spenser⟩
**²pillage** \ˈ", *esp in pres part* -ləj\ *vb* -ED/-ING/-S *vt* **1 :** to strip of money or goods by open violence **:** LOOT, SACK ⟨pirates *pillaged* the coasts —C.L.Jones⟩ **2 :** to acquire by stealing **:** take possession of unlawfully **:** PURLOIN ⟨gradually deserted, *pillaged* for building material, so that little marble remains —Claudia Cassidy⟩ ⟨the thought process which leads to the *pillaging* of an idea —L.P.Beth⟩ ⟨tobacco *pillaged* from a tin-full which his father had bought —Arthur Morrison⟩ **~** *vi* **:** to take booty **:** PLUNDER ⟨swept down . . . burning and *pillaging* —Mary Smith⟩ **syn** see RAVAGE
**pil·lag·er** \-jə(r)\ *n* -s **:** one that pillages
**¹pil·lar** \ˈpilə(r)\ *n* -s [ME *piler, piller*, fr. OF *piler*, fr. ML *pilare*, fr. L *pila* pillar, pier] **1 a :** a firm upright support for a superstructure **:** POST **b :** a column or shaft standing alone esp. for a monument **2 :** a natural pillar-shaped formation or mass ⟨to follow in the wake of another vehicle . . . was to move in a ~ of dust —Rose Macaulay⟩ ⟨little ~s of sand rose here and there —Norman Douglas⟩ **3 :** one that is a mainstay **:** a chief supporter **:** PROP ⟨a rough-hewn ~ of the . . . Church —Ben Riker⟩ ⟨the middlemen, . . . the ~s of society, the cornerstone of convention —Roy Lewis & Angus Maude⟩ **4 :** any of various vertical supporting members: as **a :** the central support of a table **:** PEDESTAL **b :** BEDPOST **c :** STANCHION **d :** the vertical hollow post of a harp frame — see HARP illustration **5 :** something regarded as a chief support **:** a fundamental fact, idea, principle, or practice ⟨science and criticism had eaten away the ~s of superstition and unreasoning faith —W.P.Webb⟩ ⟨there are five compulsory practices, or ~s of Islam —A.C.Bouquet⟩ **6 :** any of the brass posts between the two plates of a watch or clock movement that serve to keep the plates in their proper positions **7 :** a solid mass of coal, rock, or ore left standing to support the roof **8 :** the center of the volt, ring, or manege ground around which a horse turns **9 :** a body part likened to a pillar or column (as the columella of a snail shell or the margin of the external abdominal ring); *specif* **:** PILLAR OF THE FAUCES **10 :** a mailbox shaped like a pillar **11 :** a frame on which clay pipes rest while being baked in a kiln — **from pillar to post :** from one place or one situation to another **:** HITHER AND THITHER ⟨the library . . . forced to move *from pillar to post* needed a home —*Saturday Rev.*⟩

pillar 1

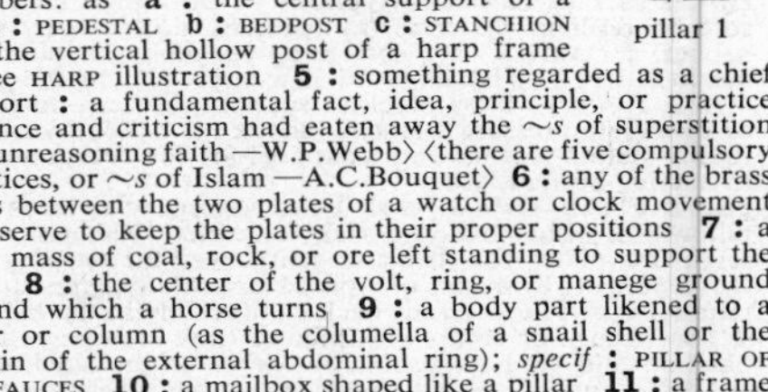

**²pillar** \ˈ"\ *vb* -ED/-ING/-S *vt* **1 :** to support or strengthen with or as if with a pillar **2 :** to embody in or represent in the form of a pillar **~** *vi* **:** to be supported by pillars

**pillar-and-breast** \'==,=\ *adj* : BORD-AND-PILLAR

**pillar and scroll** *n* : an early American shelf clock designed with slender pillars and scrolled cresting and ornamented with turned wood finials

**pillar bolt** *n* : a projecting stud bolt intended to support a part near its outer end

**pillar-box** \'=,=\ *n, Brit* : a pillar-shaped mailbox

**pillar crane** *n* : a crane the mechanism of which can be rotated about a fixed pillar

**pillar dollar** *n* : the old Spanish-American peso having on its reverse two pillars with a ribbon about them

**pillar drawing** *n* : PILLAR ROBBING

**pil·lared** \'pilə(r)d\ *adj* [ME *pilered,* fr. *piler* pillar + *-ed*] : having pillars : resembling or formed into a pillar ⟨the ~ portico —Osbert Lancaster⟩

pillar and scroll

**pil·lar·et** \'pilə,ret\ *n* -S [¹*pillar* + *-et*] : a little pillar

**pillar file** *n* : a usu. double-cut file that is rectangular in section, parallel in width with one safe edge, and tapered in thickness from the middle both ways and that is esp. suitable for narrow work

**pil·lar·ing** \'piləriŋ\ *n* -S [¹*pillar* + *-ing*] : a series of pillars; *collectively* : PILLARS

**pil·lar·ist** \'pilərəst\ *n* -S [¹*pillar* + *-ist*] *relig* : STYLITE

**pillar light** *n* : a light mounted on the pillar between doors of an automobile

**pillar lip** *n* : the inner or columellar portion of the border of the orifice of a spiral shell

**pillar mount** *n* : a mount or support in the form of a pillar for a gun in a fortification

**pillar of fire** *adj, usu cap P&F* [fr. *Pillar of Fire,* bulletin published by the founder of the sect] : of, relating to, or being a fundamentalist holiness premillenarian church beginning as an offshoot of U.S. Methodism in 1901, retaining Methodist polity, and emphasizing sanctification as a second work of grace following justification

**pillar of the diaphragm** : any of the crura of the diaphragm

**pillar of the fauces** : one of the lateral bounding folds of the fauces

**pillar of the fornix** : either of the anterior and posterior diverging extensions of the fornix of the brain

**pillar plate** *n* : the plate in watchworks that is nearest to the dial

**pillar press** *n* : a punch press with a frame of two parallel uprights through which the driving shaft passes and within which the slide works

**pillar robbing** *n* : the mining and removal of pillars after the main coal or ore body has been removed — called also *pillar drawing*

**pillar root** *n* : PROP ROOT

**pillar rose** *n* : any of various climbing roses growing to a moderate height and esp. adapted for use on low fences and walls

**pillars** *pl of* PILLAR, *pres 3d sing of* PILLAR

**pillar saint** *n* : STYLITE

**pillar shaper** *n* : a shaper whose reciprocating toolhead is mounted on a pillar, the feeding being obtained by a movement of the table to which the work is secured

**pillar-stone** \'=,=\ *n* **1** : a pillar-shaped monument or memorial of stone **2** : CORNERSTONE

**pil·lary** \'piləre\ *adj* [¹*pillar* + *-y*] : PILLARED

**pill-bearing spurge** \'=,==-\ *n* [⁴*pill*] : a dried herb (*Euphorbia pilulifera*) used esp. in folk medicine in the treatment of asthma

**pillbox** \'=,=\ *n* **1** : a box for pills; *esp* : a shallow round box of pasteboard **2** : a small low emplacement for machine guns and antitank weapons that is usu. made of reinforced concrete with overhead cover and forms part of a defensive position **3** : a small round brimless hat; *specif* : a woman's shallow hat with a flat crown and straight sides

**pill bug** *n* : WOOD LOUSE 1

**pilled** \'pild\ *adj* [ME *piled, pilled,* fr. past part. of *pilen, pillen* to pill] *dial* : having a bald or shaven head : TONSURED

**pil·ler** \'pilə(r)\ *dial var of* PILLOW

**pil·let** \'pilət\ *n* -S [ME, alter. of *pelet* pellet] : a small pill : PELLET

**pil·li·cock** \'pilə,käk\ *n* [E dial. *pillie* penis (of Scand origin, fr. the source of Norw dial. *pill* penis) + *cock*] **1** *obs* : PENIS **2** *obs* : a fine lad

**pilling** *pres part of* PILL

¹**pil·lion** \'pilyən\ *n* -S [ScGael or IrGael; ScGael *pillean,* dim. of *peall* covering, couch; ScGael & IrGael *pillin,* dim. of *peall* covering, couch; ScGael & IrGael *peall* fr. a prehistoric Goidelic word borrowed fr. L *pellis* skin, hide — more at FELL] **1 a** : a light saddle for women consisting chiefly of a cushion or pannel **b** : a pad or cushion put on behind a man's saddle chiefly for a woman to ride on **2** : a motorcycle or bicycle riding saddle for a passenger

²**pillion** \"\ *vt* -ED/-ING/-S : to seat on a pillion

³**pillion** \"\ *adv* : on or as if on a pillion ⟨ride ~ behind their sleek and slender cavaliers —Frances P. Keyes⟩

⁴**pillion** \"\ *n* -S [Corn *pylyon,* pl. of *pyl* peel, stripping, prob. fr. E *peel*] : tin left in the slags after the first smelting — compare PRILLION

**pil·li·winks** \'pilə,wiŋks\ *n pl but sing or pl in constr* [ME *pyrwykes, pyrewinkes*] : an old instrument of torture for the thumbs and fingers

**pill masser** *n* [⁴*pill*] : a machine that mixes the ingredients for pills

**pill millipede** *n* : PILLWORM

**pil·lor** \'pilə(r)\ *vt* -ED/-ING/-S [back-formation fr. ¹*pillory*] : PILLORY

**pil·lor·ize** \-lə,rīz\ *vt* -ED/-ING/-S [¹*pillory* + *-ize*] : PILLORY

¹**pil·lory** \'pilərē, -ri\ *n* -ES [ME, fr. OF *pilori*] **1** : a device for publicly punishing offenders consisting of a frame of adjustable boards erected on a post and having holes through which the head and hands of the offender were thrust — compare STOCK 4 **2** : a means by which to expose to public scorn or ridicule ⟨~ by publicity today is nationwide —R.H. Paul & Philip Mandel⟩

²**pillory** \"\ *vt* **pilloried; pilloried; pillorying; pillories 1** : to set in a pillory : punish with the pillory **2** : to expose or hold up to public contempt, ridicule, or scorn ⟨a demagogue who has risen to power by ~*ing* good men —*Newsweek*⟩

pillory

¹**pil·low** \'pi(,)lō, -lə; -ləw *or* -lō+V\ *n* -S [ME *pilwe,* fr. OE *pyle, pylu;* akin to OHG *pfuliwi* pillow; both fr. a prehistoric WGmc word borrowed fr. L *pulvinus* pillow] **1 a** : something used to support the head of a person resting or sleeping; *esp* : a sack or bag made typically of cloth and filled with a soft or resilient material (as feathers, down, hair, sponge rubber) : CUSHION **b** : something resembling a pillow ⟨the hemlock tree . . . let its ~ of new snow slip to the ground —*New Yorker*⟩ **2** : a block or support used esp. to equalize or distribute pressure : PILLOW BLOCK **3** : a cushion or pad tightly stuffed and used as a support for the design and tools in making bobbin lace

²**pillow** \"\ *vb* -ED/-ING/-S *vt* **1** : to rest or lay on or as if on a pillow ⟨his head ~*ed* on a sack —Kenneth Roberts⟩ **2** : to serve as a pillow for ⟨her arm gently ~*ed* the sleeping child⟩ **3** : to support by means of a pillow or something resembling a pillow : CUSHION ⟨~*ed* his back comfortably in the big chair⟩ **4** : to furnish or equip with pillows ⟨fine lounging chairs of bamboo and reed handsomely ~*ed* in bright blocked linen —Adria Langley⟩ ~ *vi* : to lay or rest one's head on or as if on a pillow

**pillowback** \'==,=\ *adj* [¹*pillow* + *back*] *of a chair* : having an oval-turned section in the center of the top rail suggesting a pillow in shape

**pil·low-beer** \'pilō,bi(ə)r\ *n* [ME *pilwe beer,* fr. *pilwe* pillow + *beer, bere* covering; akin to MD *-buur* covering] *chiefly dial* : PILLOWCASE

**pillow block** *n* : a block or standard to support a journal (as of a shaft) : BEARING

**pillowcase** \'==,=\ *n* : a removable covering for a pillow usu. of white linen or cotton cloth

**pillow fight** *n* **1** : a sham battle with pillows esp. among children ready for bed **2** : a sham fight or trivial argument

**pillow lace** *n* : BOBBIN LACE

**pillow lava** *n* : lava commonly basaltic in type that is congealed in rounded masses suggestive of pillows and is believed by most geologists to be indicative of submarine eruption or flow

**pillow sham** *n* : a decorative covering enclosing or laid over a pillow on a bed or couch

**pillow slip** *n* : PILLOWCASE

**pillow structure** *n* : PILLOW LAVA

**pillowwork** \'==,=\ *n* : decorative treatment of surfaces using projections resembling pillows : PULVINATION

**pil·lowy** \'piləwē\ *adj* : of, relating to, or resembling a pillow

**pill pipe** *n* [⁴*pill*] : a thin rod that is formed by rolling the mixture from a pill masser on a pill tile and is then cut into pieces of the proper size for pills

**pillroller** \'==,==\ *n* : ²MEDIC ⟨~ had missed on the diagnosis —N.C.McDonald⟩

**pills** *pl of* PILL, *pres 3d sing of* PILL

**pill tile** *n* : a flat slab of porcelain or glass on which the mixture from a pill masser is placed and rolled

**pillular** *var of* PILULAR

**pillule** *var of* PILULE

**pillwillet** *var of* PILWILLET

**pill wood louse** *n* [⁴*pill*] : WOOD LOUSE 1

**pillworm** \'=,=\ *n* [⁴*pill* + *worm*] : a millepede that curls up to protect itself

**pillwort** \'=,=\ *n* [⁴*pill* + *wort;* fr. its small globose sporocarps] : a water fern of the genus *Pilularia; esp* : a widely but locally distributed European plant (*P. globulifera*) occurring chiefly about the margins of bodies of water or in wet acid soil

**pilm** \'pilm\ *n* -S [origin unknown] *dial Eng* : DUST

**pilo-** — see PIL-

**pi·lob·o·lus** \pī'läbələs\ *n, cap* [NL, fr. Gk *pilos* felt cap, ball + *-bolos* throwing (fr. *ballein* to throw) — more at PILE (hair), DEVIL] : a genus of saprophytic fungi (order Mucorales) notable for the forcible ejection of the entire ripe sporangium

**pi·lo·car·pi·dine** \,pīlə'kärpə,dēn, ,pil-, -,dən\ *n* -S [ISV *pilocarp-* (fr. NL *Pilocarpus*) + *-idine*] : a liquid alkaloid $C_{10}H_{14}N_2O_2$ closely related to pilocarpine and occurring with it in the leaves of jaborandi (*Pilocarpus jaborandi*)

**pi·lo·car·pine** \-r,pēn, -rpən\ *n* -S [ISV *pilocarp-* + *-ine*] : an alkaloid $C_{11}H_{16}N_2O_2$ derived from imidazole and butyrolactone that is obtained from jaborandi as an oily syrup crystallizing when quite pure, that is a strong sialagogue and diaphoretic, and that is used chiefly in the form of its hydrochloride or nitrate as a miotic in glaucoma or in counteracting mydriasis caused by atropine

**pi·lo·car·pus** \,pīlə'kärpəs, ,pil-\ *n* [NL, fr. ²*pil-* + *-carpus*] **1** *cap* : a small genus of tropical American shrubs (family Rutaceae) having small greenish flowers in long racemes with versatile anthers and one-seeded loculi in the ovary **2** -ES : JABORANDI 1

**pi·lo·cystic** \,pīlō+\ *adj* [¹*pil-* + *cystic*] *of a dermoid tumor* : encysted and containing hair

**pi·lo·erection** \"+\ *n* [¹*pil-* + *erection*] : involuntary erection or bristling of hairs due to a sympathetic reflex usu. triggered by cold, shock, or fright or due to a sympathomimetic agent

**pi·lo·motion** \"+\ *n* [¹*pil-* + *motion*] : movement of cutaneous hair

**pi·lo·motor** \"+\ *adj* [ISV ¹*pil-* + *motor*] : moving or tending to cause movement of the hairs of the skin ⟨~ nerves⟩

**pilomotor muscle** *n* : ERECTOR PILI

**pilomotor nerve** *n* : an autonomic nerve supplying an erector pili

**pi·lon** \pē'lōn\ *n* -S [MexSp *pilón,* fr. Sp, mortar, sugar loaf, fr. L *pila* mortar; akin to L *pilum* pestle — more at PESTLE] *Southwest* : a bonus given with a large purchase, a trade, or a cash payment : LAGNIAPPE

**pi·lon·ci·llo** \,pēlōn'sē(,)(y)ō\ *n* -S [MexSp, dim. of Sp *pilón* — more at PILON] : unrefined sugar esp. when molded into cones or sticks

**pi·lo·ni·dal** \,pīlə'nīdᵊl\ *adj* [¹*pil-* + L *nidus* nest + E *-al* — more at NEST] **1** : containing hair nested in a cyst — used of congenitally anomalous cysts in the sacrococcygeal area that often become infected and discharge through a channel near the anus **2** : of, relating to, involving, or for use on pilonidal cysts, tracts, or sinuses

**pi·lo·ri** *or* **pilori rat** \pə'lōrē\ *n* -S [perh. of Arawakan or Cariban origin] : a Cuban hutia (*Capromys pilorides*)

**pi·lo·sa** \pə'lōsə\ *n pl, cap* [NL, fr. L, neut. pl. of *pilosus* hairy] : a division of edentate mammals comprising the sloths, anteaters, and extinct related forms

**pi·lose** \'pī,lōs\ *adj* [L *pilosus,* fr. *pilus* hair + *-osus* -ose — more at PILE] : covered with hair esp. of soft texture : HAIRY

**pi·lo·sebaceous** \,pīlō+\ *adj* [¹*pil-* + *sebaceous*] : of or relating to hair and the sebaceous glands

**pi·lo·sine** \'pīlə,sēn, -,sən\ *n* -S [ISV *pil-* (fr. *pilocarpine*) + *-ose* + *-ine*] : a crystalline alkaloid $C_{16}H_{18}N_2O_3$ occurring in the leaves of jaborandi (*Pilocarpus microphyllus*)

**pi·lo·sis** \pī'lōsəs\ *n* -ES [NL, fr. ¹*pil-* + *-osis*] : the condition of abnormal or excessive growth of hair

**pi·lo·sism** \'pīlō,sizəm\ *n* -S [L *pilosus* + ISV *-ism*] : abnormal hairiness

**pi·los·i·ty** \pī'läsəd·ē\ *n* -ES [ML *pilositat-, pilositas,* fr. L *pilosus* hairy + *-itat-, -itas* -ity — more at PILOSE] : the state of being pilose : HAIRINESS

¹**pi·lot** \'pīlət, *usu* -əd·+V\ *n* -S *often attrib* [MF *pilote,* fr. It *pilota,* alter. of *pedota,* fr. (assumed) MGk *pēdōtēs,* fr. Gk *pēda* steering oars, rudder, pl. of *pēdon* oar; akin to Gk *pod-, pous* foot — more at FOOT] **1 a** : one employed to steer a ship : HELMSMAN **b** : a person who is duly qualified and usu. licensed to conduct a ship into and out of a port or in special waters, often for fixed fees and who while in charge has the whole conduct of her navigation **c** : a book giving detailed navigational information of a body of water and the adjacent coastline **2** : a guide who leads along a difficult or unknown course : one who takes charge during dangerous or unsettled times : a leader who inspires **3** : MENOMINEE WHITEFISH **4 a** : an inclined triangular frame on the front of a railroad locomotive for removing obstacles from the track — called also *cowcatcher* **b** : a locomotive engineer assigned to assist in operating a train over track with which the regular engineer is unfamiliar **5** : one who flies or is qualified to fly an airplane — see COMMERCIAL PILOT, TRANSPORT PILOT **6 a** : a cylindrical projection at the end of a tool (as a counterbore, countersink, boring rod) to guide it **b** : a bar or simple element acting as a guide or relay for another mechanical element **c** : an auxiliary mechanism that actuates, energizes, governs, or regulates another mechanism ⟨a *pilot*-operated sliding disk valve⟩ **7** : the relatively small heading or excavation first made in the driving of a larger tunnel **8** : the manager of a baseball team

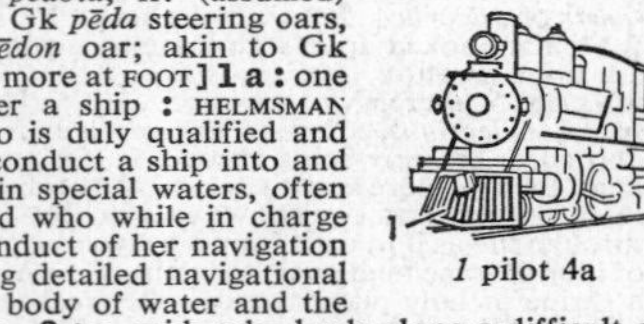
*1* pilot 4a

²**pilot** \"\ *vt* -ED/-ING/-S **1 a** : to guide along strange paths or through dangerous places ⟨a mountain man ~*ed* them through the Blackfoot country —R.H.Billington⟩ **b** : CONDUCT, ESCORT ⟨were ~*ed* . . . up to the capitol to pay our respects to the governor —A.W.Long⟩ ⟨~*s* the customers to their tables —Joseph Wechsberg⟩ **2** : to steer or set the course of (a ship) : serve as a pilot on, for, or over ⟨~*ing* ships through the canal⟩ ⟨all were charged with ~*ing* raiding parties from a British fleet —*Amer. Guide Series: Md.*⟩ **3** : to direct or lead in a straight course esp. under difficult circumstances ⟨~*ed* through the House the government's elaborate education bill —*Newsweek*⟩ **4 a** : to fly or act as pilot of (an airplane) ⟨~*ed* the huge transport plane to the west coast⟩ **b** : to drive or act as operator of (as a motor vehicle) ⟨through little lanes between huts in the village, the jeep was ~*ed* —M.R.Masani⟩ ⟨fresh as a daisy after ~*ing* a big tractor-trailer —*Motor Transportation*⟩ **5** : to lead as though showing the way to : COACH, MANAGE ⟨each dog is . . . ~*ed* by his handler and observed by the judges —W.F.Brown b.1903⟩ ⟨~*ed* the baseball team to a league pennant⟩ **syn** see GUIDE

³**pilot** \"\ *adj* : serving on a small scale as a guiding or tracing device, an activating or auxiliary unit of a full-scale contrivance, or as a trial unit in experimenting or in testing apparatus, or in checking technique or cost preparatory to full-scale activity ⟨~ studies are being made to determine the most effective ways in which local health departments can function —Thomas Parran⟩ ⟨the ~ plant provides the surest and quickest way of transmuting laboratory investigations . . . into commercial application —*Mellon Institute Report*⟩

**pi·lot·age** \'pīləd·ij\ *n* -S [F, fr. *piloter* to pilot (fr. MF *pilote* pilot) + *-age*] **1 a** : the act or business of piloting : employment of a pilot : guidance by a pilot **b** (1) : the technical knowledge or skill of a pilot : the charting or steering of a course (as for a ship) (2) : navigation of a ship or airplane by observation of landmarks directly or by means of radar — compare CONTACT FLYING **2** : the compensation made or allowed to a pilot

**pi·lo·tax·it·ic** \,pīlō,tak'sid·ik\ *adj* [ISV ²*pil-* + *taxis* + *-itic*] : having the form of or characterized by a rock structure composed of a glass-free felted mesh of slender plagioclase strips between which are enclosed the other constituent minerals in minute grains and commonly observed in finely crystallized andesites and basalts

**pilot balloon** *n* : a small unmanned balloon sent up to show the direction and speed of the wind

**pilot bird** *n* **1** : BLACK-BELLIED PLOVER **2** : an Australian bird (*Pycnoptilus floccosus*) of uncertain affinity but similar to the babbling thrushes

**pilot biscuit** *also* **pilot cracker** *n* : hardtack baked in biscuit form and served with seafood chowders and stews

**pilot black snake** *n* : a large No. American colubrid snake (*Elaphe obsoleta*) that is lustrous black with some scales edged in white — called also *mountain black snake*

**pilot boat** *n* : a strong fast seaworthy boat in which pilots meet incoming ships usu. at the mouth of rivers and harbors

**pilot bread** *n* : HARDTACK

**pilot burner** *n* : a small burner kept lighted to rekindle the principal burner (as in a flash boiler)

**pilot cell** *n* : a selected cell whose temperature, voltage, and specific gravity of electrolyte are assumed to indicate the state of charge of the entire storage battery of which the cell forms a part

**pilot chart** *n* : a chart for a navigator showing direction and strength of prevailing winds, temperature, storm paths, positions of rocks, shoals, and other information helpful to navigators

**pilot chute** *n* : a miniature parachute that is several feet in diameter and is attached to the peak of a parachute and whose function is to draw the parachute out of its pack and extend it in position for opening — see PARACHUTE illustration

**pilot cloth** *n* : a heavy twilled woolen overcoating with a thick nap used esp. for seamen's blue uniforms

**pilot coat** *n* : PEA JACKET

**pilot engine** *n* : a locomotive going in advance of a train to make sure that the way is clear

**pilot film** *n* : a sample film of a proposed television series made to induce sponsorship

**pilot fish** *n* **1** : a pelagic carangid fish (*Naucrates ductor*) that often swims in company with a shark **2** : BANDED RUDDERFISH **3** : MENOMINEE WHITEFISH

**pilot flag** *n* : a flag hoisted at the fore by a ship desiring a pilot (as the union jack in the U.S., the British union jack with a white border in Great Britain)

**pilot flame** *n* : PILOT BURNER

**pilothouse** \'==,=\ *n* : a deckhouse on a ship located forward near the bridge containing the steering wheel, compass, charts and navigating equipment, and communication systems to the engine room and other parts of the ship — called also *wheelhouse*

**piloting** *n* -S [fr. gerund of ²*pilot*] : the part of navigation concerned with directing the movement or determining the position of a ship or airplane by reference to landmarks, aids to navigation, or soundings

**pi·lot·ism** \'pīlə,tizəm\ *n* -S [¹*pilot* + *-ism*] : the practice or skill of piloting

**pilot jack** *n* : PILOT FLAG

**pilot ladder** *n* : JACK LADDER

**pi·lot·less** \'pīlətləs\ *adj* : having no pilot ⟨~ aircraft⟩

**pilot light** *n* **1** *also* **pilot lamp** : an electric light usu. used to indicate the position of a switch or circuit breaker, that a motor is in operation, or that the power is on **2** : a small permanent flame used to ignite gas at a burner

**pilot method** *n* : the method of excavating a tunnel by driving a small tunnel ahead and then enlarging its dimensions

**pilot motor** *n* : a small motor used in the automatic control of an electric circuit

**pilot nut** *n* : a tapered steel nut temporarily screwed on a bridge pin to serve as guide while the pin is being driven through the pinholes of the members it is to join

**pilot officer** *n* : an air force officer (as in the British Royal Air Force) who is equivalent in rank to a second lieutenant in the army

**pilot pin** *n* : a pin to locate a center or bearing

**pilot plow** *n* : a snowplow on a locomotive's pilot

**pi·lot·ry** \'pīlətrē\ *n* -ES [¹*pilot* + *-ry*] : PILOTISM

**pilots** *pl of* PILOT, *pres 3d sing of* PILOT

**pi·lot·ship** \-t,ship\ *n* [¹*pilot* + *-ship*] *archaic* : the function or office of a pilot

**pilot's luff** *n* : HALF BOARD

**pilot snake** *n* **1** : PILOT BLACK SNAKE **2** : BULL SNAKE **3** : COPPERHEAD 1a

**pilot train** *n* : a train that precedes another to ensure that the roadway is safe and free of obstructions

**pilot truck** *n* : LEADING TRUCK

**pilot valve** *n* : a relay valve that controls the operation of another valve

**pilotweed** \'==,=\ *n* [¹*pilot* + *weed*] : COMPASS PLANT a

**pilot whale** *n* [so called fr. the fact that the largest male acts as pilot or leader for the rest of the school] : BLACKFISH 2

**pilot wheel** *n* [so called fr. its resemblance to the wheel used in steering ships] : a wheel usu. with handles projecting from the rim for traversing the saddle of a machine tool or for operating any of the feeds by hand

**pi·lous** \'pīləs\ *adj* [L *pilosus* — more at PILOSE] : PILOSE

**pil·pul** \'pil,pül\ *n* -S [Aram & Heb *pilpūl,* fr. *pilpēl* to search, argue] : critical analysis and hairsplitting : casuistic argumentation esp. among Jewish scholars on talmudic subjects : rabbinical dialectic

**pil·pul·ist** \-ləst\ *n* -S : one who practices talmudic dialectic : a subtle reasoner — **pil·pul·is·tic** \'pil,pü'listik\ *adj*

**pil·sen** \'pilzən, -lsən\ *or* **pl·zen** \'pəl,zen, -nʸ, (,)=='=\ *adj, usu cap* [fr. *Pilsen, Plzeň,* city of Czechoslovakia] : of or from the city of Pilsen, Czechoslovakia : of the kind or style prevalent in Pilsen

**pil·sner** *also* **pil·sen·er** \'pilz(ə)nə(r), -ls(ə)-\ *n* -S *often cap* [G *pilsner,* fr. *Pilsner* of Pilsen, fr. *Pilsen,* city of Czechoslovakia] **1 a** : a light Bohemian beer with a strong hop flavor **b** : a beer of a similar type **2** *or* **pilsner glass** : a tall slender footed glass usu. used for beer

**pilt·down man** \'pilt,daün-\ *n, usu cap P* [fr. *Piltdown,* East Sussex, England] : a supposedly very early primitive modern man based on skull fragments uncovered in a gravel pit at Piltdown and used in combination with comparatively recent skeletal remains of various animals (as ape, beaver, hippopotamus, elephant) in the development of an elaborate fraud

**pil·u·lar** *or* **pil·lu·lar** \'pilyələ(r)\ *adj* [*pilule* + *-ar*] : of, relating to, or characteristic of a pill ⟨~ mass⟩

**pil·u·la·ria** \,pilyə'la(a)rēə\ *n, cap* [NL, fr. L *pilula* little ball + NL *-aria*] : a widely distributed genus of small aquatic pteridophytic plants (family Marsileaceae) having filiform fronds and globose sporocarps — see PILLWORT

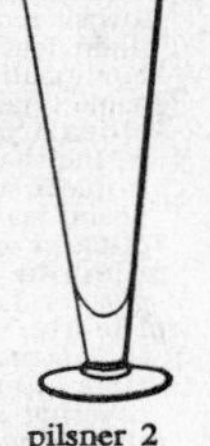
pilsner 2

**pil·ule** *or* **pil·lule** \'pil,yül\ *n* -S [MF, fr. L *pilula* little ball, pill, dim. of *pila* ball — more at PILE (hair)] : a little pill

**pi·lum** \'pīləm\ *n, pl* **pi·la** \-lə\ [L, pestle, heavy javelin] **1** : the heavy javelin of a Roman foot soldier **2** : PESTLE

**pi·lus** \'pīləs\ *n, pl* **pi·li** \-ī,lī\ [NL, fr. L — more at PILE] : a hair or a structure resembling a hair

**pil·wil·let** *or* **pill·wil·let** \pil'wilət\ *n* [imit.] **1** : WILLET **2** : an American oyster catcher (*Haematopus ostralegus palliatus*)

**¹pily** \'pīlē\ *adj* -ER/-EST [³*pile* + -*y*] : having a pile : resembling pile

**²pily** \"\ *adj* [¹*pile* + -*y*] *heraldry* : divided into piles

**¹pi·ma** \'pēmə\ *n, pl* **pima** *or* **pimas** *usu cap* **1 a** : a people of southern Arizona and northern Mexico **b** : a member of such people **2** : the Uto-Aztecan language of the Pima people

**²pima** \" *sometimes* 'pimə\ *or* **pima cotton** *n* -S *sometimes cap P* [*Pima* county, southern Arizona] **1** : a cotton with fiber of exceptional strength and firmness developed in the southwestern U.S. by selection and breeding of Egyptian cottons **2** : a fine strong cloth made from pima

**pi·man** \'pēmən\ *adj, usu cap* [¹*pima* + -*an*] **1** : constituting or relating to a language family of the Uto-Aztecan phylum containing the Pima, Tepehuan, and Papago languages **2** : of or relating to the Pima

**pim·an·threne** \pə'man,thrēn\ *n* -S [*pimaric* (in *pimaric acid*) + -*anthrene*] : a crystalline aromatic tricyclic hydrocarbon $(CH_3)_2C_{14}H_8$ obtained by dehydrogenation of various bicyclic or tricyclic diterpenes and by synthesis; 1,7-dimethylphenanthrene

**pi·mar·ic acid** \pə'mar|ik, (ˈ)pī¦m|\ *n* [*pimaric* ISV *pimar-* (fr. NL *Pinus maritima* — syn. of *Pinus pinaster*, species name of the cluster pine —, fr. *Pinus* + *maritima*, fr. L, fem. of *maritimus* maritime) + -*ic*] : either of two isomeric crystalline acids occurring esp. in oleoresins from pine trees and formerly regarded as stereoisomeric: **a** : DEXTROPIMARIC ACID **b** : LEVOPIMARIC ACID

**pim·bi·na** \pim'bēnə, 'pimbənə\ *n* -S [CanF — more at PEMBINA] : any of several plants of the genus *Viburnum; esp* : CRANBERRY BUSH 2

**pim·e·late** \'pimə,lāt, -lət\ *n* -S [ISV *pimelic* (in *pimelic acid*) + -*ate*] : a salt or ester of pimelic acid

**pi·me·lea** \pə'mēlyə *also* -lēə\ *n* [NL, fr. Gk *pimelē* lard — more at FAT] **1** *cap* : a genus of shrubs (family Thymelaeaceae) of Australia and New Zealand having small opposite leaves and clustered white, yellow, or pink flowers with two stamens succeeded by berrylike fruits — see RICE FLOWER **2** -S : any plant of the genus *Pimelea*

**pi·mel·ic acid** \pə'melik, pī-, -mēl-, -lēk-\ *n* [*pimelic* ISV *pimel-* (fr. Gk *pimelē* lard) + -*ic*] : a crystalline dicarboxylic acid $HOOC(CH_2)_5COOH$ obtained usu. by oxidation of unsaturated fats, castor oil, or cycloheptanone

**pim·e·lo·met·o·pon** \,piməlō'medə,pän\ *n, cap* [NL, fr. *pimelo-* (fr. Gk *pimelē* lard) + Gk *metōpon* forehead — more at METOPION] : a genus of Pacific wrasses closely related to *Bodianus* but distinguished by smaller scales that include the sheepshead of the California coast

**pi·ment** *also* **py·ment** \pə'ment\ *n* -S [ME, fr. OF *piment* piment, aromatic spice, fr. LL *pigmentum* plant juice] : wine flavored with spice and honey

**pi·men·ta** \pə'mentə\ *n, cap* [NL, fr. Pg, pepper, fr. LL *pigmenta*, pl. of *pigmentum* plant juice] : a genus of tropical American aromatic trees (family Myrtaceae) having large coriaceous pinnately veined leaves, small cymose flowers, and 1 to 6 pendulous ovules — see ALLSPICE, BAYBERRY

**pi·men·to** \pə'ment·(,)ō, -en·(,)tō\ *n, pl* **pimentos** *or* **pimento** [Sp *pimienta* pepper, allspice, fr. LL *pigmenta*, pl. of *pigmentum* plant juice, fr. L, pigment — more at PIGMENT] **1 a** *obs* : a small hot pepper (as a cayenne or Guinea pepper) **b** : PIMIENTO 1 **2 a** : ALLSPICE **b** *or* **pimento tree** : ALLSPICE TREE **c** : the fine-grained tough heavy pinkish wood of the allspice tree that is used chiefly for small specialty articles (as canes and umbrella handles) **3** : a vivid red that is yellower, lighter, and slightly stronger than apple red, yellower, lighter, and stronger than carmine, yellower and darker than Castilian red, yellower and lighter than madder crimson, and yellower, stronger, and slightly lighter than scarlet

**pimento cheese** *also* **pimiento cheese** *n* : a Neufchâtel, club, cream, or occas. cheddar cheese to which ground pimientos have been added

**pimento grass** *n* [so called fr. its often being found under allspice trees] : SAINT AUGUSTINE GRASS

**pi·men·ton** \,pē,men·'tōn\ *n* -S [Sp *pimentón*, aug. of *pimiento*] : SPANISH PAPRIKA 2

**pimento oil** *or* **pimenta oil** *n* : a colorless to yellow or reddish pungent essential oil obtained from allspice and used chiefly in flavoring — called also *allspice oil*

**pi-meson** \'ₓ₌,₌\ *n* [¹*pi* + *meson*] : a short-lived meson that is primarily responsible for the nuclear force and that exists in three charge states of which the positive and negative have mass 273.2 times the electron mass and the neutral has mass 264.2 times the electron mass

**pi·mien·to** \pə'ment·(,)ō, -en·(,)tō, ,pimē'e-, pəm'ye-\ *n* -S [Sp, fr. *pimienta*] **1** : any of various bluntly conical thick-fleshed sweet peppers of European origin with a distinctive mild sweet flavor that are much used as a garnish, as a stuffing for olives, and as a source of paprika **2** : a plant that bears pimientos **3** : PIMENTO 2 — not used technically

**pim·li·co** \'pimlə,kō, -lē,-\ *also* **pim·pli·coe** \'pimpl-\ *n* -S [imit.] **1** : FRIARBIRD 1 **2** : AUDUBON'S SHEARWATER

**¹pimp** \'pimp\ *n* -S [origin unknown] **1 a** : one who panders or procures; *esp* : a man who solicits for a prostitute or a house of prostitution and receives compensation therefor from the prostitute or the patron **b** : a man who cohabits with a prostitute, lives off her earnings, and often solicits for her — called also *cadet* **2 a** : a person who lends himself to some corrupting or corrupt activity : SCOUNDREL **b** *Austral* : SNEAK, INFORMER **3** *dial Eng* : a small bundle of kindling wood : FAGOT

**²pimp** \"\ *vi* -ED/-ING/-S **1** : to engage in the business or practices of a pimp **2** *Austral* : to act as an informer

**¹pim·per·nel** \'pimpə(r),nel, -nəl\ *n* -S [ME *pympernele*, fr. MF *pimprenelle*, *pimpinelle*, fr. LL *pimpinella*, a medicinal plant, perh. irreg. fr. L *piper* pepper — more at PEPPER] **1** : SALAD BURNET **2** : an herb of the genus *Anagallis; esp* : SCARLET PIMPERNEL

**²pimpernel** \"\ *n* -S *usu cap* [fr. *The Scarlet Pimpernel*, rescuer of aristocrats from the French revolutionists in the novel *The Scarlet Pimpernel* (1905) by Baroness Emmuska Orczy †1947 Eng. novelist] : a gallant dashing resourceful man given to remarkable feats of bravery and derring-do in liberating victims of tyranny and injustice ⟨lined up solidly with the *Pimpernels* and with the persecuted —Hal Lehrman⟩

**pimpernel root** *n* : the dried rhizome and roots of the burnet saxifrage formerly used as a diaphoretic and diuretic

**pimp·ery** \'pimp(ə)rē, -ri\ *n* -ES : the occupation of a pimp

**pim·pi·nel·la** \,pimpə'nelə\ *n, cap* [NL, fr. LL, a medicinal plant] : a genus of herbs (family Umbelliferae) having narrow-ribbed fruit and no calyx teeth — see BURNET SAXIFRAGE, ANISE

**pimp·ing** \'pimpiŋ, -pēŋ\ *adj* [origin unknown] **1** : PETTY, PALTRY, INSIGNIFICANT **2** *chiefly dial* : PUNY, WEAK, SICKLY

**pim·pla** \'pimplə\ *n, cap* [NL, perh. fr. L *Pimplea*, fountain in Macedonia, fr. Gk *Pimpleia*] : a common and widespread genus of ichneumon flies

**¹pim·ple** \'pimpəl\ *n* -S [ME *pinple*] **1** : a small prominent inflamed elevation of the skin : PAPULE; *esp* : PUSTULE **2 a** : a swelling or protuberance like a pimple ⟨reproduces the ~s on an orange —Olive Bell⟩ **b** : a slight elevation of the ground ⟨a nameless ~ in the middle of nowhere —Fred Majdalany⟩

**²pimple** \"\ *vt* **pimpled**; **pimpled**; **pim·pling** \-p(ə)liŋ\ **pimples** : to spot or cover with or as if with pimples ⟨surfaces *pimpled* with rivet heads —G.W.Gray b. 1886⟩

**pim·pled** \-pəld\ *adj* : having or marked by pimples

**pimple metal** *n* [so called fr. the appearance of its surface] : matte containing 77–79 percent copper

**pim·pli·ness** \'pimp(ə)lēnəs, -lin-\ *n* -ES : the condition of being pimply

**pim·ply** \-p(ə)lē, -li\ *adj* -ER/-EST : covered with pimples : PIMPLED ⟨a ~ face⟩

**pimply gut** *n* : NODULAR DISEASE

**pimply gut worm** *n* : NODULAR WORM

**¹pin** \'pin\ *n* -S [ME, pin, peg, fr. OE *pinn*; akin to MD *pin*, pinne pin, peg, OHG *pfinn* peg, and perh. to MIr *benn* peak, horn] **1 a** : a usu. cylindrical piece of wood, metal, or other material used esp. for fastening separate articles together or as a support by which one article may be suspended from another : PEG, BOLT **b** *obs* : a peg or similar object in the center of a target; *also* : the center itself **c** (1) : one of the wooden pieces constituting the target in bowling, skittles, and similar games (2) : the peg at which a quoit is pitched (3) : the staff of the flag marking a hole on a golf course (4) : one of the small upright posts on a board or billiard table used in playing bagatelle, pinball, and related games **d** : a peg for regulating the tension of the strings of a musical instrument (as a piano or harp) : WREST PIN **e** : one of a row of pegs in the side of an ancient drinking cup to mark how much each man should drink **f** (1) : DRILL PIN (2) : the part of a key stem esp. if solid that enters a lock (3) : the part of a cylinder lock that prevents turning unless the proper key is inserted — see SPOOL PIN **g** *chiefly Scot* : the latch or handle of a door ⟨gently tirled the ~ —*Ballad Book*⟩ **h** (1) : THOLEPIN (2) : BELAYING PIN **i** : the tenon of a dovetail joint **j** : a triangular rod of refractory clay that is thrust into the wall of a sagger to support glazed flatware **k** (1) : a small axle, gudgeon, or spindle on which to journal (2) : a slender post or peg acting as a stop for motion of a pointer or lever (3) : a slender post or peg that is used to locate two parts in proper relative position **l** (1) : a long slender piece of metal that is used to fasten together the ends of broken bone (2) : a metal peg that is used to fasten the artificial crown of a tooth to a prepared root **m** : the part of the bedding mortar that is forced into the holes extending through the brick **2 a** (1) : a small pointed and headed piece of brass or other wire commonly tinned and used for fastening clothes, attaching papers, and similar purposes (2) : something very small : a thing of small value : TRIFLE ⟨doesn't care a ~ for her⟩ **b** (1) : a decorative fastener in the form of a straight pointed wire with a plain or ornamented head (as a tiepin or hatpin) or a small ornamental plaque often jeweled with a fastening device on the back (as a breastpin or bar pin) (2) : an ornament (as a brooch) having a pin fastener on the back **c** (1) : BOBBY PIN (2) : HAIRPIN (3) : SAFETY PIN **d** : a needlelike device typically one of a series of perforators whose puncture in a printed sheet serves as a reference point for accurate positioning and correct folding — called also *point* **3** *archaic* : frame of mind : MOOD — usu. used in such phrases as *on a merry pin, in a merry pin* **4 a** *chiefly dial* : POINT, PINNACLE, APEX **b** *chiefly Scot* : the projecting part of the hipbone esp. of a horse **5** : LEG — usu. used in pl. ⟨pretty wobbly on his ~s⟩ **6** : a very small knot in a bow or bow stave **7** : a cask of ½ firkin capacity; *also* : this capacity as a unit of measure **8** : a handled knife with a blade of triangular section used esp. to remove the bloom from freshly tanned leather — called also *striking pin* **9** [²*pin*] : a fall in wrestling **10** : a fabric with designs as small and fine as the point, head, or width of a pin

**²pin** \"\ *vb* **pinned**; **pinned**; **pinning**; **pins** [ME *pinnen*, fr. ¹*pin*] *vt* **1 a** (1) : to fasten, join, or secure with a pin, peg, or bolt ⟨~ joists and girders⟩ ⟨~ a rose to a dress⟩ ⟨~ a fractured hip with steel needles⟩ (2) : to transfix with a pin or other sharp-pointed instrument ⟨an entomologist *pinning* a butterfly —Coleman Rosenberger⟩ **b** : to secure (hair) in place with a pin used for arranging or setting **c** : to fit (a garment) by securing adjustments of width or length with pins — usu. used with *in, out*, or *up* ⟨~ up a hem⟩ **d** : to present (a girl) with a fraternity pin as a pledge of affection ⟨she is *pinned* to the captain of the football team⟩ **2** [ME *pinnen*, perh. alter. of *pinden* to put in a pound — more at PIND] : ENCLOSE, CONFINE, PEN, IMPOUND ⟨held twice their number *pinned* within their works —J.A.Froude⟩ **3 a** *obs* : UNDERPIN **b** : to fill in (as a rubble wall) with small wedges or spalls of stone mortar **c** *obs* : to face esp. with marble **4 a** : to make absolutely dependent or contingent : attach firmly or bindingly — used with *on* or *to* ⟨~ their hope of universal salvation on some cause —M.R.Cohen⟩ ⟨*pinning* its destiny to a weak ally — *New Republic*⟩ **b** : to assign the blame or responsibility for : fix by proof or strong presumption — usu. used with *on* ⟨~ a murder on an innocent woman —*Sydney (Australia) Bull.*⟩ ⟨~s all the woes of the world on grog —John Lardner⟩ **5 a** : to hold or keep esp. as to a line of conduct or debate : keep from evading an issue — usu. used with *down* ⟨~ philosophy down and make it talk sense —Charles Frankel⟩ ⟨~ the author . . . down to a definite statement —Deems Taylor⟩ ⟨impossible to ~ him down to anything —D.G. Gerahty⟩ **b** : to define clearly or unequivocally : FIX, ESTABLISH — usu. used with *down* ⟨cannot ~ down the essence of poetry —C.I.Glicksberg⟩ ⟨the subject is not easy to ~ down —Stuart Chase⟩ **6** : to make (a chess opponent's man) unable to move without exposing the king to check or a valuable piece to capture **7 a** : to hold fast or immobile in a spot or position ⟨*pinned* his arms to his sides⟩ ⟨*pinned* an enemy to his ground by powerful infantry attacks —Tom Wintringham⟩ ⟨*pinned* down by fallen rock⟩ ⟨*pinned* down by heavy enemy shelling⟩ **b** *of a wrestler* : to secure a fall over (an opponent) **c** *of a bird dog* : to detect and show (game) ~ *vi, of a file* : to become clogged so that the adhering filings scratch the work — **pin one's ears back 1** : to administer a sound thrashing or defeat to ⟨announced that he could *pin back the ears* of any animal in the world —James Thurber⟩ **2** : to give a tongue-lashing to ⟨the blouse buyer had *her ears . . . pinned back* —*Women's Wear Daily*⟩

**³pin** \"\ *adj* [¹*pin*] **1** : of or relating to a pin **2** *of leather* : having a grain suggesting pinheads — see PIN SEAL

**pi·na** \'pēnyə, 'pinə\ *or* **pi·ña** \'pēnyə\ *n* -S [Sp *piña* residuary cone of spongy silver left after retorting, pinecone] **1** : a cone of silver amalgam prepared for retorting **2** : the residuary cone of spongy silver left after retorting

**pi·na·be·te** \,pēnə'bād·ē\ *n* -S [AmerSp, fr. Sp, silver fir, fr. Catal *pinavet*, fr. *pin-*, *pi* pine (fr. L *pinus*) + *avet* fir, fr. L *abiet-*, *abies* silver fir] : a Central American fir (*Akies religiosa*) having young shoots that are furrowed and olive green on the lower side during the first year and brown and downy later

**pinac-** *or* **pinaco-** *also* **pinak-** *comb form* [L *pinaco-* picture, fr. Gk *pinak-*, *pinako-* board, tablet, picture, fr. *pinak-*, *pinax*; akin to OHG *witufina* heap of wood, Russ *pen'* stump, stub, and prob. to Skt *pināka* staff] : tablet ⟨*pinacoid*⟩ ⟨*pinacocyte*⟩

**pi·na·ca·te bug** \,pēnə'käd·ē-\ *n* [MexSp *pinacate*, fr. Nahuatl *pinacatl*] : any of several clumsy wingless beetles of the genus *Eleodes* (family Tenebrionidae) found in arid regions of the Pacific states

**pi·na·ce·ae** \pī'nāsē,ē\ *n pl, cap* [NL, fr. *Pinus*, type genus + -*aceae*] : a family of coniferous trees and shrubs (order Coniferales) comprising plants with needle-shaped or scalelike leaves, cones with woody, fleshy, or membranous scales, and fine-grained wood that is often of great economic value and being often divided into four or more smaller families (as Araucariaceae, Taxodiaceae, and Cupressaceae) — compare TAXACEAE — **pi·na·ceous** \(ˈ)₌¦nāshəs\ *adj*

**pin·a·chrome** \'pinə,krōm\ *n* [ISV *pina-* (irreg. fr. Gk *pinak-*, *pinax* board, tablet, picture) + -*chrome*] : an isocyanine dye used in photography sensitizing to the green and orange-red regions of the spectrum

**pi·ña cloth** \'pēnyə-\ *n* [Sp *piña* piña cloth, pineapple, pinecone, fr. L *pinea* pinecone — more at PINEAL] : a lustrous transparent cloth of Philippine origin that is woven of fine silky unspun fibers from the pineapple plant and used esp. for decorative handkerchiefs and trimmings

**pin·a·coc·er·as** \,pinə'käsərəs\ *n, cap* [NL, fr. *pinac-* + -*ceras*] : a genus (the type of the family Pinacoceratidae) of compressed involute ammonites with the most highly complicated suture known

**pin·a·co·cyt·al** \¦pinəkō¦sīd·ᵊl\ *adj* : of or relating to a pinacocyte

**pin·a·co·cyte** \'₌₌₌,sīt\ *n* -S [*pinac-* + -*cyte*] : one of the flat cells covering the external surface and lining the incurrent and excurrent canals of sponges

**pin·a·coid** *also* **pin·a·koid** \'pinə,kȯid\ *n* -S [ISV *pinac-* + -*oid*] **1** : a crystal form consisting of two parallel and opposite faces **2** : a crystal form whose faces are parallel to two crystal axes

**pin·a·coi·dal** *also* **pin·a·koi·dal** \¦₌₌¦kȯid·ᵊl\ *adj* [ISV *pinacoid* + -*al*] : having only a center of symmetry — used of one class in the triclinic system; see CRYSTALLIZATION, SYMMETRY

**pin·a·col** \'pinə,kȯl, -kōl\ *n* -S [ISV *pinac-* + -*ol*; fr. the fact that it unites with water to form tabloid-shaped crystals] **1** : a liquid glycol $(CH_3)_2C(OH)C(OH)(CH_3)_2$ that forms a crystalline hexahydrate $C_6H_{12}(OH)_2.6H_2O$ and that is usu. made from acetone by reduction with amalgamated magnesium followed by hydrolysis of the intermediate magnesium derivative; 2,3-dimethyl-2,3-butanediol **2** : any of a series of tetrasubstituted derivatives of ethylene glycol obtained by reduction of ketones other than acetone — **pinacolic** *adj*

**pi·nac·o·late** \pə'nakə,lāt, ,pinə'kōlət\ *n* -S [*pinacol* + -*ate*] : a metallic derivative of pinacol — compare ALCOHOLATE

**pi·nac·o·lin** \pə'nakələn, ,pinə'kōlən\ *also* **pi·nac·o·line** \-,lēn, -,lən\ *n* -S [ISV *pinacone* + *ol-* (fr. L *oleum* oil) + -*in* — more at OIL] : PINACOLONE

**pi·nac·o·lone** \-,lōn\ *n* -S [*pinacol* + -*one*] **1** : a liquid ketone $(CH_3)_3COCH_3$ of peppermint odor formed from pinacol by treatment with acid to cause loss of water and molecular rearrangement; 3,3-dimethyl-2-butanone **2** : any of a series of ketones $R_3CCOR$ formed like pinacolone from other pinacols

**pin·a·cone** \'pinə,kōn\ *n* -S [ISV *pinac-* + -*one*] : PINACOL

**pin·a·co·the·ca** \,pinəkō'thēkə\ *n* -S [L, fr. Gk *pinakothēkē*, fr. *pinako-* (fr. *pinak-*, *pinax* board, tablet, picture) + *thēkē* case, chest; akin to Gk *tithenai* to put, place — more at PINAC-, DO] : PICTURE GALLERY

**pi·nac·u·lum** \pə'nakyələm\ *n, pl* **pinacu·la** \-lə\ [NL, fr. *pinac-* + -*ulum*] : one of the small chitinized plates on the integument of a caterpillar to which the body setae are attached

**Pin·a·cy·a·nol** \,pinə'sīə,nȯl, -nōl\ *trademark* — used for a carbocyanine dye derived from quinoline and used in photography as a sensitizer for the red portion of the spectrum

**¹pin·a·fore** \'pinə,fō(ə)r, -ō(ə)r, -ōə, -ò(ə)\ *n* -S [²*pin* + *afore*] : a covering garment worn to protect clothes from soil, made variously as an apron with or without a bib : a sleeveless low-necked wraparound garment tied or buttoned at the back

**²pinafore** \"\ *vt* -ED/-ING/-S : to dress in a pinafore

**pinak-** — see PINAC-

**pi·nak·i·o·lite** \pə'nakēə,līt\ *n* -S [G *pinakiolith*, fr. Gk *pinakion* small tablet (dim. of *pinak-*, *pinax* board, tablet) + G -*lith* -lite] : a magnesium and manganese borate $Mg_3Mn_3B_2O_{10}$ occurring in small black tabular crystals

**pinakoid** *var of* PINACOID

**pi·nal** \pē'näl\ *n, pl* **pinal** \" *or* **pina·les** \-ä(,)lās\ *usu cap* **1** : a band of San Carlos Apaches **2** : a member of the Pinal band

**pi·na·les** \pī'nā(,)lēz, pə'-\ *n pl, cap* [NL, fr. *Pinus* + -*ales*] *in some classifications* : an order of gymnospermous trees and shrubs coextensive with the order Coniferales

**pi·nane** \'pī,nān\ *n* -S [ISV *pin-* (fr. L *pinus* pine) + -*ane* — more at PINE] : a liquid saturated bicyclic hydrocarbon $C_{10}H_{18}$ occurring in stereoisomeric forms of which pinene and nopinene are unsaturated derivatives; 1,3,3-trimethyl-2,4-methylene-cyclohexane

**pi·nang** *also* **pe·nang** \pə'naŋ\ *n* -S [Malay *pinang*] **1** : BETEL PALM **2** : the fruit of the betel palm

**pi·nard** \(ˈ)pē¦när\ *n* -S [F, fr. *pineau*, *pinot* any of several vinifera grapes used esp. for wine-making (fr. MF, fr. *pine* pinecone, fr. *pin* pine, fr. L *pinus*) + -*ard* — more at PINE] : a red French table wine sometimes issued to French soldiers

**pinard yellow** *n, often cap P* : a light yellow that is greener and paler than average maize or jasmine and paler than popcorn

**pi·nas·ter** \(ˈ)pī¦nastə(r)\ *n* -S [L, wild pine, fr. *pinus* pine + -*aster*] : CLUSTER PINE

**pi·ña·ta** *or* **pi·na·ta** \pēn'yäd·ə, pin-\ *n* -S [Sp *piñata*, lit., pot, fr. It *pignatta*, fr. *pigna* pinecone, fr. L *pinea* — more at PINEAL] : a decorated pottery jar filled with candies, fruits, toys, or other gifts and usu. suspended from the ceiling that blindfolded children try to break with a stick esp. as a traditional part of Mexican Christmas festivities

**pin·a·type** \'pinə,tīp\ *n* [ISV *pina-* (irreg. fr. Gk *pinak-*, *pinax* board, tablet, picture) + -*type*] : HYDROTYPE

**pin·a·ver·dol** \,pinə'vər,dȯl, -dōl\ *n* -S [ISV *pina-* (irreg. fr. Gk *pinak-*, *pinax* board, tablet, picture) + *verd-* (fr. F *verd*, *vert* green) + -*ol* — more at VERDURE] : an isocyanine dye formerly used in photography as a sensitizer for the green and yellow portions of the spectrum

**pinball** \'₌,₌\ *n* **1** : a ball-shaped pincushion **2** : the globular flower head of the buttonbush **3** : any of various forms of bagatelle in which pins or upright posts are set in the board or table; *esp* : any of various games that are played on pinball machines

**pinball machine** *or* **pinball game** *n* : an amusement device that consists of a glass-topped cabinet in which a ball propelled by a plunger rolls down a slanting surface among an arrangement of pins and targets with each contact between ball and target scoring a number of points indicated by a system of electric lights

**pinbefore** \'₌₌,₌\ *n* -S [²*pin* + *before*, adv.] *dial Eng* : PINAFORE

**pin birch** *n* : POPLAR BIRCH

**pin block** *n* : a wooden block or plank in a piano into which the wrest pins are driven — called also *wrest plank*

**pinboard** \'₌,₌\ *n* : a board set with numerous pegs on which yarn bobbins or spools may be placed for transportation and use

**pinbone** \'₌,₌\ *n* : the hipbone esp. of a quadruped

**pinbone steak** *n* : a small sirloin steak that contains the pinbone — see BEEF illustration

**pin borer** *n* : any of various small beetles that bore minute holes into trees; *esp* : an ambrosia beetle (*Monarthrum mali*) that attacks apple trees

**pinboy** \'₌,₌\ *n* : PINSETTER

**pin bush** *n* [¹*pin* + *bush* (bushing)] : a tool for reaming or polishing small pinholes

**pinbush** \'₌,₌\ *n* [¹*pin* + *bush* (shrub)] : an Australian needlebush (*Hakea leucoptera*)

**pin buttock** *n, obs* : a thin sharp buttock

**pince-nez** \(ˈ)pan(t)¦snā, (ˈ)paⁿ¦snā, (ˈ)pin(t)¦snā *sometimes* ÷(ˈ)pin(t)¦snez\ *n, pl* **pince-nez** \-ā(z), -ezəz\ [F, fr. *pincer* to pinch (fr. OF *pincier*) + *nez* nose, fr. L *nasus* — more at PINCH, NOSE] : eyeglasses clipped to the nose by a spring

**pince-nezed** \-ād, -ezd\ *adj* : wearing pince-nez

**¹pin·cer** \'pinchə(r), -n(t)sə-; -n(t)sə- *is chiefly Brit in senses 1&2*\ *n* -S *often attrib* [ME *pynsour*, *pynceour*, prob. fr. (assumed) MF *pinceour*, fr. MF *pincier* to pinch + -*our* -or (fr. OF -*eor*, -*eur*)] **1 pincers** *pl but sometimes sing in constr* : an instrument having two short handles and two grasping jaws working on a pivot and used for gripping things — often used in the phrase *pair of pincers* **2 a pincers** *pl but sometimes sing in constr* : a grasping apparatus (as on the anterior legs of the lobster) resembling a pair of pincers : CHELA **b** : one of the central incisors of a horse or other equine **3** : one part of a double envelopment in which two forces are driven one on each side of an enemy position so as to be able by converging like the jaws of pincers to isolate and crush it ⟨caught in a ~ movement, they do not know where to turn —*Survey Graphic*⟩

pincers 1

**²pincer** \"\ *vt* -ED/-ING/-S : to pinch, nip, or torture with or as if with pincers

**pincerlike** \'₌₌,₌\ *adj* : like a pincer or a pair of pincers in appearance or action ⟨executing a ~ maneuver in an effort to wipe out the insurgents —*N.Y. Times*⟩ ⟨the ~ claw of the lobster⟩

**pin·cette** \(ˈ)pan¦set, (ˈ)paⁿ¦-\ *n* -S [MF, fr. *pincier* to pinch + -*ette*] : a small pair of pincers, tweezers, or forceps used in surgery

**¹pinch** \'pinch\ *vb* -ED/-ING/-ES [ME *pinchen*, fr. (assumed) ONF *pinchier*; akin to OF *pincier* to pinch, Sp *pinchar* to prick] *vt* **1 a** : to press hard between the ends of the finger and thumb, between teeth or claws, or between the jaws of an instrument : SQUEEZE ⟨~ed and patted my cheek —W.F. De Morgan⟩ **b** (1) : to bring into a specified state or position by pinching ⟨mountains come gradually together, and the coastal lowland is ~ed out —P.E.James⟩ (2) : to nip off or prune the tip of (a young shoot or bud) usu. to induce branching or to bring into flower at a definite time the shoots which develop after the pinching — usu. used with *out, off*, or *back* **c** : to squeeze or compress painfully ⟨complained the shoe

~*ed* his toes⟩ **d :** to cause physical or mental pain to **:** HURT, NIP ⟨how that knowledge would have ~*ed* their pride —R.P.Warren⟩ ⟨the air was so cold that it ~*ed* . . . nostrils —Marcia Davenport⟩ ⟨the tobacco hunger ~*ed* me sore —William Baucke⟩ **e** (1) **:** to cause to appear thin, shrunken, drawn, or haggard (as with pain, hunger, or strain) ⟨cruelty ~*ed* his face about the mouth —Elizabeth M. Roberts⟩ ⟨face . . . was ~*ed* with disquiet —Marcia Davenport⟩ (2) **:** to cause to shrivel or wither up ⟨a heavy frost had ~*ed* the flowers⟩ **2 a :** to subject to strict rationing or economy or severe shortage **:** STRAITEN, STINT ⟨were ready to ~ themselves for years —Samuel Butler †1902⟩ ⟨so ~*ed* for money that he often had only tea for dinner —W.A.Swanberg⟩ ⟨would be ~*ed* for supplies —*N.Y. Times*⟩ **b :** to cause distress or embarrassment to **:** VEX, HARASS; *esp* **:** to cause economic distress to ⟨the debtor who found himself ~*ed* by the shrinking supply of currency —V.L.Parrington⟩ ⟨industries like textiles . . . will be seriously ~*ed* as their contracts drop —*Market Report*⟩ ⟨is . . . true that inflation is ~*ing* some of our people now —M.G.Dilke⟩ **c :** to confine or limit narrowly **:** CONSTRICT ⟨will ~ their operating irrigation projects —Raymond Moley⟩ ⟨local prices and sales are being drastically ~*ed* by foreign imports —*Christian Science Monitor*⟩ **d :** to squeeze out (money) **:** EXTORT, WRING **3 :** to urge (a horse) to the limit **4 a :** STEAL ⟨~*ed* that box and . . . got caught —Claud Cockburn⟩ **b :** ARREST ⟨~*ed* for speeding —*Springfield (Mass.) Daily News*⟩ **5 :** to move by prying with a pinch bar **6 :** to sail (a boat) too close to the wind **7 a :** to press (the cue ball) against a billiard table with a downward stroke of the cue held more or less vertically **b :** to propel (the ball) by such a stroke **~ vi 1 :** to press or encroach so as to hem in or confine — used with *in* ⟨the hills ~ in from either side of the river —*Amer. Guide Series: Conn.*⟩ ⟨could have ~*ed* in on him at any time —Williams Forrest⟩ **2 :** to be economical **:** be miserly or closefisted ⟨~*ed* on everything, even necessities⟩ ⟨couldn't ~ and be shabby —Willa Cather⟩ **3 :** to cause pain by pressing or squeezing **:** press painfully ⟨this shoe ~*es*⟩ **4 :** NARROW, TAPER — often used with *out* ⟨a calcareous sandstone . . . which ~*es* out to the south —M.A.Clement⟩ **5 :** to form a pinch **syn** see STEAL — **pinch pennies :** to practice strict economy ⟨there weren't any *pennies pinched* when it was furnished —F.B.Gipson⟩

2**pinch** \"\ *n* -ES **1 a :** a critical point or juncture **:** EMERGENCY, STRAIT ⟨a good man to have when it comes to a ~⟩ — usu. used in the phrases *in a pinch* ⟨in a ~ it could carry half again as much —N.M.Clark⟩ and *at a pinch* ⟨at a ~, it could be supplied by sea —Richard Dimbleby⟩ **b** *obs* **:** mental or spiritual pain or distress **c** (1) **:** painful impact **:** PRESSURE, STRESS ⟨felt the ~ of chronic hunger —Dixon Wecter⟩ ⟨when the ~ of foreign competition came at last —G.M.Trevelyan⟩ ⟨again felt the ~ of blockade —F.A.Southard⟩ (2) **:** condition of hardship or privation ⟨feeling a ~ this year in that house —Pearl Buck⟩ **d :** SHORTAGE ⟨a labor ~ may be in the making —*Newsweek*⟩ ⟨the essential facts of the ammunition ~ —Elie Abel⟩ **2 a :** an act of pinching **:** NIP, SQUEEZE ⟨gave me a ~ in the leg —Margaret Deland⟩ **b :** as much as may be taken between the finger and thumb **:** a very small quantity ⟨a ~ of snuff⟩ ⟨a ~ of salt⟩ **3 :** PINCH BAR **4 :** a marked thinning of a vein or bed **5 :** a faint superficial line of crushed fibers running transversely across the belly of a bow or less commonly across part of an arrow **6 a :** THEFT **b :** a police raid **:** ARREST **7 :** pressure of the cue ball against a billiard table caused by a downward stroke of the cue **syn** see JUNCTURE — **with a pinch of salt :** with reservations

3**pinch** *adj* **1 :** SUBSTITUTE ⟨a ~ runner⟩ **2 :** made by a pinch hitter ⟨a two-run ~ single —*Springfield (Mass.) Union*⟩

**pinch·able** \ˈpinchəbəl\ *adj* **:** capable of being pinched

**pinchback** \ˈ=,=\ *adj* [1*pinch* + *back*, n.] *of a coat or jacket* **:** having a close-fitting or pleated back

**pinch bar** *n* **:** a lever having a pointed projection at one end and used esp. to roll heavy wheels — compare CROWBAR

1**pinch·beck** \ˈpinch,bek\ *n* -S [after Christopher *Pinchbeck* †1732 Eng. watchmaker who invented it] **1 :** an alloy of copper and zinc used esp. to imitate gold in cheap jewelry and ordinarily containing 10 to 15 percent of zinc **2 :** something that is counterfeit or spurious

2**pinchbeck** \"\ *adj* **1 :** made of pinchbeck **2 :** SHAM, CHEAP, SPURIOUS ⟨a ~ throne —J.A.Symonds⟩ **syn** see COUNTERFEIT

**pinchbeck brown** *n* **:** BURNISHED GOLD

**pinchbottle** \ˈ=,==\ *n* **:** a bottle with pinched or indented sides

**pinch bug** *or* **pinching bug** *n* **1 :** STAG BEETLE **2 :** HELLGRAMITE

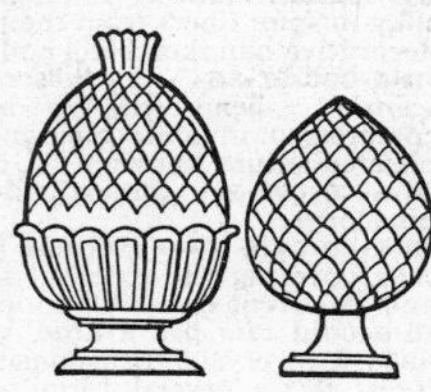

pinchbottle

**pinch clamp** *n* **:** PINCHCOCK

**pinchcock** \ˈ=,=\ *n* **:** a clamp used on a flexible tube to regulate the flow of a fluid through the tube — compare HOFFMAN CLAMP, MOHR PINCHCOCK

**pin·che** \ˈpēn(,)chā\ *n* -S [F *pinché*, fr. AmerSp *pinche*] **:** a So. American tamarin (*Leontocebus oedipus*) having a tufted head

**pincheck** \ˈ=,=\ *n* **1 :** a fine check made with different colored yarns, end-and-end, and smaller than the shepherd's check **2 :** a fabric having a pattern of pinchecks — **pinchecked** \ˈ=ˈ=\ *adj*

**pinched** \ˈpincht\ *adj* [fr. past part. of 1*pinch*] **1 :** COMPRESSED, SQUEEZED, CONTRACTED ⟨the ~ attic —Sinclair Lewis⟩ ⟨the valleys become ~ —Richard Joseph⟩ ⟨feel the effect on the consumer's ~ purse —*Wall Street Jour.*⟩ **2 :** drawn thin (as from hunger or cold) **:** WASTED, HAGGARD ⟨a small, ~ face —T.B.Costain⟩ ⟨thought he looked ~ and cold —G.G.Carter⟩ **3 :** being in straitened circumstances **:** hard up ⟨throve . . . when all their neighbors were ~ —Samuel Butler †1902⟩ — **pinched·ly** \ˈpinchədlē, -chtl-, -li\ *adv* — **pinched·ness** \-chədnəs, -ch(t)n-\ *n* -ES

**pinch effect** *n* **:** the tendency of a linear solid or fluid electrical conductor (as a rod or a column of ionized gas) to be compressed due to the action of its own magnetic field

**pinch·er** \ˈpinchə(r)\ *n* -S [ME *pynchar*, fr. *pynchen, pinchen* to pinch + *-ar, -er, -ere -er*] **1 :** one that pinches **2 pinchers** *pl* **:** PINCERS

**pin cherry** *n* **1 :** a small often shrubby shallow-rooted American wild cherry (*Prunus pensylvanica*) with small white flowers in short clusters **2 :** the bright red acid fruit of the pin cherry

**pinches** *pres 3d sing of* PINCH, *pl of* PINCH

**pinchfist** \ˈ=,=\ *n* [1*pinch* + *fist*, n.] **:** NIGGARD — **pinchfisted** \ˈ=ˈ==\ *adj*

**pinchgut** \ˈ=,=\ *n* [1*pinch* + *gut*, n.] *archaic* **:** a miserly person who starves himself or others

**pinchgut money** *or* **pinchgut pay** *n, archaic* **:** a money allowance made to sailors when food is scarce

**pinch-hit** \ˈ=ˈ=\ *vb* [back-formation fr. *pinch hitter*] *vi* **1 :** to go to bat in the place of another player esp. in an emergency when a hit is particularly needed — usu. used with *for* ⟨sent up to *pinch-hit* for the pitcher —*Scholastic Coach*⟩ **2 :** to act or serve in place of another ⟨might have to *pinch-hit* as naval officers —Sydney Connor⟩ — usu. used with *for* ⟨would *pinch-hit* for the president in the entertainment of foreign visitors —*Newsweek*⟩ **~ vt :** to make (a hit) while acting as a pinch hitter ⟨*pinch-hit* a home run in the 7th inning⟩

**pinch hit** *n* [*pinch-hit*] **:** a hit made while acting as a pinch hitter

**pinch hitter** *n* [2*pinch* + *hitter*] **1 :** a player who is sent in to bat in the place of another esp. in an emergency **2 :** a person who acts or serves in the place of another **:** SUBSTITUTE ⟨asked to fill in as a *pinch hitter* —Bernard Kalb⟩

1**pinch·ing** \ˈpinchiŋ, -chēŋ\ *n* -S [ME *pinchinge*, fr. gerund of *pinchen* to pinch] **:** the act of one that pinches; *specif* **:** the practice of severe economy or self-denial ⟨the difference between ~ and prodigality —G.B.Shaw⟩

2**pinching** *adj* [fr. pres. part. of 1*pinch*] **1 :** COMPRESSING, SQUEEZING ⟨~ shoes⟩ **2 :** causing physical or mental pain ⟨achieved at the cost of ~ self-sacrifice —*Sydney (Australia) Bull.*⟩ **3 :** NIGGARDLY, PARSIMONIOUS — **pinch·ing·ly** *adv*

**pinching bar** *n* **:** PINCH BAR

**pinchpenny** \ˈ=,==\ *adj* [fr. obs. E *pinchpenny*, n., stingy person, fr. ME *pynchepeny*, fr. *pynchen, pinchen* to pinch + *peny* penny] **:** NIGGARDLY ⟨~ economy⟩

**pinch pleat** *n* **:** a narrow short pleat usu. used in groups in the heading of curtains for controlling fullness

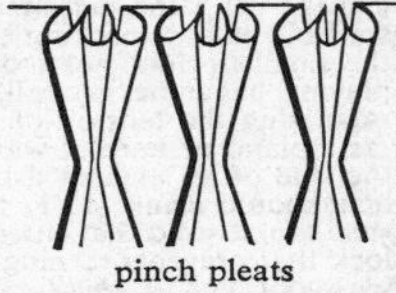

pinch pleats

**pinch roller** *n* **:** a roller of flexible material which presses the tape or wire in a magnetic recorder against the capstan for drive purposes

**pinch-spotted** *adj, obs* **:** spotted with bruises caused by pinching

**pinck·neya** \ˈpiŋknēə, piŋkˈnēyə\ *n, cap* [NL, fr. Charles C. *Pinckney* †1825 Am. statesman] **:** a genus of trees (family Rubiaceae) having showy pink and purple flowers with large colored bracts — see GEORGIA BARK

**pin cloth** *n, dial Eng* **:** PINAFORE

**pin clover** *n* **:** ALFILARIA

**pinc·ta·da** \piŋkˈtādə\ *n, cap* [NL] **:** a genus of bivalve mollusks (family Pteriidae) containing the principal pearl oysters

**pin curl** *n* **:** a curl made usu. by dampening a strand of hair with water or lotion, coiling it smoothly, and securing it in place by a hairpin or clip

**pincushion** \ˈ=,==\ *n* **1 :** a small cushion in which pins may be stuck ready for use **2 a :** SCABIOUS **b :** GUELDER ROSE **c :** a common No. American everlasting (*Antennaria plantaginifolia*) **d :** a plant of the genus *Chaenactis*

**pincushion cactus** *n* **:** a cactus of the genus *Mammillaria*

**pincushion distortion** *n* **:** distortion (as by an optical instrument or television receiver) in which the image of a straight line appears to be curved convexly toward the axis — compare BARREL DISTORTION

**pincushion flower** *n* **:** SCABIOUS 1

**pind** \ˈpind, ˈpīnd\ *vt* -ED/-ING/-S [ME *pinden* to put in a pound, dam up, fr. OE *pyndan* to dam up, fr. *pund-* enclosure, pound] *chiefly Scot* **:** to put (stray cattle) in a pound

**pin·da·ri** \pinˈdärē\ *n* -S *usu cap* [Marathi *pēḍārī, pēḍhārī* & Hindi *pindārā*] **:** one of the marauding mercenaries frequently making disastrous raids in British territory in India in the 18th century

1**pin·dar·ic** \(ˈ)pinˈdarik, -rēk\ *adj* [L *pindaricus*, fr. Gk *pindarikos*, fr. *Pindaros* Pindar †443 B.C. Greek lyric poet + Gk *-ikos* -ic] **1** *usu cap* **:** of or relating to the poet Pindar **b :** written in the manner or style characteristic of or believed to be characteristic of Pindar **2** *obs* **:** marked by irregularity or lack of restraint ⟨the beauteous strife 'twixt their cool writings and ~ life —Edward Young⟩

2**pindaric** \"\ *n* -S *usu cap* **1 :** a Pindaric ode **2 pindarics** *pl* **:** loose irregular verses that are similar to those used in Pindaric odes

**pindarical** *adj* [1*pindaric* + *-al*] *obs* **:** PINDARIC

1**pin·der** \ˈpində(r)\ *n* -S [ME *pynder*, fr. *pynden, pinden* to put in a pound + *-er*] *Brit* **:** POUNDMASTER

2**pin·der** \ˈpində(r)\ *or* **pin·da** \-də\ *or* **pin·dar** \-də(r)\ *n* -S [Kongo *mpinda*] *chiefly South* **:** PEANUT

**pin·dling** \ˈpind(ᵊ)lən, -liŋ, ˈpin(ᵊ)lən\ *adj* [perh. alter. of *spindling*] **1** *dial* **:** PUNY, DELICATE, FRAIL ⟨one . . . ~ little girl —Della Lutes⟩ **2** *dial* **:** PEEVISH, FRETFUL

**pin·do palm** \ˈpin(,)dō-\ *n* [AmerSp *pindo*, fr. Guarani *pindó*] **:** a Paraguayan coconut palm (*Cocos australis*) widely cultivated in northern greenhouses for its feathery graceful foliage

**pindot** \ˈ=,=\ *n* **:** a dot of the smallest size used in textiles — **pindotted** \ˈ=ˈ==\ *adj*

**pin drafter** *n* **:** a machine used in yarn manufacturing for combining and drafting sliver or top

**pin drill** *n* **:** a drill with a central pin or projection to fit into a hole to act as a guide while the hole is being enlarged or countersunk

**pin·dy** \ˈpindi\ *adj* [origin unknown] *dial Eng* **:** gone bad

1**pine** \ˈpīn\ *n* -S [ME, fr. (assumed) OE *pīn* punishment, torment, fr. L *poena* — more at PAIN] **1** *archaic* **:** mental suffering **:** ANGUISH, GRIEF, SORROW **2** *obs* **:** PRIVATION, WANT, FAMINE **3** *also* **pine disease :** a dietary deficiency disease of sheep or cattle marked by anemia, malnutrition, and general debility; *specif* **:** such a disease due to cobalt deficiency

2**pine** \"\ *vb* -ED/-ING/-S [ME *pinen*, fr. OE *pīnian*, fr. (assumed) OE *pīn* punishment, torment] *vt* **1 a** *obs* **:** to inflict pain upon **:** TORMENT, TORTURE **b** *chiefly dial* **:** to waste, wear out, consume, or exhaust by suffering or in grieving ⟨*pined* his flesh —Edmund Spenser⟩ **c** *archaic* **:** to grieve or mourn for **2 :** to shrink or dry (fish) esp. in curing **~ vi 1 :** to lose vigor, health, or flesh (as through grief, anxiety, or hunger) **:** become wasted (as through sorrow) **:** LANGUISH, FADE ⟨so she *pined*, and so she died forlorn —John Keats⟩ — often used with *away* ⟨sickens immediately, ~*s* away, and is soon dead —Bill Beatty⟩ **2 :** to languish with desire **:** yearn intensely — used with *for* ⟨*pined* for his native hills⟩ **3** *archaic* **:** REPINE, LAMENT **syn** see LONG

3**pine** \"\ *n* -S [ME, fr. OE *pīn*, fr. L *pinus*; akin to Gk *pitys* pine, Skt *pitu* drink, food — more at PIP] **1 :** a tree of the genus *Pinus* **2 a :** the straight-grained white or yellow usu. very durable often highly resinous wood of a pine varying from extreme softness in the white pines to hardness in the longleaf pine and related forms — compare FIR **b** *Midland & South* **:** KINDLING WOOD **3 a :** any of numerous coniferous trees of Australia: as (1) **:** a tree of the genus *Callitris* **:** CYPRESS PINE (2) **:** a tree of various other genera (as *Agathis, Podocarpus, Araucaria, Cupressus*, and *Dacrydium*) **b :** the wood of an Australian pine **4 a :** PARANÁ PINE **b :** the wood of the Paraná pine **5 :** PINEAPPLE

4**pine** \"\ *adj* **1 :** of or relating to the pine — often used in combination ⟨*pine*-clad hills⟩ **2 :** made of pine wood

**pine·al** \ˈpinēəl, ˈpīn-\ *adj* [F *pinéal*, fr. MF *pineal*, fr. L *pinea* pinecone (fr. fem. of *pineus* of the pine, fr. *pinus* pine + *-eus* -eous) + MF *-al*] **1 :** relating to or resembling a pinecone **2 :** of, relating to, or being the pineal body

**pineal body** *n* **:** a small body arising from the roof of the third ventricle and enclosed by the pia mater in all craniate vertebrates that in man and most existing vertebrates is conical, reddish gray, and suggestive of a gland or in larval lampreys and a few reptiles is raised on a stalk toward the upper surface of the head and has the essential structure of an eye and that is variously postulated to be a vestigial third eye, an endocrine organ, a time-measuring system in birds, or the seat of the soul — see BRAIN illustration

**pineal eye** *n* **:** the pineal body when eyelike in form with distinguishable lens and retina — see SPHENODON

**pin·e·a·lo·ma** \pinēəˈlōmə\ *n, pl* **pinealo·mas** \-məz\ *or* **pinealoma·ta** \-mədˑə\ [NL, fr. *pineal-* (fr. F *pinéal*) + *-oma*] **:** a tumor of the pineal body

**pine aphid** *n* **:** any of several plant lice that feed on pine; *specif* **:** PINE LEAF CHERMID

**pine·ap·ple** \ˈpī,napəl\ *n, often attrib* [ME *pinappel* pinecone, fr. *pin, pine* pine + *appel* apple, fruit] **1 :** an ornament representing a pinecone, or an ornament (as a finial on furniture) representing either a pinecone or a true pineapple **2 a :** a plant (*Ananas comosus*) native to tropical So. America but now widely cultivated in the tropics that has rigid spiny-margined recurved leaves and a short stalk with a dense oblong head of small abortive flowers **b :** the fruit of the pineapple that is a sorosis consisting of the succulent fleshy inflorescence and that ripens into a solid mass invested with the tough persistent floral bracts and crowned with a tuft of small leaves **3 a :** a dynamite bomb **b :** HAND GRENADE

pineapples 1

**pineapple cheese** *also* **pineapple** *n* **:** a cheddar type of cheese molded in the shape of a pineapple and hung in a net to give characteristic diamond-shaped markings to the outside

**pineapple cloth** *n* **:** PIÑA CLOTH

**pineapple family** *n* **:** BROMELIACEAE

**pineapple flower** *n* **:** a southern African plant of the genus *Eucomis* (family Liliaceae); *esp* **:** a bulbous plant (*E. punctata*) having a greenish fragrant flower

**pineapple guava** *n* **:** a feijoa (*Feijoa sellowiana*)

**pineapple mealybug** *n* **:** a mealybug (*Dysmicoccus brevipes*) that feeds on pineapple and other hosts chiefly in Hawaii and So. America

**pineapple oil** *or* **pineapple essence** *n* **:** an alcoholic solution of ethyl butyrate

**pineapple weed** *n* **:** an annual aromatic herb (*Matricaria matricarioides*) native to the Pacific coast of No. America but widely naturalized and having much-dissected leaves and rayless yellow flowers

**pine bark** *n* **:** the dried inner bark of a white pine (*Pinus strobus*) used in the preparation of cough syrups

**pine bark aphid** *n* **:** a plant louse (*Pineus strobi*) that lives on the bark of the white pine and produces a white flocculent deposit

**pine barren** *n* **:** a tract of sandy or peaty soil wooded with pine trees esp. in the southern U.S. with the longleaf pine or further north with a pitch pine (*Pinus rigida*)

**pine-barren sandwort** *n* **:** a white-flowered very deep-rooted perennial herb (*Arenaria caroliniana*) of the southeastern U.S. — called also *longroot*

**pine beetle** *n* **:** any of several buprestid beetles esp. of the genus *Dendroctonus* the larvae of which bore in pine trees in No. America

**pine borer** *n* **:** an insect larva that bores in pine timber: as **a :** the larva of various beetles esp. of the families Cerambycidae and Buprestidae **b :** a larval horntail

**pine bud gall** *n* **:** a gall on pine caused by the larva of a gall midge (*Contarina coloradensis*)

**pine butterfly** *n* **:** a black-and-white pierid butterfly (*Neophasia menapia*) whose larva is very injurious to young pines in western No. America

**pine cheat** *n* [so called fr. its fancied resemblance to a pine needle] **:** the leaf of a common spurry (*Spergula arvensis*)

**pine co·las·pis** \-kəˈlaspəs\ *n* [3*pine* + NL *Colaspis* (genus name of *Colaspis pini*)] **:** a chrysomelid beetle (*Colaspis pini*) having larvae that feed on pine needles in the southern U.S.

**pinecone** \ˈ=,=\ *n* **1 :** CONE **2 :** SOOT BROWN

**pinecone fish** *n* **:** a small sluggish berycoid fish (*Monocentris japonicus*) that has the body enclosed in a boxlike case made up of firmly fused large bony scales and is widely distributed in shallow waters of warm parts of the Indo-Pacific

**pinecone willow gall** *also* **pinecone gall** *n* **:** an oval imbricated gall resembling a pinecone formed on the twigs of willow by a gall midge (*Rhabdophaga strobiloides*)

**pine crab** *n* **:** a small green grapsoid crab (*Metapaulias depressus*) living in water accumulating at the leaf base of the broad-leaved pine in Jamaica

**pine creeper** *or* **pine creeping warbler** *n* **:** PINE WARBLER

**pined** *adj* [fr. past part. of 2*pine*] *archaic* **:** wasted esp. by suffering or hardship **:** GAUNT, PINCHED

**pinedrops** \ˈ=,=\ *n pl but sing or pl in constr* **1 :** a purplish brown leafless saprophytic plant (*Pterospora andromedea*) of the family Pyrolaceae with racemose drooping white flowers **2 :** BEECHDROPS

**pine engraver** *n* **:** any of several beetles of the genus *Ips* having larvae that attack pines esp. in the western U.S.; *esp* **:** a common destructive beetle (*Ips pini*)

**pine family** *n* **:** PINACEAE

**pine finch** *or* **pine linnet** *n* **:** PINE SISKIN

**pine gall weevil** *n* **:** a weevil (*Podapion gallicola*) that forms galls on pitch, scrub, and red pines

**pine grass** *n* **1 :** a bunchgrass (*Calamagrostis rubescens*) of Oregon and Washington where it forms valuable forage **2 :** a sedge (*Carex pensylvanica*) furnishing pasturage for cattle in the pine barrens of the southern U.S.

**pine green** *n* **:** a variable color averaging a dark green that is yellower and lighter than evergreen or average bottle green and bluer and paler than forest green (sense 1)

**pine grosbeak** *also* **pine bullfinch** *n* **:** a large grosbeak (*Pinicola enucleator*) of coniferous forests of northern America, Europe, and Asia that is chiefly gray with the crown, rump, and breast strongly suffused with rosy red in the adult male and yellow in the female

**pine grouse** *n* **:** DUSKY GROUSE

**pine gum** *n* **1 :** Australian sandarac **2 :** oleoresin from various pines

**pine hyacinth** *n* **:** an erect perennial herb (*Viorna baldwinii*) of Florida that is cultivated for its solitary urn-shaped pink or purplish flower

**pine knot** *n* **:** a joint of pine wood; *esp* **:** one used for fuel

**pineland** \ˈ=,=\ *n* **:** land naturally predominantly forested with pine

**pineland three-awn** *n* **:** a tufted erect perennial grass (*Aristida stricta*) that is native to the southeastern U.S. pineland and useful for grazing and has a slender panicle and appressed spikelets with long awns

**pine leaf chermid** *n* [*chermid* fr. NL *Chermidae*] **:** a pine aphid (*Pineus pinifoliae*) of western No. America — called also *pine leaf aphid, pine leaf chermes*

**pine-leaf scale** \ˈ=,=-\ *or* **pine needle scale** *n* **:** a long narrow white scale (*Phenacaspis pinifoliae*) common esp. on the leaves of pine in No. America

**pine lily** *n* **1 :** a lily (*Lilium catesbaei*) chiefly of the southeastern U.S. having flowers and narrow leaves erect **2 :** SQUAW GRASS

**pine lizard** *n* **:** a small very active iguanid lizard (*Sceloporus undulatus*) varieties of which occur in most of the U.S. and north to British Columbia — see SWIFT

**pine looper** *n* **:** any of several geometrid moths having larvae that attack pines in parts of both Europe and No. America

**pine marten** *n* **1 :** a European marten (*Martes martes*) larger than the stone marten **2 :** an American marten (*Martes americana*) closely related to the sable of Europe

**pine moth** *n* **:** any of several moths having caterpillars that feed on the leaves or bore in twigs or trunks of pine trees — compare PINE PEST

**pine mouse** *n* **:** a short-tailed glossy-furred burrowing meadow mouse (*Pitymys pinetorum*) of the eastern U.S.

**pi·nene** \ˈpī,nēn\ *n* -S [ISV *pin-* (fr. L *pinus* pine) + *-ene* — more at PINE] **:** either of two liquid isomeric unsaturated bicyclic terpene hydrocarbons $C_{10}H_{16}$ derived from pinane and found in turpentine oils: **a :** the isomer having the ethylenic double bond as part of the ring system, occurring in many essential oils (as juniper oil and eucalyptus oil), constituting in either its dextrorotatory or levorotatory form the principal component of various turpentines, and used chiefly as a solvent and chemical intermediate (as in making camphor or terpineol) — called also *alpha-pinene, 2-pinene* **b :** NOPINENE

**pine needle** *n* **1 :** one of the slender needle-shaped leaves of a pine tree **2 :** ALFILARIA

**pine needle gall** *n* **:** a gall on pitch pine caused by the larva of a gall midge (*Itonida pinirigidae*)

**pine-needle oil** *n* **:** an essential oil obtained from the needles and twigs of various pines or other conifers: as **a :** the colorless or yellowish bitter aromatic oil from the mugho pine used chiefly in medicine as an expectorant and inhalant **b :** the oil from the Siberian fir used chiefly in insecticides, soaps, and perfumes and as an inhalant

**pine nut** *n* [ME *pinnote*, fr. OE *pīnhnutu*, fr. *pīn* pine + *hnutu* nut] **1 :** PINECONE **2 :** the edible seed of any of several pines (as the neoza pine, the stone pine, or the piñon)

**pine oil** *n* **:** any of various essential oils obtained from pines or other conifers or oils similar to these oils in composition: as **a :** a colorless to light-amber liquid with an aroma of pine that contains principally terpineols and other terpenoid alcohols, is obtained from the wood esp. of the longleaf pine, boils higher than wood turpentine, and is used chiefly as a solvent, in disinfectants, deodorants, insecticides, wetting and emulsifying agents, and detergents, and in ore flotation **b :** a synthetic oil made by hydrating terpene hydrocarbons to form alcohols

**pine pandora moth** *n* **:** PANDORA MOTH
**pine pest** *n* **:** a phycitid moth (*Dioryctria zimmermani*) whose larva bores into pine trees causing exudation of pitch
**1pin·er** \'pīnə(r)\ *n* -S [ME *pynour*, fr. MD *piner*, fr. *pinen* to punish, suffer pain, work hard, fr. *pine* punishment, torment, fr. L *poena* — more at PAIN] *archaic* **:** LABORER
**2piner** \"\ *n* -S [2*pine* + *-er*] **:** one that pines; *specif* **:** an animal that suffers from pine
**3piner** \"\ *n* -S [3*pine* + *-er*] *Austral* **:** a pine-forest lumberman
**pine reproduction weevil** *n* **:** a weevil (*Cylindrocopturus eatoni*) that is a serious pest in plantations of ponderosa and Jeffrey pine in California
**pine root–collar weevil** *n* **:** a weevil (*Hylobius radicis*) having a larva that feeds in the cambium at crown level of various pines in the U. S.
**pin·ery** \'pīn(ə)rē, -ri\ *n* -ES [3*pine* + *-ery*] **1 :** a hothouse or area where pineapples are grown **2 a :** a pine forest ⟨the ruthless destruction of the Michigan *pineries*⟩ **b :** a grove of pine trees
**pines** *pl of* PINE, *pres 3d sing of* PINE
**pinesap** \'=,=\ *n* **:** any of several parasitic or saprophytic herbs of the genus *Monotropa* of the north temperate zone resembling the Indian pipe but being yellowish or reddish; *esp* **:** a fleshy tawny or reddish usu. pubescent saprophytic herb (*M. hypopithys*) growing in woodland humus of eastern No. America — called also *false beechdrops*
**pine sawfly** *n* **:** any of several sawflies (family Diprionidae) having larvae that feed on pine needles
**pine sawyer** *n* **:** any of several large beetles of the genus *Monochamus* (family Cerambycidae) whose larvae bore into the trunks of dead or dying pine trees
**pine–shoot moth** *n* **:** a small gaily colored moth (*Rhyacionia buoliana*) of the family Olethreutidae having a larva that damages pines by feeding in the young buds and shoots
**pine siskin** *n* **:** a small No. American finch (*Spinus pinus*) similar to the American goldfinch but having the plumage streaked, that breeds in the north and migrates irregularly southward in flocks in winter
**pine snake** *n* **:** BULL SNAKE
**pine spittlebug** *n* **:** a cercopid bug of the genus *Aphrophora* that attacks pines in many parts of No. America
**pine squirrel** *n* **:** FREMONT'S SQUIRREL
**pine straw** *n, chiefly Midland* **:** dried pine needles
**pine sugar** *n* **:** PINITOL
**pine swift** *n* **:** PINE LIZARD
**pine tag** *n, chiefly Midland* **:** the dried needle of the pine — usu. used in pl.
**pine tar** *n* **:** tar obtained by destructive distillation of pinewood that is a viscid dark brown phenolic liquid of empyreumatic odor and used chiefly in roofing, in rubber and plastics as a softener and plasticizer, in paints and varnishes, in soaps, and in the treatment of skin diseases
**pine–tar oil** *n* **:** a dark brown phenolic liquid of empyreumatic odor obtained by distillation of pine tar and used chiefly as a deodorant, antiseptic, and germicide and in ore flotation
**pine–tip moth** \'=,=-\ *n* **1 :** PINE PEST **2 :** a moth (*Rhyacionia frustrana*) of the family Olethreutidae with larvae that bore in the twigs of pine
**pine tortoise scale** *n* **:** a scale (*Toumeyella numismaticum*) that feeds on pines esp. in the eastern U. S.
**pine tree** *n* [ME *pine tre*, fr. OE *pīntrēow*, fr. *pīn* pine + *trēow* tree] **1 :** PINE **2 :** DUCK GREEN
**pine–tree lizard** *n* **:** PINE LIZARD
**pine tree shilling** *n* [so called fr. the representation of a pine tree on the coin] **:** a silver shilling coined in Massachusetts in the 17th century
**pine–tube moth** \'=,=-\ *n* **:** a moth (*Argyrotaenia pinatubana*) with larvae that feed within a tube of pine needles webbed together
**pine tulip** *n* **:** PIPSISSEWA
**pi·ne·tum** \pī'nēdəm\ *n, pl* **pine·ta** \-d·ə\ [L, pine grove, fr. *pinus* pine + *-etum*] **1 :** a plantation of pine trees; *esp* **:** a scientific collection of living coniferous trees **2 :** a treatise on pines
**pi·ne·us** \'pīnēəs\ *n, cap* [NL, fr. L *pineus*, adj., of the pine — more at PINEAL] **:** a genus of aphids (family Psyllidae) including several that feed on coniferous trees — see PINE BARK APHID
**pine warbler** *n* **:** a large plainly colored warbler (*Dendroica pinus*) of the eastern U. S. usu. inhabiting pinewoods
**pine webworm** *n* **:** a webworm that is the larva of a small dull-colored moth (*Tetralopha robustella*) and that attacks various pines in eastern U. S.
**pineweed** \'=,=\ *n* **:** ORANGE GRASS
**pine weevil** *n* **:** any of several weevils that attack pines; *esp* **:** a brightly metallic weevil (*Scythropus elegans*) of western No. America — called also *elegant pine weevil*
**pinewood** \'=,=\ *n* **1 :** a wood of pines ⟨this dank, dreary ~ —Christopher Isherwood⟩ — often used in pl. but sing. or pl. in constr. ⟨a ~s I was very fond of —Jean Stafford⟩ **2 :** the wood of the pine tree
**pinewoods grape** \'=,=-\ *n* **:** POST-OAK GRAPE
**pine worm** *n* **:** a larval pine sawyer
**1pi·ney** \'pīnē, -ni\ *n* -S [ME *piony* — more at PEONY] *dial* **:** PEONY
**2piney** \'pīnē, -ni\ *adj, usu* **pinier**; *usu* **piniest** [3*pine* + *-y*] **:** PINY ⟨~ smell of my bath soap —Gladys Schmitt⟩ ⟨the ~ hills —Dillon Anderson⟩
**piney dammar** *or* **piney resin** *or* **piney varnish** *n* [*piney* prob. by folk etymology (influence of 2*piney*) fr. Malayalam *payin* piney tree] **:** a pellucid fragrant acrid resin that exudes from the piney tree when wounded and is used as a varnish, in making candles, and as a substitute for incense and for amber
**pin eye** *n* **:** a primula flower in which the pistil stands above the stamens
**pin–eyed** \'=,'=\ *adj* **:** having very small eyes or spots suggesting eyes; *specif* **:** having the stigma visible at the throat of a gamopetalous corolla while the stamens are concealed in the tube — used of dimorphous flowers; compare THRUM-EYED
**piney tallow** *n* [*piney* (as in *piney dammar*) + *tallow*] **:** a solid fatty substance obtained from seeds of the piney tree and used in making candles
**piney tree** *or* **piney varnish tree** *n* [*piney tree* fr. *piney* (as in *piney dammar*) + *tree*; *piney varnish tree* fr. *piney varnish* + *tree*] **:** an East Indian tree (*Vateria indica*) that has panicles of showy white flowers and yields timber, resin, and oil
**piney woods** *n pl* **:** woodland of the southern U. S. in which pines are the dominant tree
**pinfall** \'=,=\ *n* **:** the total score made by a player or side in bowling
**1pinfeather** \'=,=-\ *n* [*pin* + *feather*] **:** a feather not fully developed; *esp* **:** a young feather just emerging through the skin and still enclosed for most of its length in a cylindrical horny sheath which is afterwards cast off — **pinfeathered** \'=,'=-\ *adj* — **pinfeathery** \'=,'=(=)=\ *adj*
**2pinfeather** \'=,==\ *vt* **:** to pluck the pinfeathers from — **pinfeatherer** \'=,===\ *n*
**1pinfire** \'=,=\ *adj* [1*pin* + *fire*, v.] **1** *of a cartridge* **:** having a movable pin projecting from the rim that when struck by a hammer explodes a cap encased in the cartridge **2** *of a firearm* **:** using a pinfire cartridge
**2pinfire** \"\ *n* **:** a pinfire firearm
**pinfish** \'=,=\ *n* **:** any of several fishes having sharp dorsal spines: as **a :** a small compressed dark green grunt (*Lagodon rhomboides*) of the Atlantic coast from Cape Cod to Cuba **b :** a related fish (*Diplodus holbrooki*)
**1pin·fold** \'pin,fōld\ *also* **pen·fold** \'pen,-\ *n* [*pinfold* fr. ME *pynfold*, *pyndefolde*, alter. (influenced by *pinden* to put in a pound and prob. by *pinnen* to enclose) of *pundfald*, fr. OE, fr. *pund-* enclosure, pound + *fald* fold, pen; *penfold* alter. (influenced by 1*pen*) of *pinfold* — more at PIND, PIN (v.)] **1 :** a pound for animals **2 :** a place of restraint **:** CONFINE
**2pinfold** \"\ *also* **penfold** \"\ *vt* **:** to enclose or confine in or as if in a pinfold
**1ping** \'piŋ\ *n* -S [imit.] **1 :** a sharp metallic sound like or suggestive of that made by a rifle bullet striking an obstruction ⟨heard the ~ of a slingshot —Frank O'Connor⟩ ⟨a bell . . . rang with a ~ —Bruce Marshall⟩ **2 :** an abnormal sound made by a gas engine usu. due to advanced spark or excessive carbon accumulation **:** KNOCK **3 :** the pulse of sound waves reflected from or emitted by a submerged object in submarine signaling or detection and heard by special apparatus
**2ping** \"\ *vi* -ED/-ING/-S **:** to make a sharp metallic sound like or suggestive of that made by a rifle bullet striking an obstruction **:** sound a ping ⟨a few mosquitoes . . . ~*ing* shrilly —John Onslow⟩ ⟨a bullet ~*ed* into the water —Henriette Roosenburg⟩
**pin game** *n* **:** PINBALL 3
**pinging** *n* -S **:** the act of one that pings; *specif* **:** DETONATION
**1pin·gle** \'piŋ(g)əl\ *vi* -ED/-ING/-S [origin unknown] **1** *chiefly Scot* **:** STRIVE, STRUGGLE **2** *chiefly Scot* **:** to dawdle or trifle esp. with one's food
**2pingle** \"\ *n* -S *Scot* **:** STRUGGLE, EFFORT
**3pingle** \"\ *n* -S [origin unknown] *dial chiefly Eng* **:** a small enclosed field
**4pingle** \"\ *n* -S [origin unknown] *Scot* **:** a long-handled cooking pot or pan
**pin·go** \'piŋ(,)gō\ *n* -S [Esk] **:** a small low mound of earth or gravel presumably due to frost action (as in arctic regions)
**Ping–Pong** \'piŋ,päŋ, -,pȯŋ\ *trademark* — used for table tennis
**pin grass** *n* **:** ALFILARIA
**pin·gue** *also* **pin·guay** \'pēŋ(,)gwā, 'piŋ-\ *n* -S [Sp *pingüe* fat, fr. L *pinguis*; akin to Gk *pimelē* lard — more at FAT] **:** a perennial glandular herb (*Actinea richardsoni*) of the family Compositae of the southwestern U. S. yielding an inferior rubber and causing poisoning of livestock
**pin·guec·u·la** \piŋ'gwekyələ\ *also* **pin·guic·u·la** \-'gwik-\ *n, pl* **pinguecu·lae** \-,lē, -,lī\ *also* **pinguicu·lae** \-,lē, -,lī\ [*pinguecula* fr. NL, alter. of *pinguicula*; *pinguicula* fr. NL, fr. L, fem. of *pinguiculus* fattish] **:** a small yellowish elevation situated near the inner or outer margins of the cornea and occurring esp. in people of advanced age
**pin·gue·fy** \'piŋgwə,fī\ *vb* -ED/-ING/-ES [L *pinguefacere*, fr. *pingue-* (as in *pinguescere* to grow fat) + *facere* to make — more at DO] *archaic* **:** FATTEN
**pin·gues·cent** \(')piŋ'gwes<sup></sup>ᵊnt\ *adj* [L *pinguescent-*, *pinguescens*, pres. part. of *pinguescere* to grow fat, fr. *pinguis* fat] *archaic* **:** FATTENING
**pin·guic·u·la** \piŋ'gwikyələ\ *n, cap* [NL, fr. L, fem. of *pinguiculus* fattish, fr. *pinguis* fat] **:** a large genus of acaulescent bog herbs (family Lentibulariaceae) having showy solitary purple, yellow, or white flowers on naked scapes and leaves that capture insects in the viscid secretion on the leaf surface and digest them
**pin·guid** \'piŋgwəd\ *adj* [L *pinguis* fat + E *-id* (as in *languid*)] **:** FAT, FATTY ⟨a ~ bullfrog —Carl Van Vechten⟩
**pin·guid·i·ty** \piŋ'gwidədē\ *n* -ES **:** FATNESS
**pin·guin** \'piŋgwən\ *n* -S [native name in the West Indies] **:** a tropical American plant (*Bromelia pinguin*) that is used in the tropics for hedges, has spiny leaves resembling aloes, reddish panicled flowers, and plum-shaped edible fruit, and yields a cordage fiber
**pin·gui·nus** \'piŋgwənəs, piŋ'gwīn-\ *n, cap* [NL, fr. F *pingouin* great auk, fr. E *penguin*] **:** a genus of very large extinct flightless seabirds (family Alcidae) containing solely the great auk
**pin·gui·tude** \'piŋgwə,tüd, -ə,tyüd\ *n* -S [L *pinguitudo*, fr. *pinguis* fat + *-tudo* -tude] *archaic* **:** FATNESS, OBESITY, OILINESS
**1pinhead** \'=,=\ *n* **1 a :** the head of a pin **b :** something very small or insignificant **2 a :** a microcephalic idiot **b :** a very dull or stupid person **:** FOOL ⟨seems an awful ~ —Wolcott Gibbs⟩ **3 :** a part of a plow containing pinholes for a pin the position of which regulates the depth of furrow **4 :** a small minnow
**2pinhead** \'=,=\ *adj* **:** PINHEADED ⟨~ philosophy . . . and abysmal ignorance —James Kelly⟩
**pinheaded** \'=,'=\ *adj* **1 :** lacking intelligence or understanding **:** DULL, STUPID ⟨a ~ young man⟩ **2 :** PIN-EYED — **pinhead·ed·ness** *n* -ES
**pin hinge** *n* **:** a hinge that uses a pin as a pivot as opposed to a loop hinge
**pinhole** \'=,=\ *n* **1 :** a hole made by or for a pin **:** PINPRICK **2 :** a small aperture or perforation resembling a hole made by a pin: as **a** *archery* **:** the center of the gold **b :** a hole through which a pin passes (as in a truss) **c :** a transparent spot on a developed photographic film or plate often caused by dust on the surface during exposure **d :** a defect in a glaze or enamel consisting of a tiny area of the body or metal that is not covered **e :** a hole in lumber caused by beetles **f :** a minute froth pit in a coated paper
**pinhole borer** *n* **:** any of various minute larval beetles (as of an ambrosia beetle) whose larvae excavate long slender burrows in timber
**pinhole camera** *n* **:** a photographic camera having a minute aperture and no lens
**pinhole pupil** *n* **:** a pupil of the eye contracted (as in opium poisoning) to the size of a pinhole
**1pinhook** \'=,=\ *n* [1*pin* + *hook*, n.] **:** a fishhook made from a pin
**2pinhook** \"\ *vi* [back-formation fr. *pinhooker*] **:** to act as a pinhooker
**pin·hook·er** \-kə(r)\ *n* [prob. fr. 1*pinhook* + *-er*] **:** a small speculator in tobacco at a local market
**pi·nic acid** \'pīnik, 'pinik-\ *n* [*pinic* fr. F *pinique*, fr. *pin* pine (fr. L *pinus*) + *-ique* -ic — more at PINE] **:** a crystalline dicarboxylic acid $HOOCC_6H_{10}CH_2COOH$ formed by oxidation of pinonic acid
**pinier** *comparative of* PINEY *or of* PINY
**pinies** *pl of* PINY
**piniest** *superlative of* PINEY *or of* PINY
**1pin·ing** \'pīniŋ, -nēŋ\ *n* -S [ME *pininge*, *pining*, fr. OE *pīnung* torment, punishment, fr. *pīnian* to torture + *-ung* -ing — more at PINE] **1 :** the act or condition of one that pines **2** *also* **pining disease :** 1PINE 3
**2pining** *adj* [fr. pres. part. of 2*pine*] **1** *archaic* **:** CONSUMING, WASTING **2 :** LANGUISHING ⟨a ~ lover⟩ — **pin·ing·ly** *adv*
**1pin·ion** \'pinyən\ *n* -S [ME *pynyon*, fr. MF *pignon*, fr. OF, prob. fr. *pignon*, *penon* pennon — more at PENNON] **1 a :** the distal part of a bird's wing including the carpus, metacarpus, and phalanges **b :** WING **c :** FLIGHT FEATHER, QUILL; *also* **:** the flight feathers **2 :** the anterior border of an insect's wing
**2pinion** \"\ *vt* -ED/-ING/-S **1 :** to restrain (a bird) from flight: **a :** to bind or confine the wings of **b :** to confine by binding the wings of **c :** to cut off the distal joint of one wing of **2 a :** to disable or restrain by binding the arms usu. to the body ⟨bodyguards had ~*ed* his attacker —Hodding Carter⟩ **b :** to disable or restrain a person by so binding (the arms) **3 :** to bind fast **:** SHACKLE ⟨this frame . . . which now is ~*ed* with mortality —George Herbert⟩
**3pinion** \",(')pēn'yōn\ *n* -S [Sp *piñón* pine nut, physic nut — more at PIÑON] **1 :** PHYSIC NUT **2** [AmerSp *piñón*, fr. Sp] **:** PIÑON
**4pinion** \"\ *n* -S [F *pignon*, fr. MF, alter. of *peignon*, fr. *peigne* comb, fr. L *pecten* — more at PECTINATE] **1 :** a gear with a small number of teeth designed to mesh with a larger wheel or rack **2 :** the smaller wheel of a pair or the smallest of a train or set of gear wheels
**1pin·ioned** \-nd\ *adj* [ME *pynyonyd*, fr. *pynyon* pinion + *-yd*, *-ed* -ed] **:** having wings or pinions
**2pinioned** *adj* [fr. past part. of 2*pinion*] **:** BOUND, FETTERED
**pinion end** *n* [obs. E *pinion* gable (fr. ME, fr. OF *pignon*, fr. assumed VL *pinnion-*, *pinnio*, fr. L *pinna* battlement, feather — alter. of *penna* feather — + *-ion-*, *-io* -ion) + E *end* — more at PEN] **:** GABLE END
**1pi·nite** \'pē,nīt\ *n* -S [G *pinit*, fr. the *Pini* mine, Saxony, Germany + G *-it* -ite] **:** a compact mineral of a dull grayish, green, or brownish color that is essentially muscovite derived from the alteration of other minerals (as cordierite)

pinion: *1* gear, *2* pinion

**2pi·nite** \'pī,nīt\ *n* -S [NL *Pinites*, form genus of fossil pines, fr. *Pinus* + *-ites*] **:** a fossil wood referred to the family Pinaceae (as to the form genera *Pinites* and *Pinoxylon*) and usu. resembling that of the recent pines
**pi·ni·tol** \'pīnə,tōl, -tōl\ *n* -S [obs. E *pinite* pinitol (fr. F, fr. *pin* pine — fr. L *pinus* — + *-ite*) + E *-ol* — more at PINE] **:** a sweet crystalline compound $C_6H_6(OH)_5OCH_3$ that is extracted esp. from the heartwood of the sugar pine and is found also in legumes and other plants; *dextro*-inositol monomethyl ether
**1pink** \'piŋk\ *vt* -ED/-ING/-S [ME *pynken* to make holes with a pointed instrument] **1 a** (1) **:** to pierce with a sword or other pointed instrument **:** STAB ⟨~*s* him neatly in the arm —*Life*⟩ (2) **:** to wound with a bullet ⟨~*ed* three times by an assassin —*Time*⟩ (3) **:** to hit with a missile ⟨gets ~*ed* so often because he crowds the plate —W.B.Furlong⟩ **b :** to wound (as pride) by insensitivity **:** wound with the weapons of irony, criticism, or ridicule ⟨television, advertising, and urban gullibility . . . are rather easily ~*ed* —John McCarten⟩ ⟨~*ed* by the small darts of political enemies —W.S.White⟩ **2 a :** to cut or perforate (cloth, leather or paper) in an ornamental pattern that often shows an underlay of a contrasting color **b :** to cut a saw-toothed edge on (cloth, paper, leather) esp. with pinking shears **3 a :** ADORN, DECORATE, DECK **b** *obs* **:** TATTOO
**2pink** *n* -S *obs* **:** a hole or eyelet made with or as if with a pinking iron
**3pink** \'piŋk\ *n* -S [ME *pynk*, fr. MD *pinke*] **1 :** a small Dutch fishing craft characterized by a full forebody narrowing to an almost pointed stern with an overhanging false counter **2 :** any of various ships having a narrow overhanging stern — called also *pinkie*
**4pink** \"\ *n* -S [alter. of earlier *penk*, fr. ME] **1** *dial Eng* **:** the European minnow **2** *Brit* **:** a newly hatched salmon or grayling
**5pink** \"\ *vi* -ED/-ING/-S [prob. fr. D *pinken* to wink, blink] **1** *chiefly dial* **:** to peer or peep with half-closed eyes **:** WINK, BLINK **2** *chiefly dial* **:** to gleam faintly **:** DIMINISH, FADE
**6pink** \"\ *adj, dial chiefly Brit, of an eye* **:** half shut **:** WINKING
**7pink** \"\ *n* -S *chiefly Scot* **:** a small gleam of light — **pink of the evening** *dial* **:** late afternoon **:** early evening ⟨enjoy the *pink of the evening* with my friends —Marie Campbell⟩
**8pink** \"\ *n* -S [origin unknown] **1 :** a plant of the genus *Dianthus*: as **a :** COTTAGE PINK **b :** CHINA PINK **2 a :** the very embodiment **:** PARAGON ⟨your new doctor is the ~ of politeness —*Encore*⟩ ⟨the ~ and pattern of a soldier —Thomas Wood †1950⟩ **b :** a member of the elite **:** a person dressed in the height of fashion **:** SWELL, EXQUISITE; *also* **:** ELITE ⟨the ~ of Victorian propriety appeared —C.W.Cunnington⟩ **c :** highest degree possible **:** HEIGHT, EXTREME ⟨dressed in the ~ of fashion —G.E. Fussell⟩ ⟨keep their house in the ~ of repair —Rebecca West⟩ — **in the pink** *or* **in the pink of condition :** in the best of health **:** in splendid physical condition ⟨delighted to see you . . . *in the pink* —James Reynolds⟩ ⟨the plants were *in the pink of condition* —Anne Dorrance⟩
**9pink** \"\ *adj* [8*pink*] **1 :** resembling the garden pink in color **:** being of the color pink ⟨tallish man with ~ wrinkly face —R.W.Brown †1956⟩ — often used in combination ⟨his fat *pink*-haired wife —Maeve Brennan⟩ **2 :** holding or believed to hold advanced liberal or moderately radical political or economic views **3 :** MOVED, ANGERED, EXCITED ⟨would get quite ~ on the subject —Graham Greene⟩ — often used as an intensive ⟨ought to be thrilled ~ that you know an aristocrat like me —Calder Willingham⟩ ⟨flattered ~ at the charge —T.O.Heggen⟩ ⟨scared ~ of . . . friends with marriage in their eye —Ethel Wilson⟩ — **pink·ness** *n* -ES
**10pink** \"\ *n* -S [9*pink*] **1 :** any of a group of colors bluish red to red in hue, of medium to high lightness, and of low to moderate saturation **2 a** (1) **:** the scarlet color of a fox hunter's coat (2) **:** a fox hunter's coat of this color (3) **:** a fox hunter **b :** pink-colored clothing ⟨dressed in ~⟩ **c pinks** *pl* **:** light-colored trousers worn with a winter semidress uniform by army officers **3 :** a person who holds advanced liberal or moderately radical political or economic views — compare RED **4 :** HUMPBACK SALMON
**11pink** \"\ *vb* -ED/-ING/-S [9*pink*] *vi* **:** to turn pink ⟨when the eastern sky was beginning to ~ —T.W.Duncan⟩ ⟨~*ing* up just a little —Victoria Case⟩ **~** *vt* **1 :** to cause to turn pink ⟨~*ed* his ears with pleased embarrassment —J.H.Wheelwright⟩ **2 :** to change the color of (a topaz) to pink by heating
**12pink** \"\ *vi* -ED/-ING/-S [imit.] **:** to make a tinkling or pinging noise **:** PING ⟨~*ing* like a hundred tiny coins —Gerald Durrell⟩ ⟨when the mixture is too rich . . . the engine ~*s* —Cyril Connolly⟩
**13pink** \"\ *n* -S [imit.] **:** CHAFFINCH
**pink–and–white shower** \'=;=;=-\ *n* **:** an ornamental leguminous tree (*Cassia javanica*) from Java and Sumatra bearing masses of pink and white flowers and having pods like those of the golden shower but ridged transversely
**pink bollworm** *n* **:** the pinkish larva of a small dark brown moth (*Pectinophora gossypiella* syn. *Gelechia gossypiella*) which bores into the flowers and bolls of cotton and is a very widespread destructive pest occurring in most cotton-growing countries including the U. S.
**pink bud stage** *n* **:** PINK STAGE
**pink calla** *n* **:** a calla (*Zantedeschia rehmannii*) that is native to southern Africa and used as an ornamental and that has lanceolate leaves and rose-colored spathes
**pink cockatoo** *n* **:** a white Australian cockatoo (*Kakatoe leadbeateri*) with the plumage flushed roseate and a large showy barred crest
**pink coral** *n* **:** a deep pink to strong yellowish pink
**pink curlew** *n* **:** ROSEATE SPOONBILL
**pink disease** *n* **1 :** a serious bark disease of rubber, cacao, citrus, coffee, and many other trees that is caused by a fungus (*Corticium salmonicolor*) and is marked by a pink covering of hyphae on the stems and branches **2 :** ACRODYNIA
**pink dogwood** *n* **:** a pink flowering dogwood
**pink–eared duck** \'=;=-\ *n* **:** an Australian duck (*Malacorhynchus membranaceus*) with a bill superficially resembling that of the shoveler
**pinked** *past of* PINK
**pink·een** \(')piŋ'kēn\ *n* -S [4*pink* + *-een*] **1** *Irish* **:** MINNOW **2** *Irish* **:** an insignificant person
**pink elephants** *n pl* **:** any of various hallucinations arising from heavy drinking, use of narcotics, or other cause — usu. used in the phrase *see pink elephants* ⟨what a drunk would see who is too pleasant to see *pink elephants* or snakes —John Mason Brown⟩
**pink·en** \'piŋkən\ *vi* -ED/-ING/-S **:** to become pink ⟨~*ed* with anger —Audrey Barker⟩ ⟨his body ~*ed* from a shower —Maritta Wolff⟩
**pinkeny** *n* -ES [alter. of earlier *pink nye*, fr. 6*pink* + obs. E *nye* eye, fr. ME — more at PIGSNEY] **1** *obs* **:** a small blinking or peering eye **2** *obs* **:** PET, DARLING
**pink·er** \'piŋkə(r)\ *n* -S **:** one that does pinking
**pin·ker·ton** \'piŋkə(r)tᵊn, -)tən *or* -)dᵊn\ *n* -S *usu cap* [after Allan Pinkerton †1884 Am. detective] **:** PRIVATE DETECTIVE
**pinkeye** \'=,=\ *n* [9*pink* + *eye*] **1 :** an acute highly contagious conjunctivitis of man and various domestic animals (as sheep and cattle) **2 :** SHIPPING FEVER 2c **3 :** PINK-EARED DUCK
**pink family** *n* **:** CARYOPHYLLACEAE
**pinkfish** \'=,=\ *n* **:** a blind goby (*Typhlogobius californiensis*) of southern California found under stones on the beaches
**pink gin** *n, chiefly Brit* **:** a mixed drink of gin and bitters
**1pin·kie** \'piŋkē, -ki\ *adj* [prob. fr. 6*pink*] *chiefly Scot* **:** SMALL
**2pinkie** \"\ *or* **pin·ky** \"\ *n, pl* **pinkies** [prob. fr. D *pinkje*, dim. of *pink* little finger] **:** LITTLE FINGER ⟨caught his ~ in the spring mechanism —S.J.Perelman⟩
**3pinkie** *also* **pinky** \"\ *n, pl* **pinkies** [prob. fr. D *pinkje* small pink, dim. of *pink*, fr. MD *pinke* — more at PINK (fishing craft)] **:** 3PINK 2
**4pinkie** \"\ *n* -S [origin unknown] **:** RABBIT BANDICOOT
**pink·ify** \'piŋkə,fī\ *vt* -ED/-ING/-ES **:** to make pink
**pink·i·ly** \-kəlē, -li\ *adv* **:** in a pinky manner **:** with a touch of pink
**pink·i·ness** \-kēnəs, -kin-\ *n* -ES **:** the quality or state of being pinky ⟨his shaven face, scarcely ruffled by the lines of his fifty years, had the same shell-like ~ —W.J.Locke⟩
**pinking** *n* -S [fr. gerund of 1*pink* & 12*pink*] **:** the act or condition of one that pinks: as **a :** a method of decorating, cutting, or finishing cloth, leather, or paper with a pinking iron or pinking shears; *also* **:** the work so done **b** *Brit* **:** DETONATION, KNOCK ⟨too much ignition advance leads to . . . ~ —B.C.MacDonald⟩
**pinking iron** *n* **:** a metal instrument for cutting or perforating designs on cloth, leather, or paper

**pinking shears** *n pl* **:** shears with a saw-toothed inner edge on the blades used chiefly for cutting cloth or finishing garments with a nonraveling zigzag edge

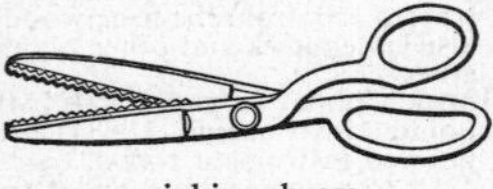
pinking shears

**pink·ish** \ˈpiŋkish, -kēsh\ *adj* **:** somewhat pink; *esp* **:** tending to be pink in politics — **pink·ish·ness** *n* -ES

**pink lady** *n* **:** a cocktail consisting of gin, brandy, fresh lemon juice, grenadine, and white of egg shaken with cracked ice and strained before serving

**pink lady's-slipper** *also* **pink lady slipper** *n* **:** a moccasin flower (*Cypripedium acaule*)

**pink laver** *n* **:** RED LAVER

**pink·ly** *adv* **:** in a pink manner **:** with a pink hue ⟨neon signs shining ~ on the snow —Morley Callaghan⟩

**pink madder** *n* **:** MADDER ROSE

**pink mahogany** *n* **:** a large evergreen West African tree (*Guarea cedrata*) with pale pinkish cedar-scented wood; *also* **:** the wood of this tree

**pink meadowsweet** *n* **:** either of two No. American spireas: **a :** HARDHACK 1 **b :** a small erect mat-forming spirea (*Spiraea densiflora*) of the western U.S. with glabrous leaves and lavender flowers

**pink needle** *n* [¹*pink* + *needle*; fr. the long tapering points of the carpels] **:** ALFILARIA

**pin knot** *n* **:** a sound knot in lumber not over ½ inch in diameter

**pinko** \ˈpiŋ(ˌ)kō\ *n* -S [⁸*pink* + -*o*] **:** ¹⁰PINK 3 ⟨pledged to purge the ~s —Addison Burbank⟩

**pink patch** *n* **:** a disease of turf grasses caused by a fungus (*Corticium fuciforme*) that mats the leaves together with reddish mycelial threads

**pink pearl** *n* **:** ROSE HERMOSA

**pink pill** *n* **:** a pink-coated pill; *also* **:** such a pill used as a proprietary medicine

**pink rhododendron** *n* **:** any pink-flowered rhododendron; *esp* **:** CALIFORNIA ROSEBAY

**pinkroot** \ˈ=,=\ *n* [⁸*pink* + *root*] **:** any of several plants of the genus *Spigelia* used as anthelmintics: as **a :** a perennial woodland herb (*S. marilandica*) of the U.S. that is sometimes cultivated for its showy red and yellow flowers — called also *Indian pink* **b :** a tropical American annual herb (*S. anthelmia*) with purplish white flowers

**pink root** *n* [⁹*pink* + *root*] **:** a disease of onion and garlic characterized by a red coloration of the roots and caused by any of several fungi esp. of the genera *Phoma* and *Fusarium*

**pink rot** *n* **1 :** a destructive disease of potato tubers caused by a fungus (*Phytophtora erythroseptica*) characterized by a wet rot and pinkish color of the cut tuber surfaces when exposed to the air **2 :** a rot of apples caused by a saprophytic fungus (*Tricothecium roseum*) **3 :** a watery soft rot of celery caused by a fungus (*Sclerotinia sclerotiorum*)

**pinks** *pres 3d sing of* PINK, *pl of* PINK

**pink salmon** *n* [⁹*pink* + *salmon*] **:** HUMPBACK SALMON

**pink salt** *n* **:** a white crystalline salt $(NH_4)_2SnCl_6$ used formerly as a mordant in dyeing for producing pink colors with madder and cochineal; ammonium chloro-stannate

**pink shower** *also* **pink shower tree** *n* **:** a tropical American tree (*Cassia grandis*) used as an ornamental having rose-colored flowers in lateral racemes

**pink slip** *n* **:** a notice from an employer that a recipient's employment is being terminated

**pink spray** *n* **:** a spray applied to fruit trees (as apple) when the flower buds are in the pink stage — compare PREPINK SPRAY

**pink stage** *n* **:** a stage in the development of the flower of an apple or other fruit tree in which the buds show pink color but are only beginning to open ⟨the *pink stage* of blossom growth⟩ — called also *pink bud stage*

**pink·ster** *or* **pinx·ter** \ˈpiŋ(k)stə(r), -ŋzt-\ *n* -S *usu cap* [D *pinkster* fr. MD *pinxter*, alter. of *pinxten*; akin to OFris *pinxtera* Whitsuntide, OS *pinkoston*, MHG *pfingesten*; all fr. a prehistoric continental WGmc word borrowed fr. Goth *paintekuste* Pentecost, fr. Gk *pentēkostē* — more at PENTECOST] **:** WHITSUNTIDE

**pinkster flower** *var of* PINXTER FLOWER

**pink-stockings** \ˈ=ˈ=\ *n pl but sing or pl in constr* **:** BLACK-NECKED STILT

**pink tea** *n* **1 :** a formal afternoon tea usu. marked by a high degree of decorum **2 :** a decorous or namby-pamby affair or proceeding ⟨do not find press relations anybody's *pink tea* —F.L.Mott⟩

**pink tint** *n* **:** a pinkish white

**pink vine** *n* **:** a climbing Mexican vine (*Antigonon leptopus*) cultivated for its racemes of coral pink flowers and its bright-colored veined fruits

**pink wax scale** *n* **:** a scale (*Ceroplastes rubens*) that attacks mandarins in Australia

**pinkweed** \ˈ=,=\ *n* **:** any of several knotgrasses with pink flowers; *esp* **:** a knotgrass (*Polygonum aviculare*) common throughout the northern U.S. and southern Canada

**pinkwood** \ˈ=,=\ *n* [⁸*pink* & ⁹*pink* + *wood*] **1 :** any of several trees and shrubs: as **a :** a Brazilian tree (*Dicypellium caryophyllatum*) of the family Lauraceae with carnation-scented bark used as a substitute for cinnamon and cloves **b :** a tree (*Physocalymma scaberrimum*) of the family Lythraceae of central So. America having hard rose-colored wood **c :** an Australian tree (*Eucryphia billardieri*) yielding cabinet wood **d :** WALLABY BUSH **2 :** the wood of a pinkwood

**pinkwort** \ˈ=,=\ *n* [⁸*pink* + *wort*] **:** a plant of the family Caryophyllaceae

¹**pinky** \ˈpiŋkē, -ki\ *adj* -ER/-EST [⁹*pink* + -*y*] **:** being of a pink cast **:** tinged with pink ⟨~ beige wool —Lois Long⟩

²**pinky** *var of* PINKIE

**pin·less** \ˈpinləs\ *adj* **:** being without a pin

**pinlock** \ˈ=,=\ *n* **:** a lock having a pin over which the pipe of the key fits

**pinmaker** \ˈ=,==\ *n* **:** one who makes pins

**pin·man** \ˈpinmən, -ˌman, -aa(ə)n\ *n, pl* **pinmen :** BOWLER

**pin mark** *n* **1 :** a slight indentation in the side of a piece of foundry type made by the pin that pushes the type from the mold **2 :** the mark on the bottom of a piece of ceramic ware made by a pin supporting it during firing

**pin money** *n* **1 a :** money allotted by a man to his wife, daughter, or sister for her personal expenses esp. for clothes ⟨this man provides *pin money* in plenty for his daughter —W. J.Weston⟩ **b :** money used or set aside for the purchase of incidentals **:** POCKET MONEY ⟨selling . . . jam and things for *pin money* —Alice S. Rivoire⟩ **2 :** a trifling sum of money ⟨worked feverishly for what would look like *pin money* to modern . . . men —D.W.Maurer⟩

**pinn-** *or* **pinni-** *comb form* [L, fr. *pinna* feather, wing, fin] **:** feather **:** fin ⟨pinnal⟩ ⟨*Pinnipedia*⟩

¹**pin·na** \ˈpinə\ *n, pl* **pin·nae** \-ˌnē, -ˌnī\ *or* **pinnas** [NL, fr. L, feather, wing, alter. of *penna*] **1 :** a leaflet or primary division of a pinnate leaf or frond **2 a :** a feather, wing, or fin or some similar part **b :** the largely cartilaginous projecting portion of the external ear — called also *auricle*; see EAR illustration

²**pinna** \ˈ"\ *n* [NL, fr. L *pinna*, *pina* pen shell, fr. Gk *pinē*] **1** *cap* **:** the type genus of Pinnidae comprising large wedge-shaped bivalves that have thin shells with a toothless hinge and linear ligament and are attached to the substrate by a long silky byssus **2** *pl* **pinnas** *or* **pinnae :** PEN SHELL

**pin·nace** \ˈpinəs\ *n* -S [MF *pinace*, prob. fr. OSp *pinaza*, fr. *pino* pine, fr. L *pinus* — more at PINE] **1 a :** a light sailing ship that is often schooner-rigged but sometimes is propelled by oars and is used largely as a tender for a warship or other large craft **b :** a doublebanked boat of a warship; *also* **:** any of various ship's boats (as a man-of-war's steam launch) **2** *obs* **a :** WOMAN **b :** PROSTITUTE, MISTRESS

¹**pin·na·cle** \ˈpinəkəl, -nēk-\ *n* -S [ME *pinacle*, fr. MF, fr. LL *pinnaculum* gable, small wing, dim. of L *pinna* battlement, feather, wing, alter. of *penna* feather, wing — more at PEN] **1 :** an upright architectural member generally ending in a small spire and used esp. in Gothic construction to give additional weight to a buttress or an angle pier **:** FINIAL **2 :** a structure or formation suggesting a pinnacle's height and tapering slenderness; *specif* **:** a lofty peak ⟨three silent ~s of aged snow —Alfred Tennyson⟩ **3 :** the highest point of development or achievement **:** ACME ⟨men who . . . reached the ~ of their profession —*advt*⟩ ⟨on a ~ of happiness —Van Wyck Brooks⟩

²**pinnacle** \ˈ"\ *vt* **pinnacled; pinnacled; pinnacling** \-k(ə)liŋ\ **pinnacles 1 :** to surmount with a pinnacle ⟨~ a pediment⟩ **2 :** to raise or rear on or as if on a pinnacle ⟨desired not to be *pinnacled* . . . but to sink into the crowd —John Buchan⟩

**pin·na·globin** \ˌpinə+\ *n* [NL ²*Pinna* + E *globin*] **:** a brown respiratory pigment in the blood of a mollusk of the genus *Pinna* that is apparently similar to hemocyanin but contains manganese in place of copper

**pin·nal** \ˈpinᵊl\ *adj* [ISV *pinn-* + -*al*] **:** relating to a pinna

**pin·nate** \ˈpiˌnāt, -ˌnət, *usu* -d·+V\ *adj* [NL *pinnatus*, fr. L, feathered, winged, fr. *pinna* + -*atus* -ate] **1 :** resembling a feather esp. in having similar parts arranged on opposite sides of an axis like the barbs on the rachis of a feather — used esp. of compound leaves; see LEAF illustration **2 :** characterized by pinnate arrangement of parts ⟨~ veining⟩ — see VENATION illustration

**pin·nat·ed** \-ˌnād·əd\ *adj* [*pinnate* + -*ed*] **:** PINNATE — **pin·nat·ed·ly** *adv*

**pinnated grouse** *n* **:** PRAIRIE CHICKEN

**pin·nate·ly** *adv* **:** in a pinnate manner

**pinnati-** *comb form* [NL, fr. *pinnatus* pinnate] **:** pinnately ⟨*pinnatisect*⟩

**pin·nat·i·fid** \pəˈnadəˌfid\ *adj* [NL *pinnatifidus*, fr. *pinnati-* + L -*fidus* -fid] **:** cleft in a pinnate manner ⟨a ~ leaf⟩ — compare PALMATIFID — **pin·nat·i·fid·ly** *adv*

**pin·na·tion** \pəˈnāshən\ *n* -S **:** the state of being pinnate

**pin·nati·sect** \pəˈnadəˌsekt\ *adj* [*pinnati-* + -*sect*] **:** cleft pinnately to or almost to the midrib

**pinned** \ˈpind\ *adj* [partly fr. ¹*pin* + -*ed*, partly fr. past part. of ²*pin*] **:** having or fastened with a pin

¹**pin·ner** \ˈpinə(r)\ *n* -S [ME, fr. ¹*pin* + -*er*] *archaic* **:** PINMAKER

²**pinner** \ˈ"\ *n* -S [²*pin* + -*er*] *Brit* **:** POUNDMASTER

³**pinner** \ˈ"\ *n* -S [²*pin* + -*er*] **1 :** a woman's cap with long lappets worn in the 17th and 18th centuries; *also* **:** one of these lappets **2 :** one whose work is inserting or removing pins, placing on pins, or fastening with pins: as **a :** a hat assembler who cuts and pins brims **b :** a worker who sticks cookies on pins of a wire rack before dipping them into icing **c :** one who rivets the pins by which knife blades are attached to handles **3** [prob. by shortening & alter.] *dial* **:** PINAFORE **4 :** a small stone used to support a large stone in masonry construction

**pinni-** — see PINN-

**pin·ni·dae** \ˈpinəˌdē\ *n pl, cap* [NL, fr. *Pinna*, type genus + -*idae*] **:** a family of chiefly tropical marine bivalve mollusks (suborder Ostreacea) that live in bottom sediment — see PINNA

**pin·ni·gra·da** \ˌpinəˈgrād·ə\ [NL, fr. *pinn-* + -*grada* (fr. L, neut. pl. of -*gradus* going) — more at -GRADE] *syn of* PINNIPEDIA

¹**pin·ni·grade** \ˈ==,grād\ *adj* [NL *Pinnigrada*] **:** walking by means of fins or flippers

²**pinnigrade** \ˈ"\ *n* -S [NL *Pinnigrada*] **:** a pinnigrade animal

**pin·ning** \ˈpiniŋ, -nēŋ\ *n* -S [ME *pynnynge* action of fastening with pegs, fr. gerund of *pynnen*, *pinnen* to pin] **1 a :** a pin or peg for fastening; *also* **:** a fastening made by pins **b :** small stones for filling masonry interstices **c :** FOUNDATION, PROP, UNDERPINNING **2 :** adhesion of the tail of the young lamb to the body due to pasting up with sticky meconium preventing passage of feces **3 :** clogging of the teeth of a file by abraded material

**pinning block** *n* [*pinning* fr. gerund of ²*pin*] **:** a metal or wooden block with pinholes used as an aid in pinning and mounting insects

**pinning end** *n* [by alter. (influence of *pinning*, gerund of ²*pin*)] **:** GABLE END

**pinning forceps** *n* **:** small forceps usu. resembling dental forceps used for inserting insect pins in boxes

¹**pin·ni·ped** \ˈpinəˌped\ *adj* [NL *Pinnipedia*] **:** of or relating to the Pinnipedia

²**pinniped** \ˈ"\ *n* -S [NL *Pinnipedia*] **:** a mammal of the family Pinnipedia **:** SEAL, WALRUS

**pin·ni·pe·dia** \ˌ==ˈpēdēə\ *n pl, cap* [NL, fr. *pinn-* + *ped-* + -*ia*, n. pl. suffix] **:** a suborder of aquatic carnivorous mammals including all the seals and the walruses

**pin·nock** \ˈpinək\ *n* -S [origin unknown] *dial Eng* **:** a small bridge

**pin·no·ite** \ˈpinəˌwīt\ *n* -S [G *pinnoit*, fr. *Pinno*, 19th cent. Ger. mining official + G -*it* -ite] **:** a hydrous magnesium borate $Mg(BO_2)_2.3H_2O$ usu. occurring in yellow nodular masses with a radiating fibrous structure (hardness 3–4, sp. gr. 2.3)

**pin·no·the·res** \ˌpinəˈthi(ˌ)rēz\ *n, cap* [NL, fr. L *pinoteres*, *pinotheres* crab living in the mantle cavity of the pen shell, fr. Gk *pinotērēs*, fr. *pino-* (fr. *pinē* pen shell) + -*tērēs* (fr. *tērein* to guard) — more at PAIN] **:** a genus (the type of the family Pinnotheridae) of small crabs (as the oyster crab and the pea crab) having usu. a thin membranous covering and living as commensals in the mantle cavity of various bivalve mollusks or in some similar cavity in other marine animals

¹**pin·no·therid** \ˌ==ˈthirəd, -ther-\ *adj* [NL *Pinnotheridae*] **:** of or relating to the genus *Pinnotheres* or the family Pinnotheridae

²**pinnotherid** \ˈ"\ *n* -S [NL *Pinnotheridae* family of crabs, fr. *Pinnotheres*, type genus + -*idae*] **:** a crab of the genus *Pinnotheres* or the family Pinnotheridae

**pin·nu·la** \ˈpinyələ\ *n, pl* **pinnu·lae** \-ˌlē, -ˌlī\ [NL, fr. L, small feather, small fin, fr. *pinna* feather, wing, fin, alter. of *penna* feather, wing — more at PEN] **1 :** PINNULE 2, 3 **2 :** a barb of a feather — **pin·nu·lar** \-lə(r)\ *adj*

**pin·nu·late** \-ˌlāt, *usu* -ād·+V\ *or* **pin·nu·lat·ed** \-ˌād·əd\ *adj* [*pinnulate* fr. *pinnule* + -*ate*; *pinnulated* fr. *pinnulate* + -*ed*] **:** having pinnules

**pin·nule** *also* **pin·ule** \ˈpin(ˌ)yül\ *n* -S [NL *pinnula*, fr. L, small feather, small fin] **1 :** a small plate (as in an alidade) pierced with a peephole **2 a :** one of the secondary branches of a plumelike organ; *specif* **:** one of the lateral parts of the arm of a crinoid or of the tentacle of an alcyonarian polyp **b :** a small detached fish fin (as behind the dorsal and anal fins of the mackerel) **:** FINLET **3 :** a secondary pinna **:** one of the ultimate divisions of a bipinnate or twice-pinnate leaf

¹**pin·ny** \ˈpinē, -ni\ *adj* -ER/-EST [¹*pin* + -*y*] **1 :** containing hard specks — used esp. of metal **2 :** PINNED — used of a file **3 :** matted together — used of wool

²**pinny** \ˈ"\ *n* -ES [by shortening & alter.] **:** PINAFORE

**pin oak** *n* [so called fr. the persistence of the bases of dead branches which resemble pins driven into the trunk] **:** any of several American oaks (as a bastard oak or laurel oak); *esp* **:** a large symmetrical pyramidal oak (*Quercus palustris*) that is native to the northeastern U. S. but widespread in cultivation and has deeply pinnatifid leaves which turn brilliant red in the fall and rather small almost hemispherical acorns — called also *swamp oak*

**pin oat** *n* **:** a very slender oat kernel that is usu. borne as the higher secondary or tertiary grain in the spikelet

**pi·no·cam·phe·ol** \ˌpīnōˈkam(p)fēˌōl, -ˌōl\ *n* -S [*pinane* + -*o-* + *camph-* + connective -*e-* + -*ol*] **:** a crystalline bicyclic terpenoid alcohol $C_{10}H_{17}OH$ occurring in hyssop oil; 3-pinan-ol

**pinoche** *or* **pinochi** *var of* PENUCHE

**pi·noch·le** *also* **pi·noc·le** \ˈpēˌnəkəl *sometimes* -năk-\ *or* **pe·nuch·le** \ˈpēˌnək-\ *n* -S [perh. modif. of G dial. (Swiss) *binokel*, fr. F dial. (Swiss) *binocle*, fr. F *binocle* pince-nez, lorgnette, fr. obs. F *binocle*, adj., binocular, fr. NL *binoculus*, fr. *bin-* + L *oculus* eye — more at EYE] **:** a card game for two, three, four or sometimes more players played with a 48-card pack containing two each of A, K, Q, J, 10, 9, in which points are scored by melding combinations of cards and by taking cards in tricks; *also* **:** the meld of queen of spades and jack of diamonds scoring 40 points in this game

**pinochle rummy** *n* **:** FIVE HUNDRED RUM

**pino·cytosis** \ˌpinō, ˌpīnō+\ *n, pl* **pinocytoses** [NL, fr. *pino-* (fr. Gk *pinein* to drink) + *cyt-* + -*osis* — more at POTABLE] **:** the taking up of fluid by living cells

**pi·no·ki** \pəˈnōkē\ *n* -S *usu cap* **:** a dialect of Chiquitoan

**pi·nol** *or* **pi·nole** \ˈpīˌnōl, -ˌnōl\ *n* -S [ISV *pin-* (fr. *pinene*) + -*ole*] **:** a liquid cyclic ether $C_{10}H_{16}O$ that is obtained by oxidation of alpha-pinene

**pi·no·le** \pəˈnōlē\ *n* -S [AmerSp, fr. Nahuatl *pinolli*] **1 :** a finely ground flour made from parched corn **2 :** any of various flours resembling pinole and ground from the seeds of other plants (as mesquite beans or chia)

**pi·no·lin** *also* **pi·no·line** \ˈpīˈnōlən; ˈpīnᵊlˌēn, -ᵊlən\ *n* -S [ISV *pin-* (fr. L *pinus* pine) + -*ol* + -*in* or -*ine* — more at PINE] **:** ROSIN SPIRIT

**pi·ñon** \(ˈ)pēnˌyōn, ˈpinyən\ *n, pl* **piñons** \-ōnz,-ənz\ *or* **piño·nes** \pēnˈyōnēz\ [AmerSp *piñón*, fr. Sp, pine nut, fr. *piña* pinecone, fr. L *pinea* — more at PINEAL] **1** *or* **piñon pine a :** any of various low-growing nut pines (as *Pinus parryana*, *P. cembroides*, *P. edulis*, and *P. monophylla*) of western No. America **b :** the nut pine of Europe **2 :** the nutlike seed of a piñon pine used esp. in confectionery

**piñon bird** *or* **piñon jay** *n* **:** a bluish corvine bird (*Gymnorhinus cyanocephalus*) of western No. America that feeds on piñon nuts

**pi·non·ic acid** \pəˈnänik-\ *n* [*pinonic* ISV *pin-* (fr. *pinene*) + -*one* + -*ic*] **:** a crystalline keto acid $CH_3COC_6H_{10}CH_2COOH$ derived from dimethyl-cyclobutane and obtained by oxidation of alpha-pinene

**pi·no·syl·vin** \ˌpīnōˈsilvən\ *n* -S [ISV *pino-* (fr. NL *Pinus* — genus name of the Scotch pine *Pinus sylvestris* —, fr. L *pinus* pine) + *sylv-* (fr. NL *sylvestris* — specific epithet of the Scotch pine *Pinus sylvestris* —, fr. L *silvestris* of a forest, fr. *silva* forest) + -*in* — more at PINE] **:** a toxic phenolic compound $C_6H_5CH{=}CHC_6H_3(OH)_2$ related to stilbene that is found in the heartwood of Scotch pine and that gives protection to the wood against fungi, insects, and chemicals (as calcium bisulfite); 5-styryl-resorcinol

**pi·not** \(ˈ)pēˌnō\ *n* -S *usu cap* [F — more at PINARD] **1 :** any of several purple or white vinifera grapes grown chiefly in California and used esp. for wine-making **2 :** a wine made from Pinot grapes

**pinot blanc** \(ˌ)=ˌ=ˈblä\ *n, usu cap P&B* [F, white Pinot] **:** a white table wine of Chablis type produced in California from a white Pinot grape

**pinot chardonnay** *n, usu cap P&C* [F, Chardonnay Pinot] **:** CHARDONNAY

**pinot noir** \(ˌ)=ˌnōn(ə)ˈwär\ *n, usu cap P&N* [F, black Pinot] **:** a dry red table wine of Burgundy type produced in California from a purple Pinot grape

**pin pallet** *n* **:** an alarm clock lever escapement in which the pallet has upright pins instead of horizontally set jewels

**pinpatch** \ˈ=,=\ *n, dial Eng* **:** PERIWINKLE

**pin perforation** *n* **:** a roulette on a stamp made of pinpricks

¹**pinpoint** \ˈ=,=\ *n* [¹*pin* + *point*, n.] **1 a :** the point of a pin ⟨left impaled upon the ~ —Marcia Davenport⟩ **b :** a very small, infinitesimal, or very sharp point ⟨a ~ of rock —Wynford Vaughan-Thomas⟩ ⟨above the town ~s of light twinkled —Eric Ambler⟩ **2 a :** something that is relatively of very small size, scope, or importance ⟨at this one ~ in the heart of the wilderness —Walter O'Meara⟩ ⟨not a ~ of difference —*Irish Digest*⟩ ⟨his interests and ideals shrink to the ~s of the commonplace —H.A.Overstreet⟩ **b** (1) **:** a precisely identified point that locates a relatively small target, a place for rendezvous, or other strategic position or locality **:** the coordinates that define such a point ⟨fussy to a fault about anchoring on the precise ~ assigned —K.M.Dodson⟩ (2) **:** a target, installation, or other place on the ground thus located **:** a pinpoint target ⟨hit his ~⟩

²**pinpoint** \ˈ"\ *vt* **1 a :** to locate with great precision or accuracy ⟨can ~ the position of his aircraft within two miles —*Time*⟩ **b :** to make (something) a specific target of bombing, shelling, or air photography by means of precision instruments ⟨~*ed* oil refineries and other strategic installations⟩ **c :** to aim or direct with great precision or accuracy ⟨~ very heavy bombs on the most vulnerable point —J.W.Angell⟩ **2 a :** to fix, determine, or identify with precision ⟨hope to ~ promising young engineers by psychometric methods —W.H. Hale⟩ ⟨~ and define the procedural rights of a citizen —*New Republic*⟩ **b :** to cause to stand out conspicuously **:** HIGHLIGHT, EMPHASIZE ⟨~*ed* the obvious fact —Nona B. Brown⟩ ⟨scenes that were supposed to ~ delicate emotional balances —Cecile Starr⟩ **3 :** to punctuate with pinpoints of light ⟨the lights of their cigarettes ~*ed* the darkness —Robert De Vries⟩

³**pinpoint** \ˈ=ˈ=\ *adj* **1 a :** extremely fine or precise ⟨functions with ~ accuracy —*Progress Thru Research*⟩ ⟨~ localization of the foreign body —*Jour. Amer. Med. Assoc.*⟩ **b :** located or fixed with great precision or accuracy ⟨~ targets⟩ **c :** directed with extreme precision ⟨~ bombardment⟩ **d :** extremely detailed or specific ⟨a revulsion against ~ planning —A.M. Schlesinger b. 1917⟩ ⟨opposed to ~ price control —*N.Y. Herald Tribune*⟩ **2 :** small as a pinpoint ⟨little ~ creatures —Anthony Standen⟩ ⟨millions of ~ holes —T.R.Ybarra⟩

**pin-point clover** *n* **:** an annual clover (*Trifolium gracilentum*) of western No. America having long-peduncled heads of reddish purple or pink flowers

**pin pool** *n* **:** any of several varieties of billiards in which small wooden pins are used; *specif* **:** a game played with two white balls, one red ball, and five small pins that are set up in diamond fashion at the center of the table and have a value according to position

¹**pinprick** \ˈ=,=\ *n* [¹*pin* + *prick*, n.] **1 :** a small puncture made by or as if by a pin **2 :** a petty irritation or annoyance; *specif* **:** a small, irritating, and antagonistic action or statement that is often repeated for the purpose of annoying ⟨the action was viewed as another ~ —Walter Sullivan⟩

²**pinprick** \ˈ"\ *vt* **:** to administer pinpricks to ⟨~*ed* and heckled the socialist leaders —John Gunther⟩ ~ *vi* **:** to administer pinpricks

**pin punch** *n* **:** a punch used to dislodge rivets and pins

**pinrail** \ˈ=,=\ *n* **:** a rail or strip fitted with pins or for holding pins: as **a :** a rail that holds belaying pins; *esp* **:** one along the bulwarks **b :** a beam at one side of a theater stage through which wooden or metal pins are driven and to which lines from the flies are fastened

**pin rod** *n* **:** a rod or plate with turned ends for connecting two parts (as brake shoes on the opposite sides of a locomotive) so that they act kinematically as one part

**pin rot** *n* **:** a rot of the heartwood of incense cedar caused by a pore fungus (*Polyporus amarus*) — called also *peckiness*

**pins** *pl of* PIN, *pres 3d sing of* PIN

**pins and needles** *n pl* **:** a pricking tingling sensation in a limb recovering from numbness — **on pins and needles :** in a very nervous or jumpy state esp. as a result of some suspense-provoking situation ⟨*on pins and needles* while awaiting the doctor's verdict⟩

**pin seal** *n* [²*pin*] **:** leather made from a very young seal

**pinsetter** \ˈ=,==\ *n* **1 :** an employee of a bowling alley who clears away deadwood, sets up pins, and returns balls to players **2 :** a mechanical device in a bowling alley for spotting the pins simultaneously

**pinson** *n* -S *obs* [ME *pynson*, perh. fr. (assumed) MF *pinçon* pincers, fr. MF *pincier* to pinch — more at PINCH] **:** a thin shoe **:** SLIPPER

**pin·sons** \ˈpin(t)sənz\ *n pl* [ME *pynsons*, perh. fr. (assumed) MF *pinçons*, pl. of (assumed) MF *pinçon* pincers] *dial chiefly Eng* **:** PINCERS

**pin spanner** *n* **:** PIN WRENCH

**pinspot** \ˈ=,=\ *n* **:** each of the spots like pinheads often forming a pattern on a textile

**pinspotter** \ˈ=,==\ *n* **:** PINSETTER

**pinstripe** \ˈ=,=\ *n, often attrib* **:** a fine stripe on a fabric; *also* **:** a fabric made with such stripes

¹**pint** \ˈpīnt\ *n* -S *often attrib* [ME *pinte*, fr. MF, fr. ML *pincta*, fr. (assumed) VL *pincta*, fem. of (assumed) VL *pinctus* painted, alter. of L *pictus*, past part. of *pingere* to paint; prob. fr. the use of a painted mark on a container to point out its capacity — more at PAINT] **1 :** any of various units of capacity equal to ½ quart: as **a :** a U. S. unit for liquids equivalent to 28.875 cubic inches **b :** a U. S. dry unit equivalent to 33.600 cubic inches **c :** a British liquid or dry unit equivalent to 34.678 cubic inches — see MEASURE table **2 a :** a pint pot or vessel **b** *chiefly Brit* **:** a pint of ale, beer, or other beverage

²**pint** \ˈ"\ *dial var of* POINT

**pin·ta** \ˈpintə, ˈpēn-\ *n* -S [AmerSp, fr. Sp, spot, mark, fr. (assumed) VL *pincta*, fem. of (assumed) VL *pinctus* painted]

: a chronic skin disease endemic in tropical America that occurs successively as an initial papule, a generalized eruption of pintids, and a patchy loss of pigment, that chiefly affects dark-skinned people, and that is caused by a spirochete (*Treponema careteum*) morphologically indistinguishable from the causative agent of syphilis

**pin table** *n, Brit* : PINBALL MACHINE

**pin·ta·do** \pin·'tä(,)dō\ *n, pl* **pintados** *or* **pintadoes** [Pg, fr. past part. of *pintar* to paint, fr. (assumed) VL *pinctare*, fr. (assumed) VL *pinctus* painted] **1** : a painted or printed chintz formerly made in India **2** *or* **pintado petrel** : CAPE PIGEON **3** *or* **pin·ta·da** \- də\ [*pintado* fr. AmerSp, fr. Sp, past part. of *pintar* to paint, fr. (assumed) VL *pinctare; pintada* fr. AmerSp, fr. Sp, fem. of *pintado*, past part. of *pintar*] : CERO

**pin·ta·do·ite** \-dō,īt\ *n* -s [*Pintado* Canyon, San Juan county, southeast Utah + E *-ite*] : a hydrous calcium vanadate $Ca_2V_2O_7.9H_2O$ occurring in a green incrustation

**pintail** \'=,=\ *n, pl* **pintails** *or* **pintail** **1 a** *or* **pin-tailed duck** : a river duck (*Anas acuta*) of Europe, Asia, and No. America having central tail feathers markedly elongated in the male and the head and neck brown, the breast white, and the upper parts grayish **b** : RUDDY DUCK **2 a** *or* **pin-tailed chicken** : SHARP-TAILED GROUSE **b** : PIN-TAILED SANDGROUSE

**pin-tailed** \'=;=\ *adj* **1** : having a tapered tail with the middle feathers longest **2** : having the tail feathers spiny

**pin-tailed sandgrouse** *or* **pin-tailed grouse** *n* : a sand grouse (*Pterocles alchata*) of Europe and Africa having elongated middle tail feathers

**pin·ta·no** \pin·'tä(,)nō\ *n* -s [AmerSp] : SERGEANT MAJOR 4

**pin thorn** *n* : COCKSPUR THORN

**pin·tid** \'pintəd\ *n* -s [*pinta* + *-id*] : one of many initially reddish, then brown, slate blue, or black patches on the skin characteristic of the second stage of pinta

**pin·tle** \'pint<sup></sup>ᵊl\ *n* -s [ME *pintel* pintle, penis, fr. OE, penis; akin to OFris & MLG *pint* penis, OE *pinn* pin, peg — more at PIN] **1** : a usu. upright pivot pin (as of a hinge or a rudder) on which another part turns **2** : a hook at the rear of a limber to receive the lunette of a gun trail, caisson, or other vehicle when the gun is limbered

**pintle chain** *n* : a chain for sprocket wheels consisting of links fastened together by pintles

**pintle valve** *n* : a short extension of the needle-valve tip to facilitate control of fluid through the valve

**¹pin·to** \'pin·(,)tō, 'pēn·(,)-\ *n, pl* **pintos** *also* **pintoes** *often attrib* [AmerSp, fr. *pinto*, adj., spotted, mottled, fr. obs. Sp, fr. (assumed) VL *pinctus* painted — more at PINT] *chiefly West* : a spotted or calico horse or pony

**²pinto** \"\ *n* -s [AmerSp (esp. in the expression *mal del pinto* pinta), fr. *pinto*, adj., spotted, mottled] : PINTA

**pinto bean** *also* **pinto** *n* [AmerSp *pinto*, fr. *pinto*, adj., spotted, mottled] : a mottled bean that resembles the kidney bean in size and shape and is grown extensively in Colorado and in other southwestern states as a field bean for food and for stock feed

**pintoes** \'=,=\ *n pl* [¹*pin* + *toes*, pl. of *toe*] : toes that turn inward ⟨a horse with ~ is never liable to strike himself —Henry Wynmalen⟩

**pinto leaf** *n* : a virus disease of some cherries characterized by a blotchy mosaic pattern on the leaves

**pint pot** *n* : a pint-measure pot or drinking vessel usu. of pewter; *also* : such a pot full of beer, ale, or other beverage

**pints** *pl of* PINT

**pintsch gas** \'pinch-\ *n, usu cap P* [after Richard *Pintsch* †1919 Ger. inventor] : a compressed oil gas obtained by cracking gas oil, consisting chiefly of hydrocarbons and hydrogen, and formerly used in lighting railroad cars and buoys

**pint-size** \'=;=\ *or* **pint-sized** \'=;=\ *adj* : SMALL, DIMINUTIVE ⟨a *pint-size* but highly efficient adding machine —*New Yorker*⟩ ⟨horse carts drawn by *pint-sized* horses —R.A.Gunnison⟩

**pin tuck** *n* : a very narrow tuck

**pin tumbler** *n* : the part of a cylinder lock that in conjunction with others prevents motion unless the proper key is used — compare LEVER TUMBLER

**pin·tu·ra** \pin·'tu̇rə\ *n* -s [Sp, painting, fr. (assumed) VL *pinctura*, alter. (influenced by assumed VL *pinctus* painted) of L *pictura* — more at PICTURE] : a symbolic or hieroglyphic manuscript of Mexico with colored characters and figures

**pi·ñue·la** \,pēnyə'wālə\ *n* -s [AmerSp, fr. Sp *piña* pineapple, pinecone, fr. L *pinea* pinecone — more at PINEAL] : any of several bromeliads or aroids (as the pineapple and the pinguin) that are often epiphytic

**pin·u·late** \'pinyə,lāt, -lət\ *adj* [*pinulus* + *-ate*] : being or having the form of a pinulus

**pinule** *var of* PINNULE

**pin·u·lus** \'pinyələs\ *n, pl* **pinu·li** \-ə,lī\ [NL *pinulus, pinnulus*, alter. of *pinnula*] : a usu. pentact sponge spicule of which one ray projects either internally or externally from the sponge and develops numerous small spines

**¹pinup** \'=,=\ *n* -s [fr. *pin up*, v., fr. ²*pin* + *up*, adv.] : something that is fastened to a wall: as **a** : a photograph of a pinup girl ⟨sprinkled with blond ~s on the walls —A.W. Baum⟩ ⟨magazine ~s⟩ **b** : a lamp or other accessory that is attached to a wall

**²pinup** \'=,=\ *adj* **1** : of or relating to pinup girls ⟨those pictures . . . give producers the idea that I am the ~ type —*Irish Digest*⟩ **2** : designed for hanging upon a wall of a room ⟨a ~ lamp⟩

**pinup girl** *n* **1** : a girl whose physical charms, attractive personality, or other glamorous qualities make her a suitable subject of a photograph pinned up on an admirer's wall ⟨the worship of the movie hero and the *pinup girl* —J.M.Barzun⟩ ⟨has been the *pinup girl* of libidinous . . . undergraduates —Bennett Cerf⟩ **2** : PINUP a

**pi·nus** \'pīnəs\ *n, cap* [NL, fr. L, pine — more at PINE] : a large and economically important genus (the type of the family Pinaceae) of coniferous trees chiefly of north temperate regions, in former classifications including pines, firs, spruces, larches and hemlocks, now restricted to the true pines, and comprising trees with primary leaves that are early deciduous, secondary needlelike leaves that are borne usu. in fascicles of one to seven, and cones that consist of imbricated woody scales enclosing winged seeds

**pin valve** *n* : NEEDLE VALVE

**pin vise** *n* : a hand vise used (as by jewelers) for holding fine work

**pinwale** \'=;=\ *adj, of a fabric* : made with extremely narrow wales

**pinweed** \'=,=\ *n* **1** : an herb of the genus *Lechea* **2** : ALFILARIA

**¹pinwheel** \'=,=\ *n, often attrib* [¹*pin* + *wheel*, n.] **1** : a contrate gear wheel in which the teeth are cylindrical pins **2 a** : a toy consisting of lightweight vanes (as of paper or plastic) attached loosely to the end of a stick so that they revolve in a breeze **b** : a fireworks device in the form of a small wheel which when the fuse is lighted is made to spin by spouts of colored fire that shoot out tangentially at various points on the wheel **3** : a revolvable cylindrical box with pins on its inner surface used for washing and softening hides in warm water or other liquid

pinwheel 2 a

**²pinwheel** \"\ *vt* : to wash and soften (hides) in a pinwheel ~ *vi* : to revolve rapidly in the manner of a pinwheel

**pin-wing** \'=,=\ *vt* : PINION

**pin wire** *n* : wire from which pins are made

**pinworm** \'=,=\ *n* **1** : any of numerous small nematode worms that have the tail of the female prolonged into a sharp point, infest the intestines esp. the cecum of various vertebrates, and belong to the family Oxyuridae — see ENTEROBIASIS, OXYURIASIS **2** : any of several rather slender insect larvae that burrow in plant material; *specif* : TOMATO PINWORM

**pin wrench** *n* : a wrench having a projecting pin to enter a hole (as in a nut or cylinder) to make a hold

**pinxter** *usu cap, var of* PINKSTER

**pinxter flower** *also* **pinxter bloom** *or* **pinxter** *or* **pinkster flower** *n* [*pinxter, pinkster* fr. D *pinkster* Whitsuntide — more at PINKSTER] : a deciduous pink-flowered azalea (*Rhododendron nudiflorum*) native to rich moist woodlands of eastern No. America — called also *wild honeysuckle*

**¹pi·ny** \'pīnē, -ni\ *n* -ES [ME *piony* — more at PEONY] *dial* : PEONY

**²piny** \'pīnē, -ni\ *adj* -ER/-EST [³*pine* + *-y*] **1** : abounding in pines ⟨~ woods⟩ **2** : of, relating to, or characteristic of pine ⟨a ~ odor⟩

**pin·yo·ca** \pēn'yōkə\ *n* -s *usu cap* : a dialect of Chiquitoan

**pi·nyon** \(')pēn,yōn, 'pinyən\ *n* -s [AmerSp *piñón* — more at PIÑON] : PIÑON

**pinyon jay** *n* : PIÑON BIRD

**pinz·gau** \'pin(t)s,gau̇\ *or* **pinz·gau·er** \-au̇(ə)r\ *n* -s *usu cap* [*pinzgau* fr. *Pinzgau*, valley in western Austria; *pinzgauer* fr. G, lit., one that is of or comes from Pinzgau, fr. *Pinzgau* + G *-er*] : an Austrian breed of heavy draft horse; *also* : a horse of this breed

**PIO** *abbr* public information office; public information officer

**piobaireachd** *var of* PIBROCH

**pi·o·let** \,pēə'lā\ *n* -s [F, fr. F dial. (Valais canton, Switzerland & Piedmont), dim. of *piola* small ax, fr. (assumed) MF dial., fr. OProv, dim of *apcha, abcha* battle-ax, of Gmc origin; akin to OHG *happa* sickle, pruning knife — more at HASH] : a two-headed ice ax used in mountaineering (as in Switzerland)

**¹pion** *vi* -ED/-ING/-S [MF *pioner, pionner*, fr. *peon, pion* foot soldier, pioneer — more at PIONEER] *obs* : to dig or excavate as a pioneer

**²pi·on** \'pī,än\ *n* -s [by contr.] : PI-MESON

**¹pi·o·neer** \,pīə'ni(ə)r, -iə\ *n* -s [MF *pionier, pionnier*, fr. OF *peonier* foot soldier, fr. *peon, pion* foot soldier (fr. ML *pedon-, pedo*) + *-ier* -er — more at PAWN] **1 a** : a member of a military unit usu. of engineers equipped and trained esp. for road building, temporary bridging, demolitions **b** *obs* : one that excavates or undermines **2** : one that begins or helps develop something new and prepares a way for others to follow: **a** : a person or group that originates or helps open up a new line of thought or activity or a new method or technical development ⟨broke decidedly with the prevailing theological views and became the ~ of a new order —C.A.Dinsmore⟩ ⟨a ~ in oceanography⟩ ⟨a ~ in the development of radar⟩ **b** : one of the first to settle in a primitive territory : an early settler **3** *usu cap* : a member of the Russian Communist youth organization for boys and girls in the 10 to 16 year age group — compare KOMSOMOL, OCTOBRIST **4** : a plant or animal capable of establishing itself in a bare or barren area (as after a burn) and initiating a new ecological cycle **5** *or* **pioneer publisher** *usu cap both Ps* : a full-time worker of the Jehovah's Witnesses

**²pioneer** \"\ *adj* **1** : first of a kind : EARLIEST, ORIGINAL ⟨a ~ model improved by later inventions⟩ ⟨one of the ~ institutions in America for the education of young women —S.P. Chase & J.K.Snyder⟩ **2** : of or relating to a pioneer; *esp* : of, relating to, or characteristic of early settlers or their time ⟨~ days⟩ ⟨a ~ village⟩ ⟨~ conditions⟩ **3** : being a pioneer ⟨settled on the frontier as a ~ merchant⟩ ⟨the ~ exponent of ballet on ice —*Current Biog.*⟩ **4** *usu cap* : of or relating to a culture in the southwestern U. S. about the beginning of the Christian era characterized by a squarish semisubterranean house having an entrance passage and a roof supported by four posts, the beginning of agriculture and pottery, and cremation

**³pioneer** \"\ *vb* -ED/-ING/-S *vi* : to act as a pioneer : lead the way ⟨group which ~*ed* in the development of the modern art movement —*Current Biog.*⟩ ~ *vt* **1** : to open or prepare (as a way or region) for others to follow : EXPLORE ⟨Portugal, which had done so much to ~ the outer ocean —Marjory S. Douglas⟩ : SETTLE ⟨a climate that encouraged colonists to ~ the wilderness⟩ **2** : to originate or take part in the development of (as a new enterprise, course of action, or style) ⟨~ some of the first big natural-gas developments in north Texas —T.H.White b. 1915⟩ ⟨she ~*ed* the short haircut for women⟩ **3** : to lead safely : GUIDE

**pioneer day** *n, usu cap P&D* **1** : July 24 observed as a legal holiday in Utah in commemoration of the arrival of Brigham Young on the present site of Salt Lake City in 1847 **2** : June 15 formerly observed as a legal holiday in Idaho as the anniversary of the acceptance of the Oregon treaty by the president and the senate in 1846

**pioneer gold** *n* : PRIVATE GOLD

**pioneer tunnel** *or* **pioneer bore** *n* : a small tunnel parallel to a main tunnel and well in advance of the completed main tunnel so that by crosscuts to the line of the main tunnel several headings can be exposed and work expedited

**pioner** *obs var of* PIONEER

**pi·on·no·tal** \,pīə'nōd·ᵊl\ *adj* : producing pionnotes

**pi·on·no·tes** \,pīə'nōd·ēz\ *n pl but sing or pl in constr* [NL, prob. irreg. fr. Gk *piōn* fat + *nothos* spurious] : a smooth or tuberculate gelatinous layer of spores (as in fungi of the genus *Fusarium*)

**pi·o·ny** \'pīənē, pē'ōnē\ *archaic var of* PEONY

**¹pi·oph·i·lid** \(')pī,äfəlәd\ *adj* [NL *Piophilidae*] : of or relating to the Piophilidae

**²piophilid** \"\ *n* -s : a fly of the family Piophilidae

**pi·o·phil·i·dae** \,pīə'filə,dē\ *n pl, cap* [NL, fr. *Piophila*, type genus (fr. *pio-* fat — fr. Gk *piōn* — + *-phila*) + *-idae*; akin to Gk *pimelē* lard — more at FAT] : a family of two-winged flies including the cheese fly

**pi·os·i·ty** \pī'äsəd·ē\ *n* -ES [fr. *pious*, after such pairs as E *religious: religiosity*] : an exaggerated or superficial piousness : an obvious manifestation of devoutness

**pi·o·tine** \'pīə,tēn\ *n* -s [G *piotin*, fr. Gk *piotēs* fattiness (fr. *piōn* fat, fatty) + G *-in* -ine] : SAPONITE

**piou·piou** \pyüpyü\ *n* -s [F, fr. F (baby talk), small chicken, of imit. origin] *slang* : a French infantryman

**pioury** *var of* PIURI

**pi·ous** \'pīəs\ *adj* [L *pius*; akin to L *piare* to appease, atone for, Oscan *pihatu* appeased, and perh. to L *purus* pure — more at PURE] **1 a** : marked by or showing reverence for deity and zealous devotion to the duties and rites of religion : DEVOUT ⟨the ~ Jewish historian, who saw in Israel's exile God's punishment for sin —J.G.Frazer⟩ ⟨one society is genuinely ~, another is worldly-minded —A.L.Kroeber⟩ ⟨~ practices such as attendance at daily mass —T.F.McNally⟩ **b** : marked by conspicuous religiosity **c** : of, relating to, or suggesting the sacred or devotional as distinct from the profane or secular : RELIGIOUS ⟨~ papers devoted to the publication of . . . offerings made at sacred shrines —D.H.Wiest⟩ ⟨a ~ opinion⟩ ⟨a ~ hush in the atmosphere —Mary McCarthy⟩ **2** : marked by or showing loyal reverence for and faithfully performing the duties owed to a person or thing (as a family, school, cause) : DUTIFUL ⟨undertaking the ~ task of writing the life of an ancestor —*Times Lit. Supp.*⟩ ⟨took me to pay a ~ visit to my old school —A.T.Quiller-Couch⟩ ⟨hangs on to his ~ Marxianism —H.A.Overstreet⟩ **3** : perpetrated for a supposed good end ⟨often the gap between the old rule and the new was bridged by a ~ fraud of a fiction —B.N.Cardozo⟩ **4** : being or relating to a use that is legally a charitable use **5 a** : characterized by pretense at propriety, virtue, benevolence, or devotion : given to or intended for the concealment of real feelings or intentions : marked by sham or hypocrisy ⟨a world of arrogant acts accompanied by ~ disclaimers —Rosemond Tuve⟩ ⟨~ noble phrases about ideals which serve only to cover up . . . iniquity —M.R.Cohen⟩ **b** : marked by politic or self-conscious virtue : VIRTUOUS ⟨sick of your ~ penny-pinching —Marcia Davenport⟩ ⟨put on ~ expressions and were altogether very superior, if not stuffy —Edison Marshall⟩ **6** : deserving commendation : COMMENDABLE, WORTHY ⟨the ~ practice of sifting the past twelve months' new books for gold —W.T.Scott⟩; *specif* : displaying an ideal, a benevolent wish, or a good intention ⟨international law was scoffed at as ~ but impotent —W.E.Jackson b. 1919⟩ ⟨a ~ hope⟩ ⟨~ platitudes⟩ **syn** see DEVOUT

**pi·ous·ly** *adv* : in a pious manner : with a pious motive or intention ⟨~ reminded them of their duty⟩ ⟨knelt ~ at the shrine⟩

**pi·ous·ness** *n* -ES : the quality or state of being pious

**¹pip** \'pip\ *n* -s [ME *pippe*, fr. MD *pip, pippe* nasal mucus, slime, pip; akin to OHG *pfiffiz, pfiffiz* pip; both fr. a prehistoric WGmc word borrowed fr. (assumed) VL *pipita*, alter. of L *pituita* nasal mucus, phlegm, pip; akin to OIr *ith* grain, Skt *pitu* drink, food, L *opimus* fat, fertile — more at FAT] **1 a** : the formation of a scale or crust on the tip and dorsal surface of the tongue of a bird often associated with respiratory diseases **b** : the scale or crust itself **2 a** : any of various ailments formerly or locally identified as syphilis, dyspepsia, a slight cough, or other ailment **b** : a fit of peevishness or feeling out of sorts : a slight nonspecific disorder : mild malaise — usu. used with *the* ⟨gives me the ~, the way some of them make a fuss about it —Dorothy Sayers⟩

**²pip** \"\ *n* -s [alter. of earlier *peep*, of unknown origin] **1 a** : one of the dots used on dice and dominoes to indicate numerical value **b** : SPOT 3c(1) **2 a** : SPOT, SPECK, PROTUBERANCE **b** : an image in the form of an inverted V or a spot of light on a radarscope or sonar screen indicating the return of radar or sound waves reflected from an object : BLIP **c** : an inverted V on the line of a graph **3 a** : the individual rootstock of the lily of the valley producing leaves and a flower stalk **b** : any of various other dormant roots or rootstocks (as of peonies and anemones) **4** : one of the segments forming the surface of a pineapple **5** : a star worn to indicate rank (as by a second lieutenant, lieutenant, or captain) in the British army ⟨the three ~s of a captain⟩

**³pip** \"\ *vb* **pipped; pipped; pipping; pips** *vt* **1** *Brit* : BLACKBALL **2** *Brit* : DEFEAT ⟨*pipped* his opponent in the race⟩ **3** *Brit* : KILL ~ *vi* : DIE — sometimes used with *out*

**⁴pip** \"\ *n* -s [short for *pippin*] **1** : a small fruit seed; *esp* : a seed of a fleshy fruit (as the orange, apple, pear) having several seeds **2** *slang* : something extraordinary of its kind : PIPPIN ⟨the gal's a ~ and I'm going to marry her —Ring Lardner⟩ ⟨created a traffic jam that was a ~ —Emmett Kelly⟩

**⁵pip** \"\ *vb* **pipped; pipped; pipping; pips** [imit.] *vi* **1** : PEEP 1 **2 a** *of a hatching bird* : to break through the shell of the egg **b** *of an egg* : to break open from pipping ~ *vt* : to break open (the shell of an egg) in hatching

**⁶pip** \"\ *n* -s [imit.] : a short high-pitched tone produced as a signal ⟨broadcast six ~s as a time signal⟩

**pi·pa** \'pēpə\ *n* [D, fr. Galibi] **1** -s : SURINAM TOAD **2** *cap* [NL, fr. D *pipa*] : a genus of toads comprising solely the Surinam toad

**pi-pa** \'pē'pä\ *n* -s [Chin (Pek) *p'i² p'a²*] : a 4-stringed Chinese musical instrument plucked like a guitar and having a large body resembling a lute and a neck with 12 or more frets that leads into the body

**pip·able** \'pīpəbəl\ *adj* : capable of being piped

**pip·age** *or* **pipe·age** \'pīpij\ *n* -s [¹*pipe* + *-age*] **1 a** : the transportation of natural gas, petroleum, or water by means of pipes **b** : the charge for such transportation **2** : PIPING, PIPES

**pi·pal** *or* **pipal tree** *or* **pi·pul** *or* **pee·pul** *also* **pee·pal** \'pēpəl\ *n* -s [Hindi *pīpal*, fr. Skt *pippala*] : a fig (*Ficus religiosa*) of India remarkable for its great size and longevity, useful as a source of lac, and distinguished from the banyan by the absence of prop roots — called also *sacred fig*

**pip card** *n* : SPOT CARD 2

**¹pipe** \'pīp\ *n* -s *often attrib* [ME, fr. OE *pīpa*; akin to OFris *pipe* pipe, OS *pīpa*, OHG *pfīfa*, all fr. a prehistoric WGmc word derived fr. (assumed) VL *pipa*, back-formation fr. L *pipare* to peep, chirp, of imit. origin like Gk *pipos, pippos* young bird, Skt *pippakā*, a kind of bird] **1 a** (1) : a wind instrument consisting of a tube of straw, reed, wood, or metal (as a flageolet, oboe) — compare PANPIPE, PITCH PIPE, SHEPHERD'S PIPE; *specif* : a small fipple flute held in and played by the left hand leaving the right hand free for beating a tabor — called also *tabor pipe* (2) : one of the open or closed tubes comprising the stops of a pipe organ — compare FLUE PIPE, REED PIPE (3) : BOATSWAIN'S PIPE (4) : BAGPIPE — usu. used in pl. **b** (1) : VOICE, VOCAL CORD — usu. used in pl. ⟨a soloist with a powerful set of ~s⟩ (2) : PIPING 1 ⟨their voices came in a shallow unison ~ —*Time*⟩ ⟨helped him with his first ~s on the flute —H.S. Canby⟩ **2 a** : a long hollow cylinder (as of metal, clay, concrete, plastic) used for conducting a fluid, gas, or finely divided solid and for structural purposes; *typically* : metal tubing in standard diameters and lengths threaded at the ends for joining and used for water, steam, and other conduits **b** *chiefly dial* : a canal or vessel of the body (as of the respiratory organs) — usu. used in pl. ⟨cleared her ~s and began to sing⟩ **c** *slang* : a coaxial cable used to transmit television or telephone signals **3 a** : a tubular or cylindrical object, part, or passage: as (1) : the tubular stem of a plant — compare PIPE TREE (2) : BURROW (3) : the hollow part of a pipe key (4) : BLOWPIPE 4 (5) : isinglass dried in the form of long hollow pieces (6) : PLAYPIPE **b** : a roughly cylindrical and vertical geological formation ⟨a firn ~⟩ ⟨a sand ~⟩: as (1) : an elongated vertical or steeply inclined body of ore (2) : one of the vertical cylindrical masses of volcanic agglomerate in which diamonds occur in So. Africa (3) : the eruptive channel opening into the crater of a volcano; *also* : the filling of such a channel (4) : the vent of a geyser **c** : a cavity in a casting (as an ingot of steel) due to unequal contraction on solidifying **d** : a small rounded molder's trowel for dressing up concave surfaces **4** : a former department of the British Exchequer charged with drawing up the pipe rolls **5** [ME, fr. MF, pipe, cask, fr. (assumed) VL *pippa*, alter. of *pipa*] **a** : a large cask of varying capacity used esp. for wine and oil **b** : any of various units of liquid capacity based on the size of a pipe; *esp* : a unit equal to 2 hogsheads **6 a** : a device usu. consisting of a tube having a bowl at one end and a mouthpiece at the other and used for smoking ⟨tobacco ~⟩ **b** : PIPEFUL **7** : any of the channels of a decoy **8 a** : a distance (as three quarters of a mile) customarily traveled in colonial New York while smoking one pipeful **b** : a distance (as six miles) customarily traveled by voyageurs or dogsledders between rests **9** *slang* **a** : PIPE DREAM ⟨might turn in a story about a sea serpent . . . but I haven't got the nerve to try 'em with a ~ like this —O.Henry⟩ **b** : something easy : SNAP ⟨both think acting on the show is a ~ —*Newsweek*⟩ **c** : something sure : CINCH ⟨a play . . . that is at least a ~ and as certain to make a fortune for anyone who invests in it as anything reasonably can be —G.S.Kaufman⟩

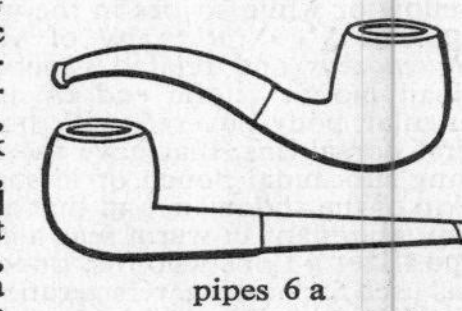

pipes 6 a

**²pipe** \"\ *vb* -ED/-ING/-S [partly fr. ME *pipen* to play on a pipe, fr. OE *pīpian*, fr. *pīpe*, n.; partly fr. ¹*pipe*] *vi* **1 a** : to play on a pipe (as a bagpipe) ⟨we *piped* to you, and you did not dance —Mt 11:17 (RSV)⟩ **b** : to convey orders by signals on a boatswain's pipe **2 a** : to speak in a high or shrill voice ⟨a thin call *piped* from the house, and he turned to wave —Ellen Glasgow⟩ ⟨his shrill voice *piped* above the hot volume of American jazz —Scott Fitzgerald⟩ **b** : to emit or have a shrill sound like that of a pipe : WHISTLE ⟨wind began to ~ around the stacks, not loud —Warren Eyster⟩ ⟨tree frogs ~ . . . before the rain —Marjory S. Douglas⟩ **3** *slang* : WEEP **4** : to become pipy **5** : to develop cavities in the interior during solidification — used esp. of cast steel ~ *vt* **1 a** : to play (a tune) on a pipe (as a bagpipe) **b** : to utter in the shrill tone of a pipe ⟨a robin . . . *piping* a few querulous notes —Washington Irving⟩ **2 a** : to cause to go or be with pipe music ⟨men of Scotland who've *piped* their men into battle —Wynford Vaughan-Thomas⟩ **b** (1) : to call or direct by the boatswain's pipe ⟨*piped* all hands on deck⟩ (2) : to receive aboard or attend the departure of from a naval vessel with side boys and piping the side ⟨~ the admiral aboard⟩ **3** : to make slips or cuttings of for propagation **4** : to trim with piping ⟨the edge of the white jacket was *piped* with navy⟩ **5** : to throw water upon from a hydraulic pipe : wash with a pipe **6** : to furnish or equip (as a building) with pipes **7 a** : to convey by means of pipes ⟨~ water from the standpipe into every house⟩ **b** : to convey as if by pipes ⟨every bit of talk in that town is *piped* into his ears —W.L.Gresham⟩; *specif* : to transmit (as current, a radio or television program) by wire or coaxial cable ⟨~ electricity from the dam to the cities⟩ ⟨~ music into restaurants, stores, and factories⟩ ⟨~ the telecast to all network stations⟩ **8** *slang* : to look at : NOTICE ⟨slapped their wrists when they *piped* the red long johns —H.D.Schwartz⟩ **9** : to put (cookie dough, frosting) on a cookie sheet or baked goods by forcing through a pastry tube **10** : to make cavities in (as

an ingot of steel) during casting — **pipe one's eye** *Brit* : WEEP — **pipe the side** : to sound on a boatswain's pipe a ceremonial signal when a commissioned officer or high official comes aboard or leaves a naval vessel
**pipeage** *var of* PIPAGE
**pipe amygdule** *n* : an elongated nodule resembling a tube in an amygdaloid
**pipe–band** \ˈ=,=\ *n* : a band of bagpipers ⟨a Scottish *pipe-band*⟩
**pipe beetle** *n* : SNOUT BEETLE
**pipe berth** *or* **pipe cot** *n* : a berth of canvas in a pipe frame that can swing up or down when not in use
**pipe clay** *n* : highly plastic and fairly pure clay of a grayish white color used in making tobacco pipes, in calico printing, for marking and scouring, and for whitening leather — called also *ball clay*
**pipe–clay** \ˈ=,=\ *vt* -ED/-ING/-S [*pipe clay*] **1** : to whiten or clean with pipe clay ⟨*pipe-clay* shoes or helmets⟩ **2** : to put in order : clean up ⟨*pipe-clay* accounts⟩
**pipe–clay·ey** \ˈ=,=ē, -i\ *adj* [*pipe clay* + *-y*] : PIPE-CLAYISH
**pipe–clay·ish** \-ish,-ēsh\ *adj* [*pipe clay* + *-ish*] **1** : manifesting cleanliness or spruceness **2** : formally and stiffly military (as in appearance, manner)
**pipe cleaner** *n* : something used to clean the inside of a pipe; *specif* : a piece of flexible wire in which tufted fabric is twisted and which is used to clean the stem of a tobacco pipe
**pi·pec·o·line** \pīˈpekə,lēn, pəˈp-, -,lən\ *n* -S [ISV, blend of *picoline* and *-pe-*] : any of the three liquid monoethyl derivatives $CH_3C_5H_9NH$ of piperidine
**pipe covering** *n* : insulating material applied around a pipe to prevent heat exchange between contents and the surroundings
**pipe cutter** *n* : a tool or machine for cutting pipe; *specif* : a hand tool comprising a grasping device and three sharp-edged wheels forced inward by screw pressure that cut into the pipe as the tool is rotated

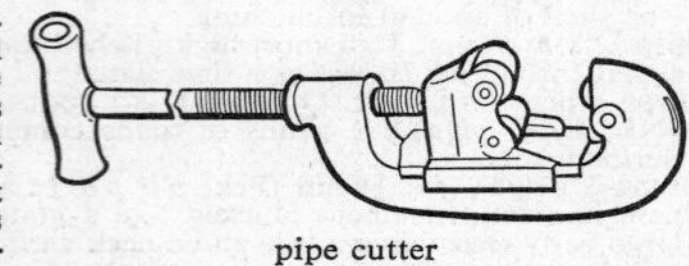
pipe cutter

**piped** \ˈpīpt\ *adj* [¹*pipe* + *-ed*] **1** *of leather* : having small pipelike wrinkles when flexed **2** *of a tailored seam* : finished with a binding to prevent raveling **3** *slang* : INTOXICATED
**pipe dance** *n* : CALUMET DANCE
**pipe die** *n* : a screw-thread die for cutting pipe threads
**pipe down** *vi* **1** : to dismiss sailors from an activity by a pipe call **2** : to become quiet : stop talking
**pipe dream** *n* [so called fr. the fantasies brought about by the smoking of opium] : an illusory or fantastic plan, hope, or story
**piped rot** *n* : a decay of oak and chestnut caused by a fungus (*Stereum hirsutum*) and characterized by the appearance of yellow or white stripes in the wood
**pipefish** \ˈ=,=\ *n* : any of various long slender fishes of *Syngnathus* and related genera that are distinguished by a small mouth at the end of an elongate tubular snout, an angular body covered with bony plates, and no pelvic and first dorsal fins, that have the eggs hatched by the male in a long subcaudal pouch or in some cases in depressions in the skin of the abdomen, and that are nearly cosmopolitan but are esp. abundant in warm seas among seaweeds
**pipe fitter** *n* : one who fits, threads, installs, and repairs piping (as used for heating, refrigerating, or air-conditioning systems)
**pipe fitting** *n* **1** : a piece (as a coupling or an elbow) used for connecting pipe lengths or as accessory to a pipe **2** : the work of a pipe fitter
**pipe·ful** \ˈpīp,fu̇l\ *n* -S : a quantity of tobacco smoked in a pipe at one time
**pipe grip** *n* **1** : PIPE WRENCH **2** : CHAIN TONGS
**pipe hanger** *n* : a bracket, clamp, clip, or loop used to suspend pipes (as from ceilings, overhead beams)
**pipe in** *vt* : to put in a word
**pipe–joint cement** *n* : a cement (as a mixture of red lead with linseed oil in a thick paste) for making a pipe joint impervious to leakage — compare DIAMOND CEMENT
**pipe key** *n* : a bit key having a hollow barrel that fits over a stem in the lock — called also *barrel key*
**pipelayer** \ˈ=,=\ *n* : one that lays conducting pipe (as for water or gas)
**pipe·less** \ˈpīpləs\ *adj* : having no pipe
**pipeless furnace** *n* : a furnace with but a single short pipe to connect it with the space to be heated
**pipe light** *n* : a twisted or folded paper used to light a pipe
**pipelike** \ˈ=,=\ *adj* : resembling a pipe or piping
¹**pipeline** \ˈ=,=\ *n* [¹*pipe* + *line*] **1** : a line of pipe connected to pumps, valves, and control devices for conveying liquids, gases, or finely divided solids **2** : a direct channel for receiving information from an inside source or for conveying messages ⟨a news ~ from the mayor's office⟩ **3** : the processes (as of transportation) through which supplies pass between the source and the user ⟨the Army estimates it will take . . . five months to activate its equipment ~ —*Newsweek*⟩
²**pipeline** \"\ *vt* : to convey by a pipeline ~ *vi* : to construct a pipeline
**pipe·lin·er** \ˈ=,=ə(r)\ *n* **1** : one of a crew who build and maintain pipelines and pumping stations **2** : a leader in the pipeline industry
**pipeline run** *n* **1** : the quantity of oil transported from one point to another by a pipeline **2** : the quantity of oil delivered by a producer to the pipeline **3** : the quantity of oil delivered by a pipeline
**pipe major** *n* : the principal player in a band of bagpipes
**pipe·man** \ˈpīpmən\ *n, pl* **pipemen 1** : one whose work is installing or repairing conduit pipes **2** : one who holds the nozzle of a hose or pipe and directs its play **3** : one who inspects and repairs the air brakes of railroad cars
**pipe metal** *n* : an alloy of tin and lead and sometimes zinc for making organ pipes
**pip em·ma** \(ˈ)pip-ˈemə\ *adv* [fr. Brit. signalmen's telephone pronunc. of *P.M.*] *Brit* : after noon
**pipe of peace** : CALUMET
**pipe–opener** \ˈ=,=(=)=\ *n* **1** *Brit* : a walk or other exercise in the open to get fresh air in the lungs **2** : a practice game or trial preliminary to a contest
**pipe organ** *n* : ORGAN 1b (1) — compare REED ORGAN
**pipe plant** *n* : INDIAN PIPE
¹**pip·er** \ˈpīpə(r)\ *n* -S [in sense 1, fr. ME, one that plays a pipe, fr. OE *pīpere*, fr. *pīpan* to play a pipe + *-ere* -er; in other senses, partly fr. ¹*pipe* + *-er*; partly fr. ²*pipe* + *-er* — more at PIPE] **1 a** : one that plays on a pipe (as a bagpipe) **b** : a young pigeon **c** [so called fr. the piping sound it makes when caught] : a European gurnard (*Trigla lyra*) having a large head with prominent nasal projections **2** : a maker, layer, or repairer of pipes ⟨a water ~⟩ **3** : a caddisworm that lives in a piece of reed **4** : a mine fissure from which gas is discharged **5 a** : a sewing machine attachment for applying piping **b** : a worker who pipes garments, shoes, or other articles
²**piper** \ˈpīpə(r), ˈpip-\ *n, cap* [NL, fr. L, pepper — more at PEPPER] : a very large genus (the type of the family Piperaceae) of tropical plants comprising the true peppers and being mostly climbing jointed shrubs with entire stipulate leaves and baccate fruit — see BETEL, BLACK PEPPER
**piper·a·ce·ae** \,pipəˈrāsē,ē, ,pīp-\ *n pl, cap* [NL, fr. *Piper*, type genus + *-aceae*] : a family of tropical plants (order Piperales) having aromatic herbage, minute naked spicate flowers, and one-celled ovary — **piper·a·ceous** \ˌ=ˈ=ˈrāshəs\ *adj*
**pipe rack** *n* **1** : a rack for pipes **2** : a rack (as for garments in a store) made of piping
**piper·a·les** \,=ˈ=ˈrā(,)lēz\ *n pl, cap* [NL, fr. *Piper* + *-ales*] : an order of apetalous dicotyledonous plants constituting the families Piperaceae, Saururaceae, and Chloranthaceae and having simple leaves and minute flowers in spikes with the perianth simple or lacking

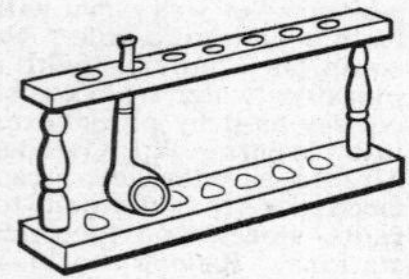
pipe rack 1

**piper·a·zine** \pīˈperə,zēn, pəˈp-, ˈpipər-\ *n* -S [ISV, blend of *piperidine* and *az-*] **1** : a crystalline heterocyclic base $C_4H_{10}N_2$ or $C_4H_{10}N_2.6H_2O$ obtained usu. by the action of ammonia on ethylene dibromide or ethylene dichloride or by reduction of pyrazine and used in medicine esp. as an anthelmintic; hexahydro-pyrazine **2** : a derivative of piperazine — compare DIKETOPIPERAZINE
**pipe reamer** *n* : a fluted conical tool for beveling or removing burrs from pipe ends
**pi·per·ic acid** \(ˈ)pīˌperik-, pəˈp-\ *n* [ISV *piper-* (fr. L *piper* pepper) + *-ic* — more at PEPPER] : a crystalline unsaturated acid $(CH_2O_2)C_6H_3(CH{=}CH)_2COOH$ formed by hydrolysis of piperine
**pip·er·idge** \ˈipərij\ *var of* PEPPERIDGE
**pi·per·i·dide** \pīˈperə,dīd, pəˈp-, -rədəd\ *n* -S [*piperidine* + *-ide*] : an amide of which piperidine is the amine constituent : an *N*-acyl derivative of piperidine
**pi·per·i·dine** \-,dēn, -dᵊn\ *n* -S [ISV, blend of *piperine* and *-ide*] : a liquid heterocyclic base $C_5H_{10}NH$ having a peppery ammoniacal odor that is obtained usu. by hydrolysis of piperine or by reduction of pyridine; hexahydro-pyridine — compare CONHYDRINE, CONIINE
**pip·er·ine** \ˈpipə,rēn, -,rən\ *n* -S [ISV *piper-* (fr. L *piper* pepper) + *-ine* — more at PEPPER] : a crystalline alkaloid $C_{17}H_{19}NO_3$ that is an active constituent of various kinds of pepper and that on hydrolysis yields piperidine and piperic acid
**pi·per·i·tone** \pīˈperə,tōn, pəˈp-\ *n* -S [ISV *piperit-* (fr. NL *piperita* — specific epithet of *Eucalyptus piperita* —, fr. L *piper* pepper + *-ita*, fem. of *-itus* -ite) + *-one* — more at PEPPER] : a liquid unsaturated cyclic ketone $C_{10}H_{16}O$ of camphoraceous odor found in various essential oils and used chiefly in making menthol and thymol; 1-*p*-menthen-3-one
**pip·er·ly** \ˈpīpə(r)lē\ *adj* : resembling or befitting a strolling piper : TRIVIAL, WORTHLESS
**pi·per·o·caine** \pīˈperə,kān, pəˈp-\ *n* -S [*piperidine* + *cocaine*] : a base $C_6H_5COO(CH_2)_3(NC_5H_9)CH_3$ derived from piperidine and benzoic acid and used in the form of its crystalline hydrochloride as a topical, infiltration, and spinal anesthetic
**pipe–rock** \ˈ=,=\ *n* : sedimentary rock containing scolites
**pip·er·oid of ginger** \ˈpipə,rȯid-\ [L *piper* pepper + E *-oid*] : an oleoresin prepared by extracting ginger with ether and removing the solvent by evaporation
**pipe roll** *n* **1** : one of the annual rolls containing the statements of the accounts of the king's revenue and various expenses and other matters affecting the British public treasury and dating from 1131 to 1833 **2** : a roller for supporting a pipe without restraining its longitudinal movement caused by expansion and contraction
**piper·o·nal** \pīˈperə,nal, pəˈp-; ˈpipər-\ *n* -S [ISV *piperine* + *-one* + *-al*] : a crystalline aldehyde $(CH_2O_2)C_6H_3CHO$ that has an odor like that of the heliotrope, that is obtained usu. by oxidation of piperic acid or isosafrole, and that is used chiefly in perfumery, cosmetics, and soaps; 3,4-methylenedioxybenzaldehyde — called also *heliotropin*
**pipe·o·nyl** \pīˈperənᵊl, pəˈp-; ˈpipərə,nil\ *n* -S [ISV *piperonal* + *-yl*] : the univalent radical $(CH_2O_2)C_6H_3CH_2$ of piperonyl alcohol; 3,4-methylenedioxy-benzyl
**piperonyl alcohol** *n* : a crystalline alcohol $(CH_2O_2)C_6H_3CH_2OH$ obtained by reduction of piperonal
**piperonyl butoxide** *n* : an insecticide $C_{19}H_{30}O_5$ derived from piperonyl alcohol and the butyl ether of diethylene glycol; *also* : an oily liquid containing this compound and related compounds used chiefly as a synergist (as for pyrethrum insecticides)
**piperonyl cyclonene** *n* : an insecticide containing as its principal components two ketones derived from cyclohexenone and related to piperonyl alcohol and used chiefly as a synergist
**piper·o·nyl·ic acid** \(ˌ)pīˌperˌəˌnilik-, pəˌperˌ, ˌpipərˌ\ *n* [ISV *piperonyl* + *-ic*] : a crystalline acid $(CH_2O_2)C_6H_3COOH$ obtained by oxidation of piperonal
**pip·er·oxan** \ˌpipər+\ *n* -S [*piperidene* + *oxan*, a gas, CNO, fr. ¹*ox-* + *-ane*] : an adrenolytic drug $C_{14}H_{19}NO_2$ containing both a piperidine and a benzodioxan nucleus used in the form of its crystalline hydrochloride to detect the presence of epinephrine-producing tumors by the transient fall in blood pressure it produces
**pipers news** *n, chiefly Scot* : already familiar news
**piper·y·lene** \pīˈperə,lēn, pəˈp-; ˈpipər-\ *n* -S [ISV *piperidine* + *-ylene*] : an oily diolefin hydrocarbon $CH_3CH{=}CHCH{=}CH_2$ isomeric with isoprene formed in the cracking of petroleum and also made synthetically (as by exhaustive methylation of piperidine); 1,3-pentadiene
¹**pipes** *pl of* PIPE, *pres 3d sing of* PIPE
²**pipes** \ˈpīps\ *n pl but sing or pl in constr* [fr. pl. of ¹*pipe*] : SCOURING RUSH
**pipe–stap·ple** \ˈpīp,stapəl\ *n* -S *Scot* : the stem of a tobacco pipe
**pipestem** \ˈ=,=\ *n* **1** : something like the stem of a tobacco pipe; *specif* : a very thin arm or leg **2** : any of several slender-stemmed plants: as **a** : FETTERBUSH **b** *also* **pipestem clematis** : a clematis (*Clematis lasiantha*) of California
**pipe still** *n* : a distillation apparatus composed of a series of pipes used esp. for petroleum oils and tar
**pipestone** \ˈ=,=\ *n* : a pink or mottled pink-and-white argillaceous stone carved by the Indians into tobacco pipes — compare CATLINITE
**pipe stop** *n* : an organ stop composed of flue pipes
**pipe tap** *n* : a tap for forming pipe threads
**pipe thimble** *n* : THIMBLE 2b
**pipe thread** *n* : a screw thread used on pipe and pipe fittings characterized by a somewhat fine pitch and usu. a tapering diameter
**pipe tomahawk** *n* : a tomahawk with a bowl in the head for use as a pipe (as in formal peace ceremonies) — compare CALUMET
**pipe tongs** *n* : a crude form of pipe wrench — compare CHAIN TONGS
**pipe tree** *n* **1** : any of various shrubs having twigs formerly used for pipe stems: as **a** : LILAC **b** : ELDER **c** : MOCK ORANGE **2** : CATALPA
¹**pi·pette** *also* **pi·pet** \(ˈ)pīˌpet *sometimes* pəˈp-; *usu* -ed·+V\ *n* -S [F *pipette*, dim. of *pipe* — more at PIPE (cask)] **1** : a small piece of apparatus with which fluids are transferred, measured, or absorbed (as in chemical operations) and which in the simplest form consists of a narrow glass tube into which the liquid is drawn up by suction and in which it is retained by closing the upper end — compare BURETTE, DROPPER 4a **2** : a funnel-shaped arrangement inserted near the middle of a barometer with the small end down to prevent air bubbles from rising to the top
²**pipette** *also* **pipet** \"\ *vt* **pipetted; pipetted; pipetting; pipettes** *also* **pipets** : to transfer, draw off, measure, or apply with a pipette
**pipe turner** *n* : one of two or more workers who take sections of green pipe from the press, turn them socket end up, and put them on a truck for removal
**pipe up** *vi* **1** : to begin to play (as on a pipe) or to sing or speak ⟨a few of us would like to *pipe up* . . . against this —C.E.Montague⟩ **2** *of the wind* : to increase in strength
**pipe vine** *n* : a climbing plant of the genus *Aristolochia*; *esp* : DUTCHMAN'S-PIPE
**pipe-vine swallowtail** *n* : an American butterfly (*Battus philenor*) having bluish green, pale-spotted wings and larvae that feed on the Dutchman's-pipe — called also *philenor butterfly*
**pipe vise** *n* : a vise shaped to hold pipe for threading, cutting, or reaming

pipettes 1: *1* dropper, *2* volumetric or transfer pipette, *3* absorption pipette

**pipewalker** \ˈ=,=\ *n* : a watchman who patrols a pipeline
**pipewood** \ˈ=,=\ *n* **1** : a white-flowered shrub (*Leucothoe populifolia*) of the southern U.S. from the wood of which pipe bowls are made **2** : FETTERBUSH
**pipework** \ˈ=,=\ *n* **1** : PIPE **2** : the various sets of wooden and metal flue and reed pipe comprising the stops in a pipe organ
**pipewort** \ˈ=,=\ *n* : a plant of the genus *Eriocaulon*
**pipe wrench** *n* : a wrench for gripping and turning a pipe or other cylindrical surface usu. by use of two serrated jaws so designed as to grip the pipe when turning in one direction only — compare CHAIN TONGS, STILLSON WRENCH
**pipey** *var of* PIPY
**pip fruit** *n* [⁴*pip*] *Austral* : POME FRUIT
**pi·pi** \ˈpēpē\ *n, pl* **pipi** *or* **pipis** [Maori] **1** : a bivalve mollusk (*Mesodesma novae-zelandiae*) used as food in New Zealand **2** : an edible Australian wedge shell (*Plebidonax deltoides*)
**pipid** \ˈpīpəd, ˈpip-\ *n* -S [NL *Pipidae*] : a toad of the family Pipidae
**pip·i·dae** \ˈpipə,dē\ *n pl, cap* [NL, fr. *Pipa*, type genus + *-idae*] : a small family of tropical toads completely lacking a tongue and comprising the Surinam toad and related forms
**pipier** *comparative of* PIPY
**pipiest** *superlative of* PIPY
**pi·pi kau·la** \,pēpēˈkau̇lə\ *n, pl* **pipi kaulas** [Hawaiian, fr. *pipi* beef (fr. E *beef*) + *kaula* rope] *Hawaii* : JERKED BEEF
**pi·pil** \pəˈpē(ə)l\ *n, pl* **pipil** *or* **pipils** *usu cap* [Sp, of AmerInd origin] **1 a** : a Nahuatlan people or group of tribes in El Salvador, Guatemala, and Honduras **b** : a member of such people **2** : the language of the Pipil people

pipe wrench

**pip·i·le** \ˈpipə,lē\ *n, cap* [NL, fr. L *pipilare* to chirp, freq. of *pipare* — more at PIPE] : a genus of large crested So. American guans comprising the piping guans
**pip·i·lo** \ˈpipə,lō\ *n, cap* [NL, prob. fr. L *pipilare* to chirp] : a genus of American birds (family Fringillidae) of terrestrial habit — see TOWHEE
¹**pip·ing** \ˈpīpiŋ, -īpēŋ\ *n* -S [in sense 1, fr. ME, fr. gerund of *pipen* to pipe; in other senses, partly fr. ¹*pipe* + *-ing*; partly fr. gerund of ²*pipe* — more at PIPE] **1 a** : the music of a pipe **b** : a sound like that of a pipe ⟨the keen ~ of a field lark —Sidney Lanier⟩ **2** : a quantity of pipe or system of pipes **3** : a cutting of a jointed-stemmed or hollow-stemmed plant (as a carnation) **4 a** (1) : a narrow fold (as of bias-cut cloth) with or without an inserted cord that is stitched in seams or along edges as a trimming for clothing, slipcovers, curtains (2) : the trimming made in this fashion **b** : dough or decorative icing forced from a pastry tube **c** : a narrow piece of fabric or leather sewed in with the seam or edge of a shoe to give it finish **5** : a pipe formed in iron or steel ingots in cooling **6** : water erosion in a layer of subsoil or under or through a dam resulting in the formation of tunnels and caving
²**piping** \"\ *adj* [fr. pres. part. of ²*pipe*] : characterized by the music of the pipe rather than of the martial drum and fife : SOFT, TRANQUIL ⟨~ times of peace —Shak.⟩
³**piping** \"\ *adv* [ME, fr. ¹*piping*] : EXTREMELY, VERY — used in the phrase *piping hot*
**piping crow** *n* : an Australian bird of the genus *Gymnorhina*; *esp* : a black and white bird (*G. tibicen*) the size of a small crow that is a good mimic and is therefore often kept in confinement
**piping frog** *n* : SPRING PEEPER
**piping guan** *n* : a guan of the genus *Pipile*
**piping hare** *n* : PIKA
**pip·ing·ly** *adv* : in a piping manner
**pip·ing·ness** *n* -ES : the quality or state of being piping
**piping plover** *n* : a small plover (*Charadrius melodus*) of eastern No. America that is smaller and paler than the semipalmated plover
**piping rock** *n* : a light olive gray that is paler than slate tan and paler and slightly redder than average covert gray — called also *gray stone, light grège*
**pip·i·ri** *also* **pip·pi·ree** \ˌpipəˈrē\ *or* **pit·ir·ri** \ˌpidəˈrē\ *n* -S [AmerSp *pipiri*, of imit. origin] : any of several West Indian flycatchers; *esp* : GRAY KINGBIRD
**pipis** *pl of* PIPI
**pip·is·trelle** *or* **pip·is·trel** \ˌpipəˈstrel\ *n* -S [F *pipistrelle*, fr. It *pipistrello*, alter. of *vispistrello*, *vipistrello*, fr. L *vespertilion-*, *vespertilio* bat — more at VESPERTILIO] : a bat of the genus *Pipistrellus*; *esp* : a brown bat (*P. pipistrellus*) of Europe
**pip·is·trel·lus** \,pipəˈstreləs\ *n, cap* [NL, fr. It *pipistrello*] : a nearly cosmopolitan genus of very small vespertilionid bats having a blunt tragus and 34 teeth
**pip·it** \ˈpipət, *usu* -əd·+V\ *n* -S [imit.] : any of various small singing birds of the family Motacillidae of nearly cosmopolitan range; *esp* : any of those belonging to the genus *Anthus*, resembling the true larks in habit, colors, and the long hind claw, and like the true larks singing on the wing — called also *titlark*; see MEADOW PIPIT, ROCK PIPIT, SPRAGUE'S PIPIT, TREE PIPIT
**pip·kin** \ˈpipkən\ *n* -S [perh. fr. ¹*pipe* (cask) + *-kin*] **1** : a small pot of earthenware or of metal usu. having a horizontal handle **2** *chiefly dial* : PIGGIN
**pipped** \ˈpipt\ *adj* [¹*pip* + *-ed*] **1** : suffering from the pip **2** *slang* : INTOXICATED
**pip·per** \ˈpipə(r)\ *n* -S [²*pip* + *-er*] : the center or bead of a ring gunsight
**pip·per·idge** \ˈipərij\ *var of* PEPPERIDGE
**pip·pin** \ˈpipən\ *n* -S [ME *pepin, pipin*, fr. OF *pepin*] **1** *chiefly Brit* : ⁴PIP 1 **2 a** : a seedling apple or an apple from a seedling clone **b** : any of numerous apples that are typically of superior dessert quality and have usu. yellow or greenish yellow skins strongly flushed with red and lightly russeted — compare CODLING, COSTARD **3** : a highly admired or very admirable person or thing
**pipping** *pres part of* PIP
**pip–pip** \(ˈ)pipˈpip\ *interj* [perh. imit. of a bicycle or automobile horn] *Brit* : so long : GOOD-BYE
**pip·ple** \ˈpipəl\ *vi* -ED/-ING/-S [perh. freq. of ²*pipe*] : to make the murmuring sound of a gentle wind or of rippling water
**pip·py** \ˈpipē\ *adj* -ER/-EST [⁴*pip* + *-y*] : full of pips
**pip·ra** \ˈpiprə\ *n* [NL, fr. Gk *pipra* woodpecker] **1** *cap* : a genus of birds (family Pipridae) containing the typical manakins **2** -S : MANAKIN
**pip·ri·dae** \ˈpiprə,dē\ *n pl, cap* [NL, fr. *Pipra*, type genus + *-idae*] : a family of birds (suborder Tyranni) consisting of the manakins and sometimes treated as a subfamily of the Cotingidae — **piprine** \ˈpi,prīn, ˈpī,p-\ *adj* — **piproid** \ˈpi,prȯid\ *adj*
**pips** *pl of* PIP, *pres 3d sing of* PIP
**pip·sis·se·wa** \pipˈsisəwə\ *n* -S [Cree *pipisisikweu*, lit., it (i.e., its juice) breaks it (i.e., a stone in the bladder) into small pieces] : an evergreen herb of the genus *Chimaphila*; *esp* : an herb (*C. umbellata*) whose astringent leaves have been used as a tonic and diuretic — called also *love-in-winter*
**pip–squeak** \ˈ=,=\ *n* [²*pip* + *squeak*] **1** : a small or insignificant person : UPSTART **2** : a small high-velocity shell used by the Germans in World War I
**pip·ta·de·nia** \,piptəˈdēnēə\ *n, cap* [NL, fr. Gk *piptein* to fall + NL *aden-* + *-ia*; fr. the deciduous antheral glands — more at FEATHER] : a large genus of tropical chiefly Brazilian shrubs and trees (family Leguminosae) with twice-pinnate leaves, small spicate flowers, and flat pods — see COHOBA
**pip·tom·er·is** \pipˈtämərəs\ [NL, fr. Gk *piptein* to fall + NL *-o-* + Gk *meris* part — more at MERIT] *syn of* JACKSONIA
**pip·to·ste·gia root** \,piptəˈstēj(ē)ə-\ *n* [NL *Piptostegia* genus of Convolvulaceae, fr. Gk *piptein* to fall + NL *-o-* + *steg-* + *-ia*] : a jalap from the root of a Brazilian bindweed (*Piptostegia pisonis*) — called also *Brazilian jalap*
**pip·tu·rus** \pipˈt(y)u̇rəs\ *n, cap* [NL, fr. Gk *piptein* to fall down + NL *-urus* — more at FEATHER] : a small genus of woody plants (family Urticaceae) of Australia and the Mascarene islands having alternate leaves, flowers in dense globular clusters, and a strong inner bark fiber — see QUEENSLAND GRASS-CLOTH PLANT
**pipul** \"\ *var of* PIPAL

**1pi·pun·cu·lid** \(ˈ)pīˈpəŋkyələd\ *adj* [NL *Pipunculidae*] **:** of or relating to the Pipunculidae

**2pipunculid** \"\ *n* -s **:** a fly of the family Pipunculidae

**pi·pun·cu·li·dae** \ˌpī(ˌ)pənˈkyüləˌdē, ˌpīˌpəŋˈk-, ˌpipənˈk-\ *n pl, cap* [NL, fr. *Pipunculus*, type genus + *-idae*] **:** a family of two-winged flies (suborder Cyclorrhapha) including small flies having very large eyes and having larvae that are parasitic on other insects

**pipy** *also* **pip·ey** \ˈpīpē\ *adj* **pipier; pipiest** [¹*pipe* + *-y*] **1 :** containing tubular formations **2 :** having the hollow form of a pipe

**pi·quance** \ˈpēkən(t)s\ *n* -s **:** PIQUANCY

**pi·quan·cy** \-nsē\ *n* -ES **1 :** the quality or state of being piquant **:** PIQUANTNESS ⟨the sense that he was watched . . . added ~ to a journey so entirely sentimental —Thomas Hardy⟩ **2 :** something that is piquant; *esp* **:** a piquant dish ⟨restaurateurs . . . scouring Italy for *piquancies* to enhance their menus —S.J.Perelman⟩

**pi·quant** *also* **pi·quante** \ˈpēkənt, -ˌkänt, -ˌkant\ *adj* [*piquant* fr. MF, fr. pres. part. of *piquer* to prick, sting, nettle, pique; *piquante* fr. MF, fem. of *piquant* — more at PIKE] **1** *archaic* **:** disagreeably sharp **:** STINGING, PROVOCATIVE, CUTTING **2 :** agreeably stimulating to the palate **:** pleasantly tart, sharp, or biting **:** PUNGENT ⟨ham . . . curing in a ~ brine —*New Yorker*⟩ **3 :** arousing or having the power to arouse pleasant mental excitement **:** engagingly provocative ⟨the writing is never dull and often ~ —*Geog. Jour.*⟩ **:** agreeably challenging ⟨his comments are always ~ and sometimes blistering —*Times Lit. Supp.*⟩; *also* **:** having a lively arch charm ⟨she made a ~ pretty show with . . . her agreeable, slightly roguish face —Arnold Bennett⟩ **syn** see PUNGENT

**piquant green** *n* **:** a moderate yellow-green that is greener, lighter, and stronger than average moss green, yellower and deeper than average pea green, and yellower, darker, and slightly less strong than apple green (sense 1)

**pi·quant·ly** *adv* **:** in a piquant manner

**pi·quant·ness** *n* -ES **:** the quality or state of being piquant **:** PIQUANCY

**piquant sauce** *n* **:** a sauce with a sharp flavor (as from lemon juice, vinegar, capers, spices)

**1pique** \ˈpēk\ *n* -s [MF, fr. *piquer*] **1** *archaic* **:** mutual animosity **:** a state of strife **2 :** offense taken by one slighted or disdained **:** vexation or anger excited by a wound to one's vanity **:** a fit of resentment ⟨go off in a ~⟩ **syn** see OFFENSE

**2pique** \"\ *vb* -ED/-ING/-S [F *piquer* to prick, sting, nettle, pique — more at PIKE] *vt* **1 :** to arouse anger or resentment in **:** NETTLE, IRRITATE ⟨the Swiss will be *piqued* at the U.S. because of the higher tariff —*Wall Street Jour.*⟩; *specif* **:** to offend by slighting ⟨~ her by his apparent indifference⟩ **2 a :** to excite or arouse by a provocation, challenge, or rebuff ⟨a possible coincidence, which ~*s* one's curiosity —Johnson O'Connor⟩ **b :** to stimulate by wounding pride or inciting jealousy or rivalry ⟨~ him to violent efforts⟩ ~ *vi* **:** to cause annoyance or irritation **syn** see PROVOKE

**3pique** \"\ *n* -s [F *pic*, fr. MF, prick, sting, game of piquet, fr. *piquer* to prick, sting — more at PIKE] **:** the making of 30 points in hand and play in piquet before the other player scores; *also* **:** the bonus of 30 points for this

**4pique** \"\ *vt* -ED/-ING/-S **:** to score a pique against in piquet ~ *vi* **:** to make a pique in piquet

**5pique** \ˈpē(ˌ)kā\ *n* -s [AmerSp, fr. Quechua *piki*] **1 :** CHIGGER **2 :** any of various ticks

**6pi·qué** *or* **pi·que** \(ˈ)pēˈkā, pəˈkā\ *n* -s [F *piqué*, fr. past part. of *piquer* to prick, pierce, quilt — more at PIKE] **1 :** a durable clothing fabric of cotton, rayon, or silk woven orig. with crosswise ribs and now also with lengthwise ribs and figured effects obtained by the interlacing of a fine surface warp and a heavy back warp **2 :** tortoise shell or ivory inlaid with a design in gold or silver dots

**7piqué** \"\ *adj* [F, fr. past part. of *piquer*] **1 :** INLAID ⟨knife handles ~ with gold⟩ **2** *of a glove seam* **:** made by lapping one raw edge over another and stitching in place **3 :** SPICCATO **4** *ballet* **:** executed by stepping on the point of the supporting foot

**8pique** \ˈpēk\ *archaic var of* PEAK

**pi·que·ria** \pəˈkirēə\ *n, cap* [NL, fr. Andrés *Piquer* †1772 Span. physician and author + NL *-ia*] **:** a small genus of tropical American plants that is closely related to and often included in *Stevia*

**pi·quero** \pēˈke(ˌ)rō, pəˈk-\ *n* -s [AmerSp, fr. Sp, pikeman, fr. *pica* pike (fr. *picar* to prick, pierce, fr. — assumed — VL *piccare*) + *-ero* -er — more at PIKE] **:** any of several gannets of the western coast of America; *esp* **:** a booby of this region

**1pi·quet** *also* **pic·quet** \(ˈ)pēˈkā, pəˈkā\ *n* -s [F, dim. of *pic* pique (at cards) — more at PIQUE] **:** a two-handed card game which is played with a piquet pack and in which points are scored for announcing some combinations of cards, for winning tricks, and for pique and repique

**2piquet** *var of* PICKET

**piquet pack** *n* [¹*piquet*] **:** a pack of 32 playing cards made by removing all cards below the sevens and used for many games

**pi·quette** \pēˈket, pəˈk-\ *n* -s [F, fr. *piquer* to prick, sting, bite (the tongue) — more at PIKE] **:** a beverage made by steeping grape marc in water

**pi·queur** \-ˈkər(·)\ *n* -s [F, fr. *piquer* to prick, sting, goad + *-eur* -or] **1 :** an attendant directing the hounds in a hunt **2 :** a servant who runs before a carriage to clear the way

**pi·quia** \ˌpēkēˈä\ *n* -s [Pg *piquiá*, fr. Tupi] **:** a tree of the genus *Caryocar*; *esp* **:** a So. American timber tree (*C. butyrosum*) bearing edible oily nuts much like typical souari nuts

**pir** \ˈpi(ə)r\ *n* -s [Hindi *pīr*, fr. Per] **:** a Muslim spiritual guide or saint in India or Pakistan

**pi·ra·cy** \ˈpīrəsē, -si\ *n* -ES [ML *piratia*, fr. LGk *peirateia*, fr. Gk *peiratēs* pirate + *-ia* -y — more at PIRATE] **1 :** robbery on the high seas **2 a** *common law* **:** an act of depredation with the intent of stealing committed on the high seas that would if committed on the land amount to a felony **:** such an act committed on unappropriated lands by a descent from the sea or using the sea as a basis of operations **b** *international law* (1) **:** an act or practice of violence or depredation that would be felonious if done ashore committed upon the high seas by one not acting under the authority of a politically organized community (2) **:** a similar act or practice committed upon unappropriated lands by a descent from the sea **3 :** an act resembling piracy; *esp* **:** an unauthorized appropriation and reproduction of another's production, invention, or conception esp. in infringement of a copyright **4 :** CAPTURE 3

**pi·rae·us** \(ˈ)pīˈrēəs\ *adj, usu cap* [fr. *Piraeus*, Greece] **:** of or from the city of Piraeus, Greece **:** of the kind or style prevalent in Piraeus

**pi·ragua** \pəˈrägwə, -rag-\ *n* -s [Sp — more at PIROGUE] **1 :** a canoe made of a hollowed tree trunk **2 :** DUGOUT **3 :** a two-masted flat-bottomed boat undecked or decked only at the ends

**pi·rai** \pəˈrī\ *n* -s [Pg *pirai, piray* & AmerSp *piray*, fr. Galibi & Guarani *pirai*] **:** CARIBE

**pir·an·del·li·an** \ˌpirənˈdelēən\ *adj, usu cap* [Luigi *Pirandello* †1936 Ital. novelist and dramatist + E *-ian*] **:** of, relating to, or befitting the writer Pirandello

**pi·ran·ga** \pəˈraŋgə\ *n, cap* [NL] **:** a genus of tanagers including the scarlet, summer, and hepatic tanagers of No. America

**pi·ra·nha** *also* **pi·ra·ña** \pəˈranyə, -rän-\ *n* -s [*piranha* fr. Pg, fr. Tupi; *piraña* fr. AmerSp, fr. Pg] **:** CARIBE

**pi·ra·ni gauge** \pəˈränē-\ *n, usu cap P* [after Marcello St. *Pirani* b1880 Brit. physicist born in Germany] **:** a hot-wire manometer in which the cooling effect on the filament is deduced from its lowered resistance

**pi·ra·ru·cu** \pəˌrärəˈkü\ *n* -s [Pg *pirarucu, pirarucú*, fr. Tupi *pirá-rucú, pirá-urucú*, lit., red fish] **:** a large-scaled osteoglossid fish (*Arapaima gigas*) of the rivers of northern So. America that is held to attain a length of 15 feet and a weight of 500 pounds and is of great importance in the diet of the natives of the area

**1pi·rate** \ˈpīrət, *usu* -əd+V\ *n* -s *often attrib* [ME, fr. MF or L; MF, fr. L *pirata*, fr. Gk *peiratēs*, fr. *peiran* to attempt, make a try at — more at FEAR] **1 :** one who commits or practices piracy: as **a :** a robber on the high seas **b :** one noted for predatory practices ⟨financial ~*s*⟩ **c :** an infringer of the law of copyright **2 :** a ship used in piracy **3 :** a stream that has captured another

**2pirate** \"\ *vb* -ED/-ING/-S *vt* **1 :** to commit piracy upon **:** ROB **2 :** to take or appropriate by piracy: as **a :** to publish (as a book) without proper authorization esp. in infringement of copyright **b :** to take over and use (as a wavelength) in violation of exclusive assignment to another **c :** to lure (a worker) away from another employer by offers of betterment ~ *vi* **:** to commit or practice piracy

**pirate bird** *n* **:** JAEGER 3

**pirate perch** *n* **:** a small fish (*Aphredoderus sayanus*) of sluggish streams from New Jersey and Minnesota southward that is remarkable for having the vent in front of the pelvic fins and with the throat perches forms the order Salmopercae

**pi·rat·i·cal** \(ˈ)pīˈradəkəl, pəˈr-, -atˌ |ēk-\ *also* **pi·rat·ic** \|ik, |ēk\ *adj* [*piratical* fr. MF *piratique* (fr. L *piraticus*) or L *piraticus* (fr. Gk *peiratikos*, fr. *peiratēs* pirate + *-ikos* -ic) + E *-al*; *piratic* fr. F *piratique* or L *piraticus* — more at PIRATE] **1 :** of, produced by, or being a pirate or piracy ⟨~ strongholds⟩ ⟨~ editions⟩ ⟨~ attackers⟩ ⟨~ enterprises⟩ **2 :** befitting or resembling a pirate ⟨a fierce ~ expression⟩ — **pi·rat·i·cal·ly** \|ək(ə)lē, |ēk-, -li\ *adv*

**pir·ca** \ˈpirkə\ *n* -s [Sp, fr. Quechua *pirka*] **:** a crude dry masonry wall of the early Inca period

**pi·ric·u·lar·ia** \pəˌrikyəˈla(a)rēə, ˌpirəkyüˈl-\ *n, cap* [NL, fr. L *pirum* pear + *-iculum*, dim. suffix + NL *-aria* — more at PEAR] **:** a form genus of imperfect fungi (family Moniliaceae) characterized by simple or slightly branched conidiophores producing terminal two-septate to many-septate solitary hyaline pear-shaped spores and including one form (*P. grisea*) that causes a leaf spot of various grasses

**piriform** *var of* PYRIFORM

**pir·i·for·mis** *or* **pyr·i·for·mis** \ˌpirəˈfȯrməs\ *n* -ES [*piriformis*, NL, alter. of *pyriformis*; *pyriformis*, NL, fr. ML *pyrum* pear (alter. of L *pirum*) + L *-iformis* -iform] **:** a muscle arising from the front of the sacrum, passing out of the pelvis through the greater sciatic foramen, and being inserted into the upper border of the great trochanter of the femur

**pir·i·piri** \ˌpirəˈpirē\ *n* -s [Maori] **1 a :** a troublesome New Zealand weed (*Acaena sanguisorbae*) bearing burs covered with hooked bristles **b :** WHITE MAPAN **2** *also* **pirijiri :** a fragrant Asiatic and Australasian herb (*Haloragis micrantha*) of the family Haloragidaceae

**pir·i·ri·gua** \ˌpirərēˈgwä\ *n* -s [Pg *piririguá*, fr. Guarani] **:** a largely buff and brown So. American cuckoo (*Guira guira*) resembling the anis in habit

**pirl** \ˈpər(·ə)l\ *vb* -ED/-ING/-S [origin unknown] **1** *archaic* **:** TWIST, TWINE **2** *chiefly Scot* **:** SPIN, REVOLVE

**pir·lie** \ˈpərlē\ *n* -s [prob. fr. *pirl* + *-ie*] **1** *Scot* **:** a small object; *specif* **:** the little finger **2** *Scot* **:** PIRLIE-PIG

**pirlie-pig** \ˈ≈≈ˌ≈\ *n, Scot* **:** a child's savings bank usu. made of crockery

**pirn** \ˈpərn, ˈpirn\ *n* -s [ME *pirne*] **1 :** QUILL 1a(1) **2** *chiefly Scot* **:** any of various devices resembling a reel

**piro** \ˈpi(ˌ)rō\ *n, pl* **piro** *or* **piros** *usu cap* [Sp, of AmerInd origin] **1 a :** a Tanoan people of Pueblo Indians in central New Mexico and the state of Chihuahua, Mexico **b :** a member of such people **2 a :** an Arawakan people of eastern Peru **b :** a member of such people **c :** the language of such people

**pi·ro·gen** \pəˈrōgən\ *or* **pi·ro·gi** \-gē\ *n pl* [Yiddish & Russ; Yiddish *pirogen*, pl. of *pirog* small filled pastry, fr. Russ *pirogi* fr. Russ, pl. of *pirog* — more at PIROSHKI] **:** PIROSHKI

**pi·rogue** \ˈpēˌrōg, ˈpiˌr-, pəˈr-, pēˈr-, ˈ≈ˌrō\ *also* **pi·roque** \-ōk, -ō\ *n* -s [F, fr. Sp *piragua*, of Cariban origin; akin to Galibi *piraua* pirogue, Carib *piraguas*] **1 :** a dugout canoe **2 :** a boat like a canoe

**pi·rol** \ˈpēˌrōl, ≈ˈ≈\ *n* -s [G, fr. MHG *piro*, of imit. origin] **:** GOLDEN ORIOLE

**pirola** *syn of* PYROLA

**pirolaceae** [NL, fr. *Pirola* (syn. of *Pyrola*) + *-aceae*] *syn of* PYROLACEAE

**pi·root** \pīˈrüt\ *vi* -ED/-ING/-S [prob. alter. (influenced by *root*) of ²*pirouette*] **1** *South & Midland* **:** to go about idly or aimlessly — often used with *around* **2** *South & Midland* **:** to nose around **:** SNOOP ⟨went ~*ing* into a cave one day —J.F. Dobie⟩

**piro·plasm** \ˈpirəˌplazəm\ *or* **piro·plas·ma** \ˌpirəˈplazmə\ *n, pl* **piroplasms** \"≈≈ˌplazəmz\ *or* **piroplas·ma·ta** \ˌ≈≈ˈplazmədə\ [NL *Piroplasma*] **:** a parasitic protozoan of the family Babesiidae — **piro·plas·mic** \ˌ≈≈ˈplazmik\ *adj*

**piro·plas·ma** \ˌpirəˈplazmə\ [NL, prob. fr. L *pirum* pear + NL *-o-* + *plasma* — more at PEAR] *syn of* BABESIA

**1piro·plas·mid** \ˌpirəˈplazməd\ *adj* [NL *Piroplasmidae* (syn. of *Babesiidae*), fr. *Piroplasma* + *-idae*] **:** of or relating to the Babesiidae

**2piroplasmid** \"\ *n* -s **:** PIROPLASM

**piro·plas·mo·sis** \ˌpirəˌplazˈmōsəs\ *n, pl* **piroplasmo·ses** \-ōˌsēz\ [NL, fr. *Piroplasma* + *-osis*] **:** infection with or disease caused by protozoans of the genus *Babesia* or the family Babesiidae including Texas fever and east coast fever of cattle, babesiasis of sheep, and malignant jaundice of the dog

**piroque** *var of* PIROGUE

**pi·rosh·ki** *also* **pi·roj·ki** \pəˈrȯshkē, -ˈräsh-\ *n pl* [Yiddish & Russ; Yiddish *pirozshke* (sing.), fr. Russ *pirozhki*, pl. of *pirozhok* small pocket of pastry, dim. of *pirog* small filled pastry, prob. fr. *pir* banquet, feast; akin to Russ *pit'* to drink, OSlav *piti* — more at POTABLE] **:** small pastry turnovers stuffed with a savory filling

**1pir·ou·ette** \ˌpirəˈwet, *usu* -ed·+V\ *n* -s [F, teetotum, pirouette, fr. MF *pirouet* teetotum, top; akin to F dial. (Béarn) *pire peg*] **1 :** a rapid whirling about of the body (as in a dance); *specif* **:** a full turn on the toe or ball of one foot in ballet **2 :** an advanced movement in horsemanship executed at a gallop in which a horse's shoulders describe a circle while his hind legs serve as a pivot

**2pirouette** \"\ *vi* -ED/-ING/-S [F *pirouetter*, fr. *pirouette*, n.] **1 :** to perform a pirouette **2 :** to turn about as if in a pirouette **:** turn about lightly and gracefully or within a narrow area ⟨vanes *pirouetted* in the wind —*Time*⟩ **syn** see TURN

**pir·ou·et·ter** \-ed·ə(r), -etə-\ *n* -s **:** one that pirouettes

**pir·quet test** *also* **pirquet reaction** \(ˈ)pirˈkā-\ *n, usu cap P* [after Baron Clemens von *Pirquet* †1929 Austrian pediatrician] **:** a tuberculin test made by applying a drop of tuberculin to a scarified spot on the skin

**pir·rau·ra** *or* **pir·rau·ru** \pəˈraůrə\ *n* -s [native name in Australia] **:** a legally designated sex mate other than husband or wife among some Australian aborigines; *also* **:** the relationship between such sex mates

**pirs** *pl of* PIR

**pirs·son·ite** \ˈpirsᵊnˌīt, ˈpər-\ *n* -s [Louis V. *Pirsson* †1919 Am. mineralogist + *-ite*] **:** a mineral $Na_2Ca(CO_3)_2.2H_2O$ consisting of a hydrous calcium sodium carbonate and occurring in white or colorless orthorhombic crystals (hardness 3, sp. gr. 2.35)

**pi·sa·ca** *or* **pi·sa·cha** \pəˈshächə\ *n* -s *usu cap* [Skt *piśāca*] **:** the Dard group of Indic languages

**pis al·ler** \pēˈzäˌlā, ˌpēˌzaˈlā, pēˈza(ˌ)lā\ *n, pl* **pis allers** \-ā(z)\ [F, lit., to go worst] **:** a last resource or device for coping with a difficulty **:** EXPEDIENT, SHIFT ⟨Poor Laws were an unhappy *pis aller*, revealing the failure of society to deal . . . with its economic problems —R.M.MacIver⟩

**1pi·san** \ˈpēzᵊn\ *adj, usu cap* [*Pisa*, Italy + E *-an*] **1 :** of, relating to, or characteristic of Pisa **2 :** of, relating to, or characteristic of the people of Pisa

**2pisan** \"\ *n* -s *cap* **:** a native or inhabitant of Pisa

**pi·sang** \pəˈsäŋ\ *n* -s [Malay, banana, plantain] **:** PLANTAIN

**pisang wax** *n* **:** a wax obtained from the leaves of a plantain (*Musa paradisiaca*)

**pi·sanite** \pəˈzäˌnīt, -zaˌn-\ *n* -s [G *pisanit*, fr. Félix *Pisani* †1920 French chemist and mineralogist + G *-it* -ite] **:** a mineral $(Fe,Cu)SO_4.7H_2O$ consisting of a hydrous iron copper sulfate isomorphous with melanterite and kirovite

**pis·ant** *var of* PISSANT

**pis·as·ter** \pəˈsastə(r)\ *n, cap* [NL, fr. L *piscis* fish + NL *-aster* (star) — more at FISH] **:** a genus of large shallow-water typically 5-rayed starfishes (family Asteriidae) including the common purple or orange starfish (*P. ochraceus*) of the Pacific coast of No. America

**pi·sau·ri·dae** \pəˈsȯrəˌdē\ *n pl, cap* [NL, fr. *Pisaura*, type genus (fr. L *Pisaurum* — Pesaro —, Italy) + *-idae*] **:** a family of hunting spiders that do not spin webs to catch their prey — compare LYCOSIDAE

**pis·can** \ˈpiskən\ *adj* [L *piscis* fish + E *-an* — more at FISH] **:** of or relating to fishes

**pis·ca·ry** \ˈpiskərē\ *n* -ES [in sense 1, fr. ME *piscarie*, fr. ML *piscaria*, fr. L, neut. pl. of *piscarius* of fish, of fishing, fr. *piscis* fish + *-arius* -ary; in sense 2, fr. ML *piscaria*, fr. L, fem. of *piscarius* — more at FISH] **1 :** FISHERY 4; *esp* **:** COMMON OF PISCARY **2 :** a fishing place

**pis·cat·a·way** \pəˈskadəˌwā\ *n, pl* **piscataway** *or* **piscataways** *usu cap* [fr. *Piscataway*, former Conoy Indian village in Prince George county, Maryland] **:** CONOY 1

**pis·ca·tion** \pəˈskāshən\ *n* -s [LL *piscation-, piscatio*, fr. L *piscatus* (past part. of *piscari* to fish, fr. *piscis* fish) + *-ion-, -io* -ion — more at FISH] **:** FISHING

**pis·ca·tor** \pəˈskād·ə(r), ˈpiˌsk-\ *n* -s [L, fr. *piscatus* + *-or*] **:** FISHERMAN, ANGLER

**pis·ca·to·ri·al** \ˌpiskəˈtōrēəl, -tȯr-\ *adj* [L *piscatorius* + E *-al*] **:** PISCATORY — **pis·ca·to·ri·al·ly** \-ēəlē, -li\ *adv*

**pis·ca·to·ry** \ˈpiskəˌtōrē, -tȯr-, -ri\ *adj* [L *piscatorius*, fr. *piscatus* + *-orius* -ory] **1 :** of or relating to fishermen or fishing ⟨the ~ life⟩ **2 :** living by or given to fishing ⟨~ tribes⟩

**pis·ces** \ˈpi(ˌ)sēz, ˈpī(ˌ)sēz *also* ˈpiˌskās *or* ˈpē(ˌ)sēz\ *n pl* [in sense 1, fr. ME, fr. ML, fr. L, a constellation, fr. pl. of *piscis* fish; in sense 2, NL, fr. L, pl. of *piscis* — more at FISH] **1** *sing in constr, usu cap* **:** the 12th sign of the zodiac — see SIGN table, ZODIAC illustration **2** *cap, in some classifications* **:** a variously limited class of vertebrates comprising all the fishes and sometimes the cyclostomes and lancelets — compare CHOANICHTHYES, TELEOSTOMI

**pisci-** *comb form* [L, fr. *piscis*] **:** fish ⟨*pisci*fauna⟩ ⟨*pisci*culture⟩

**pis·cic·o·la** \pəˈsikələ\ *n, cap* [NL, fr. *pisci-* + *-cola*] **:** a widely distributed genus of marine and freshwater leeches related to *Ichthyobdella* and living as parasites on fishes or turtles

**pis·ci·cul·tur·al** \ˌpisəˈkəlch(ə)rəl\ *adj* **:** of or relating to pisciculture — **pis·ci·cul·tur·al·ly** \-rəlē\ *adv*

**pis·ci·cul·ture** \ˈpisəˌkəlchə(r) *also* ˌ≈≈ˈ≈≈\ *n* [prob. fr. F, fr. *pisci-* + *culture*] **:** fish culture

**pis·ci·cul·tur·ist** \ˌ≈≈ˈkəlch(ə)rəst\ *n* -s **:** one who specializes in fish culture; *specif* **:** the superintendent of a state-operated fish hatchery

**pis·cid·ia** \pəˈsidēə\ *n, cap* [NL, blend of *pisci-* and *-cidia* (fr. L *caedere* to kill); fr. the fact that leaves and bark of shrubs of this genus poison fish when thrown into the water — more at CONCISE] **:** a genus of shrubs or small trees (family Leguminosae) having pink or white and red flowers in panicles and indehiscent pods with black seeds — see JAMAICA DOGWOOD

**pis·ci·fauna** \ˌpisə+\ *n* [NL, fr. *pisci-* + *fauna*] **:** the fishes of a given region

**pis·ci·na** \pəˈs(h)ēnə, -sīnə\ *n, pl* **piscinas** \-nəz\ *or* **piscinae** \-shēˌnā, -sēˌnī, -sī(ˌ)nē\ [L, fr. *piscis* fish + *-ina* -ine — more at FISH] **1 :** an artificial reservoir or tank used by the ancient Romans esp. as a fishpond or swimming pool **2** [ML, fr. L] **:** a stone basin with a drain located near the altar of a church for disposing of water from liturgical ablutions — **pis·ci·nal** \-ēnᵊl, -īn-\ *adj*

**1pis·cine** \pəˈsēn\ *n* -s [ME, fr. OF, fr. L & ML *piscina*] **:** PISCINA

**2pis·cine** \ˈpiˌsīn, ˈpīsēn, ˈpīˌsīn\ *adj* [L *piscinus*, fr. *piscis* fish + *-inus* -ine] **:** of, relating to, or having the characteristics of fish

**pis·cin·i·ty** \pəˈsinədē\ *n* -ES **:** the quality or state of being a fish

**pis·civ·o·rous** \pəˈsiv(ə)rəs\ *adj* [*pisci-* + *-vorous*] **:** feeding on fishes

**pis·co** \ˈpi(ˌ)skō, ˈpē(-\ *n* -s [Sp, fr. *Pisco*, Peru] **:** a So. American brandy that resembles French marc and is often used in cocktails

**pisco sour** *n* **:** a cocktail of Peruvian origin consisting of lime juice, pisco brandy, and sugar garnished with beaten egg white

**pi·sé** \(ˈ)pēˈzā\ *also* **pisé de terre** \(ˌ)≈ˌ≈dəˈte(ə)r\ *n, pl* **pisés** \-ā(z)\ *also* **pisés de terre** [*pisé* fr. F, fr. F dial. (Lyon), fr. MF, fr. past part. of *piser* to stomp, fr. (assumed) VL *pinsiare*, *pistiare*, alter. of L *pinsare*, *pisare* to beat, pound, crush; *pisé de terre* fr. F, lit., earth pisé; akin to L *pinsere* to pound, crush — more at PESTLE] **:** a building material consisting of stiff earth or clay rammed in between forms — compare ⁴COB, TAPIA

**pis·gah sight** \ˈpizgə\ *n, usu cap P* [fr. Mt. *Pisgah*, Palestine, from which Moses was allowed to see the Promised Land according to Deut 3:27] **:** a distant view (as of an unobtainable objective) ⟨only a *Pisgah sight* of the promised land of long-deferred discovery —I.B.Hart⟩

**1pish** \ps, psh; *often read as* ˈpish\ *interj* [origin unknown] — used to express disdain or contempt

**2pish** \ˈpish\ *vb* -ED/-ING/-ES *vi* **:** to express disdain or contempt by or as if by saying *pish* ⟨~*ed* and pshawed a little at what had happened —Thomas Hughes⟩ ~ *vt* **:** to dismiss or reject by or as if by saying *pish*

**pi·shogue** *or* **pi·shoge** \pəˈshōg\ *or* **pish·rogue** \(ˈ)piˈshrōg\ *n* -s [IrGael *piseog*] **1** *Irish* **:** a wise saw or aphorism **2** *Irish* **a :** CHARM, INCANTATION, SPELL **b :** SORCERY, WITCHCRAFT

**pish·pash** \ˈpishˌpash, -ˌpäsh\ *n* -ES [origin unknown] *India* **:** a rice broth containing bits of meat

**pish·posh** \ˈpishˌpäsh\ *n* -ES [redupl. of ¹*pish*] **:** NONSENSE

**1pi·sid·i·an** \pəˈsidēən, (ˈ)pīˈs-\ *adj, usu cap* [*Pisidia*, ancient country of southern Asia Minor + E *-an*] **1 :** of, relating to, or characteristic of ancient Pisidia **2 :** of, relating to, or characteristic of the people of Pisidia

**2pisidian** \"\ *n* -s *cap* **:** a native or inhabitant of Pisidia

**pi·sid·i·um** \-ēəm\ *n, cap* [NL, dim. of L *pisum* pea — more at PEA] **:** a genus of nearly cosmopolitan minute freshwater bivalves (family Sphaeriidae) usu. somewhat smaller than those of the genus *Sphaerium* and having the siphons united at their ends

**1pi·si·form** \ˈpīsəˌfȯrm, -īzə-\ *adj* [L *pisum* pea + E *-iform*] **:** resembling a pea in size or shape ⟨~ granules⟩

**2pisiform** \"\ *n* -s **:** a bone on the ulnar side of the carpus in most mammals and a few other vertebrates

**pi·sis·tra·te·an** \(ˌ)pīˌsistrəˈtēən, ≈ˈ≈≈ˌ≈≈\ *adj, usu cap* [*Pisistratus* †527 B.C. tyrant of Athens + E *-an*] **:** of or relating to Pisistratus or esp. the critical revision of the Homeric poems attributed to him

**pisk** \ˈpisk\ *n* -s [origin unknown] **:** the common American nighthawk

**pis·kun** \ˈpiskən\ *n* -s [Blackfoot] **:** a steep cliff sometimes with a corral or enclosure at the bottom that is used by American Indians for driving large numbers of buffalo to their slaughter

**pis·ky** \ˈpiskē\ *dial Eng var of* PIXIE

**pis·mire** \ˈpisˌmī(ə)r, -iz,m-\ *n* -s [ME *pissemire*, fr. *pisse* piss + *mire* ant, of Scand origin; akin to OSw *myr, myra* ant, ON *maurr*; akin to MD *miere* ant, MLG *mire*, Crimean Goth *miera*, L *formica*, Gk *myrmēx*, Av *maoiri-*; 1st constituent fr. the smell of anthills, due to the formic acid exuded by ants — more at PISS] **1 :** ANT **2 :** an insignificant or contemptible person ⟨what do you think I'd do with a young ~ like you —R.P.Warren⟩

**pis·mo clam** \ˈpizˌmō-\ *n, often cap P* [fr. *Pismo* Beach, Calif.] **:** a thick-shelled clam (*Tivela stultorum*) of the family Veneridae that occurs on the southwest coast of No. America and is used extensively for food

**piso·lite** \ˈpīzəˌlīt, ˈpīˌ |sə-\ *n* -s [NL *pisolithus*, fr. Gk *pisos* pea + *-lithus* -lith] **:** a limestone composed of globular concretions about the size of a pea — compare OOLITE

**piso·lith** \-ˌlith\ *n* -s [ISV *piso-* (fr. Gk *pisos* pea) + *-lith*] **:** a pisiform concretion of larger size than an oolite

**piso·lit·ic** \ˌ≈ˈlid·ik\ *adj* **:** of, relating to, or having the characteristics of pisolite

**pi·so·ne** \pəˈsōnē\ *n, pl* **pisone** *or* **pisones** *usu cap* [Sp, of AmerInd origin] **1 :** an Indian people of northeastern Mexico perhaps related to the Janambre **2 :** a member of the Pisone people

**pi·so·nia** \pəˈsōnēə, pīˈs-\ *n, cap* [NL, irreg. fr. Willem *Piso* †*ab* 1678 Dutch physician and traveler + NL *-ia*] **:** a genus of tropical often thorny trees, shrubs, and vines (family Nyctaginaceae) having small dioecious apetalous flowers and utricular fruits — see COCKSPUR 2b

**pi·so·te** \pə'sōd·ē\ *n* -s [AmerSp *pizote, pisote*, fr. Nahuatl *pitzotl*] : COATI

**¹piss** \'pis\ *vb* -ED/-ING/-ES [ME *pissen*, fr. OF *pissier*, fr. (assumed) VL *pissiare*, of imit. origin] *vi* : URINATE — usu. considered vulgar ~ *vt* **1** : to urinate in or on ⟨~ the bed⟩ — usu. considered vulgar **2** : to discharge as or as if urine ⟨~ blood⟩ — usu. considered vulgar

**²piss** \"\ *n* -ES [ME *pisse*, fr. *pissen*, v.] **1** : URINE — usu. considered vulgar **2** : an act of urinating — often used with *take;* usu. considered vulgar

**pissant** \'=,=\ *n* [¹*piss* + *ant*] *chiefly dial* : ANT

**piss away** *vt, slang* : to let flow as if of no account : fritter away ⟨enough money to *piss away* from now until the day I die —Millard Lampell⟩

**pissed** \'pist\ *adj* **1** *slang* : ANGRY, DISGUSTED **2** *slang* : DRUNK

**pissed off** *adj, slang* : ANGRY, DISAPPOINTED, DISGUSTED ⟨a lot of guys . . . are *pissed off* at me 'cause I came in after them and made corporal —Norman Mailer⟩

**pis·so·des** \pə'sō(,)dēz\ *n, cap* [NL, fr. Gk *pissa* pitch + NL *-odes* — more at PITCH] : a holarctic genus of small weevils that feed on coniferous trees — see WHITE PINE WEEVIL

**pis·soir** \(')pi¦swär, (')pē¦s-\ *n* -s [F, fr. MF, fr. *pisser* to urinate, fr. OF *pissier* — more at PISS] : a public urinal usu. located on the street in some European countries and surrounded by a shield or screen

**pisspoor** \'=¦=\ *adj* [²*piss* + *poor*] *slang* : utterly inadequate or thoroughly unsatisfactory : DEPLORABLE, WRETCHED ⟨just plain ~, mean and shiftless —James Jones⟩ ⟨that's a ~ attitude —Joseph Landon⟩

**pis·tache** \pə'stash, (')pi¦s-\ *n* -s [F, fr. L *pistacium*] : PISTACHIO

**pis·tach·io** \pə'stashē,ō, -taash-,-taish- *also* -täsh- *or* -tash- *or* -(,)shō\ *n* -s [It *pistacchio*, fr. L *pistacium*, fr. Gk *pistakion* pistachio nut, dim. of *pistakē* pistachio tree, fr. Per *pistah*] **1 a** (1) : a small tree (*Pistacia vera*) of southern Europe and Asia Minor having leaves with 3 to 5 broad leaflets, greenish brown paniculate flowers, and a large fruit (2) : the edible green seed of the pistachio tree **b** : WITCH HAZEL 2a(1) **2** *or* **pistachio green** : a light yellowish green that is yellower and paler than apple green, deeper than ocean green, and yellower and duller than crayon green

**pistachio nut** *n* : the nut of the pistachio tree containing a single oblong greenish edible seed used esp. as a flavoring substance in cookery and confectionery

**pis·ta·cia** \pə'stashēə, -tāsh-\ *n* [NL, fr. Gk *pistakē* the pistachio tree] **1** *cap* : a small genus of trees (family Anacardiaceae) native to southern Europe, Asia, and No. America having simple or pinnate leaves, small dioecious apetalous flowers, and drupaceous fruits — see MASTIC TREE, PISTACHIO, TEREBINTH **2** -s : any tree of the genus *Pistacia*

**pis·ta·cite** \'pistə,sīt\ *n* -s [G *pistazit*, fr. L *pistacium* + G *-it* -ite] : EPIDOTE

**pis·ta·reen** \¦pistə¦rēn\ *n* -s [prob. modif. of Sp *peseta* — more at PESETA] : an old Spanish 2-real piece circulating in Spain, the West Indies, and the U. S. at the debased rate of ⅕ the piece of eight or 20 cents and in the U. S. after 1827 at 17 cents

**piste** \'pēst\ *n* -s [F, fr. MF, fr. OIt *pista*, fr. *pistare* to trample down — more at PISTON] **1** : a beaten track or trail made by an animal **2** : a hard packed ski trail or course

**pis·tia** \'pistēə\ *n* [NL, fr. Gk *pistos* liquid + NL *-ia*] **1** *cap* : a genus of tropical free-floating aquatic herbs (family Araceae) having tufted leaves and few-flowered spadices — see WATER LETTUCE **2** -s : any plant of the genus *Pistia*

**pis·tic** \'pistik\ *adj* [LL *pisticus*, fr. Gk *pistikos*, fr. *pistis* faith + *-ikos* -ic; akin to Gk *peithesthai* to believe, be persuaded, obey — more at BIDE] : of, relating to, or exhibiting faith

**pis·til** \'pist³l *sometimes* -stil\ *n* -s [NL *pistillum*, fr. L, pestle — more at PESTLE] : the ovule-bearing organ of a seed plant : the ovary with its appendages (as style and stigma) — compare GYNOECIUM; see FLOWER illustration

**pistill-** *comb form* [NL *pistillum*] : pistil ⟨*pistilline*⟩ ⟨*pistilloid*⟩

**pis·til·late** \'pistə,lāt, -,lət\ *adj* [*pistill-* + *-ate*] **1** : having or producing a pistil — see AMENT illustration **2** : having pistils but no stamens — compare STAMINATE

**pis·til·line** \-,līn, -lən\ *adj* [*pistill-* + *-ine*] : of, relating to, or consisting of a pistil

**pis·til·lode** \'pistə,lōd\ *also* **pis·til·lo·di·um** \,==ˈlōdēəm\ *n* -s [NL *pistillodium*, fr. *pistill-* + Gk *-ōdēs* -ode + NL *-ium*] : a rudimentary pistil

**pis·til·lo·dy** \'pistə,lōdē\ *n* -ES [*pistill-* + *-ody*] : the metamorphosis of other organs into pistils

**pis·til·loid** \'pistə,lȯid\ *adj* [*pistill-* + *-oid*] : resembling or modified into a pistil ⟨~ sepals⟩

**¹pis·tol** \'pist³l\ *n* -s *often attrib* [MF *pistole*, fr. G, fr. MHG dial. (Silesia) *pischulle, pischol, pischczal*, fr. Czech *píšťal*, lit., pipe; akin to Russ *pishchal* shawm, shepherd's pipes, harquebus, *pishchat'* to play the pipes, prob. all of imit. origin] **1** : a short firearm intended to be aimed and fired with one hand : REVOLVER — see AUTOMATIC PISTOL **2** : a handgun whose chamber is integral with the barrel — distinguished from *revolver;* see SINGLE-SHOT PISTOL

**²pistol** \"\ *vt* **pistoled** *or* **pistolled; pistoled** *or* **pistolled; pistoling** *or* **pistolling; pistols** : to shoot with a pistol

**pistol carbine** *n* : a pistol that has a removable butt piece and is therefore capable of being used as a pistol or as a carbine

**pistol casebearer** *n* : a casebearer that makes a curved case; *specif* : one that is the larva of a small No. American moth (*Coleophora malivorella*) and that feeds on the foliage of various fruit trees

**pis·tole** \pə'stōl\ *n* -s [MF, prob. back-formation fr. *pistolet*] **1** : an old gold 2-escudo piece of Spain **2** : any of several old gold coins of Europe having about the value of a pistole

**pis·tol·eer** \¦pistə¦li(ə)r\ *n* -s [¹*pistol* + *-eer*] : one who uses a pistol; *esp* : a soldier armed principally with a pistol

**pistolet** *n* -s [MF, perh. dim. of *pistole* pistol] *obs* : any of several gold coins of European countries; *esp* : PISTOLE

**pistol grip** *n* **1** : a grip of a shotgun or rifle shaped like a pistol

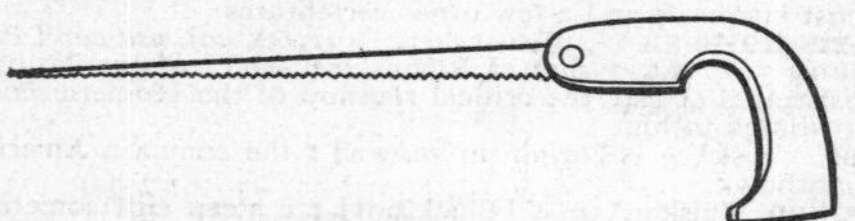

pistol grip of a keyhole saw

stock **2** : a handle (as of a saw) shaped like a pistol stock

**pis·tol·o·gy** \pə'stäləjē\ *n* -ES [Gk *pistis* faith + E *-o-* + *-logy* — more at PISTIC] : a branch of theology dealing with faith

**pistol prawn** *or* **pistol shrimp** *n* : SNAPPING SHRIMP

**pistol shot** *n* **1** : the approximate distance a pistol will shoot or send a bullet or shot ⟨came within *pistol shot*⟩ **2** : one skilled in or accustomed to pistol shooting

**pistol-whip** \'==,=\ *vt* : to beat with a pistol; *specif* : to beat the head or face of with the side of a pistol

**pis·ton** \'pistən\ *n* -s [F, fr. MF, large pestle, fr. OIt *pistone*, fr. *pistare* to beat, pound, trample down (fr. ML *pistare*, fr. L *pistus*, past part. of *pinsere* to pound, crush) + *-one*, aug. suffix — more at PESTLE] **1** : a sliding piece moved by or moving against fluid pressure and usu. consisting of a short cylinder fitting within a cylindrical vessel along which it moves back and forth — compare CYLINDER 2b,2c, SLIDE VALVE **2 a** *or* **piston valve** : a sliding valve moving in a cylinder like an engine piston in a brass wind instrument and serving when depressed by a finger knob to add a crook to the tube and hence to lower its pitch **b** *or* **piston knob** : a push button on an organ console for bringing in a preselected registration

**piston displacement** *n* : the volume displaced by a piston in a cylinder (as in a pump or an engine) in a single stroke : the product of piston travel and cross-sectional area of the containing cylinder

**piston drill** *n* : a pneumatic percussion drilling machine in which the drill forms a continuation of the piston rod

**piston engine** *n* : an engine utilizing pistons working in cylinder and usu. involving reciprocating motion

**pistonhead** \'==,=\ *n* : the part of a piston that is made fast to the piston rod

**pistonlike** \'==,=\ *adj* : resembling a piston

**pis·ton·phone** \-,fōn\ *n* [*piston* + *-phone*] : an instrument for measuring acoustic intensity by the displacement of a piston resulting from the sound pressure upon it

**piston pin** *n* : WRIST PIN

**piston pump** *n* : a pump having a reciprocating piston operating in a cylinder so as to impart motion and pressure to the fluid by direct displacement

**piston ring** *n* : a metal ring for sealing the gap between a piston and the cylinder wall

**piston rod** *n* : a rod by which a piston is moved or by which it communicates motion

**piston spring** *n* : a spring for a piston ring

**piston valve** *n* **1** : a reciprocating valve consisting of a piston or connected pistons working in a cylindrical case provided with ports that are traversed by the valve **2** : PISTON 2a

**pi·sum** \'pīsəm, -īzəm\ *n, cap* [NL, fr. L, pea — more at PEA] : a small genus of Eurasian herbaceous vines (family Leguminosae) distinguished from *Lathyrus* by the enlarged summit of the style — see PEA

**¹pit** \'pit, *usu* -id·+V\ *n* -s [ME *pitt, pit*, fr. OE *pytt;* akin to OS *putti* well, OHG *pfuzzi, pfuzza* well, ON *pyttr* well, pit, pool, cesspool; all fr. a prehistoric WGmc-NGmc word prob. borrowed fr. L *puteus* well, pit; perh. akin to L *putare* to prune — more at PAVE] **1 a** : a hole, shaft, or cavity in the ground formed naturally (as by erosion) or artificially (as by digging) : as (1) : a usu. open deep excavation or shaft that has been dug for taking a mineral deposit from the ground or for quarrying stone ⟨a gravel ~⟩ ⟨a coal ~⟩ (2) : a scooped-out place used for burning something (as charcoal, lime) (3) *dial chiefly Eng* : GRAVE ⟨thou hast kept me alive, that I should not go down to the ~ —Ps 30:3 (AV)⟩ (4) : a hole in the ground usu. covered over with something (as brushwood) and designed to serve as a trap into which wild animals may fall and so be captured (5) : a covered excavation (as in a field) used for storing produce (6) : PROPAGATING PIT (7) : an area dug out or sunk into the ground as a place of imprisonment (8) : an excavation (as beneath a furnace) for receiving cinders or ashes (9) : an area dug out as a shelter against gunfire **b** : an often sunken or depressed area designed for a particular use or purpose with reference to the surrounding or adjacent floor area : as (1) : an enclosure in which animals are kept or are made to fight each other as a sport ⟨a bear ~⟩ ⟨like a couple of gamecocks in a ~⟩ (2) *chiefly Brit* : the ground floor of a theater; *esp* : the part of this area at the rear (3) : ORCHESTRA PIT (4) : a usu. rectangular sunken area in a garage or service station designed to permit more convenient greasing of and repair work on the underside of a car — called also *grease pit* (5) : DROP PIT (6) : a sunken area in a foundry floor designed to catch cast metal (7) : a small area at one end of a bowling alley behind the pins that is designed to catch the pins when they are knocked down (8) : an area alongside an auto speedway used for refueling or repairing the cars (9) : an area in a securities or commodities exchange typically surrounded by a circle of steps in which members of one or the other branch of the exchange do the actual trading ⟨the wheat ~⟩ (10) : an area covered or filled with sawdust or similar soft material designed to cushion the impact of one (as a pole vaulter) landing on that spot after a leap (11) : an area in which gaming tables are placed in a casino **2** : an abyss conceived of as the abode of evil spirits and the damned : HELL ⟨a demon from the depths of the ~ —John Morley⟩ **3** : a hollow or indentation esp. in the surface of an animal body or plant body : a surface depression: as **a** : a natural hollow in the surface of the body; *esp* : a hollow below the lower end of the breastbone — usu. used in the phrase *pit of the stomach* **b** (1) : one of usu. several or many small more or less round indentations left as scars in the skin typically as a result of disease : POCKMARK (2) : a usu. developmental imperfection in the enamel of a tooth that takes the form of a small pointed depression **c** : one of the small depressions left in a surface (as of metal, stone) as a result of some eroding or corrosive agent dripping or spattering on it **d** : a minute depression in the secondary wall of a plant cell that is formed where secondary-wall material has not covered the primary wall and that has a function in the intercellular movement of water and dissolved material **e** : one of the small depressed lesions left in the surface of a plant by disease **4** : a plant disease that produces pits in the plants affected

**²pit** \"\ *vb* **pitted; pitted; pitting; pits** [ME *pitten*, fr. *pitt, pit*, n.] *vt* **1** : to put into or as if into a pit; *esp* : to store (as vegetables) in a pit **b** : to make pits in ⟨the field had been *pitted* by the explosions⟩; *esp* : to make small indentations (as pockmarks) in ⟨a face that had been *pitted* by smallpox⟩ ⟨packed sand that had been *pitted* by the heavy rain⟩ **2 a** : to set (as gamecocks) into or as if into a pit so as to fight ⟨*pitted* a pair of cocks against each other⟩ **b** : to set into opposition or rivalry : match against an opponent or competitor : OPPOSE ⟨*pitting* his courage and his will against terrific odds —E.O. Hauser⟩ ⟨we will be *pitted* against each other —T.B.Costain⟩ ⟨*pitting* one prizefighter against another⟩ ~ *vi* **1** : to yield to pressure (as of the finger) and temporarily retain the indentation so made ⟨tissue affected by edema will usually ~⟩ **2** : to form small indentations : become marked with pits ⟨a metal that *pitted* after contact with acid⟩

**³pit** \"\ *n* -s [D, fr. MD *pitte, pit* — more at PITH] : the stone of a drupaceous fruit (as a cherry) — compare ⁴PIP 1

**⁴pit** \"\ *vt* **pitted; pitted; pitting; pits** : to remove the pit from (a fruit)

**⁵pit** \"\ *chiefly Scot var of* PUT

**pi·ta** \'pēd·ə\ *n* -s [Sp & Pg] **1** : any of several fiber-yielding plants: as **a** : CENTURY PLANT **b** : YUCCA **c** : a Central American wild pineapple (*Ananas magdalenae*) **2 a** : the fiber of a pita **b** : any of several other fibers; *esp* : MAURITIUS HEMP

**pit·a·hau·e·rat** \,pid·ə'hau̇ə,rat\ *n, pl* **pitahauerat** *or* **pitahauerats** *usu cap* **1** : a people of the Pawnee confederacy **2** : a member of the Pitahauerat people

**pit·a·haya** \,pid·ə'hīə\ *or* **pi·taya** \pə'tīə\ *n* -s [Sp, fr. Taino *pitahaya*] **1** : any of several cacti (as *Lemaireocereus thurberi* or *Acanthocereus pentagonus*) of the southwestern U. S. and adjacent Mexico that have edible juicy fruits; *esp* : SAGUARO **2** : the highly colored fruit of a pitahaya that often is as large as a peach and has bright red juice

**pi·tan·ga** \pə'taŋgə\ *n* -s [Pg, fr. Tupi] : SURINAM CHERRY 2

**pi·tan·gua** \,pi,taŋ'gwä\ *n* -s [Pg *pitanguá*, fr. Tupi] : a large-billed flycatcher (*Megarhynchus pitangua*) of Central America and So. America

**pi·tan·gus** \pə'taŋgəs\ *n, cap* [NL, fr. Pg *pitanguá*] : a genus of tyrant flycatchers inhabiting chiefly the warmer parts of America

**pit annulus** *n* [¹*pit*] : the thicker outer rim of the membrane of some bordered pits

**¹pit-a-pat** \¦pid·ē¦pat, -it¦, ¦i¦p- *sometimes* ¦ə¦p-; *usu* -ad·+V\ *or* **pit-pat** \'pit,p-\ *also* **pitty-pat** *like* PIT-A-PAT\ *or* **pitty-patty** \¦==¦pad·ē, -at¦, ¦i\ *adv (or adj)* [imit.] **1** : with a succession of strong rapid beats (as of the heart) : PITTER-PATTER ⟨heart went *pit-a-pat*⟩ **2** : with a succession of light rapid pats (as of footfalls) ⟨came running *pit-a-pat* down the corridor in her bare feet⟩

**²pit-a-pat** \"\ *n* **1** : a pattering sound : PITTER-PATTER ⟨the *pit-a-pat* of rain on the roof⟩ **2** : an onset of palpitation (as from emotion) ⟨the *pit-a-pat* of two young hearts —John Dryden⟩

**³pit-a-pat** \"\ *vi* : to go pit-a-pat : PITTER-PATTER ⟨love *pit-a-patted* in their hearts —Donn Byrne⟩

**pit aperture** *n* [¹*pit*] : the opening from the lumen of a cell into a pit cavity in a plant

**pi·ta·rah** *also* **pat·ta·ra** \pə'tärə\ *n* -s [Hindi *piṭārā, peṭārā;* akin to Skt *piṭaka* pitarah] : a basket or box for carrying the clothing of a traveler by palanquin

**pi·tau** \'pē,tau̇\ *n* -s [Maori] : SILVER TREE FERN

**pit band** *n* : a theater or opera house orchestra ⟨the bright surface excitement of a Broadway *pit band* —*New Yorker*⟩

**pitbird** \'=,=\ *n* [¹*pit* + *bird*] : REED WARBLER

**pit border** *n* [¹*pit*] : the extension of the secondary cell wall that forms a rim and overarches the pit cavity of a bordered pit

**pit boss** *n* **1** : a foreman in charge of workers in a given section of a coal mine or one in charge of all operations at a strip coal mine — compare SHIFT BOSS **2** : one that supervises the gaming tables in a casino during play

**pit bull** *or* **pit bullterrier** *n* : BULLTERRIER

**pit·cair·nia** \pit'ka(a)rnēə\ *n, cap* [NL, fr. William *Pitcairn* †1791 Eng. physician and botanist + NL *-ia*] : a large genus of tropical often epiphytic herbs (family Bromeliaceae) that have fleshy leaves with spiny margins and flowers with showy bracts

**pit canal** *n* [¹*pit*] : the passage in a bordered pit that is between the cell lumen and the pit chamber and that is esp. prominent when both secondary wall and pit border are thick

**pit cavity** *n* [¹*pit*] : the space within a plant cell pit

**¹pitch** \'pich\ *n* -ES [ME *pich*, fr. OE *pic*, fr. L *pic-, pix;* akin to Gk *pissa, pitta* pitch, OSlav *pĭkŭlŭ* pitch, L *opimus* fat, copious — more at FAT] **1** : any of various black or dark-colored viscous semisolid to solid substances obtained as residues in the distillation of tars or other organic materials: as **a** : a soft to hard and brittle substance that is obtained by distilling coal tar, contains principally aromatic resinous compounds together with aromatic and other hydrocarbons and their derivatives, and is used chiefly in waterproofing, impregnating, and binding **b** : a bright lustrous substance that is obtained by distilling wood tar, contains resin acids, and is used chiefly in plastics and insulating materials and in caulking seams **c** : a usu. soft substance that is obtained by distilling fats, fatty oils, or fatty acids (as from the manufacture of soap or candles), contains polymers and decomposition products, and is used chiefly in varnishes and paints and in floor coverings — called also *fatty acid pitch, stearin pitch* **2** : any of various bituminous substances ⟨mineral ~⟩ **3** : a resin that is obtained from various coniferous trees and is often of medicinal value ⟨pine ~⟩ **4** : any of various artificial mixtures (as of rosin with oils or waxes) resembling resinous or bituminous pitches; *specif* : a mixture of crude pitch, powdered resin, plaster of paris, and tallow used in metalcraft to form a base for supporting and fixing work while tooling or to furnish a supporting filling for a hollow object being worked on

**²pitch** \"\ *vt* -ED/-ING/-ES [ME *pichen*, fr. OE *pician*, fr. *pic*, n.] : to cover or smear with or as if with pitch : treat with pitch : apply pitch to

**³pitch** \"\ *vb* **pitched** *or archaic* **pight** \'pīt\ **pitched** *or archaic* **pight; pitching; pitches** [ME *picchen, pichen;* perh. akin to OE *pīcung* pricking — more at PICK] *vt* **1 a** *archaic* : to fix firmly in or on something : make secure ⟨built of the round sea pebbles ~*ed* in mortar —Joseph Jekyll⟩ **b** (1) : to erect (a tent) and fix firmly in place ⟨decided to ~ their tents there for the night⟩ (2) : to set up (a camp) by erecting tents ⟨moved the camp away from where it had been ~*ed*⟩ (3) : to set up (a wicket used in the game of cricket) by driving into the ground ⟨the wickets are ~*ed* opposite and parallel to each other⟩ **c** *archaic* : to spread out (as a net, a snare) and make secure ⟨~*es* toils to stop the flight —John Dryden⟩ **2** *archaic* **a** : to locate in or move into a particular place or position so as to cause to be situated securely or permanently ⟨the abrupt hill on which the town . . . is ~*ed* —William Black⟩ **b** : to turn (as the eyes, thoughts) toward something : DIRECT ⟨~*ing* her mind among the enjoyments of Corinth —Leigh Hunt⟩ **3** : THROW, FLING: as **a** : to take up (as hay) with a pitchfork and toss to a particular area ⟨watched the farmers ~*ing* hay⟩ **b** (1) : to bowl (a cricket ball) to a particular point (2) : to deliver (a baseball) to a batter ⟨~*ed* a fast ball to him and he struck out⟩ (3) : to toss (as coins) so as to cause to fall at or near a particular mark ⟨boys ~*ing* pennies⟩ ⟨liked to ~ horseshoes⟩ **c** : HURL ⟨~*ed* the spear over their heads⟩ **4 a** *obs* : to furnish with things that are stuck in or placed on ⟨~*ing* the top with multitude of stakes —Henry Holcroft⟩ **b** *archaic* : to set (as a road, path) with a layer of pebbles or stones **5 a** *chiefly Brit* : to set out or display (goods) for sale esp. in a market **b** : to sell, peddle, or advertise (goods) esp. in a high-pressure way ⟨~*ing* a new line of refrigerators⟩ **6** *obs* : to state or establish as definite ⟨first they ~ their conclusion, and then hunt about for premises —Joseph Hall⟩ **7 a** (1) : to cause to be at a particular level ⟨~*ed* their aspirations too high⟩ or of a particular overall quality ⟨~*ing* the conversation along idealistic lines⟩ (2) : to cause (as the voice) to have a particular highness or lowness of tone : give a particular musical pitch to ⟨~*ed* her voice too high⟩ (3) : to set in a particular musical key ⟨~*ed* the melody in the key of A⟩ **b** : to cause to be set at a particular angle ⟨~*ed* the roof too steep⟩ **8** *chiefly dial* : to put into the ground to grow : PLANT **9** : to cause to be loosened and lost ⟨the ship was in danger of ~*ing* her masts in the heavy sea⟩ **10** : PIT 2b **11 a** *chiefly Brit* : NARRATE, TELL ⟨~ a yarn that not even a child would have believed⟩ **b** : to utter, state, or deliver with a glibness typically marked by exaggeration, artificial fervor, insincerity, or deceptiveness ⟨was disgusted with the line she ~*ed*⟩ **12** : to start fermentation in (as wort) by adding some substance **13 a** : to lead (a card of a specified suit) in some games **b** : to establish (trump) by such leading **14** : to make a pitch shot with (a golf ball) **15 a** : to choose and put into a particular ball game as a usu. starting pitcher ⟨the manager had a hard time deciding which player to ~⟩ **b** : to play (a game of ball) in the position of pitcher ⟨~*ed* a perfect game⟩ ⟨~*ed* the first three innings⟩ **16** : to chip (a stone) so as to have straight lines and a flat surface : SQUARE **17** : ⁵FIT 2d(6) ~ *vi* **1 a** : to fall precipitately : fall headlong heavily : plunge headlong **b** (1) *of a ship* : to have the bow alternately plunge precipitately down and rise abruptly up ⟨~ and roll in a rough sea⟩ (2) *of an airplane* : to turn about a lateral axis so that the nose rises or falls in relation to the tail (3) *of a missile or spacecraft* : to turn about a lateral axis that is both perpendicular to the longitudinal axis and horizontal with respect to the earth **c** : to plunge forward with a movement suggestive of a pitching ship **d** : BUCK 1 **2 a** : ENCAMP ⟨~*ed* on the other side of the hill⟩ **b** (1) *archaic* : to settle down in a particular place or position ⟨the first settlers ~*ed* here —Jeremy Belknap⟩ (2) : to make a choice of something usu. in a rather casual way : fix on something — used with *on* or *upon* ⟨the place which he ~*ed* upon for his trading post —Washington Irving⟩ **3** : to incline forward and downward : SLOPE, DIP ⟨a vein of ore ~*ing* 36 degrees east⟩ **4 a** : to pitch something; *esp* : to pitch a baseball or softball ⟨a pitcher that really knows how to ~⟩ **b** : to play ball as a pitcher : have the position of pitcher ⟨~*ed* for 10 years before retiring⟩ **c** : to make a pitch shot in golf **5** *cricket, of a bowled ball* : to strike the ground before being played by a batsman ⟨the ball ~*ed* short of a length⟩ **6** : to exert oneself energetically against odds : fight courageously against difficulties and opposition ⟨no matter what happened, he stayed in there ~*ing*⟩ **syn** see PLUNGE, THROW — **pitch into 1** : to attack or assail with blows or words : BELABOR, SCOLD ⟨got mad and *pitched into* him with both fists⟩ ⟨said his mother would *pitch into* him when he got home⟩ **2** : to set to work on energetically ⟨decided to *pitch into* the job and get it over with⟩ — **pitch woo** : to make love : NECK

**⁴pitch** \"\ *n* -ES **1 a** (1) : the action of pitching (2) : a particular manner of pitching **b** *Brit* : a quantity of goods displayed for sale **2 a** : degree of slope : SLOPE: as (1) : the inclination of a roof as determined by the ratio of the height to the span (2) : the inclination of a flight of stairs as determined by the angle of the nosing line with the floor (3) : the angle of setting (as of a plowshare, a carpenter's plane iron, or a propeller blade) (4) : the angle that the cutting edge of a saw tooth makes with a line parallel to the points of the teeth (5) : the angle of a shotgun barrel from the vertical when the butt of the gun is at right angles to the vertical (6) : the angle at which finger holes are bored in a bowling ball (7) : the angle at which a heel is attached to the sole of a shoe (8) : the dip or inclination of a vein or bed of a mineral; *esp* : PLUNGE 4 **b** : the distance between two points of a mechanical part or between two such parts: as (1) : the distance between a point on a gear tooth or sprocket tooth and a corresponding point on the next tooth (2) : the distance between a point on one of the threads of a screw and a corresponding point on an adjacent thread (3) : the distance between a pair of paddles on a wheel (4) : the distance between a pair of rivet holes (5) : the distance between a pair of stays (as in a steam boiler) (6) **:** the distance between two

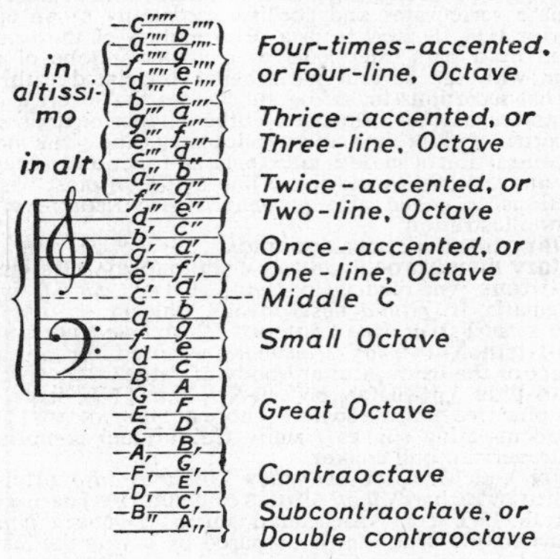

staff notation of pitch 4b

points on the circumference of an armature **c** (1) **:** the longitudinal distance between corresponding edges of successive perforations in motion-picture film (2) **:** the distance between successive grooves of a disc recording **d :** the distance advanced by a propeller in one revolution — called also *effective pitch* **e :** a unit of width of typewriter type based on the number of times a letter can be set in a linear inch ⟨elite is a 12-*pitch* type⟩ **f :** a unit of measure of carpet fineness based on the number of warp threads within a length of usu. 27 inches **g** (1) **:** the number of teeth (as of a gear) or of threads (as of a screw) per inch (2) **:** the number of grooves per inch in a disc recording **3 a** *archaic* **:** the highest point **:** SUMMIT ⟨driven headlong from the ~ of heaven —John Milton⟩ **:** the highest or most intense degree **:** ZENITH, ACME, TOP ⟨when the general hilarity was at its ~ —William Black⟩ ⟨singing at the ~ of their voices —J.H.Newman⟩ **b** *archaic* **:** ALTITUDE, ELEVATION ⟨just of his size, complexion, and ~ —Edmund Hickeringill⟩ ⟨flies at a much higher ~ —Henry Hallam⟩ **c** *archaic* **:** the tip of a piece of land (as a cape) extending into a body of water **4 a :** the relative level, intensity, or extent of some quality or state ⟨were at a high ~ of excitement⟩ **b** (1) **:** the highness or lowness of a musical tone dependent on the number of vibrations (as of the string of a musical instrument, the vocal cords) per second and the resultant corresponding number of sound waves reaching the ear per second in such a way that the greater the number of vibrations the higher the tone and the fewer the number of vibrations the lower the tone (2) **:** a tone produced by a particular number of vibrations per second and a corresponding number of sound waves per second and chosen as a standard (as in tuning musical instruments) — see ABSOLUTE PITCH, INTERNATIONAL PITCH, PHILHARMONIC PITCH **c** (1) **:** the

THE ABSOLUTE PITCHES OF THE PURE AND TEMPERED SCALES

| NOTE | VIBRATIONS PER SECOND pure | VIBRATIONS PER SECOND tempered | NOTE | VIBRATIONS PER SECOND pure | VIBRATIONS PER SECOND tempered |
|---|---|---|---|---|---|
| c′ | 264 | 261.62 | g′ | 396 | 391.99 |
| d′ | 297 | 293.66 | a′ | 440 | 440.00 |
| e′ | 330 | 329.63 | b′ | 495 | 493.88 |
| f′ | 352 | 349.23 | c″ | 528 | 523.25 |

difference in the relative vibration frequency of the human voice that contributes to the total meaning of ear-apprehended speech by being (as in Chinese) an integral part of a word and essential to the conveyance of its minimal meaning or by varying (as in English) according to the intended minimal meaning of a word with different meanings (2) **:** a definite relative pitch that is a significant phenomenon (as a phoneme) in speech — symbols 1 (highest), 2, 3, 4 (lowest) **5 :** a steep place **:** a steep ascent or descent **:** DECLIVITY **6 a :** a place where one stations oneself or where one settles down: as (1) *archaic* **:** a piece of ground selected for a place of residence **:** ABODE (2) *Brit* **:** the open-air stand of one who conducts business on the street ⟨a shoeblack, whose ~ is at the corner —*Punch*⟩ (3) **:** a place in a river chosen for angling (4) **:** the piece of ground assigned to a tributer in Cornwall **b** (1) *chiefly Brit* **:** a field used for playing some games (as soccer, cricket) (2) **:** the specially prepared part of a cricket field between the bowling creases **:** WICKET **7 :** LENGTH 10a **8 :** an all-fours game in which the first card led must be a trump; *esp* **:** AUCTION PITCH **9 a** *chiefly Brit* **:** CHAT **b** (1) **:** a typically high-pressure sales talk (2) **:** a commercial advertisement (3) **:** RECOMMENDATION, BOOST, PLUG **c :** a line of talk or way of speaking or writing marked by glibness and typically by exaggeration, artificial fervor, insincerity, or deceptiveness **10 a :** PITCH SHOT **b** (1) **:** the delivery of a baseball by a pitcher to a batter (2) **:** a baseball so thrown **c :** a pass in football

**pitch accent** *n* [[4]*pitch*] **1 :** stress deriving from the relative acuteness of musical tones and tending to be accentuated by higher pitch **2 :** prominence given to a syllable or word by means of raised pitch or change of pitch

**pit chamber** *n* [[1]*pit*] **:** the part of the pit cavity of a bordered pit enclosed by the overarching extension of the secondary cell wall

**pitch-and-run shot** \ˌ=ˈ=ˌ=-\ *or* **pitch-and-run** \ˌ=ˈ=ˌ=\ *n* [[3]*pitch*] **:** CHIP SHOT

**pitch-and-toss** \ˌ=ˈ=ˌ=\ *n* [[3]*pitch*] **:** a game in which the player who pitches coins nearest to a mark has first chance at tossing up all the coins played and winning those that fall heads up

**pitch apple** *n* [[1]*pitch*] **:** a common tropical American tree (*Clusia rosea*) that has coarse evergreen leaves, solitary white or rose flowers, and a whitish resinous fruit and that when young often grows over other trees like a vine in such a way as to strangle them — called also *strangler fig*

**pitch-black** \ˈ=ˈ=\ *adj* [[1]*pitch* + *black*, adj.] **:** of the color pitch black **:** extremely dark **:** intensely black ⟨a *pitch-black* night⟩ — **pitch-black·ness** \ˈ=ˈ=+\ *n*

**pitch black** *n* [[1]*pitch* + *black*, n.] **1 :** a dark brown that is nearly black **2 :** a deep black

**pitch·blende** \ˈpich,blend\ *n* [part trans. of G *pechblende*, fr. *pech* pitch + *blende* — more at BLENDE] **:** a massive variety of uraninite occurring in metalliferous veins that ranges in color from brown to black and has a distinctive luster and that contains a slight amount of radium and is the principal ore= mineral source of uranium

**pitch bowl** *n* **:** BULLET 3b

**pitch box** *n* **:** a shallow box of wood or metal used in metalcraft for holding pitch in order to form a bed for fixing or holding the work while tooling

**pitch circle** *n* [[4]*pitch*] **:** a pitch line in a circular gear that forms a circle concentric with the axis of the gear

**pitch coal** *n* [[1]*pitch*] **:** a brittle lustrous bituminous coal or lignite

**pitch cone** *n* [[4]*pitch*] **:** a cone that constitutes the pitch surface of an ordinary bevel gear

**pitch count** *n* [[4]*pitch*] **:** a count of 4 points for an ace, 3 for a king, 2 for a queen, and 1 for a jack (as in the game of pitch)

**pitch cylinder** *n* [[4]*pitch*] **:** a cylinder that constitutes the pitch surface of a spur gear

**pitch-dark** \ˈ=ˈ=\ *adj* [[1]*pitch*] **:** extremely dark **:** PITCH-BLACK — **pitch-dark·ness** \ˈ=ˈ=+\ *n*

**pitch diameter** *n* [[4]*pitch*] **:** the diameter of the pitch circle of a wheel

**pitched** *past of* PITCH

**pitched battle** *n* [fr. past part. of [3]*pitch*] **1 :** a battle in which the opposing forces have firm fixed positions that are clearly defined — distinguished from *skirmish* **2 :** an intensely fought battle in which the opposing forces are locked in close combat

**pitched field** *n*, *archaic* **:** PITCHED BATTLE

**[1]pitch·er** \ˈpichə(r)\ *n* -s [ME *picher*, fr. OF *pichier*, fr. ML *bicarius* goblet, beaker — more at BEAKER] **1 a** (1) **:** a relatively large container for holding and pouring out liquids that is made typically of earthenware, glass, metal, or plastic and has a wide mouth with a broad lip or spout and a handle at one side or sometimes two ears (2) *chiefly Brit* **:** JUG 1b **b :** the contents of a pitcher **:** PITCHERFUL **c :** powdered pottery shards used in ceramics in bodies and glazes to improve properties — usu. used in pl. **2 :** ASCIDIUM; *esp* **:** a modified leaf of a pitcher plant in which the hollowed petiole and base of the blade form an elongated receptacle over which the outer part of the blade usu. projects like a lid

pitcher 1a(1)

**[2]pitch·er** \ˈ"\ *n* -s [[3]*pitch* + *-er*] **1 :** one that pitches: as **a :** the player that pitches in a game of baseball or softball — see BASEBALL illustration **b :** a worker that tosses bricks to a setter or loader **c :** a worker in a tan house who cleans out vats of used tanbark **2** *chiefly dial* **a :** one that loads cars underground in a coal mine **b :** one that attends to the laying down and taking up of temporary railways at the working faces **c :** one that picks over dumps for pieces of ore **3 :** a small object (as a marble, stone) used for tossing in some games **4 :** an iron golf club with a broad face lofted more than that of a mashie niblick — called also *number seven iron;* see IRON illustration

**[3]pitcher** \ˈ"\ *n* -s [[2]*pitch* + *-er*] **:** PARAFFINER

**pitch·ered** \-chə(r)d\ *adj* [[1]*pitcher* + *-ed*] **1 :** having ascidia ⟨a ~ plant⟩ **2 :** developed into ascidia ⟨~ leaves⟩

**pitch·er·ful** \-chə(r),fu̇l\ *n*, *pl* **pitcher·fuls** *also* **pitchers·ful** \-chə(r)z,fu̇l\ **:** the quantity held by a pitcher

**pitcher house** *n* [ME *picher hous*] *obs* **:** WINE CELLAR

**pitcheri** *var of* PITURI

**pitcher molding** *n* **:** the molding of clay ware in molds made of lightly fired clay

**pitcher plant** *n* **:** any of several plants esp. of the genera *Sarracenia*, *Nepenthes*, *Cephalotus*, and *Darlingtonia* with leaves which are either wholly or partly modified into forms resembling pitchers and in which insects are trapped and digested by the plant through liquids (as acid secretions or water prob. with the aid of proteolytic enzymes) contained by the leaves: as **a :** a bog herb (*Sarracenia purpurea*) of the northeastern U. S. with leaves modified into the form of broadly winged pitchers **b :** CALIFORNIA PITCHER PLANT **c :** AUSTRALIAN PITCHER PLANT

**pitcher-plant family** *n* **1 :** NEPENTHACEAE **2 :** SARRACENIACEAE

**pitcher sage** *n* **:** a Californian mint (*Sphacele calycina*) with pubescent or woolly herbage and large white flowers

**pitcher's elbow** *n* [[2]*pitcher*] **:** pain and disability associated with the tearing of tendons from their attachment on the epicondyle of the humerus often with involvement of tissues within and around the elbow joint

**pitches** *pl of* PITCH, *pres 3d sing of* PITCH

**pitch-faced** \ˈ=ˌ=\ *adj* [[4]*pitch*] **:** having a rough quarry finish along the vertical surface except for edges faced cleanly with a pitching chisel ⟨*pitch-faced* stonework⟩

**pitch factor** *n* [[4]*pitch*] **:** the ratio of the voltage induced in a short-pitch winding to the voltage that would be induced if the winding were full pitch

**pitch-farthing** *n* [[3]*pitch*] **:** CHUCK-FARTHING

**pitch fir** *n* [[1]*pitch*] **:** PITCH PINE

**[1]pitch·fork** \ˈpich,ˌ=\ *n* [ME *pychforke*, alter. (influenced by *pichen* to pitch, throw) of *pikfork*, fr. *pik* pick + *fork* — more at PITCH, PICK, FORK] **1 :** a usu. long-handled fork typically with two or three long somewhat curved prongs for pitching hay or straw or similar material **2 a :** the fruit of an herb of the genus *Bidens* **b pitchforks** *pl but sing or pl in constr* **:** BUR MARIGOLD

**[2]pitchfork** \ˈ"\ *vt* **1 :** to lift and toss with or as if with a pitchfork ⟨~*ed* the hay into the wagon⟩ **2 :** to thrust into something suddenly and unexpectedly or without preparation **:** throw into something precipitately and by surprise ⟨was ~*ed* into the job by destiny —G.W.Johnson⟩ ⟨their very success . . . ~*ed* them into the place of world leadership —*Times Lit. Supp.*⟩ ⟨is literally ~*ed* into astounding triumphs —Wolcott Gibbs⟩

**pitchforks** *adv* **:** very hard — usu. used in the phrase *rain pitchforks*

**pitchhole** \ˈ=ˌ=\ *n* [[4]*pitch* + *hole*] **:** a recess in a stone otherwise dressed true for setting

**pitch hyperboloid** *n* [[4]*pitch*] **:** a hyperboloid that constitutes the pitch surface of a skew bevel

**pitchi** \ˈpichē\ *n* -s [native name in Australia] **:** a large shallow elongated wooden receptacle much used by Australian aborigines as a container for food and drink

**pitchier** *comparative of* PITCHY

**pitchiest** *superlative of* PITCHY

**pitch in** *vi* **1 :** to set to work energetically **:** begin something energetically **:** pitch into something ⟨had a lot to do and decided to *pitch in*⟩ **2 :** to make a contribution toward commonly shared expenses **:** chip in ⟨had *pitched in* to rent a cottage —Martin Donohue⟩

**pitch·i·ness** \ˈpichēnəs, -chin-\ *n* -ES **:** the quality or state of being pitchy

**pitching** *n* -s [fr. gerund of [3]*pitch*] **1 :** a stone facing on a slope of ground **2 :** a layer of coarse stone on a road

**pitching chisel** *or* **pitching tool** *n* **:** a chisel used for making an edge on the face of a stone

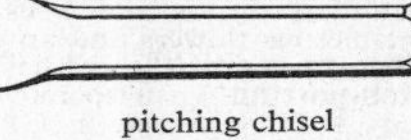
pitching chisel

**pitching moment** *n* [fr. pres. part. of [3]*pitch*] **:** a moment tending to rotate an airplane or airfoil about its lateral axis

**pitching niblick** *n* **:** an iron golf club with a loft between those of a pitcher and a niblick — called also *number 8 iron;* see IRON illustration

**pitching piece** *n* **:** a beam supporting a staircase and located at the top of the stairs — opposed to *apron piece*

**pitching yeast** *n* **:** a yeast used in pitching (as wort)

**pitch line** *n* [[4]*pitch*] **1 :** the line on which the pitch of gear teeth or sprocket teeth is measured and which consists of an ideal line in a toothed gear or rack which bears such a relation to a corresponding line in another gear with which it works that the two lines will have a common velocity (as in rolling contact) **2 :** the line from which players lag in the game of marbles

**[1]pitch·man** \ˈpichmən\ *n*, *pl* **pitchmen** [[4]*pitch* + *man*] **1 :** one who sells something **:** SALESMAN, VENDER; *esp* **:** one who vends gadgets or novelties or similar articles esp. on the streets or from a concession (as at a fair) ⟨demonstrated and hawked his product with the vigor of an oldtime ~ —*Time*⟩ **2 :** one that uses a fast line of talk to advertise and sell something or to cause something to be known and accepted ⟨frenetic commercials delivered by radio and television *pitchmen*⟩

**[2]pitchman** \ˈ"\ *n*, *pl* **pitchmen** [[1]*pitch* + *man*] **:** an operator of a machine for grinding pitch for use with coke in the manufacture of carbon electrodes

**pitch mining** *n* [[4]*pitch*] **:** the mining of steeply inclined coal beds

**pitch moth** *n* [[1]*pitch*] **:** any of several moths (as the sequoia pitch moth, the pitch twig moth) having larvae that bore into the wood of coniferous trees and so cause pitch to exude

**pitch nodule maker** *n* [[1]*pitch*] **:** a pitch moth (*Petrova albicapitana*) whose larva is esp. destructive to lodgepole pine and jack pine in No. America

**pitch ore** *n* [[1]*pitch*] **:** PITCHBLENDE

**pitch out** *vi* **:** to make a pitchout

**pitchout** \ˈ=ˌ=\ *n* [*pitch out*] **1 :** a pitch in the game of baseball that is deliberately wide of the plate so that the batter cannot hit it and that is usu. designed to enable the catcher to check or put out a base runner (as by breaking up a steal or preventing a squeeze play) **2 :** a lateral pass in the game of football made between two backs behind the scrimmage line

**pitch peat** *n* [[1]*pitch*] **:** a black homogeneous peat with a waxy luster

**pitch-penny** \ˈ=ˌ==\ *n* [[3]*pitch*] **:** PITCH-AND-TOSS

**pitch pine** *n* [[1]*pitch*] **1 a :** any of several pines that yield pitch; *esp* **:** a 3-leaved pine (*Pinus rigida*) of eastern No. America closely related to the pond pine **b :** the wood of a pitch pine **2 :** a dark grayish green that is bluer, lighter, and stronger than average ivy, yellower and slightly lighter than Persian green, and yellower and lighter than hemlock green — called also *thyme* **3** *chiefly Midland* **:** KINDLING WOOD

**pitch pipe** *n* [[4]*pitch*] **:** a small reed pipe or flue pipe that is blown with the breath to produce one or more tones used for establishing the pitch in singing or in tuning an instrument

**pitch pocket** *n* [[1]*pitch*] **:** a cavity in lumber that contains or has contained resin

**pitch point** *n* [[4]*pitch*] **:** the point of contact of the pitch lines of two gears or of a rack and pinion when in mesh

**[1]pitchpole** *also* **pitchpoll** \ˈ=ˌ=\ *n* [[3]*pitch* + *poll* (head)] **:** SOMERSAULT

**[2]pitchpole** *also* **pitchpoll** *vb* -ED/-ING/-S *vi* **:** to turn end over end **:** SOMERSAULT ~ *vt* **:** to cause to turn end over end

**pitch seam** *or* **pitch streak** *n* [[1]*pitch*] **:** a pitch-filled shake or check in lumber

**pitch shot** *n* [[4]*pitch*] **:** an approach stroke in golf in which the ball is lofted to the green with backspin so that the ball rolls very little after striking the green — compare CHIP SHOT

**pitchstone** \ˈ=ˌ=\ *n* [trans. of G *pechstein*, fr. *pech* pitch + *stein* stone] **:** a glassy rock that has a resinous luster and that contains more water than obsidian does

**pitch surface** *n* [[4]*pitch*] **:** the surface of either of two tangent imaginary friction wheels having the same axes and the same angular velocities as those of a pair of real gears in mesh

**pitch tree** *n* [[1]*pitch*] **:** any of several resinous conifers: as **a :** KAURI PINE **b :** AMBOINA PINE **c :** NORWAY SPRUCE

**pitch twig moth** *n* [[1]*pitch*] **:** a small largely reddish brown pitch moth (*Petrova comstockiana*) whose larvae attack various hard pines

**pitch-up** \ˈ=ˌ=\ *n* -s [fr. the verb *pitch up*] **:** the tendency of a climbing airplane esp. with swept-back wings to nose sharply upward beyond the control of the pilot

**pitchuri** *var of* PITURI

**pitchwoman** \ˈ=ˌ==\ *n*, *pl* **pitchwomen** [[4]*pitch* + *woman*] **:** a female pitchman

**pitchy** \ˈpichē, -chi\ *adj*, *usu* -ER/-EST [[1]*pitch* + *-y*] **1 a :** full of pitch: as (1) **:** RESINOUS ⟨~ lumber⟩ (2) **:** coated, smeared, or sticky with pitch **:** TARRY ⟨a ~ road⟩ **b :** of, relating to, or having the qualities of pitch ⟨a ~ substance⟩ **2 :** as dark or as black as pitch **:** very dark **:** PITCH-BLACK ⟨went out into the ~ night⟩ — often used with *black* or *dark* ⟨the ~ black night⟩

**pit coal** *n* [[1]*pit*] **:** coal mined from the earth **:** mineral coal — distinguished from *charcoal*

**pit committee** *n* **:** a joint committee of employer and workers dealing with the labor problems of a mine

**pit disease** *n* [[1]*pit*] **:** an often fatal disease of oysters resulting from the presence of flagellates of the genus *Hexamita* in the blood stream and involving embolism and destruction of tissues

**pit dwelling** *n* **:** PIT HOUSE

**pi·tei·ra** \pəˈterə, -tārə\ *n* -s [Pg, fr. *pita* + *-eira* -ary (fr. L *-aria*)] **1 :** GIANT CABUYA **2 :** MAURITIUS HEMP

**pit·e·ous** \ˈpid-ēəs, -itē-\ *adj* [ME *piteus*, *piteous*, alter. (influenced by *pite* pity) of *pitous*, fr. OF *piteus*, fr. *pité* pity + *-eus* -ous — more at PITY] **1 a :** arousing or deserving pity or compassion ⟨had received ~ appeals for help —F. Tennyson Jesse⟩ **b** *archaic* **:** feeling pity or compassion **:** COMPASSIONATE, MERCIFUL **2** *archaic* **:** PALTRY, MEAN ⟨~ amends —John Milton⟩ — **pit·e·ous·ly** *adv* — **pit·e·ous·ness** *n* -ES

**pitfall** \ˈ=ˌ=\ *n* [ME, fr. *pit* + *fall*] **1 :** TRAP, SNARE; *specif* **:** a pit bridged by a cover of flimsy material or otherwise concealed or camouflaged and used to capture and hold animals or men falling into it **2 :** a hidden or not easily recognized danger, error, or source of injury or destruction into which one that is unsuspecting or incautious may fall ⟨the ~*s* of ignorance⟩

**pit field** *n* [[1]*pit*] **:** an area in the wall of a plant cell in which one or more pits develop

**pit game** *n*, *pl* **pit game** *or* **pit games** [[1]*pit*] **:** PIT GAME FOWL

**pit game fowl** *n* **:** a game fowl of the Modern Game class that is bred primarily for fighting and selected for vigor, muscularity, and aggressiveness — compare EXHIBITION GAME FOWL

**[1]pith** \ˈpith, *dial* ˈpeth\ *n* -s [ME *pithe*, *pith*, fr. OE *pitha;* akin to MD & MLG *pit*, *pitte* pith, pit (of a fruit)] **1 a** (1) **:** a usu. continuous central strand of predominantly parenchymatous tissue that occurs in the stems of most vascular plants and some roots as part of the primary tissue system, is typically surrounded by vascular tissue, prob. functions chiefly in storage, and may disappear leaving a void in some plants (as many umbellifers) (2) **:** a slender soft core at the center of the heartwood of many logs consisting of the dried remains of the pith **b :** any of various loose spongy plant tissues that resemble true pith ⟨the white ~ lining the skin of an orange⟩ **c :** the soft or spongy interior of a part of the body: as (1) *archaic* **:** the spinal cord or bone marrow (2) **:** the medulla of a hair (3) **:** the spongy interior of a feather **2 a** (1) **:** the essential part of something **:** ESSENCE, CORE, MARROW ⟨individuality, which was the very ~ of liberty —H.J.Laski⟩ ⟨the ~ of greatness⟩ ⟨getting down to the ~ of the matter⟩ (2) **:** the very center **:** HEART ⟨people who live in the thick of politics and in the ~ of society —Francis Hackett⟩ **b :** substantial quality (as of meaning or content) **:** SOLIDITY, MEATINESS ⟨made a speech that lacked ~⟩ **3** *archaic* **:** VIGOR, ENERGY, STRENGTH ⟨took the ~ out of my legs —R.L.Stevenson⟩ **4 :** IMPORTANCE, WEIGHTINESS ⟨enterprises of great ~ and moment —Shak.⟩

**[2]pith** \ˈ"\ *vt* -ED/-ING/-S **1 a :** to kill (as cattle) by piercing or severing the spinal cord at or near the axis **b :** to destroy the spinal cord or entire central nervous system of (as a frog) usu. by passing a wire or needle up and down the vertebral canal **2 a :** to remove the pith from ⟨a plant stem that had been ~*ed*⟩ **b :** to draw out **:** SAP, EXTRACT ⟨could ~ so much of the vigor out of his body —C.E.Montague⟩

**pithead** \ˈ=ˌ=\ *n* **:** the top of a mining pit or coal shaft; *also* **:** the immediately adjacent ground and buildings

**pit-headed** \ˈ=ˌ==\ *adj* **:** having a pit on the surface of the head ⟨pit vipers are *pit-headed*⟩

**pit-head frame** \ˈ=ˌ=-\ *n* **:** HEADFRAME

**pit-head·man** \ˈ=ˌ=mən\ *n*, *pl* **pitheadmen 1 :** one that works about a pithead **2 :** one in charge of a pithead or pitheadmen

**pithec-** *or* **pitheco-** *comb form* [Gk *pithēk-*, *pithēko-*, fr. *pithēkos* — more at BEBUNG] **:** ape **:** monkey ⟨*pithec*an⟩ ⟨*pitheco*metric⟩

**pi·the·can** \pəˈthēkən, ˈpithək-\ *adj* [*pithec-* + *-an*] **:** of, relating to, or resembling apes, esp. the anthropoid apes

**pith·e·can·thrope** \ˌpithəˈkan,thrōp, ˈpithəkən-\ *n* -s [NL *pithecanthropus*] **:** PITHECANTHROPUS 2

**pith·e·can·throp·ic** \ˌpithə,kanˈthräpik\ *adj* [NL *pithecanthropus* + E *-ic*] **:** of, relating to, or resembling pithecanthropi

**[1]pith·e·can·thro·pid** \ˌ=ˌ=ˈkan(t)thrəpəd; -,kanˈthrōp-, -räp-\ *adj* [NL *Pithecanthropidae*] **:** PITHECANTHROPIC

**[2]pithecanthropid** \ˈ"\ *n* -s **:** PITHECANTHROPUS 2

**pith·e·can·throp·i·dae** \ˌpithə,kanˈthräpə,dē\ *n pl*, *cap* [NL, fr. *Pithecanthropus*, type genus + *-idae*] **:** a formerly recognized family containing the genus *Pithecanthropus*

**pith·e·can·thro·pine** \ˌ=ˌ=ˈkan(t)thrə,pīn, -,kanˈthrōpən\ *adj* [NL *pithecanthropus* + E *-ine*] **:** PITHECANTHROPIC

**[1]pith·e·can·thro·poid** \-ˈkan(t)thrə,pȯid\ *adj* [NL *pithecanthropus* + E *-oid*] **:** of, relating to, or resembling the pithecanthropi

**[2]pithecanthropoid** \ˈ"\ *n* -s **:** a pithecanthropoid mammal or fossil

**pith·e·can·thro·pus** \ˌpithəˈkan(t)thrəpəs, -,kanˈthrōp-\ *n* [NL, fr. *pithec-* + *-anthropus*] **1** *cap* **a :** a hypothetical group of extinct primates intermediate between man and the anthropoid apes **b :** a genus of extinct primitive men that includes two generally accepted species (*P. erectus* and *P. robustus*) known from skull and other bone fragments found in Javanese Pliocene gravels and sometimes the very similar Peking man and that comprises forms having a profile like that of an ape with very low forehead and undeveloped chin, a posture approaching that of modern man, and a brain of 900 to 1000 cubic centimeters which is larger than that of any known ape and smaller than that of any normal modern man — compare SINANTHROPUS **2** *pl* **pithecanthro·pi** \-ˌpī, -(ˌ)pē\ **:** an individual of the group or genus *Pithecanthropus*

**pi·the·cia** \pə̇'thēsh(ē)ə\ *n, cap* [NL, fr. *pithec-* + *-ia*] **:** a genus of saki monkeys of northern So. America and the Amazon basin — **pi·the·cian** \-sh(ē)ən\ *adj or n*

**pith·e·cism** \'pithəˌsizəm\ *n* -s [ISV *pithec-* + *-ism*] **:** pithecoid characteristics present in man

**1pithe·coid** \'pithə̇ˌkȯid, pə̇'thēˌk-\ *adj* [NL *Pithecia* + E *-oid*] **1 :** of or relating to *Pithecia* or closely related genera **2 a :** PITHECAN **b :** of, relating to, or resembling monkeys

**2pithecoid** \"\ *n* -s **:** a pithecoid individual

**pith·e·coi·dea** \ˌpithə̇'kȯidēə\ *n pl, cap* [NL, fr. *pithec-* + *-oidea*] *in some classifications* **:** a suborder of Primates that is coordinate with Prosinii and Anthropoidea and includes the new-world monkeys and old-world monkeys

**pith·e·co·lo·bi·um** \ˌpithə̇kə'lōbēəm\ *n, cap* [NL, fr. *pithec-* + Gk *lobion* small lobe, dim. of *lobos* lobe — more at SLEEP] **:** a large genus of tropical shrubs and trees (family Leguminosae) having bipinnate leaves and globose heads of flowers with many stamens and a twisted or coiled pod — see ALGARROBILLA, CAT'S-CLAW 1b, RAIN TREE, WILD TAMARIND

**pith·e·co·log·i·cal** \ˌpithə̇kəˌläjə̇kəl\ *adj* **:** of or relating to pithecology

**pith·e·col·o·gy** \ˌpithə̇'käləjē\ *n* -ES [*pithec-* + *-logy*] **:** the study of apes

**pith·e·co·met·ric** \ˌpithə̇kəˌme·trik\ *adj* [*pithec-* + *-metric*] **:** relating to measurements of the skeletons of apes

**pith·e·co·mor·phic** \-ˌmȯrfik\ *adj* [*pithec-* + *-morphic*] **:** resembling apes

**pith·e·co·mor·phism** \ˌ≈≈≈'≈ˌfizəm\ *n* -s **:** structural resemblance to an ape

**1pi·the·cus** \pə̇'thēkəs; 'pithə̇k-,'pithēk-\ [NL, fr. Gk *pithēkos* monkey, ape — more at BEBUNG] *syn of* MACACA

**2pithecus** \"\ [NL, fr. Gk *pithēkos* ape, monkey] *syn of* PRESBYTIS

**-pithecus** \"\ *n comb form* [NL, fr. Gk *pithēkos*] **:** ape — in generic names ⟨Siva*pithecus*⟩

**pithed** *past of* PITH

**pith fleck** *or* **pith–ray fleck** \'≈ˌ≈-\ *n* **:** a minute spot in the wood of a tree that results from injury to the cambium by the boring of small dipterous larvae

**pith·i·ly** \'pithəlē, -li\ *adv* [ME, fr. *pithy* + *-ly*] **:** in a pithy manner ⟨impressed by the way in which they can summarize ~ great tracts of life —H.J.Laski⟩

**pith·i·ness** \-thēnə̇s, -thin-\ *n* -ES **1 :** the quality or state of being pithy **2 :** a disease of celery marked by the occurrence of soft spongy stalks and hearts

**pithing** *pres part of* PITH

**pith knot** *n* **:** a sound knot of timber with a pith hole not more than ¼ inch in diameter

**pith·less** \'pithlə̇s\ *adj* **:** devoid of pith — **pith·less·ly** *adv*

**pithole** \'≈ˌ≈\ *n* [1*pit* + *hole*] *dial chiefly Brit* **:** PIT, GRAVE

**pi·thos** \'piˌthäs, 'pīˌ-\ *n, pl* **pi·thoi** \-thȯi\ [Gk — more at FISCAL] **:** a very large earthenware jar with a wide round mouth used throughout the ancient Greek world esp. for holding and storing large quantities of food (as grain) or liquids (as wine, oil) and sometimes for the burial of the dead

**pit house** *n* **1 :** a primitive habitation consisting of a pit dug in the earth and roofed over **2 :** a pit usu. with glass walls and roof for storing plants and for growing plants that prefer low temperatures

**pith ray** *n* **:** MEDULLARY RAY

**pith rush** *n* **:** STAFF RUSH

**piths** *pl of* PITH, *pres 3d sing of* PITH

**pith tree** *n* **:** AMBATCH

**pithworm** \'≈ˌ≈\ *n* **:** WIREWORM

**pithy** \'pithē, -thi, *dial* 'peth-\ *adj, usu* -ER/-EST [ME, fr. *pithe, pith* pith + *-y* — more at PITH] **1 a** (1) **:** of or resembling pith ⟨a ~ substance⟩ (2) **:** containing, filled with, or abounding in pith ⟨~ stems⟩ **b** *chiefly Scot* **:** STRONG, VIGOROUS **2 a :** containing much meaning and substance in a terse concentrated form **:** brief and to the point **:** full of significance **:** MEATY ⟨a ~ proverb⟩ ⟨a ~ summary⟩ ⟨wrote several ~ chapters⟩ **b :** marked by the use of pithy speech or writing ⟨a ~ speaker⟩ ⟨a ~ style⟩ **syn** see CONCISE

**pithy gall** *n* **:** a large rough furrowed oblong gall formed on blackberry canes by a small cynipid gall wasp (*Diastrophus turgidus*)

**piti·able** \'pid·ēəbəl, -itē-\ *adj* [ME *piteable*, fr. MF *piteable, pitiable*, fr. *pité, pitié* piety, pity + *-able* — more at PITY] **:** deserving, needing, or arousing pity **:** PITIFUL ⟨the ~ spectacle of a human being in distress —Lyman Bryson⟩ ⟨a ~ wretch⟩ ⟨a ~ attempt to be funny⟩ **syn** see CONTEMPTIBLE

**piti·able·ness** *n* -ES **:** the quality or state of being pitiable

**piti·ably** \-blē,-bli\ *adv* **:** in a pitiable manner ⟨struggle ~ for the preservation of an existence devoid of all warmth and light —M.R.Cohen⟩

**pitied** *past of* PITY

**piti·er** \'pid·ēə(r), -itē-\ *n* -s **:** one that pities

**pities** *pl of* PITY, *pres 3d sing of* PITY

**piti·ful** \'pid·|ēfəl, -it|, |əf-\ *adj, sometimes* **pitifuller**; *sometimes* **pitifullest** [ME *petefull*, fr. *pete, pite, pitie* pity + *-full, -ful* -ful — more at PITY] **1 a :** deserving or arousing pity **:** exciting or being such as to excite compassion ⟨one of those ~ refugees of which Europe was full —Upton Sinclair⟩ **b :** deserving or arousing contemptuous commiseration or pitying contempt **:** CONTEMPTIBLE ⟨the ~ wage scale —H.S. Truman⟩ **2** *archaic* **:** full of pity **:** COMPASSIONATE, MERCIFUL ⟨be ~ to my great woe —John Keats⟩

**piti·ful·ly** *adv* **:** in a pitiful manner

**piti·ful·ness** *n* -ES **:** the quality or state of being pitiful

**piti·less** \'pid·|ēlə̇s, -it|, |ᵊl-\ *adj* [ME *piteeles*, fr. *pitee, pite* pity + *-les* -less] **1 a :** devoid of or unmoved by pity and compassion **:** showing no mercy **:** MERCILESS ⟨a ~ dictator⟩ **b** *archaic* **:** exciting no pity or compassion ⟨a corpse, dog-worried, ~ —J.S.Phillimore⟩ **2 :** grimly uncompromising ⟨a ~ acceptance of fact —H.G.Wells⟩ ⟨the almost ~ clarity of intelligence —P.E.More⟩

**piti·less·ly** *adv* **:** in a pitiless manner

**piti·less·ness** *n* -ES **:** the quality or state of being pitiless

**pitirri** *var of* PIPIRI

**pit·less** \'pitlə̇s\ *adj* **:** having no pit

**pitlike** \'≈ˌ≈\ *adj* **:** resembling a pit

**pit–making scale** \'≈ˌ≈≈-\ *n* [1*pit*] **:** PIT SCALE

**pit·man** \'pitmən\ *n* **1** *pl* **pitmen :** one who works in or near a pit: as **a :** a worker in a coal mine **b :** BOTTOM SAWYER **c :** a worker in a quarry **d :** one that greases or repairs or otherwise services the underside of cars and other vehicles in a garage **e :** one that stands in a pit under the track of an electric railway system using underground and overhead power supply and attaches and detaches the underground current collector or plow at changeover points **f :** one that lays mats or planks on soft ground as a foundation for construction machines and assists with the cleaning and operation of the machines — called also *matman* **g :** one that pulls hot metal tubes through the pit of an extrusion press and straightens them **2** *pl* **pitmans :** CONNECTING ROD

**pitman chest** *n* **:** a wind-chest used in many pipe organs that has esp. fast action and stop control

**pit membrane** *n* [1*pit*] **:** a membrane of a plant pit that consists of primary wall and middle lamella and that closes the pit externally — called also *closing membrane;* compare TORUS

**pitmirk** \'≈ˌ≈\ *n* [1*pit* + *mirk*] *Scot* **:** intense darkness

**pi·tom·e·ter** \pə̇'tämәd·ə(r), pē't-\ *n* [*pitot* + *-meter*] **:** an instrument that consists essentially of two pitot tubes one of which is turned upstream and the other downstream and that is used to record autographically the velocity of a flowing liquid or gas

**pi·ton** \'pēˌtän, 'pēˌtōⁿ, 'pīˌt-, ≈'≈\ *n* -s [F, fr. MF, nail, screw eye] **1 :** a sharp peak of a mountain **2 :** a usu. iron spike, wedge, or peg that is driven into fissures or cracks (as of a rock or ice surface) so as to serve as a support (as for one climbing a mountain) and that often has an eye at one end through which safety ropes may be passed

**pit orchestra** *n* **:** PIT BAND

**pitot–static tube** \ˌpēˌtōˌ≈≈-, pēˌtōˌ≈≈-\ *n, often cap P* **:** a device that consists of a combination of a pitot tube and a static tube and that measures pressures in such a way that the relative speed of a fluid can be determined (as in an airspeed indicator) — called also *pitot tube*

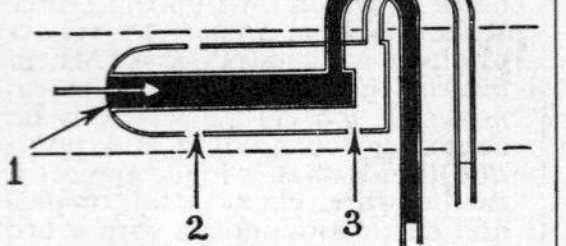

pitot-static tube: *1* pitot opening, *2* static opening, *3* drain holes

**pi·tot tube** \(')pēˌtō-\ *also* **pitot** *n* -s *often cap P* [F (*tube de*) *Pitot*, after Henri *Pitot* †1771 French physicist and engineer] **1 :** a device that consists of a tube having a short right-angled bend which is placed vertically in a moving body of fluid with the mouth of the bent part directed upstream and is used with a manometer to measure the velocity of fluid flow **2 :** PITOT-STATIC TUBE

**pit–pair** \'≈ˌ≈\ *n* [1*pit*] **:** two pits occurring opposite one another in the walls of adjacent cells of many higher vascular plants and acting together as a structural and functional unit

**pit·pan** \'pitˌpan\ *n* -s [Miskito *pitban* boat] **:** a long flat-bottomed canoe used esp. in Central America

**pit–pat** *var of* PIT-A-PAT

**pit·pit** \'pitˌpit\ *n* [imit.] **:** GUITGUIT

**pit pony** *n* [1*pit*] *chiefly Brit* **:** a pony used for packing or haulage in a mine

**pitprop** \'≈ˌ≈\ *n* [1*pit* + *prop*] **:** a usu. wooden upright used as a temporary support for a mine roof

**pi·tri** \'pi·trē\ *n, pl* **pitris** *or* **pitri** [Skt *pitṛ* father — more at FATHER] *Hinduism* **:** a deceased forefather viewed as semidivine

**pit river indian** *n, usu cap P&R&I* [fr. *Pit river*, Calif.] **:** ACHOMAWI

**pit run** *n* **:** BANK GRAVEL

**pits** *pl of* PIT, *pres 3d sing of* PIT

**pit saw** *n* **1 :** a long handsaw usu. with a handle at each end that is used chiefly for cutting a log lengthwise into planks and is worked by two men one of whom stands on or above the log and the other below it usu. in a pit **2** *or* **pit–saw file :** a single-cut file that is left uncut at the point and is used chiefly for sharpening pit saws

**pit sawyer** *n* **:** BOTTOM SAWYER

**pit scale** *n* **:** one of several scales of the genus *Asterolecanium* that cause serious injury to oaks

**pit·ta** \'pid·ə\ *n* [NL, fr. Telugu *piṭṭa* bird] **1** *cap* **:** a large genus (the type of the family Pittidae) of chiefly terrestrial nearly songless birds that are found principally in the southern part of Asia and in Australia and adjacent islands and that have short wings and tail, long legs, a stout bill, and brilliant plumage marked by sharply contrasting colors **2** -s **:** any bird of the genus *Pitta*

**pit·tance** \'pitᵊn(t)s\ *n* -s [ME *pitaunce*, fr. OF *pitance* piety, pity, allowance of food given a member of a religious house, fr. ML *pietantia, pitantia*, fr. *pietant-, pietans* (pres. part. of *pietari* to be pious, be charitable, fr. L *pietas* piety) + L *-ia* -y — more at PITY] **1 a** *archaic* **:** a gift or bequest made to a religious community (as to provide anniversary masses for a deceased person or to provide additional food or drink on festivals or similar occasions) **b :** a usu. small charitable gift (as of money, food, clothing) **:** ALMS **2 a :** a usu. small often barely sufficient portion, amount, or allowance ⟨had received a mere ~ of education⟩; *often* **:** a meager wage or remuneration ⟨lived in squalid, verminous slums, worked long hours for a ~ —W.S.Maugham⟩ **b :** a small special allowance (as of extra food or drink) apportioned out to the members of a religious community on festivals or similar occasions

**pittara** *var of* PITARAH

**pitted** *adj* [fr. past part. of 2*pit*] **:** marked with or having the form of a pit or pits ⟨the surface is very ~⟩

**pit·ten** \'pitᵊn\ *Scot past part of* PUT

**1pit·ter** \'pid·ə(r), -itə-\ *vi* -ED/-ING/-S [imit.] **1 :** CHIRR, STRIDULATE ⟨~*ing* grasshoppers⟩ **2 :** PITTER-PATTER ⟨rain ~*ing* on a rooftop⟩

**2pitter** \"\ *n* -s [4*pit* + *-er*] **:** one that pits; *specif* **:** one that removes pits ⟨the cherry ~ and the sausage meat grinder are of interest merely as curios today —*Think*⟩

**3pitter** \"\ *n* -s [1*pit* + *-er*] **:** one that takes care of gamecocks at a fight — compare HANDLER

**1pitter–patter** \ˌpid·ə(r)ˌpad·ə(r), -itə . . . atə-\ *adv* (*or adj*) [imit.] **:** PIT-A-PAT ⟨her heart went *pitter-patter*⟩

**2pitter–patter** \"\ *n* **:** a pattering sound **:** PIT-A-PAT ⟨the *pitter-patter* of raindrops on a tin roof⟩

**3pitter–patter** \"\ *vi* **pitter–pattered**; **pitter–pattered**; **pitter–pattering**; **pitter–patters :** to go pitter-patter **:** PIT-A-PAT ⟨footsteps *pitter-pattered* down the hall⟩

**pit·ti·cite** \'pid·əˌsīt\ *n* -s [G *pittizit*, irreg. fr. Gk *pitta, pissa* pitch + G *-it* -ite — more at PITCH] **:** a brown massive mineral consisting of a hydrous ferric arsenate and sulfate

**pit·ti·dae** \'pid·əˌdē\ *n pl, cap* [NL, fr. *Pitta*, type genus + *-idae*] **:** a family of passerine birds comprising the pittas and related forms

**pitting** *n* -s [fr. gerund of 2*pit*] **1 :** the action or process of forming pits ⟨~ sometimes occurs on freshly painted surfaces⟩ **2 :** a particular arrangement of pits on a surface (as of wood) ⟨studied the ~ of each kind of timber⟩ **3 :** the action of putting gamecocks into a pit to fight; *also* **:** a division or round in a cockfight

**pit·tite** \'pid·ˌīt, -īˌtīt\ *n* -s *chiefly Brit* [1*pit* + *-ite*] **:** one that frequents the pit of a theater

**pit·to** \'pid·(ˌ)ō\ *n* -s [native name in India] **:** GILLAR

**pit tomb** *or* **pit grave** *n* **:** a grave consisting of a deep pit with vertical sides and with or without a lateral niche

**pit·to·spo·ra·ce·ae** \ˌpid·əspə'rāsēˌē\ *n pl, cap* [NL, fr. *Pittosporum*, type genus + *-aceae*] **:** a family of chiefly Australian shrubs and trees (order Rosales) with regular pentamerous flowers and an ovary with many ovules — **pit·to·spo·ra·ceous** \ˌ≈≈≈ˌrāshəs\ *adj*

**pit·tos·po·rum** \pə̇'täspərəm\ *n* [Gk *pitto-* pitch (fr. *pitta, pissa*) + NL *-sporum* (fr. Gk *spora, sporos* seed) — more at PITCH, SPORE] **1** *cap* **:** a genus (the type of the family Pittosporaceae) of evergreen trees and shrubs of Asia, Africa, and Australasia that have often fragrant white or yellow flowers succeeded by berries with seeds embedded in a viscous substance — see LAUREL 4h, TARATA **2** -s **:** any tree or shrub of the genus *Pittosporum*

**pitts·burgh** *also* **pitts·burg** \'pitsˌbərg, -bə̄g,-bəig\ *adj, usu cap* [fr. *Pittsburgh*, Pa.] **:** of or from the city of Pittsburgh, Pa. ⟨*Pittsburgh* steel mills⟩ **:** of the kind or style prevalent in Pittsburgh

**pitts·burgh·er** *also* **pitts·burg·er** \-gə(r)\ *n* -s *cap* [*Pittsburgh*, Pa. + E *-er*] **:** a native or resident of Pittsburgh, Pa.

**pittsburgh ivy** *n, usu cap P* **:** an English ivy that has stiff stems and crowded leathery often ruffled leaves and that can be grown without support

**pitty–pat** *or* **pitty–patty** *var of* PIT-A-PAT

**pi·tu·i·cyte** \pə̇'tüəˌsīt, pə̇·'tyü-\ *n* -s [NL *pitui*ta + E *-cyte*] **:** one of the pigmented more or less fusiform cells of the stalk and neural lobe of the pituitary body that are usu. considered to be derived from neuroglial cells

**pitu·i·ta** \pə̇'tüəd·ə, pə̇·'tyü-; ˌpitə'wēd·ə, ˌpichə'wīd·ə\ *n, pl* **pitui·tae** \-üəˌtē, -üəˌtī, -wēˌtī, -wīˌtē\ [NL, fr. L, phlegm, nasal mucus — more at PIP] **:** PITUITARY BODY

**1pi·tu·i·tary** \pə̇'tüəˌterē, pə̇·'tyü-, -ri\ *adj* [L *pituitarius*, fr. *pituita* + *-arius* -ary] **1 a** *archaic* **:** MUCOUS **b :** of or relating to the pituitary body **2 :** of, relating to, or resembling a type of physique that is marked by one or more symptom complexes (as acromegaly) and that is produced by secretory disturbances of the pituitary body

**2pituitary** \"\ *n* -ES **1 :** PITUITARY BODY **2 :** the cleaned, dried, and powdered posterior lobe of the pituitary body of cattle that is used in the treatment of uterine atony and hemorrhage, shock, and intestinal paresis

**pituitary basophilism** *n* [2*pituitary* + *basophil* + *-ism*] **:** CUSHING'S DISEASE

**pituitary body** *or* **pituitary gland** *n* [so called fr. the former belief that it secreted nasal mucus] **:** a small oval reddish gray very vascular endocrine organ attached to the infundibulum of the brain and occupying the sella turcica that is present in all craniate vertebrates and consists essentially of an epithelial anterior lobe derived from a diverticulum of the oral cavity joined by a pars intermedia to a posterior lobe of nervous origin with the several parts being associated with various internal secretions including substances that exert a controlling and regulating influence on other endocrine organs, others concerned with growth and development, and some modifying the contraction of smooth muscle, renal function and reproduction and directly or indirectly impinging on most basic body functions — called also *hypophysis;* see NEUROHYPOPHYSIS; BRAIN illustration

**pituitary fossa** *n* **:** SELLA TURCICA

**pituitary membrane** *n, archaic* **:** SCHNEIDERIAN MEMBRANE

**pi·tu·i·tous** \pə̇'tüəd·əs, pə̇·'tyü-, -üətəs\ *adj* [L *pituitosus* phlegmatic, fr. *pituita* nasal mucus, phlegm + *-osus* -ous — more at PIP] **1** *archaic* **:** MUCOUS **2** *archaic* **:** PHLEGMATIC

**Pi·tu·i·trin** \-üə·trə̇n\ *trademark* — used for an aqueous extract of the fresh pituitary body of cattle

**pi·tu·o·phis** \pə̇'tüəfə̇s, pə̇·'tyü-\ *n, cap* [NL, irreg. fr. Gk *pitys* pine tree + *ophis* snake — more at PINE, ANGUIS] **:** a genus of rodent-eating snakes (family Colubridae) comprising the No. American bull snakes

**pit·u·ri** \'pichərē\ *or* **bed·gery** \'bejərē\ *also* **pitch·eri** *or* **pitchuri** \'pichərē\ *n, pl* **pituris** *or* **bedgeries** [native name in Australia] **1 :** an Australian shrub (*Duboisia hopwoodii*) **2 :** a narcotic drug that is prepared by drying the leaves and twigs of the pituri shrub

**pit viper** *n* **:** any of various mostly New World highly specialized venomous snakes (as the rattlesnake, copperhead, water moccasin, fer-de-lance) that have a small depression on each side of the head between the eye and the nostril which is lined with sensory epithelium and innervated by branches of the trigeminal nerve, that have hollow perforated fangs usu. folded back in the upper part of the mouth but erected in striking, and that constitute the family Crotalidae

**pitwood** \'≈ˌ≈\ *n* **:** timber used chiefly for roof props in mines

**pitwork** \'≈ˌ≈\ *n* **:** pumping apparatus used in a mine shaft

**pitwright** \'≈ˌ≈\ *n* **:** one that does carpentry in and about a mine

**1pity** \'pid·|ē, -it|, |i\ *n* -ES [ME *pite*, fr. OF *pitez, pitié, pité*, fr. L *pietat-, pietas* piety, compassion, fr. *pie-* (fr. *pius* pious) + *-tat-, -tas* -ty — more at PIOUS] **1** *archaic* **:** MERCY, CLEMENCY ⟨saw that his judge was inclining to mercy, and he renewed his appeals for ~ —J.H.Shorthouse⟩ **2 a** (1) **:** sympathetic heartfelt sorrow for one that is suffering physically or mentally or that is otherwise distressed or unhappy (as through misfortune, difficulties) **:** COMPASSION, COMMISERATION ⟨felt the deepest ~ for the prisoners⟩ (2) **:** the capacity to feel such sorrow ⟨was habitually hardhearted and without ~⟩ **b :** a somewhat disdainful or contemptuous feeling of regret over the condition of one viewed by the speaker as in some way inferior or reprehensible ⟨leaves us less with a sense of repugnance . . . than with a sense of ~ for the man who could think of nothing better —T.S.Eliot⟩ **3 :** a cause of regret **:** a condition or circumstance that is to be regretted ⟨what a ~ that you didn't get here sooner⟩ ⟨it's a ~ that we can't be friends⟩ **syn** see SYMPATHY — **for pity's sake** — used typically to express surprise, indignation, annoyance, or entreaty ⟨*for pity's sake*, what are you doing here⟩ ⟨please don't fail me, *for pity's sake*⟩ — **have pity** *or* **take pity 1 :** to be merciful **:** show mercy ⟨*have pity* on us: for we have sinned —Bar 3: 2 (DV)⟩ **2 :** to become less severe **:** RELENT ⟨begged him not to be so harsh, but he *had* no *pity* upon them⟩

**2pity** \"\ *vb* -ED/-ING/-ES *vt* **1** *chiefly dial* **:** to cause to feel pity **:** move to pity ⟨it would ~ one's heart to observe the change —William Whiston⟩ **2 :** to feel pity for ⟨*pitied* them in their distress⟩ ⟨whom everybody *pities* because his daughter has disgraced him —Edmund Wilson⟩ **~** *vi* **:** to feel pity **:** have pity ⟨will not ~, nor spare, nor have mercy —Jer 13:14 (AV)⟩

**pitying** *adj* **:** expressing or feeling pity ⟨let him perish without a ~ thought of ours wasted upon him —Thomas De Quincey⟩ — **pity·ing·ly** *adv*

**pit·y·lus** \'pid·ᵊləs\ *n, cap* [NL, fr. Gk *pitys* pine tree — more at PINE] **:** a genus of Central and So. American grosbeaks related to the cardinal bird but lacking a crest

**pit·yo·cam·pa** \ˌpid·ēō'kampə\ *n* -s [L, fr. Gk *pityokampē*, fr. *pitys* pine tree + *-o-* + *kampē* caterpillar — more at -CAMPA] **:** the larva of a European processionary moth (*Cnethocampa pityocampa*) found on pine or fir trees

**pit·y·ri·as·ic** \ˌpid·əˌrīˌasik\ *adj* [ISV *pityrias-* (fr. NL *pityriasis*) + *-ic*] **:** of or affected with pityriasis

**pit·y·ri·a·sis** \ˌpid·ə'rīəsə̇s\ *n, pl* **pityria·ses** \-īəˌsēz\ [NL, fr. Gk, fr. *pityron* bran, scurf, dandruff + *-iasis*, n. suffix — more at -IASIS] **1 :** one of several skin diseases marked by the formation and desquamation of branny scales **2 :** a disease of domestic animals marked by dry epithelial scales or scurf due to alteration of the function of the sebaceous glands and possibly associated with digestive disorders

**pit·y·ro·gram·ma** \ˌpid·ərō'gramə\ *n, cap* [NL, fr. Gk *pityron* bran + *gramma* letter — more at GRAM] **:** a small genus of terrestrial tropical ferns (family Polypodiaceae) that have fronds with a powdery yellowish or white undersurface and linear dorsal sori — see GOLD FERN, SILVER FERN

**piu** \'pyü, pē'ü\ *adv* [It *più*, fr. L *plus* — more at PLUS] **:** MORE — used to qualify another adverb or adjective that is used as a direction in music ⟨~ allegro⟩

**piu·piu** \ˌpēüˌpēü\ *n, pl* **piupiu** *or* **piupius** [Maori] **:** a short kilt made usu. of strips of flax and worn by Maoris for native dances and on ceremonial occasions

**pi·u·ri** *also* **pi·ou·ry** \pē'(y)u̇rē\ *n, pl* **piuris** *also* **piouries** [Hindi *piyūṛī;* akin to Skt *pīta* yellow] **:** INDIAN YELLOW 1a

**pi·ute** \'pīˌ(y)üt, ≈'≈\ *usu cap, var of* PAIUTE

**piute trout** *n, usu cap P* **:** a brilliantly colored cutthroat trout native to a few small upland streams in eastern California near Lake Tahoe

**pi·va** \'pēvə\ *n, pl* **pivas** \-vəz\ *or* **pi·ve** \-(ˌ)vā\ [It, fr. (assumed) VL *pipa* pipe — more at PIPE] **1 :** an ancient Italian bagpipe or shawm **2 :** a 16th-century Italian dance form in quick triple meter

**pi·val·ic acid** \(')pīˌvalik-\ *n* [ISV *pi*nacolin + *val*eric + *-ic*] **:** a crystalline acid $(CH_3)_3CCOOH$ isomeric with normal valeric acid and formed by oxidation of pinacolone; trimethyl-acetic acid

**1piv·ot** \'pivət, *usu* -əd·+V\ *n* -s [F, fr. OF, fr. an assumed word akin to OProv *pua* tooth of a flax comb, fr. (assumed) VL *puga*, perh. fr. L *pungere* to prick — more at PUNGENT] **1 a :** a usu. short shaft or pin whose pointed end forms the fulcrum and center on which something turns about, oscillates, or balances: (1) **:** the pin of a hinge (2) **:** an axle on which a wheel turns (3) **:** the shaft on which the hands of a timepiece turn (4) **:** the pin on which a pointer (as of a compass) is balanced and turns **b** (1) **:** the pointed end of such a shaft or pin (2) **:** a real or apparent point or position on which something turns about, oscillates, or balances **c :** a usu. metallic pin holding an artificial crown to the root of a tooth **2 :** something that has an important role, position, or influence **:** something on which the activity, development, or course of something else depends or to which it is closely linked **:** a central or indispensable individual, element, or factor **:** something having a major or central role, function, or effect: as **a** (1) **:** the man or group of men around whom a body of troops wheels (as in changing front or direction or making a tactical maneuver) (2) **:** a key player or position (as on a football team) (3) **:** an individual on whom the condition or future of something depends ⟨elected a man that proved to be the ~ of the organization's success⟩ ⟨as if the ~ and pole of his life . . . was his mother —D.H.Lawrence⟩ **b :** an essential or vital component part (as of a piece of machinery) **c :** a central or crucial fact or condition about which a whole series of consequences revolves **:** central point **:** HEART, CRUX ⟨the ~ of the matter is whether they will or will not agree⟩ ⟨the ~ of the controversy —J.A. Todd⟩ **d :** a central point of attraction or interest ⟨public occasions when he himself is the ~ of attention —Stewart Cockburn⟩ **3 :** the action of turning about, oscillating, or balancing on or as if on a pivot: as **a :** the turn of the body from left to right on the backswing and from right to left on the downswing in hitting a golf ball **b :** the action in the game of basketball of stepping once or more than once in any direction with the same foot while keeping the other foot at its point of contact with the floor **c** : a dance step in which the dancer rotates on one foot and completes the step by shifting the weight to the other foot

**2pivot** \"\ *vb* -ED/-ING/-S [F *pivoter*, fr. *pivot*] *vi* **1** : to turn about or oscillate or balance on or as if on a pivot ⟨the guns are mounted in such a way as to ~ easily⟩ ⟨the future ~*s* on what is done today⟩ **2** : to change card partners at fixed intervals so as to have each player as a partner at some time during a partnership game ~ *vt* **1** : to provide with, mount on, or attach by means of a pivot ⟨a ~*ed* mechanism⟩ **2** : to cause to pivot ⟨~ himself sharply about on his heel⟩ ⟨~*ing* their life on some such particular motive —D.J.Unger⟩

**3pivot** \"\ *adj* [1*pivot*] **1** : turning on or as if on a pivot ⟨a ~ gun⟩ : equipped with a pivot ⟨~ gearing⟩ **2** : PIVOTAL ⟨a ~ figure in the controversy⟩ ⟨a ~ man on a football team⟩

**1piv·ot·al** \'pivəd·ᵊl, -ətᵊl\ *adj* [ISV 1*pivot* + *-al*] **1 a** : of or relating to a pivot ⟨correct ~ dimensions⟩ **b** : constituting or functioning as a pivot ⟨a ~ shaft⟩ **2** : that vitally affects the activity or development or course of something : central in importance, function, influence, or effect ⟨holds a ~ position⟩ ⟨one of the great ~ points of the war —S.L.A.Marshall⟩

**2pivotal** \"\ *n* -S : something that is pivotal

**pivotal fault** *n* : ROTARY FAULT

**piv·ot·al·ly** \-ᵊlē, -ᵊli\ *adv* **1** : in a pivotal manner : as a pivot ⟨functioning ~⟩ **2 a** : by means of a pivot ⟨can be turned ~⟩ **b** : on a pivot ⟨is mounted ~⟩

**pivot bearing** *n* : STEP BEARING

**pivot bridge** *n* : a drawbridge in which one span turns about a central vertical axis

**piv·ot·er** \-d·ə(r), -tə-\ *n* -S [1*pivot* + *-er*] : a worker who grinds pivots to the proper shape for timepiece balance staffs

**pivot joint** *n* : an anatomical articulation that consists of a bony pivot in a ring of bone and ligament (as that of the odontoid and atlas) and that permits rotatory movement only

**pivot of maneuver** : a part of an attacking force that attempts to immobilize an enemy while another part strikes a decisive blow

**pivot pin** *n* **1** : KNUCKLE PIN **2** : KINGBOLT

**pivots** *pl of* PIVOT, *pres 3d sing of* PIVOT

**pivot stand** *n* : a part of a gun mount which is secured to the platform and in which the pivot is enclosed — called also *pedestal*

**pivot tooth** *or* **pivot crown** *n* : an artificial crown attached to the root of a tooth by a pivot

**1pix** *var of* PYX

**2pix** *pl of* PIC

**1pix·ie** *or* **pixy** \'piksē, -si\ *n, pl* **pixies** [origin unknown] **1 a** : FAIRY; *specif* : a cheerful sprite like an elf typically conceived of as playing mischievous tricks on householders or as dancing in the moonlight to the sound of crickets or frogs **b** : a playfully mischievous individual : PRANKSTER, RASCAL, ROGUE **2** : a skullcap or a small hat with a pointed crown worn by women and girls

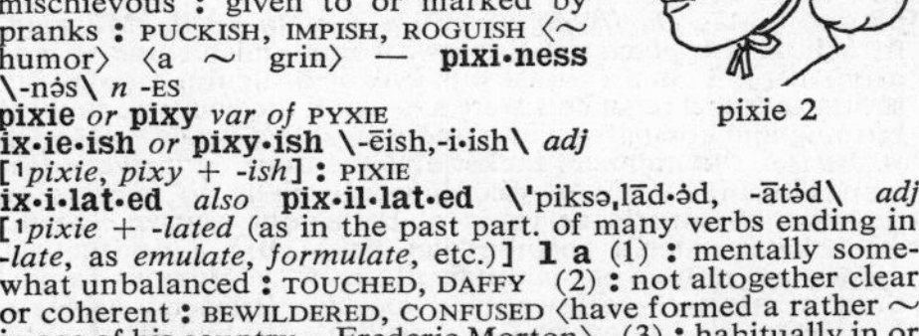
pixie 2

**2pixie** *or* **pixy** \"\ *adj* : playfully mischievous : given to or marked by pranks : PUCKISH, IMPISH, ROGUISH ⟨~ humor⟩ ⟨a ~ grin⟩ — **pixi·ness** \-nəs\ *n* -ES

**3pixie** *or* **pixy** *var of* PYXIE

**pix·ie·ish** *or* **pixy·ish** \-ēish,-iish\ *adj* [1*pixie*, *pixy* + *-ish*] : PIXIE

**pix·i·lat·ed** *also* **pix·il·lat·ed** \'piksə,lād·əd, -ātəd\ *adj* [1*pixie* + *-lated* (as in the past part. of many verbs ending in *-late*, as *emulate*, *formulate*, etc.)] **1 a (1)** : mentally somewhat unbalanced : TOUCHED, DAFFY **(2)** : not altogether clear or coherent : BEWILDERED, CONFUSED ⟨have formed a rather ~ image of his country —Frederic Morton⟩ **(3)** : habitually in or seeming to be in a mild stupor or daze : BEMUSED ⟨has been ~ of late, never quite aware of what is going on⟩ **(4)** : under or seeming to be under a magic spell : ENCHANTED, BEWITCHED ⟨a countryside with an unreal ~ charm⟩ **b** : amusingly or fancifully unconventional : WHIMSICAL ⟨a ~ comedy⟩ **c** : playfully mischievous : PUCKISH, PRANKISH, PIXIE ⟨~ leprechauns⟩ ⟨~ humor⟩ **2** : INTOXICATED, DRUNK ⟨pretty well ~ by the fourth drink⟩

**pix·i·la·tion** *also* **pix·il·la·tion** \,==ˈlāshən\ *n* -S : the quality or state of being pixilated

**pixy stool** *n* **1** *dial Eng* : TOADSTOOL **2** *dial Eng* : MUSHROOM

**piyyut** *or* **piyut** \pē'yüt\ *n, pl* **piyyu·tim** *or* **piyu·tim** \(,)pē-,yü'tēm\ [LHeb *piyyūṭ* poem, poetry, fr. *piyyēṭ* to write poetry, fr. Gk *poiētēs* poet — more at POET] : a religious poem recited in the synagogue in addition to the traditional liturgy on Jewish festivals, special Sabbaths or ceremonial occasions

**pize** \'pīz\ *n* -S [perh. by shortening fr. *pizen*, alter. of *poison*] *chiefly dial* : CURSE, MALEDICTION

**piz·za** \'pētsə\ *or* **pizza pie** *n* -S [It *pizza*, fr. (assumed) VL *picea* (perh. intended as trans. of MGk *pitta* cake, pie, fr. Gk, pitch), fr. L, fem. of *piceus* of pitch, fr. *pic-*, *pix* pitch + *-eus* -eous — more at PITCH] : a usu. large open pie made typically of thinly rolled bread dough spread with a spiced mixture (as of tomatoes, cheese, ground meat, garlic, oil) and baked

**piz·ze·ria** \,pētsə'rēə *sometimes* ,pit-\ *n* -S [It, fr. *pizza* + *-eria* -ery] : an establishment (as a bakery, restaurant, shop) where pizzas are made and sold

**1piz·zi·ca·to** \,pitsə'käd·(,)ō, -sē'-, -ká|, |(,)tō\ *adv* (*or adj*) [It, past part. of *pizzicare* to pinch, pluck (strings), play pizzicato, fr. *pizzare* to sting, prick, pinch] : by means of plucking by the fingers instead of bowing : PLUCKED — used as a direction in music ⟨marked the opening part of the movement ~⟩ ⟨a brief section is played ~⟩ ⟨a series of ~ notes⟩

**2pizzicato** \"\ *n, pl* **pizzica·ti** \|d·(,)ē, |(,)tē\ *or* **pizzicatos** : a note or passage played by plucking strings

**piz·zle** \'pizəl\ *n* -S [prob. fr. Flem *pezel*; akin to LG *pesel*, *peisel* pizzle, MD *pese* sinew, bowstring, MLG *pēse* bowstring] **1** : the penis of an animal (as a bull) **2** : a whip made of a bull's pizzle

**PJ** *abbr* **1** police justice **2** presiding judge **3** probate judge

**pj's** \(')pē¦jāz\ *n pl* [by abbr.] : PAJAMAS

**pk** *abbr* **1** pack **2** park **3** peak **4** peck

**PK** *abbr* psychokinesis

**pK** \(')pē¦kā\ *symbol* the negative logarithm of the dissociation constant K or −log K that serves as a convenient measure of the strength of an acid ⟨K for acetic acid is 0.000018 or $1.8 \times 10^{-5}$ from which *pK* is (5 − 0.25) or 4.75⟩ — compare PH

**pkg** *abbr* package

**pkge** *abbr* package

**pkmr** *abbr* packmaster

**pkr** *abbr* packer

**pkt** *abbr* **1** packet **2** pocket

**pkwy** *abbr* parkway

**pky** *abbr* pecky

**pl** *abbr* **1** pile **2** place **3** plain **4** plaster **5** plate **6** platoon **7** plural

**PL** *abbr* **1** partial loss **2** perception of light **3** phase line **4** poet laureate **5** private line **6** profit and loss **7** public law **8** public liability

**plac-** *or* **placo-** *comb form* [Gk *plak-*, *plako-* flat surface, tablet, fr. *plak-*, *plax* — more at PLEASE] : tablet : flat plate ⟨*plac*odont⟩ ⟨*placo*derm⟩

**placa·bil·i·ty** \,plakə'bilәd·ē, -ətē, -i *also* ,plāk-\ *n* -ES [L *placabilitas*, *placabilitat-*, fr. *placabilis* + *-itat-*, *-itas* -ity] : the quality or state of being placable

**placa·ble** \'plakəbəl *also* 'plāk-\ *adj* [ME, fr. L *placabilis*, fr. *placare* to soothe, placate + *-abilis* -able — more at PLEASE] **1** : of a tolerant nature : easily soothed or satisfied : PEACEABLE, TRACTABLE ⟨indignities which might move even a ~ nature to fierce . . . resentment —T.B.Macaulay⟩ ⟨young people are almost always ~ —Samuel Butler †1902⟩ **2** *archaic* : characterized by serenity : PEACEFUL, QUIET ⟨the wind blew in momentary gusts, and then became more ~ —Nathaniel Hawthorne⟩ — **placa·bly** \-blē, -li\ *adv*

**placa·ble·ness** *n* -ES *archaic* : PLACABILITY

**1plac·ard** \'pla,kärd, -,kàd, -,kə(r)d\ *n* -S [ME *placquart*, fr. MF, fr. *plaquier* to plate, plaster — more at PLAQUE] **1** *archaic* : a piece of armor plate (as a breastplate or backplate) ⟨pulled down his visor and clasped it to the ~ —Horace Smith⟩; *specif* : PLACCATE 1 **2 a** *obs* : an authorization or permit bearing an official seal **b** *archaic* : an official edict or proclamation **3 a** : a notice or announcement printed on one side of a sheet for posting in a public place : POSTER, SIGN ⟨every travel agent . . . has some sort of ~ in his window advertising one of the sightseeing tourist itineraries —Richard Joseph⟩ **b** : a small card or metal plaque ⟨a ~ on the door says "no admittance"⟩ ⟨leather belts with plain brass ~*s* or initialed —*New Yorker*⟩ ⟨a ~ on the fuselage lists performance data⟩

**2placard** \"\ *vt* -ED/-ING/-S **1 a** : to cover with or as if with posters ⟨~ a fence with advertisements⟩ ⟨ancestors whose portraits snootily ~ the . . . walls —Wyndham Lewis⟩ **b** : to post in a public place ⟨pictures of the occasion were . . . ~*ed* throughout eastern Europe —*Time*⟩ **2** : to label or announce by or as if by posting : call attention to ⟨has never been my habit to ~ my movements like a court circular —John Buchan⟩ ⟨crimes ~*ed* by the evening papers —L.P.Smith⟩

**pla·cate** \'plā,kāt *also* 'pla,- *sometimes* =ˈ= *or* plə'-, *usu* -kād+V\ *vb* -ED/-ING/-S [L *placatus*, past part. of *placare* to placate — more at PLEASE] *vt* : to soothe or mollify esp. by making concessions : APPEASE ⟨the pressure . . . put on them to ~ public opinion —A.L.Funk⟩ ~ *vi* : to be conciliatory or help to reconcile differences ⟨flattering and *placating* and yet yielding no ground —F. Tennyson Jesse⟩ **syn** see PACIFY

**pla·cat·er** \-kād·ə(r)\ *n* -S [*placate* + *-er*] : one that placates; *esp* : MEDIATOR

**pla·cat·ing·ly** *adv* [fr. *placating*, gerund of *placate* + *-ly*] : in a placating manner

**pla·ca·tion** \plā'kāshən, plə'-\ *n* -S [MF, fr. L *placation-*, *placatio*, fr. *placatus* (past part. of *placare* to placate) + *-ion-*, *-io* -ion — more at PLEASE] : an act of soothing or propitiating

**pla·ca·tive** \'plākəd·iv, 'plak-\ *adj* [*placate* + *-ive*] : PLACATORY

**pla·ca·to·ry** \'plākə,tōrē, 'plak-, -tȯr-, -ri\ *adj* [LL *placatorius*, fr. *placatus* + *-orius* -ory] : tending or intended to placate : CONCILIATORY

**plac·cate** \'plakət\ *n* -S [prob. alter. of *placard*] **1** *archaic* : an extra piece of armor worn over the lower part of the breast **2** *archaic* : a jacket or doublet lined with steel splints : BRIGANDINE

**1place** \'plās\ *n* -S [ME, fr. MF, open space in a city, space, locality, fr. L *platea* broad street, fr. Gk *plateia* (*hodos*), fr. fem. of *platys* broad, flat; akin to Skt *pṛthu* broad, L *planta* sole of the foot] **1 a** : a way for admission or transit ⟨calling "~! ~!" to clear the way for their master —G.P.R. James⟩ ⟨~ is made for it on his class schedule —H.W.Dodds⟩ **b** : physical environment : SPACE ⟨all are strangers, rootless in ~ or time —T.H.White b.1915⟩ **c** : physical surroundings : ATMOSPHERE ⟨the feeling for ~ was in him like the feeling for a personality —R.L.Cook⟩ **2 a** : an indefinite region or expanse : AREA ⟨visit the far ~*s* of the earth⟩ ⟨small supplies of foreign ore . . . brought from ~*s* like No. Africa —Samuel Van Valkenburg & Ellsworth Huntington⟩ ⟨schools continued to spring up all over the ~ —Bernard Kalb⟩ **b (1)** : a building or locality used for a special purpose ⟨~ of amusement⟩ ⟨~ of worship⟩ ⟨a secondhand car ~ —Robert Westerby⟩; *specif* : eating place ⟨found a little Italian ~ with an eighty-five cent dinner —Mary McCarthy⟩ **(2)** *archaic* : an assembly point ⟨posted upon a parade, or ~ of arms —Daniel Defoe⟩ **c** *archaic* : the three-dimensional compass of a material object ⟨in the world I fill up a ~ which may be better supplied when I have made it empty —Shak.⟩ **d** : WHERE ⟨wished he could go some ~ and run a lunchroom —*Time*⟩ ⟨has no ~ to turn for allies —M.H.Rubin⟩ ⟨the magic rests, more than any ~ else, in a sense of ambiguity —M.F. Harrington⟩ **3 a** : a particular region or center of population ⟨Britain is an ideal ~ to tour by bus —Richard Joseph⟩ ⟨Denver, Salt Lake City, and hundreds of other ~*s*, large and small —*Motor Transportation in the West*⟩ **b** : an individual dwelling or estate : HOUSE, HOMESTEAD ⟨invited them to his ~ for the evening⟩ ⟨our twenty-eight-acre ~ on the edge of Baltimore —A.W.Turnbull⟩; *specif* : FARM ⟨a few ~*s* were . . . harrowing summer fallow —H.L.Davis⟩ **c** : a fortified military post ⟨to effect the release of . . . Americans held there, a group of American settlers in Texas attacked the ~ —E.C.Barker⟩ **d** : 1SCENE 3 **4 a** : a particular portion of a surface : specific locality : SPOT ⟨worn ~ in a rug⟩ ⟨sore ~ on the back of the hand⟩ ⟨steep ~ in the road⟩ ⟨this is the right ~ —M.R.Werner⟩ **b (1)** : a passage in a piece of writing ⟨in ~*s* he might have been a little bolder in dealing with the . . . text —G.R.Crone⟩ **(2)** *obs* : a selected passage : TEXT ⟨comparing two ~*s* of Scripture —Thomas Fuller⟩ **(3)** : the point at which a reader left off ⟨dropped the book and lost her ~⟩ **c** *obs* : LOCUS CLASSICUS **5 a (1)** : relative position in the social scale : degree of prestige ⟨put the country people in their ~, and with a few tactful rebuffs . . . checked any undue familiarity —Lord Dunsany⟩ ⟨color drew a line around several million people who were thereby condemned to permanent inferiority of ~ —Oscar Handlin⟩ **(2)** : relative position of merit in any context : degree of importance ⟨the ~ of health in the life of the individual —Marie Theresa⟩ ⟨decisions which have brought our science and our engineering to their present ~ —H.S.Truman⟩ **b** : a step in a sequence ⟨in the first ~, the house . . . is haunted —Charles Lee⟩ ⟨from eleventh ~ . . . the city rose to seventh —*Amer. Guide Series: Md.*⟩ **c (1)** : one of the leading positions at the finish of a horse race — used of 1st or usu. 2d in the U.S. and of 1st, 2d, or 3d in England **(2)** : a leading position at the conclusion of any competition entitling the contestant to a prize or special recognition ⟨1st ~ in the dog show⟩ ⟨won a 2d ~ in the handcrafts division⟩ **6 a (1)** : a proper or designated niche ⟨the junior college has a ~ to fill in this emergency —L.L.Medsker⟩ ⟨scientific names are the surest way of indicating to biologists of various nations the ~*s* of insects . . . in the natural world —E.S. McCartney⟩ ⟨whenever an artist has a reasoned conception of any musical work as a unit . . . tempos naturally fall into ~ —Virgil Thomson⟩ **(2)** : a normal or suitable environment ⟨a frontier plantation . . . was no ~ to educate a boy —T.J. Wertenbaker⟩ ⟨turns to individual personality as the logical ~ to study cultural integration —H.J.Muller⟩ **b** : a fitting moment or appropriate point in a discussion ⟨this is not the ~ to discuss compensation —Robert Moses⟩ **c** *obs* : a reasonable basis : GROUND ⟨there is no ~ of doubting but that it was the very same —Henry Hammond⟩ **7 a (1)** : an available seat or accommodation ⟨~*s* were booked for him in the boat train —John Buchan⟩ ⟨has a 2-*place* sailplane⟩ ⟨Eton's 1100 nonscholarship ~*s* are booked solid until 1971 —*Newsweek*⟩; *esp* : a seat at a table ⟨a man drinking a glass of orange juice was sitting at the table . . . and two ~*s* farther along a second man was munching a piece of toast —Hamilton Basso⟩ **(2)** : PLACE SETTING ⟨seldom . . . sat down to a meal without laying one or two extra ~*s* for friends —David Garnett⟩ **b** : an empty or vacated position ⟨coffeehouses supplied in some measure the ~ of a journal —T.B.Macaulay⟩ ⟨lost his bike and had to get another in its ~⟩ **c** : a position dictated by circumstance ⟨put yourself in my ~⟩ ⟨in a tight ~ they still call on the North Wind —Alfred Duggan⟩ **8** : the position of a figure in relation to others of a row or series — used esp. of figures occurring after a decimal point ⟨carry the answer out to the third decimal ~⟩ **9 a** : remunerative employment : JOB ⟨would rather starve than take a ~ as a servant —Ellen Glasgow⟩ ⟨was offered a ~ on the *Times* to do political reporting —*Irish Digest*⟩; *esp* : public office ⟨no judge of a high court . . . views the function of his ~ so narrowly —B.N.Cardozo⟩ **b (1)** : a position of responsibility ⟨a policy imposed by a corrupt use of pension and ~ —J.H.Plumb⟩ **(2)** : a duty accompanying a position of responsibility ⟨it was not his ~ to make the final decision⟩ **c** : the prestige accorded to one in an influential position : RANK, STATUS ⟨would on no terms either collaborate with . . . or yield ~ to him —*Times Lit. Supp.*⟩ ⟨spent the remainder of her life . . . in an endless quest for preferment and ~ —*Time*⟩ **10 a** : a public square : PLAZA **b** : a short street or court; *often* : DEAD END — **in place 1** *obs* : on hand : PRESENT ⟨beholding worldly wights *in place*, leave off their work . . . to gaze on them —Edmund Spenser⟩ **2** : in an original or proper place : in situ ⟨a piece of jawbone with the teeth *in place* —R.W.Murray⟩ ⟨kicked up his heels, a kind of shuffle dance *in place* —Eugene Walter⟩ **3** : in a suitable environment : APPROPRIATE ⟨colonnaded mansions that would be more *in place* in Natchez —John Durant⟩ — **in place of** *prep* : as a substitute or replacement for : instead of ⟨*in place of* dues . . . is asked to make an annual contribution —E.B.Lyman⟩ ⟨a single executive *in place of* the former executive committee —Joseph Schafer⟩ — **out of place 1** : out of harmony with the surroundings : MISPLACED, INCONGRUOUS ⟨a prizefighter feels somewhat *out of place* at a literary tea⟩ ⟨bathing suits look *out of place* in a hotel lobby⟩ **2** : out of order : IMPROPER, INAPPROPRIATE ⟨the expression of his personal political convictions . . . is quite *out of place* and an unwarranted imposition on the reader —Hilary Corke⟩ — **place in the sun** : favorable position or status : ADVANTAGE, EMINENCE ⟨the laborer . . . toiling for a *place in the sun* —A.R.Williams⟩ ⟨Italian fiction has found its *place in the sun* —T.G.Bergin⟩ — **upon the place** *obs* : on the spot : IMMEDIATELY ⟨told him *upon the place*, I would serve his majesty —William Temple⟩

**2place** \"\ *vb* -ED/-ING/-S *vt* **1** : to distribute in an orderly manner : ARRANGE, DISPOSE, STATION ⟨the furniture has been *placed* for a definite reason —Betty Fisk⟩ ⟨before the artist put any of the black in his picture . . . he *placed* all the principal branches —Ernest Knaufft⟩ ⟨five . . . strategically *placed* seaports —R.S.Thoman⟩ ⟨shows the emperor *placing* and giving orders to his artillery —Tom Wintringham⟩ **2 a** : to put into or as if into a particular position : cause to rest or lie : SET, FIX ⟨would ~ a finger on the list of figures she was tabulating —Jane Woodfin⟩ ⟨carbide . . . is finely ground and *placed* in electric cyanamide ovens —N.R.Heiden⟩ ⟨waste . . . talent and potential leadership by *placing* higher education beyond their reach —L.M.Chamberlain⟩ ⟨the growing railroad system *placed* increasing demands on iron and coal mines —R.H.Brown⟩ ⟨we have . . . been rather better *placed* than some to weigh the particular criticisms —Barbara Ward⟩ ⟨~ our faith in knowledge —H.I.Poleman⟩ **b** : to present for consideration — used with *before* ⟨the pending debate should be *placed* before a larger audience —Leo Cherne⟩ **c** : to put into a particular condition or state ⟨~ the company in a better financial position⟩ ⟨~ a performer under contract⟩ ⟨the airlines *placed* modern equipment into service —H.G.Armstrong⟩ **d** : to direct accurately to a desired area or previously determined spot ⟨disrupted the defenses with his uncanny ability to ~ the ball —A.J.Daley⟩ ⟨the bombs were *placed* directly upon the assigned target —Tex McCrary & D.E.Scherman⟩ **e** : to cause (the voice) to produce singing or speaking tones that are free and well resonated with reference to the adjustment of the vocal organs and resonance cavities **3** : to appoint to a position ⟨was made lieutenant colonel and *placed* in command of a company —L.S.Mayo⟩ **4 a** : to find a place for: as **(1)** : to secure employment for ⟨~ the girl as a typist⟩ ⟨aims . . . to ~ all physically handicapped persons in remunerative positions —*Amer. Guide Series: Minn.*⟩ **(2)** : to find a residence for (a homeless child) ⟨boarding out with foster parents is the method to be given first consideration in *placing* a child —*Social Services in Brit.*⟩ **b (1)** : to find a publisher for (as a novel) ⟨the manuscript was . . . submitted to a literary agent in New York who was unable to ~ it —Haldeen Braddy⟩ **(2)** : to find a producer for (as a play) **5 a (1)** : to assign to a position in an order of progression : RANK ⟨of the factors of strategic intelligence . . . geography is often *placed* first —G.B. & Charlotte L. Dyer⟩ ⟨fails to sustain that mysterious quality of life which would ~ it among the real masterpieces of the novel —Carlos Lynes⟩ **(2)** : ESTIMATE ⟨the same area has iron ore reserves *placed* at 1.3 billion metric tons —*Americana Annual*⟩ **b (1)** : to assign to a chronological position ⟨the estimated time of burial was *placed* in the early Tintah stage —Meridel Le Sueur⟩ **(2)** : to assign to a category ⟨relatively profuse body hair clearly ~*s* the Caucasoids closest of all living races to the lower primates —Weston La Barre⟩ **(3)** : to recognize by identifying characteristics ⟨listening and *placing* the sounds that break the silence of a winter night —Rose Feld⟩; *specif* : to recall in context from a previous association ⟨the man looked familiar but he couldn't ~ him —Willard Robertson⟩ **c (1)** : to determine or announce the place of (contestants) in a race ⟨judges must occupy the judges' box . . . and their sole duty shall be to ~ the horses —Dan Parker⟩ **(2)** : to succeed in gaining a position for in a contest or competition ⟨*placed* two men on the . . . Olympic team —*Amer. Guide Series: Conn.*⟩ **6** *archaic* : ATTRIBUTE, ASCRIBE ⟨*placed* it all to judicious affection —Jane Austen⟩ **7 a** : to use (money) for the purchase or development of property for financial gain : INVEST ⟨~ a million dollars in bonds⟩ ⟨~ half of the capital of the firm in plane production⟩ **b (1)** : to give (an order for goods or services) to a supplier ⟨~ an order for a new generator⟩ ⟨~ an order to have the house painted⟩ **(2)** : to give an order for (a service) ⟨~ a telephone call⟩ ⟨~ a bet⟩ ⟨*placed* his insurance with another company⟩ ~ *vi* **1** : to earn a top spot in a competition ⟨only the first three men or women to ~ in each event are honored —*Collier's Yr. Bk.*⟩ ⟨*placed* third in the bridge tournament⟩; *specif* : to come in second in a horse race ⟨bet on each horse to win, ~, or show⟩ **2** : to propel an object accurately to a predetermined spot ⟨you cannot ~ to a yard by means of shoulder and arm energy alone —*Manchester Guardian Weekly*⟩ **syn** see SET

**place·able** \'plāsəbəl\ *adj* : capable of being placed

**place bet** *n* **1** : a bet on a horse to finish no worse than second in a race **2** : a bet that the shooter in a crap game will make his point or that a particular point will appear before a 7

**pla·ce·bo** \plə'sē(,)bō\ *n* -S **1** [ME, fr. L, I shall please, 1st sing. fut. indic. of *placēre* to please; from the initial word of the first antiphon, Ps 114:9 (Vulgate) — more at PLEASE] : the vespers for the dead in the Roman Catholic Church **2** [L, I shall please] **a** : an inert medicament or preparation given for its psychological effect esp. to satisfy the patient or to act as a control in an experimental series **b** : something tending to soothe or gratify ⟨the ~ of illusions —Martin Gumpert⟩

**place brick** *n* : a brick not fully burned — called also *sandal brick*; compare SAMEL

**place card** *n* : a card that marks a place reserved for occupancy ⟨airlines have in each seat pocket a *place card* to be left in the seat when leaving it temporarily⟩; *specif* : a small usu. decorated card inscribed with the name of a guest and set at the place he is to occupy at the dinner table

**place hitter** *n* : a baseball player who is able to hit a pitched ball to a chosen part of the playing field

**placeholder** \'=,==\ *n* : a symbol in a mathematical or logical expression that may be replaced by the name of any member of a class or element of an aggregate — compare VARIABLE 2a

**place isomerism** *n* : POSITION ISOMERISM

**1place-kick** \'=,=\ *also* **placement kick** *n* : the kicking of a ball (as in football) placed or held in a stationary position on the ground — compare DROPKICK, PUNT

**2place-kick** \"\ *vt* **1** : to kick (a ball) from a stationary position **2** : to score by means of a place-kick ⟨*place-kicked* the extra point⟩ ~ *vi* : to make a place-kick ⟨ability to *place*=*kick* is a great asset to a fullback⟩

**place·less** \'plāsləs\ *adj* : lacking a fixed location — **place·less·ly** *adv*

**placemaking** \'=,==\ *n* : the successive shifting of two bells in change ringing to make places

**place·man** \'plāsmən\ *n, pl* **placemen** *chiefly Brit* : a political appointee — often used disparagingly

**place mat** *n* : a small usu. rectangular table mat on which a place setting is laid

**place·ment** \'plāsmənt\ *n* -S [2*place* + *-ment*] : an act or instance of placing: as **a** : an orderly distribution or arrangement ⟨strategic ~ of artillery⟩ ⟨~ of lights for taking indoor portraits⟩ ⟨reasons for the ~ of material in a course —A.J. Flynn⟩ **b (1)** : the position of a ball set on the ground for a place-kick **(2)** : PLACE-KICK **c** : the accurate propulsion of a ball to a predetermined spot; *esp* : a tennis shot that is unreturnable by an opponent **d** : the art or practice of producing free and well-resonated voice tones ⟨the natural quality of a singing voice is enhanced by good ~⟩ **e** : the assignment of a student to a class or course on the basis of his ability or proficiency in the subject **f (1)** : the assignment of a worker to a suitable job ⟨service activities pay . . . dividends in better teacher ~ —R.H.Eckelberry⟩ **(2)** : the business of establishing contact between applicants and prospective employers

⟨~ is the province of the appointment bureau⟩ **g :** a transfer of custody (as of a minor or a defective) ⟨the effects of foster home ~ upon children's performances in intelligence tests —R.K.Merton⟩ ⟨to prevent the exploitation of a patient, the precise terms of each ~ are written out in detail —Ruth & Edward Brecher⟩ **h :** INVESTMENT ⟨foreign investors . . . have uniformly shown a preference for fixed-return ~s —R.E. Cameron⟩

**placement test** *n* **:** a test usu. given to a student entering an educational institution to determine his knowledge or proficiency in various subjects so that he may be assigned to appropriate courses or classes

**place–money** \ˈ=,==\ *n* **:** money paid to those backing a horse to place in a race

**place–name** \ˈ=,=\ *n* **:** the name of a geographical locality (as of a city or town) ⟨little trace . . . of the Celts survived except in *place-names* —*Bavarian Palatinate*⟩

**pla·cen·ta** \pləˈsentə\ *n, pl* **placentas** \-təz\ *also* **placen·tae** \-n,tē\ [NL, fr. L, flat cake, fr. Gk *plakount-, plakous,* fr. *plak-, plax* flat surface — more at PLEASE] **1 a :** the vascular organ in mammals except monotremes and marsupials that unites the fetus to the maternal uterus and intermediates the metabolic exchanges of the developing individual through a more or less intimate association of chorionic and usu. allantoic and of uterine mucosal tissues by which the fetal and maternal vascular systems are brought into intimate relation permitting exchange of materials by diffusion but without direct contact between fetal and maternal blood and which typically involves the interlocking of fingerlike or frondose vascular chorionic villi with corresponding modified areas of uterine mucosa — compare AFTERBIRTH **b :** any of various analogous organs in other animals (as some viviparous sharks and free-swimming tunicates) for the attachment of the young to the mother and its nourishment by her **2 :** a sporangium-bearing surface: as **a :** the part of the carpel of a seed plant bearing ovules — see PLACENTATION **b :** the point on a fern or fern ally leaf or sporophyll at which sporangia develop

**¹pla·cen·tal** \-tᵊl\ *adj* [NL *placentalis,* fr. *placenta* + L *-alis* -al] **1 :** of, relating to, having, or occurring by means of a placenta **2 :** of or relating to placental mammals

**²placental** \"\ *n* -s [NL *Placentalia*] **:** a placental mammal

**placental barrier** *n* **:** a semipermeable membrane made up of placental tissues and limiting the character and amount of material exchanged between mother and fetus

**plac·en·ta·lia** \,plasᵊnˈtālēə\ [NL, fr. *placenta* + *-alia*] *syn of* EUTHERIA

**¹plac·en·ta·li·an** \ˌ==ˈtālēən\ *adj* [NL *Placentalia* + E *-an*] **:** of or relating to the placental mammals

**²placentalian** \"\ *n* -s **:** PLACENTAL

**placental sign** *n* **:** a slight bloody discharge from the vagina coinciding with implantation of an embryo in the uterus

**placenta pre·via** \-ˈprēvēə\ *n, pl* **placentae previ·ae** \-vē,ē\ [NL, previous placenta] **:** an abnormal implantation of the placenta at or near the internal opening of the uterine cervix so that it tends to precede the child at birth usu. causing severe maternal hemorrhage

**plac·en·tary** \ˈplasᵊn,terē, pləˈsentərē\ *adj* [NL *placentarius,* fr. *placenta* + L *-arius* -ary] **:** PLACENTAL

**pla·cen·tate** \pləˈsen,tāt\ *adj* [NL *placentatus,* fr. *placenta* + L *-atus* -ate] **:** having a placenta

**plac·en·ta·tion** \,plasᵊnˈtāshən\ *n* -s [NL *placenta* + E *-ation*] **1 a :** the development of the placenta and attachment of the fetus to the uterus during pregnancy **b :** the morphological type of a placenta ⟨discoidal ~⟩ **2 :** the arrangement or mode of attachment of the placentas and ovules in a plant ovary

**plac·en·tif·er·ous** \ˌ==ˈtif(ə)rəs\ *adj* [NL *placenta* + E *-iferous*] *archaic* **:** having a placenta

**plac·en·ti·tis** \ˌ==ˈtīdəs\ *n, pl* **placentit·i·des** \-tidə,dēz\ [NL, fr. *placenta* + *-itis*] **:** inflammation of the placenta

**plac·en·tog·ra·phy** \-ˈtägrəfē\ *n* -ES [NL *placenta* + ISV *-o-* + *-graphy*] **:** roentgenographic visualization of the placenta after injection of an opaque medium

**pla·cen·toid** \pləˈsen,tȯid\ *adj* [NL *placenta* + ISV *-oid*] **:** resembling a placenta

**plac·en·to·ma** \,plasᵊnˈtōmə\ *n, pl* **placentomas** \-məz\ *or* **placentoma·ta** \-mədə\ [NL, fr. *placenta* + *-oma*] **:** a tumor developed from retained placental remnants

**plac·en·tome** \ˈplasᵊn,tōm\ *n* -s [NL *placenta* + E *-ome*] **:** the placenta and its adjuncts **:** the whole group of fetal and maternal tissues that are involved in placentation

**¹plac·er** \ˈplāsə(r)\ *n* -s [²*place* + *-er*] **:** one that places: as **a :** one that deposits or arranges ⟨bookbinder's ~⟩ ⟨enamel kiln ~⟩ **b :** one of the winners in a competition ⟨fifth ~ in the . . . Miss America competition —*Time*⟩

**²plac·er** \ˈplasə(r), -laas-\ *n* -s *often attrib* [Sp, fr. Catal, submarine plain, fr. *plaza* place, fr. L *platea* broad street — more at PLACE] **:** an alluvial, lacustrine, marine, eolian, or glacial deposit (as of sand or gravel) containing particles of gold or other valuable mineral — compare LODE

**³placer** \"\ *vb* -ED/-ING/-S *vt* **:** to extract (minerals) from sand or gravel by washing ~ *vi* **:** to work at placer mining

**placer mining** *n* **:** the process of extracting minerals from a placer esp. by washing, dredging, or hydraulic mining

**places** *pl of* PLACE, *pres 3d sing of* PLACE

**place setting** *n* **1 :** an arbitrary selection of dishes and flatware constituting a table service for one person **2 :** a basic purchasing unit of matched pieces usu. consisting of a dinner plate, salad or dessert plate, bread-and-butter plate, and cup and saucer in dinnerware and of a knife, fork, salad fork, soup spoon, teaspoon, and butter spreader in flatware

place setting 2 arranged on a place mat

**pla·cet** \ˈplāsət\ *n* -s [L, it pleases, 3d sing. pres. indic. of *placēre* to please — more at PLEASE] **:** an expression of approval or vote of assent; *specif* **:** EXEQUATUR 2

**place theory** *n* **:** a theory in physiology: the perception of pitch results from the ability of sounds of different pitch to stimulate different areas of the organ of Corti — compare TELEPHONE THEORY

**plac·id** \ˈplasəd, -laas-\ *adj* [L *placidus,* fr. *placēre* to please — more at PLEASE] **1 a :** marked by serenity **:** SMOOTH, TRANQUIL ⟨ribbon of sand . . . between the angry sea and the ~ bay —D.J.Lynde⟩ ⟨the ~ atmosphere of easy living —Louis Fischer⟩ **b :** free of interruption or disturbance **:** QUIET, UNEVENTFUL ⟨young men now arriving . . . at the age of forty have never known ~ times as adults —J.D.Hicks⟩ **2 a :** of a peaceable nature **:** MEEK, MILD ⟨a ~ lamb lying fast asleep —Elinor Wylie⟩ ⟨the relatively ~ crime of horse lifting —W.B.Bracke⟩ **b :** characterized by unruffled composure **:** CALM, PHLEGMATIC ⟨that ~ force . . . in many farmers —Guy McCrone⟩ ⟨so ~, so resigned that if the earth had opened at his feet he would have felt neither surprise nor fear —Herman Smith⟩; *specif* **:** COMPLACENT ⟨an air of ~ sufficiency which was the first hint . . . of the man's overweening, unmeasurable conceit —Joseph Conrad⟩ **syn** see CALM

**pla·ci·da·men·te** \plä,chēdəˈmentē\ *adv* [It, fr. *placido* calm, quiet (fr. L *placidus*) + *-mente,* adv. suffix] **:** PLACIDLY, CALMLY — used as a direction in music

**pla·cid·i·ty** \pləˈsidədē, plə'-, -ətē, -i\ *n* -ES [L *placiditas* fr. *placidus* placid + *-itat-, -itas* -ity] **:** the quality or state of being placid **:** COMPOSURE, SERENITY

**plac·id·ly** *adv* **:** in a placid manner **:** CALMLY, PHLEGMATICALLY, COMPLACENTLY

**plac·id·ness** *n* -ES [*placid* + *-ness*] *archaic* **:** PLACIDITY

**placing–out** \ˈ==ˈ=\ *n* [*placing* (fr. gerund of ²*place*) + *out*] **:** a system of caring for dependent children by placing them in private families instead of putting them in institutions (as orphanages)

**plac·it** \ˈplasət\ *n* -s [ML *placitum*] *archaic* **:** DECREE, PETITION

**plac·i·ta co·ro·nae** \ˌplasədəkəˈrō,nē\ *n pl* [ML] **:** PLEAS OF THE CROWN

**plac·i·tum** \ˈplasədəm\ *n, pl* **placi·ta** \-də\ [ML, fr. L *placitum* opinion, decision, decree — more at PLEA] *archaic* **:** a judicial proceeding or decree

**plack** \ˈplak\ *n* -s [ME *plakke,* fr. MD *placke* a coin — more at PLAQUE] **1 :** a small billon coin of Scotland issued from James III to James VI; *also* **:** a corresponding unit of value ⟨half-*plack* coin⟩ **2** *archaic* **:** a paltry bit **:** TRIFLE

**plack·et** \ˈplakət, *usu* -əd·+V\ *n* -s [origin unknown] **1** *obs* **:** PUDENDUM **2 a** *or* **placket-hole :** a finished slit in a garment (as at the top of a skirt or petticoat making it easy to put on); *esp* **:** one giving access to an inner pocket **b** *archaic* **:** a pocket esp. in a woman's skirt ⟨in a ~ at her side is an old enameled watch —Leigh Hunt⟩ **c :** a finished opening usu. in a seam or bisecting an edge (as of a slipcover) assuring a snug fit when fastened **3** *archaic* **a :** PETTICOAT **b :** WOMAN ⟨was that brave heart made to pant for a ~ —John Fletcher⟩

**plack·less** \ˈplakləs\ *adj* [*plack* + *-less*] *chiefly Scot* **:** PENNILESS

**placo-** — see PLAC-

**plac·ob·del·la** \,pla,käbˈdelə\ *n, cap* [NL, fr. *plac-* + *-bdella*] **:** a common and widely distributed genus of freshwater leeches (family Glossiphoniidae) parasitic on aquatic vertebrates

**plac·ode** \ˈpla,kōd\ *n* -s [ISV *plac-* + *-ode*] **:** a platelike thickening of embryonic ectoderm from which a definitive structure develops ⟨ear ~⟩ ⟨olfactory ~⟩ — see LENS PLACODE

**¹plac·o·derm** \ˈplakə,dərm\ *adj* [*plac-* + Gk *derma* skin — more at DERM-] **1** *also* **plac·o·der·ma·tous** \ˌ==ˈdərmədəs\ **:** having a cell wall of two or rarely more pieces and vertical pores in the wall — used of desmids of the family Desmidiaceae; distinguished from *saccoderm* **2** *or* **plac·o·der·mal** \ˌ==ˈdərməl\ [NL *Placodermi*] **:** of or relating to the Placodermi

**²placoderm** \"\ *n* -s [NL *Placodermi*] **:** a fish or fossil of the class Placodermi

**plac·o·der·mi** \ˌ=='dər,mī\ *n pl, cap* [NL, fr. *plac-* + Gk *derma* skin — more at DERM-] **:** a class of extinct fishes with an armor of large bony plates and primitive jaw structures that has been taken as equivalent to Antiarcha plus Arthrodira but is now usu. extended to include also the Acanthodii, Cycliae, and minor groups — compare CHONDRICHTHYES — **plac·o·der·moid** \ˌ=='dər,mȯid\ *adj*

**¹plac·o·dont** \ˈplakə,dänt\ *adj* [NL *Placodont-, Placodus* or *Placodontia*] **:** of or relating to the genus *Placodus* or suborder Placodontia

**²placodont** \"\ *n* -s **:** a reptile of the genus *Placodus* or suborder Placodontia

**plac·o·don·tia** \ˌ=='dänch(ē)ə\ *n pl, cap* [NL, fr. *Placodont-, Placodus,* genus of reptiles + *-ia*] **:** a suborder of Sauropterygia that is sometimes regarded as a separate order and that comprises armored Triassic reptiles resembling the turtles in many respects — see PLACODUS — **plac·o·don·tian** \ˌ=='dänch(ē)ən\ *adj*

**plac·o·dus** \ˈplakədəs\ *n, cap* [NL, fr. *plac-* + *-odus*] **:** a genus (the type of the family Placodontidae of the suborder Placodontia) comprising rather large extinct reptiles from the marine Trias of central Europe that have short broad bodies and broad flat molar teeth on the palate and dentary bones apparently adapted to crushing mollusks

**plac·o·ga·noi·dei** \,plakōgəˈnōidē,ī\ [NL, fr. *plac-* + *Ganoidei*] *syn of* PLACODERMI

**¹plac·oid** \ˈpla,kȯid\ *adj* [*plac-* + *-oid*] **1 :** consisting of a basal plate of dentine of dermal origin embedded in the skin and bearing a projecting point or spine tipped with enamel — used of an elasmobranch fish scale; compare SHAGREEN **2** [NL *Placoidei*] **:** of or relating to the Placoidei

**²placoid** \"\ *n* -s [NL *Placoidei*] **:** a fish of the group Placoidei

**pla·coi·dal** \pləˈkȯidᵊl\ *or* **pla·coi·de·an** \-dēən\ *adj* [NL *Placoidei* + E *-al, -an*] **:** PLACOID 2

**pla·coi·dei** \-dē,ī\ *n pl, cap* [NL, fr. *plac-* + *-oidei*] *in former classifications* **:** a group of fishes with placoid scales equivalent or nearly so to Chondrichthyes and sometimes including the cyclostomes

**placque** *var of* PLAQUE

**plac·u·la** \ˈplakyələ\ *n, pl* **placulas** \-yələz\ *or* **placu·lae** \-yə,lē\ [NL, fr. *plac-* + L *-ula*] **:** the flattened blastula of urochordates or a similar oligochaete embryo

**pla·cu·na** \pləˈkyünə\ *n, cap* [NL, fr. Gk *plak-, plax* flat surface] **:** a genus of large flattened tropical bivalve mollusks (order Filibranchia) with extremely thin nearly transparent shells that is related to *Anomia* but sometimes made the type of a separate family — see WINDOWPANE OYSTER

**plad·dy** \ˈpladi\ *var of* PLAIDIE

**pla·fond** \pləˈfän(d)\ *n* -s [F, fr. MF *platfonds,* fr. *plat* flat + *fonds* bottom, fr. L *fundus* — more at PLATE, BOTTOM] **1 :** a ceiling usu. of elaborate design formed by the underside of a floor **2 :** a French variant of auction bridge that is similar to contract bridge

**pla·gal** \ˈplāgəl\ *adj* [ML *plagalis,* fr. *plaga* plagal mode (prob. back-formation fr. *plagius* plagal, fr. MGk *plagios,* fr. Gk, oblique, sideways, crooked, fr. *plagos* side) + L *-alis* -al; akin to Gk *pelagos* surface of the sea, sea, L *plaga* covering, net, region — more at FLAKE] **1** *of an ecclesiastical mode or melody* **:** having the keynote on the 4th scale step — distinguished from *authentic* **2** *of a cadence* **:** having a concluding chord sequence consisting of the subdominant chord and its resolution to the tonic — see CADENCE illustration

**plage** \ˈpläzh\ *n* -s [F, beach, fr. It *piaggia,* fr. LL *plagia* beach, shore, fr. Gk *plagios* oblique, sideways — more at PLAGAL] **1 :** the beach of a seaside resort **2 :** a bright region on the sun seen in the light of calcium or hydrogen and often associated with sunspots — compare FLOCCULUS

**plagi-** *or* **plagio-** *comb form* [Gk, fr. *plagios* — more at PLAGAL] **:** oblique **:** aslant ⟨*Plagianthus*⟩ ⟨*plagio*tropic⟩

**pla·gi·an·thus** \,plājēˈan(t)thəs\ *n, cap* [NL, fr. *plagi-* + *-anthus*] **:** a genus of Australasian shrubs and trees (family Malvaceae) having small flowers without bracteoles — see RIBBON TREE

**pla·gia·rism** \ˈplājə,rizəm *sometimes* -jēə,-\ *n* -s [*plagiary* + *-ism*] **1 :** an act or instance of plagiarizing ⟨virtually a free adaptation . . . and on the face of it a straight-out ~ —Antony Alpers⟩ **2 :** a plagiarized item ⟨his book is full of ~s⟩

**pla·gia·rist** \-rəst\ *n* -s [*plagiary* + *-ist*] **:** one who plagiarizes **:** one guilty of literary or artistic theft — **pla·gia·ris·tic** \ˌ=(=)=ˈristik, -tēk\ *adj*

**pla·gia·rize** \ˈ=(=)=,rīz\ *vb* -ED/-ING/-S — *see -ize in Explan Notes* [*plagiary* + *-ize*] *vt* **:** to steal and pass off as one's own (the ideas or words of another) **:** use (a created production) without crediting the source ⟨a learned book of his . . . had been coolly *plagiarized* and issued in short version —*Times Lit. Supp.*⟩ ~ *vi* **:** to commit literary theft **:** present as new and original an idea or product derived from an existing source

**pla·gia·ry** \ˈplājē,erē, -jər-, -ri\ *n* -ES [L *plagiarius* kidnapper, plagiarist, fr. *plagium* hunting net (fr. *plaga* net) + *-arius* -ary — more at PLAGAL] **1** *obs* **:** KIDNAPPER **2** *archaic* **:** PLAGIARIST **3 :** PLAGIARISM ⟨not alone in his condemnation of literary imitation and ~ —N.F.Adkins⟩ ⟨famous *plagiaries* —*Univ. of Minn. Press Cat.*⟩

**plagii** *pl of* PLAGIUM

**pla·gi·o·ceph·a·ly** \,plājēōˈsefəlē\ *n* -ES [*plagi-* + *-cephaly*] **:** a malformation of the head marked by obliquity of the main axis of the skull and usu. caused by closure of half of the coronal suture

**pla·gi·o·chi·la** \,plājēōˈkīlə\ *n* [NL, fr. *plagi-* + Gk *cheilos* lip — more at GILL] **1** *cap* **:** a genus of mostly tropical leafy liverworts (family Jungermanniaceae) having succubous toothed or lobed leaves **2** -s **:** any liverwort of the genus *Plagiochila*

**pla·gi·o·clase** \ˈplājēə,klās\ *n* -s [ISV *plagi-* + *-clase;* orig. formed as G *plagioklas*] **:** a triclinic feldspar; *esp* **:** one of the calcium-sodium series comprising anorthite and albite and the intermediate bytownite, labradorite, andesine, and oligoclase — see MOONSTONE

**pla·gi·o·cli·nal** \ˌplājēōˈklīnᵊl\ *adj* [*plagi-* + *-clinal*] **:** oblique to the general strike of rocks in the surrounding area

**pla·gi·o·dont** \ˈplājēə,dänt\ *adj* [ISV *plagi-* + *-odont*] **:** having the palatal teeth set obliquely or in two convergent series — used of a snake

**pla·gi·o·graph** \ˈplājēə,graf, -ráf\ *n* [*plagi-* + *-graph*] **:** a pantograph that may be set at any angle to the drawing to be copied — called also *skew pantograph*

**pla·gi·o·he·dral** \ˌplājēōˈhēdrəl\ *or* **pla·gi·he·dral** \-jə'-\ *adj* [*plagi-* + *-hedral*] **:** having an oblique spiral arrangement of faces **:** GYROIDAL ⟨~ quartz crystals⟩; *specif* **:** being a group of the isometric system characterized by 13 axes of symmetry but no center or planes

**pla·gi·o·nite** \ˈplājēə,nīt\ *n* -s [G *plagionit,* fr. Gk *plagion,* neut. of *plagios* oblique + G *-it* -ite — more at PLAGAL] **:** a mineral $Pb_5Sb_8S_{17}$ consisting of a lead antimony sulfide of a blackish lead-gray color and metallic luster (sp. gr. 5.4)

**pla·gio·patagium** \ˌplājēō+\ *n, pl* **plagiopatagia** [NL, fr. *plagi-* + *patagium*] **:** an extensile membrane connecting the forelimb and hind limb (as of a bat or flying squirrel) and used when spread in flying or gliding

**pla·gi·or·chi·idae** \,plājēō(r)ˈkīə,dē\ *n pl, cap* [NL, fr. *Plagiorchis,* type genus + *-idae*] **:** a large family of digenetic trematodes that produce xiphidiocercaria — see PLAGIORCHIS

**pla·gi·or·chis** \,plājēˈórkəs\ *n, cap* [NL, fr. *plagi-* + Gk *orchis* testicle — more at ORCHIS] **:** a large genus (the type of the family Plagiorchiidae) of digenetic trematodes including parasites of the oviducts or intestine of various wild and domesticated birds and of the intestine of mammals

**pla·gi·o·rhyn·chus** \,plājēōˈriŋkəs\ *n, cap* [NL, fr. *plagi-* + *-rhynchus*] **:** a genus of acanthocephalan worms parasitic in the intestine of domestic fowls and other birds

**pla·gi·o·sto·ma·ta** \,plājēōˈstōmədə\ *also* **pla·gi·os·to·ma** \,plājēˈästəmə\ [NL, fr. *plagi-* + *-stomata, -stoma*] *syn of* PLAGIOSTOMI

**pla·gi·o·stom·a·tous** \ˌplājēōˈstämədəs, -tōm-\ *or* **pla·gi·os·to·mous** \ˌplājēˈästəməs\ *adj* [*plagiostomatous* fr. NL *Plagiostomata* + E *-ous; plagiostomous* fr. NL *Plagiostomi* + E *-ous*] **:** PLAGIOSTOME

**¹pla·gi·o·stome** \ˈplājēə,stōm\ *adj* [NL *Plagiostomi*] **:** of or relating to the Plagiostomi

**²plagiostome** \"\ *n* -s **:** a fish of the group Plagiostomi

**pla·gi·os·to·mi** \,plājēˈästə,mī\ *n pl, cap* [NL, fr. *plagi-* + *-stomi*] *in some esp former classifications* **:** a group of fishes more or less exactly equivalent to Chondrichthyes or more restrictedly an order including the existing sharks and rays as distinguished from the chimaeras and the extinct primitive groups Pleuropterygii and Ichthyotomi — compare SELACHII

**pla·gi·o·sto·mia** \,plājēōˈstōmēə\ [NL, fr. *Plagiostomi* + *-ia*] *syn of* PLAGIOSTOMI

**pla·gi·o·trop·ic** \ˌplājēōˌträpik\ *adj* [ISV *plagi-* + *-tropic;* orig. formed as G *plagiotropisch*] **:** having the longer axis inclined away from the vertical ⟨~ roots and lateral branches⟩ — compare ORTHOTROPIC — **pla·gi·o·trop·i·cal·ly** \-pək(ə)lē\ *adv*

**pla·gi·ot·ro·pism** \,plājēˈä·trə,pizəm\ *n* [ISV *plagi-* + *-tropism;* orig. formed as G *plagiotropismus*] **:** the quality or state of being or tending to be plagiotropic

**pla·gi·ot·ro·pous** \ˌ=='ä·trəpəs\ *adj* [ISV *plagi-* + *-tropous*] **:** PLAGIOTROPIC

**pla·gi·ot·ro·py** \ˌ=='ä·trəpē\ *n* -ES [ISV *plagi-* + *-tropy*] **:** PLAGIOTROPISM

**pla·gi·um** \ˈplājēəm\ *n, pl* **pla·gia** \-ēə\ [LL, prob. back-formation fr. L *plagiarius* kidnapper — more at PLAGIARY] *civil law* **:** KIDNAPPING

**¹plague** \ˈplāg *chiefly dial* ˈpleg\ *n* -s *often attrib* [ME *plage,* fr. MF, fr. LL *plaga,* fr. L, blow, wound, misfortune — more at PLAINT] **1 a :** a disastrous evil or affliction **:** CALAMITY, SCOURGE ⟨rebel regiments were a ~ upon the country, robbing, burning and committing every conceivable outrage —Kenneth Roberts⟩ ⟨the numbers racket and the dope ~ thrive —Herman Kogan⟩ — often used interjectionally to express annoyance or impatience ⟨a ~ o' both your houses —Shak.⟩ ⟨~ take it, what's keeping that boy⟩ **b :** a destructively numerous influx or multiplication of a noxious animal **:** INFESTATION ⟨~ of swarming locusts⟩ ⟨tremendous ~s of rats have devastated the rice fields —J.F.Embree & W.L. Thomas⟩ ⟨a ~ of leafworms destroyed a large part of the crops —*Amer. Guide Series: Texas*⟩ **2 a :** an epidemic disease causing a high rate of mortality **:** PESTILENCE ⟨a ~ of cholera⟩ ⟨the great ~ diseases . . . are rapidly approaching extinction —A.C.Morrison⟩ **b :** an acute contagious febrile disease caused by a bacterium (*Pasteurella pestis*), occurring in several forms, and usu. transmitted (as bubonic plague) from rats to man by the bite of infected fleas or directly (as pneumonic plague) from person to person — compare BLACK DEATH **3 a :** a cause of irritation or distress **:** NUISANCE, HARASSMENT ⟨having . . . been her husband's ~ because of the violence of her temper —W.B.Yeats⟩ ⟨wild dogs are a . . . ~ to squatters —Rachel Henning⟩ **b :** a sudden unwelcome increase or prevalence **:** OUTBREAK ⟨a ~ of broken dishes in the cafeteria —Stuart Chase⟩ ⟨a ~ of hot-dog stands and cheap amusements —*Amer. Guide Series: N.Y. City*⟩ ⟨a ~ of burglaries⟩

**²plague** \"\ *vt* -ED/-ING/-S **1 a :** to afflict with evil or calamity **:** SCOURGE, TORMENT ⟨mass poverty and unemployment continued to ~ the nation —F.L.Schuman⟩ **b :** to infect with a plague ⟨diseases that ~ mankind —*Wall Street Jour.*⟩ ⟨a disease that ~s watermelons —Jane Nickerson⟩ **2 a** (1) **:** to cause worry or distress to **:** TROUBLE, HARASS ⟨debts . . . *plagued* her after her husband's death —Ruth P. Randall⟩ ⟨back trouble . . . had been *plaguing* him increasingly in recent weeks —A.C.Spectorsky⟩ ⟨outmoded notions about race . . . still ~ this nation —Bradford Smith⟩ (2) **:** to slow up or put at a disadvantage **:** HAMPER, HANDICAP ⟨construction of the power plant . . . has been *plagued* by bad weather —*Annual Report of Ill. Power Co.*⟩ ⟨a series of injuries *plagued* the team⟩ ⟨the traffic detour . . . which has *plagued* motorists —*Springfield (Mass.) Daily News*⟩ **:** BURDEN ⟨the dance of today is *plagued* with exotic . . . mannerisms —John Martin⟩ **b :** to disturb or annoy persistently **:** BOTHER, NAG ⟨she talked, she wrote, she *plagued* him —Elizabeth Janeway⟩ ⟨something . . . every congressman is continually *plagued* to do by his constituents —*Christian Science Monitor*⟩ **syn** see WORRY

**plagu·ed** \ˈplegəd\ *adj* [fr. past part. of ²*plague*] *dial* **:** TROUBLESOME, IRRITATING

**plague grasshopper** *or* **plague locust** *n* **:** a grasshopper that may rapidly build up vast destructive swarms from a small localized population; *esp* **:** either of two Australian grasshoppers (*Chortoicetes terminifera* or *Austroicetes cruciata*)

**plague·some** \ˈplāgsəm\ *adj* [¹*plague* + *-some*] **1 :** TROUBLESOME **2 :** PESTILENTIAL

**plague spot** *n* **1 :** a hemorrhagic spot on the skin **2 :** a locality afflicted with a plague or regarded as a source of contamination

**¹pla·guey** *or* **plaguy** \ˈplāgē, -gi *chiefly dial* ˈpleg-\ *adj* [¹*plague* + *-y*] *chiefly dial* **1 :** of, relating to, or afflicted with a plague ⟨the ~ fever came aboard —*Ballad Book*⟩ **2 :** causing irritation or annoyance **:** TROUBLESOME ⟨a ~ newfangled safety rail —*Architect & Building News*⟩ ⟨no . . . ~ choice to be made —C.E.Montague⟩ — often used as an intensive ⟨no wonder the ~ fools can't talk English —J.C.Lincoln⟩

**²plaguey** *or* **plaguy** \"\ *adv* **:** to a troublesome extent **:** EXCESSIVELY ⟨it's so ~ cold —Max Peacock⟩

**pla·gui·ly** \-gəlē\ *adv* [¹*plaguey, plaguy* + *-ly*] *archaic* **:** ²PLAGUEY

**plag·u·la** \ˈplagyələ\ *n, pl* **plagu·lae** \-yə,lē\ [NL, prob. fr. L, curtain, dim. of *plaga* covering — more at PLAGAL] **:** a ventral sclerite in the pedicel of various spiders

**plaice** *also* **plaise** \ˈplās\ *n, pl* **plaice** *also* **plaise** [ME *plaice, plais,* fr. OF *plais, plaïz,* fr. LL *platensis,* prob. fr. Gk *platys* broad, flat — more at PLACE] **1 a :** a European flounder (*Pleuronectes platessa*) that grows to a weight of 8 or 10 pounds or more **b :** any of various American flatfishes; *esp* **:** SUMMER FLOUNDER **2** *dial Eng* **:** ¹FLUKE 2

**¹plaid** \ˈplad, -aa(ə)d\ *n* -s [ScGael *plaide*] **1 :** a rectangular length of tartan worn over the left shoulder by men and women as part of the Scottish national costume ⟨a ~ . . . which served him as a garment by day and a blanket by night —*Scots Mag.*⟩ **2 a :** a twilled woolen fabric with a tartan pattern used in making plaids **b :** a fabric with a woven or printed pattern of tartan or an imitation of tartan **3 a :** TARTAN 1 **b :** a woven or printed pattern of unevenly spaced stripes repeated in sequence and crossing each other at right angles ⟨the ~s of these shirts never saw the Scottish shore⟩

**2plaid** \"\ *adj* **:** having a multicolored cross-barred pattern ⟨~ vest⟩ ⟨~ blanket⟩

**plaid·ed** \-dəd\ *adj* [1*plaid* + *-ed*] **1 :** wearing a plaid ⟨~ Highlander⟩ **2 :** PLAID

**plaid·en** \'plad°n\ *chiefly Scot var of* PLAIDING

**plaid·ie** \'pladī\ *n* -s [1*plaid* + *-ie*] *Scot* **:** PLAID 1

**plaid·ing** \'pladiŋ\ *n* -s [1*plaid* + *-ing*] **:** PLAID 2

**plaid neuk** *n, Scot* **:** a pocket formed by the sewed-up corner of a plaid

**plai·do·yer** \ˌpledwə'yā\ *n* -s [F, fr. OF *plaidoyer* to plead, fr. *plaid* plea — more at PLEA] **:** an address, plea, or argument made esp. by an advocate in court

**plaik** \'plāk\ *var of* PLAYOCK

**1plain** \'plān\ *vb* -ED/-ING/-S [ME *plainen, pleynen,* fr. MF *plaindre,* fr. L *plangere* to lament — more at PLAINT] *vi* **1** *archaic* **:** COMPLAIN; *specif* **:** to make a complaint against someone **2** *archaic* **:** to make a doleful sound **:** MOURN ⟨wind went . . . *~ing* over the barren moor —Mary Linskill⟩ **~** *vt, archaic* **:** BEWAIL, BEMOAN

**2plain** \"\ *n* -s *archaic* **:** PLAINT

**3plain** \"\ *n* -s [ME *plain, pleyn,* fr. OF *plain,* fr. L *planum,* fr. neut. of *planus* level, flat] **1 a :** an extensive area of land having few inequalities of surface, being usu. fairly flat but sometimes having a considerable slope, and usu. being at low elevation though some (as the Great Plains of the U.S.) are as much as three or four thousand feet above sea level **:** a very widespread tract of level or rolling treeless country with a vegetation predominantly of short perennial grasses and annual forbs — often used in pl. ⟨from the ecological viewpoint there is no essential distinction between . . . prairie and *~s* —F.E.Clements & V.E.Shelford⟩ **b :** a smooth flat or gently sloping part of an ocean floor ⟨the ~ of the ocean floor may be broken by long deep troughs —C.M. Nevin⟩ **c :** a broad unbroken expanse ⟨looking far over the mystic ~ of the waves —William Black⟩ ⟨a flat featureless snow ~ —G. de Q. Robin⟩ **2** *archaic* **a :** a field of battle **:** BATTLEGROUND ⟨lead forth my soldiers to the ~ —Shak.⟩ **b :** 4PLANE **3 :** something that is free from artifice, ornament, or extraneous matter ⟨nature and art, the ~ and the precious —J.H.Hagstrum⟩; *specif* **:** a usu. wool or cotton fabric of plain weave and solid color ⟨fine *~s* . . . usually are finer yarn, higher thread-count cloths than print cloths —John Hoye⟩

**4plain** \"\ *adj* -ER/-EST [ME *plain, pleyn,* fr. MF *plain,* fr. L *planus* level, flat, plain — more at FLOOR] **1** *obs.* **a :** FLAT ⟨his back is ~ to his tail —Edward Topsell⟩ **b :** PLANE **2 a** *archaic* **:** having an even surface **:** LEVEL, SMOOTH ⟨make the rougher places ~ —Catherine Winkworth⟩ **b** *of a merino sheep* **:** lacking folds or wrinkles ⟨a *plain*-bodied ewe⟩ **3 a :** lacking ornament **:** UNDECORATED ⟨a New England country church is traditionally a rather ~ building with a thin spire —Robert Holland⟩ **b** *heraldry* **:** not charged or engrailed **4 :** free of extraneous matter **:** PURE, UNADULTERATED ⟨takes his whiskey with ~ water⟩ ⟨the ~ colors . . . give such freshness to her work —*Yankee*⟩; *specif* **:** free of bubbles or other imperfections — used of glass **5 a** *archaic* **:** free of obstacles **:** OPEN ⟨give . . . battle in the ~ sea —John Speed⟩ **b :** free of impediments to view **:** UNOBSTRUCTED ⟨pastured out on the moors in ~ sight of us —Martha Kean⟩ **6 a** (1) **:** evident to the mind or senses **:** distinctly recognizable **:** OBVIOUS ⟨stared at him coldly, hatred and contempt very ~ in her face —Irwin Shaw⟩ ⟨the facts are undoubted; they are ~ matters of history —E.A.Freeman⟩ ⟨she's wild about him — it's as ~ as the nose on your face⟩ (2) **:** easily understood **:** CLEAR ⟨makes it . . . ~ that events develop quite independently of the people they affect —C.H.Rickword⟩ ⟨what, in ~ words, is the morality of culture —J.C.Powys⟩ **b :** characterized by candor **:** FRANK, BLUNT ⟨to be ~ with you, I will sing none —Izaak Walton⟩ ⟨an impressive honesty and a good deal of ~ speaking —Alan Bullock⟩ **c :** devoid of elaboration or subterfuge **:** BALD, UNDISGUISED ⟨made no attempt to harangue his listeners but stuck to the ~ facts⟩ ⟨~ anger seized me —Arthur Grimble⟩ **7 a :** belonging to the great majority of mankind **:** COMMON ⟨the ~ people everywhere . . . wish to live in peace with one another —F.D.Roosevelt⟩ **b** (1) **:** lacking special distinction **:** of a routine nature **:** ORDINARY ⟨writes not for musical specialists . . . but for the ~ operagoer —Ernest Newman⟩ ⟨~ common sense tells us that . . . gold and silver are practically useless except for what they will procure —W.P.Webb⟩ (2) **:** not being trump ⟨lost only one trick in each of the ~ suits —C.H.Goren⟩ **c :** characterized by lack of vanity or affectation ⟨just ~ folks — homespun, guileless and democratic —Thomas Pyles⟩ ⟨as ~ as an old shoe in dress, mannerisms, and the way he runs his business —*Time*⟩ **d :** avoiding waste or extravagance **:** FRUGAL ⟨every cent of tax money had to be put to some good ~ use —Dorothy C. Fisher⟩ **e :** of or relating to expressions used by the Quakers ⟨the use of *thee* and *thy* is characteristic of the ~ language⟩ **8 :** characterized by simplicity **:** UNCOMPLICATED: as **a** *of musical harmony* **:** using only essential chord tones ⟨the harmonic underpinning is a little ~ —Virgil Thomson⟩ **b :** devoid of strong seasoning or exotic ingredients ⟨~ home cooking⟩ **c** *of cloth* (1) **:** made in plain weave (2) **:** having no pattern **d** *of paper or board* (1) **:** made throughout of one grade of stock (2) **:** UNCOATED **9 a :** unremarkable either for physical beauty or ugliness **:** lacking allure **:** HOMELY ⟨a ~ woman with a face as hardy and simple and serviceable as the house —Rebecca West⟩ **b** *of livestock* **:** COARSE, INFERIOR ⟨a boar with a ~ head⟩

**syn** HOMELY, SIMPLE, UNPRETENTIOUS: PLAIN stresses lack of anything likely to attract attention — lack of ornament, complexity, extraneous matter, or strongly marked characteristics ⟨had no eccentricity even to take him out of the common run; he was just a good, dull, honest, *plain* man —W. S.Maugham⟩ ⟨a *plain* two-story frame house⟩ — and may suggest elegance ⟨his brown stockings . . . were of a fine texture; his shoes and buckles, too, though *plain,* were trim —Charles Dickens⟩ or frugality ⟨a *plain* skirt of serviceable gray flannel⟩ With reference to personal appearance it suggests lack of positive characteristics, contrasting with *beautiful* but implying no positive ugliness ⟨was not a *plain* woman, and she might have been very pretty still —Ellen Glasgow⟩ In reference to houses, furniture, food, and other elements of domesticity, HOMELY sometimes suggests *homey* and may indicate comfortable informality without ostentation ⟨his secluded wife ever smiling and cheerful, his little comfortable lodgings, snug meals, and *homely* evenings, had all the charms of novelty and secrecy —W.M.Thackeray⟩ It may connote warmth and simplicity ⟨a book-learned language, wholly remote from anything personal, native, or *homely* —Willa Cather⟩ With reference to appearance HOMELY in American but not usu. in British usage often falls between *plain* and *ugly* ⟨she was certainly not bad-looking now and she could never have been so *homely* as she imagined —Edmund Wilson⟩ SIMPLE may occasionally differ slightly from PLAIN in implying choice rather than compulsive circumstance ⟨what was then called the *simple* life . . . is recognizable as the austere luxury of a very cultivated poet —Agnes Repplier⟩ ⟨a monk of Lindisfarne, so *simple* and lowly in temper that he traveled on foot on his long mission journeys —J.R.Green⟩ UNPRETENTIOUS, stressing lack of vanity or affectation, may praise a person but depreciate a possession ⟨an *unpretentious* family doctor without the specialist's curt loftiness⟩ ⟨an *unpretentious* and battered old car⟩ **syn** see in addition EVIDENT, FRANK, LEVEL

**5plain** \"\ *vt* -ED/-ING/-S [ME *plainen,* fr. 4*plain*] **1** *obs* **:** PLANE ⟨the pavement thus laid is to be *~ed* and polished —Philemon Holland⟩ **2** *of glass* **:** to free from bubbles or other imperfections **:** REFINE

**6plain** \"\ *adv* [4*plain*] **:** in a plain manner **:** without obscurity or ambiguity **:** CLEARLY, SIMPLY ⟨preached that it was just ~ wrong for some people, by tricks and wiles, to get a stranglehold on business —F.L.Allen⟩ ⟨the tiny snap as he closed the book came ~ to the colonel's ears —A.B.Mayse⟩

**7plain** \"\ *adv* [partly fr. ME *plein, playne* entire, complete, fr. MF *plein* full, fr. L *plenus;* partly fr. 6*plain* — more at FULL] *chiefly dial* **:** ENTIRELY, ABSOLUTELY ⟨the house was plumb ~ deserted, as anybody could see —Helen Eustis⟩

**plain base** *adj* [4*plain*] *of a bullet* **:** being without a gascheck

**plain bob** *n* **:** a method of ringing changes in which the treble alone has a plain hunt

**plainchant** \'ˌ=ˌ=\ *n* [F *plain-chant,* lit., plain song, trans. of ML *cantus planus*] **:** PLAINSONG

**plain chart** *n* **:** a nautical chart laid down on a Mercator projection

**plain clothes** *n* **:** unofficial clothes **:** the dress of an ordinary citizen ⟨man waiting for him was in *plain clothes* —Nancy Rutledge⟩ — opposed to *uniform*

**plainclothes** \'ˌ=ˌ=\ *adj* [*plain clothes*] **:** not in uniform ⟨was directed to a ~ recruiting sergeant —Nigel Dennis⟩

**plain·clothes·man** \(')=ˈ=mən, -ˌman, -ˌmaa(ə)n\ *n, pl* **plainclothesmen :** a policeman who wears civilian clothes while on duty **:** DETECTIVE

**plain component** *or* **plain sequence** *n* **:** the sequence of letters in a substitution alphabet that identifies the plaintext letters — compare ALPHABET 1j

**plain concrete** *n* **:** concrete containing no steel reinforcing bars or wire or containing not more than two tenths of one percent of reinforcing

**plain condensed milk** *n* **:** EVAPORATED MILK — used esp. of the bulk commercial product as distinguished from the canned pasteurized consumer product

**plain counterpoint** *n* **:** STRICT COUNTERPOINT

**plain dealing** *adj* [6*plain*] **:** STRAIGHTFORWARD ⟨a *plain dealing* honest man —M.G.J. de Crèvecoeur⟩

**plained** *past of* PLAIN

**1plainer** *comparative of* PLAIN

**2plainer** *n* [5*plain* + *-er*] *obs* **:** PLANER

**plainest** *superlative of* PLAIN

**plain-hearted** *adj* [4*plain* + *hearted*] **:** SINCERE, ARTLESS

**plain hunt** *n* [4*plain*] **:** a course followed by a single bell through a series of changes in change ringing in which the bell works from first or lead position to last place and back up again

**plain hunting** *n* **:** change ringing in which each bell has a plain hunt — see CHANGE RINGING illustration

**plaining** *n* -s [fr. gerund of 5*plain*] **:** FINING 1b

**plain·ish** \'plānish\ *adj* [4*plain* + *-ish*] **:** rather plain

**plain jane** *adj, usu cap J* [fr. the name *Jane*] **:** of the usual type **:** ORDINARY, UNREMARKABLE ⟨the plain Jane model . . . may be offered with optional trim —*Motor Life*⟩

**plain knitting** *n* **1 :** GARTER STITCH **2** *or* **plain knit :** STOCKINETTE STITCH

**plain-laid** \'ˌ=ˌ=\ *adj, of a rope* **:** consisting of three, four, or six usu. left-handed strands twisted together in a direction opposite to that of the twist in the strands — compare CABLE-LAID

**plain language** *n* **:** language unconcealed by any cryptographic process

**plain live axle** *n* **:** an axle carrying both differential and road wheels

**plain·ly** *adv* [4*plain* + *-ly*] **:** in a plain manner: as **a :** with clarity of perception or comprehension **:** DISTINCTLY, CLEARLY **b :** in unmistakable terms **:** OBVIOUSLY **c :** with candor **:** FRANKLY **d :** SIMPLY, UNPRETENTIOUSLY

**plain muscle** *n* **:** SMOOTH MUSCLE

**plain·ness** \'plānnəs\ *n* -ES [ME *playnesse, pleynnesse,* partly fr. MF *plainesse, planece* flatness, fr. L *planities* flat surface, fr. *planus* flat, level; partly fr. ME *plain* + *-nesse* -ness — more at FLOOR] **:** the quality or state of being plain

**plain of mars** *usu cap P&M* [3*plain*] **:** an area in the center of the palm between Upper Mars and Lower Mars that when well developed or crossed with many lines is usu. held by palmists to indicate the presence of sudden temper

**plain people** *n, usu cap both Ps* [4*plain*] **:** members of any of various religious groups (as Mennonites, Dunkers, Amish, or Schwenkfelders) who wear plain clothes, adhere to old customs, and practice in general a simple way of life as a means of carrying out the biblical injunction not to be conformed to this world

**1plains** *pres 3d sing of* PLAIN, *pl of* PLAIN

**2plains** \'plānz\ *adj, usu cap* [*Plains* (*Indian*)] **:** of or belonging to No. American Indians of the Great Plains or to their culture characterized by the horse, the tepee, geometric painting on tanned skin, and tailored garments decorated with beads and porcupine quills

**plain sail** *n* [4*plain*] **:** the ordinary working canvas of a sailing ship usu. including topgallant sails, royals, and a flying jib — see SAIL illustration

**plain sailing** *n* [alter. of *plane sailing*] **1 :** PLANE SAILING 1 **2 :** effortless progress over an unobstructed course **:** easy going

**plain-saw** \'ˌ=ˌ=\ *vt* [6*plain*] **:** TANGENT-SAW

**plains cottonwood** *or* **plains poplar** *n* [fr. the Great *Plains*] **:** a large poplar (*Populus sargentii*) chiefly of the Great Plains region of No. America having deeply furrowed gray bark and broadly oval leaves with coarse curved teeth and long points

**plainscraft** \'ˌ=ˌ=\ *n* [*plains* (pl. of 3*plain*) + *craft*] **:** knowledge of and skill in applying the lore of a plains environment

**plains cree** *n, usu cap P&C* **1 :** an Algonquian people formerly inhabiting the southwestern portion of the Cree territory — compare WOOD CREE **2 :** a member of the Plains Cree people

**plain seam** *n* [4*plain*] **:** a seam made with a single line of stitching inside the matched edges of two pieces of material

**plain service** *n* **:** a worship service unaccompanied with music

**plains indian** *n, usu cap P&I* [fr. the Great *Plains,* region of central No. America] **:** an Indian of the Algonquian, Athapaskan, Caddo, Kiowa, Siouan, or Uto-Aztecan nomadic peoples formerly inhabiting the Great Plains of central U.S. and Canada — called also *Buffalo Indian*

**plains·man** \'plānzmən\ *n, pl* **plainsmen** [Great *Plains* + *man*] **:** an inhabitant of the plains; *esp* **:** one skilled in plainscraft ⟨army scout and ~ —*Amer. Guide Series: Texas*⟩

**plainsong** \'ˌ=ˌ=\ *n* [trans. of ML *cantus planus*] **1 :** the ancient nonmetrical monophonic chant of the church service that is based on the ecclesiastical modes and is used today in some liturgical churches — called also *plainchant;* compare AMBROSIAN CHANT, CANTUS FIRMUS 1, GREGORIAN CHANT **2 a :** a chant melody used as a cantus firmus for contrapuntal treatment **b :** CANTUS FIRMUS 2 — compare PRICK SONG **3 :** a simple air or melody

**plainspoken** \'ˌ=ˌ=\ *adj* [6*plain* + *spoken*] **:** characterized by candor **:** FRANK, STRAIGHTFORWARD — **plainspokenness** *n* -ES

**plain·stanes** \'plānˌstānz\ *n pl* [4*plain* + pl. of *stane* stone] *Scot* **:** a flagstone sidewalk

**plain stitch** *n* [4*plain*] **:** KNIT STITCH

**plain suit** *n* [4*plain*] **:** a card suit that is not trump

**plains vizcacha** *n* [*plains* pl. of 3*plain*] **:** a large colonial vizcacha (*Lagostomus maximus*) of the grassy plains of southern So. America

**plaint** \'plānt\ *n* -s [ME, fr. MF, fr. L *planctus,* fr. *planctus,* past part. of *plangere* to strike, beat, beat one's breast, lament; akin to L *plaga* blow, Gk *plēgē* blow, *plēssein* to strike, OE *flōcan* to applaud, OHG *fluokhōn* to curse] **1 :** an audible expression of or as if of woe **:** LAMENTATION, WAIL ⟨a ~ over a lost doll⟩ ⟨did not squeal, as vulgar pigs do, but uttered a sweet little ~ —Raymond Weeks⟩ **2 a :** a critical protest **:** COMPLAINT ⟨their *~s* to the papers gave a picture of suffering which impressed contemporary students of the social scene —Roy Lewis & Angus Maude⟩ **b :** a legal written complaint esp. in county-court practice in England

**plaintext** \'ˌ=ˌ=\ *n* **:** the plain-language form of an encrypted text or of its elements ⟨PA in the cipher represents TH in the ~⟩ — compare CIPHERTEXT, 3P 4

**plaint·ful** \'plāntfəl\ *adj* [*plaint* + *-ful*] **:** MOURNFUL

**plain·tiff** \'plāntəf\ *n* -s [ME *plaintif,* fr. MF, fr. *plaintif* lamenting, complaining — more at PLAINTIVE] **1 :** one who commences a personal action or lawsuit to obtain a remedy for an injury to his rights — opposed to *defendant;* compare PROSECUTOR **2 :** the complaining party in any litigation including demandant in real actions, the complainant in equity, and the libelant in divorce

**plaintiff in error :** a party who proceeds by writ of error or statutory substitute to obtain reversal of a judgment or order for errors of law appearing in the record

**plain tire** *n* [4*plain*] **:** BALD TIRE

**plain·tive** \'plāntiv, -tēv *also* -təv\ *adj* [ME *plaintif,* fr. MF, fr. *plaint* + *-if* -ive — more at PLAINT] **1** *archaic* **:** afflicted with grief or sadness **:** LAMENTING, PINING ⟨the aimless dead ~ for Earth —Rupert Brooke⟩ **2 :** expressive of suffering or woe **:** SORROWFUL, MELANCHOLY ⟨he sighed, his voice became ~ —Aldous Huxley⟩ ⟨~ songs . . . about green hills and pines in the night wind and lonesomeness and dying away from home —R.O.Bowen⟩ ⟨the clarinet sings, in its eerie ~ tone —Sara R. Watson⟩ — **plain·tive·ly** \-təvlē, -li\ *adv* — **plain·tive·ness** \-tivnəs, -tēv- *also* -təv-\ *n* -ES

**plain turkey** *n* [3*plain*] **:** the bustard (*Choriotis australis*) of Australia that is now becoming rare because of excessive hunting for sport and table

**plain wanderer** *n* **:** a small Australian bird (*Pedionomus torquatus*) similar to the button quails

**plain weave** *n* [4*plain*] **:** the simplest form of textile weave in which the weft yarns pass alternately over and under the warp yarns to form a checkerboard pattern

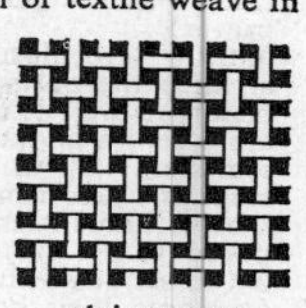

plain weave

**plain work** *n* **1 :** plain sewing **2 :** the surface produced on stone by chiseling off irregularities

**plainwoven** \'ˌ=ˌ=\ *adj* **:** made in plain weave

**1plaise** \'plāz\ *dial var of* PLEASE

**2plaise** *var of* PLAICE

**plaister** *var of* PLASTER

**1plait** \'plāt, 'plat, *usu* -d·+V\ *n* -s [ME *pleit, plait, plete,* fr. MF *pleit,* fr. (assumed) VL *plictus* fold, fr. (assumed) VL *plictus,* alter. (influenced by L *implictus, replictus*) of L *plicatus,* past part. of *plicare* to fold — more at PLY] **1 a :** a flat fold **:** PLEAT 1 **b :** one of the flattened folds on the inner wall of some gastropod shells **2 a :** a braid of hair, straw, or other material ⟨in an attractive ~ round her head —*Atlantic*⟩ ⟨wick . . . of cotton strands of good quality woven into a thin ~ —T.P.Hilditch⟩; *specif* **:** PIGTAIL ⟨used to have little bows on the ends of your *~s* before you cut your hair —Dodie Smith⟩ **b :** braided fiber esp. for straw hats ⟨a roll of ~⟩ **3** *archaic* **:** a devious twist of character or conduct **:** QUIRK ⟨a simple heart . . . without *~s* and folds —George Hakewill⟩

**2plait** \"\ *vt* -ED/-ING/-S [ME *pleiten, plaiten, pleten,* fr. *pleit, plait, plete* plait] **1 :** PLEAT 1 **2 a :** to interweave the strands or locks of **:** BRAID, INTERTWINE ⟨his hair was *~ed* in a queue —Ethel Wilson⟩ ⟨flirting her white mane . . . to draw attention to the red ribbons it was *~ed* with —George Orwell⟩ **b :** to make by plaiting ⟨~ a rug⟩ ⟨shoes often *~ed* from thongs of hemp —Herbert Harris⟩ ⟨weaverbirds . . . *~ed* their elaborate nests perfectly —E.A.Armstrong⟩ **3 :** to unite by or as if by interweaving ⟨~ . . . interrelated events into a clean-cut chronology —*Time*⟩ ⟨swallows . . . *~ing* together the summer air all day —Kenneth Rexroth⟩

**plait·ed** \-d·əd\ *adj* [ME *pleited, plaited,* fr. past part. of *pleiten, plaiten* to plait] **1 a :** PLEATED **b :** BRAIDED, INTERWOVEN **c :** PLATED 4 **2** *obs* **:** having convolutions **:** INVOLVED, DEVIOUS ⟨time shall unfold what ~ cunning hides —Shak.⟩

**plaited stitch** *n* **:** an embroidery stitch having a braided appearance, usu. made in herringbone or basket-weave patterns

**plait·er** \-d·ə(r)\ *n* -s **1 :** one that plaits ⟨straw ~⟩ ⟨basket ~⟩ **2 :** PLEATER 3

**plaiting** *n* -s [fr. gerund of 2*plait*] **1 :** PLEATING 2 **2 :** the interlacing of three or more strands (as of hair or straw) **:** BRAIDING **3 :** the knitting together of two or more yarns usu. of different colors or fibers so that one appears on the face of a fabric and the other on the back

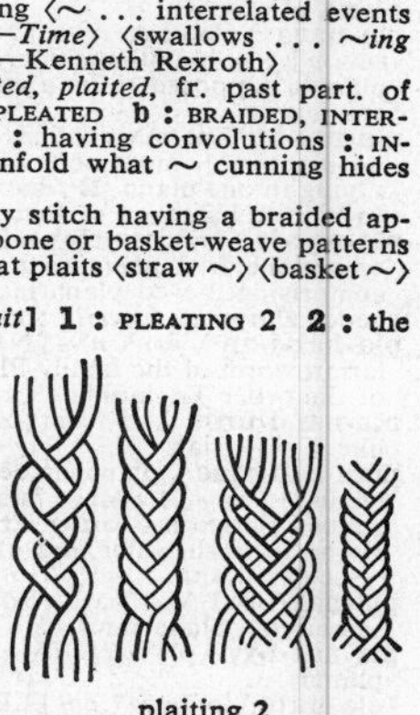

plaiting 2

**pla·kat** \plə'kat, 'plaˌkat\ *n* -s [Siamese, fighting fish] **:** BETTA

**1plan** \'plan, -aa(ə)n\ *n* -s [F, plane, foundation, ground plan, partly fr. L *planum* level ground, fr. *planus* level, flat; partly fr. *planter* to plant, fix in place, fr. LL *plantare* — more at FLOOR, PLANT] **1 :** a drawing or diagram drawn on a plane: as **a :** a top view of a machine **b :** a representation of a horizontal section of a building — see GROUND PLAN **c :** a large-scale map of a small area **2 a :** one of numerous planes conceived as perpendicular to the line of vision and interposed between the eye and pictured objects **b :** one of several possible planes in a relief sculpture raising certain figures in the design above the ground **3 a :** a method of achieving something **:** a way of carrying out a design **:** DEVICE ⟨could not avoid suspecting that it was a ~ to obtain freedom in the evenings —Arnold Bennett⟩ **b :** a method of doing something **:** PROCEDURE, WAY ⟨the usual ~ is to bring with each course the implements considered correct for handling it —Agnes M. Miall⟩ **c :** a detailed and systematic formulation of a large-scale campaign or program of action ⟨drew up a secret ~ for the defense of the country⟩ ⟨the ~ called for the establishment of flexible four-year programs for the six basic industries —*Current Biog.*⟩ **d :** a proposed undertaking or goal **:** AIM, INTENTION ⟨had just entered college with the ~ of studying medicine —J.G.Cozzens⟩ **4 a :** an orderly arrangement of parts in terms of an overall design or objective ⟨the conventional ~ of state universities throughout the country —*Amer. Guide Series: Minn.*⟩ ⟨a ~ of life so delightfully simple —J.W.Krutch⟩ ⟨detailed to him the ~ of a very moral and aristocratical novel she was preparing —T.L.Peacock⟩ **b :** a schematic table or program of related parts or items ⟨drew up a ~ of study for himself⟩ ⟨the ~ of the graduation exercises⟩ **c :** a schedule or method of payment ⟨an easy-payment ~⟩ ⟨a pay-as-you-go ~⟩

**syn** PLAN, DESIGN, PLOT, SCHEME, and PROJECT can mean, in common, a proposed method of doing or making something or of achieving an end. PLAN implies mental formulation of a method, order, or form or a graphic representation of one, sometimes applying to an already achieved order ⟨her *plan* to try hitching rides in automobiles —Millen Brand⟩ ⟨drew *plans* for factory and home sites —*Amer. Guide Series: Md.*⟩ ⟨it imposes *plan* and meaning and order on its materials —W.V. O'Connor⟩ DESIGN adds to PLAN the idea of intention in the disposition of individual parts, often suggesting definiteness of pattern or a degree of order or harmony achieved ⟨a great man by accident rather than *design* —H.J.Laski⟩ ⟨a complex moral and philosophical *design* that lay behind the surface reality —J.W.Aldridge⟩ ⟨the *design* of constitutional governments —C.L.Jones⟩ PLOT connotes a laying out in or analyzing into distinguishable, proportioned, and comprehensible sections with attention to the proper relation of parts, applying now chiefly to the fundamental design of action or narrative in a literary or dramatic work or to a clandestine plan contrived by a group as for political revolution or assassination ⟨the fundamental elements of storytelling — suspense, pace, and clean-cut *plot* —*Current Biog.*⟩ ⟨a *plot* to overthrow the government⟩ SCHEME in the sense of a plan, design, or order, especially one revealed by analysis, suggests system and careful choice or ordering of detail ⟨the place of man in the *scheme* of things —E.D.Adrian⟩ ⟨the strong and the weak places in the general *scheme* of transportation by rail —O.S.Nock⟩ ⟨the rapid development of pension *schemes* —G.O.May⟩ ⟨the long-term *schemes* for building up India's economy —*Collier's Yr. Bk.*⟩ In more recently current use, it can apply to a plan motivated by craftiness or self-seeking ⟨a *scheme* to undermine public confidence in the administration⟩ ⟨a *scheme* to take over the control of a labor union⟩ PROJECT in current use is a neutral word designating any plan or prospective or actual undertaking or enterprise, often of considerable size ⟨his pet *project* of forming a citizens' committee⟩ ⟨the *project* consists of 80 farmsteads, each having a modern five-room house, a barn, and a poultry shed —*Amer. Guide Series: La.*⟩ ⟨a man of huge *projects* but small accomplishments⟩ In the verbal uses of the terms, PLAN, PLOT, and PROJECT signify to form or contrive a plan, plot, or project as distinguished by the noun meanings ⟨*planning* a dinner without taking into account the number of guests —M.R.Cohen⟩ ⟨*planned* my life from the outset largely and spaciously —Havelock Ellis⟩ ⟨a story thus *plotted* would choke on its own melodrama —Frederic Morton⟩ ⟨arguing whether the right to *plot* revolution is un-American —S.W. Chapman⟩ ⟨although his health was rapidly failing, he *pro-*

*jected* a new book —C.A.Dinsmore⟩ ⟨a group of New Haven citizens that *projected* a railway between New Haven and Hartford and obtained a charter for it —G.S.Bryan⟩ DESIGN signifies to formulate or achieve a design or intention ⟨*design* a new gown⟩ ⟨this book is *designed* to supply some of this information —R.M.Dawson⟩ SCHEME confines itself almost exclusively to the formulation of a scheme in the more current sense distinguished above, a clandestine, usu. self-seeking, planning or plotting ⟨open-air daylight creatures like us . . . called to plot and *scheme* and hide against the frozen silliness of the world —Eden Phillpotts⟩ ⟨*scheming* for a slice of official cake —S.H.Adams⟩ ⟨*scheming* to overthrow the party in power⟩

**²plan** \"\ *vb* **planned; planned; planning; plans** *vt* **1 :** to arrange the parts of **:** DESIGN ⟨*planned* the new school for beauty as well as utility⟩ ⟨*planned* the mural to blend with the architecture of the lobby⟩ ⟨*planned* his program for the next semester⟩ **2 :** to devise or project the realization or achievement of **:** prearrange the details of ⟨*planned* and organized extensive home-missionary programs —S.G.Hefelbower⟩ ⟨prepared to ~, instead of improvise, foreign policy —*Time*⟩ **3 :** to set down the features of in a plan **:** represent by a plan ⟨explored their houses, *planned* their cities —T.E.Lawrence⟩ **4 :** to have in mind **:** INTEND ⟨the many jewels she had accumulated and which she *planned* to leave them —R.B. Gehman⟩ ⟨~*s* a movie of the salvage operations —*Current Biog.*⟩ — sometimes used with *on* ⟨*planned* on seeing him later⟩ **5 :** to devise procedures or regulations for in accordance with a comprehensive plan for achieving a given objective (as in economic development or scientific research) ⟨*planning* a more balanced if less profitable economy with the resources available —David Mitrany⟩ ⟨proposed a central authority to ~ the state's future utilization of electric power on an overall basis —*Current Biog.*⟩ ~ *vi* **1 :** to make plans **:** DEVISE, CONTRIVE, SCHEME ⟨she must ~ — plot if she must —Pearl Buck⟩ **2 :** to set up economic or social controls or regulations ⟨found *planning* necessary during the war⟩ ⟨can be prepared to scrap the whole system of *planning* when the emergency passes —*New Republic*⟩ **syn** see ¹PLAN

**¹plan-** *or* **plano-** *comb form* [prob. fr. NL, fr. Gk, wandering, fr. *planos;* akin to Gk *planasthai* to wander — more at PLANET] **:** moving about **:** motile ⟨*plan*uria⟩ ⟨*plano*gamete⟩

**²plan-** *or* **plano-** *comb form* [L *planus* flat, level — more at FLOOR] **1 :** flat ⟨*plano*meter⟩ ⟨*plano*occipital⟩ **2 :** flatly ⟨*plano*rotund⟩ **3 :** flat and ⟨*plano*-concave⟩

**plana** *pl of* PLANUM

**pla·naea** \plə'nēə\ *n* -s [NL, fr. L *planus* flat — more at FLOOR] **:** a hypothetical organism in the form of a ciliated planula supposed to be a stage in the evolution of the higher animals

**pla·nar** \'plānə(r)\ *adj* [LL *planaris*, fr. L *planum* flat surface + *-aris* -ar — more at PLANE] **1 :** of or relating to a plane **:** lying in one plane **2 :** having a flat two-dimensional quality ⟨a picture based on ~ forms⟩

**pla·nar·ia** \plə'na(a)rēə\ *n* [NL, fr. fem. of LL *planarius* lying on a plane, fr. L *planum*] **1** *cap* **:** the type genus of Planariidae comprising 2-eyed planarian worms **2** -s **:** any worm of the genus *Planaria; broadly* **:** PLANARIAN

**pla·nar·i·an** \-ēən\ *n* -s [NL *Planariidae* + E *-an*] **:** a turbellarian worm of the family Planariidae; *broadly* **:** a turbellarian of the order Tricladida **:** TRICLAD

**pla·nar·i·form** \-rə,fȯrm\ *adj* [*planarian* + *-form*] **:** shaped like a planarian

**plan·a·ri·idae** \,planə'rīə,dē\ *n pl, cap* [NL, fr. *Planaria*, type genus + *-idae*] **:** a large family of small soft-bodied usu. leaf-shaped flatworms (order Tricladida) that are almost all free-living in fresh water and often have well-developed eyespots — see PLANARIA

**pla·nar·i·oid** \plə'na(a)rē,ȯid\ *adj* [*planarian* + *-oid*] **:** resembling a planarian

**pla·nar·i·ty** \plə'narəd·ē\ *n* -ES **:** the quality or state of being planar

**¹pla·nate** \'plā,nāt\ *adj* [LL *planatus*, past part. of *planare* to flatten, level, fr. L *planus* flat — more at FLOOR] **:** FLATTENED, PLANE ⟨recognizes that there is a ~ bedrock surface beneath the gravels —K.M.Hussey⟩

**²planate** \"\ *vt* -ED/-ING/-S [back-formation fr. *planation*] **:** to erode to a plain **:** PLANE ⟨former low domes were *planated* by wave erosion —*Jour. of Geol.*⟩

**pla·na·tion** \plā'nāshən, plə'-\ *n* -s [⁴*plane* + *-ation*] **:** a process of erosion that produces flat surfaces: as **a :** lateral erosion by a meandering stream that widens its floodplain **b :** erosion by waves and currents that results in wave-cut platforms **c :** abrasive action of a glacier or of wind that planes or facets a previously rounded or irregular stone

**planch** \'planch\ *n* -ES [ME *plaunche* plank, fr. MF *planche*, fr. L *planca* — more at PLANK] **1** *dial Eng* **:** a plank floor **2 :** a flat plate (as of metal or baked clay)

**plan·ché·ite** \'plänchā,īt, ⸗'⸗,⸗\ *n* -s [F, fr. *Planché*, proper name + F *-ite*] **:** a mineral $Cu_{15}Si_{12}O_{36}(OH)_8$(?) consisting of a blue fibrous copper silicate

**plan·cher** \'planchə(r)\ *n* -s [ME, fr. MF *plancher, planchier, plancier* plank floor or ceiling, fr. *planche* plank — more at PLANCH] **1** *obs* **:** a plank floor or platform **2 :** PLANCIER

**plan·chet** \'planchət\ *n* -s [*planch* + *-et*] **1 :** a metal disk to be stamped as a coin; *also* **:** a small metal or plastic disk sometimes with a raised edge **2 :** FLAN 2

**plan·chette** \plan'shet\ *n* -s [F, lit., small board or plank, fr. *planche* plank + *-ette* — more at PLANCH] **1 :** a small usu. heart-shaped board supported on casters at two points and on a vertical pencil at a third that is believed to produce automatic writing when moved across a surface by the light pressure of the fingers of one or more persons **2 :** CIRCUMFERENTOR

**planch·ing** \'planchiŋ\ *n* -s [*planch* + *-ing*] *dial Eng* **:** a boarded floor **:** FLOORING

**planching nail** *or* **plensh·ing nail** \'plenchiŋ-\ *n* **:** a flooring nail

**planch·ment** \'planchmənt\ *n* -s [*planch* + *-ment*] **:** CEILING

**plan·cier** \plan'si(ə)r\ *n* -s [MF, plank floor or ceiling — more at PLANCHER] **:** the underside of a cornice **:** SOFFIT

**planck constant** \'pläŋk-\ *n, usu cap P* [after Max K. E. L. *Planck* †1947 Ger. physicist] **:** the constant *h* in the Planck radiation law now found also in numerous formulas concerned with quantized energy and having a value of approximately $6.624 \times 10^{-27}$ erg second ($gCm^2sec^{-1}$)

**planck distribution law** *n, usu cap P* [after Max K. E. L. *Planck*] **:** PLANCK RADIATION LAW

**planck·ian radiation** \'plaŋkēən-\ *n, usu cap P* [Max K. E. L. *Planck* + E *-ian*] **:** BLACKBODY RADIATION

**planck radiation law** *n, usu cap P* [after Max K. E. L. *Planck*] **1 :** a law in physics: radiant energy arising from processes within atoms or molecules is emitted in finite quanta each of which is equal to the product of the radiation frequency by a universal constant *h* — see PLANCK CONSTANT **2 :** a law in physics: the energy density of radiation within a blackbody cavity at absolute temperature T in terms of the wavelength λ is given by

$$\Delta P\lambda = \frac{8\pi hc}{\lambda^5[\mathrm{EXP}\frac{hc}{K\lambda T}-1]}\Delta\lambda,$$

where ΔPλ is the energy density within a given small wavelength interval Δλ, *h* is the Planck constant, and *c* the speed of light, all quantities being in cgs units

**planctonic** *var of* PLANKTONIC

**plan·dok** \'plan,däk\ *n* -s [Malay *pĕlandok*] **:** CHEVROTAIN

**¹plane** \'plān\ *vb* -ED/-ING/-S [ME *planen*, fr. MF *planer*, fr. LL *planare* to make flat, level, fr. L *planus* flat, level — more at FLOOR] *vt* **1 :** to make smooth or even **:** LEVEL ⟨what student came but that you *planed* her path —Alfred Tennyson⟩ **2 :** to produce a plane surface on by the use of a planer **3 :** to remove by or as if by planing ⟨the mountainside had come away bodily, *planed* clean —Rudyard Kipling⟩ ~ *vi* **1 a :** to work with a plane **b :** to do the work of a plane **2 :** to extend in a smooth or level line without elevations or depressions ⟨mellow farmlands ~ to the water's edge —*Amer. Guide Series: Vt.*⟩ ⟨this sea that *planed* away in all directions —T.O.Heggen⟩

**²plane** \"\ *or* **plane tree** *n* -s [ME, fr. MF, fr. L *platanus*, fr. Gk *platanos;* akin to Gk *platys* broad — more at PLACE] **:** a tree of the genus *Platanus*

**³plane** \"\ *n* -s [ME, fr. MF, fr. LL *plana*, fr. *planare* to make

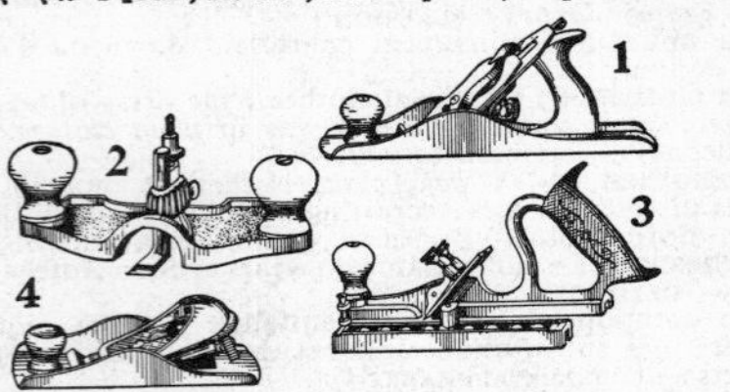


planes: *1* jack plane, *2* router plane, *3* tonguing and grooving plane, *4* block plane

level] **:** a tool for smoothing or shaping a surface of wood that consists of a smooth-soled stock as of wood or iron from the face of which projects slightly the steel cutting edge of a chisel set at an angle to the face with an aperture in the front for the escape of shavings — see BEADING PLANE, BENCH PLANE, BLOCK PLANE, BULLNOSED PLANE, CHAMFER PLANE, CIRCULAR PLANE, COMBINATION PLANE, DADO PLANE, DOVETAIL PLANE, FORE PLANE, JACK PLANE, JOINTER PLANE, MATCH PLANE, RABBET PLANE, ROUTER PLANE, SCRUB PLANE, SMOOTHING PLANE

**⁴plane** \"\ *n* -s [L *planum* level surface, fr. neut. of *planus* level, flat] **1 a** (1) **:** a surface such that the straight line that joins any two of its points lies wholly in that surface **:** a two-dimensional extent of zero curvature **:** a surface any intersection of which by a like surface is a straight line (2) **:** the graph of a linear equation in three dimensions **b** (1) **:** a flat or level material surface ⟨an inclined ~⟩ ⟨the faults have tilted a ~ to the west —*Jour. of Geol.*⟩ (2) **:** FACET ⟨the evening sunlight had begun to turn the smooth ~*s* of the prickly pears into trembling mirrors —Michael Swan⟩ **c :** an imaginary plane surface used to identify the position of a bodily organ or a part of the skull ⟨alveolocondylean ~⟩ **d :** SURFACE PLATE **e :** an inclined track (as in a coal mine) over which transportation of a string of cars or a train is effected by gravity or by external power (as by a stationary engine) **2 a :** a level of existence, consciousness, or development ⟨moved on a ~ of excited worldliness —H.S.Canby⟩ ⟨keep the conversation on an amicable ~ —P.G.Wodehouse⟩ ⟨on the intellectual ~⟩ ⟨on the religious ~⟩ **b :** any of the seven theosophical stages or states of manifestation of being **:** a sphere of existence in theosophy **c :** a stage in surgical anesthesia ⟨the patient can be brought into the second ~ of anesthesia in another location —*Jour. Amer. Med. Assoc.*⟩ **3 a :** one of the main supporting surfaces of an airplane ⟨a low-wing, all-metal single-*plane* craft —*Science News Letter*⟩ ⟨biplane⟩ **b** [by shortening] **:** AIRPLANE ⟨jet ~⟩ ⟨transport ~⟩ **c :** DIVING PLANE

**⁵plane** \"\ *adj* [L *planus* flat, level — more at FLOOR] **1 :** having no elevations or depressions **:** forming part of a plane **:** FLAT, LEVEL ⟨a ~ surface⟩ **2 :** of, relating to, or dealing with planes or two-dimensional figures only **syn** see LEVEL

**⁶plane** \"\ *vi* -ED/-ING/-S [F *planer*, fr. *plan* plane, fr. L *planum* level surface; fr. the level surface formed by the wings of a soaring bird] **1 a :** to soar on or as if on wings ⟨watching a gull ~ down in circles without moving a wing —G.W. Brace⟩ ⟨a great morpho butterfly leisurely *planing* along —H.M.Tomlinson⟩ **b** (1) *of a seaplane* **:** to move through the water at such a speed as to be supported by hydrodynamic and aerodynamic rather than by hydrostatic forces (2) *of a boat* **:** to skim across the surface of the water **:** lift partly out of the water while in motion ⟨these craft, when they reach a certain speed, ~ on the flat after sections of their hull —Peter Heaton⟩ **c :** to move downward as if on an inclined plane **:** GLIDE ⟨*planed* down toward it and in a few moments could make out that it was a ship —J.H.Marsh⟩ ⟨were pulling her stern first to keep her from diving and *planing* to the bottom —N.C. McDonald⟩ **2** [⁴*plane* (airplane)] **:** to travel by airplane ⟨had *planed*, trained and driven fifteen hundred miles —Paul Gallico⟩ **3** *of a submarine* **:** to move from one level to another ⟨will ~ down or up faster, to escape or attack —E.C.Fay⟩ ⟨ordered me to ~ upward two feet, to allow him to raise the periscope that much higher out of the water and thus see a little farther —E.L.Beach⟩

**plane angle** *n* **:** an angle formed by two intersecting lines each of which lies on a face of a dihedral angle and is perpendicular to the edge of the face

**plane at infinity** [⁴*plane*] **:** the aggregate of all points at infinity in projective geometry of three dimensions

**plane bit** *n* [³*plane*] **:** PLANE IRON

**plane chart** *n* [⁵*plane*] **:** a depiction of a small portion of the earth's surface as plane with meridians and parallels of latitude appearing as two systems of straight lines at right angles and all arc degrees as equal

**plane curve** *n* **:** a curve that lies wholly in a single plane

**plane figure** *n* **:** a geometrical configuration all of whose points lie in a plane

**plane geometry** *n* **:** a branch of elementary geometry that deals with plane figures

**plane iron** *n* [³*plane*] **:** the blade of a plane

**planeload** \'⸗,⸗\ *n* [⁴*plane*] **:** a load that fills an airplane **:** plane capacity

**plane man** *n* **:** DILLYMAN

**plane-mile** \'⸗;⸗\ *n* [⁴*plane* + *mile*] **:** a statistical unit denoting one mile traveled by one airplane

**plane·ness** \'plānnəs\ *n* -ES **:** the quality or state of being plane

**plane of defilade** [⁴*plane*] **:** a plane tangent to the mask and passing through the point from which protection (as from enemy fire or observation) is desired

**plane of incidence :** a plane containing an incident line (as a ray of light) and the normal to a surface (as of a mirror) at the point of incidence

**plane of polarization :** a plane in which the magnetic-vibration component of plane-polarized electromagnetic radiation lies

**plane of projection :** a plane that is intersected by imaginary lines drawn from the eye to every point on the object and that is therefore the plane on which the pictorial representation in perspective is formed

**plane of sight :** a vertical plane containing the line of sight of a gun

**plane of site :** a plane containing the line of site of a gun and a horizontal line perpendicular to it

**plane of symmetry** **1 :** a plane through a crystal that divides the crystal into two parts that are mirror images of each other **2 :** a vertical fore-and-aft plane that divides an airplane into symmetrical halves

**plane-parallel** \'⸗;⸗⸗,⸗\ *adj* [⁵*plane*] **:** having two opposite faces plane and parallel ⟨a *plane-parallel* sheet of glass⟩

**plane-polarized** \'⸗;⸗⸗,⸗\ *adj* [⁴*plane*] *of a moving wave* **:** vibrating in a single plane ⟨a *plane-polarized* light wave⟩ ⟨a *plane-polarized* sound wave⟩

**plan·er** \'plānə(r)\ *n* -s [¹*plane* + *-er*] **:** one that planes: as **a :** a machine tool consisting essentially of a fixed bed, a reciprocating table to which the work is secured, and a device for holding the cutting tool stationary while each cut is taken and for moving the tool in position for the succeeding cut at the end of each cutting stroke, the power for moving the table being usu. transmitted to the table from the driving shaft through a train of gears — see CLOSED PLANER, CRANK PLANER, OPENSIDE PLANER, ROTARY PLANER, SHAPING PLANER **b :** a power tool for surfacing wood by means of a cutting tool that rotates across the width of the board that is fed under it **c :** a smooth-faced block of wood that is laid on the surface of type and tapped with a mallet to level the type or make a stone proof **d :** a grader with several blades to distribute and smooth earth or pavement material **e :** a worker who planes wood, stone, or metal

**plan·era** \'planərə\ *n, cap* [NL, after J. J. *Planer* †1789 Ger. botanist] **:** a genus of trees (family Ulmaceae) of southeastern U. S. resembling the hackberry but having an oval, ribbed, nutlike fruit — see PLANER TREE

**planer center** *n* **:** one of a pair of index centers bolted to the table of a planer and used to support work which is to be planed round or in which radial slots are to be cut

**planer head** *n* **:** a part of a planer that secures the cutting tool to the crossrail or housing and that contains the mechanism which feeds it toward the work

**planer jack** *n* **:** a jack used to level up the work to be machined on a planer

**planer knife** *n* **:** PLANE IRON

**pla·ner tree** \'plānə(r)-\ *n* [after J. J. *Planer* †1789 Ger. botanist] **:** a small-leaved No. American tree (*Planera aquatica*) bearing wingless fruit — called also *hornbeam, water elm*

**¹pla·nes** \'plā,nēz\ *n, cap* [NL, fr. Gk *planēt-, planēs* wanderer — more at PLANET] **:** a genus of small pelagic crabs with hairy legs

**²planes** *pres 3d sing of* PLANE, *pl of* PLANE

**plane sailing** *n* [⁵*plane*] **1 :** the navigation or conducting of a ship by neglecting the earth's curvature and considering the earth or a part of it as a plane **2 :** PLAIN SAILING 2

**plane·shear** \'plān,shi(ə)r\ *n* -s [alter. (influenced by *plane, sheer*) of *plancher*] **:** PLANK-SHEER

**planes·man** \'plānzmən\ *n, pl* **planesmen** [⁴*plane*] **:** one who operates the bow or stern diving planes on a submarine

**plane surveying** *n* [⁵*plane*] **:** ordinary field and topographical surveying in which the curvature of the earth is disregarded — compare GEODETIC SURVEYING

**plane symmetry** *n* [⁴*plane*] **:** symmetry with respect to a plane

**¹plan·et** \'planət, *usu* -əd.+V\ *n* -s [ME *planete*, fr. OF, fr. LL *planeta*, modif. (influenced by Gk *planētēs* wanderer) of Gk *planēt-, planēs*, lit., wanderer, fr. *planasthai* to wander; akin to ON *flana* to rush around, and prob. to L *planus* flat — more at FLOOR] **1 a :** a heavenly body seeming to have a motion of its own among the fixed stars ⟨therefore is the glorious ~ Sol in noble eminence enthroned —Shak.⟩ ⟨the moon, that ~ of love and death —Gilbert Highet⟩ **b** (1) **:** one of the bodies except a comet, meteor, or satellite that revolves around the sun in the solar system

TERRESTRIAL AND MAJOR PLANETS

| SYMBOL | NAME | MEAN DISTANCE FROM THE SUN astronomical units | million miles | PERIOD IN DAYS OR YEARS | DIAMETER IN MILES |
|---|---|---|---|---|---|
| ♃ | Jupiter | 5.20 | 483 | 12 years | 86,800 |
| ♄ | Saturn | 9.54 | 886 | 29 years | 71,500 |
| ♅ | Uranus | 19.18 | 1783 | 84 years | 29,400 |
| ♆ | Neptune | 30.06 | 2794 | 165 years | 28,000 |
| ⊕ | Earth | 1.00 | 93 | 365¼ days | 7,913 |
| ♀ | Venus | 0.72 | 67 | 225 days | 7,600 |
| ♂ | Mars | 1.52 | 142 | 687 days | 4,200 |
| ♇ | Pluto | 39.52 | 3670 | 248 years | 4,000? |
| ☿ | Mercury | 0.39 | 36 | 88 days | 2,900 |

(2) **:** a similar body that may possibly revolve around another star **c :** EARTH — usu. used with *the* ⟨one of these goals is a reasonable degree of communication spread out more evenly over the ~ —I.A.Richards⟩ **2 :** a heavenly body (as a star) held to influence the fate of human beings **3 :** a person or thing of great magnitude or brilliance **:** LUMINARY ⟨a major ~ who changed the whole direction of the scientific thought of his day⟩

**²planet** \"\ *or* **pla·ne·ta** \plə'nēd·ə\ *n* -s [ML *planeta*, perh. fr. Gk *planētēs* wanderer] **:** CHASUBLE

**plane table** *n* [⁴*plane*] **1 :** an instrument for plotting the lines of a survey directly from the observations and consisting essentially of a drawing board mounted on a tripod and fitted with a ruler that is pointed at the object observed usu. with the aid of a sighting device (as a telescope) — see ALIDADE **2 :** a large surface plate **3 :** an inclined plane used as a buddle

**plane-table** \'⸗,⸗⸗\ *vb* [*plane table*] *vi* **:** to make use of a plane table ~ *vt* **:** to plot with a plane table

**plan·et·al** \'planəd·ᵊl\ *adj* [¹*planet* + *-al*] **:** PLANETARY

**¹plan·e·tar·i·an** \,planə'ta(a)rēən\ *adj* [fr. (assumed) LL *planetarius* + E *-an* — more at PLANETARY] **:** PLANETARY

**²planetarian** \"\ *n* -s **:** an inhabitant of a planet

**plan·e·tar·i·ly** \'⸗⸗'terəlē\ *adv* [¹*planetary* + *-ly*] **:** in the manner of or with reference to a planet ⟨will break through the tyranny of national boundaries and teach our children to think ~ —O.L.Reiser & Blodwen Davies⟩

**plan·e·tar·i·um** \,planə'ta(a)rēəm, -ter-, -tār-\ *n, pl* **planetariums** \-mz\ *or* **planetar·ia** \-ēə\ [*planet* + *-arium*] **1 a :** ORRERY 1 **b :** a model representing the solar system **2 a :** an optical device designed to project (as on a domed ceiling) various celestial images and effects (as the appearance of the nighttime sky) at a specific time and place **b :** a building or room housing such a device

**¹plan·e·tary** \'planə,terē, -ri\ *adj* [fr. (assumed) LL *planetarius* (whence LL *planetarius* astrologer), fr. *planeta* planet + L *-arius* -ary] **1 a :** of, relating to, or belonging to a planet ⟨~ orbit⟩ ⟨~ year⟩ **b :** caused or held to be caused by a planet ⟨a ~ plague —Shak.⟩ **c** (1) **:** ERRATIC, WANDERING ⟨a ~ vagabond⟩ (2) **:** having a motion like that of a planet **:** ORBITING **d :** IMMENSE ⟨it seemed not weeks, not even months or years, but a fantastic length of time, a ~ distance —Marcia Davenport⟩ **2 a :** of, relating to, or belonging to the earth **:** TERRESTRIAL ⟨~ rumblings and eructations —L.C.Eiseley⟩ **b :** GLOBAL, WORLDWIDE ⟨neither national nor continental but ~ —Lewis Mumford⟩ ⟨people had begun to think in ~ terms —Van Wyck Brooks⟩ **3 :** having or consisting of an epicyclic train of gear wheels ⟨~ drive⟩

**²planetary** \"\ *n* -ES **:** a planet or planetary body ⟨scanned the entire literary horizon for new *planetaries* —Carl Van Doren⟩ **2 :** PLANETARY NEBULA ⟨the observed speeds of expansion of the *planetaries* —R.H.Baker⟩

**planetary configuration** *n* **:** the apparent position of a planet in the sky in relation to its actual position in the solar system with reference to the earth and the sun

**planetary electron** *n* **:** an electron that moves about the atomic nucleus as part of an atom

**planetary gear** *or* **planetary gearing** *n* **:** PLANET DIFFERENTIAL

**planetary hour** *n* **:** HOUR 5

**planetary house** *or* **planetary mansion** *n* **:** ¹HOUSE 3b

**planetary nebula** *n* **:** a relatively small and generally ring-shaped nebula that is composed of gas expanding outward from a hot subluminous central star

**planetary transmission** *n* **:** a transmission or transmission system (as in an automobile) that uses a planet differential

**planetary wind** *n* **:** one of the major winds ⟨the trade winds, countertrades, and prevailing westerlies are *planetary winds*⟩

**planet differential** *or* **planet gear** *n* **:** an epicyclic train that has two contiguous and parallel main wheels usu. of equal diameter but of unequal number of teeth meshing with a single pinion

**plan·e·tes·i·mal** \,planə'tesəməl\ *n* -s [*planet* + *-esimal* (as in *infinitesimal*)] **:** one of numerous small solid heavenly bodies of undetermined characteristics that may have existed at an early stage of the development of the solar system

**planetesimal hypothesis** *n* **:** a hypothesis in astronomy: the planets have evolved by aggregation from planetesimals

**plan·et·oid** \'planə,tȯid\ *n* -s [¹*planet* + *-oid*] **1 :** a body resembling a planet **2 :** ASTEROID — **plan·et·oi·dal** \'⸗⸗'tȯidᵊl\ *adj*

**plane tree** *var of* PLANE

**plane-tree family** \'⸗,⸗-\ *n* [*plane tree*] **:** PLATANACEAE

**plane-tree maple** \'⸗,⸗-\ *n* [*plane tree*] **:** SYCAMORE 2

**plane trigonometry** *n* [⁵*plane*] **:** a branch of trigonometry that deals with plane triangles

**planets** *pl of* PLANET

**planet-stricken** \'⸗⸗;⸗⸗\ *or* **planet-struck** \'⸗⸗;⸗\ *adj* **1 :** affected by the supposedly harmful influence of a planet **:** BLASTED **2 :** overcome by fear **:** PANIC-STRICKEN

**planet wheel** *n* [¹*planet*] **:** a gear wheel that revolves around the wheel with which it meshes in an epicyclic train — see SUN-AND-PLANET MOTION illustration

**plane wave** *n* [⁵*plane*] **:** a wave whose wave fronts are plane surfaces corresponding to parallel rays ⟨light waves from the distant stars are virtually *plane waves* when they strike a telescope lens⟩

**planform** \'⸗,⸗\ *n* [*plan* + *form*] **:** the contour of an airplane as viewed from above

**plan·ful** \'planfəl\ *adj* [¹*plan* + *-ful*] **1 :** full of plans **:** RE-

SOURCEFUL, SCHEMING ⟨a latter-day robber baron, ~, secretive, ruthless —Wolfgang Langewiesche⟩ **2 :** according to a plan ⟨persistent and ~ arousing of the mind —Hugo Münsterberg⟩ — **plan·ful·ly** \-fəlē\ *adv* — **plan·ful·ness** *n* -ES

**plan·gen·cy** \ˈplanjənsē\ *n* -ES [*plangent* + *-cy*] **:** the quality or state of being plangent **:** EXPRESSIVENESS ⟨there is about the spoken word a poignancy, a ~, directness and intimacy that is hard to match in print —Irwin Edman⟩

**plan·gent** \-jənt\ *adj* [L *plangent-, plangens,* pres. part. of *plangere* to strike, lament — more at PLAINT] **1 :** having a loud and reverberating sound **:** RESONANT ⟨let out a ~ roar —*New Yorker*⟩ ⟨~ organ music —J.L.Lowes⟩ **2 :** having an expressive esp. plaintive quality ⟨the long ~ ripple of the harp strings —Osbert Sitwell⟩ ⟨a strange, chanting cry, slow and ~ —C.G.D.Roberts⟩ — **plan·gent·ly** *adv*

**plan·gi** \ˈplanjē\ *n* -S [Malay *kain pĕlangi* bandanna cloth gaudily colored by tie dyeing, fr. *kain* cloth + *pĕlangi* striped in gay colors] **:** a technique of cloth decoration in which a woven fabric is bunched and bound before it is dyed — compare IKAT

**plan·gor·ous** \ˈplaŋgərəs\ *adj* [L *plangor* lamentation (fr. *plangere* to lament) + E *-ous* — more at PLAINT] **:** expressive of loud lamentation **:** WAILING

**plani-** *comb form* [L *planus* — more at FLOOR] **:** flat **:** level **:** plane ⟨*plani*form⟩ ⟨*plani*graphy⟩

**-pla·nia** \ˈplānēə\ *n comb form* -S [NL, fr. Gk, act of wandering, fr. *planos* wandering + *-ia* -y — more at PLAN-] **:** a wandering of (a specified substance) into a tract not its own ⟨meno*plania*⟩

**plan·i·di·iform** \ˌplanəˈdīəˌfȯrm\ *adj* [NL *planidium* + E *-iform*] **:** resembling a planidium

**pla·nid·i·um** \pləˈnidēəm\ *n, pl* **planid·ia** \-ēə\ [NL, fr. ¹*plan-* + *-idium,* dim. suffix, fr. Gk *-idion*] **:** a first-stage legless larva of various parasitic hymenopterous and dipterous insects

**pla·ni·form** \ˈplānəˌfȯrm, ˈplan-\ *adj* [ISV *plani-* + *-form*] **:** having or being a joint with nearly flat articular surfaces

**pla·ni·gram** \ˈplānəˌgram, ˈplan-\ *n* [*plani-* + *-gram*] **:** a roentgenogram made by planigraphy

**pla·ni·graph** \-raf, -rȧf\ *n* [*plani-* + *-graph*] **:** PLANIGRAM

**pla·nig·ra·phy** \pləˈnigrəfē\ *n* -ES [ISV *plani-* + *-graphy*] **:** a roentgenographic technique that makes on a film sharp images of structures in a predetermined plane and blurs images of other structures above and below

**pla·ni·lla** \pləˈnē(y)ə\ *n* -S [AmerSp, fr. dim. of Sp *plana* level ground, fr. fem. of *plano* level, flat, fr. L *planus* — more at FLOOR] **:** a level place used as a cleaning floor at a mine

**pla·nim·e·ter** \pləˈnimәd·ə(r)\ *n* [F *planimètre,* fr. *plani-* + *-mètre* -meter] **:** an instrument for measuring the area of any plane figure by passing a tracer around its boundary line

**pla·ni·met·ric** \ˌplānəˈme-trik, ˌplan-\ *adj* [*planimetry* + *-ic*] **1 :** of, relating to, or established by planimetry **2** *of a map* **:** having no indications of contour — **pla·ni·met·ri·cal·ly** \-rək(ə)lē\ *adv*

**pla·nim·e·try** \pləˈniməˌtrē\ *n* -ES [F *planimétrie,* fr. ML *planimetria,* fr. L *planus* flat + *-metria* -metry — more at FLOOR] **1 :** the measurement of plane surfaces — distinguished from *stereometry* **2 :** the natural and cultural features of terrain excluding relief as indicated on a map

**planing machine** *n* [fr. gerund of ¹*plane*] **:** a machine that planes: as **a :** PLANER **b :** a stationary machine for planing wood — compare BUZZ PLANER, CYLINDER PLANER **c :** a portable machine for planing a floor or deck **d :** a machine for planing stone slabs **e :** a rotary hand machine that fits over an engine steam chest and is used for planing the valve seat

**planing mill** *n* **:** a woodworking establishment in which wood is smoothed, cut, matched, and fitted

**planing surface** *n* [fr. gerund of ⁶*plane*] **:** a surface of a seaplane float or hull designed to receive dynamic lift from the free water surface upon which it moves

**pla·ni·pen·nate** \ˌplānəˈpeˌnāt\ *adj* [NL *Planipennia* + E *-ate*] **:** of or relating to the Planipennia

**pla·ni·pen·nia** \ˌ==ˈpenēə\ *n pl, cap* [NL, fr. *plani-* + L *penna* wing + NL *-ia* — more at PEN] **1** *in some classifications* **:** a suborder of Neuroptera that includes most of the typical neuropterans when Neuroptera is construed as including Megaloptera **2** *in some classifications* **:** an order or other group coextensive with Neuroptera

**pla·ni·ros·tral** \ˌplānəˈrästrəl\ *adj* [*plani-* + L *rostrum* beak + E *-al* — more at ROSTRUM] **:** having a broad flat beak

**plan·ish** \ˈplanish\ *vt* -ED/-ING/-ES [MF *planiss-,* stem of *planir,* fr. *plan* level, fr. L *planus* — more at FLOOR] **:** to make smooth or plane; *specif* **:** to condense, toughen, and polish by hammering lightly with or as if with a smooth-faced hammer

**plan·ish·er** \-shə(r)\ *n* -S **:** one that planishes; *specif* **:** a tool used for planishing

**planishing hammer** *n* [fr. gerund of *planish*] **:** a hammer with slightly convex faces that is used in sheet-metal work to smooth and shape surfaces

planishing hammer

**plan·i·sphere** \ˈplanəˌsfi(ə)r\ *n* [ML *planisphaerium,* fr. L *planus* flat, plane + *sphaera* sphere — more at FLOOR, SPHERE] **:** a representation of the circles of the sphere on a plane; *esp* **:** a polar projection of the celestial sphere and the stars on a plane with adjustable circles or other appendages for showing celestial phenomena (as the position of the heavens or the time of rising and setting of stars) for any given time — **plan·i·spher·ic** \ˌ==ˈsfirik, -fer-\ *adj*

**planispiral** *var of* PLANOSPIRAL

**¹plank** \ˈplaŋk, -aiŋk\ *n* -S [ME *plank, planke,* fr. ONF *planke,* fr. L *planca;* perh. akin to Gk *plak-, plax* flat surface, tablet — more at PLEASE] **1 a :** a heavy thick board that in technical specifications usu. has a thickness of 2 to 4 inches and a width of at least 8 inches — compare TIMBER **b** (1) **:** any of various objects made of a plank or planking (as a bench, table, or narrow footbridge) (2) **:** GANGPLANK ⟨was to lift ~ at four that afternoon —R.P.Warren⟩ **c :** PLANKING **d :** a heavy usu. oak board that is grooved to catch the drip and is used in cooking and serving food (as broiled meat or fish) **e :** a flat slab of some hard material ⟨asphalt ~⟩ ⟨concrete ~⟩ **2 :** something that supports ⟨the ~*s* of the peace system —Sigmund Neumann⟩ **3 a :** an article in the platform of a political party or group ⟨with temperance and opposition to slavery as the two specific ~*s* in its platform —*Amer. Guide Series: Maine*⟩ **b :** a principal item of a policy or program ⟨a cardinal ~ in Britain's patient Far Eastern policy —Benjamin Welles⟩

**²plank** \"\ *vt* -ED/-ING/-S [ME *planken,* fr. ¹*plank*] **1 :** to cover, floor, or lay with planks ⟨~*ed* the well over —Lucy M. Montgomery⟩ ⟨the ~*ed* streets fringing the mills and factories —*Amer. Guide Series: Wash.*⟩ ⟨no use ~*ing* a boat till you got her timbered out —G.W.Brace⟩ **2 :** to set down **:** DEPOSIT ⟨~*ed* himself in the chair⟩ ⟨~ the cash on the counter for a slice of sirloin —*Saturday Rev.*⟩ **3 :** to cook and serve on a plank usu. with an elaborate garnish (as of mashed potatoes or other vegetables) ⟨~*ed* shad⟩ ⟨~*ed* steak⟩ **4 :** to extend or place so as to resemble a plank ⟨hitched up his knee and ~*ed* a most unlovely boot firmly against the edge of the table —Ngaio Marsh⟩ ⟨turned around with his back ~*ed* against the wall —H.L.Davis⟩

**plank buttress** *n* [¹*plank*] **:** BUTTRESS ROOT

**plank down** *vb* [²*plank*] *vt* **1 :** to set down forcibly or with emphasis ⟨was herded into a corner and *planked down* among five other sufferers —Thomas Wood †1950⟩ ⟨delighted to slam us all in jail and *plank down* martial law —Laura Krey⟩ **2 :** to pay or put down (money) on the spot ⟨pulled out a silver dollar and *planked* it *down* for a year's subscription —A.W.Long⟩ ⟨*planked down* a fistful of money —*Irish Digest*⟩ ~ *vi* **:** to declare oneself forcibly or unmistakably ⟨*planked* squarely *down* on the side of the government —Mollie Panter-Downes⟩

**plank·er** \-kə(r)\ *n* -S [¹*plank* + *-er*] **:** FLOAT 5 d (1)

**plank house** *n* **:** a house built of planks; *esp* **:** one of the rather large usu. rectangular and elaborately constructed buildings prevailingly used by Indians but also by some Eskimos of the northwest coast of No. America and adjacent Siberia

**planking** *n* -S [fr. gerund of ²*plank*] **1 :** the act or process of covering or fitting out with planks **2** [¹*plank* + *-ing*] **a :** a quantity of planks **b :** a covering or flooring made of planks; *specif* **:** the outer and inner covering of the timbers of a wooden ship — see SHIP illustration

**plank·less** \-kləs\ *adj* **:** having no planks

**plank owner** *n* [¹*plank;* fr. the tradition that he becomes part owner of the ship] **:** a member of the first crew to serve on a newly commissioned ship

**plank road** *n* **:** a road built of planks laid crosswise on longitudinal timbers and widely used in the U. S. in the mid 19th century

**plank root** *n* **:** BUTTRESS ROOT

**plank scraper** *n* **1 :** FLOAT 5 d (1) **2 :** a V-shaped or trapezoid-shaped drag for the leveling of land for irrigation, for the construction of border levees, and for the cleaning out of lateral distributing ditches

**plank-sheer** \ˈ=ˌ=\ *n* [alter. (influenced by *plank, sheer*) of *plancher*] **1 :** a heavy plank forming the outer edge of the deck of a vessel **2 :** the waterway (sense 2b) of a yacht

**plank·ter** \ˈplaŋktə(r)\ *n* -S [Gk *planktēr* wanderer, fr. *plang-,* stem of *plazesthai* to stray, wander — more at PLANKTON] **:** a planktonic organism

**plank·tiv·o·rous** \(ˈ)plaŋkˈtiv(ə)rəs\ *adj* [*plankton* + *-vorous*] **:** feeding on plankton

**plank·tol·o·gy** \plaŋkˈtäləjē\ *also* **plank·ton·ol·o·gy** \ˌplaŋktəˈnä-\ *n* -ES [*plankton* + *-logy*] **:** a branch of biology concerned with the study of plankton

**plank·ton** \ˈplaŋktən, -aiŋ-\ *n* -S [G, fr. Gk, neut. of *planktos* wandering, drifting, fr. *plang-,* stem of *plazesthai* to stray, drift, pass. of *plazein* to drive astray; akin to L *plangere* to strike — more at PLAINT] **:** the passively floating or weakly swimming animal and plant life of a body of water consisting chiefly of minute plants (as diatoms and blue-green algae) and of minute animals (as protozoans, entomostracans, and various larvae) but including also larger forms (as jellyfishes and salpae) that have only weak powers of locomotion — compare BENTHOS, NEKTON, TRIPTON — **plank·ton·ic** *also* **planc·ton·ic** \(ˈ)plaŋkˈtänik\ *adj*

**plankton net** *n* **:** a townet usu. made of fine-meshed silk bolting cloth that is used for the capture of plankton

**plank·tont** \ˈplaŋkˌtänt\ *n* -S [*plankton* + *-ont*] **:** PLANKTER

**plank·ways** \ˈplaŋˌkwāz\ *or* **plank·wise** \-wīz\ *adv* [¹*plank* + *-ways, -wise*] **:** in the direction of the length of timber **:** LENGTHWISE

**plan·less** \ˈplanləs\ *adj* **:** functioning or taking place without a plan or set goal ⟨a ~ course of study⟩ — **plan·less·ly** *adv*

**plan·less·ness** *n* -ES **:** the quality or state of being without plan **:** lack of system **:** DISORGANIZATION ⟨this ~, this indeterminate confusion of purpose —H.G.Wells⟩

**planned** *adj* [fr. past part. of ²*plan*] **1 :** INTENDED, PROJECTED ⟨his ~ trip abroad⟩ ⟨the ~ revision of the curriculum⟩ **2 a :** designed or carried out according to plan **:** ORDERLY ⟨a ~ highway system⟩ ⟨a ~ retreat⟩ ⟨~ migration on a vast scale —Stuart Chase⟩ **b :** not spontaneous **:** PREARRANGED ⟨a ~ demonstration⟩ ⟨a ~ outburst⟩ **3 :** subject to regulation and control in terms of a plan **:** ORGANIZED, SYSTEMATIZED ⟨all the signs are that the village of the next generation will be a ~ community —*Times Lit. Supp.*⟩

**planned economy** *n* **:** an economic system in which the elements of an economy (as labor, capital, and natural resources) are subject to government control and regulation designed to achieve the objectives of a comprehensive plan of economic development — compare FREE ECONOMY, FREE ENTERPRISE

**planned parenthood** *n* **:** the practice of measures (as contraception or the treatment of infertility) designed to regulate the number and spacing of children in a family; *broadly* **:** BIRTH CONTROL

**plan·ner** \ˈplanə(r), -aan-\ *n* -S **:** one who plans **:** DESIGNER, PROJECTOR; *specif* **:** one who supervises, participates in, or advocates social or economic planning ⟨a lawyer turned ~ who is active in New York housing and planning circles —Christopher Tunnard⟩

**planning** *n* -S [fr. gerund of ²*plan*] **:** the act or process of making or carrying out plans; *specif* **:** the establishment of goals, policies, and procedures for a social or economic unit ⟨city ~⟩ ⟨business ~⟩

**planning board** *n* **:** a body of citizens appointed to prepare or administer a plan (as for the growth and development of a city)

**pla·no** \ˈplā(ˌ)nō\ *adj* [²*plan-*] **:** having a flat surface ⟨true ~ lenses cannot produce prismatic effects —*Jour. Amer. Med. Assoc.*⟩

**plano-** — see PLAN-

**plan·o·blast** \ˈplanəˌblast\ *n* [¹*plan-* + *-blast*] **:** the medusa form of a hydroid — **plan·o·blas·tic** \ˌ==ˈblastik\ *adj*

**¹plan-occipital** \ˈplan+,=ˈ===\ *adj* [²*plan-* + *occipital*] **:** having a flattened occiput

**²planoccipital** \"\ *n* **:** a person having a planoccipital skull

**pla·no-concave** \ˌplā(ˌ)nō+\ *adj* [²*plan-* + *concave*] **:** flat on one side and concave on the other — see LENS illustration

**pla·no-convex** \"+\ *adj* [²*plan-* + *convex*] **:** flat on one side and convex on the other — see LENS illustration

**plan·o·ga·mete** \ˈplanəgəˌmēt\ *n* [ISV ¹*plan-* + *gamete*] **:** a motile gamete; *esp* **:** one that is ciliated

**plan·o·gam·ic** \ˌplanəˈgamik\ *adj* [*planogamete* + *-ic*] **:** of or relating to a planogamete

**¹plan·o·graph** \ˈplanəˌgraf, -rȧf\ *vt* -ED/-ING/-S [back-formation fr. *planography*] **:** to print by planography ⟨a ~*ed* pamphlet⟩

**²planograph** \"\ *n* [²*plan-* + *-graph*] **:** a print made by planography

**pla·no·graph·ic** \ˌ==ˈgrafik\ *adj* **:** produced by or used in planography ⟨~ printing⟩ ⟨printing from a ~ surface⟩

**pla·nog·ra·phy** \pləˈnägrəfē\ *n* -ES [²*plan-* + *-graphy*] **:** a process (as lithography or offset) for printing from a plane surface; *also* **:** matter printed by such process — compare INTAGLIO, LETTERPRESS, STENCIL

**pla·nom·e·ter** \pləˈnämәd·ə(r)\ *n* [²*plan-* + *-meter*] **:** a surface plate or other device for gauging a plane surface

**pla·nom·e·try** \-mə·trē\ *n* -ES [²*plan-* + *-metry*] **:** the art or process of producing or gauging a plane surface (as with a planometer)

**pla·no-miller** \ˈplānə+,-\ *n* [²*plan-* + *miller*] **:** a milling machine resembling a planer

**pla·no-milling machine** \ˌplānō+ . . . -\ *n* **:** PLANOMILLER

**pla·nont** \ˈplaˌnänt\ *n* -S [¹*plan-* + *-ont*] **:** a motile organism (as the amoebula of various protozoans or the gamete of some phycomycetes)

**¹pla·nor·bid** \pləˈnȯrbəd\ *adj* [NL *Planorbidae*] **:** of or relating to the Planorbidae

**²planorbid** \"\ *n* -S **:** a snail of the family Planorbidae

**pla·nor·bi·dae** \-bəˌdē\ *n pl, cap* [NL *Planorbis,* type genus, + *-idae*] **:** a family of freshwater pulmonate snails having a single pair of tentacles with an eye at the base of each and gills as well as lungs and including numerous forms important as intermediate hosts of pathogenic trematode worms — see PLANORBIS

**pla·nor·bis** \-bəs\ *n, cap* [NL, fr. L *planus* flat + *orbis* ring, disk, orb — more at FLOOR] **:** a widely distributed genus (the type of the family Planorbidae) of snails with secondarily acquired gills, a fundamentally sinistral body, and a more or less discoidal and planospiral shell that may be either dextral or sinistral

**plan·o·sol** \ˈplanəˌsȯl\ *n* -S [²*plan-* + L *solum* ground, soil — more at SOIL] **:** an intrazonal group of soils with strongly leached upper layer over a compacted clay or silt that is developed on smooth flat uplands in cool to warm humid to subhumid regions

**pla·no·spiral** \ˌplānō+\ *also* **pla·ni·spiral** \ˌplānə+\ *adj* [*planospiral* fr. ²*plan-* + *spiral; planispiral* fr. *plani-* + *spiral*] **:** having the shell coiled in one plane — used esp. of foraminifers and gastropod mollusks — **pla·no·spirally** \"+\ *adv*

**plan·o·spore** \ˈplanəˌspō(ə)r\ *n* [¹*plan-* + *spore*] **:** a motile spore **:** ZOOSPORE a

**plan position indicator** *n* **:** PPI

**plans** *pl of* PLAN, *pres 3d sing of* PLAN

**Plan·sifter** \ˈplanˌsiftə(r)\ *trademark* — used for any of several oscillating sifters arranged one above the other in a flour mill for separating and grading the stocks from the break rolls

**¹plant** \ˈplant, ˈplaa(ə)nt, ˈplaint, ˈplȧnt\ *vb* -ED/-ING/-S [ME *planten,* fr. OE *plantian,* fr. LL *plantare* to plant, fix in place, fr. L, to plant, fr. *planta* plant] *vt* **1 a :** to put in the ground and cover with soil so as to grow ⟨~ corn⟩ ⟨~ seeds⟩ **b :** to set in the ground for growth ⟨~ trees⟩ ⟨~ bushes⟩ **c :** to put plants to grow in **:** CULTIVATE ⟨cleans up and ~*s* the ground thus regained from the forest —J.G.Frazer⟩ ⟨the river overflowed the ~*ed* land —*Amer. Guide Series: Tenn.*⟩ **d :** IMPLANT ⟨the task of ~*ing* in the native-born generations a knowledge of the ancestral language —Oscar Handlin⟩ **2 a** (1) **:** to establish or institute in a particular place or region ⟨engaged in ~*ing* a colony of Germans in the valley —H.E. Scudder⟩ ⟨~*ed* the first church in that part of the colony —L. H.Beck⟩ (2) **:** to settle as a colonist ⟨~*ed* former soldiers in the border regions⟩ **b :** COLONIZE, POPULATE ⟨intending to return and ~ Delaware —John Winthrop⟩ **c :** to place (animals) in a particular locality so as to grow and multiply there ⟨underseas gardens in which the oysters are ~*ed,* cultivated, and harvested —*Amer. Guide Series: Conn.*⟩ ⟨~*ing* beavers for conservation purposes —Willis Peterson⟩ **d :** to stock with animals ⟨~*ed* his ranch with beef cattle⟩ ⟨~*ed* the stream with trout⟩ ⟨~*ed* the bay with clams⟩ **e :** INOCULATE 2 a (2) **3 a :** to place in or on the ground ⟨stakes were ~*ed* to determine the ice movement in the mountain region —G. de Q. Robin⟩ ⟨~*ed* a foot in a prairie-dog hole —F.B.Gipson⟩ **b :** to place firmly or forcibly ⟨came boiling out and ~*ed* herself in his path with her hands on her hips —Robert Murphy⟩ ⟨~*ed* a hard blow on his chin⟩ **c :** to set firmly in position **:** fix in place **:** ESTABLISH ⟨~*ed* obstruction buoys around a large coral head —K.M.Dodson⟩ ⟨remained ~*ed* in the rocker —J.C.Lincoln⟩ **4 a :** CONCEAL, HIDE ⟨the plunder was ~*ed* under the floor of a restaurant —*London Daily Chronicle*⟩ **b :** to conceal (something) temporarily where discovery may deceive or mislead ⟨~*ed* a gun in the butler's coat⟩ ⟨~*ed* gold nuggets in a worthless mine⟩ **c :** to covertly arrange publication or dissemination of ⟨politicians and officials exploit their intimacy with the press and ~ true or false stories with them —*Times Lit. Supp.*⟩ ⟨a report, undoubtedly ~*ed* by him, that he had gone to South America —Robert Shaplen⟩ **d :** to place or cause to be placed in a position under false colors ⟨~*ed* a spy on the committee's staff⟩ ⟨frequently the gang is not able to ~ a confederate inside the house —Richard Harrison⟩ **e :** to prepare beforehand **:** PREARRANGE ⟨carefully ~*s* the surprise word —*Britain Today*⟩ ⟨asked an obviously ~*ed* question⟩ **5 :** leave behind **:** ABANDON ⟨~*ed* his family and left them penniless⟩ **6 :** BURY, INTER ⟨these people believe in sealed copper coffins in vaults, and they are decidedly not ~*ed* but laid to rest —Mari Sandoz⟩ ⟨death lost some of its terrors when one could be ~*ed* neatly in a corner of one's own farm —Stuart Cloete⟩ ~ *vi* **1 :** to perform the act of planting ⟨this is perfect weather for ~*ing*⟩ **2 :** to become a plant **:** GROW

**²plant** \"\ *n* -S [ME *plante,* fr. OE, fr. L *planta,* prob. back-formation fr. (assumed) L *plantare* to tread the ground in planting, fr. L *planta* sole of the foot — more at PLACE] **1 a** (1) **:** a young tree, vine, shrub, or herb planted or suitable for planting **:** a vegetable, flower, fruit, or ornamental grown for or ready for transplanting ⟨cabbage ~*s* for sale⟩ ⟨thin the hill to four ~*s*⟩ — see HOUSEPLANT, POT PLANT, WILD FLOWER (2) *obs* **:** CUTTING, SLIP, SET **b** *archaic* **:** a sapling used as a cudgel or pole **c :** any of numerous organisms constituting the kingdom Plantae, being typically characterized by lack of locomotive movement or rapid motor response, by absence of obvious nervous or sensory organs though possessing irritability as indicated by specific response to stimuli, by possession of cell walls composed of cellulose, and by a nutritive system in which carbohydrates are formed photosynthetically through the action of chlorophyll and organic nutrients are not required, and exhibiting a strong tendency to alternation of a sexual with an asexual generation though one or the other may be greatly modified or almost wholly suppressed — see ALGA, FERN, FUNGUS, MOSS; ANIMAL, SAPROPHYTE **2 :** one thought to resemble a growing plant ⟨a sensitive ~ who must be shielded from shock⟩ **3 a :** the land, buildings, machinery, apparatus, and fixtures employed in carrying on a trade or a mechanical or other industrial business ⟨to meet the nation's telephone needs we again built a great deal of new physical ~ —C.F.Craig⟩ **b :** a factory or workshop for the manufacture of a particular product ⟨an automobile ~⟩ ⟨an ice-cream ~⟩ **c :** the total facilities available for production or service in a particular country or place ⟨a nation which both in present ~ and in natural resources is probably the richest in the world —*New Republic*⟩ ⟨not just the town's sewers but its streets, its schools — its whole ~ — had to be enlarged for the new arrivals —C.W.Thayer⟩ **d :** a piece of equipment or a set of machine parts functioning together for the performance of a particular operation ⟨a couple of experts armed with drills, an oxyacetylene ~, and other strange tools —F.W. Crofts⟩ **e** *chiefly Austral* **:** the equipment and personnel necessary for an enterprise (as stock raising or mining) ⟨such a ~ may consist of a head stockman, one or two other white men and up to twenty aboriginals —*Australian Veterinary Jour.*⟩ **f :** the physical equipment (as buildings or athletic fields) of an institution (as a college) ⟨several large bequests have enabled the school to expand its ~⟩ **4** [¹*plant*] **a :** stolen goods; *also* **:** a place for storing them **b** (1) **:** UNDERCOVER MAN ⟨joined the criminal ring as a ~⟩ (2) **:** fixed police surveillance ⟨to put a ~ on a suspect⟩ **c :** a swindling plot **:** a scheme to defraud **d** (1) **:** something deliberately placed so that its discovery may deceive or mislead ⟨left muddy footprints as a ~ to confuse the police⟩ (2) **:** something (as a news story or rumor) whose publication or dissemination is deliberately arranged by an individual or group for a particular purpose ⟨the story had all the earmarks of a propaganda ~⟩ **e** (1) **:** a seemingly casual statement or action deliberately inserted in a play to prepare the spectator for a later development or effect (2) **:** a person placed in an audience to take a seemingly spontaneous part in the proceedings **f :** a trap for wrongdoers ⟨the town has set up several ~*s* for traffic violators⟩ **5** [¹*plant*] **:** a way of standing **:** POSE ⟨took up a determined ~ in front of the door⟩ **6** [¹*plant*] **a :** a crop or growth of something planted ⟨the sugar beet is up to a good ~ once again —A.G.Street⟩ **b** (1) **:** the stocking of a place with animals (as fish or game) for conservation or sport ⟨the authorities made a small ~ of deer on the islands —C.C.Van Fleet⟩ (2) **:** an oyster that has been bedded as distinguished from one of natural growth, *also* **:** a young oyster suitable for transplanting

**plan·ta** \ˈplantə\ *n, pl* **plan·tae** \-nˌtē\ [NL, fr. L, sole of the foot — more at PLACE] **1 :** the back side of the shank of a bird's leg **2 a :** the flattened end of the proleg of a caterpillar **b :** a sclerite on the insect pretarsus

**plant·able** \ˈplantəbəl\ *adj* **:** capable of being planted ⟨~ trees⟩ ⟨~ fields⟩

**plan·tad** \ˈplanˌtad\ *adv* [L *planta* sole of the foot + E *-ad*] **:** toward the sole of the foot

**plan·tae** \ˈplanˌtē\ *n pl, cap* [NL, fr. L, pl. of *planta* plant] **:** the basic group of living things that comprises all the plants **:** PLANT KINGDOM — compare ANIMALIA, PROTISTA

**plant·age** \ˈplantij\ *n* -S [²*plant* + *-age*] *archaic* **:** VEGETATION

**plan·tag·e·net** \planˈtajənət\ *n* -S *cap* [*Plantagenet,* nickname of the family adopted as surname by Richard, Duke of York †1460] **:** a member of an English royal family founded by Geoffrey, Count of Anjou, through his marriage in 1128 with Matilda, daughter of Henry I of England, to which belonged the rulers of England from 1154 to 1485 — see ANGEVIN

**plan·ta·gi·na·ce·ae** \ˌplantəjəˈnāsēˌē\ *n pl, cap* [NL *Plantagin-, Plantago,* type genus + *-aceae*] **:** a family of dicotyledonous plants constituting the order Plantaginales and characterized by spicate or capitate tetramerous flowers with a membranous or scarious corolla and a fruit that is a pyxidium or an indehiscent nutlet — see PLANTAGO — **plan·ta·gi·na·ceous** \ˌ===ˈnāshəs\ *adj*

**plan·ta·gi·na·les** \ˌ=ˌ==ˈnā(ˌ)lēz\ *n pl, cap* [NL *Plantagin-, Plantago* + *-ales*] : an order of plants coextensive with the family Plantaginaceae

**plan·ta·go** \plan·ˈtā(ˌ)gō\ *n* [NL *Plantagin-, Plantago*, fr. L, plantain — more at PLANTAIN] **1** *cap* : a large genus (the type of the family Plantaginaceae) of acaulescent or short-stemmed chiefly dooryard or roadside weeds that have narrow or elliptic leaves and very small inconspicuous flowers in close-bracted spikes or heads — see ¹PLANTAIN, RIBGRASS **2** -s : any plant of the genus *Plantago*

**plantago seed** *n* : FLEASEED 1

¹**plan·tain** \ˈplantᵊn, -ntən, *also* -n·ˌtān\ *n* -s [ME *plauntein, plantaine*, fr. OF *plantain, plantein*, fr. L *plantagin-, plantago*, fr. *planta* sole of the foot; fr. its broad leaves — more at PLACE] : a plant of the genus *Plantago* — see BROAD-LEAVED PLANTAIN, RUGEL'S PLANTAIN

²**plantain** \"\ *n* -s [MF *plantain*, fr. ML *plantanus*, alter. (influenced by L *planta* plant) of L *platanus* plane tree — more at PLANE] : ²PLANE

³**plantain** \"\ *n* -s [Sp *plántano, plátano* plane tree, banana tree, fr. ML *plantanus* plane tree] **1** : a banana plant (*Musa paradisiaca*) **2** : the starchy fruit of the plantain that is a staple item of diet throughout the tropics when cooked and that is distinguished in appearance from the ordinary banana by its angular shape and yellowish green color

plantain

**plantain eater** *also* **plantain cutter** *n* [³*plantain*] : TOURACO

**plantain family** *n* [¹*plantain*] : PLANTAGINACEAE

**plantain lily** *n* : a plant of the genus *Hosta* distinguished by plaited basal leaves and racemose white or violet flowers

**plantain shoreweed** *n* : SHOREWEED

**plant·al** \ˈplantᵊl\ *adj* [²*plant* + *-al*] : of or relating to plants : VEGETATIVE

**plant anatomy** *n* : ANATOMY 1 b

**plant-animal** \ˈ=ˈ===\ *n* [NL *plantanimal*, trans. of Gk *zōophyton* zoophyte] : ZOOPHYTE

**plan·tar** \ˈplantə(r)\ *adj* [L *plantaris*, fr. *planta* sole of the foot + *-aris* -ar — more at PLACE] : of, relating to, or typical of the sole of the foot ⟨the ~ wart is in the skin rather than on it —H.K.Schwarzfeld⟩

**plantar artery** *n* : either of two branches into which the posterior tibial artery divides

**plantar cushion** *n* : a thick pad of fibrous tissue behind and under the navicular and coffin bones of the horse

**plantar fascia** *n* : a dense fibrous membrane of the sole of the foot that binds together the deeper structures

**plan·tar·is** \planˈta(a)rəs\ *n, pl* **plantar·es** \-ˌrēz\ [NL, fr. L *plantaris* plantar] : a small muscle of the calf of the leg that arises from the lower end of the femur and the posterior ligament of the knee joint and is inserted with the tendon of Achilles by a very long slender tendon into the calcaneus

**plantar ligament** *n* : the superficial part of the inferior calcaneocuboid ligament in the sole of the foot

**plantar nerve** *n* : either of two nerves into which the tibial nerve divides

**plantar reflex** *n* : a reflex movement of flexing the foot and toes that after the first year is the normal response to tickling of the sole — compare BABINSKI REFLEX

**plantar vein** *n* : one of the veins that accompany the plantar arteries

**plan·ta·tion** \planˈtāshən, plaan-, plȧn-, *in southern US* " *or* -nt·ˈā-\ *n* -s *often attrib* [L *plantation-, plantatio*, fr. *plantatus* (past. part. of *plantare* to plant) + *-ion-, -io* -ion] **1 a** *archaic* : the act or process of planting **b** : something that is planted ⟨plant the seeds of the harvest you want to reap in cleared, plowed soil and protect the ~ while it grows —Lincoln Steffens⟩ **2 a** : a usu. large group of plants under cultivation ⟨a ~ of nodding purple and ivory-colored lilacs —*New Yorker*⟩ **b** : GROVE ⟨screened from the converging roads by a ~ of copper beeches —Osbert Lancaster⟩ **c** : a cultivated oyster bed **3 a** : the settlement of people in a particular region : COLONIZATION ⟨forced ~s of English settlers —Seamus MacCall⟩ **b** : the founding or establishing of something : IMPLANTATION **4 a** *sometimes cap* : a settlement in a new country or region : COLONY ⟨a vessel from the overseas ~s —Leslie Thomas⟩ ⟨Rhode Island and Providence *Plantations*⟩ **b** : a minor division of local government in Maine **5 a** : a place that is planted : cultivated land ⟨the man creates the ~ by cutting down the trees of the forest, the woman turns the soil —J.G.Frazer⟩ **b** : a usu. large estate in a tropical or subtropical region that is generally cultivated by unskilled or semiskilled labor under central direction ⟨rich cotton land, cultivated in large ~s —*Amer. Guide Series: Ark.*⟩ **6** : a moderate reddish brown that is lighter, stronger, and much yellower than roan and yellower, lighter, and stronger than mahogany

**plantation rubber** *n* : natural rubber grown esp. in the Malay Peninsula, Indonesia, and Ceylon chiefly from a Brazilian tree (*Hevea braziliensis*) imported into those areas

**plantation walking horse** *or* **plantation walker** *n, usu cap P & sometimes cap W&H* : TENNESSEE WALKING HORSE

**plant band** *n* : BAND 4 e

**plant bed** *n* : an area in which plants (as tomatoes or pansies) are grown usu. from seed until ready for transplanting to other locations

**plant bug** *n* : an insect of the hemipterous family Miridae including many that are destructive pests of plants — see TARNISHED PLANT BUG

**plant cane** *n* : a stalk of sugar cane of the first growth from the cutting — compare RATOON

**plant collar** *n* : a band of tar paper or similar material placed around the base of the stem of transplanted seedlings (as plants of the cabbage family) to protect them from injury by insects

**plant cutter** *n* **1** : any of several birds of the family Phytotomidae **2** : TOURACO

**plan·té battery** \plänˈtā-\ *n, usu cap P* [after Gaston *Planté* †1889 French physicist] : a type of lead-acid storage battery

**planted** *past of* PLANT

**plant·er** \ˈplantə(r), -aan-, -ain-\ *n* -s [¹*plant* + *-er*] **1** : one that cultivates plants: as **a** (1) : FARMER (2) : one who owns or operates a plantation **b** : a planting machine **2 a** : one who settles or founds a place ⟨among the earliest ~s of York —W.M.Emery⟩; *esp* : one who helps to found a new colony or settles in it ⟨one of the ~s of Virginia⟩ **b** : one settled in Ireland on forfeited lands or in the holding of an evicted tenant **3** : one who helps to establish a doctrine or institution ⟨one of the chief ~s of democracy in his country⟩ **4** : a snag fixed at one end in a riverbed and standing almost rigidly — distinguished from *sawyer* **5** [²*plant* + *-er*] : an owner or operator of a fishing or shipping plant in Newfoundland **6** : a container (as a box, pot, or hanging basket) in which plants are grown or placed for decorative purposes — compare CACHEPOT, DISH GARDEN

**planter's punch** *n* : a punch of rum, lime or lemon juice, sugar, water, and sometimes bitters, shaken with crushed ice and garnished with slices of fruit or mint

**plant factor** *n* : the ratio of the average power load of a plant to its rated capacity

**plant food** *n* **1** : food materials used by plants **2** : FERTILIZER

**plant forcer** *n* : HOT CAP

**plant growth substance** *n* : a growth regulator for plants

**plant hopper** *n* : an insect of the hemipterous families Membracidae, Fulgoridae, and various related groups

**plant hormone** *n* **1** : a plant regulator (as indoleacetic acid or ethylene) produced by plants that usu. moves within the plant from the site of production to the site of action — called also *phytohormone* **2** : a synthetic plant regulator

**plant house** *n* : a structure in which plants are kept or grown — compare CONSERVATORY, GREENHOUSE

**plan·ti·gra·da** \ˌplantəˈgrādə, plan·ˈtigrədə\ *n pl, cap* [NL, fr. F *plantigrade*] *in former classifications* : a group consisting of the plantigrade carnivores

¹**plan·ti·grade** \ˈplantəˌgrād\ *adj* [F, fr. L *planta* sole of the foot + F *-grade*] : walking on the sole with the heel touching the ground ⟨the bear and man are both ~ animals⟩ — opposed to *digitigrade*

²**plantigrade** \"\ *n* -s : a plantigrade animal

¹**plant·ing** \ˈplantiŋ, -laan-, -lain-, -lȧn-, -tēŋ\ *n* -s [ME, fr. gerund of *planten* to plant] **1** : the act or process of setting in the ground for cultivation **2 a** : PLANTATION 2 ⟨surrounded by many ~s of elm and maple —*Amer. Guide Series: Conn.*⟩ **b** : an area where plants are grown for commercial or decorative purposes **3** : an act or instance of stocking or introducing animals (as fish, shellfish, or game) in a particular place **4** : a process of introducing additional colors in woven fabrics (as rugs) by substituting one colored thread for another at intervals

²**planting** \"\ *adj* [¹*planting*] : owning or operating a plantation ⟨the southern ~ aristocracy⟩

**planting pit** *n* [¹*planting*] : a wooden or metal box sunk at the pit end of a pole-vault runway to prevent the vaulter's pole from slipping

**planting stick** *n* : DIBBLE

**plant kingdom** *n* : the one of the three basic groups of natural objects that comprises all living and extinct plants — compare ANIMAL KINGDOM, MINERAL KINGDOM

**plant·less** \ˈplantləs\ *adj* : having no plants ⟨a ~ desert⟩

**plant·let** \-lət\ *n* -s : a little plant

**plant life** *n* **1** : FLORA, VEGETATION **2** : the mode of life of plants

**plantlike** \ˈ=ˌ=\ *adj, of an animal* : resembling a plant esp. in being fixed to a substrate and in exhibiting indeterminate growth ⟨certain ~ corals may continue to enlarge indefinitely⟩

**plantlike flagellate** *n* : any of various organisms constituting the subclass Phytomastigina, having many characteristics in common with typical algae, and being considered usu. as protozoans by protozoologists and as algae by algologists

**plant·ling** \ˈplantliŋ\ *n* -s [²*plant* + *-ling*] : PLANTLET

**plant liqueur** *n* : a liqueur made from plants, roots, herbs, and seeds first macerated in brandy and then distilled — compare FRUIT LIQUEUR

**plant louse** *n* **1** : any of numerous small insects of the family Aphididae that live on plants and suck their juices; *broadly* : APHID **2** : any of various small insects of similar habits; *esp* : JUMPING PLANT LOUSE

**plan·toc·ra·cy** \planˈtäkrəsē\ *n* -ES [*planter* + *-o-* + *-cracy*] **1** : government by planters **2** : a ruling class made up of planters

**plant out** *vb* [¹*plant*] *vt* : to transplant from a protected or enclosed place (as from a cold frame, pot, greenhouse) to the open ~ *vi* : to carry out a transplanting

**plant patent** *n* [²*plant*] : a patent granted to one who produces a new and distinctive plant by breeding or selection and propagates it asexually

**plant pathologist** *n* : a specialist in plant pathology

**plant pathology** *n* : a branch of botany that deals with the diseases of plants

**plant physiologist** *n* : a specialist in plant physiology

**plant physiology** *n* : a branch of botany that deals with plant functions

**plant regulator** *n* : a natural or synthetic organic substance (as an auxin or maleic hydrazide) other than a nutrient that acts in very small amounts to modify any physiological process in plants — compare PLANT HORMONE

**plants** *pres 3d sing of* PLANT, *pl of* PLANT

**plants·man** \ˈplantsmən\ *n, pl* **plantsmen 1 a** : one who raises or sells plants commercially : NURSERYMAN **b** : one who practices the science or art of raising plants : HORTICULTURIST **2** : one who loves plants

**plant sociology** *n* : PHYTOSOCIOLOGY

**plan·tu·la** \ˈplanchələ\ *n, pl* **plantu·lae** \-chəˌlē\ [NL, dim. of L *planta* sole of the foot — more at PLACE] : a small structure resembling a cushion found on the ventral surface of the tarsal segments of most insects — **plan·tu·lar** \-chələ(r)\ *adj*

**plant·ule** \ˈplanˌchül\ *n* -s [NL *plantula*, dim. of L *planta* plant] : an embryo plant

**plan·u·la** \ˈplanyələ\ *n, pl* **planu·lae** \-yəˌlē\ [NL, fem. dim. of L *planus* flat — more at FLOOR] : the very young free-swimming larva of a coelenterate that usu. has a flattened oval or oblong form and consists of an outer layer of ciliated ectoderm cells and an internal mass of endoderm cells — **plan·u·lar** \-yələ(r)\ *adj*

**plan·u·loid** \-yəˌlȯid\ *adj* [NL *planula* + E *-oid*] : resembling a planula

**plan·u·loi·dea** \ˌplanyəˈlȯidēə\ [NL, fr. *planula* + *-oidea*] *syn of* MESOZOA

**pla·num** \ˈplānəm\ *n, pl* **pla·na** \-nə\ [L, neut. of *planus* flat — more at FLOOR] : a flat surface of bone esp. of the skull

**plan view** *n* : the appearance of an object as seen from above

**planx·ty** \ˈplaŋkstē\ *n* -ES [origin unknown] **1** : an Irish melody for the harp written in triplets and slower than the jig **2** : a dance to a planxty

**plap·pert** \ˈpläpə(r)t\ *n* -s [G, alter. of MHG *blaffert*] : BLAFFERT

¹**plaque** *also* **placque** \ˈplak *chiefly Brit* ˈpläk\ *n* -s [F, fr. MF, solid metal sheet, fr. *plaquier* to plate, fr. MD *placken* to piece, spot, patch, beat; akin to MD *placke* piece, spot, a coin, MHG *placke* spot, patch] **1 a** : an ornamental brooch; *esp* : the badge of an honorary order **b** : a flat thin piece (as of metal, clay, or ivory) used for decoration (as on a wall or in an article of furniture) ⟨a handsome ceramic ~ hung over the fireplace⟩ **c** (1) : an inscribed usu. metal tablet placed (as on a building or post) to identify a site or commemorate an individual or event ⟨roadside ~s mark historic battles and gallant deeds of bygone days —*Time*⟩ (2) : NAMEPLATE **d** : CHIP 5a **2** : an abnormal patch or flattened area on some body part or surface: **a** : a localized patch of skin disease ⟨psoriatic ~⟩ **b** : a deposit of lipoid or fibrous matter in the wall of a blood vessel ⟨atheromatous ~s in the aorta⟩ **c** : a film of mucus harboring bacteria on a tooth **3** : BLOOD PLATELET

²**pla·qué** \(ˈ)plaˈkā\ *adj* [F, fr. past part. of *plaquer* to plate, fr. MF *plaquier*] : EN PLACARD

**pla·quette** \(ˈ)plaˈket\ *n* -s [F, fr. *plaque* + *-ette*] **1** : a small plaque **2** : a metal stamping die that is cut in relief and used to decorate the sides of leather bookbindings

¹**plash** \ˈplash, -aa(ə)sh,-aish\ *n* -ES [ME *plasche*, fr. OE *plæsc*; akin to MD *plasch, plas* pool, plash; all prob. of imit. origin] : a shallow or marshy pool : PUDDLE ⟨the bird . . . bathed itself in some ~es nearby —Hugh McCrae⟩

²**plash** \"\ *vt* -ED/-ING/-ES [ME *plashen*, fr. MF *plaissier*, fr. OF, fr. *plais* hedge, twined fence, prob. fr. (assumed) VL *plaxus* entwined, alter. of L *plexus*, past part. of *plectere* to entwine, braid — more at PLY] *Brit* : PLEACH ⟨~ a hedge⟩

³**plash** \"\ *n* -ES [prob. imit.] **1 a** : a surface agitation of water with accompanying sound ⟨the measured ~ of oars —A.C.Benson⟩ ⟨the ceaseless ~ of the waves —William Black⟩ **b** (1) : a splashing movement of water ⟨~ of the fountains from the mouths of stone dolphins —Mark Schorer⟩ (2) : a movement or sound suggestive of the splashing of water ⟨the ~ of the paintbrush against the wall —Donald Windham⟩ ⟨the ~ of bare feet made him turn his head —Josephine Pinckney⟩ **c** : a dash or blotch esp. of color or light ⟨a few ~es of white in the breast of the duck —J.H.Robinson †1935⟩ ⟨effect of the wilder ~ of irresponsible prismatic impressions which vertigo had unloosed —Florence Gould⟩ **2** *dial chiefly Eng* : a heavy fall of rain

⁴**plash** \"\ *vb* -ED/-ING/-ES [perh. fr. D *plassen*, fr. MD, of imit. origin] *vt* **1** : to break the surface of (water) so as to cause a surface agitation with an accompanying sound : SPLASH **2** : DASH, SPATTER, SPECKLE ⟨no bird on dew-*plashed* wing —Walter de la Mare⟩ ~ *vi* **1** : to dash or tumble about with a splashing or spattering sound — used esp. of water ⟨far below him ~*ed* the waters —H.W.Longfellow⟩ ⟨raindrops ~*ed* on the tile roof —Anne S. Mehdevi⟩ **2** : to cause a splashing or spattering ⟨~*ing* of hooves in water —Robinson Jeffers⟩ ⟨could hear a slight ~*ing* as the bows of the lighter forged through the water —Miles Burton⟩

**plash·ing·ly** *adv* : with plashing movement or sound

¹**plashy** \-shē, -shi\ *adj* -ER/-EST [¹*plash* + *-y*] : abounding with pools or puddles ⟨down the steep, ~ path they poured —Rudyard Kipling⟩ : MARSHY ⟨~ brink of weedy lake —W.C. Bryant⟩ ⟨the heron fishes in his ~ pool —Walter de la Mare⟩

²**plashy** \"\ *adj* -ER/-EST [³*plash* + *-y*] : marked by plashes : SPLASHING, PLASHING ⟨a ~ tramp by the side of the bridge caught the sensitive ear —Washington Irving⟩

**-pla·sia** \ˈplāzh(ē)ə\ *or* **-pla·sy** \ˌplāsē, -lasē, pləsē\ *n comb form, pl* **-plasias** *or* **-plasies** [NL *-plasia*, fr. Gk *plasis* molding + NL *-ia* -y] : development : formation ⟨*dysplasia*⟩ ⟨*heteroplasia*⟩ ⟨*homoplasy*⟩

**-pla·sis** \ˌplāsəs\ *n comb form, pl* **-pla·ses** \-āˌsēz\ [NL, fr. Gk *plasis* molding, fr. *plassein* to mold] : molding ⟨*anaplasis*⟩ ⟨*cataplasis*⟩ ⟨*paraplasis*⟩

**plasm** \ˈplazəm\ *n* -s [LL *plasma* form, mold] : PLASMA

**plasm-** *or* **plasmo-** *comb form* [F, fr. NL *plasma*] **1** : plasma ⟨*plasmapheresis*⟩ ⟨*plasmodium*⟩ **2** : cytoplasm ⟨*plasmolysis*⟩ ⟨*plasmogamy*⟩ **3** : protoplasm ⟨*plasmoptysis*⟩

**-plasm** \ˌplazəm\ *or* **-plas·ma** \ˈplazmə\ *n comb form* -s [G *-plasma*, fr. NL *plasma*] : formative or formed material (as of a cell or tissue) ⟨*cytoplasm*⟩ ⟨*karyoplasma*⟩ ⟨*metaplasm*⟩

**plas·ma** \ˈplazmə\ *n* -s [G, fr. LL, form, mold, fr. Gk, fr. *plassein* to mold — more at PLASTER] **1** : a faintly translucent cryptocrystalline variety of quartz of various shades of green **2** [NL, fr. LL, form, mold] **a** : the fluid part of blood, lymph, or milk that is distinguishable from suspended material (as fat globules or cells) and that in blood differs from serum essentially in containing the antecedent substance of fibrin in addition to the constituents of serum **b** : the juice that can be expressed from muscle **3** [NL] : PROTOPLASM **4** : a mixture of starch and glycerol used as an ointment base **5** : an ionized gas (as in the atmospheres of stars) containing about equal numbers of positive ions and electrons and differing from an ordinary gas in being a good conductor of electricity and in being affected by a magnetic field

**plas·ma·blast** \ˈplazməˌblast\ *n* -s [*plasma* + *-blast*] : a precursor of a plasma cell

**plasma cell** *n* : a mononuclear slightly amoeboid wandering cell commonly found in association with low-grade chronic inflammations or various allergic processes and believed to secrete ferments rather than to act as a phagocyte

**plas·ma·cyte** \ˈplazməˌsīt\ *n* [ISV *plasma* + *-cyte*] : PLASMA CELL

**plas·ma·cy·toid** \ˌ==ˈsīˌtȯid\ *adj* : resembling or derived from a plasma cell

**plas·ma·gel** \ˈplazmə+ˌ-\ *n* [*plasma* + *gel*] : gelated protoplasm; *esp* : the outer firm zone of a pseudopodium — compare PLASMASOL

**plas·ma·gene** \-ˌjēn\ *n* [ISV *plasma* + *-gene*] : a submicroscopic factor or determiner believed by some biologists to be present in the cytoplasm of cells and to influence physiological and hereditary phenomena of the cytoplasm much as genes are believed to do for the entire cell — compare PLASTOGENE — **plas·ma·gen·ic** \ˌ==ˈjenik\ *adj*

**plas·mal** \ˈplazməl\ *n* -s [prob. back-formation fr. *plasmalogen*] : a substance consisting of one or more aldehydes of the type of those related to palmitic acid and stearic acid obtained in the form of an acetal (as by treatment of a plasmalogen with alkali)

**plas·ma·lemma** \ˈplazmə+\ *n* [NL, fr. *plasma* + Gk *lemma* rind, husk — more at LEMMA] : the differentiated protoplasmic surface bounding a cell : PLASMA MEMBRANE

**plas·mal·o·gen** \plazˈmaləjən, -ˌjen\ *n* -s [*plasm-* + *al*kali + connective *-o-* + *-gen*] : a phosphatide that is the precursor of plasmal in tissue

**plasmal reaction** *n* : a modified Feulgen reaction designed to detect aldehyde in tissue

**plasma membrane** *n* **1** : an external semipermeable limiting layer of cell protoplasm that is commonly regarded as an oriented protein gel rich in lipoids and calcium and that is a major factor in regulating exchanges between the cell and its environment — called also *cell membrane, ectoplast*; see CELL WALL **2** : a protoplasmic surface (as a tonoplast) regarded as similar in structure or function to the plasma membrane

**plas·ma·pher·e·sis** \ˌplazməˈferəsəs\ *also* **plas·ma·phore·sis** \-ˌfəˈrēsəs, -ˈfȯrəs-\ *n, pl* **plasmaphere·ses** \-ˌsēz\ [*plasmapheresis*, NL, fr. *plasm-* + Gk *aphairesis* action of taking off, removal; *plasmaphoresis*, NL, alter. (influenced by *-phoresis*) of *plasmapheresis* — more at APHAERESIS] : an experimental technique used (as in the study of shock) for reducing the level of plasma protein by withdrawing large volumes of blood, centrifuging out the cells, and reinjecting them suspended in a protein-free but innocuous medium

**plas·ma·sol** \ˈplazmə+ˌ-\ *n* [*plasma* + *sol*] : solated protoplasm; *esp* : the inner fluid zone of a pseudopodium or amoeboid cell — compare PLASMAGEL

**plasmasome** *var of* PLASMOSOME

**plas·mat·ic** \(ˈ)plazˈmad·ik\ *adj* [*plasmatic* fr. Gk *plasmat-, plasma* + E *-ic*] : of, relating to, or occurring in plasma esp. of blood

**plasmato-** *comb form* [Gk *plasmat-, plasma*] : PLASM- ⟨*plasmatoparous*⟩

**plas·ma·top·a·rous** \ˌplazməˈtäpərəs\ *adj* [*plasmato-* + *-parous*] : discharging the protoplasmic contents of a conidium in an undivided mass that first becomes invested with a membrane or wall and then puts out a germ tube — used of various downy mildews

**plas·ma·tor·rhex·is** \ˌplazməd·əˈreksəs\ *n, pl* **plasmator·rhex·es** \-kˌsēz\ [NL, fr. *plasmato-* + *-rrhexis*] : the disruption of a cell by internal pressure due to swelling

**-plas·mia** \ˈplazmēə\ *n comb form* -s [NL, fr. *plasma* + *-ia*] : a (specified) condition of the blood plasm ⟨*oligoplasmia*⟩

**plas·mic** \ˈplazmik, -mēk\ *adj* [*plasm-* + *-ic*] : PROTOPLASMIC, PLASMATIC — **plas·mi·cal·ly** \-mək(ə)lē, -mēk-, -li\ *adv*

**plas·min** \ˈplazmən\ *n* -s [*plasm-* + *-in*] : a proteolytic enzyme that dissolves the fibrin of blood clots and that is formed by the activation of plasminogen (as by streptokinase) — called also *fibrinolysin*

**plas·min·o·gen** \plazˈminəjən, -ˌjen\ *n* -s [*plasmin* + connective *-o-* + *-gen*] : the precursor of plasmin found in blood plasma and serum — called also *profibrinolysin*

**plasmo-** — see PLASM-

**Plas·mo·chin** \ˈplazməkən\ *trademark* — used for pamaquine

**plas·mo·cy·to·ma** *or* **plas·ma·cy·to·ma** \ˌplazməsīˈtōmə\ *n, pl* **plasmocyto·mas** \-məz\ *or* **plasmocytoma·ta** \-məd·ə\ [*plasmocytoma* fr. NL, alter. of *plasmacytoma*; *plasmacytoma* fr. NL, fr. ISV *plasmacyte* + NL *-oma*] : a myeloma composed of plasma cells

**plasmod-** *or* **plasmodi-** *or* **plasmodio-** *comb form* [NL *plasmodium*] : plasmodium ⟨*plasmodiocarp*⟩ ⟨*plasmoditrophoblast*⟩ ⟨*plasmodic*⟩

**plas·mode** \ˈplazˌmōd\ *n* -s [NL *plasmodium*] : PLASMODIUM 1a

**plas·mo·des·ma** \ˌplazməˈdezmə\ *also* **plas·mo·desm** \ˈ==-ˌdezəm\ *or* **plas·mo·des·mus** \ˌ==ˈdezməs\ *n, pl* **plasmo·desma·ta** \ˌ==ˈ=məd·ə\ *or* **plasmodesmas** [*plasmodesma* fr. NL, fr. *plasm-* + Gk *desma* bond; *plasmodesm* ISV, fr. NL *plasmodesmus*; *plasmodesmus* fr. NL, fr. *plasm-* + Gk *desmos* band, bond — more at DESM-, DESMA] : a protoplasmic connection between cells : an intercellular bridge — called also *cell bridge* — **plas·mo·des·ma·tal** \ˌ==ˈ=məd·ᵊl\ *or* **plas·mo·des·mal** \ˌ==ˈ=məl\ *or* **plas·mo·des·mic** \ˌ==ˈ=mik\ *adj*

**plas·mo·di·al** \(ˈ)plazˈmōdēəl\ *also* **plas·mod·ic** \-ˈmädik\ *or* **plas·mo·di·ate** \-ˈmōdēət, -ˌāt\ *adj* [*plasmodial* ISV *plasmod-* + *-al*; *plasmodic* fr. *plasmod-* + *-ic*; *plasmodiate* fr. *plasmod-* + *-ate*] : of, relating to, or resembling a plasmodium

**plas·mo·di·a·sis** \ˌplazməˈdīəsəs\ *also* **plas·mo·di·o·sis** \(ˌ)plazˌmōdēˈōsəs\ *n, pl* **plasmodia·ses** \-əˌsēz\ *or* **plasmodio·ses** \-ōˌsēz\ [NL *Plasmodium* + *-iasis* or *-osis*] : MALARIA

**plas·mo·di·cide** \plazˈmōdəˌsīd\ *n* -s [*plasmod-* + *-cide*] : an agent used to kill malaria parasites

**plas·mo·dieresis** \ˌplaz(ˌ)mō+\ *n, pl* **plasmodiereses** [NL, fr. *plasm-* + *dieresis* dividing, fr. Gk *diairesis* — more at DIAERESIS] : CYTOKINESIS 2

**plas·mo·di·idae** \ˌplazməˈdīəˌdē\ *n pl, cap* [NL, fr. *Plasmodium*, type genus + *-idae*] : a family of sporozoans (order Haemosporidia) that comprises the malaria parasites, is distinguished by alternation between the blood system of vertebrates and the digestive system of mosquitoes, and is usu. held to include a single genus (*Plasmodium*) — see LAVERANIA

**plas·mo·di·o·carp** \plazˈmōdēəˌkärp\ *n* -s [*plasmod-* + *-carp*] : a fructification in various slime molds that consists of an elongated sometimes branched reticulate body within which spores develop and is a modification of the plasmodium — compare AETHALIUM — **plas·mo·di·o·car·pous** \¦≈¦≈≈≈¦kär-pəs\ *adj*

**plas·mo·di·oph·o·ra** \ˌplaz(ˌ)mōdīˈäf(ə)rə\ *n, cap* [NL, fr. *plasmod-* + *-phora*] : the type genus of Plasmodiophoraceae comprising minute plant parasitic fungi that are sometimes included among the slime molds — see CLUBROOT

**plas·mo·di·oph·o·ra·ce·ae** \ˌ≈(ˌ)≈≈ˌäfəˈrāsēˌē\ *n pl, cap* [NL, fr. *Plasmodiophora*, type genus + *-aceae*] : a family of fungi (order Plasmodiophorales) having a multinuclear thallus and often causing hypertrophy in seed plants — see PLASMODIOPHORA — **plas·mo·di·oph·o·ra·ceous** \¦≈(ˌ)≈≈¦≈≈¦≈shəs\ *adj*

**plas·mo·di·oph·o·ra·les** \ˌ≈(ˌ)≈≈ˌäfəˈrā(ˌ)lēz\ *n pl, cap* [NL, fr. *Plasmodiophora* + *-ales*] : an order of fungi (subclass *Oomycetes*) having spores with unequal flagella

**plas·mo·di·trophoblast** \plaz¦mōdē+\ *n* [ISV *plasmod-* + *trophoblast*] : the syncytium of a chorion

**plas·mo·di·um** \plazˈmōdēəm\ *n* [NL, fr. *plasm-* + ISV *-ode* + NL *-ium*] **1** *pl* **plasmo·dia** \-dēə\ **a** : a motile multinucleate mass of protoplasm resulting from fusion of uninuclear amoeboid cells; *also* : an organism (as a particular stage of a slime mold) consisting of such a structure — compare COENOCYTE **b** : SYNCYTIUM 1 **2 a** *cap* : the type genus of Plasmodiidae including all the malaria parasites affecting man **b** *pl* **plasmodia** : an individual malaria parasite

**plas·mod·ro·ma** \plazˈmädrəmə\ *n pl, cap* [NL, fr. *plasm-* + *-droma* (fr. Gk *-dromos* -drome)] : a subphylum of Protozoa comprising the classes Mastigophora, Sarcodina, and Sporozoa and characterized by absence of cilia and possession of nuclei of one kind only — compare CILIOPHORA

**plas·mog·a·my** \plazˈmägəmē\ *n* -ES [ISV *plasm-* + *-gamy*] : fusion of protoplasts as distinguished from fusion of nuclei — compare KARYOGAMY

**plas·mog·o·ny** \-gənē, -ni\ *n* -ES [ISV *plasm-* + *-gony*] **1** : ABIOGENESIS **2** : PLASMOGAMY

**plas·mol·y·sis** \plazˈmäləsəs\ *n, pl* **plasmoly·ses** \-əˌsēz\ [NL, fr. *plasm-* + *-lysis*] : contraction or shrinking of the cytoplasm away from the wall of a living cell (as of a plant) due to loss of water by exosmosis

**plas·mo·lyt·ic** \¦plazmə¦lid·ik, -ēk\ *adj* [ISV *plasmolyt-* (fr. NL *plasmolysis*) + *-ic*] : of or relating to plasmolysis — **plas·mo·lyt·i·cal·ly** \-ək(ə)lē, -ēk-, -li\ *adv*

**plas·mo·lyz·ability** \ˌplazməˌlīzəˈbiləd·ē\ *n* : the capability of being plasmolyzed

**plas·mo·lyz·able** \¦≈≈¦līzəbəl\ *adj* : capable of being plasmolyzed

**plas·mo·lyze** \ˈ≈≈ˌlīz\ *vb* -ED/-ING/-S *see -ize in Explan Notes* [NL *plasmolysis* + E *-ize*] *vt* : to subject to plasmolysis ~ *vi* : to undergo plasmolysis

**plas·mon** \ˈplazˌmän\ *also* **plas·mone** \-mōn\ *n* -S [G *plasmon*, fr. *plasma* — more at PLASMA] : the cytoplasm regarded as a system of hereditary determinants or agents comparable to the genomes — compare PLASMAGENE, PLASTOGENE

**plas·mop·a·ra** \plazˈmäpərə\ *n, cap* [NL, fr. *plasm-* + *-para* (fr. L *parere* to bring forth) — more at PARE] : a genus of downy mildews (family Peronosporaceae) having conidiophores that are blunt-tipped and branched at nearly right angles — see GRAPE MILDEW 2

**plas·moph·a·gous** \(ˈ)≈¦mäfəgəs\ *adj* [*plasm-* + *-phagous*] : feeding on plasma — **plas·moph·a·gy** \≈ˈ≈≈jē\ *n* -ES

**plas·mop·ty·sis** \plazˈmäptəsəs\ *n, pl* **plasmopty·ses** \-əˌsēz\ [NL, fr. *plasm-* + *-ptysis*] : the bursting forth of protoplasm from a cell through rupture of the cell wall

**plas·mo·quine** \ˈplazməˌkwin, -wēn, -ˌkwən\ *or* **plas·mo·quin** \-ˌkwən\ *n* -S [*plasm-* + *-quine* or *-quin* (fr. *quinine*)] : PAMAQUINE

**plas·mo·some** \ˈplazməˌsōm\ *or* **plas·mo·so·ma** \ˌ≈≈ˈsōmə\ *or* **plas·ma·some** \ˈ≈≈ˌsōm\ *n* -S [*plasmosome* fr. *plasm-* + *-some*; *plasmosoma* fr. NL, fr. *plasm-* + *-soma*; *plasmasome* fr. *plasma* + *-some*] **1** : a true nucleolus **2** : MICROSOME

**plas·mot·o·my** \plazˈmäd·əmē\ *n* -ES [ISV *plasm-* + *-tomy*; prob. orig. formed as G *plasmotomie*] : division of the plasmodium of a protozoan into two or more multinucleate parts

**plasms** *pl of* PLASM

**-plasms** *pl of* -PLASM

**pla·some** \ˈplāˌsōm, ˈplaˌ-\ *n* -S [G *plasom*, contr. of *plasmatosom*, fr. *plasmato-* + *-som* -some] : BIOPHORE

**plast** \ˈplast, -aa(ə)st, -aist\ *n* -S [*-plast*] : PLASTID

**-plast** \ˌplast, -aa(ə)st, -aist\ *n comb form* -S [MF *-plaste*, fr. LL *-plastus*, fr. Gk *-plastos*, fr. *plastos* formed, molded] **1 a** : thing made ⟨gypso*plast*⟩ ⟨melo*plast*⟩ **b** : plastic — esp. in names of groups of plastics ⟨pheno*plast*⟩ **2 a** : organized particle or granule : cell ⟨bio*plast*⟩ ⟨leuco*plast*⟩ **b** : formative cell : -BLAST ⟨odonto*plast*⟩

**plas·tein** \ˈplaˌstēn, -ˌstēən\ *n* -S [ISV *plast-* (fr. Gk *plastos* formed, molded) + *-ein* (as in *casein*); prob. orig. formed in G; fr. its tendency to pass over into hydrogel] : any of several substances resembling proteins precipitated by the action of proteolytic enzymes (as pepsin or papain) on the digestion products of protein

**plas·te·line** *or* **plas·ti·line** \ˈplastəˌlēn\ *also* **plas·ti·li·na** \ˌ≈≈ˈlēnə\ *n* -S [fr. *Plastilina*, a trademark] : a nonhardening modeling clay made from clay mixed with oil or wax

**¹plas·ter** \ˈplastə(r), -laas-, -lais-, -lȧs-\ *also* **plais·ter** \ˈplās-\ *n* -S [ME *plaster*, *plastre*, fr. OE, fr. L *emplastrum*, fr. Gk *emplastron*, *emplastros*, fr. *emplastos* daubed on, plastered up, verbal of *emplassein* to plaster up, make stick, fr. *em-* ²en- + *plassein* to form, mold, plaster; akin to Gk *pelanos* round flat cake, L *planus* level, flat — more at FLOOR] **1 a** : an external application of a consistency harder than ointment that is prepared for use by spreading it on cloth (as gauze) or other material and that is adhesive at the ordinary temperature of the body; *also* : the application together with the material on which it is spread — see ADHESIVE PLASTER, MUSTARD PLASTER, POROUS PLASTER, STICKING PLASTER **b** : anything applied to heal or soothe : SALVE **2** [ME *plaster*, *plastre*, fr. MF *plastre*, fr. L *emplastrum*] **a** : a cementing material that is produced by expelling a gas or liquid from a natural material (as limestone or gypsum) and has cementing properties caused by reabsorption of the gas or liquid **b** : PLASTER OF PARIS **c** : a material that is applied in a plastic state (as by troweling) and hardens upon drying, that is used esp. for coating interior walls, ceilings, and partitions, and that is usu. made by mixing sand and water with gypsum plaster, quicklime, or hydrated lime to which hair or fiber may be added to act as a binder ⟨lime ~⟩ ⟨acoustical ~⟩ — see BOND PLASTER, CEMENT PLASTER, GAUGING PLASTER, KEENE'S CEMENT; compare BROWN COAT, FINISHING COAT, SCRATCH COAT; MORTAR, STUCCO **d** : LAND PLASTER **3 a** : a coating or surface of plaster (as on a wall or ceiling) esp. when hardened ⟨drive nails into the ~⟩ ⟨cracks in the ~⟩ **b** : PARGETING, PLASTERWORK **c** : a work of art made of plaster of paris

**²plaster** \"\ *also* **plaister** \"\ *vb* **plastered**; **plastered**; **plastering** \-t(ə)riŋ\ **plasters** [ME *plasteren*, partly fr. ¹*plaster* & partly fr. MF *plastrir*, fr. *plastre* plaster] *vt* **1 a** : to overlay or cover with plaster or a similar material ⟨~ a wall⟩ **b** : to smear or bedaub as if with plaster : COAT ⟨frequently fell and rose well ~*ed* with yellow clay —R.M.Lovett⟩ ⟨when the debris is solidly ~*ed* over with snow —V.A.Firsoff⟩ **2 a** : to apply a plaster to (as a wound or sprain) **b** : SOOTHE, ALLEVIATE, REMEDY **3 a** : to cover over or conceal as if with a coat of plaster ⟨has at bottom the feelings of a gentleman, but all these are so ~*ed* over with a stiff manner —H.J.Laski⟩ : repair or redecorate superficially as if by plastering ⟨the new owners doubled its size and ~*ed* it with the panels and doors of an ancient English manor house —Van Wyck Brooks⟩ **b** : to apply as a coating or incrustation ⟨typical of the veneer of antiquity which the sixteenth century loved to ~ over everything —R.A.Hall b.1911⟩ ⟨~*ed* with jewels or decked in uniform —*Saturday Rev.*⟩ **c** : to smooth down with or as if with a sticky or shiny substance ⟨wore his black hair ~*ed* down⟩ **4** : to fasten or apply tightly to another surface ⟨~*ed* my ear again to the drawing-room window —Denton Welch⟩ ⟨rain sluicing down to ~ his ragged shirt to his body —Marcia Davenport⟩ **5** : to treat with plaster of paris: as **a** : to fertilize (as land or a crop) with plaster of paris **b** : to add plaster of paris to grapes or new wine for the purpose of improving the color or keeping qualities of the wine **6 a** : to affix to or place upon esp. conspicuously or lavishly ⟨walls ~*ed* with show bills⟩ ⟨notices with which actresses ~ their books —G.B.Shaw⟩ ⟨portrait ~*ed* on a magazine cover⟩ ⟨the more chips you ~ on the table the more likely is the ball to stop in your number —John Irwin⟩ ⟨monotonous superlatives that were ~*ed* on movie previews —Edmund Wilson⟩ **b** (1) : to cause (an area) to be saturated with posters, placards, or advertising matter ⟨run off 500 placards and ~ the town with them —Joanna Spencer⟩ ⟨~*ed* the country around New York with newspaper ads . . . and billboards —J.D.Hart⟩ (2) : to cause to become known to many throughout a wide area ⟨having ~*ed* his nasty innuendoes around —Anthony West⟩ **7** : to inflict heavy damage, injury, or casualties upon, esp. by a concentrated or unremitting attack : strike heavily and effectively ⟨warships ~*ing* the beach to clear the way for the invasion craft —C.D. Pearson⟩ ⟨plan was to ~ the positions on the forward hills —E.V.Westrate⟩ ⟨~*ed* his opponent for four rounds and then knocked him out⟩ ⟨~*ed* the opposing team⟩ ~ *vi* : to apply plaster

**³plaster** \"\ *adj* [¹*plaster*] **1** *also* **plaister** \"\ : made of plaster ⟨~ ornaments⟩ **2** : SHAM ⟨elevate the patriot leaders into ~ models of inhuman perfection —H.B.Parkes⟩

**plaster arch** *n* : an untrimmed plaster opening in a house or building

**plaster bandage** *n* : gauze bandage impregnated with plaster of paris and used to form plaster casts

**plaster base** *n* : a material (as wood lath, metal lath, woven wire fabric, or plasterboard) on which plaster is to be applied

**plasterbill** \ˈ≈≈ˌ≈\ *n* [¹*plaster* + *bill*; so called fr. the conspicuous white markings on the head] : SURF SCOTER

**plasterboard** \ˈ≈≈ˌ≈\ *n* : a board used in large sheets as a backing (as for plaster or tile) or as a substitute for plaster in walls and consisting of several plies of pulpboard, paper, or felt usu. bonded to a hardened gypsum plaster core

**plaster bond** *n* : a bituminous coating applied to the inside surface of outside walls of buildings to exclude dampness

**plaster cast** *n* **1** : a model in plaster of a person or thing **2** : a rigid dressing made from gauze impregnated with plaster of paris and used for immobilizing injured parts of the body esp. to permit the healing of bone defects

**plaster ceiling panel** *n* : a section of a ceiling that is made to appear depressed or raised by furring on the joists before lathing is done

**plaster clover** *n* : WHITE SWEET CLOVER

**plaster cove** *n* : a cove usu. between a sidewall and ceiling that is made by nailing cove brackets against each stud and the corresponding ceiling joist and running continuous lath from sidewall to ceiling

**plastered** *adj, slang* : DRUNK, INTOXICATED

**plas·ter·er** \ˈ≈st(ə)rə(r)\ *n* -S [ME, fr. *plasteren* to plaster + *-er*] : one that plasters: as **a** : one who applies plaster to cover surfaces (as walls or ceilings) or to fill in holes and rough places (as in walls, furniture, or castings) **b** : one who makes plaster casts **c** : one who molds and puts in place plaster panels and trim

**plasterer's putty** *n* : pure slaked lime made into a white paste and used in finishing plastered walls — see FINE STUFF

**plaster grounds** *n pl* : wood strips attached to a wall along the base and around windows, doors, or other openings to serve as guides for the plasterer and sometimes as nailing strips for the wood trim

**plaster head** *n* : a small strip of wood or metal used along projecting angles to protect the plaster

**plaster hook** *n* : FIRE HOOK 1

**plas·ter·i·ness** \-rēnəs\ *n* -ES : the quality or state of being plastery

**plastering** *n* -S [ME, fr. gerund of *plasteren* to plaster] **1** : the act or process of applying a plaster (as to a wound) or a coating of plaster (as to a wall) **2** : a coating of plaster or similar substance **3** : DRUBBING ⟨gave the other side a ~ they wouldn't forget⟩

**plaster key** *n* : the portion of the plaster extending through the lath

**plaster mold** *n* **1** : any of several imperfect fungi (as *Papulaspora byssina*) that invade cultivated mushroom beds and tend to form white or brown plastery patches on the surface **2** : an injury to a mushroom bed caused by a plaster mold

**plaster of paris** *often cap 2d P* [ME; fr. its originating in Paris, France] **1** : a fine white powder consisting essentially of the hemihydrate of calcium sulfate $CaSO_4.½H_2O$ or $2CaSO_4.H_2O$ that is made by calcining gypsum until it is partially dehydrated, that forms with water a paste which soon sets, and that is used chiefly for casts and molds, building materials (as plasters, tile, blocks, moldings, and stuccowork), and for surgical bandages — called also *calcined gypsum* **2** : native gypsum

**plasters** *pl of* PLASTER, *pres 3d sing of* PLASTER

**plaster saint** *n* : one depicted or regarded as a person without human failings ⟨classed as nondelinquents, although they were no *plaster saints* —*Newsweek*⟩ ⟨author's knowledge of humanity runs too deep for him to paint a *plaster saint* —Gerald Walker⟩

**plaster stone** *n* : GYPSUM

**plasterwork** \ˈ≈≈ˌ≈\ *n* : plastering used to finish architectural constructions (as for the lining of rooms) — compare PARGETING

**plas·tery** \ˈplast(ə)rē, -laas-, -lais-, -lȧs-, -ri\ *adj* : resembling or having the properties or characteristics of plaster ⟨examples in which the paint assumes almost ~ texture —Stuart Preston⟩

**¹plas·tic** \ˈplastik, -laas-, -lais-, -tēk\ *adj* [L *plasticus*, fr. Gk *plastikos*, fr. *plastos* formed, molded (verbal of *plassein* to form, mold) + *-ikos* -ic — more at PLASTER] **1 a** : giving form : having power to form or create : CREATIVE, FORMATIVE ⟨the poor ~ power, such as it is, within me set to work —Charles Lamb⟩ ⟨in these ~ moments, everything is possible —Béla Menczer⟩ **b** : giving or able to give material or sensible form to conceptions of color, shape, tone, or movement arising from the subconscious ⟨~ sensibility —Herbert Read⟩ **2 a** : capable of being modeled or shaped : susceptible of modification or change ⟨~ clay⟩ ⟨the ~ quality of concrete before it hardens⟩ **b** : easily changed or modified : PLIANT, IMPRESSIONABLE ⟨strongest impressions are registered on the ~ and emerging personality —*Diseases of the Nervous System*⟩ ⟨~ affections of children —H.G.Wells⟩ **c** : characterized by mobility, pliancy, and flow or the simulation of these qualities ⟨~ dances⟩ ⟨~ and impressionistic style of modeling —*Encyc. Americana*⟩ ⟨peasant woman of superb and ~ proportions —Hervey Allen⟩ ⟨has the ~ face and the genuine warmth of personality which should make him a television natural —D.F.Schoenbrun⟩ **3 a** (1) : relating to, composed of, or producing three-dimensional forms or movement; *esp* : showing or producing a forceful effect of three-dimensional, cohesive form : SCULPTURAL ⟨~ aim in stonework —J.J. Sweeney⟩ (2) : having or producing the illusion of sculpture or relief ⟨a ~ figure in painting⟩ ⟨of the several ~ means, he used color most sparingly —Sheldon Cheney⟩ (3) : of, relating to, or employing plastique ⟨the ~ form and architectural construction of postwar ballets —Leonide Zarine⟩ **b** : characterized by concern with or emphasis upon form, solidity, and space as depicted esp. by means of lines, colors, or planes and esp. as differentiated from concern for illustrative content or decorative detail ⟨used color not only for decorative but for ~ purposes —David Sylvester⟩ ⟨~ isolation of the objects against a uniform ground —J.T.Soby & A.H.Barr b. 1902⟩ ⟨~ light brings out the three-dimensional qualities of set, scenery, or talent —Herbert True⟩ **c** : having or producing coherency, harmony, and vitality of form : ORGANIC ⟨revolutionary sense of the ~ whole —F.L. Wright⟩ **4 a** : capable of being deformed continuously and permanently in any direction without rupture under a stress exceeding the yield value ⟨the ~ yielding of rocks —C.M. Nevin⟩ ⟨slow movement of the ~ ice —V.C.Finch & G.T. Trewartha⟩ — distinguished from *elastic* **b** : of, relating to, or produced by plastic flow ⟨existence of a limiting stress below which no ~ strain occurs —R.S.T.Kingston & L.D. Armstrong⟩ **5** *biol* **a** : capable of variation and phylogenetic change : ADAPTABLE ⟨a ~ genus⟩ ⟨a ~ species⟩ **b** : capable of growth, repair, or differentiation ⟨a ~ tissue⟩ **6** : of, relating to, involving, or by means of plastic surgery ⟨~ repair⟩ **7** : of or relating to plastics : made of a plastic ⟨~ dishes⟩ ⟨~ rope⟩ ⟨~ manufacturing⟩

**syn** PLIABLE, PLIANT, DUCTILE, MALLEABLE, ADAPTABLE: PLASTIC may describe substances soft enough to mold and often liable to subsequent hardening and becoming fixed ⟨a *plastic* tar⟩ ⟨toys made of *plastic* substances⟩ ⟨when children are small we elders in charge are apt to suppose them altogether *plastic* —H.G.Wells⟩ PLIABLE suggests something easily bent, twisted, or manipulated ⟨*pliable* willow twigs⟩ ⟨I've always been a *pliable* sort of person, and I let the ladies guide me —Upton Sinclair⟩ ⟨a sturdier quality, which made her less *pliable* to the influence of other minds —Nathaniel Hawthorne⟩ PLIANT may stress flexibility to a slightly greater degree than PLIABLE but sometimes lacks the suggestions of submissiveness of the latter word ⟨a *pliant* rod⟩ ⟨in all these countries the Norse nature, supple and *pliant*, accepted the gifts of new experience, and in return imparted strength of purpose to peoples with whom the Norsemen mingled in marriage as well as war —H.O.Taylor⟩ DUCTILE describes what can be drawn out ⟨*ductile* copper wire⟩ or easily led or induced to flow ⟨a *ductile* liquid⟩ In ref. to persons it indicates complaisance or responsiveness to formative influences ⟨he is a big dimpled child with cream and rose complexion, self-willed yet *ductile*. He can be managed, if his petulance is understood —Francis Hackett⟩ MALLEABLE refers to what may be beaten into shape ⟨thin gold leaf is very *malleable*⟩ In ref. to persons it may indicate plasticity and may but does not necessarily suggest weakness and lack of independent will ⟨children, *malleable* as yet, innocent and unformed. He may impress their minds most dangerously —Elinor Wylie⟩ ⟨long enough for the Communist overseers to spot the more *malleable* individuals and concentrate on converting them into tools —Gladwin Hill⟩ ADAPTABLE, generally complimentary, applies to a thing, condition, or person that modifies readily to adjust to circumstances ⟨an *adaptable* appliance⟩ ⟨have proved themselves an uncommonly *adaptable* people —*Amer. Guide Series: Ariz.*⟩

**²plastic** \"\ *n* -S [LL *plasticus*, n., fr. L *plasticus*, adj., plastic] **1** *archaic* : MOLDER, SCULPTOR **2** [MF *plastique*, fr. *plastique*, adj., plastic, fr. L *plasticus*] **a** : the art of modeling or sculpturing figures — often used in pl. but sing. or pl. in constr. **b** : PLASTIQUE **3 a** (1) : a substance that at some stage in its manufacture or processing can be shaped by flow (as by application of heat or pressure) with or without fillers, plasticizers, reinforcing agents, or other compounding ingredients and that can retain the new solid often rigid shape under conditions of use (2) : any of a large group of materials of high molecular weight that usu. contain as the essential ingredient a synthetic or semisynthetic organic substance made by polymerization or condensation (as polystyrene or a phenol-formaldehyde resin) or derived from a natural material by chemical treatment (as nitrocellulose from cellulose), that are molded, cast, extruded, drawn, or laminated under various conditions (as by heat in the case of thermoplastic materials, by chemical condensation in the case of thermosetting materials or polyesters, or by casting during polymerization of monomers) into objects of all sizes and shapes including films and filaments — often used in pl. but sing. in constr.; compare ELASTOMER, RESIN 2, RUBBER 2a, SYNTHETIC RUBBER **b** : an article fabricated from a plastic **4 plastics** *pl but sing or pl in constr* : PLASTIC SURGERY

**-plas·tic** \¦≈≈\ *adj comb form* [Gk *-plastikos*, fr. *-plastos* formed, molded, (fr. *plastos*, verbal of *plassein* to form) + *-ikos* -ic] **1** : developing : forming : growing ⟨hetero*plastic*⟩ ⟨xylo*plastic*⟩ **2** : of or relating to (something designated by a term ending in *-plasm*, *-plast*, or *-plasty*) ⟨rhino*plastic*⟩ ⟨proto*plastic*⟩

**plas·ti·cal·ly** \-tək(ə)lē, -tēk-, -li\ *also* **plas·tic·ly** \-kl-\ *adv* **1** : in a plastic manner ⟨ice flowing ~ downward to form the body of a glacier⟩ **2** : with respect to plastic qualities ⟨a picture considered ~⟩

**plastic art** *n* [trans. of F *art plastique*] **1** : art in which modeling is used **2** : an art (as painting or sculpture) in which substantial three-dimensional form or its effect is achieved

**plas·ti·cate** \ˈplastəˌkāt\ *vt* -ED/-ING/-S [back-formation fr. *plasticator*] : to knead by means of a plasticator : MASTICATE

**plas·ti·ca·tor** \-ˌkād·ə(r)\ *n* -S [²*plastic* + *-ator*] : a machine for plasticizing rubber or mixing thermoplastic materials by means of a revolving screw

**plastic binding** *n* : mechanical binding in which the binding device is made of plastic

**plastic cement** *n* : a material in a plastic state used to seal narrow openings often reinforced with asbestos or other fibers

**plastic cream** *n* : cream that has been centrifuged at high speed causing it to form an oil-in-water emulsion

**plastic deformation** *or* **plastic flow** *n* : a permanent deformation or change in shape of a solid body without fracture under the action of a sustained force ⟨small changes in the density of crystals due to *plastic deformation* —Louise R. Smoluchowski⟩ ⟨*plastic flow* of crystalline rocks —*Jour. of Geol.*⟩

**plastic foam** *n* : EXPANDED PLASTIC

**plas·ti·cim·e·ter** \ˌplastəˈsiməd·ə(r)\ *n* [*plasticity* + *-meter*] : a device for measuring plasticity (as of cement, lime pastes, mortars)

**Plas·ti·cine** \ˈplastəˌsēn, -aas-, -ȧs-\ *trademark* — used for a modeling paste

**plas·ti·cism** \-ˌsizəm\ *n* -S [²*plastic* + *-ism*] : the theory or practice of plastic art

**plas·tic·i·ty** \plaˈstisəd·ē, -sətē, -i\ *n* -ES **1** : the quality or state of being plastic : capacity for being molded or altered ⟨the great adaptability and ~ of man —Curt Stern⟩ **2** : the ability to retain a shape attained by pressure deformation; *specif* : the ability of particles to be displaced relatively to one another without at the same time being removed from their sphere of attraction — compare ELASTICITY **3** : the capacity of an organism for adjustment to different kinds of habitats ⟨ants exhibit ~ in building habits —*Ecology*⟩

**plasticity index** *n* : difference in moisture content of soils between the liquid and plastic limits expressed in percentage

**plas·ti·ci·za·tion** \ˌplastəsəˈzāshən, -laas-,-lais-, -ˌsīˈz-\ *n* -S : the process of plasticizing or the state of being plasticized; *specif* : BREAKDOWN 6 b

**plas·ti·cize** \ˈ≈≈ˌsīz\ *vt* -ED/-ING/-S *see -ize in Explan Notes* [²*plastic* + *-ize*] : to make plastic; *specif* : to break down (sense 3 b)

**plas·ti·ciz·er** \-zə(r)\ *n* -S : one that plasticizes; *specif* : a chemical substance added to natural and synthetic rubbers and resins to impart flexibility, workability, or distensibility — compare SOFTENER

**plastic magnesia** *n* : MAGNESIUM OXYCHLORIDE CEMENT

**plastic operation** *n* : an operation in plastic surgery

**plastic patent** *n* : a material resembling patent leather made usu. from vinyl resins

**plastic plate** *n* : a letterpress printing plate made from a molded plastic

**plastics** *pl of* PLASTIC

**plastic sulfur** *n* : sulfur in an amorphous form obtained usu. by pouring boiling sulfur into cold water and composed of molecules that are long chains of sulfur atoms

**plastic surgeon** *n* : a surgeon skilled in plastic surgery

**plastic surgery** *n* : the branch of surgery concerned with the repair or restoration of lost, injured, or deformed parts of the body chiefly by transfer of tissue

**plas·tid** \ˈplastəd\ *also* **plas·tide** \", -ˌstīd\ *n* -S [ISV, fr. Gk *plastides*, pl. of *plastis*, fem. of *plastēs* sculptor, molder, fr. *plastos* formed, molded; orig. formed as G *plastiden*, pl. — more at PLASTIC] : any of various small bodies of specialized protoplasm lying in the cytoplasm of cells (as those of plants and some protozoans), serving in many cases as organs or centers of special metabolic activities, and now generally regarded as persistent cell constituents multiplying by self-division — see CHLOROPLAST, CHROMOPLAST, LEUCOPLAST — **plas·tid·i·al** \(ˈ)plas¦tidēəl\ *adj*

**plas·tid·i·um** \plaˈstidēəm\ *n, pl* **plastid·ia** \-dēə\ [NL, fr. ISV *plastid*] : PLASTID

**plas·ti·dome** \ˈplastəˌdōm\ *n* -S [ISV *plastid* + *-ome*; orig. formed in F] : the plastids of a cell regarded as a functional unit

**plas·ti·do·zoa** \ˌplastədōˈzōə\ [NL, fr. ISV *plastid* + *-zoa*] *syn of* PROTOZOA

**plas·tid·u·lar** \(ˈ)plaˈstijələ(r)\ *adj* [ISV *plastidule* + *-ar*] : of or relating to a plastidule

**plas·tid·ule** \ˈplastəˌd(y)ül\ *n* -s [ISV *plastid* + *-ule*; orig. formed as G *plastidul*] **1** : a hypothetical ultimate unit of protoplasm : ALTMANN'S GRANULES **2** : a structural subunit of a plastid

**-plasties** *pl of* -PLASTY

**plas·ti·fi·ca·tion** \ˌplastəfəˈkāshən\ *n* -s [fr. *plastify*, after such pairs as E *identify: identification*] : PLASTICIZATION

**plas·ti·fy** \ˈplastəˌfī\ *vt* -ED/-ING/-ES [²*plastic* + *-fy*] : PLASTICIZE

**plas·ti·gel** \-ˌjel\ *n* [²*plastic* + *gel*] : a very viscous substance (as a paste resembling putty in consistency) obtained by adding a thickening agent to a plastisol

**plastiline** *also* **plastilina** *var of* PLASTELINE

**plas·tin** \ˈplastən\ *n* -s [ISV *plast-* (fr. Gk *plastos*) + *-in*; prob. orig. formed in G] **1** : an acidophilic component of protoplasm more or less coextensive with the presumed highly polymerized protein framework of cytoplasm and nucleus **2** : the substance of the true nucleolus

**plas·ti·noid** \ˈplastəˌnȯid\ *adj* [*plastin* + *-oid*] : resembling plastin

**plas·tique** \plaˈstēk\ *n* -s [F, lit., plastic, fr. MF — more at PLASTIC] **1** : slow changes of position like moving sculpture without marked rhythm or dramatic theme in dancing **2** : the technique of statuesque posing in dancing

**plas·ti·sol** \ˈplastəˌsȯl, -sōl\ *n* -s [²*plastic* + *-sol* (as in *hydrosol*)] : a relatively viscous dispersion of a powdered thermoplastic resin in a liquid plasticizer used chiefly in coatings, films, and molded products ⟨vinyl ~s⟩ — compare ORGANOSOL

**plasto-** *comb form* [Gk, fr. *plastos* formed, molded] **1** : formation : development ⟨*plasto*chron⟩ ⟨*plasto*type⟩ **2** : plasticity : plastic ⟨*plasto*meter⟩ ⟨*plasto*mer⟩ **3** : cytoplasm ⟨*plasto*gamy⟩ ⟨*plasto*mere⟩ **4** : plastid ⟨*plasto*gene⟩

**plas·to·chron** \ˈplastəˌkrän\ *n* -s [*plasto-* + Gk *chronos* time] : a unit of time corresponding to the interval between two successive similar, periodically repeated events (as the emergence of leaf primordia at any two successive nodes in a stem apex) — **plas·to·chron·ic** \ˌ==ˈkränik\ *adj*

**plas·to·cyte** \ˈ==ˌsīt\ *n* [*plasto-* + *-cyte*] : BLOOD PLATELET — **plas·to·cyt·ic** \ˌ==ˈsid·ik\ *adj*

**plas·to·gam·ic** \ˌ==ˈgamik\ *adj* : of or relating to plastogamy

**plas·tog·a·my** \plaˈstägəmē\ *n* -ES [ISV *plasto-* + *-gamy*] : PLASMOGAMY

**plas·to·gene** \ˈplastəˌjēn\ *n* [*plasto-* + *-gene*] : a submicroscopic factor or determiner reported to be present in the plastids in plant cells and to influence physiological and hereditary phenomena of the plastids — compare GENE, PLASMAGENE, PLASMON

**plas·tome** \ˈplaˌstōm\ *n* -s [by contr.] : PLASTIDOME

**plas·to·mer** \ˈplastəmə(r)\ *n* -s [*plasto-* + *-mer*] : a relatively tough usu. hard and rigid polymeric substance — compare ELASTOMER, ²PLASTIC 3

**plas·to·mere** \ˌmi(ə)r\ *n* -s [*plasto-* + *-mere*] : CHONDRIOMERE — compare CYTOMERE

**plas·tom·e·ter** \plaˈstäməd·ə(r), -mətə-\ *n* [*plasto-* + *-meter*] : an instrument for measuring plasticity or viscosity (as of rubber) — **plas·to·met·ric** \ˌplastōˈme·trik\ *adj* — **plas·tom·e·try** \plaˈstämə·trē, -ri\ *n* -ES

**plas·to·some** \ˈplastəˌsōm\ *n* -s [ISV *plasto-* + *-some*] : CHONDRIOSOME

**plas·to·type** \-ˌtīp\ *n* [*plasto-* + *type*] : an artificial specimen cast or molded directly from a type specimen (as of a fossil)

**plas·tral** \ˈplastrəl, -laas-\ *adj* [*plastron* + *-al*] : of or relating to a plastron

**plas·tron** \-trən\ *n* -s [MF, fr. OIt *piastrone*, aug. of *piastra* thin metal plate — more at PIASTER] **1 a** : a metal breastplate worn under the hauberk **b** : a quilted pad worn during fencing practice to protect the chest, waist, and side on which the weapon is held **2 a** (1) : the ventral part of the shell of a tortoise or turtle consisting typically of nine symmetrically placed bones overlaid by horny plates (2) : the ventral armor of other animals (as some extinct amphibians or glyptodonts) **b** : the modified posterior interambulacral area on the under side of a heart urchin **c** : the ventral plate of the cephalothorax of a spider — compare STERNUM **3** : a separate or attached front for a garment usu. extending from neck to waist: as **a** : a trimming like a bib for a woman's dress **b** : DICKEY 1 b **4** : a thin film of air held by hydrofuge hairs of certain aquatic insects

**plasts** *pl of* PLAST

**-plasts** *pl of* -PLAST

**-plasty** \ˌplastē, -laas-, -lais-, -ti\ *n comb form* -ES [F *-plastie*, fr. Gk *-plastia* form, mold, fr. *-plastos* -plast + *-ia* -y] : plastic surgery ⟨dermato*plasty*⟩ ⟨auto*plasty*⟩ ⟨cine*plasty*⟩

**-plasy** — see -PLASIA

**¹plat** \ˈplat, *usu* -ad·+V\ *n* -s [OE *plaett*; akin to MD *plat* slap, ME *platten* to slap, MHG *platzen*; prob. all of imit. origin] *chiefly dial* : BUFFET, SLAP; *also* : a slapping sound

**²plat** \"\ *adj* [ME *plat, platte*, fr. MF *plat*, fr. OF — more at PLATE] **1** *obs* : FLAT, LEVEL **2** *chiefly dial* : PLAIN, STRAIGHTFORWARD

**³plat** \"\ *vt* **platted; platted; platting; plats** [ME *platten*, fr. *plat, platte*, adj., flat] *chiefly dial* : FLATTEN

**⁴plat** \"\ *n* -s [ME, fr. MF, fr. *plat*, adj., flat] **1** *archaic* : a flat surface or thing (as the flat of a sword, a flat piece of stone, the sole of the foot) **2** *archaic* **a** : PLACE, LOCALITY **b** : an expanse of open level land : PLATEAU, TABLELAND **3** : a platform, floor, or surface in or about a mine used esp. for loading and unloading ore

**⁵plat** \"\ *vt* **platted; platted; platting; plats** [ME *platen*, alter. (perh. influenced by ³*plat*) of *plaiten* to plait — more at PLAIT] : to form by braiding or interweaving : PLAIT

**⁶plat** \"\ *n* -s : platted work : BRAID, PLAIT

**⁷plat** \"\ *n* -s [ME *plaite*, fr. MF *plate*, fem. of *plat* something flat, fr. *plat*, adj. flat] : a small flat-bottomed, square-sterned rowboat

**⁸plat** \"\ *n* -s [prob. alter. (influenced by ⁴*plat*) of *plot* (ground)] **1** : a small piece of ground : PLOT, QUADRAT **2** : a plan, map, or chart ⟨started forth with a ~ of my destination that I made on a large sheet of notepaper —W.A. White⟩: as **a** : a precise and detailed plan showing the actual or proposed divisions, special features, or uses of a piece of land (as a town or town site or a real estate subdivision) **b** : an accurately scaled diagram showing boundaries and subdivisions of a piece of land together with data required for accurate identification of the various parts **3** *obs* : a plan, scheme, or outline (as of a course of action or a work of fiction or art) : ARRANGEMENT, DESIGN **4** *obs* **a** : a plan for securing adequate stipends from the endowments of the pre-Reformation church for the ministry of the Reformed Church of Scotland **b** : a commission in charge of such a plan

**⁹plat** \"\ *vt* **platted; platted; platting; plats** **1 a** *obs* : to lay out : PLAN, ARRANGE **b** : to lay out a plan for the future development of (as a town or subdivision) usu. with a formally drafted plat ⟨San Francisco was *platted* as if it were a prairie town —*Time*⟩ **2** : to make a plat of ⟨an entire project is laid out and *platted* —*Amer. Builder*⟩

**¹⁰plat** \ˈplä\ *n, pl* **plats** \-ä(z)\ [F, lit., plate, fr. *plat*, adj. flat] : a dish of food : food dressed for table

**plat-** — see PLATY-

**plat** *abbr* **1** platform **2** platoon

**plat·a·can·tho·my·i·dae** \ˌplad·əˌkan(t)thəˈmīəˌdē\ *n pl, cap* [NL, fr. *Platacanthomys*, type genus (fr. *platy-* + *acanth-* + *-mys*) + *-idae*] : a small family of myomorph rodents comprising the Asiatic spiny dormice and related forms

**pla·tae·an** \plaˈtēən\ *adj, usu cap* [L *plataeeus* plataean (fr. *Plataeae* Plataea, fr. Gk *Plataiai*) + E *-an*] : of or relating to Plataea, a city of Boeotia in ancient Greece

**plat·a·le·i·dae** \ˌplad·əˈlēəˌdē\ *n pl, cap* [NL, fr. *Platalea*, type genus (fr. L *platalea* spoonbill) + *-idae*; akin to Gk *platys* flat, broad — more at PLACE] : a family of birds (order Ciconiiformes) that consists of the spoonbills and is often ranked as a subfamily of Threskiornithidae

**plat·a·le·i·form** \ˌ==ˈ==ˌfȯrm\ *adj* [L *platalea* spoonbill + E *-iform*] : resembling a spoonbill : SPOON-BILLED

**plat·an** *or* **plat·ane** \ˈplatᵊn\ *n* -s [ME *platan*, fr. L *platanus*] : ²PLANE

**plat·a·na·ce·ae** \ˌplatᵊnˈāsēˌē\ *n pl, cap* [NL, fr. *Platanus*, type genus + *-aceae*] : a family of trees (order Rosales) coextensive with the genus *Platanus* — **plat·a·na·ceous** \ˌ==ˈāshəs\ *adj*

**plat·a·nist** \ˈplatᵊnəst\ *n* -s [NL *Platanista*] : an Indian susu

**plat·a·nis·ta** \ˌplatᵊnˈistə\ *n, cap* [NL, fr. L, a fish of the Ganges, fr. Gk *platanistēs*; akin to Gk *platē* oar, *platys* flat, broad] : the type genus of Platanistidae

**plat·a·nis·ti·dae** \-təˌdē\ *n pl, cap* [NL, fr. *Platanista*, type genus + *-idae*] : a family of toothed whales comprising the susu and related extinct forms

**pla·tan·na** \pləˈtanə\ *or* **plat·hand·er** \ˈplatˌhandə(r)\ *n* -s [Afrik *platanna*, prob. alter. of *plat-hander* one who is flat-handed, fr. D, fr. *plat* flat (fr. MD, fr. OF) + *hander* (fr. *hand*, fr. MD); akin to OHG *hant* hand — more at PLATE, HAND] : a frog (*Xenopus laevis*) of southern Africa that has strongly clawed feet

**pla·ta·no** \ˈplädə(ˌ)nō\ *n* -s [Sp *plátano* — more at PLANTAIN] : BANANA, PLANTAIN

**plat·a·nus** \ˈplad·ənəs\ *n* [NL, fr. L, plane tree — more at PLANE] **1** *cap* : a genus of trees (family Platanaceae) comprising the plane trees, being native in temperate regions, and having light brown often deciduous flaky bark, large palmately lobed leaves, and small monoecious flowers in globose heads — see LONDON PLANE, SYCAMORE 3a **2** -ES : any tree of the genus *Platanus*

**platband** \ˈ=,=\ *n* [F *plate-bande*, lit., flat band, fr. MF, fr. *plate*, fem. of *plat* flat + *bande* band, strip — more at BAND] **1 a** : a horizontal band that is a member of a building and that takes the form of a lintel course, a flat arch, or one of a group of moldings **b** : ARCHITRAVE, EPISTYLE **c** : a list or fillet between the flutings of a column **2** : a border of flowers or turf

**platch** \ˈplach\ *vb* -ED/-ING/-ES [prob. imit.] *Scot* : SPLASH, SMEAR

**plat du jour** \ˌplädəˈzhü(ə)r\ *n, pl* **plats du jour** \"\ [F, lit., dish of the day] : a dish that is emphasized as a feature of a restaurant bill of fare on a particular day

**¹plate** \ˈplāt, *usu* -ād·+V\ *n* -s [ME, fr. OF, fr. *plate*, fem. of *plat*, adj., flat, fr. (assumed) VL *plattus*, prob. fr. Gk *platys* flat, broad — more at PLACE] **1 a** (1) : a smooth usu. nearly flat and relatively thin piece of metal or other material : a substantial slice or lamina (2) : a perfectly flat sheet of material of uniform thickness throughout; *esp* : a sheet of rolled iron or steel usu. a quarter of an inch or more thick (3) : a flat circular piece usu. of metal that is either perforated or provided with bubble caps and that is set horizontally as one of a series at specified distances one above another esp. in a fractionating column or tower for effecting intimate contact between rising vapors and condensed liquid falling from plate to plate — called also *tray* **b** (1) : forged, rolled, or cast metal in sheets usu. thicker than ¼ inch (2) : a very thin layer of usu. precious metal deposited on a surface of base metal by plating (as by electroplating) ⟨the ~ has worn off these spoons⟩ ⟨quadruple ~ silverware⟩ **c** (1) : one of the broad pieces of metal often on a backing (as of leather) that were used to reinforce and complete armor of linked mail (2) : one of the thin pieces making up plate armor; *also* : armor of such plates : PLATE ARMOR **d** (1) : a lamina or plaque that forms part of an animal body ⟨a carapace of bony ~s⟩; *esp* : an enlarged scale (as on the belly of a snake) (2) : the thin under portion of the forequarter of beef; *esp* : the back half of this cut as distinguished from the brisket — see BEEF illustration **e** : slaty rock or shale (as in a mine) **f** *chiefly Brit* : PLATE RAIL 1; *broadly* : any railroad rail **g** : a very light horseshoe without calks that is used esp. for racing **h** (1) : HOME PLATE (2) : a rectangular slab of whitened rubber 6 inches by 24 inches in size that is anchored flush with the ground at the spot where a softball or baseball pitcher must stand when delivering the ball to the batter — called also *box, pitcher's plate, rubber, slab*; see BASEBALL illustration **i** : the belly or the back of a violin **j** : a square or oblong piece of fur composed usu. of waste fur and small inferior pieces that are matched and sewn together and used for inexpensive garments or linings **2** [ME; partly fr. OF *plate* piece of silver, piece of metal; partly fr. OSp *plata* silver, money, metal plate, fr. (assumed) VL *plattus* flat] **a** (1) *obs* : a piece of money; *esp* : a coin of silver (2) : Spanish silver money (3) : a piece of plate money **b** : precious metal; *esp* : silver bullion ⟨the Spanish ~ ships⟩ ⟨melting coin into ~⟩ **c** : a heraldic roundel of silver **3** [ME, fr. MF, fr. fem. of OF *plat*, adj., flat] **a** (1) : domestic hollow ware (as dishes, flagons, cups) of gold or silver (2) : such vessels of base metals or of plated ware (3) *chiefly Brit* : SILVER 4 **b** (1) : a shallow usu. circular vessel (as of china, wood, or plastic) from which food is eaten (2) : an often larger vessel (as a platter or vegetable dish) from which food is served ⟨pass the meat ~⟩ ⟨a cake ~⟩ **c** (1) : an individual serving on a plate : PLATEFUL ⟨have a ~ of spaghetti⟩ (2) : a main course of a meal served in individual portions on the plate from which it is to be eaten ⟨the special ~ includes liver and onions, potatoes, with gravy, and green salad⟩ (3) : the food and service supplied to one person at a particular meal or social affair ⟨a fund-raising dinner at $100 a ~⟩ **d** (1) : a prize (as a cup or other piece of plate) given to the winner in an athletic or other contest (2) : a sports competition for a prize; *esp* : a horse race in which the contestants compete for a prize rather than for personally wagered stakes **e** (1) : a dish or pouch passed (as in a church) in taking collections (2) : a collection taken for a specific purpose or particular organization ⟨the ~ was a generous one⟩ **f** (1) : a flat glass dish used chiefly for culturing microorganisms; *esp* : PETRI DISH (2) : a film of more or less solid culture medium or a culture contained in such a dish **4 a** : a flat thin smooth piece (as of metal) on or from which something is or is to be embossed, molded, engraved, grained, deposited, or written ⟨a ~ for etching⟩ **b** : a surface from which printing is done: as (1) : a stereotype, electrotype, or plastic plate molded from a page of letterpress matter (2) : a metal or plastic sheet from which an inked image is transferred to a blanket (as in photo-offset) or direct to the paper (as in lithography) (3) : a flat and comparatively thin piece of copper or steel engraved in intaglio (as for banknotes or calling cards) — compare DIE 6h (4) : PHOTOENGRAVING **c** : a sheet of glass, metal, porcelain, or other material coated with a light-sensitive photographic emulsion; *usu* : DRY PLATE **d** : a copper plate coated with silver amalgam that is used in the amalgam process of extracting metals **e** (1) : the usu. flat or grid-formed anode of an electron tube at which electrons collect (2) : a metallic grid with its interstices filled with active material that forms one of the structural units of a storage cell or battery **5** : a supporting or reinforcing element (as of a building): as **a** (1) : a horizontal timber laid on a wall or supported on posts or corbels to carry the trusses of a roof or the rafters directly (2) : either of the horizontal members at the top and bottom of a stud partition between which the studs are placed (3) : a supporting sill (as one over or under an opening) ⟨window ~s⟩ **b** : a heavy framed mine timber **c** : the part of an artificial set of teeth that fits to the mouth and holds the teeth in place; *broadly* : DENTURE **d** : a metal tab attached to the sole or heel of a shoe as a reinforcement intended esp. to minimize wear — compare CLEAT, HEEL PLATE, TOEPLATE **e** : the flat metal framework of a timepiece containing the bearing holes and jewels into which its wheel-pivots fit **f** : the metal structure that supports the strings of a piano **g** : a flat metal surface of or attached to a machine by which work is held fast (as for locating, indexing, leveling, turning, or machining) **h** : a thin flat narrow piece of metal (as stainless steel) that is used to repair bone defects or fractures **6** : a relatively large illustration ⟨prepared the ~s on bristol board⟩; *esp* : a full-page illustration printed on different paper from accompanying text pages ⟨a book with color ~s⟩ **7** [by shortening] **a** : BOOKPLATE **b** : FASHION PLATE **c** : PLATE GLASS **8** : a small cooking stove that is usu. heated with gas or electricity, has one or more heating units, and lacks an oven : HOT PLATE 2

**²plate** \"\ *vb* -ED/-ING/-S [ME *platen*, fr. *plate*, n.] *vt* **1** : to cover or equip with plate or plates: as **a** : to overlay with metal plates ⟨the first ironclads were wooden ships *plated* with iron⟩; *esp* : to arm with armor plate **b** : to cover with an adherent layer (as of metal) mechanically, chemically, or electrically; *also* : to deposit (as a layer of metal) on the surface of something by such means **c** : to shoe (a horse) with plates **d** : to adorn or cover with metal plate ⟨~ a harness⟩ **e** : to fit with a specified kind of plate ⟨*plated* the books with her new bookplate⟩ **2** : to form into or prepare as a plate: as **a** : to beat (as metal) into thin flat sheets **b** *printing* (1) : to make a plate from ⟨for long press runs type forms are often *plated* —R.R.Karch⟩ : make plates for ⟨~ a book⟩ (2) : to equip (as a printing press) with a plate or plates — sometimes used with *up* **c** : to impart a finish to (a sheet of paper) by subjecting to very high pressure between sheets of the material whose surface is to be duplicated **d** : to inoculate and culture (microorganisms) upon a plate; *also* : to distribute (an inoculum) upon a plate or plates for cultivation — often used with *out* **e** : to collect (a particular stamp) in all of the positions that were on the original sheet, identifying the positions by a philatelic study of matching characteristics (as perforations, plate numbers, printing defects) **3 a** : to fix or secure with a plate or plates **b** : to repair (as a fractured bone) with metal plates **4 a** : to knit or weave (fabric) with a face and back of different colors or fibers **b** : to spin (yarn) with a core and outside wrapping of different fibers **~** *vi* : to perform the action of plating or undergo the process of being plated ⟨a very pure silver that ~s out well⟩ ⟨learned to ~ expertly while still a boy⟩

**plate-and-frame filter** \ˈ=;=;=-\ *n* : a filter press in which the spaces for the caked solid matter are formed by inserting hollow frames between each pair of plates instead of providing the plates with raised edges

**plate armor** *n* **1** : body armor of plates of metal — see ARMOR illustration; compare MAIL 1 b **2** : strong metal plate used esp. for protecting naval vessels or forts

**¹pla·teau** \(ˈ)plaˈtō *sometimes* pləˈt-\ *n, pl* **plateaus** *or* **plateaux** \-ōz\ [F, fr. MF, fr. *plat* flat — more at PLATE] **1 a** (1) : a flat and often galleried ornamental dish or salver (as for a tea service or condiments) (2) : an ornamental plaque (3) : a table top; *esp* : a removable and usu. decorated top (as of marble or inlay) (4) : an ornamental shelf (as in a whatnot) **b** : a woman's hat of a flat or plate-shaped style **2 a** : a usu. extensive land area having a relatively level surface raised sharply above adjacent land on at least one side and often dissected by canyons : TABLELAND ⟨the Columbia lava ~ in eastern Washington and Oregon⟩ ⟨the ~ region of central Bolivia⟩ — compare MESA **b** : a similar undersea feature **3 a** : a region of little or no change in the dependent variable of a graph; *esp* : a horizontal section of a learning curve indicating neither progress nor decline **b** : a relatively stable level, period, or condition; *esp* : one showing cessation or minimization of cyclical phenomena or of fluctuations up or down ⟨a price ~ interrupting an inflationary spiral⟩ ⟨output seems to have reached a ~⟩

**²plateau** \"\ *adj, usu cap* **1** : ANASAZI **2** : of or relating to the Indians of the No. American plateau area between the Cascade mountains and the Rocky mountains south of the great bend of the Fraser river or to their seminomadic food-gathering culture

**³plateau** \"\ *vi* -ED/-ING/-S : to reach a period or phase of stability : form a plateau : level off ⟨after initial logarithmic progress growth ~ed sharply⟩

**plateau-basalt** *n* : basalt extruded on continental areas that lacks olivine and may contain quartz

**plateband** \ˈ=,=\ *n* [by alter.] : PLATBAND 1

**plate battery** *n* : B BATTERY

**plate block** *n* : a plate number block

**plate bolt** *n* : a bolt grommeted into the foundation of a building for securing a sill or plate

**plate bone** *n* : SCAPULA

**plate budding** *n* : plant budding in which a rectangular scion with bud is inserted under a longitudinal flap of bark on the stock in such a manner as to cover the exposed wood on the stock

**plate bulb** *n* : a steel or iron plate with a thickened edge of bulbous section

**plate calender** *or* **plate-glazing calender** *n* : PLATER

**plate circuit** *n* : an electric circuit including the plate and cathode of an electron tube

**plate clutch** *n* : DISK CLUTCH

**plate column** *n* : PLATE TOWER

**plate count** *n* : a determination of the degree of bacterial contamination of a sample (as of milk or semen) made by enumeration after a period of incubation of the colonies appearing in a plate that has been inoculated with a suitable dilution of the sample

**plate culture** *n* : a culture (as of bacteria) contained on a plate; *also* : the cultivation of such a culture

**plate current** *n* : a current flowing in the plate circuit of an electron tube that is equal to the electron flow from cathode to plate

**plate cut** *n* : a notch in the undersurface of a rafter at the point where it seats on the plate

**plate cylinder** *n* : the cylinder of a rotary printing press to which the printing plates are attached

**plat·ed** \ˈplād·əd, -lātəd\ *adj* [ME, fr. past part. of *platen* to plate — more at PLATE] **1** : covered or furnished with plates or with metal (as for defense, ornament, or strength) **2** : overlaid with a different and richer material (as gold or silver) ⟨~ forks⟩ ⟨~ ware⟩ **3** : consisting of or made into thin sheets **4** *of yarn or knitted goods* : having a surface of one color or kind and a backing or core of another

**plated leather** *n* : leather that has been pressed under heat and heavy pressure to improve appearance and give polished surface; *also* : leather grained by embossing

**plated lobster** *n* : CRAYLET

**plated parquet** *n* : parquetry in which the inlays (as of selected hardwoods) are fixed on a framed deal backing

**plate finish** *n* : a finish that is applied to paper by plating; *also* : a similar finish that is produced by other means (as web glazing)

**plate-finish** \ˈ=,=\ *vt* [fr. *plate finish*, n.] : PLATE 2c

**plate·ful** \ˈplātˌfu̇l\ *n, pl* **platefuls** *also* **platesful** \-tˌfu̇lz, -ts,fu̇l\ : a quantity to fill a plate; *also* : a generous serving (as of food)

**plate gear** *n* : a gear having a solid web of material between the hub and rim

**plate girder** *or* **plate beam** *n* : a built-up girder resembling an I beam in cross section but having a rolled steel plate for a web and flanges that usu. consist of angles alone or angles and plates

**plate glass** *n* : flat glass of high quality formed by a process of continuous or semicontinuous rolling or sometimes by the rolling of metal cast on a table and then ground and polished so that the surfaces are plane and parallel

**plate-glaze** \ˈ=,=\ *vt* : PLATE 2c

**plateholder** \ˈ=,==\ *n* **1** : one that holds plates; *esp* : one that places plates for molds **2** : a flat lighttight container in which a light-sensitive photographic plate may be held in a camera and may be exposed by removal of a slide — see CAMERA illustration

**plate horse** *n* : PLATER 3

**plate keel** *n* : a ship's keel made of a flat plate or plates — compare BAR KEEL

**platelayer** \ˈ=,=(=)\ *n* [¹*plate* + *layer*] *Brit* : a railroad laborer who lays and maintains rails : TRACKLAYER

**plate·less** \ˈplātləs\ *adj* : having or requiring no plate or plates ⟨~ printing⟩

**plate·let** \-lət\ *n* -s [ISV *plate* + *-let*] : a minute flattened body; *specif* : BLOOD PLATELET

**plate letter** *n* : a letter on a note or piece of paper money indicating the position the note had on the printing plate

**platelike** \ˈ=,=\ *adj* : resembling a plate esp. in smooth flat form ⟨a ~ scale on the head of a lizard⟩

**plat·el·min·thes** \ˌplad·ˌelˈmin(t)thēz, -n,thēz\ *syn of* PLATYHELMINTHES

**plate lock** *n* **1** : a lock having the outer case of hard wood **2** : a lock whose works are pivoted on a metal plate

**plate·man** \ˈplātmən\ *n, pl* **platemen** **1** : MIDDLER 3 **2** : a worker at the breaker of a coal mine who picks rocks and oversize lumps from the coal before it is conveyed for further treatment or loading **3** : AMALGAMATOR 2b

**[1]plate mark** *n* **1 :** HALLMARK **2 :** a depression of an etching or engraving made by the pressure of the edge of the plate upon the dampened paper while printing **3 :** an impression from a flat uninked plate to smooth a rough area prior to printing or to produce a blind panel
**[2]plate mark** *vt* [*[1]plate mark*] **:** to impress with a plate mark
**plate meristem** *n* **:** a meristem in which growth occurs chiefly through cell division in two planes resulting in a flat plate of tissue — compare MASS MERISTEM, RIB MERISTEM
**plate metal** *n* **:** refined iron run in molds and broken up for remelting or for use in a mix
**plate mill** *n* **:** a rolling mill for producing relatively thick flat metal products
**plate modulation** *n* **:** modulation in radio in which the modulating voltage is introduced into the plate circuit of the tube which provides the carrier
**plate money** *n* **:** money issued in Sweden in the 17th and 18th centuries consisting of large rectangular pieces of copper with values in daler denominations stamped in the corners and in the center
**plat·en** \ˈplatᵊn\ *n* -s *often attrib* [MF *plateine*, fr. *plate* thin plate, plaque (fr. OF, fr. fem. of *plat*, adj., flat) + *-ine* — more at PLATE] **1 a :** a flat plate (as of metal) usu. designed to press or to be pressed against by something: as (1) **:** a flat surface (as on a hand press or platen press) that presses the paper against the form (2) **:** the movable table of a planer or similar machine tool (3) **:** either of two plates of a testing machine that apply a load to a specimen under test (4) **:** a diaphragm or plate in a molding machine against which the flask is forced by pressure from below (5) **:** a sometimes heated flat surface against which materials are pressed for flattening, curing, or laminating (6) **:** a circular flanged rotating plate in a phonograph turntable upon which a record rests during reproduction **b :** a hard roll that serves as a backing against which the paper is pressed when the typebars of a typewriter strike to make an imprint **2** [by alter.] *obs* **:** PATEN 1
**platen press** *n* **:** a small printing press in which a platen presses the paper against a form secured to an opposed vertical flat bed — called also *job press;* compare CYLINDER PRESS, ROTARY PRESS
**plate number** *n* **1 :** a number that is the serial number of the plate from which a sheet of postage stamps is printed and that appears in the four margins of the printed sheet, at least once on each pane **2 :** a stamp or block of stamps with plate number attached
**plate nut** *n* **:** NUT PLATE
**plate organ** *n* **:** an insect sense organ covered by an integumentary plate
**plat·e·o·sau·rus** \ˌplad·ēōˈsȯrəs\ *n, cap* [NL, fr. Gk *platē* oar + NL *-saurus;* akin to Gk *platys* flat, broad — more at PLACE] **:** a genus of moderate-sized chiefly bipedal Triassic saurischian dinosaurs on the ancestral line of the Sauropoda
**plate oven** *n* **:** a double oven one part of which is used for heating split cylinders of sheet or cylinder glass before flattened into sheets and the other chamber for annealing the sheets
**plate paper** *n* **:** a soft paper with a smooth dull finish used for printing fine-line hand-engraved plates and woodcuts
**plate press** *n* **:** a press with a flat carriage and a roller used for printing from engraved steel or copper plates
**plate printing** *n* **:** printing from engraved steel or copper plates
**plate proof** *n* **:** a first or other proof taken from a plated letterpress printing surface
**plat·er** \ˈplād·ə(r), -lātə-\ *n* -s **1 :** one that plates: as **a** (1) **:** a worker that plates metal or metal objects with gold or silver (2) **:** one that applies a protective coating of nickel or similar substance to metal objects by means of an electrolytic bath — called also *bath plater, electroplater, vatman* (3) **:** one that coats plastic articles with metal plate (4) **:** a textile worker that plates fabric or yarn **b :** an operator of a machine for impressing the weave pattern of linen fabric onto paper **c :** a worker that presses hat brims by hand **2 :** a machine for plating paper — called also *plate calender* **3 a :** a horse that runs chiefly in purse races and esp. in claiming races **b :** an inferior racehorse
**plate rail** *n* **1** *chiefly Brit* **:** a primitive type of flat rail of cast iron with an upright ledge on the outer edge to keep wheels on the rail **2 :** a rail or narrow shelf along the upper part of a wall to hold plates or ornaments
**plate resistance** *n* **:** the ratio of the potential difference between plate and cathode of a vacuum tube to the resulting current
**plat·er·esque** \ˌplad·əˈresk\ *also* **plat·e·res·co** \ˌ==ˈre(ˌ)skō\ *adj* [Sp *plateresco,* fr. *platero* silversmith (fr. *plata* silver) + *-esco* -esque — more at PLATE] **:** relating to or being a 16th century Spanish architectural style distinguished by a wealth and richness of ornamentation suggestive of silver plate

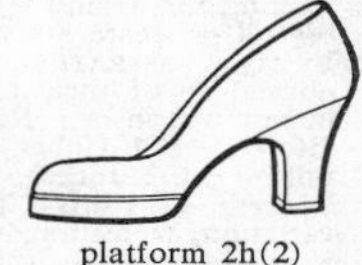
plate rail 2

**plater finish** *n* **:** PLATE FINISH
**plateroom** \ˈ==ˌ=\ *n, Brit* **:** a room set aside for the storage of table and other plate
**plates** *pl of* PLATE, *pres 3d sing of* PLATE
**platesful** *pl of* PLATEFUL
**plate ship** *n* **:** TREASURE SHIP; *esp* **:** one of the Spanish treasure ships from America
**plate system** *n* **:** a system of quick freezing in which the freezing coils are placed in platelike arrangements
**plate tower** *n* **:** a tower or column provided with plates for use esp. in fractional distillation (as of petroleum distillates) — called also *plate column*
**plate tracery** *n* **:** decorative architectural tracery consisting of a series of patterns cut through a flat plate of stone
**plate tumbler** *n* **:** SLIDING TUMBLER
**plate valve** *n* **:** an automatic valve in which a lightweight thin disk, strip, or ribbon is constrained to move between the valve seat and valve cover according to variations in fluid pressure on its sides
**plate vein** *n, archaic* **:** the cephalic vein of a horse
**plate voltage** *or* **plate potential** *n* **:** the constant component of the potential difference between plate and cathode in an electron tube
**plateway** \ˈ=ˌ=\ *n* [*[1]plate + way*] **:** a railway having plate rails
**plate wheel** *n* **:** a wheel the rim and hub of which are connected by a continuous plate of metal
**platework** \ˈ=ˌ=\ *n* **:** plated work
**plat-eye** \ˈ=ˌ=\ *n* [*plat* of unknown origin] **:** a ghost, spook, or evil spirit with fiery eyes
**[1]plat·form** \ˈplatˌfȯrm\ *n, often attrib* [MF *plate-forme,* lit., flat form, fr. *plate* (fem. of *plat* flat, fr. OF) + *forme* form, fr. OF — more at PLATE, FORM] **1 a :** a diagrammatic representation of something on the flat (as a ground plan or map) **b :** a plan of action or statement of policy **:** DESIGN, PATTERN, SCHEME: as (1) **:** a plan of ecclesiastical or religious policy or principles (2) **:** a declaration of the principles on which a group of persons or a party stand and on which they appeal for support; *esp* **:** a declaration of principles and policies of government adopted by a political party or an individual (as a candidate for political office) **2 :** a horizontal flat surface usu. higher than the adjoining area (as of floor or ground): as **a :** a permanent or temporary base for the mounting of guns **b** *obs* **:** a promenade on top of a building or wall **c** *also* **platform deck :** a light partial deck without sheer or crown on a ship **d** (1) **:** a natural or constructed terrace (2) **:** a small level space (as a ledge) on steep rocks (3) **:** a flat or nearly flat area of the earth's solid surface either above or below the surface of the sea that stands above adjacent areas on at least one side and is ordinarily smaller than a plateau — compare CONTINENTAL PLATEAU **e :** a raised flooring (as a stage or dais) in a building on which speakers, theatrical performers, or other persons show themselves to an audience **f :** an elevated ledge or shelf (as of a machine or freight station) used esp. for the reception or transfer of materials **g :** a raised area in either valve of some brachiopods to which the muscles attach **h** (1) *or* **platform sole :** a thick midsole of a shoe made of wood, cork, or other lightweight material and usu. covered with the same material as the upper — see SHOE illustration (2) *or* **platform shoe :** a shoe having a platform sole **3 a** *obs* **:** the site of or area occupied by something (as a building) **b** (1) **:** the grounds for or basis of something (as a decision, proposal, or action) (2) **:** a level of something (as conduct, discussion, or thought) **c** (1) **:** a place for public discussion (as of questions of public interest) **:** a lecture forum **:** LYCEUM ⟨during the ~ season⟩; *also* **:** public discussion of such matters (2) **:** public speaking ⟨a good ~ manner⟩

platform 2h(2)

**[2]platform** \"\ *vb* -ED/-ING/-S *vt* **1** *obs* **:** FORMULATE, OUTLINE **2 :** to furnish with a platform **3 :** to place on or as if on a platform ~ *vi* **:** to speak from or as if from a platform
**plat·form·al·ly** \-məlē\ *adv* **:** in the manner of a public speaker **:** ORATORICALLY
**platform car** *n* **:** FLATCAR
**platformed** *adj* **:** furnished with or formed as a platform **:** level on top
**platform elevator** *n* **:** ELEVATOR 1b
**plat·form·er** \ˈplatˌfȯrmə(r)\ *n* **1 :** a planner or deviser esp. of a political platform **2 :** a platform speaker
**platform frame** *n* **:** a light timber frame for buildings in which a platform is constructed at each floor and the studs for the next floor are erected on this platform usu. with an intervening soleplate — compare BALLOON FRAME
**platform harvester** *n* **:** a corn-harvesting machine having a sled platform or a wheel-mounted platform that carries knives to cut the cornstalks
**Plat·form·ing** \ˈplatˌfȯrmiŋ, -mēŋ\ *trademark* — used for a process for the reforming of gasoline with a supported catalyst containing some platinum that promotes dehydrogenation of naphthenes to aromatic hydrocarbons, isomerization and cracking of paraffin hydrocarbons, and desulfurization
**plat·form·ism** \ˌmizəm\ *n* -s **:** the making of political speeches or the exaggerated bombast characteristic of such speeches
**plat·form·less** \-ˌmləs\ *adj* **:** lacking a platform
**platform pipe** *n* **:** an Amerindian tobacco pipe found in Hopewell sites that has a thin rectangular platform on the center of which the bowl rests
**platform reef** *n* **:** a flat tabula reef more extensive than a patch reef ⟨*platform reefs* are common off the coast of Australia⟩
**platform road** *n, Brit* **:** a station track for loading railroad trains
**platform rocker** *n* **:** a chair that is so sprung on a stable platform as to be capable of motion like that of a conventional rocking chair

platform rocker

**platform scale** *or* **platform balance** *n* **:** a weighing machine with a flat platform on which objects are weighed
**platform shoe** *n* **:** PLATFORM 2h(2)
**platform sole** *n* **:** PLATFORM 2h(1)
**platform spring** *n* **:** a suspension in an automotive vehicle consisting of two longitudinal half-elliptic springs pivoted or shackled to the frame at the forward end and one transverse inverted half-elliptic spring attached to the rear of the two longitudinals by double shackles or crosses
**platform ticket** *n, Brit* **:** a ticket authorizing a person not himself traveling to go on the restricted platform at which trains arrive and depart (as to meet or speed a traveler)
**platform truck** *n* **:** a low-hung four-wheel hand truck without sides or a similar motorized vehicle for transporting heavy material
**plathander** *var of* PLATANNA
**plat·hel·min·thes** \ˌplat,helˈmin(t)thēz,-n,thēz\ *syn of* PLATYHELMINTHES
**plat·ic** \ˈplad·ik\ *adj* [LL *platicus* broad, general, fr. Gk *platikos,* fr. *platos* breadth (fr. *platys* wide, broad, flat) + *-ikos* -ic; fr. the approximation being broad and not exact — more at PLACE] *of the conjunction of two astrologic planets* **:** falling within half the sum of the orbs but not within a single degree — compare PARTILE — **plat·ic·ly** *adv*
**platier** *comparative of* PLATY
**platies** *pl of* PLATY
**platiest** *superlative of* PLATY
**pla·til·la** \pləˈtilə\ *n* -s [Sp, dim. of *plata* silver, fr. OSp — more at PLATE] **:** a white linen fabric formerly made in Silesia
**platin-** *or* **platino-** *comb form* [NL *platinum*] **1 :** platinum ⟨*platino*type⟩ ⟨*platin*iridium⟩ **2 :** platinic acid ⟨*platin*ate⟩
**[1]pla·ti·na** \pləˈtēnə, ˈplatᵊnə\ *n* -s [Sp, platinum — more at PLATINUM] **:** PLATINUM; *esp* **:** crude native platinum
**[2]platina** \"\ *adj* **:** of the color platinum — used esp. of pale bluish gray furs ⟨a fascinating mink-tail print in brown or ~ tones —Lois Long⟩
**platina fox** *n* **:** a pale white-marked bluish gray fox that is a variety of the silver fox developed under domestication
**[1]plat·i·nate** \ˈplatᵊnˌāt\ *n* -s [*platin-* + *-ate*] **:** a salt of platinic acid
**[2]platinate** \"\ *vt* -ED/-ING/-S [*platin-* + *-ate*] **:** PLATINIZE
**platina yellow** *n* **:** GOLD PHEASANT
**pla·tine** \ˈplāˌtīn\ *adj, usu cap* [*Plate* river (Río de la Plata) in Argentina and Uruguay + E *-ine*] **:** bordering upon the River Plate or its chief tributaries ⟨the ~ portions of Argentina⟩
**plating** *n* -s [fr. gerund of *[2]plate*] **1 :** the art or process or an instance of covering something with a plate or plates and esp. with a superficial covering of metal **2 :** the formation of something (as metal) into plates **3 :** a surface made by plating: as **a :** a coating of metal plates; *esp* **:** defensive armor of metal (as steel) plates **b :** a thin coating of metal laid on another metal esp. for decorative effect **c :** the plates forming the hull, decks, and bulkheads of a ship — see SHIP illustration **d :** PLAITING 3
**platini-** *comb form* [NL *platinum*] **:** platinum ⟨*platini*chloride⟩ ⟨*platini*ferous⟩
**pla·tin·ic** \pləˈtinik, -nēk\ *adj* [ISV *platin-* + *-ic*] **:** of, relating to, or containing platinum — used esp. of compounds in which this element is tetravalent — compare PLATINOUS
**platinic acid** *n* **:** a weak acid $H_2Pt(OH)_6$ obtained as a yellowish white precipitate by hydrolysis of chloroplatinic acid; hexa-hydroxo-platinic acid
**platinic chloride** *n* **1 :** a reddish brown solid salt $PtCl_4$ obtained usu. by heating chloroplatinic acid with chlorine **2 :** CHLOROPLATINIC ACID — not used systematically
**plat·i·ni·chloride** \ˌplatᵊnə+\ *n* [*platini-* + *chloride*] **:** CHLOROPLATINATE
**plat·in·iridium** \ˌplatᵊn+\ *n* [*platin-* + *iridium*] **:** a mineral consisting of a natural alloy of iridium with platinum and other related metals occurring usu. in silver-white grains (hardness 6–7, sp. gr., 22.6–22.8)
**platinite** *var of* PLATYNITE
**plat·i·nize** \ˈplatᵊnˌīz\ *vt* -ED/-ING/-S [*platin-* + *-ize*] **:** to cover, treat, or combine with platinum or a compound of platinum: as **a :** to deposit platinum upon by simple immersion **b :** to coat with platinum black by electro-deposition or by chemical precipitation
**platino-** — see PLATIN-
**plat·i·no·chloride** \ˌplatᵊnō+\ *n* [*platin-* + *chloride*] **:** CHLOROPLATINITE
**plat·i·no·cyanide** \"+\ *n* [*platin-* + *cyanide*] **:** a fluorescent complex salt (as barium platinocyanide $Ba[Pt(CN)_4].4H_2O$) formed by the union of platinous cyanide with another cyanide; tetra-cyano-platinate (II) — called also *cyanoplatinite*
**[1]plat·i·noid** \ˈplatᵊnˌȯid\ *adj* [*platin-* + *-oid*] **:** resembling platinum
**[2]platinoid** *n* -s [ISV *platin-* + *-oid*] **1 :** an alloy chiefly of copper, nickel, and zinc used for forming electrical resistance coils and standards **2 :** a metal related to platinum
**plat·i·no·type** \ˈplatᵊnōˌtīp\ *n* [*platin-* + *type*] **:** a permanent photographic print having an image of platinum black obtained by the reduction of a platinum salt by a developer containing an iron salt (as ferrous oxalate) *also* **:** the process of making such a print
**plat·i·nous** \ˈplatᵊnəs\ *adj* [*platin-* + *-ous*] **:** of, relating to, or containing platinum — used esp. of compounds in which this element is bivalent — compare PLATINIC
**[1]plat·i·num** \ˈplat(ᵊ)nəm\ *n* -s [NL, fr. Sp *platina,* platinum, dim. of *plata* silver, fr. OSp — more at PLATE] **1 :** a very heavy precious metallic element that is typically grayish white, is noncorroding, ductile, and malleable, expands only slightly when heated and fuses with difficulty, has a relatively high electric resistance, and is chiefly bivalent and tetravalent, that occurs usu. native as grains and nuggets containing alloys (as with iridium, osmium, iron, copper) in alluvial deposits often associated with nickel sulfide and gold ores, and that is used chiefly in the form of alloys in special chemical ware and apparatus (as crucibles, dishes, foil, wire), in electrical and electronic devices, as a catalyst, in dental alloys, and in jewelry — symbol *Pt;* see ELEMENT table **2 :** a moderate gray that is lighter than median gray **3 :** a furbearer (as a fox or mink) of a light color phase that occurs esp. in ranch-bred animals
**[2]platinum** \"\ *adj* **1 :** of or relating to platinum **:** made of platinum ⟨~ jewelry⟩ **2 :** of the color platinum **3 :** belonging to the platinum color phase ⟨~ foxes⟩ **4 :** suggestive of the luxury value of platinum **:** COSTLY ⟨present-day ~ prices of basic needs⟩
**platinum black** *n* **:** a soft dull black powder of finely divided metallic platinum obtained by reduction and precipitation from solutions of its salts that is capable of occluding large volumes of hydrogen, oxygen, or other gases and that is used as a catalyst for hydrogenation or oxidation
**platinum blonde** *n* **1 :** a pale silvery blonde color that in human hair is usu. produced by bleach and a bluish rinse **2 :** a person whose hair is of the color platinum blonde
**platinum metal** *n* **:** any of the six precious metallic elements including platinum and elements resembling it in chemical and physical properties that belong to group VIII of the periodic table and are often subdivided into two triads one of which is composed of ruthenium, rhodium, and palladium whose specific gravities are about 12 and the other of which is composed of osmium, iridium, and platinum whose specific gravities are over 21
**platinum paper** *n* **:** photographic paper sensitized with a solution containing potassium chloroplatinite and ferric oxalate
**platinum process** *n* **:** the platinotype process
**platinum sponge** *n* **:** metallic platinum in a gray porous spongy form that is obtained by reducing ammonium chloroplatinate, that occludes large volumes of oxygen, hydrogen, and other gases, and that is used as a catalyst
**plat·i·tude** \ˈplad·əˌtüd, -at|, |əˌtyüd\ *n* -s [F, fr. *plat* flat (fr. OF) + *-itude* (as in *altitude, rectitude*) — more at PLATE] **1 :** the quality or state of being dull or insipid **:** staleness of ideas or language **:** TRITENESS **2 :** a thought or remark that is flat, dull, trite, or weak **:** a dull, stale, or insipid truism **:** COMMONPLACE
**plat·i·tu·di·nal** \ˌ==ˈtüd(ᵊ)nəl, -ˈtyü-\ *adj* [fr. *platitude,* after such pairs as E *latitude: latitudinal*] **:** PLATITUDINOUS
**[1]plat·i·tu·di·nar·i·an** \ˌ==ˈtüdᵊnˈerēən, ˌ==ˈtyü-, -ᵊnˈa(a)r-, -ᵊnˈär-\ *n* -s [fr. *platitude,* after such pairs as E *latitude: latitudinarian*] **:** one given to platitudes
**[2]platitudinarian** \"\ *adj* **:** characterized by or addicted to platitudes
**plat·i·tu·di·nize** \ˌ==ˈtüdᵊnˌīz\ *vi* -ED/-ING/-S [*platitudinous* + *-ize*] **:** to utter platitudes **:** speak in platitudes — **plat·i·tu·di·niz·er** \-zə(r)\ *n* -s
**plat·i·tu·di·nous** \ˌ==ˈtüdᵊnəs, ˌ==ˈtyü-\ *adj* [fr. *platitude,* after such pairs as E *multitude: multitudinous*] **:** having the characteristics of a platitude **:** full of platitudes — **plat·i·tu·di·nous·ly** *adv*
**pla·to·da** \pləˈtōdə\ *or* **plat·o·dar·ia** \ˌplad·əˈda(a)rēə\ *or* **pla·to·des** \pləˈtō(ˌ)dēz\ [*platoda* fr. NL, fr. *platy-* + *-oda* -ode; *platodaria* fr. NL, fr. *platoda* + *-aria; platodes* fr. NL, fr. *platy-* + *-odes* -ode] *syn of* PLATYHELMINTHES
**plat·ode** \ˈplaˌtōd\ *n* -s [NL *Platoda*] **:** FLATWORM, PLATYHELMINTH
**plat·oid** \-ˌtȯid\ *adj* [*platy-* + *-oid*] **:** broad and flat; *esp* **:** resembling a flatworm
**pla·to·nia** \pləˈtōnēə\ *n, cap* [NL, fr. L *Platon, Plato* + NL *-ia*] **:** a small genus of So. American timber trees (family Guttiferae) with opposite pinnate veined leaves and showy usu. solitary terminal roseate flowers that are followed by globose edible single-seeded berries — see BACURY
**pla·to·nian** \pləˈtōnēən, plā-, -nyən\ *adj, often cap* [L *Platon, Plato* (fr. Gk *Platōn*) + E *-ian*] **:** PLATONIC 1
**[1]pla·ton·ic** \pləˈtänik, plā-, -nēk\ *adj* [L *platonicus,* fr. Gk *platōnikos,* fr. *Platōn* Plato †347 B.C. Greek philosopher + *-ikos* -ic] **1** *usu cap* **:** of or relating to the philosopher Plato or Platonism; *specif* **:** being in accordance with or in the manner of Plato and his works **2 a** *often cap* (1) **:** constituting or relating to subsistent, transcendent, or eternal ideas (as Platonic forms) ⟨~ entities⟩ (2) **:** constituted by such ideas or forms ⟨a ~ heaven⟩ **b** *sometimes cap* (1) **:** involving, founded on, or being in harmony with platonic love ⟨a ~ relationship⟩ (2) **:** experiencing or professing platonic love **c** *sometimes cap* **:** of a theoretical, nominal, or academic nature **:** devoid of substantiality ⟨if the majority has only a ~ belief in it, the law will break down —Walter Lippmann⟩ ⟨purely ~ protestations⟩
**[2]platonic** \"\ *n* -s **1** *archaic, usu cap* **:** a follower of Plato **:** PLATONIST **2** *often cap* **:** emotion or behavior of a platonic lover — usu. used in pl.
**pla·ton·i·cal** \-nəkəl, -nēk-\ *archaic var of* PLATONIC
**pla·ton·i·cal·ly** \-nək(ə)lē, -nēk-, -li\ *adv, sometimes cap* **:** in a Platonic manner
**platonic body** *or* **platonic solid** *n* **:** any of the five regular geometrical solids comprising the simple tetrahedron, hexahedron, octahedron, dodecahedron, and icosahedron
**pla·to·ni·cian** \ˌplād·ōˈnishən\ *n* -s *usu cap* [F *platonicien,* fr. L *platonicus* platonic + F *-ien* -ian] **:** PLATONIST
**platonic love** *n, often cap P&L* **1 :** love conceived in the philosophy of Plato as an urge to union with the beautiful, ascending from passion for the individual to ecstasy in contemplation of the universal and ideal **2 :** a close relationship between two usu. opposite-sexed persons in which an element of sexual attraction or libidinal desire has been either so suppressed or so sublimated that it is generally believed to be absent
**pla·to·nism** \ˈplātᵊnˌizəm\ *n* -s [NL *platonismus,* fr. L *platon-, Platon, Plato* †347 B.C. Greek philosopher (fr. Gk *Platōn*) + *-ismus* -ism] **1** *usu cap* **:** the philosophy of Plato stressing that ultimate reality consists of transcendent eternal universals which are the true objects of knowledge, that knowledge consists of reminiscence of these universals under the stimulus of sense perception, that objects of sense are not completely real but participate in the reality of the ideas, that man has a tripartite preexistent and immortal soul consisting of the appetitive functions, the spirited functions, and the intellect, and that the ideal state is aristocratic and made up of the three classes of artisans, soldiers, and philosopher-rulers — compare FORM, IDEALISM **2** *usu cap* **a :** the philosophic tradition established by Plato and extending through the Academy to the Alexandrian School and Plotinus — compare NEOPLATONISM **b :** any later revival of this tradition: as (1) **:** one during the Renaissance in Florence (2) **:** one in the 17th century in Cambridge University — compare CAMBRIDGE PLATONIST **c :** a particular formulation within the Platonic tradition **3** *sometimes cap* **a :** a tenet of Platonic philosophy **:** a platonic saying ⟨~s of poets⟩ **b :** any expression of idealism ⟨~ in the poetry of Shelley⟩ **4** *sometimes cap* **:** the doctrine or practice of platonic love **5** *sometimes cap* **:** a logical or mathematical theory incorporating within its language names for such abstract or higher level entities as classes — contrasted with *nominalism;* called also *terminological platonism*
**pla·to·nist** \-ˌnəst\ *n* -s *usu cap* [ML *platonista,* fr. L *platon-, Platon, Plato* Plato †347 B.C. + *-ista* -ist] **:** a follower of Plato, his philosophy, or the Platonic tradition **:** an adherent or advocate of Platonism
**pla·to·nis·tic** \ˌplātᵊnˈistik, -tēk\ *adj* **1** *often cap* **a :** characteristic of or relating to Platonists or Platonism **b :** PLATONIC 1, 2a **2** *sometimes cap* **:** being in accordance with platonism; *specif* **:** including abstract entities
**pla·to·nize** \ˈplātᵊnˌīz\ *vb* -ED/-ING/-S *usu cap* [F *platoniser,* prob. fr. LGk *platōnizein,* fr. Gk *Platōn* Plato †347 B.C. + *-izein* -ize] *vi* **:** to adopt, imitate, or conform to Platonic opinions ~ *vt* **1 :** to explain in accordance with or adapt to Platonic doctrines **2 :** to render Platonic **:** IDEALIZE

**1pla·toon** \plə'tün, pla'-\ *n* -S [F *peloton* platoon, ball — more at PELOTON] **1 a :** a small body of military personnel functioning as a unit: as (1) *archaic* **:** a body of men firing together (2) *archaic* **:** a small group drawn up in a hollow square to strengthen the angles of a formation (3) **:** a subdivision of a military unit (as a company) that normally consists of a headquarters unit and two or more squads or sections commanded by a lieutenant **b** *archaic* **:** a volley of shots **2 :** a group of persons sharing some common characteristic or activity ⟨a ~ of waiters⟩ ⟨a ~ of potential killers —Martin Levin⟩: as **a :** a squad of a police force working under a platoon system **b :** a squad of paid fire fighters on duty during a single shift **c :** a group (as of students) performing a particular activity at the same time **d :** a group of football players trained esp. for either offense or defense and intended to be sent into or withdrawn from the game as a body **3 :** a group of things of the same or similar kind existing together or viewed as a unit ⟨~*s* of empty bottles⟩

**2platoon** \"\ *vt* -ED/-ING/-S **:** to arrange in or divide into platoons ⟨the advantages from ~*ing* students in smaller schools⟩

**platoon school** *n* **:** a departmentalized school in which the pupils of each grade are organized into platoons that take turns in using the classrooms, shops, auditorium, gymnasium, and other physical resources of the school plant

**platoon sergeant** *n* **:** a noncommissioned army officer rating just below a master sergeant and above a staff sergeant

**platoon system** *n* **1 :** a system of assignment of divisions of the police of a large city to duty at stated times so that the city is equally policed at all hours **2 :** a system of football strategy in which defensive and offensive platoons are alternated in play

**plats** *pl of* PLAT, *pres 3d sing of* PLAT

**plats du jour** *pl of* PLAT DU JOUR

**platt** \'plat, 'plät\ *n* -S *usu cap* [G, by shortening] **:** PLATTDEUTSCH

**platt·deutsch** \'=,dȯich\ *n* -ES *cap* [G, fr. D *Platduitsch*, lit., Low German, fr. *plat* flat, level, low (fr. MD, fr. MF, flat) + *Duitsch* German, fr. MD *duutsch, dūtsch* — more at PLATE, DUTCH] **:** a colloquial language of northern Germany comprising a number of Low German dialects and of limited use as a literary language

**platted** *past of* PLAT

**plat·te·land** \'pläd·ə,länt\ *n, sometimes cap* [Afrik, fr. D, lit., flatland, fr. *platte, plat* flat, level, low + *land*, fr. MD; akin to OHG *lant* land — more at LAND] **:** the isolated rural sections of southern Africa **:** BACKVELD

**1plat·ter** \'plad·ə(r), -atə-\ *n* -S [ME *plater*, fr. AF, fr. OF *plat* plate — more at PLATE] **1 :** a large shallow plate used esp. for serving meat **2 a** *or* **platter hat :** a woman's low-crowned hat that is distinctly flat in silhouette **b :** any of various broad flat objects ⟨the theater is . . . a cunningly contrived ~ of steel pipes and wooden planks —*New Yorker*⟩ **c :** a phonograph record or electrical transcription record **d :** HOME PLATE — **on a platter** *adv (or adj)* **:** without the least expenditure of effort **:** without difficulty **:** very easily ⟨can have the presidency *on a platter* —Jonathan Daniels⟩

platter 2a

**2platter** \"\ *n* -S [9*plat* + -*er*] **:** one that plats ⟨subdividers and ~*s* of land⟩

**platter–faced** \'==,=\ *adj* [1*platter*] **:** having a broad flat face

**1platting** *n* -S [fr. gerund of 5*plat*] **1 :** the action of one that plats some material **:** PLAITING **2 :** material that is plaited; *also* **:** plaited work (as of straw)

**2platting** *n* -S [fr. gerund of 9*plat*] **:** the action or process of mapping a surveyed area

**platt·ner·ite** \'platnə,rīt\ *n* -S [G *plattnerit*, fr. Karl Friedrich *Plattner* †1858 Ger. metallurgist + G -*it* -ite] **:** a mineral $PbO_2$ consisting of native lead dioxide usu. occurring in iron black masses of submetallic luster

**platt·ner process** \'pla|tnə(r)-, 'plä|\ *n, usu cap 1st P* [after Karl F. *Plattner* †1858 Ger. metallurgist] **:** a process for the extraction of gold (as from ores) by chlorination, solution, and precipitation

**plat·ty** \'plad·i, -ati\ *adj* [perh. fr. 8*plat* + -*y*] *dial Eng, of a crop* **:** spotty or uneven in growth

**1platy** \'plād·ē, -ātē, -i\ *adj* -ER/-EST [1*plate* + -*y*] **:** like a plate **:** consisting of plates or flaky layers — used chiefly of soil or mineral formations

**2platy** \'plad·ē, -atē, -i\ *n, pl* **platy** *or* **platys** *or* **platies** [fr. *platy*- (in NL *Platypoecilus*)] **:** a member of a genus (*Platypoecilus*) of small stockily built fishes that are native to southern Mexico, are highly favored for the tropical aquarium, and are notably variable in captivity ranging from the grayish or olive wild type stock through brilliant color variants and modified forms all of which are usu. regarded as varieties of a single species (*P. maculatus*)

**platy-** *also* **plat-** *comb form* [LL *plat-*, fr. Gk *plat-, platy-*, fr. *platys* — more at PLACE] **:** flat **:** broad ⟨*platy*cnemic⟩ ⟨*plat*oid⟩ ⟨*platy*poda⟩

**platy·basic** \'plad·ē+\ *adj* [ISV *platy-* + *basic*] **:** relatively broad at the base ⟨a ~ skull⟩

**platy·carya** \,==+\ *n, cap* [NL, fr. *platy-* + Gk *karya* nut tree — more at CARYA] **:** a small genus of Asiatic trees (family Juglandaceae) that have alternate pinnate leaves and small monoecious flowers in catkins which are followed by a small winged nut

**platy·ce·lous** *or* **platy·coe·lous** \'plad·ē'sēləs\ *also* **platyce·lian** *or* **platycoe·lian** \-lēən, -lyən\ *adj* [*platy-* + *-cele, -coele* + *-ous* or *-an*] *of a vertebra* **:** flat or concave ventrally and convex dorsally — compare OPISTHOCOELOUS

**platy·cephalic** \'==+\ *also* **platy·cephalous** \'==+\ *adj* [*platycephalic* fr. *platy-* + *-cephalic; platycephalous* ISV *platy-* + *-cephalous*] **:** having a head flat on top ⟨the chimpanzee is more ~ than . . . the gorilla —Arthur Keith⟩

**platy·ce·phal·i·dae** \,==sə'falə,dē\ *n pl, cap* [NL, fr. *Platycephalus*, type genus + *-idae*] **:** a family of scorpaenid fishes comprising the flatheads

**platy·ceph·a·lus** \,=='sefələs\ *n, cap* [NL, fr. *platy-* + *-cephalus*] **:** the type genus of Platycephalidae

**platy·ceph·a·ly** \,=='sefəlē\ *also* **platy·ceph·a·lism** \-,lizəm\ *n, pl* **platycephalies** *also* **platycephalisms** [*platycephaly* ISV *platy-* + *cephal-* + *-y; platycephalism* fr. *platy-* + *cephal-* + *-ism*] **:** the condition of being platycephalic

**platy·cer·cus** \,=='sərkəs\ *n, cap* [NL, fr. Gk *platykerkos* flat-tailed, fr. *platy-* + *kerkos* tail] **:** a genus of chiefly Australian parrakeets comprising the rosella and related birds

**platy·ce·ri·um** \,=='sirēəm\ *n, cap* [NL, fr. *platy-* + Gk *kērion* honeycomb (fr. *kēros* wax) — more at CEREUS] **:** a genus of tropical Old World ferns (family Polypodiaceae) that are mostly epiphytic and have large flat lobed fronds often resembling the antlers of a stag — see STAGHORN FERN

**plat·ycne·mia** \,plad·ē(k)'nēmēə\ *n* -S [NL, fr. *platy-* + *-cnemia*] **:** the condition of being platycnemic

**plat·ycne·mic** \'=='nēmik\ *adj* [ISV *platy-* + *-cnemic*] *of a shinbone* **:** laterally flattened with a platycnemic index of 55 to 63

**platycnemic index** *n* **:** the ratio of the anteroposterior diameter of the shinbone to its lateral diameter multiplied by 100

**plat·ycne·my** \'==,nēmē\ *n* -ES [ISV, fr. NL *platycnemia*] **:** PLATYCNEMIA

**platy·co·don** \,plad·ē'kō,dän\ *n* [NL, fr. *platy-* + Gk *kōdōn* bell (fr. *kōos* hollow, den); akin to Gk *koilos* hollow — more at CAVE] **1** *cap* **:** a genus of perennial herbs (family Campanulaceae) having large bell-shaped blue or white flowers with stamens that are much dilated at the base and a capsule that opens by apical valves — see BALLOONFLOWER **2** -S **:** any plant or flower of the genus *Platycodon*

**platy·cra·nia** \,=='krānēə\ *n* -S [NL, fr. *platy-* + *-crania*] **:** the condition of a skull caused by artificial flattening — **platy·cra·ni·al** \'=='=nēəl\ *adj*

**plat·yc·tene** \'plad·ik'tēn\ *adj* [NL *Platyctenea*] **:** of or relating to the Platyctenea

**plat·yc·te·nea** \,=='tēnēə\ *n pl, cap* [NL, fr. *platy-* + Gk *kten-, kteis* comb — more at PECTINATE] **:** an order of ctenophores (class Tentaculata) in which the body is much flattened giving distinct dorsal and ventral surfaces — compare CTENOPLANA — **plat·yc·te·ne·an** \-nēən\ *adj or n*

**platy·dactyl** *also* **platy·dactyle** \'plad·ē+\ *or* **platy·dactylous** \"+\ *adj* [*platydactyl* fr. *platy-* + *dactyl; platydactyle* fr. *platy-* + Gk *daktylos* finger, toe; *platydactylous* ISV *platy-* + *-dactylous*] **:** having flat digits — used esp. of lizards and frogs with flattened adhesive tips to the toes

**platy·el·min·thes** \-,el'min(t)thēz, -n,thēz\ *syn of* PLATYHELMINTHES

**platy·fish** \'plad·ē+,-\ *n* **:** PLATY

**platy·gas·ter·i·dae** \,==ga'sterə,dē\ *n pl, cap* [NL, fr. *Platygaster*, type genus (fr. *platy-* + *-gaster*) + *-idae*] **:** a family of serphoid wasps that are mostly parasites of gallflies

**platy·hel·mia** \-'helmēə\ [NL, fr. *platy-* + Gk *helmis* worm + NL *-ia*] *syn of* PLATYHELMINTHES

**platy·helminth** \'==+\ *n, pl* **platyhelminths** *or* **platyhelminthes** [NL *Platyhelminthes*] **:** a worm of the phylum Platyhelminthes **:** FLATWORM

**platy·helminthes** \'==+\ *n pl, cap* [NL, fr. *platy-* + Gk *helminth-, helmis* worm — more at HELMINTH-] **:** a phylum of soft-bodied bilaterally symmetrical usu. much flattened invertebrates comprising the planarians, flukes, tapeworms, and related worms and often also the nemerteans, having the body unsegmented or composed of a series of proglottides formed by strobilation, built up of ectoderm, endoderm, and mesoderm, and without body cavity, the space between the body wall and the various organs being filled with parenchyma, and distinguished by an excretory system made up of tubules that permeate the body and usu. communicate with the exterior and that end internally in flame cells — **platy·helminthic** *adj*

**platy·hieric** \'==+\ *adj* [*platy-* + *-hieric*] **:** having a relatively wide sacrum with a sacral index of 106 or over — compare DOLICHOHIERIC, SUBPLATYHIERIC

**platy·kur·tic** \'=='kərd·ik\ *adj* [*platy-* + *kurt-* (fr. Gk *kyrtos* bulging, curved) + *-ic* — more at LEPTOKURTIC] **1** *of a frequency distribution curve* **:** being less peaked than the corresponding normal distribution curve **2 :** *of a frequency distribution* **:** being less concentrated about the mean than the corresponding normal distribution

**platy·kurtosis** \'==+\ *n* [NL, fr. E *platykurtic* + NL *-osis*] **:** the condition of being platykurtic

**platy·lep·a·did** \,=='lepədəd, -,did\ *n* -S [NL *Platylepad-, Platylepas* + E *-id*] **:** a barnacle of the genus *Platylepas*

**platy·lepas** \'==+\ *n, cap* [NL, fr. *platy-* + *Lepas*] **:** a genus of commensal barnacles common in warm seas where they live embedded in the skin of turtles, manatees, sea snakes, and fishes

**platy·me·ria** \,=='mirēə\ *n* -S [NL, fr. *platy-* + *mer-* + *-ia*] **:** the condition of being platymeric or of having platymeric femurs

**platy·mer·ic** \'=='merik\ *adj* [*platy-* + *mer-* + *-ic*] *of a thighbone* **:** laterally flattened with a platymeric index of 75 to 85

**platymeric index** *n* **:** the ratio of the anteroposterior diameter of the femur to its lateral diameter multiplied by 100

**platy·my·ar·i·an** \'==,mī'a(a)rēən\ *also* **platy·my·ar·i·al** \-rēəl\ *adj* [*platy-* + *my-* + *-aria* + *-an* or *-al*] *of nematode muscle cells* **:** having the myofibrils restricted to the region next the hypodermis — compare COELOMYARIAN

**plat·y·nite** *or* **plat·i·nite** \'plad·ə,nīt\ *n* -S [Sw *platynit*, fr. Gk *platynein* to widen, flatten (fr. *platys* broad, flat) + Sw *-it* -ite — more at PLACE] **:** a mineral $PbBi_2(Se,S)_3$ consisting of a lead and bismuth selenide and sulfide and occurring in thin iron-black metallic plates

**platy·ope** \'plad·ē,ōp\ *n* -S [back-formation fr. *platyopic*] **:** a platyopic individual

**platy·o·pia** \,plad·ē'ōpēə\ *n* -S [NL, fr. *platy-* + Gk *ōp-, ōps* face, eye + NL *-ia*] **:** broadness of face **:** the condition of being platyopic

**platy·op·ic** \'=='äpik, -'ōp-\ *adj* [*platy-* + Gk *ōp-, ōps* face, eye + E *-ic* — more at EYE] **:** having a broad flat face

**platy·pel·lic** \'=='pelik\ *adj* [*platy-* + *-pellic*] **:** having a broad pelvis with a pelvic index of less than 90 — **platy·pel·ly** \'==,pelē\ *n* -ES

**platy·pel·loid** \'=='pe,lȯid\ *adj* [*platypellic* + *-oid*] *of a pelvis* **:** broad and flat **:** approaching a platypellic condition — compare GYNECOID

**1platy·pez·id** \'=='pezəd\ *adj* [NL *Platypezidae*] **:** of or relating to the Platypezidae

**2platypezid** \"\ *n* -S [NL *Platypezidae*] **:** a fly of the family Platypezidae

**platy·pez·i·dae** \,=='pezə,dē\ *n pl, cap* [NL, fr. *Platypeza*, type genus (fr. *platy-* + Gk *peza* foot, lower part of a body) + *-idae;* akin to Skt *padya* of the foot, L *ped-, pes* foot — more at FOOT] **:** a small family of two-winged flies having larvae that breed in fungi and adults that often fly in swarms — see SMOKE FLY

**pla·typ·o·da** \plə'tipədə\ *n pl, cap* [NL, fr. *platy-* + *-poda*] **:** a division of Pectinibranchia comprising gastropod mollusks with the foot adapted for creeping — compare HETEROPODA — **pla·typ·o·dous** \-dəs\ *adj*

**platy·po·dia** \,=='pōdēə\ *n* -S [NL, fr. *platy-* + *-podia*] **:** FLAT-FOOTEDNESS

**platy·pod·i·dae** \,=='pädə,dē\ *n pl, cap* [NL, fr. *Platypod-, Platypus*, type genus (fr. Gk *platypod-, platypous* flat-footed) + *-idae*] **:** a family of ambrosia beetles occurring mainly in the tropics and subtropics

**platy·poecilia** \'==+\ *or* **platy·poecilius** \"+\ [NL, fr. *platy-* + *Poecilia*, genus of fishes — more at POECILIIDAE] *syn of* PLATYPOECILUS

**platy·poe·ci·lus** \,=='pēsələs\ *n, cap* [NL, fr. *platy-* + Gk *poikilos* many-colored — more at PAINT] **:** a genus of topminnows (family Poeciliidae) comprising the platys

**pla·typ·tera** \plə'tiptərə\ *n pl, cap* [NL, fr. *platy-* + *-ptera*] *in former classifications* **:** an order of insects including the termites, bird lice, and other forms that are now divided among several orders

**platy·pus** \'plad·əpəs, -dē-, -,pu̇s\ *n* -ES [NL, fr. Gk *platypous* flat-footed, fr. *platy-* + *pous* foot — more at FOOT] **:** a small aquatic mammal (*Ornithorhynchus anatinus*) of the order Monotremata of southern and eastern Australia and Tasmania having a fleshy bill resembling that of a duck, dense blackish brown fur, 5-toed webbed feet, and a broad flattened tail, and being an expert swimmer and diver, inhabiting burrows near the water, feeding chiefly on aquatic mollusks, and unlike most mammals being oviparous, laying eggs about three fourths of an inch long — called also *duckbill, duckmole*

**platy·pus·a·ry** *also* **platy·pus·sa·ry** \-sərē\ *n* -ES [*platypus* + *-ary* (n. suffix)] **:** a place for care and exhibition of the platypus

**platy·rhi·na** \,plad·ē'rīnə\ *or* **platyrhi·ni** *or* **platyr·rhi·ni** \-ī,nī\ *syn of* PLATYRRHINA

**platyrrhina** \"\ *n pl, cap* [NL, fr. *platy-* + Gk *-rrhina*, neut. pl. of *-rrhin* -nosed, fr. *rhin-, rhis* nose — more at RHIN-] *in many classifications* **:** a division of Anthropoidea comprising the new-world monkeys all of which have a broad nasal septum, usu. 36 teeth, and often a prehensile tail — compare CATARRHINA, CEBIDAE

**1plat·yr·rhine** \'plad·ə,rīn, -,rən\ *also* **plat·yr·rhin·i·an** \,=='rinēən\ *or* **plat·y·rhine** *or* **plat·y·rhin·i·an** *n* -S [*platyrrhine, platyrhine* fr. *platyrrhine, platyrhine*, adj.; *platyrrhinian, platyrhinian* fr. F *platyrrhinien*, fr. Gk *platyrrhin-, platyrrhis* broadnosed (fr. *platy-* + *rhin-, rhis* nose) + F *-ien* -ian] **:** a platyrrhine individual

**2platyrrhine** \"\ *also* **platyrrhinian** \"\ *or* **platyrhine** *or* **platyrhinian** *adj* [*platyrrhine* fr. NL *Platyrrhina; platyrrhinian* fr. NL *Platyrrhina* + E *-an; platyrhine* fr. NL *Platyrhina; platyrhinian* fr. NL *Platyrhina* + E *-an*] **1 :** of or belonging to the Platyrrhina **2** [*platyrrhine, platyrhine* fr. *platy-* + *-rrhine* or *-rhine; platyrrhinian, platyrhinian* fr. *platyrrhinian, platyrhinian*, n.] **:** having a short broad nose with a high nasal index

**plat·yr·rhin·ic** \'plad·ə'rinik\ *adj* [1*platyrrhine* + *-ic*] **:** PLATYRRHINE 2

**platyr·rhi·ny** \'==,rīnē\ *n* -ES [2*platyrrhine* + *-y*] **:** the condition of being platyrrhine **:** shortness and broadness of nose

**platys** *pl of* PLATY

**pla·tys·ma** \plə'tizmə\ *n, pl* **pla·tys·ma·ta** \-məd·ə\ *also* **platysmas** [NL, fr. Gk *platysma* flat piece, plate, fr. *platynein* to widen, flatten — more at PLATYNITE] **:** a broad thin layer of muscle on each side of the neck immediately under the superficial fascia that belongs to the group of facial muscles and is innervated by the facial nerve — **pla·tys·mal** \-zməl\ *adj*

**1platy·so·mid** \'plad·ē'sōməd\ *adj* [NL *Platysomidae*] **:** of or relating to the Platysomidae

**2platysomid** \"\ *n* -S [NL *Platysomidae*] **:** a fish or fossil of the family Platysomidae

**platy·som·i·dae** \,=='sämə,dē, -sōm-\ *n pl, cap* [NL, fr. *Platysomus*, type genus (fr. Gk *platysōmos* broad-bodied, fr. *platy-* + *sōma* body) + *-idae* — more at -SOME] **:** a family of Carboniferous and Permian ganoid fishes (order Archistia) having a deep compressed body covered with rhombic scales joined by peg-and-socket joints

**platy·spermic** \'==+\ *adj* [*platy-* + *-spermic*] *of a seed* **:** bilaterally symmetrical

**platy·staph·y·line** \'=='stafə,līn\ *adj* [*platy-* + *staphyl-* (fr. NL *staphylion*) + *-ine*] **:** having a broad flat palate

**platy·ste·mon** \,=='stēmən\ *n, cap* [NL, fr. *platy-* + Gk *stēmōn* warp, thread — more at STAMEN] **:** a genus of small annual herbs (family Papaveraceae) of the southwestern U.S. with linear leaves and creamy to pale yellow flowers

**plat·ys·ten·ce·phal·ic** \'plad·ə'stensə'falik\ *adj* [Gk *platystatos* (superl. of *platys* broad) + E *encephalic* — more at PLACE] **:** having a dolichocephalic head with a wide pentagonal occiput and a prognathous jaw — **plat·ys·ten·ceph·a·ly** \,==,='sefəlē\ *n* -ES

**platy·ster·ni·dae** \,plad·ē'stərnə,dē\ *n pl, cap* [NL, fr. *Platysternon*, genus name of *Platysternon megacephalum* (fr. *platy-* + Gk *sternon* chest, breast) + *-idae* — more at STERNUM] **:** a family of Asiatic freshwater turtles (suborder Cryptodira) including a single species (*Platysternon megacephalum*) characterized by a relatively huge head with hooked mandibles and a very long tail

**platy·stom·i·dae** \,=='stämə,dē\ *n pl, cap* [NL, fr. *Platystomus*, type genus (fr. *platy-* + *-stomus*) + *-idae*] **:** a family of snout beetles with short beak, trapezoidal prothorax, and flexible palpi

**1plaud** \'plȯd\ *n* -S [prob. back-formation fr. *plaudite*] *archaic* **:** PRAISE, APPLAUSE

**2plaud** \"\ *vt* -ED/-ING/-S [L *plaudere* to applaud] *archaic* **:** APPLAUD

**1plau·dit** \'plȯdət, *usu* -əd·+V\ *n* -S [L *plaudite* applaud!, 2nd pers. pl. imper. of *plaudere* to applaud] **1 :** an act of applauding (as by clapping the hands) **:** a round of applause ⟨with the ~*s* of his audience still ringing in his ears —A.C. Cole⟩ **2 :** strong and openly expressed approval **:** enthusiastic approbation ⟨the book received the ~*s* of the critics⟩

**2plaudit** \"\ *vb* -ED/-ING/-S **:** APPLAUD

**plau·di·te** \'plȯdəd·ē\ *n* -S [L, applaud!] **1 :** an appeal for applause esp. by an ancient Roman actor **2** *obs* **:** PLAUDIT

**plau·di·to·ry** \'plȯdə,tōrē, -tȯr-, -ri\ *adj* [obs. E *plauditor* one who applauds (fr. E 2*plaudit* + *-or*) + E *-y*] **:** APPLAUSIVE, LAUDATORY

**plau·si·bil·i·ty** \,plȯzə'biləd·ē, -ətē, -i\ *n* -ES **1 :** the quality or state of being plausible **2 :** something plausible

**1plau·si·ble** \'plȯzəbəl\ *adj, sometimes* -ER/-EST [L *plausibilis* deserving applause, pleasing, acceptable, fr. *plausus* (past part. of *plaudere* to applaud) + *-ibilis* -ible] **1** *obs* **a :** worthy of being applauded **b :** APPLAUSIVE, PLAUDITORY **:** expressing approval **2 :** obtaining approbation or favor **:** AGREEABLE, AFFABLE, POPULAR, SUITABLE ⟨a more ~ site for a house —E.B. White⟩ **3 a :** superficially fair, reasonable, or valuable **:** SPECIOUS ⟨a ~ pretext⟩ **b** *of a person* **:** apparently trustworthy or fair **:** superficially pleasing or persuasive **4 a :** superficially worthy of belief **:** CREDIBLE ⟨a ~ conclusion⟩ **b :** being such as may be accepted as real ⟨a jewel too big to be ~⟩ — **plau·si·ble·ness** *n* -ES

**2plausible** \"\ *n* -S **:** something (as a statement or an argument) that is plausible **:** PLAUSIBILITY

**plau·si·bly** \-blē, -li\ *adv* **:** in a plausible manner ⟨very ~ presented⟩ **:** so as to seem to accord with justice, propriety, or right ⟨delayed as long as they ~ could⟩

**plau·sive** \'plȯziv, -lȯs-\ *adj* [L *plausus* (past part. of *plaudere* to applaud) + E *-ive*] **1 :** manifesting praise or approval **:** APPLAUDING **2** *obs* **:** PLEASING, AGREEABLE **3** *archaic* **:** SPECIOUS

**plaus·tral** \'plȯstrəl\ *adj* [L *plaustrum* wagon + E *-al;* prob. akin to L *plaudere* to clap, beat, applaud] **:** of or relating to a wagon or cart

**plaus·trum** \-trəm\ *n, pl* **plaus·tra** \-trə\ *or* **plaustrums** [L] **:** an ancient Roman two-wheeled farm cart

**plau·tine** \'plȯ,tīn\ *adj, usu cap* [L *plautinus*, fr. *Plautus* †184 B.C. + L *-inus* -ine] **:** of, relating to, or in the style of the Roman comic dramatist Plautus who is noted for vivacious broad humor

**1plau·tus** \'plȯd·əs\ *n, cap* [NL, fr. L, flat, flat-footed; akin to L *plaudere* to clap, applaud] **:** a genus of auks including the dovekie

**2plautus** \"\ [NL, fr. L, flat, flat-footed] *syn of* PINGUINUS

**1play** \'plā\ *n* -S *often attrib* [ME *play, pley*, fr. OE *plega;* akin to OE *plegan* to play, MD *pleyen, playen* to frolic, play] **1 a :** an act of briskly handling, using, or plying a sword or other weapon or instrument ⟨a duelist famous for his brilliant ~⟩ ⟨indiscriminate gun ~ in the streets —Green Peyton⟩ **b** (1) *archaic* **:** a particular amusement **:** GAME, SPORT (2) **:** the conduct or carrying on of a game **:** the course of a game ⟨rain interfered with ~⟩ ⟨talking during ~ may be distracting⟩ (3) **:** a particular act, maneuver, or point in a game ⟨relied mostly on running ~*s* —G.S.Halas⟩ **:** manner or trick of playing ⟨his ~ is excellent⟩ **:** turn to play ⟨it's your ~⟩ (4) **:** the action between two downs in football (5) **:** the action in which cards are played after bidding in a card game **c** (1) *obs* **:** SEXUAL INTERCOURSE (2) **:** exchange of caresses in or as if in preparation for sexual intercourse **:** DALLIANCE ⟨sexual ~⟩ **d** (1) **:** recreational activity **:** FROLIC, SPORT; *esp* **:** the spontaneous or organized recreational activity of children ⟨in cooperative ~ children learn adjustments in a social group —Gertrude H. Hildreth⟩ (2) **:** JEST, FUN — usu. used in the phrase *in play* ⟨said it in ~, not in earnest⟩ (3) **:** the act or an instance of playing upon words or speech sounds esp. to achieve a humorous or rhetorical effect (as in punning) ⟨the title of this address is an obvious ~ upon the original meaning . . . of the term *philosophy* —C.W.Berenda⟩ ⟨take a familiar line of verse and turn it into a poem with an ironic ~ upon the original —Oscar Cargill⟩ — usu. used in the phrases *play of words* or *play on words* **e :** GAMBLING, GAMING ⟨lose a fortune in ~⟩ **f** *chiefly dial* (1) **:** HOLIDAY (2) **:** FAIR, WAKE **2 a** (1) **:** an act, way, method, or manner of proceeding **:** MANEUVER, MOVE ⟨the ~ was . . . to maintain the balance —S.H.Adams⟩ ⟨that was a ~ to get your fingerprints —Erle Stanley Gardner⟩ ⟨the ~ fell flat —*Atlantic*⟩ ⟨a very bad place for that kind of ~ —Raymond Chandler⟩ (2) **:** DEAL, VENTURE ⟨land available for any company . . . looking for a land ~ —*Edmonton (Alberta) Jour.*⟩ ⟨in this big oil ~, there are more than eighty drilling rigs —*Time*⟩ **b** (1) **:** OPERATION, EMPLOYMENT ⟨discouraged from the normal ~ of their talents —Gilbert Seldes⟩ ⟨his sense of humor was in ~ —R.M.Lovett⟩ ⟨other motives surely come into ~ —M.R.Cohen⟩ ⟨a program of reaction was put into full ~ —C.L.Jones⟩ ⟨he is above the ~ of party —Ernest Barker⟩ (2) **:** brisk, lively, or light activity involving change, variation, transition, or alternation **:** dynamic activity ⟨the ~ of a supremely fine and penetrating intelligence —F.R. Leavis⟩ ⟨accustomed to make their phrases a ~ of wit —George Meredith⟩ (3) **:** brisk, fitful, or light movement of something physical **:** movement marked by alternation or sudden transition ⟨the ~ of light and shadow on the dancing waves⟩ ⟨the gem presented a dazzling ~ of colors⟩ ⟨the ~ of a gusty wind —Amy Lowell⟩ ⟨~ of surf is most spectacular on stormy days —*Amer. Guide Series: Maine*⟩ (4) **:** free or unimpeded motion (as of a part of a machine) ⟨this type of universal joint permits shaft end ~ —Joseph Heitner⟩; *also* **:** the length or measure of such motion ⟨the cylinder has about an inch of ~⟩ (5) **:** scope or opportunity for action ⟨found ample ~ for this avocation in surrounding marshes —*Amer. Guide Series: La.*⟩ ⟨the position gave much ~ to his notable talents⟩ **c** (1) **:** temporary attention, interest, or patronage ⟨took the ~ away from puppets on television —Thomas Whiteside⟩ ⟨time was heavy on their hands and they were giving the . . . casino a great ~ —C.B.Davis⟩ (2) **:** emphasis or publicity esp. in public media of communication ⟨got very little ~ here the next day —E.J.Kahn⟩ ⟨official propaganda gives a heavy ~ to impressive statistics —*New Republic*⟩ ⟨wish the country received a better ~ in the American press —Hugh MacLennan⟩ (3) **:** a move or series of moves calculated to arouse affection, sympathy, or friendly feelings — usu. used with *make* ⟨quit making a ~ for him —James Jones⟩ ⟨made a big ~ for the girl —Will Herman⟩ ⟨since the . . . audience has the votes, it is best to make your ~ for them —B.N.Cardozo⟩ **3 a :** the representation or exhibition of some action or story on the stage or in some other medium (as radio, television, or motion pictures) **:** the performance of a comedy, tragedy, or other dramatic piece ⟨going to the ~⟩ **b :** a dramatic composition **:** DRAMA **c :** PANTOMIME **4 :** an act of playing a phonograph record through ⟨this needle should be good for hundreds of ~s⟩ **syn** see FUN, ²PLAY, ROOM — **in play 1 :** so as to be engaged or occupied ⟨enabled him to escape by holding his attackers *in play*⟩ **2 a :** in such a condition or position as to be legitimately played **:** properly in the game **:** not dead ⟨the ball is *in play*⟩ **b :** still available for play — used of a card that has not yet been played — **out of play :** not in play **:** DEAD

**²play** \"\ *vb* -ED/-ING/-S [ME *playen, pleyen,* fr. OE *plegan*] *vi* **1 a :** to engage in recreational activity **:** amuse or divert oneself **:** FROLIC, SPORT ⟨children ~*ing* in the park⟩ **b :** to have sexual relations ⟨if he ~*s* with his wife in the evening there's another baby —Pramoedya Toer⟩; *esp* **:** to have promiscuous or illicit sexual relations — usu. used in the phrases *play around* or *play around with* ⟨you've got the wrong impression . . . she doesn't ~ around —Calder Willingham⟩ ⟨girls who ~ around with men in uniform —Frederic Wakeman⟩ **c** (1) **:** to toy or move aimlessly to-and-fro ⟨hand was ~*ing* on the edge of the bed —Arnold Bennett⟩ — usu. used with *with* ⟨~*ed* disconsolately with her food —Louis Auchincloss⟩ ⟨~*ed* with his walking stick⟩ (2) **:** to deal or behave frivolously, mockingly, or playfully **:** MOCK, KID, JEST ⟨the sallies of those who ~*ed* at him in print —*Times Lit. Supp.*⟩ — usu. used with *with* ⟨don't ~ with me —Hartley Howard⟩ (3) **:** to deal in a light, speculative, or sportive manner **:** toy mentally ⟨they did not believe in ghosts, but . . . they let their fancies ~ on the border line —Van Wyck Brooks⟩ — usu. used with *with* ⟨her mind ~*ed* with absurd fancies —Ellen Glasgow⟩ ⟨liked to ~ with ideas —Peggy Durdin⟩ ⟨rather ~*s* with the allegorical form —H.O.Taylor⟩ (4) **:** to make use of the double meaning of a word or of the similarity of sound of two words for stylistic or humorous effect — usu. used in the phrase *play on words* ⟨sometimes poets ~ on words in this fashion —E.S.McCartney⟩ **d** *Brit* **:** to be out of work or idle **:** take a holiday **2 a** (1) **:** to have an effect **:** operate — used with *on* or *upon* ⟨the jungle scents ~*ed* upon my emotions —William Beebe⟩ ⟨see that direct heat does not ~ on dry enamel —*Gadgets Annual*⟩ (2) **:** to take advantage **:** make use — used with *on* or *upon* ⟨~*ing* ignobly upon selfish fears —V.L.Parrington⟩ ⟨~*ing* upon the divisive forces in the Western world —*N.Y. Times*⟩ (3) **:** to exert or seek to exert wiles or influence **:** PRACTICE — used with *on* or *upon* ⟨the enchantress ~*ing* upon him —George Meredith⟩ **b** (1) **:** to dart, spring, or fly to and fro **:** FLUTTER, FRISK ⟨watched the birds ~*ing* overhead⟩ ⟨dolphins ~*ing* about the ship⟩ (2) **:** to move, operate, or have effect in a lively or brisk and irregular, intermittent, or alternating manner ⟨had seen northern lights ~ across the autumnal skies —B.A.Williams⟩ ⟨a faint smile ~*ed* about her lips —Victoria Sackville-West⟩ ⟨muscles could be seen ~*ing* beneath his thin cotton shirt —Sherwood Anderson⟩ (3) *of a cockbird* **:** to exhibit itself (as in courtship display) **c** (1) **:** to move or function freely within prescribed limits **:** have free or full play ⟨a piston rod ~*s* within a cylinder⟩ (2) **:** to discharge, eject, or fire something or to become discharged, ejected, or fired repeatedly or so as to make a stream ⟨a stream of water ~*s* to keep the molten mass from congealing —*Monsanto Mag.*⟩ ⟨his cannon ~*ed* upon the besiegers from two sides⟩ **3 a** (1) **:** to perform on a musical instrument ⟨~ on a violin⟩ (2) **:** to sound in performance ⟨the organ is ~*ing*⟩ ⟨a chorale was ~*ing* on the phonograph —Glenn Scott⟩ (3) **:** to reproduce sound of recorded material ⟨records ~*ing* at rotational speeds of 33⅓ revolutions per minute⟩ **b** (1) **:** to act on a stage or in some other dramatic medium (as radio, motion pictures, or television) (2) **:** to be staged or presented **:** RUN ⟨what's ~*ing* at the picture shows —Shelby Foote⟩ (3) **:** to act so as to support or back up — used in the phrase *play up to* ⟨amusing to find how well they ~*ed* up to the theory of what an Oxford man ought to be —H.J.Laski⟩ ⟨amused him to ~ up to the popular idea of him —Gerald Bullett⟩ (4) **:** to make a strong effort or calculated move to gain favor, approval, or sympathy from or as if from a theater audience **:** make a play ⟨might ~ to popular prejudices to serve his political ends —V.L.Parrington⟩ ⟨sometimes inclined to ~ to their roadside audience —Norma Spring⟩ ⟨whenever he had an audience, he whined and ~*ed* for sympathy —D.H.Lawrence⟩ — often used in the phrase *play up to* ⟨when . . . they weren't ~*ing* up to their public —Bennett Cerf⟩ ⟨now they would have to ~ up to this odd-looking, homely woman —Ida A. R. Wylie⟩ (5) **:** to lend itself to performance esp. theatrical ⟨the script reads well but ~*s* badly⟩ **4 a :** to engage or take part in a game ⟨~ at chess⟩ ⟨~*ed* in every major game this year⟩ **b** *archaic* **:** to exercise or fight with weapons esp. for amusement; *specif* **:** FENCE **c :** GAMBLE, GAME ⟨~*ed* for heavy stakes⟩ **d** (1) **:** to behave or conduct oneself in a specified way ⟨don't think I've ~*ed* quite fair —E.A.McCourt⟩ ⟨some cars ~ dirty —H.W.Young⟩ ⟨best to ~ safe⟩ (2) **:** to engage in a game of make-believe **:** assume a role in or as if in sport — used with *at* ⟨the commuter ~*ing* at country squire —Bergen Evans⟩ ⟨would ~ at being well-to-do local housewives —Grace Metalious⟩ (3) **:** to feign to be in a specified state or condition ⟨the . . . fawn that she found in the woods, which ~*ed* dead —*Atlantic*⟩ ⟨don't ~ innocent⟩ (4) **:** to take part, engage, or collaborate in or assent to some activity ⟨took it for granted that he would ~ with the big industrialists —Alvin Johnson⟩ **:** COOPERATE ⟨no other nation can be sure . . . whether we will simply refuse to ~ —Robert Lekachman⟩ — often used with *along* ⟨~*ed* along until he had enough evidence to hold all three —Morris Ploscowe⟩ ⟨willing to ~ along with him —Harvey Breit⟩ (5) **:** to function or operate so as to prove advantageous to or enhance the effectiveness of another — used with *into* ⟨the horizontal lines of the . . . figure ~ into the central idea with splendid effect —Roger Fry⟩ ⟨easy thus to make one subject ~ into another —A.C.Benson⟩ esp. in the phrase *play into the hands of* ⟨decided on an unfortunate procedure that ~*ed* directly into the hands of the opposing party⟩ ~ *vt* **1 a** (1) **:** to engage in or occupy oneself with (a game or other amusement) ⟨~ baseball⟩ (2) **:** to engage in (some activity) as if in a game ⟨~ secret diplomacy and power politics —A.L.Guérard⟩ ⟨~ hooky⟩ (3) **:** to pursue a certain line of conduct toward **:** deal with, handle, or manage **:** TREAT ⟨deliberately ~*ing* the conversation as though this meal were like any other —Wirt Williams⟩ ⟨~*ed* him exactly the way I figured —J.M.Cain⟩ ⟨the law ~*s* the privilege differently —B.N.Meltzer⟩ — often used with impersonal *it* as object ⟨symptomatic . . . of the desire to ~ it safe —Norman Cousins⟩ ⟨willing to ~ it on the level —Bill Hatch⟩ (4) **:** to set in opposition **:** PIT ⟨became adept at ~*ing* Japanese civilians against the military —E.T.Hall⟩ — usu. used with *off* ⟨able to ~ off one tribe against another —C.L.Jones⟩ (5) **:** to treat, use, or work upon (a person) for a certain end or as a member of a designated class **:** EXPLOIT, MANIPULATE — usu. used with *for* ⟨think you are only ~*ing* me for what you can get out of me —James Jones⟩ ⟨the king . . . ~*ed* him for a sucker —DeLancey Ferguson⟩ **b :** to treat, practice, or deal with in a spirit of play **:** pretend to engage in **:** imitate in play ⟨children, who ~ life, discern its true law and relations more clearly than men —H.D.Thoreau⟩ ⟨the children were ~*ing* house⟩ ⟨~*ing* that they were cowboys and Indians⟩ ⟨let's ~ soldiers⟩ **c** (1) **:** to carry into execution ⟨~*ed* an important part in the affair⟩ ⟨~*ed* a strange and turbulent role —Carol L. Thompson⟩ (2) **:** to perform or execute for amusement or with a view to deceive or mock ⟨~*ing* their mischievous pranks at the maddest —J.G.Frazer⟩ ⟨~*ed* a trick on me⟩ (3) **:** to bring about (some devastating action or condition) **:** WREAK ⟨~ havoc⟩ **d** (1) **:** to assign an indicated degree of value, importance, or emphasis to — usu. used with *up* or *down* ⟨~*ing* down academic scholarship —H.W.Dodds⟩ ⟨the store also ~*s* up . . . other makes —*Retailing Daily*⟩ ⟨trying to ~ herself down to me —Williams Forrest⟩ (2) **:** to give a certain emphasis to (a news story, feature, or other item) esp. by displaying more or less prominently ⟨the popular press . . . ~*ed* this for all it was worth —C.H.Driver⟩ — usu. used with *up* or *down* ⟨interesting to see what items were ~*ed* up —Jacques Kayser⟩ ⟨urged to ~ down stories of crimes⟩ **2 a** (1) **:** to put on a performance of (a play) **:** perform as a spectacle ⟨~ an Elizabethan comedy⟩ (2) **:** to act in the character or part of **:** represent by acting ⟨a war story in which she ~*ed* a beautiful spy —*Current Biog.*⟩ (3) **:** to perform or be shown in ⟨has ~*ed* more than forty communities —R.W.Sarnoff⟩ **:** perform or be shown during or for the duration of ⟨~*ed* a tour in New England⟩ ⟨~*ed* a week in Boston⟩ **b** (1) **:** to perform or act the part of in real life **:** act or behave like or in the character of ⟨~ the fool⟩ ⟨~ truant⟩ ⟨do not expect boys of 15 to be ~*ing* the lover —H.E. Scudder⟩ (2) **:** to perform the part of (some disorganizing, disrupting, or ruinous agency) ⟨this . . . routine of yours ~*s* hell with manifests and accounting —LaSelle Gilman⟩ ⟨brawled and generally ~*ed* the devil —Kenneth Roberts⟩ **3 a** (1) **:** to contend against in a game ⟨refused to ~ the challenger⟩ (2) **:** to use as a contestant in a game ⟨~*ed* his second team in the last quarter⟩ (3) **:** to fill (a certain position) on a team ⟨regularly ~*s* third base⟩ ⟨~*ed* quarterback⟩ **b** (1) **:** to risk at play **:** wager in a game **:** STAKE ⟨~*ed* his last few dollars⟩ (2) **:** to lose or squander in gambling — usu. used with *away* ⟨~*ed* away his inheritance⟩ (3) **:** to wager on ⟨~ the races⟩ ⟨~ the ponies⟩ (4) **:** to base a decision or action on **:** operate on the basis of ⟨~ a hunch⟩ ⟨~*ing* their luck instead of their skill —Nicholas Monsarrat⟩ **c :** to dispose (an implement of a game) purposefully and usu. irrevocably according to the conditions of the game: as (1) **:** to place (a card from one's hand) on the table usu. face-up and in one's turn esp. when another player has previously made a lead (2) **:** to move (a piece) in chess, checkers, backgammon, or a similar game (3) **:** to bet (a chip or a sum of money) in roulette or a similar game (4) **:** to strike (a bowled cricket ball) with the bat; *often* **:** to strike (a bowled cricket ball) defensively with no attempt to score **4 a :** to perform (music or a piece of music) on an instrument ⟨~ a waltz⟩ **b :** to perform music upon **:** cause to sound or give forth music ⟨~ the violin⟩ **c :** to attend with accompanying music in the performance of some action or movement ⟨would ~ them down the mountain, ~ them home —Stuart Cloete⟩ **5 :** to put in action or motion: as **a :** to wield or ply briskly, vigorously, or freely ⟨~*ing* knife and fork with gusto⟩ **b :** to discharge, fire, or set off with more or less repeated or continuous effect ⟨~ a rifle upon a fort⟩ ⟨~ a hose⟩ or to eject, throw, or force out in such a way ⟨~ a stream of water⟩ **c :** to cause to move, act, or operate briskly, lightly, and irregularly or intermittently ⟨~*ed* his flashlight along the line of feet —Frank Cameron⟩ **d** (1) **:** to allow (a hooked fish) to become exhausted by pulling against the line ⟨~*ed* the poor fish until it rolled, belly up, from exhaustion —Jim Rearden⟩ (2) **:** to keep (as a suitor) in a state of suspense or uncertainty by a show of coyness or a similar stratagem **:** play with in the manner of a cat with a mouse ⟨she ~*ed* him — sometimes delicately, sometimes with a less felicitous touch —Philip Guedalla⟩

**syn** PLAY, SPORT, DISPORT, FROLIC, ROLLICK, ROMP, and GAMBOL can mean, in common, to engage in an activity as a pleasure or amusement. PLAY, the most general, suggests an opposition to *work;* it implies activity, often strenuous, but emphasizes the absence of any aim other than amusement, diversion, or enjoyment ⟨children *playing* in the yard⟩ ⟨the hard-working business man often *plays* as hard as he works⟩ SPORT and DISPORT both imply a complete release from all seriousness, suggesting engagement in a pastime ⟨shall not *sport* with your impatience by reading what he says on that point —Jane Austen⟩ ⟨porters, messengers, and elevator boys, *sporting* wherever they are, with their sharp winks and sly smiles —Lin Yutang⟩ ⟨children *sporting* on the lawn⟩ ⟨good housewives *disporting* at a church picnic⟩ ⟨the sight of a tiny fish *disporting* himself with me in the tub —William Beebe⟩ FROLIC suggests generally more gaiety, levity, and spontaneousness than PLAY, applying often to the lighthearted activity of children at active play ⟨porpoises *frolicking* in the sea⟩ ⟨*frolicking* students⟩ ROLLICK adds the idea of exuberance or reveling, applying chiefly to youths or young adults ⟨a *rollicking* ship's crew⟩ ⟨a tavern full of *rollicking* revelers⟩ ROMP suggests a carefree boisterousness as of rough but happy children, usu. connoting running or racing in play ⟨a father *romping* in the living room with his small children⟩ ⟨young lions *romping* in the spring sunshine in their cages⟩ ⟨a buxom, attractive comedienne — *romps* rowdily through the sketches —*Newsweek*⟩ GAMBOL suggests the leaping and skipping of young lambs, connoting possibly more joy than FROLIC ⟨when whales *gambolled* in the bays —W.J. Dakin⟩ ⟨in the ecstasy of that thought they *gambolled* round and round, they hurled themselves into the air in great leaps of excitement —George Orwell⟩ The nouns PLAY, SPORT, DISPORT, FROLIC, ROMP and GAMBOL each signify the activity generally, or an instance of it, implicitly distinguished in the corresponding verb forms above — **play ball 1 :** to begin or resume playing a game — used as an official direction or signal (as by an umpire) **2 :** COOPERATE ⟨you *play ball* with me and I'll *play ball* with you —E.C.Marston⟩ — **play both ends against the middle :** to play off opposing interests against each other to one's own ultimate profit — **play horse :** to play the fool ⟨don't *play horse* with me —Robert Murphy⟩ — **play old gooseberry** *dial chiefly Brit* **:** to play havoc — **play politics 1 :** to act from considerations of partisan political advantage rather than principle or the general interest ⟨refused to *play politics* with foreign policy —A.E.Stevenson b.1900⟩ **2 :** to seek to gain one's ends by scheming or intrigue ⟨*play office politics*⟩ — **play possum 1 :** to pretend to be asleep or dead ⟨after they've once drugged you, you *play possum* —Erle Stanley Gardner⟩ **2 :** to feign ignorance — **play the field :** to have dates or romantic connections with more than one member of the opposite sex **:** avoid an exclusive or permanent attachment ⟨preferred *playing the field* to going steady —Geraldine Roberts⟩ — **play the game :** to act according to some code or set of standards **:** play fair or honorably ⟨wasn't *playing the game* in giving publicity to this confidential report —John Betjeman⟩ ⟨had not *played the game* in the past toward the fruit industry —*Farmer's Weekly (So. Africa)*⟩ — **play the market :** to speculate on the stock or produce exchanges — **play to the score :** to vary one's tactics (as in a card game) according to the state of the score — **play with oneself :** to engage in autoerotic activity; *specif* **:** MASTURBATE

**pla·ya** \ˈplīə\ *n* -S [Sp, lit., beach, fr. ML *plagia* hillside, shoreline, prob. fr. Gk, sides, flanks, fr. neut. pl. of *plagios* oblique; akin to Gk *pelagos* sea — more at FLAKE] **:** the flat-floored bottom of an undrained desert basin that becomes at times a shallow lake which on evaporation may leave a deposit of salt or gypsum **:** SALT PAN ⟨in the ~*s* of southern California —J.B.Droste⟩

**play·abil·i·ty** \ˌplāəˈbiləd·ē, -lətē, -i\ *n* **:** the quality or state of being playable

**play·able** \ˈplāəbəl\ *adj* **:** capable of or suitable for being played or played on ⟨harpsichord music is readily ~ —P.H. Lang⟩

**playact** \ˈ=,=\ *vb* [back-formation fr. *playacting*] *vi* **1 a :** to take part in theatrical performances esp. professionally **:** engage in playacting **b :** to pretend to be someone else (as children in play) **:** make believe ⟨children love to ~⟩ **2 :** to engage in theatrical or insincere behavior **:** put on ⟨always felt she was ~*ing* —Eden Phillpotts⟩ ~ *vt* **:** to act out ⟨toddlers will be delighted to ~ the life of a policeman —*My Baby*⟩

**playacting** \ˈ=,==\ *n* [¹*play* + *acting*] **:** the act of one that playacts: as **a :** the activity or profession of an actor ⟨many people thought ~ was sinful —George Freedley & J.A.Reeves⟩ **b :** insincere or theatrical behavior **:** make believe **:** PRETENSE ⟨her coy clapping of her hands over mouth . . . appears to have been ~ —E.D.Radin⟩

**playactor** \ˈ=,==\ *n* [¹*play* + *actor*] **:** ACTOR

**playa lake** *n* **:** a lake in an arid or semi-arid region that evaporates during the drier months to leave a playa

**play back** *vi* **:** to use back play in cricket ~ *vt* **:** to run through (a disc or tape) recently recorded

**playback** \ˈ=,=\ *n* -S [*play back*] **1 :** an act of reproducing a disc or tape sound recording often immediately after the recording process has been completed **2** *also* **playback machine :** a tape or disc sound reproducing device **:** TURNTABLE

**playball** \ˈ=,=\ *n* **:** a sponge or inflated ball that will bounce and is suitable for playing catch or other throwing and tossing games

**playbill** \ˈ=,=\ *n* **1 :** a bill advertising a play and usu. announcing the cast **2 :** a theater program

**playbook** \ˈ=,=\ *n* **:** one or more plays in book form

**playbox** \ˈ=,=\ *n, chiefly Brit* **:** a box for a child's toys and personal belongings esp. at a boarding school

**playboy** \ˈ=,=\ *n* **1** *dial Brit* **:** a tricky untrustworthy person **2 :** a typically young and wealthy man who lives a frivolous indolent life devoted chiefly to the pursuit of pleasure ⟨the story of a ~'*s* redemption —*Saturday Rev.*⟩ ⟨many simply became ~*s*, occasionally with diverting eccentricities —Christopher Rand⟩

**playbroker** \ˈ=,==\ *n* **:** an agent who acts as middleman between dramatists and managers or actors

**play-by-play** \ˌ=,=ˈ=\ *adj* **1 :** being a running commentary on a sports event ⟨*play-by-play* descriptions . . . of all games —*Amer. Guide Series: Mich.*⟩ **2 :** circumstantially related **:** DETAILED ⟨this *play-by-play* account of the three men —J.W.Rogers⟩

**playclothes** \ˈ=,=\ *n pl* **:** comfortable, utilitarian, or informal clothing worn for leisure activities, sports, or play

**playday** \ˈ=,=\ *n* **1 :** a day of play or diversion **2 :** an informal athletic competition between teams composed of players from several participating schools

**play debt** *n, archaic* **:** a gambling debt

**play doctor** *or* **play fixer** *n* **:** a person who is called in to revise a play before its production

**playdown** \ˈ=,=\ *n* -S **:** one of a series of playoffs (as among the winning teams from different leagues or localities)

**played** \ˈplād\ *adj* [fr. *played out*, adj.] **:** PLAYED OUT

**played out** *adj* **:** worn out, finished, spent, or used up ⟨never seen a limper, dirtier, more *played out* deck of cards —Hamilton Basso⟩

**play·er** \ˈplāə(r), -le(ə)r, -leə\ *n* -S [ME *pleyer*, fr. OE *plegere*, fr. *plegan* to play + -*ere* -er — more at PLAY] **1 :** one that plays: as **a :** a person who occupies himself for diversion **:** one who engages in recreational activity or amuses himself ⟨a ~ with illusion —L.A.Fiedler⟩ **b** (1) **:** a person who plays in or makes a practice of playing a usu. specified game (2) **:** a person who undertakes to play against all others in various games (as skat) **c :** a person who plays on a musical instrument **d :** a person who makes a profession of acting **:** ACTOR **e** *Brit* **:** a professional cricketer — compare GENTLEMAN 3d **f :** a mechanical device for automatically playing a musical instrument; *esp* **:** PIANO PLAYER **g :** RECORD PLAYER **2 :** the ball to be played next in billiards, croquet, and similar games

**player piano** *n* **:** a piano that contains a mechanical piano player

**playfair cipher** *n, usu cap P* **:** a cipher involving a digraphic substitution from a single alphabet square which begins with the letters of a keyword and continues with the remaining letters of the alphabet less J

| | | | | |
|---|---|---|---|---|
| K | E | Y | W | O |
| R | D | A | B | C |
| F | G | H | I | L |
| M | N | P | Q | S |
| T | U | V | X | Z |

square for Playfair cipher

**playfellow** \ˈ=,(,)=\ *n* **:** PLAYMATE

**playfield** \ˈ=,=\ *n* **:** a playground designed for outdoor athletics and games

**play forward** *vi* **:** to use forward play in cricket

**play·ful** \ˈplāfəl\ *adj* **1 :** full of play **:** SPORTIVE ⟨a nice little, sleek ~ kitten —Bram Stoker⟩ **2 :** indulging a sportive fancy **:** HUMOROUS, JOCULAR ⟨were discovering the charm of ~ satire —V.L.Parrington⟩ — **play·ful·ly** \-f(ə)lē, -li\ *adv* — **play·ful·ness** \-fəlnəs\ *n* -ES

**playgirl** \ˈ=,=\ *n* **:** a typically young woman who lives a frivolous indolent life devoted chiefly to pleasure ⟨a hard and handsome ~ —*Manchester Guardian Weekly*⟩

**playgoer** \ˈ=,=(=)\ *n* **:** a person who frequently attends plays

**playground** \ˈ=,=\ *n* **1 :** a piece of ground used for and usu. having special facilities for recreation esp. by children **2 :** a locality suitable by nature or adaptation for vacation or holiday relaxation ⟨England's mountain ~ —L.D.Stamp⟩ **3 :** the scene or arena of a specified activity ⟨the world of nature was chaotic — a ~ of supernatural forces —R.W. Southern⟩

**playground ball** *n* **1 :** SOFTBALL **2 :** an inflatable colored rubber ball (as of 5, 6, or 8 inches in diameter) used by children in simple games and for learning ball-handling skills

**play gym** *n* **:** GYM

**playhouse** \ˈ=,=\ *n* **1 :** a building used for dramatic exhibitions **:** THEATER **2 a :** a small building, hut, or enclosed area made like one or more rooms of a house for children to play in and often built by children **b :** a toy house

**playing** *pres part of* PLAY

**playing card** *n* [*playing* fr. ME *playing, pleying,* fr. gerund of *playen, pleyen* to play — more at PLAY] **1 :** a gaming implement made usu. of pasteboard in a standard size (as 2½″ or 2¼″ x 3½″ x .009″) as one of a set of 24 to 78 cards with identical backs, marked on its face to show its rank and suit, and used in playing any of numerous games **2 :** a card of a pack in which the suits are marked with designating symbols (as of a spade, heart, diamond, and club) and ranks (as of the series A, K, Q, J, 10, 9, 8, 7, 6, 5, 4, 3, 2) **3** *pl* **:** a pack of playing cards

**playing field** *n* **:** a field for various games (as football, cricket, tennis); *esp* **:** the part of a field that is officially marked off for play

**playing piece** *n* **:** COUNTER 1b

**playing trick** *n* **:** a card or combination of cards that is expected to win a trick in bridge

**playland** \ˈ=,=\ *n* **:** PLAYGROUND ⟨the development of Alaska . . . as a tourist and vacation ~ —*U.S. Code*⟩

**play·less** \ˈplāləs\ *adj* **:** devoid of play

**play·let** \-lət\ *n* -S [¹*play* + -*let*] **:** a short or slight play ⟨a tiny four-line ~ —F.M.Whiting⟩

**playmaker** \ˈ=,==\ *n* [¹*play* + *maker*] **:** a player who leads the scoring attack upon an opponent's goal (as in basketball or hockey)

**playmate** \ˈ=,=\ *n* **:** a companion in play

**play money** *n* **:** a metal or paper device made in obvious imitation of genuine coins or paper money chiefly for use in play by children

**play·ock** \ˈplāək\ *n* -S [ME (Sc) *playok*, prob. fr. ¹*play* + -*ok* (as in ME *bullok* bullock)] *Scot* **:** PLAYTHING

**play off** *vt* **1 :** to complete the playing of (an interrupted or delayed contest) **2 :** to break (a tie) by means of a play-off ~ *vi* **:** to participate in a play-off ⟨had to *play off* against last year's winner⟩

**¹play-off** \ˈ=,=\ *n* -S [fr. *play off*, v.] **1 :** a final contest or series of contests to determine the winner among two or more contestants or teams that have tied **2 :** a series of post-season contests to determine a championship

**²play-off** \ˈ=,=\ *adj* **:** relating to a play-off

**play on** *vi* **:** to play a bowled ball onto one's wicket in cricket

**play out** *vt* **1 a :** to perform to the end ⟨*played out* . . . the guilty role assigned to them —C.J.Rolo⟩ **b :** to bring to an end **:** use up **:** FINISH ⟨the pie's *played out* —W.M.Raine⟩ ⟨that graft's *played out* —S.H.Adams⟩ **2 :** to unreel or unfold ⟨*played out* a length of line —Gordon Webber⟩ ~ *vi* **1 :** to become spent or exhausted ⟨the twister raged along for about 400 feet before it *played out* —*Springfield (Mass.) Union*⟩ ⟨the pony . . . *played out* twice —H.L.Davis⟩ **2 :** to unreel or unfold to a considerable length ⟨the possibility of a snag when hose is *playing out* —W.Y.Kimball⟩

**play-party** \ˈ=,==\ *n* **:** a social gathering esp. of young people characteristic of the rural U.S. with entertainment consisting of dramatic games and swinging plays performed to the singing of ballads and clapping usu. without instrumental accompaniment

**playpen** \'=,=\ *n* [*play* + *pen*] **:** a portable enclosure usu. consisting of a platform surrounded with a rail in which a baby or young child may safely play without direct supervision

playpen

**playpipe** \'=,=\ *n* **:** a tapering metal pipe at the end of a fire hose for playing a stream of water
**play-pretty** \'=,==\ *n, chiefly Midland* **:** PLAYTHING, TOY
**playreader** \'=,==\ *n* **:** one who reads plays in manuscript and recommends their acceptance or rejection
**playroom** \'=,=\ *n* **1 :** a room fitted out or reserved for children to play in **2 :** RUMPUS ROOM
**plays** *pl of* PLAY, *pres 3d sing of* PLAY
**play school** *n* **1 :** KINDERGARTEN **2 :** a project in parent education enabling mothers to watch their children at play in a group and later discuss their observations with a teacher and other parents
**playscript** \'=,=\ *n* **:** a manuscript of a play
**playshoe** \'=,=\ *n* **:** a shoe designed for leisure wear
**play·some** \'plāsəm\ *adj* **:** PLAYFUL, WANTON, SPORTIVE — **play·some·ly** *adv* — **play·some·ness** *n* -ES
**playsuit** \'=,=\ *n* **:** a sports and play outfit made for women and children in one, two, or three pieces consisting usu. of a blouse and shorts and sometimes a matching skirt
**play therapy** *n* **:** a technique of child psychology in which a child by acting out his feelings and conflicts in play comes to understand himself as an individual ⟨emotional problems of the retarded child may yield to *play therapy* —Abraham Levinson⟩
**plaything** \'=,=\ *n* **1 :** TOY **2 :** someone or something that is played with ⟨a ~ of unscrupulous pressure groups —P.A. Sorokin⟩
**playtime** \'=,=\ *n* **1 :** a time for play or diversion **2 :** a time for the beginning of a stage performance
**play up** *vi, of a horse* **:** to resist control **:** fight the bit **:** REAR
**play·ward** \'plāwə(r)d\ *adj, archaic* **:** inclined to sport
**playwright** \'=,=\ *n* ['*play* + *wright*] **1 :** a person who writes plays **2 :** a person who adapts material for stage, radio, television, or motion-picture production
**playwrighting** \'=,==\ *n* -s [by alter. (influence of *playwright*)] **:** PLAYWRITING
**playwriting** \'=,==\ *n* **:** the writing of plays **:** the activity or occupation of a playwright
**play yard** *n* **1 :** PLAYGROUND **2 :** PLAYPEN
**plaza** \'plazə, -lāzə, -lazə\ *n* -s [Sp, fr. (assumed) VL *plattea* broad street, plaza, fr. L *platea* street, courtyard — more at PLACE] **1 :** a public square in a city or town **:** an open square **:** MARKETPLACE **2 :** a broad paved open-air area used for the parking or servicing of motor vehicles or for the channeling of motor traffic
**pla·za de to·ros** \,plӓzədā'tȯr(,)ōs\ *n, pl* **plazas de toros** [Sp, lit., plaza of bulls] **:** BULLRING
**plaza gray** *n* **:** SHELL GRAY
**plbg** *abbr* plumbing
**plbr** *abbr* plumber
[1]**plea** \'plē\ *n* -s [ME *plaid, plait, plai, plee,* fr. OF *plaid, plait, plet* agreement, decision, decree, lawsuit, fr. ML & L; ML *placitum* court day, judicial proceeding, lawsuit, fr. L, something agreeable, opinion, judicial decision, decree, fr. neut. of *placitus,* past part. of *placēre* to please, resolve, decide, decree — more at PLEASE] **1 a** *obs* **:** an action or cause in court **:** LAWSUIT **:** the presentation of a cause to the court — see COMMON PLEAS **b** *Scot* **:** CONTENTION, QUARRELING **2 :** an allegation made by a party in support of one's cause: as **a :** an allegation of fact — distinguished from *demurrer* **b** (1) **:** a defendant's answer to a plaintiff's declaration and demand in common-law practice (2) **:** an accused person's answer to a charge or indictment against him in criminal practice **c :** SPECIAL PLEA **d :** a plea of guilty to an indictment **3 :** something alleged or used to excuse or to justify **:** PRETEXT ⟨left the party early with the ~ of a headache⟩ **4** *obs* **:** something demanded **:** CLAIM ⟨none can drive him from the envious ~ of forfeiture —Shak.⟩ **5 :** an earnest entreaty **:** APPEAL, PETITION ⟨the powerful and compelling ~ for state's rights —Carol L. Thompson⟩ ⟨resisted ~s of many of his advisers —Herbert Feis⟩ **syn** see APOLOGY, PRAYER
[2]**plea** \"\ *vb* -ED/-ING/-S [ME *playen, pleyen,* fr. *plaid, plait, plai, plee,* n.] *chiefly Scot* **:** CONTEND, QUARREL
**pleach** \'plēch\ *vt* -ED/-ING/-ES [ME *plechen,* fr. ONF *plechier,* fr. L *plexus,* past part. of *plectere* to plait, weave — more at PLY] **1 a :** to cause to meet and intertwine to form a hedge **:** INTERLACE **b :** to renew by interweaving — usu. used of a hedge ⟨is now ~*ing* the hawthorn and wild plum —Elizabeth Berridge⟩ **2 :** to make into a braid **:** PLAIT — used of hair
**pleached** *adj* **1 :** twined together **:** INTERLACED **2 :** formed by the lacing of branches **:** fenced or covered over by intertwined boughs ⟨~ bower —Shak.⟩ ⟨away from the house to the ~ walk that led ... down to the river —Louis Bromfield⟩
**plead** \'plēd\ *vb* **pleaded** \-dəd\ *or* **pled** \'pled\ **pleaded** *or* **pled; pleading; pleads** [ME *pleiden, plaiden, pleden,* fr. OF *pleidier, plaidier,* fr. ML *placitare,* fr. *placitum* plea — more at PLEA] *vi* **1 a** *obs* **:** to institute or prosecute an action in court **:** to go to law **:** LITIGATE **b** *obs* **:** to contend in debate or argument **:** WRANGLE **2 :** to make a plea or conduct pleadings in a cause or proceeding in a court **:** present an answer or pleading in defense or prosecution of an action **3 :** to argue for or against a claim **:** urge reasons for or against a thing **:** entreat or appeal earnestly **:** BEG, IMPLORE ⟨~*ed* for help —D.A.Stein⟩ ⟨he did not entreat or ~; he announced —Margaret Deland⟩ ~ *vt* **1 a** *obs* **:** to bring legal action against **b :** to urge or make a plea of (the law) in court **2 :** to discuss, defend, and attempt to maintain by arguments or reasons presented to a tribunal or person having authority to determine **:** argue at the bar **3 :** to allege or cite in or by way of a legal plea or defense **:** answer to a declaration, charge, or indictment **4 :** to allege in support or vindication **:** to offer as a plea usu. in defense, apology, or excuse ⟨~*ed* ill health and private business as reasons for delaying —W.T. Utter⟩
**plead·able** \'plēdəbəl\ *adj* [ME *pledable,* fr. OF *pleidable, plaidable,* fr. *pleidier, plaidier* to plead — more at PLEAD] **:** able to be pleaded **:** capable of being lawfully maintained or of being alleged in defense, excuse, or vindication
**plead·er** \'plēdə(r)\ *n* -s [ME *pleder,* alter. of *plaidur, plaitour, pletour,* fr. OF *plaideor,* fr. *plaidier* to plead + *-eor* -or — more at PLEAD] **1 a :** one who conducts legal pleas esp. in court **:** ADVOCATE **b :** one who files a legal pleading **2 :** one who pleads **:** INTERCESSOR
[1]**plead·ing** \'plēdiŋ, -dēŋ\ *n* -s [ME *pleiding, plaiding, pleding,* fr. gerund of *pleiden, plaiden, pleden* to plead] **1 a** *obs* **:** LITIGATION **b :** the acting as an advocate or pleader in a cause **c** (1) **:** the drawing of pleas or conducting of causes as an advocate (2) **:** the body of rules governing this **:** one of the successive statements now usu. written by which the plaintiff sets forth his cause and claim and the defendant his defense **:** the formal allegations and counter allegations made by plaintiff and defendant or by prosecutor and accused in an action or proceeding until issue is joined **2 :** the act or an instance of making a plea **3 :** a sincere entreaty or petition **:** ADVOCACY, INTERCESSION ⟨the special ~ of a friend —L.L. Biancolli⟩
[2]**pleading** \"\ *adj* [fr. pres. part. of *plead*] **:** IMPLORING, SUPPLIANT ⟨a ~ note in her voice⟩
**plead·ing·ly** *adv* **:** in a pleading manner
**plea in abatement :** a plea that postpones or defeats a cause of action not on the merits of the controversy but for some defect in or matter of form or procedure
**plea in bar :** a plea entered by the defendant that constitutes a bar to the plaintiff's action
**plea in confession and avoidance :** a plea admitting that the plaintiff once had a good cause of action as alleged but that it is barred by some subsequent or collateral matter pleaded in defense (as a repeal of the statute on which the cause of action is founded)
**pleas·able** \'plēzəbəl\ *adj* [ME *plesable,* fr. MF *plaisable,* fr. *plaisir* to please + *-able* — more at PLEASE] **:** capable of being pleased
**pleas·ance** \'plez°n(t)s\ *n* -s [ME *plesaunce,* fr. MF *plaisance* pleasure, fr. OF, fr. *plaisant*] **1 a :** a feeling of pleasure **:** DELIGHT, GAIETY ⟨youth is full of ~; age is full of care —*Oxford Bk. of English Verse*⟩ **2** *obs* **:** a disposition to please **:** pleasing behavior **:** COURTESY **3 a :** PLEASANTNESS ⟨through the garden I was drawn — a realm of ~ —Alfred Tennyson⟩ **b** *archaic* **:** a source of pleasure **:** DELIGHT ⟨more towns are planning . . . to provide ~s where visitors may walk or sit —S.P.B.Mais⟩ **4 :** a pleasant place used for rest or recreation usu. consisting of a formal garden attached to a mansion or a small park ⟨tread green turf in a walled ~ —Phyllis & John Cradock⟩
**pleas·ant** \'plez°nt\ *adj, often* -ER/-EST [ME *plesaunt,* fr. MF *plaisant,* fr. pres. part. of *plaisir* to please — more at PLEASE] **1 :** agreeable to the senses **:** having a pleasing aspect **:** SATISFYING ⟨hills that make very ~ scenery —Jane Shellhase⟩ ⟨the changes make for a ~*er* life —C.B.Palmer b. 1910⟩ **2 a :** diverting!y gay and sprightly **:** MERRY ⟨there will be wit from one auctioneer, and ~ clowning from another —Cornelius Weygandt⟩ **b** *archaic* **:** causing diversion **:** LAUGHABLE **c :** merrily tipsy **:** hilariously drunk **3 :** having or characterized by good behavior and neat appearance **:** WELL-MANNERED ⟨a ~ scoundrel who certainly knew how to avoid risking his neck —H.J.Laski⟩ ⟨a very ~ person to live with —Mary Austin⟩
**syn** PLEASING, AGREEABLE, GRATEFUL, GRATIFYING, WELCOME: these adjectives agree in meaning very acceptable to or delighting the mind or senses. PLEASANT and PLEASING are often indistinguishable in having the basic meaning of the group, although usu. PLEASANT implies an objective quality while PLEASING suggests only the effect an object has upon one ⟨a *pleasant* riverside walk —S.P.B.Mais⟩ ⟨a bottle of . . . *pleasant* red or white wine —Harry Gilroy⟩ ⟨its streamlined shape is *pleasing* to the eye and appeals to the esthetic sense —H.G.Armstrong⟩ ⟨a *pleasing* group of white clapboard houses with small lawns —*Amer. Guide Series: Pa.*⟩ AGREEABLE implies a harmony with one's tastes or likings ⟨a small room . . . simple and *agreeable,* with whitewashed walls, rusty linen curtains at the windows, and a wide inviting wooden bed —Gordon Merrick⟩ ⟨a pretty face with its *agreeable* snub nose —Ethel Wilson⟩ GRATEFUL implies both pleasing and agreeable and stresses a satisfaction and esp. relief afforded the senses or mind ⟨the log fire was a *grateful* warmth against the lingering chill of April —Lucien Price⟩ ⟨the *grateful* smell of cooking pork grew every moment more perfect —Ethel Anderson⟩ ⟨placing every instrument in its most brilliant and *grateful* register —Virgil Thomson⟩ GRATIFYING applies chiefly to what affords mental pleasure by satisfying desires, hopes, or conscience ⟨the building is aesthetically *gratifying* —*Amer. Guide Series: La.*⟩ ⟨with *gratifying* rapidity this promise was fulfilled —Allan Nevins⟩ WELCOME even more than PLEASING stresses a pleasure or satisfaction given by the thing to which the word is applied, often suggesting a prior need or longing satisfied by the thing ⟨a screen playwright and craftsman of fresh-springing wit and *welcome* intelligence —Lee Rogow⟩ ⟨the sweet trill of a toad and the voice of the peeper are a *welcome* chorus —A.F.Gustafson⟩
**pleas·ant·ly** *adv* [ME *plesauntly,* fr. *plesaunt* + *-ly*] **:** in a pleasant manner ⟨live ~ together —Henry Adams⟩ ⟨skillfully and ~ written —H.E.Starr⟩
**pleas·ant·ness** *n* -ES **1 :** the quality or state of being pleasant **2 :** the elementary feeling that is aroused by agreeable stimuli
**pleasantness-unpleasantness** \'===;'===\ *n* **:** a continuum of states of feeling or of awareness of which pleasantness and unpleasantness are opposite poles esp. in respect to the motivation of behavior
**pleas·ant·ry** \'plez°ntrē, -ri\ *n* -ES [F *plaisanterie,* fr. MF, fr. *plaisant* + *-erie* -ery — more at PLEASANT] **1 :** an agreeable playfulness in conversation **:** good-humored banter **:** FACETIOUSNESS, JOCULARITY ⟨talked with fluency and spirit, and there was an archness and ~ in his manner —Jane Austen⟩ **2 :** a humorous act or speech **:** JEST, JOKE ⟨refused to be a party to the ~ —Ruth Park⟩ **3** *archaic* **:** PLEASANTNESS, PLEASURE ⟨engaged in other matters of business or ~ —Edmund Burke⟩
**please** \'plēz\ *vb* -ED/-ING/-S [ME *plesen, plaisen,* fr. MF *plaisir,* fr. L *placēre;* akin to OE *flōh* flat piece of stone, OHG *fluoh* cliff, ON *flō* layer, L *placare* to reconcile, placate, Gk *plak-, plax* flat surface, Lith *plākanas* flat, and perh. to OE *flōr* floor — more at FLOOR] *vi* **1 :** to afford or give pleasure, delight, or agreeable satisfaction **:** be agreeable ⟨the chief object of a play should be to ~ and entertain⟩ **2 :** to feel the desire or inclination **:** LIKE, WANT, WISH ⟨the fundamental American right to think as you ~ and say as you think —Archibald MacLeish⟩ ⟨an able man licensed by the times to do pretty much as he *pleased* —J.H.Hanford⟩ **3** *archaic* **:** to have the pleasure or kindness ⟨stranger, ~ to taste these bounties —John Milton⟩ ⟨will you ~ to enter the carriage —Charles Dickens⟩ ~ *vt* **1 :** to give pleasure to **:** make glad **:** GRATIFY ⟨*pleased* them by his hard work, his calm common sense —Beverly Smith⟩ **2** *dial chiefly Eng* **:** PLACATE, SATISFY; *specif* **:** to satisfy sexually **3 :** to be the will or pleasure of — used impersonally ⟨many boys, ~ God, will make the venture —J.H.Wilson⟩ ⟨may it ~ your Majesty⟩ **4 :** to be willing to **:** be so good as to **:** choose to — usu. used in the imperative to express a polite command or request ⟨~ go to the store for a loaf of bread⟩ **5** *archaic Scot* **:** to have or take pleasure in **:** LIKE **6 :** to satisfy (oneself) in respect to something **:** behave in a manner satisfactory to (oneself) **:** SUIT ⟨~ yourself as to whether you go⟩ ⟨*pleased* himself by administering justice impatiently —R.A.Billington⟩ ⟨finding that the sources themselves were far from uniform, I have sometimes *pleased* myself —McGeorge Bundy⟩
**syn** GRATIFY, DELIGHT, REJOICE, GLADDEN, EXHILARATE, TICKLE, TITILLATE, ARRIDE, REGALE: PLEASE indicates bringing happiness ranging from absence of discontent up to elation by something agreeing with one's wishes, tastes, or aspirations ⟨*pleased* by the suggestion⟩ ⟨a guest *pleased* by the reception given him⟩ ⟨*pleased* by his son's choice of profession⟩ GRATIFY may suggest stronger although perhaps less long-lived satisfaction at or as if at some particular action or occasion ⟨it *gratified* him to hear these gentlemen admire his fine stock —Willa Cather⟩ ⟨the notice . . . taken of her from the outset had *gratified* her —Robert Grant †1940⟩ ⟨wished to *gratify* his son by these eulogies —George Meredith⟩ DELIGHT applies to pleasing to the point of keenly felt and often vividly expressed intense transporting pleasure ⟨a dinner party satisfying the highest standard of hospitality, namely, that every guest be seated between persons certain to *delight* him and sure to kindle his affection —Alan Gregg⟩ ⟨the emergency ferry established there so *delighted* the handsome young actor that he spent the whole first day of the ferry service riding back and forth —*Amer. Guide Series: R.I.*⟩ REJOICE may suggest a joy marked by enthusiastic or festive happiness ⟨of even deeper happiness springing from the stirring of those faculties through which man *rejoices* in knowledge —H.O. Taylor⟩ GLADDEN suggests bringing happiness that encourages or alleviates grief, dubiousness, or gloom ⟨the comrades of the dead girl assemble in the temple on certain days to *gladden* her spirit with songs and dances —Lafcadio Hearn⟩ ⟨the springs which are under the earth and which break forth to refresh and *gladden* the life of flowers and the life of man —Laurence Binyon⟩ EXHILARATE indicates a raising to a high pitch of joy, happiness, triumph, or euphoria, with all gloom or worry dispelled ⟨realization affects people in one of two ways. It depresses them when they think how puny Man is against the Universe — or it *exhilarates* them when they consider his courage in attempting to conquer it —A.C.Clarke⟩ ⟨likely to brag a bit when *exhilarated* —S.H. Adams⟩ TICKLE may suggest a pleasurable physical sensation, one of tingling, thrilling, provoking laughs or chuckles or a comparable mental feeling ⟨the idea of himself as a parson *tickles* him: he looks down at the black sleeve on his arm, and then smiles slyly —G.B.Shaw⟩ ⟨so *tickled* he'd have wagged a tail if he'd had one —F.B.Gipson⟩ TITILLATE indicates pleasing and also interesting or intriguing ⟨*titillated* with something novel, flamboyant and sensational —C.E. Montague⟩ ⟨all this *titillates* our nerves: we think it exquisite, perfect —Irving Babbitt⟩ ARRIDE, now little used, may apply to what pleases, amuses, and calls forth laughter ⟨merry jests such as used to *arride* our ancestors —William Hardman⟩ REGALE suggests the large-scale entertainment or enjoyment of copious feasting ⟨farmers' wives *regale* the workers with brandied cakes and scuppernong grape pies —*Amer. Guide Series: N.C.*⟩
— **if you please :** if it is your pleasure, will, desire, or humor **:** if you like **:** YES — used to express courtesy, politeness, or emphasis ⟨pass me the salt, *if you please*⟩ ⟨unbridle him for a minute, *if you please* —Thomas De Quincey⟩ ⟨he was, *if you please,* a rascal⟩
**pleased** \'plēzd\ *adj* [ME *plesed,* fr. past part. of *plesen* to please] **:** affected with or manifesting pleasure **:** CONTENTED, GRATIFIED ⟨expect your family to be ~ with your marriage —Mary Austin⟩ ⟨looking ~ —R.L.Stevenson⟩ — **pleased·ly** \-z(ə)dlē, -li\ *adv*
**pleased·ness** \-dnəs\ *n* -ES **:** the quality or state of being pleased
**pleas·er** \'plēzə(r)\ *n* -s **:** one that pleases ⟨remain the crowd ~ he had been in his last play —Leo Hughes⟩
[1]**pleas·ing** \'plēziŋ, -zēŋ\ *n* -s [ME *plesing,* fr. gerund of *plesen* to please — more at PLEASE] **:** the act of one who pleases **:** the fact of being pleased **:** the giving of pleasure
[2]**pleasing** \"\ *adj* [ME *plesing,* fr. pres. part. of *plesen* to please] **:** giving pleasure **:** capable of being enjoyed **:** attractive to the senses **:** CHARMING, FAVORABLE, PALATABLE ⟨what I found most ~ . . . is the lake with the wild fowl flying over —S.P.B.Mais⟩ ⟨large rooms with ~ wood mantels and deep fireplaces —*Amer. Guide Series: Mich.*⟩ ⟨the ~ taste of homemade bread fresh from the oven⟩ **syn** see PLEASANT
**pleas·ing·ly** *adv* [ME *plesingly,* fr. *plesing* + *-ly*] **:** in a pleasing manner
**pleas·ing·ness** *n* -ES **:** the quality or state of being pleasing ⟨the liveliness and ~ of dark eyes —T.N.Carver⟩
**pleas of the crown** [trans. of ML *placita coronae*] **1 a** *Eng & Scots law* **:** the pleas or actions of which the crown formerly claimed exclusive jurisdiction as affecting the king's peace **b** *Scots law* **:** the judicial proceedings involving murder, rape, robbery, and willful fire-raising **2** *Eng law* **:** all criminal actions or proceedings
**plea·sur·abil·i·ty** \,plezh(ə)rə'bilәd·ē\ *n* **:** the quality or state of being pleasurable
**plea·sur·able** *also* **plea·sure·able** \'plezh(ə)rəbəl, -lāzh-, -zhə(r)b-\ *adj* **1 :** capable of affording pleasure or satisfaction **:** GRATIFYING, PLEASANT ⟨full of happiness and of ~ excitement —Fred Whishaw⟩ ⟨good printing will make every book more ~ to read —Joseph Blumenthal⟩ **2** *obs* **:** seeking or loving pleasure ⟨you are very ~ —Ben Jonson⟩
**plea·sur·able·ness** *n* -ES **:** PLEASURABILITY
**plea·sur·ably** \-blē\ *adv* **:** in a pleasurable manner
[1]**plea·sure** \'plezhə(r), -lāzh-\ *n* -s *often attrib* [ME *plesure,* alter. (influenced by *-ure*) of *plesir, pleser,* fr. MF *plaisir,* fr. *plaisir* to please — more at PLEASE] **1 :** a particular desire or purpose **:** INCLINATION, WILL ⟨wait upon his ~ —Shak.⟩ ⟨it was his ~ . . . to take away the charters —Leslie Thomas⟩ **2 :** a state or condition of gratification of the senses or mind **:** an agreeable sensation or emotion **:** the excitement, relish, or happiness produced by expectation or enjoyment of something good, delightful, or satisfying ⟨the ~s which one can derive from the knowledge of literature —H.J.Fuller⟩ ⟨the ~ and pain of coming of age —Lee Rogow⟩ **3 a :** sensual gratification **b :** frivolous enjoyment or amusement **:** sensuous diversion ⟨he that loveth ~ shall be a poor man —Prov. 21:17 (AV)⟩ **4 :** a cause, source, or object of delight or joy ⟨vacations are supposed to be a ~ —Orville Prescott⟩ ⟨hill and valley making the town a ~ to see —Jane Shellhase⟩ **5 :** a quality which gives a feeling of pleasurability ⟨the ~ of tinkling ice in a tall glass⟩ **6 a :** a feeling of pleasantness accompanying release of tensions esp. from anticipatory states or instinctual needs **b :** PLEASANTNESS 2
**syn** PLEASURE, DELIGHT, JOY, DELECTATION, ENJOYMENT, and FRUITION all agree in signifying the agreeable emotion accompanying the possession, acquisition, or expectation of what is good or greatly desired. PLEASURE stresses the feeling of satisfaction or gratification, often suggesting an excitement or exaltation of the senses or mind ⟨a few beautiful things on which the eyes may dwell with *pleasure* day after day —Herbert Spencer⟩ ⟨the capacity for civilized enjoyment, for leisure and laughter, for *pleasure* in sunshine and philosophical discourse —Bertrand Russell⟩ ⟨contempt and admiration, queer sensations of disgust and *pleasure,* all mingled —John Galsworthy⟩ DELIGHT adds the idea of liveliness or obviousness in the satisfaction induced, often more unstable or less enduring than pleasure ⟨a kind of *delight* in being alive to greet the dawn —Louis Bromfield⟩ ⟨with what *delight* I find myself on this boat going home again —Katherine A. Porter⟩ ⟨my frenzy of *delight* at the possibilities of escape —Rudyard Kipling⟩ JOY can interchange with PLEASURE or DELIGHT but often implies a more deep-rooted rapturous emotion or intense happiness ⟨the thrill of *joy* that surged over him —O.E.Rölvaag⟩ ⟨the *joy,* severed from its spiritual sustenance, loses its high ecstasy —P.E.More⟩ DELECTATION suggests the reaction to pleasurable experience more or less consciously sought, received, or provided, connoting rather amusement or diversion than anything like deep-seated joy ⟨hardly ever wrote a letter that had not a smile or a laugh in it and for the *delectation* of the reader I will give a few examples of her manner —W.S.Maugham⟩ ⟨guards scatter perfume for the prisoners' *delectation* and musicians play concerts at unusual hours —C.W.Bird⟩ ⟨revived ancient, joyful customs for the *delectation* of islanders and visitors —Ernest Gruening⟩ ENJOYMENT like DELECTATION stresses the reaction to pleasurable experience but suggests a wider range of deeper pleasure from a mere transient though complete gratification to a deep-seated or long-lasting gratified happiness ⟨occasioned more amusement than *enjoyment* or a serious regard —H.V. Gregory⟩ ⟨the capacity for civilized *enjoyment,* for leisure and laughter, for pleasure in sunshine and philosophical discourse —Bertrand Russell⟩ ⟨the *enjoyment* of a full fruitful life⟩ FRUITION in an older sense now of rare occurrence signified pleasure in possession or enjoyment in attainment ⟨in love we must deserve nothing, or the fine bloom of *fruition* is gone —George Meredith⟩ ⟨no man has ever had the *fruition* of these marvels —John Buchan⟩
[2]**pleasure** \"\ *vb* **pleasured; pleasured; pleasuring** \-zh(ə)riŋ\ **pleasures** *vi* **1 :** to take pleasure **:** DELIGHT — often used with *in* ⟨get my fill of these here tropical fruits because I . . . do ~ in the flavor —C.W.Wilkinson⟩ **2 :** to seek pleasure **:** take a holiday or outing ⟨the streets are filled with plantation people . . . buying and selling and *pleasuring* around the hot catfish stands —C.B.Davis⟩ ~ *vt* **1 :** to give or afford pleasure to **:** GRATIFY, PLEASE ⟨I'll learn, just to ~ you —Elizabeth M. Roberts⟩ ⟨~*s* the actors somewhat more than it advances their education —*Newsweek*⟩ **2 :** to give sexual pleasure to
**pleasureable** *var of* PLEASURABLE
**plea·sure·ful** \-(r)fəl\ *adj* **:** full of pleasure **:** DELIGHTFUL, PLEASING ⟨language study afforded ~ relaxation —H.R. Warfel⟩
**pleasure ground** *n* **:** a ground laid out with ornamental features for pleasure ⟨build a vast *pleasure ground* and palace for himself —Clara E. Laughlin⟩ ⟨his small park and *pleasure grounds* —Clive Bell⟩
**pleasure-house** \'=,=\ *n* **:** a building used for pleasure and recreation
**plea·sure·less** \-(r)ləs\ *adj* **:** affording no pleasure ⟨the whole affair was ~ to her⟩
**pleasuremonger** \'==,==\ *n* **:** one whose only business is seeking pleasure
**pleasure-pain** \'=='=\ *n* [trans. of G *lust-unlust*] **:** PLEASANTNESS-UNPLEASANTNESS
**pleasure principle** *n* [trans. of G *lustprinzip*] **:** a tendency for man's behavior to be directed (as by the id) toward the immediate satisfaction of instinctual drives and immediate relief from pain or discomfort — compare REALITY PRINCIPLE
**plea·sur·er** \'plezh(ə)rə(r)\ *n* -s **:** one that gives or takes pleasure; *specif* **:** PLEASURE-SEEKER
**pleasures** *pl. of* PLEASURE, *pres 3d sing of* PLEASURE
**pleasure-seeker** \'==,==\ *n* **:** one who looks for enjoyment

⟨an excuse for *pleasure-seekers* to see the sun rise —Linton Wells⟩

**¹pleasuring** *n* -s [fr. gerund of ²*pleasure*] **1 :** an act or instance of taking or giving pleasure ⟨changed from earning their living from farming . . . to the business of ~ —Mary H. Vorse⟩ **2 :** a pleasure trip **:** VACATION

**²pleasuring** *adj* [fr. pres. part. of ²*pleasure*] **:** designed or used for pleasure ⟨taking their ease in great ~ grounds where the wilderness is preserved —R.M.Yoder⟩

**pleas·ur·ist** \ˈplezh(ə)rəst\ *n* -s **:** PLEASURE-SEEKER

**¹pleat** \ˈplēt, *usu* -ēd·+V\ *vt* -ED/-ING/-S [ME *pleten* — more at PLAIT] **1 :** FOLD; *esp* **:** to form, crease, or arrange in pleats or folds similar to pleats ⟨~ a skirt⟩ ⟨~ a ruffle⟩ **2 :** PLAIT 2

**²pleat** \"\ *n* -s [ME *plete* — more at PLAIT] **1 a :** a creased or uncreased fold in cloth made by doubling material over on itself to form a section of three thicknesses, stitched, attached, or held along one side from which it hangs or flares free — see BOX PLEAT, INVERTED PLEAT, KICK PLEAT **b :** something resembling such a fold ⟨a ~ of skin⟩ ⟨a great flat acreage of sand, molded into endless neat ~s by the previous night's tides —Gerald Durrell⟩ **2 :** a double fold esp. in paper or leather (as in the accordion fold used typically on endpapers and in the pockets of books)

**³pleat** \"\ *adj* **:** PLEATED

**pleated** *adj* **1 a :** made with a pleat **b :** having pleats — often of a particular style ⟨knife-*pleated* skirt⟩ **2 :** resembling pleats ⟨pine and spruce trees drape a shaggy green shawl over the ~ terrain —R.L.Neuberger⟩

**pleat·er** \ˈplēd·ə(r)\ *n* -s **1 :** one that pleats or makes pleats in cloth, paper, or other material **2 :** one that presses or irons pleats **3 :** a textile worker who folds cloth after processing **4 :** TUCKER 1a(2)

**pleater tape** *n* **:** a wide stiff tape with a series of narrow slots used in pleating the tops of curtains

**pleating** *n* -s **1 :** the act or process of making a pleat **2 :** PLEAT; *collectively* **:** the pleats of a specific article (as a garment) **3 :** a style of pleat or arrangement of pleats ⟨sunburst ~⟩ ⟨accordion ~⟩

**pleb** \ˈpleb\ *n* -s [by shortening] **:** PLEBEIAN

**plebe** \ˈplēb\ *n* -s [F *plèbe*, fr. L *pleb-, plebs*] **1** *obs* **:** PLEBS **2** *also* **pleb :** a freshman esp. at a military or naval academy

**¹ple·be·ian** *also* **ple·bi·an** \plə̇ˈbēən, plēˈ-\ *n* -s [L *plebeius* of the common people (fr. *plebes, plebs* common people) + E *-an*; akin to Gk *plēthos* throng, L *plenus* full — more at FULL] **1 :** a member of the Roman plebs **2 a :** one who is not of noble birth **b :** a member of the working class **:** one of the common people ⟨a simple ~ —C.H.Sykes⟩

**²plebeian** *also* **plebian** \"\ *adj* [L *plebeius* + E *-an*] **1 :** of or relating to the Roman plebs **2 a :** of or relating to the common people ⟨the old nobility . . . had swallowed its pride and married wholesale into ~ families —Nancy Mitford⟩ **b :** having characteristics attributed to the general populace **:** crude or coarse in manner or style **:** COMMONPLACE, EVERYDAY, HOMELY, UNDISTINGUISHED ⟨a wild ~ desire to slap the handsome girl's face —J.C.Powys⟩ ⟨his square ~ nose —G.M. Trevelyan⟩ — **ple·be·ian·ly** *adv*

**ple·be·ian·ism** *also* **ple·bi·an·ism** \-ə,nizəm\ *n* -s **:** plebeian character, manners, or style **:** CRUDENESS, VULGARITY ⟨a Greek philosopher in the midst of foreign ~ —*Irish Statesman*⟩

**ple·be·ian·ize** \-ə,nīz\ *vt* -ED/-ING/-S **:** to make plebeian, common, or vulgar

**pleb·i·fi·ca·tion** \,plebəfə̇ˈkāshən\ *n* -s [*plebs* + *-i-* + *-fication*] **:** the act of plebeianizing **:** the state of being plebeianized ⟨represents the ~ of the Romantic spirit —F.J.Mather⟩ ⟨begin with the attempt to popularize learning . . . but you will end in the ~ of knowledge —S.T.Coleridge⟩

**ple·bis·ci·tary** \plə̇ˈbisə,terē\ *also* **ple·bis·ci·tar·i·an** \=ˌ==ˈta(a)rēən\ *adj* [*plebiscite* + *-ary* or *-arian* (fr. *-ary* + *-an*)] **:** of, relating to, based on, or of the nature of a plebiscite ⟨the ~ will of the whole people —Gordon Wright⟩

**pleb·i·scite** *also* **pleb·e·scite** \ˈplebə,sīt *also* -,sət *sometimes* ˈplēbə,sīt *or* ˈplebə,sēt; *usu* -d·+V\ *n* -s [in sense 1, fr. L *plebi scitum, plebiscitum*, fr. *plebi* (gen. of *plebes* common people) + *scitum* decree, fr. neut. of *scitus*, past part. of *sciscere* to try to find out, approve, decree, incho. of *scire* to know; in other senses, fr. F *plébiscite*, fr. L *plebiscitum* — more at PLEBEIAN, SCIENCE] **1 :** PLEBISCITUM 1 **2 a :** a vote or decree of the people usu. by universal suffrage on some measure submitted to them by some person or body having the initiative — compare REFERENDUM **3 a :** a vote of the people usu. by universal adult suffrage of some specified district or region on the question put before them by a treaty of peace or by an international body as to choice of sovereignty **b :** the political machinery for expressing self-determination

**pleb·i·sci·tum** \,plebəˈsīd·əm, ,plēb-\ *n, pl* **plebisci·ta** \-d·ə\ [L] **1 :** a vote or decree made by the ancient Roman comitia orig. binding only on the plebs **2 :** PLEBISCITE 2

**plebs** \ˈplebz\ *n, pl* **ple·bes** \ˈplē,bēz\ [L — more at PLEBEIAN] **1 :** the common people of ancient Rome consisting of a composite body of native or naturalized Romans of varying social origins — compare PATRICIAN **2 :** the general populace ⟨all this talk . . . was so much claptrap, inept fabrications to hoodwink the gullible ~ —F.S.Grafford⟩

**ple·cop·tera** \plə̇ˈkäptərə\ *n pl, cap* [NL, fr. *pleco-* (fr. Gk *plekein* to plait, weave) + *-ptera* — more at PLY] **:** an order of insects constituted by the stone flies

**ple·cop·ter·an** \-rən\ *n* -s [NL *Plecoptera* + E *-an*] **:** PLECOPTERID

**¹ple·cop·ter·id** \-rə̇d\ *or* **ple·cop·ter·ous** \-rəs\ *adj* [NL *Plecoptera* + E *-id* or *-ous*] **:** of or relating to the Plecoptera

**²plecopterid** \"\ *n* -s **:** an insect of the order Plecoptera **:** STONE FLY

**plec·o·tine** \ˈplekə,tīn\ *adj* [NL *Plecotus* + E *-ine*] **:** of or relating to the genus *Plecotus*

**ple·co·tus** \plə̇ˈkōd·əs\ *n, cap* [NL, fr. Gk *plekein* to twist, plait, weave + *ōt-, ous* ear — more at PLY, EAR] **:** a genus of bats (family Vespertilionidae) consisting of the common long-eared bat of Europe and Asia

**plect-** *or* **plecto-** *comb form* [Gk *plektos*, fr. *plekein*] **:** twisted ⟨*Plect*enchyma⟩ ⟨*plecto*gnath⟩

**plec·ta·nia** \plekˈtānēə\ *n, cap* [NL, fr. Gk *plektanē* wreath, coil (fr. *plekein* to plait) + NL *-ia*] **:** a genus of ascomycetous fungi with brightly colored, stalked, and often bristly apothecia that is often included in the closely related genus *Peziza*

**plec·tas·ca·les** \,plek,taˈskā(,)lēz\ *n pl, cap* [NL, fr. *plect-* + *asc-* + *-ales*] *in some classifications* **:** an order comprising ascomycetes in which the asci are not in a hymenial layer but are scattered throughout the tissue of perithecia or similar structures

**plec·ten·chy·ma** \plekˈteŋkəmə\ *n* -s [NL, fr. *plect-* + *-enchyma*] **:** a parenchymatous tissue formed by massed and twisted filaments or tubular cells esp. in fungi and lichens — compare PROSENCHYMA, PSEUDOPARENCHYMA — **plec·ten·chym·a·tous** \ˌplek,teŋˈkimədəs\ *adj*

**¹plec·tog·nath** \ˈplek,täg,nath\ *adj* [NL *Plectognathi*] **:** of or relating to the Plectognathi

**²plectognath** \"\ *n* -s **:** a fish of the order Plectognathi

**plec·tog·na·thi** \plekˈtägnə,thī\ *n pl, cap* [NL, fr. *plect-* + *-gnathi*, pl. of *-gnathus*] **:** an order of bony fishes that generally have the maxillary bone united with the premaxillary, the posttemporal united with the skull, and the gill openings greatly reduced in size, have the ventral fins rudimentary or wanting and the body usu. covered with bony plates, spines, or small rough ossicles, and include the boxfishes, filefishes, globefishes, sunfishes, triggerfishes, and related forms — **plec·tog·nath·ic** \ˌplek,tägˈnathik\ *adj* — **plec·tog·na·thous** \(ˈ)plekˈtägnəthəs\ *adj*

**plec·to·my·ce·tes** \ˌplektō,mīˈsēd·ēz\ *also* **plec·to·my·ce·tae** \-d·ē\ *n pl, cap* [NL, fr. *plect-* + *-mycetes* or *-mycetae* (fr. Gk *mykēt-, mykēs* fungus, mushroom) — more at MYC-] *in some classifications* **:** a subclass of Ascomycetes coextensive with the order Plectascales — **plec·to·my·ce·tous** \ˌ==ˌ=ˈsēd·əs\ *adj*

**plec·top·ter** \plekˈtäptə(r)\ *n* -s [NL *Plectoptera*] **:** an insect of the order Plectoptera

**plec·top·tera** \plekˈtäptərə\ *n pl, cap* [NL, fr. *plect-* + *-ptera*] **:** an order of slender delicate insects that have membranous net-veined wings, that comprise the mayflies and related insects, and that were formerly included among the Neuroptera — see EPHEMERIDAE

**¹plec·top·ter·an** \(ˈ)plekˈtäptərən\ *or* **plec·top·ter·ous** \-rəs\ *adj* [NL *Plectoptera* + E *-an* or *-ous*] **:** of or relating to the Plectoptera

**²plectopteran** \"\ *n* -s **:** PLECTOPTER

**¹plec·to·spon·dyl** \ˌplektōˈspändəl\ *adj* [NL *Plectospondyli*] **:** of or relating to the Plectospondyli

**²plectospondyl** \"\ *n* -s **:** a fish of the order Plectospondyli

**plec·to·spon·dy·li** \ˌ==ˈspändə,lī\ *n pl, cap* [NL, fr. *plect-* + *-spondyli*] *in some classifications* **:** an order or other group comprising fishes with the anterior vertebrae modified and united and usu. being more or less coextensive with Ostariophysi — **plec·to·spon·dyl·ous** \ˌ==ˈspändələs\ *adj*

**plec·to·stele** \ˈplektə,stēl *also* ˌ==ˈstēlē\ *n* [*plect-* + *stele*] **:** an actinostele (as in a club moss) in which the xylem elements are arranged in usu. parallel plates

**plec·tre** \ˈplektə(r)\ *n* -s [F, fr. L *plectrum* — more at PLECTRUM] **:** PLECTRUM

**plec·trid·i·al** \(ˈ)plekˈtridēəl\ *adj* [NL *plectridium* + E *-al*] **:** having the form of a drumstick

**plec·trid·i·um** \plekˈtridēəm\ *n, pl* **plectrid·ia** \-ēə\ [NL, fr. L *plectrum* + NL *-idium*] **:** a hammer-shaped or drumstick-shaped cell; *esp* **:** any of various rod-shaped bacteria formerly classed as a genus *Plectridium* in which one end becomes enlarged by the production of an endospore

**plec·tron** \ˈplek,trän\ *n* -s [Gk *plēktron*] **:** PLECTRUM 1

**plec·trop·o·mus** \plekˈträpəməs\ *n, cap* [NL, fr. Gk *plēktron* + NL *-pomus* (fr. Gk *pōma* lid, cover); akin to Gk *pōy* herd, flock — more at FUR] **:** a genus comprising tropical Indo-Pacific percoid food fishes (as the coral cod of Australia) and others that are dangerously poisonous when eaten and being sometimes isolated in a separate family but usu. included among the Serranidae

**plec·trum** \ˈplektrəm\ *n, pl* **plec·tra** \-rə\ *or* **plectrums** [L, fr. Gk *plēktron* striking instrument, spur, fr. *plēk-* (stem of *plēssein* to strike) + *-tron*, suffix denoting an instrument — more at PLAINT] **1 :** a small thin piece of ivory, wood, metal, horn, quill, or other material used in playing on plucked stringed musical instruments (as the lyre, mandolin) **2** [NL, fr. L] **:** any of various anatomic parts that suggest a plectrum in form

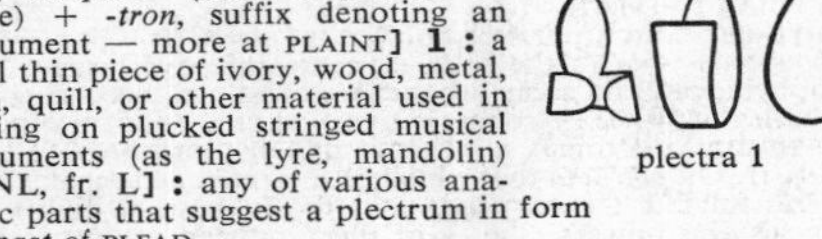

plectra 1

**pled** *past of* PLEAD

**¹pledge** \ˈplej\ *n* -s [ME *plegge*, fr. MF *plege*, fr. OF, fr. LL *plebium* security, fr. (assumed) LL *plebere* to pledge, prob. modif. (influenced by L *praebēre* to offer) of (assumed) OFrk *plegan* to be responsible for, guarantee; akin to OHG *pflegan* to take care of — more at PLIGHT, PREBEND] **1 a :** a person under early English law whose body is given as security for the performance of an obligation **:** HOSTAGE **b :** a chattel or object of personal property delivered by a debtor or obligor to a creditor or obligee to be kept by the latter until the debt or obligation is satisfied **:** an object given as security by pledge **c** (1) **:** a bailment of a chattel or object of personal property as security for the satisfaction of a debt or other obligation (2) **:** the contract, obligation, or form of property incidental to such a bailment **d :** the delivery without transfer of title of movables or objects capable of physical delivery and sharply distinguished from a common-law mortgage by the fact that in a pledge the title was not transferred while in the mortgage it was **e :** the transfer of a chose in action by delivery and transfer of title — compare MORTGAGE **2 :** the state of being held as a security or guaranty ⟨the camera spent three weeks in ~ at the shop —John Hersey⟩ **3 a :** something given or considered as a security for the performance of an act and usu. liable to forfeiture in case of nonperformance **b :** something in pawn ⟨kept the famous painting as a ~ that would be restored eventually to its original owner⟩ **4 :** something that is a token, sign, evidence, or earnest of something else ⟨the strong beat of his heart was a ~ of a vigorous life⟩ **5 :** a gage of battle ⟨threw his gauntlet as a sacred ~ —Edmund Spenser⟩ **6 :** a child that constitutes evidence of a bond between its parents **7 a :** an assurance of goodwill or favor given by drinking one's health **b :** the toasting of a person **8 a :** a promise or agreement by which one binds himself to do or forbear something ⟨in the typical Victorian romance a touch of the hand was a ~ of matrimony —M.D.Geismar⟩ **b :** a promise usu. in writing to refrain from using intoxicants or something considered harmful — usu. used with *the* ⟨takes a lifelong ~ to abstain from drinking whiskey —M.V.Reidy⟩ **9 a :** a promise to join a fraternity or secret society **b :** a person who has promised to join such a group but has not been initiated ⟨inculcating the doctrine of hospitality in all actives and ~s —J.E.Ivins⟩

**syn** EARNEST, TOKEN, PAWN, HOSTAGE: PLEDGE may apply to anything handed over as a security for fulfillment of a debt or promise or satisfaction of an obligation ⟨the pawnshop, where one waits nervously while the swarthy, shrewd-eyed attendant squints contemptuously at the *pledges* one offers —Donn Byrne⟩ ⟨property of the debtor in the creditor's possession was held as a valid *pledge* —*Harvard Law Rev.*⟩ EARNEST may designate a payment, usu. of money, serving to bind an agreement and indicate either the certainty or the likelihood of additional subsequent payments; in today's English it often indicates a reliable sign indicating a future course ⟨the boy or girl, man or woman, was hired and given the *earnest* . . . by the employer —F.D.Smith & Barbara Wilcox⟩ ⟨the gold on the surface was only an *earnest* of the gold veining the rocks beneath it —M.B.Eldershaw⟩ TOKEN may apply to any symbol or symbolizing action given as an indication of good faith, obligation, or indebtedness ⟨impossible to employ the Canadian Eskimos in the armed forces . . . (although a *token* group of four men from Aklavik has been officially enlisted) —Farley Mowat⟩ ⟨has not yet faced up to a service pay raise, though even a *token* raise could indicate to the regulars that they are held in some esteem —H. W.Baldwin⟩ PAWN indicates a person or thing given as a guaranty or security and eventually redeemable ⟨the folly of lending much money on such worthless *pawns*⟩ HOSTAGE usually refers to a person yielded into another's hands as a guaranty of the good intentions of the person or agency performing the yielding ⟨giving over their children as *hostages* to the invaders⟩

**²pledge** \"\ *vb* -ED/-ING/-S [ME *pleggen* to become surety for, fr. MF *plegier*, fr. OF, fr. *plege*, n.] *vt* **1 :** to give as a pledge **:** deposit (as a chattel) in pledge or pawn **:** make a pledge of **:** PAWN; *specif* **:** to assign as security for the repayment of a loan — compare COLLATERAL **2 :** to give assurance, promise, or evidence esp. of goodwill or favor by or in drinking to: **a** *obs* **:** to drink at the invitation of or in response to a toast proposed by **b :** to drink the health of **:** TOAST ⟨lifted his glass and *pledged* the beautiful girl⟩ **3 :** to bind by or as if by a pledge **:** PLIGHT ⟨*pledged* the signatory powers to meet the common danger —*Current Biog.*⟩ ⟨we mutually ~ to each other our lives, our fortunes, and our sacred honor —*U.S. Declaration of Independence*⟩ **4 a :** to assure or promise the performance of (as by a pledge) ⟨to ~ my vow, I give my hand —Shak.⟩ **b :** to promise seriously **:** UNDERTAKE ⟨I have *pledged* three stories —Malcolm Cowley⟩ **5 :** to cause (one) to make a pledge to join a group ⟨was *pledged* to join a fraternity⟩ ~ *vi* **1 :** to give or make a pledge **:** become surety **2 :** to drink a pledge **syn** see PROMISE

**pledg·ee** \(ˈ)pleˈjē\ *n* -s **1 :** one to whom a pledge is given **2 :** one who holds property as a pledge

**pledg·er** \ˈplejə(r)\ *n* -s **:** one that pledges

**pledges** *pl of* PLEDGE, *pres 3d sing of* PLEDGE

**pled·get** \ˈplejət\ *n* -s [origin unknown] **1 :** a compress or small flat mass usu. of gauze or absorbent cotton that is laid over a wound or into a cavity to apply medication, exclude air, retain dressings, or absorb the matter discharged **2 :** a thread of oakum used in caulking a boat

**pled·gor** *or* **pled·geor** \(ˈ)plejˈjó(ə)r, ˈplejə(r)\ *n* -s **:** PLEDGER

**pleg·a·dis** \ˈplegədə̇s\ *n, cap* [NL, fr. Gk *plēgad-, plēgas* scythe, sickle, fr. the stem of *plēssein* to strike — more at PLAINT] **:** a genus of birds (family Threskiornithidae) including the glossy ibis

**ple·gia** \ˈplēj(ē)ə\ *n* -s [*-plegia*] **:** PARALYSIS ⟨another type of ~⟩

**-plegia** \"\ *n comb form* -s [NL, fr. Gk *plēgē* blow, stroke (fr. the stem of *plēssein* to strike) + NL *-ia*] **:** paralysis of a specified nature ⟨para*plegia*⟩

**-ple·gy** \ˌplējē, -ji\ *n comb form* -ES [NL *-plegia*] **:** paralysis of a specified nature

**ple·iad** \ˈplēəd *also* ˈplīəd\ *n* -s [F *Pléiade*, a group of 7 16th cent. Fr. poets, fr. MF, fr. *Pléiade*, a group of 7 tragic poets of ancient Alexandria, fr. Gk *Pleiades, Pleiades*, pl., fr. *Pleiades, Plējades*, 7 stars in the constellation Taurus] **:** a usu. illustrious or brilliant group or cluster of persons or things usu. seven in number ⟨educated a brilliant ~ of great masters of painting —*Encyc. Americana*⟩

**ple·i·dae** \ˈplēə,dē\ *n pl, cap* [NL, fr. *Plea*, type genus (fr. Gk *plein* to sail, float, swim) + *-idae* — more at FLOW] **:** a widely distributed family of small aquatic bugs

**¹plein air** \ˈplān-\ *n* [F, lit., full air] **:** outdoor daylight ⟨to paint in *plein air*⟩ ⟨to render the high tonal values of the local *plein air*⟩

**²plein air** \"\ *adj* **1 :** relating to the method, action, or product of painting in outdoor daylight **2 :** of, relating to, or constituting a French art movement starting about 1865 which attempted to represent effects of outdoor light and air not observable in the studio

**plein·air·ism** \plāˈna(a)(,)rizəm\ *or* **plein·air·isme** \plenerēs(mᵊ), -ēz(mᵊ), -s(mə), -z(mə)\ *n* -s [F *pleinairisme*, fr. *plein air* + *-isme* -ism] **:** the study, action, or product of plein air painting; *specif* **:** the plein air art movement in France

**plein·air·ist** \-,rəst\ *or* **plein·air·iste** \-ēst\ *n* -s [F *pleinairiste*, fr. *plein air* + *-iste* -ist] **:** an adherent or follower of a theory, method, or practice of plein air painting

**plein jeu** \ˈplaⁿ-\ *n, often cap P&J* [F, lit., full play] **:** a mixture stop in a pipe organ including the unison, octave, and fifth

**pleio-** *or* **pleo-** *or* **plio-** *comb form* [*pleio-, plio-* fr. Gk *pleiōn, pleōn; pleo-* fr. LL, fr. Gk *pleon*, neut. of *pleōn* — more at PLUS] **1 :** more ⟨*Pleio*cene⟩ ⟨*pleo*morphism⟩ ⟨*pleo*mastia⟩ ⟨*Plio*cene⟩ **2 :** Pliocene ⟨*Plio*hippus⟩ ⟨*Plio*pithecus⟩

**plei·o·bar** \ˈplīə,bär\ *n* [ISV *pleio-* + Gk *baros* weight — more at GRIEVE] **1 :** an area of high barometric pressure **2 :** an isobar of high pressure

**plei·om·ery** \plīˈämərē\ *n* -ES [ISV *pleio-* + *-miery*] **:** a state of having more than the normal number of floral leaves

**pleiomorphic** *var of* PLEOMORPHIC

**plei·on** \ˈplī,än\ *n* -s [NL, fr. Gk *pleiōn* more, greater — more at PLUS] **:** a region in meteorology of positive departure from the normal of an element (as pressure, temperature, rainfall) — **plei·o·ni·an** \(ˈ)plīˈōnēən\ *adj*

**plei·o·phyl·ly** \ˈplīə,filē\ *n* -ES [ISV *pleio-* + *-phylly* (fr. *-phyll* + *-y*)] **:** an abnormal increase or excess in the number of leaves or leaflets

**plei·o·taxy** \ˈplīə,taksē\ *n* -ES [ISV *pleio-* + *-taxy*] **:** development of more than the normal number of parts (as bracts in a flower or inflorescence)

**plei·o·trop·ic** \ˌplīəˈträpik\ *adj* [*pleio-* + *-tropic*] *of a gene* **:** producing more than one effect **:** having multiple phenotypic expressions ⟨a ~ gene that induces shortening of the ear and reduces general body size has been reported in the mouse⟩ — **plei·o·trop·i·cal·ly** \-pə̇k(ə)lē\ *adv*

**plei·ot·ro·pism** \plīˈä·trə,pizəm\ *n* -s [*pleio-* + *-tropism*] **:** a condition produced by a pleiotropic gene

**plei·ot·ro·py** \-rəpē\ *n* -ES [ISV *pleio-* + *-tropy*] **:** the quality or state of being pleiotropic

**pleis·to·cene** \ˈplīstə,sēn\ *adj, usu cap* [ISV *pleisto-* (fr. Gk *pleistos* most) + *-cene*; akin to Gk *pleiōn* more — more at PLUS] **:** of, relating to, or constituting a subdivision of the Quaternary — see GEOLOGIC TIME table

**plen** *abbr* plenipotentiary

**plena** *pl of* PLENUM

**ple·na·ri·ly** \ˈplēnərəlē, ˈplen-, plə̇ˈner-\ *adv* **:** in a plenary manner

**ple·nar·ty** \ˈplēnə(r)d·ē, ˈplen-\ *n* -ES [ME *plenerte*, fr. MF *plenierté, plenerté*, fr. *plenier, plener* complete, full (fr. *plein, plen* full, fr. L *plenus*) + *-té* -ty — more at FULL] **:** the state of a benefice when occupied

**ple·na·ry** \ˈplēnərē, ˈplen-, -ri\ *adj* [LL *plenarius*, fr. L *plenus* full + *-arius*, -ary — more at FULL] **1 :** complete in every respect **:** ABSOLUTE, PERFECT, UNQUALIFIED ⟨the ~ inspiration of the Bible —M.R.Cohen⟩ ⟨a ~ state of cleanliness —Arnold Bennett⟩ **2 :** fully attended or constituted **:** including all entitled to be present ⟨a ~ session of the legislature⟩ ⟨~ assembly⟩ **3 :** including all steps in due order **:** COMPLETE ⟨a ~ proceeding⟩ — opposed to *summary*

**plenary council** *n* [trans. of LL *concilium plenarium*] **:** an assembly of the ecclesiastical authorities of a country or larger territory

**plenary indulgence** *n* [trans. of ML *plenaria indulgentia*] *Roman Catholicism* **:** a remission of the entire temporal punishment due to sin

**plenary inspiration** *n* **:** divine inspiration covering all subjects dealt with — compare VERBAL INSPIRATION

**ple·ne** \ˈplēnē\ *adj* [L *plenus* full; trans. of LHeb *mālē*] **:** having the full orthographic or grammatical form given in Masoretic texts as corrections of the defective forms that appeared in ancient biblical texts ⟨~ spelling⟩ ⟨~ writings⟩ — compare KERE, KETHIB

**ple·ne ad·mi·nis·tra·vit** \ˈplēnēəd,minəˈstrāvət\ [L] **:** he has fully administered — used at law referring to a plea in bar by an executor or administrator when sued by a creditor, heir, or legatee

**ple·ni·lune** \ˈplēnə,lün, ˈplen-\ *n* -s [ME, fr. L *plenilunium*, fr. *plenus* full + *-i-* + *-lunium* (fr. *luna* moon) — more at FULL, LUNAR] **:** the time of full moon; *also* **:** a full moon

**plen·i·po** \ˈplenə,pō\ *n* -s [by shortening] **:** PLENIPOTENTIARY

**ple·nip·o·tence** \plə̇ˈnipəd·ən(t)s\ *n* -s **:** the quality or state of being invested with authority or power to transact business

**ple·nip·o·tent** \-nt\ *adj* [LL *plenipotent-, plenipotens*, fr. L *plenus* full + *-i-* + *potent-, potens* able, powerful — more at FULL, POTENT] **:** PLENIPOTENTIARY

**plen·i·po·ten·tial** \ˌplenəpəˈtenchəl\ *adj* [LL *plenipotent-, plenipotens* + E *-ial*] **:** PLENIPOTENTIARY

**¹plen·i·po·ten·tia·ry** \-chərē, -chē,erē, -ri\ *adj* [ML *plenipotentiarius*, adj. & n., fr. LL *plenipotent-, plenipotens* + *-i-* + L *-arius* -ary] **1 :** containing or conferring full power **:** invested with full power **:** ABSOLUTE, UNLIMITED ⟨countries with ~ parliaments —E.V.Rostow⟩ **2 :** of or relating to a plenipotentiary

**²plenipotentiary** \"\ *n* -ES [ML *plenipotentiarius*] **:** a person invested with full power to transact any business; *esp* **:** MINISTER PLENIPOTENTIARY

**plen·ish** \ˈplenish\ *vt* -ED/-ING/-ES [ME (Sc dial.) *plenyssen*, fr. MF *pleniss-*, stem of *plenir*, fr. OF, fr. *plein, plen* full, fr. L *plenus* — more at FULL] **1 a :** to fill up **b** *chiefly dial* **:** REPLENISH **2** *chiefly Brit* **:** to equip (a house or farm) with furnishings

**plenishing** *n* -s [fr. gerund of *plenish*] *chiefly Scot* **:** furniture, equipment, and stock esp. as needed to run a farm

**ple·nist** \ˈplēnəst\ *n* -s [L *plenus* full, complete + E *-ist*] **:** one who maintains that there are no vacuums in nature — compare VACUIST

**plen·i·tude** \ˈplenə,tüd, -ə,tyüd\ *or* **plent·i·tude** \-ntə-\ *n* -s [*plenitude* fr. ME, fr. MF or L; MF, fr. L *plenitudo*, fr. *plenus* full + *-i-* + *-tudo* -tude; *plentitude* alter. (influenced by *plenty*) of *plenitude* — more at FULL] **1 :** the quality or state of being full **:** absolute fullness **:** COMPLETENESS ⟨death . . . in the ~ of health, vigor, and aspirations —George Grote⟩ ⟨loves and sorrows that are great are destroyed by their own ~ —Oscar Wilde⟩ **2 :** a more than ample amount or number **:** great sufficiency **:** ABUNDANCE ⟨the ~ of plants around them —Napier Devitt⟩ ⟨sea gulls gorge themselves on a ~ of fish —Renate O'Connell⟩ ⟨her long skirts are voluminous and worn over a ~ of petticoats —Mabel S. Shelton⟩ ⟨exchange . . . their Old World stone cottages and thatched barns for a ~ of lumber —*Amer. Guide Series: Minn.*⟩ **3** *of a flower* **:** DOUBLENESS **4** *heraldry* **:** fullness of the moon

**plen·i·tu·di·nous** \ˌplenəˈtüdᵊnəs, -əˈtyü-\ *adj* [L *plenitudin-, plenitudo* plenitude + E *-ous*] **1 :** characterized by plenitude ⟨with manifold and ~ life —Robert Browning⟩ **2 :** PORTLY, STOUT — used humorously

**plenshing nail** *var of* PLANCHING NAIL

**plen·te·ous** \ˈplentēəs\ *adj* [ME *plentivous, plentious*, fr. OF *plentiveus, plentivous, plentious*, fr. *plentif* abundant (fr. *plenté* abundance, plenty + -*if* -ive) + -*eus*, -*ous* -ous — more at PLENTY] **1 :** bearing or yielding abundance **:** FRUITFUL, PRODUCTIVE — usu. used with *in* or *of* ⟨the seasons had been ~ in corn —George Eliot⟩ **2 :** constituting, characterized by, or existing in plenty ⟨gathered gold and silver, and ~ . . . goods —William Morris⟩ ⟨~ grace with thee is found —Charles Wesley⟩ **3** *obs* **:** giving liberally **:** BOUNTIFUL ⟨with ~ hand, bring clover grass —John Dryden⟩ **syn** see PLENTIFUL

**plen·te·ous·ly** *adv* [ME *plentivously, plentiously,* fr. *plentivous, plentious* + -*ly*] **:** in a plenteous manner ⟨he provided for her ~ while he lived —S.H.Adams⟩

**plen·te·ous·ness** *n* -ES [ME *plentivousnesse, plentiousnesse,* fr. *plentivous, plentious* + -*nesse* -ness] **:** the quality or state of being plenteous

**plen·ti·ful** \'plentəfəl, -tēf-\ *adj* **1 :** containing or yielding plenty **:** FRUITFUL, OPULENT ⟨a ~ land⟩ ⟨a ~ supper of roast and boiled beef and mutton —W.H.Hudson †1922⟩ **2 :** characterized by, constituting, or existing in plenty **:** NUMEROUS ⟨the deer are as ~ as the vast wilderness will support —S.H. Holbrook⟩ ⟨his religion . . . summoned him to serve the ~ reform movements of the day —V.L.Parrington⟩

**syn** PLENTEOUS, AMPLE, ABUNDANT, COPIOUS: these adjectives have the common meaning of more than adequate or sufficient yet not in excess. That is PLENTIFUL or PLENTEOUS of which there is a rich or full, usu. more than full, supply ⟨a *plentiful* supply of books⟩ ⟨butter is cheap when it is *plentiful*, and dear when it is scarce —G.B.Shaw⟩ ⟨aluminum, one of the world's most *plentiful* elements —*Amer. Guide Series: Pa.*⟩ ⟨a *plenteous* number of individual poems —*College English*⟩ ⟨a *plenteous* harvest —J.G.Frazer⟩ That is AMPLE which is generously sufficient to satisfy a particular requirement ⟨manufacturers had *ample* supplies on hand to meet the emergency —*Current Biog.*⟩ ⟨provide *ample* opportunity for fieldwork with Indian tribes —D.G.Mandelbaum⟩ ⟨*ample* proof of the power of words —*advt*⟩ ABUNDANT suggests a greater or richer supply than does PLENTIFUL ⟨her unselfish and *abundant* interests —Rex Ingamells⟩ ⟨the many small denominational colleges so *abundant* throughout the Middle West —G.P. Merrill⟩ COPIOUS, not quite interchangeable with PLENTIFUL, puts emphasis upon largeness of supply more than on fullness or richness ⟨his papers were *copious* and bizarre, and it took me nearly two hours to find the will —John Cheever⟩ ⟨his *copious* flaxen curls —Richard Garnett †1906⟩ ⟨washed down with *copious* drafts of beer —Green Peyton⟩

**plen·ti·ful·ly** \-f(ə)lē, -li\ *adv* **:** in more than adequate numbers or quantity **:** ABUNDANTLY

**plen·ti·ful·ness** *n* -ES **:** the quality or state of being plentiful

**plentitude** *var of* PLENITUDE

**¹plen·ty** \'plentē, -ti\ *n* -ES [ME *plente, plentee, plentie,* fr. OF *plenté,* fr. L *plenitat-, plenitas* fullness, abundance, fr. *plenus* full + -*itat-, -itas* -ity — more at FULL] **1 a :** a more than adequate number, quantity, or amount **:** a full supply **:** enough and to spare ⟨always gave them ~ of time —Seymour Blau⟩ ⟨cowboys on the range still do ~ of roping —S.E.Fletcher⟩ ⟨would have ~ of visitors —H.E.Scudder⟩ **b :** a large number or amount of something — used with *a* ⟨a ~ of things to be done —Verne Athanas⟩ ⟨what they asked for they got, and they asked for a ~ —*Amer. Mercury*⟩ **2 a :** an abundance esp. of material things that permit a satisfactory life **:** a condition or time of abundance ⟨the general feeling of ~ in this rich land —Pearl Buck⟩ ⟨a peace that seemed to bring ~ in its train —Stringfellow Barr⟩ **b plenties** *pl* **:** plentiful amounts esp. of things that constitute material comfort ⟨drink *plenties* of this milk too —J.L.Weldon⟩ **3 :** the quality or state of being copious **:** PLENTIFULNESS — often used with *in* ⟨down by the lake the daffodils were now in their ~ —Victoria Sackville-West⟩ ⟨will . . . gain pleasure and profit in ~ —H.M. Parshley⟩

**²plenty** \"\ *adj* [ME *plente,* fr. *plente,* n.] **1 :** ample in amount or supply **:** PLENTIFUL ⟨if reasons were as ~ as blackberries —Shak.⟩ ⟨bread is never too ~ in Indian households —Willa Cather⟩ **2 a** *chiefly dial* **:** existing in large quantity or number ⟨who has conies ~ to dispose of cheap —Jeremy Bentham⟩ **b :** AMPLE, MANY **:** more than enough ⟨he could get ~ men . . . to do his bidding —W.C.Tuttle⟩ ⟨there is ~ work to be done —*Time*⟩ ⟨you'll have ~ support from the other districts —Ralph Ellison⟩

**³plenty** \"\ *adv* **:** more than sufficiently **:** ABUNDANTLY, PLENTIFULLY ⟨they will talk ~, but not about themselves —J.L.Phelan⟩ ⟨her style is ~ vigorous enough —Florence Bullock⟩ ⟨the nights were ~ cold —F.B.Gipson⟩ ⟨a transatlantic holiday is ~ exciting —T.H.Fielding⟩

**¹plenum** \'plenəm, -lēn-\ *n, pl* **plenums** \-mz\ *or* **plena** \-nə\ [NL, fr. L, neut. of *plenus* full — more at FULL] **1 a :** a space or all space every part of which is full of matter — opposed to *vacuum* **b** (1) **:** a condition in which the pressure of the air in an enclosed space is greater than that of the outside atmosphere (2) **:** an enclosed space in which such a condition exists; *esp* **:** a plenum chamber **2 a :** a general assembly of all members esp. of a legislative body **b :** the entire membership of a specific group **3 :** the quality or state of being full

**²plenum** \"\ *adj* **:** relating to or being a space in which a plenum exists ⟨a ~ chamber in a hot-air furnace⟩ ⟨the ~ system forces air into the room, causing a leakage outward although exhaust ducts may also be provided —V.M.Ehlers & E.W.Steel⟩

**plenum ventilation** *n* **:** a system of ventilation that applies the motive force at the inlets, drives the air through the rooms which become plenums, and avoids the incoming of cold drafts

**pleo-** — see PLEIO-

**pleo·chro·ic** \¦plēə¦krōik\ *adj* [ISV *pleio-* + -*chroic*] **:** of, relating to, or having pleochroism

**ple·och·ro·ism** \plē'äkrə,wizəm\ *n* -s [ISV *pleochroic* + -*ism*] **:** the property possessed by a crystal of showing different colors when viewed by light that vibrates parallel to different axes — see DICHROISM, TRICHROISM

**ple·och·ro·ous** \-rəwəs\ *adj* [*pleio-* + -*chroous*] **:** PLEOCHROIC

**ple·o·cy·to·sis** \,plēō,sī'tōsəs\ *n, pl* **pleocyto·ses** \-'tō,sēz\ [NL, fr. *pleio-* + *cyt-* + -*osis*] **:** an abnormal increase in the number of cells (as lymphocytes) in the cerebrospinal fluid

**ple·o·dont** \'plēə,dänt\ *adj* [ISV *pleo-* (fr. Gk *pleos* full) + -*odont;* akin to Gk *plērēs* full — more at FULL] **:** having solid teeth ⟨~ reptiles⟩

**ple·o·mas·tia** \,plēə'mastēə\ *n* -s [NL, fr. *pleio-* + -*mastia*] **:** a condition of having more than two mammary glands or nipples — **ple·o·mas·tic** \¦==¦mastik\ *adj*

**ple·o·ma·zia** \,==ˈmāz(h)ēə\ *n* -s [NL, fr. *pleio-* + *maz-* + -*ia*] **:** PLEOMASTIA

**ple·o·me·tro·sis** \,plēōmə'trōsəs\ *n, pl* **pleometro·ses** \-rō,sēz\ [NL, fr. *pleio-* + Gk *mētēr* queen bee, mother + NL -*osis* — more at MOTHER] **:** the occurrence of several queens in a single nest of ants

**ple·o·me·trot·ic** \¦==¦trädik\ *adj* [fr. NL *pleometrosis,* after such pairs as NL *narcosis:* E *narcotic*] **:** of, relating to, or characterized by pleometrosis

**ple·o·morph** \'plēə,mȯrf\ *n* -s [back-formation fr. *pleomorphic*] **:** POLYMORPH 1, 2

**ple·o·mor·phic** \¦==¦mȯrfik\ *also* **plei·o·mor·phic** \¦plīə-\ *adj* [ISV *pleomorphism* + -*ic*] **:** of, relating to, or characterized by pleomorphism

**ple·o·mor·phism** \,==ˈmȯ(r),fizəm\ *n* -s [ISV *pleio-* + -*morphism*] **1 :** the occurrence of more than one distinct form in the life cycle of some plants (as the rusts) **2 :** POLYMORPHISM a

**ple·o·mor·phous** \¦==¦mȯrfəs\ *adj* [ISV *pleomorphism* + -*ous*] **:** PLEOMORPHIC

**ple·o·mor·phy** \'==,mȯrfē\ *n* -ES [*pleomorphous* + -*y*] **:** PLEOMORPHISM

**ple·on** \'plē,än\ *n* -s [NL, fr. Gk *pleōn,* pres. part. of *plein* to sail; fr. the fact that it bears the swimming limbs — more at FLOW] **1 :** the abdomen of a crustacean **2 :** the telson of a king crab — **ple·o·nal** \-ēən°l\ *or* **ple·on·ic** \(')plē¦änik\ *adj*

**ple·o·nasm** \'plēə,nazəm\ *n* -s [LL *pleonasmus,* fr. Gk *pleonasmos,* fr. *pleonazein* to be more, to be in excess, to be redundant, fr. *pleon,* neut. of *pleiōn, pleōn* more] **1 a :** iteration or repetition in speaking or in writing **:** the use of more words than those necessary to denote mere sense (as *the man he said, saw with his own eyes, true fact*); *esp* **:** the coincident use of a word and its substitute for the same grammatical function **:** REDUNDANCY, TAUTOLOGY **b :** an instance or example of such iteration **2 :** SUPERFLUITY ⟨a ~ or overflow of that great kindness —Samuel Purchos⟩

**ple·o·naste** \'plēə,nast\ *n* -s [F, fr. Gk *pleonastos* abundant, fr. *pleonazein* to be more; fr. the many faces of the crystal] **:** CEYLONITE

**ple·o·nas·tic** \¦plēə¦nastik\ *adj* [fr. *pleonasm,* after such pairs as E *spasm: spastic*] **:** of, relating to, or having the characteristics of pleonasm — **ple·o·nas·ti·cal·ly** \-tək(ə)lē\ *adv*

**pleonastic genitive** *n* **:** DOUBLE POSSESSIVE

**ple·o·nex·ia** \,plēə'neksēə\ *n* -s [Gk, fr. *pleonektein* to be greedy, to have or want more, fr. *pleon,* neut. of *pleiōn, pleōn* more + *echein* to have — more at PLEIO-, SCHEME] **:** AVARICE, COVETOUSNESS

**ple·oph·a·gous** \plē'äfəgəs\ *adj* [*pleio-* + -*phagous*] **1 :** eating a variety of foods **2** *of a parasite* **:** not restricted to a single kind of host

**ple·o·pod** \'plēə,päd\ *n* -s [*pleio-* (fr. Gk *pleōn,* pres. part. of *plein* to sail) + -*pod;* fr. its being used for swimming — more at FLOW] **:** an abdominal limb of a crustacean

**ple·op·o·dite** \plē'äpə,dīt\ *n* -s [*pleopod* + -*ite*] **:** PLEOPOD

**ple·o·sponge** \'plēə,spənj\ *n* [NL *Pleospongia,* fr. *pleio-* + -*spongia*] **:** any of various Lower and Middle Cambrian calcareous, cylindrical or cup-shaped, double-walled, porous fossils that may be the remains of sponges or primordial precursors of the true corals

**ple·os·po·ra** \plē'äspərə\ *n, cap* [NL, fr. *pleio-* + -*spora*] **:** a genus of ascomycetous fungi (family Sphaeriaceae) having brown muriform ascospores in scattered or gregarious perithecia

**ple·o·spo·ra·ce·ae** \,plēəspə'rāsē,ē\ *n pl, cap* [NL, fr. *Pleospora* + -*aceae*] **:** a family of ascomycetous fungi (order Sphaeriales) that is sometimes combined with Mycosphaerellaceae and that includes parasitic fungi which cause stem or leaf spot diseases or rots of economic plants

**pler·er·gate** \pli'rər,gāt\ *n* [Gk *plērēs* full + E *ergate* — more at FULL] **:** REPLETE

**ple·ro·cer·coid** \,plirə'sər,kȯid\ *n* -s [*plero-* (fr. Gk *plērēs* full) + *cerc-* + -*oid*] **:** the solid elongate infective larva of pseudophyllidean and some other tapeworms usu. occurring in the muscles of fishes — compare CYSTICERCUS, PROCERCOID

**ple·ro·ma** \plə'rōmə\ *n, pl* **pleromas** *or* **pleromata** [LL, fullness, fr. Gk *plērōma* that which fills, fr. *plēroun* to make full, fr. *plērēs* full] **1 :** PLENITUDE: **a :** the fullness of divine excellencies and powers ⟨the ~ of the Godhead resides in Christ corporeally —Philip Schaff⟩ **b :** the fullness of being of the divine life held in Gnosticism to comprise the aeons as well as the uncreated monad or dyad from which they have proceeded **2** [NL, fr. LL, fullness] **:** PLEROME — **ple·ro·mat·ic** \¦plirə¦madik\ *adj*

**pleroma violet** *n* **:** a moderate purple that is bluer and duller than manganese violet or heliotrope (sense 4a) and bluer than average amethyst

**ple·rome** \'pli,rōm\ *also* **ple·rom** \-irəm\ *n* -s [G *plerom,* fr. LL *pleroma*] **1 :** the central core of primary meristem of a plant or plant part that according to the histogen theory gives rise to the stele **2 :** the stelar region in a root tip

**ple·roph·o·ry** \plə'räfərē\ *n* -ES [Gk *plērophoria,* fr. *plērophorein* to bring full measure, to fulfill, fr. *plērēs* full + *phorein,* freq. of *pherein* to carry — more at BEAR] *archaic* **:** complete assurance ⟨the ~ of faith —John Trapp⟩

**ple·rot·ic water** \plə'rädik-\ *n* [*plerotic* fr. L *pleroticus* filling up, fr. Gk *plērōtikos,* fr. *plēroun* to make full + -*ikos* -ic] **:** GROUNDWATER

**plesi-** *or* **plesio-** *comb form* [NL *plesi-,* fr. Gk *plēsi-, plēsio-,* fr. *plēsios,* fr. *pelas* near — more at FELT] **:** close **:** near ⟨*plesio*morphous⟩ ⟨*plesio*saurus⟩

**ple·si·an·thro·pus** \,plēsē'an(t)thrəpəs, -sē,an'thrōpəs\ *n, cap* [NL, fr. *plesi-* + -*anthropus*] **:** a genus of australopithecine apes with a distinctly humanlike skull — compare STERKFONTEIN APE-MAN

**ple·si·o·bi·o·sis** \,plēsēō,bī'ōsəs\ *n, pl* **plesiobio·ses** \-ō,sēz\ [NL, fr. *plesi-* + -*biosis*] **:** casual association of two or more colonies of social insects

**ple·si·o·saur** \'plēsə,sȯ(ə)r\ *n* -s [NL *Plesiosauria*] **:** a reptile or fossil of the suborder Plesiosauria

**ple·si·o·sau·ria** \,==='sȯrēə\ *n pl, cap* [NL, fr. *plesi-* + -*sauria*] **1** *cap* **:** a suborder of Sauropterygia comprising Mesozoic marine reptiles with dorsoventrally flattened bodies and limbs modified into paddles — compare PLESIOSAURUS **2** *in some classifications* **:** an order of Reptilia nearly coextensive with Sauropterygia — **ple·si·o·sau·ri·an** \¦===¦sȯrēən\ *adj or n* — **ple·si·o·sau·roid** \-ō,rȯid\ *adj*

**ple·si·o·sau·rus** \,==='sȯrəs\ *n* [NL, fr. *plesi-* + -*saurus*] **1** *cap* **:** a genus of marine reptiles (suborder Plesiosauria) of the Mesozoic of Europe and No. America having a very long neck, a small head, and all four limbs developed as paddles for swimming **2** *pl* **plesiosau·ri** \-ō,rī\ **:** any reptile of the genus *Plesiosaurus*

**ple·si·o·type** \'plēsēə,tīp\ *n* [*plesi-* + *type*] **1 :** a specimen that is both a homeotype and a hypotype **2 :** a specimen identified by other than the original author of a species

**ples·site** \'ple,sīt\ *n* -s [G *plessit,* prob. fr. Gk *plēsi-* plesi- + G -*it* -ite] **:** a mineral consisting of an intimate intergrowth of kamacite and taenite in meteorites

**ples·sor** \'plesə(r)\ *n* -s [by alter.] **:** PLEXOR

**ples·sy's green** \(')ple¦sēz-\ *n, usu cap P* **:** a bluish green pigment consisting essentially of hydrated chromium phosphate $CrPO_4.nH_2O$

**plet** \'plet\ *dial var of* PLAT

**pleth·o·don** \'plethə,dän\ *n* [NL *pleth-* (fr. Gk *plēthos* mass, magnitude, fr. *plēthein* to be full) + -*odon*] **1** *cap* **:** the type genus of Plethodontidae comprising New World terrestrial salamanders that lay large yolk-filled eggs and do not pass through an aquatic larval period — see RED-BACKED SALAMANDER **2** -s **:** a salamander of the genus *Plethodon*

**¹pleth·o·dont** \-nt\ *also* **pleth·o·don·tid** \¦==¦däntəd\ *adj* [NL *Plethodontidae*] **:** of or relating to the Plethodontidae

**²plethodont** \"\ *also* **plethodontid** \"\ *n* -s **:** a salamander of the family Plethodontidae

**pleth·o·don·ti·dae** \,=='däntə,dē\ *n pl, cap* [NL, fr. *Plethodont-, Plethodon,* type genus + -*idae*] **:** a large family of small chiefly No. American terrestrial or freshwater salamanders that have neither lungs nor gills as adults — see PLETHODON

**pleth·o·ra** \'plethərə *sometimes* plə'thōrə *or* -'thȯrə\ *n* -s [ML, fr. Gk *plēthōra* fullness, plethora, fr. *plēthein* to be full — more at FULL] **1 :** a bodily condition characterized by an excess of blood and marked by turgescence and a florid complexion **2 :** an often undesirable or hampering superfluity **:** EXCESS, PROFUSION ⟨a ~ of . . . attractions to look at —Janet Flanner⟩ ⟨to plow through a ~ of references —Dwight MacDonald⟩ ⟨the ~ of distracting activities —Virgil Thomson⟩ **3 :** a defect of wood resulting from excessive and uneven growth of the tissues

**pleth·o·ric** \'plethərik, plə'thȯr, -'thär-, -rēk\ *adj* [LL *plethoricus,* fr. Gk *plēthōrikos,* fr. *plēthōra* plethora + -*ikos* -ic] **1 :** marked by plethora ⟨a ~ condition⟩ **2 :** marked by excess or profusion ⟨that ~ opulence —*Asiatic Annual Register*⟩ ⟨~ volumes which slumber in decorous old libraries —J.H. Burton⟩

**pleth·o·ry** \'plethərē\ *n* -ES [fr. *plethoric,* after such pairs as E *allegoric: allegory*] *archaic* **:** PLETHORA ⟨the state of the nation is full even to ~ —Edmund Burke⟩

**pleth·ron** \'plethrən\ *n, pl* **pleth·ra** \-rə\ [Gk] **1 :** an ancient Greek unit of length equal to 100 Greek feet or 101.2 modern feet **2 :** a unit of area equal to one square plethron

**ple·thys·mo·gram** \plə'thizmə,gram, -ism-\ *n* [ISV *plethysmo-* (fr. *plethysmograph*) + -*gram*] **:** a tracing made by a plethysmograph

**ple·thys·mo·graph** \-raf, -räf\ *n* [ISV *plethysmo-* (fr. Gk *plēthysmos* multiplication, increase, fr. *plēthynein* to increase, fr. *plēthys, plēthos* mass, magnitude) + -*graph;* orig. formed as It *pletismografo*] **:** an instrument for determining and registering variations in the size of an organ or limb and in the amount of blood present or passing through it

**ple·thys·mo·graph·ic** \¦=¦==¦grafik\ *adj* **:** of, relating to, or made by means of the plethysmograph — **ple·thys·mo·graph·i·cal·ly** \-fək(ə)lē\ *adv*

**pleth·ys·mog·ra·phy** \,plethəz'mägrəfē, -thəs'-\ *n* -ES **:** the use of the plethysmograph **:** examination by plethysmograph

**ple·thys·mo·thal·lus** \plə,thizmə'thaləs, -ism-\ *n* [NL, fr. Gk *plēthysmos* multiplication + NL *thallus*] **:** a dwarf filamentous thallus occurring in the life cycle of various brown algae and bearing at what appears to be a juvenile stage either unilocular or plurilocular sporangia

**pleur-** *or* **pleuri-** *or* **pleuro-** *comb form* [NL, fr. L, fr. Gk, side, rib, fr. *pleura*] **1 a :** pleura ⟨*pleur*ectomy⟩ ⟨*pleuri*septate⟩ ⟨*pleuro*genic⟩ **b :** pleura and ⟨*pleuro*pericarditis⟩ ⟨*pleuro*pedal⟩ **2 :** side **:** lateral ⟨*pleur*ite⟩ ⟨*pleuro*centrum⟩ **3 :** rib ⟨*pleur*al⟩

**¹pleu·ra** \'plu̇rə, 'plürə\ *n, pl* **pleu·rae** \-,rē, -,rī\ *or* **pleuras** [ML, fr. Gk, side, rib — more at PLEURISY] **1 a :** either of a pair of two-walled sacs of serous membrane each lining one lateral half of the thorax, having an inner layer closely adherent to the corresponding lung, reflected at the root of the lung to form a parietal layer that adheres to the walls of the thorax, the pericardium, upper surface of the diaphragm, and adjacent parts, and containing a small amount of serous fluid that minimizes the friction of respiratory movements **b :** the membranous tissue making up the pleurae **2** [NL, fr. Gk] **:** a laterally located body part; *specif* **:** PLEURON

**²pleura** *pl of* PLEURON *or of* PLEURUM

**-pleu·ra** \'plu̇rə, 'plürə\ *n comb form* -s [NL, fr. ML *pleura*] **:** lining **:** girdle ⟨endo*pleura*⟩ ⟨epi*pleura*⟩

**pleu·ra·can·thea** \,plu̇rə'kan(t)thēə\ *or* **pleu·ra·can·thi·ni** \-rə,kan'thī,nī\ *or* **pleu·rac·an·tho·di·i** \,plu̇,rakən'thōdē,ī\ [*pleuracanthea* fr. NL, fr. *pleur-* + -*acanthea* (fr. -*acanthus*); *pleuracanthini* fr. NL, fr. *pleur-* + *acanth-* + -*ini; pleuracanthodii,* fr. NL, fr. *pleur-* + *Acanthodii*] *syn of* ICHTHYOTOMI

**pleu·ra·can·thus** \,plu̇rə'kan(t)thəs\ *n, cap* [NL, fr. *pleur-* + -*acanthus*] **:** a genus (the type of the family Pleuracanthidae) of Paleozoic sharks of the Carboniferous and Lower Permian of Europe and No. America having a subterminal mouth, long dorsal fin, and a strong serrated spine on the nape

**¹pleu·ral** \'plu̇rəl, 'plür-\ *adj* [*pleur-* + -*al*] **1 :** of or relating to the pleura or the sides of the thorax **2 :** of or relating to a pleuron or pleurite

**²pleural** \"\ *n* -s [*pleur-* + -*al*] **1 :** a bony process in a turtle lying superficial to the ribs and uniting them and thereby forming most of the carapace **2 :** a rib or long ray of bone articulating with a vertebra and extending ventrally into the abdominal wall of a fish

**pleural cavity** *n* **1 :** the space between the two layers of pleura **2 :** the chest cavity

**pleural effusion** *n* **1 :** an exudation of fluid from the blood or lymph into a pleural cavity **2 :** an exudate in a pleural cavity

**pleural ganglion** *n* [¹*pleural*] **:** either of a pair of ganglia in a mollusk that send nerves to the mantle and parts of the body wall behind the head and that often lie close to or are fused with the cerebral ganglia

**pleural muscle** *n* **:** any of several muscles that operate the insect wing

**pleural sclerite** *n* **:** any of several plates of the pleural area of the insect integument

**pleur·ap·o·phys·i·al** \plu̇¦rapə¦fizēəl\ *adj* [*pleurapophysis* + -*al*] **:** of, relating to, or having the characteristics of a pleurapophysis

**pleur·apoph·y·sis** \,plu̇rə'päfəsəs\ *n* [NL, fr. *pleur-* + *apophysis*] **:** a laterally or more or less ventrally directed process or appendage of a vertebra forming a rib or part corresponding to a rib **:** a rib that is a part of a vertebra

**pleuri-** — see PLEUR-

**pleu·ric** \'plu̇rik\ *adj* [F *pleurique,* fr. L *pleuricus* lateral, fr. Gk *pleurikos,* fr. *pleura* side, rib + -*ikos* -ic] **:** PLEURAL

**pleu·ri·sy** \'plu̇rəsē, 'plür-, -si\ *n* -ES [ME *pleresie, pluresie,* fr. MF *pleuresie,* fr. ML *pleuresis,* alter. of LL *pleurisis,* alter. of L *pleuritis,* fr. Gk, fr. *pleura* side, rib + -*itis;* prob. akin to Gk *platys* flat, broad — more at PLACE] **1 :** inflammation of the pleura with or without effusion of an exudate into the pleural cavity — see DRY PLEURISY, WET PLEURISY **2** [influenced in meaning by L *plur-, plus* more — more at PLUS] *obs* **:** EXCESS, ABUNDANCE ⟨for goodness, growing to a ~, dies in his own too much —Shak.⟩

**pleurisy root** *n* **1 :** BUTTERFLY WEED **2 :** ASCLEPIAS 3a

**pleu·rite** \'plu̇,rīt\ *n* -s [*pleur-* + -*ite*] **1 :** any of various small sclerites in the pleural area of an arthropod; *sometimes* **:** PLEURON **2 :** the membranous part of the lateral abdominal wall of some insects

**pleu·rit·ic** \(')plu̇¦rid·¦ik, (')plü¦-, plə'r-, -it¦, ¦ēk\ *adj* [modif. (influenced by *pleurisy*) of MF *pleuretique* & ML *pleureticus,* fr. LL *pleuriticus,* fr. Gk *pleuritikos,* fr. *pleuritis* + -*ikos* -ic] **:** of, relating to, or suffering from pleurisy

**pleu·ri·tis** \plü'rīdəs\ *n, pl* **pleurit·i·des** \-'ridə,dēz\ [L] **:** PLEURISY

**pleuro-** — see PLEUR-

**pleu·ro·bra·chia** \,plu̇rə'brākēə\ *n, cap* [NL, fr. *pleur-* + *brachia*] **:** a genus (the type of the family Pleurobrachiidae) of globose or ovoid relatively firm-bodied ctenophores

**pleu·ro·branch** \'plu̇rə,braŋk\ *also* **pleu·ro·bran·chia** \,==-'braŋkēə\ *n, pl* **pleurobranchs** \-ks\ *also* **pleurobranchi·ae** \-kē,ē\ [*pleurobranch* ISV *pleur-* + -*branch; pleurobranchia* fr. NL, fr. *pleur-* + -*branchia*] **:** a gill of a crustacean arising from the side of the thorax — compare PODOBRANCH — **pleu·ro·bran·chi·al** \¦==¦braŋkēəl\ *or* **pleu·ro·bran·chi·ate** \-ēət, -ē,āt\ *adj*

**pleu·ro·bronchitis** \¦plu̇rō+\ *n* [NL, fr. *pleur-* + *bronchitis*] **:** combined pleurisy and bronchitis

**pleu·ro·cap·sa** \,plu̇rə'kapsə\ *n, cap* [NL, fr. *pleur-* + L *capsa* chest, case — more at CASE] **:** a genus (the type of the family Pleurocapsaceae) of branching filamentous epiphytic blue-green algae reproducing by true endospores that is sometimes isolated in a separate order

**pleu·ro·carp** \'plu̇rə,kärp\ *n* -s [ISV *pleur-* + -*carp*] **:** a pleurocarpous moss

**pleu·ro·car·pi** \,==ˈkär,pī\ *n pl, cap* [NL, fr. *pleur-* + -*carpi* (pl. of -*carpus*)] *in some classifications* **:** a group of mosses of the order Bryales comprising the pleurocarpous forms — compare ACROCARPI

**pleu·ro·car·pous** \¦==¦kärpəs\ *also* **pleu·ro·car·pic** \-pik\ *adj* [*pleurocarpous* ISV *pleur-* + -*carpous; pleurocarpic* fr. *pleur-* + -*carpic*] *of a moss* **:** bearing the archegonia and antheridia on short lateral branches — compare ACROCARPOUS

**pleu·ro·cen·tral** \¦plu̇rə¦sen·trəl\ *adj* [NL *pleurocentrum* + E -*al*] **:** of, relating to, or constituting a pleurocentrum

**pleu·ro·centrum** \"+\ *n* [NL, fr. *pleur-* + *centrum*] **:** one of a pair of dorsal and lateral elements of the centrum of the vertebra of a fish and of an extinct amphibian representing or formed from dorsal arcualia

**pleu·roc·era** \plu̇'räsərə\ *n, cap* [NL, fr. *pleur-* + -*cera*] **:** a large genus of American freshwater snails (suborder Taenioglossa) having the mantle edge entire and the copulatory organ not developed — compare THIARA — **pleu·roc·er·oid** \-sə,rȯid\ *adj*

**pleu·ro·cerebral** \¦plu̇rō+\ *adj* [*pleur-* + *cerebral*] **:** connecting the pleural and cerebral ganglia of a mollusk

**pleu·ro·coc·cus** \,plu̇rə'käkəs\ [NL, fr. *pleur-* + -*coccus*] *syn of* PROTOCOCCUS

**pleu·ro·di·ra** \,plu̇rə'dīrə\ *n pl, cap* [NL, fr. *pleur-* + -*dira* (fr. Gk *derē, deirē* neck) — more at DER-] **:** an extensive group of freshwater turtles in which the neck cannot be retracted, but is bent laterally beneath the front of the carapace — compare MATAMATA — **pleu·ro·di·ran** \¦==¦dīrən\ *adj or n* — **pleu·ro·dire** \'==,dī(ə)r\ *adj or n*

**pleu·ro·di·rous** \¦==¦dīrəs\ *adj* [NL *Pleurodira* + E -*ous*] **1** *of a turtle* **:** bending the neck laterally **2 :** of, relating to, or being a member of the group Pleurodira

**pleu·ro·dis·cous** \¦plu̇rə¦diskəs\ *adj* [*pleur-* + *disc-* + -*ous*] **:** laterally attached to a disk — used esp. of an appendage

**¹pleu·ro·dont** \'plu̇rə,dänt\ *adj* [ISV *pleur-* + -*odont*] **:** a lizard having pleurodont teeth

**²pleurodont** \"\ *adj* [ISV *pleur-* + -*odont*] **1** *of teeth* **:** consolidated with the inner surface of the alveolar ridge without sockets — compare ACRODONT **2 :** having teeth that are pleurodont

**pleu·ro·dyn·ia** \,plu̇rə'dinēə\ *n* -s [NL, fr. *pleur-* + -*odynia*] **1 :** a sharp pain in the side usu. located in the intercostal muscles and believed to arise from inflammation of fibrous tissue **2 :** EPIDEMIC PLEURODYNIA

**pleu·ro·gen·ic** \¦plu̇rə¦jenik\ *or* **pleu·rog·e·nous** \(')plu̇¦räjənəs\ *adj* [*pleur-* + -*genic* or -*genous*] **:** originating in the pleura

**pleu·ro·loph·o·cer·cous** \ˌplu̇rəˌläfəˈsərkəs\ *adj* [*pleur-* + *loph-* + *cerc-* + *-ous*] **:** of, relating to, or being a small cercaria that has a long strong tail, a pair of fin folds, a protrusible oral sucker, and pigmented eye spots

**pleu·ro·me·ia** \plu̇ˈrōmēə\ *n, cap* [NL, fr. *pleur-* + ISV *-ome* + NL *-ia*] **:** a genus of Triassic fossil plants that is included in Lepidodendrales or isolated in a separate order, has characters in common with the genera *Sigillaria* and *Isoetes*, and is marked by an unbranched trunk arising from an enlarged lobulated root-bearing base terminating in a crown of long ligulate leaves, and bearing heterosporous cones at its apex

**pleu·ron** \ˈplu̇ˌrän\ *n, pl* **pleu·ra** \-ürə\ [NL, fr. Gk, rib, side; prob. akin to Gk *platys* flat, broad — more at PLACE] **1 a :** lateral part of a thoracic segment of an insect usu. consisting of an epimeron and an episternum **2 :** a lateral process of a somite of a crustacean between the tergum and sternum

**¹pleu·ro·nec·tid** \ˌplu̇rəˈnektəd\ *adj* [NL *Pleuronectidae*] **:** of or relating to the Pleuronectidae

**²pleuronectid** \"\ *n* -s **:** a flatfish of the family Pleuronectidae

**pleu·ro·nec·ti·dae** \ˌ==ˈnektəˌdē\ *n pl, cap* [NL, fr. *Pleuronectes*, type genus (fr. *pleur-* + *-nectes*) + *-idae*] **:** a family of flatfishes (order Heterosomata) that have the eyes on the right side, the dorsal fin extending well forward on the head, and the mouth terminal — see FLOUNDER

**pleu·ro·ne·ma** \ˌplu̇rəˈnēmə\ *n, cap* [NL, fr. *pleur-* + *-nema*] **:** a genus of holotrichous ciliates living in fresh and salt water and having an ovoid body with a folding undulating membrane — see HOLOTRICHA

**pleu·ro·pedal** \ˌplu̇rə+, (ˈ)plu̇ˈräpəd·ᵊl\ *adj* [*pleur-* + *pedal*] **:** connecting the pleural and pedal ganglia of a mollusk

**pleu·ro·pericarditis** \ˌplu̇rō+\ *n* [NL, fr. *pleur-* + *pericarditis*] **:** inflammation of the pleura and the pericardium

**pleu·ro·peritoneum** *also* **pleu·ro·peritonaeum** \"+\ *n* [NL, fr. *pleur-* + *peritoneum, peritonaeum*] **:** the membrane lining the body cavity and covering the surface of the enclosed viscera of vertebrates that have no diaphragm — compare PERITONEUM

**pleu·ro·pneumonia** \"+\ *n* [NL, fr. *pleur-* + *pneumonia*] **1 :** inflammation of the pleura and lungs **:** pleurisy complicated by pneumonia; *specif* **:** a predominantly pulmonary form of shipping fever of horses **2 :** an acute febrile and often fatal inflammation of the lungs of cattle, sheep, and related animals resulting from infection by microorganisms of the family Mycoplasmataceae — see CONTAGIOUS BOVINE PLEUROPNEUMONIA

**pleuropneumonia group** *n* **:** a group of microorganisms coextensive with the family Mycoplasmataceae

**pleuropneumonia–like organism** \ˌ====(=)=ˌ=-\ *n* **:** a microorganism of the family Mycoplasmataceae

**pleu·ro·po·di·al** \ˌplu̇rəˈpōdēəl\ *adj* [NL *pleuropodium* + E *-al*] **:** of or relating to a pleuropodium

**pleu·ro·po·di·um** \ˌ==ˈpōdēəm\ *n* -s [NL, fr. *pleur-* + *-podium*] **1 :** either of a pair of glandular organs located on the first abdominal segment of an insect and believed to represent modified appendages **2 :** either of a pair of large fleshy lobes of the mantle of a sea hare

**pleu·rop·ter·yg·i·an** \plu̇ˌräptəˈrijēən\ *adj* [NL *Pleuropterygii* + E *-an*] **:** of or relating to the subclass or order Pleuropterygii

**pleu·rop·ter·yg·ii** \=ˌ==ˈrijēˌī\ *n pl, cap* [NL, fr. *pleur-* + *-pterygii*] **:** a subclass or order of small primitive Devonian elasmobranchs including the genus *Cladoselache* in which the paired fins are supported by unjointed parallel radial cartilages extending straight outward to the fin membrane and claspers are locking

**pleu·ro·sau·rus** \ˌplu̇rəˈsȯrəs\ *n, cap* [NL, fr. *pleur-* + *-saurus*] **:** a genus of slender serpentiform aquatic-limbed reptiles from the Upper Jurassic of Europe usu. regarded as eosuchians

**pleu·ro·sig·ma** \ˌplu̇rəˈsigmə\ *n, cap* [NL, fr. *pleur-* + Gk *sigma*; fr. the shape of the diatoms] **:** a genus of diatoms of the family Naviculaceae

**pleu·ros·te·al** \plu̇ˈrästēəl\ *adj* [NL *pleurosteon* + E *-al*] **:** of or relating to a pleurosteon

**pleu·ros·te·on** \-ēˌän\ *n* -s [NL, fr. *pleur-* + *-osteon*] **:** the anterolateral piece of the sternum of a young bird

**pleu·ro·ster·ni·dae** \ˌplu̇rəˈstərnəˌdē\ *n pl, cap* [NL, fr. *Pleurosternum*, type genus (fr. *pleur-* + *sternum*) + *-idae*] **:** a family of primitive fossil turtles that includes some of the earliest testudinates

**pleu·ro·stig·ma** \ˌplu̇rəˈstigmə\ *n pl, cap* [NL, fr. *pleur-* + L *stigma*] *in some classifications* **:** a subclass of centipedes distinguished by paired tracheal spiracles in the sides of the segments — compare EPIMORPHA

**pleu·ro·thot·o·nos** \ˌplu̇rəˈthätᵊnəs\ *n* -ES [NL, fr. Gk *pleurothen* from the side (fr. *pleura* side) + NL *tonus*] **:** a tonic spasm in which the body is curved laterally

**pleu·rot·o·ma** \plu̇ˈrädəmə\ *n, cap* [NL, fr. *pleur-* + *-toma*] *syn of* TURRIS

**pleu·ro·to·mar·ia** \ˌplu̇rəd·əˈma(a)rēə\ *n, cap* [NL, fr. *pleur-* + *-toma* + *-aria*] **:** a large genus of nearly extinct two-gilled gastropods (suborder Rhipidoglossa) usu. having a trochiform nacreous shell with a broad sinus in the outer margin of the last whorl that extends back around the whorls as a raised band — **pleu·ro·to·mar·i·id** \ˌ===ˈma(a)rēəd\ *adj or n* — **pleu·ro·to·mar·i·oid** \-ēˌȯid\ *adj or n*

**pleu·ro·trema·ta** \ˌplu̇rəˈtremədə, -rēm-\ *n pl, cap* [NL, fr. *pleur-* + *-tremata*] **:** an order of Chondrichthyes comprising the sharks — compare HYPOTREMATA

**pleu·ro·tus** \plu̇ˈrōdəs\ *n, cap* [NL, fr. *pleur-* + Gk *ōt-, ous* ear; fr. the shape of some members of the genus — more at EAR] **:** a genus of white-spored agarics having the pileus laterally sessile or with an eccentric stipe — see OLIVE TREE AGARIC, OYSTER MUSHROOM

**pleu·ro·visceral** \ˌplu̇rō+\ *adj* [*pleur-* + *visceral*] **:** connecting the pleural and visceral ganglia of a mollusk

**pleu·rum** \ˈplu̇rəm\ *n, pl* **pleu·ra** \-rə\ [NL, by alter.] **:** PLEURON

**pleus·ton** \ˈplüstən\ *n* -s [ISV *pleus-* (fr. Gk *pleusis* sailing, fr. *plein* to sail) + *-ton* (as in *plankton*) — more at FLOW] **:** small but macroscopic floating organisms that form mats or layers on or near the surface of a body of water, that usu. include floatingalgae (as spirogyras), small floating spermatophytes (as the duckweeds), and associated small animals, and that usu. exclude anchored plants and larger floating spermatophytes (as the water hyacinth)—compare NEUSTON

**pleus·ton·ic** \(ˈ)plüˈstänik\ *adj* **:** of, relating to, or having the characteristics of pleuston

**plew** \ˈplü\ *n* -s [CanF *pelu*, adj., hairy, fr. F *pelu, poilu*, fr. *poil* hair, fr. OF *poil, peil*, fr. L *pilus* — more at ³PILE] *West & Canad* **:** a beaver skin

**plex·i·form** \ˈpleksəˌfȯrm\ *adj* [NL *plexus* + E *-iform*] **:** of, relating to, or having the form or characteristics of a plexus ⟨the ~ layer of the retina⟩ ⟨~ synapse⟩ ⟨ships . . . pieced together on great ~ ways by giant cranes —*Life*⟩

**Plex·i·glas** \ˈpleksəˌglas\ *trademark* — used for an acrylic resin or plastic

**plex·im·e·ter** \plekˈsimədə(r)\ *n* [Gk *plēxis* stroke (fr. *plēssein* to strike) + E *-meter* — more at PLAINT] **:** a small hard flat plate (as of ivory) placed in contact with the body to receive the blow in mediate percussion — **plex·i·met·ric** \ˌpleksəˈme·trik\ *adj* — **plex·im·e·try** \plekˈsimə·trē\ *n* -ES

**plex·o·dont** \ˈpleksəˌdänt\ *adj* [L *plexus* network, twining, braid + E *-odont*] **:** of, relating to, or having molar teeth with complicated crown patterns and multiple roots

**plex·or** \ˈpleksə(r)\ *n* -s [NL, fr. Gk *plēxis* stroke + L *-or*] **:** a small hammer with a rubber head used in medical percussion — called also *plessor*

plexor

**plex·ure** \ˈplekshə(r)\ *n* -s [L *plexus* + E *-ure*] **1 :** the act or process of weaving together **2** [NL *plexus* + E *-ure*] **:** PLEXUS

**plex·us** \ˈpleksəs\ *n* -ES [NL, fr. L, network, twining, braid, fr. *plexus*, past part. of *plectere* to braid — more at PLY] **1 :** a network of anastomosing or interlacing blood vessels or nerves **2 :** an intricately interwoven combination of elements or parts in a cohering structure ⟨the ~ of the entire . . . system and its fifty departments —M.L.Bach⟩ ⟨in the ~ of financial affairs —Frank Norris⟩ ⟨a ~ of routes between western and eastern Europe —Derwent Whittlesey⟩

**plf** *or* **plff** *abbr* plaintiff

**pli·a·bil·i·ty** \ˌplīəˈbiləd·ē, -lətē, -i\ *n* **:** the quality or state of being pliable **:** FLEXIBILITY, COMPLAISANCE ⟨the ~ of the metal⟩ ⟨with his usual ~, had yielded to their arguments —T.B. Macaulay⟩ ⟨their jocund ~, their readiness to lend themselves to improper uses —Norman Douglas⟩

**pli·a·ble** \ˈplīəbəl\ *adj* [ME *pliabylle*, fr. MF *pliable*, fr. *plier* to bend, ply + *-able* — more at PLY] **1 :** bending or creasing easily **:** FLEXIBLE, SUPPLE ⟨~ as a whip —Green Peyton⟩ ⟨~ . . . ash saplings —Ronald Duncan⟩ ⟨corduroy, as ~ as velvet —*advt*⟩ **2 :** yielding easily to the wishes or influence of others **:** COMPLAISANT, COMPLIANT ⟨a . . . self-controlled, ~ personality —Shepard Henkin⟩; *sometimes* **:** susceptible to corruption ⟨~ officials⟩ **3 :** adjustable to varying conditions **:** ADAPTABLE ⟨a culture more ~ and more ready to accept change —G.D.Taylor⟩ **syn** see PLASTIC

**pli·a·ble·ness** *n* -ES **:** PLIABILITY

**pli·a·bly** \-blē,-bli\ *adv* **:** in a pliable manner **:** DOCILELY

**pli·an·cy** \ˈplīənsē, -si\ *n* -ES [*pliant* + *-cy*] **:** the quality or state of being pliant **:** FLEXIBILITY, COMPLAISANCE ⟨for the good of his soul and the ~ of his mind —J.E.Gloag⟩ ⟨more quickness of observation and less ~ of temper than her sister —Jane Austen⟩

**pli·ant** \-nt\ *adj* [ME *pliaunt*, fr. MF *pliant*, pres. part. of *plier* to bend, ply] **1 :** yielding readily without breaking **:** bending or folding easily **:** FLEXIBLE, WORKABLE, LITHE ⟨modeled in the ~ material and then . . . hardened —Nathaniel Hawthorne⟩ ⟨a girl . . . with a slim, ~ figure —Inez Karma & Gilbert Millstein⟩ **2 :** easily influenced **:** YIELDING ⟨sees the . . . natives as a ~ mass —J.S.Redding⟩ ⟨had a ~ congressional majority —A.S.Link⟩ **3 :** SUITABLE, APT ⟨which I observing, took once a ~ hour —Shak.⟩ **4 :** lending itself to varied uses **:** ADAPTABLE ⟨a ~ style⟩ ⟨the clarinet . . . a very fluent and ~ instrument —Winthrop Sargeant⟩ **syn** see PLASTIC

**pli·ant·ly** *adv* **:** in a pliant manner

**pliantness** *n* -ES [ME *pliauntnes*, fr. *pliaunt* pliant + *-nes* -ness] **:** PLIANCY

**pli·ca** \ˈplīkə\ *n, pl* **pli·cae** \-ˌīˌkē, -ˌīˌsē\ [NL, fr. ML, fold, plait, musical ligature, fr. L *plicare* to fold — more at PLY] **1** *or* **plica po·lon·i·ca** \ˌ==pəˈlänəkə\ *pl* **plicae poloni·cae** \-nəˌkē, -nəˌsē\ [NL *plica polonica*, lit., Polish plait; fr. its frequent occurrence in Poland in the 17th century] **:** a state of the hair in which it becomes twisted, matted, and crusted, usu. as a result of neglect, filth, and infestation by vermin **2** [ML] **:** a fold or folded part: as **a :** a groove or fold of skin **b :** a longitudinal fold in a bryophyte leaf or a sporangium **3** [ML] **:** a ligature in medieval music

**plica ala·ris** \-əˈla(a)rəs\ *n, pl* **plicae ala·res** \-(ˌ)rēz\ [NL, alar fold] **:** the fold of skin along the front of a bird's wing stretching from the shoulder to the wrist joint

**plica cir·cu·la·ris** \-ˌsərkyəˈla(a)rəs\ *n, pl* **plicae circula·res** \-(ˌ)rēz\ [NL, circular fold] **:** one of numerous permanent crescentic folds of mucous membrane found in the small intestine esp. in the lower part of the duodenum and the jejunum — called also *valvula connivens*

**pli·cal** \ˈplīkəl\ *adj* [*plica* + *-al*] **:** of, relating to, or having plicae

**¹pli·cate** \ˈplīˌkāt\ *vt* -ED/-ING/-S [L *plicatus*, past part. of *plicare* to fold — more at PLY] **1 :** FOLD, PLEAT **2 :** to perform plication on

**²pli·cate** \", -kət\ *adj* [L *plicatus*, past part. of *plicare*] **1 :** folded lengthwise like a fan **:** PLAITED ⟨a ~ leaf⟩ — used esp. of vernation **2 :** FOLDED; *esp* **:** having the surface thrown up into or marked with parallel ridges (as the elytra of certain insects) — **pli·cate·ly** *adv* — **pli·cate·ness** *n* -ES

**pli·cat·ed** \-ˌkād·əd\ *adj* [fr. past part. of ¹*plicate*] **:** FOLDED, RIDGED ⟨the mouth is longitudinal with ~ lips, situated on the ventral surface —Laura Henry⟩

**pli·ca·tile** \ˈplīkəd·ᵊl, -ˌtīl, -ˌtil\ *adj* [L *plicatilis*, fr. *plicatus* (past part. of *plicare* to fold) + *-ilis* -ile] **:** capable of being folded; *specif* **:** folding lengthwise ⟨the ~ wings of certain insects⟩

**pli·ca·tion** \plīˈkāshən\ *n* -s [ME *plicacioun*, prob. fr. (assumed) ML *plication-, plicatio*, fr. L *plicatus* (past part. of *plicare* to fold) + *-ion-, -io* -ion] **1 a :** the act or process of folding **b :** the quality or state of being folded **c :** FOLD **2 a :** the tightening of stretched or weakened bodily tissues or channels by folding the excess in tucks and suturing ⟨~ of the neck of the bladder⟩ **b :** the folding of one part on and the fastening of it to another (as areas of the bowel freed from adhesions and left without normal serosal covering) **3 a :** the action or process of the folding of geological strata **b :** a fold in a stratum

**pli·cat·u·late** \(ˈ)plīˈkachələt\ *adj* [²*plicate* + *-ule* + *-ate*] **:** minutely plicate

**plica·ture** \ˈplikəˌchu̇(ə)r, -līk-, -ˌchər\ *n* -s [L *plicatura*, fr. *plicatus* (past part. of *plicare* to fold) + *-ura* -ure] **:** PLICATION

**plié** \(ˈ)plēˈā\ *n* -s [F, fr. past part. of *plier* to bend, ply — more at PLY] **:** a bending of the knees by a ballet dancer with the back held straight

**plied** *adj* [fr. past part. of ¹*ply*] **:** composed of two or more strands ⟨~ yarn⟩ ⟨~ thread⟩ — compare PLY YARN

**pli·ers** *or* **ply·ers** \ˈplī(ə)rz, -īəz\ *n pl but sing or pl in constr* [¹*ply* + *-ers* (pl. of *-er*)] **:** a small pincers usu. with long roughened jaws for holding small objects or for bending and cutting wire — often used with *pair* ⟨a pair of ~s⟩

**plies** *pres 3d sing of* PLY, *pl of* PLY

**¹plight** \ˈplīt, *usu* -īd·+V\ *vt* -ED/-ING/-S [ME *plighten*, fr. OE *plihtan* to endanger, fr. *pliht* risk, danger; akin to OE *plēon* to expose to danger, MD *plien, plegen* to be responsible for, OHG *pflegan* to take care of] **:** to put or give in pledge **:** ENGAGE ⟨~ faith⟩ ⟨~ troth⟩ ⟨a ~*ed* bride⟩ ⟨he was half engaged . . . not absolutely ~*ed* —George Meredith⟩ **syn** see PROMISE

**²plight** \"\ *n* -s **:** a solemnly given pledge **:** ENGAGEMENT ⟨women . . . not famous for keeping their ~ —Sir Walter Scott⟩

**³plight** \"\ *n* -s [ME *plit*, fr. AF, fr. (assumed) VL *plictus* fold — more at PLAIT] **1 :** CONDITION, STATE; *esp* **:** bad state or condition **:** PREDICAMENT ⟨the ~ of the unemployed⟩ ⟨ruined landowners who do not dare to face their desperate ~ —Marc Slonim⟩ ⟨the ~ of the sensitive artist in a . . . standardized society —J.W.Aldridge⟩ **2 :** physical condition ⟨the horses are in fine ~⟩ ⟨lived . . . many years after in very good ~ —Thomas Gray⟩ **3** *archaic* **:** FOLD, PLAIT **4** *archaic* **:** ATTIRE, DRESS ⟨sit in silver ~ —John Keats⟩ **syn** see PREDICAMENT

**⁴plight** *vt* -ED/-ING/-S [ME *pliten*, fr. *plit*, n.] *obs* **:** PLAIT, FOLD

**plim** \"\ *vb* **plimmed; plimmed; plimming; plims** [perh. alter. of ²*plum*] *vi, dial chiefly Eng* **:** to increase in size **:** fill out **:** SWELL ⟨her bosom *plimmed* and fell —Thomas Hardy⟩ ~ *vt, dial chiefly Eng* **:** INFLATE, SWELL ⟨*plimming* her chest towards them —Joyce Cary⟩

**plim·soll** *also* **plim·sol** \ˈplim(p)səl, -mˌsȯl, -mˌsäl\ *or* **plim·sole** \-m(p)səl, -mˌsōl\ *n* -s [prob. so called fr. a supposed resemblance between the upper edge of the mudguard and the Plimsoll mark on the side of a ship] *Brit* **:** a light shoe having a rubber sole and mudguard and a canvas top

**plimsoll mark** *also* **plimsoll line** *n, usu cap P* [after Samuel *Plimsoll* †1898 Eng. leader of shipping reform] **1 :** a circle intersected by a horizontal line that is marked amidships on the sides of a seagoing cargo ship to represent the summer load line and is accompanied by letters indicating the authority under which the ship is registered **:** the minimum summer freeboard mark — compare DRAFT MARK **2 a :** a set of load-line markings on a seagoing cargo ship including the Plimsoll mark and the graduated load lines beside it **b :** LOAD LINE 2

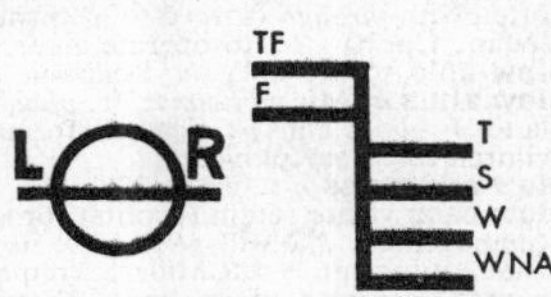


Plimsoll mark 2a: tropical freshwater mark, *TF;* freshwater mark, *F;* tropical load line, *T;* summer load line, *S;* winter load line, *W;* winter load line, North Atlantic, *WNA;* Lloyd's register of shipping, *LR*

**¹plink** \ˈpliŋk\ *vb* -ED/-ING/-S [imit.] *vi* **1 :** to make a tinkling sound **2 :** to shoot at random targets ⟨you'll probably do plenty of ~*ing* and informal target shooting —*Amer. Rifleman*⟩ ⟨people . . . who ~ with anything from a dime store bow and arrow to handmade equipment —*Sports Illustrated*⟩ ~ *vt* **1 :** to cause to make a tinkling sound ⟨~*ed* the little bell before him —Walter Goodman⟩ **2 :** to shoot at esp. in a casual manner ⟨like boys . . . ~*ing* cans from a riverbank —R.O.Bowen⟩

**²plink** \"\ *n* -s **:** a tinkling sound ⟨cricket chirp and ~ of samisens —Frederick Ebright⟩

**plink·er** \-kə(r)\ *n* -s **:** one who engages in plinking

**plinth** \ˈplin(t)th\ *n, pl* **plinths** \-n(t)s, -n(t)ths\ [L *plinthus*, fr. Gk *plinthos* plinth, brick; perh. akin to OE *flint* — more at FLINT] **1 a** (1) **:** a square vertically faced member immediately below the circular base of a column in classical architecture — see BASE illustration (2) **:** the lowest member of a pedestal **b :** the lowest member of a base **:** SUBBASE **c :** a block upon which the moldings of an architrave or trim are stopped at the bottom **2 a :** a square block serving as a base (as for a statue or vase) **b :** the squared base of something (as a vase or piece of furniture) **3 a** *or* **plinth course :** a course of stones forming a continuous foundation or base course (as of a rubble wall) **b :** a baseboard without a molded edge **4** *also* **plint** \-nt\ -s **:** a padded couch or low table used for massage or corrective physical exercises

**plin·thi·form** \ˈplin(t)thəˌfȯrm\ *adj* [*plinth* + *-iform*] **:** shaped like a plinth

**plio-** — see PLEIO-

**pli·o·cene** \ˈplīəˌsēn\ *adj, usu cap* [*pleio-* + *-cene*] **:** of or relating to a subdivision of the Tertiary — see GEOLOGIC TIME table

**Plio·film** \ˈplīə+ˌ-\ *trademark* — used for a glossy moisture-proof membrane made of rubber hydrochloride and used chiefly for making raincoats, as packaging material, and as fruit wrapping

**plio·hip·pus** \ˌplīōˈhipəs\ *n, cap* [NL, fr. *pleio-* + *-hippus*] **:** a genus of extinct one-toed horses from the No. American Pliocene having strongly hypsodont molar teeth

**plio·pithe·cus** \ˌplīōpəˈthēkəs, -ōˈpithəkəs\ *n, cap* [NL, fr. *pleio-* + *-pithecus*] **:** a genus of anthropoids found in the Upper Miocene and Lower Pliocene strata of Europe and possibly Asia having a very similar dentition to and commonly held to be ancestral to the gibbons

**plio·saur** \ˈplīōˌsȯ(ə)r\ *n* -s [NL *Pliosaurus*] **:** a reptile of the genus *Pliosaurus* or the family Pliosauridae

**plio·sau·ri·an** \ˌ==ˈsȯrēən\ *adj* [NL *Pliosaurus* + E *-an*] **:** of or relating to *Pliosaurus*

**plio·sau·rus** \ˌ==ˈsȯrəs\ *n, cap* [NL, fr. *pleio-* + *-saurus*] **:** a genus (usu. the type of the family Pliosauridae) of extinct marine reptiles that is related to *Plesiosaurus* but distinguished by a much shorter neck and larger head

**plio·thermic** \ˌplīō+\ *adj* [*pleio-* + *thermic*] **:** of or relating to a period in geological history of more than average warmth of climate

**pli·o·tron** \ˈplīəˌträn\ *n* -s [fr. *Pliotron*, a trademark] **:** a high vacuum tube containing a cathode, anode, and control grid that is used to control the flow of current in a single direction

**plique–a–jour** \ˌplē(ˌ)käˈzhu̇(ə)r\ *n* -s [F] **:** a style of enameling in which more or less transparent enamels are fused into a pierced framework so that the light passes through the enamels and enhances their color producing an effect similar to that of stained glass

**plis·kie** *or* **plis·ky** \ˈpliski\ *n, pl* **pliskies** [origin unknown] *chiefly Scot* **:** PRACTICAL JOKE, TRICK

**plis·sé** *or* **plis·se** \(ˈ)plēˈsā, pləˈsā\ *n* -s [F *plissé*, fr. *plissé*, past part. of *plisser* to pleat, fr. MF, fr. *pli* pleat, fold — more at PLY] **1 :** a textile finish that consists of forming permanently puckered designs by treating the cloth with a caustic soda solution which shrinks the treated sections and so causes the untreated parts to crinkle **2 :** a fabric usu. of cotton, rayon, or nylon that has been given a plissé finish

**plmb** *or* **plmg** *abbr* plumbing

**pln** *abbr* plain

**ploat** \ˈplōt\ *vt* -ED/-ING/-S [D *ploten* to pluck out (wool)] *chiefly Scot* **1 :** to pluck feathers from (a bird) ⟨~ your geese⟩ **2 :** CHEAT, FLEECE

**plo·ce** \ˈplō(ˌ)sē\ *n* -s [LL, fr. Gk *plokē* complication, twisting, fr. *plekein* to plait — more at PLY] **:** emphatic repetition of a word with particular reference to its special significance (as in "a wife who was a wife indeed")

**plo·ce·idae** \plōˈsēəˌdē\ *n pl, cap* [NL, fr. *Ploceus*, type genus + *-idae*] **:** a large family of Old World passerine birds that are predominantly African, somewhat resemble finches, and comprise the weaverbirds — see PLOCEUS

**plo·ce·iform** \plōˈsēəˌfȯrm\ *adj* [NL *Ploceus* + E *-iform*] **:** resembling a weaverbird

**plo·ceus** \ˈplōsēəs, -ōˌsüs\ *n, cap* [NL, fr. Gk *plokeus* braider, plaiter, fr. *plekein* to plait] **:** a genus (the type of the family Ploceidae) comprising the baya and related Asiatic birds

**¹plod** \ˈpläd\ *vb* **plodded; plodded; plodding; plods** [imit.] *vi* **1 :** to walk heavily **:** move or travel slowly but steadily **:** TRUDGE ⟨cows . . . *plodding* past a gate to be milked —Andrew Buchanan⟩ ⟨wayfarers . . . ~ on for miles without speech —Thomas Hardy⟩ ⟨a caravan ~*s* across the sweeping sands —*Univ. of Ariz. Record*⟩ **2 :** to work laboriously, steadily, and monotonously **:** DRUDGE ⟨*plodded* straight ahead, doing over and over some appointed task —Sherwood Anderson⟩ ~ *vt* **1** *obs* **:** PLOT **2 :** to tread (as a path, a course) slowly or heavily ⟨the plowman homeward ~*s* his weary way —Thomas Gray⟩ ⟨*plodded* his way back —Herman Wouk⟩ **3 :** to pass (milled soap) through a plodder

**²plod** \"\ *n* -s **1 :** a plodding walk ⟨the fathers set off . . . by the usual way, a tedious ~ —G.W.Murray⟩ **2 :** the sound of a heavy tread (as that of a horse) **:** TRAMP ⟨the tired ~ of his step —Donn Byrne⟩

**plod·der** \-ädə(r)\ *n* -s **1 :** one that plods; *esp* **:** a person who proceeds or works slowly, steadily, and unimaginatively ⟨thick-witted, insensitive ~*s* . . . unable to follow the transcendental speculations of their opponents —C.W.Shumaker⟩ ⟨the ~*s* who do exactly what they're told —Ethelbert Robinson⟩ **2 :** a machine for making ribbons or chips of milled soap into cakes by means of a spiral screw that forces the soap into a compression chamber and through a die

**plodding** *adj* **1 :** marked by slowness and heaviness of movement ⟨a . . . ~ tale —Hollis Alpert⟩ ⟨~ in his speech —Richard Llewellyn⟩ **2 :** DULL, PEDESTRIAN ⟨the naturalistic writer's ~ accumulation of detail —C.J.Rolo⟩ — **plod·ding·ly** *adv* — **plod·ding·ness** *n* -ES

**plodge** \ˈpläj\ *vi* [prob. blend of ¹*plod* and *trudge*] *dial* **:** to wade or walk heavily

**plo·dia** \ˈplōdēə\ *n, cap* [NL] **:** a genus of phycitid moths that includes the Indian meal moth — compare PHYCITIDAE

**ploi·ar·ia** \plōiˈ(y)a(a)rēə, plōˈya-\ *n, cap* [NL, prob. modif. of Gk *ploiarion* boat, dim. of *ploion* ship; akin to Gk *plein* to sail, float — more at FLOW] **:** the type genus of the family Ploiariidae comprising fragile-bodied bugs with elongated cylindrical heads, prominent eyes, raptorial forelimbs, and the remaining limbs greatly elongated and filamentous

**¹ploi·ar·i·id** \(ˈ)plōi(y)a(a)rēəd, plōˈya-\ *adj* [NL *Ploiariidae*] **:** of or relating to the Ploiariidae

**²ploiariid** \"\ *n* -s [NL *Ploiariidae*] **:** a bug of the family Ploiariidae

**ploi·a·ri·idae** \ˌplōi(y)əˈrīəˌdē, ˌplōyə-\ *n pl, cap* [NL, fr. *Ploiaria*, type genus + *-idae*] **:** a small cosmopolitan family of slender predaceous bugs related to the assassin bugs

**-ploid** \ˌplȯid\ *adj comb form* [ISV, fr. ²*diploid* & ¹*haploid*] **:** having or being a chromosome number that bears (such) a relationship to or is (so many) times the basic chromosome number characteristic of a given plant or animal group ⟨heteroploid⟩ ⟨hexaploid⟩ ⟨heptaploid⟩ ⟨crossing 12-, 9-, and 8-*ploid* western blackberries —*Biol. Abstracts*⟩

**ploi·dy** \ˈplȯidē, -di\ *n* -ES [fr. such words as *diploidy, hexaploidy*] **:** degree of replication of chromosomes or genomes

**ploi·ma** \ˈplōimə, -lōəmə\ *n pl, cap* [NL, fr. Gk *plōimos* fit for sailing; akin to Gk *plein* to sail, float] **:** a suborder of Monogononta or other large group of rotifers that are propelled by the ciliated disk only and that usu. have a forked and more or less retractile tail

**1ploi·mate** \-mət, -,māt\ *adj* [NL *Ploima* + E *-ate*] **:** of or relating to the Ploima
**2ploimate** \"\ *n* -s **:** a rotifer of the group Ploima
**ploi·ter** \ˈplȯitər\ *var of* PLOUTER
**plom·bage** \ˌpləmˈbäzh\ *n* -s [F, plombage, action of filling a tooth, fr. *plomber* to fill a tooth, apply lead to (fr. OF *plomer* to apply lead to, fr. *plon* lead, fr. L *plumbum*) + *-age* — more at PLUMB] **:** sustained compression of the sides of a pulmonary cavity against each other to effect closure by pressure exerted by packing (as of paraffin or plastic sponge)
**1plonk** *var of* PLUNK
**2plonk** \ˈpläŋk\ *n* -s [perh. modif. of F *blanc* white (in *vin blanc* white wine) — more at BLANK] *Austral* **:** cheap or inferior wine
**3plonk** \"\ *n* -s [origin unknown] *slang* **:** a socially awkward, stodgy, or pompous person **:** BORE
**ploo** \ˈplü\ *dial Brit var of* PLOW
**plook** *var of* PLOUK
**1plop** \ˈpläp\ *vb* **plopped; plopped; plopping; plops** [imit.] *vi* **1 :** to fall, drop, or move suddenly with a sound like that of something dropping into water ⟨the first large drops . . . *plopping* loudly on the tar-paper roofs —Donald Windham⟩ ⟨terrapins sliding down the mud banks and *plopping* into the water —Gerald Durrell⟩ ⟨began to shake the branches . . . oranges *plopped* down —Evelyn Eaton⟩ **2 :** to allow the body to drop heavily ⟨she *plopped* into a chair⟩ ⟨weary troops . . . *plopped* down beside their infantry kits —W.R. Moore⟩ **~** *vt* **:** to put down, drop, or throw with a plop ⟨*plopped* the tray on the coffee table —Nancy Rutledge⟩ ⟨picked up the silvery wriggling fish . . . and *plopped* them into burlap bags —J.M.Brinnin⟩
**2plop** \"\ *n* -s **:** the sound made in plopping **:** a dull faintly explosive sound ⟨the soft ~ of a fish jumping —Shirley A. Grau⟩ ⟨the ~ of a toad on the stones —Josephine Johnson⟩ ⟨the ~ of the heavy ball against the leather of the mitt —Donald Windham⟩ — often used interjectionally
**3plop** \"\ *adv* **:** with a plop **:** PLUMP ⟨emptied its contents . . . ~, from a height on to my solar plexus —Aldous Huxley⟩ ⟨~ came the ball down to the corner of the green —Harry Vardon⟩
**plosh** \ˈpläsh\ *n* -ES [by alter.] **:** 3PLASH
**plo·sion** \ˈplōzhən\ *n* -s [fr. *explosion, implosion*] **:** EXPLOSION 2d
**1plo·sive** \ˈplōs|iv, |ēv *also* -ōz| *or* |əv\ *n* -s [fr. *2explosive, 2implosive*] **:** 2EXPLOSIVE 2
**2plosive** \"\ *adj* **:** of or relating to a plosive
**1plot** \ˈplät, *usu* -äd+V\ *n* -s [ME *plot, plotte* patch, spot, plot (of ground), fr. OE *plot* plot (of ground)] **1 a :** a small area of ground or of something on the ground; *esp* **:** such an area devoted to a particular purpose ⟨a little ~ of ground⟩ ⟨a garden ~⟩ ⟨vegetable ~*s*⟩ ⟨a setting of well-kept lawns and flower ~*s*⟩ **b :** a small portion of land in a cemetery usu. containing two or more graves ⟨buried in the family ~⟩ **c :** an area of land used for scientific study or experimentation **:** QUADRAT 2 ⟨an experimental ~⟩ ⟨stems were taken at random in . . . different parts of the ~*s* —*Jour. of Economic Entomology*⟩ ⟨proper selection of the sample or census ~ —L.W.Wing⟩ **d** (1) **:** a measured parcel of land ⟨divided the tract into ~*s*⟩ ⟨houses . . . erected on ~*s* ranging from a few to as many as 40 acres —*Amer. Guide Series: Fla.*⟩ (2) **:** an assemblage of adjacent parcels forming a single land unit ⟨concentrate the small . . . holdings into bigger ~*s* —H.R. Lieberman⟩ **2** *archaic* **:** a spot or patch (as on the skin) differing from the surrounding surface **3 :** a ground plan (as of a building or area) **:** PLAT **4 a :** the plan or pattern of events or the main story of a literary work (as a novel, play, short story, or poem) comprising the gradual unfolding of a causally connected series of motivated incidents **:** narrative structure ⟨complications of the ~⟩ ⟨a detective story with an ingenious ~⟩ ⟨a novel almost without ~⟩ **b** *obs* **:** 8PLAT 3 **5** [prob. back-formation fr. *1complot*] **:** a secret plan contrived by one or more persons for accomplishing a usu. evil or unlawful end **:** CONSPIRACY, INTRIGUE ⟨a ~ to assassinate the king⟩ ⟨a ~ against the government⟩ **6 a :** a chart or map showing the movements or progress of a craft (as a ship, submarine, airplane) ⟨a ~ of the ship's course . . . should also be kept —*Manual of Seamanship*⟩ **b :** a location on a chart or map marked by the intersection of bearings or celestial lines of position **c :** a tactical, navigational, or control center aboard ship ⟨the gunnery liaison officer . . . feeding information to the fire control officer in ~ —*All Hands*⟩ **7 :** 1GRAPH 1
**syn** CONSPIRACY, CABAL, INTRIGUE, MACHINATION: PLOT suggests careful foresight in planning and a continuity or complexity of positive action by one or a number of persons of any sort ⟨the great Jesuit *plot* for the destruction of Protestant England and the invasion and conquest of the island by vast armies —S.M.Crothers⟩ CONSPIRACY differs from *plot* mainly in that it may indicate the persons involved ⟨Guy Fawkes was known as a member of the *conspiracy*⟩ It may suggest secrecy and unity within the band and carry a melodramatic effect. It may also suggest less positive action ⟨a *conspiracy* of silence⟩ or occas. philanthropic or benevolent aims. CABAL almost always endows the persons involved with a degree of eminence and is used mainly in matters political ⟨that moment at 1:20 in the morning of June, 1920, when a Senatorial *cabal*, the most venal since the days of President Grant, nominated Warren G. Harding for the Presidency —Irving Stone⟩ INTRIGUE suggests secret underhand maneuvering in an atmosphere of duplicity ⟨*intrigues* framed against the royal power and directed toward the disruption of the state —Hilaire Belloc⟩ ⟨the *intrigue* of special privilege in and upon the conquered countries —W.A.White⟩ ⟨the *intrigue* for place and the control of influence —J.H.Plumb⟩ MACHINATION suggests crafty maneuver, as though in an intrigue or plot ⟨the devilish *machinations* of an enchanter masquerading as a pious hermit —J.L.Lowes⟩ ⟨prevented authors and publishers from defeating the *machinations* of infringers —Margaret Nicholson⟩ **syn** see in addition PLAN
**2plot** \"\ *vb* **plotted; plotted; plotting; plots** *vt* **1 a :** to make a plot, map, or plan of **:** draw to scale **:** DELINEATE ⟨*plotting* this underground river —Martin Gardner⟩ **b :** to mark or note (as a site, position, or course) on or as if on a map or chart ⟨had *plotted* the reef on his chart⟩ ⟨~ . . . the exact position of the ship —Peter Heaton⟩ ⟨~ a course to that goal —*Time*⟩ ⟨~ the course of an airplane in flight from radar information⟩ **2 :** to measure out (land) in plots — usu. used with *out* ⟨new residential districts are all *plotted* out⟩ **3 a :** to locate and mark (a point) by means of coordinates **b :** to make (a curve) by marking out a number of plotted points ⟨*plotting* the thermal conductivity versus mean temperature —*Industrial Mineral Wool Products*⟩ **c :** to represent graphically (a mathematical equation) by means of a curve so constructed **4 :** to plan or contrive (as something evil or unlawful) esp. secretly ⟨*plotted* the murder of her husband⟩ **5 :** to invent or devise the plot of (a literary work) ⟨*plotted* his play carefully⟩ **~** *vi* **1 :** to scheme secretly and underhandedly **:** CONSPIRE ⟨~ for the coup d'etat —Geoffrey Bruun⟩ **2 :** to develop or outline a literary plot ⟨~*s* better than most novelists⟩ **syn** see 1PLAN
**3plot** \ˈplät\ *also* **plote** \-lōt\ *vt* **plotted; plotted; plotting; plots** *also* **plotes** [origin unknown] *chiefly Scot* **:** to subject to intense heat **:** SCALD, SCORCH
**plo·tin·i·an** \plōˈtinēən\ *adj, usu cap* [*Plotinus* †A.D.270 Rom. Neoplatonic philosopher + E *-an*] **:** of or relating to Plotinus or Plotinism
**plo·ti·nism** \plōˈtī,nizəm, ˈplōtᵊn,i-\ *n* -s *usu cap* [*Plotinus* + E *-ism*] **:** the doctrines of the philosopher Plotinus — compare NEOPLATONISM
**plo·ti·nist** \-tᵊnəst, -tᵊnə-\ *n* -s *usu cap* [*Plotinus* + E *-ist*] **:** a follower of Plotinus
**plot·less** \ˈplätləs\ *adj* **:** lacking a plot ⟨a loosely constructed comparatively ~ novel⟩
**plot·less·ness** *n* -ES **:** the quality or state of being plotless
**1plo·to·sid** \pləˈtōsəd\ *adj* [NL *Plotosidae*] **:** of or relating to the Plotosidae
**2plotosid** \"\ *n* -s [NL *Plotosidae*] **:** a catfish of the family Plotosidae
**plo·to·si·dae** \-sə,dē\ *n pl, cap* [NL, fr. *Plotosus*, type genus + *-idae*] **:** a family of chiefly tropical marine catfishes having an elongate eellike scaleless body and an arborescent movable organ of unknown function behind the vent
**plo·to·sus** \-səs\ *n, cap* [NL, prob fr. Gk *plōtos* floating, swimming + L *-osus* -ose; akin to Gk *plein* to sail, float — more at FLOW] **:** a genus (the type of the family Plotosidae) of marine catfishes
**plots** *pl of* PLOT, *pres 3d sing of* PLOT
**plot's elm** \ˈpläts-\ *or* **plot elm** *n* [prob. fr. the name *Plot*] **:** a European elm (*Ulmus plotii*) having an arching leader, pendulous branches, and subcordate bluntly serrate leaves
**plot·tage** \ˈpläd·ij\ *n* -s [*1plot* + *-age*] **1 :** the increment of value resulting from the combination of small tracts of land or lots into larger ones **2 :** the area included in a plot of land
**plotted** *past of* PLOT
**1plot·ter** \ˈpläd·ə(r), -ätə-\ *n* -s **:** one that plots: as **a :** a person who marks on a map or display board the positions of airplanes in flight **b :** a device for plotting; *specif* **:** a pencil holder in an instrument for plotting coordinates **c :** SCHEMER, CONSPIRATOR **d :** a contriver of a literary plot
**2plot·ter** \"\ *dial Eng var of* PLOUTER
**plott hound** \ˈplät-\ *n, usu cap P* [prob. after Jonathan *Plott* *fl* 1750 Am. dog breeder] **:** a large powerful usu. chiefly black hound of American origin used esp. in bear and boar hunting and believed to have resulted from crosses between German boarhounds, foxhounds, bloodhounds, and possibly other hound strains
**plotting** *pres part of* PLOT
**plotting board** *n* **:** a device for showing graphically the position of a stationary target or the periodic positions of a moving target with reference to the battery or batteries in artillery firing
**plot·ty** \ˈpläd·ē\ *adj* [*1plot* + *-y*] **:** of or relating to plot **:** marked by intricacy of plot or intrigue ⟨as long as a modern novel and ever so much more ~ —*Harper's*⟩
**plo·tus** \ˈplōd·əs\ [NL, fr. Gk *plōtos* floating, swimming] *syn of* ANHINGA
**plouk** \ˈplük\ *n* -s [ME *plowke*] *chiefly Scot* **:** a spot or blemish on the skin; *esp* **:** one caused by an infection **:** PIMPLE — **plouky** \-ki\ *adj*
**plounce** \ˈplaün(t)s\ *vb* -ED/-ING/-S [prob. imit.] *vt, chiefly dial* **:** to plunge (a person) into water usu. as a punishment for being a scold **:** DUCK **~** *vi, dial* **:** to splash about **:** FLOUNDER
**1plout** \ˈplaüt\ *n* -s [prob. imit.] *chiefly Scot* **:** a sudden splash or sudden heavy rainfall
**2plout** \"\ *vi* -ED/-ING/-S *chiefly Scot* **:** to splash or fall with a splash
**plou·ter** \ˈplaütər\ *vi* -ED/-ING/-S [prob. imit.] **1** *Scot* **:** to move about with splashing **:** WADE **2** *Scot* **:** POTTER
**plov·div** \ˈpläv,dif, -lȯv-\ *adj, usu cap* [fr. *Plovdiv*, city in southern Bulgaria] **:** of or from the city of Plovdiv, Bulgaria **:** of the kind or style prevalent in Plovdiv
**plover** \ˈpləvə(r), -lōv-\ *n, pl* **plover** *or* **plovers** [ME, fr. MF *plover, plovier*, fr. (assumed) VL *pluviarius*, fr. L *pluvia* rain + *-arius* -ary — more at PLUVIAL] **1 :** any of numerous shore-inhabiting birds of the family Charadriidae that differ from the sandpipers in having a short, hard-tipped bill and usu. a stouter, more compact build, frequent plains, grassy uplands, and beaches, are mostly gregarious and migratory, and include several well-known small birds (as the ring plovers) and some larger forms (as black-bellied plover, golden plover, dotterel, lapwing) important as game birds **2 :** any of various birds related to the plover: as **a :** TURNSTONE **b :** any of various sandpipers; *esp* **:** UPLAND PLOVER — compare CRAB PLOVER, WRYBILL **3 :** BROCCOLI BROWN
**plover page** *or* **plover's page** *n, Scot* **:** a small sandpiper sometimes accompanying the larger plovers; *esp* **:** RED-BACKED SANDPIPER
**plover quail** *n* **:** PLAIN WANDERER
**plovery** \-ərē\ *adj* **:** abounding in plovers ⟨this ~ headland —W.B.Yeats⟩
**1plow** *or* **plough** \ˈplaü\ *n* -s [ME, plow, plowland, fr. OE *plōh* plowland; akin to MD *ploech* plow, OHG *pfluog*] **1 a** *archaic* **:** PLOWLAND 1 **b** *chiefly Brit* **:** plowed land **:** arable country ⟨eight acres of ~ —*Farmers Weekly (London)*⟩ ⟨was on ~ with the clay clinging to my shoes —Ralph Hammond-Innes⟩ ⟨trotting across the ~ —Anthony Powell⟩ **2 :** an implement that is used to cut, lift, turn over, and partly pulverize the soil esp. in the preparation of a seedbed and that consists typically of a share for cutting, a moldboard for lifting and turning the soil usu. over a landside, a frog to which share, moldboard, and landside are attached, and a beam by which the implement is drawn — see DISC PLOW **3 :** any of various devices operating like a plow: as **a :** SNOWPLOW **b :** a ballast spreader **c :** an implement for unloading cars of earth or ballast **d :** a machine mounted on the side of a car body for ditching or grading at the side of the roadway **e :** a carpenter's plane for cutting a groove or rabbet **f :** a device for trimming the edges of books that consists of a knife resembling a chisel which is mounted on wood and slides between the runners of a lying press **g :** a device for making contact with the live wire or rail in a conduit **4** *plough, chiefly Brit* **:** 2FLUNK

plow 2: *1* share, *2* moldboard, *3* landside, *4* beam

**2plow** *or* **plough** \"\ *vb* -ED/-ING/-S [ME *plowen, ploughen*, fr. *plow, plough*, n.] *vt* **1 a :** to turn up, break up, or trench (the soil) with a plow **:** till with or as with a plow ⟨~ a field⟩ **b :** to make (as a furrow) with a plow ⟨a brown furrow had been ~*ed* —*Atlantic*⟩ **2 a :** to cut into, tear up, or make furrows or ridges in (a surface) with or as if with a plow ⟨gophers that ~ and loosen the prairie soil —E.W.Teale⟩ ⟨~ the roads after a snowstorm⟩ — often used with *up* ⟨tanks . . . had ~*ed* up muddy roads —*N.Y.Times*⟩ **b :** to furrow (the face) deeply with wrinkles ⟨face . . . ~*ed* with labor and sorrow —Thomas Carlyle⟩ **c** *chiefly Midland* **:** CULTIVATE — used esp. of corn ⟨~*ing* corn all day . . . with his team and cultivator —Burl Ives⟩ **d :** IMPREGNATE 1 ⟨~ a woman⟩ ⟨he ~*ed* her, and she cropp'd —Shak.⟩ **3 :** to cleave the surface of or move through (water) ⟨ships ~*ing* the seven seas⟩ **4 :** to cut a groove or rabbet in (a piece of wood) with a carpenter's plow ⟨risers are cut to size but not ~*ed* —*Building, Estimating & Contracting*⟩ **5 :** to trim (as a book or paper) with a plow **6 :** to turn over (grain) so as to expose fresh surfaces to the air and equalize temperature in malting **7** *plough, chiefly Brit* **:** 1FLUNK **~** *vi* **1 a :** to use a plow **:** till with a plow ⟨the farmer ~*ed* all day⟩ **b :** to bear or admit of plowing ⟨the land ~*s* well now —Adrian Bell⟩ **2 a :** to move in a way resembling that of a plow cutting into or going through the soil ⟨the ship ~*ed* southward⟩ — used often with *through, along, into* ⟨we ~*ed* through the snow⟩ ⟨he ~*ed* through the crowds —S.H.Holbrook⟩ ⟨~*s* along at a ten-knot rate —William Beebe⟩ ⟨a truck ~*ed* into her parked car —*N.Y.Times*⟩ **b :** to proceed steadily and laboriously **:** PLOD ⟨kept ~*ing* ahead in spite of the difficulties⟩ — used often with *through* ⟨forced to ~ through a summer reading list —Jane Cobb⟩ **3 :** to operate a carpenter's plow
**plow·able** \ˈplaüəbəl\ *adj* **:** capable of being plowed
**plow alms** *n* [ME *ploualmes*, fr. *plou, plow, plough* plow, land + *almes* alms] **:** a penny formerly paid annually to the church for every plowland
**plow and press** *n* **:** 1PLOW 3f
**plow back** *vt* **:** to retain (profits) for reinvestment in a business ⟨management . . . will *plow back* its earnings into new plant and equipment —J.R.Miller⟩ ⟨requires that 10 percent be *plowed back* into advertising —*Fortune*⟩
**plow beam** *n* [ME *plowebeme*, fr. *plowe, plow, plough* plow + *beme, beem* beam] **:** 1BEAM 1d
**plowboy** *or* **ploughboy** \ˈ=,=\ *n* **:** a boy who guides a horse in plowing **:** a country youth
**plow drill** *n* **:** a small usu. press drill that is attached behind a plow — compare 7DRILL 2, 2LISTER 2
**plow·er** *or* **plough·er** \ˈplaü(ə)r, -aüə\ *n* -s **:** one that plows **:** PLOWMAN
**plowgang** *or* **ploughgang** \ˈ=,=\ *n* [*1plow* + *gang*, n.] **:** any of various old Scottish units of land area (as a unit equivalent to a bovate)
**plowgate** *or* **ploughgate** \ˈ=,=\ *n* [*1plow* + *gate* (way)] **:** a unit of land area once used in Scotland and northern England prob. orig. equal to a plowland or carucate
**plow-hand** \ˈ=,=\ *n* **:** a hired worker who operates a plow
**plowhead** *or* **ploughhead** \ˈ=,=\ *n* [ME *ploghe hede*, fr. *ploghe, plow, plough* plow + *hede, heved, hed* head] **:** the clevis of a plow
**plow·land** *or* **plough·land** \ˈ=,land\ *n* [ME *plowlond*, fr. *plow, plough* plow + *land, lond* land] **1 :** any of various old English units of land area **:** CARUCATE ⟨division of the arable land into units called ~*s*, each . . . composed of eight "oxgangs" —F.M. Stenton⟩ **2 a :** arable land ⟨a third of the ~ —*World Report*⟩ **b :** a plot of such land ⟨a green hillock at the edge of a ~ —John Drinkwater⟩
**plow layer** *n* **:** the upper layer of soil comprising that usu. turned in plowing
**plowless farming** *n* **:** the stirring of soil for crop production with an implement (as a duckfoot, blade, chisel) that does not invert the soil or bury the crop residues
**plowline** *or* **ploughline** \ˈ=,=\ *n* **1 :** a rein to guide a plow horse **2 :** the level of the bottom of a plowed furrow
**plow·man** *or* **plough·man** \ˈ=mən\ *n, pl* **plowmen** *or* **ploughmen** [ME, fr. *plow, plough* plow + *man*] **1 :** one that plows **:** HUSBANDMAN **2 :** a field laborer **:** COUNTRYMAN
**plowman's-spikenard** *n, pl* **plowman's-spikenards :** a European aromatic herb (*Inula squarrosa*) with rough leaves and corymbose yellow flower heads
**plow monday** *n, usu cap P&M* **:** the Monday after Epiphany once celebrated in many parts of England as the first day of plowing
**plow out** *vt* **1 a :** to bring to the surface by or as if by plowing **:** plow up **:** turn up **b :** to remove or eradicate with or as if with a plow **2 :** to excavate or hollow out by plowing or by a process suggestive of plowing ⟨deep gullies *plowed out* by the heavy rains⟩
**plow packer** *n* **:** a soil packer attached behind a plow
**plow paddle** *or* **plow pattle** *or* **plow pettle** *n* [*pattle, pettle* alter. of *paddle*] **:** PLOWSTAFF
**plowpoint** *or* **ploughpoint** \ˈ=,=\ *n* **:** the point of a plowshare; *esp* **:** one that is detachable
**plow press** *n* **:** the press used with a bookbinder's plow
**plow·right·ia** \plaüˈrīd·ēə\ [NL, fr. C. B. *Plowright*, 19th cent. Eng. mycologist + NL *-ia*] *syn of* DIBOTRYON
**plows** *pl of* PLOW, *pres 3d sing of* PLOW
**plowshare** *or* **ploughshare** \ˈ=,=\ *n* -s [ME *plowghschare*, fr. *plowgh, plow, plough* plow + *schare, shaar* plowshare — more at SHARE] **:** the irregularly shaped part of a moldboard plow that cuts the furrow slice at the bottom and side, consists of a point which penetrates the soil first, a horizontal cutting edge, and a heel or outside corner, is usu. made of steel or chilled iron, and is either welded to or independent of the landside — compare BAR SHARE, SLIP SHARE, STONY SHARE
**plowshare bone** *n* **1 :** VOMER **2 :** PYGOSTYLE
**plowshoe** *or* **ploughshoe** \ˈ=,=\ *n* **:** a casing or support for a plowshare
**plow sole** *or* **plow pan** *n* **:** a compacted layer of earth at the bottom of the furrow at the same depth — compare HARDPAN
**plow spade** *n* **:** PLOWSTAFF
**plowstaff** *or* **ploughstaff** \ˈ=,=\ *n* [ME *ploustaf*, fr. *plou, plow, plough* plow + *staf* staff] **:** a spade or paddle for cleaning the plowshare
**plow steel** *n* [prob. so called fr. the use of strong wire rope in the formerly common procedure of plowing fields with a gang-plow pulled by a steam engine] **:** steel of high quality containing 0.5 to 0.95 percent carbon and used esp. for wire made into rope
**plowter** *var of* PLOUTER
**plow truck** *n* **:** a seat attachment on a pair of wheels that enables the plowman to ride
**plow under** *vt* **1 a :** to cover a green manure crop, crop residues, or barnyard manure by plowing **b :** to plow a field of a growing unharvested crop **2 :** to cause to disappear **:** BURY, OVERWHELM ⟨let us not *plow under* the family farmer —A.E. Stevenson b.1900⟩ ⟨talented students . . . were too often *plowed under* —E.A.Weeks⟩
**plow up** *vt* **1 :** to bring to the surface by or as if by plowing **:** turn, cast, or pull up with or as if with a plow ⟨had *plowed* quite a lot of arrowheads *up*⟩ ⟨*plow up* the beets —*Accent*⟩ ⟨by hard work had *plowed up* several nasty secrets⟩ **2 :** to break (ground) up by plowing
**plow-up** *or* **plough-up** \ˈ=,=\ *n* -s [*plow up*] **:** the conversion of an area of virgin sod into cropland
**plowwright** *or* **ploughwright** \ˈ=,=\ *n* [ME *plow wryhte*, fr. *plow, plough* plow + *wryhte, wrighte* wright] **:** one who makes or repairs plows
**ploy** \ˈplȯi\ *n* -s [prob. short for *2employ*] **1** *chiefly Scot* **a :** PURSUIT, ACTIVITY; *esp* **:** one that involves enterprise or finesse ⟨entered with eagerness into the new ~ —S.R.Crockett⟩ ⟨cart ropes would not hold them back from such a ~ —Sir Walter Scott⟩ **b :** RAMBLE, ESCAPADE ⟨through lots of ~*s* together —Harry Lauder⟩ **2 :** a social amusement **:** FROLIC ⟨their ~ of that week happened to be rabbit-shooting with saloon pistols —*McClure's*⟩ ⟨it's a grand ~ for young folk —John Buchan⟩ **3 :** a tactic (as in games and social debate) intended to embarrass or frustrate one's opponent ⟨~*s* and gambits for use against such rivals as fishing companions, wine experts, and fellow club members —*New Yorker*⟩
**pls** *abbr* please
**plstc** *abbr* plastic
**plstr** *or* **plstrer** *abbr* plasterer
**plt** *abbr* **1** pilot **2** plate
**pltf** *abbr* plaintiff
**pltg** *abbr* plating
**pltry** *abbr* poultry
**plu** *abbr* plural
**plu·chea** \ˈplüshēə\ *n, cap* [NL, fr. N. A. *Pluche* †1761 Fr. naturalist] **:** a genus of herbs or subshrubs (family Compositae) of warm regions comprising the marsh fleabanes and having small corymbose heads of tubular flowers and often aromatic or fetid foliage
**1pluck** \ˈplək\ *vb* -ED/-ING/-S [ME *plucken*, fr. OE *pluccian*; akin to MD *plucken, plocken* to pluck, MHG *pflücken, pflocken*; all prob. fr. a prehistoric WGmc word borrowed fr. (assumed) VL *piluccare* to pick, clean — more at PLUSH] *vt* **1 :** to pull or pick off or out **:** gather by picking ⟨~ feathers from a fowl⟩ ⟨~ grapes⟩ **2 :** to remove something from by or as if picking or pulling off or out: as **a** (1) **:** to so remove a natural covering (as of feathers, hair, or wool) from the body of ⟨~ a chicken before cleaning⟩; *also* **:** to trim the hair of (a dog) with a stripping knife (2) **:** to free (a pelt) from guard hairs in processing (3) **:** to shape (an eyebrow) by pulling some of the hairs **b :** ROB, PLUNDER, FLEECE **3 a :** to move or separate forcibly (as by pulling, dragging, snatching) — used with adverbs expressive of direction (as *out, from, down, apart*) ⟨~*ed* the map down from the wall⟩ ⟨~*ing* the portiere aside⟩ ⟨~*ed* him back from danger⟩ **b** (1) **:** to tear down **:** DEMOLISH — usu. used with *down* ⟨the chapel was ~*ed* down by the inhabitants of the village⟩ (2) **:** to make humble **:** bring low — usu. used with *down* **c :** to tear to pieces **:** pull apart **:** DISSEVER, RIVE ⟨a violent wind ~*ed* the sails to bits⟩ **4 a :** to handle with a picking or pulling motion ⟨a sick child ~*ing* at the bedclothes⟩; *esp* **:** to pull sharply or with sudden force ⟨~*ed* the strings of his guitar⟩ **b :** to seize (as a person) by a part of the body or clothing ⟨~*ed* him by the sleeve to catch his attention⟩ **c :** to make (as a musical instrument) sound by plucking **5 a** *Brit* **:** to reject (as a candidate for a degree or position) for some deficiency or misdemeanor (as for failure to satisfactorily pass an examination) ⟨expected to be ~*ed* on his tripos⟩ **b :** to select (a military officer) for involuntary retirement ⟨~*ed* after 20 years of service and sent into involuntary retirement⟩ **c :** to remove (a person) from one situation in life and transfer him to another ⟨~*ed* from his prosaic routine by the draft⟩; *esp* **:** to draft from a position of lesser to one of greater responsibility ⟨the convention ~*ed* him from the pastorate to head the foreign mission board⟩ **6** *of a glacier* **:** to break loose and bear away (solid rock) in large masses — compare ABRADE **~** *vi* **1 a :** DRAG **b** *obs* **:** GRAB, STEAL **c :** PICK *vi* 5 ⟨a paper that ~*s* badly⟩ **2 :** to make a sharp pull

or twitch : TUG — usu. used with *at* ⟨~*ing* at the folds of her skirt⟩

²**pluck** \"\ *n* -s [ME, fr. *plucken*, v.] **1 a** : an act of plucking or pulling; *esp* : a quick or sudden and forcible pull (as a twitch, tug, or jerk) **b** *obs* : SET-TO : BOUT, GO **2 a** : the heart, liver, lungs, and windpipe of a slaughtered animal esp. as an item of food **b** : the corresponding parts of a human cadaver **3** : something that is plucked or used in plucking ⟨spun out a small ~ of wool⟩ ⟨lost the ~ for his ukelele⟩ **4** : SPIRIT, COURAGE, RESOLUTION, NERVE **5** : the condition of being plucked; *esp*, *Brit* : failure in an examination **6** : DISTINCTNESS, SHARPNESS, BOLDNESS — used of a picture, drawing, or photograph **syn** see FORTITUDE

**pluck–buffet** \'plək,bəfət\ *n* [¹*pluck* + *buffet*, n.] : a former competition between archers in which the loser received a buffet

**plucked** \'pləkt\ *adj* [²*pluck* + *-ed*] *dial chiefly Eng* : having courage, spirit, or resolution ⟨what a good ~ one that boy of mine is —W.M.Thackeray⟩

**plucked·ness** \'plək(t)nəs, -kədn-\ *n* -ES : the condition of one that is plucked : BARENESS, NAKEDNESS

**plucked wool** *n* : wool plucked from the carcass of a sheep

**pluck·er** \'pləkə(r)\ *n* -s : one that plucks: as **a** : a person or machine that plucks poultry **b** : a person or machine that plucks furs

**plück·er tube** \'plü|kə(r)-, -lü|\ *n*, *usu cap P* [after Julius *Plücker* †1868 Ger. mathematician and physicist] : a gas-filled discharge tube with a narrowly constricted straight portion in which the intensified luminosity adapts the tube to use in the spectroscopy of gases

**pluck·i·ly** \'pləkəlē, -li\ *adv* : in a plucky manner : with or so as to be expressive of pluck

**pluck·i·ness** \-kēnəs, -kin-\ *n* -ES : the quality or state of being plucky

**plucking** *pres part of* PLUCK

**pluck·less** \-kləs\ *adj* : lacking pluck : feeble in courage or moral stamina — **pluck·less·ness** *n* -ES

**plucks** *pres 3d sing of* PLUCK, *pl of* PLUCK

**pluck up** *vb* [ME *plucken up*, fr. *plucken* to pluck + *up*, adv.] *vt* **1** : to assume an appearance of : bring to the fore : SUMMON ⟨*plucked* his nerve *up* to demand an explanation⟩ **2** : to eradicate by or as if by tearing up by the roots ~ *vi* **1** : to assume an appearance (as of valor) esp. in response to a particular stress

**plucky** \'pləkē, -ki\ *adj* -ER/-EST [²*pluck* + *-y*] **1** : having or marked by courage : COURAGEOUS, SPIRITED, BRAVE, RESOLUTE ⟨a ~ man⟩ ⟨a ~ stand against oppression⟩ **2** : clear in outline or detail : DISTINCT, SHARP — used esp. of a drawing or photograph **3** *of a stone or rock* : breaking with a conchoidal fracture under the hammer or chisel ⟨flint, obsidian, and some limestones are ~ rocks⟩

¹**pluff** \'pləf\ *n* -s [E dial. *pluff*, v., to puff, fire a gun, of imit. origin] *Scot* : PUFF

²**pluff** \", 'plu̇f\ *adj*, *dial* : soft and puffy

**pluff·er** \-fə(r)\ *n* -s [E dial. *pluff* to puff, fire a gun + E *-er*] *dial chiefly Brit* : POPGUN

**pluffy** \'pləfi\ *adj* [¹*pluff* + *-y*] *chiefly Scot* : puffy and fat

¹**plug** \'pləg\ *n* -s *often attrib* [D, fr. MD *plugge* plug, peg; akin to MHG *pfloc* plug, peg] **1** : a piece of wood, metal, or other material used or serving to fill a hole: as **a** : STOPPER, STOPPLE, BUNG **b** : the plunger of a pump **c** : the piece in a cock that can be turned to regulate the flow of liquid or gas **d** : PLUG GAGE **e** : an obstructing mass of material in a bodily vessel or the opening of a skin lesion ⟨necrotic ~⟩ ⟨fibrinous ~⟩ **f** : a more or less columnar mass of intrusive igneous rock : the filling of the conduit leading to a volcanic vent; *also* : a body of rock salt of similar shape — compare BYSMALITH, ¹NECK 3b(2)c **g** : a filling for a hollow tooth **h** : a reference peg driven in flush with the surface of the ground **i** : a fusible boiler plug **j** : a piece of one kind of metal inserted in a hole in the center of a coin of another kind of metal **k** : a block of wood driven or inlaid in a wall to form a nailing surface **l** : the cylindrical piece in a pin-tumbler cylinder containing the keyhole and rotated by the key — see KEY PLUG **m** : a cylindrical piece of wood or metal placed in the tubular magazine of a repeating shotgun to reduce the ammunition capacity of the magazine **n** : a separate piece of leather inserted in the upper of a shoe esp. for contrast or ornament **o** : the rotating cone within the outer shell of a jordan **2** : a flat compressed cake of tobacco **3 a (1)** : BLOW, PUNCH **(2)** *slang* : BOXING, FISTICUFFS ⟨the noble art of ~⟩ **b** : SHOT ⟨took a ~ at the deer with his rifle⟩ **4** : a small core or segment that is removed from a larger object: as **a** : a piece cut from the center of a coin **b** : a core removed from something (as a watermelon or a bale of wool) as a representative sample on which to base an estimate of the quality of the whole **c** : a bit of material removed by a punch in forming a hole **5** : something inferior or defective of its kind: as **a** : an inferior and often aged or unsound horse ⟨a race for platers and ~s⟩; *also* : a quiet steady cold-blooded horse usu. of light or moderate weight ⟨stock includes three good farm ~s⟩ **b (1)** : a slow-selling book **(2) plugs** *pl* : REMAINDERS — **c** *slang* : an incompetent telegrapher **d** : a drudging student : GRIND **e** : a slow, stupid, or ineffective person ⟨a willing worker but a dull old ~⟩ **6 a** : FIREPLUG **b** : PLUG HAT **c (1)** : SPARK PLUG **(2)** : PLUG FUSE **7 a** : an artificial angling lure used primarily for casting, made of wood or plastic, and usu. rigged with one or more sets of gang hooks ⟨an underwater ~⟩ ⟨a subsurface ~⟩ **b** *Brit* : SQUID 3 **8** : any of various devices resembling or functioning like a plug: as **a** : either the tapered parts or the key of a plug and feather **b** : a piece of soft steel impressed by a punch to form a die **c** : a wedge or key used to secure a railroad rail in a chair **d** : an extension to replace the broken section of watch or clock arbor end or pivot, filtering over the arbor or into a hole drilled in the arbor **e (1)** : a male fitting used to make an electrical connection by insertion in a receptacle or body and having one or more contact-making parts or blades that serve to close a circuit or to attach a conductor or some other piece of electrical equipment to a circuit **(2)** : a device for connecting electric wires to a jack or fuseplug **9** : a piece of favorable publicity; *esp* : personal or product advertising incorporated in general matter ⟨gave the actor a ~ in her column⟩ ⟨some radio programs have become mere strings of ~s tacked together with music⟩

²**plug** \"\ *vb* **plugged**; **plugged**; **plugging**; **plugs** *vt* **1 a** : to stop, make tight, or secure (as an opening) by or as if by insertion of a plug ⟨*plugged* the leak with tar⟩ ⟨~ the bunghole tightly⟩ : close an opening in — often used with *up* ⟨grease *plugged* up the sink⟩ **b** : to fill a cavity in (a tooth) **c** : to close (a rivet) by hammering or pressing **2** : to remove a small core or segment from ⟨~ a watermelon to test its ripeness⟩ ⟨*plugging* cotton bales⟩ **3** *slang* **a** : to hit with a bullet : put a bullet into : SHOOT **b** : to strike with the fist : PUNCH **4** : to stop (an electric motor) reversing its direction of rotation **5 a** : to break off or proportion (a piece of stone) with a plug and feather — usu. used with *off* **b** : to remove a piece from the center of (a coin) and insert a piece of baser metal **c** : to alter (as a woodcut or die) by removing a portion and inserting a plug carved with the desired substitution **6** : to advertise or publicize insistently; *esp* : to publicize (a piece of music) by very frequent performances ~ *vi* **1** : to become stopped or occluded — usu. used with *up* ⟨the drain will ~ up if you let grease settle in it⟩ **2** : to work doggedly and persistently ⟨*plugged* away at his lessons⟩ **3** : to fire a shot or shots ⟨kept *plugging* away at the can⟩ **4** : ⁴ROOT; *also* : to advertise or publicize something insistently ⟨devoted much of his talk to *plugging* for the party candidate⟩

**plug and feather** *n* : a device for splitting stones consisting of two tapered pieces and a wedge-shaped key

**plugboard** \'=,=\ *n* **1** : an electrical switchboard in which connections are made by means of plugs **2** : the part of a tabulating machine in which adjustments are made that determine the place at which a card is punched or stamped **3** : a panel in a computer or other electronic equipment having a multiplicity of female connectors into which male plugs are inserted to establish electrical control circuits

**plug casing** *n* : a casing for adapting a plug-fuse cutout base to a cartridge fuse

**plug casting** *n* : fishing by bait casting with a plug

**plug center bit** *n* : a center bit ending in a small cylinder instead of a point

**plug cock** *or* **plug bib** *n* **1** : a cock turned on or off by a plug **2** : a spigot that is merely driven into a barrel

**plug drill** *n* : a stonecutter's percussion drill

**plug flow** *n* : the slipping along of a material through a conduit without plastic shear ⟨thin clay extruded to form tile exhibits *plug flow*⟩

**plug fuse** *n* : an electric fuse that screws into a socket — compare CARTRIDGE FUSE

**plug·ga·ble** \'pləgəbəl\ *adj* : capable of or suitable for being plugged

**plug gage** *n* : a gage with an external measuring surface designed to check the contour or size of an opening

**plugged** \-gd\ *adj* **1** : furnished with a plug : BLOCKED, OBSTRUCTED ⟨suffering from a ~ sinus⟩ **2** *of a coin* : altered by the insertion of a plug of base metal

**plug·ger** \-gə(r)\ *n* -s : one that plugs: as **a** : a dental instrument used for driving and consolidating filling material in a tooth cavity **b (1)** : a steady, dogged, and usu. uninspired worker **(2)** : an enthusiastic supporter or encourager (as of a contestant) : ROOTER; *also* : one that gives insistent publicity (as to a person, product, or cause) **c** : a worker who fits plugs (as into barrels) **d** : JACKHAMMER **e** : a tool for removing plugs (as of turf)

**plug·ger·man** \-mən\ *n*, *pl* **pluggermen** : a miner who keeps ore moving through chutes as it is loaded into cars at a lower level

**plugging** *n* -s [fr. gerund of ²*plug*] **1** : the act of one that plugs; *also* : the act of stopping with a plug **2** : material used for a plug

**plug·ging·ly** *adv* [*plugging* (pres. part. of ²*plug*) + *-ly*] : so as to plug or form a plug

**plug hat** *n* : a man's stiff hat (as a bowler or a top hat) — **plug–hatted** \'=,==\ *adj*

**plughole** \'=,=\ *n* : an opening in which a plug fits

**plug in** *vi* : to establish an electric circuit by inserting a plug ⟨outlets conveniently placed for *plugging in*⟩ ~ *vt* : to attach or connect (as a lamp, an electrical device) to a service outlet ⟨*plugged* the radio *in*⟩ ⟨wired and ready to be *plugged in*⟩

¹**plug–in** \'=,=\ *adj* [*plug in*] : designed to be plugged into an electrical circuit ⟨a *plug-in* broiler⟩

²**plug–in** \'=,=\ *n* -s **1** : PLUG 8e(1) **2** : JACK 2l

**plug key** *n* : SWITCH PLUG

**plug·less** \'pləgləs\ *adj* : lacking a plug

**pluglike** \'=,=\ *adj* : resembling or functioning like a plug

**plug·man** \'pləgmən\ *n*, *pl* **plugmen 1** : the member of a gun crew (as in the U. S. Navy) whose duty is to open and close the breech plug or breechblock in firing **2** : a miner who attends pumps in a mine **3** : a plugger who fastens stoppers in bottoms of billet molds in which copper is to be cast

**plugs** *pl of* PLUG, *pres 3d sing of* PLUG

**plug switch** *n* : an electrical switch in which connection is made by means of a plug

**plug tobacco** *n* : tobacco in the form of plugs

**plugtray** \'=,=\ *n* : TRAY 3

**plug–ugly** \'=,==\ *n* -ES *often attrib* **1** : a member of a gang of disorderly ruffians often active in political pressure and intimidation ⟨the *plug-uglies* took over the polls⟩ ⟨*plug-ugly* tactics⟩ **2** : a coarse uncouth fellow : TOUGH, ROUGHNECK

**plug valve** *n* : a valve or cock opened or closed by the turning of a usu. conical plug

**plug weld** *n* : a butt weld made in the opening of a slotted lap joint

¹**plum** \'pləm\ *n* -s *often attrib* [ME *plum*, *plumme*, *plowme* plum, plum tree, fr. OE *plūme*; akin to OHG *pflūmo* plum tree; both fr. a prehistoric WGmc word borrowed fr. L *prunum* plum, fr. Gk *proumnon*] **1 a** : any of numerous trees and shrubs of the genus *Prunus* that have medium-sized globular to oval smooth-skinned fruits which are drupes enclosing a smooth elongated flattened seed and that include various improved forms cultivated for their fruits or for their ornamental flowers or foliage — compare CHERRY, PEACH; see DAMSON, GREENGAGE, PRUNE **b** : the fruit of a plum **c** : the streaked hard small-pored reddish brown wood of a plum tree esp. of the common European plum used to a limited extent for small cabinetwork and turnery **2 a** : any of various trees with edible fruits resembling plums: as **(1)** : a tree of the genus *Spondias* — see HOG PLUM **(2)** : PERSIMMON **(3)** : a tree of the genus *Flacourtia* — see GOVERNOR'S PLUM **b** : the fruit of such a tree **c** *chiefly New Eng* : any of various edible berries (as a partridgeberry, Juneberry, or huckleberry) **3 a** : a raisin when used in puddings or other dishes **b** : SUGARPLUM **4 a** *archaic* : the sum of £100,000 sterling ⟨worth half a ~ —Richard Steele⟩ **b** : something excellent or superior of its kind (as a choice passage in a book or an unusually good position) ⟨a fellowship that was the history department's ~⟩ — compare LEMON **c** : something desirable received or available as a recompense for service esp. through political patronage ⟨a senator with several ~s at his disposal⟩ **d** : an unexpected increment of property or money : WINDFALL — compare MELON **5** : a stone or mass of rock embedded in a matrix of a different kind (as a pebble in a conglomerate); *esp* : large stone added to concrete after mixing and placing but before hardening **6 a** : a variable color averaging a dark reddish purple that is bluer and duller than grape wine or royal purple (sense 1) and less strong and slightly darker than imperial **b** : a dark purple that is bluer, stronger, and slightly lighter than average prune, redder and duller than mulberry (sense 2a) and redder and less strong than mulberry purple

²**plum** \"\ *vi* **plummed**; **plummed**; **plumming**; **plums** [ME *plumen*] *dial chiefly Eng* : RISE, SWELL

³**plum** *var of* PLUMB

⁴**plum** \"\ *adj* **1** *dial Eng* : rounded out : PLUMP **2** *dial Eng*, *of a drink* : mild, smooth, and mellow

¹**plu·ma** \'plümə\ *n*, *pl* **plu·mae** \-(,)mē, -,mī\ [NL, fr. L, small soft feather — more at FLEECE] : CONTOUR FEATHER

²**pluma** \"\ *n* -s [AmerSp, fr. Sp, feather, fr. L, small soft feather] : any of several Caribbean sparid porgies (genus *Calamus*)

**plu·ma·ceous** \(')plü¦māshəs\ *adj* [NL *plumaceus*, fr. *pluma* + L *-aceus* -aceous] : PENNACEOUS

**plu·mach** \(')plü¦mash\ *n* -s [ME *plumash*, fr. MF *plumache*, fr. *plume* feather] *archaic* : an ornamental plume (as on a helmet)

**plu·mage** \'plümij, -mēj\ *n* -s [ME, fr. MF, fr. OF, fr. *plume* feather (fr. L *pluma* small soft feather) + *-age*] **1** : the entire clothing of feathers of a bird — compare PELAGE **2** : a bunch or tuft of feathers used for ornament **3** : elaborate, showy, or ceremonial dress **4** : the suite of feathery fins of some aquarium fishes (as various goldfishes and the bettas)

**plu·maged** \-jd\ *adj* : having plumage — usu. used with a descriptively qualifying adverb ⟨brilliantly ~ parrots⟩ ⟨a fully ~ young bird⟩

**plu·mas·sier** \,plüməˌsi(ə)r; plü'masē,ā, -ēər\ *n* -s [MF, fr. *plumasse* large feather (fr. *plume* feather) + *-ier* -er] : one that prepares or deals in ornamental plumes or feathers

**plu·mate** \'plü,māt, -mət\ *adj* [NL *plumatus*, fr. L, covered with feathers, fr. *pluma* small soft feather + *-atus* -ate] : having a main shaft that bears many small hairs or filamentous parts — used of bodily hairs, antennae, or similar structures

**plu·ma·tel·la** \,plüməˈtelə\ *n* [NL, fr. L *plumatus* covered with feathers + NL *-ella*] **1** *cap* : a genus (the type of the family Plumatellidae) of freshwater phylactolaematous bryozoans having a chitinous ectocyst and forming branching colonies **2** -s : any bryozoan of the genus *Plumatella*

¹**plumb** \'pləm\ *n* -s [ME *plom*, *plum*, *plumbe*, fr. (assumed) OF *plomb* lead, plummet (whence MF *plomb*), fr. OF *plon* lead, fr. L *plumbum*, of non-IE origin; akin to the source of Gk *molybos* lead, Basque *berun*] **1** : a little mass or weight of lead or other heavy material (as brass) attached to a line and used to indicate a vertical direction : PLUMMET, PLUMB BOB **2 a** : a lead or other weight: as **(1)** : a mariner's sounding lead **(2)** : a fishline sinker **(3)** : a sinker used to sound a stream or lake **(4)** : a clock weight **b** : a missile of lead — **out of plumb** *or* **off plumb** *adv* : out of the vertical : out of true

²**plumb** \"\ *also* **plum** \"\ *adv* [ME *plom*, fr. *plom*, *plum*, *plumbe*, n.] **1** : straight down or occasionally up : VERTICALLY **2** : DIRECTLY, EXACTLY; *also* : IMMEDIATELY **3** *chiefly dial* : COMPLETELY, ABSOLUTELY, UTTERLY

³**plumb** \"\ *vb* -ED/-ING/-s [ME *plomen*, fr. *plom*, *plum*, *plumbe*, n.] *vt* **1** : to weight with lead **2 a** : to sound with a plumb; *also* : to measure the depth of (as water) by sounding **b** : to ascertain a quality (as depth, dimension, propriety) of : examine minutely and critically ⟨~ one's motives⟩ ⟨there were depths . . . beneath the story that he had never ~*ed* —Van Wyck Brooks⟩ **c** : to reach the nadir of ⟨~*ing* that abyss of misery⟩ **3 a** : to adjust or test by a plumb line : cause to be perpendicular ⟨~ a wall⟩ **b** : to be or make perpendicular to **4** : to seal with or as if with lead ⟨~ a joint⟩ ⟨luggage ~*ed* by the customs inspector⟩ **5** [back-formation fr. *plumber*] **a** : to supply with a system of plumbing ⟨~ a new house⟩ **b** : to work upon (something) as a plumber : install as part of a system of plumbing ⟨had a friend ~ his sink⟩ ~ *vi* **1** : to hang or fall vertically : be perpendicular ⟨the chimney ~*s* perfectly⟩ **2** [back-formation fr. *plumber*] : to work as a plumber : do plumbing

⁴**plumb** \"\ *also* **plum** \"\ *adj* [ME *plom*, fr. *plom*, *plum*, *plumbe*, n.] **1 a** : conforming to the direction of a line attached to a plumb ⟨the wall is ~⟩ **b** : perfectly true : level and smooth — used of a cricket wicket **2** : DOWNRIGHT, COMPLETE, ABSOLUTE **syn** see VERTICAL

⁵**plumb** \"\ *dial var of* PLUMP

⁶**plumb** \"\ *dial chiefly Eng var of* ²PLUM

**plumb–** *or* **plumbo–** *comb form* [L *plumb-*, fr. *plumbum*] : lead ⟨*plumb*ate⟩ ⟨*plumbo*jarosite⟩

**plumb·able** \'pləməbəl\ *adj* : capable of being plumbed

**plum·ba·gin** \,pləm'bājən, -āgən; 'pləmbəjən\ *n* -s [ISV *plumbag-* (fr. NL *Plumbago*) + *-in*] : a yellow crystalline phenolic compound $C_{11}H_8O_3$ having antibacterial and medicinal properties that occurs esp. in the roots of shrubs of the genus *Plumbago*; 5-hydroxy-2-methyl-1,4-naphthoquinone

**plum·bag·i·na·ce·ae** \,pləm,bajə'nāsē,ē\ *n pl*, *cap* [NL, fr. *Plumbagin-*, *Plumbago*, type genus + *-aceae*] : a family of plants (order Plumbaginales) that are widely distributed esp. in saline situations and have basal or alternate leaves, small clustered tubular flowers, and a fruit which is a utricle or an achene — see PLUMBAGO — **plum·bag·i·na·ceous** \,===-'nāshəs\ *adj*

**plum·bag·i·na·les** \,=,=='nā(,)lēz\ *n pl*, *cap* [NL, fr. *Plumbagin-*, *Plumbago* + *-ales*] : a small order of shrubby or herbaceous plants that is coextensive with the family Plumbaginaceae and is often included in the order Primulales

**plum·bag·i·nous** \,pləm¦bajənəs\ *adj* [L *plumbagin-*, *plumbago* galena + E *-ous*] : resembling graphite : consisting of or containing graphite

**plum·ba·go** \,pləm'bā(,)gō\ *n* [L, galena, leadwort, fr. *plumbum* lead] **1** -s : GRAPHITE **2** [NL *Plumbagin-*, *Plumbago*, fr. L *plumbagin-*, *plumbago*] **a** *cap* : a genus (the type of the family Plumbaginaceae) of herbs, shrubs, and woody climbers that are widely distributed in warm climates and have alternate sessile leaves and spicate blue, white, or rosy red flowers with a glandular calyx and a salver-shaped corolla **b** -s : any plant of this genus

**plumbago blue** *n* : a purplish gray that is bluer, lighter, and stronger than crane and bluer, lighter, and stronger than dove gray, zinc, or cinder gray

**plumbago family** *n* : PLUMBAGINACEAE

**plumbago gray** *n* : a pale purple to purplish gray that is bluer than heliotrope gray

**plumbago slate** *n* : a grayish purple that is redder and slightly darker than telegraph blue, bluer and darker than mauve gray, and bluer and paler than average rose mauve

**plum·bane** \'pləm,bān\ *n* -s [*plumb-* + meth*ane*] **1** : a compound of lead and hydrogen; *esp* : the unstable tetrahydride $PbH_4$ **2** : a derivative of a plumbane

¹**plum·bate** \'pləm,bāt\ *n* -s [ISV *plumb*ic + *-ate*] : a salt (as calcium ortho-plumbate $Ca_2PbO_4$ or sodium hexahydroxo-plumbate $Na_2[Pb(OH)_6]$) formed by reaction of lead dioxide with basic oxides

²**plumbate** \"\ *adj* [*plumb-* + *-ate*] : of or relating to a middle American pottery with a lustrous metallic surface typically the color of lead but sometimes grayish green or orange

**plumb bob** *n* : the usu. conoidal and metal bob of a plumb line

**plumb bond** *n* : a masonry bond (as a clip bond or split bond) in which corresponding joints are precisely in line with one another; *also* : a masonry face exhibiting such a relation

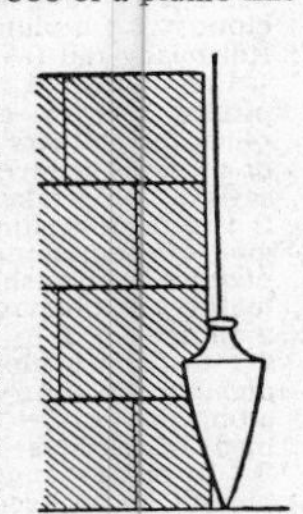

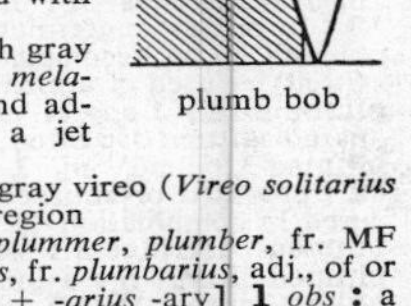

plumb bob

**plumb cut** *n* : a cut in a vertical plane; *esp* : the top cut face of a rafter that is designed to butt vertically against a ridgeboard — compare SEAT CUT

**plumbed** *past of* PLUMB

**plum·be·ous** \'pləmbēəs\ *adj* [L *plumbeus*, fr. *plumbum* lead + *-eus* -eous] **1** : consisting of or resembling lead : LEADEN **2 a** : having a dull gray color like that of lead **b** : of the color lead **3** *of a ceramic object* : finished or treated with a lead glaze

**plumbeous gnatcatcher** *n* : a bluish gray gnatcatcher (*Polioptila melanura melanura*) of the southwestern U. S. and adjacent Mexico distinguished by a jet black crown in the male

**plumbeous vireo** *n* : a dusky slaty gray vireo (*Vireo solitarius plumbeus*) of the Rocky mountain region

¹**plumb·er** \'pləmə(r)\ *n* -s [ME *plummer*, *plumber*, fr. MF *plommier*, *plombier*, fr. L *plumbarius*, fr. *plumbarius*, adj., of or relating to lead, fr. *plumbum* lead + *-arius* -ary] **1** *obs* : a dealer or worker in lead **2** : one who installs, repairs, and maintains piping, fittings, and fixtures (as toilets, sinks, baths) that are involved in the distribution and use of water in a building (as for sanitary, industrial, or domestic purposes); *broadly* : one performing these services together with those of a gas fitter and steam fitter

²**plumber** \"\ *n* -s [³*plumb* + *-er*] : one who checks the vertical condition of structural components (as of a building)

**plumb·er block** \'pləmə(r)-\ *n* [earlier spelling of *plummer block*] : PLUMMER

**plumber's friend** *also* **plumber's helper** *n* : PLUNGER 2 e

**plumber's furnace** *n* : a portable heater for melting solder and lead

**plumber's snake** *n* : a long flexible rod or cable usu. of spring steel that is used to free clogged pipes

**plumber's soil** *n* : lampblack mixed with glue and water for use as a paint to prevent adhesion of solder

**plumb·ery** \'pləmərē\ *n* -ES [ME *plomerye*, fr. MF *plommerie* leadwork, fr. *plommier* dealer or worker in lead + *-ie* -y] **1** : a workshop (as in a medieval cathedral) for plumbing or leadwork **2** : the business or work of a plumber

**plum·bic** \'pləmbik\ *adj* [ISV *plumb-* + *-ic*] : of, relating to, or containing lead — used esp. of compounds in which this element is tetravalent; compare PLUMBOUS

**plum·bif·er·ous** \,pləm¦bif(ə)rəs\ *adj* [*plumb-* + *-iferous*] : containing lead

**plumb·ing** \'pləmiŋ, -mēŋ\ *n* -s [fr. gerund of ³*plumb*] **1 a** : the act of using a plumb, plummet, or plumb line **b** : a delving in or as if in examination or scrutiny ⟨lovely ~*s* of the psyche —F.R.Leavis⟩ **2 a** : the art of craft of working in lead **b** : a plumber's occupation or trade **3 a** : LEADWORK **b (1)** : plumber's work : the pipes, fixtures, and other apparatus concerned in the introduction, distribution, and disposal of water in a building **(2)** : TOILET 5 b — used with *the* **c** : a natural or artificial system of tubes, conduits, or channels

**plumbing screw** *n* : LEVELING SCREW

**plumb·ism** \'pləm,bizəm\ *n* -s [*plumb-* + *-ism*] : LEAD POISONING; *esp* : chronic lead poisoning

**plumb·ite** \'pləm,bīt\ *n* -s [ISV *plumb-* + *-ite*] : a salt formed in solution by reaction of lead monoxide with an alkali

**plumb joint** *n* [³*plumb* + *joint*] : a soldered lap joint in sheet-metal work

**plumb bladder** *n* : PLUM POCKET

**plumb·less** \'pləmləs\ *adj* : impossible to plumb : FATHOMLESS

**plumb level** *n* : a level with a plumbing attachment (as a horizontal arm and a plumb line at right angles to the arm)

**plumb line** *n* **1 a** : a line or cord having at one end a plumb bob or other weight and used to determine verticality : PLUMMET **b** : PLUMB RULE **2 a** : a line directed to the center of gravity of the earth : a vertical line **b** *obs* : a line perpendicular to another **3** : SOUNDING LINE

**plumb–line** \ˈ⸗,⸗\ *vt* [*plumb line*] : to test the verticality or find the depth of by means of a plumb line; *broadly* : TEST, SCRUTINIZE

**plum blotch** *n* : a disease of plums caused by an imperfect fungus (*Phyllosticta congesta*) characterized by minute brown or gray angular leaf spots and irregular brown or gray blotches on the fruit

**plumb·ly** \ˈpləmlē, -li\ *adv* [⁴*plumb* + *-ly*] : straight downward

**plumb·ness** \-mnə̇s\ *n* -ES : the quality or state of being plumb or vertical

**plumbo-** — see PLUMB-

**plum·bo·ferrite** \ˌpləm(ˌ)bō+\ *n* -S [Sw *plumboferrit*, fr. *plumb-* + *ferr-* (fr. L *ferrum* iron) + *-it* -ite — more at FARRIER] : a mineral $PbFe_4O_7$ consisting of an oxide of lead and iron

**plum·bog** \ˈpləm,bäg\ *also* **plum·boy** \-bȯi\ *n* : DWARF RASPBERRY

**plum·bo·gummite** \ˌpləm(ˌ)bō+\ *n* -S [*plumb-* + *gumm-* (fr. L *gummi* gum) + *-ite* — more at GUM] **1** : a mineral $PbAl_3(PO_4)_2(OH)_5.H_2O$ consisting of a hydrous basic phosphate of lead and aluminum **2** : a group of isostructural minerals consisting of plumbogummite, gorceixite, goyazite, crandallite, deltaite, florencite, and dussertite and related to alunite and other sulfates isostructural with it

**plum·bo·jarosite** \"+\ *n* [*plumb-* + *jarosite*] : a mineral $PbFe_6(SO_4)_4(OH)_{12}$ consisting of a basic sulfate of iron and lead isostructural with jarosite

**plum·bo·niobite** \"+\ *n* [G *plumboniobit*, fr. *plumb-* + *niobit* niobite] : a niobite of complex composition resembling samarskite but containing lead and found in dark brown to black masses in pegmatite veins or massive slate

**plum·bous** \ˈpləmbəs\ *adj* [ISV *plumb-* + *-ous*] : of, relating to, or containing lead — used esp. of compounds in which this element is bivalent; compare PLUMBIC

**plumb post** *n* : one of the vertical members of a trestle bent — compare BATTER PILE

**plumb rule** *n* [ME *plomrewle*, fr. *plom, plum, plumbe*, n., plumb + *rewle, reule* rule] : a narrow board with a plumb line and bob used esp. by builders and carpenters

**plumbs** *pl of* PLUMB, *pres 3d sing of* PLUMB

**plumb–stem bow** *n* : a bow of a ship that is nearly perpendicular to the waterline

**plum·bum** \ˈpləmbəm\ *n* -S [L — more at PLUMB] : LEAD — symbol *Pb*

**plum·cot** \ˈpləm,kät, -ˌkət\ *n* -S [¹*plum* + *apricot*] : a hybrid between the plum and the apricot

**plum curculio** *n* : an American weevil (*Conotrachelus nenuphar*) that is very destructive to plums, cherries, nectarines, peaches, and other stone fruits and to apples, the adult feeding on the leaves of these trees and laying its eggs in crescent-shaped incisions made in the fruit and the larva migrating inward and feeding upon the pulp around the stone or core

**plum duff** *n* : a steamed or boiled plain flour pudding usu. containing raisins or currants

¹**plume** \ˈplüm\ *n* -S [ME, fr. MF, fr. L *pluma* small soft feather — more at FLEECE] **1** : a feather or feathers of a bird: as **a** : a large conspicuous or showy feather ⟨ostrich ~*s*⟩ **b** : a contour feather as distinguished from a down feather **c** : PLUMAGE 1 **d** : a cluster of distinctive feathers ⟨with a ~ of stiff white feathers projecting from the nape⟩ **2 a** : an ornament that consists of a feather, cluster of feathers, tuft of hair, or similar matter worn or displayed often as a symbol of position or rank ⟨wore a ~ of three ostrich feathers in her hair⟩ ⟨the horsehair ~ of an ancient helmet⟩ **b** : something that adorns or attracts attention like a plume : showy raiment and appurtenances : PLUMAGE 2 ⟨made fine with borrowed ~*s*⟩ **c** : a token of honor or prowess : a deserved prize, reward, or approval **3** : something that is felt to resemble a feather (as in shape, appearance, or lightness): as **a** (1) : a plumose appendage of a plant (as a pappus or the coma of a seed) (2) : PLUMULE 1 **b** : an elongated usu. open and mobile column or band (as of smoke, blowing sand or snow, or of cloud) **c** : a plumate part or structure on an animal; *esp* : a full bushy tail (as of a long-haired cat) **d** : a flaw in a gem (as an agate) **4** : PLUME MOTH

²**plume** \"\ *vb* -ED/-ING/-S [ME *plumen*, fr. MF *plumer* to pluck the feathers from (a bird), fr. OF, fr. *plume*, n.] *vi* **1** *obs, of a hawk* : to strip the prey of feathers **2** *obs* : to show self-satisfaction : take pride in oneself or one's accomplishments **3** : to form a plume : assume a plumose appearance; *esp* : to give off something in the form of a plume ⟨a cigarette still *pluming* in the ashtray⟩ ~ *vt* **1 a** : to provide (as a bird) with feathers or plumage : FEATHER **b** : to deck (as a helmet) with a plume **c** : to trick out (as a person) or array showily **d** : to form a plume of (as smoke) or in (as air) ⟨chimneys *pluming* the wintry sky⟩ ⟨an engine . . . *pluming* black smoke along the gray —William Sansom⟩ **2** *archaic* **a** : to strip (a bird) of feathers **b** : to rob or strip bare : DEPRIVE, DESPOIL **3** : to pride, congratulate, or take credit to (oneself) ⟨*plumed* himself on his accomplishment⟩ **4 a** : to dress the feathers of (itself) — used of a bird **b** : to preen and arrange (feathers)

**plume bird** *n* : any of various birds (as an egret or a bird of paradise) that are often hunted for their showy plumes

**plumed** \ˈplümd\ *adj* **1** *obs* : stripped of feathers : PLUCKED **2** : provided or adorned with or as if with a plume — often used in combination ⟨a white-*plumed* egret⟩

**plumed partridge** *n* : MOUNTAIN QUAIL

**plumed thistle** *n* : a thistle of the genus *Circium*

**plume–footed** \ˈ⸗;⸗\ *adj* : having the feet covered with feathers ⟨a *plume-footed* owl⟩

**plume grass** *n* **1** : a grass of the genus *Erianthus*; *esp* : RAVENNA GRASS **2** : an Australian grass of the genus *Dichelachne* with showy feathery flower panicles

**plume hyacinth** *n* : a large grape hyacinth (*Muscari comosum plumosum*) with a branched raceme of sterile flowers that have the petals very irregular, curled, and crisped forming tufts of narrow violet-blue segments

**plume hydroid** *n* : a hydrozoan of the family Plumulariidae

**plume·less** \ˈplümlə̇s\ *adj* : lacking a plume : having no feathers

**plumeless thistle** *n* : a thistle of the genus *Carduus* — compare PLUMED THISTLE

**plume·let** \ˈplümlə̇t\ *n* -S : a small tuft or plume

**plumelike** \ˈ⸗,⸗\ *adj* : resembling a plume usu. in form or texture

**plume moss** *n* : a branched feathery moss (*Hypnum crista-castrensis*) that commonly grows on decaying wood

**plume moth** *n* : any of numerous small slender moths constituting the family Pterophoridae and usu. having the wings deeply divided into two or more plumose lobes

**plume–of–navarre** \-nəˈvär\ *n* -S *often cap N* [prob. after Henry of *Navarre* (Henry IV) †1610 king of France] : WHITE-FRINGED ORCHIS

**plume poppy** *n* : any of several Asiatic herbs of the genus *Macleaya* (esp. *M. cordata*) widely cultivated for the showy plumy panicles of flowers

**plum·er** \ˈplümə(r)\ *n* -S : a person that hunts birds for their plumes

¹**plu·me·ria** \plüˈmirēə\ *n, cap* [NL, fr. *Plumerius* (latinized form of the name of Charles *Plumier*) + NL *-ia*] : a genus of tropical American shrubs or trees (family Apocynaceae) having thick fleshy branches and large highly fragrant, waxy-looking white, yellow, red, or pink flowers with a twisted corolla — see FRANGIPANI

²**plumeria** \"\ *n* -S [NL *Plumeria*] : FRANGIPANI

**plume–royal** \ˈ⸗ˈ⸗⸗\ *n* -S : PURPLE-FRINGED ORCHID b

**plum·ery** \ˈplümərē\ *n* -ES [¹*plume* + *-ery*] : PLUMES, PLUMAGE

**plumes** *pl of* PLUME, *pres 3d sing of* PLUME

**plu·met** \ˈplümə̇t, plüˈmet\ *n* -S [MF *plumete* small feather, fr. *plume* + *-ete* -et — more at PLUME] : a small tuft of feathers

**plu·me·té** \ˌplüməˌtā, ˈplüməd·ē\ *or* **plu·met·ty** \ˈplüməd·ē, (ˈ)plüˈmed·ē\ *adj* [ME *plumte*, fr. MF *plumeté* made so as to resemble a feather, prob. fr. *plumete* small feather] *heraldry* : divided into fusils marked in a manner supposed to represent feathers

**plume thistle** *n* : PLUMED THISTLE; *esp* : BULL THISTLE

**plu·me·tis** \ˌplüməˌtē\ *n, pl* **plumetis** \-ē(z)\ [F, fr. MF, hand embroidery, prob. fr. *plumete* small feather] : a fine lightweight dress fabric of cotton, wool, or rayon that is woven with raised dots or figures on a plain background producing a feathery or embroidered effect

**plu·mette** \(ˈ)plüˈmet\ *n* -S [¹*plume* + *-ette*] : PLUMET

**plum family** *n* **1** : ROSACEAE **2** : AMYGDALACEAE

**plum fir** *n* : a Chilean evergreen tree (*Podocarpus andina*) with an edible plumlike yellowish white fruit

**plum–fruited yew** \ˈ⸗,⸗⸗-\ *n* : PLUM FIR

**plum gouger** *n* : a weevil (*Anthonomus scutellaris*) with a grub that feeds in and destroys plums, cherries, and sometimes other fruits

**plum grape** *n* : FOX GRAPE c

**plu·mi·corn** \ˈplüməˌkȯrn\ *n* -S [*plumi-* (fr. L *pluma* small soft feather) + *-corn* (fr. L *cornu* horn) — more at FLEECE, HORN] : one of the tufts of lengthened feathers on the head of various owls ⟨the earlike ~*s* of a great horned owl⟩

**plu·mie·ra** \plüˈmirə, ˌplüméˈirə\ [NL, fr. Charles *Plumier* †1704 Fr. botanist] *syn of* PLUMERIA

**plu·mie·ride** \plüˈmiˌrīd, ˌplüméˈiˌr-, ˈplüméəˌr-\ *n* -S [ISV *plumier-* (fr. NL *Plumiera*) + *-ide*] : a bitter crystalline glucoside $C_{21}H_{28}O_{12}$ found in trees of the genus *Plumeria*

**plum·i·ness** \ˈplümēnə̇s\ *n* -ES : the quality or state of being plumy

**pluming** *pres part of* PLUME

**plu·mi·ped** \ˈplüməˌped\ *also* **plu·mi·pede** \-ˌpēd\ *adj* [L *plumiped-, plumipes* having feathered feet (read by some editors at Catullus 58ª, 5 for the word which is now generally taken to be *plumipedа*), fr. *plumi-* (fr. *pluma* small soft feather) + *ped-, pes* foot — more at FOOT] **1** : having feet covered with feathers **2** : having winged feet

**plum juniper** *n* **1** : SYRIAN JUNIPER **2** : a Mediterranean juniper (*Juniperus Macrocarpa*) with a large berrylike glaucous blue fruit that turns brown after ripening

**plum leafhopper** *n* : a leafhopper (*Macropsis trimaculata*) that feeds on the foliage of various fruit trees and transmits the virus of peach yellows to peach trees

**plum·less** \ˈpləmlə̇s\ *adj* : having or bearing no plums ⟨a ~ pudding⟩ ⟨barren ~ trees⟩

**plumlike** \ˈ⸗,⸗\ *adj* : resembling a plum, esp. a plum fruit

**plummed** *past of* PLUM

**plum·mer** \ˈpləmə(r)\ *also* **plummer block** *n* -S [prob. fr. the name *Plummer*] : a pillow block or bearing block

**plummer–vinson syndrome** \ˌpləmə(r)ˈvin(t)sən-\ *n, usu cap P&V* [after Henry S. *Plummer* †1937 and Porter P. *Vinson* b1890 Am. physicians] : a condition that is marked by difficulty in swallowing, atrophic changes in mouth, pharynx, and upper esophagus, and hypochromic anemia and is commonly considered to be due to a nutritional deficiency

¹**plum·met** \ˈpləmə̇t, *usu* -ə̇d·+V\ *n* -S [ME *plcmet*, fr. MF *plommet, plombet* ball of lead, fr. *plomb* lead + *-et* — more at PLUMB] **1 a** : SOUNDING LEAD **b** : PLUMB BOB; *also* : PLUMB LINE **c** *obs Scot* : a weighted knob on the pommel of a sword or dirk **d** *obs* : a leaden ball (as on the thong of a scourge) **e** : a weight for a clock **f** : a leaden weight on an angler's line **g** : a piece of lead formerly used for marking (as in ruling paper before writing) **h** : an ancient Egyptian amulet resembling a plumb bob in shape and is used to determine the specific gravity of a liquid **2** : something that weighs down or depresses

²**plummet** \"\ *vi* -ED/-ING/-S **1** : to fall perpendicularly ⟨the plane ~*ed* to earth⟩ **2** : to drop sharply and abruptly ⟨prices may ~ later⟩ ⟨blood pressure ~*ed* to 60/20⟩

**plum·met·less** \-mə̇tlə̇s\ *adj* : UNFATHOMABLE

**plum·mi·ly** \ˈpləmə̇lē\ *adv* : in a plummy manner : so as to be plummy

**plum·mi·ness** \-mēnə̇s\ *n* -ES : the quality or state of being plummy

**plum·ming** \ˈpləmiŋ\ *n* -S [¹*plum* + *-ing*, n. suffix (action)] : degradation of a silver photographic image frequently manifested by a color change (as to purplish) occurring during drying esp. at elevated temperatures — called also *bronzing*

**plum·my** \ˈpləmē\ *adj* -ER/-EST [¹*plum* + *-y*] **1 a** : full of plums ⟨a rich ~ cake⟩ **b** : CHOICE, DESIRABLE, ADVANTAGEOUS ⟨got the *plummiest* appointment in the department⟩ **2 a** : resembling a plum or resembling that of a plum ⟨a dark ~ shade⟩ **b** : soft and full ⟨~ cheeks⟩ **c** *of the voice* : rich and mellow often to the point of affectation

**plu·mose** \ˈplüˌmōs\ *adj* [L *plumosus* downy, fr. *pluma* small soft feather + *-osus* -ose — more at FLEECE] **1** : having feathers or plumes : FEATHERED **2** : PLUMATE; *also* : having hairs or other parts plumate : FEATHERY, PLUMELIKE ⟨a ~ stigma⟩ — **plu·mose·ly** *adv* — **plu·mose·ness** *n* -ES — **plu·mos·i·ty** \plüˈmäsəd·ē\ *n* -ES

¹**plump** \ˈpləmp\ *vb* -ED/-ING/-S [ME *plumpen*, of imit. origin] *vi* **1** : to drop, fall, sink, or come in contact with suddenly or heavily ⟨~*ed* to her knees in front of the fire⟩ ⟨~*ing* down with a sigh⟩ **2 a** *chiefly Brit* : to vote for only one candidate in an election in which one is entitled to vote for two or more **b** : to come out strongly in favor of something : support a point of view, aim, party, or person vigorously or as a partisan — used with *for* ⟨~*ed* for a third party ticket⟩ ⟨ready to ~ for any scheme that would improve the school system⟩ **3** : to come or go or arrive or depart suddenly, unexpectedly, or energetically ⟨~*ed* out of the house in a huff⟩ ⟨~*ed* down in this little town on a quiet Sunday⟩ ~ *vt* **1** : to drop, cast, plunge, or place all at once, suddenly and heavily, or with accurate firmness and an effect of determination ⟨~*ing* stones into the water⟩ ⟨washed and dressed the baby and ~*ed* him into his high chair⟩ **2** : to utter (as an opinion) suddenly or abruptly : blurt out **3** : to make favorable mention of : give support and favorable publicity to ⟨newspaper ads ~ the virtues of the Russian-built . . . car —*Newsweek*⟩

²**plump** \"\ *adv* **1** : with a sudden or heavy drop : suddenly and heavily ⟨fell ~ into the river⟩ **2** : straight down : VERTICALLY, PERPENDICULARLY; *also* : straight ahead : directly in front ⟨there was the deer ~ in our path⟩ **3** : without hesitation, circumlocution, or concealment : BLUNTLY, FLATLY, DIRECTLY, UNQUALIFIEDLY ⟨came out ~ for a lower tariff⟩

³**plump** \"\ *n* -S : an act of falling, plunging, or striking abruptly or heavily : a sudden plunge, heavy fall, or blow ⟨gave a ~ of his fist against the door⟩; *also* : the sound made by such an act ⟨fell into the brook with a ~⟩

⁴**plump** \"\ *adj* **1** : descending or facing directly **2** : done or made suddenly and without reservation : BLUNT, DIRECT, UNQUALIFIED **3** : paid at one time

⁵**plump** \", ˈplu̇mp\ *n* -S [ME *plumpe*] **1** *chiefly dial* : CLUSTER, GROUP, CLUMP **2** : a flock of waterfowl ⟨a ~ of ducks⟩

⁶**plump** \ˈpləmp\ *adj* -ER/-EST [MD *plomp, plump* dull, blunt, stupid] **1 a** : having ample flesh : showing rounded, buxom, and usu. pleasing fullness ⟨a woman of medium height, a little ~ but not fat —Mary McCarthy⟩ ⟨the ~ figure and portly waist . . . of a genial and humorous man —J.R.Green⟩ **b** : marked by a full rounded form ⟨~ cushions with bright covers —Blanche E. Baughan⟩ ⟨secret thickets where the ~*est* beach plums ripen —Phyllis Duganne⟩ ⟨the wind . . . having driven ~ golden clouds across the sky —Rebecca West⟩ **2** : marked by amplitude, abundance, or richness ⟨what a ~ endowment to the . . . mouth of a prelate —John Milton⟩ ⟨the book is ~ with examples and citations —C.W.Collins⟩ **syn** see FAT

⁷**plump** \"\ *vb* -ED/-ING/-S *vt* : to cause to fill or swell out : FATTEN, DISTEND ~ *vi* : to fill or swell out : become fattened or distended

**plum peach** *n, chiefly Midland* : a clingstone peach

**plump·en** \ˈpləmpən\ *vb* -ED/-ING/-S [⁶*plump* + *-en*] : ⁷PLUMP

**plump·er** \-mpə(r)\ *n* -S [⁷*plump* + *-er*] **1** : one that swells out something; *esp* : something carried in the mouth to fill out the cheeks **2** : a solution used in tanning to remove acid from a hide and thus allow the tanning material to act quickly; *also* : a worker that applies this solution

²**plumper** \"\ *n* -S [¹*plump* + *-er*] **1 a** : an act or instance of falling suddenly or heavily (as from a horse) **b** *archaic* : a heavy blow **2** *chiefly Brit* : a vote given to one candidate only when the voter might vote for more than one for the same office (as for several candidates for a county council) **3** *dial* : a downright lie

**plum pine** *n* : BROWN PINE 2

¹**plumping** *adj* [fr. pres. part. of ¹*plump*] : very large : of exceptional size ⟨won by a ~ majority⟩

²**plumping** *n* -S [fr. gerund of ⁷*plump*] : a process of softening and swelling hide fibers by immersion in solution of acid or alkali

**plump·ish** \ˈpləmpish\ *adj* : somewhat plump : moderately stout ⟨~ women in tight shorts⟩

¹**plump·ly** *adv* [⁶*plump* + *-ly*] : in a plump way ⟨a ~ pretty matron⟩

²**plump·ly** *adv* [⁴*plump* + *-ly*] : in a wholehearted manner and without hesitation or circumlocution : firmly and directly ⟨came out ~ in support of the president's stand⟩

¹**plump·ness** *n* -ES [⁶*plump* + *-ness*] : the quality or state of being plump : fullness of form : CORPULENCE

²**plump·ness** *n* -ES [⁴*plump* + *-ness*] : freedom from hesitation or circumlocution in utterance : FORTHRIGHTNESS

**plum pocket** *n* **1** : a disease of plums caused by either of two fungi (*Taphrina pruni* and *T. communis*) and characterized by abortion of the stone leaving a cavity within the swollen distorted fruit — usu. used in pl. **2** : a fruit affected with plum pockets — called also *bladder plum*

¹**plumps** *pres 3d sing of* PLUMP, *pl of* PLUMP

²**plumps** \ˈpləmps\ *n pl but sing or pl in constr* [imit.] : a game of marbles in which the marble shot must hit the one shot at before striking the ground

**plum pudding** *n* **1 a** : a boiled or steamed pudding of flour or bread crumbs, raisins, currants, and other fruits, suet, eggs, and spices and other flavoring matters **b** : a pudding containing plums **2** : a muscular fibrous tissue that permeates the blubber of the tongue of some whales

**plum–pudding** \ˈ⸗;⸗⸗\ *adj* [*plum pudding*] : suggesting plum pudding esp. in the irregular jumbling or interlocking of diverse elements or parts ⟨*plum-pudding* mahoganies⟩

**plum–pudding stone** *n* : a conglomerate rock : PUDDING STONE

**plum purple** *n* **1** : PLUM 6a **2** : a dark violet that is redder and duller than Derby blue and less strong and slightly darker than blue plum — called also *cathedral, grape*

**plumpy** \ˈpləmpē\ *adj* -ER/-EST [⁶*plump* + *-y*] : PLUMP, CHUBBY

**plums** *pl of* PLUM, *pres 3d sing of* PLUM

**plum scab** *n* : PEACH SCAB

**plum·stead peculiars** \ˈpləmz,tˌed-, -ˌtəd-, -m(ˌ)st|\ *n pl, usu cap 1st P* [*Plumstead*, parish in Woolwich metropolitan borough, London, England] : PECULIAR PEOPLE 2

**plum thrips** *n* : PEAR THRIPS

**plum tomato** *n* **1** : any of several cherry tomatoes bearing red or yellow oblong fruits **2** : the fruit of a plum tomato used esp. for salads and preserves

**plum tree** *n* [ME *plumtre*, fr. OE *plūmtrēow*, fr. *plūme* plum + *trēow* tree] **1** : PLUM 1a **2** *slang* : a source of advantage (as political favors or appointments) ⟨never one to hesitate before shaking the *plum tree* for himself or his intimates⟩

**plu·mu·la** \ˈplümyələ\ *n, pl* **plumu·lae** \-ˌlē\ [NL] : PLUMULE

**plu·mu·la·ceous** \ˌplümyəˈlāshəs\ *adj* : relating to or like a plumule

**plu·mu·lar** \ˈplümyələ(r)\ *adj* : of or relating to a plumule

**plu·mu·lar·ia** \ˌplümyəˈla(a)rēə\ *n* [NL, fr. L *plumula* small soft feather + NL *-aria*] **1** *cap* : the type genus of Plumulariidae comprising hydrozoans with sessile zooids arranged on only one side of each branching plumose stem **2** -S : any hydrozoan of the genus *Plumularia* : PLUME HYDROID — **plu·mu·lar·i·an** \ˌ⸗⸗;⸗rēən\ *adj or n*

**plu·mu·la·ri·idae** \ˌplümyələˈrīəˌdē\ *n pl, cap* [NL, fr. *Plumularia*, type genus + *-idae*] : a large and widely distributed family of calyptoblastic hydrozoans — see PLUMULARIA

**plu·mu·late** \ˈplümyəˌlāt, -lə̇t\ *adj* : finely plumose

**plu·mule** \ˈplü(ˌ)myül\ *n* -S [NL *plumula*, fr. L, small soft feather, dim. of *pluma* small soft feather — more at FLEECE] **1** : the primary bud of a plant embryo usu. situated at the apex of the hypocotyl and consisting of leaves and an epicotyl that elongates to extend the axis as a primary stem **2 a** : a down feather **b** : ANDROCONIUM

**plu·mu·li·form** \ˈplümyələˌfȯrm\ *adj* [NL *plumuliformis*, fr. L *plumula* small soft feather + *-iformis* -iform] : resembling a small downy feather

**plu·mu·lose** \ˈplümyəˌlōs\ *adj* [NL *plumulosus*, fr. *plumula* + L *-osus* -ose] : resembling or constituting a plumule

**plum violet** *n* : a dark red to purplish red — called also *canyon*

**plum–web–spinning sawfly** *n* : a sawfly (*Neurotoma inconspicua*) of the family Pamphiliidae with a larva that feeds on the foliage of plum and sand cherry

**plum weevil** *n* : PLUM CURCULIO

**plum wine** *n* : a dark reddish purple that is stronger and slightly redder and lighter than royal purple (sense 1), redder and paler than imperial, and redder, lighter, and stronger than average plum (sense 6a) or violet carmine

**plumy** \ˈplümē\ *adj* -ER/-EST [¹*plume* + *-y*] **1** : DOWNY **2** : covered or adorned with, abounding in, or resembling plumes : PLUMED, FEATHERY

**plum–yew** \ˈ⸗;⸗\ *n* : any of several evergreen trees and shrubs (genus *Cephalotaxus*) of eastern Asia that are related to the yews, have large seeds enclosed in a fleshy envelope, and are sometimes cultivated as ornamentals

¹**plun·der** \ˈpləndə(r)\ *vb* **plundered**; **plundered**; **plundering** \-d(ə)riŋ\ **plunders** [G *plündern*, fr. MHG *plundern*, fr. *plunder, blunder* household goods, clothes, fr. MLG *plunder-*; akin to MD *plunder, plonder* household goods, clothes] *vt* **1 a** : to take the goods of by force (as in war) or wrongfully : PILLAGE, SPOIL, SACK ⟨laws about the ~*ing* of nonbelligerents⟩ **b** : to take or appropriate by force or wrongfully : STEAL, LOOT ⟨the raiders ~*ed* all the cattle⟩ **2** : to make extensive use of material from (an author or his work) without acknowledgment ⟨Shakespeare and his fellow-dramatists ~*ed* the Church legends —Henry Adams⟩ ~ *vi* : to commit robbery, spoliation, or looting **syn** see ROB

²**plunder** \"\ *n* -S **1** : an act of plundering (as in war) : PILLAGING; *also* : spoliation by extortion **2** : something that is taken by open force (as from an enemy) or by theft or fraud : PILLAGE, SPOIL, BOOTY, LOOT **3** *chiefly dial* **a** : personal property and effects : BAGGAGE; *also* : a freight shipment : FREIGHT **b** : goods and equipment used in an indicated situation or activity ⟨camping ~⟩; *esp* : household goods — called also *house plunder* **c** : trade goods : items for buying or selling **d** (1) : PROFIT, GAINS (2) : something garnered or collected ⟨a boyish ~ of nuts, grapes, and crab apples⟩ **e** : miscellaneous articles : JUNK

**plun·der·able** \-dərəbəl\ *adj* : capable of being plundered : worth plundering : subject to plunder

**plun·der·age** \-rij\ *n* -S **1** : an act or instance of plundering; *esp* : embezzlement of goods on shipboard **2** : property obtained by plunderage

**plunderbund** \ˈ⸗⸗,⸗\ *n* [²*plunder* + *bund* (league)] : a league of commercial, political, or financial interests that exploits the public

**plun·der·er** \ˈplənd(ə)rə(r)\ *n* -S : one that plunders : PILLAGER

**plun·der·less** \-də(r)lə̇s\ *adj* : lacking plunder

**plun·der·ous** \-d(ə)rəs\ *adj* : given to or characterized by plundering

**plunder room** *n, chiefly Midland* : LUMBER ROOM

¹**plunge** \ˈplənj\ *vb* -ED/-ING/-S [ME *plungen, plongen*, fr. MF *plonger, plongier*, fr. (assumed) VL *plumbicare*, fr. L *plumbum* lead — more at PLUMB] *vt* **1 a** : to cause to penetrate or enter quickly and forcibly into some material medium : thrust or force into or in liquid, a penetrable substance, or a cavity : IMMERSE, SUBMERGE ⟨~ the body into water⟩ ⟨~ a dagger into the breast⟩ **b** *obs* : to baptize by immersion **c** : to sink (a potted plant) in the ground or in a bed of prepared material **2 a** : to cause to enter or force into some state or course of action usu. suddenly, unexpectedly, or violently and against opposition ⟨scoundrels that *plunged* the nation into needless war⟩ ⟨*plunging* himself into dissipation⟩ **b** *obs* : to harass or overwhelm esp. with difficulties **3 a** : to set (as the horizontal cross hair of a theodolite) in the direction of a grade in plunging a grade **b** : to turn over (as the telescope of a transit) on its horizontal transverse axis ~ *vi* **1** : to thrust or cast oneself into or as if into water : submerge oneself : dive or rush in : penetrate, sink, or enter suddenly or impetuously (as into a forest) **2 a** (1) : to pitch or throw oneself headlong or violently forward and downward (as of a horse or ship) (2) : to execute a football plunge **b** : to act with reckless haste : enter into some state or course of action usu. suddenly, unexpectedly, or unreasonably ⟨*plunged* into debt⟩ **c** : to bet or

gamble heavily and with seeming recklessness **:** risk large sums in hazardous enterprises **3 a :** to descend or dip suddenly ⟨the road *plunges* along the slope⟩ **b :** to incline downward — used esp. of a pipelike ore deposit, an anticline, or a syncline

**syn** PLUNGE, DIVE, and PITCH can mean in common to throw oneself or cause something to be thrown or thrust forward and downward with force into or as if into deep water. PLUNGE stresses the force of the movement forward and downward, often suggesting lack of intention and usu. implying a final total immersion ⟨to *plunge* bodily into the water after a forty-foot drop —C.S.Forester⟩ ⟨the schooner's bows rose dizzily to dip, then *plunge* —I.L.Idriess⟩ ⟨we are *plunged* once more into the war of nerves —*Times Lit. Supp.*⟩ ⟨horses *plunged* and tugged —Stephen Crane⟩ ⟨the singer drew breath and *plunged* into a new stanza —Florette Henri⟩ DIVE, usu. implying intention, suggests a certain skill in execution, less heaviness, and more grace ⟨an enormous water rat *dived* down from the bank —J.C.Powys⟩ ⟨the sun *dived* suddenly into the confusion of low, wooded islands along the western shore —Walter O'Meara⟩ ⟨she *dove* into the red pocketbook and, burrowing among the debris, came up at last with what she was after —Helen Howe⟩ ⟨*dive* a plane into the sea⟩ PITCH, in this comparison, usu. implies total absence of control ⟨*pitch* headlong over a cliff⟩ ⟨stumble and *pitch* forward on his face⟩ It can often apply to a plunging or tossing from side to side ⟨the ship began to *pitch* suddenly as the storm hit⟩ ⟨a horse *pitching* and plunging to dislodge a rider⟩

— **plunge a grade 1 :** to establish a grade between two points of known level by sighting a target set up at either point through a theodolite fixed at the other point, clamping the instrument, and then bringing the target into the fixed line of sight at any desired intermediate points on the grade — compare ²BONE 4 **2 :** to test (as a railroad embankment) as to its reliability or condition by prodding with a light pointed steel rod

**²plunge** \"\ *n* -S [ME, fr. *plungen, plongen,* v.] **1 :** a place for plunging or diving (as a swimming pool) **:** a deep place in water **:** a deep pool **2 :** a dive, leap, rush, or pitch into or as if into water **:** an act of pitching oneself headlong or violently forward and usu. downward ⟨take the water with a ~⟩: as **a :** a breaking of a wave **b :** a heavy fall (as of rain) **c :** a quick thrust into the line in a football game **d :** a brief swim **3 a** *chiefly dial* **:** involvement in a difficult or dangerous situation **:** STRAIT, DILEMMA **b :** an act or instance of engaging in heavy and reckless betting or hazardous speculation or expenditure **:** SPLURGE **4 :** the vertical angle between the lineation of a linear structural or textural fissure in rocks and a horizontal plane — used esp. of ore bodies, folds, or mineral orientations; compare ⁴PITCH 2a (8)

**plunge basin** *n* **:** a hollow excavated by falling water at the foot of a fall or cataract

**plunge bath** *n* **:** a bath in which the bather is immersed in or as if in a pool

**plunge pool** *n* **:** the water in a plunge basin; *also* **:** a small deep plunge basin

**plung·er** \-jə(r)\ *n* -S **1 :** a person that plunges: as **a :** DIVER **b :** a reckless gambler or speculator **c :** an operator of a pusher for moving iron and steel billets into and out of a furnace — called also *pusher* **d :** a worker who operates the guides on a rod-rolling mill **2 :** a device, piece of equipment, or apparatus that functions by plunging or is used in the plunging of something: as **a :** the rod carrying the valves in the inner assembly of an automobile tire valve unit **b** (1) **:** a sliding reciprocating piece driven by or against fluid pressure; *esp* **:** a long valveless piston used as a forcer in a force pump, as a ram in a hydraulic press, or in other similar situations (2) **:** a piece with a motion more or less like that of a ram or piston (as a device for firing the charge in a cartridge or a contact mine, the dasher of a churn, or the iron core of an electric sucking coil) **c :** a tank in which clay is worked with water to the proper consistence **:** BLUNGER **d :** the moving member that in molding ceramic or glassware by pressing forces clay or hot glass into shape **e :** a rubber suction cup attached to a wooden handle and used to free plumbing traps and waste outlets of minor obstructions

plunger 2e

**plunger bucket** *or* **plunger lift** *n* **:** a piston without a valve in a pump

**plunger elevator** *n* **:** HYDRAULIC ELEVATOR

**plunge rod** *n* **:** a leveling rod or a pointed steel rod used in plunging a grade

**plunger piston** *n* **:** PLUNGER 2b(1)

**plunger pump** *n* **:** FORCE PUMP

**plunges** *pres 3d sing of* PLUNGE, *pl of* PLUNGE

**plunging** *pres part of* PLUNGE

**plunging fire** *n* **:** direct fire from a superior elevation resulting in the projectiles striking the target (as ground) at a high angle

**plung·ing·ly** *adv* **:** in a plunging manner **:** with plunges or plunging

**plunging rod** *n* **:** PLUNGE ROD

**¹plunk** \ˈpləŋk\ *also* **plonk** \ˈpläŋk, -ȯ-\ *vb* -ED/-ING/-S [imit.] *vt* **1 :** to pluck (as the string of a musical instrument) sharply so as to produce a quick, hollow, metallic, or harsh sound ⟨~*ing* the strings on a harp⟩; *also* **:** to play (a stringed instrument) in a plunking manner ⟨~*ed* the banjo⟩ **2 a :** to act on (as an object, a surface) so as to cause to give off a plunking sound; *also* **:** to move (as an object, a person) with a sudden or forceful movement usu. oriented to a particular place ⟨~*ed* herself into the chair⟩ ⟨~*ing* the books onto the table⟩ **b :** to strike (as a person) with the fist or a bullet ~ *vi* **1 :** to make a plunking sound ⟨frogs ~*ing* in the hollow⟩ **2 :** to drop or sink abruptly or heavily **:** PLUMP, DIVE ⟨~*ed* into the pool⟩ **3 :** to come out in favor of someone or something **:** SUPPORT — used with *for* ⟨the moderates finally ~*ed* for the party candidate⟩

**²plunk** \"\ *also* **plonk** \"\ *n* -S **1 a :** an act or instance of plunking **:** BLOW **b :** a sound of or as if of a musical instrument being plunked ⟨a ~ of hoofbeats⟩ **2** *slang* **:** DOLLAR ⟨paid 10 ~*s* for a ticket⟩

**³plunk** \"\ *also* **plonk** \"\ *adv* **1 :** with a plunking sound **:** PLUMP **2 :** PRECISELY, EXACTLY ⟨~ in the center —W.R. Kuhns⟩

**plunk down** *vi* **:** to drop abruptly **:** settle into position ⟨*plunked down* on the grass⟩ ~ *vt* **1 :** to put down usu. firmly or abruptly ⟨*plunked* his paper *down* on the table⟩ **:** settle (as oneself) into position ⟨*plunked* himself *down* on the bench⟩ **2 :** to pay out ⟨*plunked* $100 *down* for a suit⟩

**plunk·er** \-kə(r)\ *n* -S **:** one that plunks — see LURE illustration

**plunky** \-kē\ *adj* -ER/-EST **:** marked or marred by a plunking sound ⟨a ~ tune⟩

**plun·ther** \ˈplən(t)thə(r)\ *vi* -ED/-ING/-S [imit.] **:** PLOD, FLOUNDER

**plup** \ˈpləp\ *n* -S [imit.] **:** PLOP

**¹plu·per·fect** \(ˈ)plü¦pərfəkt, -¦pə̄f-\ *adj* [modif. of LL *plusquamperfectus,* fr. L *plus* more + *quam* than + LL *perfectus* perfect (of a tense) — more at PLUS, QUANTITY, PERFECT] **1 :** PAST PERFECT **2 :** more than perfect or complete **:** SUPERLATIVE, UTTER — **plu·per·fect·ly** *adv* — **plu·per·fect·ness** *n*

**²pluperfect** \"\ *n* **1 :** the pluperfect tense of a language **2 :** a verb form in the pluperfect tense

**¹plu·ral** \ˈplu̇rəl, ˈplür-\ *adj* [ME *plurel, plural,* fr. MF & L; MF *plurel,* fr. L *pluralis,* fr. *plur-, plus* more + *-alis* -al] **1 :** belonging to a class of grammatical forms used to denote more than one ⟨~ noun⟩ ⟨~ pronoun⟩ ⟨~ endings⟩, used to agree with syntactically related forms denoting more than one ⟨~ verb⟩ ⟨~ adjective⟩, and used in languages (as ancient Greek) having a dual form to denote more than two — opposed to *singular* **2 :** relating to or consisting of or containing more than one ⟨~ citizenship⟩ ⟨~ winner⟩ or more than one kind or class ⟨~ population⟩ ⟨~ society⟩

**²plural** \"\ *n* -S [ME *plurel,* fr. *plurel, plural,* adj.] **:** the plural number or an inflectional form denoting it or a word in that form ⟨how such words form their ~*s*⟩

**plural executive** *n* **:** a group of officers or major officials (as a board of directors) or a committee that functions in making current decisions or in giving routine orders usu. the responsibility of an individual executive officer or official

**plu·ral·ism** \-rə,lizəm\ *n* -S **1 :** the quality or state of being plural ⟨ethical ~, which speculated on the variety of political systems that became possible once the moral value of group life was acknowledged —David Easton⟩ **2 a :** the holding by one person of two or more offices at once **b :** PLURALITY 2a **3 a :** a metaphysical theory that there are more than one or more than two kinds of ultimate reality — compare DUALISM, MONISM **b :** a metaphysical theory (as atomism or monadism) that reality is not an organic whole but is composed of a plurality of independent entities whether material or spiritual or both — contrasted with *monism* **4 a :** a state or condition of society in which members of diverse ethnic, racial, religious, or social groups maintain an autonomous participation in and development of their traditional culture or special interest within the confines of a common civilization **b :** a concept, doctrine, or policy proposing or advocating this state

**plu·ral·ist** \-ləst\ *n* **1 a :** a clergyman holding more than one benefice or living at a time **b :** a person holding two or more offices at once **2 :** one who holds a theory of pluralism or who advocates a state of pluralism

**plu·ral·is·tic** \¦==¦listik, -tēk\ *or* **plu·ral·ist** \ˈ==,ləst\ *adj* **:** of, relating to, or characterized by pluralism ⟨American culture is supremely *pluralist* in religion —Max Lerner⟩ — **plu·ral·is·ti·cal·ly** \¦==¦listək(ə)lē\ *adv*

**pluralistic idealism** *n* **:** a system of philosophical idealism emphasizing the multiplicity of selves and their individual experiences — contrasted with *monistic idealism;* compare LEIBNIZIANISM, PERSONALISM

**plu·ral·i·ty** \plu̇ˈraləd·ē, plüˈ-, plə'-, -lətē, -i\ *n* -ES [ME *pluralite,* fr. MF *pluralité* large number, fr. LL *pluralitat-, pluralitas,* fr. L *pluralis* plural + *-itat-, -itas* -ity] **1 a :** the state of being plural ⟨~ of causes⟩ ⟨noun endings expressing ~⟩ **b :** the state of being numerous **c :** a large number or quantity **:** MULTITUDE **2 a :** the holding by one person of two or more benefices or livings at one time **b :** any of the benefices or livings so held **c :** the holding by one person of two or more offices or positions at one time **3 a :** a number greater than another number **b :** an excess of votes over those cast for an opposing candidate **c :** a number of votes cast for a candidate in a contest of more than two candidates that is greater than the number cast for any other candidate but not more than half the total votes cast — distinguished from *majority*

**plu·ral·iza·tion** \,plu̇rələˈzāshən, ,plür-, -,lī'-\ *n* -S [ISV *pluralize* + *-ation*] **:** the act of pluralizing

**plu·ral·ize** \ˈplu̇rə,līz, ˈplür-\ *vb* -ED/-ING/-S *see -ize in Explan Notes* [ISV ¹*plural* + *-ize*] *vt* **:** to make plural by using a plural form **:** attribute plurality to ~ *vi* **:** to take a plural **:** assume a plural form — **plu·ral·iz·er** \-zə(r)\ *n* -S

**plu·ral·ly** \-rəlē, -li\ *adv* [ME *pluraliche,* fr. *plurel, plural* plural + *-liche, -ly* -ly] **:** in a plural manner or in the plural form

**plural marriage** *n* **:** polygamous marriage esp. as once practiced by Mormons

**plural vote** *n* **:** the casting of more than one vote or the right of casting more than one vote or of voting in more than one constituency

**plural wife** *n* **:** a wife in a plural marriage; *esp* **:** a wife in unlawful polygamy who is not the lawful one

**plu·rel** \ˈplu̇rəl\ *n* -S [irreg. fr. ¹*plural*] **:** a group or aggregate resulting from a process of categorizing or statistical analysis ⟨the age-classes of population . . . are purely nominal ~*s* with no tangible interaction —P.A.Sorokin⟩

**pluri-** *comb form* [L, fr. *plur-, plus* more — more at PLUS] **:** many **:** having or being more than one **:** MULTI- ⟨*pluri*axial⟩ ⟨*pluri*locular⟩

**plu·ri·axial** \¦plu̇rē+\ *adj* [*pluri-* + *axial*] **:** having more than one axis; *specif* **:** having flowers developed on secondary shoots — compare MONAXIAL

**plu·ri·cellular** \¦plu̇rə+\ *adj* [*pluri-* + *cellular*] **:** of, relating to, or involving several to many cells ⟨a tumor of ~ origin⟩

**plu·ri·es** \ˈplu̇rē,ēz\ *n, pl* **pluries** [ME, fr. LL, often, many times, fr. L *plur-, plus* more; fr. the use of the Latin word *pluries* in a writ of this kind] **:** any of one or more writs (as of fieri facias) issued after the first and alias writs have proved ineffectual

**plu·ri·glandular** \¦plu̇rə+\ *adj* [ISV *pluri-* + *glandular*] **:** of, relating to, affecting, or derived from more than one gland or kind of gland ⟨~ syndrome⟩ ⟨signs of ~ insufficiency —J.E. Kraus & W.A.D.Anderson⟩

**plu·ri·lateral** \"+\ *adj* [ISV *pluri-* + *lateral*] **:** MULTILATERAL

**plu·ri·lingual** \"+\ *adj* [*pluri-* + *lingual*] **:** MULTILINGUAL

**plu·ri·loc·u·lar** \¦plu̇rə¦läkyələ(r)\ *adj* [F *pluriloculaire,* fr. *pluri-* + *-loculaire* (fr. NL *loculus*)] **:** divided into chambers; *esp* **:** divided by longitudinal and transverse septa into many small chambers each producing a single diploid zoospore ⟨a ~ sporangium⟩

**plu·ri·nominal** \¦plu̇rə+\ *adj* [*pluri-* + *nominal*] **1 :** POLYNOMIAL **2 :** nominating or electing more than one representative ⟨~ district⟩

**plu·rip·a·ra** \plüˈripərə\ *n, pl* **pluripa·rae** \-pə,rē\ [NL, fr. *pluri-* + *-para*] **:** MULTIPARA

**plu·ri·potent** \¦plu̇rə+\ *adj* [*pluri-* + *potent*] *of embryonic tissue* **:** not fixed as to future developmental potentialities **:** PLASTIC

**plu·ri·potentiality** \"+\ *n* [*pluri-* + *potentiality*] **:** capacity to affect more than one organ or tissue

**plu·ri·presence** \"+\ *n* [*pluri-* + *presence*] **:** the theological notion of presence in more than one place at the same time ⟨~ of saints⟩

**plu·ris pe·ti·tio** \ˈplu̇rəspəˈtishē,ō\ *n* [L, act of asking for more] *Scots law* **:** PLUS PETITIO

**plu·ri·syllable** \¦plu̇rə+\ *n* [*pluri-* + *syllable*] **:** a word of more than one syllable — compare POLYSYLLABIC

**plu·ri·va·lent** \¦plu̇rə¦vālənt, (ˈ)plü¦rivəl-\ *adj* [ISV *pluri-* + *valent*] **:** having several degrees of power or capability; *specif* **:** consisting of several associated homologous chromosomes ⟨~ chromatin rods⟩

**plu·ri·valve** \ˈplu̇rə,valv\ *adj* [prob. fr. (assumed) NL *plurivalvis,* fr. NL *pluri-* + *-valvis* (fr. *valva* valve)] **:** MULTIVALVE

**plu·ri·verse** \ˈplu̇rə,vərs\ *n* -S [*pluri-* + *-verse* (as in *universe*)] **:** the world as conceived according to a theory of pluralism — compare MULTIVERSE

**plu·ri·vocalic** \¦plu̇rə+\ *adj* [*pluri-* + *vocalic*] **:** having more than one vowel — compare UNIVOCALIC

**plu·ri·vol·tine** \¦plu̇rə¦vōl,tēn, -tᵊn\ *adj* [*pluri-* + *-voltine* (as in *bivoltine*)] **:** having several generations a year — used esp. of a silkworm

**plu·riv·o·rous** \(ˈ)plü¦riv(ə)rəs\ *adj* [*pluri-* + *-vorous*] **:** living upon several hosts ⟨~ fungus⟩

**¹plus** \ˈpləs\ *prep* [L *plur-, plus* more; akin to Gk *pleiōn, pleōn* more, L *plenus* full — more at FULL] **1 :** increased by **:** with the addition or increment of **:** with an addition ⟨four ~ five or mathematically expressed 4 + 5⟩ ⟨the debt ~ interest⟩ — compare MINUS **2 :** possessed of **:** having gained **:** WITH ⟨came home poorer and ~ a wife and three children⟩

**²plus** \"\ *n, pl* **plus·es** *also* **plus·ses** \-səz\ **1 :** PLUS SIGN **2 :** an added quantity **:** something additional or extra **3 :** a positive quantity **:** GAIN, ADVANTAGE ⟨the quiet operation of the system was an unexpected ~⟩ **4 :** SURPLUS

**³plus** \"\ *adj* **1 a :** requiring addition ⟨the ~ sign⟩ **b :** algebraically positive ⟨a ~ quantity⟩ **2 a :** having or receiving as an addition or gain — used predicatively ⟨he was ~ a useful nag on the deal⟩ **b :** having or being in addition to what is anticipated ⟨other ~ values were the excellent schools and good neighbors⟩ **3 a :** falling high in the range (as of quality or size) specified — used postpositively ⟨a grade of C ~ in French⟩ ⟨a sheet of 12 ~ copper⟩ **b :** greater than that specified esp. in size ⟨a 100 ~ mesh⟩ ⟨a conglomerate of ~ one inch gravel⟩ **c :** possessing a specified quality to an exceptional or unanticipated degree ⟨a new higher waistline that is style ~⟩ ⟨his smile had charm ~⟩ **4 :** positively electrified **:** electrically positive **5 a :** reacting sexually to a morphologically indistinguishable but physiologically separable minus form — used of lower fungi in which maleness and femaleness are indeterminable as such; compare HETEROTHALLIC **b :** of, relating to, or exhibiting such a sexual character

**⁴plus** \"\ *vt* **plussed** \-st\ **plussed** \"\ **plus·sing** \-siŋ\ **plus·es** *also* **plusses** \-səz\ **:** to add something to **:** INCREASE ⟨hoping to ~ his sale⟩

**plus fours** *n pl* **:** knickerbockers for sports and country wear made four inches longer than ordinary knickerbockers for looseness and ease at the knees

plus fours

**¹plush** \ˈpləsh\ *n* -ES [MF *peluche,* prob. fr. (assumed) MF *peluchier* to pick, pluck, clean, fr. OF, fr. (assumed) VL *piluccare* to pick, clean, irreg. fr. L *pilare* to remove the hair from, fr. *pilus* hair — more at PILE] **1 a :** a fabric that has an even pile longer and less dense than velvet pile, is made on a cotton ground with a pile of silk, mohair, rayon, or cotton, and is used esp. for upholstery **b plushes** *pl* **:** plush breeches such as are worn by some footmen **2 :** a natural substance (as grass) that is felt to resemble plush in softness or appearance

**²plush** \"\ *adj, sometimes* -ER/-EST **1 :** relating to, like, or made of plush **2 :** notably luxurious, expensive, or easy **:** highly superior of its kind ⟨a ~ job⟩ ⟨~ apartments⟩

**plush copper** *n* **:** CHALCOTRICHITE

**plus head** *n* **:** a curved head, top, or bottom of a piece of machinery that is convex on the outside

**plushed** \ˈpləsht\ *adj* **1 :** resembling plush **2 :** covered, dressed, or finished in plush

**plush·i·ly** \-shəlē\ *adv* **:** in a plushy manner **:** so as to resemble plush ⟨~ green lawns⟩

**plushlike** \ˈ=,=\ *adj* **:** resembling plush esp. in having a soft piled surface

**plush·ly** *adv* **:** LUXURIOUSLY

**plushy** \ˈpləshē, -shi\ *adj* -ER/-EST **1 a :** having the texture or appearance of plush **:** soft and shaggy **b :** covered with plush **2 :** LUXURIOUS, RICH, SHOWY **:** PLUSH 2

**plu·sia** \ˈplüz(h)ēə\ *n* [NL, fr. Gk *plousios* rich; fr. the metallic markings on the wings; akin to Gk *ploutos* wealth] **1** *cap* **:** a large widely distributed genus (the type of the family Plusiidae) of moths that have a stout body, slender antennae, and the fore wings usu. with metallic markings **2** -S **:** any moth of *Plusia* or a closely related genus

**¹plu·si·id** \ˈplüsēəd\ *adj* [NL *Plusiidae*] **:** of or relating to the Plusiidae

**²plusiid** \"\ *n* -S **:** a moth of the family Plusiidae

**plu·si·idae** \plüˈsīə,dē\ *n pl, cap* [NL, fr. *Plusia,* type genus + *-idae*] **:** a family of moths that are closely related to and often included among the Noctuidae, have hairy eyes and larvae which move like spanworms, and include various economic pests — see PLUSIA

**plus juncture** *n* **:** OPEN JUNCTURE

**plus lens** *n* **:** CONVERGING LENS

**plus pe·ti·tio** \ˈpləspəˈtishē,ō\ *n* [LL, fr. L *plus* more + *petitio* petition — more at PLUS] *Roman, civil, & Scots law* **:** a demanding by the plaintiff in his pleading of more than he proves either in amount or as to time or condition of performance

**plus pressure** *n* **:** pressure (as in a boiler) in excess of atmospheric pressure

**plus·sage** *also* **plus·age** \ˈpləsij\ *n* -S **:** an amount over and above another amount

**plussed** *past of* PLUS

**plusses** *pl of* PLUS, *pres 3d sing of* PLUS

**plus sign** *n* **1 :** a sign + denoting addition or a positive quantity — compare MINUS SIGN **2 :** an indication of desirable qualities **:** a favorable sign ⟨her neatness is a *plus sign*⟩

**plussing** *pres part of* PLUS

**plus value** *n* **:** a card or other value that is worth less than ½ probable trick but adds somewhat to the value of the hand in some methods of evaluating the strength of a hand in contract bridge

**plut-** *or* **pluto-** *comb form* [Gk *plout-, plouto-,* fr. *ploutos;* prob. akin to Gk *plein* to sail, float — more at FLOW] **:** wealth ⟨*plut*archy⟩ ⟨*pluto*mania⟩

**plu·tarch** \ˈplü,tärk, -tåk\ *n* -S *sometimes cap* [after *Plutarch* †A.D.120? Greek biographer] **:** BIOGRAPHER

**plu·tarch·an** \-kən\ *or* **plu·tarch·ian** \(ˈ)plü¦tärkēən\ *adj, usu cap* [*Plutarch* + E *-an*] **1 :** of or relating to Plutarch, the Greek biographer **2 :** suggesting or typical of the distinguished men of whose lives Plutarch wrote ⟨a *Plutarchan* parallel⟩

**plu·tar·chy** \ˈplü,tärkē\ *n* -ES [*plut-* + *-archy*] **:** PLUTOCRACY

**plute** \ˈplüt\ *n* -S [by shortening & alter.] *slang* **:** PLUTOCRAT

**plu·te·al** \ˈplüd·ēəl\ *also* **plu·te·an** \-ēən\ *adj* [*pluteus* + *-al* or *-an*] **:** of, relating to, or being a pluteus

**plu·tel·la** \plüˈtelə\ *n* [NL, perh. fr. Gk *ploutos* wealth + NL *-ella*] **1** *cap* **:** the type genus of Plutellidae **2** -S **:** any moth of the genus *Plutella; esp* **:** CABBAGE MOTH

**¹plu·tel·lid** \-ləd\ *adj* [NL *Plutellidae*] **:** of or relating to the Plutellidae

**²plutellid** \"\ *n* -S [NL *Plutellidae*] **:** a moth of the family Plutellidae

**plu·tel·li·dae** \-lə,dē\ *n pl, cap* [NL, fr. *Plutella,* type genus + *-idae*] **:** a family of small often cryptically colored moths with narrow wings and with usu. green phytophagous larvae that include some economically important pests of cultivated plants — see PLUTELLA

**plu·te·us** \ˈplüd·ēəs\ *n, pl* **plu·tei** \-ē,ī\ *also* **pluteuses** [L] **1 a :** a low wall or parapet in ancient Roman architecture; *esp* **:** one used as a partition between the bases of columns **b :** an ancient Roman reading desk or storage place for manuscripts **2** [NL, fr. L] **:** the free-swimming bilaterally symmetrical larva of a sea urchin or ophiuran distinguished by several slender anteriorly projecting processes enclosing calcareous rods

**plu·toc·ra·cy** \plüˈtäkrəsē, -si\ *n* -ES [Gk *ploutokratia,* fr. *ploutos* wealth + *-kratia* -cracy] **1 :** government by the wealthy **:** the rule or dominion of wealth or of the rich **2 :** a controlling or influential class of rich men **:** a body of plutocrats

**plu·to·crat** \ˈplüd·ə,krat, -ütə,-, *usu* -ad.+V\ *n* -S [fr. *plutocracy,* after such pairs as E *aristocracy: aristocrat*] **:** a person with power or influence due to his wealth **:** a member of a plutocracy

**plu·to·crat·ic** \¦==¦krad·|ik, -at|, |ēk\ *also* **plu·to·crat·i·cal** \|əkəl, |ēk-\ *adj* **:** of, relating to, or characterized by plutocrats or plutocracy — **plu·to·crat·i·cal·ly** \|ək(ə)lē, |ēk-, -li\ *adv*

**plu·to·democracy** \¦plüd·ō+\ *n* [*plut-* + *democracy*] **:** a democracy held to be controlled by people of wealth rather than by the common man ⟨attacks by Fascist dictators on western *plutodemocracies*⟩

**plu·to·gogue** \ˈplüd·ə,gäg *sometimes* -,gȯg\ *n* -S [*plut-* + *-gogue* (as in *demagogue*)] **:** a person who favors the wealthy or their interests or attempts to present them to the public in a favorable light — **plu·to·gogu·ery** \-,gäg(ə)rē, ,==ˈ=(=)=\ *sometimes* -gȯg-\ *n* -ES

**plu·tol·a·try** \plüˈtälə·trē\ *n* -ES [*plut-* + *-latry*] **:** excessive devotion to wealth

**plu·tol·o·gy** \-läjē\ *n* -ES [*plut-* + *-logy*] **:** the scientific study of wealth **:** theoretical economics

**plu·to·ma·nia** \,plüd·əˈmānēə\ *n* [NL, fr. *plut-* + LL *mania*] **:** excessive or abnormal desire for wealth; *also* **:** insanity marked by delusions of wealth

**pluto monkey** \ˈplüd·(,)ō-\ *n, usu cap P* [after *Pluto,* Greek god of the subterranean world of the dead] **1 :** a long-tailed West African guenon monkey (*Cercopithecus leucampyx*) of a grizzled blackish color with a white frontal band **2 :** a red guenon (*Erythrocebus pyrrhonotus*) often kept as a pet in ancient Egypt and a favorite of present-day organ-grinders

**plu·ton** \ˈplü,tän\ *n* -S [prob. back-formation fr. *plutonic*] **:** a body of intrusive igneous rock of any size or shape; *esp* **:** one of large size that was originally deep-seated

**plu·to·ni·an** \plüˈtōnēən, ˈ====\ *adj* [L *plutonius* plutonian (fr. Gk *ploutōnios,* fr. *Ploutōn* Pluto, Greek god of the subterranean world of the dead) + E *-an*] **1** *sometimes cap* **a :** of or relating to the lower world **:** INFERNAL **b :** resembling the lower world **:** grim and gloomy **:** harsh and unpleasing ⟨a ~ darkness⟩ ⟨such ~ landscapes⟩ **2 :** PLUTONIC 1 **3 :** of or relating to the planet Pluto

**plu·ton·ic** \(ˈ)plü¦tänik, -nēk\ *adj* [L *Pluton-, Pluto* Pluto (fr. Gk *Ploutōn*) + E *-ic*] **1 a :** relating to or being the theory of the plutonists **:** IGNEOUS **b :** originating or situated deep within the earth **2** *sometimes cap* **:** of or relating to the Greek god Pluto **:** PLUTONIAN 1

**plutonic plug** *n* **:** a plug composed of holocrystalline granular igneous rock (as granite or gabbro)

**plutonic rock** *n* **:** an igneous rock (as granite) of holocrystalline granular texture regarded as having solidified at considerable depth below the surface

**plu·to·nism** \'plüt³n,izəm\ *n* -s [*plutonium* + *-ism*] **:** poisoning from exposure to or absorption of radiations from plutonium

**plu·to·nist** \'plüt³nəst\ *n* -s [*plutonic* + *-ist*] **:** an adherent of the theory that the igneous rocks have solidified from magmas, some of them at great depth below the surface — opposed to *neptunist*

**plu·to·nite** \-³n,īt\ *n* -s [ISV *plutonic* + *-ite*; orig. formed as G *plutonit*] **:** a deep-seated rock

**plu·to·ni·um** \plü'tōnēəm\ *n* -s [NL, fr. *Pluton-*, *Pluto* Pluto, most remote known planet in our solar system (fr. L *Pluton-*, *Pluto* Pluto, Greek god of the subterranean world of the dead) + *-ium*] **:** a radioactive metallic element of the actinide series that is similar chemically to uranium, that is usu. produced in nuclear reactors as the long-lived isotope of mass number 239 by spontaneous emission of an electron from neptunium obtained in turn from uranium 238, that is also found in minute quantities in pitchblende and other uranium-containing ores, that undergoes very slow disintegration with the emission of a helium nucleus to form uranium 235, and that is fissionable with slow neutrons to yield atomic energy for use in power plants or atom bombs — symbol *Pu*; see ELEMENT table, NEPTUNIUM SERIES

**plu·to·nom·ic** \,plüt³n¦ämik\ *adj* [ISV *plutonomy* + *-ic*] **:** of or relating to political economy or economics

**plu·ton·o·my** \plü'tänəmē\ *n* -ES [ISV *plut-* + *-nomy*] **:** POLITICAL ECONOMY **:** ECONOMICS

**pluvi-** *or* **pluvio-** *also* **pluvia-** *comb form* [ME *pluvy-*, fr. L *pluvi-*, fr. *pluvia*] **:** rain ⟨*pluvia*meter⟩ ⟨*pluvi*an⟩ ⟨*pluvio*graph⟩

**¹plu·vi·al** \'plüvēəl\ *adj* [L *pluvialis*, fr. *pluvia* rain (fr. fem. of *pluvius* rainy, fr. *pluere* to rain) + *-alis* -al — more at FLOW] **1 :** of or relating to rain **:** characterized by abundant rain **2** *of a geologic change* **:** resulting from the action of rain or sometimes from the fluvial action of rainwater flowing in stream channels

**²pluvial** \"\ *n* -s [ML *pluviale* ecclesiastic's cope, fr. L, neut. of *pluvialis*, adj.] **1** *archaic* **:** an ecclesiastic's cope; *also* **:** a monarch's robe of state of similar design **2** [¹*pluvial*] **:** a prolonged period of wet climate in which the moisture relations of an affected area are profoundly altered (as by the formation of lakes or glaciers)

**plu·vi·a·line** \'plüvēə,līn\ *adj* [NL *Pluvialis* + E *-ine*] **:** of or relating to the plovers

**plu·vi·a·lis** \,plüvē'āləs\ *n, cap* [NL, fr. L *pluvialis*, adj., pluvial] **:** a genus of Charadriidae including the golden plovers

**plu·vi·an** \'plüvēən\ *adj* [*pluvi-* + *-an*] **:** RAINY

**plu·vi·o·graph** \'plüvēə,graf, -räf\ *n* [ISV *pluvi-* + *-graph*] **:** a self-registering rain gage

**plu·vi·o·graph·ic** \¦==¦grafik\ *also* **plu·vi·o·graph·i·cal** \-fəkəl\ *adj* [*pluviography* or *pluviograph* + *-ic* or *-ical*] **:** of or relating to pluviography or the pluviograph

**plu·vi·og·ra·phy** \,plüvē'ägrəfē\ *n* -ES [*pluvi-* + *-graphy*] **:** a branch of meteorology that deals with the automatic registration of precipitation (as of rain or snow) **2 :** graphic presentation of precipitation data

**plu·vi·om·e·ter** \,plüvē'ämədə(r)\ *also* **plu·vi·am·e·ter** \-'am-\ *n* [*pluviometer* prob. fr. F *pluviomètre*, fr. *pluvi-* + *-mètre* -meter; *pluviameter* alter. (influenced by L *pluvia* rain) of *pluviometer*] **:** RAIN GAGE

**plu·vi·o·met·ric** \¦plüvēə¦me·trik\ *also* **plu·vi·o·met·ri·cal** \-rəkəl\ *adj* [ISV *pluvi-* + *-metric, -metrical*] **:** of, relating to, or used in the measurement of rainfall — **plu·vi·o·met·ri·cal·ly** \-rək(ə)lē\ *adv*

**plu·vi·om·e·try** \,plüvē'ämə·trē\ *n* -ES [ISV *pluvi-* + *-metry*] **:** a branch of meteorology that deals with the measurement of rainfall

**plu·vi·o·scope** \'plüvēə,skōp\ *n* [ISV *pluvi-* + *-scope*] **:** RAIN GAGE

**plu·vi·ose** \'plüvē,ōs\ *adj* [L *pluviosus*] **:** marked by or regularly receiving heavy rainfall ⟨a ~ period⟩ ⟨~ areas⟩ — **plu·vi·os·i·ty** \¦==¦äsəd·ē\ *n* -ES

**plu·vi·ous** \'plüvēəs\ *adj* [ME *pluvyous*, fr. L *pluviosus*, fr. *pluvia* rain + *-osus* -ose] **:** of or relating to rain **:** RAINY, PLUVIOSE

**¹ply** \'plī\ *vb* **plied; plied; plying; plies** [ME *plien* to bend, fold, mold, fr. MF *plier* to bend, fold, fr. L *plicare* to fold; akin to OE *flohtenfōte* web-footed, OHG *flehtan* to braid, plait, ON *flētta* to plait, Goth *flahta* braid, L *plectere* to braid, plait, Gk *plekein* to plait, Skt *praśna* plaited basket] *vt* **1 a :** BEND, FOLD, MOLD **b :** to twist together (as two or more single yarns) **2** *obs* **:** to bend in will or sense **:** ADAPT ~ *vi* **1** *obs* **:** to be pliable **:** BEND; *also* **:** TWIST **2** *obs* **:** to be pliant **:** YIELD, COMPLY

**²ply** \"\ *n* -ES [ME (Sc) *ply* condition, fr. MF *pli* pleat, fold, fr. *plier*, v.] **1** *chiefly dial* **:** physical condition ⟨in good ~⟩ ⟨out of ~⟩ **2 :** FOLD, LAYER: **a :** one of the strands in a yarn composed of two or more strands **b :** one of several layers of cloth usu. sewn or laminated together ⟨a shirt collar that has three *plies* of cloth⟩ ⟨the body of a tire has several *plies* of rubberized fabric⟩ **c :** one of the interwoven webs in some fabrics and carpets **d :** one of the veneer sheets forming plywood **e :** a layer of a paper or paperboard composed of more than one web; *also* **:** a liner or filler of a pasteboard or combination board **f :** an arbitrary measure of thickness (as of paper) **3 a** *archaic* **:** BEND, CURVATURE ⟨the ~ of an animal's limb⟩ ⟨the ~ of the arm is the elbow⟩ **b :** a trend of mind or spirit **:** INCLINATION, BIAS

**³ply** \"\ *vb* **plied; plied; plying; plies** [ME *plien*, short for *applien* to apply] *vt* **1 a :** to use or wield diligently or vigorously and steadily **:** EXERT, EXERCISE ⟨~ an ax⟩ ⟨~ your wit⟩ ⟨go ~ thy needle; meddle not —Shak.⟩ **b :** to practice or perform diligently **:** apply oneself to ⟨~*ing* his trade⟩ **2 a :** to keep after **:** assail vigorously or continually **b :** to urge something importunately on **:** keep supplying ⟨~ her with questions⟩ ⟨*plied* the man with liquor⟩ **3 a** *obs* **:** to use (a tide or other natural aid) in working a ship **b :** to make a practice or business of rowing or sailing over or on ⟨the ferryboat *plies* the river⟩ ~ *vi* **1 a :** to employ oneself or work diligently or steadily **:** apply oneself **:** be in steady action ⟨those who ~ in freedom's cause⟩ ⟨oars ~*ing* strongly against the current⟩ **b :** to wait regularly for business **:** have one's regular stand — used esp. of a porter, boatman, or other independent laborer ⟨a taxi driver ~*ing* for hire⟩ **2 a** *of a boat or its crew* **:** to work to windward **:** BEAT **b :** to direct one's course **:** STEER **c :** to go or travel more or less regularly between usu. specified points ⟨a steamer ~*ing* between opposite shores of the lake⟩ **syn** see HANDLE

**plyboard** \'=,=\ *n* **1 :** PAPERBOARD **2 :** PLYWOOD

**ply·er** \'plī(ə)r, -īə\ *n* -s [¹*ply* + *-er*] **1 :** one that plies **2 plyers** *pl* **:** a balance of timbers in the form of a St. Andrew's cross used in raising and lowering a drawbridge

**plyers** *var of* PLIERS

**ply·gain** \'pli,gīn\ *n* -s [W, lit., cockcrow; akin to L *pullus* young fowl, young of an animal and to L *canere* to sing — more at FOAL, CHANT] **:** an old Welsh custom of carol or hymn singing at cockcrow on Christmas morning

**plymetal** \'=,==\ *n* **:** plywood sheathed on both sides with aluminum and used esp. in airplane construction

**ply·mo·the·an** \,plimə'thēən\ *n* -s *cap* [irreg. fr. *Plymouth*, town in southeast Massachusetts + E *-an*] **:** a native or resident of Plymouth, Mass.

**ply·mo·thi·an** \"\ *n* -s *cap* [irreg. fr. *Plymouth*, city in southwest England + E *-an*] **:** a native or resident of Plymouth, England

**¹plym·outh** \'pliməth\ *adj, usu cap* [fr. *Plymouth*, England] **:** of or from the city of Plymouth, England **:** of the kind or style prevalent in Plymouth

**²plymouth** \"\ *n* -s *often cap* **:** FASHION GRAY

**plymouth brother** *n, pl* **plymouth brethren** *usu cap P&B* **:** a member of a religious body organized about 1830 at Plymouth, England, that takes the Bible as its sole guide, protests against sectarianism and rejects creeds and rituals, has no ordained ministry, organizes its meetings on a New Testament pattern, baptizes believers only, partakes of the Lord's Supper every Sunday, and emphasizes premillenialism

**plymouth cloak** *n, usu cap P* [fr. *Plymouth*, England; prob. fr. the idea that a returned traveler landing at Plymouth without money or adequate clothing could more easily provide himself with a staff to ward off possible beatings than with a cloak to cushion himself against them] *archaic* **:** STAFF, CUDGEL

**plymouth porcelain** *n, usu cap 1st P* **:** the first English commercial hard-paste porcelain made at Plymouth (1768–70) and continued at Bristol

**plymouth rock** *n, usu cap P&R* [fr. *Plymouth Rock*, the rock on which the Pilgrims are supposed to have landed in 1620 in Plymouth, Massachusetts] **1 :** an American breed of medium-sized single-combed dual-purpose domestic fowls that have long smooth yellow legs and occur in several color varieties (as white, barred, buff) **2 :** a bird of the Plymouth Rock breed

**plywood** \'=,=\ *n* **:** a structural material consisting of sheets of wood glued or cemented together with the grains of adjacent layers arranged at right angles or at a wide angle and being made up (1) wholly of uniformly thin veneer sheets or (2) of usu. equal numbers of veneer sheets on either side of a thicker central layer — called also (1) *all-veneer plywood* (2) *lumber-core plywood*; compare LAMINATED WOOD

**ply yarn** *n* **:** yarn made by twisting together two or more strands that are often different in fiber and color

**plzen** *usu cap, var of* PILSEN

**pm** *abbr* **1** premium **2** premolar **3** pumice

**PM** \(')pē'em\ *abbr or n* -s push money

**PM** *abbr* **1** past master **2** paymaster **3** peculiar meter **4** permanent magnet **5** *often not cap* per month **6** phase modulation **7** police magistrate **8** Pontifex Maximus **9** postmaster **10** *often not cap* [L *post meridiem*] afternoon **11** postmortem **12** prime minister **13** prize money **14** [L *pro mille*] per thousand **15** provost marshal **16** purchase money

**Pm** *symbol* promethium

**PMG** *abbr* **1** paymaster general **2** postmaster general **3** provost marshal general

**PMH** *abbr, often not cap* production per man-hour

**pmk** *abbr* postmark

**PMO** *abbr* principal medical officer

**PMS** *abbr* pregnant mare serum

**pmt** *abbr* payment

**pn** *abbr* **1** partition **2** position

**PN** *abbr* **1** *often not cap* please note **2** *often not cap* promissory note **3** psychoneurotic

**PNA** *abbr* pentose nucleic acid

**-pnea** *or* **-pnoea** \(p)(')nēə\ *n comb form* -s [NL, fr. Gk *-pnoia*, fr. *pnoia*, *pnoē* breathing, breath, fr. *pnein* to breathe] **:** breath **:** breathing ⟨hyper*pnea*⟩ ⟨poly*pnoea*⟩ ⟨oligo*pnea*⟩

**pneu** *abbr* pneumatic

**pneum** *abbr* pneumatic

**pneum-** *or* **pneumo-** *comb form* [NL, fr. Gk *pneum-*, fr. *pneuma*] **1 :** air **:** gas ⟨*pneumo*empyema⟩ ⟨*pneumo*pericardium⟩ **2 :** lung **:** pulmonary and ⟨*pneumo*gastric⟩ ⟨*pneum*ectomy⟩ **3 :** respiration ⟨*pneumo*gram⟩ **4 :** pneumonia **:** pneumonia and ⟨*pneumo*enteritis⟩ ⟨*pneumo*bacillus⟩ ⟨*pneumo*coccus⟩

**pneu·ma** \'n(y)ümə\ *n* -s [Gk, wind, air, breath, spirit] **1 a** (1) **:** an ethereal fiery stuff or universal spirit held by the ancient Stoics to be a cosmic principle (2) **:** the world soul or the spirit of God **b :** a life-giving principle in man; *specif* **:** the vital soul or spirit considered as a soul between body and spirit or as a spirit superior to both body and soul **2** [ML, fr. Gk, wind, breath] **a** (1) **:** a ligature in medieval music denoting a long florid phrase sung on one syllable or with no syllable (2) **:** a prolonged phrase sung in such manner **b :** NEUME 1

**pneumat-** *or* **pneumato-** *comb form* [LGk, fr. Gk, fr. *pneumat-*, *pneuma*] **1 :** spirit ⟨*pneumato*phobia⟩ ⟨*pneumato*graphy⟩ **2 :** air **:** vapor **:** gas ⟨*pneumato*lytic⟩ ⟨*pneumat*ize⟩ ⟨*pneumat*uria⟩ **3 :** respiration ⟨*pneumato*graph⟩ ⟨*pneumato*meter⟩ **4 :** pneumatic ⟨*pneumato*gram⟩

**¹pneu·mat·ic** \n(y)ü'mad·ik, -atik, -ēk *sometimes* nə'm-\ *adj* [L *pneumaticus*, fr. Gk *pneumatikos*, fr. *pneumat-*, *pneuma* wind, air, breath, spirit (fr. *pnein* to breathe) + *-ikos* -ic; akin to OE *fnēosan* to sneeze — more at SNEEZE] **1 a :** of, relating to, or using air, wind, or other gas: (1) **:** moved or worked by air pressure either by a percussive action or by a rotary action ⟨~ chisel⟩ ⟨~ drill⟩ (2) **:** adapted for holding compressed air **:** inflated with air ⟨~ tire⟩ **b :** of or relating to pneumatics **2 :** of or relating to the pneuma; *esp* **:** SPIRITUAL **3 :** marked by or having cavities filled with air ⟨~ system of the pelican —E.A.Armstrong⟩ **4 :** having a well proportioned feminine figure; *esp* **:** having a full bust

**²pneumatic** \"\ *n* -s **1 :** a spiritual being; *specif* **:** one held by the Gnostics as belonging to the highest of the three classes into which mankind is divided **2 :** a pneumatic tire

**pneumatic action** *n* **:** an action employing compressed air and collapsible bellows for connecting and manipulating the movable parts of a pipe organ

**pneu·mat·i·cal** \-ad·əkəl, -atə-, -ēk-\ *adj* [L *pneumaticus* + E *-al*] **:** PNEUMATIC

**pneu·mat·i·cal·ly** \-ək(ə)lē, -ēk-, -li\ *adv* **:** in a pneumatic manner **:** by means of a pneumatic device

**pneumatic caisson** *n* **:** a caisson in which air pressure is used to keep out the water

**pneumatic conveyor** *or* **pneumatic elevator** *n* **:** CONVEYER 2 a (9)

**pneumatic dispatch** *n* **:** a system of tubes through which letters, packages, and related matter are sent by air pressure

**pneumatic duct** *n* **:** the duct that connects the air bladder with the alimentary canal in physostomous fishes

**pneumatic gun** *n* **:** a gun using compressed air or gas as the propulsive force usu. to throw dynamite or other high explosives

**pneumatic hammer** *n* **:** AIR HAMMER

**pneu·ma·tic·i·ty** \,n(y)ümə'tisəd·ē\ *n* -ES **:** the quality or state of being pneumatic; *specif* **:** a condition marked by the presence of air cavities

**pneumatic physician** *n* **:** a physician of an ancient Greek school of medical thought holding that health and disease depend on the proportions of the vital principle

**pneumatic pile** *n* **:** a tubular pile or large cylinder sunk by the atmospheric pressure exerted when the air is exhausted from a chamber at its lower end

**pneumatic post** *n* **:** the transmission of mail between post offices by pneumatic dispatch

**pneumatic pump** *n* **:** an air-exhausting pump **:** FORCE PUMP

**pneu·mat·ics** \n(y)ü'mad·iks, -atiks, -ēks *sometimes* nə'm-\ *n pl but sing in constr* [*pneumat-* + *-ics*] **1 :** a branch of mechanics that deals with the mechanical properties of gases (as weight, pressure, elasticity) — compare AERODYNAMICS, AEROMECHANICS, AEROSTATICS **2** [NL *pneumatica*, fr. fem. of L *pneumaticus* pneumatic + E *-s*] **:** PNEUMATOLOGY

**pneumatic syringe** *n* **:** a stout tube closed at one end and provided with a piston for illustrating the phenomena of the compressibility of gases

**pneumatic trough** *n* **:** a trough that is filled with water or mercury for use in collecting gases

**pneumatic tube** *n* **:** a tube used in pneumatic dispatch

**pneu·ma·tique** \,n(y)ümə'tēk\ *n* -s [F, fr. *pneumatique*, adj., pneumatic, fr. L *pneumaticus*] **:** a letter or message transmitted by pneumatic dispatch

**pneu·ma·tism** \'n(y)ümə,tizəm\ *n* -s [*pneumat-* + *-ism*] **:** the manifestation of spiritual gifts; *specif* **:** observable phenomena and exterior signs frequently interpreted as indicating that one is possessed by the Holy Spirit

**pneu·ma·ti·za·tion** \,n(y)ümədə'zāshən, -ətə'z-, -ə,tī'z-\ *n* -s [ISV *pneumatize* + *-ation*] **:** the presence or development of air-filled cavities in a bone

**pneu·ma·tize** \'==,tīz\ *vt* -ED/-ING/-S [*pneumat-* + *-ize*] **:** to make pneumatic; *esp* **:** to fill with air cavities

**pneumatized** *adj* **:** having air-filled cavities

**pneumato-** — see PNEUMAT-

**pneu·ma·to·cele** \'n(y)ümədə,sēl\ *n* -s [MGk *pneumatokēlē*, a gaseous tumor, fr. Gk *pneumat-* + *kēlē* tumor] **:** a gas-filled cavity or sac occurring esp. in the lung

**pneu·ma·to·cyst** \-,sist\ *n* [*pneumat-* + *-cyst*] **1 :** the cavity of a pneumatophore **2 :** PNEUMATOPHORE 1

**pneu·ma·tode** \'n(y)ümə,tōd\ *n* -s [ISV *pneumat-* + *-ode*] **:** PNEUMATOPHORE

**pneu·ma·to·gram** \'n(y)ümədō,gram\ *n* [ISV *pneumat-* + *-gram*] **1 :** PNEUMOGRAM **2 :** a message sent by pneumatic dispatch

**pneu·ma·to·graph** \-,graf\ *n* [ISV *pneumat-* + *-graph*] **:** PNEUMOGRAPH

**pneu·ma·to·graph·ic** \¦===¦grafik\ *adj* **1 :** of or relating to pneumatography **2 :** PNEUMOGRAPHIC

**pneu·ma·tog·ra·phy** \,n(y)ümə'tägrəfē, -fi\ *n* -ES [ISV *pneumat-* + *-graphy*] **1 :** writing held to be that of spirits and produced directly without a medium or material device **2 :** descriptive pneumatology

**pneu·ma·to·logic** \¦n(y)ümədō+\ *or* **pneu·ma·to·logical** \"+\ *adj* **:** of or relating to pneumatology

**pneu·ma·tol·o·gist** \,n(y)ümə'täləjəst\ *n* -s **:** one trained or skilled in pneumatology; *specif* **:** one esp. prepared by training and experience to interpret the theological doctrine of the Holy Spirit

**pneu·ma·tol·o·gy** \-jē, -ji\ *n* -ES [NL *pneumatologia*, fr. *pneumat-* + *-logia* -logy] **1 a :** the doctrine or theory of spiritual beings (as the Holy Spirit and spirits between God and man) **b** (1) **:** the doctrine of spiritual phenomena (2) **:** magical or necromantic love **2** *archaic* **:** a theory of the nature and functions of mind and soul **:** PSYCHOLOGY **3** *archaic* **:** the science of air or gases

**pneu·ma·tol·y·sis** \,=='täləsəs\ *n* [NL, fr. *pneumat-* + *-lysis*] **:** the process by which pneumatolytic minerals are formed

**pneu·ma·to·lyt·ic** \¦n(y)ümədō¦lid·ik\ *adj* [ISV *pneumat-* + *-lytic*] **:** formed or forming by hot vapors or superheated liquids under pressure — used esp. of minerals and ores occurring in or near masses of igneous rock

**pneu·ma·to·ma·chi·an** \,===¦mākēən\ *n* -s *usu cap* [LGk *pneumatomachos* (fr. Gk *pneumat-* + *-machos* fighter — fr. *machesthai* to fight —) + E *-an*] **:** one who is hostile to or denies the divinity or personality of the Holy Spirit; *specif* **:** a member of a 4th century sect under the leadership of Macedonius, Bishop of Constantinople, holding the Holy Ghost to be a creature or created being

**pneu·ma·tom·a·chist** \,=='täməkəst\ *n* -s *usu cap* [LGk *pneumatomachos* + E *-ist*] **:** PNEUMATOMACHIAN

**pneu·ma·tom·a·chy** \-kē\ *n* -ES *usu cap* [*pneumatomachist* + *-y*] **:** denial of the deity of the Holy Spirit

**pneu·ma·tom·e·ter** \,=='täməd·ə(r)\ *n* [*pneumat-* + *-meter*] **1 :** an instrument for measuring the amount of force exerted by the lungs in respiration **2 :** SPIROMETER

**pneu·ma·tom·e·try** \-mə·trē\ *n* -ES [ISV *pneumat-* + *-metry*] **:** SPIROMETRY

**pneu·ma·to·phore** \'n(y)ümədə,fō(ə)r, n(y)ü'madə,-\ *n* -s [ISV *pneumat-* + *-phore*] **1 :** a muscular gas-containing sac that serves as a float on a siphonophore colony (as of members of the genus *Physalia*) **2 :** a submerged or exposed root often functioning as a respiratory organ of a swamp or marsh plant

**pneu·ma·toph·o·rous** \¦n(y)ümə¦täf(ə)rəs\ *adj* **:** of, relating to, or having the characteristics of a pneumatophore

**pneu·ma·toph·o·rus** \-f(ə)rəs\ *n, cap* [NL, fr. *pneumat-* + *-phorus*] **:** a genus of small warm-water mackerels including the Pacific mackerel and the chub mackerel

**pneu·ma·to·sis** \,n(y)ümə'tōsəs\ *n, pl* **pneumato·ses** \-,sēz\ [NL, fr. Gk *pneumatōsis* inflation, fr. *pneumatoun* to inflate, turn into vapor (fr. *pneumat-*, *pneuma* wind, air, breath) + *-sis* — more at PNEUMATIC] **:** the presence of air or gas in abnormal places in the body

**pneu·ma·tu·ria** \,n(y)ümə'türēə, -ə'tyü-\ *n* -s [NL, fr. *pneumat-* + *-uria*] **:** passage of gas in the urine

**pneume** *var of* NEUME

**pneu·mec·to·my** \n(y)ü'mektəmē\ *n* -ES [ISV *pneum-* + *-ectomy*] **:** the surgical removal of lung tissue

**pneumo-** — see PNEUM-

**pneu·mo·bacillus** \¦n(y)ümō+\ *n, pl* **pneumobacilli** [NL, fr. *pneum-* + *bacillus*] **:** a bacterium (*Klebsiella pneumoniae*) associated with pneumonia and other inflammations of the respiratory tract — called also *Friedländer's bacillus*

**pneu·mo·branchia** \,n(y)ümə'braŋkēə\ *or* **pneu·mo·bran·chi·a·ta** \-,braŋkē'ād·ə, -äd·ə\ *n pl, cap* [NL, fr. *pneum-* + *-branchia* or *branchiata*] *in former classifications* **:** a group of terrestrial snails (suborder Rhipidoglossa) comprising those (as members of the genus *Helicina*) in which the gills are replaced by a respiratory sac

**pneu·mo·cele** \'n(y)mə,sēl\ *n* -s [ISV *pneum-* + *-cele*] **:** PNEUMATOCELE

**pneu·mo·coc·cal** \¦==¦käkəl\ *also* **pneu·mo·coc·cic** \-¦käk(s)ik\ *adj* [NL *pneumococcus* + E *-al* or *-ic*] **:** of, caused by, or derived from pneumococci

**pneu·mo·coc·ce·mia** \,==,käk'sēmēə, -ä'kēm-\ *n* -s [NL, fr. *pneumococcus* + *-emia*] **:** the presence of pneumococci in the circulating blood

**pneu·mo·coc·cus** \,=='käkəs\ *n, pl* **pneumococ·ci** \-ä,kī, -ä(,)kē, -äk,sī, -äk(,)sē\ [NL, fr. *pneum-* + *-coccus*] **:** a bacterium (*Diplococcus pneumoniae*) that causes lobar pneumonia

**pneu·mo·co·ni·o·sis** *or* **pneu·mo·ko·ni·o·sis** \,=mō,kōnē'ōsəs\ *also* **pneu·mo·no·co·ni·o·sis** *or* **pneu·mo·no·ko·ni·o·sis** \,=mənō,k-\ *n, pl* **pneumoconio·ses** *or* **pneumokonio·ses** \-,sēz\ [*pneumoconiosis, pneumokoniosis* fr. NL, fr. *pneum-* + *-coniosis* (fr. ²*coni-* + *-osis*); *pneumonoconiosis, pneumonokoniosis* fr. NL, fr. *pneumon-* + *-coniosis* (fr. ²*coni-* + *-osis*)] **:** a disease of the lungs caused by the habitual inhalation of irritant mineral or metallic particles — compare ANTHRACOSIS, SILICOSIS

**pneu·mo·dynamic** \¦n(y)ümō+\ *adj* [*pneum-* + *dynamic*] **:** acting by the force of gases in motion **:** PNEUMATIC

**pneu·mo·encephalitis** \¦n(y)ümō+\ *n* [NL, fr. *pneum-* + *encephalitis*] **:** NEWCASTLE DISEASE

**pneu·mo·encephalogram** \"+\ *n* [*pneum-* + *encephalogram*] **:** a roentgenogram made by pneumoencephalography

**pneu·mo·encephalograph** \"+\ *n* [ISV *pneum-* + *encephalograph*] **:** PNEUMOENCEPHALOGRAM

**pneu·mo·encephalographic** \¦==+\ *adj* **:** of or relating to pneumoencephalography — **pneu·mo·encephalographically** \"+\ *adv*

**pneu·mo·encephalography** \¦==+\ *n* [ISV *pneum-* + *encephalography*] **:** roentgenography of the brain after the injection of air into the ventricles

**pneu·mo·enteritis** \¦==+\ *n* [NL, fr. *pneum-* + *enteritis*] **:** pneumonia combined with enteritis

**pneu·mo·gastric** \"+\ *adj* [*pneum-* + *gastric*] **1 :** of or relating to the lungs and the stomach **2 :** VAGAL

**pneumogastric nerve** *also* **pneumogastric** *n* **:** VAGUS NERVE

**pneu·mo·gram** \'n(y)ümə,gram\ *n* [*pneum-* + *-gram*] **:** a record of respiratory movements obtained by pneumography

**pneu·mo·graph** \-,graf\ *n* [ISV *pneum-* + *-graph*] **:** an instrument for recording the thoracic movements or volume change during respiration

**pneu·mo·graph·ic** \¦==¦grafik\ *adj* [ISV *pneum-* + *-graphic*] **:** of, relating to, or by means of pneumography — **pneu·mo·graph·i·cal·ly** \-fək(ə)lē\ *adv*

**pneu·mog·ra·phy** \n(y)ü'mägrəfē\ *n* -ES [*pneum-* + *-graphy*] **1 :** a description of the lungs **2 :** roentgenography after the injection of air into a body cavity **3 :** the process of making a pneumogram

**pneu·mo·hemothorax** *also* **pneu·mo·haemothorax** \¦n(y)ümō+\ *n* [NL, fr. *pneum-* + *hem-* + *thorax*] **:** accumulation of blood and gas in the pleural cavity

**pneu·mo·hydrothorax** \"+\ *n* [NL, fr. *pneum-* + *hydr-* + *thorax*] **:** HYDROPNEUMOTHORAX

**pneu·mol·o·gy** \n(y)ü'mäləjē\ *n* -ES [*pneum-* + *-logy*] **:** the scientific study of the respiratory organs

**pneu·mol·y·sis** \=='mäləsəs\ *n* [NL, fr. *pneum-* + *-lysis*] **:** PNEUMONOLYSIS

**pneu·mo·mycosis** \¦n(y)ümō+\ *n* [NL, fr. *pneum-* + *mycosis*] **:** a fungus disease of the lung

**pneumon-** *or* **pneumono-** *comb form* [NL, fr. Gk, fr. *pneumōn*] **:** lung ⟨*pneumon*ectomy⟩ ⟨*pneumono*cele⟩

**pneu·mo·nec·to·my** \,n(y)ümə'nektəmē\ *n* -ES [ISV *pneumon-* + *-ectomy*] **:** excision of an entire lung or of one or more lobes of a lung — compare SEGMENTAL RESECTION

**pneu·mo·nia** \n(y)ü'mōnyə, nə'm-, -ōnēə\ *n* -s [NL, fr. Gk *pneumonia*, fr. *pneumon-*, *pneumōn* lung, alter. (influenced by *pnein* to breathe) of *pleumōn* lung — more at SNEEZE, PULMONARY] **:** a disease of the lungs characterized by inflammation and consolidation followed by resolution and caused by microorganisms, viruses, chemical irritants, or foreign bodies — see BRONCHOPNEUMONIA, LOBAR PNEUMONIA, PRIMARY ATYPICAL PNEUMONIA

**pneu·mon·ic** \(')n(y)ü¦mänik, nə'm-\ *adj* [NL *pneumonicus*, fr. Gk *pneumonikos*, fr. *pneumon-* + *-ikos* -ic] **1 :** of or relating to the lungs **:** PULMONIC **2 :** of, relating to, or affected with pneumonia ⟨a ~ lung⟩ ⟨a ~ condition is also a frequent terminal state —K.F.Maxcy⟩

**pneumonic plague** *n* **:** plague of an extremely virulent form that involves chiefly the lungs and usu. is transmitted from person to person by droplet infection

**pneu·mo·ni·tis** \,n(y)ümə'nīdəs\ *n, pl* **pneumonit·i·des** \-'nidə,dēz\ [NL, fr. *pneumon-* + *-itis*] **1 :** PNEUMONIA **2 :** a disease characterized by inflammation of the lungs esp. in patchy distribution

**pneumonoconiosis** *var of* PNEUMOCONIOSIS

**pneu·mo·nog·ra·phy** \,n(y)ümə'nägrəfē\ *n* -ES [*pneumon-* + *-graphy*] **:** X-ray photography of the lungs

**pneumonokoniosis** *var of* PNEUMOCONIOSIS

**pneu·mo·nol·y·sis** \,n(y)ümə'näləsəs\ *n* [NL, fr. *pneumon-* + *-lysis*] **:** surgical freeing of the pleura so as to permit collapse of a lung involving (1) separation of the parietal pleura from the fascia of the chest wall or (2) separation of the visceral and parietal layers of pleura — called also (1) *external pneumonolysis*, (2) *internal pneumonolysis*

**pneu·mo·noph·o·ra** \,n(y)ümə'näfərə\ *or* **pneumonophorae** \-ə,rē\ *n pl, cap* [NL, fr. *pneumon-* + *-phora* or *-phorae*] *in former classifications* **:** a division of Holothurioidea comprising forms with a respiratory tree — compare APNEUMONA

**pneu·mo·no·ul·tra·mi·cro·scop·ic·sili·co·vol·ca·no·co·ni·o·sis** \¦n(y)ümə(,)nō,əltrə,mīkrə'skäpik'silə(,)kō,väl'kā(,)nō,kōnē'ōsəs\ *n* [NL, fr. *pneumon-* + ISV *ultramicroscopic* + NL *silic-* + *volcano* + *-coniosis* (fr. ²*coni-* + *-osis*)] **:** a pneumoconiosis caused by the inhalation of very fine silicate or quartz dust and occurring esp. in miners

**pneu·mo·nys·sus** \,n(y)ümə'nisəs\ *n, cap* [NL, prob. fr. *pneumon-* + Gk *hyssos* javelin; fr. the club-shaped peritreme] **:** a genus of mites (family Halarachnidae) that live in the air passages of mammals

**pneu·mo·pericardium** \¦n(y)ümō+\ *n* [NL, fr. *pneum-* + *pericardium*] **:** accumulation of air or other gas in the pericardial sac

**pneu·mo·peritoneum** \"+\ *n* [NL, fr. *pneum-* + *peritoneum*] **1 :** a state in which air or other gas is present in the peritoneal cavity **2 :** the induction of pneumoperitoneum to alter pressure relations within the body cavity and relax a tuberculous lung

**pneu·mo·peritonitis** \"+\ *n* [NL, fr. *pneum-* + *peritonitis*] **:** peritonitis with the presence of gas in the peritoneal cavity

**pneu·mo·stome** \'n(y)ümə,stōm\ *n* -S [ISV *pneum-* + *-stome*] **:** the respiratory opening of a gastropod mollusk

**pneu·mo·tachogram** \'n(y)ümō+\ *n* [*pneum-* + *tachogram*] **:** a record of the velocity of the respiratory function obtained by use of a pneumotachograph

**pneu·mo·tachograph** \"+\ *n* [ISV *pneum-* + *tachograph*] **:** a device or apparatus for measuring the rate of the respiratory function

**pneu·mo·taxic center** \¦n(y)ümə+...-\ *n* [*pneumotaxic* fr. *pneum-* + *taxic*] **:** a neural center in the upper part of the pons that provides inhibitory impulses on inspiration and thereby prevents overdistention of the lungs and helps to maintain alternately recurrent inspiration and expiration

**pneu·mo·tectic** \¦=='tektik\ *adj* [*pneum-* + L *tectus* (past part. of *tegere* to enclose, cover) + E *-ic* — more at THATCH] **:** of, relating to, or constituting late magmatic stages of mineral deposition in which solutions and gases have a leading role

**pneu·mo·thorax** \¦n(y)ümō+\ *n* [NL, fr. *pneum-* + *thorax*] **:** a state in which air or other gas is present in the pleural cavity and which occurs spontaneously as a result of disease or injury of lung tissue or puncture of the chest wall or is induced as a therapeutic measure to collapse the lung (as in tuberculosis)

**pneu·mo·trop·ic** \¦n(y)ümə¦träpik\ *adj* [*pneum-* + *-tropic*] **:** turning, directed toward, or having an affinity for lung tissues — used esp. of infective agents

**pneu·mot·ro·pism** \n(y)ü'mä·trə,pizəm\ *n* [*pneum-* + *-tropism*] **:** the quality or state of being pneumotropic

**-pneus·ta** \(p)'n(y)üstə\ *n pl comb form* [NL, fr. Gk *-pneustos* having (such) breath, fr. (assumed) Gk *pneustos* (verbal of Gk *pnein* to breathe) — more at SNEEZE] **:** animals having a (specified) mode of breathing — in higher taxa ⟨Entero*pneusta*⟩

**PNG** *abbr, often not cap* persona non grata

**pnl** *abbr* panel

**-pnoea** — see -PNEA

**pnom·penh** *or* **phnom penh** \pə'nóm¦pen\ *adj, usu cap initial Ps* [fr. *Pnompenh, Phnom Penh*, city in Cambodia] **:** of or from Pnompenh, the capital of Cambodia **:** of the kind or style prevalent in Pnompenh

**pnr** *abbr* pioneer

**pntd** *abbr* painted

**pntr** *abbr* painter

**pnxt** *abbr* [L *pinxit*] he or she painted it

**po** *abbr* **1** poetry **2** point **3** pole

**PO** *abbr* **1** personnel officer **2** petty officer **3** pilot officer **4** postal order **5** post office **6** probation officer **7** putout

**Po** *symbol* polonium

**poa** \'pōə\ *n* [NL, fr. Gk, grass; akin to Gk *pidax* spring, Lith *pieva* meadow] **1** *cap* **:** a genus of grasses that are widely distributed in temperate and arctic regions and have open panicles with 2- to 6-flowered spikelets on which the upper scales exceed the empty ones — see KENTUCKY BLUEGRASS, WIRE GRASS **2** -S **:** any grass of the genus *Poa*

**po·a·ce·ae** \pō'āsē,ē\ [NL, fr. *Poa* + *-aceae*] *syn of* GRAMINEAE

¹**poach** \'pōch\ *vt* -ED/-ING/-ES [ME *pochen*, fr. MF *pocher*, fr. OF *pochier*, lit., to put into a bag (the white of the egg being regarded as the bag in which the yolk is contained), fr. *poche* bag, pocket, of Gmc origin; akin to MD *poke* bag — more at POKE (bag)] **1 :** to cook in a liquid kept just below the boiling point ⟨trout ~*ed* in bouillon⟩ **2 :** to cook (as an egg) in a poacher

²**poach** \"\ *vb* -ED/-ING/-ES [MF *pocher*, of Gmc origin; akin to MD *poken* to poke, stick — more at POKE (to prod)] *vt* **1** *dial chiefly Eng* **:** to push, shove, or thrust roughly or forcefully **:** POKE **2 :** to trample or cut up with hoofs **:** make soft or muddy **:** make mudholes in ⟨good for grass, too, to be trodden except they ~ it, where it's sodden —John Masefield⟩ **3 a :** to trespass on ⟨a field ~*ed* too frequently by the amateur —*Times Lit. Supp.*⟩ — often used with *on* or *upon* ⟨what happens to a poet when he ~*es* upon a novelist's preserves —Virginia Woolf⟩ **b :** to take (game or fish) by illegal methods **:** STEAL ⟨men were transported with the worst felons for ~*ing* a few hares or pheasants —G.B.Shaw⟩ **4 :** POTCH **5 :** to wash free from acid, thoroughly mix, and make uniform by agitation in a boiling weakly alkaline solution followed by boiling water — used of cellulose nitrate pulp ~ *vi* **1** *dial chiefly Eng* **:** POKE **2 a :** to sink into mud or mire while walking **:** plod through mud or soft ground **:** plunge about **b :** to become soft or muddy and full of holes when trampled on ⟨swampy country that is inclined to ~ in the winter —W.G.Batt & A.V.Allo⟩ **3 :** to trespass for the purpose of stealing game **:** take game or fish illegally ⟨had taken to ~*ing* as a means of supplying fresh meat for the table —H.D.Quillin⟩ **4 :** to play a ball in a racket game that should normally be played by one's partner

**poached egg** *n* [ME *poched egg*] **1 :** an egg dropped from its shell and cooked in simmering water for about five minutes — called also *dropped egg* **2 :** an egg cooked in a poacher

¹**poach·er** \'pōchə(r)\ *n* -S [²*poach* + *-er*] **1 a :** one that trespasses or steals ⟨catches the ~ on his preserve —*Time*⟩ **b :** one who kills or takes game or fish illegally ⟨~*s* of deer —William Faulkner⟩ **2 a :** BALDPATE 2 **b :** SEA POACHER **3 :** POTCHER **4** *or* **poacher tub :** a large tank with a rotating paddle wheel for poaching cellulose nitrate pulp

²**poacher** \"\ *n* -S [¹*poach* + *-er*] **1 :** a vessel fitted with a pan containing depressions or shallow cups in each of which an egg can be cooked over steam rising from boiling water in the bottom part **2 :** a shallow baking dish in which food (as fish) can be poached

poacher 1

**poach·wood** \'pōch,wu̇d\ *n* [perh. alter. of *campeachy wood*] **:** LOGWOOD 1a(1), 1a(2)

**poachy** \'pōchē, -chi\ *adj* -ER/-EST [²*poach* + *-y*] **:** easily cut up or made muddy by the feet of cattle **:** SODDEN, SWAMPY ⟨a ~ field⟩

**po·a·les** \pō'ā(,)lēz\ [NL, fr. *Poa* + *-ales*] *syn of* GRAMINALES

**po·a·nes** \pō'ā(,)nēz\ *n, cap* [NL] **:** a genus of skipper butterflies

**POB** *abbr* post-office box

**pob·by** \'päbi\ *adj* -ER/-EST [origin unknown] *dial Brit* **:** puffed up **:** SWOLLEN

**po·bla·ción** \,pō,bläsē'ōn\ *n, pl* **poblacio·nes** \-ō(,)nās\ [PhilSp, fr. Sp, population, town, fr. LL *population-*, *populatio* people — more at POPULATION] **:** a center of a municipality in the Philippines that is usu. the barrio that gives the municipality its name and is the seat of government

**po' boy** \'pō,=\ *also* **po' boy sandwich** *n* [alter. (in the attempt to represent southern U. S. pronunc.) of *poor boy, poor boy sandwich*] **:** POOR BOY

**pobs** \'päbz\ *n pl* [prob. baby-talk alter. of *porridge*] *dial Eng* **:** PORRIDGE

**POC** *abbr, often not cap* port of call

**po·can** \'pōkən\ *or* **pocan bush** *n* [*pocan* modif. of *puccoon*, *pakon* (in some Algonquian language of Virginia) — more at POKE] **:** POKEWEED

**po·chade** \pō'shäd\ *n* -S [F, fr. *pocher* to poach (an egg), sketch roughly + *-ade* — more at POACH] **:** a rough or quickly executed sketch or study

**po·chard** *also* **poa·chard** \'pōchə(r)d\ *n, pl* **pochards** *also* **pochard** [origin unknown] **:** any of numerous rather heavy-bodied diving ducks belonging chiefly to the genus *Aythya* and having large head and feet with legs placed far back under the body; *specif* **:** a common Old World duck (*A. ferina*) that greatly resembles the American redhead

**po·ché** \(')pō'shā\ *n* -S [F, fr. past part. of *pocher* to sketch roughly] **:** the black portion of an architectural plan representing solids (as walls and columns)

**po·chéd** \-ād\ *adj* [*poché* + *-ed*] *of an architectural drawing* **:** having the parts representing solids filled in

**pocher** *var of* POTCHER

**po·chette** \pō'shet\ *n* -S [F, dim. of *poche* pocket — more at POACH] **1 :** ³KIT **2 :** HANDBAG 2 **3 :** a small envelope of thin transparent paper for holding a stamp (as in an album)

**po·chis·mo** \pō'chēz(,)mō\ *n* -S [MexSp, fr. *poche, pocho* U. S. resident of Mexican origin (prob. fr. Sp *pocho* discolored) + Sp *-ismo* -ism] **1 :** a term of U. S. origin borrowed into Mexican Spanish and used along the border between the U. S. and Mexico esp. by U. S.-born Mexicans ⟨not a single ~ has added to the beauty of our Spanish language —F.G.Beraza⟩ **2 :** a vocabulary consisting of pochismos

**po·choir** \(')pōsh¦wär\ *n* -S [F, stencil, stencil plate, fr. *pocher* to poach (an egg), sketch roughly, stencil — more at POACH] **:** a stencil process for making colored prints or adding color to a printed key illustration

**po·cho·te** \pə'chōd·ē\ *n* -S [MexSp, fr. Nahuatl *pochotl*] **1 a :** any of several trees of the genus *Ceiba*; *esp* **:** CEIBA 2a **b :** a medium-sized tree (*Cochlospermum irtifolium*) having seeds covered with long cottony white hairs **2 :** the fiber of a pochote tree used as a stuffing for mattresses

¹**pock** \'päk\ *n* -S [ME *pokke*, fr. OE *pocc*; akin to MLG & MD *pocke* pock, G dial. *pfoche* pock, L *bucca* cheek, mouth] **1 a :** a pustule on the surface of the body in smallpox and other eruptive diseases; *also* **:** a spot like such a pustule **b :** HOLE ⟨guiding the car around another ~ in the road —Peter De Vries⟩ ⟨his eyes wide ~*s* of fear in a white face —Joseph Hilton⟩ **2** *chiefly dial* **:** POX

²**pock** \"\ *vt* -ED/-ING/-S **:** to mark with or as if with pocks **:** PIT ⟨the rains of twenty centuries had ~*ed* that pure and haughty face —Compton Mackenzie⟩ ⟨the hull was ~*ed* with dents —Frank Schreider⟩

³**pock** \"\ *chiefly dial var of* ¹POKE 1a(1)

**pock-arred** \'=¦ärd, -ād\ *adj* [E dial. *pock-arr* pockmark (fr. ¹*pock* + *arr*) + *-ed*] *dial Brit* **:** POCKMARKED

¹**pock·et** \'päkət, *usu* -əd·+V\ *n* -S [ME *poket*, fr. ONF *pokete*, dim. of *poke*, *poque* bag, of Gmc origin; akin to MD *poke* bag — more at POKE] **1 :** a coarse bag or sack; *esp* **:** one used in packing produce for market ⟨the packing of green beans and peas in orange ~*s* —W.J.C. van Rensburg⟩ ⟨rice ~*s*⟩ **2 a :** a small bag carried by a person **:** PURSE ⟨Lucy Locket lost her ~⟩ **b :** a small cloth bag sewed or inserted into a garment and left open at the top or side ⟨pants ~⟩ ⟨coat ~⟩ ⟨change ~⟩ **3 :** any of various units of weight; *esp* **:** an English unit for hops equal to 168 pounds **4 :** supply of money **:** MEANS ⟨ample choice of accommodations to fit all ~*s* —*Christian Science Monitor*⟩ ⟨the real gems I have seen were beyond my ~ —H.J.Laski⟩ **5 :** something that serves as a receptacle or container: as **a :** any of the bags at the corners or sides of a billiard table **b :** a superficial pouch in some animals (as the cheek pouch of the pocket gopher) **c** (1) **:** a receptacle usu. of strong paper and open at one end attached to the inside cover of a book (2) **:** ENVELOPE **d** (1) **:** the trap of a weir or pound net (2) **:** the cod of a seine **e :** a box (as in a sorting case) or space (as on a checkerboard) for holding classified or alphabetized items or counters **6 :** a small isolated area or group distinguished (as in substance, form, contents, or condition) from a larger area or group surrounding it ⟨~*s* of unemployment, scattered across the country —*U. S. News & World Report*⟩ ⟨~*s* here and there where the population has remained unchanged since remotest centuries —G.O.Williams⟩: as **a** (1) **:** a cavity found on or beneath the surface of the ground and containing a deposit (as of gold, oil, gas, or water) ⟨china clay and china stone found in great ~*s* on the surface of the granite masses —L.D. Stamp⟩ ⟨an oil ~ underlying the city —*Amer. Guide Series: Mich.*⟩ (2) **:** a small body of ore ⟨are not uniformly ore bearing, but rather punctuated with ~*s* and sheets of iron ore —*Amer. Guide Series: Minn.*⟩ **b :** a small abnormal enclosed formation in the body ⟨a ~ is formed with a center of degenerated and infected material —Morris Fishbein⟩ **c :** a battle area or a body of soldiers surrounded or nearly surrounded by enemy forces ⟨the woods might have been planned by a master strategist to hold ~*s* of resistance —*Infantry Jour.*⟩ **d :** AIR HOLE **7 :** a hollow place or cavity: as **a :** a mountain glen or hollow ⟨small villages resting solidly in the ~*s* of northern mountains —*Amer. Guide Series: N.J.*⟩ **b :** a socket into which something (as a post, stake, or bar) fits ⟨the bars slide into ~*s* in the interior of the reactor —Leon Svirsky⟩ **c :** a cavity in a casting or a high point in a pipeline where foreign substance (as dirt or air) can collect and possibly become detrimental to intended functioning **d :** a hole or recess in a building member (as a window frame or flue) ⟨a venetian blind ~⟩ ⟨a soot ~⟩ **e :** an interspace made by sewing a strip of canvas on a sail in which a batten or a light spar can be placed **f :** a space between two bowling pins **g :** a cavity made in a piece of meat by a deep cut or removal of a bone to permit the insertion of stuffing ⟨a ~ in a shoulder of veal⟩ ⟨a ~ roast⟩ **8 :** an enclosed place or area: as **a :** a bight on a lee shore ⟨a little ~ with a stone beach at the head of it —G.W.Brace⟩ **b :** BLIND ALLEY ⟨no ~*s* or dead ends in which pupils might be trapped —*Nat'l Fire Codes*⟩ **c :** the position of a contestant in a race hemmed in by others **9 a :** a temporary extension to a foundry flask **b :** a large core of a foundry mold enclosed on three sides by metal and well pierced — **in one's pocket 1 :** very close to one **2 :** in one's control or possession ⟨sure that local law enforcers were *in his pocket* —*Time*⟩ ⟨the museum job safely *in his pocket* —Jacob Hay⟩ — **in pocket** *adv* **1 :** provided with funds **2 :** in the position of having made a profit ⟨probably find himself *in pocket* in a good year —F.D.Smith & Barbara Wilcox⟩

²**pocket** \"\ *vb* -ED/-ING/-S *vt* **1 a :** to put away in or as if in one's pocket ⟨~*ed* his change⟩ ⟨~*ed* his tools⟩ ⟨~*ed* his winnings⟩ **b :** to appropriate to one's own use **:** STEAL ⟨~*ed* the money he collected for charity⟩ ⟨fail to ring up a sale, ~ the cash —H.N.Schisler⟩ **c :** to hold under one's personal control ⟨circumvented in his attempt to ~ the legislature —E. A.Weeks⟩ **d :** to veto (a bill) by retaining it unsigned until after a legislature has adjourned ⟨the president and some governors have the power to kill a bill by ~*ing* it⟩ **2 :** to put up with **:** ACCEPT, SWALLOW ⟨if I calmly ~ the abuse, I am laughed at —Oliver Goldsmith⟩ ⟨cheerfully ~*ed* a loss in some cases —Warner Olivier⟩ **3 :** to set aside **:** forget about **:** SUPPRESS ⟨had almost of necessity ~*ed* his pride —A.J.Cronin⟩ ⟨~ his scruples⟩ **4 a :** to enclose in or as if in a pocket ⟨the ring of hills in which the town is ~*ed* —*Amer. Guide Series: Pa.*⟩ ⟨it has walls . . . high rocky ones that ~ fern and orchis —D.C.Peattie⟩ **b :** to force into a pocket **:** prevent from running or moving freely **:** hem in ⟨~ a boat in such a manner that she cannot escape or get ahead —H.A.Calahan⟩ **c :** to drive (a ball) into a pocket of a pool table **5 :** to form into a pocket or pouch **:** collect (pus) in a pocket or pouch **6 :** to create or establish pockets in ⟨~*ed* the nation here and there with jobless —*Time*⟩ ⟨a ~*ed* dress⟩ ~ *vi* **:** to form pockets ⟨an automatic press that performs shaping operations, such as bumping, heading, and ~*ing* —*Dict. of Occupations*⟩

³**pocket** \"\ *adj* **1 a :** small or flat enough to be carried in the pocket ⟨a ~ dictionary⟩ ⟨a ~ flask⟩ **b :** reduced in size **:** smaller than others of its kind **:** MINIATURE ⟨the recent bloodless ~ civil war —Paul Hofmann⟩ **c :** CONDENSED ⟨a ~ drama⟩ ⟨a ~ lecture⟩ **2 :** of or relating to money **:** MONETARY ⟨our ~ interest has something to do with our attitude —*Textbooks in Education*⟩ **3 :** carried in or paid from one's own pocket **:** used for or consisting of small cash outlays ⟨an adequate sum for ~ expenses⟩ **4 :** ISOLATED ⟨modern art is not a ~ movement —Howard Devree⟩

**pock·et·able** \-əbəl\ *adj* **:** capable of being carried or put in a pocket ⟨the format of this series, the most ~ of them all —Arthur Hesilrige⟩ — **pock·et·able·ness** *n* -ES

**pocket battleship** *n* **:** a small battleship built so as to come within treaty limitations; *specif* **:** a German vessel of World War II having 10,000 tons displacement and carrying 11-inch and 6-inch guns

**pocket beach** *n* **:** a usu. small beach at the head of a bay or other inlet

**pocket billiards** *n pl but usu sing in constr* **:** POOL 2b

**pocket bird** *n* **:** SCARLET TANAGER

**pocketbook** \'==,=\ *n* **1** *usu* **pocket book :** a small book that can be carried in the pocket; *esp* **:** a paperback sold cheaply to reach a mass market ⟨the popular novelist would be satisfied with his income from serials and scenarios and *pocket books* —Randall Jarrell⟩ **2 a :** a pocket notebook ⟨made a series of notes in his ~ —Ngaio Marsh⟩ **b** (1) **:** a pocket-size flat or folding container for money and personal papers **:** WALLET (2) **:** PURSE **c :** HANDBAG 2 ⟨held ~*s* in their laps; one of the ~*s* was black, the other of some kind of alligator skin —Millen Brand⟩ **3 a :** financial resources **:** INCOME ⟨apartment-house or cottage rentals to meet the ~*s* of the white-collar workers —*Harper's*⟩ **b :** economic interests ⟨have no intention of voting against their own ~*s* or against the party of their forebears —Elmo Roper & Louis Harris⟩ **4** *also* **pocket-book clam** \'==,=-\ **:** a freshwater mussel (*Lampsilis ventricosus*) of the upper Mississippi drainage area that yields mother-of-pearl and is used in button making

**pocket boom** *n* **:** a storage boom for sorted logs

**pocket borough** *n* **1 :** a former English parliamentary constituency controlled by a single person or family — compare CLOSE BOROUGH, ROTTEN BOROUGH **2 :** a political unit controlled by a single person or group

**pocket chronometer** *n* **:** a pocket watch with a chronometer escapement or with an observatory rating

**pocket conveyor** *n* **:** a conveyor with pockets attached to an endless moving chain

**pocket dry rot** *n* **:** PECKINESS

**pocketed bat** *n* **:** a small brown free-tailed bat (*Tadarida femorosacca*) of California

**pocket edition** *n* **1 :** POCKETBOOK 1 **2 :** a miniature form of something ⟨this famous dwarf was, when young, a very perfect *pocket edition* of a man —*Atlantic*⟩

**pock·et·ful** \'päkət,fu̇l\ *n, pl* **pocketfuls** *or* **pocketsful** \-t-,fu̇lz, -ts,fu̇l\ **:** as much or as many as the pocket will contain ⟨a ~ of money⟩ ⟨a ~ of cigars⟩

**pocket gopher** *n* **:** any of numerous No. American fossorial sciuromorph rodents (family Geomyidae) distinguished by fur-lined cheek pouches **:** GOPHER 2a

**pocket-handkerchief** \¦==+\ *n* **1 :** a handkerchief carried in the pocket **2 :** something tiny ⟨established in a hut on a *pocket-handkerchief* of land —Fletcher Pratt⟩

**pocket-hole** \'==,=\ *n* **:** an opening in an article of clothing that gives access to a pocket

**pock·et·ing** \'päkəd·iŋ, -ətiŋ, -ētŋ\ *n* -S [¹*pocket* + *-ing*] **:** any of various strong usu. cotton fabrics used for pockets esp. in suits and coats

**pocket judgment** *n* [so called fr. its summary enforcement] **:** STATUTE MERCHANT

**pocketknife** \'==,=\ *n, pl* **pocketknives :** a knife with a blade folding into the handle to fit it for being carried in the pocket

**pock·et·less** \'päkətləs\ *adj* **:** having no pocket

**pocket money** *n* **:** money for small current personal expenses ⟨provided with weekly *pocket money* to assure a feeling of financial dignity —*Amer. Guide Series: Minn.*⟩ — called also *spending money*

**pocket mouse** *n, pl* **pocket mice :** any of various nocturnal burrowing rodents resembling mice and belonging to *Perognathus* and related genera (family Heteromyidae) that are found in arid parts of western No. America and have long hind legs and tail and fur-lined cheek pouches

**pocket piece** *n* **1 :** a coin or token kept in the pocket as a charm or good-luck piece ⟨the Scout Good Turn *pocket piece* —*Boy Scout Handbook*⟩ **2 :** a movable part in a window-frame pulley stile that gives access to the enclosed weight and sash cord

**pocket pistol** *n* **1 :** a small pistol **2 :** a pocket flask for liquor

**pocket plum** *n* **:** PLUM POCKET

**pocket print** *n* **:** a detachable core print left in the mold when a pattern is lifted

**pocket rat** *n* **:** any of various rodents with cheek pouches: as **a :** POCKET GOPHER **b :** POCKET MOUSE **c :** KANGAROO RAT

**pocket rot** *n* **:** a rot found esp. in timber that produces small pockets often filled with fungus threads, cellulose, or other substances, but eventually becoming empty cavities

**pockets** *pl of* POCKET, *pres 3d sing of* POCKET

**pocket sheriff** *n* **:** an English sheriff formerly appointed by the sole authority of the crown

**pocket-size** \'==¦=\ *or* **pocket-sized** \'==¦=\ *adj* **1 :** of a size convenient for the pocket ⟨a *pocket-size* book⟩ **2 :** small in scale **:** DIMINUTIVE ⟨a *pocket-size* country⟩

**pocket veto** *n* **:** an indirect veto of a legislative bill by an executive (as by the president or a state governor) through retention of the bill unsigned until after adjournment of the legislature

**pock·ety** \'päkəd·ē, -ətē, -i\ *adj* [¹*pocket* + *-y*] **1 :** having an uneven distribution of ore — used of an ore deposit **2 :** forming, resembling, or having the characteristics of a pocket

**pocking** *pres part of* POCK

¹**pockmark** \'=,=\ *n* [¹*pock* + *mark*] **:** a mark, pit, or depressed scar caused by smallpox

²**pockmark** \"\ *vt* **:** to cover with or as if with pockmarks **:** PIT, SCAR ⟨the mines that ~*ed* the great coal and iron fields —Oscar Handlin⟩ ⟨the field was ~*ed* with bomb craters —W. D.Edmonds⟩

**pockmarked** \'=,=\ *adj* **:** marked by or as if by smallpox

**pock neuk** *or* **pock nook** *n* [³*pock* + *neuk, nook*] **1** *chiefly Scot* **:** the bottom of a bag **2** *chiefly Scot* **:** financial resources **:** MEANS

**pock pudding** *n* [³*pock*] **1** *chiefly Scot* **:** BAG PUDDING **2** *chiefly Scot* **a :** a fat overfed person **b :** ENGLISHMAN — usu. used disparagingly

**pocks** *pl of* POCK, *pres 3d sing of* POCK

**pock scab** *n* [¹*pock*] *n* **:** POWDERY SCAB

**pocky** \'päkē, -ki\ *adj* -ER/-EST [ME *pokky*, fr. *pokke* pock (mark) + *-y* — more at POCK] **1 :** covered with pocks; *specif* **:** SYPHILITIC **2 :** relating to or being a pock or the pox

**po·co** \ˈpō(ˌ)kō, ˈpȯ(-\ *adv (or adj)* [It & Sp, little, fr. L *paucus* — more at FEW] **:** in a slight degree **:** SOMEWHAT — used esp. as a direction in music ⟨~ allegro⟩

**poco a poco** \ˌ==ä'=(ˌ)=\ *adv* [It] **:** little by little **:** GRADUALLY — used as a direction in music

**po·co·cu·ran·te** \ˌpōkōkyəˈrantē\ *adj* [It *poco curante* caring little, fr. *poco* little + *curante* caring (pres. part. of *curare* to care), fr. L *curant-, curans*, pres. part. of *curare* to take care of, heal — more at CURE] **:** not concerned **:** INDIFFERENT, NONCHALANT

**po·co·cu·ran·tism** \ˌ===ˈran·ˌtizəm\ *also* **po·co·cu·ran·te·ism** \-ntē,i-\ *n* -s **:** INDIFFERENCE, NONCHALANCE ⟨keep up their appearance of calm ~ —F.M.Ford⟩

**po·co·sin** *also* **po·co·son** *or* **po·co·sen** \pəˈkōsᵊn, ˈpōkəsən\ *n* -s [Delaware *pākwesen*, fr. *pākw-* shallow + *-sen* (suffix used to designate resting in place)] **:** a swamp or marsh esp. in an upland on interfluvial area of the coastal plain of the southeastern U.S.

**¹pod** \ˈpäd\ *n* -s [origin unknown] **1 :** a bit socket in a brace **2 :** a straight groove or channel in the barrel of a pod auger or similar tool

**²pod** \"\ *n* -s [prob. alter. (influenced by the *p* of *pea*, with which it is often associated) of ¹*cod*] **1 :** a dry dehiscent seed vessel or fruit that is either monocarpellary (as a legume, silique, or follicle) or composed of two or more carpels (as a capsule); *specif* **:** LEGUME **2 a :** BAG, POUCH, SAC; *esp* **:** a musk bag **b :** a protective envelope (as a cocoon) **c :** a grasshopper egg case **3 :** a number of animals (as seals or whales) closely clustered together **:** SCHOOL ⟨we lowered for a ~ of four or five whales —Herman Melville⟩ **4 :** POTBELLY 1a **5 a :** a roughly cylindrical ore body dwindling at each end like a cigar **b :** a similarly shaped mineral aggregate in schist or gneiss **6 :** a streamlined often detachable compartment slung under the wings or fuselage of an aircraft and used as a container (as for a jet engine, cargo, or weapons) ⟨jet ~⟩ ⟨rocket ~⟩ ⟨fuel ~⟩

**³pod** \"\ *vb* **podded; podded; podding; pods** *vi* **1 :** to assemble in pods **2 :** to produce pods ⟨rows of *podding* peas on hazel sticks —H.E.Bates⟩ ~ *vt* **:** to drive (seals) into pods

**pod-** *or* **podo-** *comb form* [Gk, fr. *pod-, pous* — more at FOOT] **1 :** foot ⟨*podology*⟩ ⟨*podoscaph*⟩ **2 :** hoof ⟨*pododerm*⟩ **3 :** peduncle **:** stalk ⟨*Podocarpus*⟩ ⟨*Podophthalmia*⟩

**¹-pod** \ˌpäd\ *n comb form* -s [Gk *-pod-, -pous*, fr. *-pod-, -pous*, adj. combining form, having (such or so many) feet, fr. *pod-, pous* foot] **:** one having (such or so many) feet ⟨*chenopod*⟩

**²-pod** \"\ *adj comb form* [Gk *-pod-, -pous*] **:** having (such or so many) feet ⟨*acanthopod*⟩

**³-pod** \"\ *also* **-pode** \ˌpōd\ *n comb form* -s [NL *podium* foot — more at PODIUM] **1 a :** footlike part ⟨*pseudopode*⟩ **b :** foot ⟨*nectopod*⟩ **2 :** -PODITE ⟨*endopod*⟩

**POD** *abbr* **1** pay on delivery **2** post office department

**-po·da** \pədə\ *n pl comb form* [NL, fr. Gk, neut. pl. of *-pod-, -pous* having (such or so many) feet] **:** ones having (such or so many) feet — in taxonomic names in zoology ⟨Arthro*poda*⟩ ⟨Deca*poda*⟩ ⟨Hetero*poda*⟩; compare -PUS

**po·dag·ra** \pəˈdagrə, ˈpädəg-\ *n* -s [ME, fr. L, fr. Gk, trap for the feet, foot disease of animals, gout, fr. *pod-* + *-agra*] **1 :** gout in the feet; *broadly* **:** GOUT **2 :** a painful condition of the big toe caused by gout — **po·dag·ral** \-grəl\ *adj* — **po·dag·ric** \-rik\ *adj* — **po·dag·rous** \-rəs\ *adj*

**po·dal** \ˈpōdᵊl\ *adj* [*pod-* + *-al*] **1 :** of or relating to a foot **2 :** being membranes attached to the neuropodia and notopodia of various polychaete worms

**po·dal·ic** \pōˈdalik\ *adj* [*pod-* + *-al* + *-ic*] **:** of, relating to, or by means of the feet ⟨used ~ version in the child's delivery⟩

**po·da·li·ri·idae** \ˌpōdᵊlᵊˈrīəˌdē\ *n pl, cap* [NL, fr. *Podalirius*, type genus + *-idae*] **:** a family of large hairy long-tongued bees that are usu. solitary but include some which burrow in cliffs and form large communities

**po·da·lir·i·us** \ˌpōdᵊlˈirēəs\ *n, cap* [NL, after *Podalirius* (fr. L, fr. Gk *Podaleirios*), son of the legendary ancient Greek physician Asclepius] **:** the type genus of the family Podaliriidae

**po·dar·gi·dae** \pəˈdärjəˌdē\ *n pl, cap* [NL, fr. *Podargus*, type genus + *-idae*] **:** a family of Oriental and Australian birds (order Caprimulgiformes) comprising the frogmouths

**po·dar·gus** \-gəs\ *n, cap* [NL, fr. Gk *podargos* swift-footed, white-footed, fr. *pod-* + *argos* swift, white, shining — more at ARGENT] **:** the type genus of the family Podargidae

**po·dar·thral** \pəˈdärthrəl\ *adj* [NL *podarthrum* + E *-al*] **:** of or relating to the podarthrum

**po·dar·thrum** \-thrəm\ *n, pl* **podar·thra** \-rə\ [NL, fr. *pod-* + Gk *arthron* joint — more at ARTHR-] **:** the joint between the toes and the tarsometatarsus in a bird

**po·da·tus** \pəˈdād·əs\ *n, pl* **poda·ti** \-ād·ˌī\ [NL, fr. *pod-* + L *-atus* -ate] **:** PES

**pod auger** *n* [¹*pod*] **:** an auger having a pod

**pod·axonia** \ˌpäd+\ *n pl, cap* [NL, fr. *pod-* + *axonia*] *in some esp former classifications* **:** a group comprising the Brachiopoda, Bryozoa, and Gephyrea — **pod·ax·o·ni·al** \ˌpäˌdakˈsōnēəl\ *adj*

**pod bit** *n* [¹*pod*] **:** a bit having a pod

**pod blight** *n* [²*pod*] **:** a destructive disease of various legumes (as beans) caused by fungi of the genus *Diaporthe*

**pod borer** *n* [²*pod*] **:** an insect larva that bores into the pods of legumes — see BEAN-POD BORER

**pod corn** *n* [²*pod*] **:** an Indian corn (*Zea mays tunicata*) having each kernel as well as the whole ear enclosed in a husk — called also *cow corn, husk corn*

**podded** *adj* [fr. past part. of ³*pod*] **1 :** having or producing pods — often used in combination ⟨long-*podded*⟩ **2 :** borne in a pod ⟨~ seeds⟩

**podding** *pres part of* POD

**pod·dish** \ˈpädish, -dēsh\ *n* -ES [alter. of *pottage*] *dial Eng* **:** PORRIDGE

**¹pod·dy** \ˈpädē, -di\ *adj* -ER/-EST [²*pod* + *-y*] *chiefly dial* **:** POTBELLIED

**²poddy** \"\ *n* -ES *chiefly Austral* **:** a domestic animal (as a calf, lamb, or foal) just taken from its mother

**-pode** — see -POD

**po·de·on** \ˈpōdē,än, ˈpäd-\ *n, pl* **po·de·o·nes** \ˌ==ˈō,nēz\ [NL, fr. Gk *podeōn* ragged end (in an animal skin) where the feet or tail has been, mouth of a wineskin, fr. *pod-, pous* foot — more at FOOT] **:** the petiole of the abdomen of a hymenopteron

**po·de·sta** \ˌpōdəˈstä\ *n* -s [It *podestà, potestà*, lit., power, authority, fr. L *potestat-, potestas* — more at POTESTATE] **1 :** a chief magistrate with extensive powers elected in a medieval Italian town or republic **2 :** a subordinate judge or magistrate in some Italian towns **3 :** a chief executive of an Italian commune appointed by the central government in the Fascist regime

**po·de·tial** \pəˈdēshəl\ *adj* [*podetium* + *-al*] **:** of or relating to a podetium

**po·de·ti·iform** \-ˈ=shēə,fȯrm\ *adj* [*podetium* + *-iform*] **:** like a podetium in form or appearance

**po·de·tium** \pōˈdēsh(ē)əm\ *n, pl* **pode·tia** \-)ə\ [NL, fr. *pod-* + *-etium* (origin unknown)] **1 :** a stalk on which the ascocarp is borne in various lichens (as the genus *Cladonia*) **2 :** an organ or body resembling a stalk (as the seta of a moss)

**po·dex** \ˈpōˌdeks\ *n, pl* **pod·i·ces** \ˈpädəˌsēz\ [L; akin to *pedere* to break wind — more at PETARD] **1 :** the anal region **:** RUMP **2** [NL, fr. L] **:** the pygidium of an insect

**pod fern** *n* [²*pod*] **1 :** FLOATING FERN **2 :** OREGON CLIFF BRAKE

**podge** \ˈpäj\ *n* -s [prob. alter. of *pudge*] **:** something podgy ⟨the baby a . . . flourishing ~ of flesh —W.M.Thackeray⟩

**podg·er** \-jə(r)\ *n* -s [origin unknown] **1 :** a small drift used to bring rivet holes into alignment **2 :** TOMMY

**podg·i·ly** \ˈpäjəlē, -li\ *adv* **:** in a podgy manner

**podg·i·ness** \-jēnəs, -jin-\ *n* -ES **:** the condition of being podgy

**podgy** \ˈpäjē, -ji\ *adj* -ER/-EST [*podge* + *-y*] **:** softly fat **:** PUDGY ⟨his pink, smooth, ~ face —Angus Wilson⟩

**-po·dia** \ˈpōdēə\ *n comb form* -s [NL, fr. Gk, fr. *pod-* + *-ia* *-y*] **:** a (specified) condition of the feet **:** condition of having (such) feet ⟨platy*podia*⟩

**po·di·al** \ˈpōdēəl\ *adj* [NL *podium* + E *-al*] **1 :** of or relating to a podium **2 :** of or relating to the pleural areas of an arthropod body segment in which the limbs are implanted

**po·di·a·trist** \pəˈdīəˌtrəst, pōˈ-\ *n* -s [*podiatry* + *-ist*] **:** CHIROPODIST

**po·di·a·try** \-rē,-ri\ *n* -ES [*pod-* + *-iatry*] **:** CHIROPODY

**pod·i·cal** \ˈpädəkəl, -dēk-\ *adj* [L & NL *podic-, podex* + E *-al* — more at PODEX] **1 :** of or relating to the podex **2 :** being either of a pair of ventrolateral plates arising from the tenth abdominal segment and partially enclosing the anus of an orthopterous insect

**pod·i·ceps** \ˈpädəˌseps\ [NL, irreg. fr. L *podic-, podex* rump + *pes* foot — more at PODEX, FOOT] *syn of* COLYMBUS

**pod·i·ci·ped·i·dae** \ˌ==sə̇ˈpedəˌdē\ *or* **pod·i·cip·i·dae** \ˌ==ˈsipəˌdē\ [*Podicipedidae* fr. NL, fr. *Podiciped-, Podicipes* (syn. of *Colymbus*) (alter. of *Podiceps*) + *-idae; Podicipidae* fr. NL, fr. *Podicip-, Podiceps* + *-idae*] *syn of* COLYMBIDAE

**po·dil·e·gous** \pəˈdiləgəs\ *adj* [*pod-* + *-i-* + Gk *legein* to gather + E *-ous* — more at LEGEND] **:** gathering pollen by means of a pollen brush on the legs ⟨~ bees⟩ — compare GASTRILEGOUS

**pod·ite** \ˈpäˌdīt\ *n* -s [*-podite*] **:** a limb segment of an arthropod — **po·dit·ic** \pəˈdid·ik\ *adj*

**-po·dite** \pəˌdīt\ *n comb form* -s [ISV *pod-* + *-ite*] **:** segment of an appendage of an arthropod ⟨basi*podite*⟩ ⟨endo*podite*⟩ — **-po·dit·ic** \pəˈdid·ik, -itik\ *adj comb form*

**po·di·um** \ˈpōdēəm\ *n, pl* **podiums** \-mz\ *or* **po·dia** \-ēə\ [L — more at PEW] **1 :** a low wall serving as a foundation, substructure, or terrace wall: as **a :** a dwarf wall around the arena of an ancient amphitheater serving as a base for the tiers of seats **b :** the masonry under the stylobate of a temple **2 a :** a balcony in an ancient Roman theater containing seats for the emperor and other spectators of high rank **b :** a raised platform or pedestal **:** DAIS ⟨the police direct traffic from round *podia* elevated six feet from the ground —*Saturday Rev.*⟩ ⟨there is one conductor who practically has the downbeat ready as he steps onto the ~ —Milton Cross⟩ **c :** LECTERN ⟨pounding the ~ and talking loudly —L.W.Youngdahl⟩ **3** [NL, fr. Gk *podion* small foot — more at PEW] **:** FOOT; *specif* **:** a tube foot of an echinoderm

**-po·di·um** \ˈpōdēəm\ *n comb form* \-ēə\ [NL, fr. L *podium*] **1 :** one having a (specified kind of) foot or part resembling a foot — in generic names ⟨Cheno*podium*⟩ ⟨Lyco*podium*⟩ **2 :** footlike part ⟨pleuro*podium*⟩

**pod·ler** \ˈpädlər\ *also* **pod·ley** \-li\ *n, pl* **podlers** \-lərz\ *also* **podlies** \-liz\ *or* **po·dles** \-dᵊlz\ [prob. alter. of *podlok*, obs. var of *pollack*] *chiefly Scot* **:** a young pollock

**pod mahogany** *n* **:** a medium to large-sized African tree (*Seymeria quanzensis*) having black seeds with a red cap — called also *mahogany bean, Rhodesian mahogany*

**pod maize** *n* **:** POD CORN

**podo** \ˈpä(ˌ)dō\ *n* -s [short for *podocarpus*] **1 :** any of several East African trees of the genus *Podocarpus* **2 :** the soft wood of a podo tree widely used for building, furniture, and crates

**podo-** — see POD-

**podo·branch** \ˈpädəˌbraŋk\ *also* **podobran·chia** \ˌ==ˈbraŋkēə\ *n, pl* **podobranchs** \-ks\ *also* **podobranchi·ae** \-kiˌē\ [NL *podobranchia*, fr. *pod-* + *-branchia* (gill)] **:** a gill attached to the basal segment of a thoracic limb of a crustacean — compare ARTHROBRANCH, PLEUROBRANCH

**podo·carp** \ˈpädəˌkärp\ *n* -s [NL *Podocarpus*] **:** a plant of the genus *Podocarpus*

**podo·car·pa·ce·ae** \ˌ==kärˈpāsēˌē\ *n pl, cap* [NL, fr. *Podocarpus*, type genus + *-aceae*] *in some classifications* **:** a family of gymnosperms with simple persistent needlelike or scalelike leaves and 2-celled anthers — compare PODOCARPINEAE

**podo·car·pic acid** \ˌ==ˈkärpik-\ *n* [ISV *podocarp-* (fr. NL *Podocarpus*) + *-ic*] **:** a crystalline phenolic acid $C_{16}H_{20}$(OH)COOH that is derived from phenanthrene and related to the diterpenes and that is found esp. in resins from trees of the genus *Podocarpus*

**podo·car·pin·e·ae** \ˌ==(ˌ)kärˈpinēˌē\ *n pl, cap* [NL, fr. *Podocarpus* + *-ineae*] *in some classifications* **:** a section of the Taxaceae including *Podocarpus* and related genera — compare PODOCARPACEAE

**podo·car·pus** \ˌ==ˈkärpəs\ *n* [NL, fr. *pod-* + *-carpus*] **1** *cap* **:** a genus of evergreen trees (family Taxaceae) widely distributed in the southern hemisphere and having a pulpy fruit with one hard seed — see BLACK PINE, KAHIKATEA, MIRO, PLUM FIR, YACCA **2** -ES **:** any tree of the genus *Podocarpus*

**podo·derm** \ˈpädəˌdərm\ *n* -s [*pod-* + *-derm*] **:** the dermal or growing part of the covering of the foot of a hoofed animal as distinguished from the epidermal or horny part

**podo·dermatitis** \ˌpädō+\ *n* [NL, fr. *pod-* + *dermatitis*] **:** inflammation of the dermal tissue underlying the horny layers of a hoof: as **a :** FOOT ROT 2 **b :** LAMINITIS

**po·dog·o·na** \pəˈdägənə\ [NL, fr. *pod-* + *-gona* (fr. Gk *gonos* offspring, procreation, seed, genitals) — more at GON-] *syn of* RICINULEI

**¹po·do·lian** \pəˈdōlēən, -lyən\ *adj, usu cap* [*Podolia*, region in the southwestern Ukraine + E *-an*] **1 :** of, relating to, or characteristic of Podolia **2 :** of, relating to, or characteristic of the people of Podolia

**²podolian** \"\ *n* -s *cap* **:** a native or inhabitant of Podolia

**po·do·lite** \ˈpōdᵊlˌīt\ *n* -s [G *podolit*, fr. *Podolia* + G *-it* -ite] **:** CARBONATE-APATITE

**po·dol·o·gy** \pəˈdäləjē\ *n* -ES [*pod-* + *-logy*] **:** the scientific study of the morphology and physiology of the feet

**pod·o·mere** \ˈpädəˌmi(ə)r\ *n* -s [*pod-* + *-mere*] **:** a leg segment of an arthropod

**po·doph·rya** \pəˈdäfrēə\ *n, cap* [NL, fr. *pod-* + *-ophrya* (fr. Gk *ophrye, ophrys* crag, brow of a hill, eyebrow) — more at BROW] **:** a genus (the type of the family Podophryidae) of stalked subspherical naked suctorian protozoans common in fresh or salt water

**pod·oph·thal·ma** \ˌpäˌdäfˈthalmə\ *or* **podophthalma·ta** \-məd·ə\ [*podophthalma*, NL, fr. *pod-* + *-ophthalma; podophthalmata*, NL, fr. *pod-* + *ophthalm-* + *-ata*] *syn of* PODOPHTHALMIA

**pod·oph·thal·mia** \-mēə\ *n pl, cap* [NL, fr. *pod-* + *-ophthalmia*] **1** *in some classifications* **:** a group comprising the stalk-eyed crustaceans **2** *in former classifications* **:** a division of Malacostraca comprising forms with the eyes supported on movable stalks and coextensive with the Phyllocarida, Euphausiacea, Mysidacea, Decapoda, and Stomatopoda — **pod·oph·thal·mi·an** \ˌ=ˌ=ˈ=mēən\ *adj or n* — **pod·oph·thal·mic** \-mik\ *adj* — **pod·oph·thal·mous** \-məs\ *adj*

**pod·ophthalmite** \ˌpäd+\ *n* [*pod-* + *ophthalmite*] **:** the distal segment of the eyestalk of a crustacean — **pod·ophthalmitic** \(ˌ)päd+\ *adj*

**podo·phyl·lin** \ˌpädəˈfilən\ *n* -s [ISV *podophyll-* (fr. NL *Podophyllum*) + *-in*] **:** a bitter light brown to greenish yellow resin that is irritating to the eye and other mucous membranes, that is obtained from podophyllum, and that is used as a cathartic, applied externally in solution in the treatment of venereal warts, and also used in cytological research for its property of inhibiting the division of malignant cells — called also *podophyllum resin*

**podo·phyl·lo·tox·in** \ˌ==ˌfiləˈtäksən\ *n* [ISV *podophyllo-* (fr. NL *Podophyllum*) + *toxin*] **:** a crystalline polycyclic compound, $C_{22}H_{22}O_8$ constituting one of the active principles of the drugs podophyllum and podophyllin

**podo·phyl·lous** \ˌpädəˈfiləs\ *adj* [*pod-* + *-phyllous*] **:** of, relating to, or being the laminar dermal tissue underlying the horny layers of a hoof

**podo·phyl·lum** \ˌ==ˈfiləm\ *n* [NL, fr. *pod-* + *-phyllum*] **1** *cap* **:** a small genus of herbs (family Berberidaceae) that have poisonous rootstocks, large palmate leaves, chiefly hexamerous flowers, and large fleshy sometimes edible berries — see MAYAPPLE **2** *pl* **podophyl·li** \-ˌiˌlī\ *or* **podophyllums :** the rhizome and rootlet of the mayapple (*Podophyllum peltatum*) that is used as a cholagogue and cathartic; *also* **:** a similar product of an Indian herb (*P. emodi*) — called also *Indian podophyllum*

**podophyllum resin** *n* **:** PODOPHYLLIN

**podos** *pl of* PODO

**podo·scaph** \ˈpädəˌskaf\ *n* -s [*pod-* + Gk *skaphos* boat — more at SCAPH-] **:** one of a pair of canoe-shaped floats attached to the feet and used for walking on water with the aid of a paddle

**podo·so·ma·ta** \ˌ==ˈsōməd·ə\ [NL, fr. *pod-* + *-somata*] *syn of* PYCNOGONIDA

**podo·sphae·ra** \-ˈsfirə\ *n, cap* [NL, fr. *pod-* + *-sphaera*] **:** a genus of powdery mildews (family Erysiphaceae) having perithecia with only a single ascus and rigid usu. dichotomously branched but sometimes simple appendages

**podo·ste·ma·ce·ae** \ˌ==stəˈmāsēˌē\ [NL, fr. *Podostemon* + *-aceae*] *syn of* PODOSTEMONACEAE

**podo·ste·mad** \ˌ==ˈstēˌmad\ *n* -s [NL *Podostemon* + E *-ad*] **:** a podostemonaceous plant

**podo·ste·mon** \-mən\ *n* [NL, fr. *pod-* + Gk *stēmōn* thread-warp — more at STAMEN] **1** *cap* **:** a widely distributed genus (the type of the family Podostemonaceae) of rock-inhabiting submerged aquatic herbs having sessile involucrate flowers and poorly differentiated leaves — see RIVERWEED **2** -s **:** any plant of the genus *Podostemon*

**podo·ste·mo·na·ce·ae** \ˌ==ˌ=məˈnāsēˌē\ *n pl, cap* [NL, fr. *Podostemon*, type genus + *-aceae*] **:** a family of aquatic fleshy herbs (order Podostemonales) with leaves and stems confluent that are natives of tropical regions, are often confined to submerged ledges or rocks of waterfalls, and have small perfect apetalous flowers

**podo·ste·mo·na·ceous** \ˌ=ˈ=ˈ=ˈnāshəs\ *or* **podo·ste·ma·ceous** \ˌ==stəˈmāshəs\ *adj* [NL *Podostemonaceae* or *Podostemaceae* + E *-ous*] **:** of or relating to the Podostemonaceae

**podo·ste·mo·na·les** \ˌ==ˌstēməˈnā(ˌ)lēz\ *n pl, cap* [NL, fr. *Podostemon* + *-ales*] **:** a small order of dicotyledonous aquatic plants that comprises solely the family Podostemonaceae and is often included in the order Rosales

**podo·the·ca** \ˌpädəˈthēkə\ *n, pl* **podothe·cae** \-ēˌsē\ [NL, fr. *pod-* + *-theca*] **:** the scaly covering of the foot of a bird or reptile — **podo·the·cal** \ˌ==ˈthēkəl\ *adj*

**-po·dous** \pədəs\ *adj comb form* [Gk *-pod-, -pous* having (such or so many) feet + E *-ous* — more at -POD] **:** having (such or so many) feet **:** -footed ⟨acantho*podous*⟩ ⟨hexa*podous*⟩

**podo·za·mi·tes** \ˌpädəzəˈmīd·(ˌ)ēz\ *n, cap* [NL, fr. *pod-* + *Zamia* + L *-ites* -ite] **:** a genus of fossil plants of the Mesozoic based upon the general resemblance of the leaflets to those of the cycads of the genus *Zamia*

**pod pepper** *n* **:** a pepper of the genus *Capsicum*

**pod rot** *also* **pod rot disease** *n* **:** a disease of cacao that produces lesions on the pods and that may be caused by either of two fungi (*Diplodia theobromae* or *Phytophthora faberi*)

**pods** *pl of* POD, *pres 3d sing of* POD

**-pods** *pl of* -POD

**pod shrimp** *n* **:** a crustacean (as of the genus *Estheria*) that has a bivalve shell

**pod·snap·pery** \(ˈ)pädˈsnap(ə)rē\ *n* -ES *sometimes cap* [Mr. *Podsnap*, complacent Philistine in *Our Mutual Friend* (1864–5), by Charles Dickens †1870 Eng. novelist + E *-ery*] **:** an attitude toward life marked by complacency and a refusal to recognize unpleasant facts

**pod spot** *n* **:** a brownish spotting of bean pods caused by the anthracnose fungus

**po·dunk** \ˈpōˌdəŋk\ *n* -s *usu cap* [fr. *Podunk*, village near Worcester, Mass., or *Podunk*, locality in Conn.] **:** a small, unimportant, and isolated town

**po·du·ra** \pəˈd(y)u̇rə\ *n* [NL, fr. *pod-* + *-ura*] **1** *cap* **:** the type genus of Poduridae **2** -s **:** any insect of the genus *Podura* — **po·du·ran** \-rən\ *adj or n*

**po·du·ri·dae** \-rəˌdē\ *n pl, cap* [NL, fr. *Podura*, type genus + *-idae*] **:** a family of primitive insects (order Collembola) that lack a tracheal system and include the snow fleas and springtails

**pod·zol** *or* **podzol soil** *also* **pod·sol** *or* **podsol soil** \ˈpädˌzȯl(-), -ˌsȯl(-), ˈ=ˌ=(-)\ *n* -s [*podzol, podsol* fr. Russ *podzol*, fr. *zola* ashes; akin to OE *glōwan* to glow — more at GLOW] **:** any of a group of zonal soils that develop in a temperate to cold moist climate under coniferous or mixed forest or under heath vegetation and have an organic mat and thin organic-mineral layer above a gray leached layer resting on an illuvial dark brown horizon — **pod·zol·ic** \(ˈ)=ˈzäik\ *adj*

**pod·zol·iza·tion** *also* **pod·sol·iza·tion** \ˌ==əˈzāshən\ *n* -s **:** an important process in the formation and modification of certain soils (as pedalfers) esp. in humid regions involving principally the leaching of the upper layers of soil and the accumulation of material in the lower layers with a resultant development of characteristic horizons; *specif* **:** the development of a podzol

**pod·zol·ize** *also* **pod·sol·ize** \ˈ=ˌ=ˌīz\ *vb* -ED/-ING/-S *vt* **:** to convert into a podzol ~ *vi* **:** to undergo podzolization

**poe** *or* **poe·bird** \ˈpōˌē\ *n* -s [Tahitian *poe*, lit., pearl beads; fr. the two tufts of white in its throat] **:** TUI

**POE** *abbr* **1** port of embarkation **2** port of entry

**poecil-** *or* **poecilo-** *or* **poikil-** *or* **poikilo-** *comb form* [Gk *poikil-, poikilo-*, fr. *poikilos* — more at PAINT] **:** variegated **:** various ⟨*Poecilichthys*⟩ ⟨*poecilogony*⟩ ⟨*poikilitic*⟩ ⟨*poikiloblast*⟩

**poe·cil·ich·thys** \ˌpēsəˈlikthə̇s\ *n, cap* [NL, fr. *poecil-* + *-ichthys*] **:** a genus of No. American darters commonly found under large stones in swift streams

**¹poe·cil·i·id** \pēˈsilēə̇d\ *adj* [NL *Poeciliidae*] **:** of or relating to the Poeciliidae

**²poeciliid** \"\ *n* -s **:** a fish of the family Poeciliidae

**poe·ci·li·dae** \ˌpēsəˈlīəˌdē\ *n pl, cap* [NL, fr. *Poecilia*, type genus, fr. Gk *poikilia* condition of being marked with various colors, fr. *poikil-* poecil- + *-ia -y*) + *-idae*] **:** a large family of small New World viviparous fishes (order Microcyprini) comprising the topminnows and having the male anal fin modified as a copulatory organ — compare GUPPY, SWORDTAIL

**poecilitic** *var of* POIKILITIC

**poe·ci·lo·cyt·ta·rous** \ˌpēsəlōˈsid·ərəs\ *adj* [*poecil-* + Gk *kyttaros* cell of a honeycomb + E *-ous*] **:** of, relating to, or being a type of nest of some social wasps (family Vespidae) in which the layers of brood comb are supported by the outer covering and a central support (as the limb of a tree) — compare PHRAGMOCYTTAROUS

**poe·ci·log·o·ny** \ˌpēsəˈlägənē\ *n* -ES [ISV *poecil-* + *-gony*] **:** a supposed method of development occurring in invertebrate animals where in the same species there are two kinds of young although the adults are exactly alike

**po·em** \ˈpōəm *also* -ōˌem *or* -ˌ+ˈōm\ *n* -s [MF *poeme*, fr. L *poema*, fr. Gk *poiēma, poēma*, fr. *poiein* to make, do, create, compose — more at POET] **1 :** a composition in verse ⟨wrote his account of the ball game in the form of a ~⟩ **2 :** a piece of poetry designed as a unit and communicating to the reader the sense of a complete experience ⟨a ~ is not a syllogism, and its essential unity and progression are psychological rather than logical —John Ciardi⟩ **3 :** a composition, creation, achievement, experience, or object likened to a poem (as in expressiveness, lyric beauty, or formal grace) ⟨a prose ~⟩ ⟨a symphonic ~⟩ ⟨the house we stayed in . . . was itself a ~ —H.J.Laski⟩

**po·e·mat·ic** \ˌpōəˈmad·ik, -atik, -ēk\ *adj* [Gk *poiēmatikos*, fr. *poiēmat-, poiēma* + *-ikos* -ic] **:** POETIC

**po·eph·a·ga** \pōˈefəgə\ *n pl, cap* [NL, fr. Gk *poēphaga*, neut. pl. of *poēphagos* grass-eating, fr. *poa* grass + *-phagos* -phagous — more at POA] *in some esp former classifications* **:** a group including the kangaroos and related forms

**po·eph·a·gous** \(ˈ)=ˈ=əgəs\ *adj* [Gk *poēphagos*] **1 :** HERBIVOROUS **2** [NL *Poephaga* + E *-ous*] **:** of or relating to the Poephaga

**po·eph·a·gus** \pōˈefəgəs\ *n, cap* [NL, fr. Gk *poēphagos* grass-eating] **:** a genus of mammals (family Bovidae) that comprises the Asiatic yak and is sometimes made a subgenus of *Bos*

**poes** *pl of* POE

**po·e·sy** *also* **po·e·sie** \ˈpōəzē, -sē, -i\ *n, pl* **poesies** [ME *poisie poesie*, fr. MF *poesie*, fr. L *poesis*, fr. Gk *poiēsis, poēsis* creation, making, poem, fr. *poiein* to make, do, create, compose + *-sis* — more at POET] **1 a :** a body of poems **:** the work produced by poets **:** POEM ⟨olden songs and poesies —John Keats⟩ **b :** poetic form or composition **:** POETRY ⟨there is only the one verbal art which is ~ —Herbert Read⟩ **c :** artificial, precious, or sentimentalized poetic writing ⟨the plush curtains of melodrama have been exchanged for the dainty chintzes of ~ —Michael Williams⟩ **2 :** POSY ⟨within the hoop of the betrothal or wedding ring it was customary to inscribe sentences or *poesies* —W.T. & Kate Pavitt⟩ **3 a :** poetic inspiration **:** creative or imaginative power ⟨the bold wings of ~ —William Wordsworth⟩ **b :** an imaginative, exalted, or idealized quality or spirit ⟨of love the ~, the passion —Robert Browning⟩

**po·et** \ˈpōə̇t, *in rapid speech sometimes* ˈpōil; *usu* \|d.+V\ *n* -s [ME *poet, poete*, fr. OF *poete*, fr. L *poeta*, fr. Gk *poiētēs, poētēs* maker, composer, poet, fr. *poiein* to make, do, create, compose; akin to Skt *cinoti* he gathers, heaps up, piles in order, OSlav *činiti* to arrange; basic meaning: to pile up] **1 :** one who writes poetry **:** a maker of verses **2 :** a writer having great imaginative and expressive gifts and possessing a special sensitivity to language ⟨a ~ born, not made⟩ **3 :** a creative artist (as a composer or painter) whose work is marked by imagination, spontaneity, and lyricism ⟨a natural ~ with the camera —G.W.Stonier⟩ ⟨the first ~ of the piano in the history of music —*Time*⟩

**po·et·as·ter** \ˈpōəd·ˌastə(r), -ōəˌta-, -aas- *sometimes* ˌ==ˈ==\ *n* -s [NL, fr. L *poeta* + *-aster*] **:** a writer of worthless or inferior verses **:** a pretended poet **:** VERSIFIER ⟨indicative of the mistakes of ~*s* and would-be poets rather than of real poets —C.S. Kilby⟩

**po·et·as·ter·ing** \-t(ə)riŋ\ *n* -s **:** playing at poetry **:** dabbling in verse ⟨away with all ~ at dinner parties —W.M.Thackeray⟩

**po·et·as·tery** *or* **po·et·as·try** \-t(ə)rē\ *n* -ES **:** POETASTERING ⟨prevent young dramatists from wasting their budding talents on . . . pretentious ~ —Clare B. Luce⟩

**po·e·taz narcissus** \ˈpōəˌtaz-\ *n* [NL *poetaz* (specific epithet of *Narcissus poetaz*), blend of *poeticus* (specific epithet of *N. poeticus*, fr. L, poetic) and *tazetta* (specific epithet of *N. tazetta*, fr. It *tazzetta* small basin, small cup, dim. of *tazza* basin, cup), the two species from which it is derived — more at POETIC, TAZZA] **:** any of various narcissus that are hybrids between the polyanthus narcissus and the poet's narcissus and have flowers four or more in a cluster and with a short crown that is not crisped

**po·et·ess** \ˈpōəd·əs, -ətəs\ *n* -ES [*poet* + *-ess*] **:** a female poet

**po·et·ic** \pōˈed·|ik, -et|, |ēk\ *adj* [MF *poetique*, fr. L *poeticus*, fr. Gk *poiētikos* capable of making, creative, poetic, fr. *poiētēs* maker, composer, poet + *-ikos* -ic — more at POET] **1 a :** of or relating to poets **:** appropriate to or characteristic of poets ⟨the personality truly and naturally ~ seems to be becoming rarer —Edmund Wilson⟩ ⟨had no ~ talents at all —*Times Lit. Supp.*⟩ ⟨a ~ face⟩ **b :** given to or occupied with poetry ⟨a ~ plowman⟩ ⟨a ~ family⟩ **2 a :** written in verse ⟨a ~ version of his earlier prose drama⟩ ⟨did a ~ paraphrase of the speech⟩ **b :** of, relating to, or suitable for poetry or poems ⟨a ~ renaissance⟩ ⟨his small ~ output⟩ ⟨a ~ subject⟩ **3 :** having or expressing the qualities of poetry ⟨~ movements of the whole body —G.B.Shaw⟩ ⟨this essentially ~ mode of thought —Kathleen Raine⟩ ⟨a darkly ~ architectural scene —Carlyle Burrows⟩ **4 :** stilted and artificial in diction or style ⟨the prose is ~ in the bad sense —M.D.Geismar⟩ ⟨uses the literary and always ~ phrase —*N.Y.Herald Tribune Bk. Rev.*⟩

**po·et·i·cal** \|əkəl, |ēk-\ *adj* [ME, fr. L *poeticus* + ME *-al*] **1 :** POETIC **2 :** beyond or above the truth of history or nature **:** IDEALIZED ⟨the more ~ and elevated the ideas are which are clustered around marriage, the more probable it is that experience will produce disappointment —W.G.Sumner⟩

**po·et·i·cal·i·ty** \pōˌed·əˈkaləd·ē\ *n* -ES **:** poetic quality or expression ⟨the poem is a mere tumbled out spate . . . of *poeticalities* —F.R.Leavis⟩

**po·et·i·cal·ly** \pōˈed·|ək(ə)lē, -et|, |ēk-, -li\ *adv* **:** in a poetic manner ⟨two themes which he strove to blend ~ rather than rationally —E.S.Bates⟩

**po·et·i·cal·ness** \-kəlnəs\ *n* -ES **:** poetic quality

**po·et·i·cism** \pōˈed·əˌsizəm\ *n* -s [*poetic* + *-ism*] **:** an archaic, trite, or strained form of poetic expression ⟨the common stock of ~*s* that have fallen into public domain from the poetry of the past —John Ciardi⟩

**po·et·i·cize** \-ˌsīz\ *vt* -ED/-ING/-S [*poetic* + *-ize*] **:** to put into poetry **:** give a poetic quality to ⟨not unaware of the life of today about her, but touching it only to ~ it —*N.Y. Herald Tribune Bk. Rev.*⟩

**poetic justice** *n* **:** an outcome of a fictitious or real situation in which vice is punished and virtue is rewarded usu. in a manner peculiarly or ironically appropriate to the particular situation

**poetic license** *n* **:** LICENSE 4

**po·et·ics** \pōˈed·|iks, -et|i, |ēks *also* **po·et·ic** \-k\ *n pl but usu sing in constr* [fr. *poetic*, adj., after L *poetica*, fr. Gk *poiētikē*, fr. fem. of *poiētikos*] **1 a :** a treatise on poetry or aesthetics ⟨the best attempt yet made to write a ~ of modern art —Joseph Frank⟩ **b :** poetic theory ⟨a fascinating and often valuable essay in ~ —*Times Lit. Supp.*⟩ **2 :** poetic practice ⟨exemplifies with peculiar force the general habit and tendency of Victorian *poetic* —F.R.Leavis⟩ **3 :** poetic feelings or utterances ⟨there was no discontent . . . no ~, no strong, balked emotion —*Bookman*⟩

**po·et·i·cule** \pōˈed·ə(ˌ)kyül\ *n* -s [*poet* + *-i-* + *-cule* (as in *animalcule*)] **:** POETASTER

**po·et·ization** \ˌpōəd·əˈzāshən, -ətəˈz-, -əˌtīˈz-\ *n* -s **:** the act or an instance of poetizing

**po·et·ize** \ˈpōəd·ˌīz, -əˌtīz\ *vb* -ED/-ING/-S [MF *poetiser*, fr. *poete* poet + *-iser* -ize — more at POET] *vi* **:** to write poetry **:** write or speak poetically ⟨has *poetized* about what he has called reality and the imagination —R.H.Pearce⟩ ~ *vt* **:** POETICIZE ⟨to make anything significant one has to ~ it —Henry Miller⟩ — **po·et·iz·er** \-zə(r)\ *n* -s

**poet laureate** *n, pl* **poets laureate** *or* **poet laureates** [ME] **1 :** a poet honored (as by a university) for achievement in his art **2 :** a poet appointed for life by an English sovereign as a member of the royal household and formerly expected to compose poems for court and national occasions **3 :** one regarded by a country or region as its most eminent or representative poet

**po·et·ling** \ˈpōətliŋ, -lēŋ\ *n* -s [*poet* + *-ling*] **:** an immature or petty poet **:** POETASTER ⟨the whine of our ~*s* —Sidney Alexander⟩

**po·eto·mach·ia** \pōˌed·əˈmakēə\ *n* -s [NL, fr. L *poeta* poet + NL *-o-* + Gk *-machia* -machy — more at POET] **:** a contest of poets; *specif* **:** a literary quarrel involving a number of Elizabethan dramatists

**po·et·ress** \ˈpōə·trəs, -ət·r-\ *n* -ES [MF *poeteresse*, fem. of *poete* poet — more at POET] *archaic* **:** POETESS

**po·et·ry** \ˈpōə·trē, -ri, *also* -ət·r-, *in rapid speech sometimes* ˈpòi·t-\ *n* -ES [ME *poetrie*, fr. MF, fr. ML *poetria*, fr. L *poeta* poet, fr. Gk *poiētria*, fr. *poiētēs* poet — more at POET] **1 a :** metrical writing **:** VERSE ⟨turns out 20 lines of ~ each day for the paper⟩ **b :** the productions of a poet **:** POEMS ⟨a collection of 16th century ~⟩ ⟨picked up a volume of ~⟩ **c poetries** *pl* **:** pieces of poetry **2 :** writing that formulates a concentrated imaginative awareness of experience in language chosen and arranged to create a specific emotional response through its meaning, sound, and rhythm **3 a :** a quality that stirs the imagination or gives a sense of heightened and more meaningful existence ⟨the ~ with which an American train is surrounded —Henri Peyre⟩ ⟨what are ceremonies but the manners and ~ of the state —*N.Y. Times Bk. Rev.*⟩ **b :** a quality of spontaneity and grace ⟨her dancing is pure ~⟩ ⟨has the technique and power of a great pianist, but his playing lacks ~⟩

**poets** *pl of* POET

**poetsch process** \ˈpech-\ *n, usu cap 1st P* [after F. H. Poetsch, 19th cent. Ger. mining engineer] **:** a method of excavating in which soft water-bearing formations are first artificially frozen and then mined while still solid

**po·et·ship** \ˈpōətˌship\ *n* [*poet* + *-ship*] **:** the state or function of a poet

**poet's narcissus** *also* **poet's daffodil** *n* **:** a narcissus (*Narcissus poeticus*) having fragrant, chiefly white, and usu. solitary flowers with a very shallow corona that is crisped and reddish on its edge

**pog·a·mog·gan** \ˌpägəˈmägən\ *n* -s [of Algonquian origin;

pogamoggan of the Sioux

akin to Ojibwa *pägämägan* club, Cree *pakämâgan* hammer, lit., (something) used for striking] **:** a club used as a weapon or ceremonial object by various American Indian peoples and usu. consisting in the Great Lakes region of a flat curved club with a knobbed head and in the Plains region of a piece of stone fastened to the end of a slender stick covered with leather

**po·gey bait** *or* **po·gie bait** \ˈpōgē, -gi-\ *n* [*pogey, pogie* prob. alter. of *pogy*] *slang* **:** CANDY

**pogge** \ˈpäg\ *n* -s [origin unknown] **:** a sea poacher (*Agonus cataphractus*) of the north Atlantic

**pog·gen·dorff illusion** \ˈpägənˌdȯrf-\ *n, usu cap P* [after Johann C. Poggendorff †1877 Ger. physicist] **:** an apparent deflection of a straight line when it is interrupted by two lines parallel to each other

**pog·gy** \ˈpägē\ *n, pl* **poggies** *also* **poggy** [origin unknown] **:** a small whale

**pogie** *var of* POGY

**pogies** *pl of* POGY

**pogon-** *or* **pogono-** *comb form* [NL, fr. Gk *pōgōn-*, *pōgōno-*, fr. *pōgōn*] **:** beard **:** something resembling a beard **:** ⟨*Pogonia*⟩ ⟨*pogonotomy*⟩

**-po·gon** \pōˌgän\ *n comb form* [NL, fr. Gk *pōgōn*, perh. fr. *pō-* (akin to Gk — Cyprian dial. — *pos* on, at) + *-gōn* (akin to Gk *genys* cheek) — more at POST-, CHIN] **:** beard — in generic names ⟨*Calopogon*⟩

**po·go·na·tum** \ˌpōgəˈnād·əm, -ād·əm\ *n, cap* [NL, fr. *pogon-* + L *-atum* (neut. of *-atus* -ate)] **:** a genus of erect acrocarpous mosses (family Polytrichaceae) in which the leaves have ventral lamellae

**po·go·nia** \pəˈgōnyə, -nēə\ *n* [NL, fr. *pogon-* + *-ia*] **1** *cap* **:** a genus comprising terrestrial orchids of the north temperate zone that have a slender rootstock, one or few leaves, and a solitary terminal flower with a crested tip and being sometimes extended to include forms usu. placed in the genera *Isotria* and *Triphora* **2** -s **:** any orchid of *Pogonia* or a closely related genus

**po·go·ni·on** \-nēən\ *n* -s [NL, fr. Gk *pōgōnion* small beard, dim. of *pōgōn* beard — more at -POGON] **:** the most projecting median point on the anterior surface of the chin — see CRANIOMETRY illustration

**pog·o·nip** \ˈpägəˌnip\ *n* -s [Southern Paiute, fr. *pagina-* cloud, fog + *-pi*, n. suffix] **:** a dense winter fog containing frozen particles that is formed in deep mountain valleys of western U.S.

**pogon iris** \ˈpōˌgän-\ *n* [NL, subgenus of irises, fr. *pogon-* + *Iris*] **:** BEARDED IRIS

**po·go·nof·o·ra** \ˌpōgəˈnäfərə\ *n pl, cap* [NL, irreg. fr. Gk *pōgōnophora*, neut. pl. of *pōgōnophoros* wearing a beard, fr. *pōgōno-* pogon- + *-phoros* -phorous] **:** a group of marine worms constituting a class of uncertain systematic relationships and superficially resembling polychaetes but having a dorsal nervous system and obscure metamerism

**po·go·nol·o·gy** \ˌ==ˈnäləjē\ *n* -ES [NL *pogonologia*, fr. *pogon-* + L *-logia* -logy] **:** the study of or a treatise on beards

**po·go·no·myr·mex** \ˌpōgənōˈmərˌmeks\ *n, cap* [NL, fr. *pogon-* + Gk *myrmēx* ant — more at PISMIRE] **:** a widely distributed genus of harvester ants

**po·go·no·mys** \pəˈgōnəˌmis\ *n, cap* [NL, fr. *pogon-* + *-mys*] **:** a genus of prehensile-tailed rats of New Guinea

**po·go·not·o·my** \ˌpōgəˈnäd·əmē\ *n* -ES [*pogon-* + *-tomy*] **:** the cutting of a beard **:** SHAVING

**po·go·not·ro·phy** \ˌ==ˈnä·trəfē\ *n* -ES [Gk *pōgōnotrophia*, fr. *pōgōno-* pogon- + *-trophia* -trophy] **:** beard growing

**po·go stick** \ˈpō(ˌ)gō-\ *n* [fr. *Pogo*, a trademark] **:** an upright pole with two foot rests and a strong spring at the bottom enabling the user to propel it along the ground by jumps

**¹po·grom** \pəˈgräm, (ˈ)pōˌgräm, ˈpōgrəm *sometimes* ˈpägrəm\ *n* -s [Yiddish, fr. Russ, lit., devastation, destruction, fr. *po-* like (fr. *po* on, at, according to) + *grom* thunder; akin to OE *of* of, from, off, and to OSlav *gromŭ* thunder, OE *grimm* grim — more at OF, GRIM] **:** an organized massacre and looting of helpless people usu. with the connivance of officials; *specif* **:** such a massacre of Jews

**²pogrom** \"\ *vt* -ED/-ING/-S **:** to massacre in a pogrom

**po·grom·ist** \-məst\ *n* -s **:** one who organizes or takes part in a pogrom

**po·gy** *also* **po·gie** \ˈpōgē, -gi\ *n, pl* **pogies** [of Algonquian origin; akin to Abnaki *pôkañgan* menhaden] **1 :** MENHADEN **2** *usu* **pogie a :** BLACK PERCH d **b :** a Pacific coast surf fish (*Holconotus rhodoterus*)

**poh** *a strong often trilled* p-*sound; often read as* ˈpō\ *interj* [origin unknown] — used to express contempt

**po·ha** \ˈpō(ˌ)hä\ *n* -s [Hawaiian *pohā*] *Hawaii* **:** cape gooseberry (*Physalis peruviana*)

**po·hu·tu·ka·wa** \pōˌhüd·əˈkäwə\ *n* -s [Maori] **1 :** a New Zealand tree (*Metrosideros tomentosa*) with crimson flowers and silvery leaves below **2 :** a New Zealand variety of the sweet potato

**¹poi** \ˈpȯi, ˈpōē\ *adv* [It, fr. L *post* behind, after — more at POST-] **:** THEN, LATER, NEXT — used to qualify another word used as a direction in music ⟨adagio ~ allegro⟩

**²poi** \ˈpȯi, ˈpōē\ *n, pl* **poi** *or* **pois** [Hawaiian & Samoan] **1 :** a Hawaiian food made of taro root which is cooked and pounded and kneaded into a smooth pasty mass to which varying quantities of water are added, often allowed to ferment before being eaten, and traditionally eaten with the fingers **2 :** a Hawaiian or Samoan food made of mashed ripe bananas or pineapples to which coconut cream is usu. added

**³poi** \"\ *n, pl* **poi** *or* **pois** [Maori] **:** a small ball which is made typically of flax, grass, or rushes, to which a string of varying length is attached, and which is swung rhythmically by Maori performers in various dances and songs

**poi·e·sis** \pȯiˈēsəs\ *n, pl* **poie·ses** \-ēˌsēz\ [Gk *poiēsis* creation, making, poem — more at POESY] **:** the action or faculty of producing or doing something esp. creatively

**-poi·e·sis** \ˌpȯiˈēsəs\ *n comb form, pl* **-poie·ses** \-ēˌsēz\ [NL, fr. Gk *poiēsis*] **:** production **:** formation ⟨hemato*poiesis*⟩ ⟨leuko*poiesis*⟩

**poi·et·ic** \(ˈ)pȯiˈed·|ik, -et|, |ēk\ *adj* [Gk *poiētikos* capable of making, creative, poetic — more at POETIC] **:** of or relating to poiesis **:** CREATIVE ⟨a ~ shaper of his own destiny —C.P. Aiken⟩

**-poi·et·ic** \"\ *adj comb form* [Gk *poiētikos*] **:** productive **:** formative ⟨hemato*poietic*⟩

**poi·gnance** \ˈpȯin(y)ən(t)s\ *n* -s **:** POIGNANCY

**poi·gnan·cy** \-nsē, -si\ *n* -ES **1 :** the quality or state of being poignant ⟨acute sudden ~ of love —Havelock Ellis⟩ **2 :** an instance of poignancy ⟨experience filled with *poignancies*⟩

**poi·gnant** \-nt\ *adj* [ME *pugnaunt*, *poinaunt*, fr. MF *poignant*, pres. part. of *poindre*, fr. L *pungere* to prick, pierce, sting — more at PUNGENT] **1 a** *archaic* **:** sharp and piquant to the taste **b :** pungent and strongly pervasive in odor ⟨a ~ perfume, soft and languorous —Kenneth Roberts⟩ **2 a** (1) **:** painfully sharp with regard to the feelings **:** PIERCING, KEEN ⟨~ grief⟩ ⟨with a look of ~ regret on his face —Bram Stoker⟩ (2) **:** very moving **:** deeply affecting **:** TOUCHING ⟨the ~ spectacle of a little child without a home⟩ ⟨so many ~ memories —Havelock Ellis⟩ **b** (1) **:** STINGING, CUTTING ⟨his satire is particularly ~ —F.M.Godfrey⟩ ⟨~ sarcasm —Benjamin Disraeli⟩ (2) **:** INCISIVE, PENETRATING ⟨are revealed with ~ clarity —Joseph Frank⟩ (3) **:** making a strong impression **:** STRIKING ⟨a ~ paradox —J.T.Clark⟩ ⟨become both convincing and ~ to us —David Cecil⟩ **c :** URGENT, PRESSING, ACUTE ⟨the more ~ problems of human existence —M.R. Cohen⟩ **3** *obs* **:** having a physically sharp point **4 a :** keenly stimulating or pleasurable to the mind or feelings ⟨a more ~ felicity than he had yet experienced —Nathaniel Hawthorne⟩ ⟨ecstasy too ~ to endure —*Saturday Rev.*⟩ ⟨this kind of day . . . had a more ~ loveliness —Jan Struther⟩ **b :** deft and to the point ⟨her illustrations were apposite and ~ —Charles Lamb⟩ **:** APT, POINTED ⟨makes some brief but ~ observations —G.A.Panichas⟩ **syn** see MOVING, PUNGENT

**poi·gnant·ly** *adv* **:** in a poignant manner **:** with poignancy

**poignard** *var of* PONIARD

**poikil-** *or* **poikilo-** — see POECIL-

**poi·ki·lit·ic** \ˌpȯikəˈlid·ik\ *or* **poe·ci·lit·ic** \ˌpēsə-\ *adj* [*poecil-* + *-itic*] **:** of, relating to, or consisting of a structural pattern in igneous rocks in which a crystal of one mineral encloses smaller unoriented grains of another mineral so that a lustrous mottling effect is produced

**poi·kilo·blast** \pȯiˈkiləˌblast, ˈpȯikəlōˌb-\ *n* -s [ISV *poecil-* + *-blast*] **1 :** a nucleated poikilocyte **2 :** a large crystal of a metamorphic rock with a texture marked by the inclusion of small idioblasts — **poi·kilo·blas·tic** \=ˌ==ˈblastik, ˌ===-\ *adj*

**poi·kilo·cyte** \=ˈ==ˌsīt, ˌ===-\ *n* -s [ISV *poecil-* + *-cyte*] **:** an abnormally formed red blood cell characteristic of various anemias

**poi·kilo·cytosis** \=ˌ==, ˌ===+\ *n, pl* **poikilocytoses** [NL, fr. ISV *poikilocyte* + NL *-osis*] **:** a condition marked by the presence of poikilocytes

**poi·kil·osmotic** \ˌpȯikəl+\ *adj* [*poecil-* + *osmotic*] **:** lacking a bodily osmotic regulating mechanism and having body fluids with an osmotic pressure similar to that of the surrounding medium ⟨most lower marine invertebrates are ~⟩ — compare HOMOIOSMOTIC

**poi·kilo·therm** \pȯiˈkiləˌthərm, ˈpȯikəlōˌth-\ *n* -s [ISV *poecil-* + *-therm*; orig. formed in G] **:** an organism (as a frog) with a variable body temperature usu. slightly higher than the temperature of its environment **:** a cold-blooded organism

**poi·kilo·ther·mic** \=ˌ==ˈthərmik, ˌ===-\ *also* **poi·kilo·ther·mal** \-məl\ *or* **poi·kilo·ther·mous** \-məs\ *adj* **:** of, relating to, or typical of a poikilotherm **:** COLD-BLOODED 2

**poi·kilo·ther·mism** \=ˌ==ˈthərˌmizəm, ˈ===ˌth-\ *n* -s **:** the state of being poikilothermic

**poi·ki·lo·ther·my** \-mē\ *n* -ES **:** POIKILOTHERMISM

**poil** \ˈpȯi(ə)l\ *n* -s [F, lit., hair, fr. L *pilus* — more at PILE] **:** a thread of raw silk used as a core for tinsel

**poi·lu** \(ˈ)pwäˈlü, *F* pwalüe\ *n* -s [F, fr. *poilu* hairy, fr. MF, fr. *poil* hair] **:** a soldier in the French army; *esp* **:** a front-line French soldier in World War I

**poi·men·ics** \pȯiˈmeniks\ *n pl but usu sing in constr* [Gk *poimenikos* of a shepherd (fr. *poimen-*, *poimēn* shepherd, pastor + *-ikos* -ic) + E *-s*; akin to Gk *pōy* herd, flock — more at FUR] **:** the study or application of pastoral theology

**poin·ci·ana** \ˌpȯin(t)sēˈanə, *esp in regions where it grows* ˌp(w)än-\ *n* [NL, fr. De Poinci, 17th cent. governor of part of the French West Indies + L *-ana*, fem. of *-anus* -an] **1** *cap* **:** a small genus of ornamental tropical trees or shrubs (family Leguminosae) that have bright orange or red flowers — see PRIDE OF BARBADOS **2** -s **:** any of various trees now or formerly included in the genus *Poinciana*; *esp* **:** ROYAL POINCIANA

**poind** \ˈpȯind, ˈpind\ *vt* -ED/-ING/-S [ME (Sc dial.) *punden*, *pynden*, fr. OE *pyndan* to dam up — more at PIND] *Scot* **:** to take forceful legal possession of esp. so as to sell under warrant

**poinding** *n* -s [ME *punding*, gerund of *punden* to poind] *Scots law* **:** a process by which a creditor seizes movable property so as to become vested with its title and the right of sale or appropriation in satisfaction of a debt

**poin·set·tia** \÷pȯinˈsed·|ə, |ēə, -set|\ *n* [NL, fr. Joel R. Poinsett †1851 Am. diplomat + NL *-ia*] **1 a** *cap, in some classifications* **:** a genus of chiefly tropical American herbs or woody plants (family Euphorbiaceae) with alternate leaves and cymose inconspicuous greenish flowers subtended by brightly colored involucral leaves that is now included as a section in the genus *Euphorbia* **b** -s **:** any plant of the genus *Euphorbia* that has flower clusters marked by showy involucral bracts; *esp* **:** a showy Mexican and So. American plant (*E. pulcherrima*) with tapering scarlet petallike leaves that surround small yellow flowers **2** -s **:** a strong to vivid red that is bluer and lighter than bright cherry red

**¹point** \ˈpȯint *dial* ˈpīnt\ *n* -s [ME, partly fr. OF *point* prick, sting, small spot, dot, item, point in time or space, fr. L *punctum* small hole, spot, point in time or space, fr. neut. of *punctus*, past part. of *pungere* to prick, sting, pierce; partly fr. OF *pointe* sharp end, fr. (assumed) VL *puncta*, fr. L, fem. of *punctus*, past part. — more at PUNGENT] **1 a** (1) **:** one of the indivisible parts of an extended usu. abstract whole **:** an individual detail of a pair or group of details **:** ITEM, PARTICULAR ⟨said there were two ~*s* in the proposal that were important⟩ ⟨carefully considered each ~ of the argument⟩ ⟨said that in his new job he would have to watch a couple of ~*s*⟩ (2) **:** a distinguishing trait or feature **:** a differentiating detail **:** individualizing mark **:** CHARACTERISTIC ⟨was well aware of the teacher's good and bad ~*s*⟩ ⟨tact is one of her strong ~*s*⟩; *specif* **:** a feature of an animal's physical qualities or behavior esp. as figuring in evaluation of the animal's relative excellence of breed ⟨judges at a dog show carefully noting the ~*s* of each dog⟩ (3) **points** *pl* **:** the facial markings of a Siamese cat **:** MASK **b** (1) **:** the most important essential in some discussion or matter **:** the principal or central element **:** the precise part on which the rest turns or depends ⟨the ~ of his talk was that more effort was needed⟩ ⟨the ~ is they are doing as well as they can⟩ ⟨asked them not to digress and to keep to the ~⟩ ⟨became impatient with the witness and asked her to come to the ~⟩ (2) **:** the part of something spoken or written that gives it effectiveness or meaningfulness **:** the element on which applicability or cogency depends **:** the main idea or vital feature ⟨could not see the ~ of such a remark⟩ ⟨missed the whole ~ of the joke⟩ **c :** the quality of something spoken or written of being able to arouse interest and of being generally effective **:** pungent effectiveness arising esp. out of applicability **:** COGENCY, FORCE, PUNCH ⟨is a basically sound book but somehow lacks ~⟩ **2** *obs* **:** the state of being in a particular physical condition ⟨looked fairer and in better ~ than all the rest —John Evelyn⟩ **3 a** (1) **:** an end or object to be achieved **:** AIM, PURPOSE ⟨did not see what ~ there was in continuing the discussion⟩ (2) **:** something to be gained **:** BENEFIT, GOOD ⟨wondered whether there would be any ~ in seeing her⟩ **b :** something that one has proposed and is trying to get established or accepted **:** a particular line of argument **:** what one is driving at **:** THESIS, PROPOSITION ⟨said he was beginning to see her ~⟩ ⟨has unquestionably won his ~⟩ ⟨carried the ~ without difficulty and did as she wanted to⟩ ⟨made their ~ so that everyone was convinced⟩ **c** (1) **:** something that is the subject of discussion or attention ⟨asked what the ~ at issue was⟩ or concern ⟨with them the whole thing is a ~ of conscience⟩ **:** MATTER ⟨is a ~ of controversy⟩ ⟨a ~ of interest⟩ (2) **:** something (as a vital idea, an essential detail) that is important enough to require serious discussion or consideration ⟨told him that he had a ~ in what he said⟩ (3) **:** POINTER 8 **4 a** (1) **:** a particular narrowly limited part of a surface or of space that is singled out as occupying a usu. precisely indicated spot and that has usu. minimum extension or no relevant extension **:** a specific narrowly localized place having no relevant size or shape **:** a definite precisely indicated placement or position of something ⟨fire broke out at several ~*s* in the city⟩ ⟨walked to a ~ 50 yards north of the building⟩ ⟨struck the target at a ~ just left of center⟩ ⟨a satellite that was 200 miles from earth at its farthest ~⟩ (2) **:** a narrowly localized abstract spot used as a place of reference ⟨conceived of a line drawn from a ~ into infinity⟩ ⟨the shortest distance between any two ~*s* is a straight line⟩ (3) **:** a particular place (as a city, town, or region) **:** LOCALITY ⟨asked them what ~*s* they intended to visit⟩ ⟨stopped at a number of ~*s* along the way⟩ ⟨have come from distant ~*s*⟩ **b** (1) **:** a particular narrowly limited often critical interval of time singled out as occurring at a precisely indicated moment and having usu. minimum duration or no relevant duration **:** exact moment **:** precise instant **:** JUNCTURE ⟨at this ~ he was interrupted⟩ (2) **:** a time interval or set of circumstances occurring immediately or nearly immediately before something indicated **:** VERGE ⟨was on the ~ of refusing⟩ ⟨is at the very ~ of death⟩ ⟨found her on the ~ of hysterics⟩ **c** (1) **:** a particular narrowly limited step, stage, or degree in the condition or development of something that is typically singled out as critical or decisive or as otherwise highly significant or important ⟨had reached the ~ where nothing seemed to matter any more⟩ ⟨arrived at the ~ of perfection⟩ ⟨a high ~ of civilization⟩ (2) **:** a definite measurable position in some kind of scale ⟨water's boiling ~⟩ ⟨melting ~ of gold⟩ ⟨stock prices at their highest ~*s*⟩ **d** (1) **:** one of the undefined elements of a geometric system and esp. of a Euclidean geometric system; *also* **:** an element of an aggregate determined by an ordered set equal in number to the number of dimensions of the aggregate (2) **:** a real or complex number that is represented by a geometric point **5** *obs* **a :** CONCLUSION, TERMINATION **b :** DECISION, RESOLUTION **6 a :** the extreme terminal usu. sharp or narrowly rounded part of something (as a sword, arrow, awl, pin, hook, indicator) that is usu. formed by the gradual or abrupt decrease in width or

| a | b | c |
|---|---|---|
| | d | |
| k | e | m |
| | f | |
| g | h | j |

points 11: *a* dexter chief, *b* middle chief, *c* sinister chief, *d* honor, *e* fess, *f* nombril, *g* dexter base, *h* middle base, *j* sinister base, *k* dexter flank, *m* sinister flank

thickness of the body which it terminates and that is typically used for piercing, pricking, indicating, or for some similar function : a usu. sharp, tapering, or otherwise narrowly converging end : TIP ⟨the sharp ~ of a needle⟩ ⟨forced the government on the people at the ~ of the sword⟩ ⟨both ~s of an anchor⟩ ⟨the ~ of a fishhook⟩ ⟨a weather vane with its ~ turned toward the north⟩ **b** : something with such a point: as (1) *obs* : a weapon used for stabbing or piercing (2) : an instrument used in etching and engraving (3) : a tool used in trimming and smoothing rough stone surfaces (4) : an instrument used to test the hardness of a mineral or gem **c** (1) : a piece of stone typically having a triangular shape and used chiefly by some prehistoric peoples as a tool or sometimes as a weapon (2) : an arrowhead without cutting edges : PILE (3) : GLAZIER'S POINT **d** (1) : a short steel pin placed in a printing press to perforate a sheet and so position it for register the next time it is run through the press — called also *press point* (2) : a piece of steel placed in the furniture of a printing form to mark a sheet at a certain place as a guide for folding (3) : a short sharp piece of serrated steel fastened to the furniture or a metal base in a printing form for slitting a sheet so that it can be registered on corresponding slits of a folding machine (4) : PIN 2 d **e** (1) : a device with a tapered point that controls the increase or decrease of stitches (as in machine-knitted fabrics) (2) : one of a series of needles in a lace machine used for controlling the size of the mesh **f** : a drivepipe through which steam or water is introduced into frozen gravel to thaw it for mining or dredging **g** (1) : the contact or discharge extremity of an electric device (as a spark plug, contact break, lightning rod) (2) *chiefly Brit* : an electric outlet : SOCKET **7** : a projecting usu. tapering part of something: as **a** : a piece of land (as a promontory, cape) projecting into a body of water **b** : a sharp prominence ⟨beyond a ~ of rock⟩ : APEX, PEAK ⟨the towering ~s of a mountain range⟩ **c** : the shaped end of one of the pieces of a leaf spring **d** (1) : the tip of the chin (2) : the tip of the foot (3) : the tip of the tongue (4) : a tine of an antler (5) **points** *pl* : the extremities of an animal; *esp* : the legs, mane, and tail of a horse **e** (1) : POINT RAIL (2) : a railroad switch (3) : the tip of the angle between two rails in a railroad frog **f** : the head of the bow of a stringed instrument **8** : a short musical phrase: **a** *archaic* : a short phrase sounded as a signal (as in hunting, battle) **b** (1) : a phrase (as a fugue subject) in contrapuntal music (2) : the entry of such a phrase at one or the other part of a contrapuntal composition **9 a** (1) : a very small mark (as a dot, speck) on a surface : a tiny spot ⟨a blue background that was touched up with little ~s of gold⟩ (2) : something that in general size and appearance is suggestive of such a mark ⟨~s of light shone through the perforated paper⟩ ⟨the pupil of the eye was contracted to a minute ~⟩ **b** : a small mark used in writing or printing: as (1) : PUNCTUATION MARK; *esp* : PERIOD (2) : a simple or compound mark used as a supplementary mark (as for indicating vowels, differentiating letters similar in form, marking stress accent) in Semitic alphabets (3) : [1]DOT 2 e (4) : DECIMAL POINT (5) : one of the small raised impressions used in braille **c** : a note in medieval music : PUNCTUS **10 a** : a lace like a shoelace having aglet ends for tying parts of a garment or costume together and used esp. in the 16th and 17th centuries ⟨sleeves were joined to a bodice with ~s⟩ ⟨hose was tied to the doublet with ~s⟩ **b** : REEF POINT **c** : a short length of material (as silkworm gut, nylon) used in angling to attach an artificial fly to a leader **d** : a small piece of material (as gutta-percha, gold) used in dentistry as a temporary filling for teeth **11 a** : one of nine particular divisions of a heraldic shield or escutcheon that determine the position of a charge; *esp* : a horizontal segment located at the base of the field and bounded by two straight or concaved slanting lines that meet at or below the fess point **b** : one of the pendants of the label of a heraldic shield or escutcheon **12 a** (1) : one of the 32 precisely marked equidistant spots about the circumference of a compass card that indicate the direction in which the various parts of the horizon lie (2) : the difference of 11¼ degrees between two such successive points **b** : a part of the horizon indicated precisely or approximately by one of the points of a compass card **13** : a small detachment probing ahead of and scouting for an advance guard or following behind and protecting a rear guard **14 a** : LACE: as (1) : NEEDLEPOINT 1 (2) : BOBBIN LACE **b** *obs* : a piece of needlepoint used as a woman's head covering **c** (1) : a stitch used in the making of lace or in producing canvas work or sometimes in producing other similar work (2) : a line of fancy stitching on the back of a glove **d** : one of the stripes woven in the edge of a Hudson's Bay blanket to indicate the weight of the blanket **15** : one of 12 spaces marked off on each side of a backgammon board **16** : a unit of measurement (as of excellence, value, proficiency, extent): as **a** (1) : a unit of counting in the scoring of a game, contest, or other competition or match (2) : a unit used in evaluating the worth or strength of a hand in some card games (as bridge) **b** (1) : a unit of academic credit used in many educational institutions and granted in larger or smaller multiples according to the grade achieved in a course (2) : a unit of credit counting toward an individual's return from overseas military service or toward his release from military service and granted in larger or smaller multiples according to the length of service already done, the number of combat decorations awarded, or other qualifications **c** : a unit used in quoting prices of stocks, shares, and various commodities that is equivalent in the stock exchange of the U. S. to one dollar a share **d** : a unit that is used in Australia to measure the extent of rainfall and that is equivalent to 1/100 inch **e** : a unit that is used to measure the thickness of paper and paperboard and that is equivalent to 1/1000 inch **f** : a unit that is used to measure the size of type used in printing and that is 0.013837 or approximately 1/72 inch — see TYPE illustration **g** : a unit used to measure the weight of diamonds that is equivalent to 1/100 carat **h** : a unit of value of coupons allotted for purchase of commodities in a rationing system **17** : the action of pointing: as **a** : the action of a hunting dog that scents or sees game and stiffens into an intently rigid attitude with head and gaze directed toward the game **b** : the action (as in some dance positions or movements) of extending one leg so that it supports no body weight and so that only the tips of the toes of the extended foot touch the floor **c** : a thrust or lunge made while fencing **18 a** : a particular position of a player in some games: as (1) : an off-side fielding position in cricket near the batsman and about in line with the popping crease — see CRICKET illustration (2) : the position to the right of the goal in lacrosse **b** : the player of a particular position in some games **19 a** : a run (as a cross-country run) made straight from one place to another **b** : the terminal place to which such a run is made **20** : one of the numbers 4, 5, 6, 8, 9, 10 that if thrown on the come-out in the game of craps gives the shooter the right to continue throwing until he wins by throwing the same number or loses by throwing a 7 — **at point 1** *obs* : in readiness ⟨let him keep *at point* a hundred knights —Shak.⟩ **2** *or* **at the point** *archaic* : on the verge : on the point : very near : just about — used with a following infinitive ⟨you are *at point* to lose your liberties —Shak.⟩ ⟨am *at the point* to die —Gen 25:32 (AV)⟩ — **in point 1** *heraldry* **a** : approaching at the tips so as to touch actually or nearly ⟨two or more piles *in point*⟩ **b** : ENTÉ EN POINT 1 **2** : RELEVANT, PERTINENT — used predicatively or postpositively ⟨mentioned a case *in point*⟩ — **in point of** *prep* : with regard to : in the matter of : with reference to ⟨*in point of* law⟩ ⟨*in point of* fact⟩ — **to point** *archaic* : in the smallest detail : fully and exactly ⟨all things thus happily performed *to point* —Robert Browning⟩ — **to the point** : RELEVANT, PERTINENT, APT ⟨made a suggestion that was altogether *to the point*⟩

[2]**point** \"\ *vb* -ED/-ING/-S [ME *pointen*, fr. MF *pointer*, partly fr. *pointe* point (sharp end), partly fr. *point* prick, small spot, dot — more at [1]POINT] *vt* **1 a** : to cause to have a sharp point : SHARPEN ⟨~*ing* a pencil with a knife⟩ **b** : to give added force, emphasis, or piquancy to : give more point to ⟨occasionally ~*ed* his remarks by slyly wagging his forefinger —G.B.Shaw⟩ — often used with *up* ⟨~*ed* up his narrative with effective use of dialect⟩ **2 a** (1) : to finish (as a wall) by filling the joints with cement, mortar, or other material (2) : to scratch out the old mortar from the joints of (as a wall) and fill in with new material — often used with *up* ⟨~*ed* up the brickwork⟩ **b** : to trim and smooth the surface of (stone) with a sharp tool — often used with *down* ⟨~*ing* down the block of granite⟩ **3 a** (1) : to mark the pauses or grammatical divisions in (something written or printed) : PUNCTUATE ⟨~*ing* the text of a speech⟩ (2) : to separate (a numerical figure) into groups by inserting a dot; *esp* : to separate (a decimal fraction) from a whole number by inserting a decimal point — usu. used with *off* ⟨~*ed* off the last two figures of 125⟩ **b** : to mark (as Hebrew words or words of other Semitic languages) with vowel points or other differentiating points **4 a** (1) : to indicate the position or direction of something by extending a finger toward the thing so indicated — usu. used with *out* ⟨~*ed* out the house where he used to live⟩ ⟨~*ing* out places of interest as they drove along⟩ (2) : to direct someone's attention to : call to someone's notice ⟨~*ed* out that several mistakes had been made⟩ ⟨~*ing* out the necessity of such a step⟩ ⟨let me ~ out that I knew nothing about the matter⟩ **b** *of a hunting dog* : to indicate the presence and place of (game) by stiffening into an intently rigid attitude with head and gaze directed toward the place so indicated ⟨a setter that ~s pheasant extraordinarily well⟩ **5 a** : to cause to be turned in a particular direction or toward a particular thing : DIRECT; *specif* : to cause the tip of (as a finger, stick, weapon, vehicle) to be extended, aimed, or turned in a particular direction or toward a particular thing ⟨~*ing* the gun at the target⟩ ⟨~*ed* the boat upstream⟩ **b** : to extend (a leg) in executing a point in dancing **6 a** : to taper and finish off the end of (a cable or rope) by interweaving the nettles **b** : to insert reef points through the eyelet holes of (a sail) **c** : to brace up sharp (the yards of a ship) **7** : to insert white hairs into (furs) to improve the appearance ⟨red fox dyed and ~*ed* to imitate silver fox⟩ **8** : to locate esp. in marble essential or selected points of (a piece of statuary) by drilling a hole to the proper depth at each point ⟨~*ing* a block of marble before beginning to cut a statue⟩ ~ *vi* **1 a** : to be of such a kind as to show or tend to show fairly convincingly the fact or probability of something specified : give or tend to give a fairly good indication of something specified — used with *to* or sometimes *toward* or *at* ⟨everything ~s to a bright future for them⟩ ⟨such symptoms ~ to a serious disorder⟩ **b** : to indicate the position or direction of something esp. by extending a finger toward the thing so indicated ⟨kept ~*ing* through the window⟩ — used with *at, to,* or *toward* before a specified object ⟨~*ed* at the map on the wall⟩ ⟨~*ed* to her brother and said he was the one⟩ **c** : to point game ⟨a dog that ~s well⟩ **2 a** : to lie extended, aimed, or turned in a particular direction or toward a particular thing ⟨a directional arrow that ~*ed* to the north⟩ ⟨the boat was ~*ing* upstream⟩ ⟨an indicator that ~*ed* toward an even number⟩ **b** : to execute a point in dancing **3** *of an abscess* : to come to a head **4** *of a ship* : to sail close to the wind — often used with *up* ⟨would ~ up better on the port tack —Nelson Hayes⟩ **5** *of a horse* : to rest a forefoot on the toe or hold a forefoot forward to remove the weight of the body from it **6** : to make special intensive preparations for meeting a particular sports opponent — used with *for* ⟨the team was ~*ing* for the game with the neighboring college⟩

**point after touchdown** : EXTRA POINT

**point at infinity** : an ideal mathematical point in projective geometry that preserves the magnitudes of all angles of a transformed plane

[1]**point-blank** \ˈ;ˈ\ *n, pl* **point-blanks** [prob. fr. [2]*point* + *blank* (bull's-eye)] **1 a** : the distance that a missile (as a bullet) flies along a nearly straight horizontal line from its starting point (as the barrel of a gun) before beginning to drop appreciably below that line **b** : the point at which a missile begins to drop appreciably below its initial nearly straight horizontal line of flight **2** : a shot aimed or fired straight at its target

[2]**point-blank** \"\ *adj* **1 a** (1) : marked by no appreciable drop below an initial nearly straight horizontal line of flight toward a target ⟨a projectile following a *point-blank* trajectory⟩ (2) : consisting of or lying within the distance within which something may be aimed or fired straight at a target without having to allow for appreciable drop in the line of flight of the missile shot or to be shot ⟨estimated the *point-blank* range of the gun⟩ ⟨there were lions at *point-blank* range —*Newsweek*⟩ **b** : aimed or fired straight at a target ⟨a *point-blank* shot⟩ **2** : that is direct, plain, and unequivocal : BLUNT ⟨a *point-blank* refusal⟩

[3]**point-blank** \"\ *adv* **1 a** (1) : with aim directed straight toward a target; *esp* : with aim so directed on a horizontal plane ⟨fired *point-blank* at the traitor —Desmond Ryan⟩ (2) : without dropping appreciably below an initial nearly horizontal line of flight toward a target ⟨an arrow whistling *point-blank* toward the bull's-eye⟩ **b** *archaic* (1) : in a straight direct line : DIRECTLY ⟨led him *point-blank* to the bed —M.L. Weems⟩ (2) : WHOLLY, ALTOGETHER ⟨so *point-blank* against the common sentiment —John Norris †1711⟩ **2** : in a direct, plain, and unequivocal manner : BLUNTLY ⟨asked her *point-blank* what she wanted⟩

**point count** *n* **1** : a method of evaluating the strength of a hand in the game of bridge by counting a set number of points for each high card held and often by adding points for long suits or short suits in the hand **2** : the value of a hand as evaluated by some method of point count

**point d'an·gle·terre** \ˌpwaⁿ,däⁿglə'te(ə)r\ *n, pl* **points d'angleterre** \"\ *usu cap A* [F, lit., lace from England] : a bobbin lace of Flemish origin made with applied bobbin or needlepoint designs

**point d'ap·pui** \ˌ;ˌda;pwē\ *n, pl* **points d'appui** [F, lit., point of support] : FOUNDATION, BASE; *esp* : a base from which a military operation can be carried on

**point de gaze** \-ˌdə;gäz, -gaz\ *n, pl* **points de gaze** [F, lit., lace of gauze] : a fine needlepoint lace of Belgian origin with a gauzy net ground ornamented with floral patterns

**point d'es·pagne** \-ˌde;spanyə\ *n, pl* **points d'espagne** *usu cap E* [F, lit., lace from Spain] : a needlepoint lace of Spanish origin with usu. gold or silver threads or with heavy designs on a fine ground

**point d'es·prit** \-ˌde;sprē\ *n, pl* **points d'esprit** [F, lit., lace of spirit] : a fine bobbinet with scattered woven dots used esp. for curtains, dresses, or trimmings

[1]**point-device** \ˌpȯintdə;vīs\ *adj, archaic* [ME (*at*) *point devis*, fr. *at* + *point* + *devis* fixed, set, fr. MF, fr. L *divisus*, past part. of *dividere* to divide — more at DIVIDE] : marked by punctilious often fussy attention to detail : METICULOUS ⟨*point-device* in its accouterments —J.L.Lowes⟩

[2]**point-device** \"\ *adv, archaic* : with punctilious often fussy attention to detail : METICULOUSLY ⟨was dressed *point-device* —Sir Walter Scott⟩

**point d'hon·grie** \ˌpwaⁿ,dōⁿ;grē\ *n, pl* **points d'hongrie** *usu cap H* [F, lit., lace from Hungary] : an embroidery of zigzag designs worked in bright graduated colors and formerly much used in canvas work esp. for upholstery and rugs

**point duty** *n, Brit* : the directing of traffic by a policeman stationed typically at an intersection — compare POINTSMAN

**pointe** \ˈpwaⁿt, ˈpwant\ *n* -S [F, lit., point (sharp end) — more at [1]POINT] **1** *ballet* : the extreme tip of the toe **2** *ballet* : a position of balance on the extreme tip of the toe

[1]**point·ed** \ˈpȯintəd\ *adj* [ME, partly fr. *point* + *-ed*; partly fr. past part. of *pointen* to point — more at POINT] **1 a** : tapering to or ending in an esp. sharp point ⟨a ~ stick⟩ ⟨~ rocks jutting up from the surf⟩ **b** (1) *of an arch* : having a pointed crown ⟨Gothic architecture is characterized by the ~ arch⟩ (2) : marked by the use of the pointed arch ⟨~ architecture⟩ **2 a** : that is made so evident as to be quite conspicuous : made quite obvious ⟨her ~ lack of concern over what happened to him⟩ **b** : made quite unmistakable in meaning, reference, or application : clearly aimed or directed ⟨was disturbed by such ~ remarks⟩ ⟨a ~ allusion to what was going on⟩ **3 a** : PUNCTILIOUS, PRECISE, EXACT ⟨is described with ~ correctness —W.E.Gladstone⟩ **b** : keenly intent : CONCENTRATED, DETAILED ⟨would call for more ~ attention to the problems of colonial government —*Current Biog.*⟩ ⟨no guide to nature, humanity and much of history is more ~ than art —J.F.Dobie⟩ **4 a** : full of life and piquancy : LIVELY, ZESTFUL, STIMULATING, TANGY ⟨with just enough Irish malice to make the narrative ~ —H.J.Laski⟩ **b** : very much to the point : INCISIVE, TERSE : full of punch and effectiveness : EPIGRAMMATIC ⟨~ wit⟩ ⟨the writing is ~, vigorous —C.B.Hagan⟩ — **point·ed·ness** *n* -ES

[2]**pointed** *adj* [short for *appointed*, past part. of *appoint*] *obs* : SET, FIXED ⟨I'll not be tied to hours nor ~ times —Shak.⟩

**point·ed·ly** *adv* **1** : in a pointed manner : SIGNIFICANTLY: as **a** : in such a way as to make something clearly evident or conspicuous ⟨differing ~ therefore from the U. S. —Frank Gorrell⟩ **b** : in such a way as to make some meaning, reference, or application quite unmistakable ⟨have been so ~ uninterested —Claire Sterling⟩ ⟨~ ignored a question —Mary K. Hammond⟩ **c** : in a way that is incisive, terse, and very much to the point ⟨because it bears trenchantly and ~ on our life today —Leslie Rees⟩ ⟨discussed this situation more ~ —E.D. Canham⟩ **2** *dial* : by all means : very much : SURELY, CERTAINLY, INDEED ⟨I'm ~ shamed —Maristan Chapman⟩

**point·er** \ˈpȯintə(r)\ *n* -S [[2]*point* + *-er*] **1 a** : one that furnishes something with points: as (1) : one that points furs (2) : one that stitches points on gloves **b** : one that causes something to have a tapering end or sharp point: as (1) : one that sharpens pencils, drills, or similar objects (2) : one that tapers the teeth of combs or the ends of rods, springs, or similar objects **2** : one that indicates something : one that points out something: as **a** : a light tapered rod used typically by teachers or lecturers to call attention to details (as of material appearing on a blackboard) **b** : one of the hands of a clock or watch **c** : the indicator of a pair of scales or some similar indicator **d** : STATION POINTER **3** : a tool with a pointed end: as **a** : a bricklayer's tool used for clearing out old mortar in pointing **b** : a tool used in engraving, cutting, or boring **4** : one that points something in a particular direction; *specif* : one that raises a gun to a prescribed elevation in fixing it on a target — compare TRAINER **5 a** : a large strong slender smooth-haired gundog of Spanish origin that has usu. a white coat spotted here and there with brown or black patches, a long wide head with a marked depression between the prominent eyebrows and broad nose, soft long ears hanging close to the cheeks, and a moderately long tapered tail and that scents out and indicates the presence of game by stiffening into an intently rigid attitude with head and gaze directed toward the game and typically with the tail stretched out rigidly and with a forepaw raised and bent backward **b pointers** *pl* : MEN — distinguished from *setters* **6** : SNAKEPIECE **7** : POINT MAN **8** : a piece of information that is esp. helpful in learning to do or accomplish something : a useful suggestion or hint : TIP ⟨gave him some ~s on how to run the business⟩

**pointes** *pl of* POINTE

**point-event** \ˈ;ˌ;\ *n* : an event without extension in space or time

**point·ful** \ˈpȯintfəl\ *adj* : that is to the point : that has point : that has meaning, relevance, or force ⟨made a ~ remark⟩ — **point·ful·ly** \-fəlē\ *adv* — **point·ful·ness** \-fəlnəs\ *n* -ES

**point function** *n* : a variable (as the temperature of the air) each value of which is associated with and determined by the position of some point in space

**pointier** *comparative of* POINTY

**pointiest** *superlative of* POINTY

**poin·til·lage** \ˌpwaⁿtē;(y)äzh, -ant-\ *n* -S [F, fr. *pointiller* + *-age*] : POINTILLISM

**poin·til·lé** \-(y)ā\ *adj* [F, fr. past part. of *pointiller* to mark with dots, stipple, fr. *point* dot — more at POINT] : decorated with closely spaced usu. gold dots made with a pointed tool ⟨a ~ leather book binding⟩

**poin·til·lism** *also* **poin·til·lisme** \ˈ;tē,(y)izəm, -tᵊl,i-\ *n* -S [F *pointillisme*, fr. *pointiller* + *-isme* -ism] : the practice or technique of applying dots or tiny strokes of color elements to a surface so that when seen from a distance the dots or strokes blend luminously together

**poin·til·list** *also* **poin·til·liste** \-tē(y)əst, -tᵊlə-\ *n* -S [F *pointilliste*, fr. *pointiller* + *-iste* -ist] : one that uses pointillism

**poin·til·lis·tic** \ˌ;tē;(y)istik, -tᵊl;is-\ *adj* : of, relating to, or typical of pointillism or pointillists

**pointing** *n* -S [partly fr. [1]*point* + *-ing*; partly fr. gerund of [2]*point*] **1 a** : punctuation marks **b** : vowel points or other differentiating marks used in some Semitic languages **c** : marks used in the texts of plainsong to indicate a division of verses corresponding to the musical division **2** : the material (as mortar) used in pointing something (as a brick wall) **3** : HEAD 20a **4** : a line of ornamental stitchwork (as on the back of a glove) **5** : a stride which is esp. characteristic of the Thoroughbred horse and in which extension is emphasized rather than flexion

**point-instant** \ˈ;ˌ;\ *n* -S : the smallest unit of space-time

**point lace** *n* : NEEDLEPOINT 1

**point·less** \ˈpȯintləs\ *adj* **1 a** : lacking a point : having a blunt end : UNPOINTED ⟨my pencils are all ~ —Charles Dickens⟩ **b** : lacking any scored points : SCORELESS ⟨the game ended in a ~ tie⟩ **2 a** : devoid of meaning, relevance, or purpose : SENSELESS ⟨a ~ remark⟩ ⟨a ~ life⟩ **b** : devoid of effectiveness, force, or punch : VAPID, FLAT, INSIPID ⟨~ attempts to be funny⟩ — **point·less·ly** *adv* — **point·less·ness** *n* -ES

**point·let** \ˈpȯintlət\ *n* -S [[1]*point* + *-let*] : a very small point ⟨the ~ of a leaf⟩

**point man** *or* **point rider** *n* : one of the cowboys riding on each side of the front of a trail herd

**point mutation** *n* : GENE MUTATION

**point of addition** : a dot or similar mark used in medieval music to indicate an increase in the time value of a note

**point of aim** : an auxiliary mark or marker at which a target archer sights the arrow so as to achieve correct elevation

**point of articulation** : an immovable or relatively immovable part (as the upper teeth or lower lip) of the vocal tract that a more movable part (as the tongue) approaches or comes into contact with in an articulation

**point of departure** : a starting point esp. in a discussion ⟨chose conditions in the slums as a *point of departure*⟩

**point of impact 1** : the point at which the projectile first strikes the ground or other material object **2** : the point at the center of the pattern of a shot charge fired from a shotgun

**point of inflection** : a point on a curve that separates an arc concave upward from one concave downward and vice versa

**point of view 1 a** (1) : a particular position (as in space, time, development) from which something is considered or evaluated : STANDPOINT, VIEWPOINT ⟨from the *point of view* of a child, many things in the adult world are mysterious⟩ (2) : a particular manner of considering or evaluating something ⟨has a very peculiar *point of view*⟩ **b** : a particular reasoned mental attitude toward or opinion about something ⟨asked him to indicate his *point of view*⟩ **2** : a particular indicated matter ⟨which from the *point of view* of climate and soils is best suited to agriculture —W.B.Fisher⟩

**point plat** \(ˈ)pwaⁿ ;plä\ *n* [F, lit., flat lace] : FLAT POINT

**point rail** *n* : a tapering rail used in a railroad frog to permit switching

**points** *pl of* POINT, *pres 3d sing of* POINT

**point-set** \ˈ;ˌ\ *adj, of printing type* : cast with a width measurable in points — compare UNIT-SET

**points·man** \ˈpȯintsmən\ *n, pl* **pointsmen 1** *Brit* : a policeman stationed typically at an intersection to direct traffic — compare POINT DUTY **2** *Brit* : SWITCHMAN

**point source** *n* : a source of light or other radiation that is concentrated at a point

**point system** *n* **1** : a system of wage payment in which work is subdivided into units equivalent to the number of minutes that a task should take and the payment of the worker on the basis of the number of points of work accomplished in a given length of time — called also *Bedaux system* **2** : a system in which printing type and spacing materials are made in sizes that are exact multiples of the point

**point-to-point** \ˌ;ˈ;ˈ\ *n* -S : a cross-country horse race from one specified point to another with each rider free to choose his own course : STEEPLECHASE

point turc

**point turc** *or* **point turque** \(ˈ)pwaⁿ ;tərk\ *n, pl* **points turc** *or* **points turque** [F *point turc*, lit., Turkish lace] : an embroidery stitch done with very fine thread and a coarse needle which in passing through the fabric leaves a hole after the thread is drawn tight to resemble hemstitching and used esp. on curved lines (as in appliqué) where no threads can be drawn

**pointy** \'pȯintē\ *adj, usu* -ER/-EST [[1]*point* + *-y*] **1 :** coming to a rather sharp point **:** quite pointed ⟨a small, merry-looking man with a ~ nose —A.J.Liebling⟩ **2 :** having parts that stick out sharply here and there **:** marked by protruding points ⟨~ little firs —Jack Kerouac⟩

**pois** *pl of* POI

[1]**poise** \'pȯiz\ *vb* -ED/-ING/-S [ME *poisen* (also, to weigh), fr. MF *pois-*, stem of *peser*, fr. L *pensare* to weigh, ponder, consider — more at PENSIVE] *vt* **1** *archaic* **:** to weigh mentally **:** CONSIDER, PONDER, DELIBERATE ⟨would have seen him turn crimson in *poising* the question —A.W.Kinglake⟩ **2 :** BALANCE: **a** *archaic* **:** to bring into equilibrium with something else ⟨who ~*s* and proportions sea and land —William Cowper⟩ **b** *obs* **:** OFFSET, COUNTERBALANCE ⟨two contrary winds ~ each other —Henry Stubbe⟩ **c** (1) **:** to hold or carry in equilibrium **:** hold or carry steadily or evenly ⟨walked along gracefully with a water jar *poised* on her head⟩ ⟨*poised* a plate on the end of his finger⟩ **:** cause to be evenly or motionlessly supported or suspended ⟨for an instant the gull hung *poised* in the sky⟩ **:** hold supported or suspended without motion ⟨*poised* her fork and gave her guest a knowing look —Louis Bromfield⟩ ⟨masses of ice are *poised* at one moment and the next come crashing down —John Hunt & Edmund Hillary⟩ (2) **:** to keep (as something that is supported or suspended) in a steady position **:** keep from going one way or the other **:** STABILIZE ⟨the nonchalance with which the steersman *poised* the canoe —Ernest Beaglehole⟩ **d :** to hold or carry (as the head) in a particular way ⟨*poised* her head disdainfully —G.B. Shaw⟩ **3 :** to draw up into readiness **:** put into a position or attitude of readiness ⟨*poised* their armies for the battle⟩; *esp* **:** BRACE ⟨*poised* themselves for the ordeal awaiting them⟩ ~ *vi* **1 :** to become drawn up into readiness for something ⟨knew that they were *poising* for the encounter⟩ **2 :** HOVER ⟨the hawk *poised* momentarily and then struck⟩ **syn** see STABILIZE

[2]**poise** \"\ *n* -S [ME *poyse*, fr. MF *pois*, fr. L *pensum* weight, fr. neut. of *pensus*, past part. of *pendere* to weigh — more at PENDANT] **1 a** *obs* **:** HEAVINESS **b :** a definite mass (as a movable sliding block on a scale) used for its weight **2 a :** BALANCE, EQUILIBRIUM ⟨a watch spring in perfect ~⟩ ⟨a ~ between widely divergent impulses —F.R.Leavis⟩ **b** *archaic* **:** suspension of movement or activity ⟨the ~ of the flood tide . . . was only of brief duration —Frederick Leighton⟩ **3 a** (1) **:** easy composure of manner marked esp. by assurance and gracious dignity ⟨is a woman of ~ and charm⟩ **:** tranquil self-possession and self-confidence ⟨never lost his ~ under any circumstances⟩ ⟨have the ~ and security that goes with independence —W.F. McDermott⟩ ⟨are old enough to face them with a certain ~ —Bertrand Russell⟩ (2) **:** TRANQUILLITY, CALM, SERENITY ⟨without disturbing the ~ of a drawing room —Van Wyck Brooks⟩ ⟨is imperatively needed to give ~ to the nerves —Havelock Ellis⟩ ⟨known for his accomplishments, his ~ of mind, and his invariable courtesy —Edward Breck⟩ **b :** a particular way of carrying oneself **:** BEARING, CARRIAGE ⟨noted her very distinctive ~⟩ **syn** see BALANCE, TACT

[3]**poise** \'pwäz\ *n* -S [F, after Jean Louis Marie *Poiseuille* †1869 Fr. physician and anatomist] **:** a cgs absolute unit of viscosity that is equal to one dyne-second per square centimeter

**poised** *adj* [fr. past part. of [2]*poise*] **:** having poise: **a :** marked by balance or equilibrium ⟨as ~ as the flight of a gull —J.L. Lowes⟩ **b :** marked by easy composure of manner or bearing ⟨was perfectly ~ and sure of himself on all official occasions —E.H.Spicer⟩

**pois·er** \'pȯizə(r)\ *n* -S **1 :** one that poises; *specif* **:** one who balances the mass of a watch balance wheel about its staff **2 :** [3]HALTER

**poi·seuille's law** \(')pwä¦zə(r)z-, -zə̄z-\ *n, usu cap P* [after Jean L. M. *Poiseuille* †1869 French physician] **:** a statement in physics: the velocity of flow of a liquid through a capillary tube varies directly as the pressure and the fourth power of the diameter of the tube and inversely as the length of the tube and the coefficient of viscosity

**pois green** \'pwä-\ *n* [*pois* fr. F, pea, fr. L *pisum;* intended as part trans. of F *pois vert*, lit., green pea — more at PEA] **:** a grayish to moderate yellow green that is yellower and darker than mytho green and yellower and very slightly lighter than gage green

[1]**poi·son** \'pȯizᵊn, *dial* 'pīz-\ *n* -S [ME *poisoun*, *poison*, fr. OF *poison* drink, philter, poisonous drink, poison, fr. L *potion-*, *potio* drink, fr. *potus* (past part. of *potare* to drink) + *-ion-*, *-io* -ion — more at POTABLE] **1 a :** a substance (as a drug) that in suitable quantities has properties harmful or fatal to an organism when it is brought into contact with or absorbed by the organism **:** a substance that through its chemical action usu. kills, injures, or impairs an organism ⟨strychnine, carbon monoxide, and other ~*s*⟩ — compare ECONOMIC POISON, PESTICIDE, TOXIN, VENOM **b** (1) **:** something destructive or harmful to the success, prosperity, or happiness of something else ⟨were generally considered boxoffice ~ —Edith Isaacs⟩ ⟨are plain political ~ —J.T.Norman⟩ (2) **:** something that undermines, interferes with, or blights the progress, activity, or welfare of something else ⟨her life was ruined by the ~ of lying gossip⟩ (3) **:** something that causes something else to become tainted, corrupted, rotten, or perverted ⟨the ~ of bad example⟩ **c** (1) **:** something obnoxious, disgusting, or nauseating ⟨most stage juveniles, especially in musicals, are pure ~ —John Mason Brown⟩ (2) **:** something totally at variance with one's tastes or inclinations **:** an object of aversion or abhorrence **:** something to be avoided ⟨diversions of that kind were pure ~ to him⟩ **2** *slang* **:** alcoholic drink; *esp* **:** strong liquor **3 :** a substance that inhibits the activity of another substance or the course of a reaction or process (as catalytic action, fluorescence, thermionic emission, nuclear fission) ⟨a catalyst ~⟩ ⟨fission ~*s*⟩ **4** *or* **poison circle** *or* **poison spot :** a game in which each player of a circle of players tries to force another into a designated central area so as to make him it

**syn** VENOM, VIRUS, TOXIN, BANE: POISON now refers to any matter that is lethal or very noxious (as strychnine, arsenic, carbon monoxide) or to anything thought of as having a similar effect ⟨a populace whose emotional life has been drugged by the sugared *poison* of pseudo art —Roger Fry⟩ ⟨the nineteenth century had brought this new *poison* of mystic tribalism into the common life of Europe —Stringfellow Barr⟩ VENOM may refer to a poison interjected with fierce malignant hostility ⟨the *venom* of the rattlesnake⟩ VIRUS may refer to a submicroscopic agency of infection working with insidious deadliness or deleteriousness ⟨the *virus* of infantile paralysis⟩ TOXIN, less used in figurative senses than others in this group, may refer to a destructive toxic substance generated within a plant or animal body ⟨the bacterial *toxins*, such as those of the organisms causing diphtheria, tetanus and botulism —W.A.Hagan⟩ BANE may apply to any cause of ruin, destruction, or great tribulation; in compounds it may designate poisonous substances and things ⟨the military mania which has been the *bane* of some countries⟩ ⟨rats*bane*⟩

[2]**poison** \"\ *vb* **poisoned; poisoned; poisoning** \-z(ᵊ)niŋ\ **poisons** [ME *poisonen*, fr. *poisoun*, *poison*, n.] *vt* **1 a** (1) **:** to give poison to **:** kill or injure by means of poison ⟨was accused of ~*ing* her husband⟩ (2) **:** to put poison on or into ⟨~*ing* an arrow⟩ ⟨~*ed* the water⟩ (3) **:** to taint, infect, or impregnate with poison ⟨~*ed* the air with its fumes⟩ **b :** to produce an abnormal condition in through the action of a poison or toxic substance ⟨blood that has been ~*ed* by infection⟩ **2 a** (1) **:** to exert a baneful influence on **:** CORRUPT, VITIATE, PERVERT ⟨~*ing* minds with evil propaganda⟩ (2) **:** to cause to be unfavorably disposed toward a person ⟨malicious tales of that kind ~*ed* nearly everyone against him⟩ **b** (1) **:** to destroy, harm, or otherwise affect adversely as if by poison ⟨aching in mind and body, ~*ed* with fatigue —Felix Riesenberg⟩ (2) **:** to taint, infect, or impregnate as if with poison ⟨even such harmless pleasures were ~*ed* with suspicion —Virginia Woolf⟩ **c :** to make unfit (as for some indicated or implied use or purpose) through the addition or application of something ⟨~*ed* the soup with too much salt⟩ ⟨parts of it were so dry and ~*ed* with alkali dust that no life existed there —S.H.Adams⟩ **3 a :** to inhibit the activity of (as a catalyst) — compare PROMOTE **b :** to inhibit the course or occurrence of (as a reaction or phenomenon) ~ *vi* **:** to put poison into or on something ⟨was in the lower field next day, ~*ing* —G.S. Perry⟩

[3]**poison** \"\ *adj* [[1]*poison*] **1 :** POISONOUS ⟨a ~ plant⟩ ⟨a ~ drink⟩ **:** VENOMOUS ⟨talk about ~ tongues —Dan Wickenden⟩ **2 :** POISONED ⟨a ~ arrow⟩

[4]**poison** \"\ *adv, chiefly dial* **:** EXTREMELY, VERY ⟨was ~ pretty —Maristan Chapman⟩ ⟨felt ~ mean that week —Fitz Farrell⟩ ⟨is a ~ bad world —R.L.Stevenson⟩

**poison arum** *n* **:** a plant (*P. virginica*) of the genus *Peltandra*

**poison ash** *n* **1 :** POISON SUMAC **2 :** a torchwood (*Amyris balsamifera*) of the West Indies **3 :** FRINGE TREE

**poison bean** *n* **1 :** a shrub (*Daubentonia drummondii*) of the family Leguminosae that is found in the southern part of the U. S. and that bears poisonous seeds — called also *rattlebush* **2 :** a seed of the poison bean shrub

**poisonberry** \'⸗⸗- — *see* BERRY\ *n* **:** any of several plants with small inedible or poisonous fruits: as **a :** a shrub of the genus *Cestrum* **b :** a West Indian shrub (*Bourreria succulenta*) of the family Boraginaceae with small flowers in corymbose cymes **c :** POISONBERRY TREE **d :** BITTERSWEET 2 a

**poisonberry tree** *n* **:** an Australian shrub (*Pittosporum phillyraeoides*) with bitter berries that are reputed poisonous and herbage that is used for fodder

**poison black cherry** *n* **:** the fruit of the belladonna

**poison bulb** *n* **:** a southern African blood lily (*Haemanthus toxicarius*) with a reputedly poisonous bulb

**poison bush** *n* **:** any of several poisonous or unwholesome Australian plants: **a :** a leguminous plant of *Gastrolobium* or the related genus *Gompholobium* with poisonous herbage **b :** a poisonous desert shrub (*Myoporum deserti*) **c :** POISON PEA; *esp* **:** DARLING PEA **d :** a tree (*Trema cannabina*) that is injurious to livestock because of the large amount of fiber it contains

**poison camas** *n* **:** a common perennial death camas (*Zigadenus nuttallii*); *broadly* **:** DEATH CAMAS

**poison circle** *n* **:** POISON 4

**poison claw** *n* **:** the maxilliped of a chilopod

**poison creeper** *n* **:** a poison ivy (*Rhus taxicodendron*)

**poison cup** *n* **:** DEATH CUP

**poison darnel** *n* **:** BEARDED DARNEL

**poison dogwood** *or* **poison elder** *n* **:** POISON SUMAC

**poi·son·er** \-z(ᵊ) nə(r)\ *n* -S [ME, fr. *poisonen* to poison + *-er*] **:** one that poisons

**poison fish** *n* **1 :** any of several fishes that have venomous spines **2 :** any of several fishes whose flesh contains poisonous alkaloids

**poison flag** *n* **:** any of several American irises (as *Iris versicolor*) with blue flowers

**poison flour** *n* **:** arsenic trioxide obtained by sublimation in a floury state

**poison flower** *n* **:** BITTERSWEET 2 a

**poisonful** *adj, obs* **:** POISONOUS

**poison gas** *n* **:** a poisonous gas or a liquid or solid giving off poisonous vapors designed (as in chemical warfare) to kill, injure, or disable by inhalation or contact

**poison hemlock** *n* **1** *or* **poison parsley :** a large branching biennial poisonous herb (*Conium maculatum*) native to Eurasia and Africa and adventive in No. America that has large decompound leaves with lanceolate pinnatifid leaflets, involucels of narrow bracts, and white flowers **2 :** any of several plants of the genus *Cicuta*

**poi·son·ing** \'pȯiz(ᵊ)niŋ, -nēŋ, *dial* 'pīz-\ *n* -S [ME *poysenynge*, fr. gerund of *poisonen* to poison — more at POISON] **:** the abnormal condition produced by a poison or toxic substance ⟨suffering from acute ~⟩

**poison ivy** *n* **1 :** any of several American plants of the genus *Rhus* of climbing, shrubby, or occas. arborescent habit that have ternate leaves, greenish flowers, and white berries and that produce an acutely irritating oil which causes a usu. intensely itchy skin rash when the herbage esp. if bruised is touched; *esp* **:** a climbing plant (*R. radicans*) that is esp. common in the eastern and central U.S. — see POISON OAK **2** *or* **poison laurel :** MOUNTAIN LAUREL 1

**poison milkweed** *n* **:** FLOWERING SPURGE

**poison nut** *n* **:** NUX VOMICA

**poison oak** *n* **:** any of several shrubby sumacs that are poison ivies: as **a :** POISON SUMAC **b :** a bushy poison ivy (*Rhus diversiloba*) of the Pacific coast **c :** a bushy poison ivy (*Rhus quercifolia*) of the southeastern U.S.

**poi·son·ous** \'pȯiz(ᵊ)nəs, *dial* 'pīz-\ *adj* **1 a :** that is poison or that has the qualities or effects of poison ⟨a ~ substance⟩ ⟨a stifling ~ atmosphere —Joseph Conrad⟩ **b** (1) **:** that contains or is mixed with or impregnated with poison ⟨a ~ liquid⟩ ⟨~ fumes⟩ (2) **:** that has been dipped into or touched or smeared with poison ⟨avoided the ~ tip of the arrow⟩ **2 a :** that destroys, harms, interferes with, or otherwise adversely affects in a manner suggestive of poison ⟨a double life that would be ~ to their continued happiness⟩ ⟨is ~ to any attempt at dispassionate thinking —*Saturday Rev.*⟩ **b :** that taints, corrupts, perverts, or prejudices esp. in an evil or insidious way ⟨the ~ effects of such deception⟩ ⟨secret spreading of ~ propaganda —F.D.Roosevelt⟩ **3 :** viciously spiteful **:** full of malice **:** VENOMOUS, MALIGNANT, MALEVOLENT ⟨~ slander⟩ ⟨gave her a ~ look⟩ ⟨the most ~ hostility —Dorothy C. Fisher⟩ ⟨wrote two ~ pamphlets which preserve the gossip and scandal of the day —R.W.Southern⟩ **4 :** altogether disagreeable ⟨was in a ~ temper —Ngaio Marsh⟩ **:** OBNOXIOUS, LOATHSOME, NAUSEATING ⟨thought the weather was positively ~⟩ ⟨such children in literature are often pretty ~ —Orville Prescott⟩ — **poi·son·ous·ly** *adv* — **poi·son·ous·ness** *n* -ES

**poison out** *vt* **:** to put poison into (a body of water) so as to destroy or stupefy fishes ⟨was *poisoned out* and all rough fishes were destroyed —*Report: W. Va. Conservation Commission*⟩

**poison parsnip** *n* **1 :** WILD PARSNIP **2 :** SPOTTED COWBANE

**poison pea** *n* **:** any of several plants of the genus *Swainsona* — compare DARLING PEA

**poison-pen** \¦⸗⸗¦⸗\ *adj* **1 :** venomously written **:** written with malice and spite ⟨*poison-pen* brochures —J.R.Carlson⟩; *esp* **:** written usu. anonymously and with the intention of seriously harming or destroying another's reputation ⟨writing a *poison-pen* letter in disguised handwriting to the police —Georg Mann⟩ **2 :** marked by or given to poison-pen writing ⟨a *poison-pen* writer⟩

**poison rye grass** *n* **:** BEARDED DARNEL

**poisons** *pl of* POISON, *pres 3d sing of* POISON

**poison sego** *n* **:** DEATH CAMAS

**poison spot** *n* **:** POISON 4

**poison sumac** *n* **:** a smooth American swamp sumac (*Rhus vernix*) that has pinnate leaves and greenish flowers succeeded by greenish white berries and that produces an irritating oil like that of poison ivy and a lacquer resembling Japanese lacquer — called also *poison ash, poison dogwood*

**poison tobacco** *n* **:** HENBANE 1 a

**poison tree** *n* **1 :** BLIND-YOUR-EYES **2 :** POISON SUMAC **3 :** POISONWOOD 1

**poison vetch** *n* **:** any of several plants of the genus *Astragalus* that are poisonous to livestock — see LOCOWEED

**poison vine** *n* **:** POISON IVY

**poisonweed** \'⸗⸗,⸗\ *n* **:** any of various plants of the western U. S. with a poisonous foliage: as **a :** any of several native or naturalized larkspurs **b :** any of several lupines — see LUPINOSIS

**poisonwood** \'⸗⸗,⸗\ *n* **1 :** a caustic or poisonous tree (*Metopium toxiferum*) of the family Anacardiaceae occurring in Florida and the West Indies and having compound leaves, greenish paniculate flowers, and orange-yellow fruits **2 :** CRABWOOD **3 :** POISON SUMAC **4 :** MANCHINEEL

**pois·son bleu** \¦pwa,sōⁿ¦blə(r·), -wä,s-, -lə̄\ *n* [F, lit., blue fish] **:** BLUE CAT

**pois·son distribution** \(')pwa|¦sōⁿ-, -wä|\ *n, usu cap P* [after Siméon D. *Poisson* †1840 French mathematician and statistician] **:** a distribution in statistics that is a good approximation to the binomial distribution when the probability of success in a single trial is very small and the number of trials is very large

**poisson's ratio** *also* **poisson ratio** *n, usu cap P* [after S. *Poisson*] **:** the ratio of transverse to longitudinal strain in a material under tension

**poi·trel** \'pȯi·trəl\ *n* -S [MF *poitral*, fr. L *pectorale* breastplate, fr. neut. of *pectoralis* of the chest, pectoral — more at PECTORAL] **:** a medieval often richly decorated piece of armor used to protect the breast of a horse

**poi·vrade** \pwȧvrȧd\ *or* **poivrade sauce** *n* -S [F, fr. MF, fr. *poivre* pepper (fr. L *pipr-*, *piper*) + *-ade* — more at PEPPER] **:** a peppery sauce

**poize** *obs var of* POISE

**po·joa·que** \pō'(h)wäkē\ *n, pl* **pojoaque** *or* **pojoaques** [Sp, of AmerInd origin] **1 :** a Tanoan people formerly found in New Mexico **2 :** a member of the Pojoaque people

**po·kal** \pō'käl\ *n* -S [G, fr. It *boccale* mug, jug, jar, fr. LL *baucalis* vessel for cooling wine or water, fr. Gk *baukalis*, prob. of non-IE origin] **:** a large usu. covered goblet typically made of glass or silver

[1]**poke** \'pōk\ *n* -S [ME, fr. ONF *poke*, *poque*, of Gmc origin; akin to OE *pocca*, *pohha* bag, pocket, MD *poke* bag, MHG *pfoch* pouch, purse, ON *poki* pouch, OE *pocc* pock — more at POCK] **1 a** (1) *chiefly South & Midland* **:** BAG, SACK ⟨take the boys a ~ of candy —H.D.Skidmore⟩ (2) **:** a pouch or purse for carrying nuggets of gold or gold dust ⟨threw their thick ~*s* of gold carelessly onto the counter —E.B.Lung⟩ (3) *slang* **:** WALLET **b** *chiefly dial* **:** POCKET **2** *slang* **:** an accumulated sum of money **:** WAD ⟨spent his ~ —Chesley Wilson⟩ ⟨struck it rich and kept his ~ —*Time*⟩ **3 a** (1) **:** a swelling (as a goiter) on the neck (2) **:** a swelling appearing on sheep and associated with liver fluke infestation **b :** a disease caused by liver fluke infestation

[2]**poke** \"\ *vb* -ED/-ING/-S [ME *poken;* akin to MD *poken* to poke, stick, MLG *pōken* to stick with a knife, and perh. to OIr *būalaim* I strike] *vt* **1** *archaic* **:** INCITE, ROUSE **2 a** (1) **:** to prod or jab with or as if with the end of one's finger or the end of a stick or with the end of some similar object ⟨*poked* him in the ribs and grinned broadly⟩ ⟨*poked* the burlap bag with a broom handle⟩ (2) **:** to set into movement or push or urge along by means of prodding or jabbing ⟨all he had ever done was ~ a team or explore the trail or push cattle along —A.B. Guthrie⟩ (3) **:** to stir up (as the coals of a fire) with or as if with a poker ⟨staring into the fireplace and occasionally *poking* the glowing embers⟩ **b** (1) **:** PIERCE, STAB ⟨a straw man that had been *poked* through with a pitchfork⟩ (2) **:** to produce by piercing, stabbing, or jabbing ⟨*poked* a hole in the drum⟩ **c** (1) **:** to strike with the fist **:** HIT, PUNCH, SOCK ⟨*poked* him in the nose⟩ (2) **:** to deliver (a blow) with the fist ⟨first *poked* a right to the chin and then a left to the body⟩ ⟨threatened to ~ him one⟩ **3 a** (1) **:** to move, thrust, or shove esp. with a quick action or with sudden force ⟨*poked* his head round the corner —Dorothy Sayers⟩ (2) **:** to cause to be directed in a particular direction or toward a particular thing by or as if by thrusting or shoving ⟨had *poked* the head of a boat into the mud —Frederick Way⟩ ⟨*poked* his finger at his client —Willa Cather⟩ **b :** to cause to stick out **:** cause to project ⟨kept *poking* her head in and out of the cab window —Louis Bromfield⟩ **c :** to thrust forward in such a way as to be intrusive **:** interpose or interject in a prying or otherwise meddlesome manner **:** push forward obtrusively ⟨asked him not to ~ his nose into other people's business⟩ ⟨*poking* their great stupid faces into everything —*Times Lit. Supp.*⟩ **4 :** to confine in some stodgy poky place ⟨didn't want to stay *poked* up in that town⟩ ~ *vi* **1 a :** to make a prodding, jabbing, or thrusting movement esp. repeatedly ⟨walked up and down and *poked* among the rocks —John Masefield⟩ **b :** to strike out at something with or as if with the fist ⟨kept *poking* at him but never hit him⟩ ⟨cranks who ~ at the schools —W.L.Miller⟩ **2 a :** to go investigating, looking about, or rummaging through something inquisitively without much order or system ⟨went into the attic where they *poked* about among old boxes and trunks —Louis Bromfield⟩ ⟨they went everywhere, they *poked* into everything —G.W. Johnson⟩ ⟨if he cared to ~ about in his unconscious —Clifton Fadiman⟩ **b :** to pry into something in an intrusive or otherwise meddlesome way ⟨is notoriously hostile to people who go *poking* into his private affairs —Irving Howe⟩ **3 a :** to live in or stay about a stodgy place **:** live in or hang about a place pokily ⟨doesn't want to ~ around in that town any longer⟩ **b :** to move or act with marked slowness **:** move or act in a largely ineffective, desultory, or aimless way **:** PUTTER, DAWDLE ⟨watched the traffic *poking* along the road⟩ ⟨just *poked* around at home and didn't accomplish much⟩ ⟨talked for a while and then *poked* off⟩ **4 a** (1) **:** to become stuck out **:** undergo thrusting out **:** PROTRUDE ⟨saw his head *poking* through the window⟩ (2) **:** to become extended or thrust forward ⟨saw to it that the railroad *poked* down closer to Texas —S.E.Fletcher⟩ ⟨into the jumbled wilderness . . . ~ the beginnings of a fabulous highway —R.L.Neuberger⟩ **b :** to come into sight or notice esp. with real or apparent suddenness **:** be visible or noticeable by being extended above, beyond, or out of something ⟨bell towers ~ above the trees —*Yale Rev.*⟩ — **poke fun at :** to make fun of in a usu. lightly bantering way and esp. slyly or indirectly **:** make an object of usu. light ridicule or mockery **:** KID ⟨*poke fun at* some of the stuffed shirts who have the largest incomes —Bruce Bliven b. 1889⟩

[3]**poke** \"\ *n* -S **1 a :** a quick thrust **:** JAB, DIG ⟨felt a ~ in the ribs⟩ **b :** a blow with the fist **:** PUNCH ⟨gave him a ~ on the nose⟩ **2 a** (1) **:** SLOWPOKE (2) **:** an annoyingly stupid individual **:** DUMBBELL **b :** COWBOY 3a **3 :** a poky place ⟨wondered how people put up with living in a little ~ like that —Mary Lavin⟩ **4 :** a device designed to keep an animal (as a cow, horse) from breaking through or jumping over fences and consisting typically of a collar from which a rod or pole hangs down at an angle so as to extend ahead of the animal **5 a :** a projecting brim on the front of a woman's bonnet **b :** POKE BONNET

poke 4

[4]**poke** \"\ *n* -S [modif. of *puccoon*, *pakon* (in some Algonquian language of Virginia) any of various plants used for staining and dyeing, fr. *pak* blood] **:** POKEWEED

[5]**poke** \"\ *n* -S [by shortening] **:** SHITEPOKE

**pokeberry** \'⸗- — *see* BERRY\ *n* [[4]*poke* + *berry*] **1 :** POKEWEED **2 :** one of the berries of the pokeweed

**poke bonnet** *n* [[3]*poke* (brim)] **:** a woman's bonnet with a projecting brim at the front

**poke check** *n* [[3]*poke*] **:** an act or instance of attempting to knock the puck away from an opponent in ice hockey by jabbing or thrusting at it with the stick

**poke-easy** \'⸗,⸗⸗\ *n* -ES [[2]*poke*] *Midland* **:** one that moves about slowly and indolently and that is easy-going or lazy

**poke-in** \'⸗,⸗\ *n* -S [fr. *poke in*, v.] **:** STRANDER 2

**poke·lo·gan** \'pōk,lōgən\ *or* **poke·lo·ken** \-ōkən\ *n* -S [of Algonquian origin; akin to Ojibwa *pokenogun* stopping place, Malecite *pecelāygan* stopping place, Natick *pohki* open, clear] *NewEng* **:** a usu. stagnant inlet or marshy place branching off from a stream or lake

poke bonnet

**poke milkweed** *n* [[4]*poke*] **:** a milkweed (*Asclepias exaltata*) of the eastern U. S. with leaves resembling those of the pokeweed

**poke pudding** *n* [[1]*poke*] **:** POCK PUDDING

[1]**pok·er** \'pōkə(r)\ *n* -S [[2]*poke* + *-er*] **1 :** a rigid fairly heavy straight metal rod (as of iron, steel) that typically has one end fitted with or shaped into a handle and the other bent or hooked and that is usu. used for adjusting or stirring burning logs or coals (as in a fireplace) or similar burning material **2 :** a toothed rod attached to the bobbin rail of a spinning machine and used for giving an up-and-down movement to the bobbin rail

[2]**poker** \"\ *n* -S [prob. modif. of F *poque*, a card game somewhat similar to poker] **:** one of several card games (as draw poker, stud poker) in which a player bets that the value of the hand he holds is greater than the value of the hands held by the other players and in which each subsequent player must either equal or raise the bet already made or drop out of the game for

that deal and in which at the end of the betting the player

poker: hands in descending value: *1* royal flush, *2* straight flush, *3* four of a kind, *4* full house, *5* flush, *6* straight, *7* three of a kind, *8* two pairs, *9* one pair

holding the hand that has the highest value wins all that has been bet in that deal

**poker dice** *n pl* **1 :** dice usu. in sets of five with each one of the dice carrying on two or more of its faces the representation of a particular playing card (as the ace, king, queen, jack, ten, nine) instead of spots **2** *usu sing in constr* **:** one of several games which are played with poker dice or with regular dice and in which the object is to make and bet on winning combinations like those used in the game of poker

**poker face** *n* [²*poker*] **1 a** (1) **:** a face that does not reveal the feelings or thoughts of a person **:** a woodenly expressionless face **:** DEAD PAN ⟨conceals his emotions behind a *poker face* —P.G.Wodehouse⟩ (2) **:** a stolidly grave or solemn face ⟨they play their silly roles with *poker faces*⟩ **b :** one that has or that assumes a poker face ⟨asked why those *poker faces* had been invited to the party⟩ **2 :** stolid gravity or solemnity of manner ⟨wrote all this nonsense with a *poker face*⟩

**poker–faced** \ˈ⸗⸗¦⸗\ *adj* **1 a :** woodenly expressionless ⟨remained altogether *poker-faced* when he stepped before the judge⟩ **b :** stolidly grave or solemn ⟨described the escapade with *poker-faced* earnestness⟩ **2 :** marked by or showing a real or apparent lack of personal involvement or commitment **:** DETACHED, IMPERSONAL ⟨related every detail of the murder with *poker-faced* objectivity⟩

**pok·er·ish** \ˈpōk(ə)rish\ *adj* [fr. archaic E *poker* hobgoblin (prob. of Scand origin; akin to Norw *pokker* devil, ON *pūki*) + *-ish* — more at PUCK] *archaic* **:** that elicits a vague fear, dread, or awe **:** EERIE ⟨there is something ~ about a deserted dwelling, even in broad daylight —J.R.Lowell⟩

**pokeroot** \ˈ⸗,⸗\ *n* [⁴*poke* + *root*] **:** POKEWEED

**poker plant** *n* [¹*poker*] **:** an herb (*Kniphofia uvaria*) that is found in the southern part of Africa and that has a spike of orange-red or scarlet flowers

**poker spine** *n* **:** a stiff spinal column resulting from rheumatoid arthritis

**poker work** *n* **:** PYROGRAPHY

**pokes** *pl of* POKE, *pres 3d sing of* POKE

**poke salad** *n* [⁴*poke*] *chiefly Midland* **:** the cooked young shoots of pokeweed

**pokeweed** \ˈ⸗,⸗\ *n* [⁴*poke* + *weed*] **:** a tall coarse American perennial herb (*Phytolacca americana*) having young shoots that are edible, a thick fleshy poisonous root that yields emetic and purgative extracts, a smooth fairly succulent stem that ranges in color from green to purplish, large simple smooth leaves, small greenish white racemose flowers, and fleshy dark purple berries that contain poisonous seeds and yield emetic and purgative extracts and a crimson juice used in making an ink; *broadly* **:** a plant of the genus *Phytolacca*

**pokeweed family** *n* **:** PHYTOLACCACEAE

**pokey** *also* **poky** \ˈpōkē, -ki\ *n, pl* **pokeys** *also* **pokies** [alter. of earlier *pogie* workhouse, of unknown origin] *slang* **:** JAIL

**pok·i·ly** \ˈpōkəlē, -li\ *adv* **:** in a poky manner

**pok·i·ness** \-kēnəs, -kin-\ *n* -ES **:** the quality or state of being poky

**poking** *adj* [fr. pres. part. of ²*poke*] **:** PETTY, MEAN ⟨her face changed slowly from ~ suspicion to a brilliant . . . smile of welcome —Christopher Isherwood⟩

**poking stick** *n* **:** a small rod made of wood, bone, or metal and formerly used to stiffen the pleats of ruffs

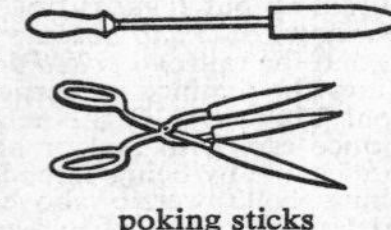

poking sticks

**pok·kah boeng** \ˈpäkə,bůŋ\ *n* [Jav, lit., damaged top] **:** a disease of sugarcane caused by an ascomycetous fungus (*Gibberella frejikuroi*) and marked by chlorosis and splitting of the young leaves and by rotting of the growing point

**po·ko·mam** \,pōkōˈmäm\ *n, pl* **pokomam** *or* **pokomams** *usu cap* **1 a :** an Indian people of southeastern Guatemala **b :** a member of such people **2 :** a Mayan language of the Pokomam people

**po·ko·mo** \pəˈkō(,)mō\ *n, pl* **pokomo** *or* **pokomos** *usu cap* **1 a :** a Bantu people of Kenya in Africa **b :** a member of such people **2 :** a Bantu language of the Pokomo people

**po·kon·chi** \pəˈkōnchē\ *n, pl* **pokonchi** *or* **pokonchis** *usu cap* **1 a :** an Indian people of north central Guatemala **b :** a member of such people **2 :** a Mayan language of the Pokonchi people

**poku** *var of* PUKU

**poky** *also* **pokey** \ˈpōkē, -ki\ *adj, usu* **pokier**; *usu* **pokiest** [²*poke* + *-y*] **1 a :** uncomfortably small or cramped and marked typically by lack of proper ventilation and lighting and by a generally unattractive appearance ⟨lived in a series of ~ houses, surrounded by a swarm of children —V.S. Pritchett⟩ ⟨~, hole-in-the-wall shops —Faubion Bowers⟩ ⟨inspected the cheerless, ~ rooms with their cheap furniture and threadbare carpets —Valentine Williams⟩ **b :** stagnating with general dullness and provincialism **:** STODGY, ONE-HORSE ⟨had no desire to remain in that ~ little town⟩ **2 a :** devoid of style, imagination, and taste **:** DOWDY ⟨was dressed in the *pokiest* way imaginable⟩ **b :** devoid of freshness, liveliness, or interest **:** UNSTIMULATING, DULL, DEAD ⟨is certainly a ~ place to go for a vacation⟩ ⟨has a ~ way of writing⟩ **3 a :** that is typical of a fuddy-duddy **:** prim and overly conservative **:** strait-laced and not up to date ⟨just a timid . . . ~ little creature worrying like a mole —Saul Bellow⟩ **b :** tediously concerned with what is obvious, trifling, or boring ⟨it feels merely ~ to say one thing more —William Empson⟩ **c :** not easily excited or aroused **:** ponderously phlegmatic ⟨is a ~ individual with little interest in the world about him⟩ **4 :** that moves or acts like a slowpoke **:** annoyingly slow **:** that pokes along ⟨infuriated with the ~ traffic⟩ ⟨is too ~ to get anything done efficiently⟩ ⟨asked her not to be so ~⟩

**pol** *abbr* **1** polar **2** polish; polished **3** political; politician; politics

**POL** *abbr* petroleum, oil, and lubricants

**po·la·bi·an** \pōˈläbēən\ *n* -S *usu cap* [*Polab* Polabian (of Slavic origin, akin to Pol *po* on and to Pol *Łaba* Elbe, river in Czechoslovakia and Germany) + *-an*] **1** *or* **po·lab** \pōˈläb\ **:** a member of a Slavic people formerly dwelling in the basin of the Elbe and on the Baltic coast of Germany **2 :** the extinct West Slavic language of the Polabians

**po·la·bish** \pōˈläbish\ *n* -ES *usu cap* [G *polabisch*, fr. *polabisch*, adj., being Polabian, fr. *polab-* Polabian (of Slavic origin; akin to Pol *po* on and to Pol *Łaba* Elbe) + *-isch* -ish (fr. OHG *-isc*)] **:** POLABIAN 2

¹**po·lac·ca** \pōˈlakə\ *n* -S [It, of unknown origin] **:** POLACRE

²**polacca** \"\ *n* -S [It, fr. fem. of *polacco* Polish, fr. Pol *Polak* Pole] **:** POLONAISE 2

¹**po·lack** *also* **po·lak** \ˈpō,läk *sometimes* -lak\ *n* -S *usu cap* [Pol *Polak*] **1** *obs* **:** ²POLE 1 ⟨the Moscovites discomfited by the *Polacks* in the battle —Thomas North⟩ **2 :** a person of Polish birth or descent — usu. used disparagingly

²**polack** *also* **polak** \"\ *adj, usu cap* **:** POLISH — usu. used disparagingly

**po·la·cre** \pōˈläkə(r)\ *n* -S [F, modif. of It *polacca*] **:** a ship with two or three masts usu. chiefly in one piece and square or sometimes lateen sails used in the Mediterranean

**po·lak** \pōˈläk\ *n* -S [origin unknown] **:** BALSA

**po·land** \ˈpōlənd\ *adj, usu cap* [fr. *Poland*, country in central Europe] **:** of or from Poland **:** of the kind or style prevalent in Poland **:** POLISH

**poland china** *also* **poland** *n, usu cap P&C* [fr. *Poland*, country in central Europe + *China*, country in Asia] **1 :** an American breed of large compact white-marked black swine of the lard type **2** -S **:** an animal of the Poland China breed

**po·land·er** \ˈpōləndə(r)\ *n* -S *cap* [*Poland*, country in central Europe + E *-er*] **:** a native or inhabitant of Poland **:** POLE

**pol·a·ni·sia** \,päləˈnizh(ē)ə, -isēə\ *n, cap* [NL, fr. *pol-* (fr. *poly-*) + ¹*anis-* + *-ia*; prob. fr. the large but varying number of stamens] **:** a genus of widely distributed herbs (family Capparidaceae) having palmate leaves and flowers with many stamens of unequal lengths — see CLAMMYWEED

¹**po·lar** \ˈpōlə(r)\ *adj* [NL *polaris*, fr. L *polus* pole + *-aris* -ar — more at POLE] **1 a :** of, relating to, or situated in the vicinity of one of the earth's two poles ⟨valley glaciers in both ~ and equatorial regions —Hugh Odishaw⟩ ⟨Antarctica is the only ~ continent —*Antarctica*⟩ **b** (1) **:** of, relating to, or suggesting the region around one of the earth's two poles ⟨~ weather⟩ ⟨~ waste⟩ ⟨~ night⟩ (2) **:** situated in, suitable for, coming from, or having the characteristics of the region around one of the earth's two poles ⟨~ air mass⟩ ⟨~ flying⟩ ⟨~ airplane⟩ ⟨~ sea⟩ **2 a :** of or relating to one or more physical poles (as of a sphere or magnet) ⟨~ magnetism⟩ **b :** having poles and as a result a property analogous to that of a magnet in that there is an associated directed line connecting the two poles at the ends of which line there are equal and opposite properties ⟨~ molecule⟩ **3 :** of, relating to, or like a polestar in serving as a guide ⟨~ principle⟩ ⟨this ~ idea provides the clue to both . . . systems —V.L.Parrington⟩ **4 :** diametrically opposite in nature, tendency, or action ⟨extreme and indefensible ~ positions —Hunter Mead⟩ ⟨for whom classicism and romanticism are not ~ but continuous —Harry Levin⟩ ⟨~ if not mutually hostile parties —Austin Warren⟩ **5 a :** ELECTROVALENT **b :** having a dipole ⟨~ compounds such as hydrogen chloride, ammonia, water⟩ ⟨alcohols and ketones are common ~ solvents⟩ **6 :** held to resemble a pole or axis around which all else revolves **:** PIVOTAL ⟨the ~ events of this informed study —Fraser Neiman⟩

²**polar** \"\ *n* -S **:** the secant of a conic through the points of tangency of the two tangents that can be drawn to the conic from an external point

**polar air** *n* **:** air that originates in a subpolar anticyclone and in regions somewhat south of those in which arctic air originates

**polar axis** *n* **1 :** the axis of rotation of an equatorial mounting that is set parallel to the earth's axis permitting a telescope to be turned in hour angle or right ascension **2 :** the reference line in polar coordinates from which the angle coordinate is measured

**polar bands** *n pl* **:** NOAH'S ARK 2

**polar bear** *n* **1 :** a large creamy white long-necked bear (*Thalarctos maritimus* or *Ursus maritimus*) inhabiting arctic regions of both hemispheres esp. along shores or among ice floes, having a long narrow skull and small molar teeth, and attaining a length of 9 feet and often a weight of 1000 pounds **2 :** a pale orange yellow to yellowish white — called also *Jersey cream*

polar bear

**polar body** *n* **1 :** any of the metachromatic granules concentrated at the ends of bacteria (as the diphtheria bacillus *Corynebacterium diphtheriae*) **2 :** one of the minute bodies or cells that separate from the oocyte during maturation

**polar cap** *n* **:** a white spot at each pole of the planet Mars varying in size with the Martian seasons

**polar capsule** *n* **:** a specialized cell of a cnidosporidian spore that produces a coiled thread that presumably serves as a temporary attachment organelle when the spore ruptures

**polar cattle** *n pl* **:** MUSK-OXEN

**polar circle** *n* **:** one of the two parallels of latitude each at a distance from a pole of the earth equal to the obliquity of the ecliptic or about 23 degrees 27 minutes — compare ANTARCTIC CIRCLE, ARCTIC CIRCLE

**polar code** *n* **:** a telegraph message code obtained by polarity reversal of a direct current

**polar coordinate** *n* **:** either of two numbers that locate a point in a plane by its distance from a fixed point along a line to the point and the angle this line makes with a fixed line

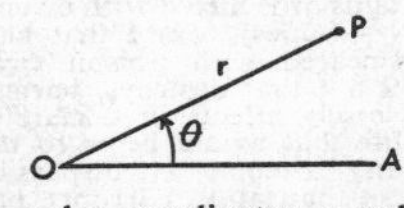


polar coordinates, *r* and *θ*; point, *P;* fixed point, *O;* distance from *O* to *P*, *r;* fixed line, *OA;* angle *AOP*, *θ*

**polar coordinate paper** *n* **:** graph paper laid out for plotting data in polar coordinates

**polar coordinate system** *n* **:** the series of points in a plane with each held to have a set of polar coordinates together with the reference elements and rules needed to locate each point by such a set of coordinates

**polar curve** *n* **:** a curve whose equation is in polar coordinates

**polar distance** *n* **:** the angular distance of any point on a sphere from one of its poles

**polar equation** *n* **:** an equation in polar coordinates

**polar fox** *n* **:** ARCTIC FOX

**polar front** *n* **:** the boundary between the cold air of a polar region and the warmer air of lower latitudes

**polar graph** *n* **:** a graph in polar coordinates

**polar hare** *n* **:** a large hare (*Lepus arcticus*) of arctic America related to the common European hares and almost completely white in winter

**po·lar·ic** \pōˈlarik\ *adj* **:** POLAR

**po·lar·im·e·ter** \,pōləˈrimәd·ə(r)\ *n* [ISV *polar* + *-i-* + *-meter*] **1 :** an instrument for determining the amount of polarization of light or the proportion of polarized light in a partially polarized ray **2 :** a polariscope equipped with graduated circles for measuring the amount of rotation of the plane of polarization esp. by liquids — compare OPTICAL ROTATION

**po·lar·i·met·ric** \pō¦larəˈme·trik\ *adj* [ISV *polarimetry* + *-ic*] **:** of or relating to polarimetry or the polarimeter ⟨~ equipment⟩

**po·lar·im·e·try** \,pōləˈrimə·trē\ *n* -ES [ISV *polar* + *-i-* + *-metry*] **:** the art or process of using the polarimeter (as in measuring the polarization of light)

**po·lar·i·scope** \pōˈlarə,skōp, pəˈ- *also* -ler-\ *n* [ISV *polar* + *-i-* + *-scope*] **1 :** an instrument for studying the properties of or examining substances in polarized light consisting essentially of two Nicol prisms or other polarizing devices — compare ANALYZER, POLARIZER **2 :** POLARIMETER 2

**po·lar·i·scop·ic** \⸗¦⸗⸗¦skäpik\ *adj* [ISV *polariscope* + *-ic*] **:** of, relating to, or obtained by the use of a polariscope ⟨~ observations⟩ — **po·lar·i·scop·i·cal·ly** \-pək(ə)lē\ *adv*

**po·lar·i·ty** \pōˈlarəd·ē, pəˈ-, -ətē, -i *also* -ler-\ *n* -ES [*polar* + *-ity*] **:** the quality or state of being polar: as **a :** the quality or condition inherent in a body that exhibits opposite properties or powers in opposite parts or directions or that exhibits contrasted properties or powers in contrasted parts or directions **:** the having of poles — compare MAGNET **b :** direction or attraction (as of inclination, feeling, or thought) toward a particular object **:** tendency or trend in a specific direction **c :** the particular either positive or negative state (as of a body) with reference to the two poles or to electrification **d** (1) **:** the observed axial differentiation of an organism or tissue into parts with distinctive properties or form (as head and tail or shoot and root) (2) **:** the underlying structural orientation held to account for orderly regeneration of lost parts of normal type in proper axial relation to the body as a whole (as in the growth of roots from the base of a cutting or the growth of a head at the anterior end of a planaria fragment) — compare GRADIENT CONCEPT **e** (1) **:** the principle, property, or condition of diametrical opposition (as in nature, tendency, or action) ⟨a cabinet system . . . produces a certain ~ in a nation —Ernest Barker⟩ ⟨the acute ~ between extreme passion and extreme control —Gilbert Highet⟩ (2) **:** an instance or case of such a relationship **:** something that is or is held to be diametrically opposite from something else **f** (1) **:** the relationship existing between two apparently opposed objects that nevertheless involve each other usu. by being dependent upon a mutual factor (as day and night or birth and death) — compare DIALECTIC 2b (2) **:** an instance or case of such a relationship

**polarity cap** *n* **:** an electric cap having knife-blade terminals so arranged that it can be inserted in its base or body in one way only

**po·lar·iz·abil·i·ty** \,pōlə,rīzəˈbiləd·ē\ *n* **1 :** the quality or state of being polarizable **2 :** the electric dipole moment per unit electric intensity of a material or a molecule

**po·lar·iz·able** \ˈ⸗⸗,rīzəbəl, ,⸗⸗ˈ⸗⸗⸗\ *adj* [ISV *polarize* + *-able*] **:** capable of being polarized ⟨an ion that can be easily distorted is highly ~⟩

**po·lar·iza·tion** \,pōlərəˈzāshən, -,rīˈ-\ *n* -S [F *polarisation*, fr. *polariser* to polarize + *-ation*] **1 :** the action of polarizing or the state of being polarized: as **a** (1) **:** the action or process of affecting light or other transverse wave radiation so that the vibrations of the wave are confined to a single plane — called also *linear polarization, plane polarization* (2) **:** the action or process of affecting light or other transverse wave radiation so that the vibrations may be regarded as confined to two mutually perpendicular planes with the components having a particular relationship between their phases and amplitudes — called also *circular polarization, elliptical polarization* (3) **:** the state of radiation affected by either of these processes **b :** the deposition of gas on one or both electrodes of an electrolytic cell increasing the resistance and setting up a counter electromotive force ⟨so-called dry cells are notably subject to ~⟩ — called also *electrolytic polarization* **c :** an effect resulting from the slight shifting of the electrons in a dielectric when placed in an electric field; *specif* **:** the electric moment thus produced per unit volume of dielectric — called also *dielectric polarization* **d :** an effect occurring in atoms and molecules wherein a slight relative shift of electrons and nuclei is produced in an electric field **e :** MAGNETIZATION — called also *magnetic polarization* **2 a :** division (as of groups, ideologies, systems, or forces) into two opposites ⟨~ . . . made between writing journalistically and writing creatively —J.T.Farrell⟩ **b :** the concentration about opposing extremes of usu. conflicting groups or interests formerly ranged on a continuum ⟨~ of all sorts of antagonisms —Isaac Deutscher⟩ ⟨as a result of this ~ between right and left, the middle-of-the-road parties . . . have lost strength —Louis Wasserman⟩ **c :** the division (as of a society or force) into two elements concentrated about opposing extremes ⟨a ~ of society into two classes —Reinhard Bendix⟩ ⟨the ~ of power between two implacable enemies —M.B.Travis⟩ ⟨the ~ of European politics between two political extremes —Barbara Ward⟩

**polarization figure** *n* **:** INTERFERENCE FIGURE

**po·lar·ize** \ˈpōlə,rīz\ *vb* -ED/-ING/-S [F *polariser*, fr. NL *polaris* polar + F *-iser* -ize] *vt* **1 :** to cause (as light waves) to vibrate in a definite pattern **:** affect by polarization **2 :** to give polarity to **:** bring into a state of physical polarization **3 :** to direct or orient toward a specific polar point (as an object or principle) ⟨the whole society was *polarized* toward financial success —W.P.Webb⟩ ⟨when a young person . . . has his interest *polarized* and his life altered —John Mason Brown⟩ **4 :** to produce or bring about a polarization of **:** subject to or cause to exhibit polarization ⟨the campaign . . . tends to ~ people —R.M.Goldman⟩ ⟨a conflict . . . which ~s political life —L.S.Feuer⟩ ⟨this tactic . . . *polarized* the political elements into Right and Left camps —*Current History*⟩ **5 :** to serve as a focal point for the concentration of ⟨a bell tower which . . . ~s a deep local pride —K.R. Greenfield⟩ ⟨groups . . . have *polarized* what is most reactionary in our economic and social system —*New Republic*⟩ ~ *vi* **1 a :** to gather or become concentrated about opposing extremes ⟨political forces had *polarized* into right and left extremes —Andrew Roth⟩ **b :** to serve as a focal point about which such concentration may take place **2 :** to adhere to or become directed toward a specific polar object or principle ⟨some individuals ~ negatively by turning into cynical sensualists —P.A.Sorokin⟩

**polarized–relay armature** *n* **:** an armature in which the moving part is a permanent magnet

**po·lar·iz·er** \ˈpōlə,rīzə(r)\ *n* -S **:** one that polarizes; *specif* **:** the part of a polariscope receiving and polarizing the light — compare ANALYZER

**polarizing angle** *n* **:** the angle at which unpolarized light or other electromagnetic radiation must be incident upon a nonmetallic surface for the reflected radiation to acquire maximum plane polarization — called also *Brewster angle;* compare BREWSTER'S LAW

**polarizing microscope** *n* **:** a microscope equipped to produce polarized light for the examination of an object

**polar lake** *n* **:** a lake in which the surface temperature never exceeds 4°C

**polar lights** *n pl* **1 :** AURORA BOREALIS **2 :** AURORA AUSTRALIS

**po·lar·ly** *adv* **:** in a polar manner, direction, or degree ⟨atomic submarines moving ~⟩

**polar maritime air** *n* **:** air coming orig. from polar regions but having humidity and temperature properties modified by passing over relatively warm oceans

**polar nucleus** *n* **:** either of two nuclei that fuse in the center of the embryo sac of a seed plant to form the primary endosperm nucleus

**po·lar·o·gram** \pōˈlarə,gram, ˈpōlərə,-\ *n* [ISV *polarization* + *-o-* + *-gram*] **:** the current-voltage diagram obtained during polarographic treatment of a solution

**Po·lar·o·graph** \-graf, -räf\ *trademark* — used for an instrument used in polarography

**po·lar·o·graph·ic** \⸗¦⸗⸗¦grafik, ¦⸗⸗⸗\ *adj* [*polarization* + *-o-* + *-graphic*] **:** of, relating to, or by means of polarography ⟨~ techniques⟩ ⟨~ waves⟩ — compare AMPEROMETRIC — **po·lar·o·graph·i·cal·ly** \-fək(ə)lē\ *adv*

**po·lar·og·ra·phy** \,pōləˈrägrəfē\ *n* -ES [ISV *polarization* + *-o-* + *-graphy*] **:** a method of qualitative or quantitative analysis used esp. in studying reversible oxidation-reduction phenomena that is based on current-voltage curves obtained during electrolysis of a test solution with a steadily increasing electromotive force between two mercury electrodes one of which is readily polarized and consists of a stream of fine mercury droplets whereas the other consists of a substantial pool of mercury into which the droplets fall

**Po·lar·oid** \ˈpōlə,rȯid\ *trademark* — used for a light-polarizing material comprising in one form oriented suspensions of dichroic particles in a light-transmitting medium and used esp. in eyeglasses and lamps to prevent glare and in various optical devices

**po·lar·on** \ˈpōlə,rän\ *n* -S [ISV *polar* + *-on*; prob. orig. formed in Russ] **:** a conducting electron in an ionic crystal together with the induced electric polarization of the surrounding lattice

**polar ox** *n* **:** MUSK-OX

**polar plant** *n* **:** COMPASS PLANT a

**polar projection** *n* **:** a cartographic projection of the sphere in which the point of sight is at the center and the plane of projection passes through one of the polar circles

**polar ray** *n* **:** an astral ray as contrasted with a spindle fiber

**polars** *pl of* POLAR

**polar telescope** *n* **:** a telescope that utilizes the polar axis for its tube and uses a mirror in front of the objective to direct the light into the tube

**polar triangle** *n* **:** a spherical triangle formed by the arcs of three great circles each of whose poles is the vertex of a given spherical triangle

**polar valence** *n* **1 :** ELECTROVALENCE **2 :** covalence characterized by unequal distribution of electrons between the atoms united

**po·lar·ward** \ˈpōlə(r)wə(r)d\ *adv* (*or adj*) **:** toward the polar regions

**polar whale** *n* **:** GREENLAND WHALE

**po·la·touche** \ˌpōlə'tüsh\ *n* -s [F, fr. Russ *poletusha*] **:** a small flying squirrel (*Sciuropterus volans*) native to northern Europe and Asia

**pol·davy** \päl'dāvē, pōl-\ *also* **pol·da·vis** \-vəs\ *n, pl* **pol·davies** *or* **poldavys** *also* **poldavis** [ME *poldavy*, prob. fr. *Pouldavid*, locality in Finistère department, northwest France] **:** a coarse canvas or sacking formerly used for sails esp. by the British

**pol·der** \'pōldə(r)\ *n* -s [D, fr. MD *polder, polre*] **:** a tract of low land reclaimed from the sea or other body of water (as by dikes or dams)

**polderboy** *or* **polderman** \'=,=\ *n, pl* **polderboys** *or* **pol·dermen :** a workman engaged in making or maintaining a polder

[1]**pole** \'pōl\ *n* -s [ME, fr. OE *pāl* pole, stake, fr. L *palus* stake; akin to L *pangere* to fasten — more at PACT] **1 a :** a long comparatively slender usu. cylindrical piece of wood or timber (as the stem of a small tree stripped of its branches) **b :** a similar typically cylindrical piece of metal or other substance **2 :** a pole of a specified nature and use: as **a :** an upright column to the top of which something is affixed or by which something is supported ⟨a birdhouse set on a ~⟩ ⟨telephone ~*s*⟩ ⟨a tent ~⟩ **b :** a long slender stick or staff manipulated by hand ⟨vault with a ~⟩ ⟨a boatman's ~⟩ **c :** one used as the handle of an implement ⟨the ~ of a harpoon⟩ **d :** an upright mast in a firehouse by which one may slide from one story to a lower story **e :** an upper part of the mast of a ship **f :** SKI POLE **g :** one of several distance markers placed ⅛ mile apart on the inner rail of a racetrack **h :** a shaft usu. of wood which extends from the front axle of a wagon between wheel horses and by which the wagon is held back **:** TONGUE **i :** a short striped column used as a sign by tradesmen; *specif* **:** BARBER POLE **j :** a usu. horizontal bar or rod from which something may be hung ⟨a curtain ~⟩ **k :** TOTEM POLE **l :** FLAGPOLE **m :** a stick usu. of a specified length used for measuring **3 a :** a unit of length varying from one locality to another; *esp* **:** one measuring 16½ feet — compare PERCH, ROD **b :** a unit of area equal to a square rod or perch **:** one measuring 30¼ square yards ⟨plots of ground averaging about ten ~*s* each —John Galsworthy⟩ **4 :** the tail of various birds and animals; *esp* **:** the tail of an otter **5 :** the flowering stalk of a plant of the genus *Agave* (as the sisal) **6 :** a tree having a breast-high diameter of from 4 to 12 inches **7 :** the inside position on a racetrack **8** *usu cap* **:** QUTB — **under bare poles :** with furled sails ⟨how could she sail upwind *under bare poles* —S.H.Adams⟩

[2]**pole** \"\ *vb* -ED/-ING/-S *vt* **1 :** to furnish with poles for support ⟨peas were brushed . . . gourds *poled* —Nora Waln⟩ **2 :** to strike with a pole; *esp* **:** to hit or pierce with the end of a carriage pole **3 :** to act upon with a pole (as in stirring or pushing) **4 :** to impel or push (as a boat or raft) by means of a pole ⟨never ~ a boat from the bow —H.A.Calahan⟩ ⟨a canoe . . . *poled* by two men —*McClure's*⟩ **5 :** to convey (as hay or reeds) on poles ⟨~ hay into a barn⟩ **6 :** to hit (as a home run) with a free powerful swing of a baseball bat ⟨*poled* his twelfth home run in the sixth inning —*N.Y. Herald Tribune*⟩ **7 :** to subject (metal) to the operation of poling **8 :** to remove dew from (as grass on a putting green) with a long slender pole **9 :** [1]FOREPOLE ~ *vi* **1 :** to propel a boat with a pole ⟨*poled* up the sheltered creek —Cameron Hawley⟩ ⟨*poled* cautiously through the shallows —Francis Birtles⟩ **2** *Austral* **:** SPONGE, IMPOSE — usu. used with *on* **3 :** FLOWER — used of a plant of the genus *Agave* **4 :** to use one's ski poles to gain additional speed ⟨*poled* vigorously down the slope⟩

[3]**pole** \"\ *adj* **1 :** of or relating to a long slender cylindrical piece of wood or other pole **2 a :** made of poles ⟨~ bridge⟩ ⟨~ fence⟩ **b :** having a foundation made of piles or poles stuck into the ground ⟨~ barn⟩ ⟨~ cabin⟩ **3 :** attached to the end of a pole ⟨~ hook⟩ ⟨~ net⟩

[4]**pole** \"\ *n* -s [ME *pool*, fr. L *polus*, fr. Gk *polos* pivot, axis, pole; akin to Gk *kyklos* circle, wheel — more at WHEEL] **1 a :** either extremity of an axis of a sphere **b :** one of the two extremities of the earth's axis — called also *geographical pole;* see NORTH POLE, SOUTH POLE **2 :** something held to resemble a physical pole: as **a :** either of two opposites (as principles, ideas, or factors) forming part of the same system ⟨oscillations of the . . . national mind between the ~*s* of sentiment and intellect —René Wellek⟩ ⟨the major ~*s* of world power —*Atlantic*⟩ **b :** a point of guidance or attraction ⟨a ~ of attraction for all the peoples . . . under Communist oppression —*European Federation Now*⟩ ⟨the ~*s* around whom the discussion was supposed to revolve —D.W.Brogan⟩ ⟨the pivot and ~ of his life . . . was his mother —D.H. Lawrence⟩ **3** *archaic* **:** FIRMAMENT, HEAVENS, SKY ⟨when the night had veil'd the ~ —William Blake⟩ **4 a :** one of the two terminals of an electric cell, battery, or dynamo so related that if the two are connected by an external conductor an electric current will flow from the pole having the higher potential to the other — see NEGATIVE POLE, POSITIVE POLE **b :** one of two or more regions in a magnetized body at which the magnetic flux density is more or less concentrated — see NORTH POLE, SOUTH POLE **c :** a unit comprising the parts of a circuit breaker or switch that control one line of a circuit **5 a :** either of two morphologically or physiologically differentiated areas that are at opposite ends of an axis in organisms or cells (as an egg cell) — see ANIMAL POLE, VEGETAL POLE **b :** an eminence, region, or point on a cell where an axis ends (as at the origin of a nerve cell process or the base of a flagellum) **c :** either end of the spindle in mitosis **6 a :** the vertex of the angle coordinate in a polar coordinate system **b :** one of the ends of the axis of a circle of a sphere **7 a :** the normal to a plane of a crystal erected through the origin of coordinates **b (1) :** the point on a unit sphere where a normal so erected intersects the sphere **(2) :** the projection usu. stereographic or gnomonic of such a point **8 :** the center of a reflecting or refracting surface that is bounded by a circle — **poles apart** *or* **poles asunder :** as far apart or as opposed as the poles of the earth **:** completely averse ⟨their characters . . . are *poles apart* —T.R.Ybarra⟩ ⟨candidates . . . *poles apart* on international relations —*Christian Science Monitor*⟩ ⟨the leisured aristocratic class . . . *poles asunder* from the typical Pharisee —G.H.Box⟩

[5]**pole** \"\ *vt* -ED/-ING/-S **:** to determine or mark the terminal polarities of (as a generator or transformer)

[6]**pole** \"\ *n* -s *cap* [G, of Slavic origin; akin to Pol *Polak* Pole] **1 :** a native or inhabitant of Poland; *esp* **:** a member of the Slavic majority ethnic group of the Polish nation who is Polish-speaking and usu. Roman Catholic **2 :** a person of Polish descent **:** a descendant of natives of Poland ⟨the clannish barriers which now separate the *Pole*, the largest minority, from the Southerner and the Negro —A.G.Mezerik⟩

**pole and satchel charge** *n* **:** POLE CHARGE

[1]**pole·ax** *or* **pole·axe** *or* **pol·lax** *or* **pol·laxe** \'pō,laks\ *n* [ME *polax, pollax*, fr. *pol, polle* head + *ax* — more at POLL] **1 a :** a battle-ax with a short handle and often a cutting edge or point opposite the blade **b :** one having a long handle and used as an ornamental weapon (as by members of a royal bodyguard) **2 :** a short ax with a strong hook at the top of the handle formerly used in naval warfare esp. by boarders **3 :** an ax made with a hammer face opposite the edge and used in slaughtering cattle

[2]**poleax** *or* **poleaxe** *or* **pollax** *or* **pollaxe** \"\ *vt* **:** to attack, strike, or fell with or as if with a poleax ⟨the oxen . . . were shot or ~*ed* —H.W.Nevinson⟩ ⟨the crowds . . . had already been ~*ed*, mentally and emotionally —Benedict Thielen⟩

**pole bean** *n* **:** any of various cultivated beans having long internodes and twining stems and forming elongated vines that are commonly trained to grow upright on poles or other supports — compare BUSH BEAN

**pole blight** *n* **:** a destructive disease of undetermined cause affecting white pines and characterized by shortening of the needle-bearing stems esp. in the upper crown, yellowing and shortening of the needles, abundant resin flow, and eventual death of the tree

**pole boat** *n* **:** a boat propelled by means of a pole

**pole borer** *n* **:** a cerambycid beetle (*Parandra brunnea*) having larvae that bore in shade trees and large poles (as telephone poles)

[1]**poleburn** \'=,=\ *n* [[1]*pole* + *burn*, n.] **:** POLE ROT

[2]**poleburn** \"\ *vi* **:** to become affected with pole rot

**pole-car** \'=,=\ *n* **:** a railroad car sometimes used in pole switching

**pole·cat** \'pōl,kat, *usu* -ad·+V\ *n, pl* **polecats** *also* **polecat** *often attrib* [ME *polcat*, prob. fr. MF *poul, pol* cock + ME *cat;* prob. fr. its habit of feeding on poultry — more at PULLET] **1 a :** a European carnivorous mammal (*Mustela putorius* syn. *Putorius foetidus*) of which the ferret is considered a domesticated variety and which is about two feet long, dark brownish above with white markings on the head, and blackish below **b :** any of several closely related animals of eastern Europe and Asia **2 :** SKUNK; *esp* **:** one of the genus *Mephitis* **3** *Africa* **:** ZORIL **4 :** the common palm civet (*Paradoxurus hermaphroditus*) **5** *archaic* **:** a vile or contemptible person; *esp* **:** PROSTITUTE ⟨out of my door, you witch, you hag, . . . you ~ —Shak.⟩

**polecat tree** *or* **polecat wood** *n* **:** YELLOW BUCKTHORN

**polecat weed** *n* **:** SKUNK CABBAGE

**pole cell** *n* [[4]*pole* + *cell*] **:** a cleavage cell of the embryo of various insects and some other invertebrates regularly undergoing early chromatin diminution in somatic cells that retains the full chromatin complement and ultimately gives rise to the germ cells **:** one that enters the posterior extremity of the egg

**pole chain** *n* **1 :** GUNTER'S CHAIN **2 :** a chain joining the pole of a wagon to a horse's collar

**pole charge** *n* **:** a quantity of fused explosives fastened to the end of a pole and used in military attacks (as against pillboxes, dugouts, and cave positions)

**pole-clipped** \'=,=\ *adj* **:** pruned or pollarded esp. with a pole type of pruner

**pole-clipt** *adj, obs* **:** POLE-CLIPPED ⟨thy *pole-clipt* vineyard —Shak.⟩

**pole compass** *n* **:** a compass raised (as on a pole) above the deck of an iron or steel ship to lessen the effect of the hull's magnetism

**poled** *past of* POLE

**pole effect** *n* **:** the minute change in wavelength and marked change in character of many spectral lines in light emanating from the central region of a metallic arc as compared with light originating near the electrodes

**pole flounder** *or* **pole fluke** *n* **:** WITCH FLOUNDER

**pole·head** \'pōl,hed\ *n* [ME *polheved*, fr. *pol, polle* head + *heved* head — more at POLL, HEAD] *archaic* **:** TADPOLE

**pole horse** *n* **1 :** a horse harnessed beside the pole of a wagon; *specif* **:** a wheeler as distinguished from a leader **2 :** the horse having a starting position next to the inside rail in a harness race

**poleis** *pl of* POLIS

**pole jack** *n* **:** a jack used to pull out poles from their setting

**pole jump** *n* **:** POLE VAULT

**pole lathe** *n* **:** a primitive lathe in which the cord passing around the work to rotate it is fastened at its ends to the treadle and to an elastic pole above

**pole·less** \'pōlləs\ *adj* [[1]*pole* & [4]*pole*] **:** having no pole ⟨~ tent⟩ ⟨~ magnet⟩

**pole·man** \'pōlmən\ *n, pl* **polemen 1 :** one that uses a pole (as in surveying, lumbering, or fighting) **2 :** one that picks up the sound from a motion-picture stage by moving a microphone mounted on the end of an adjustable boom close to the speaking actors — called also *boom man*

**pol·e·march** \'pälə,märk\ *n* -s [Gk *polemarchos*, fr. *polemos* war + *archos* ruler — more at ARCHI-] **:** a chieftain or military commander in ancient Greece; *esp* **:** the third archon in ancient Athens presiding at the court and having jurisdiction over the causes of the metics

**pole mast** *n* **:** a mast in one length or piece as distinguished from one made up of two pieces **:** a mast formed by a single spar

[1]**po·lem·ic** \pə'lemik, pō'-, -mēk\ *n* -s [F *polémique*, fr. MF *polemique*, fr. *polemique*, adj.] **1 a :** a controversial discussion or argument **:** an aggressive attack on or the refutation of the opinions or principles of another ⟨the premises of our ~ against totalitarianism —J.M.Cameron⟩ ⟨dismiss these books as cold-war ~*s* —Karl Meyer⟩ ⟨repeating old and weary ~*s* —Irving Howe⟩ **b :** the art or practice of disputation or controversy ⟨neither descended to crude ~ —Richard Hoggart⟩ ⟨his active ~ against . . . liberals —A.C.McGiffert⟩ ⟨the style too frequently descends to the level of ~*s* —M.S.Handler⟩ — usu. used in pl. but usu. sing. in constr. ⟨the book . . . is a little masterpiece of ~*s* —Martin Gardner⟩ **2 :** one that controverts an opinion, doctrine, or system **:** an aggressive controversialist **:** DISPUTANT ⟨the sarcasms and invectives of the young ~ —T.B.Macaulay⟩ **3 polemics** *pl but usu sing in constr* **:** the branch of Christian theology devoted to the refutation of errors — compare APOLOGETICS, IRENICS

[2]**polemic** \"\ *adj* [F *polémique*, fr. MF *polemique*, fr. Gk *polemikos* of or relating to war, fr. *polemos* war + *-ikos* -ic; akin to OE eal*felo* baleful, MHG *vālant* devil, ON *felms*fullr frightened, Goth us*filma* astonished, Gk *pelemizein* to shake, *pallein* to shake, brandish, hurl] **:** POLEMICAL ⟨written with a ~ purpose —A.C.McGiffert⟩ ⟨the militant and ~ position of the church in the empire —H.O.Taylor⟩ ⟨~ journalist⟩

**po·lem·i·cal** \-məkəl, -mēk-\ *adj* **1 :** of, relating to, or of the nature of a polemic or polemics **:** CONTROVERSIAL ⟨prefer their politics heated and ~ —Bernard Hollowood⟩ ⟨a regrettably ~ spirit in . . . the literature —Dexter Perkins⟩ **2 :** engaged in or addicted to polemics **:** DISPUTATIOUS ⟨~ and . . . not always fair to his opponents —K.S.Latourette⟩ ⟨~ writers⟩

**po·lem·i·cal·ly** \-mək(ə)lē\ *adv* **:** in a polemical manner **:** CONTROVERSIALLY ⟨criticism . . . too ~ stated —W.L.Miller⟩

**po·lem·i·cist** \-məsəst\ *n* -s **:** POLEMIST ⟨socialism's most suasive intellectual ~ —*Time*⟩

**po·lem·i·cize** \-mə,sīz\ *vi* -ED/-ING/-S **:** POLEMIZE ⟨*polemicized* both for and against communism —Ward Moore⟩

**po·lem·ist** \-məst *also* 'päləm-\ *n* -s [[1]*polemic* + *-ist*] **:** one skilled in or given to polemics esp. as the advocate of a partisan cause ⟨the poet who is a ~ and pamphleteer —Louise Bogan⟩ ⟨preacher, teacher . . . and ~ for freedom —*Nation*⟩

**pol·e·mize** \'pälə,mīz\ *vi* -ED/-ING/-S [[1]*polemic* + *-ize*] **:** to engage in controversy **:** dispute aggressively **:** indulge in polemics **:** argue or write polemically ⟨he did not ~ against the pleasures of the senses —S.L.Terrien⟩

**pol·e·mo·ni·a·ce·ae** \ˌpälə,mōnē'āsē,ē\ *n pl, cap* [NL, fr. *Polemonium*, type genus + *-aceae*] **:** a widely distributed family of chiefly herbaceous plants (order Polemoniales) with often showy flowers that have a 3-loculate ovary and 5 stamens inserted on the corolla tube and alternating with its lobes — **pol·e·mo·ni·a·ceous** \ˌ==ˌ==ˌāshəs\ *adj*

**pol·e·mo·ni·a·les** \ˌ==,=='ā(,)lēz\ *n pl, cap* [NL, fr. *Polemonium* + *-ales*] **:** a large order of dicotyledonous herbs, shrubs, or trees having flowers with the stamens adnate to the corolla lobes and a single superior compound ovary

**pol·e·mo·ni·um** \ˌpälə'mōnēəm\ *n* [NL, fr. Gk *polemōnion*, a plant, perh. Greek valerian] **1** *cap* **:** a genus (the type of the family Polemoniaceae) of herbs having pinnate leaves and large cymose-paniculate flowers with herbaceous calyx, declinate stamens, and mucilaginous seeds — see GREEK VALERIAN **2** -s **:** any plant of the genus *Polemonium*

**po·lem·o·scope** \pō'lemə,skōp\ *n* [NL *polemoscopium*, fr. Gk *polemos* war + NL *-scopium* -scope; fr. its suggested use in war as a device for observing the enemy] **:** an opera or field glass with an oblique mirror arranged for seeing objects not directly before the eye

**po·len·ske value** \pō'len(t)skə-\ *also* **polenske number** *n, usu cap P* [after Eduard *Polenske*, 20th cent. Ger. chemist] **:** a value similar to a Reichert value that indicates the content in butter or other fat of the volatile water-insoluble acids (as capric acid and lauric acid)

**po·len·ta** \pō'lentə\ *n* -s [It, fr. L *pollenta* pearl barley — more at POLLEN] **:** mush orig. made of chestnut meal but now principally of cornmeal or sometimes of semolina or farina ⟨the popularity of ~ among Italian peasants⟩

**pole of cold :** a place where the winter cold is the most intense usu. located in the interior of a continent

**pole of inaccessibility** *often cap P&I* **:** the central point of a polar region most difficult of penetration

**pole of the heavens :** CELESTIAL POLE

**pole piece** *n* [[1]*pole* + *piece*] **1 :** a stout harness strap connecting a horse's collar with the pole of a wagon **2 :** the ridgepole of a roof **3** [[4]*pole* + *piece*] **:** a piece of soft iron at a pole of an electromagnet usu. shaped to concentrate or direct the external flux in some desired path — see MAGNETO illustration

**pole-pile** \'=,=\ *vt* **:** to stack (as lumber for drying) on end against a center pole

**pole pitch** *n* **:** the distance measured on the circumference of the armature from the center of one pole to the center of the next pole **:** 180 electrical degrees — compare COIL, PITCH 2b(6)

**pole plate** *n* [[1]*pole* + *plate*] **1 :** a horizontal timber resting on the tie beams of a roof rather than on the wall and supporting the ends of the rafters — compare PLATE 5a(1); see ROOF illustration **2** [[4]*pole* + *plate*] **:** a condensed platelike body developed at each pole of the spindle in various forms of mitosis esp. in protozoans

**pole pruner** *n* **:** a tool for pruning with the cutting parts on the end of a rod or pole 6 to 12 feet long

**pol·er** \'pōlə(r)\ *n* -s **:** one that poles: as **a :** POLE HORSE **b :** one that poles a boat (as a punt) **c :** a worker who performs the poling in a refining furnace **d :** a textile worker who puts yarn on poles for processing **e :** a worker who builds corduroy roads for skidding logs **f :** BOATMAN 1c

**pole riding** *n* **:** the action or an instance of reducing speed on a slope by weighting one's ski poles

**pole rot** *or* **pole sweat** *n* **:** a rotting that occurs while tobacco is on poles during curing — called also *poleburn;* compare HOUSEBURN

**poles** *pl of* POLE, *pres 3d sing of* POLE

**polesaw** \'=,=\ *n* **:** a small curved saw blade mounted on a long handle and used for pruning branches beyond arm reach

polesaw

**pole screen** *n* **:** BANNER SCREEN

**pole shoe** *n* **:** an iron or steel plate sometimes attached to a field-magnet pole to support the field coil

**po·le·sian** \pō'lēzhən\ *n* -s *cap* [*Polesie*, district in southwest White Russia and northwest Ukraine, U.S.S.R. + E *-an*] **:** a member of a people inhabiting the eastern European district of Polesie and being dialectally Belorussian

**poles·man** \'pōlzmən\ *n, pl* **polesmen :** POLEMAN

[1]**polestack** \'=,=\ *vt* [[1]*pole* + *stack*, v.] **:** POLE-PILE

[2]**polestack** \"\ *n* [[1]*pole* + *stack*, n.] **:** a stack of hay hung on an upright pole or laid on poles for rapid curing

**polestar** \'=,=\ *n* -s **1 :** the conspicuous star that at any period is nearest the north celestial pole — called also *North Star* **2 a :** a directing or controlling principle **:** GUIDE ⟨drove forward . . . into the new seas of political idealism trusting to the ~ of emancipated human nature —V.L.Parrington⟩ **b :** a center of attraction ⟨Indian liberty . . . provided a new ~ in political thinking —*Amer. Indian*⟩

**pole step** *n* **:** a lag screw usu. with an L-shaped end that when screwed into a telephone or electric light pole becomes a step for climbing

**pole stock** *n* **:** lumber used in making poles for vehicles and agricultural implements

**pole strength** *n* **:** a quantity corresponding to the amount of magnetic flux emanating from a given magnetic pole and expressed in terms of the unit magnetic pole

**pole strip** *n* **:** a template for spacing holes

**pole switching** *n* **:** switching by means of a pole extended from the side of a locomotive or a pole-car in front of a locomotive with the pole being used to push a car or cut of cars on a paralleling track to a designated classification track

**pole tie** *n* **:** SLABBED TIE

**pole-timber** \'=,==\ *adj* **:** having a minimum of 10 percent pole size or larger trees of which at least half are pole size ⟨*pole-timber* forest⟩ ⟨*pole-timber* stands⟩

**pole trailer** *n* **:** a dolly or rig to carry poles in tow behind a truck

**pole transformer** *n* **:** a distribution transformer designed for mounting on a pole or crossarm

**pole trap** *n* **1 :** a trap set on a pole **2 :** a trap arranged with a bent pole to swing the animal off the ground when the trap is sprung

**pole trawl** *or* **pole seine** *n* **:** a trawlnet having the mouth spread open with a pole or beam

**pole vault** *n* **:** a vault or vaulting with the aid of a pole; *specif* **:** a field event in athletics consisting of a vault for height over a crossbar

**pole-vault** \'=,=\ *vi* [*pole vault*] **:** to attain a height by or as if by vaulting with the aid of a pole ⟨*pole-vaulted* 11 feet 4 inches⟩

**pole-vaulter** \'=,==\ *n* **:** an athlete who participates in the pole vault

**pole vaulting** *n* **:** the act or action of performing the pole vault

**pole·ward** \'pōlwə(r)d\ *also* **pole·wards** \-dz\ *adv (or adj)* **:** toward or in the direction of a pole of the earth ⟨Britain lay ~ of . . . its American colonies —R.H.Brown⟩ ⟨found in ~ areas⟩

**polewood stage** \'=,=-\ *n* **:** a stage in the development of a forest when most of the trees are poles

**po·ley** \'pōlē\ *adj* [prob. irreg. fr. [4]*poll* + *-y*] **:** POLLED, HORNLESS ⟨a ~ cow⟩

**po·leyn** \'pō,lān\ *n* -s [ME, fr. MF *polain*] **:** a piece of defensive armor usu. covering the knee

**poli-** *or* **polio-** *comb form* [NL, fr. Gk, gray, fr. *polios* — more at FALLOW] **1 :** of or relating to the gray matter of the brain or spinal cord ⟨*polio*myelitis⟩ **2 :** gray ⟨*Poli*anthes⟩

**po·li·a·nite** \'pōlēə,nīt\ *n* -s [G *polianit*, irreg. fr. Gk *poliainesthai* to become white with foam (fr. *polios* gray) + G *-it* -ite] **:** pyrolusite in well-formed crystals

**pol·i·an·thes** \ˌpälē'an(t),thēz\ *n, cap* [NL, fr. *poli-* + *-anthes*] **:** a small genus of Mexican tuberous herbs (family Amaryllidaceae) having tall stems and spikes of fragrant white flowers borne in pairs and with the tube of the perianth strongly curved

[1]**po·lice** \pə'lēs, pō'-, *in rapid speech* 'plēs\ *n, pl* **police** *often attrib* [MF, conduct of public affairs, administration of government, fr. LL *politia*, fr. L, state, fr. Gk *politeia* citizenship, administration of government, state, fr. *politēs* citizen, fr. *polis* city; akin to Skt *pur* city and prob. to L *plenus* full — more at FULL] **1** *archaic* **:** social or group organization **:** CIVILIZATION ⟨insects whose faculties, ~, and sagacity have been . . . overrated —J.R.Johnson⟩ ⟨the age . . . was far less insecure in its condition of ~ —Thomas De Quincey⟩ **2** *archaic* **:** POLICY ⟨the ~ and interests of the Roman see —John Entick⟩ **3 a (1) :** the internal organization or regulation of a political unit (as a nation or state) **:** the control and regulation of such a unit through the exercise of governmental powers **(2) :** such control and regulation with respect to matters affecting the general comfort, health, morals, safety, or prosperity of the public **b :** the control and regulation of the affairs affecting the general order and welfare of a nonpolitical unit (as a camp) or area ⟨regulations regarding the ~ of this navigation —*Congress of Vienna 1815*⟩ ⟨the ~ of the boat is superior to the best regulated tavern —Anne Royall⟩ **c :** the organization or system of laws for effecting such control **4 a :** the department of government concerned primarily with the maintenance of public order, safety, and health and the enforcement of the laws and possessing executive, judicial, and legislative powers — see POLICE POWER **b :** the department of government having as its principal function the prevention, detection, and prosecution of public nuisances and crimes **5 a :** POLICE FORCE ⟨the metropolitan ~⟩ ⟨the ~ was there in force —Arthur Morrison⟩ ⟨the ~ and other local law enforcement bodies —Jack Lait & Lee Mortimer⟩ **b :** a member of a police force or constabulary **:** POLICEMAN — usu. used in pl. ⟨ask these two ~ all the questions —Thomas Sterling⟩ ⟨detectives, plainclothesmen and uniformed ~ —*N. Y. Herald Tribune*⟩ **6 a (1) :** an organization resembling the police force of a community **:** a group of persons officially entrusted with the duty of keeping order and enforcing regulations in a usu. specified area ⟨railway ~⟩ ⟨dock ~⟩ ⟨campus ~⟩ **(2) :** a member of such an organization — usu. used in pl. **b (1) :** a group of persons held to resemble such a police force in organization or function ⟨society . . . has its code and ~ as well as governments —W.M.Thackeray⟩ **(2) :** a member of such a group — usu. used in pl. ⟨members act as volunteer thought ~ —Paul Blanshard⟩ **7 :** the action or process of cleaning and putting in order (as a building or an area) ⟨the gun commander is

responsible for the ~ of his gun position⟩ **8 :** military personnel detailed to perform a usu. specified function — see KITCHEN POLICE

**2police** \"\ *vt* -ED/-ING/-S [in sense 1, fr. MF *policer*, fr. *police*, n.; in other senses, fr. 1*police*] **1** *archaic* **:** to maintain law and order in (as a country) **:** GOVERN ⟨humane laws by which kingdoms are *policed* —John Donne⟩ **2 a :** to control, regulate, or keep in order by the use of police or a similar force or by means held to resemble the use of police ⟨a four-lane thoroughfare *policed* against speeding —*Amer. Guide Series: Texas*⟩ ⟨waters . . . *policed* by two sets of revenue officers —*Amer. Guide Series: Md.*⟩ ⟨the use of superstition for . . . *policing* the mob —Benjamin Farrington⟩ **b :** to guard or protect by means of police **3 :** to make clean and put in order (as a military camp) — often used with *up* **4 a :** to supervise the operation, execution, or administration of (as an agreement) to prevent or detect and prosecute violations of rules and regulations ⟨responsibility for *policing* the peace —Sumner Welles⟩ ⟨the role of government in *policing* welfare funds —Ed Marciniak⟩ ⟨use of an internal audit agency . . . to ~ the financial and accounting activities —H.W.Bordner⟩ **b :** to exercise such a supervision over the policies and activities of ⟨a top-level committee to ~ holders of government contracts —*New Republic*⟩ ⟨every industry has a moral obligation to ~ itself —*Advertising & Selling*⟩ **5 :** to perform the functions (as regulation or protection) of a police force in or over ⟨state police charged with *policing* rural communities —*Amer. Guide Series: Mich.*⟩ ⟨ordered his 40,000-man army . . . to ~ the land —*Current Biog.*⟩

**police action** *n* **:** a usu. localized military action undertaken by regular armed forces against persons held to be violators of the general international peace and order (as guerrillas, bandits, or aggressors) without a formal declaration of war ⟨the United Nations *police action* in Korea⟩ ⟨the war with Spain . . . was a relatively small *police action* —R.K.Burns⟩

**police burgh** *n* **:** a Scottish burgh having legally defined boundaries and possessing the privilege of having its own municipal council

**police commissioner** *n* **1 :** a member of a board of civilian officials legally charged with the making of policy for and the exercise of general supervisory powers over a police department **2 :** an appointed civilian official commissioned to regulate and control the appointment, duties, and discipline of the police and to act as the chief executive of the police department in a political unit (as a city)

**police constable** *n, Brit* **:** a policeman of the lowest rank

**police court** *n* **:** a court of record having jurisdiction over various minor offenses (as violations of motor vehicle laws or cases involving breach of the peace) corresponding to that of the justice of the peace under the common law and possessing power to bind over for trial in a superior court or for a grand jury persons accused of more serious offenses

**police department** *n* **1 :** a governmental department concerned with the administration of the police force ⟨an increased budget for the *police department*⟩ **2 :** POLICE FORCE ⟨call out the entire *police department*⟩

**police dog** *n* **1 :** a dog trained to assist police in their work esp. in tracking criminals **2 :** GERMAN SHEPHERD

**po·lice·dom** \pə'lēsdəm\ *n* -S **:** the total body of police **:** the police system

**police force** *n* **:** a professional body of trained officers and men entrusted by a government with the maintenance of public peace and order, the enforcement of laws, and the prevention and detection of crime

**police inspector** *n* **:** a superior officer of police usu. ranking next below a commissioner, superintendent, or chief

**police jury** *n* **:** the governing body of a Louisiana parish corresponding to a board of supervisors in the counties of other states

**police justice** *or* **police magistrate** *or* **police judge** *n* **:** a judge of a police court

**po·lice·less** \-sləs\ *adj* **:** lacking police

**po·lice·man** \pə'lēsmən, pō'-, *in rapid speech* 'plē-\ *n, pl* **policemen 1 a :** a member of a police force **b :** one held to resemble a member of a police force in acting to enforce rules or preserve order ⟨the priest as a moral ~ in rural life —Paul Blanshard⟩ ⟨traditional ~ over big business —T.R. Ybarra⟩ **2 :** an instrument (as a flat piece of rubber on the end of a glass rod) for removing solids from a beaker or other vessel

**policeman fly** *n* **:** any of several small Australian wasps that capture flies and store them in their burrows

**po·lice·man·ship** \-n,ship\ *n* **:** action or behavior held to characterize a policeman

**police matron** *n* **:** a woman in a municipal police department who has charge of women and children detained (as in a police station and jail)

**police motu** *n, usu cap P&M* **:** a pidgin language of the territory of Papua based on Motu

**police offense** *n* **:** a minor offense against order over which a police court may have final jurisdiction and which does not involve a right to jury trial

**police office** *n, chiefly Brit* **:** the headquarters of a municipal police department **:** POLICE STATION

**police officer** *n* **:** a member of a police force

**police power** *n* **:** the inherent power of a government to exercise reasonable control over persons and property within its jurisdiction in the interest of the general security, health, safety, morals, and welfare except where legally prohibited (as by constitutional provision)

**police reporter** *n* **:** a reporter assigned to cover crimes, arrests, and other police news

**polices** *pres 3d sing of* POLICE

**police science** *n* **:** the science dealing principally with the investigation and detection of crime — compare CRIMINOLOGY

**police state** *n* **:** a political unit (as a nation) characterized by repressive governmental control of political, economic, and social life usu. by an arbitrary exercise of power by the police and esp. secret police in place of the regular operation of the administrative and judicial organs of the government according to established legal processes **:** a totalitarian state — compare GARRISON STATE

**police station** *n* **:** the headquarters of the police for a particular locality **:** the place where the police assemble for orders and to which they take arrested persons

**po·lice·woman** \(ˌ)ˌ==ˌ==\ *n, pl* **policewomen :** a woman who is a member of the police **:** a woman doing police duty

**policing** *pres part of* POLICE

**pol·i·cize** \'pälə,sīz\ *vi* -ED/-ING/-S [1*policy* + *-ize*] **:** to act in a politic, diplomatic, or crafty manner

**pol·i·clinic** \ˌpälə+\ *n* [G *poliklinik*, fr. Gk *polis* city + G *klinik* clinic, fr. F *clinique* — more at POLICE, CLINIC] **1 :** a clinic held formerly at private houses in a city or town for treatment of patients by advanced students under supervision of a professor who receives daily reports from the students **2 :** a dispensary or department of a hospital at which outpatients are treated — compare POLYCLINIC

**1pol·i·cy** \'päləsē, -si\ *n* -ES *often attrib* [ME *policie*, fr. MF, fr. LL *politia* — more at POLICE] **1** *archaic* **:** the art or science of government **:** the conduct of public affairs **2** *archaic* **:** POLITY ⟨in well constituted *policies* provision is always made for the exercise of clemency —Joseph Gilbert⟩ **3** *archaic* **:** a wise scheme or device; *esp* **:** a cunning contrivance, stratagem, or trick **4 a :** prudence or wisdom in the management of public and private affairs **:** SAGACITY, SHREWDNESS, WISDOM, WIT ⟨decide upon . . . the ~ or impolicy of these laws —R.B. Taney⟩ ⟨had I, with greater ~, concealed my struggles —Jane Austen⟩ **b :** management, administration, or procedure based primarily on temporal or material interest **:** worldly wisdom **:** shrewdness based upon considerations of expediency **:** CRAFTINESS **5 a :** a definite course or method of action selected (as by a government, institution, group, or individual) from among alternatives and in the light of given conditions to guide and usu. determine present and future decisions **b** (1) **:** a specific decision or set of decisions designed to carry out such a chosen course of action (2) **:** such a specific decision or set of decisions together with the related actions designed to implement them **c :** a projected program consisting of desired objectives and the means to achieve them ⟨formulation of ~⟩ **6** [ME (Sc) *polesy* (influenced in meaning by L *politus* polished, refined), fr. ME *policie* — more at POLITE] *obs Scot* **a :** the improvement of an estate, town, or building **b :** the improvements so made **c :** the improved grounds (as parkland) of an estate or country house in Scotland — usu. used in pl. ⟨house stands in about 20 acres of well-wooded *policies* —*advt*⟩ ⟨the *policies* of an old country house —John Buchan⟩

**2policy** \"\ *vt* -ED/-ING/-ES [MF *policier*, fr. *policie*, n.] *archaic* **:** to organize and regulate the internal order of **:** GOVERN

**3policy** \"\ *n* -ES *often attrib* [alter. (influenced by 1*policy*) of earlier *police*, fr. MF, certificate, fr. OIt *polizza*, modif. of ML *apodixa* receipt, fr. MGk *apodeixis*, fr. Gk, proof, fr. *apodeiknynai* to point out, demonstrate + *-sis* — more at APODICTIC] **1 :** a certificate of insurance **:** a writing whereby a contract of insurance is made **:** the document containing the contract made by an insurance company with a person whose property or life is insured **:** an annuity contract or certificate of an insurance company — see BLANKET POLICY, FLOATER 8, FLOATING POLICY, LIMITED POLICY, OPEN POLICY, STANDARD POLICY, TIME POLICY, UNLIMITED POLICY, UNVALUED POLICY, VALUED POLICY, WAGER POLICY **2 a :** a daily lottery in which participants bet that certain numbers will be drawn from a lottery wheel **b :** NUMBER 11a

**policyholder** \'===,==\ *n* **:** one (as a person or firm) granted an insurance policy — used chiefly in life insurance

**policy loan** *n* **:** a loan granted by the insurer to the holder of a life insurance policy in an amount no greater than the cash value of the policy

**policy proof of interest :** a marine insurance policy provision whereby the underwriter agrees to dispense with all proof of insurable interest with the policy being stamped accordingly

**policy science** *n* **:** a social science dealing with the making and execution of policy (as in government or business)

**policy slip** *n* **:** a ticket showing the number a policy player has bet

**policy wheel** *n* **:** LOTTERY WHEEL

**policy year** *n* **1 :** a period comprising the 12 months extending usu. from noon of a given date to noon of the same date one year thereafter **2 :** a period of 24 months within which all the one-year policies written during the first 12 months thereof will have matured and the losses have become known — used in certain types of insurance accounting

**po·li·gar** \'pälə,gär\ *n* -S *usu cap* [Marathi & Telugu; Marathi *pāḷegār*, fr. Telugu *pāḷegāḍu* or Kanarese *pāḷeyagāra*] **:** a subordinate feudal chief in the former Madras Presidency of India

**po·li·gnac** \,pōlēn'yak\ *n* -S [F, fr. Auguste Jules Armand Marie, Prince de *Polignac* †1847 Fr. ultraroyalist politician] **1 :** a card game in which a principal object is to avoid winning any jack in a trick **2 :** the jack of spades in polignac and other games

**po·li·lla** \pō'lē(y)ə\ *n* -S [AmerSp, fr. Sp, clothes moth] *West Indies* **:** POWDER-POST TERMITE

**poling** *n* -S [fr. gerund of 2*pole*] **:** a process used in refining some metals (as copper) that consists of the introduction of poles of green wood into the molten metal so as to generate gases that have a reducing action on oxides

**poling board** *n* **:** a vertical board used in the poling-board method to support the sides of an excavation

**poling-board method** \'==,=-\ *n* **:** a method of excavation (as of wells or trenches) by digging sections of from four to five feet each in depth with each section being sheathed with poling boards as it is finished

**poling-boat** \'==,=\ *n* **:** a usu. long narrow shallow draft boat with a flat bottom propelled with a pole

**pol·i·ni·ces** \,pälə'nī,sēz\ *n, cap* [NL, irreg. fr. L *Polynices*, legendary Theban warrior prince, fr. Gk *Polyneikēs*] **:** a genus of predacious marine snails (family Naticidae) having rather large globose shells and feeding chiefly on other mollusks (as clams) by drilling their way through the shell with their radula and extracting the soft parts within

**po·lio** \'pōlē,ō\ *n* -S *often attrib* [by shortening] **:** POLIOMYELITIS

**polio-** — see POLI-

**po·lio·encephalitis** \ˌpōlē(,)ō+\ *n* [NL, fr. *poli-* + *encephalitis*] **:** inflammation of the gray matter of the brain

**po·lio·encephalomyelitis** \"+\ *n* [NL, fr. *poli-* + *encephal-* + *myelitis*] **:** inflammation of the gray matter of the brain and the spinal cord

**po·lio·myelitic** \"+\ *adj* [ISV *poliomyelitis* + *-ic*] **:** of, relating to, or affected with poliomyelitis

**po·lio·myelitis** \"+\ *n* [NL, fr. *poli-* + *myelitis*] **:** an acute infectious virus disease esp. of children that is characterized by fever, motor paralysis, and atrophy of skeletal muscles often with permanent disability and deformity and that results from inflammation and degeneration of the nerve cells in the anterior horns of the gray substance of the spinal cord — called also *acute anterior poliomyelitis, infantile paralysis*

**po·lio·neuromere** \"+\ *n* [*poli-* + *neuromere*] **:** a segment of gray matter of the spinal cord

**pol·i·or·cet·ic** \,pälē,ō(r)'sed·ik, -sēd-\ *adj* [Gk *poliorkētikos*, fr. *poliorkētēs* taker of cities (fr. *poliorkein* to besiege, fr. *polis* city + *herkos* fence, enclosure) + *-ikos* -ic — more at POLICE, EXERCISE] **:** of or relating to poliorcetics

**pol·i·or·cet·ics** \ˌ==ˌ='sed·iks, -sēd-\ *n pl but usu sing in constr* [modif. (influenced by *-ics*) of Gk *poliorkētika*, fr. neut. pl. of *poliorkētikos*] **:** the art of conducting and resisting sieges

**po·li·o·sis** \,pōlē'ōsəs\ *n, pl* **polio·ses** \-'ō,sēz\ [NL, fr. Gk *poliōsis* process of becoming gray, fr. *polios* gray + *-ōsis* -osis — more at FALLOW] **:** loss of color from the hair

**polio vaccine** *n* **:** a vaccine intended to confer immunity to poliomyelitis

**1po·lis** \'pōləs\ *n, pl* **po·leis** \-ō,līs\ [Gk, city — more at POLICE] **:** a Greek city-state; *specif* **:** one in its ideal form as a community embodying the organization and fulfillment of man's social relations ⟨the ~ is by nature prior to the household and to each of us —C.J.O'Neil⟩

**2polis** \"\ *Scot & Irish var of* POLICE

**-po·lis** \p(ə)ləs\ *n comb form* -ES [LL, fr. Gk, fr. *polis*] **:** city ⟨megal*opolis*⟩

**1pol·ish** \'pälish, -lēsh, *esp in pres part* -ləsh\ *vb* -ED/-ING/-ES [ME *polisshen*, fr. OF *poliss-*, stem of *polir* to polish, fr. L *polire*; prob. akin to L *pellere* to drive, beat, push — more at FELT] *vt* **1 :** to make smooth and glossy by a mechanical process usu. by friction **:** give luster to **:** BURNISH ⟨glass . . . can be highly ~*ed* and cut —G.S. & Helen McKearin⟩ ⟨cleanse and ~ the teeth⟩ — sometimes used with *up* ⟨~*ed* up the handle of the big front door —W.S.Gilbert⟩ **2 :** to smooth, soften, or refine in manners **:** free from social roughness, rudeness, crudeness, or coarseness **:** imbue with refinement or culture **:** make elegant, cultured, or polite **3 :** to bring to a highly developed, finished, or refined state **:** remove technical imperfections or crudities from **:** improve in style **:** PERFECT ⟨readers who do not understand us should ~ their wits —Stuart Chase⟩ ⟨~*ed* himself into one of the nation's most adept . . . specialists —Oscar Fraley⟩ ⟨~ our outdoor flag ceremonies —Elin Lindberg⟩ — often used with *up* ⟨~ up his knowledge of . . . law —Beverly Smith⟩ **4** *archaic* **:** to transform or eliminate by polishing ⟨an overjudicious author . . . ~*es* away the strength and energy of his thoughts —*Free-Thinker*⟩ ~ *vi* **:** to become smooth **:** take on a gloss (as from or through friction) ⟨steel ~*es* well⟩ — **polish apples :** APPLE-POLISH

**2polish** \"\ *n* -ES **1 :** a condition produced by or as if by polishing: **a :** a smooth glossy surface often produced by friction **:** GLOSS, LUSTER ⟨jade takes a high ~⟩ ⟨a table with a high ~⟩ **b :** an exterior quality characterized by refinement and culture **:** freedom from rudeness or coarseness ⟨the social class which is . . . still canine under its ~ —George Meredith⟩ ⟨acquire a . . . university ~ —Harvey Graham⟩ **c :** a state of high development or refinement **:** a high quality (as of construction, interpretation, or performance) usu. characterized by a freedom from technical imperfections or crudities ⟨a production more remarkable for high ~ than warmth of poetic feeling —Richard Garnett †1906⟩ ⟨played . . . with the magnificent dash and ~ of the true virtuoso —Winthrop Sargeant⟩ **2 :** the action or process of polishing ⟨~ is the final act of the mollusk in the building of its shell —Joyce Allan⟩ **3 :** a preparation (as a liquid, cream, or wax) that is used to produce a gloss and often a color for the protection and decoration of a surface ⟨stove ~⟩ ⟨shoe ~⟩ ⟨furniture ~⟩ **4 :** RICE POLISH

**3pol·ish** \'pōlish, -lēsh\ *adj, usu cap* [6*Pole* + *-ish*] **1 a :** of, relating to, or characteristic of Poland **b :** of, relating to, or characteristic of the Poles **2 :** of, relating to, or characteristic of the Polish language

**4polish** \"\ *n* **1** -ES *cap* **:** the Slavic language of the Poles **2 a** *usu cap* **:** a European breed of crested domestic fowls with small V-shaped combs **b** *pl* **polish,** *often cap* **:** a bird of this breed **3 a** *usu cap* **:** a breed of very small snow-white rabbits **b** *pl* **polish** *often cap* **:** a rabbit of this breed **4** -ES **:** a lace shoe being five inches or more from the heel seat to the top and having the upper higher at the back than at the front

**pol·ish·able** \'pälishəbəl\ *adj* **:** capable of being polished ⟨~ and well-grained teak —J.H.Stocqueler⟩

**1polish-american** \ˌ==ˌ==+\ *n, cap P&A* **:** an American of Polish ancestry

**2polish-american** \"\ *adj, usu cap P&A* **:** of, relating to, or having the characteristics of a Polish-American

**polish berry** *n, usu cap P* **:** a scale (*Margarodes polonicus*) of north and central Europe whose body yields a red dye

**polish carpet** *or* **polish rug** *n, usu cap P* [3*polish*] **1 :** a Persian rug of the late 16th to 18th centuries having a silk pile and usu. interwoven gold and silver threads **2 :** a tapestry-woven rug in which some metal thread is used

**polish checkers** *or* **polish draughts** *n pl but sing in constr, usu cap P* **:** checkers played usu. on a special board of 100 squares in which the men can take opposing men by jumping backward as well as forward and kings can go any distance in one move

**pol·ished** \'pälisht, -lēsht\ *adj* [ME *polisshed*, fr. past part. of *polisshen* to polish] **1 a :** subjected to polishing **:** made smooth and glossy by a mechanical process and usu. by friction ⟨~ plate glass⟩ ⟨~ granite⟩ **b** (1) **:** naturally smooth and shining ⟨her ~ cheekbones stood out with a porcelain firmness and finish —Elizabeth Pollet⟩ (2) **:** having a smooth and glossy surface produced by or as if by polishing ⟨trousers of well ~ . . . homespun —John Buchan⟩ ⟨the young man's hair was ~⟩ ⟨reflections . . . in that shining, ~, shimmering expanse —Marjory S. Douglas⟩ **2 :** marked by cultivation and urbanity **:** characterized by elegance and refinement ⟨the growth of ~ society —C.H.Grandgent⟩ ⟨the easy culture of a ~ man of rank —J.A.Froude⟩ ⟨graces in the demeanor of a ~ and noble person —R.W.Emerson⟩ **3 :** having, brought to, or characterized by a high degree of development, finish, or refinement **:** free from imperfections (as of interpretation, construction, or performance) ⟨highly ~ piece of writing —B.C.L. Keelan⟩ ⟨~ French⟩ ⟨his ~, luminous, and animated eloquence —T.B.Macaulay⟩ ⟨the most ~ actress whom this century has known —E.H.Collis⟩

**polished rice** *n* **:** white rice that is given a polish by rapidly revolving cylinders covered with pigskin

**pol·ish·er** \-shə(r)\ *n* -S **:** one that polishes: as **a :** a worker who polishes an article by hand or by machine to give it a clean smooth and usu. glossy finish **b :** a bookbinder's hand tool used hot to polish leathers, crush down leather grains, and eliminate blisters on cloth covers

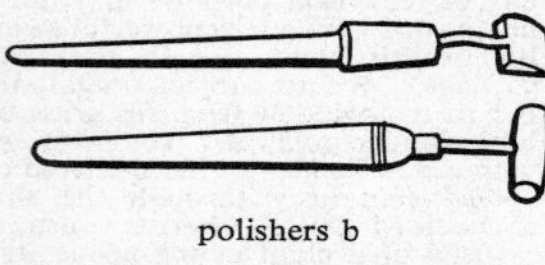

polishers b

**polishing iron** *n* **:** an iron burnisher; *esp* **:** a small smoothing iron used in laundries

**polishing wheel** *n* **:** a wheel consisting of layers of fabric impregnated with abrasive and adhesive for polishing

**polish millet** *n, usu cap P* **:** a crabgrass (*Digitaria sanguinalis*)

**polish off** *vt* **:** to finish off quickly or out of hand: as **a :** to knock out (as an opponent) ⟨handily *polished off* some of the best . . . middleweights —*Time*⟩ **b :** to dispose of summarily **:** finish off hastily **:** complete and dispense with ⟨*polished off* a volume in the evening —O.W.Holmes †1935⟩ ⟨the players *polished* this quintet *off* with a fierce brilliance⟩ **c :** to consume rapidly and completely ⟨*polished* the chicken *off* between them⟩

**polish plait** *n, usu cap 1st P* **:** PLICA 1

**polish rabbit** *n, usu cap P* **:** a rabbit of the Polish breed

**polish sausage** *n, usu cap P* **:** smoked link sausage made of coarsely ground pork and beef seasoned with garlic

**polish swan** *n, usu cap P* **:** a color phase of the mute swan having pale gray legs and feet

**polish wheat** *n, usu cap P* **:** a wheat (*Triticum polonicum*) or any of its varieties having large loose spikes with conspicuous papery glumes and very hard large long yellowish white kernels resembling those of durum wheat

**po·lis·man** \'pōləsmən\ *Scot & Irish var of* POLICEMAN

**po·lis·soir** \,pōlē'swär\ *n* -S [F, polishing implement, fr. MF, fr. *poliss-*, stem of *polir* to polish — more at POLISH] **:** a tool consisting of a flat wooden block with a long iron or steel handle and used in glass manufacturing for flattening out split cylinders of blown glass **:** an implement used for polishing or grinding

**pol·is·tes** \pə'li,stēz\ *n* [NL, fr. Gk *polistēs* founder of a city, fr. *polizein* to build a city, fr. *polis* city + *-izein* -ize — more at POLICE] **1** *cap* **:** an extensive genus of social wasps that have a spindle-shaped abdomen and wings which fold like a fan, are mostly black with yellow or brown markings, and make nests consisting of a single comb of papery material suspended by a peduncle and having no envelope **2** *pl* **polistes :** any wasp of the genus *Polistes*

**polit** *abbr* political

**pol·i·tarch** \'pälə,tärk\ *n* -S [Gk *politarchēs*, fr. *politēs* citizen + *-archēs* -arch] **:** a municipal magistrate in countries of the eastern Mediterranean under the Roman Empire ⟨the seven ~*s* who ruled the city —*United Presbyterian Mag.*⟩

**pol·it·bu·ro** *also* **pol·i·tbu·reau** \'pälət,byů(,)rō 'pōl- *also* pə'lit- *or* pə'lēt-\ *n* -S [*politburo* fr. Russ *politbyuro*, fr. *politicheskoe byuro* political bureau; *politbureau* part trans. of Russ *politbyuro*] **1 :** the principal policy-making and executive committee of a Communist party ⟨member of the Chinese ~⟩ ⟨replacement of the Russian ~ by a presidium⟩ — compare PRESIDIUM **2 :** an organized group held to resemble a Communist politburo in having a controlling position and absolute power

**po·lite** \pə'līt, pō'-, *usu* -īd·+V\ *adj*, *often* -ER/-EST [ME *polyt*, fr. L *politus*, past part. of *polire* to smooth, polish — more at POLISH] **1** *obs* **:** POLISHED 1a ⟨edifices . . . made of the *politest* stone —William Whiston⟩ **2** *obs* **:** in good order **:** well kept **:** NEAT, TIDY **3 a :** of, belonging to, or having the characteristics of advanced culture **:** exhibiting polish, cultivation, elegance, and refinement **:** characterized by elevated and preferential usages ⟨Latin . . . became the vehicle of ~ as well as official intercourse —H.O.Taylor⟩ ⟨part of a ~ schooling —F.J. Mather⟩ ⟨~ society⟩ ⟨~ languages⟩ **b :** marked by refined cultured interests and pursuits esp. in arts and belles lettres and usu. not scientific, utilitarian, or controversial in character ⟨the Revolutionary upheaval produced no ~ literature . . . comparable to its utilitarian prose —V.L.Parrington⟩ **4 a :** showing or characterized by correct social usage **:** marked by or exhibiting an appearance of consideration, tact, deference, courtesy, or grace resulting sometimes from sincere consideration of others and sometimes from mere regard for etiquette ⟨~ answer⟩ ⟨~ letter⟩ ⟨a man who thinks of living in the great world must be gallant, ~, and attentive to please the women —Earl of Chesterfield⟩ **b :** marked by a lack of roughness or crudities **:** gentle or moderate in tone **:** designed not to offend ⟨things . . . ignored or minimized in ~ history —G.G.Coulton⟩

**syn** see CIVIL

**po·lite·ful** \-ītfəl\ *adj* **:** full of politeness **:** very polite

**pol·i·teia** \,pälə'tīə\ *n* -S [Gk, constitution, citizenship, administration of government — more at POLICE] **:** CONSTITUTION; *specif* **:** the whole order of social and political relationships in a polis

**po·lite·ly** *adv* **:** in a polite manner: as **a** *obs* **:** SMOOTHLY ⟨no marble statue can be ~ carved —John Milton⟩ **b** *obs* **:** in an elegant, polished, and cultured manner ⟨a niece whom he has ~ educated in expensive finery —William Law⟩ **c :** in a courteous, socially correct, or refined manner **:** TACTFULLY ⟨~ received by the dons and fellows —Romeyn Berry⟩ ⟨ruined or

what we would now call ~ submarginal land —G.P.Musselman⟩
**po·lite·ness** *n* -ES **1 :** the quality or state of being polite: as **a** *archaic* **:** mental polish **:** intellectual culture or refinement **:** elegance and good taste (as in a literary work) ⟨renowned for the ~ of the character and editions of what he has published —John Evelyn⟩ **b :** polished or refined manners **:** courteous or socially correct behavior ⟨~ mustn't be mistaken for civility —Richard Joseph⟩ ⟨the art of chill and consummate ~ —Arnold Bennett⟩ ⟨~ forbade they should contradict him —Samuel Lover⟩ **2 :** a polite act or statement ⟨the old man, with many ~*es* . . . led him —*New Yorker*⟩ ⟨cutting ~*es* out of telegrams —Arnold Bennett⟩
**po·li·tes** \'pälə,tēz\ *n, cap* [NL, prob. fr. Gk *politēs* citizen] **:** a widely distributed genus of skipper butterflies
**po·li·tesse** \,pälə'tes\ *n* -S [F (influenced in meaning by F *poli* polished, polite, past part. of *polir* to polish), fr. MF, cleanness, neatness, fr. OIt *pulitezza*, fr. *pulito* clean, neat, polished (past part. of *pulire* to clean, polish), fr. L *politus* polished, past part. of *polire* to polish] **:** formal and cultivated politeness **:** DECOROUSNESS ⟨holding his temper on a rigid course with rules of ~ —*N.Y.Times*⟩ ⟨excel in hospitality, in ~, and . . . in kindness —*Harper's*⟩
**po·li·tian** \pō'lishən\ *n* -S [MF *policien*, fr. *policie* conduct of public affairs, administration of government + -*en* -an (fr. L -*anus*) — more at POLICY] *archaic* **:** POLITICIAN
[1]**pol·i·tic** \'pälə,tik\ *adj* [ME *politik*, fr. MF *politique*, fr. L *politicus*, fr. Gk *politikos*, fr. *politēs* citizen + -*ikos* -ic — more at POLICE] **1 :** POLITICAL ⟨their superiors in ~ and military virtues —Edmund Burke⟩ ⟨he with all his people made all but one ~ body —Philip Sidney⟩ — see BODY POLITIC **2 :** characterized by shrewdness **:** skillfully contrived **:** EXPEDIENT, JUDICIOUS ⟨this land was famously enrich'd with ~ grave counsel —Shak.⟩ ⟨neither polite nor ~ to get into other people's quarrels —Ruth Park⟩ ⟨so long as it was ~ to profess loyalty —V.L.Parrington⟩ **3 :** of, relating to, or having the nature of a constitutional as distinguished from a despotic government **:** CONSTITUTIONAL ⟨from . . . ~ government the inhabitants were brought under tyranny —Thomas Washington⟩ **4 :** sagacious in devising or promoting a policy **:** skillful or ingenious in statecraft **:** prudent in management **:** characterized by political skill and ingenuity ⟨an astute and ~ statesman⟩ **5 :** exercising, manifesting, or proceeding from craft **:** artful in address or procedure **:** shrewdly tactful **:** CUNNING, WORLDLY-WISE ⟨a ~ answer⟩ ⟨a ~ move⟩ ⟨a very ~ adversary⟩
**syn** see EXPEDIENT, SUAVE
[2]**politic** \"\ *n* -S **1** *archaic* **:** POLITICIAN ⟨amongst statesmen and ~*s* —Francis Bacon⟩ **2** *obs* **:** POLICY ⟨this did not suit with popish ~ —Richard Bentley †1742⟩ **3** *obs* **:** one that is indifferent toward religious matters **:** one concerned more with the affairs of the world than with religion ⟨worldlings and depraved ~*s* who are apt to condemn holy things —Francis Bacon⟩
[1]**po·lit·i·cal** \pə'lid·|ə̇kəl, pō'-, -it|, |ēk-, *in rapid speech* 'pli-\ *adj* [L *politicus* political + E -*al*] **1 a :** of or relating to government, a government, or the conduct of governmental affairs **b :** of or relating to matters of government as distinguished from matters of law ⟨~ sovereignty⟩ ⟨~ recognition of a new nation⟩ — compare LEGAL 3a **c :** engaged in civil as distinguished from military functions ⟨a ~ officer⟩ — see POLITICAL AGENT **d :** of, relating to, or concerned with the making as distinguished from the administration of governmental policy **2** *archaic* **:** POLITIC 2 ⟨whether it would be ~ to interfere —James Mill⟩ **3 a :** of, relating to, or concerned with politics **b :** of, relating to, or involved in party politics ⟨~ activity⟩ ⟨~ party⟩ — compare ADMINISTRATIVE, NONPARTISAN **4 :** organized in governmental terms — see POLITICAL UNIT
[2]**political** \"\ *n* -S **:** one associated with politics; *esp* **:** POLITICAL PRISONER ⟨hundreds of ~*s* . . . who had escaped from a concentration camp —Anthony West⟩
**political action** *n* **:** action designed to attain a purpose by the use of political power or by activity in political channels; *specif* **:** such action by organized labor through recognized political means (as participation in party organization, in elections, and by lobbying) — contrasted with *direct action*
**political agent** *n* **:** an official appointed by the British government to act as resident adviser to the ruler of a protected state
**political arithmetic** *n* **:** a 17th and 18th century science dealing chiefly with the economic and demographic statistics of a political unit (as a nation or state)
**political commissar** *n* **:** COMMISSAR 1a
**political crime** *or* **political offense** *n* **:** a violation of the law or of the public peace for political rather than private reasons; *specif* **:** one directed against a particular government or political system ⟨*political offenses* . . . exclude any possibility of extradition —R.G.Neumann⟩
**political economist** *n* **:** a specialist in political economy
**political economy** *n* **1 :** an 18th century branch of the art of government concerned with directing governmental policies toward the promotion of the wealth of the government and the community as a whole **2 a :** a 19th century social science comprising the modern science of economics but concerned principally with governmental as contrasted with commercial or personal economics **b :** a modern social science dealing with the interrelationship of political and economic processes
**political executive** *n* **:** the executive at the head of a government as contrasted with a chief of state
**political geography** *n* **:** a branch of geography that deals with human governments, the boundaries and subdivisions of political units (as nations or states), and the situations of cities — compare GEOPOLITICS
**po·lit·i·cal·iza·tion** \pə,lid·ə̇kələ'zāshən\ *n* -S **:** the action or process of politicalizing ⟨the total ~ of Russian arts and artists —*Saturday Rev.*⟩ ⟨the all-out ~ of economic life —J.H. Spigelman⟩
**po·lit·i·cal·ize** \pə'lid·ə̇kə,līz\ *vt* -ED/-ING/-S **:** to make political **:** imbue with politics ⟨the total state which seeks to ~ everything —*Saturday Rev.*⟩ ⟨combats the effort to ~ literature —C.I.Glicksberg⟩
**political liberty** *n* **:** the state or condition of those who are invested with the right effectually to share in framing and conducting the government under which they are politically organized — compare INDIVIDUAL LIBERTY
**po·lit·i·cal·ly** \pə'lid·|ə̇k(ə)lē, pō'-, -it|, |ēk-, -li, *in rapid speech* 'pli-\ *adv* **1** *archaic* **:** in a politic manner **:** POLITICLY ⟨~ pretended the utmost submission —Oliver Goldsmith⟩ **2 :** in political terms **:** from a political point of view ⟨basic decisions . . . must be made by ~ accountable civilian officials —D.D. Eisenhower⟩ ⟨the ~ relevant aspects of cultures —Richard McKeon⟩ ⟨~ conscious people⟩
**po·lit·i·cal·ness** *n* -ES **:** the quality or state of being political
**political party** *n* **:** [1]PARTY 3b(1)
**political prisoner** *n* **:** a person in custody or imprisoned for a political offense
**political process** *n* **:** the process of the formulation and administration of public policy usu. by interaction between social groups and political institutions or between political leadership and public opinion
**political rights** *n pl* **:** the rights that involve participation in the establishment or administration of a government and are usu. held to entitle the adult citizen to exercise of the franchise, the holding of public office, and other political activities — compare CIVIL RIGHTS
**political science** *n* **:** a social science concerned chiefly with the description and analysis of political and esp. governmental institutions and processes and making use of factual material and methods selected from other social sciences (as sociology, psychology, economics, and history) **:** the study of the phenomena of politics **:** a science dealing with the political rather than the social, ethical, or economic relations of man **:** a field of inquiry devoted to an analysis of power in society — compare COMPARATIVE GOVERNMENT, CONSTITUTIONAL LAW, INTERNATIONAL RELATIONS, POLITICAL THEORY 2, POLITICS 8b, PUBLIC ADMINISTRATION
**political scientist** *n* **:** a specialist in political science
**political theory** *n* **1 a :** a theory having to do with the political relationships among men; *specif* **:** one concerned with the organization and basis of government ⟨*political theories* are generated by social frictions —A.S.Kaufman⟩ **b :** the general body of such theories ⟨a history of *political theory*⟩ **2 :** a branch of political science concerned chiefly with the ideas of past and present political thinkers and the doctrines and proposals of political movements and groups ⟨discussion of the proper scope of governmental action . . . has usually been regarded as a proper part of *political theory* —F.W.Coker⟩
**political unit** *n* **:** a unit of territory defined by boundaries set by political authority and usu. having a separate political organization
**political verse** *n* **:** Byzantine or Modern Greek accentual verse; *esp* **:** verse of 15-syllabled iambic lines
**po·lit·i·cas·ter** \pə'lid·ə,kastə(r), ‚=‚==‚=\ *n* -S [prob. fr. [2]*politic* + -*aster*] **:** an unstatesmanlike practitioner of politics **:** a petty or contemptible politician ⟨timorous, trimming ~*s*, all for the party without thought of the state —*N.Y.Times*⟩
**pol·i·ti·cian** \,pälə'tishən\ *n* -S [[1]*politic* + -*an*] **1** *obs* **:** a politic person; *esp* **:** a shrewd or crafty schemer **2 :** one experienced in the art or science of government **:** one actively engaged in conducting the business of a government **:** one skilled or experienced in politics **:** STATESMAN ⟨a power ~⟩ ⟨the ~ and the civil servant work harmoniously together —Alexander Brady⟩ ⟨at once a barbarian potentate and an ambitious European ~ —J.A.Froude⟩ **3 :** one addicted to or actively engaged in party politics: as **a :** one engaged in party politics as a profession or as a means of livelihood **b :** one primarily interested in political offices or profits derived from them as a source of private gain — often used disparagingly **c :** one motivated by narrow (as group, sectional, or personal) and usu. short-run interests as contrasted with the long-term welfare of the people as a whole — compare STATESMAN **4** *obs* **:** POLITIQUE
**po·lit·i·cist** \pə'lid·əsəst\ *n* -S [[1]*politic* + -*ist*] **:** POLITICAL SCIENTIST
**po·lit·i·cize** \-d·ə,sīz\ *vb* -ED/-ING/-S [[1]*politic* + -*ize*] *vi* **:** to discuss or discourse upon politics ~ *vt* **:** to give a political tone or character to **:** to bring within the realm of politics ⟨we want to moralize politics and not to ~ morals —K.R.Popper⟩ ⟨attempts to ~ the civil service⟩
**pol·i·tick** \'pälə,tik\ *vi* -ED/-ING/-S [prob. back-formation fr. *politics*] **:** to engage in political discussion or activity
**pol·i·tick·er** \-kə(r)\ *n* -S **:** one that politicks ⟨a big ~ for the governor's machine —John Beecher⟩
**pol·i·tic·ly** *adv* **:** in a politic manner **:** CRAFTILY, SHREWDLY ⟨purposely and ~ selected them as a foil to himself —E.S. Barrett⟩
**pol·i·tic·ness** *n* -ES **:** the quality or state of being politic
**po·lit·i·co** \pə'lid·ə,kō, pō'-, -itə,-\ *n, pl* **politicos** *also* **politicoes** [It *politico* or Sp *político*; It *politico* fr. *politico*, adj., political, fr. L *politicus*; Sp *político* fr. *político*, adj., political, fr. L *politicus* — more at POLITIC] **:** POLITICIAN 3 ⟨cringing ~*s* who bend to their influence —E.H.Wilson⟩ ⟨some sharp ~*s* . . . think the president won't run —*Wall Street Jour.*⟩ ⟨the support of veteran ~*s* throughout the state —W.V.Shannon⟩
**politico-** *comb form* [NL, fr. L *politicus* political] **1 :** political and ⟨*politico*-diplomatic⟩ ⟨*politico*-military⟩ **2 :** politics ⟨*politico*mania⟩ ⟨*politico*phobia⟩ **3 :** political ⟨*politico*-pressure⟩ ⟨*politico*-nationalist⟩ ⟨*politico*-orthodox⟩
**pol·i·tics** \'pälə,tiks\ *n pl but sing or pl in constr* [prob. modif. (influenced by -*ics*) of Gk *politika*, fr. neut. pl. of *politikos* political — more at POLITIC] **1 a :** the art or science of government **:** a science dealing with the regulation and control of men living in society **:** a science concerned with the organization, direction, and administration of political units (as nations or states) in both internal and external affairs **:** the art of adjusting and ordering relationships between individuals and groups in a political community **b** (1) **:** the art or science concerned with guiding or influencing governmental policy (2) **:** the art or science concerned with winning and holding control over a government (as by selection of governmental personnel) — compare PARTY POLITICS **2 :** a branch of ethics concerned with the state or social organism as a whole rather than the individual person **:** a division of moral philosophy dealing with the ethical relations and duties of governments or other social organizations **:** public or social ethics **3 :** political actions, practices, or policies ⟨protested against the ~ of the Vichy government —*Current Biog.*⟩ ⟨the same ~ were followed by his successors —*New Republic*⟩ ⟨it was not good ~ . . . to present this menacing figure as an incompetent fool —Gilbert Seldes⟩ **4 a** (1) **:** political affairs or business; *specif* **:** competition between competing interest groups or individuals for power and leadership (2) **:** activities concerned with governing or with influencing or winning and holding control of a government ⟨flinch at the thought of . . . participation in partisan ~ —John Lodge⟩ ⟨a university in which ~ had no place —Marjory S. Douglas⟩ ⟨trying to understand recent French ~ —Julian Towster⟩ (3) **:** activities concerned with achieving control, advancement, or some other goal in a nongovernmental group (as a club or office) **b :** political life esp. as a principal activity or profession ⟨~ is . . . the noblest career that a man can choose —J.L.McConaughy⟩ ⟨entered ~⟩ **c :** political activities characterized by artful and often dishonest practices esp. in securing the success of political parties or candidates ⟨dirty ward ~⟩ ⟨in the underworld of ~ —H.R.Penniman⟩ **5 :** conduct of or policy in private affairs ⟨reading a lecture on . . . matrimonial ~ —Henry Fielding⟩ **6 :** the political principles, convictions, opinions, or sympathies of a person ⟨his ~ was . . . reactionary enough —Lionel Trilling⟩ ⟨changed his ~ for advancement's sake —W.B.Yeats⟩ ⟨a woman's ~ are the man she loves —Owen Rhoscomyl⟩ **7 :** the total complex of interacting and usu. conflicting relations between men living in society: as **a :** the relations between men concerned with governing or with influencing or winning and holding control over a government **b :** the relations between leaders and nonleaders in any social grouping (as a political community, church, club, or trade union) **8 a :** POLITICAL SCIENCE **b :** the branch of political science dealing with the activities of political parties and pressure groups
**pol·i·tique** \,pälə'tēk\ *n* -S *usu cap* [F, fr. MF, *politique*, adj., political, fr. L *politicus*] **:** one of a group of French moderates in the 16th century religious conflicts holding national unity of greater importance than the absolute predominance of a single sect and advocating religious toleration as the policy of the government
**pol·i·ti·za·tion** \,pälədə'zāshən\ *n* -S [irreg. fr. *politicize* + -*ation*] **:** the action or result of politicizing ⟨growing ~ and bureaucratization of the social structure —S.N.Eisenstadt⟩
**pol·i·ture** \'pälə,chu̇(ə)r\ *n* -S [It *pulitura*, fr. L *politura*, fr. *politus* polished (past part. of *polire* to polish) + -*ura* -ure — more at POLISH] *archaic* **:** [2]POLISH 1 ⟨the beauty, ~, and hardness of shells —Emanuel Mendez da Costa⟩ ⟨men who wanted the ~ and fineness of this age —John Johnson⟩
**pol·i·ty** \'pälәd·|ē, -ət|, |i\ *n* -ES [LL & L; LL *politia* conduct of public affairs, administration of government, fr. L, state — more at POLICE] **1 :** political organization **:** civil order ⟨any form of ~ is more efficient than none —Walter Bagehot⟩ **2 a :** a specific form of political organization **:** a form of government ⟨a mixed ~⟩ ⟨an equalitarian ~⟩ **b :** an Aristotelian form of political organization in which the whole body of the people govern for the good of all and that constitutes a fusion of oligarchy and democracy **3 :** the management of public or private affairs; *esp* **:** prudent, shrewd, or crafty administration ⟨I know little of stratagem and ~ —E.R.B.Lytton⟩ **4 :** a politically organized unit (as a nation, state, or community) ⟨the humanistic spirit flourished . . . under various *polities* in Greece —Norman Foerster⟩ ⟨a dispute between the temporal and spiritual powers within the universal ~ —Renzo Sereno⟩ **5 a :** the form or constitution of a politically organized unit (as a nation or state) ⟨the character of the English ~ was gradually changing —T.B.Macaulay⟩ ⟨retains in some measure the traditional ~ of the states —*Indian White Paper*⟩ **b :** the form of government or organization of a religious denomination ⟨argued for a congregational ~ —J.C.Brauer⟩ ⟨wanted to change the ~ of the Anglican church —J.E.Neale⟩ **6 :** POLICY ⟨stand up against flagrant wrongdoings . . . or against *polities* fatal to the nation —F.L.Paxson⟩
**po·litz·er bag** \'pō'litsə(r)-\ *n, sometimes cap P* [after Adam *Politzer* †1920 Austrian otologist] **:** a soft rubber bulb used to inflate the middle ear by increasing air pressure in the nasopharynx
**pol·je** \'pōlye\ *n* -S [Serbo-Croatian, lit., field; akin to OSlav *polje* field — more at FLOOR] **:** an extensive depression having a flat floor and steep walls but no outflowing surface stream and found in a region having karst topography (as in parts of Yugoslavia)
**polk** *var of* PULK
[1]**pol·ka** \'pōlkə *sometimes* 'pōkə\ *n* -S *often attrib* [Czech, fr. Pol *Polka* Polish woman, fem. of *Polak* Pole] **1 :** a vivacious couple dance of Bohemian origin with three steps and a hop in duple time **2 :** a lively Bohemian dance tune in $\frac{2}{4}$ time

rhythm of a polka

[2]**polka** \"\ *also* **polk** \'pōlk\ *vi* -ED/-ING/-S [*polka* fr. [1]*polka*; *polk* irreg. fr. [1]*polka*] **:** to dance the polka
[3]**polka** \"\ *also* **polka jacket** *n* -S [[1]*polka*] **:** a close-fitting often knitted jacket worn by women
**polka dot** \'pōkə- *also* 'pōlkə-\ *n* [[1]*polka* + *dot*, n.] **:** a dot of varying size usu. used in a pattern of one size dots evenly distributed in diamond outlines on a background of contrasting color esp. in textile design
**polka-dot** \'==,=\ *vt* [*polka dot*] **:** to spot with or as if with polka dots ⟨the tracks of mountain goats *polka-dotted* the dusty ridge —R.L.Neuberger⟩
**polka mazurka** *n* **1 :** a modified polka using a mazurka step **2 :** a dance tune in slow triple time accented on the last beat
[1]**poll** \'pōl\ *n* -S *often attrib* [ME *pol*, *polle*, fr. MLG, head, top; prob. akin to L *bulla* bubble, LGk *bylla* stuffed things, Lith *bulis* buttocks] **1 a :** [1]HEAD 1 ⟨set his hat back on his ~ —Bryan MacMahon⟩ ⟨scratching his ~ —C.G.Glover⟩ **b** *obs* **:** [1]SKULL 1 **2 :** a unit or an individual in a number ⟨a tax of forty pounds . . . per ~ to support the church —*Amer. Guide Series: Md.*⟩ **3 a** (1) **:** the hair-covered back and top of the human head ⟨all flaxen was his ~ —Shak.⟩ ⟨close-cropped ~*s* —T.B.Costain⟩ (2) **:** the region between the ears of some quadrupeds — see COW illustration **b** *obs* **:** CROWN 3a(1) **c :** [1]NAPE ⟨pierced his neck from throat to ~ —Thomas Hobbes⟩ **4 :** the broad or flat end of a hammer or similar tool **5 a** (1) **:** the casting or recording of the votes of a body of persons **:** the voting at an election ⟨on the eve of the ~ —*Canadian Forum*⟩ (2) **:** a counting of votes cast (as in an election) **b :** the place where votes are cast or recorded — usu. used in pl. ⟨at the ~*s*, a voter . . . votes the ticket of his choice —F.A.Ogg & P.O.Ray⟩ ⟨as the voter leaves the ~*s*⟩ **c :** the period of time during which votes may be cast at an election ⟨the ~ at the . . . universities is restricted to five days —T.E.May⟩ **d :** the numerical result of the counting of votes cast **:** the total number of votes recorded ⟨a heavy ~⟩ ⟨elected to Congress at the head of the ~ —C.G.Bowers⟩ ⟨topped the popularity ~ —Myles McSweeney⟩ ⟨the ~ was low —*Blackwood's*⟩ **6** *obs* **:** a counting of heads **:** CENSUS **7 :** POLL TAX ⟨an act for raising money by a ~ —*London Gazette*⟩ **8 :** the crown of a hat or cap **9 a :** a questioning or canvassing of persons usu. selected at random or by quota from various groups for obtaining information or opinions esp. to be analyzed ⟨what a ~ gains in extensiveness it loses in intensiveness —L.W.Doob⟩ **b :** a record of the information obtained in such a poll ⟨his position has shifted in popularity ~*s* —John Mason Brown⟩
[2]**poll** \"\ *vb* -ED/-ING/-S [ME *pollen*, fr. *pol*, *polle*, n.] *vt* **1 a :** to cut off or cut short the hair or wool of **:** CLIP, CROP, SHEAR ⟨~ a man⟩ ⟨~ a man's head⟩ ⟨~ sheep⟩ **b :** to cut off or cut short (as hair or wool) **2** *archaic* **:** to plunder by or as if by excessive taxation **:** practice extortion on **:** DESPOIL, FLEECE, ROB ⟨the prince doth too much ~ his subjects with heavy tributes —George Wharton⟩ **3 a :** to cut off the head or top of (as a tree or plant); *specif* **:** POLLARD 1 **b :** to cut off or cut short the horns of (cattle) **4 a :** to receive and record the votes of ⟨the first . . . election to ~ the newly enfranchised women voters —Marion Wilhelm⟩ **b** (1) **:** to call on each member of (as a jury) to answer individually as to his concurrence in a verdict rendered (2) **:** to request each member of (as a delegation at a convention) to declare his vote individually **5 :** to cut even without indentation — compare DEED POLL **6** *obs* **:** to count the heads of (as a group of persons) **:** ENUMERATE **7 :** to receive (as votes) in or as if in an election ⟨his party . . . ~*ed* nearly twelve and a half million votes —Douglas Stuart⟩ ⟨~*ed* . . . 30 to 40 percent of the general election vote —V.O. Key⟩ **8 :** to question or canvass in a poll ⟨70 percent of those ~*ed*⟩ ⟨~ attitudes on public issues⟩ ⟨~*ed* members of the delegation⟩ ~ *vi* **:** to cast one's vote at a poll **:** vote at an election ⟨a million Liberal voters ~*ed* for Conservative candidates —*Contemporary Rev.*⟩
[3]**poll** \"\ *adj* [prob. short for *polled*, past part. of [2]*poll*] **:** polled rather than indented — used of a legal document; compare DEED POLL
[4]**poll** \"\ *n* -S [prob. fr. obs. E *poll*, adj., naturally hornless, short for E [1]*polled*] **:** a polled animal ⟨a Scotch ~⟩
[5]**poll** \'päl, 'pȯl\ *n* -S [fr. *Poll*, alter. of *Moll*, nickname for *Mary*] **:** POLL PARROT
[6]**poll** \'päl\ *n* -S [Gk *polloi* many, pl. of *polys* much — more at POLY-] **1 :** a group of students (as at Cambridge University) taking a pass degree rather than honors **2** *or* **poll degree :** a pass or ordinary degree (as at Cambridge) **:** a degree without honors
**pol·lack** *or* **pol·lock** \'pälək\ *n, pl* **pollack** *also* **pollacks** *or* **pollock** *also* **pollocks** [alter. of earlier *podlok*] **:** an important and highly esteemed marine food fish (*Pollachius virens*) of both coasts of the north Atlantic related to and resembling the cods but darker and more lustrous and with a longer lower jaw — called also *bluefish*, *coalfish*, *saithe*; see WALLEYE POLLACK
**pol·lam** \'päləm\ *n* -S [Tamil *pāḷaiyam*, fr. Skt *pālayati* he guards; prob. akin to Skt *piparti* he brings over, rescues] **:** a district in India held in feudal tenure by a poligar
**pol·lan** *also* **pol·len** \'pälən\ *n, pl* **pollan** [origin unknown] **:** a whitefish (*Coregonus pollan*) of Irish lakes
[1]**pol·lard** \'pälə(r)d\ *n* -S [ME, fr. *pol*, *polle* head + -*ard* — more at POLL] **1 :** a clipped or base coin of foreign origin current in England in the late 13th century and equivalent to a penny — compare CROCARD **2** *obs* **a :** a stag that has cast its antlers **b :** a hornless animal (as a cow or sheep) **3 a :** coarse bran obtained from wheat **b :** finely ground bran together with the scourings obtained from wheat during milling and used for livestock feed **4 :** a tree that has been cut back to the trunk to promote the growth of a dense head of foliage
[2]**pollard** \"\ *adj* **:** having been pollarded **:** made into a pollard ⟨under the ~ lime trees —John Galsworthy⟩ ⟨a ~ oak⟩
[3]**pollard** \"\ *vt* -ED/-ING/-S **1 :** to remove the crown of (a tree) **:** cut back or convert into a pollard ⟨~*ed* willows⟩ **2 :** to cut or cause to become stunted in a manner suggesting a pollard
**pollax** *or* **pollaxe** *var of* POLEAX
**poll-bill** *n, obs* **:** a legislative bill providing for a poll tax ⟨levied . . . by a *poll-bill* and new assessments —David Hume †1776⟩
**pollbook** \'=,=\ *n* **1 :** an official register formerly used to record votes at an election **2 :** an official register of electors entitled to vote at an election
**poll clerk** *n* **:** a clerk employed at an election esp. in recording votes
**poll deed** *n* **:** DEED POLL
[1]**polled** \'pōld\ *adj* [ME, fr. past part. of *pollen* to poll, crop, shear — more at POLL] **1** *obs* **:** closely cropped or shaven ⟨~ heads⟩ **2 :** having no horns **:** deprived of or having shed horns ⟨a ~ stag⟩ **:** naturally hornless ⟨~ cattle⟩ **3 :** POLLARD ⟨~ trees⟩
[2]**polled** \'pōld\ *adj* [[1]*poll* + -*ed*] **:** having a poll usu. of a specified kind — used chiefly in combination ⟨a red-*polled* girl⟩
**polled angus** *n, usu cap P&A* **:** ABERDEEN ANGUS
**polled durham** *or* **polled shorthorn** *n* **1** *usu cap P&D&S* **:** a hornless variety of the cattle breed Shorthorn **2** *often cap P&D&S* **:** an animal of the Polled Durham variety
**polled·ness** *n* -ES **:** the state of being hornless ⟨~ in cattle and sheep is usu. considered to be caused by a dominant but epistatic gene⟩
**poll·ee** \(')pō'lē\ *n* -S **:** one who is questioned in a poll ⟨cited by 90 percent of the ~*s* —*N.Y. Times Bk. Rev.*⟩
[1]**pol·len** \'pälən\ *n* -S *often attrib* [L *pollin-*, *pollen* fine flour, fine dust; akin to L *pollenta* pearl barley, *pulvis* dust, Gk *palē* fine meal, dust, *poltos* porridge, and prob. to Skt *palala* ground sesame seeds] **1** *obs* **:** fine flour or meal **2** [NL

*pollin-, pollen,* fr. L] **a :** a mass of microspores in a seed plant appearing usu. as a fine dust made up of minute granular microspores typically formed in fours by reduction of a pollen mother cell with each grain consisting of a single cell that has a characteristically sculptured outer wall and gives rise on germination to a pollen tube through which its male generative element passes to the ovule for fertilization of the egg — compare TETRAD **b :** a dusty or pruinous bloom on the body of various insects

**²pollen** \"\ *vt* -ED/-ING/-S **:** to cover with pollen **:** POLLINATE

**³pollen** \"\ *var of* POLLAN

**pollen analysis** *n* **:** the identification and determination of frequency of pollen grains in peat bogs and other preservative situations as a means of dating fossil and other remains **:** the study of past vegetations and climates as indicated by the pollen content of the various layers of the earth's surface

**pol·len·ate** \ˈpäləˌnāt, *usu* -ād·+V\ *vt* -ED/-ING/-S [by alter. (influenced by ¹*pollen*)] **:** POLLINATE 1

**pol·len·ation** \ˌpäləˈnāshən\ *also* **pol·len·iza·tion** \ˌpälənəˈzāshən\ *n* -s [*pollenation* alter. (influenced by ¹*pollen*) of *pollination; pollenization* alter. (influenced by *pollenize* + *-ation*] **:** POLLINATION

**pollen basket** *n* **:** a smooth area on each hind tibia of a bee that is edged by a fringe of stiff hairs and serves to collect and transport pollen

**pollen brush** *n* **:** a scopa used in collecting pollen; *specif* **:** an arrangement of stiff hairs forming the margin of a pollen basket

**pollen catarrh** *or* **pollen fever** *n* **:** POLLINOSIS

**pollen chamber** *n* **:** a small chamber at the apex of the nucleus in some plants (as most gymnosperms) for the reception of the pollen

**pollen count** *n* **:** a count of the pollen content of the air useful in determining its infectivity in pollinosis

**pollened** *adj* [fr. past part. of ²*pollen*] **:** covered with or containing pollen

**pollen grain** *n* **:** one of the microsporic grains of which pollen is made up

**pol·len·ize** \ˈpäləˌnīz\ *vt* -ED/-ING/-S [¹*pollen* + *-ize*] **:** POLLINATE ⟨bees *pollenized* the fruit trees —Betty MacDonald⟩

**pol·len·iz·er** \-zə(r)\ *n* -s **1 :** a plant that is a source of pollen ⟨there are wild apples that are effective ~*s*⟩; *esp* **:** a plant provided (as in an orchard) primarily to supply pollen to plants of another variety that are either deficient in pollen or self-sterile **2 :** POLLINATOR a

**pollen–lethal** \ˈ⸗⸗ˌ⸗⸗\ *n* -s **:** a lethal gene acting directly on the pollen grain that contains it

**pollen mass** *n* **:** POLLINIUM

**pollen mother cell** *n* **:** a cell that is derived from the hypodermis of the pollen sac and that gives rise by meiosis to four cells, each of which develops into a pollen grain

**pol·le·noph·a·gous** \ˌpäləˈnäfəgəs\ *adj* [¹*pollen* + *-o-* + *-phagous*] **:** feeding on pollen

**pollenosis** *var of* POLLINOSIS

**pollen parent** *n* **:** a male parent

**pollen plate** *n* **:** POLLEN BASKET

**pollen profile** *n* **:** the vertical distribution or stratification of buried or fossil pollen in any horizon or other layer of the earth's surface as an indicator of ancient vegetation

**pollen sac** *n* **:** one of the sacs in a seed plant that contain the pollen and that are initially four in number but are commonly reduced to two by disintegration of the intervening walls in the mature anther

**pollen tube** *n* **:** the tube that develops from the wall of a pollen grain and that in some forms (as the cycads) acts as a haustellate organ and in seed plants provides a passage through which the male nuclei reach the embryo sac to effect fertilization

**poll·er** \ˈpōlə(r)\ *n* -s **:** one that polls: as **a** *obs* **:** one that plunders or extorts esp. by the gathering of excessive taxes **b :** one that polls or lops trees **c :** POLLSTER ⟨answers . . . collected by the ~*s* —J.W.Albig⟩ ⟨sampling techniques . . . used in recent years by public opinion ~*s* —J.R.Miller⟩

**pol·le·ra** \pəˈyerə\ *n* -s [AmerSp, fr. Sp, baby walker, chicken coop, fr. *pollo* chicken, fr. L *pullus* young fowl, young of an animal — more at FOAL] **:** a Latin-American fiesta costume usu. heavily embroidered and very full in the skirt

pollera

**poll evil** *n* **:** an inflammation identical with fistulous withers except in being located on the poll of a horse

**pol·lex** \ˈpäˌleks\ *n, pl* **pol·li·ces** \-ləˌsēz\ [NL *pollic-, pollex,* fr. L, thumb, big toe; akin to OSlav *palĭcĭ* thumb and prob. to L *pollēre* to be strong, be able] **1 :** the first digit of the forelimb **:** THUMB **2 :** the dactylopodite in the chela of a crustacean **3 :** a unit of length equal to one inch — used formerly in descriptions of invertebrate animals

**pol·li·cal** \ˈpäləkəl\ *adj* [NL *pollic-, pollex* + E *-al*] **:** of or relating to a pollex

**pol·lic·i·ta·tion** \pəˌlisəˈtāshən\ *n* -s [L *pollicitation-, pollicitatio,* fr. *pollicitatus* (past part. of *pollicitari* to promise, fr. *pollicitus,* past part. of *pollicēri* to bid, offer, promise, fr. *pol-, por-* — akin to L *per* through — + *licēri* to bid) + *-ion-, -io* -ion; akin to L *licēre* to be permitted, be for sale — more at FARE, LICENSE] **1** *archaic* **:** the action or result of promising **:** PROMISE **2 a** *Roman law* **:** an offer unaccepted or informal promise not accepted by the promisee but made enforceable as to promise of dos by late legislation **b** *civil law* **:** a promise or proposal not accepted **:** an unaccepted offer

**pollies** *pl of* POLLY

**pollin-** *or* **pollini-** *comb form* [NL, fr. *pollin-, pollen* — more at POLLEN] **:** pollen ⟨*pollinic*⟩ ⟨*polliniferous*⟩

**pol·li·nar·i·um** \ˌpäləˈna(a)rēəm\ *n, pl* **pollinar·ia** \-ēə\ [NL, fr. *pollin-* + *-arium*] **:** POLLINIUM

**pol·li·nate** \ˈpäləˌnāt, *usu* -ād·+V\ *vt* -ED/-ING/-S [*pollin-* + *-ate,* v. suffix] **1 :** to apply pollen to the stigma of (a flower or plant) ⟨insects or wind ~ the majority of plants⟩ ⟨~ each flower by hand⟩ **2 :** to mark or smudge with or as if with pollen

**pol·li·na·tion** \ˌ⸗⸗ˈnāshən\ *also* **pol·li·ni·za·tion** \ˌpälənəˈzāshən\ *n* -s [ISV *pollin-* + *-ation* or *-ization*] **1 :** the act or process of pollinating **:** the transfer of pollen from a stamen to an ovule; *broadly* **:** fertilization of a flowering plant ⟨the complex ~ mechanisms of some orchids⟩ ⟨~ of fruit trees by insects⟩ **2 :** the state of being pollinated ⟨upon ~ the petals fall⟩

**pol·li·na·tor** \ˈpäləˌnād·ə(r)\ *n* -s **:** one that pollinates: as **a :** an agent (as an insect) that pollinates flowers **b :** POLLENIZER 1

**¹poll·ing** \ˈpōliŋ, -lēŋ\ *n* -s [ME, action of cutting hair, fr. gerund of *pollen* to poll — more at POLL] **1 :** the action of one that polls; *specif* **:** the casting of ballots at an election ⟨the hours of ~ —H.R.Penniman⟩ **2 :** something that results from polling — usu. used in pl. ⟨the ~*s* of a beard⟩

**²polling** \"\ *adj* **1 :** of or relating to the registering or casting of votes (as at an election) ⟨~ day⟩ ⟨~ card⟩ **2 :** of or relating to the conduct of polls (as of public opinion) ⟨~ experts⟩ ⟨~ methods⟩

**polling book** *n* **:** POLLBOOK

**polling booth** *n* **:** a temporary structure in a polling place where the voting at an election is done

**polling place** *n* **:** the locality or the building where voters cast their ballots in an election

**polling station** *n, chiefly Brit* **:** POLLING PLACE

**pol·lin·ic** \pəˈlinik\ *also* **pol·lin·i·cal** \-nəkəl\ *adj* [*pollinic* ISV *pollin-* + *-ic; pollinical* fr. *pollinic* + *-al*] **:** of or relating to pollen

**pol·li·nif·er·ous** \ˌpäləˈnif(ə)rəs\ *adj* [prob. fr. (assumed) NL *pollinifer* polliniferous (fr. NL *pollin-* + L *-fer* -ferous) + E *-ous*] **1 :** bearing or producing pollen **2 :** adapted for the purpose of carrying pollen

**pol·li·nig·er·ous** \-ij(ə)rəs\ *adj* [*pollin-* + *-gerous*] **:** POLLINIFEROUS

**pol·lin·i·um** \pəˈlinēəm\ *n, pl* **pollin·ia** \-ēə\ [NL, fr. *pollin-* + *-ium*] **:** the coherent mass of pollen grains that characterizes members of the Orchidaceae and Asclepiadaceae and often has a stalk bearing an adhesive disk that clings to visiting insects and facilitates withdrawal of the whole pollinium from its receptacle

**pol·li·nize** \ˈpäləˌnīz\ *vt* -ED/-ING/-S [ISV *pollin-* + *-ize*] **:** POLLINATE 1

**pol·li·niz·er** \-zə(r)\ *n* -s **:** POLLENIZER

**pol·li·no·di·um** \ˌpäləˈnōdēəm\ *n, pl* **pollino·dia** \-ēə\ [NL, fr. *pollin-* + *-odium* (irreg. fr. L *-oides* -oid)] **:** a hyphal branch that functions as an antheridium esp. in fungi of the class Phycomycetes

**pol·li·nose** \ˈpäləˌnōs\ *adj* [NL *pollinosus,* fr. *pollin-* + L *-osus* -ose] *of an insect* **:** covered with pollen **:** PRUINOSE

**pol·li·no·sis** *or* **pol·le·no·sis** \ˌpäləˈnōsəs\ *n, pl* **pollino·ses** *or* **polleno·ses** \-ōˌsēz\ [*pollinosis* fr. NL, fr. *pollin-* + *-osis; pollenosis* alter. (influenced by *pollen*) of *pollinosis*] **:** an acute catarrhal disorder involving the mucous membranes of the eyes, nose, and respiratory tract often with asthmatic symptoms that recurs annually usu. in the spring or late summer and is caused by allergic sensitivity to pollens (as of ragweed, grasses, or trees) — called also *hay fever*

**pol·li·wog** *or* **pol·ly·wog** \ˈpälēˌwäg, -wȯg\ *n* -s [alter. of earlier *polwigge,* alter. of ME *polwygle,* prob. fr. *pol, polle* head + *wiglen, wigelen* to wiggle — more at POLL, WIGGLE] **1 :** TADPOLE **2 :** one who crosses the equator for the first time and undergoes an initiation (as by being tossed into seawater) by shellbacks

**poll money** *n, archaic* **:** POLL TAX

**pollock** *var of* POLLACK

**pol·loi** \pəˈlȯi\ *n pl* [Gk, many, pl. of *polys* much — more at POLY-] **:** HOI POLLOI ⟨the ribald ~ . . . became derisively familiar —*Emporia (Kans.) Gazette*⟩

**poll parrot** *n* [⁵*poll* + *parrot,* n.] **:** a tame parrot

**poll–parrot** \ˈ⸗ˌ⸗⸗\ *vb* [*poll parrot*] *vt* **:** to speak, repeat, or imitate like a parrot ⟨*poll-parroting* nonsense —H.L.Mencken⟩ ~ *vi* **:** to chatter like a parrot

**poll pick** *n* **:** a single-pointed miner's pick having a short poll or striking head

**polls** *pl of* POLL, *pres 3d sing of* POLL

**poll sickness** *n* **:** POLL EVIL

**poll·ster** \ˈpōlztə(r), -lst-\ *n* -s **:** one that conducts or asks questions in a poll (as of public opinion) or that records or compiles data obtained by a poll

**polltaker** \ˈ⸗ˌ⸗⸗\ *n* **:** POLLSTER

**poll tax** *n* **:** a tax of a fixed rather than a graduated amount per head or person which is levied on adults and payment of which is often made a requirement for voting — compare HEAD TAX

**pol·lu·cite** \pəˈlüˌsīt, ˈpälyəˌ-\ *n* -s [L *Polluc-, Pollux* Pollux + E *-ite* (after G *pollux* pollucite)] **:** a colorless transparent mineral $(Cs,Na)_2Al_2Si_4O_{12}.H_2O$ of the zeolite family consisting of hydrous cesium aluminum silicate and occurring massive or crystallizing in cubes

**pol·lu·tant** \pəˈlütᵊnt\ *n* -s **:** something that pollutes **:** a polluting substance, medium, or agent ⟨domestic wastes . . . are another chief source of ~*s* —*Pollution Problem*⟩ ⟨the great ~*s* are industrial plants and oil burners —*Automobilist*⟩

**¹pol·lute** \pəˈlüt, *usu* -üd·+V\ *vt* -ED/-ING/-S [ME *polluten,* fr. L *pollutus,* past part. of *polluere,* fr. *pol-, por-* — akin to L *per* through — + *-luere* to soil, dirty; akin to L *lutum* mud, *lustrum* cave, bog, Gk *lyma* dirt, Alb (Tosk dial.) *lum* mud — more at FARE] **1 :** to render ceremonially or morally impure **:** impair the purity of **:** destroy or violate the sanctity of **:** CORRUPT, DEFILE, DESECRATE, PROFANE ⟨~ a temple⟩ ⟨~ a person's honor⟩ **2 :** to make physically impure or unclean **:** BEFOUL, DIRTY, TAINT ⟨~ a water supply by the introduction of sewage⟩ **syn** see CONTAMINATE

**²pollute** \"\ *adj* [ME *pollut, pollute,* fr. L *pollutus,* past part. of *polluere*] *archaic* **:** POLLUTED ⟨her naked shame ~ with sinful blame —John Milton⟩

**pol·lut·ed** \-üd·əd, -ütəd\ *adj* [ME, fr. past part. of *polluten* to pollute] **1 :** made unclean or impure **:** morally corrupt or defiled **:** physically tainted ⟨change . . . a pure stream into a ~ and poisoned ditch —O.W.Holmes †1935⟩ ⟨you . . . are ~ with your lusts —Shak.⟩ **2 :** very drunk ⟨so ~ she could hardly see —Trudi Stover⟩

**pol·lut·er** \-üd·ə(r)\ *n* -s **:** one that pollutes

**pol·lu·tion** \-üshən\ *n* -s [ME *pollucioun* emission of semen at other times than in coition, defilement, uncleanness, fr. MF & LL; MF *pollution,* fr. LL *pollution-, pollutio* defilement, uncleanness, fr. L *pollutus* (past part. of *polluere* to pollute) + *-ion-, -io* -ion] **1 :** emission of semen at other times than in coition **2 :** the action of polluting or the state of being polluted **:** DEFILEMENT, DESECRATION, IMPURITY, UNCLEANNESS ⟨streams subject to ~ by . . . mill wastes —C.R.Cox⟩ ⟨the dilution of atmospheric ~ —K.H.Jehm⟩ ⟨cleanse the king and the people from the ~ of any offenses —J.G.Frazer⟩ **3 :** crossbreeding when regarded as the source of degeneration of a stock

**pol·lu·tion·al** \-shənᵊl\ *adj* **:** of or relating to pollution ⟨~ material⟩ ⟨~ source⟩

**pollux** *n* -ES [G, fr. L *Polluc-, Pollux* Pollux, one of the Dioscuri (the other being L *Castor,* Gk *Kastōr*), twin heroes or demigods of Greek mythology, fr. Gk *Polydeukēs;* fr. its appearance with castorite (previously called *castor*)] *obs* **:** POLLUCITE

**poll watcher** *n* **:** a person assigned (as by a political party or candidate) to observe activities at a polling place to guard against illegal voting, fraudulent counting of ballots, and other violations of election laws

**pol·ly** \ˈpälē\ *n* -ES [fr. *Polly,* alter. of *Molly,* nickname for *Mary*] **:** POLL PARROT

**pol·ly·an·na** \ˌpälēˈanə\ *n* -s *usu cap* [after *Pollyanna,* heroine of the novel *Pollyanna* (1913) by Eleanor Porter †1920 Am. fiction writer] **:** one having a disposition or nature characterized by irrepressible optimism and a tendency to find good in everything **:** an overly and often blindly optimistic person **:** an irritatingly cheerful person ⟨the facts on inflation are sugarcoated by the *Pollyannas* —*Atlantic*⟩ ⟨not such a *Pollyanna* as to deny the probability of recessions —*Dun's Rev.*⟩

**pol·ly·an·na·ish** \ˌ⸗⸗ˈanə·ish\ *or* **pol·ly·an·nish** \-nish\ *adj, usu cap* **:** resembling or suggesting a Pollyanna esp. by having an optimistic nature characterized by a tendency to find good in everything ⟨its *Pollyannaish* outlook and blatant self-esteem —Arthur Knight⟩

**pol·ly·an·na·ism** \ˌ⸗⸗ˈanəˌizəm\ *also* **pol·ly·an·nism** \-aˌnizəm\ *n* -s *usu cap* **:** the overly optimistic and benevolently cheerful state of mind and point of view of a Pollyanna

**polly–fox** \ˈ⸗⸗ˌ⸗\ *vi* [origin unknown] *dial* **:** to sidestep an issue esp. by equivocation or evasion

**polly mountain** *n* [origin unknown] **:** BASIL BALM 2

**pollywog** *var of* POLLIWOG

**po·lo** \ˈpō(ˌ)lō\ *n* -s *often attrib* [Balti, ball] **1 a :** a game of oriental origin played by teams of three or four players mounted on horseback and using mallets with long flexible handles to drive a wooden ball down the field and through goalposts **b :** any of several similar games (as one in which the players ride bicycles) **2 :** WATER POLO

**polo coat** *n* **:** a tailored overcoat for casual wear made of tan camel's hair cloth or other fabric in single-breasted or double-breasted style often with stitched edges and a half-belt

**po·lo·crosse** \ˈpōlōˌkrȯs\ *n* -s [*polo* + *lacrosse*] **:** a goal game combining elements of polo, lacrosse, and netball played by teams of six players mounted on horseback and using a sponge rubber ball and a stick with a head like that of a crosse and a handle and shaft like those of a polo stick

**po·lo·cyte** \ˈpōləˌsīt\ *n* -s [ISV ⁴*pole* + *-o-* + *-cyte*] **:** POLAR BODY 2

**po·lo·ist** \ˈpōlōəst\ *n* -s **:** a polo player

**¹po·lo·naise** \ˌpäləˈnāz, ˌpōl-\ *n* -s [F, fr. fem. of *polonais* Polish, fr. *Pologne* Poland, country in central Europe, fr. ML *Polonia*] **1 a :** an elaborate overdress that consists of a short-sleeved fitted waist and a draped cutaway overskirt **b** *Scot* **:** a tight-fitting jacket for boys **2 a :** a stately Polish processional dance fashionable in 19th century Europe **b :** the music for or suited to this dance in moderate ¾ time characterized typically by the rhythms of an eighth note and two sixteenths followed by either four eighths or a repetition of the rhythm of the first beat

rhythm of a polonaise

**²polonaise** \"\ *vi* -ED/-ING/-S **:** to dance a polonaise

**³polonaise** \ˌ⸗⸗ˈ⸗\ *adj, usu cap* [F, fem. of *polonais* Polish] **:** made of or dressed with browned butter and bread crumbs ⟨sauce *Polonaise*⟩ ⟨cauliflower *Polonaise*⟩

**po·lo·nay** \ˌ⸗⸗ˈnā\ *n* -s [prob. back-formation] *dial* **:** POLONAISE 1a

**po·lo·nese** \ˌ⸗⸗ˈnēz, -ēs\ *n* -s *sometimes cap* [prob. modif. of F *polonaise*] **:** POLONAISE 1a

**¹po·lo·ni·an** \pəˈlōnēən\ *adj, usu cap* [ML *Polonia* Poland + E *-an*] *archaic* **:** POLISH ⟨a *Polonian* Jew by birth —W.J. Mickle⟩

**²polonian** \"\ *n* -s *usu cap, archaic* **:** ⁶POLE 1 ⟨served against the Tartar and the *Polonian* —J.H.Burton⟩

**³polonian** \"\ *adj, usu cap* [*Polonius,* worldly-wise and long-winded old courtier in the tragedy *Hamlet* (about 1601) by William Shakespeare †1616 Eng. dramatist and poet + E *-an*] **:** resembling or held to resemble Polonius **:** having qualities or habits held to characterize Polonius

**po·lo·nism** \ˈpōləˌnizəm\ *n* -s *usu cap* [ISV *polon-* (fr. ML *Polonia* Poland) + *-ism*] **1 :** a quality or trait held to be distinctive of Poles or Polish culture **2 :** a characteristic feature of Polish occurring in another language or dialect

**po·lo·nist** \-nəst\ *n* -s *usu cap* [ML *Polonia* Poland + E *-ist*] **:** a specialist in the Polish language or Polish literature and culture

**po·lo·ni·um** \pəˈlōnēəm\ *n* -s [NL, fr. ML *Polonia* Poland + NL *-ium;* fr. the fact that Marja Skłodowska Curie †1934 Fr. physical chemist, who together with her husband Pierre Curie †1906 Fr. chemist discovered polonium, was Polish by birth] **:** a radioactive metallic element that is similar chemically to tellurium and bismuth, that occurs in pitchblende and other uranium-containing ores, in radium-lead residues, and in old radon ampuls but can be produced in much larger quantities by bombarding bismuth with neutrons in nuclear reactors, and that emits a helium nucleus to form an isotope of lead — symbol *Po;* see ACTINIUM SERIES, THORIUM SERIES, URANIUM SERIES; ELEMENT table

**po·lo·ni·za·tion** \ˌpōlənəˈzāshən\ *n* -s *often cap* **:** the act or process of polonizing or the state of being polonized ⟨resist the ~ of the Ukrainian upper classes —R. G. A. De Bray⟩

**po·lo·nize** \ˈpōləˌnīz\ *vt* -ED/-ING/-S *often cap* [ISV *polon-* (fr. ML *Polonia* Poland) + *-ize*] **1 :** to cause to acquire Polish customs or attitudes; *esp* **:** to force into conformity with Polish cultural patterns or governmental policies ⟨German cities assigned to Poland have been *polonized* —M.A.Pei⟩ ⟨the Polish clergy . . . use their influence to ~ the people — *Russian Poland*⟩ **2 :** to modify (a word or expression) to conform to characteristics distinctive of Polish ⟨difficult . . . to ~ English terms —B.W.A.Massey⟩

**¹polony** *adj, usu cap* [prob. fr. obs. E *Polony* Poland, fr. ML *Polonia*] *obs* **:** POLISH

**²po·lo·ny** \pəˈlōnī\ *n* -ES *Scot* **:** POLONAISE 1b

**³polony** \"\ *n* -ES [alter. (influenced by ¹*polony*) of *Bologna* (in *bologna sausage*) — more at BOLOGNA] *Brit* **:** a dry partly cooked sausage made of various ingredients ⟨liver ~⟩ ⟨cervelat ~⟩

**polo pony** *also* **polo mount** *n* **:** a horse trained for use as a mount in playing polo and characterized primarily by endurance, speed, courage, and docility

**pol·os** \ˈpäˌläs\ *n, pl* **po·loi** \-lȯi\ [Gk, polos, pivot, axis, pole — more at POLE] **:** a high crown or headdress of cylindrical shape, represented as worn by ancient Greek goddesses (as Demeter, Persephone, Hecate, and Aphrodite)

**polo shirt** *n* **:** a close-fitting pullover shirt for sportswear that is made of knitted cotton and has short or long sleeves and a turnover collar or a round banded neck — compare T-SHIRT

polo shirt

**po·lov·tsi·an** \pəˈläftsēən, -ävt-; ⸗ˈ-ˌ pälˈvetsēən, ⸗ˈpōl-\ *n* -s *usu cap* [Russ *Polovtsy* (pl.) Cumans + E *-an*] **:** CUMAN

**pol·ska** \ˈpōlzkə, -lskə\ *n* -s [Sw, fr. *polsk* Polish, fr. Pol *polski*] **1 :** a Swedish folk dance derived from a Polish peasant dance **2 :** music for the polska in triple time and usu. in a minor key

**pol·ster** \ˈpōlztə(r), -lst-\ *n* -s [G, lit., cushion, fr. OHG *bolstar, polstar* bolster — more at BOLSTER] **:** CUSHION PLANT

**¹polt** \ˈpōlt\ *n* -s [origin unknown] *dial Eng* **:** a hard knock **:** BLOW, THUMP ⟨fetched me an awful ~ in the right side —*Blackwood's*⟩

**²polt** \"\ *vt* -ED/-ING/-S *dial Eng* **:** to knock or thump esp. with a stick or club

**pol·ta·va** \pälˈtävə\ *adj, usu cap* [fr. *Poltava,* city in east central Ukraine, U.S.S.R.] **:** of or from the city of Poltava, U.S.S.R. **:** of the kind or style prevalent in Poltava

**pol·ter·geist** \ˈpōltə(r)ˌgīst *sometimes* ˈpäl- *or* ˈpȯl-\ *n* -s [G, fr. *poltern* to knock, rattle (fr. MHG *boldern, buldern*) + *geist* spirit, fr. OHG; akin to MLG *balderen* to make a noise — more at BOULDER, GHOST] **:** a noisy and usu. mischievous ghost **:** a spirit capable of making mysterious noises (as rappings)

**¹poltfoot** \ˈ⸗ˌ⸗\ *n, pl* **poltfeet** [prob. fr. ¹*polt* + *foot*] *archaic* **:** CLUBFOOT

**²poltfoot** \"\ *or* **poltfooted** \ˈ⸗ˈ⸗⸗\ *adj* **:** having a clubfoot

**pol·tin·nik** \pälˈtēnik\ *or* **pol·ti·na** \-ēnə\ *n* -s [*poltinnik* fr. Russ, half-ruble piece, fr. *poltina* half a ruble, fr. Old Russian *polŭtina,* prob. fr. *polŭ* half + *tina,* gen. of *tinŭ* ruble; *poltina* fr. Russ; prob. akin to L *duplus* double and to Gk *temnein* to cut — more at FOLD, TOME] **:** a Russian silver half-ruble or 50-kopeck piece

**¹pol·troon** \pälˈtrün\ *n* -s [MF *poultron,* fr. OIt *poltrone,* aug. of *poltro* colt, fr. (assumed) VL *pullitrus* (whence LL *pulletrus*), irreg. fr. L *pullus* young of an animal — more at FOAL] **:** a spiritless coward **:** a mean-spirited wretch **:** CRAVEN, DASTARD ⟨lily-livered ~*s* lacking even the meager courage of a rabbit —P.G.Wodehouse⟩

**²poltroon** \"\ *adj* **:** characterized by complete cowardice **syn** see COWARDLY

**pol·troon·ery** \-n(ə)rē\ *n* -ES [MF *poltronnerie,* fr. *poltron, poultron* poltroon + *-erie* -ery] **:** behavior characteristic of a poltroon **:** want of spirit **:** mean pusillanimity **:** COWARDICE ⟨~ among politicians —G.W.Johnson⟩

**pol·troon·ish** \-nish\ *adj* **:** resembling a poltroon **:** COWARDLY ⟨a weak, almost ~ character —*Quarterly Rev.*⟩ — **pol·troon·ish·ly** *adv*

**pol·ver·ine** \ˈpälvəˌrēn\ *n* -s [It *polverino,* fr. *polvere* dust, fr. L *pulver-, pulvis* dust — more at POLLEN] **:** a potash or pearl ash from the Levant used in making fine glass

**pol·warth** *also* **pol·worth** \ˈpōlwə(r)th\ *n* [prob. fr. *Polwarth,* county in Victoria, southeast Australia] **1** *usu cap* **:** an Australian breed of rather large medium-wooled sheep developed from crosses of Merino and Lincoln sheep and noted for ability to withstand damp and cold **2** -s *often cap* **:** a sheep of the Polworth breed

**poly** \ˈpälē, -li\ *n* -s [by shortening] **:** a polymorphonuclear leukocyte

**poly-** *comb form* [ME, fr. L, fr. Gk, fr. *polys;* akin to L *plenus* full — more at FULL] **1 a :** many **:** several **:** diverse **:** much **:** MULTI-, PLURI- ⟨*poly*tonality⟩ ⟨*poly*centric⟩ ⟨*poly*cotyledon⟩ ⟨*poly*cross⟩ ⟨*poly*arthritis⟩ **b :** excessive **:** abnormal **:** HYPER- ⟨*poly*galactia⟩ ⟨*poly*chromia⟩ ⟨*poly*dactylous⟩ **2** *chem* **a :** containing more than one and esp. more than two or three units of (a specified substance) ⟨*poly*atomic⟩ ⟨*poly*sulfide⟩ — compare OLIG- **b :** ISOPOLY- ⟨*poly*molybdate⟩ **c :** polymerized **:** polymeric **:** polymer of (a specified monomer) ⟨*poly*ethylene⟩

**poly** *abbr* polytechnic

**¹poly·acid** \ˈpälē+\ *n* [ISV *poly-* + *acid*] **1 :** an acid (as phosphoric acid) having more than one acid hydrogen atom **2 :** a complex acid of the group of isopoly or heteropoly acids

**²polyacid** \"\ *adj* **1 :** able to react with more than one molecule of a monoacid to form a salt — used esp. of bases **2 :** having more than one hydrogen atom replaceable by basic atoms or radicals — used of acids and acid salts

**poly·acrylate** \¦pälē\ *n* [ISV *poly-* + *acrylate*] **:** a polymer of an acrylate **:** a salt or ester of polyacrylic acid

**poly·acrylic acid** \"+ . . . -\ *n* [*poly-* + *acrylic*] **:** a polymer of acrylic acid **:** a polycarboxylic acid ($-CH_2CH(COOH)-$)$_x$ formed by polymerization of an acrylic ester or acrylonitrile followed by hydrolysis

**poly·acrylonitrile** \¦pälē\ *n* [ISV *poly-* + *acrylonitrile*] **:** a solid polymer of acrylonitrile ($-CH_2CH(CN)-$)$_x$ that is soluble in dimethyl-formamide from which after appropriate blending it may be spun into textile filaments — compare ACRYLIC FIBER

**poly·act** \'pälē,akt\ *adj* [*poly-* + *-act*] **:** having many rays or radii — used esp. of a sponge spicule

**poly·actinal** *or* **poly·actine** \¦==+\ *adj* [*poly-* + *-actinal* or *-actine*] **:** POLYACT

**¹poly·ad** \'pälē,ad\ *n* -s [*poly-* + *-ad*] **1 :** a group consisting of several closely related parts or elements **2 :** a polyad atom, radical, or element

**²polyad** \"\ *adj* **1** *or* **poly·ad·ic** \¦==¦adik\ **:** of, relating to, or constituting a polyad **2** [*poly-* + *-ad*] **:** POLYVALENT

**poly·adel·phia** \,==ə'delfēə\ *n pl, cap* [NL, fr. Gk, possession of many brothers, fr. *polyadelphos* with many brothers (fr. *poly-* + *adelphos* brother) + *-ia* -y] *in former classifications* **:** a class of plants having stamens united by the filaments into three or more fascicles

**poly·adel·phous** \¦==¦=fəs\ *adj* [NL *Polyadelphia* + E *-ous*] *of stamens* **:** united by the anthers into three or more groups — compare DIADELPHOUS, MONADELPHOUS

**poly·allel** \¦pälē\ *adj* [*poly-* + *-allel* (as in *diallel*)] **:** DIALLEL

**poly·alphabetic** \"+\ *adj* [*poly-* + *alphabetic*] **:** using several substitution alphabets in turn — see MULTIPLE-ALPHABET CIPHER, PROGRESSIVE-ALPHABET CIPHER, VIGENÈRE CIPHER — **poly·alphabetically** \"+\ *adv*

**poly·amide** \"+\ *n* [ISV *poly-* + *amide*] **:** a compound characterized by more than one amide group; *esp* **:** a polymeric amide (as nylon or a polypeptide or a protein)

**poly·amine** \"+\ *n* [ISV *poly-* + *amine*] **:** a compound characterized by more than one amino group

**poly·an·dria** \,pälē'andrēə\ *n pl, cap* [NL, fr. *poly-* + *-andria*] *in former classifications* **:** a class of monoclinous plants including those with many hypogynous stamens

**poly·an·dric** \¦==¦=drik\ *adj* **:** relating to or characterized by polyandry

**poly·an·drist** \'==,=drəst, ,==¦=\ *n* -s **:** one who practices polyandry **:** a polyandrous woman

**poly·an·dri·um** \,==¦=drēəm\ *also* **poly·an·dri·on** \-ē,än, -ēən\ *n* -s [LL, fr. Gk *polyandrion, polyandreion,* fr. *polyandrion* place where many people meet, fr. neut. of *polyandrios* of or connected with many men, fr. *poly-* + *andr-, anēr* man] **:** an ancient Greek burying ground esp. for men fallen in battle; *broadly* **:** CEMETERY

**poly·an·drous** \¦==¦=drəs\ *adj* [NL *Polyandria* + E *-ous*] **1 :** having many usu. free hypogynous stamens **2** [*polyandry* + *-ous*] **a :** practicing polyandry **b :** relating to or involving polyandry

**poly·an·dry** \'==,=drē\ *n* -ES [Gk *polyandria* condition of having many men, populousness, fr. *polyandros* having many men, having many husbands (fr. *poly-* + *andr-, anēr* man) + *-ia* -y — more at ANDR-] **1 a :** a marriage form in which one woman has two or more husbands at the same time — contrasted with *polygyny;* compare FRATERNAL POLYANDRY, MONANDRY, POLYGAMY **b :** the condition of having more than one male mate at one time **2 :** the state of being polyandrous

**poly·an·gi·a·ce·ae** \,pälē,anjē'āsē,ē\ *n pl, cap* [NL, fr. *Polyangium,* type genus + *-aceae*] **:** a family of myxobacteria living mostly in soils and on dung and having fruiting bodies in which the rod-shaped cells are enclosed in rounded cysts often brightly colored and covered by a membrane representing the remains of the vegetative slime

**poly·an·gi·um** \-'anjēəm\ *n, cap* [NL, fr. *poly-* + *-angium*] **:** the type genus of Polyangiaceae comprising myxobacteria with rounded usu. solitary unstalked fruiting bodies enclosed in a membrane

**poly·an·tha** \,pälē'an(t)thə\ *or* **polyantha rose** *n* -s [NL, fr. Gk *polyanthos* blooming, fr. *poly-* + *anthos* flower — more at ANTHOLOGY] **:** any of numerous dwarf hybrid bush roses derived chiefly from crosses of two species (*Rosa chinensis* and *R. multiflora*) and usu. treated in horticulture as a distinct species (*R. polyantha*) characterized by the free production of small and rarely fragrant flowers in large clusters — compare FLORIBUNDA

**poly·an·thea** \-'an(t)thēə, -,an'th-\ *n* -s [NL, fr. Gk, fem. of *polyanthēs* having many blossoms, fr. *poly-* + *anthos* flower] *archaic* **:** ANTHOLOGY

**poly·an·thus** \-'an(t)thəs\ *n, pl* **polyanthuses** \-n(t)thəsəz\ *or* **polyan·thi** \-n,thī\ [NL, fr. Gk *polyanthos* blooming] **1 :** any of various florists' primroses formerly supposed to have been derived from a species primula (*Primula elatior*) but now usu. considered a complex hybrid (*P. polyantha*) prob. derived from three primulas (*P. veris, P. elatior,* and *P. vulgaris*) **2** *or* **polyanthus narcissus :** a narcissus (*Narcissus tazetta*) having small umbeled white or yellow flowers with a spreading perianth and shallow crown and cultivated in several varieties

**poly·arch** \'pälē,ärk\ *adj* [ISV *poly-* + *-arch*] **:** having many protoxylem groups ⟨the ~ stele of a root⟩

**poly·ar·chic** \¦==¦ärkik\ *or* **poly·ar·chi·cal** \-rkəkəl\ *adj* **:** of or relating to a polyarchy ⟨tradition of ~ independence of the several ministers as department heads —C.J.Friedrich⟩

**poly·ar·chism** \'==,är,kizəm\ *n* -s **:** POLYARCHY

**poly·ar·chy** \-,kē\ *n* -ES [Gk *polyarchia,* fr. *polyarchos* ruling over many (fr. *poly-* + *archos* ruler) + *-ia* -y — more at ARCHI-] **1 :** government by many persons **:** control of esp. political leaders by their followers — compare HIERARCHY **2 :** a group of many kingdoms ⟨filled Europe with a colorful ~ of innumerable tribes —D.C.Peattie⟩

**poly·ar·gy·rite** \,pälē'ärjə,rīt\ *n* -s [G *polyargyrit,* fr. *poly-* + *argyr-* + *-it* -ite] **:** a mineral $Ag_{24}Sb_2S_{15}$(?) consisting of a sulfide of antimony and silver occurring chiefly in indistinct cuboctahedrons

**poly·arteritis** \'pälē+\ *n* [NL, fr. *poly-* + *arteritis*] **:** PERIARTERITIS NODOSA

**poly·arthritis** \"+\ *n* [NL, fr. *poly-* + *arthritis*] **:** arthritis involving two or more joints

**poly·articular** \"+\ *adj* [ISV *poly-* + *articular*] **:** having or affecting many joints ⟨~ arthritis⟩

**poly·atomic** \"+\ *adj* [ISV *poly-* + *atomic*] **:** containing more than one or usu. more than two atoms ⟨~ molecules⟩

**poly·autographic** \"+\ *adj* [*polyautography* + *-ic*] *archaic* **:** done or produced by lithography ⟨~ albums⟩ ⟨~ printing⟩

**poly·autography** \"+\ *n* [*poly-* + *autography*] *archaic* **:** LITHOGRAPHY

**¹poly·axon** *also* **poly·axone** \"+\ *n* [*poly-* + *axon, axone*] **1 :** a nerve cell having several axons **2** [*poly-* + Gk *axōn* axle, axis — more at AXIS] **:** a polyaxon sponge spicule

**²poly·axon** *or* **poly·axonic** \¦pälē+\ *adj* **:** having many axes ⟨~ spicules⟩

**poly·basic** \¦pälē, -lə+\ *adj* [*poly-* + *basic*] **1 :** having more than one hydrogen atom replaceable by basic atoms or radicals — used of acids **2 :** containing more than one atom of a univalent metal or their equivalent — used of a salt **3 :** having more than one basic hydroxyl group **:** able to react with more than one molecule of a monoacid — used of bases and basic salts — **poly·basicity** \"+\ *n*

**poly·ba·site** \,pälē'bā,sīt, -lə'b-\ *n* -s [G *polybasit,* fr. *poly-* + *basi-* + *-it* -ite] **:** an iron-black metallic-looking ore ($Ag,Cu)_{16}Sb_2S_{11}$ of silver consisting essentially of silver, copper, sulfur, and antimony

**poly·blast** \'==,blast\ *n* [ISV *poly-* + *-blast*] **:** a wandering macrophage — **poly·blas·tic** \¦==¦blastik\ *adj*

**poly·blend** \'pälē, -lə+,-\ *n* [*poly-* + *blend*] **:** a colloidal mixture of one polymer with another (as of a vinyl resin with nitrile rubber)

**po·lyb·o·rine** \pə'libə,rīn\ *adj* [NL *Polyborus* + E *-ine*] **:** of or relating to the genus *Polyborus*

**po·lyb·o·rus** \-rəs\ *n, cap* [NL, fr. Gk *polyboros* voracious, fr. *poly-* much (fr. *polys* much, many) + *boros* devouring, gluttonous, fr. *bora* food, meat — more at POLY-, VORACIOUS] **:** a genus of long-winged hawks (family Falconidae) consisting of typical caracaras

**pol·y·brid** \(')pä¦librəd; 'pälēb-, -ləb-\ *n* -s [*poly-* + *hybrid*] **:** HETEROGEN

**poly·butene** \¦pälē, -lə+\ *n* [*poly-* + *butene*] **:** POLYBUTYLENE

**poly·butylene** \"+\ *n* [*poly-* + *butylene*] **:** a polymer of one or more butylenes; *esp* **:** POLYISOBUTYLENE

**poly·ca·on** \,pälē'kā,än, -lə'k-\ *n, cap* [NL, perh. fr. *Polycaon,* in Greek legend ruler of ancient Messina] **:** a genus of beetles (family Bostrychidae) whose larvae bore into twigs and branches of various trees

**poly·carboxylic** \¦pälē, -lə+\ *adj* [*poly-* + *carboxylic*] **:** containing more than one carboxyl group in the molecule

**poly·carpellary** \"+\ *adj* [*poly-* + *carpellary*] **:** consisting of several carpels — compare MONOCARPELLARY

**poly·carpellate** \"+\ *adj* [ISV *poly-* + *carpellate*] **:** having many carpels

**poly·car·pic** \¦pälē¦kärpik, -lə¦k-\ *or* **poly·car·pous** \-rpəs\ *adj* [*polycarpic* prob. fr. NL *polycarpicus,* fr. *poly-* + *-carpicus* -carpic; *polycarpous* prob. fr. (assumed) NL *polycarpus,* fr. NL *poly-* + *-carpus* -carpous] **1 :** SYCHNOCARPOUS **2 :** having a gynoecium forming two or more distinct ovaries — **poly·car·py** \'==,=pē\ *n* -ES

**poly·car·pon** \,==¦=,pän\ *n, cap* [NL, fr. Gk *polykarpon,* a plant, fr. neut. of *polykarpos* fruitful, fr. *poly-* + *-karpos* fruit — more at HARVEST] **:** a small genus of herbs (family Caryophyllaceae) of temperate and warm regions having small white cymose flowers with 5-keeled sepals and 3 to 5 stamens

**polycaryon** *var of* POLYKARYON

**polycaryotic** *var of* POLYKARYOTIC

**poly·cen·tric** \¦pälē¦sen·trik, -lə¦s-\ *adj* [*poly-* + *-centric*] **:** having many centers: as **a** *of chromosomes* **:** having several chromomeres **b** *of cells* **:** having several centrosomes or division centers **c** *of organisms or groups* **:** having several centers of development or differentiation — compare MONOCENTRIC

**poly·cen·trop·i·dae** \,==,sen·'träpə,dē\ *n pl, cap* [NL, fr. *Polycentropus,* type genus (prob. fr. *poly-* + *centr-* + *-pus*) + *-idae*] **:** a widely distributed family of caddis flies whose larvae are mostly carnivorous and usu. live in running water

**poly·ceph·a·lous** \¦==¦sefələs\ *also* **poly·ce·phal·ic** \-sə¦falik\ *adj* [*poly-* + *-cephalous* or *-cephalic*] *of a tapeworm larva* **:** having many scolices

**poly·chae·ta** \,=='kēd·ə\ *n pl, cap* [NL, fr. Gk *polychaitēs* with much hair, fr. *poly-* much (fr. *polys* much, many) + *chaitē* long flowing hair — more at POLY- CHAETA] **:** a class of Annelida or in former classifications an order of Chaetopoda that comprises chiefly marine annelid worms usu. having paired setate appendages on most segments, a differentiated head with eyes, tactile processes and bristles, and chitinous jaws and being distinguished from the related oligochaete worms by possession of separate sexes and by a complex life history with a free-swimming trochophore larva — see ERRANTIA, SEDENTARIA

**¹poly·chaete** \'==,kēt\ *or* **poly·chae·tous** \¦==¦kēd·əs\ *adj* [*polychaete* fr. NL *Polychaeta; polychaetous* fr. NL *Polychaeta* + E *-ous*] **:** of or relating to the Polychaeta

**²polychaete** *also* **poly·chete** \'==,kēt\ *n* -s [NL *Polychaeta*] **:** an annelid worm of the class Polychaeta

**poly·cha·sium** \¦==¦kāzh(ē)əm\ *n, pl* **polycha·sia** \-(ē)ə\ [NL, fr. *poly-* + *-chasium* (as in *dichasium*)] **:** a cymose inflorescence in which each relative main axis produces more than two branches — compare DICHASIUM, MONOCHASIUM

**poly·chloroprene** \¦pälē, -lə+\ *n* [*poly-* + *chloroprene*] **:** polymerized chloroprene — compare NEOPRENE

**Poly Choke** \'==+,-\ *trademark* — used for a device fitted to the muzzle of a shotgun that replaces the choke-bored section of the barrel with an adjustable mechanism which allows the firer to select the choke he needs

**poly·choral** \¦==+\ *adj* [*poly-* + *choral*] **:** ANTIPHONAL

**poly·chord** \'==+,-\ *adj* [Gk *polychordos,* fr. *poly-* + *-chordos* -chord] *archaic* **:** having many strings — used of a musical instrument

**poly·chot·omous** \¦pälē¦käd·əməs, -lə¦k-\ *adj* [*poly-* + *-chotomous* (as in *dichotomous*)] **:** dividing or marked by division into many parts, branches, or classes; *esp* **:** dividing regularly and repeatedly into many divisions — compare DICHOTOMOUS — **poly·chot·o·my** \-mē\ *n* -ES

**polychotomous key** *n, biol* **:** a taxonomic key based on a choice between several alternative characters

**poly·chrest** \'==,krest\ *n* -s [ML *polychrestus,* fr. Gk *polychrēstos* useful for many purposes, fr. *poly-* + *chrēstos* useful — more at CHRESTOMATHY] **:** a drug or medicine of value as a remedy in several diseases — **poly·chres·tic** \¦==¦krestik\ *adj*

**poly·chres·ty** \'==,krestē\ *n* -ES [Gk *polychrēstia* great usefulness, fr. *polychrēstos* useful for many purposes + *-ia* -y] **:** a thing that has many uses; *specif* **:** POLYCHREST

**poly·chro·ic** \¦==¦krōik\ *adj* [ISV *poly-* + *-chroic*] **:** PLEOCHROIC

**poly·chro·ism** \¦==(,)krō,izəm\ *n* -s [ISV *polychroic* + *-ism*] **:** PLEOCHROISM

**poly·chro·ma·sia** \,==krō'māzh(ē)ə\ *n* -s [NL, fr. *poly-* + *-chromasia*] **:** the quality of being polychromatic; *specif* **:** POLYCHROMATOPHILIA

**poly·chromate** \¦pälē, -lə+\ *n* [ISV *poly-* + *chrom-* + *-ate*] **:** a salt containing more than one or usu. more than two atoms of hexavalent chromium in the anion

**poly·chromatic** \"+\ *adj* [Gk *polychrōmatos* polychromatic (fr. *poly-* + *chrōmat-, chrōma* color, skin) + E *-ic* — more at CHROMATIC] **1 :** showing a variety or a change of colors **:** MULTICOLORED **2** [*poly-* + *chromatic*] *of a cell or tissue* **:** exhibiting polychromatophilia

**¹poly·chromatophil** *or* **poly·chromatophile** \¦pälē, -lə+\ *n* -s [ISV, fr. NL *polychromatophilia*] **:** a young or degenerated red blood corpuscle staining with both acid and basic dyes

**²poly·chromatophil** \"\ *or* **poly·chromatophilic** \¦pälē, -lə+\ *adj* [*polychromatophil* fr. *poly-* + *chromatophil; polychromatophilic* fr. NL *polychromatophilia* + E *-ic*] **:** exhibiting polychromatophilia; *esp* **:** staining with both acid and basic dyes

**poly·chromatophilia** \¦pälē, -lə+\ *n* [NL, fr. *poly-* + *chromatophilia*] **:** the quality of being stainable with more than one type of stain; *esp* **:** stainable with both acid and basic dyes (as an abnormal red blood cell)

**¹poly·chrome** \'pälē,krōm, -lə,k-\ *n* [G *polychrom,* fr. Gk *polychrōmos* of many colors, fr. *poly-* + *-chrōmos* colored, fr. *chrōma* color] **1 :** something of many colors **2 :** variegated coloring **3** *pharmacy* **:** ESCULIN

**²polychrome** \"\ *adj* **1 :** of, relating to, or made with several colors **:** decorated in various colors ⟨~ sculpture⟩ ⟨~ molding⟩ ⟨~ weaving⟩ **2 a :** of, relating to, or constituting a style of vase painting developed in Athens in the latter part of the 6th century B.C. using various colors (as black, white, red, and yellow) to paint decorative figures and other motifs on the outer surface of ware often prepared in advance with a coat of white slip — compare BLACK-FIGURE, RED-FIGURE **b :** of, relating to, or constituting a style of prehistoric vase painting distinguished by the application of two or more colors — compare MONOCHROME

**³polychrome** \"\ *vt* **:** to decorate or variegate in polychrome style ⟨*a polychromed* ceiling⟩

**poly·chro·mia** \,=='krōmēə\ *n* -s [NL, fr. *poly-* + *-chromia*] *med* **:** excessive or abnormal pigmentation of the skin

**poly·chro·mic** \¦==¦=mik\ *adj* [*polychrome* + *-ic*] **:** POLYCHROMATIC 1

**poly·chro·my** \'==,=mē\ *n* -ES [F *polychromie,* fr. *polychrome,* n., (prob. fr. G *polychrom*) + *-ie* -y] **1 :** the art or practice of decorating (as sculpture or architectural ornaments) in combinations of several colors **2** [¹*polychrome* + *-y*] **:** a polychrome surface or effect

**poly·cir·rus** \,pälē'sirəs, -lə's-\ *n, cap* [NL, fr. *poly-* + L *cirrus* curl, ringlet, bird's nest] **:** a genus (family Terebellidae) of soft-bodied polychaete worms — see BLOODWORM

**¹poly·clad** \'==,=\ *adj* [NL *Polycladida*] **:** of or relating to the Polycladida

**²polyclad** \"\ *n* -s [NL *Polycladida*] **:** a flatworm of the order Polycladida

**poly·clad·i·da** \,pälē'kladədə, -lə'k-\ *n pl, cap* [NL, fr. *Polycladus,* type genus (fr. Gk *polyklados* with many branches, fr. *poly-* + *klados* sprout, branch, twig) + NL *-ida* — more at GLADIATOR] **:** an order of Turbellaria comprising broad flattened often brightly colored marine flatworms in which the alimentary tract has many primary branches radiating from a central cavity, the ovaries and testes are numerous, and no vitellarium is developed

**poly·clad·ine** \¦==¦kla,dīn, -lä-, -dᵊn\ *adj* [Gk *polyklados* + E *-ine*] **:** having several or many tines on the antlers

**poly·clinic** \¦pälē, -lə+\ *n* [ISV *poly-* + *clinic*] **:** a clinic treating diseases of many sorts; *also* **:** a hospital for or an institution giving clinical instruction about all kinds of diseases — compare POLICLINIC

**poly·component** \"+\ *adj* [*poly-* + *component*] **:** MULTICOMPONENT

**poly·condensation** \"+\ *n* [ISV *poly-* + *condensation*] **:** a chemical condensation leading to the formation of a compound (as a polypeptide or a polyester) of high molecular weight — compare POLYMERIZATION

**¹poly·conic** \"+\ *adj* [*poly-* + *conic*] **:** relating to or based on many cones

**²polyconic** \"\ *n* **:** POLYCONIC PROJECTION

**polyconic projection** *n* **:** a map projection based on the development of a series of concentric cones placed over a sphere so that each cone is tangent to a different parallel with only that section of each unrolled cone that lies along a common central meridian and forms a strip on both sides of the line of tangency being utilized, all parallels being arcs of nonconcentric circles, and the meridians other than the central meridian being curved lines drawn through the true divisions of the parallels

**poly·cot** \'pälē,kät, -lə,k-\ *or* **poly·cot·yl** \-kätᵊl\ *n* -s [by shortening] **:** POLYCOTYLEDON

**poly·cotyledon** \¦pälē, -lə+\ *n* [NL *polycotyledones,* pl., fr. *poly-* + *cotyledones,* pl. of *cotyledon*] **:** a plant (as the pine and other conifers) having more than two cotyledons

**poly·cotyledonary** \"+\ *adj* [*poly-* + *cotyledonary*] **:** having the placental villi in many definite groups

**poly·cotyledonous** \"+\ *adj* [NL *Polycotyledones* + E *-ous*] **:** having more than two cotyledons ⟨most gymnosperms are ~⟩

**poly·cot·y·le·dony** \,==,käd·ᵊl¦ēdᵊnē\ *n* -ES [*polycotyledon* + *-y*] **:** abnormal increase in the number of cotyledons

**poly·crase** \'==,krās, -āz\ *n* -s [G *polykras,* fr. *poly-* + *-kras* (fr. Gk *krasis* mixing, combination) — more at KRASIS] **:** a mineral (Y,Ca,Ce,U,Th)(Ti,Cb,Ta)$_2$O$_6$ consisting of a columbate and titanate of the metals of the yttrium group that is isomorphous with euxenite (hardness 5–6, sp. gr. 5)

**¹poly·cross** \'pälē, -lə+,-\ *n* [*poly-* + *cross*] **:** a cross in which the female parent is known but the male may belong to any of several available strains and which is used in the production of new lines of some economic plants (as alfalfa)

**²polycross** \"\ *adj* **:** produced by a polycross ⟨~ seed⟩ **:** producing polycrosses ⟨~ nursery⟩

**poly·crot·ic** \¦pälē¦kräd·ik, -lə¦k-\ *adj* [*poly-* + *-crotic*] *of the pulse* **:** having a complex or multiple beat and forming a curve with several secondary crests on a sphygmogram — compare DICROTIC, MONOCROTIC

**poly·crystal** \¦pälē, -lə+\ *n* [*poly-* + *crystal*] **:** a polycrystalline body or object

**poly·crystalline** \"+\ *adj* [*poly-* + *crystalline*] **1 :** characterized by or consisting of crystals variously oriented **2 :** composed of more than one crystal ⟨a ~ metal⟩

**¹po·lyc·te·nid** \pə'liktənəd, ¦pälə̄k¦tenəd\ *adj* [NL *Polyctenidae*] **:** of or relating to the Polyctenidae

**²polyctenid** \"\ *n* -s **:** a bug of the family Polyctenidae

**pol·yc·ten·i·dae** \,pälə̄k'tenə,dē\ *n pl, cap* [NL, fr. *Polyctenes,* type genus + Gk *-ktenēs* — fr. *kten-, kteis* comb) + *-idae* — more at PECTINATE] **:** a family of viviparous bugs that live as ectoparasites in the fur of bats

**poly·cyclic** \¦pälē, -lə+\ *adj* [ISV *poly-* + *cyclic*] **:** having many cycles or rounds: as **a :** containing two or more usu. fused rings in the structure of the molecule (as in anthracene) — compare POLYNUCLEAR ⟨~ hydrocarbons⟩ **b :** of, relating to, or constituting a system of electric distribution in which currents of different voltages and frequencies are superposed on the same network **c** (1) **:** having many whorls or volutions (2) **:** having many cycles of tentacles **d :** POLYPHASIC

**poly·cyesis** \"+\ *n* [NL, fr. *poly-* + *cyesis*] **:** pregnancy with more than one fetus in the uterus

**poly·cystic** \"+\ *adj* [*poly-* + *cystic*] **:** having or involving more than one cyst ⟨~ kidney⟩ ⟨~ disease⟩

**poly·cys·tis** \,pälē'sistəs, -lə's-\ *n, cap* [NL, fr. *poly-* + *-cystis*] **:** a genus of free-floating colonial blue-green algae (family Chroococcaceae) often forming netted or irregular masses and frequently causing water bloom

**poly·cyte** \'==,sīt\ *n* [*poly-* + *-cyte*] **:** a blood granulocyte of normal size but more than usu. segmented nucleus that is present in various infections — compare MACROPOLYCYTE

**poly·cy·the·mia** *also* **poly·cy·thae·mia** \,==,sī'thēmēə\ *n* -s [NL, fr. *poly-* + *-cyte* + *-emia*] **1 :** any condition marked by an abnormal increase in the number of circulating red blood cells **2** *or* **polycythemia ve·ra** \-'virə, -'verə\ **:** a disease characterized by increased concentration of hemoglobin and great absolute and relative increase in red cells accompanied by plethora, nosebleeds, and enlargement of the spleen — **poly·cy·the·mic** *also* **poly·cy·thae·mic** \-¦thēmik\ *adj*

**¹poly·dac·tyl** *also* **poly·dac·tyle** \¦==¦daktᵊl\ *adj* [Gk *polydaktylos* many-toed, fr. *poly-* + *daktylos* finger, toe] **:** having several or many digits; *esp* **:** having more than the normal number of toes or fingers ⟨~ strains of guinea pigs —*Genetics*⟩

**²polydactyl** \"\ *n* **:** one having more than the normal number of toes or fingers

**poly·dac·tyl·ism** \-ktə,lizəm\ *n* -s [ISV *polydactyl-* (fr. Gk *polydaktylos* many-toed) + *-ism*] **:** POLYDACTYLY

**poly·dac·ty·lous** \-ləs\ *adj* [*poly-* + *-dactylous*] **:** POLYDACTYL

**poly·dac·ty·lus** \,==¦=tələs\ *n, cap* [NL, fr. Gk *polydaktylos* many-toed] **:** a genus of fishes (family Polynemidae) found in warm seas

**poly·dac·ty·ly** \-lē\ *n* -ES [ISV *poly-* + *-dactyly*] **:** the condition of having more than the normal number of toes or fingers

**poly·dae·mon·ism** *also* **poly·de·mon·ism** \¦pälē¦dēmə,nizəm, -lə¦d-\ *n* -s [*poly-* + *daemon, demon* + *-ism*] **:** belief in or worship of a multitude of demons or demoniacal powers — **poly·dae·mon·is·tic** *also* **poly·de·mon·is·tic** \¦==,==¦istik\ *adj*

**poly·dem·ic** \¦pälē¦demik, -lə¦d-\ *adj* [*poly-* + *endemic*] **:** native to or occurring in several regions

**poly·dentate** \¦pälē, -lə+\ *adj* [*poly-* + *-dentate*] **:** attached to the central atom in a coordination complex by two or more bonds — used of ligands and chelating groups

**poly·dimensional** \"+\ *adj* [*poly-* + *dimensional*] **:** having many dimensions ⟨the ~ nature of documentary information —J.W.Perry⟩

**poly·dip·sia** *also* **poly·dyp·sia** \,pälē'dipsēə, -lə'd-\ *n* -s [NL, fr. *poly-* + *-dipsia,* fr. Gk *dipsa* thirst] **:** excessive or abnormal thirst — **poly·dip·sic** \¦==¦=sik\ *adj*

**poly·disk** *or* **poly·disc** \'==,disk\ *adj* [*poly-* + *disk, disc*] *of a scyphistoma* **:** producing several ephyrae at one time — compare MONODISK

**poly·disperse** \¦==+\ *adj* [*poly-* + *disperse,* adj.] **:** characterized by particles of varying size in a dispersed phase

**poly·dispersity** \"+\ *n* **:** the state of being polydisperse ⟨opalescence is a mark of ~ —J.W.McBain⟩

**po·lyd·o·mous** \pə'lidəməs\ *adj* [*poly-* + Gk *domos* house + E *-ous* — more at TIMBER] **:** inhabiting several nests — used of ant colonies; compare MONODOMOUS

**po·lyd·y·mite** \pə'lidə,mīt\ *n* -s [G *polydymit,* fr. *poly-* + *dym-* (fr. Gk *didymos* twin) + *-it* -ite — more at -DYMUS] **:** a mineral $Ni_4S_5$ consisting of a nickel sulfide that is isomorphous with linnaeite, siegenite, carrollite, and violarite

**polyecious** *var of* POLYOICOUS

**poly·ei·dic** \¦pälē¦īdik\ *adj* [*poly-* + *eid-* + *-ic*] **:** undergoing a series of conspicuous changes in form during development — used of insects exhibiting a marked metamorphosis — **poly·ei·dism** \-,dizəm\ *n* -s

**poly·electrolyte** \¦pälē+\ *n* [*poly-* + *electrolyte*] **:** a substance of high molecular weight that is an electrolyte (as an ion-exchange resin, a protein, a nucleotide)

**poly·embryonic** *also* **poly·embryonate** *or* **poly·embryonal** \"+\ *adj* [*polyembryony* + *-ic* or *-ate* or *-al*] **:** consisting of or having several embryos **:** exhibiting polyembryony

**poly·embryony** \"+\ *n* [ISV *poly-* + *embryon-* + *-y*] **:** production of two or more embryos by an ovule or egg that is typical of many seed plants and that in some insects results in the production of hundreds of individuals from a single egg

**poly·ene** \'pälē,ēn\ *n* -s [ISV *poly-* + *-ene*] **:** an organic chemical compound containing many double bonds; *esp* **:** such a compound having the double bonds in a long aliphatic hydrocarbon chain (as in carotene or vitamin A) — **poly·enic** \¦==-¦ēnik, -¦en-\ *adj*

**poly·energid** \¦pälē+\ *adj* [ISV *poly-* + *energid;* orig. formed in G] **:** comprising several or many energids ⟨a coenocyte is ~⟩

**poly·enzymatic** \"+\ *adj* [*poly-* + *enzymatic*] **:** producing or containing several different enzymes

**poly·ergus** \,==ˈərgəs\ *n* [NL, fr. Gk *polyergos* hardworking, fr. *poly-* much (fr. *polys* much, many) + *ergon* work — more at POLY-, WORK] **1** *cap* **:** a genus of ants containing the Amazon ants **2** -ES **:** any ant of the genus *Polyergus*

**poly·ester** \'==+,-\ *n* [ISV *poly-* + *ester*] **1 :** a complex ester formed by polymerization or condensation (as of a polyhydric alcohol with a polybasic acid) for use chiefly in making fibers, resins, and plastics or as a plasticizer; *esp* **:** a linear polymer formed from a glycol and a dicarboxylic acid **2 a :** POLYESTER FIBER **b :** POLYESTER RESIN

**polyester fiber** *n* **:** a synthetic fiber consisting wholly or chiefly of a polyester; *esp* **:** a quick-drying resilient fiber made in filament and staple form from ethylene glycol and terephthalic acid or its dimethyl ester and often blended with other fibers (as wool or cotton)

**poly·esterification** \"+\ *n* [*polyester* + *-ification* (as in *esterification*)] **:** the formation of a polyester

**polyester resin** *or* **polyester plastic** *n* **:** any of various synthetic resins or plastics consisting of or made from polyesters: as **a :** ALKYD **b :** a resin that has the same chemical composition as the common polyester fiber but that is extruded as a film (as for use in packaging, as electrical insulation, or as a base for magnetic recording tapes) **c :** a thermosetting resin that is made from an unsaturated polyester (as one formed from a glycol and maleic acid or fumaric acid), cured by copolymerization (as with styrene), and often reinforced with fillers (as glass fibers) and that is used chiefly in impregnating and laminating and in making cast and molded products

**poly·estrous** *or* **poly·oestrous** \¦päle+\ *adj* [*poly-* + *estrous, oestrous*] **:** having more than one period of estrus in a year

**poly·ethnic** \"+\ *adj* [*poly-* + *ethnic*] **:** formed of or inhabited by many peoples ⟨~ areas⟩

**poly·ethylene** \"+\ *n* [*poly-* + *ethylene*] **:** a polymer of ethylene; *esp* **:** one of a group of partially crystalline lightweight thermoplastics $(-CH_2CH_2-)_x$ that have good resistance to chemicals, low moisture absorption and good insulating properties, that vary from soft to hard and from tough and flexible to rigid according to the conditions of manufacture (as at high, medium, or atmospheric pressure) and the type of catalyst, and that are used chiefly in the form of film (as in food packaging and garment bags), pipe and tubing, and molded products (as squeeze bottles and other containers) and as electrical insulation esp. in cables

**polyethylene glycol** *n* **:** a member of the series of water-soluble poly-ether glycols $HOCH_2CH_2(OCH_2CH_2)_nOH$ higher than diethylene glycol and triethylene glycol that vary from water-white liquids to waxy solids as the average molecular weight increases from 200 to 6000 or more, that are usu. obtained as mixtures by condensation of ethylene oxide with water or diethylene glycol, and that are used chiefly as lubricants (as in the rubber and textile industries), solvents, softeners, bases for pharmaceutical ointments and cosmetic creams, and in the form of their fatty acid esters as surface-active agents ⟨commercially available *polyethylene glycols* are designated by numbers that approximate their average molecular weights —Franklin Johnston⟩ — compare POLYGLYCOL

**poly·foil** \'pälē, -lə̇+,-\ *n* [*poly-* + *foil*] **:** MULTIFOIL

**poly·functional** \¦==+\ *adj* [*poly-* + *functional*] **:** having many functions ⟨~ acids⟩ — **poly·functionality** \"+\ *n*

**po·lyg·a·la** \pəˈligələ\ *n* [NL, fr. L, fr. Gk *polygalon* milkwort, fr. *poly-* much (fr. *polys* much, many) + *gala* milk — more at POLY-, GALAXY] **1** *cap* **:** a genus (type of the family Polygalaceae) of herbs and shrubs of temperate and warm regions having many-colored often showy flowers with the three sometimes crested petals united below into a tube and an irregular calyx with two petaloid sepals — see GAYWINGS, MILKWORT, SENEGA ROOT **2** -s **:** any plant of the genus *Polygala*

**po·lyg·a·la·ce·ae** \==,==ˈlāsē,ē\ *n pl, cap* [NL, fr. *Polygala*, type genus + *-aceae*] **:** a family (order Geraniales) of herbs, shrubs, or small trees widely distributed throughout both hemispheres and having irregular flowers with three to five petals, monadelphous stamens, and five sepals of which the two lateral are petaloid — **po·lyg·a·la·ceous** \==¦==¦lāshəs\ *adj*

**poly·ga·lac·tia** \,pälēgəˈlaksh(ē)ə, -ālēg-, -ktēə\ *n* -s [NL, fr. *poly-* + *galact-* + *-ia*] **:** excessive milk secretion

**poly·galac·tu·ro·nase** \,pälē,ga,lakˈt(y)u̇rə,nās, -lə̇,g-, -gə-ˈlaktyər-, -āz\ *n* -s [*poly-* + *galacturonic* + *-ase*] **:** an enzyme that hydrolyzes the glycosidic linkages of polymerized galacturonic acids (as pectic acid) and that occurs esp. in microorganisms — compare PECTINASE

**poly·gal·i·tol** \,pälēˈgalə,tōl, -ālə̇ˈg-, -tōl\ *n* -s [NL *Polygala* + E *-itol*] **:** a crystalline anhydride $C_6H_{12}O_5$ of sorbitol found in species of milkwort (as *Polygala amara*); 1,5-anhydro-D-glucitol — called also *1,5-sorbitan*

**poly·gam** \'==,gam\ *n* -s [NL *Polygamia*] **:** a plant of the class Polygamia

**poly·gamia** \,==ˈgāmēə, -ˈgam-\ *n pl, cap* [NL, fr. Gk *polygamos* polygamous + NL *-ia*] *in former classifications* **:** a class of plants with both hermaphrodite and unisexual flowers on the same plant — **poly·gami·an** \¦==¦mēən\ *adj*

**poly·gam·ic** \¦==¦gamik\ *also* **poly·gam·i·cal** \-mə̇kəl\ *adj* [*polygamy* + *-ic* or *-ical*] **:** POLYGAMOUS — **poly·gam·i·cal·ly** \-mə̇k(ə)lē\ *adv*

**po·lyg·a·mist** \pəˈligəmə̇st\ *n* -s **:** one who practices polygamy — **po·lyg·a·mis·tic** \==¦==¦mistik\ *adj*

**po·lyg·a·mize** \-==,mīz\ *vi* -ED/-ING/-s *see -ize in Explan Notes* **:** to practice polygamy

**po·lyg·a·mo·dioecious** \pə¦ligə(,)mō+\ *adj* [*polygamous* + *dioecious*] **:** having some plants polygamous and some dioecious in the same species

**po·lyg·a·mous** \pəˈligəməs\ *adj* [Gk *polygamos*, fr. *poly-* + *-gamos* -gamous] **1 :** of, relating to, characterized by, or involving polygamy **:** having a plurality of wives or husbands ⟨~ marriages⟩ **2 :** bearing both hermaphrodite and unisexual flowers on the same plant **3** *zool* **:** having more than one mate at the same time — **po·lyg·a·mous·ly** *adv*

**po·lyg·a·my** \-mē,-mi\ *n* -ES [MF *polygamie*, fr. LL *polygamia*, fr. Gk, fr. *poly-* + *-gamia* (fr. *gamos* marriage + *-ia* -y) — more at BIGAMY] **1 :** the state or fact of being polygamous; *specif* **:** a marriage form in which a spouse of either sex may possess a plurality of mates at the same time — used either inclusively of both polygyny and polyandry or exclusively of polygyny ⟨among the Batak of Palawan both ~ and polyandry exist⟩ ⟨the Mormons' former practice of ~⟩; compare BIGAMY, MONOGAMY **2 :** possession of a plurality of benefices **3 :** the condition of bearing both hermaphrodite and unisexual flowers on the same plant **4** *zool* **:** the condition of having more than one mate at one time

**poly·gastric** \¦pälē, -lə̇+\ *adj* [*poly-* + *gastric*] **:** having more than one digestive cavity ⟨a ~ protozoan⟩; *also* **:** having the stomach divided into several chambers — used of ruminants

[1]**poly·gene** \'==,jēn\ *or* **poly·ge·net·ic** \¦==jə¦ned·ik\ *adj* [ISV *poly-* + *-gene;* prob. orig. formed in G] *geol* **:** originating or developing in two or more ways or at two or more times (as a limestone partly clastic and partly biochemical or a volcano built up by a succession of eruptions)

[2]**polygene** \"\ *n* [ISV *poly-* + *gene*] **:** one of a group of nonallelic genes that collectively control the inheritance of a quantitative character or modify the expression of a qualitative character, that individually are of slight effect, and that prob. are not basically different from oligogenes, but produce their dissimilar effects through interaction of all the components of the genome — compare MULTIPLE FACTOR, QUANTITATIVE INHERITANCE

**poly·genesic** \,==+\ *adj* [*poly-* + *genesic*] **:** of or relating to polygenism

**poly·genesis** \,==+\ *n* [NL, fr. *poly-* + *genesis*] **1 :** polyphyletic origin — used esp. of infrahuman species; called also *polyphylesis;* compare POLYGENY **2 :** POLYGENISM — **poly·genesist** \+ˈjenəsə̇st\ *n* -s

**poly·genetic** \¦pälē, -lə̇+\ *adj* [ISV *poly* + *genetic*] **1 :** having many distinct sources **:** originating at various places or times **2 :** of or relating to polygenesis **:** POLYPHYLETIC **3** *of a dye* **:** yielding more than one color or shade according to the mordant — **poly·genetically** \"+\ *adv*

**poly·gen·ic** \¦==¦jenik\ *adj* [ISV *poly-* + *-genic;* orig. formed as F *polygenique*] **1 :** POLYGENE **2 :** POLYGENETIC **3** [*poly-* + *genic*] **:** of, relating to, mediated by, or constituting polygenes

**polygenic system** *n* **:** a group of polygenes

**po·lyg·e·nism** \pəˈlijə,nizəm\ *n* -s [ISV *polygeny* + *-ism*] **:** the doctrine or belief that existing human races have evolved from two or more distinct ancestral types — compare MONOGENISM

**po·lyg·e·nist** \-,nə̇st\ *n* -s [ISV *polygeny* + *-ist*] **:** one who accepts the doctrine of polygenism

**po·lyg·e·nis·tic** \==¦==¦nistik\ *adj* **:** of or relating to polygenism

**poly·genome hybrid** *or* **poly·genomic hybrid** \¦pälē, -lə̇+. . .-\ *n* [*polygenome, polygenomic* fr. *poly-* + *genome, genomic*] **:** a hybrid individual that has more than two complete genomes which are derived from two or more dissimilar ancestors

**po·lyg·e·nous** \pəˈlijənəs\ *adj* [*poly-* + *-genous*] **:** consisting of or containing many kinds or elements ⟨a ~ nation⟩

**po·lyg·e·ny** \-nē\ *n* -ES [*poly-* + *-geny*] **1 :** the descent of man from two or more independent pairs of ancestors — compare MONOGENY **2 :** POLYGENISM

**poly·germ** \'pälē, -lə̇+,-\ *n* [*poly-* + *germ*] **:** a cluster of germ cells or morulae in the polyembryonic development of some parasitic insects — **poly·germinal** \¦==+\ *adj*

**poly·glandular** \¦==+\ *adj* [ISV *poly-* + *glandular*] **:** of, relating to, or involving several glands ⟨a ~ endocrinopathy⟩

**poly·glo·bu·lia** \,==,gläˈbyülēə\ *n* -s [NL, fr. *poly-* + ISV *globulin* + NL *-ia*] **:** POLYCYTHEMIA

**poly·glob·u·lism** \-ˈgläbyə,lizəm\ *n* -s [NL *polyglobulia* + E *-ism*] **:** POLYCYTHEMIA

[1]**poly·glot** \ˈpälē,glät, -lə̇,g-, *usu* -glăd.+V\ *n* -s [Gk *polyglōttos, polyglōssos* speaking many languages, many-tongued, fr. *poly-* + *-glōttos -glōssos* tongued (fr. *glōtta, glōssa* tongue, language) — more at GLOSS] **1 :** one who speaks or writes several languages **2** *usu cap* **a :** a book containing versions of the same text in several languages arranged for comparison usu. in parallel columns; *esp* **:** the Scriptures in several languages **b :** an edition of the Bible containing a monolingual text taken from a multilingual Bible **3 :** a mixture or confusion of languages or nomenclatures ⟨a ~ of diagnostic labels and systems —G.N.Raines⟩

[2]**polyglot** \"\ *adj* **1 a :** speaking or writing several or many languages **:** MULTILINGUAL ⟨a ~ traveler⟩ **b :** composed of or belonging to numerous linguistic groups ⟨a ~ population⟩ ⟨a city of sharp extremes between the rich and transient and the mass of ~ poor —*Reporter*⟩ ⟨catering to the thousands of ~ seamen —*Amer. Guide Series: N.Y.City*⟩ **2 :** containing matter in several languages ⟨a ~ sign⟩ ⟨a ~ dictionary⟩; *esp* **:** composed of correlative text in several languages often arranged in parallel columns ⟨a ~ Bible⟩ **3 :** composed of elements from different languages ⟨verbose, erudite, and ~ slang —C.H.Sykes⟩ ⟨researchers themselves have inherited a curious ~ terminology —A.G.N.Flew⟩

**poly·glot·ism** *or* **poly·glot·tism** \-glăd·,izəm, -ä,tiz-\ *n* -s **:** the use of or ability to speak many languages **:** polyglot character

**poly·glot·tal** \¦==¦glăd·ᵊl, -ät|\ *or* **poly·glot·tic** \|ik, |ēk\ *or* **poly·glot·tous** \|əs\ *adj* [¹*polyglot* + *-al* or *-ic* or *-ous*] **:** POLYGLOT — **poly·glot·tal·ly** \ᵊlē, |ᵊli\ *adv*

**poly·glycol** \ˈpälē, -lə̇+\ *n* [*poly-* + *glycol*] **:** a polyethylene glycol or related compound of the ether-glycol type containing several ether linkages that yields one or more glycols on hydrolysis of these linkages

**poly·gon** \ˈpälē,gän, -lə̇,g- *sometimes* -,gən\ *n* -s [LL *polygonum*, fr. Gk *polygōnon*, fr. neut. of *polygōnos* polygonal, fr. *poly-* + *-gōnos* (fr. *gōnia* angle, corner) — more at -GON] **1 a :** a closed figure consisting of straight lines joined end to end **b :** a closed figure on the surface of a sphere consisting of arcs of great circles joined end to end **2 a :** a polygonal or approximately polygonal object, area, or arrangement **b :** an often hexagonal block or arrangement of surficial material (as soil) forming part of a uniform pattern and often caused by alternate freezing and thawing of the crust — usu. used in pl. ⟨mud ~s⟩ ⟨stone ~s⟩ ⟨ice ~s⟩

1 2

polygons 1a: *1* convex, *2* concave

**po·lyg·o·na·ce·ae** \pə,ligəˈnāsē,ē\ *n pl, cap* [NL, fr. *Polygonum*, type genus + *-aceae*] **:** a family of herbs, shrubs, or trees (order Polygonales) chiefly of the north temperate zone having mostly entire leaves with stipules forming a sheath round the stem and flowers that are spicate and apetalous and including the buckwheats — **po·lyg·o·na·ceous** \==¦==¦nāshəs\ *adj*

**po·lyg·o·nal** \pəˈligənᵊl\ *adj* **1 :** having many sides ⟨a ~ figure⟩ ⟨the ~ assault which the coordinated natural and social sciences could make upon the problems of society —J.R. Newman⟩ **2 :** having a surface marked by a pattern of more or less polygonal blocks or spaces — see POLYGON 2 ⟨~ ground⟩ ⟨~ soil⟩ — **po·lyg·o·nal·ly** \-ᵊlē,-ᵊli\ *adv*

**po·lyg·o·na·les** \pə,ligəˈnā(,)lēz\ *n pl, cap* [NL, fr. *Polygonum* + *-ales*] **:** an order of dicotyledonous plants coextensive with the family Polygonaceae

**polygonal graph** *n* **:** a statistical diagram composed of a circle and as many radii as there are elements to be compared

**polygonal masonry** *n* **:** masonry constructed of stones dressed with smooth faces that do not meet at right angles

**polygonal number** *n* **:** FIGURATE NUMBER

**polygo·na·tion** \,pälēgəˈnāshən, -lə̇g-; pə,lig-\ *n* -s [ISV *polygon* + *-ation*] **:** the measurement of land by means of polygons — compare TRIANGULATION

**poly·gon·a·tum** \,pälēˈgänəd·əm, -lə̇ˈg-\ *n* [NL, fr. L *polygonaton* sealwort, fr. Gk *polygonaton*, fr. neut. of *polygonatos* having many joints, fr. *poly-* + *gonat-*, *gony* knee] **1** *cap* **:** a genus of herbs (family Liliaceae) of the north temperate zone having erect or arching stems, entire leaves, axillary tubular flowers often in pairs, and globular black or blue berries **2** -s **:** any plant of the genus *Polygonatum*

**po·lyg·o·nel·la** \pə,ligəˈnelə\ *n, cap* [NL, fr. *Polygonum* + *-ella*] **:** a small genus of heathlike herbs (family Polygonaceae) of eastern No. America with jointed stems, small narrow leaves, and small white or greenish apetalous flowers in panicled racemes — see JOINTWEED

**poly·go·nia** \,pälēˈgōnēə, -lə̇ˈg-\ *n* [NL, fr. *poly-* + Gk *gōnia* angle] **1** *cap* **:** a genus of anglewing butterflies including many American insects (as the comma butterfly) and having wings that are mostly tawny brown or orange above with dark spots and border and mottled on the underside with grays and browns imitative of bark or dead leaves **2** -s **:** a butterfly of the genus *Polygonia*

**poly·gon·ic** \¦==¦gänik\ *or* **po·lyg·o·nous** \pəˈligənəs\ *adj* **:** POLYGONAL — **poly·gon·i·cal·ly** \¦pälē¦gänək(ə)lē, -lə̇g-\ *adv*

**po·lyg·o·num** \pəˈligənəm\ *n* [NL, fr. Gk *polygonon* knotgrass (*Polygonum aviculare*), fr. *poly-* + *-gonon* (fr. *gony* knee) — more at KNEE] **1** *cap* **:** a large widely distributed genus (the type of the family Polygonaceae) of herbs having prominent ocreae, thickened nodes, and flowers that are solitary and axillary or in spiked racemes — see KNOTGRASS, PERSICARIA **2** -s **:** any plant of the genus *Polygonum*

**poly·gor·di·us** \,pälēˈgȯ(r)dēəs, -lə̇ˈg-\ *n, cap* [NL, prob. fr. *poly-* + *Gordius*, legendary founder of Phrygia — more at GORDIAN KNOT] **:** a genus (the type of the family Polygordiidae) comprising slender cylindrical many-segmented marine annelid worms belonging to the class Archiannelida and having the segmentation externally obscure and the sexes separate

[1]**poly·gram** \'==,gram\ *n* [Gk *polygrammos* marked with many lines, fr. *poly-* + *-grammos* (fr. *grammē* line, fr. *graphein* to write) — more at CARVE] **:** a figure determined by many lines

[2]**polygram** \"\ *n* [*poly-* (as in *polygraph*) + *-gram*] **:** a tracing made by a polygraph

**poly·graph** \-raf,-räf\ *n* [Gk *polygraphos* writing much, fr. *poly-* + *-graphos* (fr. *graphein* to write) — more at CARVE] **1 :** a voluminous or versatile writer **2 :** an instrument for recording tracings of several different pulsations simultaneously (as of the pulse, blood pressure, and respiration) — compare PATHOMETER **3 :** LIE DETECTOR — see KEELER POLYGRAPH **4 :** a cluster of two or more successive letters in cryptography

**poly·graph·ic** \¦==¦grafik\ *adj* **1 a :** VOLUMINOUS, VERSATILE ⟨a ~ writer⟩ **b** *of a book* (1) **:** dealing with a wide range of subjects ⟨a ~ treatise⟩ (2) **:** written by several authors or scribes ⟨a ~ manuscript⟩ **2 :** proceeding (as in encipherment) by groups of two or more successive letters at a time ⟨~ substitution⟩ **3 :** relating to, produced by, or employing a polygraph ⟨~ examination of the patient⟩ ⟨intelligence agency's ~ screening program —Dwight MacDonald⟩ — **poly·graph·i·cal·ly** \-fə̇k(ə)lē\ *adv*

**poly·graph·ist** \'==,grafə̇st, -räf-; pəˈligrəf-\ *n* -s **:** one skilled in the use of a polygraph

**po·lyg·ra·phy** \pəˈligrəfē\ *n* -ES [NL *polygraphia*, fr. Gk, much writing, fr. *poly-* + *-graphia* -graphy] **1** *obs* **:** CRYPTOGRAPHY **2 :** literary productiveness or versatility

**poly·groove** *or* **poly·grooved** \ˈpälē, -lə̇+\ *adj* [*poly-* + *groove* or *grooved*] **:** having many grooves ⟨a ~ rifle barrel⟩

**poly·gyn·ia** \,pälēˈjinēə, -lə̇ˈ-, -ˈg|, |īn-\ *n pl, cap* [NL, fr. *poly-* + *-gynia*] *in former classifications* **:** a class of plants comprising those having flowers with more than 12 styles

**po·lyg·y·nist** \pəˈlijənə̇st, -igə-\ *n* -s **:** one that practices or advocates polygamy

**poly·gy·noe·cial** \¦pälē|j|ə̇ˈnēs(h)ēəl, -lə̇|, |g|, |ī|-, -shəl\ *adj* [*poly-* + NL *gynoecium* + E *-al*] **:** having or made up of several or many united gynoecia ⟨collective fruits are ~⟩

**po·lyg·y·nous** \pəˈlijənəs, -igə-\ *also* **poly·gyn·ic** \¦pälē¦jinik, -lə̇ˈ-, -ˈg|, |īn-\ *or* **poly·gyni·ous** \¦==¦nēəs\ *adj* [*polygynous, polygynious* fr. *polygyny* + *-ous* or *-ious; polygynic* ISV *polygyny* + *-ic;* prob. orig. formed as F *polygynique*] **1 :** relating to, practicing, or characterized by polygyny **2 :** having many pistils **3 :** of or relating to a species maintaining a number of fecundated females in its colony — used of social bees and ants

**po·lyg·y·ny** \pəˈlijənē, -igə-\ *n* -ES [*poly-* + *-gyny*] **1 :** a marriage form in which a man has two or more wives at the same time — contrasted with *polyandry;* compare POLYGAMY, SORORAL POLYGYNY **2 :** the condition of having more than one female mate at one time **3 :** POLYGAMY 3

**poly·gyria** \,pälēˈjīrēə, -lə̇ˈj-, -jir-\ *n* -s [NL, fr. *poly-* + *gyr-* + *-ia*] **:** the condition of having an unusual number of cerebral convolutions

**poly·halide** \¦pälē, -lə̇+\ *n* [*poly-* + *halide*] **:** a halide containing more than one halogen atom in a molecule

**poly·halite** \,==ˈha,līt, -ˈhā-\ *n* -s [G *polyhalit*, fr. *poly-* + *hal-* + *-it* -ite] **:** a mineral $K_2MgCa_2(SO_4)_4.2H_2O$ occurring usu. in fibrous masses of a brick-red color due to iron but consisting essentially of hydrous sulfate of calcium, magnesium, and potassium

[1]**poly·haploid** \¦pälē, -lə̇+\ *adj* [*poly-* + *haploid*] **:** of, relating to, or constituting the gametic chromosome number of a polyploid individual

[2]**polyhaploid** \"+\ *n* **:** a polyhaploid cell or individual

**poly·haptenic** \¦pälē, -lə̇+\ *adj* [*poly-* + *haptenic*] **:** containing more than one haptenic group

**poly·harmony** \"+\ *n* [*poly-* + *harmony*] **:** a harmonic structure that characteristically introduces two or more simultaneous musical harmonies or strata of harmony

**poly·he·dral** \¦pälē¦hēdrəl, -lə̇¦h- *sometimes chiefly Brit* -hed-\ *adj* [NL *polyhedron* + E *-al*] **1 :** having the form of a polyhedron **:** having many faces ⟨a ~ solid⟩ **2 :** relating to a polyhedron

**polyhedral angle** *n* **:** a portion of space partly enclosed by three or more planes whose intersections meet in a vertex

**polyhedral disease** *n* **:** POLYHEDROSIS

**poly·he·dric** \-drik\ *also* **poly·he·dri·cal** \-drə̇kəl\ *adj* [NL *polyhedron* + *-ic* or *-ical*] **:** POLYHEDRAL

**poly·he·dron** \¦==¦hē|drən *sometimes* |,drän *or chiefly Brit* -he|\ *n, pl* **polyhe·dra** \|·drə\ *or* **polyhedrons** [NL, fr. Gk *polyedron*, neut. of *polyedros* with many seats (i.e., sides), fr. *poly-* + *hedra* seat, side — more at SIT] **1 :** a figure or solid formed by plane faces **2** *also* **polyhedral body a :** one of the angular bodies often with hornlike appendages into which the zoospores of the water net and related algae develop and within which the vegetative coenobium develops **b :** one of the refractile many-sided bodies that are present in the terminal phases of an insect polyhedrosis and are regarded as products of tissue breakdown rather than as the infective agent of the disease

a b c d e f

polyhedral angle at vertex *a* formed by lateral angles *b a c, c a d, d a e, e a f* and *f a b*

**poly·he·dro·sis** \,==,hēˈdrōsə̇s\ *n, pl* **polyhedro·ses** \-ō,sēz\ [NL, fr. *polyhedron* + *-osis*] **:** any of several virus diseases of insect larvae characterized by dissolution of tissues and accumulation of polyhedral granules in the resultant fluid — called also *polyhedral disease;* compare SILKWORM JAUNDICE, WILT 2

**poly·hi·dro·sis** \,pälē,hīˈdrōsə̇s, -lə̇-, -,hi-\ *also* **poly·idro·sis** \-ē,īˈd-, -ēəˈd-\ *n, pl* **polyhidro·ses** *or* **polyidro·ses** \-ō,sēz\ [*polyhidrosis* fr. NL, fr. *poly-* + *hidrosis; polyidrosis* fr. NL, fr. *poly-* + *-idrosis*] **:** excessive secretion of perspiration

**poly·his·tor** \,pälēˈhistə(r), -lə̇ˈh-\ *also* **poly·his·to·ri·an** \,==(,)hiˈstōrēən\ *n* -s [*polyhistor* fr. Gk *polyistōr* very learned, fr. *poly-* very (fr. *polys* very, much, many) + *histōr* judge, learned, knowing; *polyhistorian* fr. *polyhistor* + *-an* — more at HISTORY] **:** POLYMATH

**poly·his·tor·ic** \¦==(,)hiˈstȯrik\ *adj* **:** POLYMATH

**poly·his·to·ry** \¦==¦hist(ə)rē\ *n* **:** POLYMATHY

**poly·hybrid** \¦pälē, -lə̇+\ *n* [ISV *poly-* + *hybrid*] **:** a hybrid whose parents differ in a number of characters **:** an individual or group heterozygous for more than one pair of genes — **poly·hybridism** \"+\ *n*

**poly·hydramnios** \"+\ *n* [NL, fr. *poly-* + *hydr-* + *amnios*] **:** HYDRAMNIOS

**poly·hydric** \"+\ *adj* [*poly-* + *-hydric*] **1** *archaic* **:** containing more than one atom of acid hydrogen **2 :** POLYHYDROXY — used esp. of alcohols and phenols

**poly·hydroxy** \¦pälē, -lə̇+\ *adj* [*poly-* + *hydroxy*] **:** containing more than one hydroxyl group in the molecule **:** POLYHYDRIC

**poly·ide·ic** \¦pälē,īˈdēik\ *adj* [*poly-* + *idea* + *-ic*] **:** of, relating to, or characterized by polyideism

**poly·ide·ism** \,==ˈīdē,izəm\ *n* -s [*poly-* + *-idea* + *-ism*] **:** a state of absorption in a group of related ideas or memories — opposed to *monoideism*

**poly·isobutylene** \¦pälē+\ *n* [ISV *poly-* + *isobutylene*] **:** a polymer of isobutylene varying from a viscous oil to a sticky or rubbery solid; *esp* **:** an elastomer $(C_4H_8)_x$ that is formed at a low temperature (as $-100°C$) in the presence of a metal halide catalyst (as boron trifluoride) and that cannot be vulcanized unless a small amount of a proportion of isoprene or other diolefin has been incorporated with the isobutylene before polymerization — compare DIISOBUTYLENE, SYNTHETIC RUBBER

**poly·isomere** \"+\ *n* [*poly-* + *isomere*] **:** one of the simple repetitive segments characteristic of primitive organisms

**poly·isomerism** \"+\ *n* [*poly-* + *isomere* + *-ism*] **:** the tendency usu. regarded as primitive for an organism to be made up of a series of similar and equivalent parts — compare METAMERISM

**poly·isoprene** \"+\ *n* [*poly-* + *isoprene*] **:** a polymer of isoprene occurring naturally in a cis form as the rubber hydrocarbon and in the corresponding trans form as gutta and also produced synthetically in several forms

**poly·isotopic** \"+\ *adj* [*poly-* + *isotopic*] **:** of, relating to, or consisting of more than one isotope

**poly·kar·yo·cyte** \ˌpälēˈkarēəˌsīt, -lə'k-\ *n* -s [*poly-* + *kary-* + *-cyte*] **:** OSTEOCLAST — **poly·kar·yo·cyt·ic** \ˌ;==;===;sid·ik\ *adj*

**poly·karyon** *also* **poly·caryon** \"+\ *n* [NL, fr. *poly-* + *karyon*] **:** a multinuclear cell or individual

**poly·kary·ot·ic** \+;karē;äd·ik\ *adj* [*poly-* + *kary-* + *-otic*] **:** having many nuclei or cells with many nuclei

**poly·lem·ma** \ˌ;pälē;lemə, -lə;-\ *n* -s [*poly-* + *-lemma* (as in *dilemma*)] **:** an argument analogous to a dilemma in which many (as more than three) alternatives are presented in the major premise

**poly·lingual** \ˌ;pälē, -lə+\ *adj* [*poly-* + *lingual*] **:** MULTILINGUAL ⟨~ area⟩ ⟨a ~ journal⟩

**poly·literal** \"+\ *adj* [*poly-* + *literal*] **1 :** POLYGRAPHIC ⟨~ transposition⟩ **2 :** representing each letter by a polygraph ⟨~ substitution⟩

**poly·literally** \"+\ *adv* **:** in a polyliteral manner **:** so as to be polyliteral

**poly·lith** \'==ˌlith\ *n* -s [*poly-* + *-lith*] **:** a megalithic structure (as a dolmen or stone circle) made of several or many stones — compare MONOLITH

**poly·lith·ic** \;==;lithik\ *adj* [*poly-* + *-lithic*] **:** composed of several or many stones or kinds of stone ⟨a ~ deposit⟩

**poly·mas·tia** \ˌ==ˈmastēə\ *also* **poly·mas·ty** \'==ˌ=tē\ *n, pl* **polymastias** *also* **polymasties** [NL, fr. *poly-* + *-mastia*] **:** the condition of having more than the normal number of breasts — **poly·mas·tic** \;==;=tik\ *adj*

**poly·mas·ti·da** \ˌ==ˈmastədə\ *or* **poly·mas·ti·ga** \-təgə\ *or* **poly·mas·ti·go·da** \-ˌmastəˈgōdə\ *or* **poly·mas·ti·go·ta** \-ōd·ə\ [NL, irreg. fr. *Polymastig-, Polymastix*] *syn of* POLYMASTIGINA

**poly·mas·ti·gi·na** \-ˌmastəˈjīnə\ *n pl, cap* [NL, fr. *Polymastig-, Polymastix*, genus of flagellates (fr. *poly-* + Gk *mastig-, mastix* whip) + *-ina* — more at MASTIG-] **:** an order of small plastic usu. parasitic flagellates (subclass Zoomastigina) having several flagella and including various medically or economically important forms (as members of the genera *Costia, Chilomastix, Giardia, Hexamita,* and *Trichomonas*) — **poly·mas·ti·gine** \;==;mastəˌjīn\ *adj*

**¹poly·mas·ti·gote** \;==;mastəˌgōt\ *adj* [alter. of earlier *polymastigate*, fr. *poly-* + *mastig-* + *-ate*] **1 :** having many flagella **2** [NL *Polymastigota*] **:** of or relating to the Polymastigina

**²polymastigote** \"\ *n* -s **:** a flagellate of the order Polymastigina

**¹poly·math** \'==ˌmath\ *n* -s [Gk *polymathēs* knowing much, fr. *poly-* + *-mathēs* (fr. *mathein, manthanein* to learn) — more at MATHEMATICAL] **:** one of encyclopedic learning ⟨such a survey requires a heroic ~ —Douglas Bush⟩ ⟨our most ambitious critics are ~s —R.G.Davis⟩ — called also *polyhistor*

**²polymath** \"\ *or* **poly·math·ic** \;==;mathik\ *adj* **:** learned in many fields — compare ERUDITE ⟨masters of the subtle schools are controversial, *polymath* —T.S.Eliot⟩ ⟨an original, vigorous, *polymathic* mind —B.R.Redman⟩

**po·lym·a·thy** \pəˈliməthē\ *n* -ES [Gk *polymathia* much learning, fr. *polymathēs* knowing much + *-ia* -y] **:** the character or attainments of a polymath **:** encyclopedic learning ⟨scorn for mere ~ —G.W.Johnson⟩

**poly·melia** \ˌpälēˈmēlēə, -lə'm-, -mel-, -lyə\ *also* **po·lym·e·ly** \pəˈliməlē; ˈpälēˌmēlē, -ələ-, -mel-\ *n, pl* **polymelias** *also* **polymelies** [NL *polymelia*, fr. *poly-* + *-melia*] **:** the condition of having more than the normal number of limbs

**poly·menorrhea** *also* **poly·menorrhoea** \ˌ;pälē, -lə+\ *n* [NL, fr. *poly-* + *menorrhea*] **:** menstruation at abnormally frequent intervals — compare MENORRHAGIA

**poly·mer** \ˈpäləmə(r), -lēm-\ *n* -s [ISV, back-formation fr. *polymeric*; prob. orig. formed in G] **:** a natural or synthetic chemical compound or mixture of compounds formed by polymerization and consisting essentially of repeating structural units; *esp* **:** HIGH POLYMER — compare COPOLYMER, DIMER, HOMOPOLYMER, ISOMER, MONOMER; MACROMOLECULE, PLASTIC, RESIN 2a, SYNTHETIC FIBER, SYNTHETIC RUBBER

**po·lym·era** \pəˈlimərə\ *n pl, cap* [NL, fr. *poly-* + *-mera*, neut. pl. of *-merus* -merous] *in some classifications* **:** a division of invertebrate animals having the body divided into numerous clearly defined segments

**poly·me·ria** \ˌ==ˈmirēə, -məˈrīə\ *n* -s [NL, fr. Gk *polymereia* condition of having many parts, fr. *polymerēs* having many parts + *-ia* -y] **:** the condition of having supernumerary parts or accessory organs

**poly·mer·ic** \ˌ==ˈmerik, -rēk\ *adj* [ISV *polymer-* (fr. Gk *polymerēs* having many parts, fr. *poly-* + *meros* part) + *-ic* — more at MERIT] **1 :** of, relating to, or consisting of a polymer **2 a :** of, relating to, involving, or being any of a group of nonallelic identical genes that collectively control various quantitative hereditary characters — compare MULTIPLE FACTOR, POLYGENE **b :** composed of several similar parts ⟨~ chromosomes⟩ **3 :** consisting of many segments ⟨a ~ annelid worm⟩ — **poly·mer·i·cal·ly** \-rək(ə)lē, -rēk-, -li\ *adv*

**po·lym·er·ide** \pəˈliməˌrīd, -rəd\ *n* -s [ISV *polymeric* + *-ide*] *chiefly Brit* **:** POLYMER

**po·lym·er·ism** \pəˈliməˌrizəm; ˈpäləməˌrizəm, -lēm-\ *n* -s **:** the quality or state of being polymeric

**po·lym·er·iz·able** \pəˈliməˌrīzəbəl, =ˌ==ˈ===; ˈpäləm-, -lēm-, ˌ===ˈ===\ *adj* **:** capable of polymerizing

**po·lym·er·i·zate** \pəˈlimərəˌzāt; ˌpäləˈmerəˌzāt, -lēˈm-\ *n* -s [ISV, prob. back-formation fr. *polymerization*] **:** a product of polymerization **:** POLYMER

**po·lym·er·i·za·tion** \pəˌlimərəˈzāshən, ˌpäləm-, ˌpälēm-, -ˌrīˈz-\ *n* -s [ISV *polymer* + *-ization*] **1 a :** a chemical reaction in which two or more small molecules combine to form larger molecules that contain repeating structural units of the original molecules and that have the same percentage composition as the small molecules if the small ones were all of the same kind **:** the union of monomers to form polymers — see ADDITION POLYMERIZATION, CONDENSATION POLYMERIZATION, COPOLYMERIZATION; compare POLYCONDENSATION **b :** the state of being polymerized **2 :** ASSOCIATION 7 **3 :** reduplication of parts in the animal body

**po·lym·er·ize** \pəˈliməˌrīz, ˈpäləm-, ˈpälēm-\ *vb* -ED/-ING/-S *see -ize in Explan Notes* [*polymer* + *-ize*] *vt* **:** to combine (small molecules) chemically into larger or esp. very large molecules **:** subject to polymerization ~ *vi* **:** to form larger molecules from small molecules **:** undergo polymerization

**po·lym·er·iz·er** \-zə(r)\ *n* -s **:** an operator of polymerization equipment

**po·lym·er·ous** \pəˈlimərəs\ *adj* [*poly-* + *-merous*] **1 :** having many parts or members in a whorl **2** [*polymer* + *-ous*] **:** POLYMERIC 1

**polymer tempera** *n* **:** an aqueous plastic-based paint used esp. in fine arts

**po·lym·ery** \pəˈlimərē, ˈpäləˌmerē, ˈpälē-\ *n* -ES [ISV, fr. NL *polymeria*] **:** polymeric condition ⟨doubling of floral organs is a common manifestation of ~⟩

**poly·me·ter** \ˈpälēˌmēd·ə(r), -lə,m-; pəˈliməd·-\ *n* [ISV *poly-* + *-meter*] **:** any of various measuring instruments capable of indicating two or more quantities

**poly·methine** \ˌ;pälē, -lə+\ *adj* [*poly-* + *methine*] **:** consisting of or containing a series of methylidyne groups ⟨~ chain⟩

**polymethine dye** *n* **:** any of a class of dyes (as cyanines or merocyanines) characterized by a resonance structure containing a conjugated chain of carbon atoms that is at least in part an open chain [as in $-CH(=CH-CH)_n=$] attached to two polar atoms (as two amino nitrogen atoms each of which is considered to be positively charged) — see DYE table I

**poly·methylene** \"+\ *n* [ISV *poly-* + *methylene*] **1 :** a hydrocarbon constituted of methylene groups: as **a :** CYCLOPARAFFIN **b :** a polymer of high molecular weight that resembles polyethylene except for its entirely linear and unbranched structure and that is usu. made from diazomethane by loss of nitrogen **2 :** a bivalent radical $-(CH_2)_n-$ consisting of a series of methylene groups ⟨~ halides⟩

**poly·methyl methacrylate** \"+...-\ *n* [*polymethyl* fr. *poly-* + *methyl*] **:** a polymer of methyl methacrylate **:** METHYL METHACRYLATE 2

**poly·metric** \"+\ *adj* [*poly-* + *metric*] **:** relating to, exhibiting, involving, or employing a variety of meters

**po·lym·e·try** \pəˈliməˌtrē\ *n* -ES [*polymetric* + *-y*] **:** the combination of different prosodic meters; *esp* **:** the use of different meters in different lines of the same poem or the same stanza

**poly·microbic** *or* **poly·microbial** \ˌ;pälē, -lə+\ *adj* [*poly-* + *microbic* or *microbial*] **:** of, relating to, or caused by several types of microorganisms

**poly·mig·nyte** *or* **poly·mig·nite** \ˌpälēˈmigˌnīt, -ləm-\ *n* -s [Sw *polymignit*, fr. *poly-* + *mign-* (fr. Gk *mignynai* to mix) + *-it* -ite — more at MIX] **:** a mineral $(Ca,Fe,Y,etc.,Zr,Th)(Cb,Ti,Ta)O_4$ consisting of a niobate and titanate of the metals of the cerium group with iron and calcium

**poly·mix·ia** \-ˈmiksēə\ *n, cap* [NL, fr. Gk, mixture of many components, fr. *poly-* + *mixis* act of mixing (fr. *mignynai* to mix) + *-ia* -y] **:** a genus of small deep-sea berycoid fishes coextensive with the family Polymixiidae and resembling the squirrelfishes but having smooth scales and a pair of barbels on the chin — **poly·mix·i·id** \;==;=sēəd\ *n or adj*

**po·lym·nia** \pəˈlimnēə\ *n, cap* [NL, prob. fr. L *Polymnia, Polyhymnia*, one of the Greek muses, fr. Gk] **:** a small genus of American and chiefly tropical herbs (family Compositae) having large lobed leaves and corymbose heads of discoid and radiate yellow or white flowers — see LEAFCUP

**po·lym·nite** \ˈpäləmˌnīt, pəˈlim-\ *n* -s [Gk *polymnios* full of moss (fr. *poly-* + *mnion* moss, seaweed) + E *-ite* — more at MNIUM] **:** a stone marked with dendrites and black lines so disposed as to suggest rivers and marshes

**poly·molecular** \ˌ;pälē, -lə+\ *adj* [*poly-* + *molecular*] **1 :** consisting of many molecules esp. of different sizes ⟨high polymers are, in general, ~ —A.M.Sookne & Milton Harris⟩ **2 :** having a thickness of several molecules ⟨~ layers⟩ — compare MULTILAYER — **poly·molecularity** \"+\ *n*

**poly·molybdate** \"+\ *n* [*poly-* + *molybdate*] **:** any of various complex salts (as ammonium molybdate) regarded as derived from isopoly acids of molybdenum

**¹poly·morph** \ˈpälēˌmȯrf, -ləˌm-\ *n* -s [ISV, fr. *polymorphous*] **1 :** a polymorphous organism; *also* **:** one of the several forms of such an organism **2 :** any of the crystalline forms of a polymorphous substance **3 :** a polymorphonuclear leukocyte

**²polymorph** \"\ *adj* **:** POLYMORPHIC

**poly·mor·pha** \ˌ==ˈmȯrfə\ *n pl, cap* [NL, *poly-* + *-morpha*] *in some esp former classifications* **:** a suborder or other group of beetles including the Clavicornia and Serricornia

**poly·mor·phe·an** \;==;mȯrfēən, ;==ˌ=;==\ *adj* [Gk *polymorphos* multiform + E *-an*] *archaic* **:** POLYMORPHIC

**poly·mor·phic** \;==;mȯrfik\ *adj* [Gk *polymorphos* multiform + E *-ic*] **1 :** POLYMORPHOUS b **2 :** having or occurring in several distinct forms **:** exhibiting polymorphism ⟨a ~ species⟩ ⟨man is both ~ and polytypic —*New Biology*⟩ — **poly·mor·phi·cal·ly** \-fək(ə)lē\ *adv*

**poly·mor·phism** \'==ˌmȯrˌfizəm, ˌ=='===\ *n* -s [ISV *polymorphous* + *-ism*] **:** the quality or state of being polymorphous: as **a** (1) **:** capability of assuming different forms **:** capability of wide variation (2) **:** existence of a species in several forms independent of the variations of sex (as in various butterflies whose broods, appearing at different seasons, differ in size or color, or both, or in ants and termites, in which different castes exist) — compare DIMORPHISM, HETEROMORPHISM **b :** the property of crystallizing in two or more forms with distinct structures — compare ALLOTROPY

**¹poly·mor·pho·nuclear** \ˌ;pälē;mȯrfə, -lə;m- +\ *adj* [*polymorphous* + *nuclear*] **1** *of a leukocyte* **:** having the nucleus complexly lobed **2 :** being a neutrophil or other leukocyte of typical mature form with distinctly lobed nucleus

**²polymorphonuclear** \"\ *n* -s **:** a polymorphonuclear leukocyte

**poly·mor·pho·nucleate** \ˌ;pälē;mȯrfə, -lə;m-+\ *adj* [¹*polymorphonuclear* + *-ate*] **:** POLYMORPHONUCLEAR

**poly·mor·phous** \ˌ;pälē;mȯrfəs, -lə;m-\ *adj* [Gk *polymorphos* multiform fr. *poly-* + *-morphos* -morphous] **:** having or assuming various forms, characters, styles, or functions ⟨a ~ god⟩: as **a :** POLYMORPHIC 2 **b :** crystallizing with two or more different structures — **poly·mor·phous·ly** *adv* — **poly·mor·phous·ness** *n* -ES

**polymorphous–perverse** \;==;==;=, ;==;=;=,=\ *adj* **:** relating to or exhibiting infantile sexual tendencies in which the genitals are not yet identified as the sole or principal sexual organs nor coitus as the goal of erotic activity and which are a basis for pregenital libidinal fixation

**poly·mor·phy** \ˈpäləˌmȯrfē, -ləˌm-\ *n* -ES [ISV *polymorph* + *-y*] **:** POLYMORPHISM

**poly·my·ar·i·an** \;==ˌmī;a(a)rēən\ *also* **poly·my·ar·i·al** \-ēəl\ *adj* [*poly-* + *-myaria* + *-an* or *-al*] **:** having many cells in each quadrant of a cross-section — used of the arrangement of muscle cells in a nematode worm

**poly·my·ar·i·ty** \ˌ==ˌmīˈarəd·ē\ *n* -ES [*polymyarian* + *-ity*] **:** the condition of being polymyarian

**poly·my·odi** \ˌpäləˌmīˈōˌdī, -ləˌm-\ *n pl, cap* [NL, fr. *poly-* + *-myodi* (fr. Gk *myōdēs* muscular, fr. *mys* mouse, muscle) — more at MOUSE] *in former classifications* **:** a group of birds nearly equivalent to Passeres — **poly·my·odi·an** \;==;=ˈōdēən\ *or* **poly·my·odous** \-dəs\ *adj*

**poly·my·oid** \;==;mīˌȯid\ *adj* [*poly-* + *my-* + *-oid*] **1 :** having many syringeal muscles **2** [NL *Polymyodi* + E *-oid*] **:** POLYMYODIAN

**poly·myositis** \ˌ;pälē, -lə+\ *n* [NL, fr. *poly-* + *myositis*] **:** inflammation of several muscles at once

**po·lym·y·thy** \pəˈliməthē; ˈpäləˌmithē, -lə,m-\ *n* -ES [NL *polymythia*, fr. Gk *polymythos* with many legends (fr. *poly-* + *mythos* myth) + NL *-ia* -y — more at MYTH] **:** the inclusion of many or several stories or plots in one narrative or dramatic work

**poly·myx·in** \ˌpälēˈmiksən, -lə,m-\ *n* -s [ISV, fr. NL *polymyxa* (specific epithet of *Bacillus polymyxa* — fr. *poly-* + *-myxa* — ) + ISV *-in*] **:** any of several basic polypeptide toxic antibiotics that are obtained from strains of a soil bacterium (*Bacillus polymyxa*) and are active against gram-negative bacteria: as **a** *or* **polymyxin A :** one of three nephrotoxic antibiotics **b** *or* **polymyxin B :** the least toxic of the polymyxins used in the form of its sulfate chiefly in the treatment of some localized, gastrointestinal, or systemic infections

**pol·y·nee** \;==;nā\ *n* -s [Sw] **:** a tart made of rich cookie dough, filled with meringue to which ground almonds have been added, and topped with a cross made of two strips of the cookie dough

**poly·nemid** \ˌpälēˈnēməd, -nem-\ *n* -s [NL *Polynemidae*] **:** a fish of the family Polynemidae

**poly·nem·i·dae** \-ˌneməˌdē\ *n pl, cap* [NL, fr. *Polynemus*, type genus + *-idae*] **:** a family (usu. coextensive with a suborder Polynemoidea of Percomorphi) of fishes that resemble mullets but have the pectoral fin divided into two parts of which the upper is much like an ordinary fin and the lower is composed of several separate slender threadlike rays and abound on the sandy shores of warm seas, many of them being valued for food and some yielding isinglass

**¹poly·ne·moid** \;==;nēˌmȯid\ *adj* [NL *Polynemus* + E *-oid*] **:** resembling or related to the Polynemidae

**²polynemoid** \"\ *n* -s **:** a polynemoid fish

**poly·ne·moi·dea** \ˌ== nəˈmȯidēə\ *n pl, cap* [NL, fr. *Polynemus* + *-oidea*] **:** a suborder of Percomorphi coextensive with the family Polynemidae

**poly·ne·mus** \ˌpälēˈnēməs, -lə'n-\ *n, cap* [NL, fr. *poly-* + Gk *nēma* thread — more at NEEDLE] **:** a genus (the type of the family Polynemidae) of fishes resembling mullets

**poly·neph·ric** \;==;nefrik\ *adj* [*poly-* + *-nephric*] *of an insect* **:** having many Malpighian tubules

**¹poly·ne·sian** \ˌ;pälə;nēzhən, -ēsh-\ *adj, usu cap* [*Polynesia*, islands of the central Pacific ocean + E *-an*] **1 a :** of, relating to, or characteristic of Polynesia **b :** of, relating to, or characteristic of the Polynesians **2 :** of, relating to, or characteristic of the Polynesian languages **3 :** of, relating to, or being a biogeographic region or subregion of the Australian region that includes the smaller tropical Pacific islands

**²polynesian** \"\ *n* -s *cap* [*Polynesia* + E *-an*] **1 :** a member of any of the native peoples of Polynesia usu. classified as being a composite chiefly of the white, Mongoloid, and Melanesian races and described as having black wavy hair, black eyes, medium breadth of nose, medium prognathism, brown skin, tall stature, and large-boned build **2 :** a group of Austronesian languages spoken largely in Polynesia

**polynesian chestnut** *n, usu cap P* **1 :** a Polynesian tree (*Inocarpus edulis*) of the family Leguminosae **2 :** the edible kidney-shaped seed of the Polynesian chestnut

**poly·neuritic** \ˌ;pälē, -lə+\ *adj* [NL *polyneuritis* + E *-ic*] **:** of, relating to, or marked by polyneuritis

**poly·neuritis** \"+\ *n* [NL, fr. *poly-* + *neuritis*] **:** neuritis of several peripheral nerves at the same time caused by alcoholism, metallic and other poisons, infectious disease, or vitamin deficiency (as of thiamine)

**poly·neuropathy** \"+\ *n* [*poly-* + *neuropathy*] **:** a disease of nerves; *esp* **:** a noninflammatory degenerative disease of nerves usu. caused by toxins (as of lead, alcohol)

**¹pol·y·noid** \ˈpäləˌnȯid, pəˈlinəwȯd\ *adj* [NL *Polinoidae*] **:** of or relating to the Polynoidae

**²polynoid** \"\ *n* -s **:** a worm of the family Polynoidae **:** SCALE WORM

**pol·y·noi·dae** \ˌpäləˈnȯi(ˌ)dē, pəˌlinəˈwī(ˌ)dē\ *n pl, cap* [NL, fr. *Polynoe*, type genus (fr. Gk *Polynoē*, a sea nymph) + *-idae*] **:** a family of marine polychaete worms having the back covered with two rows of scales

**¹poly·no·mi·al** \ˌ;pälē;nōmēəl, -lə;n-\ *n* -s [*poly-* + *-nomial* (as in *binomial*)] **1 a :** a mathematical expression of two or more terms **b :** an algebraic function of one or more variables consisting of the sum of terms whose factors are constants or positive integral or zero powers of the variables — called also *integral rational function* **2 :** a technical name of a plant or animal consisting of a descriptive phrase of more than three words

**²polynomial** \"\ *adj* **1 :** having the character of a polynomial **2 :** consisting of many names or terms

**poly·nuclear** \ˌ;pälē, -lə+\ *adj* [ISV *poly-* + *nuclear*] **:** containing more than one nucleus: **a :** POLYCYCLIC a **b :** containing more than one central atom or ion — used of coordination complexes **c :** POLYMORPHONUCLEAR

**poly·nu·cle·o·sis** \ˌ==ˌn(y)üklēˈōsəs\ *n, pl* **polynucleo·ses** \-ōˌsēz\ [NL, fr. ISV *polynucle-* (in *polynuclear*) + NL *-osis*] **:** the presence of an excess of polymorphonuclear leucocytes (as in the circulating blood)

**poly·nucleotide** \ˌ;pälē, -lə+\ *n* [ISV *poly-* + *nucleotide*] **:** a nucleotide (as of a nucleic acid) consisting of many mononucleotides in combination

**po·lyn·ya** *also* **po·lyn·ia** \ˌ;pälən;yä\ *n* -s [Russ *polyn'ya*, fr. *polyĭ* open, hollow; akin to OSlav *polje* field — more at FLOOR] **:** an area of open water in sea ice — distinguished from *lead*

**poly·odon** \ˈpälēəˌdän\ *n, cap* [NL, fr. *poly-* + *-odon*] **:** a genus (the type of the family Polyodontidae) of fishes containing the paddlefish — **poly·odont** \-nt\ *or* **poly·odon·toid** \;==;dän·ˌtȯid\ *adj or n*

**poly·odon·tia** \ˌpälēōˈdänch(ē)ə\ *n* -s [NL, fr. *poly-* + *-odontia*] **:** the presence of more than the normal number of teeth

**poly·odon·ti·dae** \-ntəˌdē\ *n pl, cap* [NL, fr. *Polyodont-, Polyodon*, type genus + *-idae*] **:** a family of fishes (order Chondrostei) comprising the genera *Polyodon* and *Psephurus*

**polyoestrous** *var of* POLYESTROUS

**poly·oi·cism** \ˌpälēˈȯiˌsizəm, -ȯiˌki-\ *n* -s [ISV *polyoicous* + *-ism*] **:** the condition of being polyoicous

**poly·oi·cous** \;==;ȯikəs\ *or* **poly·oe·cious** \;==;ēshəs\ *also* **poly·ecious** \;==;ēshəs\ *adj* [*poly-* + Gk *oikia* house + E *-ous* — more at VICINITY] **:** having the archegonia and antheridia sometimes on the same plant and sometimes on different plants ⟨~ mosses⟩ ⟨~ liverworts⟩ — compare HETEROICOUS, PAROICOUS — **poly·oi·cous·ly** *or* **poly·oe·cious·ly** *adv* — **poly·oi·cous·ness** *or* **poly·oe·cious·ness** *n* -ES

**poly·oi·cy** \'==ˌȯisē, -ˌȯikē\ *n* -ES [ISV *polyoicous* + *-y*] **:** POLYOICISM

**poly·ol** \'==ˌȯl, -ˌōl\ *n* -s [ISV *poly-* + *-ol*] **:** a compound (as sorbitol or pentaerythritol) containing usu. several alcoholic hydroxyl groups **:** a polyhydric alcohol

**poly·olefin** \ˌ;pälē, -lə+\ *n* [*poly-* + *olefin*] **1 :** an olefin containing many double bonds **2 :** a polymer of olefin (as polyethylene)

**poly·on·y·mous** \ˌ;pälē;änəməs\ *adj* [Gk *polyōnymos*, fr. *poly-* + *-ōnymos* (fr. *onoma* name) — more at NAME] **:** having many names **:** known by various names

**poly·on·y·my** \ˌ=='änəmē\ *n* -ES [Gk *polyōnymia*, fr. *poly-* + *-ōnymia* (fr. *onoma* name + *-ia* -y)] **:** plurality of names **:** the use of various names for one thing

**poly·opia** \ˌpälēˈōpēə\ *n* -s [NL, fr. *poly-* + *-opia*] **:** perception of more than one image of a single object esp. with one eye **:** multiple vision **:** DIPLOPIA — **poly·opic** \;==;ōpik\ *adj*

**poly·or·chi·dism** \ˌ=='ȯ(r)kəˌdizəm\ *n* -s [ISV *poly-* + *-orchidism*] **:** a condition of having more than two testes

**poly·organic** \ˌ;pälē+\ *adj* [*poly-* + *organic*] **:** having many organs

**poly·os·tot·ic** \ˌ;pälēˌä;städ·ik\ *adj* [ISV *poly-* + *-ost* + *-otic*] **:** involving or relating to many bones

**poly·ovular** \ˌ;pälē+\ *adj* [*poly-* + *ovular*] **:** of, relating to, producing, or containing more than one ovum ⟨~ cycle⟩ ⟨~ follicle⟩

**poly·ovulation** \"+\ *n* [*poly-* + *ovulation*] **:** the production of several to many ova at a single ovulation ⟨~ appears to be a primitive mammalian characteristic⟩

**poly·oxy·ethylene glycol** \ˌ;pälēˌäksē + ...-\ *n* [*polyoxyethylene* fr. *poly-* + *oxy-* + *ethylene*] **:** POLYETHYLENE GLYCOL

**poly·oxymethylene** \ˌ;pälē+\ *n* [*poly-* + *oxy-* + *methylene*] **:** a polymer or hydrated polymer of formaldehyde; *esp* **:** PARAFORMALDEHYDE

**polyoxymethylene glycol** *n* **:** a linear hydrated polymer $HO(CH_2O)_nH$ of formaldehyde — see PARAFORMALDEHYDE

**pol·yp** \ˈpäləp\ *n* -s [MF *polype* octopus, nasal tumor, fr. L *polypus*, fr. Gk *polypous*, lit., many-footed, fr. *poly-* + *pous* foot — more at FOOT] **1 a** *also* **pol·ype** \"\ *archaic* **:** an animal (as an octopus, cuttlefish, or squid) having numerous feet or tentacles **b :** a typical coelenterate individual with a hollow tubular body having outer ectoderm separated from inner endoderm by mesogloea, terminating anteriorly in a central mouth surrounded by tentacles, and being posteriorly closed and attached to the substrate (as in *Hydra*) or more or less directly continuous with other individuals of a compound animal (as in *Obelia* or most corals) **:** ZOOID **2** [so called fr. the ramifications resembling the tentacles of an octopus] **a :** a projecting mass of swollen and hypertrophied mucous membrane (as in the nasal cavity) caused by chronic inflammation **b :** a pedunculated tumor (as of the lower intestine) that often undergoes malignant change

**poly·parasitism** \ˌ;pälē, -lə+\ *n* [*poly-* + *parasitism*] **:** HYPERPARASITISM 2

**pol·yp·ar·i·an** \ˌ;pälə;pa(a)rēən\ *adj* [*polypary* + *-an*] **:** of or relating to a polypary

**pol·yp·ar·i·um** \ˌ=='pa(a)rēəm\ *n, pl* **polypar·ia** \-ēə\ [NL, fr. ISV *polypary*] **:** POLYPARY

**po·lyp·a·rous** \pəˈlipərəs\ *adj* [*poly-* + *-parous*] **:** POLYTOCOUS

**pol·yp·ary** \ˈpäləˌperē\ *n* -ES [*polyp* + *-ary*] **:** the common investing structure or tissue in which the polyps of corals and other compound forms are embedded

**pol·yp·ean** \ˌ=='pēən\ *adj* [*polyp* + *-an*] **:** relating to or like a polyp

**pol·yp·ec·to·my** \ˌ=='pektəmē\ *n* -ES [*polyp* + *-ectomy*] **:** the surgical excision of a polyp

**¹poly·ped** \ˈpäləˌped, -lə,p-\ *n* -s [*poly-* + *-ped*] **:** a polyped animal

**²polyped** \"\ *adj* **:** having many feet

**poly·pe·da·tes** \ˌ==ˌpəˈdād·(ˌ)ēz\ *n, cap* [NL, prob. irreg. fr. *poly-* + Gk *pēdētēs* leaper, dancer, fr. *pēdan* to leap, jump; akin to L *ped-, pes* foot — more at FOOT] **:** a genus (the type of the family Polypedatidae) of Old World tree frogs related to the Ranidae but distinguished by cylindrical transverse sacral processes

**¹poly·pe·datid** \;===;dād·əd, -;dad·əd\ *adj* [NL *Polypedatidae*] **:** of or relating to the Polypedatidae

**²polypedatid** \"\ *n* -s **:** a tree frog of the family Polypedatid

**poly·pe·dat·i·dae** \ˌ=='dad·əˌdē\ *n, pl, cap* [NL, fr. *Polypedates*, type genus + *-idae*] **:** a family of Old World tree frogs (suborder Diplasiocoela)

**poly·peptide** \ˌ;pälē, -lə+\ *n* [ISV *poly-* + *peptide*; prob. orig.

formed as G *polypeptid*] : a polyamide that yields amino acids on hydrolysis but has a lower molecular weight than a protein and that is obtained by partial hydrolysis of proteins or by synthesis — compare PEPTIDE

**poly·petal** \"+\ adj [NL *polypetalus*] : POLYPETALOUS

**poly·pet·a·lae** \,==ˈped·ᵊl,ē\ [NL, fr. *poly-* + *-petalae*] *syn of* CHORIPETALAE

**poly·petalous** \,==+\ adj [NL *polypetalus*, fr. *poly-* + *-petalus* -petalous] *of a flower or corolla* : consisting of or having petals that are not united : CHORIPETALOUS

**poly·pet·aly** \ˌ==ˈped·ᵊlē\ n -ES [*polypetalous* + *-y*] : the condition of being polypetalous

**po·lyph·a·ga** \pəˈlifəgə\ n pl, cap [NL, fr. Gk, neut. pl. of *polyphagos* eating too much] : a suborder of Coleoptera including all the beetles except the Adephaga

**poly·phage** \ˈpälē,fāj, -lə,f-\ n -S [L *polyphagus*, fr. Gk *polyphagos* eating too much] : one eating much or many kinds of food

**poly·pha·gia** \,==ˈfāj(ē)ə\ *also* **po·lyph·a·gy** \pəˈlifəjē\ n, pl **polyphagias** *or* **polyphagies** [Gk *polyphagia*, fr. *polyphagos* eating too much + *-ia* -y] : excessive appetite or voracious eating : BULIMIA — compare HYPERPHAGIA — **poly·pha·gian** \ˌpälēˈfāj(ē)ən, -lə¦f-\ adj or n

**poly·phag·ic** \ˌpälē¦fajik, -lə¦f-\ adj [L *polyphagus* glutton + E *-ic*] : POLYPHAGOUS

**po·lyph·a·gism** \pəˈlifə,jizəm\ n -S [L *poliphagus* + E *-ism*] : the habit of feeding on a variety of plants or animals : the condition of being polyphagous

**po·lyph·a·gous** \-fəgəs\ adj [Gk *polyphagos*, fr. *poly-* (fr. *polys* many, much) + *-phagos* -phagous — more at POLY-] **1** : feeding on or utilizing many kinds of food; *specif* : feeding on various plants or animals ⟨~ insects⟩ — usu. used of an animal subsisting on a moderate variety of foods; distinguished from *omnivorous* and *pantophagous* **2** : entering several host cells ⟨the ~ thallus of a parasitic fungus⟩ — compare MONOPHAGOUS

**poly·pha·lan·gism** \,pälēfəˈlan,jizəm, -fāˈl-\ n -S [*poly-* + *phalange* + *-ism*] : the condition of having more than the normal number of phalanges in the fingers or toes

**poly·pha·lan·gy** \-njē\ n -ES [*poly-* + *phalange* + *-y*] : POLYDACTYLY

**poly·pharmacal** \ˌpälē, -lə+\ adj [*polypharmacy* + *-al*] : of or relating to polypharmacy

**poly·phar·ma·con** \,==ˈfärmə,kän\ n [NL, fr. Gk *polypharmakon*, neut. of *polypharmakos* compounded of many drugs, fr. *poly-* + *-pharmakos*, fr. *pharmakon* drug — more at PHARMACY] : a remedy compounded of many ingredients

**poly·pharmacy** \ˌ==+\ n [*poly-* + *pharmacy*] : the practice of administering many different medicines esp. concurrently for the treatment of the same disease

**poly·pharyngeal** \ˌpälē, -lə+\ adj [*poly-* + *pharyngeal*] *of a flatworm* : having several pharynges — **poly·pharyn·gy** \ˌ==fəˈrinjē, -ˈfarən-\ n -ES

**poly·phasal** \ˌ==+\ adj [*poly-* + *phasal*] : of or relating to a polyphase system : POLYPHASE

**poly·phase** \ˈ==+,-\ adj [ISV *poly-* + *-phase*] : having or producing two or more phases ⟨a ~ machine⟩ ⟨a ~ current⟩

**polyphase induction motor** n : an alternating-current motor having polyphase (as 3-phase) windings

**poly·phas·er** \"ə(r)\ n -S : a polyphase machine

**poly·phasic** \ˌpälē, -lə+\ adj [*poly-* + *phasic*] *of an animal* : having several periods of activity interrupted by intervening periods of rest in each 24 hours : POLYCYCLIC ⟨an infant is essentially ~⟩ — compare MONOPHASIC

**pol·y·pheme** \ˈpälə,fēm\ n -S *usu cap* [F *Polyphème*, a Cyclops blinded by Ulysses in the epic poem *Odyssey* ascribed to *Homer*, traditional ancient Greek poet, fr. L *Polyphemus*, fr. Gk *Polyphēmos*] : GIANT, CYCLOPS — **pol·y·phe·mi·an** \ˌ==¦fēmēən\ *or* **pol·y·phe·mic** \-mik\ *or* **pol·y·phe·mous** \-məs\ adj

**pol·y·phe·mus moth** \ˌ==¦-məs-\ n, *often cap P* [*polyphemus* fr. NL (specific epithet of *Telea polyphemus*), fr. L *Polyphemus*, a Cyclops; fr. the eyelike spot on its hind wings] : a very large American silkworm moth (*Antheraea polyphemus*) of a yellowish or brownish color with a large eyelike spot in each hind wing and a larva that is very large and bright green with silvery tubercles and with oblique white stripes on the sides and that feeds on the oak, chestnut, willow, cherry, apple, and other trees

**poly·phenol** \ˌpälē, -lə+\ n [ISV *poly-* + *phenol*] : a polyhydroxy phenol — **poly·phenolic** \"+\ adj

**poly·phenolase** \ˌpälē, -lə+\ n -S [*polyphenol* + *-ase*] : POLYPHENOL OXIDASE

**polyphenol oxidase** n : any of several copper-containing enzymes (as laccase) that catalyze the oxidation esp. of diphenols and polyphenols to quinones — compare PHENOL OXIDASE, TYROSINASE

**poly·phloes·boe·an** \ˌpälē¦fles¦bēən, ¦pälə¦-, -s bēən\ *or* **poly·phlois·boi·an** \-¦flȯis¦bȯiən\ *or* **polu·phlois·boi·an** \ˌpäl(y)ə¦-\ adj [Gk *polyphloisbos* (fr. *poly-* + *phloisbos* confused roaring noise) + E *-an*; perh. akin to Gk *aphloismos* foaming of the mouth, *phlidan* to be too moist, become soft — more at BLOAT] : loud-roaring ⟨the ~ sea⟩

**poly·phone** \ˈ==,fōn\ n [*poly-* + *-phone*] **1** : a music box that by means of perforated disks can play a number of tunes **2** : a symbol or group of symbols having more than one phonetic value (as *ea* in English, which represents \ā\ in *break* and \ē\ in *freak*)

**poly·phonemic** \ˌpälē, -lə+\ adj [*poly-* + *phonemic*] : constituting, consisting of, or standing for more than one phoneme

**poly·phon·ic** \ˌ==¦fänik\ *or* **po·lyph·o·nous** \pəˈlifənəs\ adj [Gk *polyphōnos* having many tones (fr. *poly-* + *-phōnos*—fr. *phōnē* sound—) + E *-ic* or *-ous* — more at BAN] **1 a** : consisting of or relating to two or more distinct melodies combined into a unified musical composition : CONTRAPUNTAL ⟨~ traditions of the baroque —P.H.Lang⟩ — compare MONOPHONIC **b** *of a musical instrument* : capable of giving more than one tone at a time **2** : having or consisting of many sounds or voices ⟨morning's ~ sounds⟩ **3** : being a polyphone — **poly·phon·i·cal·ly** *or* **po·lyph·o·nous·ly** adv

**polyphonic prose** n : a freely rhythmical prose employing characteristic devices of verse (as alliteration, assonance, rhyme) except strict meter

**po·lyph·o·nist** \pəˈlifənəst\ n -S [*polyphony* + *-ist*] : one skilled in polyphony : CONTRAPUNTIST

**po·lyph·o·ny** \-nē\ n -ES [Gk *polyphōnia* variety of tones, fr. *polyphōnos* having many tones + *-ia* -y] **1** : musical composition in simultaneous and harmonizing but melodically independent and individual parts or voices : COUNTERPOINT — compare HOMOPHONY **2** : multiplicity of sounds (as in reverberations of an echo) **3 a** : representation by polyphones **b** : the fact of being a polyphone

**poly·phosphate** \ˌpälē, -lə+\ n [*poly-* + *phosphate*] : a salt or ester of a polyphosphoric acid — see SODIUM TRIPOLYPHOSPHATE

**poly·phosphoric acid** \"+ . . .-\ n [*polyphosphoric* fr. *poly-* + *phosphoric*] : any of a series of condensed phosphoric acids (as pyrophosphoric acid) containing more than one atom of phosphorus

**poly·phy·le·sis** \,==fīˈlēsəs\ n, pl **polyphyle·ses** \-ē,sēz\ [NL, fr. ISV *polyphyletic*, after such pairs as ISV *genetic*: NL *genesis*] : POLYGENESIS

**poly·phy·let·ic** \ˌ==fī¦led·ik\ adj [ISV *polyphyl-* (fr. Gk *polyphylos* of many tribes, fr. *poly-* + *phylē* tribe, race) + *-etic*; orig. formed as G *polyphyletisch* — more at PHYL-] : of or relating to more than one stock : derived (as by convergence) from more than one ancestral line — opposed to *monophyletic* — **poly·phy·let·i·cal·ly** \-d·ək(ə)lē\ adv — **poly·phy·let·i·cism** \ˌ==¦led·ə,sizəm\ n -S

**polyphyletic theory** n : a theory in physiology: the several cellular elements of the blood originate in two or more distinct stem cells — compare MONOPHYLETIC THEORY

**poly·phyle·tism** \ˌ==ˈfīlə,tizəm, -ˈfil-\ n -S [ISV *polyphylet-* (fr. *polyphyletic theory*) + *-ism*] : adherence to the polyphyletic theory — **poly·phyle·tist** \-,təst\ n -S

**poly·phyle·ty** \-ləd·ē\ n -ES [*polyphyletic* + *-y*] : POLYPHYLESIS

**poly·phyl·la** \ˌpäləˈfilə, -ələˈf-\ n, cap [NL, fr. Gk *polyphyllos* with many leaves, fr. *poly-* + *phyllon* leaf — more at BLADE] : a holarctic genus of large brown beetles (family Melolonthidae) — see JUNE BEETLE

**poly·phylogeny** \ˌ==+\ n [*poly-* + *phylogeny*] : development of a group through combination and evolution of qualities derived from more than one ancestral group : POLYGENESIS

**poly·phy·ly** \ˈ==,fīlē\ n -ES [ISV *polyphyl-* (fr. Gk *polyphylos* of many tribes) + *-y*] : POLYPHYLESIS

**1poly·phy·odont** \ˌ==ˈfīə,dänt\ adj [Gk *polyphyēs* manifold (fr. *poly-* + *-phyēs*, fr. *phyein* to bring forth, produce) + *odont-*, *odous* tooth — more at BE, TOOTH] : having several or many sets of teeth in succession ⟨sharks and some teleost fishes are ~⟩ — distinguished from *diphyodont* and *monophyodont* — **poly·phy·odon·ty** \-tē\ n -ES

**2polyphyodont** \"\ n -S : a polyphyodont animal

**1polypi** *pl of* POLYPUS

**2poly·pi** \ˈpälə,pī, -ə,pē\ n pl, cap [NL, fr. L, pl. of *polypus*] *in former classifications* : a class of invertebrates more or less corresponding to Anthozoa

**pol·yp·ide** \ˈpälə,pīd\ n -S [*polyp-* + *-ide* (alter. of *-id*)] : one of the individual zooids of a bryozoan colony : POLYP

**po·lypi·dom** \pəˈlipədəm, -,däm\ n -S [*polyp* + *-i-* + Gk *domos* house — more at TIMBER] *archaic* : POLYPARY

**pol·yp·if·er·ous** \ˌpälə¦pif(ə)rəs\ *or* **pol·yp·ig·er·ous** \-ij(ə)rəs\ adj [*polyp* + *-iferous* or *-gerous*] : bearing polyps

**pol·yp·ite** \ˈpälə,pīt\ n -S [*polyp* + *-ite*] **1** : one of the zooids of a coral, hydroid, or siphonophore **2** : a feeding zooid or hydranth distinguished from a dactylozooid or other modified or degenerate zooid

**poly·pla·coph·o·ra** \ˌpälē,plaˈkäfərə, -älə,p-\ n pl, cap [NL, fr. *poly-* + *plac-* + *-phora*] : an order of Amphineura comprising the chitons all of which have the foot occupying the whole ventral surface of the body and the shell composed of eight calcified dorsal plates — **poly·pla·coph·o·ran** \ˌ==,==¦fərən\ adj or n — **poly·plac·o·phore** \ˌ==ˈplakə,fō(ə)r\ n -S — **poly·pla·coph·o·rous** \ˌ==¦plaˈkäfərəs\ adj

**poly·plastic** \ˌpälē, -lə+\ adj [*poly-* + *plastic*] : assuming or able to assume many forms

**poly·plec·tron** \ˌ==ˈplektrən, -,trän\ n, cap [NL, fr. *poly-* + *plectron*] : a genus of large showy Asiatic pheasants consisting of the peacock pheasants

**1poly·ploid** \ˈpälə,plȯid\ adj [ISV *poly-* + *ploid*] : having or being a chromosome number that is a multiple greater than two of the monoploid number ⟨a ~ cell⟩ — compare ALLOPOLYPLOID, DIPLOID, HAPLOID, HEXAPLOID — **poly·ploi·dic** \ˌ==¦plȯidik\ adj

**2polyploid** \"\ n -S : a polyploid individual

**polyploid complex** n : a complex group of interrelated hybrids produced by the intercrossing of related autopolyploids and allopolyploids that is in some respects comparable to a taxonomic genus — compare POLYPLOID SERIES

**poly·ploid·iza·tion** \ˌ==,plȯidəˈzāshən\ n -S [*polyploidize* + *-ation*] : the act or process of polyploidizing

**poly·ploid·ize** \ˈ==,plȯi,dīz\ vb -ED/-ING/-S [*polyploid* + *-ize*] vt : to cause to become polyploid ⟨~ a plant⟩ ~ vi : to induce polyploidy ⟨a *polyploidizing* agent⟩

**poly·ploid·ogen** \ˌ==ˈplȯidəjən, -,jen\ n -S [*polyploid* + *-o-* + *-gen*] : a chemical substance that is capable of inducing polyploidy in cells

**poly·ploid·ogen·ic** \ˌ==¦==¦jenik\ adj [*polyploidogen* + *-ic*] : constituting or having the capacity to induce polyploidy in the cell

**polyploid series** n : a group of related forms or species having chromosome sets that are different multiples of the same monoploid set — compare POLYPLOID COMPLEX

**poly·ploi·dy** \ˈ==,plȯidē\ n -ES [ISV *polyploid* + *-y*] : the condition of being polyploid

**pol·yp·nea** *or* **pol·yp·noea** \ˌpäləp¦nēə\ n -S [NL, fr. *poly-* + *-pnea*, *-pnoea*] : rapid or panting respiration — **pol·yp·ne·ic** *or* **pol·yp·noe·ic** \ˌ==¦nēik\ adj

**pol·yp·neus·tic** \ˌpäləp¦n(y)üstik\ adj [*poly-* + Gk *pneustikos* of breathing, fr. (assumed) Gk *pneustos* (verbal of Gk *pnein* to breathe) + Gk *-ikos* -ic — more at PNEUMATIC] *of an insect* : having at least three pairs of functional spiracles

**1poly·pod** \ˈpälē,päd, -lə,p-\ n [ME *pollypod*, prob. fr. MF *polipode*, fr. L *polypodium* polypody] : 1POLYPODY

**2polypod** \"\ adj [Gk *polypod-*, *polypous* — more at POLYP] **1** : having many feet or legs **2** [NL *polypoda*] : having abdominal limbs ⟨~ insect larvae⟩

**3polypod** \"\ n [NL *polypoda*] : a polypod animal (as an insect larva)

**po·lyp·o·da** \pəˈlipədə\ n, pl **polypo·dae** \-,dē, -,dī\ [NL, modif. of Gk *polypod-*, *polypous*] : an insect larva having abdominal legs

**poly·po·dia** \ˌpälēˈpōdēə, -ləˈp-\ n -S [NL, fr. *poly-* + *-podia*] : a condition of having more than the normal number of feet

**poly·po·di·a·ce·ae** \ˌ==,==ˈāsē,ē\ n pl, cap [NL, fr. *Polypodium*, type genus + *-aceae*] : a large family of ferns (order Filicales) having erect or creeping rootstocks with scattered or clustered fronds and the fertile bearing annulate stalked sporangia disposed in sori — **poly·po·di·a·ceous** \ˌ==,==¦āshəs\ adj

**poly·po·di·um** \ˌ==ˈpōdēəm\ n, cap [NL, fr. L, polypody, fr. Gk *polypodion*, fr. *polypodion*, dim. of *polypod-*, *polypous* many-footed] : a genus (the type of the family Polypodiaceae) of ferns containing the polypodies and distinguished by the roundish naked sori

**po·lyp·o·dous** \pəˈlipədəs\ adj [*poly-* + *-podous*] : POLYPOD

**1poly·po·dy** \ˈpälē,pōdē, -lə,p-\ n -ES [ME *polypodie*, fr. L *polipodium*] : a fern of the genus *Polypodium*; *esp* : a fern (*P. vulgare*) found throughout No. America and most of Europe and Asia that has creeping rootstocks and pinnatifid fronds with entire segments

**2polypody** \"\ n -ES [F *polypodie*, fr. Gk *polypodia*, fr. *polypod-*, *polypous* many-footed] : a condition of having many legs — used esp. of an insect embryo or larva

**polypody family** n : POLYPODIACEAE

**pol·yp·oid** \ˈpälə,pȯid\ *or* **pol·yp·oi·dal** \ˌ==¦pȯidᵊl\ adj [*polypoid* fr. ISV *polyp* + *-oid*; *polypoidal* fr. *polyp* + *-oid* + *-al*] **1** : resembling a polyp **2** : marked by the formation of lesions suggesting polyps ⟨~ degeneration⟩ ⟨~ carcinoma⟩

**po·lyp·o·ra·ce·ae** \pə,lipəˈrāsē,ē; ˌpälēp-, ˌpäləp-\ n pl, cap [NL, fr. *Polyporus*, type genus + *-aceae*] : a family of pore-bearing fungi (order Polyporales) having a soft texture when young, but commonly becoming firm, corky, or woody with age and often forming shelflike growths on trees — compare BOLETACEAE, BRACKET FUNGUS, FOMES — **po·lyp·o·ra·ceous** \pə¦lipə¦rāshəs; ¦pälēp-, ¦päləp-\ adj

**po·lyp·o·ra·les** \pə,lipəˈrā(,)lēz; ˌpälēp-, ˌpäləp-\ n pl, cap [NL, fr. *Polyporus* + *-ales*] : an order of basidiomycetous fungi (subclass Homobasidiomycetes) that is often included in Agaricales and that includes chiefly saprophytic fungi (as of wood) typically with shelflike or resupinate fruiting bodies which have a smooth or wrinkled often porose hymenium — compare CLAVARIACEAE, HYDNACEAE, POLYPORACEAE

**poly·pore** \ˈpälē,pō(ə)r, -lə,p-\ n -S [NL *Polyporus*] : PORE FUNGUS

**po·lyp·o·rite** \pəˈlipə,rīt\ n -S [NL *Polyporus* + E *-ite*] : a fossil fungus of the genus *Polyporus*; *also* : any similar or related form

**po·lyp·o·roid** \pəˈlipə,rȯid\ adj [NL *Polyporus* + E *-oid*] : relating to or resembling a pore fungus esp. of the genus *Polyporus*

**po·lyp·o·rus** \pəˈlipərəs\ n, cap [NL, fr. Gk *polyporos* with many passages, fr. *poly-* + *poros* passage, pore — more at FARE] : a genus (the type of the family Polyporaceae) of fungi having stipitate or sessile fruiting bodies and including important pathogens of various trees (as birches and conifers)

**pol·yp·ose** \ˈpälə,pōs\ adj [*polyp* + *-ose*] : POLYPOUS

**pol·yp·o·sis** \ˌpäləˈpōsəs\ n, pl **polypo·ses** \-ō,sēz\ [NL, fr. *polypus* + *-osis*] : a condition characterized by the presence of numerous polyps ⟨~ of the colon⟩ ⟨multiple ~⟩

**pol·yp·ous** \ˈpäləpəs\ adj [*polyp* + *-ous*] : relating to, of the nature of, or like a polyp

**poly·pragmatic** *also* **poly·pragmatical** \ˌpälē, -lə+\ adj [LGk *polypragmatos* (fr. Gk *polypragmatein* to be busy with many things, to be meddlesome, fr. *poly-* + *pragmat-*, *pragma* deed, affair) + E *-ic* or *-ical* — more at PRAGMATIC] : concerned with things not one's own affair : MEDDLESOME

**poly·pragmatism** \ˌ==+\ n [*polypragmatic* + *-ism*] : MEDDLESOMENESS ⟨a critique of poetical ~ —George Saintsbury⟩

**poly·pragmatist** \"+\ n [*polypragmatic* + *-ist*] : BUSYBODY

**poly·propylene** \ˌpälē, -lə+\ n [*poly-* + *propylene*] : a polymer of propylene; *esp* : a substance resembling polyethylene or polyisobutylene used chiefly in making fibers, films, and molded and extruded products

**1poly·protodont** \"+\ adj [NL *Polyprotodontia*] : of or relating to the Polyprotodontia

**2polyprotodont** \"\ n -S : a marsupial of the suborder Polyprotodontia

**poly·pro·to·don·tia** \ˌ==,prōd·əˈdänch(ē)ə\ n pl, cap [NL, fr. *poly-* + *prot-* + *-odontia*] *in some classifications* : a suborder of marsupials including the dasyures, Tasmanian wolves, opossums, bandicoots, and other largely or entirely carnivorous or insectivorous forms having specialized canines and four or five upper incisors and two or three lower incisors on each side — compare DIDACTYLA, DIPROTODONTIA

**polyps** *pl of* POLYP

**poly·psychic** *also* **poly·psychical** \ˌpälē, -lə+\ adj [ISV *poly-* + *psyche* + *-ic* or *-ical*] : having many souls or modes of intelligence

**poly·psychism** \ˌ==+\ n [ISV *poly-* + *psyche* + *-ism*] : belief in many souls in one person

**1po·lyp·ter·id** \pəˈliptərəd\ adj [NL *Polypteridae*] : of or relating to the Polypteridae

**2polypterid** \"\ n -S : a fish of the family Polypteridae

**pol·yp·ter·i·dae** \ˌpäləpˈterə,dē\ n pl, cap [NL, fr. *Polypterus*, type genus + *-idae*] : a family of primitive African fishes (order Cladistia) containing the recent genus *Polypterus* and known from fossil remains since the Upper Eocene

**po·lyp·ter·is** \pəˈliptərəs\ [NL, fr. *poly-* + *-pteris*] *syn of* GAILLARDIA

**1po·lyp·ter·oid** \-,rȯid\ adj [NL *Polypterus* + E *-oid*] : like or related to the family Polypteridae ⟨a ~ fish⟩

**2polypteroid** \"\ n -S : a polypteroid fish

**po·lyp·ter·us** \pəˈliptərəs\ n, cap [NL, fr. Gk *polypteros* many-winged, fr. *poly-* + *-pteros* -winged (fr. *pteron* wing, feather — more at FEATHER)] : the type genus of Polypteridae that comprises primitive fishes of the larger rivers of tropical Africa having an elongate body covered with rhombic enameled scales, a dorsal fin reduced to a series of finlets, pectoral fins taking the form of a rounded lobe supported on a short arm, and an air bladder functioning as an accessory breathing organ — see BICHIR, ERPETOICHTHYS

**pol·yp·to·ton** \ˌpäləpˈtō,tän\ n, pl **polypto·ta** \-ōd·ə\ [LL, fr. Gk *polyptōton*, neut. of *polyptōtos* using many cases of the same word, fr. *poly-* + *-ptōtos* (fr. *piptein* to fall, influenced in meaning by Gk *ptōsis* case) — more at SYMPTOM] : the rhetorical repetition of a word in a different case, inflection, or voice in the same sentence (as in Tennyson's "my own heart's heart, and ownest own, farewell")

**po·lyp·tych** \ˈpäləp,tik, pəˈlipt-\ n -S [Gk *polyptychos* with many folds, folded many times, fr. *poly-* + *-ptychos* (akin to Gk *ptychē* fold, layer)] : an arrangement of four or more panels (as of a painting) usu. hinged and folding together ⟨an altarpiece in the form of a ~⟩ — compare DIPTYCH, TRIPTYCH

**poly·pus** \ˈpäləpəs, -lēp-\ n [L — more at POLYP] **1** pl **poly·pi** \-,pī, -,pē\ *or* **polypuses** : POLYP 2 **2** *cap* [NL, fr. L, polyp] : a genus of octopuses

**poly·rhythm** \ˌpälē, -lə+\ n [*poly-* + *rhythm*] : the simultaneous combination of contrasting rhythms in a musical composition

**poly·rhythmic** \"+\ adj [ISV *poly-* + *rhythmic*] **1** : having many rhythms; *specif* : having many usu. varied rhythmic feet to the line ⟨~ verse⟩ **2** : having two or more rhythms proceeding simultaneously in different musical parts

**polys** *pl of* POLY

**poly·saccharide** \"+\ n [ISV *poly-* + *saccharide*] : a carbohydrate decomposable by hydrolysis into two or more molecules of monosaccharides (as glucose) or their derivatives; *esp* : one of the more complex carbohydrates ($(C_6H_{10}O_5)_x$) (as starch or cellulose) — compare OLIGOSACCHARIDE

**poly·saccharose** \"+\ n [*poly-* + *saccharose*] : POLYSACCHARIDE

**poly·saprobe** \"+\ n [ISV *poly-* + *saprobe*] : a polysaprobic individual

**poly·saprobic** \"+\ adj [ISV *poly-* + *saprobic*] : living in a medium that is rich in decomposable organic matter and nearly free from dissolved oxygen ⟨~ sewage organisms⟩

**poly·schematic** \"+\ adj [LGk *polyschematos* (fr. Gk *poly-* + *schēmat-*, *schēma* form, shape, scheme) + E *-ic*] : POLYSCHEMATIST

**poly·schematist** \"+\ *or* **poly·sche·ma·tis·tic** \"+¦skēməˈtistik\ adj [*polyschematist* fr. Gk *polyschēmatistos* multiform, composed of various metres, fr. *poly-* + *-schēmatistos* (fr. *schēmatizein* to take shape, give form — fr. *schēmat-*, *schēma* form, shape — + *-izein* -ize); *polyschematistic* fr. *polyschematist* (taken as a noun) + *-ic* — more at SCHEME] : capable of assuming many different metrical forms — used esp. of classical meters in which variations or substitutions without regard for temporal equivalence were allowed

**polyschematist dimeter** n : a classical prosodic unit of eight syllables whose first four, middle four, or last four syllables form a choriambus with the other syllables being indeterminate as to quantity and which is considered by many to be the basic figure of all rhythms of the aeolic class

**poly·scope** \ˈpälē,skōp, -lə,s-\ n [*poly-* + *-scope*] : DIAPHANOSCOPE — **poly·scop·ic** \ˌ==¦skäpik\ adj

**poly·se·mant** \ˌ==ˈsēmənt\ n -S [LGk *polysēmantos* with many meanings, fr. Gk *poly-* + *sēmantos*, verbal of *sēmainein* to mean, mark, signal, fr. *sēma* sign — more at SEMANTICS] : a word having more than one meaning — **poly·semantic** \ˌ==+\ adj

**po·ly·se·mous** \ˌpälē¦sēməs, -lə¦-; pəˈlisəm-\ adj [LL *polysemus*, fr. Gk *polysēmos* with many meanings, fr. *poly-* + *sēma* sign] : having many meanings ⟨explains that his poem is ~ —C.S.Singleton⟩ ⟨excited by the difficult, the ambiguous, the ~ —R.G.Davis⟩

**po·ly·se·my** \ˈpälē,sēmē, -lə,-; pəˈlisəm-\ n -ES [NL *polysemia*, fr. LL *polysemus* polysemous + L *-ia* -y] : multiplicity of meaning ⟨English is less exposed to ~ than French —Stephen Ullmann⟩

**poly·sepalous** \ˌpälē, -lə+\ adj [*poly-* + *-sepalous*] : having separate sepals

**poly·serositis** \"+\ n [NL, fr. *poly-* + *serositis*] : inflammation of several serous membranes (as the pleura, pericardium, and peritoneum) at the same time

**poly·si·pho·nia** \ˌ==,sīˈfōnēə\ n, cap [NL, fr. *poly-* + *siphon-* + *-ia*] : a large genus of red algae (family Rhodomelaceae) having usu. a filamentous much-branched thallus variable in shape and size but in cross section showing a single axial cell surrounded by a sheath of tubular cells at least in the axis and main branches

**poly·si·phon·ic** \ˌ==sī¦fänik\ adj [*poly-* + *siphon-* + *-ic*] : consisting of several tubes or rows of cells ⟨the ~ thallus of many red or brown algae⟩ — compare MONOSIPHONIC

**poly·somatic** \ˌ==+\ adj [*polysomaty* + *-ic*] : of, relating to, or exhibiting polysomaty

**poly·so·ma·ty** \ˌ==ˈsōməd·ē\ n -ES [ISV *poly-* + *somat-* + *-y*; orig. formed as G *polysomatie*] : the replication in somatic cells of the chromosome number through division of chromosomes without subsequent nuclear division

**1poly·so·mic** \ˌ==¦sōmik\ adj [ISV *poly-* + *-somic*] : having one or a few chromosomes present in greater or smaller number than the remaining chromosomes

**2polysomic** \"\ n -S : a polysomic individual

**poly·so·my** \ˈpälē,sōmē, -lə,s-\ n -ES [ISV *polysomic* + *-y*] : the condition of being polysomic

**poly·speed** \ˈpälē, -lə+,-\ adj [*poly-* + *speed*] : capable of several speeds ⟨~ motor⟩

**poly·sper·mic** \ˌ==¦spərmik\ adj [*poly-* + *-spermic*] : of or relating to polyspermy ⟨~ fertilization⟩

**poly·sper·my** \ˈ==,=mē\ n -ES [ISV *poly-* + *-spermy*] : the entrance of several spermatozoa into one egg — compare MONOSPERMY

**poly·spondyli** \ˌpälē, -lə+\ [NL, fr. *poly-* + *-spondyli*] *syn of* HOLOCEPHALI

**poly·spon·dyl·ic** \ˌ==spän¦dilik\ adj [*poly-* + *spondylic*] : of, relating to, or having a vertebral column (as in the chimaeroid fishes) in which the calcified portion has the form of numerous slender rings surrounding the notochord — **poly·spon·dy·lous** \-ndələs\ adj — **poly·spon·dy·ly** \-lē\ n -ES

**po·lys·po·ra** \pə'lispərə\ *n, cap* [NL, *poly-* + *-spora*] **:** a genus of imperfect fungi (family Melanconiaceae) forming minute acervuli directly over the stomata with hyaline nonseptate conidia of varying shape — see BROWNING 3a

**poly·sporangium** \ˌpälē, -lə+\ *n* [NL, fr. *poly-* + *sporangium*] **:** a sporangium containing many spores

**poly·spore** \'==ˌspō(ə)r\ *n* [ISV *poly-* + *spore*; prob. orig. formed in F] **:** one of a group of 12 to 16 spores produced instead of a tetraspore by various red algae

**poly·spored** \-ō(ə)rd\ *adj* [*poly-* + *spore* + *-ed*] **:** having many spores

**poly·spor·ic** \ˌ==ˈspōrik\ *or* **poly·spor·ous** \-rəs, pə'lispərəs\ *adj* [*poly-* + *-sporic, -sporous*] **:** POLYSPORED

**poly·stachy·ous** \ˌpälēˈstakēəs, -tāk-\ *adj* [*poly-* + *stachy-* (fr. Gk *stachys* ear of grain) + *-ous* — more at STING] **:** having many spikes ⟨~ grasses⟩

**poly·stele** \'==ˌstēl *also* ˌ==ˈstēlē\ *n* [*poly-* + *stele*] **:** a stele that consists of a number of like vascular units dispersed in parenchymatous tissue (as in a fern or monocotyledon) — see MERISTELE — **poly·ste·lic** \ˌ==ˈstēlik\ *adj* — **poly·ste·ly** \'==ˌstēlē\ *n* -ES

**poly·stemo·nous** \ˌ==ˈstēmənəs, -tem-\ *adj* [prob. fr. (assumed) NL *polystemonus*, fr. NL *poly-* + (assumed) NL *-stemonus* -stemonous] **:** POLYANDROUS

**po·lys·ti·choid** \pə'listəˌkȯid\ *adj* [NL *Polystichum* + E *-oid*] **:** resembling a fern of the genus *Polystichum*

**po·lys·ti·chous** \-kəs\ *adj* [Gk *polystichos*, fr. *poly-* + *stichos* row, line — more at DISTICH] **:** arranged in several rows ⟨the ~ spike of maize —P.C.Mangelsdorf⟩ — compare DISTICHOUS

**po·lys·ti·chum** \-kəm\ *n, cap* [NL, fr. Gk *polystichon*, neut. of *polystichos* of many rows, of many lines] **:** a genus of chiefly northern ferns (family Polypodiaceae) having lanceolate pinnate or bipinnate often evergreen fronds with the veins free and the indusia lacking sinuses and centrally peltate — see CHRISTMAS FERN, HOLLY FERN

**poly·stic·tus** \ˌpälēˈstiktəs, -lə's-\ *n, cap* [NL, fr. Gk *polystiktos* much-spotted, fr. *poly-* much (fr. *polys* much, many) + *stiktos* spotted, pricked, verbal of *stizein* to prick — more at POLY-, STICK] *in some classifications* **:** a large genus of pore fungi (family Polyporaceae) having leathery often showy annual sporophores, growing on and causing decay of wood (as timbers or wounds of trees), and being now divided among several distinct genera

**po·lys·to·ma** \pə'listəmə\ *n, cap* [NL, fr. Gk *polystomos* many mouthed, fr. *poly-* + *-stomos* -stomous] **:** a genus (the type of the family Polystomatidae) of monogenetic trematode worms including several species that occur in the urinary bladder of batrachians

**po·lys·to·mat·i·dae** \=ˌ==ˈmadəˌdē; ˌpälēstōˈm-, -ləs-\ *n pl, cap* [NL, fr. *Polystomat-, Polystoma* + *-idae*] **:** a family comprising monogenetic trematode worms with a group of strong suckers and usu. a pair of chitinous hooks at the posterior end

**poly·stomatous** \ˌpälē, -lə+\ *adj* [*poly-* + *-stomatous*] **:** having many mouths, openings, or suckers

[1]**poly·stome** \'==ˌstōm\ *n* -S [F, fr. Gk *polystomos* many-mouthed] **:** a polystomatous individual (as a monogenetic trematode worm)

[2]**polystome** \"\ *adj* **:** POLYSTOMATOUS

**poly·sto·mea** \ˌpälēˈstōmēə, -lə's-\ [NL, fr. Gk *polystomos* many-mouthed] *syn of* MONOGENEA

**poly·sto·mi·dae** \-məˌdē\ [NL, fr. *Polystoma* + *-idae*] *syn of* POLYSTOMATIDAE

[1]**poly·style** \'==+ˌ-\ *also* **poly·stylar** \ˌ==+\ *adj* [*polystyle* fr. Gk *polystylos*, fr. *poly-* + *stylos* pillar; *polystylar* fr. Gk *polystylos* + E *-ar* — more at STEER] **:** having or supported by many columns ⟨a ~ court⟩

[2]**polystyle** \"\ *n* **:** a polystyle hall or edifice

**poly·styrene** \ˌpälē, -lə+\ *n* [*poly-* + *styrene*] **:** a polymer of styrene; *esp* **:** a rigid transparent thermoplastic characterized by good physical and electrical insulating properties, low moisture absorption, and yellowing in sunlight and used either unmodified or sometimes modified (as for improving impact strength or heat resistance) chiefly in making containers and other molded products (as for radios, electrical apparatus, refrigerators) and sheet materials — compare STYRENE PLASTIC

**poly·sulfide** \"+\ *n* [ISV *poly-* + *sulfide*] **:** a sulfide containing two or more atoms of sulfur in the molecule

**polysulfide rubber** *n* **:** any of various synthetic rubbers made by the reaction of a sodium polysulfide with an organic dichloride (as ethylene dichloride or a dichloro derivative of ethyl formal), characterized in general by good resistance to oxygen, light, oils, and solvents, impermeability to gases, and poor tensile strength and abrasion resistance, and used chiefly in mechanical rubber goods, in adhesives, binders, and sealing compositions, and in coatings (as for textiles)

**poly·sulfuration** \"+\ *n* [*poly-* + *sulfuration*] **:** formation of polysulfides

**poly·syllabic** *also* **poly·syllabical** \ˌpälē, -lə+\ *adj* [ML *polysyllabus* polysyllabic (fr. Gk *polysyllabos*, fr. *poly-* + *syllabē* syllable) + E *-ic* or *-ical* — more at SYLLABLE] **1 :** having three or usu. four or more syllables ⟨penchant for ~ words —Campbell Dixon⟩ ⟨~ stem⟩ — compare PLURISYLLABLE **2 :** having or characterized by polysyllabic words ⟨a ~ statement of the obvious —A.C.Spaulding⟩ — **polysyllabically** \"+\ *adv*

**poly·syl·la·bism** \ˌ==ˈsiləˌbizəm\ *n* -S [ML *polysyllabus* + E *-ism*] **:** the use of polysyllables

[1]**poly·syllable** \'==+\ *n* [modif. (influenced by *syllable*) of ML *polysyllaba* word of many syllables, fem. of *polysyllabus*] **:** a polysyllabic word

[2]**polysyllable** \"\ *adj* **:** POLYSYLLABIC

**poly·syllogism** \ˌpälē, -lə+\ *n* [*poly-* + *syllogism*] **:** a systematic series of syllogisms

**poly·syllogistic** \"+\ *adj* [*polysyllogism* + *-istic*] **:** of, relating to, or constituting a polysyllogism

**poly·symmetrical** \"+\ *adj* [*poly-* + *symmetrical*] **:** divisible into like parts by more than one axial plane **:** ACTINOMORPHIC — used esp. of a flower — **poly·symmetrically** \"\ *adv*

**poly·syn·det·ic** \ˌ==sənˈdedˌik, -ˌsinˌde-\ *adj* [NL *polysyndeton* + E *-ic*] **:** characterized by polysyndeton — **poly·syn·det·i·cal·ly** \-d·ək(ə)lē\ *adv*

**poly·syn·de·ton** \ˌ==ˈsindəˌtän, -ˌtən\ *n, pl* **polysyndetons** \-ˌtänz, -ˌtənz\ *or* **polysynde·ta** \-ˌtə\ [NL, fr. LGk, neut. of *polysyndetos* using many conjunctions, connected, fr. Gk *poly-* + *syndetos* bound together — more at ASYNDETON] **:** repetition of conjunctions in close succession (as in *we have ships and men and money and stores*) — opposed to *asyndeton*

**poly·synthesis** \ˌpälē, -lə+\ *n* [NL, *poly-* + *synthesis*] **:** the synthesis of several elements; *specif* **:** POLYSYNTHESISM

**poly·syn·the·sism** \ˌ==+\ *n* -S [*polysynthesis* + *-ism*] **:** the uniting of many parts into one **:** a high degree of synthesis; *specif* **:** a grammatical practice of some languages (as American Indian) of combining word elements into a single word that is equivalent to a sentence in other languages

**poly·synthetic** *also* **poly·synthetical** \ˌ==+\ *adj* [LGk *polysynthetos* much compounded (fr. Gk *poly-* much — fr. *polys* much, many — + *synthetos* compounded, put together, fr. *syntithenai* to put together) + E *-ic* or *-ical* — more at POLY-, SYNTHESIS] **:** characterized by polysynthesism — **poly·synthetically** \"+\ *adv*

**poly·syn·the·tism** \ˌ==+ˈsin(t)thəˌtizəm\ *n* -S [*polysynthetic* + *-ism*] **:** POLYSYNTHESISM

[1]**poly·technic** *also* **poly·technical** \"+\ *adj* [*polytechnic* fr. F *polytechnique*, fr. Gk *polytechnos* skilled in many arts (fr. *poly-* + *technē* art, skill) + F *-ique* -ic; *polytechnical* fr. [2]*polytechnic* + *-al* — more at TECHNICAL] **:** of, relating to, or devoted to instruction in many technical arts or applied sciences ⟨a ~ institute⟩ ⟨~ research⟩

[2]**polytechnic** \"\ *n* **:** a polytechnic school

**poly·technician** \ˌ==+\ *n* [F *polytechnicien*, fr. *polytechnique* + *-ien* -ian] **:** a student or graduate of a polytechnic school esp. in France

**poly·tech·ni·za·tion** \ˌ==ˌteknəˈzāshən\ *n* -S [*poly-* + *-techny* + *-ization*] **:** practical application of scientific principles throughout a national economy

**poly·tene** \'==ˌtēn\ *adj* [ISV *poly-* + *-tene* (fr. L *taenia* band) — more at TAENIA] **:** MULTIPLE; *specif* **:** relating to, being, or having chromosomes of which the chromonemata are reduplicated — see SALIVARY CHROMOSOME — **poly·tenic** \ˌ==ˈtēnik, -ten-\ *adj* — **poly·te·ny** \'==ˌtēnē\ *n* -ES

**poly·terpene** \ˌpälē, -lə+\ *n* [ISV *poly-* + *terpene*] **:** a natural or synthetic polymer $(C_5H_8)_x$ of a terpene hydrocarbon: as **a :** RUBBER HYDROCARBON **b :** a thermoplastic resin or viscous liquid obtained by polymerization of turpentine or a nopinene fraction by means of a catalyst (as aluminum chloride) and used chiefly in adhesives and rubber goods

**poly·tetrafluoroethylene** \"+\ *n* [*poly-* + *tetrafluoroethylene*] **:** a polymer of tetrafluoroethylene; *esp* **:** a tough resin characterized by good resistance to chemicals, heat, and weathering and good electrical insulating properties and used chiefly in making molded products (as gaskets), in electrical insulation, and in coatings

[1]**poly·tha·la·mia** \ˌ==thəˈlāmēə\ [NL, fr. *poly-* + Gk *thalamos* chamber + NL *-ia* — more at THALAMUS] *syn of* TETRABRANCHIA

[2]**polythalamia** \"\ *n pl, cap* [NL, fr. *poly-* + Gk *thalamos* + NL *-ia*] **:** a division of Foraminifera including those having a many-chambered shell or sometimes including all the Foraminifera — **poly·tha·la·mi·an** \ˌ===ˈmēən\ *adj* — **poly·tha·lam·ic** \ˌ===ˈlamik\ *adj*

**poly·thal·a·mous** \ˌ==ˈthaləməs\ *adj* [*poly-* + *thalam-* (fr. Gk *thalamos* chamber), + *-ous*] **:** many-chambered; *also* **:** forming or characterized by many-chambered tests or cysts ⟨~ foraminiferans⟩ ⟨~ gall insects⟩

**poly·the·ism** \ˈpälē(ˌ)thēˌizəm, -lə(-\ *n* [F *polythéisme*, fr. LGk *polytheos* believing in many gods (fr. Gk, of many gods, fr. *poly-* + *theos* god) + F *-isme* -ism — more at THE-] **:** the belief in or worship of a plurality of gods ⟨ancient ~s of Babylon and Egypt —*Brit. Bk. News*⟩

**poly·the·ist** \-ˌthēəst\ *n* **:** one who believes in or worships a plurality of gods

**poly·the·is·tic** \ˌ==(ˌ)thēˈistik\ *also* **poly·the·is·ti·cal** \-stəkəl, -stēk-\ *adj* [*polytheist* + *-ic* or *-ical*] **:** of, relating to, or characterized by polytheism **:** believing in or worshiping a plurality of gods — **poly·the·is·ti·cal·ly** \-stək(ə)lē, -stēk-, -li\ *adv*

**poly·the·lia** \ˌ==ˈthēlēə\ *n* -S [NL, fr. *poly-* + *thel-* (fr. Gk *thēlē* nipple) + *-ia* — more at FEMININE] **:** a condition of having more than the normal number of nipples

**poly·thene** \'==ˌthēn\ *n* -S [contr. of *polyethylene*] **:** polyethylene used as a plastic

**poly·thionic acid** \ˌpälē, -lə+. . .-\ *n* [ISV *poly-* + *thionic*] **:** a thionic acid containing more than two sulfur atoms in the molecule

**po·lyt·o·cous** \pə'lid·əkəs\ *adj* [Gk *polytokos*, fr. *poly-* + *tokos* offspring, fr. *tiktein* to bear, beget — more at THANE] **:** producing many eggs or young at one time ⟨~ mammals⟩ — compare MONOTOCOUS

**poly·to·ma** \ˌpälēˈtōmə, -lə't-\ *n, cap* [NL, fr. *poly-* + *-toma* (fr. Gk *temnein* to cut) — more at TOME] **:** a common genus of colorless saprozoic plantlike flagellates (order Phytomonadina) having paired anterior flagella, lacking chromatophores, and being widely distributed in stagnant freshwater

**po·lyt·o·mous** \pə'lid·əməs\ *adj* [*poly-* + *-tomous* (as in *dichotomous*)] **1 :** divided into more than two secondary parts or branches — compare DICHOTOMOUS **2 :** PINNATIFID

**po·lyt·o·my** \-mē\ *n* -ES [ISV *poly-* + *-tomy*] **1 :** polytomous character or condition ⟨a typical ~ consists of a whorl of three to six branches surrounding an open axil —*Bryologist*⟩ **2 :** division into more members or classes than three — compare TRICHOTOMY

**poly·tonal** \ˌpälē, -lə+\ *adj* [*poly-* + *tonal*] **:** relating to or characterized by polytonality ⟨exciting rhythms and ~ harmonies —*Time*⟩ — **poly·tonally** \"+\ *adv*

**poly·ton·al·ism** \ˌ==ˈtōnᵊlˌizəm\ *n* -S [*polytonal* + *-ism*] **:** the practice or theory of using polytonal combinations in musical composition

**poly·ton·al·ist** \-ᵊləst\ *n* [*polytonal* + *-ist*] **:** one skilled in polytonality

**poly·tonality** \ˌ==+\ *n* [*polytonal* + *-ity*] **:** the simultaneous use of two or more musical keys or tonalities; *also* **:** the effect of such a combination

**poly·tone** \'==+ˌ-\ *n* [*poly-* + *tone*] **:** utterance characterized by varied tone or pitch — compare MONOTONE

**poly·tonic** \ˌ==+\ *adj* [*poly-* + *tonic*] **:** having several pitch tones ⟨~ languages⟩

**poly·topic** \"+\ *adj* [ISV *poly-* + *top-* + *-ic*] *of a kind of organism* **:** occurring or originating in two or more disjunct areas ⟨~ species⟩ — **poly·topically** \"+\ *adv*

**poly·to·pism** \'==ˌtōˌpizəm, pə'lid·əˌp-\ *n* -S [*poly-* + *top-* + *-ism*] **:** independent origin of a systematic group at more than one place presumably by identical change in scattered individuals of its precursor — compare MONOTOPISM

**poly·to·py** \-ˌpē\ *n* -ES [*polytopic* + *-y*] **:** the condition of a group that is polytopic **:** POLYTOPISM

**po·lyt·ri·cha·ce·ae** \pəˌli·trəˈkāsēˌē\ *n pl, cap* [NL, fr. *Polytrichum*, type genus + *-aceae*] **:** a family of usu. large acrocarpous mosses (order Polytrichales) that have simple or branching erect shoots growing from an underground stem, leaves with the costae bearing longitudinal lamellae of variable structure, antheridia borne in conspicuous saucer-shaped terminal rosettes, and capsules which are characteristically angular in cross section with a peristome several cells thick — see POGONATUM, POLYTRICHUM — **po·lyt·ri·cha·ceous** \ˌ==ˈkāshəs\ *adj*

**po·lyt·ri·cha·les** \ˌ==ˈkā(ˌ)lēz\ *n pl, cap* [NL, fr. *Polytrichum* + *-ales*] **:** an order of Musci that is coextensive with the family Polytrichaceae or sometimes includes this together with the genus *Dawsonia* — see DAWSONIALES

**poly·trich·i·dae** \ˌpäləˈtrikəˌdē, -lə't-\ *n pl, cap* [NL, fr. *Polytrichum* + *-idae*] **:** a small subclass of mosses comprising the orders Polytrichales and Dawsoniales

**po·lyt·ri·chous** \pə'li·trəkəs\ *adj* [Gk *polytrichos* very hairy, fr. *poly-* very, much (fr. *polys* much, many) + *-trichos* -trichous] **:** thickly covered with hairs or cilia

**po·lyt·ri·chum** \-kəm\ *n, cap* [NL, fr. L *polytrichon* golden-hair, fr. Gk, maidenhair, fr. neut. of *polytrichos* very hairy] **:** a large genus (the type of the family Polytrichaceae) of mosses chiefly of temperate and arctic regions — see HAIRCAP MOSS

**poly·troch** \'pälēˌträk, -lə't-\ *or* **po·lyt·ro·chal** \pə'li·trəkəl\ *or* **po·lyt·ro·chous** \-kəs\ *adj* [*polytroch* fr. NL *polytrochus*, fr. *poly-* + *-trochus* having (such) a ciliated band; *polytrochal* fr. NL *polytrochus* + E *-al*; *polytrochous* fr. NL *polytrochus* — more at -TROCHA] **:** having many circles of cilia ⟨~ larvae⟩

**poly·troph·ic** \ˌpälēˈträfik, -lə't-\ *adj* [*poly-* + *-trophic*] **1 :** deriving nourishment from more than one organic substance ⟨~ pathogenic bacteria⟩ **2 :** producing nutritive cells one of which is attached to each developing egg in the ovary — used of an insect or the ovary of an insect; compare ACROTROPHIC, PANOISTIC

**poly·trop·ic** \-äpik\ *adj* [*poly-* + *-tropic*] **:** visiting many kinds of flowers for nectar — used of an insect ⟨~ bees⟩; compare MONOTROPIC, OLIGOTROPIC

**poly·type** \'==ˌtīp\ *n* [*poly-* + *type*] **:** one of several polymorphic crystal structures **:** POLYMORPH

**poly·typ·ic** \ˌ==ˈtipik\ *adj* [*poly-* + *type* + *-ic* or *-ical*] **1** *also* **poly·typ·i·cal** \-pəkəl\ **:** represented by several or many types or subdivisions ⟨~ species⟩ — opposed to *monotypic* **2 :** of, relating to, or being a polytype ⟨~ crystal⟩ — **poly·typ·i·cism** \ˌ==ˈpəˌsizəm\ *n* -S

**poly·urethane** *or* **poly·urethan** \ˌpälē, -lə+\ *n* [ISV *poly-* + *urethane, urethan*] **:** any of various polymers that contain —NHCOO— linkages of the type found in carbamic esters, that are obtained by reaction of a di- or tri-isocyanate ester usu. with a polyester or a glycol (as a polyglycol), and that are used chiefly in making flexible and rigid foams, elastomers, and resins for coatings and adhesives

**poly·uria** \ˌpälēˈyu̇rēə, -lə'y-\ *n* -S [NL, fr. *poly-* + *-uria*] **:** excessive secretion of urine in physiologic or pathologic conditions

**poly·uronic acid** \ˌpälē, -lə+. . .-\ *n* [*polyuronic* fr. *poly-* + *uronic* (in *uronic acid*)] **:** a polymer of a uronic acid ⟨alginic acid is a *polyuronic acid*⟩

**poly·uro·nide** \ˌ==ˈyu̇rəˌnīd, -ˌnəd\ *n* -S [ISV *polyuronic* (in *polyuronic acid*) + *-ide*] **:** a polymeric substance consisting of uronic acid units with glycosidic linkages often in combination with monosaccharides and occurring widely in plants (as in gums and pectic substances) and in soils ⟨the ~ hemicelluloses are cell wall components widely distributed in the plant world —J.F.Bonner⟩

**poly·valence** *or* **poly·valency** \ˌpälē, -lə+\ *n* [*polyvalence* ISV, fr. *polyvalent*, after such pairs as E *absent: absence*; *polyvalency* fr. *polyvalent*, after such pairs as E *regent: regency*] **:** the state of being polyvalent

[1]**poly·valent** \"+\ *adj* [ISV *poly-* + *valent*] **:** having multiple valence: as **a** (1) **:** having a valence or oxidation state greater usu. than two ⟨~ ions⟩ (2) **:** having variable valence or oxidation state ⟨nitrogen is ~, exhibiting oxidation states of from −3 to +5 in compounds⟩ **b** (1) **:** capable of interacting with or counteracting more than one toxin, antigen, or kind of microorganism ⟨a ~ vaccine⟩ ⟨~ antivenin⟩ (2) **:** effective against or sensitive toward more than one exciting agent ⟨~ immunity⟩ ⟨~ sensitivity⟩ **c :** MULTIVALENT 2

[2]**polyvalent** \"\ *n* -S **:** a multivalent chromosome group

[1]**poly·vinyl** \ˌpälē, -lə+\ *n* [ISV *poly-* + *vinyl*] **:** a polymerized vinyl compound, vinyl resin, or vinyl plastic

[2]**polyvinyl** \"\ *adj* **:** relating to or being a polymerized vinyl compound

**polyvinyl acetal** *n* **:** any of a group of thermoplastic resins made by condensing polyvinyl alcohol with an aldehyde and used chiefly in the form of sheets and films, molded products, coatings, and adhesives; *esp* **:** the resin made from acetaldehyde

**polyvinyl acetate** *n* **:** a polymer of vinyl acetate; *esp* **:** a thermoplastic material $[-CH_2CH(OOCCH_3)-]_x$ obtained usu. in the form of a colorless to straw-colored stable solid resin or a milk-white emulsion in water and used chiefly in adhesives, textile finishes, water-base emulsion paints, and other coatings and in making polyvinyl alcohol and polyvinyl acetals

**polyvinyl alcohol** *n* **:** a polymer of vinyl alcohol; *esp* **:** a thermoplastic resin that is soluble or swells in water, that if obtained by complete hydrolysis of polyvinyl acetate has the formula $[-CH_2CH(OH)-]_x$ or if by partial hydrolysis contains some acetate groups, and that is used chiefly as emulsifiers, adhesives, and films resistant to solvents and abrasion, and in making molded and extruded products and polyvinyl acetals

**polyvinyl butyral** *n* **:** a tough flexible transparent moisture-resistant polyvinyl acetal resin made from polyvinyl alcohol and butyraldehyde and used chiefly as the interlayer in safety glass and other laminated products and as a coating for textiles

**polyvinyl chloride** *n* **:** a polymer of vinyl chloride; *esp* **:** a thermoplastic resin $(-CH_2CHCl-)_x$ that is characterized by chemical inertness, resistance to weathering, electrical resistivity, and rigidity unless it is plasticized and that is used chiefly for electrical insulation, coated fabrics, films, sheets, and pipes

**polyvinyl formal** *n* **:** a polyvinyl acetal resin made from polyvinyl alcohol and formaldehyde and used chiefly in insulating enamels and other coatings

**poly·vinylidene** \ˌpälē, -lə+\ *adj* [*poly-* + *vinylidene*] **:** relating to or being a polymerized vinylidene compound

**polyvinylidene chloride** *n* **:** a polymer of vinylidene chloride: as **a :** an insoluble crystalline thermoplastic homopolymer $(-CH_2CCl_2-)_x$ **b :** SARAN

**poly·vi·nyl·pyrrolidone** \ˌ==ˌ==+\ *n* [*poly-* + *vinyl* + *pyrrolidone*] **:** a water-soluble chemically inert solid polymer $(-CH_2CHC_4H_6NO-)_n$ made by polymerization of *N*-vinyl-pyrrolidone and used chiefly in medicine as a vehicle for drugs (as iodine) and esp. formerly as a plasma expander

**polyvinyl resin** *n* **:** VINYL RESIN

**poly·vol·tine** \ˌpälēˈvōlˌtēn, -lə'v-, -ˌtᵊn\ *adj* [*poly-* + *-voltine* (as in *bivoltine*)] **:** producing several broods in a season — used esp. of a silkworm

[1]**po·lyx·e·nid** \pə'liksənəd; ˌpäləkˈsenəd\ *adj* [NL *Polyxenidae*] **:** of or relating to the Polyxenidae

[2]**polyxenid** \"\ *n* -S **:** a millipede of the family Polyxenidae

**pol·yx·en·i·dae** \ˌpäləkˈsenəˌdē\ *n pl, cap* [NL, fr. *Polyxenus*, type genus + *-idae*] **:** a cosmopolitan family of small pselaphognathous millipedes having 10 body rings, 13 pairs of legs, and very small eyes

**po·lyx·e·nus** \pə'liksənəs\ *n, cap* [NL, fr. *poly-* + Gk *xenos* guest, host] **:** a cosmopolitan genus (the type of the family Polyxenidae) of millipedes

[1]**poly·zoa** \ˌpälēˈzōə, -lə'z-\ [NL, fr. *poly-* + *-zoa*] *syn of* BRYOZOA

[2]**polyzoa** \"\ [NL, fr. *poly-* + *-zoa*] *syn of* [2]CESTODA

**poly·zo·al** \ˌ==ˈzōəl\ *adj* [NL *Polyzoa* + E *-al*] **1 :** BRYOZOAN **2 :** CESTODE

**poly·zo·an** \-ōən\ *adj or n* [NL *Polyzoa* + E *-an*] **1 :** BRYOZOAN **2 :** CESTODE

**poly·zo·ar·i·al** \ˌ==zōˈa(a)rēəl\ *adj* [NL *polyzoarium* + E *-al*] **:** of or relating to a polyzoarium

**poly·zo·ar·i·um** \ˌ===ˈrēəm\ *also* **poly·zo·a·ry** \ˌ==ˈzōərē\ *n, pl* **polyzoar·ia** \ˌ===ˈrēə\ *also* **polyzoaries** \ˌ==ˈzōərēz\ [*polyzoarium* fr. NL, fr. *Polyzoa* + *-arium*; *polyzoary* fr. NL *Polyzoa* + E *-ary*] **:** a bryozoan colony or the supporting skeleton of such a colony

**poly·zo·ic** \ˌ==ˈzōik\ *adj* [*poly-* + *-zoic*] **1 :** composed of many zooids; *esp* **:** POLYZOOTIC **2 :** producing many sporozoites **3 :** containing many kinds of animals or many animals — used of habitats

[1]**poly·zo·oid** \-ōˌȯid\ *adj* [NL *Polyzoa* + E *-oid*] **:** resembling a polyzooid

[2]**polyzooid** \"\ *n* **:** POLYPIDE

**poly·zo·on** \ˌ==ˈzōˌän\ *n, pl* **poly·zoa** \-ōə\ *or* **polyzoons** [NL, fr. *poly-* + *-zoon*] **:** POLYPIDE

**poly·zo·ot·ic** \ˌ==ˌzəˈwäd·ik, -zōˈä-\ *adj* [*poly-* + *zo-* + *-otic*] **:** made up of numerous zooids; *specif* **:** consisting of a linear series of similar segments ⟨~ tapeworms⟩ — distinguished from *monozootic*

[1]**pom** \'päm\ *n* -S [by shortening] **1 :** POMPON **2 :** POMERANIAN

[2]**pom** \"\ *n* -S [imit.] **:** BANG ⟨the dull ~ of a distant cannon⟩ — often used interjectionally

[3]**pom** \"\ *vi* **pommed; pommed; pomming; poms** [imit.] **:** to sound with the characteristic noise of a small caliber automatic or semiautomatic cannon

**pom·ace** *or* **pum·ace** \'pəməs\ *n* -S [prob. fr. ML *pomacium* cider, fr. LL *pomum* apple, fr. L, fruit] **1 :** the substance of apples or a similar fruit crushed by grinding (as in making cider) or the residue of grape skins, seeds, and stems remaining after pressing of wine grapes **2 :** the substance of anything (as fish or castor bean) mashed or crushed to a pulpy mass

**po·ma·ce·ae** \pō'māsēˌē\ [NL, fr. LL *pomus* apple tree, fr. L, fruit tree, fr. *pomum* fruit] *syn of* MALACEAE

**pomace fly** *n* **:** FRUIT FLY

[1]**po·ma·cen·trid** \ˌpōməˈsen·trəd\ *adj* [NL *Pomacentridae*] **:** of or relating to the Pomacentridae

[2]**pomacentrid** \"\ *n* -S **:** a fish of the family Pomacentridae

**po·ma·cen·tri·dae** \ˌ==ˈsen·trəˌdē\ *n pl, cap* [NL, fr. *Pomacentrus*, type genus (fr. Gk *pōmat-, pōma* lid, cover + *kentron* sharp point) + *-idae*; akin to Skr *pāti* he protects — more at FUR, CENTER] **:** a family of small usu. brightly colored marine percoid fishes having only two spines in the anal fin and comprising the damselfishes of tropical coral reefs — **po·ma·cen·troid** \ˌ==ˈsenˌtrȯid\ *adj or n*

**po·ma·cen·trus** \ˌ==ˈsen·trəs\ *n, cap* [NL — more at POMACENTRIDAE] **:** the type genus of the family Pomacentridae

**po·ma·ceous** \pō'māshəs\ *adj* [NL *pomaceus*, fr. LL *pomum* apple (fr. L *pomum* fruit) + L *-aceus* -aceous] **1 :** of or relating to apples **:** like or typical of an apple ⟨~ harvest⟩ ⟨~ shape⟩ **2** [NL *Pomaceae* + E *-ous*] **a :** belonging to the Malaceae **b :** having the nature or appearance of a pome

[1]**po·ma·das·id** \ˌpōməˈdasəd, pō'madəs-\ *adj* [NL *Pomadasidae*] **:** of or relating to the Pomadasidae

[2]**pomadasid** \"\ *n* -S **:** a fish of the family Pomadasidae

**po·ma·das·i·dae** \ˌpōməˈdasəˌdē\ *n pl, cap* [NL, irreg. fr. *Pomadasys*, type genus + *-idae*] **:** a family of percoid fishes comprising the grunts

**po·ma·da·sy·i·dae** \ˌ==ˌdəˈsīəˌdē\ [NL, fr. *Pomadasys*, type genus + *-idae*] *syn of* POMADASIDAE

**po·ma·das·ys** \ˌ==ˈdasəs\ *n, cap* [NL, fr. Gk *pōmat-, pōma* lid + *dasys* shaggy, thick with hair — more at POMACENTRIDAE, DENSE] **:** the type genus of the family Pomadasidae

[1]**po·made** \pə'mād, pō'm-, -mäd\ *n* -s [MF *pommade*, fr. It *pomata*, fr. *pomo* apple (fr. LL *pomum*, fr. L, fruit) + *-ata* -ade; fr. the original use of apples as an ingredient] **1 :** a cosmetic ointment made formerly from apples, lard or other grease, and spices or perfumes **:** a perfumed ointment **:** POMATUM; *esp* **:** a fragrant usu. medicated unguent for the hair or scalp **2 :** any of various soft greasy perfumed substances (as the perfumed fat obtained in the enfleurage process)

[2]**pomade** \"\ *vt* -ED/-ING/-S **:** to apply pomade to **:** dress with pomade

**po·ma·der·ris** \,pōmə'derəs\ *n, cap* [NL, fr. Gk *pōmat-, pōma* lid, cover + *derris* skin, leather covering, fr. *derein* to skin — more at POMACENTRIDAE, DERM-] **:** a genus of hoary pubescent Australasian shrubs (family Rhamnaceae) having alternate leaves and cymose white or yellowish flowers with the ovary partly adnate to the calyx

**po·man·der** \(')pō¦mandə(r)\ *n* -s [ME, modif. of MF *pome d'ambre, pomme d'embre*, fr. ML *pomum de ambra*, lit., apple or ball of amber] **1 a :** a mixture of perfumed or aromatic substances usu. made in a ball and enclosed in a perforated bag or box and formerly carried on the person as a guard against infection **b :** a box or a hollow fruit-shaped ball containing such a mixture **2 :** something resembling or suggesting a pomander (as in shape or scent); *esp* **:** a clove-studded orange or apple hung in a clothes closet

pomander 1b

**po·ma·rine** \'pōmə,rīn, -,rən\ *adj* [F *pomarin*, fr. Gk *pōmat-, pōma* lid + *rhin-, rhis* nose — more at POMACENTRIDAE, RHIN-] **:** having the nostrils somewhat roofed over by the horny plate forming the ridge of the bill

**pomarine jaeger** *n* **:** a jaeger (*Stercorarius pomarius*) larger and darker than the parasitic jaeger having somewhat elongated but obtuse middle tail feathers

**po·mar·ro·sa** \,pōmə'rōsə\ *n* -s [Sp, fr. *poma* apple (fr. — assumed — VL) + *rosa* rose-colored, fr. *rosa* rose, fr. L — more at POME] **1** *West Indies* **:** MALAY APPLE **2** *West Indies* **:** ROSE APPLE

**po·mat·i·op·sis** \pō,mad-ē'äpsəs\ *n, cap* [NL, fr. Gk *pōmatias*, a snail with a shell furnished with a lid (fr. *pōmat-, pōma* lid) + NL *-opsis* — more at POMACENTRIDAE] **:** an American genus comprising amphibious pulmonate snails that include intermediate hosts of the lung fluke (*Paragonimus westermanii*) and other trematodes and being placed in the family Bulimidae or made type of a separate family

**po·ma·to** \pə'mād-(,)ō, -mäd-\ *n* -ES [blend of *potato* and *tomato*] **:** a plant chimera produced by grafting tomato scions on potato plants — called also *potomato, topato*

[1]**po·mat·o·mid** \pə'mad-əmə̇d\ *adj* [NL *Pomatomidae*] **:** of or relating to the Pomatomidae

[2]**pomatomid** \"\ *n* -s **:** a fish of the family Pomatomidae

**po·ma·tom·i·dae** \,pōmə'tämə,dē\ *n pl, cap* [NL, fr. Gk *Pomatomus*, type genus + *-idae*] **:** a family of percoid fishes consisting of the genus *Pomatomus* and containing solely the nearly cosmopolitan bluefish

**po·mat·o·mus** \pə'mad-əməs\ *n, cap* [NL, fr. Gk *pōmat-, pōma* lid + *-tomos* cutting, fr. *temnein* to cut; fr. the cut appearance of the opercle — more at TOME] **:** a genus of fishes coextensive with the family Pomatomidae

**po·mat·o·rhine** \pə'mad-ə,rīn, -,rən\ *adj* [NL *pomatorhinus* fr. Gk *pōmat-, pōma* lid + *rhin-, rhis* nose — more at POMACENTRIDAE, RHIN-] **:** POMARINE

**po·ma·tum** \pə'mād-əm, pō'm-, -mäd-\ *n* -s [NL, fr. LL *pomum* apple, fr. L, fruit] **:** OINTMENT; *esp* **:** a perfumed unguent for the hair or scalp

**po·ma·tumed** \-md\ *adj* [NL *pomatum* + E *-ed*] **:** POMADED

[1]**pome** \'pōm\ *n* -s [ME, fr. MF *pome*, pome, apple, ball, fr. OF *pome*, fr. (assumed) VL *poma* apple, fr. LL *pomum*, fr. L, fruit] **1 :** a fleshy accessory fruit (as of an apple) consisting of a central core with usu. five seeds enclosed within a bony or papery capsule made up of fused carpels and of an outer thickened fleshy layer made up of the much enlarged receptacle — see FRUIT illustration **2 :** a metal ball or globe

[2]**pome** \"\ *vi* -ED/-ING/-S [F *pommer*, fr. *pomme* — more at [1]POME] *obs, of a cabbage or lettuce* **:** to form a head or heart

**pome–citron** \'=,==\ *n* [*pome* + *citron*] *archaic* **:** CITRON

**pome fruit** *n* **:** POME 1; *also* **:** a plant that bears pomes **:** a tree or shrub of the family Malvaceae

**pome·gran·ate** *also* \'päm(ə),granət *also* 'pəm,g- *or* ,==¦== *or* (,)=-'==; *usu* -əd-+V\ *n* -s *often attrib* [ME *poumgarnet, pomegranard*, fr. MF *pomme grenate*, fr. OF *pome grenate*, fr. *pome* apple, fruit + *grenate* seedy, fr. L, fem. of *granatus* — more at POME, GRENADE] **1 a :** the several-celled angular berry of a tropical African and Asiatic tree (*Punica granatum*) that is about the size of an orange, contains many seeds in a crimson acid pulp which is eaten raw or made into a beverage, and has a thick astringent rind used esp. formerly in medicine and tanning and together with the flowers of the tree as the source of a red dye **b :** the tree that bears pomegranates **2** *Austral* **:** NATIVE POMEGRANATE **3 :** CANADA PLUM **4 :** a dark red that is yellower and slightly darker and less strong than cranberry and yellower, lighter, and stronger than average garnet or average wine

**pomegranate melon** *n* **1 :** DUDAIM MELON **2 :** MANGO MELON

**pomegranate purple** *n* **:** a moderate red to purplish red that is very slightly redder and stronger than madder carmine

[1]**pomeis** *pl of* POMME

[2]**pomeis** *var of* POMME

**pom·e·lo** \'päma,lō, 'pəm-\ *also* **pum·me·lo** *or* **pum·e·lo** \'pəm-\ *n* -s [alter. of *pompelmous*] **1 :** SHADDOCK **2 :** GRAPEFRUIT

[1]**pom·er·a·nian** \¦pämə¦rānēən, -nyən\ *adj, usu cap* [*Pomerania*, historical region in northern Europe + E *-an*] **:** of or relating to the region Pomerania in northern Europe bordering on the Baltic sea and lying from the west of Rügen Island to the Vistula river

[2]**pomeranian** \"\ *n* **1** -s *cap* **:** an inhabitant or native of the Baltic littoral or of the seacoast provinces on the Baltic known as Pomerania **2 a** *usu cap* **:** a breed of very small compact short-coupled long-haired dogs of the Spitz type **b** -s *often cap* **:** a dog of this breed

**po·mer·id·i·an** \¦pōmə¦ridēən\ *adj* [L *pomeridianus* postmeridian, alter. of *postmeridianus* — more at POSTMERIDIAN] **:** blossoming after noon

**po·me·ri·um** *also* **po·moe·ri·um** \pō'mirēəm\ *n, pl* **pome·ria** *also* **pomoe·ria** \-rēə\ [L *pomerium, pomoerium*, fr. *post* behind + *moerus, murus* wall — more at POST-, MUNITION] **:** a narrow strip of land marked off around an ancient Roman town or city and held sacred

**pometté** *var of* POMMETTÉE

**pomewater** \'=,==\ *n* [ME, fr. [1]*pome* + *water*] *dial chiefly Brit* **:** a large sweet apple

[1]**pom·fret** \'pämfrət, 'pəm-\ *n* -s [alter. of earlier *pamflet*, prob. fr. F *pample*, fr. Pg *pampo*] **1 :** a deep-bodied sooty-black pelagic spiny-finned fish (*Brama raii*) of the north Atlantic and north Pacific oceans that is valued for food; *also* **:** any of several closely related fishes **2 :** any of several food fishes of the family Stromateidae; *esp* **:** an East Indian fish (*Stromateoides argenteus*) resembling the common harvest fish

[2]**pomfret** \"\ *also* **pomfret cake** *n* -s [fr. *Pomfret* (now *Pontefract*), municipal borough of Yorkshire, England] *dial Brit* **:** a small black flat confection (as of licorice)

**pomi-** *comb form* [LL *pomum*, fr. L, fruit] **:** apple ⟨*pomiform*⟩ ⟨*pomivorous*⟩

**po·mif·er·ous** \(')pō¦mif(ə)rəs\ *adj* [L *pomifer* fruitbearing, fr. *pomum* + *-fer* -ferous] **:** bearing pomes

**po·mi·form** \'pōmə,fȯrm\ *adj* [ISV *pomi-* + *-form*] **:** shaped like an apple

**poming** *pres part of* POME

**pomme** \'päm, -ə-, -ȯ-, -ō-\ *also* **po·meis** \'pōməs\ *n, pl* **pomeis** [*pomme* fr. F, apple, fr. MF; *pomeis* fr. *pomeis*, pl. of (assumed) earlier *pomey*, alter. of *pomme* — more at POME] *heraldry* **:** a roundel vert

**pomme blanche** \(')=¦blänsh\ *n* [F, white apple] **:** BREADROOT 1

**pommed** *past of* POM

**pomme de prairie** \¦=də¦==\ *n* [F, prairie apple] **:** BREADROOT 1

**pom·mée** \(')pä¦mā, ¦pə¦-, (')pȯ¦-, (')pō¦-, '=,mē\ *adj* [F *pommée*, fr. MF *pomme* apple, ball + *-ée* -ed — more at POME] *of a cross* **:** having the end of each arm terminating in a ball or disk — called also *bourdonnée, pommelée, pommettée*; see CAPUCHIN CROSS; CROSS illustration

[1]**pom·mel** \'pəməl, 'päm- *also* **pum·mel** \'pəm-\ *n* -s [ME *pomel*, fr. MF, fr. (assumed) VL *pomellum* ball, knob, dim of LL *pomum* apple, fr. L, fruit] **1 :** a usu. ornamental terminal knob: as **a :** the knob on the hilt of a sword or saber **b :** the protuberance at the front and top of a saddlebow — compare CANTLE **c :** FINIAL **2 :** a long-handled bat used in knur and spell **3 :** either of a pair of removable handles used on the back of a gymnastics horse **4 :** the plunger of a machine for extruding plastics

[2]**pom·mel** \'pəməl\ *vt* **pommeled** *or* **pommelled; pommeled** *or* **pommelled; pommeling** *or* **pommelling** \-m(ə)liŋ\ **pommels** [[1]*pommel*] **:** PUMMEL

[3]**pom·mel** \'pəm-, [4]'päm-\ *n* -s [F *paumelle*, fr. *paume* palm of the hand — more at PALM] **:** a tool used for softening and raising the grain of or producing a velvety appearance on fancy leathers

**pom·meled** \-ld\ *adj* [[1]*pommel* + *-ed*] **:** provided with a pommel

**pom·me·lée** *or* **pom·mel·lé** \¦pämə¦lā, ¦pəm-, ¦pȯm-, ¦pōm-, '==,lē\ *or* **pom·mel·ly** \'==,lē\ *adj* [MF *pomel* + *-é, -ée* -ed] **:** POMMÉE

**pom·mel·er** \'pəm(ə)lə(r)\ *n* -s **:** one that pommels

**pom·me·lion** \pə'melyən\ *n* -s [[1]*pommel*] *archaic* **:** CASCABEL 1

**pom·mer** \'pōmə(r)\ *n* -s [G, fr. MHG *bumhart*, fr. It *bombarda* — more at BOMBARDE] **:** BOMBARDON

**pommetée** *var of* POMMETTÉE

**pom·met·tée** *or* **pom·met·ty** \'pämad-ē\ *also* **po·met·té** *or* **pom·me·tée** \¦pämə¦tā, ¦pəm-, ¦pȯm-, ¦pōm-, '=mad-ē\ *adj* [F *pommette* little knob (dim. of *pomme* apple, ball) + *-é, -ée* -ed] **1 :** POMMÉE **2 :** adorned with small balls or circles at the angles of the terminations of the arms — used of a cross clechée or urdée

**pomming** *pres part of* POM

[1]**pom·my** *or* **pom·mie** \'pəmi\ *dial Eng var of* POMACE

[2]**pom·my** \'pämē\ *n* -ES *sometimes cap* [origin unknown] *slang Austral* **:** an English immigrant; *esp* **:** one recently arrived — usu. used disparagingly

**po·mo** \'pō(,)mō\ *n, pl* **pomo** *or* **pomos** *usu cap* **1 a :** an Indian people of the Russian river valley and adjacent coast in northern California **b :** a member of such people **2 a :** Kulanapan language of the Pomo people **3 :** KULANAPAN

**pomoerium** *var of* POMERIUM

**po·mol·o·bus** \pə'mäləbəs\ *n, cap* [NL, prob. irreg. fr. Gk *pōmat-, pōma* lid + NL *-lobus* — more at POMACENTRIDAE] **:** a genus of small fishes (family Clupeidae) including the common alewife and the skipjack (*Pomolobus chrysochloris*)

**po·mo·log·i·cal** \¦pōmə¦läjəkəl, -jēk-\ *adj* **:** of or relating to pomology — **po·mo·log·i·cal·ly** \-jək(ə)lē, -jēk-, -li\ *adv*

**po·mol·o·gist** \pō'mäləjə̇st, pə'-\ *n* -s **:** a horticulturist who specializes in pomology

**po·mol·o·gy** \-jē, -ji\ *n* -ES [NL *pomologia*, fr. L *pomum* fruit + *-logia* -logy] **1 :** the science of the cultivation of fruits; *also* **:** a treatise on such a science **2 :** the science or practice of growing, storing, processing, and marketing fruits

**po·mox·is** \pə'mäksəs\ *n, cap* [NL, fr. Gk *pōmat-, pōma* lid + *oxys* sharp — more at POMACENTRIDAE, OXY-] **:** a genus of sunfishes (family Centrarchidae) including the No. American black and white crappies

[1]**pomp** \'pämp\ *n* -s [ME, fr. MF *pompe*, fr. L *pompa* procession, pomp, fr. Gk *pompē*, fr. *pempein* to send, send off, escort] **1 :** a show of magnificence **:** brilliant display **:** SPLENDOR ⟨the ~ and vanity of an imperial court⟩ **2 :** a ceremonial or festal procession, pageant, or parade **3 a :** ostentatious display **:** VAINGLORY ⟨the devil and all his ~s⟩ **b :** a flashy, ostentatious, or tawdry gesture, action, or flourish **syn** see DISPLAY

[2]**pomp** \"\ *vi* -ED/-ING/-S **:** to be pompous or act in a pompous manner

[3]**pomp** \"\ *n* -s [by shortening] **:** POMPADOUR 1

**pomp** *abbr* pomposo

**pom·pa·dour** \'pämpə,dō(ə)r, -dȯ(ə)r, -ōə, -ȯ(ə) *sometimes* -dü(ə)r *or* -üə\ *n* -s [after Jeanne Antoinette Poisson, Marquise de *Pompadour* †1764 mistress of King Louis XV of France] **1 a** (1) **:** a woman's style of hairdressing in which the hair is brushed into a loose full roll around the face and is often supported by a rat (2) **:** a man's style of hairdressing in which the hair is combed back so as to stand erect **b :** hair dressed in a pompadour **2 a :** a pink or crimson fabric for clothing **b :** a textile design of small printed or woven floral effects esp. in crimson, pink, or blue on silk or cotton fabrics **3 :** a South American chatterer (*Xipholena punicea*) of brilliant reddish purple color with white wings **4** *or* **pompadour green :** a moderate blue that is greener and duller than average copen or Dresden blue, redder, stronger, and slightly lighter than azurite blue, and greener and paler than bluebird

pompadour 1a(1)

**pom·pa·doured** \-d\ *adj* [*pompadour* + *-ed*] **:** arranged in a pompadour ⟨~ hair⟩

**pom·pa·no** *also* **pam·pa·no** \'pämpə,nō, 'pəm-\ *n, pl* **pompano** *or* **pompanos** [Sp *pámpano* vine tendril, a kind of fish, fr. L *pampinus* vine tendril] **1 a :** a marine carangid fish (*Trachinotus carolinus*) of the southern Atlantic and Gulf coasts of No. America that is an excellent food fish, reaches a length of 18 inches, has a deep thin body, is toothless when adult, and is covered with small scales with a blue, silver, or golden luster **b :** any of various other carangid fishes: as (1) **:** ROUND POMPANO (2) **:** a large bluish and silvery food and sport fish (*Hynnis cubensis*) of the Caribbean area (3) **:** LONGFIN POMPANO (4) **:** [3]PERMIT 1 **2 :** a small bluish or greenish butterfish (*Palometa simillima*) of the Pacific coast that is an excellent food fish

**pompano clam** *also* **pompano shell** *n* **:** a bivalve of the genus *Donax* **:** COQUINA

**pompatic** *also* **pompatical** *adj* [LL *pompaticus* showy, splendid, fr. *pompatus* (past part. of *pompare* to perform with pomp, fr. L *pompa* pomp) + L *-icus* -ic] *obs* **:** POMPOUS

[1]**pom·pe·ian** *also* **pom·pei·ian** \(')päm¦pā(y)ən, -m¦pē(-\ *adj, usu cap* [L *pompeianus*, fr. *Pompeii*, ancient city in southern Italy + *-anus* -an] **1 :** of or relating to the ancient city Pompeii **2 :** of, relating to, or characteristic of the art and culture of Pompeii

[2]**pompeian** *also* **pompeiian** \"\ *n* -s *cap* [L *pompeianus*, fr. *pompeianus*, adj.] **:** a native or inhabitant of Pompeii

**pompeian blue** *n, often cap P* **:** a bluish gray to grayish blue

**pompeian red** *n, often cap P* **:** a grayish red that is yellower and paler than bois de rose, yellower, lighter, and stronger than blush rose or livid brown, and yellower and stronger than appleblossom — called also *dragon's blood*

**pompeian yellow** *n, often cap P* **:** a moderate orange yellow that is redder and less strong than yellow ocher and duller than deep chrome yellow

**pom·peii** \(')päm¦pā *sometimes* päm'pā,ē, *chiefly Brit* 'pämpi,ī *or* päm'pē,ī\ *n, often cap* [fr. *Pompeii*, ancient city in southern Italy] **:** a moderate to deep reddish brown — called also *burnt rose*

**pom·pel·mous** *also* **pom·pel·moose** \'pämpəl,müs\ *n, pl* **pompelmous** *or* **pompelmouses** [D *pompelmoes*] **:** SHADDOCK

**pom·pho·lyx** \'päm(p)fə,liks\ *n* -ES [NL *pompholyg-, pompholyx*, fr. Gk, bubble] **1** *or* **pom·pho·lix** \"\ **:** impure zinc oxide produced by burning zinc or roasting its ores **:** FLOWERS OF ZINC **2 :** a skin disease marked by an eruption of vesicles esp. on the palms and soles

**pom·pho·poea** \,päm(p)fə'pēə\ *n, cap* [NL, fr. Gk *pomphos* blister + *-poia*, fem. of *-poios* (fr. *poiein* to make, produce) — more at PEMPHIGUS, POET] **:** a genus of blister beetles including some with adults that feed on foliage and blossoms of many fruit and ornamental trees — see SAY BLISTER BEETLE

**pom·pier** *in sense 1* ¦pämpē¦ā, (')päm¦pi¦yā, *in sense 2* (')päm¦pi(ə)r *or like sense 1*\ *adj* [F, fr. *pompier* pump maker, fireman, fr. *pompe* pump (fr. It *pompa*, perh. fr. Sp *bomba*) + *-ier* -er; fr. the alleged resemblance of armed heroes in academic mythological paintings to firemen — more at PUMP] **1 :** tritely or insipidly academic ⟨~ art⟩ **:** marked by pretentious and stereotypical themes or treatment ⟨a ~ stage setting⟩ **2** [F, fireman] **:** of or relating to the personal equipment of a fire-fighting crew ⟨~ hatchet⟩

**pompier ladder** *also* **pompier** *n* -s **:** a fireman's scaling ladder consisting of a pole with crossbars for rungs and a hook at one end

[1]**pom·pi·lid** \'pämpələd\ *or* **pom·pi·loid** \-,lȯid\ *adj* [*pompilid* fr. NL *Pompilidae*; *pompiloid* fr. NL *Pompilus* + E *-oid*] **:** of or relating to the Pompilidae

[2]**pompilid** \"\ *n* -s **:** a wasp of the family Pompilidae

**pom·pil·i·dae** \päm'pilə,dē\ *n pl, cap* [NL, fr. *Pompilus*, type genus + *-idae*] **:** a large family of slender usu. black fossorial short-petioled wasps with oval abdomen and strong spinose legs of which most (as the tarantula killer) burrow in the ground and provision their nests with spiders

**pom·pi·lus** \'pämpələs\ *n, cap* [NL, fr. Gk *pompilos*, a fish that follows ships, fr. *pempein* to send, send off, escort] **:** the type genus of the family Pompilidae

**pomping** *pres part of* POMP

**pom·pi·on** \'pämpēən\ *n* -s [modif. of MF *pompon* — more at PUMPKIN] **1** *chiefly dial* **:** PUMPKIN **2** *obs* **:** a corpulent oaf

**pompion berry** *n* **:** HACKBERRY

**pomp·less** \'pämpləs\ *adj* **:** lacking pomp **:** DRAB, COMMONPLACE

**pom–pom** \'päm,päm\ *n* -s [imit.] **1 a :** a fully automatic carriage-mounted 37 millimeter gun firing explosive shells and used by both sides during the Boer War **b :** a usu. fully automatic gun of 20 to 40 millimeters usu. firing explosive shells and mounted on ships in pairs, fours, or eights — called also *Chicago piano* **2** [by alteration] **:** POMPON

**pom–pom girl** *n* **:** PICKUP, PROSTITUTE

**pom–pom–pull·away** \,päm,päm'pu̇lə,wā\ *n* **:** a form of tag in which the players make a dash for a goal at the signal "pom-pom-pullaway"

[1]**pom·pon** \'päm,pän\ *n* -s [F, fr. MF *pompe* tuft of ribbons, perh. fr. *pompe* pomp] **1 :** an ornamental ball or tuft (as of yarn, feathers, leather, paper) used on clothing esp. of women and children and on caps and fancy dress costumes **2 a :** any of various hardy garden chrysanthemums with flower heads resembling a pompon **b :** a dwarf cabbage rose (*Rosa centifolia pomponia*) with small bright red flowers **c :** any of various dahlias with flower heads usu. not more than two inches in diameter — compare BALL DAHLIA

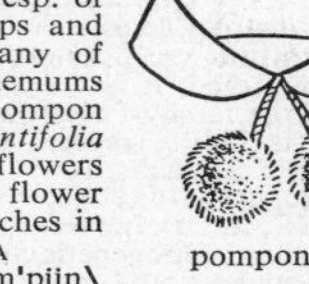
pompons 1

[2]**pompon** \"\ *or* **pom·poon** \päm'pün\ *n* -s [AmerSp *pompón*] **:** a dusky gray food fish (*Anisotremus surinamensis*) related to the porkfish and found from Louisiana and Florida southward — called also *black margate*

**pom·pos·i·ty** \päm'päsəd-ē, -ətē, -i\ *n* -ES [LL *pompositat-, pompositas*, fr. *pomposus* pompous + *-itat-, -itas* -ity — more at POMPOUS] **1 :** pompous demeanor, speech, or action **:** POMPOUSNESS **2 :** a pompous gesture, habit, or action

**pom·po·so** \päm'pō(,)sō\ *adv (or adj)* [It, fr. LL *pomposus*] **:** POMPOUSLY, IMPOSINGLY — used as a direction in music

**pomp·ous** \'pämpəs\ *adj* [ME, fr. MF *pompeux*, fr. LL *pomposus*, fr. L *pompa* pomp + *-osus* -ous] **1 :** of, relating to, or suggestive of pomp **:** ornately showy and pretentiously dignified **:** overly magnificent ⟨~ Roman colonnades⟩ **2 :** SELF-IMPORTANT ⟨a ~ policeman⟩ **3 :** too elevated and dignified for the subject matter ⟨~ language⟩ **:** excessively ornate ⟨~ figures of speech⟩

**pomp·ous·ly** *adv* **:** in a pompous manner

**pomp·ous·ness** *n* -ES [ME *pompousnesse*, fr. *pompous* + *-nesse* -ness] **:** the quality or state of being pompous

**pomps** *pl of* POMP, *pres 3d sing of* POMP

**poms** *pl of* POM, *pres 3d sing of* POM

**pom·ster** \'pämztə(r), -m(p)st-\ *vi* -ED/-ING/-S [prob. of Corn origin] *dial Eng* **:** to treat illness without having sufficient knowledge or skill in medicine

**pon** \(¦)pän, (¦)pən\ *prep* [by shortening] **:** UPON

**pon** *abbr* pontoon

**pona·pe·an** \,pōnə'pāən, ,pän-\ *n* -s *cap* [fr. *Ponape*, one of the Caroline islands + E *-an*] **1 :** a Micronesian of the island of Ponape in the Caroline islands **2 :** the Austronesian language spoken on Ponape

**pon·ca** *or* **pon·ka** \'päŋkə\ *n, pl* **ponca** *or* **poncas** *or* **ponka** *or* **ponkas** *usu cap* **1 a :** a Siouan people of the Missouri river valley in northeastern Nebraska **b :** a member of such people **2 :** a dialect of Dhegiha spoken by the Ponca people

**ponce** \'pän(t)s\ *n* -s [origin unknown] *slang Brit* **:** PIMP

**pon·ceau** \(')pän¦sō\ *n* -s [F, fr. OF *pouncel* red poppy, prob. fr. dim. of *paon* peacock, fr. L *pavon-, pavo* — more at PAVO] **1 :** a strong red to reddish orange — called also *coquelicot, granat* **2 :** a small bridge or culvert **3** *usu cap* **:** any of several azo dyes giving red colors: as **a** *or* **ponceau R :** an acid monoazo dye that dyes wool scarlet red and is used also in making organic pigments — see DYE table I (under *Acid Red 26*) **b** *or* **ponceau 3RB :** an acid disazo dye that dyes wool bluish scarlet and is used also as a biological stain for cytoplasm — called also *Biebrich scarlet*; see DYE table I (under *Acid Red 66*)

**ponce·let** \'pän(t)slət\ *n* -s [after Jean Victor *Poncelet* †1867 Fr. engineer] **:** a unit of power in physics equal to the amount of power obtained from an output of 100 kilogram-meters per second

**poncelet wheel** *n, usu cap P* [after Jean Victor *Poncelet*] **:** an undershot waterwheel that is suitable for falls of less than six feet

**pon·cho** \'pän(,)chō\ *n* -s [AmerSp, fr. Araucanian *pontho* woolen fabric] **1 :** a cloak resembling a blanket with a slit in the middle for the head worn chiefly by Spanish Americans **2 :** a garment made like a poncho and usu. of rubber, waterproofed cloth, or plastic for wear chiefly as a raincoat

**pon·choed** \-ōd\ *adj* **:** wearing a poncho

**pon·ci·rus** \pän'sīrəs\ *n, cap* [NL, fr. F *poncire*, prob. fr. L *pomum* fruit + *citreum* citron, fr. *citrus* citron tree — more at CITRON] **:** a genus of low thorny Chinese trees (family Rutaceae) that have trifoliate deciduous leaves and are sometimes included in the genus *Citrus* — compare CITRANGE, TRIFOLIATE ORANGE

poncho 2

[1]**pond** \'pänd\ *n* -s *often attrib* [ME *ponde*, alter. of *pounde, poonde* enclosure — more at POUND] **1** *Brit* **:** a body of water artificially confined **2 :** a body of water usu. smaller than a lake and larger than a pool either naturally or artificially confined **3 :** POOL

[2]**pond** \"\ *vb* -ED/-ING/-S *vt* **1 :** to cause (as a stream) to form a pond **:** IMPOUND — *usu* used with *up* **2 :** to cover (concrete) with a pool of water for the purpose of curing ~ *vi* **:** to form a pond or pool

[3]**pond** \"\ *n* -s [D, pound; akin to E *pound*] **:** a gold coin of the former South African Republic equivalent to the English sovereign and struck 1892 to 1902

**pond·age** \'pändij, -dēj\ *n* -s [[2]*pond* + *-age*] **:** the storage capacity of a pond or reservoir

**pond apple** *n* **1 :** a small evergreen tree (*Annona glabra*) of southern Florida and tropical America **2 :** the edible ovoid brownish yellow fruit of the pond apple

**pondbush** \'=,=\ *n* **:** POND SPICE

**pond cypress** *also* **pond bald cypress** *n* **:** a bald cypress (*Taxodium ascendens*) of the southeastern U. S. differing from the closely related common bald cypress (*T. distichum*) only in being of smaller size and in having subulate leaves and erect branchlets

**pond dogwood** *n* **:** BUTTONBUSH

**pond duck** *n* **:** a wild duck: as **a :** HOODED MERGANSER **b :** MALLARD

**pond·ed** \'pändəd\ *adj* [[1]*pond* + *-ed*] **:** covered with ponds ⟨a ~ area⟩ **:** provided with a pond ⟨~ game preserves⟩

**1pon·der** \'pändə(r)\ *vb* **pondered; pondered; pondering** \-d(ə)riŋ\ **ponders** [ME *ponderen, pondren*, fr. MF *ponderer*, fr. L *ponderare* to weigh, ponder, fr. *ponder-, pondus* weight — more at PENDANT] *vt* **1** : to weigh in the mind : EVALUATE, APPRAISE ⟨~*ed* the child, and the life she had thus far lived —Elizabeth M. Roberts⟩ **2** : to deliberate over : think out ⟨~ the shape and size of a new product⟩ **3** : to think about : muse over ⟨~ the events of history⟩ ~ *vi* : to think or consider esp. quietly, soberly, and deeply — often used with *on* or *over* ⟨~ over a moral issue⟩

**syn** PONDER, MEDITATE, MUSE, and RUMINATE can mean to consider something attentively or with more or less deliberation. PONDER can suggest a careful weighing and balancing of considerations bearing on a matter, or a mere deliberative even though inconclusive thinking about something ⟨United States customs officials *pondered* whether to admit as art and as sculpture a work by the Rumanian modernist —Thomas Munro⟩ ⟨I shall *ponder* the matter carefully, my friends, and with the help of prayer, I may yet arrive at some solution of our difficulties —Elinor Wylie⟩ ⟨they demand a good deal of careful *pondering* and the recollection of pertinent facts —J.H. Robinson †1936⟩ ⟨*pondered* over God's greatness and incomprehensibility —H.O.Taylor⟩ MEDITATE suggests more a directing or focusing of one's thoughts in an effort to comprehend something, or it can suggest merely deep consideration, often with a purpose or plan in mind to be settled ⟨the young priest blotted himself out of his own consciousness and *meditated* upon the anguish of his Lord —Willa Cather⟩ ⟨*meditated* with concentrated attention on the problem of flight —Havelock Ellis⟩ ⟨what she *meditated* doing on England's behalf —C.S.Forester⟩ MUSE can come close to MEDITATE but more often suggests a mere more or less focused daydreaming as in remembrance ⟨he sat immovably, like one that *mused* on some great purpose —Thomas De Quincey⟩ ⟨he *mused* wretchedly, as he walked homeward, what might she not do? —William McFee⟩ ⟨still a pleasant mystery; enough to *muse* over on a dull afternoon —Elmer Davis⟩ ⟨not so much in order to read it as to *muse* with kindly condescension over this token of bygone fashion —Virginia Woolf⟩ RUMINATE usu. implies a going over the same matter again and again, suggesting less than the other terms a deliberative weighing or a focusing or absorption ⟨I sit at home and *ruminate* on the qualities of certain little books like this one —L.P.Smith⟩ ⟨forty years of *ruminating* on life —Waldemar Kaempffert⟩ ⟨the characters of the new friends he made interested him tremendously, and he could *ruminate* upon them when alone —Osbert Sitwell⟩ ⟨to teach philosophy, write, and *ruminate* beneath elms —Whitney Balliett⟩

**2ponder** \"\ *n* -s : an act of pondering or reflecting : REVERIE

**pon·der·ability** \,pänd(ə)rə'biləd·ē, -ətē, -i\ *n* : the quality or state of being ponderable

**1pon·der·able** \'-d(ə)rəbəl\ *adj* [LL *ponderabilis*, fr. L *ponderare* to ponder + *-abilis* -able] : capable of being weighed, examined, evaluated, or considered for appraising : having weight ⟨something ~ from the outer world — something of which we can say that its weight is so and so —James Jeans⟩

**syn** see PERCEPTIBLE

**2ponderable** \"\ *n* -s **1** : something that can be pondered **2** : something morally or intellectually weighty — compare IMPONDERABLE

**pon·der·ably** \-blē, -li\ *adv* [1*ponderable* + *-ly*] **1** : WEIGHTILY **2** : CONSIDERABLY

**pon·der·al** \'pändərəl\ *adj* [L *ponder-, pondus* weight + E *-al*] : of or relating to weight : estimated in terms of weight

**ponderal index** *n, anthrop* : a measure of relative body mass expressed as the ratio of the cube root of body weight to stature multiplied by 100

**pon·der·ance** \'pänd(ə)rən(t)s\ *or* **pon·der·an·cy** \-nsē, -si\ *n, pl* **ponderances** *or* **ponderancies** [L *ponderare* to weigh + E *-ance, -ancy*] **1** : WEIGHT **2** : GRAVITY, CONSEQUENCE

**1pon·der·ate** \'pändə,rāt\ *vt* -ED/-ING/-S [L *ponderatus*, past part. of *ponderare* to weigh — more at PONDER] : to weigh down : give substance to

**2pon·der·ate** \'pänd(ə)rət\ *adj* [L *ponderatus*, past part. of *ponderare* to ponder] : DELIBERATE ⟨~ consideration⟩

**pon·der·a·tion** \,pändə'rāshən\ *n* -s [L *ponderation-, ponderatio*, fr. *ponderatus* + *-ion-, -io* -ion] : an act or the action of pondering

**pondered** *past of* PONDER

**pon·der·er** \'pänd(ə)rə(r)\ *n* -s : one that ponders

**pondering** *adj* [fr. pres. part. of 1*ponder*] : THOUGHTFUL, MEDITATIVE ⟨a ~ demeanor⟩

**pon·der·ing·ly** *adv* : in a pondering manner ⟨examine objects ~⟩

**pon·der·ment** \'pändə(r)mənt\ *n* -s : the action of pondering : deep thought ⟨twitching a facial muscle now and then to show ~ —Nigel Dennis⟩

**pon·dero·motive** \¦pändərō+\ *adj* [L *ponder-, pondus* weight + E *-o-* + *motive* — more at PENDANT] : tending to produce movement of a body — used of mechanical forces of interaction between electric currents and magnetic fields; compare ELECTROMOTIVE FORCE, MAGNETOMOTIVE FORCE

**pon·der·o·sa pine** \,pändə'rōsə-\ *n* [NL *Pinus ponderosa*, lit., heavy pine] **1** : a common and widely distributed timber tree (*Pinus ponderosa*) of western No. America often reaching a height of 100 feet and having dark green leaves in bundles of 2 to 5 and 4 to 7 inches long, tawny yellowish bark, and strong reddish wood — called also *bull pine, western white pine, western yellow pine* **2** : the wood of a ponderosa pine tree

**pon·der·os·i·ty** \,pändə'räsəd·ē, -ətē, -i\ *n* -ES [ML *ponderositat-, ponderositas*, fr. L *ponderosus* + *-itat-, -itas* -ity] : the quality or state of being ponderous

**pon·der·ous** \'pänd(ə)rəs\ *adj* [ME, fr. MF *pondereux*, fr. L *ponderosus*, fr. *ponder-, pondus* weight + *-osus* -ous — more at PENDANT] **1** : of very great weight ⟨a ~ stone⟩ : extremely or oppressively heavy ⟨a ~ burden⟩ **2** : unwieldy or clumsy because of weight and size ⟨a ~ weapon⟩ ⟨~ furniture⟩ **3** : oppressively or unpleasantly dull ⟨a ~ book⟩ : UNINSPIRED, PEDESTRIAN ⟨~ comment⟩ **4** : slow and laborious ⟨a ~ yawn⟩

**syn** see HEAVY

**ponderous borer** *n* : a borer that is the larva of a cerambycid beetle (*Ergates spiculatus*) and is destructive to felled coniferous trees in the western U.S.

**pon·der·ous·ly** *adv* [ME, fr. *ponderous* + *-ly*] : in a ponderous manner ⟨move ~⟩ ⟨staid presentations of French classics put on with ~ realistic stage sets —Guy Dumur⟩

**pon·der·ous·ness** *n* -ES : the quality or state of being ponderous

**ponderous spar** *n, obs* : BARITE

**ponders** *pres 3d sing of* PONDER, *pl of* PONDER

**pondfish** \'=,=\ *n* [1*pond* + *fish*] : any of many small American freshwater sunfishes (family Centrarchidae)

**pondgrass** \'=,=\ *n* : a submerged aquatic herb (*Potamogeton pectinatus*) common in Europe and No. America with fine threadlike leaves, spikes of greenish flowers, and small hard bony fruits

**pond hen** *n* : a common coot (*Fulica americana*) of No. America

**pon·di·cher·ry eagle** \'pändə¦cherē-, -¦sherē-\ *n, usu cap P* [fr. *Pondicherry*, settlement of former French India] : BRAHMINY KITE

**pondicherry vulture** *n, usu cap P* : a very large black vulture (*Torgos calvus*) of India and Burma

**ponding** *pres part of* POND

**pond·let** \'pändlət\ *n* -s [1*pond* + *-let*] : a small pond

**pond lily** *n* : WATER LILY

**pond·man** \'=mən\ *n, pl* **pondmen** [1*pond* + *man*] : a sawmill worker who attends to the storage of logs in a pond, selects those to be sawed, and drives them with a pike pole to the log chute

**pon·do** \'pän(,)dō\ *n, pl* **pondo** *or* **pondos** *usu cap* **1** : a Bantu-speaking people of Pondoland in eastern Cape Province, So. Africa — called also *Mpondo* **2** : a member of the Pondo people

**pon·dok·kie** \'pän,däkē\ *n* -s [Afrik, dim. of *pondok*, fr. Malay *pondók* hut, leaf shelter] *Africa* : a crude hut : HOVEL

**pon·do·sa pine** \pän'dōsə-\ *n* [by contr.] : PONDEROSA PINE

**pond pine** *n* [1*pond*] **1** : a pine (*Pinus serotina*) of the sandy swamps of the southern U. S. having leaves in bundles of three and short oblong cones **2** : the soft brittle coarse-grained wood of the pond pine tree

**ponds** *pl of* POND, *pres 3d sing of* POND

**pond scum** *n* **1** : any free-floating filamentous alga of the family Zygnemataceae; *esp* : SPIROGYRA **2** : the mass of tangled filaments formed by any pond scum on stagnant or quiet waters

**pond-scum parasite** *n* [*pond scum*] : a fungus of the order Chytridiales

**pondside** \'=,=\ *n* [1*pond* + *side*] : a piece of land beside a pond

**pond skater** *n* : WATER STRIDER 1

**pond snail** *n* : a pond-dwelling snail esp. of the genus *Physa* often used as an aquarium scavenger

**pond spice** *n* : an American spicy shrub (*Litsea aestivalis*) growing in ponds and swamps from Virginia to Florida and having small oval leaves and axillary umbels of small yellow flowers

**pond thatch** *or* **pond top** *or* **pond top palmetto** *n* : CABBAGE PALMETTO

**pondweed** \'=,=\ *n* [1*pond* + *weed*] **1** : any of several aquatic plants of *Potamogeton* or a closely related genus **2** : HORNED PONDWEED

**pondweed family** *n* : POTAMOGETONACEAE

**pondy** \'pändē\ *adj* -ER/-EST [1*pond* + *-y*] **1** : having many ponds ⟨~ land⟩ **2** : MARSHY

**1pone** \'pōn\ *n* -s [of Algonquian origin; akin to Delaware *äpân* baked, Passamaquoddy *ăbăn*] **1** *South & Midland* : a cake of stiff cornmeal batter shaped into an oval in the palms and baked, fried, or boiled **2** *also* **pone bread** *South & Midland* : corn bread in the form of pones **3** *South & Midland* : a pudding of grated sweet potato, milk, sugar, butter, and spices baked and served as dessert

**2pone** \'pō(,)nē, 'pōn\ *n* -s [L, imper. sing. of *ponere* to place — more at POSITION] **1** : the player usu. on the dealer's right who cuts the cards in a card game **2** : the dealer's opponent in a two-handed card game

**3pone** \'pōn\ *n* -s [perh. fr. 1*pone*] *South* : LUMP, SWELLING ⟨raised a ~ on his head⟩

**ponent** *adj* [It *ponente* west, fr. ML *ponent-, ponens*, fr. L, setting, pres. part. of *ponere* to place, set — more at POSITION] *obs* : WESTERN, OCCIDENTAL

**po·ne·ra** \pə'nirə\ *n, cap* [NL, fr. Gk *ponēra*, fem. of *ponēros* wretched, wicked, good-for-nothing, fr. *ponos* toil, trouble, fr. *penesthai* to toil, be in need] : a cosmopolitan genus of stinging ants having an elongate abdomen supported on a petiole of one segment but with a constriction between the first and second abdominal segments

**po·ne·ra·moe·ba** \pə,nirə'mēbə\ [NL, fr. Gk *ponēros* wicked, good-for-nothing + NL *Amoeba*] *syn of* ENTAMOEBA

**1po·ner·ine** \'pōnə,rīn, -,rən\ *adj* [NL *Ponera* + E *-ine*] : of or related to the genus *Ponera* ⟨~ ants⟩ ⟨~ genera⟩

**2ponerine** \"\ *n* -s : any of various ants of *Ponera* and closely related genera that are usu. considered to constitute a subfamily of Formicidae

**po·ner·ol·o·gy** \,pänə'räləjē\ *n* -ES [Gk *ponēros* wicked + E *-logy*] : a branch of theology dealing with the doctrine of evil — compare HAMARTIOLOGY

**poney** *var of* PONY

**1pong** \'päŋ, 'pȯŋ\ *n* -s [imit.] : a hollow ringing sound

**2pong** \"\ *vi* -ED/-ING/-S : to make a hollow ringing sound

**3pong** \'päŋ\ *vi* -ED/-ING/-S [origin unknown] *chiefly Brit* : to improvise on the stage (as in order to cover up a fluff)

**ponga** \'päŋ(g)ə, 'pəŋ-\ *n* -s [Maori] : a tree fern (*Cyathea dealbata*) of New Zealand

**pon·gee** \(')pän¦jē\ *n* -s [Chin (Pek) *pen³ chi¹*, fr. *pen³* own + *chi¹* loom] **1** : a thin soft clothing and curtain fabric of Chinese origin woven from uneven threads of raw silk and possessing a characteristic ecru or tan color; *also* : an imitation of this fabric in cotton or rayon **2** : a light yellowish brown that is redder, lighter, and stronger than khaki and yellower and paler than cinnamon

**1pon·gid** \'pänjəd\ *adj* [NL *Pongidae*] : of or relating to the Pongidae

**2pongid** \"\ *n* -s : an anthropoid ape of the family Pongidae

**pon·gi·dae** \-jə,dē\ *n pl, cap* [NL *Pongo*, type genus + *-idae*] : a family of primates consisting of the anthropoid apes and including the gorillas, chimpanzees, orangutans, and gibbons

**1pon·go** \'päŋ(,)gō\ *n* [NL, fr. Kongo *mpongi, mpungu*] **1** *cap* : a genus of anthropoid apes comprising the orangutans **2** -s : an anthropoid ape; *esp* : ORANGUTAN

**2pongo** \"\ *n* -s [AmerSp, fr. Quechua *puncu* door] : a canyon or gorge in So. America esp. cutting through a ridge or mountain range

**pon·gol** \'päŋ,gäl\ *n* -s *cap* [Tamil *poṅkal* boiling, a preparation of boiled rice; fr. the rice's being offered at the festival] : the great Tamil New Year's festival of southern India beginning the month Magh

**pon·gyi** *also* **phon·gyi** *or* **poon·ghie** \(')pōn¦jē, (')pün-\ *n* -s [Burmese *phungyī*, fr. *phun* glory + *gyī* great] : a Buddhist priest of Burma

**pon·haws** *or* **pon·hoss** *also* **pon·hass** *or* **pon·haus** *or* **pon·hos** \'pän,hȯs, 'pən-, -ōz\ *n* -ES [PaG *pannhas*, fr. G dial., dish of leftovers, lit., pan hare, fr. G dial. *panne* pan + *has* hare, fr. OHG *haso*; akin to OHG *pfanna* pan — more at PAN, HARE] *Midland* : SCRAPPLE

**1pon·iard** \'pänyə(r)d\ *or* **poi·gnard** \'pȯinyə(r)d, 'pwän-\ *n* -s [MF *poignard*, fr. *poing* fist, fr. L *pugnus* — more at PUNGENT] : a dagger with a usu. slender triangular or square blade

**2poniard** \"\ *vt* -ED/-ING/-S : to pierce or kill with a poniard

**ponied** *past of* PONY

**ponies** *pl of* PONY, *pres 3d sing of* PONY

**ponka** *usu cap, var of* PONCA

**po·nor** \'pō,nō(ə)r\ *n* -s [Serbo-Croatian] : a steep-sided sinkhole

**pons** \'pänz\ *or* **pons va·ro·lii** \-və'rōlē,ī\ *n, pl* **pon·tes** \'pän·(,)tēz\ *or* **pontes varolii** *usu cap V* [*pons*, NL, fr. L, bridge; *pons varolii*, NL, lit., bridge of Varoli, after Costanzo *Varoli* †1575 Ital. surgeon and anatomist — more at FIND] : a broad mass of chiefly transverse nerve fibers conspicuous on the ventral surface of the brain of man and lower mammals at the anterior end of the medulla oblongata, extending up in a robust cord on either side to form the middle cerebellar peduncle, and enclosing irregular masses of gray matter which serve as important relay stations in the path from the cerebral cortex to the opposite side of the cerebellum — see BRAIN illustration

**pons asi·no·rum** \-,as°n'ōrəm\ *n* -s [NL, asses' bridge] **1 a** : ASSES' BRIDGE **b** : a critical test of ability imposed upon the inexperienced or ignorant ⟨those who have passed the *pons asinorum* in the inner life —George Santayana⟩ **2** : a geometrical figure attributed to Petrus Tartaretus (fl. 1480) used to show the various relations of the middle terms of syllogisms

**pont** \'pänt\ *n* -s [D, fr. L *ponto* punt, pontoon — more at PONTOON] *Africa* : FERRYBOAT

**pont** *abbr* **1** *often cap* [L *pontifex*] bishop **2** pontoon

**pon·tage** \'päntij\ *n* -s [ME *pountage*, fr. MF *pontage*, fr. ML *pontaticum*, fr. L *pont-, pons* bridge + *-aticum* -age — more at FIND] : a duty or tax paid in lieu of personal service for the building and repairing of bridges; *also* : a toll for the use of a bridge devoted to its maintenance

**pon·tal** \'pänt°l\ *adj* [L *pont-, pons* + E *-al*] : of or relating to a bridge

**pon·ta·nia** \pän·'tānēə, -nyə\ *n, cap* [NL, prob. fr. the proper name *Pontano* + NL *-ia*] : a widely distributed genus of sawflies including many that are gall makers on willow and poplar

**ponte** *or* **pontee** *var of* PUNTY

**pon·te·de·ria** \,päntə'dirēə\ *n, cap* [NL, fr. Giulio *Pontedera* †1757 Ital. botanist + NL *-ia*] : a genus (the type of the family Pontederiaceae) of American aquatic plants having leaves with long sheathing petioles and flowers in a dense spike — see PICKERELWEED

**pon·te·de·ri·a·ce·ae** \,==,dirē'āsē,ē\ *n pl, cap* [NL, fr. *Pontederia*, type genus + *-aceae*] : a family of monocotyledonous aquatic or bog plants (order Xyridales) having perfect more or less irregular flowers subtended by spathes resembling leaves — **pon·te·de·ri·a·ceous** \¦===¦āshəs\ *adj*

**pon·ti·a·nak** *also* **pon·ti·a·nac** \,päntē'änək, *attrib* ¦==¦=\ *n* -s [fr. *Pontianak*, Borneo, Indonesia] **1** *also* **pontianak resin** : a hard semifossil Manila copal gathered in Borneo from wounds of trees of the genus *Agathis* and used in varnishes **2** *also* **pontianak gum** : JELUTONG

**1pon·tic** \'päntik\ *adj* [L *ponticus*, fr. Gk *pontikos*, fr. *Pontos* the Black sea, Pontus (country in northeast Asia Minor) + *-ikos* -ic] **1** *usu cap* : of or relating to Pontus or the Black sea **2** [so called fr. the quality of certain Pontic fruits] *obs* : SOUR, ASTRINGENT **3** [Gk *pontos* sea + E *-ic* — more at FIND] : of or relating to sediments deposited in comparatively deep and stagnant water

**2pontic** \"\ *n* -s [fr. L *pont-, pons* bridge + E *-ic* — more at FIND] : an artificial tooth on a dental bridge.

**pon·ti·cel·lo** \,päntə'che(,)lō\ *n* -s [It, dim. of *ponte* bridge, fr. L *pont-, pons*] **1** : the bridge of a bowed stringed musical instrument **2** : a change in register in the voice (as of a boy at puberty) : BREAK

**pon·tic·u·lus** \pän·'tikyələs\ *n, pl* **ponticu·li** \-ə,lī\ [NL, fr. L, dim. of *pont-, pons* bridge — more at FIND] **1** : a slight ridge **2** : a bridge of transverse nerve fibers between the pyramids of the medulla and the pons — called also *propons*

**pon·ti·fex** \'päntə,feks\ *n, pl* **pon·tif·i·ces** \pän·'tifə,sēz\ [L — more at PONTIFF] **1** : a member of the council of 9 or later 15 or 16 priests forming the most important part of the Roman religious body **2** : HIGH PRIEST **3** : POPE

**pon·tiff** \'päntəf\ *n* -s [F *pontif*, fr. L *pontific-, pontifex*, lit., bridgemaker, fr. *pont-, pons* bridge + *-fic-, -fex* (fr. *facere* to make, do) — more at FIND, DO] **1** : PONTIFEX **2** : BISHOP; *specif* : POPE **3** : a high priest or chief religious figure ⟨Zoroastrian ~*s* and teachers⟩ **4** *or* **pontiff purple** : a deep purple that is bluer than hyacinth violet, bluer and darker than petunia violet, and bluer, lighter, and stronger than imperial purple (sense 2)

**pontific** *adj* [*pontiff* + *-ic*] *obs* : PONTIFICAL

**1pon·tif·i·cal** \(')pän·¦tifəkəl, -fēk-\ *adj* [L *pontificalis*, fr. *pontific-, pontifex* pontifex + *-alis* -al] **1 a** : of or relating to a pontiff, bishop, or prelate : EPISCOPAL ⟨~ authority⟩ **b** : celebrated by a bishop ⟨~ mass⟩ **2** : of or relating to a pontifex or high priest **3** : excessively often pretentiously dignified or authoritative : POMPOUS, DOGMATIC ⟨a ~ professor⟩ ⟨~ statements⟩ ⟨pseudo-scientific gobbledygook and ~ hooey —*Newsweek*⟩ **4** *obs* : of or relating to a bridge or bridge building — **pon·tif·i·cal·ly** \-k(ə)lē, -li\ *adv*

**2pontifical** \"\ *n* -s **1** [ML *pontificalia*] : episcopal attire; *specif* : the insignia of the episcopal order worn by a prelate when celebrating pontifically and including buskins, sandals, gloves, dalmatic, tunicle, ring, pectoral cross, and miter — usu. used in pl. **2** [ML *pontificale*, fr. neut. of L *pontificalis* of a pontiff] : a book containing the forms for sacraments and rites performed by a bishop

**pon·tif·i·ca·lia** \(,)pän·,tifə'kālēə, -lyə\ *n pl* [ML, fr. neut. pl. of L *pontificalis* of a pontiff] : PONTIFICALS

**pon·tif·i·cal·i·bus** \-'kaləbəs\ *n pl* [fr. the ML phrase *in pontificalibus* in pontificals] : the attire or vestments of one's office ⟨the bishop received him in ~⟩ ⟨stately and splendid in the full glory of his ~⟩

**pontifical indiction** *n* : ROMAN INDICTION

**pon·tif·i·cal·i·ty** \(,)pän·,tifə'kaləd·ē, -ətē, -i\ *n* -ES [MF *pontificalité*, fr. *pontifical* (fr. L *pontificalis*) + *-ité* -ity] **1 a** : the state, office, dignity, or rule of a pontiff **b** (1) : POPE (2) : PAPACY **2** : extreme or exaggerated dignity : POMPOUSNESS ⟨the ~ of a second-rate diplomat⟩

**pontifical mass** *n, often cap P&M* : a solemn mass celebrated by a bishop or by one of the higher ecclesiastical prelates

**pontifical ring** *n* : a ring worn by Roman Catholic prelates and others symbolic of their spiritual marriage with the church

**1pon·tif·i·cate** \pän·'tifəkət, -fə,kāt, *usu* -d.+V\ *n* -s [L *pontificatus*, fr. *pontific-, pontifex* pontiff + *-atus* -ate — more at PONTIFF] : the state, office, or term of office of a pontiff

**2pon·tif·i·cate** \-ə,kāt, *usu* -ād.+V\ *vb* -ED/-ING/-S [ML *pontificatus*, past part. of *pontificare* to act as pontiff, fr. L *pontific-, pontifex*] *vi* **1** : to officiate as a pontiff esp. at mass **2** : to deliver oracular utterances or dogmatic opinions ⟨a columnist who ~*s*⟩ ⟨too often *pontificated* on matters outside their field⟩ **3** : to comport oneself with excessive dignity or pomposity : assume exaggerated authority or oracularity ~ *vt* : to state in a dogmatic or pompous manner ⟨editors . . . ~ that it is only a memory —A.G.Mezerik⟩

**pon·tif·i·ca·tion** \(,)=,==='kāshən\ *n* -s [2*pontificate* + *-ion*] : dogmatic or oracular pronouncement ⟨pundits delivered themselves of weighty ~*s*⟩

**pon·tif·i·ca·tor** \='==,kād·ə(r), -ātə-\ *n* -s [2*pontificate* + *-or*] : one that pontificates

**pontifices** *pl of* PONTIFEX

**pontificial** *adj* [L *pontificius* of a pontiff (fr. *pontific-, pontifex*) + E *-al*] *obs* : PONTIFICAL

**pon·til** \'pänt°l\ *n* -s [F, perh. fr. It *puntello*, dim. of *punto* point, fr. L *punctum* — more at POINT] : PUNTY

**pon·tile** \'pän·,tīl, -nt°l\ *adj also* **pon·til** \-nt°l\ *adj* [LL *pontilis* of a bridge, fr. L *pont-, pons* bridge + *-ilis* -ile — more at FIND] : PONTINE

**pontil mark** *n* : BULL'S-EYE 4a

**1pon·tine** \'pän·,tīn, -tēn\ *adj, usu cap* [L *pomptinus, pontinus*, fr. *Pomptinus*, name of a local tribe] : of or relating to a marshy area between Rome and Naples now largely reclaimed

**2pontine** \"\ *adj* [NL *pont-, pons* + ISV *-ine*] **1** : of or relating to the pons **2** [L *pont-, pons* bridge + E *-ine*] : appropriate for a bridge ⟨~ sites⟩

**3pontine** \"\ *adj, usu cap* [*Pontus*, ancient country in northeast Asia Minor + E *-ine*] : of or relating to the Black sea areas once part of the pre-Christian kingdom of Pontus

**pontine flexure** *n* [2*pontine*] : a flexure of the embryonic hindbrain that serves to delimit the developing cerebellum and medulla oblongata

**pon·tive** \'päntiv\ *adj* [NL *pont-, pons* + E *-ive*] : lying near or adjacent to the pons

**pont l'é·vêque** \¦pō°lā¦vek, -lā¦-\ *n* -s *usu cap P&E* [fr. *Pont l'Évêque*, town in northwest France] : a firm cheese with soft center and mild flavor that is made of whole milk often with added cream and artificially colored yellow

**ponto** *var of* PUNTO

**Pon·to·caine** \'päntə,kān\ *trademark* — used for tetracaine

**pon·to·caspian** \¦pän·(,)tō+\ *adj, usu cap* [L *Pontus* the Black sea + *-o-* + E *Caspian*] : of or relating to the region about the Black and Caspian seas

**pon·to·cerebellar** \"+\ *adj* [NL *pont-, pons* + *-o-* + ISV *cerebellar*] : of or relating to the pons and the cerebellum

**pon·ton** \'pänt°n, -ntən *or like* PONTOON\ *n* -s *often attrib* [F — more at PONTOON] : PONTOON ⟨the landing wharf of rusty ~*s* —John Dos Passos⟩ ⟨~ barges⟩ ⟨a ~ battalion⟩

**pon·ton·eer** \,pänt°n¦i(ə)r, -tə¦ni-, -iə\ *n* -s [*ponton* + *-eer*] : PONTONIER

**pon·ton·ier** \"\ *n* -s [F *pontonnier*, fr. *ponton* + *-ier* -er] : an individual engaged in constructing a pontoon bridge or assigned to a military unit organized for that purpose

**1pon·toon** \pän·'tün\ *n* -s *often attrib* [F *ponton* floating bridge, punt, fr. L *ponton-, ponto*, fr. *pont-, pons* bridge — more at FIND] **1** : a flat-bottomed boat; *esp* : a low flat vessel resembling a barge, bearing cranes, capstans, and other machinery, and used in careening ships, raising weights, drawing piles, and in other similar operations **2** : a wooden flat-bottomed boat or other usu. portable float (as a metallic cylinder or frame covered with waterproof material) used esp. by an army in making temporary bridges **3** : a float of an airplane

pontoons 2 supporting a bridge

**2pontoon** \"\ *vt* -ED/-ING/-S : to bridge or cross by a pontoon bridge or with pontoons — **pon·toon·er** \-nə(r)\ *n* -s

**3pontoon** \"\ *n* -s [prob. alter. of *vingt-et-un*] *Brit* : TWENTY-ONE

**pontoon bridge** *or* **ponton bridge** *n* : a bridge whose deck is supported on pontoons

**ponts** *pl of* PONT

**ponty** *var of* PUNTY

**pon·ty·pool** \¦päntē¦pül\ *adj, usu cap* [fr. *Pontypool*, urban district in Monmouthshire, England] : of, relating to, or being japanned metalware (as trays, salvers, boxes) decorated with floral and landscape designs against red, black, or other colorful backgrounds and produced in England esp. during the 18th and 19th centuries

¹**po·ny** *also* **po·ney** \ˈpōnē, -ni\ *n, pl* **ponies** *also* **poneys** [earlier *powny, powney,* prob. fr. obs. F *poulenet,* dim. of *poulain,* fr. ML *pullanus,* fr. L *pullus* young of an animal, foal — more at FOAL] **1 a :** a small horse; *esp* **:** a horse of any of several breeds of very small stocky animals noted for their gentleness and endurance (as the horses of Iceland and the Shetland islands) and usu. restricted to those not over 14 or sometimes 14¼ hands in height except for the horses used in polo which may measure up to 15 hands **b :** a bronco, mustang, or other similar horse of the western U. S. **c :** RACEHORSE — usu. used in pl. ⟨bet on the *ponies*⟩ **d** *or* **pony skin :** the skin of a pony used as fur ⟨a ~ coat⟩ **2 :** something smaller than standard: as **a :** a small liqueur or beer glass or the amount it can hold **b :** a diminutive dancer in a chorus line **3** *Brit* **:** the amount of 25 pounds **4 :** a literal line-by-line translation used as an aid in learning a foreign language or reading a foreign text — compare CRIB, TROT **5 :** a measure of liquid that is usu. half that of a jigger

²**pony** \"\ *vb* -ED/-ING/-ES *vt* **1 :** to pay (money) esp. in settlement of an account — used with *up* **2 :** to translate with the aid of a pony **3 :** to limber up (a racehorse) by galloping on a lead line or sending out with a stable pony ~ *vi* **:** to pay up — used with *up*

³**pony** \"\ *adj* **1 :** of a size smaller than usual ⟨a ~ glass of beer⟩ ⟨a ~ glass⟩ ⟨a ~ insulator⟩ **2 :** limited to a brief daily account of only the most important news sent by telegraph, telephone, or mail (as that subscribed to by many small local papers or radio stations) ⟨a ~ report⟩ ⟨a ~ service⟩

**pony backfield** *n* **:** a backfield in football composed of players who are small and fast

**pony cart** *n* **:** DONKEY CART

**pony engine** *n* **:** a small switching locomotive

**pony express** *n* **:** a rapid postal and express system operating by relays of ponies

**pony grass** *n* **:** a perennial grass (*Calamagrostis neglecta*) of the north temperate zone forming valuable forage in the Rocky mountains

**pony league** *n, often cap P&L* **:** a commercially sponsored baseball league made up of teams whose players are boys from 13 to 15 years old — compare LITTLE LEAGUE

**pony mixer** *n* **:** a machine with rotating agitators and rotating can for mixing pastes (as for paints, printing ink, pharmaceutical ointments)

**pony rougher** *n* **:** STRANDER 2

**pony support** *n* **:** a portable standard of adjustable height used as a support (as for a pipe)

**ponytail** \ˈ==,=\ *n* **:** a style of hairdressing in which the hair is arranged to resemble the tail of a horse or pony

**pony truck** *n* **:** a two-wheeled swivel truck used under the front end of a locomotive

**pony truss** *n* **:** a truss (as in bridge building) so low that overhead bracing cannot be used

ponytail

**poo** \ˈpü\ *dial var of* PULL

**POO** *abbr* post office order

¹**pooch** \ˈpüch\ *chiefly dial var of* POUCH

²**pooch** \"\ *also* **pooched** \-cht\ *adj* [*pooch,* short for *pooched,* fr. past part. of ¹*pooch*] *dial* **:** protruding abnormally **:** DISTENDED

³**pooch** \"\ *n* -ES [origin unknown] *slang* **:** DOG

**pood** *or* **poud** *or* **pud** \ˈpüd, -üt\ *n* -S [Russ *pud,* fr. ON *pund* pound — more at POUND] **:** a Russian unit of weight equal to about 36.11 pounds

¹**poo·dle** \ˈpüdᵊl\ *n* [G *pudel,* short for *pudelhund,* fr. *pudeln* to splash (fr. *pudel* puddle, fr. LG) + *hund* dog — more at PUDDLE] **1 a** *usu cap* **:** an old breed of active intelligent heavy-coated solid-colored dogs of uncertain origin but possibly derived from some type of European retriever or spaniel that are often kept as pets but also make superior gun dogs and retrievers and are readily trained as performers and that occur in toy, miniature or standard, and large varieties differing only in size and weight **b** -S *sometimes cap* **:** a dog of the Poodle breed **2** -S **:** a woolen fabric having a surface texture like a poodle's coat

²**poodle** \"\ *vt* **poodled; poodled; poodling** \-d(ᵊ)liŋ\ **poodles :** to clip the hair of in a short curly style

**poodle dog** *n* **:** POODLE; *esp* **:** any small pet dog that follows its master around

**poo·er** \ˈpüər\ *chiefly Scot var of* POWER

**poof** \ˈpüf\ *interj* [imit.] — used to express contempt, disdain, or disapproval

**poogye** *var of* PUNGI

**pooh** \ˈpü, ˈpu̇\ *or* **pooh-pooh** \ˌpü;pü\ *n* -S **:** an expression of contempt, disapproval, or impatience ⟨quietly anticipates the skeptic's every ~ —*New Yorker*⟩ ⟨a few ~s and a tush about cover that —P.G.Wodehouse⟩ — often used interjectionally

**pooh-bah** *also* **poo-bah** \ˈpü;bä\ *n* -S *often cap P&B* [*Pooh-Bah,* name of character in Gilbert and Sullivan's opera *The Mikado* (1885) bearing the title Lord-High-Everything-Else] **1 :** one holding many public or private offices ⟨the municipal treasurer . . . is usu. assigned additional duties and often becomes a veritable village *poo-bah* —J.R.Hayden⟩ **2 a :** one in high position **b :** one who gives the impression of being a person of importance

**pooh-pooh** \ˌpü;pü\ *also* **pooh** \ˈpü\ *vb* -ED/-ING/-S [¹*pooh*] *vi* **:** to express contempt or impatience esp. by saying *pooh* ~ *vt* **:** to express contempt for or impatience with **:** make light of ⟨if a traveler told a tale he was sure to *pooh-pooh* it —Virginia Woolf⟩

**pooh-pooh theory** *n* **:** a theory that language originated in interjections which gradually acquired meaning — compare BOWWOW THEORY, DINGDONG THEORY

**pooja** *or* **poojah** *var of* PUJA

¹**pook** \ˈpük\ *vt* -ED/-ING/-S [origin unknown] *dial Eng* **:** to pile (a cut crop) into heaps or small stacks

²**pook** \"\ *n* -S [origin unknown] *dial chiefly Eng* **:** a heap or small stack of a crop esp. of hay or grain that has been cut and is temporarily stored in the field during one stage of harvesting

³**pook** \"\ *vt* [origin unknown] *chiefly Scot* **:** to pluck or pull at

**poo·ka** *also* **phoo·ka** \ˈpükə\ *n* -S [IrGael *púca,* perh. fr. OE, puck] **:** a mischievous or malignant goblin or specter held in Irish folklore to appear in the form of a horse and to haunt bogs and marshes

**poo·kawn** *or* **poo·kaun** \pü'kȯn\ *n* -S [IrGael *púcān*] *Irish* **:** a small fishing boat usu. with one mast, equipped with oars as well as sails, and often lateen-rigged

**pookoo** *var of* PUKU

¹**pool** \ˈpül\ *n* -S [ME, fr. OE *pōl;* akin to MLG *pōl* pool, OHG *pfuol*] **1 a** (1) **:** a small and rather deep body of fresh water (as one fed by a spring) (2) **:** a quiet place in a stream (3) **:** a reservoir for water (4) **:** a body of water forming above a dam or the closed gates of a lock (5) **:** TIDE POOL **b :** something held to resemble a pool (as in form, depth, quiet) ⟨a ~ of silence enveloped them —Louis Bromfield⟩ ⟨rests quietly in the deep ~ of memory —William Beebe⟩ ⟨sunlight lay . . . in fresh ~s of cool light —Gordon Merrick⟩ ⟨his eyes are deep ~s of self-confession —Howard Taubman⟩ **2 :** a small body of standing or stagnant water or other liquid **:** PUDDLE ⟨saw the small ~ of blood⟩ **3 :** a continuous area of porous sedimentary rock which yields petroleum or gas on drilling **4 a :** SWIMMING POOL **b :** WADING POOL

²**pool** \"\ *vb* -ED/-ING/-S *vi* **1 :** to form a pool ⟨swift-flowing water that ~*ed* and snaked down between the rocks and ice —*Atlantic*⟩ ⟨now the drops run and ~ together —V.S. Pritchett⟩ **2** *of blood* **:** to accumulate or become static (as in the veins and capillaries of a body part or organ) ⟨become tourniquets, preventing the blood from ~*ing* —*Time*⟩ ~ *vt* **1 a :** to cut (a hole) to insert a wedge for splitting (as in mining or quarrying) **b :** to undercut or undermine (as coal) esp. in excavating **2 :** to form pools in ⟨was deeply rutted and ~*ed* with rain —Evan Coombes⟩ **3 :** to cause (blood) to pool usu. as a result of defective circulation

³**pool** \"\ *n* -S [F *poule* stakes in a card game, lit., hen — more at PULLET] **1 a** (1) **:** an aggregate stake to which each player of a game has contributed (2) **:** an old game of cards in which there is a pool ⟨sat down with her female friends to a ~ of cards and a dish of coffee —W.M.Thackeray⟩; *also* **:** a party of players for such a game **b :** all the money bet by a number of persons on the result of a particular event with the aggregate to be paid to the winner or divided among several winners according to conditions established in advance **2 a :** a game played on an English billiard table in which each of the players stakes a certain sum with the winner taking all; *also* **:** a game at a public billiard room **b :** any of various games of billiards played on a pool table having six pockets with usu. 15 object balls that may be numbered or plain and a cue ball — see CONTINUOUS POOL, FIFTEEN BALL, SNOOKER; compare CAROM BILLIARDS **3 a :** any aggregation of the interests or property of different persons made to further a joint undertaking or end by subjecting them to the same control and a common liability: as (1) **:** a common fund or combination of interests for the common adventure in buying or selling; *esp* **:** one for speculating in or manipulating the market price of securities, grain, or other commodities (2) **:** a combination between competing business houses or corporations for the control of traffic by removing competition **b :** the persons who so combine their interests or property — see TRUST **4 :** a fencing contest in which each member of a team successively engages each member of another team **5 :** a readily available supply: as **a** (1) **:** the whole quantity of material or of a particular substance present in the body and freely available for function or the satisfying of metabolic demands of the cells (as of blood in the capillaries or of neurons available to complete various neural circuits) ⟨the circulating metabolic ~⟩ ⟨the acetate ~⟩ (2) **:** a body product (as blood or one of its derivatives) collected from many donors and stored for later use (as for transfusions or a source of antibodies) **b** (1) **:** an aggregation usu. made by a group and used mutually for the benefit of all ⟨a ~ of ideas contributed by a wide range of experienced teachers —*Geog. Jour.*⟩ (2) **:** a group of separately owned objects used cooperatively for the benefit of all concerned; *esp* **:** CAR POOL **c** (1) **:** the total manpower available in an area ⟨armies . . . can be readily reinforced in case of emergency from the reserve ~ —Joseph Rosenfarb⟩ (2) **:** a group of employees held in readiness by an employer for assignment as needed ⟨a stenographic ~⟩ (3) **:** a skilled trained group esp. in a specialized field capable of being utilized ⟨a ~ of brilliant scientists who accelerate the development of atomic power —T.E.Murray⟩ ⟨a ~ of trained actors and directors who will impose less limitation on the playwright —Henry Hewes⟩ **d :** the total amount often of a strategic material or resource that is for use or in reserve ⟨new oil discoveries are wanted to replenish the ~⟩ ⟨the government with unlimited access to the paper ~ —Lucien Price⟩ ⟨its enormous ~ of patents —*New Republic*⟩ **6 :** an installation which maintains and administers a supply of something; *esp* **:** MOTOR POOL

⁴**pool** \"\ *vb* -ED/-ING/-S *vt* **:** to put together in a pool **:** contribute to a common fund or effort often on the basis of a mutual division of profits or losses or an equal share of benefits **:** make a common interest of ⟨would ~ their money now and . . . put a real show on the road —F.B.Gipson⟩ ⟨special consultants have ~*ed* their talents and knowledge —L.R.Sander⟩ ⟨teachers . . . had again ~*ed* their experiences —Lucy S. Mitchell⟩ ~ *vi* **:** to organize a pool **:** combine with others in a pool

⁵**pool** \"\ *n* -S [Russ *pul* — more at PUL] **:** PUL 1

**pool bottle** *n* **:** a leather bottle from which small numbered balls are distributed to the players in some games of pool (as to determine the order of playing)

**pool hole** *n* [²*pool*] *mining* **:** a hole cut in pooling

**poo·li** \ˈpülē\ *n* -S [Mende *puli,* a species of *Bauhinia*] **1 :** a tropical African timber tree (*Cordia platythyrsa*) **2 :** the moderately soft wood of the pooli

**poolroom** \ˈ=,=\ *n* [³*pool* + *room*] **1 :** a room in which bookmaking is carried on **2 :** a usu. public room or establishment equipped for the playing of pool and other games

**poolroot** \ˈ=,=\ *n* [¹*pool* + *root*] **:** a common perennial herb (*Eupatorium aromaticum*) of the eastern U.S. with opposite leaves and loose clusters of heads of white tubular flowers

**pools** *pl of* POOL, *pres 3d sing of* POOL

**pool selling** *n* [³*pool*] **:** the selling or distribution of chances in a betting pool

**poolside** \ˈ=,=\ *n* [¹*pool* + *side*] **:** the area surrounding a swimming pool

**pool table** *n* [³*pool*] **:** a pocketed billiard table on which pool is played — compare BILLIARD TABLE

**pool train** *n* [³*pool*] **:** a train operated by either of two or more railroads connecting the same points on which tickets of other participating railroads are accepted with revenues divided as specified in the pool agreement

**poolwort** \ˈ=,=\ *n* [¹*pool* + *wort*] **1 :** POOLROOT **2 :** WHITE SNAKEROOT

**pooly** \ˈpülē\ *adj* -ER/-EST [¹*pool* + -*y*] **:** resembling a pool **:** having many pools **:** SWAMPY

¹**poon** \ˈpün\ *or* **poon tree** *n* [Malayalam *punna*] **1 :** any of several trees (genus *Calophyllum*) of the East Indies and the Pacific islands; *esp* **:** MASTWOOD **2 :** the hard light wood of poon used esp. for masts and spars

²**poon** \ˈpu̇n\ *chiefly Scot var of* POUND

¹**poo·na** \ˈpünə\ *adj, usu cap* [fr. *Poona,* city in western India] **:** of or from the city of Poona, India **:** of the kind or style prevalent in Poona

²**poona** \"\ *n* -S [fr. Poona, India, where it originated] **:** BADMINTON

**poo·nac** \ˈpü,nak\ *n* -S [Sinhalese *punakku,* fr. Skt *piṇyāka*] **:** COCONUT CAKE

**poona pea** *n* [origin unknown] **:** PIGEON PEA

**poonghie** *var of* PONGYI

**poon·tang** \ˈpün,taŋ\ *n* -S [F *putain* prostitute, fr. OF *pute* girl, fr. (assumed) VL *putto, putta* child, fr. L *putus;* akin to L *puer* boy, child, Skt *putra* child, son — more at FEW] *slang* **:** SEXUAL INTERCOURSE

¹**poop** \ˈpüp\ *vb* -ED/-ING/-S [ME *poupen,* of imit. origin] *vi* **1 a :** to make a short jarring sound **:** toot a horn; *also* **:** GULP **b** (1) **:** to shoot a gun (2) **:** to make loud bangings (as a gun) **2 :** to emit intestinal gas — usu. considered vulgar ~ *vt* **:** to cause to discharge **:** FIRE ⟨we ~*ed* off a salvo in the direction of the sound —S.H.Baker⟩

²**poop** \"\ *n* -S **1 :** a short jarring sound **:** GULP, TOOT **2 a :** an act of defecation — usu. used with *take;* usu. considered vulgar **b :** intestinal gas expelled through the anus — usu. considered vulgar

³**poop** \"\ *n* -S [MF *poupe,* fr. L *puppis*] **1** *obs* **:** the afterpart of a ship **:** STERN **2 a :** an enclosed superstructure at the afterpart of a ship above the main deck often in ships of the 16th and 17th centuries raised to a great height **b :** POOP DECK

⁴**poop** \"\ *vt* -ED/-ING/-S **1 :** to break over the poop or stern of ⟨the huge seas are beginning to ~ her very badly —Raymond McFarland⟩ **2 :** to ship (a sea or wave) over the stern ⟨outside in the ocean there is serious danger in ~*ing* a following wave —H.A.Calahan⟩

⁵**poop** *vt* -ED/-ING/-S [origin uncommon] *obs* **:** to practice deceit upon **:** CHEAT, COZEN

⁶**poop** \ˈpüp\ *n* -S [short for *nincompoop*] **:** a foolish or useless person ⟨regarded by many as a pompous old ~ —H.A.Smith⟩

⁷**poop** \"\ *vb* -ED/-ING/-S [origin unknown] *vt, slang* **:** to put out of breath or wind thoroughly; *also* **:** to wear out **:** EXHAUST ⟨those last eight miles just ~*ed* everybody —*Infantry Jour.*⟩ ⟨found himself completely ~*ed*⟩ ~ *vi* **:** to become exhausted **:** cease completely — often used with *out* ⟨this ivy was green at a time when other ivies had ~*ed* out —*New Yorker*⟩

⁸**poop** \"\ *n* -S [origin unknown] *slang* **:** official or unofficial information ⟨gave us all the ~ he had gathered from his usual reliable sources⟩

**poop cabin** *n* [³*poop*] **:** a ship's cabin whose roof is the poop deck

**poop deck** *n* **:** a partial usu. weather deck above the main deck in the afterpart of a ship

**poop royal** *n* **:** the highest and aftermost deck over the poop in large old-time ships

¹**poor** \ˈpu̇(ə)r, -ùə, *esp South, NE, & Brit* ˈpōə *or* ˈpō(ə)r *or* ˈpȯ(ə) *or* ˈpȯ(ə)r\ *adj* -ER/-EST [ME, *povere, poure, pore,* fr. OF *povre, poure,* fr. L *pauper;* akin to L *paucus* little and to L *parere* to bring forth, *parare* to acquire — more at FEW, PARE] **1 a :** lacking material possessions **:** existing without the luxuries and often the necessities of life **:** having little money ⟨they were so ~ that they couldn't afford things —Mary Austin⟩ ⟨homes of ~*er* folk have their gardens —D.C.Buchanan⟩ **b :** of, relating to, or characterized by poverty **2 a :** wanting in amount or capacity **:** less than adequate **:** DEFICIENT, MEAGER, SCANTY ⟨they gripe . . . loudly in winters of ~ snow —R.S.Monahan⟩ ⟨was largely responsible for the ~ attendance —R.W.Southern⟩ ⟨disappointed in the ~ crop⟩ **b :** small in worth ⟨one ~ pennyworth of sugar candy —Shak.⟩ **c** *of lime* **:** LEAN 3c **3 :** worthy of being pitied **:** being in a position to excite compassionate regard ⟨the ~ guard had started to cry out —S.H.Holbrook⟩ ⟨the ~ things all got colds —Charlton Laird⟩ **4 a :** inferior in quality **:** having little distinction, value, or worth ⟨inscription painted in ~ Latin on a nearby wall —C.A.Robinson⟩ ⟨displayed very ~ sportsmanship⟩ **b :** of lowly disposition **:** HUMBLE, UNPRETENTIOUS ⟨if it would be prudent to interrupt . . . on his ~ trivial account —Thomas Hardy⟩ **c :** mentally or ethically inferior **:** mean or small of spirit ⟨neighbors seemed to him ~ fellows with too little spirit to be free men —V.L.Parrington⟩ ⟨they are base, ~, contemptible fellows —Robert Burton⟩ **d :** having little significance **:** TRIVIAL ⟨each one of those great sciences was in its dim and ~ beginning —F.W.H.Myers⟩ **5 a :** being in an emaciated condition **:** LEAN, SCRAWNY ⟨in first-class breeding condition, neither too fat nor in any way ~ —Henry Wynmalen⟩ **b** *chiefly dial* **:** lacking necessary strength **:** not in good condition **:** FEEBLE, THIN ⟨looked ~ after the hard winter⟩ **6 :** characterized by unproductiveness **:** BARREN — used of land ⟨only in the remote and ~*est* sections . . . is the dull and drudging farmwife of thirty years ago met today —*Amer. Guide Series: Minn.*⟩ **7 :** fairly unsatisfactory **:** INDIFFERENT, UNFAVORABLE ⟨the condescending . . . tone which betrays a ~ opinion of the reader —John Farrelly⟩ ⟨the business of a printer being generally thought a ~ one —Benjamin Franklin⟩ **8 :** characterized by inefficiency or failure to meet a standard ⟨drawbacks in operational use because of ~ precision —J.P.Baxter b.1893⟩

**syn** POOR, INDIGENT, NEEDY, DESTITUTE, PENNILESS, IMPECUNIOUS, POVERTY-STRICKEN, and NECESSITOUS agree in signifying having barely enough money or possessions to support life or having less money or fewer possessions than are essential. POOR is the most general, applying to both those in want and those who commonly must live below a comfortable standard of living ⟨a pretty child bought from miserably *poor* parents under a contract —Lafcadio Hearn⟩ ⟨a man may be too *poor* to maintain a wife —Edward Westermarck⟩ ⟨the resulting waste of resources can make a *poor* people in a barren land —H.W.Odum⟩ ⟨as *poor* as church mice⟩ INDIGENT and NEEDY, the first more literary than the second, both imply pressing or urgent want ⟨the depression had left a number of them *indigent,* without state or federal relief —Green Peyton⟩ ⟨the skyrocketing costs put a rapidly increasing number of people in the medically *indigent* class —J.H.Means⟩ ⟨*needy* children in migrant farm worker families —*Current Biog.*⟩ ⟨to aid *needy* and deserving students —*Official Register of Harvard Univ.*⟩ DESTITUTE implies dire and dangerous need, suggesting the calamitous and wretched ⟨left *destitute* to face the prospect of a bleak and impoverished old age —John Galsworthy⟩ ⟨soldiers who by death or illness had left their wives and children *destitute* —A.V.D.Honeyman⟩ PENNILESS and IMPECUNIOUS can be equivalent in indicating the lack of money or resources on which to live or live decently and in not carrying the immediate connotations of calamitousness or wretchedness as does *destitute.* IMPECUNIOUS differs from PENNILESS in often suggesting a habitual or chronic condition ⟨this very beautiful English girl was a *penniless* governess, left stranded in Germany by an employer —Margaret Deland⟩ ⟨remembered by his associates as the bright but *penniless* youth whose climb to fame rivaled the most incredible of the Alger stories —*Amer. Guide Series: Minn.*⟩ ⟨the *impecunious* artists and writers of New York —Jerome Mellquist⟩ ⟨my greatest treat as a small and *impecunious* Scots boy was to visit friends of my mother who were "big people" —Aylmer Vallance⟩ POVERTY-STRICKEN signifies indigent or destitute but stresses more the suffering or strain attendant upon dire poverty ⟨the bulk of the pioneers was formed by *poverty-stricken* people who migrated from densely populated areas —J.F.Embree & W.L.Thomas⟩ ⟨a *poverty-stricken* primary school —H.R.Warfel⟩ NECESSITOUS, less common than the preceding words, is equivalent to *needy,* sometimes connoting insistent demands for relief ⟨fifty *necessitous* persons are being assisted at a total annual cost of over £1,500 —*Veterinary Record*⟩ ⟨in no sense of the word were they *necessitous* or poor —Jane Austen⟩ ⟨a greedy and *necessitous* public —Edmund Burke⟩

²**poor** \"\ *n, pl* **poor :** one that is poor — usu. used collectively ⟨for you always have the ~ with you —Mt 26:11 (RSV)⟩ ⟨respected by both rich and ~⟩

³**poor** \ˈpüər\ *chiefly dial var of* POWER

⁴**poor** \ˈpu̇(ə)r\ *or* **poor cod** *n* -S [*poor,* short for *poor cod,* fr. ¹*poor* + *cod*] **:** a small European codfish (*Gadus minutus*) considered of little worth

**poor box** *n* [²*poor*] **:** a box for alms for the poor; *esp* **:** one placed near the door of a church

**poor boy** *n* [¹*poor*] **:** a sandwich made of a loaf of French bread split lengthwise, buttered, and filled with one or more meats — compare GRINDER

**poor clare** *n, usu cap P&C* **:** a nun of an order founded early in the 13th century at Assisi by St. Clare under the direction of St. Francis

**poor convict's oath** *n* **:** an oath required of a prisoner unable to pay his fine that entitles him to a release on certain conditions

**poor debtor** *n* **:** a debtor who has no property or not more than a certain small amount of property subject to execution or who has delivered up his property for the benefit of his creditors in the manner prescribed by law

**poor-debtor law** *n* [*poor debtor*] **:** a law providing relief for debtors usu. by affording them time to pay their just debts by installments, or by freeing them from arrest or imprisonment on their delivering all their property not exempt from creditors to a trustee or other public officer for the benefit of the creditors, or on their taking an oath that they have property within the amount exempted from the claims of creditors

**poor debtor's oath** *n* **:** the oath to the facts bringing a person within the purview of a poor-debtor law and required to obtain the benefit of that law

**poore** *obs var of* POOR

**poorer** *comparative of* POOR

**poorest** *superlative of* POOR

**poor farm** *n* [²*poor*] **:** a farm maintained at public expense for the support and employment of needy or dependent persons

**poorhouse** \ˈ=,=\ *n* [²*poor* + *house*] **:** a place maintained at public expense to house needy or dependent persons

**poor·ish** \ˈpu̇rish\ *adj* [*poor* + *-ish*] **:** rather poor ⟨the piano reproduction is ~ by contemporary standards —Norman Cousins⟩ ⟨brought within the means of ~ educated people the pleasures of culture and of companionship —*Australasian*⟩

**poor joe** *n* [modif. of Gullah *pojo* heron] **:** GREAT BLUE HERON

**poor john** *n, often cap P&J* [¹*poor*] **1** *archaic* **:** small cod or hake dried and salted **2** *archaic* **:** plain coarse food

**poor-land-weed** \ˈ=,=,=\ *n* **:** BUTTONWEED 1

**poor law** *n* [²*poor*] **:** a law providing for or regulating the public relief or support of the poor

¹**poor·ly** \ˈpu̇(ə)rlē, ˈpu̇əlē, -li, *esp in southern US, NE, & Brit* ˈpō(ə)r- *or* ˈpōəl- *or* ˈpȯ(ə)r- *or* ˈpȯ(ə)l-\ *adv* [ME *pourely,* fr. *poure* poor + *-ly*] **:** in a poor manner or condition: as **a :** very inadequately **:** in an inferior or imperfect way **:** INEFFECTIVELY, INSUFFICIENTLY, UNDESIRABLY ⟨millions of students can write ~ without knowing any grammar at all —James Binney⟩ ⟨a pioneer college with few buildings, ~

equipped —A.B.Noble⟩ **b :** in actual want ⟨would live as ~ now as he did more than a hundred years ago — Philip Toynbee⟩ **c** *obs* **:** without generosity **:** SHABBILY ⟨a man who ~ left me —Richard Steele⟩ **d** *archaic* **:** without spirit or courage **:** ABJECTLY ⟨to set free the minds . . . from longing to return ~ under that captivity of kings —John Milton⟩

**²poorly** \ˈ"\ *adj* **:** somewhat ill **:** not in good health **:** INDISPOSED ⟨had been ~ lately⟩ ⟨she was ~ with the slow fever —Conrad Richter⟩

**poor man's cabbage** *n* **:** a winter cress (*Barbarea verna*)

**poor man's mustard** *n* **:** GARLIC MUSTARD

**poor man's orchid** *n* **:** BUTTERFLY FLOWER

**poor man's pepper** *n* **1 :** PEPPERGRASS 1; *esp* **:** BIRD'S-PEPPER **2 :** a stonecrop (*Sedum acre*)

**poor man's shilling** *n, pl* **poor man's shillings :** HONESTY 3

**poor man's soap** *n* [so called because it will make a lather with water] **:** HARDHACK 1

**poor man's weatherglass** *n* [so called because it opens its blossoms only in fair weather] **:** SCARLET PIMPERNEL

**poormaster** \ˈ=,==\ *n* [²*poor* + *master*] **:** a supervisor of the relief of the poor

**poor mouth** *n, Midland* **:** a profession or protestation of poverty — often used with *make* ⟨when you ask him for a donation he makes a *poor mouth*⟩

**poor·ness** *n* -ES [ME *pourenesse*, fr. *poure* poor + *-nesse* -ness] **:** the quality or state of being poor

**poor pine** *n* [¹*poor*] **:** any of several pines of the southern U.S. growing in poor soil: as **a :** SPRUCE PINE 1a **b :** SHORTLEAF PINE 1

**poor preacher** *or* **poor priest** *n* **:** one of an English order of itinerant preachers founded by John Wycliffe and composed of followers who went out two by two practicing apostolic poverty and pledged but not by permanent vows to bring the Gospel to the people

**poor pussy** *n* **:** a game in which one player who represents the pussy kneels successively before the others who must refrain from laughing as they stroke his head and address him as "poor pussy"

**poor rate** *n* [²*poor*] **:** an assessment levied for the relief of the poor

**poor relation** *n* [¹*poor*] **:** one that is regarded as holding a subordinate or inferior position ⟨modern dance . . . is the *poor relation* among the theater arts —E.R.Bentley⟩ ⟨the humanities have become *poor relations* — *Report: (Canadian) Royal Commission on Nat'l Development*⟩

**poor relief** *n* [²*poor*] **:** relief or assistance usu. administered by local officials with funds from the local treasury for the aid of the needy in a community

**poor robin's plantain** *n, usu cap P&R* [¹*poor*] **1 :** ROBIN'S PLANTAIN **2 :** RATTLESNAKE WEED 1

**poor soldier** *n* **:** FRIARBIRD 1

**poor–spirited** \ˈ=ˈ===\ *adj* **:** having or showing a mean spirit **:** COWARDLY, BASE — **poor–spirited·ly** *adv* — **poor–spirited·ness** *n* -ES

**poort** \ˈpō(ə)rt, ˈpu̇(ə)-\ *n* -S [Afrik, fr. D, gate, gateway, fr. L *porta* — more at PORT] *southern Africa* **:** a pass between or across mountains

**poor·tith** \ˈpȯr,tith\ *n* -S [OF *poverteit, povretet, poverté*, fr. L *paupertat-, paupertas* poverty — more at POVERTY] *chiefly Scot* **:** POVERTY

**poor white** *n* [¹*poor*] **:** a member of an inferior or underprivileged white social group — often taken to be offensive ⟨if these bad farming practices persisted . . . some settlers were in danger of becoming *poor whites* — *Farmer's Weekly (So. Africa)*⟩

**poorwill** \ˈpü(ə)r,wil\ *n* -S [imit.] **:** a bird of the western U.S. and Mexico (*Phalaenoptilus nuttallii*) that is similar to the whippoorwill but smaller and that has a note of two syllables only

**¹poot** \ˈpüt\ *dial Brit var of* POULT

**²poot** \ˈ"\ *interj* [origin unknown] — used to express disgust

**¹pop** \ˈpäp\ *vb* **popped; popped; popping; pops** [ME *poppen*, of imit. origin] *vt* **1 a :** to strike or knock sharply **:** HIT ⟨*popped* him on the jaw and knocked him cold⟩ **b :** ASSAULT, ATTACK **c :** BREAK **2 :** to push, put, or thrust suddenly ⟨*popping* questions to his class⟩ ⟨*popping* the berry into her mouth —Virginia Woolf⟩ ⟨couldn't go out without *popping* my head round the door —Fred Majdalany⟩ **3 :** to cause to explode or burst open ⟨the corn is *popped* —Jane Nickerson⟩ ⟨*popped* his gum twice —Jean Stafford⟩ **4 :** to fire at **:** SHOOT ⟨went into the woods hoping to ~ a rabbit or two⟩ **5** *Brit* **:** HOCK, PAWN ~ *vi* **1 a :** to go, come, enter, or issue forth quickly or suddenly **:** occur or appear unexpectedly ⟨*popped* around the corner of the house and confronted me —C.B. Kelland⟩ ⟨*popped* into his head out of the blue —John Kobler⟩ **b :** to move with agility **:** DART, JUMP ⟨the private looked up startled, then *popped* to . . . attention —James Jones⟩ **2 :** to make or burst with a sharp sound **:** EXPLODE **3 :** to protrude from the sockets ⟨eyes *popping* with amazement⟩ ⟨eyes were on the point of *popping* out of his head —T.B.Costain⟩ **4 :** to shoot with a firearm ⟨~ at a target⟩ ⟨~ at a bird⟩ **5 :** to form blisters **:** BLOW — used esp. of lime and mortar **6 a :** to hit a short high fly in baseball that is easily caught ⟨*popped* to left field⟩ — often used with *up* or *out* **b** *cricket, of a bowled ball* **:** to rise sharply and travel through the air erratically after pitching — often used with *up* **7 :** BACKFIRE 2 — **pop the question :** to propose marriage

**²pop** \ˈ"\ *n* -S [ME, fr. *poppen* to pop] **1 a** *dial chiefly Eng* **:** BLOW, KNOCK, STROKE **b :** POP FLY **2 a :** a small sharp quick explosive sound ⟨the faint ~ of buttons being undone —Gordon Merrick⟩ ⟨the cork flew off with a ~⟩ **b :** the time taken by the sound of a pop **:** INSTANT **3 a (1) :** a shot from a gun ⟨when he took a ~ at you, he was playing for keeps with your life —Theodore Draper⟩ **(2) :** GUN ⟨the lad got the pistol . . . and the old man fearing he might do other mischief took the ~ away from him —D.D.Martin⟩ **b :** ATTEMPT, CRACK, EFFORT, GO, TRY ⟨about to take another ~ at matrimony —P.G.Wodehouse⟩ **4 :** a mark or spot made by a quick stroke **:** DOT **5** [so called fr. the sound made by breaking the inflated calyx] **a :** any of several West Indian plants of the genus *Physalis* **b :** the inflated calyx of a pop plant **6** [so called from the sound made by drawing the cork of the container] **:** a flavored carbonated beverage (as orange soda, root beer) **:** SODA POP ⟨picnics were held with free ~ and hamburgers —D.L.Cohn⟩ **7 a** *dial Eng* **:** REDWING **b** *Louisiana* **:** PAINTED BUNTING **8 :** a small boss with an inserted setscrew

**³pop** \ˈ"\ *adv* **:** like or with a pop **:** SUDDENLY ⟨I don't know why suddenly everything should go ~⟩ — often used interjectionally

**⁴pop** \ˈ"\ *n* -S [by shortening] **:** POPPET

**⁵pop** \ˈ"\ *n* -S [short for *poppa*] **:** FATHER — not often in formal use

**⁶pop** \ˈ"\ *n* -S [by shortening fr. *popular*] **1 pops** *pl but usu sing in constr* **:** a popular orchestra or concert ⟨went to hear the Boston *Pops*⟩ **2 :** a popular tune or recording

**⁷pop** \ˈ"\ *also* **pops** \ˈpäps\ *adj* **:** characterized by a popular tune or a mixture of popular and classical music calculated to appeal to the people in general ⟨become a singer of ~ tunes —Morroe Berger⟩

**pop** *abbr* **1** popular; popularly **2** population

**POP** *abbr* printing-out paper

**pop·a·dam** *or* **pop·a·dum** \ˈpäpədəm\ *n* -S [Tamil-Malayalam *pappaṭam*] **:** an Indian cake often eaten with curry and made of a thin strip or a ball of gluten flour or cornmeal fried in oil or other fat

**pop ash** *n* [¹*pop*] **:** a water ash (*Fraxinus caroliniana*)

**popcorn** \ˈ=,=\ *n* [contraction of *popped corn*, fr. *popped* (past part. of ¹*pop*) + *corn*] **1 a :** a variety (*Zea mays everta*) of Indian corn having small ears and small pointed or rounded kernels with very hard corneous endosperm that on exposure to dry heat are popped or everted by the explosion of the contained moisture and form a white starchy mass many times the size of the original kernel **b :** the corn when popped **2 :** a light yellow that is greener and slightly lighter than average maize and duller than chrome lemon **3** *also* **popcorn stitch :** a crochet stitch forming raised balls resembling popcorn

**popcorn flower** *n* **:** a plant of the genus *Plagiobothrys* (family Boraginaceae) usu. having crowded white flowers on a one-sided curved spike

**popdock** \ˈ=,=\ *n* [¹*pop* + *dock*] **:** FOXGLOVE

**pope** \ˈpōp\ *n* -S [ME, fr. OE *pāpa*, fr. LL *papa*, fr. Gk *pappas, papas*, title of bishops, lit., papa — more at PAPA] **1 a** *often cap* **:** the bishop of Rome as head of the Roman Catholic Church **b :** the Eastern Orthodox or Coptic patriarch of Alexandria **c :** an Eastern Orthodox priest **2 :** a spiritual head of any of various non-Christian religions ⟨the Taoist ~⟩ ⟨the Caodaist ~⟩ **3 :** one held to resemble a pope usu. in authority or position ⟨schoolmasters, professors . . . ~*s* of knowledge — Holbrook Jackson⟩ **4 :** ¹RUFF 1 **5 :** any of various birds: as **a** *dial Eng* **:** PUFFIN **b** *dial Eng* **:** BULLFINCH **c** *dial Eng* **:** RED-BACKED SHRIKE

**pope day** *n, usu cap P&D* [so called fr. the fact that the Gunpowder Plot was popularly regarded as inspired by the Pope] **:** GUY FAWKES DAY

**pope·dom** \ˈpōpdəm\ *n* -S [ME, fr. OE *pāpdōm*, fr. *pāpa* pope + *-dōm* -dom] **1 :** the office or tenure of a pope **:** PAPACY ⟨during the ~ of Vigilius⟩ **2 :** a rank or office of supreme religious authority ⟨the Caodaist ~⟩

**pope·hood** \ˈpōp,hu̇d\ *n* [ME *popehode*, fr. OE *pāpanhād*, fr. *pāpa* pope + *-hād* -hood] **:** the office or tenure of pope

**pope·ism** \ˈpō,pizəm\ *n* -S [*pope* + *-ism*] **:** POPERY

**pope joan** *n, usu cap P&J* [fr. *Pope Joan*, fictitious female pope] **:** a card game resembling Michigan and fan-tan; *also* **:** the nine of diamonds in this game

**pop·e·line** \,päpəˈlēn\ *n* -S [F, fr. E *poplin*] **:** a clothing fabric that has a silk or rayon warp and a wool filling and resembles poplin or rep

**pope·ling** \ˈpōpliŋ\ *n* -S [*pope* + *-ling*] **1** *obs* **:** PAPIST **2 :** a petty or deputy pope

**pope·ly** *adj* -ER/-EST [*pope* + *-ly*] **:** characteristic of a pope **:** PAPAL

**pope night** *n, usu cap P&N* **:** the night of Pope Day

**pop·ery** \ˈpōp(ə)rē\ *n* -ES *sometimes cap* [*pope* + *-ery*] **:** ROMAN CATHOLICISM; *esp* **:** its government and forms of worship — usu. used disparagingly

**pope's–eye** \ˈ=ˈ=\ *n, pl* **pope's–eyes :** the lymphatic gland in the thigh of an ox or sheep

**pope's head** *n* **:** a long-handled brush usu. used for dusting ceilings or washing windows

**pope·ship** \ˈpōp,ship\ *n* [ME, fr. *pope* + *-ship*] **:** POPEDOM

**pope's nose** *n* **:** the part of a bird that corresponds to the tail of a mammal and forms a broad flattened lobe bearing the tail feathers and usu. a dorsal uropygial gland — called also *parson's nose*

**pop·ess** \ˈpōpəs\ *n* -ES [*pope* + *-ess*] **:** a female pope

**pop·eye** \ˈpä,pī\ *n* [prob. back-formation fr. *popeyed*] **1 :** a staring bulging eye **2 a :** an exophthalmic condition of fishes due to infestation of the eye by larval trematode worms **b :** a fish affected with this condition

**pop·eyed** \-ˈīd\ *adj* [¹*pop* + *eyed*] **:** having eyes that bulge (as from disease, excitement) ⟨the galleries ~ with amazement —*Time*⟩ ⟨the wombat's charming but ~ offspring peer out from this pouch —Barrett McGurn⟩

**pop fly** *n* [¹*pop*] **:** a fly ball hit without much force and usu. caught easily by an infielder

**pop foul** *n* **:** a pop fly hit into foul territory in baseball

**pop goes the weasel** [³*pop*] **:** an English country longways in which each dancer in turn is popped under the arms of a couple with joined hands; *also* **:** an American square dance derived from this

**popgun** \ˈ=,=\ *n* [²*pop*] **1 :** a child's toy gun consisting of a tube and rammer for shooting ammunition (as pellets, corks) by compression of air **2 :** any firearm regarded as ridiculously inadequate

**pophole** \ˈ=,=\ *n* [¹*pop*] **:** a small opening through which an animal may pass (as a coop to an outdoor run)

**pop·i·an** *also* **pop·e·an** \ˈpōpēən\ *adj, usu cap* [Alexander *Pope* †1744 Eng. poet + *-ian, -an*] **:** of, relating to, or resembling Alexander Pope or his poetry ⟨the fashionable *Popian* couplet —George Saintsbury⟩

**po·pil·lia** \pəˈpilēə\ *n, cap* [NL, fr. L *Popillia* Roman gentile name] **:** a genus of beetles of the family Scarabaeidae — see JAPANESE BEETLE

**pop·i·nac** *also* **pop·i·nack** \ˈpäpə,nak\ *n* -S [modif. of *opopanax*] **:** HUISACHE

**pop·in·jay** \ˈpäpən,jā\ *n* [ME *papejay, papengay*, fr. MF *papegai, papejai*, fr. Ar *babghā'*] **1** *obs* **:** PARROT **2** *heraldry* **:** a parrot or parakeet usu. depicted in green with red legs and beak **3 :** one thought to resemble a parrot or parakeet (as because of excessive ostentation in clothes, senseless volubility, or vain posturing) ⟨had been stricken too sorely by the bitter struggle to be caught by military ~*s* —V.L.Parrington⟩ ⟨a curse on the tanner's grandson and his French ~*s* — Charles Kingsley⟩ **4** *dial Eng* **:** GREEN WOODPECKER

**popinjay green** *n* **:** PARROT GREEN

**pop·ish** \ˈpōpish\ *adj, sometimes cap* [*pope* + *-ish*] **:** Roman Catholic — often used disparagingly

**pop·ish·ly** *adv* **:** in a popish manner

**¹pop·lar** \ˈpäplə(r)\ *n* -S [ME *poplere*, fr. MF *pouplier*, fr. *pouple, peuple* poplar, fr. L *populus*] **1 a :** a tree of the genus *Populus* — see TREE illustration **b :** the soft light-colored nondurable wood of a poplar; *esp* **:** the wood of the aspen used for paper pulp **2 :** TULIP TREE 1

**²poplar** \ˈ"\ *adj* **1 :** of or relating to the tulip tree or the poplar **2 :** made of the wood of the tulip tree or of poplar

**poplar and willow borer** *n* **:** a grub that is the larva of a European weevil (*Sternochetus lapathi*) now established in many parts of the U.S. and that bores in stems esp. of various poplars and willows

**poplar birch** \ˈ==-\ *also* **poplar–leaved birch** \ˈ==,=-\ *n* **:** any of several white birches with leaves resembling those of the poplar; *esp* **:** AMERICAN GRAY BIRCH

**poplar borer** *n* **:** a longicorn beetle (*Saperda calcarata*) whose larva bores in and destroys various poplars

**poplar box** *n* **:** an Australian gum tree (*Eucalyptus polyanthemos*) with ashy gray bark, nearly round long-stalked leaves, and small umbellate flowers

**poplar canker** *n* **:** a branch or trunk canker of poplars esp. damaging to the Lombardy poplar and caused by a fungus (*Dothichiza populea*)

**pop·lared** \ˈpäplə(r)d\ *adj* [¹*poplar* + *-ed*] **:** planted with or abounding in poplars

**poplar goat moth** *n* **:** a large gray and black carpenter moth (*Acossus centerensis*) whose larva bores in poplar trees

**poplar hawk moth** *n* **:** a large European sphingid moth (*Smerinthus populi*) the larva of which feeds on the foliage of poplar

**pop·lar·ism** \ˈpäplə,rizəm\ *n* -S *usu cap* [*Poplar*, metropolitan borough of east London + E *-ism*] **:** a municipal policy of providing poor relief and esp. unemployment compensation in amounts held to be extravagant and productive of unjustly high taxes

**poplar leaf fig** *n* **:** a large West Indian fig (*Ficus laevigata*) having a small red fruit

**poplar tentmaker** *n* **:** a caterpillar that is the larva of a notodontid moth (*Ichthyura inclusa*) and that feeds on poplar foliage

**poplar vagabond aphid** *n* **:** an aphid (*Mordwilkoja vagabundus*) that infests poplars in the U. S. and Canada and causes galls on the twigs

**poplar worm** *n* **:** the larva of any of various lepidopterans injurious to poplar trees; *esp* **:** the larva of a dagger moth (*Acronicta lepusculina*) that feeds on the cottonwood

**pople** *var of* POPPLE

**pop·lin** \ˈpäplən\ *n* -S [F *papeline*, perh. fr. *Poperinge*, Flemish textile city] **:** a strong plainwoven fabric characterized by fine crosswise ribs that is made of various fibers singly or in combination and is used esp. for clothing and curtains

**pop·lit·e·al** *also* **pop·li·tae·al** \(ˈ)päpˈlidēəl, -itē-, ¦päpləˈtē-\ *adj* [fr. NL *popliteus* of the ham + E *-al* — more at POPLITEUS] **:** of or relating to the back part of the leg behind the knee joint

**popliteal artery** *n* **:** the continuation of the femoral artery that after passing through the thigh crosses the popliteal space and soon divides into the anterior and posterior tibial arteries

**popliteal muscle** *n* **:** POPLITEUS

**popliteal nerve** *n* **:** either of two branches into which the sciatic nerve divides usu. in the lower part of the thigh with the larger branch passing through the popliteal space and continuing downward as the tibial nerve and the smaller branch forming the peroneal nerve

**popliteal notch** *n* **:** a depression on the back of the head of the tibia between the tuberosities

**popliteal space** *n* **:** a lozenge-shaped space at the back of the knee joint

**popliteal vein** *n* **:** a vein formed by the union of the tibial veins and ascending through the popliteal space to the thigh where it becomes the femoral vein

**pop·lit·e·us** \päpˈlidēəs, -itēəs, ,päpləˈtēəs\ *n, pl* **poplit·ei** \-ē,ī\ [NL, fr. L *poplit-, poples* ham of the knee] **:** a flat muscle extending from the outer condyle of the femur to the tibia and forming part of the floor of the popliteal space

**pop·o·crat** \ˈpäpə,krat\ *n* -S *usu cap* [*populist* + *democrat*] **:** a Democrat supporting Populist policies in the last decade of the 19th century — usu. used disparagingly

**pop off** *vi* [¹*pop*] **1 a :** to leave suddenly ⟨*popped off* to town without telling anyone⟩ **b :** to die unexpectedly ⟨*popped off* at the age of forty⟩ **2 :** to talk without thinking often loudly or angrily ⟨*popping off* about taxes⟩

**pop–off** \ˈ=,=\ *n* -S [¹*pop* + *off*] **1 :** one who talks loosely or loudly ⟨is glib, volcanic . . . a *pop-off* —*Kiplinger Washington Letter*⟩ **2** *ceramics* **:** a small bit of defective enamel that loosens during drying or firing

**po·poi** \ˈpō,pȯi\ *n* -S [Marquesan] **:** a food of the Marquesas islands similar to Hawaiian poi but commonly made of both fresh and preserved cooked and pounded breadfruit

**po·po·lo·ca** \,pōpəˈlōkə\ *or* **po·po·lo·co** \-lō(,)kō\ *n, pl* **popoloca** *or* **popolocas** *or* **popoloco** *or* **popolocos** *usu cap* [MexSp, fr. Nahuatl *popoloca*] **1 a (1) :** a Popolocan people of southern Pueblo, Mexico **(2) :** a member of such people **b :** the language of such people **2 :** CHOCHO **3 :** POPOLUCA **4 :** XINCA

**po·po·lo·can** \-lōkən\ *n* -S *usu cap* [*Popoloca* + *-an*] **:** a language family of the states of Oaxaca and Pueblo in Mexico comprising Popoloca and Chocho

**po·po·lu·ca** \,pōpəˈlükə\ *n, pl* **popoluca** *or* **popolucas** *usu cap* [MexSp, alter. of *popoloca*] **1 a :** a Zoquean people of southern Vera Cruz, Mexico **b :** a member of such people **2 :** the language of the Popoluca people

**po·po·ti·llo** \,pōpəˈtē(,)(y)ō\ *n* -S [MexSp, a gnetaceous plant, fr. Nahuatl *popotl* broom] **:** MORMON TEA

**popover** \ˈ=,==\ *n* -S [¹*pop* + *over*] **:** a quick bread made from a thin batter of eggs, milk, and flour and subjected in the first stage of baking to such heat that steam expands it into a hollow shell

**po·po·vets** \pəˈpȯvəts\ *n, pl* **po·pov·tsy** \-ōftsē\ *usu cap* [Russ, fr. *popov-* (pl. stem of *pop* priest) + *-ets* agent suffix — more at BEZPOPOVETS] **:** a member of one of the major groups of the Raskolnik in Russia which maintains the hierarchical structure of episcopate and priesthood and is thereby distinguished from the priestless branch of the Bezpopovtsy — compare BEZPOPOVETS

**pop·pa** \ˈpäpə\ *n* -S [by alter.] **:** PAPA

**pop·pa·ble** \ˈpäpəbəl\ *adj* [¹*pop* + *able*] **:** capable of being popped ⟨~ corn⟩

**pop–paw** \ˈpä,pȯ\ *dial var of* PAPAW

**pop·pe·an** \ˈpäpēən\ *adj* [irreg. fr. *poppy* + *-an*] **:** of or relating to the juice of the poppy

**popped** *past of* POP

**pop·per** \ˈpäpə(r)\ *n* -S [¹*pop* + *-er*] **1 :** one that pops (as a firearm) **2 a :** a utensil for popping corn **b :** a corn variety suitable for popping **3 :** ²POP 5a **4 :** CRACKER 2b

**pop·pet** \ˈpäpət, *usu* -əd·+V\ *n* -S [ME *popet* — more at PUPPET] **1** *chiefly Brit* **:** LITTLE ONE, DEAR **2 a** *Midland* **:** DOLL **b** *obs* **:** MARIONETTE **3 a :** an upright support or guide of a machine that is fastened at the bottom only (as a lathe poppethead) **b** *or* **poppet valve :** LIFT VALVE **4 a :** one of the timber supports at the forward and after ends of a ship that form part of the launching cradle **b :** any of the small pieces of wood on a boat's gunwale supporting or forming the oarlocks

**poppethead** \ˈ==,=\ *n* [*poppet* + *head*] **1 :** a lathe tailstock or sometimes headstock **2** *Brit* **:** the headframe of a mining shaft

**pop·pied** \ˈpäpēd\ *adj* [*poppy* + *-ed*] **1 :** growing or overgrown with poppies **2 :** drugging or sleep-inducing like poppy juice **:** characterized by somnolence **:** DROWSY, INDOLENT ⟨fleeting ~ afternoons —Elizabeth Lomax⟩

**popping** *adj* [fr. pres. part. of ¹*pop*] **1 :** protruding or seeming to protrude **:** BULGING ⟨before the ~ eyes of the men at the ship's rail —T.W.Wall⟩ **2 :** INTERMITTENT, OCCASIONAL, SPORADIC ⟨the patrol was pinned down by ~ fire from a small clump of woods⟩ **3 :** full of action **:** LIVELY **:** able to pop

**popping crease** *n* [fr. gerund of ¹*pop*] *cricket* **:** a line 4 feet in front of and parallel with either bowling crease that marks the forward limit of the batsman's ground

**¹pop·ple** *also* **po·ple** \ˈpäpəl\ *n* -S [ME *popul, popil*, fr. OE *popul*, fr. L *populus*] *chiefly dial* **:** POPLAR 1 ⟨the country is big, wide, open with . . . clumps of ~ —W.F.Brown b. 1903⟩

**²popple** *also* **pople** \ˈ"\ *vi* -ED/-ING/-S [ME *poplen*, prob. of imit. origin] **1 :** to heave or toss about ⟨small trembling waves *poppled* and frothed in midstream —R.F.Burton⟩ **2 :** to bob about on or as if on agitated waters

**³popple** *also* **pople** \ˈ"\ *n* -S **1 :** a heaving of water (as from boiling or from the wind) ⟨no sound but the ~ of water against the bow —Joyce Cary⟩ **2 :** a choppy sea

**⁴popple** \ˈ"\ *dial Brit var of* POPPY

**pop·ply** \ˈpäp(ə)lē\ *adj* -ER/-EST [³*popple* + *-y*] **:** CHOPPY

**pop·py** \ˈpäpē, -pi\ *n* -ES [ME *popi*, fr. OE *popig, popæg*, modif. of (assumed) VL *papavum* (whence OF *pavo*), alter. of L *papaver*; perh. akin to L *papula* papule] **1 :** any of numerous annual, biennial, and perennial herbs or rarely subshrubs of *Papaver* or sometimes of closely related genera having showy flowers usu. of white or shades of red or yellow and including many that are cultivated as ornamentals of which the annuals are derived chiefly from the opium and corn poppies and the perennials from the Oriental poppy, alpine poppy, and Iceland poppy — see CAPSULE illustration **2 a :** an extract from the poppy used in medicines **b :** something possessing the narcotic qualities of the poppy **3** *or* **poppy red :** a strong reddish orange that is redder and lighter than paprika and redder and deeper than fire red, scarlet vermilion, or average coral red **4 :** POPPYHEAD

poppy

**poppy anemone** *also* **poppy anemony** *n* **:** a perennial tuberous European herb (*Anemone coronaria*) widely cultivated for its red, blue, or white scapose flowers

**poppy ash** *n* **:** a water ash (*Fraxinus caroliniana*)

**poppy bee** *n* **:** a leaf-cutting bee (*Osmia papaveris*) which lines its cells with pieces of poppy petals

**pop·py·cock** \ˈpäpē,käk, -pi,-\ *n* -S [D dial. *pappekak*, lit., soft dung, fr. D *pap* pap + *kak* dung, fr. *kakken* to void excrement, fr. L *cacare* — more at CACK] **:** empty talk **:** foolish nonsense **:** BOSH

**poppy day** *n, usu cap P&D* **:** a day on which contributions for war veterans are solicited and artificial red poppies are given to the contributors

**poppy family** *n* **:** PAPAVERACEAE

**poppyfish** \ˈ==,=\ *n* **:** HARVEST FISH a

**poppyhead** \ˈ==,=\ *n* **:** a raised ornament often in the form of a finial generally used on the tops of the upright ends or elbows terminating seats in Gothic churches

**poppy mallow** *n* **:** a plant of the genus *Callirrhoë*; *esp* **:** a showy often cultivated plant (*C. involucrata*) with palmately or pedately cleft leaves and red flowers borne throughout the summer

**poppy seed** *n* **:** the seed of the poppy and esp. of the opium poppy used as a food (as in bakery products) and as the chief source of poppy-seed oil — compare ⁶MAW

**poppy–seed oil** *also* **poppy oil** *n* **:** a pale to reddish drying oil obtained from the seeds esp. of the opium poppy and used chiefly as a food, in artist's colors, and in soap

poppyhead

**poppy show** *n* [alter. of *puppet show*] *chiefly dial* **:** PUPPET SHOW

**poppywort** \ˈ≈,≈\ *n* [*poppy* + *wort*] **:** a plant of the family Papaveraceae

**popquiz** *n* [²*pop*] **:** a quiz given without previous announcement or opportunity for preparation

¹**pops** *pl of* POP, *pres 3d sing of* POP

²**pops** *var of* POP

**popshop** \ˈ≈,≈\ *n* [¹*pop* + *shop*] *Brit* **:** PAWNSHOP

**Pop·s·icle** \ˈpäpsəkəl, -sēk-\ *trademark* — used for a confection made of water, flavoring, and coloring frozen on a stick without stirring

**popskull** \ˈ≈,≈\ *n* [¹*pop* + *skull*] *chiefly Midland* **:** inferior or cheap whiskey

**pop·sy** \ˈpäpsē\ *n* -ES [⁴*pop* + *-sy*] **:** GIRL, GIRL FRIEND, SWEETHEART

**pop–the–whip** \ˈ≈≈ˈ≈\ *n* [¹*pop*] **:** CRACK-THE-WHIP

**pop·u·lace** \ˈpäpyələs, *chiefly in southern U S* -pəl-\ *n* -S [MF, fr. It *popolaccio* rabble, pejorative of *popolo* the people (fr. L *populus*)] **1 :** the common people **:** the rank and file without wealth or position ("the quality" . . . had to rub shoulders with the general ~ —W.S.Clark) **2 :** the total number of people or inhabitants ⟨the ~ insists that this is the most beautiful town —Phil Stong⟩

**pop·u·la·cy** \-sē\ *n* -ES [alter. (influenced by *aristocracy*) of *populace*] *archaic* **:** POPULACE

¹**pop·u·lar** \-lə(r)\ *adj* [L *popularis* of the people, fr. *populus* the people (prob. of Etruscan origin) + *-aris* -ar] **1 :** relevant to any of the people ⟨~ action at law⟩ **2 a :** of or relating to the general public **:** constituted or carried on by the people ⟨its few noble horsemen . . . even in those days did not like ~ rebellions —Tom Wintringham⟩ ⟨in times of ~ panic . . . freedom of speech becomes important —Zechariah Chafee⟩ **b** (1) **:** of, relating to, or by the people (as of a nation or state) as a whole as distinguished from a specific class or group ⟨choosing the president by ~ suffrage rather than by majority vote of the assembly —*Current Biog.*⟩ ⟨~ government⟩ (2) **:** of, favoring, or involving participation by the common people as distinguished from a specific class or group ⟨the ~ party in provincial elections⟩ ⟨a truly ~ revolution⟩ (3) **:** based upon or alleged to be based upon the will of the people **:** involving or held to involve participation by all or the great majority of the people ⟨the Roman constitution . . . was ~ in form —J.A.Froude⟩ ⟨communist ~ democracies⟩ (4) **:** representing and usu. chosen by vote of the common people as distinguished from a specific class or group ⟨the House of Commons, not the House of Lords, is the ~ branch of the British parliament⟩ ⟨electing truly ~ representatives —*Hindustan Times*⟩ ⟨a ~ assembly⟩ **3 a** *obs* **:** being of low birth **:** PLEBEIAN **b** *archaic* **:** having low tastes **4 a :** adapted to or indicative of the understanding and taste of the majority **:** easy to comprehend **:** not abstruse, complicated, or profound **:** requiring no specialized knowledge or training to appreciate ⟨publishes excellent ~ and technical bulletins —*Amer. Guide Series: N.Y.City*⟩ ⟨drama . . . took on a more ~ form, being frequently enacted outside the churches —O.Elfrida Saunders⟩ ⟨the difficulty of writing ~ science —T.H.Savory⟩ **b :** suited to the financial means of the majority of people **:** moderate in cost **:** INEXPENSIVE ⟨there was room for a weekly journal at a ~ price —John Buchan⟩ ⟨charcoal, a ~ fuel for cooking —*Amer. Guide Series: Fla.*⟩ **5 :** marked by attempts to gain general goodwill or to curry favor at large ⟨the hypocritical ~ first acts of the usurper⟩ **6** *obs* **:** thickly inhabited **:** CROWDED, POPULOUS **7 a :** having wide or general currency esp. among the rank and file **:** PREVALENT, WIDESPREAD **:** frequently encountered or widely accepted ⟨a ~ instead of an accurate and legal conception —O.W.Holmes †1935⟩ ⟨the use of . . . homespun medicines declines, but some of the more ~ are still used —*Amer. Guide Series: Ark.*⟩ ⟨the ~ conviction that there is a poetic vision of things —Samuel Alexander⟩ **b :** well liked or admired by a particular group or circle ⟨campsites . . . are ~ with deer hunters and trout fishermen —*Amer. Guide Series: Nev.*⟩ **8 :** commonly liked or found pleasant or praiseworthy **:** APPROVED **:** given general praise, enthusiasm, liking, or support ⟨the lucidity and brevity that make a first-class ~ orator —*Times Lit. Supp.*⟩ ⟨book hotel reservations well in advance at all the most ~ places —Richard Joseph⟩ ⟨triumphantly ~ without the slightest effort on his own part —Elinor Wylie⟩ **9 :** originating among or composed or transmitted by the people, esp. by the unlettered ⟨for in all times and places, there have been ~ arts of song, dance, storytelling —John Dewey⟩ **syn** see COMMON

²**popular** \"\ *n* -S *archaic* **:** ⁶POP 1

**popular action** *n* **:** an action to recover a penalty given by a statute to anyone who sues for it — compare QUI TAM

**popular etymology** *n* **:** FOLK ETYMOLOGY

**popular front** *n, often cap P&F* **:** a working coalition of leftist and sometimes middle-of-the-road political parties against a common opponent (as fascism); *specif* **:** one sponsored and dominated by Communists as a device for gaining power ⟨ally Laborites with Communists in a *Popular Front* —*Time*⟩ ⟨official opposition to a *Popular Front* —*Manchester Guardian Weekly*⟩ ⟨Chile was ruled by a *popular front* government —W.L.Schurz⟩

**pop·u·lar·i·ty** \,≈≈ˈlarəd·ē, -rətē, -i *also* -ler-\ *n* -ES [¹*popular* + *-ity*] **1** *obs* **:** democracy as a principle or a form of government **2** [L *popularitat-, popularitas,* fr. *popularis* popular + *-itat-, -itas* -ity] **:** the act or means of currying favor with the populace ⟨the fixed professional ~ of a hotelkeeper's wife —*Saturday Rev.*⟩ **3 :** the quality or state of being popular **:** the manifest approval or esteem of many persons or of people in general ⟨his gift of friendship and charm soon won him . . . affection and ~ —F.J.Mather⟩ **4** [obs. F *popularité*, fr. LL *popularitat-, popularitas,* fr. L *popularis* of the people + *-itat-, -itas* -ity — more at POPULAR] *archaic* **:** POPULACE

**pop·u·lar·iza·tion** \,≈≈lərəˈzāshən, -,rīˈ-\ *n* -S **1 :** an act of popularizing or the state of being popularized ⟨with the ~ of the buggy . . . a demand rose for light harness —V.S.Clark⟩ **2 :** something that is popularized; *esp* **:** a publication in terms comprehensible to the average man ⟨divides the true folk tale from the ~ and that in turn from the work of art —*Yale Rev.*⟩

**pop·u·lar·ize** \ˈ≈≈lə,rīz\ *vb* -ED/-ING/-S *see -ize in Explan Notes* [¹*popular* + *-ize*] *vi* **:** to cater to popular taste ⟨insisted on a high scholastic standard; he would not ~⟩ ~ *vt* **:** to make popular: as **a :** to gain approval for **:** cause to be liked or esteemed ⟨done everything to ~ an art gallery —R.M. Yoder⟩ ⟨*popularized* literacy throughout . . . Latin America —Jerome Ellison⟩ ⟨credited with having *popularized* the island as a resort for artists —*Amer. Guide Series: Maine*⟩ **b :** to present (as a subject) in a form intelligible or interesting to those not specialists or trained thinkers ⟨synthesized a great deal of scholarship, *popularizing* . . . its results —S.C.Chew⟩ — **pop·u·lar·iz·er** \-zə(r)\ *n* -S

**pop·u·lar·ly** *adv* **:** in a popular manner ⟨science cannot be at once accurately and ~ reported —F.L.Mott⟩

**popular song** *n* **:** a song of wide appeal that is easily performed and memorized and usu. has a relatively brief vogue — compare FOLK SONG

**popular sovereignty** *n* **1 :** a doctrine in political theory that sovereignty is vested in the people as a whole rather than in a particular individual or group (as a ruling dynasty) and as a result that government is created by and subject to the will of the people ⟨establish the doctrine of *popular sovereignty* as the foundation of modern Europe — *Times Lit. Supp.*⟩ — compare LIMITED 2, MAJORITY RULE, SOCIAL CONTRACT **2 :** a principal doctrine of the pre-Civil War controversy over slavery specifying that the people of a territory like the people of a state should be free to regulate their domestic concerns without Congressional interference; *specif* **:** the doctrine asserting the right of the people living in a newly organized territory to decide by vote of their territorial legislature whether or not slavery would be permitted in the territory

**pop·u·late** \ˈ≈≈,lāt, *usu* -ād·+V\ *vb* -ED/-ING/-S [ML *populatus,* past part. of *populare* to people, fr. L *populus* people — more at POPULAR] *vt* **1 :** to have a place in **:** make up the population of **:** INHABIT, OCCUPY ⟨the galaxies *populating* the space of the universe —George Gamow⟩ ⟨characters created . . . to ~ his novel —John McCarten⟩ **2 :** to furnish or provide with inhabitants **:** PEOPLE ⟨the large rooms seemed well *populated* —E.C.Marston⟩ ⟨very heavily *populated* with all forms of wildlife —J.B.Robson⟩ ~ *vi* **:** to become populous **:** PROPAGATE

**pop·u·la·tion** \,≈≈ˈlāshən\ *n* -S [LL *population-, populatio,* fr. L *populus* people + *-ation-, -atio,* -ation] **1 a :** the whole number of people or inhabitants occupying a specific geographical locality (as an institution, a country, a world) ⟨when in operation, the building will have a daily ~ of 35,000 —*Pencil Points*⟩ ⟨the entire adult male ~ of the island except for two old men —Thor Heyerdahl⟩ **b :** the total number or amount of things esp. within a given area ⟨the tractor ~ of American farms increased —*Reporter*⟩ ⟨an enormous ~ of china, ivory, and bronze figures —Osbert Lancaster⟩ **2 :** the act or process of populating ⟨encourage ~ of colonies⟩ **3 a :** a body of persons having some quality or characteristic in common and usu. thought of as occupying a particular area ⟨a floating ~ of drifters and rogues⟩ ⟨a healthy rural ~⟩ **b** (1) **:** the organisms inhabiting a particular area or biotope ⟨an interesting xerophilic ~⟩ ⟨the Southern states have shown an average increase . . . in their beef ~s —*N.Y.Times*⟩ (2) **:** a group of interbreeding biotypes that represents the level of organization at which speciation begins — compare RACIATION **4** *math* **:** a group of individual persons, objects, or items from which samples are taken for measurement statistically — **pop·u·la·tion·al** \,≈≈ˈlāshənᵊl, -shnəl\ *adj*

**population dynamics** *n pl but sing or pl in constr* **1 :** a branch of knowledge concerned with the sizes of populations and the factors involved in their maintenance, decline, or expansion **2 :** the sequence of population changes characteristic of a particular organism

**pop·u·la·tion·ist** \,≈≈ˈlāsh(ə)nəst\ *n* -S [*population* + *-ist*] **1 :** an advocate of population control (as Malthusianism) **2 :** DEMOGRAPHER

**population pressure** *n* **:** the sum of the factors (as increase in numbers or excessive consumption of available food) arising within a population that reduce the ability of an environment to support the population and that therefore tend to result in migration and expansion of range or in extinction or decline of the population

**pop·u·lin** \ˈpäpyələn\ *n* -S [F *populine,* fr. L *populus* poplar + F *-ine* -in] **:** a sweet crystalline glucoside $C_{20}H_{22}O_8$ found in aspen bark and leaves and poplar buds; benzoyl-salicin

**pop·u·lism** \ˈ≈≈,lizəm\ *n* -S *usu cap* [*populist* + *-ism*] **:** the political and economic doctrines advocated by the Populists

¹**pop·u·list** \-ləst\ *n* -S *usu cap* [L *populus* the people + E *-ist*] **1 :** a member of a U.S. political party formed in 1891 and active esp. in the presidential campaign of 1892 primarily to represent agrarian interests and to advocate the free coinage of silver and government control of monopolies **2 :** a member of a political party purporting to represent the rank and file of the people

²**populist** \"\ *also* **pop·u·lis·tic** \,≈≈ˈlistik, -tēk\ *adj, often cap* [¹*populist*] **:** of, relating to, or advocating Populism ⟨bitter attacks upon the Court were splashed in the *Populist* press —A.F.Westin⟩

**pop·u·los·i·ty** \,≈≈ˈläsəd·ē\ *n* -ES [L *populos*us + E *-ity*] *archaic* **:** POPULOUSNESS

**pop·u·lous** \ˈ≈≈ləs\ *adj* [L *populosus,* fr. *populus* people + *-osus* -ous — more at POPULAR] **1 :** teeming with people **:** densely populated **:** thickly settled ⟨this new and ~ community —Willa Cather⟩ ⟨one of the most prosperous and ~ areas of its size in the U. S. —R.F.Weld⟩ **2 a :** large in numbers **:** NUMEROUS ⟨the Navajos would be as ~ as we are now —Henry Miller⟩ **b :** filled to capacity **:** CROWDED ⟨these narrow streets were ~ with students —A.T.Quiller-Couch⟩ ⟨a large and ~ ship —Herman Melville⟩ **3 :** of or relating to the people **:** POPULAR — **pop·u·lous·ly** *adv*

**pop·u·lous·ness** *n* -ES **:** the quality or state of being populous

**pop·u·lus** \ˈ≈≈ləs\ *n, cap* [NL, fr. L, poplar] **:** a genus of trees (family Salicaceae) that is native to the northern hemisphere, that has resinous buds, numerous stamens, incised bracts, and elongated stigmas, and that is well known in cultivation — see POPLAR; compare SALIX

¹**pop–up** \ˈ≈,≈\ *n* -S [¹*pop* + *up*] **:** one that pops up: as **a :** POP FLY **b :** a slow high shot in a racket game usu. near the net

²**pop–up** \"\ *adj* **:** of, relating to, or having a device that pops up ⟨a *pop-up* toaster⟩ ⟨a *pop-up* valve⟩

**pop valve** *n* [¹*pop*] **:** POP SAFETY VALVE

**popweed** \ˈ≈,≈\ *n* [¹*pop* + *weed*] **1 :** a common bladderwort (*Utricularia vulgaris*) of Europe **2 :** BLADDER WRACK

**por** *abbr* **1** portion **2** portrait

**POR** *abbr, often not cap* **1** payable on receipt **2** pay on return

**-po·ra** \,pərə, ˈpōrə\ *n comb form* [NL, fr. L *porus* bodily passage, pore — more at PORE] **:** one or ones having (such) a passage or pore or (such or so many) passages or pores — chiefly in generic names ⟨*Heliopora*⟩ ⟨*Millepora*⟩

**por·al** \ˈpōrəl, ˈpȯr-\ *adj* [*pore* + *-al*] **:** of or relating to the body pores

**por·bea·gle** \ˈpȯ(r),bēgəl\ *or* **porbeagle shark** \"-\ *also* **pro·bea·gle** \ˈprō,bēgəl\ *n* -S [Corn *porgh-bugel*] **:** a voracious viviparous shark (*Lamna nasus,* syn. *L. cornubica*) of the north Atlantic and Pacific oceans having a pointed nose and a crescent-shaped tail and reaching a length of about eight feet

**porc** *abbr* porcelain

**por·cate** \ˈpȯr,kāt\ *or* **por·cat·ed** \-ād·əd\ *adj* [L *porca* drainage ditch + E *-ate* — more at FURROW] **:** having furrows broader than intervening ridges

**por·ce·lain** \ˈpōrs(ə)lən, -ōrs-, -ōəs-, -ȯ(ə)s- *sometimes* -sə-,lān\ *n* -S *often attrib* [MF *porcelaine* cowrie shell, porcelain (fr. the resemblance of its finish to the surface of the shell), fr. It *porcellana,* fr. *porcello* little pig, vulva (fr. L *porcellus,* dim. of *porcus* pig, vulva) + *-ana* -an; fr. the resemblance of the shell to the female pudenda — more at FARROW] **1 a :** a hard, fine-grained, nonporous, sonorous, and usu. translucent and white ceramic ware that has a hard paste body, is fired at a high temperature, and is used esp. for table and ornamental wares, industrial and chemical wares, and esp. formerly for dentures — compare ¹CHINA, EARTHENWARE, POTTERY, STONEWARE **b :** SOFT PASTE 2 **2 :** an article of porcelain

**porcelain ampelopsis** *also* **porcelain vine** *n* **:** a woody vine (*Ampelopsis brevipedunculata*) of eastern Asia with blue or lilac berries that suggest porcelain

**porcelain blue** *n* **:** a grayish blue that is greener and paler than electric or copenhagen and greener, lighter, and stronger than Gobelin

**porcelain cement** *n* **:** a substance (as equal parts of gutta-percha and shellac mixed at a gentle heat) for causing porcelain to adhere to porcelain when applied at elevated temperatures

**porcelain clay** *n* **:** KAOLIN

**porcelain crab** *n* **:** any of several anomuran crabs of the family Porcellanidae having a smooth porcelaneous carapace

**por·ce·lained** \-nd\ *adj* [*porcelain* + *-ed*] **:** coated with or resembling porcelain

**porcelain enamel** *n* **:** VITREOUS ENAMEL

**porcelain green** *n* **:** a moderate bluish green that is greener and paler than sea blue and greener and duller than Bremen blue

**por·ce·lain·ite** \-lə,nīt\ *n* -S [*porcelain* + *-ite*] **:** baked clay or shale found in burned-out coal mines

**por·ce·lain·iza·tion** \,pōrs(ə)lənəˈzāshən, -sə,lān-, -,nīˈz-\ *n* -S **:** the act or process of porcelainizing

**por·ce·lain·ize** \ˈ≈s(ə)lə,nīz\ *vt* -ED/-ING/-S [*porcelain* + *-ize*] **:** to convert into porcelain or something resembling it; *esp* **:** to fire a vitreous coating on (steel or other metal)

**porcelain jasper** *n* **:** porcellanite resembling jasper

**por·ce·lain·ous** \ˈ≈s(ə)lənəs, -sə,lān-\ *adj* [*porcelain* + *-ous*] **:** PORCELANEOUS

**porcelain paper** *n* **:** a heavy transparent paper used in novelties and greeting cards

**porcelain stone** *n* **:** CHINA STONE 1

**por·ce·la·neous** *or* **por·cel·la·neous** \ˌ≈səˈlānēəs\ *adj* [It *porcellana* porcelain + E *-eous*] **:** of, relating to, or resembling porcelain ⟨~ shells⟩ ⟨~ glass⟩

**por·ce·lan·ic** *or* **por·cel·lan·ic** \-ˈlanik\ *adj* [It *porcellana* + E *-ic*] *of rock* **:** resembling porcelain

**por·ce·la·nous** *or* **por·cel·la·nous** \ˈ≈sələnəs, ˌ≈sˈlānəs, (ˈ)≈ˈselən-\ *adj* [It *porcellana* + E *-ous*] **:** PORCELANEOUS

**por·ce·lit·er** \ˈ≈ˌlīd·ə(r)\ *n* -S [*porcelain* + *-ite* (commercial product) + *-er*] **:** a worker who bakes vitreous enamel on castings

**por·cel·lana** \,≈≈ˈlanə, -ˈlä-,-ˈlā-\ *n, cap* [NL, fr. It, porcelain — more at PORCELAIN] **:** a cosmopolitan genus of littoral porcelain crabs that is the type of the family Porcellanidae — **por·cel·la·ni·an** \ˌ≈≈ˈnēən\ *adj or n*

¹**por·cel·lanid** \ˌ≈≈ˈnəd\ *adj* [NL *Porcellanidae*] **:** of or relating to the Porcellanidae

²**porcellanid** \"\ *n* -S **:** a crustacean of the family Porcellanidae

**por·cel·la·ni·dae** \,≈≈ˈnə,dē\ *n pl, cap* [NL, fr. *Porcellana,* type genus + *-idae*] **:** a large family of anomuran crustaceans that resemble the true crabs and comprise the porcelain crabs and related forms

**por·cel·la·nite** \ˈ≈s(ə)lə,nīt\ *n* -S [G *porzellanit,* fr. *porzellan* porcelain (fr. It *porcellana*) + *-it* -ite] **:** a hard dense siliceous rock having the appearance of unglazed porcelain on fresh fractures

**por·cel·lio** \pȯrˈselē,ō\ *n, cap* [NL *Porcellion-, Porcellio,* fr. L, wood louse, sow bug, fr. *porcellus* little pig, dim. of *porcus* pig — more at FARROW] **:** an Old World genus of terrestrial isopods that is the type of the family Porcellionidae and includes one form (*P. scaber*) which has been introduced into the U. S.

**por·cel·li·on·i·dae** \≈,≈≈ˈänə,dē\ *n pl, cap* [NL *Porcellion-, Porcellio,* type genus + *-idae*] **:** a large and widely distributed family of terrestrial isopods with 2-jointed antennae

**porch** \ˈpō(ə)rch, -ȯ(ə)rch, -ōəch, -ȯ(ə)ch\ *n* -ES [ME *porche,* fr. OF, fr. L *porticus* portico, colonnade, fr. *porta* gate, entrance — more at FORD] **1 :** a covered entrance to a building usu. with a separate roof and often large enough to serve as an outdoor seating or walking space **:** VERANDA **2** *obs* **:** a covered walk **:** COLONNADE, PORTICO **3** *dial Eng* **a :** SIDE CHAPEL **b :** TRANSEPT **4 :** a place for waiting before entering **:** ENTRANCE, PASSAGE **syn** see BALCONY

**porch box** *n* **1 :** a box containing soil for growing flowers or ornamental plants on a porch — compare WINDOW BOX **2 :** an insulated box in which bottled milk is left in house delivery

**porch climber** *n* **:** CAT BURGLAR, SECOND-STORY MAN

**porched** \-cht\ *adj* [*porch* + *-ed*] **:** having a porch

**por·cine** \ˈpȯr,sīn, -,sēn, -sᵊn\ *adj* [L *porcinus* swinish, fr. *porcus* pig + *-inus* -ine — more at FARROW] **:** of, relating to, or suggesting swine ⟨a surly and ~ sprat of a man —T.B. Costain⟩ ⟨comparison between human and ~ pleasures —Lucius Garvin⟩ ⟨~ brucellosis⟩

**por·cine·ly** *adv* **:** SWINISHLY ⟨imperially and ~ filling his clothes and the great leather couch —R.P.Warren⟩

¹**por·cu·pine** \ˈpȯrkyə,pīn, *chiefly dial* -kə,p- *or* -kē,p-\ *n* -S *often attrib* [ME *porke despyne, porkepin,* fr. MF *porc espin,* fr. OIt *porcospino,* fr. L *porcus* pig + *spina* thorn, prickle — more at SPINE] **1 a :** any of various relatively large hystricomorph rodents having stiff sharp erectile bristles mingled with the hair of the pelage and constituting the Old World terrestrial family Hystricidae and the New World arboreal family Erethizontidae — see BRUSH-TAILED PORCUPINE, CANADA PORCUPINE, LONG-TAILED PORCUPINE **b :** ECHIDNA 1 **2 a** *or* **porcupine beater** *or* **porcupine roller :** any of various rollers or cylinders covered with wire pins, card clothing, or beater blades and used for fiber preparation or spinning processes **b :** any of various other toothed mechanical devices **3 :** HEDGEHOG 4b

porcupine

²**porcupine** \"\ *vt* -ED/-ING/-S **1 :** to cause to bristle **2 :** to prick with or as if with porcupine quills

**porcupine anteater** *n* **:** ECHIDNA 1

**porcupine boiler** *n* **:** a boiler with a central drum and radiating tubes

**porcupine crab** *n* **:** a spiny anomuran crustacean (*Lithodes hystrix*) of the coast of Japan that resembles a crab

**porcupine fish** *n* **:** any of various fishes of the family Diodontidae and esp. of the genus *Diodon* that are widespread in tropical seas and have flesh which is usu. regarded as inedible or poisonous

**porcupine grass** *n* **1 :** a tall stout grass (*Stipa spartea*) of the western U.S. that has grains with long hygroscopic awns which by their twisting and untwisting often penetrate the wool and even the flesh of sheep and that affords good forage and hay **2 :** SPINIFEX 2

**porcupine rat** *n* **:** SPINY RAT 1

**porcupine wood** *n* [so called fr. the resemblance of its markings to porcupine quills] **:** the outer wood of the coconut palm

**por·cu·pin·ish** \-nish\ *adj* **:** resembling a porcupine or the spines of one **:** DEFENSIVE, PRICKLY

¹**pore** \ˈpō(ə)r, -ȯ(ə)r, -ōə, -ȯ(ə)\ *vb* -ED/-ING/-S [ME *pouren, puren*] *vi* **1 :** to gaze intently or fixedly **:** look searchingly **:** STARE ⟨*pored* on her lovely and large brown eyes —Edmund Wilson⟩ ⟨those who ~ over the microscope —R.W. Morin⟩ **2 :** to devote oneself to attentive reading **:** be deep in study — used chiefly with *over* ⟨*pored* over every single page of that thick novel —H.W.Carter⟩ **3 :** to reflect or meditate steadily **:** PONDER — used with *on* or *upon* ⟨began to ~ upon religious problems —Cecil Sprigge⟩ **4** *archaic* **:** to peer nearsightedly ~ *vt* **:** to bring to some state by poring ⟨*pored* himself blind⟩ ⟨*pored* her eyes out over his letters⟩

²**pore** \"\ *n* -S [ME *poore, pore,* fr. MF *pore,* fr. L *porus,* fr. Gk *poros* passage, pore — more at FARE] **1 a :** a minute opening esp. in an animal or plant by which matter passes through a membrane **b :** the cross section of a vessel element or tracheid often including both lumen and wall **c :** GERM PORE **2 a :** a small interstice (as in stone) admitting absorption or passage of liquid **b :** such interstices indicating density ⟨a mineral's fine ~s⟩ **3 :** one of countless minute darkish dots mottling the sun

**-pore** \,pō(ə)r, -ȯ(ə)r, -ōə, -ȯ(ə)\ *n comb form* -S [L *porus* — more at PORE] **:** opening ⟨atriopore⟩ ⟨blastopore⟩ ⟨nephridiopore⟩

**pore canal** *n* [²*pore*] **:** any of the fine cylindrical channels traversing the cuticle of an insect and often containing a process of an epidermal cell

**pored** \-ō(ə)rd, -ȯ(ə)rd, -ōəd, -ȯ(ə)d\ *adj* [²*pore* + *-ed*] **:** having pores

**pore fungus** *or* **pore mushroom** *n* [²*pore*] **:** a fungus of the family Boletaceae or Polyporaceae distinguished by having the spore-bearing surface within tubes or pores — called also *polypore*

**po·rel·la** \pəˈrelə\ *n, cap* [NL, fr. L *porus* pore + *-ella*] **:** a genus of leafy liverworts (family Jungermanniaceae) having distinct and entire underleaves and lingulate to oblong lobules and sometimes placed in a separate family because of the characteristic incomplete dehiscence of the capsule

**pore multiple** *n* [²*pore*] **:** a radial row of two or more plant pores flattened at their points of contact so as to suggest several divisions of a single pore

**pore–plate** \ˈ≈,≈\ *n* [²*pore*] **:** an olfactory sense organ of an insect

**por·er** \-ōrə(r), -ȯrə(r)\ *n* -S [¹*pore* + *-er*] **:** one that pores ⟨the author . . . is no mere ~ over maps —H.J.Rose⟩

**porge** \ˈpȯrj\ *vt* -ED/-ING/-S [Judeo-Spanish *porgar,* fr. Sp *purgar* to purge, fr. L *purgare* — more at PURGE] **:** to make (a slaughtered animal) ceremonially clean by removal of the forbidden fat, veins, and sinews according to Jewish ritual

**porg·er** \-jər\ *n* -S **:** one that porges

**por·gy** *also* **por·gie** \ˈpȯrgē, ˈpȯ(ə)g- *sometimes* ˈpōg-\ *n, pl* **porgies** *also* **porgy** *or* **porgees** *or* **porgee** [alter. of *pargo*] **1 a :** a sparid food fish (*Pagrus pagrus*) that inhabits the Mediterranean and the Atlantic coasts of Europe and America, has a compressed oblong body and strong teeth in both jaws, and is crimson with blue spots — called also *red porgy* **b :** any of various other fishes of the family Sparidae (as a scup or pinfish) — see GRASS PORGY, JOLTHEAD PORGY **2 :** any of various teleost fishes of families other than Sparidae: as **a :** MARGATE **b :** any of several surf fishes **c :** MENHADEN

**pori** *pl of* PORUS

**po·ria** \ˈpōrēə\ *n, cap* [NL, fr. L *porus* pore + NL *-ia*] **:** a genus of pore fungi (family Polyporaceae) having sporophores that are flat or that resemble a crust — see TUCKAHOE

**po·ri·ci·dal** \ˌpōrəˈsīdᵊl\ *adj* [ISV *pori-* (fr. L *porus* pore) + *-cid-* (fr. L *caedere* to cut) + *-al* — more at CONCISE] **:** dehiscing through pores — see FRUIT illustration

**po·rif·era** \pəˈrif(ə)rə, pōˈr-\ *n pl, cap* [NL, fr. L *porus* pore + *-i-* + *-fera,* neut. pl. of *-fer* -ferous] **:** a phylum of primitive invertebrate animals comprising the sponges and having a cellular grade of construction without true tissue or organ formation but with the body permeated by canals and chambers through which a current of water flows and passes in its course through one or more cavities lined with choanocytes — **po·rif·er·al** \-rəl\ *adj* — **po·rif·er·an** \-rən\ *adj or n*

**po·rif·er·ous** \-rəs\ *adj* [L *porus* pore + E *-iferous*] **1 :** provided with pores **2** [NL *Porifera* + E *-ous*] **:** of or relating to the Porifera

**po·ri·form** \ˈpōrə͵fȯrm\ *adj* [L *porus* pore + E *-iform*] **:** resembling a pore

**po·ri·na** \pəˈrīnə, -rēnə\ *or* **porina grub** *n* -s [NL] **:** a subterranean caterpillar destructive to turf in New Zealand

**poriness** *n* -ES [*pory* + *-ness*] *obs* **:** POROSITY

**¹poring** *adj* [fr. pres. part. of ¹*pore*] **:** PEERING

**²poring** *n* -s [ME *pouring*, fr. gerund of *pouren* to pore] **:** an act of peering or gazing intently

**po·ri·on** \ˈpōrē͵än\ *n, pl* **po·ria** \-ēə\ *or* **porions** [NL, fr. Gk *poros* passage + *-ion*, dim. suffix — more at FARE] **:** the midpoint on the upper margin of the external auditory meatus

**po·ri·tes** \pəˈrīd·(͵)ēz\ *n, cap* [NL, fr. L *porus* pore + NL *-ites*] **:** a genus (the type of the family Poritidae) comprising important reef-building corals with 12-rayed calyculi and a very dense skeleton that is branched or massive and globular

**¹po·ri·toid** \pəˈrīd·͵ȯid, -rid·-\ *adj* [NL *Poritidae* family of corals (fr. *Porites*, type genus + *-idae*) + E *-oid*] **:** like or related to the family Poritidae

**²poritoid** \"\ *n* -s **:** a poritoid coral

**pork** \ˈpō(ə)rk, -ȯ(ə)rk, -ōək, -ȯ(ə)k\ *n* -s *often attrib* [ME *pork, porke*, fr. OF *porc* pig, hog, fr. L *porcus* — more at FARROW] **1 :** the fresh or salted flesh of swine when dressed for food **2** *archaic* **:** HOG, SWINE **3 :** money grants, public works, or government jobs used by politicians as patronage with more regard to political advantage than to the public good ⟨talk about economy out of one side of their mouths while voting for ~ out of the other —*Newsweek*⟩

**pork barrel** *n* **:** a government project or appropriation yielding rich patronage benefits ⟨it would create an enormous *pork barrel* which, under a politically minded secretary of agriculture, would have incalculable political potency —Raymond Moley⟩

**pork-barreling** \ˈ=͵===\ *n* -s **:** the promotion of political pork barrels ⟨keeps his hold on his constituents through unashamed *pork-barreling*, busying himself getting federal money for bridges, roads, buildings, and military installations —*Newsweek*⟩

cuts of pork: *1* hind foot, *2* ham, *3* fatback, *4* loin, *5* side, *6* Boston butt, *7* picnic ham, *8* jowl, *9* forefoot

**pork·bur·ger** \ˈ=͵bərgər\ *n* -s [*pork* + *-burger*] **1 a :** ground pork **b :** a cooked patty of ground pork **2 :** a sandwich consisting of a patty of porkburger in a split round bun

**pork butcher** *n* **1 :** one that butchers hogs **2 :** a dealer in pork and pork products

**pork·chop·per** \ˈ=͵chäpə(r)\ *n* [*pork chops*, labor-union slang for economic benefits + *-er*] **:** a labor-union officer regarded by fellow unionists as motivated chiefly by self-interest

**pork·er** \-kə(r)\ *n* -s [*pork* + *-er*] **:** HOG; *esp* **:** a young pig fattened for table use as fresh pork — compare BACON HOG

**pork·et** \-kət\ *n* -s [ONF, dim. of OF *porc* pig — more at PORK] **:** a young pig **:** PORKER

**porkfish** \ˈ=͵=\ *n, pl* **porkfish** *or* **porkfishes** [*pork* + *fish*] **:** a black yellow-striped grunt (*Anisotremus virginicus*) of the western Atlantic from Florida to Brazil

**pork·ish** \-kish\ *adj* **:** SWINISH

**pork·ling** \-kliŋ\ *n* -s **:** a young pig **:** PIGLET

**pork measles** *n pl but sing or pl in constr* **:** infestation of muscles and esp. those of swine with cysticerci of the pork tapeworm

**porkpie** \ˈ=͵=\ *or* **porkpie hat** *n* [so called from its resemblance in shape to a pork pie] **:** a felt, straw, or cloth hat for informal wear having a low telescoped crown, flat top, and brim turned up all around or up in back and down in front

porkpie

**pork tapeworm** *n* **:** an armed tapeworm (*Taenia solium*) that infests the human intestine as an adult, has a cysticercal larva that typically develops in swine, and is contracted by man through ingestion of the larva in raw or imperfectly cooked pork

**¹porky** \ˈpōrkē, -ȯrk-, -ōək-, -ȯ(ə)k-, -ki\ *adj* -ER/-EST **:** of or relating to pork; *esp* **:** FAT, GREASY

**²por·ky** \ˈpȯrkē, ˈpȯ(ə)k-, -ki\ *n* -ES [*porcupine* + *-y*] **:** PORCUPINE

**por·noc·ra·cy** \pȯ(r)ˈnäkrəsē\ *n* -ES [Gk *pornē* harlot + *-cracy* — more at PORNOGRAPHY] **:** government by harlots

**por·no·crat** \ˈpȯ(r)nə͵krat\ *n* -s [fr. *pornocracy*, after such pairs as E *democracy*: *democrat*] **:** a member of a pornocracy

**por·no·graph** \ˈpȯ(r)nə͵graf, -ráf\ *n* [F *pornographe*, fr. Gk *pornographos* writing of harlots — more at PORNOGRAPHY] **1 :** PORNOGRAPHER **2** [Gk *pornē* + E *-graph*] **:** a pornographic picture or writing

**por·nog·ra·pher** \pȯ(r)ˈnägrəfə(r)\ *n* -s [Gk *pornographus* + E *-er*] **:** one that produces pornography

**por·no·graph·ic** \͵pȯ(r)nəˈgrafik, -fēk\ *adj* [*pornography* + *-ic*] **:** of or relating to licentious art or literature **:** pandering to base appetite or desire **:** descriptive or suggestive of lewdness **:** OBSCENE ⟨only the prurient could consider the sequence ~ —A.L.Mayer⟩ ⟨merely gross, a scatological rather than a ~ impropriety —Aldous Huxley⟩ — **por·no·graph·i·cal·ly** \-fək(ə)lē, -fēk-, -li\ *adv*

**por·nog·ra·phy** \pȯ(r)ˈnägrəfē, -fi\ *n* -ES [Gk *pornographos* writing of harlots (fr. *pornē* harlot + *-graphos* writing) + E *-y* — more at PAIR, -GRAPH] **1 :** a description of prostitutes or prostitution **2 :** a depiction (as in writing or painting) of licentiousness or lewdness **:** a portrayal of erotic behavior designed to cause sexual excitement — compare EROTICA

**poro-** *comb form* [Gk *poros* pore] **:** pore ⟨*porogamy*⟩

**po·ro·ceph·a·li·a·sis** \͵pōrō͵sefəˈlīəsəs\ *n, pl* **porocephaliases** [NL, fr. *Porocephalus* + *-iasis*] **:** infestation with or disease caused by a linguatulid worm of the family Porocephalidae

**po·ro·ce·phal·i·da** \-͵səˈfalədə\ *n pl, cap* [NL, fr. *Porocephalus* + *-ida*] **:** an order of tongue worms that have the female genital pore posterior and include all the tongue worms that parasitize mammals and some parasites of reptiles — compare LINGUATULA, POROCEPHALIDAE

**po·ro·ce·phal·i·dae** \-͵dē\ *n pl, cap* [NL, fr. *Porocephalus*, type genus + *-idae*] **:** a family of tongue worms (order Porocephalida) having cylindrical bodies and occurring as adults in the lungs of reptiles and as young in various vertebrates including man

**po·ro·ceph·a·lus** \-ˈsefələs\ *n, cap* [NL, fr. *poro-* + *-cephalus*] **:** the type genus of Porocephalidae

**po·ro·ches** \päˈrȯ͵kes\ *n* -ES [Yiddish *proykhes*, fr. Heb *pārokheth*] **:** PAROCHETH

**po·ro·cyte** \ˈpōrə͵sīt\ *n* -s [*poro-* + *-cyte*] **:** one of the large tubular cells that constitute the wall of the incurrent canals in some sponges

**po·ro·gam·ic** \͵pōrōˈgamik\ *or* **po·rog·a·mous** \(ˈ)pōrˈägəməs\ *adj* [*poro-* + *-gamic*, *-gamous*] **:** of, relating to, or marked by porogamy

**po·rog·a·my** \pōˈrägəmē\ *n* -ES [ISV *poro-* + *-gamy*; prob. orig. formed in G] **:** entrance of the pollen tube in a seed plant through the micropyle — compare CHALAZOGAMY

**po·ro·kai·whir·ia** \͵pōrō͵kī(h)wirēə\ *n* -s [Maori *porokaiwhiri*] **:** a small or shrubby New Zealand tree (*Hedycarya arborea*) of the family Monimiaceae with opposite short-petioled leaves and inconspicuous flowers in axillary panicles followed by bright red drupes

**po·rom·e·ter** \pəˈrämәd·ə(r)\ *n* [*poro-* + *-meter*] **:** an instrument for measuring the area of the stomatal openings of a leaf by the amount of a gas passing through a given area of it

**po·ro·plastic** \͵pōrō+\ *adj* [*porous* + *-o-* + *plastic*] **:** both porous and plastic — used of a special felt for splints, jackets, or comparable objects

**po·ro·po·ro** \ˈpōrō͵pōr(͵)ō\ *n* -s [Maori] *NewZeal* **:** KANGAROO APPLE

**po·ro·ro·ca** \͵pürəˈrōkə, ͵pōr-\ *n* -s [Pg, fr. Guarani] **:** a tidal bore esp. at the mouth of the Amazon

**po·ros** \ˈpōr͵äs\ *n* -ES [Gk *pōros* poros, chalkstone, bladder stone] **:** a coarse limestone found in the Peloponnesus and extensively used as a building material by the ancient Greeks

**po·ro·scope** \ˈpōrə͵skōp\ *n* [*poro-* + *-scope*] **:** an instrument for testing porosity

**po·ro·scop·ic** \͵pōrəˈskäpik\ *adj* [ISV *poroscopy* + *-ic*] **:** of or relating to poroscopy

**po·ros·co·py** \pəˈräskəpē\ *n* -ES [ISV *poro-* + *-scopy*] **:** examination of impressions left by the sweat pores of fingers to check or support fingerprint evidence

**po·rose** \ˈpōr͵ōs, ˈpȯ͵rōs\ *adj* [ML *porosus*, fr. L *porus* pore + *-osus* -ose] **:** POROUS; *specif* **:** divided into or so convoluted as to form a continuous series of pores ⟨a ~ hymenium⟩

**po·ro·sim·e·ter** \͵pōrōˈsimәd·ə(r)\ *n* [*porosity* + *-meter*] **:** an instrument for measuring porosity

**po·ro·sis** \pəˈrōsəs\ *n, pl* **poro·ses** \-ō͵sēz\ *or* **porosises** [NL, fr. L *porus* pore + NL *-osis*] **:** a condition (as of a bone) characterized by porosity; *specif* **:** rarefaction (as of bone) with increased translucency to X rays

**po·ros·i·ty** \pəˈräsəd·ē, pō-, pȯ-, -sətē, -i\ *n* -ES [ML *porositat-, porositas*, fr. *porosus* porous + L *-itat-, -itas* -ity] **1 :** the quality or state of being porous ⟨led to ~ and cracking in the weld zone —*Steel*⟩; *specif* **:** the ratio of the volume of interstices of a material to the volume of its mass ⟨the thimble has been made in two *porosities* —*Jour. of Research*⟩ **2 :** something that is porous **:** a porous part or area

**¹po·rot·ic** \pəˈräd·ik\ *n* -s [NL *poroticus* forming callus, fr. (assumed) Gk *pōrōtos* (verbal of Gk *pōroun* to harden, form callus, fr. *pōros* poros, chalkstone) + L *-icus* -ic] **:** a medicine favoring the formation of callus

**²porotic** \"\ *adj* [L *porus* pore + E *-otic*] **:** exhibiting or marked by porous structure or osteoporosis ⟨~ bone⟩ ⟨~ alteration of teeth⟩

**po·rous** \ˈpōrəs, ˈpȯr-\ *adj* [ME, fr. ML *porosus*, fr. L *porus* pore + *-osus* -ous] **1 a :** full of pores **:** capable of absorbing moisture **:** permeable by liquids **b :** possessing vessels or pores — compare DIFFUSE-POROUS, RING-POROUS **2 :** full of holes **:** INSUBSTANTIAL ⟨implications of such judgments are much too far-reaching to be attained by so ~ a procedure —T.A.Sebeok⟩ ⟨the largely unfenced international boundary . . . inevitably has been very ~ —Gladwin Hill⟩ — **po·rous·ly** *adv* — **po·rous·ness** *n* -ES

**porous cell** *or* **porous cup** *n* **:** a cylindrical vessel of porous earthenware used in an electrical cell to keep two liquids from mixing freely

**porous plaster** *n* **:** a commercial medicated plaster spread on perforated cloth

**por·pen·tine** \ˈpȯ(r)pən͵tīn\ *n* -s [by alter.] *obs* **:** PORCUPINE

**por·phin** \ˈpȯrfən\ *also* **por·phine** \", -͵fēn\ *n* -s [*porphyrin*] **:** a deep purple crystalline compound $C_{20}H_{14}N_4$ that is made synthetically from pyrrole and formaldehyde, contains four pyrrole rings joined by methenyl groups so as to give a heterocyclic arrangement, and forms the essential skeletal structure of the porphyrins, heme, and chlorophyll — compare STRUCTURAL FORMULA

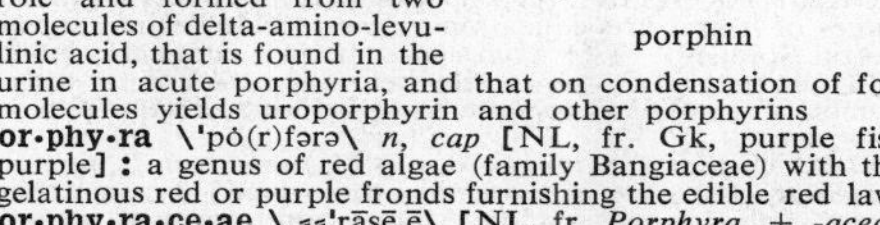

porphin

**porphobilinogen** *n* -s [prob. fr. *porphyrin* + *-o-* + *bili-* + *-in* + *-o-* + *gen*] **:** a dicarboxylic acid $H_2NCH_2(C_4H_2N)(CH_2COOH)CH_2CH_2COOH$ that is derived from pyrrole and formed from two molecules of delta-amino-levulinic acid, that is found in the urine in acute porphyria, and that on condensation of four molecules yields uroporphyrin and other porphyrins

**por·phy·ra** \ˈpȯ(r)fərə\ *n, cap* [NL, fr. Gk, purple fish, purple] **:** a genus of red algae (family Bangiaceae) with thin gelatinous red or purple fronds furnishing the edible red laver

**por·phy·ra·ce·ae** \͵==ˈrāsē͵ē\ [NL, fr. *Porphyra*, + *-aceae*] *syn of* BANGIACEAE

**por·phyr·a·tin** \pȯ(r)ˈfirətən\ *n* -s [*porphyrin* + *hematin*] **:** any of the complex compounds (as hematin) of porphyrins with metals

**por·phyr·ia** \pȯ(r)ˈfirēə, -fīr-\ *n* -s [NL, fr. ISV *porphyrin* + NL *-ia*] **:** a pathological state in man and some lower animals that is often due to genetic factors, is characterized by abnormalities of porphyrin metabolism, and results in the excretion of large quantities of porphyrins in the urine and in extreme sensitivity to light

**¹por·phyr·i·an** \(ˈ)pȯ(r)ˈfirēən\ *also* **por·phyre·an** \", ͵pȯ(r)fəˈrē-\ *adj, usu cap* [*Porphyry* 3d cent. A.D. Greek philosopher + E *-an*] **:** of or relating to the Neoplatonist Porphyry or his writings or doctrines — compare TREE OF PORPHYRY

**²porphyrian** \"\ *also* **por·phyr·i·an·ist** \-ənəst\ *n* -s *usu cap* **:** an adherent of Porphyry or of his doctrines

**porphyrian tree** *n, usu cap P* **:** TREE OF PORPHYRY

**por·phy·rin** \ˈpȯ(r)fərən\ *n* -s [Gk *porphyra* purple + ISV *-in*] **:** any of a group of reddish brown to purplish black metal-free usu. octa-substituted derivatives of porphin (as protoporphyrin or coproporphyrin) that emit an intense red fluorescence in ultraviolet light and are photosensitizing agents, that are components often in combination with proteins of most respiratory pigments of plants and animals and some enzymes (as cytochrome oxidase, catalase, and peroxidase), that are found in oil, shale, petroleum, asphalts, and coal, and that are obtained esp. from chlorophyll or hemoglobin

**porphyrine** *n* -s [Gk *porphyra* purple + ISV *-ine*] **:** an alkaloid $C_{21}H_{25}N_3O_2$ obtained as a bitter amorphous powder from Australian fever bark

**por·phy·rin·uria** \͵==rəˈn(y)ůrēə\ *n* -s [NL, fr. ISV *porphyrin* + NL *-uria*] **:** the presence of porphyrin in the urine

**por·phyr·io** \pȯ(r)ˈfirē͵ō\ *n* [NL, fr. L *porphyrion-, porphyrio* water hen, fr. Gk *porphyriōn*, fr. *porphyra* purple] **1** *cap* **:** a genus of birds (family Rallidae) consisting of the Old World purple gallinules **2** -s **:** any bird of the genus *Porphyrio*

**por·phy·rite** \ˈpȯ(r)fə͵rīt\ *n* -s [L *porphyrites* purple colored stone, porphyry, fr. Gk *porphyritēs* (*lithos*), fr. *porphyra* purple + *-itēs*, adj. suffix] **1 :** an Egyptian red porphyry **2 :** a quartz-free porphyry whose feldspar is plagioclase

**por·phy·rit·ic** \͵==ˈrid·ik\ *adj* [ML *porphyriticus*, fr. Gk *porphyritikos*, fr. *porphyritēs* (*lithos*) porphyry + *-ikos* -ic] **1 :** of or relating to porphyry ⟨a ~ column⟩ **2 :** having distinct crystals (as of feldspar, quartz, or augite) in a relatively fine-grained base that is often aphanitic, cryptocrystalline, or glassy — compare GROUNDMASS, PHENOCRYST — **por·phy·rit·i·cal·ly** \-d·ək(ə)lē\ *adv*

**por·phy·ro·blast** \pȯ(r)ˈfirə͵blast, ˈpȯ(r)fərō͵b-\ *n* [Gk *porphyra* purple + ISV *-blast*] **:** METACRYST — **por·phy·ro·blas·tic** \=͵==ˈblastik, ͵===ˈ-\ *adj*

**por·phy·ro·gene** \ˈ=ˈ==͵jēn, ˈ===͵-\ *n* -s [by shortening & alter.] **:** PORPHYROGENITE

**por·phy·rog·e·nite** \͵pȯ(r)fəˈräjə͵nīt, -fərōˈje͵n-\ *or* **por·phy·ro·gen·i·tus** \-fərōˈjenəd·əs\ *n, pl* **porphyrogenites** \-͵nīts\ *or* **porphyrogeniti** \-͵nə͵tī\ [ML *porphyrogenitus*, fr. MGk *porphyrogennētos*, fr. Gk *porphyra* purple + *gennētos* born, fr. *gennan* to bear; akin to Gk *gignesthai* to be born — more at KIN] **:** a son born after the accession of his father to the throne **:** one born in the purple

**por·phy·roid** \ˈpȯ(r)fə͵rȯid\ *n* -s [*porphyry* + *-oid*] **:** a more or less schistose metamorphic igneous or sedimentary rock with porphyritic texture

**por·phy·rop·sin** \͵pȯ(r)fəˈräpsən\ *n* -s [Gk *porphyra* purple + E *-opsin*] **:** a purple pigment in the retinal rods of freshwater fishes that resembles rhodopsin both biologically and chemically and differs structurally only in having an additional double bond in the molecule and that is bleached by light to opsin and the retinene related to vitamin $A_2$ and is regenerated in the dark

**por·phy·rous** \ˈpȯ(r)fərəs\ *adj* [Gk *-porphyros* having a purple color, fr. *porphyra* purple] **:** PURPLE

**por·phyr·oxine** \͵pȯ(r)fə͵r+͵-\ *n* [Gk *porphyra* purple + E *oxine*] **:** a crystalline opium alkaloid $C_{19}H_{23}NO_4$ whose solutions in dilute acid turn red on exposure to air

**por·phyr·u·la** \pȯ(r)ˈfir(y)ələ\ *n, cap* [NL, fr. Gk *porphyra* purple + NL *-ula*] **:** a genus of birds (family Rallidae) including the African and American purple gallinules

**por·phy·ry** \ˈpȯ(r)fərē, -ri\ *n* -ES [ME *porfurie*, fr. (assumed) AF *porfirie*, fr. ML *porphyrium*, alter. of L *porphyrites* — more at PORPHYRITE] **1 a :** an Egyptian rock consisting of feldspar crystals embedded in a compact dark red or purple groundmass much used by the ancient Romans — compare PORPHYRITE **b :** any igneous rock of porphyritic texture regardless of its mineral composition **c :** an igneous rock containing two generations of the same mineral with the minerals of one generation usu. distinctly larger than those of the other **d :** any of various igneous rocks without porphyritic texture that occur in connection with ores **2** *obs* **:** a porphyry slab; *esp* **:** one used for triturating drugs **3** *West* **:** PORPHYRY COPPER — usu. used in pl.

**porphyry copper** *n, West* **:** a large low-grade disseminated copper deposit

**porphyry shell** *n* **:** an olive shell (*Oliva porphyria*) having a dark-red or brown polished surface with light spots

**por·pi·ta** \ˈpȯ(r)pəd·ə\ *n, cap* [NL, fr. Gk *porpē* brooch; prob. akin to Gk *peirein* to pierce, *peran* to pass through — more at FARE] **:** a genus of small bright-colored siphonophores that float in the warmer parts of the ocean and have a large feeding zooid and a float in the center surrounded by smaller nutritive and reproductive zooids and by slender dactylozooids near the margin — **por·pi·toid** \-)pə͵tȯid\ *adj or n*

**¹por·poise** \ˈpȯrpəs, -ōəp-\ *n* -s [ME *porpeys, porpoys*, fr. MF *porpeis, porpois*, fr. ML *porcopiscus*, fr. L *porcus* pig + *piscis* fish — more at FARROW, FISH] **1 :** any of various small gregarious toothed whales of the genus *Phocaena* having a blunt rounded snout that does not form a projecting beak; *esp* **:** a common toothed whale (*P. phocaena*) of the north Atlantic and Pacific that is 5 to 8 feet long and usu. blackish above and whitish below — called also *harbor porpoise*; compare DOLPHIN 1a **2 :** any of various small toothed cetaceans; *esp* **:** any such cetacean with a short beak (as a member of the genus *Cephalorhynchus* of the southern hemisphere) **3 :** any of several dolphins (as the common dolphin or the bottle-nosed dolphins) **4 :** a synchronized swimming stunt consisting of a headfirst surface dive executed in either pike or tuck position to a point of complete vertical submergence

**²porpoise** \"\ *vi* -ED/-ING/-S **1 :** to leap or plunge like a porpoise ⟨penguins *porpoised* away on all sides —*Nat'l Geographic*⟩ **2** *of an underwater craft or object* **:** to break the surface of the water **:** BROACH **3** *of an airplane or surface craft* **:** to slap the surface **:** SKIP

**porpoise oil** *n* **:** a pale yellow fatty oil obtained from the body, head, or jaw of a porpoise and used esp. as a fine lubricant — compare DOLPHIN OIL

**porpoise whale** *n* **:** a New Zealand ziphioid whale (*Berardius arnuxi*)

**por·po·rate** \ˈpȯ(r)pərət\ *adj* [It *porporato*, fr. L *purpuratus*, fr. *purpura* purple + *-atus* -ate — more at PURPLE] **:** clad in purple

**por·ra·ceous** \(ˈ)pȯˈrāshəs, pəˈr-\ *adj* [L *porraceus*, fr. *porrum* leek + *-aceus* -aceous; akin to Gk *prason* leek] **:** having the clear light green color of leek leaves

**¹por·rect** \pəˈrekt, pȯˈr-\ *vt* -ED/-ING/-S [ME *porrecten*, fr. L *porrectus*, past part. of *porrigere* to stretch out, extend, fr. *por-* (akin to L *per* through) + *regere* to direct — more at FARE, RIGHT] **1** *archaic* **:** to put forward **:** stretch out **:** EXTEND **2 :** PRESENT, TENDER **3** *admiralty law* **:** to produce for examination (as a bill of costs) — **por·rec·tion** \-kshən\ *n* -s

**²porrect** \"\ *adj* [L *porrectus*] **:** extended forward **:** stretched out

**por·ret** \ˈpȯrət\ *n* -s [ME *poret*, fr. OF, fr. L *porrum* leek + OF *-et* — more at PORRACEOUS] **1** *chiefly dial* **:** LEEK, SCALLION **2** *chiefly dial* **:** a small onion **3 :** LEEK 2b

**por·ridge** \ˈpȯrij, ˈpär-, -rēj\ *n* -s [alter. (prob. influenced by ME *porray*, a kind of pottage, fr. MF *poree*, fr. ML *porrata*, fr. L *porrum* leek + LL *-ata* -ade) of *pottage*] **1 :** a soup of meat and vegetables often thickened with barley or other cereal **2 :** a soft food made by boiling meal of grains or legumes in milk or water until thick ⟨oatmeal ~⟩ ⟨bean ~⟩ **3 :** HODGEPODGE ⟨contemporary playwrights . . . produce only the thinnest ~ when they turn to undramatic prose —John Mason Brown⟩

**por·ridgy** \-jē,-ji\ *adj* **:** of, relating to, or resembling porridge ⟨a ~ modern wallpaper —Jan Struther⟩

**por·rin·ger** \-rənjə(r)\ *n* -s [alter. of *pottinger*] **1 :** a dish for porridge or similar food; *esp* **:** a low one-handled usu. metal bowl or cup from which children eat or are fed ⟨a silver ~⟩ **2 :** a hat or cap that resembles a porringer

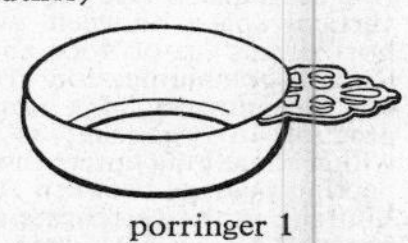

porringer 1

**por·ritch** \-rich\ *chiefly Scot var of* PORRIDGE

**por·ro prism** \ˈpȯ(͵)rō-\ *n, usu cap 1st P* [after Ignazio *Porro* †1875 Ital. engineer] **:** an optical device that inverts and reverses right and left an image viewed through it, that consists usu. of a pair of isosceles right-angled prisms so arranged that a beam of light entering the hypotenuse face of one is totally reflected twice before emerging at the same face and entering the second prism at its hypotenuse face and being again doubly reflected, and that makes possible a shortening of the physical length of the instrument in which it is used — see PRISM BINOCULAR

**¹port** \ˈpō(ə)rt, -ȯ(ə)rt, -ōət, -ȯ(ə)t, *usu* \|d· +V\ *n* -s [ME, partly fr. OE (fr. L *portus* passage, house door, port); partly fr. OF, fr. L *portus* — more at FORD] **1 a :** a place where ships may ride secure from storms **:** HARBOR, HAVEN ⟨wonder if so small a barque can . . . make the ~ —E.J.Schoettle⟩ **b** (1) **:** REFUGE (2) **:** DESTINATION, GOAL **2 a :** a harbor town or city where ships may take on or discharge cargo **:** the starting point or the destination of a voyage **:** a place to or from which goods may be shipped **b :** the entire geographical harbor area of a place ⟨the ~ of San Francisco⟩ **c :** AIRPORT ⟨the ~ is free of obstructions — no mountains or tall buildings impede an approach or takeoff —Cornelius Ryan⟩ **3 :** PORT OF ENTRY **syn** see HARBOR

**²port** \"\ *vt* -ED/-ING/-S **1** *obs* **:** to make port at **2** *obs* **:** to bring to port

**³port** \"\ *n* -s [ME *port, porte*, fr. MF *porte* gate, door, fr. L *porta* passage, gate; akin to L *portus* passage, port — more at FORD] **1** *chiefly Scot* **:** GATE, PORTAL; *esp* **:** a city gate **2** *chiefly Scot* **:** a market for hiring of laborers usu. held near the gate of a town **3 :** an opening or passageway between two woods or stones or between a wood and the jack in lawn bowling or curling **4 :** an upward curve or tongue groove in the mouthpiece of some bits to put pressure on the sensitive bars of a horse's mouth **5 a :** an opening for intake or exhaust of air, gas, steam, water, or other fluid esp. in a valve seat or valve face **b :** the area of opening in a cylinder face of a passageway for the working fluid in an engine **c :** any such passageway connecting the cylinder with the cylinder face or the latter with the exhaust **6 a :** an opening in a ship's side to admit light or air or to load cargo **:** PORTHOLE **b** *archaic* **:** the shutter or cover for a porthole **7 a :** an opening in the receiver of a firearm through which empty shells are ejected **b :** an opening in some repeating firearms through which cartridges are loaded into the magazine **8 :** a hole or slit in an armored vehicle or fortification through which guns may be fired

**⁴port** \"\ *n* -s [ME, fr. MF, fr. *porter* to carry, bear] **1 :** the manner in which one bears himself **:** BEARING, DEMEANOR, MIEN ⟨pride in their ~, defiance in their eye, I see the lords of humankind pass by —Oliver Goldsmith⟩ **2** *archaic* **:** manner or style of living **:** DIGNITY, STATE **3** *obs* **:** the action of carrying mail or the fee for it : POSTAGE **4** : the position in which a military weapon is carried when ported

**5port** \"\ *vb* -ED/-ING/-S [MF *porter* to carry, fr. L *portare* — more at FARE] *vt, obs* : CARRY, TRANSPORT ~ *vi, of a horse* : to paw the bedding and strike the floor with the forefeet — often used with *back*

**6port** \"\ *n* -S [prob. fr. ¹*port* or ³*port* (porthole)] : the left side of a ship or airplane looking forward : LARBOARD — opposed to *starboard*

**7port** \"\ *vt* -ED/-ING/-S : to turn or put (a helm or rudder) to the left

**8port** \"\ *adj* : of, relating to, or situated to port

**9port** \"\ *n* -S [fr. *Oporto, O Porto* (now Porto), city in Portugal] **1** : a fortified sweet wine of rich taste and aroma from the valley of the Douro, Portugal — see RUBY PORT, TAWNY PORT, VINTAGE PORT, WHITE PORT **2** : any of numerous wines originating in various parts of the world and resembling the port of Portugal in varying degrees ⟨California ~⟩ **3** : a very dark red that is slightly bluer than mulberry fruit

**10port** \"\ *n* -S [ScGael] *chiefly Scot* : a tune or air esp. on a bagpipe

**11port** \"\ *n* -S [by shortening] *Austral* : PORTMANTEAU

**port** *abbr* **1** portable **2** portfolio **3** portrait

**por·ta** \'pōrd·ə\ *n, pl* **por·tae** \-d·,ē, -d·,ī\ [NL, fr. L, gate — more at FORD] : HILUM 2a; *specif* : the transverse fissure of the liver — called also *porta hepatis*

**por·ta·bil·i·ty** \,pōr\|d·ə'bilad·ē, ,pó(r)\|, ,pōə\|, \|tə-, -lətē, -i\ *n* -ES : the quality or state of being portable

**1por·ta·ble** \'==,bəl\ *adj* [ME, fr. MF, fr. LL *portabilis*, fr. L *portare* to carry + *-abilis* -able — more at FARE] **1** : capable of being carried : easily or conveniently transported : light or manageable enough to be readily moved ⟨a ~ grill⟩ ⟨a ~ power drill⟩ **2** *obs* **a** : BEARABLE, SUPPORTABLE **b** : NAVIGABLE — **por·ta·bly** \-blē,-bli\ *adv*

**2portable** \"\ *n* -S : something portable: as **a** : a portable schoolhouse or other building **b** : a portable typewriter **c** : a portable radio or television set

portable b

**por·ta·ble·ness** *n* -ES : PORTABILITY

**por·ta·caval** \¦pōrd·ə+\ *also* **por·to·caval** \-rd·(,)ō+\ *adj* [²*portal* + *caval*] : extending from the portal vein to the vena cava

**portacaval shunt** *n* : a surgical shunt by which the portal vein is made to empty into the caval vein in order to bypass a damaged liver

**por·ta cipher** \¦pōrd·ə-\ *n, usu cap P* [after Giambattista della *Porta* †1615 Ital. physicist] : polyalphabetic substitution with reciprocal alphabets formed by sliding the second half of a normal alphabetic sequence against the first half

**1por·tage** \'pōr\|d·\|ij, 'pór\|, 'pōə\|, 'pó(ə)\|, \|t\|, \|ēj; *also* (')=¦täzh, -tȧzh\ *n* -S [ME, fr. MF, fr. *porter* to carry + *-age* — more at PORT] **1** : the labor of carrying or transporting ⟨force the proud young men, who ought to be warriors, to do ~, always considered woman's work —H.R.Collins⟩ **2 a** *obs* : a ship's burden : TONNAGE **b** *obs* : CARGO, FREIGHT **c** *archaic* : the cost of carriage : PORTERAGE 2 **3 a** *obs* : cargo carried for a sailor joining in a common adventure in lieu of all or part of his wages **b** *obs* : the space allotted for such cargo **c** *archaic* : a sailor's wages **4 a** : the carrying of boats or goods overland from one river or lake to another or around a rapids ⟨had to be carried over a canoe route 800 miles long with some 40 or more ~s —J.D.Leechman⟩ — called also *haulover* **b** : the route followed in making such a transfer ⟨a modest military post was established to protect the ~ —*Amer. Guide Series: La.*⟩

**2portage** \"\ *vb* -ED/-ING/-S *vt* : to make a portage with : CARRY, PACK ⟨where the falls were too angry we *portaged* our gear —Farley Mowat⟩ ~ *vi* : to make a portage ⟨we *portaged* six times —*Alaska Sportsman*⟩

**por·ta·gue** \'pōrd·ə,gyü\ *n* -S [irreg. fr. *portuguese*] : a Portuguese gold coin of the 16th century

**por·tail** \(')pōr¦tā(ə)l\ *n* -S [F, fr. MF *portal*] : PORTAL 2 a

**1por·tal** \'pōr\|d·ᵊl, 'pór\|, 'pōə\|, 'pó(ə)\|, \|tᵊl\ *n* -S [ME, fr. MF, fr. ML *portale* city gate, porch, fr. neut. of *portalis* of a gate, fr. L *porta* gate + *-alis* -al — more at FORD] **1** : DOOR, GATE, ENTRANCE; *esp* : a grand or imposing one **2 a** : the whole architectural composition surrounding and including the doorways and porches of a church ⟨the church door . . . is set in a remarkable ~ —M.C.A.Henniker⟩ **b** : a large roofed opening in a Spanish-American building : PORCH **c** : the corner of a room separated by wainscoting to form a short passage to another room **3 a** : the space between the first two principal trusses at each end of a trussed bridge **b** : any vertical space between two uprights included between two horizontals (as of floor and ceiling) which must be kept open for free communication in a building of skeleton construction **c** : the entrance to a tunnel **4** : a communicating part or area of an organism: as **a** : PORTAL VEIN **b** : the point at which something enters the body ⟨~s of infection⟩ **c** : the connecting passage between foregut and midgut and midgut and hindgut in the vertebrate embryo

**2portal** \"\ *adj* [NL *porta* + E *-al*] **1** : of or relating to the transverse fissure on the underside of the liver where most of the vessels enter **2** : of, relating to, carried out by, or being any large vein that collects blood from one part of the body and distributes it in another part through a capillary network — see PORTAL VEIN, RENAL PORTAL VEIN

**por·taled** *or* **por·talled** \-ᵊld\ *adj* [¹*portal* + *-ed*] : having a portal

**portal hypertension** *n* [²*portal*] : hypertension produced by the pressure from accumulated blood in the portal system usu. associated with cirrhotic changes in the liver and accompanied by the formation of hemorrhagic varices in the esophagus

**portal system** *n* : a system of veins that begins and ends in capillaries — compare PORTAL, PORTAL VEIN

**portal–to–portal** \¦==+==¦\ *also* **portal** *adj* [¹*portal*] : of or relating to the time spent by a workman in traveling from the entrance to his employer's property to his actual working place (as in a mine) and in returning after the work shift ⟨the basic work day was materially shortened by payment for travel time under the *portal-to-portal* principle —G.W. Stocking⟩

**portal vein** *n* [²*portal*] : a large vein formed by fusion of other veins that terminates in a capillary network and delivers blood to some area other than the heart; *specif* : a vein carrying blood from the digestive organs and spleen to the liver where the nutrients such blood carries are altered by liver cells before passing into the systemic circulation — called also *hepatic portal vein*; see RENAL PORTAL VEIN

**por·ta·men·to** \,pōrd·ə'men(,)tō\ *n, pl* **porta·men·ti** \-n(,)tē\ [It, lit., act of carrying, fr. *portare* to carry (fr. L) + *-mento* -ment — more at FARE] **1** : a continuous glide effected by the voice, a trombone, or a bowed stringed musical instrument in passing from one tone to another **2** : PORTATO

**por·tance** \'pōrtᵊn(t)s\ *n* -S [MF, fr. *porter* to carry + *-ance* — more at PORT] *archaic* : BEARING, CARRIAGE, DEMEANOR

**port arms** *n* [fr. the imper. phrase *port, arms*] : a position in the manual of arms in which the rifle is held diagonally in front of the body so that the barrel is at the left shoulder — often used as a command

port arms

**port ar·thur** \(')pōrd·¦ärthər\ *adj, usu cap P&A* [fr. *Port Arthur*, city in Manchuria] : of or from the city of Port Arthur, now forming part of Port Arthur-Dairen, Manchuria : of the kind or style prevalent in Port Arthur

**por·ta·tile** \'pōrd·ə,tīl\ *adj* [ML *portatilis*, fr. L *portatus* (past. part. of *portare* to carry) + *-ilis* -ile — more at FARE] : PORTABLE — used of an altar

**por·ta·tive** \'pōrd·əd·iv\ *adj* [ME *portatif*, fr. MF, fr. L *portatus* + *-if* -ive] : PORTABLE ⟨the ~ harp and chime —Virgil Thomson⟩

**portative organ** *n* : a small portable pipe organ formerly used in processions

**por·ta·to** \pōr'täd·(,)ō\ *n* -S [It, fr. *portato* (past part. of *portare* to carry), fr. L *portatus* — more at PORTATILE] : semidetached phrasing in musical performance

**port–au–prince** \¦pōrd·(,)ō¦prin(t)s, -¦praⁿs\ *adj, usu cap both Ps* [fr. *Port-au-Prince*, capital of Haiti] : of or from Port-au-Prince, the capital of Haiti : of the kind or style prevalent in Port-au-Prince

**port authority** *n* [¹*port*] : a governmental commission empowered to manage or construct port facilities

**port bow** *n* [⁸*port*] : the port surface of a ship's hull that curves inward to the stem — distinguished from *starboard bow*

**port captain** *n* [¹*port*] : an official of a steamship line responsible for its ships during their stay in port

**port charge** *n* : a fixed charge (as wharfage, towage, pilotage) against a ship or its cargo in port

**port·crayon** \(')pōrt+\ *n* [F *porte-crayon*, fr. *porter* to carry + *crayon* — more at PORT] *archaic* : a metal holder for a drawing or writing crayon

**1port·cul·lis** \pōrt'kələs\ *n* -ES [ME *portculis, port colice*, fr. MF *porte coleïce*, fr. OF — more at COULISSE] **1** : a large grating of iron bars or heavy timbers suspended by chains over the gateway of a fortified place and lowered between grooves to prevent passage **2** : a portcullis or a lattice used as a heraldic charge **3** : a silver halfpenny issued by Elizabeth I in 1599 having a portcullis on the obverse

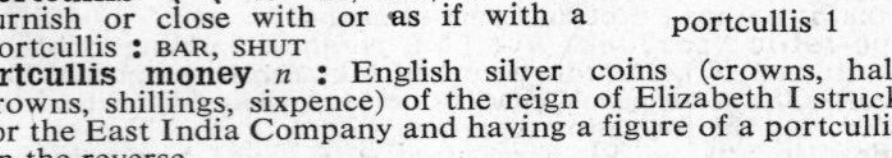

portcullis 1

**2portcullis** \"\ *vt* -ED/-ING/-ES : to furnish or close with or as if with a portcullis : BAR, SHUT

**portcullis money** *n* : English silver coins (crowns, half crowns, shillings, sixpence) of the reign of Elizabeth I struck for the East India Company and having a figure of a portcullis on the reverse

**port de bras** \¦pōrdə¦brä\ *n* [F, lit., carriage of the arm] : the practice and technique of arm movement in ballet

**port differential** *n* [¹*port*] : a differential between the freight rate from an inland point to a port and that to another port established as a basing point

**port du sa·lut** \¦pōrdəsə¦lü, -,sa¦-\ *n, usu cap P&S* [F *port-salut*, fr. *Port du Salut*, Trappist abbey in northwest France] : TRAPPIST CHEESE

**porte co·chere** \¦pōrtkō¦she(ə)r\ *n* -S [F *porte cochère*, lit. coach door] **1** *archaic* : a passageway through a building or screen-wall designed to let vehicles pass from the street to an interior courtyard **2** : CARRIAGE PORCH

**port·ed** \'pōrd·əd\ *adj* [³*port* + *-ed*] **1 a** : provided with a port **b** : shut in or closed by a gate **2** [fr. past part. of ⁵*port*] : held in the position of port — ⟨standing with rifles ~⟩

**porte·feuille** \¦pōrd·ə¦fər(·)\ *n* -S [F, fr. *porter* to carry + *feuille* leaf, sheet — more at PORT, FOIL] *archaic* : PORTFOLIO

**port eg·mont hen** \-'eg,mänt-\ *n, usu cap P&E* [fr. *Port Egmont*, Falkland islands] : a large skua (*Catharacta skua antarctica*) of the southern hemisphere

**port eliz·a·beth** \¦pōrd·ᵊl¦iz(ə)bəth\ *adj, usu cap P&E* [fr. *Port Elizabeth*, city in southern Union of So. Africa] : of or from the city of Port Elizabeth, Union of So. Africa : of the kind or style prevalent in Port Elizabeth

**porte–monnaie** \'pōrt,mənē, ='=; ¦pōrt_mo¦nā\ *n* -S [F, fr. *porter* to carry + *monnaie* coined money, fr. MF *moneie* — more at PORT, MONEY] : a small pocketbook or purse

**por·tend** \(')pōr¦tend, (')pó(ə)¦t- *also* (')pōr¦t- *or* (')pōə¦t-\ *vt* -ED/-ING/-S [ME *portenden*, fr. L *portendere* to foretell, predict, fr. *por-* (akin to L *per* through) + *tendere* to stretch — more at FARE, TEND] **1** : to give an omen or anticipatory sign of : BODE, PRESAGE ⟨~ at least the beginnings of tax relief for small business —*Nation's Business*⟩ ⟨that the appearance of the black pig ~s serious trouble in Ireland is generally believed —*Irish Digest*⟩ **2** : FORECAST, PREDICT ⟨where this process will stop no one can ~ —D.M.Friedenberg⟩ **3** : INDICATE, MEAN, SIGNIFY ⟨perhaps the present concern with the values of liberal arts education . . . ~s an intellectual anemia —Ann Spinney⟩ **4** [F *pourtendre*, fr. MF *portendre*, modif. of L *protendere*, fr. *pro* forth, before + *tendere* to stretch — more at FOR] *obs* : to stretch out before : EXTEND **syn** see FORETELL

**por·tent** \'=,tent *sometimes* ='=\ *n* -S [L *portentum*, fr. neut. of *portentus*, past part. of *portendere* to portend] **1** : something that foreshadows a coming event : OMEN, SIGN ⟨it is only natural that ~s should play a large part in the activities of crabbers, oystermen, and fishermen —*Amer. Guide Series: Md.*⟩ ⟨a hopeful ~ of the scope of discussion that may be expected to develop —Vera M. Dean⟩ **2** : prophetic indication, meaning, or significance ⟨something not yet clearly to be seen, but at least of hopeful ~ in the changing world —Martin Flavin⟩ **3** : MARVEL, PRODIGY, WONDER ⟨the old maps . . . and their ~s and monsters of the deep —Van Wyck Brooks⟩

**portentive** *adj* [L *portentus* + E *-ive*] *obs* : PORTENTOUS

**por·ten·tous** \(')=¦tentəs, *sometimes* ÷ -nchəs\ *adj* [L *portentosus*, fr. *portentum* portent + *-osus* -ous] **1** : of, relating to, or constituting a portent : pregnant with consequence or possibility ⟨the events under discussion are ~ —Philip Hamburger⟩ **2** : eliciting amazement or wonder : MARVELOUS, MONSTROUS, PRODIGIOUS ⟨the extraordinary old man gave him a second ~ wink —J.C.Powys⟩ **3** : exhibiting gravity or ponderousness : self-consciously weighty : INFLATED, POMPOUS ⟨a voice that manages to be both cozy and ~ —Gilbert Seldes⟩ ⟨regarded all these things with a ~ solemnity —H.G. Wells⟩ ⟨the style is so ~ that one expects up to the last paragraph that something of moment is about to be revealed —Dachine Rainer⟩ **syn** see OMINOUS

**por·ten·tous·ly** *adv* : in a portentous manner ⟨~, . . . the panting engines began to roll slowly toward each other —*Time*⟩

**por·ten·tous·ness** *n* -ES : the quality or state of being portentous

**por·te·ous roll** \'pōrtēəs-\ *or* **porteous** *n* -ES [ME *porthors, portous, portes*, portable breviary, manual, fr. OF *portehors*, fr. *porter* to carry + *hors* out, fr. L *foris*; akin to L *fores* door — more at PORT, DOOR] *Scots law* : a roll of offenders formerly prepared by the justice clerk

**1por·ter** \'pōr\|d·ər, 'pór\|d·ə(r, 'pōə\|d·ə(r, 'pó(ə)\|d·ə(r, \|tə-\ *n* -S [ME, fr. OF *portier*, fr. LL *portarius*, fr. L *porta* gate + *-arius* -ary — more at FORD] **1** *chiefly Brit* : a person stationed at a door or gate to admit or assist those entering ⟨at the entrance to the office block was a ~ in a blue uniform —F.W.Crofts⟩ **2** : DOORKEEPER 2

**2porter** \"\ *n* -S [ME *portour*, fr. MF *porteour*, fr. LL *portator*, fr. L *portatus* (past part. of *portare* to carry) + *-or* — more at FARE] **1** : one who carries burdens: as **a** : one who is employed to carry baggage for patrons at a hotel or transportation terminal **b** : a handler of cargo **c** *archaic* : one that conveys or carries something (as news or disease) **2** : a parlor-car or sleeping-car attendant who waits on passengers and makes up berths **3** [short for *porter's beer*; fr. its originally having been made for porters] : a weak stout that is rich in saccharine matter and contains about four percent of alcohol **4 a** *archaic* : any of various mechanical devices (as a lever or a wheeled carriage) for lifting, supporting, or moving **b** : a bar of iron or steel at the end of which a forging is made **5** *Scot* : ²BEER **6** : one who does routine cleaning of the premises, furniture, and equipment of a store, bank, school, or office building or cleans the working areas in a mill or factory **7** : BULL COOK

**3porter** \"\ *vb* -ED/-ING/-S *vt* : to transport or carry as or by a porter ~ *vi* : to act as a porter

**por·ter·age** \-ərij\ *n* -S [²*porter* + *-age*] **1** : the occupation or work of a porter : the carrying of things by human labor **2** : the charge for transportation by porter

**porteress** *var of* PORTRESS

**porterhouse** \'==,=\ *n* [²*porter* + *house*] **1** *archaic* : a house where porter and other malt liquors are sold **2** *also* **porterhouse steak** : a large steak cut from the thick end of the short loin and containing a T-shaped bone and a large piece of tenderloin — compare T-BONE; see BEEF illustration

**porterly** *adj* [²*porter* + *-ly*] *obs* : of, relating to, or resembling a porter : RUDE, VULGAR

**porter's chair** *n* [¹*porter*] : a chair with its back rising to form a hood and its sides enclosed against drafts

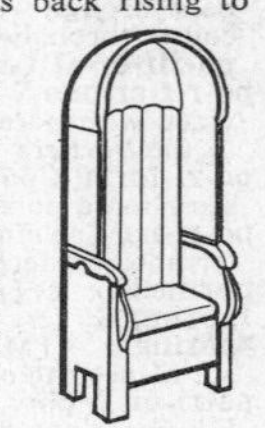

porter's chair

**portesse** *n* -S [alter. of ME *portes* — more at PORTEOUS ROLL] *obs* : BREVIARY 2a

**portfire** \'=,=\ *n* [part trans. of F *porte-feu* fr. *porter* to carry + *feu* fire — more at PORT] : a fuze or match for firing guns or fireworks: as **a** : a paper case filled with a composition of niter, sulfur, and mealed powder **b** : a slow-burning fuze (as a billet of wood impregnated with potassium nitrate) or an incendiary cord or tube for igniting fuzes of blasting charges

**port·fo·lio** \pōrt'fōlē,ō, pórt-, pōət-, pó(ə)t-, -fōl(,)yō\ *n* [alter. of earlier *porto folio*, modif. of It *portafoglio*, fr. *portare* to carry + *foglio* leaf, sheet, fr. L *folium* leaf — more at PORTAMENTO, BLADE] **1** : a flat portable case (as a briefcase, a large heavy envelope, or a loose-leaf binder) for carrying papers or drawings **2** [so called fr. the use of such a case to carry documents of state] : the office and functions of a minister of state or member of a cabinet ⟨received the ~ of war⟩ **3** : the securities held by an investor or the commercial paper held by a bank or other financial house ⟨expanded the mortgage ~⟩

**portfolio investment** *n* : investment by purchase of securities — contrasted with *direct investment*

**portgrave** *or* **portgreve** *var of* PORTREEVE

**por·thet·ria** \pō(r)'the·trēə\ *n, cap* [NL, fr. Gk *porthein* to destroy, ravage + *-tria*, fem. agent suffix; akin to Gk *perthein* to destroy, ravage — more at BOARD] : a genus of Lymantriidae including the gypsy moth

**por·theus** \'pōrthēəs, -,th(y)üs\ *n, cap* [NL, fr. Gk *porthein* + *-eus*, agent suffix] : a genus of extinct Cretaceous isospondylous fishes notable for their great size and strong teeth

**porthole** \'=,=\ *n* [³*port* + *hole*] **1** : an opening (as a window) in the side of a ship or airplane **2** : an embrasure or loophole through which to shoot **3** : ³PORT 5

**por·tia tree** \'pōrshə-\ *n, sometimes cap P* [Tamil *puraśu*] : a tropical tree (*Thespesia populnea*) that is closely related to the majaguas, has rounded cordate leaves and showy yellow and purple flowers, yields a valuable pinkish to dark red close-textured wood resistant to warping and an oil from its seeds, and is sometimes cultivated as an ornamental — called also *bendy tree, seaside mahoe, tulip tree*

**por·ti·co** \'pōr\|d\|ə,kō, 'pór\|, 'pōə\|, 'pó\|, \|t\|, \|ē,-\ *n, pl* **porticoes** *or* **porticos** [It, fr. L *porticus* — more at PORCH] : a colonnade or covered ambulatory esp. in classical architecture and usu. at the entrance of a building **syn** see BALCONY

**por·ti·coed** \-ōd\ *adj* [*portico* + *-ed*] : having a portico

**por·ti·cus** \-kəs\ *n* -ES [L] *archaic* : PORTICO

**por·tiere** \¦pōr\|d·ē¦e(ə)r, (')pōr\|ti¦e(ə)r, 'pōr\|d·ēər, (')pōr\|-¦tye(ə)r, -pór\|, -pōə\|, -pó(ə)\|, -eə,-iə,-ēə\ *n* -S [F *portière*, fr. fem. of OF *portier* doorkeeper — more at PORTER] : a curtain hanging across a doorway

**por·ti·fo·ri·um** \,pōrd·ə'fōrēəm\ *n, pl* **portiforiums** \-ēəmz\ *or* **portifo·ria** \-ēə\ [ML, fr. L *portare* to carry + *foris* out; akin to L *fores* door — more at FARE, DOOR] : BREVIARY 2a

**porting** *n* -S [³*port* + *-ing*] : the provision or arrangement of intake or exhaust openings or other ports on an engine

**por·tio** \'pōrshē,ō, -rd·ē-\ *n, pl* **porti·o·nes** \,pōrshē'ō(,)nēz, ,pōrd·ē'ō,nās\ [NL *portion-, portio*, fr. L, portion] : PART, SEGMENT, DIVISION ⟨the visible ~ of the cervix⟩

**1por·tion** \'pōrshən, -ór-, -ōə-, -ó(ə)-\ *n* -S [ME, fr. OF, fr. L *portion-, portio*; akin to L *part-, pars* part] **1** : an individual's part or share of something: as **a** : a share of an estate received by gift or inheritance ⟨Father, give me the ~ of goods that falleth to me —Lk 15: 12 (AV)⟩ **b** : DOWER 2a **c** : enough food to serve one person at one meal or enough of one kind for a helping ⟨individual ~s of meat were precisely weighed out in the restaurant kitchen⟩ **2** : the share of an individual or group in human fortune or destiny : LOT, FATE ⟨the preacher had told him hell would be his ~ —J.L.Lowes⟩ **3 a** : a part of a whole ⟨~s of this park are particularly well-adapted for picnic and camping purposes —*Amer. Guide Series: Md.*⟩ **b** : a limited amount or quantity ⟨the major ~ of our fears would be at an end —J.C.Fitzmaurice⟩ **4** : the weekly selection of the Pentateuch read in a synagogue — compare PARASHAH **syn** see FATE, PART

**2portion** \"\ *vt* **portioned**; **portioned**; **portioning** \-sh(ə)niŋ\ **portions** [ME *portionen*, fr. MF *portiouner*, fr. OF *portion* share, portion] **1** : to divide into portions : distribute in shares **2** : to allot or give to as a portion : DOWER, ENDOW **syn** see APPORTION

**portional** *adj* [ME, fr. LL *portionalis* partial, fr. L *portion-, portio* portion + *-alis* -al] **1** *obs* : PARTIAL **2** [¹*portion* + *-al*] *obs* : of, relating to, or constituting a portion or dowry

**por·tion·er** \-sh(ə)nə(r)\ *n* -S [partly fr. ²*portion* + *-er*, partly fr. ¹*portion* + *-er*] : one that portions or has a portion: as **a** *Scots law* : the owner of a portion of a decedent's estate : a small laird — see HEIR PORTIONER **b** : PORTIONIST 2

**por·tion·ist** \-sh(ə)nəst\ *n* -S [ML *portionista*, fr. L *portion-, portio* portion + *-ista* -ist] **1** : POSTMASTER 3 **2** : an incumbent of a benefice shared by two or more clergymen

**por·tion·less** \-shənləs\ *adj* : having no portion; *esp* : having no dowry or inheritance

**portion natural** *n* [¹*portion* + *natural*, adj.] *Scots law* : a child's legitim

**port jack·son fig** \-'jaksən-\ *n, usu cap P&J* [fr. *Port Jackson*, New So. Wales, Australia] : an Australian fig (*Ficus rubiginosa*) resembling the banyan, sometimes planted for ornament, and introduced into southern Africa for brushwood

**port jackson pine** *n, usu cap P&J* : an Australian cypress pine (*Callitris cupressiformis*) having globular cones with scales much dilated upward

**port jackson shark** *n, usu cap P&J* : a shark of the genus *Heterodontus*; *esp* : a small harmless shark (*H. japonicus*) of Australasian coastal waters that is brown to reddish brown and feeds chiefly on mollusks

**port·land** \'pōrtlənd, -órt-, -ōət-, -ó(ə)t-\ *adj, usu cap* **1** [fr. *Portland*, city in southwest Maine] : of or from the city of Portland, Maine ⟨*Portland* harbor⟩ : of the kind or style prevalent in Portland, Maine **2** [fr. *Portland*, city in northwest Oregon] : of or from the city of Portland, Oreg. : of the kind or style prevalent in Portland, Oreg.

**portland arrowroot** *or* **portland sago** \"-\ *n, usu cap P* [fr. Isle of *Portland*, peninsula in southern England] **1** : arum from the cuckoopint **2** : CUCKOOPINT

**portland blast–furnace slag cement** *n* [*portland cement*] : a cement produced by intimately intergrinding a mixture of portland cement clinker and granulated blast-furnace slag in widely varying proportions

**portland cement** *n* [fr. Isle of *Portland*; fr. its resemblance to Portland stone] : a hydraulic cement made by finely pulverizing the clinker produced by calcining to incipient fusion a mixture of argillaceous and calcareous materials — see ALUMINA CEMENT; compare AIR ENTRAINMENT, NATURAL CEMENT, PORTLAND BLAST-FURNACE SLAG CEMENT

**port·land·er** \'=ləndə(r)\ *n* -S *cap* [*Portland* + *-er*] : a native or resident of Portland, Oreg. or Portland, Me.

**port·land·ite** \-,dīt\ *n* -S [*portland* (*cement*) + *-ite*] : CALCIUM HYDROXIDE

**portland–pozzolan cement** \¦==¦==-\ *n* [*portland cement* + *pozzolana*] : a portland cement to which pozzolana is added during the grinding of the cement clinker

**portland stone** *n* [fr. Isle of *Portland*, peninsula in southern England, its locality] **1** *usu cap P* : a yellowish white oolitic building limestone **2** *usu cap P* [fr. *Portland*, town in southern Connecticut, its locality] : a purplish brown sandstone **3** *often cap P* : LIGHT STONE

**portland tern** *n* : ARCTIC TERN

**port·last** \'pōrt,last\ *n* -S [origin unknown] : the upper edge of a gunwale : a bulwark rail — called also *portoise*

**portledge** *n* [alter. (perh. influenced by *privilege*) of *portage*] *obs* : PORTAGE 3

**port·let** \'=lət\ *n* -S [¹*port* + *-let*] : a small harbor

**portlight** \'=,=\ *n* [³*port* + *light*] **1** : the glass pane in a ship's

porthole **2 :** a glass-paned porthole that admits light but cannot be opened **:** DEADLIGHT
**port·li·ness** \ˈpōrtlēnəs, -ȯrt-, -ōət-, -ȯ(ə)t-, -lin-\ *n* -ES **:** the quality or state of being portly
**port·ly** \-lē, -li\ *adj* [⁴*port* + *-ly*] **1** *chiefly dial* **:** DIGNIFIED, STATELY **2 :** heavy or rotund of body **:** CORPULENT, STOUT ⟨the plump figure and ~ waist were those of a genial and humorous man —J.R.Green⟩ ⟨their history has been padded out in ~ volumes —Edward Clodd⟩ **syn** see FAT
**port mac·quar·ie pine** \ˌ=mə¦kwórē-\ *n, usu cap 1st P&M* [fr. *Port Macquarie*, New So. Wales, Australia] **:** an Australian sandarac tree (*Callitris macleayana*)
**port·man** \ˈ=mən\ *n, pl* **portmen** [ME, fr. OE, fr. ¹*port* + *man*] **:** an inhabitant or burgess of a port
¹**port·man·teau** \pōrtˈmant(ˌ)ō, pȯrt-, pōət-,pȯt-, -maan-, -n,tō\ *n, pl* **portmanteaus** *or* **portmanteaux** \-ōz\ [MF *portemanteau*, fr. *porter* to carry + *manteau* mantle, fr. L *mantellum* — more at PORT] **:** TRAVELING BAG; *esp* **:** a large bag of the gladstone type
²**portmanteau** \=ˈ=(ˌ)=, ˈ=,=,=\ *adj* **:** combining more than one use or quality ⟨a ~ signature which covers a husband-and-wife collaboration —George Milburn⟩ ⟨its central character is a ~ figure whose traits are derived from several mythical heroes —D.G.Hoffman⟩
**portmanteau word** *also* **portmanteau** *n* **1 :** ³BLEND d **2 :** COUNTERWORD
**port·man·tle** \ˈpōrt,mantᵊl, =ˈ==\ *n* [part trans. of F *portmanteau*] *archaic* **:** PORTMANTEAU
**port·man·tol·o·gism** \ˌpōrt,manˈtälə,jizəm, -ˌmən-\ *n* -s [*portmanteau* (*word*) + *log-* + *-ism*] **:** ³BLEND d
**portmantua** *n, obs* [by alter.] **:** PORTMANTEAU
**port mark** *n* [¹*port*] **:** a mark showing the final destination of a shipping package
**portmote** *or* **portmoot** \ˈ=,=\ *n* [*portmote* fr. ML *portimotus*, fr. OE *port* + *gemōt* gemot; *portmoot* fr. *port* + *moot*] **:** the court of an English borough or seaport; *also* **:** a town administrative assembly
**pôrto** *adj, usu cap* [Pg] **:** OPORTO
**pôr·to ale·gre** \ˌpōrd·ōə¦legrə\ *adj, usu cap P&A* [fr. *Pôrto Alegre*, seaport city of southern Brazil] **:** of or from the city of Pôrto Alegre, Brazil **:** of the kind or style prevalent in Pôrto Alegre
**portocaval** *var of* PORTACAVAL
**port of call** [¹*port*] **1 :** an intermediate port where ships customarily stop for supplies, repairs, or transshipment of cargo **2 :** a stop included on an itinerary; *esp* **:** a place habitually visited
**port of discharge :** a port where a ship voluntarily and without cause of necessity breaks bulk and discharges part or all of its cargo
**port of entry 1 :** a place where foreign goods may be cleared through a customhouse **2 :** a place where an alien may be permitted to enter a country
**port-of-spain** \ˌ==¦=\ *adj, usu cap P&S* [fr. *Port of Spain*, seaport in northwest Trinidad] **:** of or from the city of Port of Spain, Trinidad **:** of the kind or style prevalent in Port of Spain
**por·toise** \ˈpȯrdəs, -ōz\ *n* -s [origin unknown] **:** PORTLAST
**por·to·lan** \ˈpōrd·ᵊlən\ *or* **por·tu·lan** \", -rchəl-\ *n* -s [It *portolano*] **:** PORTOLANO
**por·to·la·no** \ˌpōrd·ᵊlˈä(ˌ)nō\ *n, pl* **portolanos** \-oz\ *or* **portola·ni** \-nē\ [It, harbor official, pilot, navigation manual, fr. ML *portulanus*, harbor official, fr. L *portus* port] **:** a medieval navigation manual illustrated with charts
**por·to-no·vo** \ˌpōrd·ō¦nō(ˌ)vō\ *adj, usu cap P&N* [fr. *Porto-Novo*, seaport town in Dahomey] **:** of or relating to Porto-Novo, the capital of Dahomey **:** of the kind or style prevalent in Porto-Novo
**port or·ford cedar** \-ˈȯ(r)fə(r)d-\ *n, usu cap P&O* [fr. *Port Orford*, Curry co., Oregon] **1 :** a large evergreen timber tree (*Chamaecyparis lawsoniana*) of western No. America occas. with a trunk diameter of 12 feet and often 200 feet high **2 :** the light pale yellow to brown decay-resistant lumber of Port Orford cedar
**porto rican** *usu cap P&R, var of* PUERTO RICAN
¹**por·trait** \ˈpōr·trə̇t, ˈpȯr-, ˈpōə-, ˈpȯ(ə)-, -,trāt, *usu* \d.+V\ *vt* -ED/-ING/-S [prob. fr. obs. *portrait* portrayed, fr. ME, fr. MF, past part. of *pourtraire* to portray — more at PORTRAY] *archaic* **:** PORTRAY
²**portrait** *n* -S [MF, fr. past part. of *portraire* to portray] **1 :** PICTURE; *esp* **:** a painting, drawing, or other pictorial representation of a person usu. showing his face ⟨the best-known photographic ~s of internationally important personages —*Current Biog.*⟩ **2 :** a sculptured figure **:** BUST, STATUE ⟨has modeled some notable ~s of women —*Current Biog.*⟩ **3 :** a visible representation or likeness **:** IMAGE, SIMILITUDE ⟨seemed a veritable ~ of his father⟩ **4 :** a graphic portrayal in words **:** a verbal description ⟨such ~s reveal as clearly as the longer poems his weight of intellect —*Ency. Americana*⟩ ⟨show that in the final analysis the primary purpose of fiction is not education, not history, not even a ~ of truth, but the entertainment of the reader —F.O.Baker⟩
**portrait attachment** *n* **:** an attachment lens used on a fixed-focus camera for photographing near objects
**portrait bust** *n* **:** a bust representing the actual features of an individual
**por·trait·ist** \|d·əst, |tə-\ *n* -s [²*portrait* + *-ist*] **:** a maker of portraits (as in painting, photography, or sculpture)
**portrait lens** *n* **:** a compound photographic lens with a relatively high aperture and usu. a means for softening definition esp. in taking portraits
¹**por·trai·ture** \-,trə,chu̇(ə)r, -,chər, -trə-,tyu̇(ə)r, -trə,tu̇(ə)r, -ůə, -chə\ *n* -s [ME *portreitoure*, fr. MF *portraiture*, fr. *portrait* + *-ure*] **1 :** the making of portraits by painting, drawing, photography, or otherwise **:** PORTRAYAL **2 a :** a portrait in graphic art **b :** a sculptured portrait **3 :** depiction in words **:** verbal description ⟨faithfulness in the . . . ~ depends upon the individual writer's art —Wilfred Partington⟩ **4** *obs* **:** APPEARANCE, FORM, SHAPE
²**portraiture** \"\ *vt* -ED/-ING/-S *archaic* **:** PORTRAY
¹**por·tray** \(ˈ)pōr¦trā, (ˈ)pȯr¦-, (ˈ)pȯ(ə)¦- *also* pə(r)ˈt-\ *vt* -ED/-ING/-S [ME *portraien*, fr. MF *portraire*, fr. L *protrahere* to draw forth, to reveal, expose, fr. *pro* forth, before + *trahere* to draw — more at FOR, DRAW] **1 :** to represent by a drawing, painting, engraving **:** make a picture or image of **:** DELINEATE, DEPICT ⟨~s with sure but sparing brush strokes an unforgettable face⟩ **2 a :** to describe in words **:** present a verbal picture of ⟨a novelist who ~s life the way most of us see it —Bernice Matlowsky⟩ **b :** to play the role of **:** represent dramatically **:** ENACT ⟨a star who unquestionably conveyed to audiences the very essence of the character he was ~ing —J.F. Wharton⟩ **syn** see REPRESENT
²**portray** \", =ˈ=\ *n* -s *archaic* **:** PORTRAYAL, PORTRAIT
**por·tray·al** \=ˈtrā(ə)l *sometimes* ˈpōr-,-, ˈpȯr-,-, ˈpōə-,-, ˈpȯ(ə)-,-\ *n* -s [¹*portray* + *-al*] **1 :** the act or process of portraying **:** DESCRIPTION, REPRESENTATION **2 :** PORTRAIT
**por·tray·er** \(ˈ)=¦trāə(r), -re(ə)r, -reə\ *n* -s [ME, fr. *portraien* to portray + *-er*] **:** one that portrays
**por·tray·ment** \-rāmənt\ *n* -s [¹*portray* + *-ment*] **:** PORTRAYAL
**port·reeve** \ˈpōrt,rēv\ *or* **port·grave** \-t,grāv\ *or* **port·greve** \-t,grēv\ *n* -s [*portreeve* fr. ME *portereve*, *portreve*, fr. OE *portgerēfa*, fr. *port* + *gerēfa* reeve; *portgreve*, ME, alter. (influenced by OE *portgerēfa*) of *portreve; portgrave*, alter. (influenced by MD *portgrave* portreeve) of *portgreve*] **1 :** a bailiff or mayor charged with keeping the peace and with other duties in a port or market borough of early England **2 :** the chief officer of a seaport town
**por·tress** \ˈpōr·trə̇s\ *also* **por·ter·ess** \-ōrd·ərə̇s, -ōr·trə̇s\ *n* -ES [ME *porteresse*, fr. *porter* + *-esse* -ess] **:** a female porter: as **a :** a doorkeeper in a convent or apartment house **b :** CHARWOMAN
**port risk insurance** *n* [¹*port*] **:** marine insurance covering a ship while in port
**port roy·al·ist** \pōrt-ˈrȯiələst\ *n, usu cap P&R* [F *port-royaliste*, fr. *Port-Royal*, name of a convent near Versailles, France + *-iste* -ist] **:** a member or adherent of a 17th century French Jansenist lay community distinguished as logicians and educators
**ports** *pl of* PORT, *pres 3d sing of* PORT
**port said** \(ˈ)=¦sīd *also* ¦=sä¦ēd *sometimes* (ˈ)=¦sād\ *adj, usu cap P&S* [fr. *Port Said*, seaport city in northeast Egypt] **:** of or from the city of Port Said, Egypt **:** of the kind or style prevalent in Port Said
**port sa·lut** \ˌpȯrsə¦lü, -ˌsa¦-\ *n, usu cap P&S* [F *port-salut*, fr. *Port du Salut*, Trappist abbey in northwest France] **:** TRAPPIST CHEESE
**portside** \ˈ=,=\ *adj* [⁸*port* + *side*] **:** LEFT, LEFTIST ⟨the same ~ political tack —*Newsweek*⟩
**port·sid·er** \ˈ=ˌsīd·ə(r)\ *n* [⁸*port* + *side* + *-er*] **:** SOUTHPAW
**ports·man** \ˈpōrtsmən\ *n, pl* **portsmen** [Cinque *Ports*, group of seaport towns in southeast England + E *man*] **:** an inhabitant or citizen of one of the English Cinque Ports
**ports·mouth** \ˈpōrtsməth, -ȯrt-, -ōət-, -ȯ(ə)t-\ *adj, usu cap* [fr. *Portsmouth*, seaport and county borough in southern England] **:** of or from the county borough of Portsmouth, England **:** of the kind or style prevalent in Portsmouth
**port speed** *n* [¹*port*] **:** the speed with which a ship's cargo is handled
**port tack** *n* [⁸*port*] **:** the tack on which the wind comes from a sailing ship's port side
**por·tu·gais** \ˌpōrchə¦gā\ *n* -ES [F, Portuguese, fr. Pg *português*] **:** BLACK ANGELFISH
**por·tu·gal** \ˈpōr|chə̇gəl, ˈpȯr|, ˈpōə|, ˈpȯ(ə)|, -chēg-\ *adj, usu cap* [fr. *Portugal*, country in southwest Europe] **:** of or from Portugal **:** of the kind or style prevalent in Portugal **:** PORTUGUESE
**portugal laurel** *n, usu cap P* **:** a European evergreen shrub (*Prunus lusitanica*) with handsome foliage and white flowers
**portugee** \ˈpōrd·ə,gē, -d·ē,gē\ *n, usu cap* [back-formation fr. ²*Portuguese*, pl.] *substand* **:** PORTUGUESE
¹**por·tu·guese** \ˌpōr|chə¦gēz, ¦pȯr|, ¦pōə|, ¦pȯ(ə)|\ *adj, usu cap* [Pg *português*, fr. *Portugal* + *-ēz* -ese] **1 a :** of, relating to, or characteristic of Portugal **b :** of, relating to, or characteristic of the people of Portugal **2 :** of, relating to, or characteristic of the Portuguese language
²**portuguese** \"\ *n, pl* **portuguese** *cap* **1 a :** a native or inhabitant of Portugal **b :** a person of Portuguese descent **2 :** the Romance language of Portugal and Brazil
**portuguese bowline** *n, usu cap P* **:** a bowline knot having a large double bight producing two loops often used for hoisting a person as if in a chair seat by running one loop under the arms — called also *French bowline*

Portuguese bowline

**portuguese cypress** *or* **portuguese cedar** *n, usu cap P* **:** an ornamental Mexican evergreen tree (*Cupressus lusitanica*) long considered a native of southeastern Europe and the Azores and having pendulous branches and appressed acute leaves
**portuguese man-of-war** *n, usu cap P* **:** any of several large brilliantly colored chiefly tropical siphonophores (genus *Physalia*) that float on the surface of the sea by means of a large bladderlike pneumatophore with a crest like a sail on its upper side and with a cluster of zooids at one side of the lower surface equipped with numerous powerful nematocysts capable of causing serious injury to man and including very long tentacular dactylozooids and much shorter gastrozooids and gonozooids
**portuguese man-of-war fish** *n, usu cap P* **:** MAN-OF-WAR FISH
**portuguese red** *n, often cap P* **:** CARTHAMUS RED
**por·tu·laca** \ˌpōrchəˈlakə *sometimes* -rd·ᵊlˈa-\ *n* [NL, fr. L, purslane, fr. *portula*, dim. of *porta* gate; fr. the lid of its capsule that opens like a gate — more at FORD] **1** *cap* **:** a genus of mainly tropical succulent herbs (family Portulacaceae) having usu. yellow, pink, red, white, or purple ephemeral flowers with 4 to 6 petals and a partly inferior one-celled ovary — see PURSLANE **2** -s **:** any plant of the genus *Portulaca*; *esp* **:** a plant (*P. grandiflora*) widely cultivated for its showy flowers
**por·tu·la·ca·ce·ae** \ˌ==,ləˈkāsē,ē\ *n pl, cap* [NL *Portulaca*, type genus + *-aceae*] **:** a family of usu. succulent herbs (order Caryophyllales) having perfect regular flowers with two sepals and 4 to 5 hypogynous petals and a capsular often circumscissile fruit — **por·tu·la·ca·ceous** \¦===¦kāshəs\ *adj*
**por·tu·la·car·ia** \ˌ===ˈka(a)rēə\ *n, cap* [NL, fr. L *portulaca* purslane + *-aria* -ary] **:** a genus of southern African shrubs (family Portulacaceae) with opposite obovate fleshy leaves and small pink flowers clustered in the upper leaf axils
**portulan** *var of* PORTOLAN
¹**por·tu·nid** \pȯrˈtünə̇d, -rˈtyü-\ *adj* [NL *Portunidae*] **:** of or relating to the Portunidae
²**portunid** \"\ *n* -s **:** a crab of the family Portunidae
**por·tu·ni·dae** \=ˈ=nə,dē\ *n pl, cap* [NL *Portunus*, type genus + *-idae*] **:** a family of crabs (superfamily Brachyrhyncha) consisting of the swimming crabs and having a subquadrate carapace and the last pair of legs usu. with the terminal joint flattened like a paddle
**por·tu·nus** \-nəs\ *n, cap* [NL, fr. L, god of harbors] **:** the type genus of the family Portunidae comprising the English lady crab and related forms
**port warden** *n* [¹*port*] **1** *Brit* **:** an inspector of cargo and stowage **2 :** an administrative officer in charge of the channels, facilities, and traffic of a port **:** HARBOR MASTER
**port watch** *n* [⁸*port*] **:** the half of a ship's company that alternates with the starboard watch in working the ship in successive daily duty periods
**port-wine stain** *or* **port-wine mark** \ˈ=ˈ=-\ *n* [⁹*port*] **:** a reddish purple superficial hemangioma of the skin commonly occurring as a birthmark; *sometimes* **:** a flat vascular nevus
¹**porty** \ˈpōrd·ē\ *adj* [⁹*port* + *-y*] **:** of or relating to port wine or suggestive of port drinkers
²**por·ty** \"\ *n* -ES [F *portée*, fr. fem. of past part. of *porter* to carry — more at PORT] **:** a large core print
**por·ule** \ˈpȯ(r)ˌyül, ˈpō(r)¦ül\ *n* -s [²*pore* + *-ule*] **:** a small pore — **por·u·lose** \-ˌ(y)ə,lōs\ *adj* — **por·u·lous** \-ləs\ *adj*
**po·rus** \ˈpōrəs\ *n, pl* **po·ri** \-r,ī\ *or* **poruses** [NL, fr. L, pore] **:** a bodily pore or pit; *esp* **:** one of the pits on the body of an insect connected with the sense organs — compare TRICHOPORE
**por·wi·gle** \ˈpȯr,wigəl\ *n* -s [alter. of ME *polwygle* — more at POLLIWOG] **:** TADPOLE
**pory** \ˈpōrē\ *adj* [²*pore* + *-y*] *archaic* **:** POROUS
**por·za·na** \pō(r)ˈzänə, -zānə\ *n, cap* [NL, fr. It, crake] **:** a genus of small short-billed rails including the sora
**pos** *abbr* **1** position **2** positive **3** possession **4** possessive
**po·sa·da** \pōˈsädə, pəˈ-\ *n* -s [Sp, fr. fem. of *posado* (past part. of *posar* to put up for the night, lodge), fr. LL *pausatus*, past part. of *pausare* to halt, stop, rest — more at PAUSE] **:** an inn in Spanish-speaking countries
**po·sau·ne** \pōˈzau̇nə\ *n, pl* **posau·nen** \-nən\ [G, fr. MHG *busīne, busūne* trumpet, fr. OF *buisine, busine*, fr. L *bucina*, prob. fr. *bu-* (fr. *bos* head of cattle) + *-cina* (fr. *canere* to sing) — more at COW, CHANT] **1 :** TROMBONE **2 :** a reed stop in a pipe organ imitating the trombone tone
**POSB** *abbr* post office savings bank
¹**pose** \ˈpōz\ *vb* -ED/-ING/-S [ME *posen*, fr. MF *poser*, fr. (assumed) VL (Gaul) *pausare* (influenced in meaning by L *pos-*, perfect stem of *ponere* to put, place), fr. LL, to stop, rest — more at POSITION, PAUSE] *vt* **1 a :** to put or set in place or in a given position ⟨*posed* his spectacles, and read the obituary —Arnold Bennett⟩ ⟨this hat features an elongated . . . brim *posed* midway down on the forehead —*Women's Wear Daily*⟩ **b :** to place (as a model or sitter) in a studied attitude with attention to posture and ensemble ⟨great photographers have *posed* her —Joseph Bryan⟩ **2 a :** to put or set forth **:** PRESENT, OFFER ⟨a number of the points . . . were *posed* in an unsatisfactory way —*N. Y. Times*⟩ ⟨*posed* a resistance to the . . . concept —Roger Burlingame⟩ ⟨*posed* the greatest threat of dismemberment —E.S.Morgan⟩ **b :** PROPOUND ⟨*posing* so many puzzles —*Irish Digest*⟩ ⟨~ exactly the same issue —S.L. Payne⟩ ⟨questions which can be *posed* by the students themselves —*Bard College Bull.*⟩ ~ *vi* **1 :** to place oneself in a given posture or attitude usu. for artistic purposes ⟨~ for a photographer⟩ ⟨~ for a picture⟩ ⟨the birds were quiet and *posed* beautifully —C.L.Barrett⟩ **2 :** to assume a given attitude or character usu. with a view to deceive or impress **:** strike an attitude **:** ATTITUDINIZE ⟨*posed* in public speeches as a man of the people —G.A.Craig⟩ ⟨good poetry does not ~ —C.S.Kilby⟩
²**pose** \"\ *n* -s [F, fr. *poser*] **1 :** a fixed or sustained posture of the body or of a part of the body ⟨the free ~ of the girl —Winston Churchill⟩; *esp* **:** one assumed for artistic effect ⟨a set of about three short ~s culminating in a grand tableau —Faubion Bowers⟩ or affectation ⟨his every movement is a ~⟩ **2 a :** a mental posture **:** frame of mind ⟨the ~ of the book is one of critical detachment —A.M.Schlesinger b. 1917⟩ **b :** an attitude that is affected **:** an attitude assumed for effect **:** PRETENSE ⟨his directness was a ~, his professional ~ —Louis Auchincloss⟩ ⟨his deprecation of the human strikes us a kind of ~ —L.A.Fiedler⟩ **c :** POSING, ATTITUDINIZING ⟨an age of ~⟩ ⟨an everyday touch and a minimum of ~ —Jack Gould⟩
³**pose** \"\ *n* -s [ME *pos*, perh. of Scand origin; akin to ON *posi* pouch, purse; akin to OE *posa, pusa* bag, OHG *pfoso* pouch, and perh. to OE *pocca, pohha* bag — more at POKE] *chiefly Scot* **:** a secret treasure **:** HOARD
⁴**pose** \"\ *vt* -ED/-ING/-S [short for earlier *appose*, fr. ME *apposen*, alter. of *opposen* to oppose — more at OPPOSE] **1** *obs* **:** QUESTION **2 :** to puzzle by or as if by questioning **:** put in a quandary **:** BAFFLE, NONPLUS ⟨determined not to be *posed* —Lucy M. Montgomery⟩
¹**pos·er** \ˈpōzə(r)\ *n* -s [short for earlier *apposer*, fr. obs. *appose* + *-er*] **1** *archaic* **:** a person who questions; *specif* **:** EXAMINER **2 :** a puzzling or baffling question or problem **:** PUZZLE ⟨sets some ~s for the literary critics to answer —*Times Lit. Supp.*⟩
²**poser** \"\ *n* -s [¹*pose* + *-er*] **:** a person who poses or attitudinizes
**po·seur** *R* (ˈ)pōˈzər, + *V* -ˈzər-; *-R* -ˈzō, + *suffixal vowel* -ˈzər- *also* -ˈzōr, + *vowel in a word following without pause* -ˈzər- *or* -ˈzō *also* -ˈzōr\ *n* -s [F, fr. *poser* to pose + *-eur* -or — more at POSE] **:** a person who habitually pretends to be what he is not **:** one who is affected or insincere in his bearing and actions ⟨who he regards as ~s and cultural fakers —Hunter Mead⟩
**po·seuse** \(ˈ)pōˈzə(r)z, -zōz, -zəiz\ *n* -s [F, fem. of *poseur*] **:** a female poseur
¹**posh** \ˈpäsh\ *n* -ES [imit. of the sound made by walking through slush] *archaic* **:** a slushy mass (as of mud or broken ice) ⟨~ and ice in the river —Walt Whitman⟩
²**posh** \"\ *adj* [origin unknown] **1 :** smart or spruce in appearance **2 :** elegant or luxurious in an extreme degree ⟨a ~ finishing school⟩
³**posh** *interj* — used to express disdain or contempt
**poshteen** *var of* POSTEEN
**po·sied** \ˈpōzēd, -zid\ *adj* [*posy* + *-ed*] **1 :** inscribed with a posy or motto **2 :** provided with posies **:** FLOWERY
**posies** *pl of* POSY
**posing** *pres part of* POSE
**pos·ing·ly** *adv* **:** in a posed manner
¹**pos·it** \ˈpäzə̇t, *usu* -ə̇d·+V\ *vt* -ED/-ING/-S [L *positus*, past part. of *ponere* to place, put, lay down — more at POSITION] **1 :** to dispose or set firmly **:** place in relation to other objects **:** FIX ⟨his glance stayed ~ed on the spot —Hugh McCrae⟩ ⟨the problem so ~ed in a philosophical context —Bernard Smith⟩ **2 :** to postulate often in the absence of supporting evidence **:** take as actual **:** assume or affirm the existence of ⟨if she needs salvation, she will ~ a savior —George Santayana⟩ ⟨every code of law ~s a lawgiver —A.L.Guérard⟩ **syn** see PRESUPPOSE
²**posit** \"\ *n* -s **:** something that is posited; *specif* **:** an event or an assumption for which there is insufficient inductive evidence
¹**po·si·tion** \pəˈzishən, pōˈ-\ *n* -s [MF, fr. L *position-, positio*, fr. *positus* (past part. of *ponere* to put, place, fr. — assumed — OL *posinere*, fr. *po-* away + *sinere* to lay, let, leave) + *-ion-, -io* -ion; akin to L *post* after — more at POST-, SITE] **1 :** an act of placing or arranging: as **a :** an act of laying down or stating a proposition or thesis **:** AFFIRMATION **b :** an arranging in order (as of military forces or chess pieces) **2 a :** a proposition or thesis laid down **:** ASSERTION, STATEMENT ⟨the proper response to the ~ that atomic secrets merit unique protection is not a denial but a series of questions —J.G.Palfrey⟩ **b :** the ground or point of view adopted with reference to a particular subject **:** mental attitude **:** way of thinking about or viewing something ⟨took a radical ~ on the zoning issue⟩ ⟨took the ~ that the law must be enforced at all costs⟩ **c :** a market commitment (as in securities or commodities) ⟨had heavy ~ in steels⟩; *also* **:** the inventory of a market trader (as a security dealer) **3 :** the point or area in space actually occupied by a physical object or into which it is placed: as **a :** proper or natural location in relation to other items ⟨the ~ of the heart⟩ ⟨put the lever in operating ~⟩ **:** STAND ⟨took their ~ at the end of the line⟩ **b :** an area or locality occupied by combat units esp. in a defensive operation **:** a location (as of a battery) from which weapons are fired **c :** geographical location ⟨radioed the control tower for his ~⟩ **4 :** arrangement or ordering of parts or aspects in relation to one another or to an external source of orientation: as **a** (1) **:** bodily posture ⟨crouched in a cramped ~⟩ ⟨proper ~ is of the utmost importance in showing livestock⟩ (2) **:** any of the postures of the feet and arms on which all steps and movements of classical ballet are based ⟨the five ~s of the feet⟩ (3) **:** an arrangement of the parts of the body considered particularly desirable for some medical or surgical procedure ⟨knee-chest ~⟩ ⟨obstetrical ~⟩ **b :** any of the arrangements of surfaces with the vertical in which the movement of a timepiece is adjusted to run **c** (1) **:** the disposition of the notes or tones of a chord with reference to the lowest voice part, the uppermost voice part, or their nearness to each other in pitch ⟨open or close ~⟩ (2) **:** one of the points on the fingerboard of a stringed instrument where the strings are stopped by the fingers to produce various pitches (3) **:** one of the seven definite degrees of extension of the trombone slide **5 :** relative place, situation, or standing ⟨man's ~ in nature⟩ ⟨the economic ~ of the city⟩: as **a :** social or official rank or status ⟨a humble man satisfied with his ~⟩; *esp* **:** elevated standing ⟨a man of ~⟩ **b** (1) **:** OFFICE, EMPLOYMENT, VOCATION ⟨took a ~ in the department of state⟩ — often used to distinguish a superior or intellectual occupation from a job of labor (2) **:** the group of tasks and responsibilities making up the duties of an employee ⟨the ~ can best be filled by a college-trained man⟩ ⟨this ~ involves both bookkeeping and typing⟩ **c :** a spot, situation, or condition that conveys some advantage (as against another) ⟨maneuvering for ~⟩ **6 :** the condition in Greek or Latin prosody of having a short vowel followed by two consonants or a double consonant (as *x* or *z*) making its syllable long ⟨in *vŏlvūnt* the syllables are long by ~⟩
²**position** \"\ *vb* **positioned**; **positioned**; **positioning** \-sh(ə)niŋ\ **positions** *vt* **:** to put in a or the proper position **:** PLACE, SITUATE ⟨~ed themselves to act at once⟩ ~ *vi* **:** to assume or maintain a position
**po·si·tion·al** \-shənᵊl, -shnəl\ *adj* **1 :** of, relating to, or fixed by position **2 :** relatively immobile **:** involving little movement ⟨~ warfare⟩ **3 :** dependent on position or environment or context ⟨the front-articulated \k\ in \kē\ *key* and the back-articulated \k\ in \kül\ *cool* are ~ variants⟩
**position analysis** *n* **:** JOB ANALYSIS
**position angle** *n* **:** an angle on the celestial sphere denoting the orientation of one object or celestial body with respect to another (as the orientation of the line joining the components of a double star usu. measured from north through east up to 360 degrees, or the orientation of the axis of the sun, moon, planet, satellite, or star with respect to the north direction in the sky)
**position artillery** *n* **:** heavy artillery chiefly of fieldworks
**position buoy** *n* **:** FOG BUOY 2
**position effect** *n* **:** the part of the effect of a gene that is due to its interaction with adjacent genes and is subject to modification when the spatial relationships of the gene change (as by translocation or inversion)
**po·si·tion·er** \-sh(ə)nə(r)\ *n* -s **:** one that positions; *esp* **:** a mechanical device for placing or holding a body in position during an operation (as welding or drilling)
**position finder** *n* **:** a gunnery instrument for finding by triangulation the exact position and range of a ship or target
**positioning** *n* -s [fr. *positioning*, pres. part. of ²*position*] **:** a placing or arranging in position **:** POISING, POSING ⟨proper ~ of the masses is essential to a balanced composition⟩

**position in readiness :** location and condition in which troops are held prepared for prompt action as soon as the enemy's course of action is known

**position isomerism** *n* **:** isomerism in which a substituting atom or group occupies different positions

**po·si·tion·less** \pə'zishənləs, pō'-\ *adj* **:** lacking a position

**position light** *n* **:** any of the lights mounted on a night-flying airplane to serve as a warning to other airplanes (as a red light on the port side, a green light on the starboard side, and a white light aft)

**position light signal** *n* **:** a fixed railroad signal that gives its indications by varying the positions of two or more lights

**position line** *n* **:** LINE OF POSITION

**position micrometer** *n* **:** a filar-micrometer attachment for the equatorial telescope to measure position angles and angular separations (as of double stars)

**positions** *pl of* POSITION, *pres 3d sing of* POSITION

**position target** *n* **:** a railroad day signal that indicates by its position whether the accompanying switch is open or closed

**position vector** *n* **:** the vector of a point drawn from an origin to the point

**pos·i·ti·val** \ˌpäzəˌtīvəl\ *adj* [¹*positive* + *-al*] **:** REAL, OBJECTIVE — opposed to *ideal*

¹**pos·i·tive** \'päzəd·iv, -z(ə)tiv\ *adj, sometimes* -ER/-EST [ME, fr. OF *positif*, fr. L *positivus*, fr. *positus* (past part. of *ponere* to put, place, lay down) + *-ivus* -ive — more at POSITION] **1 a :** arbitrarily or formally laid down or imposed **:** prescribed by express enactment ⟨~ laws⟩ ⟨the formal and ~ rather than natural manners of the royal court⟩ **b :** expressed clearly, certainly, or peremptorily with no doubt, reservation, or unclarity ⟨never use them. That is ~ enough —A.T.Quiller-Couch⟩ **c** (1) **:** fully assured in opinion or utterance ⟨he is ~ that he is right⟩ (2) **:** SELF-ASSURED, DOGMATIC ⟨a very ~ man⟩ **2 a :** belonging to or constituting the degree of comparison that is expressed in English by the unmodified and uninflected form of an adjective (as *young*) or adverb (as *rapidly*) and that does not denote an increase or any specified level of the quality, quantity, or relation expressed by the adjective or adverb ⟨the ~ degree⟩ ⟨the ~ form *narrow*⟩ — compare COMPARATIVE 1, COMPARISON 3, SUPERLATIVE 1 **b** (1) **:** independent of changing circumstances or relations **:** not subject to comparison **:** free from conditions ⟨a ~ concept of nature⟩ — often distinguished from *comparative* and *relative* (2) **:** being or relating to a motion or device that is definite, unyielding, constant, or certain in its action ⟨a ~ system of levers⟩ **c :** unquestionably being the thing named **:** absolutely such ⟨~ proof⟩ **:** SHEER, UTTER — often used as an intensifier ⟨a ~ shame⟩; compare ABSOLUTE, DOWNRIGHT **3 a :** concerned with facts and matters of practical experience rather than theory or speculation ⟨~ philosophies⟩ **b :** actual or real as distinguished from fictitious ⟨a ~ phenomenon⟩ ⟨~ social tensions⟩ **c :** characterized by the performance of an active and direct role in the economic and social life of a political unit by directly undertaking functions and services (as the regulation of business and labor, establishment of agricultural price supports, provision of social security, and the conservation of natural resources) as contrasted with a restriction to the more limited functions of keeping peace and order ⟨~ government⟩ **4 a :** having or expressing condition, existence, character, or other quality actually present in a real manner or to an absolutely measurable degree as distinguished from merely lacking or failing to express an opposed quality **:** CONCRETE, GENUINE ⟨a slight ~ change in temperature over the centuries⟩ ⟨a ~ definition⟩ ⟨the people should have a more ~ voice in government⟩: as (1) **:** logically affirmative **:** capable of being constructively applied ⟨~ proposals for the betterment of society⟩ (2) **:** subject to scientific verification **:** EMPIRICAL — distinguished from *speculative* (3) **:** having rendition of light and shade similar in tone to the tones of the original subject — used esp. in photography ⟨a ~ image⟩ (4) **:** having properties required to produce a positive image ⟨a ~ film⟩ **b :** numerically greater than zero **:** not negative **:** PLUS — used of real quantities ⟨~ integers⟩ ⟨a ~ correlation⟩ **c :** reckoned, proceeding, or acting in a direction arbitrarily or customarily taken as that of increase, progressive motion, or superiority **:** opposed in character or effect to anything construed as negative ⟨the rotation of the earth is usu. taken as ~⟩ ⟨we are making some ~ progress⟩: as (1) **:** relating to, composed of, or charged with positive electricity (2) **:** losing electrons **:** ELECTROPOSITIVE 2a **:** BASIC 3a (3) **:** transmitting an ordinary ray with greater speed than an extraordinary — used esp. of a uniaxial doubly refracting crystal (as of ice or quartz) (4) **:** DEXTROROTATORY (5) **:** seeking the north — used of a magnetic pole (6) **:** oriented, directed, or moving toward a source of stimulation or characterized by such orientation, direction, or movement ⟨~ phototaxis⟩ ⟨a ~ response to light⟩ (7) **:** of, relating to, or constituting a method of steering or turning a vehicle in which the steering wheels move so that they describe concentric arcs in making a turn to ensure freedom from sideslip or harmful resistance (8) **:** characterized by or relating to upward movement or greater than average density or magnetic properties of the earth's crust ⟨~ gravity anomaly⟩ **d :** falling on a given side of a line or plane — used esp. in mathematics **5 a :** marked by acceptance or approval **:** indicating agreement or affirmation ⟨a strongly ~ response from the audience⟩ **b :** affirming the presence of that sought or suspected to be present ⟨a ~ test for blood⟩ ⟨a ~ case history⟩ **6 :** being or relating to a device giving a to-and-fro motion ⟨a ~ dobby⟩ ⟨a ~ tappet⟩ **syn** see SURE

²**positive** \"\ *n* -S **:** something that is positive: as **a** *obs* **:** POSITIVE LAW **b :** the positive degree of comparison in a language **:** a positive form of an adjective or adverb **c :** something of which an affirmation can be made **:** a real thing **:** REALITY **d** (1) **:** POSITIVE ORGAN (2) **:** POSITIVE PLATE (3) **:** POSITIVE POLE **e :** a positive photograph or a print from a negative (as on printing paper or film)

**positive acceleration** *n* **:** headward acceleration

**positive afterimage** *n* **:** a visual afterimage that retains the same light, dark, and color relationships as those appearing in the original image — opposed to *negative afterimage*

**positive birefringence** *n* **:** birefringence of a medium (as quartz) that transmits the ordinary rays with greater speed than the extraordinary

**positive block** *n* **:** a block in which only one railroad train is allowed to be at one time — compare BLOCK SYSTEM

**positive buoyancy** *n* **:** a condition of weight and mass relationships of a ship (as a submarine) in which it will float unless mechanical devices (as diving planes) are employed or unless additional weight is taken on

**positive clutch** *n* **:** CLAW CLUTCH

**positive column** *n* **:** the region in an electric discharge that extends from the anode to the Faraday dark space

**positive easement** *or* **positive servitude** *n* **:** an easement entitling its holder to do something affecting the land of another in such a way that the holder would be guilty of trespass or nuisance were it not for the easement — compare NEGATIVE EASEMENT

**positive electricity** *n* **:** electricity of which the elementary unit is the proton

**positive electron** *n* **:** POSITRON

**positive feedback** *n* **:** a feedback of such polarity and phase as to increase the net gain of an amplifier

**positive form** *n* **:** either of a pair of congruent crystal forms that together correspond to a single form in a class of higher symmetry

**positive fraud** *n* **:** FRAUD 1a(1)

**positive G** *n* **:** the G force exerted on the human body in a headward direction during acceleration

**positive law** *n* **1 :** the aggregate of legal precepts established or recognized by the authority of the state as contrasted with natural law or a body of ideal precepts **2 :** religious laws revealed by God (as the early Jewish law)

**positive lens** *n* **:** a lens that is thickest at its center and thinner toward its outer portions thus causing light which passes through it to converge **:** CONVERGING LENS

**positive light modulation** *or* **positive transmission** *n* **:** a system of television in which an increase in the brightness of the picture corresponds to an increase in the signal strength

**pos·i·tive·ly** \'päzəd·əvlē, -z(ə)tə-, *in sense 2 often* ˌ=(=)-'tiv-\ *adv* **1 :** in a positive manner **:** so as to be positive **2 :** EXTREMELY, OBVIOUSLY, NOTABLY, CERTAINLY — used chiefly to intensify a statement ⟨~ the best cake I ever ate⟩ ⟨~ shabby⟩ ⟨~ true⟩

**positive misprision** *n* **:** a misprision resulting from the commission of an act that ought not to have been committed — distinguished from *negative misprision*

**positive motion** *n* **:** motion that is transferred (as by gears, cranks, or belts) without slippage — compare FRICTION DRIVE

**pos·i·tive·ness** \'=(=)tivnəs\ *n* -ES **:** the quality or state of being positive; *esp* **:** dogmatic assertiveness

**positive optical activity** *n* **:** the optical activity of a dextrorotating medium

**positive organ** *n* **1** *obs* **:** a stationary as distinguished from a portative organ; *also* **:** CHAMBER ORGAN **2 :** a division of an organ used primarily for tonal contrast or supplement to the great organ; *sometimes* **:** CHOIR ORGAN

**positive philosophy** *n* **:** POSITIVISM 1

**positive plate** *n* **:** the electrode of a voltaic cell or storage cell that is at the higher potential when the circuit is open

**positive pole** *n* **1 :** the terminal of a voltaic cell or storage cell that is connected to the positive plate **2 :** the north-seeking pole of a magnet

**positive potential** *n* **:** an electric potential higher than that of the earth or of other conductor taken as an arbitrary zero of potential

**positive pressure** *n* **:** pressure of a gas in excess of atmospheric pressure or of an arbitrary standard ⟨inspiratory positive pressures of 5 to 15 cm $H_2O$ were employed —*Jour. Amer. Med. Assoc.*⟩

**positiver** *comparative of* POSITIVE

**positive ray** *n* **:** a stream of positively charged ions moving toward the cathode in a discharge tube

**positive religion** *n* **:** a religion that has a definite historic founder

**positive skewness** *n* **:** statistical skewness in which a distribution is skewed toward the positive side of the mean

**positivest** *superlative of* POSITIVE

**positive stability** *n* **:** the tendency of a ship to return to previous position when inclined

**positive temperature coefficient** *n* **:** a larger than 1 ratio of a quantity (as resistance or length) at a higher temperature to the corresponding value of the quantity at a lower temperature

**positive theology** *n* **1 :** theological doctrine that describes the divine nature according to positive categories **2 :** a theology that instead of beginning with the philosophy of religion takes as its content the gospel as given by biblical theology and presents it directly in systematic form

**positive valence** *n* **1 :** the valence of a positively charged ion **2 :** the number of electrons an atom can give up ⟨sodium has a *positive valence* of 1⟩

**pos·i·tiv·ism** \'päzəd·iˌvizəm, -z(ə)tiˌ-\ *n* -S [F *positivisme*, fr. *positif* positive + *-isme* -ism — more at POSITIVE] **1 a :** a system of philosophy holding that theology and metaphysics belong to earlier or imperfect modes of knowledge whereas positive knowledge is based on natural phenomena and their spatiotemporal properties and invariant relations or upon facts as elaborated and verified by the methods of the empirical sciences — compare THERAPEUTIC POSITIVISM **b :** LOGICAL POSITIVISM **2 :** the quality or state of being positive **:** DOGMATISM, CONFIDENCE, CERTAINTY ⟨exhibiting an undue ~⟩ **3 a :** the Lombrosian school of criminology or its theories **b :** the theory or doctrine that society is susceptible of analysis in purely objective mechanistic terms and that social values and normative standards are mere epiphenomena **4 :** a theory that law is restricted to the man-made statute law without ethical or ideological content as distinguished from natural law or moral law

¹**pos·i·tiv·ist** \-ˌvəst\ *n* -S [F *positiviste*, fr. *positif* + *-iste* -ist] **:** a subscriber to or adherent of positivism

²**positivist** \"\ *adj* **:** being a positivist **:** exhibiting, relating to, or characteristic of any form of positivism ⟨the spiritual barrenness of a ~ conception of reality —*Times Lit. Supp.*⟩

**pos·i·tiv·is·tic** \ˌ=(=)=ˈvistik, -tēk\ *adj* **:** of or relating to positivism or positivists **:** like or tending to positivism ⟨~ knowledge was concerned with merely physical utilities —John Dewey⟩ — **pos·i·tiv·is·ti·cal·ly** *adv* \-tək(ə)lē, -tēk-, -li\

**pos·i·tiv·i·ty** \ˌ=(=)'tivəd·ē, -ətē, -i\ *n* -ES [¹*positive* + *-ity*] **:** something that is positive **:** the quality or state of being positive **:** POSITIVENESS

**pos·i·ton** \'päzəˌtän\ *n* -S [*positive* + *-on*] **:** POSITRON

**pos·i·tor** \'päzəd·ə(r)\ *n* -S **:** one that posits; *esp* **:** the person making a statement or providing a segment of information — compare PROBAND

**pos·i·tri·no** \ˌpäzə'trē(ˌ)nō\ *n* -S [*positron* + *-ino* (as in *neutrino*)] **:** a hypothetical atomic particle similar to the neutrino and having an immeasurably small mass and a positive charge

**pos·i·tron** \'päzəˌträn\ *n* -S [blend fr. *positive electron*] **:** a positively charged particle having the same mass and magnitude of charge as the electron — called also *positive electron*

**pos·i·tro·ni·um** \ˌpäzə'trōnēəm\ *n* -S [NL, fr. ISV *positron* + NL *-ium*] **:** a short-lived system suggestive of an atom and analogous to the hydrogen atom consisting of a positron and an electron bound together

**posits** *pres 3d sing of* POSIT, *pl of* POSIT

**pos·i·tum** \'päzəd·əm\ *n* -S [L, neut. of *positus*, past part. of *ponere* to place, put, lay down — more at POSITION] **:** something that is posited or laid down

**pos·i·ture** \'päzəchə(r)\ *n* -S [L *positura* — more at POSTURE] **1** *obs* **:** PLACING, SITUATION, LOCALITY **2 a :** POSTURE **b :** CONFIGURATION

**posn** *abbr* position

¹**pos·na·nian** \(')päz'nānēən, -nyən\ *adj, usu cap* [*Poznań*, province and city in Poland + E *-ian*] **:** of or relating to the Polish province of Poznan or the city of Posen

²**posnanian** \"\ *n* -S *cap* **1 :** a native or resident of Poznan or Posen **2 :** the dialect of Poznan upon which standard Polish is based

**po·sol** \pō'sōl\ *also* **po·so·le** *or* **po·zo·le** \-ō(ˌ)lā\ *n* -S [AmerSp *posol, pozol, posole, pozole*, fr. Nahuatl *pozolli*, lit., foamy, fr. *pozol* foam] **1 :** a thick chiefly Spanish-American soup made of pork, corn, garlic, and chili **2 :** a Spanish-American drink made of cornmeal, water, and sugar ⟨began arriving with food, . . . *posole* and fruit —Oliver LaFarge⟩

**poso·logic** \ˌpäsə'läjik\ *also* **poso·log·i·cal** \-jəkəl\ *adj* **:** of or relating to posology

**po·sol·o·gy** \pə'säləjē\ *n* -ES [F *posologie*, fr. Gk *posos* how much + F *-logie* -logy; akin to L *quotus* how many — more at QUOTE] **:** a branch of medical science concerned with dosage

**po·po·li·te** \pòˈspòlyētə\ *n* -S [Pol, *pospolite* (*ruszenie*) general levy, fr. *pospolite* (neut. of *pospolity* general) + *ruszenie* movement, levy] **:** a former Polish militia in Poland consisting of the gentry called out in case of invasion

**poss** \'päs\ *vb* [ME *possen*, prob. fr. MF *pousser* — more at PUSH] *dial* **:** THRUST, PUSH, POUND

**poss** *abbr* **1** possession **2** possessive **3** possible; possibly

**pos·se** \'päsē\ *n* -S [ML *posse* (*comitatus*), fr. *posse* power (fr. L, to be able, have power) + *comitatus*, gen. of *comitatus* county — more at POTENT] **1 :** POSSE COMITATUS **2 a :** a force with legal authority **:** a detachment or body (as of police) often assigned to or brought together because of a particular emergency **b :** a crowd or throng usu. sharing some common interest **3 :** POSSIBILITY, POTENTIALITY — see IN POSSE

**posse comitatus** *n* [ML]**:** the power of a county: **a :** the entire body of the inhabitants who may be summoned by the sheriff to assist in preserving the public peace (as in a riot) or in executing a legal precept that is forcibly opposed including under the common law every male inhabitant who is above 15 years of age and not infirm **b :** a body of persons so summoned

**pos·se·man** \'päsēmən\ *n, pl* **possemen :** a member of a posse ⟨are without authority to . . . contract for the services of *possemen* —*U. S. Daily*⟩

**pos·sen·trie** \'päs°n·trē\ *n* -S [D, modif. of E *poison tree*] **:** SANDBOX TREE

**pos·sess** \pə'zes, pō|, |'ses\ *vt* -ED/-ING/-ES [ME *possessen*, fr. MF *possesser*, fr. L *possessus*, past part. of *possidēre* to own, possess (fr. *potis* able, possible + *-sidēre*, fr. *sedēre* to sit) & *possidēre* to take possession of, fr. *potis* + *sidere* to sit down, fr. the stem of *sedēre* to sit — more at POTENT, SIT] **1 a** *obs* **:** INSTALL, INSTATE **:** ESTABLISH **b :** to make (as a person) the owner or holder (as of property, power, or knowledge) **:** FURNISH — used with *of* or *with* ⟨I will ~ you of that ship and treasure —Shak.⟩ **c :** to be in possession of (something) **:** HAVE ⟨~*ed* of riches⟩ ⟨~*ed* of a strong back⟩ **2** *obs* **:** to be located or situated at **:** OCCUPY, INHABIT **3 a :** to have and hold as property **:** have a just right to **:** be master of **:** OWN ⟨~*ing* lands and money⟩ **b :** to have as a property, adjunct, attribute, or other collateral quality ⟨~*es* great patience⟩ ⟨~*ing* the respect of his fellows⟩ **c :** to have knowledge of or skill in ⟨~*ing* several languages besides his native tongue⟩ **4 a :** to take into one's possession **:** seize or gain control of **:** make one's own ⟨this the regal seat: ~ it, York —Shak.⟩ **b :** to enter into and influence powerfully or control **:** DOMINATE ⟨~*ed* of a demon⟩ ⟨what could have ~*ed* him to act so⟩ ⟨a man ~*ed* with rage⟩ **c :** to bring or cause to fall under the influence, possession, or control of some emotional or intellectual reaction ⟨periodically ~*ed* with a melancholy reserve⟩ **d :** to maintain or keep in a usu. specified condition (as of control or tranquillity) ⟨~*ing* himself firmly in the face of provocation⟩ ⟨the need to ~ one's soul in patience⟩ **e** *archaic* (1) **:** PERSUADE, INFLUENCE, CONVINCE (2) **:** to impart information to **:** INSTRUCT, ACQUAINT **f :** to copulate with **5** *obs* **:** to occupy or engross the thoughts of **syn** see HAVE

**pos·sess·able** *also* **pos·sess·ible** \-səbəl\ *adj* **:** capable of being held as or converted into a possession

**pos·sessed** \-st\ *adj* [fr. past part. of *possess*] **1** *obs* **:** held as a possession **2 a :** influenced or controlled by something (as an evil spirit or a passion) ⟨these ~ fools⟩; *often* **:** MAD, CRAZED **b :** urgently desirous to do or have something **3 :** SELF-POSSESSED, COOL, CALM **4 :** used in a construction to indicate what is possessed ⟨*dog* in the phrase "Bill's dog" is a ~ noun⟩ — usu. used of a form different from that used in other constructions (as in Hebrew and several Amerindian languages) — **pos·sessed·ly** \-sədlē, -stlē, -li\ *adv* — **pos·sessed·ness** \-sədnəs, -stnəs\ *n* -ES

**pos·sess·ing·ly** *adv* **:** so as to possess **:** in a possessing manner **:** CAPTIVATINGLY

**pos·ses·sion** \pə'zeshən, '-sesh-, pō-\ *n* -S [ME *possessioun*, fr. MF *possession*, fr. L *possession-*, *possessio*, fr. *possessus* (past part. of *possidēre* to own, possess & *possidēre* to take possession of) + *-ion-*, *-io* -ion — more at POSSESS] **1 a :** the act or condition of having in or taking into one's control or holding at one's disposal ⟨the enemy's ~ of the town⟩ ⟨have several old manuscripts in my ~⟩ **b :** actual physical control or occupancy of property by one who holds for himself and not as a servant of another without regard to his ownership and who has legal rights to assert interests in the property against all others having no better right than himself ⟨the locker shall remain in the student's ~ throughout the course⟩ — distinguished from *custody;* compare DETENTION 3 **c :** COPULATION **d :** control of the playing piece (as a ball or puck) in football, basketball, ice hockey, or other game **:** the right of a team to put such piece in play ⟨the home team took ~ on its own one yard line⟩ **2 :** something owned, occupied, or controlled **:** a thing possessed ⟨his own ~ for which he owes nothing to any man⟩: as **a possessions** *pl* **:** the aggregate of things owned **:** WEALTH **b** (1) **:** a piece of land (2) *Scot* **:** a small farmhold **c :** a territory subject to a ruler or government ⟨domestic and foreign ~*s* of the Crown⟩ **d :** an area subject to a government but not fully integrated into the nation to which the government belongs ⟨colonial and territorial ~*s*⟩ ⟨by judicial decision Puerto Rico was declared "to be appurtenant to" the U. S., albeit not a part of it — a mere ~ —Antonio Fernós-Isern⟩ **3 :** the condition or fact of being possessed by something ⟨the town's ~ by the enemy⟩: as **a :** the condition of being dominated by something (as an extraneous personality, demon, passion, idea, or purpose) ⟨there were tales of bewitchings and ~*s*⟩ **b :** a psychological state in which an individual's normal personality is replaced by another **c :** the fact or condition of being self-controlled ⟨his ~ in the emergency was absolute⟩ **4 :** an Aristotelian category having the form of a permanent disposition or state

**pos·ses·sion·al** \-shən°l, -shnəl\ *adj* **:** of or constituting possession **:** having property — **pos·ses·sion·al·ly** \-°l|ē, -əl|, |i\ *adv*

**pos·ses·sion·al·ism** \-shən°lˌizəm, -əˌli-\ *n* -S **:** the principle or practice of private ownership of property

**pos·ses·sion·ary** \-shəˌnerē\ *adj* **:** of or relating to possession **:** arising from possession

**pos·ses·sion·ate** \-shənət\ *adj* [ME, fr. ML *possessionatus* fr. L *possession-*, *possessio* possession + *-atus* -ate] **:** having possessions or endowments

**pos·ses·sioned** \-shənd\ *adj* **:** having possessions

**pos·ses·sion·er** \-sh(ə)nə(r)\ *n* -S [ME *possessiouner*, fr. *possessioun* possession + *-er* — more at POSSESSION] **1 a** *obs* **:** a property holder **b** *archaic* **:** a member of a religious order holding endowments (as of lands or buildings) — often taken as offensive **2 :** one appointed to renew boundary landmarks in the southern U. S.

**pos·ses·sion·ist** \-sh(ə)nəst\ *n* -S **:** a believer in possession by spirits

**pos·ses·sion·less** \'-shənləs\ *adj* **:** lacking possessions — **pos·ses·sion·less·ness** *n* -ES

¹**pos·ses·sive** \pə'zesiv, pō|, |'ses-|, -ēv\ *adj* [MF *possessif*, fr. L *possessivus*, fr. *possessus* (past part. of *possidēre* to own, possess) + *-ivus* -ive — more at POSSESS] **1 a :** of, relating to, or constituting a grammatical case that denotes ownership or a relation felt to be analogous to ownership ⟨in "John's hat" the word *John's* is in the ~ case⟩ — compare GENITIVE **b :** of, relating to, or constituting a word or word group that denotes ownership or a relation felt to be analogous to ownership ⟨of or relating to the possessive case ⟨a ~ construction⟩ **2 :** of or tending to possession **:** manifesting possession or the desire to possess or hold as one's own **:** POSSESSORY ⟨the ~ instinct⟩ ⟨a ~ nature⟩ **3** *of a compound word* **:** belonging to the bahuvrihi class — **pos·ses·sive·ly** \-səvlē, -sēv-, -li\ *adv* — **pos·ses·sive·ness** *n* -ES

²**possessive** \"\ *n* -S **1 :** the possessive case **2 :** a possessive word or word group

**possessive adjective** *n* **:** a pronominal adjective expressing possession (as *my* in *my hat*, *his* in *his answer*)

**possessive pronoun** *n* **:** a pronoun that derives from a personal pronoun and denotes possession and other analogous relations (as *his* in "his is better than John's")

**pos·ses·sor** \pə'zesə(r), -'ses-, pō'-\ *n* -S [ME *possessour*, fr. MF *possesseur*, fr. L *possessor*, fr. *possessus* + *-or*] **1 :** one that possesses **:** one that occupies, holds, owns, or controls **2 :** one that holds property without title — called also *naked possessor;* contrasted with *owner* **3** *usu cap* **:** JOSEPHITE

**possessoress** *n* -ES *obs* **:** a female possessor

**pos·ses·so·ri·ness** \pə'zesərēnəs, pō'-, -'ses-\ *n* -ES **:** the quality or state of being possessory

**pos·ses·sor·ship** \=ˈ==ˌship\ *n* **:** the condition of a possessor

**pos·ses·so·ry** \pə'zesərē, pō'-, -'ses-, -ri\ *adj* [LL *possessorius*, fr. *possessus* (past part. of *possidēre* to possess) + *-orius* -ory — more at POSSESS] **1 a :** of or relating to possession or a possessor **:** constituting or having the nature of possession **b :** arising out of, affecting, relating to, or confirming possession ⟨a ~ interest⟩ ⟨a ~ action at law⟩ **2 :** having or holding possession ⟨a ~ lord⟩ **3 :** characteristic of a possessor **:** POSSESSIVE ⟨a ~ spirit⟩

**possessory action** *n* **:** an action at law founded on a right of possession and brought to recover or obtain possession as: **a** (1) **:** a real action formerly used under Old English law to regain possession of a freehold (2) **:** an action founded on mere possession and sometimes used to try title indirectly **b :** a suit under admiralty law to recover possession of a ship under claim of title **c** (1) **:** an action under Scots law to vindicate and recover possession of goods heritable or movable (2) **:** an action in Louisiana to be secured in possession or restored to the possession of an immovable

¹**pos·set** \'päsət, *usu* -əd·+V\ *n* -S [ME *poshet, poshoote, possot*] **:** a hot drink consisting essentially of sweetened and spiced milk curdled with ale or wine, and sometimes thickened with bread ⟨egg ~⟩ ⟨sack ~⟩

²**posset** \"\ *vt* -ED/-ING/-S **1 :** to cause to curdle or coagulate **2 :** to pamper with delicacies ⟨cosseted and ~*ed* and prayed over — O.W.Holmes †1894⟩

**posset cup** *n* **:** a 2-handled usu. covered and spouted vessel used esp. in the 17th and 18th centuries for possets and invalid feeding

**posset pot** *n* **1 :** a two-handled vessel used for making posset **2 :** POSSET CUP

posset cup

**pos·si·bi·le** \pə'sibə,lē\ *n, pl* **pos·si·bi·lia** \,päsə'bilēə\ [NL, fr. L, neut. of *possibilis* possible — more at POSSIBLE] **:** something that is possible or conceivable without contradiction or that may or might be the case

**pos·si·bi·lism** \'päsəbə,lizəm, pə'sibə,l-\ *n* -S [F *possibilisme*, fr. L *possibilis* + F *-isme* -ism] **:** the beliefs or practices of a possibilist

**pos·si·bi·list** \-ləst\ *n* -S *often attrib* [F *possibiliste*, fr. L *possibilis* + F *-iste* -ist] **:** a member of a political party that attempts (as in the way of reform) only what is regarded as immediately possible or practicable: as **a :** one of a party of Republicans in Spain **b :** one of a party of Socialists in France

**pos·si·bil·i·tate** \,päsə'bilə,tāt\ *vt* -ED/-ING/-S [*possibility* + *-ate*] **:** to make possible

**pos·si·bil·i·ty** \-lәd·ē, -ətē, -i\ *n* -ES [ME *possibilite*, fr. MF *possibilité*, fr. L *possibilitat-, possibilitas*, fr. *possibilis* possible + *-itat-, -itas* -ity] **1 :** the character, condition, or fact of being possible whether theoretically, in general, or under a specified set of conditions ⟨the ~ of miracles⟩ ⟨the constant ~ of failure⟩ **2 :** something that is possible **:** CONTINGENCY ⟨within the range of ~⟩ **:** a particular thing that may take place, eventuate, or be manipulated to some end ⟨but one ~ remains⟩ **3** *archaic* **:** one's utmost power, capacity, or ability esp. as determined by circumstances ⟨to the ~ of thy soldiership —Shak.⟩ **4** *obs* **:** pecuniary means or pecuniary prospects — usu. used in pl. **5 possibilities** *pl* **:** potential or prospective value **:** possible uses, achievements, or other desired qualities ⟨a man of undetermined *possibilities*⟩

**possibility of reverter :** a future interest in property left to a transferor or his successor in interest that is subject to a condition precedent

**¹pos·si·ble** \'päsəbəl\ *adj, sometimes* -ER/-EST [ME, fr. MF, fr. L *possibilis*, fr. *posse* to be able + *-ibilis* -ible — more at POTENT] **1 a :** falling or lying within the powers (as of performance, attainment, or conception) of an agent or activity expressed or implied **:** being within or up to the limits of one's ability or capacity as determined by nature, authority, circumstances, or other controlling factor ⟨a ~ but difficult task⟩ — compare ACTUAL **b :** falling within the bounds of what may be done, occur, be conceived, or be attained within the framework of nature, custom, or manners ⟨a cure is still ~⟩ ⟨not ~ to see the patient⟩ **c :** being such to the utmost degree (as coarse as it was ~ to be) ⟨the largest number ~⟩ **2** *obs* **:** ABLE **3 a :** that may or may not occur **:** that may chance **:** dependent on contingency **:** neither probable nor impossible ⟨put by for ~ emergencies⟩ ⟨it is ~ that she will come⟩ **b :** LIKELY, PROBABLE — usu. used with an adverb expressing doubt ⟨scarcely ~⟩ ⟨barely ~ that it will rain⟩ **4 :** having an indicated potential by nature or circumstances **:** able or fitted to become, be used, or otherwise serve ⟨every native-born American is a ~ president⟩ ⟨a ~ site for a capitol⟩ **5 :** capable of being surmounted, traversed, or dealt with; *esp* **:** neither unacceptable nor intolerable ⟨the new neighbors were ~⟩ — often used with an adverb expressing doubt ⟨scraped together a just ~ meal⟩

**syn** PRACTICABLE, FEASIBLE: POSSIBLE is used to dispel doubt that something may or does occur or exist or may come to exist ⟨the regime of religious toleration has become *possible* only because we have lost the primal intensity of religious conviction —M.R.Cohen⟩ ⟨although he still asserts that community of goods would be the ideal institution, he reluctantly abandons it as a basis for a *possible* state —G.L.Dickinson⟩ PRACTICABLE refers to what may be readily effected, executed, practiced, used, or put into operation ⟨trial by jury — an institution in which . . . we have the very abstract and essence of all *practicable* democratic government —W.H.Mallock⟩ ⟨the only *practicable* tactics to be pursued were those of the routine police procedure —W.H.Wright⟩ FEASIBLE may designate what is likely to work out or be put into effect successfully or what in a difficult situation seems the expedient least liable to fail ⟨cheap iron and steel made it *feasible* to equip larger armies and navies than ever before —Lewis Mumford⟩ ⟨only the most simple types of utilization are *feasible* —Samuel Van Valkenburg & Ellsworth Huntington⟩ **syn** see in addition PROBABLE

**²possible** \"\ *adv, archaic* **:** POSSIBLY

**³possible** \"\ *n* -S **1 a :** POSSIBILITY, POTENTIALITY — usu. used in pl. ⟨all the infinite number of *~s* —Jonathan Edwards⟩ **b :** all that can be done **:** BEST ⟨had done my ~ . . . to gratify you —Robert Southey⟩ **2 possibles** *pl* **:** necessary things (as supplies, equipment, money) ⟨the hunters departed, each to look after his traps and *~s* —Mayne Reid⟩ **3 :** the highest attainable score for a number of rounds fired in target shooting; *broadly* **:** the highest attainable score in a competition

**pos·si·ble·ness** *n* -ES **:** the quality or state of being possible **:** POSSIBILITY ⟨the ~ of such a feat⟩

**pos·si·bly** \'päsəblē, -li\ *adv* [ME, fr. *possible* + *-ly*] **1 :** in a possible manner **:** by possible means **:** by any possibility ⟨not ~ true⟩ ⟨could you ~ agree⟩ **2 :** by merest chance **:** MAYBE, PERHAPS ⟨~ he will recover⟩

**pos·sie** *also* **pos·sy** \'päsi\ *n, pl* **possies** [alter. of *position*] *Austral* **:** POSITION, PLACE

**possn** *abbr* possession

**¹pos·sum** \'päsəm\ *n* -S [by shortening] **:** OPOSSUM

**²possum** \"\ *vb* -ED/-ING/-S *vi* **1 :** to play possum **2 :** to hunt the opossum ~ *vt* **:** FEIGN, PRETEND ⟨~*ing* surprise⟩

**possum belly** *n, slang* **:** a storage space beneath the flooring of a vehicle

**possum fruit** *also* **possum apple** *n* **:** PERSIMMON

**possum grape** *n* **1 a :** CHICKEN GRAPE **b :** a wild grape (*Vitis baileyana*) of the southeastern U.S. resembling the chicken grape but having angled branchlets and leaves with lower surfaces permanently pilose **2 :** CISSUS 2

**possum haw** *n* **1 :** BEARBERRY 3 **2 :** a withe rod (*Viburnum nudum*)

**possum oak** *n* **:** a tall water oak (*Quercus nigra*) of the southeastern U.S. that is often cultivated as a shade tree

**possum-trot plan** \'ˌ=ˌ=-\ *n* **:** a plan of a house in two parts

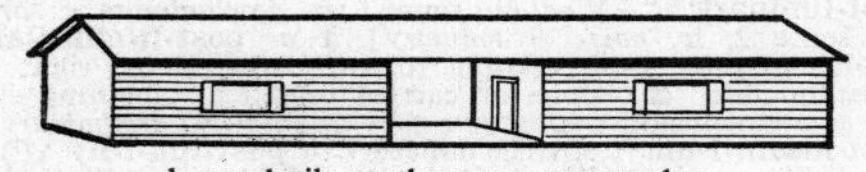

house built on the possum-trot plan

with a breezeway between — compare DOGTROT 2

**possumwood** \'==,=\ *n* **1 :** PERSIMMON **2 :** the light soft wood of the sandbox tree **3 :** OPOSSUM WOOD

**¹post** \'pōst\ *n* -S [ME, fr. OE; akin to OFris, MD, & MLG *post*, OHG *pfosto*; all fr. a prehistoric WGmc word borrowed fr. L *postis*; akin to OE *fierst, first* ridgepole, MLG *verst*, OHG *first* ridgepole, Gk *pastas* porch, colonnade, Skt *pṛstha* back, roof, top; all fr. a prehistoric IE compound whose 1st constituent is akin to Skt *pra-* before, forward, and whose 2d constituent is akin to L *stare* to stand — more at FOR, STAND] **1 :** a piece of timber or other solid substance (as metal) fixed or intended to be fixed firmly in an upright position esp. as a stay or support **:** PILLAR, PROP: as **a :** a square timber set on end to support a structural member (as a wall or girder) esp. at a corner of a building **:** UPRIGHT, COLUMN **b :** one of the pillars supporting an arch or lintel **:** DOORJAMB, GATEPOST **c :** one of the stakes of a fence or railing **:** PICKET **d :** STERNPOST **e :** one of the main upright timbers of a framed set in mining **:** STUDDLE **f :** the pin of a pinlock **g :** BINDING POST 1 **h :** BINDING POST 2 **2 :** a pole or stake set up to mark or indicate: as **a :** a boundary marker **b :** a stand for the display of public notices **c :** a pole marking the starting point or the finishing point in horse racing ⟨starting ~⟩ ⟨winning ~⟩ **3 :** an upright metal blade forming the front sight of a firearm

**²post** \"\ *vt* -ED/-ING/-S **1 :** to affix (as a paper or bill) to a post, wall, or other usual place for public notices **:** PLACARD ⟨~ the notice on the bulletin board⟩ ⟨signs are *~ed* throughout the state⟩ **2 a :** to publish, announce, or advertise by or as if by the use of a placard ⟨the students' grades are *~ed*⟩ ⟨the yardmaster . . . *~s* the track number —*Monsanto Mag.*⟩ ⟨the *~ed* price for . . . crude oil —*N.Y.Times*⟩ **b :** to denounce (as a person or institution) by public notice ⟨*~ed* the theater as unfair —Upton Sinclair⟩ ⟨harry and ~ a man for his losings —Rudyard Kipling⟩ **c :** to enter (a name) on a public listing ⟨nurses *~ed* for night duty⟩ ⟨*~ed* missing in the flood —John Blight⟩ **d :** to forbid (property) to trespassers under penalty of legal prosecution by notices placed along the boundaries ⟨~ a brook⟩ ⟨wandering around *~ed* property —Ronald Sercombe⟩ **e :** to gain recognition for (a score or performance) ⟨*~ed* a 69 to take the first-round lead⟩ ⟨*~ed* an average of 177.34 miles per hour⟩

**³post** \"\ *adj* **:** of or relating to the start or to the post at the starting point of a horse or dog race ⟨~ position⟩ ⟨~ time⟩

**⁴post** \"\ *n* -S [MF *poste* relay station, man stationed at a relay station, post, fr. OIt *posta* place assigned to a horse in a stable, relay station, fr. *posta*, fem. of *posto* (past part. of *porre* to put), fr. L *positus*, past part. of *ponere* to put, place — more at POSITION] **1 a** *obs* (1) **:** one of the men stationed or appointed in a series of places along a through road to go each from his station to the next with the state packet of dispatches and letters (2) **:** one so stationed or appointed to carry letters generally (3) **:** one appointed to furnish a change of horses to through messengers carrying such matter **b :** a special carrier of messages or letters **:** COURIER; *esp* **:** one following a fixed route **c** *chiefly Scot* **:** a postal carrier **:** POSTMAN **d :** a vehicle or ship used to carry the mails **2** *archaic* **a :** one of a series of stations for keeping horses for relays **b :** the distance between any two such consecutive stations **:** STAGE **3** *chiefly Brit* **a :** a nation's organization or system for handling the transmission of letters and other matter **:** MAIL 3a ⟨a letter delayed in the ~⟩ ⟨exchange of books by ~ —Thomas Joy⟩ **b :** the matter sent or received **:** MAIL 3b ⟨delivered his ~ to a house and moved on —Cyril Cusack⟩ **c** (1) **:** a single dispatch of mail ⟨catch the last ~ with it —Arnold Bennett⟩ (2) **:** the matter received in the mail at one time or by one person **:** MAIL 2b ⟨the ~ came with tea —Cecil Beaton⟩ **d :** POST OFFICE **e :** POSTBOX **f :** POSTAGE 3 **4 :** GENERAL POST 1 **5 :** the act of posting in horseback riding ⟨the rhythm of a ~ is not difficult once it has been achieved⟩

**⁵post** \"\ *vb* -ED/-ING/-S *vi* **1 a :** to travel with post-horses ⟨*~ing* in private carriages . . . the most comfortable and convenient method of traveling —Hugh McCausland⟩ **b :** to ride or travel with haste **:** HURRY ⟨off he *~ed* to Louisville —S.H. Adams⟩ **2 :** to rise forward and upward from a riding saddle when one diagonal pair of the horse's legs is off the ground and to return to the saddle when the opposite diagonal pair is off the ground supporting one's weight primarily by the knees and thighs **3 :** to dispatch mail ⟨not only shopped early but *~ed* early —Rose Macaulay⟩ ~ *vt* **1 a** *archaic* **:** to dispatch (a person) in haste **b** *obs* **:** to convey speedily **c** *obs* **:** to dispatch by a post or messenger **2 :** MAIL ⟨stroll down the street to ~ a letter —Elspeth Huxley⟩ **3 a :** to transfer or carry (an entry or item) from a book of original entry to the proper account in a ledger **:** transfer (an entry or item) from one record to another **b** (1) **:** to complete (a ledger) by the transfer and proper entry of all items from antecedent books — used usu. with *up* ⟨~ up the general ledger⟩ (2) **:** to make transfer entries in (all books) to complete the record ⟨~ up the books for the month⟩ **4 :** to make (a person) familiar with a subject **:** INFORM ⟨is better *~ed* than . . . his audience —A.T.Weaver⟩ ⟨keep them *~ed* as to what is going on —Shipley Thomas⟩ — used sometimes with *up* ⟨shows himself thoroughly *~ed* up —*Times Lit. Supp.*⟩

**⁶post** \"\ *adv* [⁴*post* (as in the phrase *to ride in post*)] **:** with post-horses **:** like a courier **:** at full speed **:** EXPRESS ⟨journeying ~⟩ ⟨ride ~⟩

**⁷post** \"\ *n* -S [MF *poste*, fr. OIt *posto*, fr. past part. of *porre* to put — more at ⁴POST] **1 a :** the place at which a soldier is stationed; *esp* **:** the fixed locality or stretch of ground guarded and patrolled by a sentry or outpost ⟨walking his ~ as ordered⟩ **b :** the prescribed place (as for an officer or for the colors) in a formation of troops **c :** the place at which a body of troops is stationed **:** CAMP, FORT ⟨every noncoms' club on the ~ —James Jones⟩ **d** (1) **:** a local subdivision of a veterans' organization (as the American Legion) (2) **:** a unit of five or more explorers (as of the Boy Scouts of America) corresponding to a boy scout troop **e :** one of two bugle calls sounded at tattoo (as in the British Army) ⟨last ~⟩ **2 a :** a station or position esp. to which a person is assigned ⟨~ of duty⟩ ⟨~ of danger⟩ ⟨we took ~ close to the . . . fence —S.P.B.Mais⟩ ⟨heroes still at their *~s* —Wynford Vaughan-Thomas⟩ **b :** shooting position (as in field archery or skeet) **c :** a position taken by a player in basketball as a focal point of offensive attack **3 :** an office or position to which a person is appointed ⟨a good ~ in the public service⟩ ⟨held various *~s* —*Lamp*⟩ ⟨teaching *~s* in our colleges —E.J.Simmons⟩ **4 a :** TRADING POST, SETTLEMENT ⟨sent medical supplies to the outlying ~⟩ **b :** a station on the floor of a stock exchange at which trade in a particular issue or group of issues is carried on

**⁸post** \"\ *vt* -ED/-ING/-S **1 a :** to station in a given place ⟨window where she had *~ed* herself for observation —Owen Wister⟩ ⟨repair ships . . . are *~ed* along the route —Robert Pocock⟩ **b :** to assign (a sentry) to a post ⟨*~ed* picket sentries —Charles Beadle⟩ **c :** to carry (the national flag) ceremoniously to a designated position ⟨*~ing* the colors⟩ **d :** to place (a chessman) on a square for continued occupancy ⟨the bishop and queen are badly *~ed* —*New Complete Hoyle*⟩ **2** *chiefly Brit* **:** to assign to a unit or location (as in the military or civil service) ⟨*~ed* to a regiment —Earle Birney⟩ ⟨*~ed* to his home district —*Scots Mag.*⟩ **3 a :** to lay down (as money or a deposit) **:** put up (a stake) **b :** to furnish (as bond) to the proper authority ⟨*~ed* bail for the suspect⟩ ⟨~ the collateral required⟩

**⁹post** \"\ *n* -S [origin unknown] **1 :** a pile of wet sheets of handmade paper interleaved with felt in papermaking **2 :** a charge of ore for a smelting furnace

**¹⁰post** \"\ *adv* [L — more at POST-] **:** lying behind **:** posterior in position ⟨~ diaphragmatic organs⟩

**¹¹post** \"\ *n* -S [by shortening] *slang* **:** POSTMORTEM ⟨a report on the ~⟩

**¹²post** \"\ *vt* -ED/-ING/-S *slang* **:** to conduct a postmortem on (a body) ⟨the corpse has been *~ed*⟩

**post-** *prefix* [ME, fr. L, fr. *post* (adv. & prep.); akin to Gk (Arcadian & Cyprian dial.) *pos* toward, on, at, Skt *paśca* behind, after, later, OE *of* of, from, off — more at OF] **1 a :** after **:** subsequent **:** later ⟨*post*date⟩ ⟨*post*entry⟩ ⟨*post*nati⟩ **b :** behind ⟨*post*fix⟩ **:** posterior ⟨*post*abdomen⟩ **:** following after ⟨*post*consonantal⟩ **2 a :** subsequent to **:** later than ⟨*post*-adolescence⟩ ⟨*post*classical⟩ ⟨*post*operative⟩ ⟨*post*war⟩ **b :** behind **:** posterior to ⟨*post*antennal⟩ ⟨*post*cardinal⟩ ⟨*post*ocular⟩

**post** *abbr* postal

**post·abdomen** \(ˈ)pōst+\ *n* [NL, fr. *post-* + *abdomen*] **1 :** a posterior differentiated part of the abdomen; *specif* **:** the slender posterior sting-bearing portion of the abdomen of a scorpion **2 :** a posterior part of the body beyond the abdomen proper — **post·abdominal** \¦=+\ *adj*

**post·absorptive** \¦=+\ *adj* [*post-* + *absorptive*] **:** following or typical of the period following absorption of nutrients from the alimentary canal ⟨~ blood sugar level⟩ ⟨the ~ state⟩

**post·age** \'pōstij, -tēj\ *n* -S [⁴*post* + *-age*] **1** *obs* **:** conveyance or dispatch of mail by post **2** *archaic* **:** a postal service **3 :** the fee for postal service ⟨the rate of ~ charged on the parcel —*U. S. Official Postal Guide*⟩ **4 :** adhesive stamps or printed indicia representing postal fees ⟨covers must bear ~ at the first-class rate —*Stamps*⟩

**postage currency** *n* **:** a fractional paper currency bearing the facsimiles of postage stamps; *esp* **:** one issued by the U.S. between August 1862 and May 1863

**postage–due stamp** \¦==¦=-\ *n* **:** a stamp placed by a post office on an article of mail (as on a business reply card or envelope) to indicate an amount of postage or a special service fee to be paid before the article may be received by the addressee

**postage impression** *or* **postage-paid impression** \¦==¦=-\ *n* **:** METER IMPRESSION

**postage meter** *or* **postal meter** *n* **:** a machine that prints postal indicia on pieces of mail, records the amount of postage given in the indicia, and subtracts it from a total amount which has been paid at a post office and for which the machine has been set; *also* **:** a machine that so marks mail on deposit of a coin in a slot

**postage paper** *n* **:** POSTAL PAPER

**postage stamp** *n* **:** an adhesive stamp or an imprinted stamp on a piece of postal stationery issued by a postal service for use on mail matter as evidence of prepayment of postage

**¹post·al** \'pōst°l\ *adj* [F, fr. *poste* post, mail + *-al* — more at POST (mail)] **1 :** of or relating to the posts or mails or to the post office ⟨~ service⟩ ⟨~ career⟩ ⟨~ inspector⟩ ⟨a ~ agreement between governments⟩ **2 :** of or relating to a system of carrying goods or passengers on a railroad for a uniform rate irrespective of distance ⟨the ~ principle⟩ ⟨the ~ tariff⟩ **3 :** conducted by mail ⟨~ chess⟩ ⟨~ tuition⟩

**²postal** \"\ *n* -S **:** POSTAL CARD ⟨drop a ~ to the editor —*Congressional Record*⟩

**postal bus** *n* **:** HIGHWAY POST OFFICE

**postal car** *n* **:** RAILWAY MAIL CAR

**postal card** *n* **:** POSTCARD

**postal clerk** *n* **:** a clerk in a post office; *specif* **:** one assigned to sort and distribute mail in railway post offices

**postal course** *n, Brit* **:** a course of study conducted by mail — compare CORRESPONDENCE SCHOOL

**postal currency** *n* **:** POSTAGE CURRENCY

**postal delivery zone** *or* **postal zone** *n* **:** ZONE 5c

**postal fiscal stamp** *n* **:** a stamp issued as a revenue stamp but used as a postage stamp

**post·al·ly** \'pōst°lē, -li\ *adv* [¹*postal* + *-ly*] **1 :** in a postal manner **:** for postal purposes ⟨a ~ used stamp⟩ **2 :** by or on postage stamps ⟨a ~ commemorated anniversary⟩

**postal match** *n* **:** a rifle or pistol match in which the winner is determined by comparison of targets mailed to judges for scoring

**postal money order** *n* **:** MONEY ORDER

**postal note** *n* **:** POSTAL ORDER

**postal order** *n, Brit* **:** a postal money order that is issued in fixed denominations, is payable to a particular person and at a particular office, and may be crossed for payment through a bank

**postal paper** *n* **1 :** postage stamps ⟨the *postal paper* of . . . the United States and its possessions —K.B.Stiles⟩ **2 :** POSTAL STATIONERY ⟨pioneer in issuing airmail *postal paper* —K.B. Stiles⟩

**postal savings bank** *n* **:** a savings bank conducted by a government through the local post offices

**postal stationery** *n* **:** government-issued stationery (as letter sheets, envelopes, postcards) bearing imprinted stamps

**postal storage car** *n* **:** a railroad car for transporting mail that lacks facilities for sorting or distribution en route — compare RAILWAY MAIL CAR

**postal tax stamp** *n* **:** a government stamp required on mail not for postage but for some public fund (as for a public health project)

**postal union** *n* **:** an international agreement to observe uniform regulations governing international mail

**pos·ta·ment** \'pästəmənt\ *n* -S [G, fr. (assumed) obs. It *postamento*, fr. *postare* to place, put (fr. *posto*, past part. of *porre* to put) + *-mento* -ment (fr. L *-mentum*) — more at POST] **1 a :** PEDESTAL, BASE **b :** STEREOBATE **2 :** a frame, mount, or molding for a work in relief

**post–and–lintel** \¦=¦=¦=\ *adj* **:** of or relating to a system of architectural construction based on vertical supports and horizontal beams as distinguished from systems based on arches or vaults

**post and pair** *n* [*post* prob. fr. It *posta* stake, wager, fr. fem. of *posto*, past part. of *porre* to put — more at POST] **:** a card game popular in 16th and 17th century England that was played with hands of three cards

**post–and–stall** \¦=¦=\ *adj* [¹*post*] **:** BORD-AND-PILLAR

**post·anoxic** \(ˈ)=+\ *adj* [*post-* + *anoxic*] **:** following a period of anoxia ⟨~ respiratory rhythms⟩ ⟨a ~ hyperpnea, greater than that attained during hypoxia —T.G.Bernthal⟩

**post·antennal** \(ˈ)=+\ *adj* [*post-* + *antennal*] **:** located behind the antennae of an insect ⟨~ appendage⟩ ⟨~ organ⟩ ⟨the ~ third brain segment of an insect⟩

**post·arteriolar** \¦=+\ *adj* [*post-* + *arteriolar*] **:** following after the arterioles **:** CAPILLARY ⟨~ bed⟩

**post·atomic** \"+\ *adj* [*post-* + *atomic*] **1 :** subsequent to the release of atomic energy **2 :** subsequent to the explosion of the first atomic bomb ⟨the ~ world⟩ ⟨the ~ age⟩

**post·audit** \(ˈ)=+\ *n* [*post-* + *audit*] **:** an audit made subsequent to the final settlement of a transaction — contrasted with *preaudit*

**post·axial** \"+\ *adj* [*post-* + *axial*] **:** located behind the axis of the body; *esp* **:** of or relating to the posterior side of the axis of a vertebrate limb (the ulnar side of the forelimb or fibular side of the hind limb) — **post·axially** \"+\ *adv*

**postbag** \'=,=\ *n* [⁴*post* + *bag*] **1** *chiefly Brit* **:** MAILBAG **2** *chiefly Brit* **:** a single batch of letters or other mail **:** MAIL 2 b ⟨could infer this merely from my own ~ —George Orwell⟩

**post·bellum** \(ˈ)pōs(t)¦beləm\ *adj* [L *post bellum* after the war] **:** existing after the war **:** of, relating to, or characteristic of the period following a war and esp. following the American Civil War ⟨the ~ generation⟩ ⟨the ~ South⟩ ⟨his ~ insistence on racial equality —*Va. Quarterly Rev.*⟩

**post binder** *n* [¹*post*] **:** a loose-leaf binder having metal posts designed to pass through holes punched in the sheets

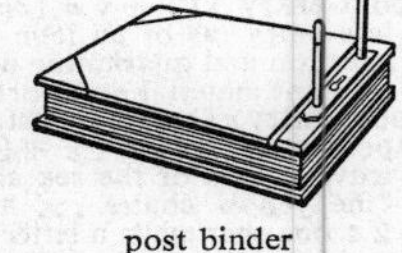

post binder

**postbox** \'=,=\ *n* [⁴*post* + *box*] **:** MAILBOX; *esp* **:** a public mailbox

**postboy** \'=,=\ *n* [⁴*post* + *boy*] **1 :** POSTRIDER **2 :** POSTILION

**post·brachium** \(ˈ)=+\ *n* [NL, fr. *post-* + *brachium*] **:** the brachium of the inferior colliculus

**post·branchial body** \(ˈ)=+-\ *n* [*post-* + *branchial*] **:** an outpocketing from the fourth visceral pouch of a vertebrate embryo that is believed to be a vestigial fifth pouch and that gives rise to all or part of the parathyroids

**post·breeding** \"+\ *adj* [*post-* + *breeding*] **:** following a period of physiological fitness for reproduction ⟨~ regressive changes⟩ — see ²COLLAPSE 5

**post·canonical** \¦=+\ *adj* [*post-* + *canonical*] **:** written subsequent to writings included in a canon esp. of Scripture

**post captain** *n* [⁷*post*] **:** a naval officer holding a captain's commission as distinguished from one bearing the courtesy title of captain

**¹postcard** \'=,=\ *n* [⁴*post* + *card*] **:** a card for bearing a message through the mail without an envelope: **a** (1) **:** a card to which an adhesive stamp must be affixed (2) **:** such a card having a decoration (as a picture) on one side **b :** a card bearing a government-imprinted stamp or official reply-paid indicia

**²postcard** \"\ *vt* **1 :** to relate by postcard ⟨~s that all is well⟩ **2 :** to communicate with by postcard ⟨~ us today⟩

**post·cardinal** \(ˈ)=+\ *adj* [*post-* + *cardinal*] **:** lying behind or caudal to the heart; *esp* **:** of, relating to, or being a vein on either side in mammalian and other embryos and in some fishes that drains the mesonephros and the portion of the trunk caudal to the heart

**post·cava** \"+\ *n* [NL, fr. *post-* + *cava*] **:** the inferior vena cava of vertebrates higher than fishes — **post·caval** \"+\ *adj*

**post cedar** *n* [¹*post*] **1 :** SOUTHERN WHITE CEDAR **2 :** INCENSE CEDAR

**post·ce·nal** *or* **post·coe·nal** \(ˈ)pōs(t)¦sēn°l\ *adj* [*post-* + L *cena* dinner + E *-al* — more at CÉNACLE] **:** occurring after dinner **:** POSTPRANDIAL

**post·central** \(ˈ)=+\ *adj* [*post-* + *central*] **:** located behind a center or central structure; *esp* **:** located behind the central sulcus of the cerebral cortex ⟨the ~ gyrus⟩ ⟨the ~ sulcus⟩

**post·centrum** \"+\ *n* [NL, fr. *post-* + *centrum*] **:** a distinct posterior part of the centrum of a vertebra in some fishes formed by coossification of the interventral and interdorsal arcualia — opposed to *precentrum*

**post chaise** *n* [⁴*post*] **:** a carriage for traveling post usu. having a closed body on four wheels and seating two to four persons

**post chariot** *n* **:** a carriage for traveling post; *specif* **:** a kind of light four-wheeled carriage with a driver's seat in front

**post·cholecystectomy syndrome** \(ˈ)=+-\ *n* [*post-* + *cholecystectomy*] **:** BILIARY DYSKINESIA

**post·ci·bal** \(ˈ)pōs(t)¦sībəl\ *adj* [*post-* + LL *cibalis* of food, fr. L *cibus* food + *-alis* -al — more at CIBARIAL] **:** occurring after a meal

**post·classic** \(ˈ)=+\ *or* **post·classical** \"+\ *adj* [*post-* + *classic, classical*] **:** of or relating to a period (as in art or literature) subsequent to one regarded as classical ⟨the sonata form is a concept created by the ~ nineteenth century —P.H. Lang⟩ — **post·classicism** \"+\ *n*

**post·climax** \(ˈ)=+\ *n* [*post-* + *climax*] **:** a relatively stable ecological community requiring a greater amount of available moisture than that generally available to a climax and occurring typically where locally abundant soil moisture compensates for a generally deficient precipitation ⟨a forest ~ on a moist northward-facing slope within a grassland climax⟩ — compare PRECLIMAX

**post·clypeus** \"+\ *n* [NL, fr. *post-* + *clypeus*] **:** the upper or proximal portion of the clypeus in some insects — compare ANTECLYPEUS

**post coach** *n* [⁴*post*] **:** STAGECOACH; *specif* **:** one used for carrying the mails

**post·coital** \(ˈ)=+\ *adj* [*post-* + *coital*] **:** occurring or existing after coitus

**post·colonial** \¦=+\ *adj* [*post-* + *colonial*] **:** having the characteristics of the American colonial style of architecture but executed in the period following the revolution

**post·commissural** \(ˈ)=+\ *adj* [*postcommissure* + *-al*] **:** of, relating to, or transmitted by the postcommissures of the brain

**post·commissure** \"+\ *n* [*post-* + *commissure*] **:** one of the bands of white matter that bound the third ventricle of the brain posteriorly

**post-common** \(ˈ)=+\ *n* [ME *post-comoun,* fr. ML *post-communio*] **:** POST-COMMUNION

**post-communion** \¦=+\ *n, often cap P&C* [ML *postcommunio,* fr. L *post-* + LL *communio* communion — more at COMMUNION] **:** the portion of a Christian communion service that follows the communicating of the congregation

**post·consonantal** \(¦)=+\ *adj* [*post-* + *consonantal*] **:** immediately following a consonant

**post·cornu** \(ˈ)=+\ *n* [NL, fr. *post-* + L *cornu* horn, something shaped like a horn — more at HORN] **:** a posterior horn of the lateral ventricle

**post·cranial** \(ˈ)=+\ *adj* [*post-* + *cranial*] **:** lying behind the head **:** of the trunk and limbs ⟨bones of the ~ skeleton⟩

**post croaker** *n* [¹*post*] **:** SPOT 7

**post·dam** \(ˈ)=+\ *n* [*post-* + *dam*] **:** a posterior extension of a full denture to accomplish a complete seal between denture and tissues

¹**post·date** \(ˈ)=+\ *n* [*post-* + *date* (n.)] **:** a subsequent date; *esp* **:** a date assigned to an event or affixed to a document that is later than its actual date ⟨a ~ on a bill of exchange⟩

²**postdate** \"\ *vt* [*post-* + *date* (v.)] **1 a :** to date (a document) as of a time subsequent to that of execution ⟨~ a check⟩ **b :** to assign (an event) to a date subsequent to that of actual occurrence ⟨*postdated* her birth⟩ **2 :** to follow (something) in time ⟨the words ~ the rest of the inscription —R.S. Rogers⟩

¹**post·dental** \(ˈ)=+\ *adj* [ISV *post-* + *dental*] *of a consonant* **:** produced with the point of the tongue at the backs of the upper front teeth

²**postdental** \"\ *n* **:** a postdental consonant

**post·depositional** \(¦)=+\ *adj* [*post-* + *depositional*] **:** occurring or produced after deposition of the sediments involved — used of a geological change or formation

¹**post·diluvian** \¦=+\ *also* **post·diluvial** \"+\ *adj* [*post-* + *diluvian or diluvial*] **:** of or relating to the period after the flood described in the Bible ⟨~ man⟩

²**post·diluvian** \(¦)=+\ *n* -s **:** one living after the flood described in the Bible

**post·disseisin** *or* **post·disseizin** \¦=+\ *n* [AF *postdisseisine,* fr. *post-* + *disseisine* disseisin — more at DISSEISIN] **:** a second disseisin by the same disseisor from lands recovered by the assize of novel disseisin; *also* **:** the writ that lay for it

**post·doctoral** \(ˈ)=+\ *also* **post·doctorate** \"+\ *adj* [*post-* + *doctoral* or *doctorate*] **:** relating to, awarded for, or engaged in advanced academic or professional work after the attainment of a doctor's degree ⟨~ training program⟩ ⟨~ student⟩ ⟨~ studies⟩

**post·ea** \ˈpōstēə\ *n* -s [L, afterward, fr. *post* after + *ea,* prob. abl. of *ea,* fem. of *is* this, that, he — more at POST-, ITERATE] **:** the entry made by the trial judge after a verdict reciting that issue was joined and summarizing the proceedings

**po·steen** \pōˈstēn\ *or* **po·shteen** \-ˈs(h)tēn\ *or* **po·stin** \-ˈstēn\ *n* -s [Per *pōstīn* of leather, fr. *pōst* skin, fr. MPer] **:** an Afghan pelisse made of leather with the fleece on

**post·embryonic** \(¦)=+\ *also* **post·embryonal** \(ˈ)=+\ *adj* [*post-* + *embryonic* or *embryonal*] **:** succeeding the embryonic stage

**post·emergence** \¦=+\ *n* [*post-* + *emergence*] **:** a stage between the emergence of a seedling and the maturity of a crop plant — used esp. of seedling stages

**post·encephalitic** \(¦)=+\ *adj* [*post-* + *encephalitic*] **:** developing after and presumably as a result of encephalitis ⟨~ parkinsonism⟩

**post·encephalitis** \¦=+\ *n* [NL, fr. *post-* + *encephalitis*] **:** symptoms or residual abnormality remaining after recovery from epidemic encephalitis

**post·encephalon** \"+\ *n* [NL, fr. *post-* + *encephalon*] **:** METENCEPHALON

**post·entry** \(ˈ)=+\ *n* [*post-* + *entry*] **1 :** a subsequent or late entry (as of an item missed in an account) **2 :** the inspection and quarantine detention period following admission of plant material at a port of entry

**post entry** *n* [³*post*] **:** a last minute entry in a race or competition

¹**post·er** \ˈpōstə(r)\ *n* -s [⁵*post* + *-er*] **1 a** *archaic* **:** a swift traveler ⟨~*s* of the sea and land —Shak.⟩ **b :** a post-horse ⟨the yellow chaise . . . and . . . four ~*s* —Charles Lever⟩ **2 :** one that mails a letter **3 a :** one that posts bookkeeping entries **b :** POSTING CLERK

²**poster** \"\ *n* -s *often attrib* [²*post* + *-er*] **1 :** a bill or placard intended to be posted in a public place; *specif* **:** one that is decorative or pictorial **2 :** POSTER STAMP

³**poster** *vt* -ED/-ING/-s **:** to affix (posters) to ⟨~*ed* the wall⟩

**poster color** *n* **:** a paint with a gum or glue-size binder sold usu. in jars — compare ⁴DISTEMPER

**poste res·tante** \¦pō,streˈstäⁿt\ *n* [F, lit., remaining (staying) mail] **:** GENERAL DELIVERY

**pos·te·ri·ad** \päˈstirē,ad\ *adv* [*posterior* + *-ad*] **:** POSTERIORLY

¹**pos·te·ri·or** \(ˈ)päˈstirēə(r), (ˈ)pō¦-, -¦stēr-\ *adj* [L, compar. of *posterus* next, following, coming after, fr. *post* after — more at POST-] **1 a :** after in time **:** SUBSEQUENT **b :** logically consequent **2 a :** situated toward the back **:** after in place — opposed to *anterior* **b :** ADAXIAL — compare ANTERIOR **c** (1) **:** situated at or toward the hinder end of the body **:** CAUDAL (2) **:** DORSAL — used of human anatomy in which the upright posture makes dorsal and caudal identical — **pos·te·ri·or·ly** *adv*

²**posterior** \"\ *n* -s **1 posteriors** *pl, archaic* **:** DESCENDANTS ⟨neither he, nor his ~*s* from generation to generation, shall sit upon it —Sir Walter Scott⟩ **2 :** a posterior thing or part: as **a :** the rear end of a quadruped **b :** BUTTOCKS ⟨smacked him on his ~ and sent him out to play⟩ — often used in pl. ⟨when she laughed, which was often, her ~*s* gave a just-perceptible upward leap —Robertson Davies⟩

**posterior femoral cutaneous nerve** *n* **:** a nerve arising from the sacral plexus of each side leaving the pelvis in company with the sciatic nerve through the greater sciatic foramen to be distributed to the skin of the perineum and of the back of the thigh and leg

**posterior foramen** *n* **:** the opening in an insect's head leading to the thoracic cavity

**posterior horn** *n* **1 :** a dorsal column of gray matter in the spinal cord **2 :** the part of a lateral ventricle of the brain that extends inward and backward

**pos·te·ri·or·ic** \(ˈ)=¦=¦=ˈōrik\ *adj* [(*a*) *posteriori* + *-ic*] **:** A POSTERIORI — **pos·te·ri·or·i·cal·ly** \-rək(ə)lē\ *adv*

**pos·te·ri·or·i·ty** \(,)=¦=¦=ˈōrəd·ē, -ˈär-\ *n* -ES [ME *posteriorite,* fr. ML *posterioritas,* fr. L *posterior* + *-itas* -ity] **1 :** the quality or state of being later or subsequent — opposed to *priority* **2** *obs* **:** INFERIORITY

**posteriormost** \=¦=¦=,=\ *adj* [¹*posterior* + *most*] **:** farthest back in time, order, or position

**posterior naris** *n* **:** the opening or one of the paired openings between the nasal cavity and the pharynx or mouth

**posterior nasal spine** *n* **:** the nasal spine that is formed by the union of processes of the two palatine bones and projects between the posterior nares

**posterior paralysis** *n* **:** progressive weakness and loss of function accompanied by modification of joints and bones of the hindquarters of young pigs receiving inadequate vitamin D and calcium

**post·er·ist** \ˈpōstərəst\ *n* -s [²*poster* + *-ist*] **:** one who designs or makes posters

**pos·ter·i·ty** \päˈsterəd·ē, -rətē, -i\ *n* -ES [ME *posterite,* fr. MF *posterité,* fr. L *posteritat-, posteritas,* fr. *posterus* coming after + *-itat-, -itas* -ity — more at POSTERIOR] **1 :** the offspring of one progenitor to the furthest generation **:** DESCENDANTS ⟨secure the blessings of liberty to ourselves and our ~ —*U.S. Constitution*⟩ **2 :** all succeeding generations **:** future time ⟨for the benefit of ~⟩ ⟨transmit to ~⟩ ⟨do the best we can . . . leaving ~ free to do better —G.B.Shaw⟩

¹**pos·tern** \ˈpōstə(r)n, ˈpäs-\ *n* -s [ME *posterne,* fr. OF, alter. of *posterle,* fr. LL *posterula* little secret door, dim. of *postera* back door, fr. fem. of L *posterus* coming after — more at POSTERIOR] **1 a :** a back door or gate **:** a private or side entrance or way **b :** an obscure or disreputable way of entrance or escape **2 :** a subterraneous passage between the ditch and the interior of either the main works or outworks of a fortification

²**postern** \"\ *adj* **:** situated at the back, rear, or side **:** PRIVATE ⟨the ~ gate of the abbey⟩ ⟨a ~ door⟩

**postero-** *comb form* [L *posterus* coming after — more at POSTERIOR] **1 :** posterior and — ⟨*postero*anterior⟩ ⟨*postero*lateral⟩ **2 :** at the back part of ⟨*postero*dorsal⟩

**pos·tero·dorsad** \¦pästərō+\ *adv* [*postero-* + *dorsad*] **:** POSTERODORSALLY

**pos·tero·dorsal** \" +\ *adj* [*postero-* + *dorsal*] **:** of or relating to the posterior part of the back — **postero·dorsally** \"+\ *adv*

**pos·tero·external** \"+\ *adj* [*postero-* + *external*] **:** posterior and external in location or direction

**pos·tero·internal** \"+\ *adj* [*postero-* + *internal*] **:** posterior and internal in position or direction

**pos·tero·lateral** \"+\ *adj* [*postero-* + *lateral*] **:** posterior and lateral in position or direction

**pos·tero·median** \"+\ *adj* [*postero-* + *median*] **:** located on or near the dorsal midline of the body or a body part

¹**pos·tero·temporal** \"+\ *adj* [*postero-* + *temporal*] **:** of or relating to the supraclavicle of a fish

²**posterotemporal** \"\ *n* **:** the supraclavicle of a fish

**pos·tero·ventrad** \"+\ *adv* [*postero-* + *ventrad*] **:** in a posterior and ventral direction **:** at once posteriorly and ventrally

**poster paint** *n* [²*poster*] **:** POSTER COLOR

**poster panel** *n* **:** an outdoor structure having a standardized size surface on which advertising posters may be posted

**posters** *pl of* POSTER, *pres 3d sing of* POSTER

**poster stamp** *or* **poster seal** *n* **:** a charity seal made in extra large size

**post·ery** \ˈpōstərē\ *adj* [²*poster* + *-y*] **:** resembling a poster in pictorial effect ⟨an irregular solid background with altogether pleasing and ~ results —*Printer's Ink*⟩ ⟨~ and rather startling —*N. Y. Times*⟩

**post exchange** *n* [⁷*post*] **:** a shop at a military installation at which merchandise and services are sold to military personnel and authorized civilians

**post·exilic** \¦=+\ *also* **post·exilian** \"+\ *adj* [*post-* + *exilic* or *exilian*] **:** existing or happening after the Exile or the Babylonian Captivity of the Jews esp. during the period of 538 B.C. to A.D. 1 ⟨~ Judaism⟩ ⟨~ Hebrew⟩

**post·exist** \¦=+\ *vi* [*post-* + *exist*] **:** to exist after death — **post·existence** \"+\ *n*

**post·face** \ˈpōs(t)fəs\ *n* [F, fr. *post-* + *-face* (as in *préface* preface) — more at PREFACE] **:** a brief article or note (as of explanation) placed at the end of a publication

**postfact** *n* [L *postfactum,* neut. of *postfactus* done afterwards, fr. *post-* + *factus,* past part. of *facere* to do — more at DO] *obs* **:** a subsequent deed or occurrence ⟨confirmed upon the ~ —Thomas Fuller⟩

**post-factum** \(ˈ)=+\ *adj* [L *post factum* after the fact] **:** occurring after the fact **:** ex post facto **:** RETROSPECTIVE ⟨*post-factum* discussions of decisions —*America*⟩

**post-fine** \ˈ=,=\ *n* [*post-* + *fine*] **:** money paid in early English law for license to levy a fine — called also *King's silver*

¹**post·fix** \ˈ=,=\ *n* -ES [*post-* + *-fix* (as in *prefix*)] **:** a letter, syllable, or word added to the end of another word **:** SUFFIX

²**postfix** \(ˈ)=¦=\ *vt* **:** to affix at the end; *specif* **:** to add (a letter or syllable) to the end of a word

**post flag** *n* [⁷*post*] **:** the national flag measuring 19 feet fly by 10 feet hoist ordinarily used at a military post (as of the U.S. Army)

**post·form** \(ˈ)=+\ *vt* [*post-* + *form*] **:** to shape subsequently (as a sheet material after laminating)

**post-free** \(ˈ)=¦=\ *adj* [⁴*post* + *free*] *chiefly Brit* **:** POSTPAID

¹**post·frontal** \"+\ *adj* [*post-* + *frontal*] **:** situated behind the frontal bone or frontal region of the skull or in reptiles the frontal shield; *specif* **:** indicating a bone behind and above the orbit of which it commonly forms part of the border that is present in many vertebrates and corresponds to the postorbital process of the frontal bone of various birds and mammals

²**postfrontal** \"\ *n* **:** a postfrontal part (as a bone or scale); *specif* **:** the sphenotic bone of a fish

**post·furca** \"+\ *n* [NL, fr. *post-* + *furca*] **:** the posterior one of the forked internal thoracic processes of the sternum of an insect — **post·furcal** \"+\ *adj*

**post·ganglionary** \(ˈ)=+\ *adj* [*post-* + *ganglionary*] **:** occurring beyond, behind, or distal to a ganglion

**post·ganglionic** \(¦)=+\ *adj* [*post-* + *ganglionic*] **:** lying behind, beyond, or distal to a ganglion — used of the axons of neurons whose cell bodies lie within an autonomic ganglion; compare PREGANGLIONIC

**post·gena** \(ˈ)=+\ *n* [NL, fr. L *post-* + *gena*] **:** the lateral part of the area of the insect cranium between the occipital and postoccipital sutures

**post·glacial** \(ˈ)=+\ *adj* [ISV *post-* + *glacial*] **:** occurring after a period of glaciation (as the Pleistocene)

¹**post·glenoid** \(ˈ)=+\ *also* **post·glenoidal** \¦=+\ *adj* [*post-* + *glenoid, glenoidal*] **:** situated behind the glenoid fossa

²**postglenoid** \"\ *n* -s **:** a flattened expansion of the squamosal part of the temporal bone lying posterior to the glenoid fossa

**post·gnathal** \(ˈ)=+\ *adj* [*post-* + *gnathal*] **:** situated behind the gnathal region of an insect's head

**post·grad** \(ˈ)=+\ *n* [by shortening] *slang* **:** POSTGRADUATE

¹**post·graduate** \(ˈ)=+\ *adj* [*post-* + *graduate*] **1 :** GRADUATE 1b **2 :** of, relating to, or engaged in study following graduation from high school usu. concentrating on preparation for college entrance

²**postgraduate** \"\ *n* **:** a student continuing his education after graduation from high school or college

¹**posthaste** \(ˈ)=¦=\ *n* [⁴*post* (courier) + *haste*] *archaic* **:** speed in traveling (as of a post or courier) **:** great haste — used chiefly in the phrase *in posthaste*

²**posthaste** \"\ *adv* **:** with great speed **:** in great haste **:** by the fastest possible means ⟨riding ~⟩ ⟨sent ~ for his lawyer⟩

³**posthaste** \"\ *adj, obs* **:** SPEEDY, IMMEDIATE ⟨requires your haste, ~ appearance —Shak.⟩

**post·heating** \(ˈ)=+\ *n* [*post-* + *heating*] **:** the process of heating a metal after welding in order to decrease the rate of cooling to room temperature

**pos·thi·tis** \(,)päsˈthīd·əs\ *n, pl* **pos·thit·i·des** \-thid·ə,dēz\ [NL, fr. Gk *posthē* penis, foreskin + NL *-itis* — more at PENIS] **:** inflammation of the prepuce

**post hoc** \(ˈ)pōst¦häk\ *adv* [L; fr. the use of the proposition *post hoc, ergo propter hoc* meaning "after this, therefore because of this" as an example of the fallacy of arguing from mere temporal sequence to cause and effect relationship] **:** after this — compare PROPTER HOC

**posthole** \ˈ=,=\ *n* [¹*post* + *hole*] **1 :** a hole sunk in the ground to hold a fence post **2 :** a shallow oil well

**post-hole digger** *n* **:** a tool for digging postholes; *esp* **:** one operated from the power takeoff on a tractor

**post horn** *n* [⁴*post*] **:** a simple straight or coiled brass or copper wind instrument with cupped mouthpiece used esp. by postilions of the 18th and 19th centuries

post horn

**post–horse** \ˈ=,=\ *n* [¹*post*] **:** a horse for use by postriders or in riding post

**posthouse** \ˈ=,=\ *n* [⁴*post* + *house*] **1 :** a house or inn for exchanging post-horses and accommodating postriders **2** *archaic* **:** POST OFFICE

**post·hu·ma** \ˈpäschəmə, päˈst(y)əmə\ *n pl* [L *postuma, posthuma,* neut. pl. of *postumus, posthumus*] **:** posthumous writings

**posthume** *adj* [MF *postume, posthume,* fr. L *postumus, posthumus*] *obs* **:** POSTHUMOUS

**post·hu·mous** \ˈpäschəməs, päˈst(y)üməs *sometimes* (ˈ)pō-\ *adj* [L *posthumus,* by folk etymology (influence of *humus* earth) fr. *postumus,* superl. of *posterus* coming after — more at HUMBLE, POSTERIOR] **1 :** born after the death of the father ⟨a ~ son⟩ **2 :** published after the death of the author ⟨a ~ volume of poems⟩ **3 :** following or occurring after one's death ⟨~ fame⟩ ⟨~ vindication⟩ — **post·hu·mous·ly** *adv* — **post·hu·mous·ness** *n* -ES

**post·hypnotic** \(¦)=+\ *adj* [ISV *post-* + *hypnotic*] **:** of, relating to, or characteristic of the period following a hypnotic trance during which the subject will still carry out suggestions made by the operator during the trance state ⟨~ suggestion⟩ — **post·hypnotically** \"+\ *adv*

**post·hypophysis** \¦=+\ *n* [NL, fr. *post-* + *hypophysis*] **:** the posterior lobe of the pituitary body

**pos·ti·cal** \ˈpästəkəl\ *also* **pos·tic** \-tik\ *adj* [L *posticus,* adj., that is behind, fr. *post* after, behind + *-icus* -ic, -ical — more at POST-] **:** POSTERIOR — **pos·ti·cal·ly** \-tək(ə)lē\ *adv*

**pos·tiche** \pä'stēsh, pȯ'-, ˈ=,=\ *n* -s [F, fr. Sp *postizo,* fr. *postizo* false, artificial, short for *apostizo,* fr. LL *appositicius* added, fr. L *appositus* (past part. of *apponere* to place near, apply to, add) + *-icius* -itious — more at APPOSITE] **:** false hair: as **a :** SWITCH **b :** TOUPEE

**pos·ti·cous** \pä'stīkəs\ *adj* [L *posticus,* fr. *post* behind, after + *-icus* -ic — more at POST-] **1 :** POSTERIOR **2 :** situated on the outer side of a filament — used of an extrorse anther

**post·ictal** \(ˈ)=+\ *adj* [*post-* + *ictal*] **:** following a sudden attack (as of epilepsy) ⟨~ drowsiness⟩

**pos·ti·cum** \pä'stīkəm\ *n, pl* **posti·ca** \-kə\ [L, rear of a building, back door, fr. neut. of *posticus* back, posterior — more at POSTICOUS] **:** a portico behind an ancient Greek or Roman temple

**post·ie** \ˈpōsti\ *n* -s [⁴*post* + *-ie*] *Scot* **:** POSTMAN

¹**pos·til** \ˈpästəl\ *n* -s [ME *postille,* fr. MF, fr. ML *postilla,* prob. fr. *post illa* (*verba textus*) after those words of the text, fr. L *post* after + *illa,* neut. acc. pl. of *ille* that — more at POST-, ALARM] **1 a :** a marginal note **:** COMMENT; *specif* **:** an explanatory marginal note in the Bible **b postils** *pl, obs* **:** COMMENTARY **2 a** *obs* **:** a short homily on a Scriptural passage; *esp* **:** one on the Gospel or Epistle for the day **b :** a collection of such homilies

²**postil** \"\ *vt* **postiled** *or* **postilled; postiled** *or* **postilled; postiling** *or* **postilling; postils** [ME *postilen,* fr. MF *postiller,* fr. ML *postillare,* fr. *postilla*] *archaic* **:** to write marginal comments in (a text) **:** ANNOTATE, GLOSS

**pos·til·ion** *or* **pos·til·lion** \pōˈstilyən, pəˈ-\ *n* -s [MF *postillon,* fr. It *postiglione,* fr. *posta* post — more at POST (mail)] **1** *obs* **:** POSTRIDER, POSTBOY, COURIER **2 :** one who rides as a guide on the near horse of a pair or of one of the pairs attached to a coach or post chaise esp. without a coachman **3 :** a woman's hat with a high narrow crown and a narrow rolled brim

postilion 3

**post·impressionism** \¦=+\ *n, usu cap* [F *postimpressionisme,* fr. *post-* + *impressionisme* impressionism — more at IMPRESSIONISM] **:** a theory or practice originating among French artists (as Cézanne, Matisse, Derain) in the last quarter of the 19th century that in revolt against impressionism stressed variously volume, picture structure, or expressionism

**post·impressionist** \"+\ *n* [F *postimpressioniste,* fr. *post-* + *impressioniste* impressionist — more at IMPRESSIONIST] **:** an adherent or follower of Postimpressionism

**post·impressionistic** \"+\ *adj* **:** of, relating to, or resembling Postimpressionism — **post·impressionistically** \"+\ *adv*

**postin** *var of* POSTEEN

¹**posting** *adj, archaic* [fr. pres. part. of ⁵*post*] **:** SPEEDY, FLEETING

²**posting** *n* -s [fr. gerund of ⁵*post*] **1 a :** the act of transferring an entry or item from a book of original entry to the proper account in a ledger **b :** the record in a ledger account resulting from the transfer of an entry or item from a book of original entry ⟨the debit ~ was made in the cash account⟩ **2 :** MAILING ⟨holiday ~*s*⟩

³**posting** *n* -s [fr. gerund of ⁸*post*] **:** appointment to a post or command ⟨my next ~ had been announced —*Atlantic*⟩

**posting box** *n, Brit* **:** a public mailbox

**posting clerk** *n* **:** one who records details of business transactions and posts entries to the proper records

**posting machine** *n* **:** a business machine esp. designed for the posting of ledgers and other business history records or the performing of similar operations (as the recording and totaling of running bank deposits and withdrawals)

**post–juvenal** \(ˈ)=+\ *adj* [*post-* + *juvenal*] **:** following or terminating the juvenal stage of a bird's life history — compare JUVENAL PLUMAGE, ²JUVENILE 2b

**post-kantian** \"+\ *adj, usu cap K* [*post-* + *Kantian*] **:** following after Kant; *specif* **:** of or relating to the school of idealists (as Fichte, Schelling, and Hegel) who followed Kant and developed some of his ideas

**post·larva** \"+\ *n* [NL, fr. *post-* + *larva*] **:** an immature fish after complete absorption of the yolk sac but before it has attained the appearance of a miniature adult **:** an advanced fry — **post·larval** \"+\ *adj*

**post·liminary** \"+\ *adj* [in sense 1, fr. *postliminium* + *-ary;* in sense 2, fr. *post-* + *liminary*] **1** *or* **post·li·min·i·ary** \¦=¦ləˈminē,erē\ **:** of, relating to, or involving the right of postliminium **2 :** done or carried on after something else or as a conclusion **:** SUBSEQUENT — opposed to *preliminary*

**post·li·min·i·um** \ˌpōs(t)ləˈminēəm\ *or* **post·lim·i·ny** \(ˈ)=ˈliməne\ *n, pl* **postlimin·ia** \ˌ=ləˈminēə\ *or* **postliminies** [L *postliminium,* fr. *post-* + *limin-, limen* threshold — more at LIMB] **1 :** a Roman legal doctrine whereby those captured by an enemy are regarded as having died freemen before capture to protect those claiming under them and whereby upon their return to the jurisdiction of Rome the captives regain their suspended property and civil rights **2 :** the right or rule of international law under which when persons or things taken by an enemy in war come again under the control of their own state they as a general rule regain the rights belonging or relating to them before capture

**post locust** *n* [¹*post*] **:** LOCUST 3a(2)

**post·lude** \ˈpōst,lüd, -ō,sl-\ *n* -s [*post-* + *-lude* (as in *prelude*)] **1 :** a closing piece of music or the closing section of a piece; *esp* **:** an organ voluntary at the end of a church service **2 :** a closing phase (as of an historical epoch or literary work) **:** EPILOGUE

**post·lu·di·um** \(ˈ)=¦=dēəm\ *n* -s [NL, fr. *post-* + *-ludium,* (as in ML *praeludium* prelude) — more at PRELUDE] **:** POSTLUDE 1

¹**post·man** \ˈpō(s)tmən, -,man, -aa(ə)n\ *n, pl* **postmen** [⁴*post* + *man*] **:** MAIL CARRIER

²**postman** \"\ *n, pl* **postmen** [¹*post* + *man;* fr. the fact that his place in the court was beside the post used as a measure of length in excise cases] **:** a junior barrister in the former English Court of Exchequer having precedence in motion except in Crown business — compare TUBMAN 1

**postman's knock** *n* **:** a British game similar to post office

¹**postmark** \ˈ=,=\ *n* [⁴*post* + *mark*] **:** an official postal marking on a piece of mail; *specif* **:** a mark showing the name of the post office and the date and sometimes the hour of

mailing and often serving as the actual and only cancellation
**²postmark** \"\ *vt* : to put a postmark on ⟨~ a letter⟩
**postmark ad** *or* **postmark advertisement** *n* : CACHET 4b
**postmaster** \ˈ=,==\ *n* [⁴*post* + *master*] **1 a :** an official in charge of posts or couriers **b :** a local official charged with carrying the mails from his station to the next **c :** a local official in charge of receiving and distributing the mail **d :** one who has charge of a post office **2 a :** one who has charge of a station for accommodation of travelers **b :** one who supplies post-horses **3 :** a holder of a scholarship (as at Merton College, Oxford) orig. entitling the recipient to an allowance of food
**postmaster general** *n, pl* **postmasters general** *also* **postmaster generals :** an official in charge of a national post office department
**post·mas·ter·ship** \-,ship\ *n* : the office of postmaster
**postmaster's stamp** *or* **postmaster stamp** *n* : a provisional postage stamp issued by a postmaster in the U.S. from 1845 to 1847 or Bermuda from 1848 to about 1856 to pay for government postal service for which government stamps had not yet been issued — compare CARRIER'S STAMP
**post-maturation** \(ˈ)=+\ *n* [*post-* + *maturation*] : changes that may occur in a fruit when it ripens on the plant
**post-maturity** \ˈ=+\ *n* [*post-* + *maturity*] : the quality or state of being past the period of maturity ⟨~ of a fetus⟩
**post·media** \(ˈ)=+\ *n* [NL, fr. *post-* + *media*] : a postmedian vein
**post·median** \(ˈ)=+\ *also* **post·medial** \"+\ *adj* [*post-* + *median* or *medial*] **1 :** located behind the middle (as of the body) **2 :** of or relating to a vein of the wing of an insect that is now regarded as a branch of the cubitus
**post·menopausal** \(ˈ)=+\ *adj* [*post-* + *menopausal*] : having undergone menopause ⟨~ women⟩ : occurring after menopause ⟨~ vaginitis⟩
**post·menopause** \(ˈ)=+\ *n* [*post-* + *menopause*] : a period of life after cessation of the menses
**post·mentum** \(ˈ)=+\ *n* [NL, fr. *post-* + *mentum*] : the part of the insect labium that is attached to the cranium
**post·meridian** \ˈ=+\ *adj* [L *postmeridianus*, fr. *post-* + *meridianus* meridian — more at MERIDIAN] : occurring after noon : of or relating to the afternoon ⟨the ~ hours of the day⟩
**post me·rid·i·em** \ˈ=mə'ridēəm, -ē,em\ *adj* [L, after noon] : being after noon — abbr. *p.m.*, *P.M.*
**post-mill** \ˈ=,=\ *n* [¹*post*] : a windmill supported by a single sturdy post about which it revolves to face the wind
**¹post·millenarian** \(ˈ)=+\ *n* [*post-* + *millenarian*] : one who holds the doctrine of postmillennialism
**²postmillenarian** \"\ *adj* : of or relating to the postmillenarians or postmillennialism
**post·millenarianism** \"+\ *n* : POSTMILLENNIALISM
**post·millennial** \ˈ=+\ *also* **post·millennian** \"+\ *adj* [*post-* + *millennial* or *millennian*] **1 :** coming after or relating to the period after the millennium **2 :** espousing the doctrine of postmillennialism
**post·millennialism** \ˈ=+\ *n* : a theological doctrine that the second coming of Christ will be after the millennium which is to come as the result of the Christianization of the world without miraculous intervention — opposed to *premillennialism*; compare AMILLENNIALISM
**post·millennialist** \"+\ *n* : an adherent of postmillennialism
**post·mineral** \(ˈ)=+\ *adj* [*post-* + *mineral*] : originating later than associated mineral deposits ⟨a ~ dike⟩
**postmistress** \ˈ=,==\ *n* [⁴*post* + *mistress*] : a female postmaster
**post·mortal** \(ˈ)=+\ *adj* [*post-* + *mortal*] : occurring after death ⟨~ wounds⟩ ⟨~ decomposition⟩ — **post·mortally** \"+\ *adv*
**post-mor·tem** \(ˈ)pōs(t)ˈmȯrtəm\ *adv* [L *post mortem*] : after death ⟨seven cases examined *post-mortem*⟩
**¹postmortem** \"\ *adj* [L *post mortem*] **1 a :** of or relating to the period after death ⟨~ changes⟩ **b :** following the event ⟨~ analysis of a bridge hand⟩ **2 :** of, relating to, or used in a postmortem examination ⟨a ~ table⟩
**²postmortem** \"\ *n* -s **1 :** POSTMORTEM EXAMINATION **2 :** an examination or analysis after the event ⟨a ~ on the election⟩ ⟨held a ~ on their bidding tactics⟩
**³postmortem** \"\ *vb* -ED/-ING/-S [²*postmortem*] *vt* : to perform a postmortem on ~ *vi* : to make a postmortem
**postmortem dividend** *n* : a dividend paid after an insured person's death representing his share in surplus for the current year
**postmortem examination** *n* : an examination of the body after death usu. with such dissection as will expose the vital organs for determining the cause of death or the character and extent of changes produced by disease : AUTOPSY
**post·naris** \(ˈ)=+\ *n* [NL, fr. *post-* + L *naris* nostril — more at NOSE] : one of the posterior nares
**¹post·nasal** \(ˈ)=+\ *adj* [*post-* + *nasal*] : lying or occurring posterior to the nose ⟨a ~ scale⟩
**²postnasal** \"\ *n* : a postnasal part; *specif* : a scale or either of a pair of scales lying behind the nasal of most lizards
**postnasal drip** *n* : flow of mucous secretion from the posterior part of the nasal cavity onto the wall of the pharynx occurring usu. as a chronic accompaniment of an allergic state (as hay fever)
**post·natal** \"+\ *adj* [ISV *post-* + *natal*] : occurring after birth ⟨~ development⟩; *specif* : of or relating to an infant immediately after birth ⟨~ care⟩ — compare NEONATAL — **post·natally** \"+\ *adv*
**post·nate** \(ˈ)pōs(t)ˈnāt\ *adj* [ML *postnatus* born after, fr. *post-* + *natus* born — more at NATION] *archaic* : arising or developing later : SUBSEQUENT
**post·na·tus** \(ˈ)pōs(t)ˈnād·əs\ *n, pl* **postna·ti** \-ā,tī\ [ML] : a person born after an event esp. with reference to the existence of political rights (as a person born in one of the 13 American colonies after the Declaration of Independence) — usu. used in pl. ⟨of the slaves only the *postnati* were freed⟩; opposed to *antenatus*
**post-nicene** \(ˈ)=+\ *adj, cap N* [*post-* + *Nicene*] : of or relating to times subsequent to the Council of Nicaea esp. within the patristic period
**post note** *n* [⁴*post*] : a bank note payable to order at a specified future time as distinguished from one payable to bearer on demand; *specif* : one issued as a circulating medium by banks and financial institutions before the American Civil War
**post·notum** \(ˈ)=+\ *n* [NL, fr. *post-* + *notum*] : a small dorsal sclerite on the insect thorax posterior to the notum — called also *postscutellum*
**post·nuptial** \(ˈ)=+\ *adj* [*post-* + *nuptial*] : made or happening after marriage or mating ⟨~ journey⟩ — **post·nuptially** \"+\ *adv*
**postnuptial settlement** *also* **postnuptial agreement** *or* **postnuptial contract** *n* : a legal settlement after marriage of property by one spouse upon the other often but not necessarily in contemplation of separation or divorce
**post oak** *n* [¹*post*] : any of several American oaks with tough moisture-resistant woods used esp. for fence posts; *esp* : a medium-sized oak (*Quercus stellata*) of the eastern and central U.S. that has a scaly fissured reddish brown bark, dark green lyrate pinnatifid leaves, and moderately large obtusely ovoid acorns — called also *box white oak, brash oak, iron oak*
**post-oak grape** *n* **1 :** a tall growing grape of the southern and central U.S. that is usu. considered a variety (*Vitis labrusca lincecumii*) of the common American fox grape **2 :** the large edible purplish black slightly bloomy fruit of the post-oak grape
**¹post-obit** \(ˈ)=+\ *adj* [L *post obitum* after death] : occurring or taking effect after death ⟨*post-obit* liquidation⟩ ⟨a *post-obit* gift⟩
**²post-obit** \"\ *n* : POST-OBIT BOND
**post-obit bond** *n* : a bond payable after a person's death; *esp* : one made by a reversioner to secure payment of a loan with a bonus and interest and to be paid out of his reversion on its vesting in him
**post·obituary** \ˈ=+\ *adj* [*post-* + *obituary*] : POST-OBIT
**post·occipital suture** \ˈ=+-\ *n* : a posterior groove on the cranium of an insect having tentorial pits at each end and forming internally a ridge on which dorsal neck and prothoracic muscles find their attachment
**post·occiput** \(ˈ)=+\ *n* [*post-* + *occiput*] : the posterior rim of the insect cranium

**¹post·ocular** \(ˈ)=+\ *adj* [ISV *post-* + *ocular*] : located behind the eye — used esp. of one or more scales in a snake or lizard
**²postocular** \"\ *n* : a part (as a shield or scale) that is postocular
**post office** *n* [⁴*post* + *office*] **1 a :** a government department charged with regulating and handling the transmission of mail in a country ⟨in the U. S. the *post office* is an executive department and its chief official, the postmaster general, is a member of the president's cabinet⟩ **b :** a section of a post office department handling the mail for a particular place (as a city or town) ⟨a list of the *post offices* of Canada⟩ **c** (1) **:** a building or a section of a building housing facilities and staff for carrying out all or some of the functions of a post-office department (2) **:** a railway car or train or a bus or truck fitted for the sorting of mail in transit **d :** a place where mail is handled for dispatch and delivery ⟨a camp *post office*⟩ ⟨a university *post office*⟩ **2 :** a game in which a player acting as postmaster or postmistress may exact a kiss from one of the opposite sex as payment for the pretended delivery of a letter
**post-office** *adj* : of, relating to, issued, or conducted by the government through the post office ⟨a *post-office* annuity⟩ ⟨a *post-office* savings bank⟩
**post-office address** *n* : an address for mail
**post-office box** *n* : a rented compartment in a post office for the keeping of mail that is not to be delivered but is to be called for by the renter — see CALL BOX 1, LOCKBOX
**post-office car** *n* : RAILWAY MAIL CAR
**post-office order** *n, Brit* : a money order issued by a post office but not bearing the name of the payee which is given on an accompanying letter of advice
**post-office red** *n* : a deep reddish orange to dark reddish brown
**post·operative** \(ˈ)=+\ *adj* [ISV *post-* + *operative*] : following a surgical operation ⟨~ care⟩ ⟨~ complications⟩ — **post·operatively** \"+\ *adv*
**post·oral** \(ˈ)=+\ *adj* [*post-* + *oral*] : situated behind the mouth
**¹post·orbital** \(ˈ)=+\ *adj* [*post-* + *orbital*] : situated behind the orbit ⟨the ~ scales of some fishes and reptiles⟩: **a :** being a downwardly directed process of the frontal bone of many mammals and birds that forms part of the outer or posterior border of the orbit and in some lower vertebrates is borne on or represented by the postfrontal bone **b :** being a bone behind and below the postfrontal in many reptiles that forms part of the boundary of the orbit
**²postorbital** \"\ *n* : a postorbital part (as a bone or scale)
**post·or·bi·to·squamosal arch** \ˈ=ˌȯ(r)bə,tō+ . . . -\ *n* [²*postorbital* + *-o-* + *squamosal*] : a bony arch made up of fused portions of the postorbital and squamosal bones that separates the two temporal openings in a diapsid reptile
**post·otic** \(ˈ)=+\ *adj* [*post-* + *otic*] : posterior to the otic vesicle
**postpaid** \(ˈ)=ˈ=\ *adv* [⁴*post* + *paid*] with postage paid by the sender and not chargeable to the receiver
**¹post·palatal** \"+\ *adj* [ISV *post-* + *palatal*] **1 :** POSTPALATINE **2 a :** articulated against the rear third or the rear half of the hard palate **b :** articulated against the rear half of the palate as a whole **:** articulated against the soft palate or velum : VELAR
**²postpalatal** \"\ *n* : a postpalatal part or sound
**¹post·palatine** \"+\ *adj* [*post-* + *palatine*] : located behind the palate or palatine bones; *specif* : of, relating to, or constituting a pair of bones now believed to be the pterygoids that are found on the skulls of some reptiles (as crocodiles)
**²postpalatine** \"\ *n* : a postpalatine part
**post·paleolithic** \(ˈ)=+\ *adj, usu cap 2nd P* [*post-* + *paleolithic*] : of, relating to, or constituting the period following the Paleolithic or initiating the Neolithic
**¹post·parietal** \ˈ=+\ *adj* [*post-* + *parietal*] : located behind parietal elements
**²postparietal** \"\ *n* : a postparietal part (as a scale)
**post·par·tum** \(ˈ)pōs(t)ˈpärd·əm\ *or* **post·par·tal** \-d·ᵊl\ *adj* [*postpartum* fr. L *post partum* after birth; *postpartal* fr. L *post partum* + E *-al*] : following parturition ⟨~ care⟩ ⟨*postpartal* examination⟩ ⟨the ~ period of 40 days —O.G.Simmons⟩
**post·petiole** \(ˈ)=+\ *n* [*post-* + *petiole*] : the second segment of the pedicel of some ants
**post·phragma** \(ˈ)=+\ *n* [NL, fr. *post-* + *phragma*] : the phragma of the postnotum of an insect
**post·pituitary** \ˈ=+\ *adj* [*post-* + *pituitary*] **1 :** situated behind the pituitary body or the sella turcica **2 :** arising in or derived from the posterior lobe of the pituitary body
**post·pon·able** \(ˈ)pōs(t)ˈpōnəbəl, ˌpəs(t)ˈp-\ *adj* : capable of being postponed
**post·pone** \(ˈ)pōs(t)ˈpōn, ˌpəs(t)ˈ-\ *vt* -ED/-ING/-S [L *postponere* to put after, neglect, postpone, fr. *post-* + *ponere* to place, put — more at POSITION] **1 :** to hold back to a later time : DEFER, DELAY ⟨~ payments for a year⟩ ⟨~ further discussion of the matter⟩ ⟨the meeting is *postponed* until next week⟩ ⟨*postponed* doing her housework for a few hours⟩ **2 a :** to place after : put nearer the end ⟨*postponing* the verb in German⟩ — used esp. of words and particles **b :** to place after in order of precedence, preference, or importance : SUBORDINATE ⟨English law in its canons of inheritance *postponed* the daughter to the son —Frederick Pollock & F.W.Maitland⟩ ⟨wish you never to ~ your business to literary trifling —G.B. Shaw⟩ **syn** see DEFER
**post·pone·ment** \-mənt\ *n* -s : the act of postponing or the condition of being postponed : DEFERMENT, DELAY ⟨ordered a 30-day ~⟩ ⟨the temporary ~ of inflation —Clark Kerr⟩
**post·pose** \(ˈ)pōs(t)ˈpōz\ *vt* [MF *postposer*, modif. (influenced by *poser* to put, place) of L *postponere* (perfect stem *postpos-*)] **1** *obs* : POSTPONE 2a,b **2 :** to place (as a particle) after a grammatically related word ⟨the articles . . . are *postposed* in Scandinavian and Rumanian —M.H.Swadesh⟩
**post·position** \ˈ=+\ *n* [F, fr. *postposer* + *-ition* (as in *position*)] **1 :** the postposing of a grammatical element **2 :** a postposed word or particle; *esp* : a word or suffix (as *-ward* in *cityward*) having the function of a preposition — **post·positional** \"+\ *adj* — **post·positionally** \"+\ *adv*
**¹post·positive** \(ˈ)=+\ *adj* [LL *postpositivus*, fr. L *postpositus* (past part. of *postponere* to put after, neglect, postpone) + *-ivus* -ive — more at POSTPONE] : placed after another word : characterized by postposition — **post·positively** \"+\ *adv*
**²postpositive** \"\ *n* -s : a postpositive particle or word
**post·prandial** \ˈ=+\ *adj* [*post-* + *prandial*] : of, relating to, or occurring in the period after a meal esp. dinner ⟨~ speeches⟩ ⟨~ nap⟩ ⟨~ air of well-being —Brendan Gill⟩ ⟨an abnormal ~ blood sugar level —*Jour. Amer. Med. Assoc.*⟩ — **post·prandially** \(ˈ)=+\ *adv*
**post·predicament** \ˈ=+\ *n* [ML *postpraedicamentum*, fr. L *post-* + LL *praedicamentum* predicament — more at PREDICAMENT] : any one of the five supplementary categories of opposition, priority, simultaneity, movement, and possession treated in the probably spurious chapters 10 to 15 of Aristotle's *Categories* — compare CATEGORY 1a
**post·primary** \(ˈ)=+\ *adj* [*post-* + *primary*] *chiefly Brit* : subsequent to primary ⟨~ education⟩ ⟨~ schools⟩
**post·pubertal** \"+\ *adj* [*post-* + *pubertal*] : occurring after puberty
**post·pubic** \(ˈ)=+\ *adj* [NL *postpubis* + E *-ic*] : of or relating to the postpubis
**post·pubis** \"+\ *n* [NL, fr. *post-* + *pubis*] : the part of the pubic bone in birds and some reptiles that lies behind the acetabulum, in birds represents the true pubis, and in reptiles is a distinct process
**post·pyramidal** \ˈ=+\ *adj* [*post-* + *pyramidal*] : lying behind the pyramids of the medulla oblongata ⟨the ~ nucleus⟩
**post race** *n* [¹*post*] : a horse or dog race in which each subscriber declares at the usual time before a race the animal he will run
**post·record** \ˈ=+\ *vt* [*post-* + *record*] : to record (voice or sound effects) after the corresponding scene has been photographed in making movies
**post·reduction** \"+\ *n* [*post-* + *reduction*] : the reduction of chromosomes in the second meiotic division
**post rem** \(ˈ)pōˈstrem\ *or* **post res** \-ˈrās\ *adv* [*post rem* fr. L, after the thing; *post res* fr. L, after the things] : logically subsequent to the existence of particulars — compare AVICENNISM
**pos·tre·mo·geniture** \pä'strēmō+\ *n* [L *postremus* last (superl. of *posterus* coming after) + E *-o-* + *geniture* — more at POSTERIOR] : ULTIMOGENITURE
**postrider** \ˈ=,==\ *n* [⁴*post* + *rider*] : a courier or mail carrier using post-horses
**post-ripeness** \(ˈ)=+\ *n* [*post-* + *ripeness*] : the condition of a fruit that has undergone changes following ripening
**post road** *n* [⁴*post*] **1 :** a road used for the conveyance of mail: as **a :** one having a series of posthouses or stations **b :** one designated to be used by official carriers of mail **2 :** a road, airway, waterway, or railway over which mail is carried during the time in transit **3 :** a city letter-carrier route
**pos·trorse** \ˈpō,strȯrs, ˈpä-\ *adj* [*post-* + *-rorse* (as in *antrorse*)] : RETRORSE — opposed to *antrorse*
**post route** *n* [⁴*post*] : a route prescribed for a mail carrier to take in his regular delivery trips
**post-runner** \ˈ=,==\ *n* [⁴*post*] **1 :** one who carries the post on foot **2 :** a speedy messenger : COURIER
**posts** *pl of* POST, *pres 3d sing of* POST
**post·scapula** \(ˈ)=+\ *n* [NL, fr. *post-* + *scapula*] : the infraspinous part of the scapula — **post·scapular** \"+\ *adj*
**post·score** \(ˈ)=+\ *vt* [*post-* + *score*] : POSTRECORD
**post·script** \ˈpōs(t)skript\ *n* [NL *postscriptum*, fr. L, neut. of *postscriptus*, past part. of *postscribere* to write after, fr. *post-* + *scribere* to write — more at SCRIBE] : a note or series of notes appended to a completed composition (as a letter, article, or book) usu. giving an afterthought or additional information ⟨added a ~ to the . . . manuscript —R.H.Gabriel⟩ ⟨included in the autobiography as a sort of ~ —*Harper's*⟩ — abbr. *PS, ps*
**post·scrip·tum** \(ˈ)pōs(t)ˈskriptəm\ *n, pl* **postscrip·ta** \-ptə\ [NL] : POSTSCRIPT
**post·scutellar** \ˈ=+\ *adj* [NL *postscutellum* + E *-ar*] : of or relating to the postnotum
**post·scutellum** \"+\ *also* **post·scutum** \"+\ *n* [NL, fr. *post-* + *scutellum*] : POSTNOTUM
**post·sphenoid** \(ˈ)=+\ *n* [*post-* + *sphenoid*] : the posterior portion of the sphenoid bone developed in five separate parts consisting of a central basisphenoid, the two alisphenoids, and the two medial pterygoid laminae
**post·spinal** \"+\ *adj* [*post-* + *spinal*] : that follows spinal anesthesia ⟨a ~ headache⟩
**post·synaptic** \ˈ=+\ *adj* [*post-* + *synaptic*] : following synapsis : belonging to the kind that exists after synaptic alteration ⟨a ~ chromosome⟩
**post·synchronization** \(ˈ)=+\ *n* [ISV *postsynchronize* + *-ation*] : the act or process of postsynchronizing
**post·synchronize** \(ˈ)=+\ *vt* [ISV *post-* + *synchronize*] : to add (speech or sound effects) in synchronism with the action after a scene has been photographed in making movies
**¹post·synsacral** \(ˈ)=+\ *adj* [*post-* + NL *synsacrum* + E *-al*] : situated behind the synsacrum
**²postsynsacral** \"\ *n* -s : a caudal vertebra in birds
**post·systolic** \ˈ=+\ *adj* [*post-* + *systolic*] : following the systole of the heart ⟨a ~ murmur⟩
**post·temporal** \(ˈ)=+\ *n* [*post-* + *temporal*] : a bone connecting the back part of the skull and the dorsal part of the pectoral arch in most teleost fishes
**post·tension** \"+\ *vt* [*post-* + *tension*] : to apply tension to (reinforcing steel) after concrete has set
**post·tibia** \"+\ *n* [NL, fr. *post-* + *tibia*] : the tibia of a hind leg of an insect
**post·tonic** \"+\ *adj* [*post-* + *tonic*] **1** *of a sound* : immediately following or constituting one of a succession of consonants immediately following a vowel having stress **2** *of a syllable* : immediately following a syllable having stress
**post town** *n* [⁴*post*] **1 :** a town having the chief post office of a local area **2** *Brit* : a town having a post office which is the distribution point for mail to the smaller local post offices in a given area and whose name must be part of the address on mail to any place within that area
**post trader** *n* [²*post*] : one of the sutlers appointed by the secretary of war for each post in the U. S. military service
**post·traumatic** \ˈ=+\ *adj* [ISV *post-* + *traumatic*] : following or resulting from trauma ⟨~ epilepsy⟩
**¹post·tympanic** \ˈ=+\ *adj* [*post-* + *tympanic*] : situated behind the tympanic bone or external auditory meatus
**²posttympanic** \"\ *n* : a posttympanic part; *specif* : a posttympanic ossicle present in some mammals
**pos·tu·lan·cy** \ˈpäschələnsē, -si\ *also* **pos·tu·lance** \-lən(t)s\ *n* -ES **1 :** the quality or state of being a postulant esp. in a religious order **2 :** the period during which a person remains a postulant
**pos·tu·lant** \-lənt\ *n* -s [F, fr. ML *postulant-, postulans*, pres. part. of *postulare*] **1 :** a candidate for admission to a religious order in the stage preliminary to the novitiate **2 :** a person on probation before being admitted as a candidate for ordination in the Protestant Episcopal Church **syn** see NOVICE
**postulata** *pl of* POSTULATUM
**¹pos·tu·late** \ˈpäschə,lāt, *usu* -ād.+V\ *vt* -ED/-ING/-S [ML *postulatus*, past part. of *postulare*, fr. L, to ask for, demand, request, fr. (assumed) *posctus*, past part. of *poscere* to ask for urgently, beg, demand; akin to OHG *forsca* question, OIr *arco* I request, Skt *prcchā* question, inquiry, L *prex* prayer, request — more at PRAYER] **1 :** to request (a higher ecclesiastical authority) to sanction the promotion of a person who is canonically disqualified : nominate (a person) subject to the sanction of a higher authority **2** [L *postulatus*, past part. of *postulare*] : DEMAND, CLAIM ⟨*postulated* . . . supremacy over this nation —William Tooke⟩ **3 :** to assume or claim as true, existent, or necessary ⟨~s that energy is expended within the plant —P.R.White⟩ : depend upon or start from the postulate of ⟨~s complete lack of respect for the . . . people —G.W. Johnson⟩ **4 :** to assume as a postulate or axiom (as in logic or mathematics) **syn** see PRESUPPOSE
**²postulate** \-lət, -,lāt, *usu* -d.+V\ *n* -s [in sense 1, fr. L *postulatum*, fr. neut. of *postulatus*, past part. of *postulare*; in other senses, fr. ML *postulatum*, fr. L] **1** *archaic* : DEMAND, STIPULATION **2 :** a proposition advanced with the claim that it be taken for granted or as axiomatic : an essential presupposition, condition, or premise (as for a train of reasoning, a philosophic system, or a school of thought) : an underlying hypothesis or assumption ⟨both science and religion have their ~s⟩ ⟨life is built upon certain ~s —Bertrand Russell⟩ ⟨three ~s of present-day income accounting —*Harvard Law Rev.*⟩ **3 :** a statement (as in logic or mathematics) that is assumed and therefore requires no proof of its validity : AXIOM ⟨the parallel ~⟩
**pos·tu·la·tion** \ˌ==ˈlāshən\ *n* -s [ME *postulacion*, fr. MF *postulation*, fr. ML *postulation-, postulatio*, fr. L, demand, request, fr. *postulatus* + *-ion-, -io* -ion] **1 a :** an act of postulating ⟨the ~ of surviving spirits might look plausible —A.G.N. Flew⟩ **b :** POSTULATE, ASSUMPTION ⟨admit as a ~⟩ **2 :** a formal petition of a plaintiff in Roman law to the praetor for leave to prosecute an action or to make an accusation
**pos·tu·la·tion·al** \ˌ==ˈlāshənᵊl, -shnəl\ *adj* : of, relating to, or involving the use of postulates ⟨science is a ~ system —C.I. Glicksberg⟩; *specif* : depending on a set of mathematical postulates ⟨the ~ method was applied to geometry —S.S. Stevens⟩ — **pos·tu·la·tion·al·ly** \-ᵊlē, -əl|, |i\ *adv*
**postulational system** *n* : AXIOM SYSTEM
**pos·tu·la·tor** \ˈpäschə,lād·ə(r), -ātə-\ *n* -s [ML, fr. L, claimant, plaintiff, fr. *postulatus*] : the official who presents a plea for beatification or canonization in the Roman Catholic Church — compare DEVIL'S ADVOCATE
**pos·tu·la·to·ry** \ˈ==lə,tōrē, -tȯr-, -ri\ *adj* [ML *postulatorius*, fr. L, petitionary, fr. *postulatus* (past part. of *postulare* to postulate) + *-orius* -ory — more at POSTULATE] : involving assumptions : HYPOTHETICAL
**pos·tu·la·tum** \ˌpäschəˈlād·əm\ *n, pl* **postula·ta** \-ād·ə\ [ML & L — more at POSTULATE] : POSTULATE
**pos·tur·al** \ˈpäschərəl\ *adj* : of, relating to, or involving posture ⟨~ tension⟩ ⟨~ albuminuria⟩ ⟨~ exercises⟩
**¹pos·ture** \ˈpäschə(r)\ *n* -s [F, fr. It *postura*, fr. L *positura*, position, fr. *positus* (past part. of *ponere* to place, put) + *-ura* -ure — more at POSITION] **1 :** relative arrangement of the

different parts esp. of the body : the characteristic position or bearing of the body or that assumed for a special purpose ⟨exercises for good ~⟩ ⟨a sitting ~⟩ ⟨~ at the table⟩; *specif* : the pose of a model or artistic figure ⟨draws her in three ~s⟩ **2** : relative place or position : SITUATION ⟨the ~ of the earth to the sun⟩ ⟨forced the English phrases into makeshift ~s —W.K.Wimsatt⟩ **3** : state or condition at a given time; *esp* : situation relative to the attitude of persons or the disposition of things involved ⟨survey the ~ of affairs —John Buchan⟩ ⟨put the country in a ~ of defense⟩ **4** : frame of mind : ATTITUDE ⟨a ~ of moral superiority —R.L. Strout⟩ **syn** see STATE

**²posture** \"\ *vb* -ED/-ING/-S *vt* **1** : to put into or make assume a given posture : POSE ⟨a ballet mistress *posturing* her dancers⟩ ⟨figures . . . *postured*, as in sculpture —Sheldon Cheney⟩ **2** *obs* : to put in place : SET ~ *vi* **1** : to assume a particular physical posture or series of postures; *esp* : to strike a pose for effect ⟨a young woman *postured* in leg-revealing shorts —*Time*⟩ **2** : to assume an artificial or pretended attitude : POSE, ATTITUDINIZE ⟨*posturing* as the friend of the oppressed⟩ ⟨you've *postured* . . . till everyone's sick of you —Stephen McKenna⟩

**pos·tur·er** \-chərə(r)\ *n* -S : one that postures: as **a** : CONTORTIONIST ⟨circus freaks and ~s⟩ **b** : POSEUR ⟨an incorrigible ~⟩

**posturing** *n* -S [fr. gerund of ²*posture*] : ceremonial pantomiming in China accompanied by music and formerly performed in a ritual manner at state sacrifices

**post·velar** \(ˈ)=+\ *adj* [*post-* + *velar*] : articulated against the rear half of the velum or soft palate

**¹post·verbal** \(ˈ)=+\ *adj* [*post-* + *verbal*] : formed after or from a verb

**²postverbal** \"\ *n* : a noun formed from a verb ⟨names of male occupations . . . from ~s —Yakov Malkiel⟩

**post·vocalic** \ˌ=+\ *adj* [ISV *post-* + *vocalic*] : immediately following a vowel

**post·war** \(ˈ)=+\ *adj* [*post-* + *war*] : occurring after a war ⟨the ~ revival of the theater⟩ : of or relating to the period after a war ⟨~ inflation⟩ ⟨the ~ scene⟩

**postwoman** \ˈ=,==\ *n, pl* **postwomen** [⁴*post* + *woman*] : a woman mail carrier

**post·zygapophysis** \(ˌ)=+\ *n* [NL, fr. *post-* + *zygapophysis*] : a posterior or inferior zygapophysis

**posy** \ˈpōzē, -zi\ *n* -ES [alter. of *poesy*] **1** : a brief sentiment, motto, or legend often in verse (as an inscription on a ring) ⟨~ at the beginning of his book . . . Commend it or Amend it —John Hoskins⟩ ⟨is this the prologue or the ~ of a ring? —Shak.⟩ **2** : BOUQUET, NOSEGAY, FLOWER ⟨a tight ~ of wild flowers —V.V.Nabokov⟩ **3** : ANTHOLOGY ⟨a ~ of funny stories —Edmund Gosse⟩

**posy pea** *n, dial* : SWEET PEA

**¹pot** \ˈpät, *usu* -äd.+V\ *n* -S [ME *pot, pott*, fr. OE *pott*; akin to OFris *pott* pot, MD *pot*, MLG *pot, put*, and perh. to OE *-pūte*, a fish with a large head — more at POUT] **1 a** : a usu. rounded metal or earthen container of varying size used chiefly for domestic purposes: as (1) : a container used for boiling or cooking — compare KETTLE (2) : a container for a beverage (3) : CHAMBER POT **b** : such a container with its contents ⟨give her a ~ and a cake —Daniel Defoe⟩ ⟨~ of tea⟩ **c** *archaic* : any of several quantities or measures ⟨a ~ of sugar weighs about 70 pounds —*Annual Register*⟩ **2 a** *chiefly Scot* : a pit or depression in the ground or in the bed of a stream **b** *archaic* : the abyss of hell **3 a** *dial Eng* : a basket or box used chiefly like one of a pair of panniers **b** : an enclosed framework of wire, wood, or wicker for catching fish, eels, or lobsters — compare POUND NET **4 a** : CRUCIBLE **1 b** : a large round metal receptacle used as part of a still **c** : a valve chamber in a compound-pressure steam pump **d** : an electrolytic cell used in recovering some metals (as aluminum) from a fused electrolyte **5** : a leather or steel protective cap or helmet worn chiefly in the 17th century **6 a** (1) : a large amount (as of money) ⟨inherited ~ of money⟩ ⟨has ~s of wealth⟩ (2) : the total prize or aggregate of bets to be won at the outcome of a particular event or contest (3) : a common resource or fund that may be created or drawn upon by a number of individuals or groups ⟨all the assets and production go into a common ~ on which they live —R.R.Nathan⟩ **b** (1) : the total of the bets made in poker or other card games on the outcome of any one deal and usu. accumulated in a pile in the center of the table : POOL (2) : a period or interval including the deal, betting, showdown, and determination of the winner in poker : one complete unit or round of play in a poker game **7** *slang Brit* : FAVORITE **8** : a paper case holding the garniture at the head of a fireworks rocket **9** [by shortening] : POTSHOT **10** [by shortening] *slang* : POTBELLY **11** : an important or prominent person ⟨they're sure to have some big ~ . . . who knows all about the house —J.D. Beresford⟩ **12** : RUIN, DETERIORATION ⟨business had gone to ~ —Alan Hynd⟩ **13** *slang* : an electronic volume control or fading device **14** [²*pot*] : a shot in which a billiard ball is potted **15** *slang* : MARIJUANA

**²pot** \"\ *vb* **potted; potted; potting; pots** *vt* **1** *slang Brit* : FOOL, DECEIVE, OUTWIT ⟨it is no hard matter to puzzle and to ~ you with authority —Richard Montagu⟩ **2** : to place or pack in a pot: **a** : to put up in a pot or sealed jar : CAN, PRESERVE **b** : to place (as a seedling or bulb) in an earth-filled pot for cultivation — often used with *up* **3** *Brit* : to pocket (an object ball) in a game of billiards or pool **4 a** : to shoot or kill (game) for food rather than as a sport **b** : POTSHOT ⟨it was nice, he thought, not to have to . . . sleep like a cat lest one be *potted* like a sitting rabbit —P.E.Lehman⟩ **5** : to make or shape (earthenware) as a potter ⟨a round bowl has an alternating panel design . . . and is well *potted* —W.E.Cox⟩ **6** : to treat (sodium nitrate) in a pot with sulfuric acid to form nitric acid **7** : to make superficially attractive by eliminating or oversimplifying difficult matters and emphasizing the exciting and attractive : GLAMORIZE ⟨a democracy, sometimes called educated, that prefers its information *potted*, pictorial, and spiced with sensation —Wilson Harris⟩ ~ *vi* **1** *obs* : to drink an intoxicating beverage from a pot **2** : to take a potshot : SHOOT ⟨we . . . *potted* at alligators in the reeds —Howard Clewes⟩

**pot** *abbr* **1** potential **2** potion **3** pottery

**po·ta·bil·i·ty** \ˌpōd·əˈbiləd·ē\ *n* : the quality or state of being potable

**¹po·ta·ble** \ˈpōd·əbəl, -ōtəb-\ *adj* [LL *potabilis*, fr. L *potare* to drink + *-abilis* -able; akin to L *bibere* to drink, Gk *pinein*, OSlav *piti* to drink, Skt *pāti, pibati* he drinks] : suitable, safe, or prepared for drinking ⟨the treatment of water supplies to make them safely ~ —A.C.Morrison⟩ — **po·ta·ble·ness** *n* -ES

**²potable** \"\ *n* -S : a liquid suitable for drinking : BEVERAGE, DRINKABLE

**po·tage** \pōˈtäzh\ *n* -S [MF, thick soup, pottage, fr. OF, pottage, fr. *pot* (of Gmc origin; akin to MD *pot*) + *-age* — more at POT] : a thick soup — compare POTTAGE

**pot·a·ger** \ˈpäd·ijə(r)\ *n* -S [F, fr. MF *potagier* cook that makes thick soup or pottage, fr. *potage* + *-ier* -er] : a cook whose specialties are soup, broth, and bouillon

**po·tag·er·ie** *or* **po·tag·ery** \pōˈtajərē\ *n, pl* **potageries** [obs. F *potagerie*, fr. MF, fr. *potage* + *-erie* -ery] : garden vegetables and herbs

**pot ale** *n* : the residue of fermented wort left in a still after whiskey or alcohol has been distilled off and used for feeding swine

**potam-** *or* **potamo-** *comb form* [L *potamo-*, fr. Gk *potam-, potamo-*, fr. *potamos*; akin to Gk *piptein* to fall — more at FEATHER] **1** : river ⟨*potamic*⟩ ⟨*potamodromous*⟩ **2** : electric current ⟨*potamometer*⟩

**pot·a·man·thi·dae** \ˌpäd·əˈman(t)thə,dē\ *n pl, cap* [NL, fr. *Potamanthus*, type genus (fr. *potam-* + *-anthus*) + *-idae*] : a small widely distributed family of mayflies

**po·tam·ic** \pəˈtamik\ *adj* [*potam-* + *-ic*] : of or relating to rivers or the navigation of rivers

**pot·a·mo·benthos** \ˌpad·əmō+\ *n* [*potam-* + *benthos*] : benthonic organisms of a river

**pot·a·mo·bi·us** \ˌpäd·əˈmōbēəs\ [NL, fr. *potam-* + *-bius*] *syn of* ASTACUS

**pot·a·mo·choe·rus** \ˌpad·əmōˈkērəs\ [NL, fr. *potam-* + *-choerus*] *syn of* KOIROPOTAMUS

**pot·a·mod·ro·mous** \ˌpäd·əˈmädrəməs\ *adj* [*potam-* + *-dromous*] *of a fish* : migratory in fresh water

**pot·a·mog·a·le** \ˌpäd·əˈmägəlē\ *n, cap* [NL, fr. *potam-* + Gk *galē* weasel — more at GALEA] : a genus (the type of a family Potamogalidae) of West African aquatic insectivores that contains the otter shrew — **pot·a·mog·a·lid** \ˌ==ˈmägələd\ *adj*

**pot·a·mo·ge·ton** \ˌpäd·əmōˈjē,tän\ *n* [NL, fr. L, pondweed, fr. Gk *potamogeitōn*, fr. *potamos* river + *geitōn* neighbor] **1** *cap* : a large genus of aquatic herbs (family Potamogetonaceae) that are found in quiet waters throughout temperate regions and have spicate flowers with a four-parted perianth and usu. floating leaves — see PONDGRASS, PONDWEED **2** -S : any plant of the genus *Potamogeton*

**pot·a·mo·ge·to·na·ce·ae** \ˌ====,jēd·əˈnāsē,ē\ *n pl, cap* [NL, fr. *Potamogeton*, type genus + *-aceae*] : a family of aquatic herbs (order Naiadales) having floating or submerged leaves, simple flowers without a perianth, and a fruit like a nut or a drupe — **pot·a·mo·ge·to·na·ceous** \ˌ=====ˈnāshəs\ *adj*

**pot·a·mog·ra·pher** \ˌpäd·əˈmägrəfə(r)\ *n* -S : a specialist in potamography

**pot·a·mo·graph·ic** \ˌpäd·əməˈgrafik\ *adj* [ISV *potamography* + *-ic*] : of or relating to potamography

**pot·a·mog·ra·phy** \ˌpäd·əˈmägrəfē\ *n* -ES [ISV *potam-* + *-graphy*] : the description of rivers

**pot·a·mo·log·i·cal** \ˌpäd·əməˈläjəkəl\ *adj* : of or relating to potamology

**pot·a·mol·o·gist** \ˌpäd·əˈmäləjəst\ *n* -S : a specialist in potamology

**pot·a·mol·o·gy** \-jē\ *n* -ES [ISV *potam-* + *-logy*] : the study of rivers

**pot·a·mom·e·ter** \ˌpäd·əˈmäməd·ə(r)\ *n* [*potam-* + *-meter*] : CURRENT METER

**pot·a·mon·i·dae** \ˌpäd·əˈmänə,dē\ *n pl, cap* [NL, fr. *Potamon*, type genus (fr. Gk *potamos* river) + *-idae*] : a family of freshwater crabs (superfamily Brachyrhyncha) whose young undergo metamorphosis in the egg and hatch as miniature adults — see RIVER CRAB

**pot·a·mo·plankton** \ˌpäd·əmō+\ *n* [ISV *potam-* + *plankton*] : plankton of rivers

**pot arch** *n* : a kiln used in preheating clay pots before they are placed in the furnace for hardening

**po·tar·ite** \pəˈtä,rīt\ *n* -S [*Potaro*, river in British Guiana + E *-ite*] : a mineral PdHg consisting of a natural alloy compound of palladium and mercury

**¹pot·ash** \ˈpäd·,ash, -ä,ta-, -aash, -aish\ *n* [sing. of *pot ashes* (fr. ¹*pot* + *ashes*, pl. of *ash*), trans. of obs. D *potaschen*, pl. (whence obs. D *potasch*, sing., now D *potas*)] **1 a** : POTASSIUM CARBONATE; *esp* : that obtained in colored impure form by leaching wood ashes, evaporating the lye usu. in an iron pot, and calcining the residue — compare PEARL ASH **b** : POTASSIUM HYDROXIDE **2 a** : potassium oxide $K_2O$ in combined form as determined by analysis (as of fertilizers) ⟨soluble ~⟩ **b** : POTASSIUM — not used systematically ⟨~ salts⟩ ⟨sulfate of ~⟩ **3** : any of several potassium salts (as potassium chloride or potassium sulfate) often occurring naturally and used esp. in agriculture and industry ⟨~ deposits⟩ ⟨~ fertilizers⟩

**²potash** \"\ *vt* : to treat with potash; *specif* : to case harden with potassium ferrocyanide

**potash alum** *n* : ALUM 1a

**potash bulb** *n* : an arrangement of glass bulbs designed to hold a solution of potassium hydroxide and used for absorbing carbon dioxide in chemical analysis — often used in pl.

**potash hunger** *n* : a potash deficiency disease of plants marked by retarded or dwarfed growth of storage organs or of terminal shoots in woody plants and by whitish or brownish spots on the leaves followed by general blighting and death of the plant

**potash soap** *n* : a soft soap made with potash

**po·tas·sa** \pəˈtasə\ *n* -S [NL, fr. E ¹*potash*] : POTASH

**pot·as·sam·ide** \ˌpäd·əˈsa,mīd, pəˈtasə,-, -,məd\ *n* [*potassium* + *amide*] : POTASSIUM AMIDE

**po·tas·sic** \pəˈtasik\ *adj* [NL *potassicus*, fr. *potassa* + L *-icus* -ic] : of, relating to, or containing potassium

**pot·as·sif·er·ous** \ˌpäd·əˈsif(ə)rəs\ *adj* [*potassium* + *-ferous*] : containing potash or other compounds of potassium ⟨~ salts⟩

**po·tas·si·um** \pəˈtasēəm, pō'-, -aas- *sometimes* -syəm\ *n* -S [NL, fr. *potassa* + *-ium*] : a silver-white soft light low-melting univalent metallic element of the alkali metal group that is more reactive than sodium, oxidizing rapidly in air and reacting violently with water with the evolution of hydrogen which takes fire, that occurs abundantly in nature in combined form in minerals (as sylvite, langbeinite, and many silicates), in sea-water and brines, and in plants and animals, that is prepared in the metallic state from several of its compounds by electrolysis or by reduction (as with sodium vapor) and must be preserved under kerosine or other inert hydrocarbon liquid, and that is used chiefly as a reducing agent and in synthesis — symbol *K*; see ELEMENT table

**potassium acid oxalate** *or* **potassium binoxalate** *n* : POTASSIUM OXALATE b

**potassium acid tartrate** *or* **potassium bitartrate** *n* : CREAM OF TARTAR

**potassium alum** *n* : ALUM 1a

**potassium amide** *n* : a crystalline compound $KNH_2$ obtained by heating potassium in ammonia

**potassium arsenite** *n* : a poisonous salt made by boiling arsenic trioxide with potassium bicarbonate solution and used chiefly in medicine — see FOWLER'S SOLUTION

**potassium bicarbonate** *or* **potassium acid carbonate** *n* : a crystalline salt $KHCO_3$ that gives a weakly alkaline reaction in aqueous solution and that is made by passing carbon dioxide into a solution of potassium carbonate; potassium hydrogen carbonate

**potassium bisulfate** *or* **potassium acid sulfate** *n* : a crystalline salt $KHSO_4$ that gives an acid reaction in solution, that is made by treating potassium sulfate with sulfuric acid, and that is used chiefly in making cream of tartar and as a flux; potassium hydrogen sulfate

**potassium bromate** *n* : a crystalline salt $KBrO_3$ used chiefly as an oxidizing agent and in improving the baking properties of flour

**potassium bromide** *n* : a crystalline salt KBr having a biting saline taste that is used chiefly in medicine as a sedative, in photography for making gelatin-silver bromide emulsions and as a restrainer in developing, and in engraving and lithography

**potassium carbonate** *n* : either of two potassium salts of carbonic acid: **a** : the deliquescent crystalline normal salt $K_2CO_3$ that gives a strongly alkaline reaction in aqueous solution, that was obtained orig. from wood ashes but is now made usu. from potassium chloride (as by electrolysis to potassium hydroxide followed by carbonation), and that is used chiefly in making hard glass, soft soap, and in other ways similarly to sodium carbonate — see POTASH 1a **b** : POTASSIUM BICARBONATE

**potassium chlorate** *n* : a crystalline salt $KClO_3$ with a cooling saline taste that is made by electrolysis of potassium chloride or by reaction of potassium chloride with another chlorate (as sodium chlorate) and that is used chiefly as an oxidizing agent in matches, fireworks, and explosives

**potassium chloride** *n* : a crystalline salt KCl occurring as the mineral sylvite in carnallite and in natural waters and used chiefly as a fertilizer and in making other potassium compounds

**potassium chromate** *n* : a yellow crystalline salt $K_2CrO_4$ having uses similar to those of sodium chromate

**potassium cobaltinitrite** *n* : a yellow crystalline salt $K_3Co(NO_2)_6$ used as a pigment and as an insoluble salt of potassium in analysis; potassium hexa-nitro-cobalt-ate(III) — see COBALT YELLOW

**potassium cyanate** *n* : a crystalline salt KOCN made by oxidizing potassium cyanide or by heating a mixture of potassium carbonate and urea and used chiefly to kill crabgrass on lawns

**potassium cyanide** *n* : an exceedingly poisonous deliquescent crystalline salt KCN made usu. by heating potassium carbonate and carbon with ammonia and used chiefly in electroplating and in the cyanide process

**potassium dichromate** *or* **potassium bichromate** *n* : a bitter poisonous orange-red crystalline salt $K_2Cr_2O_7$ used chiefly in sensitizing gelatin in photography, in textile and leather finishes, and as an oxidizing agent (as in safety matches and fireworks)

**potassium ferricyanide** *n* : a red crystalline salt $K_3Fe(CN)_6$ made by oxidizing potassium ferrocyanide with chlorine and used chiefly as a photographic bleach and in coating blueprint paper — called also *red prussiate of potash*

**potassium ferrocyanide** *n* : a tough yellow crystalline salt $K_4Fe(CN)_6$ made from the cyanogen compounds obtained as by-products in the carbonization of coal or directly by reaction of potassium cyanide with ferrous salts and used chiefly in making iron blue pigments — called also *yellow prussiate of potash*

**potassium fluoride** *n* : any of several salts made usu. by reaction of hydrofluoric acid with potassium carbonate: as **a** : the hygroscopic crystalline normal salt KF used chiefly as a solder flux and as a fluorinating agent in organic synthesis **b** *or* **potassium bifluoride** : the poisonous corrosive crystalline acid fluoride $KHF_2$ used chiefly as an electrolyte in the manufacture of fluorine and as a solder flux : potassium hydrogen fluoride

**potassium hydrate** *n* : POTASSIUM HYDROXIDE — not used systematically

**potassium hydroxide** *n* : a brittle white deliquescent solid KOH that dissolves with much heat in less than its weight of water to form a strongly alkaline and caustic solution, that is made usu. by electrolysis of a solution of potassium chloride, and that is used chiefly in making soap, in bleaching and mercerizing, and as a reagent in chemistry — called also *caustic potash*

**potassium hypochlorite** *n* : an unstable salt KOCl known chiefly in aqueous solution — see JAVELLE WATER a

**potassium iodide** *n* : a crystalline salt KI that is very soluble in water and is used chiefly in making photographic emulsions, in organic synthesis, in medicine (as in Lugol's solution), and in iodized table salt

**potassium manganate** *n* : an unstable green salt $K_2MnO_4$ readily converted into potassium permanganate

**potassium mercuric iodide** *n* : a poisonous yellow deliquescent crystalline complex salt $K_2HgI_4$ used as a disinfectant and as a chemical reagent; potassium tetra-iodomercurate(II) — see NESSLER'S REAGENT

**potassium nitrate** *n* : a soluble crystalline salt $KNO_3$ with a cooling saline taste that occurs as a product of nitrification in most arable soils esp. in hot dry countries where it is extracted by leaching but that is usu. made by reaction of potassium chloride and sodium nitrate, that decomposes on strong heating into potassium nitrite $KNO_2$ and oxygen, and that is used chiefly in making black powder, matches, and fireworks and in curing meat — called also *niter, saltpeter*

**potassium oxalate** *n* : any of three crystalline oxalates of potassium: **a** : the normal efflorescent soluble salt $K_2C_2O_4.H_2O$ used chiefly in preventing the clotting of blood (as in blood tests) and formerly in photography **b** : a bitter poisonous acid salt $KHC_2O_4.H_2O$ found esp. in oxalis and rhubarb and used chiefly in removing ink stains and scouring metals; potassium hydrogen oxalate — called also *potassium acid oxalate, salt of sorrel* **c** : POTASSIUM TETROXALATE

**potassium oxide** *n* : an oxide of potassium; *esp* : the deliquescent monoxide $K_2O$

**potassium perchlorate** *n* : a crystalline salt $KClO_4$ used chiefly in explosives and fireworks

**potassium permanganate** *n* : a salt $KMnO_4$ that crystallizes in dark purple prisms having a blue metallic luster and dissolves in water with a purple-red color, that is made usu. by reaction of manganese dioxide and potassium hydroxide and oxidation of the manganate formed, and that is used chiefly as an oxidizing and bleaching agent and as a disinfectant

**potassium persulfate** *n* : a crystalline salt $K_2S_2O_8$ used chiefly in oxidizing and bleaching and as a promoter of polymerizations (as in the manufacture of GR-S rubber)

**potassium phosphate** *n* **1** : one of the three orthophosphates of potassium analogous to the simple sodium orthophosphates **2** : a phosphate of potassium (as tetra-potassium pyrophosphate $K_4P_2O_7$) other than an orthophosphate

**potassium sodium tartrate** *n* : ROCHELLE SALT

**potassium sulfate** *n* : either of two crystalline sulfates of potassium: **a** : the normal salt $K_2SO_4$ occurring naturally esp. in complex sulfates (as langbeinite, polyhalite) and used chiefly as a fertilizer and in the manufacture of alums and other chemicals and of gypsum wallboard to accelerate the setting time **b** : POTASSIUM BISULFATE

**potassium tetroxalate** *n* : a relatively insoluble crystalline complex acid salt $KHC_2O_4.H_2C_2O_4.2H_2O$ used chiefly in removing rust marks and as a reference standard in analyzing bases and permanganates

**potassium thiocyanate** *n* : a hygroscopic crystalline salt KSCN having uses similar to those of sodium thiocyanate

**po·ta·tion** \pōˈtāshən\ *n* -S [ME *potacioun*, fr. MF *potation*, fr. L *potation-, potatio* act of drinking, fr. *potatus* (past part. of *potare* to drink) + *-ion-, -io* -ion — more at POTABLE] **1 a** : a usu. alcoholic drink or brew ⟨the root . . . whence their favorite ~ is extracted —James Cook⟩ **2 a** : the act of drinking ⟨you did rather abstain from ~ —Sir Walter Scott⟩ **b** : DRAFT 4a ⟨under the stimulus of several ~s —S.H.Adams⟩ **c** : indulgence in drinking alcoholic beverages ⟨men who were . . . the worse for ~ —Frederick Marryat⟩ ⟨the arrival of planes . . . occasioned like gourmandising and ~ —*Time*⟩

**po·ta·to** \pəˈtād·(,)ō, -ā(,)tō, -äd·ə, -ātə *sometimes* pəˈtäd·-\ *n* -ES *often attrib* [Sp *patata, batata*, fr. Taino *batata*] **1** : SWEET POTATO **2 a** (1) : an erect herb (*Solanum tuberosum*) that has compound pinnate leaves, white, yellow, blue, or purple flowers, and green, yellowish, or purplish berries, is native to the highlands of So. and Central America, and is widely cultivated esp. in the temperate regions as a garden vegetable (2) : the edible starchy tuber that is an enlargement of an underground stem of this plant — called also *Irish potato, white potato* **b** : any of several other plants of the genus *Solanum* (as Uruguay potato)

**potato alcohol** *n* : alcohol distilled from a potato mash

**potato aphid** *n* : a common aphid (*Macrosiphum euphorbiae*) that occurs on the potato and many other plants as well as on some orchard trees and that usu. overwinters on rosebushes

**potato apple** *n* : the berry of the potato

**potato ball** *n* **1 a** : a small ball cut from a potato with a special scoop **b** : a potato croquette **2** : POTATO APPLE

**potato bean** *n* **1** : YAM BEAN **2** : GROUNDNUT 2 a

**potato beetle** *or* **potato bug** *n* : an insect that attacks potato plants; *esp* : COLORADO POTATO BEETLE

**potato blight** *or* **potato disease** *also* **potato mildew** *or* **potato mold** *or* **potato murrain** *n* : a blight or decay that attacks the potato — compare EARLY BLIGHT, LATE BLIGHT

**potato cake** *n* : cold mashed potato shaped into a circular flattened cake, often rolled in flour, and fried

**potato canker** *n* **1** : POTATO WART **2** : a powdery scab in which there is destruction of the flesh of the tuber that leaves hollowed out eroded areas which are larger than the usual spots

**potato chip** *n* : a thin slice of raw white potato fried crisp in deep fat

**potato crisp** *n, chiefly Brit* : POTATO CHIP

**potato–digger** \ˈ=ˌ=,==\ *n* : a machine or implement for digging potatoes

**potato family** *n* : SOLANACEAE

**potato fern** *n* **1** : a fern (*Marattia fraxinea*) of New Zealand that has a large edible starchy rootstock **2** : a fern (*Dryopteris cordifolia*) of Australia that has small ovoid tubers which are edible

**potato flea beetle** *n* : a small oval shining black flea beetle (*Epitrix cucumeris*) that injures the leaves of various plants

**potato flour** *or* **potato starch** *n* : a flour that is prepared from potatoes which are ground to pulp and washed free of fiber

**potato fork** *n* : a hand fork with several curved tines used for digging potatoes

**potato fungus** *n* : a fungus causing late blight

**potato grub** *n* : a larva of a potato moth

**potato hook** *n* **:** a hand tool with long hooked tines used for digging potatoes and other tuber crops

potato hook

**potato leafhopper** *n* **:** a small green white-spotted leafhopper (*Empoasca fabae*) chiefly of the eastern and southern U. S. that is a serious pest on many cultivated plants causing hopperburn on potatoes and browning, yellowing, or stunting of various other plants (as beans, dahlias, or alfalfa) — called also *apple and potato leafhopper;* compare APPLE LEAFHOPPER

**potato–leaved tomato** \ˌ=ˈ==ˌ=-\ *n* **:** a tomato (*Lycopersicon esculentum grandifolium*) having large leaves with few entire-margined primary leaflets and few or no secondary leaflets

**potato masher** *n* **1 :** any of several kitchen utensils for mashing cooked potatoes **2 :** a grenade having a wooden handle by which it is thrown

**potato mosaic** *n* **:** any of various virus diseases of the potato characterized chiefly by more or less mottling of the foliage — compare AUCUBA MOSAIC, CALICO, CRINKLE, CURLY DWARF, RUGOSE MOSAIC

**potato moth** *or* **potato tuber moth** *n* **:** a grayish brown gelechiid moth (*Phthorimaea operculella*) whose larva is the potato tuberworm

**potato mottle** *or* **potato virus X** *or* **potato X virus** *n* **:** LATENT VIRUS DISEASE

**potato onion** *n* **:** MULTIPLIER ONION

**potato psyllid** *n* **:** a hemipterous insect (*Paratrioza cockerelli*) that feeds on potato and tomato plants and causes psyllid yellows

**potato race** *n* **:** a race in which each runner attempts to retrieve a series of potatoes or other small objects one at a time

**potato ring** *n* **:** a ring or hoop of ceramic or metalware used in Ireland in the 18th century as a stand for a bowl or similar article **:** DISH RING

**potato root eelworm** *also* **potato root nematode** *n* **:** GOLDEN NEMATODE

**potato rot nematode** *n* **:** a plant-parasitic nematode (*Ditylenchus destructor*) that attacks roots and tubers (as of potato or sugar beet) causing dry rugose lesions highly susceptible to secondary invasion by fungi and that has long been a serious pest of potatoes in northern Europe and is now known also from widely separated points in No. America

**po·ta·to·ry** \ˈpōd·ə,tōrē\ *adj* [LL *potatorius,* fr. L *potatus* (past part. of *potare* to drink) + *-orius* -ory — more at POTABLE] **:** of, relating to, or given to drinking

**potato scab** *n* **:** any of various diseases of the potato characterized by crusty rough spots or scabs on the tubers; *specif* **:** a disease that is characterized by lesions of brownish corky tissue, is caused by an actinomycete (*Streptomyces scabies*), and is esp. damaging in alkaline soils — called also *corky scab;* compare POWDERY SCAB

**potato set** *n* **:** a potato tuber or part of a tuber that has at least one eye and is used for planting

**potato–sick** \ˌ=ˈ==ˌ=\ *adj, of land* **:** exhausted by successive crops of potatoes

**potato slump** *n* **:** the dregs or residue from the alcoholic distillation of fermented potatoes

**potato stalk borer** *n* **:** a larva of a potato weevil

**potato tree** *n* **:** any of several arborescent or nearly arborescent plants of the genus *Solanum* (as the Brazilian *S. macranthum* and the Chilean *S. crispum*) none of which are true potatoes

**potato tuberworm** *n* **:** a small pale brown-headed caterpillar that is the larva of the potato moth and that mines in the leaves and bores in the stems of potato, tobacco, and related plants and commonly overwinters in potato tubers — called also *splitworm*

**potato vine** *n* **:** POTATO 2 a (1)

**potato wart** *n* **:** a fungous disease of potato tubers caused by a pond scum parasite (*Synchytrium endobioticum*) and characterized by dark warty spongy excrescences that are yellow or light brown when young and that originate in the eyes of the tuber

**potato weevil** *n* **:** an American weevil (*Trichobaris trinotata*) whose larva lives in the stalks of potato plants

**potato whiskey** *n* **:** whiskey distilled from potatoes

**potato wilt** *n* **:** a wilt of potatoes; *esp* **:** one caused by fungi (as *Fusarium oxysporum* or *Verticillium alboatrum*)

**potato worm** *n* **:** a large green white-striped caterpillar that is the larva of a hawkmoth (*Protoparce quinquemaculata*)

**pot–au–feu** \ˌpōd·ōˈfə̄\ *n, pl* **pot–au–feu** [F, lit., pot on the fire] **:** a French dish consisting of a thick soup of meat and many vegetables

**pot·a·wat·o·mi** *also* **pot·a·wat·a·mi** *or* **pot·ta·wat·to·mi** *or* **pot·ta·wat·ta·mi** \ˌpäd·əˈwädəmē\ *n, pl* **potawatomi** *or* **potawatomis** *usu cap* **1 a :** an Indian people of the lower peninsula of Michigan and adjoining states **b :** a member of such people **2 :** the Algonquian language of the Potawatomi people

**potbank** \ˈ=ˌ=\ *n* [1pot + bank (bench)] *dial chiefly Eng* **:** a place where pottery is made

**pot barley** *n* **:** HULLED BARLEY

**potbellied** \ˈ=ˌ==\ *adj* [1pot + bellied] **:** having a potbelly or a bulging part suggestive of a potbelly ⟨a ~ man⟩ ⟨a ~ stove⟩

**potbelly** \ˈ=ˌ==\ *n* [1pot + belly] **1 a :** an enlarged, swollen, or protruding belly or stomach **b :** a condition characterized by a potbelly and among children or animals symptomatic of disease or improper diet **2 :** a person having a protuberant belly **3 :** a stove with a rounded or bulging body

potbelly 3

**potboil** \ˈ=ˌ=\ *vi* [1pot + boil] **:** to produce potboilers ⟨the man who has to ~ for a living seldom accomplishes anything of an exceptional character —*Reynold's Newspaper*⟩ ⟨was a financial failure and . . . must go back once more to *~ing* —H.D.Piper⟩

**potboiler** \ˈ=ˌ==\ *n* [1pot + boiler] **1** *archaic* **:** POTWALLOPER **2 :** a usu. inferior work of art or literature produced chiefly for monetary return ⟨published many popular historical *~s* . . . out of which he makes a great deal of money —Harold Strauss⟩ **3 :** one that produces a potboiler ⟨several *~s* have since helped themselves to this material —*Saturday Rev.*⟩

**pot bottom** *n* **:** a boulder or concretion in a roof slate that is rounded like the bottom of a pot

**pot–bound** \ˈ=ˌ=\ *adj, of a potted plant* **:** having roots so densely matted as to allow little or no space for further growth

**potboy** \ˈ=ˌ=\ *n* **:** a boy who carries pots of ale, beer, and other drink in a public house or tavern

**pot burner** *n* **:** an oil burner in which the oil is vaporized by air entering through a perforated shell that surrounds the pot containing the oil

**1potch** \ˈpäch\ *dial Brit var of* POACH

**2potch** \"\ *vt* -ED/-ING/-ES [alter. of 2poach] **:** to bleach (pulp) in a potcher

**pot cheese** *n* **1 :** COTTAGE CHEESE **2 :** COOK CHEESE

**potch·er** *also* **poch·er** \ˈpächə(r)\ *n* -S [alter. of 1poacher] **:** an engine of the hollander type but without a bedplate used for breaking up paper stock, washing, and bleaching

**potch·er·man** \-(r)mən\ *n, pl* **potchermen :** a man who operates a potcher

**pot–clay** \ˈ=ˌ=\ *n* **:** a fireclay suitable for the manufacture of the melting pots used in glassmaking

**pot–color** \ˈ=ˌ==\ *vt* **:** to color (molten glass) in a glass pot

**pot–companion** \ˈ=ˌ==ˌ=\ *n, archaic* **:** a drinking companion

**pot culture** *n* **:** the growing of plants in flower pots

**1pote** \ˈpōt\ *vt* -ED/-ING/-S [ME *poten,* fr. OE *potian* — more at PUT] **1** *dial Eng* **:** PUSH, SHOVE, NUDGE **2** *dial Eng* **:** KICK, POKE

**2pote** \"\ *n* -S *dial Eng* **:** THRUST, KICK

**pot earth** *n* **:** POTTER'S CLAY

**pot·e·cary** \ˈpätəkərī\ *n* -ES [ME *potecarie,* short for *apotecarie* — more at APOTHECARY] *dial chiefly Eng* **:** APOTHECARY

**po·teen** \pəˈtēn, pōˈ-\ *also* **po·theen** \-ˈthēn\ *or* **pot·teen** \päˈtēn\ *n* -S [IrGael *poitín* small pot, whiskey made in a private still, fr. *pota* pot (fr. E 1pot) + *-ín* -een] **:** illicitly distilled whiskey of Ireland made variously from barley, potatoes, or sugar and molasses

**pot egg** *n, Brit* **:** a dummy nest egg for a fowl

**po·tem·kin village** \pəˈtem(p)kən-\ *n, usu cap P* [after Grigori A. *Potemkin* †1791 Russ. statesman; fr. the story that Potemkin once had impressive fake villages built along a route that Catherine the Great was to travel] **:** an imposing or pretentious facade or display designed to obscure or shield an unimposing or undesirable fact or condition **:** FALSE FRONT ⟨the visitors are shown no *Potemkin villages* but allowed to see things as they are⟩

**1po·tence** \ˈpōtᵊn(t)s\ *n* -S [ME, fr. MF, fr. L *potentia* potency, power] **1 :** POTENCY **2 :** the integrated dominance effect of a group of polygenes

**2potence** \"\ *n* -S [ME, fr. MF, crutch, gibbet, fr. L *potentia* potency, power] **1 :** CROSS, GIBBET **2 a :** the stud of a watch in which the bearing for the lower pivot of the verge is made **b :** a supporting bracket used in watchwork **3 :** a military formation in which a part of a line is thrown forward or backward at an angle to the main line

**3potence** \"\ *also* **po·ten·cee** \-nsē\ *adj* [MF *potencee,* fr. *potence* crutch, gibbet] **:** 2POTENT

**po·ten·cy** \ˈpōtᵊnsē, -si\ *n* -ES [L *potentia* potency, power, fr. *potent-, potens* potent, powerful + *-ia* -y] **1 :** the quality or state of being potent: **a :** FORCE, POWER, AUTHORITY ⟨if land armies ever lose their ~ —Green Peyton⟩ ⟨a place of ~ and sway o' the state —Shak.⟩ ⟨massed activity has a ~ which individual effort can no longer claim —John Dewey⟩ **b** (1) **:** the ability or capacity to achieve a result or effect **:** EFFECTIVENESS ⟨the ~ of prominence for good or ill is not to be denied —F. L.Mott⟩ ⟨the ~ of religious faith to deal with fear, anxiety, and tension —*Saturday Rev.*⟩ (2) **:** the ability or capacity to influence or affect thought or feeling ⟨these lines . . . have, in addition, a very remarkable ~ of suggestion —F.R.Leavis⟩ ⟨must not doubt the ~ of our ideas —C.M.Fuess⟩ ⟨the charm and emotional ~ of the music —Edward Sackville-West & Desmond Shawe-Taylor⟩ **c** (1) **:** chemical or medicinal strength or efficacy ⟨the ~ of the drink⟩ ⟨the ~ of the drug⟩ ⟨the material had lost its ~ by being exposed to light —*Current Biog.*⟩ (2) **:** physical or phenomenal intensity or force ⟨figured out that less than 100 H-bombs of 1954 ~ could lay down a saturation pattern of poisonous fallout —*New Republic*⟩ **d :** the ability to copulate — usu. used of the male **2 a :** POTENTIALITY 1 ⟨clung to our atoms as the inmost nucleus of matter and as containing the promise and ~ of life and mind —W.L.Sullivan⟩ ⟨submitted . . . only to the finest human *potencies,* which is to say, to the potentiality of being human —*New Republic*⟩ **b :** the capacity for acting or being acted upon and hence for undergoing change ⟨a ball has a ~ for being thrown⟩ ⟨a teacher is necessary to lead the student to an actual knowledge of what he knew only in ~ —Henri DuLac⟩ **c :** initial total inherent capacity for development of a particular kind prior to the establishment of limiting controls — compare COMPETENCE **3 a :** one that has power or authority ⟨it is his *~'s* wish —Rafael Sabatini⟩ **b :** a supernatural or demonic power; *specif* **:** a minor often local god ⟨pray to the *potencies* of rebirth and resurrection in nature and human love —Hans Meyerhoff⟩

**1po·tent** \ˈpōtᵊnt\ *n* -S [ME, crutch, support, modif. of MF *potence* crutch, gibbet] **1** *archaic* **:** SUPPORT, STAY **2 :** a heraldic fur consisting of rows of interlocking upright and inverted short-stemmed T-shaped panes alternately argent and azure unless other tinctures are specified and so placed one beneath another that each pane stands head to head or foot to foot with one of the other tinctures

potent 2

**2potent** \"\ *adj* [obs. E *potent,* n., crutch, fr. ME, crutch, support] *of a heraldic cross* **:** having flat bars across the ends of the arms — see CROSS illustration

**3potent** \"\ *adj* [ME (Sc), fr. L *potent-, potens* (used as pres. part. of *posse* to be able, fr. *potis esse,* fr. *potis* able, capable + *esse* to be), pres. part. of (assumed) OL *potēre* to be powerful, be able, fr. L *potis* able, capable; akin to Goth *brūthfaths* bridegroom, Gk *posis* husband, Skt *pati* master] **1 :** having or wielding strength, force, or authority **:** POWERFUL, STRONG ⟨increasing the capabilities of the ground soldier by providing him with increasingly ~ weapons —W.P.Corderman⟩ ⟨mixing the players of the first two teams would produce a ~ offensive —Eddie Beachler⟩ ⟨received the ~ machine endorsement as candidate for secretary of state —Blanton Fortson⟩ **2 a :** having or wielding influence **:** possessing the capacity to mold or alter thought or feeling **:** COGENT, AFFECTIVE ⟨a numerically inferior but intellectually ~ group —K.S.Davis⟩ ⟨still more ~ arguments for ending the struggle were found in the suffering caused by the . . . famine —W.C.Ford⟩ ⟨music is perhaps the most ~ agent for . . . inducing men to forget their differences —Jane Addams⟩ **b :** producing or capable of producing an effect or result **:** PREGNANT, INSTRUMENTAL, CAUSAL ⟨deals with what he looks upon as a ~ factor in delinquency —Winfred Overholser⟩ ⟨the most ~ and characteristic phase of the whole industrial revolution, the connection of iron with coal —G.M.Trevelyan⟩ **3 a :** chemically or medicinally effective **:** EFFICACIOUS ⟨nearly doubled the period during which the vaccine could be kept ~ —V.G.Heiser⟩ **b :** rich in a characteristic ingredient **:** STRONG ⟨~ tea⟩ ⟨a ~ drink⟩ **4 :** able to copulate — usu. used of the male

**4potent** *n* **1** *obs* **:** one having power or authority **:** POTENTATE **2** *obs* **:** a formal military order **:** WARRANT

**po·ten·tate** \ˈpōtᵊn,tāt, *usu* -ād·+V\ *n* -S [ME *potentat,* fr. LL *potentatus,* fr. L, power, fr. *potent-, potens* potent, powerful + *-atus* -ate] **1 :** one who possesses great power or sway **:** RULER, PRINCE, DICTATOR ⟨was not an oriental ~, but a modern, liberal, constitutional monarch —*Time*⟩ ⟨these great *~s* of Paris fashion —E.O.Hauser⟩ ⟨son of a mighty film ~ —Bennett Cerf⟩ **2** *archaic* **:** a powerful nation, city, or company **3 :** the chief officer of a secret fraternal order

**1potent–counterpotent** \ˈ=ˌ=ˈ=ˌ=\ *adj* **:** 2POTENT

**2potent–counterpotent** \"\ *n* **1 :** 1POTENT 2 **2 :** COUNTER-POTENT

**po·ten·tia** \pəˈtenchēə\ *n* -S [LL, fr. L, potency, power — more at POTENCY] **:** DYNAMIS

**1po·ten·tial** \pəˈtenchəl, pōˈ-\ *adj* [ME *potencial,* fr. LL *potentialis* potential, powerful, fr. LL *potentia* dynamis, state of that which is not yet fully realized & L *potentia* potency, power + L *-alis* -al] **1 a :** existing in possibility **:** having the capacity or a strong possibility for development into a state of actuality ⟨field studies of existing and ~ book markets —*Collier's Yr. Bk.*⟩ ⟨the detection of incipient or ~ disease of the nervous system —H.G.Armstrong⟩ ⟨too small to provide . . . for the ~ needs for reconstruction and development that will emerge in the postwar years —L.G.Melville⟩ ⟨~ leader⟩ ⟨~ profit⟩ ⟨~ use⟩ — compare ACTUAL **b :** having the capacity for acting or being acted upon and hence for undergoing change — compare POTENCY **2** *archaic* **:** 3POTENT **3 :** expressing possibility ⟨~ subjunctive⟩; *specif* **:** of, relating to, or constituting a verb phrase expressing possibility, liberty, or power by the use of an auxiliary (as *may, can*) with the infinitive of the verb (as in "it may rain", "he can write") **syn** see LATENT

**2potential** \"\ *n* -S **1 :** something that exists in a state of potency or possibility for changing or developing into a state of actuality ⟨industrial location in new areas will make use of labor and other *~s* which might otherwise remain untapped —*New Republic*⟩ ⟨a sound source with an unplumbed ~ for novelty and expression —*Time*⟩ ⟨in joining together at fertilization, germ cells add to the total gene ~ of an organism by the fusion of two heredities —Weston LaBarre⟩ ⟨growth ~⟩ ⟨human ~⟩ ⟨industrial ~⟩ ⟨leadership ~⟩ ⟨military ~⟩ **2 :** any of various functions (as a scalar function so related to the vector that the vector is its gradient) from which the intensity or the velocity at any point in a field may be calculated; *specif* **:** ELECTRIC POTENTIAL

**potential barrier** *n* **:** a region in which particles (as alpha particles, photoelectrons, or thermions) are decelerated or stopped by a repulsive force

**potential cautery** *n* **:** an agent (as a caustic or escharotic) used to destroy tissue by chemical action — compare ACTUAL CAUTERY

**potential coil** *or* **potential winding** *n* **:** a coil or winding connected in shunt across a circuit (as in a wattmeter)

**potential difference** *n* **:** the difference in electric potential between two points that represents the work involved or the energy released in the transfer of a unit quantity of electricity from one point to the other

**potential divider** *n* **:** VOLTAGE DIVIDER

**potential energy** *n* **:** the energy of a particle or body dependent upon its position

**potential gradient** *n* **:** the vector that represents the rate at which a potential changes with position in a specified direction; *specif* **:** the rate of change with height of the atmospheric electric potential

**potential head** *n* **:** ELEVATION HEAD

**po·ten·ti·al·i·ty** \pə,tenchēˈaləd·ē, pō,-, -ətē, -i *also* (,)pō,tenˈcha- *or* pə,tenˈcha-\ *n* -ES [ML *potentialitat-, potentialitas,* fr. LL *potentialis* potential, powerful + L *-itat-, -itas* -ity] **1 :** the capacity or possibility for changing or developing into a state of actuality ⟨the magnificent richness of human ~ and the paltriness of human achievement —Paul Pickrel⟩ ⟨economic ~⟩ ⟨growth ~⟩ ⟨propaganda ~⟩ ⟨war ~⟩ **2 :** POTENTIAL 1 ⟨present at birth as *potentialities* which later grow and develop —Abram Kardiner⟩ ⟨possible risks which have been seized upon as actualities when they have been merely *potentialities* —T.S.Eliot⟩ **3** *archaic* **:** the quality or state of being potent ⟨I have the power, the ~ of walking —S.T. Coleridge⟩

**po·ten·tial·ize** \pəˈtenchə,līz, pōˈ-\ *vt* -ED/-ING/-S **:** to make potential

**po·ten·tial·ly** \-chəlē, -li\ *adv* [ME *potencially,* fr. *potencial* potential + *-ly*] **1 :** in a potential or possible state or condition **:** with a possibility or capacity for becoming actual ⟨consider the contribution made by science both actually and still more ~ to agriculture —John Dewey⟩ ⟨~ as revolutionary . . . as the discovery of the atomic bomb —Vera M. Dean⟩ ⟨~ capable⟩ ⟨introducing ~ dangerous innovations⟩ ⟨~ most productive⟩ ⟨~ useful⟩ **2** *archaic* **:** in a powerful or authoritative manner

**po·ten·tial·ness** *n* -ES **:** POTENTIALITY

**potential temperature** *n* **:** the temperature that a sample of air attains if reduced to a pressure of 1000 millibars without receiving or losing heat to the environment

**potential well** *or* **potential hole** *n* **:** a sharply defined region of minimum potential in a field of force — compare POTENTIAL BARRIER

**po·ten·ti·ate** \pəˈtenchē,āt\ *vb* -ED/-ING/-S [L *potentia* potency, power + E *-ate;* intended as trans. of G *potenzieren*] *vt* **:** to make potent or more effective ⟨a poet's work may be *potentiated* by his experience of war and of suffering —*N.Y. Herald Tribune Bk. Rev.*⟩: as **a :** to make (as a drug) more physiologically active **b :** to cause an increase in (physiological activity or effect usu. of a drug) ⟨the effects or morphine on the stomach are *potentiated* by cholinergic drugs —B.P. Babkin & M.H.F.Friedman⟩ **~** *vi* **:** to make something potent or more effective

**po·ten·ti·a·tion** \=,==ˈāshən\ *n* -S **:** the act or process of potentiating

**po·ten·ti·a·tor** \=ˈ==,ād·ə(r)\ *n* -S **:** one that potentiates; *esp* **:** a chemical agent or drug that potentiates

**po·ten·til·la** \,pōtᵊnˈtilə\ *n* [NL, fr. ML, garden valerian, fr. L *potent-, potens* potent, powerful + ML *-illa* — more at POTENT] **1** *cap* **:** a large genus of herbs and shrubs (family Rosaceae) that are abundant in temperate regions, have alternate pinnate or palmate leaves, yellow, purple, or white flowers with a persistent bracted calyx and five petals, and a fruit consisting of many small achenes heaped on a dry receptacle, and include several which are cultivated as ornamentals — see CINQUEFOIL **2** -S **:** any plant of the genus *Potentilla*

**po·ten·ti·om·e·ter** \pə,tenchēˈäməd·ə(r)\ *n* [ISV 2*potential* + *-o-* + *-meter*] **1 :** an instrument for the precise measurement of electromotive forces by which a part of the voltage to be measured is balanced against that of a known electromotive force and computed therefrom by the law of fall of potential **2 :** VOLTAGE DIVIDER

**po·ten·ti·o·met·ric** \pə¦tenchēə¦me·trik\ *adj* [*potentiometer* + *-ic*] **:** of, relating to, or by means of a potentiometer — **po·ten·ti·o·met·ri·cal·ly** \-rək(ə)lē\ *adv*

**po·ten·ti·om·e·try** \pə,tenchēˈämə·trē\ *n* -ES [ISV 2*potential* + *-o-* + *-metry*] **:** the measurement of electromotive forces by means of a potentiometer; *also* **:** the use or application of such measurement

**po·tent·ize** \ˈpōtᵊn·,tīz\ *vt* -ED/-ING/-S **:** to make potent or effective

**po·tent·ly** *adv* **:** in a potent manner

**po·tent·ness** *n* -ES **:** the quality or state of being potent

**potents** *pl of* POTENT

**po·te·ri·um** \pōˈtirēəm\ *n, cap* [NL, fr. Gk *potērion* drinking cup (or, a plant, prob. goat's thorn); akin to Gk *pinein* to drink — more at POTABLE] **:** a small genus of thorny shrubs or herbs (family Rosaceae) with pinnate leaves and greenish flowers — see SALAD BURNET

**potes** *pres 3d sing of* POTE, *pl of* POTE

**po·tes·tal** \pōˈtestᵊl\ *adj* [*potestas* + *-al*] **:** of or relating to potestas

**po·tes·tas** \-e,stäs, -tas\ *n, pl* **potesta·tes** \,pō,teˈstä,tās, ,päd·əˈstād·(,)ēz\ [L *potestat-, potestas* power, irreg. fr. *potis* able, capable + *-tat-, -tas* -ty — more at POTENT] **:** the legal authority of a Roman citizen over his descendants and others in his household — compare PATRIA POTESTAS

**potestas ab·sti·nen·di** \-,äbztəˈnen(,)dē, -,äpst-; -,abztəˈnen(,)dē, -,dī\ *n* [L, power of refusing] **:** the right granted by the praetorian law of ancient Rome to a necessary family heir to decline the inheritance; *also* **:** the power to exercise this right — called also *beneficium abstinendi*

**potestate** *n* -S [ME *potestat,* fr. L *potestat-, potestas,* lit., power] *obs* **:** one having power or authority

**potestative** *adj* [LL *potestativus,* fr. L *potestat-, potestas* power + *-ivus* -ive] *obs* **:** having power or authority **:** POTENT

**po·tes·ta·tive condition** \ˈpōd·ə,stād·iv-\ *n* **:** a condition or term of a legal agreement that is completely within the power and control of one of the parties and that makes the agreement unenforceable for lack of mutuality of obligation

**pot–eye** \ˈ=ˌ=\ *n* **:** a ringlike device by which cloth or other textile material is guided during processing

**pot·ful** \ˈpät,fu̇l\ *n* -S [ME, fr. 1pot + *-ful*] **:** the quantity held by a pot

**pot furnace** *n* **1 :** a furnace containing several pots or crucibles in which different small batches of glass may be melted **2 :** a metallurgical furnace in which the charge is contained in a pot

**potgun** \ˈ=ˌ=\ *n* **1 a** *archaic* **:** POPGUN **b** *obs* **:** PISTOL **2** *obs* **:** a loud or boastful talker

**pothanger** \ˈ=ˌ==\ *n* **:** a rack, bar, or other device for hanging a pothook or a pot over a fire usu. in a fireplace

**pot hat** *n* **:** a hat with a stiff crown; *esp* **:** DERBY

**pothead** \ˈ=ˌ=\ *n* **1 :** BLACKFISH 2 **2 :** a form of terminal hermetically sealed to the sheath of an electric cable for making a moistureproof connection between the wires within the cable and those outside

**poth·e·cary** \ˈpäthə,kerē\ *n* -ES [alter. of *potecary*] *chiefly dial* **:** APOTHECARY

**potheen** *var of* POTEEN

**1poth·er** \ˈpäthə(r)\ *n* -S [origin unknown] **1 a :** a noisy disturbance **:** BUSTLE, COMMOTION ⟨the ~ of city traffic⟩ **b :** a vocal stir or controversy over a trivial or minor matter **:** FUSS ⟨the lack of storage facilities about which so much ~ was emitted during the campaign —Raymond Moley⟩ ⟨this ~ over a small point —B.T.Ellis⟩ ⟨the great ~ raised by civil service reform back in the 1880's —W.G.Carleton⟩ **2 :** a choking cloud or condition of dust or smoke ⟨rushed off in a terrific haste and ~ of dust —Arnold Bennett⟩ **3 :** a state of agitating worry or concern **:** TURMOIL, STEW **syn** see STIR

**2pother** \"\ *vb* -ED/-ING/-S *vt* **:** to trouble or disturb esp. about a trivial or minor matter **:** PERPLEX, VEX ⟨~*s* himself over unnecessary detail⟩ ~ *vi* **:** to trouble or concern oneself esp. with a trivial or minor matter **:** FUSS, WORRY, PUZZLE ⟨~*ed* all evening over the bus schedule⟩

**potherb** \'=,=\ *n* **1 :** an herb that is boiled for use as a vegetable; *esp* **:** wild greens gathered for food **2 :** a cultivated herb (as mint) used to season food

**poth·er·ment** \'päthə(r)mənt\ *n* -S *dial* **:** BOTHERMENT

**potholder** \'=,==\ *n* **:** a usu. cloth pad for protecting the hands against hot cooking utensils

**pothole** \'=,=\ *n* **1 a :** a circular hole formed in the rocky bed of a river or stream by the grinding action of stones or gravel whirled round by the water — called also *kettle* **b :** a pot-shaped hole in the surface of a pavement **c :** a circumscribed body of water frequented by wildfowl **2 :** a deep cave opening upward to the surface

**pot·hol·er** \'pät,hōlə(r)\ *n* **:** SPELUNKER

**pothook** \'=,=\ *n* [ME *pothoke,* fr. ¹*pot* + *hoke, hok, hook* hook] **1 :** a hook in the form of a long or short S for hanging pots over an open fire from a crane or a bar in the throat of a chimney — called also *hake* **2 :** an iron collar worn as punishment esp. by a captured runaway slave — usu. used in pl. **3 a** (1) **:** a written letter or character resembling a pothook in shape and used in teaching writing — see HANGER 4 (2) **:** writing marked by letters so formed ⟨it is impossible to decipher her ~*s*⟩ **b** *slang* **:** a nine of any suit in a pack of playing cards

pot-hooks 1

**1po·thos** \'pō,thäs\ [NL, fr. Sinhalese *pōtā* ivy-arum] *syn of* SCINDAPSUS

**2pothos** \"\ *n, pl* **pothos** *also* **pothoses :** IVY-ARUM

**pothouse** \'=,=\ *n* **:** ALEHOUSE, TAVERN 1b

**pothunter** \'=,==\ *n* **1 :** a hunter who shoots chiefly to fill his bag without regard for the rules or spirit of sport **2 :** one who contests or competes merely to win prizes **3 :** a nonprofessional archaeologist who collects archaeological objects chiefly for his own pleasure or profit; *esp* **:** one who collects such objects without maintaining an adequate record or injures or destroys an archaeological site

**pot-hunting** \'=,==\ *n* **1 :** the act of hunting chiefly to bag game without regard for the rules or spirit of sport **2 :** the act of contesting or competing chiefly for the prize or winnings **3 :** the act of hunting for archaeological findings in an amateur manner

**po·tiche** \pō'tēsh\ *n* -S [F, fr. *pot* — more at POTAGE] **:** a vase having a separate cover, a body usu. rounded or polygonal with nearly vertical sides, a rounded shoulder, and a tapered neck

**po·ti·cho·ma·nia** \,pōd·əshō'mānēə\ *also* **po·ti·chi·ma·nie** \-shē'mānē\ *n* -S [*potichomania* part trans. of F *potichomanie,* fr. *potiche* + -o- + *manie* mania, fr. LL *mania; potichimanie* alter. (influenced by *-i-*) of F *potichomanie*] **:** the art or process of imitating painted porcelain ware

**1po·tion** \'pōshən\ *n* -S [ME *pocioun,* fr. MF *potion,* fr. L *potion-, potio* potion, drink, fr. *potus* (past part. of *potare* to drink) + *-ion-, -io* -ion — more at POTABLE] **:** a liquid mixture or dose of a medicine or drug ⟨physician . . . daily prepares a nourishing ~ —*Springfield (Mass.) Union*⟩ ⟨gave him love ~*s* to increase his ardor —Willa Cather⟩ ⟨sleeping ~⟩

**2potion** \"\ *vt* -ED/-ING/-S *archaic* **:** to administer a potion to **:** DOSE, DRUG

**pot kiln** *n* **1 :** a small limekiln **2 :** a kiln for firing clay pots

**1pot·latch** *also* **pot·lach** \'pät,lach\ *n* -ES [Chinook Jargon, fr. Nootka *patshatl* giving, gift] **1 :** a ceremonial feast or festival of the Indians of the northwest coast given for the display of wealth to validate or advance individual tribal position or social status and marked by the host's lavish destruction of personal property and an ostentatious distribution of gifts that entails elaborate reciprocation **2** *Northwest* **:** a social event or celebration **:** PARTY, GET-TOGETHER

**2potlatch** \"\ *vt* **1 :** to hold or give a potlatch for (as a tribe or group) ⟨a clan . . . being ~*ed* by a neighboring clan —F.C. Hibben⟩ **2 :** to give (as a gift) esp. with the expectancy of reciprocation ⟨told her to make a start by getting friendly with her . . . uncle, even if she has to ~ a little stuff to him off the shelves —N.C.McDonald⟩ ~ *vi* **:** to hold or give a potlatch

**pot layering** *n* **:** air layering in which the rooting medium is held in a small pot

**pot lead** *n* [trans. of D *potlood*] **:** graphite esp. as used on the bottoms of racing boats

**pot-lead** \'=,=\ *vt* [*pot lead*] **:** to coat (as the hull of a racing boat) with pot lead

**potleg** \'=,=\ *n* **:** broken pieces of cast iron used as shot

**pot·lick·er** *also* **pot·lik·ker** \'pät,likə(r)\ *n* -S [¹*pot* + *licker*] *dial* **:** a mongrel dog; *esp* **:** STRAY

**potlid** \'=,=\ *n* [ME *potlede,* fr. ¹*pot* + *lede, lid* lid] **1 :** the lid or cover of a pot **2** *or* **pat·lid** \'pat,lid\ **:** a curling stone that comes to rest on the tee

**pot·lik·ker** *or* **pot·lick·er** \'pät,likə(r)\ *South & Midland var of* POT LIQUOR

**pot limit** *n* **:** a betting limit imposed in a poker game whereby no raise may be greater than the amount in the pot at the time the raise is made

**potline** \'=,=\ *n* **:** a row of electrolytic cells used in the production of aluminum

**pot liquor** *n* **:** the liquid left in a pot after cooking meat, vegetables, or greens

**potluck** \'=¦=\ *n* **1 :** the regular fare or meal available to a guest for whom no special preparations have been made ⟨tied their horses to the corral gate and came in to take ~ with us —Burges Johnson⟩ **2 :** the luck or chance of succeeding events or possibilities ⟨I should relish every hour and what it brought me, the ~ of the day —R.W.Emerson⟩ ⟨will resign and try ~ among the bigger banks —Brendan Gill⟩ ⟨season-ticket holders buy out 85% of the house in advance and take ~ —*Time*⟩

**potluck supper** *or* **potluck dinner** *n* **:** COVERED-DISH SUPPER

**pot·man** \'pätmən\ *n, pl* **potmen 1 a :** a servingman employed in a public house — compare POTBOY **b :** a worker employed by a hotel or restaurant to wash pots and pans by hand **2 :** a worker who reduces aluminum in a battery of reduction pots by an electrolytic process **3 :** a chemical worker who dehydrates concentrated caustic solutions by boiling off excess water in cast-iron pots

**pot marigold** *n* **:** a common European annual garden plant (*Calendula officinalis*) widely grown for ornament — called also *Scotch marigold*

**pot marjoram** *n* **:** WILD MARJORAM

**pot metal** *n* **1 a :** an alloy of copper and lead used esp. for making large vessels **b :** a cast iron used for making pots and other hollow ware **2 a :** glass that is melted in a pot **b :** stained glass whose colors are incorporated with melted glass in the pot

**pot of gold :** a large sum of money often obtained quickly or fabulously **:** BONANZA; *also* **:** the opportunity or prospect of making a large sum of money ⟨the *pot of gold* was seen in real estate, trade, timber, and commerce —*Amer. Guide Series: Wash.*⟩

**po·to·ma·nia** \,pōd·ə'mānēə\ *n* [NL, fr. Gk *poton* drink + LL *mania;* akin to Gk *pinein* to drink — more at POTABLE] **:** DIPSOMANIA

**po·to·ma·to** \,pōd·ə'mād·(,)ō\ *n* -ES [blend of *potato* and *tomato*] **:** POMATO

**po·tom·e·ter** \pō'tämәd·ə(r)\ *n* [Gk *poton* drink + E *-meter*] **:** an apparatus for measuring the rate of transpiration in a plant by determining the amount of water absorbed

**pot on** *vt* **:** to transplant (as a potted plant) to a larger pot

**po·too** \pō'tü\ *n* -S [imit.] **:** a large goatsucker (*Nyctibius griseus*) of So. America and the West Indies

**po·to·roo** \,pōd·ə'rü\ *n* -S [native name in New South Wales, southeast Australia] **:** RAT KANGAROO

**po·to·ro·us** \,päd·ə'rōəs\ *n, cap* [NL, fr. *potoroo* (native name in New South Wales)] **:** a genus of marsupial mammals comprising the common Australian rat kangaroos

**pot oven** *n* **:** an oven consisting of a heated iron plate covered by a pot

**potpie** \'=¦=\ *n* **1 :** meat and vegetables covered with pastry and boiled or baked in a pot **2 :** DEEP-DISH PIE

**pot plant** *n* **:** a potted plant or one suitable for growing in a pot

**pot·pour·ri** \,pōpə¦rē *sometimes* pät'pürē\ *n* -S [F *pot pourri* (trans. of Sp *olla podrida*), fr. *pot* + *pourri* rotten, past part. of *pourrir* to rot, fr. L *putrescere* — more at POTAGE, PUTRESCENT] **1 :** OLLA PODRIDA 1 **2 :** a jar of flower petals mixed with spices and used for scent or perfume **3 a :** a series of melodies arranged or played in succession **:** MEDLEY ⟨a ~ of songs, sketches, parodies, and ballets —Hollis Alpert⟩ ⟨~ of familiar American cowboy tunes —Winthrop Sargeant⟩ **b :** a group or collection of miscellaneous literary productions ⟨a ~ of stories, sketches, poetry, and drama —H.M.Gloster⟩ **c :** a general mixture of often disparate or unrelated materials or subject matter ⟨a ~ of ancient history, Asiatic lore, current power politics, violent adventure —Linton Wells⟩ ⟨the ~ of dreams, barbarities, intrigues, wars and personalities that went into the . . . new empire —H.C.Wolfe⟩ ⟨a ~ of miscellaneous observations and reflections on his travels —Barrington Moore⟩

**pot·rack** \'pä'trak\ *vi* [imit.] **:** to make the natural high shrill noise of a guinea fowl

**po·tre·ro** \pə'tre(,)rō\ *n* -S [Sp, colt pasture, fr. *potro* colt, fr. (assumed) VL *pullitrus* — more at POLTROON] *chiefly Southwest* **:** a meadow or pasture esp. on a ranch

**po·tro** \'pō·(,)trō\ *n* -S [Sp, colt] *Southwest* **:** COLT; *also* **:** an untamed bucking horse

**pot roast** *n* [¹*pot* + *roast,* n.] **:** a piece of tough beef or other meat cooked by braising usu. on top of the stove — see BEEF illustration

**pot-roast** \'=,=\ *vt* [*pot roast*] **:** to roast in a pot usu. on top of a stove

**pot-rustler** \'=,=(=)=\ *n* **:** a ranch or camp cook

**pots** *pl of* POT, *pres 3d sing of* POT

**pots·dam** \'päts,dam, -aam\ *adj, usu cap* [fr. *Potsdam,* city in eastern Germany] **:** of or from the city of Potsdam, Germany **:** of the kind or style prevalent in Potsdam

**pot seine** *n* **:** POUND NET

**pot·sherd** \'pät,shərd, -shōd, -shəid\ *n* -S [ME *pot-schoord,* fr. ¹*pot* + *schoord, shard, sherd* shard] **:** a piece of a broken earthen pot **:** a pottery fragment ⟨~*s* unearthed at an excavation⟩

**pot-shoot** \'=,=\ *vi* **:** POTSHOT ⟨there was considerable *pot-shooting* back and forth —S.L.A.Marshall⟩ — **pot-shooter** \'=,==\ *n*

**1potshot** \'=,=\ *n* [¹*pot* + *shot,* n.; fr. the idea that casual shooting is unsportsmanlike and hence characteristic of a hunter whose only object is to kill game for the cooking pot] **1 :** a shot taken in a random, casual, or sporadic manner ⟨taking ~*s* at passing rabbits —Green Peyton⟩ ⟨scattered in tall grass . . . and popped up occasionally for a ~ —Walter Karig⟩ **2 :** a critical remark or comment made in a random or sporadic manner ⟨taking clerical ~*s* at those who hold opposing views —Riley Hughes⟩ ⟨had taken a ~ at the other's way of putting the truth —J.H.Randall⟩ ⟨subjects which require serious discussion, not verbal ~*s* —C.H.Page⟩

**2potshot** \"\ *vb* **potshot** *also* **potshotted; potshot** *also* **potshotted; potshotting; potshots** *vi* **:** to attack or shoot with a potshot ⟨skirmishing and *potshotting* each other —Ray Josephs⟩ ⟨pausing periodically to ~ people who think high-flown language is better —*Time*⟩ ~ *vi* **:** to take a potshot ⟨they ~ at the carabinieri —Janet Flanner⟩ ⟨*potshotting* from 1000 yards —Georg Meyers⟩ ⟨*potshotting* at the administrative departments —*Atlantic*⟩

**pot signal** *n* **:** a small revolving fixed signal used in railroading as a substitute for a dwarf signal

**pot sleeper** *n, Brit* **:** a convex cast-iron or steel disk with a clamp on top that is used to fasten railroad rails in places where wooden ties are impractical

**pot spinning** *n* **:** a process in rayon manufacture in which the coagulated filament is fed into a revolving pot and by centrifugal force deposited on the inside in the form of a cake

**pot steel** *n* **:** a cast or crucible steel

**potstick** \'=,=\ *n* [ME *potsticke,* fr. ¹*pot* + *sticke* stick] *chiefly dial* **:** a stick for stirring the contents of a pot

**pot still** *n* **:** a still used esp. in the distillation of Irish grain whiskey and Scotch malt whiskey in which the heat of the fire is applied directly to the pot containing the mash

**potstone** \'=,=\ *n* [trans. of NL *lapis ollaris*] **1 :** a more or less impure steatite used esp. in prehistoric times to make cooking vessels **2** [¹*pot* + *stone*] **:** POT BOTTOM

**pot·sy** \'pätsē\ *n* -ES [origin unknown] **:** HOPSCOTCH; *also* **:** the object thrown in this game

**pot·tage** \'päd·ij, -ät|, |ēj\ *n* -S [ME *potage,* fr. OF — more at POTAGE] **1 :** vegetables or vegetables and meat cooked to softness and seasoned **2 :** MESS OF POTTAGE **3 :** POTAGE **4** *archaic* **:** OATMEAL

**pot·tah** \'päd·ə\ *n* -S [Hindi *paṭṭā,* fr. Skt *paṭṭaka,* fr. *paṭṭa* copper plate for grants] **:** a certificate of tenure **:** TITLE DEED **:** LEASE

**pottawattomi** *or* **pottawattami** *usu cap, var of* POTAWATOMI

**potted** *adj* **1 :** preserved in a closed pot, jar, or can **2 :** planted or grown in a pot **3 :** made easily comprehensible or superficially attractive by abridgment or glamorization **:** CANNED ⟨emitted the ~ history . . . — dates, regicides, amours, assassinations at a mile a minute —Frank Clune⟩ ⟨real scholarship and serious criticism in contradistinction to ~ "culture" —*Times Lit. Supp.*⟩ ⟨versions ~ for radio —*Times Lit. Supp.*⟩ ⟨~ pocket-book format —*Brit. Book News*⟩ **4** *slang* **:** DRUNK

**potteen** *var of* POTEEN

**1pot·ter** \'päd·ə(r), -ätə-\ *n* -S [ME *pottere,* fr. OE, fr. *pott* pot + *-ere* -er] **:** one that makes pottery ⟨for I remember stopping by the way to watch a ~ thumping his wet clay —Edward FitzGerald⟩

**2potter** \"\ *vb* -ED/-ING/-S [prob. freq. of ¹*pote*] *vi* **1** *dial chiefly Brit* **:** to poke or prod lightly and repeatedly **2 :** PUTTER ⟨bad weather finds him ~*ing* around, nailing new lobster pots, painting, repairing his gear —A.J.Cronin⟩ ⟨~*ed* around with it for a while and then gave up —*New Yorker*⟩ ⟨~*ing* about in a canoe on summer afternoons —Richard Aldington⟩ ⟨the trolley ~*ed* through that part of town in a desultory, neighborly way —*New Yorker*⟩ ⟨~*ing* among the ruins of the old casino —Alan Moorehead⟩ **3** *of a dog* **:** to quest indecisively ~ *vt* **1** *dial Eng* **:** BOTHER, IRRITATE, ANNOY **2 :** to waste by idling or trifling — often used with *away*

**3potter** \"\ *n* -S [²*pot* + *-er*] **:** POTHUNTER 1

**4potter** \"\ *n* -S [prob. fr. ¹*pot* + *-er*] **:** RED-BELLIED TERRAPIN

**potter bee** *n* **:** any of various bees (as of the genera *Anthidium* and *Megachile*) that construct nests of mud or pebbles cemented together and commonly attached to a plant stem — compare POTTER WASP

**pot·ter·er** \'päd·ərə(r)\ *n* -S **1 :** one that acts or moves in an unsystematic or ineffective manner **2 :** a hunting dog that potters

**pot·ter·ing·ly** *adv* **:** in a pottering manner

**potter's clay** *n* **:** a clay used or suitable for use by potters

**potter's field** *n* [so called fr. the mention in Mt 27:7 of the purchase of a potter's field for use as a graveyard] **:** a public burial place (as in a city) for paupers, unknown persons, and criminals

**potter's flint** *n* **:** silica in the form of powdered quartz orig. made by pulverizing flint pebbles

**potter's wheel** *n* **:** a usu. horizontal disk revolving on a vertical spindle and carrying the clay in the operation of throwing

**potter wasp** *n* **:** any of various solitary wasps usu. of the genus *Eumenes* that construct vase-shaped cells of sand and mud for their young — compare MASON WASP, POTTER BEE

**pot·tery** \'päd·ərē, -ätə-, -ä·trē, -ri\ *n* -ES [ME *poterie,* fr. OF, fr. *potier* potter (fr. *pot* + *-ier* -er) + *-ie* -y — more at POTAGE] **1 :** a place where clayware is made and fired **2 a :** the art or craft of the potter ⟨a class in ~⟩ **b :** the manufacture of clayware **3 :** CLAYWARE; *esp* **:** earthenware as distinguished on the one hand from porcelain and stoneware and on the other from brick and tile

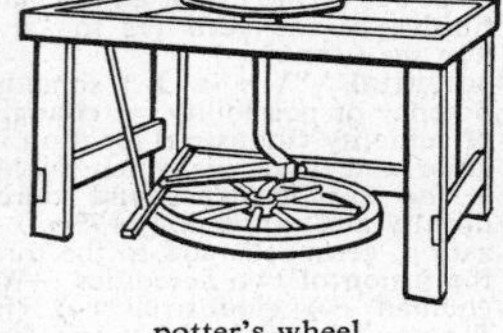

potter's wheel

**pottery-bark tree** *n* **:** a timber tree (*Licania heteromorpha*) of northern So. America characterized by exceedingly hard wood, fruit that yields a black dye, and a siliceous bark that is sometimes burned and pulverized for mixing with pottery clay

**pottery tissue** *n* **: 1** a well-glazed tissue paper used for wrapping pottery ware **2 :** tissue paper used for putting transfers on pottery ware

**pottery tree** *n* **:** a Brazilian tree (*Moquilea tomentosa*) of the family Rosaceae having a bark that is burned and pulverized for mixing with pottery clay

**pottery ware** *n* **:** POTTERY 3

**pot·ti·a·ce·ae** \,päd·ē'āsē,ē\ *n pl, cap* [NL, fr. *Pottia,* type genus (fr. J.F.*Pott* †1805 Ger. botanist + NL *-ia*) + *-aceae*] **:** a family of acrocarpous usu. low-growing mosses (order Pottiales) whose peristome when present has 16 entire or divided and often twisted teeth

**pot·ti·a·les** \-ā(,)lēz\ *n pl, cap* [NL, fr. *Pottia* + *-ales*] **:** an order of Musci comprising mosses that have gametophores with many-ranked leaves having a distinct midrib and a usu. acrocarpous sporophyte with a capsule having either a simple 16-toothed peristome or none

**potting** *n* -S **1 :** the act of one that pots: as **a** *archaic* **:** the act of drinking alcoholic beverages **b :** the making of pottery **c :** CANNING **d :** the act of planting or transplanting in a pot **2 :** the process of supplying nitrous fumes in sulfuric acid manufacture by action of sulfuric acid on a nitrate in iron pots **3 :** a wet-finishing process for giving woolens a glossy surface and a soft hand

**pot·tin·gar** \'pätiŋgər\ *n* -S [ME (Sc), alter. of ME *potecarie* — more at POTECARY] *chiefly Scot* **:** APOTHECARY

**potting compound** *n* **:** a protective insulating and sealing plastic used to embed electric coils in a container

**1pot·tin·ger** \'päd·ənjə(r)\ *n* -S [ME *potinger,* alter. of *poteger,* fr. AF *potageer,* fr. MF *potager,* adj., of or relating to pottage, fr. *potage* pottage — more at POTAGE] *chiefly dial* **:** PORRINGER

**2pottinger** \"\ *n* -S [alter. of ME *potager,* fr. MF *potagier* — more at POTAGER] **1** *archaic* **:** a maker of pottage **:** COOK **2** [influenced in meaning by *pottingar*] *archaic* **:** APOTHECARY

**pot·tle** \'päd·ᵊl\ *n* -S [ME *potel,* fr. OF, fr. *pot* + *-el*] **1 :** a liquid or dry measure equal to a half gallon **2 a :** a container holding about one pottle **b :** a pottle of wine or liquor **3 :** a vessel or small basket for holding fruit

**pottle pot** *n* [ME *potel pot,* fr. *potel* pottle + ¹*pot*] **:** a pot or tankard holding two quarts

**pot·to** \'päd·(,)ō\ *n* -S [of Niger-Congo origin; akin to Wolof *pata* tailless monkey of average size with black hair and red breast, Twi *aᵖɔ̄sɔ̄w*³ fierce animal resembling a monkey] **1 :** any of several African lorisid lemurs (genera *Arctocebus* and *Perodicticus*); *esp* **:** a West African lemur (*Perodicticus potto*) that resembles the slow loris in its nocturnal, arboreal, and slow-moving habits, is reddish gray in color, and has an index finger and tail that are vestigial **2 :** KINKAJOU

**pott's disease** \'päts-\ *n, usu cap P* [after Percivall *Pott* †1788 Eng. surgeon] **:** tuberculosis of the spine with destruction of bone resulting in curvature of the spine and occas. in paralysis of the lower extremities

**pott's fracture** *n, usu cap P* **:** a fracture of the lower part of the fibula accompanied with injury to the tibial articulation so that the foot is dislocated outward

**1pot·ty** \'päti\ *adj* [prob. fr. ¹*pot* + *-y,* adj. suffix] **1** *Brit* **:** of minor importance **:** TRIVIAL, INSIGNIFICANT ⟨just one of those ~ little country affairs —P.G.Wodehouse⟩ **2** *slang chiefly Brit* **:** slightly crazy **:** FOOLISH ⟨gone ~ on the subject —Allan Sangster⟩ ⟨driving him ~ with her demands —C.D. Lewis⟩ **3 :** haughty or supercilious in bearing or speech **:** SNOBBISH ⟨our petty rights here, our ~ dignity there —John Galsworthy⟩ ⟨a futile, ~, upper-class gentleman —Brooks Atkinson⟩ ⟨the ~, pseudocultivated tones of some . . . clubwoman —Austin Warren⟩

**2pot·ty** \'päd·ē\ *n* -ES [¹*pot* + *-y,* n. suffix] **:** a small child's pot for voiding or defecation

**potty-chair** \'==,=\ *n* **:** a child's chair having an open seat under which a pot or other receptacle is placed for toilet training

potty-chair

**pot-valiant** \'=¦==\ *adj* **:** bold or courageous under the influence of alcoholic drink

**pot-valor** \'=¦==\ *n* **:** boldness or courage resulting from alcoholic drink

**pot valve** *n* **:** a safety valve resembling an inverted pot with a recess in the crown in which the valve lever is fulcrumed

**pot·wal·lop·er** \'pä,twäləpə(r)\ *also* **pot·wal·ler** \-lə(r)\ *n* [*potwalloper* alter. (influenced by *wallop*) of *potwaller,* fr. ¹*pot* + obs. E *wall* to boil (fr. ME *wallen,* fr. OE *weallan*) + E *-er* — more at WELL] **:** a voter living in an English borough before the Reform Act of 1832 and qualifying for suffrage as a householder by the boiling of his own pot at his own fireplace

**pot-walloping** \'=¦===\ *adj* [¹*pot* + *walloping,* pres. part. of *wallop* (to boil)] *Brit* **:** qualifying for suffrage by maintaining an independent household **:** being a potwalloper **:** consisting of potwallopers ⟨*pot-walloping* constituents⟩ ⟨*pot-walloping* vote⟩ ⟨*pot-walloping* borough⟩

**potware** \'=,=\ *n* **:** POTTERY 3

**pot wheel** *n* **:** NORIA

**potwork** \'=,=\ *n* **:** POTTERY

**pou** \'pü\ *chiefly Scot var of* PULL

**1pouch** \'pau̇ch\ *n* -ES [ME *pouche,* fr. MF *pouche, poche,* of Gmc origin; akin to MD *poke* bag — more at POKE] **1 a** *archaic* **:** a small drawstring bag for carrying money **:** PURSE, POKE ⟨tester I'll have in ~ when thou shalt lack —Shak.⟩ **b :** a woman's handbag with soft sides and rounded shape usu. mounted on a frame or closed with a zipper or drawstring — compare ENVELOPE 4 **2 a :** a sack or satchel of small or moderate size for storing or transporting goods ⟨bullet ~⟩ ⟨tobacco ~⟩; *specif* **:** a bag with a locking device for the transmission of first class mail or diplomatic dispatches **b** *chiefly Scot* **:** POCKET **c :** PACKET ⟨hermetically sealed ~*es* . . . for use on such products as dry soups —N.A.Cooke⟩ **3 :** an anatomical structure felt to resemble a pouch: as **a** (1) **:** BAG 3a(4) (2) **:** CORPORATION 6 (3) **:** a fluid-filled cyst or sac **b :** MARSUPIUM 1a, 1b **c :** CHEEK POUCH **d :** the large gular space at the base of the lower mandible of a pelican **e :** a saccular plant part (as a silique or utricle)

**2pouch** \"\ *vb* -ED/-ING/-ES *vt* **1 :** to put into or as if into a pouch **:** POCKET ⟨sold justice and ~*ed* the price of every pardon —Francis Hackett⟩; *specif* **:** to put (as mail or dispatches) into locked bags ⟨the Baltimore mail was sorted . . . and ~*ed* by 4:20 A.M. —*Sat. Eve. Post*⟩ ⟨government of a twentieth-century diplomat ~*es* to him . . . a truly generous quantity of informative material —R.S.Simpson⟩ **2 a** *archaic* **:** SWALLOW ⟨allowing the fish . . . to ~ the bait —Thomas Best⟩ **b :** to store or carry in a pouch in the mouth ⟨squirrels ~*ing* acorns⟩ **3 :** to make puffy or protuberant ⟨ill health had . . . ~*ed* the loose flesh under his eyes —Ellen Glasgow⟩ ⟨up comes the great bill, ~*ed* with fish —A.J.Cronin⟩ ~ *vi* **1 :** to form a pouch **:** puff out **:** PROTRUDE ⟨snow-white hair and a ~*ing* bosom —Marguerite Steen⟩ **2 :** to transmit mail or dispatches in a locked bag

**3pouch** \'pōch\ *dial Eng var of* POACH

**pouch bone** *n* **:** MARSUPIAL BONE

**pouched** \'pau̇cht\ *adj* **:** having or forming a pouch ⟨~ mammal⟩ ⟨the ~ sagging flesh of his face —Moray Firth⟩

**pouched dog** *n* **:** TASMANIAN WOLF

**pouched frog** *or* **pouched toad** *n* **:** MARSUPIAL FROG

**pouched marmot** *n* **:** GROUND SQUIRREL 1c

**pouched mole** *n* **:** MARSUPIAL MOLE

**pouched mouse** *n* **1 a :** POCKET MOUSE **b :** POUCHED RAT c **2 :** any of numerous marsupial mice of *Phascogale* or related genera

**pouched rat** *n* **:** any of several African murid rodents with cheek pouches: as **a** *or* **pouched gopher :** POCKET GOPHER **b :** KANGAROO RAT **c :** an African rodent of *Cricetomys* or the related genus *Sarcostomus* **d :** a spiny pocket mouse (*Heteromys melanoleucus*)

**pouched stork** *n* **:** ADJUTANT BIRD

**pouch·less** \'pau̇chləs\ *adj* **:** having no pouch; *specif* **:** having no marsupium ⟨~ mammals⟩

**pouch of doug·las** \-'dəgləs\ *usu cap D* [after James *Douglas* †1742 Scot. anatomist] **:** a deep peritoneal recess between the uterus and the upper vaginal wall anteriorly and the rectum posteriorly

**pouch of rathke** *usu cap R* **:** RATHKE'S POUCH

**pouch table** *n* **:** BAG TABLE

**pouchy** \'pau̇chē\ *adj* -ER/-EST **:** having, tending to have, or resembling a pouch **:** POUCHED, PUFFY ⟨~ handbag⟩ ⟨the skin . . . is soft and a little ~ from fatigue —Walter Bernstein⟩

**poud** *var of* POOD

**pou·dre B** \¦pau̇də(r)¦bē, ¦püdrə¦bē\ *n* [F, fr. *poudre* powder + *B*, initial letter of the surname of Georges Ernest Jean Marie *Boulanger* †1891 Fr. general — more at POWDER] **:** a smokeless French rifle powder consisting essentially of about two thirds guncotton and one third pyroxylin

**poudre blue** \¦pau̇də(r)-\ *n* [alter. (influenced by F *poudre*) of *powder blue*] **:** POWDER BLUE 2a

**pou·dre de riz** \¦püdrədə¦rē\ *n* [F] **:** RICE POWDER

**pou·drette** \(')pü¦dret\ *n* -S [F, fr. *poudre* + *-ette*] **:** dried deodorized night soil mixed with various substances (as charcoal and gypsum) and used as a fertilizer

**pou·dreuse** \(')pü¦drərz, -drə̄z\ *n* -S [F, fr. *poudre* powder] **:** a small dressing table with a mirror that usu. folds down into the top

**pouf** *also* **pouff** *or* **pouffe** \'püf\ *n* -S [F, of imit. origin] **:** something that is inflated or insubstantial: as **a :** PUFF 3b(3) **b :** a bouffant or fluffy part of a garment or clothing accessory ⟨a taffeta ~ tacked on the back of a tight skirt —*Harper's Bazaar*⟩ ⟨an ivory velours . . . trimmed with a ~ of fine black plumes —*Hats*⟩ **c** (1) **:** a plumply upholstered usu. circular backless couch or hassock **:** OTTOMAN (2) **:** PUFF 3b(4) **d :** an evanescent whiff (as of smoke) often accompanied by a muffled report ⟨with a little ~, the lights went out —Anne S. Mehdevi⟩ — often used interjectionally to express extreme transience or suddenness of disappearance ⟨if you offer less, ~, he is gone —H.O.Storm⟩

**poufed** *or* **pouffed** \-ft\ *adj* [*pouf* + *-ed*] **:** PUFFED 1a(2), BLOUSED 3

**poul** *n* -S [Per *pūl*] **:** PUL

**pou·laine** \(')pü¦lān\ *n* -S [MF, fr. fem. of *poulain* Polish] **1 :** the long pointed toe of a crakow **:** PIKE **2 :** CRAKOW

**pou·larde** *also* **pou·lard** \(')pü¦lärd\ *n* -S [F *poularde*, fr. MF *pollarde*, fr. *polle*, *poule* hen — more at PULLET] **:** a pullet that has been sterilized by removing either the ovaries or a part of the oviduct usu. to produce fattening — compare CAPON

**pou·lard·ize** \-,dīz\ *vt* -ED/-ING/-S [*poularde* or *poulard* + *-ize*] **:** to make a poularde of a pullet

**poulard wheat** \"-\ *n* [part trans. of F *blé poulard*, fr. *blé* wheat + *poulard*, prob. fr. *poularde*] **:** a wheat (*Triticum turgidum*) little grown in the U. S. having 4-sided compact awned spikes that tend to branch in some varieties, rather short thick humped yellowish to red kernels, and long thick pithy or solid stems, and used chiefly for stock feed — called also *cone wheat, English wheat, rivet wheat*

**pouldron** *var of* PAULDRON

**poule** \'pül\ *n* -S [F, lit., chicken, hen] **:** PROSTITUTE

**pou·lette** \(')pü¦let\ *or* **poulette sauce** *n* -S [F *poulette* (esp. in the expression *sauce poulette* poulette sauce), lit., chick, fr. OF *polete*, fr. *pole*, *poule* hen + *-ete* -ette] **:** velouté with added egg yolk

**poulp** *or* **poulpe** \'pülp\ *n* -S [F *poulpe*, fr. L *polypus* — more at POLYP] **:** OCTOPUS

**poul·sen arc** \'pau̇lzən-, -lsən-\ *n, usu cap P* [after Valdemar *Poulsen* †1942 Dan. electrical engineer] *physics* **:** a direct-current arc formerly used for producing undamped high-frequency oscillations

**poult** \'pōlt\ *n* -S [ME *pulte* young fowl, alter. of *polet*, young chicken, young fowl — more at PULLET] **1 a :** a young turkey esp. in its early weeks **b :** a young chicken, pheasant, grouse, or other fowl **2** *chiefly Scot* **a :** CHILD **b :** one that behaves like a child

**poult-de-soie** \¦püdə¦swä; (')püd¦swä, (')pült¦s-\ *also* **poult** \'pü(lt)\ *n* -S [F *pou-de-soie*, *poult-de-soie*] **:** a plain-woven usu. solid color silk fabric with fine full ribs used for women's clothing

**poulter** *n* -S [ME *pulter*, fr. MF *pouletier*, fr. OF, fr. *polet*, *poulet* young chicken, young fowl + *-ier* -er — more at PULLET] *obs* **:** POULTERER

**poul·ter·er** \'pōltərə(r)\ *n* -S [*poulter* + *-er*] **:** one that deals in poultry

**poul·ter's measure** \'pōltə(r)z-\ *n* [so called fr. the former practice of occasionally giving one or two extra when counting eggs by dozens] **:** a meter in which lines of 12 and 14 syllables alternate

**¹poul·tice** \'pōltəs\ *n* -S [alter. of earlier *pultes*, fr. ML, pap, fr. L, pl. of *pult-*, *puls* porridge made of meal and pulse — more at PULSE] **:** a soft mass (as of bread, bran, or medicated clay) usu. heated and spread on cloth for application to sores, inflamed areas, or other lesions, to supply moist warmth, relieve pain, or act as a counterirritant or antiseptic — called also *cataplasm*; compare PLASTER

**²poultice** \"\ *vt* -ED/-ING/-S **1 :** to apply a poultice to **:** dress with a poultice **2 :** to apply a mudcap to (as an explosive or a rock surface) preparatory to surface blasting

**poul·try** \'pōl·trē, -ri\ *n* -ES *often attrib* [ME *pultrie*, fr. MF *pouleterie*, fr. OF, fr. *pouletier* + *-ie* -y] **:** domesticated birds that serve as a source of eggs or meat and that include among commercially important kinds chickens, turkeys, ducks, and geese and among kinds chiefly of local interest guinea fowl, peafowl, pigeons, pheasants, and others

**poultry bug** *n* **:** a cimicid bug (*Haematosiphon inodorus*) that is an ectoparasite on poultry and occas. on man in the southern U. S. and Mexico

**poultry flea** *n* **:** a flea (*Ceratophyllus gallinae*) that attacks poultry

**poul·try·less** \-ləs\ *adj* **:** having no poultry

**poultry louse** *n* **:** any of several biting lice (genus *Menopon*) that attack poultry; *esp* **:** SHAFT LOUSE

**poul·try·man** \-mən\ *n, pl* **poultrymen 1 a :** one that raises domestic fowls esp. on a commercial scale for the production of eggs and meat **b :** a dealer in poultry or poultry products **2 :** one employed by a hotel or restaurant to pick, clean, and cut fowls

**poultry mite** *n* **:** CHICKEN MITE

**poultry pin** *n* **:** SKEWER 1

**poultry tick** *n* **1 :** CHICKEN TICK **2 :** CHICKEN MITE

**poultry wire** *n* **:** CHICKEN WIRE

**pou·na·mu** \pō'nä(,)mü\ *n* -S [Maori] **1 :** NEPHRITE **2 :** a Maori weapon or implement made of nephrite

**¹pounce** \'pau̇n(t)s\ *vt* -ED/-ING/-S [ME *pounsen*, alter. of *pounsonen*, fr. MF *poinçonner* to stamp, fr. *poinçon* pointed tool — more at PUNCHEON] **1** *archaic* **:** to ornament with perforations ⟨a mantle of cloth of silver, *pounced* with his cipher, lined with blue velvet —W.H.Ainsworth⟩ **2 :** to ornament (metal) by hammering on the reverse side (as in repousse work) **:** EMBOSS **3** *obs* **a :** to perforate with a pointed instrument **:** PRICK, PIERCE **b :** TATTOO

**²pounce** \"\ *n* -S [ME, talon, sting, prob. by shortening & alter. fr. *punson* pointed tool, dagger — more at PUNCHEON] **1 a :** the claw of a bird of prey **:** TALON ⟨from her griping ~ the greedy prey doth rive —Edmund Spenser⟩ **b :** something capable of inflicting injury ⟨always ready with a ripping verbal ~ —Carlos Baker⟩ **2** *now dial* **:** PUNCH, POKE ⟨gave his bedfellow a ~ with his foot to waken him —S.R.Crockett⟩

**³pounce** \"\ *vb* -ED/-ING/-S *vt* **:** to seize with or as if with the talons ⟨cannot ~ the quarry on the ground —Gilbert White⟩ ~ *vi* **1 a :** to make an abrupt assault ⟨were suddenly *pounced* upon by a dozen or more ruffians with clubs —H.A.Chippendale⟩ **b :** to seize upon and make capital of something (as another's blunder or ineptitude) ⟨*pouncing* on the effect of the particular moment . . . the flicker of transient light —Eric Newton⟩ ⟨~*s* ferociously on a trivial error of fact —C.W. Shumaker⟩ **2 :** to spring suddenly or make a sudden grab ⟨ready to ~ at the phone when it rings⟩ ⟨~*s* on his riding boots . . . and begins pulling them on —G.B.Shaw⟩

**⁴pounce** \"\ *n* -S [³*pounce*] **1 :** the act of one that pounces ⟨the ~ and sparkle of the . . . wave —*Times Lit. Supp.*⟩ **2 :** a card game for from 3 to 12 players in which each person plays his own game of Canfield but may build on any of the aces in the center of the table and which is won by the one who gets rid of his stock first

**⁵pounce** \"\ *vt* -ED/-ING/-S [MF *poncer* to polish with pumice, fr. *ponce* pumice] **1 :** to put a smooth finish on (a hat) by rubbing with an abrasive ⟨felt bodies are *pounced* both inside and out —*Evolution of Hats*⟩ **2** *archaic* **:** to scatter with small particles **:** SPRINKLE, FLECK ⟨your azure robe . . . *pounced* with stars —Robert Herrick †1674⟩; *specif* **:** to dust (as paper or parchment) with a resinous powder to prevent ink or colors from spreading **3 a :** to transfer (a design) by applying powder through a perforated outline or stencil **b :** to force (powder) through the perforations of an outline or stencil

**⁶pounce** \"\ *n* -S [F *ponce* pumice, fr. LL *pomic-*, *pomex*, fr. L *pumic-*, *pumex* — more at FOAM] **1 :** a fine powder (as of sandarac with pumice or cuttlefish bone) formerly used to prevent ink from spreading on unsized paper or over an erasure and also to prepare parchment to take writing **2** [F *ponce* pounce bag, fr. (assumed) MF *ponce*, fr. MF *ponce* pumice] **a :** a fine powder (as pulverized chalk or charcoal) for use with a perforated pattern in transferring a design **b :** a perforated pattern **c** *or* **pounce bag :** a small cloth bag filled with powder for pouncing

**pounce box** *n* **:** a box with a perforated lid for holding and sprinkling pounce

**pounce paper** *n* **:** an abrasive paper that is used in pouncing hats

**pounc·er** \-n(t)sə(r)\ *n* -S **:** one that pounces; *specif* **:** a worker who pounces felt hats

**pouncet-box** \'pau̇n(t)sət-\ *n* [*pouncet-* prob. fr. (assumed) MF *poncette* small pounce bag (whence F *poncette*), fr. (assumed) MF *ponce* pounce bag (whence F *ponce*) + MF *-ette*] **1** *archaic* **:** POMANDER 1b **2** *archaic* **:** POUNCE BOX

**pounce tree** *n* **:** SANDARAC TREE 1

**pouncing** *n* -S [fr. gerund of ³*pounce*] **1 :** ⁴POUNCE 1 **2** [fr. gerund of ⁵*pounce*] **:** the process of putting a smooth finish on a felt hat

**pouncy** \'pau̇n(t)sē\ *adj* -ER/-EST [³*pounce* + *-y*] **1 :** PUNCHY **2 :** having a tendency toward abrupt assault

**¹pound** \'pau̇nd\ *n, pl* **pounds** \-n(d)z\ *also* **pound** *often attrib* [ME, fr. OE *pund*; akin to OHG *phunt* pound, ON & Goth *pund*; all fr. a prehistoric Gmc word borrowed fr. L *pondo* pound; akin to L *pondus* weight — more at PENDANT] **1 :** any of various units of mass and weight: as **a :** a unit equal to 12 troy ounces or 5760 grains or 0.3732417216 kilogram formerly used in weighing gold, silver, and a few other costly materials — called also *troy pound* **b :** a unit now in general use among English-speaking peoples equal to 16 avoirdupois ounces or 7000 grains or 0.45359237 kilogram ⟨a 7-*pound* roast⟩ — called also *avoirdupois pound*; see MEASURE table **2 a** *or* **pound sterling :** the basic monetary unit of the United Kingdom — see MONEY table **b** *or* **pound scots** *usu cap S* **:** a monetary unit of Scotland before union with England, similar to the English pound but by the time of union much debased in value **c :** any of a number of basic monetary units of other countries (as Ireland, United Arab Republic, Turkey, Israel, Lebanon, Syria, Libya, Nigeria, Cyprus) — see MONEY table **d :** a note representing one pound **e :** a gold coin worth or representing one pound unit (as a Syrian gold pound) — see SOVEREIGN **f :** LIRA — **pound of flesh :** something which is justly due but which if given inflicts great injury on the giver ⟨the *pound of flesh* which I demand of him is dearly bought, 'tis mine, and I will have it —Shak.⟩

**²pound** \"\ *vt* -ED/-ING/-S *Brit* **:** to ascertain the variation from standard of (coins) by weighing together the number that should weigh one or more pounds

**³pound** \"\ *vb* -ED/-ING/-S [alter. of ME *pounen*, fr. OE *pūnian*; prob. akin to D *puin* rubbish, rubble] *vt* **1 :** to grind with or as if with a mortar and pestle **:** PULVERIZE, CRUSH ⟨a prescription was being ~*ed* up in a mortar —William Beebe⟩ ⟨he was being ~*ed* between . . . loyalty and the howling respectability of the great world —Donald Davidson⟩ **2 a :** to strike with or as if with heavy blows **:** BEAT, HAMMER ⟨~ nails into a board⟩ ⟨~ a typewriter⟩ ⟨breakers ~ the beach⟩ ⟨peaks rose darkly, ~*ing* his senses —Florette Henri⟩ ⟨surface vessels continued to ~ enemy coastal targets —*N. Y. Times*⟩ **b :** to produce by means of repeated vigorous strokes — usu. used with *out* ⟨~ out a tune on the piano⟩ ⟨~ out a story on the typewriter⟩ **c :** to compel assimilation of by insistent repetition ⟨day after day the facts were ~*ed* home to them —Ivy B. Priest⟩ — often used with *in* or *into* ⟨~ Latin into the head of a youngster —C.M.Fuess⟩ **3 a :** to traverse or proceed along heavily or persistently **:** LUMBER, TRAMP ⟨world's heaviest aircraft, ~*ed* and blasted her way down the runway —Lou Stoumen⟩ ⟨~*ed* the pavements trying to find work —Frank O'Leary⟩ **b :** to compress by constant trampling ⟨streets . . . of reddish, clayey earth, ~*ed* to rocklike hardness by countless human feet —Tom Marvel⟩ ~ *vi* **1 a :** to strike repeated blows **:** beat or knock heavily **:** THUMP ⟨talking politely at the conference table instead of ~*ing* on it —*Newsweek*⟩ ⟨their hearts ~, and pulse rate may climb to 160 beats a minute —J.D.Ratcliff⟩ ⟨~*s* doggedly . . . at the central theme —Roger Shattuck⟩; *specif* **:** to slap the water violently and repeatedly — used of a ship ⟨if you spread the ballast out . . . she will be less likely to ~ when punching into a hard sea —Peter Heaton⟩ **b :** to keep up a battering assault ⟨these thoughts ~*ed* and hammered in her indignant consciousness —J.C.Powys⟩ ⟨all day long the sun ~*ed* down through the breathless air —T.O.Heggen⟩ ⟨the mother ~*s* at him for his drinking —Arna W. Bontemps⟩ — often used with *away* ⟨the two fleets ~*ed* away at each other until nightfall —*Amer. Guide Series: Vt.*⟩ **2 a :** to move heavily or fast usu. with an accompanying repetitive sound of impact **:** THUNDER, PELT ⟨on its rocky shore a heavy surf ~*s* ceaselessly —*Amer. Guide Series: Maine*⟩ ⟨a fast rider was ~*ing* down the road —J.D. Horan⟩ ⟨a low-flying Lancaster was ~*ing* home heavily, steadily —Earle Birney⟩ **b :** to work hard or hard and continuously — used with *away* ⟨kept ~*ing* away at his job⟩ **c :** to make a thumping noise ⟨the engine was ~*ing*⟩ **syn** see BEAT — **pound one's ear :** SLEEP ⟨each trucker driving four hours, then *pounding his ear* in the vehicle's sleeper berth while his partner drove —A.L.Davis⟩

**⁴pound** \"\ *n* -S **:** an act of pounding **:** BLOW, THUD ⟨destroys with heavy ~*s* his little caricature —Louis Auchincloss⟩ ⟨the ~ of feet in the passageway⟩

**⁵pound** \"\ *n* -S [ME, enclosure, pound, fr. OE *pund-*] **1 a :** a public enclosure for strays or unlicensed animals **:** PINFOLD ⟨dog ~⟩ **b** *dial* **:** a pen or enclosure for domestic animals (as cattle or sheep) **:** BARNYARD, CORRAL **c :** an enclosure for trapping wild animals ⟨an old buffalo ~, built of logs —*Amer. Antiquity*⟩ **d :** a depot for holding personal property until redeemed by the owner ⟨tow services and ~*s* for cars tagged for obstructing traffic —J.C.Ingraham⟩ **2 :** a place or condition of confinement ⟨find his honor in a ~, hemmed by a triple circle round —Jonathan Swift⟩ ⟨buckled straps . . . held the sleeves in ~ —P.A.Rollins⟩ **3** *dial Eng* **:** POND **4 a** (1) **:** a confine in which fish are caught or kept; *specif* **:** the inner compartment of a fish trap or pound net which retains the fish (2) **:** POUND NET **b** (1) **:** a tank full of water in which live lobsters are kept (2) **:** an establishment selling live lobsters

**⁶pound** \"\ *vt* -ED/-ING/-S [ME *pownen*, fr. *pound*, n., enclosure, pound] **1** *archaic* **:** to confine in or as if in an enclosure **:** PEN **2** *archaic* **:** to dam up (water) **:** IMPOUND

**pound·able** \-ndəbəl\ *adj* [⁶*pound* + *-able*] *obs* **:** subject to impoundment — used of livestock

**¹pound·age** \-ndij, -ndēj\ *n* -S [ME, fr. ¹*pound* + *-age*] **1 a :** a tax levied in pounds sterling ⟨payment of a ~ on profits —A.R.Wagner⟩; *specif* **:** a subsidy of twelve pence per pound on exports and imports formerly granted to the crown **b :** an agent's fee **:** COMMISSION ⟨no ~ was charged for the orders —*Manchester Guardian Weekly*⟩ **2 a :** a charge per pound of weight ⟨letters forwarded on a ~ basis —*Westminster Gazette*⟩ **b :** weight in pounds ⟨most of this ~ was around his middle —Herbert Asbury⟩; *specif* **:** the number of pounds of salt in a gallon or a cubic foot of brine

**²poundage** \"\ *n* -S [⁶*pound* + *-age*] **1 :** the act of impounding or the state of being impounded ⟨~ of cattle⟩ ⟨knows . . . the ~ of every well's water —Lawrence Durrell⟩ **2 :** a fee charged for the release of an impounded animal

**pound·al** \-ndᵊl\ *n* -S [¹*pound* + *-al* (as in *quintal*)] **:** the unit of force in the fps system equal to the force that would give a free mass of one pound an acceleration of one foot per second per second — compare DYNE

**pound brush** *n* **:** a housepainter's brush of any of the largest sizes

**pound cake** *n* [so called fr. the original method of measuring the principal ingredients in pounds] **:** a rich butter cake made with many eggs and a large amount of shortening in proportion to the amount of flour used

**pound degree** *n* **:** BRITISH THERMAL UNIT

**¹pound·er** \'pau̇ndə(r)\ *n* -S [³*pound* + *-er*] **:** one that crushes or hammers

**²pounder** \"\ *n* -S [⁶*pound* + *-er*] *archaic* **:** POUNDMASTER

**³pounder** \"\ *n* -S [¹*pound* + *-er*] **1 a :** one that weighs a usu. specified number of pounds ⟨making the ~*s* rise to the May fly —Alasdair Carmichael⟩ ⟨a helmet which protects a 200-*pounder* surely will protect a smaller man —R.M.Yoder⟩ **b :** a gun throwing a projectile of a specified weight ⟨as many as 100 guns, mostly 25-*pounders* —*Time*⟩ **2 :** something (as a bank note or a jewel) having the value of a specified number of pounds sterling ⟨the note was a ten-*pounder*⟩

**pound-foolish** \'¦=¦=\ *adj* **:** imprudent in dealing with large sums or matters — used chiefly in the phrase *penny-wise and pound-foolish*

**pound-foot** \'=,=\ *n, pl* **pound-feet :** FOOT-POUND 2

**¹pounding** *n* -S [fr. gerund of ³*pound*] **1 :** the act or process of pulverizing or compacting **:** CRUSHING **2 a :** an act or instance of striking with or as if with heavy blows **:** BEATING, HAMMERING ⟨the ~ of his gavel —Marya Mannes⟩ ⟨withstand the ~ of heavy artillery —*N. Y. Times*⟩ **b :** the action of proceeding (as by walking, riding) fast or heavily or of moving with a succession of bumps or the repetitive sound produced by such movement **:** THUDDING, THUNDERING ⟨the ~ of horses' hoofs —S.H.Holbrook⟩ ⟨~ of the waves —Joyce Cary⟩

**²pounding** \"\ *n* -S [¹*pound* + *-ing*; fr. the custom of giving a pound of sugar or some other edible commodity] *South & Midland* **:** DONATION PARTY

**poundkeeper** \'=,==\ *n* **:** POUNDMASTER

**pound-lock** \'=,=\ *n* [⁵*pound* + *lock*] **:** a lock designed to impound the water of a river

**poundmaster** \'=,==\ *n* **:** the keeper of a pound ⟨when he was ~ he tried all afternoon to lasso a dog —John Steinbeck⟩

**pound mile** *n* **:** the transport of one pound of mail or express for one mile

**pound net** *n* **:** a fish trap consisting of a long wing of net

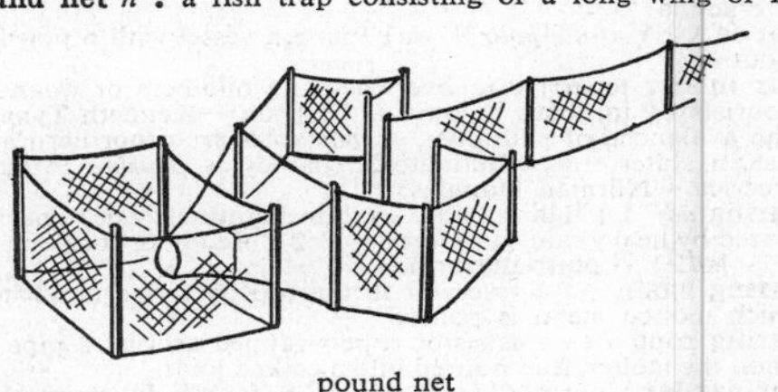

pound net

directing the fishes into the heart and on through a check valve into an inner enclosure which usu. has a closed bottom of net or wire mesh, can sometimes be raised to gather the fishes, or in other variations is equipped with spillers in which the catch is hauled to the surface — compare LEADER 1i(1), POT 3b, SEINE

**pound netter** *n* **:** one that fishes with a pound net

**pound party** *n, chiefly South & Midland* **:** DONATION PARTY

**pound scots** *n, usu cap S* **:** ¹POUND 2b

**pound sterling** *n* **:** ¹POUND 2a

**pou·part's ligament** \(')pü¦pärz-\ *n, usu cap P* [after François *Poupart* †1709 Fr. physician] **:** the thickened lower border of the aponeurosis of the external oblique muscle of the abdomen extending from the anterior superior spine of the ilium to the pubic tubercle continuous below with the fascia lata, and forming the external pillar of the external abdominal ring and a part of the anterior boundary of the femoral ring — called also *inguinal ligament*

**¹pour** \'pō(ə)r, 'pȯ(ə)r, -ōə, -ō(ə) *sometimes* 'pu̇(ə)r *or* -u̇ə\ *vb* -ED/-ING/-S [ME *pouren*] *vt* **1 a** (1) **:** to cause or allow to flow **:** emit in a steady stream **:** DIFFUSE, DISCHARGE ⟨~*ed* out torrents of water —J.G.Vaeth⟩ ⟨~ grain into an elevator⟩ ⟨ranges . . . ~ rivers down to the coast —M.B.Eldershaw⟩ ⟨summer ~*s* warm sunlight . . . into the valleys —*Amer. Guide Series: Va.*⟩ (2) **:** to dispense from a container ⟨~ a drink⟩ ⟨~ tea⟩ **b :** to supply copiously **:** convey as if through a sluice **:** CHANNEL, SPOUT ⟨~ men and money into the Netherlands —Stringfellow Barr⟩ ⟨~ out a torrent of words⟩ ⟨~*ed* ridicule on the elaborate . . . analysis —Richard Hartshorne b. 1899⟩ ⟨armies . . . that the Germans ~*ed* across Europe —Tom Wintringham⟩ ⟨sweet-tempered . . . pastors ~*ed* forth comfort and learning —Sinclair Lewis⟩ ⟨trying to ~ sympathy all over the poor man —D.B.Chidsey⟩; *specif* **:** to send in a concentrated volley ⟨~*ed* 30 bullets into his plane —Ed Cunningham⟩ **c :** to produce in abundance — used with *forth* or *out* ⟨travel-books . . . that our presses ~ forth in floods —Louise Pound⟩ ⟨keep ~*ing* out millions of cars, trucks and buses every year —*Motor Transportation in the West*⟩ **d :** to apply in liberal amounts (as for coercion or to supply motive power) ⟨~*ed* the whip into the mules —Andy Adams⟩ ⟨~*ed* on the steam⟩ ⟨began to ~ heat on the business office —*Human Organization*⟩ ⟨~*ed* in every ounce of power but couldn't make it⟩ **2 a :** to expend wholly ⟨those who most long for peace now ~ their lives on war —Muriel Rukeyser⟩ **b :** to give full expression to or a detailed account of **:** SPILL, VENT ⟨before our Father's throne, we ~ our ardent prayers —John Fawcett⟩ ⟨thrasher from cactus and mesquite ~*s* forth his song —D.C.Peattie⟩ ⟨~*s* out her troubles to them —Bosley Crowther⟩ ⟨~*ing* out his feelings in his poetry —Ruth R. Chapman⟩ **3 a :** to cause to flow or to pass as if flowing into a mold ⟨~ steel⟩ ⟨~ agar⟩ ⟨~ concrete⟩ ⟨nine sergeants were ~*ed* into plain clothes and set up in an office at Old Scotland Yard —J.D.Carr⟩ ⟨~*ed* the barefooted doctor into the coach, gave him a quart of whiskey to work on, and pulled out —F.B.Gipson⟩ **b :** to form by running plastic mixes of concrete into place in forms ⟨~ a foundation wall⟩ ~ *vi* **1 a** (1) **:** to move with a continuous flow **:** issue or glide incessantly **:** GUSH, RUN ⟨creeks ~*ing* down from the uplands —Nan McDonald⟩ ⟨wind ~*s* over the mountains —C.P. Aiken⟩ ⟨smoke . . . ~*ed* up from the blazing houses —Kenneth Roberts⟩ ⟨line ~*s* off your reel —C.C.Van Fleet⟩ (2) **:** to rain heavily **:** TEEM ⟨it was raining — but not ~*ing* —Robbie Barcroft⟩ **b :** to progress or be channeled continuously **:** move in a body **:** STREAM, SWARM ⟨Marines ~*ed* ashore and secured the beachhead —H.L.Merillat⟩ ⟨the promenading public still slowly ~*ed* up and down Fifth Avenue —Edith Wharton⟩ ⟨all this lore ~*ed* into a big filing cabinet —H.W. Thompson⟩ ⟨traffic ~*ed* over the new highway —G.R. Stewart⟩ ⟨our own stuff was ~*ing* back on them —Fred Majdalany⟩ ⟨from your farms today food ~*s* . . . to every corner of the country —A.E.Stevenson †1965⟩ **c :** to emanate in a flood ⟨a spate of English grammars began to ~ off the presses —N.C.Stageberg⟩ ⟨personality ~*s* out of him —Victor Thompson⟩ ⟨calypsos ~*ing* out of . . . jukeboxes —Paul Hofmann⟩ **d :** to preside at a tea table ⟨she was asked to ~ at a little reception for the performers after the concert⟩ **2 :** to find an outlet **:** be given full expression ⟨channels . . . through which those emotions might ~ —Oscar Handlin⟩

**syn** POUR, STREAM, GUSH, and SLUICE can mean, in common, to send forth liquid, or something suggesting liquid, copiously. POUR stresses the abundance of the issuing or sending forth, usu. implying emission in a continuous stream ⟨the torrential rain *poured* down for days⟩ ⟨to *pour* tributes on his head⟩ ⟨mail *poured* in in answer to the advertisement⟩ ⟨the crowd *poured* out of the front doors⟩ STREAM suggests a flow limited by issuance through a channel or from an opening ⟨tears *streamed* from her eyes⟩ ⟨light *streamed* through the window⟩ ⟨the rain *streamed* down the bank in small rivulets⟩ GUSH stresses a suddenness and copiousness of the pouring forth as of something released from a close confinement ⟨blood *gushed* from the wound⟩ ⟨the spring *gushed* forth⟩ ⟨words *gushed* from her in gratitude⟩ SLUICE in this comparison always implies a confining flume or a channeled abundance of liquid ⟨the rain fell with a frightening violence, . . . turning the opposite wall of the canyon into a *sluicing* cascade of muddy water —B.A.Williams⟩ ⟨the Connecticut, *sluicing* down between the Green and White mountains —R.W.Howard⟩ ⟨thrust her hands into the stream, then raised them, dripping, to *sluice* her face —Rebecca West⟩

— **pour it on 1 :** to exert maximum force or energy **:** move or cause to move at top speed or intensity ⟨didn't run at top speed for much more than a furlong, but when he did he must have *poured it on* —G.F.T.Ryall⟩ ⟨allied bombers . . . began really to *pour it on* —Alfred Friendly⟩ ⟨companies . . . taking it relatively easy on production may now be tempted to *pour it on* —J.D.Williams⟩ **2 :** to give unstinted expression to an idea or attitude ⟨gave them a ten-minute talk in which he "really *poured it on*" —*N. Y. Herald Tribune*⟩

**²pour** \"\ *n* -s **1 :** the action of pouring **:** FLOOD, STREAM ⟨seals . . . carved sheer as cameos in the moon's full ~ —E.W. Barker⟩ ⟨a great ~ of contemptuous invective —*Times Lit. Supp.*⟩; *esp* **:** a heavy fall of rain **2 a :** the action of running a plastic material into a mold or form ⟨carpenters were stripping and placing forms for the next ~ —*New Era in Concrete*⟩ **b :** the amount placed in a mold or form at one time ⟨some mechanics use two ~*s* of lead to fill the joint completely —*Building Estimating & Contracting*⟩ **3 a :** the principal opening by which molten metal enters a mold **b :** the superfluous metal adhering to the casting and resulting from the head metal in such an opening — called also *pourpiece*

**pour·abil·i·ty** \ˌpōrəˈbiləd·ē, ˌpȯr- *sometimes* ˌpu̇r-\ *n* -ES **:** adaptability to being poured ⟨the poor ~ of the material —*Modern Plastics Catalog*⟩

**pour·able** \ˈ==bəl\ *adj* **:** capable of being poured

**pour batter** *n* **:** batter of such consistency as to pour from a bowl or pitcher usu. made in a proportion of equal parts of flour and liquid — compare DROP BATTER

**pour·boire** \(ˈ)pu̇rbˈwär\ *n* -s [F, fr. *pour boire* for drinking, in order to drink, fr. *pour* for, in order to + *boire* to drink, fr. L *bibere* — more at PURCHASE, POTABLE] **:** TIP, GRATUITY

**pourcontrell** *n* -s [origin unknown] *obs* **:** OCTOPUS

**poured** *past of* POUR

**pour·er** \ˈpōrə(r), ˈpȯr- *sometimes* ˈpu̇r-\ *n* -s **:** one that pours; *specif* **:** a foundry worker who pours molten metal from a ladle or crucible

**pour·ie** \-rī\ *n* -s [¹*pour* + -*ie*] *Scot* **:** a vessel with a pouring spout

**pour in** *vi* **:** to arrive in overwhelming numbers or quantity ⟨tourists fly in, drive in, *pour in* by train —Kenneth Tynan⟩ ⟨the avalanche of petitions . . . *poured in* from northern and eastern states —R.A.Billington⟩ ⟨money is *pouring in* from America —Norman Douglas⟩

**pouring** *adj* **1 :** falling or flowing in quantities; *esp* **:** characterized by heavy rain ⟨a ~ wet day⟩ **2 :** used in or for pouring ⟨a ~ ladle⟩ — **pour·ing·ly** *adv*

**pouring basin** *n* **:** a reservoir in the top part of a mold into which molten metal is poured

**pouring rope** *n* **:** an asbestos rope wrapped around a pipe to retain the molten lead poured into a calked joint

**pour·par·ler** \ˌpu̇rˌpärˈlā, ===\ *n* -s [F, fr. MF, fr. *pourparler*, v., to discuss with a view to reaching an agreement, fr. OF, fr. *pour* for, before + *parler* to speak — more at PURCHASE, PARLEY] **:** a preliminary discussion esp. in advance of the formulation of a treaty ⟨was holding full-dress ~*s* in London —James Dugan⟩

**pourparty** *var of* PURPARTY

**pourpiece** \ˈ==\ *n* **:** POUR 3b

**pour plate** *n* **:** a plate prepared by mixing the inoculum with the cooled but still fluid medium before pouring the latter into the petri dish

**¹pour·point** \ˈpu̇rˌpȯint, -rp,want\ *n* -s [ME *purpoynt*, fr. MF *pourpoint*, fr. OF *porpoint*, fr. *porpoint*, adj., quilted, embroidered, alter. (influenced by OF *pour* for) of (assumed) VL *perpunctus*, past part. of (assumed) VL *perpungere* to perforate, fr. L *per* through + *pungere* to prick, sting, pierce — more at FARE, PURCHASE, PUNGENT] **:** a padded and quilted doublet ⟨his coat of mail . . . and the coarse linen ~ that had been worn with it —T.B.Costain⟩ — compare GAMBESON

**²pourpoint** \"\ *vt* -ED/-ING/-S **:** QUILT

**pour point** *pronunc at* ¹POUR + ˌpȯint\ *n* **:** the lowest temperature at which a substance (as a lubricating oil) flows under specified conditions

**pourpresture** *var of* PURPRESTURE

**pours** *pres 3d sing of* POUR, *pl of* POUR

**pour test** *n* **:** a test to determine the pour point by chilling a sample — compare COLD TEST

**pourtray** *archaic var of* PORTRAY

**pourveyance** *var of* PURVEYANCE

**pousse-café** \ˌpüskəˈfā, -üˌska-\ *n* [F, lit., coffee pusher, fr. *pousser* to push + *café* coffee, fr. Turk *kahve* — more at PUSH, COFFEE] **1 :** a cocktail consisting of several liqueurs of different colors and specific gravities poured so as to remain in separate layers **2 :** a small drink of brandy or a liqueur taken with black coffee following a dinner

**pous·sette** \(ˈ)püˈset\ *vi* -ED/-ING/-S [F, pushpin (game), baby carriage, fr. *pousser* to push + -*ette*] **:** to swing in a semicircle hands joined with one's partner, or as if in a country-dance

**pous·sin** \(ˈ)püˈsaⁿ\ *n* -s [F, fr. LL *pullicenus* young table fowl, dim. of L *pullus* young bird, young of an animal — more at FOAL] **:** a young chicken of about one pound weight for table use **:** a small broiler

**pou sto** \ˈpüˈstō, *chiefly Brit* ˈpau̇ˈ-\ *n* [Gk *pou stō* where I may stand; fr. a statement attributed (in various forms) to Archimedes, "Give me a place to stand (lit., where I may stand) and I will move the earth"] **:** a standing place or vantage point **:** BASE, BASIS

**¹pout** \ˈpau̇t, *usu* -au̇d·+V\ *n, pl* **pout** *or* **pouts** [prob. fr. (assumed) ME *poute*, a fish with a large head, fr. OE -*pūte*; akin to ME *pouten* to pout, MD *puut* frog, Norw *pute* cushion, Skt *budbuda* bubble; basic meaning: swelling] **1 :** BIB 2 **2 :** BULLHEAD 1b **3 :** EELPOUT

**²pout** \"\ *vb* -ED/-ING/-S [ME *pouten*] *vi* **1 a :** to show displeasure by thrusting out the lips or wearing a sullen expression ⟨~*ed* and seemed about to cry⟩ **b :** SULK ⟨the minority leader . . . held aloof, almost ~*ing*, from the fight —*New Republic*⟩ **2 a :** to swell out **:** PROTRUDE ⟨his mouth . . . ~*ed* in a way that suggested petulance and undisciplined sensuality —John Wain⟩ **b :** to jut out or become distended ⟨on a cut surface the ends of the cords ~ —J.P.Greenhill⟩ ⟨the paper ~*ed* up in vigorous flame —Shea Murphy⟩ ~ *vt* **1 a :** to push out or swell out **:** PROTRUDE ⟨~*ed* her lips for a kiss —Maurice Hewlett⟩ **b :** to fluff out or up ⟨the falcon was . . . twice his size with ~*ed* feathers —Theodora Keogh⟩ **2 :** to say with a pout ⟨"My feet are killing me," she ~*ed* —*N. Y. Herald Tribune*⟩

**³pout** \"\ *n* -s **1 :** a protrusion of the lips expressive of displeasure **2 pouts** *pl* **:** a fit of pique ⟨had the ~*s*⟩

**¹pout·er** \ˈpau̇d·ə(r), -au̇tə-\ *n* -s [²*pout* + -*er*] **1 :** one that pouts **2 :** a domestic pigeon of a breed that is characterized by long legs, slender body, erect carriage, and a remarkably distensible crop which they have a habit of dilating, and that occurs in several varieties sometimes regarded as separate breeds ⟨the ~ . . . expands its throat, almost hiding the rest of its body behind the great balloon —*All-Pets Mag.*⟩

**²pou·ter** \ˈpōtər, ˈpau̇t-, ˈpüt-\ *vb* -ED/-ING/-S [prob. by alter.] *chiefly Scot* **:** POTTER

**pou·te·ria** \pau̇ˈtirēə, püˈt-\ *n, cap* [NL] **:** a large genus of chiefly tropical American timber trees (family Sapotaceae) with flower clusters borne in the leaf axils and usu. edible fruit

**pout·ing·ly** *adv* **:** in a pouting manner

**pouty** \ˈpau̇d·ē\ *adj* -ER/-EST **1 :** looking or tending to look petulant **:** SULKY ⟨had a ~ look on his face⟩ **2 :** tending to protrude ⟨the mucous membrane . . . is ~ —*Western Osteopath*⟩

**poverish** *vt* -ED/-ING/-ES [ME *povereshen*, alter. of MF *empovriss*-, stem of *empovrir* — more at IMPOVERISH] *archaic* **:** IMPOVERISH

**pov·er·ty** \ˈpävə(r)d·ē, -)t|, |i\ *n* -ES [ME *poverte*, fr. OF *poverté*, fr. L *paupertat-, paupertas*, fr. *pauper* poor + -*tat-*, -*tas* -ty — more at POOR] **1 a :** lack or relative lack of money or material possessions **:** PRIVATION, WANT ⟨transition from a life of almost the greatest pomp and circumstance . . . to one just, but only just, above the line of genteel ~ —Geoffrey Gorer⟩ ⟨in ~, morality and even a touch of happiness was possible, never in destitution —R.A.Schermerhorn⟩ ⟨had roamed the picturesque poor quarters . . . but this ugly, barren ~ on the Spanish land was his first view of some men's helpless fate —Janet Flanner⟩ **b :** renunciation as a member of a religious order of the right as an individual to own, to receive by inheritance or gift, or to dispose of property **2 a :** meagerness of supply **:** SCARCITY, DEARTH ⟨biographer . . . is necessarily embarrassed by the ~ of personal information preserved —John Loftis⟩ ⟨the cold thin atmosphere of his work was due . . . to a ~ of ideas and sensuous imagery —V.L. Parrington⟩ **b :** poorness in kind or quality **:** INFERIORITY ⟨cannot hide ~ of form under an opulent mask of orchestral color —Hunter Mead⟩ **c :** lack of desirable elements or attributes **:** DEFICIENCY ⟨the . . . ~ of North and Northeastern Africa in river-producing power —Samuel Haughton⟩ ⟨suffered . . . from a certain ~ in our English critical vocabulary —Irving Babbitt⟩ ⟨slums cause spiritual ~ in many lives —J.T.Fanell⟩ **3 a :** debility due to malnutrition **:** FEEBLENESS, EMACIATION ⟨produce insufficient fodder . . . and one or two ranches suffered quite heavy losses from ~ —*Report: Northern Rhodesia Veterinary Dept.*⟩ **b :** lack of fertility ⟨~ of the soil⟩

**poverty grass** *n* **1 :** any of several slender grasses: as **a :** an erect American grass (*Aristida dichotoma*) with dichotomously branched culms found in dry sandy soil **b :** an oat grass (*Danthonia spicata*) **2 :** BEACH HEATHER **3 :** BROOM CROWBERRY **4 :** RABBIT-FOOT CLOVER

**poverty pine** *n* **:** JERSEY PINE

**poverty plant** *n* **:** BEACH HEATHER

**poverty poker** *n* **:** any form of poker played with the agreement that when a player has lost a specified amount he may continue to play without increasing his loss

**poverty-stricken** \ˈ===,==\ *adj* **:** afflicted by or exhibiting poverty ⟨a *poverty-stricken* immigrant in a cold-water flat⟩ ⟨the modern notion of the Elizabethan stage as a bare and *poverty-stricken* affair, "with no scenery" —Leslie Hotson⟩ ⟨beasts . . . *poverty-stricken* to the point of death —F.D. Davison⟩ **syn** see POOR

**povertyweed** \ˈ===,=\ *n* **:** any of various weedy plants growing esp. on poor soils: as **a :** COWWHEAT **b :** SPURRY **c :** a troublesome aromatic weed (*Iva axillaris*) found esp. in alkali regions of the western U. S. **d :** PEARLY EVERLASTING **e :** BUTTONWEED 1 **f :** any of several annual herbs of the genus *Monolepis*, family Chenopodiaceae; *esp* **:** a weed (*M. nuttalliana*) of the western U. S. with fleshy stems, slender-petioled narrow leaves, and small flowers in clusters in the upper axils

**po·vi·done** \ˈpōvəˌdōn\ *n* -s [*polyvinylpyrrolidone*] **:** POLYVINYLPYRROLIDONE

**po·vin·dah** \pōˈvində\ *n* -s *usu cap* **:** one of a caste or class of soldier merchants trading between northern India and central Asia

**¹pow** \ˈpō, ˈpau̇\ *n* -s [alter. of ¹*poll*] *dial* **:** HEAD, POLL ⟨blessings on your frosty ~ —Robert Burns⟩

**²pow** \ˈpau̇\ *n* -s [imit.] **:** a sound of a blow or explosion ⟨the ~ of an ax on a tree⟩ ⟨heard the ~ of a blowout —*Ethyl News*⟩

**POW** *abbr or n* -s prisoner of war

**pow·an** \ˈpōən\ *n, pl* **powan** *or* **powans** [origin unknown] **:** a whitefish (*Coregonus clupeoides*) of Loch Lomond and Lock Eck in Scotland

**¹pow·der** \ˈpau̇də(r)\ *n* -s *often attrib* [ME *poudre*, fr. OF, fr. L *pulver-, pulvis* dust — more at POLLEN] **1 :** a substance composed of fine particles: as **a :** dry pulverized earth or disintegrated matter **:** DUST **b :** the spores of lycopodium — see LYCOPODIUM POWDER **c** *or* **powder snow :** fine dry light snow ⟨five inches new ~; skiing excellent⟩ — compare CORN SNOW **2 :** a powdered preparation **:** a product in the form of discrete usu. fine particles ⟨metal ~*s*⟩: as **a :** a medicine or medicated preparation in powdered form ⟨antiseptic ~⟩ ⟨digestive ~⟩ ⟨~*s* . . . prepared extemporaneously by the pharmacist —E.F.Cook & E.W.Martin⟩ **b :** a finely ground or dehydrated condiment or food ⟨curry ~⟩ ⟨ice cream ~⟩ **c :** a usu. perfumed cosmetic esp. for the skin or hair **3 a :** any of various solid explosives used chiefly in gunnery and blasting: as (1) **:** GUNPOWDER (2) **:** BLACK POWDER (3) **:** SMOKELESS POWDER (4) **:** DYNAMITE **b :** impetus or explosive force ⟨the postponement seemed to add ~ to the . . . issue —*Newsweek*⟩

**²powder** \"\ *vb* **powdered; powdered; powdering** \-d(ə)riŋ\ **powders** [ME *poudren*, fr. OF *poudrer* to cover with dust, fr. *poudre*, n.] *vt* **1 a :** to cover with or as if with powder **:** DUST ⟨a friar . . . stood at the door, his habit and beard ~*ed* with snow —Robert Brennan⟩ ⟨mildew . . . ~*s* it as white as a clown —Andrew Young⟩ **b :** to apply a cosmetic powder to ⟨pulled out her compact and ~*ed* her nose⟩ ⟨their heads ~*ed* with gold —Effie Gray⟩ **2 :** SCATTER, BESTREW ⟨nose ~*ed* with golden freckles —Ellen Glasgow⟩ ⟨white chiffon ~*ed* with minute gold beads —*Country Life*⟩; *specif* **:** to sow with small heraldic charges ⟨~ their red mantlings with gold billets —W.H. St. John Hope⟩ — compare SEMÉ **3** *archaic* **:** to sprinkle with a condiment ⟨give you leave to ~ me and eat me too —Shak.⟩; *specif* **:** to preserve by salting **4 a :** to reduce to powder by grinding **:** COMMINUTE, PULVERIZE, TRITURATE **b :** to convert into powder by means other than grinding ~ *vi* **1 a :** to be reduced to powder **:** become pulverized **:** crumble into dust ⟨two skeletons . . . ~*ed* upon exposure, and could not be measured —C.S.Coon⟩; *specif* **:** CHALK ⟨using too thin varnish in printer's ink causes it to ~⟩ **b :** to shed powder ⟨the bulrushes . . . were ripe and ~*ing* —Rumer Godden⟩ **2 :** to apply or use cosmetic powder ⟨girls not old enough to paint and ~⟩ ⟨actors ~ with the left hand for luck⟩ **3** *slang* **:** to go away in a hurry **:** DECAMP, ESCAPE ⟨instead of ~*ing* out of town right away, I buy some new clothes —H.L. Dutkin⟩

**³powder** \"\ *n* -s [origin unknown] *chiefly dial* **:** a sudden impetuous rush or irrational hurry — often used with *in* or *with* ⟨a knocking at the gate, laid on in haste with such a ~ —Samuel Butler †1680⟩

**⁴powder** \"\ *vi* -ED/-ING/-S *chiefly dial* **:** to rush or hurry esp. impetuously ⟨gallops up to us, the groom ~*ing* afterward —W.M.Thackeray⟩

**powder bag** *n* **:** a fabric container for the propelling charge in separate-loading or semifixed ammunition

**powder barrel** *n* **:** a barrel usu. of 100-pound capacity for storing or transporting powder

**powder base** *n* **:** a cosmetic cream or other foundation for use under face powder

**powder blue** *n* **1 :** a pigment consisting of powdered smalt **2 a** *or* **powdered blue :** a variable color averaging a pale blue that is greener and paler than Sistine, greener, lighter, and stronger than average cadet gray or old blue, and greener and duller than blue flower — called also *poudre blue* **b :** the color smalt

**powder charge** *n* **:** the charge of powder for propelling a projectile

**powder coupling** *n* **:** a coupling in which the power-transmitting fluid is finely divided steel

**powder down** *n* **:** modified down feathers in some birds (as herons, parrots, tinamous, frogmouths) that grow continuously and disintegrate at the ends

**pow·dered** \ˈpau̇də(r)d\ *adj* [ME *poudred*, fr. past part. of *poudren* to powder] **1** *now dial Brit* **a :** SPICED, SEASONED **b :** PICKLED, PRESERVED **2 :** patterned or strewn with small objects ⟨the vast . . . sky, ~ with innumerable stars —W.H. Hudson †1922⟩ ⟨bindings ~ with monograms and fleurs-de-lis —Edith Diehl⟩ **3 :** reduced to a powder **:** PULVERIZED ⟨~ chalk⟩ ⟨~ coal⟩ **4** *obs* **:** subjected to sweating in a powdering tub **5 :** dressed or treated with powder ⟨the ~ coiffures of the French court —Lois Long⟩ ⟨~, weighted silks —*Atlantic*⟩

**powdered milk** *n* **:** DRIED MILK

**powdered sugar** *n* **:** sugar derived from granulated sugar by grinding to several grades of fineness with flour added to prevent caking — compare CONFECTIONERS' SUGAR

**pow·der·er** \-dərə(r)\ *n* -s **:** one that powders; *specif* **:** a worker who rubs powder onto a hat before it is lured

**powder flag** *n* **:** a red flag hoisted by a ship loading or discharging explosives or flammable fuel in bulk

**powder hole** *n* **:** DRY HOLE 2

**powder horn** *n* **1 :** a flask for carrying gunpowder; *esp* **:** one made of the horn of an ox or cow **2 :** a plant of the genus *Cerastium*

powder horn *1*

**powdering** *n* -s [ME *poudringe*, fr. gerund of *poudren* to powder] **1 :** the act or an instance of applying a powder ⟨the ~ of a wig⟩ **2 :** ornamentation with a multitude of small objects ⟨wore his mother's arms but . . . added a ~ of golden fleurs-de-lis on the silver border —H.S.London⟩ **3 :** a powdery deposit ⟨snow ~*s* in the valleys —R.S.G.Hall⟩

**powdering tub** *n* **1** *archaic* **:** a tub for salting meat **2** *obs* **:** a sweating tub for the cure of venereal disease ⟨to the spital go, and from the *powd'ring tub* of infamy fetch forth the lazar kite —Shak.⟩

**powder keg** *n* **1 :** a small usu. metal cask for holding gunpowder or blasting powder **2 :** something liable to explode ⟨merchant seamen see a tanker as a potential *powder keg*⟩ ⟨politicos . . . sitting uneasily on the *powder keg* of Arabian Nationalism —*Saturday Rev.*⟩

**pow·der·man** \-də(r)ˌman, -ˌmən\ *n, pl* **powdermen 1 :** one who works with explosives: as **a :** one whose work is blasting with powder **b :** one in charge of the storage and issuance of explosives at a mine **c :** one who screens and melts trinitrotoluene and fills projectile cases **2 :** a worker who blends and heats the powders from which plastics are molded

**powder metallurgy** *n* **:** the production of metal powders and their utilization in the production of shaped parts

**powder method** *n* **:** DEBYE-SCHERRER METHOD

**powder monkey** *n* **1 :** one who transports powder from the magazine to the guns esp. on shipboard ⟨*powder monkeys* skidded over the wet decks, their deadly burdens cradled in their desperate arms —Frank Yerby⟩ ⟨was made *powder monkey* for the artillery squad who fired the cannon at sundown —F.B.Gipson⟩ **2 :** one who carries or has charge of powder or other explosives in mining or blasting operations

**powder of al·ga·roth** \-ˈalgəˌrȯth, -räth\ *usu cap A* [part trans. of F *poudre d'algaroth*, fr. *poudre* powder + *d'* of + *algaroth* powder of algaroth, fr. It *algarotto*, fr. Vittorio *Algarotto* †1604 Ital. physician] **:** a white powder of variable composition consisting principally of antimony oxychloride formed by the action of much water on antimony trichloride and used chiefly in the preparation of tartar emetic and formerly in medicine

**powder paint** *n* **:** a paint packaged as a powder having a binder (as casein, glue, cement) for use in water solution

**powder pattern** *n* **:** a pattern of lines or arcs recorded on photographic film by the Debye-Scherrer method

**powder photograph** *n* **:** the photographic record made by the Debye-Scherrer method

**powder post** *n* **:** a defective powdery condition of wood caused chiefly by powder-post beetles — **powder-posted** \ˈ==ˌpōstəd\ *adj*

**powder-post beetle** *also* **powder-post borer** *n* **:** any of several beetles (family Lyctidae) having larvae that feed in very dry wood or lumber and reduce the interior to powder — compare ANOBIUM, FURNITURE BEETLE

**powder-post termite** *n* **:** a dry-wood termite (*Cryptotermes brevis*) that is widely distributed in warm regions and is extremely destructive of seasoned wood

**powder puff** *n* **1 :** a small fluffy pad or other device for applying cosmetic powder **2** *or* **powder puff cactus :** a globose cactus (*Mammillaria bocasana*) with yellowish white flowers and radial spines represented by long white silky hairs

**powder ring** *n* **:** a fabric ring containing an increment of the propelling charge for a weapon (as a mortar)

**powder room** *n* **1 a :** a rest room for women **b :** a small usu. prettified first floor lavatory and dressing room in a home provided esp. for the convenience of women guests **2 :** BATHROOM

**powder rose** *n* **:** a grayish yellowish pink that is redder and deeper than iris mauve

**powders** *pl of* POWDER, *pres 3d sing of* POWDER

**powder snow** *n* **:** POWDER 1c

**powder table** *n* **:** POUDREUSE

**powder train** *n* **:** an element used in some fuses to obtain time action

**pow·dery** \ˈpau̇d(ə)rē, -ri\ *adj* [ME *powdry*, fr. *powdre*, *poudre* powder + -*y*] **1 a :** resembling or consisting of powder ⟨~ dust⟩ ⟨~ snow⟩ **b :** easily reduced to powder **:** CRUMBLING, FRIABLE ⟨the trail continued under the brown and ~ carpet —R.T.Bird⟩ **2 :** covered with or as if with powder **:** DUSTY, CHALKY ⟨the ~ gray of a frightened native —Marguerite Steen⟩ ⟨Pierrot . . . sad, ~, languishing —Sheldon Cheney⟩ ⟨the frescoes are ~ —Aline B. Saarinen⟩

**powdery mildew** *n* **1 :** a perfect fungus of the family Erysiphaceae or an imperfect fungus of the genus *Oidium* distinguished by the abundant powdery conidia produced on the host **2 :** a plant disease caused by a powdery mildew — compare DOWNY MILDEW

**powdery scab** *n* **:** a disease of potato tubers caused by a fungus (*Spongospora subterranea*) and characterized by nodular discolored lesions which at maturity burst to expose a powdery mass of spores in circular pits surrounded by the lighter colored frayed remnants of the skin of the tuber — called also *pock scab*

**pow·ell·ite** \ˈpau̇əˌlīt\ *n* -s [John W. *Powell* †1902 Am. geologist + E -*ite*] **:** a mineral $CaMoO_4$ consisting of a calcium molybdate occurring in small yellow tetragonal pyramidal crystals isomorphous with scheelite

**¹pow·er** \ˈpau̇(ə)r, -au̇ə, *esp in Southern US* -au̇wə(r\ *n* -s *often attrib* [ME, fr. OF *poer*, *poeir*, fr. *poer*, *poeir*, v., to be able, fr. (assumed) OL *potēre* — more at POTENT] **1 a :** a position of ascendancy **:** ability to compel obedience **:** CONTROL, DOMINION ⟨party in ~⟩ ⟨there are no . . . assignable boundaries to sovereign ~ —J.H.Hallowell⟩ ⟨bidding for personal ~ and aiming to make himself absolute dictator —A.P.Ryan⟩ ⟨knowledge meant ~ over nature —W.A.Kaufmann⟩ **b** (1) **:** a military force or its equipment ⟨mechanized, motorized, horse and foot units . . . make the enemy a formidable ~ —Shipley Thomas⟩ ⟨sea-borne air ~ successfully challenged land-based planes —*Atlantic*⟩ (2) **:** ability to wage war ⟨his military ~ absolutely crushed —Oscar Handlin⟩ **c** *chiefly dial* **:** a large number or quantity **:** MULTITUDE, ABUNDANCE, HEAP ⟨there had been such a ~ of elderberries the year before —Mary Webb⟩ ⟨contains a ~ of fine Arizona scenery —*Newsweek*⟩ **2 a** (1) **:** capability of acting or of producing an effect ⟨purchasing ~⟩ ⟨countries behind the Iron Curtain would make the same choice if they had the ~ —A.J.Toynbee⟩ ⟨the urbane ~ of reason, and the persuasive influence of just consideration —Gilbert Parker⟩ ⟨learned more about the ~ and the beauty of clear design by reading . . . sonnets —Janna Burgess⟩ (2) **:** a mental or physical ability or aptitude **:** FACULTY, TALENT ⟨their visual sense was far more highly developed than their ~ of smell —W.E.Swinton⟩ ⟨a man who has learned the technique of scientific investigation has added a new ~ to his mind —Benjamin Farrington⟩ ⟨showed his ~ as a playwright —A.H.Quinn⟩ — often used in pl. ⟨a man of fine mental ~*s* —C.B.Fisher⟩ ⟨test your ~*s* of observation —Richard Harrison⟩ ⟨loath to believe that a bird so small . . . could possess such vocal ~*s* —John Burroughs⟩ (3) **:** performance measured without consideration of the element of speed **b :** political sway **:** social sway **:** INFLUENCE, PRESTIGE ⟨when the Democratic party regained ~ in the state, he was reappointed surrogate —H.W.H.Knott⟩ ⟨a man of ~ with the Sioux, rescued the three captives —I.B.Richman⟩ **3 a** (1) **:** a delegated right or privilege **:** PREROGATIVE ⟨invaded his ~s as commander-in-chief —Isabel Whittier⟩ ⟨not necessary for Congress to trace back every one of its ~s to some single grant of authority —F.A.Ogg & P.O.Ray⟩ (2) **:** delegated authority ⟨an emissary with ~ to negotiate⟩ **b :** a document conferring legal authority ⟨not until the end of September did the British representative . . . show satisfactory ~s to treat with the thirteen United States of America —W.C. Ford⟩ **c :** legal authority ⟨the ~ to bestow degrees was granted by the legislature in 1820 —*Amer. Guide Series: Maine*⟩ ⟨argument began over the nature of the proposed pact and whether it would deprive Congress of the ~ to declare war —L.B.Burbank⟩; *specif* **:** the ability to change legal relations — compare COLLATERAL POWER, GENERAL POWER OF APPOINTMENT, POWER APPENDANT, POWER COUPLED WITH AN INTEREST, POWER IN GROSS, POWER OF APPOINTMENT, POWER OF ATTORNEY, SPECIAL POWER **4 :** one that has influence or authority ⟨was a ~ in ecclesiastical councils —H.E.Starr⟩ ⟨the organs of justice . . . are the chief ~ in the state —Jacques Maritain⟩ ⟨I wish the ~s that be would send me out there —Rose Macaulay⟩ ⟨preferred in politics to be the ~ behind the throne —Louis Bromfield⟩; *specif* **:** a sovereign state ⟨the brutal and unprovoked assault . . . has caused reassessment of the foreign policies of the western ~s —*Army-Navy-Air Force Jour.*⟩ **5 a powers** *pl, often cap* [ME *poweris* (pl.), trans. of LL *potestates*, trans. of Gk *exousiai*] **:** the sixth order in the celestial hierarchy ⟨the ~s and Thrones above —John Keble⟩ **b :** a supernatural being or occult force or the ability to control them ⟨the sky . . . is the male ~ —J.G.Frazer⟩ ⟨a good ~ called God —*Time*⟩ ⟨shamanistic ~s . . . were associated with animal or abstract beings —M.J.Herskovits⟩ **c** *dial* **:** the religious fervor of a revivalist — used with *the* ⟨almost got the ~ with the rest of them if for no other reason than the coffee and sandwiches —H.A.Chippendale⟩ **6 a :** physical might or resources **:** STRENGTH, SOLIDITY ⟨punishment calls for clear predominance of ~ —H.D.Gideonse⟩ ⟨the dancer is . . . using only a portion of his ~ —Reginald & Gladys Laubin⟩ ⟨a great flood moving with majesty and ~ —Willa Cather⟩ ⟨the building has unusual ~ —*Amer. Guide Series: N.Y. City*⟩ **b :** mental or moral efficacy **:** VIGOR, INTENSITY ⟨laid down with great ~ and insight a spiritual philosophy —W.R.Inge⟩ ⟨the ~ of his curiosity surprised him —Morley Callaghan⟩ ⟨it is fine, sturdy stuff and more ~ to him —G.N.Shuster⟩ **c :** political or national might ⟨present-day tendency . . . to speak of the state almost exclusively in terms of ~ —*Amer. Polit. Sci. Rev.*⟩ **7 a :** the number of times as indicated by an exponent a number occurs as a factor in a product; *also* **:** the product itself **b :** the property that a mathematical aggregate has in common with all equivalent aggregates **:** the cardinal number that two or more aggregates share **8 a :** an inherent property or effect ⟨they are . . . ~s of material substances —Grace De Laguna⟩ ⟨adrenalin . . . has the ~ of constricting the blood vessels —Morris Fishbein⟩ **b** (1) **:** the phonetic value of a letter ⟨the ~ of K was usually written by C —Stanley Wemyss⟩ (2) **:** the meaning of a word or phrase **9 a** *archaic* **:** SIMPLE MACHINE **b** (1) **:** a source or means of supplying energy ⟨muscle ~⟩ ⟨tractor ~⟩ ⟨wind ~⟩ ⟨atomic ~⟩ ⟨using horses and mules for ~ —C.B.Bender⟩; *esp* **:** ELECTRICITY ⟨the shortage of ~ dims the streets —Wyndham Lewis⟩ (2) **:** energy supplied from such sources **:** MOTIVE POWER ⟨gathered their herds and started them on their own ~ in charge of cowboys —W.P.Webb⟩ ⟨ships . . . arrive, dock, and depart under their own ~ —*Amer. Guide Series: N.C.*⟩ **c :** the time rate at which work is done or energy emitted or transferred ⟨mechanical ~ of the internal combustion engine —A.C.Morrison⟩ — usu. expressed in horsepower or watts **10 a :** MAGNIFICATION 1 b **b :** the reciprocal of the focal length of a lens

**syn** CONTROL, AUTHORITY, JURISDICTION, COMMAND, DOMINION, SWAY: POWER indicates possession of the ability to wield coercive force, permissive authority, or substantial influence ⟨the Governor's position is no longer one merely of dignity and honor, but of constantly increasing *power* —*Amer. Guide Series: Mass.*⟩ ⟨the trustees have *power* to appoint and displace professors, tutors, and other officers —John Marshall⟩ or to make effective use of one's capacities ⟨the Senate had been voting according to direction for so long that they seemed to have lost the *power* of independent decisions —Robert Graves⟩ CONTROL emphasizes the power of direction or restraint ⟨his nervous exasperation had grown so much that now very often he used to lose *control* of his voice —Joseph Conrad⟩ ⟨he is likely to be the most hated man, because he exercises the greatest *control* —Abram Kardiner⟩ ⟨all such laws shall be subject to the revision and *control* of the Congress —*U. S. Constitution*⟩ AUTHORITY usu. implies the granting of power for a specific purpose and within a carefully delineated frame of reference ⟨by *authority* we mean the established right, within any social order, to determine policies, to pronounce judgments on relevant issues, and to settle controversies, or, more broadly, to act as leader or guide to other men —R.M.MacIver⟩ but may also refer to influence derived from public sanction ⟨some of the new philosophies undermine the *authority* of science, as some of the older systems undermined the *authority* of religion —W.R.Inge⟩ JURISDICTION usu. applies to official power and responsibility formally determined and demarcated ⟨in all cases affecting ambassadors, other public ministers, and consuls, and those in which a State shall be a party, the Supreme Court shall have original jurisdiction —*U. S. Constitution*⟩ ⟨there can be no doubt as to the *jurisdiction* of this court to revise the judgment of the Circuit Court, and to reverse it for any error apparent on the record —R.B.Taney⟩ ⟨many of the smaller squires and most of the larger ones had the right to private *jurisdiction;* the number of nobles with the right to put a man to death upon their own estates was appreciable —Hilaire Belloc⟩ COMMAND stresses the power to make arbitrary decisions and to compel obedience ⟨in war the president assumes *command* of the army and navy⟩ ⟨he had no *command* among the men, and people did what they pleased with him —R.L.Stevenson⟩ or it may imply self-mastery or mastery over one's resources ⟨the author's *command* of his material is admirable, and his presentation masterly —H.O.Taylor⟩ DOMINION indicates ultimate sovereignty or supreme authority ⟨neither the English nor colonial Governments claimed or exercised any *dominion* over the tribe or nation by whom it was occupied, nor claimed the right to the possession of the territory, until the tribe or nation consented to cede it —R.B.Taney⟩ ⟨the four wars between England and France for *dominion* in North America —*Amer. Guide Series: N.C.*⟩ SWAY, somewhat rhetorical in effect, indicates a sweeping extent over which dominant power or dominion is exercised ⟨it was as a successful warlord that the dictator Julius Caesar, after the defeat of Pompey at Pharsalia in 48 B.C., had brought the whole Roman world under the *sway* of one supreme military commander —P.N.Ure⟩ ⟨in 1673 the Dutch recaptured the Colony, but in 1674 it was restored by treaty to the English, who promptly resumed their *sway* —*Amer. Guide Series: N.Y.*⟩ ⟨no government, whatever its nature or form, can hold absolute *sway* in the multitudinous ramifications of human activity —*Encyc. Americana*⟩

**syn** POWER, FORCE, ENERGY, STRENGTH, MIGHT, PUISSANCE, ARM can signify the ability to exert effort for a purpose. POWER signifies ability, latent, exerted, physical, mental or spiritual, to act, be acted upon, effect or be effected, sometimes designating the thing having this ability ⟨*power*, which is any and every capacity to produce results —*Amer. Polit. Sci. Rev.*⟩ ⟨the immense property value of the slaves and the *power* of the owners to control all the political agencies of the government —W.C.Ford⟩ ⟨the *power* of the bridge to withstand great weights⟩ ⟨the precious *power* to lift the minds and hearts of children —R.H.Wittcoff⟩ ⟨the *power* to understand and be affected by music⟩ ⟨who was a *power* in marine and financial circles in New York —H.W.H.Knott⟩ FORCE stresses the actual exercise of power, often applying to something which exercises its power efficaciously ⟨to charge against a door with enough *force* to break it down⟩ ⟨a society crowded by almost every other *force* toward like-mindedness and conformity —Oscar Handlin⟩ ⟨a powerful political *force*⟩ ⟨a police *force*⟩ ENERGY contrasts with latent power, denoting the power expended or capable of being transformed into work; in common use it implies stored-up power; in the physical sciences it is conceived of as one of two possible aspects of matter (the other being mass) and signifying, roughly, the capacity for work, realized or potential ⟨how the immense *energy* of volcanoes might be harnessed for man's use —Howel Williams⟩ ⟨measuring the physical output may furnish some rough estimate of the *energy* given out by the worker —J.A. Hobson⟩ ⟨*energy* for sudden action, rapidity of decision, mystical fusion of reason and passion, which characterizes men created to act —William Troy⟩ ⟨the electrical *energy* expended in the circuit is derived from the chemical *energy* of the freshly compounded battery —K.K.Darrow⟩ ⟨*energy* and mass are two aspects of the same entity, and when the energy departs the corresponding amount of mass also departs —A. S.Eddington⟩ STRENGTH applies to the power residing in a thing as a result of qualities or properties (as health or soundness in bodily condition, or numbers or great equipment in military organization) that enable it to exert force or manifest great energy as in resistance, attack, or endurance ⟨a man of great *strength*⟩ ⟨a wall of great *strength*⟩ ⟨a political party of great *strength*⟩ ⟨a military force of great *strength*⟩ MIGHT, somewhat literary, suggests great or superhuman power or force ⟨sportsmen have risen in their articulate *might* and blasted the proposals out of legislative halls —*Amer. Guide Series: Mich.*⟩ ⟨the most savage winter in the memory of the Colonies hurled its icy *might* against the Americans at Valley Forge —F.V.W.Mason⟩ although in certain current fixed constructions it still retains its older sense of strength or force ⟨they reserve to themselves the right to curse the city's shortcomings with *might* and main —*Amer. Guide Series: Md.*⟩ ⟨Washington remonstrated with all his *might* —H.E.Scudder⟩ PUISSANCE, rhetorical and literary, is similar to MIGHT but suggests a display of power ⟨the sapience and *puissance* of the American businessman in general and the American financier in particular —G.W.Johnson⟩ ⟨their legs had lost almost all *puissance;* for minutes they would stand virtually in place, unable to coordinate their thighs and feet to move forward —Norman Mailer⟩ ARM in this connection is the figurative extension of *arm*, the human limb, and signifies operative and effective power or that in which such power resides; or it can, in related but specialized use, signify a branch of the service ⟨the strong *arm* of the law⟩ ⟨the military was a fairly good *arm* of the American people —T.D.Clark⟩ ⟨until all *arms* of the international fighting services are up to strength —A.P.Ryan⟩

[2]**power** *vb* -ED/-ING/-S *vt* **1 :** to give strength to **:** make powerful ⟨warships . . . other craft, ~*ed* by 80,000,000 horsepower —*Time*⟩ **2 a :** to supply with or propel by means of motive power ⟨tankers . . . fetch the fuel that ~s trains and trucks —Andrew Boyd⟩ ⟨are you waiting for me to ~ you out the door —F.W.Booth⟩; *esp* **:** to furnish with electricity ⟨tiny atomic batteries designed to ~ the electronic brains in guided missiles —*Newsweek*⟩ **b :** to give impetus to ⟨decision to revenge . . . his wife, is ~*ed* by a quiet, controlled anger —*Atlantic*⟩ ~ *vi* **:** to move under power ⟨we ~*ed* cautiously into a fog —Thomas Morgan⟩

**powerable** *adj* [[1]*power* + *-able*] *obs* **:** POWERFUL

**power amplifier** *n* **:** an amplifier that can produce relatively large power output usu. greater than one watt

**power appendant** *or* **power appurtenant**, *n* **:** a power coupled with an interest that the donee can exercise only out of an estate held by him (as a grant by the holder of a life estate of a lease) — distinguished from *power in gross*

**powerboat** \ˈ==ˌ=\ *n* **:** a motorboat esp. of substantial engine power

**power brake** *n* **:** automotive brake with engine power used to amplify the torque applied at the pedal by the driver

**power car** *n* **1 a :** a railroad car equipped with machinery for supplying heat and electricity to a train **b :** a railroad car having controls for operation alone or with other cars as a train **2 :** a usu. faired in structure supported from or suspended beneath the hull of an airship and carrying the engine or engines used for propulsion

**power coupled with an interest :** a power accompanying an interest of the donee in the property to which the power relates — distinguished from *collateral power*

**power dive** *n* [[1]*power* + *dive*, n.] **:** a steep dive of or as if of an airplane accelerated by the power of the engine ⟨made a succession of *power dives* upon the enemy ships —*Manchester Guardian Weekly*⟩ ⟨watched a falcon rise . . . then plummet downward in a magnificent *power dive* —H.M.Robinson⟩

**power-dive** \ˈ==ˌ=\ *vb* [*power dive*] *vi* **:** to dive steeply with the added impetus of motive power ⟨*power-dived* from 20,000 feet⟩ ~ *vt* **:** to cause to go into a power dive ⟨practically *power-dived* this old crate into the Mediterranean to get away —Lowell Bennett⟩

**power duster** *n* **:** a motor-driven agricultural machine for spreading insecticidal dusts

**powered** \ˈpaů(ə)rd, -aůəd, -aůwəd\ *adj* **:** having, producing, or propelled by means of power ⟨~ aircraft⟩ ⟨~ flight⟩ ⟨great ~ engines⟩ — often used in combination ⟨kerosine-*powered* jet-propulsion engines⟩

**power factor** *n* **:** the ratio of the mean actual power in an alternating-current circuit measured in watts to the apparent power measured in volt-amperes, being equal to the cosine of the phase difference between electromotive force and current

[1]**pow·er·ful** \ˈpaů(ə)rfəl, -aůəf-,-aůwəf-, *-R chiefly substand* -aůf-\ *adj* [ME *powerfull*, fr. [1]*power* + *-full*, *-ful* -ful] **1 a :** having great force or potency **:** STRONG, COMPELLING ⟨~ state⟩ ⟨~ leader⟩ ⟨~ physique⟩ ⟨~ solvent⟩ ⟨images that are always ~, imaginative, and solid —Whitney Balliett⟩ ⟨the . . . ~ immediacy of hunger —Lionel Trilling⟩ ⟨a ~ influence for good —C.C.Walcutt⟩ **b :** having great prestige or effect **:** INFLUENTIAL, STIMULATING ⟨~ clique⟩ ⟨~ journal⟩ ⟨the ~ Senate Foreign Relations Committee —Vera M. Dean⟩ ⟨love of the outdoors was a ~ factor in his decision to take up farming⟩ ⟨music is ~ in the building up of . . . expansiveness of personality —H.A.Overstreet⟩ **2 :** endowed with talent or ability **:** CAPABLE ⟨here is one of our most ~ performers refusing to show his power —E.R.Bentley⟩ **3** *chiefly dial* **:** great in amount or extent **:** BIG, CONSIDERABLE ⟨think if they raise 75 or a hundred bu. of wheat they have a ~ crop —A.E.Fife⟩ — **pow·er·ful·ly** \-f(ə)lē, -li\ *adv*

[2]**powerful** \"\ *adv, chiefly dial* **:** to a great degree or extent **:** VERY ⟨was ~ glad to see me —Mark Twain⟩ ⟨it was ~ dark going down through the holler —H.E.Giles⟩

**pow·er·ful·ness** \-fəlnəs\ *n* -ES *archaic* **:** POWER

**power gas** *n* **:** a cheap gas (as Mond gas) made for producing power esp. for driving gas engines

**power grid** *n* **:** a network of electrical transmission lines connecting a multiplicity of generating stations to loads over a wide area

**powerhouse** \ˈ==ˌ=\ *n* **1 a :** a building in which mechanical, electrical, or other power is generated; *specif* **:** an electric utility generating station **b :** a source of influence or inspiration ⟨protegés of party ~s —*New Republic*⟩ ⟨the meeting for worship is . . . the ~ of everything Quakerism has accomplished —W.W.Comfort⟩ **2 :** one having or wielding great power: as **a :** an individual of unusual physical or mental capacity ⟨a ~ with sandpaper lungs, stomped his foot and opened his mouth —Truman Capote⟩ ⟨a ~ of a woman teacher —*Time*⟩ ⟨no other . . . trout can boast of greater fighting qualities; he is a ~ —Alexander MacDonald⟩ **b :** an effective well-coordinated group ⟨the combo is a real ~ . . . with the authentic feeling for the music —*Christian Science Monitor*⟩; *specif* **:** an athletic team characterized by strong aggressive play ⟨two perennial ~s, Notre Dame and Army —*Americana Annual*⟩ **c :** a very strong hand held by one player in a card game **d :** a group or list of influential people ⟨has lined up a ~ to officiate at its Fiction Writers Conference —Bennett Cerf⟩

**power in gross :** collateral power exercisable by the donee only in the creation of such estates as will not attach to that which he himself holds or be satisfied out of his own interest — distinguished from *power appendant*

**power landing** *n* **:** an airplane landing in which the power is not cut until contact has been made with the landing surface

**pow·er·less** \-aů(ə)rləs, -aůəl-,-aůwəl-\ *adj* **1 :** devoid of strength or resources **:** HELPLESS, IMPOTENT ⟨~ in the hands of her remorseless . . . enemy —W.M.Thackeray⟩ **2 :** lacking the authority or capacity to act **:** UNABLE — used with following infinitive ⟨arguing that he was ~ to do away with the odious institution —Lytton Strachey⟩ ⟨became entangled in the marsh . . . and was ~ to make the attack —*Amer. Guide Series: La.*⟩ — **pow·er·less·ly** *adv*

**pow·er·less·ness** *n* -ES **:** the quality or state of being powerless **:** IMPOTENCE

**power load** *n* **:** the part of the output of an electric power plant used for the operation of motors or heating devices

**power loading** *n* **:** the weight per horsepower of an airplane usu. computed on the basis of full load and of power in air of standard density

**pow·er·man** \-aů(ə)rmən, -aůəm-,-aůwəm-, -ˌman, -ˌmaa(ə)n\ *n, pl* **powermen :** a specialist in the installation, operation, and maintenance of generating equipment for electric power

**power mower** *n* **:** a motor-driven lawn mower

**power net** *n* **:** a usu. nylon knitted elastic fabric used for corsets and girdles

**power of appointment :** a legal authority granted under a deed or will authorizing the donee to dispose of an estate in a specified manner for his own benefit or the benefit of others

**power of attorney :** a legal instrument authorizing one to act as the attorney or agent of the grantor either generally for the management of a specified business or enterprise or more often specifically for the accomplishment of a particular transaction — called also *letter of attorney*

**power of termination :** the right of a grantor or his successors in interest to enter upon an estate granted upon a condition after breach of the condition in order to terminate the granted estate and revest it in the grantor or his successors

**power-operate** \ˈ==ˈ=(=),=\ *vt* **:** to operate (as a tool, machine, device) by mechanical power

**power pack** *n* **1 :** a unit consisting typically of transformer, rectifier, and filter for obtaining a moderate steady direct current from an alternating-current service ⟨*power pack* for a camera flash⟩ ⟨*power pack* for a capacitor⟩ ⟨*power packs* for guided missiles⟩ **2** *or* **power package :** an airplane engine with cowling and accessories designed for installation or removal as a unit — compare POWER UNIT

**power plant** *n* **1 :** POWERHOUSE 1 a **2 :** an engine and related parts (as carburetion system, ignition apparatus, transmission) supplying the motive power of a self-propelled vehicle ⟨an aeroplane can be considered as being divided into two main parts, the *power plant* and the airframe —*Manual of Seamanship*⟩ ⟨a 90- or 99-inch wheelbase car . . . tough enough to take any *power plant* up to 450 horsepower —Les Nehamkin⟩

**power play** *n* **1 :** an offensive play (as in football or hockey) in which mass interference is provided at a particular point or in a particular zone **2 :** a military, diplomatic, or political action or maneuver resembling a power play in sports ⟨worked a successful *power play* . . . by sending in elements of three divisions from the northeast and elements of a fourth division from the east —*N.Y. Times*⟩

**power-political** \ˈ===ˈ===\ *adj* [fr. *power politics*, after E *politics: political*] **:** of, relating to, or having the characteristics of power politics ⟨economic policy as *power-political* weapon —Andreas Dorpalen⟩ ⟨*power-political* maneuvers by great powers —J. S. Roucek⟩

**power politician** *n* [fr. *power politics*, after E *politics: politician*] **:** one that believes in, advocates, or practices power politics

**power politics** *n pl but sing or pl in constr* [trans. of G *machtpolitik*] **:** politics based primarily on the use of power as a coercive force rather than upon ethical precepts ⟨less savory incidents of church *power politics* —W.H.Chamberlin⟩; *esp* **:** international politics characterized by attempts to advance national interests (as the achievement and maintenance of security) or to obtain concessions from rivals through coercion on the basis of military and economic strength ⟨a statesman conversant with the facts of *power politics* —E.M.Earle⟩ ⟨eliminate *power politics* and replace them with a kind of mystical international cooperation —G.L.Kirk⟩ ⟨give up our *power politics* . . . and turn instead to treaty rights and principle and law —T.K.Finletter⟩ — compare BALANCE OF POWER, MACHTPOLITIK, REALPOLITIK

**powers** *pl of* POWER, *pres 3d sing of* POWER

**power shovel** *n* **:** a power-operated shovel consisting of a boom or crane that supports a dipper handle with a dipper at the end of it and used principally for excavation and removal of debris

**power stall** *n* **:** an airplane stall with the power on usu. occurring in a pull-up or in an attempt to climb too rapidly

**power-stall landing** *n* **:** a landing made with the airplane in the normal landing attitude, with power on, at an airspeed just sufficient to maintain the lifting power of the wings

**power station** *n* **:** POWERHOUSE 1 a

**power steering** *n* **:** automotive steering with engine power used to amplify the torque applied at the steering wheel by the driver

**power stroke** *n* **:** the stroke in the cycle of an internal-combustion engine during which the piston is propelled by the pressure of the expanding steam or gases

**power supply** *n* **:** a device providing power to electronic equipment and sometimes designated *A*, *B*, or *C* according to its function of heating vacuum tube cathodes, causing a flow of electron current in plate circuits, or applying a direct voltage in grid circuits

**power take-off** *n* **:** a supplementary mechanism on a truck or tractor enabling the engine power to be used to operate nonautomotive apparatus (as winches, pumps, saws, cement mixers)

**power test** *n* **:** a psychological test of knowledge or skill in which the time taken to complete the test is not considered **:** test of ability apart from speed

**power train** *n* **1 :** the intervening mechanism (as drive shaft, coupling, clutch, transmission, differential) of a vehicle between engine and propeller or driven axle **2 :** a rail unit comprising a locomotive and power-generating equipment on cars for use at army stations or in a community emergency

**power tube** *n* **:** a vacuum tube of large output suitable for use as a generator of alternating current or as a power amplifier

**power unit** *n* **:** an engine usu. of the internal-combustion type mounted with accessories for use in portable operation of mechanical equipment — compare POWER PACK 2

**pow·ha·tan** \ˈpaůəˈtan, paůˈhatᵊn\ *n, pl* **powhatan** *or* **powhatans** *usu cap* **1 a :** an Algonkian people of eastern Virginia **b :** a member of such people **2 :** an Algonkian language of the Powhatan people

**pow·itch** \ˈpaůich\ *n, pl* **powitch** [Chinook Jargon, fr. Chinook *-páuč*] **:** OREGON CRAB APPLE

**pow·nie** \ˈpōni\ *Scot var of* PONY

**powre** *obs var of* POUR

**pows** *pl of* POW

**pow·sow·dy** \ˈpōˌsōdi, ˈpaůˌsaůdi, =ˈ==\ *n* -ES [origin unknown] *dial Brit* **:** any of various dishes ranging from sheep's head broth to an ale posset and including often incongruous mixtures

**pow·ther** \ˈpü*th*ər\ *Scot var of* POWDER

[1]**pow·wow** \ˈpaůˌwaů\ *n* -S [of Algonquian origin; akin to Natick *pauwau* conjurer, he uses divination, Narraganset *powwaw*] **1 a :** a No. American Indian conjurer or medicine man **b** (1) **:** healing by incantation or magic among the Pennsylvania Dutch (2) *or* **powwow doctor :** a practitioner of this art ⟨the richest ~ in York . . . is said to receive as much as $50 for a treatment —*Nation*⟩ **2 a :** a No. American Indian ceremony (as for the cure of disease, success in hunting, victory in war) often accompanied by great noise, feasting, and dancing **b** (1) **:** a tribal council (2) **:** a conference with an Indian leader or group ⟨held a ~ with the head medicine man —F.B.Gipson⟩ **3 a :** a social gathering or celebration; *esp* **:** a noisy one **:** FROLIC ⟨then came the ~, with the Old Man the guest of honor —H.A.Chippendale⟩ **b :** a meeting or conference for discussion **:** SESSION ⟨brought together in a two-day ~ businessmen . . . scholars, journalists, and government officials —F.L.Allen⟩ ⟨official small fry . . . that modestly take up wall space at international ~s —Janet Flanner⟩; *esp* **:** a meeting to discuss political strategy ⟨indicated here at a . . . Democratic ~ that any party presidential campaign will lean heavily on the administration foreign policy record —*Christian Science Monitor*⟩ **c :** an informal conversation or interview ⟨in Rome the year before . . . had a fine ~ with the Pope —Bruce Marshall⟩; *esp* **:** a deliberative huddle ⟨the . . . group, which held frequent little ~s, often gained time for further deliberations by bidding in smaller jumps —S.G.Thompson⟩

²**powwow** \", ˌ='=\ *vb* -ED/-ING/-S *vi* **1 :** to hold or take part in a ceremonial or conjuring session; *esp* **:** to practice healing by incantation or magic **2 :** to have a meeting or take part in a discussion ⟨invited them to stack their arms in the yard, and come inside the shack and ~ —W.A.Fraser⟩ ~ *vt* **:** to subject to treatment by incantation or magic ⟨had one of his eyes ~*ed*⟩

¹**pox** \ˈpäks\ *n, pl* **pox** *or* **poxes** [alter. of *pocks*, pl. of ¹*pock*] **1 a :** any of various virus diseases characterized by pustules or eruptions — usu. used in combination ⟨chicken *pox*⟩ ⟨cow*pox*⟩ ⟨fowl *pox*⟩ **b** *archaic* **:** SMALLPOX **c :** SYPHILIS — not often in formal use ⟨most of them had a dose of clap or ~ and some had a double dose —Bruce Siberts⟩ **2 :** an afflictive rash **:** repellent cluster **:** PLAGUE ⟨a ~ of garish neon lights —Robert Cahn⟩ ⟨a ~ of jeering urchins —*New Yorker*⟩ ⟨the world . . . is covered by a ~ of danger spots —*N.Y.Times*⟩ — often used interjectionally ⟨a ~ on the girl —Virginia Woolf⟩ **3 a :** a disease of sweet potatoes caused by actinomycetes of the genus *Streptomyces* and characterized by pitted lesions on the roots or tubers — called also SOIL ROT **b :** STORAGE SPOT

²**pox** \"\ *vt* -ED/-ING/-ES *archaic* **:** to infect with a pox and esp. with syphilis

**poxy** \ˈpäksē\ *adj* -ER/-EST **:** afflicted with or as if with a pox

**poyn·ting's theorem** \ˈpȯintiŋz-\ *n, usu cap P* [after John H. *Poynting* †1914 Eng. physicist, its originator] **:** a statement in electromagnetic theory: the transfer of energy by an electromagnetic wave is at right angles to both electric and magnetic components of the wave vibration and its rate is proportional to the vector product of their amplitudes

**poy·ou** \ˈpȯi(ˌ)(y)ü\ *n* -S [Guarani *tatu-pó-yu*, lit., armadillo with a yellow hand, fr. *tatu* armadillo + *pó* hand + *yu* yellow] **:** PELUDO

**poz·nan** \ˈpōzˌnan, -ˌnän, -ˌnən; ˈpäzˌnan, -ˌnən; ˈpȯzˌnän, -ˌnäⁿ\ *adj, usu cap* [fr. *Poznán*, city in west central Poland] **:** of or from the city of Poznan, Poland **:** of the kind or style prevalent in Poznan

**pozole** *var of* POSOL

**poz·zo·la·na** \ˌpätsəˈlänə\ *or* **poz·zo·lan** \ˈpätsələn\ *also* **poz·zu·o·la·na** \ˌpütswəˈlänə\ *or* **puz·zo·lan** \ˈpütsələn\ *or* **puz·zo·la·na** \ˌpütsəˈlänə\ *n* -S [It *pozzolana* fr. ML *putheolana*, fr. L *puteolana*, fem. of *puteolanus*, adj., of or belonging to Puteoli, fr. *Puteoli* (now *Pozzuoli*), seaport in southern Italy + L *-anus* -an] **1 :** an aggregate material (as volcanic ash, tuff) used by the ancient Romans as an ingredient of mortar **2 :** any pulverulent siliceous or siliceous and aluminous substance that reacts chemically with slaked lime at ordinary temperature and in the presence of moisture to form a cementitious compound **3 :** a mortar or hydraulic cement consisting essentially of pozzolana and slaked lime — compare PORTLAND-POZZOLAN CEMENT

**poz·zo·la·nic** \ˌpätsəˈlanik\ *also* **puz·zo·la·nic** \ˌpüt-\ *or* **poz·zu·o·la·nic** \ˌpätswəˈl-\ *adj* **:** of, relating to, or having the properties of a pozzolana

**pp** *abbr* **1** pages **2** [L *papa*] pope **3** [L *patres*] fathers **4** pianissimo

**PP** *abbr* **1** parcel post **2** parish priest **3** part paid **4** parts per **5** past participle **6** peak to peak **7** pellagra preventive **8** *often not cap* [L *per procurationem*] by proxy or by the agency of **9** personal property **10** picked ports **11** [It *più piano*] more softly **12** postpaid **13** pounds pressure **14** power plant **15** prepaid **16** privately printed **17** [L *punctum proximum*] near point

**PPA** *abbr, often not cap* per power of attorney

**p paper** *n, usu cap 1st P* **:** perfect paper — compare M PAPER, N PAPER

**PPC** *abbr* **1** [Fr *pour prendre congé*] to take leave **2** *often not cap* picture postcard

**ppd** *abbr* **1** postpaid **2** prepaid

**PPD** *abbr* purified protein derivative

**pp factor** \ˈpēˈpē-\ *n, usu cap both Ps* [pellagra-preventive *factor*] **:** PELLAGRA-PREVENTIVE FACTOR

**pph** *abbr* pamphlet

**PPI** \ˌpē(ˌ)pēˈī\ *n* -S [*p*lan *p*osition *i*ndicator] **:** a radarscope on which spots of light representing reflections of radar waves indicate the range and bearing of objects such as airplanes, ships, buildings, cliffs, and mountains

**PPI** *abbr, often not cap* **1** parcel post insured **2** policy proof of interest

**ppl** *abbr* participle

**PPM** *abbr, often not cap* parts per million

**ppn** *abbr* precipitation

**ppp** *abbr* pianissimo, double pianissimo

**PPS** *abbr* **1** parliamentary private secretary **2** [L *post postscriptum*] additional postscript **3** pulses per second

**ppt** *abbr* precipitate

**pptn** *abbr* precipitation

**PQ** *abbr* **1** personality quotient **2** previous question

**pr** *abbr* **1** pair **2** pounder **3** power **4** prayer **5** preferred **6** presbyopia **7** present **8** price **9** priest **10** primitive **11** prince **12** printed; printer **13** prior **14** private **15** pronoun **16** pronounced **17** pronunciation **18** prose **19** proved

**PR** *abbr* **1** parliamentary report **2** payroll **3** pitch ratio **4** [L *populus Romanus*] Roman people **5** press release **6** prize ring **7** proportional representation **8** [L *pro rata*] in proportion **9** public relations **10** [L *punctum remotum*] far point

**Pr** *symbol* **1** praseodymium **2** propyl

**praam** *var of* PRAM

**prab·ble** \ˈprabəl\ *n* -S [alter. of ²*brabble*] *chiefly dial* **:** QUARREL, SQUABBLE — often used in the phrase *pribbles and prabbles*

**pra·bhu** \ˈprə(ˌ)bü\ *n* -S [Skt, lit., excelling, mighty, fr. *prabhavati* he surpasses, is powerful, fr. *pra-* before + *bhavati* he becomes, is — more at FOR, BE] **1** *India* **:** LORD, CHIEF **2** *India* **:** a member of the writer caste in western India

¹**prac·tic** \ˈpraktik\ *adj* [ME *practik*, fr. MF *practique, pratique*, fr. LL *practicus* — more at PRACTICAL] **1 :** PRACTICAL **2** *obs* **:** PRACTICED, EXPERIENCED, SKILLED; *also* **:** CUNNING

²**practic** \"\ *n* -S [ME *practik*, fr. MF *practique, pratique*, fr. LL *practice*, fr. Gk *praktikē*, fr. fem. of *praktikos* practical — more at PRACTICAL] **1 :** PRACTICE **2** *also* **prac·tick** \"\ *Scots law* **:** the ancient reported decision of the Court of Session used to show the customary practices and law — usu. used in pl.

**prac·ti·ca·bil·i·ty** \ˌpraktəkəˈbilədˌē, -tēk- -lətē, -i\ *n* **1 :** the quality or state of being practicable **2 :** something that is practicable

**prac·ti·ca·ble** \ˈpraktəkəbəl, -tēk-\ *adj* [modif. (influenced by *practic*) of F *praticable*, fr. MF, fr. *pratiquer* to practice (fr. *pratique* practice) + *-able* — more at PRACTIC] **1 :** possible to practice or perform **:** capable of being put into practice, done, or accomplished **:** FEASIBLE ⟨a ~ method⟩ ⟨a ~ aim⟩ **2 a :** capable of being used **:** USABLE ⟨a ~ weapon⟩ **b** *of a theatrical property* **:** that may be used as real ⟨a ~ door at the back of the stage⟩ **syn** see POSSIBLE

**prac·ti·ca·ble·ness** *n* -ES **:** PRACTICABILITY 1

**prac·ti·ca·bly** \-blē, -li\ *adv* **:** in a practicable manner **:** so as to be practicable

¹**prac·ti·cal** \ˈpraktəkəl, -tēk-\ *adj, sometimes* -ER/-EST [LL *practicus* practical (fr. Gk *praktikos*, fr. *praktos*, verbal of *prassein, prattein* to pass through or over, experience, transact, negotiate, practice + *-ikos* -ic) + E *-al*; akin to Gk *peran* to pass through — more at FARE] **1 a :** actually or actively engaged in some course of action or occupation ⟨a ~ man but no theorist⟩ **b :** pursuing an occupation as a means of livelihood rather than as an avocation or sideline ⟨the conflicting views of ~ farmers and country gentlemen⟩ **2 a :** of, relating to, or consisting or manifested in practice or action — compare IDEAL, SPECULATIVE, THEORETICAL ⟨a ~ matter⟩ ⟨~ questions⟩ **b :** being such in practice, conduct, effect, or essential character **:** VIRTUAL ⟨our ~ freedom is better than your nominal liberty⟩ **3 :** available, usable, or valuable in practice or action **:** capable of being turned to use or account **:** USEFUL ⟨a ~ acquaintance with a language⟩ ⟨~ economy⟩ **4 a :** given or disposed to action as opposed to speculation or abstraction **b :** skillful or experienced from practice **:** evincing practice or skill **:** capable of applying knowledge to some useful end ⟨a ~ mind⟩ **c** (1) **:** qualified by practice or practical training but lacking the highest professional training ⟨the duties of ~ and graduate nurses⟩ (2) **:** designed to supplement theoretical training by experience ⟨~ work in the field or laboratory⟩ (3) *chiefly Brit* **:** concerned with or used in connection with practical training ⟨a ~ room⟩ ⟨~ examinations⟩ **5 :** aware of and willing to overlook or participate in chicaneries or irregularities **:** UNSCRUPULOUS ⟨a ~ politician who knew which side his bread was buttered on⟩ **6 :** PRACTICABLE 2b **7 :** PRACTICING ⟨a ~ Catholic⟩

²**practical** \"\ *n* -S **:** an examination requiring demonstration of some practical skill

**practical art** *n* **:** an art (as of handicraft) that serves ordinary or material needs — compare FINE ART, LIBERAL ARTS

**practical astronomy** *n* **:** a branch of astronomy dealing with the making of observations of the celestial bodies for navigation and other position-finding purposes on the earth — compare NAUTICAL ASTRONOMY

**prac·ti·cal·ism** \-kəˌlizəm\ *n* -S **:** devotion to practical matters

**prac·ti·cal·ist** \-ləst\ *n* -S **:** an advocate or adherent of what is practical

**prac·ti·cal·i·ty** \ˌpraktəˈkaləd·ē, -lətē, -i\ *n* -ES **1 :** the quality or state of being practical **2 :** a practical matter or an instance of being practical

**prac·ti·cal·ize** \ˈpraktəkəˌlīz\ *vt* -ED/-ING/-S **:** to make practical

**practical joke** *n* **:** a joke whose humor stems from the tricking or abuse of an individual placed somehow at a disadvantage

**practical joker** *n* **:** a person addicted to the perpetration of practical jokes

**practical judgment** *n* **:** a judgment as to action or fitness **:** a judgment of the practical reason **:** an ethical judgment

**prac·ti·cal·ly** \ˈpraktək(ə)lē, -tēk-, -li, *dial & rapid speech* ˈprakl-\ *adv* **1 :** not theoretically **:** REALLY ⟨~ worthless⟩ **2 :** by means of practice **:** by experience or experiment ⟨~ acquainted with a subject⟩ **3 a :** in actual practice or use **:** to all practical purposes though not entirely or absolutely **:** VIRTUALLY ⟨a ~ inert solution⟩ ⟨~ inexhaustible resources⟩ ⟨a ~ perfect fit⟩ **b :** NEARLY, ALMOST ⟨it rained ~ all night⟩ ⟨the bottle is ~ full⟩

**practical music** *n* **:** APPLIED MUSIC

**prac·ti·cal·ness** *n* -ES **:** PRACTICALITY 1

**practical nurse** *n* **:** a nurse that cares for the sick professionally without having the training or experience required of a registered nurse; *esp* **:** a person who has undergone training and obtained a license from a state or other legal authority qualifying her to provide routine care to the sick

**practical politics** *n pl but sing or pl in constr* **1 :** matter for concrete action as distinguished from theoretical discussion **2 :** political intrigue, scheming, or action involving dishonorable or dishonest dealings

**practical reason** *n* **1 :** reason concerned with the practical accomplishment of chosen ends — contrasted with *theoretical reason* **2** *Kantianism* **:** the action or office of reason in matters of the will; *specif* **:** the determination of the grounds or universal laws of voluntary action by reason

**practical theology** *n* **:** the branches of theological study that deal with the institutional activities of religion covering esp. homiletics, pastoral theology, church polity, science of church administration, and liturgics

**practical unit** *n* **:** any of various electric and magnetic units selected for convenience as to size for use in actual practical measurements

**prac·ti·cant** \ˈpraktəkənt\ *n* -S [ML *practicant-, practicans*, pres. part. of *practicare* to practice medicine, fr. *practice* practice — more at PRACTICE] **:** PRACTITIONER

¹**prac·tice** *or* **prac·tise** \ˈpraktəs\ *vb* -ED/-ING/-S [ME *practisen*, fr. MF *practiser, pratiser*, fr. *practique, pratique* practice + *-iser* -ize — more at PRACTIC] *vt* **1** *obs* **a :** to make use of **:** USE, EMPLOY **b :** FREQUENT, HAUNT **2 a :** to exercise oneself in for instruction or improvement or for the acquisition of discipline, proficiency, or dexterity ⟨*practiced* the piano every day⟩ **b :** to exercise (another) in something for similar purposes **:** TRAIN, DRILL ⟨*practicing* the children in penmanship⟩ **3 a** *archaic* **:** to carry on or engage in (an activity or process) **b** *obs* (1) **:** to work out (as a sum) (2) **:** to act in (a play) **c :** to do or perform often, customarily, or habitually **:** make a practice of **:** engage regularly in ⟨~ politeness and grace⟩ **4 a** *obs* **:** to put (as a law) into effect **b :** to give practical expression to **:** act in a manner consonant with ⟨a man who ~*s* the religion that he preaches⟩ **c :** to follow (as an art, profession, or trade) as a way of life **:** be professionally engaged in ⟨*practiced* medicine for 40 years⟩ **5** *obs* **a :** to bring about **:** be responsible for **:** cause to take place **b :** to scheme to bring about **:** PLAN, PLOT **c :** to make an effort (as to do or cause something) **:** TRY **6** *archaic* **:** CONSTRUCT ~ *vi* **1 :** ACT, OPERATE, PROCEED **2 :** to perform an act often or customarily in order to acquire proficiency or skill ⟨~ with the broadsword⟩ ⟨~ on the piano⟩ **3 :** to exercise or pursue an employment or profession (as medicine or law) actively **4** *archaic* **a :** to plan or scheme esp. for a bad purpose **:** use or try artifices or stratagems **:** PLOT, INTRIGUE ⟨he will ~ against thee by poison —Shak.⟩ **b :** to deal or treat with someone esp. for the purpose of influencing or winning over **:** NEGOTIATE **5 :** to do something habitually ⟨*practicing* is better than preaching⟩

**syn** PRACTICE, EXERCISE, and DRILL can mean in common to perform or cause to perform an act or series of acts repeatedly, esp. for the purpose of attaining dexterity. PRACTICE stresses doing, esp. habitually, regularly, or over and over, commonly for the attainment of skill ⟨*practice* good deeds⟩ ⟨*practicing* horrible customs —*Sociology & Social Research*⟩ ⟨*practice* scales on the piano⟩ ⟨*practice* golf strokes⟩ EXERCISE stresses a keeping in action or use and usu. presupposes a power which can be developed or strengthened by activity or manifest in practice ⟨*exercise* responsibility for the public safety while driving⟩ ⟨the reader is being asked to *exercise* taste —William Empson⟩ ⟨the power now contested was *exercised* by the first Congress —John Marshall⟩ It commonly also signifies practice of physical movement of some kind specifically for the attainment of health or physical vigor ⟨*exercise* each morning by walking to work⟩ DRILL connotes an intention of fixing physical or mental habits by repetition as of group movements in unison or grammatical rules ⟨*drill* a class in the fundamentals of table manners⟩ ⟨*drill* a group of army recruits in the manual of arms⟩ The distinctions between the nouns PRACTICE, EXERCISE, and DRILL may be derived from the distinctions between the corresponding verb uses ⟨the *practice* of witchcraft⟩ ⟨the *exercise* of reason⟩ ⟨an *exercise* for developing the shoulders⟩ ⟨*drill* in the manual of arms⟩ ⟨a *drill* in grammatical rules⟩

²**practice** *also* **practise** \"\ *n* -S **1 a** *obs* (1) **:** performance or operation of something **:** EXECUTION (2) **:** a mode of acting or proceeding **b :** actual performance or application of knowledge as distinguished from mere possession of knowledge **:** performance or application habitually engaged in; *usu* **:** repeated or customary action **:** USAGE ⟨the ~ of rising early or working hard⟩ **c** (1) **:** the usual mode or method of doing something ⟨the ~ is to use a local anesthetic⟩ (2) **practices** *pl* **:** habitual conduct that is socially, ethically, or otherwise unacceptable ⟨the unwholesome ~*s* of folk medicine⟩ ⟨departing these evil ~*s*⟩ **2 a** (1) *obs* **:** skillful or artful management **:** dexterity in contrivance or the use of means (2) **:** treacherous contriving; *also* **:** SCHEME, PLOT **b** *archaic* (1) **:** NEGOTIATION (2) **:** INTRIGUE **c** *archaic* **:** the act of using artifice or influence upon **:** imposing or working upon **3 a :** systematic exercise for instruction or discipline ⟨troops called out for ~⟩ ⟨~ makes perfect⟩ ⟨daily piano ~⟩ **b** *archaic* (1) **:** a practical treatise (2) **:** practical proficiency or skill acquired by systematic action or exercise ⟨this disease is beyond my ~ —Shak.⟩ **4 a :** the exercise of a profession or occupation ⟨the ~ of law⟩ **b :** professional business or work esp. as an incorporeal property ⟨a lucrative ~⟩ ⟨sold his ~⟩ **5 :** the form, manner, and order of conducting and carrying on suits and prosecutions through their various stages according to law **syn** see HABIT — **in practice** *adv* **1 a :** in actual or accepted usage **:** as a fact **b** *obs* **:** in customary or present use **:** in vogue **2 :** in such a condition as a result of practice as to be able to perform in an effective or superior manner ⟨athletes must keep *in practice*⟩ — **out of practice** *adv* **:** in such a condition as a result of lack of practice as to be unable to perform in an effective or superior way ⟨*out of practice* on the piano⟩

**practice curve** *n* **:** a graphic representation of change in performance as a function of practice

**practiced** *or* **practised** *adj* **1 :** EXPERIENCED, EXPERT, SKILLED ⟨a ~ marksman⟩ ⟨a ~ palate⟩ **2 :** tried or done habitually in order to acquire proficiency **:** learned by practice ⟨a ~ skill⟩ ⟨sat with ~ poise⟩ **3** *archaic* **:** used or frequented habitually

**prac·ticed·ness** *n* -ES **:** the quality or state of being practiced

**prac·tic·er** *or* **prac·tis·er** \-sə(r)\ *n* -S [ME *practisour*, fr. *practisen* + *-our* -or] **:** one that practices: as **a :** one that exercises a profession **:** PRACTITIONER **b :** a habitual performer of a particular act ⟨man as a maker and ~ of culture —T.D.McCown⟩; *esp* **:** an adherent of a faith or code of behavior ⟨a ~ of yogi⟩ **c :** SCHEMER, PLOTTER

**practice school** *n* **:** a demonstration school

**practice teacher** *n* **:** one doing practice teaching **:** STUDENT TEACHER

**practice teaching** *n* **:** teaching by a student preparing for a teaching career for the purpose of practicing educational skills and methods under the supervision of an experienced teacher

**prac·ti·cian** \prakˈtishən\ *n* -S [alter. (influenced by *practic*) of ME (Sc dial.) *practiciane*, fr. MF *praticien*, fr. *pratique* practice + *-ien* -ian — more at PRACTIC] **:** one acquainted or skilled by practice **:** a practiced or practical person; *also* **:** PRACTITIONER

**prac·tic·ing** *or* **prac·tis·ing** \ˈpraktəsiŋ, -sēŋ\ *adj* [ME *practesynge*, fr. pres. part. of *practisen* to practice — more at PRACTICE] **:** actively engaged in an indicated career or way of life ⟨a ~ physician⟩ ⟨~ Catholics⟩

**practick** *var of* PRACTIC

**practics** *pl of* PRACTIC

**prac·ti·cum** \ˈpraktəkəm, -tēk-\ *n* -S [G *praktikum*, fr. LL, neut. of *practicus* practical — more at PRACTICAL] **:** a unit of work done by an advanced university student that involves practical application of previously studied theory and the collection of data for future theoretical interpretation (as in practice teaching)

**practise** *var of* PRACTICE

**prac·ti·tion·er** \prakˈtish(ə)nə(r)\ *n* -S [*practition-* (alter. of *practician*) + *-er*] **1 :** one that exercises an art, science, or profession (as law, medicine, or engineering) — see GENERAL PRACTITIONER **2 :** one that does something or follows some course or regimen habitually or customarily **3** *obs* **:** one that practices something (as an art or a profession) to acquire or maintain proficiency **:** a learner or novice **4 :** one who engages in the public practice of Christian Science healing and applies its principles to human ills and problems

**prad** \ˈprad\ *n* -S [modif. of D *paard*, fr. MD *pert, paert, part*, fr. LL *paraveredus* post horse for secondary roads — more at PALFREY] *chiefly Austral* **:** HORSE

**prae·ci·pe** *or* **pre·ci·pe** \ˈprēsəˌpē, ˈpres-\ *n* -S [ME *precipe*, fr. ML, fr. L *praecipe*, imper. of *praecipere* to take beforehand, to give rules or precepts, admonish, enjoin — more at PRECEPT] **1 :** any of various legal writs commanding a person to do something or to appear and show cause why he should not **2 :** a written order addressed to the clerk or prothonotary of a court requesting the issuance of a specified writ and containing the pertinent information therefor

**praecipe in cap·i·te** \-inˈkapəˌtē\ *n* [NL] **:** a writ of right issuing from a Chancery Court in aid of a disseized tenant of land in chief holding immediately of the crown — compare PRAECIPE 1

**prae·cip·u·um** \prēˈsipyəwəm\ *n, pl* **praecip·ua** \-yəwə\ [L, fr. neut. of *praecipuus* taken beforehand, fr. *praecipere* to take beforehand — more at PRECEPT] **1** *Roman law* **:** a portion received from an inheritance before general distribution **2** *Scots law* **:** an additional share or bonus (as received by the eldest of several female heirs portioners)

**prae·co·ces** *or* **pre·co·ces** \ˈprekəˌsēz\ *n pl, often cap* [NL, fr. L *praecoces*, masc. & fem. pl. of L *praecoc-, praecox* ripe before its time, premature — more at PRECOCIOUS] **:** precocial birds

**prae·cog·ni·tum** \prēˈkägnəd·əm\ *n, pl* **praecogni·ta** \-d·ə\ [L, neut. of *praecognitus*, past part. of *praecognoscere* to foreknow — more at PRECOGNITION] **:** something known or that should be known in order to understand something else

**prae·di·al** *or* **pre·di·al** \ˈprēdēəl\ *adj* [ML *praedialis*, fr. L *praedium* + *-alis* -al] **1 :** being or made up of land or immovable property or the profits therefrom **:** LANDED — used chiefly with reference to the Roman and civil law systems and practically equivalent to the *real* of English law **2 :** of, relating to, or arising from land or landed property **:** attached to land ⟨~ slaves⟩ ⟨a ~ relationship⟩

**praedial larceny** *n* **:** theft of growing crops

**praedial servitude** *n, Roman & civil law* **:** a service, burden, or charge granted for the benefit of a tract of land affecting and exercised against another tract and resembling the easement at common law against a servient tenement in favor of a dominant tenement

**praedial tithe** *n* **:** a tithe payable out of farm produce or the products of the soil (as grain or firewood)

**prae·di·um** \ˈprēdēəm\ *n, pl* **prae·dia** \-dēə\ [L, fr. *praed-, praes* surety, bondsman — more at PREST] **:** landed property **:** a tenement of land — see PRAEDIUM RUSTICUM, PRAEDIUM URBANUM

**praedium dom·i·nans** \-ˈdäməˌnanz\ *n* [L, dominant praedium] **:** a dominant tenement, estate, or tract of land having the benefit of an easement or servitude exercisable against and affecting another tenement or tract

**praedium rus·ti·ca·num** \-ˌrəstəˈkānəm\ *n* [L, country praedium] *Roman, civil, & Scots law* **:** land upon which no building stands whether in town or country

**praedium rus·ti·cum** \-ˈrəstəkəm\ *n* [L, rustic praedium] *Roman & civil law* **:** land adapted to and used for agricultural or pastoral purposes — compare PRAEDIUM URBANUM

**praedium ser·vi·ens** \-ˈsərvēˌenz\ *n* [L, servient praedium] **:** the servient tenement, estate, or tract of land against which another dominant tenement, estate, or tract enjoys or exercises an easement or servitude

**praedium ur·ba·num** \-ˌərˈbānəm\ *n, pl* **praedia urba·na** \-nə\ [L, town praedium] *Roman, civil, & Scots law* **:** land, whether in town or country, upon which a house or other building stands and the land immediately adjacent thereto used for purposes incidental to the enjoyment of the buildings

**praefect** *var of* PREFECT

**praejudiciary** *var of* PREJUDICIARY

**praelect** *var of* PRELECT

**prae·lec·tor** *also* **pre·lec·tor** \prēˈlektə(r)\ *n* -S [NL, fr. LL *praelector* one that reads aloud and expounds upon an author, fr. L *praelectus* (past part. of *praelegere* to read aloud and expound) + *-or* — more at PRELECT] **1 :** a reader, lecturer, or professor in a college or university **2 :** a college officer (as in Cambridge University) in charge of presenting members of the college to the university for matriculation and graduation

**prae·lu·di·um** *or* **pre·lu·di·um** \prēˈlüdēəm\ *n, pl* **prae·lu·dia** *or* **pre·lu·dia** \-dēə\ [ML — more at PRELUDE] **:** PRELUDE

**praemium** *obs var of* PREMIUM

¹**prae·mu·ni·re** *or* **pre·mu·ni·re** \ˌprēmyəˈnīrē\ *n* -S [ME *praemunire (facias)*, fr. ML, that you cause to warn (prominent words in the writ), fr. *praemunire* to warn (influenced in meaning by L *praemonēre* to forewarn) (fr. L, to fortify, fr. *prae-* pre- + *munire* to fortify) + *facias* that you cause — more at PREMONITION, MUNITION] **:** a legal writ charging an offense of procuring translations, processes, excommunications, bulls, or other actions or benefits from the pope against the king, his crown, and realm

²**praemunire** \"\ *vt* -ED/-ING/-S *archaic* **:** to prosecute for or convict of praemunire

¹**prae·nes·tine** \prēˈnestən\ *adj, usu cap* [L *Praenestinus*, fr. *Praeneste*, ancient city in Latium, Italy + L *-inus* -ine] **:** relating to or characteristic of the city of Praeneste ⟨the engraved cylindrical *Praenestine* cists⟩

²**praenestine** \"\ *n* -S *usu cap* **:** a language closely related to or a dialect of Latin known from a small body of inscriptions from as early as the 6th century B.C.

**prae·no·men** *or* **pre·no·men** \(ˈ)prēˈnōmən\ *n, pl* **praenomens** \-nz\ *or* **praenom·ina** \-ˈnämənə, -ˈnōm-\ *or* **prenomens** *or* **prenomina** [L, *praenomen*, fr. *prae-* pre- + *nomen* name — more at NAME] **1 :** the first name of a person;

*esp* **:** the first of the usual three names of an ancient Roman by which he was distinguished from others of the same family ⟨in the name Marcus Tullius Cicero, Marcus is the ~⟩ — compare AGNOMEN, COGNOMEN, NOMEN **2 :** the first independent element of a name (as of a place or a biological species) ⟨in the binomial *Cynomys ludovicianus, Cynomys* is both generic name and ~⟩

**praepositor** *var of* PREPOSITOR

**prae·pos·tor** *or* **pre·pos·tor** \prē'pästə(r)\ *also* **prae·pos·i·tor** *or* **pre·pos·i·tor** \-äzət-\ *n* -s [ML *praepositor, praepostor*, fr. L *praepositus, praepostus* (past part. of *praeponere* to put in front, put in charge of) + *-or* — more at PREPOSITION] **:** a monitor at an English public school

**praeses** *var of* PRESES

**praesidium** *var of* PRESIDIUM

**prae·tax·a·tion** *or* **pre·tax·a·tion** \,prē,tak'sāshən\ *n* [ML *praetaxatus* (past part. of *praetaxare* to reckon beforehand, fr. *prae-* pre- + *taxare* to estimate, reckon) + E *-ion* — more at TAX] **:** the act or privilege of voting before others esp. as exercised by a small powerful group in selecting a monarch

**praeter-** — see PRETER-

**prae·tex·ta** *also* **pre·tex·ta** \prē'tekstə\ *n, pl* **praetex·tae** \-k,stē\ [L (toga) *praetexta*, lit., bordered toga, fr. *toga* + *praetexta*, fem. of *praetextus* bordered, fr. past part. of *praetexere* to weave in front, fringe, border — more at PRETEXT] **:** a white robe with a purple border orig. worn by an ancient Roman magistrate or priest and later by a Roman boy before he assumed the toga virilis or until about the end of his 14th year and by a girl until marriage

**prae·tor** *also* **pre·tor** \'prēd·ə(r), -ētə-\ *n* -s [ME *pretor*, fr. L *praetor*, prob. fr. *praeitus* (past part. of *praeire* to go ahead, lead the way, fr. *prae-* pre- + *ire* to go) + *-or* — more at ISSUE] **:** an ancient Roman magistrate ranking below a consul

**prae·to·ri·al** *also* **pre·to·ri·al** \prē'tōrēəl, prə'-, -tȯr-\ *adj* [L *praetorius* of a praetor + E *-al*] **:** PRAETORIAN

**¹prae·to·ri·an** *also* **pre·to·ri·an** \-rēən\ *adj* [L & LL *praetorianus*, fr. L *praetorius* of a praetor (fr. *praetor*) + *-anus* -an] **1 a :** of or relating to a Roman praetor **:** exercised by a praetor **b :** of, relating to, or created by the praetor's equitable power **2** *usu cap* **:** of, relating to, or constituting the bodyguard of a Roman emperor **3 :** resembling or characteristic of the Praetorian soldiers esp. in respect to corruption or political venality

**²praetorian** *also* **pretorian** \"\ *n* -s **1 :** a person (as an ex-praetor) of praetorian rank **2** *usu cap* **:** a soldier of the Praetorian Guard **3 :** a defender of an established order **:** CONSERVATIVE

**praetorian cohort** *n* **1 :** a picked body of troops that formed the guard of a praetor, or of a general in command of an army under the Roman republic **2** *usu cap P* **:** a cohort of the Praetorian Guard

**praetorian guard** *n, usu cap P&G* **:** a member of the bodyguard of the emperor of ancient Rome instituted by Augustus and consisting at first of 9 and later of 10 cohorts and coming to have great power in the making and unmaking of emperors until suppressed by Constantine in A.D. 312

**prae·to·ri·an·ism** \=ˈ=rēə,nizəm\ *n* -s **:** a corrupt military despotism

**praetorian law** *n* [trans. of L *jus praetorium*] *Roman law* **:** a system of equity developed by the praetors after their acquisition about 149 B.C. of criminal jurisdiction providing for their right to allow an action not provided for by law, their right to disallow an action that would strictly lie by the jus civile, and their right to allow an equitable defense where no defense was provided by law

**prae·to·ri·um** *also* **pre·to·ri·um** \prē'tōrēəm\ *n* -s [L *praetorium*, fr. neut. of *praetorius* of a praetor — more at PRAETORIAN] **1 a :** an ancient Roman general's tent in a camp **b :** a council of war held in such a tent **2 a :** the official residence of an ancient Roman governor **b :** a splendid countryseat or a palatial residence esp. in ancient Rome

**prae·tor·ship** *also* **pre·tor·ship** \'prēd·ə(r),ship\ *n* **:** the office or period of office of a praetor

**¹prag·mat·ic** \prag'mad·ik, praig-, -mat|, |ēk\ *n* -s [in sense 1, fr. LL *pragmatica (sanctio)*, fr. L *pragmatica* (fem. of *pragmaticus*, adj.) + *sanctio* decree; in sense 2, fr. L *pragmaticus*, fr. *pragmaticus*, adj.; in sense 3, fr. ²*pragmatic*] **1 :** PRAGMATIC SANCTION **2** *obs* **:** one skilled in affairs or business **3 :** an officiously busy person **:** MEDDLER, BUSYBODY

**²pragmatic** \(')=ˈ==\ *adj* [L *pragmaticus* skilled in law or business, fr. Gk *pragmatikos*, fr. *pragmat-, pragma* deed, affair (fr. *prassein, prattein* to pass through, experience, practice) + *-ikos* -ic — more at PRACTICAL] **1 :** of or relating to the affairs of a community or state — compare PRAGMATIC SANCTION **2 :** active in affairs **:** BUSY; *often* **:** OFFICIOUS, MEDDLING **3 :** stiff in one's opinion **:** CONCEITED, OPINIONATED, DOGMATIC **4 :** PRACTICAL, MATTER-OF-FACT **5 :** dealing with events in such a manner as to show their interconnection **6 a** *Kantianism* **:** prescribing the means necessary to the attainment of happiness **b :** of or relating to philosophic pragmatism; *esp* **:** of or relating to the philosophic pragmatism of Peirce, James, and Dewey

**prag·mat·i·ca** \prag'mad·əkə\ *n, pl* **pragmati·cae** \-d·ə,sē\ *or* **pragmaticas** [Sp *pragmática*, fr. LL *pragmatica (sanctio)*] **:** PRAGMATIC SANCTION

**prag·mat·i·cal** \(')prag|mad·|əkəl, -raig-, -at|, |ēk-\ *adj* [L *pragmaticus* + E *-al*] **1** *archaic* **:** PRAGMATIC 1 **2 :** of, relating to, or concerned with the practice or the practical side of anything **:** PRACTICAL, MATTER-OF-FACT **3** *obs* **:** of, relating to, or experienced in business or affairs **:** ACTIVE, BUSINESSLIKE, ENERGETIC, SKILLED **4 :** objectionably busy **:** FORWARD, OFFICIOUS, MEDDLESOME; *also* **:** CONCEITED, DOGMATIC **5 :** PRAGMATIC 6 b

**prag·mat·i·cal·i·ty** \prag,mad·ə'kaləd·ē\ *n* -ES **:** the quality or state of being pragmatical

**prag·mat·i·cal·ly** \(')prag|mad·|ək(ə)lē, -raig-, -at|, |ēk-, -li\ *adv* **:** so as to be pragmatic or pragmatical **:** in a pragmatic or pragmatical manner

**prag·mat·i·cal·ness** *n* -ES **:** the quality or state of being pragmatic

**pragmatic anthropology** *n, Kantianism* **:** practical ethics

**prag·mat·i·cism** \prag'mad·ə,sizəm\ *n* -s **1 :** PRAGMATICALNESS **2 :** the philosophic doctrine of C.S.Peirce

**prag·mat·i·cist** \-səst\ *n* -s **:** an advocate of pragmaticism

**pragmatic maxim** *n* **:** a statement of principle in the pragmaticism of Charles S. Peirce: in order to ascertain the meaning of an intellectual conception one should consider what practical consequences might conceivably result by necessity from the truth of that conception and the sum of these consequences will constitute the entire meaning of the conception

**prag·mat·ics** \prag'mad·iks\ *n pl but sing or pl in constr* **:** a branch of semiotic that deals with the relation between signs or linguistic expressions and their users — distinguished from *semantics* and *syntactics*

**pragmatic sanction** *n* [trans. of LL *pragmatica sanctio*] **1 :** an imperial constitution or decree answering a request or petition of a college, municipality, or other public body of the Byzantine Empire concerning its public affairs **2 :** a solemn decree issued by the head of a state on a weighty matter and having the force of a fundamental law

**prag·ma·tism** \'pragmə,tizəm, 'praig-\ *n* -s [²*pragmatic* + *-ism*] **1 :** pedantic assertiveness **:** DOGMATISM, OFFICIOUSNESS **2 :** practical treatment of things **:** MATTER-OF-FACTNESS **3 :** the pragmatic or philosophic method in the treatment of history or literature **4 a :** emphasis in philosophical thought on the application of ideas or the practical bearings of conceptions and beliefs **b :** an American movement in philosophy founded by Peirce and James and marked by the doctrines that the meaning of conceptions is to be sought in their practical bearings, that the function of thought is as a guide to action, and that the truth is preeminently to be tested by the practical consequences of belief

**¹prag·ma·tist** \-məd·əst, -mətəst\ *n* -s [²*pragmatic* + *-ist*] **:** one who is pragmatic: as **a :** BUSYBODY **b :** an adherent of pragmatism

**²pragmatist** \"\ *adj* **:** PRAGMATISTIC

**prag·ma·tis·tic** \ˌ==ˈtistik\ *adj* **:** of, relating to, or constituting pragmatism

**prag·ma·tize** \'==,tīz\ *vt* -ED/-ING/-s [Gk *pragmat-, pragma* deed, affair + E *-ize*] **:** to consider, represent, or embody (something unreal) as fact **:** MATERIALIZE, RATIONALIZE — **prag·ma·tiz·er** \-zə(r)\ *n* -s

**prague** \'präg *sometimes* 'prāg\ *adj, usu cap* [fr. *Prague*, Czechoslovakia] **:** of or from Prague, the capital of Czechoslovakia **:** of the kind or style prevalent in Prague

**¹pragu·i·an** \-gēən\ *adj, usu cap* [*Prague*, Czechoslovakia, the focal point of the *Cercle Linguistique de Prague* (Prague Linguistic Circle) + E *-ian*] **:** of or relating to a group of linguists and literary scholars noted for important advances in theory and procedure esp. in phonemics and textual analysis made between World War I and World War II

**²praguian** \"\ *n* -s *usu cap* **:** a member or adherent of the Praguian group of linguists and literary scholars

**prahu** *var of* PRAU

**prai·ri·al** \'prerēəl\ *adj* [F, fr. *prairie* + *-al*] **:** of or relating to prairies or to prairie land

**prai·rie** \'prerē, -ri *also* 'pra(a)r- *or* 'prār-, *chiefly substand* pə'r-\ *n* -s *often attrib* [F, fr. OF *praerie*, fr. (assumed) VL *prataria*, fr. L *pratum* meadow + *-aria* -ary; akin to L *pravus* crooked, wrong, bad, MIr *rāth, rāith* earthworks, fortification MW bed*rawt* grave mound] **1 :** a meadow or tract of grassland: as **a :** an extensive tract of level or rolling land in the Mississippi valley characterized in general by a deep fertile soil and except where cultivated by a covering of tall coarse grasses mostly without trees — compare PAMPA, PLAIN, SAVANNA, STEPPE **b :** one of the plateaus into which the prairies proper merge on the west and whose treeless state is due to dryness **c :** a low sandy wet and often water-covered grass-grown tract in the Florida pinewoods **2 :** a light yellowish brown that is stronger and slightly redder and lighter than khaki, darker and slightly yellower than walnut brown, and slightly darker than manila

**prairie acacia** *n* **:** a low thornless No. American shrub (*Acacia angustissima*) with feathery leaves and globose heads of yellow flowers

**prairie alligator** *n, chiefly Midland* **:** STICK INSECT

**prairie anemone** *n* **:** a pasqueflower (*Pulsatilla ludoviciana*)

**prairie ant** *n* **:** any of several ants inhabiting prairies; *esp* **:** a common ant (*Pogonomyrmex occidentalis*) of the central plains of the U.S.

**prairie antelope** *n* **:** PRONGHORN

**prairie apple** *n* **1 :** BREADROOT 1 **2 :** an earth plum of the genus *Geoprumnon*

**prairie aster** *n* **:** a violet-flowered perennial aster (*Aster turbinellus*) of the central U.S. having solitary heads

**prairie bass** *n* **:** BOWFIN

**prairie bean** *n* **1 :** METCALFE BEAN **2 :** BUSH PEA

**prairie beardgrass** *n* **:** a bunchgrass (*Andropogon scoparius*)

**prairie berry** *n* **:** TROMPILLO

**prairie bird** *n* **:** any of several birds that frequent open grasslands (as the horned lark or the prairie chicken)

**prairie bird's-foot trefoil** *n* **:** an annual No. American herb (*Lotus americanus*) with red or rose-colored flowers

**prairie bitters** *n pl but sing or pl in constr* **:** a drink of buffalo gall in water used in folk medicine

**prairie brant** *n* **:** WHITE-FRONTED GOOSE

**prairie breaker** *n* **:** a plow with a long low moldboard that is designed to cut a wide shallow furrow (as in virgin sod) and turn the slice completely over

**prairie brown** *n* **:** a brownish orange that is less strong and slightly yellower and lighter than spice and slightly redder and darker than Windsor tan, Titian, amber brown, or gold pheasant

**prairie button snakeroot** *n* **:** KANSAS GAY-FEATHER

**prairie chicken** *or* **prairie fowl** *or* **prairie grouse** *n* **1 a :** a grouse (*Tympanuchus cupido pinnatus*) of the Mississippi valley from Manitoba to Texas having the upper part streaked and spotted with rufous and black and the underparts white evenly barred with blackish and on each side of the neck a patch of bare inflatable skin — called also *greater prairie chicken* **b :** a smaller similar bird (*T. pallidicinctus*) of western Texas — called also *lesser prairie chicken;* compare HEATH HEN **2 :** SHARP-TAILED GROUSE

**prairie clover** *n* **:** a plant of the genus *Petalostemon*

**prairie cock** *n* **:** a male prairie chicken

**prairie coneflower** *n* **:** a plant of the genus *Ratibida; esp* **:** a rough perennial herb (*R. columnifera* or *Lepachys columnifera* or *Obelisteca columnifera*) with a yellow head of few rays but an elongated disk of tubular flowers

**prairie cordgrass** *n* **:** a cordgrass (*Spartina pectinata*) of No. America having leaves with scarious margins and glumes with long awns

**prairie crab** *or* **prairie crab apple** *n* **:** IOWA CRAB

**prairie crocus** *n, chiefly Midland* **:** PASQUEFLOWER

**prai·ried** \'prerēd\ *adj* **:** having prairies

**prairie dock** *n* **1 :** a tall weedy compass plant (*Silphium terebinthinaceum*) with broad heads of yellow ray flowers **2 :** AMERICAN FEVERFEW

**prairie dog** *also* **prairie marmot** *n* **:** a colonial American burrowing rodent (genus *Cynomys*) related to the ground squirrels and marmots; *esp* **:** a stocky gregarious rodent (*C. ludovicianus*) of the plains of western No. America from Montana to northern Mexico that is plain grayish or reddish buff with a black tip to the tail — see PRAIRIE DOG TOWN

prairie dog

**prairie dog town** *n* **:** a group of associated burrows of the prairie dog often opening from a common mound or hillock

**prairie-dog weed** *n* **:** FETID MARIGOLD

**prairie dropseed** *n* **:** a grass (*Sporobolus heterolepis*) chiefly of the prairies of No. America having ovoid panicles, very long narrow leaves, and the second glume of each spikelet with a carinate tip

**prairie falcon** *n* **:** a falcon (*Falco mexicanus*) that resembles the Old World lanner and is about 18 inches long, pale grayish brown above, and white streaked with brown below

**prairie false boneset** *n* **:** a perennial herb (*Kuhnia glutinosa*) having oblong or lanceolate 3-ribbed leaves that are densely puberulent beneath

**prairie fire** *n* **1 :** INDIAN PAINTBRUSH 1 **2 :** a fire in open grassland

**prairie flax** *n* **:** a western No. American perennial flax (*Linum lewisii*) having blue flowers in a few-flowered inflorescence

**prairie fox** *n* **:** KIT FOX

**prairie goose** *n* **:** HUTCHINS'S GOOSE

**prairie gourd** *n* **:** a perennial gourd (*Cucurbita foetidissima*) of dry parts of the central and southwestern U.S. and Mexico that has a thick fusiform taproot, ovate to slightly lobed leaves, and a small hard smooth bitter green-and-orange fruit

**prairie grain wireworm** *n* **:** a wireworm that is the larva of an elaterid beetle (*Ctenicera destructor*) and that is often highly destructive to sprouting grains, esp. wheat

**prairie grass** *n* **1 :** any of several grasses found on the prairies of the U.S. (as *Sporobolus Cryptandrus* and *Sphenopholis obtusata*) **2** *Austral* **:** RESCUE GRASS

**prairie grub** *n* **:** HOP TREE

**prairie hare** *n* **:** WHITE-TAILED JACKRABBIT

**prairie hay** *n* **:** hay made from native prairie grass

**prairie hen** *n* **1 :** PRAIRIE CHICKEN **2 :** CLAPPER RAIL

**prairie horned lark** *n* **:** a horned lark (*Otocoris alpestris praticola*) of east-central No. America with a pale yellow or whitish throat and white patches over and behind the eyes

**prairie indigo** *n* **:** a stocky glaucous white-flowered false indigo (*Baptisia leucantha*) of the Mississippi drainage

**prairie june grass** *n, usu cap J* **:** JUNE GRASS 2

**prairie lily** *n* **1 :** WESTERN RED LILY **2 :** a rough-hairy perennial herb (*Nuttallia decapetala*) with a solitary yellowish white flower **3 :** EVENING STAR 2

**prairie lotus** *or* **prairie trefoil** *n* **:** PRAIRIE BIRD'S-FOOT TREFOIL

**prairie mallow** *n* **:** MOSS ROSE 1 b

**prairie mimosa** *n* **:** a glabrous perennial herb (*Desmanthus illinoensis*) of the prairies of No. America with fruits in dense globose heads

**prairie mole** *n* **:** a large mole (*Scalopus aquaticus machrinus*) of the north-central U.S.

**prairie orchid** *n* **:** a fringed orchis (*Habenaria leucophaea*) of boggy or wet lands chiefly of the north-central U.S. that bears lax racemes of very fragrant creamy or greenish white flowers

**prairie owl** *n* **1 :** BURROWING OWL **2 :** SHORT-EARED OWL

**prairie oyster** *n* **1 :** a raw egg or egg yolk taken whole with seasoning, vinegar, and sometimes brandy esp. as a pick-me-up **2** *chiefly dial* **:** a testis of a bull calf used as food — compare MOUNTAIN OYSTER

**prairie peppergrass** *n* **:** a weedy No. American peppergrass (*Lepidium densiflorum*) chiefly of the central and western U.S.

**prairie phlox** *n* **:** a No. American perennial herb (*Phlox pilosa*) with ciliate lanceolate leaves and a terminal corymb of pink, purple, or white flowers

**prairie pigeon** *n* **1 :** UPLAND PLOVER **2 :** GOLDEN PLOVER **3 :** PECTORAL SANDPIPER

**prairie pine** *n* **:** a gayfeather (*Liatris spicata*)

**prairie pink** *n* **:** SKELETON WEED 2 a

**prairie plover** *n* **1 :** UPLAND PLOVER **2 :** GOLDEN PLOVER **3 :** MOUNTAIN PLOVER

**prairie plum** *n* **:** CHICKASAW PLUM

**prairie pointer** *n* **:** SHOOTING STAR 2

**prairie potato** *or* **prairie turnip** *n* **:** BREADROOT 1

**prairie ragweed** *n* **:** BURWEED MARSH ELDER

**prairie rattlesnake** *or* **prairie rattler** *n* **:** any of several moderate-sized rattlesnakes that are varieties of a species (*Crotalus viridis*) and are widely distributed esp. between the Mississippi river and the Rocky mountains

**prairie rocket** *n* **1 :** any of several western American cruciferous herbs of the genus *Cheiranthus* having large yellow flowers **2 :** any of several plants of the genus *Erysimum*

**prairie rose** *n* **:** a climbing rose (*Rosa setigera*) chiefly of the central U.S. having usu. trifoliolate leaves and large pink flowers that fade to white

**prairies** *pl of* PRAIRIE

**prairie sabbatia** *n* **:** a prairie herb (*Sabbatia campestris*) with ovate-lanceolate entire leaves and solitary lilac-colored flowers

**prairie sage** *n* **:** a perennial cottony-white herb (*Artemisia gnaphalodes*) with numerous small paniculate heads of yellowish flowers

**prairie sagewort** *n* **:** a wormwood (*Artemisia frigida*) that is a silky-leaved aromatic subshrub of dry northerly parts of the northern hemisphere

**prairie schooner** *or* **prairie wagon** *n* **:** a broad-wheeled covered wagon made smaller than a Conestoga wagon with a body having less upward curve toward the ends and used by pioneers in cross-country travel

prairie schooner

**prairie senna** *n* **:** SENSITIVE PEA

**prairie smoke** *n* **1 :** a No. American perennial herb (*Geum triflorum*) with basal pinnate leaves, purple flowers, and plume-tipped fruit **2 :** PASQUEFLOWER

**prairie soil** *n* **:** a zonal group of soils developed in a temperate relatively humid climate under tall grass and characterized by a dark brown or grayish brown surface horizon that grades through brown soil to the lighter colored parent material at two to five feet

**prairie spurge** *n* **:** a wiry weedy annual spurge (*Chamaesyce nuttallii*) of the central and southwestern U.S. with bright green foliage and greenish white axillary solitary flowers

**prairie squirrel** *n* **:** any of various ground squirrels (as *Citellus franklini, C. tridecemlineatus,* and *C. richardsoni*) of the prairies of western No. America

**prairie star** *n* **:** WOODLAND STAR

**prairie sunflower** *n* **1 :** an annual sunflower (*Helianthus petiolaris*) with rather slender usu. branching stems that is common in the central U.S. **2 :** SHOWY SUNFLOWER

**prairie titlark** *n* **:** a common and widely distributed pipit (*Anthus spinoletta rubescens*) of No. America

**prairie vetchling** *n* **:** an everlasting pea (*Lathyrus decaphyllus*) of the central U.S. with erect leaflets, angled stems, and showy purple flowers

**prairie violet** *n* **:** a stemless violet (*Viola pedatifida*) of central No. America with palmately divided leaves and violet-colored flowers

**prairie wake-robin** *n* **:** a perennial trillium (*Trillium recurvatum*) of the central U.S. with a dark purple sessile flower

**prairie warbler** *n* **:** a small warbler (*Dendroica discolor*) of eastern No. America that has the back olive green spotted with rufous, the underparts yellow, and the sides of the head and body streaked with black

**prairieweed** \'==,=\ *n* **:** a shrubby cinquefoil (*Potentilla fruticosa*) that is sometimes a pernicious weed esp. on wet limy soil

**prairie white-fringed orchid** *n* **:** PRAIRIE ORCHID

**prairie willow** *n* **:** a slender shrubby but highly variable willow (*Salix humilis*) of dry lands and barrens of No. America having elliptical leaves with toothed or crinkled margins

**prairie wolf** *n* **:** COYOTE

**prairie wool** *n* **:** native prairie herbage cured and dried in nature

**prai·ril·lon** \prä'rilyən, pre'rilən\ *n* -s [AmerF, dim. of F *prairie* — more at PRAIRIE] **:** a small prairie

**prais·able** \'prāzəbəl\ *adj* [ME *preisable*, fr. *preisen* to praise + *-able*] **:** PRAISEWORTHY — **prais·able·ness** *n* -ES — **prais·ably** \-blē\ *adv*

**¹praise** \'prāz\ *vb* -ED/-ING/-s [ME *preisen, praisen*, fr. MF *preisier* to prize, value, praise, fr. LL *pretiare* (often spelled *preciare* in later MSS) to value, prize, fr. L *pretium* price, value — more at PRICE] *vt* **1 a :** to express approbation of **:** EXTOL, COMMEND, APPLAUD ⟨*praised* beyond his merits⟩ **b :** to glorify (a god or a saint) by homage and ascription of perfections esp. in song **:** LAUD, MAGNIFY ⟨~ him . . . all his host —Ps 148:2 (RSV)⟩ **2 a** *archaic* **:** to determine the worth of **:** APPRAISE **b** *obs* **:** to hold in esteem **:** VALUE, PRIZE **3** *obs* **:** to win or gain praise or commendation for ~ *vi* **:** to express praise **:** make laudatory comments

**²praise** \"\ *n* -s [ME *preyse*, fr. *preisen, praisen*, v.] **1 a :** an act of praising **:** the quality or state of being praised **:** commendation for worth or excellence **:** approval expressed **:** honor rendered because of excellence or worth **:** LAUDATION **b :** the act of glorifying or extolling God or a god **:** WORSHIP; *esp* **:** worship by song as distinguished from prayer and other acts ⟨a service of ~⟩ **2** *archaic* **:** an object, subject, ground, or reason of praise ⟨he is your ~; he is your God —Deut 10:21 (RSV)⟩

**praise·ful** \-zfəl\ *adj* [ME *preiseful, praiseful*, fr. *preisen, praisen* + *-ful*] **1** *archaic* **:** meriting praise **:** LAUDABLE **2 :** full of, abounding in, or giving praise **:** LAUDATORY — **praise·ful·ly** \-fəlē, -li\ *adv* — **praise·ful·ness** *n* -ES

**praise house** *n* **:** a small meetinghouse usu. in the southeastern U.S. where religious services consisting mainly of song are held mostly during week-nights as a supplement to Sunday church services

**praise·less** \-zləs\ *adj* **:** receiving or meriting no praise

**praise meeting** *n* **:** a religious service mainly of song and often of a joyous informal nature

**prais·er** \-zə(r)\ *n* -s [ME *preiser, praiser*, fr. *preisen, praisen* to praise + *-er*] **:** one that praises: as **a** *obs* **:** APPRAISER **b :** LAUDER, EULOGIST **c :** WORSHIPER

**praise·worth·i·ly** \'prāz,wər<u>th</u>əlē\ *adv* **:** in a praiseworthy manner **:** so as to be praiseworthy or to have a praiseworthy result

**praise·worth·i·ness** \-<u>th</u>ēnəs\ *n* -ES **:** the quality or state of being praiseworthy

**praiseworthy** \'=ˌ==\ *adj* [²*praise* + *worthy*] **:** deserving of praise **:** CREDITABLE, LAUDABLE, WORTHY

**prais·ing·ly** *adv* **:** in a praising manner **:** with praise

**praiss** \'prēs\ *n* -ES [F, prob. fr. *presser* to press — more at PRESS] **:** a fluid extract of tobacco **:** the juice of tobacco **:** TOBACCO WATER

**praj·na** \'prəjnə\ *n* -S [Skt *prajñā*, fr. *prajānāti* he knows, fr. *pra-* before, forward + *jānāti* he knows — more at KNOW] **:** transcendental wisdom or supreme knowledge in Buddhism gained through intuitive insight

**pra·ka·ra·na** \prə'kərənə\ *n* -S [Skt, production, creation, discussion, topic, prakarana, fr. *prakaroti* he makes, produces, accomplishes] **:** a drama of India involving fictional situations from ordinary life

**pra·krit** \'prä,krit\ *n* -S *cap* [Skt *prākṛta*, fr. *prākṛta*, natural, usual, vulgar, fr. *prakṛti* original form, nature, fr. *prakaroti* he produces, fr. *pra-* before, forward + *karoti* he does, makes — more at FOR, KARMA] **1 :** any or all of the ancient Indic languages or dialects other than Sanskrit including Magadhi, Maharashtri, Sauraseni, Ardhamagadhi **2 :** any of the modern Indic languages

**prak·ri·ti** \'prəkrəd·ē\ *n* -S [Skt *prakṛti*] **1 :** unmanifested cosmic energy or potential matter that in Sankhya philosophy is constituted of the three gunas and that in contact with purusha produces a disequilibrium among the gunas which in turn results in the production of the manifested world **2 :** the phenomenal world **:** MATTER, NATURE

**pra·krit·ic** \prə'krid·ik\ *adj* **1** *usu cap* **:** relating to, from, or resembling Prakrit **2** *sometimes cap* **:** VERNACULAR, DIALECTIC

**pral·a·ya** \'prələyə\ *n* -S *usu cap* [Skt, lit., end, destruction] **:** a period of dissolution or destruction of the manifested universe at the end of a kalpa according to Hindu philosophy **:** the end of the world

**pra·line** \'prä,lēn, 'prā,- *also* 'prä,- *or* 'prō,- *or* ='= \ *n* -S [F, after Field Marshal César de Choiseul, Count Plessis-*Praslin* †1675 Fr. soldier whose cook invented the confection] **1 :** a confection of nut kernels **: a :** almonds roasted in boiling sugar until brown and crisp and sometimes pulverized or made into a paste **b :** a round patty of creamy brown sugar containing pecan meats **2 :** DARK BEAVER

**prall·tril·ler** \'präl-,trilə(r)\ *n* -S [G, fr. *prallen* to rebound (alter. — influenced by MHG *pralte*, past, & *gepralt*, past part. — of MHG *prellen*) + *triller* trill, fr. It *trillo*; akin to LG *prall* full, tight, OFris *prålling* testicle — more at TRILL] **:** a melodic musical grace made by a quick alternation of a principal tone with an upper auxiliary tone — called also *inverted mordent*

pralltriller: *1* as written, *2* as performed

**¹pram** *also* **praam** \'präm\ *n* -S [D *praam*, fr. MD *praem*; akin to MLG *prām* pram] **:** a small lightweight nearly flat-bottomed boat that has very broad transom and usu. squared-off bow, is of lapstrake construction or now often of molded plywood or plastic, is designed for use with oars, sail, or outboard motor, and is of Scandinavian origin though now widely used as a tender for larger boats

**²pram** \'pram\ *n* -S *often attrib* [by shortening & alter. fr. *perambulator*] **1** *chiefly Brit* **:** PERAMBULATOR **:** BABY CARRIAGE **2** *chiefly Brit* **:** HANDCART

**³pram** \"\ *vt* **prammed; prammed; pramming; prams** *chiefly Brit* **:** to air or take about (as a child) in or as if in a baby carriage

**pram·ni·an** \'pramnēən\ *adj, usu cap* [L *Pramnius* Pramnian (fr. Gk *Pramnios*) + E *-an*] **:** being a strong ancient Greek wine

**pra·na** \'pränə\ *n* -S [Skt *prāṇa*, lit., breath, fr. *pra-* before, forward + *aniti* he breathes — more at FOR, ANIMATE] **:** a life breath or vital principle in Vedic and later Hindu religion **:** any of the three or more vital currents **:** the principle of life moving in the human body

**¹prance** \'pran(t)s, -raa(ə)n-, -rain-, -rän-\ *vb* -ED/-ING/-S [ME *prauncen*] *vi* **1** *of a quadruped* **:** to spring or bound from the hind legs or move by so doing — used esp. of a mettlesome horse **2 :** to ride or drive a prancing horse **:** cause one's horse to prance while riding or driving often to attract attention or as an expression of exuberant feelings **3 a :** to walk or progress with ostentation or parade **:** SWAGGER ⟨*pranced* out of the room in a dudgeon⟩ **b :** DANCE, CAPER ~ *vt* **:** to cause (a horse) to prance

**²prance** \"\ *n* -S **:** an act or instance of prancing**:** as **a :** a prancing movement; *esp* **:** a sharp forward raising of alternate knees with well-extended toes in dancing **b :** SWAGGER

**prance·ful** \-sfəl\ *adj* **:** SPIRITED, DASHING

**pranc·er** \-sə(r)\ *n* -S **:** one that prances**:** as **a :** HORSE; *esp* **:** a mettlesome or fiery horse **b :** a rider of a spirited horse **c :** DANCER, CAPERER

**pranc·ing·ly** *adv* **:** in a prancing manner

**prancy** \-sē\ *adj* -ER/-EST **:** characterized by prancing **:** inclined to prance

**pran·di·al** \'prandēəl\ *adj* [L *prandium* late breakfast, luncheon (perh. fr. *pram-* early + *-dium*, fr. the stem of *edere* to eat) + E *-al*; akin to Goth *fruma* first — more at FOREMOST, EAT] **:** of or relating to a meal (as dinner) — usu. used in combination ⟨pre*prandial* potations⟩ ⟨post*prandial* oratory⟩

**pran·di·al·ly** \-lē\ *adv* **:** at or over a meal

**prandtl number** \'pränt^əl-\ *n, usu cap P* [after Ludwig *Prandtl* †1953 Ger. physicist; trans. of G *Prandtlsche zahl*] **:** the ratio of the product of the coefficient of viscosity and the specific heat at constant pressure to the thermal conductivity in fluid flow used esp. in the study of heat transfer in mechanical devices

**¹prang** \'praŋ\ *vb* -ED/-ING/-S [imit.] *vt* **1** *slang chiefly Brit* **:** to damage or destroy by aerial bombing ⟨~*ing* shore installations⟩ **2** *slang chiefly Brit* **:** to cause (an airplane) to crash **3** *slang chiefly Brit* **:** to bump into **:** STRIKE, HIT ⟨~*ed* the other car⟩ ⟨~*ed* his sister with a stick⟩ ~ *vi, slang chiefly Brit* **:** to perform an action of pranging; *esp* **:** to crash an airplane

**²prang** \"\ *n* -S *slang chiefly Brit* **:** CRASH

**¹prank** \'praŋk, -ai-\ *vt* -ED/-ING/-S [ME *pranken*] *obs* **:** to make pleats in **:** FOLD

**²prank** \"\ *vi* -ED/-ING/-S [origin unknown] **1** *dial chiefly Eng* **:** PRANCE **2** *obs* **:** to play tricks maliciously or in the performance of magic **3 :** to play pranks **:** cut up **:** FROLIC

**³prank** \"\ *n* -S **:** TRICK**: a** *obs* **:** a malicious or harmful act **b** *archaic* **:** a spell or act of magic or conjuring **:** a bit of sleight of hand **c :** a gay or sportive action **:** a ludicrous or mildly mischievous act **:** FROLIC, CAPER, PRACTICAL JOKE ⟨sent the child's painting to the academy as a ~⟩

**⁴prank** \"\ *vb* -ED/-ING/-S [prob. fr. D *pronken* to strut, show off, get dressed up, fr. MD; akin to MLG *prunken* to strut, show off, MHG *gebrunkel* glitter of metal] *vt* **1 :** to adorn in a gay or showy manner **:** dress or equip ostentatiously ⟨~*ed* herself out in her best⟩ **2 :** ADORN, DECK, SPANGLE ⟨flowers ~*ing* the meadow⟩ — often used with *with* ⟨a book ~*ed* with fancy devices⟩ ~ *vi* **:** to make ostentatious show

**prank·er** \-kə(r)\ *n* -S [²*prank* + *-er*] **1** *archaic* **:** PRANCER **2 :** PRANKSTER

**prank·ful** \-kfəl\ *adj* [³*prank* + *-ful*] **:** full of or given to pranks **:** MISCHIEVOUS

**prank·i·ness** \-kēnəs\ *n* -ES **:** the quality or state of being pranky

**prank·ing·ly** *adv* **:** in a pranking manner **:** SHOWILY, OSTENTATIOUSLY

**prank·ish** \-kish\ *adj* [³*prank* + *-ish*] **1 :** full of pranks **:** FROLICSOME ⟨a ~ boy⟩ **2 :** being or having the nature of a prank ⟨a ~ trick⟩ — **prank·ish·ly** *adv* — **prank·ish·ness** *n* -ES

**pran·kle** \-kəl\ *vi* [freq. of ²*prank*] *archaic* **:** to prance or caper lightly

**prank·some** \-ksəm\ *adj* [³*prank* + *-some*] **:** PRANKISH 1

**prank·ster** \-kstə(r)\ *n* -S [³*prank* + *-ster*] **:** a player of pranks; *often* **:** a somewhat malicious but not vicious trickster or practical joker ⟨~*s* deflated the tires of his car —*Life*⟩ ⟨one ~ took the police cruiser and parked it around the block⟩

**pranky** \-kē\ *adj* -ER/-EST [³*prank* + *-y*] **:** given to playing pranks **:** characterized by pranks

**prao** *var of* PRAU

**prase** \'prāz\ *n* -S [F, fr. L *prasius*, fr. Gk *prasios*, fr. *prasios*, adj., leek green, fr. *prason* leek — more at PORRACEOUS] **:** a variety of chalcedony that is translucent and leek green

**pra·seo·didymium** \¦prāzē(,)ō+\ *n* -S [NL, irreg. fr. Gk *prasios, praseios* leek green + NL *didymium*] **:** PRASEODYMIUM

**pra·seo·dym·i·um** \-'dimēəm\ *n* -S [NL, alter. of *praseodidymium*] **:** a yellowish white trivalent metallic element of the rare-earth group that occurs usu. with cerium, lanthanum, and neodymium, that forms green salts, and that is used chiefly in the form of its salts in coloring glass greenish yellow — symbol *Pr*; see DIDYMIUM; ELEMENT table

**pra·sine** \'prā,zēn, -,zⁱn, -,zīn\ *adj* [L *prasinus*, fr. Gk *prasinos*, fr. *prason* leek] **1 :** having the green color of a leek **2** *or* **pra·si·nous** \-āzⁱnəs\ **:** of the color leek

**pras·oid** \'prā,zȯid\ *adj* [ISV *prase* + *-oid*] **:** resembling prase ⟨a ~ mineral⟩

**¹prat** \'prat\ *n* -S [ME *pret, pratte*, fr. OE *prætt* — more at PRETTY] *chiefly Scot* **:** TRICK; *esp* **:** one that is low or mean

**²prat** \"\ *n* -S [origin unknown] **:** BUTTOCKS — sometimes considered vulgar

**³prat** \"\ *vt* **pratted; pratted; pratting; prats :** to nudge or push (as a person) with the buttocks — sometimes considered vulgar ⟨*pratted* him away from the ticket window⟩

**pra·tal** \'prād·^əl\ *adj* [LL *pratalis*, fr. L *pratum* meadow + *-alis* -al — more at PRAIRIE] **:** of, relating to, or growing or living in meadows

**¹prate** \'prāt, *usu* -ād·+V\ *vb* -ED/-ING/-S [ME *praten*, fr. MD; akin to MD & MLG *pratten* to pout, and perh. to Russ *bredit'* to talk nonsense, obs. Pol *brzedzić* to gossip] *vi* **1 a :** to talk at length and to little purpose **:** be loquacious **:** chatter foolishly and without real understanding ⟨*prating* of responsibility⟩ ⟨*prated* on about his wealth⟩ **b :** to speak boastingly or maliciously **2** *of an animal* **:** to make a characteristic repetitive sound ⟨the *prating* of passenger pigeons⟩ ~ *vt* **:** to utter foolishly **:** BABBLE ⟨what nonsense would the fool, thy master, ~ —John Dryden⟩

**²prate** \"\ *n* -S **:** an act of prating **:** trifling talk **:** unmeaning or idle loquacity **:** CHATTER

**prat·er** \'prād·ə(r), -ātə-\ *n* -S [ME, fr. *praten* + *-er*] **:** one that prates

**prat·fall** *also* **pratt·fall** \'prat,=\ *n* [²*prat* + *fall*] **1 :** a fall on the buttocks ⟨burlesque often relies on ~*s* for its humor⟩ **2 :** a humiliating mishap or blunder

**pra·tie** \'prād·ē\ *n* -S [by alter.] *dial* **:** POTATO

**pra·ti·mok·sha** \,prəd·ē'mōkshə\ *or* **pa·ti·mok·kha** \,pəd·ē-'mōkə\ *n* -S [Pali & Skt; Pali *patimokkha*, fr. Skt *pratimokṣa*, lit., liberation, deliverance, fr. *prati* toward, near + *mokṣa* liberation] **:** Buddhist rules of monastic discipline

**pra·tin·co·la** \prə'tiŋkələ\ [NL, fr. L *pratum* meadow + *incola* inhabitant, fr. *in-* ²in- + *-cola* (fr. *colere* to cultivate, dwell) — more at PRAIRIE, WHEEL] *syn of* SAXICOLA

**prat·in·cole** \'prat^ən,kōl, -ad·iŋ,k-\ *n* -S [NL *Pratincola*] **:** a limicoline bird of the genus *Glareola*; *esp* **:** a common bird (*G. pratincola*) of parts of Europe, Asia, and Africa, having the upper parts light brown, the throat buff bordered by a black line, the breast brownish, and the abdomen white

**pra·tin·co·line** \prə'tiŋkə,līn\ *n* -S [NL *Pratincola* + E *-ine*] **:** PRATINCOLE

**pra·tin·co·lous** \-ləs\ *adj* [L *pratum* meadow + *incola* inhabitant + E *-ous*] **:** living in meadows or low grassy situations ⟨~ ants⟩

**prating** *n* -S [ME, fr. gerund of *praten* to prate — more at PRATE] **1 :** foolish chatter **:** platitudinous discourse **:** evil speaking **2 :** recurrent chattering natural sound of an animal (as a pullet coming into lay)

**prat·ing·ly** *adv* **:** in a prating manner

**pra·tique** \pra'tēk, prə'tēk, 'prad·,ēk\ *n* -S [F *pratique* practice, intercourse, pratique — more at PRACTIC] **:** permission to hold intercourse given to a ship after compliance with quarantine regulations or on presenting a clean bill of health

**pra·tol** \'prā,tȯl, -tōl\ *n* -S [NL *pratense* (specific epithet of *Trifolium pratense*, fr. L, neut. of *pratensis* growing in meadows, fr. *pratum* meadow + *-ensis* -ese) + E *-ol* — more at PRAIRIE] **:** a crystalline phenolic flavone derivative $HOC_{15}H_8O_2OCH_3$ found in clover

**¹prat·tle** \'prad·^əl, -at^əl\ *vb* **prattled; prattled; prattling** \-d·^əliŋ, -t(^ə)liŋ\ **prattles** [LG *pratelen*, fr. MLG *prätelen*; akin to MD *praten* to prate — more at PRATE] *vi* **1 :** to talk or say much and idly **:** PRATE **2 :** to utter meaningless sounds that are suggestive of the chatter of children ⟨water *prattling* over rocks⟩ ~ *vt* **:** to say lightly and artlessly **:** BABBLE ⟨*prattled* his secret to unfriendly ears⟩

**²prattle** \"\ *n* -S **1 :** trifling or empty talk or chatter **:** trivial loquacity **:** PRATE, BABBLE **2 :** a sound (as of a brook) that is meaningless and repetitive like the chatter of children

**prat·tle·ment** \-mənt\ *n* -S [¹*prattle* + *-ment*] **:** PRATTLE

**prat·tler** \'pratlə(r), -ad·^əl-,-at·^əl-\ *n* -S **:** one that prattles; *esp* **:** a child too young to have acquired complete speech control and full vocabulary

**prat·tling·ly** *adv* **:** in a prattling manner **:** with prattle

**pratt truss** \'prat-\ *n, usu cap P* [fr. the name *Pratt*] **:** a truss having vertical members between the upper and lower members and diagonal members sloping toward the center

Pratt truss

**pra·tye·ka bud·dha** \prə-¦tyā-kə+\ *n, usu cap P&B* [Skt *pratyekabuddha*, fr. *pratyeka* single (fr. *praty-* — fr. *prati* toward, against — + *eka* alone) + *buddha* — more at BUDDHA] **:** one who having attained enlightenment enters Nirvana without turning back to teach others

**pra·ty·len·chus** \,prād·^əl'eŋkəs, ,prad·-\ *n, cap* [NL, blend of L *pratum* meadow and NL *Tylenchus* — more at PRAIRIE] **:** a genus of plant-parasitic nematodes (family Tylenchidae) associated with root rots of various economically important plants — compare MEADOW NEMATODE

**prau** \'prau̇\ *or* **pra·hu** \", 'prä(,)hü\ *or* **prao** \'prau̇\ *or* **proa** \'prōə\ *also* **prow** *or* **praw** \'prau̇\ *n* -S [Malay *pĕrahu*, prob. fr. Marathi *padāv*] **:** one of several usu. undecked Indonesian boats propelled by sails, oars, or paddles; *esp* **:** a swift light sailing craft about 30 feet long and 4 feet wide which has an upcurved equally sharp stem and stern so that sailing in either direction is possible, which has a curved windward side and a straight leeward side with a small canoe or other outrigger attached, and which has a large triangular sail attached to a long yard and hung obliquely from a short mast

**prav·i·ty** \'pravəd·ē\ *n* -ES [L *pravitas* crookedness, depravity, fr. *pravus* crooked, wrong, bad + *-itas* -ity — more at PRAIRIE] **1** *archaic* **:** DEPRAVITY, WICKEDNESS **2** *archaic* **:** BADNESS, FOULNESS; *esp* **:** physical corruption

**¹prawn** \'prȯn, -rän\ *n* -S [ME *prayne, prane*] **1 a :** any of numerous decapod crustaceans that have slender legs, long antennae, a large strong compressed abdomen, and a prominent serrated rostrum, are widely distributed in fresh and salt waters in warm and temperate regions and highly esteemed as food, and vary in size from an inch or so to the size of a lobster **b :** any of various other crustaceans**:** as (1) **:** NORWAY LOBSTER (2) **:** SHRIMP **2** *or* **prawn pink :** CREVETTE

**²prawn** \"\ *vi* -ED/-ING/-S **1 :** to fish for prawns **2 :** to fish using prawns for bait — **prawn·er** \-nə(r)\ *n* -S

**prawn killer** *n* **:** SQUILLA

**prawny** \-nē\ *adj* **:** of, relating to, or like prawns

**prax·e·an** \'praksēən\ *also* **prax·e·an·ist** \-nəst\ *n* -S *usu cap* [*Praxeas*, 2d cent. A.D. Asia Minor heretic + E *-an* or *-ist*] **:** a follower of Praxeas who was a leader of the modalistic Monarchians; *specif* **:** a modalistic Monarchian

**prax·e·o·log·i·cal** \¦praksēə¦läjəkəl\ *adj* **:** of or relating to praxeology

**prax·e·ol·o·gy** *also* **prax·i·ol·o·gy** \,praksē'äləjē\ *n* -ES [*praxeology* alter. of *praxiology*; *praxiology* fr. *praxis* + *-o-* + *-logy*] **:** the study of human action and conduct

**-prax·ia** \'praksēə\ *n comb form* -S [NL, fr. Gk *praxis* action + NL *-ia*] **:** performance of movements ⟨echo*praxia*⟩ ⟨*parapraxia*⟩

**prax·is** \'praksəs\ *n, pl* **prax·es** \-k,sēz\ [ML, fr. Gk, doing, action, fr. the stem of *prassein, prattein* to pass through, experience, practice + *-sis* — more at PRACTICAL] **:** ACTION, PRACTICE**:** as **a :** exercise or practicing of an art, science, or skill **b :** usual or conventional conduct **:** HABIT, CUSTOM

**-prax·is** \'praksəs\ *n comb form, pl* **-praxis·es** \-ksəsəz\ *also* **-prax·es** \-k,sēz\ [NL, fr. Gk *praxis* doing, action] **:** therapeutic treatment usu. by a (specified) system or agency ⟨chiro*praxis*⟩ ⟨radio*praxis*⟩

**prax·it·e·le·an** \(¦)prak¦sid·^əl¦ēən\ *adj, usu cap* [*Praxiteles*, 4th cent. B.C. Greek sculptor + E *-an*] **:** of, relating to, or having the characteristics of Praxiteles or his sculpture

**pray** \'prā\ *vb* -ED/-ING/-S [ME *preyen, prayen*, fr. OF *preier*, fr. L *precari*, fr. *prec-, prex* request, entreaty, prayer; akin to OE *gefrǣge* hearsay, report, *fricgan, frignan, frinan* to ask, inquire, OHG *frāga* question, *frāgēn* to ask, ON *frētt* question, *fregna* to inquire, find out, Goth *frailman* to find out by inquiry, Toch A *prak-* to ask, Skt *praś-* interrogation, *prcchati* he asks] *vt* **1 :** ENTREAT, IMPLORE**:** as **a :** to make supplication to (a god) **b** (1) **:** to ask (someone) to do something usu. humbly or as an inferior to a superior **:** CRAVE ⟨~*ed* the king to give them land⟩ — often used as a function word in introducing a question, request, or plea ⟨~ tell me the time⟩ ⟨~ let us hurry⟩; compare PLEASE (2) **:** to ask earnestly for (something) **:** supplicate for **:** BEG ⟨I know not how to ~ your patience —Shak.⟩ **c :** to ask (someone) for or on behalf of another ⟨we ~ you . . . be ye reconciled to God —2 Cor 5:20 (AV)⟩ **2** *obs* **:** to ask or entreat to come **:** INVITE **3 a :** to accomplish, put, or bring, by praying ⟨~ a soul out of purgatory⟩ **b :** to overcome (someone) by prayer — used with *down* or *out* ⟨he ~*ed* down his rival⟩ ~ *vi* **:** to make request with earnestness or zeal esp. for something desired **:** make entreaty or supplication **:** offer prayer to a divine being; *specif* **:** to address a god with adoration, confession, supplication, or thanksgiving — **pray in aid** *or* **pray aid :** to claim or call in aid (as when under English law calls are made upon another for assistance in proving one's title or right) — see AID 4 — **pray over :** to send up a prayer for **:** supplicate concerning; *often* **:** to publicly or ostentatiously offer prayer concerning the evil ways of ⟨*prayed over* by the elders of the church⟩

**praya** \'prīə\ *n* -S [Pg *praia*, fr. ML *plagia* hillside, shoreline — more at PLAYA] **:** BEACH, STRAND **:** WATERFRONT

**¹prayer** \'pra(a)(ə)r, 'pre(, |a\ *n* -S *often attrib* [ME *preyere, prayere*, fr. OF *preiere*, fr. ML *precaria* written petition, supplication, prayer, fr. L, fem. of *precarius* obtained by entreaty or prayer, fr. L *prec-, prex* request, entreaty, prayer + *-arius* -ary — more at PRAY] **1 a :** a solemn and humble approach to Divinity in word or thought usu. involving beseeching, petition, confession, praise, or thanksgiving ⟨devoted a moment to silent ~ before beginning his task⟩ **b :** an earnest request to someone for something**:** as (1) **:** the part of a petition or memorial (as to a legislature) that specifies the thing desired (2) **:** the part of a bill in equity or other pleading that specifies the relief sought (3) **:** a request (as by a charge to a jury) for action by the court (4) **:** a formal motion in the British Parliament to invalidate a ministerial order or regulation **c prayers** *pl* **:** earnest good wishes ⟨whatever you decide you have my ~*s*⟩ **2 :** the act or practice of praying **:** the addressing of words or thought to Divinity in petition, confession, praise, or thanksgiving ⟨public ~ was then an accepted custom⟩ ⟨friends and neighbors gathered in ~ for the dead⟩ **3 :** a religious service consisting chiefly of prayers — often used in pl. ⟨had regular family ~*s*⟩ **4 :** a set form of words used in praying **:** a formula of supplication, confession, praise, or thanksgiving addressed to God or an object of worship ⟨a book of ~*s* for different occasions⟩ **5 :** something prayed for **:** a subject of prayer ⟨God granted their ~⟩ **6 :** a slight or minimal chance (as to succeed or survive) ⟨a second-rate maritime power without a ~ of meeting military shipping needs —*N.Y. Times*⟩ ⟨hadn't a ~ to recover⟩

**syn** PRAYER, SUIT, PLEA, PETITION, APPEAL signify, in common, an earnest, usu. formal, request for something. PRAYER implies that the request is made to one in authority or power and usu. suggests humility and fervor ⟨a very long distance between what the Department of Justice asks for in its *prayer* for relief and what the courts will grant in the form of a remedy —E.S.Mason⟩ ⟨to all my tearful *prayers* —W.S.Gilbert⟩ SUIT implies a deferential and formal petition as to a court or legislative body, although the term is not common today except in legal use or in application to the addresses of a suitor to his loved one ⟨*suits* for violation of contracts are allowed against a union's funds —Philip Taft⟩ ⟨a *suit* in which the college trustees sought to defend their rights against the new political forces —A.C.Cole⟩ ⟨she returned his love, spurning the *suit* of . . . —*Amer. Guide Series: N.C.*⟩ PLEA usu. implies argument and urgent entreaty of which self-justification, a desire for vindication or support, or partisanship is often the motive ⟨his fiancée jilted him on the *plea* that he cared more for the house than for her —*Amer. Guide Series: Md.*⟩ ⟨a *plea* for postwar preparedness —*Current Biog.*⟩ ⟨a *plea* for international peace —Merle Curti⟩ PETITION implies a formal and specific request, often in writing, presented to a person or body that has power to grant it and usu. implying no humility or use of entreaty but rather the exercise of a right ⟨students who have exceeded the maximum number of absences will have a right to *petition* the Committee on Attendance for reinstatement —*Loyola Univ. Bull.*⟩ ⟨the *petition* must be addressed to the Commissioner of Patents . . . and must be signed by the inventor —*General Information Concerning Patents*⟩ ⟨divorce *petitions* —Robert Reid⟩ APPEAL implies the call for attention to and favorable consideration of one's plea, often suggesting an insistence, as in a legal appeal from an inferior to a superior court, or a plea to the emotions ⟨the *appeal* of the abandoned child —Joseph Conrad⟩ ⟨the *appeal* to sex —C.W.Cunnington⟩ ⟨make an *appeal* from the decision of the county court⟩

**²pray·er** \'prāə(r), -re(ə)r, -reə\ *n* -S [ME *preyere, prayere*, fr. *preyen, prayen* to pray + *-ere* -er — more at PRAY] **:** one that prays **:** SUPPLICANT

**prayer bead** *n* **1 prayer beads** *pl* **:** a string of beads by which prayers are counted; *specif* **:** ROSARY **2 :** JOB'S TEARS

**prayer bones** *n pl* **:** KNEES

**prayer book** *n* **1 :** a book containing prayers and often forms of worship and used in religious services or in private devotions **2** *slang* **:** a narrow piece of holystone used in the hand to scrub crevices in the deck of a ship

**prayer desk** *n* **:** PRIE-DIEU

**prayer·ful** \'pra(a)rfəl, -re|, |əf-\ *adj* **1 a :** given to prayer **:** DEVOUT **b :** characterized by or indicative of prayer **:** DEVOTIONAL **2 :** carefully thorough **:** EARNEST — **prayer·ful·ly** \-fəlē, -li\ *adv* — **prayer·ful·ness** \-lnəs\ *n* -ES

**prayerhouse** \'=,=\ *n* **:** a chapel or other place where services of prayer and worship are held

**prayer in aid :** AID PRAYER

**prayer·less** \-a(a)|rləs, -|əl-\ *adj* **:** using no prayer ⟨a ~ meeting⟩ — **prayer·less·ly** *adv* — **prayer·less·ness** *n* -ES

**prayer life** *n* **:** an individual's private practice of prayer ⟨the *prayer life* of Jesus⟩

**prayerlike** \'=,=\ *adj* **:** having the impact or form of prayer

**prayer meeting** *or* **prayer service** *n* **:** a meeting or gathering for prayer to God; *esp* **:** a Protestant Christian service of worship usu. held regularly on a week night and frequently highlighted by evangelistic or revivalistic preaching

**prayer plant** *n* **:** a maranta (*Maranta leuconeura kerchoviana*) that is native to Brazil but widely used as an ornamental foliage plant and that has large leaves with red spotting between the white purple-striped flowers

**prayer rug** *or* **prayer carpet** *or* **prayer mat** *n* **:** a small Oriental rug used by Muslims to kneel on when praying and characteristically showing the design of a mihrab

**prayers** *pl of* PRAYER

**prayer scarf** *or* **prayer shawl** *also* **prayer cloak** *n* **:** TALLITH

**prayer stick** *or* **prayer feather** *or* **prayer plume** *n* **:** a feather-decorated stick used by Indians of the southwestern U.S. to convey symbolically a ceremonial offering and a supplicatory prayer

**prayer stool** *n* **:** a stool to kneel on when praying

**prayer tower** *n* **:** MINARET

**prayer wheel** *n* **:** a cylinder of wood or metal revolving on an axis and containing written prayers that are considered efficacious by Tibetan Buddhists

**prayerwise** \'=,=\ *adv* **:** in the manner of or by way of prayer

**¹praying** *n* -S [ME *preying, praying*, fr. gerund of *preyen, prayen* to pray — more at PRAY] **:** the act, an instance, or the custom of making prayer

**²praying** *adj* [ME *preying, praying*, fr. pres. part. of *preyen*,

prayen] : habituated or devoted to prayer : accustomed to pray ⟨a ~ man⟩ — **pray·ing·ly** *adv*
**praying indian** *n, usu cap P&I* : a member of the Massachuset people converted by John Eliot and living in one of six villages in eastern Massachusetts
**praying mantis** *also* **praying mantid** *n* [so called fr. the posture of such insects, with the forelimbs extended as though in prayer] : MANTIS; *esp* : the common mantis (*Mantis religiosa*)
**praying shawl** *also* **praying scarf** *n* : TALLITH
**prays** *pres 3d sing of* PRAY
**prchst** *abbr* parachutist
**prcht** *abbr* parachute
**pre-** *prefix* [ME, fr. OF & L; OF, fr. L *prae-*, fr. *prae* — more at FOR] **1 a** (1) : earlier than : prior to : before ⟨*pre*departure⟩ ⟨*pre*historic⟩ ⟨*pre*payment⟩ ⟨*pre*-Slavic⟩ ⟨*pre*-Victorian⟩ (2) : preparatory or prerequisite to ⟨*pre*medical⟩ ⟨*pre*professional⟩ (3) : in a formative, incipient, or preliminary stage ⟨*pre*cartilage⟩ **b** : in advance : beforehand ⟨*pre*cut⟩ ⟨*pre*judge⟩ ⟨*pre*plan⟩ **2 a** : in front of : before ⟨*pre*anal⟩ ⟨*pre*axial⟩ ⟨*pre*molar⟩ **b** : at the front : anterior : constituting a front part ⟨*pre*abdomen⟩ ⟨*pre*sternum⟩ **3 a** : exceedingly ⟨*pre*noble⟩ ⟨*pre*adore⟩ **b** *petrography* : predominating in a ratio greater than 5:3 ⟨*pre*alkalic⟩ ⟨*pre*calcic⟩ ⟨*pre*chloric⟩
**pre·abdomen** \(ˌ)prē+\ *n* [*pre-* + *abdomen*] : the enlarged anterior portion of the abdomen of a scorpion
**pre·acanthella** \ˌprē+\ *n* [NL, fr. *pre-* + *acanthella*] : ACANTHELLA
**1preach** \ˈprēch\ *vb* -ED/-ING/-ES [ME *prechen*, fr. OF *preechier, prechier, precher*, fr. LL *praedicare*, fr. L, to proclaim publicly, praise, fr. *prae-* pre- + *dicare* to proclaim, dedicate — more at DICTION] *vi* **1** : to proclaim the gospel : discourse publicly on a religious subject or from a text of Scripture : deliver a sermon ⟨~*ed* on grace to a large congregation⟩ **2** : to urge acceptance or abandonment of an idea or course of action ⟨~*ed* against speculation and in favor of honest investment —Arthur Pound⟩; *specif* : to exhort in an officious or tiresome manner ⟨kept ~*ing* at his students about studying⟩ ~ *vt* **1** : to set forth in a sermon or a formal religious address ⟨the minister's duty to ~ the Word of God⟩ ⟨~ the gospel⟩ **2** : to advocate earnestly (as by public speaking or writing) ⟨~ the doctrine of states' rights⟩ : INCULCATE ⟨puppet shows that ~ safety —*Lamp*⟩ **3** : to utter publicly (as a sermon) : DELIVER ⟨~*ed* a homily on forgiveness⟩ **4** : to bring, put, or affect by preaching ⟨~*ed* the . . . church out of debt —*Amer. Guide Series: Va.*⟩
**2preach** \"\ *n* -ES : EXHORTATION
**preach·able** \-chəbəl\ *adj* : suitable for preaching from or about
**preach·er** \-chə(r)\ *n* -S [ME *prechour*, fr. OF *preecheur, precheur*, fr. *preechier, prechier* to preach + *-eur* -or — more at PREACH] **1** : one that preaches: **a** : one who discourses publicly on religious subjects : one whose function is to preach sermons : MINISTER **b** : one who inculcates or exhorts something earnestly or officiously ⟨the ~ of a nobler creed of morals —John Buchan⟩ ⟨a ~ of class hatred⟩ **2** : DOMINICAN
**preacher bird** *also* **preacher** *n* -S : RED-EYED VIREO
**preach·er·less** \-chə(r)ləs\ *adj* : having no preacher
**preach·er·ly** \-lē\ *adj* : of or befitting a preacher ⟨a ~ attitude⟩
**preach·er·ship** \-chə(r),ship\ *n* : the office of preacher ⟨appointed to a university ~⟩
**preach·i·fi·ca·tion** \ˌprēchəfəˈkāshən\ *n* -S [fr. *preachify*, after such pairs as E *edify: edification*] : an act or product of preachifying
**preach·i·fy** \ˈprēchə,fī\ *vi* -ED/-ING/-ES [*1preach* + *-ify*] : to preach ineptly or tediously
**preach·i·ly** \-chəlē\ *or* **preach·ing·ly** *adv* : in a manner suiting a sermon or preachment
**preach·i·ness** \-chēnəs\ *n* -ES : the quality or state of being preachy
**preaching** *n* -S [ME *preching*, fr. gerund of *prechen* to preach — more at PREACH] **1** : the act, practice, or art of delivering a sermon or exhortation **2** : SERMON, PREACHMENT **3** : a public religious service emphasizing a sermon
**preaching cross** *n* : a cross sometimes surmounting a pulpit erected outdoors at a preaching place
**preach·ment** \ˈprēchmənt\ *n* -S [ME *prechement*, fr. MF, fr. *precher* to preach + *-ment* — more at PREACH] **1** : the act or practice of preaching ⟨convert men to an obedience of law by ~ and moral suasion —Glenn Hegley⟩ **2** : an instance of preaching : SERMON, EXHORTATION; *specif* : a tedious or unwelcome exhortation or discourse ⟨twist the facts into a crusade or a ~ —*Current Biog.*⟩
**preachy** \-chē\ *adj* -ER/-EST : given to preaching or having a preaching style : marked by obvious moralizing : DIDACTIC ⟨have been ~ in tone and have urged Soviet people to live according to the precepts of Marxism-Leninism —F.C. Barghoorn⟩
**1pre·adamite** \prē+\ *n* [NL *praeadamita*, fr. L *prae-* pre- + *Adam* (the first man in the Bible) + *-ita* -ite] **1** : an inhabitant of the earth before Adam **2** : one who holds that men existed before Adam; *specif* : a follower of the doctrine of Isaac La Peyrère that only the Jews are descendants of Adam and that the Gentiles are descendants of men who lived before Adam
**2pre·adamite** \"+\ *or* **pre·adamic** \ˌprē¦ə+\ *or* **pre·adamical** \(ˌ)prē¦adə¦mid·əkəl\ *adj* : existing before Adam : of a time prior to that of Adam
**pre·adamitism** \prē+\ *n* : belief in the existence of preadamites
**pre·adapt** \ˌprē+\ *vt* [*pre-* + *adapt*] : to endow with preadaptation
**pre·adaptation** \(ˌ)prē+\ *n* [*pre-* + *adaptation*] **1** : adaptation prior in time to some specified change or condition **2 a** : the possession by an organism or group of characters that are not adapted to the ancestral environment but that favor its survival in some other environment **b** : a preadaptive character
**pre·adaptive** \ˌprē+\ *adj* : of, relating to, or characterized by preadaptation
**pre·admission** \ˌprē+\ *n* [*pre-* + *admission*] : admission (as of steam or a combustible mixture) to an engine cylinder before the back stroke is completed with intent to increase the cushioning
**pre·adolescence** \(ˌ)prē\ *n* [*pre-* + *adolescence*] : the period of human development just preceding adolescence; *specif* : the period between the approximate ages of 9 and 12
**1pre·adolescent** \"+\ *adj* [*pre-* + *adolescent*] **1** : of, characteristic of, or occurring during preadolescence ⟨the ~ years⟩ ⟨~ changes⟩ ⟨~ problems⟩ **2** : that is in the stage of preadolescence ⟨a ~ girl⟩
**2pre·adolescent** \"\ *n* : a preadolescent child
**pre·adult** \ˌprē+\ *adj* [*pre-* + *adult*] : preceding adulthood
**pre·agonal** \(ˈ)prē+\ *adj* [*pre-* + *agonal*] : immediately preceding the death agony
**1pre·am·ble** \ˈprē,ambəl, -,aam-, ˌ=ˈ==\ *n* -S [ME, fr. MF *preambule*, fr. ML *praeambulum*, fr. LL, neut. of *praeambulus* walking in front, fr. L *prae-* pre- + *-ambulus* (fr. *ambulare* to walk) — more at AMBLE] **1** : an introductory part (as to a book, document) : INTRODUCTION, PREFACE; *specif* : the introductory part of a statute, ordinance, or regulation that states the reasons and intent of the law or regulation or is used for other explanatory purposes (as to recite facts knowledge of which is necessary to an understanding of the law or to define or limit the meanings of words used in the law) — compare PURVIEW **2** : an introductory fact or circumstance : PRELIMINARY; *esp* : one that gives indication of what is to follow
**2preamble** \"\ *vi* -ED/-ING/-S : to make a preamble
**pre·am·bu·lar** \(ˈ)=¦byələ(r)\ *or* **pre·am·bu·lary** \-,lerē\ *or* **pre·am·bu·la·to·ry** \-lə,tōrē\ *adj* [ML *praeambulum* + E *-ar* or *-ary* or *-atory*] : of, relating to, or of the character of a preamble : INTRODUCTORY, PRELIMINARY
**pre·am·bu·late** \=ˈ=lyə,lāt\ *vi* -ED/-ING/-S [ML *praeambulum* + E *-ate*] : to make a preamble — **pre·am·bu·la·tion** \(ˌ)==,==ˈlāshən\ *n*
**pre·amp** \ˈprē,amp, =ˈ=\ *n* [by shortening] : PREAMPLIFIER
**pre·amplifier** \(ˈ)prē+\ *n* [*pre-* + *amplifier*] : an amplifier designed to amplify extremely weak signals obtained from a microphone, phonograph pickup, or television camera before the signals are fed to additional amplifier circuits

**1pre·anal** \"+\ *adj* [*pre-* + *anal*] : situated in front of the anus ⟨a ~ gland⟩
**2preanal** \"\ *n* : a preanal part (as a scale or plate)
**1pre·anesthetic** \(ˌ)prē+\ *adj* [*pre-* + *anesthetic*] : used before administration of an anesthetic ⟨~ medication⟩ ⟨~ agent⟩
**2preanesthetic** \"\ *n* : a substance used to induce an initial light state of anesthesia
**pre·animism** \(ˈ)prē+\ *n* [*pre-* + *animism*] : a theory that preceding animism there was a definite concept of the supernatural among primitive people; *specif* : ANIMATISM
**pre·apprehension** \(ˌ)prē+\ *n* [*pre-* + *apprehension*] **1** : an apprehension or opinion formed before examination or knowledge : a preconceived notion **2** : a fear of some evil that may come about : FOREBODING
**pre·arrange** \ˌprē+\ *vt* [*pre-* + *arrange*] : to arrange beforehand — **pre·arrangement** \"+\ *n*
**pre·aspirated** \(ˈ)prē+\ *adj* [*pre-* + *aspirated*] : having at the onset of articulation some degree of \h\ ⟨a ~ stop consonant⟩
**pre·aspiration** \(ˌ)prē+\ *n* [*pre-* + *aspiration*] : the addition of a preaspirated sound
**pre·assembled** \ˌprē+\ *adj* [*pre-* + *assembled*] : assembled beforehand
**pre·assigned** \"+\ *adj* [*pre-* + *assigned*] : assigned beforehand
**preatomic** \ˌprē+\ *adj* [*pre-* + *atomic*] : of or relating to a time before the use of the atom bomb and atomic energy ⟨the ~ age⟩ ⟨~ weapons⟩
**pre·audience** \(ˈ)prē+\ *n* [*pre-* + *audience*] : the right to be heard before another is heard; *specif* : precedence at the bar among barristers and law officers
**pre·audit** \"+\ *n* [*pre-* + *audit*] : an audit made prior to the final settlement of a transaction — contrasted with *postaudit*
**pre·axiad** \(ˈ)prē¦akse,ad\ *adv* [*pre-* + *axi-* + *-ad*] : PREAXIALLY
**pre·axial** \(ˈ)prē+\ *adj* [*pre-* + *axial*] : situated in front of the axis of the body
**pre·axially** \"+\ *adv* : in a preaxial manner
**preb** *abbr* prebend; prebendary
**pre·bait** \ˈprē+ˌ-\ *vt* [*pre-* + *bait*] : to attract (rodents or other animals) to a feeding site with food esp. as a preliminary to a control campaign using poisoned baits
**pre·bath** \"+ˌ-\ *n* [*pre-* + *bath*] : a fluid (as a hardening solution or wetting agent) in which exposed photographic materials are immersed before development
**preb·end** \ˈprebənd\ *n* -S [ME *prebende*, fr. MF, fr. ML *praebenda*, fr. LL, subsistence allowance granted by the state, fr. L, fem. of *praebendus*, gerundive of *praebēre* to hold forth, offer, supply, contr. of *praehibēre*, fr. *prae-* pre- + *-hibēre* (fr. *habēre* to hold, have) — more at GIVE] **1** : the stipend or maintenance granted out of the estate of a cathedral or collegiate church to a canon or member of a chapter thereof **2 a** : the land or tithe from which a prebend comes **b** : the holding of such land or tithe as a benefice **3** : PREBENDARY
**preben·dal** \prəˈbendᵊl, ˈpreban-\ *adj* : of, relating to, or being a prebend or prebendary : holding a prebend
**prebendal stall** *n* **1** : a prebendary's stall in a cathedral **2** : a prebendary's benefice
**preb·en·dary** \ˈprebən,derē\ *n* -ES [ML *praebendarius*, fr. *praebenda* prebend + L *-arius* -ary] **1 a** : a member of a cathedral or collegiate church chapter receiving a prebend in consideration for his officiating at stated times in the church **b** : an honorary canon in the Church of England with the title but not the emoluments of a prebend **2** *obs* : a prebendary's benefice or office : PREBEND
**1pre·bind** \"+ˌ-\ *vt* [*pre-* + *bind*] : to bind (a book) in durable materials esp. for circulating library use; *often* : to give (a book) a durable original binding — compare REBIND
**2pre·bind** *or* **pre·bound** \"+ˌ-\ *n* : a prebound book
**prebloom spray** \ˈprē¦=-\ *n* [*prebloom* fr. *pre-* + *bloom*] : a pesticidal spray applied to orchard trees between the time the buds show first color and the full opening of blossoms
**pre·board** \"+ˌ-\ *vt* [*pre-* + *board*] : to place (a stocking or garment) on a board before scouring and dyeing
**pre·break** \"+ˌ-\ *vt* [*pre-* + *break*] : to bend (paperboard) in score lines to aid in forming into final shape
**pre·bronchial** \(ˈ)prē+\ *adj* [*pre-* + *bronchial*] : situated in front of the bronchus; *esp* : being an air sac on each side of the esophagus of a bird
**prec** *abbr* preceding
**1pre·cambrian** \(ˈ)prē+\ *adj, usu cap* [*pre-* + *Cambrian*] : prior to the Cambrian : of or relating to all of geological history prior to the Cambrian — see GEOLOGIC TIME table
**2precambrian** \"\ *n, usu cap* : the Precambrian era or system of rocks
**precambrian shield** *n, usu cap P* : the nuclear area of Precambrian rocks present in each of the continents
**1pre·cancel** \(ˈ)prē+\ *vt* [*pre-* + *cancel*] **1** : to cancel (an adhesive or imprinted postage stamp) in advance of use usu. with printed horizontal bars and the name of the city or city and state of the user for use by special permit on certain classes of mail sent in large quantities **2** : to precancel the imprinted stamp on (a stamped envelope or postcard) — **pre·cancellation** \(ˌ)prē+\ *n*
**2precancel** \"\ *n* : a precanceled stamp
**pre·can·cer·osis** \(ˌ)prē,kan(t)səˈrōsəs\ *n, pl* **precancero·ses** \-ō,sēz\ [NL, fr. ISV *precancerous* + NL *-osis*] : a condition marked by the presence of one or more precancerous lesions
**pre·cancerous** \(ˈ)prē+\ *adj* [ISV *pre-* + *cancerous*] : that may become cancerous ⟨a ~ lesion⟩ : tending to become malignant ⟨all intestinal polyps are ~ —E.R.Fisher & R.B. Turnbull⟩
**pre·capitalist** *or* **pre·capitalistic** \"+\ *adj* [*pre-* + *capitalist* or *capitalistic*] : characterized by independent individual production and direct marketing
**pre·car·i·al** \prēˈka(a)rēəl, -ker-, -kār-\ *adj* : of, relating to, or being a precarium ⟨~ transactions⟩ ⟨~ tenure⟩
**pre·car·i·ous** \-rēəs\ *adj* [L *precarius* obtained by entreaty or prayer, obtained by mere favor, doubtful, uncertain — more at PRAYER] **1** *archaic* : depending on the will or pleasure of another : held on sufferance : liable to be changed or lost at the pleasure of another **2** : dependent upon uncertain premises : DUBIOUS **3** *obs* : IMPORTUNATE, BEGGING **4 a** : dependent on chance circumstances, unknown conditions, or uncertain developments : UNCERTAIN ⟨unfavorable weather . . . and too great dependence on a single ~ crop do not bring disaster as they once did —Samuel Van Valkenburg & Ellsworth Huntington⟩ **b** : characterized by a lack of security or stability that threatens with danger ⟨the ~ safety of an ice floe —G. de Q. Robin⟩ ⟨faced trouble inside his ~ four-party coalition government —*Time*⟩ **5** : PRECARIAL **syn** see DANGEROUS
**pre·car·i·ous·ly** *adv* : in a precarious manner ⟨perched ~ on a narrow board, sixty feet above the floor —Robert Berkelman⟩
**pre·car·i·ous·ness** *n* -ES : the quality or state of being precarious
**pre·car·i·um** \-rēəm\ *n, pl* **precar·ia** \-rēə\ [L, fr. neut. of *precarius*] **1** *Roman, civil, & Scots law* **a** : something granted or lent to be returned or redelivered at the will of the grantor **b** : a contract making a loan or grant upon such terms or the tenure by which it is held : a tenancy at will **2** *medieval European feudal law* : any of various estates or tenures that grew out of the original precarium characterized by more or less uncertainty or limitation of the duration and arduousness of the conditions of tenure — compare BENEFICE
**pre·cartilage** \(ˈ)prē+\ *n* [*pre-* + *cartilage*] : embryonic tissue from which cartilage is formed — **pre·cartilaginous** \(ˌ)prē+\ *adj*
**pre·cast** \ˈprē+ˌ-\ *vt* [*pre-* + *cast*] : to cast and finish (as concrete slabs, piles) before placing in position
**1prec·a·tive** \ˈprekəd·iv\ *adj* [LL *precativus*, fr. L *precatus* (past part. of *precari* to entreat, pray) + *-ivus* -ive — more at PRAY] **1** : PRECATORY, BESEECHING ⟨a ~ utterance⟩ **2** : of, relating to, or constituting a verb form expressing a wish or request
**2precative** \"\ *n* -S : a precative verb form
**prec·a·to·ry** \-kə,tōrē\ *adj* [LL *precatorius*, fr. L *precatus* + *-orius* -ory] : of, relating to, or expressive of entreaty : SUPPLICATORY
**precatory trust** *n* : a trust created by precatory words construed as mandatory

**precatory words** *n pl* : words of recommendation, request, entreaty, wish, or expectation employed in wills and other legal instrument and often resulting in no effective gift or rights being created
**1pre·cau·tion** \prēˈkóshən, prəˈk-\ *n* [F *précaution*, fr. LL *praecaution-, praecautio*, fr. L *praecautus* (past part. of *praecavēre* to guard against, fr. *prae-* pre- + *cavēre* to be on one's guard) + *-ion-, -io* -ion — more at SHOW] **1** : previous caution or care : caution employed foresightedly ⟨warned of the need for ~⟩ **2** : a measure taken beforehand to ward off evil or secure good or success : an act of foresight : a precautionary act ⟨take ~s against accident⟩
**2precaution** \"\ *vt* : to put (a person) on guard : FOREWARN
**pre·cau·tion·ary** \-,nerē, -ri\ *also* **pre·cau·tion·al** \-nᵊl\ *adj* : of, relating to, or having the character of a precaution : advising, suggesting, or using caution beforehand ⟨~ measures against epidemic⟩ ⟨helped avert panic by ~ advice⟩
**pre·cau·tious** \-shəs\ *adj* : using precaution : PRECAUTIONARY — **pre·cau·tious·ly** *adv* — **pre·cau·tious·ness** *n*
**pre·cava** \(ˈ)prē+\ *n, pl* **precavae** [NL, fr. *pre-* + *cava*] **1** : SUPERIOR VENA CAVA **2** : either of a pair of veins in a squid that passes through the kidney and enters the branchial heart of the same side of the body — **pre·caval** \"+\ *adj*
**precaval sinus** *n* : DUCT OF CUVIER
**pre·ced·able** \prēˈsēdəbəl, prəˈs-\ *adj* : that can be preceded
**1pre·cede** \-ēd\ *vb* -ED/-ING/-S [ME *preceden*, fr. MF *preceder*, fr. L *praecedere*, fr. *prae-* pre- + *cedere* to go — more at CEDE] *vt* **1** *obs* : to go before in quality or degree : EXCEED, SURPASS **2** : to be, go, or come before in rank, dignity, or importance : take precedence of ⟨countries that ~ ours in per capita contributions⟩ **3** : to be, go, or come before in arrangement or sequence : be, go, or move before or in front of ⟨solidly constructed mansion *preceded* by a large oval lawn —E.E.Cummings⟩ **4** : to go before in order of time : be earlier than : occur before with relation to something ⟨military penetration *preceded* settlement —*Amer. Guide Series: Minn.*⟩ **5** : to cause to be preceded : PREFACE, INTRODUCE — used with *by* or *with* before the instrumental object ⟨~ his address with a welcome to the visitors⟩ **6** : to rise earlier than and move in front of (another star) in the apparent rotation of the heavens ~ *vi* : to go or come before : have precedence ⟨the statistics for the year that *preceded*⟩
**2precede** \"\ *n* -S : a brief item placed before a newspaper story to give its latest development
**prece·dence** \÷ˈpresədən(t)s, prēˈsēdᵊn(t)s, prəˈs- *also* ÷ˈpresədᵊn- *sometimes* ÷ˈprestən-\ *n* -S **1** : the fact of preceding in time : the earlier place or occurrence : ANTECEDENCE **2** : the right or privilege of preceding others ⟨dealt cards for ~ —Evelyn Waugh⟩; *specif* : the right to superior honor on a ceremonial or formal social occasion ⟨ladies always have the ~ of gentlemen —Noreen Routledge⟩ **3** : the order of preference (as in seats of honor or initiative of departure) observed usu. according to rank on ceremonial or formal social occasions ⟨seated the officials and diplomats according to ~⟩ **4** : consideration before others : priority of importance : PREFERENCE ⟨weapons must . . . take ~ of exports —Vera M. Dean⟩ ⟨a motion to adjourn has ~ over all others⟩
**prece·den·cy** \-nsē\ *n* -ES : PRECEDENCE
**1pre·ce·dent** \(ˈ)prēˈsēdᵊnt, prəˈs-, *or like* 2PRECEDENT\ *adj* [ME, fr. MF, fr. L *praecedent-, praecedens*, pres. part. of *praecedere* to precede — more at PRECEDE] **1** : going before in time : ANTERIOR, PRECEDING, ANTECEDENT ⟨a series of ~ causes going back to infinity —C.H.Whiteley⟩ **2** : going before in order or arrangement ⟨a ~ theorem⟩
**2prec·e·dent** \ˈpresədənt *also* -əd·ᵊnt *or* -estənt *sometimes* -rēs- *or* -rez(ə)d- *or* -ə,dent\ *n* -S [ME, fr. MF, *precedent*, adj.] **1 a** : something that precedes; *esp* : an earlier occurrence of a similar character ⟨~*s* would seem to show that the reduction of armaments is conducive to war —F.A.Voigt⟩ **b** : a rough draft of a writing : ORIGINAL **c** : TOKEN, SIGN **2 a** (1) : something done or said that may serve as an example or rule to authorize or justify a subsequent act of the same or an analogous kind : an authoritative example ⟨took the exploits of the American colonists as a ~ for subversive activity⟩ (2) : the norm for subsequent practice set by such a precedent ⟨the founder also set the ~ of only paying himself a salary —*Current Biog.*⟩ (3) : prevailing custom established by long practice : CONVENTION ⟨followed historical ~ in organizing the town⟩ ⟨broke ~ when they elected a woman⟩ **b** : a judicial decision, a form of proceeding, or course of action that serves as a rule for future determinations in similar or analogous cases : an authority to be followed in courts of justice — compare DICTUM **3 a** : a person or thing serving as a model **b** *obs* : SPECIMEN, INSTANCE
**3prec·e·dent** \-ent *also* -ənt *or* -ᵊnt\ *vt* -ED/-ING/-S : to furnish with or support or justify by a precedent
**precedent condition** *n* : CONDITION PRECEDENT
**prec·e·den·tial** \ˌpresəˈdenchəl *sometimes* -rēsə- *or* -rezə-\ *adj* [*2precedent* + *-ial*] **1** : having the character of or constituting a precedent : having force as an example for imitation ⟨~ acts⟩ ⟨a ~ case⟩ **2** : having precedence : PRELIMINARY, ANTECEDENT
**prec·e·dent·less** *pronunc at* 2PRECEDENT + ləs\ *adj* : having no precedent
**prece·dent·ly** *pronunc at* 1PRECEDENT + lē *or* lī\ *adv* [*1precedent* + *-ly*] : BEFOREHAND
**preceding** \(ˈ)=¦==\ *adj* [fr. pres. part. of *precede*] **1** : that precedes : going before (as in order, rank, time, or place) ⟨had not eaten since the ~ day⟩ ⟨already stated in the ~ paragraph⟩ **2** : west of : moving in the direction toward which stars appear to travel by diurnal motion — compare FOLLOWING
**precel** *vi* **precelled; precelled; precelling; precels** [ME *precellen*, fr. L *praecellere*, fr. *prae-* pre- + *-cellere* to rise, project — more at EXCEL] *obs* : SURPASS, EXCEL
**precellence** *or* **precellency** *n* [*precellence* fr. ME, fr. LL *praecellentia*, fr. L *praecellent-, praecellens* (pres. part. of *praecellere*) + *-ia* -y; *precellency* fr. LL *praecellentia*] *obs* : EXCELLENCE, PREEMINENCE
**pre·censor** \(ˈ)prē+\ *vt* [*pre-* + *censor*] : to censor (a publication or film) before its release to the public ⟨only half a dozen states ~ movies —*Scientific Monthly*⟩
**pre·cent** \prēˈsent, prəˈs-\ *vb* -ED/-ING/-S [L *praecentare*, fr. *praecentus*, past part. of *praecinere*] *vi* : to act as precentor : lead a choir or congregation in singing ~ *vt* : to lead in singing (as a psalm)
**pre·cen·tor** \-ntə(r)\ *n* -S [LL *praecentor* leader of music, fr. L *praecentus* (past part. of *praecinere* to sing or play before — an audience —, fr. *prae-* pre- + *-cinere*, fr. *canere* to sing) + *-or* — more at CHANT] **1** : a leader of the choir in a cathedral, collegiate, or monastic church **2** : an official in a cathedral church ranking in cathedrals of the Old Foundation next to the dean and charged with various administrative duties; *esp* : one responsible for directing the arrangements for divine service **3** : the leader of congregational singing in a church having no choir and often no instrumental accompaniment **4** : CANTOR 2
**pre·cen·to·ri·al** \ˌprē,senˈtōrēəl\ *adj* : of or relating to a precentor
**pre·cen·tor·ship** \prēˈsentə(r),ship, prəˈs-\ *n* : the office, function, or term of a precentor
**pre·central** \(ˈ)prē+\ *adj* [*pre-* + *central*] **1** : situated in front of the central sulcus of the brain ⟨the ~ sulcus⟩ **2** : of or relating to a precentrum
**pre·centrum** \"+\ *n* [NL, fr. *pre-* + *centrum*] **1** : a distinct anterior portion of the centrum of a vertebra commonly bearing the neural and hemal arches in a fish that has vertebra with postcentra **2** : one of an alternate series of vertebral centra occurring in some fishes and having both hemal and neural arches
**pre·cept** \ˈprē,sept\ *n* -S [ME, fr. L *praeceptum*, fr. neut. of *praeceptus*, past part. of *praecipere* to take beforehand, give rules or precepts, admonish, instruct, fr. *prae-* pre- + *-cipere* (fr. *capere* to take, seize) — more at HEAVE] **1** : a command or principle intended as a general rule of action ⟨the dominance of his party was the most important ~ of his life —Carol L. Thompson⟩: as **a** : a commandment enjoined respecting moral conduct ⟨observe the sixth commandment not as a ~ of divine law but as a counsel of profitable prudence —W.L. Sullivan⟩ **b** : a working rule respecting the technique of an art or science ⟨by ~ and example was largely instrumental in

rescuing English poetry —Gerald Bullett⟩ **2 :** a written order or mandate issued by legally constituted authority to a person commanding or authorizing him to do something: as **a :** an order, warrant, or writ issued pursuant to law to an administrative officer; *usu* **:** a command in the nature of civil or criminal process **b :** the direction or command of a feudal superior to an agent or official to admit a tenant to occupancy ⟨the ~ of sasine in Scots law⟩ **c** *Brit* **:** an order requiring payment or collection of a local tax **syn** see LAW

**pre·cept·ee** \ˌprē,sep'tē; prē'‚‚, prə̇-\ *n* -s [*preceptor* + *-ee*] **:** one that works for and studies under a preceptor in order to obtain practical professional experience and training ⟨a ~ in urology⟩ — compare INTERN

**preceptial** *adj* [*precept* + *-ial*] *obs* **:** PRECEPTIVE

**pre·cep·tion** \prē'sepshən, prə̇s-\ *n* -s [L *praeception-, praeceptio,* fr. *praeceptus* (past part. of *praecipere* to take beforehand) + *-ion-, -io* -ion — more at PRECEPT] *Roman law* **:** the taking before general distribution of an estate of something as a legacy under an option to select granted by the will to the legatee

**pre·cept·ist** \'prē,septə̇st\ *n* -s [*precept* + *-ist*] **:** a maker of or believer in precepts **:** DOGMATIST

**pre·cep·tive** \prē'septiv, prə̇'s-, -tēv\ *adj* [ME, fr. MF *preceptif,* fr. L *praeceptivus,* fr. *praeceptus* (past part. of *praecipere* to take beforehand, give rules or precepts to, instruct) + *-ivus* -ive — more at PRECEPT] **:** giving precepts **:** having the character of a precept **:** MANDATORY, DIDACTIC ⟨the ~ parts of the Bible⟩ ⟨~ grammar⟩ — **pre·cep·tive·ly** \-tə̇vlē, -li\ *adv*

**precept of cla·re con·stat** \-,kla(a)rē'känz,tat\ [*clare constat* fr. L, it is clearly established] *Scots law* **:** a deed in which a superior recognizes the title of the heir of a deceased vassal or tenant to enter upon the superior's land — compare WRIT OF CLARE CONSTAT

**pre·cep·tor** \prē'septə(r), prə̇'s-, 'prē,s-\ *n* -s [ME *preceptur,* fr. L *praeceptor* teacher, instructor, fr. *praeceptus* (past part. of *praecipere*) + *-or*] **1 a :** TEACHER, TUTOR **b :** the headmaster or principal of a school **2** [ML *praeceptor,* fr. L] **:** the head of a preceptory of Knights Templars **3 a :** a practicing physician who takes an undergraduate medical student as a resident student and gives him personal training in the practice of medicine **b :** a specialist in a branch of medicine or surgery who takes a young physician as a resident student and gives him personal training in his specialty ⟨a ~ in obstetrics and gynecology⟩

**¹pre·cep·to·ri·al** \ˌprē,sep'tōrēəl\ *adj* [*preceptor* + *-ial*] **1 :** of or relating to a preceptor ⟨~ duties⟩ **2 :** making use of preceptors ⟨~ system⟩

**²preceptorial** \"\ *n* -s **:** a class or course given at some colleges and universities for advanced students and emphasizing independent reading, informal discussion in small groups, and individual conferences with a teacher

**pre·cep·tor·ship** \prē'septə(r),ship, prə̇'s-, 'prē,s-\ *n* **1 :** the position of a preceptor **2 :** the state of being a preceptee **:** a period of training under a preceptor

**pre·cep·to·ry** \-tərē\ *n* -ES [ML *praeceptoria,* fr. *praeceptor* preceptor (among the Knights Templars) + L *-ia* -y — more at PRECEPTOR] **1 a :** a subordinate house or community of the Knights Templars established on one of the provincial estates of the order; *broadly* **:** COMMANDERY 2a(1) **b :** COMMANDERY 3 **2 a :** the manor or estate supporting a preceptory **b :** the buildings housing a preceptory

**pre·cep·tress** \-ptrə̇s\ *n* -ES [*preceptor* + *-ess*] **:** a female preceptor

**pre·ceramic** \ˌprē+\ *adj* [*pre-* + *ceramic*] **:** of or relating to an age or culture prior to the period when pottery making appears ⟨~ epoch⟩ ⟨~ archaeological site⟩

**pre·ces** \'prē,sēz\ *n pl* [L, prayers, pl. of *prec-, prex* prayer — more at PRAY] **:** short petitions said in liturgical worship in alternation by the minister and congregation

**pre·cess** \prē'ses, prə̇'s-\ *vi* -ED/-ING/-ES [back-formation fr. *precession*] **:** to progress with a movement of precession ⟨will cause the axis to ~ about the tangent —*Nature*⟩

**pre·ces·sion** \-eshən\ *n* -s [NL *praecession-, praecessio,* fr. ML, action of preceding, fr. L *praecessus* (past part. of *praecedere* to precede) + *-ion-, -io* -ion — more at PRECEDE] **:** a comparatively slow gyration of the rotation axis of a spinning body (as a top) about another line intersecting it so as to describe a cone caused by the application of a torque tending to change the direction of the rotation axis and being a motion continuously at right angles to the plane of the torque producing it

**pre·ces·sion·al** \-shənᵊl, -shnəl\ *adj* **:** of or relating to precession ⟨~ movement⟩

**precession of the equinoxes** [trans. of NL *praecessio aequinoctiorum*] **:** a slow westward motion of the equinoctial points along the ecliptic caused by the action of sun and moon upon the protuberant matter about the earth's equator in connection with its diurnal rotation

**pre–chellean** \(ˈ)prē+\ *adj, usu cap C* [*pre-* + *Chellean*] **:** of, relating to, or constituting a Lower Pleistocene culture preceding the Abbevillian and characterized by crudely flaked stone hand axes and rostrocarinates

**pre·chelonian** \ˌprē+\ *n* [*pre-* + *chelonian*] **:** an actual or hypothetical primitive reptile considered to be ancestral to modern turtles

**pre·chlorination** \(ˌ)prē+\ *n* [*pre-* + *chlorination*] **:** chlorination of water before filtration

**pre·chordal** \(ˈ)prē+\ *adj* [*pre-* + *chordal*] **:** anterior to the notochord — used esp. of the trabeculae of an embryonic cranium

**pre–christian** \"+\ *adj, usu cap C* [*pre-* + *Christian*] **1 :** of or being a time before the beginning of the Christian era ⟨the *pre-Christian* centuries⟩ **2 :** of or being a time before the introduction or prevalence of Christianity in a locality

**pre·chrome** \"+\ *adj* [*pre-* + *chrome*] **:** CHROME-MORDANT

**pre·ci·bal** \(ˈ)prē'sībəl\ *adj* [*pre-* + LL *cibalis* of food, fr. L *cibus* food + *-alis* -al — more at CIBARIAL] **:** occurring before meals

**pré·cieuse** \(ˈ)prās¦y|ə(r)z, ¦prāsē¦ yə(r)|, |ə̄z\ *n, pl* **précieuses** \"\ [F, fr. *précieuse,* adj.] **:** an affected woman of polite society; *esp* **:** one of the literary women of the French salons of the 17th century

**¹pré·cieux** \|ə, |ər(·), |ə̄\ *or* **pré·cieuse** \|ə(r)z, |ə̄z\ *adj* [F *précieux,* masc., lit., precious (fr. OF *precios, precieus*), *précieuse,* fem. of *précieux* — more at PRECIOUS] **:** extremely or excessively refined **:** AFFECTED ⟨still a dandy, ~ to his slim finger tips —John Gunther⟩

**²précieux** \"\ *n, pl* **précieux** \"(z)\ [F, fr. *précieux,* adj.] **:** a man marked by preciosity

**pre·cinct** \'prē,siŋ(k)t, *chiefly archaic* ‚'‚\ *n* -s [ME *precincte,* fr. ML *praecinctum,* fr. L, neut. of *praecinctus,* past part. of *praecingere* to gird about, encircle, fr. *prae-* pre- + *cingere* to gird — more at CINCTURE] **1 :** a part of a territory (as a city) having definite bounds or functions and often established for administrative purposes **:** DISTRICT ⟨a school ~⟩ ⟨a bold municipal experiment in planning a whole business ~ of offices and shops —Lewis Mumford⟩: as **a :** SOCIETY 3b(1) **b :** one in colonial Massachusetts having a political status and powers partially separate from its parent town and usu. being eventually incorporated as a separate town **c :** a subdivision of a county, town, city, or ward for election purposes — called also *election district* **d :** a division of a city for police control **2 a :** an enclosure bounded by the walls or other limits of a building or place or by an imaginary line around it ⟨the ~ of the fortification —J.A.Davison⟩ ⟨demand . . . for the admission of females to the club ~*s* —F.L.Allen⟩ **b :** a sphere of thought, action, or influence **:** DOMAIN ⟨an attitude common in the ~*s* of industry⟩ **c :** a space within the grith of a house or borough where one is exempt from arrest in the customary law of the Anglo-Saxons and some other Teutons **3 :** the region immediately surrounding a place **:** ENVIRONS — usu. used in pl. ⟨the ~*s* of the inn —Thomas Hardy⟩ **4 :** a surrounding or enclosing line or surface **:** BOUND — usu. used in pl. ⟨a ruined tower within the ~*s* of the squire's grounds —T.L.Peacock⟩

**precinct captain** *also* **precinct leader** *n* **:** the party leader of an election precinct — compare COMMITTEEMAN

**pre·ci·os·i·ty** \ˌpreshē'äsə̇d·ē, -sətē, -i *sometimes* -esē-\ *n* -ES [ME *preciousite, preciosite* preciousness, fr. MF *precieusité, preciosité,* fr. L *pretiositat-, pretiositas,* fr. *pretiosus* + *-itat-, -itas* -ity] **1** *archaic* **:** something precious **2** [F *préciosité,* fr. MF *precieusité, preciosité* preciousness] **a :** fastidious or excessive refinement (as in language) ⟨he had the fastidiousness, the ~, the love of archaisms, of your true decadent —R.L.Douglas⟩; *specif* **:** the affected purism and sententiousness characteristic of the French précieuses of the 17th century **b :** an instance of preciosity ⟨uttering obtuse and outmoded *preciosities*⟩

**¹pre·cious** \'preshəs\ *adj* [ME, fr. OF *precios, precieus,* fr. L *pretiosus,* fr. *pretium* price, value + *-osus* -ous — more at PRICE] **1 :** of great value or high price: as **a :** of such extreme value that a suitable price is hard to estimate **:** PRICELESS, INVALUABLE **b** *of a gemstone* **:** of highest value commercially because of its beauty, rarity, or hardness **2 :** of great nonmaterial value **:** very highly esteemed or cherished **:** DEAR ⟨we went up the wrong valley and lost several ~ days —Heinrich Harrer⟩ ⟨a very useful report, with the ~ qualities of objectivity, balance and good humor —*advt*⟩ **3 a :** PARTICULAR, FASTIDIOUS **b :** OVERNICE, OVERREFINED ⟨divorced from the social instinct, thought . . . tends to become finicky and ~ —Bertrand Russell⟩ **c :** AFFECTED, POSING, HYPOCRITICAL ⟨have made culture appear to be a power in whose service people could grow dry, intolerant, and ~ —Katharine F. Gerould⟩ **4 a :** FINE, GREAT — used as an intensive ⟨opened the territory to some ~ scoundrels —*Amer. Guide Series: Oregon*⟩ **b :** WORTHLESS — used ironically ⟨nobody would care if he went to his ~ Rome and stayed there —L. C. Douglas⟩ **syn** see COSTLY

**²precious** \"\ *adv* **:** EXTREMELY, VERY ⟨no equipment and ~ few drugs —Nevil Shute⟩ ⟨she actually has ~ little to say about what roles she is going to play —Robert Trumbull⟩

**precious coral** *n* **:** RED CORAL

**pre·cious·ly** *adv* [ME, fr. *precious* + *-ly*] **1 :** in a precious manner **2 :** PRECIOUS

**precious metal** *n* **:** any of the less common and highly valuable metals (as gold, silver, and the platinum metals) — compare NOBLE METAL

**pre·cious·ness** *n* -ES [ME *preciousnesse,* fr. *precious* + *-nesse* -ness] **:** the quality or state of being precious

**precious stone** *n* **:** GEMSTONE

**¹precipe** *n* -s [irreg. fr. L *praecipit-, praeceps,* fr. neut. of *praecipit-, praeceps* headlong] *obs* **:** PRECIPICE

**²precipe** *var of* PRAECIPE

**prec·i·pice** \'presəpə̇s\ *n* -s [MF, fr. L *praecipitium,* fr. *praecipit-, praeceps* headlong, fr. *prae-* pre- + *-cipit-, -ceps* (fr. *caput* head) — more at HEAD] **1** *obs* **:** a sudden or headlong fall **2 :** a very steep, perpendicular, or overhanging place (as the face of a cliff) **:** an abrupt declivity **:** a sheer cliff **3 :** a hazardous situation **:** the brink of disaster

**pre·cip·i·ta·bil·i·ty** \prē,sipəd·ə'biləd·ē, prə̇,s-\ *n* **:** the quality or state of being precipitable

**pre·cip·i·ta·ble** \‚'‚pəd·əbəl\ *adj* [¹*precipitate* + *-able*] **:** capable of being precipitated

**pre·cip·i·tance** \-d·ən(t)s, tən-\ *n* -s **:** PRECIPITANCY

**pre·cip·i·tan·cy** \-nsē, -nsi\ *n* -ES **:** precipitant motion or action **:** headlong haste ⟨ran from the room with startling ~⟩ ⟨effected the changes with a ~ that stirred up resistance⟩

**¹pre·cip·i·tant** \-nt\ *adj* [F *précipitant,* fr. L *praecipitant-, praecipitans,* pres. part. of *praecipitare*] **:** PRECIPITATE ⟨steer a middle course between chronic indecision and ~ judgment —A.S.Eddington⟩ — **pre·cip·i·tant·ly** *adv* — **pre·cip·i·tant·ness** *n* -ES

**²precipitant** \"\ *n* -s **:** something causing precipitation; *specif* **:** an agent that causes the formation of a precipitate

**¹pre·cip·i·tate** \prē'sipə,tāt, prə̇'s-, *usu* -ād.+V\ *vb* -ED/-ING/-S [L *praecipitatus,* past part. of *praecipitare,* fr. *praecipit-, praeceps* headlong — more at PRECIPICE] *vt* **1 a :** to throw violently (as upon an object of attack) **:** HURL ⟨in dismay he ~*s* himself once more upon his task —Eric Blom⟩ **b :** to throw down ⟨the Congo ~*s* itself between the mountains, forming some thirty-two separate rapids and cataracts —Tom Marvel⟩ ⟨*precipitated* himself into skepticism —Kingsley Price⟩ **2 a :** to cause to move or act very rapidly **:** urge or press on with eager haste or violence ⟨the completion of the railroad . . . *precipitated* the extinction of water-borne commerce —*Amer. Guide Series: Maine*⟩ **b :** to cause to happen or come to a crisis suddenly, unexpectedly, or too soon **:** bring on quickly or abruptly ⟨that the sudden withdrawal of alcohol from a chronic alcoholic may ~ a delirium —*Ency. Americana*⟩ ⟨the power of dissolving Congress and *precipitating* a national election —A.N.Holcombe⟩ **3 a** (1) **:** to cause to separate as a precipitate ⟨water ~*s* camphor from its alcoholic solution⟩ (2) **:** to cause (vapor) to condense and fall or deposit ⟨an ice-filled glass ~*s* moisture from the air⟩ **b :** to give distinct or substantial form to **:** body forth ⟨ward membership . . . may easily ~ itself into many visible forms of behavior —Edward Sapir⟩ ~ *vi* **1 a :** to fall headlong **b :** to descend steeply **c :** to fall or come suddenly into some condition (as ruin) ⟨Fascism *precipitated* toward its agony —Cecil Sprigge⟩ **2 :** to move or act precipitately **3 :** to become separate or distinct **:** take material or observable form ⟨this desire or tendency ~*s* into observable motion whenever counteracting causes are removed —Arthur Pap⟩: as **a :** to separate from a solution as a precipitate **b :** to condense from a vapor and fall as rain or snow **syn** see SPEED

**²pre·cip·i·tate** \-pəd·ə̇t, -pətə̇, -pə,tā, *usu* |d· +V\ *n* -s [NL *praecipitatum,* fr. L, neut. of *praecipitatus,* past part. of *praecipitare*] **1 :** a substance separated from a solution in a concrete state as a result of a chemical or physical change (as by the action of a reagent or of cold); *esp* **:** an insoluble amorphous or crystalline solid that may fall to the bottom, may be diffused through the solution, or may float at or near the top and that can often be separated from the liquid by filtration **2 :** a product, result, or outcome of some process or action ⟨inductive generalizations . . . are the ~ of past experience —H.N.Lee⟩

**³precipitate** \"\ *adj* [L *praecipitatus,* past part. of *praecipitare*] **1 :** exhibiting a lack of due deliberation or care **:** acting with, done, or caused by unwise haste **:** RASH, PREMATURE ⟨Brazil was prompt, but not ~, in accommodating itself to the change —Walter Karig⟩ ⟨she was resolved to lose nothing by neglect or delay, but she also meant to do nothing ~ —H.G. Wells⟩ **2 a :** falling, flowing, or rushing with steep descent **b :** very steep **:** PRECIPITOUS ⟨bare ~ cliffs —*Amer. Guide Series: Vt.*⟩ **3 :** marked by extreme or excessive speed or haste **:** violently rapid ⟨an army in ~ flight⟩ ⟨born . . . by ~ delivery in a physician's office —*Jour. Amer. Med. Assoc.*⟩ **:** SUDDEN, ABRUPT ⟨hoping that her departure would not seem indecently ~ —Victoria Sackville-West⟩

**syn** HEADLONG, IMPETUOUS, HASTY, ABRUPT, SUDDEN: PRECIPITATE applies to what is done hurriedly or rapidly without expected expenditure of time and may suggest lack of due consideration ⟨we'll load up the equipment and pull out in the morning — why be so *precipitate* —P.B.Kyne⟩ ⟨a *precipitate* attack was launched —S.M.Wilson⟩ HEADLONG indicates tearing rush with rash lack of observation and forethought ⟨thousands and thousands of Belgians, pursuing with incredible speed and fury the Roman cavalry which soon turned in *headlong* flight —A.C.Whitehead⟩ ⟨a *headlong* leap into unconsidered undertakings —S.L.A.Marshall⟩ IMPETUOUS may apply to hasty forcible impulsiveness or impatience that precludes thoughtful prudence ⟨the *impetuous* Spaniard rushed eagerly into the water up to his armpits and drank greedily —*Amer. Guide Series: Calif.*⟩ ⟨*impetuous* rhetoric sweeps the author on to absurd generalizations —*Reporter*⟩ HASTY, in addition to stressing the notion of hurry, may suggest carelessness, thoughtlessness, or anger ⟨*hasty* makeshifts take the place of planning, and temporary adaptations become fixed as permanent maladjustments —Arthur Geddes⟩ ⟨faithful observation accompanied by reasonable inference, as opposed to the careless use of the senses and the *hasty* guessing that characterize most people —Norman Foerster⟩ ABRUPT applies to that which is done with sudden sharpness breaking away from a previous course or performed without warning or intimation ⟨the frequent *abrupt* about-face maneuvers performed by Soviet propagandists —T.P.Whitney⟩ ⟨the reasoning that leads to this conclusion should be less *abrupt.* Jumping to conclusions is not permissible even among philosophers —O. S.J.Gogarty⟩ SUDDEN may heighten the notions of unexpectedness and haste without necessarily implying a break from a previous course ⟨the car came to a stop, so *sudden* that it pitched both Clara and Hugh out of their seats —Sherwood Anderson⟩ ⟨after the southern attack on Fort Sumter, there was a *sudden* and remarkable transformation of feeling in the North —W.A.Swanberg⟩ ⟨the *sudden* rush of a fresh, strong, exhilarating, and unpredictable wind —B.R.Redman⟩

**precipitated chalk** *n* **:** precipitated calcium carbonate

**precipitated sulfur** *n* **:** sulfur obtained as a pale yellowish or grayish amorphous or microcrystalline powder by precipitation (as from the reaction of a polysulfide with an acid) and used chiefly in treating skin diseases

**pre·cip·i·tate·ly** *adv* **:** in a precipitate manner **:** HEADLONG, HASTILY, RASHLY ⟨a visitor arrived unexpectedly and we all fled ~ —Henry Miller⟩ ⟨in no danger . . . of plunging ~ into marriage —Ellen Glasgow⟩

**pre·cip·i·tate·ness** *n* -ES **:** the quality or state of being precipitate **:** PRECIPITANCY

**pre·cip·i·ta·tion** \(ˌ)prē,sipə'tāshən, prə̇,s-\ *n* -s [MF or L; MF, fr. L *praecipitation-, praecipitatio,* fr. *praecipitatus* + *-ion-, -io* -ion] **1 :** the quality or state of being precipitate **:** PRECIPITANCY, HASTE ⟨had acted with some ~ and had probably started out upon a wild-goose chase —Dorothy Sayers⟩ **2 a :** an act, process, or instance of precipitating ⟨a ~ of this issue . . . at the present time —A.H.Vandenberg⟩: as (1) **:** the process of forming a precipitate from a solution — compare COAGULATION 1b, FLOCCULATION 1 (2) **:** the process of precipitating or removing solid or liquid particles from a smoke or gas by electrical means **:** ELECTROSTATIC PRECIPITATION **b :** a deposit on the earth of hail, mist, rain, sleet, or snow; *also* **:** the quantity of water deposited **3 :** something precipitated; *specif* **:** PRECIPITATE 1

**precipitation hardening** *n* **:** the process of hardening an alloy by a heat treatment or aging method that causes a constituent to precipitate from solid solution

**precipitation heat treatment** *n* **:** a treatment involving the heating or aging of an alloy at elevated temperature to cause a constituent to precipitate from solid solution

**precipitation number** *n* **:** an index of the proportional amount of solid matter precipitated from oil under test

**precipitation static** *n* **:** static produced in airborne radio equipment by the striking of rain, snow, hail, dust particles or other particles in the atmosphere on the antenna and surfaces of an airplane

**pre·cip·i·ta·tive** \‚'‚‚,tād·iv, -,təd·-\ *adj* **:** tending to or inducing precipitation

**pre·cip·i·ta·tor** \-,tād·ə(r), -ātə-\ *n* -s **:** one that precipitates: as **a** (1) **:** a person who precipitates some act or event **:** HASTENER (2) **:** an operator of a precipitating machine (3) **:** a worker who precipitates silver or gold from cyanide solution in zinc boxes or with zinc dust **b** (1) **:** an apparatus for causing precipitation (2) **:** an apparatus used in electrostatic precipitation that contains the collecting and discharge electrodes and may be characterized by a series of parallel pipes or plates through or between which the gas passes — called also *electrical precipitator, electrostatic precipitator*

**pre·cip·i·tin** \‚'sipəd·ən\ *n* -s [ISV *precipitate* + *-in*] **:** an antibody that forms an insoluble precipitate when it unites with its antigen — compare AGGLUTININ

**pre·cip·i·tin·o·gen** \‚'‚‚¦tinəjən, -,jen\ *n* -s [*precipitin* + *-o-* + *-gen*] **:** an antigen that stimulates the production of a specific precipitin — **pre·cip·i·tin·o·gen·ic** \‚'‚‚¦jenik\ *adj*

**precipitin reaction** *n* **:** the specific reaction of a precipitin with its antigen to give an insoluble precipitate

**precipitin test** *n* **:** a serologic test using a precipitin reaction to detect the presence of a specific antigen; *specif* **:** a criminological test determining the human or other source of a blood stain ⟨show by a *precipitin test* that this is dog blood —Erle Stanley Gardner⟩

**precipitious** *adj* [L *percipitium* + E *-ous*] **:** PRECIPITOUS

**pre·cip·i·tous** \prē'sipəd·əs, prə̇'s-, -pətəs\ *adj* [F *précipiteux,* fr. MF *precipiteux,* fr. L *precipitium* precipice + MF *-eux* -ous — more at PRECIPICE] **1 :** marked by great rapidity, haste, or lack of caution **:** PRECIPITATE, HASTY, SUDDEN, RASH ⟨psychoses . . . shorter, more fleeting and more ~ in onset —I.I.Weiss⟩ **2 a :** having the character of a precipice **:** very steep, perpendicular, or overhanging in rise or fall ⟨a ~ slope⟩ ⟨a ~ bluff⟩ **b :** having very steep, perpendicular, or overhanging sides **:** containing precipices ⟨~ mountains⟩ ⟨a ~ gorge⟩ **c :** having a very steep ascent ⟨~ stairs⟩ ⟨a ~ street⟩ **syn** see STEEP

**pre·cip·i·tous·ly** *adv* **:** in a precipitous manner **:** ABRUPTLY, SUDDENLY ⟨mountains rising ~ from the shore⟩ ⟨~ increase the birthrate⟩

**pre·cip·i·tous·ness** *n* -ES **:** the quality or state of being precipitous

**Pre·cip·i·tron** \prē'sipə·,trän, prə̇'s-\ *trademark* — used for an electrostatic air-cleaning apparatus that ionizes floating particles of dust, pollen, fumes, and smoke and then precipitates the particles on charged collecting elements usu. in the form of plates

**¹pré·cis** \(ˈ)prā¦sē; 'prāsē, -si\ *n, pl* **précis** \-ēz\ [F, fr. *précis* precise] **1 :** a concise epitome or abstract (as of a book or a case) **:** a brief summary of essential points, statements, or facts ⟨a ~ of French history⟩ **2 :** the act or practice of writing such statements **syn** see COMPENDIUM

**²pre·cis** \'prēsə̇s\ *n, cap* [NL] **:** a widely distributed genus of chiefly tropical nymphalid butterflies that includes the buckeye of No. and So. America

**¹pre·cise** \prē'sīs, prə̇'s-\ *adj, sometimes* -ER/-EST [MF *precis,* fr. L *praecisus,* past part. of *praecidere* to cut off, shorten, fr. *prae-* pre- + *-cidere* (fr. *caedere* to cut) — more at CONCISE] **1 a** (1) **:** characterized by a definite often terse statement or specific meaning **:** devoid of anything vague, equivocal, or uncertain ⟨this is no time for generalities and I will venture to be ~ —Sir Winston Churchill⟩ ⟨find a more ~ term than *good* to describe the work⟩ (2) **:** measured or measuring in mathematically often minutely exact units ⟨the ~ velocity of the satellite⟩ ⟨~ figures recording the racer's time to the hundredth of a second⟩ ⟨the ~ techniques of microchemistry⟩ ⟨a ~ balance⟩ (3) **:** having distinct often close limits **:** exactly delimited ⟨energy . . . released in ~ channels, as when a current causes the glow in a bulb —E.A.Armstrong⟩ ⟨determine the ~ meaning of the term⟩ ⟨standardization through ~ control of processing⟩ (4) **:** exact to a point **:** being without deviation **:** ABSOLUTE ⟨hit the mark with ~ accuracy⟩ ⟨that totalitarianism is the ~ opposite of anarchy⟩ **b :** developed or indicated in specific or minute detail ⟨working out the ~ relationship of the languages —Edward Sapir⟩ **2 :** conforming strictly to an exact pattern or standard **:** shaped, arranged, or performed with minute conformity to a pattern ⟨flying a beautiful, tight, ~ formation —Walter Bernstein⟩ **:** rigorous in observing a rule, code, or convention **:** SCRUPULOUS, FASTIDIOUS ⟨a ~, magisterial person . . . incapable of letting the most trivial mistake go uncorrected —Gerald Bullett⟩; *specif* **:** PURITANICAL **3 :** distinguished from every other **:** VERY ⟨the ~ task for which he was born —L.P.Smith⟩ ⟨arrived just at that ~ moment⟩ **4 :** sharply distinct in appearance or sound ⟨the ~ images in the camera finder⟩ ⟨speaks . . . with a ~ British accent —*Current Biog.*⟩ **syn** see CORRECT

**²precise** \"\ *vt* -ED/-ING/-S **:** to make precise **:** state, define, or determine exactly or strictly **:** PARTICULARIZE

**pre·cise·ly** *adv* **:** in a precise manner **:** EXACTLY, EXPRESSLY, DEFINITELY, PUNCTILIOUSLY ⟨measure off ~ three yards⟩ ⟨trails off into rhetoric ~ where he should be both specific and firm —Howard M. Jones⟩ ⟨an outcome ~ opposite to his expectation⟩

**pre·cise·ness** *n* -ES **:** the quality or state of being precise (as in speech or conduct)

**pre·ci·sian** \-'sizhən\ *n* -s [¹*precise* + *-ian*] **1 :** a person who stresses or practices scrupulous adherence to a strict standard of religious observance or morality; *specif* **:** PURITAN 1 **2 :** PRECISIONIST

**pre·ci·sian·ism** \-,nizəm\ *n* -s **:** the quality or state of being a precisian **:** the practice of a precisian; *specif* **:** PURITANISM

**¹pre·ci·sion** \prē'sizhən, prə̇'s-\ *n* [in sense 1, fr. L *praecision-, praecisio* act of cutting off, fr. *praecisus* (past part. of *praecidere* to cut off) + *-ion-, -io* -ion; in other senses, fr. F *précision,* fr. L *praecision-, praecisio* act of cutting off — more at PRECISE] **1** *obs* **:** PRESCINDING, ABSTRACTION **2 a :** the quality or state of being precise **:** exact limitation **:** EXACTNESS,

DEFINITENESS ⟨defining words with utmost care, they fashioned their statements of doctrine with meticulous ~ —C.A.Dinsmore⟩ ⟨drove . . . emperors with the ~ of an automaton —Norman Douglas⟩; *esp* : the degree of refinement with which an operation is performed or a measurement stated ⟨the number, 2.42, shows a higher ~ than 2.4, but it is not necessarily any more accurate —*Amer. Society of Civil Engineers*⟩ — contrasted with *accuracy* **b** (1) : the degree of agreement of repeated measurements of a quantity (2) : the deviation of a set of estimates from their mean **3** : an instance of precision : NICETY ⟨suspicion of the ~*s* of language —F.S.C.Northrop⟩

**²precision** \"\ *adj* : marked by precision of execution or measurement ⟨a ~ landing⟩ ⟨a troop of ~ dancers⟩: as **a** : adapted for extremely fine or accurate measurement, observation, or operation ⟨a ~ level . . . will detect a variation of as little as .0025″ per foot —*Metals & Alloys*⟩ ⟨~ cartography⟩ **b** : held to low tolerance in manufacture or finishing ⟨a ~ gear⟩ ⟨a ~ finish⟩ ⟨~ parts⟩

**precision block** *n* : GAGE BLOCK

**precision bombing** *n* : the dropping of aerial bombs by means of a bombsight upon a narrowly defined target (as a ship or factory) esp. so as not to straddle or overspread — compare AREA BOMBING, PINPOINT, SATURATE

**pre·ci·sion·ist** \-zh(ə)nəst\ *n* -s : one who professes, practices, or lays great stress upon precision (as in language or ritual) : PURIST

**pre·ci·sive** \-ˈsīsiv, -īziv\ *adj* [in sense 1, fr. L *praecisus* + E *-ive*; in sense 2, fr. ¹*precision* + *-ive*] **1** : cutting off, separating, or defining one thing or person from all others ⟨~ censure⟩ ⟨~ abstraction⟩ **2** : having or marked by precision or exactness

**preclassic** *or* **preclassical** \(ˈ)prē+\ *adj* [*pre-* + *classic, classical*] **1** : of or relating to a time before the classical period (as of an art) **2** : of or being a European court dance of the 15th and 16th centuries

**pre·climax** \"+\ *n* [*pre-* + *climax*] : a relatively stable ecological community requiring a lesser amount of available moisture than that generally available to the climax and occurring typically where local soil conditions partially nullify a generally adequate precipitation ⟨a grassland ~ within a forest climax⟩ — compare POSTCLIMAX

**pre·clinical** \"+\ *adj* [*pre-* + *clinical*] **1** : of or relating to the period preceding clinical manifestations ⟨the ~ stage of a disease of slow onset⟩ **2** : of or relating to the period preceding the clinical study of medicine ⟨the ~ years⟩; *specif* : of or relating to the first two years of the prescribed medical course devoted to the study of basic sciences (as anatomy, physiology, pathology) ⟨~ studies⟩ **3** : of, relating to, or being a science basic to medicine ⟨research in the ~ sciences⟩

**pre·clud·able** \prēˈklüdəbəl, prəˈk-\ *adj* : capable of being precluded

**pre·clude** \-üd\ *vt* -ED/-ING/-S [L *praecludere*, fr. *prae-* pre- + *-cludere* (fr. *claudere* to close) — more at CLOSE] **1** *archaic* : to put a barrier before : shut up : HINDER, STOP, IMPEDE, CLOSE **2** : to shut out or obviate by anticipation : prevent or hinder by necessary consequence or implication : deter action of, access to, or enjoyment of : make ineffectual ⟨the adoption of one choice often necessarily ~*s* the use of another —C.I. Glicksberg⟩ ⟨engagements . . . ~ the principal from extending this trip —D.L.Gales⟩ **syn** see PREVENT

**pre·clu·sion** \-üzhən\ *n* -s [L *praeclusion-, praeclusio*, fr. *praeclusus* (past part. of *praecludere*) + *-ion-, -io* -ion] : an act of precluding or state of being precluded : a shutting out : prevention by anticipation

**pre·clu·sive** \-üs|iv *also* -üz|\ *adj* [L *praeclusus* + E *-ive*] : shutting out : precluding or tending to preclude : PREVENTIVE ⟨~ buying — purchasing vital materials to keep them from going to the Axis —Robert Reuben⟩ — **pre·clu·sive·ly** \|əvlē\ *adv*

**pre·coagulation** \ˌprē+\ *n* [*pre-* + *coagulation*] : chemical treatment with a coagulant before filtration

**precoces** *var of* PRAECOCES

**pre·co·cial** \prēˈkōshəl, prəˈk-\ *adj* [NL *precoces* + E *-ial*] *of a newly born or hatched individual* : capable of a high degree of independent activity from birth ⟨the chicks of gallinaceous birds are ~⟩ — compare ALTRICIAL

**pre·co·cious** \-shəs\ *adj* [L *praecoc-, praecox* early ripening, premature, precocious (fr. *prae-* + *-coc-, -cox*, fr. *coquere* to cook, ripen) + E *-ious* — more at COOK] : exceptionally early in development: **a** : flowering, fruiting, or developing before the usual time : early or prematurely ripe or developed — used of a plant or its organs **b** : manifesting at an early age some of the mental or physical characteristics usu. associated with maturity ⟨a ~ child⟩ ⟨a ~ genius⟩ **c** : characterizing, shown, or made by a precocious individual ⟨a ~ achievement⟩ ⟨at the ~ age of 25 he had written a masterpiece⟩ **d** : appropriate to a period later than that of actual occurrence ⟨a ~ culture⟩ ⟨a ~ heat wave⟩ — **pre·co·cious·ly** *adv* — **pre·co·cious·ness** *n* -ES

**pre·coc·i·ty** \-ˈkäsəd·ē, -ətē, -i\ *n* -ES [L *praecoc-, praecox* + E *-ity*] : the quality or state of being precocious: as **a** : early flowering or early ripening **b** : exceptionally early or premature development; *esp* : early development of the mental powers : FORWARDNESS **c** : early sexual maturity of poultry resulting in initiation of egg laying at an early age

**precocity theory** *n* : a theory in biology: early condensation of the chromosomes induces a characteristic prophase pairing that is the fundamental factor distinguishing meiosis from mitosis

**pre·cogitate** \(ˈ)prē, prə+\ *vt* -ED/-ING/-S [L *praecogitatus*, past part. of *praecogitare*, fr. *prae-* pre- + *cogitare* to think — more at COGITATE] : PREMEDITATE — **pre·cogitation** \(ˌ)prē, prə+\ *n* -S

**pre·cognition** \ˌprē+\ *n* [LL *praecognition-, praecognitio*, fr. L *praecognitus* (past part. of *praecognoscere* to foreknow, fr. *prae-* pre- + *cognoscere* to know) + *-ion, -io*, -ion — more at COGNITION] **1** : previous cognition : FOREKNOWLEDGE; *specif* : clairvoyance relating to a future or not yet experienced event or state **2** *Scots law* **a** : an ex parte preliminary examination (as in a criminal case) **b** : the evidence taken in such an examination

**pre·cognitive** \(ˈ)prē+\ *adj* : giving precognition ⟨a ~ dream⟩

**pre·cognize** \(ˌ)prē+\ *vt* [*pre-* + *cognize*] : to know beforehand

**pre·cognosce** \(ˌ)prē+\ *vt* -ED/-ING/-S [L *praecognoscere* to foreknow] *Scots law* : to examine in the proceeding of precognition

**pre–columbian** \ˌprē+\ *adj, usu cap C* [*pre-* + *Columbian*] : preceding or belonging to the time before the discovery of America by Columbus ⟨*pre-Columbian* times⟩ ⟨an exhibition of *pre-Columbian* art⟩

**precombustion chamber** \ˌ==ˈ==-\ *n* [*pre-* + *combustion*] : an auxiliary space in which combustible gases are ignited and combustion started ahead of the main combustion chamber of a jet or gas engine

**precombustion engine** *n* : a mixed cycle internal combustion engine with a small uncooled precombustion chamber in which a portion of the mixture is ignited and in turn ignites the cylinder charge

**pre·commissure** \(ˈ)prē+\ *n* [*pre-* + *commissure*] : the anterior commissure of the brain

**pre·compose** \ˌprē+\ *vt* [*pre-* + *compose*] : to compose beforehand

**pre·conceive** \"+\ *vt* [*pre-* + *conceive*] : to form an opinion of beforehand : form a previous notion or idea of; *esp* : to form (as an opinion) without adequate evidence or through prejudice ⟨held to his *preconceived* opinion despite the new evidence⟩

**pre·concept** \(ˈ)prē+\ *n* [*pre-* + *concept*] : a rudimentary idea intermediate between an ordinary recept and a fully developed concept

**pre·conception** \ˌprē+\ *n* [*pre-* + *conception*] : an act or an instance of preconceiving : a conception or opinion previously formed : PREJUDICE, PREPOSSESSION

**pre·conceptual** \"+\ *adj* : of, relating to, or marked by a preconception

**pre·concert** \"+\ *vt* [*pre-* + *concert*] : to arrange beforehand : settle by prior agreement

**preconcerted** *adj* : previously arranged — **pre·con·cert·ed·ly** *adv* — **pre·con·cert·ed·ness** *n* -ES

**pre·condemn** \ˌprē+\ *vt* [*pre-* + *condemn*] : to condemn before trial or without due consideration : PREJUDGE

**¹pre·condition** \"+\ *n* [*pre-* + *condition* (n.)] : something that must exist before something else can come about : CONDITION, PREREQUISITE, QUALIFICATION ⟨prepared to negotiate . . . without any ~*s* —*N.Y. Times*⟩ ⟨the indispensable ~ of success, the support of a united party —M.W.Straight⟩

**²precondition** \"\ *vt* [*pre-* + *condition* (v.)] **1** : to put (a thing) in proper or desired condition in advance or in preparation for some intended treatment or processing ⟨~ the surface of the mineral to be separated —*Science*⟩ **2** : to put (a person) in preparation for some argumentative presentation or some mental test or shock ⟨merchandisers were seeking ways to ~ the customer to buy their product —Vance Packard⟩

**preco·ni·za·tion** \ˌprekənəˈzāshən, ˌprēk-, -ˌnīˈz-\ *n* -S [ML *praeconization-, praeconizatio*, fr. *praeconizatus* (past part. of *praeconizare*) + L *-ion-, -io* -ion] : the act or process of preconizing (as a bishop)

**preco·nize** \ˈ==ˌnīz\ *vt* -ED/-ING/-S [ML *praeconizare*, fr. L *praecon-, praeco* herald, crier (prob. fr. *praedicare* to proclaim publicly) + LL *-izare* -ize — more at PREACH] **1** : to announce or commend publicly **2** : to summon publicly or by name **3** *Roman Catholicism* : to approve (a high ecclesiastical appointment) publicly by papal proclamation in consistory

**pre·conquest** \(ˈ)prē+\ *adj* [*pre-* + *conquest*] : of or relating to times before the conquest of a country or people ⟨~ Normandy⟩ ⟨~ sculptured stones —F.M.Stenton⟩

**¹pre·conscious** \"+\ *adj* [*pre-* + *conscious*] **1** : not present in consciousness but capable of being recalled without encountering any inner resistance or repression — compare CENSORSHIP **2** : preceding the development of self-consciousness or awareness — **pre·consciously** \"+\ *adv*

**²preconscious** \"\ *n* : the preconscious part of mental life or psychic content in psychoanalysis

**pre·consonantal** \(ˌ)prē+\ *adj* [*pre-* + *consonantal*] : immediately preceding a consonant

**pre·contact** \(ˈ)prē+\ *adj* [*pre-* + *contact*] : of or relating to the period before contact of a primitive people with a more advanced culture

**¹pre·contract** \"+\ *n* [ME *precontracte*, fr. *pre-* + *contracte*, *contract* contract — more at CONTRACT] : a contract preceding another; *esp* : an informal agreement of marriage made per verba de praesenti and formerly disabling one from entering into a similar contract with another person

**²pre·contract** \(ˌ)prē+\ *vt* [*pre-* + *contract* (v.)] : to contract, engage, or stipulate by precontract

**pre·cook** \(ˈ)prē+\ *vt* [*pre-* + *cook*] : to cook (food) partially or entirely before final cooking or reheating ⟨~ cereal before packaging⟩ ⟨~ meat before reheating for a meal⟩

**pre·cool** \"+\ *vt* [*pre-* + *cool*] : to cool (as fresh fruit, vegetables, or meat) artificially to refrigeration temperature before shipment

**pre·cooler** \(ˈ)prē+\ *n* : a device (as a heat exchanger) for cooling a fluid or gas before it is used (as by a mechanical device)

**pre·coracoid** \"+\ *n* [*pre-* + *coracoid*] **1** : an anterior and ventral bony or cartilaginous element of the shoulder girdle in front of the coracoid proper that occurs in many amphibians and reptiles and is often represented in the latter by a process of the coracoid **2** : MESOCORACOID

**pre·cordial** \"+\ *adj* [prob. fr. MF, fr. *pre-* + *cordial*, fr. ML *cordialis* — more at CORDIAL] : situated or occurring in front of the heart : involving the precordium

**precordial region** *n* : PRECORDIUM

**pre·cor·di·um** \prēˈkȯ(r)dēəm\ *n, pl* **precor·dia** \-ēə\ [NL, fr. *pre-* + L *cord-, cor* heart + NL *-ium* — more at HEART] : the part of the ventral surface of the body overlying the heart and stomach and comprising the epigastrium and the lower median part of the thorax

**pre·cornu** \(ˈ)prē+\ *n* [NL, fr. *pre-* + *cornu*] : the anterior cornu of a lateral ventricle

**pre–cortesian** \ˌprēˌkȯ(r)ˈtezēən, -tēzhən\ *adj, usu cap C* [*pre-* + Hernán *Cortés* (Cortez) †1547 Span. conqueror of Mexico + E *-ian*] : of or relating to the period before the conquest of Mexico by Cortez

**pre·costa** \(ˈ)prē+\ *n* [NL, fr. *pre-* + *costa*] : a small vein anterior to the costa in the wings of a primitive insect — **pre·costal** \"+\ *adj*

**pre–crag** \ˈprē+ˌ-\ *adj, usu cap C* [*pre-* + *crag* (sedimentary rock)] : of or relating to a hypothetical preglacial stage of Lower Paleolithic culture ⟨*pre-Crag* flints⟩

**pre·critical** \(ˈ)prē+\ *adj* [*pre-* + *critical*] **1** : that is prior to the development of critical capacity ⟨in ~ cultures, myths of magic . . . tend to prevail —*Amer. Anthropologist*⟩ **2** : being prior to the publication of Immanuel Kant's *Critique of Pure Reason*

**pre·crural** \"+\ *adj* [*pre-* + *crural*] : situated in front of the leg or thigh

**pre·cuneus** \"+\ *n* [NL, fr. *pre-* + *cuneus*] : a somewhat rectangular gyrus bounding the mesial aspect of the parietal lobe of the cerebrum and lying immediately in front of the cuneus

**pre·current** \"+\ *adj* [L *praecurrent-, praecurrens*, pres. part. of *praecurrere*] : occurring beforehand : ANTICIPATORY

**precurse** *n* -S [L *praecursus*, past part. of *praecurrere* to run before, precede, fr. *prae-* pre- + *currere* to run — more at CURRENT] *obs* : something that presages a future event

**pre·cur·sive** \prēˈkərsiv, prəˈk-\ *adj* : PRECURSORY, PROGNOSTICATIVE

**pre·cur·sor** \=ˈkərsər, -ˈkōsə(r, -ˈkəisə(r, ˈprēˌ==\ *n* -S [L *praecursor*, fr. *praecursus* + *-or*] **1 a** : one that precedes and indicates the approach of another ⟨headaches . . . were the ~*s* of breakdown and helpless invalidism —V.S.Pritchett⟩ **b** : one that precedes another in an office or process : PREDECESSOR, FORERUNNER ⟨Greek mathematics was the ~ to modern mathematics —Harry Lass⟩ **2** : a substance from which another substance is formed esp. by natural processes ⟨ethyl alcohol is the ~ of acetic acid in the formation of vinegar⟩ — compare PROVITAMIN, ZYMOGEN

**pre·cur·so·ry** \-sərē, -ri\ *adj* [L *praecursorius*, fr. *praecursus* + *-orius* -ory] : having the character of a precursor : PRECEDING, PRELIMINARY, PREMONITORY ⟨~ symptoms of a fever⟩

**pre·cut** \ˈprē+ˌ-\ *vt* [*pre-* + *cut*] **1** : to cut to proper dimensions (the parts of a house) **2** : to cut the parts of (a house) for prefabrication assembly

**pre·cyst** \ˈprē+ˌ-\ *n* [*pre-* + *cyst*] : a differentiated phase in many protozoans that lays down the resting cyst and is characterized by structural simplification and modified metabolic activities involving the increase of storage products and the termination of active feeding — **pre·cystic** \(ˈ)prē+\ *adj*

**pred** *abbr* predicate; predicative

**pre·da·cious** *or* **pre·da·ceous** \prēˈdāshəs, prəˈd-\ *adj* [*predacious*, fr. L *praedari* to plunder, prey upon + E *-acious* (as in *rapacious*); *predaceous*, alter. (influenced by E *-aceous*) of *predacious* — more at PREY] **1** *usu predaceous* : preying on other animals : exhibiting or relating to predatism : PREDATORY ⟨a ~ kind of animal — the early geological gangster —W.E.Swinton⟩ **2** : marked by rapacity : tending to devour or despoil — **pre·da·cious·ness** *n* -ES

**pre·dac·i·ty** \-dasəd·ē\ *n* -ES [fr. *predacious*, after such pairs as E *rapacious: rapacity*] : the quality or state of being predacious ⟨a boy . . . with plenty of drive and ~ —Max Lerner⟩

**¹pre–darwinian** \ˌprē+\ *adj, usu cap D* [*pre-* + *darwinian*] : of or relating to the period or to the beliefs prevalent before enunciation of the Darwinian theory

**²pre–darwinian** \"\ *n, usu cap D* : a holder of pre-Darwinian beliefs

**pre–darwinianism** \"+\ *n, usu cap D* : the beliefs of the pre-Darwinians

**¹pre·date** \ˈprē+ˌ-\ *vt* [*pre-* + *date*] **1** : ANTEDATE 1 **2** : to precede in date : be earlier in time than

**²pre·date** \"+,-\ *n* : an edition of a newspaper carrying a dateline later than the date of issue ⟨Sunday ~*s* of metropolitan newspapers are sent to many small towns⟩

**pre·da·tion** \prēˈdāshən, prəˈd-\ *n* -S [L *praedation-, praedatio*, fr. *praedatus*, (past part. of *praedari* to plunder) + *-ion-, -io* -ion — more at PREY] **1** : the act of preying or plundering : DEPREDATION, DESPOILMENT, RAPACITY ⟨the enlightened monarchs . . . were not averse to an occasional war of ~ —Morris Watnick⟩ **2** : a mode of life in which food is primarily obtained by killing and consuming animals ⟨~ reduces the size of the prey population, which responds by more rapid growth —*Scientific Monthly*⟩ — compare MUTUALISM, PARASITISM

**predation pressure** *n* : the effects of predation on a natural community esp. with respect to the survival of species preyed upon

**pred·a·tism** \ˈpredəˌtizəm\ *n* -S [*predatory* + *-ism*] : the habit or practice of living by predation or as a predator — used chiefly of wild animals; compare COMMENSALISM, PARASITISM

**pred·a·tive** \-dəd·iv\ *adj* [L *predatus* + E *-ive*] : PREDATORY

**pred·a·tor** \ˈpredəd·ə(r), -edətə- *also* -edəˌtȯ(ə)r *or* -ō(ə)\ *n* -S [L *praedator* plunderer, hunter, fr. *praedatus* (past part. of *praedari* to plunder, prey on) + *-or* — more at PREY] **1** : one that preys, destroys, or devours ⟨of all the man-made agents of destruction, . . . the motorcar is the most voracious ~ —Eugene Kinkead⟩ **2** : an animal that depends on predation for its food: **a** : CARNIVORE; *esp* : an animal that preys on one or more other animals that man wishes to preserve for his own use **b** : INSECTIVORE **3** *law* : an animal or bird not regarded as game and not protected by game laws

**pred·a·to·ri·al** \ˌpredəˈtōrēəl, -tȯr-\ *adj* [L *praedatorius* predatory + E *-al*] : PREDATORY

**pred·a·to·ri·ly** \ˌ==ˈrōlē, -li\ *adv* : in a predatory manner

**pred·a·to·ri·ness** \-rēnəs, -rin-\ *n* -ES : the quality or state of being predatory

**pred·a·to·ry** \ˈpredəˌtōrē, -tȯr-, -ri\ *adj* [L *praedatorius*, fr. *praedatus* (past part. of *praedari* to plunder, prey) + *-orius* -ory — more at PREY] **1 a** : of, relating to, or practicing plunder, pillage, or rapine : using violence or robbery for aggrandizement ⟨seven years of ~ warfare —*Amer. Guide Series: N.Y.*⟩ ⟨a ~ class of capitalists —J.D.Hart⟩ **b** : disposed or showing a disposition to injure or exploit others for one's own gain ⟨the girl was small, too small, with severe elegance and with a ~ face —D.C.Loughlin⟩ **2** *obs* : DESTRUCTIVE, HARMFUL, INJURIOUS **3** : living by predation : PREDACIOUS; *also* : adapted to predation

**pre·dawn** \ˈprē+ˌ-\ *adj* [*pre-* + *dawn*] : of or relating to the time just before dawn

**prede** *vb* -ED/-ING/-S [L *praeda* booty, plunder — more at PREY] *obs* : PLUNDER

**¹pre·decease** \ˌprē+\ *vb* [*pre-* + *decease*] *vt* : to die before (another person) ~ *vi* : to die first

**²predecease** \"\ *n* [*pre-* + *decease*] : prior decease

**prede·ces·sor** \ˈpredəˌsesə(r) *also* ˈprēd- *or* -edə,- *or* -edi,- *or* -se,sō(ə)r *or* -ō(ə) *or* ˌ==ˈ=(,)=\ *n* -S [ME *predecessour*, fr. MF *predecesseur*, fr. LL *praedecessor*, fr. L *prae-* pre- + *decessor* retiring governor, fr. *decessus* (past part. of *decedere* to depart, retire from office) + *-or* — more at DECEASE] **1 a** : one that precedes; *esp* : a person who has previously occupied a position or office to which another has succeeded ⟨dwell with satisfaction upon the poet's difference from his ~*s* —T.S. Eliot⟩ ⟨was my ~ in title to the house⟩ **b** : something that has been followed or displaced by another ⟨sun-dried bricks, the ~*s* of burnt brick —Fiske Kimball⟩ ⟨the edifice follows the general style and proportions of its ~ —*Amer. Guide Series: Vt.*⟩ **2** *archaic* : ANCESTOR

**pre·decide** \ˌprē+\ *vt* [*pre-* + *decide*] : to decide in advance ⟨the fiscal monster which ~*s* everything —*Life*⟩

**pre·declare** \"+\ *vt* [*pre-* + *declare*] *archaic* : to declare beforehand

**pre·define** \"+\ *vt* [*pre-* + *define*] : to define or determine in advance — **pre·definition** \(ˌ)prē+\ *n*

**pre·delinquent** \ˌprē+\ *adj* [*pre-* + *delinquent*] : behaving so as to suggest future delinquency : developing or tending toward delinquency

**pre·del·la** \prəˈdelə\ *n, pl* **predel·le** \-elē, -e(ˌ)lā\ [It, stool, prayer stool, step of an altar, prob. fr. OHG *bret* board; akin to OE *bord* board] **1 a** : a step or platform on which an altar is placed — called also *footpace* **b** : a painting or sculpture on the face of a predella **2 a** : SUPERALTAR **b** : GRADINE, RETABLE **c** : a painting or sculpture along the front of a superaltar or forming a border or frame at the foot of an altarpiece **3** : a secondary painting constituting a border or other appendage to a principal one

**pre·dental** \(ˈ)prē+\ *adj* [*pre-* + *dental*] : preliminary to or preparing for a course in dentistry

**pre·dentary** \"+\ *adj* [*pre-* + *dentary*] : of, relating to, or being a bone in the lower jaw of some dinosaurs that is situated in front of the dentary bones

**pre·den·ta·ta** \ˌprēˌdenˈtäd·ə, -tād·ə\ [NL, fr. L *prae-* pre- + *dentata*, neut. pl. of *dentatus* toothed — more at DENTATE] *syn of* ORNITHISCHIA

**pre·dentin** \(ˈ)prē+\ *n* [*pre-* + *dentin*] : immature uncalcified dentin consisting chiefly of fibrils

**pre·depression** \ˌprē+\ *adj* [*pre-* + *depression*] : of or relating to the economic situation existing before a business depression ⟨very oppressive ~ salary contracts —*Harper's*⟩

**pre·design** \"+\ *vt* [*pre-* + *design*] *archaic* : to design or plan beforehand

**pre·designate** \(ˈ)prē+\ *vt* [*pre-* + *designate*] **1** : to designate beforehand ⟨subjects were . . . to respond whenever any one of a set of eight *predesignated* letters appeared —*Biol. Abstracts*⟩ **2** : to specify (the expected character of a sample) in advance of or independently of examination of the sample in order to avoid fallacious inference — **pre·designation** \(ˌ)prē+\ *n*

**¹pre·des·ti·nar·i·an** \(ˌ)prēˌdestəˈna(a)rēən\ *adj* [*predestination* + *-arian* (as in *trinitarian*, adj.)] : of or relating to predestination : holding the doctrine of predestination

**²predestinarian** \"\ *n* -S [*predestination* + *-arian*] **1** : a believer in esp. theological predestination ⟨the nature of man is a subject for quarrels between . . . free-willers and ~*s* —J.R.Chamberlain⟩ **2** : FATALIST

**pre·des·ti·nar·i·an·ism** \(ˌ)=ˌ==ˈ==əˌnizəm\ *n* -S [²*predestinarian* + *-ism*] : the system or doctrine of the predestinarians

**¹pre·des·ti·nate** \prēˈdestənət, -ˌnāt\ *adj* [ME, fr. L *predestinatus*, past part. of *praedestinare* to determine beforehand, — more at PREDESTINE] **1** : foreordained by God's decree or eternal purpose **2** : destined, fated, or determined beforehand ⟨there is a sense of ~ inevitability about its passage . . . with its sixteen silvered cars —W.D.Edmonds⟩

**²predestinate** \"\ *n* -S : a person predestinated to eternal life

**³pre·des·ti·nate** \-ˌnāt\ *vt* [ME *predestinaten*, fr. L *praedestinatus*, past part. of *praedestinare*] **1** : to foreordain to an earthly or eternal lot or destiny (as salvation or damnation) by divine purpose or decree ⟨for whom he did foreknow, he also did ~ to be conformed to the image of his Son —Rom 8:29 (AV)⟩ **2** *archaic* : to choose, fix, or settle beforehand : PREDETERMINE

**pre·des·ti·na·tion** \(ˌ)=ˌ==ˈnāshən\ *n* [ME *predestinacion*, fr. LL *praedestination-, praedestinatio*, fr. L *praedestinatus* (past part. of *praedestinare* to predestine) + *-ion-, -io* -ion] **1** : the act of predestinating or the state of being predestinated : FATE, FOREORDINATION, DESTINY ⟨the freshman comes with a kind of fatal ~ —Irwin Edman⟩ **2** : the theological doctrine that all events throughout eternity have been foreordained by divine decree or purpose; *esp* : the foreordination by God of each individual's ultimate destiny particularly to eternal life ⟨Calvin's doctrine of ~ includes the decree of reprobation, which Lutheran confessions exclude⟩ — see ELECTION 1 d

**pre·des·ti·na·tion·al** \(ˌ)=ˌ==ˈnāshənᵊl, -shnəl\ *adj* : of or relating to predestination

**pre·des·ti·na·tion·ist** \(ˌ)=ˌ==ˈnāsh(ə)nəst\ *n* -S [*predestination* + *-ist*] : PREDESTINARIAN

**pre·des·ti·na·tor** \=ˈ==ˌnād·ə(r)\ *n* -S [*predestinate* + *-or*] **1** : one that predestinates **2** *archaic* : PREDESTINARIAN

**pre·destine** \(ˈ)prē+\ *vt* [ME *predestinen*, fr. MF or L; MF *predestiner*, fr. L *praedestinare* to determine beforehand, fr. *prae-* pre- + *destinare* to determine — more at DESTINE] : to destine, decree, determine, appoint, or settle beforehand : foreordain esp. by divine decree or eternal purpose ⟨advocates of the doctrine of double predestination maintain that God ~*s* some to eternal life and others to eternal death⟩

**pre·destiny** \"+\ *n* [*pre-* + *destiny*] : PREDESTINATION, FATE

**pre·determinate** \ˌprē+\ *adj* [LL *praedeterminatus*, fr. past part. of *praedeterminare* to predetermine] : PREDETERMINED

**pre·determination** \"+\ *n* [partly fr. *predetermine* + *-ation*, partly fr. *pre-* + *determination*] **:** the act of predetermining or the state of being predetermined: as **a** *archaic* **:** a decision made beforehand esp. without due consideration **b :** the ordaining of events beforehand **c :** PREDESTINATION ⟨the ~ of God's will⟩ **d :** a previous mental determination **:** a purpose formed beforehand **e :** a fixing or settling in advance ⟨this is not an insinuation that there was any ~ of such a sequence of developmental steps leading to ourselves —A.L. Kroeber⟩ **f :** the calculation or discovery of something beforehand ⟨~ of the cost of construction⟩

**pre·determine** \"+\ *vb* [LL *praedeterminare*, fr. L *prae-* pre- + *determinare* determine] *vt* **1 a :** FOREORDAIN, PREDESTINE **b :** to determine beforehand **:** settle in advance ⟨it is impossible to ~ the specific problems that he will meet —W.J.Reilly⟩ **2 :** to impose a direction or tendency on beforehand ~ *vi* **:** to determine or resolve beforehand

**predetermined cost** *n* **:** a cost estimated or computed in advance of production to which it applies — see STANDARD COST; compare ACTUAL COST, HISTORICAL COST

**pre·determinedly** \¦prē+\ *adv* [*predetermined* (past part. of *predetermine*) + *-ly*] **:** in a predetermined manner

**pre·determinism** \"+\ *n* [*predetermine* + *-ism*] **:** the view that the development of the individual is predetermined by heredity

**predial** *var of* PRAEDIAL

**pre·diastolic** \(¦)prē+\ *adj* [*pre-* + *diastolic*] **:** occurring or audible before the diastole of the heart ⟨a ~ murmur⟩

¹**pred·i·ca·ble** \'predəkəbəl, -dēk-\ *n* -s [ML *praedicabile*, fr. neut. of *praedicabilis* capable of being predicated, fr. LL *praedicare* to predicate + L *-abilis* -able] **:** something that may be predicated **:** a general attribute of a class; *esp* **:** one of the five most general kinds of attribution in traditional logic that include genus, species, difference, property, and accident

²**predicable** \"\ *adj* [ML *praedicabilis*] **:** capable of being predicated or asserted

**pre·dic·a·ment** \prē'dikəmənt, prə'd-, *in sense 1 usu* 'predək- *or* 'predēk-\ *n* -s [ME, fr. LL *praedicamentum*, fr. *praedicare* to *predicate* + L *-mentum* -ment; trans. of Gk *katēgoria* category] **1 :** the character, status, or classification assigned by a predication; *specif* **:** CATEGORY 1 **2** *archaic* **:** CONDITION, STATE **3 :** a difficult, perplexing, or trying situation **:** a position imposing a hard or unwelcome choice ⟨everywhere he could observe, in new shapes and sizes, the old ~*s* and follies of men —E.B.White⟩ **4 :** a near near-fall in wrestling that scores one point for the aggressor

**syn** DILEMMA, QUANDARY, PLIGHT, SCRAPE, FIX, JAM, PICKLE: PREDICAMENT suggests a difficult situation bringing perplexity about best procedure for extrication, sometimes with lack of freedom to do what one would prefer ⟨the *predicament* of our contemporary English drama, forced to deal almost exclusively with cases of sexual attraction, and yet forbidden to exhibit the incidents of that attraction or even to discuss its nature —G.B.Shaw⟩ ⟨in the *predicament* with which our civilization now finds itself confronted — the problem, namely, how to find healthy, happy leisure for all the working millions who are now being liberated by machines from their day-long toils —L.P.Smith⟩ DILEMMA may apply to a predicament extending a choice between equally unpleasant or unsatisfactory alternatives ⟨a *dilemma* arose, when the weary emigrants came to a point where the stream forked, and no one knew which fork to follow —G.R.Stewart⟩ ⟨his *dilemma* is that he can neither use his terms with the simple directness of the natural scientist pointing to physical factors, nor with the assurance of a philosopher who has some source for their meaning in the system from which he begins his deduction —R.M.Weaver⟩ QUANDARY may focus attention on puzzlement and perplexity without clear analysis between possible choices ⟨he was in a greater *quandary* than ever. Lord, Lord, he thought, what had he got into? —Theodore Dreiser⟩ PLIGHT may refer to any unfortunate, trying, or unhappy situation ⟨why then discharge the men from the electric plant and then try to support them anyway, seeing that they are not likely to get other employment, or, if they do, will displace others who would be in a similar *plight* —M.R.Cohen⟩ ⟨the *plight* of the ten million forgotten men and women living at or below the destitution level —R.H.S.Crossman⟩ SCRAPE may refer to a situation, often one in which one has involved oneself carelessly or rashly, from which he becomes disentangled with difficulty or loss, esp. one impairing his reputation ⟨other young clergymen, much greater fools in many respects than he, would not have got into these *scrapes*. He seemed to have developed an aptitude for mischief —Samuel Butler †1902⟩ ⟨he escapes from trouble only to become idiotically conceited; and in the grip of conceit he plunges dementedly into a more ghastly *scrape* than the last —F.A.Swinnerton⟩ FIX and JAM, informal words, stress involvement and entanglement from which extrication is difficult ⟨I am . . . self-employed, and when you are in that *fix* you cannot tell when you are on vacation and when you are working —Frank Sullivan⟩ ⟨they get sick and it puts them in a *jam* and they end up under a pile of bills —Hamilton Basso⟩ PICKLE, now rather dated, may refer to any particularly embarrassing or sorry situation ⟨I worked hard enough to earn my passage and my victuals. But when I was left ashore in Melbourne I was in a pretty *pickle* —G.B. Shaw⟩ **syn** see in addition CLASS

**pred·i·ca·men·tal** \¦predəkə¦ment³l, -dēk- *sometimes* prē¦dik- *or* prə¦d-\ *adj* **:** of or relating to a predicament (sense 1)

¹**pred·i·cant** \'predəkənt, -dēk-\ *n* -s [MF, fr. LL *praedicant-*, *praedicans*, pres. part. of *praedicare* to preach — more at PREACH] **1 :** PREACHER; *specif* **:** a preaching friar **:** DOMINICAN **2** [modif. of D *predikant*] **:** PREDIKANT

²**predicant** \"\ *adj* [LL *praedicant-*, *praedicans*, pres. part. of *praedicare* to preach] **:** devoted to preaching ⟨the Dominicans are a ~ order⟩

¹**pred·i·cate** \'predəkə̇t, -dēk- *sometimes* -də,kāt; *usu* \d·+V\ *n* -s [LL *praedicatum*, fr. neut. of *praedicatus*, past part. of *praedicare* to predicate, preach, fr. L, to proclaim publicly, assert — more at PREACH] **1 a :** something that is affirmed or denied of the subject in a proposition in logic ⟨in "paper is white", whiteness is the ~⟩ **b :** a term designating a property or relation **:** a propositional function of one or more arguments **2 :** the part of a sentence or clause that expresses what is said of the subject and that usu. consists of a verb with or without objects, complements, or adverbial modifiers **3 :** a title asserting something ⟨"mother of God" is a ~ of Mary⟩

²**pred·i·cate** \-də,kāt, *usu* -ād·+V\ *vb* -ED/-ING/-S [LL *praedicatus*, past part. of *praedicare* to assert, predicate, preach, fr. L, to proclaim publicly, assert — more at PREACH] *vt* **1 a :** AFFIRM, DECLARE, PROCLAIM **b** *archaic* **:** PREACH **c** *obs* **:** COMMEND, PRAISE **2 a :** to assert or affirm as a quality, attribute, or property — used with following *of* ⟨~*s* intelligence of man⟩ **b** *logic* **:** to affirm of the subject of a proposition **:** make (a term) the predicate in a proposition **3 :** FOUND, BASE ⟨any code of ethics must be *predicated* upon the basic principles of truth and honesty —H.A.Wagner⟩ **4** [by alter.] *archaic* **:** PREDICT **5 :** to convey an implication of ⟨~*s* the arrival of a revolutionary situation —George Soule⟩ ~ *vi* **:** to assert something about another thing **:** AFFIRM, DECLARE **syn** see ASSERT

³**pred·i·cate** *pronunc at* ¹PREDICATE\ *adj* **:** belonging to the predicate; *specif* **:** completing the meaning of a copula or link verb ⟨~ noun⟩ ⟨~ adjective⟩

**predicate calculus** *n* [trans. of G *prädikatenkalkül*] **:** FUNCTIONAL CALCULUS

**predicate nominative** *n* **:** a predicate noun or pronoun in the nominative or common case completing the meaning of a link verb (as *consul* in "Caesar consul erat" or "Caesar was consul")

**predicate term** *n* [¹*predicate*] **:** PREDICATE 1 a

**predicate variable** *n, logic* **:** a variable for which a predicate may be substituted

**pred·i·ca·tion** \,predə'kāshən\ *n* -s [ME *predicacion*, fr. OF *predication*, fr. L *praedication-*, *praedicatio*, act of proclaiming, fr. *praedicatus* (past part. of *praedicare* to proclaim) + *-ion-*, *-io* -ion — more at PREACH] **1** *archaic* **a :** an act of proclaiming or preaching **b :** SERMON **2 :** an act or instance of predicating **:** AFFIRMATION, ASSERTION: as **a :** the expression of action, state, or quality by a grammatical predicate **b** *logic* **:** the affirming something of another thing; *esp* **:** the attachment of a predicate to a subject, ascription of a property to an individual, or assignment of something to a class — see ESSENTIAL PREDICATION; compare SUBJECTION

**pred·i·ca·tional** \¦==¦kāshən³l, -shnəl\ *adj* [*predication* + *-al*] **:** of, relating to, or forming a predication or a predicate

**pred·i·ca·tive** \'predə,kād·|iv, -ăt|, |ēv, *chiefly Brit* pri'dikətiv\ *adj* [LL *praedicativus*, fr. *praedicatus* (past part. of *praedicare* to assert, predicate) + L *-ivus* -ive] **:** expressing affirmation or predication **:** DECLARATORY; *esp* **:** constituting a predicate or part of one — **pred·i·ca·tive·ly** \-ə̇vlē, -li\ *adv*

**pred·i·ca·tor** \'predə,kād·ə(r), -atə-\ *n* -s [MF *predicatour*, fr. LL *praedicator*, fr. L, proclaimer, fr. *praedicatus* (past part. of *praedicare* to proclaim) + *-or* — more at PREACH] **1 :** one that predicates **2** *archaic* **:** PREACHER; *esp* **:** a preaching friar

**pred·i·ca·to·ry** \'predəkə,tōrē\ *adj* [LL *praedicatorius*, fr. *praedicatus* (past part. of *praedicare* to preach + L *-orius* -ory] **:** of or relating to preaching

**pre·dict** \prē'dikt, prə'd-\ *vb* -ED/-ING/-S [L *praedictus*, past part. of *praedicere* to predict, fr. *prae-* pre- + *dicere* to say — more at DICTION] *vt* **:** to declare in advance **:** PROPHESY ⟨the katydids ~ frost in six more weeks —Corey Ford⟩ ~ *vi* **:** to make a prediction **:** PROPHESY **syn** see FORETELL

**pre·dict·abil·i·ty** \=¦=əbiləd·ē, -lətē, -i\ *n* **:** the quality or state of being predictable

**pre·dict·a·ble** \=¦==bəl\ *adj* [*predict* + *-able*] **:** capable of being foretold ⟨are clearly drifting into ~ chaos and critical dilution of standards —H.D.Gideonse⟩ — **pre·dict·a·bly** \-blē, -bli\ *adv*

**predicted firing** *n* [fr. past part. of *predict*] **:** the firing at a point at which a moving target will arrive at the same time as the projectile according to predictions based on observations — compare ²LEAD 3 g

**pre·dic·tion** \prē'dikshən, prə'd-\ *n* -s [L *praediction-*, *praedictio*, fr. *praedictus* (past part. of *praedicere* to predict) + *-ion-*, *-io* -ion] **1 a :** an act of predicting **b :** something that is predicted **:** FORECAST, PROPHECY **2** *obs* **:** PORTENT **3 :** an inference regarding a future event based on probability theory

**pre·dic·tive** \-ktiv\ *adj* [LL *praedictivus*, fr. L *praedictus* + *-ivus* -ive] **:** of, relating to, or usable or valuable for prediction — **pre·dic·tive·ly** \-tə̇vlē\ *adv*

**pre·dic·tor** \-ktə(r)\ *n* -s [ML *praedictor*, fr. L *praedictus* + *-or*] **1 :** one that predicts ⟨every hillside and prairie mile and desert ridge is a mirror of the past and a ~ of the future —R. W.Howard⟩ **2 :** a mechanism for controlling antiaircraft fire by calculating the precise position of an aircraft on arrival of a shell

**pre·dic·to·ry** \-ktərē\ *adj* [*predict* + *-ory*] *archaic* **:** PREDICTIVE, PROPHETIC

**pre·digest** \(¦)prē+\ *vt* [*pre-* + *digest*] **1 :** to subject to predigestion **:** digest beforehand **2 :** to simplify for easy use ⟨want our great works even more thoroughly ~*ed* in the form of textbooks, condensations, summaries, and the like —Crane Brinton⟩

**pre·digestion** \¦prē+\ *n* [*pre-* + *digestion*] **1** *obs* **:** premature or too rapid digestion **2 :** artificial partial digestion of food (as by enzymatic action) for use in illness or impaired digestion

**pre·di·kant** \¦prādē¦känt\ *n* -s [D, fr. MF *predicant* — more at PREDICANT] **:** PREACHER; *specif* **:** a minister of the Dutch Reformed Church

**predi·lect** \¦pred³l¦ekt, -rēd-, -ē,dī,le-\ *or* **predi·lect·ed** \-təd\ *adj* [*predilect* fr. ML *praedilectus*, past part. of *praediligere*; *predilected* fr. *predilect* + *-ed*] **:** PREFERRED, CHOSEN ⟨not the most obstinately ~ optimism can blind us to the growing canker —H.B.Alexander⟩

**predi·lec·tion** \¦pred³l¦ekshən, -də¦le- *also* -rēd³l- *sometimes* -rē,dī¦le-\ *n* -s [F *prédilection*, fr. ML *praedilectus*, (past part. of *praediligere* to prefer, love more, fr. L *prae-* pre- + *diligere* to love) + F *-ion* — more at DILIGENT] **:** a favorable prepossession **:** INCLINATION, LIKING, PREFERENCE ⟨a ~ for straight bourbon —C.V.Little⟩

**syn** PARTIALITY, PREPOSSESSION, PREJUDICE, BIAS: PREDILECTION indicates a previous liking or temperamental predisposition ⟨one or two authors of fiction for whom I have a *predilection* and whose works I look out for —A.C.Benson⟩ ⟨the person with a *predilection* for history may think of such treasured shrines as Independence Hall, Valley Forge Park, and the Gettysburg Battlefields —*Amer. Guide Series: Pa.*⟩ PARTIALITY indicates a disposition to favor a person or thing, sometimes unfairly or with partisanship or undue fondness ⟨fond *partiality* for their own daughters' performance, and total indifference to any other person's —Jane Austen⟩ ⟨sometimes newcomers to the fleet were a bit annoyed over the skipper's *partiality* toward this absentminded youth —L.C. Douglas⟩ PREPOSSESSION implies a fixed idea or notion, esp. a value judgment, that dominates and is likely to preclude objective judgment of something seeming counter to it ⟨we have not only to realise how our own *prepossessions* and the metaphysical figments of our own creation have obscured the simple realities of religion and science alike —Havelock Ellis⟩ PREJUDICE indicates a preconceived notion, a judgment before evidence is available, or an unreasoned prepossession, often an unfavorable one marked by suspicion, dislike, or antipathy ⟨but she had *prejudices* on the side of ancestry; she had a value for rank and consequence, which blinded her a little to the faults of those who possessed them —Jane Austen⟩ ⟨every one I knew well in Sligo despised Nationalists and Catholics, but all disliked England with a *prejudice* that had come down perhaps from the days of the Irish Parliament —W.B.Yeats⟩ BIAS may indicate an imbalance or distortion in judgment with a resulting unreasoned and unfair inclination for or against a person or thing ⟨we can discover some of our own peculiarities, our own particular slant or *bias* —A.J.Toynbee⟩ ⟨the personal *bias* of the brilliant founder of psychoanalysis has given the Freudian psychology more than one twist —Edward Sapir⟩

**pre·diluvian** \¦prē+\ *adj* [*pre-* + L *diluvium* flood + E *-an* — more at DELUGE] **:** ANTEDILUVIAN 1

**preding** *pres part of* PREDE

**pre·dispose** \¦prē+\ *vb* [*pre-* + *dispose*] *vt* **:** to dispose in advance **:** make susceptible **:** INCLINE ⟨there was little about this baby-faced young man to ~ people in his favor —Thomas Mann⟩ ⟨~ the miner to rheumatism —Lewis Mumford⟩ ~ *vi* **:** to bring about susceptibility ⟨exposure to cold and dampness . . . ~ to infection —H.J.Morgan⟩

**predisposed** *adj* [fr. past part. of *predispose*] **1 :** having a predisposition **:** INCLINED, SUSCEPTIBLE, TENDING **2 :** arranged or settled in advance ⟨took up his ~ place in society⟩

**pre·disposition** \(¦)prē+\ *n* [*pre-* + *disposition*] **:** a condition of being predisposed **:** INCLINATION, TENDENCY ⟨habits and ~*s* requisite to . . . painstaking work on one manuscript —Harry Bober⟩ ⟨there is less ~ to attend college in the face of discouraging odds in some homes than in others —B.G. Gallagher⟩ ⟨a certain degree of hereditary ~ to cancer is apparent in man —G.E.Wakerlin⟩

**predivine** *vb* [L *praedivinare*, fr. *prae-* pre- + *divinare* to divine] *obs* **:** to divine beforehand

**pred·most race** \pər'zhed,mōst-\ *n, usu cap P* [fr. *Předmost*, village in central Czechoslovakia] **:** BRÜNN RACE

**pred·nis·o·lone** \pred'nisə,lōn\ *n* -s [*prednis-* (as in *prednisone*) + *-ol* + *-one* (as in *prednisone*)] **:** a glucocorticoid $C_{21}H_{28}O_5$ that is a dehydrogenated analogue of hydrocortisone, is similar in biological action to prednisone, and is often used in the form of an ester or a methyl derivative

**pred·ni·sone** \'prednə,sōn\ *n* -s [prob. fr. *pregnane* + *-diene* + *cortisone*] **:** a crystalline or amorphous glucocorticoid drug $C_{21}H_{26}O_5$ that is a dehydrogenated analogue of cortisone, is more active biologically than cortisone, and is used similarly

**pre·dom·i·nance** \prē'dämənən(t)s, prə'd-\ *n* [F *prédominance*, fr. MF *predominer* to predominate + *-ance*] **1 a :** the quality or state of being predominant **:** controlling influence **:** ASCENDANCY ⟨her great tradition of continued ~ and uninterrupted empire —Hilaire Belloc⟩ **b :** numerical superiority **:** MAJORITY, PREVALENCE ⟨a ~ of water colors marked the exhibition⟩ **2 :** the power or influence over human affairs assigned in astrology to heavenly bodies

**pre·dom·i·nan·cy** \-nənsē, -si\ *n* -ES [¹*predominant* + *-cy*] **:** PREDOMINANCE

¹**pre·dom·i·nant** \-nənt\ *adj* [MF *predominant*, fr. ML *praedominant-*, *praedominans*, pres. part. of *praedominari* to predominate, fr. L *prae-* pre- + *dominari* to rule, govern — more at DOMINATE] **:** holding an ascendancy **:** having superior strength, influence, authority, or position **:** CONTROLLING, DOMINATING, PREVAILING ⟨the town and the school district were the ~ governmental units —Margie Malmberg⟩ ⟨could yield to the pressure of a ~ self-interest —J.L.Motley⟩ **syn** see DOMINANT

²**predominant** \"\ *n* **1 :** one that predominates **2 :** an organism occupying a position of marked importance in an ecological community without being a true dominant; *esp* **:** a vertebrate holding a conspicuous position in a predominantly plant community ⟨the buffalo constituted a true ~ on the western grass lands⟩

**pre·dom·i·nant·ly** *adv* **:** in a predominant manner

¹**pre·dom·i·nate** \-mənə̇t\ *adj* [alter. (influenced by *moderate*, adj.) of *predominant*] **:** PREDOMINANT ⟨the ~ gonadal sex in cases of true hermaphroditism —*Jour. Amer. Med. Assoc.*⟩ — **pre·dom·i·nate·ly** *adv*

²**pre·dom·i·nate** \prē'dämə,nāt, prə'd-, *usu* -ād·+V\ *vb* [ML *praedominatus*, past part. of *praedominari* to predominate — more at PREDOMINANT] *vi* **1** *obs* **:** to have determining astrological influence **2 a :** to exert controlling power or influence **:** exercise superiority (as in strength or authority) **:** GOVERN, PREVAIL, RULE ⟨moral and humane tendencies . . . normally ~ over the sadistic strain in human nature —Alfred Cobban⟩ **b :** to hold advantage in numbers or quantity **:** PREPONDERATE ⟨sagebrush is the *predominating* growth —G.R.Stewart⟩ ~ *vt* **:** to exert control over **:** DOMINATE, GOVERN, RULE ⟨his smile *predominated* his features —Alvin Redman⟩ ⟨hardwoods . . . ~ the forest lands there —*Subscription Books Bull.*⟩

**pre·dom·i·nat·ing·ly** \=¦==,==,==\ *adv* [*predominating* (pres. part. of *predominate*) + *-ly*] **:** PREDOMINANTLY

**pre·dom·i·na·tion** \=,=='nāshən\ *n* [*predomine* + *-ation*] **:** PREDOMINANCE

**predomine** *vb* [MF *predominer*, fr. ML *praedominari*] *obs* **:** PREDOMINATE

**pre·doom** \(ˈ)prē+\ *vt* [*pre-* + *doom*] **1** *archaic* **:** to doom or condemn beforehand **2** *archaic* **:** to condemn to (a penalty) in advance

**pre·dravidian** \¦prē+\ *n, usu cap D* [*pre-* + *Dravidian*] **:** a member of an ethnic group chiefly in India believed by some anthropologists to be a blend of Negrito and proto-Australoid or Veddoid

**pre·dreadnought** \'prē+¦-\ *n* [*pre-* + *dreadnought*] **:** the heaviest battleship carrying mixed-caliber batteries and preceding development of the dreadnought

**pre·dynastic** \¦prē+\ *adj* [*pre-* + *dynastic*] **:** of or relating to a time before dynasties, esp. before the ancient Egyptian dynasties ruling from about 3400 B.C.

**pree** \'prē\ *vt* **preed; preed; preeing; prees** [short fr. *preve*, to test, prove, fr. ME *proeven*, *preven* fr. OF *preuv-*, pres. stem of *prover* to test, prove — more at PROVE] *Scot* **:** to taste tentatively **:** SAMPLE — **pree the mouth of** *Scot* **:** KISS

**pre·echo** \(ˈ)prē+\ *n* [*pre-* + *echo*] **:** an echo in a sound recording (as a phonograph record) that is mechanically induced by a manufacturing fault and is heard before the sound causing it when the recording is played

**pre·eclampsia** \¦=+\ *n* [NL, fr. *pre-* + *eclampsia*] **:** a toxic condition developing in late pregnancy characterized by a sudden rise in blood pressure, excessive gain in weight, generalized edema, albuminuria, severe headache, and visual disturbances — **pre·eclamptic** \"+\ *adj*

**preef** \'prēf\ *chiefly Scot var of* PROOF

¹**pre·election** \¦prē+\ *n* [*pre-* + *election*] **1 a** *obs* **:** PREFERENCE **b :** PREDESTINATION **2** *archaic* **:** election in advance

²**preelection** \"\ *adj* [*pre-* + *election*] **:** preceding an election ⟨a ~ campaign leaflet —*New Yorker*⟩ ⟨~ meeting⟩ ⟨~ pledge⟩

**pre·electric** \"+\ *or* **pre·electrical** \"+\ *adj* [*pre-* + *electric* or *electrical*] **:** preceding general use of electricity

**preem** \'prēm\ *n* -s [by shortening & alter.] *slang* **:** PREMIERE 1

**pre·emergence** \¦prē+\ *adj* [*pre-* + *emergence*] **:** used or occurring before emergence of seedlings aboveground ⟨dramatic success has been achieved with ~ herbicides —*Chem. & Engineering News*⟩ ⟨no ~ injury occurred in the field —*Experiment Station Record*⟩

**preemie** *var of* PREMIE

**pre·em·i·nence** \prē'emənən(t)s\ *n* [ME, fr. LL *praeeminentia*, fr. *praeeminent-*, *praeeminens* preeminent + L *-ia* -y] **1 :** the quality or state of being preeminent **:** superiority in rank, position, or influence **:** surpassing excellence **:** dominant authority ⟨more important than any legal sanction was . . . the personal ~ he had won —John Buchan⟩ ⟨corn moved forward . . . in the race with soybeans for ~ as a chemurgic crop —*Collier's Yr. Bk.*⟩ **2** *archaic* **:** a particular distinction or honor or an outstanding quality

**pre·em·i·nen·cy** \-nənsē\ *n* [LL *praeeminentia*] *archaic* **:** PREEMINENCE

**pre·em·i·nent** \-nənt\ *adj* [LL *praeeminent-*, *praeeminens*, fr. L, pres. part. of *praeeminere* to be outstanding, excel, fr. *prae-* pre- + *eminere* to stand out — more at EMINENT] **:** having paramount rank, dignity, or importance **:** FIRST, OUTSTANDING, SUPREME ⟨was able to achieve to a ~ degree the combination of two great gifts —M.R.Cohen⟩ ⟨the ~ classic in its category —R.L.Taylor⟩ ⟨the cuisine is . . . ~ for its seafood —E.A. Weeks⟩ — **pre·em·i·nent·ly** *adv*

**pre·emphasis** \(ˈ)prē+\ *n* [*pre-* + *emphasis*] **:** the intentional alteration of the relative strengths of signals at different frequencies (as in radio and in disc recording) to reduce adverse effects (as noise) in the following parts of the system

**pre·empt** \prē'em(p)t\ *vb* -ED/-ING/-S [back-formation fr. *preemption*] *vt* **1 :** to settle upon (public land) with a right of preemption **:** take by preemption **2 :** to seize upon to the exclusion of others **:** take for oneself **:** APPROPRIATE ⟨prose has ~*ed* a lion's share of the territory once held . . . by poetry —J.L.Lowes⟩ ⟨as the immigrants ~*ed* the central areas of the cities, the older stock moved out toward the . . . suburbs —Oscar Handlin⟩ ~ *vi* **:** to make a preemptive bid in bridge **syn** see APPROPRIATE

**pre·emp·tion** \-'em(p)shən\ *n* -s [ML *praeemptus* (past part. of *praeemere* to buy beforehand, fr. L *prae-* pre- + *emere* to take, buy) + E *-ion* — more at REDEEM] **1 :** the act or right of purchasing before others: as **a :** the privilege or prerogative formerly enjoyed by the king of buying provisions at an appraised valuation for his household in preference to others **b :** the prior right belonging among some primitive peoples to persons standing in various family, tribal, or neighborhood relations to purchase property sold or proposed to be sold to a stranger at the price offered by the stranger **c :** the right of a belligerent to seize and purchase at an appraised price other contraband of war than absolute contraband belonging to a neutral and en route to an enemy in its own territory or on the high seas or in unappropriated territory **d :** a preemption right or a piece of land occupied under one **2 :** a prior seizure or appropriation **:** a taking possession before others ⟨raises the question of federal ~ of the security field —*Report: Amer. Civil Liberties Union*⟩ ⟨the agency's ~ of all . . . power and responsibility —A.G.Harper⟩

**pre·emp·tion·er** \-sh(ə)nə(r)\ *n* -s [*preemption* + *-er*] **:** the holder of a preemption right; *also* **:** PREEMPTOR

**preemption right** *n* **:** a right of preemption; *specif* **:** a right given by public land laws whereby a citizen may claim and buy under stated conditions a portion not exceeding 160 acres of public land

**pre·emp·tive** \-m(p)tiv, -tēv *also* -təv\ *adj* [ML *praeemptus* + E *-ive*] **1 :** of or relating to preemption **:** having power to preempt **:** PREEMPTING **2 :** of, relating to, or constituting a bid in bridge that is higher than necessary and is designed to shut out shifts by the partner or bids by the opponents — **pre·emp·tive·ly** \-tə̇vlē, -li\ *adv*

**preemptive right** *n* **:** the right of existing shareholders to purchase additional stock offered for sale for cash prior to its being offered for sale to others

**pre·emp·tor** \prē'em(p)tə(r) *also* -,tȯ(ə)r *or* -ȯ(ə)\ *n* -s [ML *praeemptus* + E *-or*] **:** one that preempts; *specif* **:** one that preempts land

**pre·emp·to·ry** \-m(p)t(ə)rē, -ri\ *adj* [ML *praeemptus* + E *-ory*] **:** of or relating to preemption

**preems** *pl of* PREEM

¹**preen** \'prēn\ *n* -s [ME *prene*, fr. OE *prēon*; akin to MD *priem* bodkin, MLG *prēn*, *prīm* pin, awl, MHG *pfrieme* awl] **1** *dial chiefly Brit* **a :** a metal pin ⟨needles and ~s⟩ **b :** BROOCH **2** *dial chiefly Brit* **:** something of trifling value ⟨he never cared a ~ for her —G.O.Brown⟩

**²preen** \"\ *vt* -ED/-ING/-S [ME *prenen*, fr. *prene*] *chiefly Scot* : ²PIN

**³preen** \"\ *vb* -ED/-ING/-S [ME *preinen*, alter. (influenced by ME *prenen*) of *proinen*, *prunen*] *vt* **1** : to trim or dress with or as if with the beak or the tongue ⟨pigeons ~*ed* themselves and cooed softly —D.H.Lawrence⟩ ⟨a cat ~*s* its fur⟩ **2** : to dress or smooth (oneself) up : arrange (the clothing or hair) fastidiously ⟨he ~*ed* back his hair, which lay slick and thin on his head —D.C.Loughlin⟩ **3** : to pride or congratulate (oneself) for achievement ⟨~*ed* himself on having put across another sharp deal —David Walden⟩ ⟨~*ed* himself upon his sapience —Amy Lowell⟩ ~ *vi* **1** : to make sleek : DRESS, TRIM **2** : GLOAT, SWELL ⟨~*ed* as he addressed the convention opening —*Newsweek*⟩ ⟨she ~*ed*, approving her adolescence —Virginia Woolf⟩

**pre·engage** \¦prē+\ *vb* [*pre-* + *engage*] *vt* : to engage beforehand: as **a** : to bind by a prior obligation or pledge esp. of marriage **b** : to win over or obtain beforehand : PREPOSSESS **c** : PREOCCUPY ~ *vi* : to bind or pledge oneself beforehand

**pre·engagement** \"+\ *n* [partly fr. *pre-* + *engagement*, partly fr. *preengage* + *-ment*] **1** : the act of preengaging or the state of being preengaged : a prior engagement or obligation; *esp* : a previous engagement to marry **2** : PREOCCUPATION

**pre·engineering** \(¦)=+\ *adj* [*pre-* + *engineering*] : preliminary to or preparing for an engineering course

**preen gland** *n* [³*preen*] : UROPYGIAL GLAND

**pre·equalization** \(¦)prē+\ *n* [*pre-* + *equalization*] : PREEMPHASIS

**pre·erythrocytic** \¦prē+\ *adj* [*pre-* + *erythrocytic*] : of, relating to, or being exoerythrocytic stages of a malaria parasite that occur before the red blood cells are invaded

**prees** *pres 3d sing of* PREE

**pre·essential** \¦prē+\ *n* [*pre-* + *essential*] : a prerequisite essential

**pre·establish** \"+\ *vt* [*pre-* + *establish*] : to establish beforehand

**preestablished harmony** *n* [fr. past part. of *preestablish*] : a harmony declared by the philosopher Leibniz to be established eternally in advance between all monads but esp. between mind and matter

**pre·examination** \¦prē+\ *n* [*pre-* + *examination*] : examination in advance or previously

**pre·exile** \(')prē+\ *adj* [*pre-* + *exile*] : PREEXILIAN

**pre·exilian** \¦prē+\ *or* **pre·exilic** \"+\ *adj* [*preexilian* fr. *pre-* + L *exilium* + E *-an*; *preexilic* fr. *pre-* + *exile* + *-ic*] : previous to the exile of the Jews to Babylon in about 600 B.C.

**pre·exist** \"+\ *vb* [*pre-* + *exist*] *vi* : to exist earlier ~ *vt* : to exist before (something) ⟨monuments that ~ written history⟩

**pre·existence** \"+\ *n* [*pre-* + *existence*] **1** : existence in a former state or previous to something else; *specif* : existence of the soul before its union with the body — compare TRANSMIGRATION **2 a** : existence of Jesus Christ's human soul prior to his physical conception **b** : existence of the Messiah before his first advent **c** : eternal existence of the second person of the Trinity **d** : eternal existence in God of Christ as a rational principle of self-revelation in the cosmos **e** : ideal existence of Christ in the mind and eternal purpose of God

**pre·existent** \"+\ *adj* [*pre-* + *existent*] : existing previously : existing before something

**pre·ex·ist·ent·ism** \"+,izəm\ *n* [*preexistent* + *-ism*] : a theory that the life of the soul antedates that of the body

**pre·expose** \¦prē+\ *vt* [*pre-* + *expose*] : to expose in advance or prematurely

**pre·exposure** \"+\ *n* [*pre-* + *exposure*] : a preliminary exposure; *specif* : a slight uniform exposure given to a sensitive photographic film or plate prior to the main exposure usu. to increase its sensitivity

**preeze** \'prēz\ *chiefly Scot var of* PRESS

**pref** *abbr* **1** preface **2** prefatory **3** prefect; prefecture **4** preference **5** preferred **6** prefix

**¹pre·fab** \(')prē¦fab\ *adj* [by shortening] : PREFABRICATED

**²prefab** \"\ *n* -S : a prefabricated house or structure

**pre·fabricate** \(')prē+\ *vt* [*pre-* + *fabricate*] **1** : to fabricate all or most of the parts of (as a house) at a factory so that construction consists mainly of assembling and uniting standardized parts **2** : to produce synthetically or artificially : develop in a superficially plausible or stereotyped manner ⟨the novel's circumstances and characterizations have been tailor-made to fit a *prefabricated* scheme which is essentially false and gratuitous —Jerome Stone⟩ — **pre·fabrication** \(¦)prē+\ *n*

**pre·fabricator** \(')=+\ *n* [*prefabricate* + *-or*] : one that prefabricates; *esp* : a maker of prefabricated houses

**¹pref·ace** \'prefəs\ *n* -S [ME, fr. MF, fr. ML *prefatia*, alter. of L *praefation-*, *praefatio* preliminary remarks, fr. *praefatus* (past part. of *praefari* to say beforehand, fr. *prae-* pre- + *fari* to say, speak) + *-ion-*, *-io* -ion — more at BAN] **1** *often cap* : a eucharistic prayer of thanksgiving common to most Christian liturgies forming in the Roman rite an introduction to the canon **2** : the introductory remarks of a speaker or the author's introduction to a book usu. explaining the object and scope of what follows : FOREWORD, PROLOGUE **3** : a brief paraphrase or comment formerly made upon a psalm before the singing of it in a Scottish church **4** : an approach to something : PRELIMINARY ⟨our defeat and dismay may be the ~ to our successors' victory —T.S.Eliot⟩

**²preface** \"\ *vb* -ED/-ING/-S *vi* **1** : to make introductory remarks or write a preface **2** *archaic* : to give a commentary upon a psalm about to be sung in a Scottish church ~ *vt* **1** : to say or write as preface ⟨a note *prefaced* to the score —Edward Sackville-West & Desmond Shawe-Taylor⟩ **2** : to usher in : PRECEDE, HERALD ⟨her cousin *prefaced* his speech with a solemn bow —Jane Austen⟩ ⟨whether the coming years will ~ a durable peace or another disastrous war —J.F.Dulles⟩ **3** : to introduce by or begin with a preface : furnish with a preface ⟨~*s* it with a reasoned and sagacious introduction —Anthony Powell⟩ **4** : to stand in front of : FRONT ⟨shows the entrance . . . *prefaced* by an open octagonal porch —John Summerson⟩ **5** : to go before as a preface : be a preface to ⟨its hardships and frustrations *prefaced* those of subsequent parties traveling in the same direction —T.D.Clark⟩ **6** *archaic* : to paraphrase or comment on (a psalm) in a Scottish church

**pref·ac·er** \-sə(r)\ *n* -S [*preface* + *-er*] : the maker or writer of a preface

**pre·fashion** \(')prē+\ *vt* [*pre-* + *fashion*] : to fashion beforehand

**pre·fa·tial** *or* **pre·fa·cial** \prē'fāshəl, (')prē¦f-\ *adj* [ML *prefatia* preface + E *-al*] : PREFATORY

**pref·a·to·ri·al** \¦prefə¦tōrēəl, -tȯr-\ *adj* [*prefatory* + *-al*] : PREFATORY — **pref·a·to·ri·al·ly** \-rēəlē, -li\ *adv*

**pref·a·to·ri·ly** \¦==¦=rəlē, -li\ *adv* [*prefatory* + *-ly*] : in a prefatory manner : as a preface

**pref·a·to·ry** \'prefə,tōrē, -tȯr-, -ri\ *adj* [L *praefatus* (past part. of *praefari* to say beforehand) + E *-ory* — more at PREFACE] **1** : of, relating to, or constituting a preface : INTRODUCTORY, PRELIMINARY ⟨~ statement⟩ **2** : located in front ⟨a broad ~ arch to the main apse —A.W.Clapham⟩

**pre·fect** *also* **prae·fect** \'prē,fekt\ *n* -S [ME, fr. MF, fr. L *praefectus*, fr. past part. of *praeficere* to place at the head of, fr. *prae-* pre- + *facere* to make — more at DO] **1** : any of various high officials or magistrates of differing functions and ranks placed at the head of particular commands, charges, or departments in ancient Rome **2** : a chief officer or chief magistrate : PRESIDENT ⟨~ of Paris police⟩ ⟨the ~ of one of the congregations of cardinals⟩ ⟨~ of the ladies' sodality⟩ **3** : a student monitor or praepostor in English public or secondary schools and some American private schools

**prefect apostolic** *n*, *pl* **prefects apostolic** [NL *praefectus apostolicus*] : the supervising head of a prefecture apostolic

**pre·fec·to·ral** \(')prē¦fekt(ə)rəl\ *adj* [F *préfectoral*, fr. L *praefectus* prefect + F *-oral* (as in *électoral*)] : PREFECTORIAL

**pre·fec·to·ri·al** \¦prē,fek¦tōrēəl, -tȯr-\ *adj* [LL *praefectorius* (fr. L *praefectus* prefect + *-orius* -ory) + E *-al*] : of or relating to a prefect — **pre·fec·to·ri·al·ly** \-rēəlē, -li\ *adv*

**prefect's court** *n* : a court having probate jurisdiction in New Mexico

**pre·fec·tur·al** \(')prē¦fekchərəl\ *adj* [*prefecture* + *-al*] : of or relating to a prefecture

**pre·fec·ture** \'=,=chə(r)\ *n* -S [L *praefectura*, fr. *praefectus* prefect + *-ura* -ure] **1** : the office, position, jurisdiction, or term of office of a prefect : PRESIDENCY, SUPERINTENDENCY **2** : the official residence of a prefect **3** : the district governed by a prefect (as in the Roman Empire, in France, or in Japan)

**prefecture apostolic** *n*, *pl* **prefectures apostolic** [NL *praefectura apostolica*] *Roman Catholicism* : a district of a missionary territory in its initial stage of ecclesiastical organization

**pre·fecundation** \(¦)prē+\ *n* [*pre-* + *fecundation*] : the changes or conditions preceding fecundation esp. in the female generative organs — **pre·fecundatory** \¦=+\ *adj*

**pre·fer** \R prē'fər, prə'-, + *vowel* -fər-; -R -fə̄, + *suffixal vowel* -fər- *also* -fə̄r, + *vowel in a following word* -fər- *or* -fə̄ *also* -fə̄r\ *vt* **preferred; preferred; preferring; prefers** [ME *preferren*, fr. MF *preferer*, fr. L *praeferre* to bear before, put before, prefer, fr. *prae-* pre- + *ferre* to bear, carry — more at BEAR] **1 a** *archaic* : to promote or advance to a rank or position ⟨has *preferred* me to the valuable rectory of this parish —Jane Austen⟩ **b** *archaic* : to move ahead or set forward **c** *obs* : to help bring about (a result) **2** : to have a preference for : CHOOSE : like better : value more highly ⟨*preferred* to live abroad —Edward Shils⟩ ⟨the rye grasses ~ cool and moist conditions —*Farmer's Weekly* (*So. Africa*)⟩ ⟨that peculiar taint of barbarism which makes men ~ occasional disobedience to systematic liberty —H.T.Buckle⟩ ⟨*preferred* that excellence should thrive rather than be obscured by a many-voiced mediocrity⟩ **3** : to give (a creditor) priority : pay (a creditor) before or rather than another **4** *archaic* : to put or set forward or before someone : OFFER, PRESENT, RECOMMEND, INTRODUCE **5** : to bring or lay (as a charge, complaint, or indictment) against a person ⟨*preferred* charges against him⟩ **6** : to bring forward or lay before one for consideration, decision, or action : PROPOSE ⟨the young man seems to be *preferring* some request which the elder one is indisposed to grant —Ambrose Bierce⟩ **7** : to show preference for (one of two or more card suits bid by one's partner) **syn** see OFFER

**pref·er·a·bil·i·ty** \,pref(ə)rə'bilədē, -lətē, -i\ *n* [*preferable* + *-ity*] : PREFERABLENESS

**pref·er·a·ble** \'pref(ə)rəbəl *also* -fərb- *sometimes* prē'fər- *or* prə'f-\ *adj* [F *préférable*, fr. *préférer* to prefer (fr. MF *preferer*) + *-able*] **1** : worthy to be preferred : having greater value or desirability **2** *obs* : exercising preference : PREFERENTIAL — **pref·er·a·bly** \-blē, -bli\ *adv*

**pref·er·a·ble·ness** \-bəlnəs\ *n* -ES : the quality or state of being preferable

**pref·er·ence** \'prefər(ə)n(t)s, -frən-\ *n* -S [F *préférence*, fr. ML *praeferentia*, fr. L *praeferent-*, *praeferens* (pres. part. of *praeferre* to prefer) + *-ia* -y] **1** *archaic* : PREFERABLENESS, SUPERIORITY **2 a** : the act of preferring or the state of being preferred : choice or estimation above another : higher valuation or desirability ⟨the passionate sincerity of artists and other intellectuals may still be warped by wishful ~*s* —H.J.Muller⟩ **b** : the power or opportunity of choosing ⟨gave him his ~⟩ **3** : PREFERMENT, PROMOTION ⟨the navy . . . passed him over in ~ —Taliaferro Boatwright⟩ **4 a** : the legal right to prior payment of a debt (as the expense of administration of an insolvent estate) **b** : the payment without legal justification of a debt either in full or to an extent injuring other creditors entitled to be treated on a basis of equality (as under bankruptcy or insolvency laws) **c** : DISCRIMINATION 4b **5** : someone or something that is preferred : an object of choice : FAVORITE ⟨which is your ~⟩ **6 a** : the practice of giving one or more countries legal advantages over others in international trade esp. by reduced tariffs — compare IMPERIAL PREFERENCE **b** : an advantage given one customer above others **7** : the right given by a corporation's charter to one or more classes of stocks to receive a dividend before dividends may be paid on junior shares **8 a** : a three-handed form of vint **b** : the act of bidding in bridge so as to show superior support for one of two or more suits bid by one's partner by a bid in the partner's first suit or by passing his second or third suit **syn** see CHOICE

**preference stock** *n*, *Brit* : PREFERRED STOCK

**pref·er·en·dum** \,prefə'rendəm\ *n*, *pl* **preferen·da** \-də\ [NL, fr. L, neut. of gerundive of *praeferre* to prefer] : the range of a gradient item (as light, temperature, or moisture) that seems to be positively attractive to a motile organism when a selection is available

**pref·er·ent** \'pref(ə)rənt\ *adj* [L *praeferent-*, *praeferens*, pres. part. of *praeferre* to prefer] : exhibiting or enjoying preference

**pref·er·en·tial** \¦prefə¦renchəl\ *adj* [ML *praeferentia* preference + E *-al*] **1** : of, relating to, or showing preference : offering or constituting an advantage ⟨~ treatment⟩ **2** : of, relating to, employing, or creating a preference in trade relations ⟨a ~ rate⟩ — **pref·er·en·tial·ly** \-chəlē, -li\ *adv*

**preferential ballot** *n* : a ballot listing several candidates for an office and used in preferential voting

**preferential hiring** *n* : a policy agreed to by an employer to hire qualified union members if they are available with the understanding that nonunion workers may be hired without being required to join the union when the union cannot supply men

**pref·er·en·tial·ism** \-ə,lizəm\ *n* -S [*preferential* + *-ism*] : the policy or practice of granting preferences in international trade

**pref·er·en·tial·ist** \-ləst\ *n* -S [*preferential* + *-ist*] : an adherent of preferentialism

**preferential mating** *n* : mating with a relative with whom marriage is enjoined under tribal rules — compare LEVIRATE, SORORATE

**preferential primary** *n* : PRESIDENTIAL PRIMARY

**preferential shop** *n* : a shop in which under a labor contract the management gives preference to members of the union chiefly in hiring, layoffs, and dismissals and often also in promotions and work shifts, but is free to hire outside the union membership when the union is unable to supply workers

**preferential tariff** *n* : a tariff schedule under which one or more nations are given lower rates or other advantages over others

**preferential voting** *also* **preferential system** *n* : a system of voting whereby the voter indicates his order of preference for each of the candidates listed on the ballot for a specified office so that if no candidate receives a majority of first preferences the first and second preferences and if necessary third and other preferences may be counted together until one candidate obtains a majority — called also *alternative vote;* compare HARE SYSTEM, PROPORTIONAL REPRESENTATION

**pre·fer·ment** \prē'fərmənt, prə-, -fə̄m-, *sometimes* 'prefə(r)m-\ *n* -S [ME *preferrement*, fr. *preferren* to prefer + *-ment*] **1 a** : advancement or promotion in dignity, office, or station ⟨he could see lesser musicians receiving ~, and it galled him —Howard Taubman⟩ **b** : a position or office of honor or profit **2** *obs* : an act of preference or choice **3** : priority or seniority in right esp. to receive payment or to purchase property on equal terms with others **4** : the act of making, bringing, or laying ⟨feared that ~ of charges would quickly follow discovery⟩

**¹preferred** *past of* PREFER

**²preferred** *n* -S [by shortening] : PREFERRED STOCK

**preferred creditor** *n* [¹*preferred*] : a creditor whose claim takes legal precedence over other claims

**preferred lie** *n* : an improved lie to which a golf ball may sometimes be moved in play without penalty

**preferred stock** *n* **1** : stock assured by a corporation's charter of dividends before any are paid on the common and usu. also having preference in distribution of assets **2** *Brit* : common stock that takes a specified dividend ahead of a deferred common

**pre·fer·rer** \prē'fər·ə(r), prə'- *also* -'fə̄rə(r\ *n* -S [*prefer* + *-er*] : one that prefers: as **a** : PROMOTER, PATRON **b** : one that presents or submits something

**preferring** *pres part of* PREFER

**prefers** *pres 3d sing of* PREFER

**pre·fig·u·rate** \prē'figyə,rāt\ *vt* [LL *praefiguratus*, past part. of *praefigurare* to prefigure] : PREFIGURE

**pre·figuration** \(¦)prē+\ *n* [LL *praefiguration-*, *praefiguratio*, fr. *praefiguratus* + L *-ion-*, *-io* -ion] **1** : the act of prefiguring or the state of being prefigured **2** : something that prefigures : an antecedent image or representation : FORECAST, FORESHADOWING, PROTOTYPE ⟨by that trick of lighting a ~ of age fell across her —Ngaio Marsh⟩

**pre·figurative** \(')prē+\ *adj* [ML *praefigurativus*, fr. LL *praefiguratus* + L *-ivus* -ive] : of, relating to, or showing by prefiguration : FORESHOWING, PREFIGURING — **pre·figuratively** \"+\ *adv* — **pre·figurativeness** \"+\ *n*

**pre·figure** \(')prē+\ *vt* [ME *prefiguren*, fr. LL *praefigurare*, fr. L *prae-* pre- + *figurare* to shape, picture — more at FIGURE] **1** : to show, suggest, or announce beforehand : offer or constitute an antecedent type, image, or likeness of : represent in advance ⟨children who supply us with the images by which we ~ the angelic choirs —Mary Austin⟩ **2** : to picture or imagine beforehand : FORESEE, PREDICT ⟨few writers care to ~ the future, even for so short a span —*Times Lit. Supp.*⟩

**pre·fig·ure·ment** \-mənt\ *n* -S [*prefigure* + *-ment*] : an image or likeness conceived or presented beforehand : a representation, embodiment, or typification in advance ⟨a ~ of 20th century dictatorships —Geoffrey Bruun⟩

**pre·filter** \(')prē+\ *n* [*pre-* + *filter*] : a preliminary filter

**prefine** *vt* [L *praefinire*, fr. *prae-* pre- + *finire* to limit — more at DEFINE] *obs* : to limit, determine, or define beforehand

**pre·finish** \(')prē+\ *vt* : to finish beforehand

**¹pre·fix** \'prē,fiks, prē'f-,prə'f-\ *vt* [ME *prefixen*, fr. MF *prefixer*, fr. *pre-* + *fixer* to fix, fr. *fix* fixed, fr. L *fixus*, past part. of *figere* to fix, fasten — more at DIKE] **1** *archaic* : to fix or appoint beforehand : establish (as a boundary, a decision, or a goal) in advance **2** [partly fr. ²*prefix*] : to place in front : add as a prefix ⟨it was flattering to a young man to be able to ~ the title of professor to his name —A.W.Long⟩

**²pre·fix** \'prē,fiks\ *n* -ES [NL *praefixum*, fr. L, neut. of past part. of *praefigere* to fasten before, fr. *prae-* pre- + *figere*] **1** : a sound or sequence of sounds or in writing a letter or sequence of letters occurring as a bound form attached to the beginning of a word, base, or phrase and serving to produce a derivative word or an inflectional form — compare AFFIX, INFIX, SUFFIX **2** : a title used before a person's name **3** : the quantifier or group of quantifiers preceding the matrix of a formula esp. in prenex normal form

**pre·fix·al** \'prē,fiksəl, =¦==\ *adj* [²*prefix* + *-al*] : of, relating to, or constituting a prefix — **pre·fix·al·ly** \-səlē, -li\ *adv*

**¹pre·fix·a·tion** \,prē,fik'sāshən\ *n* -S [¹*prefix* + *-ation*] : formation or inflection by means of prefixes

**²pre·fixation** \¦prē+\ *n* [*pre-* + *fixation*] : development or treatment prior to photographic fixation

**prefixed** *adj* [fr. past part. of ¹*prefix*] **1** *archaic* : settled beforehand : PREDETERMINED **2** : attached as a prefix — **pre·fixed·ly** \'prē,fiksədlē, -kstlē, -li\ *adv*

**pre·fix·ion** \prē¦fikshən\ *n* -S [MF *prefixion*, fr. *prefixer* to prefix + *-ion*] **1** *obs* : a fixing or appointing beforehand : PREAPPOINTMENT **2** : the placing of a word or particle before and usu. in combination with a word

**pre·fixture** \(')prē+\ *n* [¹*prefix* + *-ture* (as in *fixture*)] **1** : an act of prefixing **2** : PREFIX

**pre·flight** \(')prē+\ *adj* [*pre-* + *flight*] : preparing for or preliminary to flight esp. of an airplane

**pre·flood** \"+\ *adj* [*pre-* + *flood*] : of, relating to, or remaining from a time before a flood

**pre·focus** \"+\ *vt* [*pre-* + *focus*] : to focus beforehand (as automotive headlights before installation)

**¹pre·form** \"+\ *vt* [L *praeformare*, fr. *prae-* pre- + *formare* to form] **1** : to form beforehand : shape previously ⟨their natures and ~*ed* faculties —Shak.⟩ **2** : to fix or determine the form of beforehand : PREDETERMINE **3** : to bring to approximate preliminary shape and size (as a gemstone before final cutting and polishing)

**²preform** \"\ *n* : any of various objects of manufacture or handicraft after preliminary shaping: as **a** : a roughed-out gemstone **b** : BISCUIT 6a **c** : a tablet or roughly shaped unit of plastic molding composition that facilitates handling and weighing

**pre·formant** \(')prē+\ *n* [*pre-* + *formant*] : PREFORMATIVE

**pre·formation** \(¦)prē+\ *n* [*pre-* + *formation*] **1** : the act or an instance of forming beforehand : previous formation **2** : a now discredited theory in biology that every germ cell contains the organism of its kind fully formed and complete in all its parts and that development consists merely in increase in size from microscopic proportions to those of the adult — compare ENCASEMENT 1b

**pre·for·ma·tion·ism** \-shə,nizəm\ *also* **pre·form·ism** \(')prē-¦fȯ(r),mizəm\ *n* -S [*preformationism* fr. *preformation* + *-ism*; *preformism* fr. ¹*preform* + *-ism*] : PREFORMATION 2

**pre·for·ma·tion·ist** \-nəst\ *also* **pre·form·ist** \-məst\ *n* -S : an adherent of preformationism

**¹pre·formative** \(')prē+\ *adj* [L *praeformatus* (past part. of *praeformare* to preform) + E *-ive*] **1** : PREFORMING **2** [*pre-* + *formative*, adj.] : being a prefix ⟨a ~ affix⟩ : characterized by the use of preformatives ⟨the ~ conjugation⟩

**²preformative** \"\ *n* [*pre-* + *formative*, n.] : PREFIX 1 — used esp. in Semitic grammar; contrasted with *afformative*

**preformed wire rope** *n* [fr. past part. of ¹*preform*] : a wire rope of which each wire and strand has been given in advance the helical shape it will have in the rope with resultant increased safety

**pre·former** \(')prē+\ *n* -S [¹*preform* + *-er*] : one that preforms

**pre·for·mis·tic** \(¦)prē,fȯ(r)¦mistik\ *adj* [*preformist* + *-ic*] : of, relating to, or in accord with the theory of preformation or its supporters

**¹pre·frontal** \(')prē+\ *adj* [*pre-* + *frontal*] : anterior to a frontal structure ⟨a ~ bone⟩ ⟨~ convolution⟩: **a** : of or relating to a bone anterior and lateral to the frontal bone of some vertebrates ⟨the ~ ectethmoid of a teleost fish⟩ **b** : of, relating to, or being a plate or scale in the center or on each side of the head of some reptiles and fishes in front of the frontal scale **c** : of, relating to, or constituting the anterior part of the frontal lobe of the brain bounded posteriorly by the ascending frontal convolution

**²prefrontal** \"\ *n* : a prefrontal part (as a scale or bone)

**prefrontal lobe** *n* : the anterior part of the frontal lobe made up chiefly of association areas and mediating various inhibitory controls — compare LOBOTOMY

**prefrontal lobotomy** *also* **prefrontal leucotomy** *n* : lobotomy in which the frontal lobe of the brain is reached through holes drilled in the skull

**pre·ful·gence** \prē'fəljən(t)s\ *or* **pre·ful·gen·cy** \-nsē, -si\ *n* [*prefulgence* fr. *prefulgent*, after such pairs as E *benevolent: benevolence*; *prefulgency* fr. *prefulgent*, after such pairs as *efficient: efficiency*] : the quality or state of being prefulgent

**pre·ful·gent** \-nt\ *adj* [L *praefulgent-*, *praefulgens*, fr. pres. part. of *praefulgēre*, to shine forth, fr. *prae-* pre- + *fulgēre* to shine — more at FULGENT] : surpassingly fulgent : shining most brightly

**pre·game** \(')prē+\ *adj* [*pre-* + *game*] : preparatory to or preceding a game ⟨~ warm-up⟩ ⟨showered with gifts in a ~ ceremony⟩

**pre·ganglionic** \(¦)prē+\ *also* **pre·gangliar** \(')prē+\ *adj* [*preganglionic* fr. *pre-* + *ganglion* + *-ic*; *pregangliar* fr. *pre-* + *ganglion* + *-ar*] : anterior or proximal to a ganglion; *specif* : being, affecting, involving, or relating to a usu. medullated efferent nerve fiber arising from a cell body in the central nervous system and terminating in an autonomic ganglion — compare POSTGANGLIONIC

**pre·genial** \(')prē+\ *adj* [*pre-* + Gk *geneion* chin + E *-al* — more at GENIAL] : located in front of the chin; *esp* : of, relating to, or being the anterior scales of the chin in reptiles

**pre·geniculate** \¦=+\ *adj* [*pre-* + *geniculate*] : of, relating to, or arising from a lateral geniculate body

**pre·genital** \(')=+\ *adj* [*pre-* + *genital*] : of, relating to, or characteristic of the oral, anal, urethral, and phallic phases of psychosexual development — compare POLYMORPHOUS-PERVERSE

**pre·geological** \(¦)prē+\ *adj* [*pre-* + *geological*] : antedating reliable geological data or responsible theory

**pre·gestational** \(¦)prē+\ *or* **pre·gestation** \¦=+\ *adj* [*pre-* + *gestational* or *gestation*] : taking place before the commencement of pregnancy ⟨~ flushing of ewes⟩

**pre·ghie·ra** \prāg'yerə\ *n* -S [It *preghiera* prayer, fr. Prov *pregueira*, fr. ML *precaria* — more at PRAYER] : PRAYER; *specif* : a short instrumental musical composition in devotional mood

**pre·glacial** \(')prē+\ *adj* [*pre-* + *glacial*] : prior to a period of glaciation; *specif* : prior to the Pleistocene

**preg·na·ble** \'pregnəbəl\ *adj* [alter. (influenced by *pregnant*) of earlier *preignable*, alter. (influenced by such words as *reign, deign*, with silent *g*) of ME *prenable*, fr. MF — more at IMPREGNABLE] **1 :** vulnerable to capture **:** EXPUGNABLE ⟨a ~ fort⟩ **2** [*pregnate* + *-able*] **:** capable of being impregnated ⟨a ~ cat⟩

**preg·nance** \-nən(t)s\ *n* -s [fr. *pregnant*, after such pairs as E *benevolent: benevolence*] **:** PREGNANCY

**preg·nan·cy** \-nənsē, -si\ *n* -ES [*pregnant* + *-cy*] **1 a :** the condition of being pregnant **:** the state of being with young **:** GESTATION **b :** FERTILITY, FRUITFULNESS ⟨~ of the soil⟩ **2 a :** fertility or inventiveness of mind ⟨there was a depth and ~ in the Greek imagination —P.E.More⟩ **b :** significant quality **:** MEANINGFULNESS ⟨the traditional ~ of all great art —C.E.Montague⟩ ⟨phrases of homely vigor or happy ~ —J.L. Lowes⟩ **3** *obs* **:** promising quality **:** appearance of future usefulness or success **4 :** latent potentiality **:** richness in possible consequence or significance

**pregnancy disease** *n* **:** a disease of pregnant ewes that is due to carbohydrate deficiency, is marked by dullness, staggering, and collapse, and is esp. frequent in ewes carrying twins or triplets — compare KETOSIS

**pregnancy test** *n* **:** a physiological test to determine the existence of pregnancy in an individual (as the bitterling or Friedman test)

**preg·nane** \'preg,nān\ *n* -s [ISV *pregnant* + *-ane*; fr. the occurrence of its derivatives in pregnancy urine] **:** a crystalline saturated steroid hydrocarbon $C_{21}H_{36}$ that is related to cholane and is the parent compound of the corticoid and progestational hormones; 17-ethyl-androstane

**pregnanediol** \ˌ=ˌ=ˈ=ˌ=ˌ=\ *n* -s [ISV *pregnane* + *-diol*] **:** a crystalline biologically inactive dihydroxy derivative $C_{21}H_{34}(OH)_2$ of pregnane that is formed by reduction of progesterone and is found esp. in pregnancy urine in the form of its glucuronide

**¹preg·nant** \'pregnənt\ *adj* [ME *preignant*, fr. MF, fr. pres. part. of *preindre* to press, fr. OF *priembre*, fr. L *premere* — more at PRESS] *archaic* **:** COGENT, CONVINCING, FORCIBLE, PRESSING ⟨a ~ example⟩

**²pregnant** \"\ *adj* [ME, fr. L *praegnant-, praegnans*, alter. (influenced by *-ant-, -ans* -ant) of earlier *praegnat-, praegnas*, fr. *prae-* pre- + *gnat-* (fr. root of *nasci* to be born) — more at NATION] **1 a :** containing unborn young within the body **:** preparing to bring forth **:** GRAVID, GESTATING **b :** of or relating to pregnancy ⟨~ urine⟩ **c :** being about to produce or realize **:** containing as implicit **:** capable of producing ⟨the ideals with which the modern world is ~ —Walter Lippmann⟩ **2 a :** abounding in fancy, wit, or resource of mind **:** FERTILE, GERMINAL, INVENTIVE ⟨all this has been said . . . by great and ~ artists —*Times Lit. Supp.*⟩ **b** *obs* **:** full of promise **:** quick of apprehension **3 :** rich in significance or implication **:** heavy with suggestion or import **:** having possibilities of development or consequence **:** MEANINGFUL, WEIGHTY ⟨the journal brimmed over with his thoughts, many of them thin, diffuse, abstract, others nutty and ~ —Van Wyck Brooks⟩ **4 :** containing the germ or shape of future events **:** bearing latent potentialities, results, or issues ⟨the 1930s were ~ years —Gordon Bell⟩ **5** *obs* **:** OPEN, READY, RECEPTIVE ⟨my matter hath no voice, lady, but to your own most ~ and vouchsafed ear —Shak.⟩ **6 :** exhibiting fertility **:** TEEMING ⟨all nature seemed ~ with life —L.F. Herreshoff⟩ **syn** see EXPRESSIVE

**preg·nant·ly** *adv* **:** in a pregnant manner

**preg·nate** \'preg,nāt\ *vb* -ED/-ING/-S [LL *praegnatus*, past part. of *praegnare* to be pregnant, back-formation fr. L *praegnans* pregnant] *vi, obs* **:** to become fertile ~ *vt* [by shortening] **:** IMPREGNATE

**preg·nene** \'preg,nēn\ *n* -s [ISV *pregnane* + *-ene*] **:** an unsaturated derivative $C_{21}H_{34}$ of pregnane containing one double bond in the molecule

**preg·nen·in·o·lone** \ˌpreg,nē'ninᵊl,ōn\ *n* -s [ISV *pregnene* + *-in* + *-ol* + *-one*] **:** ETHISTERONE

**preg·nen·o·lone** \preg'nēnᵊl,ōn\ *n* -s [ISV *pregnene* + *-ol* + *-one*] **:** a crystalline unsaturated hydroxy steroid ketone $C_{21}H_{32}O_2$ formed by the oxidation of cholesterol (as in living cells), stigmasterol, diosgenin, or other steroids and yielding progesterone on dehydrogenation; 3-hydroxy-5-pregnen-20-one

**pre·gummed paper** \(')prē+-\ *n* [*pre-* + *gummed*] **:** postage-stamp paper that is gummed before being printed

**pregustation** *n* [L *praegustatus* (past part. of *praegustare* to taste beforehand, fr. *prae-* pre- + *gustare* to taste) + E *-ion* — more at CHOOSE] *obs* **:** a tasting in advance **:** FORETASTE

**pre·hallux** \(')prē+\ *n* [NL, fr. *pre-* + *hallux*] **:** a rudimentary extra toe or a process that appears as a rudiment of a toe on the preaxial side of the hallux (as of a frog) — called also *calcar*

**pre·halter** \(')prē+\ *n, pl* **pre·halteres** \ˌ=+\ [NL, fr. *pre-* + *halter*] **:** the squama of a dipterous insect

**pre·haps** \prē'haps, prə'-\ *dial var of* PERHAPS

**pre·harvest** \(')prē+\ *adj* [*pre-* + *harvest*] **:** occurring or used shortly before the time for harvesting ⟨a ~ drop of fruit⟩

**preharvest spray** *n* **:** a hormone spray used to prevent preharvest drop of tree fruits (as apples)

**pre·hearing** \(')prē+\ *adj* [*pre-* + *hearing*] **:** preliminary to a hearing

**pre·heat** \"+\ *vt* [*pre-* + *heat*] **:** to heat beforehand: as **a :** to heat (an oven) to a designated temperature before placing food therein **b :** to heat (an engine) to an operating temperature before operation **c :** to heat (metal) prior to a thermal or mechanical treatment

**pre·heater** \"+\ *n* [*preheat* + *-er*] **:** any of various devices for preliminary heating: as **a :** a heat exchanger used in brewing and distilling **b :** any of various devices for using waste heat for preliminary heating in petroleum refining processes

**pre–hellenic** \ˌprē+\ *adj, usu cap H* [*pre-* + *hellenic*] **:** of, relating to, or characteristic of the phases and periods of civilization in Greek lands before the rise of the Hellenic or classical Greek culture — compare AEGEAN, CYCLADIC, HELLADIC, MINOAN, MYCENAEAN

**pre·hend** \prē'hend\ *vt* -ED/-ING/-S [L *prehendere* — more at PREHENSILE] **1 :** SEIZE **2 :** APPREHEND

**pre·hen·si·ble** \prē'hen(t)səbəl\ *adj* [L *prehensus* (past part. of *prehendere*) + E *-ible*] **:** capable of being seized

**pre·hen·sile** \prē'hen(t)səl\ *adj* [F *préhensile*, fr. L *prehensus* (past part. of *prehendere* to grasp, seize, fr. *pre-* — fr. *prae-* pre- — + *-hendere* — akin to ON *geta* to get) + F *-ile* — more at GET] **1 :** adapted for seizing or grasping esp. by wrapping around ⟨the ~ tail of a monkey⟩ ⟨a ~ upper lip . . . used to pluck foliage —Grace H. Glueck⟩ **2 a :** gifted with mental grasp or moral or aesthetic insight or perception ⟨our poets — those gifted strangely ~ men —A.T.Quiller-Couch⟩ **b :** showing cupidity **:** AVARICIOUS, GREEDY ⟨increased the staff of his ~ employees —J.B.Cabell & A.J.Hanna⟩ — **pre·hen·sil·i·ty** \ˌprē(ˌ)hen'silədē\ *n* -ES

**pre·hen·sion** \prē'henchən\ *n* -s [L *prehension-, prehensio*, fr. *prehensus* + *-ion-, -io* -ion] **1 :** the act of taking hold, seizing, or grasping (as with the hand); *specif* **:** the conveyance of food or drink into the mouth **2 a :** mental apprehension **b :** an apprehension that may or may not be cognitive

**pre·hen·sive** \-n(t)siv, -sēv *also* -səv\ *adj* [L *prehensus* + E *-ive*] **1 :** PREHENSILE **2 :** of or relating to prehension

**pre·hen·so·ri·al** \ˌprē(ˌ)hen'sōrēəl, -sȯr-\ *adj* [NL *prehensorium* organ adapted for grasping (fr. L *prehensus* + *-orium*) + E *-al*] **:** PREHENSILE

**prehensorial foot** *n* **:** TOXICOGNATH

**pre·hepatic** \ˌprē+\ *adj* [*pre-* + *hepatic*] **:** anterior to or in front of the liver

**pre·he·pat·i·cus** \ˌprēhə'padəkəs\ *n* -ES [NL, fr. L *prae-* pre- + Gk *hēpat-, hēpar* liver, + L *-icus* -ic — more at HEPATIC] **:** the embryonic connective and vascular tissues from which the interstitial part of the liver is developed

**pre–hispanic** \ˌprē+\ *adj, usu cap H* [*pre-* + *hispanic*] **:** of or relating to cultures prior to Spanish conquests in the western hemisphere

**pre·historian** \"+\ *n* [*prehistory* + *-an*] **:** an archaeologist who specializes in prehistoric man and his culture

**pre·his·tor·ic** \ˌprē(h)i'stȯrik, -tär-, -rēk\ *or* **pre·his·tor·i·cal** \-rəkəl, -rēk-\ *adj* [*pre-* + *historic, historical*] **:** of, relating to, or existing in times antedating written history — **pre·his·tor·i·cal·ly** \-rək(ə)lē, -rēk-, -li\ *adv*

**prehistoric archaeology** *n* **:** the study of prehistoric human evidences (as artifacts and fossilized human remains)

**pre·history** \(')prē+\ *n* [*pre-* + *history*] **1 :** the study of prehistoric man ⟨many different sciences, notably geology, paleontology, archaeology, comparative anatomy, and even psychology, have combined to give us that body of knowledge which we call ~ —R.W.Murray⟩ **2 :** a history of the antecedents of an event or situation ⟨the ~ of existing racial tensions must be considered⟩

**prehn·ite** \'prā,nīt, 'pre,-\ *n* -s [G *prehnit*, fr. Col. Van *Prehn* 18th cent. Dutch officer who brought it from the Cape of Good Hope + G *-it* ¹-ite] **:** a pale green mineral $Ca_2Al_2Si_3O_{10}(OH)_2$ that occurs in crystalline aggregates having a botryoidal or mamillary structure but only rarely in distinct crystals and that is a basic calcium aluminum silicate (hardness 6–6.5, sp. gr. 2.80–2.95)

**prehn·i·tene** \-ˌnə,tēn\ *n* -s [ISV *prehnitic* (*acid*) + *-ene*] **:** a liquid aromatic hydrocarbon $C_6H_2(CH_3)_4$ prepared with other hydrocarbons by methylation of mesitylene or pseudocumene by means of the Friedel-Crafts reaction; 1,2,3,4-tetramethyl-benzene

**prehn·it·ic acid** \(')prā¦nid·ik-, (')pre¦-\ *n* [ISV *prehnite* + *-ic*; prob. fr. the resemblance of the crystals to the mammillae on prehnite] **:** either of two isomeric acids derived from benzene: **a :** MELLOPHANIC ACID **b b :** a crystalline acid $C_6H_2(COOH)_4$ formed esp. by oxidation of prehnitene; 1,2,3,4-benzene-tetracarboxylic acid

**pre·holiday** \(')prē+\ *adj* [*pre-* + *holiday*] **:** preceding a holiday

**pre–homeric** \ˌprē+\ *adj, usu cap H* [*pre-* + *homeric*] **:** antedating the Greek poet Homer or the Homeric writings

**¹pre·hominid** \(')prē+\ *adj* [NL *Prehominidae*] **:** of or relating to the Prehominidae

**²prehominid** \"\ *n* -s **:** one of the Prehominidae

**pre·hominidae** \ˌprē+\ *n pl, cap* [NL, fr. *pre-* + *homin-, homo* + *-idae*] **:** the extinct manlike primates when regarded (as by some anthropologists) as constituting a family

**¹pre·human** \(')prē+\ *adj* [*pre-* + *human*] **1 :** antedating the appearance of human beings **2 :** being or relating to an animal in some respects like an ape but regarded as an ancestor of human beings

**²prehuman** \"\ *n* **:** a prehuman animal

**pre·hydration** \ˌprē+\ *n* [*pre-* + *hydration*] **:** preliminary hydration

**pre·hypophysis** \"+\ *n* [NL, fr. *pre-* + *hypophysis*] **:** the anterior lobe of the pituitary body

**prei·gnac** \pren'yak\ *n* -s *often cap* [fr. *Preignac*, commune of Gironde dept., southwest France] **:** any of several aromatic fruity French red or white still wines

**pre·ignition** \ˌprē+\ *n* [*pre-* + *ignition*] **:** ignition in an internal-combustion engine occurring while the inlet valve is open or before compression is completed — compare AUTOIGNITION

**pre·imaginal** \"+\ *adj* [*pre-* + *imaginal*] **:** of, relating to, occurring in, or constituting a stage in insect development that immediately precedes the imago

**pre·imagine** \"+\ *vt* [*pre-* + *imagine*] **:** to imagine in advance **:** PRECONCEIVE

**pre–inca** \(')prē¦iŋkə\ *adj, usu cap I* [*pre-* + *inca*] **:** of or relating to the pre-Incans or their culture ⟨*pre-Inca* pottery⟩

**pre–incan** \-kən\ *n, usu cap I* [*pre-inca* + *-an*] **:** a native of Bolivia, Ecuador, or Peru of the prehistoric period preceding the rise of the Inca Empire

**pre·incarnate** \ˌprē+\ *adj* [*pre-* + *incarnate*] **:** of, relating to, or having existence before incarnation — used esp. of the second person of the Trinity

**pre·inclined** \"+\ *adj* [*pre-* + *inclined*] **:** prepared in advance **:** READY ⟨~ to accept his apology⟩

**pre·indicate** \(')prē+\ *vt* [*pre-* + *indicate*] **:** to point out in advance **:** PRESAGE, PROGNOSTICATE, FORESHOW

**pre·induction** \ˌprē+\ *adj* [*pre-* + *induction*] **:** occurring or available prior to induction into military service ⟨~ tests⟩ ⟨~ training⟩

**pre·industrial** \"+\ *adj* [*pre-* + *industrial*] **:** not based on or characterized by a preponderance of industry ⟨a ~ stage of social organization⟩ ⟨~ areas⟩

**pre·infection** \"+\ *n* [*pre-* + *infection*] **:** an infection that is established in the body but not yet clinically manifested

**pre·infective** \"+\ *adj* [*pre-* + *infective*] **:** insufficiently mature to produce infection — used esp. of helminth larvae

**pre·inform** \"+\ *vt* [*pre-* + *inform*] **:** to provide with advance information ⟨~*ed* that his wife would be there⟩

**pre·install** \"+\ *vt* [*pre-* + *install*] **:** to install (as passages for wiring or pipes) in a building during construction to provide for future changes and adaptations

**pre·insula** \(')prē+\ *n* [NL, fr. *pre-* + *insula*] **:** the anterior part of the cerebral island of Reil

**pre·intone** \ˌprē+\ *vt* [*pre-* + *intone*] **:** to intone beforehand in a low voice

**pre·invasion** \"+\ *adj* [*pre-* + *invasion*] **:** taking place in the period immediately preceding a military invasion ⟨~ diplomacy⟩

**pre·invasive** \"+\ *adj* [*pre-* + *invasive*] **:** not yet become invasive — used of malignant cells or lesions remaining in their original focus

**pre·inventory** \(')prē+\ *adj* [*pre-* + *inventory*] **:** occurring or available immediately before the taking of an inventory ⟨~ sales⟩ ⟨an excellent ~ bargain⟩

**pre–islamic** \ˌprē+\ *adj, usu cap I* [*pre-* + *islamic*] **:** existing prior to the development and acceptance of the Muslim religion ⟨*pre-Islamic* Arabs⟩ ⟨*pre-Islamic* cultures of Asia Minor⟩

**¹pre·ja·cent** \prē'jāsᵊnt\ *adj* [MF, fr. L *praejacent-, praejacens*, pres. part. of *praejacēre* to lie before, fr. *prae-* pre- + *jacēre* to lie — more at ADJACENT] **1** *obs* **:** PREEXISTING **2 :** being an antecedent proposition in logic from which another is developed

**²prejacent** \"\ *n* -s **:** a prejacent proposition in logic

**pre·je·val·sky's horse** \ˌprejə'välzkēz-, -lskēz-\ *usu cap P* [by alter.] *var of* PRZHEVALSKI'S HORSE

**pre·job** \(')prē+\ *adj* [*pre-* + *job*] **:** occurring before employment ⟨~ training⟩

**pre·judge** \(')prē¦jəj\ *vt* [MF *prejuger*, fr. L *praejudicare*, fr. *prae-* pre- + *judicare* to judge — more at JUDGE] **1 :** to judge before hearing or before full and sufficient examination **:** decide or sentence by anticipation **:** pass judgment on beforehand **2** *obs* **:** to anticipate the judgment of (another)

**pre·judg·er** \-jəjə(r)\ *n* -s **:** one who passes judgment beforehand

**pre·judg·ment** \-jəjmənt\ *n* [F *préjugement*, fr. MF *prejuger* + *-ment*] **:** an act or instance of prejudging **:** decision without adequate examination **:** PREJUDICE

**pre·ju·di·cal** \prē'jüdəkəl\ *adj* [by alter.] **:** PREJUDICIAL

**¹prejudicate** *vb* -ED/-ING/-S [L *praejudicatus*, past part. of *praejudicare* to prejudge] *vt* **1** *obs* **:** to affect in a prejudicial manner **2** *obs* **:** PREJUDGE ~ *vi, obs* **:** to form a judgment prematurely or on the basis of incomplete or imperfect evidence

**²prejudicate** *adj* [L *praejudicatus* prejudged, fr. past part. of *praejudicare*] **1** *obs* **:** decided beforehand **2** *obs* **:** PRECONCEIVED **3** *obs* **:** BIASED; PREJUDICED — **prejudicately** *adv, obs*

**pre·ju·di·ca·tion** \prē,jüdə'kāshən\ *n* -s [L *praejudicatus* (past part. of *praejudicare*) + E *-ion*] **1 :** an act of prejudging **:** opinion formed in advance of or without adequate examination of evidence **2 a :** a preliminary inquiry and determination of issues not directly involved in the merits of an action under Roman law **b :** a previous decision of a point at law **:** PRECEDENT

**prejudicative** *adj* [L *praejudicatus* + E *-ive*] *obs* **:** PREJUDGING

**¹prej·u·dice** \'prejədəs\ *n* -s [ME, fr. OF, fr. L *praejudicium* previous judgment, precedent, detriment, fr. *prae-* pre- + *judicium* judgment, fr. *judic-, judex* judge — more at JUDGE] **1 a :** injury or damage due to some judgment or action of another (as in disregard of a person's right) **:** resulting detriment — now used chiefly in phrases ⟨in the ~ of⟩ ⟨to the ~ of his own interests⟩; compare WITHOUT PREJUDICE, WITH PREJUDICE **b** *obs* **:** injury in general **:** DETRIMENT, HURT **2 a** (1) **:** preconceived judgment or opinion **:** leaning toward one side of a question from other considerations than those belonging to it **:** unreasonable predilection for or objection against something (2) **:** an opinion or leaning adverse to anything without just grounds or before sufficient knowledge **b :** an instance of such judgment or opinion **:** an unreasonable predilection, inclination, or objection **c :** an irrational attitude of hostility directed against an individual, a group, a race, or their supposed characteristics — compare *discrimination* **3** *obs* **a :** an opinion or judgment formed beforehand or without due examination **:** PREJUDGMENT **b :** PROGNOSTICATION **c :** EXPECTATION, ANTICIPATION **syn** see PREDILECTION

**²prejudice** \"\ *vt* -ED/-ING/-S [ME *prejudisen*, fr. MF *prejudicier*, fr. OF *prejudice* prejudice] **1 :** to injure or damage by some judgment or action usu. at law; *broadly* **:** to cause injury to **:** HURT, DAMAGE, IMPAIR ⟨~ a good cause⟩ **2 :** to cause to have prejudice **:** prepossess with opinions formed without due knowledge or examination **:** bias the mind of **:** give an unreasonable bent to ⟨~ a critic⟩ — not often used of favorable prejudice ⟨if anything could ~ me in her favor⟩ **3** *obs* **:** to judge beforehand usu. unfavorably **:** PREJUDGE

**prej·u·diced** \-st\ *adj* [fr. past part. of *prejudice*] **:** having a prejudice, prepossession, or bias for or against — **prej·u·diced·ly** *adv*

**prej·u·dice·less** \-sləs\ *adj* **:** free from prejudice **:** not prejudiced

**prejudiciable** *adj* [ME, fr. MF, fr. *prejudicier* to prejudice + *-able*] *obs* **:** PREJUDICIAL 1

**prej·u·di·cial** \ˌprejə¦dishəl\ *adj* [ME, fr. ML *praejudicialis*, fr. L *praejudicium* prejudice + *-alis* -al] **1 :** tending to injure or impair **:** HURTFUL, DAMAGING, DETRIMENTAL ⟨too high a temperature is ~ to the soap —T.P.Hilditch⟩ **2** *obs* **:** being or taking the form of prejudice **:** biased, possessed, or blinded by prejudices **3 :** leading to premature judgment or unwarranted opinion — **prej·u·di·cial·ly** \-shəlē, -li\ *adv* — **prej·u·di·cial·ness** *n* -ES

**pre–judicial** \ˌprē+\ *adj* [LL *praejudicialis* of a preceding judgment, fr. L *praejudicium* preceding judgment + *-alis* -al — more at PREJUDICE] **:** coming or decided prior to the hearing before the judex under Roman law

**pre·judiciary** *or* **prae·judiciary** \"+\ *adj* [L *praejudicium* prejudice + E *-ary*] **:** PREJUDICIAL

**prej·u·di·cious** \ˌprejə¦dishəs\ *adj* [L *praejudicium* + E *-ous*] **:** PREJUDICIAL 1 — **prej·u·di·cious·ly** *adv*

**preke** *n* -s [origin unknown] *obs* **:** OCTOPUS

**pre·kindergarten** \(')prē+\ *adj* [*pre-* + *kindergarten*] **1 :** designed for or characteristic of children too young for kindergarten ⟨~ problems⟩ ⟨~ training⟩ **2 :** very young, elementary, or immature ⟨~ children⟩ ⟨~ politics⟩

**pre·know** \"+\ *vt* [*pre-* + *know*] **:** to know beforehand **:** FOREKNOW — **pre·knowledge** \"+\ *n*

**pre·labial** \"+\ *adj* [*pre-* + L *labium* lip (or NL *labium*) + E *-al*] **1 :** situated before the lips or a labium **2** [NL *prelabium* + E *-al*] **:** of or relating to a prelabium

**pre·labium** \"+\ *n* [NL, fr. *pre-* + *labium*] **:** the movable distal part of the insect labium

**pre·lacteal** \"+\ *adj* [*pre-* + *lacteal*] **1 :** preceding the milk teeth — used of early rudimentary teeth of marsupials **2 a** *of an infant food* **:** taken before milk **b** *of infant feeding* **:** preceding the taking of milk

**prel·a·cy** \'preləsē, -si\ *n* -ES [ME *prelacie*, fr. AF, fr. ML *praelatia* fr. *praelatus* prelate + L *-ia* -y] **1 :** the office or dignity of a prelate **:** a benefice held by a prelate **2 :** the whole body of ecclesiastical dignitaries **:** PRELATES **3 :** church government by prelates **:** EPISCOPACY

**pre·lap·sar·i·an** \ˌprē,lap¦sa(a)rēən\ *adj* [*pre-* + L *lapsus* fall + E *-arian* (as in *infralapsarian*) — more at LAPSE] **:** characteristic of or belonging to the time or state before the fall of man

**pre·larva** \(')prē+\ *n* [*pre-* + *larva*] **:** a newly-hatched and very immature larva usu. differing markedly from the typical larva of its kind

**prel·ate** \'prelət, *usu* -əd.+V\ *n* -s [ME *prelat*, fr. OF, fr. ML *praelatus*, fr. L (suppletive past part. of *praeferre* to prefer), fr. *prae-* pre- + *latus*, suppletive past part. of *ferre* to bear — more at TOLERATE] **1 a :** an ecclesiastic of superior rank and authority **:** a dignitary of a church **b :** a member of an episcopate **c** *obs* **:** a chief priest (as of the Jews or druids) **d :** the chaplain of a fraternal society or other order **2** *obs* **:** a person in authority **:** SUPERIOR, CHIEF, LEADER **3 :** a moderate violet that is deeper and slightly bluer than Parma violet (sense 2a) and bluer than Roman purple

**prel·ate·ship** \-tship\ *n* [*prelate* + *-ship*] **:** the office or status of a prelate — sometimes used as a form of address

**prel·at·ess** \-lədəs\ *n* -ES [*prelate* + *-ess*] **1 :** a female prelate (as an abbess) **2 :** the wife of a prelate

**pre·la·tial** \prē'lāshəl\ *adj* [ML *praelatia* prelacy + E *-al*] **:** PRELATIC

**pre·lat·ic** \-lad·ik\ *or* **pre·lat·i·cal** \-dəkəl\ *adj* [*prelate* + *-ic, -ical*] **1** *usu prelatic* **:** of, relating to, constituting, or resembling a prelate or prelacy **2** *usu prelatical* **:** adhering to prelacy **:** EPISCOPAL — often used disparagingly — **pre·lat·i·cal·ly** \-dək(ə)lē\ *adv*

**pre·la·tion** \prē'lāshən\ *n* -s [ME, fr. MF, fr. L *praelation-, praelatio*, fr. *praelatus* (suppletive past part. of *praeferre* to prefer) + *-ion-, -io* -ion — more at PRELATE] **:** an act of preferring or the condition of being preferred **:** PREFERMENT, PROMOTION

**prelatish** *adj* [*prelate* + *-ish*] **:** PRELATIC

**prelatism** *n* -s [*prelate* + *-ism*] *obs* **:** episcopacy or adherence to it — usu. used disparagingly ⟨the councils . . . were foully corrupted with ungodly ~ —John Milton⟩

**prel·a·tist** \'preləd·əst\ *n* -s [*prelate* + *-ist*] **:** one who supports or advocates prelacy; *esp* **:** HIGH CHURCHMAN — usu. used disparagingly

**prel·a·tize** \-lə,tīz\ *vb* -ED/-ING/-S [*prelate* + *-ize*] *vt* **:** to make prelatical **:** bring under prelatical influence ~ *vi* **:** to be or become prelatical

**prel·at·ry** \-lətrē\ *n* -s [*prelate* + *-ry*] **:** PRELACY

**prel·a·ture** \-lə,chü(ə)r\ *n* -s [F *prélature*, fr. ML *praelatura*, fr. *praelatus* prelate + L *-ura* -ure] **1 a :** the status or dignity of a prelate **:** PRELACY 1 **b :** an order of prelates **2 :** a prelatic benefice or bishopric

**prelaty** *n* -ES [ML *praelatia* — more at PRELACY] *obs* **:** PRELACY

**pre·law** \(')prē+\ *adj* [*pre-* + *law*] **:** occurring before the commencement of studies in law **:** forming a foundation for legal studies ⟨~ studies⟩; *also* **:** taking or studying a prelaw course ⟨~ and predental students⟩

**prêle** \'prel\ *n* -s [F, alter. (resulting fr. incorrect division of *l'aprêle*) of (assumed) earlier *aprêle*, fr. OF *asprele*, fr. (assumed) VL *asperella* (whence It *asprella, sprella*), fr. L *asper* rough + *-ella*] **:** HORSETAIL, SCOURING RUSH

**pre·lect** *also* **prae·lect** \prē'lekt\ *vi* -ED/-ING/-S [L *praelectus*, past part. of *praelegere* to read aloud and expound — more at PRAELECTOR] **:** to discourse publicly **:** LECTURE ⟨would ~ over some thriving plant —R.L.Stevenson⟩

**pre·lec·tion** *or* **prae·lec·tion** \-kshən\ *n* -s [L *praelection-, praelectio*, fr. *praelectus* + *-ion-, -io* -ion] **1 :** a lecture or discourse read or delivered in public (as to students) **2** [L *prae-* pre- + *lection-, lectio* act of reading — more at LECTION] **:** a previous reading **:** a reading beforehand

**prelector** *var of* PRAELECTOR

**pre·legacy** \(')prē+\ *n* [*pre-* + *legacy*] **:** a legacy under Roman or civil law payable before the testator's estate is distributed to heirs and general legatees

**pre·legal** \"+\ *adj* [*pre-* + *legal*] **:** PRELAW

**pre·leukemic** \ˌprē+\ *adj* [*pre-* + *leukemic*] **:** occurring before the development of overt leukemia ⟨a ~ latent phase⟩

**pre·li·ba·tion** \ˌprēlī'bāshən\ *n* [L *praelibation-, praelibatio*, fr. *praelibatus* (past part. of *praelibare* to taste beforehand, fr. *prae-* pre- + *libare* to pour as an offering, to taste) + *-ion-, -io* -ion — more at LIBATION] **1 :** FORETASTE **2 :** a preliminary offering or an offering of first fruits

**pre·liberation** \ˌprē+\ *adj* [*pre-* + *liberation*] **:** existing before a liberation ⟨~ patriots⟩

**pre·license** \(')prē+\ *adj* [*pre-* + *license*] **:** occurring prior to or leading to the issuance of a license ⟨~ training⟩

**¹pre·life** \'prē,līf\ *n* [*pre-* + *life*] **:** a life conceived as lived before one's present earthly life — compare AFTERLIFE

**²prelife** \"\ *adj* [*pre-* + *life*] **:** of, relating to, or occurring during the time preceding the first appearance of life on earth

**pre·lim** \'prē,lim, prə'lim\ *n or adj* [by shortening] *slang* **:** PRELIMINARY

**pre·lim·i·nar·i·ly** \prə̇ˈlimə,nerəlē\ *adv* **:** in a preliminary manner **:** as a preliminary ⟨~ to this decision⟩

**¹pre·lim·i·nary** \prə̇ˈlimə,nerē, prē'-, -ri\ *n* -ES [F *préliminaires,* pl., fr. ML *praeliminaris,* adj.] **:** something that precedes a main discourse, work, design, or business **:** something introductory or preparatory (as a preparatory step or measure): as **a :** a preliminary scholastic examination (as of a candidate for a higher degree) **b :** a contest designed to eliminate the less qualified competitors (as in a sport) prior to a decisive contest **c preliminaries** *pl, Brit* **:** FRONT MATTER **d :** a minor match or contest that precedes the main event (as of a boxing card)

**²preliminary** \"\ *adj* [F *préliminaire,* fr. ML *praeliminaris,* fr. L *prae-* pre- + *limin-, limen* threshold + *-aris* -ar — more at LIMB] **1 :** preceding the main discourse or business **:** INTRODUCTORY, PREVIOUS ⟨~ articles to a treaty⟩ **2 :** lying before **:** leading to **:** being at the threshold of ⟨hills that are ~ to the mountains —John Burroughs⟩

**³preliminary** \"\ *adv* **:** as a preliminary

**pre·limit** \(ˈ)prē+\ *vt* -ED/-ING/-S [*pre-* + *limit*] **:** to keep within prescribed bounds **:** set the bounds of in advance ⟨the council strictly ~*ed* the scope of the committee's function⟩

**pre·lingual** \"+\ *adj* [*pre-* + *lingual*] **:** previous to the use, acquisition, or development of language ⟨an infant in the ~ stage⟩

**pre·linguistic** \ˌprē+\ *adj* [*pre-* + *linguistic*] **:** PRELINGUAL

**pre–linnaean** \ˌprē+\ *adj, sometimes cap L* [*pre-* + *linnaean*] **:** of, relating to, or dating from the period prior to the adoption of binomial nomenclature by Linnaeus

**pre·literacy** \(ˈ)prē+\ *n* [*pre-* + *literacy*] **:** the period in the life of a society or culture antedating the use of writing or the keeping of written records

**pre·literary** \"+\ *adj* **1** [*pre-* + L *litterae, literae* writing + E *-ary* — more at LETTER] **:** PRELITERATE **2** [*pre-* + *literary*] **:** preceding the development of a written literature

**¹pre·literate** \"+\ *adj* [*pre-* + *literate*] **1 :** antedating the use of writing ⟨ancient ~ cultures⟩ **2 a :** not yet having attained a level of cultural development employing a written language **b :** lacking the use of writing **:** NONLITERATE ⟨~ people now living⟩

**²preliterate** \"\ *n* **:** a preliterate person

**pre·lith·ic** \prēˈlithik\ *adj* [*pre-* + *-lithic*] **:** not yet having advanced to the use of stone implements — used of largely hypothetical stages of human culture or evolution

**pre·localization** \ˌprē+\ *n* [*pre-* + *localization*] **:** segregation in the egg or by early cleavage divisions of material destined to form particular tissues or organs

**pre·logging** \(ˈ)prē+\ *n* [*pre-* + *logging*] **:** the harvesting prior to a major logging operation of those trees that would otherwise be lost or damaged during that operation

**pre·logical** *also* **pre·logic** \"+\ *adj* [*prelogical* fr. *pre-* + *logical*; *prelogic* fr. *pre-* + L *logicus* logical, fr. Gk *logikos* — more at LOGICAL] **:** not yet logical **:** belonging to or characterized by a supposed primitive mode of thought with no regard for logical consistency — **pre·logicality** \ˌprē+\ *n* — **pre·logical·ly** *adv*

**pre·loral** *or* **pre·loreal** \(ˈ)prē+\ *adj* [*pre-* + *loral, loreal*] **:** situated in front of the lores

**¹prel·ude** \ˈprel,yüd, ˈprā,lüd, ˈpre,lüd, ˈprāl,yüd, ˈprē,lüd; *the first pronunciation is heard more often for nonmusical than for musical senses, the ā pronunciations vice versa; the ē pronunciation is rarely heard for musical senses*\ *n* -S [MF *prelude,* fr. ML *praeludium,* fr. L *praeludere* to prelude] **:** an introductory performance, action, event, or other matter, preceding and preparing for a principal or a more important matter **:** a preliminary part **:** INTRODUCTION, PREFACE: as **a :** a musical section or movement introducing the theme or chief subject (as of a fugue, suite) or serving as an introduction to an opera or oratorio **b :** an opening voluntary (as in a church service) **c :** a separate concert piece usu. for piano or orchestra and usu. based entirely on a short motive

**²prelude** \"\ *vb* -ED/-ING/-S [L *praeludere* to play beforehand, to prelude, preface, fr. *prae-* pre- + *ludere* to play — more at LUDICROUS] *vi* **:** to give or serve as a prelude **:** furnish an introduction **:** be introductory; *esp* **:** to play a musical introduction ~ *vt* **1 :** to serve as prelude to **:** precede as introductory **:** FORESHADOW **2 :** to play as a prelude **:** play or perform a prelude to

**prel·ud·er** \-də(r)\ *n* -S **1 :** one that preludes **2 :** something that constitutes a prelude

**pre·lu·di·al** \prēˈlüdēəl\ *adj* [ML *praeludium* prelude + E *-al*] **:** relating to or having the form or position of a prelude **:** INTRODUCTORY

**pre·lu·dio** \prāˈlüdyō\ *n, pl* **prelu·di** \-dē\ [It, lit., prelude, fr. ML *praeludium*] **:** a musical prelude

**pre·lu·di·ous** \prēˈlüdēəs\ *adj* [ML *praeludium* + E *-ous*] **:** PRELUDIAL — **pre·lu·di·ous·ly** *adv*

**preludium** *var of* PRAELUDIUM

**prel·u·dize** *pronunc at* ¹PRELUDE + ˌīz\ *vi* -ED/-ING/-S [¹*prelude* + *-ize*] **:** to play or compose a prelude

**pre·lumbar** \(ˈ)prē+\ *adj* [*pre-* + *lumbar*] **:** lying or occurring in front of the lumbar vertebrae or region

**pre·lu·sion** \prēˈlüzhən\ *n* -S [L *praelusion-, praelusio,* fr. *praelusus* (past part. of *praeludere* to prelude) + *-ion-, -io* -ion] **:** something going before **:** PRELUDE, INTRODUCTION

**pre·lu·sive** \-üsiv\ *or* **pre·lu·so·ry** \-üsərē\ *adj* [L *praelusus* (past part. of *praeludere* to prelude) + E *-ive, -ory*] **:** constituting or having the form of a prelude **:** INTRODUCTORY **:** indicating that something is to follow ⟨a ~ warning⟩ — **pre·lu·sive·ly** \-sə̇vlē\ *or* **pre·lu·so·ri·ly** \-sərəlē\ *adv*

**prem** *abbr* **1** premier **2** premium

**pre·makeready** \(ˈ)prē+\ *n* [*pre-* + *makeready*] **:** work constituting makeready (as underlaying low cuts) done to a printing surface before it is placed on the press

**pre·malignant** \ˌ=+\ *adj* [*pre-* + *malignant*] **:** PRECANCEROUS

**pre·man** \(ˈ)prē,man, -aa(ə)n\ *n, pl* **premen** [*pre-* + *man*] **:** a hypothetical ancient primate constituting the immediate ancestor of man **:** PREHOMINID

**pre·mandibular** \ˌprē+\ *adj* [*pre-* + *mandibular*] **:** situated in front of a mandible **:** PREDENTARY

**pre·marital** \(ˈ)=+\ *adj* [*pre-* + *marital*] **:** existing or occurring before marriage ⟨~ illusions⟩ ⟨~ experimentation⟩

**pre–marxian** \(ˈ)=+\ *or* **pre–marxist** \"+\ *adj, usu cap M* [*pre-* + *Marxian, Marxist*] **:** existing before Karl Marx or his socialistic doctrines ⟨*pre-Marxian* socialists⟩

**pre·mastery** \(ˈ)prē+\ *n* [*pre-* + *mastery*] **:** attainment of a skill or technique in advance of need

**pre·matrimonial** \(ˌ)=+\ *adj* [*pre-* + *matrimonial*] **:** occurring before marriage

**pre·maturation** \"+\ *n* [*pre-* + *maturation*] **:** unusually or abnormally early attainment of maturity

**¹pre·mature** \ˌprē *chiefly Brit* ˌpre+\ *adj* [L *praematurus* very early, too early, untimely, fr. *prae-* pre- + *maturus* ripe, mature] **1** *obs* **:** mature or ripe before the proper or usual time **2 a :** happening, arriving, existing, or performed before the proper or usual time **:** adopted, arriving, or received too soon **:** too early **:** UNTIMELY ⟨a ~ fall of snow⟩ ⟨~ reports⟩ **b** (1) *of a human infant* **:** born after a gestation period of less than 37 weeks or sometimes with a birth weight between two and five and one half pounds irrespective of the length of gestation (2) **:** of, relating to, or for the use of a premature infant ⟨~ diets⟩

**²premature** \"\ *n* -S **:** something that comes, happens, or occurs before the expected time: as **a :** an infant prematurely born **b :** a shell that bursts before the desired time

**³premature** \"\ *vi* **:** to explode prematurely — used esp. of a bomb or torpedo

**premature delivery** *or* **premature labor** *n* **:** expulsion of the human fetus after the 28th week of gestation but before the normal time

**pre·ma·ture·ly** *adv* **:** in a premature manner **:** before the proper time **:** too soon

**pre·ma·ture·ness** *n* -ES **:** the quality or state of being premature **:** PREMATURITY

**pre·maturity** \ˌprē *chiefly Brit* ˌpre+\ *n* [partly fr. F *prématurité* (fr. *pré-* pre- + *maturité* maturity, fr. L *maturitat-, maturitas*), partly fr. *premature* + *-ity*] **:** the quality or state of being premature: as **a :** early ripeness or flowering of a plant **b :** early maturity or development **:** PRECOCITY **c :** untimely maturity **:** undue earliness or haste **:** HASTINESS **d :** the condition of an infant born viable but before its proper time

**pre·maxilla** \ˌprē+\ *n* [NL, fr. *pre-* + *maxilla*] **:** either member of a pair of bones of the upper jaw of vertebrates situated between and in front of the maxillae that in man form the median anterior part of the superior maxillary bones but in most other mammals are distinct and bear the incisor teeth and in birds coalesce to form the principal part of the upper mandible — see FISH illustration

**¹pre·maxillary** \(ˌ)prē+\ *adj* [ISV *pre-* + *maxillary*] **1 :** situated in front of the maxillary bones **2 :** constituting or relating to the premaxillae

**²premaxillary** \"\ *n* [¹*premaxillary*] **:** PREMAXILLA

**¹pre·med** \(ˈ)prē¦med\ *adj* [by shortening] **:** PREMEDICAL

**²premed** \"\ *or* **pre·medic** \(ˈ)prē+\ *n* -S [short for *premedical*] **:** a premedical student or course of study

**pre·media** \(ˈ)prē+\ *n* [NL, fr. *pre-* + *media*] **:** a premedian vein (as in the wing of an insect)

**¹pre·median** \"+\ *or* **pre·medial** \"+\ *adj* [*pre-* + *median, medial*] **1 :** lying in front of the middle of the body **2** [*premedia* + *-an, -al*] **:** of, relating to, or being a vein of the wing of an insect now usu. regarded as a part of the media

**²premedian** \"\ *or* **premedial** \"\ *n* **:** a premedian vein

**pre·medical** \(ˈ)prē+\ *adj* [*pre-* + *medical*] **:** preceding and preparing for the professional study of medicine ⟨the ~ course in a university⟩ ⟨a ~ student⟩

**pre·medicate** \"+\ *vt* [*pre-* + *medicate*] **:** to administer premedication to **:** treat by premedication

**pre·medication** \(ˌ)prē+\ *n* **:** preliminary medication (as the giving of a quieting drug before an operation or before the induction of anesthesia)

**pre·medieval** \"+\ *adj* [*pre-* + *medieval*] **:** preceding the Middle Ages ⟨is almost an allegory of ~ times —*Literary Digest*⟩

**¹pre·meditate** \(ˈ)prē+\ *vb* [L *praemeditatus,* past part. of *praemeditari* to premeditate, fr. *prae-* pre- + *meditari* to meditate] *vt* **:** to think on and revolve in the mind beforehand **:** contrive and design previously **:** con over in advance ⟨with words *premeditated* thus he said —John Dryden⟩ ⟨carefully *premeditating* each step of his plan⟩ ~ *vi* **:** to think, consider, or deliberate beforehand

**²premeditate** *obs var of* PREMEDITATED

**premeditated** *adj* [fr. past part. of ¹*premeditate*] **:** characterized by fully conscious willful intent and a measure of forethought and planning **syn** see DELIBERATE

**pre·med·i·tat·ed·ly** *adv* **:** in a premeditated manner **:** with premeditation

**pre·med·i·tat·ed·ness** *n* -ES **:** the quality or state of being premeditated

**pre·med·i·tate·ly** \(ˈ)=¦medə,tātlē\ *archaic var of* PREMEDITATEDLY

**pre·med·i·tat·ing·ly** *adv* [*premeditating* (pres. part. of ¹*premeditate*) + *-ly*] **:** in the manner of one premeditating ⟨dwelt ~ on the possibility of violent action⟩

**pre·meditation** \(ˌ)prē+\ *n* [ME *premeditacion,* fr. L *praemeditation-, praemeditatio,* fr. *praemeditatus* (past part. of *praemeditari* to premeditate) + *-ion-, -io* -ion] **:** an act or instance of meditating beforehand: as **a :** previous deliberation as to action **:** planning and contriving **:** FORETHOUGHT **b :** consideration or planning of an act beforehand that shows intent to commit that act ⟨purchase of poison before a murder may evidence ~⟩

**pre·meditative** \(ˈ)=+\ *adj* [*premeditate* + *-ive*] **:** given to or characterized by premeditation

**pre·meditator** \(ˈ)prē+\ *n* [*premeditate* + *-or*] **:** one that premeditates

**pre·melting** \"+\ *n* [*pre-* + *melting*] **:** partial melting below the melting point

**pre·menarche** \ˌprē+\ *n* [*pre-* + *menarche*] **:** the period in the life of a girl preceding the establishment of menstruation — **pre·menarcheal** \"+\ *adj*

**pre–mendelian** \ˌprē+\ *adj, usu cap M* [*pre-* + *mendelian*] **:** preceding the knowledge or acceptance of Mendel's laws ⟨*pre-Mendelian* concepts of genetics⟩

**pre·menopausal** \(ˌ)prē+\ *adj* [*premenopause* + *-al*] **:** of, relating to, or being in the period just preceding menopause ⟨~ women⟩

**pre·menopause** \(ˈ)prē+\ *n* [*pre-* + *menopause*] **:** the period or physiological state that immediately precedes the menopause

**pre·menstrual** \"+\ *adj* [*pre-* + *menstrual*] **:** of or relating to the period just preceding menstruation ⟨~ changes in the uterus⟩ — **pre·men·stru·al·ly** \-əlē, -li\ *adv*

**pre·menstruum** \(ˈ)=+\ *n* [NL, fr. *pre-* + ML *menstruum* menses — more at MENSTRUUM] **:** the period or physiological state that immediately precedes menstruation

**pre·mentioned** \"+\ *adj* [*pre-* + *mentioned,* past part. of ²*mention*] **:** mentioned previously

**pre·men·tum** \prēˈmentəm\ *n* [NL, fr. *pre-* + *mentum*] **:** the part of the insect labium lying in front of the mentum and bearing a pair of lobes

**pre·meridian** \ˌprē+\ *adj* [*pre-* + *meridian*] **:** happening or being before noon

**pre–messianic** \(ˌ)=+\ *adj, often cap M* [*pre-* + *messianic*] **:** existing or occurring before the appearance of a messiah

**pre·metallic** \ˌprē+\ *adj* [*pre-* + *metallic*] **:** previous to the knowledge of the use of metals

**pre·metallized** \(ˈ)=+\ *adj, of a dye* **:** combined with chromium or other metal before addition to the dye bath

**pre·metaphase** \(ˈ)prē+\ *n* [*pre-* + *metaphase*] **:** PROMETAPHASE

**premia** *pl of* PREMIUM

**pre·mi·ate** \ˈprēmē,āt\ *vt* -ED/-ING/-S [ML *praemiatus,* past part. of *praemiare* to reward, fr. L *praemium* reward — more at PREMIUM] **:** to give a prize or premium to or for

**pre·mie** *or* **pree·mie** \ˈprēmē\ *n* -S [by shortening and alter. fr. ²*premature*] **:** a premature infant

**¹pre·mier** \(ˈ)prē¦mi(ə)r, -miə, prə̇ˈm- *sometimes* ˈpri,m- *or* (ˈ)pre¦m-; (ˈ)prā¦m-; *sometimes* ˈprē¦m(ə)r *also* ˈprem- *or* ˈprim- *sometimes* ˈprām-; *also* prəmˈyi(ə)r *or* -yiə *or* (ˈ)prem¦y- *or* ˈprim,y- *sometimes* (ˈ)prem¦y-; *also* (ˈ)prem¦ye(ə)r *or* -yeə *sometimes* prəmˈy- *or* ˈprim,y-; *sometimes* ˌpreme¦e(ə)r *or* -¦eə *or* ˈprem- *or* ˈprim-; *sometimes* ˈpremyə(r) *or* ˈprem- *or* ˈprim-; *sometimes* (ˈ)pre¦me(ə)r *or* -meə *or* (ˈ)pre¦m-\ *adj* [ME *primier, premier,* fr. MF *premier* first, chief, fr. L *primarius* of the first rank, principal — more at PRIMARY] **1 :** first in position, rank, or importance **:** CHIEF, PRINCIPAL, LEADING ⟨the ~ place⟩ ⟨a ~ angling fish — J.L.B.Smith⟩ **2 :** first in time **:** most ancient **:** EARLIEST ⟨a ~ peer is one bearing the oldest title of his degree⟩

**²premier** \"\ *n* -S [F, fr. *premier,* first, chief, fr. MF] **1 :** PRIME MINISTER ⟨the French ~⟩ ⟨the ~ of Western Australia⟩ ⟨the ~*s* of the Canadian provinces⟩ **2** *often cap* [fr. the *Premier* diamond mine, near Pretoria, south central Transvaal] **:** a diamond characterized by white color inclined toward bluish in sunlight but yellowish in artificial light **3 :** PREMIER DANSEUR

**premier danseur** *n* [F, lit., first dancer] **:** the principal male dancer in a ballet company

**¹pre·miere** \(ˈ)prim¦ye(ə)r, -yeə, prəmˈy-, (ˈ)prem¦y-, (ˈ)prēm-y- *sometimes* (ˈ)prām¦y-; (ˈ)prē¦mi(ə)r, -miə, prə̇ˈm- *sometimes* (ˈ)pre¦m-; *also* ¦prime¦e(ə)r *or* -¦eə *or* ¦prem-; *sometimes* ˈpremēə(r) *or* ˈprem- *or* ˈprim-; *sometimes* (ˈ)prem¦ye(ə)r *or* yeə *or* (ˈ)prim¦y- *or* prəmˈy-; *sometimes* (ˈ)pre¦me(ə)r *or* -meə *or* ˈpremyə(r)\ *n* -S [F *première,* fr. *première,* fem. of *premier* first, chief] **1 :** a first performance or exhibition (as of a play) **:** FIRST NIGHT **2 :** the leading lady of a group: as **a :** the chief actress of a theatrical cast **b :** PREMIERE DANSEUSE

**²premiere** \", *but* -meə(r) *is more frequent than for the noun*\ *adj* [alter. (influenced by ¹*premiere*) of ¹*premier*] **:** FIRST, OUTSTANDING, CHIEF ⟨a ~ performance⟩ ⟨the ~ dance of the program⟩

**³premiere** *or* **premier** \"\ *vb* **premiered; premiered; premiering; premieres** *or* **premiers** [¹*premiere*] *vt* **:** to give a first public performance or showing of ~ *vi* **1 :** to have a first public performance or showing **2 :** to appear for the first time as a star or featured performer (as in a play)

**premiere danseuse** *n* [F *première danseuse,* lit., first female dancer] **:** the principal female dancer in a ballet company

**pre·mier·ship** *pronunc at* PREMIER +ˌship\ *n* [¹*premier* + *-ship*] **:** the position or office of a premier

**pre·military** \(ˈ)prē+\ *adj* [*pre-* + *military*] **:** preceding military service or activity

**pre·milk** \(ˈ)=+\ *adj* [*pre-* + *milk*] **:** previous to the appearance of milk — used chiefly of a stage of seed development ⟨seeds collected in ~ . . . stages —*Experiment Station Record*⟩

**¹pre·millenarian** \(ˌ)=+\ *adj* [*pre-* + *millenarian*] **:** of, relating to, or constituting the doctrine of premillennialism

**²premillenarian** \"\ *n* **:** one that holds the doctrine of premillennialism

**pre·millenarianism** \"+\ *n* [¹*premillenarian* + *-ism*] **:** PREMILLENNIALISM

**pre·millennial** \ˌprē+\ *adj* [*pre-* + *millennium* + *-al*] **:** coming before a millennium **:** previous to the millennium ⟨an expectation that Christ's Second Advent will be ~⟩ — **pre·millennially** \"+\ *adv*

**pre·millennialism** \"+\ *n* [*premillennial* + *-ism*] **:** the doctrine that the second coming of Christ precedes and ushers in the millennium — opposed to *postmillennialism*

**pre·millennialist** \"+\ *n* [*premillennial* + *-ist*] **:** PREMILLENARIAN

**pre·mil·len·ni·al·ize** \-ə,līz\ *vi* -ED/-ING/-S [*premillennial* + *-ize*] **:** to preach premillennialism

**pre·millennian** \"+\ *adj* [*pre-* + *millennium* + *-an*] **:** PREMILLENNIAL

**pre·mineral** \(ˈ)=+\ *adj* [*pre-* + *mineral*] **:** of earlier origin than associated mineral deposits ⟨a ~ fault⟩

**premio** *n* [It, reward, prize, insurance premium, fr. L *praemium* profit, reward — more at PREMIUM] *obs* **:** PREMIUM

**pre·mis·al** \prēˈmīzəl\ *n* -S [²*premise* + *-al*] **:** the act or an instance of making or stating a premise

**¹prem·ise** *also* **prem·iss** \ˈpreməs\ *n, pl* **premises** *also* **premisses** [in sense 1, fr. ME *premisse,* fr. MF, fr. ML *praemissa,* fr. L, fem. of *praemissus,* past part. of *praemittere* to place ahead, send ahead, fr. *prae-* pre- + *mittere* to send; in other senses, fr. ME *premisses,* fr. ML *praemissa,* fr. L, neut. pl. of *praemissus* — more at SMITE] **1 :** a proposition antecedently supposed or proved **:** a basis of argument: as **a :** a proposition in logic stated or assumed as leading to a conclusion **:** either of the first two propositions of a syllogism from which the conclusion is drawn **b :** something assumed or taken for granted **:** PRESUPPOSITION; *esp* **:** something implied as a condition precedent **c** *obs* **:** a condition stated beforehand **:** STIPULATION ⟨the ~*s* observed, thy will by my performance shall be served —Shak.⟩ **2 premises** *pl* **:** matters previously stated or set forth: as **a :** the part of a deed preceding the habendum, being formerly the first of eight parts making up an old-style deed and serving to state the names and addresses of the parties and to make the recitals necessary to explain the transaction (as the consideration, the capacity of the parties to act, and the identity of the land to be conveyed) **b :** the part of a bill in equity that sets forth the causes of complaint, the parties against whom redress is sought, and other pertinent explanatory matter **3 premises** *pl a archaic* **:** property that is conveyed by bequest or deed **b :** a specified piece or tract of land with the structures on it **c :** a building, buildings, or part of a building covered by or within the stated terms of a policy (as of fire insurance) **d :** the place of business of an enterprise or institution **4** *obs* **:** an antecedent happening or circumstance — usu. used in pl.

**²premise** \", prēˈmīz\ *vb* -ED/-ING/-S [partly fr. ¹*premise,* partly fr. MF *premis, premise,* past part. of *premetre* to place ahead, fr. L *praemittere* — more at ¹PREMISE] *vt* **1 a :** to set forth beforehand or as introductory to a main subject **:** offer previously as something to explain or aid in understanding what follows (as a premise or first proposition on which rest subsequent reasonings) ⟨I ~ these particulars that the reader may know that I enter upon it as a very ungrateful task — Joseph Addison⟩ **b :** to presuppose or imply as preexistent **:** postulate as a condition precedent **2** *archaic* **:** to use, send, or do in advance or as an initial step **:** put before something else; *esp* **:** to do or use in the initial phase of a medical or surgical treatment **3 :** to introduce by or with some pertinent thing ⟨let me ~ my argument with a bit of history⟩ ~ *vi* **:** to make a premise **:** set something forth as a premise **syn** see PRESUPPOSE

**pre·mit** \prēˈmit\ *vt* **premitted; premitted; premitting; premits** [L *praemittere* to place ahead] *archaic* **:** PREMISE

**¹pre·mi·um** \ˈprēmēəm, *esp Brit* -myəm\ *n, pl* **premiums** \-mz\ *also* **pre·mia** \-mēə, -myə\ [L *praemium* booty, profit, reward, fr. *prae-* pre- + *-emium* (fr. *emere* to take, buy) — more at REDEEM] **1 a :** a reward or recompense for a particular act **:** a prize to be won for superior performance or successful competition **:** AWARD ⟨a ~ for the best yearling steer exhibited⟩ ⟨encouraging children with ~*s* for good conduct⟩ **b :** something paid over and above a fixed wage, price, or other remuneration **:** BONUS ⟨immediately after the war a new car could only be obtained by paying a considerable ~⟩ ⟨with incentive pay and other ~*s* his income was nearly double the basic wage⟩ ⟨a third shift ~⟩ **c** (1) **:** something offered or given for the loan of money usu. apart from or in addition to interest ⟨had to pay a ~ to get his mortgage⟩ (2) **:** a sum in advance of or in addition to the nominal value of something; *esp* **:** such a sum added to the face or par value of a mortgage or security usu. as a condition of redeeming it at a particular time or under specified circumstances ⟨bonds callable at a ~ of six percent⟩ **d :** something (as an article of merchandise) given without charge or at less than usual price with the purchase of a product or service **e :** BONUS 4 **2 a :** the consideration paid in money or otherwise for a contract of insurance in the form of an initiation fee, an admission fee, an assessment, or a stipulated single or periodic payment according to the nature of the insurance — see EARNED PREMIUM, GROSS PREMIUM, LEVEL PREMIUM, MINIMUM PREMIUM, NATURAL PREMIUM, NET PREMIUM, SINGLE PREMIUM, UNEARNED PREMIUM **b :** a payment made for instruction (as under an apprentice system) in a trade or profession **3 :** a high value or a value in excess of that normally or usu. expected ⟨put a ~ on accuracy⟩ ⟨gold coin had a considerable ~ over paper money⟩ ⟨selling at a ~⟩ ⟨found housing at a ~⟩ ⟨a ~ on honesty in government⟩

**²premium** \"\ *adj* **1 :** of exceptional quality or ability ⟨a ~ student⟩ ⟨~ products⟩ **2 :** commanding a higher than usual price esp. because of superior quality ⟨~ gasolines⟩

**premium loan** *n* **:** a loan made in the amount of and for the purpose of paying a premium due upon a life insurance policy and constituting a lien against the policy

**premium note** *n* **:** a note given by the insured in payment of all or a portion of the premium on an insurance policy

**premium system** *n* **:** a system for paying workmen in which the workman's hourly rate is guaranteed and a premium (as a percentage of the hourly wage) is paid for doing the work in less than the standard time specified

**¹pre·mix** \(ˈ)prē+\ *vt* [*pre-* + *mix*] **:** to mix before use ⟨possible to ~ the ore at the shipping point, thus saving time at the iron works —*Amer. Guide Series: Mich.*⟩

**²pre·mix** \ˈ=,=\ *n* **:** a mixture of ingredients (as the dry materials for a cake batter or high protein supplements for an animal ration) designed to be mixed with other ingredients (as the liquid materials for a cake batter or high carbohydrate parts of an animal ration) before use

**pre·modern** \(ˈ)prē+\ *adj* [*pre-* + *modern*] **:** antedating the modern **:** not of the current kind, form, or style

**¹pre·molar** \"+\ *adj* [*pre-* + *molar*] **:** situated in front of or preceding the molar teeth; *usu* **:** being or relating to those teeth of a mammal in front of the true molars and behind the canines when the latter are present

**²premolar** \"\ *n* **1 :** a premolar tooth that is in man one of two in each side of each jaw — called also *bicuspid* **2 :** a milk tooth that occupies the position later taken by a premolar tooth of the permanent dentition

**pre·monish** \(ˈ)prē+\ *vb* -ED/-ING/-ES [*pre-* + *monish*] *vt* **:** to admonish beforehand **:** give previous warning to ~ *vi* **:** to give warning in advance — **pre·mon·ish·ment** \-mənt\ *n* -S

**pre·mo·ni·tion** \ˌprēməˈnishən, ˌprem-\ *n* -S [MF, fr. LL *praemonition-, praemonitio,* fr. L *praemonitus* (past part. of *praemonēre* to warn in advance, fr. *prae-* pre- + *monēre* to warn) + *-ion-, -io* -ion — more at MIND] **1 :** previous warning, notice, or information **:** FOREWARNING ⟨falling leaves gave a ~ of coming winter⟩ **2 :** anticipation of an event without conscious reason **:** PRESENTIMENT ⟨felt a ~ of danger⟩

**pre·mon·i·tor** \prē'mänəd·ə(r)\ *n* [L *praemonitor*, fr. *praemonitus* + *-or*] : one that premonishes
**pre·mon·i·to·ri·ly** \-ˌmänəˌtōrəlē, -tòr-, -lē\ *adv* : in a premonitory manner
**pre·mon·i·to·ry** \-ˌ==ˌtōrē, -tòr-, -ri\ *also* **pre·mon·i·tary** \-ˌterē, -ri\ *adj* [LL *praemonitorius*, fr. L *praemonitus* + *-orius* -ory] : giving previous warning or notice ⟨~ symptoms of disease⟩
**premonstrate** *vt* [L *praemonstratus*, past part. of *praemonstrare* to show beforehand, fr. *prae-* pre- + *monstrare* to show — more at MUSTER] *obs* : to show or represent beforehand
**¹pre·mon·stra·ten·sian** \(ˌ)prēˌmän(t)strəˈtenchən\ *n* -s *usu cap* [ML *praemonstratensis*, fr. *praemonstratensis* of Prémontré (fr. *Praemonstratus* Prémontré, abbey in northern France + L *-ensis* -ese) + E *-an*] : a member of an order of regular canons founded by St. Norbert at Prémontré near Laon, France, in 1119
**²premonstratensian** \"\ *adj, usu cap* : of or relating to the Premonstratensians
**pre·mon·stra·tion** \ˌprēˌmänˈstrāshən\ *n* -s [LL *praemonstration-, praemonstratio*, fr. L *praemonstratus* (past part. of *praemonstrare* to show beforehand) + *-ion-, -io* -ion — more at PREMONSTRATE] *obs* : a showing forth in advance
**pre·moral** \(ˈ)prē+\ *adj* [*pre-* + *moral*] : existing or like that existing before the development of a moral code in society
**pre·morse** \prēˈmȯrs\ *adj* [L *praemorsus*, fr. past part. of *praemordēre* to bite off in front, fr. *prae-* pre- + *mordēre* to bite — more at SMART] : bitten off : terminated abruptly or as if bitten off : irregularly truncate ⟨a ~ root⟩
**pre·mortal** \(ˈ)prē+\ *adj* [*pre-* + *mortal*] **1** : existing prior to the presumed assumption of mortality by man **2** [*premortem* + *-al*] : existing or taking place immediately before death ⟨~ injuries⟩
**pre·mortem** \(ˈ)prēˈmȯrtəm\ *adj* [L *prae mortem* before death] : PREMORTAL 2
**pre·mortuary** \(ˈ)prē+\ *adj* [*pre-* + *mortuary*] : occurring or relating to what occurs before a funeral; *also* : prepared in advance for or as if for a funeral ⟨a ~ tribute⟩
**pre·mo·tion** \prēˈmōshən\ *n* [ML *praemotion-, praemotio*, fr. LL *praemotus* (past part. of *praemovēre* to move beforehand, fr. L *prae-* pre- + *movēre* to move) + L *-ion-, -io* -ion] : movement or excitation to action beforehand; *specif* : the inspiration or determination (as by divine power) of an action beforehand
**pre·move** \-ˈmüv\ *vt* [LL *praemovēre* to move beforehand] : to move or excite to action beforehand; *specif* : to determine (as by divine inspiration) the action of beforehand — **pre·move·ment** \-mənt\ *n*
**pre–muhammadan** \ˌ==+\ *adj, usu cap M* [*pre-* + *muhammadan*] : PRE-ISLAMIC
**pre·mundane** \(ˌ)prē+\ *adj* [*pre-* + *mundane*] : existing before the creation of the world
**pre·mune** \prēˈmyün\ *adj* [back-formation fr. *premunition*] : exhibiting premunition
**premunire** *var of* PRAEMUNIRE
**premunite** *vt* [L *praemunitus*, past part. of *praemunire* to fortify in front or beforehand] *obs* : to fortify in front or beforehand
**pre·mu·ni·tion** \ˌprēmyəˈnishən\ *also* **pre·mu·ni·ty** \prēˈmyünəd·ē\ *n, pl* **premunitions** *also* **premunities** [*premunition* fr. L *praemunition-, praemunitio* fortification in advance, fr. *praemunitus* (past part. of *praemunire* to fortify in front or beforehand, fr. *prae-* pre- + *munire* to fortify) + *-ion-, -io* -ion; *premunity* fr. *premune* + *-ity* — more at MUNITION] **1** *archaic* : PREMONITION **2 a** *archaic* : an advance provision of protection (as against military attack) **b** : resistance to a disease due to the existence of its causative agent in a state of physiological equilibrium in the host **c** : immunity to a particular infection due to the previous presence of the causative agent in the host
**pre·mu·ni·to·ry** \prēˈmyünəˌtōrē\ *adj* [L *praemunitus* (past part. of *praemunire*) + E *-ory*] : relating to or involving a praemunire
**pre·mu·nize** \ˈprēmyəˌnīz\ *vt* -ED/-ING/-S [*premune* + *-ize*] : to induce premunition in
**pre–mycenaean** \(ˌ)prē+\ *adj, usu cap M* [*pre-* + *mycenaean*] : of or relating to a civilization in Greek lands earlier than the period to which characteristic Mycenaean objects belong
**pre·myelocyte** \(ˈ)=+\ *n* [*pre-* + *myelocyte*] : a partially differentiated granulocyte in bone marrow having the characteristic granulations but lacking the specific staining reactions of a mature granulocyte of the blood
**pre·name** \ˈ=,=\ *n* [*pre-* + *name*] : FORENAME
**pre·nan·thes** \prēˈnanˌthēz\ *n, cap* [NL, fr. Gk *prēnēs* prone (akin to *pro* before, forward) + NL *-anthes* — more at FOR] : a genus of No. American and Asiatic perennial herbs (family Compositae) with lobed or pinnatifid leaves and small heads of drooping ligulate flowers — see RATTLESNAKE ROOT
**pre·narial** \(ˈ)prē+\ *adj* [*pre-* + *narial*] : relating to or situated in front of the nostrils
**pre·naris** \(ˈ)prē+\ *n, pl* **prenares** [NL, fr. *pre-* + *naris*] : either of the anterior nares
**¹pre·nasal** \"+\ *adj* [*pre-* + *nasal*] : situated in front of the nasal bones, nose, or nostrils
**²prenasal** \"\ *n* : a prenasal part (as a scale); *esp* : a bone or cartilage in the snout of various animals (as swine)
**pre·nasalization** \(ˌ)=+\ *n* [*pre-* + *nasalization*] : pronunciation of a stop sound with a brief interval of nasalization that is not ascribable to a preceding segment of speech
**pre·nasalized** \(ˈ)=+\ *adj* [*pre-* + *nasalized*] : marked by prenasalization
**pre·natal** \(ˈ)=+\ *adj* [*pre-* + *natal*] : occurring, existing, or taking place before birth : ANTENATAL ⟨~ care⟩ ⟨the ~ period⟩ — **pre·natally** \"+\ *adv*
**pre·na·tal·ist** \-ᵊləst\ *n* -s : a believer in the prenatal divinity of Jesus
**pren·der** *also* **pren·dre** \ˈprendə(r)\ *n* -s [MF *prendre* to take, fr. L *prehendere, prendere* to seize, grasp — more at PREHENSILE] : the power or right under the law of taking a thing without its being offered
**pre·neural** \(ˈ)prē+\ *adj* [*pre-* + *neural (plate)*] : situated in front of or anterior to the neural plate — used esp. of a bone forming part of the carapace of a turtle
**pre–newtonian** \ˌprē+\ *adj, usu cap N* [*pre-* + *newtonian*] : existing prior to the development of Newtonian philosophy or physics
**pre·nex normal form** \ˈprēˌneks-\ *n* [LL *praenexus* tied up or bound in front, fr. L *prae-* pre- + *nexus*, past part. of *nectere* to tie, bind — more at ANNEX] : a normal form of an expression in the functional calculus in which all the quantifiers are grouped without negations or other connectives before the matrix so that the scope of each quantifier extends to the end of the formula
**pre–noachian** \ˌprē+\ *adj, usu cap N* [*pre-* + *noachian*] : existing before the Noachian deluge
**pre·noble** \(ˈ)prē+\ *adj* [*pre-* + *noble*] : eminently noble
**pre·nodal** \"+\ *adj* [*pre-* + *nodus* + *-al*] : situated between the nodus and the base of the wing of an insect
**pre·nol·epis** \prēˈnäləpəs\ *n, cap* [NL, fr. Gk *prēnēs* prone + NL *-lepis* — more at PRENANTHES] : a large and widely distributed genus of ants
**prenomen** *var of* PRAENOMEN
**¹pre·nom·i·nal** \prēˈnämənᵊl\ *adj* [L *praenomin-, praenomen* + E *-al*] : of, relating to, or constituting a praenomen
**²prenominal** \(ˈ)prē+\ *adj* [*pre-* + L *nomin-* *nomen* name, noun + E *-al* — more at NAME] : placed or coming before a noun ⟨the ~ form of a possessive pronoun⟩
**¹prenominate** *adj* [LL *praenominatus*, past part. of *praenominare* to name before, fr. *prae-* pre- + *nominare* to name — more at NOMINATE] *obs* : previously mentioned
**²prenominate** *vt* [LL *praenominatus*, past part. of *praenominare*] *obs* : to mention previously — **prenomination** *n, obs*
**pre–norman** \(ˈ)prē+\ *adj, usu cap N* [*pre-* + *norman*] : of, relating to, or occurring in England prior to the Norman conquest
**pre·notice** \"+\ *n* [*pre-* + *notice*] : notice or warning given or received in advance
**pre·notification** \(ˌ)=+\ *n* [*pre-* + *notification*] : PRENOTICE
**pre·notify** \(ˈ)=+\ *vt* [*pre-* + *notify*] : to give prenotice to : warn or notify in advance
**pre·notion** \"+\ *n* [L *praenotion-, praenotio* previous notion, preconception, fr. *prae-* pre- + *notion-, notio* idea, conception — more at NOTION] **1** : PRESENTIMENT, PREMONITION, FOREKNOWLEDGE **2** : a preconceived idea formed without actual experience
**prent** \ˈprent\ *dial Brit var of* PRINT
**¹pren·tice** \ˈprentəs\ *n* -s [ME *prentis*, short for *apprentis* — more at APPRENTICE] **1** : APPRENTICE 1, LEARNER **2** *or* **prentice of law** *obs* : APPRENTICE 2 a
**²prentice** \"\ *adj* **1** : of, relating to, or characteristic of an apprentice ⟨~ work⟩ ⟨~ training⟩ **2** : not fully skilled : incompletely trained : INEXPERIENCED ⟨tried his ~ hand at modern drama⟩; *also* : crude and imperfect : lacking in finish or polish ⟨a ~ effort⟩ ⟨~ touches that marred the concept⟩
**³prentice** \"\ *vt* -ED/-ING/-S : APPRENTICE
**pre·nuptial** \(ˈ)prē+\ *adj* [*pre-* + *nuptial*] : ANTENUPTIAL
**pre·occasioned** \ˌ=+\ *adj* [*pre-* + *occasioned*, past part. of *²occasion*] : caused by some previous happening ⟨anger ~ by his neglect⟩
**pre·occipital** \"+\ *adj* [*pre-* + *occipital*] : situated in front of the occiput or an occipital part (as the occipital lobe of the brain) ⟨~ lesions⟩
**pre·occupancy** \(ˈ)=+\ *n* [*pre-* + *occupancy*] **1** : an act or the right of taking possession before another : PREOCCUPATION ⟨the ~ of wild land⟩ **2** [*preoccupy* + *-ancy*] : the condition of being completely busied or preoccupied
**¹pre·occupant** \(ˈ)=+\ *adj* [L *praeoccupant-, praeoccupans*, pres. part. of *praeoccupare* to occupy in advance] : occupying in advance
**²preoccupant** \"\ *n* [*pre-* + *occupant*] : one that occupies something (as a piece of land) ahead of others : a prior occupant
**preoccupate** *vt* -ED/-ING/-S [L *praeoccupatus*, past part. of *praeoccupare* to seize beforehand, anticipate] **1** *obs* **a** : to take before : ANTICIPATE **b** : SURPRISE, FORESTALL **2** *obs* : PREPOSSESS, PREJUDICE
**pre·occupation** \(ˌ)=+\ *n* [L *praeoccupation-, praeoccupatio* act of seizing beforehand, fr. *praeoccupatus* (past part. of *praeoccupare* to seize beforehand, fr. *prae-* pre- + *occupare* to seize, occupy) + *-ion-, -io* -ion — more at OCCUPY] **1 a** : an act of preoccupying or the condition of being preoccupied : PREPOSSESSION **b** : extreme or excessive concern with something : complete engrossment of the mind or interests ⟨his ~ with business left little time for his family⟩ **c** : something that causes preoccupation or engages the attention ⟨the ~s of daily life⟩ **2** *obs* : PROLEPSIS 2b
**pre·occupied** \(ˈ)=+\ *adj* [fr. past part. of *preoccupy*] **1 a** : lost in thought : ENGROSSED, ABSORBED **b** : already occupied : FILLED **2** : previously applied to some other group and therefore unavailable according to the rules of nomenclature for use in a new sense — used of a biological generic or specific name
**pre·oc·cu·pied·ly** \-pī(ə)dlē, -li\ *adv* : in a preoccupied manner
**pre·occupy** \(ˈ)=+\ *vt* [*pre-* + *occupy*] **1** : to engage, occupy, or engross the interest or attention of beforehand or preferentially : PREENGAGE, PREPOSSESS **2** : to occupy or take possession of before another ⟨~ a country not before held⟩ **3** : to fill beforehand : occupy in advance of
**¹pre·ocular** \(ˈ)=+\ *adj* [*pre-* + L *oculus* eye + E *-ar* — more at EYE] : situated in front of the eye ⟨an insect with the antennae ~ in position⟩
**²preocular** \"\ *n* : a preocular part ⟨~s and other scales of a snake⟩
**pre·oedipal** \(ˈ)=+\ *adj* [*pre-* + *oedipal*] : antedating the occurrence of oedipal conflict
**pre·operative** \"+\ *adj* [*pre-* + *operative*] : occurring during the period preceding a surgical operation — **pre·operatively** \"+\ *adv*
**pre·opercle** \(ˌ)prē+\ *also* **pre·operculum** \ˌ=+\ *n, pl* **preopercles** *also* **preopercula** [NL *preoperculum*, fr. *pre-* + *operculum*] : a flat membrane bone in the gill cover of most fishes lying immediately in front of the opercle
**pre·opercular** \ˌ=+\ *adj* [NL *preoperculum* + E *-ar*] : being or relating to a preopercle
**pre·opinion** \"+\ *n* [*pre-* + *opinion*] : an opinion previously formed : PRECONCEPTION, PREJUDICE
**pre·optic** \(ˈ)=+\ *adj* [*pre-* + *optic*] : situated in front of an optic part or region ⟨~ tracts in the brain⟩
**pre·option** \(ˈ)=+\ *n* [*pre-* + *option*] : the right or privilege of making a selection (as from available goods) before others ⟨the king having always the ~ of the spoils of war⟩
**pre·oral** \(ˈ)=+\ *adj* [*pre-* + *oral*] : situated in front of or anterior to the mouth — **pre·orally** \"+\ *adv*
**¹pre·orbital** \(ˈ)=+\ *adj* [*pre-* + *orbit* + *-al*] **1** : situated in front of the orbit ⟨the ~ membrane bone of bony fishes⟩ **2** : occurring before going into or being in orbit
**²preorbital** \"\ *n* : a preorbital part; *esp* : a large membrane bone that is situated just in front of the orbit in many teleost fishes
**pre·ordain** \ˌ=+\ *vt* [*pre-* + *ordain*] : to decree or ordain in advance : order or assure the occurrence of beforehand : FOREORDAIN
**pre·ordainment** \ˌ=+\ *n* -s [*preordain* + *-ment*] : the quality or state of being preordained
**pre·order** \(ˈ)=+\ *vt* [*pre-* + *order*] **1** : to plan out in order or arrange beforehand : FOREORDAIN **2** : to give an order for in advance ⟨it is wise to ~ very special dishes when making your reservation⟩
**preordinance** *n* [ME, fr. *pre-* + *ordinance*] *obs* : antecedent decree
**pre·ordination** \(ˌ)=+\ *n* [LL *praeordination-, praeordinatio*, fr. *praeordinatus* (past part. of *praeordinare* to preordain, fr. L *prae-* pre- + *ordinare* to order, ordain) + *-ion-, -io* -ion — more at ORDAIN] : the action or an act or instance of preordaining or foreordaining
**pre·organic** \ˌ=+\ *adj* [*pre-* + *organic*] : formed or occurring before the beginning of life ⟨~ evolution⟩
**pre·original** \ˌ=+\ *adj* [*pre-* + *original*] : occurring in or dating from a period preceding the accepted period of origin of something ⟨the curious ~ form of the [work], an unfinished but printed version —*Modern Language Notes*⟩ — **pre·originally** \"+\ *adv*
**pre·outfit** \(ˈ)=+\ *vt* [*pre-* + *outfit*] : to outfit in advance ⟨~ a party for mountain climbing⟩
**pre·ovu·la·to·ry** \(ˈ)prēˌävyələˌtōrē\ *adj* [*pre-* + *ovulate* + *-ory*] : occurring in or having the form typical of the period immediately preceding ovulation ⟨the ~ phase of the cycle⟩ ⟨~ endocrine relations⟩
**pre·oxygenation** \(ˌ)prē+\ *n* [*pre-* + *oxygenation*] : inhalation of large quantities of essentially pure oxygen usu. as a prelude to some activity (as high-level flight) in which it is desirable to minimize nitrogen and maximize oxygen in the blood and tissues
**¹prep** \ˈprep\ *n* -s [short for *preparation*] **1** *Brit* **a** : preparation of study assignments : HOMEWORK ⟨I may stay for three-quarters of an hour, and then I must go and do my ~ —Archibald Marshall⟩ **b** : a specific time or place set aside for study ⟨supposed to superintend tea and evening ~ —H.G. Wells⟩ ⟨collected their books and went into ~ —Hugh MacLennan⟩ **2** [short for *preparatory*] **a** : PREPARATORY SCHOOL **b** : a preparatory school student **3** : the act or an instance of preparing a patient for a surgical operation ⟨the floor nurse had three ~s to do⟩ **4** *horse racing* : a trial run
**²prep** \"\ *vb* **prepped; prepped; prepping; preps** *vi* **1** : to attend preparatory school ⟨the place where he *prepped* for college⟩ **2** : to engage in preparatory study or training ⟨entered medical school to ~ for the study of psychiatry —Gilbert McKean⟩ ⟨*prepped* for his new post abroad⟩ ~ *vt* **1** : to prepare for an examination, assignment, or course of study ⟨youths of higher mental caliber but not as well *prepped* —*Newsweek*⟩ **2** : to prepare for a surgical operation ⟨an orderly came in to ~ him for the appendectomy⟩
**prep** *abbr* **1** preparation; preparatory; prepare **2** preposition
**¹pre·pack** \(ˈ)=+\ *or* **pre·package** \(ˈ)=+\ *vt* [*pre-* + *pack*, v. or *package*, v.] : to enclose in a prepack
**²prepack** \"\ *or* **prepackage** \"\ *n* : a usu. transparent package (as of food or a manufactured article) prepared or wrapped beforehand for the individual consumer by a manufacturer, distributor, or retailer
**pre·paid expense** \(ˈ)=ˌ=-\ *n* : DEFERRED CHARGE
**prepaid station** *n* : a railroad station to which freight cannot be shipped C.O.D. — contrasted with *open station*
**pre·palatal** \(ˈ)prē+\ *adj* [ISV *pre-* + *palatal*] : articulated against the front third or half of the hard palate or against the front third of the palate as a whole
**pre·par·able** \prēˈpa(a)rəbəl, -ˈper-, ˈprep(ə)rə-\ *adj* : capable of being prepared
**prep·a·rate** \ˈprepərət\ *adj* [ME *preparat*, fr. L *praeparatus*, past part. of *praeparare* to prepare] : PREPARED, READY ⟨the dark entrails of the ~ earth —S.V.Benét⟩
**pré·pa·ra·teur** \ˌprepərəˈtər(·)\ *n* -s [F, lit., one that prepares, fr. LL *praeparator*, fr. L *praeparatus*, past part. of *praeparare* to prepare) + *-or*] : a laboratory assistant ⟨turned the cucumber over to my ~ and began on my fish —William Beebe⟩
**prep·a·ra·tion** \ˌprepəˈrāshən\ *n* -s [ME *preparacion*, fr. MF *preparation*, fr. L *praeparation-, praeparatio*, fr. *praeparatus* (past part. of *praeparare* to prepare) + *-ion-, -io* -ion] **1 a** : the action or process of making something ready for use or service ⟨began ~ of the land for sowing⟩ ⟨finished the ~ of the manuscript for the printer⟩ **b** : the action or process of putting something together : COMPOUNDING ⟨skilled in the ~ of home remedies⟩ ⟨spent several years in the ~ of his masterpiece⟩ ⟨has made the ~ of meals easier⟩ **c** : the action or process of getting ready for some occasion, test, or duty : TRAINING ⟨exercised regularly in ~ for the fight⟩ ⟨a period of observation in ~ for assuming the post —*Current Biog.*⟩ **2** : a state of being prepared : FITNESS, PREPAREDNESS, READINESS ⟨the car was in excellent ~ for the trip⟩ **3 a** : ritual acts and observances preceding the Jewish Sabbath or other festival ⟨it was the day of ~ for the Passover —Jn 19:14 (RSV)⟩ **b** : liturgical prayers or private devotions said by one preparing for a sacrament (as the celebration of the Eucharist) or in advance of communicating; *also* : the first part of the Communion service **4 a** : a preliminary measure or plan : an action taken to expedite or prepare the way for something — usu. used in pl. ⟨~s for new elections were started at once —*Americana Annual*⟩ **b** : the anticipation of a dissonant tone as a consonance in the preceding chord; *also* : the tone so sounded — see SUSPENSION illustration **c** (1) : work done by a teacher or student in preparing for a class; *specif* : a unit of time regularly devoted by a teacher to preparing for a class ⟨prefer teaching five sections, with three or four ~s —H.R.Douglass⟩ (2) *Brit* : PREP **d** : heavy fire delivered before an attack to disrupt the enemy's defenses and communications ⟨artillery ~⟩ **e** : a series of processes (as cataloging, shelflisting, marking) that a book is put through before it reaches the library shelves **5** : something that is prepared : something made, equipped, or compounded for a specific purpose ⟨caffeine is one of the more common ingredients found in pharmaceutical ~s —*Jour. Amer. Pharmaceutical Assoc.*⟩ ⟨a widely sold ~ for colds⟩
**preparation hymn** *n* : a hymn preceding the sermon in an order of service used by Free Churches
**prep·a·ra·tion·ist** \-sh(ə)nəst\ *n* -s : one who believes in preparedness esp. for war
**¹pre·par·a·tive** \prēˈpa(a)rəd·iv, -ˈper-, -rətiv\ *n* -s [ME *preparatif*, fr. MF, fr. L *praeparatus* (past part. of *praeparare* to prepare) + MF *-if* -ive (n. suffix)] **1 a** : something that prepares the way for or serves as a preliminary to something else : PREPARATION ⟨the best ~ in the world . . . for thoughtless, unburdened sleep —H.R.Steeves⟩ **b** *archaic* : something administered to a person to prepare him for a particular medication or course of treatment **2** : a military or naval signal to make ready
**²preparative** \"\ *adj* [MF *preparatif*, fr. ML *praeparativus*, fr. L *praeparatus* (past part. of *praeparare* to prepare) + *-ivus* -ive (adj. suffix)] : PREPARATORY
**³preparative** \"\ *adv* : PREPARATIVELY
**pre·par·a·tive·ly** \-əvlē\ *adv* : by way of preparation
**pre·par·a·tor** \prēˈparəd·ə(r), ˈprepəˌrād-·\ *n* -s [LL *praeparator* one that prepares] : one who prepares something; *specif* : one who prepares specimens for scientific use or museum display
**pre·par·a·to·ri·ly** \prēˈparəˌtōrəlē, prəˈ-, -tòr-, -li *also* -ˈper- *or* ˈprep(ə)rəˌt- *sometimes by* r-dissimilation ÷ˈprepəˌt-\ *adv* : in a preparatory manner : by way of preparation
**¹pre·par·a·to·ry** \prēˈparəˌtōrē, prəˈ-, -tòr-, -ri *also* -ˈper- *or* ˈprep(ə)rəˌt- *sometimes by* r-dissimilation ÷ˈprepəˌt-\ *adj* [ME, fr. LL *praeparatorius*, fr. L *praeparatus* (past part. of *praeparare* to prepare) + *-orius* -ory] : preparing or serving to prepare for something : INTRODUCTORY, PRELIMINARY ⟨~ education⟩ ⟨~ training⟩
**²preparatory** \"\ *n* -ES : PREPARATIVE
**³preparatory** \"\ *adv* : PREPARATORILY ⟨found the veteran cleaning out his desk ~ to departure —S.H.Adams⟩
**preparatory school** *n* **1** : a usu. private school preparing students primarily for college **2** *Brit* : a private elementary school preparing students primarily for public schools
**preparatory seminary** *n* : a Roman Catholic school for young men intending to enter the priesthood that corresponds to a high school and junior college and has a course of study emphasizing philosophy during the last two years — called also *junior seminary, minor seminary*
**pre·pare** \prēˈpa(a)(ə)r, prəˈ-, -pe(ə)r, -pa(a)ə, -peə\ *vb* -ED/-ING/-S [ME *preparen*, fr. MF *preparer*, fr. L *praeparare*, fr. *prae-* pre- + *parare* to prepare, procure — more at PARE] *vt* **1 a** : to make ready beforehand for some purpose : put into condition for a particular use, application, or disposition ⟨telling him to cut the weeds and to ~ ground for winter crops —Elizabeth M. Roberts⟩ ⟨*prepared* the guest room for their visitor⟩ ⟨*prepared* the patient for the operation⟩ **b** : to make ready for eating ⟨would rather starve to death than eat food *prepared* over such fires —J.G.Frazer⟩ **c** : to put into a suitable state of mind for something ⟨*prepared* her gradually for the shocking news⟩ ⟨*prepared* the people for a long struggle⟩ **d** : to equip with necessary knowledge and skill (as for a specific profession, occupation, or test) : EDUCATE, TRAIN ⟨*prepared* himself for the legal profession —*Current Biog.*⟩ ⟨*preparing* pupils for college entrance examinations —D.E. Smith⟩ **2 a** : to get ready beforehand : procure as suitable or necessary : PROVIDE ⟨given the job of *preparing* the equipment for the trip⟩ **b** : to work out beforehand : plan the details of : get ready ⟨*prepared* his strategy for the coming campaign⟩ **3** : to become proficient in beforehand : study or work on for a particular purpose or occasion ⟨*prepared* his assignment for the next day⟩ ⟨the players *prepared* their parts —Malcolm Muggeridge⟩ **4 a** : to put together : COMPOUND ⟨*prepared* a vaccine from live virus⟩ ⟨*prepared* the doctor's prescription⟩ **b** : MAKE, PRODUCE ⟨unsuccessful in his attempts to ~ the metal by electrolysis —*Encyc. Americana*⟩ **c** : to put into written form : draw up ⟨*prepared* and issued a vigorous manifesto —*Britain Today*⟩ ⟨directed the commission to ~ proposals for the regulation, limitation, and balanced reduction of all armed forces —*Americana Annual*⟩ **5 a** : to anticipate and modify (as a dissonance or its effect) by sounding the dissonant tone in the preceding consonant musical chord **b** : to lead up to (as a tone or an ornament) by a prefatory tone ⟨a *prepared* trill⟩ **6** : to lead up to ⟨the age of peace and prosperity that *prepared* the war —F.R.Leavis⟩ ~ *vi* **1 a** : to make oneself ready : get ready ⟨he *prepared* for teaching⟩ **b** : to arrange things in readiness : make ready ⟨the nation *prepared* for war⟩ **2** *archaic* : to get ready for a journey or expedition ⟨are actually preparing for England —Robert Bage⟩
**syn** FIT, QUALIFY, CONDITION, READY: PREPARE is a rather general term indicating a process, purposive, considered, and involving various steps whereby something is made ready ⟨*prepare* a large meal⟩ ⟨*prepare* the ground for spring crops⟩ ⟨*prepare* a patient for an operation⟩ ⟨*prepare* oneself for the ministry⟩ ⟨*preparing* a speech on the subject⟩ ⟨I had intended, when the time came, to *prepare* a second edition of this book —T.S.Eliot⟩ FIT may indicate equipping and repairing; it may apply to the process of training and gradually remedying deficiencies and acquiring skills, crafts, accomplishments, attitudes for some specific activity or situation ⟨about 60 destroyers *fitted* with echo-ranging gear —J.P.Baxter b. 1893⟩ ⟨I had *fitted* myself to do everything, from sweeping out to writing the editorials and keeping the bank account —W.A.White⟩

⟨the soldier's efforts to *fit* himself into the new world made possible by his sweat and blood —Dixon Wecter⟩ ⟨parents whose duty it is to *fit* children for carrying on life —Herbert Spencer⟩ QUALIFY may imply formal fulfillment of requirements or definite experience or accomplishment demonstrating fitness ⟨a *qualified* accountant⟩ ⟨*qualified* to practice medicine⟩ ⟨combined with a subsequent three years of seminary training, it *qualifies* graduates to enter into the ministry of the church —*Amer. Guide Series: Mich.*⟩ ⟨teams winning in the *qualifying* rounds⟩ CONDITION may indicate the steady, cumulative course or process of bringing into a certain condition, often a careful procedure for achieving a certain desired condition ⟨compulsory education, the press, the cinema, and the wireless are weapons possibly even stronger than the atom bomb, and the art of using them for the *conditioning* of men's minds and characters is much enhanced by modern developments in psychology and sociology —Walter Moberly⟩ ⟨these early circumstances and experiences profoundly *conditioned* him —Carl Van Doren⟩ ⟨the religious emotion to which I had been *conditioned* in my childhood —R.M.Lovett⟩ READY may apply to quick preliminary equipping, ordering, and preparing immediately before entering into some activity or function ⟨the whole town took part in helping to *ready* the outdoor theater —Marguerite Johnson⟩ ⟨under this great silvery dome they were *readying* the 200-inch eye for its night's vigil on the universe —G.W.Gray b. 1886⟩ ⟨the expedition *readied* itself during the summer at the little Dutch town of Helvoet Sluys —Oscar Handlin⟩

— **prepare the way** : to clear the way ⟨the orator *prepared the way* for his proposal —R.M.Weaver⟩ ⟨management has to take the time and effort needed to *prepare the way* —Bruce Payne⟩

**prepared** *adj* **1** : made ready, fit, or suitable beforehand : READY, EQUIPPED **2** : subjected to a special process or treatment ⟨~ ergot⟩ — **pre·pared·ly** \-r(ə)dlē, -li\ *adv*

**prepared bid** *n* : an opening bid in contract bridge that promises ability to rebid safely if one's partner responds with a suit-bid — compare ANTICIPATION 6

**prepared chalk** *n* : native calcium carbonate ground to a fine powder and freed of most of its impurities by elutriation — called also *drop chalk*

**pre·pared·ness** \-r(ə)dnəs\ *n* -ES : the state of being prepared : READINESS; *specif* : a state of adequate preparation in case of war

**prepared opium** *n* : raw opium that has been treated to render it fit for smoking and that contains about eight percent of morphine — called also *chandu, smoking opium*

**prepared roofing** *n* : roofing consisting of asbestos felt or rag felt saturated with asphalt and assembled with asphalt cement — called also *roll roofing*

**prepared sizes** *n pl* : the four largest sorted sizes of anthracite coal ⟨broken, egg, stove, and chestnut are *prepared sizes*⟩ — compare STEAM SIZES

**pre·parental** \ˌprē+\ *adj* [*pre-* + *parental*] : preceding parenthood ⟨~ teaching of prospective mothers and fathers⟩

**pre·par·er** \prē'pa(a)rə(r), -'per-\ *n* -S : one that prepares; *esp* : a worker who performs the preliminary or initial steps of a manufacturing process

**pre·parietal** \ˌprē+\ *adj* [*pre-* + *parietal*] **1** : situated in front of parietal structures ⟨a ~ scale in front of the parietal plate in snakes⟩ **2** : of, relating to, or constituting the anterior part of the parietal convolutions of the brain

**pre·par·tum** \(')prēˌpärd·əm\ *also* **pre·par·tal** \-d·ᵊl\ *adj* [*prepartum* fr. *pre-* + *-partum* (as in *postpartum*); *prepartal* fr. *prepartum* + *-al*] : ANTEPARTUM

**pre·patellar** \ˌprē+\ *adj* [*pre-* + *patellar*] **1** : situated in front of the patella **2** : of, relating to, or constituting a synovial bursa between the patella and the skin — compare HOUSEMAID'S KNEE

**pre·patent** \(')=+\ *adj* [*pre-* + *patent*] : existing in an unobserved state : LATENT

**prepatent period** *n* : the period between infection with a parasite and the demonstration of the parasite in the body esp. as determined by the recovery of an infective form (as oocysts or eggs) from the feces

**pre·pausal** \(')prē+\ *adj* [*pre-* + *pausal*] : preceding a pause

**pre·pay** \(')prē+\ *vt* [*pre-* + *pay*] : to pay in advance ⟨~ freight charges⟩ ⟨~ the interest on the loan⟩

**pre·payment** \"+\ *n* [*pre-* + *payment*] : payment in advance

**prepay station** *n* : PREPAID STATION

**prepd** *abbr* prepared

**pre·pectus** \(')=+\ *n* [NL, fr. *pre-* + *pectus*] : the anterior marginal sclerite of the episternum of an insect; *esp* : such a sclerite of the mesepisternum of some hymenopterons

**pre·pend** \prē'pend\ *vt* -ED/-ING/-S [*pre-* + *-pend* (as in *perpend*)] : CONSIDER, PREMEDITATE ⟨make jokes with malice ~*ed* —Charles Lamb⟩

**pre·penial** \(')prē+\ *adj* [*pre-* + *penial*] : lying in front of the penis ⟨the ~ scrotum of a marsupial⟩

**pre·pense** \(')prēˌpen(t)s\ *adj* [short for obs. E *prepensed*, alter. (influenced by E *pre-*) of obs. E *purpensed*, fr. ME, past part. of *purpensen* to premeditate, fr. MF *pourpenser* to plan, resolve, fr. OF, fr. *pour* for + *penser* to think — more at PURCHASE, PENSIVE] : deliberated, contrived, or planned beforehand : AFORETHOUGHT, PRECONCEIVED, PREMEDITATED — usu. used postpositively ⟨malice ~⟩

**pre·pense·ly** *adv* : with premeditation : DELIBERATELY

**pre·perceive** \ˌprē+\ *vt* [*pre-* + *perceive*] : to have an anticipation of or be in a state of readiness for (a perception)

**pre·perception** \"+\ *n* [*pre-* + *perception*] : readiness for or anticipation of a perception — **pre·perceptive** \"+\ *adj*

**prepg** *abbr* preparing

**pre·phenic acid** \(')prē+-\ *n* [*prephenic* fr. *pre-* + *phen-* + *-ic*] : a quinonoid dicarboxylic acid $HOC_6H_5(COOH)CH_2$-COCOOH formed as an intermediate in the biosynthesis of aromatic amino acids from shikimic acid

**pre·phragma** \(')prē+\ *n* [NL, fr. *pre-* + *phragma*] : the anterior phragma of the notum of an insect

**pre·pink spray** \(')=ˌ=-\ *n* [*prepink* fr. *pre-* + *pink*] : a spray applied esp. to apple trees after the leaves and buds show but before pinkish color is apparent — compare PINK SPRAY

**pre·placement** \(')=+\ *adj* [*pre-* + *placement*] : occurring before employment or assignment to a job ⟨~ examination⟩

**pre·placental** \ˌ=+\ *adj* [*pre-* + *placental*] : existing or arising before the formation of a placenta

**pre·plan** \(')=+\ *vb* [*pre-* + *plan*] *vt* : to plan in advance ⟨the service could not have been premeditated or *preplanned*, since no imagination could have foreseen its need —T.O. Beachcroft⟩ ~ *vi* : to make plans beforehand ⟨the damage-control officer must ~ —L.J.Levert⟩

**prepn** *abbr* preparation

**pre·pol·lent** \(')prēˌpälənt\ *adj* [L *praepollent-*, *praepollens*, pres. part. of *praepollēre* to surpass in power, fr. *prae-* pre- + *pollēre* to be strong, be able — more at POLLEX] : superior in influence or power : PREDOMINANT

**pre·pollex** \(')=+\ *n* [NL, fr. *pre-* + *pollex*] : an extra digit or rudiment of a digit on the preaxial side of a thumb

**pre·pon·der** \prē'pändə(r)\ *vi* -ED/-ING/-S [L *praeponderare*] : PREPONDERATE

**pre·pon·der·ance** \-d(ə)rən(t)s\ *n* -S [fr. *preponderant*, after such pairs as E *abundant: abundance*] **1** : a superiority in weight; *specif* : the excess of weight of the part of a cannon behind the axis of the trunnions over that in front **2** : a superiority in power, influence, importance, or strength ⟨this overwhelming ~ of American power and wealth —Barbara Ward⟩ ⟨the immense ~ of good over evil —C.W.Eliot⟩ ⟨the ~ of the evidence⟩ **3 a** : a superiority or excess in number or quantity ⟨give numerical ~ in the lower house to the uplands of the state —U.B.Phillips⟩ ⟨the ~ of small farms was also advantageous to the slave —*Amer. Guide Series: Tenn.*⟩ **b** : MAJORITY ⟨the great ~ of the animals on the road are mules —Christopher Rand⟩

**pre·pon·der·an·cy** \-nsē, -si\ *n* -ES [*preponderant* + *-cy*] : the quality or state of being preponderant : superior weight, influence, importance, or power : DOMINANCE

**pre·pon·der·ant** \-nt\ *adj* [L *praeponderant-*, *praeponderans*, pres. part. of *praeponderare* to preponderate] **1** : having superior weight, force, or influence : PREDOMINANT, PREPONDERATING ⟨the ~ tone of the residential sections . . . is that of the middle-income group —*Amer. Guide Series: N.C.*⟩ **2** : having greater prevalence ⟨always ~ in numbers, and often in influence and power —H.O.Taylor⟩ **syn** see DOMINANT

**pre·pon·der·ant·ly** *adv* : in a preponderant manner or to a preponderant extent : PREDOMINANTLY

1**pre·pon·der·ate** \-əˌrāt, *usu* -ād·+V\ *vb* -ED/-ING/-S [L *praeponderatus*, past part. of *praeponderare* to exceed in weight or influence, preponderate, fr. *prae-* pre- + *ponderare* to weigh, fr. *ponder-*, *pondus* weight — more at PENDANT] *vt* **1** *archaic* : OUTWEIGH **2** *archaic* : to weigh down : INCLINE ~ *vi* **1 a** : to exceed in weight : turn the scale ⟨when surplus energy has accumulated in such bulk as to ~ over productive energy —Brooks Adams⟩ **b** : to descend or incline downward : become weighed down **2** : to exceed in influence, power, or importance : PREDOMINATE ⟨state ownership will inevitably ~ in the heavy industries —Owen & Eleanor Lattimore⟩ **3** : to exceed in numbers : form a majority ⟨it is the first glory of this volume that such poems ~ in it —*Times Lit. Supp.*⟩

2**preponderate** \-ˌrət\ *adj* [L *praeponderatus*, past part. of *praeponderare*] : PREPONDERANT — **pre·pon·der·ate·ly** *adv*

**preponderating** *adj* : PREPONDERANT ⟨governments are not in general fully conscious of the ~ importance of science —*Endeavour*⟩ **syn** see DOMINANT

**pre·pon·der·at·ing·ly** *adv* : PREPONDERANTLY

**pre·pon·der·a·tion** \prēˌpändə'rāshən\ *n* -S [LL *praeponderation-*, *praeponderatio*, fr. L *praeponderatus* (past part. of *praeponderare*) + *-ion-*, *-io* -ion] **1** : PREPONDERANCE **2** *archaic* : the addition of weight to one side of a balance

**pre·pon·der·ous** \=ˈ=d(ə)rəs\ *adj* [*pre-* + *ponderous*] : PREPONDERANT — **pre·pon·der·ous·ly** *adv*

**pre·pontine** \(')prē+\ *adj* [*pre-* + *pontine*] : in front of the pons

**pre·pose** \(')prē'pōz\ *vt* -ED/-ING/-S [F *préposer*, fr. MF *preposer* to put in front, prefer, put in charge of, modif. (influenced by *poser* to put, place) of L *praeponere* (perfect stem *praepos-*) — more at POSE] : to place before or in front of something : PREFIX; *specif* : to place (as a particle) before a grammatically connected word ⟨the articles are *preposed* in most languages —M.H.Swadesh⟩

**prep·o·si·tion** \ˌprepə'zishən\ *n* -S [ME *preposicioun*, fr. L *praeposition-*, *praepositio* (trans. of Gk *prothesis*), fr. *praepositus* (past part. of *praeponere* to put in front, put in charge of, fr. *prae-* pre- + *ponere* to put, place) + *-ion-*, *-io* -ion — more at POSITION] **1** : a linguistic form that combines with a noun, pronoun, or noun equivalent to form a phrase that typically has an adverbial, adjectival, or substantival relation to some other word (as *of* in "they are proud of him", *with* in "the man with a red face", or *outside* in "it came from outside the house") **2** [influenced in meaning by *pre-* & *position*] : the act of placing before or the state of being placed before : position before

**prep·o·si·tion·al** \ˌ==ˌzishənᵊl, -shnəl\ *adj* [ISV *preposition* + *-al*] : of, relating to, or formed with a preposition ⟨~ phrases⟩ — **prep·o·si·tion·al·ly** \-ᵊlē, -əlē, -li\ *adv*

**prepositive** *adj* [LL *praepositivus*, fr. L *praepositus* (past part. of *praeponere* to put in front + *-ivus* -ive] : put before : PREFIXED ⟨~ particles in Mongolian⟩ — **prepositively** *adv*

**pre·pos·i·tor** *or* **prae·pos·i·tor** \prē'päzəˌtȯ(ə)r\ *n* -S [ML, fr. L *praepositus* (past part. of *praeponere*) + *-or*] : the principal who appoints an institor under Roman or Scots law

**pre·pos·i·ture** *also* **prae·pos·i·ture** \-əchə(r)\ *n* -S [ME *prepositure*, fr. ML *praepositura*, fr. LL, position of authority, fr. L *praepositus* director, chief, man in charge + *-ura* -ure] : the office or dignity of a provost of a priory or collegiate church : PROVOSTRY

**pre·pos·i·tus** *also* **prae·pos·i·tus** \prē'päzəd·əs\ *n, pl* **pre·posi·ti** *also* **praeposi·ti** \-ˌtī\ [ML, abbot, prior, provost, fr. L *praepositus* director, chief, man in charge, fr. *praepositus*, past part. of *praeponere* to put in front, put in charge of — more at PREPOSITION] **1 a** : ABBOT **b** : PRIOR 1a **2** : the head of a cathedral or collegiate chapter : PROVOST

**pre·possess** \ˌprē+\ *vt* [*pre-* + *possess*] **1** *obs* : to take previous possession of **2** : to influence or affect strongly beforehand : cause to be preoccupied with an idea, belief, or attitude ⟨was ~*ed* with the notion of his own superiority⟩ **3 a** : to influence beforehand for or against someone or something : PREJUDICE ⟨in spite of that sliding eye, which often ~*ed* one to doubt . . . he did seem to be telling the truth —C.D. Lewis⟩ **b** : to induce to a favorable opinion beforehand ⟨was not ~*ed* by his appearance —Agatha Christie⟩

**prepossessing** *adj* **1** *archaic* : creating prejudice ⟨this awkward ~ visage of mine —Oliver Goldsmith⟩ **2** : tending to please or arouse confidence : creating a favorable impression : ATTRACTIVE ⟨strong and vigorous, and of ~ appearance —E.G.Nash⟩ ⟨a ~ and engaging book —John Berryman⟩ — **pre·pos·sess·ing·ly** *adv* — **pre·pos·sess·ing·ness** *n* -ES

**pre·possession** \ˌprē+\ *n* [*pre-* + *possession*] **1** *archaic* : prior occupancy or possession **2** : an attitude, belief, or impression formed beforehand : a preconceived opinion : BIAS, PREJUDICE ⟨his moral ~*s* held his sensibility in check —C.I. Glicksberg⟩ ⟨had repeatedly to amend their ~*s* and especially their assumptions about the country —Bernard De Voto⟩ **3** : a concentration on one idea or object to the exclusion of others : PREOCCUPATION ⟨an amazing ~ with financial concerns —T.A.Sherman⟩ **syn** see PREDILECTION

**pre·pos·ter·ous** \prē'päst(ə)rəs, prə̇'-\ *adj* [L *praeposterus*, lit., reversed, fr. *prae-* pre- + *posterus* next, following — more at POSTERIOR] **1 a** : contrary to nature, reason, or common sense : ABSURD, NONSENSICAL ⟨so many seemingly incredible and ~ things were true nevertheless —Ellen Glasgow⟩ **b** : ridiculous in appearance or manner : GROTESQUE ⟨false nose and ~ spectacles —Eric Keown⟩ ⟨uses its ~ Elizabethan collar as a storehouse for food —Bill Beatty⟩ **2** : having or placing something first that should be last ⟨an infuriating book . . . a ~ one in inverting with absolute conviction a comfortable and rarely questioned order of values —*Times Lit. Supp.*⟩ **syn** see FOOLISH

**pre·pos·ter·ous·ly** *adv* **1** : NONSENSICALLY, ABSURDLY ⟨a poor but almost ~ happy government clerk —*Time*⟩ **2** : in an inverted or unnatural order or position : with the hind part foremost ⟨tumbled to earth and stayed a mighty while ~ —George Chapman⟩

**pre·pos·ter·ous·ness** *n* -ES : the quality or state of being preposterous : ABSURDITY

**prepostor** *or* **prepositor** *var of* PRAEPOSTOR

**pre·po·tence** \prē'pōtᵊn(t)s\ *n* [F *prépotence*, fr. L *praepotentia*] : PREPOTENCY

**pre·po·ten·cy** \-nsē, -si\ *n* [L *praepotentia*, fr. *praepotent-*, *praepotens* + *-ia* -y] **1** : the quality or state of being prepotent : PREDOMINANCE ⟨not a policy of self-defence but of ~ and imperialism —*Times Lit. Supp.*⟩ **2** : the ability of one individual or strain to transmit its characters to offspring to a greater extent than the other parent individual or strain because of an accumulation of homozygous dominant genes

**pre·po·tent** \-tᵊnt\ *adj* [ME, fr. L *praepotent-*, *praepotens*, pres. part. of *praeposse* to be more powerful, fr. *prae-* pre- + *posse* to be able — more at POTENT] **1 a** : having exceptional power, authority, or influence : PREEMINENT ⟨had long been ~ as an influence in taste and practice —F.R.Leavis⟩ **b** : exceeding others in power : SUPERIOR ⟨the soul may be seen as ~ over mere things —Weston La Barre⟩ **2** : exhibiting genetic prepotency : DOMINANT **3** : having priority over other response tendencies esp. by virtue of maturational primacy, recentness of emission or evocation, repetition with positive reinforcement, or greater motivational charge ⟨the ~ response is that with the greatest immediately effective habit strength⟩ — **pre·po·tent·ly** *adv*

**prepped** *past of* PREP

**prepping** *pres part of* PREP

**pre·prandial** \(')prē+\ *adj* [*pre-* + *prandial*] : of, relating to, or suitable for the time immediately before dinner ⟨a ~ drink⟩

**pre·preference** \"+\ *adj* [*pre-* + *preference*] *Brit* : having priority over preference shares or bonds either as to payment of interest or dividends or as to security for repayment of principal

1**pre·print** \(')=+\ *n* [*pre-* + *print*, n.] **1** : a printing issued in advance of book or periodical publication; *esp* : a portion of a larger work (as a chapter of a book or an article in a magazine) issued before publication of the whole ⟨~*s* of a review⟩ ⟨~*s* of an advertisement⟩ — compare FASCICLE, INSTALLMENT **2** : a printing of a speech, lecture, or paper issued before its formal delivery

2**preprint** \"\ *vt* [*pre-* + *print*, v.] : to print and issue in advance of publication or delivery

**pre·professional** \ˌ=+\ *adj* [*pre-* + *professional*] : of or relating to the period preceding specific study for or practice of a profession ⟨~ education⟩ ⟨~ interests⟩

**pre·prophetic** \"+\ *adj* [*pre-* + *prophetic*] : constituting or relating to the period preceding the writings of the Hebrew prophets ⟨~ religious observances⟩

**preps** *pl of* PREP, *pres 3d sing of* PREP

**prep school** *n* [by shortening] : PREPARATORY SCHOOL

**pre·psychotic** \ˌprē+\ *adj* [*pre-* + *psychotic*] : preceding or predisposing to psychosis : possessing recognizable features prognostic of psychosis ⟨~ behavior⟩ ⟨~ personality⟩

**pre·pub** \(')prēˌpəb\ *n* -S [by shortening] : PREPUBLICATION

**pre·pubertal** \(')prē+\ *or* **pre·puberal** \"+\ *adj* [*prepubertal* fr. *pre-* + *puberty* + *-al*; *prepuberal* fr. *pre-* + *puberal*] : of or relating to prepuberty — **pre·pu·ber·tal·ly** \-əlē\ *or* **pre·pu·ber·al·ly** \-əlē\ *adv*

**pre·puberty** \(')prē+\ *n* [*pre-* + *puberty*] : the period esp. in the life of a human being immediately preceding puberty; *broadly* : the period between infancy and the beginning of puberty in man or other higher vertebrates

**pre·pubescence** \ˌ=+\ *n* [*pre-* + *pubescence*] : PREPUBERTY

**pre·pubescent** \"+\ *adj* [*pre-* + *pubescent*] : PREPUBERAL

**pre·pubic** \(')=+\ *also* **pre·pubian** \"+\ *adj* [*prepubic* fr. *pre-* + *pubic*; *prepubian* ISV *pre-* + *pub-* (fr. NL *pubis*) + *-an*] **1** : in front of the pubis **2** [*prepubis* + *-ic* or *-an*] : relating to or constituting the prepubis

**pre·pubis** \(')=+\ *n* [NL, fr. *pre-* + *pubis*] **1** : the part of the pubis of a reptile or bird that lies in front of the acetabulum, is best developed in ornithischian dinosaurs in which it is regarded as the homologue of the true pubis of other reptiles and higher groups, and in birds is derived largely from the ilium **2 a** : EPIPUBIS **b** : an epipubic bone

**pre·publication** \(ˌ)=+\ *n* [*pre-* + *publication*] : a copy of a book or other printed work issued in advance of publication

**pre·publish** \(')=+\ *vt* [*pre-* + *publish*] : to issue in advance of publication

**pre·puce** \'prēˌpyüs\ *n* -S [ME, fr. MF, fr. L *praeputium*, fr. *prae-* pre- + *-putium* (akin to Belorussian *potka* penis); prob. akin to Skt *puṣyati* he thrives, flourishes — more at FOG] : FORESKIN; *also* : a similar fold investing the clitoris

**pre–pueblo** \(')=+\ *or* **pre–puebloan** \"+\ *adj, usu cap 2d P* [*pre-* + *pueblo* or *puebloan*] : of or belonging to a prehistoric culture in southwestern U.S. and the adjacent part of Mexico immediately preceding the Pueblo — compare BASKET MAKER, HOHOKAM

**pre·pupa** \(')=+\ *n* [NL, fr. *pre-* + *pupa*] **1** : a stage in the development of many holometabolic insects immediately preceding the change to a pupa and usu. marked by cessation of feeding **2** : an insect in the prepupal stage — **pre·pupal** \"+\ *adj*

**pre·pu·tial** *also* **pre·pu·cial** \(')prēˌpyüshəl\ *adj* [*preputial* fr. L *praeputium* + E *-al*; *prepucial* alter. (influenced by *prepuce*) of *preputial*] : of, relating to, or constituting a prepuce

**pre·pu·ti·um** \prē'pyüsh(ē)əm\ *n, pl* **prepu·tia** \-)ə\ [L *praeputium*] : PREPUCE

**pre·pyloric** \ˌprē+\ *adj* [*pre-* + *pyloric*] : situated in front of the pylorus

1**pre–raphaelite** \(')prē+\ *n, usu cap P&R* [*pre-* + *Raphael* †1520 Ital. painter + E *-ite*] **1 a** : a member of a brotherhood of artists formed in England in 1848 and dedicated to restoring in painting and propagating in criticism the artistic principles and practices (as fidelity to nature, sincerity, and delicacy of finish) regarded as characteristic of Italian art before Raphael **b** : an artist or writer influenced by the ideas or work of members of the Pre-Raphaelite brotherhood **2** : a modern artist dedicated to restoring early Renaissance ideals or methods **3** : an Italian painter active before the time of Raphael's fame and influence; *esp* : one active in the earlier part of the 14th century

2**pre–raphaelite** \"\ *adj, usu cap P&R* : of or relating to Pre-Raphaelitism or Pre-Raphaelites

**pre–raphaelitism** *also* **pre–raphaelism** \"+\ *n, usu cap P&R* [*pre-raphaelitism* fr. 1*pre-raphaelite* + *-ism*; *pre-raphaelism* fr. *pre-* + *Raphael* + E *-ism*] : the principles, practice, or style of Pre-Raphaelites

**pre·rational** \(')prē+\ *adj* [*pre-* + *rational*] : preceding the development of intelligence ⟨~ instincts⟩

**pre·record** \ˌprē+\ *vt* [*pre-* + *record*] : PRESCORE

**prerecorded tape** *n* [*prerecorded* fr. past part. of *prerecord*] : magnetic tape on which sound has been recorded before the tape is offered for sale

**pre·reduction** \ˌprē+\ *n* [*pre-* + *reduction*] : reduction of chromosomes in the first meiotic division

**pre·release** \"+\ *n* [*pre-* + *release*] : a release in advance of the usual or expected time: as **a** : a showing of a movie before the date set for its release **b** : an opening to the exhaust in a steam engine before the end of a stroke in order to minimize back pressure

**prerequire** \"+\ *vt* [*pre-* + *require*] *archaic* : to require beforehand

1**pre·requisite** \(')prē+\ *n* [*pre-* + *requisite*, n.] **1** : something that is required beforehand : something that is necessary to an end or to the carrying out of a function ⟨payment of the tax as a ~ for voting —*Amer. Guide Series: Ark.*⟩ ⟨the days before there were anesthetics, when speed was one of the ~*s* of a surgeon —O.S.J.Gogarty⟩ **2 a** : an educational requirement that a student must satisfy before he is permitted to do advanced work ⟨a bachelor's degree is a ~ for graduate work⟩ **b** : a course that a student must complete as a sensible or arbitrary requirement for another course ⟨freshman composition is a ~ for advanced composition⟩

2**prerequisite** \"\ *adj* [*pre-* + *requisite*, adj.] : required beforehand : necessary as a preliminary condition

**pre·resolve** \ˌprē+\ *vi* [*pre-* + *resolve*] *archaic* : to make up one's mind beforehand

**pre·revolutionary** \(ˌ)prē+\ *adj* [*pre-* + *revolutionary*] : of or belonging to a time before a revolution; *specif* : of or belonging to the time before the American Revolution

**pre·ripen** \(')prē+\ *vt* [*pre-* + *ripen*] : to ripen (fruit) artificially in order to facilitate its safe shipment

**pre·rog·a·ti·val** \prēˌrägəˌtīvəl\ *adj* : of or relating to a prerogative

1**pre·rog·a·tive** \prē'rägəd·iv, prə̇-, -ətiv, *by* r-*dissimilation* ÷pə'-\ *n* -S [ME, fr. MF & L; MF *prerogative*, fr. L *praerogativa* preference, privilege, Roman century chosen by lot to be the first to vote in the comitia, fr. fem. of *praerogativus* that votes first, that is first asked to express an opinion, fr. *praerogatus* (past part. of *praerogare* to ask before another, fr. *prae-* pre- + *rogare* to ask) + *-ivus* -ive — more at RIGHT] **1 a** (1) : a right attached to an office or rank to exercise a special privilege or function; *specif* : an official and hereditary right (as of a royal sovereign) that may be asserted without question and for which there is in theory no responsibility or accountability as to the fact and manner of its exercise though in practice it is usu. limited by the power of public opinion or by statute and is generally (as in England) exercised on the advice of ministers who are responsible to a legislative body (2) : a sovereign right inhering in a state or in the head of a state ⟨the ~ of the president to commute punishments and grant reprieves or pardons⟩ **b** : a special right or privilege belonging to a person, group, or class of individuals ⟨cruelty remains the special ~ of men —Christine Weston⟩ ⟨in his youth, to sit thus was the ~ of the gentry —Oscar Handlin⟩ **c** : a privilege, advantage, or precedence attaching to one who holds an office **2 a** : a special quality that gives superiority : a distinctive excellence ⟨the lively nature and gay wit which were the family ~ —*Modern Philology*⟩ **b** *obs* : PRECEDENCE, PREEMINENCE ⟨give me leave to have ~ —Shak.⟩ **3** : a right of voting first **syn** see RIGHT

2**prerogative** \"\ *adj* [ME (Sc), fr. ML *praerogativus*, fr. L, that votes first] **1** : of, relating to, or deriving from a prerogative : existing or exercised by special right or privilege : PRIVILEGED ⟨~ power⟩ ⟨~ right⟩ **2** : privileged to vote first ⟨~ century of Roman citizens⟩ **3** : of or relating to a prerogative court ⟨~ records⟩ ⟨~ procedure⟩

**prerogative court** *n* **1** : an ecclesiastical court formerly exercising probate jurisdiction with respect to wills and estates of decedents **2** : a court formerly appointed by the royal governor of an American colony **3** : ORPHANS' COURT

**pre·rog·a·tived** \-vd\ adj : endowed with a prerogative : PRIVILEGED ⟨tis the plague of great ones; ~ are they less than the base —Shak.⟩

**prerogative instance** n : a crucial instance in induction : an instance of first importance

**prerogative writ** n : any of various writs of procedendo, certiorari, mandamus, prohibition, quo warranto, and habeas corpus issued orig. in England by the exercise of the royal prerogative and now in the discretion of the courts and directed usu. to the parties whose action is to be controlled and not to the sheriff — called also extraordinary writ

**pre·rolandic** \¦prē+\ adj [pre- + rolandic] : PRECENTRAL 1

**prerotation device** \"+-\ n [prerotation fr. pre- + rotation] : a device for setting the landing wheels of an airplane in rotation prior to the initial contact with the ground in landing in order to reduce landing shock and damage to tires

**pre·rupt** \prē'rəpt\ adj [L praeruptus, past part. of praerumpere to break off in front, fr. prae- pre- + rumpere to break — more at REAVE] **1** : broken off abruptly : PRECIPITOUS, STEEP **2** : lacking an introduction : ABRUPT

**pres** abbr **1** present **2** presentation **3** presidency; president; presidential **4** pressure **5** presumptive

**pre·sa** \'prāsə\ n, pl **pre·se** \-sā\ [It, lit., action of taking, seizure, fr. fem. of preso (past part. of prendere to take, seize), fr. L prehensus, past part. of prehendere to take, grasp, seize — more at PREHENSILE] : a mark or cue (as :S: or ※) indicating the point of entry of the successive voice parts of a canon

**pre·sacral** \(')prē+\ adj [pre- + sacral] : effected by way of the anterior aspect of the sacrum ⟨~ nerve block⟩

**[1]pres·age** \'presij, -sēj\ n -s [ME, fr. L praesagium, fr. praesagire to have a presentiment of, fr. prae- pre- + sagire to perceive keenly — more at SEEK] **1** : something that foreshadows or portends a future event : a warning or indication of something about to happen : OMEN, PROGNOSTIC ⟨the coming of the swallow is a true ~ of the spring —John Worlidge⟩ ⟨sees a lunar rainbow . . . as a ~ of good fortune —Van Wyck Brooks⟩ **2** : an intuition or feeling of what is going to happen in the future : FOREBODING, PRESENTIMENT ⟨feel in his nerves the ~ of a storm —Charlton Ogburn⟩ ⟨artists whom the ~ of an early death stimulates —Roger Fry⟩ **3** archaic : an utterance foretelling something future : PREDICTION, PROGNOSTICATION ⟨expected as ill a ~ . . . from those fortune tellers —Edward Hyde⟩ **4** : foreknowledge of the future : PRESCIENCE ⟨if there be aught of ~ in the mind —John Milton⟩ **5** : AUGURY 3 ⟨hand . . . raised in ~ of volunteered information —New Yorker⟩ ⟨a firm steel bridge as ~ of what is ahead —William Sansom⟩ ⟨birds of evil ~ —Edmund Burke⟩

**[2]pres·age** \", prē'sāj, prə̇'-\ vb -ED/-ING/-S [MF presager, fr. presage omen, fr. L praesagium] vt **1 a** : to give an omen or warning of : signify beforehand by supernatural means : FORESHADOW, PORTEND ⟨evil luck was presaged . . . by a dog crossing the hunter's path —Amer. Guide Series: Ind.⟩ ⟨sensation of creeping uneasiness which presaged some kind of trouble —Marcia Davenport⟩ ⟨fiery meteors may ~ death and destruction —Christopher Marlowe⟩ **b** : to point to or indicate in advance : give prior indication of by natural means : provide a symptom of : PREINDICATE ⟨dropsy . . . almost invariably ~s cardiac failure —F.A.Faught⟩ ⟨Democratic gains aren't significant enough to ~ drastic legislative changes —Wall Street Jour.⟩ **2** : to indicate or calculate in advance : FORECAST, FORETELL, PREDICT ⟨lands he could measure, terms and tides ~ —Oliver Goldsmith⟩ **3** : to have a presentiment or prevision of : feel beforehand : FOREBODE 2 ⟨from the preliminaries . . . he was only able to ~ danger and disaster —A.W. Tourgee⟩ ~ vi **1** obs : to have a presentiment or foreknowledge **2** : to make or utter a prediction ⟨prophecy would fain ~ auspiciously —J.B.Mozley⟩ — sometimes used with of ⟨by certain signs we may ~ of heats and rains —John Dryden⟩ **syn** see FORETELL

**pres·age·ful** \'presijfəl\ adj : full of presage or presages : FOREBODING, FOREKNOWING, OMINOUS, PROPHETIC ⟨a ~ mood⟩ ⟨~ victory⟩ ⟨that . . . ~ gloom of yours —Alfred Tennyson⟩

**presagement** n -s obs : the action of one that presages : a result of presaging : FOREBODING, OMEN, PRESENTIMENT, PORTENT ⟨whether he had any ominous ~ before his end —Henry Wotton⟩

**presager** n -s obs : one that presages ⟨unusual signs, ~s of strange terrors to the world —Shak.⟩

**presaging** adj : characterized by presage ⟨~ tokens of success —Daniel Defoe⟩ ⟨a ~ intelligence⟩

**pres·ag·ing·ly** adv : in a manner full of presages or characterized by presage

**presagious** adj [MF presagieux, fr. presage omen + -ieux -ious] obs : of the nature of a presage : full of presages ⟨~ dreams —James Heath⟩

**pre·sanctified** \(')prē+\ adj [pre- + sanctified; trans. of ML praesanctificatus, trans. of MGk proēgiasmenos] : consecrated at a previous service — used of Eucharistic elements ⟨a ~ Host⟩ ⟨liturgy of the ~⟩

**presby-** or **presbyo-** comb form [NL, fr. Gk presby- older, fr. presbys old man — more at PRIEST] : old age ⟨presbyopia⟩ ⟨presbyophrenia⟩

**pres·by·cu·sis** \,prezbə'kyüsə̇s, -esb-\ or **pres·by·a·cu·sia** \-bēə'kyüzh(ē)ə\ also **pres·by·a·cou·sia** \-küzh-\ n, pl **presbycu·ses** \-ü,sēz\ or **presbyacusias** also **presbyacousias** [presbycusis fr. presby- + -cusis (fr. Gk akousis hearing); presbyacusia, presbyacousia fr. NL, fr. presby- + -acousia — more at -ACOUSIA] : a condition of hearing less acutely that occurs in old age

**pres·by·ope** \'prezbē,ōp, -esb-\ n -s [prob. fr. F, fr. presby- + -ope] : one that has presbyopia : a farsighted person

**pres·by·o·phre·nia** \,prezbēə'frēnēə, -esb-\ n -s [NL, fr. presby- + -phrenia] : a form of senile dementia occurring chiefly in women and characterized by loss of memory often to the point of disorientation with preservation of mobility, loquacity, good spirits, and considerable mental alertness — **pres·by·o·phren·ic** \¦==¦frenik\ adj

**pres·by·o·pia** \,prezbē'ōpēə, -esb-\ n -s [NL, fr. presby- + -opia] : a condition of defective elasticity of the crystalline lens of the eye usu. in old age resulting in difficulty of accommodation and inability to attain a sharp focus for near vision — compare HYPEROPIA

**[1]pres·by·op·ic** \¦==¦äpik\ adj [presbyopia + -ic] : affected by presbyopia : FARSIGHTED

**[2]presbyopic** \"\ n -s : a presbyopic person

**pres·by·ter** \'prezbəd·ə(r), -esb-, -ətə-\ n -s [LL, presbyter, elder, fr. Gk presbyteros — more at PRIEST] **1** : an official in the early Christian church vested with the task of providing leadership as an overseer usu. over a local congregation **2** : a clergyman ranking immediately below a bishop in the more liturgical churches that have episcopal polities (as the Eastern Orthodox Church and the Anglican Church) : PRIEST 1a(1) ⟨bishops, ~s and deacons consecrated or ordained in the Church of South India —Brit. Book News⟩ **3** : an elder in a Presbyterian church **4** usu cap, archaic : PRESBYTERIAN

**pres·byt·er·al** \(')prez¦bid·ərəl, -es¦-\ adj [ML presbyteralis of a priest, fr. LL, of a presbyter, fr. presbyter + L -alis -al] : PRESBYTERIAL

**pres·byt·er·ate** \='==rə̇t, -,rāt\ n -s [LL presbyteratus office of a presbyter, fr. presbyter + L -atus -ate] **1** : a body of presbyters or elders : PRESBYTERY 2 **2** : the office or position of a presbyter or elder

**pres·by·tère** \,prezbə'te(ə)r\ n -s [F, fr. MF presbitaire presbytère, group of priests serving a particular church, fr. ML presbyterium group of priests, priesthood, fr. LL, group of presbyters, office of a presbyter, presbytery (part of a church where the clergy sit) — more at PRESBYTERY] : the residence of a Roman Catholic parish priest

**pres·by·ter·ess** \'prezbəd·ərə̇s\ n -ES [part trans. of ML presbyterissa, fr. presbyter priest (fr. LL, presbyter, elder) + LL -issa -ess] **1 a** : the wife of a presbyter or priest in one of the early medieval churches; esp : one coming under the operation of the rule requiring the continence of clergymen **b** : a priest's concubine **2** : a woman serving as a presbyter or elder in one of the early medieval churches : one of a body of aged widows dedicated to the service of the church and constituting an ecclesiastical order **3** : the wife of a priest of the Eastern Orthodox Church

**[1]pres·by·te·ri·al** \¦prezbə¦tirēəl, -esb-, -tēr-\ adj [presbytery + -al] **1** usu cap, archaic : PRESBYTERIAN 2 **2** : of or relating to a presbyter or a body of presbyters ⟨a ~ title⟩ **3** : of, relating to, or based upon a local presbytery ⟨substitute a ~ . . . polity for episcopacy —W.E.Garrison⟩ **4** usu cap [[2]presbyterial] : of or relating to a Presbyterial ⟨Presbyterial officers⟩ ⟨Presbyterial meeting⟩

**[2]presbyterial** \"\ n -s usu cap : an organization of Presbyterian women associated with a presbytery — compare SYNODICAL

**pres·by·te·ri·al·ly** \-rēəlē, -li\ adv : by a presbytery : in a presbyterial manner

**[1]pres·by·te·ri·an** \-rēən\ adj [presbytery + -an] **1** often cap : having or characterized by a graded system of representative ecclesiastical bodies (as presbyteries, sessions, and a general assembly) exercising legislative and judicial powers ⟨in local affairs the churches are ~ in government —F.S.Mead⟩ — compare CONGREGATIONAL 2, EPISCOPAL 2a **2** usu cap **a** : of, relating to, or constituting a Protestant Christian church that is presbyterian in government and traditionally Calvinistic in doctrine ⟨a Presbyterian minister⟩ ⟨the Presbyterian Church of Canada⟩ — compare REFORMED **b** : characterizing or held to characterize a member of such a church ⟨a Presbyterian conscience⟩ ⟨a thorough-going Presbyterian distaste for bishops —E.R.R.Green⟩

**[2]presbyterian** \"\ n -s usu cap : a member of a Presbyterian church : a supporter of Presbyterianism

**pres·by·te·ri·an·ism** \,=='tirēə,nizəm, -tēr-\ n -s **1** usu cap **a** : the presbyterian form of church government ⟨~ declared to be the only lawful government —A.C.McGiffert⟩ **b** : belief in or adherence to such church government **2** cap : the faith and polity of the Presbyterian Church; esp : the principles of Presbyterians including the right of all members of the church to share in its government exercised through elders chosen or approved by them, the recognition of only one order in the Christian ministry with all members equal and exercising all ministerial functions, and the unity of the whole church expressed in a graded system of church courts composed of ministers and elders **3** usu cap : the whole body of Presbyterian churches

**pres·by·te·ri·an·ize** \-,nīz\ vt -ED/-ING/-S often cap : to make presbyterian ⟨resolved to Presbyterianize the university —G.C.Brodrick⟩

**pres·by·te·ri·an·ly** adv, usu cap : in a Presbyterian manner or direction ⟨a Presbyterianly inclined church⟩

**pres·by·ter·ism** \'prezbəd·ə,rizəm\ n -s usu cap [presbyter + -ism] archaic : PRESBYTERIANISM

**pres·by·ter·i·um** \,prezbə'tirēəm\ n -s [LL] **1** : PRESBYTERY 1 **2** : PRESBYTERY 6

**pres·by·ter·ship** \'prezbəd·ə(r),ship\ n [presbyter + -ship] : PRESBYTERATE 2

**pres·by·tery** \'prezbə,terē, -resb-, -ri\ n -ES [ME presbytory, fr. LL presbyterium group of presbyters, office of a presbyter, presbytery (part of a church where the clergy sit), fr. Gk presbyterion group of presbyters, office of a presbyter, fr. presbyteros presbyter, elder — more at PRIEST] **1 a** : the division in an ancient church lying east of the sanctuary and containing the seats of the bishop and clergy **b** : the part of a church (as the choir or sanctuary or both) reserved for the officiating clergy **2** : a ruling body in Presbyterian churches consisting of all the ministers of and one or more representative elders from each of the congregations within a specific district, having legislative and judicial powers, and ranking in authority above the session but below the synod — compare CLASSIS, COLLOQUY 2, CONSISTORY 2 d **3** : the district within which the congregations under the authority of a presbytery are situated : the jurisdiction of a presbytery **4** : the Presbyterian polity — compare EPISCOPACY 1, INDEPENDENCY **5** obs : PRESBYTERATE 2 **6** : a body of presbyters in an early Christian church **7** : the house of a presbyter; specif : PRESBYTÈRE

**pres·byt·ic** \(')prez¦bid·ik\ adj [ISV presbyt- (fr. NL presbytia presbyopia, fr. Gk presbytēs old man + NL -ia) + -ic] : FARSIGHTED ⟨~ eyes⟩

**pres·by·tis** \prez'bīd·ə̇s\ n, cap [NL, fr. Gk, old woman, fem. of presbytēs old man, fr. presbys old man — more at PRIEST] : a genus of old-world monkeys consisting of the langurs

**pre·scap·u·la** \prē'skapyələ\ n [NL, fr. pre- + L scapula] : the supraspinous part of the scapula

**pre·scapular** \(')prē+\ adj [pre- + scapular] **1** : situated anterior to the scapula **2** [prescapula + -ar] : of, relating to, or being the prescapula

**[1]pre·school** \(')prē+\ adj [pre- + school, n.] : of, relating to, or constituting the period in a child's life from infancy to the age of five or six ordinarily preceding attendance at elementary school but often occupied by attendance at nursery school or kindergarten

**[2]preschool** \'prē+,-\ n : NURSERY SCHOOL, KINDERGARTEN

**pre·school·er** \'prē,skülə(r)\ n -s [preschool + -er] : a child who is not old enough to attend elementary school : a pupil in a kindergarten or nursery school : KINDERGARTNER 1

**pre·science** \'prē|sh(ē)ən(t)s, 'pre|, |s(ē)-\ n -s [ME, fr. LL praescientia, fr. L praescient-, praesciens + -ia -y] **1** : foreknowledge of events: **a** : omniscience with regard to the future usu. held to be a divine attribute ⟨belief in the absolute ~ . . . of God —Frank Thilly⟩ ⟨God's certain ~ of the volitions of moral agents —Jonathan Edwards⟩ **b** : the human faculty or quality of being able to anticipate the occurrence or nature of future events : FORESIGHT ⟨the acute phatic ~ of a mother when her child is concerned —Weston La Barre⟩ ⟨country people seem to have a greater ~ of snow —Adrian Bell⟩ ⟨foresaw the great dangers . . . with far more ~ than most well-informed people —Sir Winston Churchill⟩ **2** : an instance of foreknowledge or foresight ⟨~s like these do come to us sometimes —Kenneth Roberts⟩

**pre·scient** \-nt\ adj [L praescient-, praesciens, pres. part. of praescire to know beforehand, fr. prae- pre- + scire to know — more at SCIENCE] : having or marked by prescience : having foreknowledge : characterized by foresight ⟨~ of what he was later to fulfill —H.O.Taylor⟩ ⟨some extraordinarily ~ memoranda on the probable course of postwar relationships —R.H.Rovere⟩

**pre·scientific** \(¦)prē+\ adj [pre- + scientific] **1** : preceding the development or the acquisition of scientific knowledge ⟨terms familiar to the ~ era —J.C.Swaim⟩ ⟨a ~ stage of cultural development⟩ **2** : of, belonging to, or having the characteristics of a period before the rise of modern science or a state prior to the application of scientific method ⟨~ man assumed the prevalence of a divine law —James Ward⟩ ⟨a primitive ~ view⟩ ⟨the thesis . . . that native culture is ~ —David Bidney⟩

**pre·scient·ly** adv : with prescience or foresight ⟨more ~ than those in organization they grasped the antithesis —W.H. Whyte⟩

**pre·scind** \prē'sind\ vb -ED/-ING/-S [L praescindere to cut off in front, fr. prae- pre- + scindere to cut, split — more at SHED] vt **1** archaic : to cut short, off, or away : SEVER ⟨the brevity of his reign ~ed many . . . hopes of his good government —Richard Brathwaite⟩ **2** : to abstract by an act of attention : detach for purposes of thought : separate in consideration — used with from ⟨its momentousness . . . ~ed their minds from the goat —Malcolm Lowry⟩ ⟨I cannot ~ . . . the existence of a sensible thing from being perceived —George Berkeley⟩ ~ vi : to abstract or detach oneself — used with from ⟨we have ~ed from all these concrete characteristics —Peter Dunne⟩ ⟨if we ~ entirely from any audience consideration —Quarterly Jour. of Speech⟩ **syn** see DETACH

**prescious** adj [L praescius, fr. praescire to know beforehand + -ius -ious] obs : PRESCIENT

**pre·score** \(')prē+\ vt [pre- + score] : to record (as dialogue, music, or sound effects) in advance for use when the corresponding scenes are photographed in making movies

**pres·cott scale** \'preskət-\ n, usu cap P [prob. fr. the name Prescott] : a scale (Matsucoccus vexillorum) that attacks pines in the western U.S.

**pre·scribe** \prē'skrīb, prə̇'-\ vb -ED/-ING/-S [ME prescriben to hold or possess by right of prescription, fr. ML prescribere to claim by right of prescription, fr. L praescribere to write at the beginning, order, direct, prescribe, fr. prae- pre- + scribere to write; in several senses directly fr. L praescribere — more at SCRIBE] vi **1** : to claim a title to something by right of prescription : assert a prescriptive right or claim **2** : to lay down a rule : give directions : DICTATE, DIRECT **3 a** : to write or give medical prescriptions ⟨~ for a patient⟩ **b** : to give advice in the manner of a doctor giving a medical prescription **4** : to become by prescription invalid or unenforceable ⟨various rights ~ in twenty years⟩ ~ vt **1 a** : to lay down authoritatively as a guide, direction, or rule of action : impose as a peremptory order : DICTATE, DIRECT, ORDAIN ⟨the code of behavior which the culture ~s for child training —Franz Alexander⟩ ⟨legislatures may ~ qualifications . . . for admission to the bar —H.S.Drinker⟩ ⟨rigid convention ~s that such meetings open with prayer —D.L. Cohn⟩ **b** : to specify with authority ⟨the fixed routine of prescribed duties —Oscar Wilde⟩ ⟨purchased by the department at prescribed prices —Farmer's Weekly (So. Africa)⟩ **c** : to require (as a person) to follow a direction or rule of action ⟨prescribed to take the following oath —C.W.Ferguson⟩ **2** obs : to describe in advance : foretell or make a prophecy of in writing **3** : to direct, designate, or order the use of as a remedy ⟨the doctor prescribed quinine⟩ ⟨we ~ a certain amount of art for ourselves as a kind of corrective —Louis Kronenberger⟩ **4** : to keep within limits or bounds : CONFINE, RESTRAIN ⟨prescribed to one poor solitary place — Michael Drayton⟩

**syn** ASSIGN, DEFINE: PRESCRIBE indicates authoritative dictating or commanding, with explicit clear direction ⟨a doctor prescribing medicine for a patient⟩ ⟨payment of the tax as a prerequisite for voting was prescribed by a constitutional amendment —Amer. Guide Series: Ark.⟩ ⟨the power to prescribe rules of conduct was delegated to the President —C.J.Friedrich⟩ ASSIGN may imply arbitrary or chance allotment, designation, or determination for the sake of some such end as harmonious operation, smooth routine, or proper or practical functioning or procedure ⟨assign an officer to a military unit⟩ ⟨assigned to the night shift⟩ ⟨the clause, assigning original jurisdiction to the supreme court —John Marshall⟩ DEFINE may indicate an exact delineation or demarcation to prevent confusion or conflict ⟨defining the jurisdiction of various courts⟩ ⟨defined still more clearly the extent to which the nations of this continent are willing to combine their military power to defend any American republic from an aggressor —S.G.Inman⟩ ⟨obscure symbolisms which define the relation of various age groups to each other —Edward Sapir⟩ **syn** see in addition DICTATE

**pre·scrib·er** \-bə(r)\ n -s : one that prescribes ⟨the ~ should specify the drug strength of a potent agent —W.H.Blome & C.H.Stocking⟩

**[1]pre·script** \'prē,skript, ='=\ adj [ME prescripte, fr. L praescriptus, past part. of praescribere to prescribe] : prescribed as a rule : ordained or appointed by authority ⟨a ~ form of words —Jeremy Taylor⟩

**[2]prescript** \'=,=\ n -s [L praescriptum, fr. neut. of praescriptus, past part. of praescribere] **1** : something prescribed as a rule : COMMAND, DIRECTION, INSTRUCTION, LAW, ORDINANCE, PRECEPT, REGULATION ⟨the constitution of the church . . . set down by divine ~ —John Milton⟩ ⟨according to the ~s of existing law —J.W.Burgess⟩ **2** archaic : a medical prescription ⟨your ~ is compounded of . . . delicate simples —Samuel Harsnett⟩

**pre·scrip·ti·ble** \prē'skriptəbəl\ adj [MF prescriptible, fr. ML prescriptibilis, fr. prescriptus (past part. of prescribere to claim by right of prescription) + L -ibilis -able] : depending on or derived from prescription : proper to be prescribed : subject to prescription

**pre·scrip·tion** \prē'skripshən, prə̇'-\ n -s often attrib [ME prescripcion, fr. MF prescription, fr. LL praescription-, praescriptio prescription (sense 2a), fr. L, prefatory writing, order, rule, fr. praescriptus (past part. of praescribere to write at the beginning, order, direct, prescribe) + -ion-, -io -ion; in several senses directly fr. L praescription-, praescriptio] **1 a** (1) : the establishment of a claim of title to something under common law orig. by virtue of immemorial use and enjoyment or usu. in modern times by use and enjoyment for a period fixed by statute (as 20 years) ⟨a municipal corporation can be brought into existence by ~ —J.E.Pate⟩ ⟨gaining a right by ~ —O.W.Holmes †1935⟩ (2) : the acquisition under common law of incorporeal interests in land (as easements) by such a process as distinguished from acquisition of title by adverse possession ⟨~ is based upon the legal fiction that possession was originally acquired under a grant⟩ **b** : the right or title acquired under common law by possession had during the time and in the manner fixed by law **2 a** : the operation of the Roman law whereby rights might be acquired or extinguished by limitation of the time within which the owner might have his remedy under the praetorian law — distinguished from usucapion **b** : the operation of the civil law whereby rights might be established by long exercise of their corresponding powers or extinguished by prolonged failure to exercise such powers : a civil law process in which the usucapion and prescription of Roman law are merged **3** : the action of prescribing : the process of making claim to something (as a title) by long use and enjoyment **4** : the action of prescribing : the process of laying down authoritative rules or directions ⟨~ of the duty of an individual towards others —R.M.MacIver⟩ ⟨the issue of . . . ~ or free choice in education —Sidney Hook⟩ **5 a** (1) : a written direction for the preparation, compounding, and administration of a medicine (2) : a prescribed remedy **b** : a written formula for the grinding of corrective lenses for eyeglasses **c** : a written direction for the application of physical therapy measures (as directed exercise or electrotherapy) in cases of injury or disability **d** : something resembling or held to resemble such a medical direction ⟨step-by-step ~s for improving executive performance —Dun's Rev.⟩ ⟨a useful ~ for depression unemployment —L.G.Reynolds⟩ ⟨a ~ of spiritual aspirin doled out to a nervous reader —Ben Bradford⟩ **6 a** : custom of ancient or long continued character usu. having an authoritative status ⟨morals . . . were by ~ singularly unconstrained —E.J.Simmons⟩ ⟨they had no religious reverence for ~ —T.B.Macaulay⟩ **b** : claim founded upon ancient custom or long continued use **7** obs : the action of laying down boundaries, limits, or restrictions : CIRCUMSCRIPTION, LIMITATION **8** : something prescribed; specif : PRESCRIPT 1 ⟨peremptory ~s as to the only correct use of language —E.W.Hall⟩ ⟨one year of English is a practically universal ~ —H.N.Fairchild⟩ **9** : a plea or clause placed at the beginning of the formula in an action under Roman law and limiting the scope of the claim or the remedy (as to a certain time)

**prescription drug** n : a drug that can be bought only as prescribed by a physician — compare OVER-THE-COUNTER 2

**pre·scrip·tion·ist** \-shənə̇st\ n -s : a writer or compounder of prescriptions

**pre·scrip·tive** \prē'skriptiv, prə̇'-, -tēv also -təv\ adj [in sense 1, prob. fr. [2]prescript + -ive; in other senses, fr. prescription, after such pairs as E description: descriptive] **1** : serving to prescribe : laying down rules or directions : giving precise instructions ⟨direct primary legislation is largely permissive rather than ~ —V.O.Key⟩ ⟨traditional grammarians gave ~ rules of usage —A.S.Hornby⟩ **2** : acquired by, founded upon, or determined by prescription : established in or as if in law by immemorial use and enjoyment ⟨the ~ rights and privileges of the nobles —Indian White Paper⟩ ⟨our constitution is a ~ constitution —Edmund Burke⟩ ⟨members of the upper chamber by ~ right⟩ **3** : arising from or recognized by long-standing custom : established by tradition or usage : CUSTOMARY ⟨his ~ corner at the winter's fireside —Nathaniel Hawthorne⟩ ⟨compliments to which there is no stated and ~ answer —Samuel Johnson⟩ — **pre·scrip·tive·ly** \-tə̇vlē\ adv

**pre·scrip·tiv·ist** \-tə̇və̇st\ n -s [prescriptive + -ist] : one who advocates prescriptive principles esp. in grammar ⟨learned to distrust . . . ~s —E.P.Hamp⟩

**prescrive** vb -ED/-ING/-S [ME (Sc) prescriven to become by prescription invalid or unenforceable, fr. MF prescrire to direct, prescribe, invalidate, annul (3d pers. pl. pres. indic. prescrivent), fr. ML prescribere to claim by right of prescription & L praescribere to write at the beginning, order, direct, prescribe — more at PRESCRIBE] obs Scot : PRESCRIBE

**pre·scu·tal** \(ˈ)prē¦skyüd·ᵊl\ *adj* [*prescutum* + *-al*] **:** of or relating to the prescutum

**prescutal ridge** *n* **:** an inner ridge corresponding to the outer prescutal suture on the thorax of an insect

**prescutal suture** *n* **:** a transverse groove on the mesonotum and metanotum of most insects separating the prescutum and scutum and forming the prescutal ridge on the inner surface

**pre·scutellar** \¦prē+\ *adj* [*pre-* + *scutellar*] **:** of, relating to, or situated on the area in front of the scutellum of insects

**pre·scutum** \(ˈ)prē+\ *n, pl* **prescuta** [NL, fr. *pre-* + *scutum*] **:** the anterior piece of the dorsal part or tergum of a thoracic segment of an insect

**presdl** *abbr* presidential

**prese** *pl of* PRESA

**¹pre·season** *or* **pre·seasonal** \(ˈ)prē+\ *adj* [*preseason* fr. *pre-* + *season*, n.; *preseasonal* fr. *pre-* + *seasonal*] **:** of, relating to, or during the time preceding a season ⟨~ football practice⟩ ⟨*preseasonal* treatment of hayfever⟩

**²pre·season** \ˈprē+,-\ *n* [*pre-* + *season*, n.] **:** a period of time immediately preceding a season ⟨the quietness of a summer resort during the ~⟩

**pre·select** \¦prē+\ *vt* [*pre-* + *select*] **:** to select beforehand ⟨a ~*ed* slate of candidates⟩ ⟨sets off . . . a flashing light when a ~*ed* speed is exceeded —*Motor Life*⟩

**pre·selection** \"+\ *n* [*preselect* + *-ion*] **:** selection in advance ⟨~ of the variables to be correlated —R.B.Cattell⟩

**pre·se·lec·tor** \,prēsəˈlektə(r)\ *n* [*preselect* + *-or*] **:** the part of a radio receiver and esp. a superheterodyne receiver in which the incoming signal receives its first filtering

**pre·sell** \(ˈ)prē+\ *vt* [*pre-* + *sell*] **:** to precondition (as merchandise or customers) by advertising and devices of salesmanship for a subsequent purchase

**pres·ence** \ˈprezᵊn(t)s\ *n* -s [ME, fr. MF, fr. L *praesentia*, fr. *praesent-, praesens* present + *-ia* -y — more at PRESENT] **1 a :** the fact or condition of being present **:** the state of being in one place and not elsewhere **:** the condition of being within sight or call, at hand, or in a place being thought of **:** the fact of being in company, attendance, or association **:** the state of being in front of or in the same place as someone or something ⟨the ~ of free nitrogen bubbles in the body tissues —H.G.Armstrong⟩ ⟨hidden in the jungle, their ~ undiscovered —Joseph Millard⟩ ⟨the indwelling ~ of the Divine Spirit in the human soul —W.R.Inge⟩ ⟨the effective ~ of Britain on the European political scene —Percy Winner⟩ **b :** the manner in which Christ is held in some branches of the Christian church to be present in the Eucharist — compare REAL PRESENCE **2 a :** the part of space within one's ken, call, or influence **:** the vicinity of or the area immediately near one **:** the place in front of or around a person ⟨he came into the ~ of the king⟩ ⟨in her ~ he could scarcely speak⟩ ⟨removed his hat in the ~ of ladies⟩ **b :** the vicinity of one of superior or exalted rank ⟨survey the secretary's humor before entering the ~ —R.H.Ferrell⟩; *specif* **:** the area proximate to a royal personage **c** *obs* **:** PRESENCE CHAMBER ⟨two great cardinals wait in the ~ —Shak.⟩ **3** *archaic* **:** a number of persons assembled **:** ASSEMBLY, COMPANY ⟨here is like to be a good ~ of worthies —Shak.⟩ ⟨the ~ was so numerous that little could be caught of what they said —Thomas Jefferson⟩ **4 :** the consecrated elements of the Eucharist held in some branches of the Christian church to be identical with the body and blood of Christ **5 :** one that is present: as **a :** the actual person or thing having the specified status of being present — used with possessive ⟨your royal ~*s* be rul'd by me —Shak.⟩ ⟨a fiery column charioting his Godlike ~ —John Milton⟩ **b :** a person present in the flesh; *specif* **:** one having a dignified, noble, or impressive appearance **c :** something present of a visible or concrete nature ⟨the impersonal radar reports simply a ~ —*Lamp*⟩ **d :** one having existence or influence in the present ⟨these rocks are not dead masses but ~*s* imbued with an . . . ancient life that still continues —*Times Lit. Supp.*⟩ **e :** one that is present (as in a particular area or medium) and that usu. exerts influence or holds an important position thereby ⟨not . . . as an actor on the stage but rather as a ~ behind the scenes —*Times Lit. Supp.*⟩ ⟨introduced himself in the later books as a kind of ~ —John Arthos⟩ **6 a :** the bearing, carriage, mien, or air of a person **:** personal appearance ⟨a man of heavy, uninspiring ~ but considerable eloquence —Cicely V. Wedgwood⟩; *esp* **:** fine, stately, or distinguished bearing ⟨her carriage is superb and she has ~ —John Martin⟩ ⟨a small birdlike person, of no ~ —Rose Macaulay⟩ **b :** a quality of poise and effectiveness and ease of performance that enables a performer to achieve a close and sympathetic relationship with his audience ⟨the American singer must acquire . . . the sense of ~ on a stage —Rudolf Bing⟩ ⟨that sense of a measured and boundless ~ that fine acting must afford —*New Republic*⟩ **7 :** something (as a spirit, being, or influence) felt or believed to be present ⟨an intangible, mysterious ~ seemed to be creeping closer . . . upon them —O.E.Rölvaag⟩; *esp* **:** one having a divine or spiritual nature ⟨before creation a ~ existed —Witter Bynner⟩ ⟨she could have imagined a seraphic ~ in the room —George Meredith⟩ **8 :** a quality in sound reproduction that gives a listener the illusion of being in the same room as the original source of sound rather than in the room with the sound-reproducing system ⟨music with concert-hall ~ recorded on professional equipment —*advt*⟩ **9 :** the degree of occurrence of a specific unit (as a biological species or chemical element) ⟨carbon showed a ~ of 40 percent in the samples tested⟩

**presence chamber** *n* **:** the room where a great personage (as a monarch) receives company or those entitled to come into his presence

**presence of mind** [trans. of L *praesentia animi*] **:** self-control so maintained in an emergency, in danger, or in an embarrassing situation that one can say or do the right thing **:** unshaken calmness and readiness of thought

**pre·senile** \(ˈ)prē+\ *adj* [ISV *pre-* + *senile*] **1 :** of, relating to, or constituting the period immediately preceding the development of senility in an organism or person ⟨the ~ period of life⟩ ⟨the ~ decline of vital powers⟩ **2 :** prematurely displaying symptoms of senile psychosis

**pre·se·nil·i·ty** \,prēsəˈniləd·ē\ *n* [*presenile* + *-ity*] **1 :** premature senility **2 :** the period of life immediately preceding senility

**pre·sensation** \¦prē+\ *n* [*pre-* + *sensation*] **:** a perception or feeling of something before it appears, develops, or exists **:** ANTICIPATION, FOREBODING, PRESENTIMENT

**pre·sen·sion** \prēˈsenchən\ *n* -s [L *praesension-, praesensio*, fr. *praesensus* (past part. of *praesentire* to perceive beforehand) + *-ion-, -io* -ion — more at PRESENTIENT] *archaic* **:** PRESENSATION ⟨appeared to have a very decided ~ of his untimely death —E.A.Seymour⟩

**¹pres·ent** \ˈprezᵊnt\ *n* -s [ME, fr. OF, fr. *presenter* to present] **1 :** something presented or given **:** DONATION, GIFT ⟨Christmas ~*s*⟩ ⟨brought home ~*s* for the children⟩ **2 :** PRESENTATION 1 ⟨made her a ~ of a diamond necklace⟩

**²pre·sent** \prēˈzent, prəˈ-\ *vb* -ED/-ING/-S [ME *presenten*, fr. OF *presenter*, fr. L *praesentare*, fr. *praesent-, praesens*, pres. part. of *praeesse*] *vt* **1 a :** to bring or introduce into the presence of someone (as a superior) **:** to introduce for acquaintance ⟨the ambassador was ~*ed* to the president⟩ ⟨the small boy ~*ed* himself before his father⟩ ⟨offered to ~ his friend to the attractive young lady⟩ **b :** to dedicate by bringing before or into the presence of God ⟨~*ed* Christ in the temple⟩ **c :** to introduce formally at court esp. to the sovereign **d :** to bring (a candidate) before university authorities for examination or for conferral of a degree **e :** to bring (as an entertainer) before the public **2 :** to make a present or donation to **:** furnish or provide (as a person) with something by way of a present or gift **3 a :** to lay or put before a person for acceptance **:** offer as a gift **:** give or bestow formally **b :** to offer or convey by way of message, greeting, or compliment **c :** to hand or pass over usu. in a ceremonious way **:** deliver formally for acceptance **4 a :** to lay (as a charge) before a court as an object of inquiry **:** give notice officially of (as a crime or offense) **:** find or represent judicially ⟨the grand jury ~*ed* many offenses⟩ **b** (1) **:** to bring a formal public charge against **:** charge formally **:** ACCUSE (2) **:** to bring an indictment or presentment against **5 :** to nominate (a clergyman) to a benefice **6** *archaic* **:** to represent (a character) on the stage **:** act the part of **:** PERFORM, PERSONATE **7** *obs* **:** to make an open offer of (as battle) **8 :** to aim, point, or direct so as to face something or in a particular direction ~ *vi* **1 :** to make a presentation of a clergyman to the ordinary for institution to an ecclesiastical office **2 :** to present a weapon (as a rifle) **3** *obs* **:** to blow favorably — used of the wind **4 a :** to become directed toward the opening of the uterus — used esp. of parts of a fetus ⟨premature babies which ~ by breech —*Yr. Bk. of Obstetrics & Gynecology*⟩ **b :** to project or be directed ⟨a neoplasm that ~*s* as an axillary mass⟩ **5 :** to come forward as a patient **syn** see OFFER

**³present** \"\ *n* -s **1 :** the position of a firearm ready to be fired or of a lance or similar weapon ready to be used in attack ⟨bring the rifle down to the ~⟩ **2 :** the position of present arms ⟨soldiers standing at ~⟩

**⁴pres·ent** \ˈprezᵊnt\ *adj* [ME, fr. OF, fr. L *praesent-, praesens*, pres. part. of *praeesse* to be before one, be at hand, fr. *prae-* pre- + *esse* to be — more at IS] **1 :** now existing or in progress **:** begun but not ended **:** now being in view, being dealt with, or being under consideration **:** being at this time **:** not past or future **:** CONTEMPORARY ⟨to understand the ~ institutions we must . . . comprehend something of their history —J.B. Conant⟩ ⟨12 pioneer papers have survived to the ~ day —*Amer. Guide Series: Minn.*⟩ ⟨in 1909 the . . . house again burned and the ~ hostelry of the same name was built —*Amer. Guide Series: N.H.*⟩ **2 a :** being in one place and not elsewhere **:** being within reach, sight, or call or within contemplated limits **:** being in view or at hand **:** being before, beside, with, or in the same place as someone or something ⟨both men were ~ at the meeting⟩ ⟨more beautiful than all the women ~⟩ ⟨~ company excepted⟩ — used interjectionally to indicate one's presence esp. in answer to a roll call **b :** existing in something (as a class or case) mentioned or under consideration ⟨in the Hemiptera . . . wings may be ~ or absent —T.H.Huxley⟩ **3 :** constituting the one actually involved, at hand, or being considered ⟨the ~ writer⟩ ⟨the ~ volume⟩ ⟨the ~ case⟩ **4 :** of, relating to, or constituting a verb tense that is expressive of present time or the time of speaking **5 :** existing at or belonging to the time under consideration **:** contemporaneous with a specified past time ⟨there existed in preconquest England a church . . . united to the see of Rome by ancient tradition and ~ reverence —F.M.Stenton⟩ **6** *obs* **a :** having one's mind or thoughts directed toward a matter at hand **:** intent upon something **:** ATTENTIVE **b :** having self-possession **:** COLLECTED **7** *archaic* **:** immediately accessible or available (as in providing assistance) **:** ready at hand ⟨this sum . . . was a large and ~ resource —James Mill⟩ **8** *archaic* **:** immediately operative or effective **:** IMMEDIATE, INSTANT ⟨the queen . . . demanded the ~ payment of some arrears —Thomas Fuller⟩ ⟨an ambassador . . . desires a ~ audience —Philip Massinger⟩

**⁵present** \"\ *n* -s [ME, fr. OF, fr. L *praesent-, praesens*, fr. *praesent-, praesens*, pres. part. of *praeesse*] **1 a** *obs* **:** present occasion or affair **:** business or action in hand **b presents** *pl* **:** the present words or statements **:** the present legal instrument (as a deed of conveyance, lease, or power of attorney) or other writing **:** the document in which these words are used ⟨know all men by these ~*s*⟩ **2 a :** the present tense of a language **b :** a verb form in the present tense **3 :** the present time **:** the time being or contemplated ⟨another of those periods, much like the ~ —Ruth Moore⟩ ⟨from 1700 to the ~ —*Bull. of Bates Coll.*⟩ — compare FUTURE 1, PAST — **at present** *adv* **:** at the present time **:** just now ⟨the materials *at present* within my command —Mary W. Shelley⟩ ⟨*at present* he regrets what he has done —Jane Austen⟩ — **at this present** *adv, archaic* **:** at the present time ⟨nations which *at this present* are in high repute —Marchamont Needham⟩ — **for the present** *adv* **:** for the time being **:** TEMPORARILY ⟨leave it at that *for the present* —Virgil Thomson⟩ ⟨*for the present* men are expendable, tanks aren't —Fred Majdalany⟩ — **in present** *adv, obs* **:** at the present time ⟨man's joy and pleasure rather hereafter than *in present* is —George Herbert⟩

**pre·sent·abil·i·ty** \prē,zentəˈbiləd·ē\ *n* **:** the quality or state of being presentable ⟨candidates screened for ~ on television⟩

**pre·sent·able** \prēˈzentəbəl, prəˈ-\ *adj* [²*present* + *-able*] **1 :** appropriate for or liable to legal presentment ⟨~ offenses⟩ ⟨a ~ offender⟩ **2 :** capable or admitting of being presented (as to a person or the mind) **:** suitable to be offered, set forth, or brought forward **:** appropriate for presentation ⟨ideas that are ~ in simple language⟩ ⟨emotions ~ only in music⟩ **3** *archaic* **:** admitting of the presentation of a clergyman — used of an ecclesiastical benefice **4 :** having a bearing or appearance that will satisfy or give pleasure to others **:** in condition to be seen or inspected esp. by the critical **:** suitable (as in attire or behavior) for presentation into society or company **:** fit to be seen ⟨dinner . . . at a ~ restaurant —*N.Y. Times*⟩ ⟨an adequate number of ~ domestic servants —Roy Lewis & Angus Maude⟩ ⟨give me a minute to make myself ~ —Kenneth Roberts⟩

**pre·sent·ably** \-blē\ *adv* **:** in a presentable manner

**present arms** *n* [fr. the imper. phrase *present arms*] **:** a position in the manual of arms in which the rifle is held perpendicularly in front of the center of the body ⟨*present arms* is analogous to a salute⟩ — often used as a command

present arms

**pre·sen·ta·tion** \,prē,zen·ˈtāshən, prezᵊn-, ,prēzᵊn-\ *n* -s *often attrib* [ME *presentacioun*, fr. MF *presentation*, fr. LL *praesentation-, praesentatio*, fr. L *praesentatus* (past part. of *praesentare* to present) + *-ion-, -io* -ion — more at PRESENT] **1 :** the act of presenting: as **a** (1) **:** the act, power, or privilege esp. of a patron of applying usu. by deed to the bishop or ordinary for the institution of one nominated to a benefice (2) **:** the appointment to a benefice through being so presented — compare COLLATION, NOMINATION **b :** the nomination by one ecclesiastical authority (as a vestry) of a candidate to be appointed by another (as a bishop) **c** *often cap* **:** the act of formally presenting a person before God as a ceremonial religious act ⟨the ~ of Christ in the temple⟩ **d :** the act of presenting usu. in a formal manner for acceptance **:** BESTOWAL, DELIVERY ⟨the ~ of an honors thesis —*Official Register of Harvard Univ.*⟩ ⟨~ of the colors⟩ **e :** the act of setting forth for the notice or attention of the mind **:** STATEMENT ⟨the ~ of information . . . by the executive to Congress —Vera M. Dean⟩ ⟨the military officer must learn to make staff ~*s* —Dallas Albritton⟩ ⟨limited most novelists to the ~ . . . of the life they know best —F.B.Millett⟩ **f :** the act of presenting to sight or view **:** pictorial, theatrical, or symbolic representation **:** DISPLAY, EXHIBITION, SHOW ⟨news happenings which . . . lend themselves to visual ~ —*Current Biog.*⟩ ⟨~ of a ballet⟩ **g :** the act of formally presenting a candidate (as for examination or for conferral of a degree) **h :** the formal or ceremonious introduction of a person (as to an assembly or at a royal court) ⟨~ of a nationally recognized speaker to the . . . student body —*Bull. of Meharry Med. Coll.*⟩ ⟨induce . . . one of the great ladies of the court to act as sponsor at her ~ —R.D.Benn⟩ **2 :** someone or something presented: as **a :** a symbol or image that represents something ⟨~ on a radar screen⟩ **b :** something offered or given **:** DONATION, GIFT, PRESENT ⟨make this scholarship an annual ~ —*Springfield (Mass.) Union*⟩ **c :** one set forth, represented, or delineated for the attention of the mind ⟨the author of a more formal ~ —Arthur Knight⟩ **3 :** the position in which the fetus lies in the uterus in labor with respect to the mouth of the uterus ⟨face ~⟩ ⟨breech ~⟩ **4 :** a datum of perception or sense appearance; *specif* **:** the element in the cognition of an object which is given by direct awareness as distinguished from that which is added by association or thinking ⟨a visual ~ of a baseball . . . is spatially bidimensional —Nelson Goodman⟩ **5 :** appearance in conscious experience either as a sensory product or as a memory image **6** *usu cap* **a :** CANDLEMAS 1 **b :** a church feast celebrating the presentation of the Virgin Mary in the temple observed in both Eastern Orthodox and Roman Catholic churches on November 21 **7 :** the method by which radio, navigation, or radar information is given to the operator (as the pilot of an airplane)

**pre·sen·ta·tion·al** \¦=(,)=¦tāshənᵊl, -shnəl\ *adj* **1 :** of or relating to a presentation, presentations, or presentationism in philosophy or psychology **2 :** of, characterized by, or belonging to a style of theatrical production designed to present a story in theatrical forms ⟨the ~ theater⟩ ⟨~ method⟩ **3 :** NOTIONAL 4 b (1)

**presentation copy** *n* **:** a copy of a book or a similar publication inscribed by the author and used as a presentation

**pre·sen·ta·tion·ism** \,=(,)=ˈtāshə,nizəm\ *n* -s **:** MONISM 1 b — compare REPRESENTATIONISM

**presentation piece** *n* **:** a coin or medal struck for use as a gift or prize

**presentation time** *n* **:** the minimum time of application of a given stimulus required to effect a response — compare ACTION TIME, REACTION TIME

**pre·sen·ta·tive** \prēˈzentəd·|iv, prəˈ-, -ət| *also* |əv\ *adj* [²*present* + *-ative*] **1 :** subject to ecclesiastical presentation **:** carrying with it the right of presentation ⟨a ~ benefice⟩ **2 :** of the nature of a philosophical or psychological presentation **a :** known or capable of being known directly rather than through cogitation ⟨the ~ elements in a cognition⟩ **b :** having the power or function of apprehending directly **:** INTUITIVE, PERCEPTIVE ⟨a ~ faculty⟩ **c :** of, relating to, derived from, or concerned with one or more presentations ⟨~ theories⟩ **3 :** NONREPRESENTATIONAL

**present-day** \¦==¦=\ *adj* [fr. the phrase *present day*] **:** now existing or occurring **:** CURRENT ⟨*present-day* local government is mainly concerned with . . . public services —W.E.Jackson⟩ ⟨their survival among millions of *present-day* peoples —J.H. Steward⟩ ⟨the *present-day* remains of . . . irrigation canals —R.W.Murray⟩

**presented** *past of* PRESENT

**pres·en·tee** \¦prezᵊn¦tē\ *n* -s [ME, fr. MF *presenté*, fr. *presenté*, past part. of *presenter* to present] **1 :** one that is presented; *esp* **:** a clergyman presented to a benefice ⟨rob the ~*s* of . . . their tithes —G.G.Coulton⟩ **2 :** one to whom something is presented ⟨believing ~*s* in return supplied him with small sums of money —Thomas Campbell⟩

**pre·sentence** \(ˈ)prē+\ *adj* [*pre-* + *sentence*, n.] **:** of, based upon, or constituting an investigation into the character and background of a convicted offender as a means of collecting information useful to the sentencing judge ⟨the ~ reports of probation officers may help determine a fair and proper sentence⟩

**pre·sent·er** *also* **pre·sen·tor** \prēˈzentə(r), prəˈ-\ *n* -s [*presenter* fr. ²*present* + *-er*; *presentor* fr. earlier *presentour*, fr. MF, fr. *presenter* to present + *-our, -eur* -or — more at PRESENT] **:** one that presents ⟨the best ~ for all sales ideas —D.H. McCollum⟩ ⟨the ~ merely introduced the characters —Muriel C. Bradbrook⟩ ⟨the ~ of a bank draft⟩

**pre·sen·tial** \prēˈzenchəl\ *adj* [LL *praesentialis*, fr. L *praesentia* presence + *-alis* -al — more at PRESENCE] **1 :** of, relating to, or constituting the present **:** IMMEDIATE **2 :** of, relating to, or formed from the present stem of a verb

**pre·sen·ti·al·i·ty** \prē,zenchēˈaləd·ē\ *n* -ES [ML *praesentialitat-, praesentialitas*, fr. LL *praesentialis* + L *-tat-, -tas* -ty] *archaic* **:** the quality or state of being present (as in time or place)

**presentially** *adv, obs* **:** in a presential manner ⟨exhibits the sacrifice . . . actually and ~ in heaven —Jeremy Taylor⟩

**presentiate** *vt* -ED/-ING/-S [L *praesentia* presence + E *-ate* (v. suffix)] *obs* **:** to make present (as in time or space) ⟨that place where thou art pleased to ~ thyself —Henry Hammond⟩

**pre·sen·tient** \prēˈsenchənt\ *adj* [L *praesentient-, praesentiens*, pres. part. of *praesentire* to perceive beforehand, fr. *prae-* pre- + *sentire* to feel — more at SENSE] **:** apprehensive in advance **:** having a presentiment **:** feeling or perceiving beforehand — usu. used with *of* ⟨ravenous fowls . . . ~ of their food —Robert Southey⟩

**pre·sen·ti·ment** \prēˈzentəmənt, prəˈ-\ *n* -s [obs. F *presentiment* (now *pressentiment*), fr. MF *presentiment, pressentiment*, fr. *presentir* to have a presentiment of (fr. L *praesentire* to perceive beforehand) + *-ment*] **1 a :** an impression, conviction, or feeling that something will or is about to happen **:** a vague expectation of a future event that seems to be a direct perception although it has no basis in fact ⟨I've a strong ~ it'll prove a success —J.C.Powys⟩ ⟨the almost total lack of ~ . . . of the new forces about to be released —S.T.Possony⟩ **b :** an antecedent impression or conviction of something unpleasant, distressing, or calamitous about to happen **:** an anticipatory fear **:** FOREBODING, PREMONITION ⟨a thousand ~*s* of evil to her beloved —Jane Austen⟩ **2 :** an opinion or conception formed prior to actual knowledge of something **:** PREJUDGMENT ⟨reason has a ~ of objects which possess a great interest for it —Friedrich Max Müller⟩ **syn** see APPREHENSION

**presenting** *pres part of* PRESENT

**pres·en·tist** \ˈprezᵊntəst\ *n* -s [⁴*present* + *-ist*] **:** one who holds that biblical prophecy esp. of the Apocalypse is now in course of fulfillment — compare PRETERIST, FUTURIST

**pres·ent·ly** *adv* [ME, fr. ⁴*present* + *-ly*] **1 a** *archaic* **:** without delay or hesitation **:** FORTHWITH, IMMEDIATELY ⟨and ~ the fig tree withered away —Mt 21:19 (AV)⟩ **b :** after a little while **:** before long **:** after a short time **:** BY AND BY 2, SHORTLY, SOON ⟨a long-suffering type but ~ even he becomes fed up —John McCarten⟩ ⟨leaving the older section, we ~ reached the newest development —Joseph Wechsberg⟩ ⟨I'll be there ~⟩ **2 a :** at the present time **:** at present **:** at this time **:** NOW ⟨fix it with the tools ~ at hand —T.W.Arnold⟩ ⟨the dangerous situation in which this nation ~ finds itself —Adrienne Koch⟩ ⟨expenses . . . in these categories ~ cannot be deducted —*U. S. Code*⟩ **b :** at the time indicated or referred to **:** at that time ⟨towns where, ~, the courthouses . . . were of brick —*Amer. Guide Series: Tenn.*⟩ **3** *obs* **:** IMMEDIATELY 1 ⟨~ without the chapel is the burse —Peter Heylin⟩ **4 :** by way of immediate consequence or necessity **:** as a direct result **:** by direct inference **:** CONSEQUENTLY, DIRECTLY, NECESSARILY ⟨we do not infer, nor doth it ~ follow, that the present reading is corrupt —Brian Walton⟩

**pre·sent·ment** \prēˈzentmənt, prəˈ-\ *n* -s [ME *presentement*, fr. MF, fr. OF, fr. *presenter* to present + *-ment* — more at PRESENT] **1** *archaic* **:** the act of presenting a clergyman to a benefice **2 :** the act of presenting to an authority a formal statement of a matter to be dealt with: **a :** the notice taken or statement made by a grand jury of any offense or unlawful state of affairs from their own knowledge or observation without any bill of indictment laid before them ⟨grand jury has just returned a ~ on the subject of lawlessness —*Commonweal*⟩ ⟨special grand jury . . . returned a ~ —*N. Y. Herald Tribune*⟩ **b :** a similar statement formerly made by a magistrate or constable **c :** a formal complaint made by the authorities of a parish to the bishop or archdeacon at his visitation **3 a :** representation in art of an object (as by a picture, image, or graphic description) **:** DELINEATION ⟨the actuality of ~ for which he is noted⟩ **b :** something that makes this representation (as a portrait or likeness) ⟨a curious ~ of the Trinity occurs several times in church windows —O. Elfrida Saunders⟩ **4 :** a theatrical or dramatic representation (as the performance of a play) **5 :** PRESENTATION 1d ⟨settle matters about the ~ of the petition —Edmund Burke⟩; *specif* **:** the act of producing and offering at the proper time and place a document (as a matured note, bill of exchange, or check) requiring to be accepted or paid by another **6 a :** the act of presenting to view, perception, notice, or consciousness **:** DESCRIPTION, STATEMENT, SUGGESTION **b :** something that is set forth, presented, or exhibited **7 :** the appearance, aspect, form, or mode in which something is presented **8 a :** the appearing of something before the mind **:** PRESENTATION 5 **b :** the content of a perception or a thought as it stands before the mind

**presentment of englishry** *usu cap E* **:** the presentation of proof that a slain person was of English rather than Norman birth as an excuse for not paying a fine levied by the Norman kings of England upon local governmental units for the murder of a Norman

**present money** *n* [⁴*present*] *obs* **:** READY MONEY ⟨the temptation of a pistole *present money* never faileth —George Berkeley⟩

**pres·ent·ness** *n* -ES **:** the quality or state of being present ⟨a study of the pastness of the present and . . . of the ~ of the past —R.E.Spiller⟩

**presentor** *var of* PRESENTER

**present participle** *n* **:** a participle that typically expresses present action in relation to the time expressed by the finite verb in its clause and that in English is traditionally one of the principal parts of the verb, is formed with the suffix *-ing*, and is used in the formation of the progressive tenses

1**present perfect** *adj* [4*present* + *perfect*, adj.] **:** of, relating to, or constituting a verb tense that is traditionally formed in English with *have* and that expresses action or state completed at the time of speaking

2**present perfect** *n* **1 :** the present perfect tense of a language **2 :** a verb form in the present perfect tense

**presents** *pl of* PRESENT, *pres 3d sing of* PRESENT

**present tense** *n* [ME *present tens*] **:** the tense of a verb that expresses action or state in the present time and is used of what occurs or is true at the time of speaking (as in "I am in a hurry" or "he is singing") and of what is habitual or characteristic (as in "he pays his debts" or "he dresses well") or is always or necessarily true (as in "the sun shines by day" or "a straight line is the shortest distance"), that is sometimes used to refer to action in the past (as in the historical present), and that is sometimes used for future events (as in "Christmas falls on Friday next year")

**present value** *also* **present worth** *n* **:** the principal of a sum of money payable at a future date that drawing interest at a given rate will amount to the given sum at the date on which this sum is to be paid ⟨at 6% interest the *present value* of $106 due one year hence is $100⟩ — compare ARITHMETICAL DISCOUNT

**pre·serv·able** \prē'zərvəbəl, prə̇'-\ *adj* **:** capable of being preserved

**pre·serv·al** \-vəl\ *n* -S **:** PRESERVATION ⟨~ and removal of . . . mineral beds —A.M.Bateman⟩

**pres·er·va·tion** \ˌprezə(r)'vāshən\ *n* -S [ME, fr. MF, fr. ML *praeservation-*, *praeservatio*, fr. *praeservatus* (past part. of *praeservare* to preserve) + L *-ion-*, *-io* -ion] **:** the act of preserving or the state of being preserved ⟨fostered the ~ of local speechways —Hans Kurath⟩ ⟨essential to the ~ of my regard —Jane Austen⟩ ⟨in a good state of ~ —*Amer. Guide Series: Texas*⟩

**pres·er·va·tion·ist** \-sh(ə)nə̇st\ *n* -S **:** one that advocates the preservation of a species (as of wildlife) from extinction

1**pre·serv·a·tive** \prē'zərvəd·|iv, prə̇'-, -zə̄v-, -zəiv-, -vət| *also* |əv\ *adj* [ME, fr. ML *praeservativus*, fr. *praeservatus* (past part. of *praeservare* to preserve) + L *-ivus* -ive] **:** having the power of preserving **:** tending to preserve ⟨bound together for ~ purposes —*Springfield* (*Mass.*) *Union*⟩ ⟨need for ~ action —A.N.Whitehead⟩

2**preservative** \"\ *n* -S [ME, fr. *preservative*, adj.] **:** something that preserves or has the power of preserving: as **a** *archaic* **:** a medicine designed to preserve one's health by preventing or providing a protection from disease **:** a safeguard against poison or infection ⟨hope his restoratives and his ~*s* will . . . be effectual —Samuel Johnson⟩ **b :** a preservative quality, principle, or factor ⟨accounts federalism the ~ of the American system —G.W.Johnson⟩ ⟨their pleasantest ~ from want —Jane Austen⟩ ⟨public life seems to be a good ~ . . . for congressmen —Elmer Davis⟩ **c :** a substance added to chemicals, natural products, fabrics, or food products to preserve them against decay, discoloration, or spoilage under conditions of storage or nonchemical use ⟨salt, sugar, and spice are common food ~*s*⟩ **d :** a substance impregnated into or covering wood to prevent attack by insects and other organisms **e :** a chemical (as sodium sulfite) for retarding oxidation of photographic solutions

**preservative medium** *n* **:** MEDIUM 8b

**pre·serv·a·tize** \-vəˌtīz\ *vt* -ED/-ING/-S [2*preservative* + *-ize*] **:** to treat (as food) with a preservative ⟨*preservatized* butter⟩

**preservatory** *n* -ES [ML *praeservatus* (past part. of *praeservare* to preserve) + E *-ory*] *obs* **:** a charitable house of refuge for unemployed, deserted, or destitute women and girls

1**pre·serve** \prē'zərv, prə̇'-, -zə̄v, -zəiv\ *vb* -ED/-ING/-S [ME *preserven*, fr. MF *preserver*, fr. ML *praeservare*, fr. LL, to observe, fr. L *prae-* pre- + *servare* to keep, guard — more at CONSERVE] *vt* **1 :** to keep safe from injury, harm, or destruction **:** guard or defend from evil **:** PROTECT, SAVE ⟨thornbushes . . . are *preserved* by superstition —O.S.J.Gogarty⟩ ⟨their knowledge of the Marxist conspiracy should be put to use to ~ the republic —Howard Rushmore⟩ **2 a :** to keep alive, intact, in existence, or from decay ⟨~ an old house⟩ ⟨the right of trial by jury shall be *preserved* —*U. S. Constitution*⟩ ⟨among the deeds *preserved* in the courthouse —*Amer. Guide Series: Pa.*⟩ **b :** to retain in one's possession ⟨~ my shaky dignity —Reginald Kell⟩ ⟨*preserved* their detachment —Dexter Perkins⟩ **c :** MAINTAIN ⟨~ a correspondence⟩ **3 a :** to keep or save from decomposition (as by refrigeration, curing, or treating with a preservative) ⟨~ specimens or skins to be stuffed⟩ ⟨~ milk indefinitely⟩ **b :** to can, pickle, or similarly prepare (as fruits or vegetables) for future use ⟨~ peaches⟩ **4 :** to keep up and reserve for personal or special use ⟨~ game or fish by raising and protecting it⟩ ⟨~ a stream or field⟩ ~ *vi* **1 :** to remain fresh or in its original state **:** KEEP **2 :** to make preserves **3 :** to raise and protect game for purposes of sport **4 :** to endure or stand the process of preservation (as by canning or pickling) ⟨duck eggs do not ~ satisfactorily —F.D. Smith & Barbara Wilcox⟩

2**preserve** \"\ *n* -S **1 :** something that preserves or is designed to preserve; *specif* **:** GOGGLE 2 **2 a :** fruit canned or made into jams or jellies ⟨black-currant ~⟩ — often used in pl. **b :** fruit cooked whole or in large pieces with sugar so as to keep its shape ⟨quince ~⟩ — often used in pl. ⟨strawberry ~*s*⟩ **3 :** an area (as a tract of land or body of water) restricted for the protection and preservation of animals, trees, or other natural resources ⟨our Adirondack mountains with their enormous forest ~ —Averell Harriman⟩ ⟨a wildlife ~⟩; *esp* **:** one used primarily for regulated hunting or fishing **:** RESERVE ⟨a state game ~⟩ — compare SANCTUARY 4 **4 :** something (as a place, occupation, or sphere of activity) that is sacred to or reserved exclusively for certain persons ⟨regarded the diplomatic service as a ~ for their younger sons —G.B.Shaw⟩ ⟨translation . . . has been the ~ of scholarly jargonists —Dudley Fitts⟩ ⟨recognizing . . . the Baltic states as a Soviet ~ —*Times Lit. Supp.*⟩

**pre·serv·er** \-və(r)\ *n* -S **:** one that preserves (as from destruction, injury, or decay) ⟨God the creator and ~ of all mankind —*Bk. of Com. Prayer*⟩ ⟨game ~⟩ ⟨steel ~⟩

**pre·serv·er·ess** \-vərə̇s\ *n* -ES *archaic* **:** a female preserver

**pre·service** \(ˈ)prē+\ *adj* [*pre-* + *service*, n.] **:** of, relating to, or taking place during a period of time preceding active service (as in a profession or the armed forces) ⟨the kind of ~ experiences core teachers need —J.M.Mickelson⟩ ⟨protect the veteran's right to reemployment in his ~ job —H.S.Truman⟩ — compare IN-SERVICE

**preserving melon** *n* **:** CITRON

**pre·ses** \'prēˌsēz\ *n*, *pl* **preses** [L *praesid-*, *praeses* guard, president, ruler, fr. *praesidēre* to guard, preside over] *chiefly Scot* **:** the president or presiding officer (as of a meeting or group) **:** CHAIRMAN

**pre·session** \(ˈ)prē+\ *adj* [*pre-* + *session*] **:** occurring before a session (as of a legislative body) ⟨a ~ caucus⟩

**pre·set** \"+\ *vt* [*pre-* + *set*] **:** to set beforehand ⟨a new control device that is ~ to shift the dial and change the volume at the desired time —*Time*⟩

**pre·sexual** \"+\ *adj* [*pre-* + *sexual*] **:** preceding sexual development or maturity

**pre·shrunk** \"+\ *adj* [*pre-* + *shrunk*] **:** of, relating to, or constituting a fabric subjected to a shrinking process during manufacture usu. to reduce later shrinking (as from laundering)

**pre·side** \prē'zīd, prə̇'-\ *vb* -ED/-ING/-S [L *praesidēre* to guard, preside over, fr. *prae-* pre- + *sedēre* to sit — more at SIT] *vi* **1 a :** to occupy the place of authority (as in an assembly) **:** act as president, chairman, or moderator (as of a group or meeting) **:** direct, control, or regulate proceedings as chief officer ⟨the mayor ~*s* in council meetings —F.A.Ogg & P.O. Ray⟩ ⟨the chief justice ~*s* over the supreme court⟩ ⟨~ at a public meeting⟩ **b :** to occupy a similar position or perform similar duties ⟨~ over a funeral service⟩ ⟨~ over a literary salon⟩ ⟨~ at tea⟩ **2 :** to exercise superintendence, guidance, direction, or control ⟨called to ~ over her son's bereft family —R.K.Leavitt⟩ ⟨*presided* over one of the . . . forges in the blacksmith shop —Ben Riker⟩ ⟨~ over a radio program⟩ **3 :** to occupy the most conspicuous position **:** sit or reign supreme ⟨gently rugged country *presided* over by . . . mountains —R.W.Hatch⟩ ⟨an 18th century tallboy in . . . the hall where it ~*s* in silent majesty —H.J.Laski⟩ **4 :** to occupy the position of chief or featured instrumental performer orig. as director of a group of musicians — used with *at* ⟨~ at the organ⟩ ~ *vt* **:** to exercise control or superintendence over **:** DIRECT, RULE ⟨those that were to ~ the naval affairs —Thomas Manley⟩

**pres·i·dence** \'prez(ə)dən(t)s\ *n* -S [MF, office of president, fr. ML *praesidentia*] **1 :** the action or fact of presiding **:** DIRECTION, SUPERINTENDENCE ⟨by the ~ and guidance of an unseen governing power —William Wollaston⟩ **2 :** PRESIDENCY 1a ⟨preserve both the senate and the ~ —P.G.Hamerton⟩

**pres·i·den·cy** \'prez(ə)dənsē, -si *also* -zədᵊns- *or* -zəˌden(t)s-\ *n* -ES [ML *praesidentia*, fr. L *praesident-*, *praesidens* president, ruler + *-ia* -y] **1 a :** the office of president ⟨elected to the ~ of . . . the hotel corporation —*Current Biog.*⟩ ⟨assumed the ~ of the university⟩ **b** *sometimes cap* (1) **:** the office of president of the U. S. ⟨the ~ . . . is preeminently a place of moral leadership —F.D.Roosevelt⟩ ⟨an avowed candidate for the ~ —*Nation*⟩ (2) **:** the American governmental institution comprising the office of president and the various administrative and policy-making agencies directly associated with the president of the U. S. ⟨the ~ . . . was proliferating into countless people, councils, and commissions —Douglass Cater⟩ **2 :** the term during which a president holds office ⟨the third year of his ~⟩ **3 :** the action or function of one that presides **:** SUPERINTENDENCE ⟨such a body . . . met by his advice and under his ~ —F.M.Stenton⟩ ⟨the ~ and guidance of some superior agent —John Ray⟩ **4 :** one of three great divisions (Madras, Bombay, and Bengal) of British India orig. forming a district under a president of the East India Company and later a province under the administration of a governor **5 :** a council of three in the Mormon Church consisting of a president and two counselors and having jurisdiction in spiritual or temporal matters throughout the church or a stake or within a smaller unit (as a quorum) — compare FIRST PRESIDENCY **6 :** one of the four or five former divisions of the British colony of the Leeward Islands ⟨by the Leeward Islands Act, 1956 . . . each of the 4 *presidencies* became a colony —*Statesman's Yr. Bk.*⟩

1**pres·i·dent** \-nt\ *n* -S [ME, fr. MF, fr. L *praesident-*, *praesidens* president, ruler, fr. *praesident-*, *praesidens*, pres. part. of *praesidēre* to guard, preside over] **1 :** an official chosen to preside over a meeting or assembly ⟨~ of a ball⟩ ⟨~ of a bullfight⟩ ⟨~ of the teachers' conference⟩ **2 :** an appointed governor of a subordinate political unit (as a province, colony, or city) **3 :** the chief officer of a corporation, company, institution, society, or similar organization usu. entrusted with the direction and administration of its policies ⟨colleges and universities are usu. headed by a ~ —Kenneth Holland⟩ ⟨chosen ~ of the Turkish Historical Society —*Current Biog.*⟩ ⟨~ of the nation's largest steel company⟩ **4 a :** the presiding officer of a governmental body (as an advisory council, administrative board, or legislative assembly) ⟨the constitution . . . makes the vice-president of the U. S. ~ of the senate —F.A.Ogg & P.O.Ray⟩ ⟨~ of the U. N. general assembly⟩ — compare LORD PRESIDENT OF THE COUNCIL **b :** the presiding judge or justice of a court of law ⟨~ of the Court of Session in Scotland⟩ ⟨~ of the Probate, Divorce and Admiralty Division of the Supreme Court of Judicature⟩ ⟨joint ~*s* of the shire court —F.M.Stenton⟩ **c :** the elected governor usu. serving as head of an executive council in several of the original 13 states of the U. S. during their existence as British colonies and also during the late 18th century after the Revolution ⟨~ of Pennsylvania⟩ ⟨in 1608 . . . made ~ of Virginia —*Brit. Book News*⟩ **5** *obs* **:** a presiding deity, patron, or genius **:** GUARDIAN ⟨great ~ of fire —George Chapman⟩ **6 a :** an elected official serving as both chief of state and chief political executive in a republic having a presidential government ⟨the executive power shall be vested in a ~ of the United States —*U. S. Constitution*⟩ **b :** an elected official having the position of chief of state but usu. only minimal political powers in a republic having a parliamentary government ⟨Israel's ~ . . . is not head of the executive and his actual powers are very limited —Misha Louvish⟩ ⟨the ~ of France under the Third Republic resembled a constitutional monarch⟩ **7 :** the head of the church leaders of the Mormon Church who with two counselors forms the first presidency **8** *Brit* **:** the captain of a racing crew

2**president** \"\ *adj* [ME, fr. L *praesident-*, *praesidens*, pres. part. of *praesidēre*] *archaic* **:** occupying the first rank or chief place **:** PRESIDING ⟨residence of the ~ priest of the province —Z.M.Pike⟩

**pres·i·den·te** \ˌprezə'dentē\ *n* -S [AmerSp, fr. Sp, president, fr. L *praesident-*, *praesidens* president, ruler] **:** a cocktail consisting of rum, curaçao, dry vermouth, and grenadine shaken or stirred with cracked ice

**pres·i·dent·ess** \'prez(ə)dəntə̇s\ *n* -ES **1 :** a female president **:** a woman that presides ⟨formed a tea society with the parson's wife for ~ —J.F.Cooper⟩ **2 :** the wife of a president

**president general** *n* **:** the chief presiding officer in an organized system (as a religious or fraternal order or a federation of states or provinces) usu. having subordinate officers of presidential rank or title ⟨*president general* of the Daughters of the American Revolution⟩ ⟨proposed a *president general* for the North American colonies⟩

**pres·i·den·tial** \ˌprezəˌdenchəl *sometimes* (ˈ)prezˌ-\ *adj* [ML *praesidentialis*, fr. *praesidentia* presidency + L *-alis* -al — more at PRESIDENCY] **1 a :** of, relating to, or exercised by a president ⟨a man of ~ stature —*N. Y. Times*⟩ ⟨~ patronage⟩ ⟨~ aide⟩ ⟨~ policy⟩ **b :** of or relating to the election of a president ⟨~ campaign⟩ ⟨~ convention⟩ **c :** performing functions delegated by or under the authority of a president ⟨~ agent⟩ ⟨~ commission⟩ **2** *obs* **:** having the function of presiding or watching over ⟨govern them . . . by a ~ angel —Robert Gell⟩ **3 :** of, based upon, or having the characteristics of presidential government ⟨~ system⟩ ⟨~ republic⟩

**presidential government** *n* **:** a system of government in which the position and powers of both chief of state and chief political executive are concentrated in a president who is chosen independently of the legislature for a fixed term and who in position, duties, and powers is constitutionally independent of the legislature — compare PARLIAMENTARY GOVERNMENT

**pres·i·den·tial·ly** \-chəlē\ *adv* **1 :** in the character or person of a president ⟨each of the great powers will be represented ~ —*London Daily News*⟩ **2 :** so far as concerns the president or the presidency of the U. S. ⟨states voting Republican ~ —V.O.Key⟩

**presidential primary** *also* **presidential preference primary** *n* **:** a primary in which the voters indicate preferences for nominees for president of the U. S. directly by vote or indirectly through the choice of delegates to the presidential nominating convention — called also *preferential primary*

**presidential year** *n* **:** a year in which a presidential election is held

**president pro tempore** *n*, *pl* **presidents pro tempore** **1 :** a member of the U. S. senate and usu. a leader of the majority party who is chosen to serve as presiding officer of the senate in the absence of the vice-president **2 :** a similar officer in another legislative body ⟨*president pro tempore* of the state senate⟩ ⟨*president pro tempore* of the provincial congress⟩

**pres·i·dent·ship** \'prez(ə)dəntˌship\ *n* **1 :** the office of president ⟨contests for the ~*s* and chairmanships of civic bodies —*Hindustan Times*⟩ ⟨accepted the ~ of the . . . association —*Modern Language Teaching*⟩ **2 :** the period of incumbency of a president ⟨the 17th year of his ~ —Cotton Mather⟩

**pre·sid·er** \prē'zīdə(r), prə̇'-\ *n* -S **:** one that presides

**presides** *pres 3d sing of* PRESIDE

**pre·sid·i·al** \prə̇'sidēəl\ *adj* [LL *praesidialis* of a garrison, fr. L *praesidium* defense, garrison, fortification (fr. *praesid-*, *praeses* guard, president, ruler, fr. *praesidēre* to guard, preside over) + *-alis* -al — more at PRESIDE] **1 :** of, having, or constituting a garrison ⟨three ~ castles in this city —James Howell⟩ **2** [influenced in meaning by LL *praesidalis* of a provincial governor, fr. L *praesid-*, *praeses* guard, president, ruler + *-alis* -al] **a :** PRESIDENTIAL 1 ⟨~ power⟩ ⟨~ cabinet⟩ **b :** PRESIDENTIAL 2 ⟨judgment holds in me a ~ seat —Charles Cotton⟩ **3** [F *présidial* being a presidial court, fr. MF *presidial*, alter. (influenced by LL *praesidialis* of a garrison) of *presidal*, fr. LL *praesidalis* of a provincial governor] **:** of or relating to a province **:** PROVINCIAL ⟨~ seat of justice⟩ — see PRESIDIAL COURT

**presidial court** *or* **presidial** *n* [*presidial court* part trans. of F *cour présidial*, fr. MF *cour presidial*, alter. (influenced by LL *praesidialis* of a garrison) of *cour presidal*, fr. *cour* court + *presidal* being a presidial court, fr. LL *praesidalis* of a provincial governor; *presidial* fr. F *présidial*, fr. *présidial*, adj. (in the term *cour présidial*)] **:** a court of justice under the ancien régime in French cities without a parliament

**pre·sid·i·ary** \-dēˌerē\ *adj* [L *praesidiarius*, fr. *praesidium* defense, garrison, fortification + *-arius* -ary] **:** PRESIDIAL 1 ⟨~ cohorts were stationed at every threatened point —Charles Merivale⟩

**presiding** *pres part of* PRESIDE

**presiding bishop** *n* **1 :** the president of the national council of the Protestant Episcopal Church who is elected by the general convention **2 :** the chief member of the presiding bishopric of the Mormon Church

**presiding bishopric** *n* **:** the chief office of the Aaronic priesthood in the Mormon Church filled by three persons and supervised by the first presidency

**presiding elder** *n* **:** DISTRICT SUPERINTENDENT ⟨a *presiding elder* may be an elder or a fully ordained minister⟩

**pre·sidio** \prə̇'sidēˌō, -sēd-\ *n* -S [Sp, fr. L *praesidium* defense, garrison, fortification] **:** a garrisoned place; *specif* **:** a military post or fortified settlement in areas currently or orig. under Spanish control ⟨one of the first settlements in Texas not established as a ~ —*Amer. Guide Series: Texas*⟩ ⟨a sleepy Mexican ~ with fortifications rusting —C.C.Dobie⟩

**pre·sid·i·um** \prē'sidēəm, prə̇'-, -'zi-\ *also* **prae·sid·i·um** \", prī-\ *n*, *pl* **presid·ia** \-dēə\ *or* **presidiums** [Russ *prezidium*, fr. L *praesidium* defense, garrison, fortification] **1 :** a permanent executive committee selected in Communist countries from a larger body in theory to act for the larger body when in recess but usu. regarded as exercising full powers for and in the name of the parent body ⟨the ~ . . . in practice is the effective working part of the Supreme Soviet —J.A. Corry⟩ ⟨the ~ of the central committee . . . replaced the politburo —Julian Towster⟩ ⟨the ~ of the Yugoslav parliament —M.S.Handler⟩ — compare POLITBURO 1 **2 :** a presiding or executive committee in a nongovernmental organization ⟨elected to the three-man ~ of the . . . orchestra association —*Springfield* (*Mass.*) *Union*⟩

**pre·sign** \prē+\ *vt* -ED/-ING/-S [*pre-* + *sign*] *archaic* **:** PRESIGNIFY ⟨agents of destruction . . . ~ regeneration —P.J.Bailey⟩

**pre·sig·ni·fi·ca·tion** \prēˌsignəfə̇'kāshən\ *n* [LL *praesignification-*, *praesignificatio*, fr. L *praesignificatus* (past part. of *praesignificare*) + *-ion-*, *-io* -ion] *archaic* **:** PRESAGE ⟨the broad arrow, the mysterious ~ of mischief —J.P.Kennedy †1870⟩

**pre·sig·ni·fy** \prē'signəˌfī\ *vt* -ED/-ING/-ES [L *praesignificare*, fr. *prae-* pre- + *significare* to signify] **:** to intimate or signify beforehand **:** PRESAGE ⟨a long cloud . . . *presignified* a violent storm —Richard Chandler⟩

**pre·simian** \(ˈ)prē+\ *adj* [*pre-* + *simian*] **:** existing or happening before the existence of anthropoid apes

1**pre–socratic** \ˌprē+\ *adj*, *sometimes cap P & usu cap S* [*pre-* + *socratic*] **:** of or relating to Greek philosophy or philosophers before Socrates; *esp* **:** of or relating to the members or the ideas of the Ionian, Pythagorean, and Eleatic schools, the school of the atomists, and sometimes the Sophists ⟨*pre-Socratic* thought⟩

2**pre–socratic** \"\ *n* -S *sometimes cap P & usu cap S* **:** a pre-Socratic philosopher ⟨a fundamental doctrine on which the *pre-Socratics* had been agreed —Friedrich Solmsen⟩

**pre·so·ma** \prē'sōmə\ *n* -S [NL, fr. *pre-* + *-soma*] **:** the anterior part of the body in an invertebrate in which a clearly defined head is lacking

**pre·somite** \(ˈ)prē+\ *adj* [*pre-* + *somite*] **:** occurring before the formation of somites ⟨~ period of the chick embryo⟩ **:** not yet divided into somites ⟨a ~ human embryo⟩

1**pre·sphenoid** \"+\ *n* [*pre-* + *sphenoid*] **:** a presphenoid bone or cartilage usu. united with the basisphenoid in the adult and in man forming the anterior part of the body of the sphenoid

2**presphenoid** \"\ *also* **pre·sphenoidal** \ˌprē+\ *adj* [*presphenoid* fr. 1*presphenoid; presphenoidal* fr. 1*presphenoid* + *-al*] **:** indicating or relating to a median part of the vertebrate skull anterior to the basisphenoid

**pre·sphygmic** \(ˈ)prē+\ *adj* [ISV *pre-* + *sphygmic*] **:** occurring before the pulse beat ⟨a ~ arterial thrill⟩

**pre·spi·nous** \prē'spīnəs\ *adj* [*pre-* + *spine* + *-ous*] **:** PRESCAPULAR 2

**pre·spiracular** \ˌprē+\ *adj* [*pre-* + *spiracular*] **:** anterior to the spiracle

1**press** \'pres\ *n* -ES *often attrib* [ME *presse*, *prees*, fr. OF *presse*, fr. *presser* to press — more at 2PRESS] **1 a :** a crowd of people or a crowded condition **:** MULTITUDE, THRONG ⟨there was . . . a ~ of people trying to force their way past the powerful yeomen ushers —Leslie Hotson⟩ ⟨perched on the folded-down top of a convertible, to roll down the boardwalk with a ~ of people following her car —Pete Martin⟩ **b** *archaic* **:** the crush or melee of cavalry or foot soldiers in battle **c :** a thronging or crowding forward or together ⟨had difficulty keeping his feet in the ~ and surge of the mob⟩ ⟨had been pushed out of their home territories by the ~ of white settlement —*Amer. Guide Series: Ind.*⟩ **2 a :** an apparatus or machine by which a substance is cut or shaped (as by pressing, drawing, or stamping), by which an impression of a body is taken, by which a material is compressed or packed, by which pressure is applied to a body, by which liquid is expressed, or by which a cutting tool (as a drill) is fed into the work by applied pressure — compare CHEESE PRESS, DRILL PRESS, FORMING PRESS, HYDRAULIC PRESS, PUNCH PRESS **b :** a building containing presses or a business using presses **c :** a medieval apparatus in which an accused person refusing to plead was crushed until he yielded or died **3 :** CLOSET, CUPBOARD — compare CLOTHESPRESS **4** [2*press*] **:** the act of pressing or pushing something **:** PRESSURE ⟨a ~ of a button⟩ ⟨a ~ of the hand⟩ ⟨finishes with a light ~ of the earth over the newly planted seed⟩ ⟨could no longer stand against the steady ~ of the Roman lines —A.C.Whitehead⟩ **5** [2*press*] **:** the properly smoothed and creased condition of a freshly pressed garment ⟨a fabric that keeps its ~⟩ ⟨a good ~ on these trousers⟩ **6 a :** PRINTING PRESS **b** *chiefly Brit* **:** HANDPRESS — compare MACHINE **c :** the act or the process of printing ⟨to see a book through the ~⟩ **d :** a printing or publishing establishment ⟨a university ~⟩; *also* **:** its personnel **7 a :** the gathering and publishing or broadcasting of news **:** JOURNALISM ⟨freedom of the ~⟩ **b :** newspapers, periodicals, and often radio and television news broadcasting regarded as a group ⟨the ~ has three functions: to inform, to influence, and to entertain —R.E. Wolseley⟩ ⟨the American ~⟩ ⟨the Democratic ~⟩ ⟨the religious ~⟩ **c :** news reporters, publishers, and broadcasters as a group ⟨the ~ . . . is very apt to think in the local terms of the papers that they represent —F.D.Roosevelt⟩ **d :** comment or notice in newspapers and periodicals ⟨the navy . . . is enjoying a good ~ —*Atlantic*⟩ **8 a :** any of various pressure devices (as the standing press) used to compress or hold books **b :** any of various devices used to keep sporting gear (as rackets and skis) from warping when not in use **9** [2*press*] **a :** a lift in weight lifting in which the weight is raised from the floor to shoulder height and then smoothly extended overhead — called also *military press;* compare CLEAN AND JERK, SNATCH **b :** a fencer's applying of pressure against an opponent's blade in order to force an opening for an attack **c :** a method by which a gymnast raises the body into a hand balance by using the muscles only without the aid of a kick or throw **d :** an aggressive pressuring defense employed in basketball in the half-court area of the defensive team — compare FULL-COURT PRESS **10 :** a pair of rolls between which the wet web of paper is passed to remove water and compact the sheet in papermaking **syn** see CROWD — **in press :** in the process of printing or manufacture — used of books or other printed matter

2**press** \"\ *vb* -ED/-ING/-ES [ME *pressen*, fr. MF *presser*, fr. OF, fr. L *pressare*, fr. *pressus*, past part. of *premere* to press; akin to L *prelum* press, wine press and perh. to Russ *peret'* to press] *vt* **1 a :** to bring pushing or thrusting force to bear on by means of something in direct contact : FORCE, THRUST **:** exert steady pressure on ⟨found that if a telegraph key was ~*ed* down hard a stronger current ran through the wires —Roger Burlingame⟩ **b :** to torture or put to death by the press **2 a :** to make a hostile assault on : ASSAIL, BESET, HARASS ⟨enemy forces ~*ed* the town hard on all sides⟩ ⟨single lions, past their prime . . . become now and then the quarry of a pack hard ~*ed* by hunger —James Stevenson-Hamilton⟩ **b :** to reduce to misery or distress : AFFLICT, OPPRESS ⟨the bondslaves of our day, whom dirt and danger ~ —Rudyard Kipling⟩ **c :** to weigh upon (as mind or body) so as to cause distress or pain : DEPRESS **3 a :** to squeeze out the juice or contents of : EXPRESS ⟨~ grapes⟩ **b :** to squeeze with apparatus or instruments to a desired density, smoothness, or shape **c :** to compact (as paper or bound or unbound books) in a press **4 a :** to exert influence on : CONSTRAIN, URGE ⟨my host ~*ed* me to drink —Allen Upward⟩ ⟨came from the dance for a few minutes to ~ his friend to join it —Jane Austen⟩ **b :** to importune urgently : try hard to persuade : BESEECH, ENTREAT **5 :** to move by means of pressure **6 a :** to inculcate strongly (as an attitude or opinion) : present (a claim) earnestly : EMPHASIZE, STRESS ⟨~*es* upon us similar reflections —G.G. Coulton⟩ **b :** to insist on or request urgently (an act or procedure) ⟨~ a conciliatory approach on him⟩ **7 :** to follow through (a course of action) : PROSECUTE ⟨the bridge trains were ordered to ~ the march at highest possible speed —P.W. Thompson⟩ ⟨must ~ action wherever I can, show people that I mean business when I talk about a flight across the ocean —C.A.Lindbergh b. 1902⟩ **8 :** to clasp in affection or courtesy : EMBRACE ⟨~*ed* the visitor's hand⟩ ⟨~*ed* the well loved woman to him⟩ **9 :** to make or reproduce (a phonograph record) from a matrix ~ *vi* **1 :** to crowd closely against or around someone or something : MASS ⟨hundreds ~*ed* about the performer after the show⟩ **2 :** to force or push one's way (as through a crowd or against obstruction) : strain onward : advance energetically or eagerly **3** *obs* **:** to strive earnestly : ATTEMPT, UNDERTAKE **4 a :** to seek urgently : ARGUE, CONTEND ⟨was now ~*ing* for eight dreadnoughts, rather than six —Virginia Cowles⟩ **b :** to exert effort : apply pressure : WORK ⟨~*ed* aggressively for power development⟩ **5 :** to require promptitude : call for action : create urgency ⟨time ~*es*⟩ ⟨let me know if anything ~*es*⟩ **6 :** to impose a weight or burden : lie heavily ⟨care ~*ed* upon his mind⟩ **7 :** to take or hold a press ⟨a fabric that ~*es* well⟩ **8 :** to hit a golf ball with excessive impact that impairs smoothness and coordination of the stroke

**syn** BEAR, SQUEEZE, CROWD, JAM: PRESS indicates application of pressure; it may apply to weighing down, pushing, thrusting, stamping, driving, or to constraining, compelling, persecuting, promoting, or urging ⟨*pressed* the crowd back⟩ ⟨*press* out the grapes⟩ ⟨he *pressed* the agitated girl into a seat —Thomas Hardy⟩ ⟨determined to *press* the matter —Rose Macaulay⟩ ⟨when *pressed* for details he always closed his eyes —L.C.Douglas⟩ ⟨construction was therefore *pressed* at feverish speed —*Amer. Guide Series: Fla.*⟩ ⟨the Conservatives, fearing for imperial security, *pressed* the Labor government hard —*Collier's Yr. Bk.*⟩ BEAR in the sense here discussed may apply to the application of any pressure or force, often actually or figuratively downward or backward ⟨the weight of the roof *bears* on these pillars⟩ ⟨his debts *bore* heavily on him⟩ ⟨his activity and zeal *bore* down all opposition —T.B.Macaulay⟩ ⟨Clan Alpine's best are backward *borne* —Sir Walter Scott⟩ SQUEEZE applies to pressure on all sides to flatten or crush, to force in pressing into a small circumscribed space, to pressure, to extract, elicit, or compel ⟨*squeeze* an orange⟩ ⟨to make newly joined officers *squeeze* through the narrowest shelves of a dinner wagon —J.S.Bradford⟩ ⟨to *squeeze* more education out of the G. I. bill —Louis Auchincloss⟩ ⟨large scale immigration during the 19th century *squeezed* Negro artisans and laborers out of industry —*Amer. Guide Series: N.J.*⟩ CROWD may indicate forceful pushing, pressing, or packing together of people ⟨never have more startling twists been *crowded* into the concluding scene of a melodrama —John Mason Brown⟩ ⟨I hope not too many try to *crowd* in here at once. It isn't a very big room —John Steinbeck⟩ ⟨at first volunteers *crowded* the recruiting stations, could not be used —Elsie Singmaster⟩ JAM suggests wedging in with great pressure or force, sometimes so that subsequent movement is impossible or difficult ⟨*jam* the shirts into the suitcase⟩ ⟨an upturned boat *jammed* by the current against the timbers —H.G.Wells⟩ ⟨*jammed* in the schoolhouse and standing about fifty deep outside —*Amer. Guide Series: Md.*⟩

— **press one's luck :** to push one's luck

**³press** \"\ *vb* -ED/-ING/-ES [alter. (influenced by ²*press*) of obs. E *prest* to enlist (someone) as a soldier or sailor by giving some pay in advance, fr. E ²*prest*] *vt* **1 :** to force (men) into service esp. in the army or navy : IMPRESS ⟨the cutter is often mentioned . . . with regard to revenue work and law enforcement, in seizing illegal goods, or in ~*ing* men for naval service —H.I.Chapelle⟩ **2 a :** to take by authority (as for public or emergency use) : COMMANDEER ⟨~*ed* a passing car to give chase⟩ **b :** to enlist the help of ⟨~*ed* a passerby into service to warn off traffic⟩ ~ *vi* **:** to impress men as soldiers or sailors

**⁴press** \"\ *n* -ES **1 :** impressment into service esp. in a navy **2** *obs* **:** a warrant for impressing recruits

**⁵press** *adj* [L *pressus*, past part. of *premere* to press — more at ²PRESS] *obs* **:** CONCISE, PRECISE, EXACT

**⁶press** \'pres\ *n* -ES [origin unknown] **:** an East Indian tree shrew (*Tupaia ferruginea*)

**press** *abbr* pressure

**press·able** \'presəbəl\ *adj* **:** capable of being pressed

**press agent** *n* [¹*press* + *agent*] **:** an agent employed by an individual, organization, or group to establish and maintain good public relations through publicity

**press–agent** \'=,==\ *vb* -ED/-ING/-S [*press agent*] *vt* **:** to serve as press agent to : provide publicity for : PUBLICIZE ⟨*press-agented* him as a popular hero —G.F.Milton⟩ ~ *vi* **:** to serve as press agent ⟨was *press-agenting* for several large companies⟩

**press–agent·ry** \'=,===\ *n* **:** the function or activities of press agents : PROMOTION, PUBLICITY ⟨this reputation is not wholly the product of *press-agentry* —Egon Glesinger⟩

**press association** *n* **:** an association of newspapers formed to gather and distribute news to its members — compare NEWS AGENCY

**press bed** *n* **:** a bed that is set wholly within or folds into a press or cupboard with doors

**pressboard** \'=,=\ *n* [¹*press* + *board*; fr. its use in presses for pressing and finishing knit underwear] **1 :** a strong highly glazed board resembling vulcanized fiber **2** [²*press* + *board*] **:** FULLERBOARD **3** [²*press* + *board*] **:** an ironing board; *esp* **:** a small one for sleeves

**press box** *n* **:** a space reserved for reporters (as at a game)

**press brake** *n* **:** a press used to bend metal bars or sheets

**press bureau** *n* **:** a business or a department that acts as a press agent

**press–button** \'=,==\ *n* **:** PUSH BUTTON

**press cake** *n* **:** a cake of compressed substance: as **a :** a filter cake formed in a filter press (as in the manufacture of cane sugar) **b :** an oil cake obtained by expression

**press cloth** *n* [¹*press* + *cloth*] **1 :** a cloth filter usu. of cotton or linen used in a press **2** [²*press* + *cloth*] **:** a cloth to protect a garment from direct contact with an iron in pressing

**press conference** *n* **:** an interview given by a public figure to newsmen by appointment

**press copy** *n* **:** a copy of something written made on a copying press

**press cupboard** *n* **:** a 16th and 17th century cupboard resembling a court cupboard but having drawers or doors below the main shelf

press cupboard

**press drill** *n* **:** an agricultural drill having a press wheel attachment for compacting the soil in the seeded furrows

**pressed** \'prest\ *adj* [ME, fr. past part. of *pressen* to press] **1 :** compacted or molded by pressure : squeezed together or into some form **2** *of food* **:** shaped, molded, or having liquid or juices extracted under pressure ⟨~ duck⟩ ⟨~ meat loaf⟩

**pressed amber** *n* **:** AMBEROID

**pressed brick** *n* **:** bricks subjected to pressure to free them from imperfections of shape and texture before burning

**pressed cheese** *n* **:** a hard cheese (as cheddar) that has been subjected to pressure to remove the whey, to produce physical conditions essential to ripening, and to give it a form convenient for handling

**pressed distillate** *n* **:** the oil left in petroleum refining after the paraffin has been separated from the paraffin distillate by cooling and pressing — compare PRESSED OIL

**pressed glass** *n* **:** glass given its shape in manufacture by being poured under pressure into a mold while still molten or pressed into a mold while still plastic

**pressed oil** *n* **:** an oil (as a vegetable or petroleum oil) from which the easily solidified substances have been removed by cooling and pressing — compare PRESSED DISTILLATE

**pressed steel** *n* **:** steel parts made by shaping steel sheet between dies in a mechanical or hydraulic press

**pressed ware** *n* **:** articles of glass or fired clay formed by pressing

**pressed wax** *n* **:** PRESS WAX

**presse–pâte machine** \'pre¦spät-\ *n* [prob. fr. F *presse-pâte* presse-pâte machine (fr. *presser* to press + *pâte* paste, pulp, fr. LL *pasta* dough, paste) + E *machine* — more at PASTE] **:** either of two machines used in papermaking: **a :** a machine functioning like the wet end of a paper machine **b :** a wet machine for preparing laps of pulp

**press·er** \'presə(r)\ *n* -S **:** one that presses : a worker or apparatus that presses clothing, food, or an article undergoing an industrial process: as **a :** the operator of a press for forming glassware **b :** an operator who shapes pottery or ceramic ware by hand pressing or in a mechanical press **c :** a bindery worker who stacks completed books in a vertical press after the casing-in operation **d :** a device used in spring-needle knitting to close the barb of the needle so as to permit the yarn loop to be withdrawn

**presser bar** *n* **:** a bar to which the presser foot of a sewing machine is attached

**presser foot** *n* **1 :** FOOT 7e **2 :** PRESSER SHOE

**presser shoe** *n* **:** a machine shoe or foot to hold something down (as lumber during dressing)

**presses** *pl of* PRESS, *pres 3d sing of* PRESS

**press figure** *or* **press number** *n* **:** a numeral printed at the foot of a page of some 18th century books perhaps to identify the pressman printing that part of the book — compare SIGNATURE

**press fit** *n* **:** the fit of a shaft driven into a hole slightly smaller than itself and held tight and motionless — compare LOOSE FIT

**press–forge** \'=,=\ *vt* **:** to forge on a forging press — **press forger** *n*

**press forging** *n* **:** a forging produced between dies by pressure (as of a hydraulic press or a drop hammer)

**press gallery** *n* **:** a gallery for the press esp. in a legislative chamber; *also* **:** a group or corps of reporters occupying or eligible to occupy such a gallery ⟨the Washington *press gallery*⟩

**¹press–gang** \'=,=\ *n* [⁴*press* + *gang*] **:** a detachment of men under command of an officer empowered to force men into military or more commonly naval service

**²press–gang** \"\ *vt* **:** to impress by or as if by a press-gang

**¹press·ing** \'presiŋ, -sēŋ\ *n* -S [ME *pressinge*, fr. gerund of *pressen* to press] **1 :** an exertion of pressure or a process using pressure ⟨requires only the ~ of a button⟩ ⟨the ~ of apples for cider⟩ ⟨the ~ of cheese⟩ **2 :** the product of any of numerous mechanical presses: as **a :** a metal part stamped, pierced, or formed in a press ⟨~*s* for many of the most famous names in the British motor-car industry —*Punch*⟩ **b :** a glass or ceramic article formed by forcing a tempered clay mixture or hot glass into a mold **c** (1) **:** a phonograph record made from a matrix by compression or injection molding (2) **:** the whole number of records made at one time ⟨the first ~ of her song⟩

**²pressing** \"\ *adj* [fr. pres. part. of ²*press*] **1 :** urgently important : CRITICAL ⟨the ~ necessity of earning a livelihood —*Amer. Guide Series: R.I.*⟩ ⟨I've more ~ things to think about than girls —C.B.Kelland⟩ ⟨a ~ demand⟩ **2 :** EARNEST, WARM ⟨a ~ invitation⟩ ⟨~ attentions⟩

**syn** PRESSING, URGENT, IMPERATIVE, CRYING, IMPORTUNATE, INSISTENT, EXIGENT, INSTANT can mean, in common, claiming or demanding immediate attention. PRESSING characterizes what makes an unavoidable claim upon one's concern as if pressure were applied ⟨a *pressing* need⟩ ⟨*pressing* problems⟩ URGENT is stronger than PRESSING, suggesting constraint or compulsion of one's attention ⟨his voice was *urgent* and incisive —Elinor Wylie⟩ ⟨an *urgent* seriousness underlay his words —W.H.Wright⟩ ⟨the *urgent* needs of the war —T.B. Costain⟩ ⟨*urgent* expenses⟩ IMPERATIVE puts stress upon the obligatory nature of the task, need, or duty that lays claim to attention ⟨the *imperative* need for a more spacious home —Havelock Ellis⟩ ⟨a remonstrance had become *imperative* —Samuel Butler †1902⟩ ⟨*imperative* orders —Sir Winston Churchill⟩ CRYING puts stress upon the extreme, often shocking, conspicuousness of the thing claiming attention ⟨a *crying* need to make American cities better places in which to live and work —L.E.Cooper⟩ ⟨a *crying* scandal of the times —J.T. Farrell⟩ ⟨*crying* disproportion between ambition and accomplishment —W.C.Brownell⟩ IMPORTUNATE stresses pertinacity in demanding, often to the point of annoyance or nagging ⟨a thick fringe of *importunate* hangers-on —Claudia Cassidy⟩ ⟨the troublesome and *importunate* monk —H.T.Buckle⟩ ⟨hundreds of *importunate* requests to submit to the monarch —*Time*⟩ INSISTENT is not as strong as IMPORTUNATE; it implies, however, an insisting or an unremitting claiming on attention ⟨the *insistent* friendliness of sextons —Robert Lynd⟩ ⟨the clamor of his *insistent* admirers —Saxe Commins⟩ ⟨*insistent* problems⟩ EXIGENT is close to URGENT or PRESSING but implies more an imperative demand for action than a claim upon attention ⟨outlasting the adverse circumstance, however *exigent* and oppressive —*Times Lit. Supp.*⟩ ⟨*exigent* foreign diplomats —Janet Flanner⟩ ⟨the *exigent* demands of war —Allan Nevins⟩ INSTANT is an older form in general interchangeable with INSISTENT, or esp. URGENT or IMPORTUNATE, but sometimes suggesting perseverance ⟨was *instant* that I should continue at Oxford —A.T.Quiller-Couch⟩ ⟨the *instant* need —John Buchan⟩ ⟨down the other side of High Street he walked, his eyes *instant* for suggestion and opportunity —Arthur Morrison⟩ ⟨they would teach in Sunday schools, and be *instant*, in season and out of season, in imparting spiritual instruction —Samuel Butler †1902⟩

**pressing board** *n* **:** a hardwood often metal-edged board placed between layers of bound books or between unbound sections during pressing

**pressing iron** *n* **:** IRON 2b

**press·ing·ly** *adv* **:** in an urgent or pressing manner

**press·ing·ness** *n* -ES **:** the quality or state of being pressing : URGENCY

**pres·sion** \'preshən\ *n* -S [L *pression-*, *pressio*, fr. *pressus* (past part. of *premere* to press) + *-ion-*, *-io* -ion — more at PRESS] **:** PRESSING, PRESSURE

**pres·si·ros·tral** \¦presə¦rästrəl\ *adj* [NL *Pressirostres* + E *-al*] **:** of or relating to the Pressirostres

**pres·si·ros·tres** \,==ˈrä,strēz\ *n pl*, *cap* [NL, fr. *pressi-* (fr. L *pressus*, past part. of *premere* to press) + *-rostres* (fr. L *rostrum* beak) — more at ROSTRUM] *in former classifications* **:** a group of birds having a narrow compressed bill

**pres·sive** \'presiv\ *adj* [obs. F *pressif* urgent, fr. MF, fr. *presser* to press + *-if* -ive] *archaic* **:** marked by pressure, urgency, or oppressiveness

**press juice** *n* **:** a liquid obtained by pressing ⟨*press juice* of potatoes⟩

**pressly** *adv* [⁵*press* + *-ly*] *obs* **:** EXACTLY

**press·man** \'presmən\ *n*, *pl* **pressmen 1 :** the operator of a press; *esp* **:** the operator of a printing press **2** *Brit* **:** NEWSPAPERMAN ⟨he'd fight off all the other *pressmen* —Ngaio Marsh⟩

**pressmark** \'=,=\ *n* [¹*press* (closet) + *mark*] *chiefly Brit* **:** a character or combination of characters assigned to a book to indicate its physical location (as room, case, shelf) in a library — compare CALL NUMBER

**pressmaster** *n*, *obs* **:** the officer commanding a press-gang

**press mold** *n* **:** a cast-iron mold used in glassmaking

**press money** *n* [by alter.] **:** PREST MONEY

**press–off** \'=,=\ *n* -S [fr. the phrase *press off*, fr. ²*press* + *off*] **1 :** the jumping of machine-knitted stitches from the needles (as when yarn breaks) **2 :** defective material (as an uncompleted stocking) formed by a press-off

**press of sail** *or* **press of canvas :** a greater spread of sail than a ship usu. carries in the breeze prevailing

**pres·sor** \'presə(r)\ *adj* [LL, one that presses, fr. L *pressus* (past part. of *premere* to press) + *-or*] **:** raising or tending to raise blood pressure ⟨~ substances⟩ : involving or producing an effect of vasoconstriction ⟨~ reflexes⟩ ⟨a ~ action⟩

**pres·so·receptor** \¦presō+\ *n* [ISV *presso-* (fr. L *pressura* pressure) + *receptor*] **:** a proprioceptor that responds to alteration of blood pressure

**press peach** *n*, *chiefly Midland* **:** CLINGSTONE

**press point** *n* **:** POINT 6d(1)

**press proof** *n* **1 :** the last proof submitted before a printing order is sent to press **2 :** a proof made on a printing press that is usu. the press on which the job is to be printed to show general appearance, margins, and color **3 :** REPRO PROOF

**press reader** *n* **:** a proofreader who reads press proofs

**press release** *n* **:** HANDOUT 1c

**press roll** *n* **:** a live roll that presses and holds moving lumber against the roll which feeds it into a planer or other machine

**pressroom** \'=,=\ *n* -S **:** a room in a printing plant containing the printing presses

**pressrun** \'=,=\ *n* -S **:** a continuous operation of a printing press producing a specified number of copies; *also* **:** the number of copies so printed ⟨a ~ of 1000⟩

**press sheet** *n* **1 :** CLIPSHEET **2 :** a sheet as printed during a pressrun and before folding

**press–stud** \'=,=\ *n*, *chiefly Brit* **:** SNAP FASTENER

**pres·sur·al** \'preshərəl\ *adj* **:** of, relating to, or caused by pressure ⟨a ~ tide⟩

**¹pres·sure** \'preshə(r)\ *n* -S [in sense 1, fr. ME, fr. LL *pressura*, fr. L, action of pressing, pressure, fr. *pressus* (past part. of *premere* to press) + *-ura* -ure; in other senses, fr. L *pressura* — more at PRESS] **1 a :** the burden of physical or mental distress : the oppression of adversity, grief, illness, or trouble **b :** the constraint of circumstance : the weight of social or economic imposition ⟨the ~ of poverty⟩ ⟨financial ~⟩ **c :** the operation of a factor urging toward commitment or decision ⟨the ~ of community disapproval⟩ **2 :** the application of force to something by something else in direct contact with it : COMPRESSION, PUSHING, SQUEEZING ⟨felt the quick ~ of her companion's hand⟩ **3** *archaic* **:** a mark impressed on something : IMAGE, STAMP ⟨from the table of my memory I'll wipe away all trivial fond records . . . all forms, all ~*s* past that youth and observation copied there —Shak.⟩ **4 a :** the action of a force against some opposing force : a force in the nature of a thrust distributed over a surface **b :** the force or thrust exerted over a surface divided by the area of the surface **c :** ELECTROMOTIVE FORCE **5 :** the stress or urgency of matters demanding attention : EXACTION, EXIGENCY, OBLIGATION ⟨the ~ of affairs⟩ ⟨the ~ of a family's necessities⟩ **6 :** a factor that tends to reduce a wild animal population; *esp* **:** any such factor arising from human activity ⟨hunting ~⟩ ⟨population ~*s*⟩ **7 :** ATMOSPHERIC PRESSURE **8 :** a touch sensation aroused by moderate compression of the skin — distinguished from *contact* and *pain* **syn** see STRESS

**²pressure** \"\ *vt* **pressured; pressured; pressuring** \-sh(ə)riŋ\ **pressures 1 :** to apply pressure to : bring influence to bear on : CONSTRAIN ⟨several advertisers . . . have *pressured* business papers —C.B.Larrabee⟩ **2 :** to increase or intensify pressure in : PRESSURIZE ⟨pressurized cabins are *pressured* at about 5000 feet —G.A.Smathers⟩ **3 :** to cook in a pressure cooker ⟨a box of beef or mutton bones, *pressured* until the marrow is extracted, makes excellent broth —*All-Pets Mag.*⟩

**pressure accumulator** *n* **:** a tank for storing air or gas under pressure or for absorbing the pulses in a hydraulic or pneumatic system

**pressure altimeter** *n* **:** an altimeter using an aneroid to determine altitude by measuring differences in atmospheric pressure — compare ABSOLUTE ALTIMETER

**pressure altitude** *n* **:** the altitude corresponding to a given pressure in a standard atmosphere

**pressure angle** *n* **:** the angle between the line of force and a line at right angles to the center line of two gears at the pitch point

**pressure bandage** *n* **:** PRESSURE DRESSING

**pressure bar** *n* **:** a bar that grips the edge of a metal sheet to prevent buckling or crimping during punching, stamping, or forming on a press

**pressure bottle** *n* **:** a bottle able to withstand pressures greater than atmospheric (as for holding gas under pressure or for conducting chemical digestions under pressure)

**pressure box** *n* **:** an elevated cistern fed by a flume, ditch, or pipe, and supplying water under a head

**pressure cabin** *n* **:** an airplane cabin in which near-normal atmospheric pressure can be maintained by a supercharger during high-altitude flight

**pressure canner** *n* **:** a pressure cooker for use in home canning

**pressure car** *n* **:** a tank car carrying a compressed gas (as butane) just behind a gas-fired locomotive and supplying it with fuel — compare TENDER

**pressure–cook** \'==,kůk\ *vb* [back-formation fr. *pressure cooker*] **:** to cook in a pressure cooker

**pressure cooker** *n* [¹*pressure* + *cooker*] **:** an airtight utensil for quick cooking or preserving of foods by means of superheated steam under pressure — compare AUTOCLAVE

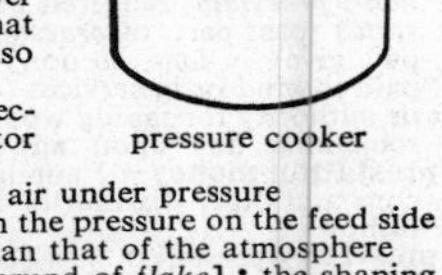

pressure cooker

**pressure distillate** *n* **:** an unrefined distillate remaining after cracking of petroleum under heat and pressure

**pressure dressing** *n* **:** a thick pad of gauze or other material placed over a wound and affixed firmly so that it will exert pressure — called also *compression dressing*

**pressure element** *n* **:** a fluid connection (as between an accumulator and a machine)

**pressure fan** *n* **:** a fan supplying air under pressure

**pressure filter** *n* **:** a filter in which the pressure on the feed side of the filter medium is greater than that of the atmosphere

**pressure flaking** *n* [*flaking* fr. gerund of *flake*] **:** the shaping of a stone implement by pressing off flakes with a pointed stick or bone — compare PERCUSSION FLAKING

**pressure gauge** *n* **:** a gauge for indicating fluid pressure : MANOMETER: as **a :** a gauge on a steam boiler to indicate steam pressure — see BOURDON GAUGE **b :** a device to measure the pressure of an explosive (as when fired in a gun)

**pressure glide** *n* **:** a fencer's attack against an opponent's blade by pressing his own sharply forward and downward toward the opponent's guard

**pressure gradient** *n* **:** the space rate of variation of pressure in a given direction; *specif* **:** such rate of variation in a direction normal to an isobar

**pressure group** *n* **1 :** a minority group seeking to influence legislation in its own interest (as by lobbying or propaganda) ⟨political scientists who tend to think that the *pressure groups* are the highest form of political organization of which Americans are capable —E.E.Schatt-Schneider⟩ **2 :** a group using tactics resembling the tactics of political pressure groups to promote its interests or affect public opinion ⟨*pressure groups* which insist that the high school maintain a winning football team —Paul Woodring⟩

**pressure gun** *n* **:** GREASE GUN 1

**pressure head** *n* **:** HEAD 14

**pressure hull** *n* **:** the inner hull of a submarine designed to withstand pressure when submerged

**pressure ice** *n* **:** ice in rough irregular ridges formed in the arctic seas when large areas of sea ice press against each other

**pressure jump line** *n* **:** a line along which an atmospheric pressure wave produces a sudden increase of pressure that often results in storms

**pressure nozzle** *n* **1** *aeronautics* **:** PITOT-STATIC TUBE **2** *aeronautics* **:** a combination of a venturi tube and either a pitot or a static tube in which each of the two tubes is joined to a differential pressure gauge the scale of which is calibrated to indicate the velocity of airflow

**pressure plate** *n* **:** a plate in an automobile dry disk clutch that is pressed against the flywheel to transmit propulsion torque to the wheels

**pressure point** *n* **:** a region of the body in which the distribution of soft and skeletal parts is such that a static position (as of a part in a cast or of a bedfast person) tends to cause circulatory deficiency and necrosis due to local compression of blood vessels — compare BEDSORE

**pressure ridge** *n* **:** a ridge produced on floating ice by buckling or crushing under lateral pressure of wind or tide or on a congealing lava flow by the continued movement of its liquid interior

**pressures** *pl of* PRESSURE, *pres 3d sing of* PRESSURE

**pressure saucepan** *n* **:** a small pressure cooker

**pressure–sensitive** \ˈ==ˌ=(=)=\ *adj* **:** responsive to pressure **:** adhering or sealing under the influence of pressure alone ⟨*pressure-sensitive* adhesives are normally used in the form of adhesive tapes —V.N.Morris, C.L.Weidner, & N. St. Landau⟩

**pressure shift** *n* **:** a change in the wavelengths of the spectrum lines of a gas that results from compressing the gas and is often accompanied by a broadening of the lines

**pressure sore** *n* **:** BEDSORE

**pressure spot** *n* **:** one of the spots on the skin peculiarly sensitive to pressure — called also *touch spot*

**pressure stage** *n* **:** the stage in the process of expansion and of energy transformation in which steam after expanding through a predetermined pressure range in a steam turbine gives up its acquired kinetic energy to the moving blades without further drop in pressure — compare VELOCITY STAGE

**pressure stop** *n, phonetics* **:** a stop in the formation of which the air behind the articulation is compressed with consequent outrush of air when the articulation is broken — compare SUCTION STOP

**pressure suit** *n* **:** an inflatable suit for high-altitude flying to protect a flier's body from the dangerous effects of low atmospheric pressure

**pressure tank** *n* **:** a tank in which a liquid or gas is stored under pressure greater than atmospheric

**pressure tube** *n* **1 :** a heavy tube containing reagents and hermetically closed so that interaction of the contents can be brought about at a much higher pressure than would be possible in an open tube **2 :** BOURDON TUBE

**pressure vessel** *n* **:** a container (as a tank, boiler, shell, cylinder) subjected in use to disruptive pressure

**pressure wave** *n* **:** a wave (as a sound wave) in which the propagated disturbance is a variation of pressure in a material medium — called also *P-wave*

**pressure welding** *n* **:** welding in which pressure is used to complete the weld

**pressuring** *pres part of* PRESSURE

**pres·sur·iza·tion** \ˌpreshərəˈzāshən\ *n* **-s :** the action or process of pressurizing or the state of being pressurized

**pres·sur·ize** \ˈpreshəˌrīz\ *vt* -ED/-ING/-S **1 :** to maintain near-normal atmospheric pressure in (as an aircraft cabin) during high-level flight by means of a supercharger **2 :** to apply pressure to **3 :** to design (as an airplane fuselage or a flier's inflatable suit) to withstand pressure **4 :** to force gas into (an oil well) to increase the flow of an adjacent well — **pres·sur·iz·er** \-zə(r)\ *n* -s

**press warrant** *n* **:** a warrant formerly given by the crown as authority to impress men into the navy

**press wax** *n* **:** the press cake from honeycombs after removal of the molten beeswax by filtration

**press wheel** *n* **:** a wheel attachment on an agricultural press drill for compacting the soil in the seeded furrows

**presswoman** \ˈ=ˌ==\ *n, pl* **presswomen** *Brit* **:** a woman news reporter or journalist

**presswork** \ˈ=ˌ=\ *n* **:** the operation, management, or product of a printing press; *esp* **:** the branch of printing concerned with the actual transfer of ink from printing surface to paper

[1]**prest** *adj* [ME, fr. OF, fr. L *praestus* ready — more at PRESTO] *obs* **:** READY, PROMPT, QUICK, PREPARED

[2]**prest** \ˈprest\ *n* -s [ME, fr. MF, loan, fr. OF, fr. *prester* to lend, give, fr. L *praestare* to be responsible for, perform, pay, give, fr. *praed-, praes* surety, bondsman (fr. *prae-* pre- + *vad-, vas* bail, security) + *stare* to stand — more at WED, STAND] **1** *obs* **a :** a loan of money; *esp* **:** a forced loan to the sovereign **b :** an advance on wages or on the cost of an undertaking **c :** PREST MONEY **2** *Eng law* **:** a duty formerly paid by the sheriff on his account into the exchequer or for money in his hands

[3]**prest** \"\ *archaic var of* PRESSED

**pre·stab·i·lism** \prēˈstabəˌlizəm\ *n* -s [G *prästabilismus*, fr. *prästabilieren* to preestablish (fr. *prä-* pre- + *stabilieren* to establish, fr. L *stabilire*) + *-ismus* -ism — more at ESTABLISH] **1 :** the Leibnizian doctrine of preestablished harmony of body and mind **2 :** the Kantian view that the living organism embodies an initial tendency implanted by the first cause whereby its kind is reproduced

**pres·ta·ble** \ˈprestəbəl\ *adj* [obs. F, capable of being lent, fr. MF, inclined to grant, fr. *prester* to lend, give + *-able*] *archaic Scot* **:** PAYABLE

**prestamp cover** \ˈprēˌstamp-\ *n* [*prestamp* fr. *pre-* + *stamp*, n.] **:** a philatelic cover of a date previous to the use of adhesive stamps **:** a stampless cover

**pres·tant** \ˈprestənt\ *n* -s [F, fr. L *praestant-, praestans*, pres. part. of *praestare* to be superior, be excellent, fr. *prae-* pre- + *stare* to stand — more at STAND] **:** PRINCIPAL 2g (1)

**pre·state** \prēˈstāt\ *vt* [L *praestatus*, past part. of *praestare* to be responsible for, perform, pay, give — more at PREST] **1** *Roman & civil law* **:** PERFORM **:** furnish pursuant to an obligation **:** UNDERTAKE **2** *Roman & civil law* **:** GUARANTEE, INDEMNIFY **3** *Roman & civil law* **:** to support by oath

**pres·ta·tion** \preˈstāshən\ *n* -s [ME, fr. MF, fr. LL *praestation-, praestatio* required payment, fr. L, warranty, fr. *praestatus* (past part. of *praestare* to be responsible for, perform, pay, give) + *-ion-, -io* -ion] **1** *feudal law* **:** a rent, tax, or due paid in kind or in services (as in return for the lord's warrant or authority for taking wood) **2** *civil law* **:** a performance of something due upon an obligation

**prestation money** *n* **:** annual dues formerly paid by archdeacons and other dignitaries of the Church of England to their bishop

**pres·ter** \ˈprestə(r)\ *n* -s [ME, fr. L, venomous snake, scorching whirlwind, fr. Gk *prēstēr* venomous snake, scorching whirlwind, neck vein swollen with anger, fr. *prēthein* to blow up, swell out, spout, blow into a flame — more at FROTH] **1** *obs* **:** a venomous snake **2** *obs* **:** a scorching whirlwind **3** *archaic* **:** a neck vein swollen with anger

**pre·sternal** \(ˈ)prē+\ *adj* [*presternum* + *-al*] **:** of or relating to the presternum

**pre·sternum** \"+\ *n* [NL, fr. *pre-* + *sternum*] **1 :** the anterior segment of the sternum of a mammal **:** MANUBRIUM **2 :** the first division of the sternum of a thoracic segment of an insect **:** the sclerite in front of the eusternum of the insect thorax

**pres·ti·dig·i·ta·tion** \ˌprestəˌdijəˈtāshən\ *n* -s [F, fr. *prestidigitateur*, after such pairs as F *créateur* creator (fr. OF *creatour*): *création* creation] **:** SLEIGHT OF HAND, LEGERDEMAIN

**pres·ti·dig·i·ta·tor** \ˌ=ˈ=ˈdijəˌtād·ə(r), -ātə-\ *n* -s [F *prestidigitateur*, alter. (influenced by *preste* quick, nimble — fr. MF, fr. OIt *presto* — & by L *digitus* finger) of *prestigiateur*, fr. L *praestigiator* — more at TOE] **:** one skilled in legerdemain **:** a performer of sleight of hand ⟨is a sort of literary ~: he can make something out of nothing, and keep any number of verbal notions in the air simultaneously —F.B.Millett⟩ — **pres·ti·dig·i·ta·to·ri·al** \ˌ=ˈ=ˌdijəd·əˈtōrēəl\ *adj* — **pres·ti·dig·i·ta·tory** \-d·əˌtōrē\ *adj*

**pres·tige** \(ˈ)preˈstēzh *also* -ēj *sometimes* ˈprestij *or* -ˌtēj\ *n* -s [F, fr. LL *praestigium*, irreg. fr. L *praestigiae* (pl.) conjurer's tricks, alter. of (assumed) L *praestrigiae*, fr. L *praestringere* to bind, tie up, blind, fr. *prae-* pre- + *stringere* to draw tight — more at STRAIN] **1** *archaic* **:** a conjurer's trick **:** ILLUSION, DECEPTION **2 :** standing or estimation in the eyes of people **:** weight or credit in general opinion **:** ASCENDANCY, HONOR, INFLUENCE, REPUTATION ⟨the power and ~ of the aristocracy and the landed gentry were unimpaired —Bertrand Russell⟩ ⟨such luster — or ~ or mana — as individual writers possess is usually owed, not to the quality of their work, but to its public acceptance —*Times Lit. Supp.*⟩ **syn** see INFLUENCE

**pres·tig·i·a·tion** \preˌstijēˈāshən\ *n* -s [LL *praestigiatus* (past part. of *praestigiare* to do conjurer's tricks, fr. L *praestigiae*) + E *-ion*] *archaic* **:** the performance of tricks of magic or illusion

**pres·tig·i·a·tor** \ˌ=ˈ==ˌād·ə(r)\ *n* -s [L *praestigiator*, fr. *praestigiae* + *-ator*] *archaic* **:** CONJURER, MAGICIAN

**pres·tig·i·ous** \(ˈ)preˈstijəs\ *adj* [L *praestigiosus* full of tricks, deceitful, fr. *praestigiae* + *-osus* -ose] **1** *archaic* **:** of, relating to, or marked by illusion, conjuring, or trickery **2 :** having an illustrious name or reputation **:** esteemed in general opinion **:** HONORED ⟨the most ~ club in town preserves a tenuous artistic tradition —A.L.Guérard⟩ ⟨the ~ or the desirable things of the earth, craved for by predatory natures —Joseph Conrad⟩ — **pres·tig·i·ous·ly** *adv* — **pres·tig·i·ous·ness** *n* -ES

[1]**pres·tis·si·mo** \preˈstisəˌmō\ *adv (or adj)* [It, fr. *presto* quick + *-issimo*, suffix denoting a high degree (fr. L *-issimus*, superl. suffix)] **:** at a very rapid tempo — used as a direction in music

[2]**prestissimo** \"\ *n* -s **:** a movement or passage performed prestissimo

**prest money** *n* [ME *prest moneye* money paid in advance, fr. [2]*prest* + *moneye* money] *obs* **:** money advanced to men enlisting in the British army or navy **:** IMPREST

[1]**pres·to** \ˈpre(ˌ)stō\ *adv (or adj)* [It, adv. & adj., quickly, quick; It *presto*, adv., fr. L *praesto* at hand, on the spot, fr. *prae-* pre- + *-sto* (perh. akin to L *situs*, past part. of *sinere* to lay, let, leave); It *presto*, adj., fr. L *praestus* ready, fr. *praesto* — more at SITE] **1 :** in haste **:** QUICKLY, IMMEDIATELY — used orig. as a magician's command **2 :** at a rapid tempo — used as a direction in music — compare PRESTISSIMO

[2]**presto** \"\ *n* -s **:** a musical passage or movement in rapid tempo

[1]**presto chan·go** \-ˈchān(ˌ)jō\ *v imper* [[1]*presto* + *chango* (fr. *change* + *-o* — as in [1]*presto*)] **:** change quickly — used orig. as a magician's command

[2]**presto chango** \"\ *n* **:** a sudden transformation as if by magic ⟨suggest that the solution of social and political ills lay in . . . a moral *presto chango* —Irwin Edman⟩

**pre·sto·mal** \prēˈstōməl\ *adj* [*prestomum* + *-al*] **:** of or relating to a prestomum

**pre·sto·mum** \-məm\ *n, pl* **presto·ma** \-ōmə\ *also* **presto·mums** [NL, fr. *pre-* + *-stomum*] **:** the cleft between the labellar lobes in front of the oral aperture in insects

**pres·ton** \ˈprestən\ *adj, usu cap* [fr. *Preston*, Lancashire, England] **:** of or from Preston, Lancashire, England **:** of the kind or style prevalent in Preston

**preston salts** *n* [prob. fr. the name *Preston*] **:** smelling salts consisting of ammonium carbonate in ammonia water with an essential oil

**pre·stress** \(ˈ)prē+\ *vt* [*pre-* + *stress*] **:** to introduce internal stresses into (a building material) to counteract the stresses that will result from applied load (as in incorporating wires or cables under tension in concrete)

**prests** *pl of* PREST

**pre·subiculum** \ˌprē+\ *n* [NL, fr. *pre-* + *subiculum*] **:** the part of the hippocampal convolution lying between the subiculum and the main olfactory region

**pre·sum·able** \prēˈz(y)üməbəl, prə̇ˈ-\ *adj* [F *présumable*, fr. MF *presumable*, fr. *presumer* to presume + *-able*] **:** capable of being presumed **:** acceptable as an assumption **:** credible on its face or without close inquiry **:** PROBABLE

**pre·sum·ably** \-blē, -li\ *adv* **:** by reasonable assumption **:** as a ready supposition **:** PROBABLY

**pre·sume** \-üm\ *vb* -ED/-ING/-S [ME *presumen* to dare, anticipate, suppose, fr. LL & MF; ME *presumen* to dare, fr. LL *praesumere*, fr. L, to anticipate, suppose, take in advance, fr. *prae-* pre- + *sumere* to take, fr. *sub-* + *emere* to buy, obtain; ME *presumen* to anticipate, suppose, fr. MF *presumer*, fr. L *praesumere* — more at REDEEM] *vt* **1 :** to take upon oneself without leave, authority, or warrant **:** undertake rashly **:** DARE ⟨men who *presumed* to guide human thought —R.E.Coker⟩ **2 :** to look confidently forward to **:** ANTICIPATE, EXPECT ⟨the reading public . . . might be *presumed* to know that dynamite and poison have a certain deadly quality —Norman Birkett⟩ **3 :** to accept as true or credible without proof or before inquiry **:** ASSUME, INFER, SUPPOSE ⟨until a man or an organization has been condemned by due process of law he or it must be *presumed* innocent —R.M.Hutchins⟩ **4 :** to raise a presumption of or that **:** take for granted **:** IMPLY ⟨they ~ a fairly high degree of sensitivity and discernment in the reader —Anthony Quinton⟩ **~** *vi* **:** to take a permission or privilege for granted **:** be brash **:** take liberties **:** act presumptuously ⟨ignorance ~*s* where understanding is reticent⟩ **syn** see PRESUPPOSE — **presume on** *or* **presume upon 1 :** to base expectations on **:** rely on ⟨it was unsafe to *presume* too much *on* their fidelity —J.A. Froude⟩ **2 :** to place presumptuous reliance on **:** count on brashly **:** dare excessively on the strength of ⟨*presumed* abominably *on* an all too brief acquaintance⟩

**pre·sumed** \-md\ *adj* **:** ASSUMED, SUPPOSED — **pre·sumed·ly** \-m(ə)dlē\ *adv*

**pre·sum·er** \-mə(r)\ *n* -s **:** one that presumes

**presuming** *adj* **:** PRESUMPTUOUS — **pre·sum·ing·ly** *adv*

**pre·sump·tion** \prēˈzəm(p)shən, prə̇ˈ-\ *n* -s [ME *presumpcioun* presumptuous attitude or conduct, assumption, fr. OF *presumption*, fr. LL *praesumption-, praesumptio* presumptuous attitude or conduct (fr. L) & L *praesumption-, praesumptio* assumption, fr. L *praesumptus* (past part. of *praesumere* to anticipate, suppose, take in advance) + *-ion-, -io* -ion — more at PRESUME] **1 :** presumptuous attitude or conduct **:** the taking of too much on oneself **:** the overstepping of limits of propriety, courtesy, or morality **:** AUDACITY, EFFRONTERY ⟨the two qualities most generally associated with Satan were acuteness of intellect and ~ of Spirit —Irving Kristol⟩ ⟨you know nothing about the . . . law, and yet you have the ~ to attempt to influence me —Kenneth Roberts⟩ **2 a :** an attitude or belief dictated by probability **:** ASSUMPTION ⟨the ~ is on the side of established moral law —J.A.Pike⟩ **b :** the ground, reason, or evidence lending probability to a belief **3** *law* **:** an inference as to the existence of the fact not certainly known from the known or proved existence of some other fact, sometimes operating as evidence, sometimes as a rule of procedure as to who must proceed with evidence on the main issue, or as to who has the burden of proof and sometimes having no effect as evidence, once evidence on the issue is in — distinguished from *fiction*

**presumption of fact** *law* **:** a presumption founded on a previous experience or general knowledge of connection between a known fact and one inferred from it — called also *logical presumption*

**presumption of innocence :** a rebuttable presumption in favor of the defendant in a criminal action imposing on the prosecution the burden of proving him guilty beyond reasonable doubt

**presumption of law :** a presumption (as of innocence) founded on a rule or policy of the law regardless of what the actual fact may be — compare IRREBUTTABLE PRESUMPTION, REBUTTABLE PRESUMPTION

**presumption of survivorship :** the legal presumption in the absence of direct evidence that of two or more persons dying in a common disaster (as a shipwreck) one survived the others because known to be younger, stronger, or otherwise more likely to survive

**pre·sump·tive** \-(p)tiv, -tēv *also* -təv\ *adj* [ML *praesumptivus*, fr. LL, presumptuous, fr. L *praesumptus* (past part. of *praesumere* to anticipate, suppose, take in advance) + *-ivus* -ive] **1 a :** giving grounds for reasonable opinion or belief ⟨~ evidence⟩ ⟨an extremely strong ~ case is made out —J.A. Hobson⟩ **b :** based on probability or presumption ⟨the ~ heir⟩ **2** [prob. fr. LL *praesumptivus*] *archaic* **:** PRESUMPTUOUS **3 :** based on inference **:** APPARENT, PRESUMED ⟨the ~ visit cannot be established as certain⟩ **4 :** of or relating to embryonic cells, tissues, or formed structures of which the normal structural destination can be predicted ⟨ectoderm overlying chordamesoderm is ~ neural tissue⟩

**presumptive evidence** *n* **:** CIRCUMSTANTIAL EVIDENCE

**pre·sump·tive·ly** \-tə̇vlē, -li\ *adv* **:** in a presumptive manner **:** by presumption **:** PRESUMABLY

**pre·sump·tu·ous** \prēˈzəm(p)chəwəs, prə̇ˈ-, -)chəs, -)sh-\ *adj* [ME, fr. MF *presumptueux*, fr. LL *praesumptuosus*, *praesumptiosus*, fr. *praesumptio* presumptuous attitude or conduct + L *-osus* -ose — more at PRESUMPTION] **:** overstepping due bounds (as of propriety in conduct) **:** assuming a prerogative, privilege, or permission without warrant **:** taking liberties **:** manifesting presumption **:** OVERWEENING ⟨enforced the doctor's orders in a way which seemed to him loud and ~ —Glenway Wescott⟩ **syn** see CONFIDENT

**pre·sump·tu·ous·ly** *adv* [ME, fr. *presumptuous* + *-ly*] **:** in a presumptuous manner

**pre·sump·tu·ous·ness** *n* -ES [ME *presumptuousnes*, fr. *presumptuous* + *-nes* -ness] **:** the quality or state of being presumptuous

**pre·supervisory** \(ˌ)prē+\ *adj* [*pre-* + *supervisory*] **:** preparing for or preliminary to supervisory work

**pre·sup·pos·al** \ˌprēsəˈpōzəl\ *n* [*presuppose* + *-al*] *archaic* **:** PRESUPPOSITION

**pre·sup·pose** \-ōz\ *vt* [ME *presupposen*, fr. MF *presupposer*, modif. (influenced by *poser* to put, place) of ML *praesupponere* (perfect stem *praesuppos-*), fr. L *prae-* pre- + ML *supponere* to suppose — more at SUPPOSE] **1 :** to suppose beforehand **:** form an opinion or judgment of in advance **:** EXPECT ⟨~*s* that we are acquainted with the general outline —Daniel George⟩ **2 :** to require as a necessary antecedent condition in logic or fact **:** IMPLY ⟨true amiability ~*s* discernment, tact, a sense for what other people really feel and want —George Santayana⟩ ⟨every act of ours . . . ~*s* a balance of thought, feeling, and will, like a correct attitude for an effective stroke in a game —Joseph Conrad⟩

**syn** PRESUME, ASSUME, POSTULATE, PREMISE, POSIT: PRESUPPOSE indicates a taking for granted of something as true or existent, ranging from hazy, casual, uncritical acceptance or belief to certainty through the requirements of logical causation ⟨Puritanism *presupposed* an intelligent clergy capable of interpreting Scripture —*Amer. Guide Series: Mass.*⟩ ⟨culture, which exists only through man, who is also a social animal, *presupposes* society —A.L.Kroeber⟩ PRESUME may imply that whatever is taken for granted is entitled to belief until disproved; broadly it may imply casual conjecture ⟨everyone charged with a penal offense has the right to be *presumed* innocent until proved guilty —*U.N. Declaration of Human Rights*⟩ ⟨nobody in Baskul had known much about him except that he had arrived from Persia, where it was *presumed* he had something to do with oil —James Hilton⟩ ASSUME indicates arbitrary or deliberate acceptance of something not proved or demonstrated or susceptible of being proved or demonstrated, or acceptance in accord with what evidence is available ⟨there are many laws at present which are inequitable, because, for example, they *assume* a freedom of choice on the part of one party which under existing social circumstances is not there —Norbert Wiener⟩ ⟨if we take the witness at his word and *assume* that he has this fear —B.N.Meltzer⟩ POSTULATE may suggest assumption acknowledged as indemonstrable but accepted as true because indispensable as the basis for some thought series or procedure ⟨the prevailing theological system is one which *postulates* the reality of guidance by a personal god —Aldous Huxley⟩ ⟨in the field of chemistry the nature philosophers *postulated* that electrical forces were responsible for the combination of chemical substances, a theory which enjoyed a considerable following when experimental evidence for the view was later discovered —S.F.Mason⟩ PREMISE indicates laying down a proposition from which an inference can be drawn or stating facts and principles fundamental to an argument ⟨Bentham's hopes for such a "hedonistic" or "felicific calculus" and for a system of legislation and jurisprudence constructed by its use were *premised* on the assumption that pleasures and pains can be compared quantitatively —Lucius Garvin⟩ POSIT may apply to something premised as a truth or declared conviction ⟨St. Thomas *posits* the composition of substance and accident as the objective basis of mathematical abstraction —F.G.Connolly⟩

**pre·sup·po·si·tion** \ˌprēˌsəpəˈzishən\ *n* [MF, fr. ML *praesupposition-, praesuppositio*, fr. *praesuppositus* (past part. of *praesupponere*) + L *-ion-, -io* -ion] **:** an act of presupposing or an assumption made in advance **:** a preliminary supposition **:** POSTULATE

**pre·sup·po·si·tion·less** \-nlə̇s\ *adj* **:** lacking presuppositions

**pre·sup·pres·sion** \ˌprēsəˈpreshən\ *n* [*pre-* + *suppression*] **:** effective work in fire control prior to any actual fire **:** forest fire control activities including both prevention and suppression

**pre·surgical** \(ˈ)prē+\ *adj* [*pre-* + *surgical*] **:** preliminary to surgery ⟨~ procedures⟩

**pre·sylvian** \(ˈ)prē+\ *adj* [*pre-* + *sylvian* (as in *sylvian fissure*)] **:** in front of the lateral fissure of the brain

**pre·systole** \"+\ *n* [NL, fr. *pre-* + *systole*] **:** the interval just preceding cardiac systole — **pre·systolic** \ˌprē+\ *adj*

**pret** *abbr* preterit

**pre·ta** \ˈprād·ə\ *n* -s [Skt, fr. *pra-* before, forward, away + *ita* gone, past part. of *eti* he goes — more at FOR, ISSUE] **1** *Hinduism* **:** a wandering spirit of a dead person who is not at rest **2** *Buddhism* **:** an unresting ghost tortured incessantly by hunger and thirst

**pre·tan** \(ˈ)prē+\ *vt* [*pre-* + *tan*] **:** to tan (leather) prior to the main tanning

**pre·tarsus** \(ˈ)prē+\ *n* [NL, fr. *pre-* + *tarsus*] **:** a terminal outgrowth of the arthropod tarsus **:** DACTYLOPODITE

**pre·taste** \ˈprē+,-\ *n* [*pre-* + *taste*] **:** FORETASTE

**pretaxation** *var of* PRAETAXATION

**pre·technical** \(ˈ)prē+\ *adj* [*pre-* + *technical*] **:** existing prior to technological development

**pre·tectal** \"+\ *adj* [*pre-* + *tectum* + *-al*] **:** situated in front of the tectum; *esp* **:** lying at the junction of the diencephalon and the tectum and being associated with analysis and distribution of visual impulses ⟨~ nucleus of nerve cells⟩ ⟨~ area⟩

**pre·temporal** \"+\ *adj* [NL *pretemporalis*, fr. *pre-* + LL *temporalis* temporal, of the temples]**:** situated in front of the temporal bone

[1]**pre·tend** \prēˈtend, prə̇ˈ-\ *vb* -ED/-ING/-S [ME *pretenden*, fr. L *praetendere* to stretch forth, spread before, bring forward as an excuse, allege, fr. *prae-* pre- + *tendere* to stretch — more at THIN] *vt* **1 a :** to hold out the appearance of being, possessing, or performing **:** PROFESS ⟨does not ~ to be a social scientist —R.G.Ross⟩ **b :** ASSERT, CLAIM ⟨in cheap years, it is ~*ed*, workmen are generally more idle —Adam Smith⟩ **2 a :** to make believe **:** FEIGN, SHAM ⟨~ to be angry⟩ ⟨~*ed* to be deaf⟩ **b :** to hold out, represent, or assert falsely **:** put forward or offer as true or real (something untrue or unreal) **:** show hypocritically or deceitfully ⟨man who ~*s* to be dead so as to evade his creditors and collect on his insurance —P.G. Wodehouse & Guy Bolton⟩ **3 a :** PRESUME, VENTURE ⟨how that vehicle got to Sidney I do not ~ to say —Rachel Henning⟩ **b** *archaic* **:** UNDERTAKE, ATTEMPT ⟨she could not ~ to go into the sea without proper attendants —Tobias Smollett⟩ **c** *archaic* **:** INTEND **4 a** *obs* **:** to hold out before one **:** EXTEND, OFFER **b** *obs* **:** to hold out as a disguise for something else **~** *vi* **1** *obs* **:** to direct one's course or efforts **:** ASPIRE ⟨those persons who ~ toward Heaven —Jeremy Taylor⟩ **2 :** to feign an action, part, or role in or as if in play **:** make believe ⟨never sincere, always ~*ing*⟩ **3 a :** to put in a claim **:** lay claim **:** allege a title — used with *to* ⟨those ~*ing* to office were theorists —C.L.Jones⟩ ⟨for the other sciences . . . I can ~ to no special competence —Stuart Chase⟩ **b** *archaic* **:** to make suit **syn** see ASSUME

[2]**pretend** \"\ *adj* **:** MAKE-BELIEVE, IMAGINARY, PRETENDED ⟨dangle our legs in the water and see who could catch the most ~ fish —H.E.Giles⟩ **:** IMITATION ⟨~ pearls⟩

**pre·tend·ant** \-dənt\ *n* -s [MF, fr. *pretendant*, pres. part. of *pretendre* to claim, aspire, fr. L *praetendere*] **:** PRETENDER, CLAIMANT

**pre·tend·ed** \-də̇d\ *adj* [ME, fr. past part. of *pretenden*] **1 a :** SO-CALLED, ALLEGED ⟨~ neutrality⟩ **b :** professed or avowed but not genuine ⟨~ loyalty⟩ ⟨a ~ friend⟩ **2** *obs* **:** INTENDED, PROPOSED ⟨notice of their . . . ~ flight —Shak.⟩ — **pre·tend·ed·ly** *adv*

**pre·tend·er** \-ndə(r)\ *n* -s **:** one that pretends: as **a :** one who lays claim or asserts a title to something **:** CLAIMANT; *specif* **:** a claimant to a throne who is held to have no just title **b :** one who makes a false or hypocritical show **:** one who simulates or feigns

**pre·tend·er·ism** \-dəˌrizəm\ *n* -s [*pretender* + *-ism*; fr. the use of the term "Old Pretender" as a nickname for James Francis Edward Stuart †1766 claimant to the throne of England by virtue of being the only son of the deposed Stuart king James II, and the use of the term "Young Pretender" as a nickname for Charles Edward Louis Philip Casimir Stuart †1788 claimant to the throne of England by virtue of being the elder son of James Francis Edward Stuart] : support or agitation for the deposed Stuart dynasty in England

**¹pre·tense** *or* **pre·tence** \prē'ten(t)s, prə'-, 'prē,t-\ *n* -s [ME, fr. MF *pretensse*, fr. (assumed) ML *pretensa*, fr. LL, fem. of *praetensus* (L *praetentus*), past part. of L *praetendere*] **1 :** a claim made or implied ⟨theory which has made the . . . greatest ~ of having a scientific foundation —John Dewey⟩; *esp* : a claim indicated outwardly but not supported by fact ⟨the ~ that one does not use theater music in religious ceremonies —Virgil Thomson⟩ **2 a :** mere ostentation : PRETENTIOUSNESS ⟨confuse dignity with pomposity and ~ —Bennett Cerf⟩ **b :** a pretentious act or assertion ⟨it would be a delight to talk without ~ —Louis Bromfield⟩ **3 :** an attempt to attain a certain condition or quality ⟨the people were so overwhelmingly ignorant that democracy could only be a ~ —C.L.Jones⟩ ⟨laboring . . . to keep some ~ of order in San Antonio —Green Peyton⟩ — often used with *at* ⟨without ~ at general inclusiveness —Frank Weitenkampf⟩ **4 a** *obs* : INTENTION, PURPOSE **b :** professed rather than real intention or purpose : COVER, PRETEXT, EXCUSE ⟨felt as though he were there under false ~*s* —Joseph Conrad⟩ ⟨under a ~ of personal devotion to a country in which he was not born —O.S.J. Gogarty⟩ **5 a :** something alleged or believed on slight grounds : an unwarranted assumption ⟨mother's affectionate ~ of his being head of the family —Mary Austin⟩ **b :** MAKE-BELIEVE, FICTION **6 :** the act of offering something false or feigned : presentation of what is deceptive or hypocritical : deception by showing what is unreal and concealing what is real : false show : SIMULATION ⟨made a ~ of searching his pockets for cigarettes⟩ ⟨saw through his ~ of indifference⟩

**²pretense** *or* **pretence** *vt* -ED/-ING/-S [prob. back-formation fr. *pretensed*] *obs* : PRETEND

**pre·tensed** \-st\ *adj* [ME, fr. LL *praetensus* (L *praetentus*) (past part. of L *praetendere*) + ME *-ed*] *archaic* : PRETENDED

**pre·tense·less** \-sləs\ *adj* : not having or making pretenses : STRAIGHTFORWARD, SINCERE

**¹pre·ten·sion** *also* **pre·ten·tion** \prē'tenchən, prə'-\ *n* -s [*pretension* fr. ML *praetension-, praetensio*, fr. LL *praetensus* (L *praetentus*) (past part. of L *praetendere* to stretch forth, spread before, bring forward as an excuse, allege) + L *-ion-, -io* -ion; *pretention* fr. ML *praetention-, praetentio*, fr. L *praetentus* (past part. of *praetendere*) + *-ion-, -io* -ion — more at PRETEND] **1 :** an assertion or declaration whose truth is questioned : an allegation of doubtful value : PRETEXT ⟨this was but an invention and ~ given out by the Spaniards —Francis Bacon⟩ **2 :** a claim or an effort to establish a claim : formal demand for recognition of a title, right, or privilege ⟨~ to the throne⟩ **3 :** a tacit, asserted, or obvious claim, right, or title : claim to attention, consideration, or honor because of real or alleged superiority, merit, or ability ⟨country estate of some ~*s*⟩ ⟨people of ~ to taste and culture⟩ **4 :** ASPIRATION, INTENTION ⟨serious ~*s* as a writer⟩ **5 :** PRETENTIOUSNESS, VANITY ⟨a quality of ~ and pseudoculture about the program that I found distasteful —Philip Hamburger⟩ ⟨the class which has the ~*s* and prejudices and habits of the rich without its money —G.B.Shaw⟩

**²pre·tension** \(')prē+\ *vt* [*pre-* + *tension*] : to prestress (reinforced concrete) by subjecting the steel reinforcement to tension before the concrete hardens

**pre·ten·sion·less** \prē'tenchənləs\ *adj* : lacking pretension : UNPRETENTIOUS

**pre·ten·sive** \prē'ten(t)siv\ *adj* [¹*pretense* + *-ive*] **1 :** having the character of a pretense ⟨~ farming carried on for instruction and experiment⟩ **2 :** PRETENTIOUS

**pre·ten·tious** \prē'tenchəs, prə'-\ *adj* [F *prétentieux*, fr. *prétention* pretension (fr. ML *praetention-, praetentio*) + *-eux* -ous] **1 :** making or possessing claims (as to excellence, superiority, greatness) : OSTENTATIOUS, SHOWY, POMPOUS ⟨~ literary style⟩ ⟨~ country house⟩ : SELF-IMPORTANT ⟨~ fraud who assumes a love of culture that is alien to him —Richard Watts⟩ **2 :** characterized by effort or strain : making demands upon one's skill, ability, or means : AMBITIOUS ⟨the ~ daring of the Green Mountain Boys in crossing the lake —*Amer. Guide Series: Vt.*⟩ — **pre·ten·tious·ly** *adv* — **pre·ten·tious·ness** *n* -ES

**preter** *adj* [by shortening] *obs* : PRETERIT

**preter-** *also* **praeter-** *comb form* [L *praeter* past, by, beyond, fr. L *prae* before — more at FOR] **1 :** past : by ⟨*preterist*⟩ **2 :** beyond the range of : surpassing ⟨*preternormal*⟩

**pre·te·ri·ent** \prē'tirēənt\ *adj* [irreg. fr. L *praetereunt-, praeteriens*, pres. part. of *praeterire* to go by, pass over] : TRANSIENT

**¹pret·er·ist** \'pred·ərəst, -rēd-\ *n* -s [*preter-* + *-ist*] : one who believes the prophecies of the Apocalypse to have been already fulfilled — compare FUTURIST, PRESENTIST

**²preterist** \"\ *adj* : of or relating to the preterists or their views

**¹pret·er·it** *or* **pret·er·ite** \'pred·ərət, -etə-, *usu* -əd.+V\ *adj* [ME *preterit*, fr. MF, fr. L *praeteritus*, past part. of *praeterire* to go by, pass over, fr. *praeter* past, by, beyond + *ire* to go — more at ISSUE] **1** *archaic* : belonging wholly to the past : BYGONE, FORMER **2 :** of, relating to, or constituting a verb tense that indicates action in the past without implication as to duration, continuance, or repetition — **pret·er·it·ness** *or* **preteriteness** *n* -ES

**²preterit** *or* **preterite** \"\ *n* -s **1 :** the preterit tense of a language **2 :** a verb form in the preterit tense

**pre·ter·i·tal** \prē'terad·ᵊl\ *adj* : of or relating to the preterit

**pret·er·i·tion** \,pred·ə'rishən\ *n* -s [LL *praeterition-, praeteritio*, fr. L *praeteritus* (past part. of *praeterire*) + *-ion-, -io* -ion] **1 :** PRETERMISSION 1 **2 :** PARALEIPSIS **3 :** the Calvinistic doctrine that having elected to eternal life such as he chose God passed over the rest leaving them to eternal death — compare REPROBATION b

**¹preterit-present** \'⸗⸗⸗'⸗⸗\ *n* [trans. of NL *praeterito-praesens*] : a preterit-present verb form

**²preterit-present** *or* **preterite-present** \"\ *adj, of a verb* : preterit in form and origin but present in meaning

**pre·ter·la·bent** \,prēd·ə(r)'lābənt\ *adj* [L *praeterlabent-, praeterlabens*, pres. part. of *praeterlabi* to glide by, fr. *praeter* past, by, beyond + *labi* to glide — more at SLEEP] *of a stream* : flowing beside or by

**pre·terminal** \(')prē+\ *adj* [*pre-* + *terminal*] : occurring before death ⟨~ rise of body temperature⟩

**pre·ter·mis·sion** \,prēd·ə(r)'mishən, -ētə(-\ *n* -s [L *praetermission-, praetermissio*, fr. *praetermissus* (past part. of *praetermittere*) + *-ion-, -io* -ion] **1 :** the act or an instance of pretermitting : OMISSION **2 :** PARALEIPSIS **3** *Roman & civil law* : a passing over in silence by a testator of an apparent heir

**pre·ter·mit** \-it, *usu* -id.+V\ *vt* **pretermitted; pretermitted; pretermitting; pretermits** [L *praetermittere* to let pass, omit, overlook, fr. *praeter* past, by, beyond + *mittere* to let go, send — more at SMITE] **1 :** to let pass without mention, notice, or attention : pass by or over : OMIT ⟨~ all personal references in an account⟩ ⟨~ children in a will⟩ **2 :** to leave undone, unsaid, unused : NEGLECT **3 :** break off : INTERRUPT, SUSPEND ⟨if only reparations were temporarily *pretermitted* —R.F.Harrod⟩

**pre·ter·nat·u·ral** \,prēd·ə(r)'nach(ə)rəl, -ētə(r)-\ *adj* [ML *praeternaturalis*, fr. L *praeter naturam* beyond nature (fr. *praeter* past, by, beyond + *naturam*, accus. of *natura* nature) + *-alis* -al] **1 :** existing outside of nature : NONNATURAL; *sometimes* : SUPERNATURAL ⟨thoughts, beliefs, and rituals of mankind . . . ~ origins for these aspects of human activity were still widely postulated —H.J.Fleure⟩ **2 :** exceeding in degree or intensity what is natural or regular in nature : ABNORMAL, EXCEPTIONAL ⟨wits trained to ~ acuteness by the debates of the law courts and the assembly —G.L.Dickinson⟩ ⟨composed her features into an appearance of ~ pleasantness —J.C.Snaith⟩ **3 :** lying beyond or outside ordinary experience : inexplicable by ordinary means ⟨~ phenomena, among which the alleged psychic phenomena are perhaps the most spectacular —Herbert Spiegelberg⟩ ⟨notions that ~ powers and human action were inextricably linked —W.V. O'Connor⟩ — **pre·ter·nat·u·ral·ly** \-rəlē, -li\ *adv* — **pre·ter·nat·u·ral·ness** *n*

**pre·ter·nat·u·ral·ism** \,⸗⸗'nach(ə)rə,lizəm\ *n* **1 :** the quality or state of being preternatural **2 :** something preternatural **3 :** belief in or recognition of the preternatural

**¹pre·test** \'prē,test\ *n* [*pre-* + *test*] : a preliminary test serving for exploration rather than evaluation: as **a :** a test given to a class to determine readiness for the material about to be taught **b :** a test given to make students aware of their own needs and prepare them for a final and decisive test **c :** a field trial of those techniques (as questionnaires, interviews, schedules) commonly used in testing the public in order to determine their efficiency as instruments of research ⟨a ~ of a public opinion poll⟩ **d :** the advance testing of something intended for public sale or intended to influence public taste in order to determine its probable reception ⟨a ~ for a new line of merchandise⟩

**²pre·test** \(')⸗'⸗\ *vt* : to subject to a pretest ~ *vi* : to give a pretest

**¹pre·text** \'prē,tekst\ *n* -s [L *praetextus*, fr. *praetextus*, past part. of *praetexere* to weave in front, fringe, adorn, assign as a pretext, fr. *prae-* pre- + *texere* to weave — more at TECHNICAL] : a purpose or motive alleged or an appearance assumed in order to cloak the real intention or state of affairs : EXCUSE, PRETENSE, COVER **syn** see APOLOGY

**²pretext** \⸗'⸗\ *vt* -ED/-ING/-S : to use or allege as a pretext ⟨~*ing* an early engagement in town next morning —W.S. Maugham⟩

**pretexta** *var of* PRAETEXTA

**pre·thin** \(')prē+\ *vt* [*pre-* + *thin*] : to thin (a heavy set of fruit) by hand or by the use of a caustic or a hormone spray in order to increase the quality of the remaining fruit and to stimulate flower bud production for the following year

**pre·thoracic** \¦prē+\ *adj* [*pre-* + *thoracic*] : situated above or anterior to the thorax; *specif* : lying above or anterior to those vertebrae bearing thoracic ribs ⟨~ vertebrae⟩

**pre·thoughtful** \(')prē+\ *adj* [*pre-* + *thoughtful*] : FORETHOUGHTFUL, PRUDENT — **pre·thought·ful·ly** *adv* — **pre·thought·ful·ness** *n*

**pre·tibial** \(')prē+\ *adj* [ISV *pre-* + *tibial*] : lying or occurring in front of the tibia ⟨a ~ skin rash⟩ ⟨~ edema⟩

**pretibial fever** *n* : a disease characterized by an eruption in the pretibial region, headache, backache, malaise, chills, and fever, and believed to be caused by a virus

**pre·til** \prā'tēl\ *n* -s [AmerSp, fr. Sp, parapet, railing, irreg. fr. L *pector-, pectus* breast — more at PECTORAL] : an adobe wall continued above the roof to form a low parapet

**pre·ti·um af·fec·ti·o·nis** \'pred·ēəm,afektē'ōnəs\ *n, pl* **pretia affectionis** \-d·ēə-\ [L, price of affection] : a factitious value placed upon a thing by its owner because of some sentimental association or a whim

**prêt-nom** \'pre'nōⁿ\ *n, pl* **prêt-noms** \"\ [F *prête-nom*, fr. *prêter* to lend (fr. OF *prester*) + *nom* name, fr. L *nomen* — more at PREST, NAME] *civil law* : one who lends his name to another in the purchase of property

**pre·tone** \'prē,tōn\ *n* [*pre-* + *tone*] : a sound or syllable immediately preceding the accented syllable

**pre·tonic** \(')prē+\ *adj* [ISV *pre-* + *tonic*] **1** *of a sound* : immediately preceding or constituting one of a succession of consonants immediately preceding a vowel having stress **2** *of a syllable* : immediately preceding a syllable having stress

**pre·tophaceous** \¦prē+\ *adj* [*pre-* + *tophaceous*] : existing before the development of tophi ⟨~ stage of gout⟩

**pretor** *var of* PRAETOR

**pre·to·ria** \prē'tōrēə, prə'-, -tȯr-\ *adj, usu cap* [fr. *Pretoria*, Union of So. Africa] : of or from Pretoria, the administrative capital of the Union of So. Africa : of the kind or style prevalent in Pretoria

**pretorial** *var of* PRAETORIAL

**pretorial court** *n* : a proprietary court of the Colony of Maryland with jurisdiction of capital crimes

**pre·treat** \(')prē+\ *vt* [*pre-* + *treat*] : to treat previously ⟨~ water with a coagulant before filtering⟩ — **pre·treat·ment** \prē'trētmənt\ *n*

**pre·trial** \'prē+,-\ *n* [*pre-* + *trial*] : a conference preliminary to a hearing or trial on the merits where a judge, referee, examiner, arbitrator, or other quasi-judicial officer endeavors to simplify the issues of law or fact in a case by ascertaining what is admitted, what is contested, whether certain matters may be stipulated thereby avoiding the expense of proof in order to save time and expense at the trial

**pret·ti·fi·ca·tion** \,prid·əfə'kāshən\ *n* -s [fr. *prettify*, after such pairs as E *ossify*: *ossification*] : the act, process, or result of prettifying ⟨an excess of ~ and sentimentality, a failure to stick to what the composer has written —Howard Taubman⟩

**pret·ti·fi·er** \'prid·ə,fī(ə)r, -itə,-\ *n* -s : one that prettifies

**pret·ti·fy** \-fī\ *vt* -ED/-ING/-ES [*pretty* + *-fy*] **1 :** to make pretty : adorn esp. in a petty or overnice way **2 :** SOFTEN, PALLIATE ⟨accounts of this series of battles have often been *prettified*⟩

**pret·ti·ly** \'prid·ᵊlē, -it\, \ᵊli, \əl-\ *adv* [ME *prattily*, fr. *prety, praty, pratty* pretty + *-ly*] **1 :** in a pretty manner : CHARMINGLY ⟨blushed ~⟩ **2 :** POINTEDLY, APTLY ⟨~ punished by the Gods for my neglect of you —Robert Graves⟩

**pret·ti·ness** \¦ēnəs, ¦in-\ *n* -ES **1 :** the quality or state of being pretty **2 a :** a pretty or prettyish action, thing, characteristic, or remark **b :** a pretty ornament : AFFECTATION

**¹pret·ty** \'prid|ē, |t|, |i *also* 'pūr|, *-R sometimes* 'pu̇l\ *adj* -ER/-EST [ME *prety, praty*, fr. OE *prættig* tricky, fr. *prætt* trick + *-ig* -y; akin to MD *perte* trick, ON *prettr*] **1 a :** marked by or calling for skillful dexterity or artful care and ingenuity esp. in coping with some difficult or complicated matter ⟨the most consummate of ~ hypocrites —Lafcadio Hearn⟩ ⟨keeping up with the elusive dictators of fashion is a ~ game —A.L.Guérard⟩ **b :** extremely fitting or suitable : PAT, APT ⟨as ~ an example . . . as one can find —Oliver La Farge⟩ **2 a :** pleasing by delicacy or grace : superficially appealing rather than impressively or strikingly beautiful ⟨~ verses⟩ ⟨~ little garden⟩ **b :** having conventionally accepted elements (as proportion, shape, color) of beauty ⟨her ~, rather vapid features⟩ **c :** enjoyable for melody, lilt, or suggestion, but not intense, grand, or complex ⟨charming to the wise youth her ~ laughter sounded —George Meredith⟩ **d :** appearing or sounding pleasant or nice : suggesting charm, grace, or delicacy, but lacking strength, force, manliness, purpose, or intensity ⟨young man with a face that was ~ in a chorus-man way —Dashiell Hammett⟩ ⟨stringing ~ words that make no sense —Elizabeth B. Browning⟩ ⟨~ fancies of snow and moonlight —Nathaniel Hawthorne⟩ **3 a** (1) : FINE, GOOD ⟨a ~ bargain on the car being traded in⟩ (2) : POOR, MISERABLE, INDEFENSIBLE — used ironically ⟨a ~ state of affairs⟩ ⟨~ mess you've made of it⟩ ⟨you're a ~ one to talk about language now —Elinor Wylie⟩ **b** *archaic Scot* : strong and brave : STOUT ⟨six to ten ~ men were chosen as town guard —Mairi A. MacDonald⟩ **4 :** moderately large : CONSIDERABLE ⟨has a ~ collection of books —Tobias Smollett⟩ ⟨it may involve a ~ sum —T.B.Costain⟩ ⟨a very ~ profit⟩ ⟨his house cost him a ~ penny⟩ **5** *of weather* : FAIR, MILD, CLEMENT ⟨a ~ day for a picnic⟩ **syn** see BEAUTIFUL

**²pretty** \'pu̇(r)|, 'pri|, ˌpə(r)| *sometimes* 'prů| *or -R* 'pu̇| *before 'near' often* 'prüt *or* 'prit\ *adv* **1 :** in some degree : MODERATELY, CONSIDERABLY, TOLERABLY, RATHER ⟨~ sure of the fact⟩ ⟨~ cold weather⟩ ⟨~ equally matched⟩ ⟨left things ~ much as they were⟩ **2** *chiefly dial* : PRETTILY, FINELY ⟨sang real ~⟩

**³pretty** *pronunc at* ¹*pretty*\ *n* -ES : a pretty person or thing : a pretty one: as **a** *chiefly South and Midland* : TOY **b pretties** *pl* : dainty clothes; *esp* : LINGERIE

**⁴pretty** \"\ *vt* **prettied; prettied; prettying; pretties :** to make pretty : make attractive or agreeable — usu. used with *up* ⟨curtains to ~ up the room⟩ ⟨once carefully tended gardens . . . have been hurriedly *prettied* up —Joseph Wechsberg⟩

**pretty-by-night** \'⸗⸗⸗'⸗\ *n* : FOUR-O'CLOCK 1a

**prettyface** \'⸗⸗,⸗\ *n* **1 :** a Californian herb (*Triteleia ixioides*) sometimes cultivated for its delicate yellow, purple-tinged flowers **2** *Austral* : WHIPTAIL

**pret·ty·ish** \'prid·ēish\ *adj* : rather pretty

**pret·ty·ism** \-ē,izəm\ *n* -s : affectation or prettiness in style or manner; *also* : an instance of such affectation

**pretty nancy** *n, usu cap N* [¹*pretty* + *Nancy* (feminine name)] : LOBEL'S CATCHFLY

**¹pretty-pretty** \¦⸗⸗¦⸗⸗\ *n* [redupl. of ³*pretty*] : a useless ornament : KNICKKNACK

**²pretty-pretty** \"\ *adj* [redupl. of ¹*pretty*] : aiming at prettiness for its own sake : inanely or inappropriately pretty

**pre·tuberculous** *or* **pre·tubercular** \¦prē+\ *adj* [*pre-* + *tubercular* or *tuberculous*] **1 :** preceding the development of lesions definitely identifiable as tuberculous **2 :** likely to develop tuberculosis ⟨undernourished and ~ children⟩

**pre·typify** \(')prē+\ *vt* [*pre-* + *typify*] : to typify earlier : PREFIGURE

**pret·zel** \'pretsəl\ *n* -s [G *brezel*, fr. OHG *brezitella*, fr. (assumed) ML *brachiatellum* (whence It *bracciatello* ring-shaped bun), fr. L *brachiatus* having branches like arms (fr. *brachium* arm + *-atus* -ate) + *-ellum* -el; perh. fr. the likeness in shape to a pair of folded arms — more at BRACE] : a brittle glazed and salted cracker made of a rope of dough typically twisted into a form resembling the letter B

pretzel

**pre·umbonal** \¦prē+\ *adj* [*pre-* + *umbonal*] : situated before the umbones of a bivalve shell

**preux** \'prə\ *adj* [F, fr. OF *prod, prud, prous* good, capable, valiant — more at PROUD] : CHIVALROUS, GALLANT ⟨while one wants on all occasions to do the ~ thing —P.G.Wodehouse⟩

**preux che·va·lier** \-shə,val'yā\ *n* [F] : a gallant knight : chivalrous fighter

**prev** *abbr* previous; previously

**pre·vail** \prē'vāl, prə'-, *esp before pause or consonant* -āəl\ *vi* -ED/-ING/-S [ME *prevailen*, modif. (prob. influenced by ME *vailen* to avail) of L *praevalēre* to be more able, prevail, fr. *prae-* pre- + *valēre* to be strong — more at WIELD, VAIL] **1** *obs* : to grow strong : increase in vigor **2 :** to gain victory by virtue of strength or superiority : win mastery : TRIUMPH — used with *over* or *against* ⟨gates of hell shall not ~ against it —Mt 16:18 (AV)⟩ ⟨the ungodly o'er the just ~*ed* —Robert Burns⟩ **3 :** to be or become effective or effectual : be successful ⟨the temptation to exploit consumers . . . usually ~*s* unless it is curbed —T.W.Arnold⟩ **4 :** to urge one successfully : succeed in persuading or inducing one — used with *on, upon,* or *with* ⟨could not ~ with her to dance with him again —Jane Austen⟩ ⟨she was ~*ed* upon to sing for the company⟩ **5** *obs* : AVAIL ⟨nothing ~*s*, for she is dead —Christopher Marlowe⟩ **6 :** to be or become common or widespread : be frequent : PREDOMINATE ⟨link between obsolete forms of life and those which generally ~ —Thomas Hardy⟩ **7 :** to be or continue in use or fashion : OBTAIN, PERSIST ⟨a custom that still ~*s* among us⟩ ⟨unable to buy at the prices now ~*ing*⟩ **syn** see INDUCE

**pre·vail·ance** \-ālən(t)s\ *n* -s [*prevail* + *-ance*] : PREVALENCE

**prevailing** *adj* **1 :** having superior force or influence : EFFICACIOUS ⟨the ~ doctrine of the age⟩ **2 a :** most frequent ⟨windows facing the ~ wind⟩ **b :** generally current : COMMON ⟨adapted a loose structure of ~ ideas to the needs of his own temperament —M.D.Geismar⟩

**syn** PREVAILING, PREVALENT, RIFE, CURRENT can apply to what is in general or wide circulation or use or what exists generally, especially in a given place or time. PREVAILING applies to what is predominant or widespread beyond others of its kind or class at a time or place indicated, implicit, or assumed to be the present ⟨the *prevailing* point of view among farmers⟩ ⟨the *prevailing* tendency to obliterate the dividing lines between all the arts —J.L.Lowes⟩ ⟨the predominant English taste, the *prevailing* English authority, of his time —H.L.Mencken⟩ ⟨anyone acquainted with the literature of the first decade after the war must have noticed a *prevailing* tone of disgust —C.D.Lewis⟩ PREVALENT applies to what is general or common over a given area at a given time, stressing less than PREVAILING an implicit comparison with other things of the same kind or class ⟨confined by the classical tradition still *prevalent* in their time —Huntington Hartford⟩ ⟨a *prevalent* feature in these compositions was a nursed and petted melancholy —Mark Twain⟩ ⟨this custom is similar to customs *prevalent* in different parts of Europe —K.D.Upadhyaya⟩ ⟨the disease is most *prevalent* in countries where there are large populations of both sheep and dogs —L.K.Whitten⟩ RIFE adds to PREVALENT the idea of great abundance or rapid spread by increase ⟨when cutthroat competition was *rife* in most industries —*Textbooks in Education*⟩ ⟨for slavery of all kinds was *rife* throughout the island —Alan Villiers⟩ ⟨disease was once more *rife* in the herds —*Farmer's Weekly (So. Africa)*⟩ ⟨literary production is *rife* in Puerto Rico —R.M.Lovett⟩ CURRENT applies especially to something that changes with time and implies existence or prevalence at the time specified or understood, chiefly the present ⟨the present vogue of racialism in the West, however, has really little to do with *current* scientific hypotheses —A.J.Toynbee⟩ ⟨caught in the drift of *current* social thinking —C.A. & Mary Beard⟩ ⟨resisted the temptation to use phrases that are merely *current* usage —L.A.Weigle⟩

**pre·vail·ing·ly** *adv* : most frequently : most commonly ⟨how far our researches are preferably individual, as they have ~ been —F.N.Robinson⟩

**pre·vail·ing·ness** *n* -ES : the quality or state of being common, frequent, or predominant

**prevailing westerlies** *n pl* : the average or normal westerly winds of the middle latitudes

**pre·vail·ment** \-lmənt\ *n* -s : power to prevail or dominate : VICTORY

**prev·a·lence** \'prev(ə)lən(t)s\ *also* **prev·a·len·cy** \-nsē, -si\ *n, pl* **prevalences** *also* **prevalencies** [*prevalence* fr. F *prévalence* superiority, fr. LL *praevalentia* greater power, fr. L *praevalent-, praevalens* (pres. part. of *praevalēre* to be more able, prevail) + *-ia* -y; *prevalency* fr. LL *praevalentia*] **1 :** the quality, condition, or fact of being prevalent : frequent occurrence : general or widespread acceptance, usage, or dissemination ⟨the ~ of burglaries⟩ ⟨~ of radios⟩ ⟨~ of rumors⟩ **2 :** the degree to which something (as a disease, an infective agent) is prevalent; *sometimes* : the percent of a population being studied that is affected with a particular disease at a given time

**¹prev·a·lent** \-nt\ *adj* [L *praevalent-, praevalens*, pres. part. of *praevalēre* to be more able, prevail — more at PREVAIL] **1** *archaic* : POWERFUL, POTENT, INFLUENTIAL, EFFICACIOUS **2 :** being in ascendancy : VICTORIOUS, DOMINANT ⟨law schools with a nominal college affiliation . . . became the ~ type —W.C.Mallalieu⟩ **3 :** generally or widely accepted, current, practiced, or favored : generally or extensively existing : WIDESPREAD ⟨places where malaria is ~⟩ **syn** see PREVAILING

**²prevalent** \"\ *n* -s : something prevalent

**prev·a·lent·ly** *adv* : very frequently : most frequently or commonly : PREVAILINGLY

**pre·var·i·cate** \prē'varə,kāt prə'- *also* -ver-, *usu* -ād.+V\ *vb* -ED/-ING/-S [L *praevaricatus*, past part. of *praevaricari* to walk crookedly, collude, fr. *prae-* pre- + *varicare* to straddle, fr. *varicus* having the feet spread apart, fr. *varus* bent, knock-kneed; prob. akin to OE *wōh* crooked, OHG *winkil* corner, *wado* calf of the leg, ON *vōthvi* muscle, Goth *unwāhs* blameless, L *vatius* bowlegged, *vagus* wandering, Skt *vañcati* he goes crooked, *vaṅgati* he limps, and perh. to Skt *ūru* thigh; basic meaning: bending] *vi* **1** *obs* : to swerve from regularity or rectitude : go astray **2 :** to deviate from the truth : speak equivocally or evasively : LIE **3** *law* : to deviate from duty and probity: as **a** *Roman & civil law* (1) : to conceal a crime (2) : to collude with the opposing party to an action in making a sham accusation or defense **b** *Old English law* (1) *of an informer or defendant* : to collude in order to conduct a sham prosecution (2) : to violate a trust secretly ~ *vt* **1** *obs* : TRANSGRESS **2** *obs* : PERVERT **syn** see LIE

**pre·var·i·ca·tion** \⸗,⸗⸗'kāshən\ *n* -s [ME *prevaricacioun* deviation from duty, fr. LL *praevarication-, praevaricatio*, fr. L, collusion, fr. *praevaricatus* (past part. of *praevaricari*) + *-ion-, -io* -ion] **1 :** the act or an instance of prevaricating; *esp* : a perversion of or a deviation from the truth **2 :** a statement that deviates from or perverts the truth; *often* : LIE ⟨the august tribunal of the skies, where no ~*s* shall avail —William Cowper⟩

**pre·var·i·ca·tive** \⸗'⸗⸗,kād·iv, -,kəd·-\ *adj* : tending to prevaricate ⟨~ writers⟩

**pre·var·i·ca·tor** \-ād·ə(r), -ātə-\ *n* -s [L *praevaricator* advocate that acts in collusion with the opposing party, fr. *praevaricatus* (past part. of *praevaricari*) + *-or*] **1** : one who evades or perverts the truth **2** : one guilty of a breach of trust ⟨such ~*s* of tithes were destined to find their part in hell —G.G. Coulton⟩ **3** : one guilty of collusion in a court of law **4** : a master of arts at Cambridge University appointed to deliver a satirical oration at commencement according to a custom abandoned since the 18th century — compare TERRAE FILIUS

**pre·var·i·ca·to·ry** \prēˈvarəkə,tōrē\ *adj* : marked by or given to prevarication ⟨~ answers⟩

**pre·velar** \(ˈ)prē+\ *adj* [*pre-* + *velar*] : articulated against the front half of the soft palate

**pré·ve·nance** \,prāvəˈnäⁿs\ *n* -s [F, fr. *prévenant* (pres. part. of *prévenir* to anticipate, fr. L *praevenire* to precede, anticipate), after such pairs as F *abondant* abundant (fr. MF *abundant*): *abondance* abundance (fr. MF *abundance*)] : attentiveness to or anticipation of others' needs or an instance of such anticipation

**pre·vene** \prēˈvēn\ *vt* -ED/-ING/-S [ME (Sc) *prevenen*, fr. L *praevenire* to precede, anticipate, prevent] **1** *obs* : FORESTALL, PREVENT **2** : to come before : PRECEDE

**pre·ven·ience** \prēˈvēnyən(t)s, -nēən-\ *n* -s [fr. *prevenient*, after such pairs as E *intelligent*: *intelligence*] **1** : PRÉVENANCE **2** : prevenient character or action

**pre·ven·ient** \-yənt\ *adj* [L *praevenient-*, *praeveniens*, pres. part. of *praevenire*] : ANTECEDENT, ANTICIPATORY — **pre·ven·ient·ly** *adv*

**prevenient grace** *n* : divine grace that is said to operate on the human will antecedent to its turning to God

**pre·vent** \prēˈvent, prə̇ˈ-\ *vb* -ED/-ING/-S [ME *preventen*, fr. L *praeventus*, past part. of *praevenire* to precede, anticipate, prevent, fr. *prae-* pre- + *venire* to come — more at COME] *vt* **1 a** *archaic* : to anticipate (as an occasion, an appointed time) by preparation or action : be in readiness for **b** *archaic* : to meet or satisfy (as a question, wish, objection) in advance **c** *archaic* : to act ahead of (another's action) **d** *archaic* : to arrive before : PRECEDE, OUTRUN **2** *archaic* : to predispose to repentance and faith by divine grace **3** : to deprive of power or hope of acting, operating, or succeeding in a purpose : FRUSTRATE, CIRCUMVENT ⟨police officials should not ~ police reporters from obtaining the news —Lou Smyth⟩ **4** : to keep from happening or existing esp. by precautionary measures : hinder the progress, appearance, or fulfillment of : make impossible through advance provisions ⟨one may ~ feeding problems quite as readily as some physical diseases —M.J.E. Senn⟩ ⟨authority . . . and purposefulness of his manner . . . ~ the role becoming a minor one —E.R.Bentley⟩ **5** : to hold or keep back (one about to act) : HINDER, STOP ⟨had to catch his arm to ~ him falling —Claud Cockburn⟩ — often used with *from* ⟨there is nothing to ~ us from going⟩ **6** *obs* : to hasten the coming of (an event) **7** *obs* : to take possession of or occupy in advance ~ *vi* **1** *obs* : to act or come before **2** : to interpose an obstacle ⟨we shall come tomorrow if nothing ~*s*⟩

**syn** ANTICIPATE, FORESTALL: PREVENT implies an advance move or provision that blocks the occurrence or possible occurrence of something (as a calamity) or the success of something (as a plan) ⟨the surest way to *prevent* aggression is to remain strong enough to overpower and defeat any who might attack —D.L. Lawrence⟩ ⟨medical science knows how to limit these evils and can do much to *prevent* their destructiveness —C.W. Eliot⟩ ⟨we can cure disease or *prevent* it —W.W.Howells⟩ ANTICIPATE stresses more the foreseeing of something that will or may take place in the future than the provision for handling it or acting appropriately in relation to it ⟨one must foresee, *anticipate* and ratify this suggestion, which will inevitably occur —Juan Gris⟩ ⟨my other architectural friends *anticipate* a great outburst of postwar activity and world-planning —E.M. Forster⟩ ⟨she *anticipated* that he would also become more exacting in his demands on her time —G.B.Shaw⟩ FORESTALL can mean to stop something from happening or to intercept and stop something in its course, but more usually stresses not a stopping but a rendering of something ineffective or harmless by forehanded action ⟨property owners own out to the edge of the sidewalk, effectively *forestalling* street widening if they want to —Hal Burton⟩ ⟨to *forestall* every risk and retain every advantage —*New Republic*⟩ ⟨a new warning device to *forestall* surprise attacks by aircraft —I.I.Rabi⟩

**syn** PREVENT, PRECLUDE, OBVIATE, AVERT, and WARD (*off*) can mean to hinder or stop (something that may occur) or, in the case of PREVENT and PRECLUDE, to stop (someone about to act, or someone's action) PREVENT implies an insurmountable obstacle or impediment ⟨measures taken to *prevent* disease⟩ ⟨no war was too serious to *prevent* frequent truces for meals or festivals —R.A.Billington⟩ ⟨by solving it he *prevents* an innocent man going to the gallows —*New Books*⟩ PRECLUDE implies a situation or condition or measures taken that effectively shut out all possibility of a thing's occurring or a person's doing something ⟨provide the mechanism to assure that atomic energy is used for peaceful purposes and *preclude* its use in war —B.M.Baruch⟩ ⟨the brevity of his stay would *preclude* the possibility of his enjoying the school pageant —C.H.Grandgent⟩ ⟨in no way *precludes* them from having a vital and extraordinary power —Montgomery Belgion⟩ Whereas PRECLUDE often suggests the operation of chance, OBVIATE usually implies the use of intelligence or forethought in clearing away (as obstacles) or disposing of (as difficulties) ⟨fruits should be washed in order to *obviate* hazard to the consumer —R.N. Shreve⟩ ⟨by reciprocally extending rights and privileges to one another's citizens . . . they may *obviate* jealousies and promote the general well-being —F.A.Ogg & P.O.Ray⟩ ⟨a single administrator can do much to *obviate* the confusion which still exists in this field —H.S.Truman⟩ AVERT and WARD (*off*) always imply the anticipation and deflection or prevention of an approaching or oncoming evil, usually by immediate and effective measures, AVERT suggesting more active measures to force back, WARD (*off*) implying more defensive measures to avoid or counteract ⟨delegates were sent to a peace conference held at Washington in an effort to *avert* hostilities —*Amer. Guide Series: N.C.*⟩ ⟨men seeking to *avert* a revolution they do not understand with weapons they don't know how to wield —H.J.Laski⟩ ⟨despite the increased chances for respiratory illness during the winter, there are many things you can do to help *ward* this *off* —*advt*⟩ ⟨most of the time he did not feel this, he *warded off* the possibility of feeling it —Marcia Davenport⟩

**pre·vent·abil·i·ty** \prē,ventəˈbiləd·ē, prə̇,-, -ətē, -i\ *n* : the quality or state of being preventable

**pre·vent·able** *also* **pre·vent·ible** \prēˈventəbəl, prə̇ˈ-\ *adj* : capable of being prevented : AVOIDABLE, AVERTIBLE ⟨conscious of ~ human suffering —A.L.Guérard⟩

**pre·vent·ative** \-təd·iv, -ətiv\ *adj or n* [*prevent* + *-ative*] : PREVENTIVE

**pre·vent·er** \-ntə(r)\ *n* -s : one that prevents: as **a** : one that forestalls or anticipates another **b** : PREVENTIVE **c** : an auxiliary rope, stay, bolt, or other contrivance ⟨~ to keep an oar from slipping through the oarlock⟩ **d** *obs* : PROLEPSIS 2b

**preventer plate** *n* : a heavy plate for holding the chains to the side of a large ship

**preventing** *pres part of* PREVENT

**pre·vent·ing·ly** *adv* [*preventing* (pres. part. of *prevent*) + *-ly*] : so as to prevent or hinder

**pre·ven·tion** \prēˈvenchən, prə̇ˈ-\ *n* -s [LL *praevention-*, *praeventio* action of overtaking or anticipating, fr. L *praeventus* (past part. of *praevenire* to precede, anticipate, prevent) + *-ion-*, *-io* -ion — more at PREVENT] **1 a** : the right under canon law of a superior ecclesiastic to claim jurisdiction over or transact a matter excluding an inferior to whom the matter normally would be entrusted **b** *Scots civil law* : the authority of one of a number of judges of concurrent jurisdiction to exercise that jurisdiction with respect to a cause of which he first takes cognizance **2** *obs* : a going before : state of being before : PRECEDENCE **3** *obs* **a** : ANTICIPATION, FORESTALLMENT **b** : PREVENTIVE, PRECAUTION **c** : OBSTACLE **d** : PRESENTIMENT **e** : PREFACE, INTRODUCTION **4** *obs* : PROLEPSIS 2b **5** : the act of preventing or hindering : obstruction or thwarting of action, access, or approach ⟨~ of forest fires⟩ ⟨~ of disease⟩ ⟨~ of war⟩ ⟨~ of cruelty to animals⟩ ⟨slum ~⟩ **6** *obs* : PREJUDICE, PREPOSSESSION

**pre·ven·tion·al** \-chənᵊl\ *adj* **1** *obs* : PRECEDING **2** : PREVENTIVE

**pre·ven·tion·ism** \-chə,nizəm\ *n* -s : a policy of prevention (as of war, fire, disease)

**pre·ven·tion·ist** \-ˌnəst\ *n* -s : one expert in or favoring or employing preventive measures

¹**pre·ven·tive** \prēˈventiv, prə̇ˈ-,-tēv *also* -təv\ *n* -s [*prevent* + *-ive*, n. suffix] : something that prevents or is preventive; *specif* : something taken to prevent disease : PROPHYLACTIC

²**preventive** \"\ *adj* [*prevent* + *-ive*, adj. suffix] **1** : making or aiming to make unlikely or impossible : devoted to or concerned with prevention : PRECAUTIONARY ⟨a ~ measure against rats⟩ ⟨~ steps against soil erosion⟩ ⟨~ penology⟩ **2** : undertaken in order to forestall or ward off hostile action ⟨~ war⟩ ⟨knock out the enemy air force with a quick ~ thrust⟩ — **pre·ven·tive·ly** \-tə̇vlē, -li\ *adv* — **pre·ven·tive·ness** \-tivnə̇s, -tēv- *also* -təv-\ *n* -ES

**preventive detention** *n, Eng law* : a sentence passed on a persistent offender under the Criminal Justice Act of 1948 in order to protect the public and to administer medical or psychiatric treatment or corrective training to the offender

**preventive law** *n* : a branch of law that endeavors to minimize the risk of litigation or to secure more certainty as to legal rights and duties

**preventive medicine** *n* : a branch of medical science dealing with methods (as vaccination) of preventing the occurrence of disease : PROPHYLAXIS

**pre·ven·tor** \-ntə(r)\ *Brit var of* PREVENTER

**pre·ven·to·ri·um** \,prēvən·ˈtōrēəm\ *n, pl* **prevento·ria** \-ōrēə\ *also* **preventoriums** [*prevent* + *-orium*] : an establishment where persons (as children) liable to develop disease (as tuberculosis) receive preventive care and treatment

**prevents** *pres 3d sing of* PREVENT

**pre·verb** \ˈprē+,-\ *n* [ISV *pre-* + *verb*] : a prefix or particle occurring before a verb base (as *be-* in *become*)

**pre·verbal** \(ˈ)prē+\ *adj* [*pre-* + *verbal*] **1** : occurring before the verb ⟨~ position of a preposition⟩ **2** : existing or occurring before speech ⟨~ stage of random articulation in infants —F.H.Allport⟩

**pre·vernal** \"+\ *adj* [*pre-* + *vernal*] **1** : early flowering or leafing — used of plants that unfold their leaves or flowers before the rest of the plants in their locality **2** : of or relating to the end of winter and the beginning of spring : occurring early in the growing season ⟨~ activity of a ground spider⟩ ⟨~ group of migratory birds⟩

**pre·vertebrate** \ˈprē+,-\ *n* [*pre-* + *vertebrate*] : a hypothetical ancestral form preceding the vertebrates

**pre·vesical** \(ˈ)prē+\ *adj* [*pre-* + *vesical*] : situated in front of a bladder and esp. the urinary bladder

¹**pre·view** \ˈprē,vyü\ *vt* [*pre-* + *view*] **1** : to see beforehand; *specif* : to view or to show in advance of public presentation **2** : to give an overall presentation of (a subject of study) before beginning systematic instruction

²**preview** *n* **1** : a view of a performance or exhibition before it is open to the public : a showing or viewing of a motion picture before it is released for commercial exhibition **2** *also* **pre·vue** \"\ *n* -s [*prevue* alter. (prob. influenced by *revue*) of *preview*] : a showing of snatches from a motion picture advertised for appearance in the near future **3** : a statement giving advance information : FORETASTE, GLIMPSE **4** : a general survey of a new subject given by a teacher before beginning systematic instruction **5** : a radio or television program rehearsal

**pre·villous** \(ˈ)prē+\ *adj* [*pre-* + *villous*] : occurring before the formation of villi ⟨an embryo in the ~ stage⟩ : not yet having villi ⟨a ~ human embryo⟩

¹**pre·vi·ous** \ˈprēvēəs\ *adj* [L *praevius* going before, leading the way, fr. *prae-* pre- + *via* way — more at VIA] **1 a** : going or existing before in time : EARLIER ⟨reverted to his ~ position⟩ **b** : preceding in spatial order ⟨shown in the photograph on the ~ page —Bernard DeVoto⟩ **c** : ANTECEDENT, PRIOR — used with *to* ⟨the period just ~ to the war⟩ **2** : acting too soon : IMPATIENT, HASTY, PREMATURE ⟨it turned out that our condemnation of him had been a little ~⟩ ⟨grew ~ and stuck my hand in there just when the wheel was moving forward —*Inland Printer*⟩

²**previous** \"\ *adv* : PREVIOUSLY — usu. used with *to* ⟨~ to this meeting . . . booksellers have been calling attention —*Publisher's Weekly*⟩

**previous examination** *n* : the first examination taken by a candidate for the B. A. degree at Cambridge University — compare INTERMEDIATE 2c, RESPONSION

**pre·vi·ous·ly** *adv* **1** : BEFOREHAND, HITHERTO, ANTECEDENTLY ⟨had served ~ in the army⟩ ⟨entered the country two years ~⟩ ⟨better than any solution ~ devised⟩ ⟨his own ~ unquestioned first principle —M.R.Cohen⟩ **2** : too soon : HASTILY, PREMATURELY

**pre·vi·ous·ness** *n* -ES **1** : ANTECEDENCE, PRIORITY **2** : undue haste : IMPATIENCE

**previous question** *n* : a parliamentary motion to put the main issue to an immediate vote without further debate or proposal of new amendments that if lost has the effect in English practice of postponing consideration of the issue until it may again be introduced and in American practice of keeping the issue before the body as if the motion had not been made

**pre·vise** \prēˈvīz, prə̇ˈ-\ *vt* -ED/-ING/-S [L *praevisus*, past part. of *praevidēre*] **1** : FORESEE **2** : to inform beforehand : WARN

**pre·vis·i·bil·i·ty** \prē,vizəˈbiləd·ē\ *n* : FORESEEABILITY, PREDICTABILITY

**pre·vis·ible** \prēˈvizəbəl\ *adj* [*previse* + *-able*] : capable of being foreseen or predicted — **pre·vis·ibly** \-blē\ *adv*

¹**pre·vi·sion** \prēˈvizhən, prə̇ˈ-\ *n* [LL *praevision-*, *praevisio*, fr. L *praevisus* (past part. of *praevidēre* to foresee, fr. *prae-* pre- + *vidēre* to see) + *-ion-*, *-io* -ion — more at WIT] **1** : FORESIGHT, FOREKNOWLEDGE, PRESCIENCE ⟨over a limited period, which is . . . as far as human ~ can go —M.R.Cohen⟩ **2** : PROGNOSTICATION, FORECAST ⟨taken aback to find in her glance an equal ~ of dislike —Clemence Dane⟩

²**prevision** \"\ *vt* **previsioned; previsioned; previsioning** \-zh(ə)niŋ\ **previsions 1** : to give or endow with prevision ⟨all who have been ~*ed* by suffering —Thomas Hardy⟩ **2** : FORESEE ⟨~*ed* herself in a position where she could repay slurs —S.H.Adams⟩

**pre·vi·sion·al** \-zhənᵊl, -zhnəl\ *adj* : marked by prevision

**pre·vi·sion·ary** \-zhə,nerē\ *adj* : PREVISIONAL ⟨collections of apparently ~ experiences, largely consisting of dreams —J.B. Rhine⟩

**pre·vocalic** \¦prē+\ *adj* [ISV *pre-* + *vocalic*] : immediately preceding a vowel : ANTEVOCALIC

**pre·vocational** \"+\ *adj* [*pre-* + *vocational*] : given or required before admission to a vocational school ⟨~ courses⟩

**prevomer** *n* [NL, fr. *pre-* + *vomer*] : the vomer of a nonmammalian vertebrate — **prevomerine** *adj*

**prevue** *var of* PREVIEW

¹**pre·war** \(ˈ)prē+\ *adj* [*pre-* + *war*, n.] : occurring or existing before a war (as the Civil War, World War I, World War II) ⟨~ levels of industrial production⟩

²**prewar** \"\ *adv* : in a prewar period or era ⟨more people can afford autos than ~ —*Time*⟩

**pre·warn** \"+\ *vt* [*pre-* + *warn*] : FOREWARN

**pre·welt method** \ˈprē¦welt-\ *n* [*prewelt* fr. *pre-* + *welt*, v.] : shoe construction used chiefly in infants' and children's shoes in which the welt is sewn to the lasting edge of the upper by means of a chainstitch seam and the outsole is attached to the welt with a lockstitch seam

**pre·wrap** \(ˈ)prē+\ *vt* [*pre-* + *wrap*] : to wrap (a manufactured article) before sale

**prexy** \ˈpreksē, -si\ *also* **prex** \-ks\ *n* -ES [*prexy* fr. *prex* + *-y*; *prex* by shortening & alter. fr. *president*] *slang* : PRESIDENT — used chiefly of a college president

¹**prey** \ˈprā\ *n* -s [ME *preye*, fr. OF *preie*, fr. L *praeda*; akin to L *prehendere* to grasp, seize — more at PREHENSILE] **1** *archaic* : something taken or got by violence (as in war) : SPOIL, BOOTY, PLUNDER **2 a** : an animal that is or may be seized by another to be devoured **b** : a person or thing helpless or unable to resist injurious attack ⟨ill fares the land, to hastening ills a ~ —Oliver Goldsmith⟩ ⟨fell a ~ to doubts⟩ **3 a** *archaic* : the act of plundering **b** : the act or habit of seizing animals to devour

**syn** see VICTIM

²**prey** \"\ *vb* **preyed; preyed; preying; preys** [ME *preyen*, fr. OF *preier*, fr. L *praedari* to plunder, prey, fr. *praeda*] *vi* **1** : to make raids for the sake of booty : commit depredations — used with *on*, *upon* ⟨pirates ~ upon the coastal shipping⟩ **2 a** : to seize and devour prey ⟨cats ~ upon robins⟩ **b** : to commit violence or robbery or fraud ⟨gamblers and confidence men, who ~*ed* upon the construction workers —*Amer. Guide Series: Ark.*⟩ **3** : to have an injurious, destructive, or wasting effect ⟨grief ~*ed* on his mind⟩ ~ *vt* **1** *obs* : to take as prey : seize and devour **2** *obs* : PLUNDER, RAVAGE, ROB

**prey·er** \-āə(r)\ *n* -s : one that preys ⟨who had said, ~*s* are preyed upon —Elizabeth Bowen⟩

**preying** *adj* : WASTING, GNAWING ⟨~ anxiety⟩ — **prey·ing·ly** *adv*

**pre·zoea** \¦prē+\ *n, pl* **prezoeae** [NL, fr. *pre-* + *zoea*] : a newly hatched decapod crustacean larva before it sheds the embryonic cuticle — **pre·zoeal** \"+\ *adj*

**pre·zon·al** \(ˈ)prē¦zōnᵊl\ *adj* [*pre-* + *zone* + *-al*] : situated anterior to the pelvic girdle

**pre·zone** \ˈprē,zōn\ *n* [*pre-* + *zone*] : PROZONE

**prf** *abbr* proof

**PRF** *abbr* pulse repetition frequency

**pri-** *comb form* [NL, fr. Gk *priōn* saw — more at PRION-] : saw : resembling a saw ⟨*Pri*acanthus⟩ ⟨*pri*odont⟩

**pri** *abbr* **1** primary **2** prison **3** private

¹**pri·a·can·thid** \¦prīə¦kan(t)thə̇d\ *adj* [NL *Priacanthidae*] : of or relating to the Priacanthidae

²**priacanthid** \"\ *n* -s : a fish of the family Priacanthidae

**pri·a·can·thi·dae** \,=ˈ=thə,dē\ *n pl, cap* [NL, fr. *Priacanthus*, type genus + *-idae*] : a family of small usu. red or rose-colored carnivorous percoid fishes of tropical seas having the body short and covered with rough scales, the eyes large, and the mouth very oblique

**pri·a·can·thus** \-thəs\ *n, cap* [NL, fr. *pri-* + *-acanthus*] : the type genus of the family Priacanthidae including the bigeye of the American coasts

**pri·al** \ˈprīəl\ *n* -s [by alter.] *chiefly dial* : PAIR ROYAL

¹**pri·a·pe·an** \¦prīə¦pēən\ *adj* [L *priapeius* of or relating to Priapus (fr. Gk *priapeios* of Priapus, fr. *Priapos* Priapus, Greco-Roman god of procreation and fertility) + E *-an*] **1** *usu cap* : PRIAPIC **2** *often cap* : of or relating to a priapean

²**priapean** \"\ *n* -s *often cap* [LL *priapeius* (fr. L, of Priapus) + E *-an*; fr. the meter having been used in Roman poems to Priapus] : a verse in classical poetry composed of a glyconic followed by a pherecratic

**pri·ap·ic** \(ˈ)prī¦apik\ *adj* [L *priapus* + E *-ic*] **1** : preoccupied with or employing the phallus symbolically : PHALLIC ⟨~ rites⟩ **2 a** : featuring or stressing the phallus ⟨a ~ statuette⟩ **b** : suggesting a phallus ⟨the ~ golden rocket bursting —William Sansom⟩ **3** : preoccupied with maleness : actively and obviously masculine; *esp* : concerned with male sexual ardor ⟨~ episodes⟩ ⟨~ victories⟩

**pri·a·pism** \ˈprīə,pizəm\ *n* -s [F & LL; F *priapisme*, fr. LL *priapismus*, fr. Gk *priapismos*, fr. *priapizein* to be lewd, to be a Priapus (fr. *Priapos*, Greco-Roman god of procreation and fertility usu. portrayed in sculpture with an erect phallus + *-izein* -ize) + *-ismos* -ism] **1** : an abnormal, more or less persistent, and often painful erection of the penis; *esp* : one caused by disease rather than sexual desire **2** : a phallic figure **3** : a lewd act or display — **pri·a·pis·mic** \¦==ˈpizmik\ *adj*

**pri·a·pi·um** \prīˈāpēəm\ *n, pl* **pria·pia** \-pēə\ [NL, fr. L *priapus* lecher (fr. *Priapus*, god of fertility) + *-ium* (n. suffix)] : PHALLUS

**pri·ap·u·la·cea** \prī,apyəˈlāsh(ē)ə\ *or* **pri·a·pu·li·da** \,prīəˈpyüləd·ə\ [NL, fr. *Priapulus*, genus of marine worms + *-acea* or *-ida*] *syn of* PRIAPULOIDEA

¹**pri·ap·u·lid** \prīˈapyələd\ *adj* [NL *Priapulida*] : of or relating to the Priapuloidea

²**priapulid** \"\ *n* -s : a worm of the group Priapuloidea

**pri·ap·u·loi·dea** \prī,apyəˈlȯidēə\ *n pl, cap* [NL, fr. *Priapulus*, genus of marine worms, fr. *priapus* phallus + *-ulus* -ule) + *-oidea*] : a group of marine worms of obscure position that are classed as a division of Gephyrea and that somewhat resemble the Sipunculoidea from which they are distinguished by the absence of tentacles and usu. by the presence of caudal gills

**pri·a·pus** \prīˈāpəs\ *n, pl* **pria·pi** \-ā,pī\ *or* **priapuses** [NL, fr. L, lecher, fr. *Priapus*, god of fertility, fr. Gk *Priapos*] : PHALLUS

**pri·a·pu·si·an** \¦prīə¦pyüsēən\ *adj, usu cap* [*Priapus* (fr. L) + E *-an*] : of or relating to the worship of the ancient Greek god Priapus

**prib·ble** \ˈpribəl\ *n* -s [alter. (influenced by *bibble-babble*) of *prabble*] *chiefly dial* : a trivial dispute or discussion

¹**price** \ˈprīs\ *n* -s *often attrib* [ME *pris*, fr. OF, fr. L *pretium* price, money, value; akin to Gk *proti* near, toward, to, OSlav *protivŭ* against, toward, Skt *prati* against, back, in return, L *per* through; basic meaning: exchange — more at FARE] **1** *archaic* : genuine and inherent value : WORTH, EXCELLENCE, PRECIOUSNESS ⟨her ~ is far above rubies —Prov 31:10 (AV)⟩ **2 a** : the quantity of one thing that is exchanged or demanded in barter or sale for another : a ratio at which commodities and services are exchanged **b** : the amount of money given or set as the amount to be given as a consideration for the sale of a specified thing ⟨the ~ of wheat is expected to rise⟩ **3** : the terms or consideration for the sake of which something is done or undertaken: as **a** : an amount or gain sufficient to bribe one : something for which one is prepared to sacrifice probity, responsibility, or other quality or duty ⟨not always easy to guess a man's ~⟩ **b** : a sum offered in reward for the apprehension or death of a person ⟨outlaws with ~*s* on their heads⟩ **4** : the cost at which something is obtained ⟨the ~ of liberty is eternal vigilance⟩ or offered ⟨the ~ of peace was more than their spirit could stomach⟩ **5** : ODDS 4b — **at a price** *adv* **1** : through heavy sacrifice : with a great or considerable cost ⟨he won but only *at a price*⟩ **2** : at more than the normal or market price ⟨housing could be obtained *at a price*⟩ — **of price** : having great value or worthiness : PRECIOUS ⟨things *of price*⟩ — **what price** : of what value or use is — used interrogatively ⟨*what price* isolation now⟩ — **without price** : beyond price : PRICELESS

²**price** \"\ *vb* -ED/-ING/-S [ME *prisen* to price, prize — more at PRIZE] *vt* **1** : to set a price on : fix the price of ⟨*pricing* his goods high⟩ **2** *obs* : to rate highly : VALUE **3** *obs* : to pay the price of **4** : to ask the price of ⟨*priced* table linens at several stores **5** : to drive by raising prices to a level at which people refuse to buy or which is too high to meet competition — usu. used with the phrase *out of the market* ⟨*priced* themselves out of the world market⟩ ⟨*priced* coal out of the competitive market⟩ ~ *vi* : to set prices

**price·able** \ˈprīsəbəl\ *adj* : capable of being priced : having a determinable price

**price concession** *n* : CONCESSION 2d

**price current** *n, pl* **prices current** : PRICE LIST — often used in pl.

**price-cutter** \ˈ=,==\ *n* : one that reduces prices esp. to a level designed to cripple competition

**priced** \¦prīst\ *adj* [fr. past part. of ²*price*] : having a price set — often used in combination ⟨high-*priced* goods⟩ ⟨a modestly-*priced* line⟩

**price discrimination** *n* **1** : the offering of similar or identical goods at different prices to different buyers **2** : the setting of a price differential on similar goods that is not based on differences in the cost of production

**price-fixing** \ˈ=,==\ *n* : the process by which prices are set in advance (as by agreement among producers or by governmental edict) rather than by operation of a free market

**price index** *n* **1** *or* **price relative** : a price expressed as a percentage of itself in some arbitrarily chosen base period **2** : the weighted average of a group of price indexes used to indicate changes in the level of prices from one period to another

**price·ite** \ˈprī,sīt\ *n* -s [Thomas *Price* 19th cent. Am. metallurgist + E *-ite*] : a mineral $Ca_4B_{10}O_{19}.7H_2O$(?) occurring as a snow-white massive calcium borate

**price leadership** *n* : leadership by a dominant firm in the determination of prices in an industry with other firms following the pattern established by the leader

**price·less** \ˈprīslə̇s\ *adj* **1 a** : having a value beyond any price : too valuable to be appraised, estimated, or adequately appreciated ⟨the ~ boon of good health⟩ **b** : excessively high-priced ⟨a sale of ~ jewels⟩ **2 a** : of intangible value : having worth in terms of other than market value ⟨such a pair of well-worn comfortable walking shoes is ~⟩ **b** : having no market value : UNSALABLE **3** : surprisingly amusing, odd, or absurd

**syn** see COSTLY

**price·less·ness** *n* -ES : the quality or state of being priceless
**price level** *n* : an average of prices at a particular time relative to that at some other time — compare PRICE INDEX
**price line** *n* : a line of merchandise available at a fixed price under a price-lining system ⟨an excellent $7.95 *price line* of sport shoes⟩
**price lining** *n* : a system of retail merchandising under which a merchant sets up fixed prices for various categories of goods and plans his buying and other expenses so as to be able to supply goods regularly at such prices ⟨*price lining* is esp. practical in stores that employ comparison shoppers⟩
**price list** *n* : a statement or list of the prevailing prices of the merchandise, stocks, specie, bills of exchange, or other matter dealt in issued statedly or occasionally by dealers to their customers and often giving other particulars (as import or export duties and drawbacks)
**pricemaker** \ˈ=,==\ *n* [¹*price* + *maker*] : a determiner of betting odds (as at a racetrack)
**price-mark** \ˈ=,=\ *vt* : to mark the retail price on (merchandise)
**price mechanism** *or* **price system** *n* : a system of price determination and allocation of goods by free market forces
**price of money** : the net rate of interest paid for borrowed money
**pric·er** \ˈprīsə(r)\ *n* -S : one that prices something: as **a** : a person that fixes prices of merchandise; *esp* : an expert that values and sets a price on specialty items (as jewels or antiques) **b** : a shopper that inquires about and compares prices often with little intention of buying **c** : a clerk who marks prices on stock and quotes prices to inquirers
**price range** *n* : the highest and lowest prices recorded within a given time on a market
**price-ring** \ˈ=,=\ *n* : a group (as of producers) acting in concert to fix or control prices
**prices** *pl of* PRICE, *pres 3d sing of* PRICE
**price support** *n* **1** : artificial maintenance of prices (as of a particular raw material) at some predetermined level usu. through government action **2** : an amount paid out in purchases or loans by which a price is maintained
**price tag** *n* **1** : a tag on merchandise showing the price at which it is offered for sale **2** : PRICE, COST ⟨the *price tag* is becoming the most important thing in medicine —Milton Silverman⟩ ⟨the *price tag* on dissent can be awfully high —J.B. Martin⟩
**price war** *n* : a period of intensive industrial or commercial competition characterized by repeated price cutting and designed to cripple or gravely handicap financially insecure competitors
**pricey** \ˈprīsi\ *adj* [¹*price* + *-y*] *Austral* : high in price : charging high prices
**pricier** *comparative of* PRICY
**priciest** *superlative of* PRICY
¹**prick** \ˈprik\ *n* -S [ME *prikke, prik,* fr. OE *prica;* akin to MD *pric, pricke* prick, ON *prik* short stick, point and perh. to ON *pikka* to peck, hack — more at PICK] **1** : a mark or shallow hole made by a pointed instrument : PUNCTURE, POINT, DOT: as **a** : a wound or flaw consisting of such a mark or hole; *esp* : an injury to a horse's hoof resulting from driving a nail into the quick in shoeing **b** : the footprint of a hare **2** : any of various small marks or points resembling a prick made by a pointed instrument: as **a** *archaic* : PUNCTUATION MARK : a diacritical mark **b** *obs* : a minute part or particle : a point in space or time **c** (1) : a mark fixed for shooting with bow and arrow : BULLSEYE, TARGET (2) *obs* : something at which one directs one's aim : OBJECTIVE, INTENT **d** (1) : a note used in medieval music (2) : a dot placed after a note or rest in musical notation **e** *obs* : a mark on the dial of a sundial or clock noting the divisions of time **3** : something that pricks or is capable of making punctures (as a pointed instrument or weapon): as **a** (1) : a sharp projecting organ or part of a plant or animal (as a thorn, prickle, or spine) (2) *obs* : the sting of a bee or other arthropod **b** *obs* : a goad for oxen **c** *obs* : a usu. nonmaterial source of distress or stimulation (as a cause of remorse or vexation or an incentive) **d** *dial chiefly Eng* : SKEWER **e** *obs* : an upright tapering object (as a spire, a tent pole, or the pricket of a candlestick) **4** : an instance of pricking or the sensation of being pricked: as **a** : a nagging or sharp feeling of remorse, regret, or sorrow (as for past deeds or omissions) **b** : a slight sharply localized discomfort ⟨felt only a ~ as the doctor made the injection⟩ **c** : a brief sharp attack : STAB ⟨a ~ of conscience⟩ **5** : PENIS — usu. considered vulgar **6** : a roll of tobacco suitable for carrying on the person **7** *slang* : a disagreeable or contemptible person
²**prick** \"\ *vb* -ED/-ING/-S [ME *prikken, priken,* fr. OE *prician;* akin to MHG *pfrecken* to prick, OE *priccan,* ON *prika;* all fr. the root of E ¹*prick*] *vt* **1** : to pierce slightly with something sharp-pointed : make a puncture in : drive a fine point into ⟨~ holes in paper⟩: as **a** (1) : to wound usu. slightly with a pointed instrument ⟨~*ed* his finger with a pin⟩ (2) : to give a slight piercing wound to ⟨the pin ~*ed* his finger⟩ **b** : to drive a nail into the quick of (a horse) in shoeing **c** : to pierce the skin of (a suspected witch) repeatedly to prove the status by finding spots that fail to bleed **2** : to affect with anguish or grief : sting with or as if with remorse **3 a** : to ride or guide with spurs or a goad **b** : to urge as if with spurs : INCITE, IMPEL — sometimes used with *on* or *off* ⟨my duty ~s me on to utter that —Shak.⟩ **4 a** *archaic* : to write down (music) in notes **b** : to mark, distinguish, or note (as an item in a list) by means of a small mark — sometimes used with *down* ⟨~*s* down each item⟩ **c** : to select (as a candidate) by such pricking **d** : to mark or outline with punctures : trace or form by pricking ⟨~ an embroidery pattern⟩ **5** *dial chiefly Eng* : to adorn the person or dress of esp. by adding some fancy bauble : PRINK — often used with *up* **6** : to search for the tracks of (a hare) : track (a hare) by its footprints **7** *obs* **a** : to make fast or take up on the point of an implement **b** : to fix or insert by the point : thrust or drive (a pointed implement) into something **c** : to fasten with a pointed implement **8 a** *obs* : to bring into a desired position or relation by or as if by pricking **b** : to remove (a young seedling) from the original container to another suitable for further growth — used with *out* or *off* or formerly with *forth* or *in* **9** : to cause to be or stand erect; *esp* : to raise or bend (the ears) into a position for optimum hearing — usu. used with *up* and esp. of a dog or horse **10** : to run a middle seam through (a sail) **11** : to cause (as wine) to undergo an acetic fermentation : spoil by acidifying ~ *vi* **1 a** : to prick something or cause a pricking sensation ⟨how those briers ~*ed*⟩; *also* : to be prickly ⟨short spines that ~ all over the back⟩ **b** (1) : to become punctured (2) : to feel a sharp pain as if from being punctured ⟨the elbow ~*ed* and tingled⟩ (3) : to give rise to such a sensation ⟨a healing wound often ~*s*⟩ **2** : to urge a horse with the spur; *also* : to ride fast : GALLOP ⟨~*ing* through the night⟩ **3** : THRUST — usu. used with *at* ⟨his neglect ~*ed* at his conscience⟩ **4** : to become sharp or acid : spoil by souring — used of beverages (as wine) **5 a** : to point or become directed upward ⟨steeples ~*ing* toward the sky⟩ **b** *of an ear* : to be in a position of attention ⟨the dog's ears ~*ed* up at the sound⟩ **6** *chiefly dial* : PRINK
**syn** see PERFORATE, URGE — **prick up one's ears** : to begin to listen intently or with increased interest
³**prick** \"\ *adj* : standing erect ⟨~ ears are a disqualification for this breed⟩ : erected in a position of attention ⟨a startled horse with sharply ~ ears⟩ : LISTENING ⟨keep your ears ~ for any information we can use⟩
**prick ear** *n* [back-formation fr. *prick-eared*] : an ear carried stiffly erect ⟨*prick ears* are required of most terriers by the breed standards⟩
**prick-eared** \(ˈ)=ˈ=\ *adj* **1** : having erect pointed ears — used esp. of a dog; compare CROP-EARED 2 **2** : having conspicuous ears
**pricked** \ˈprikt\ *adj* [ME *prikked,* fr. past part. of *prikken* to prick] : having pricks: as **a** : POINTED, DOTTED, PUNCTURED **b** *of a game bird* : slightly wounded with shot : WINGED
**pricked-up coat** *n, Brit* : SCRATCH COAT
**prick·er** \ˈprikə(r)\ *n* -S [ME *priker,* fr. *priken* to prick + *-er* — more at PRICK] **1** : one that pricks: as **a** : a rider of horses **b** : a military light horseman **c** : a mounted helper at a hunt : WHIPPER-IN — used in the phrase *yeoman pricker* **d** : one who pricks suspected witches to determine their guilt or innocence **e** : one who uses a prick or pricker in various occupations **2** : something that pricks, is prickly, or is used to prick or puncture something: as **a** : any of various sharp-pointed instruments for pricking holes : AWL; *esp* : a steel spike having the form of a small fid or marlinespike and used for punching eyelets in sailcloth **b** : BRIAR, PRICKLE, THORN **c** : a toothed roller for marking off a uniform dotted line or for pricking holes in tough material (as leather) prior to sewing **d** (1) *Brit* : a pointed bar used by miners esp. for bringing down coal from overhead (2) : ¹SNUFFER 3 **e** : an iron rod for sounding (as in a bog) **f** : CLIMBING IRON **g** : NEEDLE 8b **h** (1) : a founder's vent wire (2) : a pointed projection (as on a covering plate for a loam mold) to hold sand
**prick·et** \ˈprikət, *usu* -əd.+V\ *n* -S [ME *priket,* fr. *prik* prick + *-et* — more at PRICK] **1 a** : a spike or point on which a candle is stuck to hold it upright **b** : a candlestick with such a point **c** *obs* : a candle or taper esp. for use with a pricket holder **2** [prob. so called fr. the straightness of his horns] **a** : a buck in his second year — compare BROCKET **b** : the unbranched horn of a young male deer — called also *dag* **3** *obs* : a pointed finial or small spire

pricket 1b

**prickfoot** \ˈ=,=\ *n* : a low-growing prickly Australasian plant (*Eryngium vesiculosum*)
**prickier** *comparative of* PRICKY
**prickiest** *superlative of* PRICKY
**pricking** *n* -S [ME *priking,* fr. gerund of *priken* to prick] **1** : an act or instance of piercing or puncturing with or as if with a sharp point **2** : the condition or result of being pricked; *esp* : a sharp tingling sensation
**prick·ing·ly** *adv* : in a pricking manner : so as to prick
**pricking-up** \ˌ==ˈ=\ *n* -S : SCRATCH COAT
**pricking wheel** *n* : PRICKER 2c
**prick·ish** \ˈprikish, kēsh\ *adj* : easily irritated
¹**prick·le** \ˈprikəl\ *n* -S [ME *prikle, prikel,* fr. OE *pricle, pricel;* akin to MD *prikel* prickle; all fr. the root of E ¹*prick*] **1** : a little prick : a small sharp point : a fine sharp process or projection (as from the skin of an animal) : a small spine or thorn; *esp* : a sharp pointed emergence arising from the epidermis or bark of a plant **2 a** : a prickling sensation **b prickles** *pl* : a stinging discomfort (as from prickly heat) ⟨decided, with hot ~*s* at the back of his neck, that a girl customer was giggling at him —Sinclair Lewis⟩
²**prickle** \"\ *vb* **prickled; prickled; prickling** \-k(ə)liŋ\ **prickles** *vt* : to prick slightly (as with a prick or prickles); *also* : to produce pricks, prickles, or prickings in ~ *vi* : to pierce, prod, or cause tingling with or as if with a prick or prickles ⟨how those burrs *prickled*⟩
³**prickle** \"\ *n* -S [origin unknown] **1** : a wicker or willow basket orig. for fruit or flowers **2** : a unit of weight that equals the weight of the contents of one prickle and usu. varies about 50 pounds
**prickleback** \ˈ==,=\ *n* [¹*prickle* + *back*] : STICKLEBACK
**prickle cell** *n* : a cell found in the germinal layer of the skin having numerous spines or radiating processes ⟨*prickle-cell* layer⟩
**prickle-cone pine** \ˈ==,=-\ *also* **prickly-cone pine** \ˈ==,=-\ *n* : BISHOP PINE
**prick·led** \ˈprikəld\ *adj* : having prickles
**prickle grass** *n* : a weedy tropical grass (*Tragus racemosus*) with prickly burs introduced into Texas and Arizona
**prickle palm** *var of* PRICKLY POLE
**prick·less** \ˈprikləs\ *adj* **1** : free from prickles ⟨a ~ rose⟩ **2** : not subjected to pricking : UNPRICKED ⟨escape ~ from the briars⟩
**prick·li·ness** \ˈpriklēnəs, -lin-\ *n* -ES : the quality or state of being prickly
**prick·ling** \ˈprik(ə)liŋ, -lēŋ\ *adj* : PRICKLY
**pricklouse** *n* [¹*prick* + *louse*] *obs* : TAILOR
**prick·ly** \ˈpriklē, -li\ *adj* -ER/-EST [¹*prickle* + *-y*] **1 a** : full of sharp points or prickles : covered with prickles ⟨a ~ shrub⟩ **b** : distinguished from related kinds by the presence of prickles **2** : PRICKLING, STINGING ⟨a ~ sensation⟩ **3 a** : containing points likely to give rise to controversy : VEXATIOUS **b** : easily irritated : highly sensitive ⟨his ~ originality and sturdy independence —J.G.Robertson⟩
**prickly apple** *n* : a common West Indian thorny shrub or small tree (*Catesbaea spinosa*) — called also *lily thorn*
**prickly ash** *n* **1 a** : a prickly aromatic shrub or small tree (*Zanthoxylum americanum*) with yellowish flowers appearing with the pinnate leaves **b** : HERCULES'-CLUB 1a **2** *or* **prickly elder** : HERCULES'-CLUB 3 **3** : an Australian tree (*Orites excelsa*) of the family Proteaceae having alternate lanceolate or obovate leaves, slender axillary spikes of flowers, and woody follicles
**pricklyback** \ˈ==,=\ *n* : STICKLEBACK
**prickly beaver** *n* : PORCUPINE
**prickly broom** *n* : FURZE
**prickly bur** *n* : the fruit of a common American chestnut (*Castanea dentata*)
**prickly comfrey** *n* : a rough-leaved European herb (*Symphytum asperum*) with bluish-purple flowers that is adventive in the eastern U.S. and is sometimes used for forage
**prickly fern** *n* : PRICKLY SHIELD FERN
**prickly-fruited** \ˈ==ˈ==\ *adj* : having the fruit covered with prickles or bristles ⟨a *prickly-fruited* cactus⟩
**prickly fungus** *n* : a fungus of the family Hydnaceae
**prickly glasswort** *n* : GLASSWORT 2
**prickly gooseberry** *n* : a wild gooseberry (*Ribes cynosbati*)
**prickly heat** *n* : a miliaria that is a noncontagious cutaneous eruption of red pimples attended with intense itching and tingling, occurring usu. in hot humid weather, and caused by inflammation of the skin around the sweat ducts
**prickly juniper** *n* : an evergreen shrub or small tree (*Juniperus oxycedrus*) with spine-tipped leaves
**prickly lettuce** *n* : a European annual wild lettuce (*Lactuca scariola*) having prickly stems and yellow flower heads and being a troublesome weed in parts of the U. S.
**prickly mimosa** *n* **1** *or* **prickly wattle** : a prickly-stemmed Australian acacia (*Acacia juniperina*) **2** : KANGAROO ACACIA
**prickly moses** *n, Austral* : PRICKLY MIMOSA 1
**prickly nightshade** *n* : BUFFALO BUR
**prickly pear** *n* **1** *also* **prickly-pear cactus** : a flat-jointed cactus of the genus *Opuntia* often used as food for stock **2** : the round, pear-shaped, or barrel-shaped fruit of prickly pear widely used as food esp. in tropical America — see TUNA
**prickly pine** *n* **1** *Austral* : LEOPARD TREE **2 a** : LODGEPOLE PINE **b** : TABLE-MOUNTAIN PINE
**prickly poison** *n* : an Australian poison bush (*Gastrolobium spinosum*)
**prickly pole** *also* **prickly palm** *or* **prickle palm** *n* : a West Indian palm (*Bactris plumeriana*) having a slender trunk with many rings of long black prickles
**prickly poppy** *n* : a plant of the genus *Argemone; esp* : an annual herb (*A. mexicana*) with large yellow flowers
**prickly potato** *n* : BUFFALO BUR
**prickly saltwort** *n* : GLASSWORT 2
**prickly-seeded spinach** \ˌ==ˈ==-\ *n* : SPINACH 1 — compare ROUND-SEEDED SPINACH
**prickly shield fern** *n* : a No. American fern (*Polystichum braunii*) having its almost coriaceous more or less evergreen fronds densely chaffy with pale brown scales
**prickly sida** *n* : INDIAN MALLOW 2
**prickly sow thistle** *n* : an annual European sow thistle (*Sonchus asper*) naturalized in No. America and having clasping spiny-toothed leaves with rounded basal auricles, lemon-yellow flower heads, and 3-nerved achenes
**prickly spruce** *n* : COLORADO SPRUCE
**prickly tang** *n* : a seaweed (*Fucus serratus*) — see ³TANG
**prickly tea tree** *n* : an Australian shrub (*Melaleuca styphelioides*) with pubescent spikes of white flowers
**prickly thatch** *n* : SILVERTOP 2a
**prickly thrift** *n* : a plant of the genus *Acantholimon* having stiff and prickly foliage (esp. *A. glumaceum*)
**prickly yellowwood** *or* **prickly yellow** *n* : any of several chiefly tropical American trees of the genus *Zanthoxylum; esp* : PRICKLY ASH
**prick·mad·am** \ˈprik,madəm\ *n* -S [modif. (influenced by ¹*prick*) of MF *trique-madame*] *dial chiefly Eng* : any of several stonecrops used chiefly in folk medicine as anthelmintics
¹**prickmedainty** \ˈ=(,)=ˈ==\ *adj* [²*prick* + *me* + *dainty*] *chiefly Scot* : affectedly nice : GOODY-GOODY
²**prickmedainty** \"\ *n, chiefly Scot* : an affectedly nice person : FOP
**prick post** *n* : a secondary or side post in a framed structure; *sometimes* : QUEEN POST
**prick punch** *n* : a pointed steel punch used to mark a reference point on metal or to puncture sheet metal for the insertion of rivets or bolts
**prick-punch** \ˈ=,=\ *vt* [*prick punch*] : to mark (as machine work) with a prick punch
**pricks** *pl of* PRICK, *pres 3d sing of* PRICK
**prickseam** \ˈ=,=\ *or* **prix·seam** \"\ *n* [*prickseam* fr. ¹*prick* + *seam; prixseam* alter. of *prickseam*] : a seam stitched on the outside (as of a glove) so that both raw edges show
**prick shooting** *n* : shooting (as an arrow) at a prick
**prick song** *n* [ME *prikked song,* fr. *prikked* pricked (i.e., dotted or written) + *song* — more at PRICKED] **1** *obs* : music that is written down **2 a** : descant as distinguished from the cantus firmus **b** : contrapuntal music
**prickspur** \ˈ=,=\ *n* : an ancient spur with a single point
**prick stitch** *n* : a short backstitch used chiefly on bulky materials and covering only a thread or two on the surface of the fabric
**prick up** *vt* : to apply a scratch coat of plaster to (as a wall)
**prickwood** \ˈ=,=\ *n* **1** : SPINDLE TREE **2** : RED DOGWOOD

prickspur

**pricky** \ˈprikē, -ki\ *adj* -ER/-EST [¹*prick* + *-y*] : PRICKLY
**pricy** \ˈprīsi\ *adj* -ER/-EST [¹*price* + *-y*] *Austral* : LUXURIOUS, EXPENSIVE
¹**pride** \ˈprīd\ *n* -S [ME *pride, prude, prute,* fr. OE *prȳte, prȳde* pride, fr. *prūt, prūd* proud — more at PROUD] **1** : the quality or state of being proud: as **a** (1) : inordinate self-esteem : an unreasonable conceit of superiority (as in talents, beauty, wealth, rank) (2) *usu cap* : such pride personified as one of the deadly sins **b** : a sense of one's own worth and abhorrence of what is beneath or unworthy of oneself : lofty self-respect : a reasonable or justifiable feeling of one's position ⟨a people which takes no ~ in the noble achievements of remote ancestors —T.B.Macaulay⟩ ⟨took a proper ~ in his skill⟩ **c** : a sense of delight or elation arising from some act or possession ⟨parental ~⟩ **2** : proud or disdainful behavior or treatment : insolence or arrogance of demeanor : haughty bearing : DISDAIN ⟨let not the foot of ~ come against me —Ps 36:11 (AV)⟩ **3 a** : inordinate show : ostentatious display : MAGNIFICENCE ⟨~, pomp, and circumstance of glorious war —Shak.⟩ **b** : showy decoration or adornment : magnificent or splendid ornamentation — used of a bird (as a peacock) in full display **c** : highest pitch : elevation reached : LOFTINESS, PRIME ⟨in the ~ of one's life⟩ **4 a** : something of which one is proud or which excites pride : the best in a group or class : PICK ⟨a bold peasantry their country's ~ —Oliver Goldsmith⟩ **b** *obs* : exalted position : place such as may reasonably incite to pride **5 a** *obs* : a sense of power : fullness of animal spirits : METTLE **b** : sexual desire : LUST, HEAT — used chiefly of a female domestic animal **c** *obs* : WANTONNESS, EXCESS, EXTRAVAGANCE, OVERBOLDNESS **6 a** *of lions* : COMPANY **b** : a showy or pretentious group ⟨the queen surrounded by a ~ of gaily dressed ladies⟩ ⟨a pompous ~ of civic notables⟩ **7 prides** *pl, chiefly Midland* : the male genitals
**syn** VANITY, VAINGLORY: PRIDE may be commendatory in indicating a justified self-esteem, proper self-respect, or dislike of falling below one's standards that spurs one on, buoys one up, or checks one from base decisions ⟨civic *pride* that brings them great satisfaction and strengthens their character —J.C. Penney⟩ ⟨this *pride* as an integral feeling of self-respect —J.C. Powys⟩ It may be uncomplimentary in designating an unjustified self-esteem arising from a false, inflated, and pretentious sense of one's worth culminating in arrogant conceit ⟨it is not exactly *pride;* there is no strut or swagger in it though perhaps just a little condescension —John Burroughs⟩ ⟨this race so admirably endowed, with ambitions ever unsatisfied, modeling, in insatiable *pride,* its gods after its own likeness —Agnes Repplier⟩ VANITY indicates an unsound, ill-based false pride and self-glorifying or self-centering with specious concern about trivialities ⟨one of the troubles about *vanity* is that it grows with what it feeds on. The more you are talked about, the more you will wish to be talked about —Bertrand Russell⟩ ⟨her face was intent and fixed upon her image in the mirror; *vanity* had superseded shyness in her innocent mind —Elinor Wylie⟩ VAINGLORY may suggest excessive or meretricious pride flaunted with boastful arrogance ⟨*vainglorie*, rivalries, and earthly heats that spring and sparkle out among us in the jousts —Alfred Tennyson⟩
²**pride** \"\ *vb* -ED/-ING/-S [ME *priden, pruden,* fr. *pride, prude,* n.] *vt* **1** : to indulge (as oneself) in pride : take credit to : rate highly : PLUME ⟨~ herself upon her skill⟩ **2** : to make (as a person) feel proud : infect or fill with pride **3** *obs* **a** : ADORN, GLORIFY **b** *of a bird* : to cause (the feathers) to spread in display ~ *vi* **1** : to be or grow proud — sometimes used with *it* **2** : to pride oneself or take pride in or over something
³**pride** \"\ *n* -S [origin unknown] : SAND PRIDE; *also* : a larval lamprey
**pride·ful** \-fəl\ *adj* [ME *pridefulle,* fr. *pride* + *-fulle* -ful] : full of pride: as **a** : HAUGHTY **b** : ELATED — **pride·ful·ly** \-fəlē, -li\ *adv* — **pride·ful·ness** \-lnəs\ *n* -ES
**pride·less** \ˈprīdləs\ *adj* [ME *pridelees,* fr. *pride* + *-lees* -less] : lacking in pride; *often* : having no proper self-respect — **pride·less·ly** *adv*
**pride of barbados** *usu cap B* : a thorny shrub or small tree (*Poinciana pulcherrima*) with showy yellow to bright orange-red flowers
**pride of california** *usu cap C* : a Californian wild pea (*Lathyrus splendens*) that is cultivated for ornament and has long climbing stems and large pink or violet flowers
**pride of china** *usu cap C* : CHINABERRY 2
**pride-of-india** \ˌ==ˈ=(ə)=\ *n, usu cap I* : CHINABERRY 2
**pride of ohio** *usu cap 2d O* : the common American shooting star (*Dodecatheon meadia*)
**pride of place** : the highest or first position
**pride of the morning** : a light fog or misty dew such as often precedes a fine day
**pride-of-the-peak** \ˌ==ˈ=\ *n* : an orchid (*Habenaria paramoena*) chiefly of southeastern U.S. that has rose-purple to violet flowers with the lip shallowly erose and the terminal lobe deeply emarginate
**prides** *pl of* PRIDE, *pres 3d sing of* PRIDE
**prideweed** \ˈ=,=\ *n* **1** : HORSEWEED 1 **2** : HORSETAIL 2
**prideworthy** \(ˈ)=ˈ==\ *adj* : of a kind or quality in which one may reasonably take pride
**prid·i·an** \ˈpridēən\ *adj* [L *pridianus,* fr. *pridie* on the day before (fr. *pri-* before — as in L *prior* — + *dies* day) + *-anus* -an — more at PRIOR, DEITY] : of or relating to a previous day or to yesterday; *also* : FORMER ⟨a ~ monarchy —Hugh McCrae⟩
**prid·ing·ly** \ˈprīdiŋlē\ *adv* : with a show of pride : VAUNTINGLY, PROUDLY
**pridy** \ˈprīdē, ˈprid-, -di\ *adj* [ME (Sc), fr. *pride* + *-y*] *chiefly dial* : PROUD
**prie** \ˈprē\ *var of* PREE
**pried** *past of* PRY
**prie-dieu** \(ˈ)prēd|y|ə(r), ˈprēdē|, |ə̄\ *n, pl* **prie-dieus** *or* **prie-dieux** \-(z)\ *also* **prie-dieu** [F *prie-Dieu,* lit., pray God] **1** : a small kneeling bench designed for use by a person at prayer and fitted often with a raised shelf on which the elbows or a book may be rested and sometimes with storage space (as for articles of devotion) **2** : a low upholstered chair without arms and with a high straight back

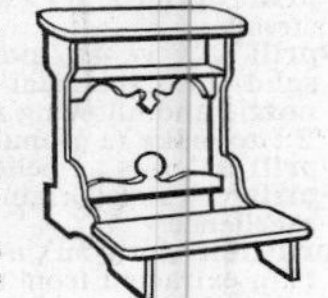

prie-dieu 1

**pri·er** *also* **pry·er** \ˈprī(ə)r, ˈprīə\ *n* -S [¹*pry* + *-er*] : one that pries : a close inquirer : an inquisitive person
**pries** *pres 3d sing of* PRY, *pl of* PRY
¹**priest** \ˈprēst\ *n* -S [ME *prest, preist,* fr. OE *prēost,* modif. of LL *presbyter,* fr. Gk *presbyteros* priest,

elder, older, compar. of *presbys* old man, fr. a prehistoric compound whose first constituent is akin to Gk *paros* before, OE *first* period, interval, delay, OHG *frist*, ON *frest* period, interval, delay, Gk *pro* before, ahead and whose second constituent is akin to Gk *bous* head of cattle; basic meaning: leader of the herd — more at FOR, COW] **1 :** one who performs sacrificial, ritualistic, mediatorial, interpretative, or ministerial functions esp. as an authorized or ordained religious functionary or official minister of a particular religion: **a** (1) **:** a member of the second order of clergy in the ancient Christian and Anglican communions ranking below a bishop and above a deacon (2) **:** a member of the highest order of clergy in the Roman Catholic Church since the Reformation and in the Eastern Orthodox Church (3) **:** a professional clergyman of a religious denomination **:** a minister of religion (4) **:** a member of the Aaronic priesthood of the Mormon Church ranking above deacon and teacher and authorized to administer the sacrament of the Lord's Supper and to baptize **b :** a religious functionary who serves at the altar or performs sacrifices at the altar of a pre-Christian or non-Christian religion ⟨ordained that the Levites should be the ~*s* of the tabernacle⟩ ⟨a ~ of Apollo⟩ **c :** a person having a specific religious or quasi religious status (as a witch doctor or seer) in his usu. primitive community **2 :** a short club used by anglers to stun or kill a captured fish **3** *often cap* **:** a breed of fancy pigeons

**²priest** \"\ *vb* -ED/-ING/-S *vt* **:** to ordain (a person) as priest **:** make a priest of ~ *vi* **:** to perform priestly offices **:** serve as a priest

**priest·al** \'prēst°l\ *adj* **:** of priests **:** PRIESTLY

**priestcraft** \'=,=\ *n* [¹*priest* + *craft*] **1 :** professional knowledge and skill in respect to the exercise of priestly functions **2 :** the scheming and machinations of priests **:** priestly intriguing

**priest·dom** \'prēs(t)dəm\ *n* -S [¹*priest* + -*dom*] **:** the dominion of priests **:** religious rule

**priest·ess** \'prēstəs\ *n* -ES [¹*priest* + -*ess*] **:** a female priest

**priestfish** \'=,=\ *n* **:** a common rockfish (*Sebastodes mystinus*) of the Pacific coast of No. America that is slaty or bluish black above fading to white on the belly and is a leading sport fish of shallow waters

**priest hole** *or* **priest's hole** *n* **:** a secret room or place of concealment for a priest (as in an English house during the proscription of Roman Catholic priests)

**priest·hood** \'prēst,hu̇d, -,stu̇d\ *n* -S [ME *presthod*, fr. OE *prēosthād*, fr. *prēost* priest + -*hād* -hood] **1 :** the office of a priest **:** priestly function **:** sacerdotal character **2 :** the order of priests **:** PRIESTS **3 :** the authority to speak and administer in the name of the Deity given in the Mormon Church by ordination; *also* **:** the body of those so ordained including those of the Aaronic as well as the Melchizedek orders

**priesthood of all believers :** a doctrine of the Protestant Christian Church: every individual has direct access to God without ecclesiastical mediation and each individual shares the responsibility of ministering to the other members of the community of believers

**priest·ian·i·ty** \,prēs(h)chē'anəd·ē *also* ,prēstē'a- *or* prēs(h)-'cha- *sometimes* prēst'ya-\ *n* -ES [¹*priest* + -*ianity* (as in *christianity*)] **:** religion that emphasizes the office or power of the priest — usu. used disparagingly

**priest·ish** \'prēstish\ *adj* **:** PRIESTLIKE

**priest·ism** \-,stizəm\ *n* -S **:** the influence, doctrines, or principles of priests — usu. used disparagingly

**priest·ist** \-,stəst\ *n* -S *usu cap* [trans. of Russ *popovets*] **:** POPOVETS

**priest-king** \(')=¦=\ *n* -S **:** a sacerdotal ruler **:** one who rules as king by right of his priestly office functioning as vice-regent of a deity

**¹priest·less** \'prēs(t)ləs\ *adj* **:** having no priest ⟨a ~ religion⟩

**²priestless** \"\ *n* -ES *usu cap* [trans. of Russ *bezpopovets*] **:** BEZPOPOVETS

**priest·let** \-s(t)lət\ *n* -S [¹*priest* + -*let*] **:** a young, new, or unimportant priest **:** PRIESTLING

**priestlike** \'=,=\ *adv (or adj)* [ME *preistlik*, fr. *preist* priest + *lik* like — more at PRIEST, LIKE] **:** like a priest **:** in the manner or character of or befitting to a priest **:** PRIESTLY

**priest·li·ness** \'prēs(t)lēnəs, -lin-\ *n* -ES [*priestly* + -*ness*] **:** the professional quality or manner of a priest **:** priestly characteristics

**priest·ling** \'prēs(t)liŋ, -lēŋ\ *n* -S [*priest* + -*ling*] **1 a :** a young priest **b :** a petty priest **2 :** one devoted to or under the influence of priests

**priest·ly** \-s(t)lē, -li\ *adj* -ER/-EST [ME, fr. OE *prēostlic*, fr. *prēost* priest + -*lic* -ly] **:** of or relating to a priest or the priesthood **:** SACERDOTAL **:** resembling or characteristic of a priest **:** befitting or becoming to a priest

**priestly blessing** *n* [trans. of LHeb *bīrkhāt kōhănīm*] **:** a Hebrew blessing of the people pronounced by a cohen or cohanim in a synagogue on festival days in accordance with the command and formula of Num 6: 22–27; *also* **:** an English translation of this blessing pronounced by a rabbi at various occasions (as at a bar mitzvah)

**priest-ridden** \(')=¦=\ *adj* **:** controlled or oppressed by a priest

**priests** *pl of* PRIEST, *pres 3d sing of* PRIEST

**priest's-crown** \(')=¦=\ *n, pl* **priest's-crowns** [ME *prestes crowne*, fr. *prestes*, gen. of *prest* priest + *crowne* crown; fr. the bald appearance of the receptacle — more at PRIEST, CROWN] **:** DANDELION 1

**priest·ship** \'prēs(t),ship, -ēs,chip, -ēsh,ship\ *n* **:** the office of a priest

**priestshire** *n* [OE *prēost-scīr*, fr. *prēost* priest + *scīr* shire — more at PRIEST, SHIRE] *obs* **:** an ecclesiastical parish

**priest's hole** *var of* PRIEST HOLE

**priest vicar** *n* **:** a vicar choral of the Church of England in priest's orders **:** MINOR CANON

**¹prig** *n* -S [ME, alter. of *sprig*] *obs* **:** a small nail **:** BRAD

**²prig** \'prig\ *vb* **prigged; prigged; prigging; prigs** *vt* [origin unknown] *chiefly Brit* **:** STEAL, FILCH, PILFER ~ *vi* **1** *chiefly Scot* **:** to haggle about or over something **:** quibble over money or price **:** drive a hard bargain **2** *chiefly Scot* **:** ENTREAT, PLEAD, BEG

**³prig** \"\ *n* **1** *obs* **:** TINKER **2 :** THIEF, PILFERER

**⁴prig** \"\ *n* [prob. fr. ³*prig*] **1** *archaic* **:** FELLOW, PERSON **2** *archaic* **:** FOP, BUCK, DANDY **3 a :** a notably or excessively punctilious person **b** *obs* **:** a nonconformist minister; *broadly* **:** PURITAN **4 :** one who offends or irritates by obvious or rigid observance of the proprieties (as in speech, manners, or conduct) **:** one self-sufficient in virtue, culture, or propriety often in a pointed manner or to an obnoxious degree

**⁵prig** \"\ *adj* **:** PRIGGISH

**prig·ger** \'prigə(r)\ *n* -S [²*prig* + -*er*] *archaic* **:** THIEF

**prig·gery** \-gərē, -ri\ *n* -ES [⁴*prig* + -*ery*] **:** PRIGGISHNESS

**prig·gish** \'prigish, -gēsh\ *adj* [⁴*prig* + -*ish*] **:** characteristic or suggestive of a prig; *esp* **:** marked by overvaluing oneself or one's ideas, habits, notions, by precise or inhibited adherence to them, and by small disparagement of others ⟨the instructor must not act like a ~ moderator with a gavel —J.M.Barzun⟩
**syn** see COMPLACENT

**prig·gish·ly** *adv* **:** in a priggish manner

**prig·gish·ness** *n* -ES **1 :** the quality or state of being priggish **2 :** a priggish act or piece of conduct

**¹prig·gism** \'pri,gizəm\ *n* -S [³*prig* + -*ism*] *archaic* **:** THIEVISHNESS, ROGUERY

**²priggism** \"\ *n* -S [⁴*prig* + -*ism*] **:** self-conscious propriety of conduct **:** stilted correctness of behavior **:** prim adherence to conventionality **:** PRIGGISHNESS

**¹prill** \'pril\ *n* -S [alter. of ³*purl*] *dial chiefly Eng* **:** a running stream

**²prill** \"\ *vt* -ED/-ING/-S [perh. fr. ¹*prill*] **1 :** to convert (a solid) into spherical pellets (as by forcing a melt through a nozzle and allowing the molten drops to solidify while falling) **2 :** to make (a granular or crystalline material) free flowing

**³prill** \"\ *n* -S **:** a pellet made by prilling

**⁴prill** \"\ *n* -S [origin unknown] **:** rich copper ore selected for excellence

**pril·lion** \'prilyən\ *n* -S [alter. (influenced by ⁴*prill*) of *pillion*] **:** tin extracted from slag — compare PILLION

**¹prim** \'prim\ *n* -S [short for obs. *primprint* privet, of unknown origin] **:** PRIVET 1a

**²prim** \"\ *vb* **primmed; primmed; primming; prims** [origin unknown] *vi* **:** to make oneself or one's expression prim **:** assume a prim manner or appearance ⟨they mince and ~ and pout —George Meredith⟩ ~ *vt* **1 :** to give a prim or demure expression to ⟨*primming* her thin lips after every mouthful of tea —John Buchan⟩ **2 :** to arrange or dress affectedly or demurely — usu. used with *up* or *out* ⟨~ her up in an old-fashioned gown⟩

**³prim** \"\ *adj, usu* **primmer;** *usu* **primmest 1 a :** formal and precise in manner or appearance **:** stiffly decorous ⟨a ~ and slightly sardonic man —W.J.Locke⟩ ⟨*prim*-lipped⟩ **b :** PRUDISH ⟨was at heart intensely ~, easily shocked —*Time*⟩ **2 :** NEAT, TRIM ⟨~ little egg saucers —Sheila Hibben⟩ ⟨~ little spicy gardens —*Amer. Guide Series: Texas*⟩

**prim** *abbr* **1** primary **2** primate **3** primitive

**¹pri·ma** \'prēmə\ *adj* [It, fem of *primo*, fr. L *primus* — more at PRIME] **:** FIRST, LEADING

**²prima** *var of* PRIMA VOLTA

**³pri·ma** \'prīmə\ *n* -S [L, fem. of *primus* first] **:** the first word of the next galley proof or page of copy marked on the corresponding page or galley; *also* **:** the word at which reading is to be resumed after an interruption — compare MARKOFF

**prima ballerina** *n* **:** the leading female dancer in a ballet company

**pri·ma·cy** \'prīməsē, -si\ *n* -ES [ME *primacie*, fr. MF, fr. ML *primatia*, fr. L *primat-*, *primas* one of the first, leader + -*ia* -y — more at PRIMATE] **1 :** the state of being first (as in importance, order, or rank) **:** PRECEDENCE, PREEMINENCE, SUPERIORITY ⟨the ~ of the deed over word and thought —Gilbert Highet⟩ ⟨too proud of the ~ of his intelligence to listen —Eliseo Vivas⟩ **2 :** the office, rank, or character of an ecclesiastical primate **:** the chief ecclesiastical station or dignity in a church; *also* **:** supreme episcopal jurisdiction

**prima don·na** \¦primə¦dänə, -rēm-\ *n, pl* **prima donnas** [It, lit., first lady] **1 :** the leading or a principal female singer in an opera or concert organization **2 :** a person who finds it difficult to work under direction or as part of a team **:** one who is impatient of restraint or criticism ⟨we are looking for good teammates, rather than *prima donnas* —*Farm Chemicals*⟩

**primaeval** *var of* PRIMEVAL

**¹pri·ma fa·cie** \¦prīmə¦fāshē,ē, -shē\ *adv* [L] **:** at first view **:** on the first appearance ⟨bears out what is *prima facie* probable —D.M.Davin⟩

**²prima facie** \"\ *adj* **1 :** based on immediate impression **:** APPARENT ⟨*prima facie* plausibility⟩ **2 :** SELF-EVIDENT ⟨a *prima facie* right⟩ ⟨*prima facie* duty⟩

**prima facie case** *n* **:** a case established by prima facie evidence

**prima facie evidence** *n* **:** evidence sufficient in law to raise a presumption of fact or establish the fact in question unless rebutted

**pri·mage** \'prīmij, -mēj\ *n* -S [prob. fr. ⁴*prime* + -*age*] **1 a :** a small payment made by shippers to the captain of a ship for his special care of their goods — called also *hat money* **b :** a small percentage added to the freight charge and paid to the owner of a ship as extra compensation **2 :** a primary ad valorem revenue duty laid by the Australian government on imports

**pri·mal** \'prīməl\ *adj* [ML *primalis*, fr. L *primus* first + -*alis* -al] **1 :** of or relating to the first period or state **:** ORIGINAL, PRIMITIVE ⟨village life continued in its ~ innocence —Van Wyck Brooks⟩ **2 :** first in importance **:** FUNDAMENTAL, PRINCIPAL ⟨paper money was a ~ necessity to the colonists —J.C.Fitzpatrick⟩

**primal cut** *n* **:** any of various wholesale cuts (as a quarter, side, or ham) into which the carcass of a food animal is divided

**pri·mal·i·ty** \prī'maləd·ē\ *n* -ES **:** the quality or state of being primal

**primal scene** *n* **:** sexual intercourse performed by parents and observed by their child ⟨permitted to . . . witness parental nakedness and *primal scenes* —Victor Eisenstein⟩

**pri·ma·quine** \'prēmə,kwēn, 'prīm-, -,kwən\ *n* -S [¹*prima* + -*quine* (fr. *quinoline*)] **:** an antimalarial drug $C_{15}H_{21}N_3O$ derived from a methoxy-quinoline and used in the form of its diphosphate

**pri·maried** \'prī,merēd, -,m(ə)rēd\ *adj* [²*primary* + -*ed*] *of a bird* **:** having primaries — usu. used in combination ⟨*ten-primaried*⟩

**pri·mar·i·ly** \(')prī¦merəlē, ,prə'm-, -li\ *adv* **1 :** first of all **:** FUNDAMENTALLY, PRINCIPALLY ⟨has now become ~ a residential town —S.P.B.Mais⟩ **2 :** in the first place **:** ORIGINALLY ⟨~ nomads, they eventually settled down to farming⟩

**pri·mari·ness** \(')prī,merēnəs, 'prīm(ə)rē-\ *n* -ES **:** the quality or state of being primary ⟨this ~ of elements, these gaseous atoms —Saul Levitt⟩

**¹pri·mary** \'prī,merē, -m(ə)rē, -ri\ *adj* [LL *primarius* basic, primary, fr. L, principal, fr. *primus* first + -*arius* -ary — more at PRIME] **1 a :** first in order of time or development **:** INITIAL **:** PRIMITIVE ⟨the ~ forest⟩ ⟨the ~ stage of civilization⟩ ⟨~ tuberculosis⟩ **b** (1) **:** of or relating to geological formations of the Paleozoic and earlier periods (2) *of minerals or ore deposits* **:** formed first; *esp* **:** formed under igneous, pneumatolytic, or hydrothermal conditions **:** HYPOGENE **2 a :** first in rank or importance **:** CHIEF, PRINCIPAL ⟨the ~ duty of safeguarding the peace of the world —P.J.Noel-Baker⟩ ⟨the ~ member of the cabinet⟩ **b :** BASIC, FUNDAMENTAL ⟨man has always used the most durable materials available for his ~ tools —R.W.Murray⟩ ⟨the family is still the ~ human association —Kimball Young⟩ **c :** of, relating to, or constituting the principal quills of a bird's wing **d :** of or relating to agriculture, forestry, and the extractive industries or their products ⟨~ economic activities⟩ ⟨~ goods⟩ ⟨world ~ prices have dipped significantly below their recent peaks —W.T.C.King⟩ **e :** expressive of present or future time — used of a grammatical tense ⟨the present, future, perfect, and future perfect indicative are the Greek ~ tenses⟩ **f :** of, relating to, or constituting the strongest of the three or the four degrees of stress recognized by most linguists **3 :** functioning or transmitted without intermediary **:** DIRECT ⟨require ~ assistance if they are to be kept from starving and freezing to death —*N.Y. Times*⟩ **4 a :** not derived from or dependent on something else **:** FIRSTHAND, INDEPENDENT, ORIGINAL ⟨a very useful ~ historical source —R.A.Hall b.1911⟩ ⟨~ research⟩ **b** *of a color* **:** not derivable from other colors **c :** preparatory to something else **:** belonging to the first stage of some continuing process or series; *specif* **:** of or relating to a primary school ⟨~ education⟩ ⟨~ grades⟩ ⟨~ instruction⟩ **d :** belonging to the first group or order in successive divisions, combinations, or ramifications ⟨~ nerves⟩ ⟨~ compounds⟩ **e :** of, relating to, or constituting the inducing current or its circuit in an induction coil or transformer ⟨the ~ voltage⟩ ⟨~ current⟩ **f :** directly derived from ore **:** VIRGIN ⟨~ aluminum⟩ ⟨~ copper⟩ **5 :** characterized by replacement in the first degree **:** resulting from the substitution of one of two or more atoms or groups in a molecule ⟨a ~ phosphate⟩; *esp* **:** being or characterized by a carbon atom united by a single valence to only one chain or ring member ⟨a ~ radical $RCH_2$— such as ethyl or benzyl⟩ — compare SECONDARY, TERTIARY

**²primary** \"\ *n* -ES **1 :** something that stands first in order, rank, or importance **:** FUNDAMENTAL — usu. used in pl. **2** [short for *primary planet*] **a :** a planet as distinguished from its satellites **b :** the brighter component of a double star **3 a** *also* **primary quill :** one of the quills on the distal joint of a bird's wing that are attached to the bones of the hand and its fingers and are usu. 9 or 10 in number — see BIRD illustration **b :** either of the forewings of an insect **c** (1) **:** one of the first formed plates in the development of the skeleton of an echinoderm after metamorphosis (2) **:** an ambulacral plate of a sea urchin extending half across the ambulacral area; *also* **:** the largest spine or one of the largest spines on any plate of the test or the tubercle bearing it — compare SECONDARY 6c **4 a** *or* **primary color :** any of a set of colors from which all other colors may be derived — see ADDITIVE PRIMARY, PSYCHOLOGICAL PRIMARY, SUBTRACTIVE PRIMARY **b :** a primary-color sensation **5 :** PRIMARY COIL **6** [trans. of F (*assemblée*) *primaire*] **a :** CAUCUS 1b **b** *or* **primary election :** an election in which qualified voters nominate or express a preference for a particular candidate or group of candidates for political office, choose party officials, or select delegates for a party convention — see CLOSED PRIMARY, DIRECT PRIMARY, NONPARTISAN PRIMARY, OPEN PRIMARY, PRESIDENTIAL PRIMARY

**primary accent** *n* **:** the first and chief accent or beat of a musical measure

**primary air** *n* **:** air admitted to the fuel stream or area ahead of the combustion zone in a burner or furnace

**primary alcohol** *n* **:** an alcohol that possesses the group $-CH_2OH$ and can be oxidized so as to form a corresponding aldehyde and acid having the same number of carbon atoms

**primary alphabet** *n* **:** an alphabetic sequence serving as a component of a substitution alphabet; *esp* **:** a mixed sequence serving as a cipher component

**primary amine** *n* **:** an amine $RNH_2$ (as methylamine) having one organic substituent attached to the nitrogen atom

**primary atypical pneumonia** *n* **:** a usu. mild pneumonia caused by a virus or a pleuropneumonia-like organism

**primary battery** *n* **:** an assembly of two or more primary cells

**primary benefit** *n* **:** the retirement benefit to which a worker is entitled at age 65 based upon credits earned in employment covered under Federal Old Age and Survivors Insurance

**primary body** *n* **:** the parts and appendages of the root and stem of a plant that are built up from apical meristems — compare SECONDARY BODY

**primary body cavity** *n* **:** BLASTOCOEL

**primary burial** *n* **:** the initial interment of a human corpse or the remains of such interment — contrasted with *secondary burial*

**primary cause** *n* **:** FIRST CAUSE

**primary cell** *n* **:** a cell that converts chemical energy into electrical energy by irreversible chemical reactions and that cannot be recharged by passing an electric current through it — compare STORAGE CELL

**primary circle** *n* **:** one of the four fundamental great circles of the celestial sphere ⟨the horizon, celestial equator, ecliptic, and galactic equator are *primary circles*⟩

**primary coil** *n* **:** the coil through which the inducing current passes in an induction coil or transformer

**primary commercial blanket bond :** a blanket bond covering any loss up to a stated amount caused by the dishonest act of an employee or group of employees

**primary constriction** *n* **:** CENTROMERE

**primary covert** *n* **:** a wing covert covering the base of a primary of a bird

**primary deposit** *n* **:** a bank deposit consisting of cash, checks, or other demands for payments — compare DERIVATIVE DEPOSIT

**primary endosperm nucleus** *n* **:** the nucleus formed by the fusion of two polar nuclei in the embryo sac of a seed plant prior to fertilization — called also *secondary nucleus;* compare ENDOSPERM NUCLEUS

**primary evidence** *n* **1 :** the evidence usu. of self-validating written documents primarily required by law as the best evidence of a fact to be proved **2 :** PRIMA FACIE EVIDENCE

**primary explosive** *n* **:** an explosive (as mercury fulminate or lead azide) that is sensitive to friction, blows, shock, or heat

**primary group** *n* **:** a social group (as a family or circle of friends) characterized by a high degree of affective interpersonal contact and exerting a strong influence on the social attitudes and ideals of the individual — contrasted with *secondary group;* compare GEMEINSCHAFT

**primary growth** *n* **:** growth by the activity of a primary meristem resulting mainly in an increase in length and the addition of appendages — compare SECONDARY GROWTH

**primary host** *n* **:** DEFINITIVE HOST

**primary humor** *n* **:** HUMOR 1b(1)

**primary infection** *n* **:** the initial infection of a host by a pathogen that has completed a resting or dormant period

**primary intention** *n* **:** FIRST INTENTION

**primary jurisdiction** *n* **:** the right or responsibility of an administrative or regulatory agency to pass initially on controversies involving matters of fact or discretion within its sphere before relief is sought in the courts

**primary lesion** *n* **:** the initial lesion of a disease (as of cancer); *specif* **:** the chancre of syphilis

**primary lookout** *n* **:** LOOKOUT 2b

**primary market** *n* **1 :** a wholesale market large enough to dominate the trade in some goods over a large area **2 :** PRIMARY POINT

**primary meeting** *n* **:** CAUCUS 1b

**primary memory** *n* **:** memory of what has just occurred

**primary meristem** *n* **:** a meristem consisting of direct derivatives of embryonic cells that are always active in growth — compare SECONDARY MERISTEM

**primary minimum** *n* **:** a depression in the light curve of an eclipsing variable that occurs when the brighter in surface brightness of the two stars is eclipsed by the fainter one

**primary narcissism** *n* **:** the stage of a child's primary concern with himself as an organism prior to awareness of external reality as a mediating factor

**primary phloem** *n* **:** the first-formed phloem; *specif* **:** phloem developed from an apical meristem

**primary pit field** *n* **:** a thin area in the walls of many cells which is esp. conspicuous in cambium initials and in which one or more pits usu. develop

**primary point** *n* **:** a large city that receives agricultural products in considerable quantities direct from country shippers

**primary protective layer** *n* **:** a layer developed within the separation layer in leaves of deciduous plants at the time of leaf fall that protects the exposed cells from desiccation and infection until the periderm forms

**primary quality** *n* **:** a quality (as bulk) that is inseparable from a physical object and is in it as in our perception of it ⟨these I call original or *primary qualities* of body, which I think we may observe to produce simple ideas in us, viz. solidity, extension, figure, motion or rest, and number —John Locke⟩ — contrasted with *secondary quality*

**primary quill** *n* **:** PRIMARY 3a

**primary rainbow** *n* **:** a rainbow in which the effective rays are refracted on entering each drop, reflected from its interior surface, and refracted again on emerging to pass to the observer's eye and in which the red is seen on the outside edge of the bow

**primary ray** *n* **:** a vascular ray developed during primary growth

**primary receipts** *n pl* **:** the daily receipt of goods at a primary point

**primary release** *n* **:** an arrow release in which the arrow and bowstring are held between the thumb and forefinger

**primary reserve** *n* **:** a bank's cash on hand and deposits in other banks

**primary road** *n* **:** a principal usu. state-maintained road in a recognized system of highways

**primary rocks** *n pl* **:** the rocks believed to have been first formed — called also *primitive rocks*

**primary root** *n* **:** the root of a plant that is the first to develop and that originates from the radicle

**primary salt** *n* **:** a salt derived from a polyacid in which only one acid hydrogen atom has been replaced by a base or basic radical

**primary school** *n* **1 a :** a school at which children receive their first formal education usu. comprising the first three grades of elementary school but sometimes also including kindergarten **b :** ELEMENTARY SCHOOL **2** *Brit* **:** a school for children from five to eleven years of age

**primary shipments** *n pl* **:** the daily shipments from a primary point

**primary spermatocyte** *n* **:** a cell of the next to last generation preceding the spermatozoon

**primary substance** *n* **:** SUBSTANCE 2a(1), 2a(4)

**primary succession** *n* **:** PRISERE

**primary syphilis** *n* **:** the first stage of syphilis marked by the development of the chancre and the spread of the causative spirochete in the tissues and organs of the body

**primary tissue** *n* **:** plant tissue developed during primary growth — compare MERISTEM

**primary triad** *n* **:** one of the triads on the first, fourth, or fifth note or tone of any major or minor musical scale

**primary type** *n* **:** one of the specimens upon which the description of a new biological species is actually based

**primary wall** *n* **:** the first-formed wall of a plant cell that is produced around the protoplast next to the middle lamella, is usu. anisotropic in polarized light, and possesses plasmodesmata — compare SECONDARY WALL

**primary xylem** *n* : the first-formed xylem; *specif* : xylem developed from an apical meristem

**1pri·mate** \ˈprīˌmāt, -ˌmət, *usu* -d·+V\ *n* -s [ME *primat*, fr. OF, fr. ML *primat-, primas* archbishop, fr. LL, archbishop, head, leader, fr. L, one of the first, leader, fr. *primus* first — more at PRIME] **1** *often cap* : a bishop who has precedence in a province, group of provinces, or a nation **2** *archaic* : one who is first in authority or rank : LEADER ⟨the prince . . . is the ~ and pearl of nobility —Richard Mulcaster⟩ **3** : a mammal of the order Primates

**2primate** \"\ *adj* : PRINCIPAL ⟨another bid for recognition as the world's ~ city —*Focus*⟩

**pri·ma·tes** \prīˈmād·(ˌ)ēz, -āˌtēz\ *n pl, cap* [NL, fr. pl. of L *primat-, primas* one of the first] : an order of eutherian mammals including man, apes, monkeys, lemurs, and living and extinct related forms that are all thought to be derived from generalized arboreal ancestors descended in turn from shrewlike precursors during the Paleocene and that are in general characterized by increasing perfection of binocular vision, specialization of the appendages for grasping, and enlargement and differentiation of the brain

**pri·mate·ship** \ˈ=(ˌ)=ˌship\ *n* **1** : the office, dignity, or position of a primate **2** : PRIMACY

**pri·ma·tial** \prīˈmāshəl\ *adj* [F, fr. MF, fr. ML *primatialis*, fr. *primatia* primacy + L *-alis* -al — more at PRIMACY] **1** : of, relating to, or characteristic of a primate ⟨was deprived of his ~ authority —F.M.Stenton⟩ **2** : having primacy : PRINCIPAL ⟨the ~ city of ancient Ireland —W.G.Carleton⟩

**primatial council** *n* : an assembly of church officials composed of representatives of an ecclesiastical province, a primatial jurisdiction, or an entire nation

**pri·mat·i·cal** \(ˈ)prīˌmad·əkəl\ *adj* [*1primate* + *-ical*] : PRIMATIAL

**pri·ma·tol·o·gist** \ˌprīməˈtäləjəst\ *n* -s : a specialist in primatology

**pri·ma·tol·o·gy** \-jē, -ji\ *n* -ES [NL *Primates* + E *-o-* + *-logy*] : the study of members of the order Primates esp. other than recent man

**pri·ma·ve·ra** \ˌprēməˈverə\ *n* -s [AmerSp, lit., spring, fr. Sp, spring, fr. LL *prima vera*, fr. fem. of L *primum ver* early spring, fr. *primus* first + *ver* spring; fr. its early flowering — more at VERNAL] **1** : a Central American timber tree (*Cybistax donnellsmithii*) with brilliant yellow flowers **2** : the hard light wood of the primavera — called also *white mahogany*

**pri·ma·ve·ral** \ˌprīməˌvirəl\ *adj* [Sp, fr. *primavera* spring + *-al* (fr. L *-alis* -al)] : of or relating to early spring ⟨took full advantage of the ~ weather —*Time*⟩

**1pri·ma vol·ta** \ˌprēməˌvòltə\ *also* **pri·ma** \ˈprēmə\ *adv* (*or adj*) [It] : at the first time — used as a direction in music to perform the first time but omit at the repetition

**2prima volta** \"\ *also* **prima** \"\ *n* : a part performed or to be performed prima volta in a piece of music

**1prime** \ˈprīm\ *n* -s [ME, fr. OE *prīm*, fr. L *prima* (*hora*) first hour, fr. *prima*, fem. of *primus* first + *hora* hour — more at HOUR] **1 a** *often cap* : a religious office constituting the first of the daytime canonical hours — compare LAUD, MATINS **b** : the first hour of the day usu. considered either as 6 a.m. or the hour of sunrise **2 a** : the beginning or earliest stage of something : the first part or age ⟨saurians of the ~ —Henry Adams⟩ **b** : SPRING ⟨the ~ of the year⟩ **c** : the spring of life : YOUTH ⟨in her ~, pretty as a lamb, a laughing girl —A.E. Coppard⟩ **3 a** : the most active, thriving, or successful stage of something ⟨patent medicines were in their ~ —Thérèse S. Westermeier⟩ ⟨the ~ of his musical career —Terry de Valera⟩ **b** : the period of greatest vigor and productivity in a person's life ⟨these two home-run sluggers, who were tremendous crowd pullers in their ~ —*Collier's Yr. Bk.*⟩ **4 a** : the chief or best individual of a group ⟨~ of the flock, and choicest of the stall —Alexander Pope⟩ **b** : the best part of something ⟨give him always of the ~ —Jonathan Swift⟩ **c** : an export grade of yellow pine lumber of very high quality that is free from defects and largely heartwood **d** : sheet metal products of the highest commercial quality **5** : PRIME NUMBER **6 a** : PRIMERO **b** : the second-highest hand in primero and related games consisting of one card of each suit **c** : a block in backgammon formed by a series of six closed points **7** : a parry in fencing defending the upper inside target in which the hand is to the left at head height in a position of pronation with the point of the blade directed downward and the forearm is across the body parallel to the ground — called also *first;* compare QUARTE **8 a** : the first note or tone of a musical scale : TONIC **b** : a tone represented by the same staff degree as a given tone **c** : the pitch relation between two such musical notes or tones or their simultaneous combination — called also *unison* **d** : PRIME TONE **9** : a symbol or accent ′ suffixed in writing or printing to distinguish one character from a related character (as *a′* from *a* or from *a″*, to indicate a relative unit (as a minute of angle or a foot), or to differentiate a mathematical function — compare DOUBLE PRIME

**2prime** \"\ *adj* [ME, fr. MF, fem. of *prin* prime, fr. L *primus;* akin to L *prior* former, prior — more at PRIOR] **1 a** : first in order of time : ORIGINAL, PRIMITIVE ⟨high heaven and earth ail from the ~ foundation —A.E.Housman⟩ **b** : having the vigor and freshness of youth : YOUTHFUL ⟨our manhood's ~ vigor —Robert Browning⟩ **2 a** (1) : of, relating to, or constituting a prime number (2) : having no common integral divisor greater than 1 ⟨12 is ~ to 25⟩ ⟨12 and 25 are relatively ~⟩ **b** (1) *of a polynomial* : not factorable (2) : having no common polynomial divisors with coefficients in the same field other than constants ⟨these two polynomials are relatively ~⟩ **3** *obs* : LECHEROUS, LUSTFUL ⟨as ~ as goats —Shak.⟩ **4 a** : first in rank or authority : CHIEF, LEADING ⟨made you the ~ man of the state —Shak.⟩ **b** : first in significance or urgency : PRINCIPAL ⟨a ~ requisite⟩ ⟨a ~ example⟩ ⟨a ~ need⟩ **c** (1) : first in excellence or importance : having the highest quality or value ⟨a ~ new plow —M.A.Hancock⟩ ⟨~ farming land —J.D.Adams⟩ ⟨a ~ fish⟩ ⟨~ television time⟩ (2) : of the highest grade — used of meat, esp. beef; compare CHOICE, COMMERCIAL, GOOD 1f(5) (3) : being in the best condition — used esp. of fur skins and hides ⟨when the deer hides are ~ —Farley Mowat⟩ **d** : having the highest credit rating ⟨~ borrowers⟩ ⟨~ commercial loans⟩ **5** : not deriving from something else : PRIMARY ⟨the ~ postulate of his philosophy⟩

**3prime** \"\ *adv* [*2prime*] : PRIMELY

**4prime** \"\ *vb* -ED/-ING/-S [prob. fr. *1prime*] *vt* **1** : FILL, LOAD ⟨*primed* the lamp with oil⟩ ⟨came to these encounters well *primed* with wine —J.B.Cabell⟩ **2** : to prepare for firing by supplying with priming or a primer ⟨~ a cannon⟩ ⟨~ a mine⟩ **3 a** : to lay the first color, coating, or preparation upon ⟨*primed* the wall with white paint⟩ ⟨an undercoater for sealing and *priming* inside surfaces —*Wall Street Jour.*⟩ **b** *archaic* : to put cosmetics on : make up ⟨every morning ~*s* her face —John Oldham⟩ **4** : to put into working order by filling or charging with something: as **a** : to pour water into the barrel or bucket of (a pump) **b** : to pour gasoline into the carburetor of (an engine) **c** : to impart a charge of static electricity to one armature of (an induction electric machine) **5 a** : to instruct beforehand : COACH ⟨*primed* the witness⟩ **b** : to make ready : PREPARE ⟨keeping their eyes *primed*, their cameras ready —Barbara B. Jamison⟩ ⟨a livestock dipping vat was *primed* with a fresh solution —F.B.Gipson⟩ **6** : to harvest (tobacco) by picking the leaves a few at a time as they ripen **7** : STIMULATE ⟨loses money in attempting to ~ the sugarcane industry —Sidney Shalett⟩ ~ *vi* **1** *archaic* : to assume precedence : DOMINEER **2** : to operate so that steam is liberated in small portions with the result that fine water particles are entrained with and carried over by steam **3** : to have a shortened tide day **4** : to become prime ⟨the hides were *priming* towards winter, heavy and well-furred —Mari Sandoz⟩ — **prime the pump** : to take steps to encourage the growth, functioning, or expression of something; *specif:* to attempt to stimulate employment or economic activity by government spending ⟨this spending has not yet *primed the pump* —T.W.Arnold⟩ — compare PUMP PRIMING

**5prime** \"\ *n* -s : the priming of a gun

**6prime** \"\ *vi* -ED/-ING/-S [origin unknown] *of a fish* : to leap from the water

**prime cost** *n* **1** : the combined total of raw material and direct labor costs incurred in production **2** : the direct or immediate cost of a commodity; *specif* : the cost or expenses of producing or obtaining a commodity exclusive of general expenses of management involved and of profit on capital

**prime factor** *n* : a factor that is a prime number

**prime·ly** *adv* : in a prime manner : EXCELLENTLY

**prime matter** *n* : MATTER 3b(5)

**prime meridian** *n* : the meridian of 0 degrees longitude which runs through the original site of the Royal Observatory at Greenwich, England, and from which other longitudes are reckoned east and west around the world to 180 degrees — compare NATIONAL MERIDIAN

**prime minister** *n* **1** : the chief minister of a ruler or state **2** : the official head of a cabinet : the chief executive of a parliamentary government

**prime-ministerial** \(ˌ)=ˌ==ˌ===\ *adj* : of or relating to a prime minister

**prime-ministership** \(ˈ)=ˌ===ˌ=\ *n* : PRIME MINISTRY

**prime ministry** *n* **1** : the office of prime minister **2** : the term of office of a prime minister

**prime mover** *n* [trans. of ML *primus motor*] **1** *in some philosophies* **a** : the self-moved being to which all motion must ultimately go back **b** *cap P&M* : GOD — compare FIRST CAUSE **2 a** (1) : an initial source of motive power (as an engine) designed to receive and modify force and motion as supplied by some natural source and apply them to drive other machinery (as a waterwheel, turbine, or steam engine) (2) : a powerful tractor or truck usu. with all-wheel drive for hauling artillery or moving stalled vehicles **b** : the original or most effective force in an undertaking or work ⟨see the *prime mover* of our increased growth in physical environment —Lawrence Farmer⟩ ⟨he was a *prime mover* in the evolution of progressive ensemble jazz —Bill Simon⟩ **3** : AGONIST **syn** see ORIGIN

**prime·ness** *n* -ES : the quality or state of being prime

**prime number** *n* : a number not divisible by any integer greater than one except its own absolute value

**1prim·er** \ˈprimə(r) *also chiefly Brit* ˈprīm-\ *n* -s [ME, fr. ML *primarium*, fr. neut. of *primarius* basic, primary, fr. LL — more at PRIMARY] **1** : a layman's prayer book of the 14th to 17th centuries containing miscellaneous prayers, psalms, and offices orig. written or printed in Latin but later mainly in English and used also in teaching children to read **2 a** : a small elementary book for teaching children to read ⟨a ~ for the first grade⟩ **b** : a usu. small introductory book on a specific subject ⟨a ~ of modern art⟩ ⟨a ~ of chemistry⟩ **3** : something that gives or is a means of giving elementary instruction or training ⟨his year as a precinct worker served as his ~ of politics⟩

**2primer** *adj* [ME, fr. MF, fr. LL *primarius*] *obs* : PRIMARY

**3prim·er** \ˈprīmə(r)\ *n* -s [*4prime* + *-er*] **1** : an instrument or device for priming: as **a** : a contrivance (as a cap, tube, or wafer containing percussion powder or other compound) used to ignite an explosive charge and itself ignited by friction, percussion, or electricity **b** : a small copper cup containing a charge of some shock-sensitive high explosive (as mercury fulminate) that initiates the propelling charge in a firearm when ignited (as in a percussion cap) by a blow from the hammer or (as in a modern cartridge or shot-shell case) by impact of the firing pin **2** : PRIMING **3 a** : one who applies priming (as of paint or varnish) **b** : a worker who gathers the prime leaves from tobacco plants **4** : a plasma gene that acts as a priming device for various reactions

**pri·mero** \prəˈme(ˌ)rō, -mi(ˌ)rō\ *n* -s [modif. of Sp *primera*, fr. fem. of *primero* first, fr. L *primarius* principal — more at PRIMARY] : an old card game popular esp. in the 16th century in which each player holds three or four cards ⟨never prospered since I forswore myself at ~ —Shak.⟩

**prim·er seisin** \ˈprimə(r), -īmə(r)-\ *n* [ME *primer cession, primer season*, fr. *2primer* + *cession, season*, alter. of *seisine* seisin — more at SEISIN] : a right of the crown to exact from the heir of a tenant in capite seised of a knight's fee one year's profits of the land in addition to the ordinary relief if the lands were in immediate possession or half a year's profits if the lands were in reversion expectant on a life estate

**primes** *pl of* PRIME, *pres 3d sing of* PRIME

**prime tone** *n* : the lowest tone of a group of overtones

**pri·meur** \(ˈ)prēˌmər, -mə̄\ *n* -s [F, fr. MF, fr. *prime* first + *-eur* -or — more at PRIME] : an early fruit or vegetable : FIRSTLING

**pri·me·val** *also* **pri·mae·val** \(ˈ)prīˈmēvəl\ *adj* [L *primaevus* of the first period of life (fr. *primus* first + *aevum* age) + E *-al* — more at PRIME, AYE] : of or relating to the earliest ages of the world or human history : ABORIGINAL, PRIMITIVE ⟨had lapsed into nearly its ~ state of wilderness —Nathaniel Hawthorne⟩ ⟨a splendid ~ rustic figure —Osbert Lancaster⟩ — **pri·me·val·ly** \-vəlē, -li\ *adv*

**pri·me·verin** \ˌprīməˈvirən, -ver-\ *n* -s [ISV *primever-* (fr. F *primevère* cowslip, fr. OF *primevoire*, lit., spring, prob. short for *flour de primevoire* spring flower, fr. *flour* flower + *de* of — fr. L, from — + *primevoire* — fr. LL *prima vera* early spring —) + *-in* — more at FLOWER, DE-, PRIMAVERA] : a crystalline glycoside $C_{20}H_{28}O_{13}$ that is found in the cowslip (*Primula veris*) and that on hydrolysis yields primeverose and a derivative of salicylic acid

**pri·me·verose** \-ˌrōs\ *n* -s [*primeverin* + *-ose*] : a crystalline disaccharide $C_{11}H_{20}O_{10}$ obtained by hydrolysis of primeverin, primulaverin, and other glycosides that yields glucose and xylose on hydrolysis

**prime vertical** *n* : the vertical circle at right angles to the celestial meridian and passing through the east and west points of the horizon

**prime vertical dial** *n* : a sundial in which the shadow is projected on the plane of the prime vertical : a vertical south dial

**prime-vertical transit** *n* : a transit instrument mounted so that its telescope revolves in the plane of the prime vertical

**pri·me·vous** \(ˈ)prīˈmēvəs\ *adj* [L *primaevus* of the first period of life] : PRIMEVAL

**prim·i·ces** \ˈpriməsəz\ *n pl* [ME, fr. OF, fr. L *primiciae, primitiae* — more at PRIMITIAE] : FIRSTFRUITS

**pri·mie·ra** \prēˈmyerə\ *n* -s [It, prob. fr. Sp *primera* — more at PRIMERO] **1** : a form of primero popular in Italy **2** : PRIME 6 b

**primigenial** *var of* PRIMOGENIAL

**pri·mi·grav·id** \ˌprīməˌgravəd\ *adj* [NL *primigravida*] : pregnant for the first time

**pri·mi·grav·i·da** \ˌ==ˈgravədə\ *n, pl* **primigravi·das** \-dəz\ *or* **primigravi·dae** \-ˌdē\ [NL, fr. *primi-* (fr. L, fr. *primus* first) + L *gravida* pregnant woman — more at PRIME, GRAVIDA] : an individual pregnant for the first time

**primi inter pares** *pl of* PRIMUS INTER PARES

**priming** *n* -s [fr. gerund of *4prime*] **1 a** : the act or action of one that primes: as (1) : the placing in position of an explosive used to fire a charge (2) : the application of a first coating (as of paint, varnish, or size) to a surface that is to be painted (3) : the action of a boiler or still in carrying water globules over with the steam generated (4) : the action of boiling over — used esp. of a still in gas manufacturing (5) : the pulling of tobacco leaves from the growing plant as they mature **b** (1) : the explosive used in priming a charge (2) : the material used in priming a surface (3) : the tobacco leaves removed by priming **2** : a strong solution of sugar added to beer to give it body and make it more palatable

**priming charge** *n* : a small charge of easily detonated explosive used to ignite a main charge (as a propelling charge in a gun)

**priming illumination** *n* : a constant low-intensity illumination of a photocathode that is used to bring the sensitivity of the cell up to a maximum

**priming needle** *n* : NEEDLE 8 b

**priming of the tide** : acceleration of the time of high or low water in the 1st and 3d quarters of the moon — opposed to *lag of the tide*

**priming wire** *n* : a pointed wire used to penetrate the vent of a firearm and pierce the cartridge before priming

**pri·mip·a·ra** \prīˈmipərə\ *n, pl* **primiparas** *or* **primiparae** [NL, individual having only one child, fr. L, individual bearing for the first time, fr. *primi-* (fr. *primus* first) + *-para* (fem. of *-parus* -parous)] **1** : an individual that has borne only one offspring **2** : an individual bearing a first offspring — **pri·mi·par·i·ty** \ˌprīməˈparəd·ē\ *n*

**pri·mip·a·rous** \(ˈ)prīˌmipərəs\ *adj* [in sense 1, fr. NL *primipara* + E *-ous;* in sense 2, fr. L *primipara* + E *-ous*] **1** : of or relating to a primipara **2** : bearing young for the first time — compare MULTIPAROUS

**pri·mip·i·lar** \(ˈ)prīˌmipələ(r), ˌprīməˌpīlə(r)\ *adj* [L *primipilaris*, fr. *primipilus* chief centurion of the third division (fr. *primus* first + *pilus* division of the third division — fr. *pilum* javelin, pestle, javelin of the Roman infantry — after the phrase *primi pili* (*centurio*) centurion of the third division) + *-aris* -ar — more at PESTLE] : of, relating to, or constituting the chief centurion of the third division of a Roman legion

**pri·mite** \ˈprīˌmīt\ *n* -s [L *primus* + E *-ite*] : the anterior member of a pair of gregarines in syzygy — compare SATELLITE

**pri·mi·ti·ae** \prīˈmishēˌē\ *n pl* [ML, fr. L, firstlings, firstfruits, fr. *primus* first + *-itiae*, fem. pl. of *-itius* -ice] : ANNATES

**pri·mi·tial** \prīˈmishəl\ *adj* [ML *primitialis* original, principal, fr. L *primitus* firstly + *-ialis* -ial] : ORIGINAL, PRIMITIVE

**1prim·i·tive** \ˈprimәd·iv, -ətiv\ *adj* [ME *primitif*, fr. L *primitivus*, fr. *primitus* firstly, originally (fr. *primus* first + *-itus*, adv. suffix) + *-ivus* -ive — more at PRIME] **1 a** : not derived from or reducible to something else : ORIGINAL, PRIMARY ⟨seeks excellence at its ~ source — nature —John Dewey⟩ ⟨an acre of one ~ color alone —J.A.Michener⟩ ⟨~ verbs⟩ **b** : AXIOMATIC, POSTULATIONAL ⟨~ formula⟩ ⟨~ concept⟩ **c** : of, relating to, or constituting the smallest possible unit cell of a space lattice; *esp* : of, relating to, or constituting such a cell having its axes normal to planes and parallel to axes of symmetry **2 a** : of or relating to the earliest age or period of something ⟨had generally shown a desire to have the church become its ~ self again —Stringfellow Barr⟩ ⟨from the moment when ~ human creatures shaped the first tools —Jacquetta & Christopher Hawkes⟩ ⟨~ Norse⟩ **b** (1) : PRIMORDIAL — opposed to *definitive* (2) : closely approximating an early ancestral type : little evolved : ARCHAIC, PERSISTENT ⟨the opossums are ~ mammals⟩ **c** : belonging to or characteristic of an early stage of development : CRUDE, RUDIMENTARY ⟨a health resort with ~ facilities has been built here —*Amer. Guide Series: Texas*⟩ ⟨a ~ but effective police inquiry —T.S.Eliot⟩ **d** : of, relating to, or constituting the assumed parent speech of related languages ⟨~ Germanic⟩ **3 a** : of or relating to the beginning of things : PRIMEVAL ⟨it runs through resort areas, rolling and rocky farmland, through ~ forests —*Amer. Guide Series: Maine*⟩ **b** : earliest formed : FUNDAMENTAL — used esp. of the Archean in geology **4 a** : of or relating to a state of nature : ELEMENTAL ⟨the noble savage endowed with ~ virtue —Oscar Handlin⟩ ⟨our ~ feelings of vengeance —John Mackwood⟩ **b** : of or relating to any unindustrialized people or culture not possessing a written language and commonly having a relatively simple technology and material culture : NONLITERATE, PRELITERATE **c** : lacking in sophistication or subtlety of thought, feeling, or expression : NAÏVE, SIMPLE ⟨neither staunchly ~ nor confidently au courant, she rarely knew where she was at —Jean Stafford⟩ **d** (1) : SELF-TAUGHT, UNTUTORED ⟨a ~ painter who has never been inside a museum or art school⟩ (2) : produced by a self-taught artist ⟨a ~ portrait⟩ **5** : of, relating to, or holding the doctrines of any of several small Protestant religious groups

**2primitive** \"\ *n* -s **1 a** : something that is primitive ⟨involves no cult of the instinctive and ~ —F.R.Leavis⟩; *specif* : a primitive idea, term, or proposition ⟨limit the number of undefined concepts to a few simple ~*s* —K.F.Leidecker⟩ **b** : a radical or root word — compare DERIVATIVE **2** *often cap* : a member of any of several small Protestant religious groups; *esp* : PRIMITIVE METHODIST **3 a** (1) : an artist active in the early period of a culture or artistic movement (2) : a later imitator or follower of such an artist **b** (1) : a self-taught artist (2) : an artist whose work is marked by directness and naïveté ⟨the simplicity of vision and of purpose that make the true ~ —Cyril Ray⟩ **c** : a work of art produced by a primitive artist **4** : a relation from which a differential equation is derived **5 a** : a member of a nonliterate or preliterate people ⟨the anthropology of the future will not be concerned above all else with ~*s* —A.L.Kroeber⟩ **b** : a simple and unsophisticated person ⟨this grand ~, shaggy and good as a dog —J.H. Allen⟩ **c** : a person whose attitudes, behavior, or mentality are those of an earlier stage of society or human development ⟨a revolt of the ~*s*, goaded by demagogues —*New Republic*⟩ ⟨a handsome, tough tavern brawler with a law degree, a kind of lowbrow intellectual ~ —*Time*⟩ **6** : a postage stamp of early issue; *also* : a philatelic cover of early date

**primitive area** *n* : a large tract within a U. S. national forest set aside for preservation in natural condition with no alteration or development beyond measures for fire prevention being permitted

**primitive axis** *n* : an elongated thickening of the mesoblastic and hypoblastic layers of the blastoderm extending forward from the anterior end of the primitive streak

**primitive baptist** *n, usu cap P&B* : a member of an ultraconservative Baptist religious group that dates from early in the 19th century but has never been formally organized as a denomination and that from its origin has represented a protest movement against missions and Sunday schools

**primitive church** *n, often cap P&C* : the early Christian church as it existed in its original character and organization for about the first three centuries A.D.

**primitive friends** *n pl, cap P&F* : a conservative group of Friends in the U. S. who in 1861 separated from the Wilburites

**primitive green** *n* : a strong green that is bluer and stronger than mintleaf (sense 1) or pepper green and yellower, lighter, and stronger than viridian

**primitive groove** *n* : a depression or groove in the epiblast of the primitive streak that extends forward to the primitive knot

**primitive knot** *n* : a knob of cells at the anterior end of the primitive streak that is the point of origin of the embryonic head process — see END BUD 2

**prim·i·tive·ly** \ˈprimәd·əvlē, -ətə-, -li\ *adv* **1** : at first : in the beginning : ORIGINALLY ⟨the two case endings may have been ~ different —Robert Shafer⟩ **2** : PRIMARILY **3** : in a primitive style or manner ⟨rather ~ operated quarries —*Amer. Guide Series: Minn.*⟩

**primitive methodist** *n, usu cap P&M* : a member of the nonepiscopal Primitive Methodist Church organized in 1812 in England and later extended to the U. S. where it now continues to emphasize basic Wesleyan doctrines and greater congregational participation in its government

**prim·i·tive·ness** \-ivnəs\ *n* -ES : the quality or state of being primitive

**primitive pit** *n* : a depression immediately behind the primitive knot in which the primitive groove ends

**primitive rocks** *n pl* : PRIMARY ROCKS

**primitive segment** *n* : any one of the transverse segments into which the body of the embryo of vertebrates becomes marked off by the formation beginning first in the neck region of a series of distinctly limited masses of mesoblast cells on each side of the neural tube — called also *protovertebra*

**primitive streak** *n* : an opaque band that appears in the blastoderm in the axial line of the future embryo but somewhat behind the place where the embryo proper begins to develop and that represents a highly modified blastopore through which the involution of chordamesoderm takes place

**primitive water** *n* : water originating within the earth

**prim·i·tiv·ism** \ˈprimәd·əˌvizəm, -mətə,-\ *n* -s **1** : primitive practices or procedures ⟨the final stage of the transition from ~ to modernism —Farley Mowat⟩ **2 a** : a belief in the superiority of a simple unsophisticated way of life esp. close to nature **b** : a belief in the superiority of early esp. nonindustrial society to that of the present **3 a** : the style of self-taught artists usu. marked by imaginative naïveté and formal simplicity and directness **b** : the style of the art of primitive peoples usu. marked by vitality, boldness, and deliberate distortion **c** : a conscious imitation by a sophisticated artist of the style of primitive artists or primitive art

**1prim·i·tiv·ist** \-ˌvəst\ *n* -s : an adherent of primitivism

**2primitivist** \"\ *or* **prim·i·tiv·is·tic** \ˌ===ˌvistik, -tēk\ *adj* : of, relating to, or characteristic of primitivism or primitivists — **prim·i·tiv·is·ti·cal·ly** \-tək(ə)lē\ *adv*

**prim·i·tiv·i·ty** \ˌpriməˈtivəd·ē\ *n* -ES : PRIMITIVENESS

**prim·i·tiv·ization** \ˌprimәd·ivəˈzāshən, -ˌvīˈz-\ *n* -s : the process of becoming primitive

**prim·ly** *adv* : in a prim manner
**primmed** *past of* PRIM
**primmer** *comparative of* PRIM
**primmest** *superlative of* PRIM
**primming** *pres part of* PRIM
**prim·ness** *n* -ES : the quality or state of being prim
**¹pri·mo** \'prē(,)mō, 'prī(,)-\ *adv* [L, fr. *primus* first — more at PRIME] : in the first place : FIRST ⟨in danger, ~, of setting down material perhaps distasteful to the reader —Lawrence Durrell⟩
**²pri·mo** \'prē(,)mō\ *n* -S [It, fr. *primo* first, fr. L *primus*] : the first or leading part (as in a duet or trio)
**pri·mo·cane** \'prīmə,kān\ *n* [¹*primo* + *cane*] : a new cane on a bramble fruit (as a blackberry or raspberry) that will flower and fruit the following year
**pri·mo·fil·i·ces** \,prī(,)mō'filə,sēz\ *n pl, cap* [NL, fr. L *primo* + NL *Filices*] *in some classifications* : a subclass of Filicineae comprising fossil forms with the axis usu. protostelic, the fronds but slightly developed, terminal or subterminal sporangia, and usu. isospores and including the order Coenopteridales and sometimes other forms of somewhat uncertain relationships
**pri·mo·genial** \¦prī(,)mō, -,mə+\ *adj* [modif. (influenced by LL *primogenitalis* primogenital) of L *primigenius* primogenial (fr. *primus* first + *-genius* — fr. *gignere* to beget —) + E *-al*] **1** *also* **pri·mi·genial** \¦prīmə+\ : first formed or generated : ORIGINAL, PRIMITIVE **2** : PRIMOGENITARY
**pri·mo·genital** \¦=(,)=+\ *adj* [LL *primogenitalis*, fr. *primogenitus* state of being firstborn (fr. L, firstborn, fr. *primus* first + *genitus*, past part. of *gignere* to beget) + L *-alis* -al] : PRIMOGENITARY
**pri·mo·gen·i·tary** \-əd·,erē\ *adj* [LL *primogenitus* state of being firstborn + E *-ary*] : of, relating to, or based on primogeniture ⟨~ rules⟩ ⟨~ succession⟩
**pri·mo·gen·i·tor** \,=(,)='jenəd·ə(r)\ *n* [LL, fr. L *primus* first + *genitor* begetter — more at GENITOR] : first ancestor ⟨this tiny, nameless ~ of all living matter —*Time*⟩; *broadly* : ANCESTOR, FOREFATHER ⟨our distant ~*s*⟩
**pri·mo·gen·i·ture** \¦prīmō¦jenə,chü(ə)r, -üə, -nəchə(r)\ *n* [LL *primogenitura*, fr. L *primus* first + *genitura* birth, fr. *genitus* (past part. of *gignere* to beget) + *-ura* -ure — more at KIN] **1** : the state of being the firstborn of the children of the same parents **2** : an exclusive right of inheritance; *specif* : a right belonging under English law to the eldest son or failing lineal descendants the eldest male in the next degree of consanguinity to take all the real estate of which an ancestor died seized and intestate to the exclusion of all female and younger male descendants of equal degree
**pri·mo·gen·i·ture·ship** \-,ship\ *n* : PRIMOGENITURE 2
**¹pri·mor·di·al** \(')prī¦mō(r)dēəl\ *adj* [ME, fr. LL *primordialis*, fr. L *primordium* beginning, origin (fr. neut. of *primordius* original, fr. *primus* first + *ordiri* to begin, begin a web) + *-alis* -al — more at PRIME, ORDER] **1 a** : existing at or from the beginning : first created or developed : EARLIEST, PRIMEVAL ⟨assuming that the sun, planets, and their satellites had all originated from a ~ mass of gas —S.F.Mason⟩ ⟨the child's ~ subconscious world —Louise Bogan⟩ **b** : earliest formed in the growth of an individual or organ : PRIMITIVE **c** : CRUDE, UNDEVELOPED ⟨a ~ theologian of the hellfire and brimstone variety —Carey McWilliams⟩ **2** : constituting a basis or starting point : existing independently : ELEMENTARY, FUNDAMENTAL, PRIMARY ⟨life's ~ reality is spirit —H.O.Taylor⟩ — **pri·mor·di·al·ly** \-əlē, -li\ *adv*
**²primordial** \"\ *n* -S : something original or fundamental : a first principle or element
**primordial meristem** *n* : PRIMARY MERISTEM
**primordial ovum** *n* : one of the large cells in the germinal epithelium and in the sexual cords or egg tubes derived from it which occur in embryos of both sexes but more abundantly in the female and from which the true eggs are believed to be derived
**primordial utricle** *n* : the cytoplasmic lining of the cell wall in a fully developed vacuolated cell
**pri·mor·di·um** \prī'mō(r)dēəm\ *n, pl* **primor·dia** \-dēə\ [L] **1** : the earliest part or stage : BEGINNING, ORIGIN ⟨regards the solar system as resulting by evolution from a ~ —H.S. Jones⟩ **2** : the rudiment or commencement of a part or organ : ANLAGE
**pri·mork** \(')prē¦mȯrk\ *n, pl* **primork** *or* **primorks** *usu cap* **1** : a people formerly occupying the region of the Sikhote Alin mountains and the adjoining Ussuri-Amur lowlands of Siberia **2** : a member of the Primork people
**primos** *pl of* PRIMO
**pri·most** \'prē,mȯst, -mōst\ *n* -S [Norw, fr. *prim* whey + *ost* cheese] : MYSOST
**primp** \'primp\ *vb* -ED/-ING/-S [perh. alter. of ²*prim*] *vt* : to dress, adorn, or arrange in a careful or finicky manner ⟨she ~*ed* her hair —Walt Sheldon⟩ ⟨seems afraid to trust the strength of his material; he ~*s* it with cute comment —*Time*⟩ ⟨~ herself⟩ ~ *vi* **1** *chiefly Scot* : to behave in a prim or affected manner **2 a** : to dress up or groom oneself carefully ⟨she's always ~*ing* in front of the mirror⟩ ⟨~*s* for hours before a date⟩ **b** : to smarten things up : arrange things neatly ⟨rearrange her magazine basket as she ~*s* for callers —W.H.Whyte⟩
**¹prim·rose** \'prim,rōz\ *n* [ME *primerose*, fr. MF, fr. OF, prob. fr. *prime* (fem. of *prin* first, prime) + *rose*, fr. L *rosa* — more at PRIME, ROSE] **1 a** : a plant of the genus *Primula* (as the cowslip or the English primrose); *esp* : any of the numerous often hybrid plants of Asiatic or European origin that are cultivated for their bright and varied flowers — see CHINESE PRIMROSE **b** : EVENING PRIMROSE **2** : the best or fairest part or example : FLOWER ⟨the Lord was pleased to work upon him in the ~ of his life —Samuel Clarke⟩ **3** : PRIMROSE YELLOW
**²primrose** \"\ *adj* **1** : of, relating to, or resembling the primrose ⟨~ color⟩ **2** : abounding in primroses : FLOWERY, GAY ⟨the ~ way⟩ ⟨a ~ bank⟩
**³primrose** \"\ *vi* -ED/-ING/-S : to look for or gather primroses ⟨*primrosing* and promise of good sport —Edmund Blunden⟩
**primrosed** *adj* : abounding in primroses
**primrose family** *n* : PRIMULACEAE
**primrose green** *n* : a pale greenish yellow that is very slightly deeper than tilleul
**primrose jasmine** *n* : an evergreen rambling Chinese shrub (*Jasminum mesnyi*) having yellow flowers with a darker eye and cultivated as an ornamental
**primrose path** *n* **1** : a path of ease or pleasure ⟨had made some progress in the *primrose path* of Epicurean wisdom —George Santayana⟩; *esp* : a path of sensual pleasure ⟨the *primrose path* of dalliance treads —Shak.⟩ **2** : a path of least resistance; *esp* : one leading to disaster ⟨leading them down the *primrose path* of military economy —*Newsweek*⟩
**primrose peerless** *or* **primrose peerless narcissus** *n* : a southern European narcissus (*Narcissus biflorus*) that is sometimes cultivated as an ornamental and has grasslike leaves and usu. paired white to greenish white flowers
**primrose willow** *n* : an annual or perennial herb of the genus *Jussiaea* with yellow flowers and principal leaves resembling those of willows — called also *water primrose*
**primrose yellow** *n* **1** : a light to moderate greenish yellow **2** : a light to moderate yellow
**prim·rosy** \'prim,rōzē\ *adj* [¹*primrose* + *-y*] : PRIMROSE
**prims** *pl of* PRIM, *pres 3d sing of* PRIM
**prim·sie** \'primsē, -mzi\ *adj* [²*prim* + connective *-s-* + *-ie*] *Scot* : PRIM
**prim·u·la** \'primyələ\ *n* [NL, fr. ML, primrose, cowslip, fr. *primula veris*, lit., firstling of spring, fr. *primula* firstling (fr. L, fem. of *primulus* first, fr. *primus* first + *-ulus* -ule) + L *veris*, gen. of *ver* spring — more at VERNAL] **1** *cap* : a genus (the type of the family Primulaceae) of chiefly European and Asiatic perennial acaulescent herbs having large tufted basal leaves and showy variously colored flowers with a salver-shaped corolla bearing five stamens within its tube — see AURICULA, CHINESE PRIMROSE, COWSLIP, OXLIP, POLYANTHUS **2** -S : any plant of the genus *Primula*
**prim·u·la·ce·ae** \,=='lāsē,ē\ *n pl, cap* [NL, fr. *Primula*, type genus + *-aceae*] : a family of herbs (order Primulales) having perfect regular flowers with a deciduous rotate or campanulate corolla and a superior ovary and being widely distributed chiefly in the northern hemisphere — **prim·u·la·ceous** \¦==¦lāshəs\ *adj*
**prim·u·la·les** \,=='lā(,)lēz\ *n pl, cap* [NL, fr. *Primula* + *-ales*] : an order of gamopetalous pentamerous dicotyledonous herbs, shrubs, or trees that includes the families Primulaceae, Theophrastaceae, and Myrsinaceae and is distinguished by the one-celled ovary with free-central placentation — see PLUMBAGINALES
**prim·u·lav·er·in** \,primyə'lavərən\ *n* -S [alter. (influenced by NL *Primula*) of ISV *primeverin*] : a crystalline glycoside $C_{20}H_{28}O_{13}$ that is isomeric with primeverin and occurs with it and that on hydrolysis yields primeverose and a derivative of gentisic acid
**prim·u·line** \'primyə,lēn, -,lən\ *n* -S [ISV *primul-* (fr. NL *Primula*) + *-ine*] : a fugitive yellow dye made by heating para-toluidine and sulfur together and sulfonating the product that can be diazotized on the fiber and coupled with a phenol or amine to yield various developed dyes (as red colors of good fastness to washing but not to light) — see DYE table I (under *Direct Yellow 59*)
**primuline yellow** *n* : YOLK YELLOW
**prim·u·li·nus** \,primyə'līnəs\ *n* -ES [NL *primulinus* (specific epithet of *Gladiolus primulinus*), fr. L *primula* (fem. of *primulus* first) + *-inus* -ine] **1** : a gladiolus (*Gladiolus primulinus*) of southeastern tropical Africa having clear primrose yellow flowers with the uppermost perianth segment much curved in a hood **2** *or* **primulinus hybrid** : any of numerous cultivated gladioli produced by hybridizing from the species primulinus and possessing its characteristic hood
**pri·mum mob·i·le** \¦prīməm'mäbə(,)lē\ *n, pl* **primum mobiles** [ME, fr. ML, lit., first moving thing] **1 a** : the ninth or in later numbering the tenth and outermost concentric sphere added in the middle ages to the system of Ptolemaic astronomy and conceived as carrying the spheres of the fixed stars and the planets in its daily revolution — compare CRYSTALLINE HEAVEN **b** *Aristotelianism* : the highest physical sphere that derives its circular motion directly from God the unmoved mover **2** : something that is a first source of motion or activity : PRIME MOVER ⟨regarded self-interest as the *primum mobile* of all human activity⟩
**pri·mus** \'prīməs\ *n* -ES *often cap* [ML, one who is first, magnate, fr. L first — more at PRIME] : the first in dignity of the bishops of the Episcopal Church in Scotland who has various privileges but no metropolitan authority
**Primus** \"\ *trademark* — used for a portable oil-burning stove
**primus in·ter pa·res** \¦==,intər'pär,ēz\ *n, pl* **pri·mi inter pares** \¦prē,mī,-\ [L] : the first among equals ⟨the prime minister's place among his colleagues as *primus inter pares* —F.A.Ogg & Harold Zink⟩
**primwort** \'=,=\ *n* [prob. fr. ¹*prim* + *wort*] : PRIVET 1a(1)
**prin** \'prin\ *chiefly Scot var of* ¹PREEN
**prin** *abbr* **1** principal; principally **2** principle
**princ** *abbr* **1** principal **2** principle
**¹prince** \'prin(t)s\ *n* -S [ME, fr. OF, fr. L *princip-, princeps* first person, chief, prince, lit., one who takes the first part, fr. *prin-* (fr. *primus* first) + *-cip-, -ceps* (fr. *capere* to take) — more at HEAVE] **1 a** : a sovereign ruler : MONARCH ⟨noblemen passed from court to court, seeking service with one ~ or another —W.M.Thackeray⟩ **b** : the ruler of a principality or state ⟨New Delhi has promised the ~*s* . . . the right to be called Your Highness —*Time*⟩ ⟨the *Prince* of Monaco⟩ **2** : a male member of a royal family; *esp* : a son or a grandson in the male line of the British king or queen **3** : a nobleman whose rank and status vary from one part of the world to another ⟨Polynesian ~*s*⟩ ⟨a Chinese ~ of the first degree⟩ **4** : an ecclesiastic of high rank; *specif* : CARDINAL **5 a** : a person at the head of a class or profession : one very outstanding in a specified respect ⟨a ~ among men⟩ ⟨that ~ of hosts who left nothing undone for the comfort of his guests⟩ ⟨a very ~ of poets⟩ — compare MERCHANT PRINCE **b** : a jolly good fellow : an open-handed and genial friend ⟨he's a real ~⟩
**²prince** \"\ *vi* -ED/-ING/-S *obs* : to play or act the part of a prince — often used with *it* ⟨showed a disposition to ~ it⟩
**prince al·bert** \-'albə(r)t, *usu* -d·+V\ *n, pl* **prince alberts** *usu cap P&A* [after *Prince Albert* Edward (later Edward VII king of England) †1910 who set the fashion of wearing it] **1** *or* **prince albert coat** : a long double-breasted frock coat for men **2** : a man's house slipper with a low counter and goring on each side

Prince Albert 1

**prince albert fir** *also* **prince albert's fir** *or* **prince albert spruce** *n, usu cap P&A* : WESTERN HEMLOCK
**prince albert's yew** *also* **prince albert yew** *n, usu cap P&A* : a small evergreen tree (*Saxe-gothaea conspicua*) of the family Taxaceae that resembles the common yews, is native to mountainous southern Chile, and is sometimes cultivated as an ornamental
**prince-bishop** \(')=¦=\ *n* : a bishop of princely rank; *esp* : one with a see constituting a feudal principality of the Holy Roman Empire
**prince charles spaniel** *n, usu cap P&C* [alter. of *King Charles spaniel*] : an English toy spaniel having a black, tan, and white coat
**prince charming** *n, sometimes cap P&C* [after *Prince Charming*, hero of the fairy tale *Cinderella* (1729), translation, by Robert Samber *fl*1729 Eng. writer, of *Cendrillon* (1697) by Charles Perrault †1703 Fr. writer] : a suitor who fulfills the dreams of his beloved; *also* : a man of often specious affability and charm toward women
**prince consort** *n, pl* **princes consort** : the husband of a reigning female sovereign
**prince·dom** \'prin(t)sdəm, -stəm\ *n* -S [*prince* + *-dom*] **1** : the jurisdiction, sovereignty, rank, or estate of a prince **2** : PRINCIPALITY
**prince ed·ward island** \-¦edwə(r)d-\ *adj, usu cap P&E&I* [fr. *Prince Edward Island*, maritime province in the Gulf of St. Lawrence in southeastern Canada] : of or from the province of Prince Edward Island : of the kind or style prevalent in Prince Edward Island
**prince elector** *n* : ELECTOR a
**prince gray** *n, often cap P* : CRANE 4
**prince·kin** \'prin(t)skən\ *n* -S [*prince* + *-kin*] : a diminutive prince
**prince·less** \-sləs\ *adj* : having no prince
**prince·let** \-slət\ *n* -S [*prince* + *-let*] : a petty prince
**prince·li·ness** \-slēnəs, -slin-\ *n* -ES **1** : princely conduct or character ⟨the ~ of his outlook⟩ **2** : LUXURY, MAGNIFICENCE, SPLENDOR ⟨the ~ of our accommodations⟩
**prince·ling** \-sliŋ, -slēŋ\ *n* -S [*prince* + *-ling*] : a petty or insignificant prince
**¹prince·ly** \-slē, -sli\ *adj, often* -ER/-EST [*prince* + *-ly* (adj. suffix)] **1** : of, relating to, or descended from a prince : ROYAL, KINGLY : of high rank or authority ⟨~ birth⟩ ⟨~ power⟩ **2** : resembling, befitting, or having the characteristics of a prince : STATELY, NOBLE : MAGNIFICENT, MUNIFICENT ⟨a message of thanks for this ~ gift —Thomas Cadett⟩ ⟨those ~ ships with long black hulls —Robert Payne⟩
**²princely** \"\ *adv* [*prince* + *-ly* (adv. suffix)] : in a princely manner : in a manner befitting a prince
**prince of wales** \-'wā(ə)lz\ *cap P&W* [ME] : the male heir apparent to the British throne — used as a title only after it has been specif. conferred by the sovereign
**prince-of-wales'-feather** \-lz(əz)-\ *n, usu cap P&W* **1** : PRINCE'S-FEATHER **2** : CRAPE FERN
**prince of wales feathers** *or* **prince of wales plumes** *usu cap 1st P&W* : a decorative motif used esp. on chair backs and consisting of three feathers derived from the crest of the Prince of Wales
**prince-of-wales'-heath** *n, usu cap P&W* : a southern African shrub (*Erica perspicua*) grown for its profusion of white flowers
**prin·ceps** \'prin,seps, -iŋ,ke-\ *n, pl* **princi·pes** \-n(t)sə,pēz, -ŋkə,pās\ [L — more at PRINCE] : one that is first: as **a** : the head of the state under the Roman Empire **b** : any of various chief officials (as the headman of a tribe) among the ancient Teutons and Anglo-Saxons **c** : a first edition of a work; *also* : a copy of this edition
**prince regent** *n, pl* **prince regents** : a prince who rules a country during the minority, absence, or disability of the nominal sovereign
**prince royal** *n, pl* **princes royal** : the eldest son of a sovereign
**prince rupert drop** *also* **prince rupert's drop** *n, usu cap P&R* [after *Prince Rupert* of Germany †1682 who first brought it to England] : RUPERT'S DROP
**prince ru·pert's metal** \-'rüpə(r)ts-\ *n, usu cap P&R* [after *Prince Rupert* †1682, its inventor] : PRINCE'S METAL
**princes** *pl of* PRINCE, *pres 3d sing of* PRINCE
**prince's-feather** \¦==¦==\ *n, pl* **prince's-feathers** **1** : a showy annual plant (*Amaranthus hybridus hypochondriacus*) often cultivated for its dense usu. red spikes of bloom **2** : a plant (*Polygonum orientale*) with broadly ovate leaves and slender drooping crimson spikes — called also *gentleman's-cane, prince's-plume* **3** : LILAC 1 a **4** : LONDON PRIDE 1
**prince·ship** \'prin(t)s,ship, -n,sh-\ *n* [*prince* + *-ship*] **1** : the dignity or position of a prince **2** : the period during which a prince (as an heir apparent) is such
**prince's lengths** *n pl, often cap P* [after *Prince* George Augustus Frederick (later George IV king of England) †1830 who prescribed them] : the three distances of 100, 80, and 60 yards in the York round at archery
**prince's metal** *n, usu cap P* [after *Prince* Rupert of Germany †1682, its inventor] : an alloy of the appearance of brass believed to be made of copper and zinc or copper and bismuth and formerly used for cheap jewelry — called also *Prince Rupert's metal*
**prince's pine** *n* **1** : JACK PINE 1 **2** : PIPSISSEWA
**prince's-plume** \¦==¦=\ *n, pl* **prince's-plumes** **1** : PRINCE'S-FEATHER **2** : DESERT PLUME
**prince's reckoning** *n, often cap P* [after *Prince* George Augustus Frederick (later George IV king of England) †1830 who prescribed it] : the standard of counting hits in archery on the target as gold 9, red 7, blue 5, black 3, white 1
**¹prin·cess** \'prin(t)səs *(before a voiced consonant sometimes* -əz), 'prin,ses, prin'ses\ *n* -ES [ME *princesse*, fr. MF, fr. OF *prince* + *-esse* -ess — more at PRINCE] **1** *archaic* : a female prince : a woman having sovereign power or the rank of a prince ⟨so excellent a ~, as the present queen —Jonathan Swift⟩ **2** : a female member of a royal family; *esp* : a daughter or a granddaughter of a sovereign ⟨the Duchess of Kent was safely delivered . . . of a ~ —*London Times*⟩ **3** : the consort of a prince **4 a** : a woman outstanding in some usu. specified respect ⟨a ~ of seamstresses⟩ **b** : something personified as female and outstanding of its kind ⟨a winding ~ of a river⟩ **5** : an attractive young woman selected to represent a commercial product, special group, or other interest publicly or to preside (as at a fair or college homecoming celebration) ⟨the new potato ~⟩ — compare QUEEN
**²princess** \"\ *vi* -ED/-ING/-ES : to act or play the princess — often used with *it*
**³princess** \"\ *or* **prin·cesse** \(')prin¦ses\ *adj* [*princesse* fr. F, princess] **1** : close-fitting and usu. with gores from neck to flaring hemline — used esp. of women's full-length garments **2** *usu princesse* : served with a garnish of asparagus usu. with artichoke hearts or truffles
**princess feather** *n* : PRINCE'S-FEATHER 2
**princess flower** *n* : TIBOUCHINA 2
**prin·cess·ly** *adj* : like, befitting, or having the characteristics of a princess
**princess pine** *n* : PRINCE'S PINE
**princess post** *n* : a post in a roofing truss that is framed in a position intermediate between the queen post and tie beam
**princess regent** *n, pl* **princess regents** **1** : a princess who rules a country during the minority, absence, or disability of the nominal sovereign **2** : the wife of a prince regent
**princess ring** *n* : a finger ring with three to five stones along the band often surrounded by smaller stones
**princess royal** *n, pl* **princesses royal** : the eldest daughter of a British or Prussian sovereign — a designation granted for life and used only after the title has been specif. conferred by the sovereign

princess ring

**princess tree** *n* : a Chinese tree (*Paulownia tomentosa*) that has soft pubescent leaves and terminal clusters of large purple irregular flowers and is introduced and naturalized esp. in eastern No. America — called also *karri-tree*
**prince·ton orange** \'prinztən-, -in(t)stən-\ *n, often cap P* [fr. *Princeton* University, N.J.] : a strong orange that is yellower, stronger, and slightly lighter than pumpkin and redder, darker, and slightly less strong than cadmium orange
**princewood** \'=,=\ *n* **1 a** : either of two tropical American timber trees (*Cordia gerascanthus* and *C. alliodora*) **b** : the hard heavy smooth elastic dark-streaked brown wood of either tree **2** : a tropical American shrub (*Exostema caribaeum*) with a bark used in the preparation of bitters
**princing** *pres part of* PRINCE
**¹prin·ci·pal** \'prin(t)səpəl, -sәbəl *also* -inzp- *or* -in(t)sp-\ *adj* [ME, fr. OF, fr. L *principalis* first, principal, fr. *princip-, princeps* first person, chief + *-alis* -al — more at PRINCE] **1** : most important, consequential, or influential : relegating comparable matters, items, or individuals to secondary rank : CONTROLLING, PRECEDING, SALIENT ⟨his chief friend and ~ ally —Anthony Trollope⟩ ⟨a chicken stew of which the ~ ingredient was not chicken but sea cucumber —John Steinbeck⟩ **2** *obs* : of or relating to a prince : PRINCELY **3** : of, relating to, or constituting principal or a principal. as **a** : CAPITAL ⟨~ costs⟩ ⟨invested a ~ sum⟩ **b** : being the person chiefly concerned in some legal proceeding **4** : MAIN 6 **syn** see CHIEF
**²principal** \"\ *n* -S [ME, fr. MF, fr. LL *principalis*, fr. L, adj., principal] **1** : a person who has controlling authority or is in a position to act independently : one who has a leading position or takes the lead: as **a** : a chief or head man or woman : one presiding as ruler, leader, superior, or lord **b** : the chief executive officer of various educational institutions ⟨the ~ of our grade school⟩ ⟨the vice-chancellor of some British universities is known as the ~⟩ **c** : one who employs another to act for him subject to his general control and instruction : the person from whom an agent's responsibility derives **d** : the chief actor or an actual participant in a crime including anyone present and actively abetting or assisting therein as distinguished from an accessory either before or after the fact **e** : the person primarily liable on a legal obligation or the one who will ultimately bear the burden because of a duty to indemnify another as distinguished from one secondarily liable (as an endorser, surety, or guarantor) **f** : one fighting or pledged to fight a duel — compare SECOND **g** : a leading performer (as in a drama, opera, orchestra, or ballet) : a person taking a chief part in a theatrical performance : STAR **h** : OFFICIAL 1 **2** : a matter or thing of primary importance : a main or most important element: as **a** (1) : a capital sum placed at interest, due as a debt, or used as a fund (2) : the corpus or main body of an estate, portion, devise, or bequest — distinguished from *income* **b** : the construction that gives shape and strength to a roof and that is generally one of several trusses of timber or iron; *also* : the most important member of a piece of framing **c** *archaic* : a fundamental point : PRINCIPLE **d** : one of the taper-bearing pillars formerly used to decorate a hearse **e** : an original (as of a writing or work of art) from which copies are, may be, or have been made **f** : either of the two outermost primaries of a hawk's wing **g** (1) : the chief open metallic stop in an English pipe organ that is an octave above the open diapason and consists of a 4-foot stop on the manual, an 8-foot stop on the pedal (2) *usu cap* : an octave or 4-foot stop — used in combination ⟨dulciana *Principal*⟩ **h** (1) : the chief motif or feature in a work of art (2) : a fugue subject — compare ANSWER **i** : a trumpet of a kind used prominently in old orchestral music (as of Handel)
**³prin·ci·pal** \¦prin(t)sə¦päl\ *n, pl* **principa·les** \,==¦pä(,)lās\ [Sp, fr. LL *principalis* chief, leading person] : a leading man or one of the first citizens of a Philippine or Latin American community
**principal axis** *n* **1 a** : any of three mutually perpendicular axes through a given point of a rigid body with respect to which the moment of inertia is either a maximum or a minimum — com-

pare PERMANENT AXIS **b :** the line with respect to which a spherical mirror or lens system is symmetrical and which passes through both the center of the surfaces and their centers of curvature **2 :** the line through a focus of a conic perpendicular to a directrix

**principal boy** *n* **:** a male character in English pantomime usu. played by a woman — compare DAME 5

**principal challenge** *n* **:** a challenge to a juror on a ground assigned that if proved true renders the juror incompetent to serve as such in the case because of his presumed malice or favor **:** a challenge for cause

**principal distance** *n* **:** the length of a perpendicular from a station point to a perspective plane taken along the principal visual ray

**principal focus** *n* **:** the focus for a beam of incident rays parallel to the axis

**principal form** *n* **:** the form that constitutes or determines a philosophical species

**principal function** *n* **:** the temporal integral of the kinetic potential **:** the integral of the kinetic less the potential energy

**prin·ci·pal·i·ty** \ˌprin(t)səˈpaləd·ē, -lətē, -i\ *n* -ES [ME *principalite*, fr. MF, fr. LL *principalitat-, principalitas* preeminence, excellence, fr. L *principalis* first, principal + *-itat-, -itas* -ity] **1 :** the quality or state of being principal **:** supreme station or power **:** HEADSHIP, PREEMINENCE ⟨your *principalities* shall come down, even the crown of your glory —Jer 13: 18 (AV)⟩ **2 a :** the state, office, or authority of a prince **:** princely dominion **:** SOVEREIGNTY **b :** the position or responsibilities of a principal (as of a school) **3 :** the territory or jurisdiction of a prince **:** the country that gives title to a prince ⟨the ~ of Wales⟩; *often* **:** a minor semi-independent state under the rule of a prince ⟨the ~ of Monaco⟩ — compare KINGDOM 2 **4** [trans. of LL *principatus*, trans. of Gk *archē*] **a :** a good or evil spiritual being of a high order ⟨for I am sure that neither death, nor life, nor angels, nor *principalities* . . . will be able to separate us from the love of God in Christ Jesus our Lord —Rom 8:38 (RSV)⟩ **b :** one of the nine orders of angels in medieval angelology

**principal line** *n* **:** the first and most intense line of a spectral line series

**prin·ci·pal·ly** \ˈprin(t)səp(ə)lē, -səb(-, -li *also* -inzp(ə)l- *or* -in(t)sp-\ *adv* [ME, fr. ¹*principal* + *-ly*] **:** in a principal manner **:** in the chief place or degree **:** PRIMARILY, CHIEFLY, MAINLY

**principal meridian** *n* **:** any of the true geographical meridians established by authority of the surveyor general of the U.S. that serves as the meridian of reference for subdividing public lands in a given region — compare GUIDE MERIDIAN

**principal moment** *n* **:** one of the three moments of inertia of a body about its principal axes of inertia at a given point

**prin·ci·pal·ness** \-pəlnəs, -bəl-\ *n* -ES **:** the quality or state of being principal

**principal parts** *n pl* **:** a series of verb forms from which all the other forms of a verb can be derived including in English the infinitive, the past tense, and the past participle (as *play, played, played* or *sing, sang, sung*)

**principal plane** *n* **:** any of the planes perpendicular to the axis and passing through the principal points of an optical system

**principal plane of symmetry :** a plane of symmetry in a crystal that includes two or more axes of symmetry

**principal planet** *n* **:** any of the nine known planets of the solar system that comprise the four terrestrial and the five major planets — distinguished from *minor planet*

**principal point** *n* **1 :** the point at which a principal visual ray intersects a perspective plane **2 :** either of two points on the axis of a lens so related that a ray from any point of the object directed toward one principal point will emerge from the lens in a parallel direction but directed through the other principal point **3 :** the point where the optical axis of the lens meets the film plane in an aerial camera

**principal quantum number** *n* **:** an integer associated with the energy of an atomic electron in any one of its possible stationary states and including both the azimuthal and the radial quantum number — called also *total quantum number*

**principal rafter** *n* **:** one of the upper diagonal members of a roof truss supporting the purlins and common rafters or those joints to which the roof boarding is secured — see ROOF illustration

**principal ray** *n* **1 :** PRINCIPAL VISUAL RAY **2 :** the one ray of the rays entering an optical instrument from any given point of the object that passes through the exact center of the aperture stop

**principals** *pl of* PRINCIPAL

**principal section** *n* **1 :** a plane passing through the optical axis of a crystal; *specif* **:** the principal plane that contains either the wave normal or the ray of light under discussion **2 :** a plane perpendicular to the edge of an optical prism

**prin·ci·pal·ship** \-pəlˌship, -bəl-\ *n* [²*principal* + *-ship*] **:** the office or condition of a principal; *esp* **:** the position of an academic principal ⟨will be asked to assume the ~ of the new high school⟩

**principal sum** *n* **:** the sum specified to be paid under the terms of an accident or health insurance policy in case of the death of the insured or the loss of limb or sight due to an accidental injury

**principal visual ray** *n* **:** a perpendicular that extends from a station point to a perspective plane and theoretically passes precisely along the visual axis of a viewing eye

**principal work** *n* **:** the open cylindrical pipes of a pipe organ that give the typical organ quality of tone

**prin·ci·pate** \ˈprin(t)səˌpāt, -sapət\ *n* -S [ME *principat*, fr. L *principatus*, fr. *princip-, princeps* first person, prince + *-atus* -ate — more at PRINCE] **1 :** princely power **:** supreme rule **2** *obs* **a :** PRINCIPALITY 4b **b :** a principal person **:** PRINCE **3 :** PRINCIPALITY 3 **4 :** the power or term of a Roman princeps

**prin·ci·pe** *It* ˈprēnchē(ˌ)pā, *Sp* ˈprēnsē(ˌ)pā *or* -nthē-, *Pg* ˈprīⁿ(n)sēpə\ *n* -S [It *principe* & Sp & Pg *príncipe*, fr. L *princip-, princeps* prince] **:** PRINCE; *esp* **:** the eldest son of a Spanish or Portuguese king — compare INFANTE

¹**principes** *pl of* PRINCEPS

²**prin·ci·pes** \ˈprin(t)səˌpēz, -iŋkəˌpās\ [NL, fr. L, princes] *syn of* PALMALES

**prin·cip·i·al** \(ˈ)prinˈsipēəl\ *adj* [L *principium* beginning + E *-al*] **:** INITIAL, PRIMARY

**principiant** *adj* [LL *principiant-, principians*, pres. part. of *principiare* to begin, fr. L *principium* beginning] *obs* **:** relating to or dealing with first principles or beginnings

**prin·cip·i·um** \prinˈsipēəm\ *n, pl* **princip·ia** \-ēə\ [L, beginning, origin, basis] **1 :** a fundamental principle **:** ultimate origin **:** BASIS, ELEMENT, FOUNDATION ⟨the *principia* of ethics⟩ **2 :** INCEPTION 2a **3 :** a general's quarters in an ancient Roman military encampment

¹**prin·ci·ple** \ˈprin(t)səpəl, -səbəl *also* -inzp- *or* -in(t)sp-\ *n* -S [ME, modif. of MF *principe*, fr. L *principium* beginning, origin, basis (in pl. *principia*, first principles, fundamentals), fr. *princip-, princeps* first, original, lit., taken as first, fr. *prin-* (fr. *primus* first) + *-cip-, -ceps* (fr. L *capere* to take) — more at PRIME, HEAVE] **1 a :** a general or fundamental truth **:** a comprehensive and fundamental law, doctrine, or assumption on which others are based or from which others are derived **:** elementary proposition ⟨the ~*s* of physics⟩ **b (1) :** a governing law of conduct **:** an opinion, attitude, or belief that exercises a directing influence on the life and behavior **:** rule or code of usu. good conduct by which one directs one's life or actions ⟨a man of no ~⟩ ⟨the honorable ~*s* to which my father reared me⟩ **(2) :** devotion to what is right and honorable esp. as a trait of character **c (1) :** natural law or laws applied to achieve a purpose or produce a result by an artificial device (as a mechanical-contrivance) **:** the laws or facts of nature underlying and exemplified in the working of an artificial device ⟨the ~ of the internal-combustion engine⟩ **(2) :** the mode of construction or working of an artificial device **2 a :** something from which another thing takes its origin **:** a basic or primary source of material or energy **:** ultimate basis or cause ⟨the ancients recognized opposed governing ~*s* as of heat and cold, moisture and dryness⟩ **b :** an original faculty or endowment **:** underlying or basic quality that motivates behavior or other activities ⟨such ~*s* of human nature as greed and curiosity⟩ **c** *obs* **:** original state **:** COMMENCEMENT, BEGINNING **3** *obs* **a principles** *pl* **:** RUDIMENTS **b :** SEED, EMBRYO **4 :** a component part **:** CONSTITUENT: as **a** *archaic* **:** ELEMENT 1a, 1b **b :** a distinguishable ingredient that exhibits or imparts a characteristic quality ⟨the bark contains a bitter ~ used in medicine⟩ ⟨the active ~ of this drug⟩ **5** *cap, Christian Science* **:** a divine principle **:** GOD ⟨the triune *Principle* of Life, Truth, and Love⟩

**syn** PRINCIPLE, AXIOM, FUNDAMENTAL, LAW, and THEOREM can mean, in common, a proposition or other formulation stating a fact, or a generalization accepted as true and basic. PRINCIPLE applies to any generalization that provides a basis for reasoning or a guide for conduct or procedure ⟨the *principle* of free speech⟩ ⟨his remarkable grasp of *principle* in the remaining field, that of historical geography —Benjamin Farrington⟩ ⟨the same hankering as their pious ancestors for a cozy universe, a closed system of certainties erected upon a single *principle* —H.J.Muller⟩ ⟨the *principle* was established that no officer or employee . . . was entitled to any classified information whatever unless it was necessary for the performance of his duties —J.P.Baxter b.1893⟩ ⟨I do not mean to assert this pedantically as an absolute rule, but as a *principle* guiding school authorities —Bertrand Russell⟩ AXIOM in an older sense applies to a principle not open to dispute because self-evident, usu. one upon which a structure of reasoning is or may be erected; in more common current usage it implies a principle universally accepted or regarded as worthy of acceptance rather than one necessarily true ⟨the journalistic *axiom* that there is nothing as dead as yesterday's newspaper —G.W.Johnson⟩ ⟨one of the *axioms* of U.S. business is that efficiency is increased by specialization —*Time*⟩ FUNDAMENTAL usu. applies to a principle, but sometimes a fact, so essential to a philosophy, religion, science, or art that its rejection would destroy the intellectual structure resting upon it ⟨the *fundamentals* of scientific research⟩ ⟨the *fundamentals* of Christian belief⟩ ⟨the simple economics *fundamental* that mechanization is the secret of America's greatness —*advt*⟩ LAW in this comparison applies to a formulation stating an order or relation of phenomena which is regarded as always holding good ⟨the conquest of nature's procreative forces, through the discovery of the *laws* of agriculture and animal husbandry —R.W.Murray⟩ ⟨the *laws* of the rain and of the seasons here are tropic laws —Marjory S. Douglas⟩ ⟨it is a *law* that no two electrons may occupy the same orbit —A.S.Eddington⟩ THEOREM applies to a proposition that admits of rational proof and, usu., is logically necessary to succeeding logical steps in a structure of reasoning ⟨theoretical economics puts the patterns of uniformity in a coherent system [of which] the basic propositions are called assumptions or postulates, the derived propositions are called *theorems* —Oscar Lange⟩ ⟨the error that was to prove most durable of all, the *theorem* that only a very short land traverse would be found necessary from Missouri to Pacific waters —Bernard DeVoto⟩

**—in principle** *adv* **:** in regard to fundamentals ⟨the idea was sound *in principle*⟩ **:** with respect to basic elements but not with respect to details ⟨prepared to accept the proposition *in principle*⟩

²**principle** \"\ *vt* -ED/-ING/-S *archaic* **:** to instill principles into **:** ground or fix in a principle **:** incite or move as an animating principle

**prin·ci·pled** \-pəld,-bəld\ *adj* [¹*principle* + *-ed*] **:** exhibiting, based on, or characterized by principle that is usu. high, righteous, or proper ⟨unprincipled expediency and ~ pragmatism —*Time*⟩ ⟨could find no ~ reason for refusing —William Phillips b.1907⟩ — often used in combination ⟨high-principled⟩ ⟨low-principled⟩

**principle of acceleration :** LAW OF ACCELERATION

**principle of association :** ASSOCIATIVE LAW

**principle of causality :** LAW OF CAUSATION

**principle of contradiction :** LAW OF CONTRADICTION

**principle of duality :** a principle in projective geometry: from a geometric theorem another theorem may be derived by substituting in the original theorem the word *point* for the word *line* in the case of a point or line in the plane or the word *point* for the word *plane* in the case of a point or plane in space and conversely

**principle of equivalence :** a principle in the general theory of relativity: the mass of a body as measured by its resistance to acceleration under the action of a force is equal to the mass as measured by the effect of a gravitational field on the body

**principle of excluded middle :** LAW OF EXCLUDED MIDDLE

**principle of identity :** LAW OF IDENTITY

**principle of least action :** a principle in physics: if the passage of a dynamic system from one configuration to another is spontaneous and without change in total energy the corresponding action has a minimum value

**principle of segregation :** the first of Mendel's laws

**principle of sufficient reason :** LAW OF SUFFICIENT REASON

**principle of utility :** GREATEST HAPPINESS PRINCIPLE

**principle of war :** any of the basic elements considered essential to success in war usu. including objective, offensive, surprise, mass or concentration, economy of force, security, movement or mobility, cooperation, and simplicity

**prin·cox** \ˈprinˌkäks, -iŋˌkä-\ *or* **princock** \-äk\ *n, pl* **princoxes** *or* **princocks** [*prin-* of unknown origin + *cox*, alter. of *cock*] *archaic* **:** a pert youth **:** COXCOMB

**prine** \ˈprīn\ *n* -S [origin unknown] *dial Eng* **:** BAR-TAILED GODWIT

**prin·gle** \ˈpriŋgəl\ *vb* -ED/-ING/-S [prob. blend of *prinkle* and *tingle*] *vi* **:** to tingle persistently or annoyingly ~ *vt* **:** to cause a tingling in

¹**prink** \ˈpriŋk\ *vi* -ED/-ING/-S [ME *prinken*] *archaic* **:** WINK

²**prink** \"\ *vb* -ED/-ING/-S [prob. alter. of ⁴*prank*] *vt* **:** to dress up **:** bedeck with finery ⟨the thousand and one emporiums which patch and ~ us —John Galsworthy⟩ ~ *vi* **:** to dress or arrange oneself for show — often used with *up*

³**prink** \"\ *vi* [perh. modif. of D *pronken* to strut — more at PRANK] *dial chiefly Eng* **:** to act or walk in an affected or mincing manner

**prink·er** \-kə(r)\ *n* -S **:** one that prinks

**prin·kle** \-kəl\ *vb* -ED/-ING/-S [prob. alter. of *prickle*] *Scot* **:** PRICKLE, TINGLE

**prinky** \-kē\ *adj* -ER/-EST [²*prink* + *-y*] **:** spruce-looking and showy **:** BEDECKED

**pri·nos** \ˈprīˌnäs, -rēˌn-\ *n, pl* **prinos** [Gk, holm oak] **1 :** WINTER BERRY **2 :** the bark of winterberry

¹**print** \ˈprint\ *n* -S [ME *printe, prente, preinte*, fr. OF *preinte*, fr. *preint*, past part. of *preindre* to press, fr. L *premere* — more at PRESS] **1 a (1) :** a mark made by impression **:** a line, character, figure, or indentation made by the pressure of one thing on another ⟨sealed with a ~ of his thumb in soft wax⟩ ⟨the delicate ~*s* of a squirrel in snow⟩ **(2) :** a mental impression **:** IMPRINT ⟨these sorrows left their ~ on his spirit⟩ **b** *obs* **:** VESTIGE **c :** something impressed with a print or formed in a mold ⟨obtained an accurate plaster ~ of the convolutions of the skull⟩ ⟨a ~ of butter⟩ **d :** an intaglio impression reproducing in reverse an original having somewhat slight relief; *also* **:** a cast or impression in relief taken from such an intaglio **e :** CORE PRINT **f :** TRACING 2c **2 :** a device or instrument (as a stamp, die, or mold) for impressing or forming a print **3 a :** printed state or form ⟨to see his name in ~⟩ ⟨put a poem into ~⟩ **b :** the printing craft or industry ⟨wise in the ways of ~⟩ **c :** TYPE ⟨set it up in ~⟩ **4 a (1) :** printed matter; *esp* **:** a printed publication **(2) prints** *pl* **:** printed papers or cards (as newspapers, pamphlets, sheet music, address cards, printing proofs, engravings) of the specifications set forth in U.S. postal regulations **b :** NEWSPRINT **5 :** printed letters **:** printed matter with regard to quality, size, or form ⟨clear ~⟩ ⟨large ~⟩ ⟨small ~⟩ **6 a :** a copy made by any printing process ⟨color ~*s*⟩ ⟨sporting ~*s*⟩ **b (1) :** a reproduction of an original painting or other work of art obtained usu. by a photomechanical process **(2) :** an artistic work sometimes with accompanying text published on a page of not more than four folds in a periodical or separately to advertise merchandise and entitled to copyright registration under English copyright law **c :** cloth with a pattern or figured design applied by printing **d :** a product of the silk-screen process **e (1) :** a photographic copy made on a sensitized surface (as from a negative or from a drawing on transparent paper) **(2) :** a photographic negative made from a positive, a negative made from a negative, or a positive made from a positive **(3) :** a developed motion picture-film containing positive images as printed from a negative **7 :** something (as a dress) made of a print fabric ⟨ruffled ~*s* for your kitchen windows⟩ **— in print 1** *chiefly dial* **:** to the letter **:** with accurateness, nice adjustment, or precision ⟨I will do it sir, *in print* —Shak.⟩ **2 :** procurable from the publisher — used esp. of a book **— out of print :** not procurable from the publisher or from ordinary new-book sources because the printed edition has been exhausted — used esp. of a book

²**print** \"\ *vb* -ED/-ING/-S [ME *printen, prenten*, fr. *printe, prente* print] *vt* **1 a :** to make an impression in or upon **:** mark with a print ⟨two small light feet that barely ~*ed* the soft soil⟩ ⟨fresh butter worked, salted, and ~*ed*⟩ **b :** to cause (as a mark) to be stamped **:** make (an impression or mark) by or as if by pressure ⟨~ his seal in wax⟩ **c :** to apply pressure with (as a stamp of the foot) so as to leave an impression **2 a :** to make a copy of by impressing paper against an inked printing surface or by an analogous method ⟨~*ing* columned pages⟩ ⟨~ bank notes⟩ — often used with *up* **b :** to perform or cause to be performed all or some of the operations necessary to the production of (as a publication, a piece of printed matter, a picture) ⟨~ greeting cards⟩ ⟨~ an edition of a newspaper⟩ **c :** to impress (as wallpaper or cloth) with a design or pattern ⟨~ cloth with linoleum blocks⟩ ⟨this air-dried tub-sized paper is easy to ~ —*Graphic Arts Monthly*⟩ **:** impress (a pattern or design) on something ⟨~*ed* gay foliage on sheer linen⟩ **d :** to publish in print ⟨"all the news that's fit to ~" —*N.Y.Times*⟩ **3 :** to form manually in unjoined characters resembling those of ordinary type ⟨~ the name and address clearly⟩ **4 a :** to make (a positive picture) on sensitized photographic paper, film, plate, or other material from a negative or a positive **b :** to make (a negative) from a negative or a positive ~ *vi* **1 a :** to use or practice the art of typography **:** work as a printer **b :** to produce printed matter ⟨the new rotary press ~*s* very rapidly⟩ **c :** to make a printed copy ⟨badly worn type ~*s* poorly⟩ **d :** to be susceptible of printing ⟨this paper ~*s* badly⟩ **2** *archaic* **:** PUBLISH; *esp* **:** to publish an article or a book **3 :** to write or hand-letter in imitation of unjoined printed characters **4** *of a firearm or a bullet* **:** to puncture a paper target

**print·abil·i·ty** \ˌprintəˈbilәd·ē\ *n* **:** the quality or state of being printable **:** printable condition ⟨the ~ of a story⟩ ⟨~ of type⟩

**print·able** \ˈprintəbəl\ *adj* **1 :** capable of being printed or of being printed from ⟨~ paper⟩ ⟨a ~ halftone⟩ **2 :** considered fit to print or publish because free from matter that is morally or legally objectionable

**prin·ta·nier** \praⁿtänyā\ *or* **prin·ta·nière** \-yeer\ *adj* [*printanier* fr. F, fr. *printanier* vernal, fr. MF, fr. *printemps* spring (fr. *prin* prime + *temps* time — fr. L *tempus*—) + *-ier* -er; *printanière* fr. F, fem. of *printanier* — more at PRIME, TEMPORAL] **:** made or dressed with diced spring vegetables ⟨a ~ soup⟩

**printcloth** \ˈ-ˌ-\ *n* [¹*print* + *cloth*] **:** plainwoven cotton gray goods suitable for converting into white fabrics (as muslin or cambric), for printing as dress or drapery goods, or for use as bagging

**print down** *vt* **:** to transfer the image from (a photographic negative) to a printing plate (as in photo-offset or gravure)

**printed circuit** *n* **:** a circuit for electronic apparatus made by depositing conductive material in continuous paths from terminal to terminal on an insulating surface

**printed matter** *n* **:** matter that is printed by any of various mechanical processes (as letterpress, lithography) and is eligible for mailing at a special rate by postal regulation which specifically excludes matter produced by various other duplicating processes (as carbon and copying-press copies)

**printed page** *n* **:** published writing — used with *the* ⟨the importance of the *printed page* in backward areas⟩

**printed paper** *n* **1 :** a class of mail in the United Kingdom comprising printed matter exclusive of newspapers not exceeding two pounds in weight **2 printed papers** *pl* **:** pieces of mail matter in international mail resembling printed paper but including newspapers and having different weight limits — compare COMMERCIAL PAPERS

**print·er** \ˈprintə(r)\ *n* -S **1 :** one whose work is printing: as **a :** one that is engaged in the art or business of printing ⟨a small commercial ~⟩; *esp* **:** a practitioner of one of the constituent skilled printing crafts (as a compositor or pressman) **b :** one who decorates materials (as textiles, pottery, wallpaper) with printed designs **2 :** a device used in printing or to print reproductions: as **a (1) :** a device containing a light source for exposing sensitive photographic material to light transmitted by a negative or positive that is either held in contact with the material (as in making a contact print) or that is not in contact with it so that a lens is used to project the image onto the material (as in making a projection print) **(2) :** a machine for printing motion-picture positives from negatives or vice versa either by contact or by optical projection **b :** an instrument that records a telegraphic message at the receiving end in printed characters

**print·ers** \-təz\ *n pl but sing or pl in constr* [fr. pl. of earlier *printer* printcloth, fr. ¹*print* + *-er*] *Brit* **:** PRINTCLOTH

**print·er's devil** \-tə(r)z-\ *n* [prob. so called fr. his becoming often black with ink] **:** a young apprentice or errand boy in a printing office

**printer's ink** *n* **1 :** ink for use in printing; *esp* **:** one of the semi-solid quick-drying black inks ordinarily used in letterpress or offset printing **2 :** printed matter ⟨the power of *printer's ink*⟩

**printer's mark** *n* **:** IMPRINT b(2)

**printer's reader** *n, chiefly Brit* **:** PROOFREADER

**printer's ream** *n* **:** a ream of 516 sheets

**printer's waste** *n* **:** imperfect or experimental postal or other official stamps that are supposed to be destroyed by the printer

**print·ery** \ˈprintərē\ *n* -ES [²*print* + *-ery*] **:** PRINTING OFFICE

**printing** *n* -S *often attrib* [ME *printing, prenting*, fr. gerund of *printen, prenten* to print — more at PRINT] **1 a :** reproduction (as on paper or cloth) of an image from a printing surface made typically by a contact impression that causes a transfer of ink — compare LETTERPRESS, INTAGLIO, PLANOGRAPHY, STENCIL, ELECTRONOGRAPHY **b :** the process of producing a positive or negative photographic image on a light-sensitive material from a negative or positive by contact or projection **:** the process of making photographic prints **c :** the process or act of decorating pottery by means of transfer papers printed with mineral colors or of gelatin sheets printed in oil with the colors being fixed by firing **2 :** the art, practice, or business of a printer **3 :** the number of copies or the amount of material printed in one continuous operation **:** IMPRESSION 6c **4 printings** *pl* **:** paper to be printed on

**printing frame** *n* **:** a holder in which a photographic negative or positive is held in uniform close contact with sensitized material for exposing the latter to light in order to make a print

**printing-in** \ˈ-ˌ-ˌ-\ *n* -S **:** a process by which cloud effects or other features not in the original negative are introduced into a photograph by printing from another negative

**printing ink** *n* **:** an ink used in printing and consisting of a pigment or pigments of the required color mixed with oil or varnish; *esp* **:** a black ink made from carbon blacks and thick linseed oil or some similar oil often with rosin oil and rosin varnish added

**printing machine** *n, chiefly Brit* **:** a power-driven printing press

**printing office** *n* **:** a business establishment in which printing (as of books, newspapers) is done

**printing-out** \ˈ-ˌ-ˌ-\ *adj* **:** relating to, used in, or being a method of photographic printing in which the image is fully brought out by the direct actinic action of light without subsequent development by means of chemicals ⟨*printing-out* paper requires fixing and toning to make the image permanent and give it a satisfactory color⟩

**printing plate** *n* **:** PLATE 4b(1), 4b(2), 4b(3)

**printing press** *n* **:** a machine that produces printed copies (as of graphic images or letterpress); *esp* **:** one that is power driven — compare COPPERPLATE PRESS, CYLINDER PRESS, PLATEN PRESS, ROTARY PRESS, WEB PRESS

**printing surface** *n* **:** a prepared surface (as set type, an electrotype, a lithographic stone, an offset or gravure plate) from which printing is done

**printing telegraph** *n* **:** PRINTER 2b

**print·less** \ˈprintləs\ *adj* **1 :** making no imprint **:** passing without a trace **2 :** bearing or taking no imprint **:** unmarked or unmarred by traces of what has passed

**printmaker** \ˈ-ˌ-\ *n* **:** one that makes prints; *esp* **:** an artist working in a graphic medium (as etching, engraving, lithography, or woodcutting)

**print-out** \'⸗,⸗\ *adj* : PRINTING-OUT

**prints** *pl of* PRINT, *pres 3d sing of* PRINT

**printscript** \'⸗,⸗\ *n* [¹*print* + *script*] : writing done in unjoined letters resembling print

**printseller** \'⸗,⸗⸗\ *n* : a seller of graphic art works; *esp* : the proprietor of a printshop (sense 1)

**printshop** \'⸗,⸗\ *n* **1** : a shop in which products of the graphic arts are sold **2** : a printing establishment; *esp* : a small one that does not have a regular schedule of publishing (as of a periodical)

**printworks** \'⸗,⸗\ *n pl but sing or pl in constr* [¹*print* + *works*] : a factory at which cloth, wallpaper, or other material is printed

**printz wood** *or* **prinz·wood** \'prin(t)s,⸗\ *n* [prob. fr. the name *Printz* or *Prinz* + E *wood*] : quartered veneer of elm

**pri·odont** \'prīə,dänt\ *adj* [*pri-* + *-odont*] : having small mandibles — used of some polymorphic insects (as various stag beetles); compare TELEODONT

**pri·odon·tes** \,prīə'dänt(,)ēz, -n(,)tēz\ *n, cap* [NL, fr. *pri-* + *-odontes*] : a genus of mammals including solely the giant armadillo

**pri·on** \'prī,än\ *n* -s [NL, fr. Gk *priōn* saw] : any of several petrels of the southern hemisphere (genus *Pachyptila*) that are bluish gray above and white below and somewhat resemble doves — see FAIRY PRION

**prion-** *or* **priono-** *comb form* [NL, fr. Gk *prion-*, fr. *priōn* saw, fr. *priein* to saw — more at PRISM] : saw : having an action or appearance like that of a saw ⟨*Priono*desmacea⟩ ⟨*priono*dont⟩

**-pri·on** \'prī,än, ,prē,än\ *n comb form* [NL, fr. Gk *priōn* saw] : creature with a (specified) kind of sawlike part — in generic names ⟨*Diprion*⟩

**pri·o·na·ce** \,prīə'nā(,)sē\ *n, cap* [NL, fr. *prion-* + *-ace*] : a genus of sharks (family Carcharhinidae) that contains the cosmopolitan blue shark

¹**pri·onid** \(')prī¦ōnəd, -¦än-; 'prīənəd, -(,)nid\ *adj* [NL *Prionidae*] : of or relating to the Prionidae

²**prionid** \"\ *n* -s : a beetle of the family Prionidae

**pri·on·i·dae** \prī'änə,dē\ *n pl, cap* [NL, fr. *Prionus*, type genus + *-idae*] : a family of large brown or black beetles having the prothorax prolonged outward into a thin more or less toothed margin and developing from larvae that burrow into the roots or wood of plants

**pri·ono·des·ma·cea** \,prīə(,)nō,dez'māsēə; prī,änō-, prī,ōnō-\ *n pl, cap* [NL, fr. *prion-* + *desm-* + *-acea*] *in some classifications* : a division of Lamellibranchia comprising comparatively primitive bivalve mollusks that typically have the hinge prionodont and being approximately equal to the combined orders Protobranchia and Filibranchia — **pri·ono·des·ma·cean** \⸗⸗(,)⸗¦⸗'māshən, ⸗¦⸗⸗¦⸗¦⸗⸗\ *n or adj* — **pri·ono·des·ma·ceous** \-shəs\ *adj*

¹**pri·on·odon** \prī'änə,dän\ *n, cap* [NL, fr. *prion-* + *-odon*] : a genus of mammals (family Viverridae) comprising the Asiatic linsangs

²**prionodon** \"\ [NL, alter. of *Priodontes*] *syn of* PRIODONTES

**pri·on·o·dont** \-dänt\ *adj* [*prion-* + *-odont*] : having a sawlike row of many simple and similar teeth

**pri·o·nop·i·dae** \,prīə'näpə,dē\ *n pl, cap* [NL, fr. *Prionops*, type genus (fr. *prion-* + *-ops*) + *-idae*] : a family of African passerine birds consisting of the helmet shrikes

**pri·o·no·tus** \,prīə'nōd·əs\ *n, cap* [NL, fr. *prion-* + *-notus*] : a genus of gurnards comprising the typical sea robins

**pri·on·urus** \,prīə'n(y)ürəs\ *n, cap* [NL, fr. *prion-* + *-urus*] : a genus of scorpions including several large venomous African scorpions of medical importance

**pri·o·nus** \prī'ōnəs, 'prīən-\ *n* [NL, fr. Gk *priōn* saw] **1** *cap* : the type genus of Prionidae including beetles whose larvae are economically important borers in the roots of various trees and shrubs and often completely hollow out the woody tissues **2** -ES : any beetle of the genus *Prionus*

¹**pri·or** \'prī(ə)r, -īə\ *n* -s [ME *prior, priour*, fr. OE *prior* & MF *prior, priour*, fr. ML *prior*, fr. LL, administrator, predecessor, fr. L, former, previous, superior] **1 a** : the superior ranking next to the abbot of a given monastery : CLAUSTRAL PRIOR **b** : the superior of a priory — called also *conventual prior* **c** : the superior of a house or group of houses of any of various religious communities **2 a** : the head of a guild **b** *Brit* : the head of a business firm

²**prior** \"\ *adj* [L, former, previous, first, superior, compar. of OL *pri* before; akin to L *priscus* ancient, *pristinus* primitive, pristine, *prae* before — more at FOR] **1** : earlier in time or order : preceding temporally, causally, or psychologically : ANTECEDENT, PREVIOUS ⟨a ~ appointment⟩ ⟨~ consideration⟩ **2 a** : taking precedence logically, methodologically, or in importance or value — usu. followed by *to* ⟨a responsibility ~ to all others⟩ **b** *of a security* : having priority as to earnings or assets over other issues of the same firm

**pri·or·able** \'prī(ə)rəbəl\ *adj* [²*prior* + *-able*] : LEGITIMATE 4b

**pri·or·al** \-ī(ə)rəl\ *adj* [¹*prior* + *-al*] : of or relating to a prior ⟨~ responsibilities⟩

**prior art** *n* : the processes, devices, and modes of achieving the end of an alleged invention that were known or knowable by reasonable diligence before and at its date — used chiefly in patent law

**pri·or·ate** \-ī(ə)rət\ *n* -s [ML *prioratus*, fr. *prior* + L *-atus* -ate] **1 a** : the office and dignity of a prior **b** : the term of office of a prior **2 a** : PRIORY **b** : a religious community under a prior

**pri·or·ess** \-ī(ə)rəs\ *n* -ES [ME *prioresse*, fr. OF, fr. ML *priorissa*, fr. *prior* + LL *-issa* -ess] : a nun whose rank in an order of women corresponds to that of prior in an order of men

**pri·or·ite** \-ə,rīt\ *n* -s [G *priorit*, fr. Granville T. *Prior* †1936 Eng. mineralogist + G *-it* -ite] : a titano-niobate of yttrium, cerium, and other rare-earth metals that is isomorphous with eschynite — called also *blomstrandine*

**pri·or·i·tied** \prī'ȯrəd·ēd\ *adj* : having a priority — usu. used in combination ⟨low-*prioritied* shipments⟩

**pri·or·i·ty** \prī'ȯrəd·ē, -rətē, -i\ *n* -ES [ME *priorite*, fr. MF, fr. ML *prioritat-, prioritas*, fr. L *prior* former, prior + *-itat-, -itas* -ity] **1** : the quality or state of being prior: as **a** (1) : antecedence in time (2) : precedence in date or position of publication — used of taxa; see LAW OF PRIORITY (3) : the quality or state of being prior logically, methodologically, or epistemologically **b** : superiority in rank, position, privilege, or other quality ⟨the ~ in law of liens on a property⟩ **2** : something that is prior or that conveys precedence: as **a** : a wartime preferential rating assigned by a government for the delivery of products according to the relative need of each for national defense and the proportionate allocation of scarce materials **b** : any preferential rating assigning rights to scarce products or materials, limited services, transportation, or surplus property or prescribing the order in which assignments are to be attended to **c** : something requiring or meriting attention prior to competing alternatives ⟨a ~ project⟩ ⟨high on our list of *priorities* is a trip to New York⟩

**pri·or·ly** \'prī(ə)rlē, -īəl-, -li\ *adv* [²*prior* + *-ly*] : in advance : PREVIOUSLY

**pri·or·ship** \-ī(ə)r,ship, -īə,sh-\ *n* [¹*prior* + *-ship*] : the office and dignity of a prior

**prior to** *prep* : in advance of : BEFORE ⟨pay the balance due *prior to* receiving the goods⟩

**pri·o·ry** \'prī(ə)rē, -ri\ *n* -ES [ME *priorie*, fr. AF, fr. ML *prioria*, fr. *prior* monastic superior + L *-ia* -y] **1** : a religious house that ranks immediately below an abbey and is either self-sustaining or dependent upon an abbey **2** : PRIORATE 1

**pris** *abbr* prisoner

**pris·able** \'prīzəbəl\ *adj* [*prise* + *-able*] : subject to prisage

**pris·age** \'prīzij, prē'zäzh\ *also* **prise** \'prīz, -rēz\ *n* -s [*prisage* fr. ME *prise* prisage + *-age*; *prise* fr. ME, fr. OF, act of taking, seizure — more at PRIZE (booty)] **1 a** : the right of the crown under old English law to take one tun of wine from every ship importing from 10 to 20 tuns and 2 tuns from every ship importing 20 or more — compare BUTLERAGE **b** : wine so taken **2** : the share of merchandise taken as lawful prize at sea that belongs to the king under old English law

**pri·sal** \'prīzəl\ *n* -s [AF *prisel*, fr. MF *prise* seizure (fr. OF) + AF *-el* -al] **1** *obs* : seizure (as of goods) under legal or customary privilege **2** *obs* **a** : the action of taking something as a prize of war **b** : something taken as a prize

**pris·can** \'priskən\ *adj* [L *priscus* ancient, old + E *-an* — more at PRIOR] : dealing with or existing in ancient times

**pris·cil·la** \prə'silə\ *n* -s *sometimes cap* [fr. *Priscilla*, a feminine name] : one of a pair of ruffled curtains with short ruffled valance attached and with tiebacks of the same material

priscillas

**pris·cil·lian** \prə'silyən\ *n* -s *usu cap* [back-formation fr. *priscillianism*] : PRISCILLIANIST 1

**pris·cil·lian·ism** \-yə,nizəm\ *n* -s *usu cap* [*Priscillian* †A.D. 385 Span. religious reformer + E *-ism*] : the teachings of Priscillian, bishop of Avila, who was condemned, put to torture, and beheaded with four companions on charges of heresy involving leanings toward Manichaeism, docetism, and modalism — see PRISCILLIANIST 1

¹**pris·cil·lian·ist** \-yənəst\ *n* -s *usu cap* [*Priscillian* †A.D.385 + E *-ist*] **1** : an adherent of Priscillianism or a follower of Priscillian **2** [*Priscilla*, prophetess associated with the founder of Montanism + E *-ist*] : MONTANIST

²**priscillianist** \"\ *adj, usu cap* : of or relating to the Priscillianists or their beliefs

**prise** *var of* PRIZE

**pri·sere** \'prī+,-\ *n* [¹*primary* + *sere* (cycle)] : the succession of vegetational stages that occurs in passing from bare earth or water to a climax community — compare SUBSERE

**pris·iad·ka** *or* **pris·jad·ka** \pris'yädkə\ *n* -s [Russ *prisyadka*] : a Slavic male dance step executed by extending the legs alternately forward from a squatting position

**prism** \'prizəm\ *n* -s [LL *prisma*, fr. Gk, anything sawn, prism, fr. *priein* to saw *pristēs* saw; akin to Gk *pristis* sawfish and perh. to Alb *priš* to break, spoil] **1 a** : a polyhedron having two faces that are polygons in parallel planes while the other faces are parallelograms — see VOLUME table **b** : something shaped like such a solid figure; *specif* : the volume of water in a stream in motion considered as a prism of chosen length in conjunction with the cross section of the channel **2 a** : a transparent body bounded in part by two plane faces that are not parallel used to deviate or disperse a beam of light **b** : an electric or magnetic field similarly used for a beam of electrons **c** : something that refracts light or produces an effect suggestive of a spectrum; *specif* : a more or less prism-shaped decorative glass luster (as for a chandelier) **3 a** : a crystal form whose faces are parallel to one axis; *specif* : one whose faces are parallel to the vertical axis — compare DOME **b** : a crystal form whose number of faces is three or more and whose intersection edges are all parallel

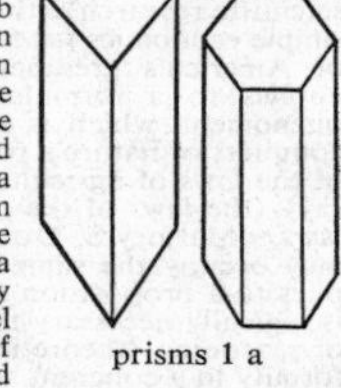

prisms 1 a

**pris·mal** \-zməl\ *adj* : PRISMATIC

**pris·mat·ic** \(')priz¦mad·|ik, -at|, |ēk\ *adj* [F *prismatique*, fr. Gk *prismat-, prisma* prism + F *-ique* -ic] **1** : of, relating to, resembling, or constituting a prism ⟨a ~ form or cleavage⟩ ⟨~ lusters on a chandelier⟩ **2 a** : formed by a prism : resembling the colors formed by the refraction of light through a prism ⟨~ effects⟩ ⟨~ spectrum colors⟩ **b** : consisting of prisms ⟨~ soil aggregates⟩ **3** : resembling a prism or its refraction of light ⟨a ~ book, sharply faceted, receiving light from many aspects and refracting the actual into the prophetic —Warren Beck⟩ : highly colored : BRILLIANT, SHOWY ⟨the ~ life⟩ ⟨~ splendor⟩ **4** : having such symmetry that a general form with faces cutting all axes at unspecified intercepts is a prism — used of a class of crystals with the highest symmetry in the monoclinic system

**pris·mat·i·cal** \|əkəl, |ēk-\ *adj, archaic* [Gk *prismat-, prisma* + E *-ical*] : PRISMATIC

**pris·mat·i·cal·ly** \|ək(ə)lē, |ēk-, -li\ *adv* : in a prismatic manner : so as to be prismatic : as if refracted by a prism

**prismatic astrolabe** *n* : a portable instrument consisting of a small telescope, a 60-degree prism, and a mercury reflecting basin by which determinations of time, latitude, and azimuth may be obtained from star observations

**prismatic coefficient** *n* : the ratio of the volume of displacement of a ship to that of a prism equal in length to the distance between perpendiculars of the ship and in cross section to that of the immersed midship section

**prismatic compass** *n* : a surveyor's hand compass provided with a triangular glass prism so adjusted that the compass can be read while taking a sight

**prismatic glass** *n* : PRISM GLASS

**prismatic layer** *n* **1** *also* **prismatic tissue** : a layer of secondary tissue developed internally by the cambium of some lycopods (as the quillworts) and interpreted as xylem, phloem, or both **2** : the middle layer of the shell of a mollusk consisting essentially of calcium carbonate arranged in prisms

**prismatic reflector** *n* : a totally reflecting prism that is usu. right-isosceles in form

**prismatic spectrum** *n* : PRISM SPECTRUM

**pris·ma·tize** \'prizmə,tīz\ *vt* -ED/-ING/-S [*prismatic* + *-ize*] : to alter into prisms ⟨*prismatized* lava⟩

**pris·ma·toid** \-tȯid\ *n* -s [NL *prismatoides*, fr. Gk *prismat-, prisma* prism + L *-oides* -oid] : a polyhedron having all of its vertices in two parallel planes — **pris·ma·toi·dal** \¦⸗⸗¦tȯid°l\ *adj*

**prism binocular** *n* : a binocular with shortened telescopic tubes in each of which light rays entering through the objective lens are reflected by two Porro prisms before passing through the eyepiece where finally an erect virtual image is formed — often used in pl.; compare FIELD GLASS

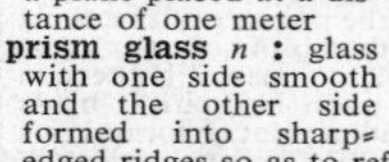

prism binocular: *1* objective lens, *2* Porro prism, *3* concave lens, *4* eyepiece, *5* focusing screw, *6* lens adjustment

**prism diopter** *n* : an arbitrary standard of prismatic deflection equal to that of a prism that deflects a beam of light one centimeter on a plane placed at a distance of one meter

**prism glass** *n* : glass with one side smooth and the other side formed into sharp-edged ridges so as to reflect the light that passes through

**prism level** *n* : a dumpy level with a mirror over the level tube and a pair of prisms so placed that the position of the level bubble can be determined by the levelman without moving his head from the eyepiece

**pris·moid** \'priz,mȯid\ *n* -s [prob. fr. (assumed) NL *prismoides*, fr. LL *prisma* prism + L *-oides* -oid] : a prismatoid whose bases have the same number of sides — **pris·moi·dal** \(')priz¦mȯid°l\ *adj*

**prism spectroscope** *n* : a spectroscope in which light is decomposed by a single prism

**prism spectrum** *n* : a spectrum obtained by use of a prism or train of prisms

**prismy** \'priz(ə)mē\ *adj* [*prism* + *-y*] : PRISMATIC — not used technically ⟨the ~ feathers of his breast —Audrey A. Brown⟩

¹**pris·on** \'priz°n\ *n* -s *often attrib* [ME *prison, prisoun, prisun*, fr. OF *prison, prisun*, fr. L *prehension-, prehensio* act of seizing, fr. *prehensus* (past part. of *prehendere* to seize, grasp) + *-ion-, -io* -ion — more at PREHENSILE] **1** : a place or condition of confinement or restraint (as of a person) : IMPRISONMENT ⟨put in ~⟩ ⟨~ seldom cures the criminal⟩ **2** : a building or other place for the safe custody or confinement of criminals or others (as formerly debtors) committed by lawful authority; *often* : an institution for the imprisonment of persons convicted of major crimes or felonies : a penitentiary as distinguished from a reformatory, local jail, or detention home

²**prison** \"\ *vt* -ED/-ING/-S [ME *prisonen*, fr. *prison*, n.] *chiefly dial* : to shut up or keep in restraint : IMPRISON, CONFINE

**prison bars** *n pl but sing or pl in constr* : PRISONER'S BASE

**prison bird** *n* : JAILBIRD

**prison breach** *or* **prison breaking** *n* : a common law crime that is now often modified by statute and that involves escape of a prisoner by force and violence from a place in which he is lawfully in custody — compare RESCUE

**prison camp** *n* **1** : a camp with minimum security for the confinement of reasonably trustworthy prisoners who are employed on farm, road, forestry, or general maintenance projects of the state or federal government **2** : a camp for prisoners of war

**pris·on·er** \-z(°)nə(r)\ *n* -s [ME, fr. MF *prisonier*, fr. OF, fr. *prison* + *-ier* -er] **1** : a person held under restraint: as **a** : a person held under arrest or in prison **b** : PRISONER OF WAR, CAPTIVE **c** : a person involuntarily restrained (as by duties, responsibilities, or possessions) ⟨the . . . star becomes the ~ of her own stardom —Delmore Schwartz⟩ ⟨was the ~ of his own suspicious nature⟩ **d** : a convert to Salvationism ⟨~*s* . . . or persons captured for the Kingdom —*Salvation Army Orders for Officers*⟩ **2 a** : a piece of metal fitted into the segments of a flywheel rim so as to hold them together and usu. held in place by taper keys or close-fitting bolts **b** : a metal link recessed on both sides so that when fitted hot into an appropriate opening in two segments of a flywheel rim the contraction of the link draws the segments together — called also *shrink link* **3** : something that is restrained as if in a prison ⟨made ~*s* of her little hands in his⟩

**prisoner at large** : a member of a naval force who is under arrest and restricted to his ship or barracks

**prisoner of war** : a person captured or interned by a belligerent power because of war with several exceptions provided by international law or agreements

**prisoner's base** *or* **prison base** *n* : a game of many variations in which players of one team seek to tag and imprison players of the other team who have ventured out of their home territory

**prison fever** *n* : TYPHUS 1a

**prison house** *n* : PRISON ⟨the idea that her present life was a *prison house* of which he held the key of escape —H.G.Wells⟩

**prisonlike** \'⸗⸗,⸗\ *adj* : resembling a prison : dreary and confining or rigidly controlled : suitable to a prison ⟨a ~ atmosphere⟩ ⟨these ~ tasks⟩

**pris·on·ment** \'priz°nmənt\ *n* -s [ME, fr. *prison* + *-ment*] : IMPRISONMENT

**pris·on·ous** \-z(°)nəs\ *adj* [¹*prison* + *-ous*] : PRISONLIKE

**prison psychosis** *n* : an apparent mental disturbance brought on by imprisonment and often manifested by pseudohallucinations, mild delusions, and paranoid trends

¹**priss** \'pris\ *vi* -ED/-ING/-ES [back-formation fr. *prissy*] *chiefly Midland* : to act or dress in a prissy or fussy manner — often used with *up* ⟨~*ing* up to impress the teacher⟩

²**priss** \"\ *n* -ES *chiefly Midland* : a prissy person — usu. used of a woman or girl

**pris·si·fied** \'prisə,fīd\ *adj* [fr. *prissy*, after such pairs as E *pretty: prettified*] : marked by prissiness ⟨~ diplomatic circles⟩

**pris·si·ly** \-sə̇lē, -li\ *adv* : in a prissy manner : with prissiness

**pris·si·ness** \-sēnəs, -sin-\ *n* -ES : the quality or state of being prissy

**pris·sy** \-sē, -si\ *adj* -ER/-EST [prob. blend of ³*prim* and *sissy*] **1** : prim and precise : affectedly proper : PRIGGISH, FINICKY **2** : lacking in masculine vigor : SISSIFIED ⟨the elevated little finger of the ~ tea drinker —Fred Majdalany⟩

**pris·tane** \'pri,stān\ *n* -s [L *pristis* shark, sawfish + E *-ane*] : a saturated liquid hydrocarbon $C_{19}H_{40}$ obtained from the liver oils of various sharks and from ambergris

**pris·tav** *also* **pris·taw** \'pri,stäf, -,stəf\ *n* -s [Russ *pristav*] : a former Russian supervisory official (as of a police force)

**pris·tel·la** \pri'stelə\ *n, cap* [NL, fr. *prist-* (prob. fr. L *pristinus* pristine) + *-ella*] : a genus of small often brightly colored So. American characin fishes that are sometimes kept in the tropical aquarium

**pris·ti·dae** \'pristə,dē\ *n pl, cap* [NL, fr. *Pristis*, type genus + *-idae*] : a small family of cartilaginous fishes closely related to the skates and rays but having the body elongated rather than flattened and distinguished by a snout elongated into a flat blade with teeth along each side and comprising the economically important sawfishes of warm seas and estuaries some of which are reputed to exceed 20 feet in length

**pris·tine** \'pri,stēn *sometimes* pri'stēn *or* 'pristən *or* 'pri,stīn\ *adj* [L *pristinus* — more at PRIOR] **1** : belonging to the earliest period or state : ORIGINAL, PRIMITIVE ⟨a ~ form of air conditioning —Lewis Mumford⟩ **2 a** : uncorrupted by civilization or the world ⟨~ innocence⟩ ⟨~ freshness⟩ **b** : free from drabness, soil, or decay : fresh and clean ⟨a ~ and fabulously wealthy residential area —Bentz Plagemann⟩ ⟨the snow which is ~ powder —*Holiday*⟩ ⟨a ~ dawn in spring⟩ — **pris·tine·ly** *adv*

**pris·tio·phor·i·dae** \,pristēə'fȯrə,dē\ *n pl, cap* [NL, fr. *Pristiophorus*, type genus (fr. *pristio-* — fr. Gk *pristēs* saw — + *-phorus*) + *-idae* — more at PRISM] : a small family of chiefly tropical sharks (suborder Squaloidea) comprising the saw sharks

**pris·tiph·o·ra** \pri'stifərə\ *n, cap* [NL, fr. *pristi-* (prob. fr. Gk *pristes* saw) + *-phora*] : a genus of sawflies (family Tenthredinidae) that includes many economic pests of forest trees — see LARCH SAWFLY

**pris·tis** \'pristəs\ *n, cap* [NL, fr. L, sawfish, fr. Gk — more at PRISM] : the type and sole recent genus of Pristidae

¹**pritch** \'prich\ *vt* -ED/-ING/-ES [ME *pricchen*, prob. alter. of *prikken, priken* to prick — more at PRICK] *chiefly dial* : to poke holes in : PRICK

²**pritch** \"\ *n* -ES [prob. alter. (influenced by ¹*pritch*) of ¹*prick*] : a pointed spike or staff put to various uses as an implement

**pritch·ar·dia** \pri'chärdēə\ *n* [NL, fr. William T. *Pritchard*, 19th cent. Eng. diplomat + NL *-ia*] **1** *cap* : a genus of showy fan palms of the Pacific islands distinguished by cuneate or flabelliform leaves having bifid segments and used for making fans and hats **2** -s : any plant of the genus *Pritchardia*

**pritch·el** \'prichəl\ *n* -s [alter. (influenced by ¹*pritch*) of ¹*prickle*] : any of various iron-pointed tools; *esp* : one used by blacksmiths for punching or enlarging nail holes in a horseshoe

**prith·ee** \'prithē, -ithē\ *interj* [fr. earlier *preythe*, fr. (*I*) *pray thee*] *archaic* — used to express a wish or request for something to be done; compare PLEASE *vt* 4

¹**prittle-prattle** \¦prid·°l¦prad·°l\ *vi* [redupl. of ¹*prattle*] : PRATTLE, CHATTER

²**prittle-prattle** \"\ *n* : empty talk : PRATTLE; *also* : CHATTERER

**pri·us** \'prīəs\ *n* -ES [L, former, previous, neut. of *prior* — more at PRIOR] : something that precedes or takes precedence : PRECONDITION

**priv** *abbr* **1** private; privately **2** privative

**pri·va·cy** \'prīvəsē, -si, *Brit sometimes* 'priv-\ *n* -ES [ME *privacie*, fr. *private* + *-cie* -cy] **1 a** : the quality or state of being apart from the company or observation of others : SECLUSION ⟨unwilling to disturb his ~⟩ **b** : isolation, seclusion, or freedom from unauthorized oversight or observation ⟨protected by law in the enjoyment of ~⟩ **2** *archaic* : a place of seclusion or retreat : private apartment ⟨remote woodland *privacies*⟩ **3 a** : private or clandestine circumstances : SECRECY **b** *archaic* : a private or personal matter : SECRET **4** *obs* : FAMILIARITY, INTIMACY **5 privacies** *pl, archaic* : GENITALIA, PRIVATES

**pri·va·do** \prə'vä(,)dō\ *n, pl* **privadoes** *also* **privados** [Sp, private, familiar, favorite, fr. L *privatus* private] *archaic* : INTIMATE, CONFIDANT

**pri·vat·do·cent** *also* **pri·vat·do·zent** \prē¦vätdō¦sent\ *n, pl* **privatdocents** \-nts\ *or* **privatdocen·ten** \-nt°n\ [G *privatdozent* (formerly spelled *privatdocent*), fr. *privat* private (fr. L *privatus*) + *dozent* (formerly spelled *docent*) teacher, lecturer — more at DOCENT] : an unsalaried university lecturer or teacher in German-speaking countries remunerated directly by students' fees

¹**pri·vate** \'prīvət, *usu* -əd+V\ *adj, sometimes* -ER/-EST [ME *privat*, fr. L *privatus* apart from the state, deprived of office, of or belonging to oneself, private, fr. past part. of *privare* to deprive, release, fr. *privus* single, private, set apart, for himself; akin to L *pro* for — more at FOR] **1 a** : intended for or restricted to the use of a particular person or group or class of persons : not freely available to the public ⟨a ~ park⟩ ⟨a ~ party⟩ **b** : belonging to or concerning an individual person,

company, or interest ‹our ~ goods› ‹~ property› ‹a ~ house› ‹~ means› **c** (1) **:** restricted to the individual or arising independently of others ‹~ views› ‹a ~ opinion› (2) **:** carried on by an individual independently rather than under institutional or organizational direction or support ‹~ research› (3) **:** being educated by independent study, under the direction of a tutor, or in a private school ‹~ students› **d** (1) **:** affecting an individual or small group **:** RESTRICTED, PERSONAL ‹~ malice› ‹for your ~ satisfaction› (2) **:** affecting the interests of a particular person, class or group of persons, or locality **:** not general in effect ‹~ act› — see PRIVATE BILL **e :** of, relating to, or receiving hospital service in which the patient has more privileges than a semiprivate or ward patient (as in having his own doctor, a room to himself, and extended visiting hours) **2 a** (1) **:** not invested with or engaged in public office or employment ‹a ~ citizen› (2) **:** not related to or dependent on one's official position **:** PERSONAL ‹~ correspondence› **b** *of military personnel* **:** of the lowest rank **:** having attained no title of rank or distinction ‹fought through the revolution as a ~ soldier› **c** (1) **:** manufactured, made, or issued by other than government means ‹~ mailing card› ‹~ stamp› (2) **:** issued by private not public authority but acceptable as money either because of intrinsic value or exchange value guaranteed by issuer ‹a ~ coin› ‹~ currency› **d** *of clothing* **:** CIVILIAN — used esp. by the Salvation Army **3 a :** sequestered from company or observation **:** withdrawn from public notice ‹a ~ retreat› **b :** free from the company of others **:** ALONE ‹let us go where we can be ~› **c :** not known publicly or carried on in public **:** not open **:** SECRET ‹~ negotiations› ‹a ~ understanding› ‹~ prayer›; *esp* **:** intended only for the persons involved ‹a ~ conversation› — compare CONFIDENTIAL **d :** having knowledge not publicly available **:** holding a confidential relationship to something ‹you are ~ to all my affairs› **e** *obs* **:** peculiar to a particular person **f :** being or considered unsuitable for public mention, use, or display — used esp. of the genital organs

[2]**private** \"\ *n* -s [ME, fr. L *privatus*, fr. *privatus*, adj., private] **1** *archaic* **:** one not in public life or office **2** *obs* **a :** a secret message **:** a private communication **b :** personal interest **:** particular business **c :** PRIVACY, RETIREMENT **d :** INTIMATE **3 privates** *pl* **:** GENITALIA, PART 1 d (3) **4 :** a person having neither commissioned nor noncommissioned rank in a group organized along military lines **:** a private soldier: as **a :** an enlistee or draftee in the army just below a private first class and above a recruit or in the marine corps at the lowest level **b :** a fire fighter in an organized force below officer rank **5 :** civilian dress for use when off duty — used by the Salvation Army — **in private** *adv* **:** PRIVATELY, SECRETLY **:** not openly or in public ‹usurp *in private* the authority she could never assert in public —Edith Wharton›

**private attorney** *n* **:** one employed by a private person rather than by a government or a subdivision thereof **:** ATTORNEY-IN-FACT

**private bag** *n, Brit* **:** a locked bag for the conveyance of postal matter between an individual and the post office esp. where direct delivery is unavailable — often used as part of a postal address ‹The Extension Officer, *Private Bag* 602, Oudtshoorn —*Farmer's Weekly* (*So. Africa*)›

**private bank** *n* **:** an unincorporated bank conducted by an individual or a partnership

**private bed** *n* **:** a bed in a hospital provided in a private room to a patient who is attended by a personal physician rather than staff physicians of the hospital

**private bill** *n* **:** a legislative bill affecting a particular individual, organization, or locality as distinguished from all the people or the whole area of a political unit (as a nation or state) ‹the power of the House of Lords to veto *private bills* —F.A. Magruder› ‹three principal categories of *private bills* introduced in Congress —S.K.Bailey & H.D.Samuel› — compare PUBLIC BILL

**private calendar** *n* **:** a legislative calendar listing private bills ‹241 bills on the *private calendar* —C.V.Woodward›

**private car** *n* **1 :** a car operated but not owned by a railroad **2 :** a passenger car assigned for private use (as of company officials)

**private carrier** *n* **:** a carrier of passengers or goods who does not hold himself out for public employment so as to be legally a common carrier

**private climate** *n* **:** the layer of air immediately surrounding and modified as to temperature and moisture by the body of a warm-blooded animal

**private company** *n* **:** a company under British law restricting the right of its stockholders to transfer their shares, limiting its members to 50 exclusive of shareholders who are present or former employees, and not inviting the public to subscribe for any shares or debentures

**private convention** *n* **:** a convention in a card game that has a meaning not revealed to the opponents and that is in most games considered unethical

**private corporation** *n* **1 :** a corporation that is not a public corporation **:** a corporation organized for the profit of its members or in which the entire interest is not held by the state **2 :** PRIVATE COMPANY

**private detective** *or* **private investigator** *n* **:** a person concerned with the maintenance of lawful conduct or the investigation of crime or other irregularities either as the regular employee of a private interest (as a hotel or store) or as contractor for fees ‹obtained a *private detective* to report on his wife's associates›

**private–duty** \¦==¦==\ *adj, of a nurse* **:** caring for a single patient either in the home or in a hospital

**private enterprise** *n* **:** FREE ENTERPRISE 2

[1]**pri·va·teer** \ˌprīvəˈti(ə)r, -tiə\ *n* -s [[1]*private* + *-eer*] **1 :** an armed private ship bearing the commission of the sovereign power to cruise against the commerce or warships of an enemy **2 :** the commander or one of the crew of a privateer **3** *archaic* **:** one fighting voluntarily as a soldier but not formally enlisted in an organized armed force **:** a free-lance soldier

[2]**privateer** \"\ *vi* -ED/-ING/-S **:** to cruise in or as a privateer

**privateering** *n* -s [fr. gerund of [2]*privateer*] **:** the career or business of a privateer ‹the narrow line between ~ and piracy›

**pri·va·teers·man** \ˌ==ˈtirzmən, -iəz-\ *n, pl* **privateersmen** [*privateers* (gen. of [1]*privateer*) + *man*] **:** PRIVATEER 2

**private eye** *n, slang* **:** a detective who is not a member of an official police force **:** PRIVATE DETECTIVE

**private first class** *n* **:** an enlistee or draftee in the army just below a corporal and above a private or in the marine corps just below a lance corporal and above a private

**private gold** *n* **:** gold coins and stamped ingots issued in the U. S. in the 19th century before the Civil War by private authority (as by the Mormons or various mining companies) — called also *pioneer gold, territorial gold*

**private insurance** *n* **:** insurance organized under private aegis — compare SOCIAL INSURANCE

**private judgment** *n* **:** the reaching of a conclusion (as in matters of religion) on the basis of personal thought and insight unhindered by political or ecclesiastical interference ‹the right of *private judgment*›

**private law** *n* **:** a branch of law treating of private matters, involving private persons, property, and relationships, and excluding those matters treated in public law

**pri·vate·ly** *adv* **1 :** in a private way **:** so as to be private **:** in private **:** SECRETLY, UNOFFICIALLY ‹some leaders of his own party hoped ~ for his defeat› **2 :** by a private person or interest ‹~ owned utilities›

**private mark** *n* **:** a distinctive and often secret identifying mark (as on an ingot of bullion or a work of art) **:** PRIVY MARK

**private member** *n, often cap P&M* **:** a member of a legislative body (as the British House of Commons) who does not belong to the ministry ‹the right of *private members* to introduce bills —D.G.Hitchner›

**private member's bill** *n, sometimes cap P&M&B* **:** a public or private bill prepared, introduced, and sponsored in the legislature by a private member ‹in New Zealand . . . *private members' bills* occasionally reach the Statute Book —Walter Nash› — compare GOVERNMENT BILL

**pri·vate·ness** *n* -ES **:** the quality or state of being private **:** PRIVACY

**private notice question** *n* **:** a parliamentary question raised following notice given privately to the speaker and the minister concerned when urgency on matters of public importance or the arrangement of business prevents scheduling on the order paper

**private nuisance** *n* **:** something constituting a nuisance in law but affecting some particular person or persons and not the general public — compare MIXED NUISANCE, PUBLIC NUISANCE

**private parts** *n pl* **:** PART 1 d (3)

**private placement** *n* **:** the sale of an issue of securities directly by the issuer to one or a few large investors (as life insurance companies) without public offering through investment bankers

**private practice** *n* **1 :** practice of a profession (as medicine or architecture) independently and not as an employee **2 :** the circle of patients depending on and availing themselves at need of the services of a physician in private practice

**privater** *comparative of* PRIVATE

**private school** *n* **:** a school that is established, conducted, and primarily supported by a nongovernmental agency — compare PUBLIC SCHOOL

**private secretary** *n* **:** a secretary who serves a single individual **:** a confidential secretary

**private siding** *n* **:** SIDING 3b

**private signal** *n* **:** a flag of unique design displayed on a yacht to identify the owner

**privatest** *superlative of* PRIVATE

**private station** *n* **:** a radio transmitting station carrying on a message service for business purposes but not open to the public

**private sweepstake** *n* **:** a sweepstake to which no money or other prize is added and which has not been advertised previous to closing

**private time** *n* **:** SUBJECTIVE TIME

**private treaty** *n* **:** a sale of property on terms determined by conference of the seller and buyer ‹got better prices by *private treaty* than his neighbors did at auction› — distinguished from *auction*

**private view** *n* **:** an invitation exhibition (as of works of art)

**private way** *n* **1 :** a right of way classified as an incorporeal hereditament of a real nature for the benefit of a person or group of persons and not the public at large to pass over land owned by another **2 a :** a way laid out by a private owner or owners and maintained at their expense, dedicated to public use, but not accepted as a public way **b :** a way laid out by public authority in New England at the request and expense of a private owner or owners, maintained by them and dedicated to public use, but not accepted as a public way

**private wrong** *n* **:** a civil injury affecting an individual or person but not the community generally **:** a wrong for which an individual has legal redress — compare PUBLIC WRONG

**pri·va·tim** \prīˈvād·əm *sometimes* -vad·-\ *adv* [L, fr. *privatus* private — more at PRIVATE] **:** in private **:** PRIVATELY

**pri·va·tion** \prīˈvāshən\ *n* -s [ME *privacion*, fr. MF *privation*, fr. L *privation-, privatio*, fr. *privatus* (past part. of *privare* to deprive) + *-ion-, -io* -ion — more at PRIVATE] **1 a :** an act or instance of depriving **:** DEPRIVATION ‹the physiological effects of complete ~ of protein› **b :** a taking away of rank or office **:** SUSPENSION 1f **2 a** (1) **:** a condition characterized by the loss of something previously or normally possessed ‹evil is a ~ of good› (2) **:** a condition characterized by the absence of a positive character ‹darkness is a negative state, a mere ~› **b :** lack of what is desired for comfort or needed for existence **:** DESTITUTION, HARDSHIP, WANT ‹a winter of hunger and ~› — usu. used in pl. ‹in spite of grief and ~s› **syn** see ABSENCE

**pri·va·tion·al** \(ˈ)prīˈvāshənᵊl, -shnəl\ *adj* **:** of or relating to privation; *esp* **:** resulting from deprivation of something

[1]**pri·va·tive** \ˈprivəd·iv\ *n* -s [L *privativus*, fr. *privatus* (past part. of *privare* to deprive) + *-ivus* -ive] **1 :** something characterized by privation **2 a :** a privative attribute, term, expression, or proposition **b :** a privative prefix or suffix **c :** a word denoting the negation of a quality otherwise inherent ‹*deaf* is a ~›

[2]**privative** \"\ *adj* **1 :** causing privation **:** DEPRIVING ‹exercise ~ power› **2 :** characterized by privation **:** not positive **:** NEGATIVE **3 :** constituting, signifying, or predicating privation, negation, or absence of a quality ‹a ~ prefix (as *a-, un-, non-*)› ‹*blind* is a ~ term›

**privative intercession** *n* **:** the assumption under Roman or civil law of a liability for a debt or obligation by the substitution of a new debtor or obligor for the old one **:** an expromission that resembles common-law novation

**privative jurisdiction** *n, Scots law* **:** exclusive jurisdiction

**priv·a·tive·ly** \-d·əvlē\ *adv* **:** in a privative manner so as to deprive **:** NEGATIVELY

**privative proposition** *n* **:** a proposition in logic stating that a particular attribute is removed from or absent from the subject

**pri·vat·iza·tion** \ˌprīvəd·əˈzāshən, -d·ˌīˈz-\ *n* -s [[1]*private* + *-ization*] **:** the tendency for an individual to withdraw from participation in social and esp. political life into a world of personal concerns usu. as a result of a feeling of insignificance and lack of understanding of complex social processes

**pri·vat·ize** \ˈprīvəd·ˌīz\ *vt* -ED/-ING/-S [[1]*private* + *-ize*] **:** to alter the status of (as a business or industry) from public to private control or ownership

**priv·et** \ˈprivət, *usu* -əd·+V\ *n* -s [origin unknown] **1 a** (1) **:** an ornamental Eurasian and northern African shrub (*Ligustrum vulgare*) that is used extensively for hedges and has half-evergreen leaves and small white flowers — called also *common privet* (2) **:** any of various other plants of the genus *Ligustrum* several of which are cultivated as ornamental or hedge plants — see AMUR PRIVET, CALIFORNIA PRIVET, IBOLIUM PRIVET, JAPANESE PRIVET **b** *also* **privet adelia :** SWAMP PRIVET **2 :** a grayish olive green that is greener and less strong than average ivy green and yellower, less strong, and slightly darker than bronze green

**privet andromeda** *n* **:** a much-branched shrub (*Lyonia ligustrina*) of the family Ericaceae with small white bell-shaped flowers in panicled racemes

**privet borer** *n* **:** a grub that is the larva of a cerambycid beetle (*Tylonotus bimaculatus*) and that mines twigs of ash and privet

**privet hawk** *n* **:** a showy Old World hawkmoth (*Sphinx ligustri*) with a larva that feeds chiefly on privet and lilac

**privet honeysuckle** *n* **:** a low Chinese evergreen shrub (*Lonicera pileata*) having foliage resembling that of a privet and violet-purple fruit

**privet mite** *n* **:** a common mite (*Brevipalpus obovatus*) that feeds on various host plants and is esp. destructive on azaleas

**-priv·ic** \ˌprivik, -vēk\ *adj comb form* [L *privus* deprived of, without, private + E *-ic*] **:** deficient in a (specified) thing or element ‹parathyro*privic*›

**privier** *comparative of* PRIVY

**privies** *pl of* PRIVY

**privies in blood :** persons related by blood and having a mutual interest in or successive relationship to the same estate or right in the same property ‹an heir and his ancestor are *privies in blood* as are coparceners among themselves›

**privies in estate :** persons having a mutual interest in or successive relationship derived at the same time out of the same original seisin to the same estate or right in the same property ‹the relationship existing between an original owner of an estate in property and one who succeeds to the same estate therein by grant or by testate or intestate succession or succession by operation of law is that of *privies in estate*›

**privies in law :** persons having by operation of special doctrines of law a mutual interest in or successive relationship to the same estate or right in the same property (as where one takes property from another by escheat) and succeeding to property with its attendant benefits and burdens

**privies in representation :** persons having by the doctrine of representation a mutual interest in or successive relationship to the same estate or right in the same property ‹an executor and his testator are *privies in representation* as are an administrator and the intestate›

**priviest** *superlative of* PRIVY

[1]**priv·i·lege** \ˈpriv(ə)lij, -lēj\ *n* -s [ME, fr. OF, fr. L *privilegium* law against or in favor of a private person, fr. *privus* private + *leg-, lex* law — more at PRIVATE, LEGAL] **1 a :** a right or immunity granted as a peculiar benefit, advantage, or favor **:** special enjoyment of a good or exemption from an evil or burden **:** a peculiar or personal advantage or right esp. when enjoyed in derogation of common right **:** PREROGATIVE **b :** such right or immunity attaching specif. to a position or an office ‹pled the ~ of his clergy› ‹the peculiar ~s of the diplomatic corps›; *esp* **:** the immunity from arrest in a civil case and enjoyment of freedom of speech during a session that is accorded to members of most legislative assemblies **c** *obs* **:** a right of asylum or sanctuary **d :** any of various fundamental or specially sacred rights considered as peculiarly guaranteed and secured to all persons by modern constitutional governments (as the enjoyment of life, liberty, and reputation, the right to acquire and possess property, the right to pursue happiness) ‹no State shall make or enforce any law which shall abridge the ~s and immunities of citizens of the United States —*U.S. Constitution*› **e :** a condition of legal nonrestraint of natural powers either generally or in respect to a particular case — compare LIBERTY **2 a :** a grant of a special right or immunity **:** FRANCHISE, PATENT ‹a ~ of printing a book› ‹a ~ granted a manor or town› **b** (1) **:** a law in ancient Rome in favor of or against a private person or after the time of Augustus a law granting a favor or immunity to some person or class of persons (2) **:** a preference to priority belonging under Roman and civil law to a creditor by reason of the nature of his claim **3 :** a customary payment or gratuity to the master of a ship by way of primage **4 :** a call, put, spread, straddle, or comparable maneuver on a stock or produce exchange; *also* **:** RIGHT 14a **syn** see RIGHT

[2]**privilege** \"\ *vt* -ED/-ING/-S [ME *privilegen*, fr. *privilege*, n.] **1 a :** to grant a privilege or privileges to **:** invest with a peculiar right, immunity, prerogative, or other benefit ‹the *privileged* classes› ‹some *privileged* institutions› **b :** to take a privilege to (oneself) ‹I ~ myself to believe› **2 :** to exempt as a privilege **:** deliver by special grace or immunity — used with *from* ‹~ legislators from arrest› **3** *archaic* **:** to give authorization for **:** EXCUSE ‹kings cannot ~ what God forbade —Samuel Daniel› ‹~ without penance or disturbance an odious crime —John Milton›

**priv·i·leged** \-jd\ *adj* [ME, fr. past part. of *privilegen* to privilege] **:** having or endowed with a privilege **:** enjoying or honored with a privilege ‹open only to the ~ few›: as **a :** not subject to the usual rules or penalties because of some special circumstance ‹a ~ statement› **b :** having a plenary indulgence attached to a mass celebrated thereon ‹~ altar› **c :** having a right of conversion or bearing a stock purchase warrant — used of a bond or preferred stock **d** *of a boat* **:** having the right of way or the right to maintain a speed and course capable of causing collision with another boat if that boat maintains its speed and course — contrasted with *burdened*

**privileged communication** *n* **1 :** a communication between parties to a confidential relation such that the recipient cannot be legally compelled to disclose it as a witness (as a communication between lawyer and client, physician and patient, husband and wife) — called also *confidential communication* **2 :** a defamatory communication the making of which does not expose the party making it to the civil or criminal liability that would follow from it if not privileged — called also *absolutely privileged communication* **3 :** a defamatory statement made by one person to another who is in a confidential relation (as that of prospective employer) or who has an interest therein that may upon proof of bad faith with actual malice be deprived of its privileged character — called also *conditionally privileged communication*

**privileged debt** *n* **:** a debt to which a preference in payment is given under civil and Scots law **:** a preferred debt

**privileged deed** *n* **:** a holograph deed that is exempted under Scots law from the statute requiring deeds to be signed before witnesses

**privileged familiarity** *n* **:** culturally sanctioned familiarity (as in a joking relationship) between persons of particular familial relations — compare AVOIDANCE

**privilege of the floor :** the right of a person to be admitted onto the floor of a legislative chamber while the legislature is in session ‹a former senator has the *privilege of the floor*›

**privilege tax** *n* **:** EXCISE 1d

**priv·i·ly** \ˈprivəlē, -li\ *adv* [ME *prively*, fr. *prive* privy + *-ly*] **:** in a privy manner **:** PRIVATELY, SECRETLY

**Priv·ine** \ˈprivən, -ˌvēn\ *trademark* — used for naphazoline

**priv·i·ty** \ˈprivəd·ē, -ətē, -i\ *n* -ES [ME *privete, privite*, fr. OF, fr. ML *privitat-, privitas*, fr. L *privus* private + *-itat-, -itas* -ity] **1 :** something that is not made public or displayed: as **a** *obs* **:** a private matter (as a plan or affair) **:** SECRET **b** *obs* **:** one's private business **c privities** *pl* **:** the external genitals **:** PART 1d(3) **2** *obs* **:** private condition (as of life or position) **:** SECLUSION, PRIVACY **3 :** private knowledge or joint knowledge with another of a private matter; *esp* **:** cognizance implying concurrence ‹all the doors were laid open for his departure, not without the ~ of the Prince of Orange —Jonathan Swift› ‹mere ~ to a crime may involve legal penalties› **4 a :** a connection between parties (as to some particular transaction) **b:** mutual or successive relationship to the same rights of property **:** the relationship between privies whereby they succeed to the same legal right or duty derived from a common source

[1]**privy** \ˈprivē, -vi\ *adj* -ER/-EST [ME *prive*, fr. OF *privé*, fr. L *privatus* private — more at PRIVATE] **1** *obs* **:** holding a close relation usu. to a person **:** INTIMATE, FAMILIAR **2 :** of, or relating to some person exclusively **:** assigned for private use or personal service esp. to an official **:** not public **:** PERSONAL ‹a ~ symbol› **3 a :** not manifest or apparent **:** withdrawn from the common knowledge or use **:** CONCEALED, PRIVATE ‹sought a ~ place to rest and think› **b :** done secretly **:** furtive in action **:** CLANDESTINE, STEALTHY ‹the grim wolf with ~ paw —John Milton› **4 :** admitted as one participating secretly or in a secret **:** privately aware as a party ‹~ to their secret›

[2]**privy** \"\ *n* -ES [ME *prive*, fr. AF, fr. OF *privé* intimate, confidant, fr. *privé*, adj.] **1 a :** any of the persons having mutual or successive relationship to the same right of property **b :** a person having an interest in any action or thing esp. deriving from a contract or conveyance to which he is not himself a party **2 a :** a small often detached building having a bench with one or more round or oval holes through which the user may defecate or urinate (as into a pit or tub) and ordinarily lacking any means of automatic discharge of the matter deposited **b :** TOILET 5b **3** *dial* **:** MATRIMONY VINE — **in privy** *adv* **:** in private **:** SECRETLY

**privy council** *n* [ME *prive counseil*, fr. *prive* privy + *counseil* council — more at COUNCIL] **1** *archaic* **:** a secret or private council ‹they'll admit me as one of their *privy council* —Oliver Goldsmith› **2** *usu cap P&C* **a :** a body of officials and dignitaries chosen by the British monarch to constitute an advisory council to the Crown that although of great historical importance now seldom meets as a body and functions principally through its committees (as the cabinet and the judicial committee) ‹His Majesty . . . by and with the advice of His *Privy Council* —E.C.E.Leadbitter› ‹the *Privy Council* in London granted him dictatorial emergency powers —S.P.Brewer› — see ORDER-IN-COUNCIL **b :** a body of officials in Canada similar in power and function to the British Privy Council ‹Canadian cabinet ministers are members of the *Privy Council*› — see GOVERNOR-GENERAL-IN-COUNCIL **3 :** a council usu. constituted by appointment to advise or assist a ruler or an executive ‹the governor of New Caledonia . . . is aided by a *privy council* —*Americana Annual*› ‹the Constitution granted Jamaica in 1944 provides for . . . a small *privy council* —A.P.Zeidenfelt›

**privy councillor** *n* **1 :** a confidential adviser **2 :** a member of a privy council

**privy mark** *or* **privy symbol** *n* **:** a symbol on a coin that identifies the minter or mintmaster — called also *private mark*

**privy parts** *n pl* **:** PART 1d(3)

**privy purse** *n* **1 :** an allowance from public revenues for the private expenses of a monarch; *esp* **:** an allowance for the private expenses of the British sovereign forming part of the civil list **2** *usu cap both Ps* **:** an officer of the British royal household who pays the private expenses of the sovereign from the civil list — called also *keeper of the privy purse*

**privy seal** *n* [ME *prive seal*, fr. *prive* privy + *seal* — more at SEAL] **1 :** a private seal: as **a :** a British royal seal used before 1885 to authorize use of the great seal (as on letters patent or pardons) or on documents not requiring the great seal (as discharges of debts) **b :** a seal used in Scotland to authenticate royal grants of personal or assignable rights **2 :** a document bearing a privy seal; *esp* **:** a warrant used by English monarchs in Stuart and earlier periods to exact a forced loan **3** *usu cap P&S* **:** LORD PRIVY SEAL

**privy verdict** *n* **:** an unsealed verdict given privily to the judge out of court, subject to later confirmation in open court, and now usu. replaced by a sealed verdict

**prix** \ˈprē\ *n, pl* **prix** \-ē(z)\ [F, fr. OF *pris* prize, price] **:** PRIZE

**prix fixe** \ˈprē¦fiks\ *n, pl* **prix fixes** \"\ [F, fixed price] **1 :** TABLE D'HÔTE **2 :** the price charged for a table d'hôte meal

**prixseam** *var of* PRICKSEAM

**priz·able** *or* **prize·able** \ˈprīzəbəl\ *adj* [¹*prize* + *-able*] **:** worthy to be prized **:** VALUABLE

**¹prize** \ˈprīz\ *n* -s [ME *pris* prize, price — more at PRICE] **1 :** something offered or striven for in competition or in contests of chance: as **a :** an honor or reward striven for in a competitive contest **:** something offered to be competed for or as an inducement to or a reward of effort ⟨a school ~⟩ ⟨the ~*s* given at an agricultural show⟩ **b :** something that may be won by chance (as in a lottery); *also* **:** a novelty or other premium given with merchandise as an inducement to buy **2 a :** something worth striving for **:** a valuable possession held or in prospect **:** ADVANTAGE, PRIVILEGE ⟨methinks, 'tis ~ enough to be his son —*Shak.*⟩ **b :** something exceptionally good or desirable of its kind **:** GEM ⟨this puppy is the ~ of the litter⟩ ⟨described her as a ~ of a wife⟩ **3** *archaic* **:** a contest for a reward **:** COMPETITION

**²prize** \"\ *adj* **1 a :** having been awarded or being worthy of a prize ⟨a ~ essay⟩ ⟨a display of ~ pumpkins⟩ **b :** awarded or intended to be awarded as a prize ⟨a ~ medal⟩ **c :** held or entered for the sake of an offered prize ⟨a ~ competition⟩ ⟨a ~ drawing⟩ **2 :** of great value ⟨the ~ argument⟩ **:** outstanding of its kind ⟨a ~ idiot⟩

**³prize** \"\ *vt* -ED/-ING/-S [ME *prisen*, fr. MF *preiser, prisier*, fr. OF, fr. LL *pretiare*, fr. L *pretium* price, money, value — more at PRICE] **1 :** to set or estimate the relative or formerly the money value of **:** APPRAISE, PRICE, RATE ⟨~ his life highly⟩ **2 :** to regard as of exceptional or great worth or excellence **:** esteem highly **:** hold as highly desirable or very precious ⟨if only rare, how this butterfly would be *prized* —Richard Jefferies⟩ ⟨~ the blessings of life around us —George Borrow⟩ **syn** see APPRECIATE

**⁴prize** \"\ *n* -s *obs* **:** ESTIMATE, VALUATION

**⁵prize** \"\ *n* -s [ME *prise, pris*, fr. OF *prise* act of taking, seizure, fr. *pris*, past part. of *prendre* to take, fr. L *prehendere* to seize, grasp — more at PREHENSILE] **1 a** (1) **:** something taken (as in war) by force, stratagem, or superior power **:** a captured thing or person **:** BOOTY, PREY; *esp* **:** property (as a ship) lawfully captured in time of war (2) **:** property seized under revenue, excise, or other laws to be taken to a court of prize jurisdiction to be forfeited **b :** an act of capturing or taking: as (1) **:** the capture of something by a belligerent exercising the rights of war; *esp* **:** the capture of a ship and its cargo at sea (2) **:** the taking from a merchant under old English law of a quantity of commodities varying from time to time for the use of the sovereign; *also* **:** the right to make such a seizure — compare PRISAGE **2** *or* **prise** \"\ **a :** a metal bar for moving heavy objects **:** LEVER, PRY **b :** PURCHASE, LEVERAGE **c :** a lever-operated press for tobacco **3** *or* **prise :** a signal blown on the horn to give notice of the killing or capture of game on a medieval hunt

**⁶prize** \"\ *also* **prise** \"\ *vb* -ED/-ING/-S *vt* **1 :** to press, force, or move with or as if with a lever ⟨trying to ~ himself out of sleep —Rebecca Caudill⟩; *esp* **:** to move in a usu. indicated direction by prying ⟨*prized* up the lid of the box⟩ ⟨*prizing* the old shingles off the roof⟩ **2 :** to force or pack (tobacco leaves) into a cask usu. by means of a prize ~ *vi* **:** to exert leverage ⟨*prizing* up with all his strength⟩

**⁷prize** \"\ *vt* -ED/-ING/-S **:** to make a prize of **:** seize as a prize ⟨the ship was *prized* for violating neutrality⟩

**prize court** *n* **1 :** a court having jurisdiction to adjudge upon captures at sea in time of war **2 :** a court having jurisdiction over seizures by revenue officers and other officials with similar authority

**prize crew** *n* **:** a detail of officers and men from the captor placed aboard a naval prize to take her into port for adjudication

**prizefight** \ˈ=,=\ *n* [back-formation fr. *prizefighter*, fr. ¹*prize* + *fighter*] **1 :** a contest between pugilists for a stake or wager **2 :** a contest between professional boxers usu. for a fixed fee or for a percentage of the money taken in (as at the gate or for radio or television rights) — **prizefighter** \ˈ=,==\ *n*

**prizefighting** \ˈ=,==\ *n* [¹*prize* + *fighting*] **:** BOXING; *esp* **:** professional boxing

**prizegiving** \ˈ=,==\ *n, chiefly Brit* **:** a formal assembly for the presentation of prizes (as at a school)

**prize·less** \ˈprīzlə̇s\ *adj* **:** having won no prize **:** lacking distinction ⟨a ~ scholar⟩

**prize·man** \-zmən\ *n, pl* **prizemen :** a winner of a prize (as an academic prize)

**prize master** *n* **:** an officer in charge of a prize crew or the prize it is handling

**prize money** *n* **1 a :** a part of the proceeds of a captured ship or other property taken as a prize that was formerly divided among the officers and men of the ship making the capture **b :** a sum formerly granted by a government to the officers and men of a ship participating in the destruction of an enemy's ship in battle **2 :** money offered in prizes

**prize package** *n* **:** something unexpectedly and surprisingly good ⟨the *prize package* was . . . when a chemical officer actually dropped a round of HE from one of his mortars into the open turret of a German tank —*Infantry Jour.*⟩

**¹priz·er** \ˈprīzə(r)\ *n* -s [ME *priser*, fr. *prisen* to prize + *-er*] **1** *obs* **:** APPRAISER **2 :** one that prizes something

**²prizer** \"\ *n* -s [¹*prize* + *-er*] **1** *archaic* **:** one that contends for a prize (as in boxing or wrestling) **2 :** PRIZEWINNER

**³prizer** \"\ *n* -s [⁶*prize* + *-er*] **:** one that exerts leverage; *esp* **:** a worker who prizes tobacco into hogsheads

**prize ring** *n* [*prize* short for *prizefight*] **1 :** a ring for a prizefight **2 a :** the system and practice of prizefighting **b :** prizefighters and their followers

prize ring 1

**priz·ery** \ˈprīzərē\ *n* -ES [⁶*prize* + *-ery*] **:** a place (as a room) adjacent to a market where recently purchased tobaccos are assembled and prized in hogsheads for shipment to redrying plants

**prizes** *pl of* PRIZE, *pres 3d sing of* PRIZE

**prizetaker** \ˈ=,==\ *n* **:** PRIZEWINNER

**prizewinner** \ˈ=,==\ *n* **:** a winner of a prize

**prizewinning** \ˈ=,==\ *adj* **:** having won or of a quality to win a prize ⟨a ~ design⟩

**prizeworthy** \ˈ=,==\ *adj* **:** meriting a prize; *often* **:** genuinely deserving of a prize won

**prizing** *pres part of* PRIZE

**prje·valsky's horse** *usu cap P, var of* PRZHEVALSKI'S HORSE

**prk** *abbr* park

**prm** *abbr* premium

**PRN** *abbr, often not cap* [L *pro re nata*] for the emergency; as occasion arises

**prntr** *abbr* printer

**¹pro** \ˈprō\ *n* -s [ME, fr. L, prep., for — more at FOR] **1 :** the arguments or evidence favoring a statement, proposition, or position **2 :** the affirmative position or one holding it **:** the affirmative side — opposed to *con* ⟨an appraisal of the ~*s* and cons⟩

**²pro** \"\ *adj* [*pro-*] **:** taking the affirmative side **:** FAVORING — opposed to *con* ⟨considered the ~ and con arguments⟩

**³pro** \"\ *adv* [*pro-*] **:** on the affirmative side **:** in favor **:** FAVORABLY — opposed to *con* ⟨much has been written on the subject ~ and con⟩

**⁴pro** \"\ *prep* [L] **:** in favor of **:** on the supporting or affirmative side of **:** FOR — opposed to *con* ⟨advanced arguments ~ and con the proposal⟩

**⁵pro** \"\ *n* -s [by shortening] **:** PROFESSIONAL ⟨a golf ~⟩

**⁶pro** \"\ *adj* [by shortening] **:** PROFESSIONAL ⟨a ~ baseball player⟩

**⁷pro** \"\ *n* -s [by shortening] **:** PROPHYLACTIC

**¹pro-** *prefix* [ME, fr. OF, fr. L, fr. Gk, fr. *pro* — more at FOR] **1 a :** earlier than **:** prior to **:** before ⟨*pro*baptismal⟩ **b :** rudimentary **:** PROT- ⟨*pro*anthropus⟩ ⟨*Pro*mammalia⟩ ⟨*pro*embryo⟩ **2 a :** situated before **:** located in front of **:** anterior to ⟨*pro*cerebrum⟩ **b :** front **:** anterior ⟨*pro*thorax⟩ **3 :** projecting ⟨*pro*gnathous⟩

**²pro-** *prefix* [L (also used esp. with verbs to mean "before", "forward", "forth", "down", "on behalf of"), fr. *pro* before, in front of, in behalf of, for, on account of — more at FOR] **1 :** taking the place of **:** substituting for ⟨*pro*cathedral⟩ ⟨*pro*-regent⟩ ⟨*pro*-treasurer⟩ **2 :** siding with **:** advocating **:** favoring **:** supporting **:** championing ⟨*pro*-British⟩ ⟨*pro*-liberalism⟩

**pro** *abbr* **1** progressive **2** pronoun **3** provost

**PRO** \¦pē,är¦ō\ *abbr or n* -s **1** public records office **2** public relations officer **3** public relations office

**proa** *var of* PRAU

**pro·ac·cel·er·in** \,prō,akˈselərən\ *n* -s [²*pro-* + *accelerate* + *-in*] **:** ACCELERATOR GLOBULIN

**pro·actinomyces** \(ˌ)prō+\ *n* [NL, fr. ¹*pro-* + *Actinomyces*] **1** *cap, in some classifications* **:** a genus comprising various actinomycetes that are now usu. included in *Nocardia* **2** *pl* **proactinomycetes** *also* **proactinomyces :** any actinomycete now or formerly included in the genus *Proactinomyces*

**pro·actinomycete** \"+\ *n* -s [¹*pro-* + *actinomycete*] **:** PROACTINOMYCES 2

**pro·al** \ˈprōəl\ *adj* [Gk *pro* before, forward + E *-al* — more at FOR] *of mastication* **:** effected by forward motion — compare ORTHAL, PALINAL, PROPALINAL

**pro·amnion** \(ˌ)prō+\ *n* [¹*pro-* + *amnion*] **:** an area in the anterior part of the blastoderm of an early amniote embryo that lacks mesoblast and gives rise to the head fold of the amnion

**pro·amniotic** \(ˌ)prō+\ *adj* [*proamnion* + *-tic* (as in *amniotic*)] **:** of or relating to a proamnion

**pro·anaphora** \(ˌ)prō+\ *n* -s *often cap* [MGk, fr. Gk *pro-* ¹pro- + LGk *anaphora* — more at ANAPHORA] **:** the part of the liturgy of the Eastern Church preceding the anaphora — **pro·anaphoral** \¦prō+\ *adj*

**pro-and-con** \¦==¦=\ *vb* **pro-and-conned; pro-and-conned; pro-and-conning; pro-and-cons :** DEBATE ⟨can discuss it and *pro-and-con* it —Gilbert Highet⟩

**pro·andric** \(ˈ)prō+\ *adj* [¹*pro-* + *andric*] *of an annelid worm* **:** retaining only the anterior pair of the primitive two pairs of testes — compare METANDRIC, PROTANDRIC

**pro·angiosperm** \"+\ *n* [¹*pro-* + *angiosperm*] **:** a fossil of a plant type held to be ancestral to the modern angiosperms — **pro·angiospermic** *or* **pro·angiospermous** \(ˌ)prō+\ *adj*

**pro·an·thro·pus** *or* **pro·an·thro·pos** \(ˈ)prō¦an(t)thrəpəs, ¦prō,an¦thrōp-\ *n* -ES [NL, fr. ¹*pro-* + *-anthropus* or Gk *anthrōpos* man — more at ANTHROP-] **:** a hypothetical prehuman primate

**pro·ar·thri** \prōˈär,thrī\ *n pl, cap* [NL, fr. ¹*pro-* + *-arthri* (fr. Gk *arthron* joint) — more at ARTHR-] *in some classifications* **:** a suborder of Cestraciontes that includes the Heterodontidae and related forms having the palatoquadrate apparatus articulated with the preorbital part of the skull

**pro·atlas** \(ˈ)prō+\ *n* [NL, fr. ¹*pro-* + *atlas*] **:** a rudimentary vertebra that lies between the atlas and the occipital bone and that occurs as a regular feature of the structure of reptiles and may occur as an anomaly in the structure of man

**pro·au·li·on** \prōˈȯlēən, -ē,än\ *n, pl* **proaulions** \-nz\ *or* **proau·lia** \-ēə\ [LGk, fr. Gk, vestibule, fr. *pro* ¹pro- + *aulion* cottage, chamber, dim. of *aulē* court, hall — more at AULA] **:** a portico or colonnade that opens into the narthex of a church or temple

**pro·avis** \(ˈ)prō¦āvə̇s, -¦äv-\ *n* -ES [NL, fr. ¹*pro-* + L *avis* bird — more at AVIARY] **:** a hypothetical primitive animal intermediate between a reptile and a bird

**prob** *abbr* **1** probable; probably **2** probate **3** problem

**prob·a·bil·i·o·rism** \,präbəˈbilēə,rizəm\ *n* -s [F *probabiliorisme*, fr. L *probabilior* (comp. of *probabilis* probable) + F *-isme* -ism — more at PROBABLE] **:** a theory that in moral questions where certainty is impossible only the more probable course may be followed

**prob·a·bil·i·o·rist** \-rə̇st\ *n* -s [F *probabilioriste*, fr. L *probabilior* + F *-iste* -ist] **:** an adherent or advocate of probabiliorism

**prob·a·bi·lism** \ˈpräbəbə,lizəm\ *n* -s [F *probabilisme*, fr. L *probabilis* probable + F *-isme* -ism — more at PROBABLE] **1 :** a theory that certainty is impossible esp. in the physical and social sciences and that probability suffices to govern belief and action **2 :** a theory that in moral questions where certainty is impossible any course may be followed that is seen as solidly probable either through clear perception of the principles involved or through awareness of the support of judicious sound authority; *esp* **:** the theory that in moral questions where certainty is impossible any solidly probable course may be followed even though an opposed course is or appears to be more probable — compare EQUIPROBABILISM, LAXISM, PROBABILIORISM, TUTIORISM

**¹prob·a·bi·list** \-lə̇st\ *n* -s [F *probabiliste*, fr. L *probabilis* + F *-iste* -ist] **:** an adherent or advocate of probabilism

**²probabilist** \"\ *adj* **:** PROBABILISTIC

**prob·a·bi·lis·tic** \¦==bəˈlistik\ *adj* **1 :** of, relating to, or based on probabilism **2 :** of, relating to, or typical of a probabilist

**prob·a·bil·i·ty** \,präbəˈbiləd·ē, -lətē, -i\ *n* -ES [MF *probabilité*, fr. L *probabilitat-, probabilitas*, fr. *probabilis* probable + *-itat-, -itas* -ity — more at PROBABLE] **1 :** the quality or state of being probable ⟨such an incredible turn of events lacks ~⟩ **2 :** something (as an occurrence, circumstance) that is probable ⟨that this will happen is a ~⟩ ⟨felt that the appointment was a decided ~⟩ **3 :** the relative frequency of the occurrence of an event based on the ratio between its occurrence and the total average number of cases necessary to ensure its occurrence when such cases are viewed as indefinitely extended ⟨when a die is rolled, the ~ that an ace will be thrown is 1 out of 6⟩ **4 :** a logical relation between statements such that any evidence confirming one necessarily confirms the other to some degree — **in all probability** *adv* **:** quite probably **:** almost certainly

**probability curve** *n* **:** a curve that represents a probability density function **:** FREQUENCY CURVE

**probability density function** *n* **1 :** a function of a discrete variate that gives the probability that a specified value will occur **2 :** a function of a continuous variate whose integral over an interval gives the probability that the variate will fall within the interval

**prob·a·bi·lize** \ˈpräbəbə,līz\ *vt* -ED/-ING/-S [L *probabilis* + E *-ize*] **:** to cause to be probable or to seem probable

**¹prob·a·ble** \ˈpräbəbəl, *in rapid speech sometimes* -bbəl\ *adj* [ME, fr. MF, fr. L *probabilis*, fr. *probare* to try, test, approve, prove + *-abilis* -able — more at PROVE] **1 a :** that is based on or arises from adequate fairly convincing though not absolutely conclusive intrinsic or extrinsic evidence or support ⟨a ~ hypothesis⟩ ⟨a ~ conclusion⟩ **b :** that can reasonably and fairly convincingly be accepted as true, factual, or possible without being undeniably so ⟨something else will seem more ~ later on —Elmer Davis⟩ ⟨indicate the ~ course of events —G.L.Dickinson⟩ ⟨pointed to him as the ~ author of the book⟩ **c :** that reasonably and fairly convincingly establishes something as true, factual, or possible but not with absolute conclusiveness ⟨advanced some highly ~ evidence⟩ **2** *archaic* **:** capable of being proved **:** DEMONSTRABLE ⟨neither proved nor ~ —George Grote⟩ **3 :** that almost certainly is or will prove to be something indicated ⟨seems to be a ~ candidate⟩

**syn** POSSIBLE, LIKELY: PROBABLE applies to that which is so supported by evidence that is adequate although not conclusive or by reason that it is worthy of belief or acceptance ⟨the *probable* cause of the explosion⟩ ⟨his actual condition or his *probable* future —George Grote⟩ ⟨far from being a madman's dream, he concluded with alarm that Burr's chance of success was uncomfortably *probable* —Hervey Allen⟩ ⟨in the light of the parallels which I have adduced the hypothesis appears legitimate, if not *probable* —J.G.Frazer⟩ POSSIBLE refers to that which is within the limit of what may happen or of what a person or thing may do, although it may not seem probable ⟨to give up the *possible* saving of millions for the immediate saving of thousands —Sinclair Lewis⟩ ⟨the stability statesmen talk about would be *possible*, there could be a new order based on vital harmony, and the earthly millennium might approach —E.M.Forster⟩ LIKELY applies to what seems to be true or to be as alleged, suggested, or represented, the chances being considerably in favor of the thing or person being as indicated ⟨a dearth of factual information to guide them in the choice of a *likely* locale for their operations —K.E. Read⟩ ⟨must the Middle East continue to be a *likely* field for the workings of Communist pressure —H.L.Hoskins⟩

**²probable** \"\ *n* -s **:** something probable: **a :** a probable situation, circumstance, or event ⟨distinguish between certainties, almost certainties, ~*s*, and possibles —S.A.B.Mercer⟩ **b :** a probable participant or candidate ⟨looked over the list of ~*s* that might be up for reelection⟩ **c :** an almost certainly destroyed airplane, ship, or other object of attack ⟨claimed thirteen kills, nine ~*s* —Wirt Williams⟩

**probable cause** *n* **:** a reasonable ground for supposing that a criminal charge is well-founded

**probable error** *n* **:** regular deviation within a determined distance on each side of the mean of a frequency curve

**probable word** *n* **:** a word whose presence in the plaintext is assumed as a step in cryptanalysis

**prob·a·bly** \ˈpräbəblē, ÷-äblē, -li\ *adv* **1** *archaic* **:** in a fairly convincing way ⟨your hypothesis . . . by which you have so ~ solved the problem of gravity —Thomas Hobbes⟩ **2 a :** insofar as seems reasonably true, factual, or to be expected **:** so far as fairly convincing evidence or indications go ⟨will ~ succeed⟩ ⟨is ~ quite happy⟩ **b :** without much doubt **:** with practical certainty **:** very likely **:** in all probability ⟨will ~ be here soon⟩

**pro·bacteriophage** \¦prō+\ *n* [¹*pro-* + *bacteriophage*] **:** PROPHAGE

**pro·band** \ˈprō,band\ *n* -s [L *probandus*, gerundive of *probare* to try, test — more at PROVE] **:** an individual actually being studied (as in a genetic investigation) ⟨the ~ had four negative sibs⟩

**pro·bang** \ˈprō,baŋ\ *n* -s [alter. (influenced by ¹*probe*) of earlier *provang*, of unknown origin] **:** a slender flexible rod (as of whalebone) with a small piece of sponge on one end that is used for removing obstructions from the esophagus or for applying medicinal preparations or for similar medical purposes

**pro·basidium** \¦prō+\ *n* [NL, fr. ¹*pro-* + *basidium*] **:** a cell in which two haploid nuclei fuse to form a diploid nucleus from which the basidium arises in some basidiomycetes

**probata** *pl of* PROBATUM

**¹pro·bate** \ˈprō,bāt, *usu* -ād+V; *chiefly Brit* -bit\ *n* -s *often attrib* [ME *probat*, fr. L *probatum*, neut. of *probatus*, past part. of *probare* to try, test, approve, prove — more at PROVE] **1 a :** the action or process of proving before a competent judicial officer or tribunal that a document offered for official recognition and registration as the last will and testament of a deceased person is genuine — compare COMMON FORM 2, SOLEMN FORM **b :** the judicial determination of the validity of a will; *specif* **:** the establishment of the prima facie validity of a will both as to manner and form of execution and as to the testator's capacity although not the validity of its provisions and also the authorization of an executor or a testamentary trustee to act **c :** the right or jurisdiction of hearing and determining questions or issues arising in matters concerning the probate of wills or the administration of decedents' estates **2 :** the officially authenticated copy of a will that together with a certificate of its having been proved is usu. delivered to the executor or administrator **3** *archaic* **:** something that proves **:** a piece of evidence **:** DEMONSTRATION, PROOF, TESTIMONY

**²probate** \"\ *vt* -ED/-ING/-S **1 a :** to make probate of (an instrument purporting to be the last will and testament of a person) **:** establish (a will) by probate as genuine and valid **b :** to grant probate of (a will) **:** determine judicially the validity of **2 :** to put (a convicted offender) on probation

**probate bond** *n* **:** a bond legally required to be given to a probate court or judge by an administrator, executor, guardian, or other fiduciary to secure the faithful performance of his duties

**probate court** *n* **1 :** a court having jurisdiction over the probate of wills and the administration of decedents' estates and in some states over the estates of minors and other legally incompetent persons and in some states having a limited jurisdiction in civil and criminal cases — called also *court of probate;* compare ORDINARY'S COURT, ORPHANS' COURT, PREFECT'S COURT, SURROGATE 1c **2 :** a British court established in 1857 with jurisdiction over the probate of wills and administration of decedents' personal estates formerly exercised by the ecclesiastical courts and also in probate matters over realty and now forming part of the probate, divorce, and admiralty division of the High Court of Justice

**probate duty** *n* **1 :** a British tax on the gross value of the personal estate of a deceased testator introduced in 1694 and merged in the estate duty in 1894 **2 :** an estate tax in some U.S. jurisdictions

**probate homestead** *n* **:** a homestead set apart by a court for the use of a surviving husband or wife and minor children out of the common property or out of the real estate belonging to the deceased

**pro·ba·tion** \prōˈbāshən\ *n* -s [ME *probacioun*, fr. MF *probation*, fr. L *probation-, probatio*, fr. *probatus* (past part. of *probare* to try, test, approve, prove) + *-ion-, -io* -ion — more at PROVE] **1 a** (1) **:** the action of critically testing and evaluating **:** critical investigation or examination ⟨our statements about them will never sustain empirical ~ —A.C.Danto⟩ (2) **:** the condition of being subjected to such testing, examination, and evaluation ⟨an educational system that has been through a long period of ~⟩ **b** (1) **:** the action of subjecting an individual to a period of testing and trial so as to be able to ascertain the individual's fitness or lack of fitness for something (as a particular job, membership in a particular organization, retention of a particular academic classification, enrollment in a particular school) ⟨an engineering company that submits all candidates for jobs to a rigorous ~⟩ (2) **:** the condition of being subjected to such testing and trial ⟨was put on ~⟩ (3) **:** the period during which an individual is subjected to such testing and trial **:** a trial period ⟨his ~ was to last one year⟩ **c** (1) **:** the action of suspending the sentence of a convicted offender in such a way that the offender is given freedom after promising good behavior and agreeing to a varying degree of supervision, to the usu. imposed condition of making a report to a particular officer or court at stated intervals, and to any other additionally specified conditions ⟨hoped that the judge would grant him ~⟩ (2) **:** the condition of one whose sentence has been suspended in such a way **:** the status of one that is being so tested ⟨knew that prison faced him if he got in trouble again during his ~⟩ (3) **:** the period during which one whose sentence has been suspended in such a way is required to fulfill the specified conditions ⟨a long ~⟩ **2** *archaic* **a :** something that constitutes proof **:** EVIDENCE **b :** the action of proving that something is what it is asserted to be **:** DEMONSTRATION

**pro·ba·tion·al** \-shənᵊl, -shnəl\ *adj* **:** PROBATIONARY — **pro·ba·tion·al·ly** \-ᵊlē, -əl|, |i\ *adv*

**¹pro·ba·tion·ary** \-shə,nerē, -ri\ *adj* [*probation* + *-ary*] **1 a :** of, relating to, or contributing toward probation ⟨a candidate for the job who has not yet completed his ~ period⟩ **b :** granted or assigned in connection with probation ⟨a ~ salary⟩ ⟨a ~ appointment⟩ **c :** done by way of or in connection with probation ⟨~ service⟩ **2 :** being tried out **:** being on a trial basis or on probation ⟨~ employees⟩

**²probationary** \"\ *n* -ES **:** PROBATIONER

**pro·ba·tion·er** \-sh(ə)nə(r)\ *n* -s **:** one that is being tried out **:** one that is on a trial basis **:** one that is on probation: as **a :** one (as a scholarship candidate, a student nurse) whose fitness is being tested during a trial period **b :** a convicted offender who has been granted freedom under the conditions of probation **syn** see NOVICE

**pro·ba·tion·er·ship** \-sh(ə)nə(r),ship\ *n* **:** the condition or position of being a probationer

**probation officer** *n* **:** an officer appointed to keep under supervision and to report on a convicted offender who is free on probation

**pro·ba·tion·ship** \-shən,ship\ *n* **1 :** the condition of being a probationer **2 :** probation **:** trial period

**proba·tive** \ˈprōbəd·iv, -räb-\ *adj* [ME *probatiffe*, fr. L *probativus* of proof, fr. *probatus* (past part. of *probare* to try, test, approve, prove) + *-ivus* -ive — more at PROVE] **1 :** serving to try out or test : EXPLORATORY ⟨a blind forward movement . . . ~ but incisive —J.K.Feibleman⟩ **2 :** that furnishes, establishes, or contributes toward proof : SUBSTANTIATING ⟨has considerable ~ force —B.N.Meltzer⟩ ⟨reasonably ~ evidence —W.W.Werntz⟩ ⟨little or no ~ value —Nathan Schachner⟩ — **proba·tive·ly** *adv* — **proba·tive·ness** *n* -ES

**pro·ba·tor** \(ˈ)prōˌbād·ə(r)\ *n* -S [L, fr. *probatus* + *-or*] : [2]APPROVER

**pro·ba·to·ry** \ˈprōbəˌtōrē\ *adj* [L *probatus* (past part. of *probare* to try, test, approve, prove) + E *-ory* — more at PROVE] : PROBATIVE

**pro·ba·tum** \prōˈbād·əm, -bäd·-\ *n, pl* **proba·ta** \-d·ə\ [L — more at PROBATE] : something conclusively established : something proved

**[1]probe** \ˈprōb\ *n* -S [ML *proba* examination, fr. LL, proof, test, fr. L *probare*] **1 a :** a surgical instrument that consists typically of a light slender fairly flexible pointed metal instrument like a small rod that is used typically for locating a foreign body (as a bullet embedded in a part of the body), for exploring a wound or suppurative tract by prodding or piercing, or for penetrating and exploring bodily passages and cavities **b :** something usu. pointed and slender that resembles or is suggestive of such an instrument and that is used to penetrate, poke, or prod in an exploratory way ⟨used a stick as a ~ to test the ice on the lake⟩ **2 a :** one of several testing devices used in electronics or other physical sciences: as (1) **:** a pointed metal tip that is attached to the free end of a conductor leading to or from an electronic instrument so as to make contact with a circuit element that is being checked (2) **:** a slender wire or some other small slender object that is inserted into something (as a flame, a discharge tube) so as to test conditions (as potential differences) at a given point (3) **:** a device (as a small special microphone attached to a larger conventional microphone) used to test a sound field with minimum disturbance of the field being tested **b :** a device (as a telescope, rocket, artificial satellite) used to penetrate into or scan an otherwise inaccessible area (as of space) **c** (1) **:** FLYING BOOM (2) **:** a pipe attached to the end of a long flexible hose which is suspended from a tanker airplane in flight and to which another plane in flight connects its gas coupling for refueling (3) **:** a pipe projecting forward from the nose of an airplane in flight that is connected with the drogue of a tanker airplane to receive fuel **d :** a small rod or similar object inserted into something as a medium of transmission or reception; *specif* **:** a metal rod used to draw energy from or inject energy into a klystron **3** [[2]*probe*] **a :** the action of probing ⟨in the midst of a leisurely ~ of his trouser pockets —Earle Birney⟩ **b :** a penetrating investigation or critical inquiry into something; *esp* **:** an investigation (as by a legislative body or specially appointed committee) designed to ferret out any evidence of illegal or corrupt practices on the part of some individual or group ⟨coupled with grand jury and legislative ~*s* —Ed Wall⟩ ⟨expected another ~ would result merely in a reshuffle in police and political circles —*Newsweek*⟩ **c :** a tentative forward exploratory push, advance, or survey (as of a reconnaissance division, a group of explorers) ⟨in three ~*s*, we covered 1383 miles in five and a half days —W.R. Anderson & Clay Blair⟩ ⟨the battalion made a couple of ~*s* to test the strength and location of the enemy⟩ **syn** see INQUIRY

**[2]probe** \"\ *vb* -ED/-ING/-S *vt* **1 a** (1) **:** to search into, search through, or explore with great thoroughness by or as if by penetrating or trying to penetrate deeply into unknown or obscure points or parts : investigate the points, parts, details, or nature of in this way : subject to intense close penetrating examination ⟨~*s* every detail of his early life and education —Stuart MacClintock⟩ ⟨*probing* the subconscious —Vance Packard⟩ ⟨attempt to ~ his sensations —Stephen Crane⟩ : carefully explore by penetrating into each section ⟨*probed* every part of the island —J.A.Michener⟩ ⟨*probed* the coastlines of both North and South America —L.A.Brown⟩ (2) **:** to subject to a penetrating investigation designed esp. to ferret out any evidence of illegal or corrupt practices : conduct a probe of ⟨spend considerable time in *probing* the actions of administrative officials —C.A.Herter⟩ **b :** to subject to one or more penetrating exploratory questions or remarks designed to elicit from another something that would otherwise remain unknown or obscure : sound out ⟨*probed* them on the matter but got no satisfactory answer⟩ ⟨~ me with that remark —Thomas Hardy⟩ ⟨I'll ~ him on the subject —W.S.Gilbert⟩ **c** (1) **:** to reach deeply into and search about all parts in a tentative exploratory way ⟨*probed* his pockets but couldn't find the keys⟩ (2) **:** to penetrate or push ahead into unknown or obscurely known parts of ⟨*probing* space with rockets and artificial satellites⟩ ⟨*probing* the wilderness with new roads⟩ (3) **:** RECONNOITER ⟨*probing* an enemy outpost⟩ (4) **:** to launch a small attack or esp. a series of small attacks against so as to discover an opponent's strength or weakness or gain some other strategic or tactical advantage ⟨*probed* enemy territory and withdrew after two or three skirmishes⟩ **2 a :** to penetrate into (as a wound, a cavity of the body) with a surgical probe (as in searching for or removing an embedded bullet, exploring the depth and direction of a sinus) ⟨*probing* a gunshot wound⟩ **b :** to penetrate into with something sharp or pointed or otherwise resembling or suggestive of a probe usu. so as to test, examine, or explore ⟨kept *probing* the crusty snow with a pole⟩ **c :** to poke esp. searchingly with some slender usu. pointed object : PROD ⟨*probed* the glowworms with a bit of stick, and rolled them over —Thomas Hardy⟩ ⟨fingered his heavy underlip as if *probing* it for a cold sore —Kenneth Roberts⟩ **3 :** to cause to move ahead with sudden force : THRUST ⟨*probed* the blade of the knife in between the logs⟩ ~ *vi* **1 :** to probe something ⟨the surgeon kept *probing* until he located the bullet in the soldier's leg⟩ **2 a :** to make a searching exploratory investigation ⟨without being able to ~ into the real nature of it —Liam O'Flaherty⟩ ⟨~ into things a little deeper —Edith Wharton⟩ ⟨always *probed* below the surface of whatever aspect of his subject he discussed —J.D. Adams⟩ **b :** to search about in a tentative exploratory way ⟨was *probing* for some way to discomfort me —Lloyd Alexander⟩ **3 a :** to reach out into something in a tentative exploratory way ⟨as far as our telescopes can ~ —George Gamow⟩ **b :** to penetrate or push ahead into unknown or obscurely known parts of something ⟨new highways are *probing* deeper into the fastnesses of the north —Harold Griffin⟩ **4 :** to force one's way forward with or as if with thrusting movements in spite of resistance : stab ahead or through : push forward ⟨were *probing* to within 20 miles of Moscow —*Time*⟩ **syn** see ENTER

**probeagle** *var of* PORBEAGLE

**prob·er** \-bə(r)\ *n* -S : one that probes

**prob·ert·ite** \ˈpräbə(r)ˌtīt\ *n* -S [Frank H. *Probert* †1940 Am. mining engineer born in England + E *-ite*] : a mineral $NaCaB_5O_9.5H_2O$ consisting of hydrous calcium sodium borate

**[1]probing** *n* -S [fr. gerund of [2]*probe*] : PROBE 3 ⟨questionings and ~*s* —Barbara Ward⟩

**[2]probing** *adj* [fr. pres. part. of [2]*probe*] **1 :** that investigates something in a tentative way : that tests or tries out something experimentally ⟨a ~ procedure⟩ **2 :** that penetrates deeply in an exploratory way to the essence of something : keen and to the point : sharply analytical : SEARCHING ⟨a ~ question⟩ ⟨a ~ study⟩

**prob·it** \ˈpräbət\ *n* -S [*prob*ability un*it*] : a statistical unit of measurement of probability based on deviations from the mean of a normal frequency distribution

**probi·ty** \ˈprōbəd·ē, -ətē, -i *also* -räb-\ *n* -ES [MF *probité*, fr. L *probitat-*, *probitas*, fr. *probus* honest, upright, virtuous + *-itat-*, *-itas* -ity — more at PROVE] : uncompromising adherence to the highest principles and ideals : unimpeachable integrity : UPRIGHTNESS, RECTITUDE ⟨a man of indisputable ~ —A.T. Quiller-Couch⟩ ⟨~ in domestic policy and wise judgment in foreign policy —A.E.Stevenson b. 1900⟩ ⟨accepted standards of sound scholarship and intellectual ~ —H.N.Fairchild⟩

**[1]prob·lem** \ˈpräbləm *sometimes* -ˌblem *or* -ˌblim; *in rapid speech often* -bᵊm *or with syllabic* l *& syllabic* m *simultaneously articulated*\ *n* -S [ME *probleme*, fr. MF, fr. L *problema*, fr. Gk *problēma* projection, protecting wall, excuse, problem, fr. *proballein* to throw forward, put forward, fr. *pro-* [1]pro- + *ballein* to throw — more at DEVIL] **1** *obs* **:** a formal public disputation based on a question proposed for academic discussion **2 a :** a question raised or to be raised for inquiry, consideration, discussion, decision, or solution ⟨mentioned the ~*s* that the speakers would discuss⟩ **b :** a proposition in mathematics or physics stating something that is to be done ⟨~: to bisect a line⟩ **c :** a constructed position in the game of chess in which a specified result (as a checkmate) is to be accomplished in a specified number of moves **3 a :** an unsettled matter demanding solution or decision and requiring usu. considerable thought or skill for its proper solution or decision : an issue marked by usu. considerable difficulty, uncertainty, or doubt with regard to its proper settlement : a perplexing or puzzling question ⟨~*s* of history —Lewis Mumford⟩ ⟨what to do now is a ~⟩ ⟨social ~*s*⟩ ⟨what happened to them remained a ~⟩ **b :** something that is a source of usu. considerable difficulty, perplexity, or worry : something that presents a perplexing or vexing problem ⟨there are no more serious ~*s* than these immature people —P.B. Gilliam⟩ : a cause of trouble or distress ⟨asked him what his ~ was⟩ **syn** see MYSTERY

**[2]problem** \"\ *adj* **1 :** that treats of or is centered about a problem of human conduct or social relationship ⟨a ~ novel⟩ **2 :** that presents a problem : that is very difficult to deal with : PROBLEMATIC ⟨a ~ neighborhood⟩ ⟨a good many ~ children who were too tough for the other schools in town —Green Peyton⟩ ⟨~ behavior⟩

**prob·lem·at·ic** \ˌpräbləˈmad·|ik, |at|, |ēk\ *or* **prob·lem·at·i·cal** \|ə̇kəl, |ēk-\ *adj* [*problematic* fr. F *problématique*, fr. LL *problematicus*, fr. Gk *problēmatikos*, fr. *problēmat-*, *problēma* problem + *-ikos* -ic; *problematical* fr. MF *problematique* + E *-al*] **1 a** (1) **:** constituting or presenting a problem : difficult to solve or to come to a decision about or to deal with : PERPLEXING, PUZZLING ⟨a ~ situation⟩ (2) **:** so full of difficulty as to make only tentative and uncertain solutions or decisions possible ⟨have arrived at a ~ impasse⟩ **b :** unclear and unsettled : being by no means definite : DUBIOUS ⟨the future remains ~⟩ **c :** open to question or debate : QUESTIONABLE ⟨whether we should do it or not is ~⟩ **2** *logic* **:** that enunciates or supports what may be but is not necessarily true ⟨a ~ proposition⟩ ⟨~ judgments concerning the existence of unicorns and zebras⟩ **syn** see DOUBTFUL

**prob·lem·at·i·cal·ly** \|ə̇k(ə)lē, |ēk-, -li\ *adv* : in such a way as to present a problem

**prob·lem·a·tist** \präˈblemətə̇st\ *n* -S [L *problemat-*, *problema* problem + E *-ist*] : PROBLEMIST

**prob·lem·ist** \ˈpräbləmə̇st\ *n* -S : one that specializes in studying or composing problems; *esp* **:** a composer or solver of chess problems

**prob·lem·ize** \-ˌmīz\ *vi* -ED/-ING/-S : to raise or discuss problems

**prob·o·la** \ˈpräbələ\ *n, pl* **probo·lae** \-ˌlē, -ˌlī\ *or* **probolas** [NL, fr. Gk *probolē* projection, prominence, fr. *proballein* to throw forward, put forward — more at PROBLEM] : one of the processes projecting from the lips of certain soil nematodes

**pro·bos·ci·dal** \prōˈbäsədᵊl\ *adj* [L *proboscid-*, *proboscis* + E *-al*] : PROBOSCIDIFORM

**pro·bos·ci·date** \-ˌdāt\ *adj* [L *proboscid-*, *proboscis* + E *-ate*] : having a proboscis

**pro·bos·cide** \-äsəd\ *n* -S [F, fr. L *proboscid-*, *proboscis*] : PROBOSCIS 1c

**[1]pro·bos·cid·ea** \ˌprōbəˈsidēə, -ˌbäˈs-; prōˌbäsəˈd-\ *n pl, cap* [NL, fr. L *proboscid-*, *proboscis*] : an order of large gravigrade mammals comprising the elephants and extinct related forms that typically have some of the teeth enlarged into tusks with corresponding modifications of the skull, that often have the nose drawn out into a trunk, and that are now limited to Africa and parts of Asia though formerly present in most parts of the world — compare MAMMOTH, MASTODON

**[2]proboscidea** \"\ [NL, fr. L *proboscid-*, *proboscis*] *syn of* MARTYNIA

**[1]pro·bos·ci·de·an** \prōˌbäsəˈdēən; ˌprōbəˌsidēən, -ˌbäˌs-\ *or* **pro·bos·cid·i·an** \ˌprōbəˌsidēən, -ˌbäˌs-\ *adj* [NL *Proboscidea* + E *-an* or *-ian*] **1 :** of or relating to the order Proboscidea **2** [L *proboscid-*, *proboscis* + E *-ean* or *-ian*] : having, relating to, or resembling a proboscis

**[2]proboscidean** \"\ *n* -S : a mammal of the order Proboscidea

**pro·bos·cid·i·al** \ˌprōbəˌsidēəl, -ˌbäsˌs-\ *adj* [L *proboscid-*, *proboscis* + E *-ial*] : PROBOSCIDATE

**pro·bos·ci·dif·er·ous** \prōˌbäsəˌdif(ə)rəs\ *adj* [L *proboscid-*, *proboscis* + E *-i-* + *-ferous* — more at PROBOSCIS] : PROBOSCIDATE

**pro·bos·cid·i·form** \ˌprōbəˌsidəˌfȯrm, -ˌbäˌs-\ *adj* [L *proboscid-*, *proboscis* + E *-iform*] : resembling a proboscis

**pro·bos·ci·ger** \prōˈbäsəjə(r)\ *n, cap* [NL, fr. *proboscis* + *-ger* -gerous] : a genus of parrots that includes the great black cockatoo

**pro·bos·cis** \prōˈbäsəs\ *n, pl* **proboscis·es** \-äsəsəz\ *also* **probosci·des** \-äsəˌdēz\ [L, fr. Gk *proboskis*, fr. *pro-* [1]pro- + *boskein* to feed — more at BOTANICAL] **1 a :** the flexible conspicuously long snout of some mammals (as tapirs, shrews); *esp* **:** the trunk of an elephant **b :** a tubular organ of varying form and use that extends or that is capable of being extended usu. from or near the oral region of many insects and some other invertebrates: as (1) **:** a sucking organ of insects (as butterflies, houseflies, mosquitoes) that is often also adapted for piercing (2) **:** the anterior muscular protrusible part of the alimentary canal of many annelids (3) **:** a prob. tactile and defensive organ of nemertean worms that can be everted through an opening above the mouth **c :** one of the complex protrusible holdfasts on the scolex of certain tapeworms — compare TRYPANORHYNCHA **2 :** the human nose esp. when very long or otherwise prominent

**proboscis flower** *n* : UNICORN PLANT

**proboscis monkey** *n* : a large Bornean monkey (*Nasalis larvatus*) with a long nose and a long tail

**pro·bou·leu·tic** \ˌprōbüˌlüd·ik, -bəˌl-\ *adj* [fr. (assumed) Gk *probouleutos* (verbal of *probouleuein* to pass a preliminary decree, fr. *pro-* [1]pro- + *bouleuein* to take counsel, deliberate, fr. *boulē* will, counsel) + E *-ic* — more at BOULE] *adj* : concerned with preliminary discussion of and deliberation on something (as a legal measure) later to be submitted to another body of voters ⟨the ~ senate of ancient Athens⟩

**proc** *abbr* **1** proceedings **2** process **3** proclamation **4** proctor

**pro·ca·cious** \prōˈkāshəs\ *adj* [L *procac-*, *procax* impudent (fr. *procare* to ask, demand, fr. *procus* suitor) + E *-ious*; akin to L *precari* to pray, entreat — more at PRAY] : IMPUDENT — **pro·ca·cious·ly** *adv*

**pro·cac·i·ty** \-ˈkasəd·ē\ *n* -ES [F *procacité*, fr. L *procacitat-*, *procacitas*, fr. *procac-*, *procax* + *-itat-*, *-itas* -ity] : IMPUDENCE

**pro·caine** \ˈprōˌkān\ *n* -S [ISV [2]*pro-* + *-caine*] : a basic ester $H_2NC_6H_4COOCH_2CH_2N(C_2H_5)_2$ of *para*-aminobenzoic acid; *also* **:** its crystalline hydrochloride that is a local anesthetic less toxic than cocaine — called also *novocaine*

**procaine amide** *n* : a base $C_{13}H_{21}ON_3$ of an amide related to procaine that is used in the form of its crystalline hydrochloride as a cardiac depressant in the treatment of ventricular and auricular arrhythmias

**pro·cambial** \(ˈ)prō+\ *adj* [NL *procambium* + E *-al*] : of, relating to, resembling, or derived from procambium

**pro·cambium** \"+\ *n* [NL, fr. [1]*pro-* + *cambium*] : the part of a plant meristem that gives rise to cambium and other primary vascular tissues

**pro·carp** \ˈprōˌkärp\ *n* -S [NL *procarpium*, fr. [1]*pro-* + *-carpium*] : a specialized female reproductive branch that is found in many red algae and that consists of carpogonium and trichogyne and usu. also auxiliary cells — compare ARCHICARP, CARPOSPORE, GONIMOBLAST

**pro·car·pi·um** \prōˈkärpēəm\ *n, pl* **procarpiums** \-ēəmz\ *also* **procar·pia** \-ēə\ [NL] : PROCARP

**pro·catalectic** \(ˌ)prō+\ *adj* [[1]*pro-* + *catalectic*] *prosody* : lacking the unaccented part of the first foot

**pro·cat·a·lep·sis** \(ˌ)prōˌkad·ᵊlˈepsə̇s\ *n* -ES [ML, fr. Gk *prokatalēpsis*, lit., art of seizing beforehand, fr. *prokatalambanein* to seize beforehand, fr. *pro-* [1]pro- + *katalambanein* to seize — more at CATALEPSY] : PROLEPSIS 2b

**pro·cat·arc·tic** \ˌprōˌkad·ˌärktik, -ōkəˌtä-\ *adj* [Gk *prokatarktikos*, fr. (assumed) *prokatarktos* (verbal of *prokatarchein* to begin first, fr. *pro-* [1]pro- + *katarchein* to make a beginning, fr. *kat-* cata- + *archein* to begin) + *-ikos* -ic — more at ARCHI-] **1** *archaic* **:** that is the immediately antecedent cause of some indicated effect **2** *archaic* **:** that is the primary cause of some indicated effect

**pro·cathedral** \ˌprō+\ *n* [[2]*pro-* + *cathedral*] : a parish church that is used as a temporary substitute for a cathedral (as in a newly created diocese)

**pro·cavia** \(ˈ)prō+\ *n, cap* [NL, fr. [1]*pro-* + *Cavia*] : a genus (the type of the family Procaviidae) that comprises all or most of the hyraxes

**[1]pro·ca·vi·id** \(ˈ)prōˌkāvēə̇d\ *adj* [NL *Procaviidae*] : of or relating to the Procaviidae

**[2]procaviid** \"\ *n* -S : a mammal of the family *Procavia*

**pro·ca·vi·idae** \ˌprōkəˈvīəˌdē\ *n pl, cap* [NL, fr. *Procavia*, type genus + *-idae*] : a family of Old World ungulate mammals that includes all recent members of the order Hyracoidea

**pro·ce·den·do** \ˌprōsəˈden(ˌ)dō\ *n* -S [L, abl. of *procedendum*, gerund of *procedere* to proceed — more at PROCEED] : a writ issuing out of a superior court to an inferior court authorizing or directing the inferior court to act upon certain matters (as the remitting of a cause for trial or the entry of a judgment in accordance with a mandate of the superior court)

**pro·ce·dur·al** \prəˈsējərəl, prōˈs-\ *adj* : of or relating to procedure ⟨~ details⟩; *esp* **:** of or relating to the procedure used by courts or other bodies (as governmental agencies) in the administration of substantive law ⟨~ due process⟩ — **pro·ce·dur·al·ly** \-rəlē, -li\ *adv*

**pro·ce·dure** \-jə(r)\ *n* -S [F *procédure*, fr. MF *procedure*, fr. *proceder* to proceed + *-ure* — more at PROCEED] **1 a :** a particular way of doing or of going about the accomplishment of something ⟨the book is lucid in its ~ —H.B.Wehle⟩ ⟨democratic ~⟩ ⟨told me he didn't especially like my ~⟩ **b** (1) **:** a particular course of action ⟨a ~ that respects the dignity and worth of the individual —W.O.Douglas⟩ (2) **:** a particular step adopted for doing or accomplishing something ⟨one of his first ~*s* was to investigate the reports⟩ (3) **:** a series of steps followed in a regular orderly definite way : METHOD ⟨surgical ~⟩ ⟨therapeutic ~⟩ ⟨scientific ~⟩ **c** (1) **:** a traditional, customary, or otherwise established or accepted way of doing things ⟨told him it was not the ~ of citizens of that country to act in that way⟩ (2) **:** PROTOCOL 4 ⟨sticklers for ~ —*Time*⟩ **d :** an established way of conducting business (as of a deliberative body): as (1) **:** the accepted usage of parliamentary bodies : established parliamentary practice : parliamentary order ⟨rules of ~⟩ (2) **:** the established manner of conducting judicial business and litigation including pleading, evidence, and practice **2 a** *obs* **:** the progress or continuation of some action or process **b** *archaic* **:** the fact of issuing from a source

**[1]pro·ceed** \prōˈsēd, prəˈs-\ *vi* -ED/-ING/-S [ME *proceden*, *proceeden*, fr. MF *proceder*, fr. L *procedere*, fr. *pro-* before, forward, forth + *cedere* to go, proceed — more at PRO-, CEDE] **1 :** ISSUE: as **a :** to come forth from a usu. specified place or thing ⟨his lips began to form some words, though no sound ~*ed* from them —Charles Dickens⟩ **b :** to come into being : take origin : ORIGINATE ⟨assuring her that his seeming inattention had only ~*ed* from his being involved in a profound meditation —T.L.Peacock⟩ **c :** to come forth by way of descent from a specified parent or ancestor ⟨a family that ~*s* from a long line of royalty⟩ **2 :** CONTINUE: as **a** (1) **:** to go on (as after a pause or an interruption) with what has been begun : go forward from a point already arrived at : go ahead ⟨let us ~ with the examination of our second main question —W.J.Reilly⟩ ⟨said he would ~ only when there was silence⟩ (2) **:** to go on with one's movement or traveling : go forward on one's way : make one's way forward ⟨had ~*ed* to the Polish capital —*Current Biog.*⟩ ⟨~*ed* from one city to another⟩ ⟨~*ed* into the next room⟩ (3) **:** to go on with what one is saying or writing : move along with the thread of one's discourse or the development of one's ideas **b :** to go on from one point to another : move along from one part of a series or sequence of things to another : pass along in an orderly regulated way usu. decided upon in advance ⟨later we shall ~ to a detailed discussion of the various parts of the country —P.E.James⟩ **3 a :** to begin and carry on some action, process, or movement : set out on a course ⟨~*ed* to wage the bloodiest war in history —M.W.Straight⟩ ⟨~*ed* to walk up and down the big and half-lit chamber —William Black⟩ ⟨~*ed* to examine his new acquaintance —W.M.Thackeray⟩ **b :** to deal with something or act toward something in a particular way ⟨~ rather harshly with themselves⟩ **c** (1) **:** to go to law : take legal action : enter upon a lawsuit ⟨threatened to ~ against him⟩ : engage in legal prosecution ⟨decided to ~ against war criminals in a more thorough fashion —R.G. Neumann⟩ (2) **:** to carry on a legal action or process ⟨the courts are now ~*ing* with the case⟩ **4 a** (1) **:** to become progressively effected or moved toward completion ⟨the job ~*ed* in the eerie glow of portable floodlights —E.J.Long⟩ ⟨an understanding of how lawmaking ~*s* —F.A.Ogg & Harold Zink⟩ (2) **:** to be in the process of being done, accomplished, or furthered : be under way ⟨negotiations now ~*ing* in the printing trade —Jack Morpurgo⟩ **b** *obs* **:** HAPPEN, OCCUR ⟨he will . . . tell you what hath ~*ed* worthy note today —Shak.⟩ **5** *Brit* **a :** to graduate as the recipient of an indicated academic degree usu. higher than a B.A. ⟨had ~*ed* M.A. at the age of 18 —*Times. Lit. Supp.*⟩ **b :** to work toward an academic degree ⟨undergraduates ~*ing* to a degree in the university —*Univ. of Toronto Cal.*⟩ **6 a :** to move along on a particular course or in a particular way or direction or toward a particular thing : move on : go along : ADVANCE ⟨her thinking probably does not ~ exactly this way —S.L.Payne⟩ ⟨as the conference ~*ed* —Vera M. Dean⟩ ⟨the highway ~*s* due south through a prosperous farm country —*Amer. Guide Series: Mich.*⟩ : make progress ⟨~*ing* steadily towards the beginning of a truly national literature —*Report: (Canadian) Royal Commission on Nat'l Development*⟩ ⟨the organization of towns ~*ed* rapidly under his jurisdiction —W.E.Stevens⟩ **b** *archaic* **:** to make out : get along : FARE ⟨make inquiry what family he has, and how they ~ —Samuel Johnson⟩ **syn** see SPRING

**[2]pro·ceed** \ˈprōˌsēd\ *n* -S *archaic* : PROCEEDS

**proceeding** *n* -S [ME *procedyng*, fr. gerund of *proceden* to proceed — more at PROCEED] **1 :** the action of proceeding **2 a :** a particular way of doing or accomplishing something ⟨is a convenient ~, but it leaves certain questions . . . unanswered —John Lardner⟩ **b :** a particular action or course of action ⟨was not quite so reckless a ~ as it might seem —G.F.Hudson⟩ : a particular way of acting ⟨his ~*s* were enough in themselves to make anyone odious —Joseph Conrad⟩ ⟨I've given up all my wild ~*s* —W.S.Gilbert⟩ : ACT, DEED ⟨everyone who took any notice of my ~*s* —H.L.Mencken⟩ **c :** a particular step or series of steps adopted for doing or accomplishing something ⟨studied each ~ necessary for bringing the case to a successful conclusion⟩ **d proceedings** *pl* **:** DOINGS, GOINGS-ON ⟨through his drunken brain the whole memory of the evening's ~*s* rushed back —Liam O'Flaherty⟩ **e** (1) **proceedings** *pl* **:** the course of procedure in a judicial action or in a suit in litigation : legal action ⟨took divorce ~*s* against him —O.S.J.Gogarty⟩ ⟨during the court ~*s*⟩ (2) **:** a particular action at law or case in litigation ⟨prosecutions and other judicial ~*s* —Zechariah Chafee⟩ **f :** a particular thing done : AFFAIR, TRANSACTION, NEGOTIATION ⟨an illegal ~⟩ ⟨business ~*s*⟩ **3 proceedings** *pl* **:** an official record or account (as in a book of minutes) of things said or done (as at a meeting or convention of a society) ⟨brought a copy of the club's ~*s* with him⟩

**pro·ceeds** \ˈprōˌsēdz\ *n pl* [fr. pl. of [2]*proceed*] **1 a :** what is produced by or derived from something (as a sale, investment, levy, business) by way of total revenue : the total amount brought in : YIELD, RETURNS ⟨the ~ from the sale of the paintings were considerable⟩ ⟨estimated that the ~ from such taxes would be enormous⟩ **b :** the net profit made on something ⟨took the ~ from the sale of his business and invested in stocks⟩ **2 :** the net sum received (as for a check, a negotiable note, an insurance policy) after deduction of any discount or charges

**[1]pro·ce·leus·mat·ic** \ˌprōsə̇ˌlüzˈmad·ik, -üˈsm-\ *n* -S [LL *proceleusmaticus*, fr. Gk *prokeleusmatikos*, adj. & n., fr. (assumed) *prokeleusmat-*, *prokeleusma* incitement (fr. *prokeleuein* to urge on, give orders to fr. *pro-* [1]pro- + *keleuein* to urge, drive on, command) + *-ikos* -ic; prob. fr. the use of proceleusmatics in ancient Greek rowing songs; akin to Gk *kellein* to beach a ship — more at CELERITY] : a metrical foot used esp. in ancient quantitative verse and consisting of four short syllables

**²proceleusmatic** \¦==¦==\ *adj* [Gk *prokeleusmatikos*] : of, relating to, or marked by the use of proceleusmatics

**pro·cel·lar·ia** \ˌprōsə'la(a)rēə\ *n, cap* [NL, fr. L *procella* storm (fr. *procellere* to throw down, fr. *pro-* forward, forth, down + *-cellere* to rise, project) + *-aria*; fr. the association of the petrels with storms at sea — more at PRO-, EXCEL] : a genus of petrels that includes the white-chinned petrels and related forms and in some classifications the shearwaters and that is the type of the family Procellariidae

**pro·cel·la·ri·idae** \ˌprōsələ'rīəˌdē, prōˌsel-\ *n pl, cap* [NL, fr. *Procellaria*, type genus + *-idae*] : a family of oceanic birds (order Procellariiformes) comprising the fulmars, shearwaters, and related birds

**pro·cel·lar·ii·for·mes** \ˌprōsəˌla(a)rēə'fȯr(ˌ)mēz\ *n pl, cap* [NL, fr. *Procellaria* + *-iformes*] : an order of predominantly pelagic birds comprising the petrels, shearwaters, albatrosses, and diving petrels

**pro·cel·lous** \prō'seləs\ *adj* [L *procellosus*, fr. *procella* + *-osus* -ous] : STORMY ⟨the dangers of that ~ sea —Rafael Sabatini⟩

**pro·cephalic** \¦prō+\ *adj* [¹*pro-* + *cephalic*] **1** : relating to, forming, or situated on or near the front of the head ⟨~ antennae⟩ **2** [Gk *prokephalos* (fr. *pro-* ¹pro- + *kephalē* head) + E *-ic* — more at CEPHALIC] *of a dactylic hexameter* : having actually or apparently an extra syllable at the beginning

**pro·cephalon** \(ˈ)prō+\ *n* -s [NL, fr. ¹*pro-* + *-cephalon* (fr. Gk *kephalē* head)] : the part of an insect's head that is in front of the segment in which the mandibles are located

**pro·ceph·a·lous** \(ˈ)prō¦sefələs\ *adj* [Gk *prokephalos*] : marked by anacrusis (sense 1)

**pro·cer·coid** \(ˈ)prō¦sərˌkȯid\ *n* -s [¹*pro-* + *cerc-* + *-oid*] : the solid first parasitic larva of pseudophyllidean and some other tapeworms that develops usu. in the body cavity of a copepod — compare PLEROCERCOID

**pro·cerebral** \(ˈ)prō+\ *adj* [NL *procerebrum* forebrain (fr. ¹*pro-* + L *cerebrum*) + E *-al*] : of or relating to the forebrain

**proc·er·ite** \'präsəˌrīt\ *n* -s [ISV ¹*pro-* + Gk *keras* horn + ISV *-ite* — more at HORN] : the flagellum of the antenna of a crustacean

**proc·er·it·ic** \¦==¦ridik\ *adj* : of or relating to a procerite

**pro·cer·i·ty** \prō'serədē\ *n* -ES [L *proceritas*, fr. *procerus* high, tall (fr. *pro-* forward + *-cerus*, fr. the stem of *crescere* to grow) + *-itas* -ity — more at CRESCENT] *archaic* : HEIGHT, TALLNESS

**proc·er·us** \'präsərəs\ *n, pl* **proc·eri** \-ˌrī\ *or* **proceruses** [NL, fr. L, high, tall] : a facial muscle arising from the nasal bone and lateral nasal cartilage and inserting in the skin at the root of the nose

**¹pro·cess** \'prä¦ˌses *also* 'prō¦ *or* ¦ˌsəs\ *n, pl* **processes** \"+əz *also* ÷¦ˌsəˌsēz *sometimes* ÷¦ˌse(ˌ)sēz\ [ME *proces, processe, process*, fr. MF *proces*, fr. L *processus*, fr. *processus*, past part. of *procedere* to proceed — more at PROCEED] **1 a** : the action of moving forward progressively from one point to another on the way to completion : the action of passing through continuing development from a beginning to a contemplated end : the action of continuously going along through each of a succession of acts, events, or developmental stages : the action of being progressively advanced or progressively done : continued onward movement ⟨the job is not finished but is still in ~⟩ ⟨many other questions are in ~ of discussion —Vera M. Dean⟩ ⟨social ~⟩ ⟨the endless interlocking chain of causation and concomitance that constitutes the ~ of history —Max Lerner & Edwin Mims⟩ ⟨in the ~ of governing people of so many races —Vernon Bartlett⟩ ⟨did his best to educate himself, and in the ~ he developed a profound respect for education —Oscar Schisgall⟩ **b** : continued onward flow : COURSE ⟨in the ~ of time⟩ **c** : something (as a series of actions, happenings, or experiences) going on or carried on : PROCEEDING ⟨standing in the cold was not a pleasant ~⟩ ⟨behind the arras I'll convey myself to hear the ~ —Shak.⟩ **d** (1) : a natural progressively continuing operation or development marked by a series of gradual changes that succeed one another in a relatively fixed way and lead toward a particular result or end ⟨the ~ of growth⟩ ⟨the ~ of digestion⟩ : a natural continuing activity or function ⟨such life ~*es* as breathing and the circulation of the blood⟩ (2) : an artificial or voluntary progressively continuing operation that consists of a series of controlled actions or movements systematically directed toward a particular result or end ⟨the ~ governing the mechanism of a clock⟩ ⟨cannot be achieved by any deductive ~ —J.H.Steward⟩ ⟨explanations of . . . how the editorial ~ worked —A.S.Link⟩ (3) : a set of facts, circumstances, or experiences that are observed and described or that can be observed and described throughout each of a series of changes continuously succeeding each other : a phenomenon or condition marked by a series of slow or rapid changes throughout a period of time ⟨the ~ of decay⟩ ⟨a pathological ~⟩ ⟨tuberculous ~⟩ (4) : a succession of related changes by which one thing gradually becomes something else ⟨a new theory of evolutionary ~⟩ **e** : a particular method or system of doing something, producing something, or accomplishing a specific result; *esp* : a particular method or system used in a manufacturing operation ⟨a ~ of making steel⟩ or other technical operation ⟨a chemical ~⟩ **2** [ME *proces, processe*, fr. MF *proces*, fr. ML *processus*, fr. L] **a** : the course of procedure in a judicial action or in a suit in litigation : legal action ⟨changed his name by legal ~ —*Current Biog.*⟩ ⟨federal ~ . . . does not have to be confined to state borders —*Va. Law Rev.*⟩ **b** (1) : a summons, mandate, or writ that serves as the means used to bring a defendant into court to answer in a judicial action or in a suit in litigation; *also* : a writ by which a court exercises its jurisdiction over the parties or subject matter of judicial action or of a suit in litigation ⟨~ for their appearance has been duly issued —*Detroit Law Jour.*⟩ (2) : the whole body of such summonses, mandates or writs **3** *obs* : REPORT, ACCOUNT ⟨the whole ear of Denmark is by a forged ~ of my death rankly abused —Shak.⟩ **4** : a part of the mass of an organism or organic structure that projects outward from the main mass ⟨a bone ~⟩ ⟨a parasite that puts forth ~*es* resembling tentacles⟩ **5** *obs* : a royal edict **6** *Roman Catholicism* : the canonical procedure followed in beatification or canonization

**²process** \"\ *vb* **processed** \"+t\ **processed** \"+t\ **processing** \"+iŋ\ **processes** \"+əz\ [in sense 1, fr. MF *processer*, fr. *proces*; in other senses, fr. ¹*process*] *vt* **1 a** : to proceed against by law : PROSECUTE ⟨the debt for which they were ~*ed* —H.W.V.Stuart⟩ **b** (1) : to take out a summons against (2) : to serve a summons on ⟨warned that they would ~ him⟩ **2** : to subject to a particular method, system, or technique of preparation, handling, or other treatment designed to effect a particular result : put through a special process: as **a** (1) : to prepare for market, manufacture, or other commercial use by subjecting to some process ⟨~*ing* cattle by slaughtering them⟩ ⟨~*ed* the milk by pasteurizing it⟩ ⟨~*ing* grain by milling⟩ ⟨~*ing* cotton by spinning⟩ (2) : to make usable by special treatment ⟨~*ing* rancid butter⟩ ⟨~*ing* waste material⟩ ⟨~*ed* the water to remove impurities⟩ **b** (1) : to subject to rapid examination and handling designed to dispose of routine details (as by recording preliminary data of or about) ⟨~*ing* books for a library⟩ ⟨efficiently ~*ed* the invoices⟩ (2) : to subject to rapid examination and handling designed to produce a preliminary classification based on apparent skills, aptitudes, and other qualifications ⟨~*ing* applicants⟩ ⟨~*ing* army recruits⟩ (3) : to take care of, attend to, or dispose of by some largely routine procedure ⟨quickly ~*ed* the loan requested by the firm⟩ (4) : to subject to examination and analysis ⟨~*ing* data radioed by a space rocket⟩ ⟨where news from everywhere is ~*ed* —F.L.Mott⟩ **3** : to produce a copy of by a mechanical or photomechanical duplicating process ⟨a ~*ed* publication⟩ ~ *vi* : to process something

**³process** \"\ *adj* [¹*process*] **1** : prepared, handled, treated, or produced by a special process: as **a** : made by some special synthetic process ⟨~ fuels⟩ ⟨~ sugar⟩ **b** : made by or used in a mechanical or photomechanical duplicating process ⟨~ publications⟩ ⟨~ ink⟩ **c** : made by special equipment or techniques so as to produce an optical effect not otherwise attainable ⟨a motion picture that has a number of remarkable ~ scenes⟩ **2 a** : used in producing special effects ⟨a ~ motion-picture camera⟩ **b** : used in making colored reproductions in almost any hue or shade by printing from halftone plates in usu. three or more colors (as red, yellow, blue)

**⁴pro·cess** \prə'ses, prō's-\ *vi* -ED/-ING/-ES [back-formation fr. ¹*procession*] : to move along : GO; *esp* : to move along in or as if in a procession ⟨~*ed* slowly through the town, conversing amiably —Thomas Wood †1950⟩

**process annealing** *n* : the process of softening steel by heating it to a temperature near but below the transformation range and then cooling slowly

**process butter** *or* **processed butter** *n* : butter that has been melted, refined, and reworked

**process chart** *n* : a chart on which are graphically shown in sequence the separate details that make up a complete process (as of a particular job operation)

**process cheese** *or* **processed cheese** *n* : a cheese made by blending several lots of cheese by heating, stirring, and emulsifying and often smoked or otherwise flavored

**processer** *var of* PROCESSOR

**processes** *pl of* PROCESS, *pres 3d sing of* PROCESS

**¹pro·ces·sion** \prə'seshən, prō's-\ *n* -s [ME *processioun*, fr. OF *procession*, fr. LL & L; LL *procession-, processio* religious procession, fr. L, act of proceeding, fr. *processus* (past part. of *procedere* to proceed) + *-ion-, -io* -ion — more at PROCEED] **1** : the action of proceeding: **a** : the action of moving along on a particular course esp. in a continuous orderly regulated often formal or ceremonial way : continuous forward movement : PROGRESSION ⟨watched the constant ~ of people passing by the building⟩ ⟨it happened during the ~⟩ ⟨the uninterrupted ~ of the clergy down the aisle⟩ **b** : the action of issuing forth; *specif* : the action of the Holy Spirit in issuing forth from another of the persons of the Trinity — see DOUBLE PROCESSION, SINGLE PROCESSION **2 a** (1) : a group of individuals (as people, animals, vehicles) moving along or about to move along on a particular course esp. in a continuous orderly regulated often formal or ceremonial way and usu. arranged in a long line ⟨formed a ~⟩ ⟨the ~ moved slowly⟩ ⟨a funeral ~⟩ (2) : the formation proper to or typical of such a group ⟨walked along in ~⟩ ⟨go in ~ round the fields —J.G.Frazer⟩ **b** : a succession, sequence, or series of things arranged or occurring in a formation or alignment like that of such a group ⟨a ~ of stately trees on each side of the avenue⟩ ⟨an endless ~ of fields broken now and then by a strip of woodland —Sherwood Anderson⟩ **3** *obs* : something (as a hymn, prayer) sung or recited during a religious procession

**²pro·ces·sion** \prə'seshən, prō's-\ *vb* -ED/-ING/-S *vi, archaic* : to move along or about in or as if in a procession ~ *vt, Midland* : to move in procession around (land, boundaries) in formally determining the limits of

**¹pro·ces·sion·al** \-shənᵊl, -shnəl\ *n* -s [ME, fr. ML *processionale*, fr. neut. of *processionalis*, adj., fr. LL *procession-, processio* + *-alis* -al] **1 a** : a book containing material (as hymns, litanies) to be sung or recited during a religious procession and often containing regulations for conducting various types of religious procession **b** : a musical composition designed for a procession: as (1) : a hymn sung during a religious procession; *esp* : a hymn sung at the entrance of a procession (as of clergy and choir) into a church at the beginning of a service (2) : an instrumental composition typically solemn in character and written as an accompaniment for a religious or other ceremonial procession **c** : the first part of a church service or some other solemn function during which a procession (as of clergy and other choir) enters the place in which the service or function is being held **2** : PROCESSION 1a,2 ⟨marched in a Sunday School ~ —K.D.Miller⟩ ⟨slow ~ of years —R.W.Howard⟩

**²processional** \"\ *adj* [F or ML; F *processionel*, fr. ML *processionalis*] **1 a** : of, relating to, or typical of a procession ⟨moved along in good ~ order⟩ ⟨the car slowed down, and at ~ pace we crept along the road —Richard Church⟩ **b** : designed for or used in a procession ⟨~ music⟩ ⟨a ~ cross⟩ ⟨~ vestments⟩ **2** : grouped or moving in or as if in a procession ⟨automobiles poking along in ~ lines of traffic⟩ — **pro·ces·sion·al·ly** \-ᵊlē, -əl, ¦ī\ *adv*

**pro·ces·sion·ary** \-shəˌnerē\ *adj* : PROCESSIONAL

**processionary caterpillar** *n* : the larva of a processionary moth

**processionary moth** *also* **processional moth** *or* **procession moth** *n* : a moth of the genus *Thaumetopoea* whose larvae make large webs on oak trees and go out in columns to feed

**pro·ces·sion·er** \-sh(ə)nə(r)\ *n* -s *chiefly Midland* : one appointed to examine and formally determine the limits of an area of land

**procession flower** *n* : any of various plants of the genus *Polygala*; *esp* : a milkwort (*P. incarnata*) of No. America

**pro·ces·sion·ist** \-sh(ə)nəst\ *n* -s : one that takes part in a procession

**pro·ces·sion·ize** \-shəˌnīz\ *vi* -ED/-ING/-S : to move along in a procession : go in procession

**pro·ces·sive** \prə'sesiv, prō's-\ *adj* [L *processus* (past part. of *procedere* to proceed) + E *-ive* — more at PROCEED] : moving forward : PROGRESSIVE

**process of tomes** \-'tōmz\ *usu cap T* [after Sir John *Tomes* †1895 Eng. dental surgeon] : one of the fine fibrils of the ameloblasts that project from the pulp of a tooth into the dentine

**proces·sor** \'prä¦ˌsesə(r) *also* -rō¦ *or* ¦ˌsəsə(r) *or* ¦ˌsəˌsȯ(ə)r\ *also* **process·er** \-ə(r)\ *n* -s : one that processes: as **a** : one that processes agricultural products, foods, or similar products **b** : one that processes films, paper, chemicals, or similar products **c** : one that processes individuals (as applicants, recruits) or data forms

**process philosophy** *n* : a theistic philosophy that views being as primarily relational, stresses emergent evolution, and criticizes or rejects nonreligious naturalism — compare NEONATURALISM

**process photography** *n* **1** : the photographic steps involved in any photomechanical reproduction process **2** *cinematography* : special printing methods or use of a background projection screen in front of which live action is photographed

**process plate** *n* : a photographic plate usu. slow in speed having the characteristics of high contrast and very fine grain and used chiefly in reproducing line drawings or in photomechanical processing

**process printer** *n* : one that does process printing

**process printing** *n* : a method of printing from halftone plates in usu. three or more colors so that nearly any hue may be reproduced

**process projection** *n* : BACKGROUND PROJECTION

**process shot** *n* : a shot made with a trick camera incorporating in the completed film matter not present in the actual scene photographed — compare PROCESS PHOTOGRAPHY 2

**process steam** *n* : steam used for heat and moisture rather than for power

**process theology** *n* : NEONATURALISM

**pro·ces·su·al** \(ˈ)prä¦seshəwəl, -rō¦s-\ *adj* [ML *processus* legal process + E *-al* — more at PROCESS] **1** : of or relating to a legal process ⟨a ~ code⟩ **2** : FUNCTIONAL, OPERATIONAL — **pro·ces·su·al·ly** \-wəlē\ *adv*

**pro·ces·sus** \prō'sesəs\ *n, pl* **processus** [L — more at PROCESS] : FUNCTIONING, OPERATION ⟨the ~ of the mind —H.F. Muller⟩ **2** : PROCESS 4

**procès-verbal** \¦prȯˌsā,verˌbäl, -rōˌs-, prō¦s-, -bal\ *n, pl* **procès-verbaux** \-bō\ [F, lit., verbal trial] : a detailed written account of things said or done that is official and authenticated: as **a** : a written statement of attested facts brought up during a legal action in court together with the official procedures adopted by the court **b** : a written record (as in a book of minutes) of the proceedings of an organized group (as a society, assembly) **c** : a written record of diplomatic negotiations

**pro·chancellor** \(ˈ)prō+\ *n* [²*pro-* + *chancellor*] : an officer of a British university who in the absence of the vice-chancellor may represent the chancellor

**pro·chein ami** *or* **pro·chein amy** \¦prōˌsheˌna¦mē, prō¦sh-, -nä¦-\ *n* [ME *prochein amy*, fr. AF *prochein ami*, lit., near friend] : one not regularly appointed that acts (as in a suit at law) for one not sui juris (as an infant, married woman) : NEXT FRIEND

**pro·chlorite** \(ˈ)prō+\ *n* [¹*pro-* + *chlorite*; fr. its being the earliest variety of chlorite distinguished] : RIPIDOLITE

**pro·cho·os** \'prōkəˌwäs, -räk-\ *n, pl* **procho·oi** \-wȯi\ [Gk *prochoos, prochous*, fr. *procheīn* to pour forth, fr. *pro-* ¹pro- + *chein* to pour — more at FOUND] : a tall slender ancient Greek jug used esp. to hold water for washing the hands

**pro·chorda** \(ˈ)prō+\ *or* **pro·chordata** \¦prō+\ [NL, fr. ¹*pro-* + *Chorda* or *Chordata*] *syn of* PROTOCHORDATA

**pro·chordal** \(ˈ)prō+\ *adj* [¹*pro-* + *chordal*] : anterior to the notochord

**¹prochordate** \"+\ *adj* [NL *Prochordata*] : PROTOCHORDATE

**²prochordate** \"\ *n* : PROTOCHORDATE

**pro·chorion** \(ˈ)prō+\ *n, pl* **prochorions** *or* **prochoria** [NL, fr. ¹*pro-* + *chorion*] : any of several structures surrounding the blastodermic vesicle in some animals (as rodents); *esp* : a gelatinous coat that is prob. a secretion of the uterine glands — **pro·chorionic** \(ˈ)prō+\ *adj*

**pro·chromosome** \(ˈ)prō+\ *n* [ISV ¹*pro-* + *chromosome*] : a condensed heterochromatic portion of a chromosome visible in the resting nucleus

**prochro·nism** \'prōkrəˌnizəm, 'präk-\ *n* -s [Gk *prochronos* anticipatory (fr. *pro-* ¹pro- + *chronos* time) + E *-ism*] : an anachronism marked by the assignment of something (as an event) to a date earlier than the actual historical one

**proci·den·tia** \ˌprōsə'dench(ē)ə, ˌpräs-\ *n* -s [L, fr. *procident-, procidens* (pres. part. of *procidere* to fall forward, fall down, fr. *pro-* forward, down + *-cidere*, fr. *cadere* to fall) + *-ia* -y — more at PRO-, CHANCE] : prolapse of an organ; *esp* : severe prolapse of the uterus in which the cervix projects from the vaginal opening

**¹procinct** *n* [ME *procincte*, fr. ML *procinctum*, alter. of *praecinctum* — more at PRECINCT] *obs* : PRECINCT

**²procinct** *n* [L *procinctus*, fr. *pro-* before, in front + *cinctus*, past part. of *cingere* to gird — more at PRO-, CINCTURE] *obs* : READINESS ⟨war he perceived, war in ~ —John Milton⟩

**pro·ci·on dye** \'prōsēən\ *n* [fr. *Procion*, a trademark] : any of several fiber-reactive dyes — see DYE table I

**prock** \'präk\ *n* -s [origin unknown] : GYASCUTUS

**¹pro·claim** \prō'klām, -rə'k-\ *vb* -ED/-ING/-S [ME *proclamen, proclaimen*, fr. MF or L; MF *proclamer*, fr. L *proclamare*, fr. *pro-* before + *clamare* to cry out, call — more at PRO-, CLAIM] *vt* **1 a** (1) : to declare openly or publicly : make widely known through speech or writing : ANNOUNCE ⟨the newspaper ~*ed* its adherence to the government's policy⟩ ⟨~*ed* that he would be a candidate⟩ (2) : to assert openly or publicly and with conviction ⟨in ringing words . . . ~*ed* the . . . right of the opposition to voice its protests —A.C.Cole⟩ **b** : to give an unmistakable indication of : clearly reveal : SHOW ⟨all these things ~ the actor in him —James Hanley⟩ **c** : to make clearly evident : demonstrate undeniably : PROVE — usu. used with a complement ⟨such conduct ~*s* him a fool⟩ **2 a** : to make known solemnly, officially, or formally ⟨~*ed* an amnesty —*Collier's Yr. Bk.*⟩ ⟨~*ed* a state of war⟩ **b** : to declare to be by solemn, official, or formal announcement ⟨is ~*ed* the panacea for many of the ills of life —E.J.Banfield⟩ ⟨~*ed* the country a republic⟩ **3 a** *archaic* : DENOUNCE **b** *archaic* : to place (as a district) under some legal restriction by official decree **4** : to bring (banns of marriage) to public notice : PUBLISH **5** : to recognize officially and publicly; *specif* : to recognize the accession of ⟨was going to help ~ a queen of Britain —John Strachey⟩ **6** : to praise or glorify openly or publicly : EXTOL ⟨loudly ~*ing* their master —*Times Lit. Supp.*⟩ ⟨had loudly ~*ed* the quality of his wife —Compton Mackenzie⟩ ~ *vi* : to make a proclamation **syn** see DECLARE

**²proclaim** \"\ *n, archaic* : the action of calling out ⟨voices of soft ~ —John Keats⟩

**pro·claim·er** \-mə(r)\ *n* -s : one that proclaims

**proc·la·ma·tion** \ˌpräklə'māshən\ *n* -s [ME *proclamacioun*, fr. MF *proclamation*, fr. L *proclamation-, proclamatio*, fr. *proclamatus* (past part. of *proclamare* to proclaim) + *-ion-, -io* -ion — more at PROCLAIM] **1 a** : the action of proclaiming ⟨laid down as a policy by ~ —Oscar Handlin⟩ **b** : the condition of being proclaimed ⟨becomes legal upon ~ —W.S.Sayre⟩ **2** : something proclaimed; *specif* : an official formal public announcement (as a public notice, edict, decree) ⟨issued a ~ announcing the cessation of war —*Amer. Guide Series: N.C.*⟩

**proclamation piece** *n* : a medal or coin issued at the same time as a proclamation (as at the accession of a ruler)

**pro·clam·a·to·ry** \prō'klaməˌtōrē\ *adj* [L *proclamatus* + E *-ory*] : of or relating to proclamation or a proclamation : proclaiming or like that of one proclaiming ⟨a ~ style of speaking⟩

**pro·climax** \(ˈ)prō+\ *n* [¹*pro-* + *climax*] : an ecological community that suggests a climax in stability and permanence but is not primarily the product of climate — compare CLIMATIC CLIMAX

**proc·li·nate** \'präkləˌnāt\ *adj* [L *proclinatus*, past part. of *proclinare* to bend forward, fr. *pro-* forward + *clinare* to bend, incline — more at PRO-, LEAN] : directed forward ⟨an insect with ~ ocellar bristles⟩

**procli·sis** \'prōkləsəs, 'präk-\ *n, pl* **procli·ses** \-ləˌsēz\ [NL, fr. ¹*pro-* + LL *-clisis* (as in *enclisis*) — more at ENCLISIS] : pronunciation as a proclitic : combination in pronunciation of an unaccented word or particle with a following accented word

**¹pro·clit·ic** \(ˈ)prō¦klid·ik, -lit, ¦ēk\ *adj* [NL *procliticus*, fr. ¹*pro-* + LL *-cliticus* (as in *encliticus* enclitic) — more at ENCLITIC] : of, relating to, or constituting a word or particle without sentence stress that is accentually dependent upon the immediately following stressed word and is pronounced with it as a phonetic unit — compare ENCLITIC — **proclitically** *adv*

**²proclitic** \"\ *n* -s : a proclitic word or particle

**proclive** *adj* [L *proclivis*, lit., sloping, fr. *pro-* forward, down + *-clivis* (fr. *clivus* slope, hill) — more at PRO-, DECLIVITY] *obs* : inclined toward something by disposition or circumstances

**pro·cliv·i·ty** \prō'klivədē, -rə'k-, -vətē, -i\ *n* -ES [L *proclivitas*, fr. *proclivis* + *-itas* -ity] : an inclination or predisposition toward something ⟨must not be forced into social activities for which they have no ~ —Philip Toynbee⟩; *esp* : a strong inherent inclination or predisposition toward something objectionable that is difficult to control and that arises from a natural tendency in that direction and esp. from particular characteristics of constitution or temperament or from frequent or habitual experience with or indulgence in the thing indicated ⟨man's ~ for violence —H.N.Maclean⟩ **syn** see LEANING

**pro·cnemial** \(ˈ)prō+\ *adj* [¹*pro-* + *cnemial*] : of, relating to, or formed on the ventral surface of the tibia

**pro·coe·la** \prō'sēlə\ *n pl, cap* [NL, fr. ¹*pro-* + *-coela*, neut. pl. of *-coelus* -coelous] : a suborder of Salientia that includes Bufonidae, Hylidae, and some families of extinct amphibians and that comprises frogs and toads with vertebrae uniformly concave in front and with sacral vertebrae united with the urostyle by a double condyle

**¹pro·coe·lia** \-lēə\ *n* -s [NL, fr. ¹*pro-* + Gk *koilia* bodily cavity — more at COELIAC] : LATERAL VENTRICLE

**²procoelia** \"\ *n pl, cap* [NL, fr. ¹*pro-* + Gk *koilia*] *in some classifications* : a division of Loricata that includes recent forms and some late fossils with dorsal vertebrae mostly concave in front

**¹pro·coe·li·an** \(ˈ)=¦=lēən\ *adj* [NL ¹*procoelia* + E *-an*] **1** : PROCOELOUS **2** [NL ²*Procoelia* + E *-an*] : of or relating to the Procoelia

**²procoelian** \"\ *n* -s : an animal of the division Procoelia

**pro·coe·lous** \(ˈ)prō¦sēləs\ *adj* [ISV ¹*pro-* + *-coelous*] **1** *of a vertebra* : concave at the anterior end of the centrum and usu. convex at the posterior end of the centrum **2** : having procoelous vertebrae

**pro con·fes·so** \¦prōkən¦fe(ˌ)sō\ *adv (or adj)* [L, as (if) confessed] *law* : in the category of what may be considered as true, factual, or valid by reason of not having been denied or rejected ⟨the matter was taken *pro confesso* since the defendant did not file an answer⟩ : as though admitted : as though confessed : on the basis of what is implicitly admitted or confessed ⟨the individual defendant was directed to appear and answer the complaint or suffer judgment to be taken *pro confesso* —*Corporation Jour.*⟩

**¹pro·consul** \(ˈ)prō+\ *n* -s [ME, fr. L, fr. the phrase *pro consule* (acting) for a consul, fr. *pro* for + *consule*, abl. of *consul* — more at FOR, CONSUL] **1** : an official in an ancient Roman province who was entrusted with most of the authority of a consul and who acted as governor or military commander in the province **2** : an official in a modern colony, dependency, or occupied area who acts as an administrator usu. with extensive powers

**²proconsul** \"\ *n* [NL, fr. L *pro-* ¹pro- + *Consul*, a chimpanzee in the London zoo] **1** *cap* : a genus of extinct primitive African Miocene anthropoid apes related to those of the genus *Dryopithecus* **2** -s : an ape of the genus *Proconsul*

**pro·consular** \"+\ *adj* [L *proconsularis*, fr. *proconsul* + *-aris* -ar] **1 :** of, relating to, or typical of a proconsul ⟨~ powers⟩ ⟨~ administration⟩ ⟨has that reserved ~ look —*Time*⟩ **2 :** governed, administered, or commanded by a proconsul ⟨a ~ province⟩

**pro·consulate** \"+\ *n* [L *proconsulatus*, fr. *proconsul* + *-atus* -ate] **1 a :** the office or position of a proconsul **b :** the term of office of a proconsul **2 :** the district governed or administered by a proconsul

**pro·consulship** \"+\ *n* **:** PROCONSULATE 1

**pro·cras·ti·nate** \prō'krastə,nāt, prə'k-, -raas-, *usu* -ād·+V\ *vb* -ED/-ING/-S [L *procrastinatus*, past part. of *procrastinare*, fr. *pro-* forward + *-crastinare* (fr. *crastinus* of tomorrow, fr. *cras* tomorrow) — more at PRO-] *vt* **:** to put off intentionally and usu. habitually and for a reason held to be reprehensible (as laziness, indifference to responsibility) **:** POSTPONE, DEFER ⟨*procrastinated* his return on various pretexts —W.H.Prescott⟩ ⟨a *procrastinated* attack⟩ ~ *vi* **:** to put off intentionally and usu. habitually and reprehensibly the doing of something that should be done **:** delay attending to something until some later time **:** be slow or late in doing or attending to things ⟨one yawns, one ~*s*, one can do it when one will, and therefore one seldom does it at all —Earl of Chesterfield⟩ **syn** see DELAY

**procrastinating** *adj* **:** given to, inclined toward, or marked by procrastination ⟨a most annoyingly ~ individual⟩ — **pro·cras·ti·nat·ing·ly** *adv*

**pro·cras·ti·na·tion** \=,=='nāshən\ *n* -S [L *procrastination-*, *procrastinatio*, fr. *procrastinatus* + *-ion-*, *-io* -ion] **:** the action, habit, or characteristic of procrastinating ⟨was infuriated by their constant ~⟩

**pro·cras·ti·na·tive** \='==,nād·|iv, -āt|, |ēv *also* |əv\ *adj* **:** PROCRASTINATING — **pro·cras·ti·na·tive·ly** \|əvlē, -li\ *adv*

**pro·cras·ti·na·tor** \|ə(r)\ *n* -S **:** one that procrastinates

**pro·cras·ti·na·to·ry** \-_nə,tōrē\ *adj* **:** PROCRASTINATING

1**pro·cre·ant** \'prōkrēənt\ *adj* [L *procreant-*, *procreans*, pres. part. of *procreare* to procreate] **:** PROCREATIVE ⟨the ~ urge of the world —Walt Whitman⟩

2**procreant** \"\ *n* -S *obs* **:** PROCREATOR

**pro·cre·ate** \-ē,āt, *usu* -ād·+V\ *vb* -ED/-ING/-S [L *procreatus*, past part. of *procreare*, fr. *pro-* forward, forth + *creare* to create — more at PRO-, CREATE] *vt* **1 :** to produce (offspring) by generation **:** BEGET, PROPAGATE, GENERATE, REPRODUCE ⟨*procreating* their kind⟩ **2 :** to give rise to **:** ORIGINATE, OCCASION ⟨*procreating* one rumor after another⟩ ~ *vi* **:** to produce offspring

**pro·cre·ation** \,=='āshən\ *n* [ME *procreacioun*, fr. MF *procreation*, fr. L *procreation-*, *procreatio*, fr. *procreatus* + *-ion-*, *-io* -ion] **:** the action of procreating or condition of being procreated ⟨with animals we share eating, sleeping, ~ —A.A. Hill⟩

**pro·cre·ation·al** \¦==¦āshən°l, -shnəl\ *adj* **:** PROCREATIVE

**pro·cre·ative** \'==,ād·|iv, -,at|, |ēv *also* |əv\ *adj* **1 :** that procreates or is capable of procreating **:** GENERATIVE ⟨a remarkably ~ people⟩ **2 :** of, relating to, or directed toward procreation ⟨the ~ process⟩ ⟨~ instincts⟩ — **pro·cre·ative·ness** \|ivnəs, |ēv- *also* |əv-\ *n*

**pro·cre·ator** \|ə(r)\ *n* [L, fr. *procreatus*, past part. of *procreare* to procreate + *-or* — more at PROCREATE] **:** one that procreates

1**pro·crus·te·an** \prō'krəstēən\ *adj*, *often cap* [*Procrustes* (fr. L, fr. Gk *Prokroustēs*), legendary robber of ancient Greece who forced his victims to fit a certain bed by stretching or lopping off their legs + E *-an*] **1 :** of, relating to, or typical of Procrustes ⟨the ~ legend⟩ ⟨*Procrustean* reasoning —Nathaniel Peffer⟩ ⟨~ determination to make the evidence fit the theory —Walter Lippmann⟩ **2 :** that is marked by complete disregard of individual differences or special circumstances and that arbitrarily often ruthlessly or violently forces into conformity with or subservience to something (as a system, policy, doctrine) ⟨~ methods⟩ ⟨~ techniques⟩ ⟨~ legislation —*Wall Street Jour.*⟩

2**procrustean** \"\ *n* -S *often cap* **:** one that is procrustean (as in actions, methods)

**procrustean bed** \"-\ *or* **pro·crus·tes bed** \-(,)stēz-\ *n*, *often cap P* **:** something (as a system, policy, doctrine) into conformity with which or subservience to which someone or something is arbitrarily and often ruthlessly or violently forced ⟨a *Procrustean bed* wherein the unsuspecting student would be cut or stretched to a preconceived pattern —Benjamin Fine⟩ ⟨might be broken by the implacable *procrustes bed* of government machinery —John Gunther⟩

**pro·cryp·sis** \prō'kripsəs\ *n* -ES [NL, fr. E *procryptic*, after E *cryptic:* Gk *krypsis* act of hiding, concealment (fr. *kryptein* to hide + *-sis*) — more at CRYPT] **:** a pattern or shade of coloring in insects that is adapted to concealing the insects from their natural enemies **:** protective coloration in insects

**pro·cryptic** \prō+\ *adj* [*pro-* (as in *protect*) + *cryptic*] **:** of, relating to, or marked by procrypsis ⟨~ coloration⟩ ⟨a ~ beetle⟩ — compare APOSEMATIC

**proct-** *or* **procto-** *also* **procti-** *comb form* [NL, fr. Gk *prōkt-*, *prōkto-*, fr. *prōktos;* perh. akin to Arm *erastank'* buttocks] **1 :** anus ⟨*procti*ger⟩ **2 :** rectum ⟨*proct*algia⟩ **:** rectum and ⟨*proto*sigmoidectomy⟩ **3 :** anus and rectum ⟨*procto*logy⟩

1**-proc·ta** \'präktə\ *n pl comb form* [NL, fr. Gk *prōktos*] **:** animals having a (specified) type of anus — in names of higher taxa ⟨Ento*procta*⟩ ⟨Ecto*procta*⟩

2**-procta** \"\ *n comb form* [NL, fr. Gk *prōktos*] **:** animal having a (specified) type of anus or buttocks — in generic names of animals ⟨Dasy*procta*⟩

**proc·tal** \'präkt°l\ *adj* [*proct-* + *-al*] **:** situated immediately in front of the cloaca ⟨a fish with a ~ pelvic fin⟩

**proct·algia** \präk'talj(ē)ə\ *n* -S [NL, fr. *proct-* + *-algia*] **:** rectal pain

**proc·ti·ger** \'präktəjə(r)\ *n* -S [NL, fr. *proct-* + *-ger* -gerous] **:** the conical reduced terminal abdominal segment of an insect in which the anus is located

**proc·ti·tis** \präk'tīd·əs\ *n* -ES [NL, fr. *proct-* + *-itis*] **:** inflammation of the anus and rectum

**proc·to·clysis** \¦präktə+\ *n*, *pl* **proctoclyses** [NL, fr. *proct-* + *clysis*] **:** slow injection of large quantities of a fluid (as a solution of salt) into the rectum in supplementing the liquid intake of the body

**proc·to·dae·al** *or* **proc·to·de·al** \¦präktə¦dēəl\ *adj* [NL *proctodae*um, *proctode*um + E *-al*] **:** of, relating to, or connected with the proctodaeum

**proc·to·dae·um** *or* **proc·to·de·um** \,=='dēəm\ *n*, *pl* **procto·daea** \-ēə\ *or* **proctodae·ums** \-ēəmz\ *or* **procto·dea** *or* **proctode·ums** [NL, fr. *proct-* + *-odaeum*, *-odeum* (fr. Gk *hodaios* on the way, fr. *hodos* way) — more at CEDE] **:** the posterior ectodermal part of the alimentary canal formed in the embryo by invagination of the outer body wall — compare MESENTERON, STOMODAEUM

**proc·to·log·ic** \¦präktə¦läjik\ *or* **proc·to·log·i·cal** \-jəkəl\ *adj* **:** of or relating to proctology ⟨a ~ disorder⟩

**proc·tol·o·gist** \präk'täləjəst\ *n* -S **:** a specialist in proctology

**proc·tol·o·gy** \-jē\ *n* -ES [*proct-* + *-logy*] **:** a branch of medicine dealing with the structure and diseases of the anus, rectum, and sigmoid colon

**proc·to·phyl·lod·i·dae** \,präk(,)tōfə'lädə,dē\ *n pl*, *cap* [NL, fr. *Proctophyllodes*, type genus (fr. *proct-* + Gk *phyllōdēs* resembling a leaf, fr. *phyll-* + *-ōdēs* -ode) + *-idae*] **:** a widely distributed family of feather mites

1**proc·tor** \'präktə(r)\ *n* -S [ME *proctour*, *procutour* procurator, proctor, alter. of *procuratour* — more at PROCURATOR] **1 :** one that by profession or by special authorization manages another's affairs or conducts proceedings for another in a court of civil or canon law **:** an attorney acting in a court of civil or canon law **2 a :** one of two officers in a British university who discharge various functions and who are esp. entrusted with the maintenance of order and the enforcement of obedience to the laws of the institution **b :** one that supervises, guides, or advises **:** SUPERVISOR, MONITOR; *specif* **:** an officer or student (as in a college or university) appointed to supervise students (as at an examination and in the dormitories) or to check on attendance or perform some similar duty **3 :** an elected representative of the clergy at a convocation in the Church of England **4 :** a collector of tithes or other ecclesiastical dues for another

2**proctor** \"\ *vb* -ED/-ING/-S **:** SUPERVISE, MONITOR

3**proctor** \"\ *adj*, *usu cap* [after Ralph R. *Proctor* †1962 Amer. civil engineer] **:** of, relating to, or determined by a procedure designed to sample and test soil to be used in fills and embankments ⟨the *Proctor* method . . . of determining the moisture content —*Military Engineer*⟩ ⟨the *Proctor* density of soil⟩

**proc·to·ri·al** \(')präk¦tōrēəl\ *adj* **:** of or relating to a proctor ⟨in defiance of ~ regulations —Max Beerbohm⟩ — **proc·to·ri·al·ly** \-əlē\ *adv*

**proc·tor·iza·tion** \,präktərə'zāshən, -,rī'z-\ *n* -S **1** *archaic* **:** the action of exercising proctorial authority or of serving as a proctor **2** *archaic* **:** the condition of being subjected to proctorial authority

**proc·tor·ize** \'==,rīz\ *vb* -ED/-ING/-S *see -ize in Explan Notes* [1*proctor* + *-ize*] *vt*, *archaic* **:** to subject to proctorial authority (as by reprimanding, disciplining) ~ *vi*, *archaic* **:** to serve in the position of a proctor

**proc·tor·ship** \'präktə(r),ship\ *n* **:** the office or function of a proctor

1**proc·to·scope** \'präktə,skōp\ *n* [ISV *proct-* + *-scope*] **:** an instrument used for dilating and visually inspecting the rectum

2**proctoscope** \"\ *vt* -ED/-ING/-S **:** to use a proctoscope on

**proc·to·scop·ic** \¦==¦skäpik\ *adj* **:** of or relating to a proctoscope or proctoscopy — **proc·to·scop·i·cal·ly** \-pək(ə)lē\ *adv*

**proc·tos·co·py** \präk'täskəpē\ *n* -ES [ISV *proct-* + *-scopy*] **:** dilation and visual inspection of the rectum

**proc·to·sigmoidectomy** \,präk(,)tō+\ *n* -ES [*proct-* + *sigmoid* (n.) + *-ectomy*] **:** complete or partial surgical excision of the rectum and sigmoid colon

**proc·to·sigmoidoscope** \"+\ *n* [*proct-* + *sigmoid* + *-o-* + *-scope*] **:** SIGMOIDOSCOPE — **proc·to·sig·moi·do·scop·ic** \,präk(,)tō,sig¦mȯidə¦skäpik\ *adj* — **proc·to·sigmoidoscopy** \,präk(,)tō+\ *n*

**proc·to·tru·pid** \¦präktə·¦trüpəd\ *or* **proc·to·tryp·id** \-·¦trip-\ *adj or n* [NL *Proctotrupidae*, *Proctotrypidae*] **:** SERPHID

**proc·to·tru·pi·dae** *or* **proc·to·tryp·i·dae** \,=='=pə,dē\ [*Proctotrupidae*, NL, fr. *Proctotrupes*, type genus (fr. *proct-* + *-trupes*, irreg. fr. Gk *trypan* to bore through, pierce) + *-idae; Proctotrypidae*, NL, fr. *Proctotypes*, type genus (syn. of *Proctotrupes;* alter. of *Proctotrupes*) + *-idae* — more at TRYPAN-] *syn of* SERPHIDAE

**proc·to·tru·poid** *or* **proc·to·tryp·oid** \¦==¦=,pȯid\ *adj or n* [NL *Proctotrupoidea*, *Proctotrypoidea*] **:** SERPHOID

**proc·to·tru·poi·dea** \,==·(,)trü'pȯidēə\ *or* **proc·to·try·poi·dea** \-·_trə'p-\ [NL, fr. *Proctotrupes* or *Proctotrypes* + *-oidea*] *syn of* SERPHOIDEA

**-proc·tous** \¦präktəs\ *adj comb form* [*proct-* + *-ous*] **:** of, relating to, or having a (specified) type of anus ⟨ento*proctous*⟩

**-proc·tus** \'präktəs\ *n comb form* [NL, fr. Gk *prōktos* anus — more at PROCT-] **:** animal having a (specified) type of anus — in generic names ⟨Mastigo*proctus*⟩

**pro·cum·bent** \(')prō¦kəmbənt\ *adj* [L *procumbent-*, *procumbens*, pres. part. of *procumbere* to fall, bend, or lean forward, fr. *pro-* forward, down + *-cumbere* to lie down — more at PRO-, INCUMBENT] **1 a :** being or having stems that trail along the ground without putting forth roots ⟨a ~ plant⟩ ⟨~ stems⟩ **b :** having the longest axis radial ⟨~ cells in a vascular ray⟩ **2 a :** lying stretched out **:** RECUMBENT ⟨the sight of this gleaming city in a lazy blue haze, ~ by the Tiber —Francis Hackett⟩ **b :** lying face down **:** PRONE, PROSTRATE ⟨~ slaves⟩ **3 :** slanting forward ⟨the ~ incisor teeth of a horse⟩

**pro·cur·abil·i·ty** \prə,kyu̇rə'biləd·ē, prō,k-, -lətē, -i\ *n* **:** the quality or state of being procurable

**pro·cur·able** \='==_bəl\ *adj* **:** capable of being procured

**proc·u·ra·cy** \'präkyərəsē\ *n* -ES [ME *procuracie*, fr. AF, fr. ML *procuratia*, alter. of L *procuratio* procuration — more at PROCURATION] **1** *archaic* **:** the office or functions of a proctor or procurator **2** *archaic* **:** management or direction of affairs for another

**pro·cur·al** \prə'kyu̇rəl, prō'k-\ *n* -S [*procure* + *-al*] **:** PROCUREMENT; *esp* **:** the action of acquiring something ⟨the ~ of new books for the library⟩

**pro·cur·ance** \-rən(t)s, 'präkyər-\ *n* -S **:** PROCUREMENT; *esp* **:** the action of furthering or bringing about the achievement of something (as by one's intervention or influence)

**proc·u·ra·tion** \,präkyə'rāshən\ *n* -S [ME *procuracioun*, fr. MF *procuration*, fr. L *procuration-*, *procuratio*, fr. *procuratus* (past part. of *procurare* to take care of) + *-ion-*, *-io* -ion — more at PROCURE] **1** *archaic* **:** management or direction of affairs for another **2 a :** POWER OF ATTORNEY **b** (1) **:** the action of appointing someone as one's agent or attorney (2) **:** the authorized action or function of one appointed as an agent or attorney **c :** the authority proper to one appointed as an agent or attorney **d :** MANDATE 2c **3 :** a particular quota of provisions or a fixed sum of money given by parochial churches of the Church of England to a bishop or archdeacon at the time of his visitation **4 a :** PROCUREMENT; *esp* **:** the action of obtaining something **b** (1) **:** the action of obtaining a loan for a client or of executing a bond for a client (2) *or* **procuration fee** *or* **procuration money :** a sum of money paid (as to a broker) by a client for a loan obtained or bond executed **c :** the act of pimping

**pro·cur·a·tive** \prə'kyu̇rəd·iv, prō'k-\ *adj* [*procure* + *-ative*] *archaic* **:** that procures or tends to procure

**proc·u·ra·tor** \'präkyə,rād·ə(r), -ātə-\ *n* -S [ME *procuratour*, fr. OF, fr. L *procurator*, fr. *procuratus* (past part. of *procurare* to take care of) + *-or* — more at PROCURE] **1 :** one that manages the affairs of another esp. by acting as the agent, deputy, proxy, or representative of the other: as **a :** one of several imperial officers of the ancient Roman empire entrusted with the management of the financial affairs of a province and often having administrative powers in a province as agents of the emperor **b :** PROCTOR 1 **c :** one that has power of attorney **d** [ML, fr. L] (1) **:** one of two or more representative officers in a medieval university having financial, electoral, and disciplinary functions (2) **:** one of several student representatives in some Scottish universities chosen to preside over the election of a rector **2 a :** one of several public magistrates or administrators (as in Italy) with varying functions **b :** PUBLIC PROSECUTOR: as (1) **:** PROCURATOR FISCAL (2) **:** PROCUREUR 2 **3 :** one that obtains or gets something esp. regularly or in an official capacity; *esp* **:** one of a group of individuals living a common life together (as in a monastic community) who is appointed to buy supplies for the group

**proc·u·ra·tor·ate** \-ərət\ *n* -S **:** the office or functions of a procurator

**procurator fiscal** *or* **procurator of the fisk** *n* **:** the public prosecutor of a local district (as a shire) in Scotland

**procurator-general** \¦==,==¦=(=)=\ *n*, *pl* **procurators-general** *or* **procurator-generals :** a procurator of high rank

**proc·u·ra·to·ri·al** \¦präkyərə¦tōrēəl\ *adj* [LL *procuratori*us procuratorial (fr. L *procurator*) + E *-al*] **1 :** of or relating to a procurator **2 :** PROCTORIAL

**proc·u·ra·tor·ship** \'prakyə,rād·ə(r),ship, -ātə-\ *n* **:** the office or function of a procurator

**proc·u·ra·to·ry** \-_rə,tōrē\ *n* -ES [LL *procuratorius*] **1** *civil law* **:** authorization of one individual to act for another **2 :** POWER OF ATTORNEY

**proc·u·ra·trix** \¦präkyə¦ra·triks\ *n* -ES [L, fem. of *procurator*] **:** a female procurator

**pro·cure** \prə'kyu̇(ə)r, prō'k-, -u̇ə\ *vb* -ED/-ING/-S [ME *procuren* to take care of, bring about, obtain, fr. LL & L; LL *procurare* to obtain, fr. L, to take care of, fr. *pro-* for, on behalf of + *curare* to take care of — more at PRO-, CURE] *vt* **1 a** (1) **:** to get possession of **:** OBTAIN, ACQUIRE ⟨*procuring* extra equipment and supplies —H.G.Armstrong⟩; *esp* **:** to get possession of by particular care or effort ⟨it fell to my lot . . . to scurry around and ~ manuscripts —A.W.Long⟩ and sometimes by devious means ⟨*procured* enormous wealth by such dealings⟩ (2) **:** GAIN, WIN ⟨the judicial qualities he developed . . . *procured* for him universal confidence and respect —H.W.H. Knott⟩ **b :** to get possession of (women) and make available for promiscuous sexual intercourse (as in a house of prostitution) **2 a** (1) **:** to cause to happen or be done **:** bring about **:** EFFECT ⟨*procured* temporary agreement⟩ **:** ACHIEVE ⟨failed to ~ a coherent theory —Joseph Conrad⟩; *esp* **:** to bring about by particular care or effort ⟨had *procured* the enactment of a more complete system of defense laws —F.L.Paxson⟩ ⟨*procuring* the release of a man in jail —Peggy Durdin⟩ and sometimes by devious means ⟨on trial for *procuring* perjury —*Time*⟩ (2) **:** to bring about by scheming and plotting **:** CONTRIVE ⟨*procured* the downfall of the government⟩ ⟨did not hesitate to ~ murder —Will Irwin & T.M.Johnson⟩ **b** *archaic* **:** to cause to be treated in an indicated way or to undergo something indicated ⟨intended by one who ~*s* another to be indicted —O.W.Holmes †1935⟩ **3 a :** to prevail upon to do something indicated **:** INDUCE ⟨*procuring* a witness to commit perjury⟩ **b** *obs* **:** to cause (as by persuading or alluring) to come to an indicated place **:** BRING ⟨what unaccustomed cause ~*s* her hither —Shak.⟩ ~ *vi* **:** to procure women for promiscuous sexual intercourse ⟨arrested on charges of *procuring* —Joachim Joesten⟩ **syn** see GET

**pro·cure·ment** \-u̇(ə)rmənt, -u̇əm-\ *n* -S [ME, fr. MF, fr. *procurer* + *-ment*] **1 :** the act of procuring ⟨~ of materials and supplies⟩ ⟨~ of personnel⟩ ⟨~ of a loan⟩ **2 :** the condition of being procured ⟨knew about the ~ of the books⟩

**procurement clerk** *n* **1 :** a clerk who edits purchase requests, invites bids from suppliers, and makes out orders for procurement of materials by an organization — called also *award clerk* **2 :** PURCHASING AGENT 1

**pro·cur·er** \-u̇rə(r)\ *n* -S [ME *procurour*, fr. MF *procureur*, fr. L *procurator* — more at PROCURATOR] **1 :** one that procures; *esp* **:** a man who procures women for promiscuous sexual intercourse **2** *obs* **:** PROCUREUR

**pro·cur·ess** \-u̇rəs\ *n* -ES [ME *procuresse*, modif. of MF *procureresse*, fr. *procureur* + *-esse* -ess] **:** a female procurer

**pro·cu·reur** \prȯkūrœ̄r\ *n* -S [MF] **1 :** an agent or representative in a French court of law **2 :** a public prosecutor in a French court of law

**pro·current** \(')prō+\ *adj* [L *procurrent-*, *procurrens*, pres. part. of *procurrere* to run forward, jut out, fr. *pro-* forward + *currere* to run — more at PRO-, CURRENT] *of a fish's fin* **:** marked by a progressively farther forward placement of rays ⟨the ~ fin of some cottids⟩

**pro·curved** \'prō+¦-\ *adj* [L *pro-* forward + E *curved* — more at PRO-] **:** curved forward

**pro·cuticle** \(')prō+\ *n* [1*pro-* + *cuticle*] **:** the chitinized part of the cuticle of an insect

**pro·cy·on** \'prōsē,än\ *n*, *cap* [NL, fr. *Procyon*, a star, fr. Gk *Prokyōn*] **:** a genus (the type of the family Procyonidae) consisting of the raccoons

**pro·cy·on·i·dae** \,prōsē'änə,dē\ *n pl*, *cap* [NL, fr. *Procyon*, type genus + *-idae*] **:** a family of plantigrade carnivorous mammals consisting of the raccoons, coatis, cacomistles, kinkajous, and sometimes the pandas

**pro·cy·on·i·for·mia** \,==,änə'fȯ(r)mēə\ *n pl*, *cap* [NL, fr. *Procyon* + L *-iformia*, neut. pl. of *-iformis* -iform] *in former classifications* **:** a subdivision of Arctoidea coextensive with Procyonidae

1**prod** \'präd\ *vb* **prodded**; **prodded**; **prodding**; **prods** [origin unknown] *vt* **1 a :** to thrust a pointed instrument into **:** prick with something sharp or blunted ⟨the animals were . . . ruthlessly *prodded* —V.G.Heiser⟩ **b :** to incite to action or thought **:** jog lightly **:** stir up **:** JOSTLE, NUDGE ⟨discretion and good judgment can be cultivated and *prodded* —*Saturday Rev.*⟩ ⟨the student was . . . *prodded* to master something —W.H. White⟩ **2 :** to poke about or stir as if with a prod ⟨refilling his pipe . . . he *prodded* the bowl with his thumb —Ellen Glasgow⟩ ⟨a fine cock rail . . . stopping to ~ the mud —D.C. Peattie⟩ ~ *vi* **:** to go poking — usu. used with *in* or *at* ⟨it is not the facts . . . which drive and ~ at my imagination —Marcia Davenport⟩ **syn** see URGE

2**prod** \"\ *n* -S **1 :** a pointed instrument used to impel, move, poke, stir, or make an electrical contact **2 :** an incitement to act **:** a sharp reminder **:** THRUST ⟨under the ~ of skepticism, there have been refinements in technique —Roland Walker⟩ ⟨a ~ on the subject of church attendance —Compton Mackenzie⟩ — **on the prod** *chiefly West* **:** in an irritable mood and ready to fight ⟨this man was *on the prod* . . . and as dangerous as a cornered cougar —P.E.Lehman⟩

3**prod** \"\ *var of* PRAD

**prod** *abbr* **1** produce; producer; produced **2** product; production

**prod·der** \-də(r)\ *n* -S **:** one that prods

**prod·dle** \'präd°l\ *vb* -ED/-ING/-S [freq. of 1*prod*] *dial Eng* **:** POTTER, FUMBLE, POKE

**prod·e·li·sion** \,präd°l'izhən\ *n* -S [L *prod-* (var. of *pro-* before) + E *elision* — more at PRO-] **:** elision of the initial vowel of a word ⟨Latin *bonum'st* for *bonum est* is an example of ~⟩

**pro·del·phic** \(')prō¦delfik\ *also* **pro·del·phous** \-fəs\ *adj* [1*pro-* + Gk *delphys* womb + E *-ic* or *-ous* — more at DOLPHIN] *of a nematode worm* **:** having the uteri parallel and anteriorly directed

**pro·democratic** \(¦)prō+\ *adj* [2*pro-* + *democratic*] **:** favoring democracy ⟨acute difficulties experienced by the ~ parties in trying to achieve governing majorities —W.R.Sharp⟩

**pro·de·nia** \prō'dēnēə\ *n*, *cap* [NL] **:** a common and widespread genus of moths (family Noctuidae) whose larvae are destructive to a great variety of plants

**pro·dentine** \(')prō+\ *n* -S [1*pro-* + *dentine*] **:** a cap of uncalcified tissue over the tooth cusps previous to the formation of dentin

1**prod·i·gal** \'prädəgəl, -dēg-\ *adj* [L *prodig*us prodigal (fr. *prodigere* to drive away, squander, fr. *prod-* — var. of *pro-* forward, forth — + *-igere*, fr. *agere* to drive) + E *-al* — more at PRO-, AGENT] **1 :** given to reckless extravagance **:** unrestrained in spending or using up one's means ⟨he had been ~ with his money —Cliff Farrell⟩ **2 :** characterized by profuse or wasteful expenditure **:** LAVISH ⟨make as much money as the most ~ editors will give him —Harrison Smith⟩ **3 :** profusely liberal **:** giving or yielding abundantly **:** LUXURIANT ⟨the lush ~ way in which the tropics announced spring —William Beebe⟩ **syn** see PROFUSE

2**prodigal** \"\ *n* -S **1 a :** one who spends or gives lavishly **:** one who is foolishly extravagant **:** SPENDTHRIFT, SQUANDERER ⟨explained what a ~ this was, what a waster —Francis Hackett⟩ **b :** a repentant wastrel **2 :** one adjudged legally incompetent to manage his property or to incur debts because of a propensity to waste his capital

3**prodigal** *adv*, *obs* **:** PRODIGALLY ⟨when the blood burns, how ~ the soul lends the tongue vows —Shak.⟩

**prod·i·gal·i·ty** \,prädə'galəd·ē, -lətē, -i\ *n* -ES [ME *prodigalite*, fr. MF *prodigalité*, fr. LL *prodigalitat-*, *prodigalitas*, L *prodigus* prodigal + *-alis* -al + *-itat-*, *-itas* -ity — more at PRODIGAL] **1 :** extravagance or an extravagant act in expenditure esp. of money **:** reckless spending of resources **:** WASTEFULNESS ⟨his ~ became a legend⟩ **2 :** profuse liberality **:** lavish supply **:** excessive abundance ⟨a sound understanding of the earth's ~ —J.R.Caceres⟩ ⟨our truly wonderful ~ of talent —J.A. Michener⟩

**prod·i·gal·ize** \'prädəgə,līz\ *vt* -ED/-ING/-S **:** to expend extravagantly

**prod·i·gal·ly** \-gəlē\ *adv* **:** in a prodigal manner **:** EXTRAVAGANTLY ⟨we are still ~ rich in natural beauty —S.P.B.Mais⟩

**prodigal son** *n* [after the *Prodigal Son* of the Biblical parable (Luke 15:11–32), who squandered his father's money] **1 :** PRODIGAL 1b **2 :** either of two marine food fishes: **a :** COBIA **b :** RAINBOW RUNNER

**pro·dig·i·o·sin** \prō,dijē'ōs°n\ *n* -S [NL *prodigiosus* (specific epithet of *Bacillus prodigiosus*, syn. of *Serratia marcescens*) (fr. L *prodigiosus* prodigious) + E *-in*] **:** a red antibiotic pigment $C_{20}H_{25}N_3O$ that is produced by a bacterium (*Serratia marcescens*), has shown activity on an experimental basis against protozoans (as the parasite of amebic dysentery) and against fungi (as the parasite of coccidioidomycosis), and is a derivative of tri-pyrryl-methane

**pro·di·gious** \prə'dijəs, prō'-\ *adj* [L *prodigiosus*, fr. *prodigium* omen, portent, monster + *-osus* -ous — more at PRODIGY] **1 a** *obs* **:** having the nature of an omen **:** PORTENTOUS ⟨never mole, harelip, nor scar, nor mark ~ . . . shall upon their children be —Shak.⟩ **b** *archaic* **:** having the appearance of a prodigy **:** ABNORMAL, STRANGE **2 :** exciting amazement or wonder **:** causing one to marvel **:** AMAZING ⟨from childhood precocious and ~ in everything —Willa Cather⟩ ⟨a ~ vision —Christopher Rand⟩ **3 :** extraordinary in bulk, extent, quantity, or degree **:** ENORMOUS, IMMENSE, VAST ⟨a ~ noise of wheels —Elinor Wylie⟩ ⟨have done a ~ amount of work —John Sparkman⟩ ⟨the amount of food provided at a party of this kind was ~ —W.S.Maugham⟩ **syn** see MONSTROUS

**pro·di·gious·ly** *adv* **:** in a prodigious manner **:** AMAZINGLY, EXTREMELY ⟨beef cattle were much in evidence . . . black and shiny, and ~ broad and fat —Christopher Rand⟩ ⟨a ~ wealthy nation —G.B.Shaw⟩

**pro·di·gious·ness** *n* -ES : the quality or state of being prodigious

**prod·i·gus** \'prädəgəs\ *n* -ES [L, fr. *prodigus*, adj., prodigal — more at PRODIGAL] *Roman law* : PRODIGAL 2

**prod·i·gy** \'prädəjē, -ji\ *n* -ES [L *prodigium* omen, portent, monster, fr. *prod-* (var. of *pro-* before) + *-igium* (akin to *aio* I say) — more at PRO-, ADAGE] **1 a** *archaic* : something out of the usual course of nature (as an eclipse or meteor) that is a portent : OMEN, SIGN **b** : something extraordinary or inexplicable : one that is abnormal or monstrous ⟨the name of the ~ was the "Ferris wheel" and thousands were scrambling to get a ride —John Kobler⟩ **2** : one that excites admiration or wonder: as **a** : an extraordinary, marvelous, or unusual accomplishment, deed, or instance — often used with *of* ⟨regarded as a worker of *prodigies* —T.B.Macaulay⟩ **b** : a highly gifted or academically talented child ⟨he was what is called an infant ~ —Bruce Bliven b.1889⟩ **syn** see WONDER

**pro·dissoconch** \(ˈ)prō+\ *n* [1*pro-* + *dissoconch*] : the rudimentary or embryonic shell of a bivalve mollusk

**pro·di·tion** \prō'dishən\ *n* -S [ME *prodycyon*, fr. MF *prodition*, fr. L *prodition-*, *proditio*, fr. *proditus* (past part. of *prodere* to bring forth, report, betray, fr. *pro-* forth + *-dere*, fr. *dare* to give) + *-ion-*, *-io* -ion — more at PRO-, DATE] : BETRAYAL, TREASON

**proditor** *n* -S [ME *proditour*, fr. MF *proditeur*, fr. L *proditor*, fr. *proditus* + *-or*] *obs* : TRAITOR ⟨thou most usurping ~ and not protector of the king —Shak.⟩

**prod·i·to·ri·ous** \ˌprädəˌtōrēəs\ *adj* [ME, fr. L *proditus* + ME *-orious*] *archaic* : apt to betray secret thoughts

**prod·ro·ma** \'prädrəmə\ *n, pl* **prodromas** \-məz\ *or* **pro·dro·ma·ta** \prō'drōmədə\ [NL, fr. F *prodrome*] : PRODROME

**prod·ro·mal** \-məl\ *or* **pro·drom·ic** \prō'drämik\ *adj* [*prodrome* + *-al* or *-ic*] : PRECURSORY; *esp* : of, relating to, or marked by prodromes ⟨the ~ stages of a disease⟩

**pro·drome** \'prōˌdrōm\ *n* -S [F, precursor, prodrome, fr. Gk *prodromos* precursor, fr. *prodromos*, adj., running ahead, fr. *pro-* 1pro- + *dromos* -drome] : a premonitory symptom of a disease

**prod·ro·mus** \'prädrəməs\ *n* -ES [NL, fr. Gk *prodromos* precursor] **1** *obs* : something that alerts or forewarns **2** : a preliminary publication or introductory work

**prods** *pres 3d sing of* PROD, *pl of* PROD

**1pro·duce** \prə'dyüs, prō'-\ *vb* -ED/-ING/-S [ME (Sc dial.) *producen*, fr. L *producere* fr. *pro-* forward + *ducere* to lead — more at PRO-, TOW] *vt* **1** : to bring forward : lead forth : offer to view or notice : EXHIBIT, SHOW ⟨the State Department *produced* the transcript —*New Republic*⟩ ⟨required to ~ his licence for inspection —Priscilla Hughes⟩ **2** : to bring forth : give birth to : BEAR, GENERATE, YIELD ⟨the greatest scientist the world has *produced* —T.B.Costain⟩ ⟨the rains ~ a quick-growing and lush herbage —N.C.Wright⟩ **3** : to extend geometrically : PROLONG — used of a line, surface, or solid ⟨~ the side of a triangle⟩ **4** : to introduce to the public : bring out as a dramatic production ⟨five new plays which were *produced* —*Current Biog.*⟩ ⟨said she would like me to ~ her in something —Mrs. Patrick Campbell⟩ **5** : to cause to have existence or to happen : bring about : ORIGINATE ⟨the sting . . . ~s violent inflammation —Richard Semon⟩ ⟨*produced* an indulgent smile —Edith Wharton⟩ **6** *obs* : ADVANCE, PROMOTE **7** : to compose, create, or bring out by intellectual or physical effort ⟨*produced* a group of poems —Naomi Lewis⟩ ⟨regularly ~s articles and drawings —*Current Biog.*⟩ **8 a** : to give being, form, or shape to : make often from raw materials : MANUFACTURE ⟨*produced* 5,002 cars in three years —*Amer. Guide Series: Mich.*⟩ **b** : to make economically valuable : make or create so as to be available for satisfaction of human wants **9** : to cause to accrue : bring in as profit ⟨money at interest ~s an income⟩ ~ *vi* : to bring forth a product or production : bear, make, or yield that which is according to nature or intention : grow, make, or furnish economically valuable products ⟨labored literally day and night to ~ —Vera M.Dean⟩ **syn** see BEAR

**2prod·uce** \'präˌd(y)üs, 'prōˌ-\ *n* -S **1 a** (1) : something that is brought forth or yielded either naturally or as a result of effort and work (2) : a result produced : CONSEQUENCE ⟨the ~ of . . . knowledge extends to the individual and to the community —Curt Stern⟩ **b** : the amount that is produced : RETURN, YIELD ⟨worth about twice as much as the annual ~ of all English mines —T.B.Macaulay⟩ **2** : agricultural products (as fresh fruits and vegetables) ⟨wagons bringing ~ . . . from farms round about —Sidney Lovett⟩ **3** : the progeny usu. of a female animal : OFFSPRING — distinguished from *get* ⟨the ~ of this fine mare includes the get of several leading stallions⟩

**produced** *adj* : extended esp. in one direction : drawn out : disproportionately elongated ⟨a ~ leaf⟩ ⟨a scale ~ into spines⟩

**1pro·du·cent** \prə'd(y)üsᵊnt\ *adj* [L *producent-* *producens*, pres. part. of *producere* to produce — more at PRODUCE] : PRODUCING

**2producent** \"\ *n* -S : one that produces (as a witness or a document)

**produce-of-dam** \'=ˌ==ˈ=\ *n* **1** : the entire progeny of a dam or a representative sample **2** : a show class for judging progenies

**pro·duc·er** \prə'd(y)üsə(r), prō'-\ *n* -S **1** : one that produces, brings forth, or generates ⟨the state is rated as the largest ~ of northern partridge —*Amer. Guide Series: Mich.*⟩ **2** : one that grows agricultural products or manufactures crude materials into articles of use — compare CONSUMER **3** : a furnace or apparatus that produces combustible gas to be used for fuel and is usu. of the updraft type which forces or draws air or a mixture of air and steam through a layer of incandescent fuel (as coke) with the resulting gas consisting chiefly of carbon monoxide, hydrogen, and nitrogen — compare GENERATOR 2b **4 a** : one who assumes responsibility for the public presentation of a theatrical entertainment (as an opera, motion picture, or play for stage or television) as an artistic and usu. also as a financial venture — compare DIRECTOR 1c **b** *Brit* : DIRECTOR 1c **5** : a well that produces ⟨the ~ is one mile east of the . . . oil pool —*Ochiltree County Herald*⟩

**produce race** *n* : a race to be run by the produce of horses named or described at the time of entry — compare FUTURITY RACE

**producer gas** *n* : gas made in a producer, consisting chiefly of carbon monoxide, hydrogen, and nitrogen, and having an average heating value of about 150 Btu — compare MOND GAS, SYNTHESIS GAS, WATER GAS

**producer goods** *n pl* : goods (as tools and raw material) that are factors in the production of other goods and that satisfy wants only indirectly — called also *auxiliary goods*, *instrumental goods*, *intermediate goods;* compare CONSUMER GOODS

**producer's surplus** *also* **producer's rent** *n* : the payment received by a producer or seller in excess of the least sum he would have been willing to accept to make the sale — compare CONSUMER'S SURPLUS

**produces** *pres 3d sing of* PRODUCE, *pl of* PRODUCE

**pro·duc·ibil·i·ty** \prəˌd(y)üsə'bilədē\ *n* -ES : the character, state, or fact of being producible

**pro·duc·ible** \prə'd(y)üsəbəl, prō'-\ *adj* [LL *producibilis*, fr. L *producere* to produce + *-ibilis* -ible] **1** : capable of being produced or brought forth or forward **2** : capable of being brought about or made : MANUFACTURABLE **3** : PRESENTABLE

**producing** *pres part of* PRODUCE

**1prod·uct** \'prä(ˌ)dəkt *sometimes* -ˌdikt *or* -ˌdēkt\ *n* -S [in sense 1, fr. ME, fr. ML *productum*, fr. L, something produced, fr. neut. of *productus*, past part. of *producere* to produce; in other senses, fr. L *productum* something produced — more at PRODUCE] **1** : the number or magnitude resulting from the multiplication together of two or more numbers or magnitudes : the result of any kind of multiplication **2 a** : something produced by physical labor or intellectual effort : the result of work or thought ⟨use for hammocks and other ~s —P.E.James⟩ ⟨even the simplest poem is the ~ of much . . . work —Gilbert Highet⟩ **b** : a result of the operation of involuntary causes or an ensuing set of conditions : CONSEQUENCE, MANIFESTATION ⟨a ~ of liberal arts education —B.W. Hayward⟩ ⟨he was a ~ of his time —Allan Nevins⟩ **c** : something produced naturally or as the result of a natural process (as by generation or growth) ⟨major ~s from forest lands . . . are mahogany and chicle —*Americana Annual*⟩ **3** : the amount, total, or quantity produced : the output of an industry or firm ⟨our national ~ . . . has quickly risen to an enormous volume —George Soule⟩ **4** : a substance produced from one or more other substances as a result of chemical change **5** : CONJUNCTION 7 — usu. used in the algebra of classes

**2pro·duct** \prə'dəkt\ *vt* -ED/-ING/-S [L *productus*, past part. of *producere*] **1** : PRODUCE **2** : to lengthen out

**3product** *n* -S [by folk etymology fr. *pratique*] *obs* : PRATIQUE

**product engineer** *n* : an engineer who specializes in designing, building, and testing the prototype of a fabricated product and controls subsequent changes in the construction and material of the product

**pro·duct·ibil·i·ty** \prəˌdəktə'bilədē\ *n* -ES [L *productus* + E *-ibility*] : the quality or state of being producible

**pro·duc·tile** \prə'dəktᵊl\ *adj* [LL *productilis*, fr. L *productus* + *-ilis* -ile] : PRODUCIBLE

**1pro·duc·tion** \prə'dəkshən, prō'-\ *n* -S [ME *produccioun*, fr. ML *production-*, *productio*, fr. L *productus* (past part. of *producere* to produce) + *-ion-*, *-io* -ion — more at PRODUCE] **1 a** : something that is produced naturally or as the result of labor and effort : PRODUCT ⟨acrid ~s poisonously irritant to throat, lungs —Emily Holt⟩ ⟨skillful artisans, whose choice ~s could secure a ready sale —H.T.Buckle⟩ **b** (1) : a literary or artistic work (2) : a theatrical representation : the staging or performing of a theatrical entertainment **c** : an action resembling an elaborate theatrical performance : one exaggerated out of all proportion to its importance ⟨taking a small child visiting . . . can be quite a ~ —Nell Dunkin⟩ ⟨have lunch and still not make a ~ of it —Richard Joseph⟩ **2 a** : the act or process of producing, bringing forth, or making ⟨chief activities . . . are maple sugar ~ and farming —*Amer. Guide Series: Pa.*⟩ ⟨lead ore was worked . . . but they ceased ~ before 1776 —T.T.Read⟩ **b** : the creation of utility : the making of goods available for human wants **3** : the act of exhibiting; *esp* : exhibiting in a court of law ⟨the appellate court went so far as to demand ~ of the grounds for refusal —*Report: Amer. Civil Liberties Union*⟩ **4** : a lengthening out or prolonging : ELONGATION, EXTENSION **5** : the total output of a commodity

**2production** \"\ *adj* : designed to provide nutrients to an animal in proportion to its production (as of milk or eggs) and being in addition to those supplied to maintain bodily condition ⟨a ~ ration of two pounds of grain for each additional gallon of milk⟩

**pro·duc·tion·al** \-shənᵊl\ *adj* : of or relating to production

**production control** *n* : systematic planning, coordinating, and directing of all manufacturing activities and influences to insure having goods made on time, of adequate quality, and at reasonable cost

**production cost** *n* : the combined total of raw material and direct labor costs and burden incurred in production

**production curve** *n* : a curve plotted to show the relation between quantities produced during definite consecutive time intervals

**production function** *n* : the technical relationship between product output and the input of factors of production

**production goods** *n pl* : PRODUCER GOODS

**pro·duc·tion·ist** \-shənəst\ *n* -S : PRODUCER

**production line** *n* : LINE 6j

**production standard** *n* : a unit of measurement that indicates the normal level of performance for an industrial operation and that is expressible as time per unit or units per hour or day

**pro·duc·tive** \prə'dəktiv, prō'-, -tēv *also* -təv\ *adj* [ML *productivus*, fr. L *productus* + *-ivus* -ive] **1** : having the quality or power of producing : bringing forth or able to bring forth esp. in abundance : CREATIVE, GENERATIVE ⟨thousands of fishermen . . . can reach some of the most ~ water —*Ford Times*⟩ ⟨more ~ ideas followed —*Phoenix Flame*⟩ **2** : effective in bringing about : CAUSATIVE, ORIGINATIVE — used with *of* ⟨their knowledge and methods were enormously ~ of new weapons —J.P.Baxter b.1893⟩ ⟨investigating committees have been ~ of much good —R.K.Carr⟩ **3** : yielding or furnishing results, benefits, or profits ⟨a ~ program of education⟩ **4 a** : effecting or contributing to effect production **b** : yielding or devoted to the satisfaction of wants or the creation of utilities **5 a** : continuing to be used in the formation of new words and constructions ⟨*un-* is a ~ prefix⟩ **b** : of or relating to a productive word element **6** : raising mucus or sputum (as from the bronchi) — used of a cough ⟨had slight ~ cough and chest pain —*Calif. Med.*⟩

**productive labor** *n* : DIRECT LABOR

**pro·duc·tive·ly** \-təvlē, -li\ *adv* : in a productive manner ⟨free to think ~ —D.H.Jenkins⟩

**pro·duc·tive·ness** \-tivnəs, -tev- *also* -təv-\ *n* -ES : the quality or state of being productive ⟨the prodigious ~ of great workers —C.W.Eliot⟩

**pro·duc·tiv·i·ty** \ˌprōˌdək'tivədē, ˌpräˌ-, -vətē, -i *also* prəˌ- *or* prōˌ- *sometimes* ˌpräd-\ *n* -ES : the ability or capacity to produce : PRODUCTIVENESS: as **a** : abundance or richness in output ⟨the remarkable ~ of novelists —E.A.Bloom⟩ **b** : the physical output per unit of productive effort **c** : the ability of land to produce a given yield of a particular crop **d** : the degree of effectiveness of industrial management in utilizing the facilities for production; *esp* : the effectiveness in utilizing labor and equipment

**product line** *n* **1** : all goods made by a manufacturing firm **2** : a group of closely related commodities made by the same process and for the same purpose and differing only in style, model, or size

**pro·duc·tor** \prə'dəktə(r)\ *n* -S [2*product* + *-or*] : PRODUCER; *specif* : a producing cause

**pro·duc·to·ry** \prə'dəktərē\ *adj* [*production* + *-ory*] : of, relating to, or characterized by production

**products** *pl of* PRODUCT, *pres 3d sing of* PRODUCT

**pro·duc·tus** \prə'dəktəs\ *n, cap* [NL, fr. L, lengthened, protracted, fr. past part. of *producere* to bring forth, produce, pull out — more at PRODUCE] : a genus of extinct articulate brachiopods characteristic of Carboniferous and Permian strata, lacking a pedicle but often anchored by spines on the shell, and including the largest known brachiopods some of which (as *P. giganteus*) attain a width of one foot

**pro·em** \'prōˌem\ *n* -S [ME *proheme*, fr. MF *proheme*, *proeme*, fr. L *prooemium*, fr. Gk *prooimion*, fr. *pro-* 1pro- + *oimē*, *oimos* song (perh. fr. *oimos* way, path) + *-ion*, dim. suffix; akin to Gk *hiesthai* to hasten — more at GAIN] **1** : a preliminary discourse to a longer piece of writing **2** : an introductory comment before a speech **3** : something that opens or begins — compare PREFACE

**pro·embryo** \(ˈ)prō+\ *n* [1*pro-* + *embryo*] : an embryonic structure developed during the segmentation of the egg or oospore before the formation of the true embryo — **pro·embryonal** \"+\ *adj* — **pro·embryonic** \(ˌ)prō+\ *adj*

**pro·emi·al** \(ˈ)prōˈēmēəl\ *adj* [ME *prohemyal*, fr. *proheme* + *-yal*, *-iol*] : of the nature of a proem : INTRODUCTORY, PREFATORY

**pro·enzyme** \(ˈ)prō+\ *n* [ISV 1*pro-* + *enzyme*] : ZYMOGEN

**pro·epimeron** \ˌprō+\ *n* [NL, fr. 1*pro-* + *epimeron*] : the epimeron of the prothorax of an insect

**pro·episternum** \"+\ *n* [NL, fr. 1*pro-* + *episternum*] : the episternum of the prothorax of an insect

**pro·erythroblast** \"+\ *n* [1*pro-* + *erythroblast*] : a hemocytoblast that gives rise to erythroblasts — **pro·erythroblastic** \"+\ *adj*

**pro·estrous** *also* **pro·oestrous** \(ˈ)prō+\ *adj* [1*pro-* + *estrous*, *oestrous*] : of or relating to proestrus

**pro·estrus** *or* **pro·estrum** *also* **pro·oestrus** *or* **pro·oestrum** \"+\ *n, pl* **proestruses** *or* **proestrums** [NL, fr. 1*pro-* + *estrus*, *estrum*, *oestrus*, *oestrum*] : a preparatory period immediately preceding estrus and characterized by growth of graafian follicles, increased estrogenic activity, and alteration of uterine and vaginal mucosa

**pro·ethical** \"+\ *adj* [2*pro-* + *ethical*] : serving the end of ethics but not ethical in nature

**pro·ethnic** \"+\ *adj* [1*pro-* + *ethnic*] : prior to a division into ethnic groups (as a race into peoples or a people into tribes) — **pro·ethnically** \"+\ *adv*

**pro·e·tus** \prō'ēdəs\ *n, cap* [NL] : a genus (the type of the family Proetidae) comprising small trilobites with nearly equal shields, smooth depressed glabella, and narrow cheeks and being common throughout the Paleozoic after the Cambrian

**pro·eutectoid** \ˌprō+\ *adj* [1*pro-* + *eutectoid*] : separating from solid solution at a temperature higher than the eutectoid

**prof** \'präf\ *n* -S [by shortening] *slang* : PROFESSOR

**prof** *abbr* **1** profession; professional **2** *often cap* professor

**pro·face** \prō'fās\ *interj* [MF (*bon*) *prou* (*vous*) *fasse*, lit., may it make you good profit] *obs* — used as a salutation in welcoming or drinking healths ⟨*Proface!* What you want in meat, we'll have in drink —Shak.⟩

**prof·a·na·tion** \ˌpräfə'nāshən\ *n* -S [MF *prophanation*, *profanation*, fr. LL *profanation-*, *profanatio*, fr. L *profanatus* (past part. of *profanare* to profane) + *-ion-*, *-io* -ion — more at PROFANE] **1** : an act of profaning : an act of violating sacred things or of treating them with contempt or irreverence : irreverent or too familiar treatment or use of what is sacred **2** : debasement or vulgarization esp. by misuse or disclosure ⟨music may be contemplated . . . happily free from all danger of ~ —C.C.Riker⟩

**syn** DESECRATION, SACRILEGE, BLASPHEMY: PROFANATION applies to any irreverent outrage shocking to those who cherish and hold sacred the thing treated; although it may suggest base callousness, it often applies to vulgar, insensible irreverence as of vandals ⟨these sages attribute the calamity to a *profanation* of the sacred grove —J.G.Frazer⟩ DESECRATION may apply to any action whereby sacred character is impaired or lost; often it indicates loss of that character through defilement, often malicious or malign and culpable ⟨*desecration* of the cathedrals by the invading barbarians⟩ ⟨the last priest, feeling there was no work to be done in such a dreary outpost, burned the chapel in 1706 to prevent its *desecration* —*Amer. Guide Series: Mich.*⟩ SACRILEGE may refer technically to reception or administration of a religious sacrament by one unworthy; it refers commonly to any outrageous profanation ⟨the execution was not followed by any *sacrilege* to the church or defiling of holy vessels —Willa Cather⟩ ⟨above all things they dread any contact with the spirits of the dead. Only a sorcerer would dare to commit such a *sacrilege*, an offense punishable with death —J.G.Frazer⟩ BLASPHEMY may refer to any strong irreverence, often one involving or suggesting reviling, defying, mocking, or otherwise treating with indignity something sacred ⟨he cooperated with me in sending the pious elders to unspeakable corners of hell; we arranged a wordless language of *blasphemy* and signaled to each other across the laps of the godly —G.W.Brace⟩

**pro·fan·a·tory** \prō'fanəˌtōrē, prə'-, -tȯr-, -ri\ *adj* [*profanation* + *-ory*] : tending to profane : DESECRATING

**1pro·fane** \prō'fān, prə'-\ *vb* -ED/-ING/-S [ME *prophanen*, fr. L *profanare*, fr. *profanus*] *vt* **1** : to violate or treat with abuse, irreverence, obloquy, or contempt (something sacred) : treat as not sacred : DESECRATE, POLLUTE ⟨the priests in the temple ~ the sabbath —Mt 12:5 (RSV)⟩ **2** : to debase by a wrong, unworthy, or vulgar use : ABUSE, DEFILE, VULGARIZE ⟨its borders have not been *profaned* by the clutter of outdoor advertising signs —Malcolm Bauer⟩ ~ *vi* : to indulge in profanity ⟨we heard a yell and then a loud *profaning*⟩

**2pro·fane** \(ˈ)prōˈfān, prə'f-\ *adj* [ME *prophane*, fr. MF, fr. L *profanus*, fr. *pro-* before + *fanum* temple — more at PRO-, FEAST] **1** : unconcerned with that which is religious or with the purposes of religion : not devoted to the sacred and the holy : SECULAR ⟨Jeremiah has been likened to several characters in ~ history —A.W.Streane⟩ ⟨the ~ world of spectators —James Joyce⟩ **2** : not holy because unconsecrated, impure, or defiled : not fit or fitted for religious uses : UNSANCTIFIED; *sometimes* : HEATHEN ⟨~ rites⟩ **3 a** : serving to debase or defile that which is holy or worthy of reverence : contemptuous of beautiful or sacred things : IRREVERENT **b** (1) : characterized by abusive language directed esp. against the name of God (2) : indulging in cursing or vituperation : marked by insulting or perverted utterance ⟨the ~ old rascal —Herman Melville⟩ **4 a** : not among the initiated esp. to religious rites **b** : not possessing esoteric or expert knowledge ⟨if a picture . . . had been injured by cleaning, or retouched by some ~ hand —Nathaniel Hawthorne⟩

**syn** PROFANE, SECULAR, LAY, and TEMPORAL can all signify not dedicated to religious ends or uses. PROFANE is mainly descriptive in opposing *sacred* and sometimes *holy*, *religious*, or *spiritual* ⟨the *profane* poet is by instinct a naturalist. He loves landscape, he loves love, he loves the humor and pathos of earthly existence. But the religious prophet loves none of these things —George Santayana⟩ ⟨*profane* men living in ships, like the holy men gathered together in monasteries, develop traits of profound resemblance —Joseph Conrad⟩ ⟨that little allegory of sacred and *profane* love —John Galsworthy⟩ SECULAR implies a relation to the world as distinguished from the church, religion, or the religious life ⟨believing that no creed, religious or *secular*, can be justified except on the basis of reason and evidence —*Times Lit. Supp.*⟩ ⟨the *secular* critics of religion —Reinhold Niebuhr⟩ ⟨anarchy in the religious society is as undesirable as it is in the *secular* world —Leo Pfeffer⟩ and is close to PROFANE ⟨*secular* and religious music⟩ but sometimes it opposes *regular* in the sense of governed by monastic rule ⟨a *secular* priest does not belong to a religious order⟩ and usu. it opposes *religious* in the sense of belonging to or serving the ends of religion or a church ⟨the parochial and *secular* schools⟩ LAY commonly applies to a person who does not belong to the clergy or sometimes to such a person's activities, interests, or duties, usu. opposing *clerical* or *ecclesiastic* ⟨the priests met with *lay* members of the parish⟩ Often the term extends to signify nonprofessional ⟨a *lay* opinion on a medical question⟩ or is often close to *average*, *mundane*, sometimes *untrained* ⟨facts in a war which either are based on military information or which cannot be explained to the *lay* mind —F.D.Roosevelt⟩ TEMPORAL, opposing *spiritual* in designating what belongs to material or worldly concerns, applies chiefly to sovereigns, rulers, or dignitaries having political authority or civil power ⟨to be ruled in *temporal* things by clerical authority —Agnes Repplier⟩ ⟨the superiority of the spiritual and eternal over the carnal and *temporal* —H.O.Taylor⟩ ⟨our *temporal* and ecclesiastical overlords⟩ ⟨the spiritual and the *temporal* ruler⟩ **syn** see in addition IMPIOUS

**3pro·fane** \prō'fān, prə'-\ *n* -S : one that is not initiated — usu. used with *the* ⟨appear . . . ridiculous to the ~ —Bernard Fay⟩

**pro·fane·ly** *adv* : in a profane manner ⟨kept wondering ~ why everything had to happen to him —Henry LaCossitt⟩

**pro·fane·ness** \-ānnəs\ *n* -ES : the quality or state of being profane ⟨did frown upon church music which savored of . . . ~ —Douglas Bush⟩

**pro·fan·er** \-ānə(r)\ *n* -S : one that profanes

**pro·fan·i·ty** \prō'fanədē, prə'-, -ətē, -i\ *n* -ES [LL *profanitas*, fr. L *profanus* profane + *-itas* -ity] **1 a** : the quality or state of being profane ⟨exploitations of the Christian religion . . . would be the ultimate ~ —Walter Moberly⟩ **b** : the use of profane language ⟨banged his gavel and fined him for ~ in court —*Amer. Guide Series: Pa.*⟩ **2** : something profane: as **a** : secular science or art ⟨a small minority studied the *profanities* —H.O.Taylor⟩ **b** : profane language

**profection** *n* -S [ML *profection-*, *profectio*, fr. L *profectus* (past part. of *proficere* to go forward, advance) + *-ion-*, *-io* -ion — more at PROFICIENT] **1** *obs* : the act of progressing : a movement forward **2** *obs* : an advance or the degree of advancement.

**pro·fec·ti·tious** \ˌprōˌfekˈtishəs\ *adj* [LL *profecticius*, *profectitius*, fr. *profectus* (past part. of *proficisci* to set out, come forth, proceed (from), fr. *pro-* forward + *-ficisci* (fr. pass. of *facere* to do, make) + *-icius*, *-itius* -itious — more at PRO-, DO] *Roman law* : DERIVED — used of property derived from an ancestor or ascendant

**profer** *vt* -ED/-ING/-S [ME *proferen*, fr. MF *proferer*, fr. L *proferre*, fr. *pro-* before + *ferre* to carry — more at PRO-, BEAR] *obs* : to put forth or before : bring forth or out

**pro·ferment** \(ˈ)prō+\ *n* -S [ISV 1*pro-* + *ferment*] : an inactive precursor of a ferment : ZYMOGEN

**pro·fert** \'prōfə(r)t\ *n* -S [L, he brings forward, 3d pers. pres. indic. of *proferre*] **1** : an allegation in a pleading or on the record that the pleader produces in open court an instrument relied upon and set forth therein **2** : the actual exhibition in court of an instrument — see DECLARATION 2a

**pro·fess** \prə'fes, prō'-\ *vb* -ED/-ING/-ES [in sense 1, fr. ME *professen*, fr. *profes*, adj., having professed one's vows, fr. OF, fr. LL *professus*, fr. L, past part. of *profitērī* to profess, confess, fr. *pro-* before + *-fitērī* (fr. *fatērī* to acknowledge, confess); in other senses, fr. L *professus*, past part. of *profitērī* — more at PRO-, CONFESS] *vt* **1 :** to receive formally into membership in a religious community through the authorized acceptance of the candidate's vows ⟨the abbot ~*ed* three of the young monks⟩ ⟨he was ~*ed* when 18 years old⟩ **2 a :** to declare or admit openly or freely : acknowledge without concealment : AFFIRM, CONFESS ⟨~*ed* great admiration for his scholarship —H.E.Starr⟩ ⟨gave me a copy of the book whose authorship he modestly ~*ed* —Sidney Lovett⟩ **b :** to declare or admit in words or appearances only : imply outwardly : aver insincerely : PRETEND, PURPORT ⟨they have become what they ~ to scorn —W.L.Sullivan⟩ ⟨doctrines that ~ to explain the human situation —D.W.Brogan⟩ **3 :** to confess one's faith in or allegiance to : recognize or embrace as a belief : FOLLOW, PRACTICE ⟨~*es* a Protestant faith —*Current Biog.*⟩ **4 a :** to proclaim oneself versed in (as a calling) : practice the profession of **b :** to teach as a professor ⟨those learned intellectual historians . . . all ~ literature —H.S.Commager⟩ ~ *vi* **1 a :** to make a profession or one's profession **b** *obs* : to profess friendship ⟨he is dishonored by a man which ever ~*ed* to him —Shak.⟩ **2 :** to follow the calling of professor **syn** see ASSERT

**pro·fess·ant** \-sᵊnt\ *n* -S : one who professes ⟨depends on the vitality of a religion in the lives of its ~*s* —P.W.Tappan⟩

**pro·fessed** \prə'fest, prō'-\ *adj* [ME, fr. *profes* professed + *-ed* — more at PROFESS] **1 :** characterized by having taken the vows of a religious order ⟨nine ~ nuns, a novice, and two postulants arrived —*Amer. Guide Series: La.*⟩ **2 a :** openly and freely declared or acknowledged : AFFIRMED ⟨failed in its ~ task —T.S.Eliot⟩ **b :** avowed with intent to deceive : HYPOCRITICAL, INSINCERE **3 :** professing to be qualified : not amateur : EXPERT ⟨a ~ philosopher —John Buchan⟩

**pro·fessed·ly** \-sədlē\ *adv* **1 :** by profession or declaration : AVOWEDLY **2 :** with pretense : ALLEGEDLY

**pro·fes·sion** \prə'feshən, prō'-\ *n* -S [ME *professioun*, fr. OF *profession*, fr. LL & L; LL *profession-*, *professio* religious profession, fr. L, public declaration, fr. *professus* (past part. of *profitērī* to profess, confess) + *-ion-*, *-io* -ion — more at PROFESS] **1 :** the act of taking the vows that consecrate oneself to special religious service **2 :** an act of openly declaring or publicly claiming a belief, faith, or opinion : an avowed statement or expression of intention or purpose : PROTESTATION ⟨his frequent ~*s* about love and friendships belie a good deal of . . . his behavior —Joseph Chiari⟩ ⟨his ~ that logic is not the sole criterion of art —Lee Strasberg⟩ ⟨welcomed by her two friends with many ~*s* of pleasure —Jane Austen⟩ **3 a :** Christian or religious conviction and purpose openly avowed **b :** the faith in which one is professed : a religion or religious system; *also* : a religious body **4 a :** a calling requiring specialized knowledge and often long and intensive preparation including instruction in skills and methods as well as in the scientific, historical, or scholarly principles underlying such skills and methods, maintaining by force of organization or concerted opinion high standards of achievement and conduct, and committing its members to continued study and to a kind of work which has for its prime purpose the rendering of a public service — see LEARNED PROFESSION **b :** a principal calling, vocation, or employment ⟨preferred to move and move again, rather than give up their old ~ of farming —G.W.Pierson⟩ ⟨men who make it their ~ to hunt the hippopotamus —J.G.Frazer⟩ **c :** the whole body of persons engaged in a calling ⟨form an association that will reflect a credit on the ~ —Thomas Pyles⟩ **5** *archaic* : professorial teaching or status

**¹pro·fes·sion·al** \-shənᵊl, -shnəl\ *adj* [*profession* + *-al*] **1 a** (1) : of, relating to, or characteristic of a profession or calling ⟨a ~ degree⟩ (2) : concerned or occupied with the training of professionals ⟨universities are ~ institutions —J.B. Conant⟩ **b** (1) : engaged in one of the learned professions or in an occupation requiring a high level of training and proficiency ⟨the ~ man or woman is expected to possess several distinctive . . . qualifications —A.E.Bestor⟩ (2) : characterized by or conforming to the technical or ethical standards of a profession or an occupation : manifesting fine artistry or workmanship based on sound knowledge and conscientiousness : reflecting the results of education, training, and experience ⟨~ courtesy⟩ ⟨they are afraid of . . . their own ~ or business standing —John Lodge⟩ ⟨it was a competent ~ job⟩ **2 a :** participating for gain or livelihood in an activity or field of endeavor often engaged in by amateurs ⟨a ~ baseball player⟩ ⟨a ~ soldier⟩ **b :** engaged or participated in by persons receiving financial return ⟨~ football⟩ **3 :** following a line of conduct or assuming a role as though it were a profession ⟨comes at times close to deserving the name of ~ southerner —Tarleton Collier⟩ ⟨become so much the ~ celebrity —Van Wyck Brooks⟩

**²professional** \"\ *n* -S **1 a :** one that engages in a particular pursuit, study, or science for gain or livelihood ⟨a small standing army largely made up of ~*s*⟩ **b :** one that competes in sports or athletics for gain or livelihood or who has taught or trained for money ⟨a golf ~⟩ — compare AMATEUR **c :** one who receives money for appearing in theatrical productions : one who is engaged professionally **2 a :** one who belongs to one of the learned professions or is in an occupation requiring a high level of training and proficiency ⟨many highly trained salaried ~*s* —R.K.Burns⟩ ⟨large corporations are absorbing more and more ~*s* —M.L.Cogan⟩ **b :** one with sufficient authority or practical experience in an area of knowledge or endeavor to resemble a professional ⟨though an amateur in politics he had been a ~ in diplomacy —*Time*⟩

**pro·fes·sion·al·ism** \-shənᵊl,izəm, -shnə,li-\ *n* -S **1 a :** the conduct, aims, or qualities that characterize or mark a profession or a professional person ⟨a moral code is the basis of ~ —Roy Lewis & Angus Maude⟩ **b :** extreme competence in an occupation or pursuit sometimes marked by absence of originality ⟨lose sight of general cultivation and fall into stark ~ —*Educational Rev.*⟩ **2 :** the following of a profession (as athletics) for gain or livelihood : the characteristics, standards, or methods of professionals esp. in sports or athletics ⟨the acceptance of money for professional services . . . is the criterion by which ~ is determined —Virgil Thomson⟩ — compare AMATEURISM

**pro·fes·sion·al·ist** \-shənᵊləst, -shnələ-\ *n* -S : one who professionalizes an occupation

**pro·fes·sion·al·iza·tion** \prə,feshənᵊlə'zāshən\ *n* -S : the act or process of making or becoming professionalized ⟨the ~ of college athletics⟩

**pro·fes·sion·al·ize** \prə'feshənᵊl,īz, prō'-, -shnə,līz\ *vb* -ED/-ING/-S [¹*professional* + *-ize*] *vt* : to give a professional character to : treat as or convert into a profession ⟨*professionalizing* the area of law dealing with civil rights —W.H. Hastie⟩ ~ *vi* : to assume a professional character : become professional

**pro·fes·sion·al·ly** \-shənᵊlē, -shnəlē, -i\ *adv* : in a professional manner ⟨a ~ equipped stage —*Key Reporter*⟩ ⟨the first ~ trained and experienced librarian to fill this position —*Current Biog.*⟩

**pro·fes·sion·ary** \-shə,nerē\ *adj* [*profession* + *-ary*] : of or relating to a profession : PROFESSIONAL

**pro·fes·sion·ist** \-sh(ə)nəst\ *n* -S [G, fr. *profession* (fr. MF) + *-ist*] **1 :** one pursuing a profession or trade **2** *chiefly Scot* : one who makes an insincere profession of religion

**pro·fes·sion·less** \-shənləs\ *adj* : lacking a profession

**pro·fes·sor** \prə'fesə(r), prō'-\ *n* -S [LL & L; LL, one that professes Christianity, fr. L, public teacher, teacher, fr. *professus* (past part. of *profitērī* to profess, confess, declare publicly, be a teacher) + *-or* — more at PROFESS] **1 a :** one who professes, avows, or declares **b** *chiefly dial* : one who professes the Christian religion openly or conspicuously and ardently **2 a :** a faculty member of the highest academic rank at an institution of higher education usu. dividing his time between scholarship and lecturing and teaching mainly advanced students — often used as an academic title with *of* ⟨~ of ancient history⟩ **b :** a teacher at a university, college, or secondary school : PEDAGOGUE **c :** one who teaches or professes special knowledge of an art, sport, or occupation requiring skill ⟨a ~ of the machine⟩ ⟨the artist was the unchallenged ~ of his art —W.A.Martin⟩ **d :** one who is conspicuous for being quiet and overly serious : one who is bookish

**pro·fes·sor·ate** \-sərət\ *n* -S [F *professorat*, fr. *professeur* professor (fr. L *professor*) + *-at* -ate] **1 :** the office, term of office, or position of a professor **2 :** PROFESSORIAT ⟨countless services to art history which have set you apart from the ~ —F.H.Taylor⟩

**pro·fes·sor·dom** \-sə(r)dəm\ *n* -S [*professor* + *-dom*] : the realm of professors; *also* : PROFESSORS

**pro·fes·so·ri·al** \¦prōfə¦sōrēəl, ¦präf-, -sȯr-\ *adj* [L *professorius* of a teacher (fr. *professor*) + E *-al*] : of, relating to, or possessing qualities thought to resemble those of a professor : as **a :** having the manner or characteristics of a professor : DIDACTIC, LEARNED ⟨eminently ~ volume —Ezra Pound⟩ **b :** composed of or produced by professors as a body ⟨the ~ board⟩ ⟨~ opinion⟩ **c :** relating to the office of professor ⟨~ duties⟩ — **pro·fes·so·ri·al·ly** \-ēəlē, -li\ *adv*

**pro·fes·so·ri·at** *or* **pro·fes·so·ri·ate** \,==¦sōrēət, -sȯr-\ *n* -S [modif. (influenced by *professorial*) of F *professorat*] **1 :** the body of college and university teachers at an institution or in society at large **2 :** the profession of college or university teaching ⟨special duty of the ~ to pursue and advance pure learning —Ernest Barker⟩ ⟨to a young man bent on entering the ~ —*Atlantic*⟩

**professor or·di·nar·i·us** \-,ȯ(r)dᵊnə'ra(a)rēəs\ *n* [NL, lit., regular professor] : a professor of the highest rank at a German university : the occupant of a chair with control over the teaching of his subject and a share in the government of the university

**pro·fes·sor·ship** \prə'fesə(r),ship, prō'-\ *n* : the office, duties, or position of an academic professor

**¹prof·fer** \'präfə(r)\ *vb* **proffered**; **proffered**; **proffering** \-f(ə)riŋ\ **proffers** [ME *profren*, fr. AF *profrer*, fr. OF *poroffrir*, fr. *por-* forth (fr. L *pro-*) + *offrir* to offer — more at PRO-, OFFER] *vt* **1 :** to present for acceptance : tentatively advance for consideration : suggest as a proposal : TENDER ⟨hovered round me . . . with their hands full of fading flowers, which they at length ~*ed* me —Samuel Butler †1902⟩ ⟨was ~*ed* the leadership but declined it —J.G.Smith⟩ ⟨return ~*ed* smiles —*Newsweek*⟩ **2 :** to propose or suggest a readiness and willingness ⟨~*ed* to lend him one —D.D.Martin⟩ ~ *vi*, *obs* : to move as if about to act : HESITATE ⟨when you see him ready to enter water, say he ~*eth* —H.J.Pye⟩ **syn** see OFFER

**²proffer** \"\ *n* -S [ME *profre*, *profer*, fr. AF *profre*, fr. *profrer*] **1 :** an offer made : something proposed for acceptance : SUGGESTION ⟨her more than generous ~ —C.G.Bowers⟩ ⟨his ~ of hospitality —Irving Bacheller⟩ **2** *obs* : a display of willingness : ATTEMPT, ESSAY

**profferer** *n* -S *obs* : one that proffers something

**pro·fibrinolysin** \¦prō+\ *n* [*pro-* + *fibrinolysin*] : PLASMINOGEN

**pro·fi·chi** \prō'fēkē\ *n, pl* **profichi** *or* **profichis** [It, pl. of *profico* caprifig, fr. L *caproficus*, alter. of *caprificus* — more at CAPRIFICATION] : the spring crop of the caprifig — compare MAMME, MAMMONI

**pro·fi·cience** \prə'fishən(t)s, prō'-\ *n* -S **1** *archaic* : an advance forward : PROGRESS **2** *archaic* : the state of progress attained : PROFICIENCY

**pro·fi·cien·cy** \-nsē, -si\ *n* -ES **1 :** advancement toward the attainment of a high degree of knowledge or skill : PROGRESS ⟨made little ~ in fashionable or literary accomplishments —T. B.Macaulay⟩ **2 :** the quality or state of being proficient : ADEPTNESS, EXPERTNESS ⟨aim at giving their students a certain ~ —W.F.Mackey⟩

**proficiency badge** *n* : a badge awarded to an intermediate girl scout for achieving knowledge or skill (as in citizenship, nutrition, dressmaking)

**¹pro·fi·cient** \-nt\ *adj* [L *proficient-*, *proficiens*, pres. part. of *proficere* to go forward, make progress, accomplish, be advantageous, fr. *pro-* forward + *-ficere* (fr. *facere* to make, do) — more at PRO-, DO] : well advanced in an art, occupation, skill, or a branch of knowledge : unusually efficient ⟨an experienced person, trained and ~ in his job —F.G.Nesbitt⟩

**syn** ADEPT, SKILLED, SKILLFUL, EXPERT, MASTERLY: these adjectives all mean having the knowledge and experience to be extremely competent in a given line of work or endeavor. PROFICIENT stresses a competence derived from training and practice ⟨a technically *proficient* pianist —Edward Sackville-West & Desmond Shawe-Taylor⟩ ⟨*proficient* in mathematics and philosophy —H.H.Shenk⟩ ⟨*proficient* in the art of self-defense —G.B.Shaw⟩ ADEPT usu. adds to PROFICIENT the idea of aptitude or cleverness ⟨*adept* at speechmaking⟩ ⟨newspapers became *adept* at handling crime news —*Amer. Guide Series: Calif.*⟩ ⟨*adept* at making up with cosmetics and dress for what nature may not have given her —Walter Le Beau⟩ SKILLED, for the most part interchangeable with PROFICIENT, usu. suggests a proficiency in the technique of an art or profession but often in industrial use signifying only that one has met a minimum standard set up for a special type of work or job ⟨contribute many *skilled* performers to the figure-skating troupes —*Amer. Guide Series: Minn.*⟩ ⟨a *skilled* musician⟩ ⟨*skilled* artisans⟩ SKILLFUL stresses dexterity in execution or performance ⟨*skillful* in sketching, pen portraiture and caricature —H.H.Reichard⟩ ⟨a fast, energetic and *skillful* campaign —G.W.Johnson⟩ ⟨*skillful* in the use of the hand tools —H.D.Burghardt & Aaron Axelrod⟩ EXPERT stresses extraordinary proficiency or adeptness ⟨an *expert* mimic —Alexander Forbes⟩ ⟨an *expert* horseman⟩ ⟨*expert* and inept raconteurs —*Yale Rev.*⟩ MASTERLY, usu. applying to the thing executed or accomplished, adds to the idea of competence and adeptness that of confident control ⟨his command of English was so *masterly* —Lucien Price⟩ ⟨in two *masterly* sentences he summed up Captain Guy's character —Herman Melville⟩ ⟨a *masterly* accomplishment in workmanship, detail, and symbolism —*Amer. Guide Series: N.Y.City*⟩

**²proficient** \"\ *n* -S **1** *obs* : one that shows signs of definite progress to his objective **2 :** one well advanced in any business, art, science, or branch of learning : ADEPT, EXPERT ⟨Shakespeare is their true ~ —I.A.Richards⟩ ⟨she was a ~ in music —T.L.Peacock⟩

**pro·fi·cient·ly** *adv* : in a proficient manner ⟨completely handed over to the experts and . . . ~ dealt with —Albert Dasnoy⟩

**proficuous** *adj* [LL *proficuus*, fr. L *proficere*] *obs* : PROFITABLE, USEFUL

**¹pro·file** \'prō,fīl\ *n* -S [It *profilo*, fr. *profilare* to draw in outline, fr. *pro-* forward (fr. L) + *filare* to spin, draw a line, fr. LL, to spin — more at PRO-, FILE] **1 :** a representation of something in outline; *esp* : a human head or face represented or seen in a side view ⟨his handsome, blunt ~ —Susan Ertz⟩ ⟨his face presented to us in ~ —Christopher Isherwood⟩ **2 :** an outline seen or represented in sharp relief : a distinctive exterior line : CONTOUR ⟨from the river as he was seeing it now, the city's ~ seemed all flat planes —Harold Sinclair⟩ ⟨some ~ of the mountains —E.H.Spicer⟩ **3 :** a side or sectional elevation: as **a :** a drawing used in civil engineering to show a vertical section of the ground along a surveyed line or graded work **b :** a drawing of the side elevation of a ship's lines or of its structure ⟨a tanker, small and neat in ~ against the blue sea —Ernest Hemingway⟩ **4 :** a ceramics shaping tool **5 :** wooden frames from which lines are stretched to establish the alignment of the face of a wall or the slope of a drainpipe or tile **6 :** a flat piece of theatrical scenery or property cut in outline **7 a :** a vertical section of a soil showing the nature and sequence of its various zones **b :** a vertical section of an organic deposit (as a peat bog) showing the sequence of its flora ⟨pollen ~*s* —*Amer. Jour. of Science*⟩ **c :** a vertical section cut through an archaeological unit (as a burial mound or village site) **8 :** a graph or curve: as **a :** a group of data representing quantitatively the extent to which an individual exhibits traits or abilities as determined by tests or ratings and usu. presented in the form of a graph **b :** a linear series of data recording the position of the piezometric surface in an artesian aquifer or groundwater basin or of the elevations of the bottom and the energy line along the axis of flow of a stream or conduit **9 a :** a concise biographical sketch depicting a personality by vivid outlining and sharp contrast **b :** a concise geographical, historical, or political sketch **c :** a concise analysis of a subject **10 a :** a linear series of recording stations or observation points for geophysical phenomena **b :** a graph or curve showing the data thus obtained **11 :** a recognizable rhythmic line characterizing a musical composition or speech utterance ⟨the classic symphonist selects a subject matter that . . . has a sharp melodic and rhythmic ~ —P.H. Lang⟩ ⟨~ of sounds⟩ **syn** see OUTLINE

profile 1

**²profile** \"\ *vb* -ED/-ING/-S [It *profilare*] *vt* **1 a :** to draw the vertical outline of : represent in profile : draw a profile of **b :** to study and design the exterior shape of (as a molding) **c :** to give a profile to **2 :** to shape the outline of (an object) by means of a cutting instrument — compare PROFILING MACHINE **3 :** to give or write a profile of ⟨try to ~ a man . . . so typical of New York —Alistair Cooke⟩ ~ *vi* : to turn in profile : present a profile; *esp* : to turn the left shoulder toward a bull in a bullfight ⟨the matador *profiled*, his thin silver blade raised —William Sansom⟩

**profile board** *n* : TEMPLATE 2

**profile cutter** *n* : a knife or machine cutter with an edge shaped to cut a definite form

**profile drag** *n*, *aeronautics* : the portion of the wing drag that is due to friction and turbulence in the fluid and that would be absent if it were nonviscous

**profile machine** *n* : PROFILING MACHINE

**profile of equilibrium** **1 :** the longitudinal profile of a stream whose smooth gradient is so adjusted to volume of water and amount and nature of load as to be maintained in approximate equilibrium while erosion and transportation continue : a graded profile **2 :** the slope away from shore of a sea floor or lake bottom having a gradient such that waves and currents neither erode it downward nor deposit sediment upon it

**profile paper** *n* : graph paper used for convenience in drawing profiles

**pro·fil·er** \-lə(r)\ *n* -S : one that profiles: as **a :** a profiling machine **b :** one that profiles metal objects by hand or on a profiling machine

**profiling machine** *n* : a vertical milling machine for milling irregular profiles by causing the spindle to move laterally by the cam action of a guide or dummy that serves as a model at the same time that the workable moves at right angles to the travel of the spindle

**pro·fil·ograph** \prō'filə,graf, -fīl-, -räf\ *n* [ISV ¹*profile* + *-o-* + *-graph*; orig. formed as F *profilographe*] **1 :** an instrument borne on wheels for recording automatically the profile of the land over which it travels **2 :** an instrument for measuring smoothness of a surface (as of a metal casting) by amplification of the minute variations from the plane or arc of smoothness

**pro·fi·lom·e·ter** \,prōfə'läməd·ə(r)\ *n* [ISV ¹*profile* + *-o-* + *-meter*; orig. formed as F *profilomètre*] : PROFILOGRAPH

**¹prof·it** \'präfət, *usu* -əd·+V\ *n* -S *often attrib* [ME, fr. MF, fr. L *profectus* advance, progress, profit, success, fr. *profectus*, past part. of *proficere* to go forward, make progress — more at PROFICIENT] **1 :** an advantage, benefit, accession of good, gain, or valuable return esp. in financial matters, education, or character development ⟨found moral ~ also in this self-study —L.P. Smith⟩ ⟨reading with ~ and delight —Havelock Ellis⟩ **2 :** the excess of returns over expenditure in a transaction or series of transactions: as **a :** the excess of the price received over the price paid for goods sold — opposed to *loss* **b :** the excess of the price received over the cost of purchasing and handling or of producing and marketing goods **3 a** (1) : net income (as in a business) usu. for a given period of time (2) : a benefit or advantage accruing from the management, use, or sale of property, from the carrying on of any process of production, or from the conduct of business **b :** the income of invested property not including an appreciation in market value **4 :** the ratio of profit for a given year to the amount of capital invested or to the value of sales **5 a :** the distributive share or compensation accruing to entrepreneurs for the assumption of risk in business enterprise **b :** entrepreneurial or employer income as distinguished from wages or rent **6 :** PROFIT A PRENDRE **syn** see USE

**²profit** \"\ *vb* -ED/-ING/-S [ME *profiten*, fr. MF *profiter*, fr. *profit*] *vi* **1 :** to make progress : become proficient : ADVANCE, IMPROVE ⟨morale, always a problem . . . has ~*ed* greatly —Greg MacGregor⟩ **2 :** to be of service or advantage : AID, FURTHER ⟨nothing ~*s* like an inquiring mind⟩ **3 :** to take advantage : make good use : derive benefit : GAIN — usu. used with *by* or *from* ⟨everyone should get as much liberal education as he can . . . absorb and ~ by —Cormac Philip⟩ ⟨would ~ greatly from a more painstaking examination of manuscripts —E.S. McCartney⟩ ~ *vt* : to be of service to : ADVANTAGE, AID, BENEFIT ⟨do not think we should ~ ourselves well if we tarried . . . to examine and dissect —Sir Winston Churchill⟩ ⟨hurry by and disregard what does not seem to ~ our own existence —Laurence Binyon⟩

**prof·it·abil·i·ty** \,präfəd·ə'biləd·ē\ *n* : the quality or state of being profitable ⟨getting things done that contribute to the ~ of the company —G.B.Hurff⟩

**prof·it·able** \'präfəd·əbəl, -f(ə)təb-\ *adj* [ME, fr. MF, fr. *profiter* to profit + *-able* — more at PROFIT] : affording profits : bringing or yielding benefits or gains : HELPFUL, LUCRATIVE, REMUNERATIVE, USEFUL ⟨he had an instinct for noting and retaining ~ detail —Audrey Barker⟩ ⟨cotton growing became increasingly ~ —*Amer. Guide Series: La.*⟩ ⟨the Press Conference . . . was a political innovation and a ~ one —Frances Perkins⟩ **syn** see BENEFICIAL

**prof·it·able·ness** *n* -ES [ME *profitablenes*, fr. *profitable* + *-nes* -ness] : PROFITABILITY

**prof·it·ably** \-blē, -li\ *adv* [ME, fr. *profitable* + *-ly*] : in a profitable manner : BENEFICIALLY ⟨very ~ study the events of Scandinavian history —L.B.Burbank⟩

**profit and loss** *n* **1 :** a summary account used at the end of an accounting period to collect the balances of the nominal accounts that the net profit or loss may be shown **2 :** a nominal account or statement of profit and loss

**profit and loss statement** *n* : INCOME ACCOUNT 2

**profit a pren·dre** *or* **profit à pren·dre** \-ä'präⁿdr(ᵊ), -d(rə)-\ *n*, *pl* **profits a prendre** *or* **profits à prendre** [AF, lit., profit to be taken] : a legal right to take a profit from something yielded or produced by land : a right to take from land a part of its soil — distinguished from *easement*

**¹prof·i·teer** \¦präfə¦ti(ə)r, -iə\ *n* -S [¹*profit* + *-eer*] : one who makes what is considered an unreasonable profit esp. on the sale of essential goods during times of emergency

**²profiteer** \"\ *vi* -ED/-ING/-S : to be a profiteer : to engage in the practice of selling essential goods for exorbitant profit

**prof·it·er** \'präfəd·ə(r)\ *n* -S : one that profits

**pro·fit·er·ole** \prə'fid·ə,rōl\ *n* -S [F, fr. *profiter* to profit — more at PROFIT] : a miniature cream puff with sweet or savory filling

**prof·it·less** \'präfətləs\ *adj* : having no profit : without benefit or value : GAINLESS ⟨let us have no part in ~ quarrels —D.D. Eisenhower⟩ — **prof·it·less·ly** *adv* — **prof·it·less·ness** *n* -ES

**profit margin** *n* : the percentage of profit realized by a business per dollar of sales — compare MARGIN 5a

**profits** *pl of* PROFIT, *pres 3d sing of* PROFIT

**profit sharing** *n* : a system or process under which employees receive a part of the profits of an industrial or commercial enterprise

**profit system** *n* : FREE ENTERPRISE

**profit taking** *n* : the selling of commodities or securities at prices in excess of cost to realize profits

**pro·flavine** \(')prō+\ *n* [²*pro-* + *flavine*] : a yellow crystalline acridine dye $C_{13}H_7N(NH_2)_2$; *also* : the orange to brownish red hygroscopic crystalline sulfate used as an antiseptic esp. for wounds — compare ACRIFLAVINE

**prof·li·ga·cy** \'präfləgəsē, -lēg-, -si\ *n* -ES [*profligate* + *-cy*] **1 :** the quality or state of being profligate ⟨the ~ of the English plays . . . and novels of that age is a deep blot on our national fame —T.B.Macaulay⟩ **2 :** a thoroughly dissolute character or way of life : continuous dissipation **3 :** reckless wastefulness and extravagance

**¹prof·li·gate** \-gət, -lə,gāt, *usu* -d·+V\ *adj* [L *profligatus*, fr. past part. of *profligare* to strike down, destroy, ruin, fr. *pro-* forward, down + *-fligare* (fr. *fligere* to strike); akin to W *blif* catapult, Gk *thlibein*, (Aeol. & Ionic dial.) *phlibein* to squeeze, Latvian *blaîzīt* to squeeze, crush — more at PRO-] **1 :** completely given up to dissipation and licentiousness : abandoned to vice and corruption : shamelessly immoral ⟨you will find us neither ~ nor ascetic —James Hilton⟩ **2 :** wildly extravagant : criminally excessive in spending or using : recklessly wasteful ⟨rescue the Empire from being gambled away by incapable or ~ aristocrats —J.A.Froude⟩ ⟨the ~ profusion with which they settled on bribery —Hartley Withers⟩

[2]**prof·li·gate** \-lə,gāt\ *vt* -ED/-ING/-S [L *profligatus*, past part.] *archaic* : to drive away : DEFEAT, OVERCOME

[3]**prof·li·gate** \-ləgət, -lēg-, -lə,gāt, *usu* -d·+V\ *n* -S [[1]*profligate*] : a profligate person

**profligated** *adj* **1** *obs* : OVERTHROWN **2** *obs* **a :** wastefully squandered **b :** abandoned to vice

**prof·li·gate·ly** *adv* : in a profligate manner ⟨has wealth of land and tills it ~ for yields so low —Harry Schwartz⟩

**prof·li·gate·ness** *n* -ES : the quality or state of being profligate

**prof·lu·ence** \ˈprä,flüən(t)s, -äfləwən-\ *n* -S [L *profluentia*, fr. *profluent-, profluens* + *-ia* -y] **1 :** a copious or smooth flowing **2 :** the quality or state of being profluent : FLUENCY

**prof·lu·ent** \-nt\ *adj* [ME, fr. L *profluent-, profluens*, pres. part. of *profluere* to flow forth, flow along, fr. *pro-* forward, forth + *fluere* to flow — more at PRO-, FLUENT] : flowing copiously or smoothly in or as if in a stream : FLUENT

**pro·flu·vi·um** \prōˈflüvēəm\ *n, pl* **proflu·via** \-ēə\ *or* **profluviums** [L, fr. *profluere*] : a flowing out : DISCHARGE

**pro·fonde** \prōˈfōⁿd\ *n* -S [F, fr. *profonde*, adj., fem. of *profond* deep, fr. L *profundus* — more at PROFOUND] : a special pocket in the tail of a magician's coat

**pro for·ma** \(ˈ)prō¦fȯrmə\ *adj* [L, for the sake of form] **1 :** set up in advance to prescribe form or describe items ⟨a *pro forma* financial statement⟩ **2 :** consisting of a memorandum invoice sent to a customer for his use or as a notice prior to actual shipment of goods ⟨a *pro forma* invoice for customs⟩ ⟨a *pro forma* invoice indicating that goods are ready for shipment⟩

**pro forma balance sheet** *n* **1 :** a balance sheet containing imaginary accounts or figures for illustrative purposes **2 :** a balance sheet that gives retroactive effect to new financing, combination, or other change in the status of a business concern or concerns

[1]**pro·found** \prəˈfau̇nd, prō'-\ *adj, usu* -ER/-EST [ME, fr. MF *profond* deep, fr. L *profundus*, fr. *pro-* before + *fundus* bottom — more at PRO-, BOTTOM] **1 a :** having intellectual depth : going thoroughly and penetratingly into a problem : possessing knowledge and insight ⟨one of the most ~ minds of this generation⟩ **b :** characterized by, exhibiting, or requiring for comprehension deep learning and insight : difficult to fathom or understand ⟨are, in their meditative depths, among the few ~ poems of our day —Louis Untermeyer⟩ **2 a :** having very great depth : extending far below the surface **b :** coming from, reaching to, or situated at a depth : not superficial : deeply seated ⟨a ~ sigh⟩ **c** (1) : bent low with humility or respect ⟨made a ~ bow to the assembled company⟩ (2) : characterized by intensity of admiration ⟨the most ~ respect⟩ **3 a :** characterized by intensity of emotion : deeply realized or felt ⟨my spirit . . . felt a ~*er* fear than ever it knew —Robert Bridges †1930⟩ ⟨have a ~ sympathy —T.S.Eliot⟩ **b :** all encompassing : COMPLETE, THOROUGH ⟨fell into a ~ sleep⟩ **c :** very deep ⟨exerts a ~ influence on legislation —S.K.Padover⟩ **syn** see DEEP

[2]**profound** \"\ *n* -S : something that is very deep: as **a :** the deeps of the sea **b :** the depth of a human mind or spirit

**pro·found·ly** *adv* [ME, fr. *profound* + *-ly*] **1 :** with keen penetration and intellectual insight ⟨inability to deal ~ with life —John Portz⟩ **2 :** at or as if at a great depth from the surface ⟨why sigh you so ~ —Shak.⟩ **3 :** very deeply ⟨I was ~ glad to see it —D.L.Busk⟩ **4 :** TOTALLY — used to indicate a degree of deafness ⟨~ deaf children go through the babbling stage —I.J. Hirsh⟩ ⟨from the ~ deaf to the partially deaf —Minnie Hill⟩

**pro·found·ness** \-n(d)nəs\ *n* -ES : PROFUNDITY

**profs** *pl of* PROF

**pro·fun·da** \prəˈfəndə\ *n, pl* **profun·dae** \-n,dē\ [NL, fr. L, fem. of *profundus* deep — more at PROFOUND] : any of various deep-seated arteries or veins: as **a :** the largest branch of the brachial artery in the upper part of the arm **b :** the deep femoral artery **c :** a tributary of the femoral vein a short distance below Poupart's ligament

**pro·fun·dal** \prōˈfəndᵊl\ *adj* [L *profundus* deep + E *-al*] : of, relating to, being, or living in the part of a thermally stratified lake that extends downward from the upper part of the hypolimnion to the bottom of the lake or in very deep lakes to 600 meters

**profunditude** *n* -S [L *profundi-* (fr. *profundus* deep) + E *-tude*] *obs* : PROFUNDITY

**pro·fun·di·ty** \prəˈfəndəd·ē, prō'-, -ətē, -i\ *n* -ES [ME *profundite*, fr. MF *profundité*, fr. L *profunditat-, profunditas* depth, fr. *profundus* deep + *-itat-, -itas* -ity — more at PROFOUND] **1 a :** intellectual depth : penetrating knowledge : keen insight and understanding ⟨the wisest theologians could not match her in ~ —Willa Cather⟩ ⟨the timeless ~ in Jesus —H.E.Fosdick⟩ **b :** a profound or abstruse matter, problem, or theory — often used in pl. ⟨mythology runs into . . . philosophical speculation, sometimes grappling with *profundities* —A.L.Kroeber⟩ **c :** a significant thought : wise saying — often used in pl. ⟨fitting either to formulate or to revere undergraduate *profundities* —F.J.Hoffman⟩ **2 a** *obs* : depth as a dimension or a physical feature **b :** the quality or state of being very deep ⟨the ~ of an abyss⟩ **c :** something resembling a very deep place ⟨through the vast ~ obscure —John Milton⟩ ⟨the ~ of the surrounding shadow —Rebecca West⟩ **3 :** extreme thoroughness : INTENSITY ⟨whether or not he understood fully the ~ of his action —M.W.Straight⟩

[1]**pro·fuse** \prəˈfyüs, prō'-\ *adj* [ME, fr. L *profusus*, past part. of *profundere* to pour forth, pour out, fr. *pro-* forth + *fundere* to pour — more at PRO-, FOUND] **1 :** pouring forth liberally : exceedingly or excessively generous : EXTRAVAGANT ⟨were both ~ in their thanks —*Collier's Yr. Bk.*⟩ **2 :** exhibiting great abundance : overly plentiful : BOUNTIFUL ⟨contains the most valuable minerals, in a ~ variety —H.T.Buckle⟩

**syn** LAVISH, PRODIGAL, LUXURIANT, LUSH, EXUBERANT: PROFUSE suggests an unrestrained abundance, often as of something poured out or gushing out very fully, freely, or copiously ⟨the milk is scanty during the first two or three days, but becomes *profuse*, in most cases, by the third and fourth day —Morris Fishbein⟩ ⟨pourest thy full heart in *profuse* strains of unpremeditated art —P.B.Shelley⟩ ⟨his court became as crowded and *profuse* as his grandfather's. Money was recklessly borrowed and as recklessly squandered —J.R.Green⟩ LAVISH may suggest an unstinted, extravagant, or munificent profusion or outpouring ⟨the *lavish* box lunch where baked ham, fried chicken, and home-baked bread are routine fare —C.W.Morton⟩ ⟨every comfort and luxury that a wealthy and *lavish* old grandfather thought fit to provide —W.M.Thackeray⟩ ⟨five hundred million dollars a year, which go into *lavish* expenditure on health, education, and economic development —Andrew Boyd⟩ PRODIGAL may apply to reckless lavishness and extravagance seeming to lead to depletion or exhaustion of supplies ⟨wildly *prodigal* of color, the new sun then sketched a wide band of throbbing red-gold across less lofty glaciers and snow fields —F.V.W.Mason⟩ ⟨the table spread with opulent hospitality and careless profusion — the baked ham at one end and the saddle of roast mutton at the other, with fried chicken, oysters, crabs, sweet potatoes, jellies, custards — a *prodigal* feast that only outdoor stomachs could manage —V.L.Parrington⟩ LUXURIANT may suggest a splendid, colorful, pleasing rich abundance ⟨a *luxuriant* growth of native iris, trumpet vines, and water hyacinths line its banks —*Amer. Guide Series: La.*⟩ ⟨rich and *luxuriant* beauty; a beauty that shone with deep and vivid tints; a bright complexion, eyes possessing intensity both of depth and glow, and hair already of a deep, glossy brown —Nathaniel Hawthorne⟩ LUSH may suggest a rich, easy, soft luxuriance ⟨a Jersey cow standing belly-deep in a *lush* meadow —Joseph Mitchell⟩ ⟨the fabulous period of the Nineties, that *lush*, plush, glittering era with all its sentimentality and opulence and ostentation —Sara H. Hay⟩ EXUBERANT suggests fruitful abundance marked by vivacity or rampant vitality ⟨an *exuberant* nature pouring out its wealth in spendthrift fashion —V.L.Parrington⟩ ⟨she was in *exuberant* spirits, and the softest colors of flame danced in her lips and eyes and informed the texture of her hair —Elinor Wylie⟩ ⟨houses frescoed, antlered, flowered and curlicued in *exuberant* outburst of Tyrolean design —Claudia Cassidy⟩

[2]**profuse** *vt* -ED/-ING/-S [L *profusus*, past part.] **1** *obs* : to pour forth or give freely **2** *obs* : to spend too liberally : LAVISH, SQUANDER

**pro·fuse·ly** *adv* : in a profuse manner : without limitation : ABUNDANTLY ⟨it is illustrated . . . ~ after the fashion that children love —Agnes Repplier⟩ ⟨the bush blossoms all too ~ —J.W.Krutch⟩

**pro·fuse·ness** *n* -ES : the quality or state of being profuse : PROFUSION ⟨it is Elizabethan in its ~ —Owen & Eleanor Lattimore⟩

**pro·fu·sion** \prəˈfyüzhən, prō'-\ *n* [L *profusion-, profusio*, fr. *profusus* (past part. of *profundere* to pour forth) + *-ion-, -io* -ion — more at PROFUSE] **1 :** the act of bestowing money or treasures without restraint : lavish expenditure : excessive liberality : EXTRAVAGANCE ⟨made himself popular by his ~ . . . in providing shows for the mob —J.A.Froude⟩ ⟨bountiful even to ~ where the interest of the navy was concerned —T.B. Macaulay⟩ **2** *obs* : the act of pouring forth or discharging **3 :** the quality or state of being profuse : a condition of superabundance : PRODIGALITY ⟨noted for their taste, hospitality, and ~ —C.G.Bowers⟩ **4 :** an overpowering quantity or amount : lavish display or supply ⟨into its columns he poured a ~ of prose and verse —Brander Matthews⟩ ⟨a ~ of clocks, tapestries, and chairs —Carlton Lake⟩ — often used with *in* ⟨grapes grow in ~ along . . . back roads —*Amer. Guide Series: N.H.*⟩ ⟨objects are piled in a chaotic ~ —David Sylvester⟩

**pro·fu·sive** \-üsiv\ *adj* : LAVISH — **pro·fu·sive·ly** \-səvlē\ *adv*

[1]**prog** \ˈpräg\ *n* -S [origin unknown] *dial Brit* : a pointed instrument (as a goad or skewer)

[2]**prog** \"\ *vt* **progged; progged; progging; progs** **1** *dial Brit* : GOAD, PROD **2** *dial Brit* : to poke at (as a hole, a log)

[3]**prog** \", ˈprōg\ *vi* **progged; progged; progging; progs** [origin unknown] **1** *chiefly dial* : to poke or search about esp. in order to steal, beg, or chance upon something profitable : FORAGE **2** *dial* : to wander about idly or aimlessly : PROWL

[4]**prog** *n* -S *chiefly dial* : food esp. when obtained by foraging, filching, or as a handout

[5]**prog** \ˈpräg\ *n* -S [by shortening & alter.] *slang Brit* : PROCTOR 2a

[6]**prog** \"\ *vt* **progged; progged; progging; progs** *slang Brit* : to subject to proctorial authority ⟨if I came in here by myself I'd get *progged* —Thomas Wolfe⟩

**prog** *abbr* **1** program **2** progress; progressive

**pro·gametangium** \¦prō+\ *n* [NL, fr. [1]*pro-* + *gametangium*] : a hyphal thread in fungi (as of the order Mucorales) at whose tip will be produced a gametangium and subsequently a gamete

**pro·gamete** \(ˈ)prō+; ,prōgəˈmēt\ *n* [ISV [1]*pro-* + *gamete*] : an oocyte or a spermatocyte

**pro·gam·ic** \(ˈ)prō¦gamik\ *adj* [[1]*pro-* + Gk *gamos* marriage + E *-ic* — more at BIGAMY] : preceding fertilization

**prog·a·mous** \ˈprägəməs\ *adj* [[1]*pro-* + Gk *gamos* marriage] : PROGAMIC

**pro·gan·o·chel·i·dae** \prō,ganəˈkelə,dē\ *n pl, cap* [NL, fr. *Proganochelys*, type genus (fr. [1]*pro-* + Gk *ganos* brightness + *chelys* tortoise) + *-idae* — more at CHELYS] : a family of extinct Triassic turtles that are the earliest known representatives of the Thecophora

**pro·gan·o·saur** \prōˈganə,sȯ(ə)r\ *n* -S [NL *Proganosauria*] : MESOSAUR

**pro·gan·o·sau·ria** \⸗,⸗⸗ˈsȯrēə\ [NL, fr. [1]*pro-* + Gk *ganos* brightness + NL *-sauria*] *syn of* MESOSAURIA

**pro·gen·er·ate** \prōˈjenə,rāt\ *vt* [L *progeneratus*, past part. of *progenerare*, fr. *pro-* forward, forth + *generare* to beget, procreate — more at PRO-, GENERATE] : BEGET, PROCREATE

**pro·genesis** \(ˈ)prō+\ *n* [NL, fr. [1]*pro-* + *genesis*] : precocious sexual reproduction in a trematode worm in which metacercariae or sometimes cercariae may lay eggs capable of repeating the life cycle — compare NEOTENY, PAEDOGENESIS

**pro·genetic** \¦prō+\ *adj* [[1]*pro-* + *genetic*] : of, relating to, or characterized by progenesis

**pro·gen·i·tal** \prōˈjenəd·ᵊl\ *adj* [*progenitor* + *-al*] : PROGENITIVE

**pro·gen·i·tive** \-d·iv\ *adj* [*progenitor* + *-ive*] : tending to or able to reproduce itself : REPRODUCTIVE — **pro·gen·i·tive·ness** *n* -ES

**pro·gen·i·tor** \prōˈjenəd·ə(r), prə'-, -nətə-\ *n* -S [ME *progenitour*, fr. MF *progeniteur*, fr. L *progenitor*, fr. *progenitus* (past part. of *progignere* to beget, fr. *pro-* before, forward, forth + *gignere* to beget) + *-or* — more at PRO-, KIN] **1 a :** an ancestor in the direct line : FOREFATHER **b :** a biologically ancestral form **2 :** one that originates or precedes : one that serves as a guide or pattern : ORIGINATOR, PRECURSOR ⟨biographical study of the ~ of the atmospheric story —*New Yorker*⟩ ⟨~*s* of socialist ideas —*Times Lit. Supp.*⟩ **syn** see ANCESTOR

**pro·gen·i·to·ri·al** \prō¦jenə¦tōrēəl\ *adj* : of or relating to a progenitor : ANCESTRAL

**pro·gen·i·tor·ship** \prōˈjenəd·ə(r),ship\ *n* : a position as a progenitor

**pro·gen·i·trix** \-nə·triks\ *also* **pro·gen·i·tress** \-rəs\ *n, pl* **progenitri·ces** \prō,jenəˈtrī¦sēz\ *also* **progenitresses** [LL, fem. of L *progenitor*] : a female progenitor

**pro·gen·i·ture** \prōˈjenəchə(r)\ *n* [F, fr. MF, fr. L *progenitus* + MF *-ure*] **1 :** a generation of offspring **2 :** PROGENY

**prog·e·ny** \ˈpräjənē, -ni\ *n* -ES [ME *progenie*, fr. OF, fr. L *progenies*, fr. *progignere* to beget] **1 a** (1) : descendants of human kind : CHILDREN (2) : a line descended from a common ancestor : CLAN, KIN (3) *archaic* : LINEAGE, PARENTAGE **b :** offspring of animals or plants — used esp. in connection with controlled breeding ⟨the ~ of a wheat cross⟩ ⟨the total ~ of a prepotent sire⟩ **2 :** something that is originated or produced : OUTCOME, PRODUCT ⟨examined one by one the marvelous ~ of the workman's art —Elinor Wylie⟩ **3 :** a body of followers, disciples, or successors

**progeny test** *n* : a test of the worth of a sire or sometimes of a dam based on the performance of its early progeny : an evaluation of the genotype of an animal in terms of its offspring — compare SIB TEST

**progeny–test** \ˈ⸗⸗⸗,⸗\ *vt* [*progeny test*] : to perform a progeny test on

**pro·ge·ria** \prōˈjirēə\ *n* -S [NL, fr. [1]*pro-* + Gk *gēras* old age + NL *-ia* — more at CORN] : premature senility; *specif* : an abnormal state showing the symptoms both of infantilism and of a developing senility

**pro·gestational** \¦prō+\ *adj* [[1]*pro-* + *gestational*] : preceding pregnancy or gestation : of, relating to, or constituting the hormonal and tissue modifications of the female mammalian system associated with ovulation and corpus luteum formation

**pro·ges·ter·one** \prōˈjestə,rōn\ *n* -S [*progestin* + *sterol* + *-one*] : a crystalline ketonic steroid progestational hormone $C_{21}H_{30}O_2$ that is obtained from corpus luteum or made synthetically, that is regarded as a biological precursor of corticoid and androgenic hormones, and that is used chiefly in treating functional uterine bleeding; 4-pregnene-3,20-dione

**pro·ges·ter·on·ic** \⸗¦⸗⸗ˈränik\ *adj* : induced by progesterone

**pro·ges·tin** \prōˈjestən\ *n* -S [L *pro* for + *gestation* + *-in* — more at FOR] : a progestational hormone; *esp* : PROGESTERONE

**progged** *past of* PROG

**progging** *pres part of* PROG

**pro·glacial** \(ˈ)prō+\ *adj* [[1]*pro-* + *glacial*] : in front of, at, or immediately beyond the margin of a glacier or ice sheet ⟨a ~ lake⟩

**pro·glot·tic** \prōˈgläd·ik\ *adj* [*proglottid* + *-ic*] : of or relating to proglottids

**pro·glot·tid** \-d·əd\ *n* -S [NL *proglottid-, proglottis*] : any of the segments of a tapeworm formed by a process of strobilation in the neck region of the worm, containing both male and female reproductive organs, and surviving briefly after breaking away from the strobila — see ECHINOCOCCUS illustration — **pro·glot·tid·e·an** \¦prō,glä¦tidēən\ *adj*

**pro·glot·tis** \prōˈgläd·əs\ *n, pl* **proglotti·des** \-d·ə,dēz\ [NL, fr. Gk *proglōssis, proglōttis* tip of the tongue, fr. *pro-* [1]*pro-* + *glōssa, glōtta* tongue — more at GLOSS] : PROGLOTTID

**prog·nath·ic** \(ˈ)präg¦nathik, -thēk\ *adj* [*prognathous* + *-ic*] : PROGNATHOUS

**prog·na·thism** \ˈprägnə,thizəm\ *also* **prog·na·thy** \-nəthē\ *n, pl* **prognathisms** *also* **prognathies** [*prognathous* + *-ism* or *-y*] : prognathic condition : the state of having protruding jaws

**prog·na·thous** \-nəthəs\ *adj* [*pro-* + NL *-gnathus* -gnathous] **1 :** having the jaws projecting beyond the upper part of the face with a gnathic index above 98 — opposed to *opisthognathous* **2** *of an insect* : having the mouthparts in front of the cranium — compare HYPOGNATHOUS

**prog·ne** \ˈprägnē\ *n, cap* [NL, irreg. after *Procne*, a woman in Greek mythology who was transformed into a swallow, fr. L, fr. Gk *Proknē*] : a genus of swallows including the purple martin and its related forms

**prog·no·sis** \prägˈnōsəs\ *n, pl* **prog·no·ses** \-ō,sēz\ [LL, fr. Gk *prognōsis*, foreknowledge, prognosis, fr. *progignōskein* to know beforehand, prognosticate, fr. *pro-* [1]*pro-* + *gignōskein* to know — more at KNOW] **1 a :** the act or art of foretelling the course of a disease **b :** the prospect of survival and recovery from a disease as anticipated from the usual course of that disease or indicated by special features of the case in question ⟨the ~ is grave; death usually occurs within one year⟩ **2 :** FORECAST, PROGNOSTICATION ⟨that ~, though wrong, then seemed justified —F.L.Schuman⟩

[1]**prog·nos·tic** \prägˈnästik, -tēk\ *n* -S [alter. (influenced by L *prognosticum*) of ME *pronostyke, pronostique*, fr. MF *pronostique*, fr. L *prognosticon, prognosticum*, fr. Gk *prognōstikon*, fr. neut. of *prognōstikos*] **1 :** something that foretells : a warning omen : PORTENT, SIGN ⟨that choice would inevitably be considered by the country as a ~ of the highest import —T.B. Macaulay⟩ **2 :** a forecast of the future based on a prognostic : PROPHECY ⟨events have caught up with his ~ —Cyril Connolly⟩

[2]**prognostic** \(ˈ)⸗¦⸗⸗\ *adj* [ML *prognosticus*, fr. Gk *prognōstikos* foreknowing, prognostic, fr. (assumed) *prognōstos* (verbal of *progignōskein* to know beforehand, prognosticate) + *-ikos* -ic — more at PROGNOSIS] : of, relating to, or serving as ground for prognostication or a prognosis : FORETELLING, PREDICTIVE

**prog·nos·ti·ca·ble** \-təkəbəl\ *adj* [ML *prognosticare* + E *-able*] : capable of being foretold

**prog·nos·ti·cal** \-kəl\ *adj* : PROGNOSTIC

**prognostically** *adv, obs* : in a prognostic manner

**prog·nos·ti·cate** \prägˈnästə,kāt, *usu* -ād·+V\ *vb* -ED/-ING/-S [ML *prognosticatus*, past part. of *prognosticare*, fr. *prognosticus* prognostic — more at PROGNOSTIC] *vt* **1 :** to foretell from signs or symptoms : PREDICT, PROPHESY ⟨*prognosticating* . . . future relations —T.S.Eliot⟩ **2 :** to give an indication of in advance : FORESHOW, PRESAGE ⟨opening new trails, they ~ renaissance and revival —Stephen Crane⟩ **~** *vi* to make a prognostication **syn** see FORETELL

**prog·nos·ti·ca·tion** \(,)präg,nästəˈkāshən *sometimes* prəg-\ *n* -S [alter. (influenced by ML *prognosticatio*) of ME *pronosticacioun*, fr. MF *pronostication*, fr. ML *prognostication-, prognosticatio*, fr. *prognosticatus* + L *-ion-, -io* -ion] **1 :** a manifestation of something that is to happen : an indication in advance : FORETOKEN ⟨if an oily palm be not a fruitful ~ —Shak.⟩ **2 a :** an act, the fact, or the power of prognosticating : a prediction of something to come : FORECAST, PROPHECY ⟨the tremendous breadth of his vision . . . as evidenced by his ~*s* and their eventual fulfillment —F.S.Crafford⟩ **b :** a premonition of something that is to or may happen : FOREBODING **3 :** PROGNOSIS 1a

**prog·nos·ti·ca·tive** \⸗ˈ⸗⸗,kād·iv, -,kəd·iv\ *adj* [MF or ML; MF *prognosticatif*, fr. ML *prognosticativus*, fr. *prognosticatus* + L *-ivus* -ive] : characterized by prognosticating : PROPHETIC

**prog·nos·ti·ca·tor** \-,kād·ə(r), -ātə-\ *n* -S [ML *prognosticator*, fr. ML *prognosticatus* + MF *-eur* -or] : one that prognosticates ⟨weather ~*s* —G.S.Perry⟩ — **prog·nos·ti·ca·to·ry** \-,kə,tōrē\ *adj*

**pro·go·ne·a·ta** \prō,gōnēˈād·ə, -ˈädə\ *n pl, cap* [NL, fr. [1]*pro-* + Gk *gonē* genitals (fr. the stem of *gignesthai* to be born) + NL *-ata* — more at KIN] *in some classifications* : a primary division of Arthropoda comprising forms with the genital apertures near the anterior end of the body and including the classes Chilopoda, Pauropoda, and Symphyla

**pro·go·ne·ate** \prōˈgōnēət, -ē,āt\ *adj* [[1]*pro-* + Gk *gonē* + E *-ate*] **1 :** having the genital opening placed near the anterior part of the body — distinguished from *opisthogoneate* **2** [NL *Progoneata*] : of or relating to the Progoneata

**pro·gra·da·tion** \,prōgrāˈdāshən\ *n* [*prograde* + *-ation*] : the process of prograding — contrasted with *retrogradation*

**pro·grade** \prōˈgrād\ *vi* [L *pro-* forward + E *grade* — more at PRO-] : to build outward toward the sea by deposition of sediment ⟨the shoreward transportation will be the dominating force, and the beach will ~ —F.P.Shepard⟩ ⟨on advancing, or *prograding*, coasts where the waves are throwing up sand —C.A.Cotton⟩

[1]**pro·gram** \ˈprō,gram, -raam, -ōgrəm\ *n* -S *or* **pro·gramme** \-,gram\ [in sense 1, fr. LL *programma*, fr. Gk, public notice, agenda, fr. *prographein* to write before, set forth as a public notice, fr. *pro-* [1]*pro-* + *graphein* to write; in sense 3, fr. NL *programma*, fr. LL; in other senses, fr. F *programme*, fr. LL *programma* — more at CARVE] **1 :** a public notice **2 a** (1) : a brief outline or explanation of the order to be pursued or the subjects embraced in a public exercise, performance, or entertainment; *esp* : a printed or written list of the acts, scenes, selections, or other features composing a dramatic, musical, or other performance with the names of the performers ⟨handed me the ~ of the concert⟩ ⟨a theater ~⟩ (2) : an order of exercises or numbers **b :** the performance or execution of a program; *esp* : a performance broadcast on radio or television ⟨listen to a brilliant ~⟩ **3 :** PROGRAMMA 2 **4 a :** a plan of procedure : a schedule or system under which action may be taken toward a desired goal : a proposed project or scheme ⟨had no ~ except to retain his job —John Gunther⟩ ⟨sets up a buying ~ —A.M.Sullivan⟩ ⟨significant characteristics of a leader are a . . . grasp of the current situation and a ~ for its solution —V.L.Albjerg⟩ ⟨the party's ~ toward socialism⟩ **b** (1) : a plan determining the offerings of an educational institution : CURRICULUM ⟨a school . . . attractive and comfortable but unsuited to the educational ~ —*Education Digest*⟩ ⟨the core ~⟩ (2) : a plan of study for an individual student over a given period : SCHEDULE ⟨had a heavy ~ in his freshman year⟩ **5 :** a catalog of projected proceedings or features : PROSPECTUS, SYLLABUS **6 :** a printed bill, card, or booklet giving a program; *specif* : a dance order ⟨a box full of yellowed ball ~*s* with faded ribbons —Marcia Davenport⟩ **7 :** a statement of an architectural problem and of the requirements to be met in offering a solution **8 :** a coherent sequence of incidents, images, thoughts, or feelings providing the background for an instrumental composition that may be inferred by an interpreter or listener, or suggested by the title of the work, or supplied in the form of a poem or exposition **9 a :** a plan for the programming of a digital computer **b :** a sequence of coded instructions for a digital computer

[2]**program** \"\ *also* **programme** \"\ *vt* **programmed** *or* **programed; programmed** *or* **programed; programming** *or* **programing; programs** *also* **programmes** **1 a :** to arrange or furnish a program of or for : BILL ⟨amount of material needed to ~ these new stations will be tremendous —*Christian Science Monitor*⟩ ⟨capable of *programming* social action with . . . confidence —R.T.La Piere⟩ **b :** to enter in a program **2 a :** to work out a sequence of operations to be performed by (an electronic computer, an accounting machine, or other automatic equipment) : code instructions or problems (as on punched cards or punched tape) to be fed to (computing equipment) **b :** to activate (such equipment) to carry through such a sequence of operations

**program clock** *n* : a master clock that rings bells or other signals at predetermined times

**program director** *n* : one that is in charge of planning and scheduling program material for a radio or television station or network

**pro·gram·ist** *or* **pro·gram·mist** \-məst\ *n* -S **1 :** a composer or advocate of program music **2 :** one who prepares or advocates a program

**pro·gram·is·tic** *or* **pro·gram·mis·tic** \¦prōgrə¦mistik\ *adj* : relating to a programist — **pro·gram·is·ti·cal·ly** \-tək(ə)lē\ *adv*

**pro·gram·ma** \prōˈgramə\ *n, pl* **programma·ta** \-məd·ə\ [LL — more at PROGRAM] **1 :** a public notice esp. if posted : DECREE, EDICT **2** [NL, fr. LL] : a preface esp. to a learned literary work **3** [NL, fr. LL] : PROGRAM 2

**pro·gram·mat·ic** \ˌprōgrəˈmad·ik, -atl, |ēk\ *adj* [Gk *programmat-, programma* + E *-ic*] **1 :** relating to program music ⟨as is found to be the case in all romantic music, ~ allusions play a big part —Beatrice Maier⟩ **2 :** of, resembling, or having a program ⟨his writing is ~ and pioneering rather than definitive —D.G.Mandelbaum⟩ ⟨the one and only party is bound to degenerate, regardless of its ~ intentions —Philip Rahv⟩ — **pro·gram·mat·i·cal·ly** \|ək(ə)lē, |ēk-, -li\ *adv*

**pro·gram·ma·tist** \prōˈgraməd·əst\ *n* -s [Gk *programmat-, programma* + E *-ist*] **:** PROGRAMIST

**programme** *var of* PROGRAM

**pro·gram·mer** \ˈprō,gramə(r), -raam-, -ōgrəm-\ *n* -s **1 :** one that programs **2 :** a component unit in a computing machine or accounting machine that stores the program and controls the sequence of operations

**programming** *or* **programing** *n* -s **:** the planning, scheduling, or performing of a program ⟨the listeners alone, can . . . actually correct shoddy or inadequate ~ —A.N.Williams b.1914⟩ ⟨more ~ is only one of many problems facing television —*Advertising Age*⟩

**program music** *n* **1 :** music that is inspired by or that suggests or characterizes something other than a musical idea or thing **:** descriptive music — compare ABSOLUTE MUSIC **2 :** instrumental music that follows the moods of a program

**program picture** *n* **:** a motion picture produced cheaply, acted by studio feature players, and usu. shown second on a double-feature program

**programs** *pl of* PROGRAM, *pres 3d sing of* PROGRAM

**pro·gravid** \(ˈ)prō+\ *adj* [¹*pro-* + *gravid*] **:** PROGESTATIONAL

**pro·gre·di·en** \prōˈgrēdēən\ *or* **pro·gre·di·ens** \-nz\ *n, pl* **progrediens** \-nz\ *or* **progredien·tes** \ˌ=ˌ=dēˈen·ˌtēz\ [NL *prогrediens*, fr. L, pres. part. of *progredi*] **:** a wingless form of an adelgid bug

¹**prog·ress** \ˈpräˌgrəs, |ˌgres, *sometimes* ˈprō|\ *n* -ES [ME *progresse*, fr. L *progressus*, fr. *progressus*, past part. of *progredi* to go forth, go forward, advance, proceed, fr. *pro-* forward + *-gredi* (fr. *gradi* to step, go) — more at PRO-, GRADE] **1 a** (1) **:** a royal journey or tour marked by pomp and pageant ⟨a staff of clerks accompanied the king on his ~*es* —F.M.Stenton⟩ (2) **:** a state procession ⟨at last all was ready for my ~ —George VI⟩ **b :** an official journey or circuit ⟨these men of law . . . on a ~ from court to court —Van Wyck Brooks⟩ **c :** a journeying forward **:** an expedition, journey, or march through a region **:** TOUR ⟨balls, dinners and crowds of beautiful women attended his ~ —*Time*⟩ **2 a :** an advance or movement to an objective or toward a goal **:** purposeful getting or going ahead ⟨when impeded in their ~, these people suddenly ceased muttering —E.A.Poe⟩ ⟨a fishing boat made a slow ~ —Elizabeth Bowen⟩ ⟨~ to the presidency and chairmanship of the board —*Current Biog.*⟩ **b :** a movement onward (as in time or space) **:** a forward course **:** PROGRESSION ⟨the daily ~ of the sun⟩ ⟨the ~ of a disease⟩ ⟨we make ~ — we pass from night to morning —Edmund Wilson⟩ **3** *Scots law* **:** succession in right to a feudal estate **:** the abstract of title with the deeds evidencing such succession **4 a :** the action or process of advancing or improving by marked stages or degrees **:** gradual betterment; *esp* **:** the progressive development or evolution of mankind ⟨there was a general belief in inevitable and universal ~ —John Berger⟩ ⟨found in civil law principles . . . the analogies that were needed to smooth the path of ~ —B.N. Cardozo⟩ **b :** a theory that change from old to new is essential to progress — **in progress :** going on **:** OCCURRING ⟨entertained troops . . . while the fighting was still *in progress* —*Current Biog.*⟩ ⟨with the beginning of healing already *in progress* —Morris Fishbein⟩

²**pro·gress** \prəˈgres, prōˈ-\ *vb* -ED/-ING/-ES [partly fr. ¹*progress;* partly fr. L *progressus*, past part. of *progredi*] *vi* **1 :** to make a journey; *esp* **:** to make a royal progress **2 :** to move forward **:** to proceed or advance from place to place, point to point, or step to step ⟨simply ~ from one place to another as her fancy dictated —Louis Bromfield⟩ ⟨the fireplace is ~*ing*, but not finished yet —Rachel Henning⟩ **3 :** to develop to a higher, better, or more advanced stage **:** make continual improvements ⟨deductive reasoning had to be combined with the methods of experimentation . . . before science could ~ —J.B.Conant⟩ **4 :** to proceed from one musical note or tone to the next ~ *vt* **1** *obs* **:** to pass over or through **2 :** to cause to progress **:** push forward **:** ADVANCE ⟨a really big housing program cannot be successfully ~*ed* —*Americana Annual*⟩

**progress chart** *n* **:** a chart showing actual performance in comparison with a predetermined schedule or estimate of expected performance

**progress clerk** *n* **:** a clerk employed to plot out and trace the progress of work from operation to operation in manufacture

**pro·gres·sion** \prəˈgreshən, prōˈ-\ *n* -s [ME *progressioun*, fr. MF *progression*, fr. L *progression-, progressio* action of going forward, advancement, progress, fr. *progressus* (past part. of *progredi* to go forward, advance) + *-ion-, -io* -ion — more at PROGRESS] **1 :** a sequence of mathematical terms in which the terms after the first are determined according to a rule **2 a :** an act of progressing **:** a movement forward **:** ADVANCE ⟨the train . . . is the most amusing means of ~ —*Nat'l Geographic*⟩ **b :** a continuous proceeding **:** a connected series (as of acts, events, steps) **:** a sequence whose continuity suggests movement or flow ⟨all the events and ~*s* of . . . life were gathered up and recorded —Victoria Sackville-West⟩ **c :** the process of advancing esp. to a better or higher condition **:** gradual development **:** PROGRESS ⟨a sphere in which spiritual ~ is impossible —Matthew Arnold⟩ ⟨an inner ~ . . . from apprehension to understanding —R.W.Southern⟩ **3 a :** succession of musical tones or chords **b :** the movement of musical parts in harmony **c :** SEQUENCE 2c **4 :** a betting system in which a player increases his bet by a given sum after each loss and decreases it after each win

**pro·gres·sion·al** \-shənᵊl\ *adj* **:** of, relating to, or characterized by progression

**pro·gres·sion·ist** \-sh(ə)nəst\ *n* -s **:** one who believes in progress; *esp* **:** one who believes in the continuous progress of the human race or of society

**prog·ress·ism** \ˈprägrə,sizəm\ *n* -s [F *progressisme*, fr. *progrès* progress (fr. L *progressus*) + *-isme* -ism — more at PROGRESS] **:** advocacy of or devotion esp. to progressive action or social and political reform ⟨illuminating observations on the political ~ of . . . the Northwest —*N. Y. Herald Tribune*⟩

**prog·ress·ist** \-,səst\ *n* -s [F *progressiste*, fr. *progrès* + *-iste* -ist] **1 :** PROGRESSIONIST **2 :** a member of a political party holding views assumed to be progressive

¹**pro·gres·sive** \prəˈgresiv, prōˈ-, -sēv *also* -səv\ *adj* [²*progress* & *progression* + *-ive*] **1 a :** of, relating to, or characterized by progress **:** devoted to or evincing continuous improvement **:** making use of or interested in new ideas, inventions, or opportunities ⟨a young man of ~ tastes —H.S.Canby⟩ ⟨he was . . . of ~ tendencies —E.H.Jenkins⟩ ⟨a practical, ~, hard-driving American city —*Amer. Guide Series: La.*⟩ ⟨the art of stage design is ~ —*Times Lit. Supp.*⟩ **b :** of, relating to, or constituting an educational theory or doctrine that opposes itself to traditional education proposing greater emphasis on the individual child, the use of projects and activities for teaching purposes, informality of classroom procedure, and encouragement of self-expression **2 :** of, relating to, or characterized by progression **:** occurring or arranged in a series **:** advancing or becoming effective by successive stages ⟨the price may be the ~ deterioration of our faculties —W.R.Inge⟩ ⟨~ changes of compressed decaying plant materials to peat . . . and finally anthracite coal —R.W.Murray⟩ ⟨the ~ complexity of business relationship —Helen Sullivan⟩ ⟨the ~ forms of that animal life were struggling for a foothold on the land —W.E. Swinton⟩ **3 :** moving forward or onward **:** ADVANCING ⟨the ~ currents, drifts, and eddies of the wide ocean —R.E.Coker⟩ **4 :** increasing in extent or severity — used of a disease, lesion, or symptom **5** *often cap* **:** of, relating to, or constituting a political party advocating or associated with the principles of political progressivism **6 :** marked by progression from one place to another: as **a** *of a card party* **:** characterized by the moving between rounds of the winners at each table to a higher or next table and the changing of partners **b** *of a meal* **:** having its courses served at different locations **7 :** of, relating to, or constituting a verb form that expresses action or state in progress or continuance at the time of speaking or a time spoken of ⟨*am seeing, had been seeing, is being seen* are ~ forms⟩ **8 :** having the nature of the second of two sounds dependent on the nature of the first ⟨~ assimilation or palatalization⟩ **9 :** of or relating to a tax or taxation imposed on an individual that increases by a given amount with increases in the tax base — used chiefly of income and death taxes **10 :** relating to or characterized by burning (as of perforated grains of smokeless powder) in which the surface increases as the burning advances — opposed to *degressive* **syn** see LIBERAL

²**progressive** \ˈ"\ *n* -s **1 a :** one that is progressive **b :** one holding political convictions based on a belief in moderate change designed to improve the condition of the majority of the people and willing to use governmental power to bring about change **:** one believing in change as a desirable means of achieving specified goals — compare CONSERVATIVE, LIBERAL **2** *usu cap* **a :** a member of a U.S. political party: as (1) **:** a member of a predominantly agrarian minor party split off from the Republicans in the early 20th century and advocating domestic reforms designed primarily to reduce the power of and eliminate abuses alleged to be perpetrated by the great industrial and financial interests; *specif* **:** BULL MOOSE (2) **:** a follower of Robert M. La Follette in the presidential campaign of 1924 (3) **:** a follower of Henry A. Wallace in the presidential campaign of 1948 (4) **:** a member of a left-wing minor party split off from the Democrats and usu. associated with essentially socialist domestic policies and a pro-Russian foreign policy **b :** a member of a primarily agrarian Canadian political party advocating low tariffs, nationalization of railways, and direct democracy (as through the use of the initiative, referendum, and recall) and achieving its chief strength in the early 1920s

**progressive-alphabet cipher** *n* **:** polyalphabetic substitution in which the choice of alphabets runs through them all in a definite order — compare MULTIPLE-ALPHABET CIPHER

¹**progressive conservative** *adj, usu cap P&C* **:** of, relating to, or constituting a major political party in Canada traditionally associated with economic nationalism and esp. a protective tariff and with advocacy of close ties with the United Kingdom and the Commonwealth

²**progressive conservative** *n, usu cap P&C* **:** a member or supporter of the Progressive Conservative party

**progressive dies** *n* **:** a compound tool used in a punch press for performing several operations (as drawing, punching, bending) in a single movement or in as few as possible successive movements

**progressive dunker** *n, usu cap P&D* **:** a member of a religious group of Brethren who because of their desire for more stress on education, a church polity that was congregational, and less rigid rules regarding plain dress left the Church of the Brethren in 1882 and formed the Brethren Church

**progressive jazz** *n* **:** jazz of the 1950s characterized by harmonic, contrapuntal, and rhythmic experimentation

**pro·gres·sive·ly** \-səvlē, -sēv-, -li\ *adv* **:** in a progressive manner **:** continuously step by step ⟨mechanization ~ opened up ever more places for the unskilled —Oscar Handlin⟩ ⟨expect little from government and ~ rely on it more —Felix Frankfurter⟩

**progressive muscular dystrophy** *n* **:** MUSCULAR DYSTROPHY

**pro·gres·sive·ness** \-sivnəs\ *n* -ES **:** the quality or state of being progressive

**progressive proof** *n* **:** a proof of a set made from plates for color printing showing each color separately and then the colors combined with one color being added at a time in the order in which they are to print

**progressive rummy** *n* **:** a variety of contract rummy

**progressive scanning** *n* **:** television scanning in which each successive line is scanned in sequence — compare INTERLACED SCANNING

**progressive sorites** *n* **:** a sorites arranged so that the predicate of each proposition that precedes forms the subject of each one that follows and the conclusion unites the subject of the first proposition with the predicate of the last proposition — compare GOCLENIAN SORITES

**progressive system** *n* **:** ALEMBERT

**pro·gres·siv·ism** \-sə,vizəm\ *n* -s **1 :** the principles or beliefs of progressives **2 :** PROGRESS 4a **3** *usu cap* **:** the political and economic doctrines advocated by the Progressives **4 :** the theories of progressive education — contrasted with *essentialism*

¹**pro·gres·siv·ist** \-,vəst\ *n* -s [¹*progressive* + *-ist*] **:** PROGRESSIVE

²**progressivist** \ˈ"\ *adj* **:** of or relating to progressivism or progressivists ⟨a tension between . . . ~ tendencies of thought and conservative . . . ones —Douglas Knight⟩

**pro·gres·siv·i·ty** \,prō,greˈsivəd·ē\ *n* -ES **:** PROGRESSIVENESS

**progress payment** *n* **:** a partial payment made under a construction contract as the project goes forward

**progs** *pres 3d sing of* PROG, *pl of* PROG

**pro·guan·il** \prōˈgwänəl\ *n* -s [iso*propyl* + *guan*ine + *-il*] **:** CHLOROGUANIDE

**progue** \ˈprōg\ *var of* PROG

**pro·gymnosperm** \(ˈ)prō+\ *n* [¹*pro-* + *gymnosperm*] **:** one of the ancestral fossil types from which modern gymnosperms are thought to have been derived — **progymnospermic** \(ˌ)prō+\ *adj* — **progymnospermous** \ˈ"+\ *adj*

**pro·haptor** \(ˈ)prō+\ *n* -s [NL, fr. ¹*pro-* + *haptor*] **:** the complex anterior attachment organ of a typical monogenetic trematode

**pro·hib·it** \prōˈhibət, prəˈ-, *usu* -bəd.+V\ *vt* -ED/-ING/-S [ME *prohibiten*, fr. L *prohibitus*, past part. of *prohibēre* to hold back, hinder, forbid, fr. *pro-* forward, forth + *-hibēre* (fr. *habēre* to hold, have) — more at PRO-, GIVE] **1 :** to forbid by authority or command **:** ENJOIN, INTERDICT ⟨the statute . . . ~*ed* the employment of workers under 16 years — *Amer. Guide Series: N.C.*⟩ **2 a :** to prevent from doing or accomplishing something **:** effectively stop ⟨children should be ~*ed* from riding bicycles on the sidewalk⟩ **b :** to make impossible **:** DEBAR, HINDER, PRECLUDE ⟨family finances ~*ed* his going to college —*Current Biog.*⟩ **syn** see FORBID

**prohibited degree** *n* **:** FORBIDDEN DEGREE

**pro·hib·it·er** \-bəd·ə(r), -bətə-\ *n* -s **:** one that prohibits

**pro·hi·bi·tion** \,prōəˈbishən, ,prōhəˈ-\ *n* -s [ME *prohibicioun*, fr. MF *prohibition*, fr. L *prohibition-, prohibitio*, fr. *prohibitus* (past part of *prohibēre* to prohibit) + *-ion-, -io* -ion — more at PROHIBIT] **1 :** WRIT OF PROHIBITION **2 :** the act of prohibiting by or as if by authority **3 :** a declaration or injunction forbidding an action **:** an order to restrain or stop ⟨enforcing many ~*s* against his settlers concerning trade, crops, and occupations —*Amer. Guide Series: Del.*⟩ ⟨don't often issue positive ~*s* in my capacity of superior officer —S.E.White⟩ **4 a :** the forbidding by law of the sale and sometimes the manufacture of alcoholic liquors as beverages **b :** the forbidding by law of the transportation as well as the manufacture and sale of intoxicating liquors except for medicinal and sacramental purposes

**pro·hi·bi·tion·ist** \-sh(ə)nəst\ *n* -s **:** one who favors the prohibition of the sale or manufacture of alcoholic liquors as beverages: as **a** *usu cap* **:** a member of a minor U.S. political party that has as its fundamental platform the prohibition by law of the manufacture, importation, transportation and sale of alcoholic beverages **b :** a supporter of the 18th Amendment to the Constitution

**pro·hib·i·tive** \prōˈhibəd·iv, prəˈ-, -bətiv\ *adj* [F *prohibitif*, fr. LL *prohibitivus*, fr. L *prohibitus* (past part. of *prohibēre* to prohibit) + *-ivus* -ive — more at PROHIBIT] **1 :** tending to prohibit or interdict **:** restraining from a desired course or action ⟨the ~ power of the police⟩ **2 :** serving to preclude the use of something — usu. used of a price or a tax ⟨the price . . . was almost ~ —A.G.DuMez⟩ ⟨the rise of ~ taxes and inheritance dues —F.B.Millett⟩

**prohibitive impediment** *n* **:** the impediment to a marriage whose existence does not nullify the marriage but subjects the parties to punishment

**pro·hib·i·tive·ly** \-əvlē\ *adv* **:** in a prohibitive manner ⟨it is ~ time-consuming —*Biol. Abstracts*⟩

**pro·hib·i·tive·ness** \-ivnəs\ *n* -ES **:** the quality or state of being prohibitive

**pro·hib·i·tor** \-bəd·ə(r), -bətə-\ *n* -s [L fr. *prohibitus* (past part. of *prohibēre* to prohibit) + *-or* — more at PROHIBIT] **:** one that prohibits

**pro·hib·i·to·ry** \-bə,tōrē, -tȯr-, -ri\ *adj* [L *prohibitorius*, fr. *prohibitus* (past part. of *prohibēre* to prohibit) + *-orius* -ory — more at PROHIBIT] **:** PROHIBITIVE

**prohibitory injunction** *n* **:** a legal injunction granted before the merits of a case are heard restraining one party from doing some act or threatened act to the injury of another party — compare MANDATORY INJUNCTION

**pro in·di·vi·so** \(ˌ)prō,indəˈvī(,)zō\ *adv* [L] **:** for or as undivided **:** in common **:** in joint tenancy or coparcenary

**pro·japygidae** \ˌprō+\ *n pl, cap* [NL, fr. *Projapyg-, Projapyx*, type genus (fr. ¹*pro-* + *Japyg-, Japyx*) + *-idae*] **:** a small but widely distributed family of the order Entotrophi comprising minute chiefly tropical subterranean insects

**pro·jeck** \prōˈjek, prəˈ-\ *dial var of* PROJECT *vi* 1

¹**proj·ect** \ˈpräˌjekt, ˈprō-, -jəkt\ *n* -s [ME *proiecte*, modif. (influenced by L *projectus*, past part. of *proicere, projicere* to throw forth) of MF *pourjet, porjet, pourject*, fr. *pourjeter, porjeter, pourjecter* to throw out, spy, get the lay of the land, plan, fr. *pour-, por-* (fr. L *porro* forward, onward) + *jeter* to throw; akin to Gk *porrō* away, forward, *pro* forward, ahead — more at PROJECTION, FOR, JET] **1 :** a specific plan or design: as **a** *obs* **:** a tabular outline **:** DRAFT, PATTERN **b :** a devised or proposed plan **:** a scheme for which there seems hope of success **:** PROPOSAL ⟨presented his ~ to the committee⟩ ⟨he discusses his ~*s* with her —*Current Biog.*⟩ **2** *obs* **:** a mental conception **:** IDEA **3 :** a planned undertaking: as **a :** a definitely formulated piece of research **b** (1) **:** an undertaking devised to effect the reclamation or improvement of a particular area of land ⟨the construction of small irrigation ~*s* —W. O.Douglas⟩ (2) **:** the area of land involved **c :** a systematically built group of houses or apartment buildings; *esp* **:** one that includes community facilities and has been socially planned with government support to serve low-income families **d :** a vast enterprise usu. sponsored and financed by a government ⟨demands made for setting up public work ~*s* —*Amer. Guide Series: N.Y.*⟩ ⟨the ~, as authorized by Congress . . . provided for a ten-year expenditure of $88 million —*Current Biog.*⟩ **4 :** PROJET 2 **5 :** a task or problem that is engaged in usu. by a group of students to supplement and apply classroom studies and that often involves a variety of mental and physical activities related to the center of interest ⟨making a model of the Shakespearean stage is a good ~ for an English class⟩ **6 :** PROJECTION 8b (1) **syn** see PLAN

²**pro·ject** \prəˈjekt, prōˈ-\ *vb* -ED/-ING/-S [modif. (influenced by L *projectus*) of MF *pourjeter, porjeter, pourjecter*] *vt* **1 :** to devise in the mind **:** plan for **:** CONTRIVE, DESIGN ⟨a road is now ~*ed* all the way along the south side —G.R.Stewart⟩ ⟨support . . . is mighty important in ~*ing* school building programs —*Education Digest*⟩ ⟨ridiculed plants of this size when they were first ~*ed* —M.W.Straight⟩ **2 :** to throw or cast forward **:** shoot forth ⟨a fountain that ~*s* its slender column of water about 75 feet in the air —*Amer. Guide Series: N.C.*⟩ ⟨plans were made to ~ iron missiles —*Current Biog.*⟩ **3 :** to put or set forth **:** present for consideration **:** exhibit the characteristics of ⟨in these volumes I was trying to ~ how this world would have appeared —F.M.Ford⟩ ⟨doing a grand job ~*ing* Britain overseas —Asher Lee⟩ **4 :** to conceive of mentally **:** IMAGINE **5 :** to cause to protrude ⟨a tiny kitchen which had no equipment . . . visibly ~*ed* —Martin Flavin⟩ **6 a :** to cause (light or shadow) to fall into space or (an image) upon a surface ⟨these pictures have been ~*ed* on screens throughout the U.S. —*Current Biog.*⟩ **b :** to cause (a figure) to stand out distinctly against a background ⟨appeared on his doorstep, darkly ~*ed* against a blaze of light —Edith Wharton⟩ **7 a :** to move in a prescribed direction (as a point, line, or area) so as to depict on a curve, a plane, or a cylindrical, spherical, or other surface so that the picture thus represented on the curve or surface is the shadow of the points, lines, or areas that would be thrown by parallel, diverging, or converging rays of light ⟨the map maker ~*ed* the world as the section of a cylinder suspended in the center of the circular vault of heaven —Tad Szulc⟩ **b :** to depict (one figure) by another figure according to a fixed correspondence between the points of the two **8 a :** to communicate or convey vividly esp. to an audience ⟨not only sang beautifully, but ~*ed* the drama very well —Robert Evett⟩ **b :** to produce with exceptional clarity and distinctness ⟨a particularly brilliant example of the singer who knows how to ~ our language —Howard Taubman⟩ ⟨his voice is not large but . . . is ~*ed* well —W.M.Clark⟩ **9 :** to externalize and regard as objective or outside oneself (as a sensation, image, or emotion) ⟨a nation is an entity on which one can ~ many of the worst of one's instincts —*Times Lit. Supp.*⟩ — opposed to *introject* ~ *vi* **1** *chiefly dial* **a :** to form a project **:** SCHEME **b :** to go about idly with no particular purpose **:** fool around ⟨I wouldn't go ~*ing* off into the woods alone —C.B.Kelland⟩ — often used with *around* **2 :** to jut out **:** extend beyond a given line **:** PROTRUDE ⟨the walls in places ~ into massive buttresses —Andrew Finn⟩ ⟨hands ~*ed* a little too far from the sleeves —J.P.Marquand⟩ **3 a :** to communicate or convey an idea or conception vividly esp. to an audience **b :** to speak with exceptional clarity and distinction ⟨don't they ~ rather oddly . . . throwing their voice —E.R.Bentley⟩ **syn** see BULGE, ¹PLAN

³**project** *adj* [L *projectus*, past part. of *proicere*, *projicere* to throw forth, reject — more at PROJECTION] *obs* **:** ABANDONED

**pro·ject·able** \-təbəl\ *adj* **:** capable of being projected

**projected** *adj* **1 :** thrown or as if thrown or cast forward ⟨the ~ scene of the mountains brought scattered applause from the audience⟩ **2 :** planned for future execution **:** CONTRIVED, PROPOSED ⟨a ~ excursion a full day long —W.F.DeMorgan⟩ ⟨~ outlays for new plant and equipment —J.G.Forrest⟩

¹**pro·jec·tile** \prəˈjektᵊl, -k,tīl, -k(,)til, prōˈ-\ *n* -s [NL *projectilis*, fr. L *projectus* (past part. of *proicere, projicere* to throw forth) + *-ilis* -ile — more at PROJECTION] **1 :** a body projected by external force and continuing in motion by its own inertia ⟨subatomic particles used as ~*s* in atom smashing⟩; *specif* **:** a missile for a firearm, cannon, or other weapon **2 :** a self-propelling weapon (as a rocket, torpedo, or guided missile)

²**projectile** \ˈ"\ *adj* [L *projectus* (past part. of *proicere, projicere*) + E *-ile*] **1 :** caused or imparted by impulse or projection **:** impelled forward ⟨~ motion⟩ **2 :** projecting or impelling forward ⟨the great injury . . . was more owing to the gravity of the stone . . . than to the ~ force of it —Laurence Sterne⟩ ⟨his family was getting on in the world and . . . he was to receive a ~ push from them —John Dollard⟩ **3 :** capable of being hurled, thrown, or projected with force similar to a missile **4 :** capable of being thrust forward — **pro·jec·tile·ly** \-l(l)ē\ *adv*

**projectile lathe** *n* **:** a lathe for turning and pointing projectiles

**projectile point** *n* **:** a point that constitutes a projectile or projectile head (as a dart or arrowhead)

**projectile vomiting** *n* **:** vomiting that is sudden, usu. without nausea, and so sufficiently vigorous that the vomitus is forcefully projected to a distance

**projecting** *adj* **:** PROTRUSIVE ⟨low ~ eaves which keep out summer heat —D.C.Buchanan⟩

**pro·jec·tion** \prəˈjekshən, prōˈ-\ *n* -s [MF, fr. L *projection-, projectio*, fr. *projectus* (past part. of *proicere, projicere* to throw forth, throw down, stretch out, jut out, fr. *pro-* forward, down + *-icere, jicere*, fr. *jacere* to throw) + *-ion-, -io* -ion — more at PRO-, JET] **1 :** a systematic presentation of intersecting coordinate lines on a flat surface upon which features from the curved surface of the earth or the celestial sphere may be mapped — compare CONIC PROJECTION, CYLINDRICAL PROJECTION, GNOMONIC PROJECTION, MERCATOR PROJECTION, ORTHOGRAPHIC PROJECTION, STEREOGRAPHIC PROJECTION **2 a :** the casting by an alchemist of a powder into a crucible containing a metal to effect its transmutation **b :** a transforming change **3 a :** the act of throwing or shooting forward **:** EJECTION ⟨watched the ~ of the arrow⟩ **b :** the state of being thrown or shot forward **4 a :** the forming of a plan **:** SCHEMING **b :** something that is planned **:** DESIGN **5 :** the representation of something against a background (as an image or shadow) **6 a** (1) **:** a jutting out or causing to jut out (2) **:** a part that projects or juts out **:** an extension beyond something else ⟨~ of earth above its natural level —Thomas Hardy⟩ ⟨~*s* . . . in the corners reveal the heavy timber framework —*Amer. Guide Series: Mich.*⟩ **b :** a view of a building or architectural element (as a front elevation) — used esp. of architectural drawings **7 a :** the operation of projecting

**b :** the picture so formed — see AXONOMETRIC PROJECTION, OBLIQUE PROJECTION, ORTHOGRAPHIC PROJECTION, TRIMETRIC PROJECTION **c :** a segment joining the projections of the ends of a given segment upon a given line or plane **d :** the foot of a perpendicular from a point upon a line or plane **8 a** (1) **:** the act of perceiving a mental object as spatially and sensibly objective or of objectifying what is primarily subjective (2) **:** a mental object or image so perceived ⟨writing from experience or from an imaginative ~ of experience —Malcolm Cowley⟩ **b :** the act of externalizing: as (1) **:** the spontaneous localization of a sensory impression or memory image either upon the surface of the body or outside in space ⟨the ~ of an afterimage upon a wall⟩ (2) **:** the attribution to other people and to objects of one's own ideas, feelings, or attitudes; *esp* **:** the externalization of blame, guilt, or responsibility for one's thoughts or actions as an unconscious mechanism to defend the ego against anxiety ⟨delusions of persecution are based on the mechanism of ~⟩ **9 a :** the display of motion pictures by projecting an image from them upon a screen for either visual or aural review **b :** the process of projecting the image of a negative or positive for viewing on a screen or for exposing a print on a light-sensitive material **10 a :** the act of communicating or conveying a vivid image esp. to an audience ⟨she excels in genuine stage ~ —Stark Young⟩ **b :** clarity and distinctness esp. of a voice ⟨sings . . . with the rugged, compelling ~ that has brought him such success —J.S.Wilson b. 1913⟩ **11 :** the functional correspondence and connection of parts of the cerebral cortex with parts of the organism ⟨the ~ of the retina upon the visual area⟩ **12 a :** the carrying forward of a trend into the future **b :** an estimate of future possibilities based on a current trend ⟨~*s* of increases in number of households —M.D.Ketchum⟩

**pro·jec·tion·al** \-shən°l, -shnəl\ *adj* **:** of, relating to, or making use of projection

**projection area** *n* **:** an area of the cerebral cortex having connection through projection fibers with subcortical centers that in turn are linked with peripheral sense or motor organs

**projection booth** *n* **:** a usu. fireproof booth in a theater or assembly hall for housing a motion-picture or other projector

**projection fiber** *n* **:** a nerve fiber connecting some part of the cerebral cortex with lower sensory or motor centers — distinguished from *association fiber*

**projection formula** *n* **:** a perspective formula projected so as to represent it in two dimensions — compare STRUCTURAL FORMULA

COOH / H—C—$NH_2$ / $CH_2OH$ — D–serine; COOH / $H_2N$—C—H / $CH_2OH$ — L–serine

projection formula

**pro·jec·tion·ist** \-sh(ə)nəst\ *n* -s **:** one who projects or makes projections: as **a :** one skilled in the process of making projections; *esp* **:** a map maker **b :** one who operates a motion-picture projector **c :** an operator of television equipment

**projection print** *n* **:** a photographic print made by projecting the image of the negative upon light-sensitive paper — compare CONTACT PRINT

**projection television** *n* **:** a television picture that is picked up from a picture tube of relatively small size and that by means of an optical system is greatly magnified and projected on a large screen

**projection welding** *n* **:** a resistance welding made by joining embossments on one or both of the parts being welded

**pro·jec·tive** \prə'jektiv, prō'-, -tēv\ *adj* [²*project* + *-ive*] **1 :** relating to or produced by projection: as **a :** of or relating to such properties of curves or surfaces as are unaltered by projection **b :** not metrical **:** not involving size and measurement but only relative position, incidences, and coincidences **c :** transformable into one another by repeated projections and sections **2 :** jutting out **:** PROJECTING **3 a :** externalizing esp. images or ideas ⟨a victim of his own ~ imagination⟩ **b :** revealing a subjective opinion ⟨~ adjectives of approval and disapproval —N.C.Stageberg⟩ **4 :** of or relating to a technique, test, or device designed to analyze the psychodynamic constitution of an individual by presenting to him unstructured or ambiguous material (as inkblots, pictures, and sentence elements) that will elicit interpretive responses revealing his personality structure — compare RORSCHACH TEST **5 :** relating to a social mechanism through which personality traits are given expression ⟨evidence of ~ material in folklore and legends⟩

**projective geometry** *n* **:** a branch of geometry that deals with the properties of geometric configurations that are unaltered by projective transformation and in which the notion of length does not appear

**pro·jec·tive·ly** \-tə̇vlē\ *adv* **:** in a projective manner

**projective transformation** *n* **:** a transformation of space that sends points into points, lines into lines, planes into planes, and any two incident elements into two incident elements

**pro·jec·tiv·i·ty** \,prō,jek'tivəd·ē, ,prä,-\ *n* -ES **:** projective character or relation **:** the quality in one geometric figure of being derivable from another by projection **:** PROJECTIVE TRANSFORMATION

**pro·jec·tor** \prə'jektə(r), prō'-\ *n* -s [²*project* + *-or*] **1 a :** one that plans a project **b :** one that promotes a chimerical project **:** SCHEMER **2 :** one that projects: as **a :** a device for projecting a beam of light ⟨a searchlight ~⟩ **b :** an optical instrument for projecting an image upon a surface (as a screen) by means of the transmission of light through a transparent slide or film or the reflection of light from an opaque object (as a photograph or postcard) **c :** a machine for projecting and showing motion pictures on a screen — compare SOUND PROJECTOR **d :** a smooth bore weapon usu. used for launching grenades or pyrotechnic signals **3 :** a projection line (as from an object to a plane of projection) — used esp. in mechanical drawing

**projects** *pl of* PROJECT, *pres 3d sing of* PROJECT

**pro·jec·ture** \prə'jekchə(r)\ *n* -s [²*project* + *-ure*] **:** the state or fact of projecting or jutting out **:** PROJECTION

**pro·jet** \(')prō¦zhā\ *n* -s [F, project, plan, sketch — more at PROJECT] **1 :** PLAN; *esp* **:** a draft of a proposed measure or treaty **2 :** a projected or proposed design esp. when developed beyond the stage of a sketch

**pro·ji·cience** \prō'jishən(t)s\ *n* -s **1 :** the property of being projicient **:** reference of a perceived quality or modification of consciousness to an external reality **2 :** PROJECTION 8b(1)

**pro·ji·cient** \-nt\ *adj* [L *projicient-, projiciens,* pres. part. of *proicere, projicere* to jut out — more at PROJECTION] **:** serving to bring an organism into relation with the environment ⟨the ~ senses⟩ ⟨~ neuromuscular system⟩ — **pro·ji·cient·ly** *adv*

**proke** \'prōk\ *vb* [ME *proken;* akin to LG *proken* to prod, poke] **:** POKE, STIR

**pro·kei·me·non** \prō'kīmə,nän\ *n, pl* **prokeime·na** \-ˌnə\ [LGk, fr. Gk, neut. of *prokeimenos,* pres. part. of *prokeisthai* to lie before, precede, fr. *pro-* ¹pro- + *keisthai* to lie — more at CEMETERY] **:** a short anthem sung in Eastern churches before the reading of a passage from the Acts, the Epistles, or the Apocalypse

**pro·ko·pevsk** \prə'kóp(y)əfsk\ *adj, usu cap* [fr. *Prokopevsk,* U.S.S.R.] **:** of or from the city of Prokopevsk, U.S.S.R. **:** of the kind or style prevalent in Prokopevsk

**prol** *abbr* prologue

**pro·la·bi·um** \prō'lābēəm\ *n* [NL, fr. ¹*pro-* + L *labium* lip — more at LIP] **:** the exposed part of a lip; *esp* **:** the protuberant central part of the upper lip

**pro·labor** \(')prō+\ *adj* [²*pro-* + *labor*] **:** favoring or supporting a labor union or organized labor ⟨~ legislation⟩

**pro·lac·tin** \prō'laktən\ *n* -s [²*pro-* + *lact-* + *-in*] **:** LACTOGENIC HORMONE

**pro·lam·in** \prō'lamən, 'prōləmən\ *or* **pro·lam·ine** \-mən, -,mēn\ *n* -s [ISV *proline* + *ammonia* + *-in, -ine*] **:** any of a class of simple proteins (as zein, gliadin, hordein) that are found esp. in seeds and are soluble in relatively strong alcohol but insoluble in absolute alcohol, water, and neutral solvents

**pro·lan** \'prō,lan\ *n* -s [G, fr. L *proles* offspring, progeny — more at PROLETARIAN] **:** either of two gonadotrophic hormones: **a** *or* **prolan A :** FOLLICLE-STIMULATING HORMONE **b** *or* **prolan B :** LUTEINIZING HORMONE

**¹pro·lapse** \prō'laps, '=,=\ *n* [NL *prolapsus,* fr. LL, fall, fr. L *prolapsus,* past part. of *prolabi* to slide forward, fall down, fr. *pro-* forward, down + *labi* to slide, fall — more at PRO-, SLEEP] **1 :** the falling down of an internal part of the body ⟨~ of the uterus⟩ **2 :** the slipping of a body part from its usual position in relation to other parts ⟨~ of an intervertebral disc⟩

**²prolapse** \"\ *vi* **:** to fall or slip forward, down, or out (as in a prolapse)

**pro·lap·sis** \prō'lapsə̇s\ *n* -ES [alter. of NL *prolapsus*] **:** PROLAPSE

**pro·lap·sus** \-səs\ *n* -ES [NL — more at PROLAPSE] **:** PROLAPSE

**pro·larva** \(')prō+\ *n* [¹*pro-* + *larva*] **:** a newly hatched fish in which the mouth parts are undeveloped and nutrition is from the yolk sac — **pro·larval** \"+\ *adj*

**¹pro·late** \prō'lāt\ *vt* [L *prolatus,* suppletive past part. of *proferre* to utter, extend] *archaic* **:** to utter or pronounce esp. with prolonged or drawling enunciation ⟨for the sake of . . . solemnity, every note was *prolated* in one uniform mode of intonation —William Mason⟩

**²pro·late** \(')prō¦lāt\ *adj* [L *prolatus* (suppletive past part. of *proferre* to bring forward, utter, extend), fr. *pro-* forward + *latus,* suppletive past part. of *ferre* to bear — more at PRO-, BEAR] **1 :** stretched out **:** EXTENDED; *esp* **:** elongated in the direction of a line joining the poles — opposed to *oblate* **2 :** PROLATIVE — **pro·late·ly** *adv* — **pro·late·ness** *n* -ES

**prolate spheroid** *n* [²*prolate*] **:** an ellipsoid of revolution generated by revolving an ellipse about its major axis

**pro·la·tion** \prō'lāshən\ *n* -s [L *prolation-, prolatio,* fr. *prolatus* + *-ion-, -io* -ion] **1** *obs* **:** UTTERANCE ⟨the ~ of the words of benediction —John Lloyd⟩ **2 :** the division of musical notes in mensural notation into duple or triple time

**pro·la·tive** \prō'lād·iv\ *adj* [L *prolatus* + E *-ive*] **:** serving to extend or complete the predication — **pro·la·tive·ly** \-ə̇vlē\ *adv*

**prole** \'prōl(i)\ *n* -s [short for *proletarian*] *chiefly Brit* **:** a member of the proletariat ⟨the ~*s* . . . perform routine tasks of work —Irving Howe⟩

**pro·leg** \'prō+,=\ *n* [²*pro-* + *leg*] **:** a fleshy leg found on the abdominal segments of the larvae of lepidopterans, sawflies, and some other insects

**pro·le·gom·e·non** \,prōlə'gämə,nän, -nən\ *n, pl* **prolegome·na** \-nə\ *sometimes sing in constr* [Gk, neut. pres. passive part. of *prolegein* to say beforehand, fr. *pro-* ¹pro- + *legein* to say — more at LEGEND] **1 :** prefatory remarks or introductory observations; *specif* **:** a formal essay or critical discussion serving to introduce and interpret an extended work ⟨the *prolegomena* to a work on Shakespeare's dramatic structure —E.T.Sehrt⟩ **2 :** a reading or group of readings or intellectual exercises leading to further understanding, development, or advance in knowledge or technique in a subject matter field **:** INTRODUCTION ⟨fundamental points . . . constitute a ~ to any future philosophy of criticism —Morris Weitz⟩ ⟨working out the *prolegomena* to a new technique of communication —*Monthly*⟩ ⟨serves as a full-length *prolegomena* to a new phase in our way of thinking about the relation of science to society —*Times Lit. Supp.*⟩

**pro·le·gom·e·nous** \¦=;=¦==nəs\ *adj* [*prolegomenon* + *-ous*] **:** of, relating to, or having the characteristics of a prolegomenon

**pro·lep·sis** \prō'lepsə̇s *chiefly Brit* -lēp-\ *n, pl* **prolep·ses** \-p,sēz\ [Gk *prolēpsis* anticipation, preconception, fr. *prolambanein* to take beforehand, anticipate, fr. *pro-* ¹pro- + *lambanein* to take — more at LATCH] **1 :** the representation or assumption of a future act or development as being presently existing or accomplished **:** PROCHRONISM ⟨that ~, or prevision and apprehension of holiness which we call faith —Wilham Sunday⟩ **2 a :** a figure in which a matter is set forth in summary before being stated or related in detail ⟨a relation by ~, anticipation of the story —L.D.Lerner⟩ **b :** a figure by which objections are anticipated in order to weaken their force ⟨thought it needful . . . by way of ~, to prevent whatsoever might be surmised in that kind —Robert Sanderson⟩ **c :** the use of an attribute to denote a future condition or development as existing or occurrent when it is actually consequential (as in "ere humane statute purged the *gentle* weal") **:** anticipative use of an adjective **3 a :** a conception or belief derived from sense perception and therefore regarded as not necessarily true **b :** an empirical general conception — used esp. in Stoicism and Epicureanism **4 :** PRESUPPOSITION, POSTULATE ⟨that nature should form real shells, without any design of covering an animal, is contrary to that innate ~ we have of the prudence of nature —John Ray⟩

**pro·lep·tic** \(')prō¦leptik *chiefly Brit* -lēp-\ *also* **pro·lep·ti·cal** \-tə̇kəl\ *adj* [*proleptic* fr. Gk *prolēptikos,* fr. (assumed) *prolēptos* (verbal of *prolambanein* to anticipate) + *-ikos* -ic; *proleptical* fr. Gk *prolēptikos* + E *-al*] **:** of, relating to, or exemplifying prolepsis ⟨a ~ justification of the line he was to take —R.F.Harrod⟩ ⟨a ~ interpretation by the prophet of the future events —Georges Florovsky⟩ ⟨and he will move breathing through us wing-linked ~ of what Eden —Denis Devlin⟩ — **pro·lep·ti·cal·ly** \-tək(ə)lē\ *adv*

**¹pro·le·tar·i·an** \,prōlə'terēən, -ta(a)r-, -tār-\ *n* -s [L *proletarius* proletarian (fr. *proles* offspring, progeny, fr. *pro-* forth + root of *-olescere* to grow) + E *-an* — more at PRO-, ADULT] **:** a member of the proletariat

**²proletarian** \"\ *adj* [¹*proletarian*] **:** of, relating to, or representative of the proletariat ⟨~ policy⟩ ⟨~ party⟩ ⟨~ literature⟩ ⟨~ background⟩ — opposed to *proprietarian*

**proletarian dictatorship** *n* **:** DICTATORSHIP OF THE PROLETARIAT

**pro·le·tar·i·an·ism** \,=;='==ə,nizəm\ *n* -s [*proletarian* + *-ism*] **:** the condition or political position of a proletarian

**pro·le·tar·i·an·i·za·tion** \,=;=;==ənə̇'zāshən, -,nī'z-\ *n* -s [*proletarianize* + *-ation*] **:** a change or shift to the status or level of the proletariat ⟨the ~ of the middle class —Daniel Lang⟩ ⟨a ~ of taste both in language and literature —Gilbert Murray⟩

**pro·le·tar·i·an·ize** \,=='==ə,nīz\ *vt* -ED/-ING/-S [¹*proletarian* + *-ize*] **:** to cause to undergo proletarianization ⟨has *proletarianized* the ruling minority —*Atlantic*⟩

**pro·le·tar·i·an·ly** *adv* **:** in a proletarian manner **:** according to proletarian sympathies or predilections

**pro·le·tar·i·an·ness** \-n(n)ə̇s\ *n* -ES **:** the quality or state of being proletarian

**¹pro·le·tar·i·at** *also* **pro·le·tar·i·ate** \,prōlə'terēə\|t, -ta(a)r-, -tār-, *sometimes* -ē,a|; *usu* |d·+V\ *n, pl* **proletariat** *also* **proletariate** [F *prolétariat,* fr. L *proletarius* proletarian + F *-at* -ate] **1 :** the lowest social and economic class in ancient Rome **2 :** the lowest social or economic class of a community ⟨a discontented ~ —*No. Amer. Rev.*⟩ ⟨savage ~ —Count Moffie⟩ **3 :** the laboring class **:** WAGE EARNERS; *specif* **:** the industrial workers — compare ARISTOCRACY, BOURGEOISIE **4** *in Marxist doctrine* **:** the class of wage earners who lack their own means of production and hence sell their labor to live

**²proletariat** *or* **proletariate** \"\ *adj* [¹*proletariat*] **:** PROLETARIAN

**pro·le·tar·i·za·tion** \,prōlə,terə̇'zāshən, -,rī'z-\ *n* -s [*proletarize* + *-ation*] **:** PROLETARIANIZATION

**pro·le·tar·ize** \,prōlə'te,rīz\ *vt* -ED/-ING/-S [*proletary* + *-ize*] **:** PROLETARIANIZE

**pro·le·tary** \'prōlə,terē\ *n or adj* [L *proletarius* — more at PROLETARIAN] **:** PROLETARIAN

**pro·let·cult** *also* **pro·let·kult** \prō'let,kəlt\ *n* -s [Russ *proletkul't,* fr. *proletarskaya kul'tura,* proletarian culture] **:** a movement in the U. S. S. R. to foster an art and a culture expressive of proletarian interests and activities

**pro·leucocyte** *or* **pro·leukocyte** \(')prō+\ *n* [F, fr. *pro-* ¹pro- + *leucocyte*] **1 :** LEUKOBLAST **2 :** a basophilic immature cell of insect blood that gives rise to other kinds of blood cells

**proli-** *comb form* [L *proles* offspring, progeny — more at PROLETARIAN] **:** offspring ⟨*prolicidal*⟩ ⟨*proligerous*⟩

**pro·lif·er·ant** \prō'lifərənt\ *adj* [fr. ¹*proliferate,* after such pairs as E *militate: militant*] **:** PROLIFIC

**¹pro·lif·er·ate** \-ə,rāt, *usu* -ād·+V\ *vb* -ED/-ING/-S [back-formation fr. *proliferation*] *vi* **1 :** to grow by proliferation ⟨the nerve tips ~ —F.A.Geldord⟩ **2 :** to increase in numbers as if by proliferation **:** BURGEON, EXPAND, MULTIPLY, SPREAD ⟨had *proliferated* into eleven subsidiary agencies —*Time*⟩ ⟨fantasies ~ where facts are few —Weston La Barre⟩ ⟨buildings which . . . ~ farther back —*Fortune*⟩ ~ *vt* **1 :** to cause to grow by proliferation **2 :** to cause to increase in numbers as if by proliferation **:** produce abundantly ⟨that fellow *proliferated* ideas —H.J.Laski⟩ ⟨tendency to ~ jobs and men —J.K.Galbraith⟩

**²pro·lif·er·ate** \-rə̇t, -,rāt, *usu* -d·+V\ *adj* [back-formation fr. *proliferation*] **:** developing a leafy shoot from a normally terminal organ — used esp. of a flower

**pro·lif·er·a·tion** \=,=='rāshən\ *n* -s [F *prolifération,* fr. *proliférer* to proliferate (fr. *prolifère* proliferous, fr. *proli-* + *-fère* -ferous) + *-ation*] **1 a :** rapid and repeated production of new parts or of buds or offspring (as in a mass of cells by a rapid succession of cell divisions or in a coral by the production of buds in quick succession) **b :** a growth so formed **2 :** the action, process, or result of increasing by or as if by proliferation ⟨the ~ of subjects taught —S.A.Rice⟩ ⟨the ~ of error —Norman Cousins⟩ ⟨~ and fragmentation of parties —Geoffrey Sawer⟩

**pro·lif·er·a·tive** \=''==,rād·iv, -ātiv\ *adj* [¹*proliferate* + *-ive*] **1 :** capable of or engaged in proliferation **2 :** of, marked by, or tending to proliferation

**pro·lif·er·ous** \-f(ə)rəs\ *adj* [*proli-* + *-ferous*] **1** *obs* **:** PROLIFIC 1a **2 a :** reproducing freely by offsets, bulbils, gemmae, or other vegetative means **b :** PROLIFERATE **3 :** PROLIFERATING; *specif* **:** producing a cluster of branchlets from a larger branch — used of coral — **pro·lif·er·ous·ly** *adv*

**pro·lif·ic** \prə¦lifik, prō¦, |fēk\ *adj* [F *prolifique,* fr. L *proles* offspring + F *-fique* -fic — more at PROLETARIAN] **1 a :** capable of reproducing or generating ⟨the domestic cat begins . . . to reproduce by the end of the first year of her life, and she is ~ to her ninth —S.G.J.Mivart⟩ **b** (1) **:** abundantly and quickly reproductive or generative **:** FECUND, FRUITFUL ⟨flying foxes are extremely ~ —J.G.Frazer⟩ ⟨the ~ hyacinth . . . is a curse to boatmen —*Lamp*⟩ (2) **:** marked by an abundance **:** copiously productive — usu. used with *in* or *of* ⟨~ of ferns —*Amer. Guide Series: Ark.*⟩ ⟨~ of illusion —H.J. Muller⟩ ⟨the waterside is ~ of such heroes —G.B.Shaw⟩ ⟨~ in the production of scientists —W.A.Noyes b. 1898⟩ **2 :** occurring or existing in large numbers **:** ABUNDANT, PROFUSE ⟨contour leather belts . . . are ~ here —Lois Long⟩ ⟨the achievements of . . . western art are both ~ and illustrious —P.A.Sorokin⟩ ⟨both books contain ~ references —W.G.V. Balchin⟩ **3** *archaic* **:** helpful to or causing abundant growth, generation, or reproduction ⟨the ~ sun, and the sudden and rank plenty which his heat engenders —R.W.Emerson⟩ **4 :** marked by abundant and often rapid productivity ⟨his ~ output as a research worker —*Chronica Botanica*⟩ ⟨a ~ writer —J.T.Adams⟩ ⟨the most ~ contributor —Lucile E. Hoyme⟩ **syn** see FERTILE

**pro·lif·i·ca·cy** \-fə̇kəsē, -fēk-, -si\ *n* -ES [*prolific* + *-acy* (as in *efficacy*)] **:** the quality or state of being prolific ⟨the emergence of paperback books in a ~ unknown on these shores —*Times Lit. Supp.*⟩; *esp* **:** the quality or state of producing young in large numbers or at frequent intervals ⟨the ~ of rabbits⟩

**prolifical** *adj* [F *prolifique* + E *-al*] *obs* **:** PROLIFIC

**pro·lif·i·cal·ly** \prə¦lifə̇k(ə)lē, prō'-, -fēk-, -li\ *also* **pro·lif·ic·ly** \-klē, -li\ *adv* [*prolifically* fr. *prolifical* + *-ly; prolificly* fr. *prolific* + *-ly*] **:** in a prolific manner

**pro·lif·i·cal·ness** *n* -ES **:** PROLIFICACY

**pro·lif·i·cate** \=''=ə,kāt\ *vt* -ED/-ING/-S [*prolific* + *-ate*] **:** to make prolific **:** FERTILIZE

**pro·lif·i·ca·tion** \=,==ə'kāshən\ *n* -s [ML *prolification-, prolificatio,* fr. *prolificatus* (past part. of *prolificare* to generate young, fr. L *proles* offspring + *-ficare* to move) + L *-ion-, -io* -ion — more at PROLETARIAN, -FICATION] **1 a :** the generation of young **b :** FECUNDITY **2 :** the quality or state of being proliferous **3 :** an apical branch arising from within an inflorescence and continuing the terminal growth of the stem (as in the male inflorescence of mosses of the genus *Polytrichum*) — compare INNOVATION

**pro·li·fic·i·ty** \,prōlə'fisəd·ē\ *n* -ES [*prolific* + *-ity*] **:** prolific power or character

**pro·lif·ic·ness** *n* -ES [*prolific* + *-ness*] **:** PROLIFICACY

**pro·lig·er·ous** \prō'lijərəs\ *adj* [ISV *proli-* + *-gerous*] **1 :** producing or believed to produce living beings **2 :** PROLIFERATIVE ⟨the cyst is typically lined with a ~ membrane that buds off daughter cysts or infective scolices⟩

**pro·line** \'prō,lēn, -lə̇n\ *n* -s [G *prolin,* fr. *pyrrolidin* pyrrolidine] **:** a heterocyclic amino acid $C_4H_8NCOOH$ that is a constituent of many proteins (as gliadin, casein, zein) and is obtained therefrom by hydrolysis; 2-pyrrolidine-carboxylic acid

**pro·lix** \(')prō¦liks\ *adj* [ME, fr. MF & L; MF *prolixe,* fr. L *prolixus* extended, copious, fr. *pro-* forward + *-lixus* (akin to *liquēre* to be fluid) — more at PRO-, LIQUID] **1** *obs* **:** marked by long duration **:** PROTRACTED ⟨if the chain of consequences be a little ~ —Isaac Watts⟩ **2 a :** unduly prolonged or drawn out **:** DIFFUSE, REPETITIOUS, VERBOSE ⟨very ~, and bursting with subordinate sentences and clauses —Arnold Bennett⟩ ⟨a sprawling book, discursive and ~ —Brendan Gill⟩ ⟨~ and often loose statements —Gail Kennedy⟩ **b :** given to verbosity and diffuseness in speaking or writing **:** LONG-WINDED ⟨the author can be awkward, stiff, and ~ —*Newsweek*⟩ ⟨was ~ with his pen —J.L.Motley⟩ **3** *archaic* **:** long or extensive in measurement ⟨with wig ~, downflowing to his waist —William Cowper⟩ **syn** see WORDY

**prolixious** *adj* [irreg. fr. L *prolixus*] *obs* **:** PROLIX

**pro·lix·i·ty** \prō'liksəd·ē, -sətē, -i\ *n* -ES [ME *prolixite,* fr. MF *prolixité,* fr. L *prolixitat-, prolixitas,* fr. *prolixus* + *-itat-, -itas* -ity] **:** the quality or state of being prolix; *esp* **:** undue lengthiness in speaking or writing ⟨his facility carried him . . . into ~ —Sir Winston Churchill⟩

**pro·lix·ly** *adv* **:** in a prolix manner

**pro·lix·ness** *n* -ES [*prolix* + *-ness*] **:** PROLIXITY

**pro·lo·bous** \(')prō¦lōbəs\ *adj* [¹*pro-* + *lobe* + *-ous*] **:** set off — used of the prostomium of an annelid worm when separated by a groove from the first true segment

**pro·loc·u·lum** \prō'läkyələm\ *or* **pro·loc·u·lus** \-ləs\ *n, pl* **prolocu·la** \-lə\ *or* **prolocu·li** \-ə,lī\ [NL, fr. ¹*pro-* + *loculus*] **:** the initial chamber of a foraminiferan test

**pro·lo·cu·tion** \,prōlə'kyüshən, ,präl-\ *n* [LL *prolocution-, prolocutio* preamble, fr. L *pro-* before + *locution-, locutio* speech — more at PRO-, LOCUTION] **1** *archaic* **:** a prefatory statement **2** [²*pro-* + *locution*] *obs* **:** intentionally ambiguous language

**pro·loc·u·tor** \prō'läkyəd·ə(r), |tə(r)\ *n* -s [L, fr. *pro-* ²pro- + *locutor* speaker, fr. *locutus* (past part. of *loqui* to speak) + *-or*] **1 a :** one who speaks, pleads, or interprets for another **:** SPOKESMAN ⟨in a national crisis one . . . ~ who spoke in the name of all the estates —T.E.May⟩ **b** *Scot* **:** an advocate or legal spokesman in a court of law **2 a :** the speaker or presiding officer of the lower house of a convocation of the Church of England through whom all resolutions of the lower house are communicated to the upper house **b :** the presiding officer or chairman of a meeting or assembly

**pro·loc·u·tor·ship** \-,ship\ *n* **:** the office of a prolocutor

**pro·log·ist** \'prō,lōgə̇st, *also* -,läg- *or* -ləjə̇st\ *also* **pro·logu·ist** \'prō,lōgə̇st *also* -läg-\ *n* -s [*prologize* + *-ist*] **:** one who writes or delivers a prologue

**pro·log·ize** \-,gīz, -,jīz\ *or* **pro·logu·ize** \-,gīz\ *vi* -ED/-ING/-S [Gk *prologizein* to speak a prologue, fr. *prologos* prologue + *-izein* -ize] **:** to write or speak a prologue

**pro·lo·gos** \'prō¦lō,gäs\ *also* **pro·lo·gus** \-,gəs\ *n, pl* **prologoi** \-,gòi\ *also* **prolo·gi** \-,jī\ [Gk *prologos,* fr. *pro-* ¹pro- + *-logos* (fr. *legein* to speak) — more at LEGEND] **:** the entire part of an ancient Greek play preceding the parodos

**¹pro·logue** *also* **pro·log** \'prō,lòg *also* -läg\ *n* -s [ME *prolog, prologe,* fr. OF *prologue, prologe,* fr. L *prologus* preface to a play, speaker of the preface, fr. Gk *prologos* prologos] **1 :** the preface or introduction to a discourse, performance, or nondramatic literary work **2 a** (1) **:** a speech often in verse addressed to the audience by one or more of the actors at the opening of a play — compare EPILOGUE (2) **:** the actor speaking such a prologue **b :** the opening scene of a play whose main action is set within a separate frame **3 :** an introductory or preceding act, event, or development ⟨in the ~ of life —W.E.Swinton⟩ ⟨a ~ to her own . . . history —Hugh Walpole⟩ ⟨sacred and solemn ~s to . . . Easter Sunday are planned Maundy Thursday and Good Friday —*Springfield (Mass.) Union*⟩

**²prologue** \"\ *vt* -ED/-ING/-S : to introduce or provide with a prologue or preface ⟨~s and epilogues the selection —*Saturday Rev. (London)*⟩

**¹pro·long** \prəˈlȯŋ, prōˈ- *also* -läŋ\ *vt* -ED/-ING/-S [ME *prolongen*, fr. MF *prolonguer*, fr. LL *prolongare*, fr. L *pro-* forward + *longus* long — more at PRO-, LONG] **1** : to lengthen in time : extend in duration : draw out : CONTINUE, PROTRACT ⟨the candidacy period for party membership can be ~*ed* one year —*Americana Annual*⟩ ⟨a chance of ~*ing* his life indefinitely —J.G.Frazer⟩ ⟨enjoying the situation and wanting to ~ it —Rose Macaulay⟩ ⟨~*ed* this anxiety⟩ **2** *archaic* : to put off : DELAY, POSTPONE ⟨and the word that I shall speak shall come to pass; it shall be no more ~*ed* —Ezek 12:25 (AV)⟩ **3** : to lengthen or draw out the pronunciation of (as a syllable or sound) ⟨no matter how long you ~ the "i" of "bit" — "b-i-i-i-t" — you never get the "i" of "police" —Weston LaBarre⟩ **4** : to lengthen in extent, scope, or range ⟨habitually ~*s* a sentence thus until it has covered the unit of its subject —R.M. Weaver⟩ ⟨the boundary . . . has . . . ~*ed* itself northward —Herbert Agar⟩ ⟨~ the list —F.L.Mott⟩ ⟨~*ing* the runways of the airfield —*Weekly Overseas Mail (London)*⟩ ⟨education . . . should be ~*ed* through adult years —C.W.Eliot⟩ **syn** see EXTEND

**²pro·long** \ˈprō,lȯŋ *also* -läŋ\ *n* -S : a prolonged part; *specif* : a cone of sheet iron placed over the end of the condenser in a furnace for recovering zinc by distillation

**pro·long·able** *pronunc at* ¹PROLONG + əbəl\ *adj* : capable of being prolonged

**pro·lon·gate** \prəˈlȯŋ,gāt, prōˈ- *also* -läŋ- *sometimes* ˈprō,=,= ; *usu* -ād.+V\ *vt* -ED/-ING/-S [LL *prolongatus*, past part. of *prolongare* to prolong] : PROLONG

**pro·lon·ga·tion** \(,)prō,lȯŋˈgāshən prə,- *also* -läŋ-\ *n* -S [MF, fr. LL *prolongation-, prolongatio*, fr. *prolongatus* + L *-ion-, -io* -ion] **1 a** : an extension or lengthening in time or duration ⟨the indefinite ~ of the Korean truce talks —Joseph & Stewart Alsop⟩ **b** : the continuation or protraction of a spoken syllable or sound ⟨the principle of ~ —H.W.Smyth⟩ **2** : an expansion or continuation in extent, scope, or range ⟨a northwesterly ~ into the plain of Lancastria —L.D. Stamp⟩ ⟨a ~ of ourselves —*Time Lit. Supp.*⟩ ⟨water and plants . . . became a part and ~ of the structures conceived by the architect —José Gómez-Sicre⟩ ⟨treats literature . . . as a ~ (of the past) rather than as an original creation —Wallace Fowlie⟩

**pro·longe** \prōˈlänj\ *n* -S [F, fr. *prolonger* to prolong, draw out, fr. MF *prolonguer*] : a rope with a hook and a toggle used chiefly for dragging a gun carriage or attaching it to the limber

**pro·long·er** \prəˈlȯŋə(r), prōˈ-\ *n* -S [*prolong* + *-er*] : one that prolongs

**pro·long·ment** \-mənt\ *n* -S [*prolong* + *-ment*] : PROLONGATION

**pro·lo·ther·a·py** \ˌprōlōˈtherəpē, -pi\ *n* [L *proles* progeny + E *-o-* + *therapy* — more at PROLETARIAN] : the rehabilitation of an incompetent structure (as a ligament or tendon) by the induced proliferation of new cells

**pro·lu·sion** \prōˈlüzhən *also* prōlˈyü-\ *n* -S [L *prolusion-, prolusio* prelude, preliminary exercise, fr. *prolusus* (past part. of *proludere* to play or practice beforehand, fr. *pro-* before + *ludere* to play) + *-ion-, -io* -ion — more at LUDICROUS] **1** : an exercise or trial preliminary to a contest or performance : PRELUDE, WARM-UP ⟨useth . . . no ~ after the manner of fencers —Daniel Featley⟩ **2** : an introductory and often tentative discourse : PREFACE, PROLOGUE ⟨~s on the Pentateuch —J.R.Lowell⟩ ⟨all this . . . ~ is only to enable you to understand —W.H.Hudson †1922⟩ ⟨his ~ on the style of the most famous among the ancient Latin poets —Joseph Addison⟩

**pro·lu·so·ry** \-üs(ə)rē, -üz(-, -ri\ *adj* [LL *prolusorius* (MS var. of *perlusorius* sportive), fr. L *prolusus* + *-orius* -ory] : of, relating to, or having the characteristics of a prolusion

**pro·lyl** \ˈprō,lil\ *n* -S [ISV *proline* + *-yl*] : the univalent acid radical $C_4H_8NCO-$ of proline

**pro·lymphocyte** \(ˈ)prō+\ *n* [¹*pro-* + *lymphocyte*] : LYMPHOBLAST

**prom** \ˈpräm\ *n* -S [short for *promenade*] **1** : a formal dance given by a high school or college class ⟨junior ~⟩ **2** *chiefly Brit* : PROMENADE CONCERT

**prom** *abbr* **1** prominent **2** promontory **3** promoted

**pro·mammal** \(ˈ)prō+\ *n* [¹*pro-* + *mammal*] **1** : an extinct reptile exhibiting definite mammalian characteristics; *esp* : a synapsid reptile **2 a** : a primitive mammal (as a platypus) not exhibiting all the characteristics of the group **b** : one of the Protomammalia

**pro·mammalia** \ˌprō+\ *n pl, cap* [NL, fr. ¹*pro-* + *mammalia*] : a hypothetical group often treated as a subclass and comprising animals immediately ancestral to the true mammals — **promammalian** \"+\ *adj*

**pro·ma·zine** \ˈprōmə,zēn\ *n* -S [*promethazine*] : a basic compound $C_{17}H_{20}N_2S$ derived from phenothiazine and administered as the hydrochloride similarly to chlorpromazine

**pro·megaloblast** \(ˈ)prō+\ *n* [¹*pro-* + *megaloblast*] : a cell that produces megaloblasts and is possibly equivalent to a hemocytoblast

**pro me·mo·ria** \ˌprōməˈmōrēə, -ˈmȯr-\ *n, pl* **pro memoria** [L, for the sake of memory] : a formal note embodying the written record of a diplomatic discussion

**¹prom·e·nade** \ˌpräməˈnād, -nād, -nȧd\ *n* -S [F, fr. *promener* to take for a walk (fr. L *prominare* to drive forward, fr. *pro-* forward + *minare* to drive) + *-ade* — more at PRO-, AMENABLE] **1** : a leisurely walk or ride esp. in a public place for pleasure, display, or exercise ⟨daily ~ through the park⟩ **2 a** : a place for strolling : a public walk **b** : a passage, gallery, or extended balcony on a building **c** : PROMENADE DECK **3 a** : a ceremonious opening of a formal ball consisting of a grand march or polonaise in which all the guests participate **b** : a square-dance figure in which the couples walk counterclockwise around the square usu. side by side with the woman on the outside **c** : PROM 1 **4** : PROMENADE CONCERT

**²promenade** \"\ *vb* -ED/-ING/-S *vi* **1** : to take or go on a promenade : stroll esp. in public **2** : to perform a promenade in a dance ~ *vt* **1** : to walk about in or on ⟨had the privilege of *promenading* the gardens —C.G.Bowers⟩ **2** : to display in or as if in a promenade : PARADE

**promenade concert** *n* : an orchestral concert during which the audience stands or promenades

**promenade deck** *n* : an upper deck or an area on a deck of a passenger ship where passengers promenade — called also *hurricane deck*; see DECK illustration

**prom·e·nad·er** \ˌ=ˈ=ˈdə(r)\ *n* -S : one who promenades

**promenade tile** *n* : QUARRY TILE

**pro·meristem** \(ˈ)prō+\ *n* [¹*pro-* + *meristem*] : the portion of a primary meristem that contains actively dividing, undifferentiated, isodiametric thin-walled cells and their most recent derivatives — compare DERMATOGEN, GROUND MERISTEM, PROCAMBIUM

**promerit** *vt* [L *promeritus*, past part. of *promerēre, promerēri* to deserve, merit, fr. *pro-* in behalf of + *merēre, merēri* to earn — more at PRO-, MERIT] *obs* : to win or deserve the favor of (God)

**pro·metaphase** \(ˈ)prō+\ *n* [*pro-* + *metaphase*] : a stage sometimes distinguished between the prophase and metaphase of mitosis and characterized by disappearance of the nuclear membrane and formation of the spindle

**pro·methazine** \"+\ *n* -S [*propyl* + *dimethylamine* + *phenothiazine*] : a crystalline antihistaminic drug $C_{17}H_{20}N_2S$ derived from phenothiazine and used chiefly in the form of its hydrochloride

**pro·me·thea moth** \prə|ˈmēthēə-,prō|\ *also* **pro·me·theus moth** \-thēəs-, -,th(y)üs-\ *n* [*promethea* fr. NL, fr. L, fem. of *prometheus* Promethean; *prometheus* fr. Gk *Promētheus*] : a large American saturniid silkworm moth (*Callosamia promethea*) having the wings and body chiefly smoky brown in the male and reddish brown in the female and a larva that feeds on sassafras, wild cherry, and other trees and suspends its cocoon from a branch by a silken band — compare CECROPIA MOTH

**pro·me·thean** \-thēən, -thyən\ *adj, usu cap* [L *prometheus* Promethean (fr. Gk *promētheios*, fr. *Promētheus* Prometheus, the Titan pioneer of civilization) + E *-an*] : of, relating to, or resembling Prometheus, his experiences, or his art; *esp* : daringly original or originative ⟨the painter's true *Promethean* craft —William Wordsworth⟩ ⟨there will always be nonconformists, bitter rebels, *Promethean* pioneers —C.I.Glicksberg⟩

**pro·me·thi·um** \-thēəm\ *n* -S [NL, fr. *Prometheus* + NL *-ium*] : a metallic element of the rare-earth group with no stable isotope occurring naturally that was discovered in radioactive form as a fission product of uranium, that has been obtained also from neutron-irradiated neodymium, and that shows chemical properties of other rare-earth elements — symbol *Pm*; see ELEMENT table

**pro mil·le** \(ˈ)prōˈmi(,)lē\ *adv* (*or adj*) [LL] : per thousand

**Pro·min** \ˈprōmən\ *trademark* — used for glucosulfone

**prom·i·nence** \ˈprämənən(t)s *sometimes* -mnə-\ *n* -S [F, fr. L *prominentia*, fr. *prominent-, prominens* prominent + *-ia* -y] **1** : the quality, state, or fact of being prominent or conspicuous : SALIENCE ⟨as the war progressed, the doctrine of national self-determination acquired greater ~ —Oscar Handlin⟩ : DISTINCTION, IMPORTANCE ⟨men of considerable ~ in the world of letters were offered the editorship —*Saturday Rev.*⟩ ⟨which syllable has the greater ~ in ordinary pronunciation⟩ **2** : something prominent : a salient point : PROJECTION, PROTUBERANCE ⟨ricochet of the whole over pits and ~*s* —Thomas Hardy⟩ **3 a** : a mass of gas that resembles a cloud, arises or erupts from the chromosphere of the sun, and is seen in monochromatic light of hydrogen or calcium as dark against the solar surface or bright if protruding from the sun's limb **b** : a similar feature of any star

**prom·i·nen·cy** \-nənsē\ *n* -ES [L *prominentia*] : PROMINENCE

**¹prom·i·nent** \-nənt\ *adj* [L *prominent-, prominens*, fr. pres. part. of *prominēre* to jut out, project, fr. *pro-* forward + *-minēre* (akin to L *mont-, mons* mountain) — more at PRO-, MOUNT] **1** : standing out or projecting beyond a surface or line : appearing in high relief : JUTTING, PROTUBERANT ⟨a very ~ nose⟩ ⟨eyes sunken under ~ brows⟩ ⟨the most ~ peak in a range⟩ **2** : distinctly manifest to the senses : readily noticeable : CONSPICUOUS, STRIKING ⟨the tower forms a ~ landmark⟩ ⟨~ diagnostic symptom⟩ ⟨~ fault in our reading and thinking —F.L.Mott⟩ **3** : NOTABLE, LEADING, EMINENT ⟨~ men of the town⟩ ⟨~ singers⟩ ⟨a family long ~ in that region⟩ **syn** see NOTICEABLE

**²prominent** \"\ *n* -S [¹*prominent*; fr. the hump or prominence on the back of the larva] : a moth of the family Notodontidae

**prom·i·nent·ly** *adv* : in a prominent manner ⟨his picture was ~ displayed in newspapers⟩

**prom·is·cu·i·ty** \ˌprämə'skyüəd·ē, ˌprō,mi'-, -ətē, -i\ *n* -ES [F *promiscuité*, fr. L *promiscuus* + F *-ité* -ity] **1 a** : indiscriminate mingling : PROMISCUOUSNESS ⟨why do we not find indicative and subjunctive interchanging in complete ~ —Adelaide Hahn⟩ **b** : a brief or random social exchange or relation ⟨in the informal *promiscuities* which followed the prize distribution —Arnold Bennett⟩ **2** : promiscuous sexual union

**pro·mis·cu·ous** \prəˈmiskyəwəs\ *adj* [L *promiscuus*, fr. *pro-* forward + *miscēre* to mix — more at PRO-, MIX] **1** : consisting of a heterogeneous or haphazard mixture of persons or things : composed of all sorts and conditions ⟨~ crowd of people⟩ ⟨~ collection of curios⟩ ⟨involving plates, cups and saucers, in one ~ ruin —T.L.Peacock⟩ **2** : not restricted to one class, sort, or person : INDISCRIMINATE ⟨~ soliciting of funds⟩ ⟨rather than a ~ acceptance of all our impulses as good —M. R.Cohen⟩ ⟨~ destruction by bombing⟩; *specif* : not restricted to one sexual partner ⟨cases where women who have abandoned the habit of ~ intercourse confine themselves to one man by marriage or cohabitation —W.W.Sanger⟩ ⟨gray squirrels are ~ in their breeding habits —R.E.Trippensee⟩ **3** : CASUAL, CARELESS, IRREGULAR, RANDOM ⟨~ eating habits⟩ — **pro·mis·cu·ous·ness** *n* -ES

**pro·mis·cu·ous·ly** *adv* : in a promiscuous manner : INDISCRIMINATELY ⟨read continually and ~⟩ ⟨cautioned about . . . riding ~ across country —W.F.Brown b. 1903⟩

**¹prom·ise** \ˈpräməs\ *n* -S [ME *promis, promise*, fr. L *promissum*, fr. neut. of *promissus*, past part. of *promittere* to send forth, promise, fr. *pro-* forth + *mittere* to send — more at PRO-, SMITE] **1 a** : a declaration that one will do or refrain from doing something specified ⟨never gave a ~ that he did not intend to keep⟩ ⟨miserable record of broken ~*s*⟩ ⟨effort of the Conservative government to validate its ~ to denationalize the steel industry —Alzada Comstock⟩ **b** : an undertaking however expressed that something will happen or that something will not happen in the future; *specif* : a declaration that gives the person to whom it is made a right to expect or to claim the performance or forbearance of a specified act — compare AGREEMENT, CAUSE, CONSIDERATION, CONTRACT, PACT **c** : a formal pledge of loyalty to various aims required by an organization ⟨the Girl Scout ~⟩ **2 a** : ground for expectation usu. of success, improvement, or excellence ⟨young poets of ~⟩ ⟨our time is . . . poised between ~ and despair —Norman Cousins⟩ **b** : appearance, character, or quality that gives or seems to give such ground of expectation ⟨book shows ~ of popular appeal —R.G. Albion⟩ **3** : something that is promised ⟨I'll claim that — at your Grace's hand —Shak.⟩

**²promise** \"\ *vb* -ED/-ING/-S [ME *promisen*, fr. *promis*, n.] *vt* **1** : to engage to do or bring about (as something desired or pleasing) : give assurance or promise of ⟨*promised* to be careful⟩ ⟨*promised* assistance whenever it should be needed⟩ ⟨*promised* his son a new bicycle⟩ ⟨*promised* the court to be ready⟩ ⟨~ me that you will tell no one⟩ **2** *archaic* : to affirm to someone the truth or certainty of (something stated) : WARRANT, ASSURE ⟨I do not like thy look, I *promise* thee —Shak.⟩ **3** *chiefly dial* : BETROTH ⟨she was happy, bein' *promised* to the son o' Farmer Brown —J. W. Riley⟩ **4** : to give ground for expecting : FORETOKEN ⟨gray skies *promising* rain⟩ ⟨~*s* to be the best game of the season⟩ **5** : to execute (as a note) as promisor ~ *vi* **1** : to give one's word to do or refrain from doing something specified ⟨you always ~, and you never do it⟩ **2** : to give ground for expectation : be imminent or threatening ⟨there had been a little rain, and more was *promising* —George Farwell⟩ ⟨the venture ~*s* well⟩

**syn** ENGAGE, PLEDGE, PLIGHT, COVENANT, CONTRACT: PROMISE indicates the giving of a stated assurance about some future act or action ⟨he *promised* to pay the bill⟩ ⟨she *promised* the child a new toy⟩ ⟨the amnesty *promised* by the king to political prisoners —*Current Biog.*⟩ Sometimes it signifies a giving of evidence or indication rather than a granting of one's word ⟨the child *promises* to be tall⟩ ⟨the night before it had rained and more rain was *promised* —Sherwood Anderson⟩ ENGAGE is used in formal or consequential situations to indicate a promising regarded as binding and one to be relied on, often concerning conduct over a period of time ⟨"You couldn't make some arrangement?" she asked. "*Engage* somebody to stay with him, or — or send him away?" —Ellen Glasgow⟩ ⟨*engaged* to be married⟩ PLEDGE, aside from uses in connection with drives and charities ⟨to *pledge* a dollar to a special church fund⟩, may apply to solemn binding assurance concerning a consequential matter ⟨I *pledge* allegiance to the Flag of the United States of America and to the Republic for which it stands —Francis Bellamy⟩ ⟨thirteen of the 26 delegates were *pledged* to bolt the convention —*Collier's Yr. Bk.*⟩ ⟨Austria swarmed with excited and angry men *pledged* to destroy the Church —Hilaire Belloc⟩ PLIGHT, indicating solemn promise, now exists mainly in stereotyped phrases ⟨to *plight* one's troth⟩ although it is occasionally used elsewhere ⟨if for America it is too violent a wrench to *plight* its fate with Europe —Nathaniel Peffer⟩ COVENANT stresses formality and seriousness of intent in promises ⟨*covenanted* to defeat the present conspiracy to set up a Home Rule Parliament in Ireland —Rose Macaulay⟩ ⟨the seller *covenants* to indemnify the purchaser if these provisions cannot be fulfilled⟩ CONTRACT may suggest definite agreements to be relied on in business and legal affairs ⟨the John Doe company has *contracted* to supply the equipment⟩ ⟨he *contracted* to pay the interest on his brother's debts⟩

**promised land** *n* [fr. past part. of ²*promise*; fr. the promise made to Abram in Gen 12:7] : a better country or condition : some place or thing that seems to promise final satisfaction or realization of hopes or dreams ⟨had himself explored the whole of the *promised land* to which he had led Italian painting —Roger Fry⟩

**prom·is·ee** \ˌprämə'sē\ *n* -S [²*promise* + *-ee*] : a person to whom a promise is made — contrasted with *promisor*

**prom·ise·ful** \ˈpräməsfəl\ *adj* [¹*promise* + *-ful*] : PROMISING : full of promise ⟨~ of better times to come⟩

**prom·is·er** \ˈpräməsə(r)\ *n* -S [²*promise* + *-er*] : one that promises

**promising** *adj* [fr. pres. part. of ²*promise*] : full of promise : likely to succeed or to yield good results : APT, AUSPICIOUS, LIKELY — **prom·is·ing·ly** *adv* — **prom·is·ing·ness** *n* -ES

**prom·i·sor** \ˌprämə'sȯ(ə)r, -ō(ə)\ *n* -S [²*promise* + *-or*] : one who engages or undertakes — contrasted with *promisee*

**pro·mis·sor** \prəˈmisə(r)\ *n* -S [L, promiser, fr. *promissus* + *-or*] **1** *obs* : PROMISOR **2** : PROMITTOR

**prom·is·so·ry** \ˈpräməˌsōrē, -sȯr-, -ri\ *adj* [ML *promissorius*, fr. L *promissus* (past part. of *promittere* to promise) + *-orius* -ory — more at PROMISE] **1** : containing or conveying a promise or assurance that something will be done or forborne or will probably be or happen ⟨~ oath⟩ ⟨~ speech⟩ **2** : stipulating or representing what is to happen or to be done subsequent to the time of making the contract of insurance — used of a representation, a warranty; compare AFFIRMATIVE

**promissory note** *n* : an unconditional written promise to pay on demand or at a fixed or determined future time a given sum of money to or to the order of a specified person or to bearer

**pro·mitosis** \ˌprō+\ *n* [NL, fr. ¹*pro-* + *mitosis*] : a primitive intranuclear mitosis in protistans characterized by absence of asters and the presence of a karyosome — compare HAPLOMITOSIS

**pro·mitotic** \"+\ *adj* [fr. NL *promitosis*, after NL *mitosis*: E *mitotic*] : of, relating to, or involving promitosis

**pro·mit·tor** \prōˈmid·ə(r)\ *n* -S [obs. *promit* to promise (fr. ME *promitten*, fr. L *promittere*) + *-or*] : a planet that promises in the root of a nativity something to be fulfilled when the line of direction shall be accomplished

**Promi·zole** \ˈprōmə,zōl, ˈpräm-\ *trademark* — used for thiazolsulfone

**pro·mne·sia** \präm'nēzhə\ *n* -S [NL, fr. ¹*pro-* + *-mnesia*] : PARAMNESIA b

**pro·monarchic** \ˌprō+\ *or* **pro·monarchical** \"+\ *adj* [²*pro-* + *monarchy* + *-ic, -ical*] : favoring monarchy

**pro·monocyte** \(ˈ)prō+\ *n* [¹*pro-* + *monocyte*] : a cell that produces monocytes : MONOBLAST

**promont** *n* -S [by shortening] *obs* : PROMONTORY

**prom·on·to·ried** \ˈprämən,tōrēd, -tȯr-, -rid\ *adj* [*promontory* + *-ed*] : furnished with or as if with a promontory

**prom·on·to·ry** \-rē, -ri\ *n* -ES [L, alter. (infl. by *mont-, mons* mountain & *-orium* -ory) of *promunturium*; akin to *prominēre* to jut out — more at PROMINENT] **1 a** : a high point of land or rock projecting into a body of water beyond the line of coast : HEADLAND **b** : a bluff or prominent hill overlooking or projecting into a lowland **c** : a low-lying cape **2** : a bodily prominence: as **a** : the angle of the ventral side of the sacrum where it joins the vertebra **b** : a prominence on the inner wall of the tympanum of the ear

**pro·morphology** \ˌprō+\ *n* [G *promorphologie*, fr. *pro-* ¹*pro-* + *morphologie* morphology] : the study of the organization of the egg esp. with reference to localization of subsequently developed embryonic structures

**pro·mot·abil·i·ty** \prə,mōd·əˈbilәd·ē\ *n* [*promotable* + *-ity*] : the quality or state of deserving promotion

**pro·mot·able** \=ˈmōd·əbəl, -ōtə-\ *adj* [*promote* + *-able*] : likely to be or deserving to be advanced in rank or position

**pro·mote** \prəˈmōt, *usu* -ōd·+V\ *vb* -ED/-ING/-S [L *promotus*, past part. of *promovēre* to move forward, promote, fr. *pro-* forward + *movēre* to move — more at PRO-, MOVE] *vt* **1 a** : to advance in station, rank, or honor : RAISE — opposed to *demote* **b** : to change (a pawn) into a piece by moving to the eighth rank **c** : to advance (a student) from one grade or class to the next usu. at the end of an academic year or semester **2** *obs* **a** : to inform against **b** : to put forward (as a claim) **3** *law* : to institute (as a prosecution or suit) as a common informer, or as one permitted by the ordinary to inaugurate a criminal proceeding — used chiefly in the phrase *to promote the office of the ordinary* **4 a** : to contribute to the growth, enlargement, or prosperity of : FURTHER, ENCOURAGE ⟨~ international understanding⟩ ⟨the fixity of inheritance laws . . . *promoted* extreme jealousy among potential heirs —Ralph Linton⟩ **b** : to bring or help to bring (as a business enterprise) into being : LAUNCH ⟨~ a mining company⟩ ⟨~ a prize fight⟩ **c** : to present (merchandise) for public acceptance through advertising and publicity **d** : to increase the activity of (a catalyst) by adding a small percentage of another substance; *also* : to accelerate (a reaction) by such an addition — opposed to *poison* **5** *slang* : to get possession of by doubtful means or by ingenuity ⟨saw what he could ~ by a little personal string pulling —J.G.Cozzens⟩ ⟨able to ~ a bottle of wine —R.M.Ingersoll⟩ ~ *vi* **1** *obs* : to incite someone (as to strife) **2** *obs* : to inform against someone **3** : to become a queen or other piece in chess ⟨a pawn automatically ~*s* when it reaches the eighth rank⟩ **syn** see ADVANCE

**pro·mot·ee** \prə,mōˈtē\ *n* -S [*promote* + *-ee*] : one who is raised in rank or position ⟨each man in the outfit punches the ~ in the arm, once for each pay grade —L.M.Uris⟩

**pro·mot·er** \prəˈmōd·ə(r), -ōtə-\ *n* -S [partly fr. earlier *promoter* (fr. MF & ML; MF *promoteur*, fr. ML *promotor*, fr. L *promotus* + *-or*); partly fr. *promote* + *-er*] **1 a** : one that forwards or advances : ENCOURAGER, ABETTOR ⟨~ of discord⟩ ⟨chief ~*s* of a congressional bill⟩ **b** : a person who alone or with others sets on foot and takes the preliminary steps in a scheme or undertaking for the organization of a company or the carrying out of a business project **c** : one who assumes the financial responsibilities of a sporting event (as a boxing match) including contracting with the principals, renting the site, collecting gate receipts **2** *obs* **a** : PROSECUTOR **b** : INFORMER 3 **3** *Eng law* : one who promotes a prosecution **4** *or* **pro·mo·tor** \"\ : an officer at various British universities who supervises the work of a student and presents him for a degree **5 a** : a substance that in very small amounts is able to increase the activity of a catalyst **b** *or* **promotor** : COLLECTOR 5

**promoter of the faith** [trans. of NL *promotor fidei*] : DEVIL'S ADVOCATE 1

**pro·mo·tion** \prəˈmōshən\ *n* -S [ME, fr. MF, fr. LL *promotion-, promotio*, fr. L *promotus* (past part. of *promovēre* to promote) + *-ion-, -io* -ion — more at PROMOTE] **1** : the act or fact of being raised in position or rank : PREFERMENT ⟨next in line for a ~⟩ ⟨the problem is solved by the ~ of a pawn to knight instead of queen⟩ **2 a** : the act of setting up or furthering a business enterprise ⟨~ of a stock company⟩ **b** : active furtherance of sale of merchandise through advertising or other publicity **syn** see PUBLICITY

**pro·mo·tion·al** \-shənᵊl, -shnəl\ *adj* : of, relating to, or serving the end of promotion ⟨~ civil service examinations⟩ ⟨fiercely accelerated advertising and ~ campaigns —Charles Lee⟩ ⟨~ pamphlets to attract settlers and investors —*Amer. Guide Series: N.Y.*⟩

**pro·mo·tive** \prəˈmōd·|iv, -ōt|, |ēv *also* |əv\ *adj* [*promote* + *-ive*] **1** : tending to further or encourage **2** : PROMOTIONAL — **pro·mo·tive·ness** *n* -ES

**pro·mo·tor** \prōˈmōd·ə(r)\ *n* -S [NL, fr. ML, one that advances — more at PROMOTER] : a muscle connected anteriorly to the base of each locomotor appendage in an onychophoran

**promotor fi·dei** \-ˈfīdē,ī\ *n, pl* **pro·mo·to·res fidei** \ˌprō,mōˈtōr,ēz, -tō,rēz\ [NL, lit., promoter of the faith] : DEVIL'S ADVOCATE 1

**pro·mo·to·ri·al** \ˌprō,mō¦tōrēəl, -tȯr-\ *adj* [ML *promotor* promoter, prosecutor + E *-ial*] : of or relating to a promoter

**promove** *vt* [ME *promoven*, fr. L *promovēre* — more at PROMOTE] *obs* : PROMOTE

**pro·mo·vent** \ˈprōməvənt\ *n* -S [L *promovent-, promovens*, pres. part. of *promovēre* to promote] : one who promotes a suit in an ecclesiastical court

**¹prompt** \ˈpräm(p)t\ *vt* -ED/-ING/-S [ME *prompten*, fr. ML *promptare*, fr. L *promptus* prompt] **1** : to move to action : INCITE, PROVOKE ⟨~*ed* by curiosity to open the closet⟩ ⟨his wife ~*ed* him to ask for a transfer to a new job⟩ **2** : to remind (one acting or reciting) of words or topics forgotten : assist by suggesting or uttering the next words of something forgotten or imperfectly learned : give a cue to **3** : to serve as the inciting cause of (an act or thought) : URGE, SUGGEST ⟨the answer shown by the . . . bank and turn indicator instead of the answer ~*ed* by his senses —H.G.Armstrong⟩ ⟨~*s* the question: has the danger of a severe recession passed —S.H.Slichter⟩

**²prompt** \"\ *adj* -ER/-EST [ME, fr. MF or L; MF *prompt*, fr. L *promptus* visible, ready, prompt, fr. past part. of *promere* to bring forth, take out, fr. *pro-* forth + *emere* to take, buy — more at PRO-, REDEEM] **1** : ready and quick to act as occasion demands : responding instantly : ALERT ⟨~ to retort to insults⟩ ⟨~ in obedience⟩ **2** : performed readily or immediately : given without delay or hesitation ⟨~ assistance⟩ ⟨~ decisions⟩ ⟨~ payment of bills⟩ ⟨~ delivery of goods⟩ **3** : of or relating to prompting actors ⟨as the young actor bowed and withdrew to the ~ corner —Laurence Irving⟩ **syn** see QUICK

**³prompt** \"\ *adv* : on time : PUNCTUALLY

**⁴prompt** \"\ *n* -s [in sense 1, fr. ¹*prompt*; in sense 2, fr. ²*prompt*] **1** : the act or an instance of prompting or reminding : REMINDER ⟨so regularly performed that there was no need of written ~*s* —Iona & Peter Opie⟩ **2** : a limit of time usu. equaling the free credit period given for payment of an account for goods purchased; *also* : the contract by which this time is fixed **3** : PROMPT SIDE

**promptbook** \ˈ=,=\ *n* [¹*prompt* + *book*] : a copy of a play with directions for performance used by a theater prompter

**prompt box** *n* [¹*prompt*] : a low box projecting above the floor of a stage with its opening toward the actors

**prompt call** *n* : a short simple square dance call serving as a reminder

**prompt copy** *n* : PROMPTBOOK

**prompt day** *n* [⁴*prompt*] : a day of settling accounts

**prompt·er** \ˈpräm(p)tə(r)\ *n* -s [¹*prompt* + *-er*] **1** : one that prompts : one who reminds another (as a reciter) of the words to be spoken next; *specif* : one responsible for prompting actors during performance **2** : CALLER a

**promp·ti·tude** \ˈpräm(p)tə,tüd, -tə,tyüd\ *n* -s [ME, fr. MF or LL; MF *promptitude*, fr. LL *promptitudo*, fr. L *promptus* prompt + *-i-* + *-tudo* -tude] : the quality or habit of being prompt : promptness or an instance of it : quickness in deciding, acting, or meeting obligations : ALACRITY ⟨reacted with exceptional ~ . . . to the challenge of another will —Hilaire Belloc⟩ ⟨the texts . . . should be published with the utmost ~ —*U.N. Dept. of Public Information*⟩

**promp·tive** \ˈpräm(p)tiv\ *adj* [¹*prompt* + *-ive*] : tending to prompt : PROVOCATIVE ⟨~ of very serious reflection⟩

**prompt·ly** \ˈpräm(p)tlē, -li, *rapid* -mpl-\ *adv* : in a prompt manner : at once : IMMEDIATELY, QUICKLY

**prompt·ness** \-nəs\ *n* -ES : the quality or habit of being prompt

**prompt note** *n* [⁴*prompt*] : a memorandum of a sale given by a seller to a purchaser specifying the sum to be paid and the time when payment is due

**promptscript** \ˈ=,=\ *n* [¹*prompt* + *script*] : PROMPTBOOK

**prompt side** *n* [¹*prompt*; fr. its being the usual station of the prompter] : the side of the stage to the right of an actor facing the audience; *broadly* : the side of the stage adjacent to the prompter's corner — abbr. *P.S.*

**promp·tu·ary** \ˈprämpchə,werē\ *n* -ES [LL *promptuarium* storehouse, fr. L, neut. of *promptuarius* serving for distribution, fr. *promptus* act of taking out (in the phrase *in promptu* visible, at hand) (fr. *promptus*, past part. of *promere* to take out) + *-arius* -ary — more at PROMPT] **1** *obs* : STOREHOUSE, REPOSITORY **2** : a book of ready reference

**promp·ture** \ˈpräm(p)chə(r)\ *n* -s [¹*prompt* + *-ure*] *archaic* : URGING, INCITEMENT ⟨hath fallen by ~ of the blood —Shak.⟩

**proms** *pl of* PROM

**promul·gate** \ˈpräməl,gāt, prəˈm-,prōˈm- *also* ˈprō(,)m-; *usu* -ād.+V\ *vt* -ED/-ING/-S [L *promulgatus*, past part. of *promulgare* to make public, perh. alter. of *provulgare*, fr. *pro-* forth + *vulgare* to publish — more at PRO-, VULGATE] **1** : to make known (as a decree, a dogma) by open declaration : PROCLAIM **2 a** : to make known or public the terms of (a proposed law) **b** : to issue or give out (a law) by way of putting into execution **c** : to make public as having the force of law **d** : to announce officially **syn** see DECLARE

**promul·ga·tion** \,präməlˈgāshən, ,prō(,)m\ *n* -s [F, fr. L *promulgation-, promulgatio*, fr. *promulgatus* + *-ion-, -io* -ion] : an act of promulgating : open declaration : public and official announcement

**promul·ga·tor** \ˈpräməl,gād·ə(r), prəˈm-, prōˈm-, ˈprō(,)m-, -ātə-\ *n* -s [LL, fr. L *promulgatus* + *-or*] : one that promulgates or publishes ⟨the original and systematic ~ of the doctrine of free, self-governing institution —John Dewey⟩

**pro·mulge** \prōˈməlj\ *vt* -ED/-ING/-S [ME *promulgen*, fr. L *promulgare*] *archaic* : PROMULGATE

**pro·mulg·er** \-jə(r)\ *n* -s [*promulge* + *-er*] *archaic* : PROMULGATOR

**pro·mus·ci·date** \(ˈ)prō¦məsə,dāt\ *adj* [LL *promuscid-, promuscis* + E *-ate*] *of an insect* : having a proboscis

**pro·mus·cis** \prōˈməsəs\ *n, pl* **promus·ces** \-ə,sēz\ *or* **pro·mus·ci·des** \-sə,dēz\ [LL *promuscid-, promuscis*, alter. of *proboscis*] : PROBOSCIS; *specif* : the proboscis of a hemipterous insect

**pro·mycelial** \¦prō+\ *adj* [NL *promycelium* + E *-al*] : of, relating to, or being a promycelium

**pro·mycelium** \(¦)prō+\ *n, pl* **promycelia** [NL, fr. ¹*pro-* + *mycelium*] : a short usu. 4-celled hyphal filament that constitutes the basidium of various heterobasidiomycetous fungi, is formed by germination of a teliospore in rusts or of a chlamydospore in smuts, and bears sporidia — called also *epibasidium*; compare AUTOBASIDIUM

**pro·myelocyte** \(ˈ)prō+\ *n* [ISV ¹*pro-* + *myelocyte*] : PREMYELOCYTE — **pro·myelocytic** \(¦)=+\ *adj*

**pro·my·shlen·nik** \,prämə'shlenək\ *n, pl* **promyshlenni·ki** \-nəkē\ [Russ, lit., trader, industrialist, fr. *promysl'* business, fr. *pro* for + *mysl'* thought; akin to L *pro* for and to OSlav *mysli* thought — more at FOR, MYTH] : a Russian trapper and fur trader of Siberia and Alaska

**pron** *abbr* **1** pronominal **2** pronoun **3** pronounced **4** pronunciation

**pro·naos** \(ˈ)prō+\ *n, pl* **pronaoi** [L, fr. Gk, fr. *pronaos* situated in front of a temple, fr. *pro-* ¹pro- + *naos* temple — more at NAOS] : the outer part of an ancient Greek temple forming a portico immediately in front of the cella and delimited by the front wall of the cella and the columns or the antae and columns; *also* : the narthex of an early church

**pro·na·tal·ist** \(ˈ)prō¦nād·ᵊləst\ *adj* [¹*pro-* + L *natus* (past part. of *nasci* to be born) + E *-al* + *-ist* — more at NATION] : encouraging an increased birthrate ⟨~ policies⟩

**pro·nate** \ˈprō,nāt, *usu* -ād.+V\ *vb* -ED/-ING/-S [LL *pronatus*, past part. of *pronare* to bend forward, bow, fr. L *pronus* prone] *vt* : to rotate (as the hand or forearm) so as to bring the palm facing downward or backward ~ *vi* : to assume a position of pronation

**pro·na·tion** \prōˈnāshən\ *n* -s [*pronate* + *-ion*] **1 a** : a medial rotation of the hand and radius around the ulna so that the palm is turned backward or downward; *also* : the position resulting from this movement — opposed to *supination* **b** : the act or state of lying face downward **2** : a faulty foot posture characterized by toeing out and usu. associated with sagging of the inner arch and inward tipping of the ankle joint

**pro·na·to·flexor** \prō¦nād·ō+\ *n* [NL, fr. *pronator* + *-o-* + *flexor*] : one of a group of muscles on the volar aspect of the forearm acting both as pronator and flexor

**pro·na·tor** \ˈprō,nād·ə(r)\ *n* -s [NL, fr. LL *pronatus* + L *-or*] : a muscle that produces pronation

**pronator qua·dra·tus** \-kwäˈdrād·əs\ *n* [NL, lit., squared pronator] : a deep muscle of the forearm passing transversely from the ulna to the radius and serving to pronate the forearm

**pronator te·res** \-ˈti,rēz\ *n* [NL, lit., smooth or rounded pronator] : a muscle of the forearm, arising from the medial epicondyle of the humerus, inserting into the lateral surface of the middle third of the radius, and serving to pronate and flex the forearm

**¹prone** \ˈprōn\ *adj* [ME, fr. L *pronus* bent forward, inclined, tending; akin to L *pro* before, forward — more at FOR] **1** : having a tendency, propensity, or inclination : DISPOSED, PREDISPOSED ⟨drivers suspected of being accident ~⟩ — used with *to* ⟨man is ~ to error⟩ ⟨those industries that are most ~ to periods of depression —J.A.Hobson⟩ ⟨when courts are so very ~ to stand upon their dignity —H.G.Wells⟩ **2** *obs* : readily followed or yielded to : EASY **3** *archaic* : ready or willing to do something specified or implied ⟨~ submission to the heavenly will —Robert Browning⟩ **4** : DOWNWARD: as **a** : having the front or ventral surface downward : standing, lying, or placed so that the face and belly are facing or upon the earth or other supporting base ⟨a ~ position⟩ ⟨the upper side of a ~ or horizontal animal —W.E.Swinton⟩ — distinguished from *supine* **b** : lying flat or prostrate — contrasted with *erect* **5** *archaic* : ANIMALLIKE, BEASTLY, BESTIAL ⟨a ~ and savage necessity, not worth the name of marriage —John Milton⟩

**syn** SUPINE, PROSTRATE, RECUMBENT, COUCHANT, DORMANT: PRONE may apply to a position with the face, chest, or abdomen lying on or turned toward the ground, floor, or other surface ⟨if we ourselves lie *prone* upon the floor we can exemplify the characteristic relationship, for our internal cavity is nearest to the floor, above it is our backbone —W.E.Swinton⟩ ⟨Her Majesty, *prone* but queenly, stretched out on the deck . . . to try her hand at target shooting —*Time*⟩ SUPINE applies to a position with the back against a supporting surface, the face upward, and suggests lethargic abjectness or inertness ⟨lying *supine* in the bottom of the canoe and staring upward at the immaculate azure of the sky —Elinor Wylie⟩ ⟨jaded people lolling *supine* in carriages —G.B.Shaw⟩ PROSTRATE applies to full-length proneness as in submission, fear, or helplessness; it may also apply to any horizontal position brought about by fall, weakness, or shock and inability to use and act ⟨*prostrate* in homage, on her face, silent —Gordon Bottomley⟩ ⟨lying *prostrate* on my chest, I took a long draught of clear cold water —W.H.Hudson †1922⟩ ⟨stood over the bloody and *prostrate* form —C.B.Nordhoff & J.N.Hall⟩ RECUMBENT may apply to lying down in any position of comfortable repose ⟨if the patient is greatly weakened or prostrated, he must be kept reasonably warm, *recumbent* —Morris Fishbein⟩ ⟨*recumbent* upon the brown pine-droppings —George Meredith⟩ COUCHANT and DORMANT, mainly technical heraldic terms in the senses here involved, apply to a prone body position, the former suggesting that the head is raised as if in watchfulness, the latter that it is lowered in sleep. **syn** see in addition LIABLE

**²prone** \"\ *n* -s [F *prône*, lit., choir screen (where the instruction was orig. delivered), fr. (assumed) VL *protinum* vestibule, screen before an entrance, alter. of L *prothyra* (pl.), fr. Gk *prothyron* space before a door, fr. *pro-* ¹pro- + *thyra* door — more at DOOR] : a short religious instruction delivered in church preceding the sermon : a brief pedagogical, hortatory, or homiletical introduction to the sermon

**prone float** *n* : DEAD MAN'S FLOAT

**prone·ly** *adv* [*prone* + *-ly*] : in a prone manner or position

**prone·ness** \ˈprōnəs\ *n* -ES : the condition or fact of being prone ⟨~ to disease⟩ ⟨possible reason for accident ~⟩

**pro·neph·ric** \(ˈ)prō¦nefrik\ *adj* [NL *pronephros* + E *-ic*] : of or relating to a pronephros

**pro·nephridiostome** \¦=+\ *n* -s [NL ¹*pro-* + *nephridium* + *-o-* + E *-stome*] : FLAME CELL

**pro·neph·ros** \(ˈ)prō¦nefrəs, -,fräs\ *also* **pro·neph·ron** \-,frən, -,frän\ *n, pl* **proneph·roi** \-,frȯi\ *also* **proneph·ra** \-frə\ [NL, fr. ¹*pro-* + Gk *nephros* kidney — more at NEPHRITIS] : one of the anterior of the three pairs of embryonic renal organs of higher vertebrates

**prone pressure method** *n* : a method of artificial respiration consisting essentially of alternate pressure and release of pressure on the back of the thorax of the prone patient by means of which water if present is expelled from the lungs and air is allowed to enter

**pro·neur** \prōˈnər(·)\ *n* -s [F *prôneur*, fr. *prôner* to exhort, praise to excess (fr. *prône* religious instruction) + *-eur* -or — more at PRONE] : FLATTERER, EULOGIST

**¹prong** \ˈprȯŋ, ˈpräŋ\ *n* -s [ME *pronge, prange*; perhaps akin to MHG *pfrengen* to press, Goth *anaprangan* to afflict, Lith *branktas* whiffletree] **1** : FORK ⟨hay ~⟩ ⟨dung ~⟩ **2** : a tine of a fork **3** : a slender pointed or projecting part: as **a** : a fang of a tooth **b** : a point of an antler **c** *South & Midland* : a branch of a stream or inlet **d** : ¹SPUR 6b **e** : a branch of a tree **f** : the projecting part or edge of a jewelry setting that holds a stone in place

**²prong** \"\ *vt* -ED/-ING/-S : to stab, pierce, or break up (as soil) with a prong : FORK

**prongbuck** \ˈ=,=\ *n* [*prong* + *buck*] **1** : SPRINGBOK **2** : PRONGHORN

**prong budding** *n* : shield budding in which a bud-bearing prong or spur is used instead of a simple bud

**prong die** *n* **1** : SPRING DIE **2** : SPLIT DIE

**pronged** \ˈprȯŋd, ˈpräŋd\ *adj* [¹*prong* + *-ed*] : having or divided into prongs : FORKED — often used in combination

**prong hoe** *n* : a hand implement equipped with two or more curved prongs and used for garden tillage or cultivation

**pronghorn** \ˈ=,=\ *also* **pronghorn antelope** \ˈ=,=-\ *or* **prong-horned antelope** \(ˈ)=-¦=-\ *n, pl* **pronghorn** *also* **pronghorns** [*pronghorn* fr. *prong-horned* (*antelope*), fr. ¹*prong* + *horned*] : a ruminant mammal (*Antilocapra americana*) of unforested parts of western No. America that is yellowish tawny above and about the neck and white below with a white rump patch and that has slightly curved horns with a lateral prong which are present in both sexes and which resemble the bovine horns in having a bony core but have a deciduous horny sheath that is replaced annually

pronghorn

**prong key** *n* [¹*prong*] : a key or spanner having two projecting pins to fit holes in the face of a circular nut : FACE SPANNER

**prongy** \ˈprȯŋē, ˈpräŋē\ *adj* [¹*prong* + *-y*] : FORKED, DIVIDED ⟨horseradish grown in poor soil may develop ~ roots⟩

**pro·no·grade** \ˈprōnə,grād\ *adj* [L *pronus* leaning forward + E *-o-* + *-grade* — more at PRONE] : walking with the body approximately horizontal ⟨most mammals except man and the higher apes are ~⟩ — compare ORTHOGRADE

**¹pro·nom·i·nal** \prōˈnämən°l, prəˈ-\ *adj* [LL *pronominalis*, fr. L *pronomin-, pronomen* pronoun + *-alis* -al — more at PRONOUN] **1** : of, relating to, or constituting a pronoun **2** : resembling a pronoun : having a meaning that resembles that of a pronoun in identifying or specifying without describing ⟨the adverb *here* is ~ in *come here*⟩

**²pronominal** \"\ *n* -s : a pronominal word

**pro·nom·i·nal·ly** \-nəlē, -li\ *adv* [¹*pronominal* + *-ly*] : in the manner of a pronoun

**pro·normoblast** \(ˈ)prō+\ *n* [ISV ¹*pro-* + *normoblast*; prob. orig. formed in G] : a cell recognized in some theories of erythropoiesis that arises from a myeloblast and gives rise to normoblasts and is approximately equivalent to the erythroblast of other theories

**pronotary** *n* -ES [by contr.] *obs* : PROTHONOTARY

**pro·notum** \(ˈ)prō+\ *n, pl* **pronota** [NL, fr. ¹*pro-* + *notum*] : the dorsal plate of an insect's prothorax

**pro·noun** \ˈprō,naůn\ *n* [MF *pronom*, fr. L *pronomin-, pronomen*, fr. *pro-* ²pro- + *nomin-, nomen* name, noun — more at NAME] **1** : a word belonging to one of the major form classes in any of a great many languages that is used as a substitute for a noun or noun equivalent, takes noun constructions and is declined, refers to persons or things named, asked for, or understood in the context, and has little or no fixed meaning except one of relation or limitation **2** : PRONOMINAL

STANDARD SIMPLE PERSONAL PRONOUNS

| *1st person* | *2d person* | *3d person* |
|---|---|---|
| | SINGULAR | |
| I | you | he, she, it |
| (mine) | (yours) | (his) (hers) (its) |
| me | you | him, her, it |
| | PLURAL | |
| we | you | they |
| (ours) | (yours) | (theirs) |
| us | you | them |

The pronouns in parentheses normally do not show possessive case relation but function nominatively (as *mine* in "mine is on the table" and "this book is mine") or objectively (as *mine* in "bring me mine" and "he mistook his coat for mine"). The forms *my, our, your,* and *their* are possessive adjectives, as are also *his, her,* and *its* when used to modify nouns.

**pro·nounce** \prəˈnaůn(t)s\ *vb* -ED/-ING/-S [ME *pronouncen, pronouncen*, fr. MF *prononcier*, fr. L *pronuntiare* to proclaim, articulate, fr. *pro-* forth + *nuntiare* to report, relate, fr. *nuntius* messenger — more at PRO-] *vt* **1** : to utter officially or ceremoniously ⟨~ a eulogy⟩ ⟨~ a death sentence⟩ : declare solemnly ⟨I now ~ you man and wife⟩ ⟨have been officially *pronounced* to be exemplars of the Christian faith —K.S. Latourette⟩ ⟨the weightiest judgment which he could ~ —H.E.Scudder⟩ **2** : to declare authoritatively or by way of a judgment, opinion, or conclusion ⟨doctors *pronounced* him fit to resume his duties⟩ ⟨*pronounced* the meeting adjourned⟩ **3 a** : to employ the organs of speech to produce (as a variety or a component of spoken language) or to produce the spoken counterpart of (as an orthographic representation of a word, syllable, speech sound, phrase) ⟨to ~ German well⟩ ⟨*chimpanzee* is *pronounced* in several ways⟩ **b** : to represent in printed or written characters the spoken counterpart of (an orthographic representation) ⟨both dictionaries ~ *clique* the same⟩ **4** : to deliver (a speech) with regard to sound or manner of utterance : RECITE ⟨speak the speech, I pray you, as I *pronounced* it to you —Shak.⟩ ~ *vi* **1** : to declare one's opinion or conclusion definitely or authoritatively : pass judgment ⟨the speaker was twice required to ~ on the subject of free speech —Guy Eden⟩ ⟨liberal platforms regularly ~ in favor of . . . antitrust enforcement —Carl Kaysen⟩ **2** : to produce the components of spoken language ⟨to ~ faultlessly⟩ ⟨why radio announcers . . . are continually under attack for the way they ~ —David Abercrombie⟩

**pro·nounce·able** \-səbəl\ *adj* : capable of being pronounced ⟨~ group of letters⟩ — **pro·nounce·able·ness** *n* -ES

**pronounced** *adj* [fr. past part. of *pronounce*] : strongly marked : DECIDED, UNMISTAKABLE ⟨~ limp⟩ ⟨~ aptitude for languages⟩ ⟨a ~ odor of fish hung about⟩ ⟨the symptoms of the disease have become steadily more ~⟩ — **pro·nounced·ly** \-n(t)sədlē, -n(t)stlē, -li\ *adv*

**pro·nounce·ment** \-n(t)smənt\ *n* -s [*pronounce* + *-ment*] **1** : a usu. formal declaration of opinion or judgment or estimation ⟨confident ~*s* of generations of literary critics⟩ ⟨~*s* of persons who know something about music but not much —Virgil Thomson⟩ **2** : an authoritative or official announcement ⟨had been making all of the important ~*s* on government policy —Don Dallas⟩

**pro·nounc·er** \-(t)sə(r)\ *n* -s [ME *pronouncere*, fr. *pronouncen* to pronounce + *-ere* -er] : one that pronounces

**pronouncing** *adj* [fr. gerund of *pronounce*] : relating to or indicating pronunciation : serving as a guide to pronunciation ⟨~ dictionary⟩ ⟨~ alphabet⟩

**pron·to** \ˈprän·(,)tō\ *adv* [Sp, quick, prompt, quickly, fr. L *promptus* prompt] : QUICKLY, PROMPTLY — not often in formal use

**pron·to·sil** \ˈpräntə,sil\ *n* -s [G] : any of three sulfonamide drugs: **a** *or* **prontosil rubrum** : a red azo dye $H_2NSO_2C_6H_4N{=}NC_6H_3(NH_2)_2$ that was the first sulfa drug tested clinically **b** *or* **prontosil album** : SULFANILAMIDE **c** *or* **prontosil soluble** : AZOSULFAMIDE

**¹pron·u·ba** \ˈpränyəbə, ˈprōn-\ [NL, fr. L, matron who attended the bride in a Roman marriage, fr. fem. of *pronubus* relating to or for marriage, fr. *pro-* ²pro- + *nubere* to marry a man — more at NUPTIAL] *syn of* TEGETICULA

**²pronuba** \"\ *n* -s [NL *Pronuba*] : YUCCA MOTH

**pro·nuclear** \(ˈ)prō+\ *adj* [NL *pronucleus* + E *-ar*] : of, relating to, or resembling a pronucleus

**pro·nucleus** \"+\ *n* [NL, fr. ¹*pro-* + *nucleus*] : a gamete nucleus after completion of maturation and entry of a sperm into the egg — compare CLEAVAGE, FERTILIZATION

**pro number** \ˈprō-\ *n* [*pro*gressive + *number*] : a number in a single continuous series of numbers assigned by a motor transportation company to successive shipments regardless of classification

**pro·nun·cia·men·to** \prō,nənchēəˈmen(,)tō, -nən(t)sēə-\ *n, pl* **pronunciamentos** *or* **pronunciamentoes** [Sp *pronunciamiento* proclamation, fr. *pronunciar* to pronounce (fr. L *pronuntiare*) + *-miento* -ment — more at PRONOUNCE] **1 a** : PROCLAMATION, EDICT, MANIFESTO; *esp* : an edict announcing a change in government **b** : military revolt **2** : PRONOUNCEMENT ⟨novels, lectures, and ~*s* on life, politics, and art —Brendan Gill⟩

**pro·nun·ci·a·tion** \prə,nən(t)sēˈāshən, *chiefly in substand speech* -naůn(t)s- *or* -nənchē-\ *n* -s [ME *pronunciacion*, fr. MF *prononciation*, fr. L *pronuntiation-, pronuntiatio*, fr. *pronuntiatus* (past part. of *pronuntiare* to pronounce) + *-ion-, -io* -ion — more at PRONOUNCE] **1 a** : the act or manner of pronouncing something : articulate utterance ⟨changes in the ~ of English⟩ **b** : the way or ways in which a unit of language is usu. spoken or on the basis of analogy probably would be spoken by persons qualified by education or otherwise to be speakers worthy of imitation **2** *obs* : DECLARATION, PRONOUNCEMENT **3** *obs* : ELOCUTION, DELIVERY

**pro·nun·ci·a·tion·al** \=¦==ˈāshən°l, -shnəl\ *adj* : relating to or dealing with pronunciation ⟨~ hints⟩ ⟨~ puns⟩

**pro·nun·ci·a·tive** \=ˈ===,ād·iv\ *adj* [L *pronuntiatus*, past part. of *pronuntiare* to declare, pronounce + E *-ive* — more at PRONOUNCE] : DOGMATIC

**pro·nun·ci·a·tor** \-,ād·ə(r)\ *n* -s [L *pronuntiatus* + E *-or*] : one that pronounces; *esp* : one who prescribes pronunciations

**pro·nun·ci·a·to·ry** \=ˈ==ə,tōrē\ *adj* [L *pronuntiatus* + E *-ory*] : of or relating to pronunciation

**pro·ny brake** \ˈprōnē-\ *n, usu cap P* [after G. C. F. M. Riche, Baron de *Prony* †1839 French engineer] : a friction brake or absorption dynamometer in which the pull on the flywheel friction blocks is measured by a spring balance or weighted lever — compare ROPE BRAKE

**pro·nymph** \(ˈ)prō+\ *n* [¹*pro-* + *nymph*] : the first postembryonic form of some insects (as the dragonfly) in which the larva is encased in a thin temporary membrane — **pro·nymphal** \(ˈ)=+\ *adj*

**pro·ode** \ˈprō,ōd\ *n* [Gk *proōidos*, fr. *pro-* ¹pro- + *ōidē* ode — more at ODE] **1** : a distich with the first line shorter than the second — opposed to *epode* **2** : a strophic unit in an ancient ode preceding the strophe and antistrophe and differing from them in structure

**pro·od·ic** \(ˈ)prō¦ädik\ *adj* [Gk *proōidikos* of or relating to a prelude, fr. *proōidos* prelude, proode + *-ikos* -ic] **1** : preceding and differing in metrical pattern from the first strophe of an ode **2** *of an ode* : preceded or introduced by a group of lines of different pattern

**pro·oe·mi·ac** \(ˈ)prō¦ēmē,ak\ *adj* [LGk *prooimiakos*, fr. Gk *prooimion* proem] : PROEMIAL

**pro·oe·mi·um** \prōˈēmēəm\ *or* **pro·oe·mi·on** \-ən\ *n, pl* **prooemiums** *or* **prooe·mia** \-ˈēmēə\ [*prooemium* fr. ME(Sc) *prohemium*, fr. L *prooemium*, fr. Gk *prooimion*; *prooemion* fr. Gk *prooimion* — more at PROEM] : PROEM

**prooestrous** *var of* PROESTROUS

**prooestrus** *or* **proœstrum** *var of* PROESTRUS

**¹proof** \ˈprüf\ *n* -s [ME *proof, prove*, alter. (influenced by *proven* to prove) of *preef, preve, preove*, fr. OF *preuve*, fr. LL *proba*, fr. L *probare* to test, prove — more at PROVE] **1 a** : the cogency of evidence or of demonstrated relationship that compels acceptance by the mind of a truth or a fact : DEMONSTRATION ⟨one who believes in you doesn't need any ~ at all —W.J. Reilly⟩ **b** : the derivation of one or more propositions or statements from one or more others in accordance with either generally recognized or specif. stipulated principles of validity **2** *obs* : something proved by common experience : knowledge acquired by experience ⟨'tis a common ~ that lowliness is young ambition's ladder —Shak.⟩ **3** : something that induces certainty or establishes validity: as **a** : a chain of statements or formulas leading logically from axioms and theorems previously established to the theorem which is the conclusion of the demonstration **b** : a mathematical process that establishes the validity of a theorem or statement **c** : an act, effort, or operation designed to establish or discover a fact or truth ⟨prepared to put his theories to the ~⟩ ⟨laboratory ~ of the presence of gold in the sample⟩ **4** *obs* : OUTCOME, RESULT **5 a** *obs* : WITNESS **b** : a leaf having its original rough outer edge or a pair of adjacent leaves still joined together at one or more edges regarded as proof that the book containing it is untrimmed — called also *witness* **6** *dial chiefly Eng* : good condition or quality : GOODNESS **7 a** *archaic* : the quality or state of having been tested or tried; *esp* : unyielding hardness or firmness ⟨armor of ~⟩ **b** *obs* : ARMOR **8** : evidence operating to determine the finding or judgment of a tribunal: as **a** *Eng law* : a written statement of the testimony which a proposed witness will give in court **b** *civil law* : a document or number of documents so established as to be legally receivable as evidence **c** *Scots law* : the evidence upon a point at issue taken before a judge or judge's representative; *also* : the taking of the evidence **d** *Scots law* : a trial by a court without a jury **9** *obs* : ATTEMPT **10 a** : an impression (as from type) taken for correction or examination; *also* : a comparable print or impression made by some other composing or printing process **b** : a proof impression of an engraving, etching, or lithograph — see OPEN-LETTER PROOF, PROOF BEFORE LETTER, REMARQUE PROOF **c** : PROOF COIN **d** : a test photographic print made from a negative **11 a** : a test applied to articles or substances to determine whether they are of standard or satisfactory quality ⟨the ~ of the pudding is in the eating⟩ **b** : a trial of ordnance, projectiles, armor, or powder to determine suitability for acceptance **c** : the process of bringing dough to a standard lightness **12 a** : the minimum alcoholic strength of proof spirit **b** : strength with reference to the standard for proof spirit **syn** see REASON

**²proof** \"\ *adj* **1** : firm or successful in resisting or repelling ⟨~ against your own moods —William Sansom⟩ : IMPENETRABLE, IMPREGNABLE — often used in combination ⟨burglar-*proof* windows⟩ ⟨bomb*proof*⟩; sometimes distinguished from *resistant* **2** : used in proving or testing : serving as a proof: as **a** : measuring or producing the greatest strain in a piece or member consistent with safety ⟨~ stress⟩ ⟨~ strength⟩ **b** *of gold or silver* : perfectly pure and kept (as in a mint or assay office) as a standard of comparison or for experiment **3** : of standard strength or quality or alcoholic content ⟨~ whiskey⟩

**³proof** \"\ *adv* [²*proof*] *archaic* : CONFIRMEDLY, THOROUGHLY, UTTERLY

**⁴proof** \"\ *vt* -ED/-ING/-S [¹*proof*] **1 a** : to make or take a proof or test of ⟨~ an etching⟩ ⟨~ a negative⟩ ⟨~ a galley of set type⟩ **b** : PROOFREAD ⟨books which I edited, ~*ed*, and supervised in production —E.G.Berenson⟩ **2** : to bring (dough) to the proper lightness **3** [²*proof*] : to give a resistant quality to : make impervious to water, gas, weather, or chemical action

**proof before letter** : a proof taken before the title or inscription has been engraved

**proof box** *n* : a cabinet for proofing dough

**proof coin** *n* : a coin not intended for circulation but struck from a new, highly-polished die on a polished planchet and sometimes in a metal different from a coin of identical denomination struck for circulation

**proof·er** \-fə(r)\ *n* -S **1** : one that pulls or makes proofs (as in letterpress printing and lithography) **2** : a bakery worker who controls the raising of dough (as in a proofer) — called also *raiser* **3** : a machine in which leavened dough is kept at a controlled temperature for raising

**proof gallon** *n* : a gallon of proof spirit

**proofhouse** \ˈ=,=\ *n* : a place for testing the barrels of firearms

**proofing** *n* -S **1** : the act or process of making proof **2** : a chemical or other substance used in proofing; *specif* : a preparation applied to fabric or incorporated in it at the time of manufacture to make it proof against weather or to prevent the passage of gas

**proof·less** \ˈprüfləs\ *adj* : lacking proof : not supported by proof ⟨~ charges⟩

**proof load** *n* : a cartridge made with a heavier charge of powder than normal ammunition for the piece and used to test the strength of chamber, barrel, and action

**proofmark** \ˈ=,=\ *n* : a distinctive symbol stamped into the metal of the barrel or other part of a firearm to indicate that testing of the part bearing the stamp by firing proof loads has been carried out

**proof·ness** *n* -ES : the state or property of being proof ⟨tested for ~ against water and corrosion⟩ : degree of being proof

**proof paper** *n* **1** : paper (as printing-out paper) for making proofs **2** : paper used in timing an exposure

**proof plane** *n* : a small metal disk attached to an insulating handle, used in testing the nature of the electrification of a body

**proof positive** *n, pl* **proofs positive** : conclusive proof

**proof press** *n* : a press used for the pulling or making of proofs

**proof·read** \ˈprü,frēd\ *vt* [back-formation fr. *proofreader*] : to read and mark corrections in (a proof or other printed or written matter)

**proofreader** \ˈ=,==\ *n* [¹*proof* + *reader*] : one that proofreads; *esp* : one whose regular occupation is proofreading — called also *corrector of the press, printer's reader, reader*

**proofroom** \ˈ=,=\ *n* **1** : a room in which proofreading is done **2** : the room where formed bread doughs are kept to rise (as in a proofer)

**proofs** *pl of* PROOF, *pres 3d sing of* PROOF

**proof spirit** *n* : alcoholic liquor or mixture of alcohol and water that contains a standard percentage of alcohol: **a** : liquor that contains nearly half alcohol by volume **b** *Brit* : liquor that weighs 12/13 of an equal measure of distilled water or contains 57.10 percent by volume of alcohol — compare OVERPROOF, UNDERPROOF

**proof stress** *n* : stress that causes a specified amount of permanent deformation in a test specimen

**proof-test** \ˈ=,=\ *vt* : to fire proof loads in (a firearm)

**proof text** *n* : a Scriptural passage adduced as proof for a theological doctrine, belief, or principle

**proof with open-letter** : OPEN-LETTER PROOF

**proof with remarque** : REMARQUE PROOF

**proofy** \ˈprüfi\ *adj* [¹*proof* + -*y*] *dial Eng* : LIKELY, PROMISING

**pro·op·ic** \(ˈ)prō¦äpik, -¦ōpik\ *adj* [¹*pro-* + Gk *ōp-, ōps* face, eye + E -*ic* — more at EYE] : having a face in which the nose and central line are prominent

**pro·os·tra·cum** \prōˈästrəkəm\ *n, pl* **proostra·ca** \-kə\ [NL, fr. ¹*pro-* + Gk *ostrakon* earthen vessel, potsherd, shell — more at OYSTER] : the anterior horny or calcareous prolongation of the phragmocone of belemnites and related cephalopods

**¹pro·otic** \(ˈ)prō+\ *adj* [*pro-* + -*otic* (of the ear)] : of or relating or adjacent to a prootic bone or center : being a prootic part

**²prootic** *n* -S : a prootic part (as a bone or cartilage)

**prootic bone** *n* : a bone or center of ossification in the front of the periotic capsule in special relation with the anterior semicircular canal

**pro·oxidant** \(ˈ)prō+\ *n* [²*pro-* + *oxidant*] : a substance that accelerates the oxidation of another substance — compare ANTIOXIDANT

**pro·oxygen** \"+\ *n* [ISV ²*pro-* + *oxygen*] : PROOXIDANT — **pro·oxygenic** \(ˈ)prō+\ *adj*

**¹prop** \ˈpräp\ *n* -S [ME *proppe*, fr. MD, stopper; akin to MLG *proppe* stopper] **1** : a rigid usu. independent and often auxiliary vertical support: as **a** : a timber for holding up the roof of a mine **b** : a pole for keeping a clothesline from sagging down **c** : a pole or stake for holding up a plant **d props** *pl* : LEGS **e** : a fired-clay piece used as a support for a shelf in a kiln **2** : something on which one leans or depends for support or strength : STAY ⟨his son was his chief ~ in old age⟩ ⟨this side of religion which has . . . become the ~ of advanced cultures and complex societies —W.W.Howells⟩ ⟨a government ~ keeping wheat from falling below a set level⟩ ⟨knocks the ~s out from under some critical theories —B.R.Redman⟩ **3** : PROP FORWARD

**²prop** \"\ *vb* **propped; propped; propping; props** [ME *proppen*, fr. *proppe*, n.] *vt* **1 a** : to prevent from falling, collapsing, sagging, or slipping by placing something under or against : shore up ⟨sat with his chin *propped* in his hands⟩ ⟨frame houses, some *propped* on stilts —*Amer. Guide Series: Pa.*⟩ — often used with *up* ⟨lay with his head *propped* up on a pillow⟩ **b** : to support by placing against something ⟨~ a ladder against a wall⟩ ⟨photographs on the mantel, *propped* up amid a clutter of china ornaments —Hamilton Basso⟩ **2** : to give support to (as by assisting, encouraging, upholding) : SUSTAIN, STRENGTHEN ⟨emphasis on *propping* economic structures abroad, rather than unduly expanding military power —*Biddle Survey*⟩ ⟨to ~ up my morale . . . a top designer had done over my office —Gary Cooper⟩ ~ *vi, Austral & Africa, of a draft animal, esp a horse* : BALK **syn** see SUPPORT

**³prop** \"\ *n* -S [origin unknown] : one of the seashells used in the game of props

**⁴prop** \"\ *n* -S [by shortening] **1** : PROPERTY 4a **2** : an article, object, or device used to provide or aid in creating a realistic effect (as of a performance, exhibit, or narrative) ⟨all the ~*s* of an espionage case are there — foreign agents, household traitors, stolen documents —J.P.Marquand⟩ ⟨camels, which they hire to visitors as ~*s* for exotic snapshots —Mollie Panter-Downes⟩

**⁵prop** \"\ *n* -S [by shortening] : PROPELLER

**prop-** *comb form* [ISV, fr. *propionic* (in *propionic acid*)] : related to propionic acid ⟨*propane*⟩ ⟨*propyl*⟩

**prop** *abbr* **1** propeller **2** proper; properly **3** property **4** proposed; proposition **5** proprietary; proprietor

**pro·pa·di·ene** \¦prōpə¦dī,ēn\ *n* -S [ISV *propane* + -*diene*] : ALLENE

**Pro·pa·drine** \ˈprōpədrən\ *trademark* — used for racemic norephedrine used in the form of its hydrochloride as a nasal vasoconstrictor

**¹pro·pae·deu·tic** \,prōpēˈd(y)üd·|ik, -üt|, |ēk\ *n* -S [fr. Gk *propaideuein* to teach beforehand (fr. *pro-* ¹*pro-* + *paideuein* to rear a child, educate, teach, fr. *paid-, pais* child), after Gk *paideuein: paideutikē* education, fr. fem. of *paideutikos* of teaching, fr. *paideutos* (verbal of *paideuein*) + -*ikos* -ic — more at FEW] : preparatory study or instruction : INTRODUCTION ⟨an essential ~ to this more philosophical task will be accomplished by our analysis —Donald Walhout⟩

**²propaedeutic** \¦==¦==\ *adj* [fr. Gk *propaideuein* to teach beforehand, after Gk *paideuein* to teach: *paideutikos* of teaching] : needed as preparation for learning or study : introductory to an art or science ⟨logic is not philosophy; it is a ~ discipline —*Times Lit. Supp.*⟩

**prop·a·ga·bil·i·ty** \,präpəgəˈbiləd·ē\ *n* : the quality or state of being propagable

**prop·a·ga·ble** \ˈpräpəgəbəl\ *adj* [ML *propagabilis*, fr. L *propagare* to propagate + -*abilis* -able] : capable of being propagated

**prop·a·gand** \ˈpräpə,gand\ *vb* -ED/-ING/-S [prob. fr. F *propagander*, fr. *propagande* propaganda] : PROPAGANDIZE

**prop·a·gan·da** \,präpəˈgandə, -gaan- *also* ,prōp- *sometimes* ˈ==,=\ *n* -S [NL (in *Congregatio de propaganda fide* Congregation for propagating the faith — an organization established by Pope Gregory XV in 1622 to take charge of Catholic missionary activity), fr. L, abl. sing. fem. of *propagandus*, gerundive of *propagare* to propagate] **1** *archaic* : a group or movement organized for spreading a particular doctrine or system of principles **2** : dissemination of ideas, information, or rumor for the purpose of helping or injuring an institution, a cause, or a person ⟨steady erosion of Socialist ~ about the wrongs done to the people —Roy Lewis & Angus Maude⟩ **3 a** : doctrines, ideas, arguments, facts, or allegations spread by deliberate effort through any medium of communication in order to further one's cause or to damage an opposing cause ⟨brushed aside the peace proposals as mere ~⟩ **b** : a public action or display having the purpose or the effect of furthering or hindering a cause ⟨distribution of free food parcels . . . is the first successful piece of ~ that the Western Powers have thought up —*New Statesman & Nation*⟩ **syn** see PUBLICITY

**prop·a·gan·dee** \¦==,gan¦dē\ *n* -S [*propagand* + -*ee*] : one subjected to propagandizing

**prop·a·gan·dism** \,==ˈgan,dizəm\ *n* -S [F *propagandisme*, fr. *propagande* propaganda (fr. NL *propaganda*) + -*isme* -ism] : the action, practice, or art of propagating doctrines or of spreading or employing propaganda ⟨untiring ~ on behalf of French contemporary music —*New Internat'l Yr. Bk.*⟩

**¹prop·a·gan·dist** \-,dəst *sometimes* ˈ==,==\ *n* -S [F *propagandiste*, fr. *propagande* propaganda + -*iste* -ist] : one engaged in propagating a belief or in producing or spreading propaganda ⟨democratic and humanitarian ~*s* succeeded in popularizing the ideal of universal elementary education —Helen Sullivan⟩

**²propagandist** \¦==¦==\ *or* **prop·a·gan·dis·tic** \¦präpə,gan¦distik\ *adj* : of, relating to, or characterized by propaganda ⟨~ writing⟩ ⟨~ plays⟩

**prop·a·gan·dis·ti·cal·ly** \-tək(ə)lē\ *adv* : in a propagandist manner : by way of propaganda ⟨~ effective play⟩

**prop·a·gan·dize** \,präpəˈgan,dīz, -gaan- *also* ,prōp- *sometimes* ˈ==,=dīz *or* -,gan-\ *vt* -ED/-ING/-S [*propaganda* + -*ize*] **1** : to disseminate (ideas, beliefs, principles) by propaganda ⟨~ the cause of states' rights⟩ **2** : to subject to propaganda ⟨~ a country⟩ ~ *vi* : to carry on propaganda

**prop·a·gant** \ˈpräpəgənt\ *n* -S [*propagate* + -*ant*] : a plant part used for vegetative propagation

**prop·a·gate** \ˈpräpə,gāt *sometimes* ˈprōp-, *usu* -ād.+V\ *vb* -ED/-ING/-S [L *propagatus*, past part. of *propagare* to set slips, propagate, extend, enlarge, fr. *propages* layer (of a plant), slip, offspring, fr. *pro* before + -*pages* (akin to L *pangere* to fix, fasten) — more at FOR, PACT] *vt* **1** : to cause to continue or increase by natural reproduction ⟨~ a breed of horses⟩ ⟨a plant unable to ~ itself in a new region⟩ ⟨~ a tree vegetatively⟩ **2** : to transmit to offspring : pass along to succeeding generations **3 a** : to cause to spread out and affect a greater number or greater area : foster the spread of : EXTEND ⟨this vast area . . . through which the Greco-Roman civilization has been *propagated* —A.J.Toynbee⟩ ⟨the evil *propagated* itself —T.B.Macaulay⟩ **b** : to make known or familiar : foster growing knowledge of, familiarity with, or acceptance of : PUBLICIZE ⟨~ the Gospel⟩ ⟨the revival meeting method of *propagating* the faith —W.P.Webb⟩ ⟨the Rights of Man, rights which the French Revolution had *propagated* —Stringfellow Barr⟩ **c** : to reproduce or accomplish incidence of elsewhere : expand the activity, intensity, or transmission of : TRANSMIT ⟨radio waves *propagated* over long distances by alternate reflections at the ground and in the ionosphere —*Technical News Bull.*⟩ ⟨sufficient to ~ the detonation through the wet earth and set off the whole line of charges —*Blasters' Handbook*⟩ ⟨~ a chain reaction⟩ ~ *vi* **1** : to have young or issue : multiply by sexual generation or by seeds, shoots, cuttings ⟨rabbits ~ rapidly⟩ **2** : to increase in extent, numbers, or influence : EXTEND ⟨cause the flame to ~ along the fiber —W.E.Shinn⟩ **syn** see SPREAD

**propagating frame** *n* : an opaque enclosed case with artificial controlled light and heat that is used for propagating plants; *broadly* : any enclosure so used : HOTBED, COLD FRAME

**propagating pit** *n* : an excavation often covered with a glass frame used for the protection of plants in cold weather or for forwarding early growth

**prop·a·ga·tion** \,==ˈgāshən\ *n* -S [ME *propagacyon*, fr. MF *propagation*, fr. L *propagation-, propagatio*, fr. *propagatus* (past part. of *propagare*) + -*ion-, -io* -ion] **1** : the act or action of propagating: as **a** : natural reproduction : production of young : natural increase (as of a kind of organism) in numbers : PROCREATION ⟨~ of a pure culture of bacteria⟩ ⟨vegetative ~ of chrysanthemums⟩ **b** : the spreading of something (as a belief, ideal, practice) abroad or into new regions : DISSEMINATION **c** : the transmission of a form of wave energy (as light, sound, radio wave) through space or along a path **d** : enlargement or extension (as of a crack) in a solid body ⟨~ under stress of a flaw in glass⟩ **2** *obs* : OFFSPRING, BREED — **prop·a·ga·tion·al** \¦==¦gāshən°l, -shnəl\ *adj*

**prop·a·ga·tive** \ˈ==,gād·|iv, -āt|, |ēv *also* |əv\ *adj* : characterized by propagation ⟨spirochetes . . . undergo . . . a ~ type of development —K.F.Maxcy⟩ : tending to propagate : relating to propagation

**prop·a·ga·tor** \|ə(r)\ *n* -S [L, fr. *propagatus* (past part. of *propagare* to propagate) + -*or*] **1** : one that propagates or disseminates ⟨find the ~ of this slander⟩ ⟨war has been the chief ~ of the machine —Lewis Mumford⟩ **2** : one that propagates plants under glass or other special structures or in the open

**prop·a·ga·tory** \ˈpräpəgə,tōrē\ *adj* **1** : PROPAGATIVE **2** : PROPAGABLE

**pro·pag·u·lum** \prōˈpagyələm\ *or* **prop·a·gule** \ˈpräpə,gyül\ *n, pl* **propag·ula** \-lə\ *or* **propagules** [NL *propagulum*, fr. L *propages* layer (of a plant), slip + -*ulum*] **1** : a propagable shoot (as an offset) **2** : a reproductive structure in brown algae

**pro·pale** \prōˈpā(ə)l\ *vt* -ED/-ING/-S [LL *propalare*, fr. L *propalam* openly, publicly, fr. *pro* before + *palam* openly; akin to OSlav *polje* field — more at FOR, FLOOR] *archaic* : DIVULGE

**pro·pal·i·nal** \(ˈ)prōˈpalən°l\ *adj* [Gk *pro* before, forward + *palin* back + E -*al* — more at FOR, PALI-] *of mastication* : effected by forward and backward motion — compare ORTHAL, PALINAL, PROAL

**pro·pam·i·dine** \prōˈpamə,dēn, -dən\ *n* [*propane* + *amidine*] : an antiseptic $CH_2[CH_2OC_6H_4C(-NH)NH_2]_2$ structurally related to propane and the amidine of benzoic acid and used chiefly in surgery for inhibiting the growth of hemolytic streptococci and staphylococci

**pro·pa·nal** \ˈprōpə,nal\ *n* -S [ISV *propane* + -*al*] : PROPIONALDEHYDE

**pro·pane** \ˈprō,pān\ *n* -S [ISV *prop-* + -*ane*] : a flammable gaseous paraffin hydrocarbon $CH_3CH_2CH_3$ that is heavier than air, occurs naturally in crude petroleum and natural gas and is also obtained by cracking, and is used chiefly as a fuel (as in liquefied petroleum gas) and in the manufacture of chemicals (as the lower nitroparaffins)

**pro·pa·no·ic acid** \¦prōpə¦nōik-\ *n* [*propanoic* ISV *propane* + -*oic*] : PROPIONIC ACID

**pro·pa·nol** \ˈprōpə,nōl, -nōl\ *n* -S [ISV *propane* + -*ol*] : PROPYL ALCOHOL

**pro·pa·none** \-,nōn\ *n* -S [ISV *propane* + -*one*] : ACETONE

**pro·par·gyl** \prōˈpärjəl\ *n* -S [ISV *prop-* + *arg-* (fr. Gk *argyros* silver) + -*yl*; fr. the possible replacement of a hydrogen atom by one of silver — more at ARGENT] : a univalent unsaturated radical $HC{\equiv}CCH_2-$ derived from methylacetylene by removal of one hydrogen atom ⟨~ alcohol⟩

**pro·par·ia** \prōˈpa(a)rēə\ *n pl, cap* [NL, fr. ¹*pro-* + Gk *pareia* cheek, cheekpiece of a helmet, prob. fr. *para-* + -*eia* (akin to Gk *ous* ear) — more at EAR] : an order of trilobites in which the posterior branch of the facial suture cuts the lateral margin of the cephalon — **pro·par·i·an** \-ēən\ *n or adj*

**¹pro·par·ox·y·tone** \¦prōpə¦räksə,tōn\ *adj* [Gk *proparoxytonos*, fr. *pro-* ¹*pro-* + *paroxytonos* having an acute accent on the penultimate syllable — more at PAROXYTONE] **1** : having or characterized by an acute accent on the antepenult **2** : having or characterized by heavy stress on the antepenult

**²proparoxytone** \"\ *n* : a proparoxytone word — **pro·par·ox·y·ton·ic** \-sə¦tänik\ *adj*

**pro·pa·ta·gi·al** \¦prōpə¦tājēəl\ *also* **pro·pa·ta·gi·an** \-ēən\ *adj* [NL *propatagium* + E -*al* or -*an*] : relating to or situated in a propatagium ⟨~ muscle⟩

**pro·patagium** \¦prō+\ *n, pl* **propatagia** [NL, fr. ¹*pro-* + *patagium*] : the membrane of a wing in front of the arm in a bird or bat; *also* : a corresponding fold of skin in a flying lemur

**prop boy** *n* : PROPERTY MAN

**pro·pel** \prəˈpel, prō-\ *vt* **propelled; propelled; propelling; propels** [ME *propellen*, fr. L *propellere*, fr. *pro* before + *pellere* to drive — more at FOR, FELT] **1** *obs* : to drive away : drive out : EXPEL **2** : to impel forward or onward : push ahead by imparting motion : give motive power to : drive onward ⟨a locomotive *propelled* by electricity⟩ ⟨the use of steam to ~ ships⟩ **3** : to give an impelling motive or impetus to : urge on ⟨had long been *propelled* by greed and ambition⟩ **syn** see PUSH

**pro·pel·la·ble** \-ləbəl\ *adj* : capable of being propelled ⟨~ by oars or sail⟩

**¹pro·pel·lant** *or* **pro·pel·lent** \-lənt\ *adj* [*propellant* fr. *propel* + -*ant*, adj. suffix; *propellent* fr. L *propellent-, propellens*, pres. part. of *propellere* to propel] : capable of propelling : used for propelling ⟨~ fuel for submarines⟩

**²propellant** *also* **propellent** \"\ *n* -S **1** : something that propels : a driving force or motive : STIMULUS **2 a** : an explosive for propelling projectiles **b** : the fuel and oxidizer carried separately or in physical combination which combine chemically to provide rocket propulsion **c** : a gas (as propane, nitrous oxide, nitrogen) placed in a pressure bottle for expelling the contents of the bottle when the pressure is released

**pro·pel·ler** *also* **pro·pel·lor** \-lə(r)\ *n* -S : one that propels: as **a** : SCREW PROPELLER **b** *obs* : a ship driven by a propeller **c** : a mechanical device having one or more blades which when rotated about a central shaft produce a forward thrust due to the aerodynamic forces acting upon them

**propeller cuff** *n* : a fairing of suitable airfoil shape used to cover the shanks of propeller blades in order to reduce the aerodynamic losses

**propeller race** *n* : SLIPSTREAM

**propeller shaft** *n* **1** : a shaft that carries a screw propeller at its end and transmits power from engine to propeller **2** : a shaft that transmits power from the transmission to the rear axle of an automotive vehicle : DRIVE SHAFT

**propeller turbine engine** *n* : TURBO-PROPELLER ENGINE

**propelling pencil** *n, Brit* : MECHANICAL PENCIL

**pro·pel·ment** \-lmənt\ *n* -S **1** : PROPULSION **2** : a propelling device in a mechanism

**propend** *vi* -ED/-ING/-S [L *propendēre*, fr. *pro* before + *pendēre* to hang — more at PENDANT] **1** *obs* : to hang downward or forward : INCLINE **2** *obs* : to become favorably inclined or disposed : TEND

**pro·pen·dent** \prōˈpendənt\ *adj* [L *propendent-, propendens*, pres. part. of *propendēre*] : hanging forward or down

**pro·pene** \ˈprō,pēn\ *n* -S [ISV *prop-* + -*ene*] : PROPYLENE

**pro·pe·no·ic acid** \¦prōpə¦nōik-\ *n* [*propenoic* ISV *propene* + -*oic*] : ACRYLIC ACID

**pro·pense** \prōˈpen(t)s\ *adj* [L *propensus*, past part. of *propendēre*] *archaic* : leaning or inclining toward : INCLINED, PRONE, DISPOSED

**pro·pen·sion** \-nchən\ *n* -S [L *propension-, propensio*, fr. *propensus* (past part. of *propendēre*) + -*ion-, -io* -ion] *archaic* : PROPENSITY

**pro·pen·si·ty** \prəˈpen(t)səd·ē, prōˈ-, -sətē, -i\ *n* -ES [*propense* + -*ity*] : a natural inclination : innate or inherent tendency ⟨~ for versifying⟩ ⟨~ to alcoholic sprees⟩ ⟨function of the wife was . . . to curb the roving *propensities* of the male —C.W. Cunnington⟩ ⟨often twitted about his ~ for having his picture taken —E.J.Kahn⟩ **syn** see LEANING

**pro·pe·nyl** \ˈprōpə,nil\ *n* -S [ISV *propene* + -*yl*] : a univalent unsaturated radical $CH_3CH{=}CH-$ derived from propylene by removal of one hydrogen atom — compare ALLYL, ISOPROPRENYL — **pro·pe·nyl·ic** \¦==¦nilik\ *adj*

**¹prop·er** \ˈpräpə(r)\ *adj, sometimes* -ER/-EST [ME *propre* proper, own, fr. OF, fr. L *proprius* own, particular] **1** : marked by suitability, fitness, accord, compatibility: as **a** : naturally suiting, complying with, or relevant to ⟨something mysterious, unreal . . . something ~ to the night —W.H.Hudson †1922⟩ ⟨keeping the body tissues in ~ condition —Morris Fishbein⟩ **b** : sanctioned as according with equity, justice, ethics, or rationale ⟨to administer ~ punishment to the perpetrators of these crimes —F.D.Roosevelt⟩ ⟨an adverse wind had so delayed him that his cargo brought but half its ~ price —Amy Lowell⟩ **c** : socially appropriate : according with established traditions and feelings of rightness and appropriateness ⟨a ~ reluctance to pronounce final judgments —*Times Lit. Supp.*⟩ ⟨the ~ ceremony, accompanied by the appropriate spell —J.G.Frazer⟩ **d** : acceptable as being qualified or competent : marked by adequate qualification, knowledge, or standards ⟨virtually all fields of human knowledge, necessary for the ~ reporting of Washington —F.L.Mott⟩ **e** : adequate to the purpose : SATISFACTORY, GOOD, PRAISEWORTHY ⟨discovered the true murderer and worked out a ~ revenge —*Time*⟩ ⟨amount of spirit . . . to give him the feeling of a ~ drink —Frank O'Connor⟩ ⟨the Department of Parks will undoubtedly build some ~ parks out there —Joseph Mitchell⟩ **f** : special to or appointed for a particular religious day or festival **2 a** : belonging to one : OWN ⟨the evidence of one's ~ nose —J.L.Lowes⟩ ⟨in the early days a leader had to be everything . . . in his own ~ person —G.W.Johnson⟩ **b** : belonging or applying to one individual only : distinguishing a person or a thing or a place from all others of the same class : naming without describing ⟨~ noun⟩ ⟨~ name⟩ —

opposed to *common* **c** *heraldry* **:** represented in natural color — abbr. *ppr.* **3 :** belonging characteristically to a species or individual **:** DISTINCTIVE, PECULIAR ⟨those high and peculiar attributes . . . which constitute our ~ humanity —S.T. Coleridge⟩ ⟨insidious ailments ~ to tropical climates —George Santayana⟩ **4 :** very good **:** EXCELLENT, CAPITAL ⟨that girl will make a ~ wife for some man⟩ **5** *chiefly Brit* **:** marked by ascribed or designated characterization to a remarkable or extreme degree **:** UTTER, ABSOLUTE ⟨that child is a ~ terror⟩ ⟨a ~ man the champion, for sure⟩ ⟨the roads are getting ~ death traps —*Time*⟩ **6** *chiefly dial* **:** becoming in appearance **:** well-formed and handsome **7 :** strictly limited or isolated to a specified thing, place, or idea **:** excluding adjuncts, concomitants, extensions, or allied matters — often used post-positively ⟨the expression "China ~" . . . applies to the eighteen provinces that lie south of the Great Wall —Owen & Eleanor Lattimore⟩ ⟨their animosity dated back to the Civil War, but the feud ~ began in 1880 —A.F.Harlow⟩ **8 :** marked by rightness, correctness, or rectitude: as **a :** strictly accurate **:** precisely applicable or pertinent **:** entirely in accordance with authority, observed facts, or other sanction **:** CORRECT ⟨various ~ ways of pronouncing a large number of words in our language —M.M.Mathews⟩ ⟨it was ~ to say that . . . most Americans belonged to the middle class —H.S.Commager⟩ **b** *archaic* **:** VIRTUOUS, RESPECTABLE ⟨a ~ gentlewoman —Shak.⟩ **c :** marked by occasionally prissy and too strict conformity to ethical standards, social conventions, or sanctioned usages ⟨mustn't sing that sort of song in company. We're oh! so ~ —George Meredith⟩ ⟨their women so ~ that no one mentioned babies until they arrived —H.S.Canby⟩ **d :** of the upper classes and correct to the point of smug priggishness ⟨she realized that ~ people go to sea as passengers on a liner, not as sailors —Hugh MacLennan⟩ ⟨ostracized by ~ folk —*Amer. Guide Series: Mass.*⟩ **9 :** that is contained in and has fewer members than a mathematical aggregate — used of a mathematical subset **syn** see DECOROUS, FIT

**²proper** \"\ *n* -s [ME *propre*, fr. *propre*, adj.] **1** *obs* **:** PROPERTY, POSSESSIONS **2** *obs* **:** essential attribute **3** *sometimes cap* **a :** the special divine office for a particular day or festival ⟨the ~ for Christmas⟩ — compare COMMON 6 **b :** the parts of the mass that vary according to the day or the feast **c :** the part of a missal or breviary containing the offices proper to certain feasts or saints ⟨the ~ of the saints⟩

**³proper** \"\ *adv* [ME *propre*, fr. *propre*, adj.] **1** *chiefly dial* **:** PROPERLY **2** *chiefly dial* **:** THOROUGHLY ⟨scolded good and ~⟩

**proper adjective** *n* **:** an adjective that is formed from a proper noun, takes its meaning from what is characteristic of the being or thing named by the noun, and is usu. capitalized in English

**properate** *vb* [L *properatus*, past part. of *properare*, fr. *properus* speedy] *obs* **:** HASTEN — **properation** *n* -s *obs*

**pro·per·din** \ˈprōpə(r)dən\ *n* -s [prob. fr. ¹*pro-* + L *perdere* to destroy + E *-in* — more at PERDITION] **:** a serum protein that acting together with complement and magnesium ions participates in the destruction of bacteria, the neutralization of viruses, and the lysis of red blood cells

**properer** *comparative of* PROPER

**properest** *superlative of* PROPER

**proper fraction** *n* **:** a fraction in which the numerator is less or of lower degree than the denominator

**pro·per·i·spome** \prōˈperə,spōm\ *n* -s [by shortening & alter.] **:** PROPERISPOMENON

**pro·per·i·spom·e·non** \prō,perəˈspämə,nän, -spōm-, -,nən\ *n, pl* **properispome·na** \-mənə\ [Gk *properispōmenon*, fr. neut. of *properispōmenos*, pres. pass. part. of *properispan* to pronounce the penultimate syllable with a circumflex accent, fr. *pro-* ¹pro- + *perispan* to pronounce with a circumflex accent — more at PERISPOMENON] **:** a word having the circumflex accent on the penult

**pro·peritoneal** \(ˌ)prō+\ *adj* [¹*pro-* + *peritoneal*] **:** lying between the parietal peritoneum and the ventral musculature of the body cavity ⟨a ~ herniated mass⟩

**prop·er·ly** \ˈpräpə(r)lē, -li, *in rapid -R speech sometimes* -pl-\ *adv* [ME *proprely*, fr. *propre* proper + *-ly*] **1 :** SUITABLY, FITLY, RIGHTLY, CORRECTLY ⟨tool ~ used⟩ ⟨~ dressed for the ceremony⟩ ⟨~ assembled machine⟩ **:** STRICTLY ⟨not ~ part of his duties⟩ **2 a :** INDIVIDUALLY **b :** INTRINSICALLY, INHERENTLY **3 a :** in an excellent or fine manner **b** *chiefly Brit* **:** EXCEEDINGLY, UTTERLY, EXTREMELY

**proper motion** *n* **:** the apparent change in position of a star usu. expressed in seconds of arc per year that results from the projection on the celestial sphere of its motion with respect to the solar system — see TANGENTIAL MOTION

**proper name** [ME *propre name*, fr. *propre* proper + *name*] *n* **1 :** PROPER NOUN **2 :** a symbol that indicates a logical subject and uniquely designates a logical simple; *specif* **:** a symbol that designates a sense-datum present and observed at the moment of the utterance of the symbol ⟨only two words which are strictly *proper names* of particulars, namely, 'I' and 'this' —Bertrand Russell⟩ — compare DESCRIPTION 1b, INCOMPLETE SYMBOL

**prop·er·ness** *n* -ES **:** the quality or state of being proper

**proper noun** *n* **:** a noun that designates a particular being or thing, does not take a limiting modifier, and is usu. capitalized in English

**proper subclass** *or* **proper subset** *n* **:** a subclass containing fewer elements than does the class to which it is subordinate

**prop·er·tied** \ˈpräpə(r)d·ēd, -)tēd\ *adj* [*property* + *-ed*] **1 :** possessing property **:** holding real estate or securities ⟨~ classes of society⟩ **2** *of a stage or scene* **:** requiring or using properties

**¹prop·er·ty** \ˈpräpə(r)d·ē, -)t|, |i, *in rapid -R speech sometimes* -pt|\ *n* -ES [ME *proprete*, fr. MF *proprieté, propriété*, fr. L *proprietat-, proprietas*, fr. *proprie-* (fr. *proprius* own, particular) + *-tat-, -tas* -ty] **1 a :** a quality or trait belonging to a person or thing; *esp* **:** a quality peculiar to an individual person or thing ⟨the eye has this strange ~: it rests only in beauty —Virginia Woolf⟩ **b :** an effect that a material object or substance has on another object or on one or more of the senses of an observer ⟨the *properties* of the objects of nature do not signify . . . anything proper to the particular objects in and for themselves, but always a relation to a second object (including our sense organs) —H.L.F. von Helmholtz⟩ ⟨alkaline *properties* of ammonia⟩ ⟨optical *properties* of a mineral⟩ **c :** special power or capability **:** VIRTUE ⟨health resort . . . popular because of the healing *properties* attributed to the water of its spring —*Amer. Guide Series: Md.*⟩ ⟨rhythm is a ~ of words —C.H.Rickword⟩ **d** (1) **:** an attribute, characteristic, or distinguishing mark common to all members of a class or species ⟨protein molecules . . . have the extraordinary ~ of being able to reproduce themselves —Gerard Piel⟩ — called also *essential property* (2) *Aristotelian logic* **:** an attribute that is common and peculiar to a species but not a part of its essence nor contained in its definition **:** PROPRIUM — called also *nonessential property;* compare PREDICABLE **2 a :** something that is or may be owned or possessed **:** WEALTH, GOODS; *specif* **:** a piece of real estate ⟨the house . . . surrounded by the ~ —G.G.Weigend⟩ **b :** the exclusive right to possess, enjoy, and dispose of a thing **:** a valuable right or interest primarily a source or element of wealth **:** OWNERSHIP ⟨all individual ~ is . . . a form of monopoly —Edward Jenks⟩ **c :** something to which a person has a legal title **:** an estate in tangible assets (as lands, goods, money) or intangible rights (as copyrights, patents) in which or to which a person has a right protected by law **3** *obs* **:** PROPRIETY, FITNESS **4 a :** any article or object used in a play or motion picture except painted scenery and actors' costumes **b** *obs* **:** a means to an end **:** TOOL ⟨impossible I should love thee, but as a ~ —Shak.⟩ **syn** see QUALITY

**²property** *vt* -ED/-ING/-ES **1** *obs* **:** to make a tool of **:** EXPLOIT **2** *obs* **:** APPROPRIATE

**property damage insurance** *n* **:** protection against the legal liability of the insured for damage caused by his automobile to the property of others

**property–increment tax** *n* **:** a tax on increase in the value of the principal of an estate as distinct from income actually realized

**property insurance** *n* **:** insurance against direct loss or damage, consequential loss, loss due to liability for damages, or loss due to dishonesty or failure of others to perform their duty

**prop·er·ty·less** \ˈpräpə(r)d·ēləs\ *adj* **:** lacking property ⟨party of the ~ proletariat —G.B.Shaw⟩

**property man** *n* **1** *or* **property master :** one who is in charge of the procuring and handling of theater or motion-picture stage properties **2 :** one who is in charge of equipment used at a coal mine

**property right** *n* **1 :** a right protected by a constitution to make contracts, conduct a business, labor, or use, enjoy, and dispose of property **2 :** a legal right or interest in or against specific property as opposed to a right enforceable against a person

**prop forward** *n* **:** either of the forwards to the right and left of the hooker in the front row of the rugby league scrum

**pro·phage** \ˈprō,fāj\ *n* -s [¹*pro-* + *phage*] **:** an intracellular form of various bacterial viruses in which the virus is harmless to the host and protects it from the attack of active viruses

**prophane** *obs var of* PROFANE

**pro·phase** \ˈprō,fāz\ *n* [ISV ¹*pro-* + *phase;* orig. formed in G] **:** the initial phase of mitosis in which chromosomes are condensed from the resting form and split into paired chromatids — **pro·pha·sic** \(ˈ)prō¦fāzik\ *adj*

**proph·e·cy** *also* **proph·e·sy** \ˈpräfəsē, -si\ *n* -ES [ME *prophecie, prophesie*, fr. OF, fr. LL *prophetia*, fr. Gk *prophēteia*, fr. *prophētēs* prophet + *-eia* -y] **1 :** the function or vocation of a prophet **:** utterance under the inspiring influence of religious experience; *specif* **:** the declaration of divine will and purpose **2 :** spoken or recorded utterance of a prophet **:** divinely inspired moral teaching (as by warning, exhorting, consoling) **:** apocalyptic revelation **3 :** a declaration of something to come **:** FORETELLING, PREDICTION **4** *obs* **:** public interpretation of Scripture **5 :** an Old Testament lection preceding the Epistle in various Christian liturgies

**proph·e·si·er** \ˈpräfə,sī(ə)r\ *n* -s **:** one that prophesies

**proph·e·sy** *also* **proph·e·cy** \-,sī\ *vb* -ED/-ING/-ES [ME *prophecien, prophesien*, fr. MF *prophecier, prophesier*, fr. OF, fr. *prophecie, prophesie*, n.] *vt* **1 :** to utter or announce by or as if by divine inspiration **2 :** PREDICT ⟨~ general disaster⟩ ⟨~ a fall in prices⟩ **3 :** FORESHOW, PREFIGURE ⟨thy very gait did ~ a royal nobleness —Shak.⟩ ~ *vi* **:** to do the work or office of a prophet: as **a :** to speak for God or a deity **:** speak under the inspiring influence of religious experience **:** speak as or as if divinely inspired **b :** to give instruction in religious matters **:** interpret or expound Scripture or religious subjects **:** PREACH, EXHORT **c :** to speak or write under strong excitement or enthusiasm **:** speak or act with prophetic frenzy **d :** to make a prediction **syn** see FORETELL

**proph·et** \ˈpräfət, *usu* -əd·+V\ *n* -s [ME *prophete*, fr. OF, fr. L *propheta*, fr. Gk *prophētēs*, fr. *pro* before, for + *-phētēs* (fr. *phanai* to say, speak) — more at FOR, BAN] **1 :** one who speaks for God or a deity **:** a divinely inspired revealer, interpreter, or spokesman: as **a :** an individual believed in ancient Israel to be possessed of clairvoyance ⟨is there no ~ of the Lord here, through whom we may inquire of the Lord? —2 Kings 3:11 (RSV)⟩ **b :** a member of a band of religious ecstatics believed in ancient Israel to be wonder workers and soothsayers ⟨a band of ~s coming down from the high place with harp, tambourine, flute, and lyre before them, prophesying —1 Sam 10:5 (RSV)⟩ **c** *often cap* **:** the writer of one of the prophetic books of the Old Testament **d :** an officer in a Christian church; *specif* **:** one in the early church interpreting God's will under the inspiration of the Holy Spirit **e** *usu cap* **:** a person regarded by a group of followers as the final authoritative revealer of God's will ⟨Muhammad, the *Prophet* of Allah to Muslims⟩ ⟨to all his followers, Zoroaster is the *Prophet*⟩ **f** *usu cap* **:** the accredited leader of a religious group (as the Mormons) **2 :** one gifted with more than ordinary spiritual and moral insight **:** SEER ⟨mighty ~ . . . on whom those truths do rest which we are toiling all our lives to find —William Wordsworth⟩; *esp* **:** an inspired poet **3 :** one who foretells future events **:** PREDICTOR ⟨in defiance of all the ~s of doom⟩ ⟨weather ~⟩ **4 :** an effective or leading spokesman for a cause, doctrine, or group ⟨the ~ of higher education for the many —J.S.Reeves⟩ ⟨one of the ~s of socialism⟩ ⟨~ of literary realism⟩ **5** *Christian Science* **a :** a spiritual seer **b :** disappearance of material sense before the conscious facts of spiritual Truth

**proph·et·ess** \-əd·əs, -ətəs\ *n* -ES [ME *prophetesse*, fr. MF, fr. LL *prophetissa*, fr. L *propheta* prophet + LL *-issa* -ess] **1 :** a female prophet **2 :** the wife of a prophet

**prophet flower** *n* [trans. of Per *gulī paighāmbar* flower of the Prophet (Muhammad †A.D.632 Arabian prophet and founder of Islam)] **:** an East Indian perennial herb (*Arnebia echioides*) having yellow flowers marked with five spots that fade after a few hours; *also* **:** a related annual (*A. griffithii*)

**proph·et·hood** \-ət,hu̇d\ *n* **:** the position or career of a prophet

**pro·phet·ic** \prəˈfed·|ik, prō'-, -et|, |ēk\ *adj* [MF *prophetique*, fr. LL *propheticus*, fr. Gk *prophētikos*, fr. *prophētēs* prophet + *-ikos* -ic] **1 :** of, relating to, or characteristic of a prophet or prophecy **:** containing or resembling prophecy **:** INTERPRETATIVE, REVELATORY ⟨~ powers⟩ ⟨~ writings⟩ **2 :** foretelling events **:** tending to indicate what is going to happen **:** PRESAGEFUL ⟨~ skirmishes on the eve of a great battle⟩

**pro·phet·i·cal** \|ək̇əl, |ēk-\ *adj* [ME, fr. MF *prophetique* + E *-al*] **:** of, pertaining to, or like a prophet or prophecy **:** containing prophecy ⟨~ books of the Old Testament⟩

**pro·phet·i·cal·i·ty** \prə,fed·əˈkaləd·ē\ *n* -ES **:** prophetical quality

**pro·phet·i·cal·ly** \prəˈfed·|ək(ə)lē, prō'-, -et|, |ēk-, -li\ *adv* **:** in a prophetic manner **:** like or characteristic of a prophet

**pro·phet·i·cal·ness** *n* -ES **:** prophetic quality

**pro·phet·i·cism** \|ə,sizəm\ *n* -s **1 :** an idea or form of words characteristic of the prophets **2 :** PROPHETISM

**prophetic lesson** *n* **:** PROPHECY 5

**proph·e·tism** \ˈpräfə,tizəm\ *n* -s **:** prophetic character, function, or authority; *specif* **:** the system or doctrines of the Hebrew prophets

**¹pro·phy·lac·tic** \ˌprōfə¦laktik, -tēk *also* ¦präf-\ *adj* [Gk *prophylaktikos*, fr. (assumed) Gk *prophylaktos* (verbal of Gk *prophylassein* to keep guard before, take precautions against, fr. *pro-* ¹pro- + *phylassein* to guard, preserve, fr. *phylak-, phylax* guard) + Gk *-ikos* -ic] **1 :** guarding from disease **:** preventing or contributing to the prevention of disease **2 :** tending to prevent or ward off **:** PREVENTIVE, CAUTIONARY ⟨the swastika . . . a very ancient ~ symbol occurring among all peoples —Victor Schultze⟩ ⟨the purpose of this volume is ~ rather than remedial —Knight Dunlap⟩

**²prophylactic** \"\ *n* -s **1 :** something (as a medicinal preparation) that prevents or helps to prevent disease **:** PREVENTIVE **2 a :** a device (as a condom) for preventing venereal infection **b :** any of a number of devices for the prevention of conception

**pro·phy·lac·ti·cal·ly** \-tək(ə)lē, -tēk-, -li\ *adv* **:** with a preventive purpose **:** so as to prevent

**pro·phy·lax·is** \ˌ==ˈlaksəs\ *n, pl* **prophylax·es** \-k,sēz\ [NL, fr. Gk *prophylaktikos* prophylactic, after such pairs as Gk *praktikos* practical **:** *praxis* doing, action] **:** the prevention of disease **:** measures necessary to preserve health and prevent the spread of disease **:** protective, preservative, or preventive treatment

**pro·phy·laxy** \ˈ==,laksē\ *n* -ES [F *prophylaxie*, fr. NL *prophylaxis*] **:** PROPHYLAXIS

**pro·phyll** \ˈprō,fil\ *also* **pro·phyl·lum** \prōˈfiləm\ *n, pl* **prophylls** \-lz\ *also* **prophyl·la** \-lə\ [NL *prophyllum*, fr. ¹*pro-* + *-phyllum*] **:** a plant structure resembling a leaf (as a bracteole) or consisting of a modified or rudimentary leaf (as a foliar primordium)

**propination** *n* -s [L *propination-, propinatio*, fr. *propinatus* (past part. of *propinare*) + *-ion-, -io* -ion] *obs* **:** the act of drinking to someone's health

**¹pro·pine** \prəˈpēn, -pīn\ *vt* -ED/-ING/-S [ME *propinen*, fr. MF *propiner*, fr. L *propinare* to present, procure, give to drink, drink to someone's health, fr. Gk *propinein* to present, drink to someone's health, drink first, fr. *pro-* ¹pro- + *pinein* to drink — more at POTABLE] **1** *chiefly Scot* **:** to present or give esp. as a token of friendship **2** *obs* **:** to pledge in drinking

**²propine** \"\ *n* -s [ME (Sc) *propyne*, fr. MF *propine*, fr. ML *propina*, fr. L *propinare*] *n, Scot* **:** a gift in return for a favor **:** TIP

**³propine** [ISV *prop-* + *-ine*] *var of* PROPYNE

**pro·pin·quant** \prōˈpiŋkwənt\ *adj* [L *propinquant-, propinquans*, pres. part. of *propinquare* to draw near, approach, fr. *propinquus* near, neighboring] **:** being in propinquity **:** NEARBY

**pro·pinque** \prōˈpiŋk\ *adj* [L *propinquus*] *archaic* **:** NEAR

**pro·pin·qui·ty** \prōˈpiŋkwəd·ē, prə'-, -ink-, -wətē, -i\ *n* -ES [ME *propinquite*, fr. L *propinquitat-, propinquitas* kinship, proximity, fr. *propinquus* near, neighboring, akin (fr. *prope* near) + *-itat-, -itas* -ity — more at APPROACH] **1 :** nearness of blood **:** KINSHIP ⟨degrees of ~⟩ **2 a :** nearness in place **:** PROXIMITY ⟨trees in close ~ to the house⟩ **b :** nearness in time **3** *archaic* **:** closeness in nature, disposition, or interests

**pro·pin·quous** \-wəs\ *adj* [L *propinquus*] **:** PROPINQUANT

**pro·pio·lactone** \ˌprōpēō+\ *or* **pro·pi·ono–lactone** \ˌprōpē¦änō, -¦ōnō+\ *n* [*propiolactone* ISV *propion-* + *lactone; propiono-lactone* fr. *propion-* + *lactone*] **:** a liquid beta-lactone $C_3H_4O_2$ made by condensation of ketene and formaldehyde

**pro·pi·ol·aldehyde** \ˌprōpē,ōl, -,ōl+\ *n* [ISV *propiolic* (in *propiolic acid*) + *aldehyde*] **:** a mobile liquid aldehyde HC≡CCHO made synthetically

**pro·pi·o·late** \ˈprōpēə,lāt\ *n* -s [ISV *propiolic* (in *propiolic acid*) + *-ate*] **:** a salt or ester of propiolic acid

**pro·pi·olic acid** \ˌprōpē¦ōlik-, -¦älik-\ *n* [*propiolic* ISV *propion-* (in *propionic acid*) + *-ol-* (prob. fr. *stearolic acid*) + *-ic;* prob. fr. the fact that the relation of propiolic acid to propionic acid is analogous to that of stearolic acid to stearic acid] **:** a pungent liquid acetylenic acid HC≡CCOOH made by carbonation of sodium acetylide that forms not only salts but also metallic derivatives like those of acetylene

**propion-** *or* **propiono-** *also* **propi-** *or* **propio-** *comb form* [ISV, fr. *propionic* (in *propionic acid*)] **:** propionic acid **:** related to propionic acid ⟨*propionyl*⟩ ⟨*propionitrile*⟩ ⟨*propiono*-lactone⟩

**pro·pi·on·aldehyde** \ˌprōpē,än+\ *n* [ISV *propion-* + *aldehyde*] **:** a volatile pungent liquid aldehyde $C_2H_5CHO$ made usu. by dehydrogenation of propyl alcohol or as a by-product in the Fischer-Tropsch synthesis of higher hydrocarbons and used in organic synthesis

**pro·pi·o·nate** \ˈprōpēə,nāt\ *n* -s [ISV *propion-* + *-ate*] **:** a salt or ester of propionic acid

**pro·pi·one** \ˈprōpē,ōn\ *n* -s [ISV *propion-* + *-one*] **:** PENTANONE b

**pro·pi·oni·bacterium** \ˌprōpē¦änə, -¦ōnə+\ *n* [NL, fr. ISV *propion-* + NL *-i-* + *bacterium*] **1** *cap* **:** a genus (the type of the family Propionibacteriaceae) of gram-positive nonmotile usu. anaerobic eubacteria that form propionic acid by fermenting lactic acid, carbohydrates, and polyalcohols and that include forms associated with the ripening of dairy products (as some hard cheeses) **2** *pl* **propionibacteria :** any bacterium of the genus *Propionibacterium*

**pro·pi·on·ic acid** \ˌprōpē¦änik-\ *n* [*propionic* ISV ¹*pro-* + *pion-* (fr. Gk *piōn, piōn* fat) + *-ic;* orig. formed as F (*acide*) *propionique* — more at PIOPHILIDAE] **:** a liquid fatty acid $C_2H_5COOH$ that has a sharp odor and is miscible with water, that occurs in milk and milk products and in distillates of wood, coal, and petroleum but that is usu. made by oxidation of propionaldehyde or propyl alcohol, and that is used chiefly in making salts (as the fungistatic calcium and sodium salts) and esters (as used for fruity and floral odors in perfumes)

**pro·pio·nitrile** \ˌprōpēō+\ *n* [ISV *propion-* + *nitrile*] **:** a toxic volatile liquid nitrile $C_2H_5CN$ that yields propionic acid and ammonia on hydrolysis and is used chiefly as a solvent — called also *ethyl cyanide*

**pro·pi·o·nyl** \ˈprōpēə,nil, -nēl\ *n* -s [ISV *propion-* + *-yl*] **:** the univalent radical $C_2H_5CO$– of propionic acid

**pro·pi·on·y·late** \ˌprōpēˈänᵊl,āt\ *vt* -ED/-ING/-S [*propionyl* + *-ate*] **:** to introduce propionyl into (a compound) usu. by reaction with propionic acid or a derivative of it

**pro·pi·the·cus** \ˌprōpəˈthēkəs\ *n, cap* [NL, fr. ¹*pro-* + *-pithecus*] **:** a genus of lemurs consisting of the sifakas

**pro·pi·ti·a·ble** \prəˈpishēəbəl, prō'- *sometimes* -isē-\ *adj* [L *propitiabilis*, fr. *propitiare* to propitiate + *-abilis* -able] **:** capable of being propitiated

**pro·pi·ti·ate** \-ē,āt, *usu* -ād·+V\ *vt* -ED/-ING/-S [L *propitiatus*, past part. of *propitiare*, fr. *propitius* propitious] **:** to appease and make favorable **:** CONCILIATE ⟨the savage hunter and fisher is careful to ~ the animals and fish which he kills —J. G.Frazer⟩ **syn** see PACIFY

**pro·pi·ti·at·ing·ly** *adv* **:** in a propitiating manner **:** so as to appease or conciliate

**pro·pi·ti·a·tion** \=,==ˈāshən\ *n* -s [ME *propiciacioun*, fr. LL *propitiation-, propitiatio*, fr. L *propitiatus* (past part. of *propitiare*) + *-ion-, -io* -ion] **1 :** the act of propitiating, appeasing, or conciliating **2 :** something that appeases or conciliates a deity **:** ATONEMENT; *specif* **:** the self-sacrifice and death of Jesus Christ to appease divine justice and to effect reconciliation between God and man

**pro·pi·ti·a·tive** \=ˈ==,ād·|iv, -āt|, |ēv *also* |əv\ *adj* **:** tending to propitiate

**pro·pi·ti·a·tor** \|ə(r)\ *n* -s [LL, fr. L *propitiatus* (past part. of *propitiare*) + *-or*] **:** one that propitiates

**pro·pi·ti·a·to·ri·ly** \prə¦pishēə¦tōrəlē, prō¦-, -tȯr-, -li *sometimes* -isē-\ *adv* **:** by way of propitiation

**¹pro·pi·ti·a·to·ry** \=ˈ===,tōrē, -tȯr-, -ri\ *n* -ES [ME *propiciatorie*, fr. LL *propitiatorium* means of atonement, mercy seat, fr. neut. of *propitiatorius*, adj.] **1 :** MERCY SEAT **2** *obs* **:** a sacrifice made in propitiation

**²propitiatory** \"\ *adj* [LL *propitiatorius*, fr. L *propitiatus* (past part. of *propitiare*) + *-orius* -ory] **1 :** of or relating to propitiation **:** EXPIATORY ⟨~ sacrifice⟩ **2 :** intended to appease or conciliate ⟨sent her flowers as a ~ gesture⟩

**pro·pi·tious** \prəˈpishəs, prō'-\ *adj* [ME *propicious*, fr. L *propitius*, fr. *pro* before + *-pitius* (akin to L *petere* to go to or toward, seek) — more at FOR, FEATHER] **1 :** favorably disposed **:** graciously inclined **:** BENEVOLENT ⟨we may succeed if the gods are ~⟩ **2 :** being of good omen **:** AUSPICIOUS, ENCOURAGING, FAVORABLE ⟨no conditions seem so ~ for a practical confederation as those of South America —Norman Angell⟩ **3 :** tending to favor or assist **:** HELPFUL, ADVANTAGEOUS, OPPORTUNE ⟨conditions ~ to the development of democracy —A.N.Christensen⟩ **syn** see FAVORABLE

**pro·pi·tious·ly** *adv* **:** in a propitious manner

**pro·pi·tious·ness** *n* -ES **:** the quality or state of being propitious

**propjet** \ˈ=,=\ *n* [⁵*prop* + *jet*] **:** TURBOPROP

**propjet engine** *n* **:** TURBO-PROPELLER ENGINE

**prop joint** *n* **:** RULE JOINT

**propl** *abbr* proportional

**pro·plasm** \ˈprō,plazəm\ *n* -s [L *proplasma*, fr. Gk, fr. *proplassein* to form or mold before, fr. *pro-* ¹pro- + *plassein* to form, mold — more at PLASTER] **:** a preliminary model (as made by a sculptor) **:** MOLD, MATRIX

**pro·plastid** \prō+\ *n* -s [ISV ¹*pro-* + *plastid*] **:** a minute cytoplasmic body from which a plastid is formed

**prop·less** \ˈpräpləs\ *adj* **:** having no support

**pro·pleu·ral** \prōˈplu̇rəl\ *adj* [*propleuron* + *-al*] **:** situated in or relating to a propleuron ⟨~ bristle⟩

**pro·pleuron** \prō+\ *n* [NL, fr. ¹*pro-* + *pleuron*] **:** a pleuron of the prothorax of an insect

**pro·plexus** \prō+\ *also* **pro·plex** \ˈprō,pleks\ *n* [NL *pro-plexus*, fr. ¹*pro-* + *plexus*] **1 :** BRACHIAL PLEXUS **2 :** CHOROID PLEXUS

**pro·pliopithecus** \prō+\ *n, cap* [NL, fr. ¹*pro-* + *Pliopithecus*] **:** a genus of small primitive short-jawed anthropoids from the Lower Oligocene of Egypt related to the gibbon but having the same dental formula as man

**propman** \ˈ=,=\ *n, pl* **propmen :** PROPERTY MAN

**propn** *abbr* proportion

**pro·pneus·tic** \prōˈn(y)üstik\ *adj* [¹*pro-* + Gk *pneustikos* of or for breathing, fr. (assumed) Gk *pneustos* (verbal of Gk *pnein* to breathe) + Gk *-ikos* -ic — more at SNEEZE] *of an insect larva* **:** having only the anterior pair of spiracles functional

**pro·po·de·al** \prōˈpōdēəl\ *adj* [*propodeum* + *-al*] **:** relating to or situated at a propodeum

**pro·po·de·um** \-ēəm\ *also* **pro·po·de·on** \-ēən\ *n, pl* **propodeums** *also* **propo·dea** \-ēə\ [*propodeum* fr. NL, alter. of *propodeon*, fr. ¹*pro-* + *podeon; propodeon* fr. NL] **:** the part of the thorax of a hymenopteran that lies immediately over and partly surrounding the insertion of the petiole of the abdomen and represents a basal abdominal segment which has become fused with the thorax

**pro·po·di·al** \-ēəl\ *adj* [NL *propodialis*, fr. *propodium* + L *-alis* -al] **1 :** of or relating to the propodium **2 :** of or relating to a propodiale or the propodialia

**pro·po·di·a·le** \prō,pōdē'ālē\ *n, pl* **propodia·lia** \-lēə\ [NL, fr. neut. of *propodialis*] : the proximal bone of a limb : HUMERUS, FEMUR

**prop·o·dite** \'präpə,dīt\ *n* -s [ISV 1*pro-* + *-podite*] : the sixth or penultimate joint of a leg (as a walking leg) of a crustacean (as a decapod) — **prop·o·dit·ic** \¦==¦did·ik\ *adj*

**pro·po·di·um** \prō+\ *n, pl* **propodia** [NL, fr. 1*pro-* + *podium*] : the anterior portion of the foot of a mollusk

**prop·o·dus** \'präpədəs\ *n, pl* **propo·di** \-pə,dī\ [NL, fr. 1*pro-* + *-podus* (fr. Gk *pod-, pous* foot — more at FOOT)] : PROPODITE

**prop·o·lis** \'präpələs\ *n* -ES [L, fr. Gk, fr. *pro-* 1pro- + *polis* city — more at POLICE] : a brownish resinous material of waxy consistency collected by bees from the buds of trees and used as a cement — called also *bee glue*

**prop·o·lize** \'präpə,līz\ *vt* -ED/-ING/-S [F *propoliser*, fr. *propolis* (fr. L) + *-iser* -ize] : to fill or cover up with propolis

**pro·pone** \prō'pōn\ *vt* -ED/-ING/-S [ME (Sc) *proponen*, fr. L *proponere* to display, declare, propound — more at PROPOUND] 1 *Scot* : PROPOSE, PROPOUND 2 *Scot* : to bring or put forward (a defense, an excuse) : set forth

**1pro·po·nent** \prə'pōnənt, prō'-\ *n* -s [L *proponent-, proponens*, pres. part. of *proponere*] 1 : one who makes a proposal : one who lays down and defends a proposition : one who argues in favor of something (as an institution, a policy, a legislative measure, a doctrine) : ADVOCATE, SUPPORTER — opposed to *opponent* 2 : the propounder of a legal instrument (as a will for probate)

**2proponent** \"\ *adj* [L *proponent-, proponens*, pres. part. of *proponere*] : that proposes, advocates, or defends ⟨peculiar element in Zionism is that its ~ Jews are not a full nationality —A.L.Kroeber⟩

**pro·pons** \'prō,pänz\ *n, pl* **propon·tes** \prō'pän,tēz\ [NL *propont-, propons*, fr. 1*pro-* + *pont-, pons* pons] : PONTICULUS 2

**pro·pon·tic** \prō'päntik\ *adj, cap* [*Propontis*, sea in northwest Turkey between Europe and Asia + E *-ic*] : of or relating to the ancient Propontis or modern Sea of Marmara

**1pro·por·tion** \prə'pōrshən, prō'-, -pȯr-, -pōəsh-, -pȯ(ə)sh-; *sometimes by* r-*dissimilation* pə'-\ *n* -s [ME *proporcioun*, fr MF *proportion*, fr. L *proportion-, proportio*, fr. *pro* for + *portion-, portio* part, share, portion — more at FOR, PORTION] 1 a : the relation of one part to another or to the whole with respect to magnitude, quantity, or degree : relative size : RATIO ⟨the ~s of local, domestic, governmental, and foreign news have never been set —F.L.Mott⟩ ⟨winter rainfall decreases, and . . . summer rainfall increases, until at the eastern margin the ~ is reversed —F.E.Egler⟩ b *archaic* : COMPARISON, ANALOGY 2 a : harmonious relation of parts to each other or to the whole : BALANCE, SYMMETRY ⟨finely molded cornice in correct classic ~ —*Amer. Guide Series: Minn.*⟩ b : reasonable or desirable estimation or assignment of relative value ⟨the more responsible . . . journals will either redress the wrong or treat it with ~ and humor —Jean Hills⟩ 3 : the equality of two ratios : a relation among quantities such that the quotient of the first divided by the second equals that of the third divided by the fourth (as 4:2=10:5 or 4/2=10/5 or 4:2::10:5) — called also *geometrical proportion* 4 a : proper or equal share : LOT ⟨the ~ of sago flour allotted to different members of the . . . labor group —R.W.Firth⟩ b : a portion or share of an actual or implied whole having a size or value relative to other portions or shares : QUOTA, PERCENTAGE ⟨felt anger and fear in equal ~s⟩ ⟨a much higher ~ of young people are going to high school and beyond —Walter Lippmann⟩ 5 a *archaic* : FORM, SHAPE b : SIZE, DEGREE, DIMENSION ⟨eddies, some of which are small and some of oceanic ~s —R.E.Coker⟩ 6 : the act of dividing proportionately; *specif* : the modification of the normal note values in mensural notation of music by diminution or augmentation according to a fractional arithmetic ratio — **in proportion** 1 : of the extent, size, or degree demanded (as by a relationship, comparison, or sense of fitness) ⟨a large house, with rooms *in proportion*⟩ 2 : to the same degree : INSOFAR ⟨man is free *in proportion* as his surroundings have a determinate nature —R.M.Weaver⟩ — **out of proportion** : DISPROPORTIONATELY, EXCESSIVELY ⟨as the speed of a plane approaches . . . 750 miles an hour the amount of power needed . . . increases *out of* all *proportion* —G.R.Harrison⟩

**2proportion** \"\ *vt* **proportioned; proportioned; proportioning** \-sh(ə)niŋ\ **proportions** [ME *proporciounen*, fr. MF *proportionner*, fr. *proportion*, n.] 1 : to adjust (a part or thing) in size relative to other parts or things : regulate the relative size of the parts of ⟨the duty of the older man to ~ his pace to the . . . course of his master —Francis Hackett⟩ 2 : to make the parts of harmonious or correspondent or symmetrical : give pleasing or appropriate proportions to 3 *obs* : to be proportionate to : equal in value or importance ⟨his ransom, which must ~ the losses we have borne —Shak.⟩ 4 *obs* : to divide into or distribute in shares 5 *obs* : APPORTION 6 *obs* : to estimate the proportions of : COMPARE

**pro·por·tion·able** \-nəbəl\ *adj* [ME *proporcionable*, fr. LL *proportionabilis*, fr. L *proportion-, proportio* proportion + *-abilis* -able] *archaic* : PROPORTIONAL, PROPORTIONATE

**pro·por·tion·ably** \-blē\ *adv* [ME *proporcionably*, fr. *proporcionable* + *-ly*] *archaic* : in proportion : PROPORTIONATELY ⟨to make the being of a gigantic stature, . . . about eight feet in height, and ~ large —Mary W. Shelley⟩

**1pro·por·tion·al** \-shənᵊl, -shnəl\ *adj* [ME *proporcional*, fr. L *proportionalis*, fr. *proportion-, proportio* proportion + *-alis* -al] 1 a : being in proportion : corresponding in size, degree, or intensity : PROPORTIONATE — used with *to* ⟨rushed into freedom and enjoyment . . . with an energy ~ to their previous restraint —G.L.Dickinson⟩ b : having the same or a constant ratio 2 : of, relating to, or used in determining proportions ⟨windows were widened for ~ consideration⟩ ⟨~ compasses⟩ 3 : regulated or determined in size or degree with reference to proportions ⟨~ system of immigration quotas⟩ — **pro·por·tion·al·ly** \-shənᵊlē, -shnəlē, -i\ *adv*

**2proportional** \"\ *n* -s 1 : a number or quantity in a proportion 2 *obs* : EQUIVALENT 2

**proportional counter** *n* : a counting tube operated at voltages below the threshold voltage whose discharge pulses are proportional to the amount of ionization produced by the ionizing particles

**proportional dividers** *n pl* : dividers having two legs pointed at both ends and joined by an adjustable pivot so that distances measured between the points at one end can be laid off in the same proportion by the points at the opposite end

proportional dividers

**pro·por·tion·al·ism** \-shənᵊl,izəm, -shnə,li-\ *n* -s : the principle or practice of electing officials by proportional representation

**pro·por·tion·al·ist** \-shənᵊləst, -shnələ-\ *n* -s : a believer in or advocate of proportional representation

**pro·por·tion·al·i·ty** \prə,pōrshə'naləd·ē\ *n* -ES [LL *proportionalitat-, proportionalitas*, fr. L *proportionalis* proportional + *-tat-, -tas* -ty] : the quality, state, or fact of being proportional

**proportionality constant** *n* : the constant ratio of one variable quantity to another to which it is proportional

**proportional limit** *n* : ELASTIC LIMIT 2

**proportional parts** *n pl* : fractional parts of the difference between successive entries in a table that are arranged in a supplementary table for use in linear interpolation

**proportional rate** *n* : a freight rate for use only as a factor in making a combination through rate

**proportional representation** *n* : an electoral system designed to represent in a legislative body each political group or party in optimum proportion to its actual voting strength in a community — abbr. *P.R.*; see CUMULATIVE VOTING, HARE SYSTEM, LIST SYSTEM; compare PREFERENTIAL VOTING, SINGLE-MEMBER DISTRICT

**proportional tax** *n* : a tax in which the tax rate remains constant regardless of the amount of the tax base

**1pro·por·tion·ate** \prə'pōrsh(ə)nət, prō'-, -pȯr-, -pōəsh-, -pȯ(ə)sh-, *sometimes by* r-*dissimilation* pə'-, *usu* -əd·+V\ *adj* [ME *proporcionate*, fr. LL *proportionatus*, fr. L *proportion-, proportio* proportion + *-atus* -ate] : being in proportion : proportionally adjusted : adequately proportioned ⟨representation ~ to the population⟩ ⟨returns ~ to your efforts⟩ ⟨additions to his family meant a ~ increase in his expenses⟩ — **pro·por·tion·ate·ly** *adv* — **pro·por·tion·ate·ness** *n* -ES

**2proportionate** \-shə,nāt, *usu* -ād·+V\ *vt* -ED/-ING/-S : to make proportionate : distribute or determine proportionally : give due proportions to : PROPORTION ⟨~ punishments to crimes⟩

**pro·por·tioned** \-shənd\ *adj* [ME *proporciouned*, fr. past part. of *proporciounen* to proportion] : having such proportions ⟨he was small and slight . . . but well-*proportioned*, and his short stature did not catch the eye —John Buchan⟩ : made or treated with regard for proper proportion ⟨give their readers a ~ and honest view of the world —Alan Barth⟩; *specif* : made in several standard lengths suited to body height classifications ⟨women's slips ~ for tall, medium, short⟩

**pro·por·tion·er** \-sh(ə)nə(r)\ *n* -s : one that proportions : a device for securing proportions in a mixture ⟨pumping liquid foam through a ~ and smothering the fire in the gasoline hatch —K.M.Dodson⟩

**proportioning** *pres part of* PROPORTION

**pro·por·tion·less** \-shənləs\ *adj* : lacking in proportion : UNSYMMETRICAL, DISTORTED

**pro·por·tion·ment** \-nmənt\ *n* -s : a state of being proportioned : PROPORTIONING

**proportions** *pl of* PROPORTION, *pres 3d sing of* PROPORTION

**pro·pos·al** \prə'pōzəl, prō'-\ *n* -s [*propose* + *-al*] 1 : an act of putting forward or stating (a scheme, an offer, an intention) for consideration ⟨sincere ~ of friendship⟩ 2 a : something put forward for consideration or acceptance : SUGGESTION, MOTION ⟨~s for mutual disarmament⟩ ⟨~ to build a new bridge⟩ ⟨legislative ~s⟩ b : an offer to perform or undertake something : BID ⟨~ of marriage⟩ ⟨the union rejected the companies' wage ~s⟩

**proposal bond** *n* : BID BOND

**pro·pos·ant** \-zᵊnt\ *n* -s [F, candidate for the Protestant ministry, fr. *proposant*, pres. part. of *proposer* to propose] : one who proposes himself as a candidate (as for the ministry)

**pro·pose** \prə'pōz, prō'-\ *vb* -ED/-ING/-S [ME *proposen*, fr. MF *proposer*, modif. (influenced by *poser* to put, place) of L *proponere* to display, declare, propound (perfect stem *propos-*) — more at PROPOUND, POSE] *vi* 1 : to form or declare a plan or intention ⟨man ~s, but God disposes⟩ 2 *obs* : to engage in talk or discussion : CONVERSE ⟨there shalt thou find my cousin . . . *proposing* with the prince —Shak.⟩ 3 : to make an offer of marriage 4 : to make a prescribed statement in a card game indicating that one's hand is weak: as a : to undertake the lowest contract in solo b : to offer the drawing of additional cards in écarté ~ *vt* 1 a : to set before the mind : bring forward : PROPOUND b : INTEND ⟨to China, where she *proposed* to spend some time with her friends —H.E.Salisbury⟩ c *obs* : CONFRONT, FACE d *obs* : SUPPOSE, IMAGINE ⟨be now the father, and ~ a son —Shak.⟩ e : to picture in the mind : IMAGE 2 *obs* : to set forth : EXHIBIT, SHOW 3 : to offer for consideration, discussion, acceptance, or adoption ⟨~ terms of peace⟩ ⟨~ a legislative measure⟩ ⟨~ a topic for debate⟩ ⟨~ an alliance⟩ ⟨~ a friend for a club⟩ 4 : to set up or declare as a formed purpose ⟨*proposed* to himself to achieve what hitherto he had been promised in vain, the title of cardinal —Hilaire Belloc⟩ 5 a : to offer as a toast ⟨*proposed* the health of all the ladies present⟩ b : to suggest drinking (a toast) 6 : to use (a taxonomic name for a new or reclassified species) for the first time in a publication **syn** see INTEND

**pro·pos·er** \-zə(r)\ *n* -s : one that proposes ⟨the original ~ of this theory —L.C.Douglas⟩; *specif* : one who applies for life insurance

**pro·pos·i·ta** \prō'päzəd·ə\ *n, pl* **proposi·tae** \-zə,tē\ [NL, fem. of *propositus*] : a female propositus

**pro·po·si·tio** \,prōpə'sid·ē,ō\ *n, pl* **propositi·o·nes** \,==,==-'ō,nās\ *or* **propositios** [L *proposition-, propositio*] : PROPOSITION 3

**1prop·o·si·tion** \,präpə'zishən\ *n* -s [ME *proposicioun*, fr. MF *proposition*, fr. L *proposition-, propositio* representation, proposition, major premise, fr. *propositus* (past part. of *proponere* to display, declare, propound) + *-ion-, -io* -ion — more at PROPOUND] 1 a *obs* : the act of proposing something for discussion or development (as by argument, narration) b : something proposed or offered for consideration, acceptance, or adoption : PROPOSAL ⟨the ~ to extend the . . . act spurred him to a defense of . . . institutions —S.H.Adams⟩ c : the point to be discussed or maintained in argument usu. stated in sentence form near the outset d (1) : a formal statement of a mathematical truth to be proved or demonstrated : THEOREM (2) : a mathematical statement of an operation to be performed : PROBLEM 2 a *obs* : the act of setting or showing forth b *obs* : the act of offering : OFFER ⟨allures us by the ~ of rewards —Jeremy Taylor⟩ 3 a : a declarative sentence : an expression in language, symbols, or signs of something capable of being believed, doubted, or denied : a verbal expression that is either true or false — called also *statement* b : the objective meaning of a statement c : a statement together with its objective meaning 4 a : a project, plan, undertaking, or situation requiring some action (as dealing with, managing, operating, carrying out) with reference to it : BUSINESS, AFFAIR ⟨a wounded bull is a nasty ~ to tackle —*Manchester Guardian Weekly*⟩ ⟨writing is essentially a two-way ~ —S.E. Fitzgerald⟩ ⟨the scheme . . . has come up against a political snag and is at the moment not a practical ~ —W.B.Fisher⟩ ⟨it looked as if the mine would never become a paying ~⟩ b : a person requiring to be dealt with ⟨a tough ~⟩ ⟨a queer ~⟩ c : a proposed conditional bargain, agreement, deal, or settlement of a difficulty

**2proposition** \"\ *vt* -ED/-ING/-S : to make a proposal to : offer a scheme to; *specif* : to suggest sexual intercourse to ⟨had a habit of pinching and ~*ing* the nurses —Alan Hynd⟩

**prop·o·si·tion·al** \¦==¦zishənᵊl, -shnəl\ *adj* : of, relating to, or resembling a proposition ⟨these poems are sometimes too thinly ~ —David Daiches⟩ — **prop·o·si·tion·al·ly** \-shənᵊlē, -shnəlē, -i\ *adv*

**propositional calculus** *n* : a fundamental branch of symbolic logic dealing with propositions or statements as wholes, with their combinations, with the connectives that interrelate them, and with their transformation rules — compare TRANSFORMATION RULE, TRUTH TABLE

**propositional function** *n* 1 : SENTENTIAL FUNCTION 2 : something that is designated or expressed by a sentential function

**proposition bet** *n* : a bet in craps that a certain number or combination of numbers will or will not appear during a specified series of rolls

**pro·pos·i·tus** \prō'päzəd·əs\ *n, pl* **proposi·ti** \-zə,tī\ [NL, fr. L, past part. of *proponere* to display, declare, propound] 1 a : one whose relations and pedigree are sought to be ascertained by a genealogical table b : PROBAND 2 : the person immediately concerned : SUBJECT ⟨the personal law of persons domiciled in India varies with the religion of the ~ —J.H.C. Morris⟩

**pro·pound** \prə'paund, prō'-\ *vb* -ED/-ING/-S [alter. of earlier *propoun*, alter. (influenced by obs. E *compoun* — var. of E 1*compound* — & obs. E *expoun* — var. of E *expound*) of *propone*, fr. ME (Sc) *proponen*, fr. L *proponere* to display, declare, propound, fr. *pro* before + *ponere* to put, place — more at FOR, POSITION] *vt* 1 : to offer for consideration, deliberation, or debate : put for solution : set forth ⟨~ a doctrine⟩ : PROPOSE ⟨~ a question⟩ ⟨~ a hypothesis⟩ 2 : to propose or name as a candidate (as for admission to communion with a church or for an office) 3 *obs* : to set before one's own mind or another's as an incentive, motive, aim, representation, or idea ⟨darest thou to the Son of God ~ to worship thee —John Milton⟩ ~ *vi* : to make a proposal : put a question

**pro·pound·er** \-də(r)\ *n* -s : one that propounds

**propoxy-** *comb form* [*prop-* + *oxy-*] : containing the univalent group $CH_3CH_2CH_2O$— composed of propyl united with oxygen ⟨*propoxy*acetanilide⟩

**propped** *past of* PROP

**prop·per** \'präpə(r)\ *n* -s : one that props : SUPPORTER

**propping** *pres part of* PROP

**propr** *abbr* proprietor

**pro·prae·tor** *or* **pro·pre·tor** \prō'prēd·ə(r)\ *n* [L *propraetor*, fr. *pro-* (as in *proconsul*) + *praetor*] : a praetor of ancient Rome sent out to govern a province

**pro·prae·to·ri·al** *or* **pro·pre·to·ri·al** \¦prōprē¦tōrēəl, -tȯr-\ *adj* : of or relating to a propraetor — **pro·prae·to·ri·an** \-ən\ *adj*

**propria** *pl of* PROPRIUM

**propriate** *adj* [L *propriatus*, past part. of *propriare* to make one's own, fr. *proprius* own, particular] 1 *obs* : APPROPRIATED 2 *obs* : PARTICULAR, PECULIAR

**pro·pri·e·tage** \prə'prīəd·ij\ *n* -s [*proprietor* + *-age*] : the body of property owners

**1pro·pri·e·tar·i·an** \prə,prīə'ta(a)rēən\ *n* -s [1*proprietary* + *-an*] 1 : an advocate of proprietary government 2 [*propriety* + *-arian*] : a stickler for the proprieties

**2proprietarian** \=¦=¦==\ *adj* [fr. *proprietariat*, after E *proletariat: proletarian*] : relating or belonging to or characteristic of the propertied class — opposed to *proletarian* ⟨sending proletarian winners of scholarships to ~ public schools . . . and absorbing them into the service of the capitalist class —G.B. Shaw⟩

**pro·pri·e·tar·i·at** \=,=='ta(a)rēət\ *n* -s [1*proprietary* + *-at* (as in *proletariat*)] : the proprietorial class — opposed to *proletariat*

**pro·pri·e·tar·i·ly** \=¦==¦terəlē\ *adv* : in a proprietary manner

**1pro·pri·e·tary** \prə'prīə,terē, prō'-, -ri, *by* r-*dissimilation* pə'-\ *n* -ES [ME *proprietarie*, fr. LL *proprietarius*, fr. *proprietarius*, adj.] 1 : one who has exclusive title to a thing : one who possesses the ownership of a thing in his own right : PROPRIETOR, OWNER; *specif* : an owner or grantee of a proprietary colony 2 [ME *proprietarie*, fr. ML *proprietarius*, fr. LL] *obs* : a monk holding property in violation of his vow of poverty 3 a : a privately owned piece of property b : PROPRIETARY COMPANY 4 : right of property : OWNERSHIP 5 : a body of proprietors 6 [2*proprietary*] a : a drug that is protected by secrecy, patent, or copyright against free competition as to name, product, composition, or process of manufacture b : an ethical drug c : a nonprescription drug or medicine designed for self-medication and required to be accompanied by a list of all active ingredients and directions for safe use ⟨aspirin is a ~⟩

**2proprietary** \"\ *adj* [LL *proprietarius*, fr. L *proprietas* property + *-arius* -ary — more at PROPERTY] 1 a : held as the property of a private owner ⟨~ right of manufacture⟩ : relating or belonging to a proprietor ⟨~ control of mineral resources⟩ ⟨~ government⟩ b : characteristic of or appropriate to an owner ⟨the lawyers' . . . normal ~ feeling about the law courts —Walter Goodman⟩ 2 : made and marketed by a person or persons having the exclusive right to manufacture and sell ⟨~ baby food⟩ ⟨~ medicine⟩ 3 : privately owned and managed usu. without public control or supervision ⟨in the 19th century there were many ~ medical schools in America⟩ ⟨~ hospital⟩

**proprietary colony** *n* : a colony granted to some individual or individuals with the fullest prerogatives of government — compare CHARTER COLONY, ROYAL COLONY

**proprietary company** *n* 1 : a corporation owning all or a controlling number of the shares of another corporation 2 : a company owning land that it leases or sells to other corporations 3 *Brit* : a privately owned company the shares of which are not offered to the public : CLOSE CORPORATION

**proprietary library** *n* : a library supported and usu. controlled by stockholding proprietors as well as by subscribers

**proprietary stamp** *n* : a revenue stamp for use on proprietary articles

**pro·pri·e·tor** \prə'prīəd·ə(r), prō'-, -ətə-, *by* r-*dissimilation* pə'-\ *n* -s [alter. (influenced by *-or*) of 1*proprietary*] 1 : an owner or grantee of a proprietary colony : PROPRIETARY 2 a : one who has the legal right or exclusive title to something whether in possession or not : OWNER ⟨~ of a store⟩ ⟨protection of the rights of authors and other copyright ~s —*Universal Copyright Convention*⟩ b : one having an interest (as control, present use, or usufruct) less than absolute and exclusive right

**pro·pri·e·to·ri·al** \prə,prīə¦tōrēəl, prō¦p-, -tȯr-\ *adj* 1 : of or relating to a proprietor or proprietorship : PROPRIETARY ⟨~ rights⟩ 2 : arising from or manifesting consciousness of ownership : appropriate to an owner ⟨showed them around the place with ~ pride⟩ ⟨adopted a ~ attitude towards the entire hill —John Morrison⟩

**pro·pri·e·to·ri·al·ly** \-ēəlē\ *adv* : in a proprietorial capacity or manner

**pro·pri·e·tor·ship** \prə'prīəd·ə(r),ship\ *n* 1 a : the state or fact of being a proprietor : OWNERSHIP b : an exclusive legal right for a definite or indefinite time to the profitable use of corporeal or incorporeal property upon agreed terms ⟨~ of a drug product⟩ ⟨~ of a copyright⟩ 2 : a holding in land ⟨numerous small pleasant ~s⟩ 3 : proprietor's equity : NET ASSETS

**pro·pri·e·to·ry** \-īə,tōrē\ *n or adj* [by alter. (influence of *-ory*)] : PROPRIETARY

**pro·pri·e·tous** \-īəd·əs\ *adj* [*proprietor* + *-ous*] : disposed to assume a proprietor's rights : PROPRIETORIAL ⟨now look . . . old girl, I won't have you adopting that ~ tone —G.J.W. Goodman⟩

**pro·pri·e·tress** \-īə·trəs\ *also* **pro·pri·e·trix** \-riks\ *n* -ES [*proprietress* fr. *proprietor-* + *-ess; proprietrix* fr. *proprietor*, after such pairs as E *executor: executrix*] : a female proprietor ⟨~ of a school for girls⟩

**pro·pri·e·ty** \prə'prīəd·ē, prō'-, -ətē, -i, *by* r-*dissimilation* pə'-\ *n* -ES [ME *propriete*, fr. MF *proprieté* quality or trait belonging to a person or thing, property — more at PROPERTY] 1 a *obs* : peculiar, proper, or true nature, character, or condition ⟨the baseness of thy fear that makes thee strangle thy ~ —Shak.⟩ b *obs* : special nature : PECULIARITY 2 a *obs* : private ownership : PROPRIETORSHIP b *obs* : privately owned possessions : PROPERTY 3 a *obs* : a special characteristic of a language : IDIOM b *obs* : precise literal or strict sense 4 : the quality or state of being proper or fitting : SUITABILITY, FITNESS, APPROPRIATENESS ⟨not so easy to see the ~ in an image which divests a snake of "winter weeds" —T.S.Eliot⟩ ⟨~ and necessity of preventing interference with the course of justice by premature statement, argument, or intimidation —O.W. Holmes †1935⟩ 5 a : the standard of what is socially acceptable in conduct, behavior, speech : DECORUM ⟨passionately, deeply devoted to ~ . . . one of the most formal high U.S. officers in Europe —*Time*⟩ ⟨many of the topics denied by ~ to the newspaper's columns are considered suitable in a barbershop atmosphere —G.S.Perry⟩; *often* : prudent regard for or fear of offending against conventional rules of behavior esp. as between the sexes ⟨a long-ago love affair and the dead Welsh girl who was too innocent-hearted for his ~ —*Time*⟩ ⟨in her re-creation of the Victorian age she antedates . . . the victory of bourgeois ~ over the more raffish and glaring manners of the Regency —R.E.Roberts⟩ b **proprieties** *pl* : the customs and manners of polite society : conventionally correct behavior — used with *the* ⟨they talked the stupid, polite conversation that occurs between strangers; and then, the *proprieties* satisfied, . . . drifted back into the realm of music —Louis Bromfield⟩ ⟨feels compelled to observe the established *proprieties* of textbook writing —J.C.Cooley⟩

**pro·pri·o·cep·tion** \,prōprēō'sepshən\ *n* -s [fr. *proprioceptive*, after E *receptive: reception*] : the reception of stimuli produced within the organism — see PROPRIOCEPTOR

**pro·pri·o·cep·tive** \¦==¦septiv\ *adj* [*proprio-* (fr. L *proprius* own, particular) + *-ceptive* (as in *receptive*)] : activated by, relating to, or being stimuli produced within the organism (as by movement or tension in its own tissues) — compare EXTEROCEPTIVE, INTEROCEPTIVE

**pro·pri·o·cep·tor** \-tə(r)\ *n* -s [*proprio-* (fr. L *proprius* own, particular) + *-ceptor* (as in *receptor*)] : a sensory receptor that is located deep in the tissues (as in skeletal or heart muscle, tendons, the gastrointestinal wall, or the carotid sinus) and that functions in proprioception (as in response to changes of physical tension or chemical condition within the body proper)

**pro·prio mo·tu** \¦prōprē,ō'mō(,)tü\ *adv* [L, by one's own motion] : by one's own motion : on one's own initiative

**pro·prio·spinal** \¦prōprēō+\ *adj* [*proprio-* (fr. L *proprius* own, particular) + *spinal*] : distinctively or exclusively spinal ⟨a ~ reflex⟩

**proprio vi·go·re** \-və'gō(,)rā\ *adv* [L, by its own force] : of or by its own force independently

**pro·pri·um** \'prōprēəm\ *n, pl* **pro·pria** \-ēə\ [L, possession, characteristic, fr. neut. of *proprius* own, particular] 1 : PROP-

ERTY, ATTRIBUTE; *esp* : an attribute belonging inseparably to every member of a species 2 : the principle of individuation in personality : SELFHOOD

**pro·proctor** \prō+\ *n* [²*pro-* + *proctor*] : an assistant or deputy proctor (as at an English university)

**prop root** *n* : a root that serves as a prop or support to the plant (as in maize or mangrove) — called also *brace root;* see ROOT illustration

¹**props** *pl of* PROP, *pres 3d sing of* PROP

²**props** *n pl but sing in constr* [fr. pl. of ³*prop*] : a game similar to dicing played with four sea shells

³**props** *n pl but sing in constr* [fr. pl. of ⁴*prop*] : PROPERTY MAN

**prop·ter af·fec·tum** \'präptərə'fektəm\ *adv* [ML] : on account of partiality ⟨challenge a juror *propter affectum*⟩

**propter de·fec·tum** \-də'fektəm\ *adv* [ML] : on account of a defect ⟨the disqualification of a juror *propter defectum*⟩

**propter defectum san·gui·nis** \-'saŋgwənəs\ *adv* [ML, on account of lack of blood kin] : for lack of an heir ⟨escheat an estate *propter defectum sanguinis*⟩

**propter de·lic·tum** \-də'liktəm\ *adv* [ML, on account of a crime] : on account of conviction for a crime ⟨disqualify a juror *propter delictum*⟩

**propter delictum te·nen·tis** \-tə'nentəs\ *adv* [ML] : on account of the tenant's crime ⟨property declared forfeit *propter delictum tenentis*⟩

**propter hoc** \-'hōk\ *adv* [L] : because of this — compare POST HOC

**propter ho·no·ris re·spec·tum** \-hə'nōrəsrə'spektəm\ *adv* [ML] : on account of respect for rank ⟨a lord may claim exemption from ordinary jury duty *propter honoris respectum*⟩

**prop·ter·yg·i·al** \¦präptə¦rijēəl\ *adj* [*propterygium* + *-al*] : of, relating to, or being a propterygium

**prop·ter·yg·i·um** \,==¦rijēəm\ *n, pl* **propteryg·ia** \-ēə\ [NL, fr. ¹*pro-* + Gk *pterygion* fin, lit., small wing — more at PTERYGIUM] : the anterior of the three principal basal cartilages in the paired fins of some fishes (as sharks and rays) — compare BASIPTERYGIUM

**prop·tosed** \'präp,tōst\ *adj* [*proptosis* + *-ed*] : affected by proptosis ⟨a ~ eye⟩

**prop·to·sis** \präp'tōsəs\ *n, pl* **propto·ses** \-ō,sēz\ [NL, fr. LL, prolapse, falling forward, fr. Gk *proptōsis*, fr. *propiptein* to fall forward, fr. *pro-* ¹pro- + *piptein* to fall — more at FEATHER] : forward projection or displacement esp. of the eyeball : EXOPHTHALMOS

**propugnation** *n* -s [L *propugnation-, propugnatio*, fr. *propugnatus* (past part. of *propugnare* to fight for, defend, fr. *pro* before, for + *pugnare* to fight) + *-ion*, *-io* -ion — more at FOR, PUGNACIOUS] *obs* : means of defense : DEFENSE ⟨what ~ is in one man's valor —Shak.⟩

**propugnator** *n* -s [ME *propugnatoure*, fr. L *propugnator*, fr. *propugnatus* (past part. of *propugnare*) + *-or*] *obs* : DEFENDER, VINDICATOR

**pro·pul·sion** \prə'pəlshən, prō'-\ *n* -s [L *propuls*us (past part. of *propellere* to drive away, propel) + E *-ion* — more at PROPEL] 1 *obs* : the action of driving out or forth : EXPULSION, EJECTION 2 : the action of driving forward or ahead : action or process of propelling ⟨~ of ships by steam turbine⟩ ⟨problems of rocket ~⟩ 3 : something that propels : a driving or inciting force or influence ⟨in the ~ and in the excitement that can be provoked by forceful and expert pianists —Arthur Berger⟩ 4 : tendency to fall forward in walking (as in paralysis agitans)

**pro·pul·sive** \-lsiv, -sēv *also* -səv\ *adj* [L *propuls*us (past part. of *propellere*) + E *-ive*] : tending or having power to propel : driving onward or forward : impelling to action or motion ⟨gunpowder was well established as a ~ agent in war weapons —H.J.J.Winter⟩ ⟨the faster the jet plane goes, the greater its ~ efficiency —Harland Manchester⟩ ⟨universities . . . have . . . been the seats of ~ thought —Amy Loveman⟩ — **pro·pul·sive·ness** *n* -ES

**propulsive coefficient** *n* : the ratio between the indicated horse power of a ship's engine and the effective horsepower

**pro·pul·sor** \-sə(r)\ *n* -s [L *propuls*us (past part. of *propellere*) + E *-or*] : one that propels or produces a propulsive force ⟨use of hydrazine as a rocket ~⟩

**pro·pul·so·ry** \-sərē\ *adj* [L *propuls*us (past part. of *propellere*) + E *-ory*] : PROPULSIVE

**pro·pupa** \(')prō+\ *n* [NL, fr. ¹*pro-* + *pupa*] 1 : PREPUPA 2 : any of various insects in the late stage of incomplete metamorphosis in which the rudiments of external wings appear — **pro·pupal** \"+\ *adj*

**prop wash** *n* : SLIPSTREAM

**prop word** *n* : a noun or pronoun of very indefinite meaning that takes the qualification of an adjective with the effect of giving the latter a virtual noun construction (as *things* in "review books, manuscripts, and other literary things" or *one* in "two apples, a red and a green one")

**pro·pygidium** \,prō +\ *n* [NL, fr. ¹*pro-* + *pygidium*] : the dorsal plate of the segment that precedes the pygidium in beetles and some other insects

**pro·pyl** \'prōpəl, -ō,pil\ *n* -s [ISV *prop-* + *-yl*] : either of two isomeric alkyl radicals $C_3H_7$ derived from propane and isopropane: **a** : the normal radical $CH_3CH_2CH_2$— — called also *n-propyl* **b** : ISOPROPYL

**pro·py·lae·um** \,präpə'lēəm\ *n, pl* **propy·laea** \-ēə\ [L, fr. Gk *propylaion* (usu. in pl. *propylaia*), fr. neut. of *propylaios* situated before the gate, fr. *pro-* ¹pro- + *pylē* gate] : a vestibule or entrance of architectural importance before a building or enclosure — often used in pl.

**propyl alcohol** *n* : either of two isomeric liquid alcohols $C_3H_7OH$: **a** : the normal alcohol $CH_3CH_2CH_2OH$ occurring in fusel oil but usu. obtained synthetically (as by oxidation of mixtures of propane and butane) that is used chiefly as a solvent (as in brake fluid compositions) and in organic synthesis; 1-propanol **b** : ISOPROPYL ALCOHOL

**pro·pyl·amine** \,prōpələ'mēn, -pə'lamən\ *n* [ISV *propyl* + *amine*] 1 : either of two flammable isomeric liquid bases $C_3H_7NH_2$ of ammoniacal fishy odor; *esp* : the normal amine $CH_3CH_2CH_2NH_2$ 2 : an amine in which propyl is attached to the nitrogen atom

**pro·pyl·ate** \'prōpə,lāt\ *vt* -ED/-ING/-S [*propyl* + *-ate*] : to introduce propyl into (a chemical compound) — **pro·pyl·ation** \,==¦lāshən\ *n* -s

**pro·pyl·ene** \'prōpə,lēn\ *n* -s [*propyl* + *-ene*] 1 : a flammable gaseous olefin hydrocarbon $CH_3CH{=}CH_2$ obtained usu. in petroleum refineries by cracking petroleum hydrocarbons and used chiefly in organic synthesis of compounds (as isopropyl alcohol, allyl chloride, cumene, propylene tetramer) with which benzene is alkylated for making detergents — called also *propene;* see POLYPROPYLENE 2 : the bivalent radical $-CH(CH_3)CH_2-$ derived from propane by removal of two hydrogen atoms from adjacent carbon atoms or from propylene by breaking of the double bond — compare TRIMETHYLENE

**propylene glycol** *n* : a sweet hygroscopic viscous liquid $CH_3CHOHCH_2OH$ made usu. from propylene or propylene oxide and used chiefly as a solvent, humectant, and preservative, as an antifreeze, and in hydraulic brake fluids; 1,2-propane-diol

**propylene oxide** *n* : a flammable liquid cyclic ether $C_3H_6O$ similar to ethylene oxide that is made by chlorinating propylene to its chlorohydrin then adding alkali and is used chiefly as a solvent and in organic synthesis

**pro·pyl·ic** \(')prō¦pilik\ *adj* [ISV *propyl* + *-ic*] : of, relating to, or containing propyl

**pro·pyl·i·dene** \prō'pilə,dēn, 'prōpələ,-\ *n* -s [ISV *propyl* + *-idene*] : a bivalent hydrocarbon radical $CH_3CH_2CH<$ analogous to ethylidene — compare ISOPROPYLIDENE

**prop·y·lite** \'präpə,līt\ *n* -s [*propylon* + *-ite*] : an altered form of andesite important for its connection with certain ore deposits and orig. supposed to mark the beginning of Tertiary eruptive activity — **prop·y·lit·ic** \¦==¦lid·ik\ *adj*

**prop·y·lit·iza·tion** \,präpə,lid·ə'zāshən\ *n* -s [*propylite* + *-ization*] : the alteration of an igneous rock to propylite

**prop·y·lon** \'präpə,län\ *n, pl* **propy·la** \-lə\ [L, fr. Gk, fr. *pro-* ¹pro- + *pylē* gate] : an outer monumental gateway standing before a main gateway (as of a temple)

**pro·pyl·par·a·ben** \,prōpəl'parə,ben\ *n* -s [*propyl* + *-paraben* (as in *methylparaben*)] : a crystalline ester $HOC_6H_4COOC_3H_7$ used as a preservative in pharmaceutical preparations; propyl *para*-hydroxy-benzoate

**pro·pyl·thiouracil** \¦prōpəl+\ *n* [*propyl* + *thiouracil*] : a crystalline compound $C_7H_{10}N_2OS$ used as an antithyroid drug in the treatment of goiter — called also *6-propyl-2-thiouracil*

**pro·pyne** *also* **pro·pine** \'prō,pīn\ *n* -s [ISV *prop-* + *-yne* or *-ine*] : METHYLACETYLENE

**pro·quaes·tor** \prō'kwestə(r)\ *n* [LL, fr. L *pro quaestore*, fr. the phrase *pro quaestore* (acting) for a quaestor, fr. *pro* for + *quaestore*, abl. of *quaestor* — more at FOR, QUAESTOR] : one acting for a quaestor; *esp* : a magistrate associated with a proconsul in the administration of an ancient Roman province

¹**pro ra·ta** \(')prō'rād·ə, -rät, -rāt, |tə\ *adv* [L] : proportionately according to some exactly calculable factor (as share, liability, period of time) : in proportion

²**pro rata** \"\ *adj* : divided, distributed, or assessed pro rata

¹**pro·rate** \(')prō¦rāt, *usu* -ād·+V\ *vb* -ED/-ING/-S [¹*pro rata*] *vt* : to divide, distribute, or assess proportionately ⟨in the sale of real estate, it is usual to ~ the taxes between the seller and the buyer —*Jour. of Accountancy*⟩ ~ *vi* : to make a pro rata distribution **syn** see APPORTION

²**prorate** \'=,=\ *n* -s : an amount determined pro rata

**pro·rat·er** \(')prō¦rād·ə(r)\ *n* -s : one that prorates; *specif* : one who acts as an agent for a debtor in making payments to his creditors

**pro·ra·tion** \prō'rāshən\ *n* -s [¹*prorate* + *-ion*] : the act or an instance of prorating; *specif* : the limitation of production of crude oil or gas to some fractional part of the total productive capacity of each producer

**prore** \'prō(ə)r\ *n* -s [prob. fr. MF, fr. L *prora* — more at PROW] *archaic* : PROW

**pro·rec·tor** \prō'rektə(r)\ *n* [NL, fr. ²*pro-* + ML *rector*] : a deputy rector in a university

**pro·rec·tor·ate** \-tərət\ *n* [ISV *prorector* + *-ate*] : the office of prorector

**pro·rep·til·ia** \,prō,rep'tilēə\ *n pl, cap* [NL, fr. ¹*pro-* + *Reptilia*] *in some classifications* : a division of reptiles containing various extinct forms regarded as connecting the reptiles and amphibians — **pro·rep·til·i·an** \¦=,=¦tilēən\ *adj*

**pro·rhinal** \(')prō+\ *adj* [¹*pro-* + *rhinal*] : in front of the nasal cavities

**pro·rhip·i·do·glos·so·mor·pha** \prō,ripədō,gläsə'mȯrfə\ *n pl, cap* [NL, fr. ¹*pro-* + *Rhipidoglossa* + *-o-* + *-morpha*] *in some classifications* : a primary division of Mollusca including the classes Gastropoda, Scaphopoda, and Lamellibranchia

**pro·ro·cen·trum** \,prōrə'sen·trəm\ *n, cap* [NL, fr. *proro-* (fr. L *prora* prow) + L *centrum* center — more at CENTER] : a genus of marine dinoflagellates that occas. cause local outbreaks of red water

**pro·ro·gate** \'prōrə,gāt\ *vt* -ED/-ING/-S [ME *prorogaten*, fr. L *prorogatus*, past part. of *prorogare*] 1 : PROROGUE 2 *Scots law* : to extend (a judge's jurisdiction) by consent

**pro·ro·ga·tion** \,==¦gāshən\ *n* -s [ME *prorogacion*, fr. L *prorogation-, prorogatio* prolongation, deferring, fr. *prorogatus* (past part. of *prorogare*) + *-ion-*, *-io* -ion] : the act of proroguing or state of being prorogued ⟨only one debate, that on foreign affairs, before the ~ on Friday —*Manchester Guardian Weekly*⟩

**pro·ro·ga·tor** \'==,gād·ə(r)\ *n* -s [LL, dispenser, fr. *prorogatus* (past part. of *prorogare* to pay in advance, fr. L, to prolong, defer) + L *-or*] : HYLEG

**pro·rogue** \prō'rōg, prə'-\ *vb* -ED/-ING/-S [ME *prorogen*, fr. MF *proroguer*, fr. L *prorogare* to prolong, defer, fr. *pro* before + *rogare* to ask — more at FOR, RIGHT] *vt* 1 *archaic* : to extend the duration of : PROLONG, PROTRACT 2 : DEFER, POSTPONE ⟨this discussion was *prorogued* until those troubles were over and the Court had been reconstructed —C.P.Curtis⟩ 3 **a** : to adjourn (as a parliament) to a specific day by prerogative act of the British crown **b** : ADJOURN 2 ⟨Massachusetts legislative leaders are apparently giving up on previous plans to ~ the 1951 legislative session by the coming weekend —*Christian Science Monitor*⟩ ~ *vi* : to suspend or end a legislative session ⟨the Vermont Legislature *prorogued* yesterday after setting a number of new records —*Springfield (Mass.) Daily News*⟩

**pro·ruminal** \(')prō+\ *adj* [¹*pro-* + *ruminal*] : situated in front of or coming before the rumen

**pro·rupt** \prō'rəpt\ *or* **pro·rupt·ed** \-təd\ *adj* [*prorupt* fr. L *proruptus*, past part. of *prorumpere* to burst forth, fr. *pro* before + *rumpere* to break; *prorupted* fr. L *proruptus* + E *-ed* — more at FOR, REAVE] : not compact : PROTUBERANT ⟨possesses not only a panhandle but two additional protuberances as well, making that state markedly *prorupted* in form —C.L. White & G.T.Renner⟩

**pro·rup·tion** \-pshən\ *n* -s [LL *proruption-, proruptio* action of bursting forth, fr. L *proruptus* (past part. of *prorumpere*) + *-ion-*, *-io* -ion] : a bursting forth : the state of being protuberant or distended ⟨~ in form reduces the labor efficiency of the farm —C.L.White & G.T.Renner⟩

**pros** *pl of* PRO

**pros** *abbr* 1 prosecuting; prosecutor 2 prosody

**pros-** *prefix* [LL, fr. Gk, fr. *pros* near, toward, to, prob. alter. (influenced by Gk dial. *pos* toward) of *proti* — more at PRICE, POST-] 1 : near : toward ⟨*pros*enchyma⟩ 2 [prob. influenced in meaning by Gk *pro* before — more at FOR] : in front ⟨*pros*encephalon⟩

**pro·sa·ic** \prō'zāik, prə'-, -āek\ *adj* [LL *prosaicus*, fr. L *prosa* prose + *-icus* -ic — more at PROSE] 1 **a** : of or relating to prose : written in prose **b** : belonging to or characteristic of prose as distinguished from poetry : FACTUAL, LITERAL ⟨the poetic is in the same way an exacter speech than the ~ —Hugh Kenner⟩ ⟨the intention is a ~ statement of weather conditions —John Dewey⟩ **c** : having a dull, flat, unimaginative quality of style or expression ⟨~ dullness, excessive and mere factuality —E.R.Bentley⟩ ⟨something provincial, mean, and ~ —Matthew Arnold⟩ 2 : belonging to or suitable for the everyday world : COMMONPLACE, DOWN-TO-EARTH, MATTER-OF-FACT ⟨the more ~ business of testing boilers —Richard Thruelsen⟩ ⟨a far more robust, more religious and, in a good sense, more ~ heritage —Douglas Bush⟩ — **pro·sa·ic·ness** *n* -ES

**pro·sa·i·cal** \-āәkəl, -aek-\ *adj* [LL *prosaicus* + E *-al*] : PROSAIC — **pro·sa·i·cal·ness** *n* -ES

**pro·sa·i·cal·ly** \-āәk(ə)lē, -aek-, -li\ *adv* : in a prosaic manner : MATTER-OF-FACTLY ⟨apply my attention ~ to my routine at the museum —Edmund Wilson⟩

**pro·sa·i·cism** \-āə,sizəm\ *n* -s : PROSAISM

**pro·sa·ism** \-ā,izəm\ *n* -s [F *prosaïsme*, fr. *prosaïque* prosaic (fr. LL *prosaicus*), after such pairs as F *archaïque* archaic: *archaïsme* archaism (fr. NL *archaismus*)] 1 : a prosaic manner, style, or quality ⟨a disinclination to interest himself in what may be called the ~s of the female world —Carlos Baker⟩ 2 : a prosaic phrase or expression ⟨prose in a poem seems offensive to me when . . . the ~s are sharp, obvious, individual —F.A.Pottle⟩

**pro·sa·ist** \-āəst\ *n* -s [L *prosa* prose + E *-ist*] 1 : a prose writer ⟨a beauty no present-day poet or ~ has yet attained —Kate W. Tibbals⟩ 2 : a prosaic person

**pros·ar·thri** \prä'sär,thrī\ [NL, alter. (influenced by *pros-*) of *Proarthri*] *syn of* PROARTHRI

**pro·sa·teur** \¦prōzə¦tər\ *n* -s [F, fr. It *prosatore*, fr. ML *prosator*, fr. L *prosa* prose + *-ator*] : a writer of prose ⟨other literary vices quite as widespread among our representative ~s —*Yale Rev.*⟩

¹**pro·sau·ro·pod** \prō'sȯrə,päd\ *adj* [NL *Prosauropoda*] : of or relating to the Prosauropoda

²**prosauropod** \"\ *n* -s [NL *Prosauropoda*] : a reptile of the division Prosauropoda

**pro·sauropoda** \,prō+\ *n pl, cap* [NL, fr. ¹*pro-* + *Sauropoda*] : a division of Saurischia comprising bipedal Triassic reptiles ancestral to the sauropod dinosaurs

**pros·bul** \'präz,bu̇l\ *n* -s [Mishnaic Hebrew *perōzbōl, perōsbōl*, prob. fr. Gk *prosbolē* application, approach, fr. *prosballein* to strike against, apply, fr. *pros-* + *ballein* to throw — more at DEVIL] : a rabbinical enactment circumventing the biblical law remitting debts during the sabbatical year by transferring a creditor's claims to the court

**pro·scap·u·la** \prō'skapyələ\ *n* [NL, fr. ¹*pro-* + L *scapula*] : the clavicle of a teleost fish — **pro·scap·u·lar** \-lə(r)\ *adj*

**pro·sce·ni·um** \prə'sēnēəm, prō'-\ *n* -s [L, fr. Gk *proskēnion*, fr. *pro-* ¹pro- + *skēnē* tent, scene — more at SHINE] 1 **a** : the stage of an ancient theater — see THEATER illustration **b** : the part of a modern stage in front of the curtain : FORESTAGE **c** : the wall that separates the stage from the auditorium in a modern theater ⟨as a frame is to a painting, as a ~ to a play —*Atlantic*⟩ 2 : the front part : FOREGROUND ⟨these thoughts . . . kept possession of the ~ of his mind —Thomas Carlyle⟩

**proscenium arch** *n* : the arch that encloses the opening in the proscenium wall through which the spectator sees the stage : the frame of the stage picture

**proscenium box** *n* : a box in or near the proscenium : STAGE BOX

**pro·sciut·to** \prō'shüd·(,)ō\ *n, pl* **prosciut·ti** \-d·ē\ *or* **prosciuttos** [It, alter. (influenced by It *pro-* before, fr. L) of obs. It *presciutto*, fr. *pre-* (fr. L *prae-* pre-) + *-sciutto* (fr. L *exsuctus* dried up, sucked out, past part. of *exsugere* to suck out, fr. *ex-* + *sugere* to suck) — more at PRO-, SUCK] : dry-cured spiced ham

**pro·scolex** \prō+\ *n* [NL, fr. ¹*pro-* + *scolex*] : ONCHOSPHERE

**pros·cop·i·nous** \(')prä¦skäpənəs\ *adj* [*proscopin-* (irreg. fr. Gk *proskopion* visor) + *-ous*] : having supraorbital ridges ⟨most primitive hominids are ~⟩

**pros·cop·i·ny** \=¦==nē\ *n* -ES [*proscopinous* + *-y*] : the condition of being proscopinous

**pro·scribe** \prō'skrīb\ *vt* -ED/-ING/-S [L *proscribere* to publish, proscribe, fr. *pro* before + *scribere* to write — more at FOR, SCRIBE] 1 **a** *Roman & civil law* : to post or publish the name of (a person) as condemned to death with his property forfeited to the state **b** : to put outside the law : OUTLAW ⟨lasting pacts *proscribing* warfare exist between many primitive societies —*Notes & Queries on Anthropology*⟩ 2 : to condemn or forbid as harmful : PROHIBIT ⟨any definition of security gets to be so broad as to ~ practically any free-flowing news —J.S.Pope⟩ — **pro·scrib·er** \-bə(r)\ *n* -s

**pro·script** \'prō,skript\ *n* [L *proscriptus*, fr. *proscriptus*, past part. of *proscribere*] : one that is proscribed : OUTLAW

**pro·scrip·tion** \prō'skripshən\ *n* -s [ME *proscripcioun*, fr. L *proscription-, proscriptio*, fr. *proscriptus* (past part. of *proscribere*) + *-ion-*, *-io* -ion] 1 : the act of proscribing or state of being proscribed : condemnation to death or exile : OUTLAWRY ⟨by ~ and bills of outlawry —Shak.⟩ 2 : an imposed restraint or restriction : INTERDICTION, PROHIBITION ⟨the ~ of solicitation and advertising and of enticing another's clients —H.S.Drinker⟩

**pro·scrip·tive** \-ptiv, -tēv *also* -təv\ *adj* [L *proscriptus* (past part. of *proscribere*) + E *-ive*] : given to proscribing or serving to proscribe ⟨a ~ tribunal⟩ ⟨a ~ law⟩ — **pro·scrip·tive·ly** \-təvlē\ *adv* — **pro·scrip·tive·ness** \-tivnəs\ *n* -ES

**pro·scu·tel·lar** \¦prōskyü¦telə(r)\ *adj* [*proscutellum* + *-ar*] : of, relating to, or constituting a proscutellum

**pro·scu·tel·lum** \,==¦teləm\ *n* [NL, fr. ¹*pro-* + *scutellum*] : the scutellum of the prothorax of an insect

¹**prose** \'prōz\ *n* -s [ME, fr. MF, fr. L *prosa*, fr. fem. of *prosus* straightforward, direct, being in prose, fr. *prorsus*, fr. *proversus*, past part. of *provertere* to turn forward, fr. *pro* before + *vertere* to turn — more at FOR, WORTH] 1 **a** : the ordinary language of men in speaking or writing : language intended primarily to give information, relate events, or communicate ideas or opinions **b** : a literary medium distinguished from poetry by its greater irregularity and variety of rhythm, its closer correspondence to the patterns of everyday speech, and its more detailed and factual definition of idea, object, or situation — compare VERSE 2 [ME, fr. ML *prosa*, fr. L] : SEQUENCE 1 3 : a prosaic style, quality, character, or condition : ORDINARINESS, MATTER-OF-FACTNESS, PLAINNESS ⟨it was to escape from the ~ of existence that they had left America —Van Wyck Brooks⟩ 4 **a** : a piece of prose : a prose exercise or composition ⟨got his ~s past . . . the heavy-lidded cold grey eye —Thomas Wood †1950⟩ **b** : a flat, tedious, unimaginative speech or piece of writing ⟨delivered a long ~, full of platitudes⟩ **c** : a friendly conversation : CHAT

²**prose** \"\ *vb* -ED/-ING/-S [ME *prosen*, fr. *prose*, n.] *vt* 1 : to write, translate, or paraphrase in prose 2 : to lecture, write, or talk in a specified state ⟨*prosed* them to death⟩ ~ *vi* 1 : to write prose ⟨*prosing* or versing —John Milton⟩ 2 : to write or speak in a dull, prosy manner ⟨don't ~ to me about duty and stuff —W.A.Butler †1902⟩

³**prose** \"\ *adj* [¹*prose*] 1 : of, relating to, or written in prose ⟨~ style⟩ ⟨~ drama⟩ 2 : MATTER-OF-FACT, PROSAIC ⟨dry, ~ people of superior intelligence object to feeling what they are supposed to feel in the presence of marvels —Mary McCarthy⟩

**pro·sect** \prō'sekt\ *vt* -ED/-ING/-S [back-formation fr. *prosector*] : to dissect (an anatomic specimen) for demonstration — **pro·sec·tion** \-kshən\ *n*

**pro·sec·tor** \-ktə(r)\ *n* -s [prob. fr. F *prosecteur*, fr. LL *prosector* anatomist, fr. L *prosectus* (past part. of *prosecare* to cut away, cut off, fr. *pro* before + *secare* to cut) + *-or* — more at SAW] : one that makes dissections for anatomic demonstrations — **pro·sec·to·ri·al** \¦prōsek¦tōrēəl\ *adj*

**pro·sec·tor·ship** \prō'sektə(r),ship\ *n* -s : the position of prosector

**pros·e·cut·able** \'präsə,kyüd·əbəl, ,==¦==\ *adj* : subject to prosecution ⟨a ~ offense⟩

**pros·e·cute** \'präsə,kyüt, -sē,-, *usu* -üd·+V\ *vb* -ED/-ING/-S [ME *prosecuten*, fr. L *prosecutus*, past part. of *prosequi* to follow, follow after, pursue — more at PURSUE] *vt* 1 **a** : to follow to the end : press to execution or completion : pursue until finished ⟨was now ordered to ~ the war with the utmost vigor —Marjory S. Douglas⟩ ⟨determined to ~ the investigation⟩ **b** : to develop in detail : go further into : INVESTIGATE ⟨its central topic, sensation . . . continued to be *prosecuted* wherever the young science took root —F.A.Geldard⟩ 2 : to engage in or proceed with : carry on : PERFORM ⟨long-lining is *prosecuted* mainly by Cornish fishermen —G.A.Steven⟩ ⟨*prosecuted* wool-growing on a large scale —H.E.Starr⟩ 3 [LL *prosecutus*, past part. of *prosequi*, fr. L] **a** : to institute legal proceedings against; *esp* : to accuse of some crime or breach of law or to pursue for redress or punishment of a crime or violation of law in due legal form before a legal tribunal ⟨*prosecuted* them for fraud⟩ **b** : to institute legal proceedings with reference to ⟨~ a claim⟩ ⟨~ an application⟩ ⟨~ an action⟩ ⟨~ a crime⟩ ~ *vi* : to institute and carry on a legal suit or prosecution : SUE ⟨~ for public offenses⟩

**prosecuting attorney** *n* : an attorney who conducts proceedings esp. of a criminal nature in a court on behalf of the government : PUBLIC PROSECUTOR, DISTRICT ATTORNEY

**prosecuting witness** *n* : a private person who initiates criminal proceedings and appears as a witness therein

**pros·e·cu·tion** \,==¦kyüshən\ *n* -s [ML *prosecution-, prosecutio*, fr. LL, continuation, retinue, fr. L *prosecutus* (past part. of *prosequi*) + *-ion-*, *-io* -ion] 1 **a** : the carrying out of a plan, project, or course of action to or toward a specific end ⟨the successful ~ of a policy of developing the primary industries —George O'Brien⟩ ⟨the feverish ~ of expansion and internal improvement —*Amer. Guide Series: N.Y.*⟩ **b** : the performance or management of an occupation or activity ⟨salmon-spearing is a culturally higher type of activity . . . because there is normally no sense of spiritual frustration during its ~ —Edward Sapir⟩ 2 *obs* : PURSUIT ⟨see behind me the inevitable ~ of disgrace and horror —Shak.⟩ 3 : INVESTIGATION, STUDY ⟨facilities are provided for the ~ of research problems by qualified medical students —*Bull. of Meharry Med. Coll.*⟩ 4 **a** : the institution and carrying on of a suit or proceeding in a court of law or equity to obtain or enforce some right or to redress and punish some wrong : the carrying on of a judicial proceeding in behalf of a complaining party; *specif* : the institution and continuance of a criminal suit involving the process of exhibiting formal charges against an offender before a legal tribunal and pursuing them to final judgment on behalf of the state or government (as by indictment or information) — compare DEFENSE **b** : the party by whom criminal proceedings are instituted or conducted

¹**pros·e·cu·tive** \'==,kyüd·iv\ *adj* [*prosecute* + *-ive*] : of or relating to prosecution ⟨~ action⟩ ⟨~ function⟩

²**prosecutive** \"\ *adj* [L *prosecutus* (past part. of *prosequi* to follow after, pursue, proceed, continue) + E *-ive*] : of, relating to, or constituting a grammatical case (as in Eskimo) that denotes motion along

³**prosecutive** \"\ *n* -s : the prosecutive case of a language or a prosecutive form

**pros·e·cu·tor** \-üd·ə(r), -ütə-\ *n* -s [ML, fr. LL, escort of goods in transit, fr. L *prosecutus* (past part. of *prosequi*) + *-or*] **1 :** a person who institutes an official prosecution before a court often by appearing as the chief witness before a grand or petit jury or before a magistrate **2 :** PROSECUTING ATTORNEY

**pros·e·cu·to·ry** \'präsəkyə,tōrē\ *adj* [*prosecute* + *-ory*] **:** of, relating to, or concerned with prosecution ⟨~ functions⟩ ⟨~ officials⟩

**pros·e·cu·trix** \,präsə'kyü·triks\ *n, pl* **prosecutri·ces** \-rə-,sēz\ *or* **prosecutrixes** [fr. *prosecutor*, after such pairs as E *executor: executrix*] **:** a female prosecutor

**prosed** *past of* PROSE

**¹pros·e·lyte** \'präsə,līt, *usu* -īd·+V\ *n* -s [ME *proselite*, fr. LL *proselytus* proselyte, alien resident, fr. Gk *prosēlytos*, fr. *pros* near, toward, to + *-ēlytos* (akin to *elthein* to come, go, suppletive aor. of *erchesthai* to come, go); akin to Gk *elan* to drive — more at PROS-, ELASTIC] **1 :** one who has been converted from one religious faith to another **:** NEOPHYTE; *specif* **:** a convert to Judaism who performs all the religious duties required of Jews and enjoys all the privileges **2 :** one who has been converted from one belief, attitude, or party to another **:** CONVERT ⟨a ~, a traditionalist who has only recently been converted to the modern credo of the glossematicians —Bjarne Ulvestad⟩

**²proselyte** \"\ *vb* -ED/-ING/-S *vt* **:** to convert from one religion, belief, opinion, or party to another **:** make a proselyte of ⟨the efforts of early missionaries to ~ Minnesota Indians were largely unproductive —*Amer. Guide Series: Minn.*⟩ ~ *vi* **1 :** to make or attempt to make proselytes ⟨left . . . to secure religious liberty and to ~ among heathen —A.D.Graeff⟩ **2 :** to recruit members for an institution, team, or group esp. by the offer of special inducements ⟨though it does not engage in *proselyting*, the college usually turns out fine basketball teams⟩

**pros·e·lyt·er** \-īd·ə(r)\ *n* -s **:** PROSELYTIZER

**pros·e·lyt·i·cal** \¦==¦lid·əkəl\ *adj* **:** of, relating to, or given to proselytism

**pros·e·lyt·ism** \'==,lī,tizəm, -,lə,-\ *n* -s **1 :** the act of becoming or condition of being a proselyte **:** CONVERSION ⟨his ~ inspired him to convert others⟩ **2 :** the act or process of proselyting ⟨represent sections detached from these ancient Churches, sometimes by ~ —B.J.Kidd⟩

**pros·e·lyt·ist** \'==,līd·əst, -,ləd·-\ *n* -s **:** PROSELYTIZER — **pros·e·lyt·is·tic** \¦==,lī¦tistik, -,lə¦-\ *adj*

**pros·e·lyt·iza·tion** \,==,līd·ə'zāshən\ *n* -s **:** PROSELYTISM

**pros·e·lyt·ize** \'präs(ə)lə,tīz\ *vb* -ED/-ING/-S *see -ize in Explan Notes* **:** PROSELYTE

**pros·e·lyt·iz·er** \-zə(r)\ *n* -s **:** one that proselytizes **:** one that makes or tries to make proselytes

**prose·man** \'prōzmən\ *n, pl* **prosemen :** a prose writer — opposed to *poet* ⟨our 18th century *prosemen* whom some uphold as our greatest —H.E.Cory⟩

**pro·seminar** \(¦)prō+\ *n* [¹*pro-* + *seminar*] **:** a directed course of study conducted in the manner of a graduate seminar but often open to advanced undergraduate students

**pros·en·ce·phal·ic** \¦präs'nsə¦falik\ *adj* [*prosencephalon* + *-ic*] **:** of, relating to, or derived from the forebrain

**pros·en·ceph·a·lon** \,präs'n'sefə,län\ *n* [NL, fr. *pros-* + *encephalon*] **:** FOREBRAIN

**pros·en·chy·ma** \präs'eŋkəmə\ *n, pl* **prosenchym·a·ta** \,präs'n'kiməd·ə\ *or* **prosenchymas** [NL, fr. *pros-* + *-enchyma*] **:** any of various tissues of higher plants composed of elongated usu. pointed cells mostly with little or no protoplasm and including tissues specialized for conduction and support — compare PARENCHYMA, PLECTENCHYMA — **pros·en·chym·a·tous** \¦präs'n¦kiməd·əs\ *adj*

**prose poem** *n* **:** a work in prose that has some of the technical or literary qualities of a poem (as regular rhythm, definitely patterned structure, or emotional or imaginative heightening)

**prose poet** *n* **:** a writer of prose poems

**pros·er** \'prōzə(r)\ *n* -s **1 :** a writer of prose **:** PROSAIST 1 ⟨the outsider, the ~, even if he is modest and sensitive, goes wrong in the poetry world very quickly —E.M.Forster⟩ **2 :** one who talks or writes tediously ⟨an insufferable ~ who bored everyone⟩

**pro·ser·pi·na·ca** \prō,sərpə'nakə\ *n, cap* [NL, fr. L, a plant, prob. knotweed, fr. *Proserpina*, goddess of the subterranean world of the dead, fr. Gk *Persephonē*] **:** a genus of No. American aquatic or marsh herbs (family Haloragaceae) having finely divided or pinnatifid leaves, tiny perfect but apetalous axillary flowers, and small bony angled fruit — see MERMAID WEED

**proses** *pl of* PROSE, *pres 3d sing of* PROSE

**pros·ethmoid** \(')präs+\ *or* **prosethmoid bone** *n* [*pros-ethmoid* fr. *pros-* + *ethmoid*] **:** the median anterior bone of the upper part of the skull of a teleost fish **:** ETHMOID

**pro·seu·che** \prə's(y)ükē\ *or* **pro·seu·cha** \-kə\ *n, pl* **proseu·chae** \-ü,kē\ [L & Gk; L *proseucha*, fr. Gk *proseuchē* proseuche, prayer, fr. *proseuchesthai* to pray to, fr. *pros* near, toward, to + *euchesthai* to pray — more at PROS-, VOW] **1 :** an ancient place of prayer **:** ORATORY **2 :** an ancient synagogue

**prosier** *comparative of* PROSY

**prosiest** *superlative of* PROSY

**pros·i·fy** \'prōzə,fī\ *vb* -ED/-ING/-ES [¹*prose* + *-ify*] *vt* **:** to make prosaic ⟨his summary *prosifies* the poem⟩ ~ *vi* **:** to write prose ⟨*prosifies* as well as versifies⟩

**pros·i·ly** \-zəlē\ *adv* **:** in a prosy manner ⟨somewhat ~ and repetitively expounded —Anthony Quinton⟩

**pro·sim·ia** \prō'simēə\ *or* **prosimi·ae** \-ē,ē\ [NL, fr. ¹*pro-* + *-simia* or *-simiae* (fr. L *simia* ape)] *syn of* PROSIMII

**¹pro·sim·i·an** \-ēən\ *adj* [ISV *prosimi-* (fr. NL *Prosimii*) + *-an*, adj. suffix] **:** of or relating to the Prosimii

**²prosimian** \"\ *n* -s [ISV *prosimi-* (fr. NL *Prosimii*) + *-an*, n. suffix] **:** one of the Prosimii

**prosim·ii** \-mē,ī\ *n pl, cap* [NL, fr. ¹*pro-* + *-simii* (fr. L *simia* ape) — more at SIMIAN] *in some classifications* **:** a suborder of Primates that includes the less progressive primates (as the tarsiers and lemurs) and is coextensive with Lemuroidea and Tarsioidea of other classifications

**pro·simulium** \,prō+\ *n, cap* [NL, fr. ¹*pro-* + *Simulium*] **:** a genus of blackflies

**pros·i·ness** \'prōzēnəs\ *n* -ES **:** the quality or state of being prosy ⟨his occasional ~, his lapses into mere talk —*Va. Quarterly Rev.*⟩

**¹prosing** *n* -s [fr. gerund of ²*prose*] **1 :** writing in prose ⟨has poetic ambitions but ~ suits him better⟩ **2 :** tedious discourse ⟨half-baked opinionating and self-consciously . . . awkward ~s on life —John Farrelly⟩

**²prosing** *adj* [fr. pres. part. of ²*prose*] **:** PROSY — **pros·ing·ly** *adv*

**pros·ist** \'prōzəst\ *n* -s **:** a prose writer **:** PROSAIST

**pro·sit** \'prōsət, -ōzət\ *or* **prost** \'prōst\ *interj* [G, fr. L *prosit* may it be beneficial, 3d pers. sing. pres. subj. of *prodesse* to be useful, be beneficial — more at PROUD] — used to wish good health esp. before drinking

**pro·slavery** \(')prō+\ *adj* [²*pro-* + *slavery*] **:** favoring slavery; *specif* **:** favoring the continuance of or noninterference with Negro slavery ⟨the ~ states of the era before the Civil War⟩

**pro·slav·ery·ism** \prō'slāv(ə)rē,izəm\ *n* -s [*proslavery* + *-ism*] **:** the advocacy of slavery

**pro·so** \'prō(,)sō\ *or* **proso millet** *n* -s [Russ *proso*; perh. akin to Gk *perknos* dusky, dark colored — more at PERCH] **:** MILLET 1a

**proso-** *comb form* [NL, fr. Gk *prosō* forward, fr. *proti* near, toward, to — more at PRICE] **1 :** in front ⟨*Proso*branchia⟩ **2 :** in a forward direction **:** onward ⟨*proso*plasia⟩

**¹pros·o·branch** \'präsə,braŋk\ *adj* [NL *Prosobranchia*] **:** of or relating to the Streptoneura

**²prosobranch** \"\ *n* -s [NL *Prosobranchia*] **:** a gastropod of the subclass Streptoneura

**pros·o·bran·chia** \,==='braŋkēə\ *or* **pros·o·bran·chi·a·ta** \,==,braŋkē'äd·ə\ [*Prosobranchia* fr. NL, fr. *proso-* + *-branchia*; *Prosobranchiata* fr. NL, fr. *proso-* + L *branchia* gill + NL *-ata*; fr. the usual location of the gills anterior to the heart — more at BRANCHIA] *syn of* STREPTONEURA

**pros·o·bran·chi·ate** \¦==¦braŋkēət, -ē,āt\ *adj or n* [NL *Prosobranchiata*] **:** PROSOBRANCH

**pros·o·coel** *also* **pros·o·cele** *or* **pros·o·coele** \'präsə,sēl\ *n* -s [*proso-* + *-coele*] **:** the primitive undivided cavity of the forebrain of an early vertebrate embryo

**pros·o·deme** \'präsə,dēm\ *n* -s [*prosody* + *-eme*] **:** SUPRASEGMENTAL PHONEME

**pros·o·det·ic** \¦präsə¦ded·ik\ *adj* [*proso-* + *-detic* (as in *amphidetic*)] **:** situated in front of the beak — used of the ligament of a bivalve mollusk; compare AMPHIDETIC, OPISTHODETIC

**¹pro·so·di·ac** \prə'sōdē,ak\ *or* **pros·o·di·a·cal** \¦präsə-¦dīəkəl\ *adj* [*prosodiac* fr. LL *prosodiacus*, fr. Gk *prosōidiakos* (prob. only a MS var. of *prosodiakos*), fr. *prosōidia*; *prosodiacal* fr. LL *prosodiacus* + E *-al*] **:** PROSODIC — **pros·o·di·a·cal·ly** \-iək(ə)lē\ *adv*

**²prosodiac** \"\ *n* -s [Gk *prosodiakos*, adj., used in a prosodion, fr. *prosodion*] **:** the verse used in a prosodion consisting of an enoplion followed by a long or short syllable

**pro·so·di·al** \prə'sōdēəl\ *adj* [*prosody* + *-al*] **:** PROSODIC — **pro·so·di·al·ly** \-ēəlē\ *adv*

**pro·so·di·an** \-ēən\ *n* -s [*prosody* + *-an*] **:** PROSODIST

**pro·sod·ic** \prə'sädik, prō'-, -dēk\ *or* **pro·sod·i·cal** \-dəkəl, -dēk-\ *adj* [*prosodic* fr. F *prosodique*, fr. *prosodie* prosody (fr. L *prosodia*) + *-ique* -ic; *prosodical* fr. *prosodic* + *-al*] **1 :** of or relating to prosody **2 :** of or relating to suprasegmental phonemes — **pro·sod·i·cal·ly** \-dək(ə)lē\ *adv*

**pro·so·di·on** \prə'sōdē,än\ *n, pl* **proso·dia** \-ēə\ [Gk, fr. neut. of *prosodios* processional, fr. *prosodos* procession, fr. *pros-* + *hodos* way, journey — more at CEDE] **:** an ancient Greek processional hymn sung by a chorus approaching the temple or altar of a god

**pros·o·dist** \'präsədəst\ *n* -s [*prosody* + *-ist*] **:** a specialist in prosody

**pros·o·dus** \'präsədəs\ *n, pl* **proso·di** \-sə,dī\ *or* **prosoduses** [NL, fr. Gk *prosodos* approach, procession] **:** a small canal in a sponge leading from an incurrent canal to a flagellated chamber

**pros·o·dy** \'präsədē, -di\ *n* -ES [ME *prosodye*, fr. L *prosodia* accent of a syllable, fr. Gk *prosōidia* song sung to instrumental music, modulation of the voice, accent, fr. *pros* near, toward, to, in addition to + *ōidē* song, ode — more at PROS-, ODE] **1 a :** the study of versification; *esp* **:** the systematic study of metrical structure **:** METRICS — compare CADENCE, FOOT, METER, RHYTHM **b :** a treatise on versification ⟨the best ~ yet written⟩ **c :** a particular system or theory of versification ⟨although the nominal basis of his ~ is both accentual and syllabic, the latter element is really its defining principle —A.D.Culler⟩ **d :** a method or style of versification ⟨the ~ of Milton⟩ ⟨the ~ of Gerard Manley Hopkins⟩ **2 :** the rhythmic aspect of language ⟨the ~ of the English language —H.J.Murrill⟩

**pros·o·gas·ter** \¦präsə¦gastə(r)\ *n* -s [NL, fr. *proso-* + *-gaster*] **:** FOREGUT

**proso·gyrate** \¦präsə+\ *adj* [*proso-* + *gyrate*] **:** curving toward the anterior — used esp. of the umbones of a bivalve mollusk; compare MESOGYRATE, OPISTHOGYRATE

**pro·so·ma** \prō'sōmə\ *n* -s [NL, fr. ¹*pro-* + *-soma*] **:** the anterior region of the body of various invertebrates (as of some mollusks) when it cannot be readily analyzed into its primitive segmentation; *esp* **:** CEPHALOTHORAX — **pro·so·mal** \-məl\ *adj*

**proso millet** *var of* PROSO

**prosop-** *or* **prosopo-** *comb form* [LL *prosopo-*, fr. Gk *prosōp-*, *prosōpo-* person, fr. *prosōpon*, fr. *pros-* + *-ōpon* (fr. *ōp-*, *ōps* face, eye) — more at EYE] **1 :** person ⟨*prosopo*graphy⟩ **2 :** face ⟨*prosop*algia⟩ ⟨*Prosopo*thrips⟩

**pro·sop·ic** \prə'säpik, -sōp-\ *adj* [*prosop-* + *-ic*] **:** of or relating to the face — **pro·sop·i·cal·ly** \-pək(ə)lē\ *adv*

**pros·o·pid·i·dae** \,präsə'pidə,dē\ *n pl, cap* [NL, fr. *Prosopid-*, *Prosopis*, type genus + *-idae*] **:** a small but widely distributed family of small black hairy bees

**¹pro·so·pis** \prə'sōpəs\ *n, cap* [NL, fr. Gk *prosōpis* burdock, perh. fr. *prosōpon* face] **:** a genus of tropical or subtropical branching shrubs or trees (family Leguminosae) having small flowers in axillary cylindrical spikes succeeded by large pods — see MESQUITE

**²prosopis** \"\ *n, cap* [NL *Prosopid-*, *Prosopis*, perh. irreg. fr. Gk *prosōpon* face] **:** the type genus of Prosopididae

**pros·o·pite** \'präsə,pīt\ *n* -s [G *prosopit*, fr. *prosop-* (fr. Gk *prosōpeion* mask, fr. *prosōpon* face) + *-it* -ite; fr. its occurrence as a pseudomorph] **:** a mineral $CaAl_2(F,OH)_8$ consisting of a basic fluoride of calcium and aluminum

**pro·so·pi·um** \prə'sōpēəm\ *n, cap* [NL, fr. Gk *prosōpeion* mask] **:** a genus of whitefishes including the Menominee whitefish, Rocky Mountain whitefish, and related forms

**pros·o·pla·sia** \¦präsə¦plāzh(ē)ə\ *n* -s [NL, fr. *proso-* + *-plasia*] **1 :** differentiation of tissue; *esp* **:** abnormal differentiation **2 :** organization of tissue toward a more complex state

**pros·o·plas·tic** \¦==¦plastik\ *adj* [*proso-* + *-plastic*] **:** relating to or produced by prosoplasia

**pros·o·pog·ra·phy** \,präsə'pägrəfē\ *n* -ES [NL *prosopographia*, fr. LL *prosopo-* prosop- + L *-graphia* -graphy] **1 :** a description of a person's appearance, character, and career **2 a :** a collection of biographical sketches **b :** the activity of producing such a collection

**pro·so·po·lep·sy** \prə'sōpə,lepsē\ *n* -ES [Gk *prosōpolēpsia*, fr. *prosōpon* person, face + *-lēpsia* (fr. *lēpsis* act of taking hold or receiving, acceptance + *-ia* -y) — more at -LEPSY] **:** PARTIALITY

**pro·so·pon** \prə'sō,pän\ *n* -s [NL, fr. Gk *prosōpon*] **:** the younger nymphal stage of an insect that undergoes an incomplete metamorphosis

**pro·so·po·poe·ia** \prə,sōpə'pēə\ *n* -s [L, fr. Gk *prosōpopoiia* dramatization, prosopopoeia, fr. *prosōpon* person, face + *-poiia* (fr. *poiein* to make + *-ia* -y) — more at POET] **1 :** a figure of speech in which an absent person is represented as speaking or a dead person as alive and present ⟨the whole speech, a ~ spoken as by the poor man —*Quarterly Jour. of Speech*⟩ **2 :** PERSONIFICATION ⟨a ~ by which virtue becomes a knight in shining armor⟩

**pros·o·po·thrips** \¦präsəpō+\ *n, cap* [NL, fr. *prosop-* + *Thrips*] **:** a genus of thrips including several that attack wheat

**pros·o·pyle** \'präsə,pīl\ *n* -s [*proso-* + *-pyle*] **:** the aperture between incurrent and radial canals in some sponges

**pro·sorus** \prə+\ *n* [NL, fr. ¹*pro-* + *sorus*] **:** the initial thallus cell that produces a vesicle in which the sporangia are formed in some Chytridiales

**pros·o·sto·ma·ta** \,präsə'stōməd·ə\ *n pl, cap* [NL, fr. *proso-* + *-stomata*] *in some classifications* **:** an order of Digenea comprising trematode worms with the mouth at or near the anterior end of the body and including all the Digenea except members of the family Bucephalidae

**pros·o·stome** \'==,stōm\ *n* -s [NL *Prosostomata*] **:** a worm of the order Prosostomata

**¹pros·pect** \'prä,spekt *sometimes* -,spikt *or* -,spēkt\ *n* -s [ME *prospecte*, fr. L *prospectus* lookout, distant view, sight, fr. *prospectus*, past part. of *prospicere* to look forward, look into the distance, exercise foresight, fr. *pro* before + *specere* to look — more at FOR, SPY] **1 :** relative aspect **:** EXPOSURE 2d ⟨their ~ was toward the south —Ezek 40: 44 (AV)⟩ **2 a** (1) **:** an extensive view **:** a sight from a commanding position ⟨here, just above 1000 feet above sea level, our ~ embraces a dozen counties —S.W.Wooldridge⟩ (2) **:** a mental consideration **:** SURVEY ⟨on a nearer ~, all the circumstance of greatness vanished into shadow —A.C.Benson⟩ **b :** a place or station that commands an extensive view **:** LOOKOUT ⟨God beholding from his ~ high —John Milton⟩ **c :** something extended to the view **:** SCENE ⟨climbing onto a huge block of stone, began gazing at the wide ~ spread out before me —W.H.Hudson †1922⟩ **d** *archaic* **:** a sketch or picture of a scene ⟨a ~ of Yale College in New Haven, neatly engraved —*Boston Evening Post*⟩ **3** *obs* **:** an appearance presented by something ⟨it were a tedious difficulty . . . to bring them to that ~ —Shak.⟩ **4 a :** act of looking forward **:** ANTICIPATION, FORESIGHT ⟨its later development justified his ~ of its future value⟩ **b :** a mental picture of something to come **:** VISION ⟨attracted by the fascination of discovery and the ~ of spiritual conquest —*Amer. Guide Series: Minn.*⟩ **c :** something that is awaited or expected **:** POSSIBILITY ⟨air-conditioned cars are a happy ~ for some commuters —*Collier's Yr. Bk.*⟩ ⟨her sadness at the small ~ of seeing him again, old as she was —Archibald Marshall⟩ **d prospects** *pl* (1) **:** financial expectations ⟨as a young man with ~s he married the girl —Dixon Wecter⟩ ⟨without any ~s in the world except those which he could make for himself —R.W.Southern⟩ (2) **:** CHANCES ⟨improved corn ~s in other areas —*Wall Street Jour.*⟩ **5 a :** a place showing signs of containing a mineral deposit **b :** a partly developed mine **c** (1) **:** a sample of ore or gravel tested for mineral content (2) **:** the mineral yield of such sample **6 a :** a potential buyer or customer ⟨called on ten ~s but failed to make a sale⟩ **b :** a likely candidate for some appointment, job, or position ⟨a good ~ for the Supreme Court⟩ ⟨the coach has come up with several fine ~s for the team⟩ — **in prospect :** in view **:** ANTICIPATED, EXPECTED ⟨new medical advances are *in prospect*⟩

**²pros·pect** \'prä,spekt *sometimes* prə's-\ *vb* -ED/-ING/-S *vi* **1 a :** to explore an area for mineral deposits ⟨~*ing* for gold⟩ ⟨~*ing* for uranium⟩ **b :** to make a search or investigation ⟨fat robins ~*ing* in the spaded earth of the flower beds —John & Ward Hawkins⟩ **2 :** to give indications of mineral yield ⟨this ore ~s well⟩ ~ *vt* **1 a :** to explore or inspect (a region) for mineral deposits **b :** to make preliminary developments and tests of (as a mine, an ore deposit) to determine its probable value **2 :** to make a careful investigation of **:** EXPLORE ⟨cautiously ~*ed* the highway —John Buchan⟩ ⟨today the principal tools for ~*ing* the brain are electrical —G.W.Gray b.1886⟩

**prospect glass** *n, dial chiefly Eng* **:** TELESCOPE

**pro·spec·tion** \prə'spekshən\ *n* -s [LL *prospection-*, *prospectio*, fr. L *prospectus* (past part. of *prospicere*) + *-ion-*, *-io* -ion] **1 :** the act of anticipating **:** FORESIGHT **2 :** the act of viewing **3 :** the act of exploring (as for gold)

**¹pro·spec·tive** \prə'spektiv, -təv *also* (')prä¦s- *or* -təv *sometimes* prō's-\ *adj* [LL *prospectivus*, fr. L *prospectus* (past part. of *prospicere*) + *-ivus* -ive] **1** *archaic* **:** commanding an extensive view **2** *archaic* **:** FORESIGHTED, FORWARD-LOOKING **3 :** concerned with or relating to the future **:** effective in the future ⟨the statute which I have proposed is solely ~ in its operation —*Jour. of Accountancy*⟩ **4 :** of the future **:** in prospect **:** EXPECTANT, EXPECTED ⟨a ~ mother⟩ ⟨a ~ teacher⟩ ⟨a ~ heir⟩ ⟨the announcement declaring his candidacy is ~⟩ — **pro·spec·tive·ly** \-tə̇vlē, -tēv-, -li\ *adv* — **pro·spec·tive·ness** \-tivnəs\ *n* -ES

**²prospective** \"\ *n* -s **1** *obs* **:** PROSPECTIVE GLASS **2 :** a scenic picture **:** PERSPECTIVE ⟨the scene again changed to a ~ of porticoes —E.K.Chambers⟩

**prospective glass** *n* **1** *obs* **:** a crystal or mirror used to predict the future ⟨in Time's long and dark *prospective glass*, foresaw what future days should bring to pass —John Milton⟩ **2 :** a small portable telescope

**pros·pect·less** \'prä,spektləs\ *adj* **:** having no prospect

**pros·pec·tor** \'prä,spektə(r) *sometimes* prə's-\ *n* -s [²*prospect* + *-or*] **:** one that prospects; *esp* **:** a person who explores a region for valuable mineral deposits

**prospects** *pl of* PROSPECT, *pres 3d sing of* PROSPECT

**pro·spec·tus** \prə'spektəs\ *n* -ES [L, lookout, distant view, sight — more at PROSPECT] **:** a preliminary printed statement describing a business or other enterprise and distributed to prospective buyers, investors, or participants: as **a** (1) **:** a booklet or leaflet describing a forthcoming publication (2) **:** a book containing samplings and descriptions of the contents of a set of books (as of an encyclopedia) **b :** a description of a new security issue supplied to prospective purchasers and giving detailed information concerning the company's business and financial standing **c** *Brit* **:** a school catalog

**pros·per** \'präspə(r)\ *vb* **prospered; prospered; prospering** \-p(ə)riŋ\ **prospers** [ME *prosperen*, fr. MF *prosperer*, fr. L *prosperare* to cause to succeed, fr. *prosperus*, adj., favorable, prob. fr. *prospere*, adv., favorably, according to hope, prob. fr. (assumed) OL *pro spere* according to hope, fr. L *pro* before, for, according to + (assumed) OL *spere*, abl. of L *spes* hope — more at FOR, SPEED] *vi* **1 a :** to succeed in an enterprise or activity **:** do well ⟨again reunited in spirit, the church ~*ed* from that time on —*Amer. Guide Series: Conn.*⟩; *esp* **:** to achieve economic or financial success ⟨after years of poverty, began to ~⟩ **b :** to turn out successfully ⟨his first venture into politics ~*ed* and he was soon considered for higher office⟩ **2 :** to become strong and flourishing **:** THRIVE ⟨there are lawns which do not ~ —R.M.Yoder⟩ ⟨moist yeast ~s at around 80 to 83 degrees —Dorothy Dean⟩ ~ *vt* **:** to cause to succeed or thrive ⟨whatever ~s my business is good —Lincoln Steffens⟩ **syn** see SUCCEED

**pros·per·i·ty** \prä'sperəd·ē, -ətē, -i\ *n* -ES [ME *prosperite*, fr. OF *prosperité*, fr. L *prosperitat-*, *prosperitas*, fr. *prosperus* favorable + *-itat-*, *-itas* -ity] **1 a :** the condition of being successful or thriving **:** a state of good fortune; *esp* **:** financial success ⟨since ~ has come to him he has added some conveniences to his cottage —*Current Biog.*⟩ **b :** a state of vigorous and healthy growth **:** WELL-BEING ⟨chlorophyll, apparently essential to plant ~ —*Crops in Peace & War*⟩ **2 :** a state of high general economic activity marked by relatively full employment, an increasing use of resources, and a high level of investment — compare DEPRESSION 3c

**pros·per·ous** \'prasp(ə)rəs\ *adj* [ME, fr. MF *prospereux*, fr. *prosperer* to prosper + *-eux* -ous] **1 :** conducive to success **:** AUSPICIOUS, FAVORABLE ⟨await a more ~ moment⟩ **2 a :** attended with or marked by good fortune **:** SUCCESSFUL, THRIVING ⟨was longing to publish his ~ love —Jane Austen⟩ ⟨a ~ voyage⟩ **b :** attended with or marked by economic well-being ⟨~ times⟩ ⟨a ~ businessman⟩ ⟨a ~ nation⟩ **c :** enjoying a vigorous and healthy growth **:** FLOURISHING ⟨never had leaves been more green or ~ —Osbert Sitwell⟩ — **pros·per·ous·ly** *adv* — **pros·per·ous·ness** *n* -ES

**pros·pho·ra** \¦präsfə¦rä\ *n, pl* **prospho·rae** \-¦rä, ¦rē\ [LGk, fr. Gk, offering, fr. *prospherein* to present, offer, fr. *pros-* + *pherein* to carry — more at BEAR] **:** one of several loaves of bread each with special seals on the upper side used in the Eastern Church in the preparation of the Eucharistic elements

**pro·spi·cience** \prō'spishən(t)s\ *n* -s [L *prospicientia*, fr. *prospicient-*, *prospiciens* (pres. part. of *prospicere* to look forward) + *-ia* -y — more at PROSPECT] **:** the act of looking forward **:** FORESIGHT

**pro·sporangium** \,prō+\ *n* [NL, fr. ¹*pro-* + *sporangium*] **:** the initial cell that gives rise to a thin-walled vesicle in which the zoospores are formed in some fungi

**pross** \'präs\ *vi* -ED/-ING/-ES [origin unknown] *chiefly Scot* **:** to put on airs

**prost** *var of* PROSIT

**pros·tal** \'präst'l\ *n* -s [NL *prostalia* (pl.) prostals, fr. ¹*pro-* + *-stalia* (fr. L *stare* to stand + *-alia*, neut. pl. of *-alis* -al) — more at STAND] **:** a spicule that projects beyond the body of a living sponge

**pro·sta·sis** \prō'stāsəs\ *n* -ES [Gk, portico, fr. *proïstanai* to put in front, fr. *pro-* ¹pro- + *histanai* to cause to stand — more at STAND] **:** the space between the antas of a portico in antis

**prostat-** *or* **prostato-** *comb form* [NL, fr. *prostata*] **1 :** prostate ⟨*prostat*ectomy⟩ ⟨*prostat*itis⟩ **2 :** prostate and ⟨*prostato*vesical⟩

**¹pros·tate** \'prä,stāt, *chiefly in substandard speech* -trāt, *usu* -ād·+V\ *n* -s [NL *prostata*, fr. Gk *prostatēs* one in front, fr. *proïstanai* to put in front] **:** PROSTATE GLAND

**²prostate** \"\ *also* **pros·tat·ic** \(')prä¦stad·ik\ *adj* [*prostate* fr. ¹*prostate*; *prostatic* prob. fr. (assumed) NL *prostaticus*, fr. NL *prostata* + L *-icus* -ic] **:** of or relating to or being the prostate gland

**pros·ta·tec·to·my** \,prästə'tektəmē\ *n* -ES [ISV *prostat-* + *-ectomy*] **:** surgical removal of the prostate gland

**prostate gland** *n* **1 a :** a pale firm partly muscular partly glandular body that surrounds the base of the male urethra in man and other mammals and discharges its viscid opalescent secretion through ducts opening into the floor of the urethra **b :** a corresponding group of glands about the female urethra of some mammals commonly considered a rudimentary or vestigial homologue of the male gland **2 :** any of various glandular bodies associated with genital ducts of male invertebrates and like or likened to the mammalian prostate

**pros·tat·i·co·vesical** \prä¦stad·ə̇kō+\ *or* **pros·ta·to·vesical** \¦prästəd·ō+\ *adj* [*prostaticovesical* fr. *prostatic* + *-o-* + *vesical*; *prostatovesical* fr. *prostat-* + *vesical*] **:** of, relating to, or adjoining the prostate and the bladder ⟨the ~ venous plexus about the base of the bladder and prostate⟩

**prostatic utricle** *n* **:** a small blind pouch that projects from the posterior wall of the urethra into the prostate

**pros·ta·tism** \'prästə,tizəm\ *n* -s [ISV *prostat-* + *-ism*] **:** disease of the prostate; *esp* **:** a condition resulting from obstruction of the bladder neck by an enlarged prostate

**pros·ta·ti·tis** \,==¦tīd·əs\ *n* -ES [NL, fr. *prostat-* + *-itis*] **:** inflammation of the prostate gland

**pro·stem·mat·ic** \\,prō,steˈmad·ik\\ *also* **pro·stem·mate** \\prōˈste,māt\\ *adj* [*prostemmatic* fr. ¹*pro-* + NL *stemmat-, stemma* one of the simple eyes of an insect, ocellus + E *-ic; prostemmate* fr. ¹*pro-* + *-stemmate* (fr. NL *stemmat-, stemma*) — more at STEMMA] **:** of, relating to, or constituting a minute sense organ in front of the eyes of collembolan insects

**pro·ster·nal** \\prōˈstərn³l\\ *adj* [ISV *prosternum* + *-al*] **:** of or relating to the prosternum

**pros·ter·na·tion** \\,prästə(r)ˈnāshən\\ *n* -s [ML *prosternation-, prosternatio,* fr. L *prosternere* to prostrate + *-ation-, -atio* -ation — more at PROSTRATE] **:** PROSTRATION

**pro·sternum** \\ˈprō+\\ *n* [NL, fr. ¹*pro-* + *sternum*] **:** the ventral plate of the prothorax of an insect

**pros·the·ca** \\präsˈthēkə\\ *n, pl* **prosthe·cae** \\-ē(,)sē\\ *or* **prosthecas** \\-ēkəz\\ [NL, fr. Gk *prosthēkē* appendage, addition, fr. *prostithenai* to put to, add] **:** a small sclerite articulated to the base of the mandible in some insects

**pros·the·sis** \\ˈprästhəsəs, *in sense 2* präsˈthēsəs\\ *n, pl* **prosthe·ses** \\-thə,sēz, -ˈthē,sēz\\ [LL, fr. Gk, lit., addition, fr. *prostithenai* to put to, add, fr. *pros* near, toward, to + *tithenai* to place, put — more at PROS-, DO] **1 a :** the addition of a sound or syllable to a word esp. by prefixing (as in *newt, beloved*) **b :** the addition of one or more syllables at the beginning of a member or verse — used esp. in ref. to Greek and Latin prosody; compare APHAERESIS **2 :** an artificial device to replace a missing part of the body (as a suction socket to replace a lower leg or a dental restoration)

**pros·thet·ic** \\(ˈ)präsˈthed|ik, -et|, |ēk\\ *adj* [Gk *prosthetikos* adding, furthering, fr. *prosthetos* put to, added (fr. *prostithenai* to add) + *-ikos* -ic] **1 :** added to a word esp. by prefixing ⟨a ~ letter⟩ ⟨a ~ sound⟩ **2 :** of or relating to prosthesis or prosthetics ⟨~ hand⟩ ⟨~ research⟩ **3 :** of, relating to, or constituting a group or radical of a different kind attached to or substituted in a compound; *esp* **:** of, relating to, or constituting a nonprotein group of a conjugated protein ⟨the ~ nucleic acid group of a nucleoprotein⟩ — compare COENZYME — **pros·thet·i·cal·ly** \\|ək(ə)lē\\ *adv*

**prosthetic dentistry** *n* **:** PROSTHODONTICS

**pros·thet·ics** \\präsˈthed·|iks, -et|, |ēks\\ *n pl but sing or pl in constr* [fr. *prosthetic,* after such pairs as E *economic: economics*] **:** the surgical and dental specialties concerned with the artificial replacement of missing parts — compare PROSTHODONTICS, RECONSTRUCTIVE SURGERY

**pros·the·tist** \\ˈprästhəd·əst\\ *n* -s [*prosthetic* + *-ist*] **:** a specialist in prosthetics

**pros·thi·on** \\ˈprästhē,än\\ *n* -s [NL, fr. Gk, neut. of *prosthios* foremost, fr. *prosthen* before, in front; akin to Gk *proti* near, toward, to — more at PRICE] **:** ALVEOLAR POINT — see CRANIOMETRY illustration

**pros·tho·don·tia** \\,prästhəˈdänch(ē)ə\\ *n* -s [NL, fr. *prosth-* (as in *prosthesis*) + *-odontia*] **:** PROSTHODONTICS

**pros·tho·don·tics** \\-ntiks\\ *n pl but sing or pl in constr* [*prosthodontia* + *-ics*] **:** the dental specialty concerned with the making of artificial replacements of missing parts of the mouth and jaws

**pros·tho·don·tist** \\;==ˈdäntəst\\ *n* -s [*prosthodontia* + *-ist*] **:** a specialist in prosthodontics

**pros·tho·gon·i·mus** \\,prästhəˈgänəməs\\ *n, cap* [NL, fr. *prosth-* (fr. Gk *prosthen* before, in front) + *-o-* + Gk *gonimos* productive, fertile; akin to Gk *gignesthai* to be born — more at KIN] **:** a genus of trematode worms (family Plagiorchiidae) parasitic in the oviducts and bursa of Fabricius and rarely in the intestine or esophagus of domestic and other birds

**pros·tho·mere** \\ˈprästhə,mi(ə)r\\ *n* -s [*prosth-* (fr. Gk *prosthen* before, in front) + *-o-* + *-mere*] **:** a segment anterior to the mouth in arthropods

**pro·stig·ma·ta** \\,prō,stigˈmäd·ə, -mād·ə\\ *n pl, cap* [NL, fr. ¹*pro-* + *stigma* + *-ata*] **:** a large group of mites having a respiratory system with the stigmal opening near the base of the chelicerae — **pro·stig·mat·ic** \\;=,=ˈmad·ik\\ *or* **pro·stig·mat·id** \\-d·əd\\ *adj*

**pro·stig·min** *or* **pro·stig·mine** \\prōˈstigmən, -g,mēn\\ *n* -s [fr. *Prostigmin,* a trademark] **:** NEOSTIGMINE

¹**pros·ti·tute** \\ˈprästə,tüt, -ə,tyüt, *usu* -üd·+V\\ *vb* -ED/-ING/-S [L *prostitutus,* past part. of *prostituere* to expose publicly to prostitution, prostitute, fr. *pro* before + *statuere* to set, station — more at FOR, STATUTE] *vt* **1 :** to offer indiscriminately for sexual intercourse esp. for payment ⟨do not ~ thy daughter, to cause her to be a whore —Lev 19:29 (AV)⟩ ⟨~ herself⟩ **2 :** to devote to corrupt or unworthy purposes or ends **:** DEBASE ⟨to mix culture with personal charm or advertisement is to ~ culture —Virginia Woolf⟩ ⟨men who ~ science in the name of profits —Harrison Brown⟩ ~ *vi* **:** to act as a prostitute **:** prostitute oneself ⟨while she was *prostituting* for him he married another woman —*Washington Post*⟩

²**prostitute** \\"\\ *adj* [L *prostitutus,* past part. of *prostituere*] **1** *archaic* **:** sexually promiscuous **:** LICENTIOUS **2 :** devoted to corrupt purposes or ends **:** PROSTITUTED

³**prostitute** \\"\\ *n* -s [L *prostituta,* fr. fem. of *prostitutus,* past part. of *prostituere*] **1 a :** a woman who engages in promiscuous sexual intercourse esp. for payment **:** HARLOT, STRUMPET, WHORE **b :** a male who engages in homosexual practices for payment **c :** a member of a group of women or sometimes men dedicated to a god who practice prostitution in association with the temple rites of the cult **2 :** a person who deliberately debases himself for money or other consideration; *specif* **:** a creatively gifted person (as a writer or painter) who deliberately lowers his standards for financial gain ⟨turns literary ~ and starts writing "poisoned pap" that sells well —*Time*⟩

**pros·ti·tu·tion** \\,prästəˈtüshən, -əˈtyü-\\ *n* -s [LL *prostitution-, prostitutio,* fr. L *prostitutus* (past part. of *prostituere*) + *-ion-, -io* -ion] **1 :** the act or practice of indulging in promiscuous sexual relations esp. for payment **2 :** the state of being prostituted **:** CORRUPTION, DEBASEMENT ⟨early-nineteenth-century houses, in various stages of destitution and ~ —Lewis Mumford⟩ ⟨political ~⟩ ⟨literary ~⟩

**pros·ti·tu·tor** \\ˈprästə,tüd·ə(r)\\ *n* -s [LL, fr. L *prostitutus* (past part. of *prostituere*) + *-or*] **:** one that prostitutes

**pro·sto·mi·al** \\prōˈstōmēəl\\ *adj* [*prostomium* + *-al*] **:** of or relating to the prostomium

**pro·sto·mi·ate** \\-ē,āt\\ *adj* [*prostomium* + *-ate*] **:** having a prostomium

**pro·sto·mi·um** \\-ēəm\\ *n, pl* **prosto·mia** \\-ēə\\ [NL, fr. ¹*pro-* + *-stoma* + *-ium*] **:** the portion of the head of various worms and mollusks situated in front of the mouth and commonly held to be nonmetameric

¹**pros·trate** \\ˈprä,strāt *sometimes* -ästrət, *usu* -d·+V\\ *adj* [ME *prostrat,* fr. L *prostratus,* past part. of *prosternere* to prostrate, fr. *pro* before + *sternere* to spread out, throw down — more at STREW] **1 a :** stretched out with face on the ground in adoration or submission ⟨smite the tax-gatherer, but fall ~ at the feet of the contemptible prince for whom the tax-gatherer plies his trade —H.T.Buckle⟩ **b :** lying prone or supine **:** extended in a horizontal position **:** FLAT ⟨quickly stooping I once more drove my weapon to the hilt in his ~ form —W.H.Hudson †1922⟩ **c :** knocked down **:** OVERTHROWN ⟨clambered over half-visible rocks, fell over ~ trees —Willa Cather⟩ **2 :** lacking in vitality or will **:** powerless to rise **:** laid low **:** OVERCOME ⟨~ with fear⟩ ⟨a whole continent ~ and impoverished —Andrew Shonfield⟩ **3 :** trailing on the ground **:** PROCUMBENT ⟨a subalpine species, usually shrubby or ~ in habit —William Dallimore & A.B.Jackson⟩ **syn** see PRONE

²**pros·trate** \\ˈprä,strāt, *usu* -äd·+V\\ *vt* -ED/-ING/-S [ME *prostraten* to prostrate oneself, fr. L *prostratus,* past part. of *prosternere* to prostrate] **1 :** to throw into a prostrate position **:** knock down **:** lay flat ⟨*prostrated* his opponent with one blow⟩ **2 a :** to extend (oneself) in a prostrate position ⟨half *prostrated* himself in something between an obeisance and an embrace —Claud Cockburn⟩ **b :** to put (oneself) in a humble and submissive posture or state ⟨the whole town had to ~ itself in official apology —Claudia Cassidy⟩ **3 a :** to reduce to submission or helplessness **:** render powerless **:** lay low ⟨the financial panic that had *prostrated* the East with the suddenness of a natural catastrophe —*Amer. Guide Series: Mich.*⟩ **b :** to subject to an emotional shock **:** OVERCOME ⟨*prostrated* with grief⟩ ⟨*prostrated* by the loss of his wife —C.S.Lewis⟩ **c :** to put into a state of extreme bodily exhaustion **:** DEBILITATE, WEAKEN ⟨*prostrated* by an attack of bilious fever —E.S.Bates⟩

**prostrate juniper** *n* **:** DWARF JUNIPER b

**prostrate pigweed** *n* **:** a prostrate or decumbent annual plant (*Amaranthus blitoides*) native to western No. America but established as a weed elsewhere esp. in waste places and neglected fields having alternate simple spatulate leaves and small greenish flowers in axillary clusters

**pros·tra·tion** \\präˈstrāshən\\ *n* -s [MF, fr. ML *prostration-, prostratio,* fr. LL, overthrow, defeat, fr. L *prostratus* (past part. of *prosternere*) + *-ion-, -io* -ion] **1 a :** the act of assuming a prostrate position esp. as a ceremonial or submissive gesture ⟨a number of young girls enter, make the customary ~ of greeting —Lafcadio Hearn⟩ **b :** the state of being in a prostrate position **:** ABASEMENT, SUBMISSIVENESS **2 a :** complete physical or mental exhaustion **:** COLLAPSE ⟨~ in influenza⟩ **b :** SHOCK, STUPEFACTION ⟨brought no incoherent cry of pity or ~ —C.E.Montague⟩ ⟨leaves the lay reader with a sense of ~ —A.G.Mazour⟩ **3 :** the process of being made powerless or the condition of powerlessness ⟨the ~ of the country before any invading and conquering army —Hilaire Belloc⟩ ⟨the general ~ of business after the war —Samuel Van Valkenburg & Ellsworth Huntington⟩

**pros·tra·tor** \\ˈprä,strād·ə(r)\\ *n* -s [LL, fr. L *prostratus* (past part. of *prosternere*) + *-or*] **:** one that prostrates

¹**pro·style** \\ˈprō,stīl\\ *adj* [L *prostylos* having pillars in front, fr. Gk, fr. *pro-* ¹*pro-* + *stylos* pillar — more at STEER] **:** marked by columniation consisting of free columns in a front portico only and across the full front of the structure — compare AMPHIPROSTYLE, PSEUDOPROSTYLE; see COLUMNIATION illustration

²**prostyle** \\"\\ *n* -s **:** a prostyle building

**pro·suspensor** \\,prō+\\ *n* [NL, fr. ¹*pro-* + *suspensor*] **:** the portion of the undifferentiated proembryo that gives rise to the suspensor

**prosy** \\ˈprōzē, -zi\\ *adj* -ER/-EST [¹*prose* + *-y*] **1 :** of, relating to, or having the characteristics of prose **:** COMMONPLACE, PROSAIC ⟨a dull ~ description of some of the exhibits —Sam Pollock⟩ ⟨the ~, shapeless frame houses without architectural charm or dignity —C.G.Bowers⟩ **2 :** tedious in speech or manner ⟨all ~ dull society sinners, who chatter and bleat and bore —W.S.Gilbert⟩

**pro·syl·lo·gism** \\prōˈsilə,jizəm\\ *n* [ML *prosyllogismus,* fr. Gk *prosyllogismos,* fr. *pro-* ¹*pro-* + *syllogismos* syllogism] **:** a syllogism with a conclusion that becomes a premise of a following syllogism

**prot-** *or* **proto-** *comb form* [ME *protho-,* fr. MF, fr. LL *proto-,* fr. LGk *prōt-, prōto-,* fr. Gk, fr. *prōtos;* akin to Gk *pro* before, ahead — more at FOR] **1 a :** first in time ⟨*proto*historic⟩ ⟨*proto*nymph⟩ **b :** first in status **:** chief in rank or importance **:** principal ⟨*proto*cerebrum⟩ ⟨*proto*cone⟩ **c :** beginning **:** tending toward **:** giving rise to ⟨*proto*fascism⟩ ⟨*proto*planet⟩ **2** *chem* **a :** first or lowest of a series **:** member of a series having or supposed to have the smallest relative amount of the element or radical indicated in the name to which it is prefixed ⟨*proto*xide⟩ ⟨*proto*chloride⟩ **b :** substance held to be the parent of the substance to the name of which it is prefixed ⟨*proto*actinium⟩ **c :** first or primary product of decomposition ⟨*proto*proteose⟩ **3** *biol* **a :** archetypal ⟨*proto*morph⟩ ⟨*proto*nephros⟩ **b :** first formed **:** primary ⟨*proto*derm⟩ ⟨*proto*xylem⟩ **4** *usu cap* **:** belonging to or constituting the recorded or assumed language that is ancestral to a language or to a group of related languages or dialects — usu. spelled *proto-* and joined to a capitalized second element with a hyphen ⟨*Proto*-Arabic⟩ ⟨*Proto*-Indo-European⟩

**prot** *abbr* **1** protected; protection **2** protectorate **3** *usu cap* Protestant

**prot·actinium** \\;prōd·+\\ *or* **pro·to·actinium** \\;prōd·(,)ō+\\ *n* [NL, fr. *prot-* + *actinium*] **:** a shiny metallic radioelement of relatively short life that is formed in nature by loss of an alpha-particle and a beta-particle from uranium 235, that disintegrates into actinium and ultimately into lead, and that is pentavalent in compounds and shows close chemical resemblance to tantalum but differs in that its pentoxide is exclusively basic with no acidic characteristics — symbol *Pa;* see ACTINIUM SERIES, URANIUM SERIES; ELEMENT table

**pro·ta·gon** \\ˈprōd·ə,gän\\ *n* -s [G, fr. *prot-* + Gk *agōn* gathering, assembly] **:** a white crystalline powder consisting of a mixture of lipides obtained from the brain

**pro·tag·o·nism** \\prōˈtagə,nizəm\\ *n* -s [*protagonist* + *-ism*] **:** the state, character, or activity of a protagonist

**pro·tag·o·nist** \\-nəst\\ *n* -s [Gk *prōtagōnistēs,* fr. *prōt-* prot- + *agōnistēs* competitor at games, debater, actor, fr. *agōnizesthai* to compete for a prize, contend, fr. *agōn* gathering, assembly at games, contest — more at AGONY] **1 a :** one who takes the leading part in a drama — opposed to *antagonist* **b :** the chief character of a novel or story in or around whom the action centers **2 a :** the spokesman or leader for a cause **:** the principal mover **:** CHAMPION ⟨was not only the ~ of his age; he was the symbol of all its inner meaning —W.O.Douglas⟩ **b :** an active participant **:** the supporter of an idea or action **:** ADVOCATE ⟨there remains a problem of market power that the ~s of big business . . . have not understood —E.S.Mason⟩ **3 :** a muscle that by its contraction actually causes a particular movement

**pro·tag·o·re·an** \\prō;tagəˈrēən\\ *adj, usu cap* [*Protagoras,* 5th cent. B.C. Greek philosopher + E *-an*] **:** of or relating to Protagoras or his teachings

**pro·tag·o·re·an·ism** \\-ə,nizəm\\ *n* -s *usu cap* **:** the teachings of the Sophist Protagoras of Abdera — compare HOMO MENSURA

**prot·amine** \\(ˈ)prōd·+\\ *n* [ISV *prot-* + *amine;* orig. formed in G] **:** any of a class of simple proteins (as clupeine or salmine) that are strongly basic, not coagulable by heat, and soluble in water and dilute ammonia, that yield large amounts of basic amino acids on hydrolysis, and that occur combined with nucleic acid in the sperm of fish; *esp* **:** SALMINE — compare HISTONE

**protamine zinc insulin** *n* **:** a combination of protamine, zinc, and insulin used in suspension in water for subcutaneous injection in place of insulin because of its prolonged effect

**prot·an·dric** \\prōdˈandrik, -aan-\\ *adj* [ISV *protandry* + *-ic*] **:** PROTANDROUS

**prot·an·drous** \\-drəs\\ *adj* [*prot-* + *-androus*] **:** exhibiting protandry

**prot·an·dry** \\-drē\\ *n* -ES [ISV *prot-* + *-andry*] **1 :** a state in hermaphroditic systems that is characterized by the development of male organs or maturation of their products before the appearance of the corresponding female product thus inhibiting self-fertilization and that is encountered commonly in mints, legumes, and composites and among diverse groups of invertebrate animals — compare PROTOGYNY **2** [*prot-* + *andr-* + *-y*] **:** the appearance of male insects earlier in the season than females of the same species

**prot·anomalous** \\;prōd·+\\ *adj* [*prot-* + *anomalous*] **:** exhibiting protanomaly

**prot·anomaly** \\"+\\ *n* [ISV *prot-* + *anomaly;* prob. orig. formed as G *protanomalie*] **:** trichromatism in which an abnormally large proportion of red is required to match the spectrum — compare DEUTERANOMALY, TRICHROMAT

**pro·ta·nope** \\ˈprōd·ə,nōp\\ *n* -s [back-formation fr. NL *protanopia*] **:** an individual affected with protanopia

**pro·ta·no·pia** \\,==ˈnōpēə\\ *n* -s [NL, fr. *prot-* + ²*a-* + *-opia*] **:** red-green blindness believed due to a defect in the receptive mechanism of the retina of the eye and marked by confusion of red and blue-green — compare DEUTERANOPIA

**pro·ta·nop·ic** \\;==ˈnäpik\\ *adj* [ISV *protanop-* (fr. NL *protanopia*) + *-ic*] **:** characterized by or affected by protanopia ⟨~ vision⟩ ⟨a ~ person⟩

**pro tan·to** \\prōˈtan·(,)tō\\ [LL] **:** for so much **:** to a certain extent

**prot·argentum** \\;prōd·+\\ *n* [NL, fr. *prot-* (fr. ISV *protein*) + L *argentum*] **:** SILVER PROTEIN b

**pro·tar·gin** \\prōˈtärjən\\ *n* -s [NL *protargentum* + ISV *-in*] **:** SILVER PROTEIN

**Pro·tar·gol** \\-,gōl, -gōl\\ *trademark* — used for strong silver protein

**pro·tarsal** \\(ˈ)prō+\\ *adj* [NL *protarsus* + E *-al*] **:** of or relating to a protarsus

**pro·tarsus** \\"+\\ *n, pl* **protarsi** [NL, fr. ¹*pro-* + *tarsus*] **1 :** the tarsus of the front leg of an insect **2 :** the tibia of the leg of a spider

**prot·a·sis** \\ˈpräd·əsəs\\ *n, pl* **prota·ses** \\-ə,sēz\\ [LL, fr. Gk, fr. *proteinein* stretch out before, put forward, fr. *pro-* ¹*pro-* + *teinein* to stretch — more at THIN] **1 a :** the first part of an ancient drama in which the characters are introduced and the argument explained **b :** the opening lines esp. of a drama or narrative poem **:** the part preceding the epitasis **:** INTRODUCTION — compare CATASTASIS **2 :** CONDITION 2a(2) — contrasted with *apodosis* **3 :** a proposition that serves esp. as a premise in a syllogism or in reasoning **:** ANTECEDENT, CONDITIONAL

**pro·tas·pid** \\prōˈtaspəd\\ *adj* [NL *protaspid-, protoaspis*] **:** relating to or being a protaspis

**pro·tas·pis** \\-pəs\\ *n, pl* **protaspi·des** \\-pə,dēz\\ [NL, fr. *prot-* + *-aspis*] **:** the minute discoid or oval first larval form of a trilobite that has a well-marked axial lobe, large head region, and but little segmentation

**pro·tat·ic** \\prōˈtad·ik\\ *adj* [LL *protaticus,* fr. Gk *protatikos,* fr. *protasis* + *-ikos* -ic] **:** of or relating to the protasis of a play **:** INTRODUCTORY — **pro·tat·i·cal·ly** \\-ək(ə)lē\\ *adv*

**prot·axial** \\(ˈ)prōd·+\\ *adj* [NL *protaxis* + E *-al*] **:** of or relating to the protaxis

**prot·axis** \\"+\\ *n* [NL, fr. *prot-* + *axis*] **:** the line of initial uplift or the core in a mountain system or range

**prote-** *or* **proteo-** *comb form* [ISV, fr. F *protéine* protein — more at PROTEIN] **:** protein ⟨*proteo*lysis⟩ ⟨*prote*ose⟩

**pro·tea** \\ˈprōd·ēə\\ *n* [NL, fr. L, *Proteus,* sea god who had the power of assuming different shapes, fr. L; fr. the great variety of forms it exhibits] **1** *cap* **:** a genus (the type of the family Proteaceae) of shrubs with alternate rigid leaves, dense flower heads resembling cones, and a fruit that is a hairy nut — see HONEYFLOWER b **2** -s **:** any plant of the genus *Protea*

**pro·te·a·ce·ae** \\,prōd·ēˈāsē,ē\\ *n pl, cap* [NL, fr. *Protea,* type genus + *-aceae*] **:** a family of chiefly Australian and southern African dicotyledonous shrubs and trees (order Proteales) that has coriaceous leaves and clustered bracteate mostly tetramerous flowers — **pro·te·a·ceous** \\;==ˈāshəs\\ *adj*

**pro·te·a·les** \\,==ˈā(,)lēz\\ *n pl, cap* [NL, fr. *Protea* + *-ales*] **:** an order of plants that is coextensive with the family Proteaceae

¹**pro·te·an** \\ˈprōd·ēən, -ōtē-, prōˈtēən\\ *adj, sometimes cap* [*Proteus,* legendary sea god in the service of Neptune who had the power of assuming different shapes (fr. L, fr. Gk *Prōteus*) + E *-an*] **1 :** characteristic of or resembling Proteus **:** capable of change **:** exceedingly variable ⟨the eyes . . . were of that baffling ~ gray which is never twice the same —Jack London⟩ **2 :** readily assuming different shapes or forms ⟨an amoeba is a ~ animalcule⟩ **3 :** capable of acting many different roles ⟨the company was led by a ~ actor⟩ **4 :** displaying great diversity **:** possessed of infinite variety ⟨one of our most ~ artists; he has been an architect, a painter, an engraver —*New Yorker*⟩ ⟨he is so many-sided, so ~ that he refuses to be pigeonholed —*Times Lit. Supp.*⟩

²**pro·te·an** \\ˈprōd·ēən\\ *n* -s [*prote-* + *-an*] **:** any of various insoluble primary protein derivatives that result from a slight modification of the protein molecule esp. by the incipient action of water, very dilute acids, or enzymes

**pro·te·ase** \\ˈprōd·ē,ās, -āz\\ *n* -s [ISV *prote-* + *-ase*] **:** any of the class of proteolytic enzymes comprising the proteinases and the peptidases

**protea veld** *n* **:** BUSHVELD

**pro·tect** \\prəˈtekt\\ *vt* -ED/-ING/-S [L *protectus,* past part. of *protegere* to cover in front, to defend, protect, fr. *pro-* ¹*pro-* + *tegere* to cover — more at THATCH] **1 :** to cover or shield from that which would injure, destroy, or detrimentally affect **:** secure or preserve usu. against attack, disintegration, encroachment, or harm **:** GUARD ⟨the ring of old forts which so far had ~*ed* the city successfully —P.W.Thompson⟩ ⟨hands half ~*ed* by shabby woolen mittens —F.V.W.Mason⟩ ⟨his invention was ~*ed* by a patent⟩ ⟨the scanty vegetation was insufficient to ~ the light soil from blustery winds —R.H. Billington⟩ ⟨both led happy ~*ed* lives —Kathleen Freeman⟩ **2** *obs* **:** to act as protector for ⟨the King had virtuous uncles to ~ his Grace —Shak.⟩ **3 :** to guard, shield, or foster by a protective tariff or other form of trade control **4 :** to render (a lyophobic colloid) stable by the addition of a protective colloid **5 a :** to warn (the crew of an approaching train) that the track ahead is not clear **b :** to flag or signal to stop **syn** see DEFEND

**pro·tect·ant** \\-tənt\\ *n* -s [*protect* + *-ant*] **:** a protecting agent; *specif* **:** a pesticidal spray that is applied to a plant before the arrival of the spore or other agent of infection — compare ERADICANT

**protected** *adj* [fr. past part. of *protect*] **:** guarded or shielded to prevent accidental contact or injury — used esp. of machinery

**protected state** *n* **:** an internationally recognized state under the protection of another usu. larger and more powerful state; *specif* **:** a state having a relatively stable and traditional government that has entered into treaty relations with the British Crown to avail itself of British protection and that while giving the British government certain rights and responsibilities usu. retains supervision of its domestic affairs while placing its foreign relations under British control ⟨the two British Settlements and the nine *protected states* which together form the Federation of Malaya —M.E.Cooper⟩ — compare PROTECTORATE

**protecting** *adj* **1 :** serving to protect or shield ⟨a good part of this game-filled plain lies within the ~ confines of the . . . National Park —Tom Marvel⟩ **2 :** serving to prevent sale at a price below a minimum — **pro·tect·ing·ly** *adv*

**pro·tec·tion** \\prəˈtekshən\\ *n* -s [ME *proteccioun,* fr. MF *protection,* fr. LL *protection-, protectio,* fr. L *protectus* (past part. of *protegere* to protect) + *-ion-, -io* -ion] **1 :** a writing that protects or secures from molestation or arrest **:** PASSPORT, SAFE-CONDUCT **2 :** the act of protecting **:** the state or fact of being protected **:** shelter from danger or harm ⟨a sense of ~ and security in the life of his home —Archibald Marshall⟩ ⟨huddled in the lee of the rock, trying to get a little ~ from the wind —H.D.Quillin⟩ **3 a :** one that protects ⟨an umbrella is ~ in a sudden shower⟩ **b :** the oversight or support usu. of one that is smaller and weaker ⟨government ~ for small business⟩ ⟨her brother's ~ was very welcome on the way home from school⟩ **4 a :** the freeing of the producers of a country from foreign competition in their home market by the imposition of high duties, quantitative trade controls, or exchange controls to restrict the importation of goods of foreign origin **b :** the theory, policy, or system favoring or practicing the imposition of such controls — compare AMERICAN SYSTEM, FREE TRADE **5 a :** immunity from prosecution obtained by some criminal classes (as proprietors of gambling houses) through bribes to officials or political bosses **b :** money paid to racketeers under threat of depredation ⟨sold ~ to everyone from the proprietors of the neighborhood delicatessens to the owners of the town's plushiest clubs —Polly Adler⟩ **6 :** COVERAGE 2c **7 :** a plant-disease control measure in which a protectant is used

**pro·tec·tion·al** \\-shən³l, -shənəl\\ *adj* **:** of, relating to, or serving for protection

**protection and indemnity insurance** *n* **:** insurance for ship owners against loss due to legal liability arising from damage to cargo, injury to passengers and crew, and other legal liabilities not assumed under the regular forms of hull insurance

**protection forest** *n* **:** a forest whose value lies in the regulating of stream flow and the preventing of erosion and avalanches rather than in its timber

**pro·tec·tion·ism** \\-shə,nizəm\\ *n* -s [¹*protectionist* + *-ism*] **:** the doctrine or policy of protectionists

¹**pro·tec·tion·ist** \\-sh(ə)nəst\\ *n* -s [*protection* + *-ist*] **:** one who favors protection; *esp* **:** one who advocates or supports a governmental policy that imposes trade restrictions on competitive foreign goods

²**protectionist** \\"\\ *adj* **:** favoring or maintaining protection; *esp* **:** favoring trade restrictions on competitive foreign goods ⟨the surprise when the voting began was the extent of new ~ sentiment —*Atlantic*⟩

**protection line** *n, usu cap P* **:** LINE OF MARS

¹**pro·tec·tive** \\prəˈtektiv, -tēv *also* -əv\\ *adj* [*protect* + *-ive*] **1 :** protecting or intended to protect **:** affording or serving as a safeguard **:** providing a defense or shelter against danger or harm **:** tending to shield ⟨many shore animals have ~ color and patterns which enable them to blend with their surround-

ings —W.H.Dowdeswell⟩ ⟨failure to use ~ masks in the numerous grinding operations —Lewis Mumford⟩ ⟨she felt ~ towards him —Olive Johnson⟩ ⟨~ force of soldiers —*Amer. Guide Series: Ariz.*⟩ **2 :** based on or relating to the economic principles of protection **:** affording or designed to afford protection ⟨~ duties⟩ **3 :** imposed as a means of or under the guise of insuring protection from possible hostility ⟨~ arrest⟩ ⟨if he's tight, return him to his ship under ~ custody —D.R. Morris⟩

**²protective** \"\ *n* -s **1 :** something that serves for protection **2 :** an agent (as a medicine or a dressing) that protects the body or one of its parts (as from irritation or injury) ⟨vitamins are ~s against certain deficiency diseases⟩

**protective coating** *n* **:** a type of paint, varnish, or lacquer used more to protect than decorate

**protective colloid** *n* **:** a lyophilic colloid (as gelatin, a natural gum, or a cellulose derivative) that when present in small quantities renders lyophobic colloids stable toward the coagulating action of electrolytes ⟨gelatin acts in part as a *protective colloid* in photographic emulsions⟩

**protective coloration** *n* **:** coloration by which an organism is actually or apparently made less visible or less attractive to predators

**protective cover** *n* **:** a permanent outer container used to protect a book against atmospheric and handling damage

**protective deck** *n* **:** the most heavily armored and usu. convexly shaped deck of a warship

**protective department** *n* **:** SALVAGE CORPS

**protective foods** *n* **:** foods (as leafy or yellow vegetables, citrus fruits, meat, milk, eggs) that contain adequate amounts of vitamins, minerals, and high quality proteins and that protect against development of a deficiency disease (as pellagra, beriberi, scurvy)

**protective liability insurance** *n* **:** insurance that protects an owner or contractor against liability for injury or damage caused by independent contractors doing work in his behalf

**pro·tec·tive·ly** \-tə̇vlē, -li\ *adv* **:** in a protective manner

**pro·tec·tive·ness** \-tivnə̇s, -tēv- *also* -əv-\ *n* -ES **:** the quality or state of being protective ⟨could not escape his mother's ~⟩

**protective resemblance** *n* **:** resemblance of an animal to its environment (as by coloration) that causes it to blend with the substrate and become hidden from its enemies

**protective system** *n* **:** PROTECTION 4b

**protective tariff** *n* **:** a tariff that protects domestic producers; *esp* **:** one primarily designed to secure protection and not revenue — compare REVENUE TARIFF

**pro·tec·tor** \prə'tektə(r)\ *n* -s [ME *protectour*, fr. MF, fr. LL *protector*, fr. L *protectus* (past part. of *protegere* to protect) + *-or* — more at PROTECT] **1 a :** one that protects or shields esp. from danger or harm **:** GUARDIAN, PATRON **b :** something serving or designed to protect **:** a device used to prevent injury **:** GUARD ⟨the chest ~ of the baseball catcher —*Selected Team Sports for Men*⟩ **2 :** one having the care of the kingdom during the king's minority **:** REGENT

**pro·tec·tor·al** \-t(ə)rəl\ *adj* **:** of or relating to a protector or protectorate

**pro·tec·tor·ate** \-t(ə)rə̇t *sometimes* -tə,rāt, *usu* -d·+V\ *n* -s **1 a :** government by a protector (as of a kingdom) ⟨conditions in England under the Cromwellian ~⟩ **b :** the rank, office, or period of rule of a protector ⟨during the ~⟩ ⟨succeeded to the ~⟩ **2 a :** the relationship of superior authority assumed by one power or state over a dependent political unit ⟨conceded to Russia a virtual ~ over Manchuria —J.A.S.Grenville⟩ **b :** the period during which such a relationship is maintained **c :** the authority assumed by the predominant state in such a relationship **d :** the dependent political unit in such a relationship: (1) **:** a territorial unit under the political control and protection of a larger and more powerful state esp. in the areas of defense and foreign relations (2) **:** a dependent territory usu. having only rudimentary political institutions over which a larger and more powerful country exercises the powers of government without having legal possession; *specif* **:** one having in effect although not in law the status of a British colony and as a result governed in both internal and external affairs by the British government although technically not constituting a part of the dominions of the crown (3) **:** PROTECTED STATE

**protectorian** *adj, obs* **:** of or relating to a protector **:** PROTECTORAL

**pro·tec·to·ry** \prə'tekt(ə)rē\ *n* -ES **:** an institution for the protection and care usu. of homeless or delinquent children

**pro·tec·tress** \-trə̇s\ *n* -ES [*protector* + *-ess*] **:** a female protector

**pro·tec·trix** \-triks\ *n* -ES [ML, fem. of *protector*, fr. LL] **:** PROTECTRESS

**protects** *pres 3d sing of* PROTECT

**pro·té·gé** \'prōd·ə,zhā, -ōtə-, ,==' =\ *n* -s [F, fr. past part. of *protéger* to protect, fr. L *protegere*] **1 :** a man under the care and protection of an influential person (as a sponsor, instructor, or patron) usu. for the furthering of his career (as in art, politics, sport) **:** PUPIL ⟨big-business ~s —*Harper's*⟩ ⟨a ~ of the Institute's famous professor —Jack Goodman⟩ ⟨~ of many popes —*Mentor*⟩ **2 a :** a resident of one country (as a colony or a protectorate) under the juridical protection of another government **b :** one protected by a foreign country under extraterritorial rights

**pro·té·gée** \"\ *n* -s [F, fem. of *protégé*] **:** a female protégé ⟨by way of example to her ~s, won more national championships than any other player in the history of the sport —H.W. Wind⟩

**pro·tegulum** \(')prō+\ *n* -s [NL, fr. ¹*pro-* + L *tegulum* covering, fr. *tegere* to cover + *-ulum* (neut. of *-ulus* -ule) — more at THATCH] **:** the embryonic shell of a brachiopod that is biconvex and smooth and has a wide posterior gape

**protei** *pl of* PROTEUS

**pro·te·ic** \prō'tēik\ *adj* [ISV *prote-* (fr. F *protéine* protein) + *-ic*] **:** PROTEINACEOUS

**pro·teid** \'prō,tēd, -ōd·ēə̇d\ *n* -s [ISV *prote-* + *-id*; orig. formed in G] **:** PROTEIN 2

**pro·te·i·da** \prō'tēədə\ *n pl, cap* [NL, fr. *Proteus* (genus of olms) + *-ida*] **:** a suborder of Caudata comprising aquatic salamanders with persistent gills and two pairs of weak limbs and usu. regarded as including the single family Proteidae and consisting of the European olms and the American mud puppies

**pro·te·i·dae** \-ə,dē\ *n pl, cap* [NL, fr. *Proteus* (genus of olms) + *-idae*] **:** a family of amphibians coextensive with the suborder Proteida

**pro·te·ide** \'prōd·ē,īd, -ēə̇d\ *n* -s [ISV *prote-* + *-ide*; orig. formed in G] **:** PROTEIN 2 — used of a subdivision of protides

**pro·te·i·form** \prō'tēə,fȯrm\ *adj* [F *protéiforme*, fr. *Protée* Proteus (fr. L *Proteus*) + *-iforme* -iform — more at PROTEAN] **:** PROTEAN

**¹pro·tein** \'prō,tēn *also* -ōd·ēən *or* -ōtēən\ *n* -s [F *protéine*, fr. LGk *prōteios* primary (fr. Gk *prōtos* first) + F *-ine* — more at PROT-] **1** *archaic* **:** an alkali metaprotein supposed to be the basis of all albuminous substances **2 :** any of a very large class of naturally occurring extremely complex combinations of amino acids containing the elements carbon, hydrogen, nitrogen, oxygen, usu. sulfur, occasionally phosphorus, iron, or other elements that are essential constituents of all living cells both animal and vegetable and also of the diet of the animal organism, that are both acidic and basic and usu. colloidal in nature although many have been crystallized, that are hydrolyzable by acids, alkalies, proteolytic enzymes, and putrefactive bacteria to polypeptides, simpler peptides, and ultimately to alpha-amino acids, that have been classified by biological functions, by chemical composition as simple or conjugated, by solubility in water and salt solutions, or by the shape of the molecule as fibrous or fibrillar (as those forming structural elements of animal tissue) or as corpuscular or globular (as those involved in animal metabolism) — compare CONJUGATED PROTEIN, DENATURE 2, ENZYME, SCLEROPROTEIN, SIMPLE PROTEIN **3 :** the total nitrogenous material in vegetable or animal substances; *esp* **:** CRUDE PROTEIN

**²protein** \"\ *adj* **:** of or containing protein

**pro·tein·a·ceous** \,prō,tē'nāshəs, ¦prōd·ēə̇'n-\ *adj* [¹*protein* + *-aceous*] **:** of, relating to, or of the nature of a protein

**pro·tein·ase** \'prō,tē,nās, -ōd·ēə̇,n-, -āz\ *n* -s [ISV ¹*protein* + *-ase*] **:** any of a group of enzymes (as pepsin, papain) that hydrolyze proteins esp. to peptides **:** ENDOPEPTIDASE — often distinguished from *peptidase;* compare PROTEASE

**pro·tein·ate** \-,nāt\ *n* -s [ISV ¹*protein* + *-ate*] **:** a compound of a protein — not used systematically ⟨silver ~⟩

**protein–bound iodine** *n* **:** the amount of iodine expressed in micrograms per 100 milliliters of blood serum that is precipitated with serum proteins and that serves as a measure of the activity of the thyroid gland ⟨the *protein-bound iodine* in the normal human being ranges from 4 to 8 micrograms, in hypothyroidism falls below this range, and in hyperthyroidism rises above it⟩

**protein crystal** *n* **:** CRYSTALLOID 2

**protein hydrolysate** *n* **:** a mixture containing amino acids and often other substances (as peptides) obtained by the hydrolysis of various animal and vegetable proteins (as lactalbumin or soybean protein) and used as sources of amino acids, as seasoning agents, and in nutrition

**pro·tein·ic** \(')prō¦tēnik, ¦prōd·ē¦inik\ *adj* [¹*protein* + *-ic*] **:** PROTEINACEOUS

**protein milk** *n* **:** a modified milk having a relatively high content of protein and low content of carbohydrate and fat

**pro·tei·nous** \prō'tēnəs\ *adj* [¹*protein* + *-ous*] **:** PROTEINACEOUS

**protein paint** *n* **:** a paint that may be either powder, paste, or ready-mixed with casein or protein for its binder

**protein shock** *n* **:** a severe reaction produced by the injection of protein (as bacterial, animal, or plant proteins or protein-containing organic extracts) and marked by chill, fever, bronchial spasm, acute emphysema, and vomiting and diarrhea

**protein silver** *n* **:** SILVER PROTEIN

**protein therapy** *n* **:** therapeutic injection of protein (as casein or a bacterial vaccine)

**pro·tein·uria** \,prō,tē'n(y)u̇rēə, ,prōd·ēə̇'n-\ *n* -s [NL, fr. ¹*protein* + *-uria*] **:** the presence of protein in the urine — **pro·tein·uric** \¦=,=¦=rik, ¦==¦=\ *adj*

**prot·e·les** \'präd·ə,lēz\ *n, cap* [NL, fr. ¹*pro-* + *-teles* (fr. Gk *telos* completion, maturity, end); fr. the degree of development of the forefeet — more at WHEEL] **:** a genus of mammals (family Hyaenidae) consisting of the aardwolf — compare PROTELIDAE

**¹pro·tel·id** \prə'telə̇d\ *adj* [NL *Protelidae*] **:** of or relating to the Protelidae

**²protelid** \"\ *n* -s **:** a mammal of the family Protelidae **:** AARDWOLF

**pro·tel·i·dae** \prə'telə,dē\ *n pl, cap* [NL, fr. *Proteles*, type genus + *-idae*] *in some esp. former classifications* **:** a family closely related to and now usu. included in the Hyaenidae that includes the aardwolf and related extinct mammals

**pro·tely·trop·tera** \prə,telē'träpt(ə)rə\ *n pl, cap* [NL, fr. *prot-* + *elytron* + *-ptera*] **:** an order of extinct insects related to the Dermaptera, known only from the Permian, and characterized by slender elytra with a reduced venation and by broad hind wings resembling those of the Dermaptera — **pro·tely·trop·ter·an** \-t(ə)rən\ *n or adj* — **pro·tely·trop·ter·on** \-tə,rän\ *n* -s — **pro·tely·trop·ter·ous** \-t(ə)rəs\ *adj*

**¹pro tem** \(')prō¦tem\ *adj* [by shortening] **:** PRO TEMPORE

**²pro tem** \"\ *adv* **:** for the time being ⟨accepting *pro tem* that hypothesis consistent with the facts —J.W.Krutch⟩

**pro tem·po·re** \-'tempə(,)rē\ *adj* [L, for the time being] **:** chosen to occupy a position either temporarily or during the absence of a regularly elected official **:** appointed for the time being ⟨designated him to act as consul *pro tempore* —H.H. Fiske⟩ — compare PRESIDENT PRO TEMPORE

**pro·tend** \prō'tend\ *vb* -ED/-ING/-S [ME *protenden*, fr. L *protendere*, fr. *pro-* ¹pro- + *tendere* to stretch — more at THIN] *vt* **1 :** to hold out **:** stretch forth **2 :** EXTEND ~ *vi* **:** to stick out **:** PROTRUDE ⟨his staff ~*ing* like a hunter's spear —William Wordsworth⟩

**pro·ten·sion** \-'tenchən\ *n* -s [LL *protension-*, *protensio*, fr. L *protensus* (past part. of *protendere* to protend) + *-ion-*, *-io* -ion] **:** a protending esp. forward

**pro·ten·si·ty** \-n(t)sə̇d·ē\ *n* -ES [L *protensus* (past part. of *protendere*) + E *-ity*] **1 :** the quality or character of being protensive **2 :** the duration of a sensation — compare EXTENSITY

**pro·ten·sive** \-n(t)siv\ *adj* [L *protensus* (past part.) + E *-ive*] **1 :** having continuance in time **:** having duration even though very slight **2 :** having lengthwise extent or extensiveness — **pro·ten·sive·ly** \-sə̇vlē\ *adv*

**proteo-** — see PROTE-

**¹pro·teo·ceph·a·lid** \¦prōd·ē(,)ō¦sefələ̇d, -,lid\ *adj* [NL *Proteocephalidae*] **:** of or relating to the Proteocephalidae

**²proteocephalid** \"\ *n* -s **:** a tapeworm of the family Proteocephalidae

**pro·teo·ce·phal·i·dae** \,===sə'falə,dē\ *n pl, cap* [NL, fr. *Proteocephalus*, type genus + *-idae*] **:** a family of tapeworms that are parasites of fishes, have scolices resembling those of members of the Cyclophyllidea and reproductive organs like those of members of the Tetraphyllidea, and are sometimes placed in either of these orders but now more usu. isolated in a separate order

**pro·teo·ceph·a·loid** \¦==(,)=¦sefə,lȯid\ *adj* [NL *Proteocephalus* + E *-oid*] **:** resembling or related to *Proteocephalus* or to the Proteocephalidae

**pro·teo·ceph·a·lus** \,==(,)='sefələs\ *n, cap* [NL, fr. *Proteus*, sea god who could assume different shapes (fr. L) + NL *-cephalus* — more at PROTEAN] **:** a very large genus comprising tapeworms parasitic in the intestines of various fishes and being the type of the family Proteocephalidae

**pro·teo·clas·tic** \¦prōd·ēə¦klastik\ *adj* [*prote-* + *-clastic*] **:** PROTEOLYTIC

**pro·te·og·e·nous** \¦prōd·ē¦äjənəs\ *adj* [*prote-* + *-genous*] **:** of or relating to a substance obtained from a protein ⟨a ~ amine⟩

**pro·teo·lipide** \¦prōd·ēə+\ *or* **pro·teo·lipid** \"+\ *n* [*prote-* + *lipide, lipid*] **:** any of a class of proteins that contain a considerable percentage of lipide and are soluble in lipides and insoluble in water — compare LIPOPROTEIN

**pro·te·ol·y·sin** \,prōd·ē'äləsə̇n, ,==¦līsᵊn\ *n* [ISV *prote-* + *lysin*] **:** a lysin (as an enzyme) producing proteolysis

**pro·te·ol·y·sis** \,=='äləsə̇s\ *n* [NL, fr. *prote-* + *-lysis*] **:** the hydrolysis of proteins or peptides with formation of simpler and soluble products (as in digestion)

**pro·teo·lyt·ic** \¦==¦lid·ik\ *adj* [ISV *prote-* + *-lytic*] **:** of, relating to, or producing proteolysis

**pro·teo·myxa** \,==='miksə\ *n pl, cap* [NL, fr. *Proteus*, sea god who could assume different shapes + NL *-myxa*] **:** a small order of obscure rhizopods of uncertain relationships usu. possessing flagella at some stage of their life

**pro·te·ose** \'prōd·ē,ōs, -ōtē-\ *n* -s [ISV *prote-* + *-ose*] **:** any of various protein derivatives that are formed by the partial hydrolysis of proteins (as by enzymes of the gastric and pancreatic juices), that are not coagulated by heat, and that are soluble in water but are precipitated from solution by saturation with ammonium sulfate — compare ALBUMOSE, PEPTONE

**¹prot·ephemerid** \¦prōd·+\ *adj* [NL *Protephemerida*] **:** of or relating to the Protephemerida

**²protephemerid** \"\ *n* -s **:** an insect of the order Protephemerida

**prot·ephemerida** \(¦)prōd·+\ *n pl, cap* [NL, fr. *prot-* + *Ephemerida*] **:** an order of extinct insects related to the Plectoptera, known only from the Upper Carboniferous, and characterized by long cerci and homonomous wings with numerous crossveins

**prot·ephem·er·oi·dea** \,prōd·ə,femə'rȯidēə\ [NL, fr. *prot-* + *Ephemera* + *-oidea*] *syn of* PROTEPHEMERIDA

**proter-** *or* **protero-** *comb form* [NL, fr. Gk *proter-*, *protero-*, fr. *proteros*; akin to Gk *pro* before, ahead — more at FOR] **:** before **:** earlier **:** former ⟨*proterozoic*⟩ ⟨*proteranthous*⟩

**proter·an·dric** \¦prädə¦randrik, ¦prōd·ə¦-, -raan-\ *adj* [ISV *proterandr-* (fr. *proterandry*) + *-ic*] **:** PROTANDROUS

**proter·an·dri·ous** \-drēəs\ *adj* [*proter-* + *andr-* + *-ious*] **:** PROTANDROUS

**proter·an·drous** \-drəs\ *adj* [ISV *proter-* + *-androus*] **:** PROTANDROUS — **proter·an·drous·ly** *adv* — **proter·an·drous·ness** *n* -ES — **proter·an·dry** \'==,=drē\ *n* -ES

**proter·an·thous** \¦==¦ran(t)thəs\ *adj* [*proter-* + *-anthous*] **:** having flowers appearing before the leaves — **proter·an·thy** \'==,ran(t)thē\ *n* -ES

**¹protero·glyph** \'präd·ərə,glif, prō'terə,-\ *adj* [NL *Proteroglypha*] **:** of or relating to the Proteroglypha

**²proteroglyph** \"\ *n* -s **:** a snake of the group Proteroglypha

**protero·glypha** \,==='glifə\ *n pl, cap* [NL, fr. *proter-* + *-glypha* (fr. Gk *glyphē* carved work); fr. the grooved fangs — more at GLYPH] **:** a group of venomous snakes comprising forms that have in the front of the upper jaw and preceding the ordinary teeth permanently erect fangs with an open or a nearly closed groove associated with a venom gland and including the families Elapidae and Hydrophidae widely distributed in the warmer parts of the world — compare OPISTHOGLYPHA — **protero·glyph·ic** \¦===¦glifik\ *adj* — **protero·glyph·ous** \-fəs\ *adj*

**proterog·y·nous** \¦präd·ə¦räjənəs\ *adj* [ISV *proter-* + *-gynous*] **:** PROTOGYNOUS — **proterog·y·ny** \-nē\ *n* -ES

**protero·saur** \'präd·ərə,sȯ(ə)r\ *var of* PROTOROSAUR

**protero·sau·ria** \-rēə\ [NL, fr. *proter-* + *-sauria*] *syn of* PROTOROSAURIA

**protero·sau·rus** \,==='sȯrəs\ [NL, alter. of *Protorosaurus*] *syn of* PROTOROSAURUS

**proteroth·e·sis** \,=='räthəsə̇s\ *n* -ES [NL, fr. *proter-* + Gk *thesis* setting, position — more at THESIS] **:** the laying of female-producing eggs in the first cells constructed by some solitary wasps and bees after which male-producing eggs are laid

**protero·type** \'==rə,tīp\ *n* [*proter-* + *type*] **:** a primary type

**¹protero·zo·ic** \¦===¦zōik\ *adj, usu cap* [ISV *proter-* + *-zoic*] **:** of or relating to a grand division of geological history that includes the entire interval from the beginning of the Huronian to the close of the Keweenawan, perhaps exceeds in length all of subsequent geological time, and is marked by rocks that contain a few fossils indicating the existence of animals as highly organized as annelid worms and of blue-green and brown algae — see GEOLOGIC TIME table

**²proterozoic** \"\ *n* -s *usu cap* **:** the Proterozoic era or system of rocks

**pro·ter·vi·ty** \prə'tərvəd·ē\ *n* -ES [L *protervitas*, fr. *protervus* forward, bold, impudent, flighty (prob. alter. of *propterus*, fr. *pro-* forward + *-pterus* — akin to Gk *petesthai* to fly) + *-itas* -ity — more at PRO-, FEATHER] **1 :** a petulant manner **:** PEEVISHNESS **2 :** insolent sauciness

**¹pro·test** \'prō,test\ *n* -s *often attrib* [ME, fr. MF, fr. *protester* to protest] **1 :** an affirmative statement **:** a frank and open avowal **:** ACKNOWLEDGMENT **2 a** (1) **:** a solemn declaration in writing made in due form usu. by a notary public under his notarial seal on behalf of the holder of a bill or note announcing refusal of payment or acceptance upon presentment and protesting against all parties to the instrument and declaring their liability for any loss or damage arising from such action (2) **:** a formal notarial notice to all parties of the insolvency or other condition of the acceptor of a bill warranting the supposition that payment will not be made when due that is employed for better security against the drawer and endorsers — used chiefly in English practice (3) **:** the action of making or procuring to be made such a declaration with due service of notice of dishonor **b :** a declaration made by the master of a ship before a notary, consul, or other authorized officer upon his arrival in port after a disaster stating the particulars of it and showing that any damage or loss sustained was not owing to the fault of the ship, her officers, or crew but to the perils of the sea and protesting against them **c :** a declaration made by a party esp. before or while paying a tax or duty or performing an act demanded of him which he deems illegal, denying the justice of the demand, and asserting his rights and claims to show that his action is not voluntary **3 a :** a solemn declaration of disapproval **:** a formal or public remonstrance ⟨saved from execution by ~s from other countries —*Current Biog.*⟩ ⟨the constitutional right of the opposition to voice its ~ —A.C. Cole⟩ **b :** a complaint, objection, or display of unwillingness usu. to an idea or a course of action ⟨went . . . under ~ to hear some Negro spirituals —H.J.Laski⟩ **c :** a gesture of extreme disapproval ⟨always threatening to resign in ~ of what he considered to be the radical views of some of the club members —*Saturday Rev.*⟩ **4 :** an objection lodged with a sports official or a governing body (as against a player because of ineligibility, a play because of illegality, a referee or umpire because of a decision)

**²pro·test** \prə'test, (')prō¦test\ *vb* -ED/-ING/-S [ME *protesten*, fr. MF *protester*, fr. L *protestari*, fr. *pro-* ¹pro- + *testari* to be a witness — more at TESTAMENT] *vt* **1 :** to make solemn declaration or affirmation of **:** AVER ⟨he would have to ~ his affection —Robertson Davies⟩ ⟨he never ~*ed* his friendship —Morley Callaghan⟩ **2** *obs* **:** to declare publicly **:** PROCLAIM, PUBLISH ⟨do me right or I will ~ your cowardice —Shak.⟩ **3 :** to promise solemnly **:** VOW ⟨if you entreat me . . . I will ~ you with my favorite vow —Edna S. V. Millay⟩ **4 :** to make or procure to be made a notarial protest of (as a bill) **5 :** to make a protest against ⟨~ a witness or a commercial instrument⟩ **6 :** to object to **:** remonstrate against ⟨some of the subscribers complained of their inadequacy while others ~*ed* their cost —John Lawler⟩ ⟨it has become customary . . . to ~ the seating —P.C.Jessup⟩ ~ *vi* **1 :** to make a protestation **:** declare the truth solemnly ⟨you don't have to ~ so much —Saul Bellow⟩ **2 :** to make or enter a protest **:** object formally and often strongly ⟨she ~*ed* about the expense —Edmund Wilson⟩ ⟨noted the number of people who were ~*ing* against the morals of the time —Gilbert Seldes⟩ **syn** see ASSERT, OBJECT

**prot·es·tan·cy** \'präd·əstənsē\ *n* -ES [¹*protestant* + *-cy*] **:** PROTESTANTISM

**¹prot·es·tant** \'präd·əstənt, 'prätə-; *also* prə'testənt *in sense 2b*\ *n* -s [MF, fr. L *protestant-*, *protestans*, pres. part. of *protestari* to protest] **1** *usu cap* **a :** one of the German princes favoring the Lutheran movement who presented at the Diet of Spires in 1529 a protest opposing the annulment of an earlier decree allowing each prince to manage the religious affairs of his territory and defending freedom of conscience and the right of minorities **b** *archaic* **:** a member of the Anglican Church **c :** a member of a Protestant religious body **d :** a Christian not of a Catholic or an Eastern church **2 a :** one who makes a declaration ⟨a ~ on behalf of the life of reason —J.M.Grossman⟩ **b :** one who makes or enters a protest ⟨the percentage of ~s seems pitifully inadequate for the needs of the hour —M.L.Cooke⟩ ⟨~s against these books —W.M. Houghton⟩ ⟨the ~s against war throughout the country —W.A.White⟩ **3** *sometimes cap* **:** one who applies Protestant principles elsewhere than in religion ⟨a history which reflects a peculiarly ~ attitude . . . evolved, quite peacefully, from liberal theology —*Times Lit. Supp.*⟩ ⟨moral ~s like their religious counterparts —H.D.Aiken⟩

**²protestant** *see pronunc of noun*\ *adj* [F, fr. MF, fr. *protestant*, n.] **1** *usu cap* **:** of or relating to one of the Christian churches separating from the Roman Catholic Church in the Reformation of the 16th century or from another Protestant church to defend beliefs and practices held vital (as the Reformation principles of justification by faith, the priesthood of all believers, the authority and sufficiency of the Bible, and the right and duty of individual judgment in matters of faith), usu. rejecting as unscriptural the ceremonial reverence of the saints, monasticism, clerical celibacy, and all but two sacraments, and marked by nonliturgical worship featuring preaching, emphasis on individual salvation or morality or on social reform, and sectarian divisions based on points of doctrine or observance **2 :** making or sounding a protest ⟨the two ~ ladies up and marched out —*Time*⟩ ⟨it is still merely a ~ movement . . . whereby students mass themselves to protest — Nathaniel Peffer⟩

**protestant existentialism** *n, usu cap P* **:** CHRISTIAN EXISTENTIALISM

**prot·es·tant·ish** \'präd·əstəntish, 'prätə-\ *adj, often cap* [¹*protestant* + *-ish*] **:** inclined to Protestant Christianity — **prot·es·tant·ish·ly** *adv, often cap*

**prot·es·tant·ism** \-n·,tizəm\ *n* -s [F *protestantisme*, fr. *protestant* + *-isme* -ism] **1 a :** the quality or state of being protestant **b** *usu cap* **:** Protestant principles or practice ⟨distinguish classical from radical *Protestantism*⟩ — compare FUNDAMENTALISM, LIBERALISM, MODERNISM **2** *usu cap* **:** the body of Protestant Christians ⟨representatives of American *Protestantism*⟩

**prot·es·tant·ize** \-n·,tīz\ *vt* -ED/-ING/-S *sometimes cap* [¹*protestant* + *-ize*] **:** to make Protestant **:** convert to Protestantism

**protestant reformation** *n, usu cap P&R* : REFORMATION 2

**protes·ta·tion** \ˌpräǀd·ə'stāshən, -rōǀ, ǀtə-, -rō,te's- *sometimes* -rä,te- *or* -räd·ˌe- *or* -rōd·ˌe-\ *n* -s [ME *protestacioun*, fr. MF *protestation*, fr. LL *protestation-, protestatio*, fr. L *protestatus* (past part. of *protestari* to protest) + *-ion-, -io* -ion — more at PROTEST] **1 :** the act of protesting or solemnly declaring existent or true **:** a public avowal **:** serious assertion ⟨with some proper ~*s* of modesty —W.H.White⟩ **2 :** a declaration in common-law pleading by which the party interposes an oblique allegation or denial of some fact protesting that it does or does not exist or is or is not sufficient in law and at the same time avoiding the duplicity of a direct affirmation or denial **3 :** a formal or documentary declaration of dissent, disapproval, or objection ⟨organizes these data around eight specific ~*s* —R.L.Roy⟩

**protested** *adj* [fr. past part. of [2]*protest*] **:** PROTESTANT

**pro·test·er** \prə'testə(r), (')prō¦t-\ *n* -s **1** *obs* **:** one that makes an affirmation ⟨state with ordinary oaths my love to every new ~ —Shak.⟩ **2 :** one that disagrees or disapproves ⟨all their friends were ~*s* and rebels and seceders —H.G.Wells⟩ ⟨even the town ~ thinks of things he would have liked in school —*Education Digest*⟩ **3** *usu cap* **:** one of a party among the Covenanters that protested against the resolution of 1650 that all persons not professed enemies to the Covenant or excommunicated should be allowed to serve in the army — compare RESOLUTIONER **4 :** one that protests a bill of exchange or a note

**pro·tes·tor** \"\ *n* -s [MF *protesteur*, fr. *protester* to protest + *-eur* -or — more at PROTEST] **:** PROTESTER

**pro·teus** \'prōd·ēəs, -ō,tüs, -ō·ˌtyüs\ *n* [fr. *Proteus*, sea god who could assume different shapes, fr. L — more at PROTEAN] **1** -ES *often cap* **:** one that is capable of infinite change **:** one having a great diversity of interests or abilities ⟨a true *Proteus* of literature . . . has been successively a dramatist, a sociologist, a highly successful writer of historical novels —William Du Bois⟩ ⟨a *Proteus*, a master of disguise, an impersonator —*Times Lit. Supp.*⟩ **2** [NL, fr. *Proteus*, sea god, fr. L] **a** (1) *cap* **:** the type genus of the family Proteidae comprising solely the olm (2) -ES **:** OLM **b** -ES **:** AMOEBA **3** *cap* [NL, fr. *Proteus*, sea god] **a :** a genus of aerobic gram-negative bacteria (family Enterobacteriaceae) that ferment glucose but not lactose, decompose urea, that are usu. motile by means of peritrichous flagella, and that include saprophytes in decaying organic matter as well as forms obscurely related to gastrointestinal disorders and several strains antigenically linked to the rickettsias of typhus **b** *pl* **pro·tei** \-d·ē,ī\ **:** any bacterium of the genus *Proteus*

**prot·evan·gel·i·um** \ˌprōd·ˌē,van'jelēəm\ *n* -s [NL, fr. *prot-* + LL *evangelium* evangel — more at EVANGEL] **:** a messianic interpretation of a text (as Gen 3:15 RSV) presaging man's ultimate triumph over sin through a coming Savior — used as the first anticipation of the gospel

**pro·tha·la·mi·on** \ˌprōthə'lāmēən, -ē,än\ *or* **pro·tha·la·mi·um** \-mēəm\ *n, pl* **prothala·mia** \-mēə\ [NL, fr. [1]*pro-* + *-thalamion* (as in *epithalamion*)] **:** a song in celebration of a marriage

**pro·thal·li·al** \(')prō¦thalēəl\ *also* **pro·thalline** \(')prō+\ *adj* [NL *prothall*ium + E *-al* or *-ine*] **:** of or relating to a prothallium

**prothallial cell** *n* **:** one of the cells produced by the first division of the microspore in a gymnosperm and believed to be a vestige related to the fern prothallus

**pro·thal·lic** \(')prō+\ *adj* [NL *prothall*ium + E *-ic*] **:** PROTHALLOID

**pro·thallium** \(')prō+\ *n, pl* **prothallia** [NL, fr. [1]*pro-* + *thallus* + *-ium*] **1 :** the gametophyte of a fern or other pteridophyte that is typically a small flat green thallus attached to the soil by rhizoids but is sometimes filamentous and branching, that occasionally forms a subterranean tuberous mass, or that rarely (as in the club mosses) develops within the megaspore by which it is produced **2 :** any of various structures (as several cells of the pollen grain or in gymnosperms of the megaspore) that in seed plants correspond to the pteridophyte prothallium

**pro·thalloid** \"+\ *adj* [NL *prothall*ium + *-oid*] **:** resembling a prothallium

**pro·thallus** \"+\ *n, pl* **prothalli** [NL, fr. [1]*pro-* + *thallus*] **:** PROTHALLIUM

[1]**pro·than·ic** \(')prō¦thanik\ *adj* [[1]*pro-* + *than-* (fr. *thanat-*) + *-ic*] **:** subject to early death — used of an embryo that fails to complete development due to severe anomalies

[2]**prothanic** \"\ *n* -s **:** a prothanic embryo

**pro·theca** \"+\ *n, pl* **prothecae** [NL, fr. [1]*pro-* + *theca*] **:** the basal and first-formed part of the calyculus of a coral

**proth·e·sis** \'präthəsəs\ *n, pl* **prothe·ses** \-ə,sēz\ [Gk, presentation of the shewbread, lit., act of placing before, fr. *protithenai* to put before, fr. *pro-* [1]pro- + *tithenai* to place, put — more at DO] **1 a :** the preparation of the bread and the wine in the liturgy of the Eastern Church **b :** the table on which this preparation is done **:** CREDENCE **c :** the northern part of the bema where this preparation occurs **2** [LL, fr. Gk, prefixation, act of placing before] **:** PROSTHESIS 2 **3 :** the addition of an inorganic sound to the beginning of a word (as in Old French *estat* and English *estate* from Latin *status*)

**pro·the·tely** \'prōthə,telē\ *n* -ES [fr. (assumed) Gk *prothe*tos (verbal of Gk *protithenai* to put before) + Gk *tel*os end, completion, maturity + E *-y* — more at WHEEL] **:** relatively precocious differentiation of a structure that is usu. associated with a later stage of development — compare HYSTEROTELY, NEOTENY

**pro·thet·ic** \prə'thed·ik\ *adj* [Gk *prothetikos*, fr. (assumed) Gk *prothetos* + Gk *-ikos* -ic] **:** of, relating to, or exhibiting prothesis ⟨a ~ vowel⟩ — **pro·thet·i·cal·ly** \-ək(ə)lē\ *adv*

**pro·thono·tar·i·al** \prə¦thänə¦ta(a)rēəl, -¦terē-\ *adj* **:** of or relating to a prothonotary

**pro·thono·tary** \prə'thänə,terē, ˌprō,thə'näd·ərē, -ri\ *or* **pro·tono·tary** \prə'tän-, ˌprōd·ə'-\ *n* [ME *prothonotarie*, fr. LL *protonotarius*, fr. *prot-* + L *notarius* notary, secretary — more at NOTARY] **1 a :** a chief clerk in the English Court of King's Bench or in a court of common pleas **b :** a similar official of the supreme court of New South Wales, Australia, and Nova Scotia **c :** a register or chief clerk of a court in some states of the U.S. **2** *usu protonotary* **:** any of various high ecclesiastical officials: **a :** one of the seven members of the College of Protonotaries Apostolic of the curia of the Roman Catholic Church whose chief duties are to keep the records of consistories and canonizations and to sign papal bulls **b :** the chief secretary of the ecumenical patriarch of Constantinople **3 :** a principal court secretary in some European countries

**pro·thono·tary·ship** \-ˌship\ *n* **:** the office of a prothonotary

**prothonotary warbler** *n* **:** a showy chiefly rich orange-golden warbler (*Protonotaria citrea*) of the southeastern U.S. with olivaceous back and blue-gray wings

**pro·thoracic** \¦prō+\ *adj* [NL *prothorac-*, *prothorax* + E *-ic*] **:** of or relating to the prothorax

**pro·thorax** \(')prō+\ *n* [NL, fr. [1]*pro-* + *thorax*] **:** the first or anterior segment of the thorax of an insect bearing the first pair of legs — see INSECT illustration

**pro·thrombase** \(')prō+\ *n* [ISV [1]*pro-* + *thrombase*] **:** PROTHROMBIN

**pro·thrombic** \"+\ *adj* [*prothromb*in + *-ic*] **:** of or resembling that of a prothrombin

**pro·thrombin** \"+\ *n* [ISV [1]*pro-* + *thrombin*] **:** a protein that is produced in the liver in the presence of vitamin K, is present in blood plasma, and is converted into thrombin by the action of various activators (as thromboplastin, blood platelet factors, accelerator globulin, and calcium ions) in the course of the clotting of blood — compare ANTIPROTHROMBIN

**prothrombin time** *n* **:** the time required for a particular specimen of prothrombin to induce blood-plasma clotting under standardized conditions in comparison with a time of between 11.5 and 12 seconds for normal human blood

**pro·tide** \'prō,tīd, -ˌtəd\ *n* -s [ISV, alter. of *proteide;* orig. formed in F] **:** any of a class of compounds comprising the amino acids and the proteides

**pro·tist** \'prōd·əst\ *n* -s [NL *Protista*] **:** one of the Protista

**pro·tis·ta** \prə'tistə\ *n pl, cap* [NL, fr. Gk *prōtista*, neut. pl. of *prōtistos* primary, principal, superl. of *prōtos* first — more at PROT-] **:** the unicellular and acellular organisms comprising bacteria, protozoa, many algae and fungi, and sometimes viruses and constituting a kingdom or other division of living beings distinct from multicellular plants and animals — compare ANIMALIA, PLANTAE, PROTOZOA — **pro·tis·tan** \-tən\ *adj or n* — **pro·tis·tic** \-tik\ *adj* — **pro·tis·ton** \-tən\ *n* -s

**pro·tis·to·logical** \prə¦tistə¦läjəkəl\ *adj* [*protistology* + *-ical*] **:** of or relating to protistology

**pro·tis·tol·o·gist** \ˌprō,ti'stäləjəst\ *n* -s [*protistology* + *-ist*] **:** one who specializes in protistology

**pro·tis·tol·o·gy** \-jē\ *n* -ES [ISV *protisto-* (fr. NL *Protista*) + *-logy*] **:** biology dealing with the Protista

[1]**pro·ti·um** \'prōd·ēəm, -ōshē-\ *n, cap* [NL, perh. fr. *prot-* + *-ium*] **:** a large genus of chiefly tropical American trees (family Burseraceae) having pinnate leaves and slender-pediceled paniculate flowers that are succeeded by globose drupes — see CARANNA, ELEMI

[2]**protium** \"\ *n* -s [ISV *prot-* + *-ium*] **:** the ordinary light hydrogen isotope of atomic mass 1 — symbol $H^1$ or $^1H$; compare DEUTERIUM, PROTON, TRITIUM

**proto-** — see PROT-

**protoactinium** *var of* PROTACTINIUM

**pro·to·as·ca·les** \ˌprōd·(ˌ)ōə'skā(ˌ)lēz\ *n pl, cap* [NL, fr. *prot-* + *asc-* + *-ales*] *in some classifications* **:** an order of fungi coextensive with the subclass Hemiascomycetes

**pro·to·as·co·my·ce·tae** \ˌ=(ˌ)=ˌa,skōmī'sēd·ˌē\ [NL, alter. of *Protoascomycetes*] *syn of* PROTOASCOMYCETES

**pro·to·ascomycetes** \¦==+\ *n pl, cap* [NL, fr. *prot-* + *Ascomycetes*] *in some classifications* **:** a subclass of Ascomycetes characterized by the lack of an ascocarp, by the production of asci directly from the fertilized ascogonium, and by a small and definite number of spores in each ascus — compare EUASCOMYCETES, HEMIASCOMYCETES

[1]**pro·to-australoid** \¦==+\ *adj, usu cap A* **:** of, relating to, or constituting a generalized type of prehistoric man characterized by long narrow head, broad nose, and medium long face

[2]**proto-australoid** \"\ *n* -s *usu cap A* **:** an individual of the proto-Australoid type

**pro·to·ba·sid·i·ae** \ˌprōd·(ˌ)ōbə'sidē,ē\ *or* **pro·to·ba·sid·ii** \-dē,ī\ [NL, fr. *prot-* + *basidiae* or *basidii* (fr. *basidium*)] *syn of* HETEROBASIDIOMYCETES

**pro·to·basidiomycetes** \¦prōd·(ˌ)ō+\ [NL, fr. *prot-* + *Basidiomycetes*] *syn of* HETEROBASIDIOMYCETES

**pro·to·basidium** \"+\ *n, pl* **protobasidia** [NL, fr. *prot-* + *basidium*] **:** a basidium (as a promycelium) that is divided into four cells each of which gives rise to a single basidiospore and that is characteristic of the subclass Heterobasidiomycetes — compare AUTOBASIDIUM, HEMIBASIDIUM

**pro·to·blast** \'prōd·ə,blast\ *n* [ISV *prot-* + *-blast;* prob. orig. formed in G] **1 :** a naked cell without a cell wall **2 :** a blastomere of the segmenting egg that is the parent cell of a definite part or organ — **pro·to·blas·tic** \¦==¦blastik\ *adj*

**pro·to·blat·toid** \¦=(ˌ)=¦bla,tȯid\ *adj* [NL *Protoblattoidea*] **:** of or relating to the Protoblattoidea

**pro·to·blat·toi·dea** \ˌ=(ˌ)=ˌbla'tȯidēə\ *n pl, cap* [NL, fr. *prot-* + *Blatta* + *-oidea*] **:** a polyphyletic group of extinct families of insects related to the Blattaria and Protorthoptera, known only from the Upper Carboniferous and Permian, and formerly regarded as an order

**pro·to·branchia** \ˌ=(ˌ)=+\ *n pl, cap* [NL, fr. *prot-* + *-branchia*] **:** an order of Lamellibranchia comprising primitive bivalve mollusks in which the gills consist of a double row of simple lamellae not reflected or united — **pro·to·branchiate** \¦=(ˌ)=+\ *adj*

**pro·to·branchiata** \¦=(ˌ)=+\ [NL, fr. *prot-* + *branchiata*] *syn of* PROTOBRANCHIA

**pro·to·canonical** \¦prōd·(ˌ)ō+\ *adj* [NL *protocanonic*us protocanonical (fr. *prot-* + LL *canonicus* belonging to the canon of Scripture) + E *-al* — more at CANONIC] **:** of, relating to, or constituting those books of the Bible accepted early into the biblical canon without serious controversy — compare DEUTEROCANONICAL

**pro·toc·a·ris** \prə'täkərəs\ *n, cap* [NL, fr. *prot-* + *-caris*] **:** the oldest known branchiopod genus found in the Lower Cambrian of Vermont and consisting of small crustaceans resembling *Triops*

**pro·to·catechualdehyde** \¦prōd·(ˌ)ō+¦==ˌ=¦==ˌ=\ *or* **pro·to·cat·e·chu·ic aldehyde** \"+¦kad·ə¦chüik, -¦shüik, -¦kyüik-\ *n* [*protocatechualdehyde* ISV *protocatechu*ic acid + *aldehyde*] **:** a crystalline compound $C_6H_3(OH)_2CHO$ which is synthetically prepared and the monomethyl ether of which is vanillin; 3,4=dihydroxy-benzaldehyde

**protocatechuic acid** *n* [*protocatechuic* ISV *prot-* + *catechu* + *-ic*] **:** a crystalline acid $C_6H_3(OH)_2CO_2H$ produced from various resins and other plant products by fusion with alkali; 3,4-dihydroxy-benzoic acid

**pro·to·cephalon** \¦prōd·(ˌ)ō+\ *n, pl* **protocephala** [NL, fr. *prot-* + *cephalon*] **1 :** the part of an insect embryo that consists of the prostomium and the first postoral somite **2 :** the primitive arthropod head corresponding to the sensory as distinguished from the feeding portion of the head of higher forms — compare GNATHOTHORAX

**pro·toc·er·as** \prə'täsərəs\ *n, cap* [NL, fr. *prot-* + *-ceras*] **:** a No. American Miocene genus of ungulates related to the chevrotains

**pro·to·ceratops** \¦prōd·(ˌ)ō+\ *n, cap* [NL, fr. *prot-* + *Ceratops*] **:** a genus of small hornless ceratopsian dinosaurs from the Cretaceous of Mongolia that is unique in that all stages of growth from the egg to the adult are represented by fossils

**pro·to·cerebral** \¦prōd·(ˌ)ō+\ *adj* [NL *protocerebr*um + E *-al*] **:** of or relating to the protocerebrum

**pro·to·cerebrum** \"+\ *n* [NL, fr. *prot-* + *cerebrum*] **1 :** the first segment of the brain in an insect innervating the compound eyes **2 :** the ganglion in a lower crustacean giving rise to the optic nerve

**pro·to-chimu** \"+\ *adj, usu cap C* **:** MOCHICA

**pro·to·chlorophyll** \"+\ *n* [*prot-* + *chlorophyll*] **:** a green magnesium-containing pigment that is present in etiolated leaves and seedlings which develop in the dark and that is converted to chlorophyll by reduction under the influence of light

**pro·to·chorda** \"+\ [NL, fr. *prot-* + *chorda* (fr. *Chordata*)] *syn of* PROTOCHORDATA

**pro·to·chordata** \"+\ *n pl, cap* [NL, fr. *prot-* + *Chordata*] *in some classifications* **:** a major division of Chordata comprising the Hemichordata, Urochorda, and usu. the Cephalochordata — **pro·to·chordate** \"+\ *adj or n*

**pro·to·ciliata** \"+\ *n pl, cap* [NL, fr. *prot-* + *Ciliata*] **:** a subclass of Ciliata comprising endozoic forms that have two to many similar nuclei and that reproduce sexually through fusion of gametes — compare EUCILIATA — **pro·to·ciliate** \"+\ *adj or n*

**pro·to·clas·tic** \¦prōd·ə¦klastik\ *adj* [G *protoklastisch*, fr. *prot-* + *-klastisch* -clastic] **:** of, relating to, or constituting the texture of an igneous rock whose earlier crystals show deformation and granulation produced before the complete solidification of the magma

**pro·toc·neme** \'prō,täk,nēm\ *n* -s [NL, fr. *prot-* + Gk *knēmē* shin — more at HAM] **:** one of the 12 primary mesenteries recognizable in an actinozoan

**pro·to·coccaceae** \¦prōd·(ˌ)ō+\ *n pl, cap* [NL, fr. *Protococcus*, type genus + *-aceae*] **:** a family of unicellular green algae that is coextensive with the genus *Protococcus* and is now usu. placed in the order Ulotrichales but is sometimes isolated in a separate order or esp. formerly included in Chlorococcales or Chaetophorales

**pro·to·coc·cal** \¦prōd·ə¦käkəl\ *adj* [NL *Protococcus* + E *-al*] **:** of or relating to the genus *Protococcus*

**pro·to·coc·ca·les** \ˌprōd·(ˌ)ōkə'kā(ˌ)lēz, -kä'k-\ *n pl, cap* [NL *Protococcus* + *-ales*] *in some classifications* **:** an order of algae coextensive with the family Protococcaceae

**pro·to·coc·coid** \¦prōd·ə¦kä,kȯid\ *adj* [NL *Protococcus* + E *-oid*] **:** resembling the genus *Protococcus*

**pro·to·coc·cus** \ˌ=='käkəs\ *n, cap* [NL, fr. *prot-* + *-coccus*] **:** a genus of unicellular globose chiefly terrestrial green algae (family Protococcaceae) that in former classifications included most such aerial algae but is now usu. restricted to forms with a single large peripheral chloroplast that divide in two planes to form thin filmy colonies (as on damp rocks or the bark of trees) — compare CHLOROCOCCUM

[1]**pro·to·col** \'prōd·ǀə,kȯl, 'prōtǀ *also* -ˌkäl *or* -ˌkōl *or* ǀəkəl *or* ǀēkəl\ *n* -s *often attrib* [earlier *prothocoll*, fr. MF *prothocole*, fr. ML *protocollum*, fr. LGk *prōtokollon* first sheet of a papyrus roll bearing the authentication and date of manufacture of the papyrus, fr. Gk *prōt-* prot- + LGk *-kollon* (fr. Gk *kollēma* papyrus roll, sheets of papyrus glued together, lit., that which is glued together, fr. *kollan* to glue together, fr. *kolla* glue); akin to OSlav *klějĭ* glue, MD *helen* to glue] **1 :** an original draft, minute, or record of a document or transaction; *specif* **:** the original record kept by a notary of documents or transactions from which he certifies copies **2 a :** a preliminary memorandum (as of discussions and resolutions arrived at in negotiation) often signed by diplomatic negotiators as a basis for a final convention or treaty ⟨the London ~ of 1852⟩ **b :** the records or minutes of a diplomatic conference or congress that show officially the agreements arrived at by the negotiators **3 :** an official statement or account of a proceeding; *esp* **:** the notes or records relating to a case, an experiment, or an autopsy **4 :** a rigid long-established code prescribing complete deference to superior rank and strict adherence to due order of precedence and precisely correct procedure (as in diplomatic exchange and ceremonies and in the military services) **5 :** PROTOCOL STATEMENT

[2]**protocol** \"\ *vb* **protocolled** *or* **protocoled**; **protocolled** *or* **protocoled**; **protocolling** *or* **protocoling**; **protocols** *vi* **:** to write or issue protocols ~ *vt* **:** to state in a protocol

**pro·to·col·ar** \¦==¦kälə(r)\ *or* **pro·to·col·a·ry** \-lərē\ *also* **pro·to·col·ic** \-lik\ *adj* [[1]*protocol* + *-ar* or *-ary* or *-ic*] **:** of or relating to a protocol

**pro·to·coleoptera** \¦prōd·(ˌ)ō+\ *n pl, cap* [NL, fr. *prot-* + *Coleoptera*] *in some classifications* **:** an order of extinct insects that are now usu. regarded as belonging to the order Protelytroptera — **pro·to·co·le·op·ter·an** \-tərən\ *adj or n* — **pro·to·coleopteron** \¦prōd·(ˌ)ō+\ *n* -s — **pro·to·coleopterous** \"+\ *adj*

**pro·to·col·ist** *pronunc at* PROTOCOL + əst\ *n* -s [[1]*protocol* + *-ist*] **1 :** one who drafts protocols **2 :** a stickler for protocol

**pro·to·col·ize** \-ˌlīz\ *vb* -ED/-ING/-S [[1]*protocol* + *-ize*] **:** PROTOCOL

**protocol statement** *n* [trans. of G *protokollsatz*] **:** a basic observational sentence; *esp* **:** a statement that reports the uninterpreted results of observations and provides the basis for scientific confirmation

**pro·to·conch** \'prōd·ə+ˌ-\ *n* [ISV *prot-* + *conch*] **1 :** the embryonic shell of a mollusk (as a univalve) **2 :** the apical chamber or whorl of an ammonite or gastropod — **pro·to·conchal** \¦==+\ *adj*

**pro·to·cone** \"+ˌ-\ *n* [*prot-* + *cone*] **:** the central of the three cusps of a primitive upper molar that in higher forms is the principal anterior and external cusp

**pro·to·co·nid** \"+¦kōnəd\ *n* -s [*protocone* + *-id* (structural element)] **:** an anterior and external cusp of a lower molar that corresponds to the protocone

**pro·to·conule** \¦prōd·(ˌ)ō+\ *n* [*protocone* + *-ule*] **:** the anterior intermediate cusp between protocone and paracone of an upper molar

**pro·to·cooperation** \"+\ *n* [*prot-* + *cooperation*] **:** automatic or involuntary interaction by different kinds of organisms through which they mutually benefit (as by provision of debris habitats by trees and stirring of the forest floor by microfauna living in or on the debris) — **pro·to·cooperative** \"+\ *adj*

**pro·to-corinthian** \"+\ *adj, usu cap C* **:** primitively Corinthian — used of a type of decoration on painted vases

**pro·to·corm** \'prōd·ə+ˌ-\ *n* [ISV *prot-* + *corm*] **1 :** a tuber=shaped body with rhizoids that is produced by the young seedlings of various orchids and some other plants having associated mycorhizal fungi **2** [*prot-* + *-corm* (fr. NL *cormus*) — more at CORMUS] **:** the part of an insect embryo posterior to the protocephalon — **pro·to·cor·mic** \¦==¦kȯrmik\ *adj*

**protocorm theory** *n* **:** a theory in botany: the sporophyte of a vascular plant is derived from a transition form comparable to the protocorm of some club mosses — compare CAULOID THEORY

**pro·to·derm** \'prōd·ə,dərm\ *n* -s [ISV *prot-* + *-derm*] **:** DERMATOGEN — **pro·to·der·mal** \¦==¦dərməl\ *adj*

**prot·odonata** \(¦)prōd·+\ *n pl, cap* [NL, fr. *prot-* + *Odonata*] **:** an order of extinct insects related to the Odonata, known mainly from the Upper Carboniferous and Permian, and characterized by a full but specialized venation with numerous crossveins — **prot·odona·tan** \-d·ən\ *adj or n* — **prot·odonate** \(')prōd·+\ *adj*

**pro·to-doric** \¦prōd·(ˌ)ō+\ *adj, usu cap D* **:** primitively Doric ⟨*proto-Doric* capital⟩ ⟨*proto-Doric* column⟩

**pro·to·dynastic** \"+\ *adj* [*prot-* + *dynastic*] **:** of or relating to the earliest dynasties of Egypt

**pro·to·enstatite** \"+\ *n* [G *protoenstatit*, fr. *prot-* + *enstatit* enstatite] **:** an unstable product of the decomposition of talc by heating that has the composition of enstatite and is convertible thereto esp. by grinding or by heating to a high temperature

**pro·to·fascism** \"+\ *n* [*prot-* + *fascism*] **:** a political movement or program tending toward or imitating fascism

**pro·to·fascist** \"+\ *n, often attrib* [*protofasc*ism + *-ist*] **:** one who adheres to, advocates, or practices protofascism

**pro·to·gas·ter·a·ce·ae** \ˌprōd·(ˌ)ō,gastə'rāsē,ē\ *n pl, cap* [NL, fr. *Protogaster*, type genus (fr. *prot-* + *-gaster*) + *-aceae*] **:** a family of homobasidiomycetous fungi (order Hymenogastrales) characterized by having only one glebal cavity in each basidiocarp

**pro·to·gas·tra·les** \ˌprōd·(ˌ)ō(ˌ)ga'strā(ˌ)lēz\ *n pl, cap* [NL, fr. *Protogaster* + *-ales*] **:** *in some classifications* **:** an order of fungi coextensive with the family Protogasteraceae

**pro·to·gen** \'prōd·əjən, -ˌjen\ *n* -s [*proto-* (fr. *protozoa*) + *-gen;* fr. its being a microbial growth factor] **:** LIPOIC ACID

**pro·tog·e·nal** \prō'täjənᵊl\ *adj* [NL *protogen*es + E *-al*] **:** of or relating to a protogene

**pro·to·gene** \'prōd·ə+ˌ-\ *n* [*prot-* + *gene*] **1 :** a dominant gene or factor **2** [ISV, fr. NL *protogenes* primeval, firstborn, fr. Gk *prōtogenēs*, fr. *prōt-* prot- + *-genēs* born — more at -GEN] **:** a hypothetical mutable primary unit that is capable of reduplication, is held to have differentiated from nonliving matter, and is regarded as a precursor of living beings

**pro·to·genesis** \¦prōd·ə+\ *n* [NL, fr. *prot-* + *genesis*] **1 :** ABIOGENESIS **2 :** reproduction by budding

**pro·to·genetic** \"+\ *adj* **:** of, relating to, or exhibiting protogenesis

**pro·to·gen·ic** \¦prōd·ə¦jenik\ *adj* [*prot-* + *-genic*] **:** formed by crystallization or solidification of molten magma

**pro·to·geometric** \¦prōd·(ˌ)ō+\ *adj, often cap* [*prot-* + *geometric*] **:** of, relating to, or characteristic of the earliest phase of geometric art in Greece

[1]**pro·to-germanic** \"+\ *n, cap P&G* **:** the assumed ancestral language of the Germanic languages

[2]**proto-germanic** \"\ *adj, usu cap P&G* **:** of or belonging to Proto-Germanic

**pro·to·gine** *also* **pro·to·gene** \'prōd·ə,jēn\ *n* -s [*protogine* fr. F, fr. *prot-* + *-gine* (fr. Gk *-genēs* born); *protogene* alter. (influenced by *-gene*) of *protogine*] **1 :** a granite that is esp. prevalent in the central Alps and that has a gneissoid texture prob. due to dynamic action **2 :** a rock with authigenic constituents

**pro·to·graph** \'prōd·ə,graf\ *n* [*prot-* + *-graph*] **:** an original writing **:** HOLOGRAPH

**pro·tog·y·ne** \prə'täjə(ˌ)nē\ *n* -s [back-formation fr. *protogynous*] **:** a protogynous individual

**pro·to·gy·nous** \¦prōd·ə¦jīnəs, -¦gī-\ *also* **pro·to·gynic** \¦==¦jīnik, -jin-\ *adj* [*protogynous* ISV *prot-* + *-gynous; protogynic* fr. *protogyny* + *-ic*] **:** characterized by protogyny

**pro·tog·y·ny** \prō'täjənē\ *n* -ES [ISV *protogyn*ous + *-y*] **:** a state in hermaphroditic systems that is characterized by development of female organs or maturation of their products before the appearance of the corresponding male product thus inhibiting self-fertilization and that is encountered in apples, pears, figworts, and among several groups of invertebrate animals — compare PROTANDRY

**pro·to-hattic** \¦prōd·(ˌ)ō+\ *n, usu cap H* **:** HATTIC

**pro·to·hematin** \"+\ *n* [ISV *prot-* + *hematin*] **:** HEMATIN 2a

**pro·to·heme** \'prōd·ə+ˌ-\ *n* [*prot-* + *heme*] **:** HEME 1

**pro·to·hemin** \¦prōd·(ˌ)ō+\ *n* [ISV *prot-* + *hemin*] **:** HEMIN 1a

**pro·to·hemiptera** \"+\ *n pl, cap* [NL, fr. *prot-* + *Hemiptera*] **:** an order of extinct insects known only from the Upper Carboniferous and Permian, formerly considered ancestral to the Hemiptera but now usu. regarded as closely related to the Palaeodictyoptera, and characterized by suctorial mouthparts and by a wing venation like that of the Palaeodictyoptera — **pro·to·hemipteran** \"+\ *adj or n* — **pro·to·hemipteron** \"+\ *n* -s — **pro·to·hemipterous** \"+\ *adj*

**pro·to·hip·pus** \ˌprōd·ə'hipəs\ *n, cap* [NL, fr. *prot-* + *-hippus*] : a genus of Pliocene horses approximating donkeys in size and having two small vestigial lateral toes that do not touch the ground

**pro·to·historian** \ˌprōd·(ˌ)ō+\ *n* [*protohistory* + *-an*] : a specialist in protohistory

**pro·to·historic** \"+\ *adj* [ISV *prot-* + *historic*] : of or relating to the times just preceding the period of recorded history

**pro·to·history** \"+\ *n* [ISV *prot-* + *history*] **1** : the study of man during the times that just antedate the beginning of recorded history **2** : the times immediately preceding historical times

**pro·to·hittite** \"+\ *n, usu cap H* : HATTIC

[1]**pro·to·human** \"+\ *adj* [*prot-* + *human*] : of, relating to, or resembling an early primitive human or a prehominid

[2]**protohuman** \"\ *n* : a protohuman individual

**pro·to·hydra** \"+\ *n, cap* [NL, fr. *prot-* + *Hydra*] : a genus of marine coelenterates similar to *Hydra* but having no tentacles

**pro·to·hymenoptera** \"+\ *n pl, cap* [NL, fr. *prot-* + *Hymenoptera*] *in some classifications* : an order of extinct insects known only from the Permian and now usu. included in the order Megasecoptera — **pro·to·hymenopteran** \"+\ *adj or n* — **pro·to·hymenopteron** \"+\ *n* — **pro·to·hymenopterous** \"+\ *adj*

[1]**proto–indo–european** \"+\ *n, cap P&I&E* : the assumed ancestral language of the Indo-European languages

[2]**proto–indo–european** \"\ *adj, usu cap P&I&E* : of or relating to Proto-Indo-European

**pro·to·language** \"+\ *n* [*prot-* + *language*] : the assumed or recorded ancestral language of a language or group of languages ⟨in reconstructing the vocabulary of a ~ —H.M. Hoenigswald⟩ ⟨must have been a suffix verb form in the ~ —C.T.Hodge⟩ — compare URSPRACHE

**pro·to·lignin** \ˌprōd·(ˌ)ō+\ *n* [*prot-* + *lignin*] : LIGNIN 1

**pro·to·lith·ic** \ˌprōd·əˌlithik\ *adj* [*prot-* + *-lithic*] : of or relating to the earliest period of the Stone Age : EOLITHIC

**pro·to·log** \'prōd·əlˌȯg *also* -ˌäg\ *n* -s [*prot-* + *-log*] : the original description of a species

**pro·to·loph** \'prōd·əlˌäf\ *n* -s [*prot-* + *-loph*] : a crest on a lophodont molar that extends from the ectoloph to the protocone

**pro·to·ma** \prə'tōmə\ *or* **pro·to·me** \-(ˌ)mē\ *n* -s [NL, fr. Gk *protomē* head of a decapitated animal, lit., front part cut off, fr. *protemnein* to cut off in front, fr. *pro-* [1]pro- + *temnein* to cut — more at TOME] : the representation of the head and neck of an animal often used decoratively in architecture

**pro·to–malay** \ˌprōd·(ˌ)ō+\ *n* -s *usu cap M* : a Malaysian whose physical appearance distinguishes him from the more Mongoloid deutero-Malay and from Veddoid or negritoid types but who is sometimes described as having early Asiatic characteristics — called also *Indonesian* — **pro·to–malayan** \"+\ *adj, usu cap M*

**pro·to·mammal** \ˌprōd·(ˌ)ō+\ *n* [*prot-* + *mammal*] : PROMAMMAL — **pro·to·mammalian** \"+\ *adj*

**pro·to·martyr** \"+\ *n* [ME *prothomartir*, fr. MF, fr. LL *protomartyr*, fr. LGk *prōtomartyr-, prōtomartys*, fr. Gk *prōt-* prot- + *martyr-, martys* martyr — more at MARTYR] : the first martyr in any cause — used esp. of the Christian martyr Stephen

**pro·to·mas·tig·i·da** \ˌ=(ˌ)=ma'stijədə\ [NL, fr. *prot-* + *mastig-* + *-ida*] *syn of* PROTOMONADINA

**pro·to·meristem** \"+\ *n* [*prot-* + *meristem*] : primary meristem

**pro·tom·er·ite** \prō'tämərˌīt\ *n* -s [ISV *prot-* + *mer-* + *-ite*] : the smaller anterior part of the trophozoite of a gregarine that is subdivided into two sections and is often prolonged anteriorly by an epimerite on which attachment organelles are located

[1]**pro·tom·o·nad** \prō'tämə,nad\ *adj* [NL *Protomonadina*] : of or relating to the Protomonadina

[2]**protomonad** \"\ *n* : one of the Protomonadina

**pro·to·mo·nad·i·da** \ˌprōd·(ˌ)ōmə'nadədə\ [NL, fr. *Protomonad-, Protomonas*, genus of flagellates + *-ida*] *syn of* PROTOMONADINA

**pro·to·mon·a·di·na** \-ˌmänə'dīnə, -dēnə\ *n pl, cap* [NL, fr. *Protomonad-, Protomonas*, genus of flagellates (fr. *prot-* + *-monad-, -monas*) + *-ina*] : an order comprising small plastic flagellates (subclass Zoomastigina) with one or two flagella and including many colonial or solitary and naked or loricate free-living freshwater forms as well as numerous species (family Trypanosomatidae) of medical or veterinary importance — compare LEISHMANIA, TRYPANOSOMA

**pro·to·mor·phic** \ˌprōd·ə'mȯrfik\ *adj* [*prot-* + *-morphic*] : PRIMITIVE

**pro·to·my·ce·ta·les** \ˌ=(ˌ)=ˌmīsə'tā(ˌ)lēz\ [NL, fr. *prot-* + *mycet-* + *-ales*] *syn of* HEMIASCOMYCETES

**pro·ton** \'prōˌtän\ *n* -s [Gk *prōton*, neut. of *prōtos* first — more at PROT-] **1** : ANLAGE **2** : an elementary particle that is identical with the nucleus of the hydrogen atom, that along with neutrons is a constituent of all other atomic nuclei, that carries a positive charge numerically equal to the charge of an electron, and that has a mass of $1.672 \times 10^{-24}$ gram — **pro·ton·ic** \prō'tänik\ *adj*

**pro·ton·ate** \'prōt°nˌāt\ *vt* -ED/-ING/-S [*proton* + *-ate* (v. suffix)] : to add a proton to

**pro·to·ne·ma** \ˌprōt°n'ēmə\ *n, pl* **protonema·ta** \-məd·ə\ [NL, fr. *prot-* + *-nema*] : the primary and usu. transitory growth or thalloid stage of the gametophyte in mosses and in some liverworts that corresponds somewhat to the prothallium in ferns, that is usu. a filamentous body resembling an alga though sometimes flat and platelike, that originates from the germination of an asexual spore, that is capable of independent growth, and that gives rise by budding to the moss plant proper or to the second stage of the gametophyte — **pro·to·ne·mal** \ˌ==ˌ'ēməl\ *adj* — **pro·to·ne·ma·tal** \-məd·°l\ *adj* — **pro·to·ne·ma·toid** \-məˌtȯid\ *adj*

**pro·to·nemertini** \ˌprōd·(ˌ)ō+\ *n pl, cap* [NL, fr. *prot-* + *Nemertini*] *in some classifications* : an order of unarmed nemertine worms in which the brain and lateral nerves lie outside the musculature

**pro·to·nephridial** \"+\ *adj* [NL *protonephridium* + E *-al*] : resembling a protonephridium in nature or function

**pro·to·nephridium** \"+\ *n* [NL, fr. *prot-* + *nephridium*] **1** : the duct of a flame cell **2** : a nephridium equipped with a solenocyte — compare METANEPHRIDIUM

**protonotary** *var of* PROTHONOTARY

**proton–synchrotron** \'=ˌ=ˌ'==ˌ=\ *n* : a synchrotron in which protons are accelerated by means of frequency modulation of the radio-frequency accelerating voltage so that they have energies of billions of electron volts — called also *bevatron, cosmotron*

**pro·to·nymph** \'prōd·ə+ˌ-\ *n* [*prot-* + *nymph*] : any of various acarids in their first developmental stage — compare DEUTONYMPH — **pro·to·nymphal** \ˌ==+\ *adj*

**pro·to·papas** \ˌprōd·ə'papəs, -päp-\ *n* -ES [MGk *prōtopapas* chief priest — more at PROTOPOPE] : PROTOPOPE

**pro·to·par·ce** \ˌprōd·ə'pärsē\ *n, cap* [NL, fr. *prot-* + *-parce* (perh. fr. L *parcus* sparing, frugal) — more at PARSIMONY] : a genus of New World hawkmoths with larvae that are hornworms — see TOBACCO HORNWORM, TOMATO HORNWORM

**pro·to·par·ia** \ˌprōd·ə'pa(a)rēə\ *n pl, cap* [NL, fr. *prot-* + Gk *pareia* cheek — more at PROPARIA] : a cosmopolitan order of Lower Cambrian trilobites with the facial suture marginal, the eyes large, and the pygidium small and rudimentary

**pro·to·path·ic** \ˌ==ˌ'pathik\ *adj* [ISV *protopath-* (fr. MGk *prōtopathēs* affected first, fr. Gk *prōt-* prot- + *-pathēs* — fr. *pathos* experience, suffering) + *-ic* — more at PATHOS] **1** *of cutaneous reception* : responsive only to rather gross stimuli (as of heat, cold, and pain) **2** *of a cutaneous sensory receptor* : adapted to or subserving protopathic reception **3** *of cutaneous reactivity* : dependent on protopathic reception or receptors — compare EPICRITIC

**pro·to·pectin** \"+\ *n* [ISV *prot-* + *pectin*] : any of a group of water-insoluble pectic substances occurring in plants and yielding pectin or pectinic acids on hydrolysis

**pro·to·pectinase** \"+\ *n* -s [*protopectin* + *-ase*] : an enzyme that accelerates the change of protopectin into soluble pectin or pectinic acids with the resultant separation of plant cells from one another

**pro·to·perithecium** \ˌprōd(ˌ)ō+\ *n* [NL, fr. *prot-* + *perithecium*] : a primordium that when fertilized develops into a perithecium

**pro·to·perlaria** \"+\ *n pl, cap* [NL, fr. *prot-* + *Perlaria*] : an extinct order of insects related to the Plecoptera, known only from the Permian, and characterized by primitive plecopterid features and a pair of prothoracic lobes resembling small wings — **pro·to·perlarian** \"+\ *adj or n*

**pro·to·phloem** \ˌprōd·ə+\ *n* [*prot-* + *phloem*] : the first-formed part of the primary phloem that develops from the procambium and consists of narrow thin-walled cells usu. capable of a limited amount of stretching and usu. associated with a region of rapid growth in length — compare METAPHLOEM

**pro·toph·y·ta** \prə'täfəd·ə\ *n pl, cap* [NL, fr. *prot-* + *-phyta*] : a major category of lower plants: as **a** *in former classifications* : a division or other group comprising the algae, fungi, and lichens **b** *in some esp. former classifications* : a division or other group comprising unicellular plants and including bacteria, yeasts, slime molds, blue-green algae, and various simple green algae — often used as a term of convenience rather than strict taxonomy; compare PROTISTA **c** *in some classifications* : a division comprising unicellular and noncellular organisms and including blue-green algae, bacteria, rickettsias and related organisms, and viruses — used chiefly in bacteriological taxonomy

**pro·to·phyte** \'prōd·əˌfīt\ *n* -s [NL *Protophyta*] **1** : a plant of the Protophyta **2** : a unicellular plant — compare METAPHYTE — **pro·to·phyt·ic** \ˌ==ˌ'fid·ik\ *adj*

**pro·to·pine** \'prōd·əˌpēn, -pən\ *n* -s [ISV *prot-* + *opium* + *-ine*] : a crystalline alkaloid $C_{20}H_{19}NO_5$ found in small quantities in opium and in many papaveraceous plants

**pro·to·planet** \ˌprōd·ə+\ *n* [*prot-* + *planet*] : a whirling gaseous eddy within a giant cloud of gas and dust rotating around a sun believed to give rise to a planet

**pro·to·plasm** \'prōd·ə, -ōtə+ˌ-\ *also* **pro·to·plasma** \"+\ *n* [G *protoplasma*, fr. *prot-* + *-plasma* -plasm (fr. NL *plasma*) — more at PLASMA] **1** : organized living matter : the more or less fluid colloidal complex of protein, other organic and inorganic substances, and water that constitutes the living nucleus, cytoplasm, plastids, and mitochondria of the cell, that is regarded as the only form of matter in which or by which the vital phenomena (as metabolism and reproduction) are manifested, that is often designated the physical basis of life, and that sometimes exhibits under the microscope a variety of appearances but typically shows a relatively fluid hyaline ground substance in which various granules and formed elements are suspended — see ALVEOLAR THEORY, GRANULAR HYPOTHESIS, RETICULAR THEORY **2** : CYTOPLASM 2

**pro·to·plasmal** \ˌ==+\ *or* **pro·to·plasmatic** \"+\ *adj* [*protoplasmal* fr. *protoplasm* + *-al*; *protoplasmatic* ISV *protoplasm* + *-atic* (as in *plasmatic*)] : PROTOPLASMIC

**pro·to·plasmic** \ˌ==+\ *adj* [ISV *protoplasm* + *-ic*] : of, relating to, consisting of, or resembling protoplasm ⟨some chemicals . . . tend to damage tissue universally and are referred to as ~ poisons —W.W.Jetter⟩

[1]**pro·to·plast** \'prōd·əˌplast, -aa(ə)st, -aist, 'prōtə,-\ *n* -s [MF *protoplaste*, fr. LL *protoplastus* first man, fr. Gk *prōtoplastos* first formed, created first, fr. *prōt-* prot- + *plastos* formed, molded, verbal of *plassein* to mold — more at PLASTER] **1** : one that is formed first : PROTOTYPE **2 a** : the living content of a cell : the nucleus, cytoplasm, and plasma membrane constituting a living unit distinct from ergastic substances and inert walls **b** : ENERGID **c** *archaic* : PLASTID — **pro·to·plastic** \ˌ==ˌ'plastik, -aas-, -tēk\ *adj*

[2]**protoplast** \"\ *n* -s [NL *protoplastes*, fr. *prot-* + Gk *plastēs* molder, modeler, fr. *plassein* to mold] *archaic* : the original maker or creator ⟨a complete imitation of the copy set by the Protoplast —Isaac Newton⟩

[1]**pro·to·pod** \'prōd·əˌpäd\ *n* -s [*prot-* + *-pod*] : PROTOPODITE — **pro·to·po·di·al** \ˌ==ˌ'pōdēəl\ *adj*

[2]**protopod** \"\ *adj* [NL *protopoda*] : of or relating to the early undifferentiated stage of an insect embryo

**pro·top·o·da** \prə'täpədə\ *n pl, usu cap* [NL, fr. *prot-* + *-poda*] : a category of insect larvae that emerge early in their embryological development and that are then only partially differentiated

**pro·top·o·dite** \-ˌdīt\ *n* -s [*prot-* + *-podite*] : the basal part of a typical limb of a crustacean consisting of two more or less consolidated segments and bearing at its distal extremity an exopodite or endopodite or both — **pro·top·o·dit·ic** \ˌ=ˌ==ˌ'did·ik\ *adj*

**pro·to·pope** \'prōd·əˌpōp\ *n* [Russ *protopop*, fr. MGk *prōtopapas* chief priest, fr. Gk *prōt-* prot- + MGk *papas* priest, fr. Gk, title of bishops, lit., papa — more at PAPA] : the first in rank of the priests of a cathedral in the Eastern Church who administers the diocese during the absence of the bishop or a vacancy in the see

**pro·to·porphyrin** \ˌprōd·(ˌ)ō+\ *n* [ISV *prot-* + *porphyrin*] : a purple porphyrin acid $C_{32}H_{32}N_4(COOH)_2$ that is obtained from hemin or heme by removal of bound iron (as with formic acid and iron filings); tetramethyl-divinyl-porphin-di-propionic acid

**pro·to·presbyter** \"+\ *n* -s [NGk *prōtopresbyteros*, fr. Gk *prōt-* prot- + *presbyteros* priest — more at PRIEST] : PROTOPOPE

**pro·to·proteose** \"+\ *n* [ISV *prot-* + *proteose*] : any of a class of proteoses formed as primary products in digestion of proteins

[1]**pro·top·ter·an** \prə'täptərən\ *or* **pro·top·ter·ous** \-t(ə)rəs\ *adj* [NL *Protopterus* + E *-an* or *-ous*] : of or relating to the genus *Protopterus* or a protopterus

[2]**protopteran** \"\ *n* -s : PROTOPTERUS 2

**pro·top·ter·us** \-rəs\ *n* [NL, fr. *prot-* + *-pterus*] **1** *cap* : a genus of dipnoan fishes of the rivers and swamps of central and western Africa that reach a length of six feet, that bury themselves in the mud during the dry season, that are closely related to lepidosirens but have a stouter body and five branchial clefts and differently constructed paired fins, and that are sometimes placed in a separate family but are usu. placed in the same family as *Lepidosiren* **2** -ES : any fish of the genus *Protopterus*

**pro·top·tile** \(')prō'täpˌtəl\ *n* -s [*prot-* + *-ptile*] : one of the first set of down feathers in young birds having two sets of down

**prot·ore** \'prōd·+ˌ-\ *n* [*prot-* + *ore*] : metalliferous material before it becomes ore through enrichment

[1]**pro·to–romance** \ˌprōd·(ˌ)ō+\ *n, cap P&R* : the partly recorded and partly assumed ancestral language of the Romance languages : VULGAR LATIN

[2]**proto–romance** \"\ *adj, usu cap P&R* : of or relating to Proto-Romance

**pro·to·ro·saur** \'prōd·ərəˌsȯ(ə)r\ *or* **pro·to·ro·sau·ri·an** \ˌ===ˌ'sȯrēən\ *also* **pro·te·ro·saur** \'===ˌsȯ(ə)r\ *n* -s [NL *Protorosauria*] : a reptile or fossil of the order Protorosauria

**pro·to·ro·sau·ria** \ˌ===ˌ'sȯrēə\ *n pl, cap* [NL, fr. *Protorosaurus* + *-ia*] : an order of Synaptosauria comprising rather small Permian and Triassic reptiles — see PROTOROSAURUS

**pro·to·ro·sau·ri·an** *or* **pro·tero·sau·ri·an** \ˌ===ˌ'sȯrēən\ *adj* [NL *Protorosauria, Proterosauria* + E *-an*] : of or relating to the Protorosauria

**pro·to·ro·sau·roid** *also* **pro·tero·sau·roid** \-ˌrȯid\ *adj* [NL *Protorosaurus, Proterosaurus* + E *-oid*] : resembling or related to the Protorosauria

**pro·to·ro·sau·rus** \ˌ===ˌ'sȯrəs\ *n, cap* [NL, irreg. fr. *proter-* + *-saurus*] : a genus of upper Permian reptiles (order Protorosauria) resembling lizards and attaining a length of several yards

**prot·orthoptera** \ˌprōd·+\ *n pl, cap* [NL, fr. *prot-* + *Orthoptera*] : an order of extinct insects related to the Orthoptera, known only from the Upper Carboniferous and Permian, and characterized by numerous venational features recalling the Orthoptera — **prot·orthopteran** \"+\ *adj or n* — **prot·orthopteron** \"+\ *n* — **prot·orthopterous** \"+\ *adj*

**pro·to·selachii** \ˌprōd·(ˌ)ō+\ [NL, fr. *prot-* + *Selachii*] *syn of* NOTIDANI

[1]**proto–semitic** \"+\ *n, cap P&S* : the assumed ancestral language of the Semitic languages

[2]**proto–semitic** \"\ *adj, usu cap P&S* : of or relating to Proto-Semitic

**pro·to–sinaitic** \"+\ *adj, usu cap S* : of or relating to an early Semitic alphabet known only from fragmentary inscriptions from Sarabit el Khadem in the Sinai peninsula and thought to date from about 1500 B.C.

**pro·to·siphon** \"+\ *n, cap* [NL, fr. *prot-* + Gk *siphōn* siphon, tube, pipe] : a genus (the type of the family Protosiphonaceae) of unicellular multinucleate freshwater green algae consisting of a single form (*P. botryoides*) that is broadly tubular or more or less balloon-shaped and grows often confusingly mingled with *Botrydium* attached to mud by a single rarely branching rhizoid — **pro·to·siphonaceous** \"+\ *adj*

**pro·to·sphargis** \"+\ *n, cap* [NL, fr. *prot-* + *Sphargis*] : a genus of gigantic turtles from the Upper Cretaceous of Italy including one form (*P. veronensis*) with a shell about nine feet long

**pro·to·spon·dy·li** \ˌ=(ˌ)='spändəˌlī\ [NL, fr. *prot-* + *-spondyli*] *syn of* CYCLOGANOIDEI

**pro·to·spon·dy·lous** \ˌ=(ˌ)=ˌ'==ləs\ *adj* [NL *Protospondyli* + E *-ous*] : of or relating to the Cycloganoidei

**pro·to·star** \'prōd·ə+ˌ-\ *n* [ISV *prot-* + *star*] : a hypothetical flat circular gaseous cloud of dust and atoms in space believed to develop into a star

**pro·tos·te·ga** \prə'tästəgə\ *n, cap* [NL, fr. *prot-* + Gk *stegē* roof; akin to L *tegere* to cover — more at THATCH] : a genus of large marine turtles from the Upper Cretaceous of No. America having a carapace and plastron somewhat like those of the leatherback

**pro·to·stele** \'prōd·əˌstēl, ˌ==ˌ'stēlē\ *n* [*prot-* + *stele*] : a stele that has the form of a solid rod or column with the phloem surrounding the xylem — called also *monostele*; compare SIPHONOSTELE — **pro·to·ste·lic** \ˌ==ˌ'stēlik\ *adj*

[1]**pro·to·stome** \'prōd·əˌstōm\ *adj* [NL *Protostomia*] : of or relating to the Protostomia

[2]**protostome** \"\ *n* -s [NL *Protostomia*] : one of the Protostomia

**pro·to·sto·mia** \ˌ=='stōmēə\ *n pl, cap* [NL, fr. *prot-* + *-stomia*] : animals in which the definitive mouth develops directly from the blastopore (as most worms, bryozoans, brachiopods, mollusks, and arthropods) — compare DEUTEROSTOMIA

**pro·to·strongyle** \ˌ==+\ *n* -s [NL *Protostrongylus*] : a worm of the genus *Protostrongylus*

**pro·to·strongylin** \"+\ *n* -s [NL *Protostrongylus* + E *-in*] : PROTOSTRONGYLE

**pro·to·strongyline** \"+\ *adj* [NL *Protostrongylus* + E *-ine*] : of or relating to the genus *Protostrongylus*

**pro·to·strongylus** \"+\ *n, cap* [NL, fr. *prot-* + *Strongylus*] : a genus of lungworms (family Metastrongylidae) parasitic in ruminants and rodents

**pro·to·syllabic** \ˌprōd·ə+\ *adj* [*prot-* + *syllabic*] *of the heaviest stress in a word* : falling on the first syllable

**pro·to·symphyla** \"+\ *n pl, cap* [NL, fr. *prot-* + *Symphyla*] : a hypothetical class of arthropods held to be ancestral to the Insecta and Symphyla

**pro·to·taxic** \"+\ *adj* [*prot-* + *-taxic* (as in *parataxic*)] : lacking in self-awareness and in perception of temporal sequence : cognitively inchoate : PRECONCEPTUAL ⟨~ symbols⟩ ⟨in the first year of life the ~ mode is operating —G.S. Blum⟩ — contrasted with *parataxic* and *syntaxic*

**pro·to·taxites** \ˌ==+\ *n, pl* **prototaxites** [NL, fr. *prot-* + *tax-* + *-ites*] : NEMATOPHYTON

**pro·to–teutonic** \ˌprōd·(ˌ)ō+\ *adj or n, cap P&T* : PROTO-GERMANIC

**pro·to·the·ca** \ˌprōd·ə'thēkə\ *n, pl* **protothe·cae** \-ē(ˌ)sē\ [NL, fr. *prot-* + *theca*] : the cup-shaped structure forming the first part of the skeleton in the Madreporaria — **pro·to·the·cal** \ˌ=(ˌ)=ˌ'thēkəl\ *adj*

**pro·to·there** \'prōd·əˌthi(ə)r\ *n* -s [NL *Prototheria*] : one of the Prototheria

**pro·to·the·ria** \ˌ==ˌ'thirēə\ *n pl, cap* [NL, fr. *prot-* + *-theria*] : a subclass of Mammalia that is coextensive with Monotremata or in some classifications includes both Monotremata and Allotheria and that is represented in the recent fauna solely by the egg-laying platypus and echidnas

**pro·to·tonic** \ˌprōd·ə+\ *adj* [*prot-* + *tonic*] : characterized by accent on the first syllable — contrasted with *deuterotonic*

**pro·to·tracheata** \ˌprōd·(ˌ)ō+\ [NL, fr. *prot-* + *Tracheata*] *syn of* ONYCHOPHORA

**pro·to·troch** \'prōd·əˌträk\ *n* -s [*prot-* + *-troch*] : the ciliated band or ring characteristic of trochophore larvae — **pro·tot·ro·chal** \prō'tä·trəkəl\ *adj*

**pro·to·troph** \'prōd·əˌträf, -rōf\ *n* -s [back-formation fr. *prototrophic*] : a prototrophic individual

**pro·to·trophic** \ˌ==ˌ'träfik, -rōf-\ *adj* [ISV *prot-* + *-trophic*] **1** : deriving nutriment from inorganic sources — used esp. of those bacteria that do not require organic media for growth **2** : requiring no specific growth substances for normal metabolism and reproduction — used esp. of the wild types of various molds

**pro·to·trop·ic** \ˌ==ˌ'träpik\ *adj* [*prototropy* + *-ic*] : of or relating to prototropy

**pro·tot·ro·py** \prə'tä·trəpē\ *n* -ES [*proton* + *-tropy*] : tautomerism involving the migration of a proton esp. to a location three atoms distant in an organic molecule — compare ANIONOTROPY, KETO-ENOL TAUTOMERISM

**pro·to·typ·al** \ˌprōd·əˌ'tīpəl\ *adj* [*prototype* + *-al*] : of, relating to, or constituting a prototype : ARCHETYPAL

**pro·to·type** \'==ˌtīp\ *n* [F, fr. MF, fr. Gk *prōtotypon* archetype, fr. neut. of *prōtotypos* original, primitive, fr. *prōt-* prot- + *typos* type — more at TYPE] **1 a** (1) : an original on which a thing is modeled : PATTERN ⟨romantically identifying the new republic with the ancient ~ —*Amer. Guide Series: N.Y.*⟩ (2) : one of the ideas or patterns in the divine mind after the likeness of which created things are made — compare ARCHETYPE, IDEA 1a **b** : an individual that exhibits the essential features of a later individual or species : PRECURSOR ⟨metal-wheeled chariots, the ~ of the tanks of modern warfare —R.W.Murray⟩ **c** : an individual, quality, or complex that exemplifies or serves as a standard of the essential features of a group or type : EXEMPLAR ⟨the gangster ~ the movies have shown the world —Polly Adler⟩ ⟨mathematics is the ~ of logical thinking⟩ ⟨~ kilogram⟩ **d** (1) *also* **prototype airplane** : the first full-scale piloted flying model of a new type of airplane (2) : the first full-scale model of a new type or design of furniture, machinery, or vehicle ⟨~ chair⟩ ⟨~ of a new tractor engine⟩ ⟨~ of a new medium tank⟩ **2 a** : an ancestral form **b** : primary type **3** : an individual that exemplifies an earlier prototype ⟨the modern ~ of Catherine the Great —Thomas Wolfe⟩

**pro·to·typ·i·cal** \ˌ==ˌ'tipəkəl, -pēk-\ *also* **pro·to·typ·ic** \-pik, -pēk\ *adj* [*prototypical* fr. *prototype* + *-ical*; *prototypic* ISV *prototype* + *-ic*] : PROTOTYPAL — **pro·to·typ·i·cal·ly** \-pək(ə)lē, -ēk-, -li\ *adv*

**pro·to·veratrine** \ˌprōd·(ˌ)ō+\ *n* [ISV *prot-* + *veratrine*] : a toxic crystalline alkaloid or a mixture of two closely related alkaloids distinguished as protoveratrine A and B obtained from the white hellebore and used in the treatment of hypertension

**pro·to·vertebra** \"+\ *n* [NL, fr. *prot-* + *vertebra*] **1** : PRIMITIVE SEGMENT **2** : MYOTOME — **pro·to·vertebral** \"+\ *adj*

**prot·oxide** \(')prōd·+\ *n* [ISV *prot-* + *oxide*] : the one of a series of oxides exclusive of suboxides that has the lowest proportion of oxygen

**pro·to·xylem** \ˌprōd·(ˌ)ō+\ *n* [*prot-* + *xylem*] : the first part of the primary xylem that differentiates from the procambium and that is distinguished from the notaxylem by smaller diameter and the annular, spiral, or occasionally scalariform wall thickenings

**protoxylem point** *n* : the protoxylem strand in cross section

**protoxylem strand** *n* : a group of protoxylem elements forming a longitudinal strand in the stele

**pro·to·zoa** \ˌprōd·ə'zōə, -ōtə-\ *n pl, cap* [NL, fr. *prot-* + *-zoa*] : a phylum or subkingdom of animals that have an essentially acellular structure though varying from simple uninucleate protoplasts (as most amoebas) to cell colonies (as volvox), syncytia (as pelomyxa), or highly organized protoplasts (as various higher ciliates) far more complex in organization and differentiation than most metazoan cells, that consist of a protoplasmic body either naked or enclosed in a test, fixed to the substrate or free, and immobile, creeping by means of pseudopodia or protoplasmic flow, or freely motile by cilia or flagella, that are similarly varied in physiological characteristics with nutrition holophytic, saprophytic, or holozoic, with reproduction asexual involving nuclear division usu. by more or less modified mitosis associated with cytoplasmic binary fission or with multiple fission or exogenous or endogenous budding or sexual by means of conjugation, of isogamous or anisogamous hologamy or of processes approaching the fertilization processes of metazoans, and with a life cycle simple (as in an amoeba) or extremely complex (as in many sporozoans), that are represented by one form or another in almost every kind of habitat (as fresh or salt water, soil, sewage, the latex of plants, and the bodies of living animals), and that include parasitic forms which are among the gravest plaguers of man and his domestic animals — compare MALARIA PARASITE, TRYPANOSOME; CILIOPHORA, PLASMODROMA; EIMERIA, METAZOA, PARAZOA, PROTISTA

**pro·to·zo·a·ci·dal** \¦==¦==¦sīdᵊl\ *adj* [*protozoacide* + *-al*] **1 :** destroying protozoans **2 :** of or relating to a protozoacide

**pro·to·zo·a·cide** \,==ˈ=ə,sīd\ *n* -S [NL *Protozoa* + E *-cide*] **:** an agent that destroys protozoans

**pro·to·zo·al** \¦==¦zōəl\ *adj* [NL *Protozoa* + E *-al*] **:** PROTOZOAN

**¹pro·to·zo·an** \-ən\ *n* -S [NL *Protozoa* + E *-an*] **:** one of the Protozoa

**²protozoan** \"\ *adj* **:** of or relating to the Protozoa

**pro·to·zoea** \¦prōd·ə+\ *n* [NL, fr. *prot-* + *zoea*] **:** a larval stage preceding the zoea in some decapod Crustacea — **pro·to·zoean** \"+\ *adj*

**pro·to·zo·i·a·sis** \,prōd·ə(,)zōˈīəsəs\ *n, pl* **protozoia·ses** \-ə,sēz\ [NL, fr. *Protozoa* + *-iasis*] **:** infection with or disease caused by protozoan parasites

**pro·to·zo·ic** \¦prōd·ə¦zōik\ *adj* [NL *Protozoa* + E *-ic*] **1 :** PROTOZOAN **2 :** containing or belonging to the period of remains of the earliest discovered life

**pro·to·zoological** \"+\ *adj* [*protozoology* + *-ical*] **:** of or relating to protozoology

**pro·to·zoologist** \"+\ *n* [*protozoology* + *-ist*] **:** a specialist in protozoology

**pro·to·zoology** \"+\ *n* [ISV *protozoo-* (fr. NL *Protozoa*) + *-logy*] **:** a branch of zoology concerned with the study of the Protozoa

**pro·to·zo·on** \,prōd·əˈzō,än, -ōtəˈ-\ *n, pl* **protozoa** [NL, sing. of *Protozoa*] **:** PROTOZOAN — **pro·to·zo·on·al** \¦==¦zōənᵊl\ *adj*

**pro·tracheata** \(¦)prō+\ [NL, fr. ¹*pro-* + *Tracheata*] *syn of* ONYCHOPHORA

**pro·tracheate** \(ˈ)=+\ *adj or n* [NL *Protracheata*] **:** ONYCHOPHORAN

**pro·tract** \prōˈtrakt, prə-ˈ-\ *vt* -ED/-ING/-S [L *protractus*, past part. of *protrahere* to draw before, protract, fr. *pro-* ¹pro- + *trahere* to draw — more at TRACE] **1** *archaic* **:** to put off to a later time **:** DELAY, DEFER ⟨attempted, however, to prevent, or at least to ~, his ruin —Edward Gibbon⟩ **2 :** to draw out or lengthen in time or space **:** CONTINUE, PROLONG ⟨the trial must not be ~*ed* in duration by anything that is obstructive or dilatory —R.H.Jackson⟩ **3 :** to draw to a scale **:** lay down the lines and angles of with scale and protractor **:** PLOT **syn** see EXTEND

**pro·tract·ed·ly** *adv* **:** in a protracted manner

**protracted meeting** *n* **:** a series of revival meetings extending over a period of time ⟨in the spring when they had the big *protracted meetings* and the foot washings —J.H.Stuart⟩

**pro·tract·ed·ness** *n* -ES **:** the quality or state of being protracted

**pro·tract·er** \-tə(r)\ *n* -S [by alter.] **:** PROTRACTOR

**pro·tract·ible** \-təbəl\ *adj* **:** capable of being protracted

**pro·trac·tile** \prōˈtraktᵊl, prə-ˈ-, -,tīl, -(,)til\ *adj* **:** capable of being thrust out **:** PROTRUSILE — compare RETRACTILE — **pro·trac·til·i·ty** \,prō,trakˈtiləd·ē, -lətē, -i\ *n* -ES

**pro·trac·tion** \-ˈtrakshən\ *n* -S [LL *protraction-, protractio*, fr. L *protractus* (past part. of *protrahere* to protract) + *-ion-, -io* -ion] **1 :** the act or an instance of protracting **:** EXTENSION, PROLONGATION, DELAY ⟨the ~ of a debate⟩ **2 a :** the drawing to scale of an area of land **b :** a plan drawn to scale of an area **:** PLOT **3 :** the prolonging of a syllable in a Greek or Latin poem beyond its normal length

**pro·trac·tive** \-ktiv\ *adj* [L *protractus* + E *-ive*] **:** that protracts **:** DELAYING

**pro·trac·tor** \-tə(r)\ *n* -S [ML, fr. L *protractus* (past part. of *protrahere* to protract) + *-or*] **1 :** one that protracts **:** as **a** *obs* **:** one that prolongs **:** RETARDER, DELAYER **b :** a muscle that extends a part — opposed to *retractor* **2 a :** an instrument made for laying down and measuring angles on paper and used in drawing and plotting **b :** a similar instrument for locating distant forest fires

bevel protractor

**pro·trema·ta** \prōˈtremədə, -rēm-\ *n pl, cap* [NL, fr. ¹*pro-* + *-tremata*] **:** an order of articulate brachiopods having the peduncle opening restricted to the ventral valve or absent — **pro·tremate** \-mət\ *n* -S — **pro·trema·tous** \(ˈ)=¦tremədəs, -rēm-\ *adj*

**¹pro·trep·tic** \prōˈtreptik\ *n* -S [LL *protrepticus* hortatory, encouraging, fr. Gk *protreptikos*, fr. (assumed) Gk *protreptos* (verbal of *protrepein* to turn forward, urge on, fr. *pro-* ¹pro- + *trepein* to turn) + *-ikos* -ic — more at TROPE] **:** EXHORTATION

**²protreptic** \"\ *also* **pro·trep·ti·cal** \-təkəl\ *adj* [*protreptic* fr. LL *protrepticus*; *protreptical* fr. LL *protrepticus* + E *-al*] **:** HORTATORY, PERSUASIVE

**pro·triaene** \(ˈ)prō+\ *n* [¹*pro-* + *triaene*] **:** a triaene in which the cladi point in a direction opposite to that of the shaft

**pro·troch·u·la** \prōˈträkyələ\ *n* -S [NL, fr. ¹*pro-* + *troch-* + *-ula* (fem. of *-ulus* -ule)] **:** a hypothetical free-swimming primitive organism resembling a simple trochophore and regarded as indicating the way of transition from radial to bilateral symmetry

**pro·trud·able** \prōˈtrüdəbəl\ *adj* **:** PROTRUSIBLE

**pro·trude** \-ˈtrüd\ *vb* -ED/-ING/-S [L *protrudere*, fr. *pro-* ¹pro- + *trudere* to thrust — more at THREAT] *vt* **1** *archaic* **:** to thrust forward **:** drive or force along **2 :** to thrust out through or as if through a narrow orifice **:** cause to project or stick out ⟨to ~ one's tongue⟩ ~ *vi* **:** to jut out beyond the surrounding surface or context ⟨tall apartment buildings perch on the top of rocky cliffs or ~ from hillsides —*Amer. Guide Series: N.Y. City*⟩ ⟨memories *protruded* into his consciousness⟩ **syn** see BULGE

**pro·trud·ent** \-dᵊnt\ *adj* [L *protrudent-, protrudens*, pres. part. of *protrudere* to protrude] **:** PROTRUDING, PROJECTING, BULGING

**pro·tru·si·ble** \prōˈtrüsəbəl, -üzə-\ *adj* [*protrusion* + *-ible*] **:** capable of being protruded

**pro·tru·sile** \prōˈtrü,|s|il, -|s|əl, -(,)|s|il, |z|\ *adj* [*protrusion* + *-ile*] **:** so made that it can be protruded ⟨a ~ proboscis⟩ — **pro·tru·sil·i·ty** \,prō,trüˈsiləd·ē, -ˈzil-\ *n* -ES

**pro·tru·sion** \prōˈtrüzhən\ *n* -S [L *protrusus* (past part. of *protrudere* to protrude) + E *-ion*] **1 :** the quality or state of protruding **:** PROJECTION ⟨the ~ of a jaw⟩ **2 :** something that protrudes ⟨a roof with many ~*s*⟩

**pro·tru·sive** \prōˈtrüsiv, (ˈ)prō¦t-, -üziv\ *adj* [L *protrusus* (past part. of *protrudere* to protrude) + E *-ive*] **1** *archaic* **:** that thrusts forward or pushes along **:** PROPULSIVE **2 :** that protrudes **:** PROTUBERANT ⟨a ~ jaw⟩ ⟨to pull a ~ manuscript from one's pocket⟩ **3 :** characterized by obtrusiveness **:** that forces attention ⟨a ~ boisterous manner⟩ — **pro·tru·sive·ly** \-əvlē\ *adv* — **pro·tru·sive·ness** \-ivnəs\ *n* -ES

**pro·tu·ber·ance** \prōˈt(y)üb(ə)rən(t)s\ *n* -S [L *protuberare* to bulge out + E *-ance*] **1 :** the quality or state of being protuberant ⟨lessen the ~ of an underjaw by an operation⟩ **2 :** something that is protuberant **:** PROTRUSION, BULGE ⟨a ~ on the forehead⟩ ⟨a cancerous ~⟩

**pro·tu·ber·an·cy** \-nsē, -si\ *n* -ES [LL *protuberare* + E *-ancy*] *archaic* **:** PROTUBERANCE

**pro·tu·ber·ant** \-nt\ *adj* [LL *protuberant-, protuberans*, pres. part. of *protuberare* to bulge out] **1 :** bulging beyond the surrounding or adjacent surface **:** PROMINENT ⟨a ~ joint⟩ ⟨~ eyes⟩ **2 :** forcing itself into consciousness **:** OBTRUSIVE ⟨one of the most ~ facts of the history of the past twenty years —Elmer Davis⟩ — **pro·tu·ber·ant·ly** *adv*

**pro·tu·ber·ate** \-ə,rāt\ *vi* -ED/-ING/-S [LL *protuberatus*, past part. of *protuberare* to bulge out, fr. L *pro-* ¹pro- + *tuber* bump, swelling, tumor — more at TUBER] **:** to swell beyond a surface **:** form a protuberance **syn** see BULGE

**prot·ungulata** \(¦)prōd·+\ *n pl, cap* [NL, fr. *prot-* + *Ungulata*] **1 :** a hypothetical group ancestral to the ungulate mammals **2** *in some classifications* **:** a major division of Eutheria comprising extinct mammals of the orders Condylarthra, Litopterna, Notoungulata, and Astrapotheria together with the recent and extinct Tubulidentata — **prot·ungulate** \(ˈ)=+\ *adj or n*

**pro·tu·ra** \prəˈtyu̇rə\ *n pl, cap* [NL, fr. *prot-* + *-ura*] **:** a group of very minute primitive wingless blind arthropods that lack antennae, have the mouth parts concealed within the head, undergo no noticeable metamorphosis except an increase in the number of abdominal segments, and are sometimes considered to form an order of Insecta or more often in current classification treated as a distinct class — **pro·tu·ran** \-rən\ *adj or n*

**pro·tutor** \(ˈ)prō+\ *n* [LL *protutela* vice-tutelage (fr. L *pro-* ¹pro- + *tutela* tutelage) + E *-or* (as in *tutor*)] **:** one who acts as tutor without legal appointment or one who marries a tutoress and is equally responsible with her

**pro·tu·tory** \-üd·ərē\ *n* -ES [*protutor* + *-y*] **:** the office or tenure of office of a protutor

**pro·tyl·o·pus** \prōˈtiləpəs\ *n, cap* [NL, fr. ¹*pro-* + *-tylopus* (fr. *Tylopoda*)] **:** a genus of camels no larger than jackrabbits found in the Upper Eocene of No. America and having teeth that form a continuous series, unfused lower leg bones, and four functional toes on the front feet

**pro·type** \ˈprō+,-\ *n* [¹*pro-* + *type*] **:** the first intact described specimen of a fossil species previously known only from an incomplete type

**proud** \ˈprau̇d\ *adj* -ER/-EST [ME, fr. OE *prūd, prūt*, prob. fr. OF *prod, prud, prut, prou* good, capable, brave, fr. LL *prode* advantageous, advantage, fr. L *prodesse* to be useful, be beneficial, fr. *prod-* (var. of *pro-* before, forward) + *esse* to be — more at PRO-, IS] **1 :** feeling or showing pride: as **a :** having or displaying inordinate self-esteem ⟨goaded the ~ baronage —J.R.Green⟩ ⟨his cold and ~ nature —A. Conan Doyle⟩ **b :** highly satisfied or pleased **:** deeply gratified **:** ELATED, EXULTANT ⟨~ to have such men —Sherwood Anderson⟩ ⟨a ~ boy . . . he has made something with his own hands —*Better Homes & Gardens*⟩ — often used with *of* ⟨~ of his success⟩ ⟨a record to be ~ of⟩ **c** *chiefly Midland* **:** GLAD, DELIGHTED ⟨we'd be ~ to have you stay for supper⟩ **d :** marked by a proper or becoming self-respect ⟨too ~ to fight —Woodrow Wilson⟩ ⟨brought a ~ . . . efficiency to everything she did —Fred Majdalany⟩ **2 a :** marked by stateliness or magnificence **:** SPLENDID ⟨~ princes and humble peasants —Vicki Baum⟩ ⟨~ old castles —E.O.Hauser⟩ **b :** giving reason or occasion for pride **:** GLORIOUS ⟨a ~ heritage⟩ ⟨our ~*est* feat —Joyce Cary⟩ ⟨his ~*est* moment —Paul Pickrel⟩ **3 :** marked by great vitality or power **:** VIGOROUS, EXUBERANT: as **a** *of an animal* **:** full of spirit **:** METTLESOME ⟨a ~ steed⟩ **b** *of a body of water* **:** overflowing its banks **:** SWOLLEN ⟨the ~ stream⟩ **c** (1) *of granulation tissue* **:** growing exuberantly ⟨~ growth in an old wound⟩ (2) *of a plant, Brit* **:** LUXURIANT ⟨~ corn⟩ **4 :** arising from or produced by pride ⟨a ~ look⟩ **5** *chiefly dial, of a female animal* **:** sexually excited **:** in heat **6 a** *chiefly dial Brit* **:** PROTUBERANT — used esp. of construction ⟨~ . . . jointings may have to be pared down —*Choice of Careers: Furniture Manufacturing*⟩ ⟨~ base edges —F.W.Mann⟩ **b** *of a cutting tool* **:** having a large amount of top rake

**syn** PROUD, ARROGANT, HAUGHTY, LORDLY, INSOLENT, OVERBEARING, SUPERCILIOUS, DISDAINFUL can mean in common showing a sense of one's superiority and scorn for what one regards as beneath him. PROUD may stress less the idea of one's sense of superiority than the idea of one's sense of accomplishment, often genuine, or strong self-respect, often justified, although it often implies an assumed superiority or suggests a loftiness or manifest self-congratulation in manner or appearance ⟨*proud* to publish a group of excellent reference works —*Saturday Rev.*⟩ ⟨he was too *proud* to admit failure and withdraw —Aldous Huxley⟩ ⟨he had a mild impersonal manner and was *proud* of having no rancor for any of the criminals he arrested —Morley Callaghan⟩ ⟨she is *proud* of everything of which she should be ashamed —H.T.Buckle⟩ ⟨a *proud* and objectionable bearing toward colleagues⟩ ARROGANT implies a claiming for oneself, often domineeringly or offensively, more consideration, importance, or worth than is warranted ⟨he was not, however, disagreeably *arrogant* or contemptuous in a cutting way as I am afraid I had been at that age —Edmund Wilson⟩ ⟨vain, *arrogant*, blustering, trying to keep leadership of his associates —Amy Loveman⟩ ⟨an *arrogant* disregard for the popular will —D.D.McKean⟩ HAUGHTY stresses an obvious consciousness of superior position or character and an obvious scorn of things regarded as beneath one ⟨supercilious and *haughty*, they turn this way and that, like the dowagers of very aristocratic families at a plebeian evening party —Aldous Huxley⟩ ⟨a cold and *haughty* stare⟩ LORDLY implies behavior or bearing befitting a nobleman but can also suggest pure pompousness or an arrogant display of power or magnificence ⟨these *lordly* archbishops who once ranked second to the emperor himself —Claudia Cassidy⟩ ⟨she had collected — or rather had received — almost with the air of a domestic, four= fifty per week from a *lordly* foreman in a shoe factory — a man who, in distributing the envelopes, had the manner of a prince doling out favors to a servile group of petitioners —Theodore Dreiser⟩ ⟨a *lordly* condescension⟩ INSOLENT implies an improper and manifest contemptuousness, suggesting a will to insult or affront ⟨vile food, vile beyond belief, slapped down before their sunken faces by *insolent* waiters —Katherine A. Porter⟩ ⟨searching the crowd until he found the face from which that *insolent* jeering came —O.E.Rölvaag⟩ ⟨an *insolent* familiarity⟩ OVERBEARING suggests a bullying or tyrannical disposition or manifest preemption of power, or an intolerable insolence ⟨backcountry militiamen whose rough *overbearing* manners sorely tried the Indians' patience —*Amer. Guide Series: Tenn.*⟩ ⟨he was arrogant, *overbearing*, conceited, and passionate — without any rank which could excuse pride, or any acquirement that could justify conceit —Anthony Trollope⟩ ⟨whose temper was so *overbearing*, that he could not restrain himself from speaking disrespectfully of that young lady at this desk —Charles Dickens⟩ SUPERCILIOUS stresses an outward appearance of patronizing haughtiness though it also suggests inner conceit and often not only scorn but also incivility ⟨he looks upon the whole struggle with the *supercilious* contempt of an indifferent spectator —Leslie Stephen⟩ ⟨his dislike of me gleamed in his blue eyes and in his *supercilious*, cold smile —Rose Macaulay⟩ DISDAINFUL implies a more contemptuous and more manifest scorn than SUPERCILIOUS ⟨nor grandeur hear with a *disdainful* smile the short and simple annals of the poor —Thomas Gray⟩ ⟨a little vanity and a little sensuality, says a *disdainful* French moralist, is about all that enters into the makeup of the average man —Irving Babbitt⟩

**proud flesh** *n* [ME] **:** an exuberant growth of granulation tissue in a wound or ulcer

**proud·ful** \-dfəl\ *adj* [ME, fr. *proud* + *-ful*] *chiefly dial* **:** marked by or full of pride ⟨a delegation of ~ citizens —Bennett Cerf⟩

**proudhearted** \ˈ=¦==\ *adj* [ME *proudherted*, fr. *proud* + *herted* hearted — more at HEARTED] **:** proud in spirit **:** HAUGHTY ⟨~ wretch⟩

**proud·ish** \ˈprau̇dish\ *adj* **:** somewhat proud

**proud·ly** *adv* [ME, fr. OE *prūtlīce*, fr. *prūd, prūt* proud + *-līce* -ly — more at PROUD] **:** in a proud manner **:** with elation ⟨a ceremonial dish . . . borne ~ into a banquet —Geoffrey Boumphrey⟩

**proust·ian** \ˈprüstēən\ *adj, usu cap* [Marcel *Proust* †1922 Fr. novelist + E *-ian*] **:** of, relating to, or having the characteristics of Proust or his writings ⟨the familiar atmospheres of the *Proustian* world —J.M.O'Brien⟩ ⟨*Proustian* resonances of the recalled past —Irwin Edman⟩

**proust·ite** \ˈprü,stīt\ *n* -S [F, fr. Joseph L. *Proust* †1826 Fr. chemist + F *-ite*] **:** a mineral $Ag_3AsS_3$ that is isomorphous with pyrargyrite and consists of a silver arsenic sulfide of a cochineal red occurring in rhombohedral crystals and also massive

**proust's law** \ˈprüsts-\ *n, usu cap P* [after J. L. *Proust*] **:** LAW OF DEFINITE PROPORTIONS

**prout's brown** \ˈprau̇ts-\ *n, often cap P* [after Samuel *Prout* †1852 Eng. artist] **:** BROWN SUGAR 2

**prout's hypothesis** \ˈprau̇ts-\ *n, usu cap P* [after William *Prout* †1850 Eng. chemist and physician] **:** a hypothesis in chemistry: the atomic weights of all other elements are exact multiples of that of hydrogen and hence hydrogen is the primary substance from which the other elements have been formed

**prov** *abbr* **1** proverb; proverbial **2** provided **3** province; provincial **4** provision **5** provisional **6** provost

**prov·abil·i·ty** \,prüvəˈbiləd·ē\ *n* -ES **:** the quality or state of being provable

**prov·able** \ˈprüvəbəl\ *adj* [ME, fr. MF, fr. L *probabilis* that which may be believed, fr. *probare* to test, prove + *-abilis* -able — more at PROVE] **:** capable of being proved ⟨practical truth ~ to all men —Walter Bagehot⟩ — **prov·able·ness** *n* -ES — **prov·ably** \-blē\ *adv*

**prov·and** \ˈprävənd\ *or* **prov·ant** \-nt\ *n* -S [ME *provande, provant*, fr. MD & MLG; MD *provande* & MLG *provande, provant*, fr. OF *provende* — more at PROVENDER] **1** *archaic* **:** supply of food **:** PROVISIONS **2** *chiefly dial* **:** PROVENDER 2

**pro·vascular** \(ˈ)prō+\ *adj* [¹*pro-* + *vascular*] **:** of or relating to procambial tissue

**prove** \ˈprüv\ *vb* **proved; proved** \-vd\ *or* **prov·en** \-vən\ **proving; proves** [ME *proven*, fr. OF *prover*, fr. L *probare* to test, prove, fr. *probus* good, fr. *pro-* before, forward + *-bus* (fr. the root of *fui* I have been) — more at PRO-, BE] *vt* **1** *archaic* **:** to know by trial **:** EXPERIENCE, SUFFER ⟨be my love and we will all the pleasures ~ —Christopher Marlowe⟩ **2 a :** to test the quality of **:** try out ⟨~ all things; hold fast that which is good —1 Thess 5:21 (AV)⟩ **b :** to subject to a technical testing process **:** ascertain (as by analysis or experiment) conformity with a standard or with stipulated requirements ⟨~ coal⟩ ⟨~ gold⟩ ⟨~ a new weapon⟩ ⟨~ a meter⟩ ⟨~ a new car model⟩ **c :** PROOF 1a — often used with *up* ⟨decided to draw and ~ up a small section —*Publishers' Weekly*⟩ **d :** to determine the alcoholic content of (a liquid) **e :** to determine the worth of (a sire) by progeny testing **f** (1) **:** to make a test of (as a mineral vein) — usu. used with *up* or *out* ⟨*proved* up the . . . copper deposit —*Time*⟩ (2) **:** to establish the presence of oil under — often used with *up* (3) **:** to establish the presence of (oil) — often used with *up* ⟨*proved* up . . . 12 billion in reserves —*Time*⟩ **3 a :** to establish the truth of (as by argument or evidence) **:** DEMONSTRATE, SHOW ⟨these . . . statements can be *proved* —*William & Mary Quarterly*⟩ ⟨no charge against him was ever *proven* in court —S.H.Adams⟩ **b :** to establish the validity of (as by mathematical demonstration) ⟨could ~ the forty-seventh proposition —R.L. Stevenson⟩ **c :** to verify the correctness of (as an arithmetic operation) ⟨showed her pupils how to ~ their answers⟩ **4 :** to ascertain the genuineness of **:** VERIFY ⟨such acts, records, and proceedings shall be *proved* —*U.S.Constitution*⟩ ⟨photographic copies of the check . . . were then *proved* and admitted in evidence —*Criminal Law Rev.*⟩; *specif* **:** to obtain probate of (a will) **5 :** to raise (dough) to a desired lightness ~ *vi* **:** to turn out esp. after trial or test ⟨the medicine *proved* to be salutary⟩; *also* **:** to turn out to be ⟨the report of the war's end *proved* false⟩

**syn** TRY, TEST, DEMONSTRATE: PROVE is now likely to stress ascertainment as certain, true, genuine, or worthy by means of evidence, tests, or logic ⟨to become a writer was, however, in Thoreau's mind; his verses *prove* it, his Journal *proves* it —H.S.Canby⟩ ⟨he *proves* the superior importance of plot over other elements in dramatic poetry —Irving Babbitt⟩ TRY in this sense is now likely to stress subjection to experiences or tests calculated to discern the good from the bad, the strong from the weak ⟨I crumbled common crackers into the pea soup and *tried* it. It was good pea soup —Kenneth Roberts⟩ ⟨the young man should be *tried* and tested —George Meredith⟩ TEST likewise stresses subjection to tests and trials, in general to specific, planned, and regular tests calculated to reveal any deficiencies ⟨the first time he made a helmet, he *tested* its capacity for resisting blows, and battered it out of shape —Bertrand Russell⟩ ⟨he gives us the background of these witnesses, *tests* their reliability, shifts, summarizes, and collates the main portions of their evidence —*Christian Science Monitor*⟩ DEMONSTRATE is likely to stress conclusive proof or resolution and its orderly presentation with many details ⟨to *demonstrate* and popularize the Copernican hypothesis —Stringfellow Barr⟩ ⟨*demonstrated* that art did not imitate nature —F.B.Millet⟩ **syn** see INDICATE

**pro·vect** \prōˈvekt\ *vt* -ED/-ING/-S [L *provectus*, past part. of *provehere* to carry forward, convey onward, fr. *pro-* forward + *vehere* to carry, convey — more at PRO-, VEHICLE] **:** to change (a consonant) by provection

**pro·vec·tion** \-kshən\ *n* -S [L *provectus* + E *-ion*] **1 :** CONSONANT SHIFT **2 a :** a phonetic change in Celtic languages whereby in contact with other consonants (as homorganic sonants) fricatives become the corresponding homorganic stops and voiced stops become voiceless **b :** a mutation in some Celtic languages (as Breton and Cornish) whereby a voiced consonant becomes unvoiced **3 :** the carrying forward of a final sound or letter to a following word (as in *a nickname* for *an ekename*)

**proved** *past of* PROVE

**pro·ved·i·tor** \prōˈvedəd·ə(r)\ *n* -S [It *proveditore, provveditore*, fr. *provedito, provveduto* (past part of *provedere, provvedere* to provide, purvey, fr. L *providēre* to provide) + *-ore* -or — more at PROVIDE] **1 :** a functionary in the Venetian republic having oversight of public services and government of provinces or acting as military adviser **2 :** one employed to procure supplies (as for an army, company, ship) **:** PURVEYOR

**prov·e·dore** *also* **prov·e·dor** *or* **prov·i·dore** \ˈprävə,dō(ə)r, -dȯ(ə)r\ *n* -S [It dial (Venice) *providore*, var. of *proveditore*] **:** PURVEYOR, PROVEDITOR

**proven** *past part of* PROVE

**prov·e·nance** \ˈprävənən(t)s\ *n* -S [F, fr. *provenant* coming from, originating in, fr. pres. part. of *provenir* to originate, come (from), fr. L *provenire* to come forth, originate — more at PROVENIENCE] **:** place of origin **:** SOURCE, PROVENIENCE ⟨the ~ of a lot of seed⟩ ⟨the ~ of the minerals⟩ ⟨tapestry . . . of Italian ~ —W.M.Milliken⟩ ⟨the date and ~ of the scrolls —Harold Roberts⟩ ⟨the ~ of these concepts —Gilbert Ryle⟩ **syn** see ORIGIN

**¹pro·ven·çal** \¦prōvən¦säl, ¦präv-\ *adj, usu cap* [MF, fr. *Provence*, region of southeastern France (fr. L *Provincia*, lit., province) + *-al* — more at PROVINCE] **1 :** of, relating to, or characteristic of Provence, a region of France **2 :** of, relating to, or characteristic of the people of Provence

**²provençal** \"\ *n, pl* **provençals** *or* **proven·çaux** \-sō(z)\ *cap* [MF, fr. *provençal*, adj.] **1 a :** a native or inhabitant of Provence in France **b :** a native speaker of the Provençal language **2 :** a Romance language spoken in southeastern France

**pro·ven·çale** \"\ *adj, usu cap* [F, fem. of *provençal*] **:** cooked with garlic, onion, olive oil, mushrooms, and herbs ⟨frogs' legs ~⟩ ⟨~ sauce⟩

**prov·ence rose** \ˈprä,ven(t)s-\ *n, usu cap P* [*Provence* alter. of *Provins*, town in northern France; trans. of F *rose de Provins*] **:** CABBAGE ROSE

**pro·ven·cial** \prōˈvenchəl\ *archaic var of* PROVENÇAL

**prov·end** \ˈprävənd\ *n* -S [ME *provende*, fr. MF — more at PROVENDER] **1** *archaic* **:** PREBEND 1 **2 :** PROVENDER

**¹prov·en·der** \ˈprävəndə(r)\ *n* -S [ME *provendre, provender*, fr. MF *provende, provendre*, fr. ML *provenda*, alter. (influenced by L *providēre* to provide) of *praebenda* prebend — more at PROVIDE, PREBEND] **1 :** FOOD, PROVISIONS ⟨how much ~ a . . . girl of fifteen could pack into her slender person —Harvey Fergusson⟩ **2 :** dry food for domestic animals (as hay, straw, corn, oats, or a mixture of ground grain) **:** FEED

**²provender** \"\ *vt* -ED/-ING/-S **:** to provide with provender

**pro·ve·nience** \prōˈvēnyən(t)s, prəˈ-, -nēən-\ *n* -S [by alter. (influence of L *provenient-, proveniens*, pres. part. of *provenire* to come forth, originate, fr. *pro-* forth + *venire* to come) — more at PRO-, COME] **:** PROVENANCE **syn** see ORIGIN

**prov·en·ly** *adv* : in a proven manner ⟨~ valuable methods —*Atlantic*⟩

**pro·ven·tric·u·lar** \ˌprōven·ˈtrikyələ(r)\ *adj* [NL *proventriculus* + E *-ar*] : of or relating to a proventriculus

**pro·ven·tric·u·li·tis** \ˌ==ˌtrikyəˈlīd·əs\ *n* -ES [NL, fr. *proventriculus* + *-itis*] : inflammation of the proventriculus of a bird usu. due to nutritional deficiencies or to parasitism

**pro·ven·tric·u·lus** \ˌ=ˈ=trikyələs\ *also* **pro·ven·tri·cule** \prōˈven·trəˌkyül\ *n, pl* **proventricu·li** \-yəˌlī\ *also* **proventricules** [NL *proventriculus*, fr. ¹*pro-* + *ventriculus*] **1** : the glandular or true stomach of a bird situated between the crop when a crop is present and the gizzard and usu. separated from the gizzard by a constriction **2** : a muscular dilatation of the foregut in front of the midgut in most mandibulate insects that is usu. armed internally with chitinous teeth or plates for triturating food **3** : the thin-walled sac in front of the gizzard of an earthworm : CROP

**prove out** *vi* : to turn out to be as stated, believed, planned, expected, hoped : measure up esp. under testing ⟨in the face of the sternest handicaps, down east individualism was still *proving out* —*Time*⟩ ⟨if . . . the selected key word does not *prove out*, the compilations on possible key letters can be carried farther —Fletcher Pratt⟩ : turn out well : PROSPER, SUCCEED, THRIVE ⟨wants to wait until the five now on order . . . *prove out* —*Newsweek*⟩

**prov·er** \ˈprüvə(r)\ *n* -S [ME, fr. *proven* to prove + *-er* — more at PROVE] : one that proves; *specif* : PROOFER

**¹prov·erb** \ˈpräˌvərb, -vəb, -vəib *sometimes* -ä̱ˌvə(r)b\ *n* -S [ME *proverbe*, fr. MF, fr. L *proverbium*, fr. *pro-* before + *verbum* word — more at PRO-, WORD] **1 a** : a brief epigrammatic saying that is a popular byword : an oft-repeated pithy and ingeniously turned maxim : ADAGE, SAW ⟨referred her to the ~ "marry in haste, repent at leisure"⟩ **b** : a profound or oracular maxim; *esp* : a truth couched in obscure language : PARABLE **2** : one (as a name or person) that has become a matter of common talk : BYWORD ⟨~s for places no one could ever see —*Manchester Guardian Weekly*⟩ **3 proverbs** *pl but sing or pl in constr* : a game in which one player tries to guess a proverb that the others have chosen by asking questions and finding one word of the proverb in each answer — **to a proverb** *adv* : in a degree that is proverbial : PROVERBIALLY ⟨ridiculous even *to a proverb* —Tobias Smollett⟩

**²proverb** \"\ *vt* -ED/-ING/-S **1** *obs* : to provide with a proverb ⟨I am ~*ed* with a grandsire phrase —Shak.⟩ **2** : to turn into a proverb or byword ⟨~*ed* for a fool in every street —John Milton⟩

**pro-verb** \ˈprō+,-\ *n* [²*pro-* + *verb*] : a form of the verb *do* used to avoid repetition of a full verb (as *do* in "my brother smokes and I do too")

**pro·ver·bi·al** \prəˈvərbēəl, -vəb-, -vəib-\ *adj* [L *proverbialis*, fr. *proverbium* proverb + *-alis* -al — more at PROVERB] **1** : of, relating to, or resembling a proverb ⟨the ~ style⟩ ⟨~ wisdom⟩ ⟨~ comparisons⟩ **2** : that has become a proverb or byword : commonly spoken of ⟨the ~ restlessness of sailors —Herman Melville⟩ — **pro·ver·bi·al·ly** \-ēəlē, -li\ *adv*

**pro·ver·bi·al·ist** \-ləst\ *n* -S : one that makes, collects, or uses proverbs

**proves** *pres 3d sing of* PROVE

**prove up** *vi* **1** : to measure up to expectations : turn out well : prove out ⟨the spots where these prospector dreams *proved up* —*Amer. Guide Series: Ariz.*⟩ **2** : to bring proof of one's right to something; *specif* : to show that the requirements for receiving a patent for government land have been satisfied

**prov·i·ant** \ˈprävēənt\ *n* -S [G, fr. It *provianda*, fr. ML *provenda* — more at PROVENDER] : PROVENDER 1

**pro·vicar** \(ˈ)prō+\ *n* [²*pro-* + *vicar*] : an administrator of a vicariate apostolic

**pro-vice-chancellor** \ˈprō+\ *n* [²*pro-* + *vice-chancellor*] : a deputy appointed by the vice-chancellor of a British university on his election

**pro·vide** \prəˈvīd, prōˈ-\ *vb* -ED/-ING/-S [ME *providen*, fr. L *providēre*, to foresee, provide, provide for, fr. *pro-* before, forward + *vidēre* to see — more at PRO-, WIT] *vi* **1 a** : to take precautionary measures : make provision — used with *against* or *for* ⟨~ against an inflationary economy⟩ ⟨~ for the common defense —*U.S.Constitution*⟩ **b** *obs* : to make ready : make preparation ⟨men . . . *providing* to live another time —Alexander Pope⟩ **2** : to make a proviso or stipulation ⟨*provided* for the adoption of collective measures —Vera M. Dean⟩ **3** : to supply what is needed for sustenance or support ⟨the Lord will ~⟩ ⟨we'll have to ~ for him —Ellen Glasgow⟩ ~ *vt* **1** *archaic* : to procure in advance : get ready beforehand : PREPARE ⟨~ us all things necessary —Shak.⟩ **2 a** : to fit out or fit up : EQUIP — used with *with* ⟨*provided* the children with the books they needed⟩ ⟨~ the car with a radio⟩ **b** : to supply for use : AFFORD, YIELD ⟨olives . . . ~ an important item of food —W.B.Fisher⟩ ⟨the preface . . . ~s a hint —L.R.McColvin⟩ **3** : STIPULATE ⟨the contract ~s that the work be completed by a given date⟩ **4** *obs* : to appoint to an ecclesiastical benefice esp. before it is vacant

**syn** SUPPLY, FURNISH: PROVIDE and SUPPLY are often interchangeable. PROVIDE may suggest equipping, stocking, or giving in the interest of preparing with foresight ⟨to *provide* for one's wife and children⟩ ⟨*provide* the safeguard we need against the abuse of mankind's scientific genius for destructive ends —Vera M. Dean⟩ ⟨to *provide* military aid and missions for friendly countries —*Current Biog.*⟩ SUPPLY may apply to providing what is needed, sometimes to making up a deficiency, replacing losses or depletions, filling a gap ⟨the book would be incomplete without some such discussion as I have tried to *supply* —W.R.Inge⟩ ⟨an age which *supplied* the lack of moral habits by a system of moral attitudes and poses —T.S.Eliot⟩ ⟨doctors or others *supplying* medical care to assistance recipients —*Americana Annual*⟩ FURNISH, also often interchangeable with PROVIDE and SUPPLY, may sometimes apply to equipping or giving something needed in a particular situation ⟨the first attempt in history to *furnish* the international society of nations with a permanent and organic system of international political institutions —P.J.Noel-Baker⟩ ⟨our failure, he believes, is not a failure to furnish education for the average —*College English*⟩

**¹provided** *adj* [fr. past part. of *provide*] **1** *obs* : PREPARED, READY ⟨a sharp ~ wit —Shak.⟩ **2** : supplied with necessaries : EQUIPPED, FURNISHED ⟨although he never did a lick of work, was always well ~ —J.F.Dobie⟩

**²provided** *conj* [fr. past part. of *provide*] : on condition that : with the understanding : if only ⟨~ the deductions are logical —G.H.Lewes⟩ ⟨~ benefits are not claimed under any other part of this policy —*Mutual of Omaha*⟩ ⟨any hole . . . ~ only it be small and narrow —J.G.Frazer⟩

**provided school** *n, Brit* : COUNCIL SCHOOL

**¹prov·i·dence** \ˈprävədən(t)s *also* -dᵊn- *or* -ˌden-\ *n* -S [ME, fr. MF, fr. L *providentia*, fr. *provident-, providens* (pres. part. of *providēre* to foresee, provide, provide for) + *-ia* -y — more at PROVIDE] **1** *often cap* **a** : divine guidance or care ⟨the notion of the detailed ~ of a rational personal God —A.N.Whitehead⟩ **b** : an act or instance of such guidance or care ⟨a special ~ in the fall of a sparrow —Shak.⟩ **2** : the quality or state of being provident or of exercising foresight : PRUDENCE, THRIFT ⟨the intellectual ~ to acquire . . . vast stores of dry information —Walter Bagehot⟩ ⟨the peasant in his traditional ~ —Bernard Pares⟩ **3 a** *usu cap* : one who exercises providential power **b** *cap* : God conceived as that ultimate reality whose sustaining power and ordering activity provide continual guidance over the matters of human destiny ⟨a redeeming *Providence* presides over the rise and fall of civilizations —S.P.Cadman⟩ **syn** see PRUDENCE

**²providence** \"\ *adj, usu cap* [fr. *Providence*, Rhode Island] : of or from Providence, the capital of Rhode Island ⟨a *Providence* silversmith⟩ : of the kind or style prevalent in Providence

**prov·i·dent** \-nt\ *adj* [ME, fr. L *provident-, providens*, pres. part. of *providēre* to foresee, provide, provide for — more at PROVIDE] **1** : taking thought of the end in view : making provision for the future : prudent in anticipating conditions or needs : THRIFTY ⟨wild squirrels are ~⟩ ⟨the ~ and subtle statesman —John Buchan⟩ **2** : prudent in the use of resources : FRUGAL, SAVING ⟨can say with certainty that he is both ~ and generous —Eric Linklater⟩

**prov·i·den·tial** \ˌprävəˈdenchəl\ *adj* [L *providentia* providence + E *-al* — more at PROVIDENCE] **1** *archaic* : FORESIGHTED, PRUDENT ⟨the ~ raven —Thomas Hood †1845⟩ **2** : of, relating to, or determined by Providence ⟨~ guidance⟩ ⟨~ mission⟩ ⟨~ disposition of events⟩ ⟨theologic assumption that nature operates only according to a ~ plan —M.R.Cohen⟩ **3** : occurring by or as if by an intervention of Providence : highly opportune : MIRACULOUS, LUCKY ⟨~ escape⟩ ⟨seemed ~ that he should arrive at just that moment⟩ ⟨what a ~ return to sanity —W.J.Locke⟩ **syn** see LUCKY

**prov·i·den·tial·ly** \-chəlē, -li\ *adv* : in a providential manner: as **a** : by divine foresight ⟨a ~ destined role —H.P.Van Dusen⟩ **b** : PRUDENTLY ⟨~ absented himself —*Time*⟩ **c** : LUCKILY ⟨the weather ~ remained clear —*Saturday Rev.*⟩

**prov·i·dent·ly** *adv* [ME, fr. *provident* + *-ly*] : in a provident manner : PRUDENTLY

**pro·vid·er** \prəˈvīd·ə(r), prōˈ-\ *n* -S **1** : one that provides : PURVEYOR ⟨the government . . . is a reluctant subsidy ~ —M.H.Curtis⟩ ⟨famed ~ of borrowed finery —*Time*⟩; *esp* : one that provides for his family ⟨a man might be a great lover but a poor ~ —W.J.Reilly⟩ **2** : an iron or steel worker who makes up production schedules based on the amounts of materials needed to fill outstanding orders

**providing** *conj* [fr. pres. part. of *provide*] : on condition that : in case : PROVIDED ⟨~ they pay the fixed rent —John Ruskin⟩ ⟨deal with whomever they wish ~ they conform to the agreement —*Canadian Forum*⟩ ⟨~ he decided not to keep it a secret —J.F.Powers⟩

**providore** *var of* PROVEDORE

**prov·ince** \ˈprävən(t)s *sometimes* -ä̱ˌvin-\ *n* -S [F, fr. L *provincia*; perh. akin to Goth *frauja* lord, master — more at FRAU] **1 a** : a country or a more or less remote region brought under the control of the ancient Roman government **b** : an administrative district or division of a country or empire ⟨the ~s of old Spain⟩ ⟨the ~s of Canada⟩ **c** (1) : a portion of a country; *esp* : one remote from or outside of the capital or largest city (2) **provinces** *pl* : all of a country outside of the metropolis — usu. used with *the* ⟨a shabby theatrical troupe which tours *the provinces* —Donald Heiney⟩ **2** [ME, fr. MF, fr. ML *provincia*, fr. L] **a** : any of the principal ecclesiastical divisions of a country forming the jurisdiction of an archbishop or metropolitan ⟨the ~ of Canterbury⟩ **b** : a territorial division of a religious order ⟨the general of the order administers several ~s⟩ **c** : a Salvation Army administrative unit smaller than a territory and larger than a division **3 a** : a biogeographic division of less rank than a region; *esp* : a primary division of a subregion **b** : an area throughout which geological history has been essentially the same or which is characterized by particular structural, petrographical, or physiographical features **4 a** : proper or appropriate business or scope (as of a person or body) : SPHERE, JURISDICTION ⟨semantic questions . . . are outside his ~ —*English Language Teaching*⟩ **b** : a department of knowledge or activity ⟨humanitarianism invaded one ~ of life after another —G.M. Trevelyan⟩ **syn** see FIELD, FUNCTION

**¹pro·vin·cial** \prəˈvinchəl, prōˈ-\ *n* -S [in sense 1, fr. ME, fr. MF or ML; MF, fr. ML *provincialis*, fr. *provincia* ecclesiastical province + L *-alis* -al; in other senses, fr. L *provincialis*, fr. *provincia* province + *-alis* -al — more at PROVINCE] **1** *sometimes cap* : a religious superior in the Roman Catholic Church who has direction under the general of his order of all religious houses in a province of the order **2 a** : one living in or coming from a province ⟨delegations of ~s —Robert Graves⟩; *specif* : a soldier recruited from a province (as a Roman province or an American colony before the Revolution) — usu. used in pl. ⟨3500 ~s . . . moved north against Crown Point —Arthur Pound⟩ **b** : a person of local or restricted interests or outlook ⟨the true ~'s attachment to a region —Milton Rugoff⟩ **c** : one who exhibits mainly the special characteristics (as of speech and customs) of a section of a country ⟨classifies the four novelists as ~s —James Gray⟩ **d** : a person lacking the polish and refinement of urban society

**²provincial** \"\ *adj* [ME, fr. *provincial*, adj.] **1 a** : of or relating to a province ⟨a ~ government⟩ ⟨a ~ dialect⟩ ⟨our greater ~ libraries —*Notes & Queries*⟩ **b** *obs* : having the subordinate relationship of a province ⟨the aforesaid country . . . now ~ to Denmark —William Warner⟩ **2** : confined to a province or region : limited in scope : NARROW, SECTIONAL ⟨~ interests⟩ ⟨a ~ attitude of mind⟩ ⟨helps free us from the ~ and the merely local —E.J.McGrath⟩ **3 a** : exhibiting the ways and manners of a province or rural district : COUNTRIFIED, UNSOPHISTICATED ⟨~ airs and graces —T.B.Macaulay⟩ ⟨no ~ twang in their writings —H.O.Taylor⟩ **b** : of, relating to, or constituting a decorative style (as in furniture and architecture) that is of country rather than courtly origin and is usu. marked by simplicity in design, informality in character, and relative plainness in decoration ⟨a French ~ style house⟩ ⟨~ chest of . . . faded walnut —*Antiques*⟩ ⟨~ designs . . . in hooked rugs —Mildred J. O'Brien⟩

**pro·vin·cial·ate** \-chələt, -chəˌlāt\ *n* -S **1 a** : the office of a provincial **b** : the term of office of a provincial **2** : the motherhouse of a provincial

**provincial court** *n* : the court of an archbishop within his province or jurisdiction ⟨the *provincial court* of Canterbury⟩

**pro·vin·cial·ism** \-chəˌlizəm\ *n* -S **1** : a dialectal or local word, phrase, or idiom ⟨answers come back in . . . slang, ~s, profanity —S.L.Payne⟩ **2** : the quality or state of being provincial: as **a** : exclusive attachment to one's own province, region, or country ⟨tourists shedding their ~⟩; *specif* : devotion to provincial autonomy ⟨went back to the pub to argue ~ —*Sunday Express (Johannesburg) So. Africa*⟩ **b** : indifference to what is alien, unfamiliar, or diverse : narrowness or limitation (as in interests, views, or thought) — contrasted with *cosmopolitanism* ⟨intellectual ~⟩ ⟨relation between temporal . . . cultural or national ~ —*Jour. of Philosophy*⟩ ⟨a newspaper steeped in ~ —Herbert Brucker⟩

**pro·vin·cial·ist** \-ləst\ *n* -S **1** : a native or inhabitant of a province : PROVINCIAL **2** : an advocate of provincialism esp. in politics ⟨the electorate was divided into centralists and ~s —Alexander Brady⟩

**pro·vin·ci·al·i·ty** \prəˌvinchēˈaləd·ē, prō,-, -ətē, -i\ *n* -ES **1** : the quality or state of being provincial : PROVINCIALISM ⟨lack of intercourse with others . . . with a consequent increase in his aloofness and ~ —J.T.Adams⟩ ⟨the ~ of his thought —Winthrop Sargeant⟩ ⟨the whole scene, paltry, confined, and dull . . . the extreme of ~ —Arnold Bennett⟩ **2** : an act or instance of provincialism ⟨biased . . . by the *provincialities* of groups —A.N.Whitehead⟩

**pro·vin·cial·iza·tion** \prəˌvinchələˈzāshən\ *n* -S : the act or process of provincializing ⟨practiced a further ~ of provincial styles —*Antiques*⟩

**pro·vin·cial·ize** \prəˈvinchəˌlīz, prōˈ-\ *vt* -ED/-ING/-S [¹*provincial* + *-ize*] : to make provincial : bring under provincial influence or control ⟨tended to divide, to ~, and to brutalize mankind —*Harper's*⟩ ⟨every branch of expenditure . . . was *provincialized* —*Pall Mall Gazette*⟩

**pro·vin·ci·ate** \prəˈvinchēˌāt\ *vt* -ED/-ING/-S [L *provincia* province + E *-ate* — more at PROVINCE] : to convert into a province : give a provincial status to

**pro·vinculum** \prō+\ *n* [NL, fr. ¹*pro-* + *vinculum*] : a primitive hinge composed of minute teeth developed before the permanent dentition in some bivalve mollusks

**pro·vine** \prōˈvīn\ *vt* -ED/-ING/-S [ME *provinen*, fr. MF *provigner*, fr. *provain* layer (of plants), fr. L *propagin-, propago*, fr. *propages* — more at PROPAGATE] : LAYER

**proving** *pres part of* PROVE

**proving ground** *n* **1** : a place or area for scientific experimentation or testing (as of aircraft, vehicles, weapons) ⟨the laboratories, pilot plants, and *proving grounds* of the nation —H.S.Truman⟩ **2** : a place where something new is tried out ⟨the *proving ground* for one of the most comprehensive social experiments —*Amer. Guide Series: Tenn.*⟩

**proving press** *n* : a small usu. hand-operated press for pulling printer's proofs

**proving ring** *n* : an elastic-shell ring used to calibrate testing machines by means of change in diameter undergone upon application of force along the diameter

**pro·virus** \(ˈ)prō+\ *n* [NL, fr. ¹*pro-* + *virus*] : a noninfectious intracellular form of a virus that behaves in the host cell as though it were a plasmagene

**¹pro·vi·sion** \prəˈvizhən, prōˈ-\ *n* [ME, fr. MF, fr. LL & L; LL *provision-, provisio* action of providing, provisions, fr. L, foresight, fr. *provisus* (past part. of *providēre* to foresee, provide, provide with) + *-ion-, -io* -ion — more at PROVIDE] **1 a** : promotion to office by an ecclesiastical superior; *esp* : appointment to a benefice not yet vacant ⟨through . . . a papal ~ he was made bishop —G.C.Sellery⟩ **b** : *Scots law* : a gift by will or deed to one as heir who would not be heir otherwise — compare HEIR OF PROVISION **c** *usu cap* : any of various laws enacted in the 13th and early 14th centuries by the assemblies of the English prelates and nobles or issued by the king with their consent ⟨*Provisions of Oxford*⟩ **2 a** : the act or process of providing ⟨the ~ of a play area for the children⟩ ⟨the ~ of free speech is . . . a weapon of enlightenment —Lucius Garvin⟩ **b** : the quality or state of being prepared beforehand ⟨cast upon the world without ~ —J.H.Newman⟩ **c** : a measure taken beforehand : PREPARATION ⟨~ . . . for decentralization —Vera M. Dean⟩ ⟨~ for inserting . . . die slings —*Steel*⟩ **3** : a stock of needed materials or supplies ⟨caravans expecting water or ~ at a designated spot —Irving Stone⟩; *esp* : a stock of food : VICTUALS — usu. used in pl. ⟨a basket of ~s — Green Peyton⟩ **4** : a stipulation (as a clause in a statute or contract) made in advance : PROVISO ⟨bequeathed the house with the ~ that it be preserved⟩ ⟨this ~ is one of fundamental importance in our legal . . . system —E.N.Griswold⟩ **syn** see CONDITION

**²provision** \"\ *vt* : to supply with provisions : VICTUAL ⟨trips to ~ the island —Ben Holt⟩ ⟨have an amply ~*ed* look that betrays their bucolic childhood —*Amer. Mercury*⟩

**provision account** *n* : RESERVE ACCOUNT 1

**¹pro·vi·sion·al** \-zhənᵊl, -zhnəl\ *adj* [¹*provision* + *-al*] **1** : provided for a temporary need : suitable or acceptable in the existing situation but subject to change or nullification : TENTATIVE, CONDITIONAL ⟨a ~ government set up in territory freed from enemy control⟩ ⟨a ~ appointment⟩ ⟨a ~ classification⟩ ⟨a ~ interpretation of the data⟩ ⟨their beliefs are relative and ~ —Walter Lippmann⟩ **2** *archaic* : marked by foresight : PROVIDENT ⟨this ~ care in every species —Oliver Goldsmith⟩ **3** : of or relating to special or extraordinary legal acts or proceedings allowed before final judgment to protect the interests of one or more parties to an action at law (as under the code procedure of New York and some other states remedies had by order of arrest, warrant of attachment, temporary injunction, or appointment of a receiver) **4** *of a postage stamp* : overprinted or issued for temporary use esp. as a substitute for a regular issue that has not yet been made or that has not yet been received in the country or territory where it is to be used — contrasted with *definitive* — **pro·vi·sion·al·ly** \-zhənᵊlē, -zhnəlē, -i\ *adv*

**²provisional** \"\ *n* -S : a provisional postage stamp

**provisional order** *n* : an order (as on a matter of local concern normally dealt with by a private bill) issued by a British governmental agency under powers granted by parliament and having the force of law subject to specific parliamentary confirmation by means of a provisional orders confirmation bill

**pro·vi·sion·ary** \-zhəˌnerē, -ri\ *adj* [¹*provision* + *-ary*] : PROVISIONAL

**pro·vi·sion·er** \-zh(ə)nə(r)\ *n* -S : a furnisher of provisions : PURVEYOR, VICTUALLER ⟨the . . . farmers were the chief ~s of the armies —A.D.Graeff⟩

**pro·vi·sion·ment** \-zhənmənt\ *n* -S : supply of provisions ⟨carrying little ~ —Willa Cather⟩

**provision tree** *n* : a tropical American tree (*Pachira aquatica*) of the family Bombacaceae having large heavy russet fruits with edible brown seeds

**pro·vi·so** \prəˈvī(ˌ)zō, prōˈ-\ *n, pl* **provisos** *or* **provisoes** [ME, fr. L, provided (abl. of *provisum*, neut. of *provisus*, past part. of *providēre* to provide), in *proviso quod* provided that, a phrase with which clauses in medieval legal documents often began — more at PROVIDE] **1** : an article or clause (as in a statute, contract, or grant) that introduces a condition, qualification, or limitation and usu. begins with the word *provided* ⟨a ~ . . . to modify the operation of that part of the statute —G.D.Oxner⟩ — compare PURVIEW **2** : a conditional stipulation : RESERVATION ⟨expresses the belief only with a skeptical ~ —H.R.Finch⟩ **syn** see CONDITION

**pro·vi·sor** \prəˈvīzə(r)\ *n* -S [ME *provisour*, fr. AF, ML, & L; AF *provisour* ecclesiastical provisor, fr. ML *provisor* ecclesiastical provisor, guardian, administrator, fr. L, one that provides, fr. *provisus* (past part. of *providēre* to provide) + *-or* — more at PROVIDE] **1** : one having a provision esp. papal to a benefice not yet vacant — compare PROVISION 1a **2** : one having charge of getting provisions (as for an army or a religious house) : PURVEYOR, STEWARD **3** *obs* : one who provides (as care, protection, sustenance) : GUARDIAN **4** : a cleric acting as an assistant to or vicar for an archbishop or bishop : an ecclesiastical deputy

**pro·vi·so·ri·ly** \-zərəlē\ *adv* : in a provisory manner

**pro·vi·so·ry** \-zərē, -ri\ *adj* [F or ML; F *provisoire*, fr. ML *provisorius*, fr. L *provisus* (past part. of *providēre* to provide) + *-orius* -ory — more at PROVIDE] **1** : containing or subject to a proviso : CONDITIONAL ⟨a ~ clause⟩ **2** : PROVISIONAL 1 ⟨human institutions as ~ and precarious —Edmund Wilson⟩

**pro·vitamin** \(ˈ)prō+\ *n* [¹*pro-* + *vitamin*] : a precursor of a vitamin that can be converted into a vitamin in the organism ⟨ergosterol is a ~ of vitamin $D_2$⟩

**provitamin A** *n* : a provitamin of vitamin A; *esp* : CAROTENE

**provn** *abbr* provision

**pro·vo** \ˈprō(ˌ)vō\ *archaic var of* PROVOST

**provocateur** *n* [F (*agent*) *provocateur*] : AGENT PROVOCATEUR

**prov·o·ca·tion** \ˌprävəˈkāshən\ *n* -S [ME *provocacioun*, fr. MF *provocation*, fr. L *provocation-, provocatio*, fr. *provocatus* (past part. of *provocare* to call forth, provoke) + *-ion-, -io* -ion — more at PROVOKE] **1** : the act or process of provoking : STIMULATION, INCITEMENT ⟨~s to further thought about our own dilemmas —E.R.May⟩ ⟨ready to smash them to pieces on the slightest ~ —Havelock Ellis⟩ ⟨her every movement was a ~ —S.B.Kaiser⟩ **2 a** *archaic* : APPEAL; *esp* : an appeal to a higher court **b** : the right of a Roman citizen condemned in a criminal action to appeal to the Roman people or the emperor

**¹pro·voc·a·tive** \prəˈväkəd·iv, prōˈ-, -ət| *also* |əv\ *n* -S [ME, fr. MF *provocatif*, adj.] **1** *archaic* : something that arouses desire or appetite; *esp* : APHRODISIAC ⟨greedy after vicious ~s —S.T. Coleridge⟩ **2** : something that provokes : STIMULUS, INCENTIVE ⟨a ~ to mirth —A.D.White⟩ ⟨his society tends to supply few ~s —Abram Kardiner⟩ ⟨prove suitable . . . as a ~ for allergic tests —R.T.Leiper⟩

**²provocative** \"\ *adj* [F *provocatif*, fr. LL *provocativus* calling forth, eliciting, fr. L *provocatus* + *-ion-, -io* -ion] : serving or tending to provoke: as **a** : calling forth a desired feeling or action ⟨~ Irish tunes which . . . compel the hearers to dance —Anthony Trollope⟩ **b** : pleasantly stimulating : APPEALING, PIQUANT ⟨her features are ~ and lively —J.K.Newnham⟩ **c** : exciting sexual desire ⟨her gestures and postures became . . . more wanton and ~ —C.B.Nordhoff & J.N.Hall⟩ **d** : exciting irritation, resentment, or anger ⟨prepared for war without being ~ —*Atlantic*⟩ **e** : arousing curiosity or anticipation ⟨~ glimpses of characters —Carol Field⟩ **f** : stimulating discussion or controversy ⟨one of the most ~ . . . novels —*Saturday Rev.*⟩ ⟨toss a ~ political comment into the conversation —R.C.Doty⟩ — **pro·voc·a·tive·ly** \|əvlē, -li\ *adv* — **pro·voc·a·tive·ness** \|ivnəs\ *n* -ES

**pro·voc·a·to·ry** \-kəˌtōrē\ *adj* [L *provocatorius*, fr. *provocatus* + *-orius* -ory] : PROVOCATIVE

**pro·voke** \prəˈvōk, prōˈ-\ *vt* -ED/-ING/-S [ME *provoken*, fr. MF *provoquer*, fr. L *provocare*, fr. *pro-* forth + *vocare* to call — more at PRO-, VOCATION] **1 a** *archaic* : to stir to a desired feeling or action : move deeply : AROUSE ⟨your zeal hath *provoked* very many —2 Cor 9:2 (AV)⟩ **b** : to incite to anger : INCENSE ⟨enough to ~ a saint⟩ ⟨loved to . . . make his brakes screech just to ~ her —H.H.Reichard⟩ **2** *archaic* : SUMMON, EVOKE ⟨can honor's voice ~ the silent dust? —Thomas Gray⟩ **3 a** : to call forth (an emotion, action, activity) : bring on : EVOKE ⟨a device that *provoked* an unfailing roar of laughter —*Saturday Rev.*⟩ ⟨his candor *provoked* a storm of controversy —*Times Lit. Supp.*⟩ ⟨no area of school learning ~s as much concern —*Education Digest*⟩ **b** : to stir up on purpose : bring about deliberately ⟨had foreseen and even *provoked* this invasion —Francis Hackett⟩ ⟨did his best to ~ an argument —Lester Atwell⟩ **c** : to provide the needed stimulus for : call

into being ⟨*provoking* a vigorous development of logical studies —*Times Lit. Supp.*⟩ ⟨not merely anticipated the new methods but actually *provoked* them —Bryan Morgan⟩ **d :** to induce (a physical reaction) ⟨~ vomiting by tickling the throat⟩ ⟨the hit . . . may ~ the nucleus to eject a particle —G.W.Gray b. 1886⟩
**syn** EXCITE, STIMULATE, PIQUE, QUICKEN: PROVOKE may center attention on the fact of rousing to action or calling forth a response; often it implies little about cause, manner, or result, but is often used in connection with angry or vexed reactions ⟨his personal emotions, the emotions *provoked* by particular events in his life —T.S.Eliot⟩ ⟨to imagine the emotions and the actions of which she might *provoke* a man —B.A.Williams⟩ ⟨it was not until the end of October that Turkey, by bombarding Russian Black Sea ports, *provoked* the Allies into declaring war on her —C.E.Black & E.C.Helmreich⟩ EXCITE, sometimes close to provoke, may suggest a more active stirring up, moving profoundly, awakening lively interest, or rousing to marked activity ⟨feeling, which had drugged her until only half of her being was awake, had *excited* him into an unusual mental activity. He was animated, eager, weaving endless impracticable schemes —Ellen Glasgow⟩ ⟨they were interested and *excited* by this prophetic voice calling for a renaissance in American political life —Bruce Bliven b. 1889⟩ ⟨your letter as usual *excites* my envy at the description of your finds —O.W.Holmes †1935⟩ STIMULATE applies to the heightening of activity or the rousing of the dominant or quiescent by something that spurs or incites or overcomes whatever makes for inactivity ⟨increasing the supply of liquid assets in order to *stimulate* spending —W.M.Dacey⟩ ⟨extra iron may be supplied to *stimulate* the formation of red blood cells —Morris Fishbein⟩ ⟨his own thought was clarified by the impulse to coherent intelligibility which good teaching *stimulates* —M.R.Cohen⟩ PIQUE suggests provoking by mild irritation, slight, challenge, rebuff, or inciting curiosity or jealousy ⟨one's interest is *piqued* but not captured by the chronicle of this weak-willed man —*N.Y.Times*⟩ ⟨the contrast between the pair held puzzles that *piqued* the inquisitive —Arnold Bennett⟩ QUICKEN applies to a general vivifying, stimulating, or making active, often beneficially ⟨the sound of tuning strings combined with the hum of voices and the flutter of programs to *quicken* yet more the thrill of expectancy that ran down her veins —Clive Arden⟩ ⟨his response was *quickened* and deepened by his mystical temperament —*Times Lit. Supp.*⟩ ⟨with his feeling of history *quickened* and sharpened, he was to find another stimulus to follow up this interest —Van Wyck Brooks⟩ **syn** see in addition IRRITATE

**pro·vok·ing** *adj* **:** PROVOCATIVE; *esp* **:** EXASPERATING ⟨will find the lack of any index . . . ~ —L.S.Hall⟩ — **pro·vok·ing·ly** *adv*

**pro·vo·la** \ˈprōvələ\ *n* -S [It, prob. fr. ML *probula* cheese made from buffalo milk] **:** a small round flaky cheese made of plastic curd and hung in a net to cure

**pro·vo·lette** \ˌprōvəˈlet\ *n* -S [*provola* + *-ette*] **:** a small round or pear-shaped cheese of stringy texture hung in a net to cure

**pro·vo·lo·ne** \ˌprōvəˈlōnē\ *also* **provolone cheese** *n* -S [It *provolone*, aug. of *provola*] **:** an often pear-shaped cheese of stringy texture made of plastic curd, molded in various forms, and hung in a net to cure

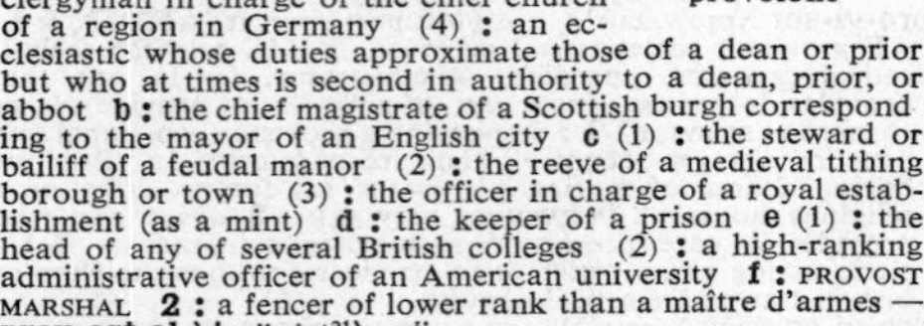
provolone

**pro·vost** \ˈprōˌvōst, ˈprävəst, ˈprōvəst, *esp as attributive* ˈprō(ˌ)vō\ *n* -S [ME *provost*, *provest*, partly fr. OE *prafost*, *profast*, *profost*, fr. ML *propositus*, alter. (influenced by L *propositus*, past part. of *proponere* to display, declare, propound) of ML *prepositus*, *praepositus* abbot, prior, provost & L *praepositus* director, chief, man in charge; partly fr. OF *provost*, fr. ML *propositus* — more at PROPOSE, PREPOSITUS] **1 :** a person appointed to superintend, preside over, or be the official head of (as an institution or corporate body): as **a** (1) **:** the head of a cathedral or collegiate chapter (2) **:** the head of a newly-constituted cathedral church (3) **:** a Protestant clergyman in charge of the chief church of a region in Germany (4) **:** an ecclesiastic whose duties approximate those of a dean or prior but who at times is second in authority to a dean, prior, or abbot **b :** the chief magistrate of a Scottish burgh corresponding to the mayor of an English city **c** (1) **:** the steward or bailiff of a feudal manor (2) **:** the reeve of a medieval tithing borough or town (3) **:** the officer in charge of a royal establishment (as a mint) **d :** the keeper of a prison **e** (1) **:** the head of any of several British colleges (2) **:** a high-ranking administrative officer of an American university **f :** PROVOST MARSHAL **2 :** a fencer of lower rank than a maître d'armes —

**prov·ost·al** \ˈprävəstᵊl\ *adj*

**provost court** *n* **:** a military court usu. for the trial of minor offenses and of limited jurisdiction within an occupied hostile territory

**provost guard** *n* **:** a police detail of soldiers under the authority of the provost marshal — compare MILITARY POLICE

**provost marshal** *n* **:** an officer who supervises the military police of a command esp. in keeping order among military personnel outside areas patrolled by an interior guard and who as a staff officer advises the commander on military police matters

**prov·ost·ry** \ˈprävəstrē\ *n* -ES [ME *provostrie*, fr. *provost*, *provest* provost + *-rie* -ry — more at PROVOST] **1 :** the office or authority of a provost of a cathedral or collegiate church **2 a :** an ecclesiastical foundation (as a cathedral or collegiate church) **b :** the revenue from such a foundation

**pro·vost·ship** *pronunc at* PROVOST + ˌship\ *n* **:** the office or jurisdiction of a provost (as of the provost of an ecclesiastical or educational college or of a Scottish burgh)

**1prow** \ˈprau̇\ *adj* -ER/-EST [ME, fr. MF *prou*, *preu*, like MF *prou*, *preu* profit, advantage fr. LL *prode* — more at PROUD] *archaic* **:** VALIANT, GALLANT ⟨the *~est* knight that ever field did fight —Edmund Spenser⟩

**2prow** \ˈ"\ *n* -S [MF, fr. OF *proe*, prob. fr. OIt (Genoese dial.) *prua*, fr. L *prora*, fr. Gk *prōira*; perh. akin to Gk *peran* to pass through — more at FARE] **1 :** the bow of a ship **:** STEM, BEAK ⟨stepped firmly to the boat's ~ —Charles Spielberger⟩ **2 :** a pointed projecting front part (as of a racing skate, airplane, chariot) ⟨turned the snowshoe sled so its ~ was headed down canyon —W.V.T.Clark⟩ ⟨other toques . . . have visor *~s* —Lois Long⟩

**3prow** \ˈ"\ *var of* PRAU

**prow·ess** \ˈprau̇əs\ *n* -ES [ME *prouesse*, *prowesse*, fr. OF *proece*, *proesse*, fr. *prod*, *prud*, *prou* good, capable, brave — more at PROUD] **1 :** distinguished bravery **:** GALLANTRY; *esp* **:** military valor and skill ⟨supposed warlike exploits . . . details of their imaginary ~ —J.G.Frazer⟩ **2 :** extraordinary ability **:** EXCELLENCE ⟨the politician's ~ in debate⟩ ⟨his ~ on the football field⟩ ⟨power derived from . . . technical ~ —Raymond Aron⟩ ⟨his ~ with a forty-five —Green Peyton⟩

**1prowl** \ˈprau̇l, *esp before pause or consonant* -au̇əl\ *vb* -ED/-ING/-S [ME *prollen*] *vi* **:** to move about or wander stealthily in the manner of a wild beast seeking prey **:** roam in search or as if in search of whatever may be found **:** pace restlessly back and forth ⟨submarines were *~ing* along our coast —Owen Wister⟩ ⟨the fear still *~s* in her consciousness —Ellen Glasgow⟩ ⟨the foreman . . . *~ing* constantly about —Theodore Dreiser⟩ ⟨*~s* as he talks —T.R.Ybarra⟩ ⟨loved to ~ about the city⟩ ~ *vt* **:** to roam over (an area) in a predatory manner ⟨wolves ~ the forest⟩ ⟨the bloodthirstiest villain that ever *~ed* the Western highways —Herbert Asbury⟩

**2prowl** \ˈ"\ *n* -S **:** an act or instance of prowling ⟨his jubilant ~ through . . . attics —C.G.Poore⟩ — often used in the phrase *on the prowl* ⟨a rapacious divorcee on the ~ —Helen Howe⟩

**prowl car** *n* **:** SQUAD CAR

**prowl·er** \-lə(r)\ *n* -S **:** one that prowls ⟨a ~ through junk shops —H.H.Martin⟩ ⟨car *~s* . . . agog for a pickup —*Harper's*⟩; *esp* **:** SNEAK THIEF ⟨*~s* made off with . . . men's clothing —*Edmonton (Alberta) Jour.*⟩

**prox** \ˈpräks\ *n* -ES [short for *proxy*] *NewEng* **:** BALLOT

**prox** *abbr* proximo

**prox·e·nete** \ˈpräksəˌnēt\ *also* **prox·e·net** \-net\ *n* -S [F or L; F *proxénète*, fr. L *proxeneta*, fr. Gk *proxenētēs*, fr. *proxenein* to do something for someone else, fr. *proxenos*] **:** a person who negotiates on another's behalf; *specif* **:** MARRIAGE BROKER

**prox·e·nus** \ˈpräksənəs\ *also* **prox·e·nos** \-ksəˌnäs\ *n, pl* **proxe·ni** \-ksəˌnī\ *also* **proxe·noi** \-ksəˌnoi\ [NL, fr. Gk *proxenos*, fr. *pro* before, for + *xenos* stranger, guest — more at FOR] **:** a citizen of a city state in ancient Greece appointed by another state to have charge of its interests and the welfare of its citizens while in his state

**proxied** *past of* PROXY

**proxies** *pl of* PROXY, *pres 3d sing of* PROXY

**prox·i·mad** \ˈpräksəˌmad\ *adv* [L *proximus* + E *-ad*] **:** PROXIMALLY

**prox·i·mal** \ˈpräksəməl\ *adj* [L *proximus* + E *-al*] **1 :** situated close to ⟨the magnetic compass . . . in ~ polar areas —*Scientific Monthly*⟩ **2 :** next to or nearest the point of attachment or origin, a point conceived of as central, or the point of view ⟨the ~ was . . . better than the peripheral stump for a graft —*Annual Rev. of Med.*⟩ ⟨more sediment is deposited on the ~ . . . slopes —P.H.Kuenen⟩; *esp* **:** located toward the center of the body ⟨the ~ end of a bone⟩ — opposed to *distal* **3 :** sensory rather than physical or social ⟨~ stimuli —D.W.Hamlyn⟩ — opposed to *distal*

**proximal convoluted tubule** *n* **:** the convoluted portion of the vertebrate nephron that lies between the Malpighian corpuscle and the loop of Heule, is made up of a single layer of cuboidal cells with striated borders, and is believed to be concerned esp. with the resorption of sugar, sodium and chloride ions, and water from the glomerular filtrate — see DISTAL CONVOLUTED TUBULE

**prox·i·mal·ly** \-məlē, -li\ *adv* **:** toward or near a proximal part or point

**prox·i·mate** \ˈpräksəmət, *usu* -əd.+V\ *adj* [L *proximatus*, past part. of *proximare* to come near, approach, fr. *proximus*, nearest, next, superl. of *prope* near — more at APPROACH] **1 a :** very near **:** immediately adjoining **:** CLOSE ⟨being . . . at the too ~ candle —J.W.Krutch⟩ ⟨a playwright so ~ to the century mark —Dan Laurence⟩ **b :** soon forthcoming **:** IMMINENT, NEXT ⟨news of his ~ arrival⟩ ⟨the ~ possibility of space travel —Pius Walsh⟩ ⟨on Tuesday ~ —George Meredith⟩ **2 :** next immediately preceding or following (as in a chain of causes or effects) ⟨an interest in ~, rather than ultimate, goals —Reinhold Niebuhr⟩ ⟨the ~ cause of their disaster —Elmer Davis⟩ ⟨one of the ~ effects will be to increase consumer spending —James Tobin⟩ — compare REMOTE, ULTIMATE **3 :** nearly accurate or correct **:** APPROXIMATE ⟨make a ~ estimate⟩ ⟨a ~ graduation scale —H.J.Wegrocki⟩ ⟨the figures . . . give at least a ~ explanation of price behavior —James Tobin⟩ **4 :** determined by proximate analysis as opposed to ultimate analysis ⟨~ composition⟩ **5** *of a grammatical form* **:** denoting the first of two third persons referred to in a context (as in the construction in some languages corresponding to "John caught sight of Albert and *he* [John] told him the news") — compare OBVIATIVE — **prox·i·mate·ly** *adv* — **prox·i·mate·ness** *n* -ES

**proximate analysis** *n* **:** quantitative analysis of a mixture (as food, coal) in which the percentage of components is determined

**proximate cause** *n* **:** a cause that directly or with no mediate agency produces an effect; *specif* **:** a cause arising out of a wrongdoer's negligence or conduct deemed under the rules of law applicable to the case and under the extent of his duty sufficient to hold him liable for the particular harm in fact resulting therefrom as distinguished from a remote cause or any supervening or concurring cause for which he is not deemed chargeable under those rules

**proximate matter** *n* **1 :** matter ready for the reception of a form — compare MATTER 3b **2 :** MATTER OF A SYLLOGISM 1

**proximate principles** *or* **proximate substances** *n pl* **:** compounds occurring naturally in animal and vegetable tissues and separable by analytical methods ⟨the *proximate principles* of food are proteins, fats, carbohydrates, mineral salts, and water⟩

**prox·ime** \ˈpräksəm\ *adj* [L *proximus* nearest, next — more at PROXIMATE] *archaic* **:** PROXIMATE

**prox·im·i·ty** \präkˈsimədē, -ətē, -i\ *n* -ES [MF *proximité*, fr. L *proximitat-*, *proximitas*, fr. *proximus* nearest, next + *-itat-*, *-itas* -ity — more at PROXIMATE] **:** the quality or state of being proximate, next, or very near (as in time, place, relationship) **:** immediate or close propinquity **:** NEARNESS ⟨research facilitated by ~ to a great library⟩ ⟨marriages in ~ of blood⟩

**proximity effect** *n* **:** the mutual effect of the currents in closely adjacent conductors (as the turns of a coil) producing an apparent increase in resistance esp. with high-frequency alternating current

**proximity fuze** *n* **:** an electronic device that detonates a projectile within effective range of the target by means of the radio waves sent out from a tiny radio set in the nose of the projectile and reflected back to the set from the target — called also *radio proximity fuze*, *variable time fuze*, *VT fuze*

**prox·i·mo** \ˈpräksəˌmō\ *adj* [L *proximo* (*mense*) in the next (month), fr. abl. sing. masc. of *proximus* nearest, next — more at PROXIMATE] **:** of or occurring in the next month after the present — abbr. *prox.* ⟨to be held on the 6th *prox.*⟩; compare INSTANT, ULTIMO

**proximo-** *comb form* [*proximal*] **:** proximal ⟨*proximo*buccal⟩ — opposed to *dist-*

**1proxy** \ˈpräksē, -si\ *n* -ES [ME *procusie*, *prokecye*, *proccy*, contr. of *procuracie* procuracy — more at PROCURACY] **1 :** the act or practice of a person serving (as in voting or marrying) as an authorized agent or substitute for another **:** the agency, function, or office of a deputy or procurator — used chiefly in the phrase *by proxy* ⟨vote by ~⟩ ⟨appear by ~⟩ ⟨marriage by ~⟩ **2 a :** authority or power to act for another **b :** a document giving such authorization; *specif* **:** a power of attorney given and signed by a stockholder authorizing a specified person or persons to vote corporate stock ⟨send *proxies* for the directors' meeting⟩ **3 a :** a person authorized to act for another **:** PROCURATOR **b :** something serving to replace another thing or substance **:** SUBSTITUTE ⟨books . . . were not *proxies* for experience —Frederick Mayer⟩ **4 :** PROCURATION 3 **5** *NewEng* **a :** BALLOT **b proxies** *pl* **:** ELECTION

**2proxy** \ˈ"\ *adj* **1 a :** taking the place of another ⟨a ~ mother of several large families —Booth Tarkington⟩ **b** *of a mineral* **:** occurring where another mineral would normally be expected **2 :** carried on by proxy ⟨~ voting⟩ or by solicitation and control of proxies ⟨a ~ war for control of a corporation⟩

**3proxy** \ˈ"\ *vi* -ED/-ING/-ES **:** to occur as a proxy mineral ⟨the gold . . . may ~ for iron ions in a growing pyrite crystal —*Economic Geology*⟩

**proxy marriage** *n* **:** a marriage that is celebrated in the absence of one of the contracting parties who however authorizes a proxy or substitute to represent him at the ceremony for the purpose of entering into marriage with the other and is valid in some, voidable in some, and void in other states of the U.S.

**pro·zone** \ˈprōˌzōn\ *n* [*pro-* + *zone*] **:** the portion of the range of concentration of antibody-antigen mixtures in which one of them although present in excess does not produce its characteristic effect (as agglutination or precipitation)

**prs** *abbr* present

**prsfdr** *abbr* press feeder

**prsmn** *abbr* pressman

**prtr** *abbr* printer

**PRU** *abbr* photographic reconnaisance unit

**1prude** \ˈprüd\ *n* -S [F, wise or good woman, prudish woman, short for *prudefemme* wise or good woman, fr. MF, alter. of *preudefemme*, fr. OF *prode femme*, fr. *prode* (fem. of *prod*, *prud*, *prou* good, capable, brave) + *femme* woman — more at PROUD, FEMME] **:** a person who is excessively or priggishly attentive to propriety or oversensitive to slight breaches of decorum ⟨not a book for *~s* —*Saturday Rev.*⟩ ⟨"you're *~s* . . . this and that can't be discussed before you" —Henry Green⟩; *esp* **:** a woman who shows or affects extreme modesty or reticence (as in speech, behavior, or dress) ⟨cold, heartless, a ~, he called her —Virginia Woolf⟩ ⟨a ~ . . . virtuously flies from the temptation of her desires —Ambrose Bierce⟩

**2prude** \ˈ"\ *adj* [F, back-formation fr. *prudefemme*] *archaic* **:** PRUDISH

**pru·dence** \ˈprüdᵊn(t)s\ *n* -S [ME, fr. MF, fr. L *prudentia*, alter. of *providentia* foresight, providence — more at PROVIDENCE] **:** the quality or state of being prudent: as **a :** wisdom shown in the exercise of reason, forethought, and self-control ⟨the blessed virtue of ~ —*Liturgical Arts*⟩ **b :** sagacity or shrewdness in the management of affairs (as of government or business) shown in the skillful selection, adaptation, and use of means to a desired end **:** DISCRETION ⟨acted with considerable ~ —W.M.Thackeray⟩ ⟨the hard ~ of statesmen —G.M. Trevelyan⟩ **c :** providence in the use of resources **:** ECONOMY, FRUGALITY ⟨wealth due to ~ during prosperous times⟩ ⟨the ~ and economic value of the extended coverage —J.V.Herd⟩ **d :** attentiveness to possible hazard or disadvantage **:** CIRCUMSPECTION, CAUTION ⟨~ not to go . . . unescorted —W.A. Swanberg⟩ ⟨conservative from ~ —T.S.Eliot⟩ ⟨~ dictated by self-regard —Felix Frankfurter⟩
**syn** PRUDENCE, PROVIDENCE, FORESIGHT, FORETHOUGHT, and DISCRETION can apply in common to a quality in a person that enables him to choose a sensible course, especially in managing his practical affairs. PRUDENCE, the most comprehensive, implies a habitual deliberateness, caution, and circumspection in action ⟨she had not *prudence* enough to hold her tongue before the servants —Jane Austen⟩ ⟨we can dream that the future will realize all our hopes, though *prudence* might suggest that as it is not yet born, it is too early to baptize it —W.R.Inge⟩ ⟨man is believed to show the highest degree of pecuniary *prudence*, scheming craftily to get the most for his money at every turn —C.E.Ayres⟩ PROVIDENCE implies thought for and provision in advance for the difficulties and needs of the future ⟨enough *providence* to save something out of one's pay for emergencies⟩ FORESIGHT stresses the ability to divine and prepare for what is going to happen ⟨not want of feeling so much as want of *foresight*. They will not look ahead. A famine ceasing, a rebellion crushed, they jog on as before —George Meredith⟩ ⟨it is essential to remember . . . that no man, whatever his diplomatic genius and *foresight*, can conceive the future —Hilaire Belloc⟩ FORETHOUGHT suggests due consideration for contingencies ⟨*forethought*, which involves doing unpleasant things now for the sake of pleasant things in the future —Bertrand Russell⟩ ⟨dry clothes . . . which . . . *forethought* had provided —B.A.Williams⟩ DISCRETION implies such qualities as good judgment, caution, and self-control that make for prudence or prudent action ⟨she administered her little patrimony and her savings with shrewd *discretion* and had enough put by for any number of rainy days that might occur —Gamaliel Bradford⟩ ⟨permitted her sympathy to outrun her *discretion*⟩ ⟨to administer public funds with fairness and *discretion*⟩

**pru·dent** \-ᵊnt\ *adj* [ME, fr. MF, fr. L *prudent-*, *prudens*, alter. of *provident-*, *providens*, pres. part. of *providēre* to foresee, provide — more at PROVIDE] **:** characterized by, arising from, or showing prudence: as **a :** marked by wisdom or judiciousness ⟨~ rulers⟩ ⟨~ laws⟩ ⟨the wise in heart shall be called ~ —Prov 16:21 (AV)⟩ ⟨a man . . . of notably liberal, ~, and humane views —*Times Lit. Supp.*⟩ **b :** shrewd in the management of practical affairs ⟨a ~ politician⟩ ⟨a ~ . . . businessman who never does anything except for a useful end —M.R. Cohen⟩ **c :** circumspect (as in conduct) **:** DISCREET, CAUTIOUS ⟨~ hesitation —Derek Patmore⟩ ⟨more ~ to hide than to fight —V.G.Heiser⟩ **d :** PROVIDENT, FRUGAL ⟨the ~ use and development of . . . resources —D.D.Eisenhower⟩ ⟨had been a ~ and thrifty wife —W.M.Thackeray⟩ **syn** see WISE

**1pru·den·tial** \prüˈdenchəl\ *adj* [L *prudentia* prudence + E *-al*] **1 :** of, relating to, or proceeding from prudence ⟨the use of ~ in addition to scientific judgment —David Easton⟩ ⟨code of ~ morality —*Saturday Rev.*⟩ ⟨the ~ timidity of their . . . representative —W.L.Sperry⟩ **2 :** exercising prudence **:** having administrative discretion esp. in business matters ⟨some churches turn over their business affairs to ~ committees⟩ —

**pru·den·tial·ly** \-chəlē, -li\ *adv*

**2prudential** \ˈ"\ *n* -S **1 :** a matter involving the exercise of administrative or financial discretion — usu. used in pl. ⟨the *~s* of the college⟩ **2** *archaic* **:** a prudential consideration — usu. used in pl. ⟨*~s* restrain him —Daniel Defoe⟩

**pru·den·tial·ism** \-chəˌlizəm\ *n* -S **:** a prudential philosophy or doctrine

**prudent investment** *n* **:** investment valuation esp. for rate-making purposes (as of a public utility) on the basis of original cost subject to adjustment for unwise investment decision as distinguished from cost of reproduction

**pru·dent·ly** *adv* [ME, fr. *prudent* + *-ly*] **:** in a prudent manner ⟨~ desisted in view of the damaging evidence —*Times Lit. Supp.*⟩ ⟨bear themselves ~ —E.C.Marchant⟩

**prudent man rule** *n* **:** a rule that gives a large measure of discretion to trustees in selecting investments for trust funds where the trust agreement calls for purchase of legal investments and that allows stocks to be purchased as well as bonds though in some states only up to a specified limit

**prud·ery** \ˈprüd(ə)rē, -ri\ *n* -ES [F *pruderie*, fr. *prude* prudish + *-erie* -ery — more at PRUDE] **:** the quality or state of being prudish **:** excessive or priggish modesty or decorousness **:** PRIMNESS ⟨sexual ~⟩ ⟨a ~ which wished to conceal the body —*Horizon*⟩

**prud·ish** \-dish, -dēsh\ *adj* [ˈprude + *-ish*] **:** marked by prudery **:** PRIM, PRIGGISH ⟨a very straight-laced, ~ girl⟩ ⟨is sexually not so much chaste as ~ —Virginia Woolf⟩ ⟨~ contemporary criticism —W.C.DeVane⟩ — **prud·ish·ly** *adv* —

**prud·ish·ness** *n* -ES

**pru·i·nate** \ˈprüəˌnāt\ *adj* [L *pruina* hoarfrost + E *-ate*] **:** PRUINOSE

**pru·i·nes·cence** \ˌprüəˈnesᵊn(t)s\ *n* -S [L *pruina* + E *-escence*] **:** the state of being pruinose; *also* **:** the dust or bloom causing this condition

**pru·i·nose** \ˈprüəˌnōs\ *adj* [L *pruinosus* covered with frost, fr. *pruina* hoarfrost + *-osus* -ose — more at FREEZE] **:** covered with whitish dust or bloom

**pru·i·nos·i·ty** \ˌprüəˈnäsədē\ *n* -ES **:** PRUINESCENCE

**pru·i·nous** \ˈprüənəs\ *adj* [L *pruinosus* covered with frost] **:** FROSTY, PRUINOSE

**pru·lau·ra·sin** \prüˈlȯrəsən\ *n* -S [ISV *prulauras-* (fr. NL *Prunus laurocerasus* cherry laurel) + *-in*] **:** a crystalline beta-glucoside $C_6H_5CH(CN)OC_6H_{11}O_5$ that is the chief active component of the leaves of the cherry laurel and is derived from glucose and racemic benzaldehyde cyanohydrin — compare AMYGDALIN

**pru·na·ce·ae** \prüˈnāsēˌē\ [NL, fr. *Prunus*, type genus + *-aceae*] *syn of* AMYGDALACEAE

**pru·nase** \ˈprüˌnās\ *n* -S [ISV *prunasin* + *-ase*] **:** an enzyme that accelerates the hydrolysis of prunasin, is found in yeast and in bitter almonds, and is one of two enzymes concerned in the hydrolysis of amygdalin

**pru·na·sin** \ˈprünəsən\ *n* -S [ISV *prunas-* (fr. NL *Prunus serotina* black cherry) + *-in*] **:** a crystalline beta-glucoside $C_6H_5CH(CN)OC_6H_{11}O_5$ found in various plants of the genus *Prunus* and obtained by partial hydrolysis of amygdalin by the enzyme prunase

**1prune** \ˈprün\ *n* -S [ME, fr. MF, fr. (assumed) VL *pruna*, fr. L, pl. of *prunum* plum — more at PLUM] **1 :** a plum that is capable of being dried or that has been dried without the development of fermentation even though the pit is not removed from the fruit and that when fresh is typically a moderate sized fruit with firm dark blue prunisne skin and a rather solid somewhat bland pulp **2 :** a variable color averaging a dark purple that is redder and duller than mulberry, mulberry purple, or plum and less strong and slightly redder than prune purple **3 :** a dull, unattractive, or stupid person

**2prune** \ˈ"\ *vt* -ED/-ING/-S [ME *proinen*, *preinen*, *prunen*] *archaic* **:** PREEN

**3prune** \ˈ"\ *vb* -ED/-ING/-S [ME *prouynen*, fr. MF *proignier*, *proognier*, prob. alter. of *provigner* to layer — more at PROVINE] *vt* **1 a :** to cut down or reduce (as a literary composition) by eliminating what is useless, burdensome, or superfluous ⟨~ an essay⟩ ⟨a severely *pruned* style⟩ ⟨*pruned* of its redundancies —Samuel Butler †1902⟩ **b :** to remove (something) as superfluous ⟨~ away all ornamentation⟩ **c :** to cut back or reduce (as a budget) **:** RETRENCH ⟨the drive to ~ appropriations —Gardner Patterson & J.N.Behrman⟩ **2 :** to lop or cut off the superfluous parts, branches, or shoots of (a plant) for better shaped or more fruitful growth **:** shape or smooth by trimming **:** TRIM ⟨*pruned* all the trees along the boulevard⟩ ⟨vines were *pruned* —*Experiment Station Record*⟩ **3 :** to cut off or cut out (as dead branches from a rosebush) — see ROOT-PRUNE ~ *vi* **:** to cut away what is superfluous or excessive ⟨selfishness plants best, *~s* best —R.W.Emerson⟩ ⟨the best time to ~⟩

**¹pru·nel·la** \prüˈnelə\ *n, cap* [NL, fr. *prunella, brunella* quincy, angina (trans. of G *bräune*, fr. *braun* brown), fr. ML *brunus* brown (fr. OHG *brūn*) + L *-ella*, dim. suffix; fr. the belief that herbs of this genus healed quinsy — more at BROWN] **:** a small genus of perennial largely Eurasian herbs (family Labiatae) having terminal spikes or heads of small purple or white flowers with the corolla tube inflated and its limb strongly 2-lipped — see SELF-HEAL

**²prunella** \"\ *also* **pru·nelle** \-el\ *n* -s [F *prunelle*, lit., sloe; fr. the dark color — more at PRUNELLE] **1 a :** a silk or woolen fabric formerly in use for gowns (as of clerics, scholars, barristers) **b :** a twilled woolen dress fabric **2 a :** a heavy woolen fabric used for the uppers of shoes **b prunellas** *pl* **:** a pair of shoes made of prunella

**³prunella** \"\ *n, cap* [NL] **:** a genus (the type of the family Prunellidae) of passerine birds that resemble thrushes and comprise the accentors — see HEDGE SPARROW

**pru·nelle** \prüˈnel\ *n* -s [F, sloe, wild plum, sloe-flavored brandy, dim. of *prune* plum, prune — more at PRUNE] **1 :** a small yellow dried plum packed without the skin **2 :** a sweet brown French liqueur having a grape brandy base and flavored chiefly with the sloe

**pru·nel·lo** \prüˈne(ˌ)lō\ *n* -s [modif. of It *prunella* small plum, dim. of *pruna* plum, fr. (assumed) VL — more at PRUNE] **:** PRUNELLE 1

**prune purple** *n* **:** a dark purple that is stronger and slightly bluer than average prune, redder and deeper than mulberry or plum, and redder and duller than mulberry purple — called also *loganberry*

**prun·er** \ˈprünə(r)\ *n* -s [³*prune* + *-er*] **:** one that prunes: as **a :** a worker employed to prune dead and excess branches from trees **b :** a tool for use in pruning operations **c :** any of several beetles whose larvae gnaw the branches of trees so as to cause them to fall; *esp* **:** OAK PRUNER

**prunes and prisms** *n pl* **:** affected, primly precise, or priggish speech or behavior ⟨go atiptoe and talk *prunes and prisms* —C.G.D.Roberts⟩ ⟨their *prunes and prisms* young daughters —Bruce Marshall⟩

**pru·ne·tin** \ˈprünəd·ən\ *n* -s [ISV *prunet-* (fr. NL *Prunus emarginata*) + *-in*] **:** a crystalline phenolic isoflavone $C_{15}H_7O_2(OH)_2OCH_3$ obtained by hydrolysis of prunitrin

**pru·ne·tol** \-üne,tōl, -tōl\ *n* -s [ISV *prunetin* + *-ol*] **:** GENISTEIN

**prune tree** *n* **:** a tree yielding fruits that are or are used for prunes

**prune worm** *n* **:** a larva of a phycitid moth (*Mineola scitulella*) that infests plum, prune, and other fruit trees

**¹pruning** *n* -s [fr. gerund of ³*prune*] **1 :** the act or process of one that prunes **2 :** something pruned off — usu. used in pl.

**²pruning** *adj* [fr. pres. part. of ³*prune*] **:** that prunes

**pruning hook** *n* **:** a pole or rod with curved blade attached for removing spent or superfluous bramble canes

**pruning knife** *n* **:** a knife resembling a common jackknife but having a curved or hooked blade

**pruning saw** *n* **:** a saw that has a usu. tapering straight or curved blade and either a closed or an open and sometimes folding handhold and that may or may not be attached to a pole

**pruning shears** *n pl* **:** shears with strong blades used in the light pruning of any kind of woody plant

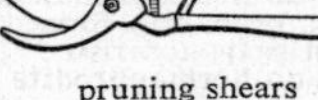
pruning shears

**pru·ni·trin** \ˈprünə·trən\ *n* -s [ISV *pruni* (fr. NL *prunus*, genus name of *prunus emarginata*) + *-trin* (as in *dextrin*)] **:** a crystalline glucoside $C_{22}H_{24}O_{11}$ found in the bitter cherry of western and in the chokecherry of eastern No. America that on hydrolysis yields glucose and prunetin

**prunt** \ˈprənt\ *n* -s [origin unknown] **:** a small glass ornament attached by fusing to a glass pattern (as on a vase)

**prunt·ed** \-təd\ *adj* **:** ornamented with prunts

**pru·nus** \ˈprünəs\ *n, cap* [NL, fr. L, plum tree, fr. Gk *proumnē*] **:** a genus of trees and shrubs (family Rosaceae) widely distributed in temperate regions that have usu. serrate leaves often with glands along the petiole or at the base of the blade and have flowers usu. in umbellate clusters or racemes which appear in spring and often before the leaves and are succeeded by a smooth globose fruit often with a bloom on its surface — see ALMOND, APRICOT, CHERRY, PEACH

**pru·ri·ence** \ˈprürēn(t)s, ˈprür-\ *n* -s **:** the quality or state of being prurient

**pru·ri·en·cy** \-ənsē, -si\ *n* -ES **:** PRURIENCE ⟨the ~ of curious ears —Edmund Burke⟩

**pru·ri·ent** \-nt\ *adj* [L *prurient-, pruriens*, pres. part. of *prurire* to itch, long for, be wanton; akin to L *pruna* glowing coal, Skt *ploṣati* he singes, burns, and prob. to L *pruina* hoarfrost — more at FREEZE] **1 a :** marked by restless craving **:** itching with curiosity ⟨the reading public . . . in its usual ~ longing after anything like personal gossip —Charles Kingsley⟩ **b :** having or easily susceptible to lascivious thoughts or desires ⟨titillated ~ people by its frank discussion of sexual experience⟩ **c :** tending to excite lasciviousness ⟨the japes about sex . . . being ~ rather than funny —John McCarten⟩ **2 :** exhibiting abnormally rapid or excessive growth ⟨pinching off the ~ bud —Nathaniel Paterson⟩ — **pru·ri·ent·ly** *adv*

**pru·rig·i·nous** \prüˈrijənəs\ *adj* [LL *pruriginosus*, fr. L *prurigin-, prurigo* + *-osus* -ous] **:** like or caused by prurigo **:** affected by prurigo **:** constituting prurigo

**pru·ri·go** \prüˈrī(ˌ)gō\ *n* -s [NL, fr. L, itching, itch, fr. *prurire* to itch — more at PRURIENT] **:** a chronic inflammatory skin disease marked by a general eruption of small itching papules

**pru·rit·ic** \prüˈrid·ik\ *adj* [*pruritus* + *-ic*] **:** relating to, marked by, or producing pruritus

**pru·ri·tus** \-rīd·əs\ *n* -ES [L, fr. *prurire* to itch] **:** localized or generalized itching due to irritation of sensory nerve endings from organic or psychogenic causes

**pru·si·a·no** \ˌprüsēˈä(ˌ)nō\ *n* -s [MexSp, fr. Sp, Prussian, fr. *Prusia* Prussia + *-ano* -an] **:** VARIED BUNTING

**prus·ik knot** \ˈprəsik-\ *n, usu cap P* [fr. the name *Prusik*] **:** a knot that is used in mountaineering for tying a small sling to a climbing rope as an aid to one who has fallen into a crevasse and that holds fast when weighted but is movable when unweighted

**prusik sling** *n, usu cap P* **:** a small movable sling fastened to a climbing rope by means of a Prusik knot

Prusik knot

**¹prus·sian** \ˈprəshən\ *adj, usu cap* [*Prussia*, region in northern Germany + E *-an*] **1 :** of, relating to, or characteristic of Prussia **2 :** of, relating to, or characteristic of the Prussians

**²prussian** \"\ *n* -s *cap* **:** a native or inhabitant of Prussia: **a :** one of a people once living in Prussia esp. in the old provinces of West and East Prussia and related to the Lithuanians **b :** a native or inhabitant of modern Prussia

**prussian blue** *n* [trans. of F *bleu de Prusse*] **1** *usu cap P* **a :** any of numerous iron blue pigments formerly regarded as ferric ferrocyanide; *esp* **:** one characterized by dark masstones and reddish tints — compare CHINESE BLUE 1a, TURNBULL'S BLUE **b :** a dark blue crystalline salt $Fe_4[Fe(CN)_6]_3.xH_2O$ obtained by precipitation from a solution of ferrocyanic acid or a ferrocyanide treated with a ferric salt and used as a test for ferric iron; ferric ferrocyanide **2** *often cap P* **:** any of the colors produced with Prussian blue, averaging a moderate to strong blue that is greener than orient — called also *Berlin blue, bronze blue, Brunswick blue, Chinese blue, Hortense blue, Milori blue, Paris blue, steel blue*

**prussian brown** *n* **1** *usu cap P* **:** an orange-brown iron oxide pigment obtained by calcining Prussian blue **2** *often cap P* **:** GOLD PHEASANT

**prussian carp** *n, usu cap P* **:** CRUCIAN CARP

**prus·sian·ism** \-shə,nizəm\ *n* -s *usu cap* **:** the ideas, practices, or policies (as the advocacy of militarism, ruthless discipline, and despotism) commonly held to be typically Prussian; *also* **:** allegiance to or partiality for such ideas, practices, or policies

**prus·sian·ize** \-nīz\ *vt* -ED/-ING/-S *often cap* **:** to make Prussian in character or principle (as in authoritarian control or rigid discipline) ⟨~ education⟩

**prussian knight** *n, usu cap P&K* **:** NOACHITE

**prussian red** *n, often cap P* **1 :** INDIAN RED 2a **2 :** COLCOTHAR 2

**prus·si·ate** \ˈprəs(h)ēət, -ē,āt\ *n* -s [F, fr. (*acide*) *prussique* prussic acid + *-ate*] **1 :** a salt of hydrocyanic acid **:** CYANIDE **2 a :** FERROCYANIDE **b :** FERRICYANIDE

**prussiate of potash** *n* **:** POTASSIUM CYANIDE

**prus·sic acid** \ˈprəsik-, -sēk-\ *n* [part trans. of F *acide prussique*, fr. *acide* acid + *prussique* prussic, fr. (*bleu de*) *Prusse* Prussian blue + *-ique* -ic] **:** HYDROCYANIC ACID

**pru·tah** *or* **pru·ta** \prüˈtä\ *n, pl* **pru·toth** *or* **pru·tot** \-tōt(h), -tōs\ [NHeb *pĕrūṭāh*, fr. Mishnaic Heb, lepton] **1 :** a monetary unit of the Republic of Israel equal to ¹⁄₁₀₀₀ of a pound — see MONEY table **2 :** a coin representing one prutah

**pruve** \ˈprüv\ *chiefly Scot var of* PROVE

**¹pry** \ˈprī\ *vi* **pried; pried; prying; pries** [ME *prien*] **:** to look closely or inquisitively **:** peer curiously **:** PEEP ⟨~ into every corner of the house⟩; *esp* **:** to make a searching or presumptuous inquiry or investigation ⟨no need to ~ for psychopathological causes —T.S.Eliot⟩ — usu. used with *into* ⟨~ into people's secrets —Virginia Woolf⟩ ⟨*pried* curiously into the meaning of nature —V.L.Parrington⟩

**²pry** \"\ *vt* **pried; pried; prying; pries** [back-formation (*prize* being taken as 3d sing. pres.) fr. ⁶*prize*] **1 :** to raise, move, or pull apart with a pry or lever **:** PRIZE ⟨~ up a floorboard⟩ ⟨~ the lid off a can⟩ ⟨~ away a large stone blocking the entrance⟩ ⟨~*ing* the heavy slabs apart⟩ **2 :** to extract, detach, or open with difficulty ⟨~ military information out of a prisoner⟩ ⟨deputies he was able to ~ away from the . . . leadership —Paul Johnson⟩ ⟨try to ~ loose that 10 percent on the . . . deal —Bennett Cerf⟩ ⟨have *pried* open enough pocketbooks —D.C.Morrill⟩

**³pry** \"\ *n* -ES [back-formation (*prize* being taken as pl.) fr. ⁶*prize*] **1 :** a tool (as a lever or crowbar) for prying or prizing; *esp* **:** one with a claw end for removing spikes **2 :** LEVERAGE

**pryer** *var of* PRIER

**prying** *adj* [fr. pres. part. of ¹*pry*] **:** inspecting closely or impertinently **:** officiously curious **:** PEEPING ⟨will not bare my soul to their shallow ~ eyes —Oscar Wilde⟩ ⟨adopt a ~, suspicious, inquisitorial attitude —*Orient Bk. World*⟩ **syn** see CURIOUS

**pry·ing·ly** *adv* **:** in a prying manner **:** INQUISITIVELY

**pry·ler** \ˈprīlə(r)\ *n* -s [origin unknown] **:** one who sweeps scale from bars and sheets in a sheet rolling mill

**prypole** \ˈ=,=\ *n* [²*pry* + *pole*] **:** a pole that forms the prop of a hoisting gin and stands facing the windlass

**pryt·a·ne·um** \,pritᵊnˈēəm\ *n* -s [L, fr. Gk *prytaneion*, fr. *prytaneia*] **:** a public building or hall in an ancient Greek city containing the state hearth and serving as the place of meeting and dining for the prytanes and sometimes of official hospitality for distinguished citizens and visitors

**pryt·a·nis** \ˈpritᵊnəs\ *n, pl* **pryt·a·nes** \-ᵊn,ēz\ [L, fr. Gk, ruler, lord, prytanis, of non-IE origin] **1 :** a member of a prytany **2 :** a chief official in various ancient Greek states (as Lycia, Miletus, or Rhodes) after the abolition of monarchies

**pryt·a·ny** \-ᵊnē\ *n* -ES [Gk *prytaneia*, fr. *prytanis* + *-eia* -y] **1 :** the presidential office of the Athenian senate held successively during the year by each of the ten sections into which the senate was divided **2 :** one of the ten divisions of the Athenian senate during its presidency **3 :** the period during which a section of the senate held the office of president

**przhe·val·ski's horse** *or* **prze·wal·ski's horse** *or* **pre·je·val·sky's horse** *or* **prje·val·sky's horse** \ˌpərzhəˈ|välzkēz-, ˈprezhə'|, (p)sheˈ|\ *n, usu cap P* [after Nikolai M. *Przhevalski* †1888 Russian soldier and explorer] **:** a wild horse (*Equus przewalskii*) of central Asia intermediate between the true horse and the ass and having a dun-colored coat with a brown mane, the lower half of the tail covered with long hairs, callosities on all four legs, and broad hoofs

**ps** *abbr* **1** pieces **2** pseudo **3** pseudonym

**PS** *abbr* **1** passenger steamer **2** permanent secretary **3** police sergeant **4** [L *postscriptum*] postscript **5** private secretary **6** privy seal **7** prompt side **8** public sale **9** public school **10** public stenographer

**p's** *or* **ps** *pl of* P

**psal·li·o·ta** \,salēˈōd·ə\ [NL, prob. fr. Gk *psallion* chain (perh. akin to Gk *psallein* to pull) + L *-ota* -ote] *syn of* AGARICUS

**psal·loid** *also* **psal·oid** \ˈsa,lȯid\ *adj* [NL *psalloides*, fr. Gk *psallein* to play upon a stringed instrument + L *-oides* -oid; fr. the lines on the fornix suggesting strings] **:** of, relating to, or constituting the fornix (sense 1c)

**¹psalm** \ˈsä|m, ˈsȧ| *also* |lm, *archaic* ˈsam\ *n* -s [ME *psalm, salm*, fr. OE *psealm, salm*, fr. LL *psalmus*, fr. Gk *psalmos* song sung to the harp, psalm (trans. of Heb. *mizmōr* song, psalm), fr. *psallein* to pull, twitch, play upon a stringed instrument; prob. akin to L *palpare* to caress — more at FEEL] **:** a sacred song, poem, or poetical composition used in the praise or worship of the Deity: as **a** *often cap* **:** one of the biblical hymns collected in the Book of Psalms **b** *often cap* **:** a modern metrical version of one of the biblical psalms used as a liturgical hymn in public worship

**²psalm** \"\ *vt* -ED/-ING/-S [ME *psalmen, salmen*, fr. *psalm, salm* psalm] **:** to sing or extol in psalms **:** pray over with psalms ~ *vi* **:** to sing psalms **:** HYMN ⟨walk in the fields, ~ with the birds —C.E.S.Wood⟩

**psalmbook** \ˈ=,=\ *n* [ME *salm boc*, fr. *salm* psalm + *boc* book, fr. OE *bōc* — more at BOOK] **1 :** a book consisting of a version of the Psalms **:** PSALTER **2 :** any book of sacred poems or songs for use in public worship

**psalm·ic** \-mik\ *adj* [*psalm* + *-ic*] **:** of, relating to, or like a psalm ⟨~ wails —Israel Zangwill⟩

**psalm·ist** \-məst\ *n* -s [LL *psalmista*, fr. LGk *psalmistēs*, fr. *psalmizein* to sing psalms, fr. Gk *psalmos* psalm + *-izein* -ize] **1 :** a writer or composer of sacred songs; *esp* **:** one of the authors of the Psalms **2 :** a precentor, cantor, or member of the lower ranks of the clergy who leads or sings the music in public worship (as in the Eastern Orthodox Church)

**psalm·is·ter** \-məstə(r)\ *n* -s [ME *psalmistre*, fr. MF, fr. LL *psalmista* psalmist + MF *-re* -er] **:** PSALMIST 2

**psalm·ist·ry** \-trē\ *n* -ES [*psalmist* + *-ry*] **:** use of psalms in devotion **:** PSALMODY

**psalm·less** \-mləs\ *adj* **:** unaccompanied by a psalm

**psalmo·di·al** \(ˈ)sä(l)ˈmōdēəl, (ˈ)sȧ(l)ˈm-, (ˈ)salˈm-\ *adj* [*psalmody* + *-ial*] **:** PSALMODIC

**psalmod·ic** \-ˈmädik\ *also* **psalmod·i·cal** \-dəkəl\ *adj* [*psalmody* + *-ic* or *-ical*] **:** of or relating to psalmody ⟨repetitive ~ plainsong —M.F.Bukofzer⟩

**psalmo·dist** \ˈ=,mədəst\ *n* -s **1 :** one versed in psalmody **2 :** one that composes psalms or sacred songs **:** PSALMIST

**psalmo·dize** \-,mə,dīz\ *vi* -ED/-ING/-S [ML *psalmodizare*, fr. LL *psalmodia* psalmody + *-izare* -ize] **:** to practice psalmody

**¹psalmo·dy** \-,mədē\ *n* -ES [ME *psalmodie*, fr. LL *psalmodia*, fr. LGk *psalmōidia*, fr. Gk, singing to the harp, fr. *psalmos* psalm + *ōidē* song, ode + *-ia* -y — more at ODE] **1 :** the act, practice, or art of singing psalms or sacred songs in worship **2 :** a collection of psalms (as for liturgical use)

**²psalmody** \"\ *vb* -ED/-ING/-ES [ME *psalmodien*, fr. *psalmodie* psalmody] *vt* **:** HYMN ~ *vi* **:** PSALMODIZE, HYMN

**psalm of ascents** *usu cap P&A* **:** SONG OF ASCENTS

**psalmograph** *n* [LL *psalmographus*, fr. LGk *psalmographos*, fr. Gk *psalmos* psalm + *-graphos* -grapher (fr. *graphein* to WRITE) — more at PSALM, CARVE] *obs* **:** PSALMIST 1

**psalmog·ra·phy** \sä(l)ˈmägrəfē, sȧ(l)ˈm-, salˈm-\ *n* -ES **:** the act or practice of writing psalms

**psalm singer** *n* **:** one holding that the Psalms and not hymns should be sung in worship

**psalm tone** *n* **:** a tone or melody in Gregorian chant used for the singing of the Psalms

**psalm tune** *n* **:** the melody to which a metrically arranged psalm is sung

**psaloid** *var of* PSALLOID

**psal·ter** \ˈsȯltə(r)\ *n* -s [ME *psalter, salter, sauter*, fr. OE & OF; OE *psaltere, saltere* & OF *psautier, sautier, psaltier*, fr. LL *psalterium*, fr. LGk *psaltērion*, fr. Gk, stringed instrument, psaltery, fr. *psallein* to play upon a stringed instrument — more at PSALM] **1 :** a translation or version of the Psalms ⟨an English ~⟩ ⟨a metrical ~⟩ **2 :** a book containing the Psalms separately printed or esp. arranged for liturgical or devotional use: as **a** *sometimes cap* **:** the Psalms as printed in the Book of Common Prayer **b** *sometimes cap* **:** the part of a breviary containing the Psalms set for each day of the week **3** *archaic* **:** PSALTERY **4 :** PSALTERIUM

**psal·ter·er** \-tərə(r)\ *n* -s [ME *sawtrer*, fr. *sautre* psaltery + *-er*] **:** a player on the psaltery

**psal·teri·al** \(ˈ)sȯlˈtirēəl, -ter-\ *adj* [NL *psalterium* + E *-al*] **:** of or relating to the psalterium

**psal·teri·on** \=ˈ=rēən, -ē,än\ *n* -s [Gk *psaltērion*] **:** PSALTERY

**psal·teri·um** \-ēəm\ *n, pl* **psal·teria** \-ēə\ [NL, fr. LL, psalter; fr. the resemblance of the folds to the pages of a book] **1 :** OMASUM **2 :** LYRA 2

**psal·tery** \ˈsȯltərē, -l·trē\ *also* **psal·try** \-l·trē\ *n* -ES [ME *psalterie, sautrie*, fr. MF *psalterie, sautere*, fr. L *psalterium*, fr. Gk *psaltērion*] **:** an ancient and medieval stringed musical instrument that consists of a soundboard over which a number of strings are stretched and that is played by plucking with or without a plectrum ⟨praise him with the ~ and harp —Ps 150:3 (AV)⟩

**psal·tress** \-l·trəs\ *n* -ES [*psalterer* + *-ess*] **:** a female psalterer

**psamm-** *or* **psammo-** *comb form* [Gk, fr. *psammos* — more at SAND] **:** sand ⟨*psammo*biotic⟩ ⟨*psammo*phile⟩

**psam·mite** \ˈsa,mīt\ *n* -s [F, fr. *psamm-* + *-ite*] **:** a rock composed of sandy particles **:** SANDSTONE — compare PELITE, PSEPHITE — **psam·mit·ic** \(ˈ)saˈmid·ik\ *adj*

**psam·mo·biotic** \ˈsa(,)mō+\ *adj* [*psamm-* + *-biotic*] **:** living or thriving in sandy areas or in the psammon

**¹psam·moch·a·rid** \(ˈ)saˈmäkərəd\ *adj* [NL *Psammocharidae*] **:** of or relating to the Pompilidae

**²psammocharid** \"\ *n* -s **:** a wasp of the family Pompilidae

**psam·mo·char·i·dae** \,saməˈkarə,dē\ [NL, fr. *Psammochares*, genus of wasps (fr. *psamm-* + Gk *chairein* to rejoice) + *-idae* — more at YEARN] *syn of* POMPILIDAE

**psam·mo·ma** \saˈmōmə\ *n, pl* **psammomas** \-ōməz\ *or* **psammoma·ta** \-ōməd·ə\ [NL, fr. *psamm-* + *-oma*] **:** a hard fibrous tumor of the meninges of the brain and spinal cord containing calcareous matter — **psam·moma·tous** \(ˈ)saˈmōməd·əs, -mäm-\ *adj*

**psam·mon** \ˈsa,män\ *n* -s [NL, fr. Gk *psammos* sand] **:** an ecological community consisting of the typically minute plants and animals that live in the water filling the interstices of sand adjacent to a body of fresh water; *also* **:** the habitat utilized

**psam·mo·phile** \ˈsamə,fīl\ *n* -s [ISV *psamm-* + *-phile*] **:** an organism that prefers or thrives in sandy soils or areas — **psam·moph·i·lous** \(ˈ)saˈmäfələs\ *adj*

**psam·mo·phis** \ˈsaməfəs\ *n, cap* [NL, fr. *psamm-* + *-ophis*] **:** a genus of No. African and Asiatic back-fanged snakes comprising the sand snakes

**psam·mo·phyte** \ˈsamə,fīt\ *n* -s [ISV *psamm-* + *-phyte*] **:** a plant thriving on or requiring sandy soil — **psam·mo·phyt·ic** \ˌ==ˈfid·ik\ *adj*

**psam·mo·sere** \ˈsamə,si(ə)r\ *n* [*psamm-* + *sere*] **:** a sere that originates in sand

**p's and q's** \ˌpēzᵊnˈkyüz\ *n pl* **:** something (as one's manners) about which one ought to be careful or circumspect **:** best behavior — usu. used with *mind* or *watch* ⟨exhorting the older democracies to mind their *p's and q's* —A.S.Bokhari⟩ ⟨just better watch his *p's and q's* when I get a six-gun of my own —Jean Stafford⟩ ⟨being on her *p's and q's* for two solid days was too much for her —Guy McCrone⟩

**psa·ro·ni·us** \səˈrōnēəs\ *n, cap* [NL, fr. L, a precious stone; fr. its speckled appearance when polished] **:** a genus of fossil ferns based on tree fern trunks with a vascular system that is a polycyclic dictyostele — see STARLING STONE

**PSC** *abbr* **1** *often not cap* per standard compass **2** public service commission

**pschent** \ˈ(p)skent\ *n* -s [Gk, fr. Egypt *p-skhent*, fr. *p* the + *skhent* double crown] **:** the headdress of the later Egyptian pharaohs formed of the two crowns worn by the respective pharaohs of Upper Egypt and Lower Egypt before the union of the country under one rule

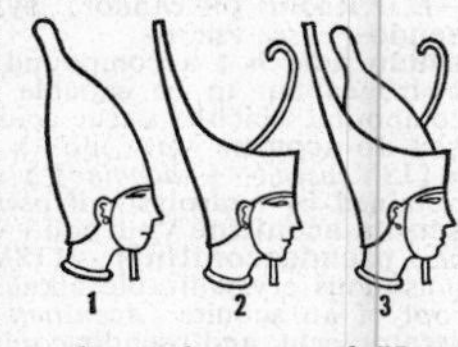

pschent: *1* crown of Upper Egypt, *2* crown of Lower Egypt, *3* double crown of Egypt

**psech·ri·dae** \ˈsekrə,dē\ *n pl, cap* [NL, fr. *Psechrus*, type genus (fr. Gk *psēchros* ground fine, fr. *psēchein* to rub down) + *-idae*; akin to Gk *psēn* to rub — more at SAND] **:** a family of chiefly Old World spiders

**pse·de·ra** \səˈdirə, ˈsedərə\ [NL] *syn of* PARTHENOCISSUS

**¹psel·a·phid** \ˈseləfəd\ *adj* [NL *Pselaphidae*] **:** of or relating to the Pselaphidae

**²pselaphid** \"\ *n* -s **:** a beetle of the family Pselaphidae

**pse·laph·i·dae** \səˈlafə,dē\ *n pl, cap* [NL, fr. *Pselaphus*, type genus + *-idae*] **:** a family of small beetles related to the rove beetles but with abdomen inflexible

**pse·laph·ognath** \səˈlafə(g),nath\ *n* -s [NL *Pselaphognatha*] **:** a millipede of the subclass Pselaphognatha

**psel·a·phog·na·tha** \,seləˈfägnəthə\ *n pl, cap* [NL, fr. *pselapho-* (fr. Gk *psēlaphan* to grope about) + *-gnatha*] **:** a small subclass of soft-bodied millipedes with tufts and rows of bristles — compare CHILOGNATHA, POLYXENUS

**psel·a·phog·na·thous** \ˌ==ˈfägnəthəs\ *adj* [NL *Pselaphognatha* + E *-ous*] **:** of or relating to the Pselaphognatha

**psel·a·phus** \ˈseləfəs\ *n, cap* [NL, fr. Gk *psēlaphan* to grope about, feel, touch; akin to Gk *psallein* to pull, twitch — more at PSALM] **:** a genus (the type of the family Pselaphidae) of small beetles

**pse·phism** \ˈsē,fizəm\ *also* **pse·phis·ma** \səˈfizmə\ *n, pl* **psephisms** \-,fizəmz\ *also* **psephismas** \-ˈfizməz\ *or* **psephis·ma·ta** \-ˈfizməd·ə\ [Gk *psēphisma*, fr. *psēphizein* to count, reckon, cast one's vote with a pebble, fr. *psēphos* pebble + *-izein* -ize — more at SAND] **:** a decree of an ancient popular assembly (as of the ecclesia of Athens)

**pse·phite** \ˈsē,fīt\ *n* -s [F *pséphite*, fr. *pséph-* (fr. Gk *psēphos* pebble) + *-ite*] **:** a coarse fragmental rock composed of rounded pebbles (as conglomerate) — compare PELITE, PSAMMITE — **pse·phit·ic** \sēˈfid·ik\ *adj*

**pse·pho·log·i·cal** \ˌsēfəˈläjəkəl\ *adj* **:** of or relating to psephology

**pse·phol·o·gist** \sēˈfäləjəst\ *n* -s **:** one who specializes in psephology

**pse·phol·o·gy** \-jē\ *n* -ES [Gk *psēphos* pebble + E *-logy*; fr. the use of pebbles by the ancient Greeks in voting] **:** the scientific study of elections

**pse·pho·man·cy** \ˈsēfə,man(t)sē\ *n* -ES [Gk *psēphos* pebble + E *-mancy*] **:** divination by pebbles

**pse·phu·rus** \səˈfyürəs\ *n, cap* [NL, fr. Gk *psēphos* pebble + NL *-urus*] **:** a genus of ganoid fishes of the larger rivers of China that includes solely the Chinese paddlefish (*P. gladius*), is closely related to the American genus *Polyodon*, and is distinguished by a narrow high snout and greatly developed clavicular fulcra

**pset·ta** \ˈsed·ə\ *n, cap* [NL, fr. Gk *psētta*, a flatfish; perh. akin to Gk *psēchein* to rub down] **:** a genus of large flatfishes including the European turbot

**¹pset·to·did** \ˈsed·ədəd\ *adj* [NL *Psettodidae*] **:** of or relating to the Psettodidae

**²psettodid** \"\ *n* -s **:** a flatfish of the family Psettodidae

**pset·tod·i·dae** \seˈtädə,dē\ *n pl, cap* [NL, fr. *Psettodes*, type genus (fr. Gk *psētta* flatfish + NL *-odes*) + *-idae*] **:** a small family (coextensive with the genus *Psettodes*) of tropical flatfishes that are in several respects intermediate between the more specialized flatfishes and the typical bony fishes

**pseud-** *or* **pseudo-** *comb form* [ME *pseudo-*, fr. LL *pseud-, pseudo-*, fr. Gk, fr. *pseudēs*, fr. *pseudein* to lie, cheat, falsify] **1 :** false: **a :** sham **:** feigned **:** fake ⟨*pseudo*dramatic⟩ ⟨*pseudo*serious⟩ **b :** counterfeit **:** spurious ⟨*pseudo*antique⟩ **c :** quack ⟨*pseudo*analyst⟩ **d :** fictitious ⟨*pseudo*biography⟩ **e :** unreal **:** illusory ⟨*pseudo*hallucination⟩ **2 a :** substance deceptively resembling (a specified thing) ⟨*pseudo*malachite⟩ **b :** temporary or substitute formation similar to (a specified thing) ⟨*pseudo*branchia⟩ ⟨*pseudo*podium⟩ **3 :** chemical compound resembling, isomeric with, or related to (a specified compound) ⟨*pseud*embryo⟩ ⟨*pseud*ovum⟩ **4 :** abnormal **:** aberrant ⟨*pseud*arthrosis⟩

**pseud** *abbr* pseudonym; pseudonymous
**pseudaconine** *var of* PSEUDOACONINE
**pseudaconitine** *var of* PSEUDOACONITINE
**pseu·da·le·tia** \ˌsüdəˈlēsh(ē)ə\ *n, cap* [NL, fr. *pseud-* + Gk *aletēs* grinder + NL *-ia*] : a genus of noctuid moths whose larvae are armyworms
**pseud·amphora** \(ˈ)süd+\ *n* [NL, fr. *pseud-* + *amphora*] : a Mycenaean vase with a spheroidal body, an arched handle at the top supported by a false neck, and a spout in the shoulder
**pseud·an·dry** \ˈsüˌdandrē\ *n* -ES [*pseud-* + *andr-* + *-y*] : use of a masculine name by a woman as a pseudonym — compare PSEUDOGYNY
**pseud·aposematic** \(ˌ)süd+\ *adj* [*pseud-* + *aposematic*] : imitating in coloration or form another animal having dangerous or disagreeable qualities
**pseud·apospory** \"+\ *n* [*pseud-* + *apospory*] : production of diploid spores by the sporophytes (as in ferns of the genus *Marsilea*) — compare APOSPORY

pseudamphora

**pseud·apostle** \ˌsüd+\ *n* [LL *pseudapostolus*, fr. Gk *pseudapostolos*, fr. *pseud-* + *apostolos* apostle — more at APOSTLE] : one falsely claiming to be an apostle
**pseud·arthrosis** \"+\ *also* **pseu·do·arthrosis** \ˌsü(ˌ)dō+\ *n* [NL, fr. *pseud-* + *arthrosis*] : the formation of a false joint (as by fibrous tissue between the ends of a fractured bone which has not perfectly united); *also* : a false joint or abnormal union between parts of bone
**pseud·atoll** \(ˌ)süd+\ *n* [*pseud-* + *atoll*] : an island or reef shaped like an atoll but not formed of true coral-reef limestone
**pseud·axis** \(ˈ)süd+\ *n* [NL, fr. *pseud-* + *axis*] : SYMPODIUM
**pseud·echis** \"+\ *n, cap* [NL, fr. *pseud-* + Gk *echis* viper — more at ECHIS] : a genus of large Australian elapid snakes including the semiaquatic black snake (*P. porphyriacus*)
**pseud·emys** \"+\ *n, cap* [NL, fr. *pseud-* + *Emys*] : a genus of turtles (family Testudinidae) comprising the sliders and including several species used for food in the southeastern U.S.
**pseud·epigraph** \"+\ *n* [NL *pseudepigrapha*] : one of the pseudepigrapha
**pseud·epig·ra·pha** \ˌsüdəˈpigrəfə\ *n pl, sometimes cap* [NL, fr. Gk, neut. pl. of *pseudepigraphos* falsely ascribed, with a false title, fr. *pseud-* + *epigraphein* to ascribe, inscribe — more at EPIGRAM] : spurious works purporting to emanate from biblical characters — compare ¹CANON 3a, APOCRYPHA
**pseud·epigraphic** \(ˌ)süd+\ *or* **pseud·epig·ra·phal** \ˌsüdəˈpigrəfəl\ *also* **pseud·epigraphical** \(ˌ)süd+\ *or* **pseud·epig·ra·phous** \ˌsüdəˈpigrəfəs\ *adj* [NL *pseudepigrapha* + E *-ic* or *-al* or *-ical*, or *-ous*] : of or relating to pseudepigraphy or pseudepigrapha : falsely or wrongly attributed
**pseud·epigraphy** \ˌsüd+\ *n* -ES [NL *pseudepigrapha* + E *-y*] : the ascription of false names of authors to works
**pseud·episcopacy** \"+\ *n* [alter. (influenced by *episcopacy*) of *pseudepiscopy*] : spurious episcopacy
**pseud·epis·co·py** \ˌsüdəˈpiskəpē\ *n* -ES [LGk *pseudepiskopos* false bishop (fr. Gk *pseud-* + *episkopos* bishop) + E *-y* — more at BISHOP] *archaic* : PSEUDEPISCOPACY ⟨a long usurpation and convicted ~ of prelates —John Milton⟩
**pseud·imago** \"+\ *n* [NL, fr. *pseud-* + *imago*] : SUBIMAGO
**pseu·do** \ˈsü(ˌ)dō\ *adj* [ME, fr. *pseudo-*] : SHAM, FEIGNED, SPURIOUS ⟨decorative ribbing of ~ wirework —*Univ. of Ariz. Record*⟩ ⟨the delicious and sometimes ~ rusticity of the eighteenth century —Christopher Morley⟩ ⟨distinction between true and ~ humanism —K.F.Reinhardt⟩ ⟨~ literary mannerisms —E.D.Radin⟩ ⟨~ candor⟩ **syn** see COUNTERFEIT
**pseudo-** — see PSEUD-
**pseudo acid** *n* : a compound believed not to contain acid hydrogen but to be capable of changing into an isomeric compound which is a true acid
**pseu·do·aconine** \ˌsü(ˌ)dō+\ *or* **pseud·aconine** \(ˈ)süd+\ *n* [ISV *pseud-* + *aconine*] : a crystalline base $C_{25}H_{41}NO_8$ obtained by hydrolysis of pseudoaconitine and indaconitine
**pseu·do·aconitine** \ˌsü(ˌ)dō+\ *or* **pseud·aconitine** \ˌsüd+\ *also* **pseudoaconitin** *n* -S [ISV *pseud-* + *aconitine*] : a very poisonous crystallizable alkaloid $C_{36}H_{51}NO_{12}$ found in the root of an aconite (*Aconitum ferox*) that yields acetic acid, veratric acid, and pseudoaconine on alkaline hydrolysis
**pseu·do·adiabatic** \ˌsü(ˌ)dō+\ *adj* [*pseud-* + *adiabatic*] : of or relating to processes whereby the temperature of a rising sample of saturated air as it undergoes volume or pressure variations changes without loss or gain of heat except that due to condensation of water vapor and all condensed material drops out as soon as formed — used of the cooling of rising air in which precipitation occurs
**pseu·do·aethalium** \"+\ *n* [NL, fr. *pseud-* + *aethalium*] : the densely clustered group of distinct sporangia in various myxomycetes
**pseu·do·allele** \"+\ *n* [*pseud-* + *allele*] : one of two or more closely linked genes that appear to act as a single member of an allelic pair — **pseu·do·allelic** \"+\ *adj* — **pseu·do·allelism** \"+\ *n*
**pseu·do·alum** \"+\ *n* [*pseud-* + *alum*] : any of various double sulphates of aluminum and a bivalent metal (as magnesium or zinc) that are not isomorphous with common alum
**pseu·do·aquatic** \"+\ *adj* [*pseud-* + *aquatic*] : growing in moist or wet places but not truly aquatic
**pseudoarthrosis** *var of* PSEUDARTHROSIS
**pseudo base** *n* : a compound that though not itself containing basic hydroxyl ion is capable of isomerizing into a true base that does contain hydroxyl ion
**pseu·do·benthonic** \ˌsü(ˌ)dō+\ *adj* [NL *pseudobenthos* + E *-on* (as in *plankton*) + *-ic*] : of, relating to, or being pseudobenthos
**pseu·do·benthos** \"+\ *n* [NL, fr. *pseud-* + *benthos*] : PSEUDOPLANKTON
**pseu·do·boleite** \"+\ *n* [F *pseudoboléite*, fr. *pseud-* + *boléite* boleite] : A hydrous basic chloride of lead and copper $Pb_5Cu_4Cl_{10}(OH)_8.2H_2O$
**pseu·do·branch** \ˈsüdōˌbraŋk\ *or* **pseu·do·bran·chia** \ˌ==ˈbraŋkēə\ *or* **pseu·do·bran·chi·um** \-ēəm\ *n, pl* **pseudobranchs** \-ks\ *or* **pseudobranchi·ae** \-kēˌē\ *or* **pseudobran·chia** \-kēə\ [*pseudobranch* fr. NL *pseudobranchia*; *pseudobranchia* fr. NL, fr. *pseud-* + ²*-branchia*; *pseudobranchium* fr. NL, fr. *pseudobranchia*] : an accessory or spurious gill (as on the inner surface of the operculum in various fishes) that is usu. small and is sometimes completely hidden beneath the epithelium — **pseu·do·bran·chi·al** \ˌ==ˈbraŋkēəl\ *or* **pseu·do·bran·chi·ate** \-ēət,-ēˌāt\ *adj*
**pseu·do·bran·chus** \ˌ==ˈbraŋkəs\ *n, cap* [NL, fr. *pseud-* + *-branchus* -branch] : a genus comprising amphibians closely related to the sirens but with thickened functionless gills and with only three toes on each foot and consisting of a single form (*P. striatus*) of Georgia and Florida that reaches a length of about 18 inches
**pseu·do·brookite** \ˌsü(ˌ)dō+\ *n* [G *pseudobrookit*, fr. *pseud-* + *brookit* brookite] : an iron titanium oxide $Fe_2TiO_5$ occurring in small brown or black orthorhombic crystals (sp. gr. 4.4–4.98)
**pseu·do·bulb** \ˈsüdō+ˌ-\ *n* [*pseud-* + *bulb*] : a solid bulbous enlargement of the stem (as found in many epiphytic orchids)
**pseu·do·bulbar** \ˌsü(ˌ)dō+\ *adj* [ISV *pseud-* + *bulbar*] : simulating that caused by lesions of the medulla oblongata
**pseu·do·bulbil** \ˌsü(ˌ)dō+\ *n* [*pseud-* + *bulbil*] : a pear-shaped oophytic outgrowth in various ferns replacing the sporangia and characterizing a phase of apospory
**pseu·do·bulbous** \"+\ *adj* [*pseudobulb* + *-ous*] : relating to or having a pseudobulb
**pseu·do·carbamide** \"+\ *n* [*pseud-* + *carbamide*] : PSEUDOUREA
**pseu·do·carp** \ˈsüdō+ˌ-\ *n* -S [*pseud-* + *-carp*] : ACCESSORY FRUIT — **pseu·do·car·pous** \ˌ==ˈkärpəs\ *adj*
**pseud·ocel·lus** \ˌsüd+\ *n, pl* **pseudocelli** [NL, fr. *pseud-* + *ocellus*] **1** : one of a pair of minute structures of unknown function on the head of a proturan **2** : one of the simple eyes of a larval insect
**pseu·do·cen·trous** \ˌsüdōˈsen·trəs\ *adj* [NL *pseudocentrum* + E *-ous*] : having a pseudocentrum
**pseu·do·centrum** \ˌ==(ˌ)=+\ *n, pl* **pseudocentra** [NL, fr. *pseud-* + *centrum*] : the body of a vertebra formed by fusion of the dorsal or dorsal and ventral arcualia (as in tailed amphibians)
**pseu·do·ceratite** \"+\ *n* [NL *Pseudoceratites*] : an ammonite of the group Pseudoceratites
**pseu·do·ceratites** \"+\ *n pl, cap* [NL, fr. *pseud-* + *Ceratites*] *in some classifications* : a group of Cretaceous ammonites with sutures similar to those of Ceratites — **pseu·do·ceratitic** \"+\ *adj*
**pseu·do·cercus** \"+\ *n* [NL, *pseud-* + *cercus*] : a process on the terminal segments of various insect larvae — called also *urogomphus*
**pseu·do·ceryl alcohol** \"+. . .-\ *n* [*pseud-* + *ceryl alcohol*] : CERYL ALCOHOL
**pseu·do·chromesthesia** \ˌsü(ˌ)dō+\ *n* [NL, fr. *pseud-* + *chromesthesia*] : association of sounds with certain colors; *specif* : the production of a colored visual sensation in response to certain sounds
**pseu·do·cilium** \"+\ *n* [NL, fr. *pseud-* + *cilium*] : one of two or four long hairlike immobile protoplasmic processes extending from the outer surface of each vegetative cell in various colonial algae (as of the genus *Tetraspora*) and often having a dense mucilaginous sheath that may extend beyond the envelope of the colony
**¹pseu·do·classic** *also* **pseu·do·classical** \"+\ *adj* [*pseud-* + *classic* or *classical*] : pretending to be or erroneously regarded as classic
**²pseudoclassic** \"+\ *n* : something (as a work of art) that is pseudoclassic
**pseu·do·classicism** \"+\ *n* [*pseud-* + *classicism*] : imitative representation of classicism in literature and art (as in the 18th century)
**pseudo-clementine** \"+\ *adj, usu cap P&C* [*pseud-* + *clementine*] : CLEMENTINE a
**pseu·do·coccidae** \"+\ *n pl, cap* [NL, fr. *Pseudococcus*, type genus + *-idae*] : a family of hemipterous insects (suborder Homoptera) comprising the mealybugs — see PSEUDOCOCCUS
**pseu·do·coccus** \"+\ *n, cap* [NL, fr. *pseud-* + *Coccus*] : a genus (type of the family Pseudococcidae) of mealybugs including several that are economically important — see CITROPHILUS MEALYBUG, CITRUS MEALYBUG, COMSTOCK MEALYBUG
**pseu·do·coel** *also* **pseu·do·cele** *or* **pseu·do·coele** \ˈsüdōˌsēl\ *or* **pseu·do·coelom** \ˌsü(ˌ)dō+\ *n* -S [*pseud-* + *-coel, -cele, -coele* or *coelom*] : a body cavity that is not the product of gastrulation and is not lined with a well-defined mesodermal membrane (as in rotifers and various worms) — compare COELOM — **pseu·do·coe·lic** \ˌ==ˈsēlik\ *adj*
**pseu·do·coelomata** \ˌsü(ˌ)dō+\ *n pl, cap* [NL, fr. *pseud-* + *Coelomata*] *in some classifications* : a group comprising lower invertebrates in which there is a body cavity that either lacks a mesodermal lining or has one derived from wandering mesenchymal cells, including rotifers, nematodes, bryozoans, and related forms, and being basically equivalent to Aschelminthes
**pseu·do·coelomate** \ˌsü(ˌ)dō+\ *adj* [*pseudocoelom* + *-ate*] : having a body cavity that is a pseudocoel ⟨~ animals⟩ — compare EUCOELOMATE
**pseu·do·conch** \ˈsüdō+ˌ-\ *n* -S [*pseud-* + *conch*] : an eminence found above and dorsal to the concha in crocodiles
**¹pseu·do·cone** \"+ˌ-\ *adj* [*pseud-* + *cone*] : being an insect eye in which the crystalline cone is formed by a vitreous secretion of the cone cells — compare EUCONE
**²pseudocone** \"\ *n* : a pseudocone eye
**pseu·do·conhydrine** \ˌsü(ˌ)dō+\ *n* [*pseud-* + *conhydrine*] : a poisonous crystalline alkaloid $C_8H_{17}NO$ that is found in hemlock and is isomeric with conhydrine which it closely resembles
**pseu·do·copulation** \"+\ *n* [*pseud-* + *copulation*] : close association of individuals of opposite sex for the bringing together (as in the amplexus of a frog) of the eggs and sperm without actual intromission
**pseu·do·cortex** \"+\ *n* [NL, fr. *pseud-* + *cortex*] : CORTEX 3c, 3d
**pseu·do·cotunnite** \"+\ *n* [It, fr. *pseud-* + *cotunnite*] : a mineral consisting of potassium lead chloride $K_2PbCl_4$(?) found in Vesuvian fumaroles after the volcanic eruptions of 1872 and 1906
**pseu·do·crystal** \"+\ *n* [ISV *pseud-* + *crystal*] : a solid body that looks crystalline even under a microscope but fails to produce a diffraction pattern indicating true crystallinity ⟨the carbon film . . . is made up of sharply oriented ~s —L.H.Germer⟩ — **pseu·do·crystalline** \"+\ *adj*
**pseu·do·cumene** \"+\ *n* [ISV *pseud-* + *cumene*] : a liquid hydrocarbon $C_6H_3(CH_3)_3$ isomeric with mesitylene and cumene that is found in coal tar and petroleum; 1,2,4-trimethyl-benzene
**pseu·do·cumidine** \"+\ *n* [ISV *pseud-* + *cumidine*] : a crystalline base $C_6H_2(CH_3)_3NH_2$ isomeric with cumidine; 2,4,5-trimethyl-aniline
**pseu·do·cumyl** \"+\ *n* [*pseud-* + *cumyl*] : any of three trimethyl-phenyl radicals $(CH_3)_3C_6H_2$ that are derived from cumene
**pseu·do·cyesis** \"+\ *n* [NL, fr. *pseud-* + *cyesis*] : a psychosomatic state marked by involuntary simulation of pregnancy and often accompanied by clear-cut physical symptoms (as cessation of menses, enlargement of the abdomen, and apparent fetal movements) and changes in endocrine balance of the same type as but less marked than those accompanying pregnancy — called also *false pregnancy*
**pseu·do·cyst** \ˈsüdō+ˌ-\ *n* [*pseud-* + *cyst*] **1** : a cluster of toxoplasms in an enucleate host cell **2** : CYSTOID 1
**pseu·do·deltidium** \ˌsü(ˌ)dō+\ *n* [NL, fr. *pseud-* + *deltidium*] : DELTIDIUM 1
**pseu·do·derm** \ˈsüdōˌdərm\ *n* -S [*pseud-* + *-derm*] : an outer covering in various sponges of the class Calcispongiae formed by outgrowth from the peripheral portions of the incurrent canals — **pseu·do·der·mic** \ˌ==ˈdərmik\ *adj*
**pseu·do·diphtheria bacillus** \ˌsü(ˌ)dō+. . .-\ *n* [*pseudodiphtheria* fr. NL, fr. *pseud-* + *diphtheria*] : a nonpathogenic bacterium (*Corynebacterium pseudodiphthericum*) that closely resembles the organism causing diphtheria but occurs in healthy throats
**pseu·do·dipteral** \ˌsü(ˌ)dō+\ *adj* [Gk *pseudodipteros* + E *-al*] : marked by columniation that is falsely or imperfectly dipteral in that the inner row of columns is omitted but the space for them is preserved — see COLUMNIATION illustration
**pseu·do·dipteros** \"+\ *n* [NL, fr. Gk, pseudodipteral, fr. *pseud-* + *dipteros* dipteral — more at DIPTERA] : a pseudodipteral building
**pseu·do·dominance** \"+\ *n* [*pseud-* + *dominance*] : appearance of a recessive phenotype in a heterozygote containing the dominant factor on one chromosome and a deficiency on the other — called also *mock-dominance*
**pseud·odont** \ˈsüdəˌdänt\ *adj* [*pseud-* + *-odont*] : having spurious or horny teeth ⟨monotremes are ~⟩
**¹pseu·do·dox** \-ˌäks\ *n* -ES [Gk *pseudodoxos* holding a false opinion, fr. *pseudodoxein* to hold a false opinion, fr. *pseud-* + *doxa* opinion — more at DOXOLOGY] : a false opinion or doctrine
**²pseudodox** \"\ *adj* : false esp. in opinion or doctrine
**pseu·do·doxy** \-sē\ *n* -ES [Gk *pseudodoxia* false opinion, fr. *pseudodoxein* to hold a false opinion + *-ia* -y] : an erroneous belief; *also* : the holding of erroneous beliefs ⟨a splendid list of contemporary *pseudodoxies*, mostly old-country beliefs —*Times Lit. Supp.*⟩
**pseu·do·ephedrine** \ˌsü(ˌ)dō+\ *n* [*pseud-* + *ephedrine*] : a poisonous crystalline alkaloid $C_{10}H_{15}NO$ occurring with ephedrine and isomeric with it
**pseu·do·farcy** \"+\ *n* [*pseud-* + *farcy*] : EPIZOOTIC LYMPHANGITIS
**pseu·do·fertilization** \"+\ *n* [*pseud-* + *fertilization*] : a process substituting for normal fertilization (as fusion of egg and polar body in various coccids or pseudogamy in a nematode)
**pseudo-foot-and-mouth disease** *n* : VESICULAR STOMATITIS
**pseudo-fowl pest** *n* : NEWCASTLE DISEASE
**pseu·do·galena** \ˌsü(ˌ)dō+\ *n* [NL, fr. *pseud-* + *galena*] : SPHALERITE
**pseu·do·gam·ic** \ˌsüdōˈgamik\ *adj* : of, relating to, or being pseudogamy
**pseu·dog·a·my** \süˈdägəmē\ *n* -ES [ISV *pseud-* + *-gamy*] **1** : activation of an egg by a sperm without accompanying nuclear fusion **2** : diploid parthenogenesis
**pseu·do·gastrula** \ˌsü(ˌ)dō+\ *n* [NL, fr. *pseud-* + *gastrula*] : AMPHIBLASTULA
**pseu·do·generic name** \"+. . .-\ *n* [*pseudogeneric* fr. *pseud-* + *generic*] : a designation used in the manner of a generic name but without taxonomic validity to group organisms too imperfectly known to permit valid classification ⟨*Sparganum, Tornaria, Cysticercus* are *pseudogeneric names*⟩ — compare FORM GENUS
**pseu·do·glanders** \"+\ *n pl but sing or pl in constr* [*pseud-* + *glanders*] : an infectious lymphangitis of horses and other equines caused by the bacterium (*Corynebacterium pseudotuberculosis*) responsible for caseous lymphadenitis of sheep, marked by ulcerating nodules of the lymph nodes of the legs, and readily mistaken for cutaneous glanders
**pseu·do·globulin** \"+\ *n* [ISV *pseud-* + *globulin*] : a simple protein insoluble in half-saturated ammonium sulfate or sodium sulfate solutions but soluble in pure water — distinguished from *euglobulin*
**pseu·do·glottis** \"+\ *n* [NL, fr. *pseud-* + *glottis*] : the space between the false vocal cords
**pseu·do·graph** \ˈsüdōˌgraf, -ˌräf\ *n* [LL *pseudographus*, fr. LGk *pseudographos* writer of falsehoods, fr. Gk *pseudographein* to write false statements, fr. *pseud-* + *graphein* to write — more at CARVE] : a false writing : a spurious document : FORGERY, PSEUDEPIGRAPH — **pseu·dog·ra·pher** \süˈdägrəfə(r)\ *n* -S
**pseu·dog·ra·phy** \süˈdägrəfē\ *n* -ES [*pseud-* + *-graphy*] *archaic* : incorrect writing or printing of words : wrong or bad spelling
**pseu·do·grasserie** \ˌsü(ˌ)dō+\ *n* [*pseud-* + *grasserie*] : a disease of the gypsy moth and other caterpillars thought to be due to a virus
**pseu·do·gry·phus** \ˌsüdōˈgrīfəs\ [NL, fr. *pseud-* + L *gryphus* griffin — more at GRIFFIN] *syn of* GYMNOGYPS
**pseu·do·gyne** \ˈsüdōˌjīn\ *n* -S [ISV *pseud-* + *-gyne*] **1** : an insect (as an aphid) that reproduces parthenogenetically **2** : an abnormal form of worker ant with a well-developed body approaching that of the fertile female esp. in the shape of the thorax — **pseu·dog·y·nous** \(ˈ)süˈdäjənəs\ *adj*
**pseu·dog·y·ny** \süˈdäjənē\ *n* -ES [*pseud-* + *-gyn* + *-y*] : use of a feminine name by a man as a pseudonym — compare PSEUDANDRY
**pseu·do·halide** \ˌsü(ˌ)dō+\ *n* [*pseud-* + *halide*] : a binary compound of a pseudohalogen analogous to a halide
**pseu·do·hallucination** \"+\ *n* [ISV *pseud-* + *hallucination*] : an externalized sensory image vivid enough to be a hallucination but recognized as unreal
**pseu·do·hallucinatory** \"+\ *adj* [*pseudohallucination* + *-ory*] : characterized by or tending to produce pseudohallucinations
**pseu·do·halogen** \"+\ *n* [ISV *pseud-* + *halogen*] : any of several radicals (as cyanogen and the cyanate, thiocyanate, and azide groups) that resemble halogens in reactions
**pseu·do·hemophilia** \"+\ *n* [NL, fr. *pseud-* + *hemophilia*] : a bleeding tendency occurring in both males and females marked by a prolonged bleeding time despite a normal number of blood platelets but often with an inability of injured capillaries to contract properly after minor injury — compare HEMOPHILIA
**pseu·do·hermaphrodism** \"+\ *n* [ISV *pseud-* + *hermaphrodism*; prob. orig. formed as F *pseudohermaphrodisme*] : PSEUDOHERMAPHRODITISM
**pseu·do·hermaphrodite** \"+\ *n* [ISV *pseud-* + *hermaphrodite*; prob. orig. formed in F] : an individual exhibiting pseudohermaphroditism
**pseu·do·hermaphroditic** \"+\ *adj* [*pseudohermaphrodite* + *-ic*] : relating to or exhibiting pseudohermaphroditism
**pseu·do·hermaphroditism** \"+\ *n* [ISV *pseud-* + *hermaphroditism*] : the condition of having the gonads of one sex and the external genitalia and other sex organs so variably developed that the sex of the individual is uncertain
**pseu·do·hexagonal** \"+\ *adj* [*pseud-* + *hexagonal*] *of a crystal or axis* : approximating in form to the hexagonal type
**pseu·do·hieroglyphic script** \"+. . .-\ *n* [*pseud-* + *hieroglyphic*] : a syllabic form of writing related to Egyptian hieroglyphics and used esp. at Byblos before 1500 B.C.
**pseu·do·hyoscyamine** \"+\ *n* [*pseud-* + *hyoscyamine*] : an alkaloid $C_{17}H_{23}NO_3$ obtained from the leaves of a corkwood (*Duboisia myoporoides*) and used as a sedative and antispasmodic like atropine
**pseu·do·hypertrophic** \"+\ *adj* [ISV *pseud-* + *hypertrophic*] : falsely hypertrophic : exhibiting increase in size without true hypertrophy — **pseu·do·hypertrophy** \"+\ *n*
**pseu·do·insoluble** \"+\ *adj* [*pseud-* + *insoluble*] : of, relating to, or constituting a substance that is not dissolved by the usual acid reagents but that is soluble in some specific solvent
**pseu·do·is** \ˈsüdəwəs, ˈsüˌdōis, süˈdōəs\ *n, cap* [*pseud-* + *ois* (perh. contr. of *Ovis*)] : a genus that comprises the bharal
**pseu·do·isatin** \ˌsü(ˌ)dō+\ *n* [*pseud-* + *isatin*] : the isomeric lactam form of isatin
**pseudo-isidorian** *or* **pseudo-isidorean** \"+\ *or* **pseudo-isidoran** \ˌ=(ˌ)=ˌizəˈdōrən\ *adj, often cap P & usu cap I* : of, relating to, or constituting a 9th century collection of decretals, decisions of councils, and letters consisting chiefly of forged documents held to have been compiled by St Isidore of Seville
**pseu·do·isochromatic plate** \ˌsü(ˌ)dō+. .-\ *n* [*pseudoisochromatic* fr. *pseud-* + *isochromatic*] : one of a set of colored plates that include some which appear isochromatic to individuals with color-vision abnormality and that are widely used as a test for color blindness — compare ISHIHARA TEST
**pseu·do·jervine** \ˌsü(ˌ)dō+\ *n* [*pseud-* + *jervine*] : a crystalline alkaloid $C_{29}H_{43}NO_7$ resembling jervine and occurring with it
**pseu·do·keratin** \"+\ *n* [ISV *pseud-* + *keratin*] : a protein (as neurokeratin) that occurs esp. in the skin and nerve sheaths and that like keratins is insoluble but is less resistant to enzyme action than keratins
**pseu·do·labial** \"+\ *adj* [NL *pseudolabium* + E *-al*] : simulating a lip : having or being a pseudolabium ⟨a ~ process⟩
**pseu·do·labium** \"+\ *n* [NL, fr. *pseud-* + *labium*] : a lip-like process esp. on a nematode worm
**pseu·do·lamellibranchia** \"+\ *n pl, cap* [NL, fr. *pseud-* + *Lamellibranchia*] *in some classifications* : an order of Lamellibranchia comprising bivalve mollusks (as scallops, pearl oysters, true oysters) having gills with interfilamentary and interlamellar junctions poorly developed, the mantle edges entirely open, and the anterior adductor muscle usu. wanting — **pseu·do·lamellibranchiate** \"+\ *adj*
**pseu·do·lamellibranchiata** \"+\ [NL, fr. *pseud-* + *Lamellibranchiata*] *syn of* PSEUDOLAMELLIBRANCHIA
**pseu·do·larix** \"+\ *n, cap* [NL, fr. *pseud-* + *Larix*] : a genus of Chinese coniferous deciduous trees (family Pinaceae) having the staminate flowers clustered and the cone scales deciduous — compare LARIX; see GOLDEN LARCH
**pseu·do·leucite** \"+\ *n* [ISV *pseud-* + *leucite*] : a mixture of orthoclase and nepheline pseudomorphic after leucite
**pseu·do·leukemia** \"+\ *n* [NL, fr. *pseud-* + *leukemia*] : any abnormal state (as Hodgkin's disease) resembling leukemia in its anatomical changes but lacking the changes in the circulating blood characteristic of the latter — **pseu·do·leukemic** \"+\ *adj*
**pseu·do·log·i·cal** \ˌsüdᵊlˈäjəkəl\ *adj* [*pseudology* + *-ical*] : fantastically or romantically falsified ⟨accounts of it are doubtless somewhat ~ —F.C.Prescott⟩
**pseu·dol·o·gist** \süˈdäləjəst\ *n* -S [Gk *pseudologistēs*, fr. *pseudologein* to speak falsely (fr. *pseudologos* speaking falsely) + *-istēs* -ist] : LIAR
**pseu·do·logue** \ˈsüdᵊlˌȯg *also* -ˌäg\ *n* -S [prob. fr. F, fr. Gk *pseudologos*] : a pathological liar
**pseu·dol·o·gy** \süˈdäləjē\ *n* -ES [Gk *pseudologia*, fr. *pseudologos* speaking falsely (fr. *pseud-* + *logos* speech) + *-ia* -y — more at LEGEND] : FALSEHOOD, LYING

**pseu·do·looper** \¦sü(ˌ)dō+\ *n* [*pseud-* + *looper*] **:** the caterpillar of a moth (*Plusia argentifera*) that damages tobacco and other plants in Australia

**pseu·do·lyn·chia** \ˌsüdō'liŋkēə\ *n, cap* [NL, fr. *pseud-* + *Lynchia*, genus of flies] **:** a genus of hippoboscid flies including the pigeon fly

**pseu·do·malachite** \¦sü(ˌ)dō+\ *n* [G *pseudomalachit*, fr. *pseud-* + *malachit* malachite] **:** a hydrous basic copper phosphate $Cu_5(PO_4)_2(OH)_4.H_2O$(?) resembling malachite — called also *dihydrite*

**pseu·do·man·cy** \'südəˌman(t)sē\ *n* -ES [LGk *pseudomanteia*, fr. *pseud-* + Gk *manteia* divination — more at -MANCY] **:** false or counterfeit divination — **pseu·do·man·tic** \¦==¦mantik\ *adj*

**pseu·do·mat** \'südō+ˌ-\ *adj* [*pseud-* + *mat*] *of a ceramic glaze* **:** having a mat surface because of incomplete fusion

**pseu·do·membrane** \¦sü(ˌ)dō+\ *n* [*pseud-* + *membrane*] **:** FALSE MEMBRANE — **pseu·do·membranous** \"+\ *adj*

**pseu·do·metameric** \"+\ *adj* [*pseudometamer*ism + *-ic*] **:** of, relating to, or exhibiting pseudometamerism ⟨a ~ worm⟩

**pseu·do·metamerism** *also* **pseu·do·metamery** \"+\ *n* [*pseud-* + *metamerism* or *metamery*] **:** false segmentation

**pseu·do·mix·is** \¦=(ˌ)=¦miksə̇s\ *n, pl* **pseudomix·es** \-k(ˌ)sēz\ [NL, fr. *pseud-* + *-mixis*] **:** pseudofertilization involving fusion of cells other than gametes and resulting in embryo formation

**pseu·dom·o·nad** \sü'däməˌnad\ *n* [NL *Pseudomonad-*, *Pseudomonas*] **:** PSEUDOMONAS 2

**pseu·dom·o·na·da·ce·ae** \süˌdämənə'dāsēˌē, ˌsüdəˌmänə'd-\ *n pl, cap* [NL, fr. *Pseudomonad-*, *Pseudomonas*, type genus + *-aceae*] **:** a large family of rod-shaped or somewhat spiral usu. aerobic and gram-negative bacteria (order Pseudomonadales) that do not form endospores, are commonly motile by polar flagella, and include saprophytes in soil and water and important plant and animal pathogens — see PSEUDOMONAS, XANTHOMONAS

**pseu·dom·o·na·da·les** \süˌdämənə'dā(ˌ)lēz, ˌsüdəmänə'd-\ *n pl, cap* [NL, fr. *Pseudomonad-*, *Pseudomonas* + *-ales*] **:** a large order of spherical, rod-shaped or spiral eubacteria which are usu. motile by polar flagella and some of which contain photosynthetic pigments — compare ATHIORHODACEAE, CAULOBACTERACEAE, NITROBACTERACEAE, PSEUDOMONADACEAE, SPIRILLACEAE, THIORHODACEAE

**pseu·dom·o·nas** \sü'dämənəs, -ˌnas\ *n* [NL, fr. *pseud-* + *-monas*] **1** *cap* **:** a genus (the type of the family Pseudomonadaceae) comprising short rod-shaped bacteria many of which produce greenish fluorescent water-soluble pigment and including saprophytes, a few animal pathogens, and numerous important plant pathogens — see XANTHOMONAS **2** *pl* **pseudo·mon·a·des** \ˌsüdə'mänəˌdēz\ **:** any bacterium of the genus *Pseudomonas*

**pseu·do·monocotyledonous** \¦sü(ˌ)dō+\ *adj* [*pseud-* + *monocotyledonous*] **:** having the two cotyledons coalesced or one of them aborted — used of a normally dicotyledonous embryo

**pseu·do·monotropy** \"+\ *n* [*pseud-* + *monotropy*] **:** monotropy in which the transition point lies below the melting points of the two forms

[1]**pseu·do·morph** \'südəˌmȯrf\ *n* -S [prob. fr. F *pseudomorphe*, fr. *pseud-* + *-morphe* -morph] **1 :** a mineral (as a piece of quartz) having the characteristic outward form of another species (as the cubic form of fluorite) or of some object (as a shell) ⟨limonite occurs as a ~ after pyrite⟩ ⟨unidentified trunks are preserved as ~*s* —G.W.Sinclair⟩ **2 :** something formed in the manner of a pseudomorph ⟨the concept of the cultural ~ —Lewis Mumford⟩

[2]**pseudomorph** \"\ *vt* -ED/-ING/-S **:** PSEUDOMORPHOSE ⟨glauberite ~*ed* to selenite —*Ward's Natural Science Bull.*⟩

**pseu·do·morphine** \¦sü(ˌ)dō+\ *n* [ISV *pseud-* + *morphine*; orig. formed in F] **:** a nonpoisonous crystalline alkaloid $C_{34}H_{36}N_2O_6$ obtained from opium and by oxidation of morphine

**pseu·do·mor·phism** \¦südə¦mȯrˌfizəm\ *n* -S [prob. fr. F *pseudomorphisme*, fr. *pseudomorphe* pseudomorph + *-isme* -ism] **:** the property of crystallizing as a pseudomorph

**pseu·do·mor·phose** \¦==¦mȯrˌfōz, -ōs\ *vt* -ED/-ING/-S [F *pseudomorphose*, n., mineral form resulting from pseudomorphosis, fr. *pseudomorphe* + *-ose* -osis] **:** to transform into a pseudomorph

**pseu·do·mor·pho·sis** \ˌsüdə'mȯrfəsə̇s, -ˌmȯr'fōs-\ *n, pl* **pseudomorpho·ses** \-ōˌsēz\ [NL, fr. ISV *pseudomorph* + *-osis*] **:** transformation into a pseudomorph

**pseu·do·mor·phous** \¦==¦mȯrfəs\ *or* **pseu·do·mor·phic** \-fik\ [*pseudomorphous*, fr. *pseud-* + *morph-* + *-ous*; *pseudomorphic* prob. fr. F *pseudomorphique*, fr. *pseud-* + Gk *morphē* form + F *-ique* -ic — more at FORM] **:** of, relating to, or being a pseudomorph **:** exhibiting pseudomorphism

**pseu·do·mycelial** \"+\ *adj* [NL *pseudomycel*ium + E *-al*] **:** of, relating to, or producing pseudomycelium

**pseu·do·mycelium** \"+\ *n* [NL, fr. *pseud-* + *mycelium*] **:** a cellular association occurring in various higher bacteria and yeasts in which cells cling together in chains resembling small true mycelia

**pseu·do·myr·mex** \ˌsüdō'mərˌmeks\ *n, cap* [NL, fr. *pseud-* + Gk *myrmēx* ant] **:** a neotropical genus of ants

**pseu·do·neuroma** \¦sü(ˌ)dō+\ *n* [NL, fr. *pseud-* + *neuroma*] **:** NEUROMA 2

**pseu·do·neuropter** \¦sü(ˌ)dō+\ *n* -S [NL *Pseudoneuroptera*] **:** an insect of the division Pseudoneuroptera

**pseu·do·neuroptera** \"+\ *n pl, cap* [NL, fr. *pseud-* + *Neuroptera*] *in some esp former classifications* **:** a division of insects having reticulate wings like those of the Neuroptera among which they have sometimes been included but undergoing an incomplete metamorphosis and including the dragonflies, mayflies, termites, psocids and book lice, bird lice, caddis flies, scorpion flies, stone flies, and others that are now placed in separate orders — **pseu·do·neuropteran** \"+\ *adj or n* — **pseu·do·neuropterous** \"+\ *adj*

**pseu·do·ni·trole** \¦==¦nī·ˌtrōl\ *n* -S [G *pseudonitrole*, fr. *pseud-* + *nitr-* + *-ole*] **:** any of a class of compounds of the general formula $RR'C(NO)NO_2$ formed by the action of nitrous acid on a disubstituted nitromethane $RR'CHNO_2$ as pungent-odored, colorless, solid dimers that when fused or dissolved depolymerize into the monomers of intense and characteristic blue color — compare NITROLIC ACID

**pseu·do·nitrosite** \¦sü(ˌ)dō+\ *n* [*pseud-* + *nitrosite*] **:** any of a class of compounds isomeric with nitrosites and characterized by the grouping $-C(NO)C(NO_2)$

**pseu·do·nucleolus** \"+\ *n* [NL, fr. *pseud-* + *nucleolus*] **:** KARYOSOME

**pseud·onychium** \¦süd+\ *n, pl* **pseudonychia** [NL, fr. *pseud-* + *-onychium*] **:** PARONYCHIUM

**pseu·do·nym** *also* **pseu·do·nyme** \'südᵊnˌim\ *n* -S [F *pseudonyme*, fr. Gk *pseudōnymos* falsely named, fr. *pseud-* + *onyma*, *onoma* name — more at NAME] **:** a fictitious name assumed (as by an author) for the time **:** PEN NAME

**pseu·do·nym·i·ty** \ˌsüdᵊn'imədˌē, -mətē, -i\ *n* -ES [*pseudonym* + *-ity*] **:** the use (as by an author) of a pseudonym; *also* **:** the fact or state of being signed (as of a book or other writing) with a pseudonym

**pseu·don·y·mous** \(')sü¦dänəməs\ *also* **pseu·do·nym·ic** \¦südᵊn¦imik\ *adj* [*pseudonymous* fr. Gk *pseudōnymos*; *pseudonymic* fr. F *pseudonyme* + E *-ic*] **:** bearing or using a false or fictitious name **:** identified by a pseudonym ⟨a ~ work⟩ ⟨a ~ author⟩; *also* **:** being a pseudonym — **pseu·don·y·mous·ly** *adv* — **pseu·don·y·mous·ness** *n* -ES

**pseu·do·paralysis** \¦sü(ˌ)dō+\ *n* [NL, fr. *pseud-* + *paralysis*] **:** apparent lack or loss of muscular power (as that produced by pain) unattended by paralysis

**pseu·do·parasite** \"+\ *n* [ISV *pseud-* + *parasite*] **:** something (as a normally free-living organism, a spore, or a bit of food debris) that appears in a specimen (as of blood or feces) and is mistaken for a parasite — **pseu·do·parasitic** \"+\ *adj*

**pseu·do·parenchyma** \"+\ *n* [NL, fr. *pseud-* + *parenchyma*] **:** a tissuey aggregation of compactly interwoven short-celled filaments in a thallophyte that somewhat resembles the parenchyma of higher plants — compare PLECTENCHYMA — **pseu·do·parenchymatous** \"+\ *adj*

**pseu·do·pelletierine** \"+\ *n* [ISV *pseud-* + *pelletierine*] **:** a crystalline bicyclic alkaloid $C_9H_{15}NO$ found with pelletierine

**pseud·opercular** *or* **pseud·operculate** \¦süd+\ *adj* [NL *pseudopercul*um + E *-ar* or *-ate*] **:** of or relating to a pseudoperculum

**pseud·operculum** \"+\ *n* [NL, fr. *pseud-* + *operculum*] **:** EPIPHRAGM 1

**pseu·do·perianth** \¦sü(ˌ)dō+\ *n* [*pseud-* + *perianth*] **:** a thin cuplike or saclike protective envelope one cell thick that develops after fertilization around the archegonium in some liverworts

**pseu·do·peridium** \"+\ *n* [NL, fr. *pseud-* + *peridium*] **:** a membranous cup enclosing the aeciospores in various rust fungi

**pseu·do·peripteral** \"+\ *adj* [*pseud-* + *peripteral*] **:** marked by columniation that is falsely or imperfectly peripteral with the lateral or lateral and rear columns engaged — compare PERISTYLAR; see COLUMNIATION illustration

**pseu·do·peziza** \"+\ *n, cap* [NL, fr. *pseud-* + *Peziza*] **:** a genus of fungi (family Mollisiaceae) having smooth waxy ascocarps and thin-walled asci that bear hyaline unicellular spores, containing one form (*P. medicaginis*) that causes a leaf spot of alfalfa and another (*P. ribis*) that causes anthracnose of currants, and including some species that were formerly included in the form genera *Colletotrichum*, *Gloeosporium*, and *Marssonina*

**pseu·do·phyl·lid·ea** \ˌsü(ˌ)dōfə̇'lidēə\ *n pl, cap* [NL, fr. *pseud-* + *phyll-* + *-idea*] **:** an order of Cestoda comprising tapeworms with two sucking grooves on the unarmed scolex and the vitelline glands scattered throughout the parenchyma and including numerous parasites of fish-eating vertebrates (as the medically important fish tapeworm of man) — **pseu·do·phyl·lid·e·an** \¦=(ˌ)==¦=dēən\ *adj or n*

**pseudo–pindaric ode** \¦sü(ˌ)dō+. . .-\ *n, usu cap 2d P* **:** IRREGULAR ODE

**pseu·do·pionnotes** \¦sü(ˌ)dō+\ *n pl but sing or pl in constr* [NL, fr. *pseud-* + *pionnotes*] **:** pionnotes that are buttery instead of gelatinous

**pseu·do·placenta** \"+\ *n* [NL, fr. *pseud-* + *placenta*] **:** a membranous organ occurring in a few insects and functioning as a placenta — **pseu·do·placental** \"+\ *adj*

**pseu·do·plague** \'südō+ˌ-\ *n* [*pseud-* + *plague*] **:** NEWCASTLE DISEASE

**pseu·do·plankton** \¦sü(ˌ)dō+\ *n* [NL, fr. *pseud-* + *plankton*] **:** organisms (as bryozoans, barnacles, corals, or corallines) that attach themselves to floating vegetation or debris and are thus effectively a part of the plankton — **pseu·do·planktonic** \"+\ *adj*

**pseu·do·plasm** \'südōˌplazəm\ *n* [ISV *pseud-* + *plasm*; prob. orig. formed in G] **:** an apparent neoplasm that disappears spontaneously **:** PHANTOM TUMOR

**pseu·do·plasmodium** \¦sü(ˌ)dō+\ *n* [NL, fr. *pseud-* + *plasmodium*] **:** an aggregation of myxamoebas resembling a plasmodium but without protoplasmic fusion (as in members of the genus *Acrasia*)

**pseu·do·plastic** \"+\ *adj* [*pseud-* + *plastic*] **1 :** lacking the capacity for major modification or evolutionary differentiation — compare EURYPLASTIC, STENOPLASTIC **2 :** characterized by or being flow in which the rate of flow (as of solutions of rubber or gelatinous substances) increases faster than normally in relation to the shearing stress — **pseu·do·plasticity** \"+\ *n*

**pseu·do·pod** \'südəˌpäd\ *also* **pseu·do·pode** \-pōd\ *n* [in sense 1, fr. NL *pseudopodium*; in other senses, fr. *pseud-* + *-pod*, *-pode*] **1** *also* **pseudopode :** PSEUDOPODIUM **2 :** a supposed or apparent psychic projection (as from a medium's body) **3 :** something resembling a pseudopodium: as **a :** a slender extension from the edge of a wheal at the site of injection of an allergen **b :** one of the slender processes of some tumor cells extending out from the main mass of a tumor **4 :** the paired unsegmented abdominal legs of caterpillars and sawfly larvae

**pseu·dop·o·dal** \(')sü¦däpədᵊl\ *or* **pseu·do·po·di·al** \¦südə¦pōdēəl\ *adj* **:** of, relating to, or resembling a pseudopod or pseudopodium

**pseu·do·pod·ic** \¦südə¦pädik\ *adj* [ISV *pseudopod* + *-ic*] **:** PSEUDOPODAL

**pseu·do·po·di·um** \ˌsüdə'pōdēəm\ *n, pl* **pseudopo·dia** \-ēə\ [NL, fr. *pseud-* + *-podium*] **1 a :** a temporary protrusion or retractile process of the protoplasm of a cell (as a unicellular organism or a leukocyte of a higher organism) often having a fairly definite filamentous form, sometimes fusing with others to form a network, and serving esp. as an organ of locomotion or for taking up food — see AXOPODIUM, FILOPODIUM, LOBOPODIUM, MYXOPODIUM **b :** one of the amoeboid protrusions of an active myxomycete plasmodium **2 :** a slender leafless branch of the gametophyte in various mosses that often bears gemmae **3 :** the foot of a rotifer

**pseu·do·pore** \'südəˌpō(ə)r\ *n* [ISV *pseud-* (in *pseudoderm*) + *pore*; prob. orig. formed in F] **:** a pore in the pseudoderm of a sponge

**pseu·do·porphyritic** \¦sü(ˌ)dō+\ *adj* [*pseud-* + *porphyritic*] *of a rock* **:** having a porphyritic appearance caused by the more rapid growth of various crystals but not being a true porphyry

**pseu·do·pregnancy** \"+\ *n* [*pseud-* + *pregnancy*] **1 :** PSEUDOCYESIS **2 :** an anestrous state resembling pregnancy that occurs in various mammals (as the dog, ferret, rabbit) usu. following an infertile copulation — compare CLOUDBURST 3, PSEUDOCYESIS — **pseu·do·pregnant** \"+\ *adj*

**pseu·do·proposition** \"+\ *n* [*pseud-* + *proposition*] **:** PSEUDOSTATEMENT

**pseu·do·prostyle** \"+\ *adj* [*pseud-* + *prostyle*] **:** marked by columniation that is falsely or imperfectly prostyle with the portico columns less than an intercolumniation from the front wall or engaged in it

**pseud·optics** \(')süd+\ *n pl but usu sing in constr* [*pseud-* + *optics*] **:** the study of optical illusions

**pseu·do·pupa** \¦sü(ˌ)dō+\ *n* [NL, fr. *pseud-* + *pupa*] **:** resting stage that intervenes in any of various insects between two of the larval stages of hypermetamorphosis; *also* **:** an individual in this stage — **pseu·do·pupal** \"+\ *adj*

**pseu·do·purpurin** \"+\ *n* [ISV *pseud-* + *purpurin*] **:** a red crystalline compound $C_{14}H_4O_2(OH)_3COOH$ obtained from madder root and also made synthetically that decomposes in boiling water into purpurin and carbon dioxide and whose alumina lake is a fine red pigment; purpurin-carboxylic acid

**pseu·do·rabies** \"+\ *n* [NL, fr. *pseud-* + *rabies*] **:** an acute febrile virus disease of domestic animals (as cattle, swine) marked by cutaneous irritation and intense itching followed by encephalomyelitis and pharyngeal paralysis and commonly terminating in death within 48 hours — called also *mad itch*; see BULBAR PARALYSIS

**pseu·do·racemic** \"+\ *adj* [*pseud-* + *racemic*] **:** of or relating to optically inactive mixed crystals containing equal quantities of the dextro and levo forms of an active compound

**pseu·do·ramose** \"+\ *adj* [*pseud-* + *ramose*] **:** forming false branches

**pseu·do·raphe** \"+\ *n* [NL, fr. *pseud-* + *raphe*] **:** an axial area on the valve of various diatoms that lacks markings but simulates the true raphe

**pseu·do·reduction** \"+\ *n* [*pseud-* + *reduction*] **:** an apparent halving of the number of chromosomes by synapsis

**pseu·do·reminiscence** \"+\ *n* [*pseud-* + *reminiscence*] **:** an error of memory consisting in illusory recall of an experience that one has not had — compare CONFABULATION

**pseu·do·saccharomycetaceae** \"+\ *n pl, cap* [NL, fr. *Pseudosaccharomycet-*, *Pseudosaccharomyces*, type genus (fr. *pseud-* + *sacchar-* + *mycet-*, *-myces*) + *-aceae*] **:** a family of yeastlike fungi (order Moniliales) that do not germinate by repetition

**pseu·do·salt** \'südō+ˌ-\ *n* [*pseud-* + *salt*] **:** a compound (as stannic chloride or mercuric cyanide) analogous in formula to a salt and sometimes called a salt but not ionized as such

**pseu·do·scarus** \¦sü(ˌ)dō+\ *n, cap* [NL, fr. *pseud-* + *Scarus*] **:** a widely distributed genus of parrot fishes

**pseu·do·science** \"+\ *n* [*pseud-* + *science*] **:** a system of theories, assumptions, and methods erroneously regarded as scientific

**pseu·do·scientific** \"+\ *adj* [*pseud-* + *scientific*] **:** of, relating to, or having the characteristics of a pseudoscience or pseudoscientists

**pseu·do·scientist** \"+\ *n* [*pseud-* + *scientist*] **:** a practitioner of a pseudoscience

**pseud·oscines** \(')süd+\ *n pl, cap* [NL, fr. *pseud-* + *Oscines*] *in some classifications* **:** a superfamily equivalent to the suborder *Menurae* — **pseud·oscinine** \"+\ *adj*

**pseu·do·scolex** \¦sü(ˌ)dō+\ *n* [NL, fr. *pseud-* + *scolex*] **:** an altered group of anterior segments that in some tapeworms replaces the scolex and serves as a holdfast

**pseu·do·scope** \'südəˌskōp\ *n* [*pseud-* + *-scope*] **:** an optical instrument that exhibits objects with their proper relief reversed, thus producing an effect opposite to that of the stereoscope — **pseu·do·scop·ic** \¦==¦skäpik\ *adj* — **pseu·do·scop·i·cal·ly** \-pə̇k(ə)lē\ *adv*

**pseu·dos·co·py** \sü'däskəpē\ *n* -ES [ISV *pseudoscope* + *-y*] **:** the production of the effect of reversed relief (as by the pseudoscope)

**pseu·do·scorpion** \¦sü(ˌ)dō+\ *n* [NL *Pseudoscorpiones*] **:** an arachnid of the order Pseudoscorpiones

**pseu·do·scorpiones** \"+\ *n pl, cap* [NL, fr. *pseud-* + *Scorpiones*] **:** an order of Arachnida comprising the book scorpions

**pseu·do·scorpionida** *or* **pseu·do·scorpionidea** \"+\ [NL, fr. *pseud-* + *Scorpionida* or *Scorpionidea*] *syn of* PSEUDOSCORPIONES

**pseu·do·segmentation** \"+\ *n* [*pseud-* + *segmentation*] **:** external annulation of the body of a nonmetameric animal (as a nematode) so that it appears segmented

**pseu·do·segmented** \"+\ *adj* [*pseud-* + *segmented*, past part. of [2]*segment*] **:** having a superficial annulation that simulates metameric segmentation ⟨~ nematodes of the genus *Desmoscolex*⟩

**pseu·do·septate** \"+\ *adj* [*pseud-* + *septate*] **:** apparently septate ⟨~ spores⟩

**pseu·do·septum** \"+\ *n* [NL, fr. *pseud-* + *septum*] **:** a septum that is perforated by one or more openings (as in various algae and fungi)

**pseu·do·skeleton** \"+\ *n* [*pseud-* + *skeleton*] **:** a sponge skeleton consisting of foreign bodies not secreted by the animal — opposed to *autoskeleton*

**pseu·do·social** \"+\ *adj* [*pseud-* + *social*] **:** marked by or reflecting loyalty to a small group that is usu. predatory and parasitic on society

**pseu·do·solution** \"+\ *n* [*pseud-* + *solution*] **:** a colloidal solution

**pseu·do·sophisticated** \"+\ *adj* [*pseud-* + *sophisticated*] **:** marked by a false or feigned sophistication

**pseu·do·sperm** \'südōˌspərm\ *n* [NL *pseudospermium*] **:** PSEUDOSPERMIUM

**pseu·do·sper·mi·um** \ˌsüdō'spərmēəm\ *n, pl* **pseudospermia** [NL, fr. *pseud-* + *-spermium* (fr. Gk *sperma* seed) — more at SPERM] **:** a small indehiscent seedlike fruit (as an achene) — **pseu·do·sper·mous** \¦==¦=məs\ *adj*

**pseu·do·sphaeriaceae** \¦sü(ˌ)dō+\ *n pl, cap* [NL, fr. *pseud-* + *Sphaeriaceae*] **:** a family of ascomycetous fungi (order Dothideales) having separate stromata resembling perithecia and each bearing a single ascus

**pseu·do·sphaeriales** \"+\ *n pl, cap* [NL, fr. *pseud-* + *Sphaeriales*] *in some classifications* **:** an order of ascomycetous fungi including forms (as those of the family Pseudosphaeriaceae) in which one ascus develops in each stromatic cavity

**pseu·do·sphere** \'südō+ˌ-\ *n* [ISV *pseud-* + *sphere*; prob. orig. formed as It *pseudosfera*] **:** a surface of constant negative curvature (as generated by the revolution of a tractrix about its axis)

**pseu·do·statement** \¦sü(ˌ)dō+\ *n* [*pseud-* + *statement*] **1 :** a statement that cannot be empirically verified; *esp* **:** a statement made in a poem **2 :** a sentence that is grammatically correct yet fails to express a total sense (as in the sentence "the true is more identical than the beautiful")

**pseu·do·stereoscopic** \"+\ *adj* [*pseud-* + *stereoscopic*] **:** giving the impression of three-dimensional relief by other means (as movement, color, perspective) than binocular vision

**pseu·dos·to·ma** \sü'dästəmə\ *n* [NL, fr. *pseud-* + *stoma*] **1 :** a stigma in serous membrane filled by intercellular substance or otherwise closed **2 :** the temporary mouth of a larval echinoderm **3 :** the osculum of a sponge — **pseu·do·stoma·tous** \¦südə¦stōmədˌəs, -täm-\ *or* **pseu·dos·to·mous** \(')sü¦dästəməs\ *adj*

**pseu·do·succinea** \¦sü(ˌ)dō+\ *n, cap* [NL, fr. *pseud-* + *Succinea*] **:** a genus of freshwater snails (family Lymnaeidae) including important New World intermediate hosts of a liver fluke (*Fasciola hepatica*)

**pseu·do·su·chia** \ˌsüdō'sükēə\ *n pl, cap* [NL, fr. *pseud-* + Gk *souchos* crocodile + NL *-ia*] **:** a suborder of Thecodontia comprising small slender generalized Triassic reptiles probably near the common ancestry of dinosaurs, birds, and crocodilians — **pseu·do·su·chi·an** \¦==¦=kēən\ *adj or n*

**pseu·do·syllogism** \¦sü(ˌ)dō+\ *n* [*pseud-* + *syllogism*] **:** a formal fallacy in which the conclusion does not follow from the premises

**pseu·do·symmetric** *or* **pseu·do·symmetrical** \"+\ *adj* [*pseudosymmetry* + *-ic* or *-ical*] **:** exhibiting pseudosymmetry

**pseu·do·symmetry** \"+\ *n* [ISV *pseud-* + *symmetry*] **:** the apparent symmetry in crystals that come to resemble (as in the apparently hexagonal prisms of aragonite) forms of another system

**pseu·do·tachylyte** \"+\ *n* [ISV *pseud-* + *tachylyte*] **:** a rock consisting of glass in which are included numerous fragments of the adjacent rock and which is supposed to have been formed by the partial fusion of crush breccia or mylonite

**pseu·do·tetramera** \"+\ *n pl, cap* [NL, fr. *pseud-* + *Tetramera*] **:** a division of beetles having the fifth tarsal joint minute and obscure so that there appear to be but four joints — **pseu·do·tetrameral** *or* **pseu·do·tetramerous** \"+\ *adj*

**pseu·do·trachea** \"+·-\ *n* [NL, fr. *pseud-* + *trachea*] **:** one of a series of chitinous tubes in the labella of dipterans (suborder Brachycera) through which liquid food is taken into the mouth — **pseu·do·tracheal** \"+·-\ *adj*

**pseu·do·trim·era** \ˌsüdō·'trimərə\ *n pl, cap* [NL, fr. *pseud-* + *tri-* + Gk *meros* part — more at MERIT] **:** a division of beetles having 4-jointed tarsi but with the 4th joint very small and hidden by the 3d — **pseu·do·trim·er·al** \¦==¦=mərəl\ *or* **pseu·do·trim·er·ous** \-mərəs\ *adj*

**pseu·do·tropine** \¦sü(ˌ)dō+·-\ *n* [*pseud-* + *tropine*] **:** a crystalline alkaloid $C_8H_{15}NO$ stereoisomeric with tropine and formed by hydrolysis of tropacocaine

**pseu·do·trunk** \'südō+·ˌ-\ *n* [*pseud-* + *trunk*] **:** a column like a trunk formed by overlapping leafstalks (as in the abaca)

**pseu·do·tsu·ga** \¦sü(ˌ)dō(t)¦sügə\ *n, cap* [NL, fr. *pseud-* + *Tsuga*] **:** a genus of American and Asiatic evergreen trees (family Pinaceae) having whorled branches, linear flat leaves, monoecious flowers, and pendulous rather large cones that have the bracts longer than the cone scales and the midrib of each produced into a rigid awn and two pointed lobes — see BIG-CONE SPRUCE, DOUGLAS FIR

**pseu·do·tubercle** \¦sü(ˌ)dō+\ *n* [*pseud-* + *tubercle*] **:** a nodule or granuloma resembling a tubercle of tuberculosis but due to other causes

**pseu·do·tuberculosis** \"+\ *n* [NL, fr. *pseud-* + *tuberculosis*] **:** any of several diseases characterized by the formation of granulomas resembling tubercular nodules but not caused by the tubercle bacillus: as **a :** SARCOIDOSIS **b :** CASEOUS LYMPHADENITIS **c :** any of various pasteurelloses of birds and mammals **d :** JOHNE'S DISEASE

**pseu·do·turbinal** \"+\ *n* [*pseud-* + *turbinal*] **:** an inversion of the lateral wall of the nose of a reptile or bird

**pseu·do·type** \'südōˌtīp\ *n* [*pseud-* + *type*] **:** an invalid type in biology; *esp* **:** an invalid genotype — **pseu·do·typ·ic** \¦==¦tipik\ *adj*

**pseu·do·urea** \¦sü(ˌ)dō+\ *n* [NL, fr. *pseud-* + *urea*] **:** the tautomeric enol form $HN{=}C(OH)NH_2$ of urea known in the form of its esters — called also *isourea*

**pseu·do·uric acid** \"+...-\ *n* [*pseudouric* ISV *pseud-* + *uric*] **:** a crystalline acid $C_5H_6N_4O_4$ related to uric acid; 5-ureido=barbituric acid

**pseu·do·vitellus** \"+\ *n* [NL, fr. *pseud-* + *vitellus*] **:** a mycetome consisting of a mass of fatty cells in the abdomen of an aphid

**pseu·do·volcano** \"+\ *n* [*pseud-* + *volcano*] **:** a false volcano **:** an eruptive vent not emitting lava like a true volcano

**pseud·ovum** \(')süd+\ *n* [NL, fr. *pseud-* + *ovum*] **:** an egg capable of developing without fertilization **:** a parthenogenetic egg

**pseu·do·wavellite** \¦sü(,)dō+\ *n* [*pseud-* + *wavellite*] : CRANDALLITE

**pseu·do·yohimbine** \"+\ *n* [*pseud-* + *yohimbine*] : a crystalline alkaloid $C_{21}H_{26}N_2O_3$ isomeric with yohimbine and occurring with it

**pseu·do·zoea** *also* **pseu·do·zoaea** \"+\ *n* [NL, fr. *pseud-* + *zoea, zoaea*] : a larval stage in the Stomatopoda similar to the decapod zoea

**PSF** *abbr, often not cap* pounds per square foot

**psgr** *abbr* passenger

**pshav** \ˈ(p)shäv, -äf\ *n, pl* **pshav** *or* **pshavs** *usu cap* : a member of a mountain people of the Caucasus

**psha·vi·an** \-ävēən\ *adj, usu cap* : of or relating to the Pshav

**¹pshaw** *any of various sounds or successions of sounds expressing any of the emotions named in the definition, among them* ˈshō *esp when* ō *precedes; usu read as* ˈshō\ *interj* — used to express irritation, disapproval, contempt, or disbelief

**²pshaw** \ˈshō\ *n* -s : an exclamation of *pshaw* ⟨a few episodical poohs and ~*s* —Sir Walter Scott⟩

**³pshaw** \"\ *vb* -ED/-ING/-S *vi* : to express irritation, disapproval, or disbelief by saying *pshaw* ⟨no doubt the government contractors ~*ed* and pished over it —Charles Hasler⟩ ~ *vt* : to say *pshaw* at

**psi** \ˈ(p)sī, ˈpsē\ *n* -s [LGk, fr. Gk *psei*] **1** : the 23d letter of the Greek alphabet — symbol Ψ or ψ; see ALPHABET table **2** : PSI PHENOMENA

**PSI** *abbr, often not cap* pounds per square inch

**PSIA** *abbr, often not cap* pounds per square inch absolute

**psi·cose** \ˈsī,kōs *also* -ōz\ *n* -s [alter. (influenced by *psi*) of *pseudofructose*, fr. *pseud-* + *fructose*] : ALLULOSE

**psid·i·um** \ˈsidēəm\ *n, cap* [NL, prob. fr. Gk *psidion* armlet] : a genus of tropical American trees (family Myrtaceae) having pubescent leaves and cymose flowers with broad calyx tube and 4- or 5-celled ovary becoming in fruit a pulpy, many-seeded berry — see GUAVA

**PSIG** *abbr, often not cap* pounds per square inch gauge

**psil-** *or* **psilo-** *comb form* [Gk, fr. *psilos*; akin to Gk *psēn* to rub, wipe — more at SAND] : mere : bare ⟨*psilo*melane⟩ ⟨*Psil*opsida⟩

**psi·la** \ˈsīlə\ *n, cap* [NL, fr. L, shaggy covering, fr. Gk *psilos* bare] : a genus of small slender two-winged flies some of whose larvae attack the roots and crown of umbelliferous plants — see CARROT RUST FLY

**psil·anthropic** \¦sīl+\ *adj* [*psilanthrop*ist + *-ic*] : relating to or embodying psilanthropy

**psil·an·thro·pism** \sīˈlan(t)thrə,pizəm\ *n* -s [LGk *psilanthrōpos* + E *-ism*] : PSILANTHROPY

**psil·an·thro·pist** \-,pəst\ *n* -s [LGk *psilanthrōpos* merely human (fr. Gk *psil-* + *anthrōpos* human being) + E *-ist* — more at ANTHROP-] : one who believes that Christ was a mere man

**psil·an·thro·py** \-,pē\ *n* -ES [fr. *psilanthropist*, after such pairs as E *philanthropist: philanthropy*] : a doctrine of the merely human existence of Christ

**psi·late** \ˈsī,lāt\ *adj* [*psil-* + E *-ate*] : lacking ornamentation — used esp. of pollen grain walls

**psi·lo·mel·ane** \,sīlōˈme,lān\ *n* -s [*psil-* + *-melane*] : a basic oxide of barium and bivalent and quadrivalent manganese probably $BaMnMn_8O_{16}(OH)_4$ — compare HOLLANDITE, CORONADITE

**psi·lo·pae·des** \,sīlōˈpē(,)dēz\ *n pl* [NL, fr. *psil-* + Gk *paides*, pl. of *pais* child — more at FEW] *archaic* : ALTRICES

**psi·lo·phy·ta·ce·ae** \,sīlō,fīˈtāsē,ē\ *n pl, cap* [NL, fr. *Psilophyton*, type genus + *-aceae*] : a family of Paleozoic plants (order Psilophytales)

**psi·lo·phy·ta·les** \-ā(,)lēz\ *n pl, cap* [NL, fr. *Psilophyton* + *-ales*] : an order of Paleozoic simple dichotomously branched plants of Europe and eastern Canada including the oldest known land plants with vascular structure

**psi·lo·phyte** \ˈ==,fīt\ *n* -s [NL *Psylophyton*] **1** : a plant of the order Psilophytales **2** : a savanna plant

**psi·loph·y·ton** \sīˈläfə,tän\ *n* [NL, fr. *psil-* + *phyton*] **1** *cap* : a genus (the type of the family Psilophytaceae) of small wiry herbaceous Paleozoic plants with underground rhizomes and apical sporangia **2** -s : any plant or fossil of the genus *Psilophyton*

**¹psi·lop·sid** \(ˈ)sī¦läpsəd\ *adj* [NL *Psilopsida*] : of or relating to the Psilopsida ⟨~ land plants⟩

**²psilopsid** \"\ *n* -s : a plant of the subdivision Psilopsida

**psi·lop·si·da** \sīˈläpsədə\ *n pl, cap* [NL, fr. *psil-* + *-opsida* (as in *lycopsida*)] : a subdivision of Tracheophyta comprising vascular plants with no roots, leaves only partially differentiated or lacking, no leaf traces, a usu. protostelic vascular cylinder, and the sporangia merely terminal enlargements of the stem — compare LYCOPSIDA, PTEROPSIDA, SPHENOPSIDA

**psi·lo·sis** \sīˈlōsəs\ *n, pl* **psilo·ses** \-ō,sēz\ [NL, fr. Gk *psilōsis*, fr. *psiloun* to strip bare, leave naked, pronounce without aspiration, (fr. *psilos* bare) + *-sis*] **1 a** : a falling out of hair : DEPILATION **b** : SPRUE **2** : failure to pronounce aspirate sounds

**psi·los·tro·phe** \sīˈlästrə(,)fē\ *n, cap* [NL, fr. *psil-* + Gk *strophē* act of turning — more at STROPHE] : a genus of herbs or low shrubs (family Compositae) of the rangelands of southwestern U.S. having persistent papery yellow flowers

**psi·lo·ta·ce·ae** \,sīlōˈtāsē,ē\ *n pl, cap* [NL, fr. *Psilotum*, type genus + *-aceae*] : a family of plants that are usu. placed in order Psilotales and are characterized by nearly naked stems, minute scalelike leaves, and 2- or 3-celled sporangia — compare PSILOTUM, TMESIPTERIS — **psi·lo·ta·ceous** \¦==¦tāshəs\ *adj*

**psi·lo·ta·les** \,==ˈtā(,)lēz\ *n pl, cap* [NL, fr. *Psilotum* + *-ales*] : an order of lower tracheophytes (subdivision Psilopsida) having a dichotomously branched sporophyte that is divided into aerial shoot and rhizome, lacks true roots, and has few or minute leaves, and having a gametophyte that is subterranean and free from chlorophyll — see PSILOTACEAE

**psi·lot·ic** \(ˈ)sī¦läd·ik, -lōd-·\ *adj* [Gk *psilōtikos*, fr. (assumed) *psilōtos* (verbal of Gk *psiloun* to strip bare) + *-ikos* -ic] : of or relating to psilosis

**psi·lo·tum** \sīˈlōd·əm\ *n, cap* [NL, prob. fr. LGk *psilōton*, a plant, perh. fr. Gk *psilon* down, soft feather, alter. of *ptilon*; akin to Gk *pteron* wing, feather — more at FEATHER] : a genus (the type of the family Psilotaceae) of chiefly tropical fern allies with terrestrial or epiphytic habit, slender branching stems, and sessile 3-celled sporangia usu. in spikes

**psi phenomena** *n pl* : the aggregate of parapsychological functions of the mind including extrasensory perception, precognition, and psychokinesis

**psis** *pl of* PSI

**psith·y·rus** \ˈsithərəs\ *n* [NL, fr. Gk *psithyros* whispering, twittering] **1** *cap* : a genus of large bees resembling bumblebees but lacking the pollen-collecting apparatus and the worker caste and being parasitic in the nests of bumblebees **2** *pl* **psithy·ri** \-,rī\ : any bee of the genus *Psithyrus*

**psit·ta·ceous** \səˈtāshəs\ *adj* [NL *Psittacus* + E *-eous*] **1** : PSITTACINE **2** : like a parrot ⟨~ chatter⟩

**psit·ta·ci** \ˈsid·ə,sī, -ə,kī\ [NL, fr. *Psittacus*] *syn of* PSITTACIFORMES

**psit·tac·i·dae** \səˈtasə,dē, -akə-\ *n pl, cap* [NL, fr. *Psittacus*, type genus + *-idae*] : a family of birds coextensive with the order Psittaciformes

**psit·ta·ci·for·mes** \,sid·əsəˈfȯr(,)mēz, -əkə-\ *n pl, cap* [NL, fr. *Psittacus* + *-iformes*] : an order of zygodactyl birds comprising the parrots and related birds (as the amazons, cockatoos, lorikeets, lories, macaws, parrakeets)

**¹psit·ta·cine** \ˈsid·ə,sīn, -,kīn\ *adj* [L *psittacinus* of or relating to a parrot, fr. *psittacus* parrot + *-inus* -ine] : of or relating to the Psittacidae

**²psittacine** \"\ *n* -s : a bird of the family Psittacidae

**psit·ta·cism** \ˈsid·ə,sizəm\ *n* -s [NL *psittacismus*, fr. L *psittacus* parrot + *-ismus* -ism] : automatic speech without thought of the meaning of the words spoken

**psit·ta·co·mor·phae** \,sid·əkōˈmȯr(,)fē\ [NL, fr. *Psittacus* + *-morphae*] *syn of* PSITTACIFORMES

**psit·ta·co·sis** \,sid·əˈkōsəs, -d·ēˈk-\ *n, pl* **psittaco·ses** \-ō,sēz\ [NL, fr. L *psittacus* parrot + *-osis*] : an infectious disease of birds that is caused by a rickettsia (*Miyagawanella psittaci*), is marked by diarrhea and wasting, and is transmissible to man in whom it is usu. manifested as an atypical pneumonia accompanied by high fever; *esp* : the form of this disease that originates in psittacine birds — see ORNITHOSIS

**psit·ta·cot·ic** \¦==¦käd·ik\ *adj* [fr. NL *psittacosis*, after such pairs as NL *narcosis*: E *narcotic*] : of, relating to, characteristic of, or affected with psittacosis

**psit·ta·cus** \ˈsid·əkəs\ *n, cap* [NL, fr. L, parrot, fr. Gk *psittakos*] : a type genus of Psittacidae formerly extensive but now usu. restricted to the African gray

**p slip** *n* [*p* prob. abbr. of *postal*; fr. its being the same size as former small-sized U.S. postal cards] : a slip of paper approximately three by five inches in size used in library filing

**psn** *abbr* position

**pso·as** \ˈsōəs\ *n, pl* **pso·ai** \-ō,ī\ *or* **pso·ae** \-ō,ē\ [NL, fr. pl. of *psoa* psoas, fr. Gk, muscle of the loins] : either of two internal muscles of the loin that together form the tenderloin of animals used as food of which the larger arises from the anterolateral surfaces of the lumbar vertebrae and passes beneath Poupart's ligament to insert with the iliacus into the lesser trochanter of the femur and of which the smaller muscle often absent arises from the last dorsal and first lumbar vertebrae and inserts into the brim of the pelvis — called also respectively *psoas major* or *psoas magnus* and *psoas minor* or *psoas parvus*

**pso·at·ic** \(ˈ)sō¦ad·ik\ *adj* : of or relating to a psoas

**¹psocid** \ˈsōsəd, ˈsäs-\ *adj* [NL *Psocidae*] : of or relating to the Psoidae or to psocids

**²psocid** \"\ *n* -s : an insect of the family Psocidae; *broadly* : any of various usu. winged insects of the order Corrodentia

**psoci·dae** \-ōsə,dē, -äs-\ *n pl, cap* [NL, fr. *Psocus*, type genus + *-idae*] : a family of small soft-bodied winged insects (order Corrodentia) related to the book lice, widely distributed, and feeding upon lichens, fungi, and decaying vegetation — **pso·cine** \-ō,sīn, ä,s-\ *adj*

**pso·cop·tera** \sōˈkäptərə\ [NL, fr. *Psocus* genus of book lice + *-ptera*] *syn of* CORRODENTIA

**psopho·car·pus** \,säfəˈkärpəs\ *n, cap* [NL, fr. Gk *psophos* noise + NL *-carpus*; fr. the sound made by the ripe pod when it springs open] : a genus of tropical Asiatic and African tuberous-rooted herbs (family Leguminosae)

**pso·phom·e·ter** \sōˈfämod·ə(r)\ *n* [Gk *psophos* noise + E *-meter*] : a device for measuring the volume of noise — **psopho·met·ric** \¦säfə¦me·trik, ¦sōf-\ *adj*

**psor-** *or* **psoro-** *comb form* [NL, fr. L, fr. Gk, fr. *psōra*] : itch ⟨*psor*ergates⟩ ⟨*psoro*sperm⟩

**pso·ra** \ˈsōrə\ *n* -s [L, itch, mange, fr. Gk *psōra*] : PSORIASIS

**pso·ralea** \səˈrālēə, -ral-\ *n, cap* [NL, fr. Gk *psōraleos* scabby, itchy, fr. *psōra* itch] : a large widely distributed genus of herbs and shrubs (family Leguminosae) with glandular compound leaves and spicate or racemose purple or white flowers — see BREADROOT

**psor·er·gates** \səˈrərgə,tēz\ *n, cap* [NL, fr. *psor-* + Gk *ergatēs* worker — more at ERGAT-] : a genus of parasitic mites including an itch mite (*P. ovis*) troublesome to sheep in Australia

**pso·ri·a·si·form** \səˈrīəsə,fȯrm\ *adj* [ISV *psorias-* (fr. NL *psoriasis*) + *-iform*] : like psoriasis

**pso·ri·a·sis** \səˈrīəsəs\ *n, pl* **psoria·ses** \-ī̶ə,sēz\ [NL, fr. Gk *psōriasis*, fr. *psōrian* to have the itch (fr. *psōra* itch, mange) + *-iasis*; prob. akin to Gk *psēn* to rub — more at SAND] : a chronic skin disease characterized by circumscribed red patches covered with white scales

**pso·ri·at·ic** \¦sōrē¦ad·ik\ *adj* [fr. NL *psoriasis*, after such pairs as L *emphasis*: E *emphatic*] : of, relating to, affected with, or accompanied by psoriasis

**²psoriatic** \"\ *n* -s : one affected with psoriasis

**pso·ric** \ˈsōrik\ *adj* [L *psoricus*, fr. Gk *psōrikos*, fr. *psōra* psora + *-ikos* -ic] : of or relating to psoriasis

**pso·roph·o·ra** \səˈräfərə\ *n, cap* [NL, fr. *psor-* + *-phora*] : a genus of large showy mosquitoes having the palpi of dissimilar length in the two sexes and the scutellum 3-lobed

**pso·rop·tes** \səˈräp(,)tēz\ *n, cap* [NL, fr. *psor-* + *-optes* (as in *Sarcoptes*)] : a genus (the type of the family Psoroptidae) of mites having piercing mandibles and suckers with jointed pedicels, living on and irritating the skin of various mammals, and resulting in the development of scab — **pso·rop·tic** \səˈräptik\ *adj*

**psoroptic mange** *n* : mange caused by mites of the genus *Psoroptes*

**pso·ro·sis** \səˈrōsəs\ *n, pl* **psoro·ses** \-ō,sēz\ [NL, fr. *psor-* + *-osis*] : a virus disease of citrus trees affecting sweet oranges, tangerines, and grapefruit and characterized by scaly bark and exudation of gum and in the later stages retarded growth, small yellow leaves, and dieback of twigs — called also *scaly bark*; compare LEPROSIS

**pso·ro·sperm** \ˈsōrə,spərm\ *n* [*psor-* + *sperm*] **1** : a myxosporidian spore **2** : any of various minute parasitic organisms probably mostly sporozoans — **pso·ro·sper·mi·al** \¦==¦spərmēəl\ *or* **pso·ro·sper·mic** \-mik\ *adj*

**PSS** *abbr* [L *postscripta*] postscripts

**PSSO** *abbr, often not cap* pass slip stitch over

**PST** *abbr* Pacific standard time

**psych** \ˈsīk\ *vt* -ED/-ING/-S [short for *psychoanalyze*] **1** *slang* : PSYCHOANALYZE **2** *slang* : to analyze (as a problem or opponent) psychologically ⟨I ~*ed* it all out by myself and decided —David Hulburd⟩; *also* : to overcome (an opponent) as the result of analyzing psychologically ⟨~ a tennis opponent⟩

**psych** *abbr* **1** psychic; psychical **2** psychological; psychologist; psychology

**psych-** *or* **psycho-** *comb form* [Gk, fr. *psychē* life, spirit, soul, self] **1** : soul : spirit ⟨*psycho*gram⟩ ⟨*psycho*pannychism⟩ ⟨*psycho*theism⟩ **2 a** : mind : mental processes and activities ⟨*psycho*dynamic⟩ ⟨*psycho*logy⟩ ⟨*psycho*metric⟩ **b** : psychological methods ⟨*psycho*analysis⟩ ⟨*psycho*technology⟩ ⟨*psycho*therapy⟩ **c** : cerebral ⟨*psycho*surgery⟩ ⟨*psycho*tropic⟩ **d** : mind and : psyche and ⟨*psycho*galvanic⟩ ⟨*psycho*physical⟩

**psy·cha·gog·ic** \¦sīkə¦gäjik\ *adj* [Gk *psychagōgikos*, fr. *psychagōgia* persuasion, winning of souls + *-ikos* -ic] **1** : ATTRACTIVE, PERSUASIVE, INSPIRING **2** : of or relating to psychagogy

**psy·cha·gogue** \ˈsīkə,gäg *sometimes* -,gōg\ *n* -s [Gk *psychagōgos* leading souls to the lower world, fr. *psych-* + *agōgos* leading, fr. *agein* to lead — more at AGENT] : a believer in or practicer of psychagogy

**psy·cha·gogy** \-,gäjē, -,gōjē\ *n* -ES [LGk *psychagōgia* evocation of souls from the lower world, fr. Gk, persuasion, winning of souls, fr. *psychagōgos* leading the soul + *-ia* -y] **1** : guidance of the soul esp. of a departed one **2** [Gk *psychagōgia* persuasion, winning of souls] : a method of influencing behavior by suggesting desirable life goals

**psy·chal** \ˈsīkəl\ *adj* [*psych-* + *-al*] : PSYCHICAL ⟨whatever the ~ reactions to the camera and the moving picture —Lewis Mumford⟩ — **psy·chal·ly** \-əlē\ *adv*

**psy·chal·gia** \sīˈkalj(ē)ə\ *n* -s [NL, fr. *psych-* + *-algia*] : mental distress

**psychanalysis** *var of* PSYCHOANALYSIS

**psych·asthenia** \(ˈ)sīk+\ *n* [NL, fr. *psych-* + *asthenia*] : a state of characterological weakness such that one feels unable to resolve doubts or uncertainties or to resist phobias, obsessions, or compulsions even though aware of their irrational nature ⟨most cases formerly classed as ~ are today considered psychoneuroses⟩ — **psychasthenic** *adj or n*

**psy·che** \ˈsī(,)kē\ *n* [Gk *psychē* life, spirit, soul, self; akin to Gk *psychein* to breathe, blow, make cold, Skt *babhasti* he blows] **1** -s **a** : the vital principle of corporeal matter that is a distinct mental or spiritual entity coextensive with but independent of body or soma : SOUL, SELF, PERSONALITY — compare ÉLAN VITAL **b** : the specialized cognitive, conative, and affective aspects of a psychosomatic unity : MIND; *specif* : the totality of the id, ego, and superego including both conscious and unconscious components **2** -s [F *psyché*, fr. *Psyché*, in Greco-Roman mythology a beautiful maiden personifying the soul who was loved by the god of love Eros, fr. L *Psyche*, fr. Gk *Psychē*, fr. *psychē* soul; perh. fr. the full-length painting of Psyche by Raphael †1520 Ital. painter] : CHEVAL GLASS **3** *cap* [NL, fr. Gk *psychē* butterfly, moth, soul] : the type genus of Psychidae **syn** see MIND

**psy·che·an** \ˈsīkēən, (ˈ)sī¦k-\ *adj, usu cap* [*Psyche*, beloved of Eros + E *-an*] : of or relating to Psyche

**psyche knot** *n, usu cap P* [after *Psyche*, who in works of art is often represented with this hair style] : a woman's hair style in which the hair is brushed back and twisted into a conical coil usu. just above the nape — compare CHIGNON

**psy·che·om·e·try** \,sīkēˈämə·trē\ *n* -ES [prob. fr. NL *psycheometria*, irreg. fr. *psych-* + *-metria* -metry] : the theory or science of the mathematical cognition of the human mind

**psy·chi·ana** \,sīkēˈanə, -ˈänə *also* -ˈānə\ *n* -s *cap* [NL, fr. *psych-* + *-ana*] : a religion disseminated principally through lessons and publications sent out on a mail-order basis from its headquarters in Moscow, Idaho and based on a central message that each individual is capable of discovering and utilizing the spiritual power within him to achieve his own requisites (as health, happiness, and financial success)

**psy·chi·a·ter** \səˈkīəd·ə(r), sīˈk-\ *n* -s [prob. fr. F *psychiatre*, fr. *psych-* + Gk *iatros* healer, physician — more at IATRIC] *archaic* : PSYCHIATRIST

**psy·chi·at·ric** \¦sīkē¦a·trik, -rēk\ *also* **psy·chi·at·ri·cal** \-rəkəl, -rēkəl\ *adj* [*psychiatric* ISV *psychiatr-* (fr. — assumed — NL *psychiatria*) + *-ic*; orig. formed as G *psychiatrisch*; *psychiatrical* fr. *psychiatry* + *-ical*] **1** : relating to, employed in, or of concern to psychiatry ⟨~ disorders⟩ ⟨~ rejections⟩ ⟨~ drugs⟩ ⟨~ immaturity —Weston LaBarre⟩ **2** : engaged in the practice of psychiatry : dealing with cases of mental disorder ⟨~ experts⟩ ⟨~ nursing⟩ ⟨~ ward⟩ — **psy·chi·at·ri·cal·ly** \-rək(ə)lē, -rēk-, -li\ *adv*

**psy·chi·a·trist** \səˈkīə·trəst *also* sīˈk-\ *n* -s [*psychiatry* + *-ist*] : a physician specializing in psychiatry — distinguished from *neurologist*

**psy·chi·a·try** \-·trē, -ri\ *n* -ES [prob. fr. (assumed) NL *psychiatria*, fr. *psych-* + *-iatria* -iatry] **1** : a branch of medicine that deals with the science and practice of treating mental, emotional, or behavioral disorders esp. as originating in endogenous causes or resulting from faulty interpersonal relationships **2** : a treatise or text on or theory of the etiology, recognition, treatment, or prevention of mental, emotional, or behavioral disorder or the application of psychiatric principles to any area of human activity ⟨social ~⟩ **3** : the psychiatric service in a general hospital ⟨this patient should be referred to ~⟩

**¹psy·chic** \ˈsīkik, -kēk\ *adj* [Gk *psychikos* of the soul, of life, fr. *psychē* soul, life + *-ikos* -ic] **1** : of, arising in, or relating to the psyche : PSYCHOGENIC ⟨terrorism and fear create a low ~ state —Lewis Mumford⟩ ⟨~ disturbances⟩ **2** : not physical or organic : lying outside the sphere of physical science or knowledge : governed by, concerned with, or acting on the psyche or self ⟨a momentary fusion of my own being with the souls of others brought into a ~ intimacy by some affinity of emotion or thought —G.W.Russell⟩ **3** : sensitive to nonphysical forces and influences : marked by extraordinary or mysterious sensitivity, perception, or understanding ⟨the naval battle . . . was recorded in all the guide books and required no ~ powers to reveal —Upton Sinclair⟩ **4** : physically delicate; *specif, of a hand* : long and narrow often fragile in appearance with slender tapering fingers and long almond-shaped nails usu. held by palmists to indicate a visionary gentle trusting nature lacking in practical or worldly qualities — compare MIXED **syn** see MENTAL

**²psychic** \"\ *n* -s **1 a** : a person apparently sensitive to nonphysical forces **b** : one serving or capable of serving as a spiritualistic medium **c** : MENTALIST **2 a** : psychic phenomena **b psychics** *pl but sing in constr* : the study of purely psychic, mental, or spiritual phenomena and laws **3** *Gnosticism* : a being endowed with soul and belonging to the second of the three classes into which mankind was divided — compare PNEUMATIC 1 **4** : PSYCHIC BID

**psy·chi·cal** \ˈsīkəkəl, -kēk-\ *adj* [Gk *psychē* life, soul + E *-ical* — more at PSYCHE] **1** : PSYCHIC **2** : of or relating to the mind : MENTAL — contrasted with *physical*

**psychical distance** *or* **psychic distance** *n* : AESTHETIC DISTANCE

**psy·chi·cal·ly** \-īkək(ə)lē, -īkēk-, -li\ *adv* : in a psychic manner

**psychical research** *or* **psychic research** *n* : investigation of phenomena that appear contrary to physical laws and suggest the possibility of mental activity apart from body

**psychic bid** *n* : a bid in contract bridge made on a hand or suit that is not conventionally strong enough to bid for the purpose of misleading the opponents

**psych·ich·thys** \sīˈkikthəs\ *n, cap* [NL, fr. *psych-* + *-ichthys*] : a genus of chimaeras differing from *Chimaera* in having no anal fin

**psychic income** *n* **1** : imputed income **2** : rewards (as in prestige, leisure, or pleasant surroundings) not measurable in terms of money or goods but serving as an incentive to work in certain occupations or situations

**psy·chi·cism** \ˈsīkə,sizəm\ *n* -s [*psychic* + *-ism*] : PSYCHICAL RESEARCH

**psy·chi·cist** \-kəsəst\ *n* -s : one interested in or concerned with psychical research

**psychic monism** *n* : a view that the psychic, spiritual, or mental constitutes the only ultimate reality

**psychic unity** *n* : a posited unity of mental structure in mankind that leads to the independent development of similar technologies, traits, and institutions

**¹psy·chid** \ˈsīkəd\ *adj* [NL *Psychidae*] : of or relating to the Psychidae

**²psychid** \"\ *n* -s : a moth of the family Psychidae

**psychi·dae** \ˈsīkə,dē, ˈsik-\ *n pl, cap* [NL, fr. *Psyche*, type genus + *-idae*] : a family of moths the males of which have thinly scaled or nearly transparent wings while the females are wingless and wormlike

**psy·chism** \ˈsī,kizəm\ *n* -s [F *psychisme*, fr. *psych-* + *-isme* -ism] **1** : a doctrine that there is a fluid universally diffused and equally animating all living beings **2** [*psych-* + *-ism*] : psychic nature or character : mental fact or process **3** : PSYCHICAL RESEARCH

**psy·chis·tic** \(ˈ)sī¦kistik\ *adj* : of or related to psychism

**¹psy·cho** \ˈsī(,)kō\ *n* -s [by shortening] **1** *slang* : PSYCHOANALYSIS **2** [short for *psychoneurotic*] *slang* : one who has developed an emotional disorder (as a psychoneurosis) esp. while in military service

**²psycho** \"\ *adj* [by shortening] **1** *slang* : PSYCHIATRIC ⟨~ ward⟩ **2** *slang* : PSYCHONEUROTIC ⟨~ cases⟩

**³psycho** \"\ *vt* -ED/-ING/-S *slang* : PSYCHOANALYZE

**psycho-** — see PSYCH-

**psy·cho·acoustic** \¦sī(,)kō+\ *adj* [ISV *psych-* + *acoustic*] : of or relating to psychoacoustics

**psy·cho·acoustics** \"+\ *n pl but sing in constr* : a branch of science dealing with hearing, the sensations produced by sounds, and the problems of communication

**psy·cho·analysis** \"+\ *also* **psych·analysis** \¦sīk+\ *n* [ISV *psych-* + *analysis*; orig. formed as G *psychoanalyse*] **1** : a method of investigating (as through free association and dream analysis) psychic content and mechanisms not readily accessible to voluntary exploration by the conscious mind **2** : a method of psychotherapy esp. with psychoneurotics designed to bring unconscious and preconscious material into consciousness and carried out largely through the analysis of resistance and through the establishment and analysis of a transference neurosis **3** : a body of empirical findings and a set of theories on human motivation, behavior, and personality development : METAPSYCHOLOGY **4** : an area of psychotherapeutic practice : an institutionalized school (as founded by Sigmund Freud) of psychology, psychiatry, and psychotherapy **5** : a method or the practice of interpreting data obtained from nonpsychiatric sources (as from anthropology, art, literature) in the light of theories based on clinical observation

**psy·cho·analyst** \¦sī(,)kō+\ *also* **psych·analyst** \(ˈ)sīk+\ *n* [ISV, fr. *psychoanalysis*, *psychanalysis*, after such pairs as ISV *analysis: analyst*] : one who practices or adheres to the principles of psychoanalysis; *specif* : a psychotherapist trained at an established psychoanalytic institute

**psy·cho·analytic** *or* **psy·cho·analytical** \¦sī(,)kō+\ *also* **psych·analytic** *or* **psych·analytical** \(¦)sīk+\ *adj* [*psychoanalytic* ISV, fr. *psychoanalysis*, *psychanalysis*, after such pairs as ISV *analysis: analytic*; orig. formed as G *psychoanalytisch*; *psychoanalytical*, *psychanalytical* fr. *psychoanalysis*, *psychanalysis* after such pairs as E *analysis: analytical*] : of or relating to psychoanalysis : employing the principles or techniques of psychoanalysis — **psychoanalytically** *adv*

**psy·cho·analyze** \¦sī(,)kō+\ *vt* [ISV, fr. *psychoanalysis*, after such pairs as ISV *analysis: analyze*] **:** to treat in accordance with the principles of psychoanalysis

**psy·cho·biochemistry** \"+\ *n* [*psych-* + *biochemistry*] **:** biochemistry applied to the problems of psychology and psychiatry

**psy·cho·biological** *or* **psy·cho·biologic** \"+\ *adj* [*psychobiology* + *-ical* or *-ic*] **:** of or relating to psychobiology

**psy·cho·biologist** \"+\ *n* [*psychobiology* + *-ist*] **:** a specialist in psychobiology

**psy·cho·biology** \"+\ *n* [ISV *psych-* + *biology;* orig. formed as G *psychobiologie*] **:** the study of mental life and behavior in relation to other biological processes

**psy·cho·catharsis** \"+\ *n* [NL, fr. *psych-* + *catharsis*] **:** CATHARSIS 3

**psy·cho·cultural** \"+\ *adj* [*psych-* + *cultural*] **:** of or relating to the interaction of psychological and cultural factors in the individual's personality or in the characteristics of a group ⟨a ~ study of suicide⟩ ⟨the ~ approach in ethnology⟩ — **psy·cho·culturally** \"+\ *adv*

**psy·cho·da** \sī'kōdə\ *n, cap* [NL, fr. Gk *psychē* butterfly, moth + NL *-oda* (prob. fr. Gk *-ōdēs* -ode) — more at PSYCHE] **:** the type genus of Psychodidae

**psy·cho·diagnosis** \ˌsī(ˌ)kō+\ *n* [NL, fr. *psych-* + *diagnosis*] **:** diagnosis employing the principles and techniques of psychodiagnostics

**psy·cho·diagnostic** \"+\ *adj* [*psych-* + *diagnostic*] **:** of, relating to, or employing psychodiagnostics

**psy·cho·diagnostics** \"+\ *n pl but sing in constr* [ISV *psych-* + *diagnostics;* orig. formed as G *psychodiagnostik*] **:** the science or practice of accomplishing a personality evaluation or of diagnosing a mental disorder esp. by the techniques of clinical psychology

[1]**psy·chodid** \(ˈ)sīˈkōdəd, -kăd-\ *adj* [NL *Psychodidae*] **:** of or relating to the Psychodidae

[2]**psychodid** \"\ *n* -s **:** a fly of the family Psychodidae

**psy·chodi·dae** \sīˈkădəˌdē, -kōd-\ *n pl, cap* [NL, fr. *Psychoda*, type genus + *-idae*] **:** a family of very small two-winged flies (suborder Nematocera) having hairy wings resembling those of moths and larvae that develop in moss and damp vegetable matter — see PHLEBOTOMUS

**psy·cho·drama** \"+\ *n* [*psych-* + *drama*] **:** a usu. unrehearsed dramatic play designed to afford catharsis and social relearning for one or more of the participants from whose life history the plot is abstracted — compare SOCIODRAMA — **psy·cho·dramatic** \"+\ *adj*

**psy·cho·dynamic** \"+\ *adj* [*psych-* + *dynamic*] **:** relating to or concerned with mental or emotional forces or processes developing esp. in early childhood and their effects on behavior and mental states — **psy·cho·dynamically** \"+\ *adv*

**psy·cho·dynamics** \"+\ *n pl but sing in constr* [*psych-* + *dynamics*] **1 :** the study of psychology from a psychodynamic point of view **2 :** explanation or interpretation (as of behavior or of mental states) in terms of mental or emotional forces or processes **3 :** motivational forces acting esp. at the unconscious level

**psy·cho·dynamism** \"+\ *n* [*psych-* + *dynamism*] **:** a dynamism that is psychological

**psychoed** *past of* PSYCHO

**psycho-ethical** \"+\ *adj* [*psych-* + *ethical*] **:** of or relating to innate ethical principles

**psy·cho·galvanic** \"+\ *adj* [ISV *psych-* + *galvanic*] **:** relating to or involving electrical changes in the body as dependent on mental or emotional processes

**psychogalvanic reflex** *or* **psychogalvanic response** *n* **:** a momentary decrease in the apparent electrical resistance of the skin resulting from activity of the sweat glands in response to exciting stimuli

**psy·cho·galvanometer** \"+\ *n* [*psych-* + *galvanometer*] **:** a galvanometer used to detect the psychogalvanic reflex — **psy·cho·galvanometric** \"+\ *adj*

**psy·cho·genesis** \ˌsīkō+\ *n* [NL, fr. *psych-* + *genesis*] **1 :** the origin and development of the mind or of a mental function or trait **2 :** development from psychic as distinguished from somatic origins **3 :** development from mental factors operating through the central nervous system ⟨the ~ of an illness⟩ — compare PSYCHOSOMATICS

**psy·cho·genetic** \ˌsīkō+\ *adj* [fr. NL *psychogenesis*, after such pairs as L *genesis:* E *genetic*] **1 :** of or relating to psychogenesis **2 :** PSYCHOGENIC — **psy·cho·genetically** \"+\ *adv*

**psy·cho·genetics** \"+\ *n pl but sing in constr* **:** the study of psychogenesis

**psy·cho·gen·ic** \ˌsīkōˈjenik\ *adj* [*psych-* + *-genic*] **:** originating in the mind or in mental or emotional conflict ⟨hysterical paralyses are thought to be ~ in origin⟩ — distinguished from *somatogenic;* compare FUNCTIONAL, HYSTERICAL, ORGANIC, PSYCHOSOMATIC — **psy·cho·gen·i·cal·ly** \-nək(ə)lē\ *adv* — **psy·cho·ge·nic·i·ty** \ˌ==jəˈnisədē\ *n* -ES

**psy·chog·e·ny** \sīˈkäjənē\ *n* -ES [ISV *psych-* + *-geny*] **:** PSYCHOGENESIS 2

**psy·chog·no·sis** \ˌsīkəgˈnōsəs\ *also* **psy·chog·no·sy** \sīˈkägnəsē\ *n, pl* **psychogno·ses** \-ōˌsēz\ *also* **psychognosies** \-əsēz\ [*psych-* + *-gnosis* or *-gnosy*] **:** the study of the psyche esp. as concerned with the individual character ⟨the biognosis and ~ of group life —J.W.Powell⟩ — compare PSYCHOANALYSIS

**psy·chog·nos·tic** \ˌsīkəgˈnästik\ *adj* **:** of or relating to psychognosis

**psy·cho·gram** \ˈsīkəˌgram\ *n* [*psych-* + *-gram*] **1 :** a message supposed to have been sent by a spirit **2 :** a description of the mental life of an individual; *esp* **:** the pattern of responses to a projective technique (as the Rorschach test) **3 :** PROFILE 8a

**psy·cho·graph** \-raf,-räf\ *n* [*psych-* + *-graph*] **1 a :** an instrument intended to record psychic processes; *esp* **:** an instrument for spirit writing **b :** a device used in automatic writing or drawing **:** AUTOSCOPE, PLANCHETTE **2 :** an image felt to have been produced upon a photographic plate without a camera by the influence of a spirit **3 :** PROFILE 8a **4 :** a biography written from a psychodynamic point of view **:** a character analysis ⟨not to treat them too seriously but rather to expose them to pitiless publicity in ~s which reveal their essential absurdity —*N. Y. Herald Tribune Bk. Rev.*⟩

**psy·chog·ra·pher** \sīˈkägrəfə(r)\ *n* -s [*psych-* + *-grapher*] **:** the writer of a psychograph **:** a psychological biographer

**psy·cho·graph·ic** \ˌsīkəˈgrafik\ *adj* [*psychography* + *-ic*] **1 :** of or relating to the psychograph **2 :** of or relating to psychography — **psy·cho·graph·i·cal·ly** \-fək(ə)lē\ *adv*

**psy·chog·ra·phy** \sīˈkägrəfē\ *n* -ES [*psych-* + *-graphy*] **1 :** automatic writing used for spiritualistic purposes **2 :** the production of images of spirits upon sensitive plates without the use of a camera held to be accomplished by means of spiritualistic forces **3** [F *psychographie*, fr. *psych-* + *-graphie* -graphy] **:** the description of an individual's mental characteristics and their development **:** psychological biography

**psy·choid** \ˈsīˌkȯid\ *n* -s [ISV *psych-* + *-oid*] **:** a hypothetical vital principle directing the behavior of an organism

**psychoing** *pres part of* PSYCHO

**psy·cho·ki·ne·sia** \ˌsī(ˌ)kōkəˈnēzh(ē)ə, -ōˌkīˈn-\ *n* -s [NL, fr. *psych-* + *-kinesia*] **:** a fit of violent maniacal action resulting from defective inhibition

**psy·cho·kinesis** \ˌsī(ˌ)kō+\ *n* [NL, fr. *psych-* + *-kinesis*] **:** the production or alteration of motion by influence of the mind without somatic intervention in objects discrete from the subject's body — compare PRECOGNITION, TELEKINESIS

**psy·cho·kinetic** \ˌsī(ˌ)kō+\ *adj* [fr. NL *psychokinesis*, after such pairs as NL *kinesis:* E *kinetic*] **:** of or relating to psychokinesis or to psychokinetics — **psy·cho·kinetically** \"+\ *adv*

**psy·cho·kinetics** \"+\ *n pl but sing in constr* **:** the science that deals with psychokinesis

**psy·cho·kyme** \ˈsīkōˌkīm\ *n* -s [*psych-* + Gk *kyma* wave — more at CYME] **:** the neural energy operative in any mental activity

**psy·cho·lep·sy** \ˈsīkōˌlepsē\ *n* -ES [ISV *psych-* + *-lepsy*] **:** an attack of hopelessness and mental inertia esp. following elation and occurring typically in psychasthenic individuals

**psy·cho·lep·tic** \ˌ==ˈleptik\ *adj* **:** of or relating to psycholepsy

**psy·cho·linguistic** \ˌsī(ˌ)kō+\ *adj* [*psych-* + *linguistic*] **1 :** of or relating to psycholinguistics **2 :** of or relating to the psychological aspects of language

**psy·cho·linguistics** \"+\ *n pl but usu sing in constr* [*psych-* + *linguistics*] **:** the study of linguistic behavior as conditioning and conditioned by psychological factors including the speaker's and hearer's culturally determined categories of expression and comprehension

**psy·cho·log·i·cal** \ˌsīkəˈläjəkəl, -jēk-\ *also* **psy·cho·log·ic** \-jik\ *adj* [*psychology* + *-ic* or *-ical*] **1 a :** relating to, characteristic of, directed toward, influencing, arising in, or acting through the mind esp. in its affective or cognitive functions ⟨~ phenomena⟩ ⟨the ~ aspects of a problem⟩ ⟨~ climate⟩ ⟨organize the material on a ~ rather than a logical basis —A.G.Schmidt⟩ **b :** directed toward the will or toward the mind specif. in its conative function ⟨~ warfare⟩ ⟨~ strategy⟩ **2 :** relating to, concerned with, deriving from, or used in psychology ⟨~ research⟩ ⟨~ tests⟩ ⟨~ criticism⟩ ⟨~ clinic⟩ ⟨~ assistant⟩ **3 :** dealing with mental phenomena esp. as interpreted or elucidated by the application of principles of psychology ⟨~ drama⟩ ⟨~ films⟩ ⟨~ novels⟩

**psychological act** *n* **:** ACT 1c

**psychological distance** *n* **:** AESTHETIC DISTANCE

**psychological hedonism** *n* **:** the theory that conduct and esp. all human behavior is fundamentally motivated by the pursuit of pleasure or the avoidance of pain — distinguished from *hedonism*

**psy·cho·log·i·cal·ly** \ˌsīkəˈläjək(ə)lē, -jēk-, -li\ *adv* [*psychological* + *-ly*] **1 :** in a psychological manner ⟨solve a problem ~⟩ ⟨a ~ sound practice⟩ **2 :** MENTALLY ⟨war which caught them in its toils either ~ or physically —G.P.Meyer⟩ **3 a :** from the standpoint of psychology **:** in terms of psychology ⟨attempt to classify poetry ~ —Gerald Brenan⟩ ⟨a drastic and a ~ dangerous experiment in planned migration —Stuart Chase⟩ **b :** by employing psychology ⟨has all the time to nurse them ~ —*Trained Nurse & Hospital Rev.*⟩

**psychological medicine** *n* **1 :** medicine studied or practiced from the standpoint of the patient as an individual **:** PSYCHOSOMATICS **2 :** PSYCHIATRY

**psychological moment** *n* **:** the occasion when the mental atmosphere is most certain to be favorable to the full effect of an action or event ⟨wait for the *psychological moment* to present a bold proposal⟩

**psychological primary** *n* **:** one of a set of six object colors comprising red, yellow, green, blue, black, and white in terms of which all other object colors may be described

**psy·chol·o·gism** \sīˈkäləˌjizəm *sometimes* səˈk-\ *n* -s [ISV *psychology* + *-ism*] **1 :** a doctrine or theory that emphasizes psychological conceptions outside the field of psychology proper (as in history or in philosophy) **2 :** an expression or term used in psychology **3 :** a theory that explains the usual normative formal principles of logic as psychological and descriptive laws — opposed to *logicism*

**psy·chol·o·gist** \-jəst\ *n* -s [*psychology* + *-ist*] **1 :** a student of the mind or of behavior **2 :** a specialist in one or more branches of psychology; *esp* **:** a practitioner of clinical psychology, counseling, or guidance

**psy·chol·o·gis·tic** \(ˌ)sīˌkäləˈjistik *sometimes* səˌk-\ *adj* [ISV *psychologism* + *-istic*] **:** tending toward psychologism; *specif* **:** attempting to introduce psychological explanations of social phenomena

**psy·chol·o·gize** \sīˈkäləˌjīz *sometimes* səˈk-\ *vb* -ED/-ING/-S *see -ize in Explan Notes* [*psychology* + *-ize*] *vt* **:** to explain or interpret in mentalistic, psychological, or psychodynamic terms ⟨~ religion⟩ ~ *vi* **:** to speculate in psychological terms or upon psychological motivations

**psy·cho·logue** \ˈsīkəˌlōj *also* -läg\ *n* -s [F, prob. fr. *psych-* + *-logue*] **:** one devoted to psychology or to psychologism

**psy·chol·o·gy** \sīˈkäləjē, -ji *sometimes* səˈk-\ *n* -ES [NL *psychologia*, fr. *psych-* + *-logia* -logy] **1 a :** the science of mind or of mental phenomena and activities **:** systematic knowledge about mental processes **:** a method of obtaining knowledge about mental processes **b :** the science of behavior **:** the study of the interactions between the biological organism (as man) and its physical and social environment; *also* **:** systematic knowledge gained through such study **2 :** the mental, attitudinal, motivational, or behavioral characteristics of an individual or of a type, class, or group of individuals ⟨the ~ of the fighting man⟩ ⟨mob ~⟩; *also* **:** such principles pertinent to a particular field of knowledge or activity ⟨color ~⟩ ⟨the ~ of power and leadership —Norman Cousins⟩ ⟨the ~ of learning⟩ **3 :** a treatise on or a school, system, or branch of psychology

**psy·chom·a·chy** \-ämәkē\ *n* -ES [LL *psychomachia* conflict of the soul, prob. fr. Gk *psych-* + *-machia* -machy] **:** a conflict of the soul (as with the body or between good and evil)

**psy·chom·e·ter** \-mәd·ә(r)\ *n* [back-formation fr. *psychometry*] **1 :** one who practices the occult art of psychometry **2** [ISV *psych-* + *-meter*] **:** a timing or measuring instrument used in mental measurement

**psy·cho·met·ric** \ˌsīkəˈme·trik\ *adj* [ISV *psych-* + *-metric*] **1 :** relating to the measurement of mental or subjective data **2 :** relating to or being a mental test or psychological method whose results are expressed quantitatively rather than qualitatively — **psy·cho·met·ri·cal·ly** \-rәk(ә)lē\ *adv*

**psy·chom·e·tri·cian** \(ˌ)sīˌkäməˈtrishən *sometimes* səˌk-\ *n* -s [*psychometric* + *-an*] **1 :** a person (as a clinical psychologist) who is skilled in the administration and interpretation of objective psychological tests (as of intelligence or of personality) **2 :** a psychologist who devises, constructs, and standardizes psychometric tests — compare PSYCHOTECHNICIAN

**psy·cho·met·rics** \ˌsīkəˈme·triks\ *n pl but sing in constr* [*psychometric* + *-s*] **1 :** a branch of clinical or applied psychology dealing with the use and application of mental measurement **2 :** the technique of mental measurements **:** the use of quantitative devices for assessing psychological trends

**psy·chom·e·trist** \sīˈkämәˌtrәst *sometimes* səˈk-\ *n* -s [*psychometry* + *-ist*] **:** PSYCHOMETRICIAN

**psy·chom·e·trize** \-ˌtrīz\ *vb* -ED/-ING/-S [*psychometry* + *-ize*] *vt* **:** to interpret by the occult art of psychometry ~ *vi* **:** to practice divination by means of psychometry

**psy·chom·e·try** \-ˌtrē\ *n* -ES [*psych-* + *-metry*] **1 :** divination of facts concerning an object or its owner through contact with or proximity to the object **2 :** PSYCHOMETRICS

**psy·cho·mi·idae** \ˌsīkəˈmīəˌdē\ *n pl, cap* [NL, fr. *Psychomia*, type genus (fr. *psych-* + *-myia*) + *-idae*] **:** a small family of caddis flies

**psy·cho·mor·phism** \-ˈmȯrˌfizəm\ *n* -s [*psych-* + *-morphism* (as in *anthropomorphism*)] **:** the attribution of mental processes (as feeling and purpose) to animals or to inanimate objects

**psy·cho·motility** \ˌsī(ˌ)kō+\ *n* [ISV *psych-* + *motility*] **:** the power of bodily movement as dependent on mental processes

**psy·cho·motion** \"+\ *n* [*psych-* + *motion*] **:** PSYCHOMOTILITY

**psy·cho·motor** \ˌsīkə+\ *adj* [ISV *psych-* + *motor*] **:** of or relating to muscular action believed to ensue from prior esp. conscious mental activity

**psy·chon** \ˈsīˌkän\ *n* -s [*psych-* + *-on*] **:** an ultimate particle of psychic nature

**psy·cho·neural** \ˌsī(ˌ)kō+\ *adj* [*psych-* + *neural*] **:** of or relating to the interrelationship of nervous system and consciousness **:** relating to the mental functions of the central nervous system

**psy·cho·neurosis** \"+\ *n* [NL, fr. *psych-* + *neurosis*] **1 :** a neurosis based on emotional conflict in which an impulse that has been blocked seeks expression in a disguised response or symptom — distinguished from *actual neurosis* **2 :** NEUROSIS 1

[1]**psy·cho·neurotic** \"+\ *adj* [fr. NL *psychoneurosis*, after such pairs as NL *neurosis:* E *neurotic*] **1 :** of or relating to psychoneurosis **2 :** affected with psychoneurosis

[2]**psychoneurotic** \"\ *n* **:** one who is psychoneurotic

**psy·cho·nom·ic** \ˌsīkəˈnämik\ *adj* [*psychonomy* + *-ic*] **:** relating to or constituting the laws of mental life

**psy·cho·nom·ics** \ˌ==ˈnämiks\ *n pl but sing in constr* **:** the science of the laws relating the mind to the organism's internal and external environment **:** PSYCHOLOGY

**psy·chon·o·my** \sīˈkänəmē\ *n* -ES [*psych-* + *-nomy*] **:** PSYCHONOMICS

**psy·cho·pan·nych·i·an** \ˌsīkōˌpaˈnikēən\ *n* -s [*psychopannychy* + *-an*] **:** PSYCHOPANNYCHIST

**psy·cho·pan·ny·chism** \ˌ==ˈpanəˌkizəm\ *n* -s [*psychopannychy* + *-ism*] **:** the theological doctrine that the soul falls asleep at death and does not wake until the resurrection of the body

**psy·cho·pan·ny·chist** \ˌ==ˈpanəkəst\ *or* **psy·cho·pan·ny·chite** \-nəˌkīt\ *n* -s [NL *psychopannychia* + *-ist* or *-ite*] **:** one who believes in or supports the doctrine of psychopannychism

**psy·cho·pan·ny·chis·tic** \ˌ==ˌpanəˈkistik\ *adj* **:** of or relating to psychopannychism

**psy·cho·pan·ny·chy** \-nəkē\ *n* -ES [NL *psychopannychia*, fr. *psych-* + Gk *pannychios* all night long, (fr. *pan-* + *nychios* nightly, of the night, fr. *nykt-, nyx* night) + NL *-ia* -y — more at NIGHT] **:** psychopannychistic slumber

**psy·cho·path** \ˈsīkəˌpath, -paa(ə)th, -paith\ *n* -s [ISV *psych-* + *-path*] **1 :** a mentally ill or unstable person **:** one with a poorly balanced personality structure **:** ECCENTRIC **2 :** PSYCHOPATHIC PERSONALITY 2

**psy·cho·path·ia** \ˌ==ˈpathēə\ *n* -s [NL, fr. *psych-* + *-pathia* -pathy] **:** PSYCHOPATHY

[1]**psy·cho·path·ic** \ˌ==ˈpathik, -ˈpaath-, -ˈpaith-, -thēk\ *adj* [ISV *psych-* + *-pathic;* orig. formed as G *psychopathisch*] **:** of, relating to, or characterized by psychopathy — **psy·cho·path·i·cal·ly** \-thək(ə)lē, -thēk-, -li\ *adv*

[2]**psychopathic** \"\ *n* -s **:** PSYCHOPATH

**psychopathic hospital** *n* **:** a hospital for the observation, examination, treatment, or temporary retention of patients showing evidence of mental disturbance

**psychopathic personality** *n* **1 :** a disorder of behavior toward other individuals or toward society in which reality is usu. clearly perceived except for an individual's social responsibilities or moral obligations, which is often manifested hedonistically (as by criminal acts, drug addiction, sexual perversion, or activity leading to immediate personal gratification esp. when it is believed that punishment can be avoided), by passive indifference (as by shiftlessness, untrustworthiness, or vagabondism), or in contrast by fanatical pseudosocial zealousness, and which is usu. a more or less permanent way of life refractory to treatment and hence often considered a constitutional disorder **2 :** an individual having a psychopathic personality

**psychopathic ward** *n* **:** a ward in a general or other hospital serving the same purpose as a psychopathic hospital

**psy·chop·a·thist** \sīˈkäpəthəst\ *n* -s [*psychopathy* + *-ist*] **:** PSYCHOPATHOLOGIST

**psy·cho·pathological** *or* **psy·cho·pathologic** \ˌsī(ˌ)kō+\ *adj* [*psychopathology* + *-ical* or *-ic*] **:** of, relating to, or exhibiting psychopathology

**psy·cho·pathologist** \"+\ *n* [*psychopathology* + *-ist*] **:** a specialist in psychopathology

**psy·cho·pathology** \"+\ *n* [ISV *psych-* + *pathology;* orig. formed as G *psychopathologie*] **1 :** the study of psychologic and behavioral dysfunction occurring in mental disorder or in social disorganization **2 :** disordered psychologic and behavioral functioning (as in a mental disease)

**psy·chop·a·thy** \sīˈkäpəthē\ *n* -ES [ISV *psych-* + *-pathy;* orig. formed as G *psychopathie*] **1 :** mental disorder **2 :** PSYCHOPATHIC PERSONALITY 1

**psy·cho·pharmacologic** *or* **psy·cho·pharmacological** \ˌsī(ˌ)kō+\ *adj* [*psychopharmacology* + *-ic* or *-ical*] **:** of, relating to, or used in psychopharmacology ⟨~ agent⟩ ⟨tranquilizers are ~ drugs⟩

**psy·cho·pharmacology** \"+\ *n* [*psych-* + *pharmacology*] **:** the study of the effects of drugs on mental states

**psy·cho·pho·bia** \ˌsīkəˈfōbēə\ *n* [NL, fr. *psych-* + *-phobia*] **:** an aversion to psychological considerations

**psy·cho·phon·asthenia** \ˌsī(ˌ)kōˌfōn+\ *n* [*psych-* + *phon-* + *asthenia*] **:** a hysterical symptom in which the voice becomes tremulous, choked, and irregular in pitch with overall difficulty in vocalization

**psy·cho·physical** \ˌsī(ˌ)kō+\ *adj* [*psychophysics* + *-al*] **1 :** of or relating to psychophysics **2 :** interrelating or existing between the physical and the psychic **3 :** partaking of both physical and psychical ⟨the ~ organism⟩ ⟨a ~ disposition⟩ — compare PSYCHOSOMATIC — **psy·cho·physically** \"+\ *adv*

**psychophysical method** *n* **:** any of the experimental and statistical methods (as of just-noticeable differences, of constant stimuli, or of average error) developed for studying the perception of physical magnitudes

**psychophysical parallelism** *n* **1 :** a philosophical theory that the parallel physical and psychical events do not interact — compare DOUBLE-ASPECT THEORY, INTERACTIONISM **2 :** DOUBLE-ASPECT THEORY 2

**psy·cho·physicist** \ˌsī(ˌ)kō+\ *n* [*psychophysics* + *-ist*] **:** a specialist in psychophysics

**psy·cho·physics** \"+\ *n pl but sing in constr* [ISV *psych-* + *physics;* orig. formed as G *psychophysik*] **:** a branch of science that deals with the problems (as the interrelations of the physical processes that constitute stimuli and the mental processes that result from their impingement on the living organism) common to physics and psychology — compare PHYSIOLOGICAL PSYCHOLOGY, PSYCHOSOMATICS

**psy·cho·physiological** *or* **psy·cho·physiologic** \"+\ *adj* [*psychophysiological* fr. *psychophysiology* + *-ical; psychophysiologic* ISV *psychophysiology* + *-ic*] **1 :** of or relating to physiological psychology **2 :** combining, interrelating, or involving mental and bodily processes — **psy·cho·physiologically** \"+\ *adj*

**psy·cho·physiologist** \"+\ *n* [ISV *psychophysiology* + *-ist*] **:** a specialist in physiological psychology

**psy·cho·physiology** \"+\ *n* [ISV *psych-* + *physiology*] **:** PHYSIOLOGICAL PSYCHOLOGY

**psy·cho·plasm** \ˈsīkōˌplazəm\ *n* [ISV *psych-* + *-plasm*] **:** a primordial substance held to supply the basis of the psychical as well as of the physical

**psy·cho·pomp** \ˈsīkōˌpämp\ *or* **psy·cho·pom·pos** \ˌ==ˈpämpəs, -m,päs\ *n, pl* **psychopomps** \ˈ==ˌpämps\ *or* **psychopompoi** \ˌ==ˈpämˌpȯi\ [Gk *psychopompos*, fr. *psych-* + *pompos* conductor, fr. *pempein* to send, conduct] **:** a conductor of souls to the afterworld

[1]**psy·chop·sid** \(ˈ)sīˈkäpsəd\ *adj* [NL *Psychopsidae*] **:** of or relating to the Psychopsidae

[2]**psychopsid** \"\ *n* -s **:** a lacewing of the family Psychopsidae

**psy·chop·si·dae** \sīˈkäpsəˌdē\ *n pl, cap* [NL, fr. *Psychopsis*, type genus (fr. Gk *psychē* butterfly + NL *-opsis*) + *-idae* — more at PSYCHE] **:** a small family of chiefly tropical lacewings occurring in Australia and part of So. America

**psy·chor·rhag·ic** \ˌsīkəˈrajik\ *adj* [*psychorrhagy* + *-ic*] **:** of or relating to psychorrhagy

**psy·chor·rha·gy** \sīˈkȯrəjē\ *n* -ES [*psych-* + *-rrhagy*] **:** temporary manifestation of a person's soul to other persons at a distance from his body

**psychos** *pl of* PSYCHO, *pres 3d sing of* PSYCHO

**psy·cho·scope** \ˈsīkəˌskōp\ *n* [*psych-* + *scope*] **:** a means of observing mental processes

**psy·cho·sensorial** \ˌsī(ˌ)kō+\ *adj* [ISV *psychosensory* + *-al*] **:** PSYCHOSENSORY

**psy·cho·sensory** \"+\ *adj* [*psych-* + *sensory*] **1 :** of, relating to, or constituting sensory consciousness not directly mediated by the sense organs **:** HALLUCINATORY **2 :** of or relating to sense perception

**psy·cho·sexual** \"+\ *adj* [*psych-* + *sexual*] **1 :** of or relating to the mental, emotional, and behavioral aspects or consequences of the biological process of sexual differentiation **2 :** of or relating to the complex of mental or emotional attitudes concerning sexual activity **3 :** of or relating to the physiological psychology of sex — **psy·cho·sexually** \"+\ *adv*

**psy·cho·sexuality** \"+\ *n* [*psych-* + *sexuality*] **:** the psychic factors of sex

**psy·cho·sis** \sīˈkōsəs\ *n, pl* **psycho·ses** \-ōˌsēz\ [NL, fr. *psych-* + *-osis*] **1 :** profound disorganization of mind, personality, or behavior that results from an individual's inability to tolerate the demands of his social environment whether because of the enormity of the imposed stress or because of primary inadequacy or acquired debility of his organism esp. in regard to the central nervous system or because of combinations of these factors and that may be manifested by disorders of perception, thinking, or affect symptoms of neurosis, by criminality, or by any combination of these — distinguished from *neurosis;* compare INSANITY **2 :** extreme mental unrest of an individual or of a social group esp. in regard to situational factors of grave import ⟨mass ~⟩ ⟨war ~⟩ — compare HYSTERIA 2 **syn** see INSANITY

**psy·cho·social** \ˌsī(ˌ)kō+\ *adj* [*psych-* + *social*] **1 :** involving both psychological and social aspects ⟨a stable marriage requires ~ adjustment⟩ **2 :** combining clinical psychological and social services ⟨the ~ team of a child guidance clinic⟩ **3 :** relating social conditions to mental health ⟨~ medicine⟩

**psy·cho·sociological** \"+\ *adj* [*psych-* + *sociological*] **:** dealing with or measuring both psychological and sociological variables ⟨a ~ survey⟩ **:** concerned with the psychological characteristics of a race or people

**psy·cho·sociologist** \"+\ *n* **:** a specialist in psychosociology

**psy·cho·sociology** \"+\ *n* **:** a study of problems common to psychology and sociology

**psy·cho·so·ma** \ˌsīkəˈsōmə\ *or* **psy·cho·some** \ˈ==ˌsōm\ *n* -s [*psychosoma* fr. NL, fr. *psych-* + *-soma*; *psychosome* fr. *psych-* + *-some*] **:** the mental and physical organism **:** mind and body as a functional unit

[1]**psy·cho·somatic** \ˌsī(ˌ)kō+\ *adj* [ISV *psych-* + *somatic*] **1 :** of or relating to psychosomatics ⟨~ research⟩ **2 :** relating to, involving, or resulting from the interaction between mind or emotions and body **:** relating to or involving both mind and body ⟨~ medicine⟩ **3 :** resulting from the influence of emotional stress or conflict on a predisposed somatic area, organ, or bodily system ⟨a ~ disorder⟩ **4 :** evidencing bodily symptoms or bodily and mental symptoms as a result of emotional conflict ⟨a ~ patient⟩ **5 :** relating to neurotic symptoms resulting from or secondary to organic disease or injury **6 :** PSYCHOGENIC — **psy·cho·somatically** \"+\ *adv*

[2]**psychosomatic** \"\ *n* -s **:** one who evidences bodily symptoms or bodily and mental symptoms as a result of mental conflict

**psy·cho·so·mat·i·cist** \ˌsī(ˌ)kōsəˈmad·əsəst\ *n* -s [[1]*psychosomatic* + *-ist*] **:** a specialist in psychosomatics

**psy·cho·so·mat·ics** \-d·iks\ *n pl but sing in constr* [ISV *psychosomat-* (fr. [1]*psychosomatic*) + *-ics*] **:** a branch of medical science that deals with the interrelationships between mental or emotional and somatic processes and esp. with the manner in which intrapsychic conflict influences somatic symptomatology **:** psychosomatic medicine — compare PHYSIOLOGICAL PSYCHOLOGY, PSYCHOPHYSICS

**psy·cho·sta·sia** \ˌsīkōˈstāzh(ē)ə\ *n* -s [Gk, fr. *psych-* + *stasis* act of weighing, (fr. *histanai* to make to stand, weigh) + *-ia* -y — more at STAND] **:** a weighing of lives or souls ⟨the judgment of Osiris under the New Kingdom consisted essentially of the ceremony of the ~ —J.E.M.White⟩

**psy·cho·static** *also* **psy·cho·statical** \ˌ¦sīkō+\ *adj* [*psychostatic* back-formation fr. *psychostatics*; *psychostatical* fr. *psychostatics* + *-al*] **:** of or relating to psychostatics — **psy·cho·statically** \"+\ *adv*

**psy·cho·statics** \ˌsīkō+\ *n pl but sing in constr* [*psych-* + *statics*] **1 :** the study of the conditions of mental processes **2 :** a theory that conscious states consist of elements subject to separation and fusion without loss of essential character

**psy·cho·surgery** \ˌ¦sī(ˌ)kō+\ *n* [*psych-* + *surgery*] **:** cerebral surgery employed in treating psychic symptoms; *esp* **:** LOBOTOMY

**psy·cho·synthesis** \"+\ *n* [NL, fr. *psych-* + *synthesis*] **:** the integrative or synthetic process in psychotherapy as contrasted with the abreactive or cathartic

**psy·cho·synthetic** \"+\ *adj* **:** of or relating to psychosynthesis

**psy·cho·taxis** \ˌsīkō+\ *n* [NL, fr. *psych-* + *-taxis*] **:** an involuntary adjustment of one's modes of thought and action for keeping the agreeable and avoiding the disagreeable as a mechanism of ego defense

**psy·cho·technical** *also* **psy·cho·technic** \ˌ¦sī(ˌ)kō+\ *adj* [*psych-* + *technical* or *technic*] **:** of or relating or devoted to the practical applications (as industrial or military problems) of psychology

**psy·cho·technician** \"+\ *n* [*psych-* + *technician*] **:** one specializing in the practical application of psychology (as in the use of psychological tests) — compare PSYCHOMETRICIAN

**psy·cho·technics** \ˌsīkō+\ *n pl but sing in constr* [ISV *psych-* + *technics*; prob. orig. formed as G *psychotechnik*] **:** PSYCHOTECHNOLOGY

**psy·cho·technological** \ˌ¦sī(ˌ)kō+\ *adj* [*psychotechnology* + *-ical*] **:** of or relating to psychotechnology

**psy·cho·technologist** \"+\ *n* [*psychotechnology* + *-ist*] **:** a specialist in psychotechnology

**psy·cho·technology** \"+\ *n* [*psych-* + *technology*] **:** the application of psychological methods and results to the solution of practical problems esp. in industry — compare INDUSTRIAL PSYCHOLOGY

**psy·cho·the·ism** \ˈsīkō(ˌ)thēˌizəm\ *n* [*psych-* + *theism*] **:** the doctrine that God is pure spirit

**psy·cho·therapeutic** \ˌ¦sī(ˌ)kō+\ *adj* [ISV *psych-* + *therapeutic*] **:** relating to or involving psychotherapeutics or psychotherapy — **psy·cho·therapeutically** \"+\ *adv*

**psy·cho·therapeutics** \"+\ *n pl but usu sing in constr* **:** the science and art of psychotherapy

**psy·cho·therapeutist** \"+\ *n* **:** PSYCHOTHERAPIST

**psy·cho·therapist** \"+\ *n* [*psychotherapy* + *-ist*] **:** one (as a psychiatrist, clinical psychologist, psychiatric social worker, or clergyman) who is a practitioner of psychotherapy

**psy·cho·therapy** \"+\ *n* [ISV *psych-* + *therapy*] **1 :** treatment of mental or emotional disorder or maladjustment by psychological means esp. involving verbal communication (as in psychoanalysis, nondirective psychotherapy, reeducation, hypnosis, or prestige suggestion) **2 :** any alteration in an individual's interpersonal environment, relationships, or life situation brought about esp. by a qualified therapist and intended to have the effect of alleviating symptoms of mental or emotional disturbance **3 a :** the process whereby a patient or other subject becomes aware of the content and mechanisms of his unconscious mind esp. through free association **b** (1) **:** an interpersonal relationship in which a person seeking help develops a transference neurosis toward the analyst who subjects to interpretive analysis both the transference and his own countertransference phenomena (2) **:** an emotional experience in which the analysand's interpersonal attitudes as evidenced in his transference neurosis are corrected or modified through transactions with the analyst

[1]**psy·chot·ic** \(ˈ)sī¦kädˌ|ik, -ät|, |ēk\ *adj* [ISV, fr. NL *psychosis*, after such pairs as NL *narcosis*: E *narcotic*] **:** of, relating to, or marked by psychosis — **psy·chot·i·cal·ly** \|ək(ə)lē, |ēk-, -li\ *adv*

[2]**psychotic** \"\ *n* -s **:** a psychotic individual

**psy·cho·tria** \sīˈkō·trēə, -kä-\ *n, cap* [NL, prob. fr. MGk *psychotria* vivifying, fr. Gk *psychē* life — more at PSYCHE] **:** a very large genus of chiefly So. American shrubs, trees, or rarely herbs (family Rubiaceae) having corymbose flowers with a 5-lobed corolla and a fruit that is a berrylike drupe with two nutlets

**psy·cho·trine** \ˈsīkəˌtrēn, -ˌtrən\ *n* -s [ISV *psychotr-* (fr. NL *Psychotria*) + *-ine*] **:** a yellow crystalline alkaloid $C_{28}H_{36}N_2O_4$ having a blue fluorescence and found in ipecac

**psy·cho·trop·ic** \ˌ¦sīkə¦träpik\ *adj* [*psych-* + *-tropic*] *of a drug* **:** acting on the mind — compare TRANQUILIZER

**psy·cho·zo·ic** \ˌ¦sīkə¦zōik\ *adj, usu cap* [*psych-* + *-zoic*] **:** of or relating to the period beginning with the appearance of man on the earth **:** QUATERNARY

**psychro-** *comb form* [Gk, fr. *psychros*, fr. *psychein* to make cold — more at PSYCHE] **:** cold ⟨*psychrometer*⟩

**psy·chro·energetic** \ˌ¦sī(ˌ)krō+\ *adj* [*psychro-* + *energetic*] **:** of or relating to the relationship between environmental climatic conditions and the efficiency of utilization of foodstuffs esp. by domestic animals

**psy·chro·graph** \ˈsīkrōˌgraf, -ràf\ *n* [*psychro-* + *-graph*] **:** a self-recording psychrometer giving simultaneous readings of the dry-bulb and wet-bulb thermometer

**psy·chrom·e·ter** \sīˈkrämәd·ə(r)\ *n* [ISV *psychro-* + *-meter*] **:** a hygrometer whose operation depends on two similar thermometers with the bulb of one being kept wet so that it is cooled as a result of evaporation and shows a temperature lower than that of the dry-bulb thermometer and with the difference between the thermometer readings constituting a measure of the dryness of the surrounding air — **psy·chro·met·ric** \ˌ¦sīkrə¦me·trik\ *adj*

**psychrometric chart** *n* [*psychrometric* fr. *psychrometry* + *-ic*] **:** a graphic representation of the properties of mixtures of air and water vapor

**psy·chrom·e·try** \sīˈkrämə·trē\ *n* -ES [ISV *psychrometer* + *-y*] **1 :** the use of the psychrometer **2 :** a science dealing with the physical laws governing air and water mixture — compare HYGROMETRY

**psy·chro·phile** \ˈsīkrōˌfīl\ *n* -s [ISV *psychro-* + *-phile*] **:** a psychrophilic organism — compare MESOPHILE, THERMOPHILE

**psy·chro·phil·ic** \ˌ¦sīkrō¦filik\ *also* **psy·chro·phile** \ˈ==ˌfīl\ *adj* [*psychrophilic* fr. *psychro-* + *-phil* + *-ic*; *psychrophile* fr. *psychro-* + *-phile*] **:** thriving at a relatively low temperature ⟨~ bacteria⟩

**psy·chro·phyte** \ˈ==ˌfīt\ *n* -s [ISV *psychro-* + *-phyte*] **:** a plant suited to arctic or alpine conditions

**psy·dra·cious** \(ˈ)sī¦drāshəs\ *adj* [NL *psydracium* + E *-ous*] *archaic* **:** of or relating to a psydracium

**psy·dra·cium** \sīˈdrāsh(ē)əm\ *n, pl* **psy·dra·cia** \-)ə\ [NL, fr. Gk *psydrakion*, fr. *psydrak-* *psydrax* blister on the tongue (fr. *psydros* lying, untrue, fr. *pseudein* to lie, falsify) + *-ion* (n. suffix)] *archaic* **:** PIMPLE, PUSTULE

**psyk·ter** *also* **psyc·ter** \ˈsiktə(r)\ *n* -s [Gk *psyktēr*, fr. *psychein* to make cold — more at PSYCHE] **:** a jar used in ancient Greece for cooling wine

psykter

**psyl·la** \ˈsilə\ *n* [NL, fr. Gk, flea; akin to L *pulex* flea, Lith *blusà*, Skt *pluṣi*] **1** *cap* **:** a genus of jumping plant lice that is often considered synonymous with *Chermes* **2** -s **:** any insect of the family Psyllidae **:** JUMPING PLANT LOUSE

**psylla wax** *n* **:** a waxy varnish deposited on alder branches by a psyllid (*Psyllia alni*)

**psyl·lia** \ˈsilēə\ *n, cap* [NL, fr. *Psylla* + *-ia*] **:** a genus of jumping plant lice containing many economically important pests of cultivated plants — see PEAR PSYLLA

[1]**psyl·lid** \ˈsiləd\ *adj* [NL *Psyllidae*] **:** of or relating to the Psyllidae

[2]**psyllid** \"\ *n* -s **:** PSYLLA 2

**psyl·li·dae** \-ləˌdē\ *n pl, cap* [NL, fr. *Psylla*, type genus + *-idae*] **:** a family of homopterous insects comprising the jumping plant lice and having long usu. 10-jointed antennae, forewings that are thickened and often feathery, and the femora thickened and adapted for leaping

**psyllid yellows** *n pl but sing or pl in constr* **:** a virus disease of potatoes characterized by rolling and yellowish discoloration of the leaflets and transmitted by the potato psyllid

**psyl·li·um** \ˈsilēəm\ *n* -s [NL, fr. Gk *psyllion*, fr. *psylla* flea] **1 :** FLEAWORT **2** *or* **psyllium seed :** FLEASEED 1

**psylly** *n* -ES [NL *psillium*] *obs* **:** FLEAWORT

**psy·war** \ˈsī+ˌ-\ *n* [*psychological warfare*] **:** psychological warfare

**pt** *abbr* **1** part **2** payment **3** peseta **4** pint **5** point **6** port

**PT** *abbr* **1** Pacific time **2** [L *Paschale tempore*] Easter time **3** *often not cap* past tense **4** physical training **5** postal telegraph **6** *often not cap* post town **7** private terms **8** pro tempore **9** *often not cap* pupil teacher

**Pt** *symbol* platinum

**pta** *abbr* peseta

**PTA** *abbr or n* -s **1 :** PARENT-TEACHER ASSOCIATION **2 :** a member of a parent-teacher association

[1]**ptar·mic** \ˈtärmik\ *n* -s [LL *ptarmicum*, fr. Gk *ptarmikon*, neut. of *ptarmikos* causing to sneeze, fr. *ptarmos* act of sneezing + *-ikos* -ic — more at STERNUTATION] **:** a substance that causes sneezing

[2]**ptarmic** \"\ *or* **ptar·mi·cal** \-mәkəl\ *adj* [*ptarmic* fr. LL *ptarmicus*, fr. Gk *ptarmikos*; *ptarmical* fr. [1]*ptarmic* + *-al*] **:** STERNUTATORY

[1]**ptar·mi·ca** \-mәkə\ *n* -s [NL, fr. Gk *ptarmikē*, fr. *ptarmikos* causing to sneeze] **:** SNEEZEWORT

[2]**ptarmica** \"\ [NL, lit., sneezewort] *syn of* ACHILLEA

**ptar·mi·gan** \ˈtärmәgən, -mēg-\ *n, pl* **ptarmigan** *or* **ptarmigans** [modif. of ScGael *tàrmachan*] **:** any of various grouses of the genus *Lagopus* of northern regions having completely feathered feet, winter plumage that is chiefly or wholly white except in the British red grouse, and summer plumage that is largely grayish, brownish, or blackish and variously barred and vermiculated

**ptbl** *abbr* portable

**pt boat** \ˈpēˈtē-\ *also* **pt** [patrol torpedo] *n* -s *usu cap P&T* **:** MOTOR TORPEDO BOAT

**PTC** *abbr* postal telegraph cable

**ptd** *abbr* **1** painted **2** pointed **3** printed

**pte** *abbr, often cap* private

**ptelea** \ˈtelēə, ˈtēl-\ *n, cap* [NL, fr. Gk *ptelea* elm; perh. akin to L *tilia* linden] **:** a small genus of No. American shrubs or small trees (family Rutaceae) having 3- to 5-foliolate leaves and panicles of small greenish flowers with 4 or 5 imbricated petals and a rounded samara — see HOP TREE

**pteno·glos·sa** \ˌtenəˈgläsə, ˌtēn-, -lȯsə\ *n pl, cap* [NL, fr. Gk *ptēnos* winged (akin to Gk *petesthai* to fly) + NL *-glossa* — more at FEATHER] *in some classifications* **:** a division of Pectinibranchia comprising the gastropod families Janthinidae and Epitoniidae in which the median tooth is very small or wanting and the lateral teeth are strong and hooked and largest at the outside of each row — **pteno·glos·sate** \ˌ¦==¦=ˌsāt, -ˌsət\ *adj*

**pter-** *or* **ptero-** *comb form* [NL, fr. Gk, fr. *pteron* — more at FEATHER] **:** feather **:** wing ⟨*pteridium*⟩ ⟨*pterodactyl*⟩

**-p·tera** \-pt(ə)rə\ *n comb form* [NL, fr. Gk, neut. pl. of *-pteros* -pterous] **:** organism or organisms having (such or so many) wings or winglike parts — in taxonomic names esp. in zoology ⟨Hemi*ptera*⟩ ⟨Physalo*ptera*⟩

**pte·ra·li·um** \təˈrālēəm, teˈr-\ *n, pl* **ptera·lia** \-ēə\ [NL, irreg. fr. Gk *pteron* feather, wing] **:** a sclerite in the articular region of an insect's wing

**pter·an·o·don** \-ˈranəˌdän\ *n* [NL, fr. *pter-* + Gk *anodont-*, *anodōn* toothless, fr. *an-* + *odōn* tooth — more at TOOTH] **1** *cap* **:** a genus of Cretaceous pterosaurs having a long toothless beak, a backwardly directed bony crest on the skull, and a wingspread of up to 25 feet **2** -s **:** any pterosaur of *Pteranodon* or a closely related genus

[1]**pter·an·o·dont** \-nt\ *adj* [NL *Pteranodont-*, *Pteranodon*] **:** of or relating to *Pteranodon* or a closely related genus

[2]**pteranodont** \"\ *n* -s **:** PTERANODON 2

[1]**pte·ras·pid** \-ˈraspəd\ *adj* [NL *Pteraspidae*] **:** of or relating to the Pteraspidae

[2]**pteraspid** \"\ *n* -s **:** an ostracoderm of the family Pteraspidae

**pte·ras·pi·dae** \-pəˌdē\ *n pl, cap* [NL, fr. *Pteraspid-*, *Pteraspis*, type genus + *-idae*] **:** a family of widespread Silurian and Lower Devonian ostracoderms (class Heterostraci) — see PTERASPIS

**pte·ras·pis** \-pəs\ *n, cap* [NL, fr. *pter-* + *-aspis*] **:** the type genus of Pteraspidae comprising small ostracoderms in which the dorsal armor is made up of 7 large plates

**pter·ergate** \tər, (ˈ)ter+\ *n* [*pter-* + *ergate*] **:** an abnormal worker ant with minute wings

**pte·re·tis** \təˈrēd·əs\ *n, cap* [NL, irreg. fr. *pteris* fern] **:** a genus of ferns (family Polypodiaceae) that are sometimes included in *Onoclea* but distinguished by the vaselike clumps of fronds with feathery pinnate fertile fronds surrounded by or clustered among much taller sterile lanceolate fronds — see OSTRICH FERN

**pter·ic** \ˈterik\ *adj* [ISV *pter-* + *-ic*] **:** of, relating to, or resembling a wing

**pter·ich·thy·o·des** \tәˌrikthēˈō(ˌ)dēz, (ˌ)teˌr-\ *n, cap* [NL, fr. *pter-* + *ichthy-* + *-odes*] **:** a genus of ostracoderms (subclass Antiarcha) from the Devonian rocks of Scotland having the head covered with bony plates and bearing the orbits close together on its dorsal surface with the anterior half of the body encased in a buckler of large bony plates

**pterid-** *or* **pterido-** *comb form* [Gk *pterid-*, *pteris* — more at PTERIS] **:** fern ⟨*pteridography*⟩ ⟨*pteridoid*⟩

**pte·rid·e·ous** \təˈridēəs, (ˈ)te¦r-\ *adj* [NL, fr. *Pterid-*, *Pteris* + E *-eous*] **:** of or relating to *Pteris* or a closely related genus

**pter·i·dine** \ˈterəˌdēn, -ˌdᵊn\ *n* -s [ISV *pter-* + *-id* + *-ine*; orig. formed as G *pteridin*; fr. its being a factor in the pigments of butterfly wings] **:** a yellow crystalline bicyclic base $C_6H_4N_4$ that is a fundamental constituent in important natural products (as folic acid, leucopterin, xanthopterin); 1,3,5,8-tetraaza-naphthalene

**pte·rid·i·um** \təˈridēəm, teˈr-\ *n, cap* [NL, fr. *Pterid-*, *Pteris* + *-ium*] **:** a genus of ferns that are related to and sometimes included in *Pteris* and that have in addition to the false indusium formed by the frond margin a true indusium on the inner side of the sori — see BRACKEN

**pter·i·dog·ra·phy** \ˌterəˈdägrəfē\ *n* -ES [ISV *pterid-* + *-graphy*] **:** the description of ferns

**pter·i·doid** \ˈterəˌdȯid\ *adj* [*pterid-* + *-oid*] **:** of, relating to, or resembling a fern

**pter·i·do·log·i·cal** \ˌterədəˈläjəkəl\ *adj* [*pteridology* + *-ical*] **:** of or relating to pteridology or pteridologists

**pter·i·dol·o·gist** \ˌterəˈdäləjəst\ *n* -s [*pteridology* + *-ist*] **:** a specialist in pteridology

**pter·i·dol·o·gy** \-jē\ *n* -ES [*pterid-* + *-logy*] **:** the study of ferns

**pter·i·doph·y·ta** \ˌterəˈdäfəd·ə\ *n pl, cap* [NL, fr. *pterid-* + *-phyta*] *in some classifications* **:** a division of vascular plants coordinate with Bryophyta and Spermatophyta and coextensive with the subdivisions Psilopsida, Lycopsida, Sphenopsida and the class Filicineae of the Pteropsida

**pte·rid·o·phyte** \təˈridəˌfīt, ˈterəd-\ *n* -s [NL *Pteridophyta*] **:** a plant of the division Pteridophyta **:** a fern or fern ally

**pte·rid·o·phyt·ic** \tə¦ridə¦fid·ik, ¦terəd-\ *or* **pter·i·doph·y·tous** \¦terə¦däfəd·əs\ *adj* [NL *Pteridophyta* + E *-ic* or *-ous*] **:** of, relating to, or characteristic of the Pteridophyta

**pte·rido·sperm** \təˈridəˌspərm, ˈterəd-\ *n* [ISV *pterid-* + *sperm*] **:** a fossil plant of the order Cycadofilicales **:** SEED FERN

**pter·i·do·sper·mae** \ˌterədōˈspər(ˌ)mē\ [NL, fr. *pterid-* + *-spermae*] *syn of* PTERIDOSPERMAPHYTA

**pter·i·do·spermaphyta** \ˌterə(ˌ)dō+\ *n pl, cap* [NL, fr. *pterid-* + *Spermaphyta*] *in some classifications* **:** a group of fossil plants coextensive with the order Cycadofilicales but treated as coordinate with Gymnospermae and Angiospermae — **pter·i·do·sper·ma·phyt·ic** \¦==(ˌ)=¦spərmə¦fid·ik\ *adj* — **pter·i·do·sper·mous** \-məs\ *adj*

**pte·ri·idae** \təˈrīəˌdē, teˈr-\ *n pl, cap* [NL, fr. *Pteria*, type genus (fr. *pter-* + *-ia*) + *-idae*] **:** a family of bivalve mollusks (group Pectinaceae) most prominent in the Paleozoic and surviving chiefly in warm seas, including the pearl oysters, and having the right valve smaller and lower, the hinge line long and straight, the shell attached by a byssus, and the foot reduced

**pter·in** \ˈterən\ *n* -s [ISV *pter-* + *-in*; orig. formed in G; fr. its being a factor in the pigments of butterfly wings] **:** a compound containing the pteridine ring system

**pteri·on** \ˈterēˌän, ˈtir-\ *n* -s [NL, fr. *pter-* + *-ion* (as in *inion*)] **:** the suture of the frontal, parietal, and temporal bones with the greater wing of the sphenoid — see CRANIOMETRY illustration

**pteris** \ˈterəs, ˈtir-\ *n, cap* [NL, fr. Gk *pterid-*, *pteris* fern; akin to Gk *pteron* feather, wing — more at FEATHER] **1 :** a genus of coarse ferns (family Polypodiaceae) having variously divided or rarely simple fronds with a marginal linear continuous sorus and an indusium composed of the reflexed margin of the frond — see PTERIDIUM **2** -ES **:** RIBBON FERN

**-p·ter·is** \pt(ə)rəs\ *n comb form* [NL, fr. Gk, fr. *pteris*] **:** fern — in generic names ⟨Glosso*pteris*⟩ ⟨Ornitho*pteris*⟩

**ptero-** — see PTER-

**ptero·branch** \ˈterəˌbraŋk\ *n* -s [NL *Pterobranchia*] **:** a member of the order Pterobranchia

**ptero·bran·chia** \ˌterəˈbraŋkēə\ *n pl, cap* [NL, fr. *pter-* + *-branchia*] **:** an order of Hemichordata or an independent phylum of uncertain affinities that comprises two genera (*Cephalodiscus* and *Rhabdopleura*) of small deep-sea tube-dwelling animals that commonly reproduce by budding

**ptero·car·pous** \ˌ¦terə¦kärpəs\ *adj* [*pter-* + *-carpous*] **:** having winged fruit

**ptero·car·pus** \ˌterəˈkärpəs\ *n, cap* [NL, fr. *pter-* + *-carpus*] **:** a genus of tropical trees (family Leguminosae) with alternate pinnate leaves, yellow flowers, and a broad legume having a membranous-winged margin — see KINO

**ptero·car·ya** \-ˈka(a)rēə\ *n, cap* [NL, fr. *pter-* + Gk *karya* nut tree, fr. *karyon* nut — more at CAREEN] **:** a genus of Asiatic trees (family Juglandaceae) having thin-shelled nuts subtended by bracteoles that become enlarged in the two-winged fruit

**ptero·cau·lon** \ˌterəˈkȯlən, -ˌlän\ *n, cap* [NL, fr. *pter-* + *-caulon* (fr. Gk *kaulos* stem, stalk — more at COLE] **:** a small genus of vigorous woolly or downy perennial herbs (family Compositae) with alternate decurrent leaves and flower heads in dense terminal clusters — see BLACK ROOT, GOLDEN CUDWEED

**pte·roc·era** \təˈräsərə, teˈr-\ *also* **pte·roc·er·as** \-sərəs, -ˌras\ [NL, fr. *pter-* + *-cera* or *-ceras*] *syn of* LAMBIS

**ptero·cla·dia** \ˌterəˈklādēə\ *n, cap* [NL, fr. *pter-* + *clad-* + *-ia*] **:** a genus of red algae (family Gelidiaceae) having thalli suggestive of fern fronds

**ptero·cle·tes** \ˌterəˈklēd·(ˌ)ēz\ *n pl, cap* [NL, irreg. fr. *Pterocles*, genus of sandgrouse] **:** a suborder of Columbiformes coextensive with the Pteroclididae

**ptero·clid·i·dae** \ˌterəˈklidəˌdē\ *n pl, cap* [NL, fr. *Pteroclid-*, *Pterocles*, type genus (fr. *pter-* + Gk *kleid-*, *kleis* key) + *-idae* — more at CLEID-] **:** a family of birds (suborder Pterocletes) consisting of the sandgrouses

**ptero·dac·tyl** \ˌ¦terə¦daktəl\ *n* -s [NL *Pterodactylus*] **:** any of numerous extinct flying reptiles constituting the order Pterosauria, known from the Lower Jurassic nearly to the close of the Mesozoic, and having no feathers, a wing membrane extending from the side of the body along the arm to the end of the greatly enlarged fourth digit, and a tail usu. rather short but sometimes expanded and resembling a rudder — **ptero·dac·tyl·i·an** \ˌ¦==¦=¦tilēən\ *adj or n* — **ptero·dac·tyl·ic** \-lik\ *adj* — **ptero·dac·tyl·id** \ˌ¦==¦=ˌtələd\ *adj or n* — **ptero·dac·ty·loid** \-ˌlȯid\ *adj* — **ptero·dac·ty·lous** \-ləs\ *adj*

**ptero·dac·ty·li** \ˌterəˈdaktəˌlī\ [NL, fr. *pter-* + *dactyli*] *syn of* PTEROSAURIA

**ptero·dac·ty·lus** \-ləs\ [NL, fr. *pter-* + *dactylus*] *syn of* ORNITHOCEPHALUS

**pte·rod·ro·ma** \təˈrädrəmə, teˈr-\ *n, cap* [NL, fr. *pter-* + *-droma* (fr. Gk *dromos* course, race) — more at -DROME] **:** a large genus of petrels found chiefly in southern seas that are dark-colored often with a white tail and under parts

**pte·rog·ra·pher** \-ägrəfə(r)\ *n* -s [*pterography* + *-er*] **:** a specialist in pterography

**ptero·graph·ic** \ˌ¦terə¦grafik\ *or* **ptero·graph·i·cal** \-fәkəl\ *adj* [*pterography* + *-ic* or *-ical*] **:** of or relating to pterography

**pte·rog·ra·phy** \təˈrägrəfē, teˈr-\ *n* -ES [*pter-* + *-graphy*] **:** the description of feathers

**pte·ro·ic acid** \təˈrōik-, (ˈ)te¦|\ *n* [*pteroic* fr. *pterin* + *-oic*] **:** a crystalline amino acid $H_2NC_6HN_4(OH)CH_2NHC_6H_4COOH$ derived from *para*-aminobenzoic acid and pteridine and formed along with glutamic acid by hydrolysis of folic acid or other pteroylglutamic acids

**pteroid** \ˈteˌrȯid, ˈtiˌr-\ *adj* [*pter-* + *-oid*] **1 :** WINGLIKE **2** [Gk *pteris* fern + E *-oid* — more at PTERIS] **:** FERNLIKE

**pter·ois** \ˈterəwəs, -eˌrȯis\ *n, cap* [NL, prob. fr. Gk *pteroeis* feathered, winged, fr. *pteron* feather, wing] **:** a genus of small brilliantly colored scorpion fishes including the lion-fishes

**pter·o·li·chus** \ˌterəˈlīkəs\ *n, cap* [NL, fr. *pter-* + *-lichus* (prob. irreg. fr. Gk *lichēn* lichen) — more at LICHEN] **:** a genus of feather mites occurring on various birds

**pte·ro·ma** \təˈrōmə, teˈr-\ *n, pl* **pteroma·ta** \-məd·ə\ [L, fr. Gk *pterōma* fr. *pteron* feather, wing + *-ōma* -ome] **:** the enclosed space of a stoa, portico, or peristyle including the stylobate and the space to the solid wall behind the portico (as in a Greek temple)

[1]**pte·rom·a·lid** \təˈräməld, ¦terə¦mal-\ *adj* [NL *Pteromalidae*] **:** of or relating to the Pteromalidae

[2]**pteromalid** \"\ *n* -s **:** a chalcid fly of the family Pteromalidae

**pter·o·mal·i·dae** \ˌterəˈmaləˌdē\ *n pl, cap* [NL, fr. *Pteromalus*, type genus (fr. *pter-* + Gk *homalos* even, level) + *-idae*; akin to Gk *homos* same — more at SAME] **:** a large family of chalcid flies having larvae that are parasitic on the larvae of other insects (as of the orders Lepidoptera and Coleoptera) and some that are hyperparasites

**ptero·mys** \ˈterəˌmis\ [NL, fr. *pter-* + *-mys*] *syn of* PETAURISTA

**pteron** \ˈteˌrän, ˈtiˌr-\ *n* -s [L, fr. Gk, lit., wing, feather — more at FEATHER] **:** a side (as of a temple) in classical architecture

[1]**ptero·nar·cid** \ˌ¦terə¦närsəd\ *adj* [NL *Pteronarcidae*] **:** of or relating to the Pteronarcidae

[2]**pteronarcid** \"\ *n* -s **:** a stone fly of the family Pteronarcidae

**ptero·nar·ci·dae** \,==ˈnärsə,dē\ *n pl, cap* [NL, fr. *pter-* + *narc-* + *-idae;* fr. the sluggish flight] **:** a widely distributed family of stone flies

**ptero·pae·des** \,terəˈpē(,)dēz\ *n pl* [NL, fr. *pter-* + Gk *paides,* pl. of *pais* child — more at FEW] **:** birds (as the megapodes) able to fly shortly after hatching

**ptero·pae·dic** \ˌ==ˈpēdik\ *adj* [NL *pteropaedes* + E *-ic*] **:** of or relating to the pteropaedes

**ptero·pe·gal** \ˌterəˈpēgəl\ *or* **ptero·pe·gous** \-gəs\ *adj* [NL *pteropegum* + E *-al* or *-ous*] **:** of or relating to the pteropegum

**ptero·pe·gum** \,==ˈ=gəm\ *n* -s [NL, fr. *pter-* + Gk *pēgon,* neut. of *pēgos* solid, strong, fr. *pēgnynai* to fasten together — more at PACT] **:** an articular socket of the wing of an insect

**¹pte·roph·o·rid** \təˈräfərəd, (ˈ)teˌr-; ˌterəˈfōr-\ *adj* [NL *Pterophoridae*] **:** of or relating to the Pterophoridae

**²pterophorid** \"\ *n* -s **:** a plume moth of the family Pterophoridae

**pter·o·phor·i·dae** \,terəˈfōrə,dē\ *n pl, cap* [NL, fr. *Pterophorus,* type genus (fr. *pter-* + *-phorus*) + *-idae*] **:** a family of moths comprising the plume moths and having larvae that are usu. leaf rollers

**pte·rop·i·dae** \təˈräpə,dē, teˈr-\ [NL, fr. *Pteropus* + *-idae*] *syn of* PTEROPODIDAE

**¹ptero·pod** \ˈterəˌpäd\ *adj* [NL *Pteropoda*] **:** of or relating to the Pteropoda

**²pteropod** \"\ *n* -s **:** a mollusk of the division Pteropoda

**pte·rop·o·da** \təˈräpədə, teˈr-\ *n pl, cap* [NL, fr. *pter-* + *-poda*] **:** a division of Tectibranchia formerly ranked as a separate class of Mollusca comprising small hermaphroditic gastropod mollusks having the anterior lobes of the foot developed in the form of broad thin winglike organs with which they swim at or near the surface of the sea, usu. lacking gills, and frequently lacking a shell

**ptero·pod·i·dae** \,terəˈpädə,dē\ *n pl, cap* [NL, fr. *Pteropod-, Pteropus,* type genus + *-idae*] **:** a family of fruit bats coextensive with the suborder Megachiroptera

**ptero·po·di·um** \,terəˈpōdēəm\ *n, pl* **pteropo·dia** \-ēə\ [NL *pterop-* (fr. *Pteropoda*) + *-podium*] **:** a pteropod's foot

**pte·rop·o·dous** \təˈräpədəs, (ˈ)teˌr-\ *adj* [NL *Pteropoda* + E *-ous*] **:** of or relating to the Pteropoda

**pte·rop·sid** \təˈräpsəd, teˈr-\ *n* -s [NL *Pteropsida*] **:** a plant of the subdivision Pteropsida

**pte·rop·si·da** \-sədə\ *n pl, cap* [NL, fr. *Pteropsis,* genus of ferns (fr. *pter-* + *-opsis*) + *-ida*] **:** a subdivision of Tracheophyta comprising vascular plants (as the ferns and flowering plants) with well-developed and typically large leaves, leaf gaps usu. present in the primary vascular cylinder, and sporangia abaxial on normal or modified leaves and including the classes Filicineae, Gymnospermae, and Angiospermae — compare LYCOPSIDA, PSILOPSIDA, SPHENOPSIDA

**ptero·pus** \ˈterəpəs\ *n, cap* [NL, fr. Gk *pteropous* wing-footed, fr. *pter-* + *pous* foot — more at FOOT] **:** the type genus of Pteropodidae comprising the common fruit bats

**ptero·saur** \ˈterə,sȯ(ə)r\ *n* -s [NL *Pterosauria*] **:** one of the Pterosauria **:** a flying reptile

**ptero·sau·ria** \,==ˈsȯrēə\ *n pl, cap* [NL, fr. *pter-* + *-sauria*] **:** an order of Archosauria comprising flying reptiles flourishing from the Jurassic to late Cretaceous times and including the pterodactyls and related forms

**ptero·sper·mum** \-ˈspərməm\ *n, cap* [NL, fr. *pter-* + *-spermum*] **:** a genus of shrubs and trees (family Sterculiaceae) of southeastern Asia and the East Indies including several that yield economically important timbers — see MAYENG

**ptero·ste·mon** \-ˈstēmən\ *n, cap* [NL, fr. *pter-* + Gk *stēmōn* warp, thread — more at STAMEN] **:** a genus of Mexican shrubs (family Saxifragaceae) having pubescent twigs, alternate dentate leaves, showy white perfect flowers in cymes, and capsular fruit

**ptero·stigma** \ˌterə+\ *n, pl* **pterostigmata** [NL, fr. *pter-* + L *stigma*] **:** an opaque thickened spot on the costal margin of the wing of an insect — **ptero·stigmal** *adj* — **ptero·stigmatic** *or* **ptero·stigmatical** \ˌterə+\ *adj*

**ptero·theca** \ˌterə+\ *n* [NL, fr. *pter-* + *theca*] **:** the part of the pupa case that covers the rudimentary wing of an insect

**ptero·thorax** \"+\ *n* [NL, fr. *pter-* + *thorax;* fr. its being the wing-bearing segment] **:** the mesothorax and metathorax of an insect

**¹pte·rot·ic** \təˈräd·ik, (ˈ)teˌr-\ *adj* [*pter-* + ²*-otic;* fr. the bone being winglike] **:** of, relating to, or constituting a bone between the prootic and epiotic in the dorsal and outer part of the periotic capsule of a fish

**²pterotic** \"\ *n* -s **:** the pterotic bone

**-p·ter·ous** \pt(ə)rəs\ *adj comb form* [Gk *-pteros* -winged, fr. *pteron* wing, feather — more at FEATHER] **:** having (so many or such) wings or winglike parts ⟨aniso*pterous*⟩ ⟨hexa*pterous*⟩ ⟨tricho*pterous*⟩

**pter·o·yl** \ˈterəwəl, -,wil\ *n* -s [*pter-* (in *pteroic acid*) + *-yl*] **:** the radical ($C_{13}H_{11}N_6O$)CO— of pteroic acid

**pter·o·yl·glutamic acid** \ˌ==(,)=+...-\ *n* [*pteroylglutamic* ISV *pteroyl* + *glutamic*] **1 :** an acid that is a conjugate of one molecule each of pteroic acid and glutamic acid; *esp* **:** FOLIC ACID 1 **2 :** any of several acids (as pteroyl-hepta-glutamic acid found in yeast) that are conjugates of pteroic acid with more than one molecule of glutamic acid

**pter·o·yl·mono·glutamic acid** \ˌ==(,)=+=+...-\ *n* [*pteroylmonoglutamic* fr. *pteroyl* + *mon-* + *glutamic*] **:** FOLIC ACID 1

**-p·ter·us** \pt(ə)rəs\ *n comb form* [NL, fr. Gk *-pteros* -pterous] **:** one having (such) wings or winglike structures — in generic names ⟨Chaeto*pterus*⟩ ⟨Tracho*pterus*⟩

**pteryg-** *or* **pterygo-** *comb form* [Gk, fr. *pteryg-, pteryx;* akin to Gk *pteron* wing, feather — more at FEATHER] **1 :** wing **:** fin ⟨*pterygo*blast⟩ ⟨*pterygo*branchiate⟩ ⟨*pterygo*steum⟩ **2 :** pterygoid and ⟨*pterygo*malar⟩

**¹pte·ryg·ial** \təˈrij(ē)əl, (ˈ)teˌr-\ *adj* [NL *pterygium* + E *-al*] **:** of or relating to a pterygium

**²pterygial** \"\ *n* -s **:** a pterygial bone or cartilage; *specif* **:** ACTINOST

**-p·te·ryg·ii** \ptəˈrijē,ī\ *n pl comb form* [NL, fr. Gk *pteryg-, pteryx* wing, fin] **:** winged ones **:** finned ones — in taxonomic names ⟨Chrondro*pterygii*⟩ ⟨Neo*pterygii*⟩ ⟨Pleuro*pterygii*⟩

**pte·ryg·io·phore** \təˈrijēə,fō(ə)r, teˈr-\ *n* -s [*pteryg-* + *-phore*] **:** one of the cartilaginous or bony elements (as basalia and radialia) by which rays of the fin of a fish are supported **:** ACTINOST

**pte·ryg·i·um** \-jēəm\ *n, pl* **pterygiums** \-mz\ *or* **pteryg·ia** \-ēə\ [NL, fr. Gk *pterygion* little wing, fin, fr. *pteryg-* + *-ion* (dim. suffix)] **1 a :** a triangular fleshy mass of thickened conjunctiva occurring usu. at the inner side of the eyeball, covering part of the cornea, and causing a disturbance of vision **b :** a forward growth of the cuticle over the nail **2 :** a generalized limb of a vertebrate **3 :** one of the lobes at the end of the snout of a weevil

**pter·y·go·branchiate** \ˌterəgō+\ *adj* [*pteryg-* + *branchiate*] **:** having plumose gills — used of an isopod crustacean

**pter·y·gode** \ˈterə,gōd\ *n* -s [NL *pterygoda*] **:** PATAGIUM 2a

**pter·y·go·dum** \,terəˈgōdəm\ *n, pl* **pterygo·da** \-də\ [NL, fr. Gk *pterygōdes* winglike, fr. *pteryg-* + *-ōdēs* -ode] **:** PATAGIUM 2a

**pter·y·go·ge·nea** \,terəgōˈjēnēə\ [NL, fr. *pteryg-* + *-genea* (fr. Gk *genos* race, kind) — more at GEN-] *syn of* PTERYGOTA

**¹pter·y·goid** \ˈterə,gȯid\ *also* **pter·y·goi·dal** \ˌ==ˈgȯidᵊl\ *adj* [*pterygoid* prob. fr. (assumed) NL *pterygoides,* fr. Gk *pterygoeidēs* winglike, fr. *pteryg-* + *-oeidēs* -oid; *pterygoidal* fr. ²*pterygoid* + *-al*] **:** of, relating to, being, or lying in the region of the inferior part of the sphenoid bone of the vertebrate skull — see PTERYGOID BONE

**²pterygoid** \"+\ *n* -s **:** a pterygoid element (as a muscle, nerve, or bone)

**pterygoid artery** *n* **:** a branch of the internal maxillary artery supplying the pterygoid muscles

**pterygoid bone** *n* **:** a horizontally placed often more or less rodlike bone or group of bones of the upper jaw or roof of the mouth in most lower vertebrates connecting the palatine in front and the quadrate behind and forming part of the palatoquadrate arch

**pterygoid canal** *n* **:** a canal in the sphenoid bone transmitting the Vidian nerve and artery

**pter·y·goi·de·us** \,terəˈgȯidēəs\ *n, pl* **pterygoi·dei** \-ē,ī\ [NL, fr. (assumed) NL *pterygoides* pterygoid] **:** PTERYGOID MUSCLE

**pterygoid fossa** *n* **1 :** a depression on the outer and posterior aspect of the pterygoid process of the sphenoid bone **2 :** a depression on the lower jawbone for the insertion of the external pterygoid muscle

**pterygoid lamina** *n* **:** one of the two vertical plates making up a pterygoid process of the mammalian sphenoid bone

**pterygoid muscle** *n* **:** either of two muscles extending from the sphenoid bone to the lower jaw: **a :** an external muscle that arises from the greater wing of the sphenoid and from the outer surface of the lateral pterygoid lamina, is inserted into the condyle of the mandible and the interarticular disk, and acts as an antagonist of the masseter, temporal, and internal pterygoid muscles **b :** an internal muscle that arises from the inner surface of the lateral pterygoid lamina and the palatine and maxillary bones, is inserted into the angle and ramus of the mandible, cooperates with the masseter and temporal in elevating the lower jaw, and controls certain lateral and rotary movements of the jaw

**pterygoid nerve** *n* **:** either of two branches of the mandibular nerve chiefly supplying the pterygoid muscles and other muscles of mastication

**pterygoid notch** *n* **:** an angular notch separating the pterygoid laminae of each pterygoid process

**pterygoid plate** *n* **:** PTERYGOID LAMINA

**pterygoid plexus** *n* **:** a plexus of veins draining the region of the pterygoid muscles and emptying chiefly into the internal maxillary and anterior facial veins

**pterygoid process** *n* **1 :** a process extending downward from each side of the sphenoid bone in man and other mammals consisting of a pair of pterygoid laminae separated by a pterygoid notch and having a deep depression on its outer and posterior aspect **2 :** PTERYGOID LAMINA **3 :** a process on the palatine bone fitting into the pterygoid notch

**pterygoid ridge** *n* **:** a transverse ridge on the sphenoid bone marking the separation of the temporal and infratemporal fossae

**pter·y·go·mandibular** \ˌterə(,)gō+\ *adj* [*pteryg-* + *mandibular*] **:** of, relating to, or linking the pterygoid process and mandible

**pter·y·go·palatine fossa** \"+...-\ *n* [*pterygopalatine* ISV *pteryg-* + *palatine*] **:** a small triangular space beneath the apex of the orbit bounded in front by the maxilla, medially by the palatine bone, and behind by the pterygoid process of the sphenoid and lodging among other structures the sphenopalatine ganglion

**pte·rygo·phore** \təˈrigə,fō(ə)r, ˈterəgō,f-\ *n* -s [*pteryg-* + *-phore*] **:** ACTINOST

**pter·y·go·po·di·um** \,terəgōˈpōdēəm\ *n, pl* **pterygopo·dia** \-ēə\ [NL, fr. *pteryg-* + *-podium*] **:** the clasper of an elasmobranch

**pter·y·go·quadrate** \ˌterə(,)gō+\ *adj* [*pteryg-* + *quadrate*] **:** of, relating to, or constituting the upper half of the first branchial arch that gives rise in lower vertebrates to most of the upper jaw

**¹pter·y·go·so·mal** \+ˈsōməl\ *n* -s [NL *Pterygosoma* + E *-al*] **:** a mite of the family Pterygosomidae

**²pterygosomal** \"\ *adj* **:** of or relating to the Pterygosomidae

**pter·y·go·so·mi·dae** \,==(,)=ˈsōmə,dē\ *n pl, cap* [NL, fr. *Pterygosoma,* type genus (fr. *pteryg-* + *-soma*) + *-idae*] **:** a family of mites mostly parasitic on lizards

**pter·y·go·ta** \,terəˈgōd·ə\ *n pl, cap* [NL, fr. Gk, neut. pl. of *pterygōtos* winged, fr. *pteryg-, pteryx* wing — more at PTERYG-] **:** a subclass of Insecta consisting of the winged and secondarily wingless insects — compare APTERYGOTA

**pter·y·gote** \ˈterə,gōt\ *or* **pter·y·go·tous** \ˌ==ˈgōd·əs\ *adj* [*pterygote* fr. NL *Pterygota; pterygotous* fr. NL *Pterygota* + E *-ous*] **:** of or relating to the subclass Pterygota

**pter·y·la** \ˈterələ\ *n, pl* **ptery·lae** \-,lē, -,lī\ [NL, fr. *pter-* + Gk *hylē* wood, forest — more at HYLE] **:** one of the definite areas of the skin of a bird on which feathers grow — called also *feather tract;* contrasted with *apterium*

**pter·y·lo·graph·ic** \ˌterəlōˈgrafik\ *or* **pter·y·lo·graph·i·cal** \-fəkəl\ *adj* [*pterylography* + *-ic* or *-ical*] **:** of or relating to pterylography

**pter·y·log·ra·phy** \,terəˈlägrəfē\ *n* -ES [ISV *pterylo-* (fr. NL *pteryla*) + *-graphy;* orig. formed as G *pterylographie*] **:** the study or description of the pterylae of birds

**pter·y·lo·log·i·cal** \ˌterəlōˈläjəkəl\ *adj* [*pterylology* + *-ical*] **:** of or relating to pterylology

**pter·y·lol·o·gy** \,terəˈläləjē\ *n* -ES [NL *pterylosis* + *-logy*] **:** the study of pterylosis

**pter·y·lo·sis** \,terəˈlōsəs\ *n, pl* **pterylo·ses** \-ō,sēz\ [NL, fr. *pteryla* + *-osis*] **:** the arrangement of feathers in definite areas of growth ⟨birds . . . at least three years old judging from the ~ of the head —*Amer. Midland Naturalist*⟩

**-p·ter·yx** \ptə(,)riks\ *n comb form* [NL, fr. Gk, fr. *pteryx* wing — more at PTERYG-] **:** winged one **:** finned one — in generic names ⟨Di*pteryx*⟩ ⟨Odonto*pteryx*⟩

**ptg** *abbr* printing

**ptil-** *or* **ptilo-** *comb form* [NL, fr. Gk *ptilon;* akin to Gk *pteron* feather — more at FEATHER] **:** down **:** feather ⟨*Ptilo*cercus⟩

**-p·tile** \ptəl, p,tīl\ *n comb form* -s [Gk *ptilon*] **:** feather ⟨neosso*ptile*⟩ ⟨teleo*ptile*⟩ ⟨proto*ptile*⟩

**ptil·ich·thy·i·dae** \,ti,likˈthīə,dē\ *n pl, cap* [NL, fr. *Ptilichthys,* type genus (fr. *ptil-* + *-ichthys*) + *-idae*] **:** a family of blennies comprising the quillfishes

**pti·li·i·dae** \təˈlīə,dē\ [NL, fr. *Ptilium,* genus of beetles (fr. *ptil-* + *-ium*) + *-idae*] *syn of* TRICHOPTERYGIDAE

**pti·lim·ni·um** \təˈlimnēəm\ *n, cap* [NL, fr. *ptil-* + *limn-* + *-ium*] **:** a genus (family Umbelliferae) of widely distributed annual herbs having finely dissected leaves, compound umbels of minute white flowers, and angled or winged fruits — see MOCK BISHOP'S-WEED

**pti·li·nal** \təˈlīnᵊl\ *adj* [NL *ptilinum* + E *-al*] **:** of or relating to the ptilinum

**pti·li·num** \-nəm\ *n, pl* **ptili·na** \-nə\ [NL, prob. fr. *ptil-* + L *-inum* (neut. of *-inus* -ine)] **:** a vesicular organ on the front of the head of flies that assists in rupturing the pupa case and shortly afterward shrinks away

**ptilo·cer·cus** \,tīlōˈsərkəs, ,tīl-\ *n, cap* [NL, fr. *ptil-* + Gk *kerkos* tail] **:** a genus of insectivores comprising the pentails

**ptil·o·no·rhyn·chi·dae** \,tilənōˈriŋkə,dē\ *n pl, cap* [NL, fr. *Ptilonorhynchus,* type genus (fr. Gk *ptilon* feather, down + *-rhynchus*) + *-idae*] **:** a family of passerine birds that comprises the bowerbirds and is often included as a subfamily in Paradiseidae

**ptilo·pod** \ˈtilə,päd, ˈtīl-\ *adj* [*ptil-* + *-pod*] **:** having the feet feathered ⟨~ domestic fowls⟩

**pti·lo·sis** \təˈlōsəs, tīˈl-\ *n, pl* **ptilo·ses** \-ō,sēz\ [NL, fr. Gk *ptilōsis* plumage, fr. *ptil-* + *-ōsis* -osis] **:** plumage irrespective of pterylosis

**pti·lo·ta** \-ōd·ə\ *n, cap* [NL, fr. Gk, fem. sing. of *ptilōtos* winged, feathered, fr. *ptilon* feather] **:** a genus of marine red algae (family Ceramiaceae) having flat feathery fronds

**¹pti·nid** \ˈtīnəd\ *adj* [NL *Ptinidae*] **:** of or relating to the Ptinidae

**²ptinid** \"\ *n* -s **:** a serricorn beetle of the family Ptinidae

**ptin·i·dae** \ˈtinə,dē\ *n pl, cap* [NL, fr. *Ptinus,* type genus + *-idae*] **:** an extensive family of serricorn beetles of small size and usu. brown color that live mostly on dead animal and vegetable matter

**pti·nus** \ˈtīnəs\ *n, cap* [NL, perh. fr. Gk *phthinein* to decay, wane — more at PHTHISIS] **:** the type genus of Ptinidae comprising predominantly brown often hirsute beetles and including several pests of stored products — see SPIDER BEETLE

**pti·san** \təˈzan, ˈtizᵊn\ *n* -s [ME *tisane,* fr. MF, fr. L *ptisana* peeled barley, barley water, fr. Gk *ptisanē,* fr. *ptissein* to peel, crush — more at PESTLE] **:** a decoction of barley with other ingredients; *broadly* **:** TEA, TISANE

**PTM** *abbr* pulse-time modulation

**PTO** *abbr* please turn over

**ptol·e·ma·ic** \ˌtäləˈmāik, -āēk\ *also* **ptol·e·mae·an** \-mēən\ *adj, usu cap* [in sense 1, fr. L *Ptolemaeus* Ptolemy 2d cent. A.D. geographer and astronomer of Alexandria (fr. Gk *Ptolemaios*) + E *-ic* or *-an;* in sense 2, *ptolemaic* fr. Gk *ptolemaikos,* fr. *Ptolemaios* Ptolemy, any of the Greco-Egyptian rulers of Egypt + *-ikos* -ic; *ptolemaean* fr. L *Ptolemaeus* Ptolemaean (fr. *Ptolemaeus* Ptolemy, Greco-Egyptian ruler of Egypt, fr. Gk *Ptolemaios*) + E *-an*] **1 :** of or relating to Ptolemy the geographer and astronomer **2 :** of or relating to the Greco-Egyptian rulers of Egypt from 323 B.C. to 30 B.C.

**ptolemaic system** *n, usu cap P* [after Ptolemy *fl* 2d cent. A.D. who maintained it] **:** the system of planetary motions according to which the earth is at the center with the sun, moon, and planets revolving around it and each orbit except for the sun and moon is composed of a principal circle upon which moves a smaller circle carrying the planet — compare COPERNICAN SYSTEM, DEFERENT, ECCENTRIC 1, EPICYCLE

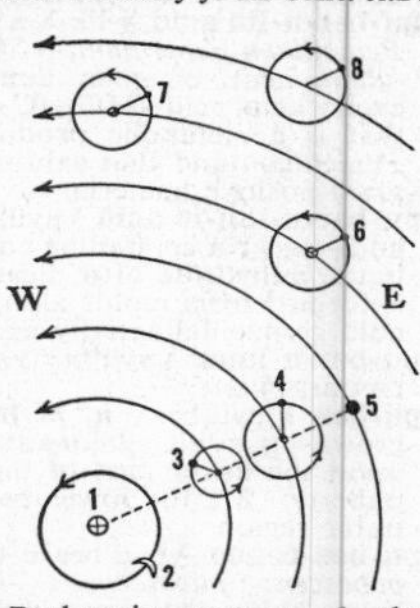

Ptolemaic system: *1* the Earth, *2* Moon, *3* Mercury, *4* Venus, *5* Sun, *6* Mars, *7* Jupiter, *8* Saturn

**ptol·e·ma·ism** \ˌ==ˈmā,izəm\ *n* -s *usu cap* [*ptolemaic* + *-ism*] **:** the principles of the Ptolemaic system

**ptol·e·ma·ist** \-āəst\ *n* -s *usu cap* [*ptolemaic* + *-ist*] **:** a supporter of the Ptolemaic system

**ptol·e·my** \ˈ==,mē, -mi\ *n* -ES *cap* [after *Ptolemy,* name given to various kings of Egypt, esp. fr. 323–30 B.C., fr. L *Ptolemaeus,* fr. Gk *Ptolemaios*] **:** a ruler of the Macedonian dynasty of Egypt

**pto·maine** \(ˈ)tōˌmān\ *n* -s [It *ptomaina,* fr. Gk *ptōma* fall, fallen body, corpse (fr. *piptein* to fall) + It *-ina* -ine — more at FEATHER] **:** any of various organic bases some of which (as cadaverine or putrescine) are poisonous and which are formed by the action of putrefactive bacteria on nitrogenous matter — compare LEUCOMAINE

**ptomaine poisoning** *n* **:** FOOD POISONING

**pto·ma·tine** \ˈtōmə,tēn, -,tən\ *n* -s [ISV *ptomat-* (fr. Gk *ptōmat-, ptōma* corpse) + *-ine*] **:** PTOMAINE

**ptosed** \ˈtōzd\ *or* **ptot·ic** \ˈtäd·ik\ *adj* [*ptosed* fr. NL *ptosis* + E *-ed; ptotic* ISV, fr. NL *ptosis,* after such pairs as L *synthesis:* E *synthetic*] **:** affected with or subject to ptosis

**pto·sis** \ˈtōsəs\ *n, pl* **pto·ses** \-ō,sēz\ [NL, fr. Gk *ptōsis* fall, falling, fr. *piptein* to fall] **:** a sagging or prolapse of an organ or part (as one of the abdominal viscera) ⟨renal ~⟩; *specif* **:** drooping of the upper eyelid (as from paralysis of the oculomotor nerve)

**ptr** *abbr* **1** painter **2** printer

**p trap** *n, cap P* **:** a P-shaped trap used esp. for sinks and lavatories

**ptrnmkr** *abbr* patternmaker

**pty** *abbr* **1** party **2** *often cap* proprietary

**ptyal-** *or* **ptyalo-** *comb form* [NL, fr. Gk, fr. *ptyalon* spittle, saliva, fr. *ptyein* to spit — more at SPEW] **:** saliva ⟨*ptyal*agogue⟩ ⟨*ptyal*orrhea⟩

P trap: *1* intake, *2* outlet, *3* cleanout

**pty·al·a·gogue** \tīˈalə,gäg *sometimes* -gōg\ *n* -s [ISV *ptyal-* + *-agogue*] **:** SIALAGOGUE

**pty·a·lin** \ˈtīələn\ *n* -s [ISV *ptyal-* + *-in*] **:** an alpha-amylase found in the saliva of many animals including man but not in that of horses, dogs, or cats **:** salivary amylase

**pty·a·lism** \ˈtīə,lizəm\ *n* -s [NL *ptyalismus,* fr. Gk *ptyalismos,* fr. *ptyalizein* to salivate, fr. *ptyalon* spittle, saliva + *-izein* -ize] **:** an excessive flow of saliva

**pty·as** \ˈtīəs\ *n, cap* [NL, fr. Gk, spitter, fr. *ptyein* to spit] **:** a genus of Colubridae comprising the Indian rat snake

**ptych-** *or* **ptycho-** *comb form* [Gk *ptych-,* fr. *ptychē,* fr. *ptyssein* to fold] **:** fold **:** layer ⟨*Ptycho*sperma⟩

**pty·chod·era** \tīˈkädərə\ *n, cap* [NL, prob. fr. *ptych-* + Gk *derē* neck, throat] **:** a widely distributed genus (the type of the family Ptychoderidae) of enteropneusts

**¹pty·choder·id** \(ˈ)tīˈkädərəd, ˌtīkōˈder-\ *adj* [NL *Ptychoderidae*] **:** of or relating to the Ptychoderidae

**²ptychoderid** \"\ *n* -s **:** an enteropneust of the family Ptychoderidae

**pty·cho·der·i·dae** \,tīkōˈderə,dē\ *n pl, cap* [NL, fr. *Ptychodera* + *-idae*] **:** a nearly cosmopolitan family of enteropneusts that includes *Balanoglossus* and related genera

**pty·cho·par·ia** \,tīkōˈpa(a)rēə\ *n, cap* [NL, fr. *ptych-* + Gk *pareia* cheek] **:** a genus of Middle and Upper Cambrian trilobites with small prominent glabella, long narrow thorax, and strongly segmented pygidium

**¹pty·cho·par·i·id** \-rēəd\ *n* -s [NL *Ptychoparia* + E *-id*] **:** a trilobite of the genus *Ptychoparia*

**²ptychopariid** \ˌ==ˈ=rēəd\ *adj* **:** of or relating to the genus *Ptychoparia*

**pty·chop·ter·i·dae** \,tī,käpˈterə,dē\ *n pl, cap* [NL, fr. *Ptychodera,* type genus + *-idae*] **:** a family of very delicate two-winged flies (suborder Nematocera) with long black-and-white-barred legs and larvae with a prolonged caudal respiratory tube comprising the phantom crane flies

**pty·cho·pterygial** \ˌtīkō+\ *adj* [NL *ptychopterygium* + E *-al*] **:** of or relating to a ptychopterygium

**pty·cho·pterygium** \"+\ *n, pl* **ptychopterygia** [NL, fr. *ptych-* + Gk *pterygion* little wing, fin — more at PTERYGIUM] **:** a primitive fin consisting of a low triangular flap supported by a series of unbranched rays

**pty·cho·sper·ma** \,tīkōˈspərmə\ *n, cap* [NL, fr. *ptych-* + *-sperma*] **:** a genus of pinnate-leaved palms that are native chiefly to Australasia and have pinnatisect leaves with segments cuneate and erose on the margin and small monoecious flowers borne in a slender branched spadix

**pty·cho·tis oil** \(ˈ)tīˌkōd·əs-\ *n* [ISV *ptychotis* (fr. NL *Ptychotis,* of unknown origin) + *oil*] **:** AJOWAN OIL

**-p·ty·sis** \ptəsəs\ *n comb form, pl* **-pty·ses** \-ptə,sēz\ [NL, fr. Gk, act of spitting, fr. *ptyein* to spit — more at SPEW] **:** spittle **:** spit ⟨hemo*ptysis*⟩ ⟨plasmo*ptysis*⟩

**ptyx·is** \ˈtiksəs\ *n, pl* **ptyx·es** \-k,sēz\ [NL, fr. Gk, act of folding, fr. *ptyssein* to fold] **:** the disposition of a single leaf in the bud

**pu** \ˈpü\ *chiefly Scot var of* PULL

**PU** *abbr* pickup

**Pu** *symbol* plutonium

**pua hemp** \ˈpüə-\ *n* [*pua* of unknown origin] **1 :** an East Indian shrub (*Maoutia puya*) of the family Urticaceae the bast fiber of which is used for cordage **2 :** the fiber of the pua hemp shrub

**pub** \ˈpəb\ *n* -s [short for *public*] **1** *chiefly Brit* **:** PUBLIC HOUSE **2 :** any of various establishments (as bars, taverns, cocktail lounges) where alcoholic beverages are sold and consumed

**pub** *abbr* **1** public **2** publication **3** published; publisher; publishing

**pub·ble** \ˈpəbəl\ *adj* [origin unknown] *dial chiefly Eng* **:** FAT, PLUMP

**pub crawl** *n* **:** a tour of bars and public houses usu. with a pause for one drink at each ⟨moved from café to café in a regular *pub crawl* —A.L.Mikhelson⟩

**pub-crawl** \ˈ=,=\ *vi* **:** to make a pub crawl ⟨went *pub-crawling* again, and by night . . . had a fine load on —T.G.Horton⟩ ~ *vt* **:** to make the rounds of (a series of bars) ⟨took off to *pub-crawl* the cafés of flag-decked Omdurman —*Time*⟩

**pub crawler** *n* **:** one that goes from bar to bar

**pu·ber·tal** \ˈpyübə(r)d·ᵊl, -)tᵊl *sometimes* ˈpüb-\ *also* **pu·ber·al** \-ərəl\ *adj* [*pubertal* fr. *puberty* + *-al; puberal* fr. ML *puberalis,* fr. L *puber* + *-alis* -al] **:** of or relating to puberty

**pu·ber·ty** \-ə(r)d·ē, -)tē, -i\ *n* -ES [ME *puberte,* fr. L *pubertas,* fr. *puber* grown up, adult + *-tas* -ty; perh. akin to L *puer* boy — more at PUERILE] **:** the condition of being or the period of becoming first capable of reproducing sexually marked by maturing of the genital organs, development of secondary sex characteristics, and in the human and in higher primates by the first occurrence of menstruation in the female; *broadly* **:** the age at which puberty occurs being typically between 13 and 16 years in boys and 11 and 14 in girls and often construed legally as 14 in boys and 12 in girls **syn** see YOUTH

**pu·ber·u·lent** \pyü'ber(y)ələnt\ *adj* [L *puber* grown up, adult, downy + E *-ulent* (as in *pulverulent*)] *biol* **:** minutely downy **:** covered with fine pubescence

**pu·ber·u·lic acid** \-lik-\ *n* [NL *puberulum* (specific epithet of *Penicillium puberulum*, fr. L *puber* grown up, adult, downy + *-ulum*, neut. of *-ulus*, dim. suffix) + E *-ic*] **:** a crystalline cyclic keto acid $(HO)_3(C_7H_2O)COOH$ related to tropolone that is a metabolic product of several molds of the genus *Penicillium* and that exhibits some germicidal activity against gram-positive bacteria

**pu·ber·u·lon·ic acid** \pyü¦berya¦länik-\ *n* [blend of *puberulic* and *-one*] **:** a crystalline compound $(HO)_2C_7HO(CO)_2O$ that is the anhydride of a dicarboxylic acid related to tropolone, is formed from molds along with puberulic acid, and exhibits mild germicidal activity against gram-positive bacteria

**pu·ber·u·lous** \pyü'ber(y)ələs\ *adj* [L *puber* + E *-ulous*] **:** PUBERULENT

**pu·bes** \'pyü,bēz\ *n, pl* **pubes** [L; akin to L *puber*, *pubes* grown-up, adult — more at PUBERTY] **1 :** the hair that appears upon the lower part of the hypogastric region at the age of puberty **2 :** the lower part of the hypogastric region **:** the pubic region

**pu·bes·cence** \pyü'bes°n(t)s\ *n* -s [ML *pubescentia*, fr. L *pubescent-, pubescens* + *-ia* -y] **1 :** the quality or state of being pubescent; *esp* **:** pubertal development of genital hair **2 a :** an epidermal covering of soft short hairs or down (as on the surfaces of leaves and stems or the bodies of insects) **b :** FUZZINESS **syn** see YOUTH

**pu·bes·cent** \-nt\ *adj* [L *pubescent-, pubescens*, pres. part. of *pubescere* to reach puberty, fr. *puber* grown up, adult + *-escere* (suffix forming inchoative verbs) — more at PUBERTY] **1 :** arriving at or having reached puberty **:** characteristic of or relating to this state — compare ADOLESCENT **2 :** having a fuzzy surface; *specif* **:** covered with fine soft short hairs — compare HIRSUTE, HISPID, LANATE, SERICEOUS, TOMENTOSE, VILLOUS

**pu·bic** \'pyübik, -bēk\ *adj* [*pubes* + *-ic*] **:** of, relating to, or lying in the region of the pubes or the pubis

**pubic arch** *n* **:** the arch formed at the front of the pelvis by the conjoined pubic bones

**pubic bone** *n* **:** PUBIS

**pubic crest** *n* **:** the border of the pubis between the pubic tubercle and the pubic symphysis

**pubic louse** *n* **:** CRAB LOUSE

**pubic symphysis** *n* **:** the rather rigid articulation of the two pubic bones in the midline of the lower anterior part of the abdomen

**pubic tubercle** *also* **pubic spine** *n* **:** a rounded eminence on the upper margin of each pubic bone near the symphysis

**pubio-** *comb form* [NL, fr. *pubis*] **:** pubis

**pu·bi·ot·o·my** \,pyübē'ädəmē\ *n* -ES [ISV *pubio-* + *-tomy*] **:** surgical division of the pubic bone esp. to facilitate delivery

**pu·bis** \'pyübəs\ *n, pl* **pu·bes** \-,bēz\ [NL (*os*) *pubis*, fr. L *os* bone + *pubis* of the groin, gen. of *pubes* pubes, groin — more at PUBES] **:** the ventral and anterior of the three principal bones composing either half of the pelvis, in man consisting of two branches or rami diverging posteriorly, the superior branch extending to the acetabulum, of which it forms a part, and uniting there with the ilium and ischium, and the inferior branch uniting with the ischium below the obturator foramen — compare PREPUBIS, POSTPUBIS

**publ** *abbr* **1** public **2** publication **3** published; publisher; publishing

[1]**pub·lic** \'pəblik, -lēk\ *adj* [ME *publique*, fr. MF *public*, *publique*, fr. L *publicus*, prob. alter. (influenced by *puber*, *pubes* grown up, adult) of *poplicus*, fr. *populus* people + *-icus* -ic — more at PUBERTY, PEOPLE] **1 a :** of, relating to, or affecting the people as an organized community **:** CIVIC, NATIONAL ⟨~ affairs⟩ ⟨~ holiday⟩ ⟨~ authority exists primarily to regulate . . . social and economic life —M.S.Kendrick⟩ — compare PUBLIC LAW **b :** of or relating to the international community or to mankind in general **:** COMMON, UNIVERSAL ⟨~ philosophy has . . . always been a political ideology —H.J.Morgenthau⟩ **c :** authorized or administered by or acting for the people as a political entity **:** GOVERNMENT ⟨~ expenditures⟩ ⟨~ subsidy⟩ ⟨~ agency⟩ ⟨~ prosecutor⟩ **d :** provided for, used by, or containing the records of a government agency ⟨the post office and other ~ buildings⟩ ⟨~ documents⟩ **2** *Brit* **:** of, relating to, or representing a university as a whole rather than one of its colleges or departments ⟨the office of . . . ~ Orator —*Cambridge Univ. Cal.*⟩ **3 a :** of or relating to business or community interests as opposed to private affairs **:** SOCIAL, IMPERSONAL ⟨~ morality⟩ ⟨leading from these private confessions of his poetry . . . toward a more ~ form of expression —Hans Meyerhoff⟩ **b :** of, relating to, or in the service of the community or nation ⟨an eminent figure in ~ life⟩ ⟨housewives volunteering for ~ work in charitable institutions⟩; *specif* **:** holding political office ⟨~ official⟩ **c :** devoted to the general or national welfare **:** PATRIOTIC, HUMANITARIAN ⟨debt the legal profession . . . owe to the publishers for their ~ spirit in producing these records —Norman Birkett⟩ ⟨all Greek thinkers were ~ men —C.P.Rodocanachi⟩ **4 a :** accessible to or shared by all members of the community ⟨~ hearing⟩ ⟨~ park⟩ ⟨~ water supply⟩ ⟨tourist passengers enjoy 16 ~ rooms aboard the magnificent new . . . flagship —*N.Y.Times*⟩ **b :** supported by or for the benefit of the people as a whole ⟨~ education⟩ ⟨~ welfare agencies⟩ **c :** COMMON 2d **d :** of, by, for, or directed to the people **:** GENERAL, POPULAR ⟨~ sentiment⟩ ⟨~ spokesman⟩ ⟨a book which increases ~ awareness —E.S.Furniss b. 1918⟩ ⟨effective use of the property in the ~ interest —C.V.Shields⟩ ⟨philanthropic activities keep him in the ~ eye⟩ **e :** providing services to the people on a business basis under some degree of civic or state control ⟨wrote with force on . . . railroads as ~ agents —W.C.Ford⟩ ⟨right of women to smoke in restaurants and other ~ places —Frances Perkins⟩ **5 a :** exposed to general view **:** CONSPICUOUS, OPEN ⟨a rather too ~ affair with another woman —William Sansom⟩ **b :** WELL-KNOWN, PROMINENT ⟨stage stars and ~ figures —James Dowdall⟩ **c :** of an observable or perceptible nature **:** EXTERNAL, MATERIAL ⟨belief in tables and chairs existing as ~ . . . objects independently of his sense impressions of them —F.S.C.Northrop⟩ ⟨the conventional or ~ aspect of language can encroach upon the . . . symbolical aspect —R.M.Weaver⟩

[2]**public** \"\ *n* -s [ME *publique*, fr. *publique*, adj.] **1 :** a place accessible or visible to all members of the community — usu. used in the phrase *in public* ⟨resent the . . . attempt to usurp in private the authority she could never assert in ~ —Edith Wharton⟩ **2 a :** an organized body of people **:** COMMUNITY, NATION ⟨the western European statesmen and ~s alike seem equally agreed that the slightest infringement of their national sovereignty is . . . abhorrent —Patrick McMahon⟩ **b :** the people as a whole **:** POPULACE, MASSES ⟨the ~ . . . in many cities have become apathetic to hit-and-run accidents —Ray Ashworth⟩ **3 :** a group of people distinguished by common interests or characteristics ⟨protecting movie stars from their ~s —*New Yorker*⟩ ⟨two books . . . different in scope, and aimed at different ~s —T.G.Bergin⟩ ⟨places before farmers, homemakers, and the rural ~ information on currently important agricultural situations —*U.S. Govt. Manual*⟩ **4** *Brit* **:** PUBLIC HOUSE

**public accountant** *n* **:** an accountant whose services are available to the public — compare CERTIFIED PUBLIC ACCOUNTANT

**public accounting** *n* **:** accounting performed by a public accountant

**public account system** *n* **:** a system under which the state buys raw materials for processing in prison factories and sells the products in the open market — compare CONVICT LABOR SYSTEM

**public act** *n* **:** PUBLIC LAW

**public–address system** \¦==¦=-\ *n* **:** an apparatus including one or more microphones or other pickup devices, an audio-frequency amplifier, and one or more loudspeakers used for broadcasting speech, music, or other sounds to a large audience (as in an auditorium or out of doors) — called also *PA system*

**public administration** *n* **:** a branch of political science dealing primarily with the structure and workings of agencies charged with the administration of governmental functions

**public administrator** *n* **1** *in many jurisdictions* **:** an officer appointed to administer the estate of a decedent where there is no one else entitled and willing to act — compare GENERAL ADMINISTRATOR **2** *in some states* **:** the custodian of an estate pending settlement of a dispute or doubt as to the person entitled to letters

**publically** *var of* PUBLICLY

**pub·li·can** \'pəblәkən, -lēk-\ *n* -s [ME, fr. MF *publicain*, *publican*, fr. L *publicanus*, fr. *publicum* public revenue (fr. neut. of *publicus* public) + *-anus* -an — more at PUBLIC] **1 a :** a Jewish tax collector for the ancient Romans ⟨~s were outcasts among the Jews, because, having accepted the office under the Roman government . . . they were regarded as traitors —F.W. Robertson⟩ **b :** one estranged from the church ⟨I firmly believe this church . . . has power to exclude him and to hold him as a ~ and heathen —A.C.McGiffert⟩ **c :** any collector of taxes or tribute ⟨outrages and exactions such as have, in every age, made the name of ~ a proverb for all that is most hateful —T.B.Macaulay⟩ **2** *chiefly Brit* **:** the keeper of a public house ⟨the local ~ produced trays of foaming stout —E.J.Gates⟩

**public assistance** *n* **:** aid provided to the needy aged, dependent children, and blind and disabled persons under the Federal Social Security Act of the U.S.

**pub·li·cate** \'pəblə,kāt\ *vt* -ED/-ING/-S [L *publicatus*, past part. of *publicare* — more at PUBLISH] *archaic* **:** PUBLISH

**pub·li·ca·tion** \,pəblə'kāshən, -blē'-\ *n* -s [ME *publicacioun*, fr. MF *publication*, fr. LL *publication-, publicatio*, fr. L *publicatus* (past part. of *publicare* to announce, proclaim, publish) + *-ion-, -io* -ion — more at PUBLISH] **1 :** communication (as of news or information) to the public **:** public announcement **:** PROCLAMATION ⟨radio is a . . . great method of communication and ~ —G.C.Chandler⟩; *specif* **:** legal notification **2 a :** the act or process of issuing copies (as of a book, photograph, or musical score) for general distribution to the public ⟨the firm is engaged in the ~ of text books⟩ ⟨the date of ~⟩ ⟨prior to the first general ~ the owner of the common law copyright . . . may enjoy the benefit of a restricted publication —R.R.Shaw⟩ **b :** a published work ⟨study of . . . the journals of social science, the ~s of the learned generally —B.N. Cardozo⟩ ⟨among his many ~s was a volume of light verse⟩ **3 :** the distribution in print esp. in technical journals of a taxonomic name (as of a species or genus) together with such descriptive or illustrative material as will characterize and distinguish the organism or group named

**public bill** *n, sometimes cap P&B* **:** a legislative bill affecting the community (as a nation or state) at large ⟨the First Reading of a *public bill* . . . is usually a formality —*Brit. Parliament*⟩ — compare PRIVATE BILL

**public bond** *n* **:** a bond issued by a government (as a nation or state) or by a subsidiary incorporated governmental authority or by a municipality

**public charge** *n* **:** one that is supported at public expense

**public corporation** *n* **1 :** MUNICIPAL CORPORATION **2 :** a government-owned corporation organized to carry on a particular governmental activity, managed according to business principles by an appointed board, and often to some extent financially independent of the government — called also *government corporation*

**public day** *n* **1 :** a day when a private institution is opened to the public or when an official devotes himself to hearing direct public business **2 :** HOLIDAY 3a

**public debt** *n* **:** NATIONAL DEBT

**public defender** *n* **:** a lawyer usu. holding public office whose duty is to defend accused persons unable to pay for legal assistance

**public domain** *n* **1 :** land owned or controlled by the U.S. government ⟨on this *public domain* the national government, as proprietor, can lease grazing lands —F.A.Ogg & P.O.Ray⟩ **2 :** the realm embracing property rights belonging to the community at large, subject to appropriation by anyone; *specif* **:** status unprotected by copyright or patent

**public enemy** *n* **:** one that constitutes a menace to society; *specif* **:** a criminal whose crimes have so aroused the police or public as to result in an intensive effort to apprehend him with the aid of wide publicity

**public funds** *n pl* **:** FUND 4d

**public health** *n* **:** the art and science dealing with the protection and improvement of community health by organized community effort and including preventive medicine and sanitary and social sciences

**public highway** *n* **:** HIGHWAY 1a

**public house** *n* **1 :** INN, HOSTELRY **2** *chiefly Brit* **:** a licensed saloon or bar

**public housing** *n* **:** low-rent housing owned, sponsored, or administered by a government

**pu·bli·ci ju·ris** \¦pəblə,sī'jürəs, -jür-\ *adj* [L] **:** belonging to the public **:** subject to a right of the public to enjoy

**pub·li·cist** \'pəbləsəst\ *n* -s [F *publiciste*, fr. *public* + *-iste* -ist] **1 a :** an expert in international law ⟨judicial decisions of the most highly qualified ~s of the various nations —*Basic Facts about the U.N.*⟩ **b :** an expert or commentator on public affairs **:** political pundit ⟨the self-constituted party of property owners, ~s, and professional men that framed the Federal Constitution —S.E.Morison & H.S.Commager⟩ ⟨cocksure materialist at whom . . . contemporary ~s are wont to fling their dialectical brickbats —Aldous Huxley⟩ **2 :** one that publicizes ⟨effective ~ of the slum problem —J.G.Hill⟩ ⟨task of the scientist as ~ to make sure that science is science, and not magic, to the public at large —Irwin Edman⟩; *specif* **:** PRESS AGENT ⟨something more lasting than a pretty face, attractive figure or a persuasive ~ —J.K.Newnham⟩

**pub·lic·i·ty** \(,)pə'blisəd·ē, -sətē, -i\ *n* -ES *often attrib* [F *publicité*, fr. *public* + *-ité* -ity] **1 :** the quality or state of being obvious or exposed to the general view **:** accessibility to the public ⟨wide open ranks . . . of desks kept everyone working by mere ~ —Christopher Morley⟩ ⟨the ~ of the courtroom —*Saturday Rev.*⟩ **2 a :** an act or device designed to attract public interest ⟨regards a whistle-stop tour as good ~⟩; *specif* **:** information with news value issued as a means of gaining public attention or support ⟨his job is producing ~ for child welfare organizations⟩ ⟨the flood of ~ and promotional material that now overloads the desk of everybody in the news business —Elmer Davis⟩ **b :** the dissemination of information or promotional material esp. by the press and other mass media ⟨felt that the recent wave of ~ on her work . . . had hurt her professionally —*Time*⟩ **c :** paid advertising ⟨the object of all commercial ~ is to persuade someone to exchange his money for what the advertiser has for sale —H.H.Smith⟩ **d :** public attention or acclaim ⟨~ came . . . unsought; he was a man who attracted attention —V.G.Heiser⟩ ⟨received considerable ~ because of their refusal to accept a . . . grant for school purposes —*Amer. Guide Series: Pa.*⟩ **e :** the practice or profession of producing promotional material ⟨~ is a one-way street; public relations, a two-way street —E.L.Bernays⟩

**syn** BALLYHOO, PROMOTION, PROPAGANDA: PUBLICITY refers to any effort to attract public attention whether by furnishing information for dissemination through regular news channels or by paid advertising ⟨recipients of this announcement are requested to give it immediately the widest possible *publicity* —*Amer. Council of Learned Soc. Scholars*⟩ ⟨"*publicity*" was not mainly an art for causing the world to take notice of, and think well of, goods; or of policies which the makers of goods wished to make popular. The word was coming to be synonymous with advertising —Mark Sullivan⟩ ⟨actresses bathing in champagne and other *publicity* stunts⟩ BALLYHOO may refer to sensational, strident, or noisy publicity ⟨the patient blindly follows the *ballyhoo* of the medical charlatan —*Police Gazette*⟩ PROMOTION suggests concentrated efforts to publicize something new or persuade the public to accept it ⟨attractive *promotions* of spring clothing helped to allay the usual post-Easter drop in retail volume —*Dun's Rev.*⟩ PROPAGANDA, the strongest term, usu. carries the suggestion of manipulation of public opinion whether through acceptable educational processes or by direct and coercive indoctrination ⟨*propaganda* means the planned use of all kinds of communications to influence the actions of other peoples —*Combat Forces Jour.*⟩

**pub·li·cize** \'pəblə,sīz\ *vt* -ED/-ING/-S [ˈ*public* + *-ize*] **:** to bring to the attention of the public **:** give publicity to **:** ADVERTISE

**public land** *n* **:** land owned by a government, esp. a national government; *specif* **:** that part of the U.S. public domain subject to sale or disposal under the homestead laws

**public law** *n* **1 a :** an enactment of a legislature affecting the public at large throughout the entire territory (as state or nation) subject to the jurisdiction of the legislature **:** GENERAL LAW — called also *public act, public statute* **b :** an enactment of a legislature (as a municipal charter) affecting the public at large within a particular subdivision of the legislative jurisdiction **2 :** the division of law that adjusts the relations of individuals with the state and regulates the organization and conduct of the machinery of government — contrasted with *private law* **3 :** international law regulating the relations among sovereign states or nations as distinguished from private international law

**public liability insurance** *n* **:** insurance to protect businessmen (as owners or landlords) against loss due to legal liability for injury or damage to the persons or property of the public

**public library** *n* **:** a nonprofit library maintained for public use and usu. supported in whole or in part by local taxation

**pub·lic·ly** \'pəbliklē, -lēk-, -li\ *also* **pub·li·cal·ly** \-lək(ə)lē, -lēk-, -li\ *adv* **1 :** in public **:** in a manner observable by or a place accessible to the public **:** OPENLY, OBVIOUSLY ⟨claims that many of them are privately on his side, but cannot support him ~ —*Time*⟩ ⟨attributes . . . directly and ~ observable —C.G.Hempel⟩ **2 :** by the public **:** by the people generally **:** COMMUNALLY ⟨every corporation is deemed ~ held unless 10 or fewer shareholders own stock —*U.S.Code*⟩; *specif* **:** by a government ⟨~ provided medical care starts with the school medical service —Moses Abramovitz & Vera Eliasberg⟩

**public member** *n* **:** a member (as of a labor relations board) not representing the special interest groups involved

**pub·lic·ness** *n* -ES **:** the quality or state of being public

**public nuisance** *n, law* **:** a nuisance (as obstructing a highway) that causes harm or annoyance to persons in a particular locality in violation of their rights as members of the community — compare MIXED NUISANCE, PRIVATE NUISANCE

**public officer** *n* **:** a person holding a post to which he has been legally elected or appointed and exercising governmental functions

**public official bond** *n* **:** a surety bond providing indemnity for failure of a public official to perform faithfully the duties of his office

**public opinion** *n* **1 :** the predominant attitude of a community **:** the collective will of the people ⟨a fluctuation in *public opinion* may redirect national policy⟩ **2 :** a summation of public expression regarding a specific issue or event ⟨*public opinion* on racial segregation falls into two main categories⟩

**public policy** *n* **1 :** the governing policy within a community as embodied in its legislative and judicial enactments which serve as a basis for determining what acts are to be regarded as contrary to the public good **2 :** the principle of law by virtue of which acts contrary to the public good are held invalid

**public prints** *n pl* **:** newspapers and periodicals ⟨led to much talk in the *public prints*⟩

**public prosecutor** *n* **:** a public official charged with the investigation and prosecution of punishable acts on behalf of the state or an international commission

**public record** *n* **:** a record required by law to be made and kept: **a :** a record made by a public officer in the course of his legal duty to make it **b :** a record filed in a public office and open to public inspection

**public relations** *n pl but usu sing in constr* **1 :** the promotion of rapport and goodwill between a person, firm, or institution and other persons, special publics, or the community at large through the distribution of interpretative material, the development of neighborly interchange, and the assessment of public reaction ⟨*public relations* are designed . . . to give a business a good reputation with the public —A.W.Page⟩ ⟨*public relations* of a resort may be only a portion of the duties of the . . . general manager —*Jour. Amer. Med. Assoc.*⟩ ⟨if the officer is civil . . . he gets a lot more done, both in correcting the driver and in doing good *public relations* for his town —Fred Sharpe⟩ ⟨took a pioneering step in *public relations* by asking . . . brokers to report the various attitudes toward the exchange they encountered generally —*Newsweek*⟩ **2 a :** the degree of understanding and goodwill achieved between an individual, organization, or institution and the public ⟨little favors, a helping hand, a brief visit, a kindly word, all add up to good *public relations* —S.I.Stuber⟩ ⟨in a sense *public relations* is the measure of the extent to which an organization has adapted itself . . . to society —E.A. Cunningham⟩ **b :** application of the techniques for achieving this relationship ⟨persuaded the President that it would be bad *public relations* to stay away from his White House desk more than two weeks at a time —*New Republic*⟩ **3 a :** the art or science of developing reciprocal understanding and goodwill ⟨universities offered courses in *public relations* —E.L.Bernays⟩ **b :** the professional staff entrusted with this task ⟨*public relations* collects, prepares and distributes information to . . . the consuming public —*Preview of Amer. Viscose Corp.*⟩ ⟨why do the Air Forces Group people in *public relations* fire that upstairs when they don't know whether it's true or not —J.G. Cozzens⟩

**public rights** *n pl* **:** the rights under law of the state over the subject and of the subject against the state

**publics** *pl of* PUBLIC

**public sale** *n* **:** AUCTION 1

**public school** *n* **1 a :** any of various endowed secondary boarding schools in Great Britain offering a classical curriculum and preparing boys esp. for the ancient universities or for public service **b :** a similar school for girls **2 a :** a tax-supported school controlled by a local governmental authority; *specif* **:** an elementary or secondary school in the U.S. providing free education for the children of residents of a specified area **b :** the building housing a public school

**public servant** *n* **1 :** a holder of public office **2 :** an individual or corporation (as a bus company) rendering a public service

**public service** *n* **1 a :** a publicly or privately owned enterprise (as a waterworks, railway, telephone company) conducted for the benefit of the community as a whole **b :** a service rendered in the public interest ⟨the program is not sponsored but is presented by the network as a *public service*⟩ **2 :** governmental employment; *esp* **:** CIVIL SERVICE ⟨first appointment to the *public service* is usually on a temporary basis —*Employment Opportunities in the Civil Service*⟩

**public–service corporation** *n* **:** a corporation providing services essential to the general public convenience or safety

**public speaker** *n* **:** one skilled in public speaking

**public speaking** *n* **1 :** the act or process of making speeches in public **2 :** the art or science of effective oral communication with an audience ⟨took a course in *public speaking*⟩

**public–spirited** \¦==¦===\ *adj* **:** motivated by devotion to the general or national welfare ⟨the trustees of our American universities are, as a class, *public-spirited* citizens . . . trying to promote the public good —M.R.Cohen⟩ — **public–spiritedness** *n* -ES

**public statute** *n* **:** PUBLIC LAW 1

**public store** *n* **:** a warehouse where dutiable goods are appraised or held under bond

**public time** *n* **:** OBJECTIVE TIME

**public utility** *n* **1 :** a business organization deemed by law to be vested with public interest usu. because of monopoly privileges and so subject to public regulation such as fixing of rates, standards of service and provision of facilities **2 :** a stock or bond issued by a public utility

**public vessel** *n* **:** a ship belonging to a government and not engaging in trade

**public warehouse** *n* **:** a privately owned warehouse for public use

**public waters** *n pl* **:** waters open of right to the use of the general public; *specif* **:** navigable waters

**public way** *n* **:** any passageway (as an alley, road, highway, boulevard, turnpike) or part thereof (as a bridge) open as of right to the public and designed for travel by vehicle, on foot, or in a manner limited by statute (as by excluding pedestrians or commercial vehicles) — compare PRIVATE WAY

**public works** *n pl* **:** fixed works (as schools, highways, docks) constructed for public use or enjoyment esp. when financed and owned by the government; *specif* **:** government sponsored public improvements (as parks or playgrounds) as distinguished from work of a routine nature such as the grading and lighting of streets

**public works and ways system** *n* : a plan or system for employing convict labor on public works and highways — compare CONVICT LABOR SYSTEM

**public wrong** *n* **1** : a crime, misdemeanor, tort, or breach of a duty owed to and prejudicing the interests of the community at large — compare PRIVATE WRONG **2** : a breach of duty owed to any person by the state or one of its political subdivisions

**pub·lish** \ˈpəblish, -lēsh, *esp in pres part* -ləsh\ *vb* -ED/-ING/-ES [ME *publishen*, fr. MF *publiss-*, stem of *publier*, fr. L *publicare*, fr. *publicus* public — more at PUBLIC] *vt* **1 a** : to declare publicly : make generally known : DISCLOSE, CIRCULATE ⟨~ glad tidings, tidings of peace —Mary A. Thomson⟩ ⟨the plan of action has not been ~*ed* in detail —D.S.Campbell⟩; *specif* : to impart or acknowledge to one or more persons ⟨a slander is not actionable unless it is ~*ed* to a third person —T.F.T.Plucknett⟩ ⟨do ~ and declare this to be my last will and testament⟩ **b** : to proclaim officially : PROMULGATE ⟨~ an edict⟩ **c** : to make public announcement of (banns of marriage) **d** : PUBLICIZE ⟨mourning . . . by which a widow ~*ed* her single-minded grief —Margery Sharp⟩ ⟨first Neolithic site to be thoroughly excavated and ~*ed* in Macedonia —G.E.Mylonas⟩; *specif* : to give publication to (a taxonomic name) **2 a** : to make a public evaluation of; *specif* : CENSURE ⟨stewards have power to ~ at their discretion any person subject to their control either by suspension . . . or by fine —Dan Parker⟩ **b** *obs* : to call to the attention of the public : ADVERTISE ⟨goods found shall be ~*ed* by the finder —Nathaniel Bacon⟩ **3 a** : to place before the public (as through a mass medium) : DISSEMINATE ⟨adopted and ~*ed* a statement of principles —H.E.Starr⟩ ⟨does not pay but ~*es* significant poetry —*Author & Journalist*⟩; *specif* : UTTER ⟨~ a forgery⟩ **b** : to produce for publication or allow to be issued for distribution or sale ⟨they write brilliantly at times, have ~*ed* long passages that . . . interest the intelligent reader —H.C. Webster⟩ **c** : to reproduce for public consumption ⟨the number of companies . . . ~*ing* LP recordings —Roland Gelatt⟩; *specif* : PRINT ⟨the pictures and stories ~*ed* in these pages are selections from previous issues —*New England Journeys*⟩ **d** : to release (a product of creative work) for public distribution or sale usu. with the consent of the copyright holder ⟨a shilling volume of 96 pages written, printed and ~*ed* within a month —*Modern Churchman*⟩ ⟨in 1837 were ~*ed* four engraved charts, the first issued by the Navy Department —C.L.Lewis⟩ ⟨his five ~*ed* symphonies —Irving Kolodin⟩ ⟨~*ed* in manuscript the first Lusatian grammar —R. G. A. De Bray⟩ **e** : to issue the work of (as an author) ⟨latest of the younger Italian novelists to be ~*ed* in the U.S. —*Time*⟩ ~ *vi* **1** : to put out an edition or circulate it to the public ⟨the only daily newspaper in the borough did not ~ yesterday because of a strike —*N.Y.Times*⟩ **2 a** : to have one's work accepted for publication or allow it to be reproduced for public consumption ⟨pressure put on faculty members . . . to ~ as a condition of appointment or promotion —H.M.Silver⟩ **b** : to reproduce the work of an author and release it to the public ⟨his first novel became a best seller and several firms offered to ~ for him⟩ **3** : to become manifest : give public witness ⟨so much joy . . . I felt it ~ in my eye —Emily Dickinson⟩ **syn** see DECLARE

**pub·lish·able** \-shəbəl\ *adj* : allowable or suitable for publication ⟨there must not . . . be any censorship of legally ~ materials —D.H.Clift⟩ ⟨investigations have not been carried far enough to yield ~ results —T.H.Johnson⟩ ⟨it was not a ~ book —Harrison Smith⟩

**pub·lish·er** \-shə(r)\ *n* -S [ME, fr. *publishen* + *-er*] **1 a** *archaic* : one that makes public : ANNOUNCER, PROCLAIMER; *specif* : TOWN CRIER **b** : a member of Jehovah's Witnesses who is expected to devote at least 60 hours of his time each month to the propagation of his faith on a house-to-house visitation basis **2 a** : the reproducer of a work intended for public consumption ⟨found it impossible to trace the ~ of the underground pamphlet⟩ **b** (1) : one whose business is publishing ⟨textbook ~⟩ ⟨greeting-card ~⟩ ⟨two new record ~*s* have recently become active —Edward Sackville-West & Desmond Shawe-Taylor⟩; *specif* : the owner and operator of a newspaper or periodical ⟨editorials tend to reflect the views of the ~⟩ (2) *Brit* : a newspaper circulation manager

**publisher's binding** *n* : EDITION BINDING

**publisher's statement** *n* : a sworn statement of circulation for a specified period (as a year) made by a publisher of a newspaper or periodical

**publishing** *n* -S : the business or profession of the commercial production and issuance of literature esp. in book form for public distribution or sale ⟨~ as a business apart from book selling is of comparatively modern date —J.A.Holden⟩ ⟨entered ~ with the Oxford University Press —*Publishers' Weekly*⟩

**pub·lish·ment** \ˈ⸗⸗mənt\ *n* -S *archaic* : PUBLICATION; *specif* : public announcement of banns of marriage

**pubs** *pl of* PUB

**PUC** *abbr* public utilities commission

**pu·ca·ra** \ˌpükəˈrä\ *adj, usu cap* [Sp *pucará*, fr. *Pucará*, district in Peru, fr. Quechua *pukára* fort] : of or relating to a culture of the southern Andes in Peru during the Tiahuanaco period characterized by a black and yellow-on-red pottery with sharp narrow incisions outlining the color areas

**pucca** *var of* PUKKA

**puc·cin·ia** \pəkˈsinēə\ *n, cap* [NL, fr. Tommaso *Puccini* †1735 It. anatomist + NL *-ia*] : a very large genus (the type of the family Pucciniaceae) that is sometimes separated into four genera and consists of heteroecious parasitic fungi having 2-celled teliospores whose pedicels do not gelatinize and aecia with a pseudoperidium and including many forms that are destructive to various economic plants — see WHEAT RUST — **puc·cin·oid** \-ˌnȯid\ *adj*

**puc·cin·i·a·ce·ae** \ˌpək,sinēˈāsē,ē\ *n pl, cap* [NL *Puccinia*, type genus + *-aceae*] : a large important family of rust fungi (order Uredinales) having stalked teliospores either separate or united in sori, being mostly heteroecious, and exhibiting in the complete forms four spore stages usu. upon two or more distinct hosts followed by an independent promycelial stage upon the germination of the teliospores — see PUCCINIA; compare SHORT-CYCLED — **puc·cin·i·a·ceous** \(ˌ)⸗⸗⸗ˈāshəs\ *adj*

**puc·coon** \pəˈkün\ *n* -S [fr. *puccoon* (in some Algonquian language of Virginia) — more at POKE] : **1** : any of several American plants yielding a red or yellow pigment: as **a** : BLOODROOT 1 **b** : any of several plants of the genus *Lithospermum* (as *L. carolinense* or *L. canescens*) — see HOARY PUCCOON **c** : GOLDENSEAL 1 **2** : the pigment obtained from a puccoon plant

**puce** \ˈpyüs\ *n* -S [F, lit., flea, fr. L *pulic-, pulex* — more at PSYLLA] : a dark red that is yellower and less strong than cranberry, paler and slightly yellower than average garnet, bluer, less strong, and slightly lighter than pomegranate, and bluer and paler than average wine — called also *eureka red, flea, Victoria lake*

**pu·cel·las** \pyəˈseləs\ *n pl but sing or pl in constr* [modif. of It

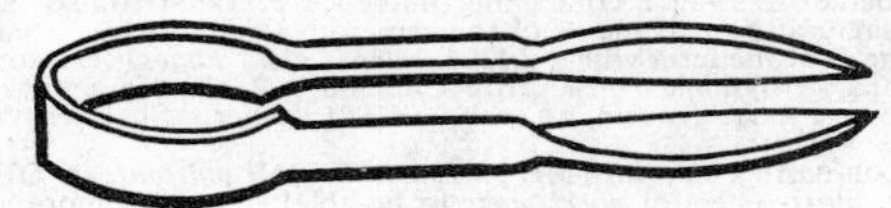

pucellas

*procello*] : a spring tool resembling tongs and used for shaping molten glass — called also *steel jack* ⟨next in importance to the blowpipe is the ~ —F.W.Hunter⟩ ⟨the top of the glass may be opened up with ~ —Karen Gillespie⟩

**pu·cher·ite** \ˈpükə,rīt\ *n* -S [G *pucherit*, fr. the *Pucher* mine, Schneeberg, Saxony + G *-it* -ite] : a mineral $BiVO_4$ consisting of a bismuth vanadate occurring in small reddish brown orthorhombic crystals

**pu·che·ro** \püˈche,rō\ *n* -S [Sp, lit., pot, fr. L *pultarius* vessel for porridge, cooking or drinking vessel, fr. *pult-, puls*, a kind of thick porridge + *-arius* -ary — more at PULSE] : a Latin American boiled dinner or stew containing beef, sausage, bacon, and various vegetables

**¹puck** \ˈpək\ *n* -S *often cap* [ME *puke, pouke*, fr. OE *pūca*; akin to Fris *puk* goblin, ON *pūki* devil, Norw & Sw dial. *puke* goblin, and prob. to OE *pocc* pock — more at POCK] **1 a** *archaic* : an evil or malicious spirit : DEVIL, DEMON ⟨nor let the ~, nor other evil spirits . . . fright us —Edmund Spenser⟩ **b** : a mischievous or rascally sprite : IMP, HOBGOBLIN **2** : a prankish person ⟨was also a ~ who loved to disconcert any classification —Ernest Barker⟩

**²puck** \"\ *vt* -ED/-ING/-S [alter. of ²*poke*] *dial chiefly Brit* : POKE, STRIKE

**³puck** \"\ *n* -S **1** *dial chiefly Brit* : BLOW, POKE ⟨hit him a ~ in the jaw —Liam O'Flaherty⟩ **2 a** : a vulcanized rubber disk 3 inches in diameter used in the game of ice hockey as the object to be driven through the goals **b** : a disk of resilient material used on a vehicle or a reciprocating machine to absorb shock and vibration **c** : a pressure roller in a magnetic recorder

**pucka** *var of* PUKKA

**¹puck·er** \ˈpəkə(r)\ *vb* **puckered; puckered; puckering** \-k(ə)riŋ\ **puckers** [prob. alter. of ¹*poke* + *-er* (freq. suffix)] *vi* **1** : to become wrinkled or constricted : present an uneven appearance : CONTRACT, FURROW, WRINKLE ⟨lips ~*ed* into a low whistle —Don Davis⟩ ⟨in humid weather . . . the finished print may have a tendency to ~ —C.E.Dunn⟩ **2** : to assume an expression of earnest concentration : FROWN ⟨an envious body will ~ as if he had never heard the name —G.D.Brown⟩ ~ *vt* **1** : to contract into folds or corrugations : draw together so as to wrinkle or crimp : CONSTRICT, FURROW ⟨spasms gnarl the hands . . . and ~ the face —A.C.Fisher⟩ ⟨the effort of thought ~*ed* his brow⟩ — often used with *up* ⟨~*ed* up my lips for . . . a good-bye kiss —Glenway Wescott⟩; *esp* : to produce (an uneven surface consisting of a series of small bulges and depressions) in a fabric by alternating groups of slack and tight yarns or by finishing with a shrinking treatment that affects only one set of yarns ⟨~*ed* nylon sport shirts need no ironing —*advt*⟩ **2** : to produce fullness in (a sewn article) by drawing stitches tight or by gathering a longer edge to a shorter one ⟨~ a blouse for smocking⟩ ⟨moccasins . . . ~*ed* to a single seam in front —*Museum of the Amer. Indian (N.Y.)*⟩

**²pucker** \"\ *n* -S **1 a** : a crimp in a normally even surface : WRINKLE, FURROW ⟨screwed her pretty mouth into a ~ of exasperation —Walter O'Meara⟩ ⟨the folds and ~*s* of the unexpanded wings of certain moths —E.B.Ford⟩; *specif* : a slight unevenness in a fabric ⟨~*s* are usually due to the presence of nonuniformly drawn yarns —C.M.Whittaker & C.C. Wilcock⟩ **b** : a fabric having a puckered finish ⟨the newest all-nylon cloth to be added is a ~ in a plaid design —*Women's Wear Daily*⟩ **2** *archaic* : a state of agitation or distraction : TIZZY

**puckerbush** \ˈ⸗⸗,⸗\ *n* : WAX MYRTLE

**puck·ery** \ˈpək(ə)rē, -ri\ *adj, sometimes* -ER/-EST **1** : characterized by puckers or having a tendency to pucker ⟨~ cloth⟩ **2** : causing a pucker ⟨a ~ quince⟩

**puck-fist** \ˈpək,fist, -fist\ *n* [¹*puck* + *fist*] **1** : PUFFBALL 1 **2** : BRAGGART

**puck·ish** \ˈpəkish, -kēsh\ *adj* [¹*puck* + *-ish*] : of, relating to, characteristic of, or resembling a puck : IMPISH, WHIMSICAL ⟨is wayward, ~, inconsistent —Gerald Abraham⟩ ⟨takes a ~ delight in shocking the smug and complacent —S.E.Morison⟩ ⟨her little heart-shaped face, with its . . . pointed chin and ~ nose —Sheila Kaye-Smith⟩ — **puck·ish·ly** \-kəshlē, -kēsh-, -li\ *adv*

**puck·ish·ness** \-kishnəs, -kēsh-\ *n* -ES : the quality or state of being puckish ⟨a charming ~ which helps to explain the wide range of his friendships —Mason Wade⟩

**puck·le** \ˈpəkəl\ *Scot var of* ⁴PICKLE 2

**pucksey** *var of* PUXY

**puck·ster** \ˈpəkstə(r)\ *n* -S [³*puck* + *-ster*] : an ice hockey player

**¹pud** *var of* POOD

**²pud** \ˈpəd\ *n* -S [origin unknown] : the hand of a child or the paw of an animal

**³pud** \ˈpu̇d\ *n* -S [short for *pudding* "sausage," "penis"] : PENIS — usu. considered vulgar

**pud** *abbr* pudding

**PUD** *abbr* **1** pickup and delivery **2** public utility district

**pud·den·ing** \ˈpu̇d(ᵊ)niŋ\ *n* -S [*pudden* (alter. of *pudding*) + *-ing*] *chiefly Brit* : PUDDING 3

**pud·der** \ˈpədə(r)\ *archaic var of* POTHER

**pud·ding** \ˈpu̇diŋ, -dēŋ\ *n* -S *often attrib* [ME; perh. akin to OE *puduc* wart, LG *puddek* sausage, *puddig* swollen] **1 a** : BLOOD SAUSAGE **b** *obs* : sausage stuffing for roast meat ⟨that roasted . . . ox with the ~ in his belly —Shak.⟩ **c** *dial Eng* : GUTS — usu. used in pl. **2 a** (1) : a boiled or baked unsweetened soft food usu. having a cereal base and a texture resembling custard and eaten either as a main course or as a side dish ⟨Virginia chicken ~⟩ ⟨corn ~⟩ — compare HASTY PUDDING, YORKSHIRE PUDDING (2) : a usu. boiled or baked sweetened dessert of a soft, spongy, or thick creamy consistency ⟨bread ~⟩ ⟨rice ~⟩ ⟨chocolate ~⟩ **b** : an unsweetened dish often containing suet or having a suet crust and orig. boiled in a bag but now often steamed or baked ⟨fig ~⟩ ⟨beefsteak and kidney ~⟩ — compare PLUM PUDDING **c** : something that resembles a pudding ⟨~ bolster⟩ ⟨the low bogs . . . had been churned to chocolate-colored ~*s* of ancient peat —Farley Mowat⟩ **3 a** : a tapered fender usu. made of rope yarn or canvas and attached to the stern of a ship ⟨the bow of your dinghy should be protected by a big, soft ~ —H.A.Calahan⟩ **b** : a soft padding esp. a binding around a metal ring used to prevent parts of a ship's rigging from chafing **4 a** : inherent quality : ability to measure up to expectations : ADEQUACY, MERIT ⟨proved his ~ commercially —*Newsweek*⟩ ⟨the proof of the ~ is in the eating⟩ **b** : tangible support or profit ⟨truth with gold she weighs, and solid ~ against empty praise —Alexander Pope⟩

**puddingberry** \ˈ⸗⸗ — *see* BERRY\ *n* **1** : DWARF CORNEL **2** : the fruit of a dwarf cornel

**pudding grass** *n* : a pennyroyal (*Hedeoma pulegioides*) formerly used to flavor stuffing for roast meat

**puddingheaded** \ˈ⸗⸗ˈ⸗⸗\ *adj* : FATHEADED

**pudding-pipe tree** \ˈ⸗⸗,⸗-\ *n* : DRUMSTICK TREE

**pudding stone** *n* : CONGLOMERATE

**pudding time** *n, archaic* **1** : dinner time ⟨as it was *pudding time* with us, our visitor was . . . invited to sit and eat —J.K. Townsend⟩ **2** : an auspicious moment ⟨here he comes in *pudding time* to resolve the question —John Dryden & W.C. Newcastle⟩

**puddingwife** \ˈ⸗⸗,⸗\ *n, pl* **puddingwives** [fr. obs. E, woman who sells sausage, fr. ME *podyngwyf*, fr. *podyng*, pudding blood sausage + *wyf, wif* woman — more at PUDDING, WIFE] : a large blue and bronze wrasse (*Iridio radiata*) of Florida and the West Indies south to Brazil

**pud·dingy** \ˈpu̇diŋē, -dēŋē\ *adj* : resembling a pudding

**¹pud·dle** \ˈpədᵊl\ *n* -S *often attrib* [ME *podel, pothel*; akin to OE *pudd* ditch, LG *pudel* puddle, and perh. to OE *puduc* wart — more at PUDDING] **1 a** (1) : a shallow depression full of water and esp. of muddy or dirty water ⟨a hard rain leaves ~*s* in the road⟩ (2) : a little pool of any kind ⟨prodded a little ~ of beer by his glass —Earle Birney⟩ ⟨~*s* of moonlight on the floor —T.W.Duncan⟩ **b** *archaic* : ditch water ⟨fresh was my only food, foul ~ all my drink —John Crowne⟩ **c** *obs* : POND, MARSH ⟨near to a long ~ or moorish ground, of some four miles long —Edward Barton⟩ **2 a** (1) : something that resembles a puddle in form ⟨most men live in a little ~ of light thrown by the gig-lamps of habit —Aldous Huxley⟩ ⟨a small ~ of minced veal on toast —Robert Standish⟩ (2) : something suggestive of a puddle of foul or dirty liquid : a contaminating circumstance or condition : MESS, SINK ⟨would have us believe . . . that in spite of all the ~*s* through which the priestly politician splashed to reach his ends, no spot or stain ever smutched his gown —V.L.Parrington⟩ **b** : MUDDLE ⟨stand and look over the little ~ of empty desks —W.A.White⟩ **3 a** (1) : an earthy mixture (as of clay, sand and gravel) worked while wet into a compact mass that becomes impervious to water when dry (2) : TAMPER c **b** : a thin mixture of soil and water for puddling plants **4** : the molten portion of a weld

**²puddle** \"\ *vb* **puddled; puddled; puddling** \-d(ᵊ)liŋ\ **puddles** [ME *podelen, pothelen*, fr. *podel, pothel*, n.] *vi* **1 a** : to dabble or wade around in a puddle ⟨in the ooze . . . a brood of goslings *puddled* —Rockwell Kent⟩ **b** : to dawdle or mess around : PUTTER ⟨children spent yesterday afternoon *puddling* in paint, plasticene, and paste —*Springfield (Mass.) Union*⟩ **2 a** : to make a puddle ⟨spray heaved in over the side, *puddling* on the slippery deck —Irwin Shaw⟩; *specif* : URINATE ⟨baby . . . alternately dozed and *puddled* —Ann Leighton⟩ **b** : to become a puddle ⟨slithering on the *puddling* brown snow —William Sansom⟩ ~ *vt* **1 a** : to stir up : make muddy or turbid : MUDDLE, ROIL ⟨great pails of *puddled* mire —Shak.⟩ ⟨the bartender went on *puddling* an old-fashioned —E.B. White⟩ **b** *archaic* : to make murky : BEFUDDLE, CONFUSE ⟨something sure of state . . . hath *puddled* his clear spirit —Shak.⟩ **c** : to immerse in a liquid ⟨the crystals are *puddled* with syrup to make a fluid mass —*Oil-Power*⟩; *specif* : to separate (ore) from sticky clay by washing in a shallow tank **2 a** (1) : to work (a wet mixture of earth or concrete) into a dense impervious mass ⟨hand methods of compacting concrete mixtures include *puddling*, spading, and tamping —J.H. Bateman⟩; *specif* : to combine with water into an impervious cover or lining ⟨a dew pond . . . constructed of straw and *puddled* clay —Norman Wymer⟩ (2) *archaic* : to cover or line with puddle ⟨~ the seams of the rock on that side of the well —Henry Stephens⟩ **b** (1) : to work (metal) while molten ⟨enabling the iron to be *puddled* into a bloom —Juliusz Slaski⟩; *specif* : to form (molten metal) into a desired shape ⟨carefully *puddled* ingots of aluminum into "contemporary amorphic baroque" blobs, then welded them to the steeple's base —*Time*⟩ (2) : to subject (iron) to the process of puddling **c** : to texture (stage scenery) by running together small colored puddles of paint **3 a** : to strew or pock with puddles ⟨meltwater ~*s* the flat sea ice⟩ ⟨cattle ~ the soft ground around the water hole with their hooves⟩ **b** : to render (soil) hard and dense by compacting ⟨splash erosion . . . ~*s* surface soils and causes surface seals —*Scientific Monthly*⟩ ⟨once soils are *puddled* badly, it may require several seasons to restore them to good tilth —A.F.Gustafson⟩ **c** (1) : to dip the roots of (a plant) in a thin mud before transplanting (2) : to saturate the soil around (a plant) in order to settle the dirt around the roots or to supply moisture, nutriment, or an insecticide

**puddle ball** *n* : the lump of pasty wrought iron taken from the puddling furnace to be hammered or rolled

**puddle bar** *n* : an iron bar made at a single heat from a puddle ball by hammering and rolling

**puddle duck** *n* : DABBLER 2

**puddle jumper** *n* **1** *slang* **a** : a small usu. antiquated car or truck **b** : LIGHTPLANE; *esp* : a military airplane used for low level observation or liaison and sometimes equipped with bazookas **2** *slang* : an outboard motorboat

**pud·dler** \ˈpəd(ᵊ)lə(r)\ *n* -S : one that puddles: as **a** : one who converts pig iron into wrought iron by puddling **b** : a rabble used in puddling **c** : PUDDLING FURNACE

**puddle wall** *or* **puddle core wall** *n* : a core wall of a dam made of puddled clay — called also *hearting*

**puddling** *n* -S **1 a** : the act or process of working a wet mixture of earth or concrete into a solid impervious mass **b** (1) : the compacting of a soil surface by water (2) : the dipping of roots into thin mud before transplanting **2** : the art or process of converting pig iron into wrought iron or now rarely steel by subjecting it to heat and frequent stirring in a small reverberatory furnace in the presence of oxidizing substances by which it is freed from most of its carbon and other impurities

**puddling furnace** *n* : a small reverberatory furnace in which iron is puddled

**pud·dly** \ˈpəd(ᵊ)lē, -li\ *adj* -ER/-EST **1** *archaic* : MUDDY, MURKY **2** : full of puddles ⟨considering a dash down the ~ path to the stable —Nora Waln⟩

**pud·dock** \ˈpədək\ *chiefly dial var of* ¹PADDOCK

**pud·dy** \ˈpədē\ *adj* -ER/-EST [perh. akin to LG *puddig* swollen, pudgy — more at PUDDING] : PUDGY

**pu·den·cy** \ˈpyüdᵊnsē\ *n* -ES [L *pudentia*, fr. *pudent-, pudens* (pres. part. of *pudēre* to be ashamed) + *-ia* -y — more at PUDIC] : MODESTY, PRUDISHNESS

**pu·den·dal** \pyüˈdendᵊl\ *adj* [NL *pudendum* + E *-al*] : of, relating to, or lying in the region of the external organs of generation ⟨a ~ artery⟩ ⟨~ nerve⟩ ⟨~ veins⟩

**pu·den·dum** \-dəm\ *n, pl* **pu·den·da** \-də\ [NL, back-formation fr. LL *pudendua*, fr. L, neut. pl. of *pudendus*, gerundive of *pudēre* to be ashamed — more at PUDIC] : the external genital organs of a human being and esp. of a woman — usu. used in pl.

**pudge** \ˈpəj\ *n* -S [origin unknown] : one that is pudgy

**pudg·i·ly** \ˈpəjəlē, -li\ *adv* : in a pudgy manner

**pudg·i·ness** \ˈpəjēnəs, -jin-\ *n* -ES : the quality or state of being pudgy

**pudgy** \-jē, -ji\ *adj* -ER/-EST [*pudge* + *-y*] **1** : short and plump : tending toward corpulence : CHUBBY, SQUAT ⟨has its share of ~ cupids —Sheila Hibben⟩ ⟨the man behind the lectern was ~ and stocky, with a fleshy face —Hans Meyerhoff⟩ **2** : BULKY ⟨a good winter glove, warm but not ~ —*New Yorker*⟩

**pu·di·bund** \ˈpyüdə,bənd\ *adj* [L *pudibundus*, fr. *pudēre* to be ashamed + *-bundus* (as in *moribundus* moribund) — more at PUDIC, MORIBUND] : PRUDISH

**pu·di·bun·di·ty** \ˌ⸗⸗ˈbəndədē\ *n* -ES : PRUDISHNESS

**pu·dic** \ˈpyüdik\ *adj* [F *pudique*, fr. L *pudicus* modest, fr. *pudēre* to be ashamed; perh. akin to L *pavire* to beat, strike — more at PAVE] : PUDENDAL

**pu·dic·i·ty** \pyüˈdisədē\ *n* -ES [MF *pudicité*, fr. L *pudicus* + MF *-ité* -ity] : MODESTY, CHASTITY

**pudor** *n* [L, fr. *pudēre* + *-or*] *obs* : MODESTY

**pu·du** \ˈpü,dü\ *n* -S [Sp, fr. Mapuche] : a small reddish deer (*Pudu pudu*) of the Chilean Andes having simple antlers resembling spikes and standing only 12 or 13 inches high

**pue** \ˈpyü\ *n* -S [ME — more at PEW] *archaic* : ¹PEW

**pueb·la** \p(y)üˈeblə, ˈpweblə\ *adj, usu cap* [fr. *Puebla*, Mexico] : of or from the city of Puebla, Mexico : of the kind or style prevalent in Puebla

**¹pueb·lo** \p(y)üˈe(,)blō, ˈpwe(,)-\ *n* -S [Sp, people, village, fr. L *populus* people — more at PEOPLE] **1 a** : a Latin-American community; *esp* : an Indian town or village ⟨typical street in a ~ of northwestern Venezuela —W.E.Rudolph⟩ **b** : a town founded by Mexican Spanish settlers in the southwestern U.S. esp. in California ⟨it was founded as San Jose de Guadalupe . . . the first ~ to be established in Alta California —Aubrey Drury⟩ **2 a** : the communal dwelling of an Indian village of Arizona, New Mexico, and adjacent parts of Mexico and Texas typical of the Anasazi culture and consisting of contiguous flat-roofed stone or adobe houses in groups sometimes several stories high and built in receding terraces with access to the lowest story orig. only by trap doors in the roof which was reached by ladders that could be drawn up for defense **b** : an Indian village of the southwestern U.S. ⟨all ~*s* have their religious societies, priests, warriors, medicine men and women —*Amer. Guide Series: N.Mex.*⟩ ⟨many members of modern ~*s* are abandoning the imposing citadels of their ancestors in favor of individual housing⟩ **3** *usu cap* **a** : a group of Indian peoples of Arizona and New Mexico **b** : a member of any of such peoples **4** *usu cap* : the languages spoken by the Pueblo peoples comprising the Keresan, Shoshonean, Tanoan, and Zuñian language families

**²pueblo** \"\ *adj, usu cap* **1** : of or relating to a culture of the plateau area of the southwestern U.S. following and forming one cultural development with the Basket Maker, developing in five stages, and characterized in its earliest stage by true masonry buildings and loom weaving and at its zenith by fine masonry, large communal towns, and buildings set under overhanging cliffs or in the open — see ANASAZI, DEVELOPMENTAL PUEBLO, GREAT PUEBLO **2** : of, relating to, or imitating the decorative and architectural style of the Pueblo Indians of New Mexico

**pueb·lo·an** \-ləwən\ *adj or n, usu cap* [¹*pueblo* + *-an*] : PUEBLO

**pueb·loid** \-,blȯid\ *adj* [¹*pueblo* + *-oid*] **1** : resembling a pueblo **2** : having characteristics similar to those of the Pueblo people or their culture

**puel·che** \ˈpwelchē\ *n, pl* **puelche** *or* **puelches** *usu cap* [Sp, fr. Araucanian] **1 a** : a people of the Argentine pampas **b** : a member of such people **2 a** : the language of the Puelche people **b** : a language stock comprising the Puelche language — **puel·che·an** \-chēən\ *adj, usu cap*

**¹pu·er** \ˈpyü(ə)r\ *n* -S [alter. of ⁴*pure*] : a mixture (as of dogs' dung in water) formerly used by tanners for bating hides and skins after liming

**²puer** \"\ *vt* -ED/-ING/-S [alter. of *³pure*] **:** to bate (hides) in a solution of fermented dog dung

**pu·e·rar·ia** \ˌpyüəˈra(a)rēə\ *n, cap* [NL, fr. Marc N. *Puerari* †1845 Swiss botanist + NL *-ia*] **:** a genus of chiefly Asiatic herbaceous or woody vines (family Leguminosae) with trifoliolate leaves, blue or purple racemose flowers, and long narrow many-seeded pods — see KUDZU

**pu·er·er** \ˈpyü(ə)rə(r)\ *n* -S **:** BATER

**pu·er·i·cul·ture** \ˈpyü(ə)rəˌkəlchə(r)\ *n* [F *puériculture,* fr. L *puer* + F *-iculture* (as in *agriculture*) — more at AGRICULTURE] **:** the rearing or hygienic care of children; *specif* **:** the prenatal care of unborn children through attention to the health of pregnant women

**pu·er·ile** \ˈpyü(ə)rəl, -ˌrīl\ *adj* [F or L; F *puéril,* fr. L *puerilis,* fr. *puer* boy, girl, child + *-ilis* -ile; akin to Gk *pais* child — more at FEW] **1 a :** of or relating to childhood **:** BOYISH ⟨~ humility . . . we used to show to the world —Corra Harris⟩ ⟨mocking is the first ~ form of wit, playing with surfaces without sympathy —George Santayana⟩ **b :** unworthy of an adult **:** IMMATURE, CHILDISH ⟨the ~ and half-educated mind —Bernhard Berenson⟩ ⟨great affairs of men in society are carried on as if they were . . . ~ and degrading farces —R.P.Blackmur⟩ **2 :** characteristic of or resembling that of children — used of respiration ⟨~ breathing is louder than normal vesicular breathing —R.M.Goepp & H.F.Flippin⟩ **syn** see YOUTHFUL

**pu·er·ile·ly** \-l(l)ē\ *adv* **:** in a puerile manner

**pu·er·il·ism** \-ˌrəˌlizəm\ *n* -S [ISV *puerile* + *-ism*] **:** childish or infantile behavior esp. as a psychiatric symptom of mental disorder

**pu·er·il·i·ty** \ˌpyüəˈriləd·ē, -lətē, -i\ *n* -ES [MF or L; MF *puerilité,* fr. L *puerilitat-, puerilitas,* fr. *puerilis* + *-itat-, -itas* -ity] **1 a :** the quality or state of being a child; *specif* **:** the status under civil law of a child between infancy and puberty defined as from 7 to 14 years of age in boys and from 7 to 12 years of age in girls **b :** IMMATURITY, CHILDISHNESS ⟨the ballet comic in its ~ and ugliness —Arnold Bennett⟩ **2 :** an act, instance, or product of an immature mind ⟨where he has committed the ~ of employing more words than are necessary, he now has the one correct word —*College English*⟩ ⟨pettiness, juvenilities, and . . . *puerilities* become not a great assembly like this —John Adams⟩

**pu·er·pera** \pyüˈərp(ə)rə\ *n, pl* **puerper·ae** \-pəˌrē\ [L] **:** a woman in childbirth or in the period immediately succeeding

**pu·er·per·al** \(ˈ)═ˈ══rəl\ *adj* [L *puerpera* woman in childbirth (fr. *puer* child + *-pera,* fr. *parere* to give birth to) + E *-al* — more at PUERILE, PARE] **:** of or relating to parturition ⟨~ infection⟩

**puerperal fever** *or* **puerperal sepsis** *n* **:** an abnormal condition that results from infection of the placental site following delivery or instrumental abortion and is characterized in mild form by fever of not over 100.4°F but may progress to a localized endometritis or spread through the uterine wall and develop into peritonitis or pass into the blood stream and produce septicemia — called also *childbed fever*

**pu·er·pe·ri·um** \ˌpyü(ə)rˈpirēəm\ *n, pl* **puerpe·ria** \-rēə\ [L, fr. *puerpera*] **1 :** the condition of a woman immediately following childbirth **2 :** the period between childbirth and the return of the uterus to its normal size

**¹puer·to ri·can** \ˌpwerd·(ˌ)ōˈrēkən, -rd·əˈ-\ *also* **por·to rican** \ˌpōrd·(ˌ)ō-, -rd·əˈ-\ *adj, usu cap P&R* [*Puerto Rico* or *Porto Rico,* island in the West Indies + E *-an*] **1 :** of, relating to, or characteristic of Puerto Rico **2 :** of, relating to, or characteristic of Puerto Ricans

**²puerto rican** \"\ *also* **porto rican** \"\ *n, pl* **puerto ricans** *also* **porto ricans** *cap P&R* **:** a native or inhabitant of Puerto Rico

**puer·to ri·co** \-ˈrē(ˌ)kō\ *adj, usu cap P&R* [fr. *Puerto Rico,* island in the West Indies] **:** of or from Puerto Rico **:** of the kind or style prevalent in Puerto Rico **:** PUERTO RICAN

**¹puff** \ˈpəf\ *vb* -ED/-ING/-S [ME *puffen,* fr. OE *pyffan,* of imit. origin] *vi* **1 a :** to blow in short gusts **:** exhale forcibly or escape in a cloud ⟨a fresh salt breeze ~*s* across the bay⟩ ⟨the gatherer ~*s* lightly into the blowpipe to shape the molten glass⟩ ⟨the dust almost ~*ed* out of the door when we opened it —Molly L. Bar-David⟩ **b :** to breathe hard because of exertion **:** PANT ⟨was ~*ing* heavily when he reached the top⟩ **c :** to emit a series of little whiffs or clouds (as of smoke or steam) often as an accompaniment to vigorous action ⟨~ at a pipe⟩ ⟨the kettle ~*ing,* and the tea all set out —Adrian Bell⟩ ⟨snorting, ~*ing* river steamers that churned their way to the city —*Amer. Guide Series: Maine*⟩ **d :** to discharge a powdery cloud of spores ⟨changes in temperature or humidity may cause some ascomycetes to ~⟩ **2 :** to speak or act in a scornful or conceited manner **:** BLUSTER, POOH-POOH ⟨a ~*ing* turkey-cock of a man, full of himself and of false patriotism —E.S.Morgan⟩ ⟨it is . . . to defy Heaven to ~ at damnation —Robert South⟩ **3 a :** to become distended **:** SWELL — usu. used with *up* ⟨a sprained ankle ~*s* up⟩ **b :** to open or appear in or as if in a puff **:** ERUPT, EXPLODE, EXPAND, POP ⟨the spin chute ~*s* out behind the hurtling plane⟩ ⟨flak was ~*ing* all around —F.V. Drake⟩ ⟨twice, little spot fires ~*ed* up on the wrong side —G.R.Stewart⟩ **c :** to make exaggerated statements or claims **:** BRAG ⟨a considerable amount of ~*ing* . . . was part of the sales talk that induced the marriage —Morris Ploscowe⟩; *specif* **:** to advertise in glowing terms ⟨~*ing* . . . is well understood by a public immunized to the superlatives of the marketplace —F.V.Harper⟩ ~ *vt* **1 a :** to propel or agitate by means of short gusts **:** blow in whiffs or spurts **:** WAFT ⟨people who eat peppermint and ~ it in your face —W.S.Gilbert⟩ ⟨a brisk breeze ~*s* the clouds away⟩ ⟨bullets . . . ~*ed* up the white dust all around him —A. Conan Doyle⟩ **b :** to extinguish by blowing — used with *out* ⟨~ out a candle⟩ **c** (1) **:** to say breathlessly **:** PANT ⟨"wait for me," he ~*ed,* doing his best to keep up with the bigger boys⟩ (2) **:** to render breathless **:** wear out ⟨twisted the rope round faster and faster, until he was ~*ed* —Dannie Abse⟩ **d :** to draw on (as a pipe or cigarette) with intermittent exhalations of smoke ⟨found that when people ~ two cigarettes alternately, they cannot in fact tell the difference between them —Martin Mayer⟩ **e :** to apply with a diffusing device (as a powder puff) ⟨neck, still white with the powder she had ~*ed* there after her bath —Wright Morris⟩ **2 a** (1) **:** to distend with or as if with air or gas **:** INFLATE, SWELL ⟨green lizards ~ out their throats like thin red bubbles —Marjory S. Douglas⟩ ⟨~*ed* out his chest and pranced around the chair —Daniel Curley⟩ (2) **:** to fluff up or pad out **:** EXPAND, STUFF ⟨the ~*ed* and tufted furniture —Norman Mailer⟩ ⟨the manuscript of her work had been submitted . . . for this one to prune and that one to ~ out —Wilfred Partington⟩; *specif* **:** to arrange (hair) in puffs **b** (1) **:** to make proud or conceited **:** ELATE, GRATIFY ⟨public acclamation ~*s* his ego⟩ ⟨might have become morally ~*ed* up if a healthy corrective had not been administered —A.W.Long⟩ (2) **:** to cause to swell with anger **:** ROUSE ⟨audience ~*s* itself to storm the gates —D.M.Friedenberg⟩ **c :** to praise extravagantly **:** OVERRATE, EXTOL ⟨hit too many homers and people start ~*ing* you up —Willie Mays⟩ ⟨do not ~ impossible trash, but they do let people . . . know what is interesting and worth reading —Mary C. Fair⟩; *specif* **:** ADVERTISE ⟨traders . . . still ~ their goods as if the whole aim of their toils were just to achieve a single transaction —C.E. Montague⟩

**²puff** \"\ *n* -S [ME *puf, puffe,* fr. OE *pyff,* fr. *pyffan*] **1 a :** an act or instance of puffing **:** WHIFF, GUST ⟨storm which set out as a mere ~ of wind thousands of miles away —Carey Longmire⟩; *specif* **:** CAT'S-PAW 1 ⟨when you reef for a land breeze study the duration of the ~*s* —Peter Heaton⟩ **b :** a slight explosive sound accompanying a puff **:** HUFF ⟨let out an irrepressible little ~ of laughter —Marguerite Steen⟩ ⟨listen to the ~ of a distant locomotive⟩ **c :** a perceptible cloud or aura emitted in a puff ⟨let ten ~*s* of his pipe eddy away —F.M.Ford⟩ ⟨sat back . . . in a fluff of soft fur and a ~ of expensive scent —Anne Panish⟩ **d :** something that resembles a puff ⟨a clear blue sky with only a few ~*s* of cloud sailing in it —Clifton Cuthbert⟩ ⟨can all be blown away with one ~ of clear common sense —Stuart Hampshire⟩ **e :** PUFFBALL **2 a :** a hollow or airy substance: as (1) **:** a dish that puffs in cooking ⟨corn ~⟩ ⟨potato ~⟩; *esp* **:** a light pastry that rises high in baking (2) **:** a tall drink that consists of an alcoholic liquor, milk, and soda water ⟨brandy ~⟩ ⟨gin ~⟩ **b** (1) **:** a disease of the tomato of unknown cause characterized by fruits that are light in weight and hollow (2) **:** WINDGALL 1 **3 a :** a slight swelling **:** PROTUBERANCE **b :** a fluffy mass: as (1) **:** POUF b ⟨a dainty ~ of sleeve at the shoulder⟩ ⟨great ~*s* of blue hydrangea blossoms —Placide Martin⟩ ⟨bird didn't even have time to get its wings open before pellets ripped it into a ~ of feathers —Barnaby Conrad⟩ (2) **:** POWDER PUFF (3) **:** a soft loose roll of hair usu. wound over a pad and pinned in place — called also *pouf* (4) **:** a quilted or tufted bed covering filled with down or fiber — called also *pouf* **c :** a padded ridge or piece of wadding; *specif* **:** TOE PUFF **4 a :** an exhibition of arrogance or ostentation **:** BLUFF, SHOW ⟨showing off for each other . . . like housewives putting on a ~ at a party —John Steinbeck⟩ **b** *archaic* **:** one that exhibits arrogance or ostentation **:** BRAGGART, SHOW-OFF **c :** LADIES' MAN ⟨thought actors were a lot of ~*s* —Stewart Granger⟩ **5 :** a commendatory notice or review ⟨pleasant letters came to me on my birthday . . . and one or two ~*s* in the newspapers —O.W.Holmes †1935⟩ ⟨interested in political ~*s,* not news —W.A.Swanberg⟩ ⟨the play got ~*s* from several critics⟩; *specif* **:** BLURB ⟨~*s* . . . with which booksellers sometimes embroider their catalogs —John Carter⟩ ⟨firm does not favor . . . publicity stunts or ~*s* for goods on sale —*Persuasion*⟩

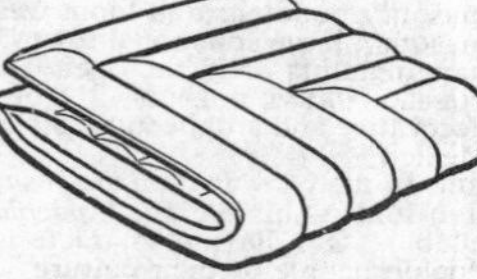

puff 3b(4), folded

**³puff** \"\ *adj* **1 :** PUFFED ⟨~ sleeve⟩ **2 :** of, relating to, or designed for promotion or flattery ⟨~ writer⟩ ⟨~ biography⟩

**⁴puff** *a strongly articulated* p-*sound sometimes trilled & sometimes with a vowel sound following; usu read as* ˈpüf\ *interj* [ME *puf*] — used to express disdain or to indicate transience

**puff adder** *n* **1 a :** a thick-bodied exceedingly venomous widely distributed African viper (*Bitis arietans*) that inflates its body and hisses loudly when disturbed **b :** a similar smaller snake (*B. inornata*) that occurs only in southern Africa **2 :** HOGNOSE SNAKE

**puffback** \ˈ═,═\ *n* **1** *or* **puffback shrike :** any of several African shrikes of the genus *Dryoscopus* that are chiefly black and white or buffy in color and have the feathers of the lower back long, fluffy, and erectile **2 :** a strike-back of the flame in a stove or oil burner

**puffball** \ˈ═,═\ *n* **1 a :** any of various basidiomycetous fungi of the family Lycoperdaceae that have a globose shape, discharge the ripe spores in a smokelike cloud when pressed or struck, and are often edible **b :** any of various similar fungi (as of the families Sclerodermataceae and Tulostomaceae) **2 :** the feathery head of achenes in the dandelion

**puffbird** \ˈ═,═\ *n* **:** any of numerous So. American and Central American zygodactyl birds of the family Bucconidae that are related to the jacamars and often sit with the feathers of the head fluffed out — called also *barbet*

**puffed** *adj* **1 a** (1) **:** BLOATED, SWOLLEN ⟨her face pale, ~, streaked with weeping —Ethel Wilson⟩ (2) **:** gathered or stiffened for protruding fullness ⟨~ sleeves⟩ **b** (1) **:** INFLATED (2) **:** heated in a closed container until the moisture in the grain turns to steam that causes the kernel to expand when the pressure is suddenly released ⟨~ rice⟩ ⟨~ wheat⟩ **2 :** exhibiting or expressive of vanity or conceit **:** PRETENTIOUS, ARROGANT ⟨are but ~ minds that bubble thus above inferiors —Owen Feltham⟩

**puff·er** \ˈpəfə(r)\ *n* -S **1 a :** one that emits puffs: as (1) **:** SMOKER 1b (2) *chiefly Scot* **:** a small steam-powered cargo ship used in coastal trade (3) **:** a small engine used in coal mines for hoisting and hauling **b :** the operator of a small engine for hauling mine cars or hoisting coal or rock **2 a :** one that extols; *esp* **:** a writer of commendatory or promotional material ⟨reviewing is done largely by people who are not critics but simply ~*s* —James Laughlin⟩ **b :** BY-BIDDER **3 a :** one that stuffs or swells; *specif* **:** an operator of a machine for raising designs on manufactured articles (as leather goods, gloves, draperies) **b** (1) **:** PUFF IRON (2) **:** BALLER 2 **4 a** (1) **:** GLOBEFISH 1 (2) **:** any of various other fishes of the order Plectognathi **b :** HARBOR PORPOISE

**puff·ery** \-fərē, -ri\ *n* -ES **:** flattering publicity **:** extravagant commendation esp. for promotional purposes; *specif* **:** ADVERTISING

**puff-fish** \ˈ═,═\ *n* **:** PUFFER 4a

**puff·i·ly** \ˈpəfəlē, -li\ *adv* **:** in a puffy manner

**puf·fin** \ˈpəfən\ *n* -S [ME *poffoun, pophyn*] **1 :** any of several sea birds of the genera *Fratercula* and *Lunda* (family Alcidae) having a short neck and a deep grooved parti-colored laterally compressed bill, nesting in burrows or crevices, and laying a single white or nearly white egg **2 :** SHEARWATER; *esp* **:** MANX SHEARWATER

**puff·i·ness** \ˈpəfēnəs, -fin-\ *n* -ES **:** the quality or state of being puffy

**puffing** *n* -S **1 :** an act or instance of puffing: as **a :** puffed decoration or trimming esp. on clothing **b :** extravagant praise or commendation; *specif* **:** seller's or dealer's talk in praise of the virtues of something offered for sale **c :** the action of a puffer in bidding up the price at an auction **2 :** PUFF 2b (1)

**puffing adder** *n* **:** HOGNOSE SNAKE

**puff·ing·ly** *adv* **:** with puffing ⟨labored ~ up one flight of stairs —J.B.Benefield⟩

**puffing pig** *n* **:** HARBOR PORPOISE

**puf·fi·nus** \ˈpəfənəs\ *n, cap* [NL, fr. E *puffin*] **:** a genus of oceanic birds (family Procellariidae) that comprises the shearwaters and is sometimes included in the genus *Procellaria*

**puff iron** *n* **:** an electrically heated metal form of irregular shape used by dry cleaners to press parts of garments (as gathers or flounces) difficult to iron by hand

**puff-leg** \ˈ═,═\ *n* **:** any of numerous hummingbirds of the genus *Eriocnemis* having tufts of downy feathers on the legs

**puff paste** *n* **:** a very rich flaky pastry composed usu. of equal parts of flour and butter, processed by repeated rolling and folding after each addition of butter, and baked at high temperature which causes it to puff in leaves or flakes ⟨make patty shells of *puff paste*⟩

**puffs** *pl of* PUFF, *pres 3d sing of* PUFF

**puffy** \ˈpəfē, -fi\ *adj* -ER/-EST **1 :** characterized by vanity or ostentation **:** POMPOUS, SHOWY ⟨a ~ pretentious man⟩ ⟨the scenes are more ~ than pointed —Leslie Rees⟩ **2 a :** blowing in puffs **:** GUSTY ⟨a ~ northeast wind⟩ **b :** BREATHLESS, SHORT-WINDED ⟨were ~ long before they reached the summit⟩ **3 a :** swollen or tending to swell in size **:** BLOATED, CHUBBY ⟨his face . . . aside from a few ~ bruises, looked fit —Gordon Merrick⟩ ⟨two Englishmen, one ~, one rangy —Sinclair Lewis⟩ **b :** resembling a puff **:** BOUFFANT, FLUFFY ⟨a ~, floor-length underskirt —Lois Long⟩ ⟨~ pillow⟩ ⟨~ clouds⟩

**¹pug** \ˈpəg, ˈpu̇g\ *n* [ME *pugge*] *archaic* **:** ¹CHAFF 1

**²pug** \ˈpəg\ *n* -S [perh. alter. of ¹*puck*] **1** *obs* **a :** a dear one **:** SWEETHEART, PET **b :** MISTRESS, PROSTITUTE **2** *obs* **a :** HOBGOBLIN **b :** MONKEY **3 a :** a small sturdy compact dog of a breed introduced from Asia into Europe by the Dutch with a short sleek coat silvery or fawn marked with black or all black, a tightly curled tail, broad wrinkled face and rounded head with button ears, and strong straight legs **b :** something that is short and squat: as (1) **:** PUG NOSE (2) **:** a close knot or coil of hair **:** BUN **4 :** PUG MOTH

**³pug** \"\ *vt* **pugged; pugged; pugging; pugs** [perh. alter. of ²*puck*] **1 :** to plug or pack with a compacted substance (as clay or mortar); *esp* **:** to fill (the space under a floor) with sound-deadening material **2 :** to work into a desired consistency by kneading or churning; *esp* **:** to wedge (clay) for making bricks or pottery **3** *chiefly Brit* **:** to trample (wet ground) into a sticky mass — used of cattle

**⁴pug** \"\ *n* -S **1 a :** a compacted mass of a plastic substance; *esp* **:** a large lump of tempered clay for making pottery **b :** a mixture of clay and manure sometimes with chopped hay or cow hair added used for covering grafts **c :** GOUGE 4 **2 :** PUG MILL

**⁵pug** \"\ *n* -S [by shortening & alter. fr. *pugilist*] **:** BOXER, PRIZEFIGHTER

**⁶pug** \"\ *n* -S [Hindi *pag* foot] **:** FOOTPRINT; *esp* **:** a print of a wild mammal **:** TRACK, SPOOR ⟨the great ~*s,* pressed deep, led from the trees on their left —Jon Godden⟩

**⁷pug** \"\ *vt* **pugged; pugged; pugging; pugs :** to track by pugs ⟨~ a tiger⟩ ⟨~ a criminal⟩

**pug-dog** \ˈ═,═\ *n* **:** ²PUG 3a

**pu·get sound pine** \ˈpyüjət-\ *n, usu cap 1st P & S* [fr. *Puget Sound,* arm of the Pacific ocean extending southward into Washington state] **:** DOUGLAS FIR

**pu·get·tia** \pyüˈged·ēə\ *n, cap* [NL, fr. *Puget* Sound + NL *-ia*] **:** a genus of spider crabs (family Majidae) common along the Pacific coast of No. America

**pug·ga·ree** *or* **pug·a·ree** \ˈpəg(ə)rē\ *or* **pug·gree** *also* **pug·ree** *or* **pa·gri** \ˈpəgrē\ *n* -S [Hindi *pagṛī*] **1 :** a turban worn in India **2 :** a light usu. printed or colored scarf wrapped around a sun helmet often with a piece hanging down in back as a protection from the sun or used as a hatband esp. for a straw hat

**pug·ger** \ˈpəgə(r)\ *n* -S [³*pug* + *-er*] **:** one that pugs clay (as for pottery or brick); *esp* **:** an operator of a pug mill

**pugging** *n* -S [fr. gerund of ³*pug*] **1 :** the working and tempering of clay usu. by machine to make it plastic and of uniform consistency **2 :** DEAFENING 2

**pug·gish** \ˈpəgish\ *adj* [²*pug* + *-ish*] **1** *archaic* **a :** characteristic of a monkey **b :** PUCKISH **2 :** SNUBBY

**pug·gle** \ˈpəgəl\ *vt* -ED/-ING/-S [freq. of ³*pug*] *chiefly dial* **:** to clear out or stir up by poking

**¹pug·gy** \ˈpəgē, -gi\ *n* -ES [²*pug* + *-y* (n. suffix)] **1 :** SWEETHEART, PET **2** *Scot* **:** MONKEY

**²puggy** \"\ *adj* -ER/-EST [²*pug* + *-y* (adj. suffix)] **:** PUGGISH 2

**³puggy** \"\ *adj* [E dial. *pug* to sweat + *-y*] **1** *dial Eng* **:** perspiring or causing perspiration **:** SWEATY **2** *dial Brit* **:** clammy, damp, and sticky ⟨tuberous plants won't do well in soggy, ~ soils —*Sydney (Australia) Bull.*⟩

**⁴pug·gy** *also* **pug·gi** \ˈpəgē\ *n, pl* **puggies** [Hindi *pagī,* fr. *pag* foot] **:** TRACKER; *esp* **:** a member of a caste in India trained to track criminals by their footprints

**¹pugh** *a strongly articulated* p-*sound sometimes trilled & sometimes with a vowel sound following; usu read as* ˈpü\ *interj* [imit. of the sniff of disdain caused by a bad smell] — used to express disgust or disdain

**²pugh** \ˈpyü\ *n* -S [by alter.] **:** ⁵PEW

**pugil** *n* -S [L *pugillus* handful, fr. *pugnus* fist — more at PUGNACIOUS] *archaic* **:** ²PINCH 2b

**pu·gi·lant** \ˈpyüjələnt\ *adj* [L *pugilant-, pugilans* pres. part. of *pugilare, pugilari* to fight with fists, fr. *pugil* boxer — more at PUGILISM] **:** PUGILISTIC

**pu·gi·lism** \-jəˌlizəm\ *n* -S [L *pugil* pugilist, boxer + E *-ism;* akin to L *pugnus* fist — more at PUGNACIOUS] **:** ²BOXING

**pu·gi·list** \-ləst\ *n* -S [L *pugil* + E *-ist*] **:** FIGHTER; *esp* **:** a professional boxer

**pu·gi·lis·tic** \ˌ═══ˈlistik, -tēk\ *adj* **:** of or relating to pugilism ⟨ended his ~ career by retiring undefeated⟩ — **pu·gi·lis·ti·cal·ly** \-tək(ə)lē, -li\ *adv*

**pugmark** \ˈ═,═\ *n* [⁶*pug* + *mark*] **:** ⁶PUG ⟨your eye notes ~*s* telling of a hungry wolf or lynx that climbed the dome —W.J.Long⟩

**pug mill** *n* [³*pug*] **:** a machine consisting of a shaft armed with blades revolving in a drum or trough and used for mixing or tempering a plastic substance into a desired consistency ⟨brick-clay . . . might need sieving, weathering, and mincing in the *pug mill* before it could be worked —Katharine S. Woods⟩ ⟨clay . . . and mixed by hand, foot, or *pug mill* to the right consistency for throwing —Bernard Leach⟩ ⟨rubber compound . . . thinned down with naphtha to suitable consistency in a *pug mill* —H.P.Stevens & Clayton Beadle⟩; *esp* **:** CEMENT MIXER

**pug moth** *n* [²*pug*] **:** any of various small geometrid moths of *Chloroclystis* and related genera

**pug·na·cious** \ˌpəgˈnāshəs\ *adj* [L *pugnac-, pugnax* pugnacious (fr. *pugnare* to fight, fr. *pugnus* fist) + E *-ious* — more at PUNGENT] **:** having a quarrelsome or belligerent nature **:** thriving on challenge **:** AGGRESSIVE, TRUCULENT ⟨bushpigs are most courageous and ~ animals . . . capable of putting up a successful fight even against a leopard —James Stevenson-Hamilton⟩ ⟨~ spirits . . . lamented that there was so little prospect of an exhilarating disturbance —Herman Melville⟩ ⟨equally ~ when it came to fighting for human rights —P.V.D. Stern⟩ ⟨not a ~ enough mediocrity to earn a larger salary —V.A.Young⟩ **syn** see BELLIGERENT

**pug·na·cious·ly** *adv* **:** in a pugnacious manner

**pug·na·cious·ness** *n* -ES **:** PUGNACITY

**pug·nac·i·ty** \ˌpəgˈnasəd·ē, -sətē, -i\ *n* -ES [L *pugnacitas,* fr. *pugnac-, pugnax* + *-itas* -ity] **:** fighting instinct **:** ready response to challenge **:** COURAGE, AGGRESSIVENESS, TRUCULENCE ⟨some children . . . seem to be born fighting and never wish to repudiate their native ~ —Margaret Hay⟩ ⟨retain . . . the ~ developed in their struggle for full civil status —William Petersen⟩

**pug nose** *n* [²*pug*] **:** a nose having a slightly concave bridge and flattened nostrils **:** SNUB NOSE

**pug-nosed** \(ˈ)═ˈ═\ *adj* **:** having a blunt nose

**pug-nosed eel** *n* **:** a deep-sea eel (*Simenchelys parasiticus*) having a shorter and stouter body than the common eel and a short blunt nose and burrowing into the bodies of other fishes

**pugree** *var of* PUGGAREE

**pugs** *pl of* PUG, *pres 3d sing of* PUG

**pu·ha** \ˈpühə\ *n* -S [Maori] *New Zealand* **:** a sow thistle (*Sonchus oleraceus*) that is commonly used as a potherb ⟨~ turned up with practically everything, corned beef, boiled bacon, baked rabbit —Ruth Park⟩

**pu·hoe** \(ˈ)püˈhōē\ *n* -S [*Tahitian*] **:** an outrigger paddling canoe of the Society islands

**pui·na·ve** \pwēˈnävē\ *n, pl* **puina·ve** \"\ *or* **puina·vis** \-vēz\ *usu cap* **1 a :** a people of eastern Colombia **b :** a member of such people **2 a :** the language of the Puinave people **b :** the Puinavean language family comprising Puinave and Macú

**pui·na·ve·an** \-vēən\ *adj, usu cap* **:** of or relating to the Puinave or their language

**puir** \ˈpü(ə)r\ *Scot var of* POOR

**puis dar·rein continuance** \pwisˈdarən-, -ˌdaˈrān-\ *n* [AF, lit., since the last continuance] **:** a pleading introducing new matter after plea has already been made and issue joined but preceding trial

**¹puis·ne** \ˈpyünē, -ni\ *adj* [AF, fr. OF *puisné* born afterwards — more at PUNY] **1** *or* **puisny** \"\ *obs* **:** of little consequence or experience **:** INSIGNIFICANT, PETTY ⟨a ~ tilter, that spurs his horse but on one side —Shak.⟩ **2 a :** of lesser age or importance **:** JUNIOR, SUBORDINATE **b** *law* **:** ASSOCIATE ⟨a ~ judge of the superior court⟩ **3** *law* **:** of subsequent date **:** LATER

**²puisne** \"\ *n* -S [AF, fr. *puisne,* adj.] **1 :** one who is a junior or subordinate **2 :** a puisne judge ⟨the other ~ doubted, but agreed that the case must be discussed —O.W.Holmes †1935⟩

**pu·is·sance** \ˈpyüəsᵊn(t)s, pyüˈis-, ˈpwis-\ *n* -S [ME *puissaunce,* fr. MF *puissance,* fr. OF, fr. *puissant*] **1 :** ability to coerce or sway **:** controlling influence **:** STRENGTH, POWER ⟨samurai bow to the ~ of the emperor⟩ ⟨legislators . . . fear the ~ of the farm vote —*Los Angeles (Calif.) Times*⟩ ⟨extraordinary rhythmic ~ —Aaron Copland⟩ **2** *obs* **:** a military force **:** ARMY ⟨cousin, go draw our ~ together —Shak.⟩ **syn** see POWER

**pu·is·sant** \-nt\ *adj* [ME *puissaunt,* fr. MF *puissant,* fr. OF, fr. *puiss-* (stem of *poer, poeir* to be able) + *-ant* — more at POWER] **:** of great force or vigor **:** STRONG, POWERFUL ⟨one of the nation's most ~ labor leaders —*Time*⟩ ⟨called on all the ~ stamina of her mother —Adria Langley⟩ ⟨though not a ~ colorist, secured some . . . beautiful effects —Royal Cortissoz⟩ — **pu·is·sant·ly** *adv*

**pu·ja** *also* **poo·ja** *or* **poo·jah** \ˈpüjə\ *n* -S [Skt *pūjā,* prob. of Dravidian origin; akin to Tamil *pūcu* to anoint, besmear] **1 :** a Hindu act of worship or propitiation ⟨the priest advised us to do ~ and make offerings . . . for relief from our terrible problem —*New Yorker*⟩ **2 :** a Hindu rite or religious festival ⟨some engage in ~ and some perform salat —J.C.Archer⟩

**pu·ju·nan** \püˈjünən\ *n* -S *usu cap* **:** a language family of the Penutian stock in California comprising four languages all known as Maidu — called also *Maidu*

**¹pu·ka** \ˈpükə\ *n* -S [Maori] **1 :** a rare New Zealand tree (*Meryta sinclairii*) of the family Araliaceae with large resinous leaves and dioecious flowers in panicles **2 :** either of two New Zealand trees of the genus *Griselinia* that are sometimes epiphytic: **a :** a tree (*G. lucida*) with long thick shining leaves and green or yellow flowers in axillary panicles **b :** KAPUKA

**²puka** \"\ *n* -s [*Hawaii*] *Hawaii* **:** HOLE, TUNNEL ⟨if . . . I ever get the giant African snails out of their favorite ~*s*, I shall really enjoy the gardening —*Honolulu Star-Bull.*⟩

**pu·ka·tea** \ˌpükəˈtāə\ *n* -s [Maori] **:** a lofty New Zealand forest tree (*Laurelia novae-zealandiae*) of the family Monimiaceae having a light-colored wood that is soft but strong

**pu·ka·teine** \ˌpükəˈtāˌēn, -ə̄n\ *n* -s [ISV *pukatea* + *-ine*] **:** a crystalline alkaloid $C_{18}H_{17}NO_3$ found in pukatea bark

**¹puke** \ˈpyük\ *n* -s [ME *pewke, puke,* fr. MD *puuc, puyc;* akin to D *puik* excellent, Fris *pûk, pük*] **:** a woolen fabric of good quality used esp. for gowns in 15th century England

**²puke** \"\ *vb* -ED/-ING/-S [perh. of imit. origin] *vi* **1 a :** VOMIT 1 — often considered vulgar **b :** to spill over because of the faulty mixing of slugs of liquid with the expelled vapors — used of a petroleum fractionating column **2 :** to become revolted ⟨a frame of mind that makes me ~ —O.W.Holmes †1935⟩ ~ *vt* **1 :** to throw up **:** VOMIT — often considered vulgar **2 :** to cause to vomit ⟨purged me and *puked* me and charged me two shillings —S.H.Adams⟩

**³puke** \"\ *n* -s **1 a** *archaic* **:** an act of vomiting induced by an emetic **b** *archaic* **:** EMETIC **c :** an attack of nausea ⟨had the ~*s*⟩ — often considered vulgar **d :** VOMIT 1b — often considered vulgar **2** *usu cap* **:** MISSOURIAN — used as a nickname **3 :** a disgusting or contemptible person ⟨backboneless little ~*s* —H.L.Davis⟩

**pu·ke·ko** \pü'kā(ˌ)kō\ *also* **pu·ke·ka** \-ākə\ *n* -s [Maori] **:** a handsome blue, black, and white gallinule (*Porphyrio melanotus*) of New Zealand, Australia, and adjacent islands

**puk·er** \ˈpyükə(r)\ *n* -s [²*puke* + *-er*] **1** *archaic* **:** EMETIC **2 :** one that vomits — often considered vulgar

**pukeweed** \ˈ=,=\ *n* **:** INDIAN TOBACCO 1

**pukh·tun** \pük'tün\ *n, pl* **pukhtun** *or* **pukhtuns** *cap* [Pashto] **:** AFGHAN 1

**puk·ka** *or* **pucka** *also* **puc·ca** \ˈpəkə\ *adj* [Hindi *pakkā* cooked, ripe, solid, fr. Skt *pakva;* akin to Skt *pacati* he cooks — more at COOK] **:** of a genuine or total nature **:** absolutely first class **:** AUTHENTIC, COMPLETE ⟨~ sahib⟩ ⟨never did . . . have ~ quarters, with a swarm of servants —P.A.Waring⟩ ⟨the smabur is not regarded as a really ~ trophy compared with tiger —Edison Marshall⟩

**puk·ras** \ˈpəkrəs\ *or* **pukras pheasant** *n* -ES [*pukras* fr. native name in India] **:** any of several pheasants of northern India and the Himalayas constituting the genus *Pucrasia* and being in the males mostly crested with long black ear tufts — called also *koklas*

**pu·ku** \ˈpü(ˌ)kü\ *also* **po·ku** \ˈpō(ˌ)-\ *or* **poo·koo** \ˈpü(ˌ)kü\ *n* -s [native name in Africa] **:** a reddish African antelope (*Adenota vardoni*) related to the waterbuck

**¹pul** \ˈpül\ *n, pl* **puls** \-z\ *or* **pu·li** \-ü(ˌ)lē\ [Russ *pulo, pul,* fr. Turk *pul* small coin, fr. LGk *phollis* bellows, a small coin, fr. L *follis* bellows, bag — more at FOOL] **1 :** a Russian copper coin issued from the 15th century to 1810 **2** [Per *pūl,* fr. Turk *pul*] **a :** a unit of value of Afghanistan equal to ¹⁄₁₀₀ afghani — see MONEY table **b :** a coin representing this unit

**pu·la·han** \ˌpüləˈhän\ *n, pl* **pulaha·nes** \-(ˌ)näs\ [Tag, fr. *pulá* red; fr. the color of the dress of the insurgents] **:** a member of a 19th century band of Tagalog insurgents esp. in Leyte and Samar organized in opposition to domination of the Philippines by the Spanish friars

**pulas** *var of* PALAS

**pu·la·san** *or* **pu·las·san** \ˌpüləˈsän\ *n* -s [Malay] **1 :** an East Indian fruit tree (*Nephelium mutabile*) **2 :** the fruit of the pulasan tree that resembles the closely related rambutan but is sweeter and less juicy

**pu·las·ki** \pəˈlaskē\ *n* -s *usu cap* [after Edward C. *Pulaski,* 20th cent. Am. forest ranger, its inventor] **1** *also* **pulaski tool :** a single-bit axe with an adze-shaped grub hoe extending from the back **2 :** HAZEL HOE

Pulaski

**pul·chri·tude** \ˈpəlkrəˌtüd, -əˌtyüd\ *n* -s [ME *pulcritude,* fr. L *pulchritudo,* fr. *pulchr-, pulcher* beautiful + *-i-* + *-tudo* -tude; perh. akin to Gk *perknos* dusky, dark — more at PERCH] **:** physical comeliness **:** BEAUTY ⟨the May queen and her court making a dazzling assemblage of ~⟩ ⟨a he-man, handsome with a certain bull-like ~ —W.A.White⟩

**pul·chri·tu·di·nous** \ˌ==ˈ=dᵊnəs\ *adj* [L *pulchritudin-, pulchritudo* + E *-ous*] **:** having or marked by pulchritude ⟨~ movie stars⟩ **syn** see BEAUTIFUL

**pule** \ˈpyül\ *vb* -ED/-ING/-S [prob. of imit. origin] *vi* **1 :** to make a plaintive moaning sound **:** WHINE, WHIMPER **2** *obs* **:** to chirp weakly **:** PEEP ~ *vt, archaic* **:** to utter in a plaintive manner

**pu·le·gol** \ˈpyüləˌgȯl, -gōl\ *n* -s [ISV *pulegone* + *-ol*] **:** a viscous liquid alcohol $C_{10}H_{17}OH$ obtained by reduction of pulegone; 2-isopropylidene-5-methyl-cyclohexanol

**pu·le·gone** \-ˌgōn\ *n* -s [ISV *puleg-* (fr. NL *pulegium,* specific epithet of *Mentha pulegium,* fr. L *puleium, pulegium* pennyroyal) + *-one*] **:** a fragrant liquid terpenoid ketone $C_{10}H_{16}O$ derived from menthenone that is the principal constituent of pennyroyal oil and yields menthol on hydrogenation

**pul·er** \ˈpyülə(r)\ *n* -s *archaic* **:** one that pules

**pulesati** *usu cap, var of* PURASATI

**pu·lex** \ˈpyüˌleks\ *n, cap* [NL, fr. L, flea — more at PSYLLA] **:** a genus (the type of the family Pulicidae) of fleas including the most common flea (*P. irritans*) that regularly attacks man

**¹puli** *pl of* PUL

**²pu·li** \ˈpülē, ˈpyülē\ *n, pl* **pu·lik** \-k\ *also* **pulis** [Hung] **:** an intelligent vigorous medium-sized farm dog of a Hungarian breed with long profuse coat tending to mat into a corded appearance

**¹pu·li·cid** \ˈpyüləsə̇d\ *adj* [NL *Pulicidae*] **:** of or relating to the Pulicidae

**²pulicid** \"\ *n* -s **:** a flea of the family Pulicidae

**pu·lic·i·dae** \pyüˈlisəˌdē\ *n pl, cap* [NL, fr. *Pulic-, Pulex,* type genus + *-idae*] **:** a large and nearly cosmopolitan family of fleas that includes many of the common fleas attacking man and his domestic animals — see PULEX

**pu·li·ci·dal** \ˌpyüləˈsīdᵊl\ *adj* [blend of L *pulic-, pulex* flea and E *-cidal* — more at PSYLLA] **:** destructive to fleas

**pu·li·cide** \ˈpyüləˌsīd\ *n* -s [blend of L *pulic-, pulex* flea and E *-cide*] **:** an agent used for destroying fleas

**pu·li·cose** \-ˌkōs\ *or* **pu·li·cous** \-ləkəs\ *adj* [L *pulicosus,* fr. *pulic-, pulex* + *-osus* -ose, -ous] *archaic* **:** infested with or caused by the bite of fleas

**puling** *adj* [fr. pres. part. of *pule*] **1 :** of an abject or plaintive nature **:** SPIRITLESS, WHINING ⟨~ coward⟩ ⟨~ hypochondriac⟩ **2 :** of a feeble or sickly nature **:** SPINDLY, LANGUISHING ⟨~ hybrids between rhododendrons and azaleas —W.H.Camp⟩ ⟨glanced with . . . favor on a ~ milkmaid —W.S.Gilbert⟩ — **pul·ing·ly** *adv*

**pulitzer** \ˈpu̇lə̇tsə(r)-, ˈpyül-\ *n* -s *usu cap* [after Joseph *Pulitzer* †1911 Am. newspaper publisher] **:** any of several annual awards for outstanding literary or journalistic achievement or public service established by the will of Joseph Pulitzer

**pulk** \ˈpu̇lk\ *n* -s [ME *polk, pulk,* perh. dim. of *pool* — more at POOL] **1** *dial chiefly Eng* **:** a muddy pond **2** *dial chiefly Eng* **:** MUDHOLE

**pul·ka** \ˈpəlkə\ *n* -s [Finn *pulkka* & Lapp *pulkke*] **:** a one-man Lapp sledge shaped like half a canoe and resting on a broad board or on several runners

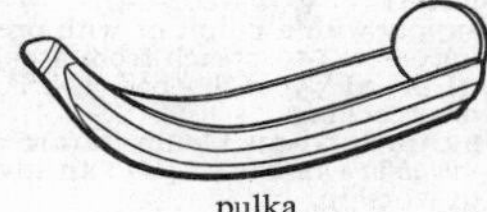

pulka

**¹pull** \ˈpu̇l\ *vb* -ED/-ING/-S [ME *pullen,* fr. OE *pullian;* prob. akin to Fris *pûlje* to shell, MLG *pulen* to shell, cull, perform a laborious task, MD *pulen, puilen, pullen* to bulge, protrude, Norw dial. *pulla* to bubble up, Icel *pūla* to work hard, push hard] *vt* **1 a** (1) **:** to draw out from the skin **:** PLUCK ⟨we'll ~ his plumes —Shak.⟩; *specif* **:** to remove (as the wool or hair) from hides or skins usu. by means of a blunt knife, scraper, or rotating spiral knife ⟨as the wool is ~*ed* it is put into containers by grade —A.L. Anderson⟩ (2) *chiefly dial* **:** PLUCK ⟨~ poultry⟩ **b :** to pick from a tree or plant **:** GATHER ⟨handed me a gay bouquet of roses ~*ed* in the rain —Katherine Mansfield⟩ ⟨~ corn from the stalk⟩ **c** (1) **:** to take out of the ground by the roots ⟨ate plenty of green food, all home-grown and freshly ~*ed;* lettuce and radishes and young onions —Flora Thompson⟩ (2) **:** to dig out **:** UPROOT ⟨immigrants were planting garden plots and ~*ing* stumps as the forest wall receded —*Amer. Guide Series: Oregon*⟩ **d :** EXTRACT ⟨had two teeth ~*ed*⟩ **2 a :** to exert force upon so as to cause or tend to cause motion toward the force **:** tug at ⟨the engine ~*ed* a long line of freight cars⟩ ⟨~*ed* the sled with a rope⟩ ⟨~*ed* his hair⟩ ⟨~ off a ring⟩ — opposed to *push* **b** (1) **:** to change the state or condition of by exerting a tugging force ⟨the major ~*ed* open a zipper on the corner of the oxygen tent —Raymond Boyle⟩ ⟨~*ed* the door shut behind him⟩ (2) **:** to stretch (cooling candy) repeatedly in order to produce a desired color, texture, and flavor (3) **:** to strain or stretch abnormally ⟨~ a muscle⟩ ⟨~ a tendon⟩ **c :** to exert an influence on **:** IMPEL ⟨driven by ambitions, ~*ed* by private sentiments —Carl Van Doren⟩ ⟨through his affection for his brother, was ~*ed,* now this way, now that —Edith Sitwell⟩ **d :** to hold back (a racehorse) from running at full speed and winning ⟨told track stewards he was approached by gamblers to ~ his mount —*Springfield (Mass.) Daily News*⟩ **e** (1) **:** to draw (an oar) through the water ⟨~*ed* an oar in the winning shell⟩ (2) **:** ROW ⟨~*ed* a dinghy across the star-bright water to the lugger —Olaf Ruhen⟩ **f :** to set in action or operation ⟨~*ed* a fire alarm⟩ ⟨some positive safeguard was required against the chance of signalmen ~*ing* the wrong levers —O.S.Nock⟩ ⟨~ the trigger⟩ **g** (1) *baseball* **:** to hit (a pitched ball) into or toward left field from a right-handed batting stance or into or toward right field from a left-handed batting stance ⟨some left-handed batters are shallow left field hitters but may ~ the ball a mile to right —Lou Boudreau⟩ (2) *cricket* **:** to hit (a bowled ball) to the on side with a stroke resembling a drive in which the bat swings downward and approximately parallel to the popping crease (3) *golf* **:** to hit (a ball) toward the left from a right-handed swing or toward the right from a left-handed swing **3 :** to draw apart **:** REND, TEAR ⟨hath turned aside my ways, and ~*ed* me in pieces —Lam 3:11 (AV)⟩ ⟨~*ed* his opponent's arguments to bits⟩ **4 a :** to make (as a proof or impression) by printing **b :** to make a proof or impression of (as a type form, lithographic stone, etching) **5 a :** to remove or cause to be removed from a place, enclosure, or situation ⟨started ~*ing* the wounded out of the vehicles —J.P.O'Neill⟩ ⟨get the prop off, ~ that tail shaft and put in the spare —K.M.Dodson⟩ ⟨~*ed* the pitcher in the third inning⟩ ⟨traveling gagman who ~*s* jokes out of his inside pockets —Lee Rogow⟩ **b :** to bring (a weapon) into the open ready for use esp. by removing from a sheath **:** DRAW ⟨~*ed* a gun on his partner —Erle Stanley Gardner⟩ ⟨~*ed* a knife on me and tried to slash my face —William Goyen⟩ **c :** to draw from a barrel or other container ⟨~*ing* pints of porter for the men off the boats —Frank Ritchie⟩ **d :** to remove (a bullet) from a cartridge **e :** to remove the old construction from (a book) preparatory to rebinding **f** (1) **:** to call out on strike ⟨~*ed* all the workers out of the plant⟩ (2) **:** to call a strike in ⟨~*ed* the plant⟩ (3) **:** to call (a strike) into effect ⟨~*ed* a strike in the plant⟩ **g :** to break up ⟨they ~*ed* camp and headed for home⟩ **6 a :** to carry out with daring and imagination ⟨~*ed* another coup, sailing his fleet out under cover of darkness —*Amer. Guide Series: Vt.*⟩ ⟨~*ed* a play that was entirely unexpected —F.G.Lieb⟩ **b** (1) **:** to put (a crime) into execution **:** COMMIT ⟨concluded that the same bandit probably had ~*ed* all three holdups —Al Spiers⟩ (2) **:** to be guilty of ⟨~ a boner⟩ (3) **:** to do, perform, or say with a deceptive intent **:** PERPETRATE ⟨had been ~*ing* all this stuff for years and getting away with it —Richard Bissell⟩ ⟨~ a fast one⟩ **c :** to draw or carry out as an assignment or duty ⟨was ~*ing* KP when his discharge papers came through —Mack Morriss⟩ ⟨~*ed* 23 combat missions⟩ **7 a :** to put on **:** ASSUME ⟨~*ed* a reluctant grin as he rode away —L.C. Douglas⟩ **b** *slang* **:** to act or behave in the manner of ⟨~ a Simon Legree⟩ **8 a :** to draw the support or attention of **:** ATTRACT ⟨~*ed* more votes than his running mates⟩ ⟨~*ed* the largest crowds in baseball history⟩ **b :** OBTAIN, SECURE ⟨~*ed* an A in his English course⟩ ⟨the motorist who dawdles at less than forty ~*s* a ticket —Noel Houston⟩ **9 :** to demand or obtain an advantage over someone by the assertion of (as a real or fancied superiority) ⟨~*ed* his scientific authority on me —Saul Bellow⟩ ⟨liked to ~ his rank on his inferiors⟩ ~ *vi* **1 a :** to exert a pulling force or perform a pulling action ⟨the second button of his dark blue coat . . . was strained, ~*ing* on the threads that held it —Stuart Cloete⟩ ⟨somebody was ~*ing* again and again at the rusty knob —Marcia Davenport⟩ **b :** to move to or from a particular place or in a particular direction esp. through the exercise of mechanical energy or physical force ⟨the train ~*ed* into the platform⟩ ⟨the car ~*ed* out of the driveway⟩ ⟨the rowers ~*ed* clear of the ship⟩ ⟨~*ed* into town last night⟩ ⟨decided to ~ south to avoid pursuit⟩ **c** (1) **:** to take a drink ⟨~*ed* at rum bottles —S.T. Williamson⟩ (2) **:** to puff or draw hard in smoking ⟨~*ed* at his pipe and stared at the fire —Kathleen Freeman⟩ **d** *of a horse* **:** to strain against the bit **e** *of a hawk* **:** to feed by tearing or snatching ⟨~ upon a stump⟩ **f :** to draw a gun ⟨without warning he ~*ed* and fired⟩ **g :** to pull a ball ⟨he'd be a better hitter if he could learn to ~⟩ **2 a :** to admit of being pulled ⟨these roots ~ easily⟩ **b** *of type* **:** to become pulled out of a form (as by an ink roller) — often used with *out* **3 :** to attract attention or influence people esp. to buy a particular product ⟨this ad ~*ed* better than any other we have run⟩ ⟨the clearance sale is ~*ing* well⟩ **4 :** to feel or express strong sympathy **:** vigorously encourage or support **:** ROOT ⟨nearly always ~*s* for the underdog —*Time*⟩ ⟨was ~*ing* for his team to win⟩

**syn** DRAW, DRAG, HAUL, HALE, TUG, TOW: PULL is a general term meaning to move in the direction of the person or thing exerting force ⟨locomotives *pulling* the train⟩ ⟨*pulling* the drowning child from the water⟩ ⟨*pulling* the box off the shelf⟩ DRAW, often interchangeable with PULL, may sometimes apply to lighter action marked by smooth continuity or dexterity ⟨*draw* up a chair⟩ ⟨*draw* the curtains⟩ ⟨*draw* off the fluid with a pipette⟩ DRAG may suggest a slow, heavy, labored, rough pulling against resistance, over an uneven surface, or of something that does not readily roll or glide ⟨*dragging* the overturned car off the road⟩ ⟨a ship *dragging* her anchor⟩ ⟨*dragging* the rocks out of the field⟩ HAUL may apply to steady forceful heavy pulling or dragging; it may apply to transporting of heavy bulky materials, often those undergoing rough handling ⟨*haul* the trunk up the stairs⟩ ⟨he made a rope fast round the body and it was unceremoniously *hauled* aboard —Nevil Shute⟩ ⟨*haul* the coal from the mines⟩ ⟨*hauling* the bricks from the town upon his wheelbarrow —Pearl Buck⟩ ⟨*hauled* in, the fish are dumped into bins partially filled with cracked ice —*Amer. Guide Series: Fla.*⟩ HALE, once a fairly common synonym of HAUL, is now most likely to be used of the constraining, compelling, and dragging involved in arresting someone resisting ⟨natives, *haled* long distances to court as liquor witnesses —Elbridge Colby⟩ TUG applies to strenuous pulling, sometimes steady but more often in marked spasmodic bursts ⟨*tugging* at the ropes⟩ ⟨*tug* the rug out from under the furniture⟩ TOW applies to pulling along behind one with a rope, chain, cable, or bar ⟨tugs *towing* strings of barges⟩ ⟨a plane *towing* a glider⟩ ⟨*towing* the wrecked car to the garage⟩ — **pull a face :** to make a face **:** GRIMACE ⟨*pulled a face* as he tasted the bitter medicine⟩ — **pull a lone oar :** to work on one's own **:** proceed without help ⟨despite offers of assistance, he insists on *pulling a lone oar*⟩ — **pull a punch 1 :** to hit an opponent with less than one's full power **2 :** to act or express oneself in a cautious or guarded manner **:** PUSSYFOOT ⟨she has *pulled* no *punches* in coming directly to the extreme issues involved —Sara H. Hay⟩ — **pull caps :** QUARREL — **pull devil, pull baker** — used as a command (as in a tug of war) for each of two opposing sides to do its utmost in pulling against the other ⟨a sorry makeshift, a compromise arrived at by the familiar *pull devil, pull baker* method —S.H.Adams⟩ — **pull fodder** *Midland* **:** to gather fodder — **pull in one's horns :** draw in one's horns — **pull leather** *chiefly West* **:** to hang on to the saddle — **pull oneself together :** to regain one's self-possession **:** collect one's faculties ⟨it took some time for him to recover from the shock and *pull himself together*⟩ — **pull one's freight** *slang* **:** DEPART, LEAVE — **pull one's leg :** to deceive or hoodwink someone **:** play a trick or prank upon someone ⟨admit he had been *pulling my leg* —*London Calling*⟩ ⟨unaware that *their legs* were being *pulled* —O.S.J.Gogarty⟩ — **pull one's teeth :** to deprive one of weapons **:** render one harmless or defenseless — **pull one's weight :** to do one's full share of the work in a joint enterprise ⟨was dropped from the committee because he wasn't *pulling his weight*⟩ — **pull stakes** *or* **pull up stakes :** to move out **:** LEAVE ⟨*pulled up stakes* and went abroad to live⟩ — **pull strings** *or* **pull wires 1 :** to exert influence (as political influence) or control over others without publicity **2 :** to accomplish or seek to accomplish one's ends through usu. secret influence or connections ⟨*pulled wires* to get the position for his son⟩ — **pull the string** *of a baseball pitcher* **:** to throw a slow ball or change-of-pace pitch

**²pull** \"\ *n* -s *often attrib* [ME *pul,* fr. *pullen,* v.] **1 a :** the act or an instance of pulling ⟨gave a quick ~ on the rope⟩ ⟨supposed to hold the man's foot in a certain position and keep a steady straight ~ on it —R.H.Newman⟩ ⟨a candy ~⟩: as (1) **:** a draft of liquid or an inhalation of smoke **:** DRAG ⟨paused to take a long ~ on his stein of beer —Warner Bloomberg⟩ ⟨the old man would take a ~ at his pipe —Donn Byrne⟩ ⟨taking a ~ of milk from the can on the window sill —B.T. Cleeve⟩ (2) **:** a pull on the bridle of a horse to check its speed ⟨in race after race he won in a gallop, under a ~ —*Collier's Yr. Bk.*⟩ ⟨to avoid a collision our young friend has to take a ~ —Geoffrey Brooke⟩ (3) **:** the act of pulling at an oar; *broadly* **:** an excursion in a rowboat ⟨enjoyed the ~, though the river is very desolate-looking down there —Rachel Henning⟩ (4) **:** the act or an instance of pulling a ball (as in golf, cricket) ⟨a powerful ~ to leg⟩ ⟨a ~ stroke⟩ ⟨a ~ shot⟩ (5) **:** the change of course of a curling stone as it moves down the ice **b** (1) **:** a force or effort exerted in pulling ⟨its ~ is only one third that of the earth —J.G.Vaeth⟩ ⟨the sun's sideward ~ —*Newsweek*⟩ (2) **:** the effort expended in moving forward or upward ⟨a long ~ uphill⟩ ⟨his long hard ~ to get where he had got in her uncle's firm —Louis Auchincloss⟩ (3) **:** the force required to overcome the resistance to pulling of a specific object (as a bow or the trigger of a firearm) ⟨a bow with a 30 pound ~⟩ ⟨a trigger with a four pound ~⟩ (4) **:** the resistance of a paint to brushing **:** drag under the brush **2 a :** something (as a quality, attainment, or circumstance) that favors an individual in a comparison or contest **:** ADVANTAGE ⟨people who have had a classical education do start with a ~ —Archibald Marshall⟩ ⟨the old families, with all the ~ of their name and possessions —A.L.Rowse⟩ **b :** special influence exerted or capable of being exerted on behalf of a person or group ⟨got that job through ~ —W.J. Reilly⟩ ⟨has come up from the ranks without any ~ or family backing —*Current History*⟩ **3 :** PROOF 10a **4 :** a device (as a knob, cord, handle) for pulling something or for operating (as in opening, closing, or lifting) by pulling ⟨a plastic ~ for a window shade⟩ ⟨a bell ~⟩ ⟨a wooden ~ for a desk drawer⟩ **5 a :** a force that attracts, compels, or influences **:** ATTRACTION ⟨writes of the natural world with scientific accuracy and the ~ of humor —N.J.Berrill⟩ ⟨a being constantly torn between the ~ of desires on the one hand and the demands of reason on the other —O.A.Johnson⟩ **b :** the ability to arouse public interest or stimulate public demand ⟨an actress with great box-office ~⟩ ⟨an advertising slogan with tremendous ~ over a long period⟩ **c :** a response to an advertisement or advertising campaign ⟨a mail ~ heavy enough to make any sponsor drool —*New Republic*⟩ **6 :** the length of a shotgun stock measured by the distance between the front of the trigger and the center of the butt plate **7 a** — used as a skeet shooter's command for the release of the high-house target; compare ¹MARK 1c(7) **b** — used as a trapshooter's command for the release of the target

**pull·able** \-ləbəl\ *adj* **:** capable of being pulled

**pullaway** \ˈ==,=\ *n* -s [by shortening] **:** POM-POM-PULL-AWAY

**pull away** *vi* **:** to draw oneself back or away ⟨*pulled away* from a high inside pitch⟩ ⟨was hard for him to *pull away* from the ties of home⟩

**pullback** \ˈ=,=\ *n* -s [fr. *pull back,* v.] **1 a :** something that holds back **:** a restraining force **:** CHECK, DRAWBACK **b :** one that pulls back **:** REACTIONARY ⟨the diehards, the ~*s,* the enemies of progress —*Newsweek*⟩ **2 :** a pulling or drawing back; *esp* **:** an orderly withdrawal of troops from a particular position or area ⟨a ~ of troops from the frontier —*Wall Street Jour.*⟩ ⟨the long-awaited, long-planned ~ from overseas of American troops —*Newsweek*⟩ **3 a :** an iron hook fixed to a casement to pull it shut or to hold it partly open at a fixed point **b :** something that returns a machine part to an initial position **c :** HAULBACK 1 **4 :** a skirt style marked by fullness drawn to the back

**pullboat** \ˈ=,=\ *n* **:** a heavy flatboat provided with winding drums and used to pull logs to the water's edge

**pull box** *n* **:** a metal box with a blank cover that is installed in an accessible place in a run of conduit to facilitate the pulling in of wires or cables

**pulldevil** \ˈ=,==\ *n* **:** a gang of fishhooks fastened back to back to be pulled through the water to catch fish

**pull·doo** \ˈpu̇lˌdü\ *n* -s [LaF *poule d'eau,* lit., water hen] **:** AMERICAN COOT

**pull down** *vt* **1 a :** DEMOLISH, DESTROY ⟨the wreckers *pulled* the building *down*⟩ **b :** to hunt down **:** OVERCOME ⟨together *pulling down* game too powerful for one to master alone —C.G.D.Roberts⟩ **2 a :** to bring to a lower level (as in price or value) **:** REDUCE ⟨the panic *pulled* stock prices *down*⟩ **b :** to depress in health, strength, or spirits **:** ENFEEBLE ⟨since his illness, he is very much *pulled down*⟩ **3 :** to catch (a ball) esp. after a hard run ⟨*pulled* the ball *down* in deep right field⟩ **4 :** to draw as wages or salary **:** receive as compensation or reward ⟨he's got to be good to *pull down* that kind of money —Richard Llewellyn⟩ ⟨*pulling down* the highest grades in the academy's history —*Time*⟩

**¹pulldown** \ˈ=,=\ *n* -s [*pull down*] **1 :** a movable arm set over a jigger to hold the profile that shapes ceramic ware on the mold **2 :** a mechanism for rapidly moving a series of motion-picture film frames into place successively in the camera gate or at the aperture of a printer or a projector **3 :** one of two or more samples of printing ink smeared on paper for purposes of comparison

**²pulldown** \(ˈ)=ˈ=\ *adj* [*pull down*] **:** capable of being pulled down or intended to be pulled down ⟨a ~ bed⟩ ⟨a ~ seat⟩

**pulled** *past of* PULL

**pulled bread** *n* **:** bread pulled from the inside of a loaf in irregular pieces and browned lightly

**pulled figs** *n pl* **:** figs that are drawn into a flat disk by the fingers with the blossom end in the center of the disk before they are packed in layers in boxes

**pulled wool** *n* **:** wool removed from the pelt of a slaughtered sheep (as by sweating or a depilatory) — called also *skin wool*

**pul·len** \ˈpu̇lə̇n\ *n* -s [ME *pullan, pullayn,* fr. OF *poleing* young cock, fr. LL *pullinus* of a chicken, fr. L, of a young animal, fr. *pullus* young of an animal, foal, chick + *-inus* -ine — more at FOAL] *dial chiefly Brit* **:** POULTRY

**pull·er** \ˈpu̇lə(r)\ *n* -s [ME, fr. *pullen* to pull + *-er* — more at PULL] **:** one that pulls ⟨proud setter up and ~ down of kings —Shak.⟩: as **a :** an instrument or device for pulling or extracting something ⟨a tack ~⟩ ⟨a cork ~⟩ **b** (1) **:** one that stretches, softens, and removes flesh from fur pelts (2) **:** one that removes wool from sheepskins (3) **:** a worker who pulls metal parts from a heat-treating furnace (4) **:** a shoe worker who stretches and fastens uppers into the proper shape and position for lasting (5) **:** a laundry worker who pulls articles from a washing machine and takes them to the extractor (6) **:** a textile worker who bunches bleached yarn skeins **c :** a horse that habitually thrusts its head forward against the bit and so maintains a pull on the reins **d :** one that releases clay targets from a trap for skeet shooters and trapshooters **e :** a long-handled stout elliptical knife used in turpentining for opening a face that is beyond ordinary reach **f :** one that draws business ⟨this ad is an excellent ~⟩

**pull·er-in** \'=ˌ=ˌ=\ *n, pl* **pullers-in** [*pull in* + *-er*] **:** one that pulls in; *specif* **:** a man who stands in front of a store or place of entertainment and tries sometimes forcibly to get passersby to enter

**pull·ery** \'pu̇lərē\ *n* -ES [¹*pull* + *-ery*] **:** an establishment for removing wool from sheep skins

**pul·let** \'pu̇lət, *usu* -ȧd·+V\ *n* -S [ME *polet, pulett* young chicken, young fowl, fr. MF *poulet, pollet,* fr. OF, dim. of *poul* cock, fr. LL *pullus,* fr. L, young of an animal, foal, chick — more at FOAL] **:** a young hen; *specif* **:** a hen of the common fowl less than a year old

**pullet disease** *n* **:** BLUE COMB

¹**pul·ley** \'pu̇lē, -li\ *n* -S [ME *poley, pouley,* fr. MF *polie,*

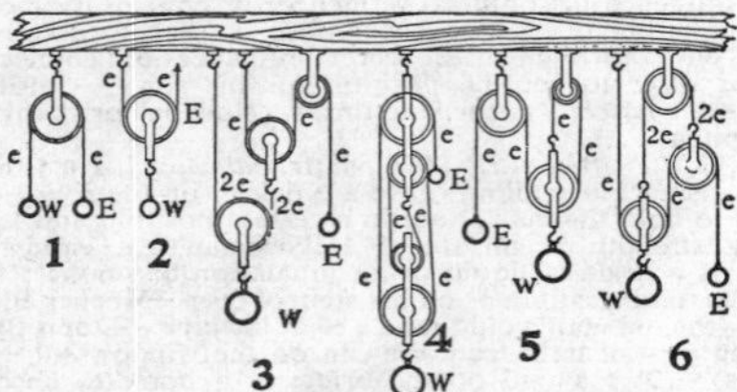


pulley 1b: various tackles showing theoretical ratios of weight lifted, *W,* to effort, *E,* and tensions in various cords, *e: 1* W=E; *2* W=2E; *3, 4, 6,* W=4E; *5* W=3E

*poulie,* fr. (assumed) VL *polidium,* prob. fr. (assumed) LGk *polidion,* dim. of Gk *polos* pivot, axis, pole — more at POLE (extremity of an axis)] **1 a :** a small wheel with a grooved rim **:** SHEAVE **b :** a sheave with the pin on which it turns, the frame in which it runs, and the flexible rope, cord, or chain passing through the groove that is used singly to change the direction and point of application of a pulling force applied at one end of the rope, cord, or chain and singly or in any of various definite combinations to increase the applied force esp. for lifting weights — see TACKLE **2 a :** a single pulley or a combination of pulleys with the necessary ropes to form a tackle regarded as one of the simple machines or mechanical powers **b :** a wheel of any size with a flat, curved, or grooved rim often of considerable width revolvable on its axis and supported by a bearing or bearings that is used to transmit power by means of a band or belt passing over its rim or a cord, rope, or chain or several of them running in its groove or grooves — see CONE PULLEY, EXPANDING PULLEY, IDLER PULLEY, MULE PULLEY, SPLIT PULLEY, TENSION PULLEY; compare DRUM, SPROCKET WHEEL **3 :** TROCHLEA

²**pulley** \"\ *n* -S [alter. (influenced by ¹*pulley*) of ME *puleyn,* fr. MF *poulain,* lit., foal, fr. LL *pullamen,* fr. L *pullus* young of an animal — more at FOAL] **:** a slideway for barrels

**pulley block** *n* **:** BLOCK 4a

**pulley bone** *n* [¹*pull* + *-ey*] *chiefly Midland* **:** WISHBONE

**pulley frame** *n* **:** HEADFRAME

**pulley lathe** *n* **:** a lathe for turning and crowning pulleys

**pulley stile** *n* **:** the upright of a window frame into which a pulley is fixed and along which the sash slides

**pulley tap** *n* **:** a tap with a long shank for tapping setscrew holes in the hubs of pulleys

**pull hitter** *n* **:** a baseball batter who consistently pulls the ball

**pulli** *pl of* PULLUS

**pul·li·cat** \'pələkət, -lēˌkat\ *or* **pul·li·cate** \-lə̇kət, -lēˌkāt\ *n* -S [fr. *Pulicat,* town of the southeastern coast of India] **:** BANDANNA

**pull in** *vt* **1 :** CHECK, RESTRAIN ⟨*pull* a horse *in*⟩ ⟨begin to *pull in* its expenses without overmuch damaging its charm —Harold Hobson⟩ ⟨*pull in* resolution —Shak.⟩ **2 :** ARREST ⟨was *pulled in* for questioning in connection with the crime⟩ ⟨took one look and *pulled* him *in*⟩ ~ *vi* **:** to arrive at a destination or come to a stop ⟨the train *pulled in* on time⟩ ⟨when a car *pulled in* he would go out to it, dressed in a white coverall —Robert McLaughlin⟩

¹**pull-in** \'(ˌ)=ˌ=\ *adj* [*pull in*] **:** used for or having the effect of pulling in

²**pull-in** \"\ *n* -S [*pull in*] *Brit* **:** a roadside eating place **:** DRIVE-IN ⟨supposes that you can always stop at any *pull-in* . . . and be given a delicious meal for a small sum —Anthony Powell⟩ — called also *pull-up*

**pulling** *pres part of* PULL

**pulling boat** *n* **:** ROWBOAT

**pull-in torque** *n* **:** the maximum constant torque under which a motor will accelerate from rest to approximate normal speed

¹**pull·man** \'pu̇lmən\ *n* -S *often cap* [after George M. *Pullman* †1897 Am. inventor] **:** a railroad passenger car with specially comfortable furnishings for day or esp. for night travel — used orig. of a parlor or sleeping car operated by a particular manufacturer

²**pullman** \"\ *adj* **1 :** of, relating to, or suitable for use in a pullman ⟨~ ticket⟩ ⟨~ case⟩ **2 :** designed for compactness and efficiency ⟨~ kitchen⟩

**pullman conductor** *n* **:** a railroad employee who supervises the porter and maid service and provides for the comfort of passengers in the sleeping, parlor, buffet, and observation cars

**pull off** *vt* **:** to carry out despite difficulties **:** complete successfully against great odds ⟨*pulled* the scheme *off*⟩ ⟨the only man in our time to have *pulled off* the miracle of writing a verse comedy —W.F.Kerr⟩

¹**pull-on** \'(ˌ)=ˌ=\ *adj* [fr. *pull on,* v.] **:** designed to be put on by being pulled on ⟨*pull-on* sports hat in gaily colored felts —*Women's Wear Daily*⟩

²**pull-on** \"\ *n* -S **:** an article of clothing (as a glove, girdle, sweater) that is pulled on to be worn and is usu. made without a placket or similar opening

**pul·lo·rum disease** \pə'lōrəm-, -lȯrəm-\ *also* **pullorum** *n* -S [L *pullorum,* gen. pl. of *pullus* young of an animal, foal, chick — more at FOAL] **:** salmonellosis of the chicken and less commonly of other birds that is caused by infection with a bacterium (*Salmonella pullorum*) transmitted both through the egg and from chick to chick, that is highly fatal in the young and is marked by weakness, lassitude, lack of appetite, and commonly by white or yellowish diarrhea, and that is frequently symptomless in mature birds but persists as an infection in the ovary resulting in lowered egg production and infertility and passing of the infection to the next generation — see BACILLARY WHITE DIARRHEA

**pull out** *vi* **1 :** LEAVE ⟨the troops *pulled out* for home⟩ **2 :** WITHDRAW ⟨one or the other of the two big unions might eventually *pull out* —*N.Y.Times*⟩

¹**pullout** \'(ˌ)=ˌ=\ *n* -S [*pull out*] **1 :** something that can be pulled out: as **a :** an outsize leaf that is secured between and folded to the same size as the ordinary leaves of a book or magazine ⟨a ~ carrying an illustration 3 pages wide⟩ **b :** readily removable printed matter placed between the leaves of a magazine and often attached by a wire stitch **2 :** the act or an instance of pulling out: as **a :** an instance of the accidental pulling out of type (as by an inking roller) from a form that is being printed or proofed — compare DROPOUT, WORK-UP **b :** a maneuver in which an airplane goes from a dive to horizontal flight **c :** a withdrawal (as of troops) from a particular area

²**pullout** \"\ *adj* [*pull out*] **:** used for or having the effect of pulling out **:** capable of being pulled out ⟨the ~ seat of this new space-saver desk —*Retailing Daily*⟩

**pull-out torque** *n* **:** the maximum torque a motor will carry without an abrupt drop in speed

**pull over** *vi* **:** to steer one's vehicle to the side of the road ⟨the trooper ordered him to *pull over*⟩ ~ *vt* **:** to locate (the forepart of a shoe) in correct position on the last and secure to the insole or to the sole in the case of a turned shoe

¹**pullover** \'(ˌ)=ˌ=\ *adj* [*pull over*] **:** designed to be put on by being pulled over the head ⟨consists of a ~ parka with a hood —Farley Mowat⟩

²**pullover** \"\ *n* -S **:** a garment (as a sweater, shirt, or blouse) that is put on by being pulled over the head and is usu. made without a placket or similar opening

pullover

**pull pin** *n* **:** a pin that when pulled disconnects or unlocks two parts of a machine and usu. reverses the process when pushed

**pull round** *vt* **:** to restore to good health ⟨the doctor *pulled* him *round*⟩ ~ *vi* **:** to regain one's health ⟨after two days of high fever, he began to *pull round*⟩

**pulls** *pres 3d sing of* PULL, *pl of* PULL

**pullshovel** \'=ˌ=ˌ=\ *n* **:** BACKHOE

**pull socket** *n* **:** a lamp socket with a pull switch

**pull station** *n* **:** a fire-alarm apparatus operated by pulling a handle or hook

**pull strap** *or* **pull tab** *n* **:** a leather or fabric loop or tab attached to the top of a shoe or boot to help in drawing it on — compare BACKSTRAP

**pull switch** *n* **:** a snap switch operated by pulling a chain or cord

**pull through** *vt* **:** to help through a dangerous or difficult period or situation ⟨new capital is needed to *pull* the business *through* its difficulties⟩ ~ *vi* **:** to survive a dangerous or difficult period or situation ⟨was so ill that no one thought he would *pull through*⟩

**pull-through** \'(ˌ)=ˌ=\ *n* -S [fr. *pull through,* v.] **:** something that is pulled through; *specif* **:** a cord fitted at one end with a weight and at the other with a brush and used for cleaning the bores of small arms

**pull-through torque** *n* **:** PULL-IN TORQUE

**pull together** *vi* **:** to work in harmony **:** COOPERATE ⟨learned to *pull together* for the good of all⟩

**pull toy** *n* **:** a toy designed to be pulled along the ground and usu. having moving parts that make sounds as it is pulled

**pul·lu·lant** \'pəlyələnt\ *adj* [L *pullulant-, pullulans,* pres. part. of *pullulare*] **:** SPROUTING, BUDDING

**pul·lu·lar·ia** \ˌpəlyə'la(a)rēə\ *n, cap* [NL, fr. L *pullulare* + NL *-aria*] **:** a genus of fungi (family Pseudosaccharomycetaceae) forming yeastlike colonies that are at first dirty white, then streaked with dark green or black, and eventually wholly black and more or less leathery and including a form (*P. pullulans*) that causes discoloration of pulp and paper

**pul·lu·late** \'pəlyəˌlāt, *usu* -ād·+V\ *vi* -ED/-ING/-S [L *pullulatus,* past part. of *pullulare* to sprout, fr. *pullulus* young of an animal, chick, sprout, dim. of *pullus* young of an animal — more at FOAL] **1 a :** to send out shoots or show signs of growth **:** BUD, GERMINATE **b :** to breed rapidly **:** produce abundantly ⟨his muse ~*s* with dizzying speed —Victor Purcell⟩ **2 a :** to increase rapidly **:** become abundant **:** MULTIPLY ⟨in the course of the argument, the most enormous errors of fact . . . simply ~ —George Saintsbury⟩ **b :** SWARM, TEEM ⟨the bleak ground ~*s* with jackrabbits —A.J.Liebling⟩ ⟨the pavements of hell ~ with liars, thieves, murderers —Bruce Marshall⟩

**pul·lu·la·tion** \ˌ=ˌ='lāshən\ *n* -S **1 :** the act or an instance of pullulating ⟨I like ~; everything ought to increase and multiply as hard as it can —Aldous Huxley⟩ **2 :** GEMMATION

**pull up** *vt* **1 :** to bring up short **:** CHECK, REBUKE ⟨*pulled* him *up* for speaking in an insulting tone⟩ **2 :** to bring to a stop **:** HALT ⟨the kids *pulled up* their pony and sat watching —Ross Annett⟩ ~ *vi* **1 a :** to check oneself ⟨was advised by his doctor to *pull up* and take it easy⟩ **b :** to come to a halt **:** STOP ⟨*pulled up* at the gas station⟩ **2 :** to draw even with or to go ahead of others in a race or contest ⟨coming into the stretch, the big horse was third, but he began to *pull up* and won by a nose⟩

**pull-up** \'(ˌ)=ˌ=\ *n* -S [fr. *pull up,* v.] **1 :** the act or an instance of pulling up: as **a :** a maneuver in which an airplane in level flight is forced into a short climb **b :** an arm strengthening exercise in which a person pulls himself up from an extended hanging position until his chin is higher than the supporting bar or rings **2** *Brit* **:** PULL-IN ⟨the place used to be a *pull-up* for lorry drivers —*Punch*⟩

**pul·lus** \'pələs\ *n, pl* **pul·li** \-əˌlī\ [NL, fr. L, young of an animal, chick — more at FOAL] **:** a young bird in the downy stage

**pully-haul** \'pu̇lēˌ=\ *vi* [¹*pull* + *-y* + *haul*] **:** to pull and haul with one's full strength or with combined strength

**pulmo-** *comb form* [L *pulmo* — more at PULMONARY] **1 :** lung ⟨*pulmometry*⟩ **2 :** pulmonic and ⟨*pulmogastric*⟩

**pul·mo·branchia** \ˌpəl(ˌ)mō+\ *n, pl* **pulmobranchiae** [NL, fr. *pulmo-* + *-branchia*] **1 :** a gill or similar organ so modified as to breathe air **2 :** a book lung (as of a spider) — **pul·mo·branchial** \ˌ=ˌ=+\ *adj* — **pul·mo·branchiate** \"+\ *adj or n*

**pul·mo·cutaneous** \ˌ=(ˌ)=+\ *adj* [*pulmo-* + *cutaneous*] **:** of or relating to the lungs and the skin

**pulmocutaneous artery** *or* **pulmocutaneous arch** *n* **:** either of the posterior pair of arterial arches that arise from the truncus arteriosus in amphibians, divide into pulmonary and cutaneous arteries, and transport venous blood to the respiratory surfaces of the skin, buccal cavity, and lungs

**pul·mo·gastric** \ˌ=(ˌ)=+\ *adj* [*pulmo-* + *gastric*] **:** relating to the lungs and stomach

**pul·mom·e·ter** \(ˌ)pəl'mäməd·ə(r)\ *n* [*pulmo-* + *-meter*] **:** SPIROMETER

**pul·mom·e·try** \-ə·trē, -ri\ *n* -ES [*pulmo-* + *-metry*] **:** the determination of the capacity of the lungs

**pulmon-** *also* **pulmoni-** *or* **pulmono-** *comb form* [L *pulmon-, pulmo* — more at PULMONARY] **:** lung ⟨*pulmonal*⟩ ⟨*pulmoniferous*⟩ **:** pulmonary and ⟨*pulmonocardiac*⟩

**pul·mo·nal** \'pəlmənᵊl\ *adj* [*pulmon-* + *-al*] **:** PULMONARY

¹**pul·mo·nar·ia** \ˌpəlmə'na(a)rēə\ *n, cap* [NL, fr. L, fem. of *pulmonarius*] **:** a genus of European herbs (family Boraginaceae) having large basal leaves, cymose blue flowers with a 5-lobed funnel-shaped corolla, and large nutlets — see BETHLEHEM SAGE, LUNGWORT

²**pulmonaria** \"\ *n pl, cap* [NL, fr. L, neut. pl. of *pulmonarius*] *in some esp former classifications* **:** a group comprising the pulmonate arachnids (as the scorpions and spiders)

³**pulmonaria** \"\ [NL, fr. L, neut. pl. of *pulmonarius*] *syn of* PULMONATA

¹**pul·mo·nary** \'pu̇lməˌnerē, 'pəl-, -ri\ *adj* [L *pulmonarius,* fr. *pulmon-, pulmo* lung + *-arius* -ary; akin to Gk *pleumōn* lung, Skt *klōman* right lung, Lith *plaučiai* lungs, and perh. to Gk *plein* to sail, float; fr. the fact that lungs float in water — more at FLOW] **1 :** of, relating to, or associated with the lungs **2 :** resembling or functioning like a lung **3 :** PULMONATE **4 :** carried on by the lungs

²**pulmonary** \"\ *n* -ES [NL ¹*Pulmonaria*] **:** LUNGWORT

**pulmonary arch** *n* **:** the fetal left fifth aortic arch that persists as the pulmonary artery

**pulmonary artery** *n* **:** an artery that conveys venous blood from the heart to the lungs and in man arises from the right ventricle, runs upward and backward, and divides into the right pulmonary artery which passes under the arch of the aorta and goes to the right lung and the left pulmonary artery which goes to the left lung with further division into branches that accompany the bronchial tubes

**pulmonary circulation** *n* **:** the passage of venous blood from the right auricle of the heart through the right ventricle and pulmonary arteries to the lungs where it is oxygenated and its return via the pulmonary veins to enter the left auricle and participate in the systemic circulation — used of man and animals with a complete double circulation

**pulmonary heart** *n* **:** the right atrium and right ventricle — compare SYSTEMIC HEART

**pulmonary plexus** *n* **:** either of two nerve plexuses that are superficial and deep and lie on either aspect of the bronchi and distributing fibers mainly from the vagus to the lungs

**pulmonary sac** *also* **pulmonary cavity** *n* **:** a hollow organ having a contractile exterior opening and lined with a network of blood vessels that functions as a lung in most land mollusks

**pulmonary valve** *n* **:** a valve consisting of three crescentic cusps separating the pulmonary artery from the right ventricle

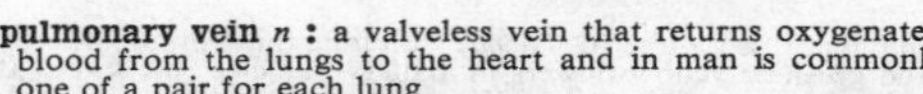

**pulmonary vein** *n* **:** a valveless vein that returns oxygenated blood from the lungs to the heart and in man is commonly one of a pair for each lung

¹**pul·mo·na·ta** \ˌ=ˌ='nād·ə, -ād·ə\ *n pl, cap* [NL, fr. *pulmon-* + *-ata*] **:** a very large order of Gastropoda (subclass Euthyneura) comprising most land snails and slugs and many freshwater snails that are distinguished by lacking gills which are usu. replaced by a lung or respiratory sac formed by the modification of the mantle cavity and communicating with the exterior by a contractile orifice capable of being entirely closed in which blood vessels line the walls and by having no true operculum and a nervous system that is concentrated and not twisted — see BASOMMATOPHORA, STYLOMMATOPHORA

²**pulmonata** \"\ [NL, fr. *pulmon-* + *-ata*] *syn of* PNEUMOBRANCHIA

³**pulmonata** \"\ [NL, fr. *pulmon-* + *-ata*] *syn of* PULMONARIA

¹**pul·mo·nate** \'pəlmənət, -ˌnāt\ *adj* [*pulmon-* + *-ate*] **1 :** having lungs or organs resembling lungs **2** [NL ¹*Pulmonata*] **:** relating to the Pulmonata or Pulmonifera

²**pulmonate** \"\ *n* -S **:** a gastropod of the order Pulmonata

**pul·mo·nat·ed** \'=ˌ=ˌnād·əd\ *adj* [*pulmon-* + *-ate* + *-ed*] **:** PULMONATE 1

**pul·mo·nec·to·my** \ˌ=ˌ='nektəmē\ *n* -ES [*pulmon-* + *-ectomy*] **:** PNEUMECTOMY

**pulmoni-** *or* **pulmono-** — see PULMON-

**pul·mon·ic** \(ˌ)pəl'mänik, -nēk\ *adj* [F *pulmonique,* fr. MF, fr. *pulmon-* + *-ique* -ic] **1 :** relating to or affecting the lungs **:** PULMONARY **2 :** of or relating to the pulmonary artery or to the junction between this artery and the right ventricle ⟨~ stenosis may be associated with pulmonary atherosclerosis⟩ **3 :** having inner closure at the bottom of the lungs — used of a phonetic stop or stop articulation ⟨consonants which include ejective and ~ variants of the characteristic lateral affricate —W.K.Matthews⟩

**pul·mon·i·fer** \(ˌ)=ˈmänəfə(r)\ *n* -S [NL *Pulmonifera*] **:** one of the Pulmonifera

¹**pul·mo·nif·era** \ˌpəlmə'nif(ə)rə\ [NL, fr. *pulmon-* + L *-fera* (neut. pl. of *-fer*)] *syn of* PULMONATA

²**pulmonifera** \"\ *n pl, cap* [NL, fr. *pulmon-* + L *-fera*] **:** a group of terrestrial snails (suborder Taenioglossa) having the gill replaced by a pulmonary sac

**pul·mo·nif·er·ous** \ˌ=ˌ='nif(ə)rəs\ *adj* [*pulmon-* + *-ferous*] **:** PULMONATE

**pul·mo·no·cardiac** \ˌpəlmə(ˌ)nō+\ *adj* [*pulmon-* + *cardiac*] **:** of, relating to, or involving both heart and lungs ⟨~ failure⟩

**pul·mo·tor** \'pu̇lˌmōd·ə(r), 'pəl-, -ōtə-\ *n* [fr. *Pulmotor,* a trademark] **:** a respiratory apparatus for pumping oxygen or air or a mixture of the two into and out of the lungs

**pul·mo·trachearia** \ˌpəlmō+\ [NL, fr. *pulmo-* + *Trachearia*] *syn of* PULMONARIA

¹**pulp** \'pəlp\ *n* -S *often attrib* [MF *poulpe,* fr. L *pulpa* solid flesh, pulp] **1 :** a moist slightly cohering mass consisting of soft undissolved animal or vegetable matter: as **a** (1) **:** the soft succulent part of fruit ⟨the ~ of a grape⟩ ⟨orange ~⟩ (2) **:** the soft pith of various stems (3) **:** PULPWOOD **b :** a soft mass of vegetable matter (as of apples or sugarcane) from which most of the water has been extracted by pressure **c :** a cellulosic material prepared by chemical or mechanical means chiefly from wood but also from rags and other materials and used in making paper and cellulose products (as rayon and cellulose acetate) — compare STOCK, STUFF **d** (1) **:** a tissue or part resembling pulp; *esp* **:** DENTAL PULP (2) **:** the characteristic somewhat spongy tissue of the spleen (3) **:** the fleshy portion of the fingertip **2 a :** pulverized ore mixed with water so as to resemble mud **b :** dry crushed ore **3 a :** pulpy condition or character **b :** something in such a condition or having such a character ⟨hammering his face in a way to make ~ —Arthur Morrison⟩ ⟨reduced to a shapeless ~ by concussion —Liam O'Flaherty⟩ **c :** something without strength or in a condition of fatigue or nervous exhaustion ⟨a life that would have reduced a lesser woman to a ~ —E.A. Weeks⟩ **4 :** a thick mass of white lead and water that settles to the bottom of a suspension of white lead in water and that when dry is commercial dry white lead **5 a :** a magazine or book using rough-surfaced paper made of wood pulp and often dealing with sensational material — compare SLICK **b :** tawdry or sensational writing ⟨other ~*s* that give the outside world such an odd picture of the American way of life —Joan Comay⟩

²**pulp** \"\ *vb* -ED/-ING/-S *vt* **1 :** to reduce to pulp **:** cause to appear pulpy **2 :** to form (material) into a pulp **3 :** to deprive of the pulp **4 :** to produce or reproduce (written matter) in pulp form ~ *vi* **:** to become pulp or pulpy

**pulp·al** \'pəlpəl\ *also* **pulp·ar** \-p(ə)r\ *adj* **:** of or relating to pulp esp. of a tooth ⟨a ~ abscess⟩ — **pulp·al·ly** \-pəlē\ *adv*

**pulpboard** \'=ˌ=\ *n* **:** a solid board or a combination board made from various fibers (as wood)

**pulp canal** *n* **:** the part of the pulp cavity lying in the root of a tooth

**pulp cavity** *n* **:** the central cavity of a tooth containing the dental pulp and being made up of the pulp canal and the pulp chamber

**pulp chamber** *n* **:** the part of the pulp cavity lying in the crown of a tooth — see TOOTH illustration

**pulp color** *n* **:** a pigment that is prepared by precipitation in water, filtered, and pressed but not dried and that is marketed in the water paste form — compare ⁴DISTEMPER 2c, DRY COLOR, FLUSH COLOR, ⁴LAKE 1b

**pulp·ec·to·my** \ˌpəl'pektəmē\ *n* -ES [¹*pulp* + *-ectomy*] **:** the removal of the pulp of a tooth

**pulp engine** *n* **:** BEATER 1n

**pulp·er** \'pəlpə(r)\ *n* -S **:** one that makes, grinds, mixes, or removes pulp **:** one that reduces something (as fruit or guncotton) to pulp; *specif* **:** a machine that reduces (as broke and waste paper) to pulp in the presence of water in papermaking

**pul·pe·ria** \ˌpu̇lpə'rēə\ *n* -S [AmerSp *pulperia,* fr. Sp *pulpa* pulp, meat, fruit, candied fruit (fr. L, solid meat, pulp) + *-eria* -ery — more at PULP] **:** a Spanish American rural grocery store often functioning also as a drinking establishment

**pulpier** *comparative of* PULPY

**pulpies** *pl of* PULPY

**pulpiest** *superlative of* PULPY

**pulp·ify** \'pəlpəˌfī\ *vt* -ED/-ING/-ES [¹*pulp* + *-ify*] **:** to make pulp of **:** PULP ⟨to ~ wood fiber⟩

**pulp·i·ly** \-pəlē\ *adv* **:** in a pulpy manner

**pulp·i·ness** \-pēnəs, -pin-\ *n* -ES **:** the quality or state of being pulpy

¹**pul·pit** \'pu̇lˌpit, 'pəl-, -ˌpət, *usu* -d·+V\ *n* -S *often attrib* [ME, fr. LL *pulpitum,* fr. L, scaffold, stage, platform] **1 a :** a usu. enclosed elevated platform or a high reading desk used in preaching or conducting a service of worship ⟨an ornate medieval ~ with a flight of steps and a sounding board⟩ ⟨read from the large Bible on the ~⟩ **b :** an elevated structure for a machine operator ⟨an operator in the control ~ pressed a button —*Newsweek*⟩ **2** [ME, fr. L *pulpitum*] *obs* **:** an elevated platform for a public speaker **3 a :** the clergy as a profession **:** PREACHERS ⟨the power of the ~⟩ **b :** the ministry of preaching a religious faith **:** a preaching position ⟨called to a city ~⟩ **4 :** a support for a harpooner on the end of the bowsprit in a whaling ship

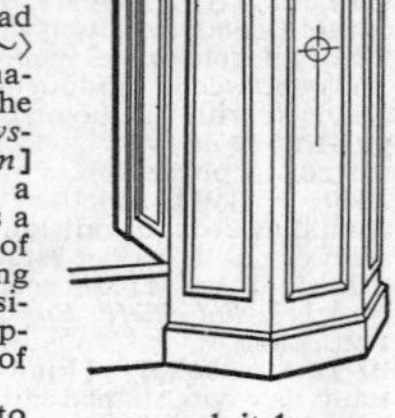

pulpit 1a

²**pulpit** \"\ *vb* -ED/-ING/-S *vt* **:** to supply with a pulpit or with preaching ~ *vi* **:** to preach from a pulpit

**pul·pit·al** \-ˌpid·ᵊl, -ˌpəd·ᵊl, -tᵊl\ *adj* **:** of or relating to a pulpit or preaching

¹**pul·pi·tar·i·an** \ˌpu̇lpə¦ta(a)rēən, ¦pəl-, -ter-\ *n* -S [¹*pulpit* + *-arian*] **:** PREACHER; *also* **:** an advocate of preaching as essential to worship

²**pulpitarian** \"\ *adj* **:** of, relating to, or characteristic of preaching

**pulpit bible** *n, usu cap B* **:** a large Bible traditionally kept open on the pulpit or lectern of many Protestant churches

**pulpit cloth** *or* **pulpit hanging** *n* **:** the antependium of a pulpit
**¹pul·pi·teer** \ˌpu̇lpəˈti(ə)r, ˌpəl-, -iə\ *n* -s [¹*pulpit* + *-eer*] **:** one who speaks in or delivers sermons from a pulpit **:** PREACHER ⟨an eloquent ~⟩
**²pulpiteer** \ˈ"\ *vi* -ED/-ING/-S **:** PREACH, SERMONIZE ⟨~*ed* against the wets —*Newsweek*⟩
**pul·pit·er** \ˈpu̇l,pid·ə(r), ˈpəl-, -ˌpəd·-\ *n* -s [¹*pulpit* + *-er*] **:** PREACHER
**pulp·i·tis** \ˌpəlˈpīd·əs\ *n, pl* **pulpit·i·des** \-ˈpid·əˌdēz\ [NL, fr. E ¹*pulp* + NL *-itis*] **:** inflammation of pulp esp. of a tooth
**pul·pit·ism** \ˈpu̇l,pid·ˌizəm, ˈpəl-, -ˌpəd·-\ *n* -s **:** a characteristic, idea, or custom of preachers or preaching
**pul·pit·less** *pronunc at* PULPIT + ləs\ *adj* **:** having no pulpit
**pulpit man** *n* **:** an operator of a steel and iron rolling mill
**pulpit rock** *n* **:** CHIMNEY ROCK
**pul·pit·ry** \ˈpu̇l,pitrē, ˈpəl-, -ˌpətrē\ *n* -ES **:** the teaching of the pulpit **:** PREACHING ⟨the platitudes of conventional ~ —John Beaufort⟩
**pulp·less** \ˈpəlpləs\ *adj* **:** having no pulp ⟨~ teeth⟩
**pulp·ot·o·my** \ˌpəlˈpäd·əmē\ *n* -ES [*pulp* + *-o-* + *-tomy*] **:** removal in a dental procedure of the coronal portion of the pulp of a tooth in such a manner that the pulp of the root remains intact and viable
**pulp·ous** \ˈpəlpəs\ *adj* [L *pulposus* fr. *pulpa* solid flesh, pulp + *-osus* -ous — more at PULP] **:** PULPY — **pulp·ous·ness** *n* -ES
**pulps** *pl of* PULP, *pres 3d sing of* PULP
**pulpstone** \ˈ⸗,⸗\ *n* **1 :** a massive grindstone used in the mechanical reduction of wood to pulp in papermaking **2 :** a lump of calcified tissue within the dental pulp
**pulpwood** \ˈ⸗,⸗\ *n* **1 :** any of various woods (as aspen, hemlock, pine, spruce) used in making pulp for paper; *also* **:** this wood after being macerated **2 :** the trees used for pulpwood
**¹pulpy** \ˈpəlpē, -pi\ *adj* -ER/-EST [¹*pulp* + *-y*] **:** resembling or consisting of pulp **:** SOFT, FLABBY, FLESHY ⟨the ~ substance of a peach⟩ ⟨men with streaks of flintlike obstinacy within their ~ exteriors —C.S.Forester⟩
**²pulpy** \ˈ"\ *n* -ES **:** PULP 5a
**pulpy kidney disease** *or* **pulpy kidney** *n* **:** a destructive enterotoxemia of lambs caused by clostridia (esp. *Clostridium welchii*) and characterized by softening and degeneration of the kidneys and often by accumulation of fluid about the heart
**pulpy nucleus** *n* **:** a very elastic but somewhat soft body of connective tissue that forms the central part of an intervertebral disk and is surrounded by the fibrous ring
**pul·que** \ˈpül(ˌ)kā, -ˌkē, ˈpu̇lkē\ *n* -s [MexSp, prob. fr. an obs. Nahuatl word derived fr. *poliuhqui, puliuhqui* decomposed, spoiled; fr. the fact that it spoils 24 to 36 hours after its preparation] **:** fermented drink that is made in Mexico from the juice of various magueys (esp. *Agave atrovirens*) and is the source of mescal
**pul·que·ria** \ˌpülkəˈrēə, ˌpu̇l-\ *n* -s [MexSp *pulqueria*, fr. *pulque* + Sp *-eria* -ery] **:** a Mexican shop that sells pulque
**puls** *pl of* PUL
**pul·sant** \ˈpəlsənt\ *adj* [L *pulsant-, pulsans,* pres. part. of *pulsare*] **:** PULSATING ⟨the hall is . . . ~ with men and women massed in the bands of the tango —Waldo Frank⟩
**pul·sa·tance** \ˈpəlsəd·ən(t)s, -sətən-, -setᵊn-\ *n* -s **:** the angular velocity that may be associated with a periodic motion **:** 2 π times the frequency of a periodic motion
**pul·sate** \ˈpəl,sāt *chiefly Brit* ˌ⸗ˈ⸗, *usu* -ād·+V\ *vi* -ED/-ING/-S [L *pulsatus*, past part. of *pulsare* to beat, strike — more at PUSH] **1 :** to exhibit a pulse **:** BEAT ⟨an artery ~*s*⟩ **2 :** to throb or move rhythmically **:** vibrate esp. with life, activity, feeling ⟨a *pulsating* population which expands and contracts with changes in religious beliefs —M.D.Brockie⟩ ⟨behind every line . . . ~ the rhythms of the authors' hatred or contempt or scorn —L.O.Coxe⟩ ⟨the country is alive and *pulsating* with beauty —Alice Duncan-Kemp⟩ ⟨the river breeze *pulsated* warmly upward —Harriet La Barre⟩
**syn** PULSE, BEAT, THROB, PALPITATE: PULSATE suggests a rhythmic regular movement, typically that of the heart in alternate dilation and constriction ⟨the heart *pulsating*⟩ ⟨a motor *pulsating*⟩ It is often used figuratively in reference to healthy or vigorous action or inspiration ⟨great effort *pulsating* from the heart of this small island —Sir Winston Churchill⟩ PULSE applies to what flows or is thought of as flowing in a regular spurting rhythm ⟨through the tensed veins on his forehead the blood could be seen to *pulse* in nervous, stacatto bounds —Donn Byrne⟩ ⟨a small fountain *pulsed* in the court —Harry Sylvester⟩ ⟨her excitement, that *pulsed* with interest and curiosity —Robert Hichens⟩ BEAT is a nontechnical term for PULSE or PULSATE; it often applies to rhythmic motion with an audible effect ⟨the *beating* of the patient's heart⟩ ⟨drums *beating*⟩ THROB indicates strong pulsation, often abnormally strong, sometimes as though caused and accompanied by passion or agitation ⟨the planes' motors *throbbed* steadily, powerfully, on the field —Kay Boyle⟩ ⟨western Christendom *throbbed* to the news of the French Revolution —Stringfellow Barr⟩ ⟨the love which fills the letter, which *throbs* and burns in it, which speaks and argues in it —H.O.Taylor⟩ PALPITATE applies to rapid throbbing or vibrating, sometimes quivering or fluttering ⟨planet-ridden space, filled with the ether, *palpitating* with strange vibrations, like light and heat and wireless —W.E.Swinton⟩ ⟨the worshiper, *palpitating* emotionally after the performance of some anthem —A.T.Davison⟩
**pul·sa·tile** \ˈpəlsəd·əl, -əˌtil\ *adj* [ML *pulsatilis*, fr. L *pulsatus* + *-ilis* -ile] **1 :** PULSATING, THROBBING ⟨a ~ vascular tumor⟩ **2 :** vibrating when beaten or struck **:** PERCUSSIVE ⟨drums are ~ instruments⟩
**pul·sa·til·la** \ˌpəlsəˈtilə\ *n, cap* [NL, fr. L *pulsatus* + *-illa*, dim. suffix] *in some classifications* **:** a genus now usu. included as a section in *Anemone* that comprises the pasqueflowers which differ from the typical anemones chiefly in their very long feathery styles
**pulsating current** *n* **:** a direct current that has recurring more or less regular variations in magnitude
**pulsating organ** *n* **:** a minute muscular organ functioning as an accessory heart in various insects
**pulsating star** *n* **:** a star that alternately increases and decreases in size usu. with corresponding changes in brightness
**pulsating vacuole** *n* **:** CONTRACTILE VACUOLE
**pul·sa·tion** \ˌpəlˈsāshən\ *n* -s [L *pulsation-, pulsatio*, fr. *pulsatus* (past part. of *pulsare* to beat, strike) + *-ion-, -io* -ion — more at PUSH] **1 a :** a beating or throbbing esp. of the heart or of an artery **b :** a single beat of the heart or pulse **2 a :** rhythmical throbbing, contraction and expansion, moving, vibration, or undulation ⟨long heavy ~ of aeroplanes passing over —Angela Thirkell⟩ ⟨a ~ of the star as a whole —Leon Campbell & L.G.Jacchia⟩ ⟨at low frequencies, such as 10 per sec., ~ is sensed rather than vibration —R.S.Woodworth⟩ ⟨a slow ~, like the quiver of invisible wings, in the air —Ellen Glasgow⟩ **b :** a distinct step in such a series of rhythmical movements **:** BEAT, VIBRATION ⟨two ~*s* of continental glaciation —J.C.Frye & A.B.Leonard⟩ ⟨the island was elevated in a series of ~*s* —D.J.Miller⟩ ⟨in the course of these ~*s* in dominance the male may not actually move up the social scale —W.C.Allee⟩ ⟨the ~*s* of its engine had died away —Arnold Bennett⟩ **3 :** a periodically recurring alternate increase and decrease of pressure, volume, voltage, or other quantity **4** *Roman law* **:** a touching of another's body willfully or in anger
**pul·sa·tion·al** \-shənᵊl, -shnəl\ *adj* **:** of, relating to, or characterized by a pulsation
**pulsation theory** *n* **:** a theory that explains the peculiar features of such stars as the Cepheid variables by assuming an expansion and contraction of the star as a whole in a regular periodic pulsation
**pul·sa·tive** \ˈpəlsəd·iv\ *adj* [ME *pulsatif*, fr. MF, fr. L *pulsatus* + MF *-if* -ive] **:** BEATING, THROBBING, PULSATILE — **pul·sa·tive·ly** \-əvlē\ *adv*
**pul·sa·tor** \ˌpəlˈsād·ə(r), ˈ⸗,⸗⸗\ *n* -s [L, fr. *pulsatus* + *-or*] **1 :** BEATER, STRIKER **2 :** something that beats or throbs in working: as **a :** PULSOMETER **b :** a device for producing pulsations in a reaction chamber by periodic discharges of gas or vapor
**pul·sa·to·ry** \ˈpəlsə,tōrē, -tȯr-, -ri\ *adj* **:** capable of pulsating **:** characterized by pulsation **:** THROBBING
**¹pulse** \ˈpəls *also* -l(t)s\ *n* -s [ME *pols, puls*, fr. OF *pols, pouls, pous* porridge, fr. L *pult-, puls* porridge made of meal and pulse, prob. fr. Gk *poltos* porridge — more at POLLEN] **1 :** the edible seeds of various leguminous crops (as peas and beans) **2 a :** a plant yielding pulse **b :** pulse plants
**²pulse** \ˈ"\ *n* -s *often attrib* [ME *pous, puls*, fr. MF *pous, pouls, pols*, fr. L *pulsus* beating, striking, pulse, fr. *pulsus*, past part. of *pellere* to drive, beat, push — more at FELT] **1 a :** a regularly recurrent wave of distention in arteries that results from the progress through an artery of blood injected into the arterial system at each contraction of the ventricles of the heart **b :** the palpable beat resulting from such pulse as detected in a superficial artery (as the radial artery) ⟨a very soft ~⟩; *often* **:** the number of such beats in a specified period of time (as one minute) ⟨a resting ~ of 70⟩ **2 a :** underlying sentiment, opinion, or drift esp. as discoverable by tact or skill in perception rather than by open inquiry; *also* **:** an indication of such ⟨one may feel the social, economic, and political ~ of the State —*Amer. Guide Series: Maine*⟩ ⟨one felt the ~ of the village in the pub —S.P.B.Mais⟩ ⟨the ~ of the wisdom and genius of the age —T.L.Peacock⟩ ⟨the ~ of international political purpose —Herbert Feis⟩ ⟨these farmers, owners of their land, are the ~ of anticommunism —George Weller⟩ **b :** feeling of life **:** throb of emotion **:** sensation of excitement **:** VITALITY ⟨new industry has quickened the ~ of the people —*Amer. Guide Series: Texas*⟩ ⟨stirred the ~ of mankind —M.R.Cohen⟩ ⟨awakened love's deep ~*s* —Vachel Lindsay⟩ **3 a :** pulsing movement **:** rhythmical beating, vibrating, or sounding ⟨the driller . . . feels the ~ of a bit far below his feet by the kick in his hand —*Lamp*⟩ ⟨the ~ of its drama is deep and slow —George Farwell⟩ ⟨the ~ of an engine⟩ **b :** PULSATION, BEAT, THROB; *specif* **:** a beat or stress in music or poetry **4 a :** a transient variation of electrical current, voltage, or some other quantity whose value is normally constant — often used of current variations produced artificially and repeated either with a regular period or according to some code **b :** an electromagnetic wave or modulation thereof having brief duration **c :** a brief disturbance transmitted through a medium ⟨a ~ of light⟩ ⟨a ~ of sound⟩ ⟨a ~ of pressure⟩ **5 :** a sudden sharp upswing in numbers (as of a kind of organism) usu. occurring at regular intervals ⟨annual plankton ~*s*⟩
**³pulse** \ˈ"\ *vb* -ED/-ING/-S *vi* **:** to exhibit a pulse or pulsation **:** THROB **:** move in pulses, beats, or periodic spurts **:** vibrate with life, sound, light ⟨an environment that ~*s* and glows —H.L.Mencken⟩ ~ *vt* **1 :** to drive by or as if by a pulsation **:** cause to pulsate ⟨the echoes had *pulsed* themselves to silence —Florette Henri⟩ ⟨a gentle surf *pulsed* the air —Ward Taylor⟩ **2 a :** to produce or modulate (as electromagnetic waves) in the form of pulses ⟨*pulsed* waves⟩ **b :** to cause to be emitted in pulses ⟨*pulsed* light⟩ **c :** to cause (an apparatus) to produce pulses ⟨a transmitter *pulsed* by an electron tube⟩ **syn** see PULSATE
**pulsebeat** \ˈ⸗,⸗\ *n* **1 a :** PULSE 1b **b :** regular rhythm ⟨the ~ of the universe⟩ **2 :** an indication of an underlying sentiment, opinion, or drift ⟨every ~ of that distrust which filled the souls of . . . people —Upton Sinclair⟩
**pulse code modulation** *n* **:** modulation of a radio wave or signal in which the intelligence is conveyed by a code or order of pulses of the wave that are usu. all of the same size and shape and that are transmitted at multiples of a standard time interval
**pulse deficit** *n* **:** the difference in a minute's time between the number of beats of the heart and the number of beats of the pulse observed in diseases of the heart
**pulse duration modulation** *n* **:** PULSE LENGTH MODULATION
**pulse family** *n* **:** LEGUMINOSAE
**pulse frequency modulation** *n* **:** modulation of a radio wave or signal in which the intelligence is conveyed by varying the frequency or repetition rate of the pulses of the wave
**pulse–jet engine** \ˈ⸗,⸗-\ *n* **:** a jet engine having in its forward end intermittent air-inlet valves designed to produce a pulsating thrust by the intermittent flow of hot gases
**pulse length modulation** *n* **:** modulation of a radio wave or signal in which the intelligence is conveyed by varying the length or duration of the pulses of the wave
**pulse·less** \ˈpəlsləs\ *adj* **:** having no pulse **:** lacking energy, animation, or purpose — **pulse·less·ly** *adv* — **pulse·less·ness** *n* -ES
**pulse modulation** *n* **:** modulation of a radio wave or signal by pulses
**pulse position modulation** *n* **:** modulation of a radio wave or signal in which the intelligence is conveyed by varying the time relationship of the pulses of the wave
**pulse pressure** *n* **:** the pressure that is characteristic of the arterial pulse and represents the difference between diastolic and systolic pressures of the heart cycle
**puls·er** \ˈpəlsə(r)\ *n* -s **:** a device to generate pulses or apply pulses for control
**pulse radar** *n* **:** radar that operates by emitting and receiving pulses at signal
**pulse rate** *n* **:** the rate of the arterial pulse usu. observed at the wrist and stated in beats per minute
**pulses** *pl of* PULSE, *pres 3d sing of* PULSE
**pulse time modulation** *n* **:** modulation of the time intervals between successive pulses of constant duration and amplitude in accordance with a signal; *specif* **:** a system of multiplex high-frequency transmission using this method of modulation
**pulse–warmer** \ˈ⸗,⸗⸗\ *n* **:** WRISTER 1
**pulse wave** *n* **:** the wave of increased pressure started by the ventricular systole radiating from the semilunar valves over the arterial system at a rate varying between 20 and 30 feet a second in different arteries
**pulse width modulation** *n* **:** PULSE LENGTH MODULATION
**pul·sif·ic** \ˌpəlˈsifik\ *adj* [²*pulse* + *-i-* + *-fic*] **:** exciting the pulse **:** causing pulsation
**pul·sim·e·ter** \ˌpəlˈsimad·ə(r)\ *n* [²*pulse* + *-i-* + *-meter*] **:** an instrument for measuring the pulse esp. for force and rate
**pulsing** *pres part of* PULSE
**pul·sion** \ˈpəlshən\ *n* -s [LL *pulsion-, pulsio*, fr. L *pulsus* (past part. of *pellere* to beat, drive, push) + *-ion-, -io* -ion — more at FELT] **:** the act or action of pushing or driving **:** PROPULSION ⟨these undirected and hence uncoordinated ~*s*, so prevalent in childhood —H.A.Murray⟩ — opposed to *traction*
**pulsion diverticulum** *n* **:** a diverticulum pushed out from a hollow organ by pressure from within; *specif* **:** a diverticulum of the esophagus as a result of the pressure from within resulting in herniation of the mucosa
**pul·sive** \ˈpəlsiv, -sēv *also* -səv\ *adj* [L *pulsus* (past part. of *pellere*) + E *-ive*] **:** impelling or tending to impel **:** PROPULSIVE — **pul·sive·ness** *n* -ES
**pul·som·e·ter** \ˌpəlˈsämad·ə(r), -mətə-\ *n* [ISV ²*pulse* + *-o-* + *-meter*] **1 :** a displacement pump with valves for raising water by steam partly by atmospheric pressure and partly by the direct action of the steam on the water without intervention of a piston — called also *vacuum pump* **2 a :** SPHYGMOGRAPH, PULSIMETER **b :** a watch with special dial used by physicians in determining the pulse rate
**pul·ta·ceous** \ˌpəlˈtāshəs\ *adj* [L *pult-, puls* porridge made of meal and pulse + E *-aceous* — more at PULSE] **:** having a consistency like that of porridge **:** MACERATED, PULPY
**pul·ton** *or* **pul·tun** \ˈpəltᵊn *also* -tən\ *n* -s [Hindi *palṭan*, fr. E *battalion*] **:** an infantry regiment in India
**pu·lu** \ˈpü,lü\ *n* -s [Hawaiian, fr. *pulu* wet, soaked] **:** a soft elastic yellowish brown vegetable wool obtained in Hawaii from the young fronds of tree ferns of the genus *Cibotium* (esp. *C. menziesii*) and formerly exported for mattress and pillow stuffing
**pulv** *abbr* **1** pulverized; pulverizer **2** [L *pulvis*] powder
**pul·ver·a·ble** \ˈpəlv(ə)rəbəl\ *adj* [L *pulverare* to bestrew with dust, pulverize (fr. *pulver-, pulvis* dust, powder) + E *-able* — more at POLLEN] **:** capable of being pulverized
**pul·ver·ant** \ˈpəlvərənt\ *adj* [L *pulverant-, pulverans*, pres. part. of *pulverare*] **:** PULVERIZED ⟨~ gypsum⟩
**Pul·ver·a·tor** \-ˌrād·ə(r)\ *trademark* — used for a device that reduces material to fine bits
**pul·ver·iz·able** \-ˌrīzəbəl, ˌ⸗⸗ˈ⸗⸗⸗\ *adj* **:** capable of being pulverized
**pul·ver·i·za·tion** \ˌpəlvərəˈzāshən, -ˌrīˈz-\ *n* -s [F *pulvérisation*, fr. MF *pulverisation*, fr. *pulveriser* + *-ation*] **:** the act or process of pulverizing ⟨avoiding the ~ of individual liberty and dignity —*New Republic*⟩
**pul·ver·ize** \ˈpəlvə,rīz\ *vb* -ED/-ING/-S *see -ize in Explan Notes* [MF *pulveriser*, fr. LL *pulverizare*, fr. L *pulver-, pulvis* dust, powder + *-izare* -ize — more at POLLEN] *vt* **1 :** to reduce (as by crushing, beating, or grinding) to very small particles (as in fine powder or dust) **:** ATOMIZE ⟨~ the soil with steel implements —Russell Lord⟩ ⟨mower . . . ~*s* grass clippings —*Star Weekly*⟩ **2 :** to destroy by or as if by smashing into fragments **:** DISINTEGRATE, ANNIHILATE, DEMOLISH, VANQUISH ⟨buildings *pulverized* by a tornado⟩ ⟨a bomb that could ~ a city⟩ ⟨if in the east Socialism has been *pulverized* by the totalitarian state —*Times Lit. Supp.*⟩ ⟨started as a slashing journalistic critic . . . joyfully *pulverizing* every kind of conventional nonsense —Edgar Johnson⟩ ~ *vi* **:** to become pulverized
**pulverized sugar** *n* **:** standard powdered sugar derived from granulated sugar by grinding and usu. after adding flour to prevent caking
**pul·ver·iz·er** \-zə(r)\ *n* -s **:** one that pulverizes; *specif* **:** ACME HARROW
**pul·ver·ous** \ˈpəlvərəs\ *adj* [L *pulver-, pulvis*, dust, powder + E *-ous* — more at POLLEN] **:** POWDERY
**pul·ver·u·lent** \(ˌ)pəlˈveryələnt\ *adj* [L *pulverulentus*, fr. *pulver-, pulvis* dust + *-ulentus* -ulent — more at POLLEN] **:** consisting of or reducible to fine powder **:** covered or looking as if covered with dust or powder **:** DUSTY, CRUMBLY ⟨if a mineral is ~, granular, or splintery —C.S.Hurlbut⟩ ⟨baking powder is a white ~ or finely granular compounded material —C.S. Bryan⟩ — **pul·ver·u·lent·ly** *adv*
**pul·vic acid** \ˈpəlvik-\ *n* [ISV *pulvic*, anagram of *vulpic*] **:** PULVINIC ACID
**pul·vil** \ˈpəl(ˌ)vil\ *or* **pul·vil·io** \ˌpəlˈvilē(ˌ)ō\ *n* -s [It *polviglio*, fr. Sp *polvillo*, dim. of *polvo* dust, powder, fr. (assumed) VL *pulvus*, alter. of L *pulvis* — more at POLLEN] *archaic* **:** cosmetic or perfumed powder
**pul·vil·lar** \ˌpəlˈvilə(r), ˈpəlvəl-\ *adj* [NL *pulvillus* + E *-ar*] **:** of or relating to a pulvillus
**pul·vil·li·form** \ˌpəlˈvilə,fȯrm\ *adj* [NL *pulvillus* + E *-iform*] **:** having the shape or appearance of a pulvillus
**pul·vil·lus** \ˌpəlˈviləs\ *n, pl* **pulvil·li** \-ˌi,lī\ [NL, fr. L, small cushion, dim. of *pulvinus* cushion] **:** a pad often covered with short hairs or an organ or process resembling or functioning like a cushion or sucker that occurs on an insect's foot between the claws of the last segment and often forms an adhesive organ
**¹pul·vi·nar** \ˌpəlˈvīnə(r)\ *n* -s *see sense 2* [L, cushioned seat, couch, fr. *pulvinus* cushion] **1 :** CUSHION **2** *pl* **pul·vi·nar·ia** \ˌpəlvəˈna(a)rēə\ **:** a cushioned couch reserved for the gods in Roman antiquity; *also* **:** a cushioned seat at a public spectacle **3** [NL, fr. L] **:** a prominence on the back of the thalamus
**²pulvinar** \ˈ"\ *adj* [NL *pulvinus* + E *-ar*] **:** resembling a cushion; *specif* **:** relating to or resembling a pulvinus
**pul·vi·nar·ia** \ˌpəlvəˈna(a)rēə\ *n* [NL, fr. L *pulvinus* cushion + NL *-aria*; fr. the appearance of the egg case] **1** *cap* **:** a genus of scales in which the females are large, flat, and nearly circular and secrete a cottony egg case — see COTTONY MAPLE SCALE **2** -s **:** any insect of the genus *Pulvinaria*
**pul·vi·nate** \ˈpəlvə,nāt, *usu* -ād·+V\ *or* **pul·vi·nat·ed** \-ˌnād·əd\ *adj* [L *pulvinatus*, fr. *pulvinus* cushion + *-atus* -ate, -ated] **1 :** curved convexly or swelled ⟨a ~ frieze⟩ **2 a :** cushion-shaped **b :** having a pulvinus **:** PULVINAR — **pul·vi·nate·ly** *adv*
**pul·vi·na·tion** \ˌ⸗⸗ˈnāshən\ *n* -s **:** a convex curve or swelling (as on a frieze)
**pul·vin·ic acid** \ˌpəlˈvinik-\ *n* [ISV, blend of *pulvic* and *-in*] **:** an orange crystalline lactonic acid ($C_{17}H_{11}O_3$)COOH obtained from lichens and by hydrolysis of vulpinic acid
**pul·vi·no** \ˌpəlˈvē(ˌ)nō\ *n, pl* **pulvi·ni** \-ˌnī\ [It, fr. L *pulvinus* cushion] **:** DOSSERET
**pul·vin·u·lus** \ˌpəlˈvinyələs\ *n, pl* **pulvinu·li** \-əˌlī\ [NL, dim. of L *pulvinus*] **:** PULVILLUS
**pul·vi·nus** \ˌpəlˈvīnəs\ *n, pl* **pulvi·ni** \-ī,nī\ [NL, fr. L, cushion] **:** a cushionlike enlargement of the base of a petiole or petiolule consisting of a mass of large thin-walled cells surrounding a vascular strand and functioning in turgor movements of leaves or leaflets by reversible volume changes in the cells
**pul·vi·plume** \ˈpəlvē+,-\ *n* [L *pulvis* dust, powder + E *plume* — more at POLLEN] **:** POWDER DOWN
**pul·war** \(ˌ)pəlˈwär\ *n* -s [Hindi *palwār*] **:** a light keelless riverboat used in India
**pu·ma** \ˈp(y)ümə\ *n, pl* **pumas** *also* **puma** [Sp, fr. Quechua] **:** COUGAR; *also* **:** the fur or pelt of a cougar sometimes used for rugs

pulwar

**pumace** *var of* POMACE
**pumelo** *var of* POMELO
**pu·mex** \ˈpyü,meks\ *n* -ES [L — more at FOAM] **:** PUMICE
**¹pum·ice** \ˈpəməs\ *or* **pumice stone** *n* -s [ME *pomis*, fr. MF *pomis*, fr. L *pumic-, pumex* — more at FOAM] **1 :** a white, gray, yellowish, brownish, or rarely red volcanic glass that is light in weight because it is full of cavities produced by the expulsion of water vapor at a high temperature as lava comes to the surface and that is used esp. in powder form for smoothing and polishing **:** hardened volcanic froth **2 :** a piece of pumice esp. for use in polishing, blotting, or erasing **3** *obs* **:** something that is as dry as pumice
**²pumice** \ˈ"\ *vt* -ED/-ING/-S **:** to clean, smooth, or treat with pumice
**pumiced sole** *or* **pumiced foot** *n* [¹*pumice* + *-ed*] **:** a horse's hoof in which the horny laminae have become spongy and soft
**pu·mi·ceous** \pyüˈmishəs\ *adj* [L *pumiceus*, fr. *pumic-, pumex* pumice + *-eus* -eous] **1 :** of, relating to, or consisting of pumice **2 :** resembling pumice in structure
**pum·ic·er** \-sə(r)\ *n* -s **:** one that pumices
**pumice soap** *n* **:** a hard soap charged with a gritty powder (as silica, alumina, powdered pumice)
**pum·i·cite** \ˈpəmə,sīt\ *n* -s [*pumice* + *-ite*] **1 :** PUMICE 1 **2 :** a volcanic dust that is similar in composition to pumice and used for abrasive purposes
**¹pum·mel** \ˈpəməl\ *vb* **pummeled** *or* **pummelled; pummeled** *or* **pummelled; pummeling** *or* **pummelling** \-m(ə)liŋ\ **pummels** [alter. of ²*pommel*] **:** THUMP, POUND, POMMEL ⟨he ~*ed* and slapped and scrubbed the somewhat obese nudity of his companion —John Buchan⟩ ⟨~*ing* away most unmercifully —Samuel Lover⟩ **syn** see BEAT
**²pummel** *var of* POMMEL
**pummelo** *var of* POMELO
**pum·mies** \ˈpəmēz\ *n pl but sing or pl in constr* [by alter.] *dial* **:** POMACE 1
**¹pum·my** \ˈpəmē\ *dial var of* ¹PUMICE
**²pummy** \ˈ"\ *chiefly dial var of* POMACE
**¹pump** \ˈpəmp\ *n* -s [ME *pumpe, pompe*, fr. MLG *pumpe* or MD *pompe*, prob. fr. Sp *bomba*, of imit. orig.] **1 a :** a device or machine that raises, transfers, or compresses fluids or that attenuates gases esp. by suction or pressure or both — see CENTRIFUGAL PUMP, DISPLACEMENT PUMP, JET PUMP, PISTON PUMP, ROTARY PUMP **b :** a part of an animal organism that functions as a mechanical pump; *specif* **:** HEART ⟨the doctor in Washington said I had a good ~ —O.W.Holmes †1935⟩ **2 a :** an act or the process of pumping **b :** a stroke of a pump **3 :** one that pumps esp. for information **4 :** PUMP GUN
**²pump** \ˈ"\ *vb* -ED/-ING/-S *vt* **1 :** to raise (as water) with a pump — often used with *up* or *out* **2 a :** to pour forth, eject, deliver, force, or draw in the manner of a pump or one using a pump ⟨spring ~*s* mildly sulfurous hot water into a deep pool —J.A.Michener⟩ ⟨the blood is ~*ed* into the running and fighting muscles —H.A.Overstreet⟩ ⟨~*ed* bullets into five congressmen —*U.S. News & World Report*⟩ ⟨knowledge ~*ed* into their resisting skulls —H.F. & Katharine Pringle⟩ ⟨~*ed* fresh life into art . . . by using his own raw experiences —L.B. Nicolson⟩ **b :** to direct, assign, or influence the flow of (money) for stimulating or building up something (as agriculture, trade, or a business) ⟨the power of the Federal Reserve system to ~ cash into the commercial banks —R.S.Sayers⟩ ⟨foreign aid programs which have ~*ed* dollars into world trade channels —*Introduction to Doing Import & Export Business*⟩ ⟨~ extra capital into the land —*Economist*⟩ **3 a :** to subject to efforts intended to draw out, obtain, or extract (as

information, secrets, money) **:** ply persistently with urgings and questions in order to elicit something ⟨had been ~*ed* long ago for biographical material —*Times Lit. Supp.*⟩ **b :** to draw out, elicit, or extract by such efforts ⟨tried to ~ out from his memory reminiscences of his youth —H.S.Canby⟩ **4 :** to draw water, air, or other fluid from **:** free from water by means of a pump ⟨~ a well dry⟩ ⟨~ out a ship⟩ **5 a :** to manipulate as or as if a pump handle ⟨he ~*ed* Daniel's hand —Walter O'Meara⟩ ⟨just ~ the lever and shoot it —Ernest Hemingway⟩ **b :** to operate by so manipulating a lever or handle ⟨a parcel-conveying system . . . which he operated by ~*ing* the sewing-machine treadle —Clarence Woodbury⟩ ⟨~ a handcar⟩ ⟨~ a bicycle⟩ **6 :** to reduce by exertion to a breathless or panting condition — often used with *out* ⟨after the race he was all ~*ed* out⟩ **7 :** to fill with air by means of a pump or bellows ⟨~ up a tire⟩ **8 :** to inject a preservative solution into (ham or other meat) by means of a needle and pump **~** *vi* **1 :** to work a pump **:** raise or move water or other fluid with a pump ⟨mill ~*ing* away on an almost still day —Laura Krey⟩ **2 :** to drive, eject, or pour forth contents in the manner of a pump ⟨rifles ~*ed* continuously⟩ **3 a :** to exert oneself to pump something or somebody ⟨constricting the throat muscles, instead of ~*ing* more vigorously with the abdominal muscles —A.T.Weaver⟩ ⟨never tell our secrets to people that ~ for them —O.W. Holmes †1894⟩ **b :** to throb heavily ⟨heart ~*ed* hard —Marcia Davenport⟩ **4 a :** to move up and down like a pump handle ⟨with a ~*ing* of wings the birds were gone —Shirley A. Grau⟩ ⟨bicycled by . . . her knees ~*ing* furiously —Lael Tucker⟩ ⟨a handcar operated by ~*ing*⟩ **b :** to run, fly, or move as the result of such movement esp. of legs or wings ⟨a man came ~*ing* up the road on a bicycle —Nelson Hayes⟩ ⟨we would stand up in the swing and ~ —Gordon Wilson⟩ ⟨runner was rounding second, ~*ing* for third —George Barrett⟩ **5 :** to spurt out intermittently ⟨blood ~*s* from a cut artery⟩ **6** *of a mechanical or electrical device* **:** HUNT 3, PULSATE, SEESAW **7 :** to take a full windup before pitching a baseball — **pump by heads :** to pump (a well producing a small quantity) intermittently by allowing the contents to accumulate to a certain depth and then emptying the well

**³pump** \"\ *n* -s [origin unknown] **:** a low shoe not fastened on and gripping the foot chiefly at the toe and heel

pump

**pump·abil·i·ty** \ˌpəmpəˈbiləd-ē\ *n* **:** the quality, state, or degree of being pumpable

**pump·able** \ˈpəmpəbəl\ *adj* **:** capable of being pumped ⟨a heavy but still ~ mud fluid —F.J.Williams⟩

**pump–action** \ˈ=,==\ *adj* [¹*pump* + *action*] *of a shotgun or rifle* **:** having an action that by the backward and forward motion of a sliding lever extracts and ejects the empty case, cocks the piece, and loads in a new round

**pump·age** \ˈpəmpij\ *n* -s [²*pump* + *-age*] **:** the amount raised by pumping or the work done by pumping ⟨the ~ of an oil well⟩

**pump bob** *n* [¹*pump*] **:** a bell crank or similar device for converting rotary into reciprocating motion

**pump brake** *n* **1 :** ⁵BRAKE 2 **2 :** a hydraulic brake (as for controlling the recoil of a gun) operating on the principle of the cataract

**pump cylinder** *n* **1 :** the cylinder of a pump **2 :** a sliding telescopic gage used by chronometer makers

**pump dale** *n* **:** the discharge spout of a bilge pump

**pump doctor** *n* **:** an expert charged with supervision and repair of pumps (as in a coal mine or copper mine)

**pump dredge** *n* **:** a dredge that delivers excavated material by pipeline usu. for dikes or fill

**pump drill** *n* **:** a primitive drill in which the shaft is revolved by working up and down a bow or bar carrying a cord attached at the center to the upper end of the shaft

**pum·pel·ly·ite** \ˌpəmˈpelē,īt\ *n* -s [Raphael *Pumpelly* †1923 Am. geologist + E *-ite*] **:** a mineral $Ca_4(Al,Mg,Fe)_6Si_6O_{23}(OH)_3.2H_2O(?)$ consisting of a hydrous calcium aluminosilicate probably related to clinozoisite

**pump·er** \ˈpəmpə(r)\ *n* -s **1 :** one that pumps or operates a pump (as for pumping oil) **2 :** an instrument or machine used in pumping; *esp* **:** a fire truck equipped with a pump **3 :** an oil well that has to be pumped

**pumper company** *n* **:** an engine company of a fire department

**pumper–ladder** \ˈ==ˈ=\ *n* **:** a fire truck equipped as both a pumper and a ladder truck

**pum·per·nick·el** \ˈpəmpə(r),nikəl\ *n* -s [G] **:** a sourdough bread made by fermentation using unbolted rye flour for the dark variety and various proportions of rye and wheat flours for the lighter kinds

**pum·pet** \ˈpəmpət\ *or* **pumpet ball** *n* -s [MF *pompette* wart, pimple, fr. *pompe* tuft of ribbons + *-ette* — more at POMPON] **:** INK BALL

**pump gun** *n* [²*pump*] **:** a pump-action shotgun or rifle

**pump handle** *n* [¹*pump*] **1 :** the handle of a pump esp. of a house well or cistern **2 :** a handshake in which the arm is moved as though it were a pump handle

**pump house** *n* **:** a building in which are located and operated the pumps of an irrigation system (as a spa) **:** a pumping station

**pumping** *n* -s [fr. gerund of ²*pump*] **:** the action produced by heavy traffic whereby free water rises through joints and cracks in a pavement carrying with it fine-grained soil whose removal causes voids and subsequent subsidence and cracking of the pavement

**pumping engine** *n* **:** an engine used for pumping: as **a :** a steam engine and pump combined for raising water **b :** a fire truck equipped with a pump

**pumping jack** *n* **:** a device over a deep well for operating a pump by belt power

**pumping of the barometer :** a rather rapid rise and fall of the column of the mercurial barometer due to inertia attending changes in the rate of vertical motion **:** a corresponding oscillation of the index of the aneroid barometer or of the recording pen of the barograph due to various causes (as change of pressure)

**pump·kin** \ˈ÷ˈpəŋkən, ˈpəm(p)kən\ *or* **pun·kin** \ˈpəŋkən\ *n* -s *often attrib* [alter. (influenced by *-kin*) of *pumpion, pompion,* modif. of MF *popon, pompon* pumpkin, melon, fr. L *pepon-, pepo,* fr. Gk *pepōn* an edible gourd, fr. *pepōn* cooked by sun, ripe, fr. *peptein, pessein* to cook, ripen, digest — more at COOK] **1 a :** any of various usu. firm-rinded fruits of vines of the genus *Cucurbita* that are widely cultivated as a vegetable, for pies, and for livestock feed: (1) **:** any of numerous usu. large rounded, and deep yellow to orange fruits produced by plants that are horticultural varieties of the natural species (*C. pepo*); *also* **:** SUMMER SQUASH (2) **:** a fruit similarly used that is produced by horticultural varieties of the natural species (*C. moschata*) **:** a winter crookneck squash **:** CUSHAW — called also *squash* (3) *Brit* **:** any of various large-fruited winter squashes that are produced by horticultural varieties of the natural species (*C. maxima*) **b** *or* **pumpkin vine :** a plant that bears pumpkins and is usu. a strong-growing prickly vine with large lobed leaves and with yellow flowers having erect corolla lobes **2 a :** a lumbering person or body **:** CHUMP **b :** a very important person or place — usu. used in pl. and chiefly in the phrase *some pumpkins* ⟨a man of learning is supposed to be some ~*s* —J.F.Dobie⟩ **3 :** a strong orange that is lighter than mandarin orange, redder, less strong, and slightly darker than Princeton orange, redder and duller than cadmium orange, and redder and deeper than cadmium yellow

**pumpkin ash** *n* **1 :** a timber tree (*Fraxinus tomentosa*) of the central and southeastern U.S. having hairy twigs and leafstalks **2 :** the wood of the pumpkin ash tree

**pumpkin ball** *n* **:** a solid ball or rifled slug used as shotgun ammunition for large game animals

**pumpkin beetle** *n* **:** a chrysomelid beetle (*Aulacophora hilaris*) that damages fruits and vegetables in parts of Australia

**pumpkin bread** *n* **:** bread made of ground dried pumpkin or mashed boiled pumpkin mixed with cornmeal

**pumpkin bug** *n* **:** SQUASH BUG

**pumpkin head** *n* **1** *archaic* **:** a New England Puritan **2 :** DOLT, BLOCKHEAD **3 :** a pumpkin-sized head — **pumpkin–headed** \ˈ==ˈ==\ *adj*

**pumpkin pine** *n* **1 :** the homogeneous close-grained wood of especially fine old trees of the white pine (*Pinus strobus*) **2 :** WHITE PINE 1a

**pumpkinseed** \ˈ==,=\ *n* **1 :** a small brilliantly colored No. American freshwater sunfish (*Lepomis gibbosus*) or the related bluegill **2 :** BUTTERFISH a

**pumpknot** \ˈ=,=\ *n* [origin unknown] *Midland* **:** a lump or swelling on the head usu. from a blow

**pum·ple** \ˈpəmpəl\ *archaic var of* PIMPLE

**pump·less** \ˈpəmpləs\ *adj* **:** having no pump

**pump log** *n* [¹*pump*] **:** a hollowed-out log used as a conduit

**pump·man** \ˈpəmpmən\ *n, pl* **pumpmen** [¹*pump* + *man*] **:** one who tends, operates, or cares for a pump

**pump priming** *n* [¹*pump*] **:** investment expenditures by government designed to induce a self-sustaining expansion of economic activity

**pump rod** *n* **:** the rod to which the bucket of a pump is fastened and which is attached to the brake or handle **:** PISTON ROD

**pump room** *n* **:** PUMP HOUSE; *specif* **:** a hall or casino at a spa provided for the treatment of and as a gathering place for its patrons

**pumps** *pl of* PUMP, *pres 3d sing of* PUMP

**pump sole** *n* [³*pump*] **:** a thin single sole generally with beveled edges that is common on men's and women's shoes (as pumps)

**pump up** *vt* [²*pump*] **:** to work up by artificial means or by great effort ⟨*pumping up* a poem till it means everything —N.E. Nelson⟩ ⟨*pumping up* his smile —Edwin O'Connor⟩

**pump well** *n* [¹*pump*] **:** WELL 3a

**¹pun** \ˈpən\ *vt* **punned; punned; punning; puns** [ME *pounen* — more at POUND] *chiefly dial* **:** to beat with telling force **:** POUND ⟨would ~ thee into shivers with his fist —Shak.⟩

**²pun** \"\ *n* -s [perh. fr. It *puntiglio* quibble, fine point — more at PUNCTILIO] **:** the humorous use of a word in such a way as to suggest different meanings or applications or of words having the same or nearly the same sound but different meanings **:** a play on words ⟨never knew an enemy to ~*s* who was not an ill-natured man —Charles Lamb⟩ ⟨any man who would make such an execrable ~ would not scruple to pick my pocket —John Dennis⟩

**³pun** \"\ *vb* **punned; punned; punning; puns** *vi* **:** to make puns **~** *vt* **:** to persuade or drive by the use of puns

**pun** *abbr* puncheon

**pu·na** \ˈpünə\ *also* **pu·no** \ˈpü(,)nō\ *n* -s [AmSp *puna,* fr. Quechua] **1 :** a bleak desolate region; *specif* **:** a treeless windswept tableland or basin in the higher Andes **2 :** a cold mountain wind in Peru

**²puna** \"\ *n, pl* **puna** *or* **punas** *usu cap* [AmSp, of AmerInd origin] **1 a :** an Indian people chiefly of the island of Puna in the Gulf of Guayaquil, Ecuador **b :** a member of such people **2 :** the language of the Puna people

**pu·naise** \pyüˈnāz\ *or* **pu·nese** \-nēz\ *n* -s [MF *punaise,* fr. fem. of *punais* stinking, fr. (assumed) VL *putinasius* stinking from the nose, fr. L *putēre* to stink + *nasus* nose — more at FOUL, NOSE] **:** BEDBUG

**pu·na·lua** \ˌpünəˈlüə\ *n* -s [Hawaiian] **1 :** a group marriage formerly practiced in Hawaii in which a group of brothers is married to a group of sisters or in which the husbands are of the same kinship group and the wives are members of another kinship group **2 :** the two or more husbands of a wife or the two or more wives of a husband in such a group marriage **3 :** the relationship of the persons in such a form of marriage

**pu·na·lu·an** \ˌ==ˈlüən\ *adj* **:** of or relating to punalua ⟨a ~ family⟩

**pu·nan** \pü'nän\ *n, pl* **punan** *or* **punans** *usu cap* [native name in Borneo] **1 :** a Dayak people living as forest nomads in the remote interior of Borneo **2 :** a member of the Punan people

**punc** *abbr* punctuation

**punce** \ˈpən(t)s\ *dial Eng var of* POUNCE

**¹punch** \ˈpənch\ *vb* -ED/-ING/-ES [partly fr. ME *punchen,* fr. MF *poinçonner* to prick, stamp, fr. *poinçon* pointed tool; partly fr. ³*punch* — more at PUNCHEON] *vt* **1 a :** to prod with a stick or other blunt object **:** POKE ⟨was ~*ed* with her umbrella⟩ ⟨rod to ~ out the empty shells —W.F.Harris⟩ **b :** to act as herdsman of **:** DRIVE 1c **c :** to push (material) through a foundation piece with a needle ⟨in some carpets the pile is ~*ed* through the foundation⟩ **2 a :** to strike with a hard and usu. quick forward thrust esp. with the fist ⟨the boxer ~*ed* his opponent on the nose⟩ ⟨check the dough temperature, relieve it of excess gases through ~*ing* it —Mary K. Moore⟩ ⟨began to ~ a pillow into shape —Berton Roueché⟩ **b :** to drive or push rapidly and forcibly by or as if by punching ⟨roads ~*ed* out of the wilderness by massive bulldozers —*Spokane (Wash.) Spokesman Rev.*⟩ ⟨a rocket could ~ its way out of the atmosphere —*N.Y.Times*⟩ ⟨~*ed* over a touchdown —C.B. Wilkinson⟩ ⟨ideals are ~*ed* over in anger —A.L.Guernsey⟩ **3 :** to emboss, cut, or operate on by means of a punch: as **a :** to stamp with perforations **:** PERFORATE, PUNCTURE ⟨a postage stamp ~*ed* with round holes⟩ ⟨~ a ticket⟩ **b :** to record (data) by perforating a card or tape ⟨the machine reads the factors, adds, subtracts . . . and ~*es* the results —H.C. Zeisig & P.T.Martin⟩ **c :** to make by perforating or puncturing ⟨holes can be ~*ed* in glass by forcing a sharp steel pin through —C.J.Phillips⟩ **d :** to make (a foundry-type matrix) by stamping with a punch ⟨most matrices are stamped or ~*ed,* rather than engraved —*Foundry Type*⟩ **4 :** to strike sharply so as to make a printed or other record or produce some other intended effect ⟨~ the keys of a typewriter⟩; *also* **:** to press or strike sharply the activating mechanism (as a button, key, or plunger) of ⟨~ a typewriter⟩ ⟨~ a time clock⟩ ⟨~ the throttle⟩ **5 :** to deliver (as a spoken line) or render (as a musical phrase) with strong emphasis ⟨jokes were ~*ed* with an assist from a thud on the bass drum —Henry Hewes⟩ ⟨lectures on how to ~ their lines —Jane Woodfin⟩ **~** *vi* **1 :** to perform the action of punching something ⟨after the damage to his hand, the fighter could no longer ~⟩ ⟨~*ing* away at a typewriter⟩ **2 :** to penetrate the paper being printed — used of a part of a printing surface ⟨the very first thing a pressman will do when he looks at the back of a printed sheet is to start cutting out the points which ~ —*Graphic Arts Monthly*⟩ **3 :** to conduct oneself esp. against odds or difficulties with continued effort, determination, and morale ⟨after months of discouragement, he was still in there ~*ing*⟩ **syn** see PERFORATE, STRIKE

**²punch** \"\ *n* -ES **1 :** the action of punching **2 :** a quick thrust or a blow with or as if with the fist ⟨land a ~ on the jaw⟩ ⟨has thrown verbal ~*es* at many a government bigwig —*Time*⟩ ⟨the searing ~ of cloud to ground lightning —J.C.Dillon⟩ ⟨neither could expect to win a one ~ war —H.E.Salisbury⟩ **3 :** energy or vigor that commands or arrests attention **:** effectively aimed force **:** EFFECTIVENESS ⟨this book has a ~ —W.L.Dorn⟩ ⟨put more science and ~ into salesmanship —*Systems Mag.*⟩ ⟨verbs that have ~ —Bruce Westley⟩ ⟨a team with a terrific ~ —*Sporting News (St. Louis, Mo.)*⟩ **4 :** PUNCH LINE; *also* **:** a word that has the same effect **syn** see VIGOR — **to the punch :** to the first blow or decisive action in a competition — used esp. with *beat* ⟨beats you *to the* conversational *punch* by having his say before you have a chance to open your mouth —W.J.Reilly⟩

**³punch** \"\ *n* -ES [prob. short for *puncheon*] **1 a :** a tool usu. in the form of a short rod of steel that is either solid or hollow and sharp-edged and that is variously shaped at one end for different operations (as perforating, blanking, cutting, forming, drawing, bending, coining, embossing, seaming, trimming): as (1) **:** PRICK PUNCH (2) **:** CENTER PUNCH (3) **:** a short tapering steel rod for driving the heads of nails or brads below the surface — called also *nail set* (4) **:** a tool for driving a bolt or other object out of a hole — called also *starting punch* (5) **:** FORCE 8a (6) **:** ²HOB 4a (4) (7) **:** a steel die faced with a letter in relief that is forced into a softer metal (as copper) to form an intaglio matrix from which foundry type is cast **b :** a device or machine for performing the operations of a hand punch: as (1) **:** a hand-operated device for cutting holes or notches in paper or cardboard (2) **:** PUNCH PRESS (3) **:** KEY PUNCH **2 :** a stonecutter's point **3 :** a part having on its surface a figure or design in relief so that it is suitable for impressing an intaglio design on wax or other plastic material **4 :** a hole or notch resulting from a perforating operation esp. of a card or tape

**⁴punch** \"\ *n* -ES [perh. fr. Hindi *pāc* five, fr. Skt *pañca;* fr. the number of ingredients — more at FIVE] **1 :** a hot or cold beverage varying greatly in composition but usu. composed of wine, spirituous liquor, or ale or a combination thereof and citrus juice, spices, tea, and water and often served from a large bowl ⟨hot rum ~⟩ ⟨whiskey ~⟩; *also* **:** a beverage composed of fruit juices and other nonalcoholic liquids (as tea, ginger ale) and usu. served cold **2 :** a drink or serving of punch **3 :** a social affair at which punch is served

**⁵punch** \"\ *n* -ES [prob. short for *punchinello*] *dial chiefly Eng* **:** a short stocky person or animal

**⁶punch** \"\ *adj, dial Brit* **:** SHORT, THICKSET

**⁷punch** \"\ *n* -ES [by shortening & alter.] **:** PANCHAYAT

**punch·able** \ˈpənchəbəl\ *adj* **1 :** capable of being punched **2 :** made esp. for being punched — used of a card

**punch–and–judy show** \ˈpənchənˈjüdē-\ *n, usu cap P&J* [fr. *Punch* and *Judy,* traditional names of the principal characters] **:** a puppet show in which the principal character quarrels with his wife and does various outrageous and tragic things in a ludicrous way

**punchayet** *var of* PANCHAYAT

**punchball** \ˈ=,=\ *n* [¹*punch* + *ball*] **:** a game similar to baseball but played with a tennis ball that is struck with a closed fist instead of a bat

**punchboard** \ˈ=,=\ *n* [¹*punch* + *board*] **:** a small board usu. 6″x6″x½″ to 15″x15″x¾″ that has many holes each filled with a rolled-up printed slip to be punched out on payment of a nominal sum in an effort to obtain a slip bearing a lucky name or number that entitles the player to a designated prize — called also *pushcard*

**punch bowl** *n* [⁴*punch*] **1 :** a large bowl from which a beverage (as punch or lemonade) is served **2 :** something suggestive of a punch bowl; *esp* **:** a cuplike hollow in a hilly region — often used in place names

**punch cutter** *n* [³*punch*] **:** one that cuts typefounders' punches

**punch–drunk** \ˈ=,=\ *adj* [²*punch* + *drunk*] **1 :** suffering cerebral injury as a result of many minute brain hemorrhages following repeated head blows received in prizefighting **2 :** affected as if punch-drunk **:** DAZED, DAZZLED, CONFUSED ⟨a country *punch-drunk* from war losses⟩ — **punch–drunkenness** \ˈ=,===\ *n*

punch bowl with cups and ladle

**punched** *past of* PUNCH

**punched card** *or* **punch card** *n* [¹*punch*] **:** a data card with holes punched in particular positions having particular assigned significations singly or in combination for automatic sorting, selecting, arranging, or computing in electrically operated tabulating or accounting equipment or computers; *also* **:** a similar card with holes and notches cut along the edge so that a slender rod may be used to sort, select, and arrange a group of such cards by hand

**punched tape** *n* [fr. past part. of ¹*punch*] **:** paper tape punched with holes in such a way as to convey information

**¹pun·cheon** \ˈpənchən\ *n* -s [ME *ponchon, ponson, punson* pointed tool, dagger, king post, fr. MF *poinchon, poinçon* pointed tool, king post (perh. fr. its being marked by the builder with a pointed tool), fr. (assumed) VL *punction-, punctio* pointed tool, fr. (assumed) *punctiare* to prick, fr. L *punctus,* past part. of *pungere* to prick — more at PUNGENT] **1 :** a pointed tool for piercing or for working on stone **2 a :** a short upright piece of timber in framing **:** a short post **:** an intermediate stud **b :** a split log or heavy slab with the face smoothed ⟨a ~ floor⟩ ⟨a ~ door⟩ **3 :** a figured stamp, die, or punch used esp. by goldsmiths, cutlers, and engravers

**²puncheon** \"\ *n* -s [ME *poncion,* fr. MF *ponchon, poinçon,* of unknown origin] **1 :** a large cask of varying capacity **2 :** any of various units of liquid capacity (as a unit equal to 70 gallons or one of 72 gallons)

**punch·er** \ˈpənchə(r)\ *n* -s **:** one that punches or operates a punch: as **a :** COWBOY **b :** a telegraphic perforator **c :** an operator of a punch press or drill press

**punches** *pres 3d sing of* PUNCH, *pl of* PUNCH

**punch in** *vi* [¹*punch*] **:** to record the time of one's presence (as for work) by punching a time clock ⟨arrive at the plant in time for a cup of coffee before *punching in* at eight o'clock —Elizabeth Ward⟩

**pun·chi·nel·lo** \ˌpənchəˈne(ˌ)lō\ *n, pl* **punchinellos** *or* **punchinelloes** [alter. of earlier *polichinello,* fr. It dial. *polecenella,* dim. of It *pulcino* chicken, fr. LL *pullicenus,* dim. of L *pullus* young of an animal, chicken — more at FOAL] **1 :** a clown or buffoon suggestive of a fat short humpbacked character in Italian puppet shows **2 :** one resembling a punchinello esp. in grotesqueness

**punch·i·ness** \ˈpənchēnəs\ *n* -ES **:** the quality, condition, or state of being punchy

**punching** *n* -s [fr. gerund of ¹*punch*] **1 :** a piece or burr removed (as from a steel plate) by a punch **2 :** an ornamental perforation (as in leather)

**punching bag** *n* **:** a stuffed or inflated bag usu. suspended but sometimes supported on a flexible rod to be punched for exercise or for training in boxing

**punch·less** \ˈpənchləs\ *adj* **:** lacking punch ⟨a ~ fighter⟩

**punch line** *n* [²*punch*] **:** a sentence, statement, or phrase in a play, musical comedy, speech, cartoon, humorous story, or advertisement that drives home the point ⟨a poem that found its *punch line* at the very finish —M.H.Cane⟩

**punch loom** *n* [¹*punch*] **:** a machine with needles for punching loose fiber or fabric pieces through a mesh fabric background

**punch mark** *n* [³*punch*] **:** a small counterstamp on a coin or other metal object

**punch out** *vi* [¹*punch*] **:** to record the time of one's stopping work or departure by punching a time clock ⟨*punched out* and went home at five o'clock⟩

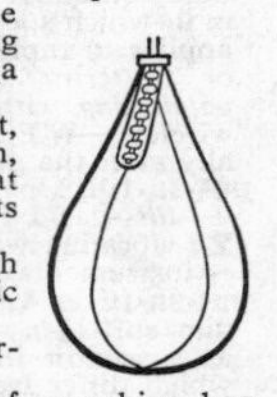

punching bag

**punch–out** \ˈ=,=\ *n* -s [¹*punch* + *out*] **:** a part of a surface marked off by perforations so that it may be forced out **:** KNOCKOUT

**punch pliers** *n pl* [¹*punch*] **:** pliers for perforating material (as leather, paper)

**punch press** *also* **punching press** *n* **:** a press for working on metal or other materials by the use of cutting, shaping, or combination dies consisting essentially of a frame in which one or more slides or rams are made to move up and down, of a bed to which the die shoe or bolster plate is bolted, and of means for applying power to the slide usu. through a crank, cam, eccentric shaft, toggle joint, knuckle joint, and rack and pinion, or other device

**punchwork** \ˈ=,=\ *n* [partly fr. ¹*punch,* partly fr. ³*punch*] **1 a :** an openwork embroidery with patterns of holes formed by separating threads of the cloth and stitching them in place **b :** a tufted embroidery of cut or uncut loops made by pushing a heavy thread through cloth and used esp. for bedspreads **2 :** a small repetitive allover pattern made with a steel punch (as on furniture or for the background on a carved decorative panel)

**¹punchy** \ˈpənchē, -chi\ *adj* -ER/-EST [⁵*punch* + *-y*] **:** having a short and thick or fat body

**²punchy** \"\ *adj* -ER/-EST [²*punch* + *-y*] **:** having or characterized by punch **:** FORCEFUL ⟨his characters all converse with the ~ drive of professional wits —*Saturday Rev.*⟩ ⟨thanked the admiral for his ~ interview —Joseph Driscoll⟩ ⟨short, ~ one-sentence paragraphs —*Newsweek*⟩ ⟨~ prose⟩

**³punchy** \"\ *adj* -ER/-EST [²*punch* + *-y*] **1 :** physically groggy from a punch or series of punches ⟨a ~ fighter⟩ **2 :** PUNCH-DRUNK 2 ⟨tendency of the bull moose to stagger around, ~ but on his feet even with a mortal hit —Warren Page⟩ ⟨men already ~ from combat —*Time*⟩

**punct** \ˈpəŋkt\ *n* -s [L *punctum* — more at POINT] **1 :** POINT **2 :** an element held in Whitehead's philosophy of nature to be analogous to a point in a geometric system

**¹puncta** *pl of* PUNCTUM

**²punc·ta** \ˈpəŋ(k)tə\ *n, pl* **punc·tae** \-),tē\ [NL, fr. LL, pricking, puncture, fr. L *punctus,* past part. of *pungere* to prick — more at PUNGENT] **:** any of various thin places arranged in characteristic pattern in the frustule wall of pennate diatoms — compare AREOLE

**punc·tar·i·a·les** \ˌpəŋ(k),ta(a)rēˈā(ˌ)lēz\ *n pl, cap* [NL, fr. *Punctaria,* type genus (fr. L *punctum* point + *-aria* -ary) + *-ales*] **:** an order comprising brown algae that resemble members of and are sometimes included in the order Dictyosiphonales but are distinguished by the lack of any marked internal tissue differentiation

**punc·tate** \'pəŋ(k),tāt\ *adj* [NL *punctatus*, fr. L *punctum* point + L *-atus*, -ate — more at POINT] **1 :** ending in a point **:** resembling a point **:** small and round like a dot **2 :** applied to a point ⟨a ~ stimulation of the skin⟩ **3 :** dotted with minute spots or depressions ⟨a ~ leaf⟩ ⟨a ~ fossil shell⟩ **4 :** marked by dots or points — used esp. of a skin lesion or disease

**punc·tat·ed** \-ād·əd\ *adj* [*punctate* + *-ed*] **:** PUNCTATE

**punc·ta·tion** \,pəŋ(k)'tāshən\ *n* -s [ML *punctatus* (past part. of *punctare* to point, fr. L *punctum*) + E *-ion*] **1 :** the action of making punctate, perforated, or marked by points or dots **:** the condition of being punctate **2 :** a minute spot or depression (as on a plant, animal, or piece of pottery) **3** *civil law* **:** a preliminary statement in writing presenting matters proposed to be put into a contemplated contract

**punc·tic·u·lar** \,pəŋ(k)'tikyələ(r)\ *or* **punc·tic·u·late** \-lət, -,lāt\ *adj* [(assumed) NL *puncticulum* (dim. of L *punctum* point) + E *-ar*, *-ate*] **:** PUNCTULATE

**punc·ti·form** \'pəŋ(k)tə,fȯrm\ *adj* [L *punctum* point + E *-iform*] **1 :** having the form or character of a point **2 :** marked by or composed of points or dots **:** PUNCTATE **3 :** of or relating to tangible points or dots used for representing words for reading by the blind

**punc·til·i·ar** \,pəŋ(k)'tilēə(r)\ *adj* [*punctilio* + *-ar*] **:** of or relating to a point of time

**punc·til·io** \,pəŋ(k)'tilē,ō\ *n, pl* **punctilios** [It & Sp; It *puntiglio* small point, point of honor, scruple, fr. Sp *puntillo*, fr. dim. of *punto* point, fr. L *punctum* — more at POINT] **1 a :** an instant of time **b :** a small detail **2 :** a nice detail of conduct in a ceremony, a procedure, or in the observance of a social or moral code **:** a point of behavior about which one is fastidious ⟨his ~, and love of ceremonious manners —Osbert Sitwell⟩ ⟨no ~ would keep him from telling what he knew —Carl Van Doren⟩ ⟨not accustomed to give much regard to the ~*s* of law —Oscar Handlin⟩ ⟨treat them with the ~*s* of the duelist's code —H.F.Armstrong⟩

**punc·til·i·ous** \,pəŋ(k)'tilēəs\ *adj* [*punctilio* + *-ous*] **:** attentive to punctilios **:** marked by precise exact accordance with the details of codes or conventions ⟨fussy about the ~ observance of orders —Willa Cather⟩ ⟨uncivilized people often pay ~ attention to rules of etiquette about salutations, visits, meetings —W.G.Sumner⟩ **syn** see CAREFUL

**punc·til·i·ous·ly** *adv* **:** in a punctilious manner

**punc·til·i·ous·ness** *n* -ES **:** the quality or state of being punctilious

**punc·tion** \'pəŋ(k)shən\ *n* -s [L *punction-*, *punctio*, fr. *punctus* (past part. of *pungere* to prick) + *-ion-*, *-io*, -ion — more at PUNGENT] **:** PRICKING, PUNCTURE

**punc·to·graph·ic** \;pəŋ(k)tə'grafik\ *adj* [fr. L *punctum* point + E *-o-* + *-graphic* — more at POINT] **:** of or relating to point writing or printing for the blind

**punc·tu·al** \'pəŋ(k)ch(əw)əl, -(k)sh-\ *adj* [ML *punctualis*, fr. L *punctus* pricking, point (fr. *punctus*, past part. of *pungere* to prick) + *-alis* -al — more at PUNGENT] **1 a :** of or relating to a point **b :** of or relating to punctuation **2 :** having the nature or a property of a point ⟨a ~ light source⟩: as **a :** belonging to a definite point of time ⟨achievements . . . are of a continuous rather than ~ nature —J.J.Obermann⟩ **b :** having fixity ⟨a ~ point in space⟩ **:** confined to a locale **:** CONCENTRATED ⟨a ~ seat of the soul —James Ward⟩ **c :** lacking extent or duration ⟨the particles which result from a quantizing of a wave equation appear to be ~ —Werner Heisenberg⟩ **3 :** pointed in expression or conception **:** being to the point **:** DEFINITE, EXPLICIT, ACCURATE; *also* **:** dealing or dealt with point by point **:** DETAILED ⟨with ~ care —William Wordsworth⟩ **4 :** marked by attention to small details and nice points **:** particular about minutiae **:** PUNCTILIOUS **5 a :** marked by exact adherence to an appointed time ⟨~, commonplace, keeping all appointments —L.P.Smith⟩ ⟨attracted notice by his ~ discharge of his duties —J.A.Froude⟩ **b :** marked by a regular predictable time schedule without unexpected deviation ⟨in a land of ~ trains —Alzada Comstock⟩ ⟨~ revolution of the seasons —Osbert Sitwell⟩ **6 :** PERFECTIVE 2 **syn** see CAREFUL

**punc·tu·al·i·ty** \,pəŋ(k)chə'waləd·ē, -(k)sh-, -lətē, -i\ *n* -ES [*punctual* + *-ity*] **1 :** the quality or state of being punctual; *esp* **:** the characteristic of being prompt in keeping engagements **2** *obs* **a :** a fine or nice point **:** an instance of precision, scrupulosity, fastidiousness, or punctiliousness **b :** a requisite of behavior or etiquette **:** PUNCTILIO **3 :** punctilious observance **:** PUNCTILIOUSNESS ⟨strictest ~ to the family hours would be expected —Jane Austen⟩

**punc·tu·al·ly** \'pəŋ(k)ch(əw)əlē, -(k)sh-, -li\ *adv* **1 :** in a punctual manner **:** PRECISELY **2 :** PROMPTLY

**punc·tu·al·ness** *n* -ES [*punctual* + *-ness*] **:** PUNCTUALITY, EXACTNESS

**[1]punc·tu·ate** \'pəŋ(k)chə,wāt, -(k)sh-, *usu* -ād.+V\ *vb* -ED/-ING/-S [ML *punctuatus*, past part. of *punctuare* to point, fr. L *punctus* pricking, point, fr. *punctus*, past part. of *pungere* to prick — more at PUNGENT] *vt* **1 :** to mark or divide (written or printed matter) with punctuation marks in order to clarify the meaning and separate structural units **2 :** to break into or interrupt at intervals ⟨the steady click of her needles *punctuated* the silence —Edith Wharton⟩ ⟨she *punctuated* his petitions with Amens —Alan Paton⟩ ⟨meetings *punctuated* by brief recesses —Lindesay Parrott⟩ ⟨her career was *punctuated* by a series of mishaps —*Harper's*⟩ ⟨the many odysseys which have *punctuated* his life —Polly Adler⟩ **3 :** to set off by contrast **:** ACCENTUATE, EMPHASIZE ⟨her heels . . . *punctuated* the declaration of finality as they clicked along the sidewalk —Helen Howe⟩ ⟨raising of a finger *punctuating* the lively lingo of the auctioneer —*Amer. Guide Series: La.*⟩ ⟨the music . . . with enough beat to ~ it —Harold Sinclair⟩ ⟨copious tears ~ their bitter tale of financial woe —B.B.Seligman⟩ ⟨brilliant solid color is *punctuated* by the blackest black —Rosamund Frost⟩ ⟨dress with beige top and caramel skirt, *punctuated* at the waistline with a black patent belt —*Women's Wear Daily*⟩ ⟨the sun was *punctuating* the sky —Sabine Gova⟩ ~ *vi* **:** to use punctuation marks

**[2]punc·tu·ate** \-,wət, -,wāt\ *adj* [L *punctus* point + E *-ate*] **:** PUNCTATE, DOTTED

**punc·tu·a·tion** \,pəŋ(k)chə'wāshən, -(k)sh-\ *n* -s [ML *punctuation-*, *punctuatio*, fr. *punctuatus* (past part. of *punctuare* to point) + *-ion-*, *-io* -ion — more at PUNCTUATE] **1 :** the act or an instance of punctuating **:** the character of being punctuated ⟨the ~ of the infinite stretch of time by periodic world conflagration —Catherine Rau⟩ ⟨the emotional impact of explosions used as a ~ —*Modern Music*⟩ ⟨the occasional ~ of a siren call, as either a squad car or an ambulance dashes through —Burns Mantle⟩ **2 :** the act, practice, or system of inserting various standardized marks or signs in written or printed matter in order to clarify the meaning and separate structural units **:** the division of written or printed matter (as into sentences or clauses) by means of punctuation marks **3 :** a system of vowel points and accents used in writing Hebrew and other Semitic languages

**punc·tu·a·tion·al** \;=='wāshənᵊl, -āshnəl\ *adj* [*punctuation* + *-al*] **:** of or relating to punctuation

**punctuation mark** *n* **:** any of various standardized marks or signs used in punctuation — compare APOSTROPHE, BRACE, BRACKET, COLON, COMMA, DASH, DIAGONAL, ELLIPSIS, EXCLAMATION POINT, HYPHEN, PARENTHESIS, PERIOD, QUESTION MARK, QUOTATION MARK, SEMICOLON, VIRGULE

**punc·tu·a·tive** \'==,wād·iv\ *adj* [*punctuate* + *-ive*] **:** PUNCTUATIONAL

**punc·tu·a·tor** \-d·ə(r)\ *n* -s [*punctuate* + *-or*] **:** one that punctuates

**punc·tu·late** \'pəŋ(k)chələt, -(k)sh-, -,lāt\ *adj* [NL *punctulatus*, fr. L *punctulum* (dim. of *punctum* puncture, point) + *-atus* -ate — more at POINT] **:** marked with small spots; *specif* **:** minutely punctate

**punc·tu·lat·ed** \-,lād·əd\ *adj* [*punctulate* + *-ed*] **:** PUNCTULATE

**punc·tu·la·tion** \,==ˈlāshən\ *n* -s [*punctulate* + *-ion*] **:** the state of being punctulate

**punc·tu·lum** \'pəŋ(k)chələm, -(k)sh-\ *n, pl* **punctu·la** \-lə\ [NL, fr. L, small puncture, small point — more at PUNCTULATE] **:** PUNCTURE

**punc·tum** \'pəŋ(k)təm\ *n, pl* **punc·ta** \-tə\ [L, puncture, point — more at POINT] **1** *obs* **:** POINT **2 :** a small area marked off in any way from a surrounding surface **:** DOT, PUNCTURE ⟨a ~ in a fossil shell⟩ ⟨insect bites . . . may show the central tiny hemorrhagic ~ —*Jour. Amer. Med. Assoc.*⟩ **3 :** a neume indicating a single note which is usu. higher than that preceding

**punc·tur·able** \'pəŋ(k)chərəbəl, -(k)sh-\ *adj* **:** capable of being punctured

**punc·tur·ation** \,pəŋ(k)chə'rāshən, -(k)shə'-\ *n* -s [[2]*puncture* + *-ation*] **1 :** an act or process of puncturing or state of being punctured **2 :** form or arrangement of punctures ⟨~ fine, the punctures separated by slightly more than their own diameter —*Jour. of the N.Y. Entomological Society*⟩

**[1]punc·ture** \'pəŋ(k)chə(r), -(k)sh-\ *n* -s [L *punctura*, prick, puncture, fr. *punctus* (past part. of *pungere* to prick) + *-ura* -ure — more at PUNGENT] **1 :** act of puncturing **:** perforation with something pointed **2 :** a hole, slight wound, or other perforation made by puncturing ⟨the ~ of a hypodermic needle⟩ ⟨a ~ wound made by a thorn⟩; *specif* **:** an accidental perforation in a pneumatic tire **3 :** a minute depression like one made by a point ⟨a shallow ~ on an insect's thorax⟩

**[2]puncture** \"\ *vb* **punctured; punctured; puncturing** \-chəriŋ, -sh(ə)riŋ\ **punctures** *vt* **1 :** to pierce with a pointed instrument or object **:** PRICK **:** make a puncture in ⟨~ the skin with a needle⟩ **2 :** to suffer a puncture of ⟨*punctured* his new tire⟩ **3 :** to deflate or make useless or absurd as if by a puncture **:** DESTROY ⟨~ one's ego⟩ ⟨~ an illusion⟩ ⟨~ a fallacy⟩ ⟨~ pretensions⟩ **4 :** to pass a spark discharge through (an insulator) ~ *vi* **:** to become punctured **syn** see PERFORATE

**punc·tured** \-(r)d\ *adj* [[1]*puncture* + *-ed*] **:** having the surface covered with minute indentations or dots **:** PUNCTATE ⟨an insect with scutellum obsoletely ~⟩

**punctured stamp** *n* [fr. past part. of [2]*puncture*] **:** a postage stamp with perforated initials

**punc·ture·less** \-(r)ləs\ *adj* **1 :** being without punctures **2 :** incapable of being punctured

**puncture vine** *or* **punctureweed** \'==,=\ *n* [[2]*puncture*] **:** a caltrop (*Tribulus terrestris*) having prickly fruits that puncture tires

**puncture voltage** *n* **:** the voltage at which an insulator is punctured electrically when subjected to a gradually increasing voltage

**punc·tus** \'pəŋ(k)təs\ *n* -ES [ML, fr. L, point — more at PUNCTUAL] **1 :** melody or melodic division in medieval music **2 :** DOT 2e(1)

**punctus con·tra punc·tum** \-,kän·trə'pəŋ(k)təm\ *adv* [ML] **:** melody against melody — used of early musical part writing; compare COUNTERPOINT

**pund** \'pu̇n(d)\ *dial var of* POUND

**pun·dit** \'pəndət, *usu* -əd.+V\ *n* -s [Hindi *paṇḍit*, fr. Skt *paṇḍita* learned, wise] **1 :** PANDIT **2 :** a learned man **:** TEACHER ⟨the fantastic ~ who was his tutor —John Gunther⟩ **3 :** an authority or one who announces judgments, opinions, or conclusions in an authoritative manner **:** CRITIC ⟨according to the ~*s*, the odds favor a breakout on the low, rather than the high, side of the market —*Wall Street Jour.*⟩ ⟨the ~*s* — most of the nationally known political reporters —*New Republic*⟩ ⟨when . . . the journalistic ~ talks commercial diplomacy —Norman Angell⟩ ⟨a staid and dependable literary ~ —*Times Lit. Supp.*⟩ ⟨musical ~*s* —R.G.Hubler⟩ ⟨the novel . . . has had moments at which the ~*s* have prophesied its decay —*Saturday Rev.*⟩

**pun·dit·ic** \,pən'did·ik\ *also* **pun·dit·i·cal** \-d·əkəl\ *adj* **:** of or relating to a pundit — **pun·dit·i·cal·ly** \-d·ək(ə)lē\ *adv*

**pun·dit·ry** \'pəndətrē\ *n* -ES [*pundit* + *-ry*] **:** the learning, methods, or pronouncements of pundits

**pun·do·nor** \,pu̇ndə'nō(ə)r\ *n, pl* **pundono·res** \-ō,rās\ [Sp, contr. of *punto de honor*] **:** a point of honor

**pu·nee** \'pünā·ä\ *n* -s [Hawaiian *pūne'e*] *Hawaii* **:** a movable couch

**punese** *var of* PUNAISE

**pung** \'pəŋ\ *n* -s [by shortening fr. earlier *tom-pong*, *tow-pong*, of Algonquian origin; akin to Micmac *tobâgun* drag made of skin — more at TOBOGGAN] *NewEng* **:** a rude oblong box on runners **:** a sleigh with a box-shaped body

**pun·ga·pung** \,pəŋ'gä,pəŋ\ *n* -s [Tag *pungapong*] **:** a Philippine aroid (*Amorphophallus campanulatus*) that has a putrid odor

**pun·gence** \'pənjən(t)s\ *n* -s [fr. [1]*pungent*, after such pairs as E *benevolent*: *benevolence*] **:** PUNGENCY ⟨smell, oily and a little fishy, with some ~ in it of herbs —Marjory S. Douglas⟩

**pun·gen·cy** \-jənsē, -si\ *n* -ES [[1]*pungent* + *-cy*] **1 :** the quality or state of being pungent **:** KEENNESS, SHARPNESS, POIGNANCY ⟨smoldering cigarettes have a harsh ~ of their own —Frances & Richard Lockridge⟩ ⟨the ~ of an aphorism⟩ ⟨~ of dialogue⟩ **2 :** something that is pungent (as an odor, taste, statement)

**[1]pun·gent** \-jənt\ *adj* [L *pungent-*, *pungens*, pres. part. of *pungere* to prick, sting; akin to L *pugio* dagger, *pugnus* fist, *pugnare* to fight, Gk *pygmē* fist, *peukedanos* sharp, piercing, *peukē* pine tree, OHG *fiuhta*] **1 :** having a stiff and sharp point **:** prickly-pointed ⟨a ~ ray on a fish⟩ ⟨~ leaves of holly⟩ **2 :** sharply painful **:** PENETRATING, PIERCING, STABBING, ACUTE ⟨our sympathy becomes so ~ —Leslie Stephen⟩ **3 a :** CAUSTIC, STINGING, BITING ⟨a ~ editorial⟩ ⟨~ humor⟩ ⟨a ~ truth⟩ **b :** POINTED, TELLING, STIMULATING ⟨fewer pages and shorter paragraphs help make it more ~ —H.T.Moore⟩ ⟨compiled a collection which should serve as a ~ antidote to much of the fuzzy thinking —R.B.Morris⟩ ⟨has drawn, with ~ finesse, the interior of a slum bistro —*Books of the Month*⟩ ⟨a place of ~ contrasts — of dull monotony and indiscreet adventure —E.M.Lustgarten⟩ **4 :** causing a sharp sensation **:** PRICKING, IRRITATING, ACRID ⟨the autumn's ~ smell of burning leaves⟩ ⟨tasting the ~ acidulous wood sorrel —John Burroughs⟩ ⟨some half-forgotten but still ~ memories —Virginia Woolf⟩ ⟨singers with coarse, ~ voices —H.F.Mooney⟩

**syn** PIQUANT, POIGNANT, RACY, SPICY, SNAPPY: PUNGENT may designate a sharp, piercing, stinging, biting, or penetrating quality, esp. of odors; it may suggest power to excite or stimulate keen interest or telling force and cogency ⟨the *pungent* odor of untanned leather⟩ ⟨the *pungent* reek of a strong cigar —A. Conan Doyle⟩ ⟨his *pungent* pen played its part in rousing the nation to its later struggle with the Crown —J.R.Green⟩ ⟨the mob needs concrete goals and the *pungent* thrill of hate in order to give vent to its destructive impulses —M.R.Cohen⟩ PIQUANT may indicate an interesting or appetizing tartness, sharpness, or pungency that stimulates or a zestful, arch, provocative, challenging, or exciting quality that is individual or peculiar ⟨a *piquant* sauce⟩ ⟨*piquant* with the tart sweet taste of green apples and sugar —Silas Spitzer⟩ ⟨*piquant* touch of innocent malice in his narration —G.G.Coulton⟩ ⟨those *piquant* incongruities, which are the chief material of wit —C.E.Montague⟩ POIGNANT may describe what is sharply or piercingly effective upon the senses or stirring to one's inmost consciousness or deepest emotions ⟨the air of romantic poverty which Rosalie found so tragically *poignant* —Elinor Wylie⟩ ⟨with *poignant* finality, as a lover might put away a rose from a lost romance —Agnes S. Turnbull⟩ ⟨a vague but *poignant* sense of discouragement that the sacrifices of the war had not been justified by its results spread over the country —Oscar Handlin⟩ RACY may suggest verve, dash, tang, or vitality manifested with lively free heartiness ⟨everybody who loves the language enough to want to keep it always young and *racy* ought to turn out too and keep the pedants from running amok —C.E.Montague⟩ ⟨a rare and *racy* sense of humor —W.S.Maugham⟩ SPICY describes what is seasoned or made redolent of spice; in extended uses it may suggest the piquant, smart, spirited, sensational, or scandalous ⟨flair for a *spicy* zestful vernacular in dialogue —Leslie Rees⟩ ⟨*spicy* tales of the type which usually appear in paperbound copies, in which bishops are forced to visit nudist camps in their underwear —Robertson Davies⟩ SNAPPY suggests briskness, animation, dash, wit, or risqué quality ⟨spoken in a *snappy*, matter-of-fact way —Vachel Lindsay⟩ ⟨the renditions, if not especially lovely, were at all times spirited, neat, and *snappy* —Virgil Thomson⟩

**[2]pungent** \"\ *n* -s **:** a pungent substance ⟨surprise is like a thrilling ~ upon a tasteless meat —Emily Dickinson⟩

**pun·gent·ly** *adv* **:** in a pungent manner ⟨write swiftly and ~, every word doing its work —Robert Payne⟩ **:** so as to be pungent ⟨~ flavored⟩

**pung·ey** *or* **pungy** \'pəŋgē\ *n, pl* **pungeys** *or* **pungies** [origin unknown] **1 :** a two-masted schooner for oyster dredging or fishing in Chesapeake Bay **2 :** CHESAPEAKE CANOE

pungey 1

**pun·gi** \'püŋgē\ *also* **poo·gye** \'pügē\ *n* -s [Hindi *pūgī*, *pūṅgī*] **:** a Hindu reed pipe with a globular mouthpiece and often a drone — called also *bin*

**pungitive** *adj* [ME, fr. ML *pungitivus*, irreg. fr. *pungere* to prick + *-ivus* -ive — more at PUNGENT] *obs* **:** tending to prick or sting **:** PUNGENT

**pun·gle** \'pəŋgəl\ *vb* -ED/-ING/-S [Sp *póngale* put it down] *vt* **:** to make a contribution or payment of (money) — usu. used with *up* ⟨Congress would ~ up that much money —*Time*⟩ ~ *vi* **:** to pay or contribute money — usu. used with *up* ⟨must ~ up for his fare —R.L.Neuberger⟩

**pun·gled** \'pəŋgəld\ *adj* [origin unknown] **:** SHRIVELED, SHRUNKEN — used esp. of grain robbed of its juices by insects

**pungs** *pl of* PUNG

**[1]pu·nic** \'pyünik, -nēk\ *adj, usu cap* [L *punicus*, fr. OL *poenicus*, fr. *Poenus* inhabitant of the Phoenician colony of Carthage (irreg. fr. Gk *Phoinix* Phoenician) + *-icus* -ic — more at PHOENICIAN] **1 :** of, relating to, or characteristic of the ancient Carthaginians **:** CARTHAGINIAN **2 :** FAITHLESS, TREACHEROUS

**[2]punic** \"\ *n* -s *usu cap* **:** the Phoenician dialect of ancient Carthage

**pu·ni·ca** \'pyünəkə\ *n, cap* [NL, fr. L *punicum* pomegranate, fr. *punicum malum*, lit., Punic apple] **:** a genus (coextensive with the family Punicaceae of the order Myrtales) comprising shrubs or small trees with showy solitary white to deep red sometimes double flowers that have numerous stamens and an ovary with the cells in two rows and are followed by an edible fruit which is technically a berry — see POMEGRANATE

**pu·nic·ic acid** \pyü'nisik-\ *n* [NL *punicum* pomegranate + E *-ic*] **:** a crystalline unsaturated fatty acid $C_4H_9(CH{=}CH)_3(CH_2)_7COOH$ that is a geometrical isomer of eleostearic acid and is obtained from oil of pomegranate

**pu·ni·cin** \'pyünəsən\ *n* -s [L *punicum* + ISV *-in*] **:** PELARGONIN

**punie** *obs var of* PUNY

**punier** *comparative of* PUNY

**punies** *pl of* PUNY

**puniest** *superlative of* PUNY

**pu·ni·ly** \'pyünᵊlē\ *adv* **:** in a puny manner

**pu·ni·ness** \-nēnəs\ *n* -ES **:** the quality or state of being puny

**pun·ish** \'pənish, -nēsh, *esp in pres part* -nəsh\ *vb* -ED/-ING/-ES [ME *punissen*, fr. MF *puniss-*, stem of *punir*, fr. L *punire*, fr. OL *poenire*, irreg. fr. *poena* penalty — more at PAIN] *vt* **1 :** to impose a penalty (as of pain, suffering, shame, strict restraint, or loss) upon for some fault, offense, or violation: **a :** to afflict (a person) with such a penalty for an offense ⟨the respectable not only obey the law, but ~ . . . those who refuse to do so —*Times Lit. Supp.*⟩ **b :** to inflict a penalty for (an offense) in retribution or retaliation ⟨the Sedition Act of 1798, designed to ~ attacks on the federal administration —Zechariah Chafee⟩ **2 a :** to deal with roughly or harshly ⟨the wife . . . who ~*ed* him with frenetic fits of nerves —Oscar Handlin⟩ **b :** to inflict injury or loss upon **:** HURT ⟨the ships were considerably ~*ed* by the batteries —P.G.Mackesy⟩ ⟨if you fined or imprisoned a man you ~*ed* his wife and children —Arnold Bennett⟩ **c :** DEPLETE, CONSUME ⟨a ~ a bottle of port⟩ **3 :** to score freely from (bowling or a bowler) **:** FLOG — used of a batsman in cricket ~ *vi* **:** to inflict punishment ⟨a ~*ing* race⟩ ⟨a ~*ing* defeat⟩

**syn** CHASTISE, CHASTEN, DISCIPLINE, CORRECT, CASTIGATE: PUNISH indicates some retribution inflicted after a fault, disobedience, or wrongdoing, usu. conscious or purposive; it may refer to any kind of transgression and any kind of penalty ⟨looked after a little more strictly than other children, and perhaps *punished* more —Margaret Deland⟩ ⟨no misdemeanor should be *punished* more severely than the most atrocious felonies —T.B.Macaulay⟩ CHASTISE is likely to suggest infliction of corporal pain, esp. by a parent, elder, or superior, and with the hope of effecting a reformation ⟨the father had to go over and give them a box or two on the ears, to quiet them down, but it turned into skylarking instead of *chastising* —O.E. Rölvaag⟩ CHASTEN is likely to suggest any affliction or trial, ranging from corporal punishment to worry, chagrin, tribulation, or duress, which leaves one humbled, more moderate, less extreme ⟨to devise means for *chastening* the stubborn heart of her husband —Rudyard Kipling⟩ ⟨heavier fines and jail sentences followed by disqualification from driving for life . . . would *chasten* most reckless and drunken drivers —Priscilla Hughes⟩ DISCIPLINE may involve punishing; it always suggests action in the interest of order, regularity, rule, or control by authority ⟨among the first recorded motions of the magistrates of the new court was the *disciplining* of Thomas Williams, who had said he did not see why the Duke of York had been such a fool as to make them the judges —*Amer. Guide Series: Del.*⟩ CORRECT may indicate chastening or punishing in the interest of amending or reforming, of guiding away from errors and lapses ⟨must know how to *correct* without wounding —J.M.Barzun⟩ CASTIGATE is likely to indicate a bitter, tongue-lashing denunciation or reprimand rather than any other form of punishment ⟨courageously patronizes democracy in England, and with equal courage *castigates* it at home —W.C.Brownell⟩

**punish·abil·i·ty** \,pənishə'biləd·ē\ *n* **:** PUNISHABLENESS

**pun·ish·able** \'pənishəbəl, -nēsh-\ *adj* [perh. fr. MF *punissable*, fr. *puniss-* (stem of *punir*) + *-able* — more at PUNISH] **:** deserving of, or liable to, punishment **:** capable of being punished by law or right ⟨~ offenders⟩ ⟨a ~ offense⟩ — **pun·ish·ably** \-blē\ *adv*

**pun·ish·able·ness** *n* **:** the quality or state of being punishable

**pun·ish·er** \'pənishə(r)\ *n* -s [ME *punisere*, fr. *punissen* to punish + *-ere* -er] **:** one that inflicts punishment

**pun·ish·ment** \'pənishmənt, -nēsh-\ *n* -s [ME *punisshement*, fr. MF *punissement*, fr. *puniss-* (stem of *punir* to punish) + *-ment*] **1 :** the act of punishing **:** the infliction of a penalty **2 a :** retributive suffering, pain, or loss **:** PENALTY ⟨rewards and ~*s* serve as the incentives to learning —L.W.Doob⟩ **b :** a penalty inflicted by a court of justice on a convicted offender **:** a penalty for an offense and for reformation and prevention; *broadly* **:** any damage or pain inflicted on an offender through judicial procedure aiming at either prevention, retribution, or reformation — compare CRUEL AND UNUSUAL PUNISHMENT **3 :** severe, rough, or disastrous treatment ⟨the fighter had been subjected to heavy ~ in his losing bout —*N.Y.Times*⟩ ⟨parts in your automobile take thousands of miles of ~ without becoming tired —*Hot-Metal Magic*⟩ ⟨the aggressor would receive terrific ~ which might well destroy the whole of his warmaking potential —A.P.Ryan⟩

**pu·ni·tion** \pyü'nishən\ *n* -s [ME *punicion*, fr. MF *punition*, fr. L *punition-*, *punitio*, fr. *punitus* (past part. of *punire*) + *-ion-*, *-io* -ion — more at PUNISH] **:** PUNISHMENT ⟨smarting from her latest ~ —Rosamond Lehmann⟩

**pu·ni·tive** \'pyünəd·|iv, -ət|\ *adj* [F *punitif*, fr. ML *punitivus*, fr. L *punitus* + *-ivus* -ive] **1 :** inflicting, awarding, or involving punishment or penalties **:** aiming at punishment ⟨a ~ law⟩ ⟨~ justice⟩ ⟨a ~ expedition⟩ **2 :** constituting or serving as a severe or discriminatory penalty ⟨~ taxes⟩ — **pu·ni·tive·ly** \|əvlē, -li\ *adv* — **pu·ni·tive·ness** \|ivnəs\ *n* -ES

**punitive damages** *n pl* **:** damages awarded in excess of compensatory damages or nominal damages to punish a defendant for a gross wrong — called also *exemplary damages*

**pu·ni·to·ry** \'pyünə,tōrē, -tȯr-, -ri\ *adj* [L *punitus* + E *-ory*] **:** having the nature of a punishment **:** PUNITIVE

**[1]pun·ja·bi** \,pən'jäbē, -jabē\ *n* -s *cap* [Hindi *pañjābī*, adj. & n.] **1 :** a native or inhabitant of the Punjab region of northwestern India **2 :** PANJABI 2

**[2]punjabi** \"\ *adj, usu cap* [Hindi *pañjābī*, fr. Per, fr. *Pañjāb* Punjab, region of northwestern India] **:** of or relating to the Punjab or its inhabitants

**[1]punk** \'pəŋk\ *n* -s [origin unknown; in sense 2, prob. partly fr. [3]*punk*] **1** *archaic* **:** PROSTITUTE, STRUMPET **2 a :** something or someone worthless or inferior **b :** NONSENSE, BUNKUM

⟨these flowers are a lot of ~ —Roger Williams⟩ ⟨~ about feeding tired skins —*Books of the Month*⟩ **3 a :** a young and inexperienced person **:** BEGINNER, NOVICE; *esp* **:** a young man **:** BOY **b :** a young gangster, hoodlum, or ruffian **:** a petty criminal **c** *slang* **:** a youth used as a homosexual partner ⟨the young boy, known in prison parlance as a ~ —N.K.Teeters & J.O.Reinemann⟩ **d :** a young tramp **e :** a stupid, naïve, or foolish person **:** JERK **4 :** a young untrained circus elephant

**2punk** \"\ *adj* -ER/-EST **:** very poor in quality **:** BAD, INFERIOR, MISERABLE ⟨meanwhile went from poor to ~ —*Time*⟩ ⟨looked ~ in a bathing suit —D.C.Loughlin⟩ ⟨a ~ liar —Josephine Johnson⟩

**3punk** \"\ *n* -s [perh. alter. (infl. by Delaware *punk* fine ashes, powder) of *spunk*] **1 :** wood that is so decayed as to be very dry, crumbly, and useful for tinder **2 :** a dry spongy substance prepared from the sporophores of various fungi of the genus *Fomes* (esp. *F. fomentarius* and *F. igniarius*) by removing the outer rind, slicing and pounding the sporophore until soft and flexible, dipping or sometimes boiling in a solution of potassium nitrate, and then drying and forming into molded sticks that are used to ignite fuses esp. of fireworks **3 :** the leathery or woody sporophore of a polypore **:** CONCH

**4punk** \"\ *adj* **1 :** having a dry flavorless flesh — used of fruits and vegetables **2 :** PUNKY

**pun·kah** *also* **pun·ka** \'pəŋkə\ *n* -s [Hindi *pākhā* fan, fr. Skt *pakṣa* wing; akin to Skt *pakṣas* wing — more at PECTORAL] **:** an Indian device for fanning a room consisting of a frame covered with cloth and suspended from the ceiling or a large fan held in the hand; *also* **:** a fanning device (as an electric fan)

**punkah wal·lah** \-'wälə\ *n* **:** the operator of a punkah

**punk·ie** *also* **punky** \'pəŋkē\ *n, pl* **punkies** [D dial. (New Amsterdam) *punki*, fr. Delaware *punk*, lit., fine ashes, powder] **:** BITING MIDGE

**punkin** *var of* PUMPKIN

**punk oak** *n* [1*punk*] **:** POSSUM OAK

**punk out** *vi* [1*punk* + *out*] **:** to back out

**punk tree** *n* [1*punk*] **:** CAJEPUT 1

**punkwood** \'=,=\ *n* **:** rotten wood; *esp* **:** wood permeated by the mycelium of pore fungi and frequently luminescent — compare 3PUNK 1

**punky** \'pəŋkē\ *adj* -ER/-EST [1*punk* + *-y*] **1 :** of, relating to, or like punk ⟨a ~ splintering of water-soaked wood —Ruth Moore⟩ **2 :** SMOLDERING **:** SLOW-BURNING

**pun·less** \'pənləs\ *adj* **:** lacking puns

**punned** *past of* PUN

**1pun·ner** \'pənə(r)\ *n* -s [1*pun* + *-er*] **:** one that rams, tamps, packs, or consolidates by ramming; *specif* **:** a ramming tool

**2punner** \"\ *n* -s [3*pun* + *-er*] **:** PUNSTER

**punner bar** *n* [1*punner*] **:** a combined punner and crowbar

**pun·net** \'pənət\ *n* -s [origin unknown] *chiefly Brit* **:** a chip basket or berry basket for fruit (as strawberries)

**punning** *pres part of* PUN

**pun·ning·ly** *adv* **:** in a punning manner

**pun·ny** \'pənē\ *adj* -ER/-EST [2*pun* + *-y*] **:** constituting or involving a pun ⟨a ~ slogan⟩ ⟨a ~ farce⟩

**puno** *var of* PUNA

**puns** *pl of* PUN, *pres 3d sing of* PUN

**pun·ster** \'pənztə(r), 'pən(t)st-\ *n* -s [2*pun* + *-ster*] **:** one who puns; *esp* **:** one who is skilled in or addicted to punning

**1punt** \'pənt\ *n* -s [fr. (assumed) ME, fr. OE, fr. L *ponton-*, *ponto* floating bridge, punt — more at PONTOON] **1 a :** a long narrow flat-bottomed boat with square ends usu. propelled with a pole **b :** a flat-bottomed boat esp. of broad beam **2 :** KICK 8 ⟨many bottles . . . have a concave bottom, or ~, to give added strength —O.A.Mendelsohn⟩

**2punt** \"\ *vb* -ED/-ING/-S *vt* **1 :** to propel (as a punt) by pushing with a pole against the bottom **2 :** to convey in a punt ~ *vi* **:** to boat or hunt in a punt

**3punt** \"\ *n* -s [F or Sp; F *ponte*, fr. Sp *punto* point, fr. L *punctum* — more at POINT] **1 :** a point in some games of chance (as basset) **2 :** 1PUNTER a **3 :** a play made against the banker (as in faro)

**4punt** \"\ *vi* -ED/-ING/-S [F *ponter*, fr. *ponte*] **1 :** to play at a gambling game against the banker **2** *Brit* **:** GAMBLE, BET ⟨in the baccarat room, ~*ing* —Max Beerbohm⟩ ⟨arguing horses in the morning, ~*ing* on them by phone and radio during . . . afternoon —Leslie Rees⟩

**5punt** \"\ *vb* -ED/-ING/-S [origin unknown] *vt* **:** to kick (a ball) in football, soccer, or rugby before the ball dropped from the hands hits the ground ~ *vi* **:** to punt a ball ⟨unable to advance after receiving the kickoff and ~*ed* —*N.Y.Times*⟩

**6punt** \"\ *n* -s **1 :** the act or an instance of punting a ball: as **a :** a kick used by the goalkeeper in soccer to clear the ball **b :** a kick in football made esp. on fourth down to gain ground when relinquishing possession of the ball **2 :** a punted ball ⟨returned a ~ 67 yards for a touchdown —*N.Y.Times*⟩

**1punt·er** \'pəntə(r)\ *n* -s [4*punt* + *-er*] **:** one that gambles: as **a :** a player who bets against the banker in a gambling game **b :** one that bets against a bookmaker ⟨~*s* who keep Britain's £1,500,000-a-week pools booming —*Australian Monthly*⟩ **c** *Brit* **:** SCALPER c(1)

**2punter** \"\ *n* -s [1*punt* + *-er*] **1 :** one that uses a punt for boating or shooting **2 :** SERVITOR 4

**3punter** \"\ *n* -s [5*punt* + *-er*] **:** one that punts a ball (as a football)

**punt formation** *n* [5*punt*] **:** an offensive football formation in which a back making a punt stands approximately 10 yards behind the line and the other backs are in blocking position close to the line of scrimmage

**punt gun** *n* [1*punt*] **:** a smooth-bored gun firing a large charge of shot fixed on a swivel in a punt and used in killing waterfowl

**pun·til** \'pənt<sup></sup>l\ *n* -s [F *pontil* — more at PONTIL] **:** PUNTY

**pun·til·la** \pün·'tē(y)ə\ *n* -s [MexSp, dim. of Sp *punta*, *punto* point, fr. L *punctum* — more at POINT] **:** a dagger used to sever a bull's spinal cord in bullfighting

**pun·ti·lle·ro** \,püntē'ye(,)rō\ *n* -s [MexSp, fr. *puntilla* + Sp *-ero* -er] **:** one who delivers the coup de grace to a dying bull in bullfighting

puntilla

**punt·latsh** \'pənt,lach\ *or* **pent·latch** \'pen-\ *n, pl* **puntlatsh** *or* **puntlatshes** *or* **pentlatch** *or* **pentlatches** *usu cap* **1 a :** a Salishan people of the east coast of Vancouver Island, British Columbia **b :** a member of such people **2 :** the language of the Puntlatsh people

**punt·man** \'pəntmən\ *also* **punts·man** \-tsm-\ *n, pl* **puntmen** *also* **puntsmen** [1*punt* + *man*] **:** 2PUNTER 1

**1pun·to** \'pən·(,)tō\ *n* -s [It, fr. L *punctum* — more at POINT] **1 :** a hit in fencing **:** POINT **2** *obs* **:** a point of punctilio

**2pun·to** \'pün·(,)tō\ *or* **pon·to** \'pän-\ *n* -s [Sp, lit., point, fr. L *punctum*] **:** the ace of trumps when trumps are red (as in ombre)

**3pun·to** \'pün(,)tō\ *n* -s [It, fr. L *punctum* point] **:** POINT, STITCH — used esp. in combination of lace or embroidery of Spanish or Italian origin

**punts** *pl of* PUNT, *pres 3d sing of* PUNT

**pun·ty** *also* **pon·tee** *or* **pun·tee** *or* **pon·ty** \'pəntē, 'pän-\ *n, pl* **punties** *also* **pontes** *or* **pontees** *or* **puntees** *or* **ponties** [F *pontil* — more at PONTIL] **:** a solid metal rod used for fashioning hot glass to which it is attached by a button of glass first gathered on the rod — called also *pontil*

**pu·nuk** \'pü,nük\ *adj, usu cap* [fr. *Punuk*, group of islets southeast of Saint Lawrence Island in the Bering sea] **:** of or belonging to an Eskimo culture of northeastern Siberia, northwestern Alaska, and St. Lawrence Island of about A.D. 500–1000 characterized by sea-mammal hunting, knives and carving tools with iron points, and a circle and dot decorative design

**1pu·ny** \'pyünē, -ni\ *adj* -ER/-EST [MF *puisné* younger, lit., born afterward, fr. *puis* afterward (fr. — assumed — VL *postius*, compar. of L *post* after, afterward) + *né* born — more at POST-, NÉ] **1** *obs* **a :** PUISNE **b :** JUNIOR **c :** RECENT, SUBSEQUENT **d :** INEXPERIENCED, UNSKILLED **2 :** slight or inferior in power, vigor, size, or importance **:** lacking in force or vitality **:** WEAK, INSIGNIFICANT, SICKLY ⟨was cowed by their indifference to him, and felt ~ —G.D.Brown⟩ ⟨man's mechanical skill has permitted him to raise to the nth power his ~ strength —E.A.Hooton⟩ ⟨pitted my ~ opinion against the judgment of the medical world —V.G.Heiser⟩ ⟨the sun is not the only heavenly body which ~ man attempts to coerce by his magic —J.G.Frazer⟩ **syn** see PETTY

**2puny** *n* -ES [MF *puisné* younger son, fr. *puisné*, adj.] *obs* **:** PUISNE, JUNIOR, NOVICE, SUBORDINATE

**pun·ya** \'pənyə\ *n* -s [Skt *puṇya*, fr. neut. of *puṇya* auspicious, beautiful, good] *Jainism* **:** GOOD, MERIT — compare 6PAPA

**1pup** \'pəp\ *n* -s [short for 1*puppy*] **1 a :** a young dog **:** PUPPY **b :** one of the young of various other animals esp. of the dog family or of some marine mammals (as seals or sea otters) **2 :** an inexperienced or objectionably brash person ⟨men did the work in those days; these young ~*s* hardly knew the meaning of the word —John Galsworthy⟩ ⟨loathed going to this red-haired young ~ for supplies —Joseph Whitehill⟩ **3** *slang* **:** a prospect of apparent promise that fails of realization; *esp* **:** an investment that turns out to be relatively worthless ⟨had sold him a racehorse for $1,600 which turned out to be a ~ —*Time*⟩

**2pup** \"\ *vi* **pupped; pupped; pupping; pups** [short for 2*puppy*] **:** to bring forth pups or young

**pu·pa** \'pyüpə\ *n, pl* **pu·pae** \-ü,pē\ *or* **pupas** [NL, fr. L *pupa* girl, doll — more at PUPIL] **1 :** an insect in an intermediate usu. quiescent form that is assumed by an insect with complete metamorphosis between the larval and the imaginal stages, is enclosed in a hardened cuticle and often in a cocoon or case formed by the larva, and is characterized by internal dedifferentiation of larva structures and their replacement by structures typical of the imago which arise from imaginal disks — see CHRYSALIS; ANT illustration **2 :** the stage in an insect's life cycle in which it is a pupa

**pupa co·arc·ta·ta** \-,kō,ärk'täd·ə\ *n, pl* **pupae coarcta·tae** \-d·,ē\ [NL, lit., coarctate pupa] **:** a pupa in which the larval skin is retained as a pupal covering — compare COARCTATE

**pu·pal** \'pyüpəl\ *adj* **:** of, relating to, or characteristic of a pupa

**pupa li·be·ra** \-'libərə\ *n, pl* **pupae libe·rae** \-bə,rē\ [NL, lit., free pupa] **:** a typical pupa in which the limbs are free

**pupa ob·tec·ta** \-äb'tektə\ *n, pl* **pupae obtec·tae** \-k,tē\ [NL, lit., obtected pupa] **:** a typical pupa (as the chrysalis of most lepidopterans) in which the appendages are closely bound to the body

**pu·par·i·al** \pyü'pa(a)rēəl\ *adj* [NL *puparium* + E *-al*] **:** of, relating to, or having the characteristics of a puparium

**pu·par·i·um** \-ēəm\ *n, pl* **pupar·ia** \-ēə\ [NL, fr. *pupa* + L *-arium*] **:** the outer shell formed from the larval skin that covers a coarctate pupa

**pupa shell** *n* **:** a small pupa-shaped shell of the family Pupillidae or a related form

**pu·pate** \'pyü,pāt\ *vi* -ED/-ING/-S [NL *pupa* + E *-ate*] **1 :** to become a pupa **2 :** to pass through a pupal state

**pu·pa·tion** \pyü'pāshən\ *n* -s **:** the act or process of pupating

**pupfish** \'=,=\ *n* [1*pup* + *fish*] **:** either of two tiny cyprinodont fishes (*Cyprinodon nevadensis* and *C. diabolis*) of warm streams and springs of Nevada

**pu·pi·dae** \'pyüpə,dē\ [NL, fr. *Pupa*, type genus (fr. *pupa*) + *-idae*] *syn of* PUPILLIDAE

**pu·pif·er·ous** \(')pyü'pif(ə)rəs\ *adj* [NL *pupa* + E *-iferous*] **:** producing sexual individuals — used of the parthenogenetic generation of an aphid

**pu·pi·form** \'pyüpə,fórm\ *adj* [NL *pupa* + E *-iform*] **:** shaped like a pupa **:** PUPAL

**pu·pig·e·nous** \(')pyü'pijənəs\ *adj* [NL *pupa* + *-i-* + E *-genous*] **:** PUPIPAROUS

**pu·pig·er·ous** \-j(ə)rəs\ *adj* [NL *pupa* + E *-igerous*] **:** bearing or containing a pupa — used of dipterous larvae that do not molt when the pupa is formed within them but retain the larval skin as a pupal covering

**1pu·pil** \'pyüpəl\ *n* -s [ME *pupille*, fr. MF, fr. L *pupillus* male ward, *pupilla* female ward; L *pupillus* fr. dim. of *pupus* boy; L *pupilla* fr. dim. of *pupa* girl, doll, puppet; prob. akin to L *puer* boy — more at PUERILE] **1 :** *Roman & Scots civil law* **:** a boy or a girl under the age of puberty and in the care of a guardian **2 :** a child or young person in school or in the charge of a tutor or instructor **:** STUDENT 1a **3 :** one who has been taught or influenced by a person of fame or distinction **:** DISCIPLE ⟨was a ~ of the great Stoic philosopher . . . and wrote a voluminous commentary to a work of his —Benjamin Farrington⟩

**2pupil** \"\ *n* -s [MF *pupille* pupil of the eye, fr. L *pupilla*, fr. dim. of *pupa* girl, doll, puppet; fr. the tiny image of oneself seen reflected in another's eye] **1 :** the contractile aperture in the iris of the eye that is round in most vertebrates whether enlarged or contracted but in foxes and cats becomes elliptical like a slit when contracted — see EYE illustration **2 :** the central dark spot of an ocellus

**pu·pil·age** *or* **pu·pil·lage** \-lij\ *n* -s [1*pupil* + *-age*] **:** the condition or period of being or of being like a pupil

**1pu·pil·ar** *also* **pu·pil·lar** \-lə(r)\ *adj* [1*pupil* + *-ar*] **:** 1PUPILLARY

**2pupilar** *also* **pupillar** \"\ *adj* [2*pupil* + *-ar*] **:** 2PUPILLARY

**pu·pil·ize** *or* **pu·pil·lize** \-pə,līz\ *vb* -ED/-ING/-S [1*pupil* + *-ize*] *archaic* **:** TEACH, COACH

**pu·pil·lar·i·ty** *also* **pu·pi·lar·i·ty** \,pyüpə'larəd·ē\ *n* -ES [MF *pupillarité* state of being a minor ward, fr. *pupillaire* pupillary + *-ité* -ity] **:** the period of growth before puberty

**1pu·pil·lary** \'pyüpə,lerē, -ri\ *adj* [F *pupillaire*, fr. L *pupillaris* of a ward, fr. *pupillus* ward + *-aris* -ar — more at PUPIL] **:** of or relating to a pupil or ward

**2pupillary** *also* **pu·pi·lary** \"\ *adj* [L *pupilla* pupil of the eye + E *-ary*] **:** of or relating to the pupil of the eye

**pupillary reflex** *n* [2*pupillary*] **:** the contraction of the pupil in response to light entering the eye

**pupillary substitution** *n* [trans. of L *substitutio pupillaris*] *Roman & civil Law* **:** the substitution by a father in his will of another heir for his own descendant instituted heir who is below the age of puberty and under the father's power for the purpose of having the substitute heir succeed to his own and the descendant's property if the descendant declines the inheritance or dies before attaining puberty when he could make his own will — compare QUASI-PUPILLARY SUBSTITUTION

**pu·pil·late** *also* **pu·pil·ate** \'pyüpə,lāt, -lət\ *adj* [NL *pupillatus*, fr. L *pupilla* pupil of the eye + *-atus* -ate] **:** OCELLATED — used of a color spot

**pu·pil·less** \'pyüpəlləs\ *adj* **:** having no pupil

**pu·pil·li·dae** \pyü'pilə,dē\ *n pl, cap* [NL, fr. *Pupilla*, type genus (fr. dim. of *pupa*) + *-idae*] **:** a large family of usu. small pulmonate land snails having a long spiral often somewhat cylindrical shell generally with a narrowed and more or less toothed aperture — compare PUPA SHELL

**pupillo-** *comb form* [L *pupilla* pupil of the eye] **:** pupil ⟨*pupillodilator*⟩

**pupil load** *n* [1*pupil*] **:** the total number of pupils assigned to a single teacher in a school for classroom or other instruction

**pu·pil·lo·dilator** \;pyüpəlō+\ *adj* [*pupillo-* + *dilator*] **:** having a dilative effect on or involving dilation of the pupil of the eye

**pu·pil·lom·e·ter** \,pyüpə'lämәd·ə(r)\ *n* [*pupillo-* + *-meter*] **:** an instrument for measuring the diameter of the pupil of the eye — **pu·pil·lom·e·try** \-mə·trē\ *n* -ES

**pu·pil·lo·motor** \;pyüpəlō+\ *adj* [*pupillo-* + *motor*] **:** having a motor influence on or involving alteration of the pupil of the eye ⟨~ nerve fibers⟩ ⟨a ~ reflex⟩

**pupil teacher** *n* [1*pupil*] **:** STUDENT TEACHER

**pu·pin system** \pyü'pēn-\ *n, usu cap P* [after Michael I. *Pupin* †1935 Am. physicist and inventor] **:** a telephone communication system in which the fidelity of the transmission is increased by introducing inductance coils in the line at definite equal intervals

**pu·pip·a·ra** \pyü'pipərə\ *n pl, cap* [NL, fr. *pupa* + *-i-* + *-para* (fr. L, neut. pl. of *-parus* -parous)] **:** a division of Diptera in which the young are born as mature maggots ready to become pupae (as of the sheep ked or horse tick)

**pu·pip·a·rous** \-rəs\ *adj* [NL *pupa* + *-i-* + E *-parous*] **1 :** producing mature larvae that are ready to pupate at birth ⟨~ insects⟩ **2 :** of or relating to the Pupipara ⟨~ anatomy⟩

**pu·poid** \'pyü,pòid\ *adj* [NL *pupa* + E *-oid*] **:** PUPIFORM

**pupped** *past of* PUP

**pup·pet** \'pəpət, *usu* -əd·+V\ *n* -s *often attrib* [ME *popet*, fr. MF *poupette* little doll, dim. of (assumed) *poupe* doll (whence F *poupée* doll), fr. (assumed) VL *puppa*, alter. of L *pupa* girl, doll, puppet — more at PUPIL] **1 a :** a small-scale figure of a human or other living being often constructed with jointed limbs, appropriately painted and costumed, and moved usu. on a small stage by a rod or by hand from below or by strings or wires from above — see MARIONETTE **b** *obs* **:** an actor in a play or pantomime **2 a** *archaic* **:** IDOL 1a **b :** DOLL 1a **3** *archaic* **:** a vain gaudily dressed person **4 :** one whose acts are controlled by an outside force or influence ⟨is no longer the arbiter of his own situation, but rather the ~ of circumstance —Joseph Furphy⟩ ⟨felt that they were after all mere ~*s*, creatures he could use —Sherwood Anderson⟩: **a :** a political or governmental official acting in an ostensibly independent or discretionary capacity but actually carrying out instructions from another authority or source ⟨eager to succeed, yet empty of policy and the ~ of his country's enemies —Hilaire Belloc⟩ ⟨their satellites and ~*s* and collaborators have indisputably recorded the actual nature of their governance —Walter Millis⟩ **b :** a character in literature that serves chiefly as an agent of the author's designs without exhibiting or developing a distinct personality or a logical motivation ⟨his personages are mere ~*s*, or, at best, incarnations of abstract qualities, or idealizations of disembodied grace or beauty —Richard Garnett †1906⟩ ⟨they are not characters; they are ~*s* needed to establish certain information —John Van Druten⟩ **5** *obs* **:** PUPPY **6 :** a lathe poppet

**1pup·pe·teer** \,pəpə'ti(ə)r, -iə\ *n* -s [*puppet* + *-eer*] **:** one who manipulates puppets or marionettes

**2puppeteer** \"\ *vi* -ED/-ING/-S **:** to perform the functions or work of a puppeteer ⟨in whose show she ~*ed* —Paul McPharlin⟩

**puppet government** *n* **:** a government which is endowed with the outward symbols of authority but in which direction and control are exercised by another power

**pup·pet·ize** \'pəpə,tīz\ *vt* -ED/-ING/-S **:** to make into or like a puppet ⟨tendency . . . to ~ his characters —*Nineteenth Century*⟩

**puppet master** *n* **:** one who makes and entertains with puppets

**puppet player** *n* **:** one that manages puppets in a puppet show

**pup·pet·ry** \'pəpətrē, -ri\ *n* -ES [*puppet* + *-ry*] **1** *archaic* **:** MUMMERY 2 ⟨the low ~ of thrones —S.T.Coleridge⟩ **2 :** the production or creation of puppets or puppet shows ⟨this yearbook . . . is one of the outstanding contributions to ~ —*Quarterly Jour. of Speech*⟩ ⟨a thriving center of ~ —Barry Carman⟩ **3 :** the creation or presence in a literary work of an inadequately motivated character or group of characters ⟨a great modern writer . . . capable in activity of presenting thoughtful women, thinking men, groaned over his ~, that he dared not animate them —George Meredith⟩

**puppet show** *or* **puppet play** *n* **:** a usu. dramatic performance staged with puppets with the dialogue or music provided by a puppeteer

**puppet valve** *n* **:** LIFT VALVE

**pup·pi·ly** \'pəpəlē\ *adj* [1*puppy* + *-ly*] *archaic* **:** PUPPYISH

**pupping** *pres part of* PUP

**1pup·py** \'pəpē, -pi\ *n* -ES [ME *popi*, fr. MF *popée*, *poupée* doll, toy, fr. (assumed) *poupe* doll — more at PUPPET] **1** *obs* **:** a small dog used esp. as a woman's pet **2 a :** a young domestic dog; *specif* **:** one less than a year old **b :** PUP 1b **3 :** PUP 2 **4 :** a small ball of crude rubber softened by means of kerosine to a gelatinous consistency and used by stampers to clean surplus gold from book covers after finishing or stamping — called also *rubber dog*

**2puppy** \"\ *vi* -ED/-ING/-ES *archaic* **:** PUP

**pup·py·dom** \-dəm\ *n* -s [1*puppy* + *-dom*] **:** PUPPYHOOD

**puppy drum** *n* **:** a young drumfish

**puppyfish** \'==,=\ *n* **:** MONKFISH

**puppyfoot** \'==,=\ *n, pl* **puppyfeet :** a card of the club suit in a pack of playing cards

**pup·py·hood** \'pəpē,hùd\ *n* **:** the state or period of being a puppy

**pup·py·ish** \-ēish\ *adj* **:** of, relating to, or characteristic of a puppy ⟨whimpering and wailing in a ~ sort of way —Jack London⟩

**pup·py·ism** \-ē,izəm\ *n* -s **:** the quality or state of being a puppy

**puppy love** *n* **:** CALF LOVE

**puppy shark** *n* **1 :** CUB SHARK **2 :** a young or small shark

**puppytrack** \'==,=\ *n* **:** PUPPYFOOT

**pups** *pl of* PUP, *pres 3d sing of* PUP

**pup tent** *n* **:** a wedge-shaped shelter tent usu. without flooring, sidewalls, or window

**pu·pu·nha** \pü'pünyə\ *n* -s [Pg, fr. Tupi] **:** a pinnate-leaved palm (*Guilielma speciosa*) that occurs in northern Brazil and Venezuela and has red starchy edible fruit

**pu·qui·na** \pü'kēnə\ *n, pl* **puquina** *or* **puquinas** *usu cap* **1 a :** a people inhabiting the shores of Lake Titicaca in Bolivia **b :** a member of such people **2 :** the language of the Puquina people

pup tent

**pur** *archaic var of* PURR

**pur** *abbr* **1** purchase; purchaser; purchasing **2** purification **3** pursuit

**pu·ra·na** \pü'ränə\ *n* -s *often cap* [Skt *purāṇa*, lit., ancient, an ancient tale, fr. *purā* formerly; akin to OE 1*fore*] **1 :** an ancient legendary tale of India **2 :** the third class of shastras or a text of this class — **pu·ra·nic** \-nik\ *adj, often cap*

**pu·ra·sa·ti** \,p(y)ùrə'säd·ē\ *or* **pu·le·sa·ti** \,p(y)ülə-\ *n, pl* **purasati** *or* **pulesati** *usu cap* [Egypt *prst*] **:** a Mediterranean people wearing a distinctive armor and feather crest believed to have been refugees from Crete migrating to Palestine and there becoming the Philistines

**pu·rau** \'pü,raů\ *n* -s [Tahitian] **:** MAJAGUA a

**pur au·tre vie** \pù,rōd·ə(r)'vē, -ō·trə-\ [AF] **:** for the life of another — used of an estate the tenancy of which is measured by the life of a person other than the tenant; compare LIFE ESTATE

**1pur·blind** \'pər, 'pə +,-\ *adj* [ME *pur blind*, *pure blind*, fr. 2*pure* + *blind*] **1 a** *obs* **:** wholly blind ⟨~ Argus, all eyes and no sight —Shak.⟩ **b :** partly blind **:** DIM-SIGHTED, SHORT-SIGHTED ⟨like a morning eagle . . . ~ amid foggy, midnight wolds —John Keats⟩ ⟨~ with cataracts —Gerald Kersh⟩ **2 :** comprehending or discerning imperfectly or obscurely **:** lacking in vision, insight, or understanding **:** characterized by obtuseness ⟨this ~ policy of social legislation⟩ ⟨shooting pheasants . . . in their ~ pomp of pelf and power —James Joyce⟩ — **pur·blind·ly** *adv* — **pur·blind·ness** *n* -ES

**2purblind** \"\ *vt* **:** to make purblind

**pur·chas·able** *also* **pur·chase·able** \'pərchəsəbəl, 'pəch-, 'pəich-\ *adj* **1 :** capable of being purchased **:** available on the market **2 :** VENAL, CORRUPT

**1pur·chase** \-chəs\ *vb* -ED/-ING/-S [ME *purchacen*, fr. OF *porchacier*, *purchacier* to seek to obtain, fr. *por*, *pur*, *pour* for (modif. — perh. influenced by L *per* through — of L *pro* for) + *chacier* to pursue, chase — more at FOR, CHASE] *vt* **1 a** *archaic* **:** to get into one's possession **:** GAIN, ACQUIRE ⟨your accent is something finer than you could ~ in so removed a dwelling —Shak.⟩ **b :** to acquire (real estate) by any means other than descent or inheritance **c** *archaic* **:** to obtain (as a license) from authority **d :** to obtain (as merchandise) by paying money or its equivalent **:** buy for a price ⟨*purchased* a new suit⟩ **e :** to obtain (something desired) by an outlay (as of labor, danger, sacrifice) ⟨~ one's life at the expense of one's honor⟩ **:** WIN, EARN ⟨his place was dearly *purchased*⟩ **2** *obs* **:** to cause to occur **:** EFFECT, PROCURE **3 a :** to haul in or up with or as if with a mechanical device or rope **b :** to apply to (as something to be moved or lifted) a device for obtaining a mechanical advantage **:** get a purchase upon or apply a purchase to; *also* **:** to move (as a cannon) by a purchase **4 a** *obs* **:** to serve as a ransom for **b :** to constitute the means or medium for buying (something) ⟨our dollars ~ less each year⟩ ⟨expert flattery may ~ an honest man⟩ **~** *vi* **1 a** *obs* **:** to acquire wealth or property **b :** to make a purchase or purchases **:** BUY **2** *obs* **:** to exert oneself **:** expend effort toward some end

**2purchase** \"\ *n* -s [ME *purchas*, *porchas*, fr. OF, fr. *porchacier* to purchase] **1 :** an act or instance of purchasing: as **a** *obs* (1) **:** the taking or seizing of prey (as in hunting)

(2) : the taking of something into one's possession violently or with force of arms : PLUNDERING, PILLAGE **b** *obs* : the seeking, procuring, or taking into possession of something : ACQUISITION; *also* : an act of instigating : CONTRIVANCE **c** : the acquiring of lands or tenements by any means other than descent or inheritance **d** : the acquiring of title to or property in anything for a price : a buying for money or its equivalent ⟨the ~ of shares in a business⟩ **2 a** (1) : something gotten into one's possession by any means honest or dishonest : GAIN, BOOTY; *esp* : the prize of a privateer (2) : something obtained for a price in money or its equivalent ⟨showed her ~*s* with pride⟩ **b** (1) : annual yield in rent (2) : value or potentiality for use or service in something or the hypothetical or figurative cash value of such or of a specified increment of such ⟨a life not worth a day's ~⟩ **c** : something bought considered with reference to its price or value : BARGAIN, BUY ⟨will find him a dearer ~ than she thought⟩ ⟨a good ~⟩ **3** *chiefly Scot* : means of acquiring property : RESOURCES **4 a** (1) : a mechanical hold or advantage applied to the raising or moving of heavy bodies (as by a lever, tackle, capstan) (2) : an apparatus or device by which the advantage is gained (as a pulley tackle) **b** (1) : an advantage used in applying one's power in any effort (2) : position or means of exerting power **5** : an unorganized minor territorial division in New Hampshire consisting of land that was originally laid off and sold by the state to an individual or individuals

**pur·chase·less** \-sləs\ *adj* : giving no purchase ⟨straining through the ~ mud⟩

**purchase money** *n* : the consideration paid or to be paid by the purchaser of property

**purchase-money mortgage** *n* : a mortgage to secure part or all of the purchase price of the property mortgaged given by the buyer to the seller or to a third person furnishing a loan to the buyer

**purchase prize** *n* : an award of being purchased (as by an established collection or museum) conferred upon a work of art in a competitive exhibition

**pur·chas·er** \-sə(r)\ *n* -s [ME *purchasour*, fr. AF, fr. OF *purchacier* to purchase + AF *-our* -or] : one that purchases: as **a** *obs* : one that makes provision esp. for his material welfare : a mercenary person **b** : one that acquires an estate in lands by his own act or agreement or takes or obtains an estate by any means other than by descent or inheritance **c** (1) : one that acquires property for a consideration (as of money) : BUYER, VENDEE (2) : PURCHASING AGENT

**purchase shears** *n pl but sing or pl in constr* : very powerful shears with removable steel cutters of rectangular section

**purchase tax** *n* : a tax imposed in Great Britain upon various commodities at rates graduated according to the degree of luxury or necessity of the particular commodity

**purchase warrant** *n* : WARRANT 2e(2)

**purchasing agent** *n* [fr. gerund of 1*purchase*] **1** : an employee who purchases materials and supplies to be used by a business (as a manufacturer) **2** : a middleman who makes purchases for clients

**purchasing power** *n* : capacity to buy: as **a** : capacity of an individual, group of individuals, or the aggregate of prospective buyers as determined primarily by current income and savings — called also *buying power* **b** : the worth of money as determined by what it can buy at a given time in comparison with what it could buy at a specified previous time ⟨decline in the *purchasing power* of the dollar⟩

**purchasing power parity** *n* : the ratio between the currencies of two countries at which each currency when exchanged for the other will purchase the same quantity of goods as it purchases at home excluding customs duties and costs of transport —compare PAR

**pur·dah** *also* **par·dah** \'pərdə\ *n* -s [Hindi *parda*, lit., screen, veil, fr. Per] : a practice inaugurated by Muslims and later adopted by various Hindus and found esp. in India that involves the seclusion of women from public observation by means of concealing clothing including the veil and by the use of high-walled enclosures, screens, and curtains within the home

**pur·do·ni·um** \,pər'dōnēəm\ *also* **pur·do·ni·an** \-ēən\ *or* **pur·do·ni·on** \-ēən\ *n* -s [prob. fr. *Purdon*, name of its inventor] *Brit* : a container for coal in the form of a box with removable metal lining

**pur·dy** \'pərdi\ *adj* [origin unknown] *dial Eng* : disagreeably self-important

**1pure** \'pyu̇(ə)r, -u̇ə\ *adj* -ER/-EST [ME *pur*, fr. OF, fr. L *purus* clean; akin to Skt *punāti* he cleanses, MIr *ūr* fresh, green, Welsh *ir*] **1 a** *of physical matter* (1) : unmixed with any other thing : free from admixture : containing no added, substitute, or foreign substance ⟨~ gold⟩ ⟨the *purest* silk obtainable⟩ (2) : free from dust, dirt, or taint : containing nothing that impairs or is hurtful ⟨~ spring water rich in minerals⟩ ⟨~ food and abundant rest⟩ (3) : perfectly clear to the eye : optically clear : SPOTLESS, STAINLESS ⟨a ~ bubbling brook⟩ ⟨fresh ~ linens⟩ **b** (1) : free from harshness or roughness and in tune — used of a musical tone (2) : perfect mathematically ⟨~ harmony⟩ ⟨a ~ interval⟩ — compare TEMPERED (3) : ABSOLUTE 11a **c** *of a vowel* : characterized by no appreciable alteration of articulation or acoustic effect during the utterance : not diphthongized **2 a** (1) : being such and no other : SHEER, SIMPLE ⟨acted so from ~ necessity⟩ ⟨the *purest* malice⟩ (2) : being nothing less than : COMPLETE, UNALLOYED, ⟨~ folly⟩ **b** (1) : taken in its essential character and apart from relations and applications : concerned basically with theory rather than practice or application : ABSTRACT ⟨~ science⟩ ⟨~ mechanics⟩ (2) : neither biased by practical considerations nor directed toward the exposition of demonstrable realities or the solution of practical problems ⟨~ literature⟩; *esp* : nonobjective and to be appraised on formal and technical qualities only — used esp. of a work of art **3 a** (1) : free from what harms, vitiates, weakens, or pollutes : faultless and uncontaminated : PERFECT — used of concepts, actions, and other immaterial matters ⟨the ~ religion of our fathers⟩ ⟨a critic of ~ if somewhat narrow taste⟩ (2) : containing nothing that does not properly belong : free from alteration, error, or foreign increment ⟨the ~ and original text⟩ ⟨spoke a very ~ French⟩ **b** : free from moral fault or guilt : INNOCENT, GUILTLESS ⟨moved only by the *purest* feelings⟩ ⟨a ~ and upright man⟩ **c** : marked by chastity : CONTINENT ⟨a ~ relationship between the sexes⟩ **d** (1) : of pure blood : having an unmixed ancestry ⟨a ~ Arab horse⟩ (2) : HOMOZYGOUS ⟨mice ~ for the dilution factor⟩ (3) : breeding true for one or more characters **e** *obs* : belonging to a religious group that stresses personal purity and precision of conduct — used usu. disparagingly of Puritans and Quakers **f** : ritually clean : suitable for use in holy services **g** : free from empirical elements : A PRIORI ⟨~ intuition⟩ ⟨~ ego⟩ **4** *chiefly dial* : having good health and spirits : FINE

**syn** ABSOLUTE, SIMPLE, SHEER: these words are alike in stressing the notion that the essential character of a thing, unmixed, unalleviated, and undiminished, is being spoken of. PURE may stress lack of intermixture, adulterating, or obscuring the essence of a matter ⟨the founders of American political democracy were not so naively devoted to *pure* theory that they were unaware of the necessity of cultural conditions for the successful working of democratic forms —John Dewey⟩ ⟨a wider opening of the hospitable American doors to the oppressed of Europe seemed to the divines and social reformers an exercise of *pure* magnanimity —Roger Burlingame⟩ ABSOLUTE may further emphasize lack of admixture or stress lack of dependence, relationship, or reservation ⟨for Christianity aims at nothing less than *absolute* truth —W.R.Inge⟩ ⟨the obstinacy, the ferocity, the treachery of the aristocracy, had compelled Caesar to crush them; and the more desperate their struggles the more *absolute* the necessity became —J.A. Froude⟩ ⟨it was horrid, that pitiful, forlorn cry of pain and of *absolute* despair coming from such a giant —Liam O'Flaherty⟩ SIMPLE stresses isolation from complicating or obscuring factors; it may indicate that further resolution or analysis is unnecessary or impossible ⟨the assumption that the exposure of an error is identical with the discovery of the truth — that error and truth are *simple* opposites —H.L.Mencken⟩ ⟨the *simple* truth, so hard to come by anywhere, implies, of course, a lucid statement of it —H.V.Gregory⟩ SHEER has more intensifying force and less suggestion of shades of meaning than others in this group; it may stress the palpable revelation or obvious display of whatever is being spoken of ⟨the "Ancient Mariner," . . . is a work of *sheer* imagination —J.L.Lowes⟩ ⟨is there anything that, for *sheer* simplicity of pathos . . . can be said to equal or even approach the last act of Christ's passion —Oscar Wilde⟩ ⟨the *sheer* dynamism of the totalitarian promise acquires a glistening certainty which few men can stand up against —A.M.Schlesinger b. 1917⟩ **syn** see in addition CHASTE

**2pure** \"\ *adv* [ME *pur*, fr. *pur*, adj.] : PURELY: as **a** : without admixture — usu. used in combination with an adjective ⟨a *pure*-white linen⟩ ⟨*pure*-silk shirtings⟩ **b** *chiefly dial* : to a notable degree : EXCEEDINGLY, THOROUGHLY ⟨~ miserable with a toothache⟩ ⟨most of the track was ~ muddy⟩

**3pure** \"\ *vt* -ED/-ING/-S [ME *puren*, fr. *pur*, adj.] **1** *obs* : PURIFY, REFINE **2** : PUER

**4pure** \"\ *n* -s [in sense 1, fr. 1*pure;* in sense 2, fr. 3*pure*] **1 a** : PURITY **b** : something that is pure **2** : PUER

**5pure** \'pür\ *Scot var of* POOR

**pure and simple** *adj* : of the clearest kind : MERE, PLAIN, ABSOLUTE — used postpositively for emphasis ⟨a pointer word *pure and simple* —Frederick Bodmer⟩ ⟨he is an adventurer *pure and simple*⟩

**1pureblood** \'ˌ=ˌ=\ *or* **pure-blooded** \'=¦==\ *adj* [1*pure* + *blood, blooded*] of unmixed ancestry : PUREBRED

**2pureblood** \"\ *n* : a pureblood individual : PUREBRED ⟨a beef sire that is a ~ of excellent ancestry⟩; *esp* : a member of one of the non-Caucasian divisions of mankind (as a Negro or American Indian) — compare MIXED-BLOOD

**1purebred** \'=¦=\ *adj* [1*pure* + *bred*] : bred from members of a recognized breed, strain, or kind without admixture of other blood over many generations — used chiefly of livestock ⟨~ cattle⟩ ⟨~ poultry⟩; compare GRADE, THOROUGHBRED

**2purebred** \'=ˌ=\ *n* -s : a purebred animal esp. of a lineage established by registration records

**pure christiania** *n, often cap C* : PARALLEL CHRISTIANIA

**pure color** *n* **1** : a color evoked by homogeneous spectral light **2** : a color of a colorimetric purity approximating that of the colors of the physical spectrum

**pure culture** *n* **1** : a culture containing a growth of a single kind of organism free from other organisms **2** : a culture containing the descendants of a single organism whether free from all organisms of other kinds or not

**puredee** *also* **pure-D** \'=¦=\ *adj* [1*pure* + *dee*] *South* : THOROUGHGOING, UNMITIGATED ⟨a fit of ~ jealousy —Eudora Welty⟩

**pure-dye** \'=ˌ=\ *adj* [1*pure* + *dye*] : having very little or no weighting — used of dyed silk

**1pu·ree** \pyü'rā, pyu̇'-,pyə'- *sometimes* pə'- *or* -'rē\ *n* -s [F, fr. past part. of MF *purer* to cleanse, strain vegetables, fr. L *purare* to cleanse, fr. *purus* clean — more at PURE] **1** : a paste or thick liquid suspension of a food (as liver, peas, chestnuts) usu. produced by rubbing the cooked food through a sieve **2** : a thick soup of smooth texture having pureed vegetables as a base ⟨a tomato ~⟩ ⟨~ of dried peas⟩

**2puree** \"\ *vt* **pureed; pureed; pureeing; purees** : to prepare in the form of a puree : boil soft and then rub through a sieve ⟨~*ing* vegetables for soup⟩

**pure endowment** *n* : an insurance contract promising to pay the insured a stated sum if he survives a specified period with nothing payable in case of prior death — compare ENDOWMENT INSURANCE

**pure experience** *n* : experience unqualified by conception or association : immediate apprehension

**pure-food law** *n* : a legislative act prohibiting the adulteration or misbranding of any article of food

**pure forest** *n* : a forest in which at least 80 percent of the trees are of the same species

**purehearted** \'=¦=\ *adj* [1*pure* + *hearted*] : having the heart free from guile or evil

**pure imaginary** *n* : a complex number of the form $ai$ where $a$ is any real number and $i=\sqrt{-1}$

**pure interest** *n* : interest on capital excluding payment for risk

**pure land** *n, usu cap P&L* **1** : a paradise into which according to Amidism anyone is reborn who calls in faith on the name of the deified Buddha Amitabha and in which one can attain Buddhahood free from the hindrances of earth — called also *Sukhavati, Western Paradise* **2** : AMIDISM

**pure line** *n* [trans. of G *reine linie*] : a homogeneous line of descent: as **a** : a group of closely related individuals of identical genetic constitution (as the offspring of a homozygous self-fertilized parent) : a line of descent theoretically realizable from the inbreeding of completely homozygous and comparable parents **b** : the descendants of a single individual esp. by vegetative multiplication : CLONE

**pure·ly** *adv* : in a pure manner: as **a** : without admixture of anything injurious, inharmonious, foreign, or otherwise undesirable or divergent ⟨a ~ bred strain⟩ ⟨to speak French ~⟩ **b** : MERELY, SIMPLY, SOLELY ⟨a ~ formal courtesy⟩ **c** : CHASTELY, INNOCENTLY ⟨live ~⟩ **d** (1) : COMPLETELY, WHOLLY ⟨a ~ experimental study⟩ (2) *chiefly dial* : in the highest degree : EXCEEDINGLY — usu. used prepositively ⟨I ~ hate a haircut —Helen Eustis⟩

**pure minor scale** *n* : NATURAL MINOR SCALE

**pure-mixed** \'=¦=\ *adj* : free from related organisms; *esp* : containing the desired organism together with one or more others that are necessary for its growth ⟨a *pure-mixed* culture of paramecium⟩

**pure·ness** *n* -ES [ME *puernesse*, fr. *pur, puer* pure + *-nesse* -ness] : the quality or state of being pure : PURITY

**pure premium** *n* : NET PREMIUM

**pure profit** *n* : profit less the unremunerated cost of services furnished by the owner for which payment would be received if supplied elsewhere

**pure proposition** *n* : a proposition that asserts or denies without qualification

**1pur·er** \'pyu̇rə(r)\ *comparative of* PURE

**2purer** \"\ *n* -s [3*pure* + *-er*] : BATER

**pure reason** *n, Kantianism* : the faculty that embraces the a priori forms of knowledge and is the source of transcendental ideas — compare INTUITIVE REASON

**pures** *pres 3d sing of* PURE, *pl of* PURE

**pure spectrum** *n* : a spectrum in which the dispersion is highly discriminative so that at each point the light is practically monochromatic

**purest** *superlative of* PURE

**pure stand** *n* : a plant population consisting exclusively or largely of members of one species, variety, or type ⟨a *pure stand* of oak⟩

**pure tone** *n* : a musical tone of a single frequency produced by simple harmonic vibrations and without overtones

**pure wave** *n* : a radio wave produced by a transmitting set that is substantially free from harmonics or any frequency except the fundamental

**pur·ey** \'pyu̇rē\ *n* -s [1*pure* + *-y*] : a child's solid-colored glass marble

**1pur·fle** \'pərfəl, 'pə̄f-,'pəif-\ *vt* **purfled; purfled; purfling** \-f(ə)liŋ\ **purfles** [ME *purfilen*, fr. MF *porfiler* to interweave, border, fr. (assumed) VL *profilare*, fr. L *pro-* forward + LL *filare* to spin — more at PRO-, FILE] **1** : to ornament the border of : trim the edge or edges of **2** : to decorate with embroidery : ornament with metallic threads, jewels, or fur ⟨a goodly lady clad in scarlet red *purfled* with gold and pearl of rich assay —Edmund Spenser⟩ : to ornament (as cabinetwork) with tracery, inlay, or similar treatment esp. around the edges ⟨~ a violin body⟩

**2purfle** \"\ *n* -s [ME *porfil, purfil*, fr. MF *porfil*, fr. *porfiler* to border] **1** : a decorated border; *esp* : an embroidered edge of a garment **2** : a heraldic border (as of fur)

**purfled** *adj* [ME *purfiled*, fr. past part. of *purfilen* to purfle] : having trimming or decoration (as of embroidery or tracery); *also* : BORDERED

**purfled work** *n* : delicate esp. Gothic tracery (as in architectural ornamentation)

**purfling** *n* -s [ME *purfiling*, fr. gerund of *purfilen* to border] : ornamentation on a border; *esp* : an inlaid border of a musical instrument (as a violin)

**pur·ga** \'pu̇(ə)rgə\ *n* -s [Russ, fr. Karelian *purgu* snowstorm; akin to Finn *purku* snowstorm] : an intense arctic snowstorm occurring usu. in flat open country and characterized by severe cold and wind-driven snow

**purgament** *n* -s [L *purgamentum*, fr. *purgare* + *-mentum* -ment] *obs* : EXCRETION

**pur·ga·tion** \,pər'gāshən, pə̄'g-,pəi'g-\ *n* -s [ME *purgacioun*, fr. MF *purgation*, fr. L *purgation-, purgatio*, fr. *purgatus* (past part. of *purgare* to cleanse) + *-ion-, -io* -ion — more at PURGE] **1 a** : the act of purging; *specif* : vigorous evacuation of the bowels (as from the action of a purgative or an infective agent) **b** : administration of or treatment with a purgative **c** *obs* : MENSTRUATION **2** : ceremonial cleansing : PURIFICATION **3 a** : moral or spiritual purification : destruction of the influences of sin : a freeing from moral evil **b** : the first stage in a mystic's progress to perfection consisting of conscious moral purification by self-discipline, subjugation of distracting desires, ascetic practices, and similar measures — called also *purgative way* **4** : the clearing of oneself from alleged guilt ⟨let him put me to my ~ —Shak.⟩ — see CANONICAL PURGATION, VULGAR PURGATION

**1pur·ga·tive** \'pərgəd·|iv, 'pə̄g-,'pəig-, -gət|\ *adj* [ME *purgatif*, fr. MF, fr. LL *purgativus*, fr. L *purgatus* + *-ivus* -ive] **1** : purging or tending to purge : CATHARTIC **2** : cleansing or purifying esp. from sin or sinful inclinations : PURGATORIAL, EXPIATORY ⟨a ~ ceremony⟩ **3** : freeing legally from fault or blame : clearing from guilt ⟨a ~ answer⟩ ⟨~ evidence⟩

**2purgative** \"\ *n* -s : a purging medicine : CATHARTIC — compare LAXATIVE

**pur·ga·tive·ly** \|əvlē, -li\ *adv* : so as to purge : in a purgative manner

**purgative way** *n* : PURGATION 3

**pur·ga·to·ri·al** \¦==¦tōrēəl, -¦tȯr-\ *adj* [in sense 1, fr. LL *purgatorius* cleansing + E *-al;* in sense 2, fr. ML *purgatorium* purgatory + E *-al* — more at PURGATORY] **1** : cleansing of sin or sinful influences : EXPIATORY, PURIFYING **2** : of, relating to, or resembling purgatory ⟨a ~ experience⟩ ⟨~ fires⟩

**1pur·ga·to·ri·an** \ˌ==¦=rēən\ *n* -s [1*purgatory* + *-an*] : a believer in the existence of a purgatory

**2purgatorian** \"\ *adj* [1*purgatory* + *-an*] : PURGATORIAL 2

**1pur·ga·to·ry** \'pərgə,tōrē, 'pə̄g-,'pəig-, -tȯr-, -ri\ *n* -ES *sometimes cap* [ME, fr. AF or ML; AF *purgatorie*, fr. ML *purgatorium*, fr. neut. of LL *purgatorius* cleansing, purging, fr. L *purgatus* (past part. of *purgare* to purge) + *-orius* -ory — more at PURGE] **1** : an intermediate state after death for expiatory purification; *specif* : a place or state of punishment wherein according to Roman Catholic doctrine the souls of those who die in God's grace may expiate venial sins or satisfy divine justice for the temporal punishment still due to remitted mortal sin **2 a** : a place or state like purgatory : a condition of prolonged and usu. penitential suffering : temporary torture or punishment : acute misery ⟨the return trip was absolute ~⟩ **b** : an expiation or means of expiation **3 a** : a chasm or cleft in a cliff or wall of rock differing from a flume in not having a stream **b** *chiefly dial* : SWAMP; *esp* : a swamp that is dangerous or difficult to cross

**2purgatory** \"\ *adj* [ME, fr. LL *purgatorius*] *archaic* : PURGATIVE, PURGATORIAL

**3purgatory** \"\ *vt* -ED/-ING/-ES [1*purgatory*] : to put into a purgatory or a purgatorial situation : subject to prolonged suffering

**purgatory hammer** *n* [1*purgatory*] : a prehistoric stone hammer that was formerly popularly supposed to have been buried with the dead for use in knocking at the gates of purgatory

**1purge** \'pərj, 'pə̄j, 'pəij\ *vb* -ED/-ING/-S [ME *purgen*, fr. OF *purgier*, fr. L *purgare* to cleanse, purify, purge, fr. OL *purigare*, fr. *purus* clean, pure + *-igare* (fr. *agere* to lead, drive, do) — more at PURE, ACT] *vt* **1 a** (1) : to clear (as oneself or another) from a charge or doubt : remove a stigma from the name of : demonstrate the innocence of : free from a charge by purgation ⟨the committee heard his attempt to ~ himself of a charge of heresy⟩ (2) : to demonstrate (as oneself) to be free from guilt by submission to ordeal under a medieval code of legal procedure **b** : to make free of physical impurities : make clean by removing whatever is foreign, soiling, or superfluous ⟨~ metal of dross⟩ ⟨*purging* water by distillation⟩ **c** : to make morally or spiritually clean : free from moral or ceremonial contamination or defilement **2** : to remove by a process of cleansing : take off or out by or as if by washing ⟨~ away dross from metal⟩ ⟨let us ~ our sins with prayer⟩ **3 a** : to cause evacuation of or from (the bowels) ⟨drugs that ~ the bowels⟩ or of or from the bowel of ⟨*purged* himself with calomel⟩ **b** : to free (itself) of suspended matter usu. by sedimentation : DEFECATE — used of a liquid **c** : to free (as a boiler) of sediment or relieve (as a steampipe) of trapped air by bleeding **d** : to rid (as a state or party) by a purge : get rid of (as disloyal or suspect elements from a group or undesirable material in a publication) : ELIMINATE **4** : to make submission or atonement in order to relieve oneself of (as a legal offence or sentence) ⟨a restitution that *purged* the previous seizure⟩ or in order to relieve (as oneself) from liability or penalty ⟨*purged* himself of contempt of court⟩ ~ *vi* **1** : to become free of impurities, excess, or other unwanted matter (as by clearing, discharging, washing) **2 a** : to have or produce frequent evacuations from the intestines (as by means of a purgative) **b** : to take a purge or purgative **3** : to cause or bring about purgation, purification, or similar effects **syn** see RID

**2purge** \"\ *n* -s **1 a** : an act or instance of purging : PURGATION **b** : a ridding (as of a nation or party) of elements or members regarded as treacherous, disloyal, or suspect **2** : something that purges; *esp* : PURGATIVE

**purge·able** \-jəbəl\ *adj* : capable of being purged : subject to purging

**purg·ee** \¦pər¦jē, (')pə̄¦-, (')pəi¦-\ *n* -s [1*purge* + *-ee*] : a person (as a political opponent) eliminated in a purge

**purg·er** \'=jə(r)\ *n* -s [ME, fr. *purgen* to purge + *-er*] : one that purges ⟨the ~*s* of yesterday have become the purgees of today —Michael Padev⟩

**purg·ery** \-jərē\ *n* -ES [F *purgerie*, fr. *purger* to purge (fr. OF *purgier*) + *-erie* -ery] : the part of a sugarhouse where molasses is drained from the sugar

**purging** *n* -s [fr. gerund of 1*purge*] **1** : the act or process of cleansing or purifying **2** : the evacuation of large amounts of usu. loose or unformed feces whether as a result of disease or of purgation

**purging agaric** *n* [fr. pres. part. of 1*purge*] : a common white pore fungus (*Fomes officinalis*) of Europe and America that causes a heart rot of various conifers and has been used as a purgative in human medicine — called also *white agaric*

**purging buckthorn** *n* : a common arborescent European buckthorn (*Rhamnus cathartica*) that is widely naturalized in the eastern U.S. and has purgative black berries and bark

**purging cassia** *n* **1** : DRUMSTICK TREE **2** : CASSIA FISTULA

**purging croton** *n* : an East Indian shrub or small tree (*Croton tiglium*) whose seeds yield croton oil

**purging flax** *n* : a European annual herb (*Linum catharticum*) with white or yellowish white flowers followed by seeds that are cathartic and diuretic — called also *fairy flax;* see 1LININ

**purging house** *n* [fr. gerund of 1*purge*] : PURGERY

**purging root** *n* [fr. pres. part. of 1*purge*] : the root of the flowering spurge

**pu·ri** \'pu̇rē\ *n* -s [Hindi, fr. Skt *pūrī;* akin to Skt *piparti* he fills, nourishes, sates, *pūrṇa* full — more at FULL] : a very light fried wheat cake of India

**pu·rif·i·cant** \pyü'rifəkənt\ *n* -s [L *purificant-, purificans*, pres. part. of *purificare*] : a purifying agent

**pu·ri·fi·ca·tion** \,pyu̇rəfə'kāshən\ *n* -s [MF, fr. L *purification-, purificatio*, fr. *purificatus* (past part. of *purificare* to purify) + *-ion-, -io* -ion — more at PURIFY] **1** : an act of purifying : the act or operation of removing impure, noxious, or foreign matter **2 a** : the act or operation of cleansing ceremonially by removing any pollution or defilement **b** : a cleansing from guilt or the pollution of sin : extinction of sinful desires or deliverance from their dominating power : spiritual or moral purgation ⟨~ through repentance⟩ **3** : the ceremony of bathing performed by Jewish women after menstruation in accordance with biblical law

**pu·ri·fi·ca·tor** \'=====,kād·ə(r)\ *n* -s [L *purificatus* + E *-or*] : one that purifies : PURIFIER: as **a** : a linen cloth used to wipe the chalice after celebration of the Eucharist **b** : a cloth-wrapped sponge used similarly to wipe the hands of the officiating clergy

**1pu·rifi·ca·to·ry** \pyü'rifəkə,tōrē, 'pyůrəf-, *chiefly Brit* ,pyů(ə)rəfə'kātəri *or* -ā·tri\ *adj* [LL *purificatorius*, fr. L *purificatus* + *-orius* -ory] **:** serving, tending, or intended to purify **:** PURIFYING

**2purificatory** \"\ *n* -ES [ML *purificatorium*, fr. neut. of LL *purificatorius* serving to purify] **:** PURIFICATOR

**pu·ri·fi·er** \'pyůrə,fī(ə)r, -īə\ *n* -S [ME, fr. *purifien* to purify + *-er*] **:** one that purifies or cleanses (as an apparatus for purifying coal gas or a machine for separating fine bran particles from flour middlings) **:** CLEANSER, REFINER

**pu·ri·form** \'pyůrə,fórm\ *adj* [L *pur- pus* pus + E *-iform*] **:** constituting or resembling pus ⟨a ~ discharge⟩ **:** PURULENT

**pu·ri·fy** \'pyůrə,fī\ *vb* -ED/-ING/-ES [ME *purifien*, fr. MF *purifier*, fr. L *purificare*, fr. *purus* pure + *-ificare* -ify] *vt* **1 :** to make pure: as **a :** to clear from material defilement or imperfection **:** free from impurities or noxious matter ⟨~*ing* air by filtration⟩ ⟨*purified* the house with soap, and water, and sweat⟩ **b :** to free from guilt or moral blemish ⟨~ the heart⟩ **c :** to cleanse ceremonially ⟨and Moses . . . *purified* the altar —Lev 8:15 (RSV)⟩ **d :** to free from anything that is alien, extraneous, improper, corrupting, or otherwise damaging ⟨~ a language of barbarisms⟩ ⟨*purified* the state of traitors⟩ **2** *Scots law* **:** to free (a condition) from defect or imperfection by performance or fulfillment **~** *vi* **:** to grow or become pure or clean

**pu·rim** \'půrəm, 'pü-, '(,)rim, pů'rim\ *n* -S *usu cap* [Heb *pūrīm*, lit. the lots, fr. pl. of *pūr* lot; fr. the casting of lots by Haman to destroy the Jews, Esth 9:24-26] **:** a Jewish festival celebrated on the 14th of Adar and instituted to commemorate the deliverance of the Jews from the machinations of Haman — called also *Feast of Lots*

**pu·rine** \'pyů,rēn, -,rən\ *n* -S [G *purin*, fr. L *purus* pure + NL *uricus* uric (fr. E *uric*) + G *-in* -ine] **1 :** a crystalline base $C_5H_4N_4$ composed of a pyrimidine ring fused with an imidazole ring that is prepared from uric acid and is the parent of compounds (as allantoin and alloxan) derived from uric acid — compare STRUCTURAL FORMULA **2 :** a derivative of purine; *esp* **:** PURINE BASE

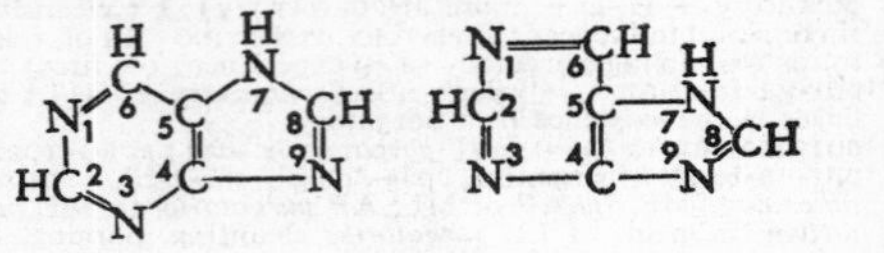

purine

**purine base** *n* **:** any of a group of crystalline bases comprising purine and bases derived from it (as adenine, caffeine, guanine, theobromine, or xanthine) some of which are components of nucleosides and nucleotides

**pu·ri·ri** \pə'rirē\ *n* -S [Maori] **:** a New Zealand ironwood (*Vitex littoralis*) yielding a very durable hard strong dark brown wood

**puris** *pl of* PURI

**pur·ism** \'pyů,rizəm\ *n* -S [F *purisme*, fr. *pur* pure (fr. L *purus*) + *-isme* -ism] **1 :** rigid adherence to or insistence on purity or nicety (as in literary style or use of words) **2 :** an example of purism; *esp* **:** a word or phrase or a sense of a word or phrase that is used chiefly by purists ⟨readers who find a usage stigmatized as ~ have a right to know the stigmatizer's place in the purist scale —H.W.Fowler⟩ **3 :** a theory and practice in art originated about 1918 by Amédée Ozenfant and Le Corbusier that reduces all natural appearances to a geometric simplicity characteristic of machines

**1pur·ist** \-,rəst\ *n* -S [F *puriste*, fr. *pur* + *-iste* -ist] **:** a person solicitous or oversolicitous about purity or nicety (as of conduct or usage): as **a :** one preoccupied with the purity of a language and its protection from the ingress of foreign or altered forms **b :** a sport fisherman who uses exclusively one method and who will give serious consideration to no other ⟨a dry fly ~⟩ ⟨a squidding ~⟩

**2purist** \"\ *adj* [1*purist*] **:** PURISTIC

**pu·ris·tic** \pyů'ristik, pyə'r-,pyü'r-\ *also* **pu·ris·ti·cal** \-tėkəl, -tēk-\ *adj* [1*purist* + *-ic*, *-ical*] **:** of, relating to, or characteristic of purists or purism ⟨a ~ outlook⟩ **:** marked by purism ⟨a ~ style⟩ — **pu·ris·ti·cal·ly** \-tėk(ə)lē, -tēk-, -li\ *adv*

**1pu·ri·tan** \'pyůrət°n, -rəd·ən,-rətən\ *n* -S [prob. fr. LL *puritas* purity + E *-an*] **1** *usu cap* **:** a member of a group of 16th and 17th century Protestant Christians in England opposing the traditional and formal usages of the Church of England who during the Commonwealth period (1649-59) became a powerful political party and who emigrated in large numbers to New England **2** *sometimes cap* **a :** one who (as because of adherence to a religious sect) practices or preaches a more rigorous or professedly purer moral code than that which prevails **b :** one who on religious or ethical grounds inveighs against current practices, pleasures, or indulgences which he regards as lax, impure, or corrupting **:** PRECISIAN ⟨she would make a ~ of the Devil —Shak.⟩

**2puritan** \"\ *adj* **:** of or relating to puritans, the Puritans, or puritanism

**puritan father** *n, often cap P&F* **:** one of the early Puritan settlers of New England

**puritan gray** *n, sometimes cap P* **:** a bluish gray that is less strong than clair de lune, greener and paler than average dusk (sense 3a), and paler than Medici blue

**pu·ri·tan·ic** \,pyůrə'tanik, -nēk\ *adj* [1*puritan* + *-ic*] **:** PURITANICAL

**pu·ri·tan·i·cal** \-nəkəl, -nēk-\ *adj* [1*puritan* + *-ical*] **1** *often cap* **:** of or relating to the Puritans or their doctrines and practice **2 :** manifesting the influence of puritan beliefs or practices **:** morally rigorous **:** STRICT ⟨a ~ woman⟩ ⟨strict ~ restraint⟩ — **pu·ri·tan·i·cal·ly** \-nək(ə)lē, -nēk-, -li\ *adv* — **pu·ri·tan·i·cal·ness** \-nəkəlnəs, -nēk-\ *n* -ES

**pu·ri·tan·ism** \'pyůrət°n,izəm, -rəd·ə,ni-, -rətə,ni-\ *n* -S **1** *usu cap* **:** the beliefs and practices of or characteristic of the Puritans **2** *sometimes cap* **:** strictness and austerity esp. in matters of religion or conduct

**pu·ri·tan·ize** \-°n,īz, -ə,nīz\ *vb* -ED/-ING/-S *sometimes cap* [1*puritan* + *-ize*] *vi* **:** to practice puritanism **:** conform to puritan beliefs **~** *vt* **:** to make puritan **:** give a puritan character to

**pu·ri·tan·ly** *adv* **:** in a puritan manner **:** toward the Puritans or their beliefs or practices ⟨~ inclined⟩

**pu·ri·tano** \,p(y)ůrə'ta(,)nō, -tä(-\ *n* -S [AmerSp, fr. Sp *puritano* puritan, fr. E *puritan*] **:** a medium-sized cigar that resembles a perfecto and is pointed at both ends

**pu·ri·ty** \'pyůrəd·ē, -ətē, -i\ *n* -ES [ME *purete*, fr. OF *pureté*, fr. LL *puritat-*, *puritas*, fr. L *purus* pure + *-itat-*, *-itas* -ity] **1 :** the quality or state of being pure ⟨a chemical of extreme ~⟩ ⟨lead a life of perfect ~⟩ ⟨the ~ of his intent was manifest⟩ ⟨spoke a French of great ~⟩ **2 a :** the fraction of spectrum component in a mixture of achromatic and spectrum colors that is required to match the color being considered and that constitutes an approximate psychophysical correlate of saturation **b :** SATURATION 4a — not used technically **3 :** ability to breed true **:** HOMOZYGOSITY ⟨the ~ of a strain⟩ — compare PURE LINE

**purity rubric** *n* **:** an authoritative statement (as in the U.S. Pharmacopoeia and the National Formulary) defining the purity of a drug or chemical for medicinal use

**pur·kin·je afterimage** \(,)pər'kin(,)jē-, 'půrkən,yā-\ *n, usu cap P* [after Johannes E. *Purkinje* †1869 Czech physiologist] **:** a second positive afterimage in a succession of visual afterimages resulting from a brief light stimulus and appearing most distinctly in a hue complementary to that of the original sensation

**pur·kin·je·an** \(,)pər'kinjēən, ,půrkən'yāən\ *adj, usu cap* [J. E. *Purkinje* + E *-an*] **:** relating to, discovered by, or named after the Czech physiologist J. E. Purkinje (1787–1869)

**purkinje cell** *n, usu cap P* **:** any of numerous nerve cells occupying the middle layer of the cerebellar cortex and being characterized by a large globose body with massive dendrites that are directed outward and a single slender axon that is directed inward

**purkinje fiber** *n, usu cap P* **:** any of the modified cardiac muscle fibers with few nuclei, granulated central cytoplasm, and sparse peripheral striations, that make up the Purkinje's network

**purkinje phenomenon** *or* **purkinje shift** *also* **purkinje effect** *n, usu cap 1st P* **:** a shift of the region of apparent maximal spectral luminosity from yellow with the light-adapted eye toward violet with the dark-adapted eye that is presumably associated with predominance of cone vision in bright and rod vision in dim illumination

**purkinje's figure** *or* **purkinje figure** *n, usu cap P* **:** any of the shadowy figures of the network of retinal vessels that may be made visible in one's own eye (as by light from a pinhole close to the eye

**purkinje's network** *or* **purkinje's system** *or* **purkinje's tissue** *n, usu cap P* **:** a network of intracardial conducting tissue made up of syncytial Purkinje fibers that lie in the myocardium and constitute the atrioventricular bundle and other conducting tracts which spread out from the sinus node — compare SINOVENTRICULAR SYSTEM

**1purl** \'pərl, *esp before pause or consonant* 'pər·əl; 'pəl, 'pəil\ *n* -S [*pirl*] **1 :** gold or silver thread or wire used for embroidering or edging **2** *Brit* **:** 4PEARL **3 a** *obs* **:** a lace frill on a ruff **b :** a ruffled or indented edge (as on a leaf) **4 :** PURL STITCH **5 :** the intertwist of thread knotting a stitch usu. along an edge ⟨the single ~ typical of blanket stitch⟩ ⟨the double ~ of buttonhole stitch⟩

**2purl** \"\ *vb* -ED/-ING/-S *vt* **1 a :** to embroider with gold or silver thread **b :** to edge or border with gold or silver embroidery ⟨cloth . . . powdered with red roses ~*ed* with fine gold —Edward Hall⟩ **2** *Brit* **:** 5PEARL **3 :** to knit (as a garment) in purl stitch **~** *vi* **:** to do knitting in purl stitch

**3purl** \"\ *n* -S [perh. of Scand origin; akin to Norw *purla* to ripple, Sw *porla*] **1 :** a purling or swirling stream or rill **2 a :** a gentle murmuring sound **b :** a gentle movement (as of purling water)

**4purl** \"\ *vi* -ED/-ING/-S [perh. of Scand origin; akin to Norw *purla* to ripple, Sw *porla*] **1 :** to run swiftly around (as in ripples or about obstructions) **:** move in circles or undulations **:** EDDY, SWIRL, CURL ⟨a brook ~*ing* over mossy stones⟩ ⟨thin winding breath which ~*ed* up to the sky —Shak.⟩ **2 :** to make a soft murmuring sound like that of a purling stream

**5purl** \"\ *n* -S [origin unknown] **1 :** an infusion of bitter herbs (as wormwood) in hot malt liquor used formerly as a tonic **2** *chiefly Brit* **:** hot beer or ale mixed with gin and sometimes sugar and spices esp. for use as a pick-me-up

**6purl** \"\ *vb* -ED/-ING/-S [alter. of *pirl*] *vi* **1** *chiefly dial* **:** to spin like a top **:** WHIRL, WHEEL **2** *chiefly dial* **:** to tip over **:** tumble or plunge forward in a fall (as from a horse) **:** CAPSIZE, UPSET **~** *vt* **:** to cause to overturn or take a tumble

**7purl** \"\ *n* -S **:** a spill that sends one whirling **:** CAPSIZING, UPSET

**1purl·er** \-lə(r)\ *n* -S [6*purl* + *-er*] *chiefly Brit* **:** SPILL, CROPPER, TUMBLE

**2purler** \"\ *n* -S [2*purl* + *-er*] **:** a worker who finishes raw edges of knitted garments with decorative stitching

**purlhouse** \'=,=\ *n* [5*purl* + *house*] *chiefly Brit* **:** a drinking place selling purl

**1pur·li·cue** *or* **pur·lie·cue** \'pərlə,kyü\ *n* -S [origin unknown] *chiefly Scot* **:** a résumé of a series of sermons or addresses given at the close (as of a communion season) **:** PERORATION

**2purlicue** *or* **purliecue** \"\ *vi* -ED/-ING/-S *chiefly Scot* **:** to give a purlicue

**pur·lieu** \'pərl(,)yü, -(,)lü\ *n* -S [ME *purlewe*, modif. (influenced by MF *lieu* place) of AF *puralé*, *puralee* perambulation, fr. OF, past part. of *puraler*, *poraler* to go through, fr. *pur*, *por* for, through + *aler* to go — more at PURCHASE, ALLEY, LIEU] **1 :** afforested land severed from an English royal forest by perambulation and disafforested so as to rèmit to the former owners their rights subject to various forest laws and restrictions **2 a :** a place of resort **:** HAUNT **b purlieus** *pl* **:** CONFINES, BOUNDS **3 a :** a locality, region, or other place just beyond or sometimes just within given bounds **:** an outlying or adjacent district **b purlieus** *pl* **:** ENVIRONS, NEIGHBORHOOD

**pur·lin** \'pərlən\ *also* **pur·line** \", -,līn\ *n* -S [origin unknown] **:** a horizontal member in a roof supported on the principals and supporting the common rafters — see ROOF illustration

**pur·loin** \pə(r)'lóin, (')pər'l-, (')pə'l-, (')pəi'l-\ *vb* -ED/-ING/-S [ME *purloinen*, fr. AF *purloigner*, fr. OF *porloigner* to put off, delay, fr. *por* for + *loing* at a distance, fr. L *longe*, fr. *longus* long — more at PURCHASE, LONG] *vt* **1** *obs* **:** to set aside **:** render inoperative or ineffectual **2 :** to take away for oneself **:** appropriate wrongfully and often under circumstances that involve a breach of trust **:** FILCH **~** *vi* **:** to practice theft **syn** see STEAL

**pur·loin·er** \-nə(r)\ *n* -S **:** one that purloins **:** THIEF, PILFERER

**purl stitch** *n* [1*purl*] **:** a basic knitting stitch usu. made with the yarn at the front of the work by inserting the right needle into the front part of a loop on the left needle from the right side, catching the yarn with the point of the right needle, and bringing it through the first loop to form a new loop — compare KNIT STITCH

**pu·ro** \'p(y)ů(,)rō\ *n* -S [Sp, fr. *puro* pure, fr. L *purus;* fr. its being all tobacco, unlike a cigarette] **:** CIGAR

**pu·ro·my·cin** \,pyůrə'mīs°n\ *n* -S [*pur*ine + *-o-* + *-mycin*] **:** a trypanocidal and amebicidal antibiotic $C_{22}H_{29}N_7O_5$ obtained from an actinomycete (*Streptomyces alboniger*)

**purp** \'pərp\ *dial var of* PUP

**pur·part** \'pər,pärt\ *n* [ML *purpart-*, *purpars*, fr. OF *pur* for + L *part- pars* part, portion] **:** PURPARTY

**pur·par·ty** \-rd·ē\ *or* **pour·par·ty** \'půr-\ *n* [ME *purpartie*, *pourpartie*, fr. AF, fr. OF *pur*, *pour*, *por* for + *partie* division — more at PURCHASE, PARTY] **:** a share or portion of an estate allotted by a partition to a coparcener

**1pur·ple** \'pərpəl, 'pəp-'pəip-\ *adj, sometimes* -ER/-EST [ME *purpel*, *purpil*, alter. of *purper*, *purpre*, fr. OE *purpuran* of purple, gen. of *purpure* purple color, fr. L *purpura* purple color, purple fish, fr. Gk *porphyra*] **1 a** *archaic* **:** of a color reserved for the use of a royal or imperial ruler **b :** of, belonging to, or worn by those of royal or imperial rank **:** IMPERIAL, REGAL ⟨a ~ tyrant⟩; *also* **:** dressed in royal raiment or colors **2 a :** of a color approaching crimson — presently used almost wholly in vernacular names of plants or animals; compare PURPLE BELLS, PURPLE FINCH **b :** of the color purple **c** *archaic* **:** colored or stained by or as if by blood ⟨I view a field of blood and Tiber rolling with a ~ flood —John Dryden⟩ **3 a :** marked by brilliant coloring **:** SHOWY **b** (1) **:** highly rhetorical **:** ornately and showily phrased or expressed ⟨a ~ patch of writing⟩ (2) **:** marked by undue pungency and profanity ⟨his language . . . is so ~ they had to stop broadcasting the meetings —*Newsweek*⟩ **c :** having the countenance overspread with tinting of purple resulting from or as if from ill-suppressed anger

**2purple** \"\ *n* -S [ME *purpil*, fr. *purpil*, adj.] **1 a** (1) *archaic* **:** any of various rich deep crimsons or scarlets; *specif* **:** the crimson obtained by dyeing textile fibers with a dye obtained from mollusks **:** TYRIAN PURPLE 1 (2) **:** any of various colors that in hue fall about midway between red and blue; *also* **:** the hue of such a color (3) **:** a nonspectral color **b** (1) **:** cloth dyed purple (2) **:** a garment of such color; *esp* **:** a purple robe worn as an emblem of rank or authority (as by a Roman emperor) **c** (1) **:** a mollusk yielding a purple dye; *specif* **:** a gastropod mollusk of *Purpura* or a related genus (as *Thais*) with an adrectal gland that yields the Tyrian purple of ancient times (2) **:** a pigment or dye that colors purple **2 a :** imperial or regal rank or power — compare PORPHYROGENITE **b :** exalted station **:** great wealth **3** *archaic* **:** a purplish blotch or discoloration (as of the skin)

**3purple** \"\ *vb* **purpled; purpled; purpling** \-p(ə)liŋ\ **purples** [1*purple*] *vt* **:** to make purple **:** dye or tint with purple ⟨the setting sun *purpled* the clouds⟩ **~** *vi* **:** to become or turn purple ⟨*purpling* with fury⟩

**purple apricot** *n* **:** a hybrid apricot (*Prunus dasycarpa*) having purplish twigs and white flowers and a dark purple bloomy fruit of inferior quality

**purple avens** *n* **1 :** WATER AVENS **2 :** PRAIRIE SMOKE 1

**purple azalea** *n* **:** PINXTER FLOWER

**purple bacterium** *n* **:** any of various free-living bacteria that contain bacteriochlorophyll marked by purplish or sometimes reddish or brownish pigments — compare PURPLE SULFUR BACTERIUM

**purple beech** *n* **:** COPPER BEECH

**purple bells** *n pl but sing or pl in constr* **:** a Mexican climbing herb (*Rhodochiton atrosanguineum*) of the family Scrophulariaceae that is sometimes cultivated for its showy dark red bell-shaped flowers

**purple bent** *n* **1 :** RHODE ISLAND BENT **2 :** an American grass (*Calamovilfa brevipilis*) found in the pine barrens from New Jersey to No. Carolina

**purple betony** *n* **:** a somewhat hairy perennial Old World betony (*Betonica officinalis*) that is sometimes cultivated for its spikes of showy reddish purple flowers

**purple bladderwort** *n* **:** an aquatic herb (*Utricularia purpurea*) that is common in ponds of the eastern U.S. and has submerged finely dissected leaves and showy emersed very irregular reddish purple flowers

**purple blotch** *n* **:** a fungous disease of onions, garlic, and shallots caused by a fungus (*Alternaria porri*) and characterized at first by small white circular to irregular spots which increase and become large purplish blotches sometimes surrounded by orange or salmon bands

**purple boneset** *n* **:** a joe-pye weed (*Eupatorium purpureum*)

**purple bonnet** *n* **:** WATER SHIELD 1

**purple bottle** *n* **:** a moss of the genus *Splachnum* (esp. *S. ampullaceum*) in which the flask-shaped apophysis is highly colored

**purple brown** *n* **:** OXIDE BROWN

**purple cane** *n* **:** PURPLE RASPBERRY

**purple carmine** *n* **:** MUREXIDE

**purple chamber** *n* **:** a royal accouchement chamber — see PORPHYROGENITE

**purple chokeberry** *n* **:** a chokeberry (*Aronia prunifolia*) of eastern No. America with a globular purplish black fruit

**purple cinquefoil** *n* **:** MARSH CINQUEFOIL

**purple clematis** *n* **:** PURPLE VIRGIN'S-BOWER

**purple cliff brake** *n* **:** a small cliff brake (*Pellaea atropurpurea*) with purplish stipes

**purple clover** *n* **1 :** RED CLOVER **2 :** a western American clover (*Trifolium involucratum*) with purple-flowered heads **3 :** an Australian herb (*Kennedya tabacina*) used for forage

**purple cockle** *n* **:** CORN COCKLE

**purple coneflower** *n* **:** a plant of the genus *Echinacea* (esp. *E. purpurea*)

**purple copper ore** *n* **:** BORNITE

**purple crab** *n* **:** a small rounded red and purple shallow-water crab (*Randallia ornata*) of the California and Mexican Pacific coast

**purple cress** *n* **:** a small perennial herb (*Cardamine douglasii*) of the cooler regions of No. America with dentate roundish leaves and racemose purple flowers

**purple cudweed** *n* **:** an annual or biennial cudweed (*Snaphalium purpureum*) with brown to chestnut or purplish flowers

**purpled** *past of* PURPLE

**purple daisy** *n* **:** either of two coneflowers of the genus *Echinacea* (*E. purpurea* and *E. angustifolia*)

**purple dogwood** *n* **:** BLUE DOGWOOD

**purple emperor** *n* **:** a large European nymphalid forest butterfly (*Apatura iris*) that in the male has the wings shaded with purple

**purple-faced langur** \'==,=-\ *n* [*purple* + *faced*] **:** a common monkey (*Presbytis senex*) of eastern Asia having purplish brown facial skin

**purple fig** *n* **:** a rough-leaved Australian fig tree (*Ficus scabra*) with inedible fruit

**purple finch** *n* **:** an American finch (*Carpodacus purpureus*) the male of which has the head and breast raspberry red

**purple fish** *n, archaic* **:** PURPLE 1c(1)

**purple-flowering raspberry** \'==,=(=)=-\ *n* **:** FLOWERING RASPBERRY

**purple foxglove** *n* **:** a common biennial foxglove (*Digitalis purpurea*) of western Europe from which most cultivated foxgloves are derived

**purple-fringed orchid** \'==,=-\ *or* **purple-fringed orchis** *n* **:** either of two orchids of the genus *Habenaria* with the lip deeply cleft into three lobes and usu. fringed and lacerate: **a :** a No. American orchid (*H. psycodes*) with fragrant purplish-fringed flowers **b :** a closely related orchid (*H. fimbriata*) with larger paler flowers

**purple fringeless orchid** *also* **purple fringeless orchis** *n* [1*purple* + *fringe* + *-less*] **:** an orchid (*Habenaria peramoena*) of northeastern and alpine eastern No. America that is closely related to the large-flowered purple-fringed orchid but has rosy purple to purple violet flowers with the lip divisions denticulate

**purple-fruited chokeberry** \'==,==-\ *n* [*purple* + *fruit* + *-ed*] **:** PURPLE CHOKEBERRY

**purple gallinule** *n* **:** any of various gallinules with showy blue and greenish plumage: as **a :** a gallinule (*Porphyrio porphyrio*) of southern Europe **b :** a gallinule (*Porphyrula martinica*) of tropical America and the southern U.S.

**purple goatsbeard** *n* **:** SALSIFY

**purple grackle** *n* **:** a No. American grackle (*Quiscalus quiscula*) with black and in the full-plumaged male purplish iridescent plumage — see BRONZED GRACKLE, FLORIDA GRACKLE

**purple granadilla** *n* **:** a commonly cultivated Brazilian passionflower (*Passiflora edulis*) grown all over the tropical world for its edible deep purple fruit which is used for sherbets, icing, confectionery, and beverages

**purple grass** *n* **:** any of various herbs (as red clover or spotted medic) having purple flowers or purplish spotted foliage

**purple hairstreak** *n* **:** a hairstreak butterfly that has the wings marked with iridescent purple: as **a :** a European forest hairstreak (*Thecla quercus*) **b :** a large American hairstreak (*Atlides halesus*) with metallic spots on the largely bluish purple to greenish wings — called also *giant purple hairstreak*

**purple haw** *n* **:** BLUEWOOD 1

**purpleheart** \'==,=\ *n* **:** a strong durable elastic purplish timber that is obtained in tropical America from leguminous trees of the genus *Peltogyne* (esp. *P. purpurea*) and that is used esp. in fancy veneers

**purple heron** *n* **:** an Old World heron (*Ardea purpurea*) chiefly grayish with a black crown and maroon breast

**purple-hinged scallop** *n* \'==,=-\ **:** a rock oyster (*Hinnites giganteus*)

**purple lake** *n* **:** BURNT CARMINE

**purple laurel** *n* **:** CATAWBA RHODODENDRON

**purple laver** *n* **:** an edible red alga (*Porphyra vulgaris*)

**purpleleaf sand cherry** \'==,=-\ *n* **:** a hybrid sand cherry that is sometimes cultivated for its reddish leaves, pedicels, and calyces and for its white flowers and blackish purple fruits

**purple-leaved plum** \'==,=-\ *n* **:** a plum that is a garden variety (*Prunus cerasifera pissardi*) of the cherry plum and is cultivated chiefly for its showy purplish foliage and white flowers

**purple locoweed** *or* **purple loco** *n* **:** WOOLLY LOCOWEED

**purple loosestrife** *n* **:** a marsh herb (*Lythrum salicaria*) of Europe and the eastern U.S. having a long spike of purple flowers

**purple marshlocks** *n pl but sing or pl in constr* **:** MARSH CINQUEFOIL

**purple martin** *n* **:** a large swallow (*Progne subis*) widely distributed in No. America and formerly abundant in towns and villages but tending to disappear from localities where the house sparrow has become abundant

**purple meadow parsnip** *n* **:** a perennial usu. yellow-flowered herb (*Thaspium trifoliatum*) of the eastern U.S. with ternately compound leaves

**purple melic grass** *n* **:** MOOR GRASS 2

**purple milkweed** *n* **:** a tall No. American perennial herb (*Asclepias purpurascens*) with a terminal umbel of red or purple flowers

**purple milkwort** *n* **:** a showy low annual herb (*Polygala viridescens*) of eastern No. America with compact spikes of rose-purple or rarely greenish flowers

**purple mite** *n* **:** CITRUS RED MITE

**purple mombin** *n* **:** MOMBIN

**purple moor grass** *n* **:** MOOR GRASS 2

**purple mullein** *n* **:** a Eurasian mullein (*Verbascum phoeniceum*) having showy purple or pink flowers

**purple navy** *n* **:** MARINE BLUE

**purple needlegrass** *n* **:** a tall needlegrass (*Stipa pulchra*) with loose nodding panicles and purplish glumes

**pur·ple·ness** *n* -ES **:** the quality or state of being purple
**purple nightshade** *n* **:** TROMPILLO
**purple of cas·sius** \-ˈkash(ē)əs, -ˈkäsēəs\ *usu cap C* [after Andreas *Cassius* †1673? German physician] **:** a purple pigment prepared usu. by precipitation from solutions of gold chloride and stannous chloride, consisting of colloidal gold and stannic oxide, and used chiefly in coloring ceramic glazes and ruby glass and in a very delicate test for gold
**purple of the ancients :** TYRIAN PURPLE 1
**purple orchid** *n* **:** a strong reddish purple that is bluer and stronger than average fuchsia purple and bluer and deeper than phlox purple
**purple orchis** *also* **purple-hooded orchis** \ˈ==,==-\ *n* **:** SHOWY ORCHIS
**purple osier** *n* **:** PURPLE WILLOW
**purple oxide** *n* **1 :** a natural or synthetic ferric oxide pigment varying in hue from reddish red-yellow to bluish red **2 :** OXIDE BROWN
**purple passage** *also* **purple patch** *n* [trans. of L *pannus purpureus* purple patch; fr. the traditional splendor of purple cloth as contrasted with more shabby materials] **1 :** a passage conspicuous for brilliancy or effectiveness in a work that is characteristically dull, commonplace, or uninspired **2 :** a piece of obtrusively ornate writing
**purple ragwort** *n* **:** a southern African annual herb (*Senecio elegans*) grown for its purple-rayed flowers
**purple raspberry** *n* **1 :** a raspberry with purplish fruits; *esp* **:** any of several cultivated raspberries that are hybrids between red and black raspberries **2 :** a raspberry with purplish canes
**purple rocket** *n* **1 :** an American herb (*Iodanthus pinnatifidus*) of the family Cruciferae with purple flowers and long slender fruits **2 :** FIREWEED b
**purples** *pl of* PURPLE, *pres 3d sing of* PURPLE
**purple sage** *n* **1 :** a silvery-leaved California herb (*Salvia leucophylla*) having purple flowers **2 :** a shrubby sagebrush (*Artemisia tridentata*) having the silvery leaves mostly 3-toothed at the apex and flowers in panicles
**purple sandpiper** *n* **:** a sandpiper (*Erolia maritima*) of the coasts of northern Europe and northeastern America that has the upper parts in winter purplish black and the underparts white
**purple sandwort** *n* **:** a sand spurry (*Spergularia rubra*)
**purple saxifrage** *n* **:** a low densely tufted perennial saxifrage (*Saxifraga oppositifolia*) growing on cool wet rocks in northern regions and having purplish imbricated keeled leaves and a solitary terminal purple flower
**purple scale** *n* **:** a brownish or purplish armored scale (*Lepidosaphes beckii*) destructive to citrus fruits
**pur·ples·cent** \ˌpərpəˈlesᵊnt\ *adj* [¹*purple* + *-escent*] **:** approaching purple **:** growing or becoming purple
**purple shell** *or* **purple snail** *n* **1 a :** a gastropod mollusk that is a source of purple dye **:** PURPLE 1c(1) **b :** JANTHINA 2 **2 :** the shell of a purple shell
**purple shore crab** *n* **:** a shore crab (*Hemigrapsus nudus*) of the Pacific coast with variable markings of yellowish green, reddish brown, or esp. purple and red-spotted chelae
**purple spurge** *n* **:** a devil's milk (*Tithymalus peplus*)
**purple star thistle** *n* **:** STAR THISTLE a
**purple-striped jellyfish** \ˈ==,strīpt-\ *n* **:** any of several large scyphozoan jellyfishes (genus *Pelagia*) with the umbrella more or less striped and mottled with purple
**purple sulfur bacterium** *n* **:** any of numerous sulfur bacteria (as of the family Thiorhodaceae) appearing reddish or purplish due to the combination of bacteriochlorophyll and carotenoid pigments in the cell
**purple thorn apple** *n* **:** a jimsonweed (*Datura stramonium tatula*) that is sometimes cultivated for its purplish leaves and stems and showy violet purple flowers
**purpletop** \ˈ==,=\ *also* **purpletop grass** *n* **:** a sticky grass (*Triodia flava*) of the eastern U.S. with purple panicles
**purple-top** *also* **purple-top wilt** *n* **:** an insect-transmitted and often fatal disease of potato plants caused by the same virus that produces aster yellows and characterized by a purplish or chlorotic discoloration of the top shoots, swelling of axillary branches, and severe wilting
**purple trillium** *n* **:** a birthroot (*Trillium erectum*) of eastern No. America having pink to purple or rarely white ill-scented flowers and an astringent root sometimes used in folk medicine
**purple veil** *n* **:** the egg raft of the angler (sense 2) consisting of a gelatinous sheet containing eggs which on hatching give it a purple color
**purple vetch** *n* **1 :** a European vetch (*Vicia benghalensis*) with whitish purple flowers that is grown for green manure and forage esp. on the Pacific coast of No. America **2 :** AMERICAN VETCH
**purple virgin's-bower** *n* **:** a partly woody vine (*Clematis verticillaris*) of northeastern No. America with waxy purplish blue flowers — called also *purple clematis*
**purple willow** *n* **:** a Eurasian osier willow (*Salix purpurea*) having a bark rich in tannin and salicin — called also *purple osier*
**purple wine** *n* **:** a variable color averaging a dark grayish purple that is bluer than raisin black and bluer and stronger than old lavender (sense 2)
**purple wing** *n* **:** any of several chiefly tropical small to medium-sized butterflies that constitute a genus (*Eunica*) of the family Nymphalidae and are often dark-colored but with blue or purple iridescence
**purple wood** *n* **1 :** a So. American tree (*Copaifera bracteata*) the bark of which yields phenin **2 :** PURPLEHEART
**purplewort** \ˈ==,=\ *n* **1 :** MARSH CINQUEFOIL **2 :** a white clover with dark-colored leaves that is a variant form of the white Dutch clover **3 :** PURPLE GRASS
**purple wreath** *n* **:** a tropical American woody vine (*Petrea volubilis*) with a profusion of showy racemes of purplish violet or blue flowers
**purpling** *pres part of* PURPLE
**pur·plish** \ˈpərp(ə)lish, ˈpə̄p-, ˈpəip-, -lēsh\ *adj* [¹*purple* + *-ish*] **:** being somewhat purple **:** having a tinge of purple ⟨a ~ red⟩
**pur·ply** \-(ə)lē, -li\ *adj* [²*purple* + *-y*] **:** PURPLISH
**purpoint** *archaic var of* POURPOINT
¹**pur·port** \ˈpər,pō(ə)rt, ˈpə̄,-, ˈpəi,-, -,pȯr|, -,pōə|, -,pȯ(ə)|, *usu* |d.+V; *chiefly Brit* -pət\ *n* -S [ME, fr. AF, content, tenor, fr. *purporter* to contain, fr. OF *porporter* to carry, convey, fr. *pur* for + *porter* to carry — more at PURCHASE, PORT] **1 a :** meaning conveyed, professed, or implied **:** IMPORT, TENOR ⟨a look so piteous in ~ —Shak.⟩ **b :** meaning synthesized or synopsized **:** SUBSTANCE, GIST ⟨gave the ~ of their talk in a few words⟩ **2** *obs* **:** DISGUISE, COVERING **3 :** INTENTION, PURPOSE, DESIGN
²**pur·port** \ˌpərˈpō(ə)r|d, -ˈpȯ(ə)r|, -ˈpōə|, -ˈpȯ(r)| *sometimes* ˌpər|- *or* (ˈ)pə̄|- *or* (ˈ)pəi|-; *usu* |d.+V; *chiefly Brit* ˈ=pət\ *vt* -ED/-ING/-S **1 :** to convey, imply, or profess outwardly (as meaning, intention, or true character) **:** have the often specious appearance of being, intending, claiming (something implied or inferred) **:** IMPART, PROFESS ⟨a letter that ~s to express public opinion⟩ ⟨a law that ~s to be in the interest of morality⟩ ⟨men ~*ing* to be citizens⟩ **2 :** to have in mind **:** INTEND, PURPOSE
**purported** *adj* [fr. past part. of ²*purport*] **:** suspected of being **:** REPUTED, RUMORED ⟨~ foreign spies⟩ ⟨a ~ biography⟩ — **pur·port·ed·ly** *adv*
**pur·port·less** *pronunc at* ¹PURPORT *or* ²PURPORT +ləs\ *adj* [¹*purport* + *-less*] **:** lacking purpose or meaning ⟨~ questioning⟩
¹**pur·pose** \ˈpərpəs, ˈpə̄p-, ˈpəip-\ *n, pl* **purposes** \-pəsə̇z, *in rapid speech sometimes* -psə̇z\ [ME *porpos, purpos*, fr. OF, fr. *porposer* to purpose] **1 a :** something that one sets before himself as an object to be attained **:** an end or aim to be kept in view in any plan, measure, exertion, or operation **:** DESIGN ⟨it was our ~ to get home before the storm⟩ ⟨his ~ was above reproach⟩ **b :** RESOLUTION, DETERMINATION ⟨infirm of ~ —Shak.⟩ **2 :** an object, effect, or result aimed at, intended, or attained ⟨energy applied to little ~⟩ **3 :** a subject under discussion or an action in course of execution **4** *obs* **a** (1) **:** PROPOSAL, PROPOSITION (2) **purposes** *pl* **:** a game like conundrums or riddles **b :** DISCOURSE, TALK, CONVERSATION **c :** PURPORT, INTENT, MEANING **5 :** an old Scots dance in which the couples talked together in an affectedly secretive manner **syn** see INTENTION — **in purpose** *adv* **1 :** in one's mind as a purpose **2 :** on purpose — **of purpose** *or* **of set purpose :** on purpose — **on purpose** *adv* **1 :** by deliberate intent and not by accident **:** INTENTIONALLY, DESIGNEDLY **2 :** in order to attain an end ⟨did it *on purpose* to fool his friends⟩ — **to the purpose :** to the point ⟨little . . . said that is at all *to the purpose* —Clive Bell⟩
²**purpose** \"\ *vb* -ED/-ING/-S [ME *purposen*, fr. MF *purposer, porposer*, fr. OF, modif. (influenced by *poser* to put, place) of L *proponere* to put forward, propose — more at PROPOSE] *vt* **1 :** to propose as an aim to oneself **:** determine upon **:** resolve to do or bring about ⟨did nothing ~ against the state —Shak.⟩ ⟨*purposing* to write an account of the tragedy⟩ **2** *obs* **:** to set forth **:** PROPOUND **3** *obs* **:** DESIGN, DESTINE ~ *vi* **1 :** to have a purpose **2** *obs* **:** to proceed to a destination **:** to be bound for some place **3** *obs* **:** DISCOURSE, TALK **syn** see INTEND
**pur·posed·ly** \-pəstlē, -sədlē\ *adv* [*purposed* + *-ly*] **:** PURPOSELY, DELIBERATELY
**pur·pose·ful** \-pəsfəl\ *adj* **1 :** full of determination **:** guided by a definite aim ⟨he was a ~ man⟩ **2 :** serving as, being directed to, or indicating the existence of a purpose or object **:** not aimless or meaningless ⟨~ activities⟩ ⟨ornament is often both decorative and ~⟩ — **pur·pose·ful·ly** \-fəlē, -li\ *adv* — **pur·pose·ful·ness** *n* -ES
**pur·pose·less** \-pəsləs\ *adj* **:** having no purpose **:** not purposeful or purposive **:** AIMLESS, MEANINGLESS — **pur·pose·less·ly** *adv* — **pur·pose·less·ness** *n* -ES
**pur·pose·like** \ˈ==,=\ *adj* [¹*purpose* + *like*] *chiefly Scot* **:** PURPOSEFUL
**pur·pose·ly** \-pəslē, -li\ *adv* [¹*purpose* + *-ly*] **:** with a deliberate or an express purpose **:** on purpose **:** INTENTIONALLY, DESIGNEDLY, EXPRESSLY
**purpose-made** \ˈ==ˈ=\ *adj* **:** designed and constructed to serve a particular purpose
**pur·pos·er** \-sə(r)\ *n* -S **:** one that purposes
**pur·pos·ive** \-siv\ *adj* [²*purpose* + *-ive*] **1 :** serving or effecting a useful end or function though not necessarily as a result of deliberate design ⟨a work of art may be without a purpose, yet ~⟩ **2 :** having, constituting, or tending to fulfill a conscious purpose or design **:** PURPOSEFUL ⟨~ action⟩ **3 :** of or relating to purposivism ⟨~ psychology⟩ — **pur·pos·ive·ly** \-səvlē, -li\ *adv* — **pur·pos·ive·ness** \-sivnəs\ *n* -ES
**pur·pos·iv·ism** \-si,vizəm\ *n* -S [*purposive* + *-ism*] **:** any of various theories of nature or of human and animal behavior that regard purpose or conscious intent as a basal fact
**pur·pos·iv·ist** \-sivəst\ *n* -S [*purposive* + *-ist*] **:** an adherent or proponent of a theory of purposivism
**pur·pres·ture** \(,)pərˈpres(h)chər\ *or* **pour·pres·ture** \pu̇r-\ *n* -S [ME, fr. MF, alter. of *purpresure, propresure*, fr. *porprendre* to seize, occupy, enclose fr. *por* for + *prendre* to take, fr. L *prehendere* — more at PURCHASE, PREHENSILE] **1 :** wrongful appropriation of land subject to the rights of others: as **a :** an encroachment upon or enclosure of real estate subject to common or public rights (as highways, rivers, harbors, forts) **b** *Brit* **:** encroachment upon the royal domain (as the royal forests) **2 :** property enclosed or seized by purpresture
**pur·pri·sion** \-ˈprizhən\ *n* -S [ME, fr. MF *porprison*, fr. *porpris* (past part. of *porprendre*) + *-on* -ion] *obs* **:** PURPRESTURE 1
**pur·pu·ra** \ˈpərpyərə\ *n* [NL, fr. L, purple color — more at PURPLE] **1** -S **:** any of several hemorrhagic states characterized by extravasation of blood into the skin and mucous membranes resulting in patches of purplish discoloration — see PURPURA HEMORRHAGICA **2** *cap* [NL, fr. L, purple fish — more at PURPLE] **:** a genus of marine snails (family Muricidae) including some that yield a purple dye and formerly comprising many forms now usu. placed in the genus *Thais*
**purpura hem·or·rhag·i·ca** \-,heməˈrajəkə\ *n* [NL, lit., hemorrhagic purpura] **1 :** a condition of unknown cause that is characterized by bleeding into the skin with the production of petechiae or ecchymoses and by hemorrhages into mucous membranes and other tissues and that is associated with a reduction in circulating blood platelets and prolonged bleeding time **2 :** an acute or subacute toxemic state in horses that is commonly secondary to an infectious disease and is characterized by dropsical swellings of the legs, abdomen, and head and by small purple hemorrhages in these swellings and in the mucous membranes — called also *petechial fever*
¹**pur·pu·rate** \ˈpərpyərət, -,rāt\ *adj* [L *purpuratus* clothed in purple, fr. *purpura* purple + *-atus* -ate] *obs* **:** purple-colored; *also* **:** ROYAL
²**pur·pu·rate** \-,rāt\ *vt* -ED/-ING/-S [L *purpuratus*, past part. of *purpurare* to purple, fr. *purpura* purple] *archaic* **:** to make purple **:** robe in purple
³**pur·pu·rate** \-,rət, -,rāt\ *n* -S [*purpuric acid* + *-ate*] **:** a salt or ester of purpuric acid
**pur·pure** *or* **pur·pur** *also* **pur·pour** \ˈpərp(y)ər\ *n or adj* [ME, fr. OE *purpure* — more at PURPLE] **:** PURPLE — used chiefly in heraldry
**pur·pu·re·al** \ˌpərˈpyu̇rēəl\ *also* **pur·pu·re·ous** \-ēəs\ *or* **pur·pu·re·an** \-ēən\ *adj* [L *purpureus* fr. L *purpureus*, fr. *purpura* purple color + *-eus* -eous; *purpureal, purpurean* fr. L *purpureus* + E *-al, -an*] **:** PURPLE
**purpureo-** *comb form* [L *purpureus* purple] **:** of a purple or purple-red color — in names of purple or purple-red coordination complexes (as of cobalt or chromium) containing five molecules of ammonia ⟨*purpureo*-cobaltic chloride $[CoCl(NH_3)_5]Cl_2$⟩
**pur·pu·res·cent** \ˌpərpyəˈresᵊnt\ *adj* [L *purpura* purple color + E *-escent*] **:** tinged with purple **:** PURPLISH
**purpuri-** *comb form* [L *purpura*] **:** purple ⟨*purpuri*parous⟩ ⟨*purpuri*ferous⟩
**pur·pu·ric** \ˌpərˈpyu̇rik\ *adj* [NL *purpura* + E *-ic*] **:** of, relating to, or affected with purpura
**purpuric acid** *n* [L *purpura* purple + E *-ic*] **:** a nitrogenous acid $C_8H_5N_5O_6$ related to barbituric acid that yields alloxan and uramil on hydrolysis and is known esp. in purple-red salts (as murexide) from which it is obtained as an orange-red powder
**pur·pu·rin** \ˈpərpyərən\ *n* -S [L *purpura* + E *-in*] **1 :** an orange or red crystalline compound $C_{14}H_5O_2(OH)_3$ obtained from madder root along with alizarin or by oxidation of alizarin and used in dyeing; 1,2,4-trihydroxy-anthraquinone **2** *also* **pur·pu·rine** \", -,rēn\ **:** any of various colored compounds obtained from chlorophyll or related compounds by the action of cold alcoholic alkali and oxygen and closely related to the chlorins
**pur·pu·rine** \-,rīn, -,rēn\ *adj* [F *purpurin*, fr. L *purpura* + F *-in* -ine] **:** of purple color **:** PURPLISH
**pur·pu·rite** \-,rīt\ *n* -S [L *purpura* purple + E *-ite*] **:** a mineral $(Mn,Fe)PO_4$, consisting of ferric-manganic phosphate isomorphous with heterosite and having a dark reddish or purple color
**pur·pu·ro·gal·lin** \,pərpyərōˈgalən\ *n* -S [L *purpura* purple + E *-o-* + *pyrogallol* + *-in*] **:** a red crystalline phenolic ketone dye $C_{11}H_4O(OH)_4$ that occurs naturally in various plant galls as the diglucoside and is made synthetically by oxidation of pyrogallol
**pur·pu·rog·e·nous** \,pərpyəˈräjənəs\ *adj* [L *purpura* purple + E *-o-* + *-genous*] **:** giving rise to a purple color or producing a purple product ⟨a ~ gland⟩
**pur·pu·ro·xanthin** \,pərpyə(,)rō+\ *n* [L *purpura* + ISV *-o-* + *xanthin*] **:** a reddish yellow crystalline compound $C_{14}H_6O_2(OH)_2$ obtained from madder root or by reduction of purpurin; 1,3-dihydroxy-anthraquinone — called also *xanthopurpurin*
¹**purr** *R* ˈpər, + *vowel* ˈpər-; *–R* ˈpə̄, + *suffixal vowel* ˈpər- *also* ˈpər, + *vowel in a following word* ˈpər- *or* ˈpə̄ *also* ˈpər\ *n* -S [imit] **1 a :** a low vibratory murmur of a cat that appears to indicate contentment or pleasure and is believed to result from the streaming of air over the false vocal cords **b :** a similar sound of another animal **2 :** a sound resembling the purr of a cat ⟨the soft ~ of a passing motor⟩
²**purr** \"\ *vb* -ED/-ING/-S [imit.] *vi* **1 :** to utter or give forth a purr **2 a :** to speak as if purring **b :** to speak in a light but catty manner ~ *vt* **:** to signify or express by purring or in a lightly catty manner
**purre** \"\ *n* -S [imit.] *dial Eng* **:** a dunlin in winter plumage
**pur·ree** \ˈpu̇rē, ˈpərē\ *n* -S [Hindi *piūṛī*; akin to Skt *pīta* yellow] **:** INDIAN YELLOW 2
**purre.maw** *n, dial Eng* **:** ROSEATE TERN
**purr·er** \ˈpər·ə(r), *–R also* ˈpərə(r\ *n* -S **:** one that purrs
**purr·ing·ly** *adv* **:** in a purring manner **:** with a purr
**purring spider** *n* **:** a moderate-sized wolf spider (*Lycosa gulosa* syn. *L. kochii*) of the eastern U.S. that often drums on dead leaves with its palpi
**purry** \ˈpər·|ē, |i, *–R also* ˈpər|\ *adj* -ER/-EST [¹*purr* + *-y*] **:** like a purr
**pur sang** \(ˈ)pu̇(ə)rˈsäⁿ\ *adj* [F *pur-sang* thoroughbred animal, fr. *pur* pure + *sang* blood, fr. L *sanguis*] **:** being such beyond a doubt or to the utmost degree **:** PURE-BLOODED — used postpositively ⟨the contemplative poet *pur sang* —Louise Bogan⟩ ⟨denounce him as a fascist *pur sang* —Thomas Mann⟩
¹**purse** \ˈpərs, ˈpə̄s, ˈpəis, *dial* ˈpəs\ *n* -S [ME *purs*, fr. OE, modif. (perh. influenced by OE *pusa, posa* bag) of ML *bursa*, fr. LL, oxhide, fr. Gk *byrsa*] **1 a :** a small bag closed with a drawstring and used to carry money; *broadly* **:** a receptacle (as a handbag, pocketbook, or wallet) used to carry money and often other small objects about with one **b :** a pouch or other receptacle (as in a fishing net) that suggests a purse in form **c** (1) *archaic* **:** a normal or abnormal bodily structure in the form of a pouch (2) **:** SCROTUM — used chiefly of domestic animals **2 a :** a money purse with its contents; *also* **:** a sum of money **:** MEANS, RESOURCES, FUNDS ⟨live within one's ~⟩ ⟨all shared the common ~⟩ ⟨charities from his private ~⟩ **b** (1) **:** a sum of money offered as a prize or as a present ⟨a race with a ~ of $3000⟩ ⟨collected a ~ to help the flood victims⟩ (2) **:** PURSE RACE **c** *archaic* **:** a definite sum of money in the Muslim Orient ⟨in imperial Turkey a ~ of silver equaled 500 piasters, a ~ of gold, 10,000⟩ **3 :** a splinter or spark that pops from an open fire

purse 1a

²**purse** \"\ *vb* -ED/-ING/-S [ME *pursen*, fr. *purs* purse] *vt* **1 :** to put into a purse ⟨I will . . . ~ the ducats —Shak.⟩ **2** *obs* **:** to enclose and hold as if in a purse **:** shut up or off **:** CONFINE **3 a :** to draw up or contract into folds or wrinkles like the mouth of a purse **:** PUCKER, KNIT ⟨didst contract and ~ thy brow —Shak.⟩ **b :** to draw closed (the mouth of a purse seine) ~ *vi* **:** to become puckered **:** draw some part (as one's lips or brow) up or together
**purse bearer** *n* [ME *pursberer*, fr. *purs* purse + *berere, berer* bearer] **1 :** the bearer of a purse **:** TREASURER, BURSAR **2 :** an official of the British crown office who bears the great seal before the lord chancellor
**purse crab** *n* **:** a large anomuran land crab (*Birgus latro*) that is widely distributed about islands of the tropical Indian and Pacific oceans where it burrows in the soil and feeds on coconuts and is related to the hermit crabs but distinguished by its large size and its broad symmetrical abdomen the oily flesh of which is esteemed a delicacy by natives of the region — called also *palm crab, robber crab, tree crab*
**purse cutter** *n* **:** CUTPURSE
**purse-cutting** \ˈ=,==\ *n* **:** the practice of a cutpurse **:** thievery or pilfering from the person of the victim
**purse·ful** \ˈ=,fu̇l\ *n* -S [*purse* + *-ful*] **:** all that is or can be contained in a purse
**purse isinglass** *n* **:** isinglass made from unopened bladders of fish
**purse-leech** \ˈ=,=\ *n* **:** one that is excessively greedy for money
**purse·less** \ˈ=ləs\ *adj* **:** lacking a purse **:** having no money
**purselike** \ˈ=,=\ *adj* **:** resembling a purse esp. in pouched rounded form ⟨wattles in the form of ~ outgrowths⟩
**purse line** *n* **:** a rope by which a purse seine is pursed
**purse pride** *n* **:** pride of money **:** the condition of the purse-proud
**purse-proud** \ˈ=,=\ *adj* **:** proud or arrogant because of one's wealth esp. in the absence of other distinctions
**purs·er** \ˈpərsər, ˈpə̄sə(r, ˈpəisə(r\ *n* -S [ME, fr. *purs* purse + *-er*] **1** *archaic* **:** a maker of purses **2 a** *archaic* **:** an official in charge of and keeping records of disbursements and receipts **:** TREASURER **b** *obs* **:** a paymaster in the British or U.S. Navy **c** (1) **:** an official on a ship responsible for all papers and accounts and on a passenger ship also for the comfort and welfare of the passengers (2) **:** a similar official on an airliner
**purse race** *n* **:** a race for a fixed purse to which entries usu. close less than six weeks before the first day of the meet in which the race is to be run — compare STAKE RACE
**purse rat** *n* **:** POCKET GOPHER
**purse ring** *n* **1 :** a ring or one of the rings to which purse strings are attached **2 :** one of the rings on a purse seine through which the purse line passes
**purs·er·ship** \ˈ==,ship\ *n* [*purser* + *-ship*] **:** the office or duties of a purser
**purses** *pl of* PURSE, *pres 3d sing of* PURSE
**purse seine** *also* **purse net** *n* [*purse seine* fr. ¹*purse* + *seine*; *purse net* fr. ME *pursnette*, fr. *purs* purse + *nette* net] **:** a large seine designed to be set by two boats around a school of fish and so arranged that after the ends have been brought together the bottom can be closed, ranging typically from 250 to 400 yards in length and from 18 to 20 yards in depth, having the upper edge supported by floats and the lower edge weighted by brass rings through which the purse line passes, and being closed below when the ends of the net have been brought together by the dropping of a heavy lead weight that is attached over pulleys to the ends of the purse line and that by its descent puckers together the bottom of the net

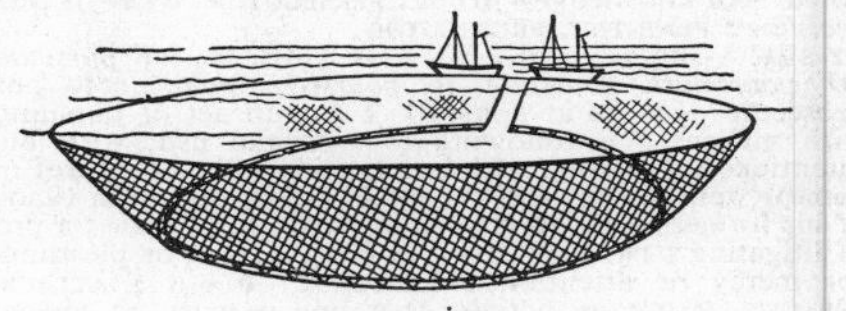

purse seine

**purse sein·er** \ˈ=,sānə(r)\ *n* [*purse seine* + *-er*] **1** *also* **purse boat :** a usu. power-driven fishing boat equipped or used for fishing with a purse seine **2 :** a fisherman who uses a purse seine **:** a member of the crew of a purse seiner
**purse silk** *n* **:** a smooth tightly twisted silk thread used esp. for embroidery or knitting
**purse string** *n* [ME, fr. *purs, purse* purse + *string*] **1 :** one of the drawstrings of a purse by which its mouth is opened or closed **2 purse strings** *pl* **:** financial resources ⟨those who have control of our municipal *purse strings*⟩ ⟨*purse strings* will thus continue to control the distribution of . . . documents —*Economist*⟩
**purse-string** \ˈ=,=\ *adj* [*purse string*] **1 :** formed or drawn in the manner of a purse string ⟨a wind-tight *purse-string* closure about the neck⟩ — see PURSE-STRING SUTURE **2 :** involving control of financial matters **:** acting through financial control ⟨committee would have *purse-string* power to enforce the decisions —*The Nat'l Jewish Monthly*⟩
**purse-string suture** *n* **:** a surgical suture passed as a running stitch in and out along the edge of a circular wound in such a way that when the ends of the suture are drawn tight the wound is closed like a purse
**pursevant** *obs var of* PURSUIVANT
**purseweb spider** \ˈ=,=-\ *also* **purse spider** *n* **:** a spider (*Atypus abbotti*) that forms a purse-shaped web at the base of tree trunks
**purse weight** *n* **:** the tom of a purse seine
**pur·shia** \ˈpərshēə, ˈpu̇r-\ *n, cap* [NL, fr. Frederick *Pursh* †1820 Ger. botanist and horticulturist in America + NL *-ia*] **:** a genus of western American shrubs (family Rosaceae) having small solitary yellow flowers and pubescent achenes and being important browse plants in dry parts of the southwestern U.S.
**pursh's plantain** \ˈpə|rshəz-, ˈpu̇|\ *or* **pursh plantain** *n, usu cap 1st P* [after Frederick *Pursh*] **:** a tufted annual plantain (*Plantago purshii*) of central and western No. America with whitish woolly spikes and foliage and small whitish flowers
**pursier** *comparative of* PURSY

**pursiest** *superlative of* PURSY

**pur·si·ly** \'pəsəlē, -li, 'pərs-,'pə̄s-,pəis-\ *adv* **:** in a pursy manner

**pur·si·ness** \-sēnəs, -sin-\ *n* -ES [ME *pursynes*, fr. ¹*pursy* + *-nes* -ness] **:** the quality or state of being pursy **:** a condition of being swollen or puffed up (as with pride, self-importance, flatulence)

**pursing** *pres part of* PURSE

**pur·sive** \'pərsiv\ *adj* [AF *pursif* — more at PURSY] **:** SHORT-WINDED, PURSY

¹**purs·lane** \'pərslən, 'pə̄s-,'pəis-, -,slān\ *n* -S [ME *purcelan, purslane*, fr. MF *porcelaine*, fr. LL *porcillagin-, porcillago*, alter. (influenced by such plant names as *plantagin-, plantago* plantain) of L *porcillaca*, alter. of *portulaca*] **:** a plant of the family Portulacaceae; *esp* **:** an annual herb (*Portulaca oleracea*) with fleshy succulent obovate leaves that is widely distributed in both hemispheres, is a troublesome weed in some areas, and is used as a potherb and for salads

²**purslane** *or* **purslaine** *obs var of* PORCELAIN

**purslane family** *n* **:** PORTULACACEAE

**purslane speedwell** *n* **:** a No. American annual herb (*Veronica peregrina*) that has small white flowers and is widely naturalized as a weed in So. America and the Old World

**purslane sphinx** *n* **:** WHITE-LINED SPHINX

**purslane tree** *n* **:** a southern African fleshy shrub (*Portulacaria afra*) with foliage that is used as fodder

**purs·ley** \'pə(r)slē, 'pə̄s-,'pəis-, -li\ *n* -S [by shortening and alter.] **:** PURSLANE

**pur·su·able** \pə(r)'süəbəl\ *adj* [*pursue* + *-able*] **:** subject to pursuit

**pur·su·al** \-üəl\ *n* -S [*pursue* + *-al*] **:** the act or an instance of pursuing **:** PURSUIT

**pur·su·ance** \-üən(t)s\ *n* -S [*pursue* + *-ance*] **1 a :** the act of pursuing (as by chasing, seeking after, continuing, following up) ⟨the ~ of truth⟩ **b :** a carrying out or into effect **:** the action of executing **:** PROSECUTION ⟨engaged in ~ of his researches⟩ ⟨immediate ~ of his orders⟩ **2 a :** something that is pursuant **:** CONSEQUENCE **b :** SEQUENCE; *specif* **:** the body of a discourse

¹**pur·su·ant** \-nt\ *n* -S [ME *poursuiant, pursuant*, fr. MF *poursuiant, poursuivant* follower, pursuer, prosecutor, fr. OF, fr. pres. part. of *poursivre, poursuir* to pursue, prosecute — more at PURSUE] **1** *obs* **:** PROSECUTOR **2 :** PURSUER

²**pursuant** \"\ *adj* [*pursue* + *-ant*] **:** that is in pursuit **:** PURSUING ⟨a ~ and powerful grandee —Lon Tinkle⟩ ⟨a ~ reek of the stables⟩

**pur·su·ant·ly** *adv* [²*pursuant* + *-ly*] **:** CONSEQUENTLY

**pursuant to** *prep* [²*pursuant*] **:** in the course of carrying out **:** in conformance to or agreement with **:** according to ⟨*pursuant to* the proposals of this note⟩ ⟨acted *pursuant to* their agreement⟩

**pur·sue** \pə(r)'sü\ *vb* -ED/-ING/-S [ME *pursuen*, fr. AF *pursuer*, fr. OF *poursivre, poursuir*, fr. (assumed) VL *prosequere*, fr. L *prosequi* to follow, follow after, pursue, fr. *pro-* forward + *sequi* to follow — more at PRO-, SUE] *vt* **1 a :** to follow with enmity **:** PERSECUTE, BEDEVIL **:** persist in harassing, afflicting, or aggrieving ⟨*pursued* with peculiar animosity —T.B.Macaulay⟩ **b :** to follow usu. determinedly in order to overtake, capture, kill, or defeat ⟨the hounds *pursued* the stag⟩ ⟨*pursued* the fleeing Indians⟩ **c :** to attend, follow, and seek to attract ⟨was *pursuing* two girls at the time —Oliver La Farge⟩ **2 a :** to seek to follow, obtain, attain to, or accomplish **:** find or employ measures to obtain or accomplish ⟨losing the pearl of great price while *pursuing* lesser ends —W.R.Inge⟩ **b :** to follow or seek by judicial proceedings **:** PROSECUTE ⟨*pursued* his legal remedies⟩ **3 :** to proceed along or act in, according to, or in compliance with **:** FOLLOW ⟨U.S. 220 ~*s* an irregular north-south course —*Amer. Guide Series: Pa.*⟩ ⟨a compact little village, astir with the same activity it has *pursued* . . . since the 17th century —*Amer. Guide Series: N.H.*⟩ **4 :** to follow up or proceed with **:** CONTINUE **:** engage oneself with **:** PRACTICE ⟨the ordinary rigorous canons of scientific evidence *pursued* by the scholarly historian —M.R.Cohen⟩ ⟨*pursuing* the game of high ambition —John Buchan⟩ ⟨placidly *pursuing* her tasks without heeding the surrounding clamor⟩ **5 :** to follow with or as if with one's eyes, senses, or mind ⟨his thoughts also followed or, rather, *pursued* the slim woman —Ethel Wilson⟩ **6 a :** to attempt to arrive at (as a point, a place, an end) ⟨moving toward the point it has so energetically *pursued* —Henry Adams⟩ **b** *obs* **:** to follow in order to avenge or punish **~** *vi* **1 :** to go in pursuit **:** follow after someone or something ⟨where only the strongest dared ~⟩ **2** *Scots & eccl law* **:** to bring suit **:** PROSECUTE — often used with *for* **3 :** to keep on doing or saying **:** press on (as in argument or speech) **syn** see FOLLOW

**pur·su·er** \-süə(r), -sü̇ə)r, -süə\ *n* -S [ME *pursuere*, fr. *pursuen* to pursue + *-ere* -er] **:** one that pursues: as **a :** one that chases or follows after ⟨that canine ~ of the rabbit⟩ ⟨a devoted ~ of knowledge⟩ **b** *obs* **:** PERSECUTOR **c** *chiefly Scots & eccl law* **:** PLAINTIFF, PROSECUTOR

**pur·suit** \-süt, *usu* -üd·+V\ *n* -S [ME, fr. AF *purseute*, fr. OF *poursieute, poursuite*, fr. *poursivre, poursuir* to pursue, prosecute — more at PURSUE] **1 a :** an act of pursuing (as with malice) **:** a following to overtake usu. with hurtful intentions **:** a chasing with haste (as to kill or capture) ⟨~ of game⟩ ⟨went out in ~ of the thief⟩ ⟨spent his life in vicious ~ of his former rival⟩ **b** (1) *chiefly Scots & eccl law* **:** a process of litigating **:** PROSECUTION (2) *obs* **:** a suing or pleading esp. for mercy or attention **:** ENTREATY **c** *obs* **:** ATTACKING, ASSAULT **2 a :** an activity that one pursues or engages in seriously and continually or frequently as a vocation or profession or as an avocation ⟨except in the arts, letters, or other unprofitable ~*s* —H.S.Canby⟩ **:** a way of life **:** OCCUPATION ⟨the law, being a profession, was accounted a more gentlemanly ~ than business —Edith Wharton⟩ **b :** an end pursued **:** OBJECTIVE **3 :** a following with a view to reach, accomplish, or obtain **:** an endeavor to attain to, gain, or achieve ⟨the ~ of knowledge⟩ ⟨mad ~ of pleasure⟩ **4 :** PURSUIT PLANE **syn** see WORK

**pursuit curve** *n* **:** the interception curve made by an interceptor maintaining continuous fire on a moving airplane from a position to the rear and side — compare LEAD-COLLISION COURSE

**pur·suit·me·ter** \-'=,mēd·ə(r)\ *n* [*pursuit* + *-meter*] **:** a device for testing the coordination of eyes and hand in respect to ability to maintain a manually operated test object in a given position or along a changing course

**pursuit plane** *n* **:** FIGHTER; *esp* **:** a fighter plane designed for pursuit of and attack on enemy airplanes

**pursuit race** *n* **:** a bicycle race in which riders spaced at equal intervals at the start attempt to eliminate other contestants by overtaking them

¹**pur·sui·vant** \'pərs(w)əvənt, -)ēv-\ *n* -S [ME *pursevant*, fr. MF *poursuivant*, *poursuivant*, lit., follower, pursuer — more at PURSUANT] **1** *also* **pursuivant of arms** *or* **pursuivant at arms a :** an inferior heraldic functionary attendant on medieval European heralds and learning the profession of heraldry **:** a neophyte herald **b :** an officer of arms ranking below a herald but having similar duties **2** *archaic* **:** a royal or state messenger **:** one with power to execute a warrant **3 a :** FOLLOWER, ATTENDANT **b :** one that seeks out and follows or delves into ⟨the literary ~ of the Renaissance —Delbert Clark⟩; *sometimes* **:** one that seeks out to entrap or seize

²**pursuivant** *vt* -ED/-ING/-S *obs* **:** to deliver to or by a pursuivant **:** PURSUE

¹**pur·sy** \'pəsē, 'pərs-,'pə̄s-,'pəis-, -si\ *or* **pus·sy** \'pəs-\ *adj* -ER/-EST [ME *pursy*, fr. AF *pursif*, alter. of MF *polsif*, fr. *polser* to push, beat, breathe with difficulty + *-if* -ive — more at PUSH] **1 a :** tending to be or habitually short-winded or asthmatic **:** short-breathed esp. because of corpulence **b :** FAT, PUFFY, OBESE **2 :** made large or self-important with pampering or luxurious living **:** characterized by or arising from arrogance of wealth, self-indulgence, or luxury

²**pursy** \'pərsē, 'pə̄s-,'pəis-, -si, *dial* 'pəs-\ *adj* -ER/-EST [¹*purse* + *-y*] **1 :** puckered up ⟨a ~ mouth⟩ **2 :** having and usu. excessively aware of having an abundance of material possessions **:** wealthy and purse-proud

**pur·te·nance** \'pərt°nən(t)s\ *n* -S [ME *purtenaunce*, lit., that which belongs to something, modif. (prob. influenced by OF *por, pur* for) of MF *partenance, pertinence* — more at PURCHASE, PERTINENCE] **:** the heart, liver, and lungs of an animal **:** ENTRAILS, PLUCK

**pu·ru·há** \,pürə'hä, -rə'wä\ *n, pl* **puruhá** \"\ *or* **puruha·es** \,==',äs\ *usu cap* [Sp, of AmerInd origin] **1 a :** an Indian people of central Ecuador **b :** a member of such people **2 :** the extinct language of the Puruhá people

**pu·ru·lence** \'pyür(y)ələn(t)s\ *also* **pu·ru·len·cy** \-nsē,-nsi\ *n* -S [LL *purulentia*, fr. L *purulentus* purulent + *-ia* -y] **1 :** the quality or state of being purulent **2 :** PUS; *also* **:** the formation of pus

**pu·ru·lent** \-nt\ *adj* [L *purulentus*, fr. *pur-, pus* pus + *-ulentus* -ulent — more at FOUL] **1 :** consisting of or being pus ⟨a ~ discharge⟩ **2 a :** containing pus ⟨a ~ lesion⟩ **b :** accompanied by the formation of pus ⟨~ meningitis⟩

**pu·ru·loid** \-,lȯid\ *adj* [*purul*ent + *-oid*] **:** resembling pus

**pu·ru·sha** \'pürəshə\ *n* -S [Skt *puruṣa*, lit., man] **:** the soul that with prakriti constitutes the primary cause of phenomenal existence according to Sankhya philosophy; *specif* **:** an individual soul of an infinite number of like, discrete, and eternal souls

**pur·ves flue** *or* **purves tube** \'pərvəs-\ *n, usu cap P* [after *Purves*, 19th cent. Eng. engineer, its inventor] **:** a boiler flue with thickened transverse ribs or corrugations rather widely spaced

¹**pur·vey** \pə(r)'vā *sometimes* ¦pər¦v- *or* (')pə¦v- *or* (')pəi¦v-\ *vb* -ED/-ING/-S [ME *purveien, porveien*, fr. MF *porveir, porveioir* to foresee, provide, fr. L *providēre* — more at PROVIDE] *vt* **1 :** to make available (something wanted or needed) **:** obtain or supply for use ⟨information ~*ed* by government bulletins⟩; *esp* **:** to provide (food or other provender) usu. as a matter of business ⟨mine host ~*ed* us a sumptuous feast⟩ **2** *archaic* **:** to provide (as a person) with something needed or wanted (as provisions, supplies, equipment) **~** *vi* **1 :** to make provision or preparations **2 :** to serve as a purveyor; *esp* **:** to supply provisions **3 :** to provide or convey something essential **:** lend necessary assistance **:** serve as a source of supply — used with *to* or *for* ⟨the function of the eye is now purely ministerial; it merely ~*s* for the ear —Sidney Lanier⟩

²**pur·vey** *n* -S *obs* **:** an act of purveying **:** something purveyed

**pur·vey·ance** \(,)='vāən(t)s\ *also* **pour·vey·ance** \pür'v-\ *n* -S [ME *porveance, purveiaunce* foresight, provision for the future, fr. OF *porveance*, fr. *porveeir* to provide + *-ance* — more at PURVEY] **1 a :** the act or fact of providing in advance **:** PREPARATION **:** prudent direction or management **b :** the act or process of purveying or procuring (as provisions) ⟨the ~ of supplies for an army⟩ ⟨dedicated to the ~ of dreams —J.W.Aldridge⟩; *specif* **:** the providing of supplies or services for a sovereign or for the crown by preemption or impressment at a valuation fixed by appraisers appointed by the purveyors or by the purveyors themselves and usu. below the market value as a royal prerogative **2** *obs* **:** something (as supplies or provisions) that is purveyed

**pur·vey·or** \(,)='vāə(r), '=,==\ *n* -S [ME *purveour*, fr. OF *porveour*, fr. *porveeir* to provide + *-eur* -or] **:** one who purveys, provides, or procures: as **a :** one who provides victuals or whose business is to make provisions for the table **:** VICTUALER, CATERER **b** *obs* **:** an official functioning in the securing of necessary supplies (as for a city or an army) **c :** a former officer of the British government providing or exacting provision under the right of purveyance

**pur·view** \'pər,vyü, 'pə̄,v-, 'pəi,v-\ *n* [ME *purveu, purvewe*, fr. AF *purveu (est)* it is provided (opening phrase of a statute), fr. OF *porveu*, past part. of *porveeir* to provide — more at PURVEY] **1 a :** the body of a statute or the part that begins with "*Be it enacted*" and ends before the repealing clause — compare PREAMBLE, PROVISO, SAVING CLAUSE **b :** the limit or scope of a statute **:** the whole extent of its intention or provisions **2 :** the range or limit of authority, competence, responsibility, concern, or intention ⟨actively under the ~ of the Federal Trade Commission —*Jour. Amer. Med. Assoc.*⟩ ⟨the problem in Indonesia . . . does not fall within the ~ of the Security Council —*N.Y.Times*⟩ **3 :** range of sight, vision, understanding, cognizance, or knowledge ⟨persuaded that there is . . . no human destiny outside the ~ of their system —Bertrand Russell⟩ **syn** see RANGE

**pur·voe** \pə(r)'vō\ *n* -S [Marathi *parbhū*, fr. Skt *prabhu* — more at PRABHU] **:** a writer caste of India

**pur·wan·nah** \pə(r)'wänə\ *n* -S [Hindi *parwāna*, fr. Per] *India* **:** a written pass or permit **:** ORDER; *also* **:** a royal grant

¹**pus** \'pəs\ *n* -ES [L *pur-, pus* — more at FOUL] **:** thick opaque usu. yellowish white fluid matter formed in connection with an inflammation due to the invasion of the body by an infective microorganism (as a bacterium) and composed of fluid exudate containing degenerating leukocytes, tissue debris, and living or dead microorganisms — see SUPPURATION

²**pus** \'püs\ *n, usu cap* [Skt *puṣya*] **:** a month of the Hindu year — see MONTH table

**-pus** \,pəs\ *n comb form* [NL *-pod-, -pus*, fr. Gk *-pod-, -pous*, fr. *pod-, pous* foot — more at FOOT] **:** creature having (such) a foot or feet ⟨*monopus*⟩ ⟨*Lycopus*⟩ — chiefly in generic names in zoology ⟨*mastigopus*⟩ ⟨*Pygopus*⟩; compare -PODA

**pu·san** \(')pü¦sän\ *adj, usu cap* [fr. *Pusan, Fusan*, city of southern Korea] **:** of or from the city of Pusan, Korea **:** of the kind or style prevalent in Pusan

**pus basin** *n* **:** a kidney-shaped metal basin used in sickrooms and hospitals to catch body discharges (as pus or sputum)

pus basin

**pus cell** *n* **:** a polymorphonuclear leukocyte

**pusch·kin·ia** \püsh'kinēə\ *n* [NL, fr. A.A.Mussin-*Puschkin* †1805? Russ. scientist + NL *-ia*] **1** *cap* **:** a small genus of Asiatic spring-blooming bulbous herbs (family Liliaceae) having solitary or racemose flowers with a 6-parted blue-veined white perianth and connate filaments **2** -S **:** any plant of the genus *Puschkinia*

**pu·sey·ism** \'pyüzē,izəm, -üsē-\ *n, usu cap* [E.B.*Pusey* 1800–1882, Eng. theologian + E *-ism*] **:** TRACTARIANISM

**pu·sey·ite** \-,īt\ *n* -S *usu cap* [E.B.*Pusey* + E *-ite*] **:** an adherent of Puseyism **:** HIGH CHURCHMAN

¹**push** \'pu̇sh\ *vb* -ED/-ING/-ES [ME *posshen, pusshen*, fr. OF *polser, pouser* to push, beat, fr. L *pulsare*, fr. *pulsus*, past part. of *pellere* to drive, push — more at FELT] *vt* **1 a :** to exert physical force upon so as to cause or tend to cause motion away from the force **:** to cause to move or tend to move away or ahead by steady pressure in contact ⟨~ a baby carriage⟩ ⟨~ a door open⟩ ⟨~ a boat off⟩ ⟨~ him out of the way⟩ ⟨~*ed* back his chair⟩ ⟨dunes that the ice ~*ed* up⟩ — opposed to *pull* **b** *archaic, of an animal* **:** to butt or thrust against with the head or horns **c :** to force to go (as by driving or displacing) ⟨~ the enemy troops into the sea⟩ ⟨my crew will ~ your cattle across the creek tomorrow —Luke Short⟩ ⟨~*ed* the worry to the back of her mind⟩ ⟨~ the job onto someone else⟩ **:** CROWD ⟨a local sensation that ~*ed* the foreign news off the front page⟩ ⟨cleared fields that ~ back the wilderness⟩ **d :** to make, effect, or accomplish by forcing aside obstacles or opposition ⟨~ his way to the front of the crowd⟩ ⟨~*ed* the new road into the wilderness⟩ **2 a :** to put in a projecting position **:** STICK ⟨~*ed* out his lower lip⟩ ⟨~ her nose into their affairs⟩ **b :** to cause to extend against resistance or with vigorous effort **:** put forth ⟨plants that ~ their roots deep into the soil⟩ **:** send out ⟨~*ed* an army across the river to intercept the enemy⟩ **c :** to cause to change in quantity or extent ⟨costs of municipal government are still rising, ~*ing* up . . . taxes —Ed Cony⟩ ⟨as the frontier was ~*ed* westward —*Amer. Guide Series: Va.*⟩; *esp* **:** INCREASE ⟨~ the production of consumer goods to record levels⟩ **3 a :** to press (a person) to do something ⟨~ her son to pursue a musical career⟩ **b :** to urge or force to greater speed or activity or beyond usual limits ⟨~*es* his horse to the front of the race⟩ ⟨~*ed* the truck to a breakneck speed⟩ ⟨cruises at 200 but can hit 250 if ~*ed*⟩ ⟨~*es* her voice a little too hard —Edward Sackville-West & Desmond Shawe-Taylor⟩ **c :** to bring (a person) to a point, state, or position by severe pressure ⟨fancied slights . . . ~*ed* men to the breaking point —Oscar Handlin⟩ ⟨the students . . . frequently ~ the professors into extreme views —Dallas Finn⟩; *esp* **:** to reduce to straits (as by lack of money, time) ⟨~ smaller companies into bankruptcy⟩ ⟨~*ed* for time⟩ **d :** to bid for the purpose of inducing (an opponent in a card game) to make a higher and possibly unsafe bid **e :** to direct the course of ⟨~*ed* his horse into the opening⟩ ⟨~ a pencil⟩ **:** OPERATE ⟨~*es* a taxi for a living⟩ **4 :** to develop (as an idea or system) more fully or to an extreme ⟨~*es* the argument one step further —Robert Strausz-Hupé⟩ ⟨~*es* his historical interpretation as far as it will go —S.F.Damon⟩ **5 a :** to promote or carry out with vigor **:** urge or press the advancement, adoption, or practice of ⟨~*ed* his protégé in university circles⟩ ⟨~ the bill in the legislature⟩; *specif* **:** to make aggressive efforts to sell ⟨a heavy consumer drive to ~ canned foods —*Printers' Ink*⟩ **b :** to engage in the illicit sale of (narcotics) **6 :** to approach in age or number ⟨the old man was ~*ing* seventy-five —Saul Bellow⟩ ⟨the crowds are ~*ing* 200,000 —Ken Purdy⟩ **~** *vi* **1** *archaic a of an animal* **:** to butt a person or object with the head or horns **b :** to thrust with a pointed weapon **c :** to make a hostile advance **2 a :** to exert oneself continuously, vigorously, or obtrusively to gain a desired end **:** work or drive hard ⟨unions ~*ing* for higher wages⟩ **b :** to peddle narcotics **3 a :** to exert a steady force against something ⟨watched the crowd ~ against the gate until it broke⟩ **b :** to move by pushing or being pushed ⟨took the raft pole and ~*ed* out into the stream⟩ ⟨the door ~*ed* open —Erle Stanley Gardner⟩ ⟨fillers that ~ out easily⟩ **c :** to make one or more bids that push an opponent **4 :** to press forward against obstacles or opposition or with energy **:** advance persistently or courageously ⟨encouraged adventurous Portuguese captains to ~ out into the Atlantic —G.C.Sellery⟩ **5 a :** to stick out **:** PROJECT ⟨a dock that ~*es* far out into the lake⟩ **:** EXTEND ⟨a road that ~*es* toward the mountains⟩ **b :** to change in quantity or extent; *esp* **:** INCREASE ⟨corn acreage ~*ed* into first place —*Amer. Guide Series: Minn.*⟩ — **push one's luck :** to take a rash risk **:** venture against increasingly adverse odds ⟨*pushed his luck* too far when he deliberately insulted a churchman —Louis Simpson⟩ — **push up daisies** *or* **push daisies** *slang* **:** to lie dead and buried ⟨if a shell has my number on it, I'll soon be *pushing daisies* —Dixon Wecter⟩

**syn** PUSH, SHOVE, THRUST, and PROPEL can mean, in common, to use force upon a thing so as to make it move ahead or aside. PUSH implies the application of force by a body already in contact with the thing to be moved onward, aside, or out of the way ⟨*push* a wheelbarrow⟩ ⟨*push* a man off a seat⟩ ⟨*push* a card across the table⟩ ⟨*push* a man into a high political position⟩ SHOVE implies a strong, usu. fast or rough, pushing of something usu. along a surface, as the ground or a floor ⟨*shove* a piano a few feet back⟩ ⟨*shove* a handkerchief into one's pocket⟩ ⟨*shove* a plate away from one⟩ THRUST stresses a rapidity or violence rather than any continuousness or steadiness in the application of force, often implying the sudden and forcible pushing of a weapon or instrument into something ⟨*thrust* a hand into a box⟩ ⟨*thrust* a sword through the arras⟩ ⟨*thrust* a grievance out of one's mind⟩ PROPEL implies a driving forward or onward by a force or power ⟨*propel* a hoop along the sidewalk⟩ ⟨boats *propelled* by the wind⟩ ⟨the engine *propels* the car at over a hundred miles an hour⟩ ⟨a man *propelled* by hunger to an enemy's house⟩

²**push** \"\ *n* -ES **1 :** a vigorous effort to attain a desired end **:** DRIVE ⟨a strong Congressional ~ for restoring high, rigid supports —Eric Sevareid⟩: as **a :** a strong organized military attack **:** ASSAULT, OFFENSIVE ⟨on the Russian front the spring ~ had finally begun —*Time*⟩ **b :** an advance overcoming obstacles ⟨the big scientific ~ into the south polar region —*Springfield (Mass.) Union*⟩ **c :** an active campaign to promote the sale of a product ⟨his sales picture on this product may be influenced by a heavy ~ on another product —J.K. Blake⟩ **2 :** a condition or occasion of stress **:** an urgent state **:** a time for action **:** EMERGENCY, PINCH ⟨when it came to the ~, I found, I had forgot all I intended to say —Thomas Gray⟩ **3 a** (1) **:** a sudden forcible act of pushing **:** SHOVE ⟨gave the boy ahead of him an impatient ~ and knocked him down⟩ (2) **:** a thrust with a pointed weapon or the horn of an animal **b** (1) **:** a physical force steadily applied in a direction away from the body exerting it ⟨gave the car a ~ around the block to start it⟩ ⟨driven by the ~ of the wind on the sails⟩ ⟨the ~ of the water against the walls of the tank⟩ (2) **:** a nonphysical pressure **:** INFLUENCE, COMPULSION, URGE ⟨the ~ and pull of conflicting emotions⟩ **c :** aggressive energy **:** vigorous enterprise ⟨it was the ~ . . . of a reinvigorated government that carried the program through —F.A.Ogg & Harold Zink⟩ **4 a :** an exertion of influence to promote another's interests **b :** stimulation or encouragement to vigorous activity **:** BOOST, IMPETUS ⟨war gave weather forecasting a tremendous ~ —J.D.Ratcliff⟩ **5 a :** CROWD, BUNCH ⟨hurry and get ready, . . . the whole ~ of you —*Atlantic*⟩ **b** *Austral* **:** a gang of rowdies or toughs **6 :** a part to be pushed; *esp* **:** PUSH BUTTON **7** *slang* **:** a foreman in a lumber camp **8** *Brit* **:** DISMISSAL — used in the phrase *get the push* or *give the push* ⟨when the Mayor makes his replacements . . . all I do is put the finger on the guy who's to get the ~ —Hartley Howard⟩ **9 :** a bid in a card game that pushes an opponent

³**push** \"\ *adj* **1 :** that pushes **:** used to communicate a push ⟨~ pole⟩ ⟨~ pedal⟩ **2 :** operated or propelled by pushing ⟨a ~ mower⟩ ⟨a ~ feed⟩

⁴**push** \"\ *n* -ES [origin unknown] **1** *dial chiefly Eng* **:** PUSTULE, PIMPLE **2** *dial chiefly Eng* **:** BOIL, CARBUNCLE

**push along** *vi* **:** to push on ⟨*pushed along* on their journey after a rest of a few hours⟩

**push and pull** *var of* PUSH-PULL

**push around** *vt* **:** to subject to impositions, unfair discrimination, or rough or contemptuous treatment **:** impose on **:** HECTOR ⟨serving the public instead of *pushing* it *around* —J.E.Gloag⟩ ⟨a people whose history for centuries has been one continuous resistance to being *pushed around*, dominated, or swallowed —Marcia Davenport⟩

**push-away** \'==,=\ *n* **:** PUSHOVER 5

**pushball** \'=,=\ *n* **1 :** a game in which each of two sides endeavors to push an inflated leather-covered ball about six feet in diameter across its opponents' goal **2 :** the ball used in a game of pushball

**push bar** *n* **:** a bar placed usu. transversely on a door at hand height (as for the protection of a screen or glass panel)

**push-bar conveyor** *or* **push-bar elevator** *n* **:** an endless-chain conveyor in which crossbars propel or lift the load by direct engagement or push the load over rollers or a flat surface

**push-bike** \'=,=\ *also* **push bicycle** *or* **push cycle** *n, Brit* **:** a pedal bicycle — distinguished from a motor bicycle

**push boat** *n* **:** a powerboat used esp. for pushing a tow of barges

**push bolt** *n* **1 :** a door bolt moved by pushing with the hand instead of with a key **2 :** a cylinder lock (as on a filing cabinet) that locks by pushing but must be unlocked with a key

**push broom** *n* **:** a brush for sweeping that has a long handle attached and is pushed

**push button** *n* **:** a small button or knob that when pushed operates something or sets it in operation ⟨lock the door by pressing the *push button* in the center of the knob⟩; *specif* **:** one that actuates a switch by making or breaking an electric circuit ⟨an elevator operated by *push buttons*⟩

**push-button** \'=,==\ *adj* [*push button*] **1 :** operated, carried on, or done by means of push buttons or as if by such means **2** *of warfare* **:** using complex and more or less self-operating mechanisms that accomplish missions against enemy airplanes, troops, ships, and installations when put in operation by a simple act comparable to pushing a button ⟨the idea formed in the public mind by such phrases as *push-button* war is a war of robots, a war of machines —E.A.Fitzpatrick⟩

**push-button yard** *n* **:** a mechanized classification yard in which an operator by pushing buttons or levers may accomplish the switching of cars and makeup of trains

**push car** *n* **1 :** a railway work car for transporting materials that is usu. towed behind a motorcar **2 :** an intermediate car connecting a locomotive and a train to be pushed on to a ferryboat

**pushcard** \'=,=\ *n* **:** PUNCHBOARD ⟨an order prohibiting the interstate sale of . . . ~*s* and other lottery devices —*Federal Trade Comm. Releases*⟩

**pushcart** \'=,=\ *n* **:** a cart or barrow pushed by hand ⟨a vendor with a ~ of fresh fruit⟩ ⟨loaded a self-service ~ in the supermarket⟩

pushcart

**pushchair** \'=,=\ *n, Brit* **:** STROLLER

**push–down** \'=,=\ *n* -S **:** a maneuver in which an airplane in level flight is forced into a short dive

**pushed** *past of* PUSH

**push·er** \'pu̇shə(r)\ *n* -S [[1]*push* + *-er*] **1 :** one that pushes ⟨ate using a piece of bread as a ~⟩: as **a** (1) **:** a machine part or implement for pushing something ⟨a cuticle ~⟩ (2) **:** a machine with parts having a thrusting action (3) **:** a watchmaker's tool used in a staking set to push friction jewels in place (4) **:** a soft metal rod used to insert or eject bushings (5) **:** a hard-pointed tool used to remove case pins, lugs, or bars (6) **:** a button on top of a watch crown or on the side of a watchcase for activating the hands of a chronograph or stopwatch (7) **:** a slide on the edge of a watch case for releasing an internal action **b** (1) **:** an aggressive person ⟨stiff competition from a real ~⟩; *esp* **:** a very aggressive salesman (2) **:** an illicit peddler of narcotics **c** (1) **:** an auxiliary locomotive used behind a train on steep grades (2) **:** PUSH BOAT **d :** the foreman of a crew of workers **:** STRAW BOSS **e :** a miner who pushes loaded cars to the place from which they will be hauled to the shaft or surface by locomotive — called also *headsman, putter, trailer, trammer, wheeler* **f :** PLUNGER **2 :** a chamois toe sock worn by a track athlete **3 a :** an airplane with the propeller located behind the wing — compare TRACTOR **b** *or* **pusher engine :** a piston engine with the propeller mounted behind

**pusher furnace** *n* **:** a continuous furnace in which pieces of work are pushed at proper speed for completion at the exit

**pusher grade** *n* **:** a railroad grade that is steeper than the ruling grade and requires a pusher locomotive to be used with a train of normal weight

**pusher propeller** *n* **:** a propeller operating at the trailing rather than the leading edge of the wing

**pushes** *pres 3d sing of* PUSH, *pl of* PUSH

**push fit** *n* **:** a fit of mating machine parts that can be made with moderate hand pressure by the assembler and is used where occasional disassembly is expected

**push·ful** \'pu̇shfəl\ *adj* [[2]*push* + *-ful*] **1 :** marked by push **:** ZEALOUS, ENERGETIC, ENTERPRISING **2 :** intrusively aggressive ⟨a ~ insurance agent⟩ **syn** see AGGRESSIVE

**push·ful·ly** \-fəlē\ *adv* **:** in a pushful manner

**push·ful·ness** \-fəlnə̇s\ *n* -ES **:** the quality or state of being pushful

**push hoe** *n* **:** SCUFFLE HOE

**push·i·ly** \-shəlē\ *adv* [*pushy* + *-ly*] **:** PUSHINGLY

**push·i·ness** \-shēnə̇s\ *n* -ES [*pushy* + *-ness*] **:** PUSHINGNESS

**pushing** *adj* [fr. pres. part. of [1]*push*] **1 :** marked by ambition, energy, enterprise, and initiative **2 :** marked by tactless forwardness, officious intrusion, and snobbish aspiration **syn** see AGGRESSIVE

**push·ing·ly** *adv* **:** in a pushing manner

**push·ing·ness** *n* -ES **:** the quality or state of being pushing

**push joint** *n* **:** a joint formed by placing a brick on a thick bed of mortar and pushing the brick against another brick in the same course in such a way as to fill the space between the bricks — called also *shoved joint*

**push key** *n* **:** a key that operates a lock by inward rather than rotary motion — called also *thrust key*

**push·mo·bile** \'pu̇shmō,bēl\ *n* -S [[1]*push* + *-mobile*] **:** a toy vehicle resembling an automobile and propelled by pushing

**push money** *n* **:** a commission paid (as by a manufacturer) to a sales person to push the sale of a particular item or line of merchandise — called also *PM, spiff*

**push moraine** *n* **:** a moraine pushed by a glacier into a ridge at its front

**push net** *n* **:** a small triangular fishing net with a rigid frame that is pushed along the bottom in shallow waters and is used in parts of the southwestern Pacific for taking shrimps and small bottom-dwelling fishes

**push off** *vi* **:** to go away **:** get out **:** set out ⟨I'd better *push off* and see about it —Dorothy Sayers⟩ ⟨about time to *push off*⟩

**push–off** \'=,=\ *n* -S [fr. *push off,* v.] **1 a :** the action of pushing off **b :** SEND-OFF **2 :** a rod or tube in compression used for keeping a trolley wire in its proper position

**push–off sweep rake** *n* **:** a tractor-mounted power sweep rake with a frame that pushes the hay from the teeth instead of merely allowing it to slide off from the force of gravity

**push on** *vi* **:** to continue on one's way **:** PROCEED ⟨instead of *pushing on* I stayed —Thomas Skelton⟩

**pushover** \'=,==\ *n* -S [[1]*push* + *over*] **1 :** an opponent easy to defeat or a victim capable of no effective resistance and succumbing or sure to succumb readily to force or guile ⟨so kind, warmhearted and open that she's . . . a ~ for rivals —Virginia Bird⟩ **2 :** someone unwilling or unable to resist the power of a particular attraction or appeal **:** SUCKER ⟨I'm a ~ for any pocket-size atlas and buy them as fast as they appear —*Saturday Rev.*⟩ **3 :** something accomplished without resistance or difficulty **:** SNAP ⟨snow is a painting ~, a surefire subject for the amateur —Joseph Alger⟩ **4 :** the beginning of a dive in flying; *specif* **:** the moment at which the control stick is pushed forward **5 :** a canoeing stroke in which the boat is moved broadside away from the paddle by bracing the shaft against the gunwale, the blade parallel to the side of the canoe, then pulling down on the handle — called also *push-away*

**push–pad** \'=,=\ *n* **:** a circular pad attached to a door at hand height for use in opening it

**push–piece** \'=,=\ *n* **:** a stud on the side of a watchcase to activate a special mechanism (as a repeater, chronograph) inside the watch

**pushpin** \'=,=\ *n* **1 :** a children's game in which one player tries to maneuver his pin over that of another player **2 :** a steel point having a projecting glass or metal head for sticking into a wall or board and used chiefly as a picture hook or as an indicator on a map

**push plate** *n* **:** HAND PLATE

**[1]push–pull** \'=¦=\ *adj* [[1]*push* + *pull*] **1 :** constituting or relating to an arrangement of two electron tubes such that an alternating input causes them to send current through a load alternately ⟨a *push-pull* circuit⟩ ⟨a *push-pull* amplifier⟩ **2 :** belonging to or being a linkage for exerting both push and pull at somewhat remote distances ⟨*push-pull* rods⟩ ⟨a *push-pull* control system⟩ **3** *or* **push and pull :** that may be pushed or pulled ⟨a *push-pull* toy⟩ ⟨a *push-pull* latch⟩

**[2]push–pull** \"\ *n* [[1]*push-pull*] **:** a push-pull arrangement ⟨connect electron tubes in *push-pull*⟩

**pushrod** \'=,=\ *n* **:** a rod actuated by a cam to open or close the valves of an internal combustion engine

**push shot** *n* **1 :** a billiards or pool shot in which the cue remains in contact with the cue ball until the cue ball has touched the object ball or one in which the cue strikes the cue ball twice **2 :** a golf shot in which a player having his weight forward on the left foot and his wrists firm hits the ball a descending blow thus producing a low ball which stops quickly **3 :** a one-hand basketball shot similar to the lay-up but executed farther from the basket

**pushtu** *or* **pushto** *cap, var of* PASHTO

**push–up** \'=,=\ *n* -S **1 :** an exercise for strengthening arm and shoulder girdle muscles that consists of bending and extending the elbows while the body is kept in a prone position with the back flat and is supported only on the hands and toes **2 :** a mass of frozen aquatic vegetation placed by muskrats over a hole in the ice that they use for access to the water

**push wave** *n* **:** a seismic disturbance consisting of longitudinal vibrations of the earth's crust

**pushy** \'pu̇shē, -shi\ *adj* -ER/-EST [[1]*push* + *-y*] **1 :** PUSHING, AGGRESSIVE **2** *chiefly dial* **:** unpleasantly eager or anxious

**pu·sil·la·nim·i·ty** \,pyüsələ'nimədˑē, -mətē, -i *sometimes* -üzə-\ *n* -ES [ME *pusillanimite,* fr. MF *pusillanimité,* fr. LL *pusillanimitat-, pusillanimitas,* fr. *pusillanimis* pusillanimous + L *-itat-, -itas* -ity] **:** the quality or state of being pusillanimous **:** weakness of spirit **:** COWARDLINESS

**pu·sil·lan·i·mous** \¦==¦lanəməs\ *adj* [LL *pusillanimis,* fr. L *pusillus* very small (dim. of *pusus* small child) + *animus* soul, mind, spirit; akin to L *puer* child, Skt *putva* child, son — more at FEW, ANIMATE] **:** lacking or showing a lack of courage and manly strength and resolution **:** marked by mean-spirited and contemptible timidity ⟨the policy of watchful waiting denounced as ~ —Allan Nevins & H.S.Commager⟩ **syn** see COWARDLY

**pu·sil·lan·i·mous·ly** *adv* **:** in a pusillanimous manner

**pu·sil·lan·i·mous·ness** *n* -ES **:** the quality or state of being pusillanimous **:** PUSILLANIMITY

**[1]puss** \'pu̇s\ *n* -ES [origin unknown] **1 a :** CAT **b** *dial Brit* **:** HARE **2 :** a young woman **:** CHILD — usu. used in affection or reproach

**[2]puss** \"\ *n* -ES [IrGael *pus* lip, mouth, fr. MIr *bus,* prob. of imit. origin — more at BUSS] *slang* **:** FACE ⟨couple of guys who need a poke in the ~ —Michael Fessier⟩ **syn** see FACE

**puss caterpillar** *n* [[1]*puss*] **:** a caterpillar that is the larva of a flannel moth (*Megalopyge opercularis*) chiefly of the southeastern U.S. and that has urticating hairs

**puss in the corner :** a game in which all players but one occupy goals (as the corners of a room) and at a signal try to exchange places before the one having no place of his own can reach one of the vacant goals — called also *pussy wants a corner*

**puss·ley** *or* **pus·ley** *also* **puss·ly** \'pəslē, -li\ *n* -S [alter. of *pursley*] **:** PURSLANE

**puss moth** *n* [[1]*puss*] **:** a light-colored stout-bodied European notodontid moth (*Cerura vinula*) whose larva feeds on poplar and willow leaves; *broadly* **:** any moth of the genus *Cerura*

**[1]pussy** \'pu̇sē, -si\ *n* -ES [[1]*puss* + *-y,* dim. suffix] **1 a :** GIRL **b :** CAT **c** *dial Brit* **:** HARE **2 a :** a catkin of the pussy willow **b :** RABBIT-FOOT CLOVER

**[2]pus·sy** \'pəsē, -si\ *adj* -ER/-EST [[1]*pus* + *-y,* adj. suffix] **:** full of or like pus

**[3]pus·sy** \"\ *var of* PURSY

**[4]pussy** \'pu̇sē, -si\ *n* -ES [earlier *puss* vulva (perh. of LG or Scand origin) + *-y,* dim. suffix; akin to ON *pūss* pocket, pouch, Icel *pussa* vulva, LG *pūse* vulva, OE *pusa, posa* bag, Gk *byein* to stuff, plug] **1 :** female genitals; *esp* **:** VULVA — usu. considered vulgar **2 :** SEXUAL INTERCOURSE — usu. considered vulgar

**pussycat** \'==,=\ *n* [[1]*pussy* + *cat*] **1 :** CAT **2 :** PUSSY WILLOW **3 :** RABBIT-FOOT CLOVER

**pussy clover** *n* [[1]*pussy*] **:** RABBIT-FOOT CLOVER

**[1]pussy·foot** \'pu̇sē,fu̇t, -si,f-, *usu* -u̇dˑ+V\ *vi* [[1]*pussy* + *foot*] **1 :** to tread or move warily or stealthily **2 :** to refrain from committing oneself (as in regard to a question at issue) **:** make guarded or equivocal statements of one's views

**[2]pussyfoot** \"\ *n, pl* **pussyfoots** [fr. *Pussyfoot,* nickname of W. E. Johnson †1945 Am. law enforcement officer and prohibition advocate] **:** PROHIBITIONIST

**[3]pussyfoot** \"\ *n, pl* **pussyfoots** [[1]*pussy* + *foot*] **:** any of several plants having leaf clusters or flower heads that suggest a cat's foot in shape: as **a :** PUSSY-PAW **b :** PUSSYTOE

**pussyfooted** \'==,==\ *also* **pussyfoot** \'==,=\ *adj* [*pussyfooted* fr. *pussyfoot,* adj. + *-ed; pussyfoot* fr. [1]*pussy* + *foot*] **:** characterized by pussyfooting

**pussy·foot·er** \'==,=ə(r)\ *n* -S [[1]*pussyfoot* + *-er*] **1 :** one that pussyfoots **2 :** an advocate or adherent of prohibition

**pussy–paw** *also* **pussy's–paw** \'==,=\ *n* **:** a Californian herb (*Calyptridium umbellatum*) of the family Portulacaceae with a scapose spike of pink or white flowers rising from a dense rosette of leaves — usu. used in pl.

**pussytoe** *or* **pussy's toe** \'==,=\ *n* **:** a cat's-foot of the genus *Antennaria; esp* **:** a cat's foot (*A. plantaginifolia*) of eastern and central No. America with foliage suggesting that of a plantain and usu. crimson flower heads subtended by purple white-marked involucres — usu. used in pl.

**pussy wants a corner :** PUSS IN THE CORNER

**pussy willow** \¦==¦=(,)=\ *n* **:** a willow having large cylindrical silky catkins; *esp* **:** a small arboreal American willow (*Salix discolor*) with usu. lanceolate leaves that are bright green above and glaucous to whitish on the undersurface

pussy willow

**pussywillow gray** *n* **:** a pinkish gray that is redder, lighter, and stronger than gull (sense 2b)

**[1]pus·tu·lant** \'pəschələnt, -st(y)ə-\ *adj* [LL *pustulant-, pustulans,* pres. part. of *pustulare* to blister — more at PUSTULATE] **:** producing pustules

**[2]pustulant** \"\ *n* -S **:** an agent (as a chemical) that induces pustule formation

**pus·tu·lar** \-lə(r)\ *adj* [*pustule* + *-ar*] **1 :** of, relating to, or of the character of pustules ⟨~ prominences⟩ ⟨~ eruptions⟩ **2 :** covered with pustular prominences **:** PUSTULATE

**[1]pus·tu·late** \-,lāt\ *vb* -ED/-ING/-S [LL *pustulatus,* past part. of *pustulare* to blister, fr. L *pustula* pustule, blister] *vt* **:** to cause to form into pustules ~ *vi* **:** to become pustulous

**[2]pus·tu·late** \-,lə̇t, -,lāt\ *or* **pus·tu·lat·ed** \-,lādˑə̇d\ *adj* [*pustulate* fr. LL *pustulatus* blistered, fr. past part. of *pustulare; pustulated* fr. past part. of [1]*pustulate*] **:** covered with pustules or similar prominences

**pus·tu·la·tion** \,=='lāshən\ *n* -S [LL *pustulation-, pustulatio,* fr. *pustulatus* (past part. of *pustulare*) + L *-ion-, -io* ion] **1 :** the action of producing pustules or state of being pustulated **2 :** PUSTULE

**pus·tu·la·tous** \¦==¦lādˑəs, '==,lədˑ-\ *adj* [[2]*pustulate* + *-ous*] **:** PUSTULAR 2

**pus·tule** \'pəs(,)chül, -,st(y)ül\ *n* -S [ME, fr. L *pustula, pussula;* akin to Gk *physa* bellows, bladder, bubble, Lith *puslė* bladder — more at FOG] **1 :** a small circumscribed elevation of the skin containing pus and having an inflamed base **2 :** any small elevation or spot on a plant resembling a blister; *esp* **:** a mark on a leaf due to the rupture of surface tissues overlying spore masses or fruiting structures of a parasitic fungus **3 a :** a wart or dermal excrescence in some amphibians (as toads) **b :** a colored point or a swelling resembling a blister (as on the integument of an insect)

**pus·tu·li·form** \'pəschələ̇,fȯrm, -st(y)əl-\ *adj* [NL *pustuliformis,* fr. L *pustula* + *-iformis* -iform] **:** having the form of a pustule

**pus·tu·lose** \-,lōs\ *adj* [L *pustulosus,* fr. *pustula* + *-osus* -ose] **:** PUSTULAR

**pus·tu·lous** \-ləs\ *adj* [L *pustulosus*] **:** resembling, covered with, or characterized by pustules **:** PUSTULATE, PUSTULAR ⟨~ skin⟩ ⟨a ~ disease⟩

**pusz·ta** \'pu̇,stȯ\ *n* -S [Hung, fr. *puszta* deserted, bare, bleak] **:** a treeless plain in Hungary **:** STEPPE

**[1]put** \'pu̇\|t *chiefly dial* 'pə\|t, *usu* \|dˑ+V\ *vb* **put** \"\ *or dial* **put·ten** \-tᵊn\ **put** *or dial* **putten; putting; puts** [ME *putten, puten;* akin to OE *put*ung instigation, *potian* to push, MD *poten* to plant, graft, Icel *pota* to poke] *vt* **1 a :** to place or cause to be placed in a specified position or relationship **:** LAY, SET ⟨~ the roof on the house⟩ ⟨~ the plant near the window⟩ ⟨two tumblers of brandy had been enough to ~ him under the table —Van Wyck Brooks⟩ **b :** to move in a specified direction or into or out of a specified place ⟨~ the hands of the clock back⟩ ⟨~ the book down⟩ ⟨~ his arm through the sleeve⟩ ⟨~ the car into the garage⟩ ⟨~ the cat out of the house⟩ **c** (1) **:** to send (as a weapon or missile) into or through something **:** THRUST ⟨a sharpshooter ~ a ball through the old captain's head —Frank Yerby⟩ ⟨~ a knife between his ribs⟩ (2) **:** DRIVE ⟨~ a nail into the wall⟩ (3) **:** to throw with an overhand pushing motion ⟨~ the shot 63 feet 6 inches —*Newsweek*⟩ **d** (1) **:** to bring into or establish in a specified state or condition ⟨when his father had died he had ~ her into mourning —F.M.Ford⟩ ⟨~ one in the proper mood to enjoy the local operettas —Horace Sutton⟩ ⟨~ the motor into working order⟩ ⟨~ her to shame⟩ ⟨~ it to use⟩ ⟨~ the matter right⟩ (2) **:** to bring into a state of dependence esp. upon a specified regimen — usu. used with *on* ⟨~ him on a salt-poor diet⟩ ⟨~ them on bread and water⟩ **e :** to carry or cause to be taken across a body of water ⟨you could ask anybody to ~ you across a river —Archibald Marshall⟩ ⟨the twenty-knot speed that would ~ a ship across the Atlantic in . . . seven days —Edward Ellsberg⟩ **f :** to remove from a specified state, condition, or situation ⟨~ its competitor out of business⟩ ⟨~ the idea from his mind⟩ **g :** FOCUS ⟨~ his glasses on the group —F.W.Booth⟩ **2 a :** to cause to endure or suffer something **:** SUBJECT — usu. used with *to* ⟨~ him to death⟩ ⟨~ them to the sword⟩ ⟨~ him to the expense of a new roof⟩ ⟨~ him to the shame of revealing his poverty⟩ **b :** IMPOSE, INFLICT — usu. used with *on* or *upon* ⟨~ a special tax on luxuries⟩ ⟨~ a heavy strain on his resources⟩ ⟨if I ~ any tricks upon 'em —Shak.⟩ ⟨~ numerous insults on him⟩ **3 a :** to set before one for judgment or decision **:** bring to the attention ⟨~ the question of a special dividend before the board of directors⟩ ⟨~ the problem of downtown parking before the mayor⟩ ⟨it was a question that her life had never permitted her to ~ to herself —Laura Krey⟩ **b :** to call for a formal vote on ⟨the chairman is not supposed to say anything except to ~ the motion —Dorothy C. Fisher⟩ ⟨the question of adjournment was then ~, and carried by a large majority —T.L.Peacock⟩ **4 a** (1) **:** to turn into language or literary form — usu. used with *in* or *into* ⟨found it difficult to ~ his feelings in words⟩ ⟨~ the story of his life into a novel⟩ (2) **:** to translate into another language or style — usu. used with *into* ⟨~ the poem into English⟩ ⟨~ the play into modern idiom⟩ (3) **:** ADAPT ⟨witty lyrics ~ to tuneful music⟩ **b :** EXPRESS, STATE ⟨that's *putting* it mildly⟩ ⟨~ his proposal awkwardly⟩ **5 a :** to devote (oneself) to an activity or end — usu. used with *to* ⟨~ himself to the study of law⟩ ⟨~ himself to winning back their confidence⟩ **b :** to set to use **:** employ actively **:** APPLY ⟨~ his mind to the problem⟩ ⟨~ all his strength into the fight⟩ ⟨~ all his resources behind the candidate⟩ **c :** to set to some employment or function **:** ASSIGN — usu. used with *to* ⟨~ him to mixing the salad⟩ ⟨~ her to filing letters⟩ ⟨~ them to work⟩ **d :** to set in a particular place or position for the purpose of carrying out an activity or performing a function ⟨~ him to school⟩ ⟨~ the children to bed⟩ ⟨~ the play on the stage⟩ **e** (1) **:** to cause to perform an action or clear an obstacle **:** URGE ⟨~ the horse over the fence⟩ ⟨~ the boy through his exercises⟩ (2) **:** to set into sudden or violent movement or activity **:** IMPEL, INCITE ⟨~ the prowler to flight⟩ ⟨~ them into a frenzy⟩ (3) **:** to compel (a person) to some course of action or behavior ⟨you ~ me to forget a lady's manners —Shak.⟩ — now used only in legal phrases ⟨the husky handyman was not immediately ~ to plea and no date was set for the arraignment —*Springfield* (*Mass.*) *Union*⟩ **6 a :** to bring into the power or under the protection or care of someone ⟨~ him into the hands of his enemies⟩ ⟨~ themselves in good hands⟩ ⟨~ him under the care of a specialist⟩ **b :** REPOSE, REST — usu. used with *in* ⟨~*s* his trust in God⟩ ⟨~*s* his faith in reason⟩ **c :** INVEST — usu. used with *in* or *into* ⟨~ all his money in the company⟩ ⟨~ his savings into stocks⟩ **d** *archaic* **:** to set as a beginner **:** APPRENTICE — usu. used with *to* **7 a :** to give as an estimate ⟨the medical examiner ~ the time as about a quarter past eleven —Mary R. Rinehart⟩ ⟨~ the number at 500,000 —Roy Lewis & Angus Maude⟩ **b :** ATTACH, ATTRIBUTE — usu. used with *on* or *upon* ⟨~*s* a wrong construction on his actions⟩ ⟨~*s* a high value on his friendship⟩ ⟨~*s* a high premium on leisure —H.W.Glidden⟩ **c :** IMPUTE — usu. used with *on* ⟨~ the blame for the illegal actions on his partner⟩ ⟨~ the responsibility for the accident on the other driver⟩ **d :** to ascribe to or base upon a particular cause or foundation — usu. used with *on* or *upon* ⟨~*s* morality on the basis of self-interest⟩ ⟨~*s* his conclusion on the evidence of the fossil remains⟩ **e :** to represent as being in a particular place ⟨he ~*s* "episcopal buildings along the crest" of Quebec before the first bishop set foot in the country —A.L. Burt⟩ ⟨the poet ~*s* his enemies in hell⟩ **8 :** to establish or cause to take effect (a limit or restraint) ⟨~ an end to his suffering⟩ ⟨~ a limit on the betting⟩ ⟨~ a check on his enthusiasm⟩ **9 :** ASSUME, SUPPOSE ⟨~ the absurd impossible case, for once —Robert Browning⟩ **10 a :** to affix (a signature or other mark) to a written or printed document ⟨they did not dare to ~ their names to what they wrote —Virginia Woolf⟩ ⟨~ a check next to the name of each course he had taken⟩ **b :** to enter as part of a list or group of related items — usu. used with *on* ⟨asked to have his name ~ on the list of candidates⟩ ⟨~ the telephone call on my bill⟩ ⟨let's plan to ~ it on the menu for tomorrow⟩ **11 :** PLACE, SUBSTITUTE ⟨before you condemn him, ~ yourself in his place⟩ **12 :** to bring (an animal) together with one of the opposite sex for breeding — usu. used with *to* ⟨consider seriously *putting* some of your ewes to longwool rams —E.F.Fricke⟩ **13 :** BET, WAGER — usu. used with *on* ⟨~ two dollars on the favorite⟩ ~ *vi* **1** *chiefly dial* **:** BUTT **2 a :** to start out; esp **:** to leave in a hurry **:** make off **:** DECAMP ⟨caught his squaw by one arm and ~ for the timber with her —H.L.Davis⟩ **b** *of a ship* **:** to take a specified course ⟨~ into the bay to avoid the storm⟩ ⟨~ down the river⟩ **3** *chiefly dial* **:** to shoot up **:** GROW, SPROUT — used of plants **4 :** to flow in or out of a body of water ⟨the river ~*s* into a lake⟩ **syn** see SET — **put forth** [ME *putten forth,* fr. *putten* to put + *forth*] **1 a :** ASSERT, PROPOSE ⟨has *put forth* a new theory of the origin of the solar system⟩ **b :** to make public **:** ISSUE ⟨has *put forth* a new set of parking regulations⟩ **2 :** to bring into action **:** EXERT ⟨had to *put* all his strength *forth* to get the measure through⟩ **3 :** to produce or send out (a growth) ⟨*put forth* leaves⟩ **4 :** to come into leaf, bud, or flower ⟨other things might *put forth;* but never again that wild beauty —Ellen Glasgow⟩ **5 :** to start out **:** begin a voyage ⟨*put forth* alone upon the great inland ocean —Jackson Rivers⟩ — **put forward 1 :** to advance to a position of prominence or responsibility ⟨was *put forward* as spokesman for the party —S.H.Adams⟩ ⟨the shortage of qualified people gave him the opportunity to *put* himself *forward*⟩ **2 :** to offer for consideration **:** PROPOSE ⟨any single fact to *put forward* in support of these fantastic charges —Kathleen Freeman⟩ ⟨the organic theory of nature which I have been tentatively *putting forward* —A.N.Whitehead⟩ — **put in an appearance :** to be present; *esp* **:** to appear at a formal or planned gathering usu. for a brief time only ⟨the candidate *put in an appearance* at five rallies in one night⟩ — **put in mind :** REMIND ⟨*put* him *in mind* of his father⟩ — **put one on to :** to call one's attention to **:** alert one to ⟨it was his suspicious manner that first *put me on to* him⟩ ⟨*put me on to* a good book⟩ — **put one's finger on :** DISCOVER, IDENTIFY ⟨*put his finger on* the cause of the trouble⟩ — **put out of the way 1 :** [1]KILL 1a ⟨hired a gunman to *put* his competitor *out of the way*⟩ **2** *also* **put out of one's way** *Brit* **:** to cause inconvenience or trouble to — often used with a reflexive object ⟨cannot *put* themselves *out of their way* on any account —William Hazlitt⟩ — **put paid to** *Brit* **:** to finish off **:** wipe out ⟨a tempest had *put paid to* their efforts —David Masters⟩ ⟨*puts paid to* whatever chances you had of coming first —Roy Saunders⟩ — **put the arm on** *slang* **1 :** to ask for money ⟨*put the arm on* a rich alumnus and got enough for a new gymnasium⟩ **2 :** to hold up **:** HIJACK ⟨*put the arm on* a big load of furs⟩ — **put the bee on** *or* **put the bite on** *slang* **:** to ask for a loan or to get money from ⟨some smooth hoodlum *puts the bee on* his daughter for two thousand bucks —Hartley Howard⟩ — **put the finger on :** to point out or identify to the police or other authorities **:** inform on ⟨*put the finger on* the other members of the gang⟩ — **put to bed :** to make the final preparations for printing (a newspaper or magazine) — **put to it :** to give difficulty to **:** press hard ⟨had been *put to it* to keep up with her even with her own famous big flat stride —Elizabeth Bowen⟩ — **put to rights :** to put into shape **:** make tidy **:** ARRANGE ⟨a new commanding officer who *put* the company *to rights*⟩ — **put two and two together :** to draw the proper inference from given premises or related circumstances ⟨sharp enough wits to *put two and two together* —T.B.Costain⟩ — **put up to 1 :** INCITE, INSTIGATE ⟨he was the ringleader who *put* the others *up to* mischief⟩ **2 :** to make acquainted with **:** inform of ⟨*put* him *up to* a good buy in stocks⟩ — **put up with 1 :** to suffer (as an insult or injury) without open resentment or attempted reprisal ⟨must live among his unruly parishioners and even *put up with* physical assault from them —Peter Forster⟩ **2 :** to endure (as something harmful or unpleasant) without complaint **:** TOLERATE ⟨we do not *put up with* string quartets playing transcriptions of piano music —Virgil Thomson⟩

**[2]put** \"\ *n* -S [ME, fr. *putten, puten* to put — more at [1]PUT] **1 :** a throw made with an overhand pushing motion; *specif* **:** the act or an instance of putting the shot **2** *dial Brit* **:** a thrust made in attack or in coming to someone's assistance **:** PUSH, SHOVE **3 :** an option to sell a specified amount of stock, grain, or other commodity at a fixed price at or within a given time — compare CALL 3d

**[3]put** \"\ *adj* [fr. past part. of [1]*put*] **:** being in place **:** FIXED, SET ⟨stayed ~ under the stove —E.B.White⟩

**⁴put** \ˈpət\ *n* -s [origin unknown] **:** BLOCKHEAD, DOLT

**put about** *vi, of a ship* **:** to change direction **:** go on another tack ~ *vt* **1 a :** to place (a sailing ship) on another tack ⟨the pinnace was *put about*, and run towards a certain dark speck —William Black⟩ **b :** to cause to change course or direction **:** cause to turn back or around ⟨*put* the horse *about* and headed for the corral⟩ **2 :** to cause to be talked about **:** CIRCULATE, RUMOR ⟨it was *put about* in Paris that he was tired of aristocratic mistresses —Nancy Mitford⟩ **3 a :** to cause difficulty or trouble for **:** INCONVENIENCE ⟨I don't want to *put* you *about*, telling falsehoods for me —John Galsworthy⟩ **b :** DISCONCERT, DISTRESS ⟨I thought the poor man would break down into tears at last, he was so *put about* —Mary Deasy⟩

**put across** *vt* **1 :** to achieve or carry through by deceit or trickery ⟨acts as a restraint on all the nations from trying to *put across* illicit enterprises —*Harper's*⟩ **2 a :** to convey effectively or forcefully ⟨knows how to *put* a song *across* —*Time*⟩ **b :** to cause to be accepted or acted upon ⟨tells how to *put* yourself *across* as a man of the world —*Saturday Rev.*⟩ ⟨was so heart-and-soul in the project that I was able to *put* the idea *across* to our group of twenty-five women —Winona Sparks⟩

**pu·ta·men** \pyüˈtāmən\ *n, pl* **putam·i·na** \-tamənə\ [NL, fr. L, that which falls off in pruning, shells, peels, fr. *putare* to cut, prune — more at PAVE] **1 :** an outer reddish layer of gray matter in the lenticular nucleus **2 :** a tough membrane that lines the shell of a bird's egg — **pu·tam·i·nous** \-tamənəs\ *adj*

**put-and-take** \ˌ==ˈ=\ *n* **:** any of various games of chance played with a special top or with dice or cards in which the players contribute to a pool or take from it — see TEETOTUM

top used in put-and-take

**pu·ta·tive** \ˈpyüd·əd·iv\ *adj* [ME, fr. LL *putativus*, fr. L *putatus* (past part. of *putare* to consider, think) + *-ivus* -ive — more at PAVE] **1 :** commonly accepted or supposed **:** REPUTED ⟨a few of us are a little dubious about these ~ human superiorities —E.A.Hooton⟩ ⟨the ~ father⟩ **2 :** assumed to exist or to have existed **:** HYPOTHESIZED, INFERRED ⟨they can recognize rock strata capable of producing oil, and look for the ~ product —*Time*⟩ ⟨traced back to a postulated form in a ~ parent language —J.B.Carroll⟩ — **pu·ta·tive·ly** \-d·əvlē\ *adv*

**putative marriage** *n, canon & civil law* **:** a duly formalized marriage that is invalid because of various impediments (as consanguinity) though recognized in some states as valid for certain purposes if contracted in good faith by at least one of the parties to it

**put away** *vt* [ME *putten away*, fr. *putten* to put + *away*] **1 a :** DISCARD, RENOUNCE ⟨to *put* grief *away* is disloyal to the memory of the departed —H.A.Overstreet⟩ **b :** DIVORCE ⟨incurring the risk of being *put away* by her husband on discovery of her previous immorality —Morris Ploscowe⟩ **2 :** to eat or drink up **:** CONSUME ⟨has been known to *put away* a couple of pounds of sausage at a single sitting —*New Yorker*⟩ **3 a :** to confine esp. in a mental institution ⟨poor demented creature, she thought, how many months would it be before they *put* her *away?* —Ellen Glasgow⟩ **b :** BURY ⟨*put away* their dead in seated position in pits roofed with bark —*Amer. Guide Series: Md.*⟩ **c :** KILL ⟨every man you *put away* has friends —Maxwell Anderson⟩ ⟨take an incurably sick dog to the vet to be *put away* —G.S.Perry⟩

**put by** *vt* [ME *putten by* to reject, fr. *putten* to put + *by*] **1** *obs* **:** to give up **:** DISCONTINUE ⟨*put by* this barbarous brawl —Shak.⟩ **2** *archaic* **a :** to turn aside **:** AVERT **b :** to cause to abandon a project **3 :** to lay aside **:** SAVE ⟨enough money *put by* for when he retires —M.A.Abrams⟩

**putch·er** \ˈpəchə(r), ˈpu̇ch-\ *n* -s [origin unknown] *dial Eng* **:** a wicker trap used in catching salmon

**put down** *vb* [ME *putten doun*, fr. *putten* to put + *doun* down] *vt* **1 a :** to do away with **:** ABOLISH, DESTROY ⟨indicted on charges of failure to *put down* gambling —Meyer Berger⟩ ⟨assist in *putting down* the pestilences —*Current History*⟩ **b :** to bring to an end by force (as an outbreak against authority) **:** SUPPRESS, CRUSH ⟨stern military measures *put down* the rioting —Jean & Franc Shor⟩ **c** *Brit* **:** to give up **:** discontinue using **2 :** DEGRADE, DEPOSE ⟨has *put down* the mighty from their thrones, and exalted those of low degree —Lk 1:52 (RSV)⟩ **3 :** to make ineffective **:** CHECK, SNUB ⟨*put down* gossip that she will again be a mama by labeling it the truth —*Time*⟩ **4 :** to do away with (as an injured, sick, or aged animal) **:** put to death **:** DESTROY, KILL ⟨with the veterinary means . . . at our disposal, I would always decide to have a sufferer from this disease *put down* —Henry Wynmalen⟩ **5 a :** to write down **:** put in writing ⟨was careful to *put down* only what he knew from first-hand experience —Granville Hicks⟩ **b :** to enter in a list ⟨one of the largest subscribers, *putting* his name *down* initially for £1,000 —W.P.Webb⟩ ⟨*putting down* the industrialist's son at birth for Eton —Roy Lewis & Angus Maude⟩ **6 a :** to place in a specified category ⟨I *put* him *down* as a hypochondriac —O.S.J.Gogarty⟩ ⟨I'd have *put* her *down* as being just on the far side of forty-five —Hamilton Basso⟩ **b :** ATTRIBUTE ⟨prepared to *put* these "shortcomings" *down* to inexperience —C.H.Dewhurst⟩ **7 :** to make by digging or drilling (as a well or pit) **:** SINK ⟨began *putting down* experimental bores —Margaret Clarke⟩ **8 :** to cause (a fish) to swim near the bottom (as from alarm) ⟨the noisy activity quickly *put down* the fish —F.C.Craighead b.1916 & J.J. Craighead⟩ **9 a :** GROOM ⟨much practice will be needed to *put* your dog *down* properly —Winnie Barber⟩ **b :** to eliminate (a show animal) from consideration in a competition ⟨even the ideal cat may be *put down* if it is not shown in perfect condition —P.M.Soderberg⟩ **10 :** to take in as food or drink ⟨poured a stiff jolt of whiskey and *put* it *down* —Raymond Chandler⟩ ⟨was now *putting down* helping after helping of the dinner —Carson McCullers⟩ **11 :** to pack or preserve for future use (as meats in brine, eggs in waterglass) ⟨*put down* a whole cask of pickles⟩ **12** *cricket* **:** to break (a wicket) with a fielded ball ~ *vi, of an airplane or airplane pilot* **:** LAND ⟨*put down* at the airport on time⟩ ⟨despite the rain, he *put down* in a perfect landing⟩

**pute** \ˈpyüt\ *adj* [L *putus*, fr. *putare* to cut, prune, cleanse — more at PAVE] **:** PURE, UNADULTERATED ⟨you and I chance to be ~ asses —Rudyard Kipling⟩

**put·e·lee** *or* **put·e·li** \ˈpəd·əˌlē\ *n* -s [Hindi *paṭelī*, dim. of *paṭelā*] **:** a bulky flat-bottomed boat used on the Ganges river in India

**puteng** *usu cap, var of* PHUTENG

**puth·ery** \ˈpu̇thərī\ *adj, dial* **:** MUGGY, SULTRY

**pu·tid** \ˈpyüd·əd\ *adj* [L *putidus*, fr. *putēre* to stink, be rotten — more at FOUL] **:** ROTTEN, WORTHLESS — **pu·tid·ly** *adv*

**put in** *vb* [ME *putten in*, fr. *putten* to put + *in*] *vt* **1 :** to make a formal offer or declaration of ⟨*put in* a plea of guilty⟩ ⟨*put* his claim *in* for damages⟩ **2 :** to come in with **:** INTERPOSE ⟨blocked his opponent's blows and then *put in* a sudden right to the jaw⟩ ⟨thought it opportune to *put in* a defensive word for his elder brother —L.C.Douglas⟩ — often used with quoted words as object ⟨another *put in*, "Pigmy-minded senators!" —Margaret A. Barnes⟩ **3 :** to lay in a supply of ⟨ran a small store, starting out with selling soft drinks . . . then he *put in* candy, cigarettes and bread —B.J.Siegel⟩ **4 :** to spend (a specified amount of time) esp. at some occupation or job ⟨*put in* their customary six or seven hours at the office —Jerome Weidman⟩ **5 :** PLANT ⟨all we got to do now is *put in* that next year's crop —William Faulkner⟩ ~ *vi* **1 :** to call at or enter a place ⟨a lot of the boys *put in* here on account of the good water —Edwin Corle⟩; *esp* **:** to enter a harbor or port ⟨the dune-locked harbors . . . where vessels frequently *put in* —*Amer. Guide Series: Mich.*⟩ **2 :** to make an application, request, or offer ⟨had to retire and *put in* for a pension —Seymour Nagan⟩ ⟨*put in* for this share of new production —*Time*⟩

**put·log** \ˈpu̇tˌlȯg, ˈpət- *also* -ˌläg\ *also* **put·lock** \-ˌläk\ *n* [*putlog* prob. by folk etymology (influence of *log*) fr. *putlock*, perh. fr. ³*put* + *lock*] **:** one of the short pieces of timber that directly support the flooring of a scaffold and that have one end resting on the ledger of the scaffold and the other in a hole left in the wall temporarily for the purpose

**put·nam scale** \ˈpətnəm-\ *also* **putnam's scale** *n, usu cap P* [prob. fr. the name *Putnam*] **:** a scale (*Aspidiotus ancylus*) that feeds on various trees and shrubs throughout most of the U.S.

**put off** *vb* [ME *putten of*, fr. *putten* to put + *of* off] *vt* **1 :** DISCONCERT, REPEL ⟨don't be *put off* by the ghastly jacket —B.C.L.Keelan⟩ ⟨in this way you may *put off* as many as you persuade —A.P.Herbert⟩ **2 a :** DELAY, POSTPONE ⟨many girls tend to *put off* marriage until they are older —Robert Reid⟩ ⟨somehow the time for departure must be *put off* —Lyle Saxon⟩ **b :** to get rid of for the time being or to induce to wait ⟨*put* the bill collector *off* for another month⟩ ⟨I'd forgotten it was that night . . . can't you *put* him *off?* —Nigel Balchin⟩ **c :** to turn the attention of from some design or purpose **:** DISSUADE, ELUDE, FRUSTRATE ⟨had *put* a robber *off* with a show of unconcern⟩ ⟨was so importunate it was impossible to *put* him *off*⟩ **3 a :** to take off **:** rid oneself of ⟨*put* his coat *off*⟩ ⟨you had your choosing, and it's time you'd *put off* your flightiness —Mary Deasy⟩ **b :** to dispose of ⟨second litters can be *put off* in autumn as porkers —A.Longwill⟩ **c :** to sell or pass fraudulently ⟨a moon-eyed roan that some slick trader had *put off* on him —F.B.Gipson⟩ ⟨*put off* a counterfeit ten-dollar bill⟩ **4 :** to push or send off (a boat) from land or another boat ⟨the pinnace was *put off* from the yacht —William Black⟩ ⟨let me cut the cable, and when we are *put off*, fall to their throats —Shak.⟩ ~ *vi* **:** to leave land ⟨the inhabitants then *put off* in boats and salvaged the cargo of the wrecked boat —*Amer. Guide Series: N.J.*⟩

**put-off** \ˈ(ˌ)=ˌ=\ *n* -s [*put off*] **:** the act or an instance of evasion or delay **:** EXCUSE, POSTPONEMENT

**put on** *vb* [ME *putten on*, fr. *putten* to put + *on*] *vt* **1 :** to impose as a burden **:** INFLICT ⟨known for *putting on* heavy fines⟩ **2 a :** to dress oneself in **:** DON ⟨at night would *put on* courtly garb —R.A.Hall b.1911⟩ ⟨*put* her new dress *on*⟩ **b :** to invest oneself with **:** take on ⟨*put on* the flesh and bones of a creature and walked His own earth —Alan Paton & Liston Pope⟩ **c :** to make part of one's appearance or behavior **:** ADOPT ⟨seems to feel the necessity of *putting on* a good deal of professional dignity —A.W.Long⟩ **d :** to assume misleadingly **:** FEIGN ⟨looked so pretty, *putting on* an ugly face —Andrew Young⟩ ⟨*put* a saintly manner *on*⟩ **3 a :** to cause to act or operate **:** APPLY ⟨*put on* a sprint of speed to make it —Donn Byrne⟩ **b :** to assign to some job or activity ⟨were *put on* with mattocks at chipping over the whole of the bare area —A.F. Ellis⟩ ⟨*put* extra salesmen *on* for the holiday rush⟩ **c** *cricket* **:** to direct (a player) to bowl **4 a :** ADD ⟨has been *putting on* weight⟩ **b :** EXAGGERATE, OVERSTATE ⟨he's *putting* it *on* when he makes such claims⟩ **5 :** to push forward (as the hands of a clock) **:** ADVANCE **6 :** PERFORM, PRODUCE ⟨*put on* an entertaining act⟩ ⟨*put on* a spectacular production of the play⟩ **7 :** to deceive in a good-natured way **:** KID ⟨you're *putting* me *on*⟩ ~ *vi, chiefly Scot* **:** to dress oneself ⟨slowly slowly raise she up and slowly *put* she *on* —*Barbara Allen*⟩

**¹put-on** \ˈ(ˌ)=ˌ=\ *adj* [fr. past part. of *put on*] **1 :** ASSUMED, PRETENDED ⟨in a *put-on* childish voice —Barnaby Conrad⟩ **2** *Scot* **:** CLOTHED

**²put-on** \"\ *n* -s [*put on*] **:** a false or pretentious manner, appearance, or mode of behavior **:** AFFECTATION ⟨all the *put-on* had gone out of their faces — they were left with what God gave them at the beginning —Shelby Foote⟩

**pu·to·ri·us** \pyüˈtōrēəs, -tȯr-\ *n, cap* [NL, fr. L *putēre* to stink + *-orius* -ory — more at FOUL] *in some classifications* **:** a genus of Mustelidae comprising the Old World polecats and now usu. considered a subgenus of *Mustela*

**put out** *vb* [ME *putten out*, fr. *putten* to put + *out*] *vt* **1 :** EXERT, USE ⟨*put out* all his strength to move the piano⟩ **2 :** EXTINGUISH ⟨*put out* the light⟩ ⟨*put* the fire *out*⟩ **3 a :** PUBLISH, ISSUE ⟨*puts out* the only newspaper in town⟩ ⟨*puts* a new catalog *out* every year⟩ **b :** PRODUCE, PROVIDE ⟨*puts out* an excellent line of inexpensive coats⟩ ⟨*putting out* a table d'hôte tourist menu that will run cheaper than à la carte dinners —Henry Giniger⟩ **4 :** INVEST ⟨couldn't *put* it *out* at profit, now —Joseph Hergesheimer⟩ **5 a :** to upset the composure of **:** DISCONCERT, EMBARRASS ⟨is never *put out* by unexpected problems⟩ ⟨such is outback hospitality that they were not in the least *put out* by our arrival —George Farwell⟩ **b :** to put into a bad temper **:** ANNOY, IRRITATE ⟨nothing *puts* him *out* so much as a chattering bridge partner⟩ **c :** to create difficulties for **:** INCONVENIENCE ⟨don't *put* yourself *out* for us⟩ ⟨will it *put* you *out* to take me to the station?⟩ **6 :** to cause to be out (as in baseball or cricket) **:** RETIRE ~ *vi* **1 :** to set out from shore ⟨a boat *puts out* with fishermen every morning⟩ **2** *slang* **:** to exert oneself **:** make an effort ⟨the only GI who deserves criticizing is the one who isn't *putting out* —*Infantry Jour.*⟩ **3** *slang, of a female* **:** to indulge in promiscuous sexual intercourse

**putout** \ˈ(ˌ)=ˌ=\ *n* -s [*put out*] **1 :** the retiring of a base runner or batter by a defensive player in baseball ⟨make the ~ on a throw to first⟩ **2 :** the official credit given a baseball player for making a putout ⟨leads the league in ~s⟩

**put over** *vt* **1 :** DELAY, POSTPONE ⟨consideration of this bill also was *put over* to the next session —Alzada Comstock⟩ **2 :** to put across ⟨*puts over* a feeling of power and bulk —Rosamund Frost⟩ ⟨*put over* a deliberate deception⟩ ⟨chose an unknown candidate and *put* him *over*⟩

**¹put-put** *or* **putt-putt** \ˈpətˌpət, *usu* -ˌpəd·+V\ *n* -s [imit.] **1 :** a sound made by or suggestive of the operation of a small gasoline engine ⟨the *put-put* of its motor —Kay Boyle⟩ ⟨occasionally there would be the rapid *put-put* of conversation —Donn Byrne⟩ **2 :** a small gasoline engine or a vehicle or boat equipped with one ⟨a phonograph and a radio and a flivver and a *put-put* for the canoe —Fannie Kilbourne⟩ ⟨experimenting with fast-flying combat planes to replace the slow-flying *put-puts* now used for the job —*Time*⟩

**²put-put** *or* **putt-putt** \"\ *vi* **put-putted** *or* **putt-putted**; **put-putted** *or* **putt-putted**; **put-putting** *or* **putt-putting**; **put-puts** *or* **putt-putts 1 :** to make put-puts **:** make the flat regularly repeated explosive sound of a small gasoline engine ⟨his angry style, which keeps *put-putting* in a series of equal explosions like a one-cylinder gasoline engine —Malcolm Cowley⟩ **2 :** to proceed or operate with or as if with put-puts **:** travel in a vehicle or boat that put-puts ⟨the launch went *put-putting* across the darkening harbor —William Irish⟩ ⟨*put-put* off across the water to visit the alligators —J.L.Jolley⟩

**pu·tre·fa·cient** \ˌpyü·trəˈfāshənt\ *adj* [L *putrefacient-, putrefaciens*, pres. part. of *putrefacere*] **:** PUTREFACTIVE

**pu·tre·fac·tion** \ˌ==ˈfakshən\ *n* -s [ME *putrefaccion*, fr. LL *putrefaction-, putrefactio*, fr. L *putrefactus* (past part. of *putrefacere*) + *-ion-, -io* -ion] **1 :** the decomposition of organic matter; *esp* **:** the typically anaerobic process of splitting of proteins by the agency of bacteria and fungi with the formation of foul-smelling incompletely oxidized products (as mercaptans and alkaloids) — compare DECAY 5a **2 :** the state of being putrefied **:** CORRUPTION, DECAY ⟨his mind was in a state of advanced ~ —Norman Douglas⟩

**pu·tre·fac·tive** \ˌ==ˈfaktiv, -tēv *also* -təv\ *adj* [MF *putrefactif*, fr. L *putrefactus* (past part. of *putrefacere*) + MF *-if* -ive] **1 :** of or relating to putrefaction **2 :** causing or tending to promote putrefaction

**pu·tre·fi·able** \ˌpyü·trəˈfīəbəl\ *adj* **:** PUTRESCIBLE

**pu·tre·fier** \ˈ==ˌfī(ə)r, -īə\ *n* -s **:** something (as a bacterium) that causes putrefaction

**pu·tre·fy** *also* **pu·tri·fy** \-ˌfī\ *vb* -ED/-ING/-ES [ME *putrefien, putryfyen*, fr. MF & L; MF *putrefier*, fr. L *putrefacere*, fr. *putrēre* to be rotten + *facere* to make — more at DO] *vt* **:** to make putrid **:** cause to decay offensively **:** produce putrefaction in ⟨flesh in that long sleep is not *putrefied* —John Donne⟩ ~ *vi* **:** to become putrid ⟨they will not ~ but rather ferment —Jane Nickerson⟩ **syn** see DECAY

**pu·tresce** \pyüˈtres\ *vi* -ED/-ING/-S [L *putrescere*] **:** to become putrescent or putrid **:** PUTREFY

**pu·tres·cence** \-sᵊn(t)s\ *n* -s [prob. fr. (assumed) NL *putrescentia*, fr. L *putrescent-, putrescens* + *-ia* -y] **:** the state of being putrescent **:** ROTTENNESS

**pu·tres·cen·cy** \-nsē\ *n* -ES [prob. fr. (assumed) NL *putrescentia*] **:** PUTRESCENCE

**pu·tres·cent** \-nt\ *adj* [L *putrescent-, putrescens*, pres. part. of *putrescere* to grow rotten, putrefy, incho. of *putrēre* to be rotten] **1 :** undergoing putrefaction **:** becoming putrid ⟨there was a continuous band of ~ carcasses —Mari Sandoz⟩ ⟨the scandal concerning all the ~ world which contains her intimate friends —W.J.Locke⟩ **2 :** of, relating to, or characteristic of putrefaction ⟨sweetmeats colored violet pink and ~ yellow —Nadine Gordimer⟩

**pu·tres·ci·bil·i·ty** \(ˌ)pyüˌtresəˈbiləd·ē\ *n* -ES [F *putrescibilité*, fr. *putrescible* + *-ité* -ity] **:** susceptibility to putrefaction

**pu·tres·ci·ble** \pyüˈtresəbəl\ *adj* [F or LL; F, fr. LL *putrescibilis*, fr. L *putrescere* + *-ibilis* -able] **:** capable of being putrefied **:** liable to become putrid

**pu·tres·cine** \-ˌsēn, -sᵊn\ *n* -s [ISV *putresc-* (fr. L *putrescere*) + *-ine*] **:** a crystalline slightly poisonous ptomaine $NH_2(CH_2)_4NH_2$ found esp. in putrid fish or flesh and in abnormal urine and also made synthetically; 1,4-butane-diamine

**pu·trid** \ˈpyü·trəd\ *adj* [L *putridus*, fr. *putrēre* to be rotten, fr. *puter, putris* rotten; akin to L *putēre* to stink, be rotten — more at FOUL] **1 a :** in an advanced state of putrefaction **:** ROTTEN ⟨horrible like raw and ~ flesh —W.S.Maugham⟩ **b :** of, relating to, indicative of, or due to putrefaction or decay **:** FOUL ⟨a ~ smell⟩ ⟨~ decomposition⟩ **2 a :** morally corrupt **:** DEPRAVED, VICIOUS ⟨knows the ~ atmosphere of the Court —Karl Polanyi⟩ ⟨teaches that pacifism is as ~ as Fascism is wicked —M.W.Straight⟩ **b :** totally disagreeable or objectionable **:** LOUSY, VILE ⟨from the practical aspect, it was ~ politics —*Time*⟩ ⟨I wanted to see them look a little more cheerful even if world events did look ~ —Henry Miller⟩ **3** *of soil* **:** easily decomposable **:** FRIABLE ⟨the hoof shakes the ~ field —Aldous Huxley⟩ — **pu·trid·ly** *adv* — **pu·trid·ness** *n* -ES

**pu·trid·i·ty** \pyüˈtridəd·ē, -ətē, -i\ *n* -ES **:** the quality or state of being putrid ⟨the ~ of vice and crime that reeked up from among the pestilent alleys —Newton Arvin⟩

**pu·tri·fact·ed** \ˈpyü·trəˌfaktəd\ *adj* [irreg. (influenced by E *putrify*) fr. L *putrefactus* (past part. of *putrefacere*) + E *-ed*] **:** PUTREFIED

**pu·tri·lage** \ˈpyü·trəlij\ *n* -s [LL *putrilagin-, putrilago* rottenness, fr. L *puter, putris* rotten] **:** matter that is undergoing putrefaction **:** the products of putrefaction — **pu·tri·lag·i·nous** \ˌ==ˈlajənəs\ *adj* — **pu·tri·lag·i·nous·ly** *adv*

**puts** *pres 3d sing of* PUT, *pl of* PUT

**putsch** \ˈpu̇ch\ *n* -ES [G, fr. G (Swiss dial.), lit., thrust, fr. MHG (Swiss dial.), of imit. origin] **:** a secretly plotted and suddenly executed attempt to overthrow a government or governing body ⟨was opposed to opportunistic plots and ~*es* —M.R.Konvitz⟩ — compare COUP D'ETAT **syn** see REBELLION

**putsch·ism** \-u̇ˌchizəm\ *n* -s **:** the advocacy or organization of a putsch

**putsch·ist** \-ˌchəst\ *n* -s **:** one who advocates or organizes a putsch

**¹putt** \ˈpət, *usu* -əd·+V\ *n* -s [origin unknown] *dial Eng* **:** a heavy cart used on a farm

**²putt** \"\ *n* -s [alter. of ²*put*] **:** a golf stroke made on or near a putting green to cause the ball to roll into or near the hole

**³putt** \"\ *vb* -ED/-ING/-s [alter. of ¹*put*] *vt* **:** to strike (a golf ball) in playing a putt ~ *vi* **:** to play a putt

**put·tee** \ˌpəˈtē, ˌpu̇ˈ-, ˈpəd·ē\ *n* -s [Hindi *paṭṭī* strip of cloth, bandage, fr. Skt *paṭṭikā*, fr. *paṭṭa* cloth, silk, bandage] **:** a covering for the leg from ankle to knee consisting of a narrow cloth wrapped spirally around the leg or a fitted leather legging secured by a strap, catch, or laces

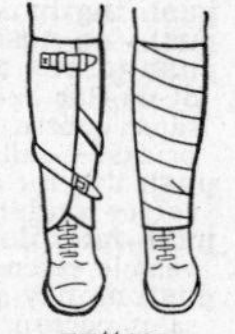
puttees

**putten** *dial past of* PUT

**¹put·ter** \ˈpu̇d·ə(r), -u̇tə-\ *n* -s [ME *puttere*, fr. *putten* to put + *-ere* -er] **1 :** one that puts ⟨a ~ of questions⟩ **2 :** PUSHER 1e

**²putt·er** \ˈpəd·ə(r), -ətə-\ *n* -s [³*putt* + *-er*] **1 :** a golf club with a short shaft and almost perpendicular face that is used in putting **2 :** one that putts

**³put·ter** \ˈpəd·ə(r), -ətə-\ *vi* -ED/-ING/-s [alter. of ²*potter*] **1 a :** to move or act without plan or purpose **:** occupy oneself aimlessly — usu. used with *about* or *around* ⟨rising now and then to ~ about the room —Laura Krey⟩ ⟨if he sold the business, what would he do with himself all day? *Putter* around —*Scribner's*⟩ **b :** to move or act slowly or lackadaisically **:** DAWDLE ⟨a slow train that ~*ed* along on a narrow-gage track —Christopher Rand⟩ ⟨you're always ~*ing* . . . now I want you to hustle —Sherwood Anderson⟩ **2 :** to look casually **:** BROWSE ⟨it is as much fun to ~ through as a family album or a municipal museum —Helen B. Woodward⟩ **3 :** to work at random **:** TINKER ⟨was ~*ing* with a small stove —Joseph Wechsberg⟩ ⟨so enthusiastic are they about the work that they return to ~ even on their days off —*Nat'l Geographic*⟩ — **put·ter·er** \-ərə(r)\ *n* -s

**⁴putter** \"\ *vi* -ED/-ING/-s [imit.] **:** to proceed or operate by means of a small gasoline engine ⟨motor whaleboats ~*ed* back and forth between the anchorage and the beach —*New Yorker*⟩ ⟨they ~*ed* on upon a steady course towards the west —Nevil Shute⟩ ⟨~*ing* motors —W.H.Hale⟩

**putter-in** \ˌ==ˈ=\ *n, pl* **putters-in** [*put in* + *-er*] **:** one that puts in; *esp* **:** a worker engaged in any of various operations (as feeding, filling, or guiding) involving the action of putting in

**put·ter·ing·ly** *adv* **:** in a puttering manner **:** AIMLESSLY

**putter-on** \ˌ==ˈ=\ *n, pl* **putters-on** [*put on* + *-er*] **:** one that puts on; *esp* **:** a worker engaged in any of various operations (as in textile printing or glue making) in which one thing is placed on something else

**putter-out** \ˌ==ˈ=\ *n, pl* **putters-out** [*put out* + *-er*] **:** one that puts out; *esp* **:** SETTER 2h

**putter-up** \ˌ==ˈ=\ *n, pl* **putters-up** [*put up* + *-er*] **:** one that puts up; *esp* **:** PACKER

**put through** *vt* **1 :** to carry to a successful conclusion **:** bring to completion ⟨the thing has to be done and the job *put through* and finished —Sir Winston Churchill⟩ ⟨in the latter office he *put through* a number of reforms —*Current Biog.*⟩ **2 a :** to make a telephone connection for ⟨the operator *put* him *through* to his party without delay⟩ **b :** to obtain a connection for (a telephone call) ⟨*put through* a long-distance call one evening —Anna Wright⟩

**put·ti·er** \ˈpəd·ēə(r), -ətē-\ *n* -s **:** one that putties **:** GLAZIER

**putting** *pres part of* PUT *or of* PUTT

**putting cleek** *n* **:** a putter having a long narrow blade with very little loft

**putting green** *n* **:** a closely cropped and rolled grassy area of a golf course located at the end of a fairway and containing the hole into which the ball must be played

**put to** *vb* [ME *putten to* to shut, fr. *putten* to put + *to*] *vt* **1** *chiefly dial* **:** SHUT ⟨*put* the door *to*⟩ **2 :** to close off (a fox earth) with the fox inside on the morning of a hunt ~ *vi, of a ship* **:** to put in to shore (as for shelter)

**put·to** \ˈpüd·(ˌ)ō\ *n, pl* **put·ti** \-üd·(ˌ)ē\ [It, lit., boy, fr. L *putus*; akin to Skt *putra* son, child — more at FEW] **:** a figure of a young boy (as a cupid) frequently used in decorative painting and sculpture esp. of the Renaissance — usu. used in pl.

**put·tock** \ˈpəd·ək\ *n* -s [ME *puttok*] **:** any of several birds of prey: **a :** a kite (*Milvus milvus*) **b :** BUZZARD **c :** MARSH HARRIER

**put together** *vt* [ME *putten togeder* to place together, fr. *putten* to put + *togeder, togedere* together] **1 :** to create as a unified whole **:** CONSTRUCT ⟨civilization is *put together* not by machines but by thought —*Saturday Rev.*⟩ ⟨*put* the book *together* in his spare time⟩ **2 :** ADD, COMBINE ⟨thought he knew more than all his teachers *put together*⟩

**puttoo** *var of* PATTU

**putt-putt** *var of* PUT-PUT

**putts** *pl of* PUTT, *pres 3d sing of* PUTT

**¹put·ty** \ˈpəd·|ē, -ət|\ *n* -ES [F *potée* putty, potful, fr. OF, potful, fr. *pot* — more at POTAGE] **1 :** LIME PUTTY **2 :** PUTTY POWDER **3 a :** a cement usu. made of whiting and boiled linseed oil beaten or kneaded to the consistency of dough and used in fastening glass in sashes and stopping crevices in woodwork **b :** any of various substances resembling such cement in appearance, consistency, or use: as (1) **:** IRON PUTTY (2) **:** RED-LEAD PUTTY (3) **:** the sticky mud at the bottom of shallow navigable water **4 a :** a variable color averaging a grayish yellow green **b :** a pale to grayish yellow **c** *of textiles* **:** a light brownish gray to light grayish brown **5 :** one who is easily manipulated **:** a soft and pliable person

⟨a grotesque fool who foolishly spoilt her, yet refused to be the ~ she desired —Rex Ingamells⟩ ⟨is ~ in her hands⟩

²**putty** \"\ *vt* -ED/-ING/-ES **:** to use putty on or apply putty to

**puttyblower** \'==,==\ *n, dial* **:** PEASHOOTER

**putty coat** *n* **:** HARD FINISH

**putty eye** *n* **:** an eye surrounded by thick fleshy tissues (as in various pigeons)

**putty gloss** *n* **:** a high polish imparted to stonework by a final polishing with putty powder

**putty knife** *n* **:** a knife with a broad flexible steel blade that is used for laying on and smoothing putty

putty knife

**putty powder** *n* **:** a polishing material (as for glass or marble) containing chiefly stannic oxide — called also *jewelers' putty*

**puttyroot** \'==,=\ *n* **:** a No. American orchid (*Aplectrum hyemale*) having a slender naked rootstock which produces each year a solid corm of which two or three remain strung together and sending up in late summer a single plaited evergreen leaf and in spring a scape of brown flowers

**put up** *vb* [ME *putten up*, fr. *putten* to put + *up*] *vt* **1 a :** to place in a container or receptacle ⟨*put* his lunch *up* in a brown paper bag⟩ **b :** to put away (a sword) in its scabbard **:** SHEATHE ⟨*put up* your swords; you know not what you do —Shak.⟩ **c :** to pack with something **:** make up into a container or package ⟨had with him a basket his mother had *put up* —Winston Churchill⟩ **d :** to prepare so as to preserve for later use: as (1) **:** to prepare (perishable foodstuffs) by canning ⟨*put up* several quarts of peaches⟩ ⟨*put* enough preserves *up* to last the year⟩ (2) **:** to cure and store (as hay or fodder) ⟨*put up* hay for wintering my saddle horses —Bruce Siberts⟩ **e :** to make up (as a medicine, prescription) **:** COMPOUND, PREPARE **f :** to put away out of use ⟨*put* her car *up* then and began spending her days cooped in . . . her hundred thousand dollar home —John Faulkner⟩ **2 :** to start (game) from cover **:** ROUSE ⟨saw birds, which my dog *put up* on one side of the river, cross to the other bank —Douglas Carruthers⟩ ⟨*put up* a herd of eleven wild deer who . . . only glided noiselessly a few yards into the woods —S.P.B.Mais⟩ **3** *archaic* **:** to put up with **:** ENDURE ⟨persuaded to *put up* in peace what already I have foolishly suffered —Shak.⟩ **4 a :** to nominate for election to a position or membership in an association ⟨his colleagues *put up* his name for premier —Neal Stanford⟩ ⟨*put* her name *up* for the sorority⟩ **b :** to select for some function or duty ⟨I was *put up*, at eight or nine, to propose some family toast —Joyce Cary⟩ ⟨catechized each man *put up* to serve on the jury —David Masters⟩ **5 :** to offer up (a prayer) **:** present (a petition) for action or consideration ⟨were really *putting up* — and in vain — a supplication for mercy —Havelock Ellis⟩ ⟨he's going to *put up* prayers for rain in church next Sunday —Ellen Glasgow⟩ **6 :** to set (hair) usu. in pin curls **7 a :** to make public or ask to be made public — used esp. of banns ⟨*put up* their banns for the third time⟩ **b :** to offer for public sale ⟨some farmer decides to pull up stakes and *puts* his possessions *up* for auction —*Amer. Guide Series: Texas*⟩ **c :** to present publicly **:** EXPOSE ⟨an idea which has been occupying me of late I would like to *put up* for criticism —Lucien Price⟩ **8 a :** to give food and shelter to (a horse) ⟨*put up* his horse for the night at the only stable in town⟩ **b :** to provide lodgings for **:** ACCOMMODATE ⟨suggested I go to his club, where he was *putting* me *up*, and have the bath —Marcia Davenport⟩ **9 :** to arrange (as a plot or scheme) with others **:** PRECONCERT ⟨*put up* a job to steal the jewels⟩ **10 :** BUILD, ERECT ⟨before the present building was *put up*, a smaller stone structure occupied the same site —C.J.Allen⟩ **11 a :** to make a display of **:** EXHIBIT, SHOW ⟨swallows can *put up* very good flight performances —David Gunston⟩ ⟨desperate as he was, he *put up* a brave front⟩ ⟨*put up* a bluff⟩ **b :** to carry on ⟨has *put up* a bitter struggle against great odds⟩ ⟨had *put up* a losing fight against erosion⟩ **12 a :** CONTRIBUTE, PAY ⟨was supposed to *put up* enough money to finish the film —Moore Raymond⟩ **b :** to offer as a prize or stake ⟨a bet of $25 was *put up* —*Amer. Guide Series: Minn.*⟩ **13 :** to increase the amount of **:** RAISE ⟨this sellers' cartel *put up* the price of rubber for a time —D.W.Brogan⟩ ⟨mechanical handling is one of the things which are *putting up* industrial productivity —Bertram Mycock⟩ ~ *vi* **:** LODGE ⟨two seasons ago I *put up* at a farmhouse —T.H.White b.1906⟩ **syn** see RESIDE

¹**put–up** \(')=¦=\ *adj* [fr. past part. of *put up*] **:** underhandedly arranged esp. with the cooperation of insiders **:** PLOTTED, PRECONCERTED ⟨a *put-up* piece of legal chicanery, fit only to arouse derisive laughter —*Time*⟩ ⟨a *put-up* job⟩

²**put–up** \"\ *n* -S [fr. past part. of *put up*] **:** something that is put up for marketing **:** PACKAGE; *esp* **:** any of various cones, tubes, or bobbins of yarn or thread

**put–upon** \'==¦=\ *adj* [fr. the past part. form of the phrase *put upon*] **:** imposed upon **:** taken advantage of **:** ABUSED, VICTIMIZED ⟨a deceived, anguished, *put-upon* girl —Anthony West⟩ ⟨identifies herself with the characters who are most *put-upon*, most noble, most righteous —James Thurber⟩

**pu·ture** \'pyüchə(r)\ *n* -S [AF, food, fr. OF *pouture*, fr. *pou*, *pouls* porridge — more at PULSE] *Eng law* **:** the customary right of keepers of forests and some bailiffs of hundreds to take food for man, horse, and dog from land of various tenants within the forest or hundred

**putwari** *var of* PATWARI

**putz** \'pu̇ts\ *n* -ES [PaG, fr. G, decoration, finery, fr. *putzen* to adorn, clean] **:** a decoration built around a representation of the Nativity scene and traditionally placed under a Christmas tree in Pennsylvania Dutch homes **:** CRÈCHE

¹**puxy** *also* **puck·sey** \'pəksi\ *n* -ES [origin unknown] *dial Eng* **:** swampy ground **:** QUAGMIRE

²**puxy** \"\ *adj, dial Eng* **:** SWAMPY

**puy** \'pwē\ *n* -S [F, fr. L *podium* balcony — more at PEW] **:** one of the hills of volcanic origin common in the Auvergne district of France

**pu·ya** \'püyə\ *n, cap* [NL, fr. AmerSp *puya* (plant of the genus *Puya*), perh. fr. Sp *puya* goad, perh. fr. (assumed) VL *puga*; akin to L *pungere* to prick, sting — more at PUNGENT] **:** a genus of terrestrial plants (family Bromeliaceae) found mostly in Peru and Chile that have basal spiny leaves and showy bracteate flowers in terminal racemes that may be 30 feet in height — see CHAGUAL GUM

**puy·al·lup** \pyü'aləp\ *n, pl* **puyallup** *or* **puyallups** *usu cap* **1 a :** a Salishan people of the east coast of Puget Sound and Vashon Island, Washington **b :** a member of such people **2 :** a dialect related to Skagit

¹**puz·zle** \'pəzəl\ *vb* **puzzled; puzzled; puzzling** \-z(ə)liŋ\ **puzzles** [origin unknown] *vt* **1** *obs* **:** to make it difficult for (a person) to choose or carry out a course of action **:** BEWILDER, CONFOUND ⟨more *puzzled* than the Egyptians in their fog —Shak.⟩ **2 a :** CONFUSE, PERPLEX ⟨~ my sad brains about life —L.P.Smith⟩ **b :** to bewilder mentally **:** confuse or nonplus the understanding of ⟨a malignant fever which *puzzled* the doctors —John Buchan⟩ ⟨are often *puzzled* and sometimes annoyed by the ways of other peoples who are strange to us —W.A.Parker⟩ **3** *archaic* **:** to make intricate **:** COMPLICATE, ENTANGLE ⟨disentangle from the *puzzled* skein —William Cowper⟩ **4 :** to proceed along in a mentally laborious manner ⟨teen-age boys who ~ their way through geometry —*Newsweek*⟩ ~ *vi* **1 a :** to be uncertain as to action or choice **:** become bewildered or perplexed ⟨we *puzzled* for two moons about where to put you —Nora Waln⟩ **b :** to exercise one's mind **:** attempt a solution of a puzzle ⟨I *puzzled* over her words and sought to attach to them some intelligent meaning —Rafael Sabatini⟩ **2 :** to search in a confused manner **:** GROPE ⟨*puzzled* about in his desk for the missing file of letters⟩

**syn** MYSTIFY, PERPLEX, BEWILDER, DISTRACT, NONPLUS, CONFOUND, DUMBFOUND: these verbs in the uses here compared all signify to disturb mentally, baffle, or throw into mental disorder or immobility. PUZZLE and MYSTIFY both suggest a complication or intricacy difficult to understand or explain, MYSTIFY suggesting more often a complication purposely created as by the concealment or obscuring of essential fact ⟨the questions which doubtless *puzzle* most of us —*Town Jour.*⟩ ⟨the secret of the enigma that *puzzled* me —L.P.Smith⟩ ⟨it was the riddle of life that was *puzzling* and killing her —Arnold Bennett⟩ ⟨why more visitors to South America do not take this memorable river trip *mystifies* my wife and me —L.A.Keating⟩ ⟨once prescriptions were written almost altogether in Latin. This was not done to *mystify* the patient —Morris Fishbein⟩ ⟨historical paraphernalia with which to *mystify* their unsuspecting clients —*Amer. Guide Series: N.Y.*⟩ PERPLEX and BEWILDER add the ideas of uncertainty and, often, worry to that of puzzlement, BEWILDER implying a consequent and usually complete intellectual disorder ⟨on their arrival they were *perplexed* by radical differences in language, customs, and environment —*Amer. Guide Series: R.I.*⟩ ⟨Gates was greatly *perplexed* to know what to do —H.E.Scudder⟩ ⟨they were *perplexed*, vexed and worried —Ernie Pyle⟩ ⟨textbooks in *bewildering* variety confronted the pioneer teacher —*Amer. Guide Series: Wash.*⟩ ⟨the *bewildering* confusion of our times —Matthew Arnold⟩ ⟨a character *bewildered* by a confusion of values —R.B.West⟩ DISTRACT suggests the perturbation of an uncertain though not necessarily puzzled or bewildered mind, implying, rather, strongly conflicting preoccupations or interests ⟨his fury is that of a temporarily *distracted* boy —Walter Goodman⟩ ⟨a man *distracted* between two spiritual homes —*Time*⟩ ⟨that conflict of races and religions which had so long *distracted* the island —T.B.Macaulay⟩ NONPLUS suggests a blankness of mind often attendant upon complete bafflement ⟨the pilots write: — "It was imperative that we should not find ourselves *nonplussed* in an emergency in the air . . ." —*Times Lit. Supp.*⟩ ⟨the problem which *nonplusses* the wisest heads on this planet . . . What is reality? —L.P.Smith⟩ ⟨she was utterly *nonplussed* by the pair of them . . . What on earth were they? —Elizabeth Goudge⟩ CONFOUND implies a mental confusion attendant upon astonishment or complete abashment ⟨professional critics . . . should be *confounded* by the book's evidence of careful research —Beka Doherty⟩ ⟨someone who can furnish him with the sort of evidence of the authenticity of his picture that would satisfy a special juryman and *confound* a purchasing dealer —Clive Bell⟩ DUMBFOUND may be interchangeable with CONFOUND but usually suggests a stronger effect, a confounding to the point of mental paralysis or wonderment ⟨to be so *dumbfounded* as to be unable to speak for a moment⟩ ⟨apparently too *dumbfounded* by the insane assault to interfere seriously —Al Newman⟩ ⟨his schoolmates are astonished; his fellow-soldiers are *dumbfounded* —J.M.Brinnin⟩

²**puzzle** \"\ *n* -S **1 :** the state of being puzzled **:** mental embarrassment **:** PERPLEXITY ⟨the transition from a state of ~ and perplexity to rational comprehension —William James⟩ **2 a :** something that puzzles **:** a difficult question or problem ⟨it is more a ~ than a comfort to see those children growing so fine and straight —Claudia Cassidy⟩ ⟨this young man was an unaccountable ~ —J.H.Powers⟩ **b :** a question, problem, toy, or contrivance designed for testing ingenuity — see CHINESE PUZZLE, CROSSWORD, JIGSAW PUZZLE **syn** see MYSTERY

**puzzle box** *n* **:** a cage used in experiments on animal learning from which the animal learns to escape by operating a button, hook, or other device

**puzzle canon** *n* **:** RIDDLE CANON

**puz·zled·ly** *adv* **:** in a puzzled manner

**puzzleheaded** \¦==¦==\ *adj* **:** having or based on confused attitudes or ideas ⟨the professional philosopher is a help and an inspiration even when he is somewhat ~ —J.A.Macy⟩ ⟨a kind of ~ conservatism —*Spectator*⟩ — **puz·zle·head·edness** *n* -ES

**puzzle jug** *n* **:** a ceramic pitcher or jug with pierced neck that will pour without spilling only if certain holes are covered with the fingers

**puzzle lock** *n* **:** COMBINATION LOCK

**puz·zle·ment** \'pəzəlmənt\ *n* -S **1 :** the state of being puzzled **:** BEWILDERMENT, PERPLEXITY ⟨frowns of deep ~ —J.D. Williams⟩ ⟨expressing his interest in and frank ~ at the ways of the world —C.L.Sulzberger⟩ **2 :** something that puzzles **:** PUZZLE ⟨the affair . . . will long be a ~ —*New Yorker*⟩

**puzzle out** *vt* **:** to solve, discover, or work out by mental effort or ingenuity ⟨*puzzled* it *out* and made a translation of it —Van Wyck Brooks⟩ ⟨don't bother to combine the symptoms in their own mind and *puzzle out* the diagnosis —A.J.Cronin⟩

**puzzlepated** \¦==¦==\ *adj* **:** PUZZLEHEADED

**puz·zler** \'pəz(ə)lə(r)\ *n* -S **1 :** one that puzzles **2 :** a person devoted to solving puzzles

**puz·zling·ly** *adv* **:** in a puzzling manner ⟨such was the object on which she ~ challenged him —Henry James †1916⟩

**puzzolan** *or* **puzzolana** *var of* POZZOLANA

**PV** *abbr* **1** par value **2** pipe ventilated **3** post village **4** priest vicar

**PVA** *abbr* **1** polyvinyl acetate **2** polyvinyl alcohol

**PVC** *abbr* polyvinyl chloride

**PVP** *abbr* polyvinylpyrrolidone

**pvt** *abbr, often cap* private

**PW** *abbr* **1** packed weight **2** prisoner of war **3** public works

**p–wave** \'=,=\ *n, usu cap P* **1 :** PRESSURE WAVE **2** *usu* **p wave :** a deflection in an electrocardiographic tracing that represents auricular activity of the heart — compare T WAVE

**pwd** *abbr* powder

**pwe** \'pwā\ *n* -S [Burmese] **:** a Burmese open-air festival consisting of dancing, singing, and dramatization

**pwo** \'pwō\ *n, pl* **pwo** *or* **pwos** *usu cap* **1 a :** a Karen people of the Irrawaddy delta region **b :** a member of such people **2 :** the language of the Pwo people

**pwr** *abbr* power

**pwt** *abbr* pennyweight

**PX** \(')pē¦eks\ *abbr or n, pl* **PXs** \-eksəz\ post exchange

**PX** *abbr* **1** please exchange **2** private exchange

**pxt** *abbr* [L *pinxit*] he or she painted it

**py–** *or* **pyo–** *comb form* [Gk, fr. *pyon* pus — more at FOUL] **1 :** marked by the presence of pus in or with **:** pussy ⟨*pyo*lymph⟩ ⟨*pyo*ureter⟩ ⟨*py*emia⟩ **2 :** due to or associated with a pus-producing infection **:** suppurative ⟨*pyo*nephritis⟩ ⟨*pyo*phthalmia⟩

**pya** \pē'ä, 'pyä\ *n* -S [Burmese] **1 :** a Burmese monetary unit equal to 1/100 kyat — see MONEY table **2 :** a coin representing one pya

**pyaemia** *var of* PYEMIA

**py·al** \(')pī¦äl\ *n* -S [Pg *poyal* mounting stone, stone bench, fr. *poyo* bench, block, fr. L *podium* platform — more at PEW] **:** the raised platform or veranda of an Indian house

**py·arthrosis** \¦pī+\ *n* [NL, fr. *py-* + *arthrosis*] **:** the formation or presence of pus within a joint

**pycn–** *or* **pycno–** *comb form* [L, fr. Gk *pykn-*, *pykno-*, fr. *pyknos*; akin to Gk *pyka* thickly, Alb *puth* kiss, Av *pusā-* headband; basic meaning: pressed together] **:** close **:** compact **:** dense **:** bulky ⟨*pycn*ic⟩ ⟨*pycn*idium⟩ ⟨*pycno*gonid⟩

**pyc·nan·the·mum** \pik'nan(t)thəməm\ *n, cap* [NL, fr. *pycn-* + *-anthemum*] **:** a genus of No. American aromatic herbs (family Labiatae) with small white or purple-dotted flowers — see BASIL MINT, MOUNTAIN MINT

**pyc·ni·al** \'piknēəl\ *adj* [NL *pycnium* + E *-al*] **:** of or relating to a pycnium **:** characterized by the presence or development of pycnia

**pycnic** *var of* PYKNIC

**pyc·nid** \'piknəd\ *also* **pyc·nide** \", -,nīd\ *n* -S [ISV, fr. NL *pycnidium*] **:** PYCNIDIUM

**pyc·nid·i·al** \(')pik¦nidēəl\ *adj* [NL *pycnidium* + E *-al*] **:** of, relating to, or characterized by the production of pycnidia

**pyc·nid·io·spore** \pik'nidēō+,-\ *n* [NL *pycnidium* + E *-o-* + *-spore*] **:** a conidium formed in a pycnidium

**pyc·nid·i·um** \pik'nidēəm\ *n, pl* **pycnid·ia** \-ēə\ [NL, fr. *pycn-* + *-idium*] **1 :** a flask-shaped spore fruit that bears conidiophores and pycnidiospores on the interior and is typical of various imperfect fungi (as of the order Phyllostictales) and ascomycetes **2 :** PYCNIUM

**pyc·nio·spore** \'piknēō+,-\ *n* [NL *pycnium* + E *-o-* + *-spore*] **:** a haploid pycnial spore of a rust fungus that by fusion with a haploid hypha of opposite sex produces aecia and dikaryotic aeciospores — see PYCNIUM

**pyc·nite** \'pik,nīt\ *n* -S [F, fr. *pycn-* + *-ite*] **:** a massive columnar topaz

**pyc·ni·um** \'piknēəm\ *n, pl* **pyc·nia** \-ēə\ [NL, fr. *pycn-* + *-ium*] **:** one of the small flask-shaped fruit bodies of a rust fungus formed in clusters just beneath the surface of the host tissue, produced as a result of infection by a single basidiospore, and producing haploid flexuous hyphae and pycniospores

**pyc·noc·o·ma** \pik'näkəmə\ *n, cap* [NL, fr. *pycn-* + *-coma*] **:** a small genus of shrubs or trees (family Euphorbiaceae) of tropical Africa and the Mascarene Islands having monoecious flowers and numerous stamens with hairlike elongated filaments

¹**pyc·no·dont** \'piknə,dänt\ *adj* [NL *Pycnodontidae*] **:** of or relating to the Pycnodontidae

²**pycnodont** \"\ *n* -S **:** a fish or fossil of the family Pycnodontidae

**pyc·no·don·ta** \,piknə'däntə\ *n, cap* [NL, fr. *pycn-* + *-odonta*] **:** a genus of large tropical oysters having strongly scalloped shells with crinkled ridges on each side of the hinge and occurring chiefly on coral reefs

**pyc·no·don·ti** \,piknə'dän,tī\ *n pl, cap* [NL, fr. *Pycnodont-*, *Pycnodus*] *in some classifications* **:** an order or other group coextensive with the family Pycnodontidae

**pyc·no·don·ti·dae** \-äntə,dē\ *n pl, cap* [NL, fr. *Pycnodont-*, *Pycnodus*, type genus (fr. *pycn-* + *-odont-*, *-odus*) + *-idae*] **:** a large family that is segregated in the order Pycnodonti or now more usu. included in Cycloganoidei and that includes Mesozoic and Tertiary ganoid fishes having a deep compressed body typically covered with rhomboidal scales, a homocercal tail, and strong blunt crushing teeth

¹**pyc·no·don·toid** \¦==¦dän,tȯid\ *adj* [NL *Pycnodont-*, *Pycnodus* + E *-oid*] **:** resembling or related to the family Pycnodontidae

²**pycnodontoid** \"\ *n* -S **:** a pycnodontoid fish or fossil

¹**pyc·nog·o·nid** \(')pik¦nägənəd, ¦piknə¦gän-\ *adj* [NL *Pycnogonida*] **:** of or relating to the Pycnogonida

²**pycnogonid** \"\ *n* -S **:** an arthropod of the class Pycnogonida

**pyc·no·gon·i·da** \,piknə'gänədə\ *n pl, cap* [NL, fr. *Pycnogonum*, genus of sea spiders (fr. *pycn-* + Gk *gony* knee) + *-ida* — more at KNEE] **:** a class of marine arthropods that superficially resemble spiders with the body relatively very thin and small, the legs usu. excessively long and slender, and the abdomen rudimentary, that have typically seven pairs of appendages of which the posterior four pairs are legs and contain diverticula of the intestine and reproductive organs and of which the first two or three pairs are often absent, a triangular mouth at the end of a tubular proboscis, no organs of respiration, and separate sexes, and that produce young which usu. pass through a metamorphosis

**pyc·nom·e·ter** *also* **pic·nom·e·ter** *or* **pyk·nom·e·ter** \pik'nämədə(r)\ *n* [ISV *pycn-* + *-meter*] **:** a standard vessel often provided with a thermometer for measuring and comparing the densities of liquids or solids — **pyc·no·met·ric** \¦piknə¦me·trik\ *adj* — **pyc·nom·e·try** \pik'nämə·trē\ *n* -ES

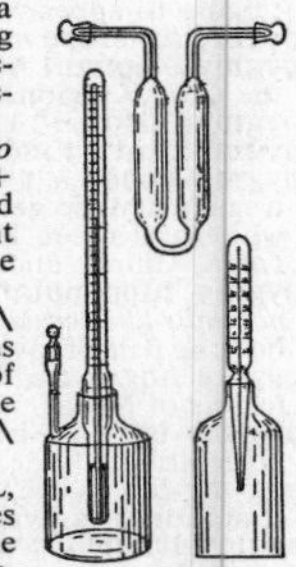

pycnometers

**pyc·no·mor·phic** \¦piknə¦mȯrfik\ *also* **pyc·no·mor·phous** \-fəs\ *adj* [*pycn-* + *-morphic* or *-morphous*] **:** compactly formed **:** characterized by compact arrangement of stainable parts — used esp. of nerve cells

**pyc·no·noti·dae** \,piknə'näd·ə,dē, -nōd-\ *n pl, cap* [NL, fr. *Pycnonotus*, type genus (fr. *pycn-* + *-notus*) + *-idae*] **:** a family of Old World passerine birds consisting of the bulbuls — **pyc·no·no·tine** \¦==nō,tīn\ *adj*

**pyc·no·po·dia** \,piknə'pōdēə\ *n, cap* [NL, fr. *pycn-* + *-podia*] **:** a genus of starfishes (family Asteriidae) including only the large 20-rayed sunflower star (*P. helianthoides*) of the littoral zone of the western coast of No. America

**pyc·nos·ce·lus** \pik'näsələs\ *n, cap* [NL, fr. *pycn-* + Gk *skelos* leg — more at CYLINDER] **:** a genus of cockroaches that includes one (*P. surinamensis*) which is the intermediate host of the eye worm (*Oxyspirura mansoni*) of poultry

**pyc·no·sis** *or* **pyk·no·sis** \pik'nōsəs\ *n* -ES [NL, fr. Gk *pyknōsis* condensation, fr. *pyknoun* to condense (fr. *pyknos* dense, thick) + *-ōsis* -osis — more at PYCN-] **:** a degenerative condition of a cell nucleus marked by clumping of the chromosomes, hyperchromatism, and shrinking of the nucleus

**pyc·no·spore** \'piknə+,-\ *n* [ISV *pycn-* + *-spore*] **:** PYCNIOSPORE

¹**pyc·no·style** \-,stīl\ *adj* [Gk *pyknostylos* with the pillars close together, fr. *pykn-* pycn- + *stylos* pillar — more at STEER] **:** having or constituting an intercolumniation of one and one-half diameters

²**pycnostyle** \"\ *n* -S **:** a pycnostyle colonnade

**pyc·not·ic** *or* **pyk·not·ic** \(')pik¦näd·ik\ *adj* [ISV, fr. NL *pycnosis*, *pyknosis*, after such pairs as NL *narcosis*: E *narcotic*; orig. formed as G *pyknotisch*] **:** of, relating to, or exhibiting pycnosis

**pyc·nox·yl·ic** \¦pik,näk¦silik\ *adj* [*pycn-* + *oxylic*] **:** having dense hard wood because of a high proportion of secondary xylem

**pye** *var of* PIE

**pye book** *n, obs* **:** ³PIE 2

**pye–dog** *also* **pi–dog** *or* **pie–dog** \'pī,=\ *n* [Anglo-Indian, prob. by shortening and alter. fr. *pariah dog*] **:** a half-wild dog of uncertain ancestry and ownership that is common about villages throughout much of southern and eastern Asia

**pyel–** *or* **pyelo–** *comb form* [NL, fr. Gk, trough, vat, fr. *pyelos*; akin to Gk *plynein* to wash, *plein* to sail, float — more at FLOW] **1 :** pelvis ⟨*pyelo*metry⟩ ⟨*pyel*ic⟩ **2 :** renal pelvis ⟨*pyelo*gram⟩ ⟨*pyel*itis⟩

**py·el·ectasis** \¦pīəl+\ *n* [NL, fr. *pyel-* + *ectasis*] **:** dilatation of the pelvis of a kidney

**py·el·ic** \(')pī¦elik\ *adj* [ISV *pyel-* + *-ic*] **:** of, relating to, or affecting the renal pelvis

**py·elit·ic** \¦pīə¦lid·ik\ *adj* [NL *pyelitis* + E *-ic*] **:** of, relating to, or constituting pyelitis

**py·eli·tis** \,pīə'līd·əs\ *n* -ES [NL, fr. *pyel-* + *-itis*] **:** inflammation of the pelvis of a kidney

**py·elo·gram** \pī'elə,gram, 'pīəlō,-\ *also* **py·elo·graph** \-raf, -räf\ *n* [ISV *pyel-* + *-gram* or *-graph*] **:** a roentgenogram made by pyelography

**py·elo·graph·ic** \pī¦elə¦grafik, ¦pīəlō¦-\ *adj* [*pyelography* + *-ic*] **:** of, relating to, or involving the use of pyelography

**py·elog·ra·phy** \,pīə'lägrəfē\ *n* -ES [ISV *pyel-* + *-graphy*] **:** roentgenographic visualization of the kidney pelvis after injection of a radiopaque substance through the ureter or into a vein

**py·elo·nephritic** \¦pīə(,)lō+\ *adj* [NL *pyelonephritis* + E *-ic*] **:** of, relating to, or caused by pyelonephritis

**py·elo·nephritis** \"+\ *n* [NL, fr. *pyel-* + *nephritis*] **:** inflammation of both the pelvis and the substance of the kidney

**py·elo·nephrosis** \"+\ *n* [NL, fr. *pyel-* + *nephrosis*] **:** disease of the kidney and its pelvis

**py·elo·ureterogram** \"+\ *n* [*pyel-* + *ureterogram*] **:** a roentgenogram of a kidney pelvis and the corresponding ureter

**py·emia** *or* **py·ae·mia** \pī'ēmēə\ *n* -S [NL, fr. *py-* + *-emia*] **:** septicemia accompanied by multiple abscesses and secondary toxemic symptoms and caused by pus-forming microorganisms (as the bacterium *Staphylococcus aureus*) — compare BACTEREMIA — **py·emic** \(')pī¦ēmik\ *adj*

**py·emo·tes** \,pīə'mōd·(,)ēz\ *n, cap* [NL] **:** a genus of mites that are usu. ectoparasites of insects but that include one (*P. ventricosus*) which causes grain itch in man when transferred (as in harvesting) to the skin

**pyengadu** *var of* PYINKADO

**py·esis** \pī'ēsəs\ *n* -ES [NL, fr. *py-* + *-esis*] **:** SUPPURATION

**pyg–** *or* **pygo–** *comb form* [NL, fr. Gk *pygē* — more at FOG] **:** rump **:** buttocks ⟨*pyg*algia⟩ ⟨*pygo*style⟩

**–py·ga** \'pīgə\ *or* **–py·gia** \'pijēə\ *n comb form* [-*pyga* fr. NL, fr. Gk *pygē* rump; *-pygia* fr. NL, fr. Gk *pygē* + NL *-ia*] **:** creature having (such) a rump — in generic names in zoology ⟨Eury*pyga*⟩ ⟨Macro*pygia*⟩

¹**py·gal** \'pīgəl\ *adj* [*pyg-* + *-al*] **:** of, relating to, or located in the region of the rump or posterior end of the back ⟨~ plates in the carapace of a turtle⟩

²**pygal** \"\ *n* -S **:** a pygal part

**pygarg** *also* **pygargus** *n, pl* **pygargs** *also* **pygarguses** [L *pygargus*, an antelope, an eagle, fr. Gk *pygargos*, lit., white rump, fr. *pyg-* + *argos* white — more at ARGENT] **1** *obs* **:** a white-rumped ungulate (as an addax) **2** *obs* **:** SEA EAGLE

**py·gid·i·al** \(ˈ)pīˈjidēəl\ *adj* [NL *pygidium* + E *-al*] **:** of, relating to, or constituting a pygidium

**py·gi·di·idae** \ˌpījəˈdīəˌdē\ *n, cap* [NL, fr. *Pygidium*, type genus (fr. Gk *pygidion*) + *-idae*] *in some classifications* **:** a family of usu. small and often parasitic So. American catfishes that lack an adipose fin and have the dorsal fin located far back toward the tail

**py·gid·i·um** \pīˈjidēəm\ *n, pl* **pygid·ia** \-ēə\ [NL, fr. Gk *pygidion* small rump, fr. *pygē* rump + *-idion* -idium] **:** a caudal structure or the terminal body region of various invertebrates: as **a :** the caudal plate of a trilobite **b :** the terminal tergite of an insect's abdomen

**¹pygmaean** *or* **pygmean** *n* -s [*pygmaean* fr. L *pygmaeus* dwarfish + E *-an*; *pygmean* fr. L *pygmaeus* + E *-an*] *obs* **:** PYGMY

**²pyg·mae·an** *or* **pyg·me·an** \(ˈ)pigˈmēən, ˈpigˌm-\ *adj* **:** PYGMY

**pyg·ma·lion** \pigˈmālyən, -lēən\ *n* -s *often cap* [fr. *Pygmalion*, legendary sculptor of Cyprus] **:** CENTENNIAL BROWN

**pyg·ma·lion·ism** \-ˌnizəm\ *n* -s *often cap* [ISV *pygmalion-* (fr. *Pygmalion*, legendary king and sculptor of Cyprus who fell in love with the statue that he had made of a woman and at whose request Aphrodite gave the statue life, fr. Gk *Pygmaliōn*) + *-ism*] **:** sexual responsiveness directed toward a statue or other representation

**pyg·moid** \ˈpigˌmȯid\ *adj* [*pygmy* + *-oid*] **:** resembling or partaking of the characteristics of the Pygmies

**¹pyg·my** *also* **pig·my** \ˈpigmē, -mi\ *n* -ES [ME *pigmei*, fr. L *pygmaeus* of a pygmy, dwarfish (n. pl. *pygmaei*, fr. Gk *pygmaioi*), fr. Gk *pygmaios* of a pygmy, fr. *pygmē* fist, measure of length, distance from the elbow to the knuckles — more at PUNGENT] **1** *often cap* **:** one of a fabled race of dwarfs described by ancient Greek authors **2** *usu cap* **:** one of a small people of equatorial Africa ranging under five feet in height, having dark skin but lighter than that of true Negroes, poorly developed chins, moderately round heads, and broad noses, practicing a crude hunting culture, using the languages of their nearest neighbors, and being prob. most closely related to the Negritos **3 a :** a short insignificant person **:** DWARF **b :** ELF, GNOME, PIXY **c :** a thing very small for its kind **4** *obs* **:** a chimpanzee or other anthropoid ape

**²pygmy** \ˈ\ *adj* **1 :** of or relating to the Pygmies or a pygmy **2 :** resembling a pygmy **:** DWARFISH **:** very small

**³pygmy** *also* **pigmy** \ˈ"\ *vt* -ED/-ING/-ES **:** to make a pygmy of **:** cause to appear small or insignificant **:** DWARF

**pygmy antelope** *n* **:** ROYAL ANTELOPE

**pygmy elephant** *n* **:** a small elephant (*Loxodonta pumilio*) of the Congo region that rarely exceeds six feet at the shoulder

**pygmy falcon** *n* **:** FALCONET 2a

**pygmy flint** *n* **:** MICROLITH

**pygmy goose** *n* **:** any of several very small short-billed extremely aquatic geese (genus *Nettapus*) that have considerable white and green in their plumage and are native to Africa, India, China, and Australia

**pygmy hippopotamus** *n* **:** a small hippopotamus (*Hippopotamus liberiensis* or *Choeropsis liberiensis*) of Liberia having but one pair of lower incisors

**pygmy hog** *n* **:** a very small wild pig (*Sus salvanius*) of the forests of Nepal

**pyg·my·ish** \-mē·ish, -mi·ish\ *adj* [¹*pygmy* + *-ish*] **:** DWARFISH, STUNTED

**pyg·my·ism** \-mēˌizəm, -miˌiz-\ *n* -s [¹*pygmy* + *-ism*] **:** the condition of a pygmy **:** a stunted or dwarfish state

**pygmy lemur** *n* **:** a dwarf lemur (esp. *Microcebus murinus*)

**pygmy locust** *n* **:** GROUSE LOCUST

**pygmy marmoset** *n* **:** a So. American marmoset (*Callithrix pygmaeus*) that is the smallest of all monkeys standing about two and one half inches high and weighing less than five ounces

**pygmy musk deer** *n* **:** CHEVROTAIN

**pygmy nuthatch** *n* **:** a small nuthatch (*Sitta pygmaea*) of western No. America that is largely bluish gray above with white chin and neck patch and whitish underparts

**pygmy owl** *n* **:** any of various small and usu. rather dark-colored owls (genus *Glancidium*) that are sometimes day-flying and chiefly insectivorous — called also *gnome owl*

**pygmy parrot** *n* **:** any of various small parrots (genus *Micropsitta*) of New Guinea and adjacent islands having a thick bill with a cere, very long claws, and brilliant plumage in the male

**pygmy-pipes** \ˈ==,=\ *n pl but sing or pl in constr* **:** SWEET PINESAP

**pygmy possum** *n* **:** MOUSE OPOSSUM

**pygmy rattler** *or* **pygmy rattlesnake** *n* **:** a rattlesnake of the genus *Sistrurus* — see MASSASAUGA

**pygmy rose** *n* **:** FAIRY ROSE

**pygmy shrew** *n* **1 :** a small European shrew (*Sorex minutus*) **2 :** a small No. American shrew (*Microsorex hoyi*)

**pygmy sperm whale** *n* **:** any of several small whales (genus *Kogia*) that are chiefly of southern seas, approximate 15 feet in length, and have a falcate dorsal fin and crescentic blowhole

**pygmy squirrel** *n* **:** any of numerous minute African and Asiatic tree squirrels (as of the genus *Myosciurus*)

**pygmyweed** *or* **pigmyweed** \ˈ==,=\ *n* **:** a small annual aquatic herb (*Tillaea aquatica*) of the family Crassulaceae that occurs along the coasts of No. America, Europe, and northern Africa and has very small solitary axillary greenish flowers

**pygmy whale** *n* **:** a small whalebone whale (*Neobalaena marginata*) of New Zealand waters

**pygo-** — see PYG-

**py·go·fer** \ˈpīgəfə(r)\ *n* -s [*pyg-* + *-fer*] **:** the last segment of the abdomen of some insects; *also* **:** the side margin of this segment

**py·gop·a·gus** \pīˈgäpəgəs\ *n* -ES [NL, fr. *pyg-* + *-pagus*] **:** a twin fetal monster joined in the sacral region

**¹py·go·pod** \ˈpīgəˌpäd\ *adj* [NL *Pygopodes*] **:** of or relating to the Pygopodes

**²pygopod** \ˈ"\ *n* -s **:** a bird of the order Pygopodes

**³pygopod** \ˈ"\ *n* -s [*pyg-* + *-pod*] **:** one of the paired appendages of the tenth abdominal segment of an insect

**py·gop·o·des** \pīˈgäpəˌdēz\ *n pl, cap* [NL, fr. *pyg-* + Gk *pod-*, *pous* foot — more at FOOT] *in some esp former classifications* **:** an order of diving birds comprising the loons, grebes, and sometimes the auks

**py·gop·o·did** \(ˈ)pīˈgäpədəd\ *adj* [NL *Pygopodidae*, family of lizards, fr. *Pygopod-*, *Pygopus*, type genus + *-idae*] **:** of or relating to the genus *Pygopus* or to the family Pygopodidae

**py·go·po·di·um** \ˌpīgəˈpōdēəm\ *n, pl* **pygopo·dia** \-ēə\ [NL, fr. *pyg-* + *-podium*] **:** a fleshy process on the terminal abdominal segment of various beetle and fly larvae

**py·gop·o·dous** \(ˈ)pīˈgäpədəs\ *adj* [*pyg-* + *-podous*] **:** having the feet set far back ⟨grebes and penguins are typical ~ birds⟩

**py·go·pus** \ˈpīgəpəs\ *n, cap* [NL, fr. *pyg-* + *-pus*] **:** a genus (the type of the family Pygopodidae) of pleurodont snake-shaped Australian and Tasmanian lizards without forelimbs and with rudimentary hind limbs

**py·go·style** \ˈpīgəˌstīl\ *n* -s [*pyg-* + *-style*] **1 :** a plate of bone that forms the posterior end of the vertebral column in most birds and is formed by the union of vertebrae **2** *obs* **:** VOMER

**py·go·styled** \-ld\ *adj* [*pygostyle* + *-ed*] **:** having a pygostyle

**py·go·sty·lous** \ˌpīgəˈstīləs\ *adj* [*pygostyle* + *-ous*] **:** of, relating to, or constituting a pygostyle **:** PYGOSTYLED

**pyin·ka·do** \pēˈiŋkəˌdō, ˈpyi-\ *or* **pyin·ga·do** \-ŋgə-\ *or* **pyen·ga·du** \pēˈeŋ-,ˈpyeŋ-\ *n* -s [Burmese *pyeng-kadō*] **1 a :** a tall Asiatic tree (*Xylia dolabriformis*) that is often confused with the acle and that has very heavy hard durable wood **b :** the wood of pyinkado **2 :** ACLE

**pyin·ma** \pēˈinˌmä, ˈpyi-\ *n* -s [native name in Burma] **:** the light red to reddish brown smooth lustrous and moderately hard heavy durable wood of the queen's crape myrtle

**py·ja·mas** \pəˈjäməz *sometimes* piˈj-, *archaic* pīˈj-\ *chiefly Brit var of* PAJAMAS

**pyke** \ˈpīk\ *n* -s [Hindi *pāyik*, *pāyak* messenger, fr. Per] *dial Eng* **:** a civilian at whose expense a soldier is treated or entertained

**¹pyk·nic** *also* **pyc·nic** \ˈpiknik\ *adj* [ISV *pykn-*, *pycn-* pycn- + *-ic*; orig. formed as G *pyknisch*] **:** characterized by shortness of stature, broadness of girth, and powerful muscularity **:** ENDOMORPHIC — compare ASTHENIC, ATHLETIC

**²pyknic** *also* **pycnic** \ˈ"\ *n* -s **:** a person of pyknic build

**pykno-** *comb form* **:** PYCN-

**pyk·no·epilepsy** \ˌpik(ˌ)nō+\ *n* [ISV *pycn-* + *epilepsy*; orig. formed as G *pyknoepilepsie*] **:** PYKNOLEPSY

**pyk·no·lep·sy** \ˈpiknəˌlepsē\ *n* -ES [ISV *pycn-* + *-lepsy*; orig. formed as G *pyknolepsie*] **:** a condition marked by epileptiform attacks resembling petit mal

**pyknometer** *var of* PYCNOMETER

**pyknosis** *var of* PYCNOSIS

**pyknotic** *var of* PYCNOTIC

**pyk·rete** \ˈpīˌkrēt\ *n* -s [Geoffrey *Pyke*, 20th cent. Eng. inventor who invented it + *-rete* (as in *concrete*)] **:** a frozen mixture of water and wood pulp that gives a tough resistant product used experimentally in arctic military structures

**pyl-** *or* **pyle-** *or* **pylo-** *comb form* [NL, fr. Gk, fr. *pylē* gate — more at PYLON] **:** portal vein ⟨*pyle*thrombophlebitis⟩

**py·la** \ˈpīlə\ *n, pl* **pylas** \-ləz\ *or* **py·lae** \-(ˌ)lē\ [NL, fr. Gk *pylē* gate] **:** the opening from the third ventricle into the aqueduct of Sylvius in higher vertebrates including man; *also* **:** a corresponding opening on either side from the cavity of the optic lobe in some lower vertebrates — **py·lar** \-lə(r)\ *adj*

**pyla·gore** \ˈpiləˌgō(ə)r, ˈpīl-\ *n* -s [Gk *pylagoras*, fr. *Pylai* Pylae, Thermopylae, meeting place of the amphictyonic council + Gk *-agoras* (fr. *ageirein* to collect, assemble) — more at GREGARIOUS] **:** a deputy of a state at the council of the Delphic Amphictyony of ancient Greece

**py·lan·gi·um** \pīˈlanjēəm\ *n, pl* **pylan·gia** \-ēə\ [NL, fr. *pyl-* + *-angium*] **:** the highly muscular portion of the arterial trunk in immediate connection with the ventricle of the heart in some lower vertebrates — compare SYNANGIUM

**pyle** *chiefly Scot var of* PILE

**-pyle** \ˌpīl\ *n comb form* -s [ISV, fr. Gk *pylē* gate] **:** opening **:** orifice ⟨micro*pyle*⟩ ⟨apo*pyle*⟩

**py·le·phlebitis** \ˌpīlə+\ *n* [NL, fr. *pyl-* + *phlebitis*] **:** inflammation of the portal vein usu. secondary to intestinal disease and with suppuration

**py·lic** \ˈpīlik\ *adj* [*pyl-* + *-ic*] **:** of or relating to a portal vein

**py·lon** \ˈpīˌlän, -lən\ *n* -s [Gk *pylōn* gateway, fr. *pylē* gate; perh. akin to Skt *gopura* town-gate, gate] **1 a :** a usu. massive gateway often with flanking towers — compare PROPYLON **b :** an ancient Egyptian gateway building having a truncated pyramidal form; *broadly* **:** two such truncated pyramids with a gateway between **c :** a monumental mass placed so as to flank an entrance way (as an approach to a bridge) **2 :** a tower (as of steelwork) for supporting either end of a wire (as for a telegraph line) over a long span **3 a :** a post, tower, or other projection marking a prescribed course of flight for an airplane **b :** a structure for supporting the propeller on the side of a rigid airship or for attaching an auxiliary fuel tank, a bomb, or other external stores carried by an airplane

pylons 1b

**pylon antenna** *n* **:** a slotted tubular radio antenna

**pylor-** *or* **pyloro-** *comb form* [LL *pylorus* — more at PYLORUS] **:** pylorus ⟨*pylor*algia⟩ ⟨*pyloro*cleisis⟩

**py·lor·ic** \(ˈ)pīˈlȯrik, pəˈl-, -lär-, -rēk\ *adj* [*pylor-* + *-ic*] **:** of, relating to, lying in the region of, or involving the pylorus or the part of the stomach from which the intestine leads

**pyloric artery** *n* **:** a branch of the hepatic artery supplying the pyloric end and lesser curvature of the stomach

**pyloric caecum** *n* **1 :** one of the tubular pouches opening into the alimentary canal in the pyloric region of most fishes **2 :** one of the tubular pouches opening into the ventriculus of an insect **3 :** one of the paired tubes in each ray of a starfish that have lateral glandular diverticula, that constitute the liver, and that communicate in pairs by a common duct with the pyloric sac

**pyloric glands** *n* **:** one of the short more or less tortuous glands of the mucous coat of the stomach occurring chiefly near the pyloric end

**pyloric ring** *n* **:** PYLORUS 1

**pyloric sac** *n* **:** an aboral division of the stomach of a starfish

**pyloric stenosis** *n* **:** narrowing of the pyloric opening (as from congenital malformation or contraction of scar tissue)

**pyloric valve** *or* **pyloric sphincter** *n* **1 :** the circular fold of mucous membrane containing a ring of circularly disposed muscle fibers that closes the vertebrate pylorus **2 :** the valvular fold of the pylorus of an invertebrate

**py·lo·ro·plas·ty** \pīˈlōrəˌplastē, pəˈl-\ *n* -ES [ISV *pylor-* + *-plasty*] **:** a plastic operation on the pylorus (as to enlarge a stricture)

**py·lo·ro·spasm** \-rəˌspazəm\ *n* [ISV *pylor-* + *-spasm*] **:** spasm of the pylorus often associated with other conditions (as ulcer of the stomach) or occurring in infants and marked by pain and vomiting

**py·lo·rus** \pīˈlōrəs, pəˈl-, -lȯr-\ *n, pl* **pylo·ri** \-ˌōrˌī, -ōˌrī\ *also* **pyloruses** [LL, fr. Gk *pylōros* gatekeeper, pylorus, fr. *pylē* gate — more at PYLON] **1 :** the opening in a vertebrate from the stomach into the intestine — see PYLORIC VALVE **2 :** a posterior division of the stomach or midgut in some invertebrates commonly separated from the posterior intestine by a valvular fold or sphincter

**pyl·stert** \ˈpīlˌstert\ *n* -s [Afrik, fr. D *pijlstaart* pintail duck, lit., arrow-tail, fr. *pijl* arrow (fr. MD *pijl*, *pile*, fr. L *pilum* javelin) + *staart* tail (fr. MD *stert*) — more at PESTLE, START] *southern Africa* **:** any of various rays

**pymander** *obs var of* POMANDER

**pyment** *var of* PIMENT

**pymt** *abbr* payment

**pyo** \ˈpī(ˌ)ō\ *n* -s [short for *pyocyanase*] **:** any of several crystalline fractions possessing antibiotic activity that are obtained from pyocyanase and distinguished from each other as pyo Ib, Ic, II, III, IV

**pyo-** — see PY-

**pyo·bacillosis** \ˌpī(ˌ)ō+\ *n* [NL, fr. *py-* + *bacillosis*] **:** infection with or disease caused in sheep, swine, or rarely cattle by a bacterium (*Corynebacterium pyogenes*) that is usu. marked by abscess formation but in sheep commonly takes the form of chronic purulent pneumonia accompanied by extensive fibrosis, pleurisy, and joint lesions

**pyo·cele** \ˈpīōˌsēl\ *n* -s [ISV *py-* + *-cele*] **:** a pus-filled cavity (as of the scrotum)

**pyo·coc·cus** \ˌpīōˈkäkəs\ *n* [NL, fr. *py-* + *-coccus*] **:** any coccoid bacterium that tends to form pus

**pyo·cy·a·nase** \ˌpīōˈsīəˌnās, -āz\ *n* -s [NL *pyocyaneus* (specific epithet of *Bacillus pyocyaneus*, syn. of *Pseudomonas aeruginosa*) (fr. *py-* + *cyaneus* cyaneous) + E *-ase*] **:** a mixture of antibiotics once regarded as a specific bacteriolytic enzyme that is obtained from the bacillus of green pus (*Pseudomonas aeruginosa*) and that is a soluble, yellowish green, alkaline, amorphous substance capable of digesting various other bacteria (as those of typhoid fever, diphtheria, and cholera)

**pyo·cy·a·ne·ous** *or* **pyo·cy·a·ne·us** \ˌpīōˌsīˈānēəs\ *also* **pyo·cy·an·ic** \-īˈanik\ *or* **pyo·cy·a·ne·al** \-īˈānēəl\ *adj* [*pyocyaneous*, *pyocyaneus* fr. NL *pyocyaneus*; *pyocyanic* fr. NL *pyocyaneus* + E *-ic*; *pyocyaneal* fr. NL *pyocyaneus* + E *-al*] **:** of, relating to, or produced by a bacterium (*Pseudomonas aeruginosa*) — compare PYOCYANASE

**pyo·cy·a·nin** \ˌpīōˈsīənən\ *or* **pyo·cy·a·nine** \ˈ", -īəˌnēn\ *n* -s [ISV *pyocyan-* (fr. NL *pyocyaneus*) + *-in* or *-ine*] **:** a toxic blue crystalline pigment $C_{13}H_{10}N_2O$ found in green pus and formed in the metabolism of a bacterium (*Pseudomonas aeruginosa*) that is a quinone imine related to phenazine and has antibiotic activity esp. toward gram-positive bacteria

**pyo·der·ma** \-ˈdərmə\ *also* **pyo·der·mia** \-mēə\ *n* -s [NL, fr. *py-* + *-derma* or *-dermia*] **:** an inflammatory skin disease caused by pus-forming microorganisms (as staphylococci) and marked by pus-containing lesions — **pyo·der·mic** \ˌ==ˈ=mik\ *adj*

**py·o·gen** \ˈpīəjən, -ˌjen\ *n* -s [ISV *py-* + *-gen*] **:** a pus-producing microorganism

**py·o·gen·ic** \ˌ==ˈjenik\ *adj* [ISV *py-* + *-genic*] **:** producing pus ⟨~ staphylococcus⟩ **:** marked or characterized by pus production ⟨~ meningitis⟩

**pyogenic membrane** *n* **:** the limiting layer of an abscess or other region of suppuration formerly supposed to secrete the pus

**py·oid** \ˈpīˌȯid\ *adj* [ISV *py-* + *-oid*] **:** resembling or made up of pus

**pyo·me·tra** \ˌpīōˈmētrə\ *n* -s [NL, fr. *py-* + *-metra*] **:** an accumulation of pus in the uterine cavity

**pyo·nephritis** \ˌpī(ˌ)ō+\ *n* [NL, fr. *py-* + *nephritis*] **:** inflammation of the kidney attended with suppuration

**pyo·nephrosis** \ˈ"+\ *n* [NL, fr. *py-* + *nephrosis*] **:** a collection of pus in the kidney

**pyo·nephrotic** \ˈ"+\ *adj* [fr. NL *pyonephrosis*, after such pairs as NL *nephrosis*: E *nephrotic*] **:** of, relating to, or affected with pyonephrosis

**pyong·yang** \pēˈ(ˌ)ȯŋˌyäŋ, ˈpyˌ, ˌəŋ-, -yaŋ\ *adj, usu cap* [fr. *Pyongyang*, No. Korea] **:** of or from Pyongyang, the capital of No. Korea **:** of the kind or style prevalent in Pyongyang

**pyopneumo-** *comb form* [NL, fr. *py-* + *pneum-*] **:** containing or characterized by the presence of both pus and gas ⟨*pyopneumo*cyst⟩ ⟨*pyopneumo*peritonitis⟩

**pyo·pneu·mo·thorax** \ˌpīōˌn(y)ümō+\ *n* [NL, fr. *pyopneumo-* + *thorax*] **:** a collection of pus and air or other gas in the thorax

**pyo·poiesis** \ˌpīō+\ *n* [NL, fr. *py-* + *poiesis*] **:** the formation of pus

**py·or·rhea** *also* **py·or·rhoea** \ˌpīəˈrēə\ *n* -s [NL, fr. *py-* + *-rrhea*, *-rrhoea*] **1 :** a discharge of pus **2 :** PYORRHEA ALVEOLARIS

**pyorrhea al·ve·o·lar·is** \-ˌalvēōˈla(a)rəs\ *n* [NL, alveolar pyorrhea] **:** an inflammatory condition involving the gingival tissues and periodontal membrane often associated with a discharge of pus from the alveoli and loosening of the teeth in their sockets

**py·or·rhe·al** \ˌpīəˈrēəl\ *or* **py·or·rhe·ic** \-ˈrēik\ *also* **py·or·rhet·ic** \-ˈredˌik\ *adj* [*pyorrheal*, *pyorrhetic* fr. NL *pyorrhea* + E *-al* or *-etic*; *pyorrheic* ISV *pyorrh-* (fr. NL *pyorrhea*) + *-ic*] **:** of, relating to, or constituting pyorrhea

**pyos** *pl of* PYO

**pyo·salpinx** \ˌpīō+\ *n* [NL, fr. *py-* + *salpinx*] **:** a collection of pus in an oviduct

**pyo·septicemia** \ˌpī(ˌ)ō+\ *n* [NL, fr. *py-* + *septicemia*] **:** pyemia and septicemia combined — **pyo·septicemic** \ˈ"+\ *adj*

**pyo·thorax** \ˈ"+\ *n* [NL, fr. *py-* + *thorax*] **:** EMPYEMA

**pyo·xan·those** \ˌpīōˈzanˌthōs *also* -ōz\ *n* -s [ISV *py-* + *xanth-* + *-ose*] **:** a greenish yellow crystalline coloring matter in pus

**pyr-** *or* **pyro-** *comb form* [ME *pyro-*, fr. MF *pyr-*, *pyro-*, fr. LL, fr. Gk, fr. *pyr* — more at FIRE] **1 a :** fire **:** heat ⟨*pyro*meter⟩ ⟨*pyr*heliometer⟩ **b :** pyrogenous and ⟨*pyro*magnetic⟩ **2 a :** derivative by the action of heat; *esp* **:** derived from the corresponding ortho acid by loss usu. of one molecule of water from two molecules of acid — in names of inorganic acids ⟨*pyro*phosphoric acid⟩; compare META- 4c, ORTH- 3a **b :** due to or attributed to the action of fire or heat ⟨*pyro*chlore⟩ ⟨*pyro*metamorphism⟩; *also* **:** of fiery color ⟨*pyro*phanite⟩ **3 :** fever **:** fever producing ⟨*pyro*toxin⟩ ⟨*pyro*gen⟩

**pyr·acanth** \ˈpirəˌkan(t)th, ˈpīr-\ *n* -s [LL *pyracanthe*, a tree, prob. fire thorn, fr. Gk *pyrakantha*] **:** FIRE THORN

**pyr·acan·tha** \ˌ==ˈkan(t)thə\ *n* [NL, fr. Gk *pyrakantha*, a tree, prob. fire thorn, fr. *pyr-* + *akantha* thorn — more at ACANTH-] **1** *cap* **:** a small genus of Eurasian thorny evergreen or half-evergreen shrubs (family Rosaceae) with alternate leaves, white flowers in compound corymbs, and small red or orange pomes — see FIRE THORN **2** -s **:** any plant of the genus *Pyracantha*

**pyra·cene** \ˈpirəˌsēn, ˈpīr-\ *n* -s [ISV *pyr-* + *ace-* + *-ene*] **:** a tetracyclic parent hydrocarbon $C_{16}H_{12}$ regarded as derived from acenaphthene

**pyr·al** \ˈpīrəl\ *adj* [*pyre* + *-al*] **:** of or relating to a pyre

**pyrales** [NL, fr. *pyr-* + *-ales*] *obs syn of* PYRALIDOIDEA

**py·ral·i·dae** \pəˈraləˌdē, pīˈr-\ [NL, fr. *Pyralis* + *-idae*] *syn of* PYRALIDIDAE

**¹py·ral·i·did** \-lədəd, ˌpirəˈlidəd\ *or* **pyr·a·lid** \ˈpirələd\ *adj* [*pyralidid* fr. NL *Pyralididae*; *pyralid* fr. NL *Pyralidae*] **:** of or relating to the Pyralididae

**²pyralidid** \ˈ"\ *or* **pyralid** \ˈ"\ *n* -s **:** a moth of the family Pyralididae

**pyr·a·lid·i·dae** \ˌpirəˈlidəˌdē\ *n pl, cap* [NL, fr. *Pyralid-*, *Pyralis*, type genus + *-idae*] **1 :** a family of moths comprising a vast and heterogeneous assemblage of small or medium-sized plainly colored slender-bodied and long-legged moths in which the costal vein of the hind wing approaches close to or unites with the subcostal vein near the middle of the wing **2** *in some classifications* **:** a small family of moths comprising typical members of the superfamily Pyralidoidea

**pyr·a·li·doi·dea** \ˌpirələˈdȯidēə, pəˌral-\ *n pl, cap* [NL, fr. *Pyralid-*, *Pyralis* + *-oidea*] *in some classifications* **:** a superfamily of moths coextensive with the family Pyralididae (sense 1)

**Pyr·a·lin** \ˈpirələn\ *trademark* — used for a plastic

**pyr·a·lis** \ˈpirələs\ *n* [L, fr. Gk, fr. *pyr* fire — more at PYR-] **1** *pl* **pyralides** *obs* **:** a fly fabled as born from or living in fire **2** [NL, fr. L] **a** *cap* **:** the type genus of the family Pyralididae — see MEAL MOTH **b** *pl* **pyralis·es** \-ləsəz\ *or* **py·ral·i·des** \pəˈraləˌdēz, pīˈr-\ **:** any moth of the genus *Pyralis*

**pyr·a·loid** \ˈpirəˌlȯid\ *adj* [NL *Pyralis* + E *-oid*] **:** related to or resembling the genus Pyralis **:** PYRALIDID

**pyr·a·me·is** \ˌpirəˈmēəs\ *n* [NL, prob. fr. L *pyramis* pyramid] *syn of* VANESSA

**¹pyr·a·mid** \ˈpirəˌmid, *in rapid speech sometimes* -rˌm-\ *n* -s [L *pyramid-*, *pyramis*, fr. Gk] **1 a :** an ancient massive structure of huge stone blocks found esp. in Egypt having typically a square ground plan, outside walls in the form of four triangles that meet in a point at the top, and inner sepulchral chambers **b :** any architectural structure (as a spire or pinnacle) of similar form **c :** an ancient truncate pyramidal structure found in Mexico and Central America that served as a foundation for a building or a platform for an altar **2 :** a polyhedron having for its base a polygon and for its other faces triangles with a common vertex — see VOLUME table **3 :** an object or figure of pyramidal form or with the shape or profile of a pyramid ⟨a ~ of cartons⟩ ⟨the frosty ~ of a well-shaped blue spruce⟩: as **a :** a tree pruned and trained in pyramidal shape **b :** a crystalline form each face of which intersects the vertical axis and either two lateral axes or in a tetragonal system one lateral axis — compare DIPYRAMID **c :** an anatomical structure resembling a pyramid: as (1) **:** a petrous bone (2) **:** a conical projection making up the central part of the inferior vermis of the cerebellum (3) **:** PYRAMID OF THE MEDULLA (4) **:** MALPIGHIAN PYRAMID **d :** one of the five large vertical sections of the Aristotle's lantern of a sea urchin **e :** PYRAMID SHELL **4 a :** verse in which the succeeding lines increase in length **b :** a graphic representation of a statistical distribution (as of a population on the basis of age and sex categories) that has essentially the form of a triangle or wedge **c :** a tridimensional diagrammatic representation representing sensory relationships **5 :** an English pool game played with 15 red balls and a white cue ball in which the player pocketing the most balls wins but loses a point each time he pockets the white ball or misses his aim **6 a :** an immaterial structure built upon a broad supporting base and narrowing gradually to an apex (as of power, dominance, or significance) ⟨families at the base of a socioeconomic ~⟩ **b** (1) **:** a group of holding companies superimposed one on another to give those in control of the top holding company control over the whole pyramid with a small investment (2) **:** the series of operations involved in pyramiding on an exchange **c :** CHAIN LETTER

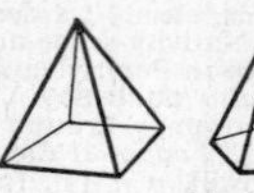

pyramids 2

**²pyramid** \ˈ"\ *vb* -ED/-ING/-S *vi* **1 :** to assume or to become disposed in the form of a pyramid **2 a :** to enlarge one's holdings on an exchange on a continued rise by using paper profits as margin to buy additional amounts **b :** to superimpose holding companies so as to reduce the investment required to control enterprises **3 :** to increase rapidly and progressively step by step on a broadening base that supports a concomitant upward trend ⟨demand for more efficient insecticides continues to ~⟩ ~ *vt* **1 :** to arrange, place, build up, or construct in a pyramidal form or as if upon the base of a pyramid : heap up ⟨~ arguments upon a hypothesis⟩ ⟨~ed his gains by careful reinvestment⟩ **2** : to use or to deal in (as a stock or commodity) in a pyramiding transaction

**¹py·ram·i·dal** \pə'ramədᵊl, ÷ ¦pirə¦mid³l\ *adj* [ML *pyramidalis*, fr. L *pyramid-*, *pyramis* + *-alis* -al] **1 a** : of, relating to, or having the form of a pyramid **b** : having symmetry such that the general form is a pyramid ⟨a ~ crystal⟩ **2** : sloping like a face of a pyramid ⟨the sheer ~ side of the cliff⟩ **3** : HUGE, ENORMOUS, IMPOSING **4** : affecting, involving, or connecting with an anatomical pyramid esp. of the central nervous system ⟨a crossed ~ lesion⟩ ⟨the inferior ~ tracts⟩

**²pyramidal** \"\ *n* -s [NL *pyramidale*] **1** : PYRAMIDAL BONE **2** : a pyramidal tent

**pyramidal bone** *n* : the third bone in the proximal row of the carpus — called also *triquetrum*

**pyramidal cell** *n* : one of numerous large multipolar cells in the cerebral cortex of higher vertebrates

**py·ram·i·dale** \pə,ramə'da(,)lē, ,pirəmə'd-, -dā(-, -dä(-\ *n* -s [NL, short for *os pyramidale* pyramidal bone, fr. L *os* bone + ML *pyramidale*, neut. of *pyramidalis* pyramidal — more at OSSEOUS] : PYRAMIDAL BONE

**py·ram·i·dalis** \-ləs\ *n, pl* **pyrami·dales** \-(,)lēz\ *or* **pyramidalises** [NL, fr. ML, pyramidal] : a small triangular muscle of the lower front part of the abdomen situated in front of and in the same sheath with the rectus

**py·ram·i·dal·ism** \=ˌ===, ,=='== (*see* ¹PYRAMIDAL) + ,izəm\ *n* -s *usu cap* [¹*pyramidal* + *-ism*] : lore concerned with the Egyptian pyramids

**py·ram·i·dal·ist** \-əst\ *n* -s *usu cap* : an exponent of Pyramidalism; *esp* : one who holds positive views as to the mystic and predictional import of the Egyptian pyramids

**py·ram·i·dal·ly** *pronunc at* ¹PYRAMIDAL + ē *or* ī\ *adv* : in the form or manner of a pyramid

**pyramidal tent** *n* : a pyramidal canvas shelter capable of holding six or more persons

**pyramidal tract** *n* : any of four columns of motor fibers that run in pairs on each side of the spinal cord and that are continuations of the pyramids of the medulla

**pyramid ant** *n* : a common household ant (*Dorymyrmex pyramicus*) of California

**pyramided** *past of* PYRAMID

**¹py·ram·i·del·lid** \pə¦ramə¦deləd, ¦pirəmə¦d-\ *adj* [NL *Pyramidellidae*] : of or relating to the Pyramidellidae

**²pyramidellid** \"\ *n* -s : a snail of the family Pyramidellidae

**py·ram·i·del·li·dae** \=,=='del,dē, ,===-\ *n pl, cap* [NL, fr. *Pyramidella*, type genus (fr. L *pyramid-*, *pyramis* pyramid + *-ella*) + *-idae* — more at PYRAMID] : a large family of marine snails (suborder Taenioglossa) having a conical or turreted dextrally coiled shell but with the apical whorls or embryonic shell sinistrally coiled, a long retractile proboscis, and no radula

**pyr·a·mid·er** \'pirə,mid·ə(r)\ *n* -s [²*pyramid* + *-er*] : one that pyramids (as on a stock exchange)

**pyramid flower** *n* **1** : AMERICAN COLUMBO **2** : the flower of American columbo

**pyramid head** *n* : a printed heading with matter so arranged that the lines form an inverted and truncated pyramid

**pyr·a·mid·i·cal** \¦pirə¦midəkəl\ *also* **pyr·a·mid·ic** \-dik\ *adj* [*pyramidical* fr. *pyramid* + *-ical*; *pyramidic* prob. fr. Gk *pyramidikos*, fr. *pyramis* + *-ikos* -ic] : resembling a pyramid : PYRAMIDAL — **pyr·a·mid·i·cal·ly** \-dək(ə)lē\ *adv* — **pyr·a·mid·i·cal·ness** \-kəlnəs\ *n* -ES

**pyramiding** *pres part of* PYRAMID

**pyr·a·mid·i·on** \,pirə'midē,än, -ēən\ *n, pl* **pyramidions** \-nz\ *also* **pyramid·ia** \-dēə\ [NL, dim. of L *pyramid-*, *pyramis* pyramid — more at PYRAMID] : a small pyramid (as at the top of an obelisk or at the apex of a large pyramid)

**pyr·a·mid·ist** \'pirə,midəst, pə'ramәd-\ *n* -s *often cap* : PYRAMIDALIST

**pyramido-** *comb form* [NL, fr. L *pyramid-*, *pyramis* pyramid] **1** : pyramidally ⟨*pyramido*attenuate⟩ **2** : pyramidal and ⟨*pyramido*prismatic⟩

**pyramid of numbers** : a concept in ecology: an organism forming the base of a food chain is numerically very abundant each succeeding member of the chain being represented by successively fewer individuals and the final large predator being always numerically rare

**pyramid of the cerebellum** : PYRAMID 3c(2)

**pyramid of the medulla** : either of two large bundles of motor fibers from the cerebral cortex reaching the medulla through the cerebral peduncles and pons and continuous with the pyramidal tracts of the spinal cord

**py·ram·i·doi·dal** \pə¦ramə¦dȯidᵊl, ¦pirə(,)mi¦d-\ *adj* [NL *pyramidoides* figure resembling a pyramid (fr. L *pyramid-*, *pyramis* + *-oides* -oid) + E *-al*] : like a pyramid

**py·ram·i·dol·o·gist** \=,=='däləjəst, ,=='(,)=-\ *n* -s [*pyramidology* + *-ist*] : PYRAMIDALIST

**py·ram·i·dol·o·gy** \-jē\ *n* -ES *often cap* [*pyramido-* + *-logy*] : PYRAMIDALISM

**Py·ram·i·don** \pə'ramə,dän\ *trademark* — used for aminopyrine

**pyramid plant** *n* : AMERICAN COLUMBO

**pyramid roof** *n* : a roof having four slopes that meet at a peak

**pyramids** *pl of* PYRAMID, *pres 3d sing of* PYRAMID

**pyramid shell** *n* [*pyramid* short for ¹*pyramidellid*] : a mollusk of the family Pyramidellidae or its shell

pyramid roof

**pyramidwise** \'==,=\ *adv* : in the manner of or so as to have the form of a pyramid ⟨arranging the bunches of grapes ~ on a platter⟩

**pyramis** *n, pl* **pyramides** [L — more at PYRAMID] : PYRAMID 3c(2)

**py·ran** \'pī,ran\ *n* -s [ISV *pyr-* + *-an*] : either of two parent cyclic compounds $C_5H_6O$ that contain five carbon atoms and one oxygen atom in the ring: **a** : the alpha isomer — called also *2H-pyran* **b** : the gamma isomer — called also *4H-pyran*; see PYRONE; compare CHROMAN, XANTHENE

**pyra·noid** \'pirə,nȯid, 'pīr-\ *adj* [*pyran* + *-oid*] : resembling pyran in chemical structure : characterized by the presence of the furan ring

**pyra·nom·e·ter** \,pirə'nämәd·ə(r), ,pīr-\ *n* [ISV *pyr-* + *ano-* + *-meter*] : an instrument for measuring radiation from the sky by comparing the heating effect of such radiation upon two blackened metallic strips with that produced in the same strips when heated by means of an electric current

**pyra·nose** \'pirə,nōs, 'pīr- *also* -ōz\ *n* -s [ISV *pyran* + *-ose*] : a glycose sugar in the form of a cyclic hemiacetal containing a 6-member ring

**py·ran·o·side** \pə'ranə,sīd, pī'r- -,sәd\ *n* -s [*pyranose* + *-ide*] : a glycoside containing the ring characteristic of a pyranose

**pyr·an·threne** \pə'ran,thrēn, pī'r-\ *n* -s [ISV *pyr-* + *-anthrene*] : a green-yellow crystalline aromatic hydrocarbon consisting of eight compactly but unsymmetrically fused benzene rings in three tiers

**pyra·nyl** \'pirə,nil, 'pīr-\ *n* -s [*pyran* + *-yl*] : any of several univalent radicals $C_5H_5O$ derived from the pyrans by removal of one hydrogen atom

**pyr·ar·gy·rite** \pī'rärjə,rīt, pə'r-\ *n* -s [G *pyrargyrit*, fr. *pyr-* + *argyr-* + *-it* -ite] : a silver antimony sulfide $Ag_3SbS_3$ that is isomorphous with proustite, occurs in rhombohedral crystals or massive, and has a dark-red or black color with a metallic adamantine luster — called also *dark red silver ore, ruby silver*

**py·raus·ta** \pə'rȯstə\ *n, cap* [NL, fr. Gk *pyraustēs* moth that gets singed in fire, fr. *pyr-* + *-austēs* (fr. *auein* to get a light, start a fire)] : a genus (the type of the family Pyraustidae) of inconspicuously colored moths with larvae that feed on foliage or bore in the stems of plants — see CORN BORER

**py·raus·ti·dae** \-tə,dē\ *n pl, cap* [NL, fr. *Pyrausta*, type genus + *-idae*] : a family closely related to Pyralididae and comprising small or medium-sized rather slender moths with larvae that are webworms or leaftiers or that bore in the stems and roots of plants — see PYRAUSTA

**pyr·a·zin·amide** \,pirə'zinə,mīd, -məd\ *n* [*pyrazine* + *amide*] : a tuberculostatic drug $C_4H_3N_2CONH_2$; pyrazinecarboxamide

**pyr·azine** \'pirə,zēn, -zən\ *n* [ISV *pyr-* + *azine*] : a crystalline feeble heterocyclic base $C_4H_4N_2$ obtained usu. by distilling piperazine with zinc dust — called also *paradiazine*

**pyr·azole** \'pirə,zōl, -zȯl\ *n* [ISV *pyr-* + *azole*; orig. formed as G *pyrazol*] **1** : a crystalline feeble heterocyclic base $C_3H_4N_2$ isomeric with imidazole obtained usu. by action of acetylene on diazomethane; 1,2-diazole **2** : a derivative of pyrazole

**pyr·az·o·line** \pə'razə,lēn, pī'r-, -,lən\ *n* -s [ISV *pyrazole* + *-ine*] **1** : a dihydro derivative $C_3H_6N_2$ of pyrazole; *esp* : a liquid compound obtained usu. by the action of hydrazine on acrolein **2** : a derivative of pyrazoline

**py·raz·o·lone** \-,lōn\ *n* -s [ISV *pyrazole* + *-one*] **1** : any of three isomeric carbonyl compounds $C_3H_4N_2O$ derived from pyrazoline **2** : any of numerous derivatives of the pyrazolones some of which (as antipyrine) are used as analgesics and antipyretics and others (as 3-methyl-1-phenyl-5-pyrazolone) in making azo dyes and as developers

**py·raz·o·lyl** \-,lil\ *n* -s [*pyrazole* + *-yl*] : any of four univalent radicals $C_3H_3N_2$ derived from pyrazole by removal of one hydrogen atom

**pyre** \'pī(ə)r, -īə\ *n* -s [L *pyra*, fr. Gk, fr. *pyr* fire — more at FIRE] : a combustible heap (as of wood) for burning a dead body as a funeral rite; *broadly* : a pile to be burnt

**pyren-** *or* **pyreno-** *comb form* [NL, fr. Gk *pyrēn-*, *pyrēno-*, fr. *pyrēn* — more at FURZE] **1** : stone of a fruit ⟨*pyreno*carp⟩ **2** : nucleolus ⟨*pyren*ematous⟩ ⟨*pyren*in⟩

**py·re·na** \pī'rēnə\ *n, pl* **pyre·nae** \-(,)nē\ [NL, fr. Gk *pyrēn*] : PYRENE

**¹py·rene** \'pī,rēn, ='=\ *n* -s [NL *pyrena*] : the stone of a drupelet (as in the fruit of the huckleberry); *broadly* : a small hard nutlet

**²py·rene** \'pī,rēn\ *n* -s [*pyr-* + *-ene*] : a pale yellow crystalline hydrocarbon $C_{16}H_{10}$ that fluoresces blue in solution, that is obtained from coal-tar distillation, from petroleum cracking, and from stupp and is also made synthetically, and that consists structurally of a cluster of four compactly fused benzene rings

**¹py·re·ne·an** \¦pirə¦nēən\ *adj, usu cap* [L *pyrenaeus* Pyrenean (fr. *Pyrene*, the Pyrenees, mountain range along the French-Spanish border from the Bay of Biscay to the southwestern coast of the Gulf of Lions, fr. Gk *Pyrēnē*, beloved of Hercules in Greek mythology who was believed to be buried upon the Pyrenees) + E *-an*] : of or relating to the Pyrenees separating France and Spain

**²pyrenean** \"\ *n* -s *cap* : a native or inhabitant of the Pyrenees

**pyrenean mountain dog** *n, usu cap P* : GREAT PYRENEES

**py·ren·em·a·tous** \¦pīrə¦nemәd·əs\ *adj* [*pyren-* + *hemat-* + *-ous*] : having nucleated red blood corpuscles

**py·renic acid** \(')pī¦rē¦nik-, -rel\ *n* [*pyrenic* ISV *pyrene* + *-ic*] : a yellow crystalline tricyclic keto dicarboxylic acid $C_{13}H_6O(COOH)_2$ formed by the oxidation of pyrene

**py·ren·i·dae** \pī'renə,dē\ [NL, fr. *Pyrena*, genus of dove shells (fr. Gk *pyrēn* pit of a fruit) + *-idae*] *syn of* COLUMBELLIDAE

**py·re·nin** \pī'rēnən\ *n* -s [*pyren-* + *-in*] : PLASTIN

**py·re·no·carp** \pī'rēnə,kärp\ *n* -s [*pyren-* + *-carp*] **1** : PERITHECIUM **2** : DRUPE — **py·re·no·car·pic** \(¦)=¦=='kärpik\ *or* **py·re·no·car·pous** \-pəs\ *adj*

**py·re·no·car·pe·ae** \=,=='kärpē,ē\ *n pl, cap* [NL, fr. *pyren-* + *-carpeae* (fr. *-carpus* -carpous)] *in some classifications* : a group of lichens comprising those whose fruiting body is closed — compare GYMNOCARPEAE

**py·re·no·chae·ta** \-'kēd·ə\ *n, cap* [NL, fr. *pyren-* + *-chaeta*] : a genus of imperfect fungi (family Sphaeropsidaceae) characterized by setose pycnidia and unicellular hyaline ovate to elongate or cylindric pycnospores

**py·re·noid** \pī'rē,nȯid, 'pīrə,n-\ *n* -s [ISV *pyren-* + *-oid*; prob. orig. formed in G] : one of the colorless highly refractive proteid bodies found within the chromatophores of various low organisms (as algae of the order Zygnematales) and serving as centers for the deposition of starch

**py·re·no·lichen** \pī¦rēnə+\ *n* [ISV *pyren-* + *lichen*] : an ascolichen of the subgroup Pyrenolichenes — compare BASIDIOLICHEN

**py·re·no·lichenes** \"+\ *n pl, cap* [NL, fr. *pyren-* + *Lichenes*] : a subgroup of ascolichens having a closed spore fruit — compare DISCOLICHENES

**py·re·no·my·ce·ta·les** \pī,rē(,)nō,mīsə'tā(,)lēz\ [NL, fr. *pyren-* + *mycet-* + *-ales*] *syn of* PYRENOMYCETES

**py·re·no·my·cete** \pī'rēnō'mī,sēt, -¦renō,mī¦sēt\ *n* -s [NL *Pyrenomycetes*] : a fungus of the subclass Pyrenomycetes

**py·re·no·my·ce·tes** \=,==,='sēd·ēz\ *n pl, cap* [NL, fr. *pyren-* + *-mycetes*] *in some classifications* : a subclass of fungi (class Ascomycetes) including those that produce a typical perithecium and comprising the orders Sphaeriales, Perisporiales, Hypocreales, and Dothideales — **py·re·no·my·ce·tous** \=¦==¦=¦sēd·əs\ *adj*

**py·re·no·peziza** \pī¦rē(,)nō+\ *n, cap* [NL, fr. *pyren-* + *Peziza*] : a genus of fungi (family Mollisiaceae) that is similar to *Pseudopeziza* except in having dark-colored apothecia and that includes several parasites of economic plants

**pyres** *pl of* PYRE

**pyret-** *or* **pyreto-** *comb form* [Gk, fr. *pyretos* burning heat, fever, fr. *pyr* fire — more at FIRE] : fever ⟨*pyreto*genesis⟩ ⟨*pyret*etiology⟩

**py·re·thrin** \pī'rēthrən *also* -reth-\ *n* -s [ISV *pyrethr-* (fr. NL *Pyrethrum*) + *-in*; orig. formed as F *pyréthrine*] : either of two oily liquid esters $C_{21}H_{28}O_3$ and $C_{22}H_{28}O_5$ of pyrethrolone having high insecticidal properties and occurring esp. in pyrethrum flowers — called also respectively *pyrethrin I, pyrethrin II*

**py·re·thro·lone** \-thrə,lōn\ *n* -s [ISV *pyrethrin* + *-ol* + *-one*] : a viscous oily keto alcohol $C_{11}H_{14}O_2$ closely related to cinerolone and obtained by hydrolysis of the pyrethrins

**py·re·thrum** \pī'rēthrəm *also* -reth-\ *n* [NL, fr. L, pellitory, fr. Gk *pyrethron*, fr. *pyr* fire; fr. the spicy taste of the root] **1 a** *cap, in some esp former classifications* : a genus of composite plants with finely divided leaves that are now usu. included in the genus *Chrysanthemum* **b** -s : any of various chrysanthemums with finely divided and often aromatic leaves: as (1) : a chrysanthemum (as *C. coccineum* or *C. cinerariaefolium*) that is a source of insecticides (2) : any of several garden perennials that are derived from the Asiatic species (*C. coccineum*) and have white, pink, red, or rarely lilac flowers in late spring — called also *painted daisy* **2** -s **a** *or* **pyrethrum flowers** : an insecticide consisting of the dried powdered flowers of a Dalmatian pyrethrum (*Chrysanthemum cinerariaefolium*) or either of two Asiatic pyrethrums (*C. coccineum* and *C. marschallii*) — called also respectively *Dalmatian insect powder, Persian insect powder* **b** *or* **pyrethrum extract** : an extract of the powdered flowers containing pyrethrins and cinerins and used in insecticidal sprays

**pyrethrum yellow** *n* : a moderate yellow that is greener and deeper than colonial yellow, greener, lighter, and stronger than brass, and greener, stronger, and slightly lighter than mustard yellow — called also *golden-feather yellow*

**py·ret·ic** \(')pī¦red·ik\ *adj* [NL *pyreticus*, fr. Gk *pyretikos*, fr. *pyret-* + *-ikos* -ic] : of or relating to fever : FEBRILE

**pyr·e·to·gen·ic** \¦pīrətō¦jenik, ¦pī,red·ə¦j-\ *also* **pyre·tog·e·nous** \¦pīrə¦täjənəs, ¦pī'r-\ *adj* [*pyret-* + *-genic* or *-genous*] : inducing fever

**pyr·e·to·therapy** \¦pīrətō, ¦pīrətō, pī¦red·ə+\ *n* [ISV *pyret-* + *therapy*] : FEVER THERAPY

**Py·rex** \'pī,reks\ *trademark* — used for glass and glassware resistant to heat, chemicals, or electricity

**py·rex·ia** \pī'reksēə\ *n* -s [NL, fr. *pyrex-* (fr. Gk *pyressein* to be feverish, fr. *pyretos* fever) + L *-ia* -y] : elevation of body temperature to an abnormal level : FEVER — **py·rex·i·al** \(')pī¦reksēəl\ *adj* — **py·rex·ic** \-sik\ *adj*

**py·rex·in** \pī'reksən\ *n* -s [NL *pyrexia* + E *-in*] : a nitrogenous heat-stabile factor that is possibly a polypeptide, is found in inflammatory discharges, and may be responsible for the fever which accompanies inflammation — compare NECROSIN

**pyr·ge·om·e·ter** \,pī(ə)rjē'ämәd·ə(r), ,pi(-\ *n* [ISV *pyr-* + *ge-* + *-meter*] : an instrument for determining the radiation from the earth's surface into space ⟨the equipment of a modern observatory, including . . . ~s —*Science*⟩

**pyr·go·cephalic** \,pər(,)gō+\ *adj* [F *pyrgocéphalie* pyrgocephaly (fr. Gk *pyrgos* tower + F *-céphalie* -cephaly) + E *-ic*] : having a skull with a high vertex — **pyr·go·ceph·a·ly** \,=='sefəlē\ *n* -ES

**pyr·gus** \'pərgəs\ *n, cap* [NL, fr. LL, tower, fr. Gk *pyrgos*, perh. of Gmc origin; akin to OHG *burg* fortified place — more at BOROUGH] : a widely distributed genus of skipper butterflies usu. having the wings largely checkered

**pyr·heliometer** \¦pī(ə)r, ¦pi(-+\ *n* [ISV *pyr-* + *heli-* + *-meter*] : an instrument for measuring the sun's total radiant energy as received at the earth in order to determine the solar constant

**pyr·heliometric** \"+\ *adj* [ISV *pyrheliometry* + *-ic*] : of or relating to pyrheliometry

**pyr·heliometry** \"+\ *n* [*pyrheliometer* + *-y*] : a branch of study dealing with the measurement of the heat of the sun's rays

**Pyri·ben·za·mine** \,pirə'benzə,mēn\ *trademark* — used for tripelennamine

**pyr·i·bole** \'pirə,bōl\ *n* -s [*pyroxene* + *amphibole*] : a constituent of a rock that is either pyroxene or amphibole or both

**pyric** \'pīrik, 'pir-\ *adj* [F *pyrique*, fr. *pyr-* + *-ique* -ic] : resulting from, induced by, or associated with burning ⟨a ~ ecological climax⟩

**pyrid-** *or* **pyrido-** *comb form* [fr. *pyridine*] : pyridine ⟨*pyr*-*idone*⟩ ⟨*pyrido*-indole⟩

**py·rid·azine** \pī'ridə,zēn, ,pirə'da,z-, -,zən\ *n* [ISV *pyrid-* + *azine*] **1** : a liquid feeble heterocyclic base $C_4H_4N_2$; 1,2-diazine — called also *ortho-diazine* **2** : a derivative of pyridazine

**pyr·i·dine** \'pirə,dēn, -,dən\ *n* -s [*pyr-* + *-id* + *-ine*] : a toxic

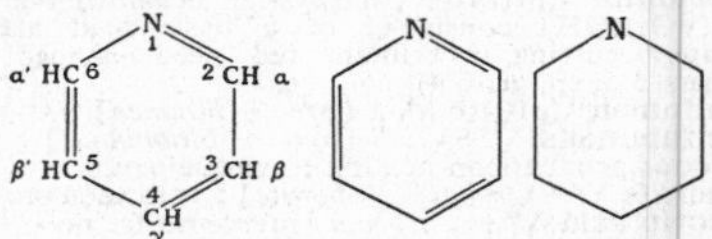


structural formula for pyridine (three methods of representation, the hexagon without double bonds being acceptable only when it cannot be mistaken for piperidine)

water-soluble flammable liquid heterocyclic base $C_5H_5N$ that has a disagreeable odor, that is obtained by distillation of bone oil or now usu. as a by-product of coking either by distillation of coal tar or by recovery from gas liquor, that is analogous to benzene in structure except that it contains a nitrogen atom and five carbon atoms in the ring, that is the parent of many naturally occurring organic compounds including alkaloids (as nicotine) and the vitamins nicotinamide and pyridoxine, and that is used chiefly as a solvent, as a denaturant for alcohol, and in the manufacture of pharmaceuticals (as antiseptics and antihistamine drugs) and waterproofing agents for textiles — compare PIPERIDINE, STRUCTURAL FORMULA

**pyridine base** *n* : any of several bases derived from pyridine and obtained with it as by-products of the coking process or made synthetically — compare COLLIDINE, LUTIDINE, METHYLETHYLPYRIDINE, PICOLINE

**pyridine nucleotide** *n* : a nucleotide characterized by a pyridine derivative as a nitrogen base; *esp* : a dinucleotide having nicotinamide as the pyridine base and adenine as the second base — compare DIPHOSPHOPYRIDINE NUCLEOTIDE, FLAVOPROTEIN, TRIPHOSPHOPYRIDINE NUCLEOTIDE

**py·ri·din·i·um** \,pirə'dinēəm\ *n* -s [NL, fr. ISV *pyridine* + NL *-ium*] : a univalent ion $[C_5H_5NH]^+$ or radical $C_5H_6N$ that is analogous to ammonium and is derived from pyridine

**pyr·i·done** \'pirə,dōn\ *n* -s [ISV *pyrid-* + *-one*] : any of several isomeric carbonyl compounds $C_5H_5NO$ derived from pyridine: as **a** : the crystalline alpha isomer — called also *2-pyridone, 2(1H)-pyridone* **b** : the crystalline gamma isomer — called also *4-pyridone, 4(1H)-pyridone*

**pyr·i·dox·al** \,pirə'däksəl, -,sal\ *n* -s [ISV *pyridoxine* + *-al*] : a crystalline aldehyde $C_8H_9NO_3$ obtainable by oxidation of pyridoxine that is a member of the vitamin $B_6$ group and occurs in the form of a phosphate active as a coenzyme (as in decarboxylation and transamination); 3-hydroxy-5-(hydroxymethyl)-2-methyl-isonicotinaldehyde — compare CODECARBOXYLASE

**pyr·i·dox·amine** \,pirə'däksə,mēn, -mən\ *n* [ISV *pyridoxine* + *amine*] : a crystalline amine $C_8H_{12}N_2O_2$ obtainable from pyridoxine that is a member of the vitamin $B_6$ group and occurs in the form of a phosphate active as a coenzyme in transamination

**pyr·i·dox·ic acid** \¦pirə¦däksik-\ *n* [*pyridoxic* fr. *pyridoxine* + *-ic*] : a crystalline acid $C_8H_9NO_4$ isolated from urine and held to be formed by oxidation of pyridoxal as the major end product of vitamin $B_6$ metabolism — called also *4-pyridoxic acid*

**pyr·i·dox·ine** \,pirə'däk,sēn, -,sən\ *also* **pyr·i·dox·in** \-,sən\ *n* -s [*pyrid-* + *ox-* + *-in* or *-ine*] : a crystalline phenolic alcohol $C_8H_{11}NO_3$ derived from pyridine that is a member of the vitamin $B_6$ group convertible in the organism into pyridoxal and pyridoxamine, that occurs esp. in cereals but is usu. made synthetically, and that is administered chiefly in the form of its hydrochloride; 3-hydroxy-4,5-bis(hydroxymethyl)-2-methyl-pyridine; *broadly* : VITAMIN $B_6$

**pyr·i·dyl** \'pirə,dil\ *n* -s [ISV *pyrid-* + *-yl*] : any of three univalent radicals $C_5H_4N$ derived from pyridine by removal of one hydrogen atom

**pyr·i·form** \'pirə,fȯrm\ *adj* [NL *pyriformis*] : having the form of a pear : PEAR-SHAPED

**pyriform aperture** *n* : the anterior opening of the nasal cavities in the skull

**pyriformis** *var of* PIRIFORMIS

**pyriform lobe** *or* **pyriform area** *n* : the lateral olfactory gyrus and the hippocampal convolution taken together

**py·ril·amine** \pī'rilə,mēn, -mən\ *n* [*pyril-* (contr. of *pyridyl*) + *amine*] : an oily liquid base $C_{17}H_{23}N_3O$ or its bitter crystalline maleate $C_{21}H_{27}N_3O_5$ used as an antihistamine drug in the treatment of various allergies

**py·rim·i·dine** \pī'rimə,dēn, -,dən; 'pirəmə,dēn\ *n* -s [ISV, alter. of *pyridine*; prob. orig. formed as G *pyrimidin*] **1** : a crystalline feeble heterocyclic base $C_4H_4N_2$ of penetrating odor that is usu. prepared indirectly from barbituric acid; 1,3-diazine — compare PURINE, STRUCTURAL FORMULA **2** : a derivative of pyrimidine; *esp* : a base (as cytosine) that is a component of nucleosides and nucleotides

HC 6 1 N 2 CH / HC 5 4 C 3 N / H

pyrimidine

**py·rim·i·dyl** \pī'rimәdᵊl, 'pirəmə,dil\ *or* **py·rim·i·din·yl** \pī'rimə,dēnᵊl\ *n* -s [ISV *pyrimidine* + *-yl*] : any of three univalent radicals $C_4H_3N_2$ derived from pyrimidine by removal of one hydrogen atom

**pyr·it·a·ceous** \¦pī,rid¦āshəs, ¦pirə¦tā-\ *adj* [*pyrite* + *-aceous*] : PYRITIC

**py·rite** \'pī,rīt\ *n* -s [L *pyrites*] **1** *obs* : PYRITES 1 **2** : a common mineral that consists of iron disulfide $FeS_2$, has a pale brass-yellow color and brilliant metallic luster, crystallizes in isometric forms (as the cube and pyritohedron), and is burned in making sulfur dioxide and sulfuric acid (hardness 6–6.5, sp. gr. 4.95–5.10) — called also *fool's gold, iron pyrites*

**py·rites** \pə'rīd·(,)ēz, -ī(,)tēz *also* pī'r-; *also* ÷'pī,rīts\ *n, pl* **pyrites** \"\ [L, fr. Gk *pyritēs* of or in fire (in *pyritēs lithos* stone that strikes fire, pyrites), fr. *pyr* fire — more at FIRE] **1** *obs* : a stone that may be used for striking fire **2** : any of various metallic-looking sulfides of which pyrite is the commonest — usu. used with a qualifying term indicating the component metal ⟨copper ~⟩ ⟨tin ~⟩

**pyrite yellow** *also* **pyrite green** *n* : a dark grayish to dark yellow that is slightly lighter than sulphine yellow or bister green

**py·rit·ic** \(')pī¦rid·ik\ *also* **py·rit·i·cal** \-d·əkəl\ *adj* [*pyrite* + *-ic* or *-ical*] : of, relating to, or resembling pyrites ⟨~ ores⟩

**pyritic smelting** *n* : a process of smelting pyritic ores without previous roasting and with little or no fuel by utilizing the heat resulting from the combustion of their high sulfur content

**py·rit·if·er·ous** \,pī,rid·'if(ə)rəs\ *adj* [*pyrites* + *-iferous*] : containing or producing pyrites

**py·rit·iza·tion** \ˌpīˌrīd·əˈzāshən\ *n* -s [*pyritize* + *-ation*] : development of pyrite in a solid rock

**py·rit·ize** \ˈpīˌrīd·ˌīz\ *vt* -ED/-ING/-s [ISV *pyrite* + *-ize*] : to convert into pyrite : introduce pyrite into ⟨*pyritized* plant remains⟩

**py·ri·to·he·dral** \pəˈrīd·əˈhēdrəl, (ˌ)pīˈr- *sometimes chiefly Brit* -hed-\ *adj* [NL *pyritohedron* + E *-al*] : of, relating to, or consisting of pyritohedrons

**py·ri·to·he·dron** \-drən *sometimes* -ˌdrän\ *n, pl* **pyritohedrons** *or* **pyritohedra** [NL, fr. *pyrito-* (fr. ISV *pyrite*) + *-hedron*] : a pentagonal dodecahedron that is a hemihedral form of the isometric system of crystalline symmetry common to pyrite

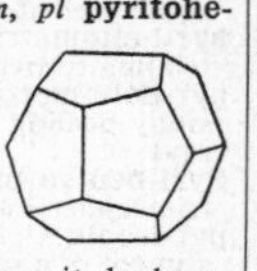

pyritohedron

**¹py·rit·oid** \ˈpīˌrīd·ˌȯid\ *adj* [ISV *pyrite* + *-oid*] : like pyrite

**²pyritoid** \"\ *n* -s [*pyrite* + *-oid*] : PYRITOHEDRON

**py·ri·tous** \pəˈrīd·əs, (ˈ)pīˈr-\ *adj* [*pyrite* + *-ous*] : PYRITIC

**py·ro** \ˈpī(ˌ)rō\ *n* -s [by shortening] **1** : PYROCELLULOSE **2** : PYROGALLOL — used esp. in photography **3** : PYROMANIAC

**pyro-** — see PYR-

**pyro** *abbr* pyrotechnic; pyrotechnics

**py·ro·aurite** \ˌpīrōˈȯˌrīt\ *n* -s [Sw *pyroaurit*, fr. *pyr-* + L *aurum* gold + Sw *-it* -ite; fr. its resemblance to gold after being heated — more at ORIOLE] : a mineral $Mg_6Fe_2(OH)_{16}CO_3.4H_2O$ that is a hydrous basic carbonate of magnesium and iron

**py·ro·belonite** \ˌpī(ˌ)rō+\ *n* [*pyr-* + *belonite*] : a mineral $MnPb(VO_4)(OH)$ consisting of a basic lead manganese vanadate occurring in brilliant red needle-shaped crystals (hardness 3.5, sp. gr. 5.4)

**py·ro·bitumen** \ˌpī(ˌ)rō+\ *n* [*pyr-* + *bitumen*] : ASPHALT

**py·ro·bituminous** \"+\ *adj* [*pyr-* + *bituminous*] : yielding bituminous products on heating : PYROGENEOUS

**py·ro·borate** \"+\ *n* [*pyr-* + *borate*] : TETRABORATE

**py·ro·boric acid** \"+ . . .-\ *n* [*pyroboric* fr. *pyr-* + *boric*] : TETRABORIC ACID

**py·ro·catechin** \"+\ *n* [ISV *pyr-* + *catechin*] : PYROCATECHOL

**py·ro·catechol** \"+\ *n* [ISV *pyr-* + *catechol*] : a crystalline phenol $C_6H_4(OH)_2$ obtained by pyrolysis of catechin, resins, lignins, and other natural substances but usu. made synthetically (as by alkaline fusion of *ortho*-chlorophenol or *ortho*-phenolsulfonic acid) and used chiefly as a photographic developer, as a developer in fur dyeing, as an intermediate in organic synthesis, and as an analytical reagent; *ortho*-dihydroxy-benzene — called also *catechol*

**py·ro·cat·e·chu·ic acid** \ˌpīrōˌkad·əˈchüˌik-, -əˈshü|, -əˈkyü|\ *n* [*pyrocatechuic* fr. *pyr-* + *catechu* + *-ic*] : a crystalline acid $C_6H_3(OH)_2COOH$ derived from pyrocatechol; 2,3-dihydroxy-benzoic acid

**py·ro·cellulose** \ˌpī(ˌ)rō+\ *n* [*pyr-* + *cellulose*] : cellulose nitrate that is of lower degree of nitration than guncotton and that is used in smokeless powders

**py·ro·chemical** \"+\ *adj* [*pyr-* + *chemical*] : relating to or involving chemical activity at high temperatures ⟨a ~ decomposition product⟩ — **py·ro·chemically** \"+\ *adv*

**py·ro·chlore** \ˈpīrəˌklō(ə)r\ *n* -s [G *pyrochlor*, fr. *pyr-* + Gk *chlōros* greenish yellow — more at YELLOW] : a brown or dark reddish mineral $NaCaCb_2O_6F$ that is isomorphous with microlite and is an oxide and fluoride of sodium, calcium, and columbium

**py·rochro·ite** \ˌpīrəˈkrōˌīt, pīˈräkrəˌwīt\ *n* -s [Sw *pyrochroit*, fr. *pyr-* + Gk *chrōs* color + Sw *-it* -ite; fr. the fact that it becomes colored when heated — more at CHROMATIC] : a mineral $Mn(OH)_2$ that is a natural manganous hydroxide

**py·ro·cinchonic acid** \ˌpī(ˌ)rō+ . . .-\ *n* [*pyrocinchonic* ISV *pyr-* + *cinchonic*] : an unstable dicarboxylic acid $C_4H_6(COOH)_2$ obtained usu. in the form of its crystalline anhydride by pyrolysis of cinchonic acid; dimethyl-maleic acid

**py·ro·clast** \ˈpīrōˌklast\ *n* -s [*pyr-* + *-clast*] : a fragment of detrital volcanic material that has been expelled aerially from a vent

**¹py·ro·clas·tic** \ˌ==ˈklastik\ *adj* [*pyr-* + *-clastic*] : formed by fragmentation as a result of volcanic or igneous action ⟨~ rocks⟩

**²pyroclastic** \"\ *n* -s : a volcanic rock composed of pyroclasts

**py·ro·coll** \ˈpīrōˌkäl\ *n* -s [ISV *pyr-* + *-coll*] : a crystalline tricyclic inner amide $C_{10}H_6N_2O_2$ obtained by the distillation of gelatin, glue, or leather scrap or by the dehydration of pyrrole-carboxylic acid with acetic anhydride

**py·ro·collodion** \ˌpī(ˌ)rō+\ *n* [*pyr-* + *collodion*] : pyroxylin containing a high percentage of nitrogen

**py·ro·condensation** \"+\ *n* [*pyr-* + *condensation*] : chemical condensation brought about by heat

**py·ro·conductivity** \"+\ *n* [*pyr-* + *conductivity*] : electrical conductivity induced by application of heat

**py·ro·cotton** \"+\ *n* [*pyr-* + *cotton*] : cellulose nitrate containing about 12.6 percent nitrogen and used in smokeless powders — compare PYROCELLULOSE

**py·ro·crystalline** \"+\ *adj* [*pyr-* + *crystalline*] : crystallized from a molten magma

**¹py·ro·electric** \"+\ *adj* [ISV, back-formation fr. *pyroelectricity*] : of, relating to, or exhibiting pyroelectricity

**²pyroelectric** \"\ *n* : a pyroelectric substance

**py·ro·electricity** \ˌpī(ˌ)rō+\ *n* [ISV *pyr-* + *electricity*] **1** : electrification produced on various crystals by change of temperature **2** : a branch of science that deals with the phenomenon of pyroelectricity

**py·ro·gallate** \"+\ *n* [*pyr-* + *gallate*] : a salt or ether of pyrogallol

**py·ro·gallic acid** \"+...-\ *n* [*pyrogallic* ISV *pyr-* + *gallic*; orig. formed as F *pyrogallique*] : PYROGALLOL

**py·ro·gal·lol** \ˌpīrōˈgaˌlȯl, -ˌlōl\ *n* -s [ISV *pyrogallic* + *-ol*] : a poisonous bitter crystalline phenol $C_6H_3(OH)_3$ with weak acid properties that is obtained usu. by pyrolysis of gallic acid with water and is used chiefly as a photographic developer, in alkaline solution as an absorbent for oxygen in gas analysis, in making dyes and in dyeing, and in medicine in treating skin diseases; 1,2,3-trihydroxy-benzene

**py·ro·gen** \ˈpīrəjən, -ˌjen\ *n* -s [ISV *pyr-* + *-gen*] **1 a** *obs* : an element (as sulfur or phosphorus) characterized by great flammability **b** : a substance produced by the action of heat **2** : a fever-producing substance (as various thermostable products of bacterial metabolism)

**py·ro·ge·na·tion** \ˌpīrəjəˈnāshən\ *n* -s [ISV *pyrogen* + *-ation*] : subjection to heat ⟨~ of formic acid⟩

**py·ro·genesis** \ˌpīrō+\ *n* [NL, fr. *pyr-* + *genesis*] **1** : the production of heat **2** : production of some product by the action of heat

**py·ro·genetic** \ˌpī(ˌ)rō+\ *adj* [ISV *pyr-* + *-genetic*] : of, relating to, or produced by pyrogenesis — **py·ro·genetically** \"+\ *adv*

**py·ro·gen·ic** \ˌpīrōˈjenik\ *adj* [ISV *pyr-* + *-genic*] **1** : producing or produced by heat **2 a** : of igneous origin ⟨~ strata⟩ **b** : formed by the action of magmatic heat **3** : producing or due to fever

**py·ro·ge·nic·i·ty** \ˌpīrōjəˈnisəd·ē\ *n* -ES [*pyrogenic* + *-ity*] : the quality or state of being pyrogenic; *esp* : capacity to produce fever

**py·rog·e·nous** \(ˈ)pīˈräjənəs\ *adj* [*pyr-* + *-genous*] : PYROGENIC

**py·ro·glazer** \"+\ *n* [*pyr-* + *glazer*] : one that hand paints on glass with ceramic colors that are later fused on in a kiln

**py·ro·gno·mic** \ˌpīrəˈnōmik, -rägˈn-, -nām-\ *adj* [*pyr-* + Gk *gnōmon* knower, discerner, index + E *-ic* — more at GNOMON] : readily becoming incandescent when heated due to rapid exothermic recrystallization — used of metamict minerals (as gadolinite)

**py·rog·nos·tic** \ˌpīrägˈnästik\ *adj* [ISV *pyr-* + *-gnostic*] : relating to or developed by the use of heat esp. as applied by a blowpipe

**py·rog·nos·tics** \ˌ==ˈ=stiks\ *n pl but sing or pl in constr* : the characteristics (as the degree of fusibility or the flame coloration) of a mineral observed by the use of the blowpipe

**¹py·ro·graph** \ˈpīrəˌgraf, -ˌräf\ *vb* [back-formation fr. *pyrography*] *vi* : to employ or engage in pyrography ~ *vt* : to decorate by pyrography

**²pyrograph** \"\ *n* : a production of pyrography

**py·rog·ra·pher** \pīˈrägrəfə(r)\ *n* -s : one that pyrographs

**py·ro·graph·ic** \ˌpīrəˈgrafik\ *adj* [*pyr-* + *-graphic*] **1** : of, relating to, or produced by pyrography **2** : marked by fire or burning

**py·rog·ra·phy** \pīˈrägrəfē\ *n* -ES [ISV *pyr-* + *-graphy*] **1** : the art or process of producing designs or pictures (as on wood or leather) by burning or scorching with hot instruments **2** : ornamentation or a picture of ornamentation produced by pyrography

**py·ro·gra·vure** \ˌpīrōgrəˈvyu̇(ə)r\ *n* [ISV *pyr-* + *gravure*; prob. orig. formed in F] : PYROGRAPHY

**py·ro·la** \ˈpīrōlə\ *n* [NL, prob. fr. L *pyrum*, *pirum* pear + *-ola* -ole] **1** *cap* : a genus (the type of the family Pyrolaceae) of short-stemmed perennial herbs that have basal persistent leaves and racemes of white, pink, or purple pentamerous flowers containing 10 straight or declined stamens and that are natives of temperate or cool regions — see FALSE WINTERGREEN, SHINLEAF, WINTERGREEN 1 **2** -s : any plant of the genus *Pyrola*

**py·ro·la·ce·ae** \ˌpīrəˈlāsēˌē\ *n pl, cap* [NL, fr. *Pyrola*, type genus + *-aceae*] : a family that comprises mostly evergreen herbs (order Ericales) of regions with pentamerous regular flowers succeeded by loculicidal capsules and that is sometimes included in Ericaceae — **py·ro·la·ceous** \ˌ==ˈlāshəs\ *adj*

**py·rol·a·ter** \pīˈräləd·ə(r)\ *n* -s [*pyr-* + *-later*] : a fire worshiper

**py·rol·a·try** \-lə·trē\ *n* -ES [*pyr-* + *-latry*] : FIRE WORSHIP

**py·ro·lig·ne·ous** \ˌpīrōˈlignēəs\ *adj* [F *pyroligneux*, fr. *pyr-* + *ligneux* woody, fr. L *lignosus*, fr. *lign-* + *-osus* -ose] : obtained by destructive distillation of wood ⟨~ liquor⟩ — compare PYROLIGNEOUS ACID

**pyroligneous acid** *n* : an acid reddish brown aqueous liquid of empyreumatic odor obtained by destructive distillation of hardwood and containing chiefly acetic acid, methanol, wood oils, and tars

**py·ro·lig·nic** \-nik\ *adj* [*pyr-* + *lign-* + *-ic*] : PYROLIGNEOUS

**py·ro·lig·nite** \ˌ==ˈ=ˌnīt\ *n* [F, fr. *pyroligneux* + *-ite*] : a crude acetate produced by treating pyroligneous acid with a metal or basic compound

**pyrolignite of iron** : IRON LIQUOR

**py·ro·lig·nous** \ˈ==ˈ=nəs\ *adj* [F *pyroligneux*] : PYROLIGNEOUS

**py·ro·luminescence** \ˌpī(ˌ)rō+\ *n* [*pyr-* + *luminescence*] : the characteristic spectral radiation (as produced by vaporized salts in a flame) of a gas or vapor excited by high temperature

**py·ro·lu·site** \ˌpīrəˈlüˌsīt\ *n* -s [G *pyrolusit*, fr. *pyr-* + Gk *lousis* washing (fr. *louein* to wash) + G *-it* -ite; fr. its use as glass soap — more at LYE] : a mineral $MnO_2$ that is of an iron-black or dark steel-gray color and metallic luster usu. soft native manganese dioxide and is the most important ore of manganese — see GLASS SOAP

**py·rol·y·sis** \pīˈräləsəs\ *n* [NL, fr. *pyr-* + *-lysis*] : chemical decomposition or other chemical change brought about by the action of heat regardless of the temperature involved — compare CARBONIZATION, CRACKING, DESTRUCTIVE DISTILLATION, THERMAL CRACKING

**py·ro·lyt·ic** \ˌpīrəˈlid·ik\ *adj* [*pyr-* + *-lytic*] : of, relating to, or produced by means of pyrolysis — **py·ro·lyt·i·cal·ly** \-d·ək(ə)lē\ *adv*

**py·rol·y·zate** \pīˈrälәˌzāt, -zət\ *n* -s [*pyrolyze* + *-ate*] : a product formed during pyrolysis

**py·ro·lyze** \ˈpīrəˌlīz\ *vt* -ED/-ING/-s [*pyr-* + *-lyze*] : to subject to pyrolysis

**py·ro·magnetic** \ˌpī(ˌ)rō+\ *adj* [*pyr-* + *-magnetic*] : THERMOMAGNETIC 1

**py·ro·man·cy** \ˈpīrōˌman(t)sē\ *n* -ES [ME *piromancie*, fr. MF *pyromancie*, fr. LL *pyromantia*, fr. Gk *pyromanteia*, fr. *pyr* fire + *manteia* divination — more at FIRE, -MANCY] : divination by means of fire or flames

**py·ro·mania** \ˌpīrō+\ *n* [NL, fr. *pyr-* + *mania*] : an irresistible impulse to start fires — **py·ro·maniac** \"+\ *n* — **py·ro·maniacal** \ˌpī(ˌ)rō+\ *adj*

**py·ro·meconic acid** \ˌpī(ˌ)rō + . . .-\ *n* [*pyromeconic* ISV *pyr-* + *meconic* (*acid*); orig. formed as F *pyroméconique*] : a crystalline acid $C_5H_4O_3$ formed by heating meconic acid or comenic acid; 3-hydroxy-4-pyrone

**py·ro·mellitic acid** \"+... -\ *n* [*pyromellitic* ISV *pyr-* + *mellitic*] : a crystalline acid $C_6H_2(COOH)_4$ that is formed by the distilling of mellitic acid; 1,2,4,5-benzene-tetracarboxylic acid

**py·ro·metallurgical** \"+\ *adj* [*pyrometallurgy* + *-ical*] : of or relating to pyrometallurgy

**py·ro·metallurgy** \"+\ *n* [ISV *pyr-* + *metallurgy*] : chemical metallurgy that depends on heat action (as roasting and smelting)

**py·ro·metamorphic** \"+\ *adj* [*pyrometamorphism* + *-ic*] : of, relating to, or produced by pyrometamorphism ⟨~ changes in sedimentary rock⟩

**py·ro·metamorphism** \"+\ *n* [*pyr-* + *metamorphism*] : change produced in rocks by the action of heat but without the action of pressure or mineralizers — compare DYNAMOMETAMORPHISM

**py·ro·metasomatic** \"+\ *adj* [*pyr-* + *metasomatic*] : of, relating to, or involving high temperature metamorphism that results in important changes in chemical composition ⟨~ magnetite deposits⟩

**py·rom·e·ter** \pīˈräməd·ə(r)\ *n* [ISV *pyr-* + *-meter*] : an instrument for measuring temperatures (as beyond the range of thermometers) usu. by the increase of electric resistance in a metal when heated, by the generation of electric current by a thermocouple when acted upon by direct heat or focused radiation, or by the increase in intensity of light radiated by an incandescent body as its temperature increases — see OPTICAL PYROMETER, RADIATION PYROMETER

**py·ro·met·ric** \ˌpīrəˈme·trik\ *also* **py·ro·met·ri·cal** \-trəkəl\ *adj* [ISV *pyrometry* + *-ic*; prob. orig. formed as F *pyrométrique*] : of or relating to pyrometry; *also* : determined by a pyrometer : used in the measurement of high temperatures — **py·ro·met·ri·cal·ly** \-ək(ə)lē\ *adv*

**pyrometric cone** *n* : any of a series of small cones of different substances that soften and arch over successively as the temperature rises, that together form a scale of fusing points and that are used in finding approximately the temperature (as of a kiln) — called also *Seger cone*

**py·rom·e·try** \pīˈräm·ə·trē\ *n* -ES [ISV *pyr-* + *-metry*] : the techniques and methods of measuring high temperatures; *esp* : the art of using a pyrometer

**py·ro·mor·phi·dae** \ˌpīrəˈmȯrfəˌdē\ *n pl, cap* [NL, fr. *Pyromorpha*, type genus (fr. *pyr-* + *-morpha*) + *-idae*] : a family of day-flying moths with smoky or translucent wings that are sometimes marked with metallic colors

**py·ro·mor·phite** \-ˌfīt\ *n* -s [G *pyromorphit*, fr. *pyr-* + *morph-* + *-it* -ite; fr. the crystalline appearance it assumes from being heated] : a mineral $Pb_5(PO_4)_3Cl$ consisting of a lead chloride and phosphate isomorphous with mimetite and vanadinite and occurring in green, yellow, brown, gray, or white crystals or masses — called also *green lead ore*

**py·ro·mor·phous** \ˌ==ˈ=fəs\ *adj* [*pyr-* + *-morphous*] : crystallizing from a molten state

**py·ro·motor** \ˌpīrə+\ *n* [*pyr-* + *motor*] : a motor driven directly by heat or heat waves

**py·ro·mucic acid** \"+... -\ *n* [*pyromucic* ISV *pyr-* + *mucic* (*acid*); orig. formed as F *pyromucique*] : alpha-furoic acid

**py·rone** \ˈpīˌrōn\ *n* -s [ISV *pyr-* + *-one*] **1** : either of two isomeric carbonyl compounds $C_5H_4O_2$ derived from pyran: **a** : an oily liquid delta-lactone; 2*H*-pyran-2-one — called also *alpha-pyrone*, *2-pyrone*; compare COUMALIN, COUMARIN **b** : a hygroscopic crystalline compound; 4*H*-pyran-4-one — called also *gamma-pyrone*, *4-pyrone*; compare CHROMONE; STRUCTURAL FORMULA **2** : a derivative of either of the pyrones

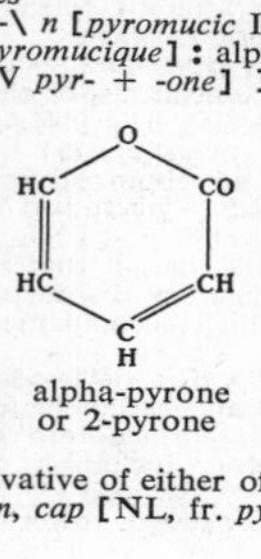

alpha-pyrone or 2-pyrone — gamma-pyrone or 4-pyrone

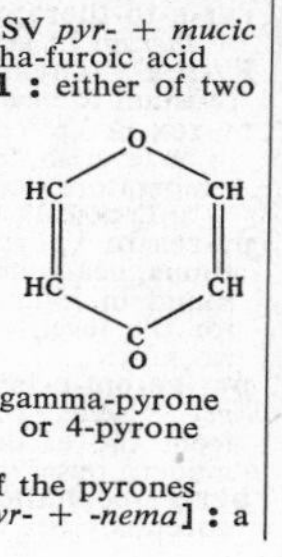

**py·ro·ne·ma** \ˌpīrəˈnēmə\ *n, cap* [NL, fr. *pyr-* + *-nema*] : a genus of saprophytic soil fungi (family Pezizaceae) that produce numerous small often bright pink apothecia which frequently form conspicuous masses on burned soil where brush heaps or logs have been fired

**py·ro·nine** \ˈpīrəˌnēn, -ˌnən\ *n* -s [ISV *pyr-* + *-on* + *-ine*; orig. formed as G *pyronin*] : any of several basic xanthene dyes derived from diphenylmethane and used chiefly as biological stains

**py·ro·ni·no·phil·ic** \ˌpīrəˌnēnəˈfilik\ *adj* [*pyronine* + *-o-* + *-philic*] : staining selectively with pyronines

**py·rope** \ˈpīˌrōp\ *n* -s [ME *pirope*, fr. MF, fr. L *pyropus*, a red bronze, fr. Gk *pyrōpos*, lit., fiery-eyed, fr. *pyr-* + *ōp-*, *ōps* eye — more at EYE] **1** *obs* : a bright red gem (as a ruby or a carbuncle) **2** : a magnesium-aluminum garnet that is deep red in color and is frequently used as a gem — compare CAPE RUBY

**py·ro·pen** \ˈpīrōˌpen\ *n* [*pyr-* + *pen*] : the heated stylus with which designs are burned in pyrography

**py·roph·a·nite** \pīˈräfəˌnīt\ *n* -s [G *pyrophanit*, fr. *pyr-* + *-phane* + *-it* -ite] : a mineral $MnTiO_3$ that is a manganese titanate isomorphous with geikielite and occurs in blood-red tabular rhombohedral crystals

**py·roph·a·nous** \(ˈ)pīˈräfənəs\ *adj* [*pyr-* + *-phane* + *-ous*] : becoming translucent or transparent when heated

**py·ro·phile** \ˈpīrōˌfīl\ *n* -s [*pyr-* + *-phile*] : one enthusiastic over fire or fireworks

**py·roph·i·lous** \(ˈ)pīˈräfələs\ *adj* [*pyr-* + *-philous*] : growing or thriving on burned or fired substrata ⟨~ fungi⟩ — compare PYRONEMA

**py·ro·pho·bia** \ˌpīrəˈfōbēə\ *n* [NL, fr. *pyr-* + *phobia*] : morbid dread of fire — **py·ro·phobic** \ˌ==ˈfōbik *also* -ˈfäb-\ *adj*

**py·ro·phor·ic** \ˌpīrəˈfȯrik\ *also* **py·roph·o·rous** \(ˈ)pīˈräfərəs\ *adj* [NL *pyrophorus* + E *-ic* or *-ous*] : igniting spontaneously ⟨finely divided ~ iron⟩

**pyrophoric alloy** *n* : an alloy (as ferrocerium) that has the property of emitting sparks when scratched or struck with steel and that is used in lighter flints

**py·roph·o·rus** \pīˈräfərəs\ *n* [NL, fr. Gk *pyrophoros* fire-bearing, fr. *pyr-* + *-phoros* -phorous] **1** *pl* **pyrophori** : any of several substances or mixtures (as a carbonized mixture of alum and sugar, or finely divided lead or iron) that ignite spontaneously on exposure to air **2** *cap* : a genus of large tropical American beetles (family Elateridae) bearing a pair of large luminous organs on the prothorax — see FIRE BEETLE

**py·ro·phos·pha·tase** \ˌpīrōˈfäsfəˌtās, -āz\ *n* [ISV *pyrophosphate* + *-ase*] : an enzyme that catalyzes the hydrolysis of a pyrophosphate to form orthophosphate — compare PHOSPHATASE

**py·ro·phosphate** \ˌpīrō+\ *n* [ISV *pyrophosphoric* (in *pyrophosphoric acid*) + *-ate*] : a salt or ester of pyrophosphoric acid — called also *diphosphate* — **py·ro·phosphatic** \"+\ *adj*

**py·ro·phosphoric acid** \"+... -\ *n* [*pyrophosphoric* ISV *pyr-* + *phosphoric*] : a crystalline acid $H_4P_2O_7$ that is formed when orthophosphoric acid is heated and is prepared in the form of salts by heating acid salts of orthophosphoric acid and that dissociates above its melting point into orthophosphoric acid and polyphosphoric acids — called also *diphosphoric acid*

**py·ro·photography** \ˌpī(ˌ)rō+\ *n* [*pyr-* + *photography*] : a process combining the use of photography and heat (as in producing fired-on pictures on porcelain)

**py·ro·photometer** \"+\ *n* [*pyr-* + *photometer*] : an optical pyrometer in which light from an incandescent body whose temperature is to be measured is passed through ruby glass and the red rays thus isolated are compared with those similarly received from a standard flame — compare PYROMETER

**py·ro·phyl·lite** \ˌpīrōˈfiˌlīt, pīˈräfəˌl-\ *n* -s [G *pyrophyllit*, fr. *pyr-* + *phyll-* + *-it* -ite] : a mineral $AlSi_2O_5(OH)$ that is a usu. white or greenish hydrous aluminum silicate, resembles talc, and occurs in a foliated form or in compact masses — compare AGALMATOLITE

**py·ro·phyte** \ˈpīrōˌfīt\ *n* -s [*pyr-* + *-phyte*] : a woody plant with unusual resistance to fire because of exceptionally thick bark

**py·ro·phy·tic** \ˌ==ˈfid·ik\ *adj* [*pyrophyte* + *-ic*] : of, relating to, or made up of pyrophytes

**pyropus** *n, pl* **pyropi** [L, a red bronze — more at PYROPE] *obs* : PYROPE

**py·ro·racemic acid** \ˌpī(ˌ)rō + . . . -\ *n* [ISV *pyr-* + *racemic*] : PYRUVIC ACID

**pyros** *pl of* PYRO

**py·ro·scope** \ˈpīrəˌskōp\ *n* [*pyr-* + *-scope*] : any of various devices (as a pyrometric cone or an optical pyrometer) for determining the temperature of a furnace or kiln

**py·ro·sis** \pīˈrōsəs\ *n* -ES [NL, fr. Gk *pyrōsis* burning, inflammation, fr. *pyroun* to burn, fr. *pyr* fire — more at FIRE] : HEARTBURN

**py·ros·ma·lite** \pīˈräzməˌlīt\ *n* -s [G *pyrosmalit*, fr. *pyr-* + *osma-* (fr. Gk *osmē* odor) + *-lit* -lite; fr. the odor it gives off before the blowpipe — more at ODOR] : a mineral $(Mn,Fe)_4Si_3O_7(OH,Cl)_6$ consisting of a pale-brown, gray, or grayish green chiefly basic iron manganese silicate

**¹py·ro·so·ma** \ˌpīrəˈsōmə\ *n, cap* [NL, fr. *pyr-* + *-soma*] : a genus (coextensive with the family Pyrosomatidae of the order Ascidiacea) of chiefly tropical free-swimming brilliantly bioluminescent pelagic compound tunicates whose colony forms a hollow cylinder that is closed at one end and is often several feet long

**²pyrosoma** \"\ [NL, fr. *pyr-* + *-soma*] *syn of* BABESIA

**py·ro·some** \ˈ==ˌsōm\ *n* -s [NL *Pyrosoma*] : an ascidian of the genus *Pyrosoma*

**py·ro·sphere** \-ˌsfi(ə)r\ *n* [ISV *pyr-* + *sphere*] **1** : the hot central portion of the earth **2** : a hypothetical spherical zone of molten magma that is held to intervene between the crust of the earth and a solid nucleus and to supply lava to volcanoes

**py·ro·stat** \-ˌstat\ *n* -s [ISV *pyr-* + *-stat*] **1** : any of various automatic devices that when exposed to heat, light, smoke, or some other manifestation of fire actuate a mechanism for giving a warning or for setting in operation a means of extinguishing such a fire — compare THERMOSTAT **2** : THERMOSTAT; *esp* : one for use with high temperatures

**py·ro·ste·gia** \ˌpīrōˈstēj(ē)ə\ *n* -s [NL, fr. *pyr-* + *steg-* + *-ia*] : FLAME VINE

**py·ro·stilp·nite** \-tilpˌnīt\ *n* -s [*pyr-* + Gk *stilpnos* glistening + *-ite* — more at STILBUM] : a mineral $Ag_3SbS_3$ that is a silver antimony sulfide polymorphous with pyrargyrite and occurs in tufts of hyacinth-red monoclinic crystals

**py·ro·sulfate** \ˌpī(ˌ)rō+\ *n* [ISV *pyrosulfuric* (in *pyrosulfuric acid*) + *-ate*] : a salt of pyrosulfuric acid — called also *disulfate*

**py·ro·sulfite** \"+\ *n* [ISV *pyr-* + *sulfite*] : METABISULFITE — used in the nomenclature adopted by the International Union of Pure and Applied Chemistry

**py·ro·sulfuric acid** \"+ . . . -\ *n* [ISV *pyr-* + *sulfuric*] : an unstable, crystalline acid $H_2S_2O_7$ that is usu. handled commercially as a thick oily fuming liquid, that is formed by the union of sulfur trioxide with sulfuric acid, that is a chief component of fuming sulfuric acid, and that is converted to sulfuric acid when mixed with water — called also *disulfuric acid*; compare OLEUM

**py·ro·sulfuryl** \"+\ *n* [ISV *pyrosulfuric* + *-yl*] : the bivalent radical, $S_2O_5$, of pyrosulfuric acid

**py·ro·tartaric acid** \"+ . . . -\ *n* [ISV *pyr-* + *tartaric*; orig. formed as F *pyrotartarique*] : a crystalline acid $HOOCCH_2CH(CH_3)COOH$ obtained by pyrolysis of tartaric acid or pyruvic acid and occurring in dextro, levo, and racemic forms; methyl-succinic acid

**¹py·ro·tech·nic** \ˌpīrəˈteknik, -rōˌt-, -nēk\ *also* **py·ro·tech·ni·cal** \-nəkəl, -nēk-\ *adj* [*pyrotechnic* prob. fr. F *pyrotechnique*, fr. *pyrotechnie* pirotechny + *-ique* -ic; *pyrotechnical* fr. *pyrotechny* + *-ical*] : of or relating to pyrotechnics ⟨~ smokes⟩ — **py·ro·tech·ni·cal·ly** \-nək(ə)lē, -nēk-, -li\ *adv*

**²pyrotechnic** \"\ *n* -s **1** **pyrotechnics** *pl but sing or pl in constr* : the art of making or the manufacture and use of fireworks (as for display, military signaling, or illumination) : PYROTECHNY **2** **pyrotechnics** *pl* **a** : materials (as fireworks, powders, and ammunition) for flares or signals **b** : a display of fireworks **3** : a spectacular and usu. highly emotional display (as of oratory, rhetoric, anger, wit, or extreme virtuosity) ⟨pages of glittering ~ —Gamaliel Bradford⟩ — usu. used in pl.

**py·ro·tech·ni·cian** \ˌ==ˈnishən\ *n* [*pyrotechnic* + *-an*] : PYROTECHNIST

**py·ro·tech·nist** \ˌ==ˌ=ˌnəst\ *n* -s [*pyrotechny* + *-ist*] : one skilled in or given to pyrotechnics; *esp* : a manufacturer or an expert in the use and handling of fireworks

**py·ro·tech·ny** \ˈ==ˌ=nē, -ni\ *n* -ES [MF *pyrotechnie*, fr. *pyr-* + Gk *technē* art, skill + MF *-ie* -y — more at TECHNICAL] **1** *archaic* : the use and application of fire in science and the arts **2** : PYROTECHNIC 1

**py·ro·terebic acid** \ˌpī(ˌ)rō + . . . -\ *n* [ISV *pyr-* + *terebic*] : a liquid unsaturated acid $(CH_3)_2C{=}CHCH_2COOH$ obtained by pyrolysis of terebic acid; 4-methyl-3-penten-oic acid

**py·ro·the·ria** \ˌpīrōˈthirēə\ *n pl, cap* [NL, *pyr-* + *-theria*] : an order of Paenungulata or in some classifications a suborder of Ungulata comprising large So. American ungulates of Lower Tertiary age that have incisors like tusks and the cheek teeth all much alike and having two parallel transverse ridges

**py·ro·toxin** \ˌpīrō+\ *n* [ISV *pyr-* + *toxin*] : a toxin (as various bacterial endotoxins) that is capable of inducing fever

**py·ro·tri·tar·ic acid** \ˌpīrōˌtrīˌtarik-\ *also* **py·ro·tri·tar·tar·ic acid** *n* \-ī,tärˌtarik-\ [*pyrotritaric* ISV *pyr-* + *tri-* + *tartaric; pyrotritartaric* fr. *pyr-* + *tri-* + *tartaric*] : a crystalline acid $(C_6H_7O)COOH$ formed esp. by heating tartaric acid; 2,5-dimethyl-3-furoic acid

**py·rox·ene** \pīˈräkˌsēn, pəˈr-\ *n* -s [F *pyroxène*, fr. *pyr-* + *-xène* -xene; prob. fr. the mistaken belief that it was alien to igneous rocks] **1** : a mineral of the pyroxene group usu. occurring in monoclinic short thick prismatic crystals or in square cross section or massive, often laminated, varying in color from white to dark green or black or rarely blue and constituting a common constituent of igneous rocks (hardness 5–6, sp. gr. 3.2–3.6) **2** : a member of the pyroxene group

**pyroxene group** *n* : a group of silicate minerals closely related in crystal form and having the general formula $ABSi_2O_6$ where A represents usu. Ca or Na and B is usu. Mg, Fe, or Al that includes the orthorhombic species enstatite and hypersthene and several monoclinic species (as diopside, spodumene, jadeite, acmite, and augite)

**py·rox·en·ic** \ˌpīˌräkˈsenik\ *adj* [ISV *pyroxene* + *-ic*] : relating to, containing, or composed of pyroxene

**py·rox·e·nite** \pīˈräksəˌnīt, pəˈr-\ *n* -s [ISV *pyroxene* + *-ite*] : an igneous rock that is free from olivine, is composed essentially of pyroxene, and occurs in numerous varieties — **py·rox·e·nit·ic** \(ˌ)=ˌ==ˈnid·ik\ *adj*

**py·rox·man·gite** \ˌpīˌräkˈsmanˌgīt\ *n* -s [ISV *pyroxene* + *mangan-* + *-ite*] : a rhodonite containing about 20 percent of manganese

**py·rox·y·lin** \pīˈräksələn, pəˈr-\ *also* **py·rox·y·line** \", -ˌlēn\ *n* -s [ISV *pyr-* + *xyl-* + *-in* or *-ine*; orig. formed as F *pyroxyline*] **1** : a substance that consists of lower-nitrated cellulose nitrate, usu. contains less than 12.5 percent nitrogen, is soluble in alcohol, a mixture of ether and alcohol, or other organic solvents, is flammable but less explosive than guncotton, and is used chiefly in making plastics (as celluloid), lacquers and other coatings, photographic films, and cements — called also *collodion cotton, soluble guncotton, soluble nitrocellulose* **2** : a product containing pyroxylin ⟨*pyroxylin*-coated fabric⟩

**pyrrh-** *or* **pyrrho-** *also* **pyrro-** *comb form* [Gk *pyrrh-, pyrrho-*, fr. *pyrrhos* red, tawny, fr. *pyr* fire — more at FIRE] : red : tawny ⟨*pyrrhite*⟩ ⟨*pyrrhotite*⟩

**¹pyr·rhic** \ˈpirik, -rēk\ *n* -s [L *pyrrhicha*, fr. Gk *pyrrhichē*] : an ancient Greek martial dance in quick time performed to the accompaniment of the flute

**²pyrrhic** \"\ *adj* [L *pyrrhichius*, fr. Gk *pyrrhichios*, fr. *pyrrhichē* pyrrhic dance] : of, belonging to, or constituting the pyrrhic dance

**³pyrrhic** \"\ *n* -s [L (*pes*) *pyrrhichius*, fr. Gk *pous pyrrhichios* pyrrhic foot, fr. *pous* foot + *pyrrhichios* pyrrhic — more at FOOT] : a foot in prosody consisting of two short or unaccented syllables

**⁴pyrrhic** \"\ *adj* : of or relating to a pyrrhic : composed of pyrrhics ⟨~ verse⟩

**⁵pyrrhic** \"\ *adj, usu cap* [*Pyrrhus* †272 B.C. king of Epirus who sustained heavy losses in defeating the Romans at Asculum in Apulia in 279 B.C. (fr. L, fr. Gk *Pyrrhos*) + E *-ic*] : of, relating to, or resembling that of Pyrrhus

**pyr·rhich·i·us** \pəˈrikēəs\ *n* -ES [L] : ³PYRRHIC

**pyrrhic victory** *n, usu cap P* [⁵*pyrrhic*] : a victory won at excessive cost

**pyr·rhite** \ˈpiˌrīt\ *n* -s [G *pyrrhit*, fr. *pyrrh-* + *-it* -ite] : PYROCHLORE

**¹pyr·rhoc·o·rid** \pəˈräkərəd\ *adj* [NL *Pyrrhocoridae*] : of or relating to the Pyrrhocoridae

**²pyrrhocorid** \"\ *n* -s : a bug of the family Pyrrhocoridae

**pyr·rho·cor·i·dae** \ˌpirəˈkōrəˌdē\ *n pl, cap* [NL, fr. *Pyrrhocoris*, type genus (fr. *pyrrh-* + Gk *koris* bedbug) + *-idae* — more at COREIDAE] : a family of moderately large often brightly colored bugs comprising the firebugs, having four-jointed beak and antennae and no ocelli, and sucking the juices of plants — compare COTTON STAINER, DYSDERCUS

**¹pyr·rho·ni·an** \pəˈrōnēən\ *also* **pyr·rhon·ic** \-ränik\ *n* -s *usu cap* [*pyrrhonian* fr. L *pyrrhoneus*, n., pyrrhonian (fr. *pyrrhon-, Pyrrho fl* 4th cent. B.C. Greek philosopher) + E *-an; pyrrhonic* fr. L *pyrrhoneus* + E *-ic*] : PYRRHONIST

**²pyrrhonian** \"\ *also* **pyrrhonic** \"\ *adj, usu cap* [*pyrrhonian* fr. L *pyrrhoneus*, adj., pyrrhonian + E *-an; pyrrhonic* fr. L *pyrrhoneus* + E *-ic*] : of or relating to Pyrrho or Pyrrhonism : SKEPTICAL

**pyr·rho·nism** \ˈpirəˌnizəm\ *n* -s *usu cap* [F *pyrrhonisme*, fr. *Pyrrhon* Pyrrho (fr. Gk *Pyrrhōn*) + *-isme* -ism] **1** : the doctrines of the founder of a school of skeptics in Greece (about 365–275 B.C.) who taught that all perceptions are of doubtful validity, that the external circumstances of life are therefore unimportant to the wise man, and that he should consequently always preserve tranquillity of mind **2** : skepticism esp. when total or radical

**pyr·rho·nist** \ˈpirənəst\ *n, usu cap* [L *pyrrhoneus* pyrrhonian (fr. *pyrrhon-, Pyrrho* 4th cent. B.C. Greek philosopher, fr. Gk *Pyrrhōn*) + E *-ist*] **1** : a follower of Pyrrho or an adherent of Pyrrhonism **2** : SKEPTIC

**pyr·rho·tism** \ˈpirəˌtizəm\ *n* -s [Gk *pyrrhotēs* redness (fr. *pyrrhos* red) + E *-ism* — more at PYRRH-] : the condition or characteristic of having red hair

**pyr·rho·tite** \-ˌtīt\ *also* **pyr·rho·tine** \-ˌtēn, -ˌtən\ *n* -s [*pyrrhotite* alter. (influenced by *-ite*) of *pyrrhotine; pyrrhotine* fr. G *pyrrhotin*, fr. Gk *pyrrhotēs* redness + G *-in* -ine] : a bronze-colored mineral FeS of metallic luster consisting of ferrous sulfide usu. with a slight deficiency of iron, attracted by the magnet, and sometimes found in hexagonal crystals but usu. massive (hardness 3.5–4.5, sp.gr., 4.58–4.64) — called also *magnetic pyrites*

**pyr·rhu·loxia** \ˌpir(y)ə+\ *n* [NL, fr. *Pyrrhula*, genus of finches (fr. Gk *pyrrhoulas*, a red-colored bird, perh. the bullfinch, fr. *pyrrhos* red) + *Loxia*] **1** *cap* : a genus of large showy finches related to the cardinal, having short thick bills, a prominent crest, and gray and red plumage, and nesting through much of Mexico north to Texas **2** -s : any bird of the genus *Pyrrhuloxia*

**pyrro-** — see PYRRH-

**pyrrol-** *or* **pyrrolo-** *comb form* [fr. *pyrrole*] : pyrrole ⟨*pyrrolidine*⟩ ⟨*pyrrolopyridine*⟩

**pyr·role** \ˈpiˌrōl, pəˈr-\ *n* -s [*pyrrh-* + *-ole*] **1** : a colorless toxic liquid heterocyclic compound $C_4H_5N$ that contains four carbon atoms and one nitrogen atom in the ring, that has an odor suggestive of chloroform, that darkens in air and forms red polymers in the presence of acids, that is obtained by distillation of coal tar or bone oil or by synthesis (as by reaction of ammonia with furan over alumina), and that is the parent of many natural compounds (as the bile pigments, porphyrins, heme, chlorophyll, indigo, a few amino acids, and a few alkaloids) — compare INDOLE, STRUCTURAL FORMULA **2** : a derivative of pyrrole; *esp* : a homologue of pyrrole (as cryptopyrrole or hemopyrrole) — **pyr·rol·ic** \(ˈ)piˈrōlik, pəˈr-, -ˈräl-\ *adj*

NH
α′HC5 1 2CH α
β′HC4 3CH β
pyrrole

**pyr·rol·idine** \pəˈrōləˌdēn, -ˈräl-, -ˌdən\ *n* -s [ISV *pyrrol-* + *-idine*] : a flammable fuming liquid heterocyclic secondary amine $C_4H_9N$ obtained from pyrrole by reduction and also prepared synthetically; *tetrahydro-pyrrole*

**pyr·rol·idone** \-ˌdōn\ *n* -s [ISV *pyrrolidine* + *-one*] : a crystalline or liquid lactam $C_4H_7NO$ made by a series of steps using acetylene, formaldehyde, and ammonia and used chiefly in making polyvinylpyrrolidone; 2-pyrrolidin-one — called also *2-pyrrolidone*

**pyr·rol·idyl** \-(ˌ)dil, -ˌdᵊl\ *or* **pyr·rol·idin·yl** \=ˌ==ˌdenᵊl\ *n* -s [*pyrrolidine* + *-yl*] : any of three univalent radicals $C_4H_8N$ that are derived from pyrrolidine by removal of one hydrogen atom

**pyr·ro·line** \ˈpirəˌlēn, -lən\ *n* -s [ISV *pyrrol-* + *-ine*] : either of two bases $C_4H_7N$ intermediate between pyrrolidine and pyrrole; dihydro-pyrrole; *esp* : a fuming liquid obtained by reduction of pyrrole; 2,5-dihydro-pyrrole

**pyr·roph·y·ta** \pəˈräfəd·ə\ *n pl, cap* [NL, fr. *pyrrh-* + *-phyta*] : a division or other category of lower plants comprising yellow-green algae that are mostly unicellular and biflagellate, that form starch, starchy compounds, or oil as food reserves, and that include the dinoflagellates and cryptomonads

**pyr·ro·porphyrin** \ˌpi(ˌ)rō+\ *n* [ISV *pyrrh-* + *porphyrin*] : a dark red crystalline pigment $C_{32}H_{36}N_4O_2$ with a violet metallic luster that is the lower homologue of phylloporphyrin and that differs from most porphyrins in being a hepta-substituted derivative of porphin rather than an octa-substituted derivative

**pyr·ryl** \ˈpirᵊl\ *or* **pyr·ro·lyl** \-rəˌlil\ *n* -s [ISV *pyrrole* + *-yl*] : any of three univalent radicals $C_4H_4N$ derived from pyrrole by removal of one hydrogen atom

**py·ru·la** \ˈpir(y)ələ\ [NL, fr. L *pyrum, pirum* pear + *-ula* -ule] *syn of* FICUS

**py·ru·lar·ia** \ˌ==ˈla(a)rēə\ *n, cap* [NL, prob. fr. L *pyrum, pirum* pear + *-ula* + NL *-aria*] : a small genus of chiefly Asiatic parasitic or half-parasitic shrubs (family Santalaceae) having alternate deciduous leaves, small green racemose apetalous flowers, and pear-shaped drupes with oily seeds — see RABBITWOOD

**py·rus** \ˈpīrəs\ *n, cap* [NL, fr. L *pyrus, pirus* pear-tree; akin to L *pyrum, pirum* pear — more at PEAR] : a genus of trees (family Rosaceae) native to the Old World that are distinguished by leaves which are mostly glabrous, hard and glossy at maturity, and involute in the bud but which have some or all the flower stalks in each cluster arising from a stout central column, by styles usu. separate at the base, and by fruit with abundant grit cells — compare MALUS; see PEAR

**pyruv-** *or* **pyruvo-** *comb form* [ISV *pyruvic*] : pyruvic acid ⟨*pyruvate*⟩ ⟨*pyruvyl*⟩

**pyr·uv·aldehyde** \ˌpīˌrüv, ˌpiˌrüv, ˌpirˌyüv+\ *n* [*pyruv-* + *aldehyde*] : a yellow pungent volatile oil $CH_3COCHO$ that polymerizes readily and is formed as an intermediate in the metabolism or fermentation of carbohydrates and lactic acid — called also *methylglyoxal, pyruvic aldehyde*

**py·ru·vate** \pīˈrüˌvāt, pəˈrü-, pirˈyü-\ *n* -s [*pyruv-* + *-ate*] : a salt or ester of pyruvic acid

**py·ru·vic acid** \(ˈ)=ˌ=vik-\ *n* [ISV *pyr-* + L *uva* grape + *-ic* — more at UVULA] : a liquid keto acid $CH_3COCOOH$ that has an odor like acetic acid, that is obtained by the dry distillation of racemic or tartaric acid or by mild oxidation of lactic acid, and that is an important intermediate in metabolism and fermentation; acetyl-formic acid — see PHOSPHOPYRUVIC ACID

**py·ru·vo·yl** \=ˈ=vəˌwil\ *or* **pyr·u·vyl** \-vəl\ *n* -s [ISV *pyruv-* + *-yl*] : the univalent radical $CH_3COCO—$ of pyruvic acid

**py·ryl·i·um** \pīˈrilēəm\ *n* -s [NL, irreg. fr. ISV *pyran*] : a univalent ion $C_5H_5O^+$ of the oxonium type that is related to pyran

**¹py·thag·o·re·an** \pəˌthagəˈrēən, (ˌ)pīˌth-, -thaig-\ *n* -s *usu cap* [L *pythagoreus* Pythagorean (fr. Gk *pythagoreios*, fr. *Pythagoras*, 6th cent. B.C. Greek philosopher and mathematician) + E *-an*] **1** : a follower of Pythagoras **2** : a member of a school of philosophers and secret society named after Pythagoras and maintaining its organization in southern Italy until the middle of the 4th century B.C.

**²pythagorean** \(ˌ)=ˌ==ˈ==\ *adj, usu cap* : of or relating to the Greek philosopher Pythagoras, his philosophy, or the Pythagoreans

**pythagorean comma** *n, usu cap P* : DITONIC COMMA

**py·thag·o·re·an·ism** \(ˌ)=ˌ==ˈ=əˌnizəm\ *n* -s *usu cap* [*pythagorean* + *-ism*] : the doctrines and theories of Pythagoras and the Pythagoreans who developed some basic principles of mathematics and astronomy, originated the doctrine of the harmony of the spheres, and believed in a theory of metempsychosis, the eternal recurrence of things, and a number mysticism

**pythagorean proposition** *n, usu cap 1st P* : a theorem in geometry: the square on the hypotenuse of a right triangle equals the sum of the squares on the other sides

**pythagorean scale** *n, usu cap P* : a musical scale with its intervals regulated by mathematical ratios rather than by consonances

**pythagorean semitone** *n, usu cap P* : LIMMA 2

**pyth·a·gor·ic** \ˌpithəˈgȯrik\ *also* **pyth·a·gor·i·cal** \-rəkəl\ *adj, usu cap* [L *pythagoricus*, fr. Gk *pythagorikos*, fr. *Pythagoras* 6th cent. B.C. Greek philosopher and mathematician + *-ikos* -ic] : PYTHAGOREAN

**py·thag·o·ri·cian** \pəˌthagəˈrishən, (ˌ)pīˌth-\ *n* -s *usu cap* [*pythagoric* + *-an*] *archaic* : PYTHAGOREAN

**py·thag·o·rism** \=ˈ==ˌrizəm\ *n* -s *usu cap* [Gk *pythagorismos*, fr. *pythagorizein* to be a follower of Pythagoras] : PYTHAGOREANISM

**py·thag·o·rist** \-ˌrəst\ *n* -s *usu cap* [Gk *pythagoristēs*, fr. *pythagorizein* to be a follower of Pythagoras] : PYTHAGOREAN

**py·thag·o·rize** \-ˌrīz\ *vi* -ED/-ING/-S *usu cap* [Gk *pythagorizein* to be a follower of Pythagoras, fr. *Pythagoras* 6th cent. B.C. Greek philosopher and mathematician + *-izein* -ize] : to philosophize in the manner of the Pythagoreans

**pyth·i·a·ce·ae** \ˌpithēˈāsēˌē\ *n pl, cap* [NL, fr. *Pythium*, type genus + *-aceae*] : a family of fungi (order Peronosporales) having sporangia usu. borne successively and singly at the tips of branching sporangiophores which differ little if any from assimilative hyphae — see PHYTOPHTHORA, PYTHIUM — **pyth·i·a·ceous** \ˌ==ˈāshəs\ *adj*

**pyth·i·a·cys·tis** \ˌpithēəˈsistəs\ *n, cap* [NL, fr. *pythia-* (fr. *Pythium*) + *-cystis*] *in former classifications* : a genus of fungi (family Pythiaceae) comprising a single species (*P. citrophthora*) that causes brown rot of citrus fruits and gummosis of citrus and other fruits and is now usu. included in *Phytophthora*

**pyth·i·ad** \ˈpithēˌad\ *n* -s *usu cap* [Gk *Pythia*, the Pythian games (fr. *Pythō* Pytho, early name of the town of Delphi in southern Greece where the Pythian games were held + *-ia* -y) + E *-ad*] : the four-year period between celebrations of the Pythian games in ancient Greece

**pyth·iam·bic** \ˌpithēˈambik, -ˌthīˈa-\ *n* -s *usu cap* [NL *pythiambicus*, fr. L *pythius* pythian + *iambicus* iambic — more at IAMBIC] : an epodic distich in Greek and Latin prosody composed of a Pythian verse and an iambic dimeter or trimeter

**¹pyth·i·an** \ˈpithēən\ *n* -s *usu cap* [L *pythius*, adj., pythian (fr. Gk *pythios*, fr. *Pythō* Pytho, Delphi) + E *-an*] **1** : a native or inhabitant of Delphi **2 a** : a priestess of Apollo at Delphi **b** : one who is phrenetic

**²pythian** \"\ *adj, usu cap* [L *pythius* pythian + E *-an*] **1 a** : of or relating to the ancient Greek god Apollo esp. as patron deity of Delphi **b** : being or relating to games celebrated at Delphi every four years in the third year of the Olympiad about the middle of August and forming one of the four great Panhellenic festivals **2** : like a Pythian priestess : ECSTATIC, PHRENETIC

**pythian verse** *n, usu cap P* : dactylic hexameter

**pyth·ic** \ˈpithik\ *adj, usu cap* [L *pythicus*, fr. Gk *pythikos*, fr. *Pythō* + *-ikos*, -ic] : PYTHIAN

**pyth·i·um** \ˈpithēəm\ *n* [NL, fr. Gk *pythein* to cause to rot + NL *-ium* — more at FOUL] **1** *cap* : a genus of destructive root-parasitic fungi (family Pythiaceae) having filamentous sporangia, smooth-walled spherical oogonia, and stalked antheridia and including forms (as *P. debaryanum*) that cause damping-off **2** -s : any fungus of the genus *Pythium* ⟨~ root necrosis⟩

**pytho·gen·ic** \ˌpīthəˈjenik, ˌpith-\ *adj* [*pytho-* (fr. Gk *pythein* to cause to rot) + *-genic*] : produced by or originating from decomposition or filth ⟨typhoid has been considered a ~ fever⟩

**py·thon** \ˈpīˌthän, -thən\ *n* [L *Python*, monstrous serpent that dwelt in the caves of Mount Parnassus near Delphi and that was killed there by Apollo, fr. Gk *Pythōn*] **1** -s : a large constricting snake (as a boa or anaconda) **2** *cap* [NL, fr. L *Python*] : a genus of large nonvenomous snakes of the family Boidae that includes the largest of recent snakes — see CARPET SNAKE, INDIAN PYTHON, RETICULATED PYTHON, ROCK PYTHON

**pytho·ness** \ˈpīthənəs, ˈpith-\ *n* -ES [ME *Phitonesse*, fr. MF *phitonise, pithonisse*, fr. LL *pythonissa*, fr. Gk *Pythōn* spirit of divination, fr. *Pythō* Delphi, where the Delphic oracle was located + LL *-issa* -ess] **1** : a woman supposed to have a spirit of divination **2** : a priestess of Apollo held to have prophetic powers

**py·thon·ic** \(ˈ)pīˈthänik, *in sense 1* " *or* pəˈth-\ *also* **py·thon·i·cal** \-nəkəl\ *adj* [*pythonic* fr. LL *pythonicus*, fr. Gk *Pythōn* spirit of divination + L *-icus* -ic; *pythonical* fr. LL *pythonicus* + E *-al*] **1 a** : of, relating to, or like a Pythian priestess or other pythoness **b** : pretending to foretell events : ORACULAR **2** [*Python*, monstrous serpent killed by Apollo near Delphi (fr. L) + E *-ic*] **a** : of, relating to, or like a python **b** : HUGE, MONSTROUS

**py·tho·nid** \ˈpīthənəd, -ˌnid\ *n* -s [NL *Pythonidae*] : a snake of the family Pythonidae; *broadly* : PYTHON 1

**py·thon·i·dae** \pīˈthänəˌdē\ *n pl, cap* [NL, fr. *Python*, type genus + *-idae*] *in some classifications* : a family comprising nonvenomous snakes closely related to the boas but having a supraorbital bone and usu. teeth on the premaxilla and the subcaudal scales mostly in two rows, including *Python* and closely related genera, and being now usu. treated as a subfamily of Boidae

**py·tho·nine** \ˈpīthəˌnīn\ *adj* [NL *Python* + E *-ine*] : of or relating to the genus *Python* or the family Pythonidae

**pytho·nism** \ˈpīthəˌnizəm, ˈpith-\ *n* -s [LL *python-, pytho* pythonic spirit (fr. Gk *Pythōn* spirit of divination) + E *-ism*] **1** : possession by or intercourse with a pythonic deity or spirit **2** : the art and practice of prophecy or divination

**pytho·nis·sa** \ˌ==ˈnisə\ *n* -s *usu cap* [LL] *archaic* : PYTHONESS

**pytho·nist** \ˈ==ˌnəst\ *n* -s [LL *python-, pytho* pythonic spirit + E *-ist*] : a person who professes to prophesy through some divine or esoteric inspiration : SOOTHSAYER

**py·tho·noid** \ˈpīthəˌnȯid\ *adj* [F *pythonoïde*, fr. *python* (fr. L *Python*, monstrous serpent killed by Apollo) + *-oïde* -oid] : like a python

**¹py·thono·morph** \pīˈthänəˌmȯrf, ˈpīthən-\ *or* **py·thono·mor·phic** \(ˌ)=ˌ==ˈmȯrfik, ˌ=(ˌ)=ˌ==-\ *also* **py·thono·mor·phous** \-fəs\ *adj* [*pythonomorph* fr. NL *Pythonomorpha; pythonomorphic, pythonomorphous* fr. NL *Pythonomorpha* + *-ic* or *-ous*] : of or relating to the Pythonomorpha

**²pythonomorph** \"\ *n* -s : a pythonomorph reptile or fossil

**py·thono·mor·pha** \(ˌ)pīˌthänəˈmȯrfə, ˌpīthən-\ *n pl, cap* [NL, fr. L *Python*, monstrous serpent killed by Apollo + NL *-morpha*] *in some classifications* : a suborder of Squamata or other group of large marine reptiles of the Cretaceous of No. America and Europe having a long snakelike scaly body, a head like that of a lizard with strong recurved teeth, and two pairs of paddle-shaped limbs

**py·uria** \pīˈyu̇rēə\ *n* -s [NL, fr. *py-* + *-uria*] : the presence of pus in the urine; *also* : a condition (as pyelonephritis) characterized by pus in the urine

**¹pyx** \ˈpiks\ *n* -ES [ME *pyxe, pix*, fr. ML *pyxis*, fr. L, box, fr. Gk — more at BOX] **1** : the vessel, tabernacle, or container used ecclesiastically to hold the reserved sacrament on the altar or Holy Table or to carry the Eucharist to the sick **2** *also* **pix** \"\ **a** *or* **pyx chest** : a box used in the British mint as a place of deposit for sample coins reserved for testing of weight and fineness — see TRIAL OF THE PYX **b** : a similar box in the U.S. Mint **3** : a small chest or coffer : BOX

**²pyx** \"\ *also* **pix** \"\ *vt* -ED/-ING/-ES **1** : to put into or preserve or carry in a pyx **2** : to assay (a coin) at the trial of the pyx : test (a coin) for weight and fineness

**pyx·id·an·thera** \ˌpiksəˈdan(t)thərə\ *n, cap* [NL, fr. L *pyxid-, pyxis* box + NL *-anthera*] : a monotypic genus of low evergreen shrubs (family Diapensiaceae) containing solely the pyxie

**pyx·i·date** \ˈpiksəˌdāt\ *adj* [L *pyxid-, pyxis* box + E *-ate*] : resembling or constituting a pyxidium

**pyx·id·i·um** \pikˈsidēəm\ *n, pl* **pyxid·ia** \-ēə\ *or* **pyxidiums** [NL, fr. Gk *pyxidion*, dim. of *pyxis* box] **1** : a capsular fruit (as in the plantain) that dehisces around its circumference so that the upper portion falls off like a cap — compare CIRCUMSCISSILE **2** : CAPSULE 2b

**pyx·ie** *also* **pix·ie** *or* **pixy** \ˈpiksē\ *n, pl* **pyxies** *also* **pixies** [by shortening and alter. (influence of *-ie*) fr. NL *Pyxidanthera* (genus name of *Pyxidanthera barbulata*), fr. L *pyxid-, pyxis* box + NL *-anthera*] : a creeping evergreen shrub (*Pyxidanthera barbulata*) of the family Diapensiaceae that grows in the pine barrens of New Jersey and No. Carolina and has narrow imbricated leaves and mostly white early-blooming star-shaped flowers

**pyx·is** \ˈpiksəs\ *n, pl* **pyxi·des** \-ksəˌdēz\ [L] **1** : ACETABULUM 2a **2** [ML, fr. L, box] **a** : an often cylindrical and ornately decorated covered container used in ancient Greece and Rome (as for the storage of salves and toiletries) **b** : PYX 1 **3** [NL, fr. L, box] **a** : PYXIDIUM 1 **b** : SCYPHUS 2

**pyx–jury** \ˈ=ˌ==\ *n* [¹*pyx*] : a committee of goldsmiths that makes the trial of the pyx

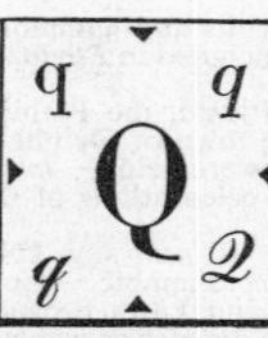

[1]**q** \'kyü\ *n, pl* **q's** *or* **qs** *often cap, often attrib* **1 a :** the 17th letter of the English alphabet **b :** an instance of this letter printed, written, or otherwise represented **c :** a speech counterpart of orthographic *q* (as *q* in *quick, Iraq*) **2 :** a printer's type, a stamp, or some other instrument for reproducing the letter *q* **3 :** someone or something arbitrarily or conveniently designated *q* esp. as the 16th or when j is used for the 10th the 17th in order or class **4 :** something having the shape of the letter Q

[2]**q** \"\ *n, pl* **q's** *usu cap* [fr. initial letter of *quality factor*] **:** the ratio of the reactance to the resistance of an oscillatory circuit ⟨one of the primary factors in determining the degree of selectivity of a tuned circuit is the ~ —J.F.Rider & S.D. Uslan⟩

[3]**q** *abbr, often cap* **1** [L *quadrans*] farthing **2** [L *quaere*] inquire **3** quantity **4** quart **5** quarter; quarterly **6** quartermaster **7** quarto **8** quasi **9** queen **10** query **11** question **12** quetzal **13** quick **14** quintal **15** quire

[4]**q** *symbol, cap* **1** [fr. initial letter of *quality factor*] quality factor **2** [fr. initial letter of G *quelle* source] second source — used in biblical criticism to designate material belonging to a hypothetical written source used in addition to Mark and perhaps other sources in writing the Gospels of Matthew and Luke

**qabbala** *or* **qabbalah** *var of* CABALA

**qad·a·rite** *also* **kad·a·rite** \'kadə,rīt\ *n* -s [Ar *qadarīy* qadarite (fr. *qadar* fate, destiny, divine preordination) + E *-ite*] *usu cap* **:** a member of an early Muslim philosophical school asserting the doctrine of free will in opposition to the Jabarites

**qa·di** *also* **ca·di** *or* **ka·di** *or* **ka·dhi** \'kädē\ *or* **qa·zi** \'käzē\ *n* -s [Ar *qāḍī*] **:** a Muslim judge who interprets and administers the religious law of Islam — compare SHARI'A

**qaid** *var of* CAID

**qaimaqam** *or* **qaimmaqam** *var of* KAIMAKAM

**qantar** *var of* KANTAR

**qaraqalpaq** *usu cap, var of* KARAKALPAK

**qar·ma·ti·an** *or* **kar·ma·ti·an** \kär'mād·ēən\ *or* **kar·ma·thi·an** *also* **car·ma·thi·an** \-āthēən\ *n* -s *cap* [Hamdan *Qarmat*, 9th cent. Iraqi peasant who founded the sect + E *-an*] **:** a Muslim Shi'ite sect founded in the 9th century and flourishing during the middle ages as a communistic secret society that in time expanded to a small independent state on the Persian gulf from which its members raided neighboring lands

**qash·qai** *also* **quash·qai** \'käsh,kī\ *n, pl* **qashqai** *or* **qashqais** *usu cap* **1 :** a migratory Turkic-speaking people of the Zagros mountains situated east of the Bakhtiari **2 :** a member of the Qashqai people

**qa·si·da** *or* **ka·si·da** \kə'sēdə\ *n, pl* **qasida** *or* **kasida** [Ar *qaṣīdah*] **:** a laudatory, elegiac, or satiric poem in Arabic, Persian, or any of various related Oriental literatures

**qat** *or* **q'at** *var of* KAT

**qat·a·ba·ni·an** *also* **kat·a·ba·ni·an** \,kad·ə'bänēən\ *n* -s *usu cap* [*Qataban, Kataban*, ancient district of southern Arabia + E *-ian*] **1 :** a native or inhabitant of the ancient South Arabian kingdom of Qataban **2 :** the Sabaean language of the Qatabanians

**qazaq** *usu cap, var of* KAZAK

**QB** *abbr* **1** quarterback **2** Queen's Bench

**q–boat** \'=,=\ *n, usu cap Q* **:** an armed ship disguised as a merchant or fishing ship and used to decoy enemy submarines into gun range — called also *mystery ship*

**QC** *abbr* **1** Quartermaster Corps **2** Queen's Counsel

**q–celtic** \'=;==\ *n, cap Q&C* **:** those Celtic languages in which the Indo-European labiovelars are found as velars **:** GOIDELIC

**QD** *abbr* **1** *often not cap* [L *quaque die*] every day **2** quarterdeck **3** *often not cap* [L *quater die*] four times a day

**QDA** *abbr, often not cap* quantity discount agreement

**QE** *abbr, often not cap* [L *quod est*] which is

**QED** *abbr* [L *quod erat demonstrandum*] which was to be demonstrated

**QEF** *abbr* [L *quod erat faciendum*] which was to be done

**QEI** *abbr* [L *quod erat inveniendum*] which was to be found out

**qere** *var of* KERE

**qeri** *var of* KERI

**QF** *abbr* quick-firing

**q factor** *n, usu cap Q* [*quality factor*] **:** [2]Q

**q fever** *n, usu cap Q* [*q* fr. initial letter of *query*] **:** a disease somewhat like but much milder than typhus that is characterized by high fever, chills, and pains in the muscles and is commonly accompanied by an atypical pneumonia, that is caused by a microorganism (*Coxiella burnetii*) apparently widespread in ruminants and transmitted by raw milk, by contact, or by ticks, and that is widely distributed in No. America, Europe, and parts of Africa

**QH** *abbr* [L *quaque hora*] every hour

**qib·la** *or* **qib·lah** *also* **kib·la** *or* **kib·lah** \'kiblə\ *n* -s [Ar *qiblah*] **:** the direction of the Kaaba shrine in Mecca toward which all Muslims turn in ritual prayer

**QID** *abbr, often not cap* [L *quater in die*] four times a day

**qinah** *var of* KINAH

**qin·tar** \kin'tär\ *n* -s [Alb] **:** a monetary unit of Albania equal to $\frac{1}{100}$ lek — see MONEY table

**qi·yas** \kē'yäs\ *n* -ES [Ar *qiyās* analogy] **:** the principle of analogy applied in the interpretation of points of Muslim law not clearly covered in the Koran or sunna **:** analogical inference or deduction

**ql** *abbr* quintal

**QL** *abbr, often not cap* [L *quantum libet*] as much as you please

**qlty** *abbr* quality

**QM** *abbr* **1** quartermaster **2** *often not cap* [L *quo modo*] in what manner

**QMC** *abbr* Quartermaster Corps

**q–meter** \'=,==\ *n, usu cap Q* **:** an instrument for measuring the Q of an oscillatory circuit

**QMG** *abbr* quartermaster general

**qmr** *abbr* quartermaster

**QMS** *abbr* quartermaster sergeant

**qn** *abbr* **1** question **2** quotation

**QN** *abbr, often not cap* [L *quaque nocte*] every night

**qoph** *or* **koph** *also* **coph** \'kōf\ *n* -s [Heb *qōph*] **1 :** the 19th letter of the Hebrew alphabet — symbol ק; see ALPHABET table **2 :** the letter of the Phoenician or of any of various other Semitic alphabets corresponding to Hebrew qoph

**qoran** *usu cap, var of* KORAN

**QP** *abbr* **1** [L *quantum placet*] as much as you please **2** queen post

**qq** *abbr* questions

**qq v** *abbr* [L *quae vide*] which see

**qr** *abbr* **1** quarter **2** quire

**qre** *var of* KERE

**q'ri** *or* **qri** *var of* KERI

**qrly** *abbr* quarterly

**qrs complex** *n, usu cap Q&R&S* **:** the deflections in an electrocardiographic tracing that represent ventricular activity of the heart

**qrtly** *abbr* quarterly

**QS** *abbr* **1** *often not cap* [L *quantum sufficit*] as much as suffices **2** quarter section **3** quarter sessions

**q's** *or* **qs** *pl of* Q

**q–ship** \'=,=\ *n, usu cap Q* **:** Q-BOAT

**q signal** *n, usu cap Q* **:** any of various conventional code signals employed in radiotelegraphy that is a combination of three letters the first of which is Q (as QRS for "send slower", QSD for "your keying is bad")

**qt** \'kyü'tē\ *n* -s *often cap Q&T* [abbr. of *quiet*] **:** QUIET — usu. used in the phrase *on the qt* ⟨met several times on the ~⟩ ⟨has to visit him at his home on the ~ —Henry Miller⟩

**qt** *abbr* **1** quantity **2** quart

**qtd** *abbr* quartered

**qtly** *abbr* quarterly

**qto** *abbr* quarto

**qtr** *abbr* quarter; quarterly

**qtrs** *abbr* quarters

**qty** *abbr* quantity

**qtz** *abbr* quartz

**qu** *abbr* **1** quart; quarter; quarterly **2** quasi **3** query **4** question

[1]**qua** \'kwā, 'kwä\ *prep* [L, fr. abl. sing. fem. of *qui* who — more at WHO] **:** in the character, role, or capacity of **:** AS ⟨his business ~ historian —*Modern Language Notes*⟩ ⟨the music ~ music . . . produces an impression of strength —Aaron Copland⟩ ⟨the renouncement of love ~ passion —Wilhelmine Delp⟩ ⟨belief that all men ~ men have certain essential rights —W.K.Frankena⟩ ⟨for art to use geometric forms, ~ geometric forms —Edgar Levy⟩

[2]**qua** \'kwä\ *var of* QUAW

[3]**qua** \'kwä, 'kwò\ *n* -s [imit.] **:** a European night heron

**quabird** \'=,=\ *n* [[3]*qua* + *bird*] **:** BLACK-CROWNED NIGHT HERON

[1]**quack** \'kwak\ *vi* -ED/-ING/-S [imit.] **1 :** to make the characteristic cry of a duck **2 :** to make a noise resembling the cry of a duck

[2]**quack** \"\ *n* -s **1 :** the cry of the duck or a sound in imitation of it **2 :** a hoarse quacking noise ⟨the brisk ~ of the radio —Sinclair Lewis⟩

[3]**quack** \"\ *n* -s [short for *quacksalver*] **1 :** a pretender to medical skill **:** medical charlatan **:** ignorant or dishonest practitioner ⟨one of the most notorious cancer-cure ~s of the day —*Jour. Amer. Med. Assoc.*⟩ **2 :** one who professes skill or knowledge in any matter of which he knows little or nothing **:** CHARLATAN ⟨a ~, both as scientist and as historian —G.W. Johnson⟩ ⟨to distinguish between the expert and the ~ —Walter Moberly⟩

[4]**quack** \"\ *vb* -ED/-ING/-S *vi* **1 :** to make vain and loud pretensions esp. of medical ability **:** play the quack **2 :** to talk pretentiously without sound knowledge of the subject discussed ~ *vt* **:** to make extravagant claims for as a cure-all **:** advertise with fraudulent boasts

[5]**quack** \"\ *adj* **:** relating to or marked by boasting and unfounded pretension **:** used by quacks **:** pretending to cure diseases ⟨a ~ medicine⟩ ⟨a ~ doctor⟩ ⟨~ claims⟩ ⟨~ theology⟩ ⟨~ weather prophet⟩

**quack·ery** \'kwak(ə)rē, -ri\ *n* -ES **:** the practice, methods, or pretensions of a quack **:** CHARLATANRY ⟨religious ~⟩ ⟨political ~⟩ ⟨medical ~⟩ ⟨half-baked thinking which verges close to ~ —Lewis Mumford⟩

**quack grass** *also* **quack** *n* [*quack grass* alter. of *quick grass*; *quack* alter. of [5]*quick*] **:** COUCH GRASS 1a

**quack·ish** \-kish, -kēsh\ *adj* **:** resembling a quack **:** boasting and fraudulent — **quack·ish·ly** *adv* — **quack·ish·ness** *n* -ES

**quack·ism** \-a,kizəm\ *n* -s **:** QUACKERY

[1]**quack·le** \'kwakəl\ *vi* -ED/-ING/-S [imit.] *of a duck* **:** QUACK

[2]**quackle** \"\ *vb* -ED/-ING/-S [imit.] *dial Brit* **:** SUFFOCATE, CHOKE

**quack·sal·ver** \'kwak,salvə(r)\ *n* -s [obs. D *quacksalver* (now *kwakzalver*), fr. MD *quacsalver*, perh. alter. (influenced by MD *quacken, quaken* to quack, croak — of imit. origin — & *salven* to apply salve to, anoint) of *quicsilver* quicksilver; fr. the use of mercury in folk medicine — more at QUICKSILVER, SALVE] **:** CHARLATAN, QUACK

**quacksalving** *adj* [fr. *quacksalver*, after such pairs as E *goer: going*] **:** relating to, characteristic of, or like a quack **:** QUACKISH

**quack·ster** \'kwakstə(r)\ *n* -s [[4]*quack* + *-ster*] **:** QUACK

**quacky** \'kwakē\ *adj* -ER/-EST [[3]*quack* + *-y*] **:** QUACKISH

[1]**quad** \'kwäd *sometimes* 'kwòd\ *var of* QUOD

[2]**quad** \"\ *n* -s [by shortening] **:** QUADRANGLE

[3]**quad** \"\ *n* -s [short for [1]*quadrat*] **:** a block of type metal of the same belly-to-back size as the letters but not as high and ½, 1, 2, or 3 or more ems in width that is used in spacing and blank lines — compare SPACE

[4]**quad** \"\ *vb* **quadded; quadded; quadding; quads** *vt* **:** to fill out (as a typeset line) with quads; *also* **:** to blank out (a line) mechanically in machine composition by using a quadder — often used with *out* ~ *vi* **:** to become quadded ⟨short lines will automatically ~ —*Intertype Streamlined Composing Machines*⟩

[5]**quad** \"\ *adj* [short for [3]*quadruple*] **1 :** being a size of paper four times as large as a specified size ⟨~ royal (40″ x 50″) is four times as large as royal (20″ x 25″)⟩ **2 :** QUADRUPLE ⟨~ cities⟩

[6]**quad** \"\ *n* -s [by shortening] **1 :** QUADRUPLET **2 :** a structural unit of four separately insulated wires twisted together used in cable construction **3 :** an assembly of four units having matched electrical characteristics (as varistors) **4 :** a group of four weapons (as machine guns) on one mount

**quad** *abbr* quadrant

**quad·ded** \-dəd\ *adj* [[6]*quad* + *-ed*] **:** having some wires arranged in quads ⟨a ~ cable⟩

**quad·der** \-ädə(r)\ *n* -s [[4]*quad* + *-er*] **:** a device in a composing machine that permits automatic blanking out of lines (as on each side of centered matter)

**quad·dle** \'kwädᵊl, 'kwòdᵊl\ *n* -s [imit.] *dial Eng* **:** GRUMBLER

**qua·di** \'kwä,dī\ *n pl, usu cap* [L] **:** an ancient Germanic people living between the headwaters of the Oder and the Danube — see HERMINONES

**quadr-** — see QUADRI-

**quad·ra** \'kwädrə\ *n, pl* **quad·rae** \-ä,drē\ [L, square, plinth, fillet; akin to L *quattuor* four] **1 :** the plinth of a pedestal, podium, or water table **2 :** FILLET, LISTEL **3 :** a square frame or border (as about a bas-relief)

[1]**quad·ra·ge·nar·i·an** \,kwädrəjə'na(a)rēən\ *n* -s [L *quadragenarius* of forty, forty years old (fr. *quadrageni* forty each — fr. *quadraginta* forty — + *-arius* -ary) + E *-an*, n. suffix] **:** a person who is 40 or more and less than 50 years old

[2]**quadragenarian** \;===;===\ *adj* **:** 40 or between 40 and 50 years old

**quad·ra·ge·nar·i·ous** \-ēəs\ *adj* [L *quadragenarius*] **:** QUADRAGENARIAN

**qua·drag·e·nary** \(')kwä'drajə,nerē\ *adj* [L *quadragenarius*] **:** based on the number 40

**quad·ra·ges·i·ma** \,kwädrə'jesəmə, -jāzəmə *sometimes* ,kwòd-\ *n* -s *usu cap* [LL, Lent, first Sunday in Lent, fr. L, fem. of *quadragesimus* fortieth, fr. *quadraginta* forty, fr. *quadra-* (akin to L *quattuor* four) + *-ginta* (akin to L *-ginti* in *viginti* twenty) — more at FOUR, VICENARY] **1** *or* **quadragesima sunday :** the first Sunday in Lent **2 :** the 40 days of Lent

**quad·ra·ges·i·mal** \;==;==məl\ *adj* [LL *quadragesimalis*, fr. *quadragesima* + L *-alis* -al] **1** *usu cap* **:** of, relating to, or used in Lent **:** LENTEN **2 :** consisting of 40 — used esp. of a fast (as the Lenten fast) originally lasting for 40 days

**quad·ra·ges·i·mo–oc·ta·vo** \,kwädrə'jesəmō,äk'tā(,)vō\ *n* -s [L *quadragesimo octavo*, abl. of *quadragesimus octavus* forty-eighth, fr. *quadragesimus* fortieth + *octavus* eighth — more at OCTAVE] **:** FORTY-EIGHTMO — symbol *Fe*; see BOOK tables

**quad·ran·gle** \'kwä,draŋgəl, -raiŋ- *sometimes* 'kwò,-\ *n* -s [ME, fr. MF, fr. LL *quadrangulum*, *quadriangulum*, fr. L, neut. of *quadrangulus, quadriangulus*, fr. *quadri-* + *angulus* angle — more at ANGLE] **1 :** a plane figure having four angles and consequently four sides **:** any figure having four angles **2 a :** a square or quadrangular enclosure or court esp. when surrounded by buildings (as in some schools and colleges) **b :** the building or group of buildings enclosing a quadrangle **c :** a building or mass of buildings quadrangular in form **3 :** the tract of country represented by one of the atlas sheets published by the U. S. Geological Survey and measuring in densely populated regions 15′ in latitude by 15′ in longitude mapped on a scale of $\frac{1}{62,500}$ and elsewhere 30′ × 30′ mapped on a scale of $\frac{1}{125,000}$ or 1° × 1° on a scale of $\frac{1}{250,000}$; *also* **:** a sheet representing such a tract ⟨the determination of latitude and longitude is difficult without the possession of a U.S.G.S. ~ (for most small maps lack parallels and meridians) —*Chronica Botanica*⟩ **4** *often cap* **:** a rectangular area on the palm bounded by the lines of Head and Heart and usu. held by palmists to indicate a person's attitude toward others (as broad-mindedness or bigotry) ⟨a star in any portion of the ~ is an excellent sign —Louis Hamon⟩ — **in quadrangle :** placed one in each quarter of the field — used of four heraldic charges

**quad·ran·gled** \-ld\ *adj* [*quadrangle* + *-ed*] **1 :** QUADRANGULAR **2 :** enclosing or having a quadrangle

**qua·dran·gu·lar** \(')kwä'draŋgyələ(r), -raiŋ- *sometimes* (')kwò;-\ *adj* [LL *quadrangularis*, fr. *quadrangulum* quadrangle + L *-aris* -ar] **:** having four angles and consequently four sides **:** TETRAGONAL ⟨the interior structure was composed of a ~ skeleton of stout poles lashed together —*Amer. Anthropologist*⟩ — **qua·dran·gu·lar·ly** *adv*

**quad·rans** \'kwä,dranz\ *n, pl* **quadran·tes** \kwä'dran,tēz\ [L *quadrant-, quadrans*, lit., fourth part] **:** a bronze coin of the Roman republic worth ¼ of an as

[1]**quad·rant** \'kwädrənt *sometimes* 'kwòd-\ *n* -s [ME, fr. L *quadrant-, quadrans* fourth part, quarter; akin to L *quattuor* four — more at FOUR] **1 :** something shaped like a quarter-circle: as **a :** an instrument for measuring altitudes variously constructed and mounted for different specific uses (as in astronomy, surveying, gunnery) and consisting commonly of a graduated arc of 90° with an index or vernier and either plain or telescopic sights and usu. having a plumb line or spirit level for fixing the vertical or horizontal direction **b :** a device resembling a bell crank for converting the horizontal reciprocating motion of an engine piston rod into the vertical up-and-down movement of a pump rod **c :** a dial or an indexing sector of approximate quarter-circle range; *also* **:** a lever that moves over such a range **d :** a device on a spinning mule for controlling the winding of the yarn **2 a :** a quarter of a circle, an arc of 90°, or an arc subtending a right angle at the center **b :** the area bounded by a quadrant and two radii **3 a :** any of the four parts into which a plane is divided by rectangular coordinate axes lying in that plane **b :** any of the four more or less equal parts into which something is divided by two real or imaginary lines that intersect each other at right angles **:** QUARTER ⟨the upper left ~ of a page⟩ ⟨a building in the southeast ~ of the city⟩ ⟨most hurricanes . . . are not symmetrical — the winds are much stronger in some ~s —R.C.Gentry & R.H.Simpson⟩ **c :** a group comprising all the cells resulting from divisions of one of the first four blastomeres in spirally cleaving eggs with determinate cleavage **d :** any of four more or less equivalent segments into which an anatomic structure or surface may be divided by vertical and horizontal partitioning through its midpoint — used chiefly of the abdomen ⟨severe pain in the lower right ~⟩ **e :** the sector between the equisignal zones of a four-course aural radio range

quadrants 2

[2]**quadrant** *adj* [prob. alter. (influenced by [1]*quadrant*) of [1]*quadrate*] *obs* **:** SQUARE, QUADRATE

**qua·dran·tal** \(')kwä;drantᵊl\ *adj* [L *quadrantalis* containing the fourth part of a measure, fr. *quadrant-, quadrans* fourth part + *-alis* -al] **:** of or relating to a quadrant **:** included in or in the shape of a fourth part of a circle ⟨~ open-tiered stand —*Parke-Bernet Galleries Catalog*⟩

**quadrantal correctors** *n pl* **:** two spheres of iron attached to the port and starboard sides of the binnacle to correct the quadrantal deviation

**quadrantal deviation** *n* **:** the part of the compass deviation due to the transient magnetism induced in the horizontal soft iron of a ship by the horizontal component of the earth's magnetism

**quadrantal error** *n* **:** a directional error of a radio compass caused by reradiated fields created around the metallic parts of the airplane

**quadrantal point** *n* **:** INTERCARDINAL

**quadrantal triangle** *n* **:** a spherical triangle with one side equal to a quadrant

**quadrant electrometer** *n* **:** a sensitive electrometer consisting of a needle independently charged and suspended within a flat cylindrical metal box divided into four quadrants, those diametrically opposite being connected to each other and each pair being connected to one of two bodies whose potential difference is to be measured by means of the deflection of the needle toward one pair of quadrants through an angle approximately proportional to the difference of potential

**quadrantes** *pl of* QUADRANS

**quadrant plate** *n* **:** a slotted plate for carrying the change gears of a lathe in any desired position

**quadrants** *pl of* QUADRANT

[1]**quad·rat** \'kwädrət\ *n* -s [alter. of [2]*quadrate*] **1 a :** [3]QUAD **b quadrats** *pl but sing in constr* **:** a game in which printer's quads are thrown like dice **2 :** a small usu. rectangular plot laid off (as in a forest, range, pasture or cultivated field) for the study of vegetation or animals

[2]**quadrat** \"\ *vt* **quadratted; quadratted; quadratting; quadrats :** to lay out (a plot of land) in quadrats **:** divide into quadrats

[1]**quad·rate** \'kwä,drāt, -ädrət *sometimes* 'kwò,-; *usu* -d·+V\ *adj* [ME, fr. L *quadratus*, past part. of *quadrare* to square, make square, fit; akin to L *quattuor* four — more at FOUR] **1 :** square or approximately square in form ⟨a roughened ~ area near the apex —L.F.Edwards⟩ ⟨the ~ masses of the rooftops —G.C.Vaillant⟩ **2** *obs* **:** SQUARE — used of numbers **3** *obs* **a :** SQUARED, BALANCED, CORRESPONDENT **b :** PERFECT, IDEAL **4 :** expanded into a square at the junction of the arms — used of a heraldic cross **5 :** being or relating to a bony or cartilaginous element of each side of the skull to which the lower jaw is articulated in most vertebrates below mammals

[2]**quadrate** \"\ *n* -s [ME, fr. L *quadratum*, fr. neut. of *quadratus*] **1 a :** SQUARE **b :** something more or less resembling a square (as a rectangular space or enclosure) **2 :** an object square or cubical in form or approximately so **3** *obs* **:** the aspect of two celestial bodies that are 90 degrees apart **4 :** a quadrate bone

[3]**quadrate** \-,drāt\ *vb* -ED/-ING/-S [L *quadratus*, past part. of *quadrare*] *vi* **:** SQUARE, AGREE, SUIT, CORRESPOND — usu. used with *with* ~ *vt* **1 :** to make square **:** divide into squares or cubes **2 :** to make accordant **:** cause to conform ⟨are all novels but an imperative that could ~ them would be a little astonishing —Bernard DeVoto⟩

**quadrate lobe** *or* **quadrate lobule** *n* **1 :** PRECUNEUS **2 :** a small lobe of the liver on the under surface of the right lobe to the left of the fissure for the gallbladder

[1]**qua·drat·ic** \(')kwä'drad·|ik, -at|, |ēk *sometimes* (')kwò;-\ *adj* [[2]*quadrate* + *-ic*] **1 :** of, relating to, or resembling a square **:** SQUARE **2 :** having terms of second degree as the highest ⟨a ~ equation is one in which the highest power of the unknown quantity is a square⟩ **3 :** TETRAGONAL ⟨~ system in crystallography⟩

[2]**quadratic** \"\ *n* -s **1 :** a quadratic polynomial or polynomial equation ⟨$3x^2+4x-1=0$ is a ~⟩ **2 qua·drat·ics** \kwä'drad·iks\ *pl but sing or pl in constr* **:** a branch of algebra treating of quadratic equations

**qua·drat·i·cal** \|əkəl\ *adj* [[1]*quadratic* + *-al*] **:** QUADRATIC — **qua·drat·i·cal·ly** \|ək(ə)lē\ *adv*

**quadratic formula** *n* **:** a formula used to solve a quadratic equation in a single variable

**quadratic mean** *n* **:** the square root of the arithmetic mean of the squares of the quantities

[1]**qua·dra·to·jugal** \kwä;drād·ō+\ *adj* [[1]*quadrate* + *-o-* + *jugal*] **1 :** of, relating to, or joining the quadrate and jugal bones **2 :** being a quadratojugal

[2]**quadratojugal** \"\ *n* **:** a small membrane bone that connects the quadrate and jugal bones on each side of the skull in many lower vertebrates

**qua·dra·to·mandibular** \"+\ *adj* [[1]*quadrate* + *-o-* + *mandibular*] **:** relating to the quadrate bone and the lower jaw

**quadrats** *pl of* QUADRAT, *pres 3d sing of* QUADRAT

**quadratted** *past of* QUADRAT

**quadratting** *pres part of* QUADRAT

**quad·ra·ture** \'kwädrəchə(r), -rə,chü(ə)r, -,chüə *sometimes* 'kwòd-\ *n* -s [L *quadratura* act of making square, fr. *quadratus* (past part. of *quadrare* to square) + *-ura* -ure — more at QUADRATE] **1** *obs* **:** square shape; *also* **:** something (as a place or region) square in shape **:** SQUARE, SQUARENESS **2 a :** the act or process of making square or of determining areas; *specif* **:** QUADRATURE OF THE CIRCLE **b :** the process of evaluating integrals **3 a :** a configuration in which two celestial bodies have a separation of 90 degrees ⟨the first quarter moon is in ~ to the sun⟩ **b :** either of two points on an orbit in a middle position between the syzygies **4 a :** a phase difference of one quarter cycle (as that between the currents in a two-phase power-distribution system) **b :** the angular distance between two points on an armature winding separated by one half the pole pitch or 90 electrical degrees

**quadrature of the circle :** a problem in mathematics that consists of finding the side of a square exactly equal in area to a given circular area and that has been shown to be impossible of solution by geometric methods limited to the use of ruler and compass alone

**qua·dra·tus** \kwä'drād·əs, -ātəs\ *n, pl* **quadra·ti** \-ād·,ī, -ā,tī\ [NL, fr. L, past part. of *quadrare* to square] **:** any of several skeletal muscles more or less quadrangular in outline

**quadrel** *n* -s [It *quadrello*, fr. (assumed) VL *quadrellum* building stone — more at QUARREL] **:** a square block (as of brick, tile, plastic)

1**qua·dren·ni·al** \(')kwä¦drenēəl, -nyəl *sometimes* (')kwȯ¦-\ *adj* [alter. of *quadriennial*] **1 :** comprising or lasting through four years ⟨a ~ period⟩ **2 :** occurring once in four years or at the end of every four years ⟨~ elections⟩

2**quadrennial** \"\ *n* -s **1 :** a quadrennial period ⟨a political organization . . . functions not by ~ but by decades and generations —W.A.White⟩ **2 :** a fourth anniversary or its celebration

**quad·ren·ni·al·ly** \-əlē, -li\ *adv* **:** every fourth year ⟨it is the election of the President that unites the scattered elements ~ —W.E.Binkley⟩

**qua·dren·ni·um** \kwä'drenēəm *sometimes* kwȯ'-\ *n, pl* **quadrenniums** \-ēəmz\ *or* **quadren·nia** \-ēə\ [alter. of *quadriennium*] **:** a period of four years

**quadri-** *or* **quadr-** *or* **quadru-** *comb form* [ME, fr. L; akin to L *quattuor* four — more at FOUR] **1 a :** four ⟨*quadri*literal⟩ ⟨*quadru*al⟩ **b :** square ⟨*quadr*ic⟩ **c :** TETRA- ⟨*quadri*basic⟩ **2 :** fourth ⟨*quadri*centennial⟩ **3 :** quadric ⟨*quadri*cone⟩

1**quad·ric** \'kwädrik\ *adj* [ISV *quadr-* + *-ic*] **:** of or relating to the second degree — used where there are more than two variables (as in solid geometry)

2**quadric** \"\ *n* -s **1 :** a quantic of the second degree **2 :** a surface whose equation in Cartesian coordinates is of the second degree

**quadric chain** *or* **quadric crank chain** *n* **:** a chain consisting of four links joined by four turning pairs

**quad·ri·centennial** \¦kwädrə+\ *n* [*quadri-* + *centennial*] **:** a 400th anniversary or anniversary celebration

**quad·ri·ceps** \'kwädrə,seps\ *also* **quadriceps extensor** *or* **quadriceps femoris** *n* -ES [NL *quadricipit-*, *quadriceps*, fr. *quadri-* + *-cipit-*, *-ceps* (as in *bicipit-*, *biceps* biceps)] **:** the great extensor muscle of the front of the thigh divided above into four parts which unite in a single tendon to enclose the patella as a sesamoid bone at the knee and insert as the patellar ligament into the tuberosity of the tibia

**quad·ri·cip·i·tal** \¦==¦sipəd·əl\ *adj* [NL *quadricipit-*, *quadriceps* + E *-al*] **:** of, relating to, or being a quadriceps

**quad·ri·color** \'kwädrə+,-\ *adj* [ISV *quadri-* + *color*] **:** FOUR-COLOR

1**quad·ri·cy·cle** \'kwädrə,sīkəl\ *n* [*quadri-* + *-cycle* (as in *tricycle*)] **1 :** a four-wheeled cycle or velocipede for pedal propulsion on roads or railroads **2 :** a motor vehicle with a live two-wheeled axle, a bicycle seat for the driver, and a two-wheeled forecarriage steered by handlebars

2**quadricycle** \"\ *adj* **:** four-wheeled ⟨a ~ landing gear⟩

**quad·ri·en·ni·al** \¦kwädrə¦enēəl\ *adj* [L *quadriennium* + E *-al*] **:** QUADRENNIAL

**quad·ri·en·ni·um** \,=='enēəm\ *n, pl* **quadrienniums** \-ēəmz\ *or* **quadrien·nia** \-ēə\ [L, fr. *quadri-* + *-ennium* (fr. *annus* year) — more at ANNUAL] **:** QUADRENNIUM

**quadriennium uti·le** \-'yüd·əl,ē\ *n* [ML or NL, lit., four-year period of equity] *Scots law* **:** the period of four years following attainment of majority within which the former minor or in case of his death his executor may act to avoid his contracts, gifts, or conveyances

**quad·ri·fid** \'kwädrə,fid\ *adj* [L *quadrifidus*, fr. *quadri-* + *-fidus* -fid] **:** divided into four parts ⟨a ~ petal⟩

**quad·ri·filar** \¦kwädrə+\ *adj* [*quadri-* + *filar*] **:** four-threaded **:** involving the use of four threads

**quad·ri·form** \'kwädrə,fȯrm\ *adj* [LL *quadriformis*, fr. L *quadri-* + *-formis* -form] **:** having a fourfold form or character

**qua·dri·ga** \kwä'drīgə\ *n, pl* **quadri·gae** \-ī,jē\ [L, back-formation fr. *quadrigae* (pl.) quadriga, contr. of *quadrijugae*, fem. pl. of *quadrijugus* of a team of four, fr. *quadri-* + *jugum* yoke, team — more at YOKE] **:** an ancient Roman car or chariot drawn by four horses abreast together with the horses drawing it; *sometimes* **:** the four horses without the chariot or the chariot alone

**qua·drig·a·mist** \kwä'drigəməst\ *n* -s [*quadri-* + *-gamist* (as in *bigamist*)] **:** one who has married four times **:** one who has four wives or four husbands at the same time

**quad·ri·gem·i·nal bodies** \¦kwädrə¦jemənəl-\ *or* **quad·ri·gem·i·nate bodies** \-mənət-, -mə,nāt-\ *n pl* [*quadrigeminal bodies* fr. *quadrigeminal* (fr. L *quadrigeminus* fourfold — fr. *quadri-* + *geminus* twin — + E *-al*) + *bodies*, pl. of *body; quadrigeminate bodies* fr. *quadrigeminate* (fr. L *quadrigeminus* + E *-ate*) + *bodies;* both intended as trans. of NL *corpora quadragemina* — more at GEMINATE] **:** CORPORA QUADRIGEMINA

1**quad·ri·lat·er·al** \¦kwädrə¦lad·ərəl, -atərəl, -a·trəl *sometimes* ¦kwȯd-\ *adj* [prob. fr. (assumed) NL *quadrilateralis*, fr. L *quadrilaterus* quadrilateral (fr. *quadri-* + *later-*, *latus* side) + *-alis* -al — more at LATERAL] **1 :** having four sides — used esp. of a plane figure **2 :** shared by four parties ⟨~ control by foreign powers⟩

2**quadrilateral** \"\ *n* -s **1 :** a plane figure of four sides and consequently four angles **:** a quadrangular figure **:** a plane figure formed by four lines — see COMPLETE QUADRILATERAL **2 :** something resembling or suggesting a quadrilateral; *specif* **:** an area defended by four fortresses supporting each other

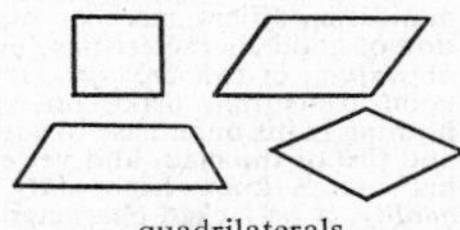

quadrilaterals

**quad·ri·lingual** \¦kwädrə+\ *adj* [*quadri-* + *lingual*] **1 :** using or made up of four languages ⟨a ~ inscription⟩ **2 :** speaking or having knowledge of four languages ⟨a ~ interpreter⟩ — **quad·ri·lin·gual·i·ty** \,kwädrəliŋ'gwaləd·ē\ *n* -ES

1**quad·ri·literal** \¦kwädrə+\ *adj* [*quadri-* + *literal*] **:** consisting of four letters — used esp. of a Semitic root having four consonants instead of three

2**quadriliteral** \"\ *n* -s **:** a word of four letters; *specif* **:** a Semitic quadriliteral root

**qua·dril·lage** \kwä'drilij\ *n* -s [F, fr. *quadrille* lozenge, small square + *-age*] **:** a system of quadrille reference lines on a map ⟨overprinted a network of even kilometer squares upon their maps, in which ~ each line was numbered from a zero point in the southwest of the war zone —Erwin Raisz⟩

1**qua·drille** \kwä'dril, k(w)ə'- *sometimes* kwȯ'-\ *n* -s [F, four-handed form of ombre, group of knights engaging in a carrousel] **:** a four-handed form of ombre popular in the 17th and 18th centuries

2**quadrille** \"\ *n* -s [F, group of knights engaging in a carrousel, troop of cavalry, fr. Sp *cuadrilla* troop, gang, group of horsemen at a tourney — more at CUADRILLA] **1 a :** one of four groups of knights engaging in a tournament or carrousel **b :** CARROUSEL 1a **2 a :** a square dance for four couples that is made up of five or six figures in various rhythms but chiefly in 6/8 and 2/4 time **b :** music for this dance **3 :** CUADRILLA

3**quadrille** \"\ *vi* -ED/-ING/-S **:** to dance a quadrille

4**quadrille** \"\ *adj* [F *quadrillé*, fr. *quadrille* lozenge, small square, group of knights engaging in a carrousel] **1 :** marked with squares or rectangles **:** having or consisting of thin lines crossing at right angles and usu. at equal intervals ⟨~ pattern⟩ ⟨a ~ design⟩ **2 :** crossing at right angles so as to form a quadrille pattern ⟨~ lines⟩ ⟨~ ruling⟩

5**quadrille** \"\ *n* -s **1 :** a quadrille pattern or ruling **2 :** QUADRILLE PAPER

**quad·rilled** \-ld\ *adj* [F *quadrillé* + E *-ed*] **:** QUADRILLE ⟨albums with pages overlaid with faint gray ~ lines —Al Burns⟩

**quadrille paper** *n* **:** paper having quadrille ruling **:** GRAPH PAPER; *specif* **:** laid paper having quadrille watermarks and used esp. for postage stamps

**qua·dril·lion** \kwä'drilyən\ *n* -s *often attrib* [F, fr. MF, fr. *quadri-* + *-illion* (as in *million*)] — see NUMBER table

1**qua·dril·lionth** \-n(t)th\ *adj* **1 :** being number one quadrillion in a countable series — see NUMBER table **2 :** being one of a quadrillion equal parts into which anything is divisible

2**quadrillionth** \"\ *n* -s **:** one of a quadrillion equal parts of anything

**qua·drip·a·rous** \kwä'dripərəs\ *adj* [*quadri-* + *-parous*] **:** having given birth to four children

**quad·ri·par·tite** \¦kwädrə¦pär,tīt\ *adj* [ME, fr. L *quadripartitus*, fr. *quadri-* + *partitus*, past part. of *partire* to divide — more at PART] **1 :** consisting of or divided into four parts ⟨split which causes the chromosome pairs . . . to be actually ~ —C.H.Waddington⟩ **2 :** drawn up in four consecutive parts ⟨~ contract⟩ ⟨~ indenture⟩ **3 :** shared or participated in by four parties or persons ⟨~ government by foreign powers⟩ ⟨a ~ agreement⟩ ⟨~ supervision⟩ **4 :** being a vaulting in which the vault over each rectangle is divided into four parts — **quad·ri·par·tite·ly** *adv*

**quad·ri·par·ti·tion** \,kwädrəpär'tishən\ *n* [L *quadripartition-*, *quadripartitio*, fr. *quadripartitus* quadripartite + *-ion-*, *-io* -ion] **:** division into four parts

**quad·ri·ple·gia** \,kwädrə'plēj(ē)ə\ *n* -s [NL, fr. *quadri-* + *-plegia*] **:** paralysis of both arms and both legs — called also *tetraplegia*

**quad·ri·ple·gic** \-jik\ *n* -s [*quadriplegia* + *-ic*] **:** a person who is paralyzed in both arms and both legs

**quadripole** *var of* QUADRUPOLE

**quad·ri·por·ti·cus** \,kwädrə'pōrd·əkəs\ *also* **quad·ri·por·ti·co** \-də,kō\ *n, pl* **quadriporticuses** [*quadriporticus* fr. LL, fr. L *quadri-* + *porticus* portico; *quadriportico* fr. It, fr. LL *quadriporticus* — more at PORCH] **:** a nearly square atrium surrounded by colonnaded porticoes

**quad·ri·reme** \'kwädrə,rēm\ *n* -s [L *quadriremis*, fr. *quadri-* + *-remis* (fr. *remus* oar) — more at REMI-] **:** a galley with four banks of oars

**quad·ri·sect** \-,sekt\ *vt* -ED/-ING/-S [*quadri-* + *-sect*] **:** to divide into four equal parts

**quad·ri·syllabic** \¦kwädrə+\ *adj* [ISV *quadri-* + *syllabic*] **:** having four syllables **:** of or relating to quadrisyllables

**quad·ri·syllable** \"+\ *n* [*quadri-* + *syllable*] **:** a word of four syllables

1**quad·ri·valent** \"+\ *adj* [ISV *quadri-* + *valent*] **:** TETRAVALENT

2**quadrivalent** \"\ *n* -s **:** a tetravalent chromosome group

**qua·driv·i·al** \kwä'drivēəl\ *adj* [ML *quadrivialis*, fr. LL *quadrivium* + L *-alis* -al] **1 :** of or belonging to the quadrivium **2 :** having four ways or roads meeting in a point; *also* **:** leading in four directions

**qua·driv·i·als** \-lz\ *n pl* **:** the four liberal arts making up the quadrivium

**qua·driv·i·um** \-ēəm\ *n, pl* **quadriv·ia** \-ēə\ [LL, fr. L, crossroads, place where four roads meet, fr. *quadri-* + *via* way, road — more at VIA] **:** a group of studies in the Middle Ages consisting of arithmetic, music, geometry, and astronomy, constituting the higher division of the seven liberal arts, and forming the course for the three years of study between the B.A. and M.A. degrees — compare *trivium*

**quad·ri·vol·tine** \¦kwädrə¦vōl,tēn, -ltən\ *adj* [*quadri-* + *-voltine* (as in *bivoltine*)] **:** producing four generations in one year — used of silkworms

**qua·droon** \(')kwä¦drün *sometimes* (')kwȯ¦-\ *n* -s [alter. (influenced by *quadri-*) of earlier *quarteron*, fr. Sp *cuarterón*, fr. *cuarto* fourth, fr. L *quartus;* akin to L *quattuor* four — more at FOUR] **1 :** the offspring of a mulatto and a white person **:** a person of quarter Negro ancestry **2 :** a person whose racial background resembles that of a quadroon; *esp* **:** one with a quarter aboriginal (as Indian) ancestry

**quadru-** — see QUADRI-

1**quad·ru·al** \'kwädrəwəl\ *adj* [*quadri-* + *-al*] **:** being or relating to forms of pronouns or nouns denoting four (as in certain Austronesian languages) — compare TRIAL

2**quadrual** \"\ *n* -s **1 :** the quadrual number **2 :** a form denoting the quadrual number or a word in that form

**quad·ru·la** \'kwädrələ\ *n, cap* [NL, fr. LL, small square, fr. L *quadra* square + *-ula;* akin to L *quattuor* four] **:** a genus of freshwater mussels (family Unionidae) having a thick shell and often being approximately square in shape — see NIGGERHEAD

**qua·dru·ma·na** \kwä'drümənə\ *n pl* [NL, fr. *quadri-* + *-mana* (fr. L *manus* hand) — more at MANUAL] **:** primates excluding man considered as a group distinguished by hand-shaped feet — compare BIMANA — **qua·dru·ma·nal** \-nəl\ *adj* — **quad·ru·mane** \'kwädrə,mān\ *adj or n*

**qua·dru·ma·nous** \kwä'drümənəs\ *adj* [NL *Quadrumana* + E *-ous*] **1 :** having four hands **2 :** relating to the quadrumana

**qua·drum·vir** \kwä'drəmvə(r)\ *n* -s [back-formation fr. *quadrumvirate*] **:** a member of a quadrumvirate

**qua·drum·vi·rate** \-vərət, -və,rāt\ *n* -s [*quadri-* + *-umvirate* (as in *triumvirate*)] **:** a group or association of four men

1**quad·ru·ped** \'kwädrə,ped *sometimes* 'kwȯd-\ *n* -s [L *quadruped-*, *quadrupes*, fr. *quadruped-*, *quadrupes*, adj., having four feet, fr. *quadri-* + *ped-*, *pes* foot — more at FOOT] **:** an animal having four feet (as most mammals and many reptiles and amphibians) — usu. used of mammals

2**quadruped** \"\ *adj* [L *quadruped-*, *quadrupes*] **:** having four feet **:** QUADRUPEDAL — compare BIPED

**quad·ru·pe·dal** \(')kwä¦drüpədəl, ¦kwädrə¦pedəl\ *adj* [ML *quadrupedalis*, fr. LL, having four metrical feet, fr. L *quadruped-*, *quadrupes* + *-alis* -al] **1 :** having four feet **:** using four limbs in walking **2 :** relating to a quadruped

**quadrupl** *abbr* quadruplicate

**quad·ru·plane** \'kwädrə,plān\ *n* [*quadri-* + *plane*] **:** an airplane with four main supporting surfaces one above another

1**quad·ru·ple** \(')kwä¦drüpəl *also* -rəp- *or* kwə'd- *or* 'kwädrəp- *sometimes* (')kwȯ¦- *or* 'kwȯdrəp-\ *vb* **quadrupled; quadrupled; quadrupling** \-p(ə)liŋ\ **quadruples** [ME (Sc) *quadruplen*, fr. L *quadruplare*, fr. *quadruplus* fourfold, quadruple] *vt* **:** to make four times as much, many, or great ~ *vi* **:** to become four times as much, many, or great

2**quadruple** \"\ *n* -s [MF, fr. *quadruple*, adj.] **1 :** a sum four times as great as another **:** a fourfold amount **:** the fourth multiple **2** *obs* **:** a coin worth four pistoles

3**quadruple** \"\ *adj* [MF or L; MF *quadruple*, fr. L *quadruplus*, fr. *quadri-* + *-plus* multiplied by — more at DOUBLE] **1 :** consisting of four **:** being four times as great or as many **:** FOURFOLD **2 :** taken by fours or in groups of four; *specif* **:** having four beats per measure ⟨~ time⟩ ⟨~ rhythm⟩

**quadruple amputee** *n* **:** a person who has lost all or part of both legs and both arms

**quadruple counterpoint** *n* **:** four-part counterpoint in which the parts are interchangeable without violating contrapuntal rules

**quad·ru·ple·ness** *n* -ES **:** the quality or state of being quadruple

**quadruple point** *n* **:** a point representing a set of conditions under which four phases of a physical-chemical system can exist in equilibrium

**quadruple star** *n* **:** four stars appearing as one

**quad·rup·let** \(')kwä¦drəplət, kwə'd-, -rüp-, 'kwäd- *sometimes*

quadruplet 3

'kwä,drəp- *or* (')kwȯ¦- *or* 'kwȯd-; *usu* -əd·+V\ *n* -s [fr. 3*quadruple*, after such pairs as E *double: doublet*] **1 a :** one of four children or offspring born at one birth **b quadruplets** *pl* **:** a group of four offspring born at one birth **2 :** a combination of four of a kind **3 :** a group of four musical notes to be performed in the time ordinarily given to three of the same kind **4 :** a bicycle for four riders

**quadruple thread** *n* **:** four equal threads any point of each of which at any right section is one quarter of a circumference in advance of the corresponding point of the next succeeding thread — compare DOUBLE THREAD

**quad·ru·plex** \'kwädrə,pleks\ *adj* [L *quadruplic-*, *quadruplex* fourfold, fr. *quadri-* + *-plic-*, *-plex* — more at SIMPLE **:** being or relating to a system of telegraphy by which two messages in each direction may be sent simultaneously over one wire

1**qua·dru·pli·cate** \(')kwä¦drüplәkәt, kwə'd-, -plēk- *sometimes* (')kwȯ¦- *or* -lə,kāt, *usu* -d·+V\ *adj* [L *quadruplicatus*, past part. of *quadruplicare*] **1 :** made in four identical copies **:** FOURFOLD **2 :** FOURTH — used of one of a set of printed copies ⟨the duplicate and triplicate copies . . . transmitted to the court to which the petition is to be transferred, and the ~ copy transmitted to the district director —*U. S. Code*⟩

2**qua·dru·pli·cate** \-lə,kāt, *usu* -ād·+V\ *vt* -ED/-ING/-S [L *quadruplicatus*, past part. of *quadruplicare*, fr. *quadruplic-*, *quadruplex*] **:** to multiply by four **:** QUADRUPLE **:** reproduce thrice; *specif* **:** to make at one time an original and three carbon copies of

3**qua·dru·pli·cate** \-ləkət, -lēkət *sometimes* -lə,kāt, *usu* -d·+V\ *n* -s [1*quadruplicate*] **1 :** a fourth thing like three others of the same kind **2 :** four copies all alike — used with *in* ⟨typed in ~⟩

**qua·dru·pli·ca·tion** \kwä,drüplə'kāshən\ *n* -s [LL *quadruplication-*, *quadruplicatio*, fr. L *quadruplicatus* (past part. of *quadruplicare*) + *-ion-*, *-io* -ion] **1 :** the act, process, or result of quadrupling **2** [ML *quadruplication-*, *quadruplicatio* (influenced in meaning by LL *replication-*, *replicatio* reply), fr. LL, act of quadrupling — more at REPLICATION] **:** a rebuttal pleading of the respondent or libelee corresponding to a common law rebutter with the original exception or answer having been followed by the replication or reply, duplication or rejoinder, triplication or surrejoinder

**quad·ru·plic·i·ty** \,kwädrə'plisəd·ē\ *n* -ES [fr. 3*quadruple*, after E *simple: simplicity*] **:** the state of being quadruple

**quad·ru·ply** \'kwädrəplē\ *adv* **:** in a quadruple manner

**quad·ru·pole** *also* **quad·ri·pole** \'kwädrə,pōl\ *n* [ISV *quadri-* + *pole*] **:** a system composed of two electric dipoles of equal but oppositely directed electric moment

**quads** *pl of* QUAD, *pres 3d sing of* QUAD

**quae·re** \'kwirē\ *n* -s [L, imper. of *quaerere* to seek, ask] *archaic* **:** QUERY, QUESTION ⟨the great ~ is, when he will come again —Thomas Browne⟩

**quae·si·tum** \kwē'sīd·əm\ *n, pl* **quaesi·ta** \-d·ə\ [L, neut. of *quaesitus*, past part. of *quaerere* to seek, ask] **1 :** something sought for **:** END, OBJECTIVE ⟨our intuition that one of the ideas . . . is, at last, our ~ —William James⟩ **2 :** the true or actual value of a quantity — compare ERROR 5a

**quaes·tio** \'kwīstē,ō\ *n, pl* **quaes·ti·o·nes** \,=='ō,nās\ [L *quaestion-*, *quaestio* question, quaestio — more at QUESTION] **1 :** a criminal inquisition or trial under Roman law **2** *quaestiones pl* **:** the commissions for the trial of various offenses under Roman law or the proceedings before such commissions; *also* **:** criminal courts or tribunals

**quaes·tor** *or* **ques·tor** \'kwestə(r), 'kwēs-\ *n* -s [ME *questor*, fr. L *quaestor*, fr. *quaesitus*, *quaestus* (past part. of *quaerere* to seek, ask) + *-or*] **1 a :** any of various Roman officials in charge of public monies (as a treasurer of state or paymaster of troops) **b :** a public judge or prosecutor in a criminal trial in early Rome **2** [ME *questor*, fr. ML, fr. L *quaestor*] **:** an agent of a pope or bishop appointed formerly as a public preacher, charged with the mission of collecting alms, and authorized to grant indulgences to those contributing **3** [modif. (influenced by L *quaestor*) of F *questeur*, fr. L *quaestor*] **:** QUESTEUR

**quaes·to·ri·al** \kwe'stōrēəl, kwē'-, -tȯr-\ *adj* [L *quaestorius* quaestorial (fr. *quaestor* + *-ius* -ious) + E *-al*] **:** of or relating to a quaestor or a quaestorship

**quaes·tor·ship** \'kwestə(r),ship, 'kwēs-\ *n* **:** the office of quaestor

1**quaes·tu·ary** \'kwes(h)chə,werē, 'kwēs-\ *adj* [MF *questuaire*, fr. LL *quaestuarius*, fr. L *quaestus* way of making money, trade, gain, profit (fr. *quaestus*, past part. of *quaerere* to seek, gain, ask) + *-arius* -ary] *archaic* **:** interested in or undertaken for monetary gain or profit ⟨this may be termed the ~ class, this being the end which they aim at —J.F.Ferrier⟩

2**quaestuary** *n* -ES [ML *questuarius*, fr. *questuarius*, adj., of the collection of alms, fr. LL *quaestuarius*] *obs* **:** QUAESTOR 2

1**quaff** \'kwäf, 'kwaf, 'kwaa(ə)f, 'kwaif, 'kwȧf\ *vb* -ED/-ING/-S [origin unknown] *vi* **:** to drink freely or copiously; *specif* **:** to drink an intoxicating beverage in such a manner ⟨holding our glasses, we ~*ed*, and we sat down —Emily Hahn⟩ ~ *vt* **1 :** to drink (a beverage or liquid) freely or copiously ⟨was aghast to see citizens ~*ing* a brew as an eye-opener —Horace Sutton⟩ *specif* **:** to swallow (a drink) in large drafts ⟨I ~*ed* a cocktail without flinching —Oscar Wilde⟩ **2 :** to affect in a specified way by drinking ⟨~*ed* himself into drowsiness⟩

2**quaff** \"\ *n* -s **:** a drink quaffed ⟨each guest having taken a ~ of ale —G.R.Gissing⟩

**quaff·er** \-fə(r)\ *n* -s **:** one that quaffs

**quaff·ing·ly** *adv* [*quaffing* (pres. part. of 1*quaff*) + *-ly*] **:** in a free, copious, or bibulous manner

1**quag** \'kwag, 'kwaa(ə)g, 'kwäg, 'kwaig\ *n* -s [origin unknown] **:** MARSH, BOG, QUAGMIRE ⟨the feet of the horse that slopped through sandy ~*s* —Elizabeth M. Roberts⟩

2**quag** \"\ *vi* **quagged; quagged; quagging; quags** [prob. imit.] *archaic* **:** QUAKE, QUIVER, SHAKE

**quag·ga** \'kwagə\ *n, pl* **quaggas** *also* **quagga** [obs. Afrik *quagga* (now *kwagga*), prob. of Bantu origin; akin to Xhosa *i-qwara* something striped or speckled, Zulu *qwara*] **:** a wild ass (*Equus quagga*) of southern Africa related to the zebras but having its upper parts striped reddish brown, the posterior part plain grayish brown, and the belly and legs whitish, the ears smaller and the tail more heavily haired than in most asses and zebras

**quag·gy** \'kwagē, 'kwaagē, 'kwägē, 'kwaigē, -gi\ *adj* -ER/-EST [1*quag* + *-y*] **1 :** having the characteristics of a quagmire **:** BOGGY, MARSHY **2 :** characterized by flabbiness **:** SOFT, YIELDING

1**quagmire** \'kwag,mī(ə)r, 'kwaag-, 'kwäg-, 'kwaig-, -mīə\ *n* [1*quag* + *mire*] **1 a :** soft wet miry land that shakes or yields under the foot ⟨the tamarack swamp . . . was too big and filled with bogs and ~*s* —Howard Troyer⟩ **b :** a usu. dry area of land converted into an expanse of soft wet ground by heavy rain or flooding ⟨a trampled ~ of mud under the never-ceasing downpour —G.R.Stewart⟩ ⟨rain had turned the prairie trails into ~*s* —Lyn Harrington⟩ **2 :** something flabby, soft, or yielding ⟨foggy ~*s* of fat and dropsy —Thomas Brown⟩ **3 :** a complex or precarious position where disengagement is difficult ⟨from a ~ of false nonsense to a firm island of reality —John Baker⟩ ⟨a ~ of perplexing problems —Fletcher Pratt⟩ ⟨sunk to the ears in a ~ of tedium and indifference —Claud Cockburn⟩ ⟨bogged down in the ~ of mediocrity —F.C.Neff⟩ ⟨lost in ~*s* of negotiation⟩

2**quagmire** \"\ *vt* -ED/-ING/-S **:** to ensnare in or as if in a quagmire ⟨a man is never ~*ed* till he stops —W.S.Landor⟩

**quag·miry** \-īrē\ *adj* -ER/-EST **:** resembling or consisting of a quagmire **:** QUAGGY ⟨a most hideous swamp, so thick with bushes and so ~ —John Winthrop⟩

1**qua·hog** *also* **qua·haug** *or* **quo·hog** *or* **quo·haug** \'kwȯ,hȯg, 'k(w)ō,-, -,häg\ *n* -s *often attrib* [Narraganset *poquaûhock*, fr. *pohkeni* dark, closed + *hogki* shell] **1 :** a thick-shelled American clam (*Mercenaria mercenaria*) — called also *round clam* **2 :** a north Atlantic clam (*Cyprina islandica*) with a blackish brown periostracum — called also *black quahog*

2**quahog** *also* **quahaug** \"\ *vi* **quahogged** *or* **quahauged; quahogged** *or* **quahauged; quahogging** *or* **quahauging; quahogs** *or* **quahaugs :** to seek or dig quahogs

**qua·hog·ger** *or* **qua·haug·er** \-gə(r)\ *n* -s **:** one that digs, gathers, or drags for quahogs

**quai** \'kā\ *n* -s [F — more at QUAY] **:** QUAY; *esp* **:** one lying along the river Seine in Paris

**quaich** *or* **quaigh** \'kwāk\ *n, pl* **quaichs** *or* **quaiches** *or* **quaighs** [ScGael *cuach*] *chiefly Scot* **:** a small shallow vessel or drinking cup typically made of wood, pewter, or silver and having ears for use as handles

quaich

1**quail** \'kwāl, *esp before pause or consonant* -āəl\ *n, pl* **quail** *or* **quails** [ME *quaile*, *quaille*, fr. MF *quaille*, fr. ML *quaccula*, of imit. origin] **1 a** (1) **:** a migratory gallinaceous game bird (*Coturnix coturnix* syn. *C. communis*) of Europe, Asia, and Africa that is about seven inches long and has the upper parts brown and black marked with buff, the throat black and white, the breast reddish buff, and the belly whitish (2) : any of various other birds of the genus *Coturnix* chiefly inhabiting eastern Asia, southern Africa, India, or Australia **b** : any of various small American game birds of the order Galliformes: as (1) : BOBWHITE (2) : any of various birds related to the bobwhite — often used in combination ⟨California ~⟩ ⟨mountain ~⟩ ⟨valley ~⟩ — see MASSENA QUAIL **c** : BUTTON QUAIL **2 a** *obs* : COURTESAN **b** *slang* : a young woman or girl; *specif* : one attending a coeducational institution **3** : HAIR BROWN

**²quail** \"\ *vb* -ED/-ING/-S [ME *quailen*, fr. MF *quailler*, fr. L *coagulare* — more at COAGULATE] *vi* **1** *dial chiefly Eng* : CURDLE, COAGULATE **2** *chiefly dial* **a** : to waste away : WITHER, DECLINE ⟨length of time causeth man and beast to ~ —Thomas Howell⟩ **b** : to break down : give way : WITHER ⟨the religion . . . ~*ing* into abject superstition —H.H.Milman⟩ **3** : to lose courage : become cowed or fearful : WEAKEN ⟨eminent men invariably ~*ed* before him —Bertrand Russell⟩ ⟨no wonder his enemies ~*ed* —Stringfellow Barr⟩ ⟨the strongest ~ before financial ruin —Samuel Butler †1902⟩ ~ *vt* **1** *obs* : to affect harmfully : SPOIL, WASTE, WITHER **2** *archaic* : to make fearful : COW, DAUNT ⟨as thunder ~*s* the inferior creatures —John Wilson †1854⟩ **syn** see RECOIL

**³quail** \"\ *dial Eng var of* COIL

**quail·berry** \ˈkwā(ə)l- — *see* BERRY\ *n* : WOLFBERRY 1

**quail brush** *n* **1** : any of various mountain mahoganies of the western U. S. **2** *also* **quail bush** : a spiny shrub (*Atriplex lentiformis*) that has scurfy foliage and is found on the alkali plains of the southwestern U. S. and adjacent Mexico

**quail call** *or* **quail pipe** *n* [*quail call* fr. ¹*quail* + *call*; *quail pipe* fr. ME *quaile pipe*, fr. *quaile* quail + *pipe*] : a call or pipe imitating the characteristic note of a quail for the purpose of luring the birds into a net or within range

**quail disease** *n* : an ulcerative enteritis of quails, turkeys, or other birds

**quail dove** *n* : any of various tropical American pigeons of terrestrial habits of the genera *Geotrygon, Oreopeleia,* and *Starnoenas* several of which occur in the West Indies and on the Florida Keys

**quail hawk** *n* **1** : BUSH HAWK **2** : COOPER'S HAWK

**quailhead** \ˈ=,=\ *n* [so called fr. the similarity of its head markings to those of a quail] : LARK SPARROW

**quail snipe** *n* **1** : DOWITCHER **2** : SEED SNIPE

**quaily** \ˈkwālē\ *n* -ES [¹*quail* + -*y*] : UPLAND PLOVER

**¹quaint** \ˈkwānt\ *adj* -ER/-EST [ME *queinte, cointe*, fr. OF *cointe* expert, elegant, fr. L *cognitus*, past part. of *cognoscere* to become acquainted with, know — more at COGNITION] **1** *obs* **a** : marked as cunning, scheming, crafty, artful, or wily ⟨the ~ smooth rogue —Thomas Otway⟩ **b** : characterized by knowledge, skill, or learning; *esp* : skilled in the use of language ⟨how ~ an orator —Shak.⟩ **2 a** : characterized by cleverness or ingenuity : skillfully wrought or artfully contrived ⟨the arming of each joint, in every piece how neat and ~ —Michael Drayton⟩ ⟨~ with many a device in India ink —Herman Melville⟩ ⟨set in the close-grained wood were ~ devices —Amy Lowell⟩ **b** : marked by beauty or elegance of appearance : HANDSOME ⟨a body so fantastic, trim, and ~ in its deportment and attire —William Cowper⟩ ⟨the ~, powerful simplicity which sculptors sometimes had —Nathaniel Hawthorne⟩ **c** : marked by ingenuity or refinement of language ⟨a new thought or conceit dressed up in smooth ~ language —Richard Steele⟩ **3 a** (1) : unusual or different in character or appearance : ODD, STRANGE ⟨came forth a ~ and fearful sight —Sir Walter Scott⟩ ⟨my stroll was marked . . . by only one ~ happening —William Beebe⟩ (2) : so unusual or different as to be bizarre, eccentric, or incongruous ⟨the head terminating in the ~ duck bill which gives the animal its vernacular name —Bill Beatty⟩ ⟨this horse . . . with so many ~ points and characteristics —Johnston Forbes-Robertson⟩ **b** : uncommon, old-fashioned, or unfamiliar but often agreeable or attractive in character, appearance, or action : PICTURESQUE ⟨a vaulted roof supporting a ~ chimney, much admired —Aubrey Drury⟩ ⟨dresses with a ~ old-fashioned elegance —*Current Biog.*⟩ ⟨a ~ pronunciation of English words that delighted her listeners —C.B.Nordhoff & J.N.Hall⟩ ⟨to make our present knowledge seem incomplete and ~ —Alan Gregg⟩ **c** : affectedly or artificially unfamiliar, old-fashioned, or picturesque ⟨a tendency to be a little too ~ —Jerome Stone⟩ ⟨they appeal to tourists as ~ —C.K.Kluckhohn⟩ ⟨the summer folk . . . left the land to the ~ natives —W. G.O'Donnell⟩ **4** *obs* : overly discriminating or needlessly meticulous : FASTIDIOUS ⟨being too ~ and finical in his expression —Roger L'Estrange⟩ **5** : highly incongruous, inappropriate, or illogical : NAIVE, UNREASONABLE — usu. used ironically ⟨out of a ~ sense of honesty —Paul Engle⟩ ⟨the ~ notion that a speaker should be heard as well as understood —H.F. & Katharine Pringle⟩ ⟨~ notion that it is a writer's business to write —J.K.Hutchens⟩ **syn** see STRANGE

**²quaint** \"\ *vb* [ME *coynten, quainten*, short for *acoynten, aquainten* to acquaint — more at ACQUAINT] *chiefly dial* : ACQUAINT

**quaint·ish** \-tish\ *adj* : marked somewhat by quaintness

**quaint·ly** *adv* [ME *queinteliche, queintely*, fr. *queinte* quaint + -*liche*, -*ly* -ly] : in a quaint manner

**quaint·ness** *n* -ES [ME *queyntnesse*, fr. *queynt, queinte* quaint + -*nes*, -*nesse* -ness] : the quality or state of being quaint

**quais** *pl of* QUAI

**quait** \ˈkwāt\ *dial var of* QUOIT

**¹quake** \ˈkwāk\ *vb* -ED/-ING/-S [ME *quaken*, fr. OE *cwacian*; akin to OE *cweccan* to shake, vibrate] *vi* **1 a** : to shake, vibrate, or tremble usu. from shock or convulsion ⟨boughs that ~*ed* at every breath —Sir Walter Scott⟩ ⟨ample bosom *quaked* mirthfully —Gerald Beaumont⟩ ⟨the earth *quaked* as if it had been struck a fantastic blow —Robert O'Brien⟩ **b** : to shake or shiver from the cold or other physical cause ⟨~ in the present winter's state, and wish that warmer days would come —Shak.⟩ ⟨with legs *quaking* —E.K.Kane⟩ **2** : to tremble or shudder inwardly often in anticipation of difficulty or danger : QUAIL ⟨my heart did never ~, or courage faint —Christopher Marlowe⟩ ⟨it was a bold thing to say, and I *quaked* —Winston Churchill⟩ ~ *vt*, *obs* : to cause to quake ⟨humble and ~ us for our sins —Henry Greenwood⟩

**²quake** \"\ *n* -S [ME, fr. *quaken*, v.] **1** : an instance of shaking or trembling : a tremulous agitation or convulsion **2** : something that causes quaking; *esp* : EARTHQUAKE

**quake grass** *n* **1** : QUAKING GRASS **2** : COUCH GRASS 1a

**quake ooze** *n* : soft boggy ground : MARSH

**quakeproof** \ˈ=,=\ *adj* : able to withstand damage or destruction by an earthquake

**¹quak·er** \ˈkwākə(r)\ *n* -S *often attrib* [¹*quake* + -*er*] **1** : one that quakes **2** *usu cap* : FRIEND 6 **3 a** (1) : an Australian night heron (*Nycticorax caledonicus*) (2) : the sooty albatross **b** : a grasshopper or locust of the genus *Oedipoda* **c** *or* **quaker moth** : any of several English noctuid moths (as *Graphiphora castanea*) **4** *often cap* : ART GRAY **5** : QUAKER GUN **6** *or* **quaker aspen** : ASPEN **7** *cap* : PENNSYLVANIAN — used as a nickname **8** : an immature or blighted coffee bean found in inferior grades of coffee — usu. used in pl.

**²quaker** \"\ *vi* [freq. of ¹*quake*] *dial Brit* : QUAKE

**quakerbird** \ˈ==,=\ *n* : SOOTY ALBATROSS

**quaker blue** *n*, *often cap Q* : a nearly neutral slightly bluish black that is lighter and slightly redder than lampblack

**quaker bonnet** *n*, *usu cap Q* : BLUET 1c(1)

**quak·er·dom** \ˈkwākə(r)dəm\ *n* -S *usu cap* : QUAKERISM

**quaker drab** *n*, *often cap Q* : a nearly neutral slightly purplish medium gray that is very slightly redder than frost gray

**quak·er·ess** \-kərəs\ *n* -ES *usu cap* : a female Quaker

**quaker gray** *n*, *often cap Q* : a light grayish olive color that is greener and paler than hemp, lighter than twine, and redder and darker than average citron gray — called also *acier, gray drab*

**quaker green** *n*, *often cap Q* : a moderate olive green that is yellower, stronger, and slightly lighter than forest green (sense 2), yellower, lighter, and stronger than cypress green, and stronger than Lincoln green

**quaker gun** *n*, *usu cap Q* [so called fr. the Friends' opposition to war] : a dummy piece of artillery that is usu. made of wood

**quak·er·ish** \-kərish\ *adj*, *usu cap* : similar to or having the characteristics of a Friend ⟨~ tidiness of her black dress and white collar —Ngaio Marsh⟩ ⟨~ notions —Frederick Chase⟩

**quak·er·ism** \-kə,rizəm\ *n* -S *usu cap* : the religious beliefs or practices of the Friends

**quaker-ladies** \ˈ==,==\ *n pl*, *often cap Q* : BLUETS

**quak·er·ly** *adj*, *usu cap* : of, relating to, or characteristic of a Friend : QUAKERISH ⟨~ meditation⟩

**quaker meeting** *n*, *usu cap Q* **1** : a society or congregation of Friends **2 a** : a meeting of Friends for worship in which prolonged periods of silence often occur **b** : a social gathering marked by little or no conversation or by conversation with long pauses

**quakes** *pres 3d sing of* QUAKE, *pl of* QUAKE

**quaketail** \ˈ=,=\ *n* : YELLOW WAGTAIL

**quak·i·ness** \ˈkwākēnəs\ *n* -ES : the quality or state of being quaky

**quak·ing** \ˈkwākiŋ, -kēŋ\ *adj* [ME, fr. pres. part. of *quaken* to quake] **1** : SHAKING, VIBRATING, TREMBLING **2** *usu cap* : QUAKERISH — **quak·ing·ly** *adv*

**quaking aspen** *also* **quaking ash** *or* **quaking asp** *n* : ASPEN

**quaking bog** *n* : a bog of forming peat that is wholly or partially floating and that shakes when walked on

**quaking grass** *n* **1** : any of several grasses of the genus *Briza* having slender-stalked and pendulous ovate spikelets that quake and rattle in the wind **2** : RATTLESNAKE GRASS

**quaky** \ˈkwākē\ *adj* -ER/-EST [¹*quake* + -*y*] : QUAKING, SHAKY, TREMBLING

**qual** *abbr* **1** qualification; qualified; qualify **2** qualitative; quality

**qua·le** \ˈkwālē\ *n*, *pl* **qua·lia** \-ēə\ [L, neut. sing. of *qualis* of what kind — more at QUALITY] **1 a** : a quality that is an independent object ⟨establish . . . the vague form or ~ of spatiality —William James⟩ **b** : something that has a quality ⟨could never adjust ourselves to a universe in which we saw *qualia* or data but never objects —Campbell Crockett⟩ **2** : a sense-datum or feeling having its own particular quality without meaning or external reference ⟨a ~ . . . such as, say, a certain shade of purple occurring in the presentation of a certain piece of cloth in a particular light —C.G.Hempel⟩

**qual·i·fi·ca·tion** \,kwäləfəˈkāshən *sometimes* ,kwȯl-\ *n* -S [ML *qualification-, qualificatio*, fr. *qualificatus* (past part. of *qualificare* to qualify) + L -*ion-*, -*io* -ion — more at QUALIFY] **1** : something that qualifies or restricts : LIMITATION, MODIFICATION ⟨~*s* amounting . . . to correctives —V.C.Aldrich⟩ ⟨the statement stands without ~⟩ **2 a** *obs* : distinctive character : NATURE ⟨the English tradesman . . . his ~ —Daniel Defoe⟩ **b** *archaic* : CHARACTERISTIC, TRAIT ⟨the ~*s* of the . . . nation —Joseph Addison⟩ **c** *archaic* : a specific capacity or attainment : ACCOMPLISHMENT ⟨every ~ is raised . . . to more than its true value —Jane Austen⟩ **3 a** : an endowment or acquirement that fits a person (as for an office) ⟨a person of outstanding ~*s* —*U.S. Code*⟩ ⟨physical ~*s* for pilots —H.G.Armstrong⟩ **b** : a condition precedent that must be complied with (as for the attainment of a privilege) ⟨residence ~*s* for membership —F.A.Ogg & P.O.Ray⟩

**¹qual·i·fi·ca·tive** \ˈkwäləfə,kād·iv\ *n* -S [ML *qualificatus* (past part. of *qualificare*) + E -*ive*, n. suffix] : a qualifying word ⟨~*s* . . . to describe the kinds of historical relationships —D.M.Taylor⟩

**²qualificative** \"\ *adj* [ML *qualificatus* (past part. of *qualificare*) + E -*ive*, adj. suffix] : QUALIFYING ⟨the ~ concords in four languages —Guy Atkins⟩

**qual·i·fi·ca·tor** \-d·ə(r)\ *n* -S [ML, fr. *qualificatus* (past part. of *qualificare*) + L -*or*] : an officer whose business it is to examine and prepare causes for trial in the ecclesiastical courts of the Roman Catholic Church

**qual·i·fi·ca·tory** \ˈkwäləfəkə,tōrē\ *adj* [ML *qualificatus* (past part. of *qualificare*) + E -*ory*] : QUALIFYING, LIMITING

**qualified** *adj* **1 a** : fitted (as by endowments or accomplishments) for a given purpose : COMPETENT, FIT ⟨~ to govern the country —G.B.Shaw⟩ ⟨poorly ~ officers —*Magazine Intelligence*⟩ **b** : having complied with the specific requirements or precedent conditions (as for an office or employment) : ELIGIBLE, CERTIFIED ⟨~ by age and residence to run for the office⟩ ⟨lacks two credits of being fully ~⟩ **2** *obs* **a** : having certain qualities; *esp* : possessed of good qualities : ACCOMPLISHED ⟨the fine ~ gentleman —Thomas Nash⟩ **b** : belonging to the aristocracy ⟨not ~ but . . . common and ordinary persons —Andrew Willet⟩ **3** : limited or modified in some way ⟨properly ~ conclusions —W.J.Reilly⟩ ⟨the author's outlook . . . is one of ~ optimism —P.B.Sears⟩; *specif* : modified by the attachment of conditions ⟨a ~ acceptance of a bill of exchange⟩ **syn** see ABLE

**qualified endorsement** *n* : an endorsement passing title to a commercial paper but disclaiming liability of the indorser should the party primarily liable fail to pay when due

**qualified fee** *n* : a defeasible estate in fee that may come to an end (as for breach of a condition or on account of an executory limitation on a stated event); *specif* : a base or determinable fee simple — compare FEE SIMPLE CONDITIONAL

**qual·i·fied·ly** *adv* : in a qualified manner

**qual·i·fied·ness** *n* -ES : the quality or state of being qualified

**qualified privilege** *n* : a privilege that arises and is available in the law of libel and slander when there are facts justifying the statement written or spoken but that may not be available when the words are uttered with malice or without good faith — compare ABSOLUTE PRIVILEGE

**qualified property** *n* **1** : ownership that is not absolute and complete **2** : property the subject matter of which by nature is not permanent (as wild animals reduced to possession but not in captivity)

**qual·i·fi·er** \ˈkwälə,fī(ə)r, -īə *sometimes* ˈkwȯl-\ *n* -S **1** : one that qualifies: as **a** : one that satisfies requirements or meets a specified standard (as of performance in an athletic contest) ⟨paced the ~*s* . . . in the trial heats —*N.Y. Times*⟩ **b** : a word (as an adjective or adverb) or word group that qualifies or restricts another word or word group ⟨resolved never to use a ~ again when . . . reviewing a book —Harvey Breit⟩ **2** : QUALIFICATOR

**¹qual·i·fy** \-fī\ *vb* -ED/-ING/-ES [MF *qualifier*, fr. ML *qualificare*, fr. L *qualis* of what kind + -*ficare* -fy — more at QUALITY] *vt* **1 a** : to reduce from a general, undefined, or comprehensive to a particular or restricted form : MODIFY, LIMIT ⟨statements were explained and *qualified* in the author's lectures —H.O.Taylor⟩ **b** : to make less harsh or strict : MODERATE, SOFTEN ⟨time *qualifies* the spark and fire —Shak.⟩ ⟨the power to regulate commerce could not be cut down or *qualified* —O.W.Holmes †1935⟩ **c** *obs* : to maintain in proper condition : CONTROL **d** : to alter the strength or flavor of (a liquid) ⟨coffee *qualified* with cognac⟩ ⟨an infusion useful to ~ the rest —Havelock Ellis⟩ **e** : to limit or modify the meaning of (as a noun or verb or adjective) **2** : to characterize by naming an attribute : DESCRIBE, DESIGNATE ⟨cannot ~ it as . . . either glad or sorry —T.S.Eliot⟩ **3 a** : to give the required qualities to : fit esp. for an office or privilege ⟨his skills ~ him for the job⟩ ⟨the cisterns ~ the farms for a Class A . . . rating —Don Cunnion⟩ **b** *obs* : to endow with qualities ⟨a mind excellently *qualified* —Robert Greene⟩ **c** (1) : to declare competent or adequate as meeting set standards : CERTIFY ⟨~ every candidate who can meet the requirements —H.G. Armstrong⟩ ⟨certificates . . . ~*ing* their meat —S.N.Behrman⟩ (2) : to invest (a person) with legal capacity : LICENSE ⟨*qualified* to practice law in this state⟩ (3) : to give legal power to by administering an oath : swear in ⟨~ a jury⟩ ~ *vi* **1** : to become fit (as for an employment) : become capable : measure up to or meet a set standard or requirement ⟨expects to ~ for the position⟩ ⟨*qualifies* as a complete man of letters —Selden Rodman⟩ ⟨approved land drainage *qualifies* for a government grant —F.D.Smith & Barbara Wilcox⟩ **2** : to obtain legal or competent power or capacity by taking oath or giving bond or complying with the necessary forms or conditions ⟨*qualifies* by court order as an executor —R.B.Gehman⟩ ⟨have just *qualified* as barristers —*Brit. Book News*⟩ **3 a** : to exhibit in a game or sport a required degree of ability in one or more preliminary contests (as heats in a race or rounds in a golf tournament) **b** : to fire a score that makes one eligible for the award of a marksmanship badge **syn** see MODERATE, PREPARE

**²qualify** \"\ *n* -ES : a gambling game played with five dice usu. for merchandise or small cash prizes in which the caster tries in five rolls to amass as many as possible of as high a number as possible

**qualifying** *adj* : that qualifies — **qual·i·fy·ing·ly** *adv*

**qualifying heat** *or* **qualifying round** *or* **qualifying game** *n* : a preliminary contest (as in a race or tournament) the winner of which may enter the final contest

**qual·i·ta·tive** \ˈkwälə,tād·iv, -ät|, |ēv *also* |əv *sometimes* ˈkwȯl-\ *adj* [LL *qualitativus*, fr. L *qualitat-, qualitas* + -*ivus* -ive] : of, relating to, or involving quality or kind ⟨~ change⟩ ⟨~ data⟩ — contrasted with *quantitative* — **qual·i·ta·tive·ly** \|əvlē, -li\ *adv*

**qualitative analysis** *n* : a branch of chemistry whose scope is to detect and characterize the elements or radicals in a pure substance or to identify the components of a mixture — compare ANALYSIS 4b

**qualitative character** *n* : a discrete heritable character that has transmitted well-defined limits and is in a simple alternate manner : a typical Mendelian character — compare QUANTITATIVE CHARACTER

**qual·i·tied** \ˈkwälēd·ēd, -ətēd *sometimes* ˈkwȯl-\ *adj* [¹*quality* + -*ed*] : having qualities : endowed with a quality ⟨he was well ~ —George Chapman⟩

**¹qual·i·ty** \-əd·ē, -ətē, -i\ *n* -ES [ME *qualite*, fr. OF *qualité*, fr. L *qualitat-, qualitas* (trans. of Gk *poiotēs*), fr. *qualis* of what kind + -*tat-*, -*tas* -ty; akin to L *qui* who — more at WHO] **1 a** : peculiar and essential character : NATURE, KIND ⟨differences in the ~ of the two temperaments —M.D.Howe⟩ ⟨self-interest and sympathy, opposite in ~ —John Dewey⟩ ⟨the ~ of mercy is not strained —Shak.⟩ ⟨the offender knew the nature and ~ of the act —B.N.Cardozo⟩ ⟨take on the ~ of animate life —H.V.Gregory⟩ **b** : a distinctive inherent feature : PROPERTY, VIRTUE ⟨the *qualities* of the circle⟩ ⟨has the . . . ~ that its color and spectrum fade out —Albert Szent-Györgyi⟩ ⟨herbs . . . and their true *qualities* —Shak.⟩ **c** : a character, position, or role usu. assumed temporarily : CAPACITY — usu. used in the phrases *in quality of, in the quality of* ⟨I make this inquiry in ~ of an antiquary —Thomas Gray⟩ ⟨in the ~ of reader and companion —Joseph Conrad⟩ **2 a** (1) : degree of excellence : GRADE, CALIBER ⟨decline in the ~ of students —H.L.Creek⟩ ⟨the ~ of the soil —J.M.Mogey⟩ ⟨manufactured in only one ~ —*Catalog of Plumbing Fixtures*⟩ ⟨the ~ of the . . . golfer's game —Judson Philips⟩ (2) : degree of conformance to a standard (as of a product or workmanship) **b** (1) : inherent or intrinsic excellence of character or type : superiority in kind ⟨merchandise of ~⟩ ⟨proclaimed the ~ of his wife —Compton Mackenzie⟩ ⟨colt with . . . plenty of ~ —G.F.T. Ryall⟩ (2) *of livestock* : refinement or excellence of appearance with close adherence to the standards of a breed (3) : fineness of texture (as of meat or plumage) (4) : the characteristics (as texture, marbling, color) of uncooked meat that influence tenderness and palatability **3 a** : social status : RANK ⟨your name, your ~ —Shak.⟩; *esp* : high social position ⟨a man of ~⟩ ⟨solicited a person of ~ for the appointment⟩ ⟨the colored people of ~ —Oscar Handlin⟩ **b** : persons of high social status : ARISTOCRACY ⟨companions . . . among the highest ~ in the land —*Fashion Digest*⟩ — usu. used with *the* ⟨flaunting themselves . . . as if they were the ~ —David Garnett⟩ **c** *obs* : a group of persons having distinctive character : FRATERNITY, PARTY, PROFESSION ⟨you are not of our ~ —Shak.⟩; *esp* : the acting profession ⟨players, I love yee, and your ~ —John Davies⟩ **4 a** : a special or distinguishing attribute : CHARACTERISTIC ⟨the boy has many fine *qualities*⟩ ⟨*qualities* of naïveté and inexperience—Peter Foster⟩ ⟨more than any other ~ . . . gregariousness —W.H.Whyte⟩ ⟨the man was much greater than the sum of his *qualities* —Willa Cather⟩; *esp* : a desirable trait : EXCELLENCE ⟨a man without *qualities* —Frederic Morton⟩ ⟨the defect as well as the *qualities* of its . . . origins —*Times Lit. Supp.*⟩ **b** : the character in a logical proposition of being affirmative or negative — see OPPOSITION 2a(2) **c** : the character of an estate as determined by the manner in which it is to be held or enjoyed **d** *archaic* : an acquired skill : ACCOMPLISHMENT ⟨she hath more *qualities* than a water spaniel —Shak.⟩ **5 a** : something that serves to identify a subject of perception or thought in the respect in which it is considered **b** : something from the possession of which a thing is such as it is : PREDICATE — see PRIMARY QUALITY, SECONDARY QUALITY, TERTIARY QUALITY **c** (1) : something that exists or can exist only as a qualification of something else (2) : an attribute that obtains only after a certain level has been reached and in a certain complex fitted to receive it ⟨in the theory of emergent evolution life and mind are *qualities*⟩ **6** : manner of action — usu. used in the phrase *adverb of quality* **7 a** : vividness of hue : SATURATION CHROMA **b** : a property of a musical tone that distinguishes it from another tone having the same pitch and loudness and that is determined by the number and prominence of the overtones mixed with the fundamental — called also *timbre* **c** : the identifying character of a vowel sound determined chiefly by the resonance of the vocal chambers in uttering it **d** : the character of an X-ray beam that determines its penetrating power and is dependent upon its wavelength distribution **e** : the attribute of an elementary sensation that makes it different in kind and not simply in intensity, duration, or extent from any other sensation ⟨red, sweet, and cold are *qualities* of certain sensations⟩ **8** : the ratio by weight of water vapor in wet steam to vapor and suspended liquid droplets together usu. expressed as a percentage

**syn** QUALITY, STATURE, and CALIBER are often interchangeable as indicating, when used in constructions without grammatical modifiers, merit or superiority because of a combination of good characteristics ⟨our candidate is a man of *quality*, of *stature*, of *caliber*⟩ QUALITY may stress inherent, enduring good traits that make one somewhat superior ⟨there was nothing in his outer case to suggest the fierceness and fortitude and fire of the man, and yet even the thick-blooded Mexican half-breeds knew his *quality* at once —Willa Cather⟩ ⟨had *quality*, if he lacked character —Ellen Glasgow⟩ ⟨as those of *quality* do, not as the vulgar —George Washington⟩ STATURE is likely to suggest height reached or development attained to and to connote considerations of prestige and eminence ⟨in time the expanding vitality attains its full *stature* —Ellen Glasgow⟩ ⟨men of *stature* and local prestige formed the personnel of these committees —C.G.Bowers⟩ Unlike QUALITY, STATURE is freely used with notions of increase or decrease ⟨probings in the realms of life and matter have seemed to diminish man's *stature* and to belittle his dignity —J.P. Marquand⟩ CALIBER may connote an unusual but measurable range, scope, breadth of intellectual capacity or of other ability ⟨it is true that, in the early years of George III's reign, there were Britons of the intellectual *caliber* of Hume and Gibbon who were avowed skeptics —G.M.Trevelyan⟩ ⟨in practically every country there is a decrease in the intellectual and moral *caliber* of those who carry the responsibility of public affairs —*Times Lit. Supp.*⟩

**syn** PROPERTY, CHARACTER, ATTRIBUTE, ACCIDENT: QUALITY is a general term applicable to any trait or characteristic; it is frequently used in relation to inherent traits not immediately apparent and ascertained only after experience or examination ⟨my intolerance is reserved for *qualities* and not for externals —A.C.Benson⟩ ⟨the persistent contemporariness that is a *quality* of all good art —Aldous Huxley⟩ ⟨there was only one *quality* in a woman that appealed to him — charm —John Galsworthy⟩ PROPERTY may refer to a peculiar or distinctive trait, often an essential or intrinsic one, which can be used to describe a species or type ⟨since ether is not material it has not any of the usual characteristics of matter — mass, rigidity, etc. — but it has quite definite *properties* of its own —A.S. Eddington⟩ ⟨weight is only an apparently invariable *property* of matter —Havelock Ellis⟩ CHARACTER may stress an identifying property ⟨hauynite and noselite show *characters* like sodalite, but they differ from it in containing the radical $SO_4$ in the place of chlorine —L.V.Pirsson⟩ ⟨deserves credit for having preserved the *character* and characteristics of his original —B.R.Redman⟩ ATTRIBUTE indicates a characteristic, often an essential concomitant, with which a person or thing has been endowed ⟨this Confederation had none of the *attributes* of sovereignty in legislative, executive, or judicial power —R.B.Taney⟩ ⟨the harder a writer tries to add beauty to clearness, the more surely does he feel himself to be held off from perfection by *attributes* of language which he did not make and cannot do away with —C.E.Montague⟩ ACCIDENT refers to an additional, concomitant trait, one nonessential and usu. noninherent in the thing under consideration

⟨certainly many mystics have been ascetic. But that has been the *accident* of their philosophy, and not the essence of their religion —Havelock Ellis⟩

**²quality** \"\ *adj* **1 :** of or relating to high society **:** ARISTOCRATIC ⟨~ folks⟩ ⟨bring ~ people to the wedding —Padraic Colum⟩ **2 :** of, relating to, or marked by good quality **:** EXCELLENT ⟨~ goods⟩ ⟨~ meat⟩ ⟨~ stocks⟩ ⟨~ leather⟩ ⟨this ~ revolution in . . . buying habits —*N.Y.Times*⟩ ⟨make it a ~ operation —Virgil Thomson⟩

**quality control** *n* **:** an aggregate of functions designed to insure adequate quality in manufactured products by initial critical study of engineering design, materials, processes, equipment, and workmanship followed by periodic inspection and analysis of the results of inspection to determine causes for defects and by removal of such causes

**quality control chart** *n* **:** a chart to determine whether or not the number of defectives in a daily industrial operation exceeds reasonable expectation

**quality factor** *n* **1 :** QUALITY 8 **2 :** ²Q

**qual·i·ty·less** \'kwäləd·ēləs\ *adj* **:** lacking quality or qualities

**quality magazine** *n* **:** a periodical containing material designed to appeal esp. to readers of superior education or culture

**quality point** *or* **quality credit** *n* **:** one of the points or credits earned in a course according to a system by which the academic credit allotted to the course is multiplied by a factor that varies with the grade received ⟨an A in a 3-credit course gives the student 9 *quality points*⟩

**qualm** \'kwä\|m, 'kwål *also* 'kwȯl *sometimes* \|lm; *archaic* 'kwam\ *n* -s [origin unknown] **1 :** a usu. sudden attack of illness, faintness, or esp. nausea ⟨a jerk in the pit of his stomach caused him a severe internal ~ —G.B.Shaw⟩ **2 a :** a spasm of fear **:** a sudden misgiving or faintheartedness ⟨the memory gave him almost a ~ of terror —Anne D. Sedgwick⟩ ⟨had ~*s* about setting forth over the treacherous waters —V.G.Heiser⟩ **b :** a sudden access of disturbing sensation or emotion ⟨a little ~ of homesickness —C.S.Forester⟩ ⟨a ~ of tenderness shook his unstable heart —D.C.Peattie⟩ **3 :** a feeling of uneasiness about a point of conscience, honor, or propriety **:** COMPUNCTION ⟨their claims are formulated without any ~*s* of modesty —Herbert Read⟩ ⟨he could drop her without a ~ —Lester Atwell⟩ ⟨have no ~*s* at all in committing adultery —*Books of the Month*⟩ **syn** see SCRUPLE

**qualm·ish** \-mish, -mēsh\ *adj* **1 a :** having or tending to have qualms esp. of nausea **:** NAUSEATED ⟨my dear angel has been ~ of late —Tobias Smollett⟩ **b :** affected by scruples or compunction **:** SQUEAMISH ⟨~ . . . he refused to kill a spider —John Hersey⟩ **2 :** of, relating to, or likely to produce qualms ⟨a ~ . . . feeling in his stomach —Gladys Schmitt⟩ ⟨the ~ nightmare —J.G.Cozzens⟩ — **qualm·ish·ly** *adv* — **qualm·ish·ness** *n* -ES

**qualmy** \-mē\ *adj* -ER/-EST **:** QUALMISH

**quamash** *var of* CAMAS

**qua·ma·sia** \kwə'māzhēə, -āsēə\ *syn of* CAMASSIA

**quam diu** \(')kwäm'dē(,)ü\ *adv* [L, so long as] **:** so long as; *specif* **:** during good behavior — usu. used of the tenure of a judge

**quam·o·clit** \'kwamə,klit\ *n* [NL, perh. alter. of Nahuatl *cuauh-mochitl* camachile] **1** *cap* **:** a small genus of twining vines (family Convolvulaceae) of warm regions distinguished from *Ipomoea* by the salverform corolla and exserted stamens and style — see STAR IPOMOEA **2** -s **:** any plant of the genus *Quamoclit; esp* **:** CYPRESS VINE

**quan·da·ry** \'kwänd(ə)rē, -ri *sometimes* 'kwȯn-\ *n* -ES [origin unknown] **:** a state of perplexity or doubt **:** DILEMMA ⟨in a ~ as to where my road should lie —Clyde Higgs⟩ **syn** see PREDICAMENT

**quan·dong** *also* **quan·dang** *or* **quon·dong** \'kwän,däŋ\ *or* **quan·tong** \-n,täŋ\ *n* -s [native name in Australia] **1 a :** a small or shrubby Australian tree (*Fusanus acuminatus* or *Elaeocarpus grandis*) of the family Santalaceae that has lanceolate leaves and small flowers in terminal panicles followed by round edible red drupes **b :** the fruit of the quandong tree — called also *native peach;* see QUANDONG NUT **2 :** BRISBANE QUANDONG

**quandong nut** *n* **:** the edible seed of the large hard pitted stone of the quandong

**quan·dy** \'kwandē\ *n* -ES [perh. imit.] *NewEng* **:** OLD-SQUAW

**¹quant** \'kwant, 'kwänt\ *n* -s [ME *quante*] *dial Eng* **:** a punting pole with a flange near the end

**²quant** \'kwänt\ *n, pl* **quants** \-ts\ *or* **quan·ta** \-tə\ [ISV, by shortening] **:** QUANTUM 3 — used esp. in the phrase *light quant*

**quant** *abbr* quantitative

**quanta** *pl of* QUANTUM

**quan·tal** \'kwänt^əl\ *adj* [L *quantus* how much + E *-al*] **:** of or relating to data in sensitivity experiments in which there are only two categories (as dead or alive, all or none)

**¹quan·tic** \'kwäntik\ *n* -s [L *quantus* how much + E *-ic*, n. suffix] **:** a homogeneous polynomial in two or more variables

**²quantic** \"\ *adj* [ISV *quantum* + *-ic*, adj. suffix] **:** of or relating to a quantum

**quan·ti·fi·abil·i·ty** \,kwäntə,fīə'biləd·ē\ *n* **:** the quality or state of being quantifiable

**quan·ti·fi·able** \'==,fīəbəl, ,=='===\ *adj* **:** capable of being quantified

**quan·ti·fi·ably** \-blē\ *adv* **:** in a quantifiable manner

**quan·ti·fi·ca·tion** \,kwäntəfəkāshən\ *n* -s [fr. *quantify*, after E *qualify: qualification*] **1 a :** the operation of quantifying in logic: as (1) *Hamiltonism* **:** the process of making the quantity of a predicate explicit by prefixing it with *all* or *some* ⟨by ~ "all men are mortals" becomes "all men are some mortals"⟩ (2) **:** the operation in symbolic logic of forming a statement by prefixing a quantifier to a sentential function **b :** a statement formed by quantification **2 :** the introduction of the element of quantity; *specif* **:** the transformation of qualitative into quantitative data in scientific methodology ⟨a thermometer is used in the ~ of temperature⟩ — **quan·ti·fi·ca·tion·al** \¦===¦kāshən^əl\ *adj* — **quan·ti·fi·ca·tion·al·ly** \-^əlē\ *adv*

**quan·ti·fi·er** \'kwäntə,fī(ə)r\ *n* -s **1 :** a word (as a numeral) expressive of quantity (*two, thirty, many,* and *much* are ~*s*) **2 :** a prefix that binds the variables in a logical formula by specifying their quantity — see EXISTENTIAL OPERATOR, UNIVERSAL QUANTIFIER

**quan·ti·fy** \'kwäntə,fī *sometimes* 'kwȯn-\ *vt* -ED/-ING/-ES [ML *quantificare*, fr. L *quantus* how much + *-ficare* -fy — more at QUANTITY] **1 a :** to qualify (a term in a logical proposition) by indicating the logical quantity ⟨the word "all" *quantifies* "men" in the proposition "all men are mortal"⟩ **:** bind (a variable in a sentential function) by prefixing a quantifier **b :** to make (the logical quantity of a term) explicit (as by transforming "the Chinese are industrious" into "most Chinese are industrious") — compare QUANTIFICATION, QUANTIFIER **2 a :** to determine, express, or measure the quantity of **b :** to transform or translate from the qualitative into the quantitative

**quan·tim·e·ter** \kwän·'timəd·ə(r)\ *n* [ISV *quantity* + *-meter*] **:** a device that is used to measure the quantity of X rays

**quan·ti·tate** \'kwän(t)ə,tāt *sometimes* 'kwȯn-\ *vt* -ED/-ING/-S [back-formation fr. *quantitative*] **:** to measure or estimate the quantity of **:** express in quantitative terms ⟨the doctor can . . . ~ the best formula for each infant —*Jour. Amer. Med. Assoc.*⟩ ⟨inability to ~ such a procedure —*Psychosomatic Medicine*⟩

**quan·ti·ta·tion** \,=='tāshən\ *n* -s [*quantitate* + *-ion*] **:** the act or process of quantitating ⟨ratio . . . used for ~ —*Chem. Abstracts*⟩

**quan·ti·ta·tive** \'==,tād·\|iv, -āt\|, \|ēv *also* \|əv\ *adj* [ML *quantitativus*, fr. L *quantitat-, quantitas* quantity + *-ivus* -ive] **1** *archaic* **:** having quantity (as mass, magnitude, extent in space, or duration in time) **2 :** of, relating to, or expressible in terms of quantity ⟨~ relation⟩ ⟨~ aspect⟩ ⟨export wheat without ~ limitation —*Sydney (Australia) Bull.*⟩ **3 :** of, relating to, or involving the measurement of quantity or amount — contrasted with *qualitative* ⟨dearth of ~ studies —W.O.Aydelotte⟩ **4 :** based upon quantity; *specif* **:** based upon temporal quantity or duration of sounds — used of a rhythmic system in which the base is some arrangement of elements distinguished as *long* and *short* (as in typical verse of the classical periods in Greek, Latin, Sanskrit, Arabic, and Persian); contrasted with *accentual;* compare QUANTITY 4a, SYLLABIC — **quan·ti·ta·tive·ly** \\|əvlē, -li\ *adv* — **quan·ti·ta·tive·ness** \\|ivnəs\ *n* -ES

**quantitative analysis** *n* **:** a branch of chemistry whose scope is to determine the amounts of elements or groups in a pure substance or to determine the percentage of components in a mixture — compare ANALYSIS 4b

**quantitative character** *n* **:** a heritable character that has indefinite limits and is transmitted as a continuous variation **:** a polygenic character — see QUANTITATIVE INHERITANCE; compare MULTIPLE FACTOR, QUALITATIVE CHARACTER

**quantitative inheritance** *n* **:** particulate inheritance of any quantitative character mediated by groups of multiple factors each allelic pair of which adds or subtracts a specific increment of the collectively controlled character (as height or skin color in man) so that each increment is essentially a qualitative character inherited in purely particulate fashion although the character as a whole appears to exhibit blending inheritance

**quan·ti·tive** \'kwän(t)əd·iv\ *adj* [by contr.] **:** QUANTITATIVE — **quan·ti·tive·ly** \-d·əvlē\ *adv*

**¹quan·ti·ty** \'kwän(t)əd·ē, -ətē, -i *sometimes* 'kwȯn-\ *n* -ES [ME *quantite*, fr. OF *quantité*, fr. L *quantitat-, quantitas*, fr. *quantus* how much, how large + *-itat-, -itas* -ity; akin to L *quam* than, how, *quando* when, *qui* who — more at WHO] **1 a :** an indefinite amount or number ⟨a ~ of interesting information —Roy Lewis & Angus Maude⟩ ⟨a ~ of pleasure —I.V.Morris⟩ ⟨an impressive ~ of lawbooks —David Williamson⟩ **b :** a determinate or estimated amount ⟨the ~ of flour called for in the recipe⟩ ⟨measuring *quantities* of heat —K.K. Darrow⟩ **c :** total amount or number ⟨the ~ of shoes produced by the company⟩ ⟨the ~ of tone —Warwick Braithwaite⟩ ⟨the ~ of her devotion —Mark Van Doren⟩ **d** (1) **:** a great or very considerable amount or number **:** LOT, BULK ⟨a ~ of bright shawl . . . about her head —Charles Dickens⟩ ⟨bought a ~ of plants —Rachel Henning⟩ ⟨merchandise sold in ~⟩ (2) **quantities** *pl* **:** great amounts or numbers **:** SCADS ⟨~ of money⟩ ⟨~ of tan-backed girls —Edmund Wilson⟩ **e** *obs* **:** a small amount **:** MITE ⟨retaining but a ~ of life —Shak.⟩ **f** *obs* **:** relative amount **:** PROPORTION ⟨women's fear and love holds ~ —Shak.⟩ **2** *archaic* **:** a definite surface or extent in space ⟨grant of a sufficient ~ of . . . land —Edmund Burke⟩ **3 a :** the character of something that makes it possible to measure or number it or to determine that it is more or less than something else ⟨a matter of ~ of production rather than quality⟩ **b :** something that may be operated upon according to fixed mutually consistent mathematical laws — see MAGNITUDE 5 **4 a :** duration and intensity of sounds as distinct from their individual quality or phonemic character; *specif* **:** the relative length or brevity of sounds usu. indicated (as for Greek and Latin prosody) by a macron for the long, a breve for the short, and a combination of macron and breve for the common that may be either long or short **b** *archaic* **:** the relative length or duration of a musical tone **c :** the relative duration or time length of a speech sound or sound group **d :** the character of an estate as determined by its time of continuance or degree of interest (as in fee, for life, or for years) **5 a :** the extent in which a term in a given logical proposition is to be taken; *esp* **:** such extent as indicated by *all, some,* or *no* **b :** the character of a logical proposition as universal, particular, or singular **c :** the extension, intension, or information of a logical term **syn** see SUM

**²quantity** \"\ *adj* **:** of, relating to, or involving quantity ⟨~ basis⟩ ⟨~ production⟩

**quantity of light :** luminous energy that is the product of mean luminous flux by time (*quantity of light* expressed in lumen-hours)

**quantity surveyor** *n* **:** one that estimates or measures building quantities

**quantity theory** *or* **quantity theory of money** *n* **:** a theory in economics: changes in the price level and the value of money vary with changes in the amount of money in circulation

**quan·ti·za·tion** \,kwäntə'zāshən, -än-,tī'-\ *n* -s **:** the act or process of quantizing: as **a :** subdivision into quanta **b :** expression in terms of quantum theory

**quan·tize** \'kwän-,tīz\ *vt* -ED/-ING/-S [*quantum* + *-ize*] **1 :** to express as multiples of a definite quantity **2 a :** to subdivide (as energy) into small finite increments **b :** to calculate or express (as the phenomena of radiation or photoelectric action) in terms of quantum mechanics **c :** to put into a definite quantum state ⟨a *quantized* molecule⟩

**quantong** *var of* QUANDONG

**quants** *pl of* QUANT

**quan·tum** \'kwäntəm *sometimes* 'kwȯn-\ *n, pl* **quan·ta** \-tə\ [L, neut. of *quantus* how much — more at QUANTITY] **1 a :** QUANTITY, AMOUNT ⟨the ~ of proof needed⟩ ⟨the ~ of damages to be assessed⟩ ⟨the tiny ~ of popular knowledge on any matter —John Buchan⟩ ⟨the ~ of the sin —Robert Burns⟩ **b :** a certain or an allotted amount **:** PORTION ⟨in almost all men . . . are *quanta* of love and tenderness —Levon West⟩ ⟨the Indian blood ~ of the population —D.P.Delorme⟩ **c :** gross quantity **:** AGGREGATE, BULK ⟨the total ~ of securities . . . that circulate in the economy —H.V.R.Iengar⟩ ⟨neither the ~ nor the season rainfall —Patricia McBride⟩ ⟨increase the ~ of material well-being —H.J.Laski⟩ **2** *obs* **:** something having quantity **:** BODY **3 a :** one of the very small increments or parcels into which many forms of energy are subdivided and which are always associated directly or indirectly with a frequency $\nu$ such that the quantum is equal to $\nu$ multiplied by Planck constant **b :** one of the small subdivisions of a quantized physical magnitude (as molecular spin, angular velocity, magnetic moment) — compare LIGHT QUANTUM, MAGNETON, PHONON, PHOTON

**quantum efficiency** *also* **quantum yield** *n* **:** the ratio of the number of photoelectrons released in a photoelectric process to the number of radiation quanta absorbed

**quantum electrodynamics** *n pl but usu sing in constr* **:** quantum mechanics applied to electrical interactions (as between nuclear particles)

**quantum-equivalence law** *n* **:** a principle of photoelectric action: when a quantum of radiation is involved in a photoelectric process its whole energy reappears in other forms since photoelectric processes do not absorb fractional quanta as do some other processes (as Compton effect)

**quantum evolution** *n* **:** comparatively rapid transition from one stable type of biological adaptation to another distinctly different type under the influence of some strong selection pressure

**quantum jump** *or* **quantum transition** *n* **:** an abrupt transition (as of an electron, an atom, or a molecule) from one discrete energy state to another with absorption or emission of a quantum of energy

**quantum liquid** *n* **:** HELIUM II

**quantum-mechanical** \¦==¦===\ *adj* **:** of or relating to quantum mechanics ⟨the *quantum-mechanical* theory of nuclear motion —*Physical Rev.*⟩

**quantum mechanics** *n pl but sing or pl in constr* **1 :** the mechanics of phenomena to which the quantum theory may be applied — called also *old quantum mechanics* **2 :** a general mathematical theory dealing with the interactions of matter and radiation in terms of observable quantities only (as the intensities and frequencies of spectral lines) — called also *new quantum mechanics;* compare ATOMIC THEORY, MATRIX MECHANICS, WAVE MECHANICS

**quantum me·ru·it** \-'merəwət\ *n* [L, as much as he deserved] **:** a count in a legal action grounded on a promise that the defendant would pay to the plaintiff for the plaintiff's work or labor as much as he should deserve

**quantum number** *n* **:** one of a set of integral or half-integral numbers used to define the magnitude of a quantity (as energy or angular momentum) that takes on only discrete values

**quantum of action :** PLANCK CONSTANT

**quantum theory** *n* **:** an extensive branch of physical theory based on Max Planck's concept of radiant energy subdivided into finite quanta and applied to a large number of processes involving transference or transformation of energy in an atomic or molecular scale — see QUANTUM 3

**quantum unit of spin :** a constant used as a unit of measurement for particle spin and equal to the Planck constant divided by $2\pi$

**quantum va·le·bant** \-və'lē,bant\ *n* [L, as much as they were worth] **:** a count in a legal action of assumpsit to recover for goods sold or materials furnished as much as they were worth

**qua·paw** *also* **kwa·pa** \'kwȯ,pȯ\ *n, pl* **quapaw** *or* **quapaws** *usu cap* [Quapaw *Ugákhpa*, lit., downstream people] **1 a :** a Siouan people of the Arkansas river valley, Arkansas **b :** a member of such people **2 :** a dialect of Dhegiha

**¹qua·qua·ver·sal** \¦kwākwə¦vərsəl\ *adj* [L *quaqua versus* turned in every direction (fr. *quaqua* wherever, in whatever direction, in every direction — fr. abl. fem. of *quisquis* whoever, every, redupl. of *quis* who — + *versus*, past part. of *vertere* to turn) + E *-al* — more at WHO, WORTH] **:** dipping from a center toward all points of the compass ⟨a ~ domal structure⟩ — used esp. of geological formations; opposed to *centroclinal;* contrasted with *partiversal;* compare DOME 7a — **qua·qua·ver·sal·ly** \-səlē\ *adv*

**²quaquaversal** \"\ *n* -s **:** a quaquaversal dome, ridge, or structure

**quar** *abbr* quarter; quarterly

**quarantain** *n* -s [F *quarantaine*, lit., period of forty days, fr. OF] *obs* **:** QUARANTINE

**quar·an·tin·able** \¦kwȯrən¦tēnəbəl, -wär-\ *adj* **1 :** liable to be quarantined **:** subject to quarantine ⟨a ~ immigrant⟩ **2 :** constituting grounds for quarantine **:** subjecting one to quarantine ⟨a ~ disease⟩

**¹quar·an·tine** \'kwȯrən-,tēn, -wär-, ,=='=\ *n* -s [in sense 1, fr. ML *quarentena*, fr. OF *quarantaine* period of forty days, fr. *quarante* forty, fr. L *quadraginta;* in other senses, fr. It *quarantina, quarantena* period of forty days, quarantine (of a ship), fr. MF *quarantaine* period of forty days, fr. OF — more at QUADRAGESIMA] **1 a :** the period often of 40 days during which a widow is permitted by law to remain in her deceased husband's principal home without being obliged to pay rent to the heirs **b :** a widow's right of quarantine **2 :** a period of 40 days **3 a :** a term (as of 40 days) during which a ship arriving in port and suspected of carrying serious contagious disease is forbidden all intercourse with the shore **b :** a regulation restraining a ship from intercourse with the shore while suspected of offering a threat of contagion **c :** a place where a ship is detained during quarantine **d :** a stoppage of travel, communication, or intercourse imposed as a precaution against contagion or infection or the spreading of plant or animal pests **4 :** a restraint or interdiction placed upon the transportation of animals, plants, or goods suspected of being carriers of disease or other pest **5 :** a place (as an isolation hospital) in which persons under quarantine are kept **6 :** a section of a prison or reformatory in which new arrivals are detained for examination and observation before being permitted to mingle with other prisoners **7 :** isolation enforced as a social or political penalty **:** SANCTION ⟨four South American countries refused to join a diplomatic ~ —R.W. Van Alstyne⟩ ⟨sheer vulgarity . . . is so blatant as to isolate itself and proclaim its own ~ —Louis Kronenberger⟩

**²quarantine** \"\ *vb* -ED/-ING/-S *vt* **1 :** to isolate as a precaution against contagious disease **:** detain in quarantine **2 :** to exclude by quarantine **3 :** to isolate or cut off from normal relations or intercourse as a social or political penalty or sanction ⟨brave words in regard to *quarantining* the aggressor —R.M.Lovett⟩ ~ *vi* **:** to establish or declare a quarantine

**quarantine flag** *n* **:** a yellow flag hoisted by all ships to request pratique on entering a harbor, by a ship to show that it has contagious or infectious disease aboard, or by a ship that has been quarantined — called also *yellow flag, yellow jack*

**quarantine period** *n* **:** a period of time that must elapse before those exposed to or attacked by a contagious disease can be considered as incapable respectively of developing or transmitting the disease

**quar·an·tin·er** \-ēnə(r)\ *n* -s **1 :** one that quarantines **2 :** one that is quarantined

**quaranty** *n* -ES [It *quarantia*, fr. *quaranta* forty, fr. L *quadraginta*] *obs* **:** a court of 40 magistrates in the Venetian republic

**quare** \'kwa(a)(ə)r, -we(ə)r, -wär\ *dial var of* ¹QUEER

**qua·re clau·sum fre·git** \,kwärē,klausəm'frāgət\ *n* [L, why he broke the close] **:** a writ for land trespass

**quare im·pe·dit** \-'impədət\ *n* [L, why he hinders] *Eng law* **:** a writ by which a common-law action for deciding a disputed right of presentation to a benefice begins

**quar·en·tene** *like* ¹QUARANTINE\ *n* -s [ML *quarentena*, fr. OF *quarantaine* period of forty days, set of forty — more at QUARANTINE] *archaic* **:** FURLONG, ROOD

**qua·res·ma** \kwä'rezmə\ *n* -s [Pg, lit., Lent, fr. LL *quadragesima* — more at QUADRAGESIMA] **:** BRAZILIAN SPIDERFLOWER

**quark** \'kwȯrk\ *vi* [imit.] *archaic* **:** CROAK

**quarl** *or* **quarle** \'kwȯrl, *esp before pause or consonant* -rəl\ *n* -s [alter. of ¹*quarrel*] **:** a large brick or tile; *esp* **:** a curved firebrick used to support melting pots for zinc and retort covers

**quarled** \-ld\ *var of* QUARRELED

**¹quar·rel** \'kwȯr(ə)l, -wär-\ *n* -s [ME, fr. OF *carrel, quarrel* square-headed arrow for an arbalest, building stone, fr. (assumed) VL *quadrellum*, fr. L *quadrum* square + *-ellum* -el; akin to L *quattuor* four — more at FOUR] **1 :** a square-headed bolt or arrow; *esp* **:** one for a crossbow or arbalest **2** [ME, square of glass, fr. MF, square of glass, building stone, fr. OF *carrel, quarrel* building stone] **:** a small quadrangular building member: as **a :** a square of glass esp. when set diagonally **b :** a small opening in window tracery of which the general form is nearly square **c :** a square or lozenge-shaped paving tile **3 :** a glazier's diamond **4 :** a stonecutter's chisel

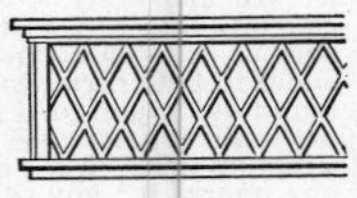

quarrels 2a

**²quarrel** \"\ *n* -s [ME *querele*, fr. MF, complaint, fr. L *querela* fr. *queri* to complain — more at WHEEZE] **1 a :** a ground of complaint **:** an occasion for dislike or hostility **:** a cause of dispute or contest ⟨it is the apparent absence of this faith which is part of my ~ with those critics —J.D.Adams⟩ **b :** a conflict between antagonists **:** a moral or physical contest **:** DISPUTE, STRIFE ⟨so it would be prudent for both of us to agree now upon some compromise with each other, and not to push our postwar ~ to extremes —A.J.Toynbee⟩ **2 :** a cause or side in a dispute ⟨a just ~⟩ **3** *obs* **a :** an occasion to act **b :** AVERSION, DISLIKE **c :** QUARRELSOMENESS

**syn** WRANGLE, ALTERCATION, SQUABBLE, BICKERING, SPAT, TIFF: QUARREL usu. indicates a verbal contention with anger, hurt feeling, vexation, and recrimination ⟨she hated any kind of *quarrel* . . . she shuddered at raised voices and quailed before looks of hate —Jean Stafford⟩ WRANGLE may indicate noisy, insistent, discordant, futile disputation ⟨spent three hours in an inconclusive *wrangle* over what was to be included in the communiqué to the press —J.P.Lash⟩ ⟨pleaded against any changes that might produce a partisan *wrangle* —*N.Y. Times*⟩ ALTERCATION usu. indicates a determined verbal contention or dispute ⟨a rapid *altercation*, in which they fastened upon each other various strange epithets —Stephen Crane⟩ ⟨the fights and violent *altercations* which grew out of impassioned discussion of the day's doings —Herbert Asbury⟩ SQUABBLE may indicate a silly, puerile, wrangle over something petty ⟨*squabbles* with his fellow faddists —L.P.Smith⟩ BICKERING implies continuing irritable petulant verbal sparring ⟨the *bickering* and squabbles of the state parties —Gerald Priestland⟩ ⟨whose *bickerings* with her husband become tiresome —Leslie Rees⟩ SPAT may suggest a short lively dispute, perhaps over something trivial and perhaps ending quickly ⟨had short *spats* with Hughie when he came in unnecessarily drunk —Ruth Park⟩ TIFF refers to a trivial ill-humored dispute, often without consequence ⟨was just a passing *tiff* and that matters would speedily adjust themselves —P.G.Wodehouse⟩

**³quarrel** \"\ *vb* **quarreled** *or* **quarrelled; quarreled** *or* **quarrelled; quarreling** *or* **quarrelling; quarrels** [ME *querelen*, fr. *querele*, n.] *vi* **1 :** to find fault **:** CAVIL, COMPLAIN ⟨I have no compulsion to ~ with a society that has permitted me to work for what I believe —M.W.Straight⟩ **2 :** to contend or dispute actively **:** CLASH, STRIVE, STRUGGLE ⟨~*ed* with his new stepmother —Carl Bridenbaugh⟩ ⟨~*ed* frequently with his superiors —*London Calling*⟩ ~ *vt* **1** *obs* **:** to dispute or question the rightness or validity of **:** CHALLENGE **2** *Scot* **:** to find fault with **:** REBUKE **3** *obs* **:** to force by quarreling

**⁴quarrel** \"\ *n* -s [ME *quarelle*, alter. of *quarere, quarrere* — more at QUARRY (excavation)] *dial chiefly Eng* **:** a stone quarry

**quar·reled** *or* **quar·relled** *or* **quarled** \-r(ə)ld\ *adj* **:** made with or into quarrels (as a window)
**quar·rel·er** *or* **quar·rel·ler** \-r(ə)lə(r)\ *n* -s [alter. (influenced by *-er*) of ME *querelour*, fr. *querelen* to quarrel + *-our* -or] **:** one that quarrels
**quarreling** *or* **quarrelling** *adj* **1 :** engaged in a quarrel **2 :** QUARRELSOME — **quar·rel·ing·ly** *or* **quar·rel·ling·ly** *adv*
**quarrelous** *or* **quarrellous** *adj* [ME *querelous*, fr. MF, fr. LL *querelosus*, fr. L *querela* complaint + *-osus* -ose — more at QUARREL] **1** *obs* **:** QUERULOUS **2** *obs* **:** QUARRELSOME
**quar·rel·some** \'kwȯr(ə)lsəm, -wär-\ *adj* **:** apt or disposed to quarrel **:** CONTENTIOUS ⟨becoming more ~ as the campaign progressed⟩ **syn** see BELLIGERENT
**quar·rel·some·ly** *adv* **:** in a quarrelsome manner
**quar·rel·some·ness** *n* -ES **:** the quality or state of being quarrelsome
**quar·ri·able** *also* **quar·ry·able** \'kwȯrēəbəl, -wär-, -riə-\ *adj* **:** capable of being quarried
**quar·ried** \-rēd,-rid\ *adj* [fr. past part. of [4]*quarry*] **1 :** dug from a stone quarry **2** [[3]*quarry* + *-ed*] **:** having stone quarries
**quar·ri·er** \-rēə(r), -riə-\ *n* -s [ME *quaryere*, fr. MF *quarrier*, fr. (assumed) OF *quare* + OF *-ier* -er] **:** one that quarries (as stone) **:** a quarry worker **:** QUARRYMAN
**quar·ri·on** \-rēən\ *n* -s [prob. native name in Australia] **:** COCKATIEL
[1]**quar·ry** \'kwȯrē, -wär-, -ri\ *n* -ES [ME *querre*, *quirre* part of the entrails of a beast taken in hunting that is given to the hounds esp. by being placed on the beast's skin for them to eat, fr. MF *cuiree*, fr. OF, prob. alter. (influenced by *cuir* leather, skin, fr. L *corium*) of *coree* breast viscera, entrails, fr. LL *corata* (pl.), fr. L *cor* heart — more at HEART, CUIRASS] **1** *obs* **a :** a part of the entrails of a beast taken in hunting that is given to the hounds; *also* **:** a similar reward to a hawk that has killed a bird **b :** a heap of the game killed **2** *obs* **:** a heap of dead bodies (as on a battlefield) **3 a :** a game bird hunted with hawks **b :** the prey of any predatory bird or animal **c :** an animal, bird, or fish sought by a hunter or fisherman **:** the object of the chase **:** GAME **4 :** an object pursued or hunted ⟨city detectives kept the ~ under surveillance for weeks⟩ ⟨thinks of a woman as a ~ —Guy Fowler⟩ **5** *obs* **:** a falcon's attack or swoop on its prey **syn** see VICTIM
[2]**quarry** \"\ *vb* -ED/-ING/-ES *vt* **1** *obs* **:** to teach (a hawk) to seize quarry **2** *archaic* **:** to hunt down (a game animal) ~ *vi*, *obs* **:** to seize quarry — used with *on* or *upon*
[3]**quar·ry** \", *chiefly dial* -wer- *or* -war-\ *n* -ES [ME *quarey*, alter. of *quarere*, *quarrere*, fr. MF *quarrere*, *quarriere*, fr. OF, fr. (assumed) OF *quarre* squared stone (akin to OProv *cayre* squared stone), fr. L *quadrum* square — more at QUARREL (arrow)] **1 :** an open excavation usu. for obtaining building stone, slate, or limestone — compare [1]BANK, [4]MINE, PIT **2 :** a source from which material may be extracted **:** LODE ⟨other dramatists also found his books a workable ~ —*Times Lit. Supp.*⟩ **3 :** a large mass (as of stone or slate) fit for quarrying
[4]**quarry** \"\ *vb* -ED/-ING/-ES *vt* **1 :** to dig or take from or as if from a quarry ⟨had *quarried* limestone there for decades⟩ ⟨I have from time to time *quarried* out bits from the history of a special science to assist my exposition —J.B.Conant⟩ **2 :** to make a quarry in ⟨*quarried* the land industriously⟩ **3 :** to remove fragments of rock by impact (as in stream erosion) or by pressure and dragging (as in glacial erosion) **:** PLUCK ~ *vi* **:** to delve in or as if in a quarry ⟨never has to ~ to fill even the largest or most unusual order —*Amer. Guide Series: Vt.*⟩
[5]**quar·ry** \'kwȯr-, 'kwär-\ *n* -ES [alter. of [1]*quarrel*] **1** *obs* **:** a square-headed bolt or arrow **2 a :** a diamond-shaped pane of glass **:** LOZENGE **b :** QUARRY TILE ⟨stood barefoot in front of him on the cold *quarries* —Mary Webb⟩ **c :** any of the four-sided units in a simple allover decorative pattern formed by two sets of straight lines intersecting at regular intervals; *also* **:** this pattern
[6]**quarry** \"\ *vt* -ED/-ING/-ES **:** to glaze or pave with quarries
**quarry bed** *n* **:** QUARRY FACE
**quarry face** *n* **:** the freshly split face of ashlar squared off for the joints only as it comes from the quarry and used esp. for massive work — distinguished from *rock face* — **quarry-faced** \¦==¦=\ *adj*
**quarry-hawk** \'==,=\ *n* **:** MAKE-HAWK
**quarrying** *n* -s **:** the business, occupation, or act of extracting stone, marble, or slate from quarries
**quarry light** *n* **:** a diamond-shaped pane of glass designed to be set in leads
**quar·ry·man** \'==mən\ *n*, *pl* **quarrymen :** one who quarries stone or performs other duties at a quarry **:** QUARRIER
**quarrystone bond** *n* **:** RUBBLEWORK
**quarry tile** *n* **:** machine-made unglazed tile
**quarry water** *n* **:** the moisture content of freshly quarried stone esp. if porous
[1]**quart** \'kwȯr|t, -wȯ(ə)|, *usu* |d·+V\ *n* -s *often attrib* [ME, fr. MF *quarte*, fr. OF, fr. fem. of *quart*, adj., fourth, fr. L *quartus*; akin to L *quattuor* four — more at FOUR] **1 :** any of various units of capacity: as **a :** a British liquid or dry unit equal to ¼ imperial gallon or 69.355 cubic inches **b :** a U.S. liquid unit equal to ¼ gallon or 57.75 cubic inches **c :** a U.S. dry unit equal to 1/32 bushel or 67.200 cubic inches — see MEASURE table **2 a :** a vessel or measure having a capacity of one quart **b :** any of various units for bottled wine; *esp* **:** a unit for champagne containing 26 fluid ounces **3 a** [Sp *cuarto*, lit., fourth part, fr. *cuarto*, adj., fourth, fr. L *quartus*] **:** a token issued in 1802 or a coin struck in 1842 for Gibraltar equivalent to the Spanish ½-real piece; *also* **:** a corresponding unit of value ⟨2-*quart* token⟩ ⟨½-*quart* coin⟩ **b** [F, lit., fourth part, fr. MF, fr. *quart*, adj., fourth, fr. OF, fr. L *quartus*] **:** a Swiss silver coin of the 16th and 17th centuries equal to three deniers
[2]**quart** \'kär|t, 'kȧ|, *usu* |d·+V\ *n* -s [F *quarte* quart (in fencing), quart (in cards), fr. fem. of *quart*, adj., fourth] **1** *usu* **quarte** \"\ **:** a fencer's parry or guard position defending the upper inside left target in which the hand is at chest height with thumb up and fingernails to the left and the tip of the blade is directed at the opponent's eyes — compare PRIME **2 :** a sequence of four playing cards of the same suit

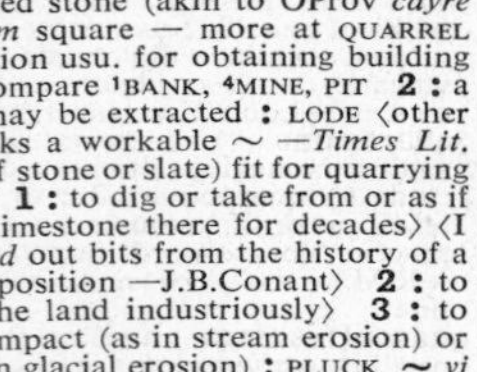

quart 2

[3]**quart** \"\ *vb* -ED/-ING/-S [F *quarter*, fr. *quarte*, n.] *archaic* **:** to assume or place in position for quart in fencing
**quart-** *comb form* [L, fr. *quartus*] **:** fourth ⟨*quartic*⟩
[1]**quar·tan** \'kwȯrt°n, -wȯ(ə)t-\ *adj* [ME *quarteyne*, fr. OF *quartaine* (in the phrase *fievre quartaine* quartan fever), fr. L *quartana* (in the phrase *febris quartana* quartan fever), fem. of *quartanus* of the fourth, fr. *quartus* fourth + *-anus* -an] **:** occurring every fourth day reckoning inclusively; *specif* **:** recurring at approximately 72-hour intervals — used chiefly of malariae malaria ⟨~ chills and fever⟩; compare TERTIAN
[2]**quartan** \"\ *n* -s [ME *quarteyne*, fr. MF *quartaine*, fr. OF, fr. L *quartana*, fr. fem. of *quartanus* of the fourth] **:** an intermittent fever that recurs at approximately 72-hour intervals
**quartan malaria** *n* **:** MALARIAE MALARIA
**quar·ta·tion** \kwȯr'tāshən\ *n* -s [*quart-* + *-ation*] **:** the alloying with silver of a button rich in gold in order to reduce the gold to such a proportion that the acid used in parting may act as desired
[1]**quar·ter** *R* 'kwȯr|d·ər, |tər *sometimes by* r-*dissimilation* -ō|; -*R* -ō(ə)|d·ə(r, |tə(r\ *n* -s [ME, fr. OF *quartier*, fr. L *quartarius*, fr. *quartus* fourth + *-arius* -ary — more at QUART] **1 :** one of four equal parts into which anything is divisible **:** a fourth part or portion ⟨a ~ of a pound⟩ **2 :** any of various units of capacity or weight equal to or derived from one fourth of some larger unit (as a hundredweight, imperial bushels, or a chaldron) **3 a :** any of various units of length or area equal to one fourth of some larger unit (as a yard) **b :** QUARTER SECTION **4 :** the fourth part of a measure of time: as **a :** one of a set of four 3-month divisions of a calendar or fiscal year **b :** a school or college term of about 12 weeks resulting when an academic year is divided into four parts one of which is taken up by the long summer vacation or used for summer school — compare SEMESTER 2 **c :** QUARTER HOUR 1 ⟨a ~ to six⟩ **5 a :** a coin worth a quarter of a dollar (as a U.S. or Canadian 25-cent piece) **b :** the sum of 25 cents **6 a :** one limb of a quadruped with the adjacent parts **:** one fourth part of the carcass of a slaughtered animal including a leg ⟨had a sack of flour and a ~ of a fine fat beef in his sleigh —Hamlin Garland⟩ — compare FIFTH QUARTER, FOREQUARTER, HINDQUARTER **b :** one of the four parts of a human body similarly divided (as in an execution for treason) **7 a :** the territory, region, or direction lying under any of the four divisions of the horizon conceived as corresponding to the cardinal points of the compass **b :** one of the four parts into which the horizon is divided or the cardinal point corresponding to it **c :** a compass point or direction other than the cardinal points ⟨the wind is in that ~⟩ **d** (1) **:** a person or group not definitely specified ⟨had his instructions from a very high ~⟩ (2) **:** a point, direction, or place not identified ⟨trade from that ~ is only a trickle —*Sydney (Australia) Bull.*⟩ ⟨procuring the release of a man in jail, by dropping a word in the right ~ —Peggy Durdin⟩ **8 a :** a district of a town or city devoted to a special purpose or activity, occupied by a particular group, or found notable for a conspicuous feature ⟨the market ~ of Paris⟩ ⟨the wholesale clothing ~ of New York⟩ ⟨a residential ~⟩ **b :** the inhabitants of such a quarter regarded as a group ⟨the ~ was aroused and indignant⟩ **9 a :** an assigned station or post; *esp* **:** the station assigned to a member of a ship's crew for a particular purpose — usu. used in pl. ⟨battle ~s⟩ ⟨collision ~s⟩ **b quarters** *pl* **:** an assembly of a ship's company for purposes of ceremony, drill, or emergency **c quarters** *pl* **:** living accommodations: as (1) **:** the living space of the crew aboard ship (2) **:** the lodgings of soldiers or sailors or their families (3) **:** the rooms, housing, or residence occupied by an individual, a family, or some other group ⟨bachelor ~s⟩ ⟨club ~s⟩ ⟨found ~s for his family⟩ **10 a :** the clemency of not putting to death a defeated enemy **:** FORBEARANCE, MERCY ⟨no ~ was asked or given; three women, two children, and a Negro servant survived —Oscar Handlin⟩ **b :** consideration shown to an opponent, antagonist, or fellow contestant by refraining from pressing advantages of superior strength or skill ⟨she had climbed trees and shot marbles and played ball with them, and neither expected nor received any ~ —Gertrude Schweitzer⟩ **11** *archaic* **a :** one of the four parts of a road marked out by horse tracks and wheel ruts **b :** the shoulder of a highway **12** *obs* **:** relations or attitude to another person — used esp. in the phrase *to keep good quarter with* **13** *archaic* **:** an upright wood framing member in a partition or wall **:** SCANTLING, STUD **14 a :** a fourth part of the moon's period — see MOON illustration **b :** QUADRATURE 3 **15 :** the side of a horse's hoof between the toe and the heel **16 a** (1) **:** any of the four parts into which a heraldic field is divided by horizontal and vertical lines through the fess point (2) **:** one of the parts into which a shield is divided by quartering — see GRAND QUARTER **b :** a bearing or charge occupying the first fourth part or thereabouts of a heraldic field — compare [1]CANTON 4 **17** *obs* **:** a garden bed or plot **18 :** the state of two machine parts that are exactly at right angles to one another or are spaced about a circle so as to subtend a right angle at the center of the circle ⟨the crankpin holes are out of ~⟩ **19 a :** the afterpart of a ship's side usu. corresponding in extent with the quarterdeck — see SHIP illustration **b :** the part of the yardarm outside of the slings **c** *archaic* **:** a fourth of a fathom **d** *or* **quarter point :** a fourth of the distance from one point of the compass to another reckoned as a fourth of 11°15′ or nearly 2°49′ **20 :** one side of the upper of a shoe or boot from heel to vamp — see SHOE illustration **21 a :** QUARTERBACK **b :** one of the four equal periods into which the playing time of some games (as football) is divided **:** one of the two subdivisions of a half ⟨romped to victory, scoring touchdowns in every ~⟩ **22 :** one teat together with the part of a cow's udder that it drains ⟨normal milk from all four ~s⟩ ⟨a three-~ cow⟩
[2]**quarter** \"\ *vb* -ED/-ING/-S [ME *quarteren*, fr. *quarter*, n.] *vt* **1 a :** to divide into four equal or nearly equal parts **b :** to separate into either more or fewer than four parts ⟨~*ed* an orange⟩ **c :** to divide (a human body) into four parts **:** DISMEMBER ⟨the traitor was hanged and ~*ed*⟩ **2 :** to provide with lodging or shelter; *esp* **:** to assign (troops) to a lodging place — often used with *on* or *upon* ⟨~*ed* his men on the inhabitants⟩ **3 :** to pass back and forth across (an area) in many directions **:** cross and recross **:** search intensively ⟨the bombers had conducted a 300-mile search, ~*ing* and requartering the area —A.R.Griffin⟩ ⟨larger animals not only eat larger pieces of food, but also ~ more territory to find it —Orlando Park⟩ **4 a :** to arrange or bear (as different coats of arms) quarterly on one escutcheon **b :** to add (a coat of arms) to another or others on one escutcheon **:** arrange alternately and quarterly — often used with *with* **5 :** to adjust or locate (as cranks) at right angles in a machine **6 :** to groom (a horse) lightly ~ *vi* **1 :** to occupy a residence **:** LODGE ⟨the family ~*ed* in a big old house⟩ **2 :** to crisscross a district **:** range back and forth over an area like a dog in search of game ⟨our attack force had to ~ for them —Fletcher Pratt⟩ **3 :** to drive a vehicle so as to straddle the ruts in the road **4 :** to change from one quarter to another — used of the moon **5 a :** to strike or blow on a ship's quarter — used of the wind **b :** to sail with the wind on the quarter
[3]**quarter** \"\ *adj* [[1]*quarter*] **1 :** consisting of or equal to a quarter **2 :** of or relating to the part in the mechanism of a clock or repeating watch governing the striking of the quarter hours — see QUARTER SNAIL **3 a :** placed at a right angle to another similar machine part ⟨a ~ crank⟩ **b :** having a branch at right angles to another ⟨a ~ crankshaft⟩ **4 :** of or relating to the quarter of a ship
**quar·ter·age** \-d·ərij, -tə-\ *n* -s [ME, fr. [1]*quarter* + *-age*] **1 :** a quarterly payment or allowance, tax, pension, or wage paid or received **2 a :** LODGING, SHELTER **b :** the provision of quarters (as for troops) or the cost of it
**quarter ail** *n* **:** [1]BLACKLEG 1
[1]**quarterback** \'==,=\ *n* **:** a backfield player in football who usu. lines up behind the center, calls the signals, and directs the offensive play of his team
[2]**quarterback** \"\ *vt* **1 :** to call the signals and direct the offensive play of (a football team) **2 :** to give executive direction to **:** issue orders to **:** BOSS ⟨~*ed* the original buying syndicate —*Time*⟩ ~ *vi* **:** to serve as quarterback ⟨~*ed* for his high school team⟩
**quarterback sneak** *n* **:** a quick or delayed run by a football quarterback inside the defensive guards or tackles
**quarter belt** *n* **:** a belt connecting pulleys whose axles are at right angles
**quarter bend** *n* **:** a bend changing direction 90 degrees (as in piping)
**quarter bill** *n* **:** a list specifying the stations to be taken by a ship's officers and crew in time of action or for given evolutions and the names of the men assigned to each — compare STATION BILL

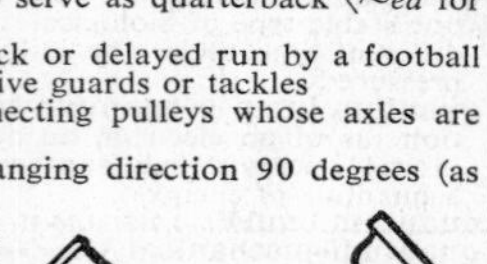

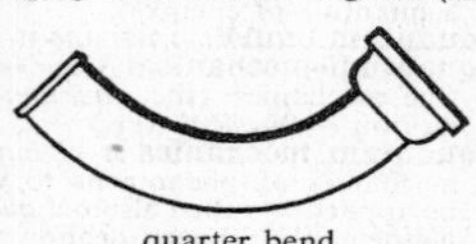

quarter bend

**quarter binding** *n* **:** a book binding in which the material of the backbone (as leather) is different from that of the sides and extends upon the boards one quarter their width or less — compare FULL BINDING, HALF BINDING, THREE-QUARTER BINDING
**quarter blanket** *n* **:** a blanket used under a horse's harness to cover from the tail to beyond the saddle
**quarter block** *n* **:** a block fitted under the quarters of a yard on each side of the slings through which clew lines and sheets are rove
**quarter blood** *n* **:** a median grade of wool fineness — compare BLOOD 7, BRAID, [3]FINE, HALF BLOOD
**quarter boards** *n pl* **:** boards raised above the bulwarks along a ship's quarter — called also *topgallant bulwarks*
**quarter boat** *n* **1 :** a boat hung on davits at a ship's quarter **2 :** a boat (as a houseboat) providing living quarters for a work crew
**quarter boom** *n* **:** a boat boom near the stern
**quarter boot** *n* **:** a boot for an overreaching horse's forefoot as a protection against injury by striking it with the hind foot
**quarter-bound** \¦==¦=\ *adj* **:** having a quarter binding — used of a book
**quarter box** *n* **:** a bearing housing with four adjustable brasses
**quarter-breed** \'==,=\ *n* **:** a person with three grandparents of one and the fourth from another race; *specif* **:** a person one fourth American Indian and three fourths white
**quarter butt** *n* **:** a billiard cue that is shorter than the ordinary cue
**quarter cask** *n*, *archaic* **:** a cask that holds about ¼ of a hogshead
**quarter-cleft** \¦==¦=\ *adj*, *archaic* **:** QUARTERSAWED
**quarter court** *n*, *obs* **:** a court sitting every three months
**quarter crack** *n* **:** a sand crack usu. in a horse's forefoot
**quarter-cut** \¦==¦=\ *adj* **:** QUARTERSAWED
**quarter day** *n* [ME, fr. [1]*quarter* + *day*] **:** the day beginning a quarter of the year and often used as the date when a quarterly payment (as rent) falls due ⟨every *quarter day* Madame wept before the landlord —Philip O'Connor⟩
[1]**quarterdeck** \'==,=\ *n* **1 :** the afterpart of a ship's upper deck sometimes including the poop deck when raised and often reserved for officers and cabin passengers **2 :** a part of a deck on a naval vessel set aside for ceremonial and official use
[2]**quarterdeck** \"\ *vi* **:** to stride back and forth on or as if on a quarterdeck
**quar·ter·deck·er** \"ə(r)\ *n* [[1]*quarterdeck* + *-er*] **1 :** a naval officer who cares more for regulations and etiquette than efficiency **2 :** SLIPPER LIMPET
**quarter dollar** *n* **:** a 25-cent piece
**quarter eagle** *n* **:** a $2.50 gold piece of the U.S. first issued in 1796 and last issued in 1929 — see EAGLE
**quartered** *adj* [fr. past part. of [2]*quarter*] **1 :** divided into or containing heraldic quarters or quarterings **2 a :** divided into four equal parts, sections, or regions **:** cut into quarters **b :** QUARTERSAWED — used of lumber (as oak) **c :** cut in four successive layers from the same piece of wood and placed so that each piece forms one quarter of the whole surface thus producing a symmetrical pattern ⟨~ veneer⟩ **3 :** furnished with quarters **:** provided with shelter **:** LODGED, LOCATED
**quar·ter·er** \-d·ərə(r), -tə-\ *n* -s **:** one that quarters: as **a :** LODGER **b :** a clay target or live bird flying to a shooter's right or left
**quarter evil** *or* **quarter ill** *n* **:** BLACKLEG 1
**quarter face** *n* **:** a face turned away (as in a portrait) so that but one quarter is visible
**quarter fast** *n* **:** QUARTER ROPE
[1]**quarterfinal** \¦==¦=\ *adj* **:** of or relating to the round in a sports contest just before the semifinal
[2]**quarterfinal** \"\ *n* **1 :** a quarterfinal match **2 quarterfinals** *pl* **:** a quarterfinal round
**quar·ter·fi·nal·ist** \"əst\ *n* **:** a contestant qualified for or participating in a quarterfinal
**quarter gallery** *n* **:** a balcony projecting from the quarter of a large sailing ship
**quarter galley** *n* **:** a small galley **:** a light sailing cruiser
**quarter grabbing** *n* [*grabbing* fr. gerund of *grab*] **:** an overreaching by a horse
**quarter grain** *n* **:** the grain of quartersawed wood (as oak)
**quarter guard** *n*, *Brit* **:** INTERIOR GUARD
**quarter gunner** *n*, *archaic* **:** GUNNER'S MATE
**quarter hoop** *n* **:** BULGE HOOP
**quarter horse** *n* [so called fr. its high speed for distances up to a quarter of a mile] **:** an alert cobby muscular horse developed on the ranges of the U.S. for great endurance under the saddle and now commonly recognized as a distinct breed — compare CUTTING HORSE
**quarter hour** *n* **1 a :** 15 minutes **b :** any of the quarter points of an hour ⟨listened apprehensively as the clock chimed successive *quarter hours*⟩ **2 :** an hour a week for an academic quarter devoted to class meetings — compare SEMESTER HOUR
[1]**quartering** *n* -s [fr. gerund of [2]*quarter*] **1 a :** the division of an escutcheon into four or more compartments showing coats of arms brought in by family alliances **b :** a quarter of an escutcheon or the coat of arms on it **2 a :** a dividing into quarters **:** a cutting or separation into four parts **b :** a division into some other number of parts **3 a :** the provision or assignment of quarters (as for soldiers) **b :** LODGING **4 a :** the use of quarters in building construction **b :** studding in place in a building **5 :** a ranging to and fro over an area **:** an intensive search or close coverage **:** CRISSCROSSING **6 :** the passing of the moon from one quarter to another **7 :** the adjustment (as of cranks or wrist pins) at right angles with each other **8 :** the sampling of crushed ore or other material by dividing it into quarters two of which are mixed and again quartered and repeating the operation until a sample of the desired size is obtained
[2]**quartering** \"\ *adj* [fr. pres. part. of [2]*quarter*] **1 a :** coming from a point well abaft the beam of a ship but not directly astern — used of wind, waves, or any moving object ⟨the canoe danced and lurched over a ~ sea —C.S.Forester⟩ **b** (1) *archery* **:** oblique with reference to the target and the archer — used of the wind (2) **:** moving away diagonally to a shooter's right or left — used of a clay target or live game bird **c :** lying at right angles ⟨~ cranks of a locomotive⟩ **:** lying in planes forming a right angle with each other **2** [[1]*quartering*] **:** of, relating to, or used in quartering
**quartering machine** *n* **:** a machine for simultaneously boring parallel holes (as the crankpin holes of locomotive driving wheels) so that the center line of one will be 90 degrees ahead of the center line of the other
**quartering sea** *n* **:** a sea striking a ship's quarter at an angle of about 45 degrees to its heading — compare FOLLOWING SEA, HEAD SEA
**quartering wind** *n* **:** a wind blowing obliquely to a specified direction (as of a ship's heading or of the shooting on a target range)
**quarter iron** *n* **1 :** a boom iron on the quarter of a yard **2 :** the iron band around the quarter of a sailing ship's yard to which the boom iron is screwed
**quarter-jack** \'==,=\ *n* **:** a clock jack that strikes the quarter hours
**quarter lift** *n* **:** a lift running to the quarters of a sailing ship's yard or to the after but not extreme end of a boom
**quarter light** *n*, *Brit* **:** a side window in a closed carriage or automobile as distinguished from those in the doors
**quarter line** *n* **1 :** QUARTER ROPE **2 :** an extra hauling line fastened to the underside of a long seine
[1]**quar·ter·ly** *R* 'kwȯr|d·ərlē, |tər-, -li *sometimes by* r-*dissimilation* -ō|; -*R* -ōd·|əl-, -ȯt|, |°l-\ *adv* [ME, fr. [1]*quarter* + *-ly*, adv. suffix] **1 a :** in heraldic quarters or quarterings **:** in four or more divisions — used of an escutcheon **b :** in diagonally opposite quarters of an escutcheon ⟨two coats of arms borne ~⟩ **2 :** at three-month intervals **:** every quarter ⟨interest is compounded ~⟩
[2]**quarterly** \"\ *adj* [[1]*quarter* + *-ly*, adj. suffix] **1 :** computed for or payable at three-month intervals ⟨a ~ insurance premium⟩ **:** recurring, issued, or spaced at three-month intervals ⟨a ~ meeting⟩ ⟨a ~ notice⟩ **2** *archaic* **:** moving in an oblique or quartering direction ⟨a ~ wind⟩ **3 :** divided into heraldic quarters or quarterings and specified by number if other than four ⟨~ of six⟩
[3]**quarterly** \"\ *n* -ES **:** a periodical that is published four times a year
**quarterly court** *n* **:** a county court held (as in Kentucky) every three months and having original and appellate jurisdiction in petty civil cases and in lesser crimes
**quarterly meeting** *n*, *usu cap Q&M* **1 :** an organizational unit of the Society of Friends usu. composed of several Monthly Meetings — compare YEARLY MEETING **2 :** a session of a Quarterly Meeting
**quarterly quartered** *adj* **1** *heraldry* **:** COUNTERQUARTERED **2** *heraldry* **:** quartered in the center and having each arm divided down the middle with the divisions of alternate tinctures **:** quartered as a saltire
**quar·ter·man** \'==mən\ *n*, *pl* **quartermen :** a foreman in a shipbuilding yard who has charge of several groups of men doing the same kind of work
**quartermaster** \'==,==\ *n* [ME *quarter maister*, fr. [1]*quarter* + *maister* master] **1 :** a petty officer who attends to a ship's helm, binnacle, and signals under the master or navigator

**2 :** a commissioned officer of the U. S. Army Quartermaster Corps **:** a commissioned officer whose duty is to provide clothing and subsistence for a body of troops
**quartermaster general** *n* **:** the U. S. Army major general commanding the Quartermaster Corps
**quar·tern** \R ˈkwȯr|d·ərn, |tərn *sometimes by r-dissimilation* -ō|; —R -ō(ə)d·ən, -)tən, -tᵊn\ *n* -s [ME *quarteroun, quartron,* fr. OF *quarteron* fourth of a pound, fourth of a hundred, fr. *quartier* quarter — more at QUARTER] **1 :** a fourth part **:** QUARTER **2 :** a fourth of various units of measure (as of a pint, a gill, a peck, or a stone) **3 :** the fourth part of a sheet of paper **4** *Brit* **:** a loaf of bread weighing about four pounds
**quarter nelson** *n* **:** a wrestling hold gained when one wrestler kneeling beside a prone opponent places his far hand on the opponent's head and passes his near arm under the opponent's adjacent arm and grasps the wrist of his own far arm — compare FULL NELSON, HALF NELSON, THREE-QUARTER NELSON
**quarter nettings** *n pl* **:** hammock nettings along a ship's quarter rails
**quarter note** *n* **:** a musical note equal in time value to a fourth of a whole note or a half of a half note **:** CROTCHET

quarter notes

**quarteron** *or* **quarteroon** *archaic var of* QUADROON
**quarterpace** \ˈ==,=\ *n* **:** a staircase landing where the stair turns at a right angle — compare HALFPACE
**quarter–phase** *adj* **:** of or relating to a combination of two circuits energized by alternating electromotive forces that differ in phase by a quarter of a cycle or by 90 degrees **:** of or relating to a four-wire two-phase system or apparatus having the neutral points of the two phases at the same potential **:** TWO-PHASE
**quarter pieces** *n pl* **:** the timbers of a ship's quarters where they meet the stern
**quarter–pierced** \ˈ==¦=\ *adj, of a cross* **:** having the central square at the intersection of the arms cut out
**quarter point** *n* **:** QUARTER 19d
**quarter post** *n* **:** a post marking a corner of a quarter section of land
**quarter race** *n* **:** a quarter-mile race between two horses
**quarter rack** *n* **:** a rack regulating a clock's striking of the quarters
**quarter rail** *n* **:** a rail reaching from a ship's gangway to its stern — compare MONKEY RAIL
**quarter rest** *n* **:** a musical rest corresponding in time value to a quarter note
**quarter rope** *n* **:** a mooring rope from a ship's quarter
**quarter round** *n* **:** an ovolo presenting the profile of a quarter circle **:** ECHINUS
**quarter run** *n* **:** a contract providing for display of an advertising card in a fourth of the subway or trolley cars, railroad coaches, or buses in a district — compare FULL RUN, HALF RUN
**quarters** *pl of* QUARTER, *pres 3d sing of* QUARTER
**quartersaw** \ˈ==,=\ *vt* **:** to saw (a log) radially into quarters and then into boards or planks in which the annual rings are at or nearly at right angles to the wide face to secure lumber that will warp relatively little, will not be likely to check, and will show the grain advantageously — compare TANGENT-SAW
**quarter screw** *n* **:** any of the four regulating screws in a common kind of compensation watch or chronometer balance
**quarter seal** *n* **:** a seal that in shape and impression is a fourth part of the great seal of the nation
**quarter section** *n* **:** a fourth of a section **:** a piece of land 160 acres in area in a U. S. public-land survey
**quarter sessions** *n pl* [so called fr. its meeting quarterly] **1 a :** an English local court of record having original and appellate jurisdiction over petty crimes and less serious felonies and sometimes also over petty civil cases and local matters involving the public interest (as licenses and the repair of roads and bridges) and presided over usu. by two justices of the peace or by a magistrate or judge sitting with a jury in a county or by a recorder in a borough — compare PETTY SESSIONS **b :** a local Scottish court held quarterly by justices of the peace chiefly for review and appeal **c :** an intermediate court in parts of Australia (as New South Wales) having original and appellate criminal jurisdiction and consisting of a judge sitting with a jury **2 :** a local court with criminal jurisdiction and sometimes administrative functions (as the care of roads and bridges) in some states of the U.S. (as Pennsylvania)
**quarter sling** *n* **:** a sling supporting a yard at one of a ship's quarters
**quarter snail** *n* **:** the snail used in the quarter part of a clock or repeater
**quarterstaff** \ˈ==,=\ *n* **:** a long stout staff used as a weapon and wielded with one hand in the middle and the other between the middle and the end
**quarter strap** *n* **1 :** either of the straps leading from a cavalry saddle to the ring to which the cinch strap is made fast **2 :** a strap around a yard at a ship's quarter often supporting a ring or grommet
**quarterstretch** \ˈ==,=\ *n* [so called fr. its extent of about a quarter of a mile] **:** HOMESTRETCH
**quarter timber** *n* **:** either of the two main timbers in the stern of a sailing ship with the fashion piece forming the main framework of the counter
**quarter tone** *n* **1** *or* **quarter step a :** a musical interval of one half a half step **b :** a tone at such an interval **2 :** a coarse-screen cut made from an enlarged photograph of a proof from a fine-screen halftone
**quarter–turn drive** *n* **:** a belt drive between pulleys whose axes are at right angles
**quartervine** \ˈ==,=\ *n* [so called fr. the ease with which the stem can be divided into quarters] **:** CROSS VINE 1
**quarter waiter** *n, obs* **:** a gentleman usher on duty in the English court for three months of each year
**quarter watch** *n* **:** a watch including one half of a full watch or one fourth of the ship's crew
**quarter–wave plate** *n* **:** a crystal plate that changes the phase difference between the two components of polarized light traversing it by one-fourth cycle — compare HALF-WAVE PLATE
**quarter–witted** \ˈ==¦==\ *adj* **:** half as bright as a half-wit
**quarter–yearly** \ˈ==¦==\ *adv (or adj)* **:** at three-month intervals
**quar·tet** *or* **quar·tette** \(ˈ)kwȯrˈtet, -ō(ə)¦t-, *usu* -ed·+V\ *n* -s [alter. (influenced by *-et* or *-ette*) of *quartetto*] **1 a :** a musical composition or movement in four parts each performed by a single voice or instrument; *specif* **:** an instrumental piece in sonata form usu. for four stringed instruments ⟨composed a ~⟩ **b :** the group of four performers of such four-part music ⟨woodwind ~⟩ **c :** a performance of such a composition **2 :** a group consisting of four ⟨a ~ of articles —*Times Lit. Supp.*⟩ ⟨in some places no murder trial is complete without its pair or ~ of differing experts —Walter Goodman⟩ **3 :** any one of the four sets of micromeres cut off in spirally cleaving eggs with determinate cleavage in sequence from the four macromeres produced by the first two cleavage divisions
**quartet table** *n* **:** a nest of four small tables
**quar·tet·to** \=ˈted·(,)ō\ *n* -s [It, dim. of *quarto* fourth, fr. *quarto*, adj., fourth, fr. L *quartus*; akin to L *quattuor* four — more at FOUR] **:** QUARTET
**¹quar·tic** \ˈkwȯrd·ik\ *n* -s [ISV *quart-* + *-ic*, n. suffix] **:** a quartic polynomial or equation
**²quartic** \"\ *adj* [*quart-* + *-ic*, adj. suffix] **:** of the fourth degree
**quartic equation** *n* **:** BIQUADRATIC EQUATION
**¹quar·tile** \ˈkwȯr,tīl, -rd·ᵊl, -(,)tīl\ *n* -s [ML *quartilis*, adj., constituting or related to the aspect of two celestial bodies that are ninety degrees apart, fr. L *quartus* fourth + *-ilis* -ile (adj. suffix)] *archaic* **:** the aspect of two celestial bodies that are 90 degrees apart
**²quartile** \"\ *n* -s [ISV *quart-* + *-ile*, n. suffix] **:** any one of the three values that divide the items of a frequency distribution into four classes of one quarter each of the total number of items so that the values corresponding to the items in one class are less than the first quartile, those in a second class are greater than the first quartile and less than the second, those in a third class are greater than the second quartile and less than the third, those in a fourth class are greater than the third quartile
**quartile deviation** *n* **:** one half of the difference obtained by subtracting the first quartile from the third quartile in a frequency distribution
**quarting** *pres part of* QUART
**quar·to** \ˈkwȯr|d·(,)ō, -ō(ə)|, |(,)tō\ *n* -s [L, abl. of *quartus* fourth] **1 :** the size of a piece of paper cut four from a sheet; *also* **:** paper or a page of this size — abbr. *4to*; symbol *4°*; see BOOK tables **2 :** a book printed on quarto pages ⟨the volume is a ~, bound on the narrow side —Walter Millis⟩
**quar·to·dec·i·man** \,=(,)=ˈdesəmən\ *n* -s [LL *quartodecimanus*, fr. L *quartus decimus* fourteenth (fr. *quartus* fourth + *decimus* tenth) + *-anus* -an; akin to L *quattuor* four — more at FOUR, DIME] **1** *usu cap* **:** one of a group in the early church esp. in Asia Minor who during the 2d century and until the Nicene council in 325 observed Easter on the 14th of Nisan when the Jews slaughtered the Passover lamb no matter on what day of the week that date occurred **2 :** one of the Celtic Christians in the British Isles in the 7th century who followed a different mode of calculating the date of Easter from that used on the continent
**quar·tole** \ˈkwȯr,tōl\ *also* **quar·to·let** \ˈkwȯrd·ᵊlˈet\ *n* -s [*quartole* ISV *quart-* + *-ole*; *quartolet* ISV *quartole* + *-et*] **:** QUADRUPLET 3
**quart pot** *n* [ME, fr. ¹*quart* + *pot*] **:** a vessel holding a quart; *esp* **:** an Australian tin vessel used for cooking and as a drinking cup
**quarts** *pl of* QUART, *pres 3d sing of* QUART
**quartz** \ˈkwȯrts, -ō(ə)ts\ *n* -ES [G *quarz*, fr. MHG, perh. of Slav origin; akin to Czech *tvrdý* quartz, fr. *tvrdý*, adj., hard; akin to Gk *seira* cord, rope, Lith *tverti* to hold, contain] **1 :** a mineral $SiO_2$ consisting of a silicon dioxide that occurs in usu. colorless and transparent but sometimes yellow, brown, purple, or green hexagonal crystals, that occurs also in crystalline masses of vitreous luster and in cryptocrystalline massive forms, and that next to feldspar is the commonest mineral (hardness 7, sp. gr. of crystals 2.65–2.66) **2 :** gold or sometimes silver ore that is either broken or in place as distinguished from auriferous gravel
**quartz battery** *or* **quartz mill** *n* **:** STAMP MILL
**quartz–crystal clock** *or* **quartz clock** *n* **:** a clock in which the high uniform piezoelectric vibrations of a quartz crystal induced by current from a constant frequency generator are used to control the rate of a synchronous motor clock
**quartz–diorite** \ˈ=ˈ==,=\ *n* **:** diorite containing appreciable amounts of quartz
**quartz flint** *n* **:** POTTER'S FLINT
**quartz glass** *n* **:** VITREOUS SILICA
**quartz·ic** \-sik\ *adj* [ISV *quartz* + *-ic*] **:** QUARTZIFEROUS
**quartz·if·er·ous** \(ˈ)kwō(r)tˈsif(ə)rəs\ *adj* [*quartz* + *-iferous*] **:** bearing or containing quartz
**quartz·ite** \ˈkwȯrt,sīt\ *n* -s [ISV *quartz* + *-ite*] **:** a compact granular rock composed of quartz that is a metamorphosed sandstone in which the siliceous cement is often so blended with the quartz grains as to give the rock a nearly homogeneous texture
**quartz·it·ic** \(ˈ)=ˈsid·ik\ *adj* **:** containing quartzite
**quartz lamp** *n* **:** a mercury-vapor lamp in a tube of quartz glass that transmits most of the ultraviolet radiation
**quartz mining** *n* **:** the mining of gold on veins or ore bodies in place as distinguished from surface digging or washing **:** underground mining in rock — compare PLACER MINING
**quartz·oid** \ˈkwȯrt,sȯid\ *n* -s **:** a crystal that is common with quartz and consists of a combination of the hexagonal prism and dipyramid
**quartz·ose** \-,sōs\ *or* **quartz·ous** \-səs\ *adj* [*quartzose* fr. *quartz* + *-ose*; *quartzous* prob. fr. F *quartzeux*, fr. *quartz* (fr. G *quarz*) + *-eux* -ous] **:** containing, consisting of, or resembling quartz
**quartz plate** *n* **:** a piece of quartz crystal cut in such a way as to be active piezoelectrically; *specif* **:** such a plate mounted with metal electrodes applied to its surfaces so that the combination is or resembles a condenser — compare PIEZOELECTRIC OSCILLATOR
**quartz porphyry** *n* **:** a porphyritic extrusive or dike rock in which quartz with more or less corroded crystals and orthoclase and usu. mica, amphibole, or pyroxene occur as phenocrysts in a groundmass that is felsophyric, granophyric, or vitrophyric
**quartz sand** *n* **:** a sand formed from quartz
**quartz schist** *n* **:** a metamorphosed schistose rock composed essentially of quartz often with some mica or tourmaline or both
**quartz spectrograph** *n* **:** a spectrograph having prisms and lenses of quartz and used for ultraviolet spectroscopy
**quartz vein** *n* **:** a vein filled with quartz either of igneous origin or deposited from solution
**quartz wedge** *n* **:** a piece of quartz cut in a thin wedge and used in the optical determination of minerals and in the study of polarized light
**quartzy** \-sē\ *adj* **:** QUARTZOSE
**qua·ru·ba** \kwəˈrübə\ *n* -s [prob. fr. Pg] **:** any of several trees of the genus *Vochysia*
**¹quas** *var of* KVASS
**²quas** *pl of* QUA
**¹quash** \ˈkwäsh *also* -ō-\ *vt* -ED/-ING/-ES [ME *quassen*, fr. MF *quasser, casser* to discharge, annul, partly fr. L *quassare* to shake, break into pieces and partly fr. LL *cassare* to annihilate, annul, fr. L *cassus* empty, void, without effect; L *cassus* akin to L *carēre* to be without — more at CASTE] *law* **:** to put an end to **:** make void **:** ABATE, ANNUL, OVERTHROW ⟨~ a writ⟩ ⟨~ a service⟩ ⟨~ an indictment⟩ ⟨amnesty decree to ~ or cut sentences of wide range of convicts —*N.Y.Times*⟩
**²quash** \"\ *vb* -ED/-ING/-ES [ME *quashen*, fr. MF *quasser, casser* to break, fr. L *quassare* to shake, break into pieces, fr. *quassus*, past part. of *quatere* to shake; akin to OE *hūdenian* to shake, MHG *hotzen* to set in motion, Icel *hossa* to bounce (a child) on one's knee, and perh. to Gk *passein* to sprinkle] *vt* **1 :** to beat down or in pieces **:** dash forcibly **:** SQUASH ⟨carts going by would ~ 'em —Lascelles Abercrombie⟩ **2 :** to suppress or extinguish summarily and completely **:** crush out **:** SUBDUE, QUELL ⟨~ a rebellion⟩ ~ *vi, obs* **:** to make a noise of splashing **syn** see CRUSH
**qashqai** *usu cap, var of* QASHQAI
**quashy** \ˈkwäshē\ *adj* -ER/-EST [²*quash* + *-y*] **:** MARSHY, SWAMPY, WET ⟨~ ground⟩
**¹qua·si** \ˈkwā,zī; *also* -äzē, -ā,sī, -äsē; *sometimes* -āzē, -ōzē, -ōsē; *or* -i *instead of* -ē\ *adv* [L, fr. *quam* than, how, as + *si* if — more at QUANTITY, SO] **1 :** as if **:** as it were **:** in a manner **:** in some sense or degree **:** SEEMINGLY, ALMOST ⟨the legatee was ~ an heir —O.W.Holmes †1935⟩ — usu. joined to second element with a hyphen ⟨a *quasi*-historical narrative⟩ ⟨*quasi*-universal literacy⟩ ⟨the *quasi*-diamond-shaped mouthpiece —William Yeomans⟩ ⟨served *quasi*-officially⟩ **2** \ˈkwäzē, -i\ [It, fr. L] **:** in effect ⟨andante ~ allegro⟩ **:** APPROXIMATELY ⟨~ largo⟩ — used to qualify a musical direction
**²quasi** \"\ *adj* **1 :** having some resemblance (as in function, effect, or status) to a given thing **:** SEEMING, VIRTUAL ⟨a ~ argument⟩ ⟨its economic power gave it a position of ~ government —Fritz Tarnow⟩ ⟨in dance band orchestrations, the arranger develops into a ~ composer —Claude Lapham⟩ — often joined to second element with a hyphen ⟨a *quasi*-shawl⟩ ⟨*quasi*-republicanism⟩ **2 :** having a given legal status only by operation or construction of law and without reference to any intent of the party in interest (as the obligee or owner) ⟨~ crime⟩ ⟨a ~ trustee⟩ ⟨a ~ right⟩
**quasi contract** *n* **1 :** an obligation similar to that upon contract, enforced by action as upon contract, and imposed by law for reasons of justice and independently of the will of the person obliged — called also *contract quasi, implied contract* **2 :** an obligation imposed by law to prevent unjust enrichment of one at another's expense **:** RESTITUTION
**quasi corporation** *n* **:** a public or municipal body or organization (as a county) not specifically incorporated or vested with all the usual powers of a corporation but exercising certain corporate functions and rights in connection with public duties
**quasi delict** *n* [LL *quasi delictum*, fr. L *quasi* + *delictum* fault — more at DELICT] **1** *Roman law* **:** a wrong not arising out of a contract and implied and made actionable by praetorian edict though not previously recognized as a delictum **2** *civil & Scots law* **:** a wrong not arising out of a contract, implied under the circumstances, and made actionable as a matter of public policy rather than on account of any deliberately wrongful conduct or intention
**quasi deposit** *n* **:** a deposit or bailment implied in law from the circumstances whereby one coming into possession of another's personal property by chance or mistake is deemed to be a bailee in order to do justice between the parties and to prevent unjust enrichment **:** a constructive or quasi bailment
**quasi easement** *n* **:** APPARENT EASEMENT
**quasi ex con·trac·tu** \-,ekskən·ˈtrak(,)t(y)ü\ *adv (or adj)* [L] **:** as if from or by contract — compare QUASI CONTRACT
**quasi in rem** \-ənˈrem\ *adv (or adj)* [L, as if against a thing] **:** as if against a thing (as a right, status, property) ⟨proceedings and judgments are *quasi in rem* when they are in a court having no jurisdiction over the person of the defendant, not seeking to adjudicate a right, title, or status as against all in the world, but seeking to apply specific property within the power of the court insofar as that property is available in satisfaction of a personal action or claim against the defendant⟩ — compare IN PERSONAM, IN REM
**quasi–judicial** \ˈ¦=(,)=+\ *adj* **1 :** having a partly judicial character by possession of the right to hold hearings on and conduct investigations into disputed claims and alleged infractions of rules and regulations and to make decisions arrived at and enforced after the general manner of procedures in courts ⟨*quasi-judicial* bodies such as the National Labor Relations Board —*Atlantic*⟩ **2 :** essentially judicial in character but not within the judicial power or function nor belonging to the judiciary as constitutionally defined ⟨*quasi-judicial* functions⟩ ⟨some method of *quasi-judicial* review is desirable —*Harvard Law Rev.*⟩ — **quasi–judicially** \"+\ *adv*
**quasi–legislative** \"+\ *adj* **1 :** having a partly legislative character by possession of the right to make rules and regulations having the force of law ⟨the Interstate Commerce Commission is a *quasi-legislative* agency⟩ **2 :** essentially legislative in character but not within the legislative power or function or belonging to the legislative branch of government as constitutionally defined ⟨*quasi-legislative* powers⟩ ⟨*quasi-legislative* authority⟩
**qua·si·mo·do** \,kwäzəˈmō(,)dō, -äsə-\ *n* -s *usu cap* [L *quasi modo* as if just now; fr. part of the opening words of the introit for that day (based on 1 Pet 2:2), *quasi modo geniti infantes* as newborn babes] **:** LOW SUNDAY
**quasi–optical** *pronunc at* ¹QUASI +\ *adj* **:** resembling light in character or behavior — used of ultrashort hertzian waves
**quasi partner** *n* **:** NOMINAL PARTNER
**quasi–public** \ˈ¦=(,)=+\ *adj* **:** essentially public (as in services rendered, functions performed, or source of income received) although under private ownership or control **:** affected with a public interest ⟨*quasi-public* enterprises like railroads⟩
**quasi–pupillary substitution** \"+...-\ *n, Roman law* **:** substitution of another heir upon the incapacity of an insane heir first named to take an inheritance
**quasi rent** *n* **:** revenue in excess of cost received from a service other than land use
**quasi–reorganization** \ˈ¦=(,)=+\ *n* **:** a corporate procedure whereby recapitalization is achieved by the elimination of the existing deficit and the establishment of a new earned surplus account for future earnings only and without resort to the legal formalities of a complete reorganization
**quasi–tangent arc** \"+...-\ *n* **:** CIRCUMZENITHAL ARC
**quasi usufruct** *n* **:** IMPERFECT USUFRUCT
**quas·ky** \ˈkwäskē\ *n* -ES [perh. irreg. fr. *oquassa*] **:** OQUASSA
**quass** *var of* KVASS
**quas·sia** \ˈkwäsh(ē)ə, -äsēə\ *n* [NL, fr. *Quassi*, 18th cent. Surinam Negro slave who discovered the medicinal value of Surinam quassia + NL *-ia*] **1** *cap* **:** a genus of shrubs or trees (family Simaroubaceae) having pinnate leaves with winged petioles and large racemose scarlet flowers **2** -s **:** a drug consisting of the heartwood of various tropical trees of the family Simaroubaceae used in medicine as a bitter tonic and as a remedy for roundworms in children, as an insecticide, and in brewing as a substitute for hops — see JAMAICA QUASSIA, SURINAM QUASSIA
**quas·sin** \ˈkwäsᵊn\ *n* -s [ISV *quass-* (fr. NL *Quassia*) + *-in*] **:** the bitter crystalline principle of quassia
**¹quat** \ˈkwät, -at\ *vb* **quatted; quatted; quatting; quats** [ME *quaten*, fr. MF *quatir* to beat, fr. (assumed) *coactire* to press together — more at DECATING] *vt, dial chiefly Eng* **1 :** beat down **:** SQUASH **2 :** GLUT, SATIATE ~ *vi, chiefly dial* **:** SQUAT
**²quat** \"\ *adj* [ME, fr. past part. of *quaten*] *chiefly dial* **:** pressed close **:** SQUAT ⟨the rest lay so ~ and close that they could not be apprehended —John Bunyan⟩
**³quat** \"\ *Scot var of* QUIT
**⁴quat** \"\ *n* -s [origin unknown] **1** *dial chiefly Eng* **:** an eruption of the skin (as a pimple, boil, sty) **2** *chiefly dial* **:** UPSTART, WHIPPERSNAPPER
**⁵quat** *var of* KAT
**quat** *abbr* [L *quattuor*] four
**qua·te·nus** \ˈkwätənəs, -,ten-\ *prep* [L, how far, to what extent, fr. *qua* where, as, insofar as + *tenus* as far as, up to; akin to L *tendere* to stretch — more at QUA, THIN] **:** in the quality or capacity of **:** AS
**quater–** *comb form* [ISV, fr. L *quater* four times] **:** TETRA- — esp. in names of organic compounds to denote the quadrupling of a radical or molecule ⟨*quater*phenyl⟩ ⟨*quater*thiazole⟩
**quater·centenary** \ˈkwäd·ə(r), -wäd-+\ *n* [L *quater* four times + E *centenary*] **:** a four-hundredth anniversary
**¹quater·nary** \ˈkwäd·ər,nerē, kwäˈtərnərē\ *n* -ES [ME, fr. L *quaternarius*, adj., consisting of four each, fr. *quaterni* four each (fr. *quater* four times) + *-arius* -ary] **1 a :** a group of four **b :** a member of a fourth group **2** *usu cap* **:** the Quaternary period or system of rocks
**²quaternary** \"\ *adj* [L *quaternarius* consisting of four each] **1 :** consisting of four parts or components **:** by fours or in sets of four ⟨a ~ compound⟩ **2 a :** fourth in order **b** *usu cap* **:** of or relating to the geological period from the end of the Tertiary to the present time — see GEOLOGIC TIME table **3 :** characterized by replacement in the fourth degree: as **a :** united to four carbon atoms in organic radicals ⟨a ~ carbon atom⟩ **b :** consisting of or containing an atom (as nitrogen) united by four bonds to carbon atoms in organic radicals ⟨~ ammonium [R₄N]⁺⟩ ⟨~ salts⟩
**quaternary ammonium compound** *also* **quaternary** *n* -ES **:** any of a large class of strong bases and their salts that may be regarded as compounds of ammonium in which all four hydrogen atoms are replaced by organic radicals and that in many cases are used as surface-active agents, as disinfectants and germicides, and as drugs — compare CATIONIC DETERGENT, METHONIUM
**quaternary silver** *n* **:** silver containing three alloying elements and used for coinage ⟨former British coinage of *quaternary silver* containing 50 percent silver, 40 percent copper, 5 percent nickel, and 5 percent zinc⟩
**quater·nate** \ˈkwäd·ər,nāt, kwäˈtərnət\ *adj* [prob. fr. (assumed) NL *quaternatus*, fr. L *quaterni* four each + *-atus* -ate] **:** composed of or arranged in sets of four ⟨~ leaves⟩
**qua·ter·ni·on** \kwəˈtərnēən, -wäˈt-\ *n* -s [ME *quaternioun*, fr. LL *quaternion-, quaternio*, fr. L *quaterni* four each (fr. *quater* four times) + *-ion-, -io* -ion; akin to L *quattuor* four — more at FOUR] **1 :** a set of four parts, things, or persons **:** TETRAD ⟨delivered him to four ~s of soldiers —Acts 12:4 (AV)⟩ ⟨the leading ~ of publishers —*Times Lit. Supp.*⟩ **2 a** (1) **:** *archaic* **:** a sheet of paper folded twice (2) **:** QUIRE 1a **b :** a sheet that is folded once to form two leaves or four pages and nested together with other sheets (as in ancient books) to form a section **3 :** a generalized complex number that is the sum of a real number and a vector and that depends on one real and three imaginary units the third of which is the product of the first two and also the negative of this product when the order of the factors is reversed so that multiplication over the field of quaternions is not commutative
**qua·ter·ni·ty** \kwäˈtərnəd·ē\ *n* -ES [LL *quaternitat-, quaternitas*, fr. L *quaterni* four each + *-itat-, -itas* -ity] **:** a union or group of four persons, things, or parts; *specif* **:** the union of four individuals in one godhead — compare TRINITY
**quater·ni·za·tion** \,kwäd·ə(r)nəˈzāshən, -wäd-, -,nīˈz-\ *n* -s **:** the process of quaternizing

**quater·nize** \ˈ==,nīz\ *vt* -ED/-ING/-S [²*quaternary* + *-ize*] **:** to convert (as an amine) into a quaternary compound

**qua·ter·phenyl** \ˌ==+\ *n* [ISV *quater-* + *phenyl*] **:** any of several crystalline aromatic hydrocarbons $C_6H_5(C_6H_4)_2C_6H_5$ that contain a sequence of four benzene rings in the molecule; *esp* **:** the isomer whose central rings are attached at para positions and which is made by pyrolysis of biphenyl

**quaters** *var of* CATERS

**qua·tor·zain** \kəˈtȯr,zān, kaˈt-, -ˌzⁿn; ˈkad·ər,zān\ *n* -S [MF *quatorzaine* group of fourteen, fr. OF, period of fourteen days, fr. *quatorze* fourteen] **:** a poem of fourteen lines; *specif* **:** a poem resembling a sonnet but lacking strict sonnet structure

**qua·torze** \kəˈtȯ(ə)rz, kaˈt-\ *n* -S [F, lit., fourteen, fr. OF, fr. L *quattuordecim*, fr. *quattuor* four + *-decim* (fr. *decem* ten) — more at FOUR, TEN] **:** a set of 4 aces, kings, queens, jacks, or tens held in a hand at piquet and scoring 14 points

**qua·train** \ˈkwä,trān *also* =ˈ= *sometimes* ˈkwä·trən *or* kwəˈtrān *or with* ō *for* ä\ *n* -S [F, fr. MF, fr. *quatre* four, fr. L *quattuor*] **:** a verse unit of four lines ⟨a ~ rhyming *abab*⟩

**quatreble** *n* -S [ME, fourfold amount, fr. *quatreble*, adj., quadruple, modif. (influenced by ME *treble*) of MF *quadruple*] *obs* **:** a musical voice part one octave higher than the mean

**qua·tre·foil** \ˈkad·ə(r),fȯil, ˈka·trə,f-\ *n* [ME *quaterfoil* set of four leaves, fr. MF *quatre* four + ME *-foil* (as in *trefoil*)] **1 :** a conventionalized representation of a flower with four petals or of a leaf with four leaflets ⟨an allover pattern of tiny emerald green ~*s* —*Parke-Bernet Galleries Catalog*⟩; *specif* **:** a heraldic representation of a flower with four petals **2 :** a figure enclosed by four joined foils; *specif* **:** a 4-lobed foliation in Gothic tracery — **qua·tre·foiled** \-ld\ *adj*

quatrefoils 2

**quatrible** *n* [alter. (influenced by obs. E *trible* treble, fr. ME) of ME *quatreble* fourfold amount — more at TREBLE] *obs* **:** a descant in fourths

**quatroon** *archaic var of* QUADROON

**quats** *pres 3d sing of* QUAT, *pl of* QUAT

**quatted** *past of* QUAT

**quatting** *pres part of* QUAT

**quat·tri·no** \kwäˈtrē(,)nō\ *n, pl* **quattri·ni** \-nē\ [It, fr. *quattro* four] **:** an old coin of several of the Italian states

**quat·tro·cen·tist** \ˌkwä·trōˈchentəst\ *n, pl* **quattrocentists** *or* **quattrocenti·sti** \-,chenˈtē(,)stē, -ˈtistē\ [It *quattrocentista*, fr. *quattrocento* + *-ista* -ist (fr. L)] **1 :** an Italian of the quattrocento; *esp* **:** a poet or artist of this period **2 :** a student of the art or literature of the quattrocento

**quat·tro·cen·to** \-ˈchen·(,)tō\ *n, sometimes cap* [It, lit., four hundred (abbr. of fourteen hundred), fr. *quattro* four (fr. L *quattuor*) + *cento* hundred, fr. L *centum* — more at FOUR, HUNDRED] **:** the 15th century; *specif* **:** the 15th century period in Italian literature and art

**quat·tuor·decillion** \ˌkwäd·ə,wȯr, -ä,tw- +\ *n, often attrib* [L *quattuordecim* fourteen + E *-illion* (as in *million*)] — see NUMBER table

**quat·uor** \ˈkwäd·ə,wȯr, -ä,tw-\ *n* -S [F, fr. L *quattuor* four] **:** QUARTET

**quauk** \ˈkwȯk\ *Scot var of* QUAKE

¹**qua·ver** \ˈkwāvə(r)\ *vb* **quavered; quavered; quavering** \-v(ə)riŋ\ **quavers** [ME *quaveren*, freq. of *quaven* to tremble] *vi* **1 :** TREMBLE, VIBRATE, SHAKE ⟨was ~*ing* inwardly with nervousness —Marcia Davenport⟩ **2 :** to trill with the voice or on a musical instrument **3 :** to utter sound in tremulous uncertain tones ⟨the full voice ~*ed* and broke —Zane Grey⟩ ~ *vt* **:** to utter with quavers; *esp* **:** to sing with trills or quavers ⟨eldest inhabitants . . . ~ out folk songs —Max Beerbohm⟩

²**quaver** \"\ *n* -S **1 :** EIGHTH NOTE **2 :** a trill in singing **3 :** a tremulous uncertainty of tone (as in the voice due to emotion, old age)

**qua·ver·ing·ly** *adv* **:** in a quavering manner

**qua·very** \ˈkwāv(ə)rē, -ri\ *adj* [¹*quaver* + *-y*] **:** characterized by quavering **:** TREMBLING, UNSTEADY

**quaw** \ˈkwȯ\ *n* -S [origin unknown] *chiefly Scot* **:** QUAGMIRE

¹**quawk** \ˈkwȯk, -wäk\ *vi* [imit.] *chiefly dial* **:** CAW, SQUAWK

²**quawk** \ˈkwȯk\ *n* -S **1 :** ²QUACK **2 :** NIGHT HERON

¹**quay** \ˈkē, ˈk(w)ā\ *n* -S [alter. (influenced by F *quai* quay, fr. OF *cai*) of earlier *key*, fr. ME, fr. MF *cai*, fr. OF, of Celt origin; akin to Corn *kē* hedge, fence — more at HEDGE] **:** a stretch of paved and strengthened bank or a solid artificial landing place (as of stone) made along or parallel to the side of a navigable water for convenience in loading and unloading ships **syn** see WHARF

²**quay** \"\ *vt* -ED/-ING/-S **:** to furnish with a quay

**quay·age** \-ij, -ēj\ *n* -S [alter. (influenced by F *quayage*, fr. OF *caiage*) of earlier *keyage*, fr. ME, fr. MF *caiage*, fr. OF, fr. *cai* quay + *-age*] **1 :** a charge for use of a quay **:** quay dues **:** WHARFAGE **2 :** room on or for quays ⟨the total ~ of the port⟩ **3 :** a system of quays ⟨reconstructed their harbor ~⟩

**quayside** \ˈ=,=\ *n* **:** land bordering on or adjacent to a quay **:** the neighborhood of the quays ⟨the waterfront with its long, paved ~ —Steven Runciman⟩

**queach** \ˈkwēch\ *n* -ES [ME *queche*] *dial chiefly Eng* **:** THICKET

**queachy** \-chē, -chi\ *adj* [obs E, forming a dense growth, fr. *queach* + *-y*] *dial chiefly Eng* **:** BOGGY, MARSHY

**queak** \ˈkwēk\ *vb* -ED/-ING/-S [imit.] *dial* **:** SQUEAK

**quean** \ˈkwēn\ *n* -S [ME *quene*, *quen*, fr. OE *cwene* woman, female serf, prostitute; akin to OHG *quena* woman, wife, ON *kona*, Goth *qino* woman, wife, OE *cwēn* woman, wife, queen — more at QUEEN] *also* **queen** \"\ **:** a disreputable woman; *specif* **:** PROSTITUTE ⟨a lively ~ who can dance, weep and love —*Time*⟩ **2 a** *chiefly Scot* **:** WOMAN; *esp* **:** one that is young or unmarried **b** *dial Brit* **:** a little girl

**quean-cat** \ˈ=,=\ *n, dial Eng* **:** a female cat

**queanish** *adj, obs* **:** of, relating to, or resembling a quean

**quea·si·ly** \ˈkwēz(ə)lē, -li\ *adv* **:** in a queasy manner

**quea·si·ness** \-zēnəs, -zin-\ *n* -ES **:** the quality or state of being queasy

**quea·sy** *also* **quea·zy** \ˈkwēzē, -zi\ *adj* -ER/-EST [ME *coysy*, *qwesye*, *quasy*] **1 :** full of doubt **:** UNSETTLED, HAZARDOUS ⟨last week's ~ market —*Time*⟩ ⟨the lightly rooted life upon one ~ planet —D.C.Peattie⟩ **2 a :** causing nausea **:** NAUSEATING ⟨~ motion of the waves⟩ ⟨a ~ mess upon the plate⟩ **b :** tending to be sick at the stomach **:** NAUSEATED **3 a :** causing qualms or uneasiness **b** (1) **:** easily disturbed **:** DELICATE, FASTIDIOUS, SQUEAMISH ⟨a ~ conscience⟩ (2) **:** experiencing a feeling of uneasiness **:** ill at ease ⟨how ~ we become in the presence of anyone who supposes that he has "charm," when he really has none —Clifford Bax⟩

¹**que·bec** \kwəˈbek, kwē- *sometimes* kāˈ-\ *adj, usu cap* [fr. *Quebec*, Canada] **1 :** of or from Quebec, capital of the province of Quebec **:** of the kind or style prevalent in Quebec **2 :** of or from the province of Quebec **:** of the kind or style prevalent in Quebec

²**quebec** \"\ *usu cap* [fr. *Quebec*, Canada] — a communications code word for the letter *q*

**quebec deal** *n, usu cap Q* **:** timber of any width and three inches or more in thickness — used esp. in the export trade

**que·bec·er** *or* **que·beck·er** \-kə(r)\ *n* -S *cap* [*Quebec*, Canada + E *-er*] **:** a native or resident of Quebec city or province, Canada

**que·bec·ois** *or* **qué·bec·ois** \ˌkā,beˈkwä\ *n, pl* **quebecois** *or* **québecois** \-(z)\ *cap* [F *Québecois*, fr. *Québec*, Canada] **:** QUEBECER

**quebec standard deal** *n, usu cap Q* **:** a deal board 3 inches by 11 inches by 12 feet

**que·brach·a·mine** \kāˈbrachə,mēn, kəˈ-, -mən\ *n* [ISV *quebracho* + *amine*] **:** a crystalline alkaloid $C_{19}H_{26}N_2$ obtained from aspidosperma

**que·brach·ine** \-chən\ *n* -S [ISV *quebracho* + *-ine*] **:** YOHIMBINE

**que·brach·i·tol** \-chə,tȯl, -tōl\ *n* -S [ISV *quebracho* + *-ite* + *-ol*] **:** a sweet crystalline compound $C_6H_6(OH)_5(OCH_3)$ occurring esp. in quebracho bark and in the latex of hevea rubber; *levo*-inositol monomethyl ether

**que·bra·cho** \-(,)chō\ *n* -S [AmerSp, alter. of *quiebracha*, *quiebrahacha*, fr. Sp *quiebra* it breaks (3d sing. pres. indic. of *quebrar* to break, fr. L *crepare* to rattle, crack, creak) + *hacha* ax, fr. F *hache* — more at RAVEN, HASH] **1 :** any of several tropical American trees with notably hard wood: as **a :** a tree (*Aspidosperma quebracho*) of Chile and Argentina that yields quebracho bark —called also *white quebracho* **b :** a tree (*Schinopsis lorentzii*) that is native to Argentina and is used as a source of tannin and in dyeing — called also *red quebracho* **c :** a So. American tree (*Iodina rhombifolia*) of the family Santalaceae used in tanning and dyeing **d :** any of several Central American and Mexican leguminous trees (as *Lysiloma divaricata*, *Caesalpinia platyloba*, *Pithecolobium arboreum*) **2 :** the wood of a quebracho **3 :** or **quebracho bark :** ASPIDOSPERMA 2

**que·bra·da** \kāˈbrädə\ *n* -S [Sp, fr. fem. of *quebrado*, *past part.* of *quebrar* to break — more at QUEBRACHO] **1 :** RAVINE; *esp* **:** one that is normally dry or nearly dry but is filled by a torrent during a rain **2 :** BROOK

**quech·ua** \ˈkechwə\ *also* **qui·chua** \ˈkēch-\ *or* **kech·ua** *or* **ki·chua** *n, pl* **quechua** *or* **quechuas** *usu cap* [Sp, fr. Quechua *kkechúwa* plunderer, despoiler, robber] **1 a :** a people of central Peru believed to be originally Aymara **b :** a member of such people **2 :** a group of peoples constituting the dominant element of the Inca empire **3 a :** the language of the Quechua people that is also widely spoken by other Indian peoples of Peru, Bolivia, Ecuador, Chile, and Argentina **b :** a language family comprising the Quechua language

¹**quech·uan** *also* **qui·chuan** \-wən\ *n, pl* **quechuan** *or* **quechuans** *usu cap* [*Quechua* + *-an*] **:** QUECHUA

²**quechuan** *also* **quichuan** \"\ *adj, usu cap* **:** of or relating to the Quechua language family

**queechy** \ˈkwēchē\ *adj* [origin unknown] *dial Eng* **:** SICKLY, PUNY

**queem** \ˈkwēm\ *Scot var of* QUEME

¹**queen** \ˈkwēn\ *n* -S [ME *quen*, *quene*, fr. OE *cwēn* woman, wife, queen; akin to OS *quān* wife, ON *kvæn*, *kvān*, Goth *qens* wife, OIr *ben* woman, Gk *gynē*, Arm *kin*, Skt *jani*] **1 a :** the wife or widow of a king **b :** the wife or widow of a chief of a tribe (as of Indians) **2 a :** a woman who is the sovereign of a kingdom **:** a female monarch **b :** CHIEFTAINESS ⟨~ of the Iroquois⟩ ⟨gypsy ~⟩ **3 a :** a woman eminent in rank, power, or attractions ⟨a ~ in society⟩ ⟨movie ~⟩ **b :** a goddess or a thing personified as female and having supremacy in a specified realm ⟨Venus, ~ of love⟩ ⟨Paris, ~ of cities⟩ ⟨a new liner to join the ocean ~*s*⟩ **c :** a strikingly attractive girl or woman; *esp* **:** the winner of a beauty contest **4 :** the most privileged piece in a set of chessmen having the power to move as either a rook or a bishop **5 :** a playing card marked with a stylized figure of a queen and usu. the initial letter Q **6 :** the fertile fully developed female of social bees, ants, and termites whose function in the colony is to lay eggs — compare SOLDIER, WORKER; see HONEYBEE illustration **7 :** a mature female cat; *specif* **:** one kept for breeding **8** *slang* **:** HOMOSEXUAL — **to the queen's taste :** to the satisfaction of an extremely discriminating person

queen 4

²**queen** \"\ *vb* -ED/-ING/-S *vi* **1 :** to act like a queen **:** behave in a queenly manner **:** put on airs ⟨~*s* in and makes with a production —Julian Halevy⟩ — usu. used with formulary *it* ⟨another woman ~*ing* it in the new penthouse —Helen Howe⟩ **2 :** to reign as queen **3 :** to become a queen in chess ~ *vt* **1 :** to promote (a pawn) to a queen in chess **2 :** to reign over as queen **3 :** to make a queen of ⟨to ~ a woman⟩ **4 :** to provide a queen for (as a hive of bees)

³**queen** \"\ *usu cap* [¹*queen*] — a communications code word for the letter *q*

⁴**queen** *var of* QUEAN

**queen anne** \-ˈan, -aa(ə)n\ *adj, usu cap Q&A* [after *Queen Anne* of England †1714] **1 :** of, relating to, or having the characteristics of a style of furniture prevalent in England under Dutch influence esp. during the first half of the 18th century that is marked by extensive use of upholstery, marquetry, and Oriental fabrics, attention to comfort (as in shapes of chair backs), general use of walnut and of the cabriole, and the introduction of such pieces as the bureau bookcase and separate mirrors ⟨*Queen Anne* sofa⟩ ⟨*Queen Anne* stool⟩ **2 a :** of, relating to, or having the characteristics of a style of English building prevalent in the early 18th century characterized by modified classic ornament, generally unpretentious design, the use of red brickwork in which even relief ornament is carved, and general fitness for domestic architecture **b :** of, relating to, or characteristic of a style of wooden cottages developed in England and the U. S. during the last quarter of the 19th century

**queen anne green** *n, often cap Q&A* **:** TEA GREEN

**queen anne's lace** *n, pl* **queen anne's lace** *also* **queen anne's laces** *usu cap Q&A* [after *Queen Anne* of England] **:** WILD CARROT

**queen bee** *n* **1 :** the fertile fully developed female of a social bee (as the honeybee) — compare QUEEN 6 **2 :** a woman who dominates or leads a group (as in a social activity)

**queen blue** *or* **queen's blue** *n* **:** a moderate blue that is redder and duller than average copen, azurite blue, or Dresden blue and redder and less strong than bluebird

**queen bolt** *n* **:** a rod serving as a queen post in a roof truss

**queen butterfly** *also* **queen** *n* -S **:** a large brown white-spotted butterfly (*Danaus glippus*) of the warmer parts of America that is closely related to the monarch butterfly

**queen cage** *n* **:** a small container to hold a queen bee (as for shipment)

**queen cell** *n* **:** one of the large irregular thick-walled special cells usu. attached to the base of a brood comb in which the larvae of the queen bees are reared

**queen closer** *or* **queen closure** *n* **:** a closer that is less than half a brick; *specif* **:** a brick of full length and thickness but half width that is used at the end of a course next to the quoin header — compare KING CLOSER

**queen conch** *n* **:** a large yellowish conch (*Cassis madagascarensis*) with brown markings that is much used in cameo making; *also* **:** any of several other large conchs or helmet shells (as the king conch)

**queen consort** *n, pl* **queens consort :** the wife of a reigning king

**queen crab** *n* **:** a large edible crab (*Carpilius corallinus*) of the family Xanthidae that frequents shallow water from the Bahamas to Brazil and is usu. pale red marked with scarlet, white, and yellow

**queen-cup** \ˈ=,=\ *n* **:** a perennial herb (*Clintonia uniflora*) of the Rocky Mountain region sometimes cultivated for its white flowers

**queen·dom** \ˈkwēndəm\ *n* -S **1 :** the state or territory ruled by a queen **2 :** the position of a queen

**queen dowager** *n* **:** the widow of a king

**queen excluder** *n* **:** a device usu. of perforated metal that shuts off the queen bee from some parts of a hive but permits the workers to pass

**queen fern** *n* **:** ROYAL FERN

**queenfish** \ˈ=,=\ *n* **:** any of several marine fishes: as **a :** a common small California sciaenid fish (*Seriphus politus*) silvery blue above with the sides and belly silvery **b :** ³WAHOO **c :** any of several large carangid food and game fishes (genus *Chorinemus*) widespread in the tropical Indo-Pacific

**queen·hood** \ˈkwēn,hu̇d\ *n* **:** the rank, dignity, or state of being of a queen

**queen-in-council** \ˈ=ˈ==\ *n, pl* **queens-in-council** *often cap Q&C* **:** KING-IN-COUNCIL — used when the British monarch is a queen

**queen-in-parliament** \ˈ=ˈ=ˈ==\ *n, pl* **queens-in-parliament** *often cap Q&P* **:** KING-IN-PARLIAMENT — used when the British monarch is a queen

**queen·ite** \ˈkwē,nīt\ *n* -S *usu cap* **:** one who supports or upholds a queen; *specif* **:** an adherent of Queen Isabella II of Spain against the Carlists

**queen·less** \ˈkwēnləs\ *adj* **:** lacking a queen

**queen·let** \-lət\ *n* -S **:** a petty queen

**queenlike** \ˈ=,=\ *adj* **:** QUEENLY

**queen lily** *n* **:** a plant of the genus *Phaedranassa*

**queen·li·ness** \ˈkwēnlēnəs, -lin-\ *n* -ES **:** the quality or state of being queenly

¹**queen·ly** \-lē, -li\ *adj* -ER/-EST [¹*queen* + *-ly*] **1 :** belonging to or befitting a queen ⟨clad in her ~ raiment —William Morris⟩ **2 :** resembling a queen **:** MAJESTIC, REGAL, HAUGHTY ⟨the ~ poise of her head —Jack London⟩

²**queenly** \"\ *adv, often* -ER/-EST **:** in a queenly manner

**queen mother** *n* **:** a queen dowager who is mother of the reigning sovereign

**queen of may** *or* **queen of the may** *usu cap Q&M* **:** MAY QUEEN

**queen of the meadow 1 :** a meadowsweet (*Filipendula ulmaria*) **2 :** any of several plants of the genus *Spiraea* **3 :** MARSH MILKWEED

**queen of the night :** a tropical American climbing cactus (*Selenicereus grandiflorus*) with triangular branches that is often cultivated for its large showy night-blooming flowers

**queen of the prairie :** an American perennial herb (*Filipendula rubra*) with ample clusters of pale pink flowers

**queen olive** *n* **:** any of various olives grown esp. in the region of Seville, Spain, and having large oblong fruits with a small but long pit that are usu. cured green and are characterized by good keeping quality and delicate flavor

**queen pigeon** *n* **:** any of several crowned pigeons (as *Goura victoria*)

**queenpin** \ˈ=,=\ *n, slang* **:** QUEEN BEE 2

**queen post** *n* **:** one of two vertical tie posts in a truss (as of a roof)

**queen post truss** *n* **:** QUEEN TRUSS

**queen regent** *n, pl* **queens regent :** a queen ruling in behalf of another or in her own right

**queen regnant** *n, pl* **queens regnant :** a queen reigning in her own right

queen posts

**queenright** \(ˈ)=ˈ=\ *adj, of a colony of bees* **:** having a queen in the hive

**queen rod** *n* **:** QUEEN BOLT

**queenroot** \ˈ=,=\ *n* **:** QUEEN'S DELIGHT

¹**queens** *pl of* QUEEN, *pres 3d sing of* QUEEN

²**queens** \ˈkwēnz\ *adj, usu cap* [fr. *Queens* borough, New York, N.Y.] **:** of or from the borough of Queens, New York, N.Y. **:** of the kind or style prevalent in Queens

**queen's arm** *n* **:** MUSKET

**queen's bench** *n, usu cap Q&B* **:** COURT OF KING'S BENCH — used when the British monarch is a queen

**queensberry rules** *n pl, usu cap Q* **:** MARQUIS OF QUEENSBERRY RULES

**queen's birthday** *n, usu cap Q&B* **:** KING'S BIRTHDAY — used when the British monarch is a queen

**queen's blue** *var of* QUEEN BLUE

**queen's champion** *n, usu cap Q&C* **:** KING'S CHAMPION — used when the British monarch is a queen

**queen's color** *n, often cap Q&C* **:** KING'S COLOR — used when the British monarch is a queen

**queen's counsel** *n, usu cap Q&C* **:** KING'S COUNSEL — used when the British monarch is a queen

**queen's crape myrtle** *n* **:** a tree (*Lagerstroemia speciosa*) that is native to Asia, Australia, and the East Indies where it provides timber and that is used elsewhere as an ornamental for its large showy mauve to pink or purple flowers in large terminal clusters — see PYINMA

**queen's-delight** \ˈ=ˈ=ˈ=\ *n, pl* **queen's-delights :** a perennial herb (*Stillingia sylvatica*) with a root that is used as an alterative and more recently shows promise as the source of a drying oil for paints and varnishes

**queen's english** *n, usu cap Q&E* **:** KING'S ENGLISH — used when the British monarch is a queen

**queen's evidence** *n, usu cap Q* **:** KING'S EVIDENCE — used when the British monarch is a queen

**queen's fettle** *n* **:** a monkshood (*Aconitum napellus*)

**queen's-flower** \(ˈ)=ˈ=\ *n, pl* **queen's-flowers :** QUEEN'S CRAPE MYRTLE

**queen·ship** \ˈkwēn,ship\ *n* **1 :** QUEENHOOD **2 :** QUEENLINESS

**queens-in-council** *pl of* QUEEN-IN-COUNCIL

**queens-in-parliament** *pl of* QUEEN-IN-PARLIAMENT

**queens·land** \ˈkwēnz,land, -,laa(ə)nd, -lənd\ *adj, usu cap* [fr. *Queensland* state, Australia] **:** of or from the state of Queensland, Australia **:** of the kind or style prevalent in Queensland

**queensland beech** *n, usu cap Q* **1 :** an Australian timber tree (*Gmelina leichardtii*) with purplish white tubular flowers **2 :** the hard heavy wood of the Queensland beech

**queensland cherry** *n, usu cap Q* **1 :** an Australian shrub or small tree (*Antidesma dallachianum*) of the family Euphorbiaceae **2 :** the red edible acid fruit of the Queensland cherry

**queens·land·er** \-də(r)\ *n* -S *cap* [*Queensland* state + E *-er*] **:** a native or inhabitant of the state of Queensland, Australia

**queensland fruit fly** *n, usu cap Q* **:** a trypetid fly (*Dacus tryoni*) that is a serious pest of fruits in New So. Wales

**queensland grass-cloth plant** *n, usu cap Q* **:** an Australian plant (*Pipturus argenteus*) whose fiber is used in making cloth

**queensland hemp** *n, usu cap Q* **:** an herb (*Sida rhombifolia*) of wide distribution in the tropics, that has a fine soft bast fiber superior to jute in strength, is used for forage and medicinally as a demulcent, and in some areas is an aggressive weed — called also *jellyleaf*

**queensland hickory** *n, usu cap Q* **:** an Australian evergreen tree (*Flindersia ifflaiana*) with yellow close-grained hard wood used typically for heavy construction and machine bearings — called also *Cairn's ash*

**queensland kauri** *n, usu cap Q* **:** any of various trees of the genus *Agathis*; *specif* **:** DUNDATHU PINE

**queensland maple** *n, usu cap Q* **1 :** an Australian tree (*Flindersia brayleana*) **2 :** the light-red wood of the Queensland maple that resembles mahogany

**queensland nut** *n, usu cap Q* **1 :** MACADAMIA 2a **2 :** MACADAMIA NUT

**queensland silver wattle** *n, usu cap Q* **:** a shrubby Australian wattle (*Acacia podalyriifolia*) with downy ash-colored or silvery phyllodes and globose golden yellow heads of flowers in axillary racemes

**queensland trumpeter** *n, usu cap Q* **:** a marine food fish (*Pomadasys hasta*) of the tropical Indo-Pacific

**queensland walnut** *n, usu cap Q* **:** AUSTRALIAN WALNUT

**queen's mark** *n, usu cap Q* **:** KING'S MARK — used when the British monarch is a queen

**queen's metal** *n* **:** an alloy somewhat resembling pewter or britannia metal and consisting essentially of tin with an admixture of antimony, zinc, and lead or copper

**queen snake** *n* **:** a harmless colubrid snake (*Natrix septemvittata*) of the central, eastern, and southern U. S.

**queen's peace** *n, sometimes cap Q&P* **:** KING'S PEACE — used when the British monarch is a queen

**queen's proctor** *n, usu cap Q&P* **:** KING'S PROCTOR — used when the British monarch is a queen

**queen's regulations** *n pl, usu cap Q&R* **:** KING'S REGULATIONS — used when the British monarch is a queen

**queen's remembrancer** *n, usu cap Q&R* **:** KING'S REMEMBRANCER — used when the British monarch is a queen

**queen's-root** \(ˈ)=ˈ=\ *n, pl* **queen's-roots :** QUEEN'S-DELIGHT

**queen's scholar** *n, usu cap Q&S* **:** a student in an English school or college who is supported by a foundation created by or under the auspices of a queen

**queen's scout** *n, usu cap Q&S* **:** KING'S SCOUT — used when the British monarch is a queen

**queen's shilling** *n* **:** KING'S SHILLING — used when the British monarch is a queen

**queensware** \ˈ=,=\ *n* **1 :** glazed English earthenware of a cream color **2 :** cream-colored Wedgwood ware

**queenswood** \ˈ=,=\ *n* **:** AUSTRALIAN WALNUT

**queen's wreath** *n* **:** PURPLE WREATH

**queen's yellow** *n* **1 :** MIMOSA 3 **2 :** CALOMEL

**queen triggerfish** *n* **:** a triggerfish (*Balistes vetula*) widely distributed in the tropical Atlantic and Indian oceans — called also *Bessy cerka*, *oldwench*, *oldwife*

**queen truss** *n* **:** a truss framed with queen posts

**queen turtle** *n* **:** an edible No. American soft-shelled turtle (*Trionyx mutica*)

**1queer** \'kwi(ə)r, -iə, *dial* -wa(a)|(ə)r, -we|, |ə, -wīr, -wā(r\ *adj* -ER/-EST [origin unknown] **1 a :** differing in some odd way from what is usual or normal **:** STRANGE, CURIOUS, PECULIAR, UNEXPECTED ⟨deep fireplaces and ~ andirons —Austin Dobson⟩ ⟨spoke in a ~, kindly, foreign voice —Alan Tomkins⟩ ⟨~ bird rustlings and cries in the trees lull me to sleep —S.P.B.Mais⟩ **b** (1) **:** ECCENTRIC, UNCONVENTIONAL ⟨a likable but somewhat ~ folk —R.H.Shryock⟩ ⟨individuals who do not follow this routine are regarded as ~ —Ralph Linton⟩ ⟨looked like a gentleman, though he was as ~ a duck as you could meet —Mary McCarthy⟩ ⟨regarded him as a foreigner, and a ~ fish —Nevil Shute⟩ (2) **:** mildly insane **:** TOUCHED **c :** OBSESSED, HIPPED ⟨seems to be ~ for these early-morning conferences —Budd Schulberg⟩ ⟨~ on the subject of first editions⟩ ⟨~ about the circus⟩ **d** *slang* **:** sexually deviate **:** HOMOSEXUAL **2 a** *slang* **:** WORTHLESS, SPURIOUS, COUNTERFEIT ⟨~ money⟩ **b :** QUESTIONABLE, SUSPICIOUS ⟨a ~ transaction⟩ ⟨~ goings-on⟩ **3 :** not quite well **:** FAINT, GIDDY, QUEASY ⟨gave her a ~ sensation to think of standing in that room again —J.C.Powys⟩ **4** *Scot* **:** DROLL, AMUSING, COMICAL ⟨told his ~*est* stories —Robert Burns⟩ **syn** see STRANGE

**2queer** \"\ *adv* -ER/-EST **:** QUEERLY

**3queer** \"\ *vt* -ED/-ING/-S **1 :** to spoil the effect or success of **:** interfere with ⟨bad weather ~*ed* our plans⟩ **:** JEOPARDIZE, HARM, DISRUPT ⟨the old man may have ~*ed* his own promotion —J.A.Michener⟩ ⟨the spring lock had snapped, ~*ing* his exit —*Time*⟩ ⟨blurring of focus and muddled misdirection of attention: consequences of ~*ing* one discipline with the habits of another —F.R.Leavis⟩ **2 :** to put or get into an embarrassing or disadvantageous situation **:** put in a bad light ⟨~*ed* himself with the authorities by his lack of cooperation⟩ ⟨the giving of such perquisites, the exercise of such influence, ~*s* the profession —Virginia Woolf⟩ — **queer one's pitch** *or* **queer the pitch :** to spoil something planned, arranged, or attempted ⟨I answered rather cautiously so as not to *queer your pitch* —Stephen Haggard⟩

**4queer** \"\ *n* -S **1** *slang* **:** one that is queer; *esp* **:** a usu. male homosexual **2** *slang* **:** counterfeit money — usu. used with *the* ⟨jailed for passing the ~⟩

**queer cuffin** *n* **:** CHURL

**queer·ish** \-rish, -rēsh\ *adj* [1queer + -ish] **:** rather queer ⟨a ~ deal in imported crabmeat —*Pacific Fisherman*⟩ — **queer·ish·ly** *adv* — **queer·ish·ness** *n* -ES

**queer·i·ty** \-rəd·ē\ *n* -ES [1queer + -ity] *chiefly dial* **:** QUEERNESS

**queer·ly** *adv* **:** in a queer manner **:** ODDLY, STRANGELY ⟨a ~ inscribed stone —R.W.Murray⟩ ⟨behaved ~⟩ ⟨just inside the door stood a constable, looking ~ at home without his helmet —Ngaio Marsh⟩

**queer·ness** \-rnəs\ *n* -ES **1 :** the quality of being queer **:** ODDITY, ECCENTRICITY ⟨his actions for some weeks had given indication of ~ —S.H.Adams⟩ **2 :** a queer characteristic ⟨much liked despite his ~*es* —Mary Johnston⟩

**queer street** *n, usu cap Q&S* **:** an embarrassing situation or condition; *esp* **:** a condition marked by financial difficulties ⟨those commitments will put us in *Queer Street* next year —John Galsworthy⟩

**queest** \'kwēst\ *n* -S [ME *quyshte, quyste,* fr. OE *cūscote, cūcsceote*] **:** RINGDOVE

**queet** \'kwēt\ *n* -S [by alter.] *Scot* **:** 2COOT

**quekchi** *usu cap, var of* KEKCHI

**quelch** \'kwelch, -lsh\ *vb* -ED/-ING/-ES [by alter.] *dial* **:** SQUELCH

**que·lea** \'kwēlēə\ *n* [NL, prob. fr. a native name in Africa] **1** *cap* **:** a genus of African weaverbirds **2** -S **:** any bird of the genus *Quelea; esp* **:** a red-billed bird (*Q. quelea*) often kept as a cage bird

**que·li·te** \kä'lēd·ē\ *n* -S [MexSp, fr. Nahuatl *quilitl* edible green] *Southwest* **:** any of various plants (as lamb's-quarters or purslane) cooked as greens **:** POTHERB

**1quell** \'kwel\ *vt* -ED/-ING/-S [ME *quellen,* fr. OE *cwellan;* akin to OS *quellian* to torture, kill, OHG *quellen* to torture, kill, ON *kvelja* to torment, torture; causative fr. the root of OE *cwelan* to die; akin to OE *cwalu* killing, murder, OHG *quelan* to suffer pain, *quāla* pain, torment, ON *kvöl* pain, torment, W *ballu* to die, Gk *dellithes* wasps, *belonē* sharp point, needle, Arm *kełem* I torment, OSlav *žėlja* pain] **1** *archaic* **:** KILL, SLAY ⟨never ~*ed* an enemy save in my just defense —Lord Byron⟩ **2 :** to put down **:** OVERPOWER, SUPPRESS, EXTINGUISH ⟨only step being taken to ~ the disturbances in the city —T.B.Costain⟩ ⟨emotions ~*ed* the conscious exercise of reason —H.O.Taylor⟩ **3 :** QUIET, ALLAY, PACIFY ⟨these generated fears must be ~*ed* —Henry Wallace⟩ ⟨curb our evil instincts and ~ our anguish —A.L.Guérard⟩ **syn** see CRUSH

**2quell** \"\ *n* -S [ME, fr. *quellen,* v.] *archaic* **:** KILLING, SLAUGHTER ⟨sooner than we would choose, bread will melt, water will burn, and the great ~ begin —W.H.Auden⟩; *also* **:** the power of quelling ⟨a sovereign ~ is in his waving hands —John Keats⟩

**quell·able** \-ləbəl\ *adj* **:** capable of being quelled ⟨a noise ~ only by maddened protest —F.A.Swinnerton⟩

**quell·er** \-ə(r)\ *n* -S [ME, fr. OE *cwellere* killer, fr. *cwellan* to kill + *-ere* -er — more at QUELL] **:** one that quells

**quel·lung** \'kweləŋ\ *n* -S [G, lit., swelling, fr. *quellen* to well, gush, swell (fr. OHG *quellan*) + *-ung* -ing (fr. OHG *-unga, -ung*) — more at DEVIL] **:** swelling of the capsule of a microorganism after reaction with antibody ⟨~ phenomena⟩ ⟨~ reaction⟩

**quel·que–chose** \¦kelkə'shōz\ *n* -S [F *quelque chose,* lit., something, anything] **:** KICKSHAW

**que·ma·de·ro** \¦kāmə'de(ˌ)rō\ *n* -S [Sp, fr. *quemado* (past part. of *quemar* to burn, fr. — assumed — VL *caimare,* alter. — perh. influenced by Gk *kaiein* to burn — of L *cremare* to burn up) + *-ero* -ary (fr. L *-arius*) — more at CAUSTIC, HEARTH] **:** a place of execution by burning

**queme** \'kwēm\ *adj* [ME, fr. OE *gecwēme;* akin to MD *bequame* pleasant, fitting, OHG *biquāmi* fitting, suitable, ON *kvæmr* coming; derivative fr. the root of E *come*] **1** *dial chiefly Eng* **:** PLEASANT, AGREEABLE, COMFORTABLE **2** *dial chiefly Eng* **:** COMELY, ATTRACTIVE **3** *dial chiefly Eng* **:** HANDY

**quem quaer·i·tis** \¦kwem'kwerəd·əs\ *n, usu cap 1st Q* [L, whom do you seek?] **:** an Easter introit trope derived from the account of the visit to Christ's tomb by the women, acted in the 10th century by ecclesiastics, and in its amplified dramatized form being the earliest known liturgical drama

**que·na** *also* **cue·na** \'kānə\ *n* -S [AmerSp *quena,* fr. Quechua *kkhina*] **:** a primitive vertical reed flute of the So. American Indians

**1quench** \'kwench\ *vb* -ED/-ING/-ES [ME *quenchen,* fr. (assumed) OE *cwencan* (as in *ācwencan* to quench, extinguish), causative fr. the root of (assumed) OE *cwincan* to become extinguished (as in *ācwincan* to vanish, be extinguished); akin to OFris *quinka* to vanish] *vt* **1 a :** to put out (as a fire or light) ⟨for three days after . . . the fire may not be ~*ed* —J.G. Frazer⟩ ⟨the signal among the palms was ~*ed* —William Beebe⟩ **b :** to put out the fire or light of (a source of heat or light) ⟨~ a fireplace⟩ ⟨~ a lamp⟩ **2 :** SUBDUE, OVERCOME ⟨~ hatred⟩ **3 :** DESTROY ⟨~ a rebellion⟩ ⟨the praise that ~*es* all desire to read the book —T.S.Eliot⟩ ⟨whose eagerness for culture was not ~*ed* by the toil of bringing up a family —C.A. Dinsmore⟩ **4 :** SLAKE, SATISFY ⟨~ a thirst⟩ **5 :** to cool (as heated steel) suddenly by immersion esp. in water or oil ⟨crushed ore melted and ~*ed* in cold water —C.L.Mantell⟩ **6 a :** SUPPRESS, INHIBIT ⟨~ luminescence⟩ ⟨~ a portion of a spectrum⟩ **b :** to arrest (as the discharge of an ion counter or the oscillation of an amplifier tube) by applying voltage ~ *vi* **1 :** to become extinguished **:** COOL ⟨the fire ~*es*⟩ **2 :** to become calm **:** SUBSIDE ⟨the bustle and the talking ~*ed* —W.B. Ready⟩ **syn** see CRUSH

**2quench** \"\ *n* -ES **:** the act of quenching or state of being quenched ⟨the sudden ~ of the white light —Saul Bellow⟩ ⟨the tube works without ~ and utilizes a gas that is 90 percent argon —*Scientific Monthly*⟩

**quench·able** \-chəbəl\ *adj* **:** capable of being quenched

**quench·able·ness** *n* -ES **:** the quality or state of being quenchable

**quench aging** *n* **:** aging of an alloy induced by rapid cooling from a high temperature

**quenched gap** *n* **:** a kind of spark gap used in radio transmitting apparatus and so designed as to extinguish the spark quickly after it starts thus opening the primary circuit and leaving the secondary circuit free to produce oscillating current

**quench·er** \-chə(r)\ *n* -S [ME *quenchere,* fr. *quenchen* to quench + *-ere* -er — more at QUENCH] **1 :** one that quenches **2 :** a satisfying drink

**quench hardening** *n* **:** hardening of a ferrous alloy induced by rapid cooling from a temperature above the transformation range

**quenching bath** *n* **:** water, oil, or other liquid in which heated metal is plunged for hardening

**quench·less** \-chləs\ *adj* **:** UNQUENCHABLE ⟨her ~ defiance of the inquisition —*Time*⟩ ⟨quick wit and ~ curiosity —Max Lerner⟩ — **quench·less·ly** *adv* — **quench·less·ness** *n* -ES

**quen·da** \'kwendə\ *n* -S [native name in Australia] **:** a widely distributed Australian bandicoot (*Thylacis obesula*)

**que·nelle** \kə'nel\ *n* -S [F, fr. G *knödel* dumpling — more at KNÖDEL] **:** a ball or oval of forcemeat mixture cooked in boiling water or stock and served as a garnish or as a separate dish

**que·nouille training** \kə'nüy-\ *n* [*quenouille* fr. F, distaff, tree trained by quenouille training, fr. LL *conucla,* alter. of *colucula,* dim. of L *colus* distaff — more at COLULUS] **:** a method of training trees or shrubs in the shape of a cone or distaff by tying down the branches

**quen·sel·ite** \'kwen(t)s°lˌīt\ *n* -S [Sw *quenselit,* fr. Percy D. *Quensel* b1881 Swed. mineralogist + Sw *-it* -ite] **:** a mineral $PbMnO_2(OH)$ consisting of basic lead manganese oxide and occurring in black monoclinic crystals

**quen·stedt·ite** \'kwenˌsteˌtīt\ *n* -S [G *quenstedtit,* fr. Friedrich A. *Quenstedt* †1889 Ger. mineralogist + G *-it* -ite] **:** a mineral $Fe_2(SO_4)_3.10H_2O$ consisting of a hydrous ferric sulfate

**que·ran·dí** *or* **que·ren·dí** *also* **que·ren·dy** \ˌkärən'dē\ *n, pl* **querandí** *or* **querandís** *or* **querendí** *or* **querendís** *usu cap* [Sp *querandí, querendí,* fr. Guarani, fr. *quira* grease + *-ndí,* suffix denoting possession] **1 :** a people of uncertain linguistic affiliation on the right bank of the lower Plata and Paraná rivers **2 :** a member of the Querandí people

**quer·ce·ta·gé·tin** \ˌkwərsə'tajətᵊn\ *n* -S [blend of *quercetin* and NL *Tagetes;* fr. its color's resembling that of quercetin] **:** a pale-yellow crystalline flavonol pigment $C_{15}H_4O_2(OH)_6$ obtained from African and French marigolds

**quer·ce·tag·e·trin** \-jə·trən\ *n* -S [ISV *quercetagetin* + *-itrin* (as in *quercitrin*)] **:** a crystalline glucoside $C_{24}H_{20}O_{13}$ obtained from African marigolds that yields quercetagetin on hydrolysis

**quer·ce·tin** *also* **quer·ci·tin** \'kwərsətᵊn\ *n* -S [ISV *quercet-, quercit-* (fr. L *quercetum* oak forest, fr. *quercus* oak + *-etum*) + *-in* — more at FIR] **:** a yellow crystalline flavonol pigment $C_{15}H_5O_2(OH)_5$ occurring usu. in the form of glycosides (as quercitrin and rutin) in various plants and in the form of the dihydro derivative in Douglas fir

**quer·ci·mer·i·trin** \ˌ≈≈'merə·trən\ *n* -S [ISV *quercimer-* (fr. *quercetin, quercitin* + Gk *meros* part) + *-itrin* (as in *quercitrin*) — more at MERIT] **:** a yellow crystalline glucoside $C_{21}H_{20}O_{12}$ occurring in cotton flowers and leaves and sunflowers and yielding quercetin and glucose on hydrolysis

**quer·ci·tannin** \¦≈≈+\ *n* [L *quercus* oak + E *-i-* + *tannin*] **:** a tannin isolated from oak bark as a reddish white powder

**quer·ci·tol** \'kwərsəˌtȯl, -ˌtōl\ *n* -S [ISV *quercitin* + *-ol*] **:** a sweet crystalline pentahydroxy cyclic alcohol $C_6H_7(OH)_5$ found in acorns and oak bark and in viburnums and other plants; deoxy-inositol

**quer·ci·trin** \'kwərsəˌtrin\ *n* -S [ISV *quercitron* + *-in*] **:** a bitter pale yellow crystalline glycoside $C_{21}H_{20}O_{11}$ obtained esp. from quercitron bark and yielding quercetin and rhamnose on hydrolysis

**quer·cit·ron** \'kwərˌsi·trən, -sə·t-, (ˌ)kwər'si·t-\ *n* -S [ISV, blend of NL *Quercus* and ISV *citron* (color)] **1 a** *or* **quercitron oak :** a black oak (*Quercus velutina*) **b :** the bark of this oak that is rich in tannin and yellow coloring matter and is used in tanning and dyeing **c :** a yellow dye consisting of finely divided quercitron bark — see DYE table I (under *Natural Yellow 10*), QUERCITRIN **2 :** ORPIMENT 2

**quercitron lake** *n* **:** YELLOW OCHER

**quer·cus** \'kwərkəs\ *n, cap* [NL, fr. L, oak — more at FIR] **:** a genus of hardwood often evergreen trees or shrubs (family Fagaceae) comprising the typical oaks and being widely distributed in the northern hemisphere but most abundant in temperate regions, having alternate linear to elliptical entire or variously lobed leaves, drooping staminate catkins, and pistillate flowers that are solitary in each involucre and succeeded in fruit by a characteristic acorn — see CORK OAK, LIVE OAK, WHITE OAK; LITHOCARPUS; compare FAGUS

**que·re·cho** \kə'rā(ˌ)chō\ *n, pl* **querecho** *or* **querechos** *usu cap* [Sp, of AmerInd origin] **:** an Apache esp. of the Jicarilla, Lipan, or Mescalero people

**que·re·la** \kwə'relə\ *n, pl* **quere·lae** \-ēˌlē\ [ML, fr. L, complaint — more at QUARREL] *civil & eccl law* **1 :** an action in a court **2 :** the bill of complaint in a court action

**que·ren·cia** \kā'rensyə\ *n* -S [Sp, fondness, haunt of an animal, favorite spot, querencia, fr. *querer* to want, like, love (fr. L *quaerere* to seek, gain, obtain, ask) + *-encia* -ence (fr. L *-entia*)] **:** an area in the arena taken by the bull for a defensive stand in a bullfight

**1que·rent** \'kwirənt\ *n* -S [L *quaerent-, quaerens,* pres. part. of *quaerere* to seek, ask] **:** INQUIRER; *specif* **:** one who consults an astrologer

**2querent** \"\ *n* -S [L *querent-, querens,* pres. part. of *queri* to complain — more at WHEEZE] *archaic* **:** COMPLAINANT, PLAINTIFF

**quer·flö·te** \'kwerˌflœd·ə, -flərd·ə\ *n* -S [G, fr. *quer* transverse, diagonal (fr. OHG *dwerah, twerh*) + *flöte* flute — more at THWART, BLOCKFLÖTE] **:** FLAUTO TRAVERSO 2

**que·ri·da** \kā'rēdə, ke'-\ *n* -S [Sp, fr. fem. of *querido,* past part. of *querer* to love — more at QUERENCIA] *chiefly Southwest* **:** a female sweetheart

**que·ri·er** \'kwirēə(r)\ *also* -wer-, -wēr-\ *n* -S **:** QUERIST

**quer·i·ma·na** \kwerə'manə\ *also* **quer·i·man** \-'män\ *n* -S [D Creole (Surinam) *kweriman,* fr. Galibi *kweriman,* prob. fr. Tupi *curemá*] **:** a young mullet having only two anal spines rather than the three characteristic of the adult

**quer·i·mo·ni·ous** \¦kwerə¦mōnēəs\ *adj* [ML *querimoniosus,* fr. L *querimonia* complaint (fr. *queri* to complain) + *-osus* -ous — more at WHEEZE] **:** COMPLAINING, QUERULOUS — **quer·i·mo·ni·ous·ly** *adv* — **quer·i·mo·ni·ous·ness** *n* -ES

**que·rist** \'kwirəst *also* -wer-, -wēr-\ *n* -S [L *quaerere* to seek, ask + E *-ist*] **:** one who inquires **:** one who asks questions

**querk** \'kwərk, -wək, -wəik\ *chiefly dial var of* QUIRK

**querk·en** \-kən\ *vt* -ED/-ING/-S [ME *querkenen;* akin to OFris *querka, quertza* to choke, MLG *querken,* ON *kyrkja, kvirkja;* denominatives fr. the root of ON *kverk* throat — more at GORGE] *dial chiefly Eng* **:** to cause to gasp **:** CHOKE

**querl** \'kwərl, *esp before pause or consonant* 'kwər·əl; 'kwəl, 'kwəil\ *chiefly Midland var of* CURL

**quern** \'kwərn, 'kwən, 'kwəin\ *n* -S [ME, fr. OE *cweorn;* akin to OHG *quirn, quirna* hand mill, millstone, ON *kvern* hand mill, Goth *-qairnus* millstone, OIr *brāu* millstone, OSlav *žrŭny* mill, and prob. to Goth *kaurjos* (nom. pl.) heavy — more at GRIEVE] **1 :** a primitive mill for grinding grain consisting of two circular stones with the upper one being turned by hand **2 :** a small hand mill (as for grinding spices or nuts) **3 :** METATE

**quernstone** \'≈ˌ≈\ *n* [ME *quernston,* fr. OE *cweornstān,* fr. *cweorn* quern + *stān* stone — more at STONE] **:** MILLSTONE

**quer·sprung** \'kf|er,shprùŋ, kə'v|, |ār-\ *n* -S [G, fr. *quer* transverse, diagonal + *sprung* jump, fr. OHG, fr. the stem of *springan* to jump — more at QUERFLÖTE, SPRING] **:** a maneuver for avoiding obstacles in skiing executed by turning at right angles in the air using one pole as a pivot

**1quer·u·lent** *also* **quer·u·lant** \'kwer(y)ələnt\ *adj* [*querulent* fr. *querulous* + *-ent* (as in *truculent*); *querulant* alter. of *querulent*] **:** abnormally given to suspicion and accusation **:** QUERULOUS

**2querulent** \"\ *n* -S **:** one that is querulent

**quer·u·len·tial** \¦≈≈¦lenchəl\ *adj* **:** QUERULOUS

**quer·u·list** \'≈≈ləst\ *n* -S [*querulous* + *-ist*] **:** COMPLAINER

**quer·u·lous** \-ləs\ *adj* [L *querulus,* fr. *queri* to complain — more at WHEEZE] **1 :** apt to find fault **:** disposed to murmur **:** habitually complaining ⟨~ disappointed old age —W.M. Thackeray⟩ ⟨the ~ boredom of a child that possesses too many toys —Lewis Mumford⟩ **2 :** expressing or suggestive of complaint **:** FRETFUL, WHINING ⟨somewhat ~ remarks about his own countrymen —*Geographical Jour.*⟩ ⟨sung in a subdued but ~ soprano —Nigel Dennis⟩ ⟨the ~ eyebrows, the thin peevish lips —D.B.W.Lewis⟩ **3 :** making a sound suggesting complaint ⟨one ~ rook —Charles Dickens⟩ ⟨the ~ sea —J.B.Cabell⟩ **syn** see IRRITABLE

**quer·u·lous·ly** *adv* **:** in a querulous manner **:** PEEVISHLY

**quer·u·lous·ness** *n* -ES **:** the quality or state of being querulous **:** PEEVISHNESS

**1que·ry** \'kwirē, -ri *also* -wer-, -wēr-\ *n* -ES [alter. of earlier *quere, quaere,* fr. L *quaere,* imper. of *quaerere* to seek, gain, obtain, ask] **1 :** QUESTION, INQUIRY ⟨my ~ as to the name of the pond —Frances H. Eliot⟩ ⟨to answer either ~ in detail would require an investigation beyond the scope of this appraisal —R.S.Thoman⟩ ⟨looking down in dazed and inarticulate ~ —Kay Boyle⟩ — sometimes used to introduce a question or a debatable proposition ⟨~, if this would be honorable⟩ **2 :** a question in the mind **:** DOUBT **3 a** *or* **query mark :** QUESTION MARK **b :** a notation (as ? or *qy*) written on a printer's proof to question the accuracy of something in the proof

**2query** \"\ *vt* -ED/-ING/-ES [alter. of earlier *quere,* fr. L *quaere,* imper. of *quaerere*] **1 :** to put as a question ⟨"can I buy two tickets?" he *queried*⟩ **2 :** to ask questions about esp. with an indication of doubt and with desire for a definite, clear, or certain statement or demonstration ⟨standard operating procedure would be to ~ the order —J.G.Cozzens⟩ **3 :** to ask questions of esp. with a certain formality or with desire for authoritative information ⟨*queried* some eminent authors for advice —*N.Y. Herald Tribune Bk. Rev.*⟩ **4 :** to mark with a query **syn** see ASK

**que·ry·ing·ly** *adv* **:** in a querying manner **:** INQUIRINGLY

**que·ry·ist** \-rēəst\ *n* -S **:** QUERIST

**ques** *abbr* question

**que·sa·di·lla** \ˌkāsə'dēyə\ *n* -S [Sp, dim. of *quesada* cheese turnover, fr. *queso* cheese (fr. L *caseus*) + *-ada* -ade (fr. LL *-ata*) — more at CHEESE] **:** a turnover made usu. with a cheese filling

**quesal** *var of* QUETZAL

**1que·si·ted** \kwē'sīd·əd\ *adj* [L *quaesitus* (past part. of *quaerere* to seek, ask) + E *-ed*] *archaic* **:** sought or inquired about

**2quesited** \"\ *n* -S *in astrology* **:** a person or thing sought or inquired about

**1quest** \'kwest\ *n* -S [ME, fr. MF *queste,* fr. (assumed) VL *quaesta,* fr. L *quaesita, quaesta,* fem. of *quaesitus, quaestus* past part. of *quaerere* to seek, ask] **1 a** *chiefly dial* **:** an official inquiry **:** INQUEST **b :** a jury of inquest ⟨what lawful ~ have given their verdict up? —Shak.⟩ **c :** INVESTIGATION ⟨a long spiritual ~ into the entire Spanish past —Bohdan Chudoba⟩ ⟨limitations set to the child's sex ~ —*Structure & Meaning of Psychoanalysis*⟩ **2 a :** the action or an act or instance of seeking: (1) **:** EXPEDITION, PURSUIT, VENTURE ⟨the ~ for Neanderthal fossils —R.W.Murray⟩ ⟨all his work is a ~ for values —C.J.Rolo⟩ ⟨our united ~ of a just and lasting peace —D.D.Eisenhower⟩ (2) **:** a chivalrous enterprise in medieval romance usu. involving an adventurous journey **b** (1) *archaic* **:** a search (as by hounds) for game (2) *dial* **:** the baying of hounds in pursuit or barking on seeing game **3** *obs* **:** those who search or make inquiry ⟨hath sent about three several ~*s* to search you out —Shak.⟩ **4 :** collection of alms or donations esp. for religious uses — **in quest of** *prep* **:** in search of **:** SEEKING ⟨cast her eyes round the room *in quest of* some amusement —Jane Austen⟩ ⟨an expedition up the river *in quest of* fruit —Rachel Henning⟩

**2quest** \"\ *vb* -ED/-ING/-S [ME *questen,* fr. MF *quester,* fr. *queste*] *vi* **1** *of a dog* **a :** to search a trail (as of game) ⟨the dog after a little understood and ~*ed* —Robinson Jeffers⟩ **b :** to give tongue **:** BAY ⟨~*ing* like a hound on a broken trail —Rudyard Kipling⟩ **2 :** to make a search **:** go in pursuit **:** go on a quest **:** SEEK, ASK ⟨still ~*ing* for sultry love and high adventure —Henry Cavendish⟩ ⟨this indolence of the body while the soul is ~*ing* —H.S.Canby⟩ ⟨~*ing* ceaselessly for improvements —*Newsweek*⟩ ⟨giraffes come ~*ing* through the trees to take their turn to drink —Alan Moorehead⟩ ⟨things that die with their eyes open and ~*ing* —Ben Hecht⟩ **3 :** to go about soliciting alms esp. for religious uses ~ *vt* **1 :** to search for **:** EXAMINE, PURSUE ⟨hounds . . . should spread to ~ as individuals all the covert's fastnesses —E.G.W.W.Harrison⟩ ⟨baffled eyes ~*ing* more information —L.C.Douglas⟩ **2 :** to ask for **:** DEMAND ⟨~*ing* . . . your prayers —Augusta Gregory⟩

**questant** *n* -S *obs* **:** QUESTER

**quest·er** \'kwestə(r)\ *n* -S **:** one that quests ⟨a jester and a ~ and a bard —Louis MacNeice⟩ ⟨competent ~*s* who are hot on the trail —E.G.Lowry⟩

**ques·teur** \ke'stər(·)\ *n* -S [F, fr. L *quaestor* — more at QUAESTOR] **:** one of three members of either branch of the French parliament chosen as financial officers in charge of payment of senators or deputies and of expense accounts

**questhouse** \'≈ˌ≈\ *n, archaic* **:** a house for holding the inquests in a ward or parish

**quest·ing·ly** *adv* **:** in the manner of one that quests **:** INQUIRINGLY, SEARCHINGLY

**1ques·tion** \'kwes(h)chən, ÷-eshən\ *n* -S [ME *questioun,* fr. MF *question,* fr. L *quaestion-, quaestio,* fr. *quaesitus, quaestus* (past part. of *quaerere* to seek, ask) + *-ion-, -io* -ion] **1 a** (1) **:** an interrogative expression ⟨ask ~*s* about the candidates⟩ — see RHETORICAL QUESTION (2) **:** an interrogative sentence or clause (3) **:** an interrogative expression used to test knowledge (as in a written or oral examination) — compare 1ANSWER 1b **b :** a subject or aspect that is in dispute, open for discussion, or to be inquired into **:** ISSUE ⟨the ~ whether or not the people of any time have ever considered their civilization with complete satisfaction —Virgil Jordan⟩ ⟨the ~ of whether some form of verse is a necessary condition of poetry —Alice Bensen⟩ ⟨the tariff ~⟩ ⟨raise the ~ of adequate financing⟩; *broadly* **:** PROBLEM, MATTER ⟨the ~ of how mankind will use the leisure —A.R.Sweezy⟩ ⟨the ~ of buying a car⟩ ⟨the ~*s* of where one lives and of the nature and quality of the common life in which one participates —N.M. Pusey⟩ ⟨composing is a ~ of paper and a pen full of ink —J.D.Cook⟩ **c** (1) **:** a subject or point of debate or a proposition to be or being voted on in a meeting (as of a legislative body) ⟨the ~ before the senate⟩ (2) **:** the bringing of such a subject or proposal to a vote ⟨loud cries for the ~⟩ ⟨put the matter to the ~⟩ — see PREVIOUS QUESTION **d :** the specific point at issue or under discussion ⟨a remark that was beside the ~⟩ **e :** something the correctness or existence of which is open to doubt ⟨no longer a ~ but an established fact⟩ ⟨an open ~ whether the addition is an improvement⟩ **2 a :** the action or an instance of asking **:** INQUIRY ⟨a long glance of sulky ~ —William Sansom⟩ ⟨this kind of division could not support very close ~ —T.S.Eliot⟩ **b :** examination with reference to a decisive result **:** INTERROGATION; *specif* **:** a judicial or official investigation **c :** torture as part of an examination ⟨he that was in ~ for the robbery —Shak.⟩ ⟨searched for something or put him to the ~ —C.B.Child⟩ **d** (1) **:** OBJECTION, DISPUTE ⟨obey without ~⟩ ⟨true beyond ~⟩ ⟨words that could without ~ be used —S.L.Payne⟩ ⟨one ~ remains unanswered⟩ (2) **:** room for doubt or objection ⟨no ~ about the official's honesty⟩ ⟨seemed little ~ that it would be able to count on government support —*Collier's Yr. Bk.*⟩ ⟨there is no ~ but that there will be a general rise in wages —E.A.Lahey⟩ (3) **:** possibility of or opportunity for a particular action **:** CHANCE — used in negative constructions ⟨there is no ~ of bypassing a statutory procedure —*Current History*⟩ ⟨there was no ~ of refusing to sit on any of these committees —Andrzej Panufnik⟩ ⟨no longer even any ~ of escape —John Farrelly⟩ — **in question 1 :** of such a nature or in such a position as to be subject to doubt **:** in dispute **:** at issue ⟨the dates are not *in question* —Herbert Read⟩ ⟨particularly *in question* were the federal security program, the granting of passports —*Annual Report: Amer. Civil Liberties Union*⟩ ⟨such interrogations put *in question* the very meaning of life —H.M.Parshley⟩ **2 :** being referred to or discussed **:** under consideration **:** CONCERNED, RELEVANT ⟨on the Sunday *in question* —Osbert Sitwell⟩ ⟨open at the page *in question* —Louis Auchincloss⟩ ⟨voice from behind the door of the room *in question* —

Edward Bok〉 — **into question** *adv* **:** up for or subject to discussion in which doubt is cast — usu. used with *bring* or *call* or *come* 〈bring several of the current beliefs of this sort *into question* —Ralph Linton〉 〈only natural that all the former systems of classifying ancient as well as more recent fossil men should be brought *into question* —R.W.Murray〉 — **out of question** *archaic* **:** UNQUESTIONABLY 〈*out of question*, 'tis Maria's hand —Shak.〉 — **out of the question 1 :** alien to the question or subject being discussed **2 :** not worthy of consideration **:** not to be thought of 〈such a course is *out of the question*〉 **3 :** IMPOSSIBLE 〈sleep during this interval was *out of the question* —T.L.Peacock〉

**²question** \"\ *vb* **questioned; questioned; questioning** \-es(h)chəniŋ, ÷ -esh(ə)n-\ **questions** [MF *questionner*, fr. *question*, n. — more at ¹QUESTION] *vt* **1 :** to ask a question of or about 〈~*ed* the Indians as to the river's name —*Amer. Guide Series: Minn.*〉 〈~ the absence of a club member〉 **2 a :** to subject to judicial or police examination 〈~ a suspect〉 **b :** to call to account **:** ACCUSE, CHARGE **3 a** (1) **:** to express doubt about **:** demonstrate lack of conviction about **:** CHALLENGE, DISPUTE 〈the honesty of these writers is unimpeachable, however much their competency may be ~*ed* —Edward Clodd〉 (2) **:** to feel doubts about **:** DOUBT 〈~*ed* her wisdom in staying on the farm —E.T.Thurston〉 **b :** to subject to analysis **:** EXAMINE, RESEARCH, PONDER, CONSIDER 〈Babylonian sages who ~*ed* the stars in their efforts to measure time —W.K.Ferguson〉 〈no more accustomed to ~ language itself than to ~ the weather —Stuart Chase〉 ~ *vi* **1 :** to ask questions **:** INQUIRE 〈a ~*ing* mind〉 **2** *obs* **:** TALK, CONVERSE, ARGUE **syn** see ASK

**ques·tion·able** \-es(h)chənəbəl, ÷ -esh(ə)n-\ *adj* **1** *obs* **:** admitting of being questioned **:** inviting or seeming to invite inquiry **2** *obs* **:** liable or amenable to judicial inquiry or action **3 :** affording reason for being doubted, questioned, or challenged **:** not certain or exact **:** not acceptable immediately or without examination **:** PROBLEMATICAL, UNCERTAIN, UNSAFE 〈the illustration is ~ but the notion implied may be sound —Samuel Alexander〉 〈canners had taken in any ~ type of fruit at top prices —*Farmer's Weekly (So. Africa)*〉 〈a highly ~ exercise of executive authority —A.F.Westin〉 〈a general storm area . . . making even a daylight flight a ~ venture —C.A. Lindbergh b.1902〉 **4 :** attended by well-grounded suspicions of being immoral, crude, false, or unsound **:** DUBIOUS 〈the propriety . . . was at least ~ —G.B.Shaw〉 〈the habit of living in ~ neighborhoods —M.D.Geismar〉 〈a ~ insurance broker —Milton Silverman〉 **syn** see DOUBTFUL

**ques·tion·able·ness** \-bəlnəs\ *n* -ES **:** the state of being questionable

**ques·tion·ably** \-blē, -bli\ *adv* **:** in a questionable manner **:** DOUBTFULLY, DUBIOUSLY, SUSPICIOUSLY 〈estates her husband had ~ acquired —*Brit. Book News*〉

**¹ques·tion·ary** \'kwes(h)chə,nerē\ *n* -ES [¹*question* + -*ary* (n. suffix)] **:** a collection of questions; *esp* **:** QUESTIONNAIRE 〈a ~ circulated two years ago to about 5000 laboratories —*Lancet*〉 〈~ containing 102 phrases and locutions —Wallace Rice〉

**²questionary** \"\ *adj* [¹*question* + -*ary* (adj. suffix)] **:** put in the form of a question **:** asking or involving questions

**¹question-begging** \'≈≈,≈≈\ *adj* **:** that involves the fallacy of petitio principii **:** that involves an assumption of something whose truth may be questioned 〈*question-begging* arguments〉 〈*question-begging* epithets〉 — compare BEG *vt* 3b

**²question-begging** \"\ *n* -S **:** something that involves an assumption whose truth may be questioned 〈most of us may think this *question-begging* —*Manchester Guardian Weekly*〉

**ques·tion·ee** \¦≈≈¦ē\ *n* -S **:** one that is questioned

**ques·tion·er** \'kwes(h)chənə(r), ÷ 'kwesh(ə)n-\ *n* -S **:** one that questions

**¹questioning** *n* -S [fr. gerund of ²*question*] **:** the asking of questions **:** examination by question **:** INTERROGATION 〈an age of disillusion, of doubt and ~ —Jawaharlal Nehru〉 〈our ~*s* lose some of their point —Jacob Kohn〉 〈~*s* of suspects〉

**²questioning** *adj* [fr. pres. part. of ²*question*] **1 :** expressing or implying a question 〈a ~ look〉 **2 :** INQUIRING, INQUISITIVE 〈a keen ~ mind —C.I.Glicksberg〉

**ques·tion·ing·ly** *adv* **:** in a questioning manner 〈looked ~ at the doctor —G.G.Carter〉

**ques·tion·ist** \-nəst\ *n* -S **1 a :** one that questions esp. intensively or habitually **b** *obs* **:** SCHOOLMAN 1 **2** *archaic* **:** a candidate for the bachelor's degree in certain British universities during the last term before final examinations

**¹ques·tion·less** \'≈≈ləs\ *adj* [¹*question* + -*less*] **1 :** not to be questioned **:** INDUBITABLE 〈remained always its born and ~ master —J.R.Lowell〉 **2 :** UNQUESTIONING 〈clear mind and ~ faith —Lew Wallace〉

**²questionless** \"\ *adv, archaic* **:** UNQUESTIONABLY, UNDOUBTEDLY 〈can ~ write a good hand —George Eliot〉

**ques·tion·less·ly** *adv* **:** in a questionless manner

**question mark** *n* **1 :** the mark ? used in writing and printing at the conclusion of a sentence to indicate a direct question or in parenthesis after a particular to indicate conjecture or uncertainty or by editors and proofreaders to indicate a queried detail **2 :** something unknown, unknowable, or uncertain 〈the future of the controversial movie . . . will remain a *question mark* at least until today —*Springfield (Mass.) Union*〉 **3 :** VIOLET TIP

**¹ques·tion·naire** *also* **ques·tion·aire** \¦kwes(h)chə¦na(ə)-\|(ə)r, -ne|, |ə\ *n* -S [F *questionnaire*, fr. *questionner* to question + -*aire* -ary — more at QUESTION] **1 :** a set of questions for obtaining statistically useful or personal information from an individual 〈filled out a consumer's preference ~〉 〈devise a special ~ on children's reading habits〉 〈a telephone ~ addressed to six authors —J.K.Hutchens〉 **2 :** a sheet of paper containing a questionnaire 〈fill out a ~〉 **3 :** a survey made by the use of a questionnaire 〈tabulate the results of a ~〉

**²questionnaire** \"\ *vt* -ED/-ING/-S **:** to send a questionnaire to or obtain information from by means of a questionnaire 〈has begun to ~ scientifically trained men —*Textile World*〉

**question of fact :** FACT IN ISSUE

**question of law :** ISSUE OF LAW

**question of privilege :** a question that concerns the rights or privileges of a legislative body or of any of its members

**question time** *n* **:** a period in a session of a British parliamentary body during which members may put to a minister questions on matters concerning his department 〈*question time* . . . is one of parliament's most valuable institutions —*Brit. Parliament*〉

**quest·man** \'≈mən\ *n, pl* **questmen** [ME, fr. *quest* + *man*] *archaic* **:** one legally empowered to solicit alms; *specif* **:** SIDESMAN 1

**questor** *var of* QUAESTOR

**questrist** *n* -S [*quester* + -*ist*] *obs* **:** SEEKER, PURSUER 〈his knights, hot ~*s* after him —Shak.〉

**quests** *pl of* QUEST, *pres 3d sing of* QUEST

**quet** \'kwet\ *n* -S [origin unknown] *dial Eng* **:** the common guillemot

**quetch** \'kwech\ *vi* -ED/-ING/-ES [ME *quecchen, quicchen*, fr. OE *cweccan* to shake, shake off, move, vibrate — more at QUAKE] **1** *chiefly dial* **:** TWITCH, STIR 〈~*ing* with pain〉 **2 :** to break silence **:** utter a sound

**quête** \'ket\ *n* -S [F, search, quest, collection, fr. OF *queste* — more at QUEST] **:** a collection of money (as for use as a payment to street musicians or strolling players)

**¹quetsch** \'kwech, 'kve-\ *n* -ES [G, fr. G dial. (Alsace) *quetsch, quetsche* plum, fr. a F dial. word akin to OF *davoisne* damson plum, fr. (assumed) VL *damascena*, fr. pl. of L (*prunum*) *Damascenum* — more at DAMSON] **:** a dry white Alsatian brandy distilled from fermented plum juice

**²quetsch** \"\ *n* -ES [G *quetsche* press, roller, fr. *quetschen* to squeeze, crush, flatten, fr. MHG *quetzen, quetschen* to strike, squeeze, crush; akin to MLG *quetsen, quessen* to strike against, MD *quetsen, quetschen* to injure, wound, break up] **1 :** a vat equipped with rollers for applying chemical solutions or sizing to yarn or cloth and used esp. in the slashing process **2 :** one of the rollers in a quetsch

**quet·ta** \'kwed·ə\ *adj, usu cap* [fr. *Quetta*, town in Baluchistan, Pakistan] **:** of or belonging to a culture of northern Baluchistan of about the fourth millennium B.C. characterized by pottery decorated in geometric designs with purplish brown or black paint on a buff ground or occas. black on a gray ground

**quet·zal** \ket'säl, -sal\ *also* **que·zal** *or* **que·sal** \kä's-\ *n, pl* **quetzals** \-lz\ *or* **quetza·les** \-(,)läs\ [AmerSp, fr. Nahuatl *quetzalli* large brilliant tail feather] **1** *also* **quetzal bird :** a large Central American trogon (*Pharomachrus mocino*) having a compressed crest, brilliant plumage with the upperparts and throat iridescent greenish and the underparts crimson, and in the male upper tail coverts often exceeding two feet in length **2** *pl usu* **quetzales a :** the basic monetary unit of Guatemala — see MONEY table **b :** a silver coin representing one quetzal **c :** a note representing one quetzal **3** *quetzales pl but often sing in constr, or* **quetzal dance :** a men's longways dance of the Mexican Totonacs dedicated in pre-Columbian times to the quetzal bird as sun symbol and still suggesting the sun with huge disk headdresses

**¹queue** \'kyü\ *n* -S [MF, fr. OF *coe, coue* — more at COWARD] **1 :** a taillike braid of natural or artificial hair usu. worn hanging at the back of the head and sometimes as part of a wig or as an addition to a hat **2 :** a line esp. of persons or vehicles 〈most of us in the customs ~ —Nancy Debenham〉 〈pedicabs wait for custom . . . in great dead ~*s* —G.S.Gale〉 〈gave up places in the production ~ —*Sperryscope*〉 **3 :** a metal piece attached to the side of the breastplate of a suit of armor and used as a rest for the butt of a lance **4 :** the tailpiece of a violin or other stringed instrument **5 :** the tail of a musical note

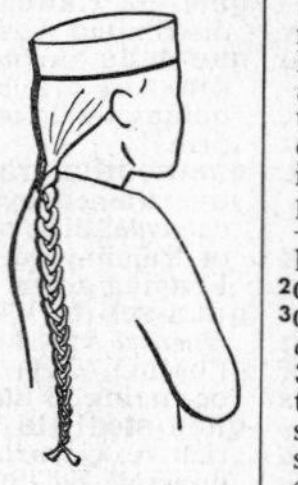

queue 1

**²queue** \"\ *vb* **queued; queued; queuing** *or* **queueing; queues** *vt* **:** to arrange or form in a queue ~ *vi* **:** to line up or wait in a queue 〈the everlasting *queuing* for whatever food was available —J.G.Winant〉 〈the salmon ~*s* to jump the weir —Edward Hyams〉 — often used with *up* 〈you had to ~ up at the bus stop —Joseph Wechsberg〉

**queu·er** \-ü(ə)r, -üə\ *n* -S **:** one that queues 〈~*s* were hoping for standing room —*Time*〉

**que·venne's iron** \kə'venz-\ *n, usu cap Q* [after Theodore *Quevenne*, 19th cent. Fr. pharmacist] **:** REDUCED IRON

**quey** \'kwā\ *n* -S [ME *quy, quee*, of Scand origin; akin to Dan *kvie* heifer, Sw & Norw *kviga*, ON *kvīga*; prob. akin to ON *kȳr* cow — more at COW] *dial Brit* **:** HEIFER

**queyn** \'kwān\ *Scot var of* QUEAN

**que·zon city** \'kā,sōn-\ *adj, usu cap Q&C* [fr. *Quezon City*, Philippines] **:** of or from Quezon City, capital of the Philippines **:** of the kind or style prevalent in Quezon City

**quia·quia** \¦kēə¦kēə\ *n* -S [AmerSp *quiaquia*, prob. fr. *quiaquia*, a kind of rattle made from a tortoise shell, of imit. origin] **:** ROUND SCAD

**¹quib·ble** \'kwibəl\ *n* -S [prob. dim. of obs. *quib* quibble, perh. fr. L *quibus*, dat. & abl. pl. of *qui* who, which (often used in legal documents) — more at WHO] **1** *archaic* **:** PUN **2 a** (1) **:** something (as a line of reasoning adopted, an objection made, a distinction drawn, a point advanced) that evades, shifts from, or obscures the real point at issue in some discussion or argument by reason of centering on what is relatively unimportant and often petty or totally irrelevant and that is marked typically by hedging or equivocation 〈produces more ~*s* and qualifications than it does direct answers —S.L.Payne〉 (2) **:** a minor objection or piece of criticism arising typically from an exaggerated tendency to find fault 〈had a few ~*s* about the quality of the performance〉 **b :** argumentation, protestation, or criticism marked by or consisting of quibbles 〈in discussing this situation there is no room for ~ —W.H.Camp〉 〈a procedure that is open to ~〉

**²quibble** \"\ *vb* **quibbled; quibbled; quibbling** \-b(ə)liŋ\ **quibbles** *vi* **1** *archaic* **:** PUN **2 a** (1) **:** to make use of, indulge in, or resort to quibbles 〈had no desire to ~ when decisive action was called for〉 (2) **:** to object to something or criticize something on minor grounds that typically reflect an exaggerated tendency to find fault **:** CAVIL, CARP 〈was a peevish critic, always ready to ~〉 **b :** to indulge in argumentation, protestation, or criticism marked by or consisting of quibbles **:** BICKER 〈the usual *quibbling* over what should be included in the humanities —W.H.Whyte〉 ~ *vt* **:** to subject to quibbles 〈aren't inclined to ~ the point —S.E.Hyman〉

**quib·bler** \-b(ə)lə(r)\ *n* -S **:** one that quibbles

**¹quibbling** *n* -S [fr. gerund of ²*quibble*] **1 :** the action of one that quibbles **2 :** an instance of quibbling 〈theological ~*s* —Corra Harris〉

**²quibbling** *adj* [fr. pres. part. of ²*quibble*] **:** marked by or consisting of quibbles **:** CARPING, CAVILING 〈had no patience with ~ criticism〉 — **quib·bling·ly** *adv*

**qui·ca** \'kēkə\ *n* -S [Pg *cuica*, fr. Tupi] **:** FOUR-EYED OPOSSUM

**¹qui·che** \(')kē¦chā\ *n, pl* **quiche** *or* **quiches** *usu cap* [Sp *quiché*, of AmerInd origin] **1 a :** an Indian people of south central Guatemala **b :** a member of such people **2 :** the Mayan language of the Quiche people

**²quiche** \'kēsh\ *n* -S [F, fr. G dial. (Lorraine) *küche*, dim. of *kuche, kuchen* cake, fr. OHG *kuocho* — more at CAKE] **:** a pastry shell sprinkled with bits of fried bacon and grated cheese, filled with custard, and baked

**qui·choid** \'kē,chȯid\ *n* -S *usu cap* [¹*Quiche* + -*oid*] **:** a linguistic subdivision of the Mayan of Guatemala, El Salvador, and Mexico

**quichua** *usu cap, var of* QUECHUA

**quichuan** *usu cap, var of* QUECHUAN

**¹quick** \'kwik\ *adj, usu* -ER/-EST [ME *quik, quike*, fr. OE *cwic, cwicu*; akin to OFris & OS *quik* alive, OHG *quec*, ON *kvikr*, Goth *qiwai* (nom. pl.) L *vivus* alive, *vivere* to live, Gk *zōē* life, *bios* mode of life, Lith *gyvas* living, Skt *jīva*] **1 a** *archaic* **:** marked by the presence of life **:** not dead **:** LIVING, ALIVE, ANIMATE 〈shall judge the ~ and the dead —2 Tim 4:1 (AV)〉 **b** *archaic* **:** arrived at a stage of pregnancy at which the motion of the fetus is perceptible 〈women . . . ~ with child —Oliver Goldsmith〉 **c** *chiefly Brit* **:** formed of living plants 〈a ~ hedge〉 **2 :** that moves, functions, or is accomplished or obtained swiftly and with vigor, energy, and promptness or that is capable of so moving or functioning or of being so accomplished or obtained **:** RAPID, SPEEDY: as **a** (1) **:** fast in understanding, thinking, or learning **:** speedy in mental processes **:** mentally agile **:** mentally nimble 〈a ~ mind〉 〈~ thinking〉 〈~ students〉 (2) **:** reacting to stimuli with speed and keen sensitivity **:** delicate and sharp in perception 〈a ~ sense of the tactful thing to do〉 〈a ~ eye for beauty〉 (3) **:** aroused immediately and intensely 〈~ resentment〉 〈a ~ temper〉 **b** (1) **:** fast in development or occurrence 〈a ~ succession of events〉 (2) **:** done or taking place with rapidity **:** done or taking place within only a small interval of time 〈gave her a ~ kiss〉 〈a ~ finish to the race〉 〈gave them a ~ look〉; *esp* **:** begun and ended in an instant 〈a ~ flash of lightning〉 (3) **:** rapidly often almost instantaneously accomplished or achieved 〈a ~ profit〉 〈a ~ victory〉 (4) **:** consumed rapidly or hurriedly 〈had a ~ bite to eat〉; *esp* **:** swallowed rapidly or hurriedly 〈had a ~ drink at the bar〉 **c** (1) **:** marked by speed, readiness, or promptness of action 〈did a ~ job〉 〈finished it with ~ efficiency〉 (2) **:** marked by speed, readiness, or promptness of physical movement 〈walked with ~ steps〉 **d** (1) **:** inclined to hastiness of action or treatment **:** OVERHASTY 〈must not be too ~ in the experiment〉 (2) **:** inclined to impatience or anger **:** easily aroused to impatience or anger 〈was too ~ with her students〉 **3** *archaic* **a :** not stagnant **:** RUNNING, FLOWING 〈gently winding valleys, with clear, ~ water —Walter Pater〉 〈sweet and ~ stream —John Evelyn〉 **b :** extremely soft and mobile from being mixed with water so as to tend to suck down an object touching the surface 〈the patch of ~ ground —P.H.Emerson〉 〈~ mud〉 **4 a** (1) *archaic* **:** burning with intense heat **:** FIERY 〈the ~ flames —P.B. Shelley〉 **:** GLOWING 〈a ~ coal —George Herbert〉 (2) *obs* **:** rapidly combustible 〈~ sulfur —Edmund Spenser〉 **b** *of soil* **:** readily absorbing heat by reason of being highly porous in composition **5** *obs* **:** full of activity **:** BUSY, BRISK 〈the markets were very ~ —Henry Best〉 **6** *obs* **a :** bitingly sharp in taste or odor **:** PUNGENT **b :** stingingly severe **:** CAUSTIC **7 :** turning, curving, or bending at a sharp angle 〈a ~ turn in the road〉 **8 :** IMBUED, FILLED, CHARGED, INSTINCT 〈a speech ~ with passion〉

**syn** PROMPT, READY, APT: QUICK describes ability to respond instantly or rapidly, often an ability native rather than acquired, or a marked capacity for speedy perception or learning 〈examined the hall and the men who passed, with the same *quick*, sharp cunning with which he had examined the street —Liam O'Flaherty〉 〈a *quick* and brilliant student . . . was elected to Phi Beta Kappa and was the valedictorian of his graduating class —*Current Biog.*〉 PROMPT may apply to speedy response, often due to training, discipline, preparation, or extreme willingness to serve, sometimes servilely 〈*prompt* to spring forward when anything was wanted —R.L.Stevenson〉 〈like a competent man of affairs, he was *prompt* in meeting engagements —V.L.Parrington〉 〈a people, gentle, submissive, *prompt* to obey, and accustomed . . . to the inexorable demands of tyranny —Agnes Repplier〉 READY may suggest speed in response or compliance coupled with willingness, vigilance, impetus, skill, or facility 〈the young lady proved to be as *ready* as the squire, and the preliminaries [of the marriage] were arranged in little more than five minutes —T.L. Peacock〉 〈their *ready* guns begin to bark —E.L.Beach〉 〈not a *ready* speaker, and so . . . he had written out what he had to say —H.E.Scudder〉 APT may focus attention on the fact of possession of qualities, such as intelligence or talent, facilitating speedy response 〈have proved themselves not only *apt* pupils, but in many cases . . . have outstripped their teachers —D.C.Buchanan〉 〈to become *apt* in argument —C.T.Copeland〉 **syn** see in addition FAST

**²quick** \"\ *adv, usu* -ER/-EST [ME *quik*, fr. *quik*, adj.] **:** QUICKLY

**³quick** \"\ *n* -S [ME *quik, quike*, fr. OE *cwic, cwicu*, fr. *cwic, cwicu*, adj.] **1** *obs* **:** a living thing **2** *chiefly Brit* **:** QUICKSET 1 **3** [prob. of Scand origin; akin to ON *kvikva, kvika* quick (of the flesh), fr. *kvikr* alive — more at ¹QUICK] **a :** a raw painfully sensitive spot or area of exposed flesh: as (1) **:** the extremely sensitive flesh underlying a fingernail or toenail (2) **:** the extremely sensitive flesh underlying a corn, bunion, or callus (3) **:** the extremely sensitive part of a sore or wound (4) **:** the sensitive layers of tissue underlying the epidermis **b :** the inmost sensibilities of an individual 〈felt hurt to the ~ by their remark〉 **c :** the very center of something **:** the vital center **:** HEART 〈the ~ of the matter〉 **4** *archaic* **:** LIFE 12 **5 :** QUICKSILVER **6 :** QUICKIE

**⁴quick** \"\ *vb* -ED/-ING/-S [ME *quiken*, fr. OE *cwician*, fr. *cwic, cwicu*, adj.] *archaic* **:** QUICKEN

**⁵quick** \"\ *n* -S [ME (northern dial.) *quike*, prob. of Scand origin; akin to Sw dial. *kvicka, kveka*, couch grass, Norw dial. *kvika* — more at QUITCH] **:** COUCH GRASS 1a

**quick assets** *n pl* **:** cash, accounts receivable, and other current assets excluding inventories

**quick bead** *n* **:** a bead that is flush with the surface of a molding — compare COCK BEAD

**quickbeam** \'≈,≈\ *n* [fr. (assumed) ME *quikbeem*, fr. OE *cwicbēam*, fr. *cwic* alive + *bēam* tree — more at QUICK, BEAM] **:** ROWAN TREE 1

**quick bread** *n* **:** a bread (as corn bread, muffins, biscuits) made with a leavening agent (as baking powder, soda) that permits immediate baking of the dough or batter mixture

**quick-break** \(')≈¦≈\ *adj* **:** designed to break an electric circuit automatically and quickly esp. so as to shorten arcing and burning 〈a *quick-break* switch〉

**quick-change** \(')≈¦≈\ *adj* **:** that changes quickly or that is adapted to changing or being changed quickly (as from one function to another) 〈a *quick-change* tool part〉

**quick-change artist** *n* **:** an individual adroit at quickly switching from one thing to another; *esp* **:** a performer skilled at quickly changing costume and makeup

**quick decline** *n* **:** a disease of grafted citrus trees with bitter orange rootstocks that is identical with or closely related to tristeza in cause and symptoms

**¹quick·en** \'kwikən\ *vb* **quickened; quickened; quickening** \-k(ə)niŋ\ **quickens** [ME *quickenen*, fr. *quik, quike* quick + -*nen* -en — more at QUICK] *vt* **1 a :** to make alive **:** REVIVE 〈warm spring days that ~ the earth〉 **b :** to cause to be enlivened **:** AROUSE, STIMULATE, EXCITE 〈~*ing* their interest with vivid details〉 **2** *archaic* **a :** KINDLE **b :** to cause to burn more brightly or more intensely **3 :** to make rapid or more rapid **:** HASTEN, ACCELERATE 〈~*ed* her steps〉 **4 a :** to make (a curve) sharper **b :** to make (a slope) steeper **5 :** to treat (articles to be plated) with a quickening liquid ~ *vi* **1 :** to quicken something **2 :** to come to life **:** become alive **:** become charged with life 〈seed that ~*s* and becomes ripe grain〉 **3 :** to reach the stage of gestation at which motion of the fetus is first begun or felt **4 :** to shine brightly or more brightly 〈watched the dawn ~*ing* in the East〉 **5 :** to become rapid or more rapid 〈her pulse ~*ed* at the sight〉

**syn** QUICKEN, ANIMATE, ENLIVEN, VIVIFY mean, in common, to make alive or lively. QUICKEN chiefly stresses the renewal of suspended life or growth or the arousing to full activity, usu. suddenly 〈its characters never *quicken* with the life one feels lurks somewhere within them —Jerome Stone〉 〈grand aspirations which *quicken* the energies of men —M.R.Cohen〉 〈he felt his own blood *quicken* —Elyne Mitchell〉 ANIMATE emphasizes the imparting of motion and activity, esp. lifelike, to something mechanical or artificial 〈all living creatures, human and animal, are *animated* by souls or spirits —Frederica de Laguna〉 〈almost every gathering is *animated* by spontaneous folk dancing —*Amer. Guide Series: Mich.*〉 〈a child's *animated* doll〉 ENLIVEN suggests a stimulus that kindles, exalts, or brightens something usu. dulled, depressed, or torpid 〈*enliven* the meal by a few foolish jokes —Ellen Glasgow〉 〈the crowded chapel was *enlivened* with bright colors —Josephine Y. Case〉 〈a barrel of home brew on a sledge to *enliven* the occasion —Roderick Finlayson〉 VIVIFY suggests the renewal of vitality, a freshening or energizing 〈the room was dead. The essence that had *vivified* it was gone —O.Henry〉 〈the vital force which was *vivifying* the nation at the expense of an occasional lapse from good taste —Agnes Repplier〉 **syn** see in addition PROVOKE, SPEED

**²quicken** \"\ *or* **quicken tree** *n* -S [ME (northern dial.) *quikentre*, fr. *quik, quike* alive, quick + *tre* tree — more at QUICK, TREE] **:** ROWAN TREE 1

**¹quickening** *adj* [ME, fr. pres. part. of *quickenen* to quicken — more at QUICKEN] **:** that quickens 〈as ~ as the ideas . . . that had followed in the wake of the French Revolution —Donald Davidson〉

**²quickening** *n* -S [ME, fr. gerund of *quickenen* to quicken] **:** the first motion of a fetus in the uterus felt by the mother usu. somewhat before the middle of the period of gestation

**quickening liquid** *n* **:** a solution of a salt of mercury in which articles to be plated with silver are plunged before being put into the silver bath

**quicker** *comparative of* QUICK

**quickest** *superlative of* QUICK

**quick fire** *n* **:** the firing of shots in rapid succession; *esp* **:** marksmanship fire employed when bobbing targets are specified

**quick-fire** \(')≈¦≈\ *or* **quick-firing** \(')≈¦≈≈\ *adj* **:** firing or adapted for firing in rapid succession 〈a *quick-fire* rifle〉

**quick-firer** \(')≈¦≈≈\ *n* -S **:** a quick-fire gun

**¹quick-freeze** \'≈¦≈\ *vb* [²*quick* + *freeze*] *vt* **:** to freeze (food) so rapidly for preservation that ice crystals formed are too small to impair seriously the composition of the cells and consequently natural juices and flavor are preserved ~ *vi* **1 :** to quick-freeze something **2 :** to become quick-frozen

**²quick-freeze** \"\ *also* **quick-freezer** \'≈¦≈≈\ *n* **:** FREEZER 1d(1)

**quick grass** *n* **:** COUCH GRASS 1a

**quick·hatch** \'kwik,hach\ *n* -ES [of Algonquian origin; akin to Cree *kwikkwâhaketsh, kikkwâhakes* wolverine, Ojibwa *qwīngwâage*, Algonquian Montagnais *karkajou*; derivatives fr. a stem represented by Cree *kwikkw, kikkw* to graze (with a shot)] **:** WOLVERINE

**quick·ie** *also* **quicky** \'kwˈikē, -ki\ *n, pl* **quickies** [¹*quick* + -*ie*, -*y*] **:** something done or made in a hurry: as **a** (1) **:** a hurriedly and cheaply produced motion picture or play (2) **:** a book or other publication hurriedly written and published **b :** a hurriedly planned and executed program (as of studies) **c :** a hurried trip or other activity **d :** a sudden often unauthorized brief strike of workers **e :** QUICK ONE

**quick-in-the-hand** \¦≈≈≈'≈\ *n* **:** JEWELWEED b

**quicklier** *archaic comparative of* QUICKLY

**quickliest** *archaic superlative of* QUICKLY

**quicklime** \'≈,≈\ *n* **:** the first solid product obtained by calcining limestone **:** ¹LIME 2a

**quick-lunch** \'≈¦≈\ *n* **:** an eating establishment (as a lunch stand, sandwich shop) specializing in light quickly prepared dishes

**quick·ly** \'kwiklē, -li\ *adv* [ME *quikly*, fr. *quik, quike* quick + *-ly* — more at QUICK] **1 :** in a quick manner: as **a :** RAPIDLY, SPEEDILY ⟨had got rich ~ —J.D.Hart⟩ **b :** without delay : SOON ⟨said she would hear from him ~⟩ **2** *archaic* **:** in a sensitively responsive manner : with sensitivity ⟨the language was still too rich and stiff to turn and twist ~ and freely upon half a sheet of notepaper —Virginia Woolf⟩

**quick march** *n* **:** a march in quick time

**quick match** *n* **:** a wick of cotton impregnated with a flammable mixture (as a paste of black powder and starch) that is used in lighting and carrying fire from one part to another in fireworks and flares

**quick·ness** \'kwiknəs\ *n* -ES [ME *quiknesse*, fr. *quik, quike* quick + *-nesse* -ness] **:** the quality or state of being quick

**quick one** *n* **:** a usu. alcoholic drink hurriedly tossed off

**quick oven** *n* **:** HOT OVEN

**quick return** *n* **:** a device used in a machine tool to cause the return stroke (as of a reciprocating tool) to be faster than the cutting stroke

**quicks** *pl of* QUICK, *pres 3d sing of* QUICK

**quicksand** \'ˌ=ˌ=\ *n, often attrib* [ME *qwykkesand*, fr. *quik, quike* quick + *sand* — more at QUICK, SAND] **1 a** (1) **:** a bed of sand which is usu. saturated with upward flowing water and made up of smooth rounded grains with little tendency to mutual adherence and in which the admixture of smooth grains and water constitutes a soft highly mobile shifting mass that yields easily to pressure and that tends to suck down and engulf objects resting on its surface (2) **:** an area marked by the presence of one or more such beds **b :** sand of the kind found in such a bed **2 :** something treacherously shifting and mobile that tends to entrap and destroy ⟨the ~s of human existence —Dorothy C. Fisher⟩ — **quicksandy** \(')=¦==\ *adj*

**quickset** \'=ˌ=\ *n* [ME *quyksette*, fr. *quyk, quik* quick + *sette, set set* — more at QUICK, SET] **1 a :** living slips or cuttings of a plant set in the ground to grow; *esp* **:** slips or cuttings (as of hawthorn) used for a hedge ⟨enclosed the ground with a single row of ~ —Robert Southey⟩ **b :** a single slip or cutting of a plant ⟨when a ~ of a vine is planted in a vineyard —Philemon Holland⟩ **2** *chiefly Brit* **:** QUICKSET HEDGE

**quick-set** \"\ *n* [²*quick* + *set*, past part. of *set*] **:** a quick= setting material

**quickset hedge** *n, chiefly Brit* **:** a hedge or thicket planted for ornamentation or as a boundary marker and typically made up of English hawthorn

**quick-setting** \(')=¦==\ *adj* **:** that is made so as to set more quickly than is usual ⟨*quick-setting* concrete⟩

**quick-sighted** \(')=¦==\ *adj* **:** marked by keen quickly responsive sight ⟨*quick-sighted* as a cat⟩ or sharp quickly responsive discernment ⟨*quick-sighted* into the faults of the time —Leonard Bacon⟩ **:** quick to see or discern : SHARP-SIGHTED — **quick-sight·ed·ness** *n* -ES

¹**quicksilver** \'=ˌ==\ *n* [ME *quiksilver*, fr. OE *cwicseolfor*, fr. *cwic* alive + *seolfor* silver; trans. of L *argentum vivum* like MD *quicsilver* quicksilver, OHG *quecsilbar* — more at QUICK, SILVER] **1 :** MERCURY 1a **2 :** something resembling or suggestive of quicksilver : something mercurial

²**quicksilver** \"\ *adj* **:** resembling or suggestive of quicksilver : MERCURIAL

³**quicksilver** \"\ *vt* **:** to overlay with or as if with quicksilver; *esp* **:** to coat (glass) with an amalgam of quicksilver and tin in making mirrors

**quicksilvering** \'=¦=(=)=\ *n* **:** the amalgam that forms the reflecting surface of some mirrors

**quicksilver rock** *n* **:** an altered serpentine consisting mainly of dark opal and chalcedony and commonly associated with the ore in mercury deposits in serpentine

**quicksilver vermilion** *n* **:** VERMILION 1a

**quicksilver water** *n* **:** a solution of mercury nitrate used in gilding

**quicksilver weed** *n* **:** EARLY MEADOW RUE

**quicksilvery** \(')=¦=(=)=\ *adj* **:** resembling or suggestive of quicksilver : MERCURIAL

**quickstep** \'=ˌ=\ *n* **1 :** a spirited march tune; *esp* **:** a spirited march tune designed to accompany a military march in quick time **2 :** a combination of short rapid dance steps

**quick stick** *also* **quick sticks** *adv, archaic* **:** QUICKLY

**quick study** *n* **:** one that can speedily learn the essentials of something to be done; *esp* **:** a performer (as an actor, musician) with a gift for learning with remarkable speed new material (as lines, stage business, scores)

**quick-tempered** \(')=¦==\ *adj* **:** easily aroused to anger : IRASCIBLE

**quickthorn** \'=ˌ=\ *n* **:** the common European hawthorn (*Crataegus oxyacantha*)

**quick time** *n* **:** a rate of marching in which 120 steps each 30 inches in length are taken in one minute

**quick trick** *n* **:** HONOR TRICK

**quickwater** \'=ˌ==\ *n* **1 :** QUICKSILVER WATER **2 a :** the part of a stream that has a strong current **b :** an artificial current or bubbling patch of water just astern of a moving boat

**quick-witted** \(')=¦==\ *adj* **:** quick in perception and understanding : mentally nimble and wide-awake : brightly alert : SHARP ⟨a *quick-witted* opponent⟩ ⟨a *quick-witted* answer⟩ ⟨saved an embarrassing situation with *quick-witted* tact⟩ **syn** see INTELLIGENT

**quick-wit·ted·ly** *adv* **:** in a quick-witted manner

**quick-wit·ted·ness** \-nəs\ *n* -ES **:** the quality or state of being quick-witted

**quickwork** \'=ˌ=\ *n, archaic* **:** one of several sections of planking or plating in the upper or sometimes the lower part of a ship's hull

**quicky** *var of* QUICKIE

¹**quid** \'kwid\ *n* -S [L, what, anything, something, neut. of *quis* who, anyone — more at WHO] **1 :** QUIDDITY **2** [L (as in *quid pro quo*)] **:** something given or received for something else ⟨bilateral deals that would ensure us a large ~ for every single quo —W.L.Thorp⟩

²**quid** \"\ *n, pl* **quid** *also* **quids** [origin unknown] *slang Brit* **:** POUND STERLING, SOVEREIGN

³**quid** \"\ *n* -S [E dial., cud, fr. ME *quide*, fr. OE *cwidu* — more at CUD] **:** a cut or wad of something to be chewed but not swallowed; *esp* **:** a cut of chewing tobacco

⁴**quid** \"\ *vi* **quidded; quidded; quidding; quids** *of a horse* **:** to drop chewed food from the mouth

**quiddany** *n* -ES [modif. of obs. F *codignat* (now *cotignat*), fr. MF, fr. OProv *codonat, codonhat*, fr. *codon* quince, fr. L *cotoneum* — more at QUINCE] *obs* **:** a jelly or syrup made from fruit (as quinces)

**quid·da·tive** *also* **quid·di·tive** \'kwidəd·iv\ *adj* [*quiddative* irreg. fr. *quiddity* + *-ative*; *quidditive* fr. *quiddity* + *-ive*] **:** QUIDDITATIVE

**quid·der** *or* **quid·dor** \'kwidə(r)\ *n* -S [⁴*quid* + *-er* or *-or*] **:** a horse that quids

**quid·dit** \'kwidət, *usu* -əd·+V\ *n* -S [ML *quidditas, quiditas*] *archaic* **:** a quibbling subtlety

**quid·di·tas** \'kwidəˌtas\ *n, pl* **quiddita·tes** \ˌ==ˈtäd·(ˌ)ēz, -ā,tēz\ [ML] **:** QUIDDITY 1a

**quid·di·ta·tive** \'==ˌtād·iv\ *adj* [*quiddity* + *-ative*] **:** of, relating to, or constituting the essential nature of something

**quid·di·ty** \'kwidəd·ē, -ətē, -i\ *n* -ES [ML *quidditas, quiditas*, fr. L *quid* what, anything + *-itas* -ity — more at QUID] **1 a** (1) **:** a quibbling subtlety : a trifling point : QUIBBLE (2) **:** an inclination to quibble **b :** an odd little feature : ECCENTRICITY ⟨his own personality, with all its quirks and *quiddities* —Clifton Fadiman⟩ **2 :** the essential nature or ultimate form of something : what makes something to be the type of thing that it is — compare HAECCEITY

¹**quid·dle** \'kwidᵊl\ *vb* **quiddled; quiddled; quiddling** \-d(ᵊ)liŋ\ **quiddles** [prob. blend of *quiddity* and *fiddle* or *twiddle*] *chiefly dial* **:** DAWDLE, TRIFLE

²**quiddle** \"\ *n* -S *chiefly dial* **:** a fussy or fastidious person

**quid·nunc** \'kwidˌnəŋk\ *n* -S [L *quid nunc* what now?] **:** one that is avidly curious and given to speculating esp. about ephemeral or petty things : an inquisitive usu. small-minded individual : NEWSMONGER, BUSYBODY, GOSSIP

**quid pro quo** \ˌkwidˌprō¦kwō\ *n, pl* **quid pro quos** *or* **quids pro quos** *also* **quids pro quo** [L, something for something (else)] **:** something given or received for something else ⟨would be folly to grant that increase without insisting on some *quid pro quo* —*Newsweek*⟩

**quie·bra·cha** \kyāˈbrächə\ *or* **quie·bra·ha·cha** \ˌ=ˌbrä-ˈhächə\ *n* -S [AmerSp — more at QUEBRACHO] **:** QUEBRACHO

**qui·esce** \kwīˈes, kwēˈ-\ *vi* -ED/-ING/-S [L *quiescere* to be quiet — more at QUIET] **:** to become quiet, calm, or silent

**qui·es·cence** \kwīˈesᵊn(t)s, kwēˈ-\ *n* -S [LL *quiescentia*, fr. L *quiescent-, quiescens* + *-ia*] **:** the quality or state of being quiescent

**qui·es·cen·cy** \-ᵊnsē\ *n* -ES [LL *quiescentia*] **:** QUIESCENCE

¹**qui·es·cent** \-nt\ *adj* [L *quiescent-, quiescens*, pres. part. of *quiescere* to be quiet — more at QUIET] **1 a :** marked by a state of inactivity or repose : tranquilly at rest : MOTIONLESS, QUIET ⟨the ~ melancholy of the town —Arnold Bennett⟩ **b** (1) **:** ARRESTED ⟨~ tuberculosis⟩ (2) **:** causing no symptoms ⟨~ gallstones⟩ **2** *of a letter* **:** not pronounced : SILENT — compare MOVABLE **syn** see LATENT

²**quiescent** \"\ *n* -S **:** a silent letter (as in Hebrew)

**qui·es·cent·ly** *adv* **:** in a quiescent manner

¹**qui·et** \'kwīət, *usu* -əd·+V\ *n* -S [ME, fr. L *quiet-, quies* rest, quiet — more at WHILE] **:** the quality or state of being quiet : TRANQUILLITY, REPOSE, STILLNESS — often used as a command — **at quiet :** at rest ⟨began . . . to grow more *at quiet* with himself —R.L.Stevenson⟩ — **on the quiet** *adv* (*or adj*) **:** in a secret or underhand manner ⟨bought the goods *on the quiet*⟩

²**quiet** \"\ *adj, usu* -ER/-EST [ME, fr. MF *quiet, quiete*, fr. L *quietus*, fr. past part. of *quiescere* to be quiet, fr. *quies* rest, quiet] **1 a** (1) **:** marked by little or no motion or agitation : making little stir : CALM ⟨the ~ waters of a lagoon⟩ (2) **:** marked by little or no activity ⟨during the morning, business was ~⟩ **:** not moving about : INACTIVE ⟨a ~ throng of onlookers⟩ **b :** causing no trouble or disturbance : not turbulent : GENTLE ⟨a ~, peace-loving people⟩ **c** (1) **:** not excited, anxious, or wrought up : SETTLED ⟨leading a ~ life⟩ ⟨went about her work with ~ efficiency⟩ (2) **:** not disturbed, bothered, or annoyed : not interfered or meddled with ⟨decided to do a little ~ reading⟩ **:** enjoyed in peace and relaxation ⟨a ~ cup of tea⟩ (3) **:** free of strife, bustle, and commotion : PLACID ⟨a ~ countryside⟩ **2 a** (1) **:** making no noise or uproar : acting, moving, or resting in silence ⟨the class was ~ and listened intently⟩ (2) **:** free from noise or uproar : SILENT, STILL, HUSHED ⟨the room was dark and ~⟩ **b :** not marked by extremes : not such as to attract undue attention : not showy or obtrusive ⟨clothes that were in ~ good taste⟩ **3 :** RETIRED, SECLUDED ⟨a ~ nook⟩ **4** *of a volcanic eruption* **:** marked by the extrusion of lava without violent explosions

³**quiet** \"\ *adv, usu* -ER/-EST **:** QUIETLY

⁴**quiet** \"\ *vb* -ED/-ING/-S [LL *quietare* to set free, calm, fr. L *quietus* quiet — more at ²QUIET] *vt* **1 :** to cause to be quiet : PACIFY, CALM ⟨had no trouble in ~*ing* the crowd⟩ **2 :** to put at rest by freeing the fact of ownership from dispute or question usu. used in the phrase *to quiet title* ~ *vi* **:** to become quiet — usu. used with *down* ⟨had been excited but soon ~*ed* down⟩ **syn** see CALM

**quiet day** *n* **:** a day set apart in the Anglican church for special devotions, meditations, and instructions

**qui·et·en** \'kwīətᵊn, -ətᵊn\ *vb* **quietened; quietened; quietening** \-t(ᵊ)niŋ\ **quietens** [²*quiet* + *-en*] *chiefly Brit* **:** QUIET **syn** see CALM

**qui·et·ism** \'kwīəˌtizəm\ *n* -S [It *quietismo*, fr. *quieto* quiet (fr. L *quietus*) + *-ismo* -ism — more at QUIET] **1 a :** a 17th century Christian mysticism that stressed passive self-annihilation through religious meditation and complete absorption in the contemplation of God and ethical antinomianism based on the view that in the state of perfect surrender the soul is indifferent to the demands of sense, desire, virtue, or morality **b :** a nonactivistic mysticism stressing passive contemplation, concentration on the interior life, and nonparticipation in affairs of the world **2 :** a state of calmness or passivity

¹**qui·et·ist** \-əd·əst\ *n* -S [It *quietista*, fr. *quieto* + *-ista* -ist] **:** one that advocates or practices quietism

²**quietist** \"\ *or* **qui·et·is·tic** \¦==ˈtistik\ *adj* **:** of, relating to, or typical of quietists or quietism

**qui·e·tive** \'kwīəd·iv\ *n* -S [⁴*quiet* + *-ive*] **:** something that has a tranquilizing effect : SEDATIVE ⟨~*s* rather than incentives will be in demand —Helmut Kuhn⟩

**qui·et·ly** *adv* **:** in a quiet manner

**qui·et·ness** *n* -ES [ME *quietnes*, fr. *quiet* + *-nes* -ness] **:** the quality or state of being quiet : TRANQUILLITY, REPOSE, STILLNESS

**qui·et·some** \'kwīətsəm\ *adj* [²*quiet* + *-some*] *archaic* **:** TRANQUIL

**quiet-spoken** \¦==¦==\ *adj* **:** marked by or using quiet speech ⟨a *quiet-spoken* young woman —Ethel Wilson⟩

**qui·e·tude** \'kwīəˌtüd, -ə,tyüd\ *n* -S [MF, fr. ML *quietudo*, fr. L *quietus* quiet — more at QUIET] **:** QUIETNESS

**qui·e·tus** \kwīˈēd·əs, -ētəs\ *n* -ES [ME *quietus (est)*, fr. ML, (he is) discharged, acquitted] **1 a :** final discharge or acquittance (as from debt or obligation) : final settlement : EXTINCTION ⟨obtained a ~ of the sum owed⟩ **b** *archaic* **:** discharge from office or duty **c :** RELEASE; *specif* **:** a proceeding in a probate court whereby an administrator obtains a full discharge **2 :** removal from or extinction of activity; *esp* **:** DEATH ⟨met their ~ without protest⟩ **3 :** something that produces a cessation of activity : something that quiets or represses ⟨this disaster . . . had the effect of a ~ —Susan E. Ferrier⟩ **4 :** a state of inactivity ⟨the long ~ of thirty years —C.R.Anderson⟩

¹**quiff** \'kwif\ *n* -S [alter. of *whiff*] **1 :** a puff of tobacco smoke **2 :** a puff of air

²**quiff** \"\ *n* -S [origin unknown] *Brit* **:** a prominent forelock of hair

³**quiff** \"\ *n, pl* **quiff** *also* **quiffs** [origin unknown] *slang* **:** GIRL, FEMALE

**qui·i·na** \kwēˈīnə\ *n, cap* [NL] **:** a genus (the type of the family Quiinaceae) of tropical American shrubs and trees

**qui·i·na·ce·ae** \ˌkwīəˈnāsēˌē\ *n pl, cap* [NL, fr. *Quiina*, type genus + *-aceae*] **:** a family of tropical American shrubs and trees (order Parietales) with opposite coriaceous leaves, small verticillate flowers in terminal spikes or racemes, and baccate one-seeded fruit

**qui·la** \'kēlə\ *n* -S [AmerSp, fr. Araucan *cula*] **:** a grass (*Chusquea quila*) of the southern part of So. America that resembles bamboo, is used as forage, and has a fiber used in making paper

**quile** \'kwī(ə)l\ *dial var of* ⁴COIL

**quil·e·ute** *or* **quil·la·yute** \¦kwilə¦yüt\ *n, pl* **quileute** *or* **quileutes** *or* **quillayute** *or* **quillayutes** *usu cap* **1 a :** a Chemakuan people of the western part of the state of Washington **b :** a member of such people **2 :** the language of the Quileute people

¹**quill** \'kwil\ *n* -S [ME *quil*; akin to MHG *kil* quill (feather), LG *quiele*] **1 a** (1) **:** a bobbin, spool, or spindle on which filling yarn is wound before insertion into a shuttle in the process of weaving (2) **:** a hollow shaft often surrounding another shaft and used in various mechanical devices **b** (1) **:** a hollow stem (as a reed) used for producing musical tones (2) **:** PANPIPE (3) **:** WHISTLE **c :** a roll of dried bark ⟨a ~ of cinnamon⟩ **2 a** (1) **:** the hollow horny barrel of a feather (2) **:** a bird's feather; *esp* **:** one of the large stiff feathers of a bird's wing or tail **b :** one of the hollow sharp spines of a porcupine or hedgehog **3 :** one of various articles made from or resembling the quill of a feather: as **a :** a pen for writing **b :** a plectrum for plucking the strings of a harpsichord, lute, or similar instrument **c :** TOOTHPICK **d :** QUILL FLY **4 :** a float for a fishline **5 :** something in its truest, purest, or best state : the real thing : MCCOY — usu. used with *pure* ⟨fine old liquor that was the pure ~⟩

²**quill** \"\ *vt* -ED/-ING/-S **1 a :** to remove quills from **b :** to pierce with or as if with quills **2 a :** to wind (thread or yarn) on a quill **b :** to make a series of small rounded ridges in (cloth)

**quil·la·cin·ga** \ˌkwiləˈsiŋgə\ *n, pl* **quillacinga** *or* **quillacingas** *usu cap* [Sp, of AmerInd origin] **1 a :** a people of southwestern Colombia and northern Ecuador **b :** a member of such people **2 :** the language of the Quillacinga people

**qui·llai** \kēˈ(y)ī\ *or* **qui·llaia** *or* **qui·llia** \-īə\ *n* -S [AmerSp *quillai, quillay*, fr. Mapuche] **:** SOAPBARK

**quil·la·ic acid** \kwəˈlāik-\ *n* [*quillai* + *-ic*] **:** a poisonous crystalline triterpenoid sapogenin $C_{30}H_{46}O_5$ obtained by hydrolysis of the saponin from soapbark

**quil·la·ja** \kwiˈlāyə, -jə\ *n, cap* [NL, fr. AmerSp *quillai, quillay*] **:** a genus of trees (family Rosaceae) native to Brazil, Peru, and Chile and distinguished by their saponaceous bark — see SOAPBARK

**quillback** \'=ˌ=\ *or* **quillback carpsucker** *n, pl* **quillback** *or* **quillbacks 1 :** a small carpsucker (*Carpiodes velifer*) that has the dorsal fin distinguished by a very long first ray and that is widely distributed esp. in larger streams of central and eastern No. America **2 :** any of several fishes related to the quillback; *esp* **:** the common carpsucker (*Carpiodes carpio*)

**quill bark** *n* **:** a roll of dried cinchona bark

**quill bit** *n* **:** a long pod bit

**quill drive** *n* **:** a drive used on electric locomotives in which the motors are mounted on a nonrotatable quill that surrounds the axle of the driving wheels and which transmits power to the wheels by means of pins on the armature structure that engage the spokes of the driving wheels

**quill-driver** \'=ˌ==\ *n* **:** one that works with a pen : WRITER, CLERK

**quilled** *adj* **1 :** that has the shape of a quill: as **a** (1) **:** rolled into the form of a quill ⟨~ cinchona bark⟩ (2) **:** fluted into rounded folds ⟨~ cloth⟩ **b :** having nearly tubular corollas or florets ⟨the ~ flowers of the cactus dahlia⟩ **2 :** that is furnished with a quill ⟨the ~ jack of a harpsichord⟩

**quill embroidery** *n* **:** QUILLWORK

**quill·er** \'kwilə(r)\ *n* -S [¹*quill* + *-er*] **1 :** a machine used in transferring yarn from spools and cones to quills **2 :** the operator of a quiller

¹**quil·let** \'kwilət, *usu* -əd·+V\ *n* -S [origin unknown] *chiefly dial* **:** a small tract of land

²**quillet** \"\ *n* -S [prob. short for obs. *quillity*, alter. of *quiddity*] *archaic* **:** a subtle distinction : QUIBBLE

³**quill·et** \"\ *n* -S [¹*quill* + *-et*] *archaic* **:** a small tube (as of paper)

**quill fern** *n* **:** MARSH FERN 1

**quillfish** \'=ˌ=\ *n* **:** any of various small very slender blennies of the north Pacific of the family Ptilichthyidae

**quill fly** *n* **:** an artificial angling fly with a quill body

**quill gear** *n* **:** an arrangement consisting of a gear wheel made integral with a hollow spindle or shaft; *esp* **:** a hollow shaft with a gear wheel on each end used in the back gear of a lathe or other machine tool

**quilling** *n* -S [in sense 1, fr. gerund of ²*quill*; in sense 2, fr. ¹*quill* + *-ing*] **1 :** the process of quilling yarn or cloth **2 :** a strip of quilled cloth

**quill mite** *n* **:** a mite (*Syringophilus bipectinatus*) that lives in the shafts of the primary wing feathers of poultry

**quil·lon** \kēyōⁿ\ *n* -S [F, fr. MF, dim. of *quille* bowling pin, fr. MHG *kegel*, fr. OHG *kegil* stake, club — more at KEG] **:** an arm of the cross guard of a sword

**quill pig** *n* **:** PORCUPINE

**quills** *pl of* QUILL, *pres 3d sing of* QUILL

**quilltail** \'=ˌ=\ *or* **quilltail coot** *n* **:** RUDDY DUCK

**quillwork** \'=ˌ=\ *n* **:** ornamentation of skins, bark, or fabrics by overlaying with porcupine quills

**quillwort** \'=ˌ=\ *n* **1 :** a plant of the genus *Isoetes* **2 :** MARSH MILKWEED

¹**quilt** \'kwilt\ *n* -S [ME *cowete, quilte*, fr. OF *coilte, cuilte, coute* quilt, mattress, fr. L *culcita* mattress, bed, cushion; perh. akin to Skt *kūrca* beard, bunch, bundle of grain] **1 a** *obs* **:** MATTRESS **b :** a bed coverlet made of two layers of cloth of which the top one is usu. pieced or appliquéd and having a filling of wool, cotton, or down held in place by stitched designs or tufts worked through all thicknesses **c :** a bedspread with a woven design resembling quilting **d :** a design or figure formed by quilting **2 a :** a piece of thick padding resembling a quilt and usu. used as a protective covering; *esp* **:** a pad formerly worn under or in place of armor **b** *obs* **:** POULTICE **c :** a heat-insulating material consisting of fibrous materials matted together and stitched or quilted between two layers of heavy paper **3 :** the core of a cricket ball or of a field-hockey ball

²**quilt** \"\ *vb* -ED/-ING/-S *vt* **1 a :** to fill, pad, or line with material like that used in quilts ⟨a helmet whose interior had been ~*ed*⟩ **b** (1) **:** to stitch, sew, or cover with lines or patterns like those used in quilts ⟨~*ed* the surface with a scroll pattern⟩ (2) **:** to stitch (designs) through layers of cloth **c :** to bind up or cover with interlacings (as of cord) ⟨a short pipe ~*ed* over with string —Charles Dickens⟩ **d :** to fasten or sew up between two pieces of material ⟨~*ed* money in his belt⟩ **2 a :** to make (a quilt) by stitching or usu. by sewing together two layers of cloth with some padding between them **b :** to make (a garment) in quilted work **3 :** to compile (as a book) by piecing together items or scraps from various sources : do in a patchwork way ⟨~*ed* together a collection of verse⟩ **4** *chiefly dial* **:** BEAT, THRASH, WHIP ~ *vi* **1 :** to make quilts **2 :** to do quilted work

³**quilt** \"\ *vb* -ED/-ING/-S [origin unknown] *dial Eng* **:** GULP, SWALLOW

**quilted** *adj* **1 :** furnished with a quilt **2 :** resembling a quilt in design ⟨embossed cottons with ~ effect —*Women's Wear Daily*⟩ **3 :** padded like a quilt

**quilted maple** *n* **:** OREGON MAPLE

**quilt·er** \'kwiltə(r)\ *n* -S **1 :** one that quilts **2 :** a sewing machine attachment for quilting

**quilting** *n* -S **1 :** the process of quilting **2 a :** material that is quilted or that is used for making quilts or for doing other quilted work **b :** stitching usu. worked in designs that holds two or more layers of cloth together **c :** a covering made of sennit **3 :** QUILTING PARTY

**quilting party** *or* **quilting bee** *n* **:** a social gathering of women at which they work together at making quilts or doing other quilted work

**quim·baya** \kimˈbīə\ *n, pl* **quimbaya** *or* **quimbayas** *usu cap* **1 a :** an extinct people of western Colombia **b :** a member of such people **2 :** a language of the Quimbaya people that is probably Cariban

**quim·per** \(')kaⁿ¦pe(ə)r, -am¦p-\ *n* -S *often cap* [*Quimper ware*] **:** a grayish blue that is redder, lighter, and slightly stronger than electric, greener and stronger than copenhagen or old china, and redder, stronger, and slightly lighter than Gobelin

**quimper ware** *n, usu cap Q* [fr. *Quimper*, France, where it is produced] **:** glazed pottery decorated esp. with peasant figures and conventionalized floral patterns

**quin** \'kwin\ *n* -S [by shortening] **:** QUINTUPLET

**quin-** *or* **quino-** *comb form* [Sp *quina* cinchona bark — more at QUININE] **1 :** quina : cinchona bark ⟨*quino*tannic⟩ ⟨*quin*oline⟩ ⟨*quin*oid⟩ ⟨*quin*ine⟩ **2 :** quinic acid ⟨*quin*ate⟩ **3 :** quinoline ⟨*quino*cyanine⟩ **4 :** quinone ⟨*quin*itol⟩ ⟨*quin*oid⟩

**qui·na** \'kēnə\ *n* -S [Sp] **:** CINCHONA

**quin·a·crine** \'kwinəˌkrēn, -ˌkrən\ *also* **chin·a·crin** *or* **chin·a·crine** \'kin-\ *n* -S [*quinacrine*, fr. *quin-* + *acridine*; *chinacrin, chinacrine*, fr. *Chinacrin*, a trademark] **:** an antimalarial drug derived from acridine and used chiefly in the form of its bitter yellow crystalline dihydrochloride $C_{23}H_{30}ClN_3O.2HCl.2H_2O$

**quin·al·dic acid** \(')kwiˌnaldik-\ *or* **quin·al·din·ic acid** \¦kwiˌnal¦dinik-\ *n* [ISV *quinaldine* + *-ic*] **:** a crystalline acid $C_9H_6NCOOH$ obtained esp. by oxidation of quinaldine and used in chemical analysis; 2-quinoline-carboxylic acid

**quin·al·dine** \kwiˈnalˌdēn, -ˌdən\ *n* [ISV *quin-* + *ald-* + *-ine*] **:** an oily liquid base $CH_3C_9H_6N$ of a slightly pungent odor obtained by condensation of acetaldehyde and aniline and occurring also in coal tar that is used chiefly in the manufacture of dyes and pharmaceuticals; 2-methyl-quinoline

**quin·al·din·i·um** \ˌkwiˌnalˈdinēəm\ *n* -S [NL, fr. ISV *quinaldine* + NL *-ium*] **:** a univalent ion $[C_{10}H_9NH]^+$ that is analogous to ammonium and is derived from quinaldine

**quin·alizarin** \¦kwin+\ *n* [ISV *quin-* + *alizarin*] **:** a red crystalline compound $C_{14}H_4O_2(OH)_4$ with green metallic luster used chiefly in chemical analysis; 1,2,5,8-tetrahydroxyanthraquinone

**quin·a·mine** \'kwinəˌmēn, -mən\ *n* [ISV *quin-* + *amine*] **:** a crystalline alkaloid $C_{19}H_{24}N_2O_2$ in various cinchona barks

**qui·naph·thol** \(')kwi+\ *n* [blend of *quin-* and *naphthol*] **:** CHINAPHTHOL

**qui·nar·i·us** \kwiˈna(a)rēəs\ *n, pl* **quinar·ii** \-ē,ī\ [L, fr. *quinarius*, adj., quinary] **1 :** a roman silver coin issued occasionally from the 3d century B.C. and equivalent to ½ denarius **2 :** a gold ½-aureus piece of imperial Rome

**¹qui·na·ry** \'kwīnərē, -win-\ *adj* [L *quinarius,* fr. *quini* five apiece + *-arius* -ary; akin to *quinque* five — more at FIVE] **1 :** consisting of five : arranged by fives : QUINTUPLE ⟨the ~ system is based on counting the fingers of one hand —H.J. Spinden⟩ **2 :** of the fifth order or rank

**²quinary** \"\ *n* -ES : a quinary group or system

**¹qui·nate** \'kwī,nāt\ *adj* [L *quini* five apiece + E *-ate*] : arranged in or composed of sets of five — used esp. of compound leaves with five leaflets

**²quinate** \", 'kwi,n-\ *n* -S [ISV *quin-* + *-ate*] : a salt or ester of quinic acid

**qui·nault** *or* **qui·naielt** \kwə'nȯlt\ *n, pl* **quinault** *or* **quinaults** *or* **quinaielt** *or* **quinaielts** *usu cap* **1 a :** a Salishan people of the valley of the Quinault river and contiguous Pacific coast, Washington **b :** a member of such people **2 :** the language of the Quinault people

**quin·az·o·line** \kwə'nazə,lēn, -lən\ *n* -S [ISV *quin-* + *azole* + *-ine;* orig. formed as G *chinazolin*] : a yellow crystalline compound $C_8H_6N_2$ with an odor like that of naphthalene regarded as derived from quinoline by substitution of a nitrogen atom for a methylidyne group in the 3-position; *also* **:** a derivative of this compound

**quince** \'kwin(t)s\ *n* -S [ME *quynce,* pl., quinces, fr. *quyn, coyn* quince, fr. MF *coin, cooin,* fr. L *cotoneum, cydoneum, cydonia, cydoneum (malum),* fr. Gk *kydōnion,* prob. fr. neut. of *kydōnios* Cydonian, fr. *Kydōnia* Cydonia, ancient city on the north coast of Crete] **1 :** the fruit of a widely cultivated central Asiatic tree (*Cydonia oblonga*) somewhat resembling a large yellow apple, differing in having many seeds in each carpel and a hard acid flesh that is used for marmalade, jelly, and preserves, and producing seeds that are covered with a mucilaginous material which is used in making a mucilage and in the preparation of toilet lotions **2 :** the tree that bears quinces and is often used as a dwarfing stock for the pear — see CHAENOMELES, FLOWERING QUINCE

**quince curculio** *n* : a small gray and yellow curculio (*Conotrachelus crataegi*) whose larva burrows in quinces

**¹quin·centenary** \(ˌ)kwin+\ *n* [L *quinque* five + E *centenary*] : a 500th anniversary or its celebration

**²quincentenary** \"\ *adj* : of or relating to a 500th anniversary

**quin·centennial** \ˌkwin+\ *adj or n* [L *quinque* five + *centennial*] : QUINCENTENARY

**quince yellow** *n* : a moderate yellow that is greener and darker than colonial yellow, greener and stronger than mustard yellow, and greener, lighter, and stronger than brass — called also *capucine, copper yellow*

**quinc·ke tube** \'kw|iŋkə-, 'kv|\ *n, usu cap Q* [after Georg H. *Quincke* †1924 Ger. physicist] : a glass tube sounded like a bottle by blowing across its mouth and used for obtaining high notes in experiments on difference tones

**quin·cun·cial** \(ˈ)kwin¦kənchəl\ *or* **quin·cunx·ial** \-əŋ(k)sēəl\ *adj* [*quincuncial* fr. L *quincuncialis,* fr. *quincunc-, quincunx* + *-alis* -al; *quincunxial* fr. L *quincunx* + E *-al*] **1 :** relating to, consisting of, or arranged in a quincunx or quincunxes **2 a :** having the members so imbricated that two are exterior, two are interior, and the other has one edge exterior and one interior — used of a pentamerous calyx or corolla ⟨~ estivation⟩ **b :** PENTASTICHOUS — **quin·cun·cial·ly** \-chəlē\ *adv*

**quin·cunx** \'kwin,kəŋ(k)s\ *n* -ES [L, lit., five twelfths, fr. *quinque-* + *uncia* twelfth part, ounce — more at OUNCE] **1 :** an arrangement of five things with one at each corner and one in the middle of a square **2 a :** an arrangement of plants (as trees) with one at each corner and one at the center of a square or rectangle **b :** a planting in the form of a series of squares or rectangles with a plant at the center of each **3 :** a quincuncial arrangement of the parts of a flower in estivation

quincunx 2b

**quin·decagon** \(ˈ)kwin+\ *n* [L *quindecim* fifteen + E *-agon* (as in *heptagon*)] : a usu. plane polygon with 15 angles and 15 sides

**quin·deca·syllabic** \(ˌ)kwin¦dekə+\ *adj* [*quindeca-,* modif. (influenced by *deca-*) of L *quindecim* fifteen + E *syllabic*] : having 15 syllables

**quin·decemvir** \ˌkwin+\ *n* [L *quindecemvir,* fr. *quindecim* fifteen + *vir* man — more at VIRILE] : one of a commission, council, or ruling body of 15; *specif* : a member of a college of priests in ancient Rome having charge of the sibylline books

**quin·decemvirate** \"+\ *n* [*quindecemvir* + *-ate*] **1 :** the office or government of quindecemvirs **2 :** a body of quindecemvirs

**quin·decillion** \"+\ *n, often attrib* [L *quinque* five + E *decillion*] — see NUMBER table

**quin·de·cim** \'kwində,sim\ *n* -S [ME *quindesin, quindecime,* fr. LL *quindecima,* fem. of *quindecimus* fifteenth, fr. L *quindecim* fifteen, fr. *quinque-* + *decem* ten — more at TEN] **1** *obs* : a tax of one fifteenth **2 :** QUINDENE

**quin·dec·i·ma** \kwin'desəmə\ *n* -S [ML, fr. LL, fem. of *quindecimus*] **1 :** FIFTEENTH 4b **2 :** a pipe-organ stop whose tones are two octaves above the notes

**quin·dene** \'kwin,dēn\ *n* -S [ML *quindena,* fr. fem. of L *quindeni* fifteen each, fr. *quini* five each + *deni* ten by ten, ten each — more at QUINARY, DENIER] : the 15th or in modern reckoning 14th day after a church festival

**quine** \'kwēn\ *Scot var of* QUEAN

**-quine** \ˌkwēn, ˌkwən\ *n comb form* -S [fr. *quinoline*] : quinoline ⟨prima*quine*⟩ ⟨penta*quine*⟩

**qui·ne·tum** \kwī'nēd·əm, kwə'n-\ *n* -S [*quin-* + L *-etum* (n. suffix denoting a garden or group of plants)] : a mixture of the alkaloids in varying proportions as they occur naturally in the bark of red cinchona used as an antiperiodic

**quin·gen·ten·a·ry** \¦kwin,jen·¦tenərē, kwin'sent³n,erē\ *n* -ES [L *quingenti* five hundred (alter. of *quincenti,* fr. *quinque-* + *centum* hundred) + *-enary* (as in *centenary*) — more at HUNDRED] : QUINCENTENARY

**quin·hy·drone** \kwin'hī,drōn, '⸗,⸗⸗\ *n* -S [ISV *quin-* + *hydro*quin*one*] **1 :** a green crystalline compound $C_6H_4O_2.C_6H_4(OH)_2$ with metallic luster formed by combination of equimolecular amounts of *para*-quinone and hydroquinone or in the oxidation of hydroquinone or the reduction of quinone **2 :** any of a class of highly colored compounds similar to quinhydrone

**quinhydrone electrode** *n* : an electrode consisting of a platinum wire in a solution containing quinhydrone used to determine hydrogen-ion concentration

**quinible** *n* -S [ME, fr. L *quini* five each, five + ME *-ible* (as in *trible* treble) — more at TREBLE] **1** *obs* : a musical descant in fifths **2** *obs* : a voice part one octave higher than the treble

**quinic acid** \'kwi|nik-, 'kwī|\ *n* [*quinic* fr. *quin-* + *-ic*] **1 :** a crystalline acid $C_6H_7(OH)_4COOH$ obtained from cinchona bark, coffee beans, and other plant products and synthetically by hydrolysis of chlorogenic acid; 1,3,4,5- tetrahydroxycyclohexane-carboxylic acid **2 :** QUININIC ACID

**quin·i·cine** \'kwinə,sēn, -sən\ *n* -S [ISV *quinic* (in *quinic acid*) + *-ine;* orig. formed in F] : a bitter poisonous reddish yellow amorphous alkaloid $C_{20}H_{24}N_2O_2$ isomeric with quinine and obtained from cinchona bark or by heating a salt of quinine — called also *quinotoxine*

**quin·i·dine** \'kwinə,dēn, -dən\ *also* **chin·i·dine** \'ki-\ *n* -S [ISV *quin-* or *chin-* + *-idine;* prob. orig. formed as F *quinidine*] : a crystalline dextrorotatory alkaloid $C_{20}H_{24}N_2O_2$ stereoisomeric with quinine found in some species of cinchona and used sometimes in place of quinine but chiefly in the form of its sulfate in the treatment of auricular fibrillation

**qui·nie·la** \kēn'yelə\ *or* **qui·nel·la** \-ē'nelə\ *n* -S [AmerSp *quiniela,* a game of chance, quiniela] **1 :** a betting pool in which the bettor selects the contestants to finish in first and second place but need not designate their order of finish **2 :** a wager in a quiniela

**qui·nine** \'kwī,nīn *also* 'kwi,nīn *or* kwə'nīn *sometimes* kwə'nēn *or* 'kwi,nēn *or* kə'nēn *or* 'kwinən; *Brit usu* kwə'nēn\ *n* -S [Sp *quina* cinchona bark (short for *quinaquina, quinquina,* fr. Quechua, perh. modif. of NL *Cinchona*) + E *-ine* — more at CINCHONA] **1 :** a bitter efflorescent crystalline levorotatory alkaloid $C_{20}H_{24}N_2O_2$ obtained from cinchona bark that is a diacid base forming two series of salts and is derived from methoxy-quinoline and quinuclidine and that is used in medicine esp. in the form of salts **2 :** any of the salts of quinine (as the hydrochlorides or sulfates) used as a febrifuge, antimalarial, antiperiodic, and bitter tonic

**quinine bush** *n* **1 :** a western American shrub of the genus *Garrya; esp* : BEAR BRUSH **2 :** CLIFF ROSE 2 **3** *Austral* : BITTERBARK 1a(1)

**quinine cherry** *n* : BITTER CHERRY

**quinine flower** *n* : a bitter herb (*Sabbatia elliottii*) of the southern U. S. that has star-shaped white flowers and is said to possess antiperiodic properties and to have been used as a substitute for quinine

**quinine tree** *n* **1 :** HORSERADISH TREE **2 :** HOP TREE **3 :** NATIVE QUINCE

**quinine water** *n* : a carbonated beverage flavored with a small amount of quinine, lemon, and lime

**qui·nin·ic acid** \(ˈ)kwī¦ninik, kwə'|\ *n* [*quininic* ISV *quinine* + *-ic*] : a yellowish crystalline acid $CH_3OC_9H_5NCOOH$ obtained by oxidation of quinine or quinidine; 6-methoxycinchoninic acid

**quin·i·tol** \'kwinə,tōl, -tōl\ *n* -S [*quin-* + *-itol*] : a crystalline cyclic glycol $C_6H_{10}(OH)_2$ obtained by reduction of hydroquinone in cis and trans forms having a sweet taste with a bitter aftertaste; 1,4-cyclohexane-diol

**qui·niz·a·rin** \kwə'nizərən\ *n* -S [ISV *quin-* + *alizarin*] : a red crystalline compound $C_{14}H_6O_2(OH)_2$ isomeric with alizarin made from phthalic anhydride and either hydroquinone or *para*-chlorophenol and used as a dye intermediate and organic pigment; 1,4-dihydroxy-anthraquinone — see DYE table I (under *Pigment Violet 12*)

**quink** \'kwiŋk\ *or* **quink goose** *n* -S [imit.] : BRANT

**quin·nat salmon** \'kwinət-\ *also* **quinnat** *n* -S [*quinnat* fr. Interior Salish *t'kwinnat*] : KING SALMON

**quin·ni·pi·ac** \'kwinəpē,ak, ⸗⸗⸗'⸗\ *n, pl* **quinnipiac** *or* **quinnipiacs** *usu cap* **1 a :** an extinct Algonquian people of central Connecticut **b :** a member of such people **2 :** the Algonquian language of the Quinnipiac people

**quino-** — see QUIN-

**qui·noa** \kē'nōə\ *or* **qui·nua** \'kēn,wä\ *n* -S [Sp, fr. Quechua *quinua*] **1 :** a pigweed (*Chenopodium quinoa*) of the high Andes of So. America **2 :** the seeds of the quinoa plant that are ground for food and widely used as a cereal in Peru

**quino·cyanine** \¦kwi(,)nō+\ *n* [*quin-* + *cyanine*] : a simple cyanine dye containing two quinoline rings

**¹quino·id** \'kwi,nȯid\ *var of* QUINONOID

**²quinoid** \"\ *n* -S : a quinonoid compound — **qui·noi·dal** \(ˈ)kwi¦nȯid³l\ *adj*

**qui·noi·dine** \kwə'nȯi,dēn, -d³n\ *or* **qui·noi·din** \-d³n\ *n* -S [ISV *quin-* + *-oid* + *-ine* or *-in*] : a bitter brownish resinous mixture often molded into sticks of amorphous alkaloids obtained as a by-product in the extraction of cinchona bark for crystalline alkaloids and formerly used as a substitute for quinine

**quin·ol** \'kwi,nōl, -nōl\ *n* -S [*quin-* + *-ol*] : HYDROQUINONE

**quinolin-** *or* **quinolino-** *comb form* [ISV *quinoline*] : quinoline : quinolinic acid ⟨*quinolinic*⟩ ⟨*quinolinonitrile*⟩

**quin·o·line** \'kwin³l,ēn, -³lən\ *also* **chin·o·line** \'kin-\ *n* -S [ISV *quin-* or *chin-* + *-ol* + *-ine*] **1 :** a pungent oily nitrogenous base $C_9H_7N$ that is obtained usu. by the distillation of coal tar or by synthesis from aniline, that is oxidized to quinolinic acid and nicotinic acid, and that is the parent compound of many alkaloids (as quinine), antimalarial drugs, amebicides, and dyes — compare ISOQUINOLINE, SKRAUP SYNTHESIS, STRUCTURAL FORMULA **2 :** a derivative of quinoline

quinoline

**quinoline blue** *n* : CYANINE 3

**quinoline dye** *n* : any of a small class of dyes derived from quinoline — see DYE table I

**quinoline yellow** *n, often cap Q&Y* : any of several quinoline dyes — see DYE table I (under *Acid Yellow 2* and *3, Direct Yellow 5,* and *Solvent Yellow 33*)

**quin·o·lin·ic acid** \¦kwin³l¦inik-\ *n* [*quinolinic* fr. *quinolin-* + *-ic*] : a crystalline acid $C_5H_3N(COOH)_2$ made by oxidizing quinoline and yielding nicotinic acid when heated; 2,3-pyridine-dicarboxylic acid

**quin·o·lin·i·um** \¦kwin³l'inēəm\ *n* -S [NL, fr. *quinolin-* + *-ium*] : a univalent ion $[C_9H_7NH]^+$ that is analogous to ammonium and is derived from quinoline

**quin·o·lin·ol** \'kwin³lə,nōl, -,nōl\ *n* -S [*quinolin-* + *-ol*] : HYDROXYQUINOLINE

**quin·o·lin·yl** \-,nil\ *n* -S [*quinolin-* + *-yl*] **1 :** the bivalent radical $C_9H_5N(CO-)_2$ derived from quinoline **2 :** QUINOLYL

**qui·nol·o·gist** \kwī'näləjəst, kwə'n-\ *n* -S [ISV *quinology* + *-ist*] : a specialist in quinology

**qui·nol·o·gy** \-jē\ *n* -ES [ISV *quin-* + *-logy*] : the science dealing with the cultivation, chemistry, and medicinal use of the cinchonas

**quin·o·lyl** \'kwin³l,il\ *n* -S [ISV *quinoline* + *-yl*] : any of seven univalent radicals $C_9H_6N$ derived from quinoline by removal of one hydrogen atom

**qui·none** \kwə'nōn, 'kwi,nōn\ *also* **chi·none** \kə'-, 'kwi,-\ *n* -S [ISV *quin-* or *chin-* + *-one;* orig. formed as G *chinon*] **1 :** either of two isomeric cyclic crystalline compounds $C_6H_4O_2$ that are diketo derivatives of dihydro-benzene: **a :** the pungent yellow para isomer obtained by oxidation of quinic acid or hydroquinone but usu. made by oxidation of aniline (as in the manufacture of hydroquinone) and used chiefly as an oxidizing agent — called also *benzoquinone, para-benzoquinone, p-benzoquinone, para-quinone, p-quinone;* compare QUINHYDRONE, STRUCTURAL FORMULA **b :** the red or colorless ortho isomer made by oxidation of pyrocatechol — called also *ortho-benzoquinone, o-benzoquinone, ortho-quinone, o-quinone* **2 :** any of various compounds containing quinone structures that are usu. yellow to orange (as in the para isomers) and orange to red (as in the ortho isomers) — compare ANTHRAQUINONE, NAPHTHOQUINONE

para isomer ortho isomer

quinone 1

**quinone di·imine** \-'dīə,mēn\ *n* [*diimine* fr. *di-* + *imine*] **1 :** a colorless crystalline compound $HN=C_6H_4=NH$ regarded as derived from quinone (sense 1a) by replacement of both oxygen atoms by imino groups but made by oxidation of *para*-phenylenediamine — called also *p-benzoquinone diimine, p-phenylene diimine* **2 :** a compound derived from a quinone by replacement of both oxygen atoms by imino groups

**quinone imine** *or* **qui·non·imine** \kwə'nōnə,mēn, -,mən\ *n* [ISV *quinone* + *imine*] **1 :** a colorless crystalline compound $O=C_6H_4=NH$ regarded as derived from quinone (sense 1a) by replacement of one oxygen atom by the imino group but made by oxidation of *para*-aminophenol — called also *p-benzoquinone imine, p-quinonimine* **2 :** a compound derived from a quinone by replacement of one or both oxygen atoms by the imino group

**quinone oxime** *n* : an oxime of a quinone; *esp* : the monoxime $O=C_6H_4=NOH$ of quinone (sense 1a) that is tautomeric with the para isomer of nitrosophenol

**qui·non·iza·tion** \kwə,nōnə'zāshən, ,kwi,nō-\ *n* -S [*quinonize* + *-ation*] : the formation of a quinone

**qui·non·ize** \kwə'nō,nīz, 'kwi,nō-\ *vt* -ED/-ING/-S *see -ize in Explan Notes* [*quinone* + *-ize*] : to cause to form a quinone

**qui·no·noid** \kwə'nō,nȯid, 'kwinə,nȯid\ *or* **quin·oid** \'kwi,nȯid\ *adj* [*quinonoid* fr. *quinone* + *-oid; quinoid* ISV *quin-* + *-oid*] : resembling quinone; *esp* : having a structure characterized by a benzene nucleus containing two instead of three double bonds within the nucleus and two external double bonds attached to the nucleus either at ortho or para positions (as in the two carbonyl groups of quinones) ⟨anthraquinone and related ~ dyes⟩

**qui·no·nyl** \kwə'nōn³l, 'kwinə,nil\ *n* -S [*quinone* + *-yl*] : the univalent radical $C_6H_3O_2$ derived from quinone by removal of one hydrogen atom

**quin·o·phan** \'kwinə,fan\ *n* -S [*quin-* + *-phan* (irreg. fr. *phenyl*)] : CINCHOPHEN

**quino·tannic acid** \¦kwinə+...-\ *n* [*quinotannic* ISV *quin-* + *tannic*] : a light yellow tannin found in cinchona bark

**quino·toxine** \¦kwinō+\ *n* [ISV *quin-* + *toxine*] : QUINICINE

**qui·no·va·tannic acid** \kwə'nōvə+...-\ *n* [ISV *quinova-* (fr. *quinovic*) + *tannic*] : a tannin obtained from the bark of a cinchona

**qui·no·vic acid** \kwə'nōvik-\ *also* **quin·o·va·ic acid** \¦kwinə-,¦vāik-\ *or* **chi·no·vic acid** \kə'nōvik-\ *n* [ISV *quinov-, quinova-, chinov-* (contr. of NL *quina nova, china nova,* tree whose bark yields quinovin, fr. *quina, china* + *nova,* fem. of L *novus* new) + *-ic;* orig. formed as F *kinovique* — more at NEW] : a crystalline triterpene acid $C_{30}H_{46}O_5$ obtained by hydrolysis of quinovin

**qui·no·vin** \kwə'nōvən\ *also* **chi·no·vin** \kə'n-\ *n* -S [ISV *quinovic* (in *quinovic acid*) + *-in*] : a bitter crystalline glycoside found in cinchona and other barks

**qui·no·vose** *also* **chi·no·vose** \-vōs *also* -vōz\ *n* -S [*quinovin* + *-ose*] : a deoxy-hexose sugar $CH_3(CHOH)_4CHO$ formed by hydrolysis of quinovin; 6-deoxy-D-glucose

**qui·nox·a·line** \kwə'näksə,lēn, -lən\ *also* **qui·nox·a·lin** \-lən\ *n* -S [ISV *quin-* + *glyoxal* + *-ine* or *-in*] **1 :** a crystalline feebly basic compound $C_8H_6N_2$ made by condensing *ortho* phenylenediamine with glyoxal and regarded as derived from quinoline by substitution of a nitrogen atom for a methylidyne group in the 4-position **2 :** a derivative of quinoxaline

**¹quin·qua·ge·nar·i·an** \¦kwinkwəjə¦na(a)rēən, (ˌ)kwin¦kwäj-\ *adj* [L *quinquagenarius* of fifty, fifty years old (fr. *quinquageni* fifty each — fr. *quinquaginta* fifty — + *-arius* -ary) + E *-an*] : fifty years old : characteristic of a person of such an age

**²quinquagenarian** \"\ *n* -S : a quinquagenarian person

**¹quin·quag·e·nary** \kwin'kwäjə,nerē\ *n* -ES [L *quinquagenarius*] : a fiftieth anniversary

**²quinquagenary** \"\ *adj* [L *quinquagenarius*] : QUINQUAGENARIAN

**quin·qua·ges·i·ma** \¦kwinkwə'jesəmə, -jāzəmə\ *n* -S *usu cap* [ML, fr. L, fiftieth, fr. *quinquaginta* fifty, fr. *quinqua-* (akin to L *quinque* five) + *-ginta* (akin to L *-ginti* in *viginti* twenty) — more at FIVE, VICENARY] **1** *obs* : the period extending from the Sunday before Lent to Easter Sunday or the first week of this period **2 :** the Sunday before Lent or the seventh before Easter in the church year observed by various branches of the Christian Church — called also *Quinquagesima Sunday, Shrove Sunday*

**quin·qua·ges·i·mal** \¦⸗⸗¦⸗⸗məl\ *adj* [ML *quinquagesima* + E *-al*] : occurring in a season of fifty days : consisting of fifty days ⟨the ~ period between Easter and Pentecost⟩

**quin·quan·gle** \'kwin,kwaŋgəl\ *n* -S [LL *quinquangulus* five-cornered, fr. L *quinque-* + *angulus* corner, angle — more at ANGLE] *archaic* : PENTAGON

**quin·quan·gu·lar** \(ˈ)kwin¦kwaŋgyələ(r)\ *adj* [LL *quinquangulus* + E *-ar*] *archaic* : PENTAGONAL

**quin·quar·tic·u·lar** \¦kwin,kwär¦tikyələ(r)\ *adj* [NL *quinquarticularis,* fr. L *quinque-* + *articulus* joint, division of a discourse, article + *-aris* -ar — more at ARTICLE] : relating to five articles or points ⟨~ dispute between Arminians and Calvinists⟩

**quinque-** *or* **quinqu-** *comb form* [L, fr. *quinque* five — more at FIVE] **1 :** five ⟨*quinque*capsular⟩ ⟨*quinque*lateral⟩ **2 :** into five parts ⟨*quinque*section⟩

**quin·que·foliolate** \¦kwinkwə+\ *adj* [*quinque-* + *foliole* + *-ate*] : having five leaflets

**¹quin·que·literal** *or* **quin·qui·literal** \¦kwinkwə+\ *adj* [*quinque-* + *literal*] : consisting of five letters or consonants — used esp. of Hebrew roots

**²quinqueliteral** *or* **quinquiliteral** \"\ *n* : a quinqueliteral character

**quin·quen·a·ry** \(ˈ)kwin¦kwenərē, 'kwinkwə,nerē\ *adj* [*quinque-* + *-nary* (as in *quinary*)] : QUINARY

**quin·quen·na·lia** \¦kwinkwə'nālēə\ *n pl* [L, neut. pl. of *quinquennalis,* fr. *quinquennium* period of five years + *-alis* -al] : public games celebrated in ancient Rome every five years

**quin·quen·ni·ad** \kwin'kwenē,ad\ *n* -S [L *quinquennium* + E *-ad*] : QUINQUENNIUM

**¹quin·quen·nial** \(ˈ)kwin¦kwenēəl, -enyəl\ *adj* [ME *quinqueniale,* fr. MF *quinquennial,* fr. L *quinquennium* period of five years (fr. *quinque-* + *-ennium,* fr. *annus* year) + MF *-al* — more at ANNUAL] **1 :** occurring once in five years ⟨~ enumeration⟩ : occurring at the end of every five years **2 :** lasting five years ⟨a ~ grant⟩ ⟨has a place in the ~ and annual economic plans of the country —J.P.M.Somerville⟩

**²quinquennial** \"\ *n* -S : a quinquennial term or office

**quin·quen·nial·ly** \-əlē, -əli\ *adv* : every five years

**quin·quen·ni·um** \kwin'kwenēəm\ *n, pl* **quinquenniums** \-ēəmz\ *or* **quinquen·nia** \-ēə\ [L] : a period of five years

**quin·que·reme** *also* **quin·qui·reme** \'kwinkwə,rēm\ *n* -S [MF, fr. L *quinqueremis,* lit., having five banks of oars, fr. *quinque-* + *remus* oar — more at ROW] : an ancient galley propelled by five banks of oars

**quin·que·valent** *also* **quin·qui·valent** \¦kwinkwə+\ *adj* [*quinque-* + *valent;* trans. of G *fünfwertig*] : PENTAVALENT

**quin·que·vir** \'kwinkwə,vi(ə)r\ *n, pl* **quinquevirs** \-rz\ *or* **quin·quev·i·ri** \kwin'kwevə,rī\ [L, fr. *quinque-* + *vir* man — more at VIRILE] : one of a commission, council, or ruling body of five (as in ancient Rome)

**quin·quev·i·rate** \kwin'kwevərət, -,rāt\ *n* -S [L *quinqueviratus,* fr. *quinquevir* + *-atus* -ate] **1 :** the office or government of quinquevirs **2 :** a body of quinquevirs

**quin·que vo·ces** \¦kwiŋ(,)kwā'wō,kās\ *n pl* [L, five words] : the five predicables of traditional logic

**quin·qui·na** \kin'kēnə\ *n* -S [Sp — more at QUININE] *archaic* : CINCHONA

**quins** *pl of* QUIN

**quin·sied** \'kwinz|ēd, |id *sometimes* -n(t)s|\ *adj* : affected with quinsy

**quin·sy** \|ē, |i\ *n* -ES [ME *quinsie, quinesie* inflammation of the throat, modif. of MF *quinancie,* fr. LL *cynanche,* fr. Gk *kynanchē* sore throat, dog's quinsy, fr. *kyōn* dog + *anchein* to strangle — more at HOUND, ANGER] : PERITONSILLAR ABSCESS

**quinsyberry** \'⸗⸗— *see* BERRY\ *n* **1 :** an Old World black currant (*Ribes nigrum*) that yields a jelly used esp. formerly as a remedy for quinsy **2 :** NORTHERN BLACK CURRANT

**¹quint** \'k(w)int, 'kant, 'kaⁿt\ *n* -S [in sense 1, fr. MF, lit., fifth, fr. L *quintus;* in other senses, fr. F *quinte,* fem. of *quint* fifth, fr. MF; akin to L *quinque* five — more at FIVE] **1** *or* **quinte** \"\ *archaic* : a tax of one fifth **2 :** a sequence of 5 playing cards of the same suit ⟨a ~ in piquet⟩ **3** *or* **quinte a :** the musical interval of a fifth **b :** a pipe-organ stop giving tones a fifth higher than the normal pitch of the digitals **c :** the smallest of the three kinds of viola da braccio **d :** the E string of a violin **e :** QUINTON

**²quint** \'kwint\ *n* -S [by shortening] : QUINTUPLET

**³quint** \"\ *n* -S [by shortening] : QUINTET 2c

**quint** *abbr* **1** quintuple **2** [L *quintus*] fifth

**quint-** *or* **quinti-** *comb form* [ME, fr. MF, fr. L, fr. *quintus;* akin to L *quinque* five — more at FIVE] **1 :** fifth ⟨*quint*illion⟩ **2 :** QUINQUE- ⟨*quint*iped⟩ **3 :** a (specified) musical instrument having its pitch a fifth above the normal

**quin·ta** \'kintə, 'kēn-\ *n* -S [Sp & Pg, quinta, ranch, farm rented at one fifth of its income, fr. L, fem. of *quintus* fifth] : a country or suburban house with a garden, vineyard, or orchard : ESTATE, VILLA

**quin·ta·de·na** \¦kwintə'dēnə\ *also* **quin·ta·dene** \'⸗⸗,dēn\ *n* -S [NL *quintadena,* prob. fr. L *quintus* fifth + NL *-dena* twelfth (fr. L *duodeni* twelve each); fr. its sounding of the twelfth, or fifth of the second octave — more at DUODENARY] : a pipe-organ stop of narrow covered metal or wood pipes giving with its own fundamental a pronounced harmonic fifth in the second octave above and of 4-foot, 8-foot, or 16-foot pitch

**1quin·tain** \'kwint°n\ *n* -s [ME *quintaine*, fr. MF, fr. L *quintana* street in a Roman camp separating the fifth maniple from the sixth where military exercises were performed, fr. fem. of *quintanus* fifth in rank, fr. *quintus* fifth + *-anus* -an] **1 :** an object to be tilted at; *esp* **:** a post with a crosspiece having at one end a broad board and at the other end a sandbag used esp. in the middle ages in a sport the object of which was to strike the board with a lance while riding under and to get past without being hit by the sandbag **2 :** the sport of tilting at a quintain

**2quintain** *n* -s [*quinti-* + *-ain* (as in *quatrain*)] *obs* **:** a five-line stanza

**quin·tal** \'kwint°l\ *n* -s [ME, hundredweight, metric weight of 100 kilograms, fr. MF, fr. ML *quintale*, fr. Ar *qinṭār* — more at KANTAR] **1 :** any of various units of weight used esp. in Latin American and Mediterranean countries and equal to from 100 to about 130 pounds **:** HUNDREDWEIGHT **2 :** a metric unit equal to 100 kilograms — see METRIC SYSTEM table

**quin·tan** \'kwint°n, -tən\ *adj* [L *quintanus*, fr. *quintus* fifth + *-anus* -an] **:** occurring as the fifth after four others; *also* **:** occurring every fifth day reckoning inclusively ⟨a ∼ fever⟩

**quin·tant** \-nt°nt,-ntənt\ *n* -s [*quint-* + *-ant* (as in *quadrant*)] **:** a portable instrument similar to a sextant but with an arc of 72 degrees and capable of measuring angles of twice that

**quin·ta·to** \kwin·'täd·(,)ō\ *n* -s [alter. of *quintaton*] **:** QUINTADENA

**quin·ta·ton** \'kwintə,ˌtōn, ˌ≈≈'≈\ *also* **quin·ta·ten** \ˌten\ *n* -s [*quintaton* fr. G, modif. (influenced by *ton* tone, fr. MHG *tōn*, fr. L *tonus*) of NL *quintadena*; *quintaten* prob. modif. of G *quintaton* — more at TONE] **:** QUINTADENA

**quinte** \'kant, 'kaⁿt\ *n* -s [F, fr. L *quinta*, fem. of *quintus* fifth; akin to L *quinque* five; fr. its being the fifth of the eight parrying positions — more at FIVE] **1 :** a parry with a foil or épée that defends the lower inside target with the hand to the left at waist height in a position of pronation with the tip of the blade higher than the hand — compare SEPTIME **2 :** a parry with a saber that protects the head with the hand and forearm raised above the head and the hand held to the right in a position of pronation with the point of the blade to the left and higher than the hand

**quin·ter·ni·on** \kwin·'tərnēən\ *n* -s [*quint-* + *-ernion* (as in *quaternion*)] **:** five sheets of paper combined into a set or section

**1quin·tes·sence** \kwin·'tes°n(t)s *archaic* 'kwintəsən-\ *n* [ME, fr. MF *quinte essence*, fr. ML *quinta essentia* (trans. of Gk *pemptē ousia*), fr. L *quinta* (fem. of *quintus* fifth) + *essentia* essence — more at ESSENCE] **1 a :** the fifth or last and highest essence in ancient and medieval philosophy above fire, air, water, and earth that permeates all nature and is the substance composing the heavenly bodies **:** ETHER 1b **b** *old chem* **:** an alcoholic tincture obtained by extraction **2 :** the essence of an esp. immaterial thing in its purest and most concentrated form **:** the most perfect or rarest distillation or extract ⟨the ∼ of music is, after all, melody —Winthrop Sargeant⟩ ⟨gets his articles down to digests and his digests down to ∼s in single paragraphs or sentences —F.L.Mott⟩ **3 :** the most typical example or representative **:** the consummate instance (as of a quality or class) ⟨the ∼ of pride⟩ ⟨the ∼ of all the heroines of fiction —*Saturday Rev.*⟩

**2quintessence** \"\ *vt* -ED/-ING/-S **:** QUINTESSENTIALIZE ⟨love *quintessenced* and alembicated till it hardly knows itself —Gamaliel Bradford⟩

**1quin·tes·sen·tial** \ˌkwintə̇ˌsenchəl\ *adj* [fr. *1quintessence*, after E *essence: essential*] **:** being a quintessence **:** purest of its kind **:** TYPICAL ⟨∼ extract of mediocrity —George Eliot⟩ ⟨the task of defining primary or ∼ literary value —C.W.Shumaker⟩ ⟨no aristocrats, but ∼ proletarians —M.S.Dworkin⟩ — **quin·tes·sen·ti·al·i·ty** \ˌ≈≈ˌ≈chē'aləd·ē\ *n* — **quin·tes·sen·tial·ly** \ˌ≈≈ˌsench(ə)lē\ *adv*

**2quintessential** \"\ *n* **:** a quintessential element — usu. used in pl. ⟨compendium of the essentials and the ∼s of originality —J.L.Lowes⟩ ⟨compress the ∼s of the metropolis's metabolism into a book —Cleveland Rodgers⟩

**quin·tes·sen·tial·ize** \ˌ≈≈'senchə,līz\ *vt* [*quintessential* + *-ize*] **1 :** to distill or extract as a quintessence **2 :** to extract the quintessence of

**quin·tet** *also* **quin·tette** \(')kwin·ˌtet, *usu* -ed·+V\ *n* -s [*quintet* fr. It *quintetto*, dim. of *quinto* fifth, fr. *quinto*, adj., fifth, fr. L *quintus*; *quintette* fr. F, fr. It *quintetto*] **1 :** a musical composition or movement for five singers or five instrumentalists with or without accompaniment **2 a :** a group of five persons who sing or play five-part music **b :** any group or set of five ⟨a ∼ of names seldom found in isolation —*Irish Statesman*⟩ ⟨took a rough bearing and led the surviving ∼ across the hard flat ground —Fred Majdalany⟩ ⟨as the ∼ came up the sidewalk —Peggy Bennett⟩ **c :** a male basketball team **3 :** a game similar to tenpins except that only five pins arranged triangularly are used

**quin·tet·to** \kwin·'ted·(,)ō\ *n* -s [It] **:** QUINTET ⟨this amiable and enlightened ∼ —T.L.Peacock⟩

**quinti-** — see QUINT-

**1quin·tic** \'kwintik\ *adj* [*quint-* + *-ic*] **1 :** of the fifth degree **2 :** having five links ⟨a ∼ chain⟩

**2quintic** \"\ *n* -s **:** a polynomial or polynomial equation of the fifth degree

**quin·tile** \'kwin·ˌtil, -nt°l, -n(ˌ)til\ *n* -s [*quint-* + *-ile*] **1** *archaic* **:** the aspect of planets when separated a fifth part of a circle or 72 degrees **2 :** any of the four values that divide the items of a frequency distribution into five classes each containing one fifth of the total number of items such that the values corresponding to the items in one class are less than the first quintile, those in a second class are greater than the first quintile and less than the second quintile, and so on throughout

**quin·til·lian** \kwin·'tilyən\ *n* -s *usu cap* [*Quintilla*, believed to be a prophetess of the sect + E *-ian*] **:** one of a party of Montanists of the 2d century A.D.

**quin·til·lion** \"\ *n* -s *often attrib* [*quint-* + *-illion* (as in *million*)] — see NUMBER table

**1quin·til·lionth** \(')≈ˌ≈yən(t)th\ *adj* **1 :** being number one quintillion in a countable series — see NUMBER table **2 :** being one of a quintillion equal parts into which anything is divided

**2quintillionth** \"\ *n, pl* **quintillionths** \-yən(t)s, -n(t)ths\ **:** one of a quintillion equal parts of anything

**quin·tin·ia** \kwin·'tinēə, kan-\ *n, cap* [NL, after Jean de la *Quintinie* †1688 Fr. botanist] **:** a small genus of New Zealand and in some classifications Philippine shrubs and trees (family Saxifragaceae) with alternate leaves and axillary or terminal racemes of white or lilac flowers — see KUMARAHOU b, OPOSSUM WOOD

**quin·tole** \'kwin·ˌtōl\ *or* **quin·to·let** \ˌkwint°l'et\ *n* -s [*quintole* fr. *quint-* + *-ole* (dim. suffix); *quintolet* fr. *quintole* + *-et*] **:** QUINTUPLET 3

**quin·ton** \kaⁿtōⁿ\ *n, pl* **quintons** \-(z)\ *n* -s [F, fr. *quint* fifth, fr. MF — more at QUINT] **:** a five-stringed violin tuned g, d', a', d'', g''

**quin·troon** \(')kwin·ˌtrün\ *n* -s [Sp *quinterón*, fr. *quinto* fifth, fr. L *quintus*] **:** the offspring of an octoroon and a white person

**quints** *pl of* QUINT

**1quin·tu·ple** \(')kwin·ˌt(y)üpəl *also* -təp- *or* 'kwin·təp-\ *adj* [MF, fr. LL *quintuplex*, fr. L *quintus* fifth (akin to L *quinque* five) + *-plic-, -plex* -fold — more at FIVE, SINGLE] **1 a :** consisting of five **:** being five times as great or as many **:** FIVEFOLD **b :** taken by fives or in groups of five **2 :** having five beats — used of a musical measure

**2quintuple** \"\ *n* -s **:** a sum five times as great as another **:** a fivefold amount **:** the fifth multiple

**3quintuple** \"\ *vb* **quintupled; quintupled; quintupling** \p(ə)liŋ\ **quintuples** *vt* **:** to make five times as much or as many ∼ *vi* **:** to become five times as much or as many

**quintuple point** *n* **:** a point representing a set of conditions under which five phases of a physical-chemical system can exist in equilibrium

**quin·tu·plet** \(')kwin·ˌtəplət, -ˌt(y)üp- *sometimes* -n·təp-; *usu* -əd·+V\ *n* -s [*1quintuple* + *-et*] **1 :** a combination of five of a kind **2 a :** one of five children or offspring born at one birth **b quintuplets** *pl* **:** a group of five such offspring **3 :** a group of five musical notes to be played or sung in the time of four of the same value

**1quin·tu·pli·cate** \(')kwin·ˌtüpləkə̇t, -lēk- *sometimes* -lə-ˌkāt; *usu* |d·+V\ *adj* [L *quintuplicatus*, past part. of *quintuplicare* to quintuplicate, fr. *quintuplic-, quintuplex* quintuple] **:** made in five identical copies **:** FIVEFOLD

**2quintuplicate** \"\ *n* -s **1 :** a fifth thing like four others of the same kind **2 :** five copies all alike — used with *in* ⟨typed in ∼⟩

**3quin·tu·pli·cate** \-lə,kāt, *usu* -ād·+V\ *vt* -ED/-ING/-S **:** to multiply by five **:** QUINTUPLE **:** reproduce four times; *specif* **:** to make at one time an original and four carbon copies of

**quin·tu·ply** \(')kwin·ˌt(y)üplē, -li *also* -təp- *or* 'kwin·təp-\ *adv* **:** in a quintuple manner **:** in fivefold quantity

**quin·tus** \'kwintəs\ *n* -ES [ML, fr. L, fifth] **:** a fifth voice or part in medieval music

**quinua** *var of* QUINOA

**qui·nu·cli·dine** \kwə̇'nüklə,dēn, -ˌdə̇n\ *n* -s [*quinine* + *nucl-* (fr. *nucle-*) + *-idine*] **:** a crystalline bicyclic base $C_7H_{13}N$ of which quinine and related alkaloids are derivatives

**quin·yie** \'kēnē\ *n* -s [alter. of *cunyie* coin, corner, fr. ME *cunye* — more at CUNYIE] **1** *Scot* **:** COIN **2** *Scot* **:** CORNER

**quin·zaine** \(')kaⁿ'ˌzān, (')kanˌ-\ *n* -s [F, fr. MF, fr. *quinze* fifteen, fr. L *quindecim* — more at QUINDECIM] **:** a period of 15 days; *specif* **:** an ecclesiastical period comprising a feast day and the fortnight after or (as at Easter) the week before and the week after

**quin·zième** \(')kaⁿz'yem, (')kanz-\ *n* -s [ME *quinsime*, fr. MF *quinzime* fifteenth, fr. *quinze* fifteen] *archaic* **:** a tax of a fifteenth

**1quip** \'kwip\ *n* -s [earlier *quippy*, perh. fr. L *quippe* indeed, to be sure (often ironical), fr. *quid* what, anything, something — more at QUID] **1 a :** a clever usu. taunting remark **:** GIBE ⟨a political candidate getting off ∼s at his rival's expense⟩ **b :** a witty or funny observation or response usu. made on the spur of the moment ⟨the ∼s and puns of poor comedians⟩ **2 :** QUIBBLE, EQUIVOCATION **3 :** something strange, droll, curious, or eccentric **:** ODDITY **syn** see JOKE

**2quip** \"\ *vb* **quipped; quipped; quipping; quips** *vi* **:** to make quips **:** SCOFF, GIBE — often used with *at* ⟨*quipping* at people making critical remarks⟩ ∼ *vt* **:** to jest or gibe at **:** assail with quips

**quip·per** \-pə(r)\ *n* -s **:** one that quips

**quip·pish** \-pish\ *adj* [*quip* + *-ish*] **:** witty or taunting esp. in response — **quippishness** *n* -ES

**quip·ster** \-pstə(r)\ *n* -s [*quip* + *-ster*] **:** a person adept in making quips

**qui·pu** \'kē(ˌ)pü\ *also* **qui·po** \-pō\ *n* -s [Sp *quipo*, fr. Quechua *quipu*] **:** a contrivance consisting of a main cord with smaller varicolored cords attached and knotted and employed by the ancient Peruvians for calculating and record keeping (as of important facts and events)

**qui·ra** \'kērə\ *n* -s [AmerSp] **1 :** any of several tropical American trees constituting a genus (*Platymiscium*) of the family Leguminosae, having pinnate leaves and yellow flowers, and including several (as *P. polystachyum* and *P. pinnatum*) that yield economically important timber **2 :** the reddish brown heavy wood of a quira — see PANAMA REDWOOD

**1quire** \'kwī(ə)r, -īə\ *n* -s [ME *quair*, fr. MF *quaer*, fr. (assumed) VL *quadernum*, alter. (influenced by L *quadrum* square) of L *quaterni* set of four, four each, fr. *quater* four times; akin to L *quattuor* four — more at FOUR] **1 a :** four sheets (as of paper) folded together into eight leaves **b :** a set of folded sheets (as of a book) fitting one within another **2 :** a collection of 24 or sometimes 25 sheets of paper of the same size and quality either not folded or having a single fold — compare REAM **3** *obs* **:** a small book or pamphlet consisting or as if consisting of a quire **:** a work (as a poem or essay) that is or might be contained in a quire — **in quires :** in sheets **:** UNBOUND ⟨a book *in quires*⟩

**2quire** \"\ *vt* -ED/-ING/-S **:** to make or divide into quires or so that folded sheets may be placed one within another ⟨∼ sheets for a catalog⟩; *also* **:** to fold (paper) in half when packing in reams

**3quire** *var of* CHOIR

**quirewise** \'≈,≈\ *adv* [*quire* + *wise*] **:** in quires so as to allow one sheet to be fitted within another ⟨print a pamphlet ∼⟩

**quir·is·ter** \'kwirəstə(r)\ *n* -s [ME *querister* — more at CHORISTER] **:** CHORISTER

**qui·ri·tar·i·an** \ˌkwirə̇ˌterēən\ *adj* [ML *quiritarius* of Roman civil law (fr. L *Quirit-*, *Quiris* Roman citizen — prob. fr. (assumed) OL *coviriom* assemblage of citizens, fr. L *co-* + *-virius*, fr. *vir* man — + *-arius* -ary) + E *-an* — more at VIRILE] **1 :** of, relating to, or constituting the old law of Rome as distinguished from the law introduced by the praetor on equitable principles **2 :** conforming to or enforced by the quiritarian law **:** legal as opposed to equitable or beneficial

**quir·i·tary** \'kwirəˌterē\ *adj* [ML *quiritarius*] **:** QUIRITARIAN

**1quirk** \'kwərk, -wə̄k, -wəik\ *n* -s [origin unknown] **1 :** a triangular shaped area: as **a** (1) *dial Eng* **:** a hosiery clock (2) **:** a small gusset set in at the base of a thumb or the fingers of a glove **b :** a diamond-shaped windowpane **2 :** an abrupt turn, twist, or curve of other deviation from a regular course or pattern **:** BEND, CROOK: as **a** (1) **:** a turn of a pen in writing **:** FLOURISH (2) *obs* **:** a sudden whimsical turn or phrase in music **b** (1) **:** a clever retort **:** CONCEIT, QUIP (2) **:** a clever or cunning evasion **:** SUBTERFUGE, QUIBBLE **c :** a peculiarity of action, behavior, or bearing **:** MANNERISM **3** *obs* **:** a sudden fit **:** short paroxysm **4 a :** a small channel or groove separating a bead or other molding from the adjoining members — see QUIRK MOLDING **b :** the bead or fillet of a grooving plane in woodworking

**2quirk** \"\ *vb* -ED/-ING/-S *vt* **1 :** to subject to quirks or quips **2 :** to give a quirk to ⟨holding her skirts with ∼*ed* fingers —Rosamond Lehmann⟩ ⟨a peculiarly ∼*ed* mouth⟩; *specif* **:** to fashion (as molding) with quirks **3 :** to strike with a sharp sudden jerk of a whip ⟨the coachman lets fly his whip and ∼s his off-wheeler on the thigh —Amy Lowell⟩ ∼ *vi* **:** to make or exhibit a quirk ⟨Annie's mouth ∼*ed* a little —G.W.Brace⟩; *specif* **:** to speak or act with a quirk of manner

**quirk bead** *or* **quirked bead** *n* **:** a bead and groove at the edge of a board or panel — compare COCK BEAD, RETURN-COCKED BEAD; see BEAD illustration

**quirk·i·ly** \-kə̇lē\ *adv* **:** in a quirky manner ⟨a ∼ entertaining way⟩ ⟨a ∼ humorous personality⟩

**quirk·i·ness** \-kēnə̇s\ *n* -ES **:** the quality or state of being quirky

**quirk molding** *n* **:** a molding distinctly set off by quirks

**quirky** \-kē\ *adj* -ER/-EST **1 :** full of quirks **:** TRICKY ⟨a ∼ lawyer⟩ **2 :** having, exhibiting, or suggesting sharp or unexpected turns, features, or qualities ⟨the inns of New England, indeed, have a ∼ character all their own —B.M.Bowie⟩ ⟨∼ and individualistic music —Irving Kolodin⟩

quirk molding

**quirl** \'kwər(-ə)l\ *chiefly Midland var of* CURL

**quir·quin·cho** \kir'kin(ˌ)chō\ *n* -s [AmerSp, fr. Quechua *quirquinchu* armadillo] **1 :** 1PICHI **2 :** PELUDO

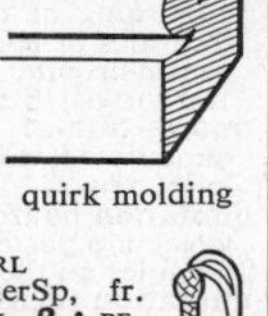

**1quirt** \'kwər|t, -wə̄|, -wəi|, *usu* |d·+V\ *n* -s [MexSp *cuarta* quirt, whip, prob. fr. *cuarta* lead mule, lead mule of a four-mule team, fr. Sp, fem. of *cuarto* fourth, fr. L *quartus* — more at QUART] **:** a riding whip used esp. in the western U. S. and consisting of a short handle (as of wood or leather) to which is attached a rawhide lash

**2quirt** \"\ *vt* -ED/-ING/-S **:** to strike, coerce, or drive with or as if with a quirt

**quis** \'kwis\ *n* -ES [perh. fr. L, who] **:** a European woodcock

**qui·sle** \'kwizəl\ *vi* -ED/-ING/-S [back-formation fr. *quisling*] **:** to serve or act as a quisling

**quis·ler** \-z(ə)lə(r)\ *n* -s [*quisle* + *-er*] **:** QUISLING

**quis·ling** \'kwizliŋ, -lēŋ\ *n* -s [after Vidkun *Quisling* †1945 Norw. politician] **:** a traitorous national who aids the invader of his country and often serves as chief agent or puppet governor

**quis·ling·ism** \-ŋ,izəm\ *n* -s [*quisling* + *-ism*] **:** TREASON; *esp* **:** the betrayal by a national of his own country followed by his enjoyment of high position under the protection of the alien occupying power

quirt

**quis·qual·is** \kwə̇'skwäləs\ *n, cap* [NL, fr. L *quis* who + *qualis* of what kind — more at WHO, QUALITY] **:** a small genus of tropical Asiatic, Indo-Malayan, and African woody vines (family Combretaceae) having red or orange spicate flowers with a superior calyx whose limb is deciduous from the long tube and a fruit possessed of five wings — see RANGOON CREEPER

**quis·que·ite** \'kiskē,īt\ *n* -s [*Quisque*, district near Mina Ragra, Pasco, Peru, its locality + E *-ite*] **:** a brittle black lustrous substance mostly composed of sulfur and carbon and accompanying the vanadium ores of Peru **:** sulfurous asphaltum

**qui·sutsch** \'kē,səch\ *n* -ES [native name in Kamchatka and Alaska] **:** SILVER SALMON

**1quit** \'kwit, *usu* -id·+V\ *adj* [ME *quit, quite*, fr. OF *quite*] **1 :** released from obligation, charge, or penalty **:** ABSOLVED, ACQUITTED; *esp* **:** FREE ⟨∼ of unnecessary fears⟩ **2** *obs* **:** DESTITUTE, BEREFT — used with *of* **3** *obs* **:** QUITS

**2quit** \"\ *vb* **quit** *also* **quitted; quit** *also* **quitted; quitting; quits** [ME *quiten, quitten*, fr. MF *quiter, quitter*, fr. OF, fr. *quite* free of, released, calm, fr. L *quietus* calm, quiet — more at QUIET] *vt* **1 :** to set free **:** RELIEVE, RELEASE ⟨∼ me of fear⟩ **2 :** to pay up **:** DISCHARGE ⟨may fairly ∼ the debt —William Cowper⟩ **3 :** CONDUCT, ACQUIT ⟨youths ∼ themselves like men⟩ **4 :** to leave or leave off from: as **a :** to depart from or out of ⟨as soon as she *quitted* the room he returned to it —W.H. Hudson †1922⟩ ⟨*quitted* Cambridge . . . before being formally ejected —Douglas Bush⟩ **b :** to leave esp. peremptorily the company of ⟨the hero *quitted* him with some contempt —George Meredith⟩ **c :** to give over (as a way of thought, acting, or living) **:** RELINQUISH, ABANDON, FORSAKE ⟨a tribe that *quitted* the plains for the mountains⟩ **d :** to terminate (as an action, activity, or employment) esp. with finality **:** LEAVE ⟨∼ a job⟩ ∼ *vi* **1 :** to leave off or cease normal, expected, or necessary action ⟨the engine coughed, sputtered, and ∼⟩ **2 :** to give up employment **:** stop working **:** LEAVE ⟨a worker *quitting* because of poor pay⟩ **3 :** to give up **:** admit defeat **:** stop struggling, fighting, or contending ⟨despairing creatures who have given up on life —*Time*⟩ **syn** see BEHAVE, GO, STOP

**3quit** \"\ *n* -s **1 :** the act or action of quitting ⟨a factory with many ∼s per year among its workers⟩ **2 :** tendency to quit ⟨a fighter with little ∼ in him⟩

**4quit** \"\ *n* -s [prob. imit.] **:** any of various small passerine birds chiefly of the West Indies (as banana quit and grassquit)

**qui tam** \'kwī'tam\ *or* **qui tam action** *n* -s [LL, lit., who as much, who as well; fr. the first words of the clause referring to the plaintiff as one who sues as much for the state as for himself] **:** an action to recover a penalty under a statute that gives part of the penalty to the one bringing the action and the rest to the state or a public body — compare POPULAR ACTION

**quitch** \'kwich\ *or* **quitch grass** *n* -ES [fr. (assumed) ME *quicche*, fr. OE *cwice*; akin to MD *queke* couch grass, OHG *quecca*, Sw dial. *kvicka, kveka*, Norw dial. *kvika*; all fr. a prehistoric Gmc word derived fr. the adj. represented by OE *cwic* alive — more at QUICK] **:** COUCH GRASS 1a

**1quitclaim** *vt* [ME *quite-claimen*, fr. MF *quiteclamer*, lit., to declare free, fr. OF, fr. *quite* free, free of + *clamer* to declare, claim — more at CLAIM] **1** *obs* **:** ACQUIT **2 :** to release or relinquish a legal claim to; *esp* **:** to release a claim to or convey by a quitclaim deed

**2quit·claim** \'kwit,klām\ *n* [ME *quite-claim*, fr. MF *quiteclame*, fr. *quiteclamer* to quitclaim] **:** a release of a claim **:** a deed of release; *specif* **:** a legal instrument by which some right, title, interest, or claim by one person in or to an estate held by himself or another is released to another and which is sometimes used as a simple but effective conveyance for making a grant of lands whether by way of release or as an original conveyance

**1quite** \'kwīt, *usu* -īd·+V\ *adv* [ME, fr. *quite, quit*, adj., released, free — more at QUIT] **1 :** COMPLETELY, WHOLLY, TOTALLY ⟨work not ∼ done⟩ ⟨∼ mistaken⟩ ⟨not ∼ master of himself⟩ **2 :** to an extreme **:** POSITIVELY ⟨∼ the rage⟩ ⟨∼ drunk⟩ ⟨∼ so⟩ **3 :** to a considerable extent **:** PRETTY, RATHER ⟨∼ near⟩ ⟨∼ ill⟩ ⟨∼ rich⟩

**2qui·te** \'kē(ˌ)tā\ *n* -s [Sp, lit., act of taking away, fr. *quitar* to take away, release, prob. fr. LL *quietare* to set free, calm — more at QUIET] **:** a series of passes made by a matador with his cape to draw the bull away from a horse or fallen picador

**quitely** *adv* [ME, fr. *quit, quite*, adj., free + *-ly*] *obs* **:** ENTIRELY, QUITE

**qui·to** \'kē(ˌ)tō\ *adj, usu cap* [fr. *Quito*, Ecuador] **:** of or from Quito, the capital of Ecuador **:** of the kind or style prevalent in Quito

**quit·rent** \'kwit·ˌrent\ *n* [ME *quiterent*, fr. *quite, quit* free + *rent*] **:** a fixed rent usu. small in amount and payable by a freeholder or copyholder to his feudal superior in commutation of services; *specif* **:** a fixed rent due from a socage tenant

**1quits** \'kwits\ *adj* [ME, released from liability, prob. fr. ML *quittus* quit, free, fr. L *quietus* free, calm, fr. L, calm, quiet — more at QUIET] **1** *obs* **:** released or cleared from liability **2 :** even or equal with another or each other by repayment of an obligation or by requital (as of a favor or injury)

**2quits** \"\ *n pl* **:** RECOMPENSE, RETALIATION

**3quits** *pres 3d sing of* QUIT, *pl of* QUIT

**quittal** *n* -s [*2quit* + *-al*] *obs* **:** REQUITAL; *also* **:** ACQUITTAL

**1quit·tance** \'kwit°n(t)s\ *n* -s [ME *quitance, quetaunce*, fr. OF *quittance*, fr. *quitter* to release, quit + *-ance* — more at QUIT] **1 a :** the act of freeing or releasing; *specif* **:** discharge from a debt or an obligation **b :** a document evidencing quittance **2 :** RECOMPENSE, REQUITAL ⟨money received in ∼ of wrongs⟩

**2quittance** *vt, obs* **:** REPAY, REQUITE; *also* **:** to give up

**quitted** *past of* QUIT

**quitted trick** *n* **:** a trick in card games after all of the cards composing it have been irrevocably played and it has been stacked with the cards in it facedown

**1quitter** *n* -s [ME *quittere, quiture* pus, quittor] **1** *obs* **:** matter discharged from a sore **:** PUS **2 :** slag from tin smelting

**2quit·ter** \'kwid·ə(r), -itə-\ *n* -s [*2quit* + *-er*] **1 :** one that quits a task, danger, or trial **:** COWARD **2 :** a young male fur seal making its first entrance upon the breeding grounds from which it may easily be driven by old bulls already established

**quitting** *pres part of* QUIT

**quit·tor** \'kwid·ə(r), -itə-\ *n* -s [ME *quittere, quiture* pus, quittor, prob. fr. OF *quiture, cuiture* act of boiling, act of cooking, fr. L *coctura*, fr. *coctus* (past part. of *coquere* to cook, boil) + *-ura* -ure — more at COOK] **:** a purulent inflammation (as a necrobacillosis) of the feet of horses and other solidungulates occurring chiefly in a cartilaginous form characterized by a chronic persistent inflammation of the lateral cartilage of the foot leading to suppuration and the formation of one or more fistulous openings above the coronet and causing marked lameness or a cutaneous form characterized by an inflammation of the soft tissues just above the hoof involving suppuration and sloughing of the skin before healing

**1quiv·er** \'kwivə(r)\ *adj* [ME *quiver, cwiver*, fr. (assumed) OE *cwifer*] *archaic* **:** FAST-MOVING, AGILE, LIVELY

**2quiver** \"\ *n* -s [ME, fr. AF *quiveir*, fr. OF *quivre, cuevre*, of Gmc origin; akin to the root of E *1cocker*] **1 :** a case for carrying arrows; *also* **:** the arrows in a quiver **2 :** a container capable of holding a set or number of units; *also* **:** a large group or array

**3quiver** \"\ *vb* **quivered; quivered; quivering** \-v(ə)riŋ\ **quivers** [ME *quiveren*, prob. fr. *1quiver*] *vi* **:** to shake or move with slight tremulous motion **:** TREMBLE ⟨∼*ing* branches⟩ ∼ *vt* **:** to cause to quiver

quiver 1

**4quiver** \"\ *n* -s **1 a :** the act or action of quivering **:** TREMOR ⟨the ∼ of a leaf⟩ ⟨a ∼ of excitement⟩ **b :** QUAVER ⟨a slight ∼ in his voice —Carleton Beals⟩ **2 :** a sudden radiance **:** FLASH ⟨a ∼ of lightning⟩

**5quiver** \"\ *vi* -ED/-ING/-S [*2quiver*] **:** to come to rest — used of an arrow ⟨the arrow ∼s in a tree⟩

**quiv·ered** \-və(r)d\ *adj* **1 :** equipped with or carrying a quiver ⟨the ∼ warriors of antiquity⟩ **2** [fr. past part. of *5quiver*] **:** sheathed in or as if in a quiver ⟨whose quills stand ∼ —Alexander Pope⟩

**quiv·er·er** \-vərə(r)\ *n* -s **:** one that quivers
**quiv·er·ful** \ˈkwivə(r),fu̇l\ *n, pl* **quiverfuls** *or* **quiversful** [²*quiver* + *-ful*] **1 :** as many as a quiver will hold ⟨a ~ of arrows⟩ **2 :** a good number **:** LOT ⟨a ~ of children⟩
**quivering** *adj* **:** TREMBLING, QUAKING ⟨~ leaves⟩
**quiv·er·ing·ly** *adv* **:** in a quivering manner
**quiverleaf** \ˈ==,=\ *n* [³*quiver* + *leaf;* fr. its tremulousness] **:** ASPEN; *esp* **:** AMERICAN ASPEN
**quiv·er·ness** \-)nəs\ *n* -ES **:** the quality or state of being shaky or atremble
**quiver tree** *n* [trans. of Afrik *kokerboom;* fr. its hollowed stems being used by natives for arrow quivers] **:** a tall much-branched southern African aloe (*Aloe dichotoma*)
**quiv·ery** \ˈkwiv(ə)rē, -ri\ *adj* **:** that quivers **:** TREMBLING
**qui vive** \kēˈvēv\ *n* [F, lit., long live who? (i.e., whom do you favor?); fr. the challenge of a French sentry or patrol] **1 :** CHALLENGE **2 :** ALERT, LOOKOUT — used in the phrase *on the qui vive* ⟨on the *qui vive* for errors⟩
**quix·ote** \ˈkwiksət, -ˌsōt\ *n* -s *often cap* [after Don *Quixote* de la Mancha, chivalrous hero of the satiric novel *Don Quixote de la Mancha* (1605, 1615) by Miguel de Cervantes Saavedra †1616 Span. novelist] **:** a quixotic person
**quix·ot·ic** \(ˈ)kwikˈsäd·ik, -ät\, |ēk\ *also* **quix·ot·i·cal** \|ək̇əl, |ēk\ *adj* [*quixote* + *-ic* or *-ical*] **:** idealistic and utterly impractical; *esp* **:** marked by rash lofty romantic ideas or chivalrous action doomed to fail ⟨~ as a restoration of medieval knighthood —M.R.Cohen⟩ **syn** see IMAGINARY
**quix·ot·i·cal·ly** \|ək(ə)lē, |ēk-, -li\ *adv* **:** in a quixotic manner
**quix·o·tism** \ˈkwiksə,tizəm\ *n* -s [*quixote* + *-ism*] **:** quixotic action or thought; *also* **:** an example of such action or thought
**quix·o·tize** \-,tīz\ *vb* -ED/-ING/-S [*quixote* + *-ize*] **:** to make or to be quixotic
**quix·o·try** \ˈkwiksətrē\ *n* -ES [*quixote* + *-ry*] **:** QUIXOTISM
**¹quiz** \ˈkwiz\ *n, pl* **quizzes** [origin unknown] **1 a :** an odd or eccentric person **b :** a person who ridicules or mocks ⟨she was a light-hearted girl, and a born ~ —George Dangerfield⟩ **2 :** PRACTICAL JOKE; *also* **:** a jesting or joking piece (as of prose or conversation) ⟨a novel that was a ~ upon the silly romances of the day⟩ **3 :** the act or action of quizzing; *specif* **:** a short oral or written test often taken without special preparation
**²quiz** \"\ *n, pl* **quizzes :** BANDALORE
**³quiz** \"\ *vb* **quizzed; quizzed; quizzing; quizzes** *vt* **1 :** to ridicule wittily **:** MOCK ⟨when they see you standing up with somebody else, they will ~ me famously —Jane Austen⟩ **2 :** to peer at esp. mockingly **3 :** to give a quiz to ⟨~ a class⟩ **4 :** to question seriously, soberly, or methodically ⟨~ murder suspects⟩ ~ *vi* **:** to conduct or give a quiz **syn** see ASK
**quiz·ee** *also* **quiz·zee** \(ˈ)kwiˈzē\ *n* -s **:** a person who is quizzed; *esp* **:** a participant in a quiz game ⟨intelligent questions directed at carefully selected ~*s* —W.V.T.Clark⟩
**quiz game** *n* **:** a form of entertainment often used on radio or television in which the members of a panel compete in answering questions
**quiz kid** *n* **:** a prematurely intelligent or knowing child
**quizmaster** \ˈ=,==\ *n* **:** one who puts the questions to the contestants in a quiz game
**quiz program** *or* **quiz show** *n* **:** a quiz game presented on radio or television
**quiz·zer** \ˈkwizə(r)\ *n* -s **:** one that quizzes; *also* **:** a quiz game, program, or show
**quiz·zi·cal** \ˈkwizək̇əl, -zēk-\ *adj* [¹*quiz* + *-ical*] **1 a :** slightly and amusingly eccentric **:** ODD ⟨a ~ old man⟩ **b :** WHIMSICAL ⟨~ understatement⟩ **2 :** marked or characterized by mockery or banter ⟨a ~ smile⟩ **3 :** QUESTIONING, CURIOUS ⟨a ~ look⟩
**quiz·zi·cal·i·ty** \,kwizəˈkaləd·ē\ *n* -ES **:** QUIZZICALNESS ⟨~ mixed with slow amiable shrewdness —R.P.Warren⟩
**quiz·zi·cal·ly** \ˈkwizək(ə)lē, -zēk-, -li\ *adv* **:** in a quizzical manner ⟨sitting with her . . . head ~ tilted —John Updike⟩
**quiz·zi·cal·ness** \-kəlnəs\ *n* -ES **:** the quality or state of being quizzical ⟨the ~ of a policeman's stare⟩
**quizzing glass** *n* **:** a small eyeglass (as a monocle with a handle)
**qung** *also* **kung** \ˈku̇ŋ\ *n, pl* **qung** *or* **qungs** *usu cap* **1 :** a southern African people of the Omatako river **2 :** a member of the Qung people

quizzing glass

**¹quo** \ˈkwō\ *var of* QUOTH
**²quo** \"\ *n* -s [L *quid pro quo*] **:** something received or given for something else ⟨the exchange of quids for ~*s* out of the public's sight and hearing —R.H.Rovere⟩
**quoc-ngu** \ˌkwäkˈŋgü, ˈkwäkˈnü\ *n* -s [Vietnamese *quốc ngữ,* lit., national language] **:** a writing system based on the Roman alphabet with additional letters and diacritics and used for the Vietnamese language
**¹quod** \ˈkwōd\ *var of* QUOTH
**²quod** \ˈkwäd\ *n* -s [origin unknown] *slang Brit* **:** PRISON
**³quod** \"\ *vt* **quodded; quodded; quodding; quods** *slang Brit* **:** to put in prison
**quod com·pu·tet** \kwädˈkämpyə,tet\ *n* [LL, lit., that he account] **:** a legal judgment ordering a defendant to account
**quod·dy** \ˈkwädē\ *also* **quoddy boat** *n* -ES [fr. Passama*quoddy* Bay, inlet between New Brunswick, Canada, and Maine] **:** an open sloop-rigged sailboat once used esp. for fishing along the Maine coast
**quod·li·bet** \ˈkwädlə,bet\ *n* -s [ME, fr. ML *quodlibetum,* fr. L *quod libet* what you will, as you please, fr. *quod* (neut. of *qui* who) + *libet* it pleases, fr. *libēre* to please — more at WHO, LOVE] **1 a :** a subtle or debatable point; *esp* **:** a theological or scholastic question proposed for argument or disputation **b :** a scholastic or theological debate over such a question **2 a :** a humorous musical medley or fantasia **b :** a whimsical harmonic combination of melodies
**quod·li·bet·ic** \ˌ==ˈbed·ik\ *also* **quod·li·bet·i·cal** \-d·ək̇əl\ *adj* [*quodlibet* + *-ic* or *-ical*] **:** consisting or of the nature of a quodlibet **:** purely academic; *also* **:** characterized by or fond of academic discussion — **quod·li·bet·i·cal·ly** \-d·ək(ə)lē\ *adv*
**quohog** *or* **quohaug** *var of* QUAHOG
**quoil** \ˈkwȯi(ə)l\ *dial var of* COIL
**¹quoin** \ˈk(w)ȯin\ *or* **coign** \ˈkȯin\ *n* -s [alter. of *coin*] **1 :** ANGLE, CORNER **2 :** any of various wedges: as **a :** a beveled wooden block or a mechanically expandable metal device used by printers to lock up a form within a chase or to secure type on a galley **b :** a wedge used on ships to keep casks from rolling or to raise or depress the muzzles of guns **c :** the keystone or a voussoir of an arch **3 :** one of the stone, brick, or wood members forming the exterior angle or corner at the juncture of two walls or planes which are distinguished from the adjoining surfaces or the units which form them by material, texture, color, size, or projection **4 :** LOZENGE 2d(1)

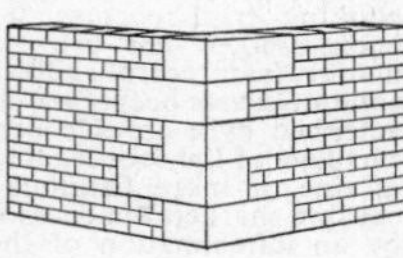
quoins 3 of stone set in brickwork

**²quoin** \"\ *or* **coign** \"\ *vt* -ED/-ING/-S **1 :** to place quoins in (a form) in printing (as between the chase and imposed matter) preparatory to locking up — often used with *up* **2 :** to provide with quoins or distinctive corners ⟨~*ed* walls⟩
**quoin·ing** \-niŋ\ *n* -s **:** the architectural members which form a distinctive corner at the juncture of two walls or planes
**quoin post** *n* **:** a corner post; *specif* **:** the vertical member at the hinged end of a gate in a navigation lock
**¹quoit** \ˈkwā|t, ˈk(w)ȯi|, *usu* |d·+V; *chiefly dial* ˈkwāk\ *n* -s [ME *coite,* perh. fr. MF *coite, coute* quilt, mattress — more at QUILT] **1 :** a flattened ring of iron or circle of rope used in a throwing game **2 quoits** *pl but sing in constr* **:** a game played with quoits that are thrown from a mark toward a pin in an attempt to ring the pin or to come as near to it as possible **3 :** the stone cover of a cromlech or cist; *also* **:** CROMLECH, CIST

quoits 1

**²quoit** \"\ *vb* -ED/-ING/-S [ME *coiten,* fr. *coite* quoit] *vi* **:** to play quoits ~ *vt* **:** to throw like a quoit ⟨~ a hat across a room⟩
**quoit·er** *pronunc at* ¹QUOIT +ə(r)\ *n* -s [ME *coiter,* fr. *coiten* + *-er*] **:** one who plays quoits
**quok·ka** \ˈkwäkə\ *n* -s [native name in Australia] **:** a stocky Australian pademelon (*Setonix brachyurus*) with a short tail — called also *short-tailed wallaby*
**quo·mi·nus** \ˈkwōmənəs\ *n* [L, whereby the less, that not; fr. the clause in the writ alluding to the plaintiff's diminished ability to pay his crown debts] **1 :** a writ under old English law for preventing waste of a wood by one having housebote and haybote therein **2 :** a writ formerly used to found jurisdiction in the Exchequer Court alleging the plaintiff's diminished ability to pay his crown debts
**quo·mo·do** \ˈkwōmə,dō\ *n* -s [L, in what manner, how, fr. *quo* (abl. of *qui* who, what) + *modo,* abl. of *modus* manner — more at METE] **:** MEANS, MANNER ⟨the ~ with which to pay off debts⟩
**quon·dam** \ˈkwändəm, -,dam\ *adj* [L, at one time, formerly, fr. *quom, cum* when (akin to L *qui* who) + *-dam* (akin to L *de* from, down, away) — more at WHO, DE-] **:** having been formerly **:** FORMER, SOMETIME ⟨a ~ friend⟩
**quondong** *var of* QUANDONG
**quonk** \ˈkwäŋk\ *or* **quonk·ing** \-ŋkiŋ\ *n* -s [imit.] **:** noise (as from conversation) that disturbs or disrupts a television or radio program because of its proximity to the microphones or cameras
**Quon·set** \ˈkwän(t)sət- *also* -wȯn- *or* -nzət-\ *trademark* — used for a prefabricated shelter set on a foundation of bolted steel trusses and built of a semicircular arching roof of corrugated metal insulated with wood fiber
**quop** \ˈkwäp\ *vi* [earlier *quap,* fr. ME *quappen*] *chiefly dial* **:** THROB
**quor·a·te·an** \,kwȯrəˈtēən\ *n* -s *usu cap* [Gurok *Quoratem,* area near Salmon River, Idaho + E *-an*] **:** a language family of the Hokan stock in California comprising Karok
**quo·rum** \ˈkwōrəm, -wȯr-\ *n* -s [ME, fr. L, of whom, gen. pl. of *qui* who; fr. the wording of the commission once issued to justices of the peace in England — more at WHO] **1 :** a select number of English justices of the peace formerly required to be present at sessions to constitute a lawful bench ⟨justices of the ~⟩ **2 :** a select group ⟨the deepest sot among the topers of the ~ —T.H.Green⟩ **3 :** the number of the members of an organized body of persons (as a legislature, court, or board of directors) that when duly assembled is legally competent to transact business in the absence of the other members **:** a usu. specified number of members (as an absolute majority) in the absence of which an organized body cannot act legally **4 :** a general council or local section of those having the same office in the Mormon priesthood
**quorum call** *n* **:** the action of calling off a list of names (as of the members of a legislature) to determine whether a quorum is present
**quos** *pl of* QUO
**quot** *abbr* quotation; quoted
**¹quo·ta** \ˈkwōd·ə, -ōtə\ *n* -s [ML, fr. fem. of L *quotus* of what number, how many — more at QUOTE] **1 :** a proportional part **:** SHARE; *esp* **:** the share or proportion assigned to each in a division or to each member of a body ⟨the ~ of troops required for an area⟩ **2 :** the share or proportion received, granted, or necessary to a person as being one of a certain number entitled to a part; *specif* **:** the smallest number of votes in proportional political representation required for election and sometimes determined by dividing the total number of votes cast by one more than the number of seats to be filled and rounding off to the next higher full number **3 :** the number of immigrants allowed to enter a country in a particular year and sometimes determined by the proportionate numbers of foreign-born groups in a given census **4 :** a fixed number or percentage of minority group members who may be admitted into some activity or institution ⟨gradual desegregation by ~⟩
**²quota** \"\ *vt* -ED/-ING/-S **:** to divide or fix by quotas ⟨an institution with a ~*ed* admission policy⟩ **:** assign a quota to
**quot·abil·i·ty** \,kwōd·əˈbiləd·ē, -ōtə-, -lət̄ē, -i *also* ÷,kō-\ *n* [*quotable* + *-ity*] **:** the quality or state of being quotable
**quot·able** \ˈ==bəl\ *adj* [¹*quote* + *-able*] **1 :** capable of being quoted; *esp* **:** effective or adapted to quotation ⟨a ~ phrase⟩ ⟨a ~ author⟩ **2 :** fit to be repeated or published ⟨what was said was funny but not ~⟩
**quot·able·ness** *n* -ES [*quotable* + *-ness*] **:** QUOTABILITY
**quota immigrant** *n* **:** an immigrant subject to the quota restrictions imposed by various U. S. immigration laws
**quo·ta·tion** \kwōˈtāshən *also* ÷kō- *sometimes chiefly Brit* kwəˈt-\ *n* -s [ML *quotation-, quotatio-* numeration, numbering of references, division by numbers, fr. *quotare* to divide by numbers, mark the number of + *-ion-, -io* -ion] **1** *obs* **:** a marginal reference or note in a book **2 a :** something that is quoted; *esp* **:** a passage referred to, repeated, or adduced esp. as evidence or illustration **b :** a striking, distinctive, or popular passage suitable for quoting ⟨a book of ~*s*⟩ **3 :** the act or process of quoting ⟨his ~ of prices⟩; *esp* **:** the naming or publishing of current bids and offers or current prices of securities or commodities; *also* **:** the bids, offers, or prices so named or published **4 a :** QUOTATION FURNITURE **b :** QUOTATION QUAD **5 :** QUOTATION MARK
**quo·ta·tion·al** \-āshən³l,-āshnəl\ *adj* **:** of the nature of a quotation **:** indicating quotation — **quo·ta·tion·al·ly** \-³lē, -əlē\ *adv*
**quotation board** *n* **:** a large board (as in a broker's office) on which are posted the current prices of stocks, bonds, or commodities on the several exchanges
**quotation furniture** *n* [prob. so called fr. its being used orig. to fill between marginal notes] **:** metal printing furniture cast hollow with the bottom side open which closely resembles quotation quads and whose dimensions are usu. given in picas
**quotation mark** *n* **:** one of a pair of punctuation marks " ", ' ', „ ", or ‚ ' used to indicate the beginning and the end of a quotation in which the exact phraseology of another or of a text is directly cited — usu. used to enclose the titles of poems, paintings, lectures, articles, and parts of books and sometimes used to enclose technical terms expected to be unfamiliar to the reader, words used in an unusual, ironical, or eye-catching sense, or words (as slang expressions) for which a writer offers a slight apology
**quotation noun** *or* **quotation word** *n* **:** HYPOSTASIS 7b
**quotation quad** *n* **:** a hollow printing quad with the bottom side open whose dimensions are usu. given in points
**¹quote** \ˈkwōt *also* ÷ˈkō-; *usu* -ōd·+V\ *vb* -ED/-ING/-S [ML *quotare* to divide into chapters by numbers, mark references by numbers, mark the number of, fr. L *quotus* of what number, how many, fr. *quot* how many, as many as; akin to L *quis* who — more at WHO] *vt* **1 a :** to speak or write (a passage) from another's work verbatim and with due acknowledgment or with the supposition that the fact of unoriginality will be apparent ⟨*quoting* an epigram from the poem⟩ **b :** to speak or write a passage from esp. in substantiation, illustration, or adornment ⟨~ the Bible⟩ **2 :** to adduce (material) in illustration ⟨~ instances⟩ ⟨~ cases⟩ **3** *obs* **a :** to give a reference to **:** supply a source for **b :** to write down or record **c :** NOTICE, MARK **4 a** (1) **:** to name the current price of (a commodity stock, or bond) (2) **:** to name (the current price) of a commodity, stock, or bond **b :** to give (the current bid and asked prices) for a commodity, stock, or bond **5 :** to set off (as a written or printed passage) by quotation marks ~ *vi* **:** to warn a hearer or reader that matter following is quoted ⟨the president said ~ you need have no fear of unemployment unquote⟩
**syn** CITE, REPEAT: QUOTE usu. involves a use of another's words, commonly with faithful exactness or an attempt at it, for some special effect like adornment, illustration, close examination ⟨I will *quote* a passage which is unfamiliar enough to be regarded with fresh attention —T.S.Eliot⟩ CITE is likely to stress the idea of adducing, bringing forward, or mentioning for a particular reason, like substantiation or proof, with or without the idea of uttering another's words ⟨the critic *cited* in the opening of this chapter —F.R.Leavis⟩ REPEAT stresses the fact of a saying or writing over again of someone else's words; it may suggest lack of the dignified reasons for the procedure attached to QUOTE and CITE ⟨unrealistic to go on *repeating* phrases about the connection of industry with personal independence —John Dewey⟩
**²quote** \"\ *n* -s **1 :** QUOTATION **2 :** QUOTATION MARK
**quoted** *past of* QUOTE
**quoted price** *n* [*quoted* fr. past part. of ¹*quote*] **:** the bid and offered prices of a security on a stock exchange at a given time
**quot·ee** \(ˈ)k(w)ōd·ˈē, -ōˈtē\ *n* -s [*quote* + *-ee*] **:** one who is quoted
**quote mark** *n* **:** QUOTATION MARK
**quot·er** \ˈk(w)ōd·ə(r), -ōtə-\ *n* -s [*quote* + *-er*] **:** one that quotes; *specif* **:** a clerk who keeps a record of insurance policy dividends and figures the interest due on them
**quotes** *pres 3d sing of* QUOTE
**quoth** \ˈkwōth\ *vb past* [ME, past of *quethen* to say, fr. OE *cwethan, cwethan;* akin to OHG *quethan, quedan* to say, ON *kvetha,* Goth *qithan*] *archaic* **:** SAID — used chiefly in the first and third persons with a postpositive subject
**quotha** \ˈkwōthə\ *interj* [alter. of *quoth he*] *archaic* — used to express surprise, contempt, or assertive self-affirmation
**quotid** *abbr* [L *quotidie*] every day
**¹quo·tid·i·an** \kwōˈtidēən\ *adj* [ME *cotidian,* fr. MF, fr. L *cotidianus, quotidianus,* fr. *cotidie, quotidie* each day, daily (fr. *quot* as many as, how many + *dies* day) + *-anus* -an — more at QUOTE, DEITY] **1 :** occurring every day ⟨~ fever⟩ **2 :** belonging to everyday ⟨~ routine⟩ **3 :** COMMONPLACE, ORDINARY ⟨~ drabness⟩
**²quotidian** \"\ *n* -s [ME *cotidian,* fr. *cotidian,* adj.] **:** something that occurs each day (as an intermittent fever)
**quo·tient** \ˈkwōshənt\ *n* -s [ME *quocient,* modif. (influenced by *-ent,* n. suffix) of L *quoties, quotiens* how many times, how often, as often as (taken as a pres. part. stem in *-ent-*), fr. *quot* how many, as many as; akin to L *quis* who — more at WHO] **1 :** the number resulting from the division of one number by another **:** the result of a process inverse to multiplication **:** the quantity such that the product of it and the divisor equals the dividend or such that the product of it and the divisor plus the remainder equals the dividend **2 :** the numerical ratio usu. multiplied by 100 between a test score and a measurement on which that score might be expected largely to depend ⟨intelligence ~⟩ ⟨accomplishment ~⟩ **3 :** PROPORTION, QUOTA
**quotient verdict** *n* **:** a verdict in a legal action for damages wherein the amount assessed by the jury is reached by striking an average of amounts suggested by each juryman
**quoting** *pres part of* QUOTE
**quot·li·bet** \ˈkwätlə,bet\ *n* -s [by alter.] **:** QUODLIBET 2
**quo·tum** \ˈkwōd·əm\ *n* -s [L, neut. of *quotus* of what number — more at QUOTE] **:** PROPORTION, PART
**quo war·ran·to** \ˌkwōwəˈrän·(ˌ)tō, -ran-·\ *n* [ML, by what warrant] **1 a :** an English writ of right formerly issued on behalf of the crown requiring a person to show by what authority he exercises his office, franchise, or liberty **b :** the entire pleadings that such a writ calls forth or the action or proceeding itself **2 a :** a legal proceeding that is brought by the state, sovereign, or public officer, has a purpose similar to that of the ancient writ of quo warranto, is usu. criminal in form and sometimes authorizes the imposition of a fine but is essentially civil in nature and seeks to correct often at the relation or on the complaint of a private person a usurpation, misuser, or nonuser of a public office or corporate or public franchise, and may result in judgments of ouster against individuals and of ouster and seizure against corporations **b :** the pleadings in such a proceeding
**quoz** \ˈkwäz\ *n* -ES [prob. alter. of *quiz*] *archaic* **:** something queer or absurd
**qu·raish** *or* **qu·raysh** *or* **ko·reish** \kəˈrīsh\ *n, pl* **quraish** *or* **quraishes** *or* **quraysh** *or* **qurayshes** *or* **koreish** *or* **koreishes** *usu cap* [Ar *Quraish*] **1 :** an Arab people of which Muhammad was a member and which from the 5th century was distinguished by a religious preeminence associated with its hereditary provision of the pre-Islamic custodians of the Kaaba at Mecca **2 :** a member of the Quraish people
**qu·raish·ite** *or* **qu·raysh·ite** *also* **ko·reish·ite** \-ī,shīt\ *n* -s *usu cap* **:** a member of the Quraish people
**qur'an** *or* **quran** *usu cap, var of* KORAN
**qursh** \ˈku̇(ə)rsh\ *or* **qu·rush** \ˈku̇rəsh\ *n* -ES [Ar *qirsh* (pl. *qurūsh*)] **1 :** a monetary unit of Saudi Arabia equal to 1/20 riyal — see MONEY table **2 :** a coin representing one qursh
**qutb** \ˈku̇d·əb\ *n* -s [Ar *quṭb*] *usu cap* **:** an Islamic saint who has attained the highest degree of sanctity and has become within some areas of Islamic mysticism responsible for the invisible government of the world
**QV** *in sense 2* ˈkyüˈvē *or* ˈ(h)wichˈsē\ *abbr, often not cap* **1** [L *quantum vis*] as much as you will **2** [L *quod vide*] which see
**q–value** \ˈ=,=(ˌ)=\ *n, usu cap Q* **:** ²Q
**q wedge** *n* -s *usu cap Q* **:** QUARTZ WEDGE
**qy** *abbr* query
**qyrghyz** *usu cap, var of* KIRGHIZ
**qz** *abbr* quartz

r r
R
r R

**¹r** \'är, 'ä\ *n, pl* **r's** *or* **rs** \'ärz, 'äz\ *often cap, often attrib* **1 a :** the 18th letter of the English alphabet **b :** an instance of this letter printed, written, or otherwise represented **c :** a speech counterpart of orthographic *r* (as *r* in *run, fry, arid, far-off,* Spanish *para, rey,* French *rire,* or German *rohr*) **2 :** a printer's type, a stamp, or some other instrument for reproducing the letter *r* **3 :** someone or something arbitrarily or conveniently designated *r* esp. as the 17th or when j is used for the 10th the 18th in order or class **4 :** something having the shape of the letter R **5** *cap* **:** one of the three R's ⟨controversy over the first *R*⟩

**²r** *abbr, often cap* **1** rabbi **2** racemic **3** radical **4** radio **5** radius **6** railroad; railway **7** rain **8** range **9** rank **10** rare; rarity **11** ratio **12** real **13** rear **14** Reaumur **15** received **16** recipe **17** reconnaissance **18** recto **19** rector **20** red; reddish **21** refraction **22** refrigerator **23** [L] regina **24** registered **25** regulating **26** reigned **27** republic; republican **28** reserves **29** reside; residence; resident **30** resistance; resistor **31** respiration **32** respond; response **33** [F *retarder*] slow **34** retired **35** retree **36** returning **37** [L] rex **38** rifle **39** right **40** ring **41** riser **42** riss **43** river **44** road **45** rod **46** roentgen **47** roman **48** rood **49** rook **50** rotor **51** rough **52** route **53** royal **54** rubber **55** ruble **56** rule **57** run **58** runic **59** rupee

**³r** *symbol* **1** correlation coefficient **2** *cap* gas constant **3** *cap* radical — used esp. of a univalent hydrocarbon radical (as alkyl); compare GENERAL FORMULA **4** *cap* recipe — often ℞ **5** *cap* registered trademark — often enclosed in a circle **6** *cap* Reynold's number **7** *cap* Rydberg constant **8 a** *cap* a relation in a logical or mathematical proposition **b** a proposition in a logical operation

**RA** *abbr* **1** radioactive **2** rate of application **3** rear admiral **4** reduction of area **5** refer to acceptor **6** regular army **7** [L *reverendus admodum*] very reverend **8** right ascension

**Ra** *symbol* radium

**¹raad** \'räd\ *n, pl* **ra·den** \-dᵊn\ [D, lit., counsel, council; akin to OE *rǣd* advice, counsel, council — more at READ] **:** a legislative assembly in one of the Boer republics of So. Africa before the establishment of British administration — compare HEEMRAAD, VOLKSRAAD

**²ra·ad** \rə'äd, 'räd\ *n* -s [Ar *ra''ād,* lit., threatener, striker] **:** ELECTRIC CATFISH

**raad·zaal** \'räd,zäl\ *n, pl* **raad·za·len** \-lən\ [D *raad* + *zaal* hall, fr. MD *sale* — more at SALOON] **:** the assembly hall of a raad ⟨left the ~ in a rage —Manfred Nathan⟩

**raan** \'rän\ *n* -s [origin unknown] *chiefly Scot* **:** BROWN HEART 2b

**rab** \'rab\ *n* -s [F *rabot*] **:** a beater for mixing hair with mortar

**ra·ban·na** \rə'banə\ *n* -s [Malagasy *rebana*] **:** a coarse matting handwoven from raffia fibers in Madagascar

**¹ra·bat** \'rabē, rə'bat\ *n* -s [MF, turndown collar, rabat, fr. *rabattre* to turn back down, to reduce — more at REBATE] **:** a short cloth breast piece fitted to a Roman collar and worn chiefly by Roman Catholic and Anglican clergymen — called also *rabbi*

rabat

**²rab·at** \'rabət\ *n* -s [F, fr. MF *rabattre* to reduce] **:** a polishing material made from imperfectly fired potter's clay

**³ra·bat** \rə'bät\ *adj, usu cap* [fr. *Rabat,* capital of Morocco] **:** of or from Rabat, the capital of Morocco **:** of the kind or style prevalent in Rabat

**ra·ba·to** \rə'bä(,)d·(,)ō, -bā|, |(,)tō\ *n* -s [modif. of MF *rabat* — more at RABAT] **1 :** a wide lace-edged collar of the early 17th century worn turned down to lie across the shoulders or stiffened to stand high at the back and often open in front **2 :** a stiff support (as of wire) for a ruff or standing collar of the early 17th century

**rabb** *abbr* rabbinic

**rab·ban** \'rabən, rə'bän\ *n, pl* **rabba·nim** \rə'bänəm, ,räbə'nēm\ [Heb *rabbān,* fr. Aram] **:** TEACHER, MASTER — used as a Jewish title of honor higher than *rabbi* and given to heads of the Sanhedrin

**¹rab·bet** \'rabət, *usu* -əd·+V\ *also* **re·bate** \(')rē¦bāt, 'rabət, *usu* -d·+V\ *n* -s [ME *rabet,* fr. MF *rabat* act of beating down, fr. OF *rabattre* to beat down, reduce — more at REBATE] **1 a :** a channel, groove, or recess cut out of the edge or face of any body; *esp* **:** one intended to receive another member (as a panel) so as to break or cover the joint or more easily to hold the members in place **b :** strips of material joined to the trim of a structure or to a member received by the structure (as to serve as a stop for a door or to make dustproof) **2 a :** RABBET JOINT **b :** RABBET PLANE

**²rabbet** \"\ *vb* -ED/-ING/-S [ME *rabeten,* fr. *rabet,* n.] *vt* **1 :** to cut a rabbet in **:** furnish with a rabbet **2 :** to unite the edges of (as boards) in a rabbet joint ~ *vi* **:** to be joined by means of a rabbet

**rabbeted lock** *n* [fr. past part. of ²*rabbet*] **:** a lock whose front conforms to a rabbet on the edge of a door

**rab·bet·er** \-bəd·ə(r)\ *n* -s [²*rabbet* + *-er*] **:** one that rabbets; *esp* **:** an operator of a sticker for grooving wooden door or window parts for the inset of glass or panels

**rabbet joint** *n* [¹*rabbet*] **:** a joint formed by fitting together rabbeted boards or timbers — see MITER JOINT illustration

**rabbet plane** *n* **:** an openside plane with the plane iron extending to the outer edge of the open side to permit planing of sharp corners and grooves

rabbet joint

**¹rab·bi** \'ra,bī\ *n* -s [LL, fr. Gk *rhabbi,* fr. Heb *rabbī* my master, fr. *rabh* great one, master + *-ī* my] **1 :** MASTER, TEACHER — used by Jews as a term of address ⟨they said to him, "*Rabbi,* when did you come here"—Jn 6:25 (RSV)⟩ **2 a :** a Jew qualified by study of the Jewish civil and religious law forming esp. the halakah to expound and apply it (as by deciding legal questions on request or filling an administrative or judicial office) ⟨naturally the ~s or their disciples who were members of the congregation or . . . visitors were preferred as preachers because of their greater fitness —G.F.Moore⟩ **b** *often cap* **:** one of the scholars who developed the Talmudic basis of orthodox Judaism during the first centuries of the Christian era — see AMORA, SABORA, TANNA; compare SCRIBE **3 :** a Jew of modern times trained and ordained by another rabbi or group of rabbis (as the faculty of a theological school) for professional religious leadership; *specif* **:** one acting as the official leader of a Jewish congregation and performing various duties (as preaching, officiating at weddings and funerals)

**²rab·bi** \'rabē\ *n* -s [alter. of ¹*rabat*] **:** ¹RABAT

**rab·bin** \'rabən\ *n* -s [F, perh. fr. Aram *rabbīn,* pl. of *rab* master; akin to Heb *rabh* master] **:** RABBI 2

**rab·bin·ate** \'rabənət, -bə,nāt\ *n* -s [*rabbin* + *-ate*] **1 :** the office or tenure of office of a rabbi ⟨studying for the ~⟩ ⟨during his ~⟩ **2 :** a group of rabbis ⟨the Reform ~⟩ ⟨the American ~⟩

**¹rab·bin·ic** \rə'binik, ra'-, -nēk\ *or* **rab·bin·i·cal** \-nəkəl, -nēk-\ *adj* [*rabbin* + *-ic, -ical*] **1 a :** of or relating to rabbis or their writings ⟨the Catholic interracial council and the *rabbinical* association have issued statements —*Christian Century*⟩ **b** *usu cap* **:** of or relating to the rabbis of the Talmudic periods ⟨the *Rabbinic* period⟩ ⟨*Rabbinic* Judaism⟩ **2 :** characterized by preoccupation with minute analysis or hypothetical casuistry ⟨the textual criticism . . . concentrates its *Rabbinical* attention on details of prosody and grammar that have no value and no meaning in themselves —*Times Lit. Supp.*⟩ **3 :** of or preparing for the rabbinate ⟨train rabbis and *rabbinical* students in psychiatry —*Current Biog.*⟩ **4 :** comprising or belonging to any of several sets of Hebrew characters simpler than the square Hebrew letters ⟨commentaries printed in ~ type⟩ — **rab·bin·i·cal·ly** \-nək(ə)lē, -nēk-, -li\ *adv*

**²rabbinic** \"\ *n* -s *usu cap* **:** RABBINIC HEBREW

**rabbinical literature** *n* **:** the literature of Hebrew theology and philosophy including the Talmud and its exegesis

**rabbinic hebrew** *n, usu cap R&H* **:** Hebrew as used by the rabbis particularly in the medieval period

**rab·bin·ics** \-ks\ *n pl but sing or pl in constr, sometimes cap* [*rabbin* + *-ics*] **:** the study of rabbinical literature

**rab·bin·ism** \'rabə,nizəm\ *n* -s [*rabbin* + *-ism*] **1 :** a rabbinic expression or phraseology **:** a peculiarity of the language of the rabbis **2 :** the teachings and traditions of the rabbis **3 :** the quality or state of being rabbinic in analysis or casuistry

**rab·bin·ite** \'rabə,nīt\ *or* **rab·bin·ist** \-ənəst\ *or* **rab·ban·ite** \-ə,nīt\ *or* **rab·ban·ist** \-ənəst\ *n* -s *usu cap* [*rabbin* or *rabban* + *-ite* or *-ist*] **:** a Jew adhering to the Talmud and the traditions of the rabbis in opposition to the Karaites — **rab·bin·it·ic** \¦rabə¦nid·ik\ *or* **rab·bin·is·tic** \-nistik\ *adj, usu cap*

**¹rab·bit** \'rabət, *usu* -əd·+V\ *n* -s *see sense 1, often attrib* [ME *rabet,* prob. fr. Walloon *robett, robete,* fr. MD *robbe* rabbit + Walloon *-ett, -ete* -et] **1** *pl also* **rabbit a :** a small grayish brown mammal (*Oryctolagus cuniculus*) that differs from the related hares in its burrowing habits and in having the young born naked and helpless, is native to southern Europe and northern Africa but has been introduced into various other regions where it is often a pest because of its rapid reproduction, and has developed under domestication many varieties differing from the wild form in size, conformation, and coloring and variously adapted to the production of meat and fur or for pet and show stock **b :** any of various hares — often used in combination ⟨jack*rabbit*⟩ **c :** the fur of the rabbit often processed and dyed to imitate other furs **2** *Brit* **:** a weak player (as in tennis); *specif* **:** a cricketer who is not a good batsman **3 :** WELSH RABBIT **4 :** BROCCOLI BROWN **5 a :** a figure of a rabbit sped mechanically along the edge of a dog track as an object of pursuit **b :** a small container usu. moved pneumatically for transferring radioactive samples in an atomic-energy plant or laboratory

**²rabbit** \"\ *vi* -ED/-ING/-S **:** to hunt rabbits

**³rabbit** \"\ *vt* -ED/-ING/-S [perh. alter. of ³*rat*] **:** CONFOUND, DRAT — used as an expletive

**rabbit ball** *n* **:** a baseball held to be lively

**rabbit bandicoot** *n* **:** a bandicoot of the genus *Thylacomys; esp* **:** a long-eared bandicoot (*T. lagotis*)

**rab·bit·berry** \'rabət- — *see* BERRY\ *n* [*rabbit* + *berry*] **:** BUFFALO BERRY

**rabbit brush** *also* **rabbit bush** *n* **1 :** any of various plants of the genus *Chrysothamnus; esp* **:** a common shrub (*C. graveolens*) of western No. America that covers vast areas affording a retreat for jackrabbits **2 :** RABBITWEED

**rabbit cat** *n* **1 a :** ABYSSINIAN CAT **b :** MANX CAT **2 :** a reputed hybrid between cat and rabbit

**rabbit–ear** \'==,=\ *n* **1 :** TOADFLAX **2** *also* **rabbit ears cactus :** a cactus (*Opuntia microdasys*) with erect much branched flat branches covered with prominent bristles

**rabbit–ear faucet** *n* **:** a self-closing faucet opened by squeezing together two small handles

**rabbit ear mite** *n* **:** a mite that is a variety of the scab mite and attacks the ear of rabbits

**rabbit ears** *n pl but sing in constr* **:** a condition in a sports player of sensitive awareness to criticism

**rab·bit·er** \'rabəd·ə(r)\ *n* -s [²*rabbit* + *-er*] **:** one that rabbits; *specif* **:** one who traps or destroys rabbits as a means of livelihood ⟨the official ~ of an Australian sheep station⟩

**rabbiteye** \'==,=\ *or* **rabbiteye blueberry** *n* [*rabbit* + *eye*] **:** a blueberry (*Vaccinium ashei*) native to the southeastern U.S. and grown commercially esp. for the canning industry

**rabbit fever** *n* **:** TULAREMIA

rabbit-ear faucet

**rabbitfish** \'==,=\ *n* [*rabbit* + *fish;* fr. the rabbitlike nose] **1 :** a chimaera (*Chimaera monstrosa*) having a long tail and occurring in deep waters of the Atlantic ocean **2 a :** GLOBEFISH **b :** a slender elongated steel-blue marine food fish (*Promethichthys prometheus*) related to the escolar and widely distributed in warm regions **c** *southern Africa* **:** any of several small slimy-skinned compressed fishes of the genus *Siganus* — compare SIGANIDAE

**rabbit flea** *n* **:** any of several fleas (esp. *Hoplopsyllus affinis*) that attack rabbits

**rabbit flower** *n* **1 :** TOADFLAX **2 :** FOXGLOVE 1

**rabbit–foot** \'==,=\ *or* **rabbit's foot** *n* **:** the hind foot of a rabbit carried as a good-luck piece

**rabbit–foot clover** *also* **rabbit foot** *n* **:** a European clover (*Trifolium arvense*) naturalized in the U. S. having soft and hairy flower heads that resemble rabbits' paws — called also *old-field clover*

**rabbit–foot grass** *or* **rabbit's foot** *n* **:** an Old World annual weedy grass (*Polypogon monspeliensis*) common in California and having bristly greenish yellow spikes

**rabbit–hunting** \'==,==\ *n* **:** examination of undealt cards by a poker player who has dropped to see what he would have received if he had stayed in

**rabbitlike** \'==,=\ *adj* [*rabbit* + *like*] **:** resembling a rabbit or that of a rabbit ⟨~ ears⟩

**rabbit louse** *n* **:** a common louse (*Haemodipsus ventricosus*) that infests rabbits and hares in Europe and No. America and is one of the carriers of tularemia

**rabbit–meat** \'==,=\ *n* **:** RED ARCHANGEL

**rabbit moth** *n* **:** a moth (*Megalopyge opercularis*) of the southern Atlantic states the larva of which feeds on the orange and other trees and bears stinging spines

**rabbit–mouthed** \¦==¦=\ *also* **rabbitmouth** \'==,=\ *adj* **:** HARELIPPED

**rabbit pea** *also* **rabbit's pea** *n* **:** CATGUT 3

**¹rabbit punch** *n* [fr. the manner in which a rabbit is stunned prior to being killed and butchered] **:** a short chopping blow delivered to the back of the neck or the base of the skull with the edge of the hand opposite the thumb

**²rabbit punch** *vt* **:** to strike with a rabbit punch

**rabbit rat** *n* **1 :** a small Australian rodent (*Conilurus albipes*) **2 :** RABBIT BANDICOOT

**rab·bit·ry** \'rabətrē\ *n* -ES [*rabbit* + *-ry*] **:** a place where domestic rabbits are kept; *also* **:** a rabbit-raising enterprise

**rabbits** *pl of* RABBIT, *pres 3d sing of* RABBIT

**rabbit's–ear** \'==,=\ *n, pl* **rabbit's–ears :** HARE'S-EAR 1

**rabbit's–foot fern** *n* **:** SERPENT FERN

**rabbit's–mouth** \'==,=\ *n, pl* **rabbit's–mouths :** SNAPDRAGON

**rabbit squirrel** *n* **:** MOUNTAIN VIZCACHA

**rabbit's–root** \'==,=\ *n, pl* **rabbit's–roots :** WILD SARSAPARILLA 1

**rabbit stick** *n* **:** a flat curved club resembling a boomerang and used by the Hopi Indians in hunting small game

**rabbit syphilis** *n* **:** a venereal disease of rabbits that is caused by a spirochete (*Treponema cuniculi*) resembling that of human syphilis but infective only for the rabbit and is marked by superficial nodule formation and ulceration with edematous swelling of surrounding tissues esp. about the external genitalia — called also *vent disease*

**rabbit–tail grass** *n* **:** HARE'S-TAIL GRASS

**rabbit thorn** *n* **:** a rough thorny shrub (*Lycium pallidum*) of the desert regions of the southwestern U.S. having numerous zigzag branches, bell shaped white or lavender flowers, and globose greenish fruit

**rabbit tick** *n* **:** a tick (*Haemaphysalis leporis-palustris*) common throughout America and living chiefly on rabbits and birds

**rabbit tobacco** *n, Midland* **:** a balsamweed (*Gnaphalium obtusifolium*) sometimes used for smoking

**rabbit vine** *n* **:** GROUNDNUT 2a

**rabbit warren** *n* **:** WARREN 3

**rabbitweed** \'==,=\ *n* [*rabbit* + *weed*] **:** a stiff woody herb (*Gutierrezia sarothrae*) of the central and southwestern U.S. with paniculate heads of small yellow flowers

**rabbitwood** \'==,=\ *n* [*rabbit* + *wood*] **:** a shrub (*Pyrularia pubera*) that is parasitic on the roots of the hemlock and has greenish racemose flowers and pulpy drupaceous fruits — see BUFFALO NUT

**rab·bity** \'rabəd·ē\ *adj* [*rabbit* + *-y*] **1 :** overrun with rabbits ⟨a ~ region⟩ **2 :** resembling (as in appearance) a rabbit or that of a rabbit ⟨~ teeth⟩ **3 :** TIMID, SHY ⟨a ~ little clerk⟩

**¹rab·ble** \'rabəl\ *n* -s [ME *rabel;* perh. akin to ⁴*rabble*] **1 :** a pack, string, or swarm of animals or insects ⟨great ~s of rats roamed the streets —Elizabeth Enright⟩ **2 a** *dial chiefly Eng* **:** a confused or meaningless string of words **:** RIGMAROLE **b :** a heterogeneous, disorganized, or confused collection of things ⟨giant trees under whose dense canopy the alien and tangled ~ of the jungle does not thrive —P.B.Sears⟩ **3 a :** a disorganized or disorderly crowd of people ⟨a mere ~ of field hands pretending to be soldiers —Kenneth Roberts⟩ **:** MOB ⟨besieged by a ~ of small children —Sacheverell Sitwell⟩ **b :** a group, class, or body regarded with contempt ⟨a ~ of nobility . . . conspires to mount a gruesome charade —*Time*⟩ **c :** the lowest class of people ⟨in the Civil War, the ~ made common cause with the . . . nobility against the middle classes —Roy Lewis & Angus Maude⟩ **:** persons of the lowest class ⟨the London ~, chimney sweepers, watermen, costermongers, thieves —E.G.Johnson⟩

**²rabble** \"\ *adj* **1 :** of, relating to, or forming a rabble ⟨those were the enemy, a ~ crew —S.L.Gwynn⟩ **2 :** resembling or suited to a rabble ⟨to burn the jails . . . was a good ~ trick —Samuel Johnson⟩

**³rabble** \"\ *vt* **rabbled; rabbled; rabbling** \-b(ə)liŋ\ **rabbles 1 :** to insult or assault by a mob **:** MOB **2 :** to mob and drive out ⟨members of the Scottish Episcopalian clergy were often ~*ed* during the English Revolution⟩

**⁴rabble** \"\ *vb* -ED/-ING/-S [ME *rablen;* akin to D *rabbelen* to chatter, rattle, LG *rabbeln*] *dial chiefly Brit* **:** BABBLE

**⁵rabble** \"\ *n* -s [F *râble* fire shovel, fr. MF *roable,* fr. ML *rotabulum,* fr. L *rutabulum,* fr. *rutus,* past part. of *ruere* to dig up, rake up — more at RUG] **1** *obs* **:** a charcoal burner's shovel **2 a :** an iron bar with the end bent for use like a rake used in puddling iron **b :** any similar device (as a rotating arm with a scraper) for skimming the bath in a melting or refining furnace or for stirring the ore in a roasting furnace by hand or mechanically

rabbles 2b

**⁶rabble** \"\ *vt* -ED/-ING/-S **:** to stir, skim, or gather with a rabble

**rab·ble·ment** \-lmənt\ *n* -s [¹*rabble* + *-ment*] **1 :** RABBLE **2 :** DISTURBANCE, TUMULT

**¹rab·bler** \'rab(ə)lə(r)\ *n* -s [³*rabble* + *-er*] **:** one that rabbles another or is part of a rabble

**²rabbler** \"\ *n* -s [⁶*rabble* + *-er*] **1 :** a workman who uses a rabble **2 :** an instrument for rabbling

**rabble–rouse** \'==,=\ *vi* [back-formation fr. *rabble-rouser*] **:** to stir up public sentiment by emotionalism **:** AGITATE ⟨ashamed of indignation, ashamed to *rabble-rouse* —T.J.Haas⟩

**rabble–rouser** \'==,==\ *n* [¹*rabble*] **:** one who stirs up the masses of the people (as to hatred or violence) **:** DEMAGOGUE

**rab·bo·ni** \ra'bō,nī, -ōnē\ *n* [Aram *rabbānī* my master, teacher, fr. *rabbān* master + *-ī* my; akin to Heb *rabh* master] **:** MASTER, TEACHER — used as a Jewish title of respect applied esp. to spiritual instructors and learned persons

**rab·e·lai·si·an** \¦rabə¦lāzēən, -zhən\ *adj, usu cap* [François *Rabelais* †1553 French humorist + E *-ian*] **1 :** of, relating to, or characteristic of Rabelais or his works **2 :** marked by or manifesting a gross robust humor, an extravagance of caricature, or a bold naturalism similar to that distinguishing the satire of Rabelais

**rab·fak** *or* **rab·fac** \'rab,fak\ *n* -s [Russ *rabfak,* fr. *rabochiĭ fakul'tet,* fr. *rabochiĭ* of labor (fr. *rabota* labor, work) + *fakul'tet* faculty, college, fr. G *fakultät,* fr. ML *facultat-, facultas;* akin to OHG *arbeit, arabeit* need, work, Goth *arbaiths* distress, need, L *orbus* bereft — more at ORPHAN, FACULTY] **:** a Soviet school giving preliminary university training to workers

**¹ra·bi** \'rəbē\ *n* -s *usu cap* [Ar *rabī'* spring] **:** one of two months called Rabi I and Rabi II of the Muhammadan year — see MONTH table

**²rabi** \"\ *adj* [Urdu *rabī* spring crop, fr. Ar *rabī'* spring] **:** of, relating to, or constituting India's spring and major crop that includes wheat, barley, millet, peas, and mustard and is planted in autumn — compare KHARIF

**rab·ic** \'rabik\ *adj* [ISV *rabies* + *-ic*] **:** of or relating to rabies ⟨~ virus⟩ ⟨~ symptoms⟩

**rab·id** \'rabəd\ *adj* [L *rabidus* raving, mad, fr. *rabere* to rave — more at RAGE] **1 a :** extremely violent **:** FURIOUS, RAGING ⟨was made . . . ~ by the gout —Charles Dickens⟩ **:** VIRULENT ⟨a country . . . that may again be tempted by ~ nationalism —*New Republic*⟩ **b :** having some feeling, interest, or view in a violent degree **:** going to extreme or unreasonable lengths in expressing or pursuing a feeling or opinion ⟨a ~ baseball fan⟩ ⟨~ on the subject of capital punishment⟩ ⟨~ for their candidate⟩ ⟨~ in his hatred of his rival⟩ **2 :** affected with rabies ⟨a ~ fox⟩ — **ra·bid·i·ty** \rə'bidəd·ē\ *n* -ES — **rab·id·ly** *adv* — **rab·id·ness** *n* -ES

**ra·bies** \'rā|bēz *sometimes* 'ra| *or* |,b-\ *n, pl* **rabies** [NL, fr. L, rage, madness, fr. *rabere* to rave] **:** an acute virus disease of warm-blooded animals that attacks chiefly the nervous system, is uniformly fatal when untreated, and is transmitted with infected saliva usu. through the bite of a rabid animal — see DUMB RABIES, FURIOUS RABIES, PASTEUR TREATMENT

**ra·bi·form** \'rābə,fórm\ *adj* [NL *rabies* + E *-form*] **:** resembling or characteristic of rabies ⟨~ symptoms⟩

**rab·i·net** \'rabə,net\ *n* -s [alter. of *robinet*] **:** a small piece of ordnance used in the 16th, 17th, and 18th centuries

**rabious** *adj* [L *rabiosus,* fr. *rabies* + *-osus* -ous] *obs* **:** FIERCE, RABID

**ra·bi·ru·bia** \,räbə'rübēə\ *n* -s [AmerSp *rabirrubia,* fr. Sp *rabo* tail (fr. L *rapum* turnip, knob formed by a tree root) + *rubia,* fem. of *rubio* yellow, fr. L *rubr-, ruber* red — more at RAPE, RED] **:** YELLOWTAIL e

**rabs** *pl of* RAB

**rab·u·lis·tic** \¦rabyə¦listik\ *adj* [L *rabula* brawling advocate (prob. of Etruscan origin) + E *-istic*] **:** characterized by railing or pettifoggery

**raccommode** *vt* -ED/-ING/-S [F *raccommoder,* fr. *re-* + *accommoder* to adapt, fr. L *accommodare* — more at ACCOMMODATE] *obs* **:** to set right

**rac·coon** *also* **ra·coon** \(')ra¦kun *sometimes* rə'-\ *n, pl* **raccoon** *or* **raccoons** *also* **racoon** *or* **racoons** [*ärähkun* (in some Algonquian language of Virginia), fr. *ärähkuněm* he scratches with his hands] **1 a :** a carnivorous nocturnal mammal (*Procyon lotor*) related to but much smaller than the bear that inhabits most of No. America, lives largely in trees, and is chiefly gray with black and white facial markings, a bushy ringed tail, and coarse fur much used in furriery **b :** CRAB-EATING RACCOON **2 :** any of various animals somewhat similar to or related to the raccoon: as **a :** CACOMISTLE **b :** PANDA

**rac·coon·berry** \(')=¦=- — *see* BERRY\ *n* [*raccoon* + *berry*] **:** MAYAPPLE 2

**raccoon dog** *n* **:** a small short-muzzled canid (*Nyctereutes procyonides*) having dark facial markings like those of the raccoon, short legs, and a short bushy tail and being widely distributed in eastern Asia and Japan and reputedly bred as a furbearer in Russia

**raccoon family** *n* **:** PROCYONIDAE

**raccoon fox** *n* **:** CACOMISTLE

**raccoon grape** *n* **1 :** FOX GRAPE **2 :** a climbing or erect shrub (*Ampelopsis cordata*) chiefly of the southeastern U. S.

**raccoon oyster** *n* **:** COON OYSTER

**raccoon perch** *n* **:** YELLOW PERCH

**rac·croc stitch** \ra'krō+\ *n* [F *raccrocher* to hook up again, fr. *re-* + *accrocher* to hook up, attach, get hold of, fr. MF *acrochier* — more at ACCROACH] **:** an invisible stitch for joining lace or net

**¹race** \'rās\ *n* -s [ME *ras, rase,* fr. ON *rās;* akin to OE *rǣs* rush, running leap, MLG *rās* strong current, MHG *rasen* to storm, rage, L *rorarii* skirmishers, Gk *erōē* rush, impetus] **1** *chiefly Scot* **:** the act of rushing onward **:** RUN **2 a :** a strong or rapid current of water that flows through a narrow channel **b :** a heavy or choppy sea; *esp* **:** one produced by the meeting of two tides **c :** a watercourse (as a brook or run) used or made for an industrial purpose (as for mining or for turning the waterwheel of a mill) **d :** the current flowing in such a course **3 a :** a set course (as of the sun) or duration of time : PERIOD **b :** the course of life : CAREER **4 a :** a running in competition : a contest of speed (as in running, riding, sailing) **b races** *pl* **:** a meeting for contests in the running esp. of horses ⟨attended the ~s⟩ — compare HANDICAP, PURSE RACE, STAKE RACE, SWEEPSTAKE **c :** a contest involving progress toward a goal (as election to public office or a winning total of games in a season's play) ⟨three-cornered ~ for governor⟩ ⟨finished second in the professional hockey league ~⟩ **5 :** a fenced lane or passageway; *specif, Austral* **:** a passageway in a sheep drafting yard **6 :** a track or channel in which something rolls or slides: as **a :** a slide on the lay of a loom for a shuttle **b :** a groove for the balls in a ball bearing or rollers in a roller bearing — see ROLLER BEARING illustration **c :** a groove in a pulley in which a rope runs **7 :** SLIPSTREAM

**2race** \"\ *vb* -ED/-ING/-S *vi* **1 :** to run or engage in a race : compete in speed ⟨eight horses will ~ for the cup⟩ **2 :** to go, move, or run at top speed or out of control esp. through urgency, compulsion, or zest ⟨we'll move out . . . and send the rebels *racing* for safety —Kenneth Roberts⟩ ⟨his mind *raced* ahead to guess the full import of the message —Gordon Merrick⟩ **3 :** to run too fast under a diminished load ⟨the propeller *raced* wildly as the stern rose⟩ ~ *vt* **1 :** to engage in a race with : contest with in speed ⟨offered to ~ him to the big tree⟩ **2 a :** to enter in a race : cause to contend in a race ⟨~ a maiden horse against a winner⟩ **b :** to race against ⟨*racing* the clock⟩ **c :** to drive at high speed ⟨*raced* his car across the desert⟩ **d :** transport or propel at maximum speed and haste ⟨fast-sailing ships . . . built expressly to ~ tea from China —*Brit. Bk. Centre*⟩ **3 :** to speed (as an engine or motor) without a working load or in disengagement from the transmission **syn** see RUN

**3race** \"\ *vb* [ME *racen*, short for *aracen*, fr. ONF *aracier*, modif. (influenced by OF *a-* off, away — fr. L *ab*) of L *eradicare* to pluck out by the roots — more at OF, ERADICATE] *obs* **:** TEAR, PLUCK, SNATCH

**4race** \"\ *n, dial chiefly Eng* **:** PLUCK 2a

**5race** \"\ *vt* -ED/-ING/-S [ME *racen*, alter. of *rasen* to rase] **1 :** to cut, scratch, or score with a sharp point **2** *obs* **:** ERASE

**6race** \"\ *n* -S **:** a shallow cut : SCRATCH, SLASH

**7race** \"\ *n* -S [MF, generation, family, fr. It *razza*] **1 a** *obs* **:** GENERATION **b** *obs* **:** the act of breeding or producing offspring ⟨male he created thee, but thy consort female for ~ —John Milton⟩ **c :** a breeding stock of animals ⟨~ of mares⟩ **2 a :** the descendants of a common ancestor : a family, tribe, people, or nation belonging to the same stock ⟨the impoverished scion of a noble ~⟩ **b :** a class or kind of individuals with common characteristics, interests, appearance, or habits as if derived from a common ancestor ⟨the ~ of doctors⟩ ⟨the whole ~ of mankind —Shak.⟩ ⟨the Anglo-Saxon ~⟩ ⟨the Jewish ~⟩ **3 :** any of various infraspecific taxonomic groups: as **a :** MICROSPECIES **b :** SUBSPECIES **c :** a permanent or fixed variety **d :** BREED **e :** PHYSIOLOGIC RACE **f :** a division of mankind possessing traits that are transmissible by descent and sufficient to characterize it as a distinct human type ⟨Caucasian ~⟩ ⟨Mongoloid ~⟩ **4** *obs* **:** inherited temperament or disposition ⟨now I give my sensual ~ the rein —Shak.⟩ **5 a :** distinctive flavor, taste, or strength (as of wine) **:** the quality indicating origin or kind **b** *archaic* **:** RACINESS

**syn** RACE, NATION, and PEOPLE, even though in technical use they are commonly differentiated, are often used popularly and interchangeably to designate one of a number of great divisions of mankind, each made up of an aggregate of persons who are thought of, or think of themselves, as comprising a distinct unit. In technical discriminations, all more or less controversial and often lending themselves to great popular misunderstanding or misuse, RACE is anthropological and ethnological in force, usu. implying a distinct physical type with certain unchanging characteristics, as a particular color of skin or shape of skull ⟨the Caucasian *race*⟩ ⟨the Malay *race*⟩ ⟨the Ethiopian *race*⟩ although sometimes, and most controversially, other presumed common factors are chosen, as place of origin ⟨the Nordic *race*⟩ or common root language ⟨the Aryan *race*⟩. In popular use RACE can apply to any more or less clearly defined group thought of as a unit usu. because of a common or presumed common past ⟨the Anglo-Saxon *race*⟩ ⟨the Celtic *race*⟩ ⟨the Hebrew *race*⟩ NATION, primarily political in force, usu. designates the citizenry as a whole of a sovereign state and implies a certain homogeneity because of common laws, institutions, customs, or loyalty ⟨the British *nation*⟩ ⟨the French *nation*⟩ ⟨the house must have been built before this country was a *nation* —Allen Tate⟩ ⟨what is a *nation?* A group of human beings recognizing a common history and a common culture, yearning for a common destiny, assuming common habits, and generally attached to a specific piece of the earth's surface —David Bernstein⟩ Sometimes it is opposed to *state* ⟨a state is accidental; it can be made or unmade; but a *nation* is something real which can be neither made nor destroyed —J.R.Green⟩ and often not clearly distinguishable from RACE in comprising any large group crossing national boundaries and with something significantly in common ⟨the children of the world are one *nation*; the very old, another —Jan Struther⟩ ⟨for the two *nations* that alone inhabit the earth, the rich and the poor —Edith Sitwell⟩ ⟨the Gypsy *nation*⟩ PEOPLE, sometimes interchangeable with NATION though stressing a cultural or social rather than a national unity, can apply to a body of persons, as a whole or as individuals, who show a consciousness of solidarity or common characteristics not wholly comprised by RACE or NATION, suggesting a common culture or common interests or ideals and a sense of kinship ⟨the Mexican *people* —Virginia Prewett⟩ ⟨the British and American *peoples* —Sir Winston Churchill⟩ ⟨we, the *people* of the United States —*U. S. Constitution*⟩ ⟨we, the *peoples* of the United Nations —*U. N. Charter*⟩ ⟨a new government, which, for certain purposes, would make the people of the several states one *people* —R.B.Taney⟩ **syn** see in addition VARIETY

**8race** \"\ *n* -S [origin unknown] **:** an elongate white mark on the face of a horse or dog

**9race** \"\ *n* -S [MF *rais* root, fr. L *radic-, radix* — more at ROOT] **:** a root of ginger

**10race** \"\ *adj* [F *ras* shaven, flat, fr. L *rasus*, past part. of *radere* to scrape — more at RAT] *of a ship* **:** designed to lie low in the water

**raceabout** \'==,=\ *n* -S [*2race* + *about*] **1 :** a small sloop usu. having a keel and derived from the knockabout but having finer lines and carrying more sail **2 :** a roadster with body lines simulating those of a racing car

**race-baiter** \'=,==\ *n* **:** one who baits a racial group

**race-baiting** \'=,==\ *n* [*7race* + *baiting*] **:** the making of malicious attacks (as through taunts and insinuations) upon the members of a racial group

**race board** *n* **:** RACE 6a

**racecourse** \'=,=\ *n* [*1race* + *course*] **1 :** a course for racing; *esp* **:** a turf course for steeplechase or cross-country racing **2 :** RACEWAY 1

**raced** *past of* RACE

**race ginger** *n* [*9race*] **:** GINGERROOT

**race glass** *n* [*1race*] **:** a field glass for use at races

**racegoer** \'=,==\ *n* **:** one who goes regularly to horse races

**racehorse** \'=,=\ *n* [*1race* + *horse*] **1 :** a horse bred and trained for racing esp. under saddle — compare HARNESS HORSE, THOROUGHBRED **2 :** STEAMER DUCK

**racehorse grass** *n* **:** JOHNSON GRASS

**racehorse keno** *n* **:** a lottery game in which each player may select 10 numbers out of 80 and wins if his 10 numbers are among 20 numbers drawn at random

**race knife** *n* [*5race*] **:** a cutting tool with a blade hooked at the tip used for marking outlines on boards or metal

**raceline** \'=,=\ *n* [*1race* + *line*] **:** an artificial channel for conveying water

**rac·e·mase** \'rasə,mās\ *n* -S [*racemic* + *-ase*] **:** any of various enzymes that catalyze racemizations and occur esp. in bacteria ⟨alanine ~⟩

**rac·e·mate** \-āt\ *n* -S [ISV *racemic* + *-ate*] **1 :** a salt or ester of racemic acid **2 :** a racemic compound or mixture

**racemation** *n* -S [LL *racemation-, racematio*, fr. L *racematus* (past part. of *racemari* to glean, fr. *racemus* cluster of grapes) + *-ion-, -io* -ion] **1** *obs* **:** the gathering or gleaning of grapes **2** *obs* **:** CLUSTER

**ra·ceme** \rā'sēm, rə'-\ *n* -S [L *racemus* cluster of grapes or berries] **1 :** an inflorescence (as in the currant and lily-of-the-valley) in which the flowers are borne on stalks of about equal length along an elongated axis that continues to grow during flowering and open in succession from below — compare CYME, CORYMB; see INFLORESCENCE illustration **2 :** something (as a synaptic nerve ending) that resembles a racemose inflorescence

**ra·cemed** \-md\ *adj* [*raceme* + *-ed*] **:** bearing or forming a raceme

**race meeting** *n* [*1race*] *chiefly Brit* **:** a number of horse races held at a particular track on the same day or on several successive days

**race memory** *n* [*7race*] **:** the body of experiences, beliefs, and general recollections transmitted from one generation of mankind or of a race to another : racial tradition

**ra·ce·mic** \rā'sēmik, rə'-, -sem-, -mēk\ *adj* [F *racémique*, fr. L *racemus* + F *-ique* -ic] **1 :** relating to or derived from racemic acid **2 :** of, relating to, or constituting a compound or mixture that is composed of equal amounts of dextrorotatory and levorotatory forms of the same compound and hence is optically inactive toward polarized light — compare DL-, MES-

**racemic acid** *n* **:** optically inactive tartaric acid that consists of equal parts of *dextro-* and *levo-* tartaric acids into which it can be separated, is often found with *dextro*-tartaric acid in the juice of grapes, and is formed by oxidation of mannitol or dulcitol and in other ways

**rac·e·mif·er·ous** \,rasə,mif(ə)rəs\ *adj* [L *racemifer* bearing clusters, fr. *racemus* + *-fer* -ferous] **:** bearing racemes

**ra·ce·mi·form** \rā'sēmə,fȯrm\ *adj* [ISV *raceme* + *-iform*] **:** having the form of a raceme

**rac·e·mism** \'rasə,mizəm\ *n* -S [*racemic* + *-ism*] **:** the quality or state of being racemic

**race·mi·za·tion** \,rasəmə'zāshən; rā,sēm-, rə,s-\ *n* -S [*racemize* + *-ation*] **:** the action or process of changing from an optically active compound into a racemic compound or mixture — opposed to *resolution*

**rac·e·mize** \'rasə,mīz, rā'sē,-, rə'sē,-\ *vb* -ED/-ING/-S [ISV *racemic* + *-ize*] *vt* **:** to subject to racemization ~ *vi* **:** to undergo racemization

**rac·e·mose** \'rasə,mōs\ *adj* [L *racemosus* full of clusters, fr. *racemus* + *-osus* -ose] **1 :** relating to, occurring in the form of, or resembling a raceme ⟨a ~ inflorescence⟩ **2** *of a gland* **:** compound with freely branching ducts that end in acini so that the whole somewhat resembles a compact cluster of grapes ⟨the pancreas and salivary glands are ~ glands⟩ — **rac·e·mose·ly** *adv*

**rac·e·mous** \-səməs\ *adj* [L *racemosus*] **:** RACEMOSE — **rac·e·mous·ly** *adv*

**race of the propeller** [*1race*] **:** SLIPSTREAM

**rac·e·phed·rine** \,rasə'fedrən\ *n* [*racemic* + *ephedrine*] **:** synthetic racemic ephedrine

**race plate** *n* **1 :** RACE 6a **2 :** TRAVERSE CIRCLE

**race prejudice** *n* [*7race*] **:** prejudice against or hostility toward people of another race or color or of an alien culture

**race problem** *n* **:** a political or social problem that arises out of a mixture of or conflict between races in a country or region

**race psychology** *n* **1 :** FOLK PSYCHOLOGY **2 :** COMPARATIVE PSYCHOLOGY 2

**rac·er** \'rāsə(r)\ *n* -S [*2race* + *-er*] **1 :** one that races **:** something designed or adapted chiefly or solely for speed or used for racing **2 :** RACING CRAB **3 :** any of various snakes of the genera *Coluber* and *Mastigophis*: as **a :** BLACK RACER **b :** BLUE RACER **4 :** a poor, thin, or spent fish **5 :** a fast running part in a machine **6 a :** TRAVERSE CIRCLE **b :** a turntable to which the chassis of a coast artillery gun is secured and used in traversing the gun **7 :** RACING SKATE

**race riot** *n* [*7race*] **:** a riot animated by racial dissensions or hatreds; *specif* **:** such a conflict between whites and Negroes

**race rotation** *n* [*1race*] **:** the rotary motion given to the slipstream by the action of the propeller

**race runner** *n* **:** a No. American lizard (*Cnemidophorus sexlineatus*) noted for swiftness of movement — called also *sand lizard, striped lizard*

**races** *pl of* RACE, *pres 3d sing of* RACE

**race suicide** *n* [*7race*] **:** the gradual extinction of a people or racial strain through a tendency to restrict voluntarily the rate of reproduction

**racetrack** \'=,=\ *n* [*1race* + *track*] **:** a usu. oval course over which races are run; *esp* **:** a dirt track for flat or harness races

racetrack: diagram of a regulation mile track (R=radius)

**raceway** \'=,=\ *n* [*1race* + *way*] **1 a :** a canal for a current of water (as a millrace or a mining race) **b :** FISHWAY **2 :** a channel designed for loosely holding electrical wires or cables in buildings **3 :** RACE 6b **4 :** a track for harness racing

**race-wide** \'=;=\ *adj* [*7race* + *wide*] **:** extending or existing throughout a race

**rach** or **rache** \'rach\ *n, pl* **raches** [ME *racche, ratche*, fr. OE *ræcc*; akin to ON *rakki* dog] *dial chiefly Brit* **:** a dog that hunts by scent : HOUND

**ra·chel** \rə'shel\ *n* -S [after Mlle. *Rachel* (Élisa Félix) †1858 Fr. actress] **:** a tannish face powder with pink undertones

**rachet** *var of* RATCHET

**rachi-** or **rachio-** *also* **rhachi-** or **rhachio-** *comb form* [Gk *rhachi-*, fr. *rhachis* lower part of the back, spine, backbone; akin to Gk *rhachos* thorn hedge, MIr *fracc* needle, Lith *ražas* stubble, tine of a fork] **:** spine **:** spinal **:** spinal and ⟨*rachi*centesis⟩ ⟨*rachio*dont⟩ ⟨*rachio*meter⟩

**ra·chi·al** \'rākēəl\ *or* **ra·chid·i·al** \rə'kidēəl\ *adj* [*rachial* fr. *rachi-* + *-al*; *rachidial* fr. NL *rachid-, rachis* + E *-ial*] **:** RACHIDIAN

**ra·chi·a·nec·tes** \,rākēə'nek,tēz\ *syn of* RHACHIANECTES

**ra·chi·centesis** \,rākē+\ *n* [NL, fr. *rachi-* + *centesis*] **:** LUMBAR PUNCTURE

**rachides** *pl of* RACHIS

**-ra·chid·ia** \rə'kidēə\ *n comb form* -S [NL, fr. *rachid-, rachis* + *-ia*] **:** condition of the spine ⟨atelo*rachidia*⟩

**ra·chid·i·an** \-ēən\ *adj* [F *rachidien*, fr. NL *rachid-, rachis* + F *-ien* -ian] **:** of or relating to a rachis; *sometimes* **:** SPINAL ⟨~ nerves⟩

**ra·chi·form** \'rākə,fȯrm\ *adj* [*rachi-* + *-form*] **:** having the form of a rachis

**ra·chi·glos·sa** \,rākē'gläsə\ *n pl, cap* [NL, fr. *rachi-* + *-glossa*] **:** a division of Stenoglossa (order Pectinibranchia) comprising marine mostly carnivorous gastropods having typically a long retractile proboscis, a distinct siphon, and the radula with three or one longitudinal series of teeth of which each may bear many cusps and including many of the large ornamental shells (as the miter shells, murices, olive shells, volutes, and whelks) — **ra·chi·glos·sate** \'==;glä,sāt\ *adj or n*

**ra·chil·la** \rə'kilə\ *n, pl* **rachil·lae** \-i,lē\ [NL, dim. of *rachis*] **:** a small or secondary rachis; *specif* **:** the axis of a spikelet of a grass or sedge

**rachio-** — see RACHI-

**ra·chi·o·dont** \'rākēə,dänt\ *adj* [*rachi-* + *-odont*] **:** having gular teeth consisting of modified ventral vertebral spines ⟨~ egg-eating snake⟩

**ra·chi·om·e·ter** \,rākē'ämәd·ə(r)\ *n* [*rachi-* + *-meter*] **:** an instrument for measuring spinal curvatures

**ra·chi·on** \'rākēən\ *n* -S [NL, fr. Gk *rhachia* surf, rocky shore, reef, fr. *rhachis* spine, ridge — more at RACHI-] **:** the marginal line of a lake at which maximum wave action and undertow turmoil occur

**ra·chis** \'rākəs\ *n, pl* **rachises** \-səz\ *or* **rach·i·des** \'rakə,dēz, 'rāk-\ [NL *rachid-, rachis*, modif. of Gk *rhachi-, rhachis* — more at RACHI-] **1 :** VERTEBRAL COLUMN, SPINE **2 :** any of various axial structures: as **a** (1) **:** the elongated axis of an inflorescence (2) **:** the extension or prolongation of the petiole bearing the leaflets of a compound leaf **b** (1) **:** the distal part of the shaft of a feather that bears the web (2) **:** the central cord in the stem of a crinoid (3) **:** the median part of the radula of a mollusk that bears the central teeth (4) **:** a central cord of the ovary of nematodes (5) **:** the distal part of the shaft of a sea pen or similar organism

**ra·chis·chi·sis** \rə'kiskəsəs\ *n, pl* **rachischi·ses** \-kə,sēz\ [NL, fr. *rachi-* + *-schisis*] **:** cleft spine **:** congenital failure of union of the paired vertebral arches : SPINA BIFIDA

**ra·chit·ic** \rə'kid·ik, -it|, |ēk\ *adj* [NL *rachitis* + E *-ic*] **1 :** of, relating to, or affected by rickets **2 :** resembling or suggesting the condition of one suffering from rickets : RICKETY ⟨natives with over-valued ~ currencies —*Time*⟩ ⟨a tall, narrow-shouldered and ~ house in a little obscure square —Aldous Huxley⟩

**rachitic rosary** *n* [so called fr. its resemblance to a string of beads] **:** BEADING f

**ra·chi·tis** *also* **rha·chi·tis** \rə'kīd·əs, -ītəs\ *n, pl* **ra·chit·i·des** \-kid·ə,dēz\ [NL, fr. Gk *rhachitis* disease of the spine, fr. *rhachis* + *-itis*] **:** RICKETS

**rach·i·to·gen·ic** \,rakəd·ō;jenik\ *adj* [*rachit-* (fr. NL *rachitis*) + *-o-* + *-genic*] **:** leading or tending to the development of rickets ⟨a ~ diet⟩

**ra·chit·o·mi** \rə'kid·ə,mī\ [NL, pl. of *rachitomus* rhachitomous] *syn of* RHACHITOMI

**rachitomous** *var of* RHACHITOMOUS

**rachy·cen·tron** \,rakē'sen,trän\ *n, cap* [NL, irreg. fr. *rachi-* + Gk *kentron* sharp point — more at CENTER] **:** a genus (coextensive with the family Rachycentridae) of pelagic marine percoid fishes comprising solely the cobia

**ra·cial** \'rāshəl\ *adj* [*7race* + *-ial*] **1 :** of, relating to, or based on a race ⟨~ evolution⟩ ⟨~ traits⟩ ⟨~ group⟩ ⟨~ segregation⟩ **2 :** existing or occurring between races ⟨~ conflict⟩ ⟨~ differences⟩ — **ra·cial·ly** \-shəlē, -li\ *adv*

**ra·cial·ism** \-shə,lizəm\ *n* -S [*racial* + *-ism*] **1 :** racial prejudice or discrimination : race hatred **2 :** RACISM

**ra·cial·ist** \-ləst\ *n* -S [*racial* + *-ist*] **1 :** one animated by or practicing racialism **2 :** one who advocates or believes in racism

**ra·cial·is·tic** \,rāshə'listik, -tēk\ *adj* [*racial* + *-istic*] **:** of, relating to, or based on racialism ⟨~ hysteria⟩ ⟨~ vices⟩

**ra·ci·al·i·ty** \,rāshē'aləd·ē\ *n* -ES [*racial* + *-ity*] **:** racial quality

**ra·cial·iza·tion** \,rāshələ'zāshən\ *n* -S [*racial* + *-ization*] **:** the act or process of imbuing a person with a consciousness of race distinctions or of giving a racial character to something or making it serve racist ends

**ra·cial·ize** \'rāshə,līz\ *vt* -ED/-ING/-S [back-formation fr. *racialization*] **:** to subject to racialization ⟨to ~ science and art⟩

**racial unconscious** *n* **:** COLLECTIVE UNCONSCIOUS

**ra·ci·a·tion** \,rāshē'āshən\ *n* -S [irreg. (influenced by *speciation*) fr. *7race* + *-ation*] **:** differentiation of local infraspecific groups within a population through continued selection for ecologically useful variations under conditions of at least partial isolation — compare SPECIATION

**r acid** *n, usu cap R* **:** a crystalline sulfonic acid $HOC_{10}H_5(SO_3H)_2$ derived from beta naphthol and used as a dye intermediate; 2-naphthol-3,6-disulfonic acid

**racier** *comparative of* RACY

**raciest** *superlative of* RACY

**rac·i·ly** \'rāsəlē, -li\ *adv* [*1racy* + *-ly*] **:** in a racy manner **:** with raciness ⟨his work, which includes . . . beer and cider jugs and mugs . . . has a ~ native character, without any affectation —Charles Marriott⟩ ⟨~ vernacular in speech⟩

**rac·i·ness** \-sēnəs, -sin-\ *n* -ES [*1racy* + *-ness*] **:** the quality of being racy : EARTHINESS ⟨with a more polite, standardized speech a lot of the ~ has departed from the London streets —H.V.Morton⟩ ⟨an idiomatic ~ of speech, expressing a strong vitality —F.R.Leavis⟩

**1racing** *n* -S [fr. gerund of *2race*] **1 :** the sport or profession of engaging in or holding races **2 :** horse races as a sport or a business

**2racing** *adj* **:** relating to or used in racing ⟨~ boat⟩ ⟨~ clothes⟩ ⟨~ club⟩ ⟨~ swimming stroke⟩

**racing colors** *n pl* **:** the registered colors of a jockey's cap and jacket designating the horse's owner

**racing crab** *n* [fr. pres. part. of *2race*] **:** any of several swift-running crabs of the family Ocypodidae

**racing form** *n* [*2racing*] **:** an information sheet giving pertinent data about horse races including entries, post positions, jockeys, probable odds, and past records of horses

**racing glass** *n* **:** RACE GLASS

**racing iron** *n* [fr. gerund of *5race*] **:** an iron or a steel bar for racing grindstones

**racing plate** *n* [*2racing*] **:** a very light horseshoe used for racehorses

**racing-sheet** \'==,=\ *n* **:** RACING FORM

**racing skate** *n* **:** a skate with a long blade projecting beyond the toe and heel of the shoe and with a thin steel tube brazed to the blade for added strength — called also *racer*

racing skate

**ra·ci·ol·o·gy** \,rāsē'äləjē\ *n* -ES [irreg. fr. *race* + *-o-* + *logy*] **:** the study of human races

**rac·ism** \'rā,sizəm\ *n* -S [prob. fr. F *racisme*, fr. *race* + *-isme* -ism] **1 :** the assumption that psychocultural traits and capacities are determined by biological race and that races differ decisively from one another which is usu. coupled with a belief in the inherent superiority of a particular race and its right to domination over others **2 a :** a doctrine or political program based on the assumption of racism and designed to execute its principles **b :** a political or social system founded on racism **3 :** RACIALISM 1

**1rac·ist** \'rāsəst\ *n* -S [prob. fr. F *raciste*, fr. *race* + *-iste* -ist] **:** one who advocates or believes in racism

**2racist** \"\ *adj* **1 :** of, relating to, or based on racism ⟨~ ideas⟩ **2 :** advocating or practicing racism ⟨a ~ leader⟩

**1rack** \'rak\ *n* -S [ME *rac, rak*; prob. of Scand origin; akin to Norw & Sw dial. *rak* wreck, wreckage; akin to OE *wrecan* to drive — more at WREAK] **1 a** *obs* **:** shock of meeting : RUSH, CHARGE **b** *obs* **:** a sound as of a collision : CRASH **2 a :** a wind-driven mass of high often broken clouds **b** *obs* **:** a driving mist or fog

**2rack** \"\ *vi* -ED/-ING/-S **:** to fly or scud in high wind

**3rack** \"\ *n* -S [ME *rekke, racke*, prob. fr. MD *rec* framework; akin to OE *reccan* to stretch, OHG *recchen*, ON *rekja* to spread out, Goth *ufrakjan* to stretch out, Gk *oregein* — more at RIGHT] **1** *dial chiefly Eng* **:** a bar or a set of bars esp. for supporting a roasting spit **2 :** a framework for holding fodder for livestock usu. with upright partitions so placed as to leave room only for one animal's head between them **3 a :** an instrument of torture formerly much used in Europe and consisting of a frame having rollers at each end to which the limbs are fastened and between which the body is stretched **b :** a framework for stretching leather to a certain specified pull used for purposes of official measurement of the area and thickness of skins and hides **c :** an instrument for bending a crossbow **4 a :** a cause of anguish or pain or the resulting suffering ⟨the ~ of gout⟩ **b :** RACK RENT **c :** a straining or wrenching ⟨a tree twisted by the ~ of storms⟩ **5 :** a framework, stand, or grating on or in which articles are placed (as for keeping or for display) ⟨clothes ~⟩ ⟨cake ~⟩ ⟨bottle ~⟩: as **a :** a frame fitted to a wagon or truck for carrying hay, straw, grain, tobacco on the stalk, or other bulky loads **b :** a series of bins or compartments into which items may be sorted ⟨mail ~⟩ **c :** any compartmented container for holding type cases, galleys, forms, leads, or furniture **d :** a stationary inclined

rack 8a and pinion

frame or table on which ores are washed **6 :** a frame placed in a stream to stop the passage of fish and floating or suspended matter **7** *or* **rack block :** a piece or frame of wood having several sheaves through which the running rigging of a ship passes **8 a :** a bar with teeth on one face for gearing with those of a pinion, bevel wheel, or worm gear **b :** a notched bar used as a ratchet to engage with a pawl, click, or detent **c :** a sector-gear pivoted to contact a snail and regulate the number of hammer blows in a striking clock or repeater watch **9 :** a support with springs to offset vibration on which the camera and the subject are fastened in process photography; *also* **:** a support for holding several films or plates during processing **10 :** a pair of antlers **11 :** a wooden triangular frame used to set up the balls for the opening shot in pool games; *also* **:** the balls as set up when the triangle has been removed — **at rack and manger** *archaic* **:** in abundance **:** in an extravagant fashion ⟨living *at rack and manger* —Thomas Carlyle⟩ — **on the rack** *adv (or adj)* **:** under great mental or emotional stress **:** in acute anxiety or uncertainty — **to rack and manger** *archaic* **:** to waste and destruction **:** to wrack and ruin ⟨the moment my back is turned everything goes *to rack and manger* —Henry Fielding⟩

4**rack** \"\ *vb* -ED/-ING/-S [partly fr. ME *rakken*, prob. fr. MD *recken* to stretch (akin to OE *reccan* to stretch); partly fr. 3*rack*] *vt* **1 :** to torture on the rack **:** inflict pain or punishment by pulling or straining **2 a :** to afflict with torture, pain, or anguish comparable to that suffered on a rack ⟨her heart went out to this ~*ed* girl —Adria Langley⟩ ⟨~*ed* with jealousy⟩ **b :** to afflict and agitate very much with or as if with trouble, stress, anxiety, doubt, unpleasant emotion, or illness ⟨the Greco-Roman world had been ~*ed* by revolutions —A.J.Toynbee⟩ ⟨was obviously ~*ing* his brains as his answer . . . disclosed —Robert Grant †1940⟩ **3 a :** to stretch, strain, or extend violently **b :** to twist the meaning of **:** pervert the sense of **c :** to raise (rents) oppressively **d :** to harass or oppress with high rents, exactions, or extortions **4** *chiefly Brit* **a :** to supply a rack with feed for (as a horse) — used with *up* **b :** to fasten (an animal) in place at the rack **5 :** to work, stretch, or treat (material) on a rack ⟨~ leather⟩ ⟨~ rubber⟩ ⟨~ ore⟩ **6 :** to work by a rack and pinion or worm so as to extend or contract ⟨~ a camera⟩ **7 :** to seize (as parallel ropes of a tackle) together so as to prevent running through the block **8 :** to place (as pool balls) in a rack — often used with *up* ~ *vi* **1 a :** to become forced out of shape or out of plumb **b :** to sway together from side to side of their proper position relative to the keel — used of a ship's sides **2** *Scot* **:** to undergo straining or stretching **:** lengthen or give under tension **syn** see AFFLICT

5**rack** \"\ *vt* -ED/-ING/-S [ME *rakken* fr. OProv *arraca*, fr. *raca* stems and husks of grapes after pressing] **1 :** to draw off (as wine) from the lees or sediment into new casks — used often with *off* **2 :** to fill (trade casks) with ale or stout

6**rack** \"\ *vi* -ED/-ING/-S [prob. alter. of 1*rock*] *of a horse* **:** to use either gait called a rack

7**rack** \"\ *n* -S **:** either of two gaits of a horse: **a :** PACE 5b **b :** a fast showy usu. artificial four-beat gait in which the feet leave the ground in the same sequence as in the walk but faster and with higher action — called also *single-foot*

8**rack** \"\ *n* -S [perh. fr. 3*rack*] **1 a :** the neck and spine of a forequarter of veal, pork, or esp. mutton **b :** the rib section of a foresaddle of lamb used for chops and roasts — see HOTEL RACK; LAMB illustration **2 :** the side planking or side buffer of a ferry slip **3 :** RACKABONES

9**rack** \"\ *var of* WRACK

10**rack** \"\ *n* -S [by shortening] **:** ARRACK

11**rack** \"\ *n* -S [perh. alter. of 4*rake*] *dial* **:** the path or track made by a moving object or animal — **by rack of eye** *dial Eng* **:** by gauging with the eye alone ⟨working *by rack of eye*⟩

12**rack** \"\ *dial Brit var of* RECK

13**rack** \"\ *n* -S [origin unknown] **:** a nearly full-grown young rabbit; *also* **:** its skin

**rack·a·bones** \ˈrakə,bōnz\ *n pl but sing in constr* [alter. of *rack of bones*] **:** a very lean person or animal; *esp* **:** a lean horse

**rack·an** \ˈrakən\ *also* **reck·an** \ˈrekən\ *n* -S [ME *racand*, fr. OE *racente*; akin to OHG *rahchinza* chain, ON *rekendi*] **1** *obs* **:** CHAIN, FETTER **2** *dial chiefly Eng* **:** a hook for hanging pots over a fire

**rack-and-lever jack** \ˈ==ˈ==-\ *n* [3*rack*] **:** RATCHET JACK

**rack-and-pinion press** \ˈ==ˈ==-\ *n* **:** a punch press in which the pressure is applied to the slide by a rack-and-pinion mechanism

**rack-and-pinion railway** *n* **:** RACK RAILWAY

**rack and snail** *n* [3*rack*] **:** a mechanical arrangement in striking timepieces that allows the hands to be advanced to correct time without waiting for the striking to run through — compare 3RACK 8c

**rack back** *vt* [4*rack*] *slang* **:** REPRIMAND

**rack bar** *n* [3*rack*] **1 :** 3RACK 8a **2 :** a stick of wood used to bouse taut a rope binding something together

**rack block** *n* **:** 3RACK 7

**rack body** *n* **:** a truck body with latticed sides

**rack car** *n* **:** a freight car having end racks but no sides and used primarily for hauling pulpwood loaded crosswise on the car

**racked** *past of* RACK

**racked rubber** *n* [fr. past part. of 4*rack*] **:** rubber stretched to a much elongated thin strip that contracts only partially when warmed

**rack·er** \ˈrakə(r)\ *n* -S [4*rack* + -*er*] **:** one that racks: as **a :** a worker who puts articles on racks, as for drying, cooling, storage, transportation, or further processing — called also *rackman* **b :** a worker who lays out on a rack the sections of a chain of pocketed springs for an innerspring mattress and sews them together **c :** one who racks pool balls

1**rack·et** *also* **rac·quet** \ˈrakət, *usu* -əd·+V\ *n* -S [MF *raquette*, fr. Ar *rāḥah* palm of the hand] **1 a :** a light bat consisting of a catgut, nylon, or formerly, cord netting stretched in a somewhat oval open frame with handle attached used for striking the ball in tennis and in similar games **b :** a small round paddle with a squat handle used in table tennis **2** *usu* **racquets** *pl but sing in constr* **:** a game for two or four played with ball and racket on a four-walled court — compare SQUASH RACQUETS **3 a :** SNOWSHOE **b :** a broad wooden shoe for a man or horse for walking on soft ground

rackets 1: *1* badminton, *2* racquets, *3* tennis, *4* court tennis, *5* table tennis

2**racket** \"\ *vt* -ED/-ING/-S *obs* **:** to strike with or as if with a racket **:** BANDY

3**racket** \"\ *n* -S [prob. of imit. origin] **1 a :** confused clattering noise ⟨the ~ of the lunchroom⟩ ⟨~ of a street repair gang⟩ **b :** noisy, disturbing, or objectionable talk or activity **:** CLAMOR ⟨made such a ~ that she couldn't nap⟩ ⟨the dogs set up a terrific ~⟩ **2 a :** social whirl or excitement **:** REVELING, MERRYMAKING **b :** a large noisy party ⟨used to give at least one ~ a year⟩ **c :** the strain of exciting or trying experiences or ordeals — used with *the* ⟨getting too old to stand the ~⟩ **3 a :** a fraudulent scheme, enterprise, or activity ⟨to him everything was a ~ —God, education, radio, marriage, children, Communism, astronomy . . . osteopathy, Hollywood —*Time*⟩ ⟨sees through pompous ~ of the publicity campaign —Hans Meyerhoff⟩ ⟨fashion is a ~ to sell clothes —*New Yorker*⟩ **b :** a usu. illegitimate enterprise or activity that is made workable by coercion, bribery, or intimidation ⟨narcotics ~⟩ ⟨numbers ~⟩ ⟨officials consorting with mobsters, protecting the ~*s* and getting in return a share of the take —*N.Y.Times*⟩ **c :** a system of obtaining money or other advantage illegally, fraudulently, or underservedly usu. with the outward consent of the victims ⟨the fortune-telling ~⟩ **d :** an easy and lucrative means of livelihood **e** *slang* **:** OCCUPATION, BUSINESS **syn** see DIN

4**racket** \"\ *vi* -ED/-ING/-S **1 :** to engage in active social life or pleasure seeking — used usu. with *about* or *around* ⟨woman of the type often referred to as "gallant" mostly because she's done more than her share of ~*ing* around —*New Yorker*⟩ ⟨~*ed* round in my car, had no aim or ambition —G.W.Brace⟩ **2 :** to move with or make a racket ⟨~*ing* along in bus or train —K.W.Slifer⟩ ⟨a machine gun would start ~*ing* in the jungle —Norman Mailer⟩

1**rack·e·teer** \ˌrakəˈti(ə)r, -iə\ *n* -S [3*racket* + -*eer*] **:** one who extorts money or advantages by threats of violence or by blackmail or by threatened or actual unlawful interference with business or employment **:** one who engages in a racket

2**racketeer** \"\ *vb* -ED/-ING/-S *vi* **:** to carry on a racket **:** use fraud or intimidation in extorting money or commercial or political advantage ~ *vt* **:** to practice extortion on ⟨these peddlers are frequently ~*ed* by gangsters —D.W.Maurer⟩

1**rack·et·er** \ˈrakəd·ə(r)\ *n* -S [1*racket* + -*er*] **:** one who uses a racket: as **a :** one who plays tennis, squash, badminton **b :** one who uses snowshoes

2**racketer** \"\ *n* -S [3*racket* + -*er*] **1 :** one who makes a racket or noisy disturbance **2** *obs* **:** RACKETEER, SWINDLER

**racketlike** \ˈ==,=\ *adj* [1*racket* + -*like*] **:** resembling a racket; *specif* **:** having or consisting of a flat expanded rounded part at the end of a straight shaft ⟨a ~ feather⟩

**rack·et·ry** \ˈrakətrē\ *n* -ES [3*racket* + -*ry*] **:** RACKET, UPROAR, EXCITEMENT

**racket store** *n* [prob. fr. 3*racket*] *chiefly Midland* **:** VARIETY STORE

**rack·ett** \ˈrakət\ *n* -S [G] **:** an obsolete bass instrument of the oboe family having its tube bent upon itself in short lengths that are enclosed in a cylinder — called also *sausage bassoon*

**rackettail** \ˈ==,=\ *also* **racket-tailed hummingbird** \ˈ==,=-\ *n* [1*racket* + *tail*] **:** any of several hummingbirds of the genera *Ocreatus* and *Discosura* having two of the tail feathers very long and racket-shaped

**racket wheel** *n* [by alter.] **:** RATCHET WHEEL

**rack·ety** *also* **rack·et·ty** \ˈrakəd·ē, -ətē, -i\ *adj, sometimes* -ER/-EST [3*racket* + -*y*] **1 :** NOISY ⟨~ streetcar⟩ **:** EXCITING **2 :** addicted to or characterized by racketing or reveling **:** GAY, DISSIPATED, ROWDY, RAFFISH ⟨rather ~ but class-conscious world of sport —*Times Lit. Supp.*⟩ **3 :** RICKETY ⟨his memory was even more ~ —E.C.Wagenknecht⟩

**rack·ful** \ˈrak,fu̇l\ *n* -S [3*rack* + -*ful*] **:** the quantity contained in a rack ⟨~*s* of highly elaborate gowns —*New Yorker*⟩

**rack·ing** \ˈrakiŋ\ *n* -S [4*rack* + -*ing*] **1 :** the setting back slightly of the end of each course of brick or stone as it is laid near the junction with another wall so that each course is shorter than the one below **2 :** spun yarn or other seizing used in racking ropes **3 :** the motion of a knitting machine that controls the needle position for dropping, transferring, or changing stitches

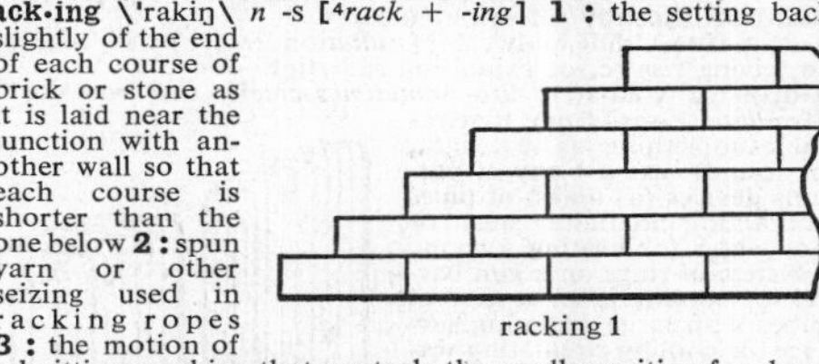

racking 1

**rack·ing·ly** *adv* [*racking* (pres. part. of 4*rack*) + -*ly*] **:** in a racking manner **:** so as to shake or strain

1**rack·le** \ˈrakəl\ *adj* [ME *rakel, rakil*] *chiefly Scot* **:** IMPETUOUS, HEADSTRONG — **rack·le·ness** *n* -ES *obs*

2**rackle** \"\ *vb* -ED/-ING/-S [imit.] *dial Brit* **:** RATTLE

**rack·less** \ˈrakləs\ *dial var of* RECKLESS

**rack·man** \ˈrakmən\ *n, pl* **rackmen** [3*rack* + *man*] **1 :** a power plant or mill worker who cleans the racks that screen fish, weeds, and other foreign matter from river water before it enters machines **2 :** one who working from a raised loading rack fills tank cars, trucks, or ships with petroleum products **3 :** a worker who places starting blanks between anodes in electrolysis tanks before the deposition of copper starting sheets on the blanks **4 :** RACKER a

**rack-o'-bones** \ˈrakə,bōnz\ *n pl but sing in constr* **:** RACKABONES

**rack punch** *n* [3*rack*] **:** MULTIPLE-DIE PRESS

**rack rail** *n* **:** COGRAIL

**rack railway** *or* **rack railroad** *n* **:** a railway having between its rails a rack that meshes with a gear wheel or pinion of the locomotive for climbing grades too steep for traction through ordinary adhesion of the wheels to the rail

**rack rent** *n* [4*rack*] **:** a rent equal or nearly equal to the full annual value of the property **:** an excessive or unreasonably high rent

**rack-rent** \ˈ=,=\ *vt* **:** to subject (as a farm or a tenant) to rack rent

**rack-renter** \ˈ=ˌ==\ *n* **1 :** one who pays rack rent **2 :** one who exacts rack rent

**racks** *pl of* RACK, *pres 3d sing of* RACK

**rack up** *vt* [4*rack*] **:** ACHIEVE, SCORE ⟨*racked* 30 points *up* in the first half⟩ ⟨*racked up* his fourth straight victory of the season⟩

**rackway** \ˈ=,=\ *n* [3*rack* + *way*] **:** RACK RAILWAY

**rack wheel** *n* **:** GEAR WHEEL

**rackwork** \ˈ=,=\ *n* **:** a mechanism (as a rack and pinion) having a rack

**ra·con** \ˈrā,kän, -ākən\ *n* -S [*radar* + *beacon*] **:** a radar beacon that sends out a coded signal in response to the proper radar signal received from a ship or aircraft and thus enables the navigator to identify the beacon as well as to determine his own range and bearing from it

**rac·on·teur** *R* ,ra,kän·ˈtər, -akən-, +V -ˈtər·; -*R* -ˈtə, + *vowel in a word following without pause* -ˈtər· *or* -ˈtə *also* -ˈtər\ *n* -S [F, fr. MF, fr. *raconter* to tell (fr. OF, fr. *re-* + *aconter* to tell, count) + -*eur* — more at ACCOUNT] **:** one who excels in telling anecdotes **:** STORYTELLER

**rac·on·teuse** \-ˈtərz, -ˈtəz, -ˈtüz, -ˈtəz\ *n* -S [F, fem. of *raconteur*] **:** a female raconteur

**racoon** *var of* RACCOON

1**ra·co·vi·an** \rəˈkōvēən\ *adj, usu cap* [*Raków*, village in southeast Poland + E -*ian*] **:** of or relating to Raków or to the Polish Socinians whose intellectual center in the 17th century was Raków

2**racovian** \"\ *n* -S *usu cap* **:** a Polish Socinian

1**racquet** *var of* 1RACKET

2**rac·quet** \ˈrakət\ *n* -S **:** GAZELLE 2

1**racy** \ˈrāsē, -si\ *adj* -ER/-EST [7*race* + -*y*] **1 :** having the distinctive or characteristic flavor, quality, or excellence of a race or kind **:** manifesting the quality of a thing in its native, original, genuine, or most characteristic form or state **:** NATURAL, UNSPOILED, FRESH ⟨~ morsels of the vernacular —Walter Pater⟩ **2 a :** full of life, zest, or vigor **:** LIVELY, SPIRITED **b :** PIQUANT, PUNGENT, EXHILARATING ⟨written with energy and with ~ humor —H.S.Commager⟩ **c :** RISQUÉ, SUGGESTIVE ⟨~ anecdotes⟩ **syn** see PUNGENT

2**racy** \"\ *adj* -ER/-EST [partly fr. 1*racy*; partly fr. 2*race* + -*y*] **1 :** having a build fitted for racing **2** *of an animal* **:** long-bodied and lean

1**rad** \ˈrad\ *adj* [ME, fr. OE *hræd* — more at RATHE] *dial* **:** QUICK, READY, EAGER; *also* **:** ELATED, EXHILARATED

2**rad** \"\ *adj* [ME, of Scand origin; akin to ON *hræddr* afraid, *hrathr* quick, rash — more at RATHE] *Scot* **:** AFRAID

3**rad** \"\ *n* -S [short for *radiation*] **:** a unit of absorbed dose of ionizing radiation equal to an energy of 100 ergs per gram of irradiated material

**rad** *abbr* **1** radial **2** radian **3** radiant **4** radiator **5** radical **6** radio **7** radium **8** radius **9** [L *radix*] root

**ra·dar** \ˈrā,där, -dä(r\ *n* -S *often attrib* [*ra*dio *d*etecting *a*nd *r*anging] **:** a radio device or system for locating an object by means of emitting radio signals usu. in the form of pulses of an ultrahigh frequency and observing and analyzing the minute signals reflected from the object and received at or near the point of transmission in such a way that range, bearing, and other characteristics of the object may be determined

**radar beacon** *n* **:** a radar transmitter that upon receiving a radar signal emits a signal which reinforces the normal reflected signal or which introduces a code into the reflected signal esp. for identification purposes

**ra·dar·man** \-mən, -,man\ *n, pl* **radarmen :** an operator of a radar device

**ra·dar·scope** \-,skōp, -,də(r)-\ *n* [*radar* + oscillo*scope*] **:** an oscilloscope having a cathode-ray tube whose fluorescent end serves as the visual indicator in a radar receiver — called also *scope*

1**rad·dle** \ˈradᵊl\ *n* -S [prob. alter. of 1*ruddle*] **:** RED OCHER; *also* **:** other coloring matter used for marking animals

2**raddle** \"\ *vt* -ED/-ING/-S **1 :** to mark or paint with or as if with raddle **:** color highly with rouge **:** RUDDLE ⟨people who never *raddled* their faces with greasepaint —*Times Lit. Supp.*⟩ ⟨a *raddled* barmaid —Janet Tobitt⟩ ⟨*raddled* tile floor —Flora Thompson⟩ ⟨*raddled* with the paint of pokeberry juice —Ellen Glasgow⟩ **2** *Austral* **:** to mark the brisket of a ram with raddle to identify the ewes he serves **3 :** PIT, SCAR ⟨when they kept to the open sea . . . his broadsides *raddled* them —*Time*⟩ ⟨poverty-haunted, crime-*raddled* neighborhood —Edmund Fuller⟩

3**raddle** \"\ *n* -S [MF *rudelle, redelle* stout pole, rail of a cart, prob. fr. MHG *reitel*] **1** *chiefly dial* **:** a long supple stick, rod, or branch often interwoven with others in making a hedge or fence or plastered with clay to make a wall **2** *chiefly dial* **:** a structure made with raddles **3 :** a bar usu. of wood having pegs between which warp yarns are guided while being wound on the beam

4**raddle** \"\ *vt* -ED/-ING/-S **1 :** to twist together **:** make by interlacing **:** INTERWEAVE **2 :** to regulate by means of a raddle

5**raddle** \"\ *vt* [perh. fr. 3*raddle*] *Scot* **:** BEAT, THRASH

**rad·dled** \-ᵊld\ *adj* [origin unknown] **1 :** CONFUSED, BEFUDDLED ⟨if you'd been as ~ as I was last night —Norman Douglas⟩ ⟨a ~ old man⟩ **2 :** WORN, BROKEN, BROKEN-DOWN ⟨factories lay like ~ skeletons —*Time*⟩ ⟨that ~ but still noble face —Esther Forbes⟩ ⟨battered trumpets . . . ~ radios —*New Yorker*⟩ ⟨the mouth was firm . . . in the loose, ~ flesh about it —Eric Ambler⟩

**rad·dle·man** \-ᵊlmən\ *n, pl* **raddlemen** [1*raddle* + *man*] **:** RUDDLEMAN

**rade** [ME, fr. OE *rād*] *chiefly dial past of* RIDE

**raden** *pl of* RAAD

**ra·di·a·bil·i·ty** \,rādēəˈbiləd·ē\ *n* [*radiation* + -*ability*] **:** the capability of transmitting radiation esp. X rays ⟨the ~ is altered by differences in thickness of the bone —K.H.Thoma⟩

**ra·di·ac** \ˈrādē,ak\ *n* -S [*ra*dioactivity *d*etection *i*dentification *a*nd *c*omputation] **:** the act or process of detecting, identifying, and measuring the nuclear radiation at a given place

1**ra·di·al** \ˈrādēəl\ *adj* [ML *radialis*, fr. L *radius* ray, beam + -*alis* -al — more at RAY] **1 :** issuing in rays **:** relating to rays of light ⟨intense ~ heat is applied —*Chem. Abstracts*⟩ **2 a :** arranged or having parts arranged like rays ⟨~ blades in a blower⟩ ⟨most cities show a ~ pattern of main highways leading outward from their center —C.L.White & G.T. Renner⟩ ⟨young dome mountains and volcanoes have ~ drainage lines —A.K.Lobeck⟩ ⟨~ seating in an auditorium⟩ **b :** being an architectural plan in which the disposition is radial as distinguished from longitudinal ⟨~ plan of a church⟩ **3 a :** relating to or placed like a radius ⟨~ blocks for chimney-construction —L.A.Harding⟩ **:** moving or taking place along a radius **:** having the direction of a radius ⟨~ acceleration⟩ ⟨~ velocity⟩ **b :** characterized by divergence from or as if from a center **4 a :** of, relating to, or adjacent to a bodily radius (as the bone of the forearm or the ray of a starfish) **b :** being any of various plates of a crinoid that lie between the basal and brachial plates **5 a :** developing uniformly around a central axis — opposed to *dorsiventral* **b :** relating to a ray or ray flower **c :** having the xylem and phloem lying on alternate radii of the axis usu. separated by nonvascular tissue ⟨a ~ actinostele⟩

2**radial** \"\ *n* -S **1 a :** radial part: as (1) **:** a bar at right angles to a curved part (as in an arch) (2) **:** the radial arm or quadrant on which the change wheels are secured in a screw-cutting lathe **b :** any of a system of radial lines **:** RAY; *specif* **:** a line of position radiating from a radio navigational aid transmitter **2 a :** a body part (as an artery, nerve, or plate) lying near or following the course of the radius; *sometimes* **:** RADIALE **b :** HYPERCORACOID **3 :** RADIAL ENGINE

**radial arm** *n* **:** a device for changing the direction of a pipeline when the angle is less than 30 degrees

**radial artery** *n* **:** the smaller of the two branches into which the brachial artery divides just below the bend of the elbow and which passes along the radial side of the forearm to the wrist then winds backward around the outer side of the carpus and enters the palm between the first and second metacarpal bones to form the deep palmar arch — see PULSE

**radial bearing** *n* **:** a ball bearing in which the direction of action of the load transmitted is radial to the axis of the shaft

**radial brick** *n* **:** brick with tapering sides to form a circular wall (as of a chimney or tower)

**radial canal** *n* **1 :** one of the numerous minute canals lined with choanocytes which radiate from the paragastric cavity in some sponges and end just below the surface of the sponge **2 :** one of the canals extending through the substance of the umbrella from the gastric cavity to the marginal circular canal in jellyfishes **3 :** a tube extending outward along each ambulacral area from the circumoral canal in most echinoderms

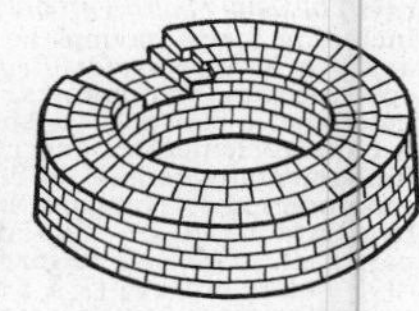

radial brick used in chimney construction

**radial drill** *n* **:** a drilling machine with the drill spindle in a toolhead and saddle that are movable along a projecting arm which itself can be rotated about a vertical column

**ra·di·a·le** \,rādēˈa(,)lē, -ˈā(-, -ˈä(-\ *n, pl* **radi·alia** \-ˈlēə\ [NL, fr. ML, neut. sing. of *radialis* radial] **1 a :** a bone or cartilage of the carpus that articulates with the radius; *specif* **:** the navicular in man **b :** a bone in the carpus of a bird made up of the radiale fused with either the intermedium or the centrale **2 :** a radial plate of a crinoid **3 :** a bone or cartilage distal to the basale and directly supporting a ray in a fish's fin; *also* **:** ACTINOST

**radial engine** *n* **:** a usu. internal-combustion engine having cylinders arranged radially like the spokes of a wheel; *specif* **:** such an engine in which the cylinders are stationary and the crankshaft revolves — see ROTARY ENGINE

**radial-flow** \ˈ;==ˈ;=\ *adj* **:** having the working fluid flowing mainly along the radii of rotation ⟨a *radial-flow* turbine⟩ — compare AXIAL-FLOW

**radial gate** *n* **:** a device used for controlling the flow of water over spillways or into canals by having the upstream face curved in the form of an arc the center of which is at the center of the gate hinge — called also *tainter gate*

**radial head** *n* **:** a rounded eminence by which the humerus articulates with the radius

**ra·di·al·ly** \ˈrādēəlē, -li\ *adv* **:** in a radial manner

**radial nerve** *n* **:** a large nerve that arises from the posterior cord of the brachial plexus and passes spirally down the humerus to the front of the lateral epicondyle where it divides into a superficial branch distributed to the skin of the back of the hand and arm and a deep branch to the underlying extensor muscles

**radial quantum number** *n* **:** an integer associated with the radial component of the momentum of an atomic electron in one of its possible stationary states — compare AZIMUTHAL QUANTUM NUMBER, PRINCIPAL QUANTUM NUMBER

**radial saw** *n* **:** a circular saw in which the saw wheel is suspended from a traverse head in turn suspended from a rotatable arm

**radial sector** *n* **:** a vein in the wings of most insects that usu. arises from the radius

**radial shield** *n* **:** one of a pair of plates situated on the disk at the base of each ray of an ophiuran

**radial symmetry** *n* **:** the condition of having similar parts regularly arranged about a central axis (as in a starfish)

**radial vein** *n* **1 :** a superficial vein ascending along the radial side of the forearm and uniting with the median cephalic vein to form the cephalic vein **2 :** a vein accompanying a radial artery

**radial velocity** *n* **1 :** the component of velocity of a particle in the direction of its radius vector **2** *or* **radial motion :** the velocity of relative approach or recession of an observer and a celestial body or other sources of radiation in the line connecting the two **:** speed in the line of sight

**ra·di·an** \ˈrādēən\ *n* -s [*radius* + *-an*] **:** a unit of plane angular measurement equal to the angle at the center of a circle subtended by an arc equal in length to the radius ⟨since the circumference of a circle is equal to 2π times its radius, the number of ~*s* in an angle of 360 degrees or in a complete turn is 2π, so that 1 ~ equals about 57.29 degrees⟩

**ra·di·ance** \ˈrādēən(t)s\ *also* **ra·di·an·cy** \-nsē, -nsi\ *n, pl* **radiances** *or* **radiancies** [*radiance* fr. [1]*radiant*, after such pairs as E *attendant: attendance; radiancy* fr. [1]*radiant* + *-cy*] **1 :** the quality or state of being radiant **:** vivid brightness **:** SPLENDOR ⟨the sun touched the tops of the still trees, and poured its ~ over the hill —Charles Dickens⟩ ⟨light up the family story with the ~ of great events —E.E.Morison⟩ ⟨in the ~ of that old summer —Ellen Glasgow⟩ ⟨pulling a cap over the ~ of her hair —C.B.Kelland⟩ **2 :** the flux density of radiant energy per unit solid angle and per unit projected area of radiating surface **3 :** a deep pink that is bluer, lighter, and stronger than average coral (sense 3b), deeper than fiesta, and yellower and deeper than begonia **4 :** GLORY ⟨a figure of the Virgin Mary with the child standing on a crescent and surrounded by a ~ —W. de G. Birch⟩

[1]**ra·di·ant** \-nt\ *adj* [ME, fr. L *radiant-, radians*, pres. part. of *radiare* to emit rays, radiate — more at RADIATE] **1 a :** radiating rays of light **:** emitting or reflecting beams of light **b :** radiating or diffusing splendor, glory, or a similar quality **:** vividly bright and shining **:** GLOWING, BRILLIANT ⟨~ as a double dawn in sky and water —Elinor Wylie⟩ ⟨his hands are ~ with rings — diamonds and sapphires —Truman Capote⟩ ⟨the fields . . . were ~ with early summer —Nancy Hale⟩ ⟨the ~ images of religion and of art as well as of science —Havelock Ellis⟩ **2 :** RAYONNANT 1 **3 :** marked by or expressive of joy, pleasure, love, confidence, or happiness **:** seeming to radiate some quality esp. good ⟨~, like a schoolboy who has received an unexpectedly large tip —Christopher Isherwood⟩ ⟨one of the most ~ lyrics in the language —W.Y.Tindall⟩ ⟨gray eyes full of a ~ curiosity —Scott Fitzgerald⟩ ⟨~ with idealism —V.L.Parrington⟩ **4 a :** emitted or transmitted by radiation **b :** emitting or relating to radiant heat ⟨a ~ lamp⟩ ⟨a ~ type radiator⟩ ⟨a ~ baseboard⟩ **5 :** of or relating to a biological radiant or biological radiation **syn** see BRIGHT

[2]**radiant** \"\ *n* -s **:** something that radiates: as **a :** the point in the heavens at which the visible paths of meteors appear to meet when traced backward or whence they appear to radiate although in reality the paths of the meteors are parallel **b :** a straight line proceeding from a given point or fixed pole about which it is conceived to revolve **c :** a point or object from which light emanates **d :** the part of a gas or electric heater that becomes incandescent and emits radiant heat **e :** an organism or group of organisms (as a species) that has reached its present geographical location as the result of a dispersal from a primary place of origin — compare RADIATION

**radiant energy** *n* **:** energy traveling as a wave motion; *specif* **:** the energy of electromagnetic waves (as radio waves, infrared rays, visible light, ultraviolet rays, X rays, and gamma rays) — compare LUMINOUS ENERGY

**radiant flux** *n* **:** the rate of emission of radiant energy or of its transmission through a specified region usu. expressed in watts — compare LUMINOUS FLUX

**radiant-flux density** *n* **:** the radiant energy in a beam of electromagnetic, thermal, or acoustic radiation passing through a unit normal section per unit time — called also *intensity of radiation*

**radiant glass** *n* **:** glass that is usu. in panels and contains radiant heating elements

**radiant heat** *n* **:** heat transmitted by radiation as contrasted with that transmitted by conduction or convection ⟨electrical ceiling cables that provide invisible *radiant heat* from above — just like the sun —*Sweet's Catalog Service*⟩

**radiant heater** *n* **:** a heating unit emitting radiant energy; *esp* **:** such a heater in which a refractory is heated to incandescence by a gas flame

**radiant heating** *n* **:** PANEL HEATING

**radiant intensity** *n* **:** the radiant energy that is emitted by a source per unit time per unit solid angle in a given direction under conditions that the source may be considered as sensibly a point source and that is measured in units of watts per steradian

**ra·di·ant·ly** *adv* **:** in a radiant manner ⟨the bride smiled ~⟩

**radiant point** *n* **:** RADIANT b

**radiant yellow** *n* **:** CADMIUM YELLOW

**ra·di·a·ta** \ˌrādēˈād·ə, -ˈäd·ə\ *n pl, cap* [NL, fr. L, neut. pl. of *radiatus* furnished with rays, fr. past part. of *radiare* to emit rays] *in some classifications* **:** a major category of invertebrates including forms having the parts arranged radially about an axis: **a** *in former classifications* **:** all the radiate animals (as coelenterates, ctenophores, and echinoderms) together with a heterogeneous group (as sponges, bryozoans, and flatworms) **b :** the coelenterates and ctenophores which are regarded as fundamentally radiate in contrast to the secondarily radiate echinoderms — compare BILATERIA, DIPLEURULA

[1]**ra·di·ate** \ˈrādēˌāt, *usu* -ād·+V\ *vb* -ED/-ING/-S [L *radiatus*, past part. of *radiare* to furnish with rays, emit rays, fr. *radius* ray — more at RAY] *vi* **1 :** to send out rays of or as if of light **:** shine brightly ⟨in the last white-hot phase of its collapse, the sun would begin to ~ as a star —F.L.Whipple⟩ ⟨a *radiating* focus of goodwill —R.L.Stevenson⟩ **2 :** to issue in rays or as if in rays **:** move, traverse, emanate or be sent out from a focal point ⟨light ~*s*⟩ ⟨heat ~*s*⟩ ⟨influences *radiating* from Paris —H.O.Taylor⟩ ⟨the system of patronage . . . provided a fixed center from which their work could ~ over society —C.D. Lewis⟩ **3 :** to proceed or be arranged in a direct line from or toward a center in the manner of a radius ⟨the web of little wrinkles that *radiated* from the corners of her eyes —Hamilton Basso⟩ ⟨streets *radiating* from a square⟩ **4 :** to evolve by radiation ⟨remarkably endowed creatures . . . *radiated* with amazing rapidity into a diversity of forms —L.C.Eiseley⟩ ~ *vt* **1 :** to send out in or as if in rays ⟨the sun ~*s* light and heat⟩ ⟨his blithe, buoyant personality *radiated* joy of life and goodwill —F.H.Garrison⟩ ⟨seems to ~ power and vitality —James Hewitt⟩ ⟨include . . . a man *radiating* peace, joy and wisdom —Henry Miller⟩ **2 :** IRRADIATE **3 :** to spread abroad or around as if from a center **:** DISSEMINATE, DIFFUSE ⟨each center would then ~ influence until proper methods in science should gradually spread throughout the educational system —D.S. & Jessie K. Jordan⟩ **4 :** to broadcast by radio or television ⟨to ~ a program⟩ **syn** see SPREAD

[2]**ra·di·ate** \-ēə̇t, -ēˌāt, *usu* |d·+V\ *adj* [L *radiatus* furnished with rays, fr. past part. of *radiare* to furnish with rays, emit rays] **:** having rays or radial parts **:** RADIATED, RADIAL: as **a :** having ray flowers — used of the head in many plants of the family Compositae; compare DISCOID 2 **b** (1) **:** characterized by radial symmetry ⟨a ~ structure in an animal⟩ (2) **:** relating to the Radiata **c :** RADIAL 2b

[3]**radiate** \"\ *n* -s [NL *Radiata*] **:** one of the Radiata

**radiated** *adj* [fr. past part. of [1]*radiate*] **1 :** emitted in rays or direct lines **2 :** formed of or arranged like rays or radii **:** having radial parts or markings ⟨a ~ group of crystals⟩ ⟨oriental crowns, the points alternately ~ —*Burke's Peerage*⟩ **3 :** exposed to radiation; *specif* **:** treated with X rays or radium ⟨~ body parts⟩

**ra·di·ate·ly** *adv* **:** in a radiate manner ⟨a ~ ribbed sea shell⟩

**ra·di·ate·ness** *n* -ES **:** the quality or state of being radiate ⟨the ~ in a starfish⟩

**ra·di·a·tion** \ˌrādēˈāshən\ *n* -s [L *radiation-, radiatio*, fr. *radiatus* (past part. of *radiare* to radiate) + *-ion-, -io* -ion] **1 a :** the act or process of radiating ⟨with ~ of the pain there may be tenderness over the sciatic nerve —J.A.Key⟩ ⟨~ of a radio program⟩ ⟨the ~ of their world-conquering culture —*Harper's*⟩ ⟨his smile . . . is a ~ of light —*Saturday Rev.*⟩ **b :** the process of emitting radiant energy in the form of waves or particles ⟨~ is easily distinguished from other forms of heat transfer . . . by its speed of propagation which equals that of light, and by the fact that no intervening medium is required for its transmission —J.G.Charney⟩; *also* **:** the combined processes of emission, transmission, and absorption of radiant energy **2 a :** something that is radiated ⟨the real apostolic ~ which goes out from a contemplative monastery springs from the interior purity of the monks' own souls —Thomas Merton⟩ ⟨believe in the presence of ~*s* which stream to earth from mysterious realms beyond —Edward Sapir⟩ **b :** energy radiated in the form of waves or particles (as sound waves, electromagnetic waves, and corpuscular emissions that include alpha rays, beta rays, and neutrons released in atomic nuclear changes as well as cosmic rays) ⟨the essential identity of light, heat, and other electromagnetic ~ —D.L.Harms⟩ ⟨an antenna in free space . . . sends out ~ in all directions —J.C.Slater⟩ **3 :** radial arrangement; *also* **:** a radial thing or part **4 a :** the spreading into different environments accompanied by divergent change of structure in the evolution of a group of organisms ⟨adaptive ~ in which new species arise better fitted to live under certain new conditions than in the ancestral habitat⟩ **b :** the totality of new species, varieties, or other groups produced by radiation **5 :** a method of surveying in which the field is triangulated by lines radiating from a central point **6 :** a tract of nerve fibers within the brain; *esp* **:** one concerned with the distribution of impulses arising from sensory stimuli to the relevant coordinating centers and nuclei **7 :** a device for radiating heat

**ra·di·a·tion·al** \ˌ==ˈāshən³l, -shnəl\ *adj* **:** of or relating to radiation

**radiation belt** *n* **:** VAN ALLEN RADIATION BELT

**radiation chemistry** *n* **:** chemistry that deals with the chemical effects of nuclear and other radiations on matter

**radiation field** *n* **:** a region traversed by radiation of any kind

**radiation fog** *n* **:** an evening fog over damp grounds or valleys resulting from cooling by radiation

**radiation pressure** *n* **:** the pressure exerted by light or other electromagnetic radiation upon matter in its path or the pressure due to the incidence of acoustic energy

**radiation pyrometer** *n* **:** a pyrometer that measures the intensity of radiation from a body having an extremely high temperature

**radiation resistance** *n* **:** the component of antenna resistance that accounts for the power radiated into space and is equal in ohms to the radiated power in watts divided by the square of the effective current in amperes at the point of power supply

**radiation sickness** *also* **radiation syndrome** *n* **:** sickness resulting from exposure to radiation (as in radiotherapy or the explosion of an atom bomb) commonly marked by fatigue, nausea, vomiting, loss of teeth and hair, and in more severe cases by damage to blood-forming tissue with decrease in red and white blood cells and with bleeding

**radiation therapy** *n* **:** RADIOTHERAPY

**ra·di·a·tive** \ˈrādēˌād·iv\ *adj* [*radiation* + *-ive*] **:** of, relating to, giving rise to, or exhibiting radiation

**ra·di·a·tor** \-ād·ə(r), -ātə- *sometimes chiefly dial* ˈrad-\ *n* -s [[1]*radiate* + *-or*] **:** one that radiates something (as heat, light, or sound): as **a :** any of various devices (as a nest of pipes containing circulating steam or hot water for heating a room, a system of rings on a gun barrel for cooling it, or a nest of tubes with large radiating surface for cooling circulating water) for heating external objects or for cooling an internal substance by radiation **b** (1) **:** TRANSMITTER a (2) **:** TRANSMITTER b (3) **:** a transmitting antenna **c :** a radioactive substance

radiators a

**ra·di·a·to·ry** \ˈrādēəˌtōrē\ *adj* [[1]*radiate* + *-ory*] **1 :** RADIATING **2 :** of or relating to radiation

[1]**rad·i·cal** \ˈradə̇kəl, -dēk-\ *adj* [ME, fr. LL *radicalis*, fr. L *radic-, radix* root + *-alis* -al — more at ROOT] **1 :** of or relating to the root **:** proceeding directly from the root: as **a** (1) **:** of or proceeding from the root of a plant ⟨~ tubers⟩ (2) **:** proceeding from the base of a stem, from a rootlike stem, or from a stem that does not rise above the ground ⟨~ leaves⟩ — compare CAULINE **b :** of, relating to, or constituting a linguistic root ⟨a ~ verb form⟩ **c :** of or relating to the root of a nativity or an election in astrology **d :** of or relating to a mathematical root **e :** designed to remove the root of a disease or all diseased tissue ⟨~ surgery⟩ — compare CONSERVATIVE **2 :** of or relating to the root or origin **:** ORIGINAL **:** FUNDAMENTAL **:** INHERENT ⟨differences that may be ascribed to ~ peculiarities of mind —Robert Bridges †1930⟩ ⟨the ~ trouble is that man is by nature a liar —Henry Adams⟩ ⟨~ differences in English and Navaho language structure —J.B.Carroll⟩ ⟨her ~ unfitness for an ascetic regimen —George Santayana⟩ ⟨reacting against the ~ faults of man and society —C.W.Hendel⟩ **3 a :** marked by a considerable departure from the usual or traditional **:** EXTREME, THOROUGHGOING, DRASTIC ⟨the most ~ proposals have called for the abandonment of the bicameral system —A.N.Holcombe⟩ ⟨to seek education for women at a time when the idea was considered a dangerously ~ doctrine —*Current Biog.*⟩ ⟨the ~ music written between 1910 and 1930 —*New Republic*⟩ **b :** tending or disposed to make extreme changes in existing views, habits, conditions, or institutions ⟨observation will reveal many people who are ~ in politics and conservative in religion —D.D.McKean⟩ ⟨the truly ~ party, the party of the destroyers of traditional values —*New Republic*⟩ **c :** of, relating to, or constituting a political group associated with views, practices, and policies of extreme change: as (1) *usu cap* **:** of, relating to, or constituted by the British radicals of the 19th century (2) *usu cap* **:** of, relating to, or constituted by the Radical Republicans **syn** see LIBERAL

[2]**radical** \"\ *n* -s **1 a :** a root part ⟨some ~ of our being which is persistent —H.B.Alexander⟩ **b :** basic principle **:** BASIS, FOUNDATION, SUPPORT **2 a :** an uncompounded word or element without prefix, infix, suffix, or inflectional ending **:** ROOT **b :** a sound or letter belonging to a radical; *esp* **:** an original unchanged initial consonantal sound in Celtic languages or one of the three original consonants forming the triliteral roots in Semitic languages **c :** one of 214 Chinese characters that represent categories of sense and are combined with phonetics to form phonograms whose meaning they suggest **3 a :** a radical expression in mathematics ⟨the expression $\sqrt[n]{a}$ is called a ~ of order *n* —R.S.Underwood & F.W.Sparks⟩ **b :** RADICAL SIGN **4 :** one that is radical: as **a :** one that advocates a decided and often extreme change from existing, usual, or traditional views, habits, conditions, or methods ⟨a literary ~ at heart, he was fighting . . . for a reevaluation of values —R.E.Spiller⟩ ⟨regarded as something of a ~ in anthropological circles . . . when he proposed that Neanderthal man might be classified as *Homo sapiens* —R.W. Murray⟩ ⟨the young ~*s* . . . who met regularly to discuss the new musical theories —Edward Sackville-West & Desmond Shawe-Taylor⟩ **b :** one that advocates radical and sweeping changes in laws, institutions, and methods of government with the least delay: as (1) **:** a member of the extreme wing of the British Liberal party in the 19th century (2) **:** a member of a group in the North favoring extreme measures against the South during the Civil War (3) **:** a member of a group in the North favoring a policy of reconstruction in the South after the Civil War **5** [F, fr. *radical*, adj., fr. LL *radicalis*] **:** a fundamental constituent of a chemical compound: **a** *according to Lavoisier* **:** the part of an acid that does not contain oxygen and that in combination with the acidifying principle oxygen constitutes the acid **b :** a single replaceable atom of the reactive atomic form of an element **c :** a group of atoms that is replaceable by a single atom or that is capable of remaining unchanged during a series of reactions, that need not be isolable (as acetyl, tertiary butyl, methylene, cyanogen, hydroxyl) but that sometimes is isolable, or that may show a definite transitory existence in the course of a reaction

**radical axis** *n* **1 :** a straight line that is the locus of points from which tangents drawn to two given circles are equal **2 :** a straight line common to the three radical planes of three given spheres taken in pairs

**radical center** *n* **:** a point from which tangents drawn to three given circles or four spheres are equal

**radical empiricism** *n* **:** an epistemological theory excluding from its formulations any elements not derived from experience and considering relations to be experienceable

**radical expression** *n* **:** a mathematical expression involving radical signs

**rad·i·cal·ism** \-kəˌlizəm\ *n* -s **1 :** the quality or state of being radical **2 a :** the doctrines or principles of radicals **b :** a radical movement **3 :** the will or the effort to uproot and reform that which is established

**rad·i·cal·i·ty** \ˌradəˈkaləd·ē\ *n* -ES **1 :** the quality or state of being fundamental **2 :** RADICALISM

**rad·i·cal·iza·tion** \ˌradə̇kələ̇ˈzāshən, -dēk-, -ˌlīˈz-\ *n* -s [*radicalize* + *-ation*] **:** the act or process of radicalizing or the condition of being radicalized

**rad·i·cal·ize** \ˈ===ˌlīz\ *vt* -ED/-ING/-S **:** to make radical esp. in politics

**rad·i·cal·ly** \ˈradə̇k(ə)lē, -dēk-, -li\ *adv* **1 :** as regards root or source **:** in origin or essence **:** NATURALLY ⟨the Romance languages are ~ from the Latin vernacular⟩ **2 :** in a radical manner **:** in a thoroughgoing or extreme manner **:** FUNDAMENTALLY ⟨follows the same route at periodical intervals, unless ~ disturbed —*How to Catch More Fur*⟩ ⟨a civilization ~ different from our own⟩ ⟨the destroyers zigzagged ~ —Walter Karig & Welbourn Kelley⟩

**rad·i·cal·ness** \-kəlnə̇s\ *n* -ES **:** the quality or state of being radical

**radical plane** *n* **:** a plane that is the locus of points from which tangents drawn to two given spheres are equal

**radical republican** *n, usu cap both Rs* **:** a Republican favoring drastic and usu. repressive measures against the southern states in the period following the Civil War

**radical sign** *n* **:** the sign √ placed before an expression to denote that the square root is to be extracted (as $\sqrt{a}$, $\sqrt{a+b}$, $\sqrt{2}$) or that some other root is to be extracted when a corresponding index (as ³ to indicate a cube root) is placed over the sign

**rad·i·cand** \ˈradəˌkand, ˌ==ˈ=\ *n* -s [L *radicandum*, neut. of *radicandus*, gerundive of *radicare, radicari* to take root] **:** the quantity under a radical sign

[1]**rad·i·cate** \ˈradəˌkāt\ *vb* -ED/-ING/-S [ME *radicaten*, fr. L *radicatus*, past part. of *radicare, radicari* to take root, fr. *radic-, radix* root — more at ROOT] *vt* **1 :** to cause to take root **:** plant deeply and firmly **2 :** to fix or establish firmly ⟨the missionary function of the Church is *radicated* in . . . God's Providence —J.D.Hassett⟩ ~ *vi, obs* **:** to take root

[2]**radicate** *adj* [L *radicatus*, past part. of *radicare, radicari* to take root] *obs* **:** RADICATED

**rad·i·ca·tion** \ˌradəˈkāshən\ *n* -s [ML *radication-, radicatio*, fr. L *radicatus*, past part. + *-ion-, -io* -ion] *archaic* **:** the process or condition of radicating **:** a taking root

**radices** *pl of* RADIX

**rad·i·cic·o·lous** \ˌradəˈsikələs\ *adj* [ISV *radici-* (fr. L *radic-, radix* root + *-i-*) + *-colous*] **:** living on or in roots ⟨~ flora⟩

**rad·i·cle** \ˈradə̇kəl, -dēk-\ *n* -s [L *radicula* little root, dim. of *radic-, radix* root] **1 a :** the lower portion of the axis of a plant embryo or seedling; *specif* **:** its extremity or root portion **b :** the hypocotyl and the root **:** HYPOCOTYL **2 :** the rootlike beginning of an anatomical vessel or part ⟨the ~ of a lacteal in a villus of the intestine⟩ ⟨the ~ of a lung⟩ **3** [by alter.] **:** RADICAL ⟨a chemical ~⟩

**ra·dic·o·la** \rəˈdikələ, raˈ-,rāˈ-\ *n, pl* **radico·lae** \-ˌlē, -ˌlī\ [NL, fr. L *radic-, radix* root + NL *-cola*] **:** the stage or an individual of a phylloxeran that attacks roots

**ra·dic·o·lous** \(ˈ)raˈdikələs, (ˈ)rāˈ-\ *adj* [by contr.] **:** RADICICOLOUS

**ra·dic·u·la** \=ˈ=kyələ\ [NL, fr. L, little root, dim. of *radic-, radix* root] *syn of* NASTURTIUM

**ra·dic·u·lar** \(ˈ)=ˈ==lə(r)\ *adj* [ISV *radicul-* (fr. L *radicula* little root) + *-ar*] **1 :** of or relating to the radicle or the root of a plant **2 :** of, relating to, or involving a nerve root ⟨~ lesions are typically responsible for severe sciatic pain⟩

**ra·dic·u·lec·to·my** \rəˌdikyəˈlektəmē, (ˌ)ra,-, (ˌ)rā,-\ *n* -ES [L *radicula* little root + E *-ectomy*] **:** RHIZOTOMY

**ra·dic·u·li·tis** \-lə̇d·ə̇s\ *n* -ES [NL, fr. L *radicula* little root + NL *-itis*] **:** inflammation of a nerve root

**ra·dic·u·lose** \(ˈ)raˈdikyəˌlōs, (ˈ)rāˈ-\ *adj* [ISV *radicul-* (fr. L *radicula* small root, dim. of *radic-, radix* root) + *-ose* — more at ROOT] **:** producing numerous rootlets

**ra·dif·er·ous** \(ˈ)rāˈdif(ə)rəs\ *adj* [ISV *radium* + *-ferous*] **:** containing radium

**radii** *pl of* RADIUS

[1]**ra·dio** \ˈrādēˌō *sometimes esp formerly* ˈrad-\ *n* -s [short for *radiotelegraphy*] **1 a :** the transmission and reception of electric impulses or signals by means of electric waves without a connecting wire ⟨~ includes wireless, television, and radar⟩ **b :** the use of these waves for the wireless transmission of electric impulses into which sound is converted — often distinguished from *television* **2 :** a radio message **:** RADIOGRAM **3 :** a radio receiving set **4 a :** a radio sending station **b :** a radio broadcasting organization ⟨a national ~⟩ **c :** the radio broadcasting industry ⟨became the youngest announcer in ~ —*Current Biog.*⟩ **d :** radio as a medium of communication ⟨jurisdiction over press, ~, and film —*Current Biog.*⟩

[2]**radio** \"\ *adj* **1 :** of, relating to, employing, or operated by radiant energy esp. of electric waves **:** relating to or employed in radiotelegraphy or radiotelephony or other applications of radio waves ⟨~ communication⟩ **2 :** of or relating to electric currents or phenomena of frequencies between about 15,000 and (10)¹¹ per second **3 a :** of, relating to, or used in radio or a radio set ⟨~ transformer⟩ ⟨~ dial⟩ **b :** specializing in radio or employed in or associated with the radio industry ⟨~ engineer⟩ **c** (1) **:** transmitted by radio ⟨~ message⟩ ⟨~ concert⟩ (2) **:** making or participating in radio broadcasts ⟨~ announcer⟩ ⟨~ commentator⟩ ⟨~ entertainers⟩ **d :** controlled or directed by radio

[3]**radio** \"\ *vb* -ED/-ING/-S *vt* **1 :** to send or communicate by radio ⟨the sound . . . is ~*ed* back automatically to the ship —Erwin Raisz⟩ **2 :** to send a radio message to ~ *vi* **:** to send or communicate by radio

**radio-** *comb form* [F, fr. L *radius* ray — more at RAY] **1 a :** radial **:** radially ⟨*radio*symmetrical⟩ ⟨*radio*litic⟩ **b :** radial and ⟨*radio*bicipital⟩ **2 a :** radiant energy **:** radiation ⟨*radio*active⟩ ⟨*radio*dermatitis⟩ **b :** radioactive ⟨*radio*element⟩ **c :** radium **:** X rays ⟨*radio*therapy⟩ **d :** radioactive isotope esp. as produced artificially ⟨*radio*carbon⟩ **e :** radio ⟨*radio*telegraphy⟩ ⟨*radio*photograph⟩

**ra·dio·acoustics** \ˈrādē(ˌ)ō+\ *n pl but sing in constr* [*radio-* + *acoustics*] **:** the study of the production, transmission, and effects of sounds as carried and reproduced by radio

**ra·dio·actinium** \"+\ *n* [NL, fr. *radio-* + *actinium*] **:** the radioactive isotope of thorium of mass number 227 formed by disintegration of actinium — symbol *RdAc* or $Th^{227}$; — see ACTINIUM SERIES

**ra·dio·activate** \"+\ *vt* [*radioactive* + *-ate*] **:** to make radioactive

**ra·dio·active** \"+\ *adj* [ISV *radio-* + *active*] **:** of, relating to, caused by, or exhibiting radioactivity ⟨~ element⟩ ⟨~ decay⟩ ⟨~ isotope⟩

**radioactive chain** *n* **:** RADIOACTIVE SERIES

**radioactive constant** *n* **:** a constant of radioactivity represented by λ in the equation $I_t = I_0e^{-\lambda t}$, where $I_0$ is initial activity, $I_t$ activity after time *t*, and *e* the natural logarithmic base

**radioactive equilibrium** *n* **:** the condition in which a radioactive species and its successive radioactive products have attained such relative proportions that they all disintegrate at the same numerical rate and therefore maintain their proportions constant

**ra·dio·actively** \"+\ *adv* **:** in a radioactive manner

**radioactive series** *n* **:** a series of elements that are formed by disintegration of a long-lived parent (as actinium, thorium, or uranium) through the successive loss of alpha or beta particles sometimes by alternative routes and that are all radioactive except the end products which are stable isotopes of lead or bismuth — compare NEPTUNIUM SERIES

**ra·dio·activity** \ˌrādē,ō+\ *n* [ISV *radio-* + *activity*] **:** the emission of radiant energy **:** the property, possessed by some elements (as radium, uranium, thorium, and their products) whether free or combined of spontaneously emitting alpha or beta rays and sometimes also gamma rays by the disintegration of the nuclei of atoms

**radio altimeter** *n* **:** an altimeter utilizing the lag between the time of transmission of a radio wave from an airplane and the time of reception of the same wave after reflection from the ground

**ra·dio·assay** \¦rādē(,)ō+\ *n* [*radio-* + *assay*] **:** an assay (as of ore) based on examination of the sample in terms of radiation components

**radio astronomer** *n* **:** a specialist in radio astronomy

**radio astronomy** *n* **:** a branch of astronomy dealing with electromagnetic radiations of radio frequency received from outside of the earth's atmosphere (as from the sun, a star, or a galaxy) or with investigations of celestial bodies (as meteors or the moon) by means of radar waves

**ra·dio·au·to·gram** \,rādē(,)ō'ȯd·ə,gram\ *n* [*radio-* + *aut-* + *-gram*] **:** AUTORADIOGRAPH

**¹ra·dio·autograph** \¦rādē(,)ō+\ *n* [*radio-* + *autograph*] **:** AUTORADIOGRAPH — **ra·dio·autographic** \"+\ *adj* — **ra·dio·autography** \"+\ *n*

**²radioautograph** \"\ *vt* **:** to make an autoradiograph of

**radio balloon** *n* **:** a small unmanned sounding balloon carrying diminutive radio sets for transmitting meteorological recordings to ground observers or for measuring cosmic rays in the stratosphere

**radio beacon** *n* **:** a radio transmitting station that transmits special radio signals for use (as on a landing field or ship) in determining the direction or position of those receiving them

**radio beam** *n* **:** BEAM 2e

**radio bearing** *n* **:** the angle between the observed direction of incoming radio waves and a fixed line (as the axis of a ship)

**ra·dio·biological** *or* **ra·dio·biologic** \¦rādē(,)ō+\ *adj* [*radiobiology* + *-ical* or *-ic*] **:** relating to, produced by, or employing radiobiology

**ra·dio·biologist** \"+\ *n* [*radiobiology* + *-ist*] **:** a specialist in radiobiology

**ra·dio·biology** \"+\ *n* [*radio-* + *biology*] **:** a branch of biology dealing with the interaction of biological systems and radiant energy or radioactive materials

**ra·dio·broadcast** \"+\ *vt* [*radio-* + *broadcast*] **:** BROADCAST 3 — **ra·dio·broadcaster** \"+\ *n*

**radio car** *n* **:** an automobile (as a police car) equipped with radio for communication

**ra·dio·carbon** \"+\ *n* [ISV *radio-* + *carbon*] **:** radioactive carbon; *esp* **:** CARBON 14

**ra·dio·cast** \'rādēō+,-\ *vt* [*radio-* + broad*cast*] **:** BROADCAST 3 — **ra·dio·caster** \"+,-\ *n*

**ra·dio·chemical** \¦rādē(,)ō+\ *adj* [*radio-* + *chemical*] **:** of, relating to, or using the methods of radiochemistry

**ra·dio·chemist** \"+\ *n* [back-formation fr. *radiochemistry*] **:** a specialist in radiochemistry

**ra·dio·chemistry** \"+\ *n* [*radio-* + *chemistry*] **1 :** the chemistry of radioactive substances and phenomena including tracer studies — called also *nuclear chemistry* **2 :** RADIATION CHEMISTRY

**ra·dio·cobalt** \"+\ *n* [*radio-* + *cobalt*] **:** radioactive cobalt; *esp* **:** COBALT 60

**ra·dio·colloid** \"+\ *n* [*radio-* + *colloid*] **:** a colloidal aggregate consisting of or containing a radioactive element — **ra·dio·colloidal** \"+\ *adj*

**radio compass** *n* **:** a direction finder used in navigation

**radio control** *n* **:** control of mechanisms other than signaling apparatus at a distance by radio waves

**radio–control** \¦rādē(,)ō+\ *vt* [*radio control*] **:** to operate by radio control ⟨*radio-controlled* airplane⟩

**ra·dio·dermatitis** \"+\ *n* [NL, fr. *radio-* + *dermatitis*] **:** dermatitis resulting from overexposure to sources of radiant energy (as X rays or radium)

**ra·dio·detector** \"+\ *n* [*radio-* + *detector*] **:** DETECTOR e

**radio direction finder** *n* **:** DIRECTION FINDER

**ra·di·odon·tia** \,rādēō'dänch(ē)ə\ *n* -s [NL, fr. *radio-* + *-odontia*] **:** the making and interpreting of radiographs of teeth and related adjacent structures — **ra·di·odon·tic** \¦rādēō¦däntik\ *adj* — **ra·di·odon·tist** \,rādēō'däntəst\ *n* -s

**radioed** *past of* RADIO

**radio electrician** *n* **:** a warrant officer (as in the U.S. Navy) whose specialty is supervision of the maintenance and operation of radio and other electronic equipment

**ra·dio·element** \¦rādē(,)ō+\ *n* [ISV *radio-* + *element*] **:** a radioactive element whether formed naturally or produced artificially — compare RADIOISOTOPE

**radio engineering** *n* **:** a branch of electrical engineering concerned with the construction, operation, and maintenance of radio equipment

**radio field intensity** *or* **radio field strength** *n* **:** the electromagnetic field intensity consisting of an electric and a magnetic field intensity produced by a radio wave and commonly expressed in millivolts per meter or microvolts per meter

**radio fix** *n* **1 :** the location of a radio transmitter by means of direction-finding equipment **2 :** a fix obtained by radio

**radio frequency** *n* **:** an electromagnetic wave frequency intermediate between audio frequencies and infrared frequencies used in radio and television transmission

RADIO FREQUENCIES

| CLASS | ABBREVIATION | RANGE |
|---|---|---|
| very low frequency | vlf | 10 to 30 kilocycles |
| low frequency | lf | 30 to 300 kilocycles |
| medium frequency | mf | 300 to 3000 kilocycles |
| high frequency | hf | 3 to 30 megacycles |
| very high frequency | vhf | 30 to 300 megacycles |
| ultrahigh frequency | uhf | 300 to 3000 megacycles |
| superhigh frequency | shf | 3000 to 30,000 megacycles |
| extremely high frequency | ehf | 30,000 to 300,000 megacycles |

**radio–frequency** \¦==(,)=¦===\ *adj* [*radio frequency*] **:** operating at radio frequency **:** using or having a radio frequency ⟨*radio-frequency* heating⟩

**radio–frequency amplification** *n* **:** amplification of current of radio frequency that in receiving sets is in the stages preceding the detector

**ra·dio·genetics** \¦rādē(,)ō+\ *n pl but sing or pl in constr* [*radio-* + *genetics*] **:** a division of radiobiology dealing with genetic systems

**ra·dio·gen·ic** \¦rādēō¦jenik\ *adj* [*radio-* + *-genic*] **1 :** produced by radioactivity ⟨~ lead⟩ **2 :** eminently suitable for broadcast by radio — **ra·dio·gen·i·cal·ly** \-nək(ə)lē\ *adv*

**ra·dio·goniometer** \¦rādē(,)ō+\ *n* [ISV *radio-* + *goniometer*] **:** DIRECTION FINDER

**ra·dio·goniometric** \"+\ *adj* [*radiogoniometry* + *-ic*] **:** relating to, using, or determined by radiogoniometry

**ra·dio·goniometry** \"+\ *n* [ISV *radio-* + *goniometry*] **:** the art or science of measuring the direction from which radio waves come

**ra·dio·gram** \'rādēə,gram, -ēō,-, -raa(ə)m\ *n* [*radio-* + *-gram*] **1 :** RADIOGRAPH **2 :** a message transmitted by radiotelegraphy **3** *or* **ra·dio·gramophone** \¦rādē(,)ō+\ [*radiogram* short for *radiogramophone; radiogramaphone* fr. *radio-* + *gramophone*] *Brit* **:** a combined radio receiver and record player

**¹ra·dio·graph** \'rādēə,graf, -ēō,-, -gráf\ *n* [*radio-* + *-graph*] **:** a picture produced upon a sensitive surface (as of a photographic film) by a form of radiation other than light; *specif* **:** an X-ray or gamma ray photograph

**²radiograph** \"\ *vt* **:** to make a radiograph of

**³radiograph** \"\ *vt* [*radio-* + *telegraph*] **:** to send (a person) a radiogram

**ra·di·og·ra·pher** \,rādē'ägrəfə(r)\ *n* -s [²*radiograph* + *-er*] **:** one who radiographs; *specif* **:** an X-ray technician

**ra·dio·graph·ic** \¦rādēə¦grafik, -ēō¦-\ *adj* [ISV *radiography* + *-ic*] **:** of or relating to radiography; *specif* **:** of or relating to the process that depends on the differential absorption of rays transmitted through heterogeneous media — **ra·dio·graph·i·cal·ly** \-fək(ə)lē\ *adv*

**ra·di·og·ra·phy** \,rādē'ägrəfē\ *n* -ES [ISV ¹*radiograph* + *-y*] **:** the art, act, or process of making radiographs

**ra·dio·halo** \¦rādē(,)ō+\ *n* [*radio-* + *halo*] **:** a halo usu. of microscopic dimensions in a mineral or a rock produced by radioactive emanations from an included small grain of some other mineral

**ra·dio·humeral bursitis** \"+ . . . -\ *n* [*radiohumeral* fr. *radio-* + *humeral*] **:** TENNIS ELBOW

**radiohumeral index** *n* **:** the ratio of the length of the radius of the human arm to the length of the humerus multiplied by 100

**radioing** *pres part of* RADIO

**ra·dio·iodide** \"+\ *n* [*radio-* + *iodide*] **:** an iodide containing radioactive iodine

**ra·dio·iodine** \¦rādē(,)ō+\ *n* [*radio-* + *iodine*] **:** radioactive iodine; *esp* **:** IODINE 131

**ra·dio·iron** \"+\ *n* [*radio-* + *iron*] **:** radioactive iron; *esp* **:** a heavy isotope having the mass number 59 produced in nuclear reactors or cyclotrons and used chiefly in biochemical and metallurgical tracer studies

**ra·dio·isotope** \"+\ *n* [ISV *radio-* + *isotope*] **:** a radioactive isotope — compare RADIOELEMENT

**radio knife** *n* **:** a needlelike surgical instrument using high-frequency oscillations in the form of a tiny electric arc at the point for cutting through or cutting away tissue and at the same time sterilizing the edges of the wound and sealing cut blood vessels

**ra·di·o·lar·ia** \,rādēō'la(a)rēə\ *n pl, cap* [NL, fr. LL *radiolus* small sunbeam (dim. of L *radius* ray, beam) + NL *-aria* — more at RAY] **:** a large order of rhizopods having protoplasm that is divided into an inner nucleated portion enclosed in a perforated membrane of chitinous material and an outer vacuolated portion from which radiate threadlike pseudopodia, usu. a horny or siliceous skeleton composed of spicules that may unite to form a basket-shaped structure, and numerous symbiotic unicellular yellow algae scattered in the protoplasm — compare ZOOXANTHELLA

**¹ra·di·o·lar·i·an** \¦===¦=rēən\ *adj* [NL *Radiolaria* + E *-an*, adj. suffix] **:** of or relating to the Radiolaria

**²radiolarian** \"\ *n* -s [NL *Radiolaria* + E *-an*, n. suffix] **:** a rhizopod of the order Radiolaria

**radiolarian ooze** *n* **:** siliceous mud of the bottom of deep seas composed largely of skeletal remains of radiolarians

**ra·di·o·lar·ite** \,===ᵊ=,rīt\ *n* -s [ISV *radiolar-* (fr. NL *Radiolaria*) + *-ite*] **1 :** a fossil radiolarian shell **2 :** a sediment or earth composed of the skeletal remains of radiolaria

**ra·dio·lead** \¦rādēō¦led\ *n* [*radio-* + *lead*] **:** lead formed in the disintegration of radium (as in the uranium series); *esp* **:** a radioactive isotope of lead

**radio link** *n* **:** a radiophone circuit connecting two fixed points (as interconnections with sections of ordinary wire circuit)

**¹ra·di·o·lite** \'rādēō,līt\ *n* -s [NL *Radiolites*] **:** a fossil of the genus *Radiolites* or family Radiolitidae

**²radiolite** \"\ *n* -s [G *radiolith*, fr. *radio-* + *-lith* -lite] **:** a spherulite made up of radiating needles

**ra·di·o·li·tes** \,rādēō'līd·(,)ēz\ *n, cap* [NL, fr. LL *radiolus* small sunbeam + NL *-ites*] **:** a genus (the type of the family Radiolitidae) of Cretaceous lamellibranchs with the lower valve conical and the upper nearly flat

**ra·di·o·lit·ic** \¦rādēō¦lid·ik\ *adj* [ISV *radio-* + *-litic*] **:** of or relating to a texture of igneous rock that is not truly spherulitic but that shows only sectors of spherulites or radial fanlike groupings of needles

**¹ra·di·o·li·tid** \-līd·əd, -lid-\ *adj* [NL *Radiolitidae*, family of lamellibranchs, fr. *Radiolites* + *-idae*] **:** of or relating to the genus *Radiolites* or the family Radiolitidae

**²radiolitid** \"\ *n* -s **:** a radiolitid lamellibranch or fossil

**ra·dio·location** \¦rādē(,)ō+\ *n* [*radio-* + *location*] **:** the method or process of detecting the position and course of distant objects by radar

**ra·dio·locator** \"+\ *n* [*radio-* + *locator*] **:** RADAR — used by the British before official adoption of *radar*

**ra·di·o·log·i·cal** \¦rādēə¦läjəkəl\ *or* **ra·di·o·log·ic** \-jik\ *adj* [*radiological* fr. *radiology* + *-ical; radiologic* ISV *radiology* + *-ic*] **1 :** of or relating to radiology ⟨~ treatment⟩ **2 :** of or relating to esp. nuclear radiation ⟨~ physics⟩; *specif* **:** producing or capable of producing casualties by nuclear radiation ⟨~ warfare⟩ ⟨~ hazards⟩ — **radiologically** *adv*

**ra·di·ol·o·gist** \,rādē'äləjəst\ *n* -s [ISV *radiology* + *-ist*] **:** a specialist in the use of radiant energy (as X rays or radium) in the diagnosis or treatment of disease

**ra·di·ol·o·gy** \-jē\ *n* -ES [*radio-* + *-logy*] **:** the science of radioactive substances, X rays, and other high-energy radiations; *specif* **:** the use of sources of radiant energy (as X rays and radium) in the diagnosis and treatment of disease

**ra·dio·lucence** \¦rādēō¦lüsᵊn(t)s\ *or* **ra·dio·lu·cen·cy** \-nsē\ *n, pl* **radiolucences** *or* **radiolucencies** [*radiolucense* fr. *radiolucent*, after such pairs as E *different: difference; radiolucency* fr. *radiolucent* + *-cy*] **:** the quality or state of being radiolucent

**ra·dio·lu·cent** \-nt\ *adj* [*radio-* + *lucent*] **:** partly or wholly permeable to X rays or other forms of radiation ⟨~ tissues⟩ ⟨~ areas⟩ — contrasted with *radiopaque*

**ra·dio·luminescence** \¦rādē(,)ō+\ *n* [ISV *radio-* + *luminescence*] **1 :** luminescence excited by impact of radioactive particles **2 :** luminescence excited by either electromagnetic or corpuscular radiation — **ra·dio·luminescent** \"+\ *adj*

**ra·di·ol·y·sis** \,rādē'äləsəs\ *n, pl* **radioly·ses** \-lə,sēz\ [NL, fr. *radio-* + *-lysis*] **:** chemical decomposition by the action of radiation — compare PHOTOLYSIS

**ra·dio·man** \'rādē,ō,man\ *n, pl* **radiomen** [¹*radio* + *man*] **1 :** a radio operator or technician **2 :** an employee of an electric company who locates the sources of trouble in defective power lines or equipment by means of a radio-equipped car

**radio marker** *n* **:** a radio transmitter of low power emitting a characteristic signal to indicate course positions with respect to a landing field or an airway — compare FAN MARKER

**ra·dio·metallography** \¦rādē(,)ō+\ *n* [*radio-* + *metallography*] **:** the determination of the structure of metal by means of X rays **:** the study of metals and alloys by X rays

**radio meteor** *n* **:** a meteor detected by the methods of radio astronomy (as by the reflection of radio waves from the ionized path it leaves in the upper atmosphere)

**ra·dio·meteorograph** \¦rādē(,)ō+\ *n* [*radio-* + *meteorograph*] **:** RADIOSONDE — **ra·dio·meteorography** \"+\ *n*

**ra·di·om·e·ter** \,rādē'äməd·ə(r)\ *n* [*radio-* + *-meter*] **:** an instrument for detecting and measuring the intensity of electromagnetic or acoustic radiation

**ra·dio·met·ric** \¦rādēō¦me·trik\ *adj* [ISV *radio-* + *-metric*] **1 :** relating to, using, or measured by the radiometer ⟨~ analysis⟩ ⟨~ data⟩ **2 :** of or relating to the measurement of geologic time by means of the rate of disintegration of radioactive elements — **ra·dio·met·ri·cal·ly** \-rək(ə)lē\ *adv*

**radiometric magnitude** *n* **:** the magnitude of a star as determined by the radiometer or a similar instrument

**ra·di·om·e·try** \,rādē'ämə·trē\ *n* -ES [ISV *radio-* + *-metry*] **:** the use of the radiometer **:** the measurement of radiation

**ra·dio·micrometer** \¦rādē(,)ō+\ *n* [ISV *radio-* + *micrometer*] **:** an exceedingly sensitive thermoelectric radiometer consisting of a D'Arsonval galvanometer with suspended coil replaced by a short-circuited thermocouple forming a loop

radiometer

**ra·dio·mimetic** \"+\ *adj* [ISV *radio-* + *mimetic*] **:** producing esp. biological effects similar to those produced by radiation

**radio navigation** *n* **:** the process of conducting an airplane or ship from one point to another by means of radio aids (as beacons, direction finders, or radioed bearings)

**ra·dio·necrosis** \"+\ *n* [NL, fr. *radio-* + *necrosis*] **:** ulceration or destruction of tissue resulting from irradiation

**ra·dio·necrotic** \"+\ *adj* **:** of or relating to radionecrosis

**ra·di·on·ic** \¦rādē¦änik\ *adj* [*radio-* + electr*onic*] **:** ELECTRONIC

**ra·di·on·ics** \,rādē'äniks\ *n pl but sing in constr* [*radio-* + electr*onics*] **:** ELECTRONICS

**ra·dio·nuclide** \¦rādē(,)ō+\ *n* [*radio-* + *nuclide*] **:** a radioactive nuclide

**radio observatory** *n* **:** an observatory concerned esp. with radio astronomy

**ra·di·opacity** \,rādē+\ *n* [*radio-* + *opacity*] **:** the quality or state of being radiopaque

**ra·di·opaque** \¦rādē+\ *adj* [*radio-* + *opaque*] **:** being opaque to X rays or other forms of radiation **:** not transmitting radiant energy ⟨barium sulfate is ~⟩ — contrasted with *radiolucent*

**ra·dio·phare** \'rādēō+,-\ *n* [*radio-* + *phare*] **:** a radiotelegraphic station used for determining the position of ships

**ra·dio·phone** \'rādēə,fōn\ *n* [*radio-* + *-phone*] **1 :** an apparatus (as the photophone) for the production of sound by the action of radiant energy **2 a :** a transmitting set for radiotelephony **b :** a receiving set for radiotelephony

**ra·dio·phosphorus** \¦rādē(,)ō+\ *n* [NL, fr. *radio-* + *phosphorus*] **:** radioactive phosphorus; *esp* **:** PHOSPHORUS 32

**ra·dio·photo** \"+\ *vt* [*radiophoto*, n.] **:** to send (a picture) by radio

**ra·dio·photograph** *or* **ra·dio·photo** \"+\ *n* [*radio-* + *photograph* or *photo*] **:** a picture transmitted by radio

**radio proximity fuse** *n* **:** PROXIMITY FUSE

**radio range** *n* **:** a radio facility providing means for aiding in the navigation of airplanes

**radio range beacon** *n* **:** a radio beacon that transmits in such a way as to mark out a fixed straight line (as for directing the course of airplanes to or from a landing field)

**radio range station** *n* **:** a radio transmitter that provides the signals used in a radio range

**radio receiver** *n* **:** a radio receiving set

**radio relay** *n* **:** a radio station that receives and retransmits a signal

**ra·dio·resistant** \¦rādē(,)ō+\ *adj* [ISV *radio-* + *resistant*] **:** resistant to the effects of radiant energy — used esp. of cells (as cancer cells) that are not destroyed by radiation; compare RADIOSENSITIVE

**radios** *pl of* RADIO, *pres 3d sing of* RADIO

**ra·dio·scope** \'rādēə,skōp\ *n* [*radio-* + *-scope*] **1 :** a device for detecting the presence of a radioactive substance **2 :** FLUOROSCOPE

**ra·dio·scop·ic** \¦rādēə¦skäpik\ *or* **ra·dio·scop·i·cal** \-pəkəl\ *adj* [*radioscopic* ISV *radioscopy* + *-ic; radioscopical* fr. *radioscopy* + *-ical*] **:** of or relating to radioscopy — **ra·dio·scop·i·cal·ly** \-pək(ə)lē\ *adv*

**ra·di·os·co·py** \,rādē'äskəpē\ *n* -ES [ISV *radio-* + *-scopy*] **:** direct observation of objects opaque to light by means of some other form of radiant energy (as X rays)

**ra·dio·sensitive** \¦rādē(,)ō+\ *adj* [*radio-* + *sensitive*] **:** sensitive to the effects of radiant energy — used of cells (as cancer cells) that can be destroyed by radiation; compare RADIORESISTANT — **ra·dio·sensitivity** \"+\ *n*

**radio set** *n* **1 :** a radio receiving set **2 :** a radio transmitting set

**radio silence** *n* **:** a condition that exists when radios are not transmitting; *also* **:** the period of time during which this condition exists

**ra·dio·sodium** \¦rādē(,)ō+\ *n* [NL, fr. *radio-* + *sodium*] **:** radioactive sodium; *esp* **:** a heavy isotope having the mass number 24, produced in nuclear reactors, and used in the form of a salt (as sodium chloride) chiefly in biochemical tracer studies

**ra·dio·sonde** \'rādēō+,-\ *n* -s [ISV *radio-* + *sonde*] **:** a miniature radio transmitter with instruments that is carried aloft (as by an unmanned balloon) for broadcasting by means of precise tone signals or other suitable method the humidity, temperature, and pressure every few seconds

**radio source** *n* **:** a region of the sky exclusive of the sun and members of the solar system from which microwave energy is received

**radio spectrum** *n* **1 :** the region of the electromagnetic spectrum usu. including frequencies below thirty thousand megacycles in which radio or radar transmission and detection techniques may be used **2 :** the molecular absorption spectrum of a substance in the radio-spectrum region

**radio star** *n* **:** a radio source of very small dimensions and relatively strong radiation and sometimes identified with certain small nebulosities and galaxies

**ra·dio·strontium** \¦rādē(,)ō+\ *n* [NL, fr. *radio-* + *strontium*] **:** radioactive strontium; *esp* **:** STRONTIUM 90

**radio sun** *n* **:** the sun as observed in the radio region of the spectrum

**ra·dio·surgery** \¦rādē(,)ō+\ *n* [*radio-* + *surgery*] **:** surgery by means of the radio knife

**ra·dio·symmetrical** \"+\ *adj* [*radio-* + *symmetrical*] **:** radially symmetrical; *specif* **:** ACTINOMORPHIC — compare MONOSYMMETRICAL

**ra·dio·technology** \"+\ *n* [*radio-* + *technology*] **1 :** the technology of radio **2 :** the application of X rays to industrial problems **3 :** the application of any form of radiation to industrial problems

**ra·dio·telegram** \"+\ *n* [ISV *radio-* + *telegram*] **1 :** RADIOGRAM 2 **2 :** a message transmitted by radiotelegraphy to or from a ship or other mobile station

**¹ra·dio·telegraph** *also* **ra·dio·telegraphy** \"+\ *n* [ISV *radio-* + *telegraph* or *telegraphy*] **:** telegraphy carried on by the aid of radio waves and without connecting wires

**²radiotelegraph** \"\ *vt* **:** to send (a message) by radiotelegraphy

**ra·dio·telegraphic** \¦rādē(,)ō+\ *adj* [*radiotelegraphy* + *-ic*] **:** of, relating to, or transmitted by means of radiotelegraphy

**ra·dio·telegraphist** \"+\ *n* [ISV ¹*radiotelegraph* + *-ist*] **:** one licensed to operate radiotelegraph equipment

**ra·dio·telephone** \"+\ *n* [ISV *radio-* + *telephone*] **:** RADIOPHONE 2

**ra·dio·telephony** \"+\ *n* [ISV *radio-* + *telephony*] **:** telephony carried on by the aid of radio waves without connecting wires

**radio telescope** *n* **:** a radio receiver-antenna combination used for observations in radio astronomy

**ra·dio·therapeutic** \"+\ *adj* [*radio-* + *therapeutic*] **:** of or relating to radiotherapy

**ra·dio·therapeutics** \"+\ *n pl but sing in constr* [*radio-* + *therapeutics*] **:** RADIOTHERAPY

**ra·dio·therapeutist** \"+\ *n* [*radio-* + *therapeutist*] **:** RADIOTHERAPIST

**ra·dio·therapist** \"+\ *n* [*radiotherapy* + *-ist*] **:** a specialist in radiotherapy

**ra·dio·therapy** \"+\ *n* [ISV *radio-* + *therapy*] **:** treatment of disease by means of X rays or radioactive substances (as radium)

**ra·dio·ther·mics** \,rādēō'thərmiks\ *n pl but sing in constr* [*radiothermy* + *-ics*] **:** the science of heat generation by radio-frequency currents or by radio waves

**ra·dio·ther·my** \'===,=mē\ *n* -ES [*radio-* + *-thermy*] **:** diathermy by means of a shortwave radio machine

**ra·dio·thorium** \¦rādē(,)ō+\ *n* [NL, fr. *radio-* + *thorium*] **:** the radioactive isotope of thorium of mass number 228 formed from mesothorium 2 — symbol *RdTh* or $Th^{228}$; see THORIUM SERIES

**ra·dio·toxicity** \"+\ *n* [*radio-* + *toxicity*] **:** the toxicity of radioactive substances

**ra·dio·tracer** \"+\ *n* [*radio-* + *tracer*] **:** a radioactive tracer

**radio transmitter** *n* **:** a radio transmitting set

**ra·dio·tri·cian** \,rādēō'trishən\ *n* -s [*radio-* + *electrician*] **:** one who specializes in radio work

**ra·dio·trop·ic** \¦rādēō¦träpik\ *adj* [*radio-* + *-tropic*] **:** of, relating to, or characterized by radiotropism

**ra·di·ot·ro·pism** \,rādē'ä·trə,pizəm\ *n* [*radio-* + *tropism*] **:** a tropism in which some form of radiation is the orienting factor

**radio tube** *n* **:** a vacuum tube for radio

**radious** *adj* [L *radiosus*, fr. *radius* ray + *-osus* -ous — more at RAY] *obs* **:** RADIANT, RADIATING

**ra·dio·vi·sion** \¦rādēō¦vizhən\ *n* [*radio-* + *television*] **:** television carried on by radio waves without connecting wires

**radio wave** *n* **:** an electromagnetic wave having radio frequency

**rad·ish** \'radish, ÷'red-\ *n* -ES [ME, alter. of OE *rǣdic*, fr. L *radic-*, *radix* root, edible root, radish — more at ROOT]

**1 :** the pungent fleshy root of a plant (*Raphanus sativus*) eaten raw as a relish **2 :** the plant that produces radish roots

**radish tree** *n* **:** an Australian shrub or small tree (*Codonocarpus cotinifolius*) of the family Phytolaccaceae with pale glaucous foliage and small unisexual flowers in racemes

**¹ra·di·um** \ˈrādēəm\ *n* -s [NL, fr. L *radius* ray, beam + NL *-ium* — more at RAY] **:** an intensely radioactive shining white metallic element of the alkaline-earth group that resembles barium chemically, that occurs in combination in minute quantities in pitchblende, carnotite, and other uranium minerals principally as the isotope of mass number 226 formed from uranium 238, having a half-life of 1620 years, and emitting alpha particles and gamma rays to form radon, and that is used chiefly in luminous materials (as paint made by admixture with zinc sulfide or other phosphor), in medicine esp. in the treatment of cancer, and in radiography — symbol *Ra;* see ACTINIUM SERIES, ELEMENT table, THORIUM SERIES, URANIUM SERIES

**²radium** \"\ *n* -s [fr. *Radium*, a trademark] **:** a smooth lustrous supple fabric made of silk or rayon in plain weave and used esp. for women's clothing and curtains

**radium clock** *n* **:** an electroscope alternately charged by the accumulation of alpha particles from radium in a closed tube and discharged by automatic grounding at regular intervals

**radium dial** *n* **:** a clock, watch, or instrument dial having figures coated with luminous paint

**radium emanation** *n* **:** RADON 1

**ra·di·um·ize** \ˈrādēə,mīz\ *vt* -ED/-ING/-S [¹*radium* + *-ize*] *see -ize in Explan Notes* **:** to subject to the action of radium ⟨the green effect in *radiumized* diamonds —*Time*⟩

**radium needle** *n* **:** a hollow radium-containing device shaped like a needle and used esp. in medical treatment

**radium pack** *n* **:** radium in a pack for therapeutic application

**radium series** *n* **:** URANIUM SERIES

**radium therapy** *n* **:** RADIOTHERAPY

**radium vermilion** *n* **:** a red lead that is coated with an organic color

**¹ra·di·us** \ˈrādēəs\ *n, pl* **ra·dii** \-ē,ī\ *also* **radiuses** [L, radius, ray, rod, spoke — more at RAY] **1 a :** the preaxial bone of the human forearm or of the corresponding part of the forelimb of vertebrates above fishes that in man is movably articulated with the ulna at both ends so as to admit of partial rotation about that bone, that bears on its inner anterior aspect near the head a prominence for the insertion of the biceps tendon, and that has the lower end broadened for articulation with the proximal bones of the carpus so that rotation of the radius involves also that of the hand — compare PRONATION, SUPINATION **b :** HYPERCORACOID **c :** HYPOCORACOID **2 :** a line segment extending from the center of a circle or sphere to the curve or surface **3 :** one of a number of rods, bars, or lines extending usu. in a single plane out from a center or hub ⟨*radii* of a wheel⟩ **4 a :** the distance of a radius ⟨a ~ of 10 miles from home⟩ ⟨truck with a short turning ~⟩ **b :** the circular area implicated by a stated radius ⟨40 inland lakes within a ~ of 20 miles —*Amer. Guide Series: Mich.*⟩ **c :** a bounded or circumscribed area **:** a limited range ⟨at the limit of the operating ~ of any fleet from Europe —S.L.A.Marshall⟩ **d :** a range of operation, activity, influence, concern, or knowledge ⟨a modern hospital that serves a wide ~ —*Amer. Guide Series: Vt.*⟩ ⟨the ~ of action of an airplane⟩ ⟨all who had come within the ~ of his kind if somewhat stern influence —F.S.Betten⟩ **5 :** a part analogous to the radius of a circle **:** a radial part (as the movable limb of a sextant or other angle-measuring instrument or a wheel spoke) **6 :** the distance from a center line or point to an axis of rotation **:** THROW, ECCENTRICITY **7 a :** an imaginary radial plane dividing the body of a radially symmetrical animal into similar parts — compare ADRADIUS, INTERRADIUS, PERRADIUS **b :** any of five radiating ossicles in the Aristotle's lantern of a sea urchin **c :** a main vein in the wing of an insect **:** the third and usu. largest vein of an insect's wing — see RADIAL SECTOR **d :** one of the grooves extending from the focus of a fish scale toward the margin **8 :** a rounded part (as an edge or fillet) produced by radiusing ⟨put a $\frac{1}{64}$ inch ~ on the cutting tip of this lathe tool⟩ **syn** see RANGE

**²radius** \"\ *vt* -ED/-ING/-ES **:** to cut (as a fillet or rounded-off edge) on an arc of a circle ⟨faceted and ~*ed* tool edges —Paul Grodzinski⟩ ⟨chamfering or ~*ing* of the bearings —*Aero Products*⟩

**radius bar** *n* **:** RADIUS ROD

**radius clause** *n* **:** a clause in an agreement with an employer by which a trainee engages not to seek employment with another company for a stated period

**radius gage** *n* **:** a gage for determining the curvature of internal and external fillets

**radius of curvature :** the reciprocal of the curvature of a curve

radius gage

**radius of gyration :** the radius of a cylindrical surface coaxial with the axis of rotation of a body such that if the entire mass of the body were concentrated in that surface the moment of inertia and energy of rotation would be unchanged ⟨the *radius of gyration* equals the square root of the quotient of the moment of inertia of the body divided by its mass⟩

**radius of torsion :** the reciprocal of the torsion of a space curve

**radius rod** *n* **:** a bar for preserving an invariable distance between two pieces of a mechanism and permitting one to move around the other as a fixed point

**radius vector** *n, pl* **radii vec·to·res** \-,vekˈtōr(,)ēz\ **1 :** a straight line segment or its length from a fixed point, pole, or center to a variable point **:** the linear polar coordinate of a variable point **2 :** a straight line joining the center of an attracting body (as the sun) with that of a body (as a planet or comet) describing an orbit around it

**ra·dix** \ˈrādiks\ *n, pl* **radi·ces** \ˈradə,sēz, ˈrād-\ *or* **radixes** \ˈrādiksəz\ [L, root — more at ROOT] **1 :** BASE 6d ⟨10 is the ~ of the common system of logarithms⟩ **2** *obs* **:** ROOT 4a **3 :** the primary source **:** the originating cause **4** *archaic* **:** ETYMON, ROOT 6 **5 :** the root of a plant **6 :** RADICLE 1; *esp* **:** a root of a cranial or spinal nerve

**radix gra·mi·nis** \-ˈgramənəs\ *n* [L, root of grass] **:** the rootstock of a couch grass (*Agropyron repens*) formerly used as a diuretic and aperient

**rad·knight** \ˈrad,nīt\ *n* [OE *rādcniht*, lit., riding knight, fr. *rād* riding + *cniht* military follower — more at ROAD, KNIGHT] **:** one of a class of feudal tenants in some parts of England holding on condition of doing service on horseback besides other services (as plowing) — called also *radman;* compare ESQUIRE

**radm** *abbr, often cap R&A & sometimes cap D & M* rear admiral

**rad·man** \-,mən\ *n, pl* **radmen** [(assumed) OE *rādman*, fr. OE *rād* riding + *man* — more at MAN] **:** RADKNIGHT

**rad·nor·shire** \ˈradnər,shi(ə)r, -,shər\ *or* **rad·nor** \-nər, -,nȯ(ə)r\ *adj, usu cap* [fr. *Radnorshire* or *Radnor*, county in Wales] **:** of or from the county of Radnor, Wales **:** of the kind or style prevalent in Radnor

**ra·dome** \ˈrā,dōm\ *n* [*radar dome*] **:** a usu. dome-shaped plastic housing used (as on the exterior surfaces of an airplane) to shelter the antenna assembly of a radar

**ra·don** \ˈrā,dän\ *n* -s [NL, fr. *rad-* (fr. *radium* + *-on*] **1 :** a heavy radioactive gaseous element of the group of inert gases formed by disintegration of radium and used similarly to radium in medicine — called also *radium emanation* — symbol *Rn;* see ELEMENT table, URANIUM SERIES **2 :** an isotope of radon: as **a :** ACTINON **b :** THORON

**radon seed** *n* **:** radon packed in a container for local application in cancer — compare SEED 4b

**ra·doph·o·lus** \rəˈdäfələs\ *n, cap* [NL] **:** a genus of chiefly tropical plant-parasitic nematodes (family Tylenchidae) including pests of the roots of sugarcane, rice, and other economically important plants

**rads** *pl of* RAD

**rad·u·la** \ˈrajələ\ *n, pl* **radu·lae** \-,lē, -,lī\ [NL, fr. L, scraper, fr. *radere* to scrape — more at RAT] **:** a chitinous band in nearly all mollusks except bivalves that bears numerous usu. very minute teeth on its dorsal surface and slides backward and forward by special muscles over a more or less protrusible prominence on the floor of the mouth and serves to tear up the food and draw it into the mouth — see ODONTOPHORE — **rad·u·lar** \-lə(r)\ *adj*

**radular sac** *n* **:** the posterior extension of the radula forming a narrow curved pouch opening on the floor of the mouth

**rad·u·late** \-,lət, -,lāt\ *adj* [NL *radula* + E *-ate*] **:** having a radula

**radu·li·form** \rəˈd(y)ülə,fȯrm, ˈrajəl-\ *adj* [L *radula* scraper + E *-iform*] **:** like a rasp **:** CARDIFORM

**rad·zi·mir** \ˈradzə,mi(ə)r\ *n* -s [prob. modif. of F *ras de Saint-Maur* short-napped cloth of Saint Maur] **1** *archaic* **:** a silk fabric usu. black for mourning clothes **2 :** a firm silk or rayon fabric for women's clothing often made with lengthwise ribs or a broken twill weave

**raetam** *var of* RETEM

**raeto-romance** *var of* RHAETO-ROMANCE

**ra·fale** \rəˈfal\ *n* -s [F, lit., squall, gust of wind, prob. fr. MF *rafle, raffe* act of snatching — more at RAFFLE] **:** a burst of artillery fire consisting of several rounds discharged as rapidly as possible from each gun of a battery

**¹raff** \ˈraf, ˈraa(ə)f, ˈraif\ *n* -s [ME *raf*, perh. fr. MF *raffe, rafle* act of snatching, sweeping — more at RAFFLE] **1** *dial Brit* **a :** HODGEPODGE, JUMBLE **b :** RUBBISH, TRASH **2 a :** RIFFRAFF **b :** a coarse disreputable person

**²raff** \ˈraf\ *n* -s [G dial. *raf, raffe;* akin to ON *raptr* rafter — more at RAFTER] *dial Eng* **:** LUMBER

**raffaelesque** *usu cap, var of* RAPHAELESQUE

**raffe** \ˈraf\ *or* **raf·fee** \raˈfē\ *n* -s [origin unknown] **:** a usu. triangular topsail set above a square lower sail

**raf·fia** \ˈrafēə, -fyə\ *n* -s [Malagasy *rafia, raofia, rofia*] **1 :** the fiber of the raffia palm of Madagascar used for tying plants and making articles (as baskets or hats) **2 :** RAFFIA PALM

**raffia palm** *n* **1 :** a pinnate-leaved palm (*Raphia ruffia*) native to Madagascar that is of considerable economic importance on account of the strong fiber obtained from its leafstalks — see RAFFIA 1 **2 :** JUPATI

**raffia wax** *n* **:** a hard light-brown wax obtained as a by-product from the leaves of the raffia palm or similar palms native to tropical Africa and So. America

raffe

**raf·fi·nase** \ˈrafə,nās\ *n* -s [ISV *raffin-* (fr. *raffinose*) + *-ase*] **:** an enzyme that catalyzes the hydrolysis of raffinose and occurs in various molds (as *Aspergillus niger*) and yeasts

**raf·fi·nate** \-āt\ *n* -s [F *raffiner* to refine (fr. *re-* + *affiner* to make fine) + ISV *-ate* — more at AFFINE] **:** a liquid product resulting from extraction of a liquid with a solvent; *also* **:** the less soluble residue that remains after extraction (as in refining lubricating oil)

**raff·ing** \ˈrafən, -fiŋ\ *adj* [origin unknown] *Scot* **:** RIP-ROARING

**raf·fi·nose** \ˈrafə,nōs\ *n* -s [F, fr. *raffiner* to refine + *-ose* — more at RAFFINATE] **:** a crystalline slightly sweet nonreducing trisaccharide sugar $C_{18}H_{32}O_{16}$ that is obtained by aqueous extraction of cottonseed meal but also found in small quantities in sugar beet, eucalyptus manna, and many cereals and that yields on hydrolysis D-fructose and melibiose

**raff·ish** \ˈrafish, ˈraaf-, ˈraif-, -fēsh\ *adj* [¹*raff* + *-ish*] **1 :** marked by or suggestive of flashy vulgarity, crudeness, or rowdiness **:** TAWDRY, UNKEMPT ⟨a *raffish*-looking old man with stringy gray hair, angry eyes, wrinkled stockings —Kenneth Roberts⟩ ⟨a district of ~ lodging houses —T.W.Duncan⟩ ⟨the ~ locutions of their dialogue —*Times Lit. Supp.*⟩ **2 :** marked by a careless or carefree unconventionality or disreputableness **:** DEVIL-MAY-CARE, RAKISH ⟨a cocktail party given by some . . . ~ bachelors —Crary Moore⟩ ⟨sported a ~ handlebar moustache —Anthony West⟩ — **raff·ish·ly** *adv* — **raff·ish·ness** *n* -ES

**¹raf·fle** \ˈrafəl\ *n* -s [ME *rafle*, fr. MF] **1 a :** a game with three dice in which the winner of the stakes is the player who throws all three alike or the highest pair if no triplet is thrown **b :** any three of a kind in chuck-a-luck with the banker taking all bets not on triplets **2 :** a lottery in which each participant buys a ticket for an article put up as a prize with the winner being determined by a random drawing ⟨selling tickets for a ~ on a new car⟩

**²raffle** \"\ *vb* **raffled; raffled; raffling** \-f(ə)liŋ\ **raffles** *vi* **:** to engage in a raffle ⟨~ for a watch⟩ ~ *vt* **:** to dispose of by means of a raffle — used often with *off* ⟨*raffled* off a sewing machine at the bazaar⟩

**³raffle** \"\ *n* -s [prob. fr. F *rafle* act of snatching, sweeping, fr. MF *rafle, raffe*, fr. MHG *raffen* to snatch; akin to OE *hreppan* to touch, ON *hreppa* to catch, receive, OE *hearpe* harp — more at HARP] **1 :** RABBLE, RIFFRAFF **2 :** REFUSE, RUBBISH; *specif* **:** a jumble or tangle of nautical material (as cordage or spars) ⟨her decks forward covered with ~ —W.C.Russell⟩

**⁴raffle** \"\ *vt* -ED/-ING/-S [prob. alter. of ¹*ruffle*] **:** SERRATE ⟨~ a leaf⟩

**⁵raf·fle** \"\ *vt* -ED/-ING/-S [alter. of ¹*ravel*] *dial Brit* **:** ENTANGLE

**raf·fles** \ˈrafəlz\ *n* -ES *often cap* [fr. *Raffles*, hero of the story *The Amateur Cracksman* (1899) by E. W. Hornung †1921 Eng. novelist] **:** an amateur or gentleman burglar

**raf·fle·sia** \rəˈflēzh(ē)ə, raˈ-, -zēə\ *n* [NL, fr. Sir Thomas S. *Raffles* †1826 Eng. colonial administrator + NL *-ia*] **1** *cap* **:** a genus (the type of the family Rafflesiaceae) of Malaysian stemless leafless plants having huge dioecious apetalous flowers that grow parasitically on the stems and roots of various plants of the genus *Cissus*, have a calyx of five spreading fleshy lobes, and usu. exhale an odor like that of carrion **2** -s **:** any plant of the genus *Rafflesia*

**raf·fle·si·a·ce·ae** \rə,flēz(h)ēˈāsē,ē, ra,-\ *n pl, cap* [NL, fr. *Rafflesia*, type genus + *-aceae*] **:** a family of endotrophic parasitic plants (order Aristolochiales) found chiefly in warm regions of the Old World and sometimes in Mexico that lack stems, have imbricated scales in place of leaves, and have apetalous flowers emerging from the host and having five to ten calyx lobes — **raf·fle·si·a·ceous** \-ˈāshəs\ *adj*

**raff·man** \ˈrafmən\ *n, pl* **raffmen** [alter. of *raftman*] **:** ³RAFTER

**raffs** *pl of* RAFF

**ra·fraî·chis·soir** \rə,freshəˈswär\ *n* -s [F, wine cooler, fr. *rafraîchiss-* (stem of *rafraîchir* to refresh, cool, fr. *re-* + *a-* ad- + *frais* fresh, cool, fr. OF *freis*) + *-oir* -ory — more at FRESH] **:** a small table or stand having a marble top with wells sunk into it esp. for containing plants or flowers

**¹raft** *archaic past of* REAVE

**²raft** \ˈraft, ˈraa(ə)ft, ˈraift, ˈraft\ *n* -s [ME *rafte*, fr. ON *raptr* rafter — more at RAFTER] **1** *archaic* **:** RAFTER, SPAR **2 a :** a collection of usu. logs or timber fastened together for transportation by floating ⟨great ~*s* of logs . . . for the English market —*Amer. Guide Series: Vt.*⟩ **b :** a flat structure for support or conveyance (as of people or cargo) on a body of water ⟨floating down the river on a ~⟩ ⟨rubber ~*s* filled with men —K.M.Dodson⟩ **c :** a floating platform; *esp* **:** one used by swimmers **:** FLOAT 4c(1) ⟨in the park pool swimming out to the ~ —Donald Windham⟩ **d :** a rubber lifesaving apparatus that is inflated for use usu. in emergency landings of airplanes on water ⟨the ~ resembled an overlarge bedroll —E.K.Gann⟩ ⟨get out fast and inflate the ~ —Howard Hunt⟩ **3 a :** a mass of floating logs, driftwood, or debris that impedes or blocks navigation of a watercourse ⟨the ~ covered the stream from shore to shore —*Amer. Guide Series: Ark.*⟩ **b :** a floating cohesive mass (as of seaweed or insect eggs) **c :** an aggregation of waterfowl (as ducks) resting on the water ⟨estuaries . . . where ~*s* of wildfowl lie offshore —N.C. Stevenson⟩ **4 :** MAT 3d ⟨~ foundation⟩ ⟨~ construction⟩

**³raft** \"\ *vb* -ED/-ING/-S *vt* **1 a :** to transport (as logs or timber) in the form of a raft by floating ⟨~*ed* his logs down the lakes —*Amer. Guide Series: Mich.*⟩ **b :** to convey (as people or cargo) on or by means of a raft ⟨~*ed* them across the stream⟩ ⟨freight ~*ed* down the river —*Amer. Guide Series: La.*⟩ **2 :** to make into a raft ⟨~ the logs at hand⟩ **3 :** to go along or across (a watercourse) on a raft ⟨~ a river⟩ **4 :** to transport (land-derived debris, boulders, or silt) embedded in floating ice or in masses of floating organic material (as seaweed) to places not reached by the currents of rivers, lakes, or seas ~ *vi* **1 :** to manage a raft **:** travel by raft ⟨~*ing* across rivers —Jack Kelsey⟩ **2 :** RAFTER

**⁴raft** \"\ *n* -s [alter. (influenced by ²*raft* mass of logs) of ¹*raff*] **:** a large and often motley collection (as of people or things) **:** a great amount or number **:** LOT, SLEW ⟨a ~ of shiftless brothers and sisters —W.L.Gresham⟩ ⟨had a ~ of patients —Carson McCullers⟩ ⟨assembled a ~ of facts and figures —*New Yorker*⟩ ⟨sold a ~ of bathtubs —*advt*⟩

**raft dog** *n* [²*raft*] **:** an iron bar with bent-down sharpened ends that fastens together the logs forming a raft — compare DOG 3a

**raft duck** *n* [²*raft;* fr. its swimming in dense flocks] **1 :** SCAUP DUCK **2 :** REDHEAD 2b

**¹raf·ter** \ˈraftə(r), ˈraaf-, ˈraif-, ˈråf-\ *n* -s [ME, fr. OE *ræfter;* akin to MLG *rafter, rachter* rafter, ON *raptr*] **1 :** one of the often sloping beams that support a roof — compare HIP RAFTER, JACK RAFTER, VALLEY RAFTER; see ROOF illustration **2** *or* **rafter bird :** SPOTTED FLYCATCHER

**²rafter** \"\ *vb* -ED/-ING/-S *vt* **1 :** to furnish (as a house) with rafters **2** *dial Eng* **:** to plow so as to turn the grass side of each furrow upon an unplowed ridge **:** RIDGE 2a ~ *vi* **:** to override and underrun one another — used of pieces of ice under pressure

**³raft·er** \"\ *n* -s [³*raft* + *-er*] **:** one who by walking on floating logs or booms or working from a boat maneuvers logs into position and binds them into rafts that can be towed to a mill — called also *boom man, raffman, raftsman*

**⁴rafter** \"\ *n* -s [⁴*raft* + *-er*] **:** FLOCK — used esp. of turkeys

**rafter dam** *n* [¹*rafter*] **:** a dam formed by long horizontal timbers set at an angle to the banks and meeting in the center of the stream like the rafters of a roof principal

**rafting auger** *n* [fr. gerund of ³*raft*] **:** an auger turned by a bar placed through an eye in the end of the shank and used for boring large and deep holes in heavy timbers

**raft port** *n* [²*raft*] **:** a large square port forward or aft in a ship for loading or unloading bulky material (as timber)

**rafts·man** \ˈraftsmən\ *also* **raft·man** \-tm-\ *n, pl* **raftsmen** *also* **raftmen** [²*raft*] **1 :** one who engages in rafting ⟨intrepid *raftsmen* crossing the Pacific⟩ **2 :** ³RAFTER

**raf·ty** \ˈrafti\ *adj* [origin unknown] **1** *dial Eng* **:** DAMP, RAW — used of weather **2** *dial Eng* **a :** MUSTY, FUSTY 1 **b :** RANCID — used of bacon

**¹rag** \ˈrag, ˈraa(ə)g, ˈraig\ *n* -s [ME *ragge*, fr. (assumed) OE *ragg* (whence OE *raggig* raggy), fr. ON *rögg* tuft, shagginess — more at RUG] **1 a :** a waste piece of cloth torn or cut off (as from a fabric or garment) **:** TATTER **b rags** *pl* **:** remnants of used or unused cloth and discarded clothing **c rags** *pl* **:** CLOTHES ⟨sumptuous ~*s* . . . cover her emaciated body —Otis Fellows⟩ ⟨his neat black suit . . . among the colored ~*s* of the other passengers —Dan Jacobson⟩; *esp* **:** poor or ragged clothing — often used in the phrase *in rags* ⟨accosted by a beggar in ~*s*⟩ **d :** a small cloth; *esp* **:** one devoted to a particular use — usu. used in combination ⟨wash*rag*⟩ ⟨dish*rag*⟩ **2 a :** an unevenly shaped or torn fragment **:** SHRED ⟨~*s* of meat⟩ ⟨a ~ of cloud⟩ ⟨~*s* of land⟩ ⟨~*s* of bark⟩ **b :** SCRAP, REMNANT ⟨still clinging . . . to some ~ of honor —R.L. Stevenson⟩ ⟨tearing their arguments to ~*s*⟩ ⟨not a ~ of legality⟩ ⟨not a ~ of evidence against him⟩ **3 :** something resembling a rag in appearance: as **a :** SAIL ⟨a clipper with every ~ set —J.R.Lowell⟩ **b :** the stringy axis of and the white fibrous membrane investing the pulp and sectional divisions of a citrus fruit **c :** something without strength or stamina ⟨kept . . . on the jump and left her a ~ —W.D.Steele⟩ **4 :** something resembling a rag in low worth or repute: as **a :** a person held in low esteem ⟨washed-out ~ he'd been dragging to dances —Martin Dibner⟩ **b :** depreciated paper money **c :** a low or worthless playing card **5 a :** a ragged edge; *specif* **:** one left by a cutting tool in metalworking **b :** a fin or burr on cast metal **6 :** NEWSPAPER, PERIODICAL

**²rag** \"\ *n* -s [origin unknown] **1 :** any of various hard rocks (as a quartzose mica schist used for whetstones or a hard limestone used in building) ⟨coral ~⟩ ⟨walls of yellowish, gravelly ~ —F.D.Ommanney⟩ **2 :** a large roofing slate left rough on one side

**³rag** \"\ *vb* **ragged** \-gd\; **ragged; ragging; rags** [origin unknown] *vt* **1 :** to rail at **:** SCOLD ⟨*ragging* the government —J.A. Michener⟩ ⟨*ragging* a waiter because the toast was cold —Leonard Merrick⟩ **2 a :** to persecute in petty ways **:** TORMENT, ANNOY ⟨gave my form a punishment for *ragging* him —R.G.G.Price⟩ **b :** to make fun of or find fault with goodnaturedly **:** TEASE, CHAFF ⟨*ragged* each other about that all day long —F.M.Ford⟩ ~ *vi, chiefly Brit* **:** to engage in horseplay (as in a school dormitory) ⟨~ in the corridors at night —Cyril Connolly⟩

**⁴rag** \"\ *n* -s **1** *chiefly Brit* **a :** an outbreak of boisterous and usu. mischievous merrymaking (as of students in the streets after a football match) **:** a student riot **b :** a traditional student revel at British universities marked by playful disorder, comic pageantry, and mockery of the authorities **2** *chiefly Brit* **:** PRANK, HOAX ⟨~*s* and japes —Thomas Wood †1950⟩ ⟨quite serious . . . no ~ —E.F.Benson⟩

**⁵rag** \"\ *vt* **ragged; ragged; ragging; rags** [origin unknown] **1 :** to break (ore) into lumps for sorting **2 :** to cut or dress roughly (as a grindstone)

**⁶rag** \"\ *n* -s [by shortening] **1 :** RAGTIME **2 :** a dance in ragtime

**⁷rag** \"\ *vb* **ragged; ragged; ragging; rags** *vt* **:** to play (a musical composition) in ragtime ~ *vi* **:** to dance to ragtime music

**ra·ga** \ˈrägə\ *n* -s [Skt *rāga*, lit., color, musical tone; akin to Skt *rajyati* it is dyed, Gk *rhezein* to dye] **1 :** one of the ancient traditional melodic patterns of Hindu music **2 :** an improvisation on the notes of a traditional raga

**rag·a·bash** \ˈragə,bash\ *also* **rag·a·brash** \-brash\ *n* -ES [prob. fr. ¹*rag* + *-abash, -abrash*, of unknown origin] *dial Brit* **:** RIFFRAFF

**rag·a·muf·fin** \ˈragə,məfən\ *n* -s [fr. *Ragamoffyn*, name of a demon in *Piers Plowman* (1393), attributed to William Langland †1400? Eng. poet] **1 :** a ragged dirty man or boy ⟨friendly . . . little ~, full of impulsive energies —Peggy Bennett⟩; *esp* **:** a disreputably tattered person ⟨have led my ~*s* where they are peppered —Shak.⟩ ⟨a ~ brigade of women and children and dogs —*Scribner's*⟩ **2 :** a child in masquerade costume (as for Halloween) ⟨~*s* ringing doorbells⟩

**rag-and-bone man** \,==ˈ=-\ *n, chiefly Brit* **:** a usu. itinerant dealer in things of small value (as secondhand clothes and old newspapers) **:** OLD-CLOTHESMAN

**rag baby** *n* **:** RAG DOLL 1 ⟨looked like an adorable old *rag baby* —W.A.White⟩

**ragbag** \ˈ=,=\ *n* [¹*rag* + *bag*] **1 :** a bag in which scraps or worn-out pieces of cloth are kept for future use or disposal ⟨~ of ends and tufts of brocade —R.W.Emerson⟩ **2 :** a heterogeneous collection of usu. trivial or useless objects ⟨a ~ of prejudices —J.R.Newman⟩

**rag bolt** *n* **1 :** a joining piece with a barbed shank hindering withdrawal when driven into wood — called also *barb bolt* **2 :** JAG BOLT

**rag doll** *n* **1 :** a stuffed and usu. painted cloth doll **2 :** a device for testing the germination of seed consisting of a strip of cloth that has numbered squares on which the seeds are placed and that is rolled into a bundle and kept moist during the test; *also* **:** a modification of this device used for inoculation of seed by disease organisms (as for tests of disease resistance)

**¹rage** \ˈrāj\ *n* -s [ME, fr. MF, fr. LL *rabia*, fr. L *rabies* rage, madness, fr. *rabere* to rave, be mad; akin to Skt *rabhas* violence, impetuosity] **1 a :** violent and uncontrolled anger often accompanied with raving **:** FURY ⟨overcome with a mighty ~⟩ ⟨out of this helplessness and ~ comes the will to endure —Leon Edel⟩ **b :** a fit of violent wrath ⟨fell into an appalling ~ and started out to destroy everything in sight —T.R.Ybarra⟩ **c** *archaic* **:** INSANITY ⟨mornings which presage the loss of reason and conclude in ~ —John Dryden⟩ **2 a :** violent action of the elements (as wind or sea) ⟨river hurled itself in thundering lacy-white ~ against jagged boulders —F.V.W.Mason⟩ **b :** a furious storm **:** TEMPEST ⟨a ~ on the bar kept seaside dwellers indoors⟩ **3 a :** extreme force of feeling **:** PASSION, FRENZY ⟨a ~ for order⟩ ⟨a ~ for power⟩ ⟨a ~ to live⟩ ⟨convulsed with a ~ of grief —Nathaniel Hawthorne⟩ ⟨the old man is in a ~ of excitement —Clemence Dane⟩ **b :** a state or feeling of exalted fervor (as of enthusiasm or inspiration) ⟨chill penury repressed their noble ~ —Thomas Gray⟩ ⟨that sacred ~ . . . we associate with the great novels on social issues —*New Republic*⟩ **4 :** something eagerly and usu. excessively sought after or pursued **:** CRAZE, VOGUE ⟨the current ~ for . . . how-to-do-it material —W.I.Nichols⟩ — often used in the phrase *all the rage* ⟨a period when cures and taking the waters were all the ~ —Peter Forster⟩ **syn** see ANGER, FASHION

**²rage** \"\ *vi* -ED/-ING/-S [ME *ragen*, fr. OF *ragier*, fr. *rage* anger] **1 :** to be in a rage **:** be furious **:** RAVE ⟨a person who everlastingly ~*s* —H.A.Overstreet⟩ — usu. used with *over, at,* or *against* ⟨*raging* over the waste of her small capital —*Amer. Guide Series: Tenn.*⟩ ⟨*raged* at him for his carelessness⟩ ⟨~ at the imposed weight —Arnold Bennett⟩ **2 a :** to become stirred up violently **:** be in a tumult ⟨the storm still *raging* outside —W.H.Hudson †1922⟩ ⟨the wind might ~ unbridled —C.G.D. Roberts⟩ **b :** to move wildly or turbulently **:** go on a rampage ⟨sent his brother *raging* after women —G.K.Chesterton⟩ ⟨the winds of doctrine . . . ~ through the land —V.L.Parrington⟩ ⟨rivers ~ through fertile bottom lands —*Amer. Guide Series: N. C.*⟩ **3 a :** to be intense or overwhelming **b :** to prevail uncontrollably **:** spread with destructive effect ⟨yellow fever was *raging* —W.P.Webb⟩ ⟨for two weeks . . . the controversy *raged* —A.L.Funk⟩ ⟨the fallacies . . . which ~ in the world —H.L.Mencken⟩

**rage·ful** \-jfəl\ *adj* **:** full of rage **:** FURIOUS

**rag engine** *n* **:** a beater used in converting rags into pulp

**ra·geous** \ˈrājəs\ *adj* [ME, fr. MF *rageux*, fr. *rage* anger + *-eux* -ous — more at RAGE] *dial chiefly Eng* **:** ENRAGED, FURIOUS

**rag fair** *n* **:** a street market where old or secondhand clothing is sold

**rag felt** *n* **:** a heavy paper that is made from rags impregnated with asphalt and is used for roofing and shingles

**ragfish** \ˈ=,=\ *n* [¹*rag* + *fish*] **:** a marine fish of the family Icosteidae remarkable for the soft skeleton

**rag·ged** \ˈragəd\ *adj, sometimes* -ER/-EST [ME, fr. *ragge* rag + *-ed*] **1 :** roughly unkempt **:** SHAGGY ⟨~ sheep —John Dryden⟩ ⟨~ rust-colored hair —Willa Cather⟩ **2 a :** having an irregular edge or broken outline **:** having sharp indentations, notches, or projections **:** JAGGED ⟨a ~ wound⟩ ⟨a ~ . . . shoreline —*Amer. Guide Series: Va.*⟩ ⟨a ~ edge of corrugated iron —B.J.Haimes⟩ ⟨almost choked . . . on a ~ bone —D.C.Allen⟩ **b :** RAGULY **c :** not flush **:** not justified **:** UNEVEN — used of the ends of lines of text in printing ⟨set left-hand margins flush, right-hand margins ~⟩ **3 a :** torn or worn to tatters **:** having the texture broken **:** TATTERED, FRAYED ⟨a ~ flag⟩ ⟨a ~ sail⟩ ⟨discarded and ~ garments —Jack London⟩ **b :** almost exhausted from stress and strain **:** worn out ⟨drove us ~ with questions that revealed the most fantastically confused sources of information —Verna C. Millan⟩ — compare RUN RAGGED **4 :** wearing tattered clothes ⟨men ~ as the tramps, but going back to cold houses —Josephine Johnson⟩ **5 a :** irregularly strung out **:** STRAGGLY ⟨a ~ grove of palms —T.E. Lawrence⟩ **b :** executed or performed in an irregular, uneven, or uncoordinated manner **:** UNPOLISHED ⟨a rambling, ~ . . . book —*Times Lit. Supp.*⟩ ⟨send up a ~ cheer —Arnold Hill⟩ ⟨~ play on defense —*N.Y.Times*⟩ **c** *of a sound* **:** HARSH, DISSONANT ⟨a voice ~ with anxiety —Alan Sullivan⟩ ⟨the engine sounded ~ —H.H.Arnold & I.C.Eaker⟩ — **on the ragged edge :** in a state of anxiety or foreboding **:** on the verge of something dreaded ⟨a year lived *on the ragged edge* —Harlan Cleveland⟩ ⟨*on the ragged edge* of want —F.L.Allen⟩

**ragged cup** *n* **:** CUP PLANT

**ragged fringed orchid** *n* **:** RAGGED ORCHIS

**ragged jack** *n* **:** RAGGED ROBIN

**ragged jacket** *n* **:** a harp seal during its first molt

**ragged lady** *n* **1 :** SCARLET GAURA **2 :** LOVE-IN-A-MIST 1

**rag·ged·ly** *adv* **:** in a ragged manner: as **a :** ROUGHLY, SHAGGILY ⟨a white beard, ~ cut —Charles Dickens⟩ **b :** IRREGULARLY, STRAGGLINGLY ⟨the line of volunteers crawled forward ~ —Marjory S. Douglas⟩ ⟨stone walls trail ~ through the woods —*Amer. Guide Series: Vt.*⟩ **c :** without coordination **:** UNEVENLY ⟨a band struck up ~ —Lawrence Durrell⟩

**rag·ged·ness** *n* -ES **:** the quality or state of being ragged

**ragged orchis** *or* **ragged orchid** *n* **:** a fringed orchid (*Habenaria lacera*) of the eastern U. S. having a greenish flower with the lip deeply lacerate — called also *green fringed orchis*

**ragged robin** *n* **:** a perennial herb (*Lychnis floscuculi*) cultivated for its pink flowers with petals cut into narrow lobes

**ragged sailor** *n* **1 :** CORNFLOWER 1b **2 :** PRINCE'S-FEATHER 2 **3 :** a moderate purplish blue that is lighter and stronger than marine blue, bluer and less strong than average cornflower, and bluer, lighter, and stronger than gentian blue

**ragged school** *n* **:** a free school for destitute English children

**ragged staff** *n* [ME *ragged staffe*, fr. *ragged* + *staffe* staff] **:** a staff with knobs on each side

**ragged–tooth shark** \ˈ==,=-\ *n* **:** a medium-sized grayish sand shark (*Carcharius taurus*) widely distributed in warm seas and in some regions regarded as a dangerous man-eater

**rag·gedy** \ˈragədē, -di\ *adj* [*ragged* + *-y*] **:** marked by or tending to raggedness **:** somewhat ragged ⟨a ~ man⟩ ⟨~ hair⟩ ⟨you look starved and ~ —Saul Bellow⟩ ⟨making ~ yellow and black patterns —Richard Llewellyn⟩ ⟨~ carnival tune —Truman Capote⟩

**rag·gee** *also* **rag·gi** *or* **rag·gy** *or* **ra·gi** \ˈragē\ *n* -S [Hindi *rāgī*] **:** an East Indian cereal grass (*Eleusine coracana*) from whose seeds is ground a somewhat bitter flour that is a staple food in the Orient — called also *finger millet, korakan*

**rag·ger** \ˈragə(r)\ *n* -S [¹*rag* + *-er*] **:** an engine-lathe operator who rough-turns hardened steel rolls

**rag·gety** \ˈragədˑē\ *adj* [alter. of *raggedy*] *dial* **:** RAGGED

**ragging** *n* -S [fr. gerund of ⁵*rag*] **1 :** grains of heavy material placed on the sieve of a jig to form an artificial bed in ore dressing **2 :** the act or process of breaking lumps of ore with a heavy sledge

**¹rag·gle** \ˈragəl\ *vt* -ED/-ING/-S [origin unknown] **:** to cut a raggle in (stone)

**²raggle** \"\ *n* -S **1 :** a groove cut in masonry; *esp* **:** one that receives the upper edge of a flashing above a roof **2 :** a manufactured building unit provided with a groove into which metal flashing can be fitted

**rag·gle–tag·gle** \ˌragəlˈtagəl\ *adj* [irreg. fr. *ragtag*] **:** MOTLEY ⟨*raggle-taggle* gypsies⟩ ⟨a forlorn, *raggle-taggle* show —Edwin Corle⟩

**¹rag·gy** \ˈragē\ *adj* -ER/-EST [ME, fr. OE *raggig*, fr. (assumed) *ragg* rag + *-ig* -y — more at RAG] **:** RAGGED, ROUGH

**²raggy** \"\ *adj* -ER/-EST [⁶*rag* + *-y*] **:** of, relating to, or marked by ragtime ⟨the ~ early brass band jazz —Rudi Blesh⟩

**raging** *adj* [fr. pres. part. of ²*rage*] **1 :** that rages **2 :** causing great pain or distress ⟨troubled with a ~ tooth —Shak.⟩ **3 :** VIOLENT, WILD ⟨the ~ passion of the victors —Laurence Binyon⟩ **4 :** EXTRAORDINARY, TREMENDOUS ⟨a ~ beauty —William Plomer⟩ ⟨a ~ success —Leslie Rees⟩ — **rag·ing·ly** *adv*

**rag·lan** \ˈraglən\ *n* -S [after F.J.H.Somerset, Baron *Raglan* †1855 Brit. field marshal] **:** any of various loose overcoats with raglan sleeves

**raglan sleeve** *n* [*raglan* + *sleeve*] **:** a sleeve extending to the neckline and so having slanted seams from the underarm to the neck in front and back

raglan sleeve

**rag·let** \ˈraglət\ *n* -S [origin unknown] **:** RAGGLE 1

**rag·man** \ˈ=,man, -,maa(ə)n, -mən\ *n, pl* **ragmen** [¹*rag* + *man*] **:** a man who collects or deals in rags and refuse

**rag·man roll** \ˈragmən-\ *or* **ragman's roll** *n* [ME *Ragmane rolle*, roll used in a medieval game and containing verses describing various characters, fr. AF *Ragemon le bon*, lit., Ragemon the good (fr. the name of one of the characters serving as title of the verses) + ME *rolle* roll] **1** *obs* **:** a long list (as on a scroll or document) **:** CATALOG ⟨the whole *ragman roll* of fasting days —Thomas Nash⟩ **2 :** a series of rolls of deeds on parchment in which the Scottish nobility and gentry subscribed allegiance to Edward I of England in 1291 and esp. in 1296 during Edward's progress through Scotland and at the parliament of Berwick — usu. used in pl.

**rag·mat·i·cal** \(ˈ)ragˈmadˑəkəl\ *adj* [origin unknown] *archaic* **:** TURBULENT, RIOTOUS ⟨~ fellow —Tobias Smollett⟩

**ra·gout** \raˈgü\ *n* -S [F *ragoût*, fr. *ragoûter* to revive the taste, fr. *re-* + *a-* ad- + *goût* taste, fr. L *gustus;* akin to L *gustare* to taste — more at CHOOSE] **:** meat and vegetables well seasoned and cooked in a thick rich usu. brown sauce

**rag paper** *n* **:** a paper made wholly or partly from rags

**ragpicker** \ˈ=,==\ *n* **:** one that picks up rags and refuse (as from rubbish cans or public dumps) as a means of livelihood

**ragpicker's disease** *or* **ragsorter's disease** *n* **:** pulmonary anthrax caused by inhalation of spores of the anthrax bacillus from contaminated wool or other hair

**rag rug** *n* **:** a hand-woven or machine-woven rug made with a heavy cotton warp and a filling of rags torn into strips whose ends are tied or sewed together

**rags** *pl of* RAG, *pres 3d sing of* RAG

**ragshag** \ˈ=,=\ *n* -S [¹*rag* + *shag*] **:** a person in ragged or masquerade dress ⟨a ~ parade⟩

**ragsorter** \ˈ=,==\ *n* **:** one that sorts and prepares rags and old clothing for new uses (as in papermaking)

**ragstone** \ˈ=,=\ *n* [²*rag*] **:** any of various hard rocks **:** RAG

**ragtag** \ˈ=,=\ *n* [¹*rag* + *tag*] **:** a motley crowd ⟨a ~ of admiring youngsters at his heels —Paul Gallico⟩

**rag, tag, and bobtail** *or* **ragtag and bobtail** *n* **:** RABBLE, RIFFRAFF ⟨the *rag, tag, and bobtail* of the city —Kenneth Roberts⟩ ⟨a *ragtag and bobtail* army —F.V.W.Mason⟩

**rag·time** \ˈrag,tīm\ *n* [prob. fr. *ragged* + *time*] **1 :** rhythm characterized by strong syncopation in the melody with a regularly accented accompaniment **2 :** music having ragtime rhythm

**rag·tim·er** \-mə(r)\ *n* [*ragtime* + *-er*] **:** a person who composes or plays ragtime ⟨the first . . . ~*s* were piano syncopators of decided originality —Wilder Hobson⟩

**rag·timey** \-mē\ *adj* **:** of, relating to, or like ragtime

**rag·u·ly** \ˈragyəlē\ *also* **rag·u·lé** \ˌragyəˈlā\ *adj* [perh. fr. ¹*rag* + *-uly, -ulé* (as in *nebuly, nebulé*)] **:** notched in regular oblique breaks — used of a heraldic line of partition or charge (as a cross or saltier)

**ragweed** \ˈ=,=\ *n* [¹*rag* + *weed;* fr. the ragged shape of the leaves] **1 :** TANSY RAGWORT **2 :** any of various chiefly No. American weedy herbaceous plants that constitute the genus *Ambrosia* and produce highly allergenic pollen responsible for much hay fever and asthma: as **a :** an annual weed (*A. artemisiifolia*) with finely divided foliage that is common on open or cultivated ground in much of No. America and is introduced elsewhere by accident **b :** GREAT RAGWEED **c :** an annual to perennial highly variable weed (*A. psilostachya*) chiefly of dry barren lands of the southwestern U. S. and Mexico **3 :** FRANSERIA 2

**ragweed family** *n* **:** AMBROSIACEAE

**rag wheel** *n* **1 :** SPROCKET WHEEL **2 :** a polishing wheel made of disks of cloth clamped together

**ragwork** *n* **:** rubblework of thin small stones

**rag worm** *n* **:** any of various aquatic worms used as bait

**ragwort** \ˈ=,=\ *n* [ME, fr. *ragge* rag + *wort;* fr. the ragged shape of its leaves] **:** any of several herbs of the genus *Senecio; esp* **:** TANSY RAGWORT — see GOLDEN RAGWORT, PURPLE RAGWORT

**¹rah** \ˈrä, ˈrȯ\ *interj* [short for *hurrah*] — used esp. in a cheer and usu. reduplicated to express joy, approbation, or encouragement

**²rah** \"\ *n* -S **:** HURRAH

**³rah** \"\ *vi* -ED/-ING/-S **:** HURRAH

**ra·han·wein** \ˈrähən,wēn\ *n, pl* **rahanwein** *or* **rahanweins** *usu cap* **:** one of a group of peoples in Somaliland characterized esp. by a strong Negroid mixture

**rah·dar** \ˈrä,där, =ˈ=\ *n* -S [Hindi *rāhdār*, fr. Per] *India* **:** a keeper of a toll road

**¹rah–rah** \ˈ=ˈ=\ *adj* [fr. redupl. of ¹*rah*] **1 :** given to cheering (as at games) **:** demonstrative in the expression of college spirit ⟨the pennant-waving, *rah-rah* boy —*Badger Report*⟩ **2 :** relating to the boisterous or enthusiastic expression of college spirit ⟨typical college *rah-rah* activities —Clyde Kennedy⟩

**²rah–rah** \"\ *vi* -ED/-ING/-S **:** HURRAH

**ra·ia** \ˈrā(y)ə\ [NL, fr. L, ray] *syn of* RAJA

**ra·iae** \ˈrā,(y)ē\ [NL, fr. L, pl. of *raia* ray] *syn of* BATOIDEI

**¹raid** \ˈrād\ *n* -S [Sc dial., fr. OE *rād* ride, raid — more at ROAD] **1 a :** a hostile or predatory incursion by mounted men ⟨a border ~⟩ **b :** a sudden and rapid invasion or military operation esp. on a small scale **:** FORAY, INROAD ⟨a ~ specifically designed to capture one or more prisoners —*Combat Forces Jour.*⟩; *specif* **:** a surprise attack made usu. by a small force (as of airplanes, fast naval craft, or ground or amphibious forces) and with no intention of holding the territory or area invaded — compare AIR RAID **c :** an attack upon enemy or neutral merchant ships in shipping lanes **2 a :** a brief expedition or hurried movement into a place or situation outside one's usual sphere esp. for the purpose of obtaining something ⟨a ~ upon the neighborhood shops⟩ **b :** a sudden attack or invasion by officers of the law (as for the purpose of making arrests or seizing illicit stores) ⟨a ~ upon a gambling house⟩ **c :** a venture by wild animals or birds onto cultivated land esp. for food ⟨on its early morning ~*s* on the peas in adjacent gardens —*Brit. Birds in Colour*⟩ ⟨~*s* by baboons⟩ **d :** a daring or unorthodox operation against a competitor or rival (as to gain recruits or exert pressure) ⟨signed many baseball stars in a ~ of the major leagues⟩; *specif* **:** an effort by one union to win as members workers already belonging to another union **3 :** the act of mulcting esp. public money (as by graft or pork-barrel appropriations) ⟨forestall a ~ on the treasury⟩ **4 :** an attempt by professional operators to depress prices of stocks by concerted selling

**²raid** \"\ *vb* -ED/-ING/-S *vt* **:** to make a raid upon or into ⟨amassed their cattle and horses by ~*ing* the herds of other clans —*Current Biog.*⟩ ⟨rear-area units ~*ed* of their physically fit —*Time*⟩ ⟨the sinking fund was ~*ed* year after year for ever-increasing amounts —J.H.Plumb⟩ ⟨when the barn owl ~*s* sparrow roosts —W.H.Dowdeswell⟩ ⟨~ the icebox⟩ ~ *vi* **:** to conduct or take part in a raid **:** MARAUD ⟨300 Indians were sent . . . to ~ on the settlers —Louise Koier⟩ ⟨~*ing* parties crossed the border repeatedly⟩

**raid·er** \ˈrādə(r)\ *n* -S **1 :** one that raids **:** one that leads or participates in a raid **2 :** a fast unarmored lightly armed ship designed to capture or destroy merchant shipping — called also *commerce raider* **3 :** an airplane engaged in raiding ⟨most of the ~*s* were two-engined fighter-bombers —*Newsweek*⟩ **4 :** a member of a battalion (as of U. S. Marines) specially trained for close-range fighting — compare COMMANDO, RANGER

**raie ul·time** \ˌrā,ülˈtēm\ *n, pl* **raies ultimes** \"\ [F, lit., ultimate line] **:** one of the observed lines of the spectrum of an element which are the last to disappear as the quantity of the element is decreased — called also *ultimate line*

**ra·ii·dae** \ˈrā(y)ə,dē\ [NL *Raia*, type genus + *-idae*] *syn of* RAJIDAE

**¹raik** \ˈrāk\ *vi* [ME *raiken* to go, stroll, wander, fr. ON *reika*] *archaic* **:** ³RAKE

**²raik** \"\ *n* -S [ME, act of going, wandering, ground over which animals move, fr. ON *reik*, act of wandering] *archaic* **:** ⁴RAKE

**¹rail** \ˈrāl, *esp before pause or consonant* ˈrāəl\ *n* -S [ME *reil*, fr. OE *hrægl* garment, cloak; akin to OFris *hreil* garment, OHG *hregil*] **1** *archaic* **:** a loose garment worn in varying styles by women since the early medieval period **2** *obs* **:** a neckerchief for women

**²rail** \"\ *n* -S [ME *raile*, fr. MF *reille* ruler, bar, fr. L *regula* straight piece of wood, ruler, fr. *regere* to keep straight, direct, rule — more at RIGHT] **1 a :** a bar usu. of timber or metal extending from one post or support to another as a guard or barrier (as in a fence, balustrade, or staircase); *specif* **:** one made by splitting a small log and used esp. in making rail fences — compare RIDER 6a **b :** a horizontal structural member in a frame or paneling (as in furniture, woodwork, or stage flats) — compare NEWEL, STILE; see DOOR illustration **c :** a long piece of wood or other material serving as a structural member or support (as in a piano action or an automobile frame) ⟨curtain ~⟩ ⟨the side ~*s* of a ladder⟩ ⟨the brass ~ in a saloon⟩ **2 a :** a construction of bars and posts **:** FENCE, RAILING **b** (1) **:** the stout narrow plank that forms the top of the bulwarks of a ship (2) **:** a light structure of wood or metal serving as a guard at the outer extremity of a deck — often used in combination ⟨poop ~⟩ ⟨forecastle ~⟩ — see SHIP illustration (3) **:** a section of planking with holes for belaying pins (as around a mast or across the shrouds) — see FIFE RAIL; compare PINRAIL **a c :** a fence bounding a racetrack ⟨the inner ~⟩ ⟨the outer ~⟩ **3 a :** a bar orig. of wood but now usu. of rolled steel forming a track for vehicles whose wheels run in a depression in the bar (as in street railways) or on the top of the bar ⟨piers carry the overhead crane ~*s* —*Architectural Rev.*⟩ — compare BULLHEADED 3b, FLANGE RAIL, T RAIL **b** (1) **:** railroad rails in bulk ⟨trend toward the use of heavier ~ —*Yrbk. of Railroad Information*⟩ (2) **:** a continuous line of railroad rails ⟨boys walking on the ~⟩ ⟨lay ~⟩ (3) **:** TRACK ⟨the meanest stretch of ~ ever spiked —A.W.Somerville⟩ — usu. used in pl. ⟨a sleek and shining streamliner hurrying along the ~*s* —*Stories Behind the Pictures*⟩ ⟨network of ~*s* sharply divides the industrial section —*Amer. Guide Series: Texas*⟩ **c :** RAILROAD ⟨travel or ship by ~⟩ ⟨the ~*s* want more liberal treatment as to tax write-offs for depreciation —*Sat. Eve. Post*⟩ ⟨the terminal of the central ~ —Irene S. van Dongen⟩ **4 rails** *pl* **:** stocks or bonds of railroad companies **5** *slang* **:** a railroad employee **6 :** CARRIAGE RAIL **7 :** the cushioned rim around the bed of a billiard, pool, or crap table — **on the rails 1 :** progressing satisfactorily or rapidly **:** well under way ⟨got the joint European defense effort *on the rails* —*Christian Science Monitor*⟩ **2 :** on the proper course ⟨weak men would apparently take to crime who had previously been kept *on the rails* by a certain balance existing in society —Herbert Butterfield⟩ — **over the rail** *adv* **:** over the side of a ship ⟨paused a second and then went *over the rail* —L.M.Uris⟩

**³rail** \"\ *vt* -ED/-ING/-S [ME *railen*, fr. *raile* rail] **1 :** to provide with rails or a railing **:** FENCE ⟨being ~*ed* away solicitously from small precipices —Elizabeth Bowen⟩ — often used with *in* or *off* ⟨~ in a space⟩ **2** *chiefly Brit* **:** to transport by railroad ⟨apricots and plums, ~*ed* in large containers —*Farmer's Weekly (So. Africa)*⟩

**⁴rail** \"\ *adj* **:** of or relating to railroads ⟨~ connections for various points⟩

**⁵rail** \"\ *n, pl* **rail** *or* **rails** [ME *rale, raile*, fr. MF *raale*] **:** any of numerous precocial wading birds structurally related to the cranes but of small or medium size having short rounded wings, a short tail, and usu. very long toes that enable them to run on the soft mud of swamps and constituting a distinct subfamily of Rallidae; *broadly* **:** a bird of the family Rallidae — see BLACK RAIL, CLAPPER RAIL, CORNCRAKE, KING RAIL, SORA, WATER RAIL

**⁶rail** \"\ *vb* -ED/-ING/-S [ME *railen*, fr. MF *railler* to ridicule, mock, fr. OProv *ralhar* to babble, joke, fr. (assumed) VL *ragulare* to bray, fr. LL *ragere* to neigh] *vi* **1 :** to revile or scold in harsh, insolent, or vituperative language **:** utter reproaches, abuse, or angry complaints **:** RANT ⟨listened to herself ~ on —Clae Waltham⟩ ⟨cursed and ~*ed*, and finally declared he was going to trail the raiders —Zane Grey⟩ ⟨went abroad to ~ at the insecurity and poverty —Edmund Wilson⟩ ⟨made their listeners aware of the very things they were ~*ing* against —J.G.Harrison⟩ **2** *obs* **:** SCOFF, JEST, BANTER ~ *vt, archaic* **:** to move, effect, or influence by railing ⟨noble natures . . . are not ~*ed* into vice —Sir Thomas Browne⟩ **syn** see SCOLD

**⁷rail** \"\ *n* -S **:** RAILING, TAUNTING, SCOLDING

**rail·age** \ˈrālij\ *n* -S [³*rail* + *-age*] *Brit* **:** railroad transportation **:** the charge for conveyance by rail

**rail anchor** *n* [²*rail*] **:** a device to help maintain the proper line and gage of track by resisting the longitudinal movement of rails under traffic and maintaining proper expansion allowance at joint gaps for temperature changes

**railbed** \ˈ=,=\ *n* **:** the roadbed of a railroad track ⟨crossed a ~ buried in the snow —Wright Morris⟩

**railbird** \ˈ=,=\ *n* [⁵*rail* + *bird*] **1 :** RAIL; *esp* **:** SORA **2** [²*rail* + *bird*] **:** a racing enthusiast who sits on or near the track rail to watch a race or workout

**rail bond** *n* [²*rail*] **:** an electric jumper around a joint in the rails of a track to insure continuity of conductivity for signal currents

**rail bus** *n* **:** a passenger car with an automotive engine for operation on rails

**railcar** \ˈ=,=\ *n* **:** a self-propelled railroad car carrying passengers, baggage, mail, goods, or combinations of these — compare RAIL DIESEL CAR

**rail carrier** *n* **:** a company whose business is transporting persons or goods or both by railroad

**rail chair** *n* **:** CHAIR 5a

**rail clamp** *n* **:** a device for clamping on rails to prevent or halt the movement of railroad cars past a given point (as at platforms or on stub tracks)

**rail clip** *n* **1 :** a metal plate projecting over the base of a rail for bolting the rail to its support **2 :** an anchor for fastening the rear of a derrick car or a crane to the rails of a track to keep the crane from tipping while lifting a heavy load **3 :** a metal support bolted or clamped to a rail for carrying a detector bar

**rail creep** *n* **:** the longitudinal movement of rail produced by the passage of trains over it

**rail diesel car** *n* **:** a self-propelled railroad car powered by a diesel engine and capable of operating as a single unit or in combination with other rail diesel cars as a train — abbr. *RDC;* compare RAILCAR

**railed** *past of* RAIL

**rail·er** \ˈrālə(r)\ *n* -S [⁶*rail* + *-er*] **:** one that rails **:** REVILER

**railfan** \ˈ=,=\ *n* [²*rail* + *fan*] **:** one whose hobby is railroads or model railroads **:** a railroad enthusiast

**rail fence** *n* [²*rail*] **:** a fence of posts and usu. split rails — compare WORM FENCE

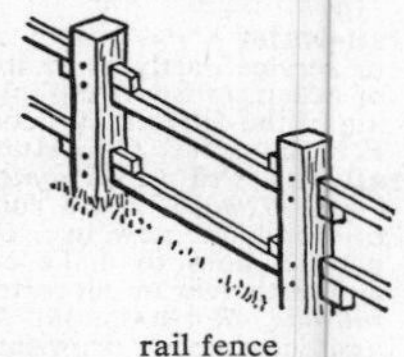

rail fence

**rail–fence cipher** *n* **:** a zigzag transposition method in which alternate letters of the plaintext are juxtaposed (as in the encipherment $^{b}r_{i}d^{g}e$=birgde)

**rail fork** *n* **:** a bar with a forked end for turning railroad rails

**rail guard** *n* **:** a vertical metal device attached to the front of a locomotive ahead of either front wheel to clear the rail of obstructions

**railhead** \ˈ=,=\ *n* **1 a** (1) **:** a point on a railroad at which traffic may originate or terminate (2) **:** a point on a railroad in a theater of operations at which supplies for troops are unloaded for distribution and forwarding **b :** the end of a railroad line (as of one under construction) **2 :** the top portion of the rail that carries the wheels of rolling stock

**¹railing** *n* -S [fr. gerund of ³*rail*] **1 :** a barrier (as a fence or balustrade) consisting of a rail and supports **2 :** RAILS; *also* **:** material for making rails **3 :** a strip of wood covering the roughed ends or edges of a board or piece of plywood

**²railing** *n* -S [fr. gerund of ⁶*rail*] **:** INVECTIVE, RANTING ⟨his self-pity and his ~*s* at fate —*Times Lit. Supp.*⟩

**³railing** *n* -S [fr. gerund of ³*rail*] *Brit* **:** a shipment by rail ⟨potato ~*s* were well maintained —*Farmer's Weekly (So. Africa)*⟩

**rail·ing·ly** *adv* [²*railing* + *-ly*] **:** in a railing manner

**rail·lery** \ˈrālərē, -ri\ *n* -ES [F *raillerie*, fr. MF *railler* to rail + *-erie* -ery — more at RAIL] **1 :** good-natured ridicule **:** pleasantry touched with satire **:** BANTER, CHAFFING, MOCKERY ⟨mistaking bustle for style, ~ for badinage, and noise for gaiety —Benjamin Disraeli⟩ ⟨know when delicate ~ was properly called for —Jane Austen⟩ ⟨actually refers to you without fury, even with ~ —G.B.Shaw⟩ **2 :** an instance of good-natured ridicule **:** JEST

**rail·less** \ˈrālləs\ *adj* [²*rail* + *-less*] **:** being without rails or railing **:** UNRAILED ⟨~ trolley⟩ ⟨sit on the ~ porch —James Jones⟩ ⟨a thousand ~ miles —T.H.White b. 1915⟩

**rail·leur** \raˈyər\ *n* -S [F, fr. MF *railler* + *-eur* -or] **:** one given to raillery

**rail·lie·ti·na** \ˌrālyəˈtīnə\ *n, cap* [NL, fr. A. *Railliet*, 19th cent. Fr. biologist + NL *-ina*] **:** a large genus of armed tapeworms (family Davaineidae) having the adults parasitic in birds, rodents, or rarely man and the larvae in various insects

**raillike** \ˈ=,=\ *adj* **:** resembling a rail

**rail lugger** *n* [perh. alter. of *rail hugger*, fr. ²*rail* + *hugger*] *slang* **:** a horse or dog that bears toward or runs close to the inside rail in a race

**rail·ly** \'rālē\ *vb* [F *railler*, fr. MF — more at RAIL] *vt, archaic* : JEST, MOCK ~ *vi, archaic* : RALLY, RIDICULE

**rail·man** \'=mən\ *n, pl* **railmen 1 :** a cable hand **2 :** a dock worker who signals from the ship's rail during loading and unloading **3 :** one employed on a railroad

**rail-motor** \'='==\ *adj* **:** relating to service or rates involving transportation partly by railroad and partly by highway vehicle

[1]**rail·road** \'rā(ə)l,rōd *sometimes* 'rāu̇,- *or* 'reu̇,-\ *n, often attrib* [[2]*rail* + *road*] **1 :** RAILWAY 1, 3 **2 a :** a permanent road having a line of rails fixed to ties and laid to gage usu. on a leveled or graded ballasted roadbed and providing a track for freight cars, passenger cars, and other rolling stock designed to be drawn by locomotives or sometimes propelled by self-contained motors — see ELEVATED RAILROAD, LIGHT RAILWAY; compare TRAMWAY **b :** such a road together with all the lands, buildings, rolling stock, franchises, and other assets relating thereto and constituting a single property **:** a railroad company ⟨~ shares⟩ **3 railroads** *pl* **:** the securities of railroad transportation companies **4 :** a split in bowling in which there is a greater than one-pin distance between the pins left standing making it necessary to hit one pin on the side to slide it across the intervening space to hit another pin in order to make a spare ⟨6-7-10 ~⟩ ⟨8-10 ~⟩

[2]**railroad** \"\ *vt* **1 :** to build railroads in ⟨~ a country⟩ **2 :** to transport by railroad **3 a :** to send or put through in great haste or without due consideration (as for private benefit) ⟨~ the measure through the legislature⟩ **b** (1) **:** to send (type matter) to press before reading and correction (2) **:** to send (copy) to the composing room without careful editing **4 :** to convict and send esp. to prison with undue haste and usu. by the use of false charges or insufficient evidence **:** FRAME ⟨a convicted person who claims to have been ~*ed* by evidence that was improperly procured —O.K.Fraenkel⟩ ⟨being ~*ed* into a booby hatch —Sidney Howard⟩ ⟨~*ed* two radicals to death —Lawrence Elliott⟩ ~ *vi* **1 :** to become employed on a railroad **2 :** to travel by rail **3 :** to build a railroad ⟨this new, raw land was well worth ~*ing* into —*Amer. Guide Series: Wash.*⟩

[3]**railroad** \"\ *adj, of a card game* **:** adapted for play by commuters on railroads with the rules of the game modified to produce quick decisions ⟨~ bridge⟩ ⟨~ euchre⟩

**railroad board** *n* **:** a coated or uncoated board used for show-cards, tickets, car signs, and tags

**railroad bridge** *n* **:** a bridge constructed for the exclusive or chief purpose of carrying railroad traffic

**railroad car** *n* **:** CAR 1c

**railroad engineer** *n* **:** RAILWAY ENGINEER

**railroad engineering** *n* **:** RAILWAY ENGINEERING

**rail·road·er** \-də(r)\ *n* -s [[1]*railroad* + *-er*] **:** a railroad employee or official

**railroad flat** *or* **railroad apartment** *n* **:** an apartment in a substandard building having a series of narrow rooms arranged in line usu. with each room forming the corridor to the next and with only the front and rear rooms having windows

**railroad furniture** *n* **:** metal printing furniture that resembles railroad rails in shape and is used mostly to fill gutters

**rail·road·i·ana** \,rāl,rōdē'anə\ *n pl* [[1]*railroad* + *-ana*] **1 :** literature of or relating to railroads **2 :** the history or lore of railroads

**railroading** *n* [fr. gerund of [2]*railroad*] **:** construction or operation of a railroad line **:** the business of managing a railroad or of working as an employee of a railroad

**railroad jack** *n* **1 :** a portable jack used for heavy lifting **2 a :** a 4-screw or 6-screw hoist operated by electric motors for lifting locomotives off their wheels while they are undergoing repairs **b :** a hydraulic lift device operated either by hand lever or motor

**railroad man** *n* **:** RAILROADER

**railroad manila** *n* **:** a cheap yellow writing paper containing groundwood and used for school writing tablets, sales books, and order blanks

**railroad sickness** *n* **:** a disease of cattle resembling milk fever presumably due to comparable metabolic imbalance and occurring esp. in cows in advanced pregnancy and in fat cows or steers during or after a long drive or journey by rail or truck — compare GRASS TETANY

**railroad spike** *n* **:** a hook-headed spike for securing the rails of a railroad to the ties

**railroad station** *n* **:** a building containing accommodations for railroad passengers or freight — called also *depot*

**railroad vine** *n* **:** a creeping or climbing vine (*Ipomea pes-capri*) of the coastal sand dunes from Florida to Texas having flowers with a purple corolla limb and suborbicular leaves with an apical notch

railroad spike

**railroad worm** *n* **1 :** APPLE MAGGOT **2 :** the larva or wingless female of any of several So. American beetles (genus *Phrixothrix*) of the family Cantharidae

**rails** *pl of* RAIL, *pres 3d sing of* RAIL

**railside** \'=,=\ *adj* [[2]*rail* + *side*] **:** situated beside a railroad track or right of way

**rail-splitter** \'=,==\ *n* **:** one that makes logs into fence rails

**rail sweep** *n* **:** a device on the front of a railcar for brushing easily removable obstructions from the surface of the railhead

**rail tongs** *n pl* **:** tongs used by trackmen for lifting rails

**rail train** *n* **:** a train of rolls in a rolling mill for making railroad rails

**rail-water** \'='==\ *adj* **:** of or relating to transportation rates or service partly by railroad and partly by inland waterway or ocean transport esp. by through bill of lading ⟨the narrowing of the differential between all-rail and *rail-water* routes —E.R.Johnson & G.G.Huebner⟩

**rail·way** \'rā(ə)l,wā *sometimes* 'rāu̇, *or* 'reu̇,-\ *n, often attrib* [[2]*rail* + *way*] **1 :** a runway or track formed of rails orig. of wood but now usu. of steel laid end to end usu. in two parallel lines to make a permanent way for cars **:** a way laid with two or more tracks in such manner — called also *railroad* **2 :** RAILROAD 2; *often* **:** a railroad operating with light equipment or within a small area — compare STREET RAILWAY **3 :** a line of track providing a runway for wheels ⟨a cash or parcel ~ in a department store⟩ ⟨the ~ of a traveling crane⟩

**rail·way·ac** \-wā,ak\ *n* -s [*railway* + mani*ac*] *Brit* **:** RAILFAN

**railway artillery** *n* **:** artillery mounted on and fired from artillery cars

**railway bridge** *n* **:** RAILROAD BRIDGE

**railway engineer** *n* **:** an engineer whose training or occupation is in railway engineering

**railway engineering** *n* **:** a branch of civil engineering dealing with the location, construction, and maintenance of railroads

**rail·way·less** \-wālə̇s\ *adj* **:** lacking railways ⟨the all but roadless, ~ deserts —Joseph Wechsberg⟩

**railway letter** *n, Brit* **:** a letter carried on a railway or ship by the railway service instead of by the postal service and received by the railway from the sender and delivered by the railway to the addressee either directly at a railway station or through a post office

**railway mail car** *n* **:** a railroad car carrying mail that is sorted in transit — compare POSTAL STORAGE CAR

**railway mail clerk** *n* **:** one who sorts and classifies mail in a railway mail car

**rail·way·man** \'==,man, -,maa(ə)n, -mən\ *n, pl* **railwaymen** [*railway* + *man*] **:** RAILROADER

**railway post office** *n* **:** RAILWAY MAIL CAR

**railway station** *n* **:** RAILROAD STATION

[1]**rai·ment** \'rāmənt\ *n* -s [ME *rayment*, short for *arrayment, arayment*] **1 :** CLOTHING, VESTURE, GARMENTS ⟨if these strangers were of important air and costly ~ —Brian O'Nolan⟩ ⟨had no change of ~ —John Buchan⟩ ⟨bore necessities of life, such as food and ~ and shelter —*New Yorker*⟩ **2** *obs* **:** an article of dress

[2]**raiment** \"\ *vt* -ED/-ING/-S **:** CLOTHE, GARB, APPAREL ⟨was ~*ed* in silks⟩

**rai·ment·less** \-tlə̇s\ *adj* **:** lacking raiment

[1]**rain** \'rān\ *n* -s *often attrib* [ME *reyn*, fr. OE *regn*, *rēn*; akin to OHG *regan* rain, ON *regn*, Goth *rign*, and perh. to ON *raki* dampness, L *rigare* to water] **1 a :** water falling in drops condensed from vapor in the atmosphere — compare DRIZZLE, MIST **b :** the descent of water in drops esp. from the clouds **c :** water that has fallen as rain **:** RAINWATER ⟨the ~ on the door log had turned to ice —Conrad Richter⟩ **2 a :** a fall of rain esp. heavier or of longer duration than a shower **:** RAINSTORM ⟨the roads . . . can be used in summer only and then if there are no unusual ~*s* —W.E.Rudolph⟩ ⟨spring ~*s*⟩ **b rains** *pl* **:** the rainy season (as in India) **3 :** rainy weather ⟨a week of ~⟩ **4 a :** a falling or driving of numerous particles or bodies ⟨a ~ of petals⟩ ⟨a ~ of soot⟩ ⟨warships maintained a steady ~ of fire —H.L.Merillat⟩; *also* **:** multitudinous onset ⟨a ~ of protests⟩ ⟨a ~ of abuse⟩ **b :** falling or driven particles ⟨an average pollen ~ for a locality —S.A.Cain⟩ **5 :** a scratch or marking running lengthwise of a motion picture film that on projection appears as a vertical streak **6 rains** *pl* **:** regions of calms and heavy rainfalls ⟨the ~*s* of the north Atlantic⟩

[2]**rain** \"\ *vb* -ED/-ING/-S [ME *reynen*, fr. OE *regnian;* akin to OHG *reganōn* to rain, ON *regna*, Goth *rignjan;* all fr. a prehistoric Gmc verb derived fr. the ancestor of OE *regn* rain] *vi* **1 :** to fall as water in drops from the clouds ⟨care must be taken that such materials are dry and not ~*ed* on —*Bull. of Amer. Inst. of Architects*⟩ — often used with *it* ⟨it may ~⟩ ⟨it is ~*ing* in at the window⟩ **2 :** to send down rain ⟨caused the clouds to ~ —Norman Douglas⟩ **3 a :** to fall or drop like rain ⟨bombs, grapeshot, and cannonballs ~*ed* upon the defenseless town —*Amer. Guide Series: Maine*⟩ **b :** to occur in a multitudinous onset ⟨conflicting thoughts ~ thick and fast —*Saturday Rev.*⟩ **4 :** to be in a form or arrangement suggestive of falling rain ⟨gray hair ~*ing* down over his eyebrows —Anna Ortese⟩ ⟨trunks whose lower boughs were out of sight among the ~*ing* aerial roots as fine as hairs —D.C.Peattie⟩ ~ *vt* **1 :** to pour from or as if from the clouds **:** shower down ⟨behold, I will ~ bread from heaven for you —Exod 16:4 (RSV)⟩ ⟨petals are ~*ed* down upon them from windows and balconies —John Kobler⟩ **2 :** to bestow profusely or abundantly **:** yield or shed copiously ⟨more blows were ~*ed* on him —T.B.Costain⟩ ⟨~ favors⟩

**rain area** *n* **1 :** the area indicated on a weather map over which rain fell within a period of time **2 :** the area over which rain is falling **3 :** the most rainy portion of a cyclonic storm

**rainband** \'=,=\ *n* **:** a dark band in the yellow portion of the solar spectrum near the sodium lines caused by watery vapor in the atmosphere and therefore sometimes used in weather predictions

**rain barrel** *n* **:** a barrel of or for rain water; *esp* **:** a barrel placed so as to catch water from eaves

**rain beetle** *n* **:** any of several black hairy beetles (genus *Pleocoma*) related to the scarab beetles

**rain belt** *n* **:** a region of relatively heavy rainfall

**rain·belt·er** \'rān,beltə(r)\ *n* -s [*rain belt* + *-er*] *West* **:** a new settler who takes up farming in a semiarid region during a rainy season

**rainbird** \'=,=\ *n* **:** any of numerous birds chiefly of the family Cuculidae whose cries are popularly believed to augur rain: as **a :** RAIN CROW **b :** a West Indian lizard cuckoo (*Saurothera vetula*) **c :** a koel (*Eudynamys scolopacea*) of India **d :** a So. American cuckoo of the genus *Piaya* **e** *dial Eng* **:** GREEN WOODPECKER

**rain boot** *n* **:** an ankle-high overshoe of rubber or plastic for wear in rain and mud

[1]**rain·bow** \'rān,bō\ *n* [ME *reinbowe*, fr. OE *rēnboga;* akin to OHG *reginbogo* rainbow, ON *regnbogi;* all fr. a prehistoric WGmc-NGmc compound whose first constituent is represented by OE *regn, rēn* rain and whose second constituent is represented by OE *boga* bow — more at RAIN, BOW] **1 a :** a circle or from the usual viewpoint an arc of a circle exhibiting in concentric bands the several colors of the spectrum and formed opposite the sun by the refraction and reflection of the sun's rays in drops of rain — see PRIMARY RAINBOW, SECONDARY RAINBOW **b :** a phenomenon similar to a rainbow in formation and appearance — see FOGBOW, MOONBOW, WHITE RAINBOW **2 a :** an arrangement of the colors of the spectrum **:** a multicolored or glittering array ⟨horizontal stripes in a ~ of colors —*New Yorker*⟩ ⟨silken cloak and a ~ of medals —E.T.Gilliard⟩ **b :** a wide assortment **:** a broad or complete range **:** GAMUT ⟨party was a catchall large enough to hold a ~ of opinions —E.O.Hauser⟩ **3 a :** ILLUSION, WILL-O'-THE-WISP ⟨families chasing the ~ of better fortune ever westward —Dixon Wecter⟩ ⟨proof that the early owners were not following a ~ —Allan Forbes & R.M.Eastman⟩ **b :** attainment of success or fortune **4 :** any of several brilliantly colored fork-tailed Andean hummingbirds of the genus *Coeligena* **5 :** RAINBOW TROUT

[2]**rainbow** \"\ *adj* **:** having the colors of the rainbow **:** MULTICOLORED ⟨shining robes, and wonderful ~ wings —Mark Twain⟩ ⟨~ effect⟩

[3]**rainbow** \"\ *vt* -ED/-ING/-S **:** to produce rainbows on **:** cause to be like a rainbow (as in coloring or form) **:** span as or like a rainbow ⟨~*ed* mists of the mountains —Frank Yerby⟩ ⟨under the ~*ed* prisms of the great chandelier —Winston Churchill⟩ ~ *vi* **:** to appear like a rainbow (as in coloring or in arrangement of colors ⟨stripes of color ~*ing* along Varadero Beach —Budd Schulberg⟩

**rainbow bird** *n* **:** an Australian bee-eater (*Merops ornatus*)

**rainbow boa** *n* **:** a moderate-sized iridescent boa (*Epicrates cenchris*) of the American tropics

**rainbow cactus** *n* **:** a stout cylindric cactus (*Echinocereus rigidissimus*) of the southwestern U.S. and adjacent Mexico with spines partly red and partly white, showy red flowers, and edible red fruit

**rainbow chaser** *n* **:** VISIONARY

**rainbow-colored** \'=,=¦==\ *adj* **:** exhibiting the colors of the spectrum **:** MULTICOLORED

**rainbow darter** *n* **:** a bright-colored darter (*Poecilichthys caeruleus*) of the Mississippi drainage and north and east into Ontario and New York

**rainbow drops** *n pl but sing or pl in constr* **:** a plant of the genus *Viscaria*

**rainbow duck** *n* **:** WOOD DUCK 1

**rainbow fish** *n* **1 :** any of numerous brilliantly colored wrasses and parrot fishes of tropical seas **2 :** GUPPY **3 :** a small brilliantly striped Australian freshwater silversides (*Melanotaenia nigrans*) sometimes kept in the tropical aquarium

**rainbow herring** *n* **:** a brilliantly colored smelt (*Osmerus dentex*) of the Bering sea region

**rainbow moss** *n* **:** a Chinese club moss (*Selaginella uncinata*) cultivated for its feathery blue-green foliage

**rainbow parrot fish** *n* **:** a large variably colored heavy-bodied parrotfish (*Pseudoscarus guacamaia*) of the tropical western Atlantic that is esp. common about Bermuda and may attain a length of four feet

**rainbow perch** *n* **:** a small surf fish (*Hypsurus caryi*) of the Pacific coast of No. America that is brilliantly striped in red, orange, and light blue and is of some importance as a market fish; *also* **:** a similar but larger and duller fish (*Taeniotoca lateralis*) of the same region

**rainbow pink** *n* **:** CHINA PINK

**rainbow rock cress** *n* **:** a plant of the genus *Aubrietia*

**rainbow roof** *n* **:** a pitched roof whose slopes are slightly convex giving it a delicately rounded appearance

rainbow roof

**rainbow runner** *n* **:** a large brilliantly marked blue and yellow carangid food and sport fish (*Elagatis bipinnulatus*) nearly cosmopolitan in warm seas

**rainbow serpent** *n* **:** a widely recognized serpent deity of contemporary primitive societies symbolized by the rainbow which is mythically interpreted as a great snake

**rainbow shower** *n* **:** a showy hybrid ornamental tree (*Cassia javanica* x *C. fistula*) developed in Hawaii and having flowers that range in color from cream to orange and red

**rainbow snake** *n* **:** a shy burrowing No. American colubrid snake (*Abastor erythrogrammus*) that is brightly colored in red, blue, and yellow — called also *hoop snake*

**rainbow trout** *n* **:** a large stout-bodied and sometimes anadromous trout (*Salmo gairdnerii*) of still and flowing waters of the Pacific coast of No. America from southern California to Alaska that has a large head and small mouth, that in the typical freshwater form is greenish above and white on the belly with a pink, red, or lavender stripe more or less developed along each side of the body and usu. profusely sprinkled with black dots, and that is highly esteemed as a sport and food fish although in parts of Alaska considered a pest because of its destruction of salmon eggs — see STEELHEAD

**rainbowweed** \'=,=,=\ *n* [*rainbow* + *weed*] **:** PURPLE LOOSESTRIFE

**rain·bowy** \'rān,bōē\ *adj* **:** like a rainbow

**rain cape** *n* **:** a cape of waterproof or water-resistant material for wear in the rain

**rain check** *n* **1 :** the stub of a ticket (as to a baseball game) retained by the spectator and good for admission to a later performance if the scheduled performance is interrupted during its early part (as, in baseball usu. before 4½ innings are over) by rain or bad weather **2 :** an extension of the offer of a favor or privilege until a more appropriate or convenient time ⟨decided to pass up the invitation for the moment, but told him we wanted a *rain check* for transportation across with the last officers who would leave the city —R.A.Gunnison⟩ ⟨who smiles, confers a *rain check* to an untoward hour —Marsden Hartley⟩ — often used with *take* or *give* ⟨take a *rain check* on that dinner⟩

**rain cloud** *n* **:** a cloud (as a nimbus) bringing rain

**raincoat** \'=,=\ *n* **:** a coat of waterproof or water-resistant material for wear in the rain

**rain crow** *n* **1 :** the black-billed or the yellow-billed cuckoo **2** *or* **rain dove :** MOURNING DOVE

**rain dance** *n* **:** a dance forming part of a ritual for invoking rain (as the ancient hula of Hawaii and the surviving corn dances of American Indians)

**rain doctor** *n* **:** a priest or sorcerer among nonliterate peoples who employs magic rituals and incantations for the purpose of producing rain

**raindrop** \'=,=\ *n* [ME *reindrope*, fr. OE *rēndropa*, fr. *regn, rēn* rain + *dropa* drop] **:** a drop of rain ⟨the ~*s* were falling more thickly —J.C.Lincoln⟩

**rained** *past of* RAIN

**rai·nette green** \rā'net-\ *n* [F *rainette* tree frog, dim. of *raine* frog, fr. L *rana*, prob. of imit. origin] **:** a moderate yellow green that is paler than average moss green and yellower and duller than average pea green or apple green (sense 1)

**rain·ey's corpuscle** \'rānēz-\ *n, usu cap R* [after George *Rainey* †1884 Eng. anatomist] **:** the crescent-shaped spore of a sarcosporidian

**rainfall** \'=,=\ *n* **1 :** a fall of rain ⟨there was another ~ that night —Dan Wickenden⟩ **2 a :** the water or amount of water that falls in rain usu. measured by the depth in inches ⟨~ increases steadily from the desert margin toward the south —P.E.James⟩ **b :** an amount of precipitation esp. during a given time ⟨having a ~, including snowfall, of from sixty to eighty inches —*Economic Geology*⟩

**rain forest** *n* **1 :** a tropical woodland that has an annual rainfall of at least 100 inches and often much more, is typical of but not wholly restricted to certain lowland areas, is characterized by lofty broad-leaved evergreen trees forming a continuous canopy, lianas, and herbaceous and woody epiphytes and by nearly complete absence of low-growing or understory ground-rooted plants — called also *tropical rain forest* **2 :** TEMPERATE RAIN FOREST

**rainfowl** \'=,=\ *n* [ME *reynfowle*, fr. *reyn* rain + *fowle, foul* fowl] **1 :** CHANNELBILL **2** *dial Eng* **:** GREEN WOODPECKER

**rainfrog** \'=,=\ *n, chiefly South & Midland* **:** a small green frog

**rain·ful** \'rānfəl\ *adj* **:** full of rain **:** RAINY ⟨nearing the base of the clouds . . . I felt . . . a faint distaste for climbing into their cold, ~ interior —J.L.Rhys⟩

**rain gage** *n* **:** an instrument for measuring the quantity of precipitation that falls at a given place and time

**rain glass** *n* **:** BAROMETER

**rainier** *comparative of* RAINY

**rainiest** *superlative of* RAINY

**rain·i·ly** \'rānəlē\ *adv* **:** in a rainy manner

**rain·i·ness** \-nēnə̇s\ *n* -ES **:** the quality or state of being rainy

**raining** *pres part of* RAIN

**rain insurance** *n* **:** insurance against loss from cancellation of a scheduled event because of rain

**rain leader** *or* **rain pipe** *n* **:** DOWNSPOUT

**rain·less** \'rānlə̇s\ *adj* **:** lacking rain **:** lacking precipitation ⟨a ~ month⟩ — **rain·less·ness** *n* -ES

**rain lily** *n* **:** any of several plants of the southwestern U.S. that frequently flower after rain: as **a :** EVENING STAR; *also* **:** a related plant (*Cooperia pedunculata*) **b :** ATAMASCO LILY

**rainmaker** \'=,==\ *n* **:** one that seeks to produce rain: as **a :** an American Indian medicine man who uses incantations and magic rituals for the purpose of producing rain **b :** a person who attempts rainmaking

**rainmaking** \'=,==\ *n* **:** the act or process of attempting by some scientific or other artificial means to produce rain or to make rain fall earlier or in greater amounts than it would fall naturally

**rain or shine 1 :** whatever the weather may be **:** without fail ⟨the auction will be held *rain or shine*⟩ **2 :** whatever the circumstances ⟨always cheerful, *rain or shine*⟩

**rain out** *vt* **:** to interrupt or prevent by rain ⟨the afternoon's game was *rained out* —Mary Deasy⟩ ⟨educational and social events in this area have been *rained out* right and left —*Springfield (Mass.) Daily News*⟩

**rain pie** *n, Brit* **:** GREEN WOODPECKER

**rainpool** \'=,=\ *n* **:** a pool of water formed in the rainy season or after a rain ⟨moringa trees in blossom grew by a great ~ —G.W.Murray⟩

**rain print** *n* **:** a small shallow depression formed by the impact of a raindrop in fine sand, mud, or clay and sometimes preserved on the bedding planes of sedimentary rocks

[1]**rainproof** \'=¦=\ *adj* [[1]*rain* + *proof*] **:** impervious to rain ⟨a ~ bag⟩ — compare SHOWERPROOF, WATERPROOF

[2]**rainproof** \"\ *n* **:** a rainproof coat or cape

[3]**rainproof** \"\ *vt* **:** to make rainproof — **rain·proof·er** \'rān¦prüfə(r)\ *n*

**rain quail** *n* **:** a migratory Indian quail (*Coturnix coromandelica*)

**rain rot** *n* **:** a severe weeping dermatitis accompanied by swelling of the skin and loss of wool occurring in heavy-wooled sheep exposed to rain for prolonged periods — called also *fat scab, wool rot*

**rains** *pl of* RAIN, *pres 3d sing of* RAIN

**rain shadow** *n* **:** a region of reduced rainfall to the lee of high mountains

**rainspout** \'=,=\ *n* **:** WATERSPOUT

**rainsquall** \'=,=\ *n* **:** a squall accompanied by rain ⟨a thick ~ passed over the two boats —Joseph Conrad⟩ ⟨a black ~ makes up from windward —S.E.Morison⟩

**rainstone** \'=,=\ *n* **:** a stone used in rainmaking magic

**rainstorm** \'=,=\ *n* **:** a storm of or with rain

**raintight** \'=¦=\ *adj* **:** so tight as to exclude rain ⟨an aluminum ~ window⟩

**rain toad** *n* **:** a tree toad (*Hyla versicolor*) whose call is popularly supposed to predict rain

**rain tree** *n* [so called fr. the belief that it exudes water from its leaflets] **:** an ornamental tropical American tree (*Pithecolobium saman*) having bipinnate leaves, globose clusters of flowers with crimson stamens, and sweet-pulp pods eaten by cattle

**rainwash** \'=,=\ *n* **1 :** the washing away of material by rain ⟨some solid material is carried into streams by ~ —C.A. Cotton⟩ **2 :** material washed away by rain ⟨eventually the ~ is swept into rills and streams —Arthur Holmes⟩

**rainwater** \'=,==\ *n* [ME, fr. OE *rēnwæter*, fr. *regn, rēn* rain + *wæter* water] **:** water fallen as rain that has not had an opportunity to collect soluble matter from the soil and is therefore quite soft — compare SPRINGWATER

**rainwater fish** *n* **:** a very small American killifish (*Lucania parva* or a related species) living in swamps and brackish water along the eastern and southern Atlantic coast and being of considerable value as a destroyer of mosquito larvae

**rainwater head** *n* : LEADER HEAD

**rainwear** \'ˌ=ˌ=\ *n* : waterproof or water-resistant clothing (as a raincoat) for bad weather wear

**rainworm** \'=ˌ=\ *n* [prob. trans. of G *regenwurm;* fr. its habit of appearing above ground esp. during a heavy rain] **1** : EARTHWORM **2** : an adult mermithid worm

**rainy** \'rānē, -ni\ *adj* -ER/-EST [ME *reyny*, fr. *reyn* rain + *-y*] **1** : abounding with or characterized by rain : WET, SHOWERY ⟨~ weather⟩ ⟨a ~ spell⟩ ⟨~ regions⟩ **2** : being a time when much rain falls ⟨the ~ season in a tropical land⟩ **3** : bringing rain ⟨~ winds⟩ ⟨~ clouds⟩ **4** : affected by rain : like rain ⟨very dark by contrast even with the subdued, ~ light of the woods —H.M.Rideout⟩

**rainy day** *n* : a period of want or need ⟨imperative that a couple should so live as to set something aside for a *rainy day* —*Saturday Rev.*⟩

**¹ra·ioid** \'rā,(y)ȯid\ *adj* [L *raia* ray + E *-oid*] : resembling or related to a ray : BATOID ⟨a ~ fish⟩

**²raioid** \"\ *n* -S : ¹RAY

**rai·on** \rī'ōn\ *n* -S [Russ *raĭon*, district, province, fr. F *rayon* honeycomb, department of a store, fr. OF *ree, raie* honeycomb, of Gmc origin; akin to OHG *rāza* honeycomb, MD *rāte*, and perh. to L *cratis* wickerwork, hurdle — more at HURDLE] : a political subdivision in the U.S.S.R. comparable to the U.S. county : DISTRICT

**¹rais** *or* **reis** \'rīs\ *n, pl* **rais** *or* **reis** [F *reis*, fr. Ar *ra'īs* chief, fr. *ra's* head] **1** : a Muslim ship's captain **2** : a Muslim chief or ruler

**²rais** \"\ *n pl, usu cap* : a Mongoloid people of Nepal who speak Kiranti

**rais·able** *also* **raise·able** \'rāzəbəl\ *adj* [¹*raise* + *-able*] : capable of being raised ⟨some questions . . . are not . . . ~ in an action between parties —James Bryce⟩

**¹raise** \'rāz\ *vb* -ED/-ING/-S [ME *reisen, raisen*, fr. ON *reisa* to raise, cause to rise — more at REAR] *vt* **1 a** : to lift or restore to or set in an erect position : set upright : cause or help to stand ⟨caught the fallen child's hand and *raised* her up⟩ **b** *archaic* : to rouse from bed or from sleep : BESTIR : WAKEN **c** : to rouse (a game bird or mammal) for a hunter's pursuit : FLUSH **d** : to rouse or incite to action or effort : summon to resist or repel injury : call to war, struggle, or conflict ⟨~ the countryside at the threat of invasion⟩ **e** : to impart strength, courage, or cheer to (the mind or heart) : ENCOURAGE, INSPIRIT **f** (1) : to bring up (as a familiar spirit or the spirit of one departed) from a lower world : evoke or summon from the world of spirits (2) : to bring back from the dead : restore to life : RESURRECT ⟨why is it thought incredible by any of you that God ~*s* the dead —Acts 26:8 (RSV)⟩ **g** *chiefly Scot* : to make (one) angry or excited **2 a** : to put up (a building) : ERECT, CONSTRUCT ⟨those arts which were destined to ~ our Gothic cathedrals —G.G.Coulton⟩ **b** *obs* : to draw (a mathematical figure) on a given base **3 a** *archaic* : to bring (children) into existence : BEGET **b** : to give (children) a parent's fostering care : bring up : NURTURE, REAR **c** : to breed and care for (animals) to maturity ⟨*raised* dogs as a hobby⟩ **d** : to practice the cultivation of (plants or crops) : GROW, PRODUCE ⟨*raised* great acreages of wheat⟩ **4 a** : to bring into being : cause to arise or appear ⟨I will ~ up for them a prophet —Deut 18:18 (RSV)⟩ **b** : to bring about : stir up : set in motion ⟨*raised* a storm over his fancied injustices⟩ ⟨*raised* prejudices difficult to dispel⟩ **5 a** : to utter loudly or vehemently ⟨*raised* a hue and cry⟩ ⟨*raised* the alarm throughout the district⟩ ⟨*raised* the shout of victory⟩ **b** : VOICE ⟨he *raised* a sigh so piteous and profound as it did seem to shatter all his bulk —Shak.⟩ **c** : to strike up : SING ⟨*raised* a song of sheer jubilation⟩ **d** : to make (the voice) heard ⟨voices were *raised* widely in opposition⟩ **6 a** : to promote or advance (one) to some dignity, office, or rank : EXALT, HONOR ⟨was *raised* to a baronetcy for his services to the nation —*Current Biog.*⟩ ⟨was *raised* to the priesthood —R.J.Purcell⟩ **b** : to elevate the moral or mental state of : UPLIFT ⟨detected the law of gravitation, and in so doing, *raised* his power of thought—ours with it—above the mere multitudinousness and opacity of separate things —H.A. Overstreet⟩ **c** : to lift higher : draw up : cause to rise : ELEVATE ⟨*raised* a fist to strike⟩ ⟨*raised* the flag each morning outside the barracks⟩ ⟨*raised* the general standard of living⟩ **7 a** : to cause the beginning of : touch off : START ⟨*raised* a smile even from his friends —*Times Lit. Supp.*⟩ **b** : INSTITUTE, CREATE, ESTABLISH **8** : to bring together : COLLECT, GATHER, LEVY ⟨the government *raised* large sums for highway construction by a tax on gasoline sales⟩ ⟨the budget . . . is *raised* by registration fees, ticket sales, and grants —Hartzell Spence⟩ ⟨difficult to ~ enough money to pay for campaign expenses⟩ ⟨*raised* a company of minutemen from his county —E.K. Alden⟩ **9** : to lift (a siege or blockade) by withdrawing the besieging troops or by forcing the besieging troops to withdraw **10** : to cause to ascend (as dust or smoke) **11 a** : to cause to increase in height, level, bulk, size, amount, or value ⟨heavy rains *raised* the river stage⟩ ⟨*raised* the price to retailers a cent a gallon⟩ **b** : to make light and spongy (as bread by leavening with yeast) or thicker (as hides by steeping in a fermenting liquor) **c** : to multiply (a quantity) by itself a specified number of times — compare CUBE, POWER, SQUARE **d** : to lift to a higher degree according to some scale ⟨~ the temperature⟩ ⟨*raised* the instrument's pitch⟩ **e** : to make keener : HEIGHTEN, INTENSIFY, SHARPEN ⟨~*s* ordinary joys to an agonized ecstatic pitch⟩ **f** : to make hotter, brighter, or faster ⟨~ the metal to white heat⟩ ⟨*raised* his pulse to a drumbeat⟩ **g** : to bring up the nap of (cloth) with teasels or wire cards **12 a** : to come in view of : SIGHT ⟨they *raised* the islands after two hours of hard running —Arthur Mayse⟩ **b** : to cause (an object) to appear above the horizon or to seem to grow higher by coming nearer at sea — compare LAY, SETTLE **13** *obs* : OBTAIN, WIN **14** : to bring up for consideration : introduce into discussion : offer as an objection, a problem, or a significant point ⟨all these new views of the world *raised* problems for scholars as well as statesmen —R.W. Southern⟩ ⟨~*s* the moral question —E.M.Woolf⟩ ⟨~*s* the issue of the failure to distinguish between normal and abnormal —Abram Kardiner⟩ **15** : to cause to come up (as mucus from the lungs or gas from the stomach) **16** : to add fraudulently to the face value of (a bank check or other negotiable paper) by altering the writing, figures, or printing in which the sum payable is shown **17 a** (1) : to increase (a poker bet or pot) by a specified amount (2) : to bet more than (a previous bettor) — compare CALL **b** : to make a higher bridge bid in (a partner's suit) **18** : to move (a curling stone) ahead in the line of direction by a hit from behind with another stone **19** : to form (hollow ware) from a flat sheet of metal by alternately hammering and annealing **20 a** : to elevate (a part of the tongue) closer to the palate in uttering a vowel **b** : to utter (a vowel) with the tongue in a higher position **21** : to establish radio communication with : elicit a response from (a station being called) ⟨next time you ~ the ship, tell them I'm on my way —K.M.Dodson⟩ ~ *vi* **1** *dial* : RISE, ARISE **2 a** : to make a poker bet that increases the stake **b** : to make a higher bridge bid in a partner's suit **3** : to drive a raise in a mine **syn** see BUILD, LIFT

**²raise** \"\ *n* -S **1** : an act or method of raising : a lifting up : ELEVATION ⟨firemen are taught ~*s* of several kinds to get their ladders up⟩ **2** : a rising stretch of road : an upward grade : RISE **3** : an increase in amount ⟨opposed the administration's request for a ~ in the national debt limit —*New Republic*⟩: as **a** : an increase in wages or salary ⟨braced the boss for a ~⟩ **b** (1) : the act of increasing a bet (2) : the amount of such increase **4** : a vertical or inclined opening or passageway driven to connect one mine working place with another at a higher level — called also *rise, riser* **5** : the spinning of a curling stone toward a target circle

**³raise** \"\ *n* -S [ME *rase*, fr. OE *rǣs*] *dial Eng* : CAIRN, MOUND — used esp. in place names

**raiseable** *var of* RAISABLE

**raised** *adj* [fr. past part. of ¹*raise*] **1 a** : having a pattern or design in relief ⟨~ metalwork⟩ ⟨~ needlework⟩ ⟨~ textiles⟩ ⟨~ braille lettering⟩ **b** : NAPPED ⟨a ~ fabric⟩ **2** : leavened with yeast rather than with baking powder or soda ⟨~ doughnuts⟩

**raised band** *n* : a ridge across the backbone of a hand-sewn book produced when the cords or bands are not sawed in; *also* : a similar ridge raised on a machine-sewn book by applying a heated die — compare SUNKEN CORD

raised bands

**raised beach** *n* : a beach formed by a sea or lake and subsequently elevated above high-water level either by local crustal movements or by lowering of sea level

**raised cottage** *n* : a cottage built on stilts (as brick piers) for protection against flood waters

**raised initial** *n* : a cockup initial

**raised point** *n* : needlepoint lace chiefly of Venetian origin with padded floral designs in high relief — called also *gros point*

**raised printing** *n* : printing in which the letters or image are raised above the surface of the paper (as by embossing)

**raised table** *n* : a raised or projecting member of a flat architectural or sculptural surface that is large in proportion to the projection

**raise·man** \'=mən\ *n, pl* **raisemen** [²*raise* + *man*] : a miner who works in a raise

**rais·er** \'rāzə(r)\ *n* -S [ME, fr. *raisen* to raise + *-er*] **1** : one that raises ⟨a sheep ~⟩ ⟨a cotton ~⟩ ⟨a fund ~⟩ ⟨a check ~⟩ **2** : LETTERER d **3** : PROOFER 2 **4** : one that sets up the staves for barrels, shapes the barrels, and drives on the forming hoops

**raises** *pres 3d sing of* RAISE, *pl of* RAISE

**¹rai·sin** \'rāzᵊn\ *n* -S *often attrib* [ME *raisin, reisin*, fr. MF, grape, fr. L *racemus* cluster of grapes or berries, of non-IE origin; akin to the source of Gk *rhag-, rhax* berry, grape] **1** : any of various grapes dried in the sun or by artificial heat, containing a high sugar percentage, and having a flavor quite different from that of the fresh grape **2** : a dark purplish red that is bluer and duller than pansy purple, bluer and lighter than dahlia purple (sense 1), bluer and paler than Bokhara, and bluer and less strong than redgrape

**²raisin** \"\ *vi* -ED/-ING/-S *of grapes* : to dry on the vine and take on an appearance like that of raisins

**raisin black** *n* : a dark grayish purple that is redder than average purple wine and redder and stronger than old lavender (sense 2)

**rai·si·né** \ˌrāzə'nā\ *n* -S [F, fr. *raisin* grape] : a preserve esp. of pears with quinces or of grapes with quinces cooked slowly in sweet wine or cider

**rais·ing** \'rāziŋ, -zēŋ\ *n* -S [ME, fr. gerund of *raisen* to raise] **1** : the act or process of lifting : ELEVATION ⟨attempted idly to guess what that ~ of her finger had meant⟩ **2** : a party or bee for raising the frame of a building ⟨came the day of the ~ . . . all the men from the village and the near farms gathered to help make a home for the newcomers —Irving Bacheller⟩ **3 a** : the fostering care of parents for children : NURTURE, UPBRINGING **b** : the breeding and care of animals ⟨turkey ~⟩ ⟨cattle ~⟩ **c** : the growing of plants : CULTIVATION ⟨wheat ~⟩ **4** : the driving of a raise in a mine

**raising hammer** *n* : a hammer with a rounded face used in raising sheet metal

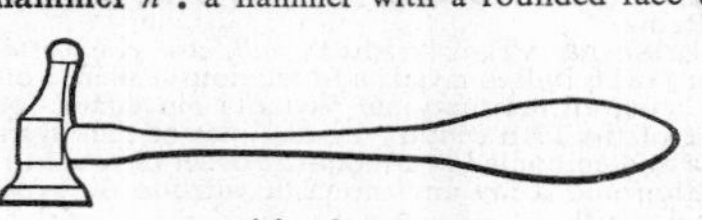
raising hammer

**raising plate** *n* : PLATE 5a(1)

**raisin grape** *n* : a grape grown primarily for making raisins

**raisin moth** *n* : a phycitid moth (*Cadra figulilella*) the larva of which attacks dried fruits and cereal products

**raisin purple** *n* : a dark reddish purple that is redder and less strong than patriarch or amaranth

**raisin–seed oil** *n* : GRAPE-SEED OIL

**raisin tree** *n* : RED CURRANT 1a(1)

**raisin wine** *n* : a usu. inferior wine made by the fermentation of an infusion of raisins

**rai·siny** \'rāzᵊnē\ *adj* : containing or resembling raisins

**rai·son d'être** \ˌrā,zōⁿ'det(rə), -zōⁿ-, -zän'-, -tr(ᵊ)\ *n, pl* **raisons d'être** [F] : reason or justification for existence

**rais·ty** \'rāstē\ *var of* REASTY

**raith** \'rāth\ *n* -S [ScGael *rāith*] *Scot* : a quarter of a year

**rai·vel** \'rāvəl\ *chiefly Scot var of* RAVEL

**raiyat** *var of* RYOT

**raiyatwari** *var of* RYOTWAR

**raj** \'räj\ *n* -ES [Hindi *rāj*, fr. Skt *rājya*, fr. *rājati* he rules; akin to Skt *rājan* king] : REIGN, RULE

**¹ra·ja** *or* **ra·jah** \'räjə\ *n* -S *often cap* [Hindi *rājā*, fr. Skt *rājan* — more at ROYAL] **1 a** : an Indian prince or king **b** : a petty chief or dignitary **c** : the bearer of a title of nobility among the Hindus **2** : a Malay prince, ruler, or chief

**²ra·ja** \'rāth\ *n, cap* [NL, fr. L *raia* ray] : a genus (the type of the family Rajidae) of skates with the body angular in outline

**ra·jab** \rə'jab\ *n* -S *usu cap* [Ar] : the seventh month of the Muhammadan year — see MONTH table

**ra·jah** \'räjə\ *n* -S [fr. *Rajah*, a trademark] : a silk clothing fabric with a rough surface somewhat similar to pongee

**rajah rat** *n* [NL *rajah* (specific epithet of *Rattus rajah*), fr. E *rajah*] : a reddish often spiny rat (*Rattus rajah*) occurring in numerous races that are widely distributed in southeastern Asia and the East Indies

**ra·jas** \'rəjəs\ *n* -ES [Skt, lit., darkness, dust; akin to ON *rökkr* darkness, Goth *riqis*, Gk *erebos*] : the extension or passion that constitutes one of the three gunas of Sankhya philosophy — compare SATTVA, TAMAS

**ra·ja·ship** *or* **ra·jah·ship** \'räjə,ship\ *n* : the dominion or the rank of a raja

**ra·ja·stha·ni** \ˌräjə'stänē\ *n* -S *usu cap* [Hindi *Rājasthānī* Rajputana, region of northwest Indian Union] : the Indic colloquial language of Rajasthan — compare HINDI

**raja–yoga** \'==ˌ==\ *n* [Skt *rājayoga*, fr. *rājan* king + *yoga* — more at YOGA] : a yoga discipline that consists of eight stages leading to self-realization and liberation — compare ASANA, DHYANA, SAMADHI; HATHA-YOGA, JNANA-YOGA, KARMA-YOGA

**raj·ban·si** \räj'bən(t)sē\ *n* -S [Hindi *rājbāsī* of royal race, fr. Skt *rājan* king + *vaṁśa* lineage] : a member of an extensive Koch caste of Assam and Bengal

**raj·i·dae** \'rajə,dē\ *n pl, cap* [NL, fr. ²*Raja*, type genus + *-idae*] : a family of elasmobranch fishes consisting of the skates

**raj·ma·hal creeper** \ˌräjmə'häl-\ *n, usu cap R* [fr. *Rajmahal* Hills, Bihar prov., India] : a woody vine (*Marsdenia tenacissima*) the stems of which yield a fiber — see RAJMAHAL HEMP

**rajmahal hemp** *n, usu cap R* : a strong silky fiber derived from the stems of the Rajmahal creeper and used in India for bowstrings and cordage

**raj·pra·mukh** \'räjprə,mu̇k\ *n* -S [Hindi *rājpramukh*, fr. Skt *rājapramukha*, fr. *rājan* king + *pramukha* chief, fr. *pra-* before + *mukha* face, mouth — more at FOR] : the constitutional head of a state of India formed from several former princely states who is elected by a council of rulers

**raj·put** *or* **raj·poot** \'räj,püt, -pu̇t\ *n* -S *usu cap* [Hindi *rājpūt*, fr. Skt *rājaputra* king's son, fr. *rājan* king + *putra* son — more at FEW] : a member of a dominant military caste of Kshatriya rank and Indo-Aryan race numerous in northern India

**ra·k'a** *or* **ra·k'ah** \'rəkə\ *n* -S [Ar *rak'ah*] : a fixed series of ritual movements and formulas (as bowings and recitations) repeated in the daily prayers of Muslims

**¹rake** \'rāk\ *n* -S [ME, fr. OE *raca, racu;* akin to OHG *rehho* rake, ON *reka* spade, shovel, Goth *rikan* to heap up, collect, and perh. to Gk *oregein* to stretch out — more at RIGHT] **1 a** : a hand tool consisting usu. of a bar with projecting prongs that is set transversely at the end of a long handle and used for gathering grass, leaves, or other material or for loosening or smoothing the surface of the ground **b** : a machine rake for gathering hay — compare DUMP RAKE, SIDE-DELIVERY RAKE **2** : any of various implements resembling a rake or a hoe (as for mixing plaster or scraping hides) **3 a** : a small steel tool formerly used by hand binders to scratch the backs of books during forwarding permitting glue to permeate deeper and so strengthening the binding **b** : a wire-toothed wooden tool similar to a lawn rake used to make patterns in a bookbinder's marbling vat **4 a** : a device for studying pressure distribution in a flow field by means of tubes arranged like rake teeth and connected with pressure-indicating devices

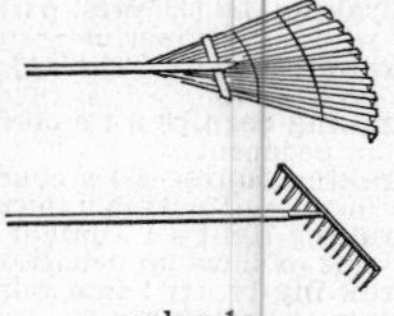
rakes 1a

**²rake** \"\ *vb* -ED/-ING/-S [ME *raken*, fr. ¹*rake*] *vt* **1 a** : to collect, gather, or separate with or as if with a rake ⟨*raked* the grass from the lawn after mowing⟩ ⟨*raked* the stuff into separate piles⟩ **b** : to stir up, loosen, or make even or smooth with or as if with a rake ⟨*raked* the soil level after spading and seeding⟩ ⟨*raked* the fire and added coal⟩ **c** : to clean or purify as if by raking ⟨~ a fatty oil⟩ **2** *obs* : to cover over or bury by or as if by raking **3** : to bank (a fire) with cinders **4** : to remove obstructing excrement from the rectum of (a costive horse) with the hand : BACK-RAKE **5** : to gain (wealth or possessions) rapidly or in abundance — usu. used with *in* ⟨had *raked* the cash in night after night for years at a small strategically placed stand⟩ **6 a** : to scrape or scratch as if with a rake : pass over lightly : RUB, TOUCH ⟨like clouds that ~ the mountain summits —William Wordsworth⟩ ⟨the blade *raked* the other's cheek⟩ **b** : to censure severely : attack verbally : administer a dressing down to — often used with *over* **7 a** : to search through : SCOUR, RANSACK ⟨the statesman ~*s* the town to find a plot —Jonathan Swift⟩ **b** : to dig out and present (as unfavorable evidence) — usu. used with *up* ⟨*raked* up long buried scandal to discredit his enemy⟩ **8 a** : to fire in a direction with the length of : ENFILADE ⟨blockhouses at opposite corners enabled watchers to ~ the walls with rifle fire —*Amer. Guide Series: Tenn.*⟩ ⟨*raked* each wave of advancing troops with gunfire⟩ **b** : to sweep (a length or area) with gunfire, shells, or bombs ⟨*raked* the area with a dive-bombing and strafing attack —Merle Miller⟩ **9** *of a falcon* : to attack while flying **10** : to glance over rapidly : SCAN, SURVEY ⟨a three-decker pulpit from which the preacher can ~ his congregation from end to end —Charles Gordon⟩ ⟨*raked* the leaden sky with his binoculars —J.E.Macdonnell⟩ **11** : to scrape off (loose mortar) preparatory to pointing : remove (green mortar) to a uniform depth from the face of a wall — often used with *out* ~ *vi* : to do a task with or as if with a rake : COLLECT, SCRAPE, SEARCH — **rake over the coals** : to censure severely : REPRIMAND, SCOLD ⟨was *raked over the coals* for his habitual lateness⟩

**³rake** \"\ *vi* -ED/-ING/-S [ME *raken*, fr. OE *racian*] **1** *chiefly dial* : to move forward esp. swiftly : run rapidly **2** *chiefly dial* : ROAM, ROVE **3** *of a hawk* : to fly after game — **rake out** *or* **rake off** *or* **rake away** *falconry* : to fly wide of the quarry

**⁴rake** \"\ *n* -S [ME *rake*, fr. ON *rāk* streak, stripe; akin to ON *reka* to drive — more at WREAK] **1** *dial Eng* **a** : WAY, PATH; *esp* : a cattle path **b** : pasture land **2** *dial Eng* **a** : a trip esp. for bringing something back : GO **b** : as much as can be carried in one trip : LOAD **3** *chiefly Scot* : GASH VEIN

**⁵rake** \"\ *vb* -ED/-ING/-S [origin unknown] *vi* : to incline from the perpendicular ⟨the roof of the dwelling *raked* sharply —Willard Robertson⟩ ~ *vt* : to cause to incline from the perpendicular

**⁶rake** \"\ *n* -S **1 a** : inclination from the perpendicular (as of a mast or funnel); *esp* : the overhang of a ship's bow or stern **b** : the slope of a ship's sternpost or of the forepart of the rudder **2** : inclination from the horizontal (as of a stage or auditorium floor) **3** : the angle between the top cutting surface of a cutting tool (as on a lathe) and a plane which is perpendicular to the surface of the work and to the direction of motion of the tool with respect to the work — compare CUTTING ANGLE, SIDE RAKE **4** : PLUNGE 4 **5** : an inclined edge of a building ⟨the ~ of a cornice⟩ ⟨the ~ of a gable⟩ **6** : the angle between a wing-tip edge that is sensibly straight in planform and the plane of symmetry of an airplane

**⁷rake** \"\ *n* -S [short for ²*rakehell*] : a dissolute or licentious man or woman : LIBERTINE ⟨turned his attention to the pleasures of this life and a more perfect ~ has seldom existed —Nancy Mitford⟩

**⁸rake** \"\ *vi* -ED/-ING/-S : to act the rake : lead a dissolute or licentious life ⟨swear and rant and ~ . . . with the best of them —George Farquhar⟩

**rake angle** *n* : ⁶RAKE 3

**raked** *adj* [fr. past part. of ⁵*rake*] : slanted from the perpendicular or horizontal : INCLINED ⟨drop-leaf table . . . ~ square tapering legs —*Parke-Bernet Galleries Catalog*⟩

**raked joint** *n* [fr. past part. of ²*rake*] : a masonry joint from which the mortar is raked out to a specified depth while still green — see JOINT illustration

**¹rake·hell** \'rāk,hel\ *or* **rake·helly** \-lē\ *adj* [*rakehell* perh. alter. (influenced by the phrase *to rake hell*) of earlier *rackle* rash, impetuous, headstrong, fr. ME *rakel, rakil; rakehelly* fr. ²*rakehell* + *-y*] : of, relating to, or characteristic of a rakehell : DISSOLUTE, LICENTIOUS, RASCALLY ⟨ready to abjure the ~ life —Lee Rogow⟩ ⟨~ amours⟩

**²rakehell** \"\ *n* : a dissolute or profligate person : LIBERTINE, RAKE, RASCAL ⟨the favorite resort of the courtesans and the ~*s* —W.S.Clark⟩

**rake·hell·ish** \-lish\ *adj* : RAKEHELL

**rake·man** \'=mən\ *n, pl* **rakemen** [¹*rake* + *man*] : a rackman who uses a rake

**rake–off** \'ˌ=ˌ=\ *n* -S [²*rake* + *off;* fr. the use of a rake by a croupier to collect the operator's profits in a gambling casino] : a percentage or cut (as of winnings, profits, or loot) taken or retained by an operator or enterpriser or by a gang boss ⟨take kindly to organized oppressions of industries, to the collection of *rake-offs* —*Harper's*⟩ ⟨a big private *rake-off* on government purchases —*Atlantic*⟩ ⟨gamblers . . . get their share of the *rake-off* —Lewis Mumford⟩

**rak·er** \'rākə(r)\ *n* -S [²*rake* + *-er*] **1** : one that rakes: as **a** : one that gathers clams with a rake **b** : one that rakes dead leaves and other debris from around turpentine trees to lessen fire hazards **c** : ¹GUMMER 1 **d** : an iron bar with pointed steel ends bent at right angles in opposite directions that is used for raking out old mortar in walls before pointing **e** : a raft dog similarly shaped **f** : one of a number of short teeth with deep gullet and considerable rake that are interspersed among the other teeth in some saws to clean out the kerf **2** [⁵*rake* + *-er*] : any of a number of shores except the bottom innermost one that prop up a wall **3** : GILL RAKER

**raker tooth** *n* : an unset sawtooth that cleans out the bottom of a cut

**rak·ery** \'rāk(ə)rē\ *n* -ES [⁷*rake* + *-ery*] *archaic* : DEBAUCHERY, LEWDNESS

**rakes** *pl of* RAKE, *pres 3d sing of* RAKE

**rakeshame** \'=ˌ=\ *n* [²*rake* + *shame*] *archaic* : a base or degraded person

**rake's progress** *n* [fr. *The Rake's Progress* (1735), series of engravings by William Hogarth †1764 Eng. artist] : a reckless course : a steady deterioration ⟨while a painful policy of deflation is being pursued in some countries, the inflationary *rake's progress* is going merrily on —*Irish Statesman*⟩

**rake·steel** *or* **rake·stele** \'rāk,stēl\ *n* [¹*rake* + *stele* (handle)] *dial chiefly Eng* : a rake handle

**rake vein** *n* [⁴*rake*] *chiefly Scot* : GASH VEIN

**ra·ki** \rə'kē, 'rakē, 'rākē\ *n* -S [Turk] : a Turkish liqueur distilled usu. from fermented raisins but occas. from figs or dates and flavored with aniseed

**ra·ki·ja** *or* **ra·kia** \'rākē(y)ə\ *n* -S [Serbo-Croatian *rakija*] : a brandy made in Yugoslavia

**¹raking** *n* -S [fr. gerund of ²*rake*] **1** : a raked area **2** : the stuff gathered with a rake

**²raking** *n* -S [fr. gerund of ⁸*rake*] : dissolute conduct : LICENTIOUSNESS

**³raking** *adj* [fr. pres. part. of ⁸*rake*] : DISSOLUTE

**⁴raking** *adj* [fr. pres. part. of ⁵*rake*] : inclined from the per-

pendicular or horizontal ⟨shadows and markings revealed in the ~ light of dawn or sunset —C.M.Lerici⟩
**5raking** *adj* [fr. pres. part. of *3rake*] **:** SPEEDY, SWIFT ⟨a fellow with . . . a powerful ~ stride —John Buchan⟩
**raking bond** *n* [*4raking*] **1 :** DIAGONAL BOND **2 :** HERRINGBONE BOND
**raking cornice** *n* **:** a cornice that follows the slope of a gable or pediment
**raking course** *n* **:** a course of bricks laid diagonally between the face courses in a thick wall to strengthen it
**raking light** *n* **:** a bright light directed at a painting from the side to show up details of painting technique
**rak·ing·ly** *adv* **:** in a raking manner **:** OBLIQUELY
**raking molding** *n* **:** a slanted molding (as in a pediment)
**raking piece** *n* **:** a peaked or sloping piece of theatrical scenery
**raking shore** *n* **:** RAKER 2
**raking shot** *n* **:** a shot fired (as at game) from an acute angle
**1rak·ish** \'rākish, -kēsh\ *adj* [*7rake* + *-ish*] **:** of or relating to a rake **:** LICENTIOUS, WANTON ⟨he combined the studies and the ~ life —P.E.More⟩
**2rakish** \"\ *adj* [prob. fr. *5rake* + *-ish;* fr. the raking masts of pirate ships] **1 :** having a smart stylish appearance suggestive of speed ⟨a ~ ship⟩ ⟨in his battered, ~ roadster —MacKinlay Kantor⟩ **2 :** negligent of convention or strict formality **:** CARELESS, JAUNTY, SPORTY ⟨the languid ~ habit of wearing a hat indoors at his desk —*Amer. Guide Series: N. C.*⟩
**rak·ish·ly** *adv* **:** in a rakish manner
**rak·ish·ness** *n* -ES **:** the quality or state of being rakish
**rak·sha·sa** \'räkshəsə\ *n* -S [Skt *rākṣasa,* fr. *rakṣas,* lit., injury; akin to Gk *erechthein* to rend, break] **:** a demon or evil spirit of Hindu mythology
**ra·ku ware** \'rä(,)kü-\ *n* [Jap *raku* enjoyment; fr. the engraving of this word on the gold seal with which the original ware was stamped] **:** a soft low-fired, lead-glazed, and often hand-modeled Japanese pottery used since the 16th century esp. for teabowls
**rale** \'ral, 'räl, 'rȧl\ *n* -S [F *râle,* fr. *râler* to make a rattling sound in the throat] **:** an abnormal sound heard accompanying the normal respiratory sounds on auscultation of the chest ⟨the ~*s* produced when air passes through mucus-clogged bronchioles⟩ — compare RHONCHUS
**ra·leigh** \'rólē, 'rälē, -li\ *adj, usu cap* [fr. *Raleigh,* capital of No. Carolina] **:** of or from Raleigh, the capital of No. Carolina ⟨a *Raleigh* club⟩ **:** of the kind or style prevalent in Raleigh
**1ral·len·tan·do** \¦rälən·¦tän(,)dō, ¦ralən·¦tan-\ *adv (or adj)* [It, lit., slowing down, verbal of *rallentare* to relax, slow down again, fr. *r-* re- + *allentare* to slow down, fr. LL, fr. L *al-* ad- + *lentus* pliant, tough, slow — more at LITHE] **:** with a gradual decrease or slackening in tempo **:** RITARDANDO — used as a direction in music
**2rallentando** \"\ *n* -S **1 :** a gradually slackening musical tempo **2 :** a musical passage or movement gradually decreasing in tempo
**ral·len·ta·to** \¦rälən·¦täd·(,)ō\ *adv (or adj)* [It *rallentato,* past part. of *rallentare*] **:** RALLENTANDO — used as a direction in music
**rallery** *n* -ES [modif. of F *raillerie* raillery] **1** *obs* **:** RAILLERY **2** *obs* **:** a playful act
**ral·li cart** \'ralē-\ *n, often cap R* [fr. *Ralli,* name of its first purchaser] **:** a light two-wheeled horse-drawn cart for four persons having the body brought rather low by shafts fastened within rather than below it — compare DOGCART, GOVERNESS CART
**ral·li·dae** \'ralə,dē\ *n pl, cap* [NL, fr. *Rallus,* type genus + *-idae*] **:** a family of gruiform birds consisting of the rails, crakes, wekas, coots, gallinules, and related forms
**ral·li·er** \'ralēə(r)\ *n* -S **:** one that rallies
**ral·li·form** \'ralə,fórm\ *adj* [ML *rallus* rail + E *-iform* — more at RALLUS] **:** resembling or related to the rails
**ral·line** \'ra,līn\ *adj* [ML *rallus* rail + E *-ine*] **:** of, relating to, or resembling the rails
**rallo** *abbr* rallentando
**ral·lus** \'raləs\ *n, cap* [NL, fr. ML *rallus* rail, fr. MF *raale*] **:** the type genus of Rallidae comprising slender-billed rails (as the European water rail, the clapper rail, and the king rail)
**1ral·ly** \'ralē, -li\ *vb* -ED/-ING/-ES [F *rallier,* fr. OF *ralier,* fr. *re-* + *alier* to unite — more at ALLY] *vt* **1 a :** to muster, call up, or summon for a common purpose ⟨they knew well that he would ~ his friends and pursue them —H.E.Scudder⟩ **b :** to recall (a scattered force or group) to order or unity **:** REGATHER, REUNITE ⟨would permit the chancellor to ~ the drifting and disillusioned voters once more around the . . . banner —F.E. Hirsch⟩ **2 a :** to stir up (a power of mind or body) **:** COLLECT ⟨*rallied* his tired wits to face this fresh problem⟩ ⟨*rallied* his energies and struck again⟩ **b :** to rouse (one) from depression or weakness **:** restore the spirits or courage of ⟨felt she had to be salty to ~ him⟩ **3 :** to strengthen the price of (as securities) after a decline **:** cause to rise in price ⟨the news *rallied* an unsteady market⟩ **4 :** to haul or let run (a sail) sharply in a specified direction ~ *vi* **1 :** to reunite so as to renew an effort (as a battle) **:** recoup forces **:** REASSEMBLE ⟨the soldiers . . . *rallied* at the top of a high hill —O.G.Libby⟩ **2 :** to unite as supporters or followers **:** join in a common cause ⟨upwards of 700 people *rallied* to him —G.H.Genzmer⟩ **3 a :** to collect one's vital powers **:** RECUPERATE, REVIVE ⟨*rallied* after months of prostration from grief and shock⟩ **b :** to rebound in price ⟨stocks *rallied* after brief uncertainty⟩ **c :** to regain offensive strength **:** recapture initiative **:** come back — used esp. of an athletic contestant or team **4 a :** to engage in a court rally **b :** to practice or warm up by exchanging shots (as in tennis) with an opponent **syn** see STIR
**2rally** \"\ *n* -ES **1 a :** a recouping or reuniting of forces: as (1) **:** a mustering together of scattered forces to renew an effort or contest (2) **:** a summoning up of strength or courage after weakness, sickness, or dejection **b :** a recovery of price after a decline ⟨a sharp ~ lent buoyancy to the market before closing⟩ **2 :** a mass meeting intended to arouse group enthusiasm or support (as for a political candidate or a school team) **3 :** a series of strokes that are interchanged between players (as in tennis) before a point is won **4** *also* **ral·lye** \"\ -S **:** a competitive long-distance automobile run esp. of sport cars over public roads and under ordinary traffic rules with the object of maintaining a specified exact average speed between checkpoints over a route unknown to the participants until the start of the run
**3rally** \"\ *vb* -ED/-ING/-ES [F *railler,* fr. MF — more at RAIL] *vt* **:** to attack with raillery **:** BANTER, RIDICULE ⟨*rallied* him on his overweening pretensions⟩ ~ *vi, archaic* **:** to indulge in raillery, pleasantry, or derision **syn** see RIDICULE
**rallying cry** *n* [fr. gerund of *1rally*] **:** SLOGAN
**ral·ly·ing·ly** *adv* [*rallying* (fr. pres. part. of *3rally*) + *-ly*] **:** BANTERINGLY
**rallying point** *n* [fr. gerund of *1rally*] **:** a point, place, or principle at or upon which scattered forces unite or opposing groups come together
**ral·ston·ite** \'rólztə,nīt, -lst-\ *n* -S [J. Grier *Ralston,* 19th cent. Am. clergyman + E *-ite*] **:** a mineral $NaMgAl_5F_{12}(OH)_6.3H_2O$ consisting of a hydrous basic fluoride of aluminum, sodium, and magnesium in octahedral crystals
**1ram** \'ram, 'raa(ə)m\ *n* -S [ME, fr. OE *ramm;* akin to MLG, MD, & OHG *ram,* and prob. to ON *rammr, ramr* strong, bitter, sharp, OIr *remor* thick, fat, OSlav *ramĕnŭ* violent] **1 a :** a male sheep **b** *southern Africa* (1) **:** a male goat (2) **:** the male of any of numerous small antelopes **:** BUCK **2 a** (1) **:** BATTERING RAM (2) **:** something resembling or used as a battering ram **b** (1) **:** a warship fitted with a heavy steel or iron beak at the prow for piercing or cutting an enemy's ship (2) **:** the prow of a ship fitted with such a beak **3 :** any of various guided pieces for exerting considerable pressure or for driving or forcing something by impact: as **a :** the plunger of a hydrostatic press, hydraulic elevator, or force pump **b :** the reciprocating arm or piece carrying the tool head in a shaping or a slotting machine **c :** the weight which strikes the blow esp. in a pile driver or steam hammer **4 :** HYDRAULIC RAM **5 :** RAM EFFECT
**2ram** \"\ *vb* **rammed; rammed; ramming; rams** [ME *rammen,* prob. fr. *ram,* n.] *vi* **1 :** to pound earth in order to make it hard and solid **2 :** to strike with violence **:** CRASH ⟨three perished when their auto *rammed* into a tree —*Pasadena (Calif.) Independent*⟩ **3 :** to move with extreme rapidity and force ⟨a passenger train *ramming* past in the final heat of its run from Chicago —H.L.Davis⟩ **4 :** to produce a ram effect in the pressure of a fluid (as by driving, pressing, or pushing upon air ~ *vt* **1 a :** to force down usu. by driving, pressing, or pushing ⟨~ fence posts into the ground⟩ ⟨*rammed* his hat over his ears⟩ ⟨~ the mix little by little into the mold with a mallet —F.H.Norton⟩ **b :** to make compact (as earth) esp. by pounding or stamping ⟨*rammed* earth construction is not new —*New Republic*⟩ **2 :** to stop up **:** block to prevent passage ⟨*rammed* the mouse hole with a tin can⟩ **3 a :** to press or push in the contents of **:** fill firmly ⟨*rammed* his pipe with his finger⟩ **b** (1) **:** to force ammunition into (a gun) (2) **:** to force (as ammunition) into a gun **c :** to force recognition of (as a point of view) — usu. used with *home* ⟨he despaired of his ability to ~ home the reality of the beauty of the Church —Bruce Marshall⟩ ⟨~*s* home the pure and shrieking insanity of war —Clifton Fadiman⟩ **4 :** to thrust into **:** press closely and tightly together ⟨*rammed* the clothes into a packing case⟩ ⟨his hands were *rammed* hard in his pants' pockets —E.V. Roberts⟩ ⟨great slices of meat onto his fork and *ramming* them into his mouth —Bruce Marshall⟩ **5 :** to fill up **:** CRAM ⟨the closet was *rammed* with the children's toys⟩ **6 :** to butt or strike against violently **:** drive against or through **:** crash into ⟨side-swiped one parked machine then *rammed* the rear of another —*Springfield (Mass.) Daily News*⟩ **7 :** to drive forcefully and with extreme rapidity ⟨was *ramming* his airplane across the U. S. at eight miles a minute —Horace Sutton⟩ **syn** see PACK — **ram down one's throat :** to force (one) to accept ⟨there is no attempt to *ram* . . . ideas *down* other people's *throats* —T.O.Beachcroft⟩
**3ram** \'ram\ *adj* [of Scand origin; akin to Sw dial. *ram* strong-smelling, strong or unpleasant to the taste, Dan dial., strong, biting, ON *rammr, ramr* strong, bitter, sharp — more at *1*RAM] *dial Eng* **:** RANCID
**ra·ma** \'rämə\ *n, pl* **rama** *or* **ramas** *usu cap* [Sp, of AmerInd origin] **1 a :** a Chibchan people of southeastern Nicaragua **b :** a member of such people **2 :** the language of the Rama people
**ramack** *var of* RAMMACK
**ra·ma·da** \rə'mädə, -madə\ *n* -S [Sp, fr. *rama* branch (alter. of *ramo,* fr. L *ramus*) + *-ada* (fr. L *-ata* -ate) — more at RAMIFY] **1 :** a structure resembling a pergola **:** ARBOR **2 :** an open porch
**ram·a·dan** \¦ramə¦dän\ *or* **ram·a·zan** \-'zän\ *also* **ram·a·dhan** \-'dän\ *n* -S *usu cap* [Ar *Ramaḍān*] **1 :** the 9th month of the Muhammadan year observed as a sacred month on each day of which strict fasting is practiced from dawn to sunset — see MONTH table **2 :** the fasting observed in Ramadan
**1ramage** *adj* [ME, fr. OF, living in the branches of trees, wild, fr. *ram, raim* branch (fr. L *ramus*) + *-age* (as in *salvage* savage) — more at RAMIFY] *obs* **:** UNTAMED, WILD
**2ram·age** \'ramij\ *n* -S [F, fr. OF, fr. *ram, raim* branch + *-age*] **1 :** the boughs or branches of a tree **2 :** the cry of birds ⟨grew from the ~ of birds to the hurry of wind —Hugh McCrae⟩ **3 :** a genealogical tree of a segmentary unilateral descent group
**ramage hawk** *n* **:** *1*BRANCHER
**ra·ma·ism** \'rämə,izəm\ *n* -S *usu cap* [*Rama,* Hindu epic hero (fr. Skt *Rāma*) + E *-ism*] **:** the worship of the Hindu epic hero Rama as an incarnation of the god Vishnu
**ra·ma·ite** \-,īt\ *n* -S *usu cap* [*Rama* + E *-ite*] **:** one who worships Rama
**ra·ma·krish·na** \¦rämə¦krishnə\ *adj, usu cap* [after *Ramakrishna* †1886 Indian mystic and religious leader] **:** of, relating to, or being an international Vedanta movement founded at the end of the 19th century by disciples of the mystic Ramakrishna and embodied in a monastic order devoted to spiritual cultivation and a lay and monastic mission devoted to philanthropic work
**ra·mal** \'rāməl\ *adj* [NL *ramus* + E *-al*] **:** of or relating to a ramus
**ram·a·li·na** \,ramə'līnə\ *n, cap* [NL, fr. L *ramale* twigs, brushwood (fr. *ramus* branch + *-ale,* neut. of *-alis* -al) + NL *-ina* — more at RAMIFY] **:** a genus of fruticose lichens (family Usneaceae) that have a thallus with flattened usu. tufted lobes which are more or less dichotomously branched and that include several (as *R. fraxinea*) which are sources of dyes or perfume
**ra·man** \'rämən\ *adj, usu cap* [*Rama,* Hindu epic hero + E *-an*] **:** of or relating to Rama
**ra·ma·nas rose** \'ramənəs-\ *n* [perh. fr. Jap *ramman* blooming profusely] **:** a red-flowered cultivated rose that is a variety of the Japan rose
**ra·man effect** \'rämən-\ *n, usu cap R* [after Sir Chandrasekhara V. *Raman* b1888 Indian physicist] **:** a change in frequency undergone by a portion of the light that has been scattered in passage through a transparent liquid, solid, or gas whose characteristics determine the amount of change
**raman spectrum** *n, usu cap R* **:** the characteristic array of frequencies of light that are observed when a fixed single frequency of light is scattered by a pure substance — compare RAMAN EFFECT
**ra·ma·pi·the·cus** \,rämәpә'thēkəs, -mə'pithəkəs\ *n, cap* [NL, fr. *Rama,* Hindu epic hero + *-pithecus*] **:** a genus of Upper Pliocene Indian apes related to those of the genus *Dryopithecus* but exhibiting almost human dentition and dental arch
**ra·mark** \'rā,märk\ *n* -S [*radar marker*] **:** a continuously transmitting radar beacon that provides bearing information for ships and airplanes
**ramass** *vt* -ED/-ING/-ES [MF *ramasser,* fr. *re-* + *amasser* to amass — more at AMASS] *obs* **:** to collect together **:** GATHER
**ra·mate** \'rā,māt\ *adj* [L *ramus* branch + E *-ate* — more at RAMIFY] **:** characterized by the presence of branches **:** BRANCHED
**ram·bla** \'rämblə\ *n* -S [Sp, fr. Ar *ramlah*] **1 :** a dry ravine ⟨in the adjoining ~ the birds assemble in their hundreds —*Manchester Guardian Weekly*⟩ **2 :** a very broad street
**1ram·ble** \'rambəl, -aam-\ *vb* **rambled; rambled; rambling** \-b(ə)liŋ\ **rambles** [perh. alter. of *romble,* fr. ME *romblen,* freq. of *romen* to roam — more at ROAM] *vi* **1 a :** to move usu. by walking from place to place without conscious aim or goal **:** stroll here and there **:** ROVE, WANDER ⟨*rambling* till suppertime through the orderly avenues between the lines of English walnut trees —Jean Stafford⟩ ⟨to ~ through the country and to talk about books —J.P.Marquand⟩ **b :** to explore without any particular purpose ⟨most students *rambled* around among a lot of different subjects —Sloan Wilson⟩ **2 :** to talk or write in a desultory fashion ⟨this essay ~*s* a great deal, darting . . . from point to point —*Saturday Rev.*⟩ ⟨great temptation . . . to ~ on interminably in praise of the delights of sailing —E.J. Schoettle⟩ **3 a :** to grow at random ⟨roses that ~ over our summer house —Nora Waln⟩ **b :** to extend or stretch seemingly without design or plan ⟨a little tame wood which *rambled* up from the village —Audrey Barker⟩ ⟨roads and drives ~ past great estates —*Amer. Guide Series: N. C.*⟩ ~ *vt* **:** to wander over **:** ROAM ⟨*rambling* the streets of London —Virginia Woolf⟩ ⟨*rambling* the woods with his father on quiet Sunday afternoons⟩
**2ramble** \"\ *n* -S **1 :** the act of rambling **:** a walk taken without a specific aim or goal **:** leisurely excursion for pleasure ⟨in my ~*s* about the city —John Reed⟩ **2 :** an informal discursive piece of writing ⟨cannot in this short ~ give a simple and sincere account of my new life —E.B.White⟩
**ram·bler** \-b(ə)lə(r)\ *n* -S **1 :** one that rambles ⟨still time to save this ancient hunting ground of Norman kings for the woodland ~ —S.P.B.Mais⟩ **2** *or* **rambler rose :** any of various climbing roses with rather small often double flowers in large clusters: as **a :** CRIMSON RAMBLER **b :** any of several yellow-flowered or white-flowered relatives of the crimson rambler **3 :** RANCH HOUSE
**rambler rose** *n* **:** a deep pink to moderate purplish red that is yellower and less strong than peachblossom (sense 2)
**rambling** *adj* **1 :** moving about from one place to another **:** wandering without purpose ⟨envied the ~ deer⟩ **2 :** straying from subject to subject **:** often incoherent **:** MEANDERING ⟨the ~ quality of the average medieval tale —G.C.Sellery⟩ ⟨talked . . . in his smiling ~ way —Hugh Walpole⟩ ⟨talked in a ~ excited manner about her marriage —Ellen Glasgow⟩ **3 :** stretching or spreading irregularly without or as if without plan ⟨a ~ dispersed series of streamlets flowing erratically —L.C.Eiseley⟩ ⟨the ridges along the valley climb into low ~ mountains —*Amer. Guide Series: Vt.*⟩ **4 :** informally designed **:** LARGE, SPRAWLING ⟨a ~ old manor house —James Stern⟩ ⟨lovely old Saxon church and ~ vicarage —Sam Pollock⟩
**ram·bling·ly** *adv* **:** in a rambling manner
**ram·bong** \'ram'bäŋ\ *n* -S [Atjehnese] **:** a rubber plant (*Ficus elastica*)
**rambong rubber** *or* **rambong** *n* -S **:** rubber obtained from the rambong
**ram·bouil·let** \¦rambə¦lā, räⁿbüye\ *n* [fr. *Rambouillet,* Dept. Seine-et-Oise, France] **1** *usu cap* **:** a French breed of large sturdy plain-bodied sheep developed by selection for both mutton and wool production from Spanish merino sheep **2** -S *often cap* **:** an animal of the Rambouillet breed
**ram bow** *n* **:** a strongly built extension below water of the bow of a ship for the purpose of piercing the hull of an enemy
**ram·bunc·tious** \(')ram'bəŋ(k)shəs, (')raam-\ *adj* [prob. alter. of *rumbustious*] **1 :** outrageously flamboyant in behavior **:** excessively exuberant **:** WILD, UNCONTROLLABLE, UNRULY ⟨ever since she got out of college she's been too ~ to live with —Sinclair Lewis⟩ **2 :** difficult to manage or bring under control **:** UNTAMED ⟨the ~ region on which this young man was to have so much influence —S.H.Holbrook⟩
**ram·bunc·tious·ly** *adv* **:** in a rambunctious manner ⟨heard him shout ~ from the front door as he entered⟩
**ram·bunc·tious·ness** *n* -ES **:** the quality or state of being rambunctious ⟨the traditional ~ of the fraternities —*Time*⟩
**ram·bu·tan** \ram'büt°n\ *or* **ram·bo·tan** *or* **ram·boe·tan** *or* **ram·bou·tan** \'rambə,tan\ *also* **ram·bus·tan** \-bə,stan\ *n* -S [Malay *rambutan,* fr. *rambut* hair; fr. the hairy integument of the fruit] **1 :** a bright red oval Malayan fruit that has a pleasant acid pulp and is covered with long soft spines **2 :** a tree (*Nephelium lappaceum*) that is closely related to the litchi and bears fruits which are rambutans
**ram cat** *n* **:** a male cat
**ram·dohr·ite** \'räm,dō,rīt\ *n* -S [G *ramdohrit,* fr. Paul *Ramdohr* b1890 Ger. mineralogist + G *-it* -ite] **:** a mineral $Pb_3Ag_2Sb_6S_{13}$ consisting of a rare compound of lead, silver, antimony, and sulfur
**ra·me·an** \'rāmēən\ *adj, usu cap* [Petrus *Ramus* + E *-ean* — more at RAMISM] **:** RAMIST
**ramee** *var of* RAMIE
**ram effect** *n* -S **:** the compressing effect obtained by locating the entrance to an air-intake duct in an airplane in the air stream in such a manner as to take advantage of the relative velocity between the air intake and the air stream by increasing the static pressure in the system to aid in compressing the charge air or to maintain the flow of air through a cooling system
**ram·e·kin** *or* **ram·e·quin** \'ramәkən\ *n* -S [F *ramequin,* fr. LG *ramken,* dim. of *ram* cream, fr. MLG *rōm, rōme* — more at REAM] **1 :** a preparation of cheese usu. with bread crumbs, puff paste, or eggs baked in a mold or shell **2 :** an individual baking dish in which food is baked and served ⟨oysters in ~*s*⟩
**ram·el·lose** \'ramə,lōs\ *adj* [L *ramus* branch + *-ellus,* dim. suffix + E *-ose*] **:** bearing little branches
**ra·ment** \'rāmənt\ *n* -S [NL *ramentum*] **:** RAMENTUM 2
**ram·en·ta·ceous** \¦ramən·¦tāshəs\ *or* **ra·men·tal** \rə'ment°l\ *adj* [NL *ramentum* + E *-aceous* or *-al*] **:** covered with, consisting of, or resembling ramenta
**ram·en·tif·er·ous** \¦ramən·¦tif(ə)rəs\ *adj* [NL *ramentum* + E *-iferous*] **:** bearing ramenta
**ra·men·tum** \rə'mentəm\ *n, pl* **ramen·ta** \-tə\ [L, fr. *radere* to scratch, scrape + *-mentum* -ment — more at RAT] **1 :** something scraped off **:** a minute particle **:** SHAVING **2** [NL, fr. L] **a :** any of the thin brownish often fringed or laciniate scales that are borne upon the leaves or young shoots of many ferns and that consist of a single layer of cells **b :** the armor of a fossil cycad stump that suggests in appearance the ramenta of existing ferns
**ra·me·ous** \'rāmēəs\ *adj* [L *rameus,* fr. *ramus* branch — more at RAMIFY] **:** RAMAL
**rames** \'rāmz\ *n pl* [fr. pl. of ME *rame* skeleton, prob. fr. MD *raem, rame* frame; akin to MLG *rame* frame, OHG *rama* pillar, support, weaver's frame, OE *rima* rim — more at RIM] *dial chiefly Eng* **:** BONES, SKELETON ⟨tis said I be only the ~ of a man —Thomas Hardy⟩
**ram·e·se·um** \,ramə'sēəm\ *n* -S *usu cap* [*Rameses* (*Ramses*) + E *-eum* (as in *museum*)] **:** a temple erected by or in honor of a Ramesside king; *specif* **:** a temple erected in honor of Ramses II at Thebes in Egypt
**1ram·es·side** \'ramə,sīd, -,səd\ *also* **ram·es·sid** \-,səd\ *adj, usu cap* [irreg. (influence of the Gk form *Rhamessēs*) fr. *Rameses* (*Ramses*), the name of 12 kings of ancient Egypt that reigned intermittently fr. *ab*1315–1090 B.C. + E *-ide, -id*] **:** of or relating to the kings of ancient Egypt named Ramses; *esp* **:** of or relating to the kings of the XXth dynasty founded by Ramses III about 1200 B.C.
**2ramesside** \"\ *also* **ramessid** \"\ *n* -S *usu cap* **:** a king of the XXth Egyptian dynasty
**ra·met** \'rāmət\ *n* -S [L *ramus* branch + E *-et* — more at RAMIFY] **:** a plant that is an independent member of a clone — compare ORTET
**ram·fee·zled** \ram'fēzəld\ *adj* [origin unknown] *Scot* **:** worn out **:** EXHAUSTED
**ramhead** *n* **1** *obs* **:** a stupid or dull-witted person **:** BLOCKHEAD **2** *obs* **:** an arm or hook of a crane
**rami** *pl of* RAMUS
**ram·i·corn** \'ramə,kórn\ *adj* [L *ramus* branch + E *-i-* + *-corn* — more at RAMIFY] **:** having branched antennae
**ram·ie** *or* **ram·ee** \'ramē, 'rāmē\ *n* -S [Malay *rami*] **1 :** a tall perennial herb of eastern Asia (*Boehmeria nivea*) having dark green rather thick broad leaves that are white and woolly on the undersurface and being commercially cultivated in China, Japan, the Philippines, and more recently the southern U.S. for its fiber **2 a :** the strong lustrous bast fiber of ramie capable of being spun or woven **b :** any of the various strong smooth lustrous fabrics of ramie often similar to linen or silk made in various weights usu. for underwear, household linens, upholstery, or curtains
**ramie hemp** *n* **:** RAMIE 2a
**ram·i·fi·ca·tion** \,raməfə'kāshən\ *n* -S [F, fr. MF, fr. ML *ramificatus* (past part. of *ramificare*) + MF *-ion*] **1 :** the act or process of branching; *specif* **:** the mode of arrangement of branches **2 a :** a branch or offshoot from a main stock or channel ⟨the ~ of an artery⟩ **b :** the resulting branched structure ⟨make visible the whole ~ of the dendrite⟩ **3 :** something that springs from another in the manner of a branch **:** OUTGROWTH, SUBDIVISION **:** an extension of a basically simple idea, plan, or problem **:** a resulting development **:** CONSEQUENCE ⟨a university whose daily life abounds with events of far-reaching ~*s* —T.D.Durrance⟩ ⟨his banking house had ~*s* throughout Europe —R.A.Hall b.1911⟩ ⟨his mind brooded on the ~*s* of clans and tartans —W.B.Yeats⟩
**ram·i·form pit** \'ramə,fórm-\ *n* [L *ramus* branch + E *-iform*] **:** a branched pit formed by the coalescence of the cavities of two or more simple pits (as in the walls of brachysclereids)
**ram·i·fy** \'ramə,fī\ *vb* -ED/-ING/-ES [MF *ramifier,* fr. ML *ramificare,* fr. L *ramus* branch + *-ificare* -ify; akin to L *radix* root — more at ROOT] *vt* **1 :** to cause to branch **:** spread out **2 :** to separate into divisions or ramifications ~ *vi* **1 :** to split up into branches or constituent parts **2 :** to send forth branches, outgrowths, shoots, or extensions resembling them ⟨closely spaced veinlets of quartz . . . ~ in all directions —A.M.Bateman⟩ **3 :** to extend by means of branches or divisions ⟨a long-range industrial research program . . . should ~ into the field of substitute materials —W. H.Camp⟩ **syn** see BRANCH
**ram·il·lie** *or* **ram·i·lie** \'ramәlē\ *also* **ram·il·lies** *or* **ram·i·lies** \-ēz\ *n, pl* **ramillies** *or* **ramilies** *sometimes cap* [fr. *Ramillies,* Belgium, in commemoration of a battle in 1706 when the British defeated the French] **:** an 18th century wig with a long plait in back that is tied top and bottom with bows

ramillie

**ra·mism** \'rā,mizəm\ *n* -S *usu cap* [F *ramisme,* fr. Petrus *Ramus* (Pierre de La Ramée) †1572 Fr. philosopher and mathematician + F

*-isme* -ism] **:** the doctrines of Petrus Ramus who opposed scholasticism and advocated Calvinism as well as a logic more informal than Aristotelian and designed to be amalgamated with rhetoric

**¹ra·mist** \ˈrāməst\ *n* -s *usu cap* [F *ramiste*, fr. P. *Ramus* + F *-iste* -ist] **:** an advocate of Ramism

**²ramist** \"\ *or* **ra·mis·tic** \rəˈmistik\ *adj, usu cap* **:** of or relating to Petrus Ramus or to Ramism

**ramjet engine** \ˈ=,=-\ *or* **ramjet** *n* [²*ram* + *jet*] **:** a jet engine having in its forward end a continuous inlet of air so that there is a compressing effect produced on the air taken in while the engine is in motion with the compressed air that enters the combustion chamber and the constant burning of the fuel resulting in a continuous jet of hot gases

**ram·ko·ka·mek·ra** \ramˈkōkə,mekrə\ *n, pl* **ramkokamekra** *or* **ramkokamekras** *usu cap* **1 a :** a Ge people of northeastern Brazil **b :** a member of such people **2 :** the language of the Ramkokamekra people

**ram leather** *n* **:** CUP LEATHER

**ramline** \ˈ=,=\ *n* **:** a line used to mark a straight middle line (as on a spar or mast)

**ram·mack** *also* **ram·ack** \ˈramək\ *vi* -ED/-ING/-S [origin unknown] *dial* **:** to rush around

**rammed** *past of* RAM

**ram·mel** \ˈraməl\ *n* -s [ME *ramell, ramail*, fr. MF *ramaille*, fr. *ram, rame, raim* branch — more at RAMAGE] **1** *dial chiefly Eng* **:** UNDERBRUSH **2** *dial chiefly Eng* **:** TRASH **3** *dial chiefly Eng* **:** hard barren soil

**ram·mels·berg·ite** \ˈraməlz,bər,gīt\ *n* -s [Karl F. *Rammelsberg* †1899 Ger. mineralogist + E *-ite*] **:** a mineral $NiAs_2$ consisting of a native nickel diarsenide related to loellingite and polymorphous with pararammelsbergite

**ram·mer** \ˈramə(r)\ *n* -s [ME, fr. *rammen* to ram + *-er* — more at RAM] **:** one that rams: as **a :** an instrument for driving something (as stones, piles, earth) with force **b :** a rod made chiefly of wood and operated by hand or entirely of metal and operated by power that is used for ramming home the projectile or the charge of a gun **c :** a worker who compacts sand around mold patterns

**ramming** *pres part of* RAM

**ramming effect** *or* **ramming** *n* -s **:** RAM EFFECT

**ram·mish** \ˈramish\ *adj* [ME *rammissh*, fr. ¹*ram* + *-issh*, *-ish* -ish] **1 :** resembling a ram **2** *chiefly dial* **:** rank in smell or taste

**ram·mish·ness** *n* -ES **:** the quality or state of being rammish

**ram·my** \-mē\ *adj* -ER/-EST [¹*ram* + *-y*] **:** RAMMISH

**ra·mon** \rəˈmōn\ *n* -s [AmerSp *ramón*, fr. Sp, browse, aug. of *ramo* branch, twig — more at RAMADA] **:** BREADNUT 1

**ra·mo·na** \rəˈmōnə\ [NL, prob. after *Ramona*, heroine of a novel (1884) of the same name by Helen Hunt Jackson †1885 Am. writer] *syn of* AUDIBERTIA

**ra·mo·neur** \,raməˈnər\ *n* -s [F, fr. MF, fr. *ramoner* to sweep (fr. OF, fr. *ramon* broom, dim. of *ram, raim* branch) + *-eur* -or — more at RAMAGE] *Brit* **:** CHIMNEY SWEEP

**ra·mont·chi** \rəˈmänchē\ *n* -s [origin unknown] **:** GOVERNOR'S PLUM

**ramoosi** *usu cap, var of* RAMUSI

**ra·mose** \ˈrā,mōs, raˈmōs\ *adj* [L *ramosus*, fr. *ramus* branch + *-osus* -ose — more at RAMIFY] **:** consisting of or having branches or lateral divisions **:** BRANCHED — **ra·mose·ly** *adv* — **ra·mos·i·ty** \rəˈmäsəd-ē\ *n* -ES

**ra·mos gin fizz** *also* **ra·mos fizz** \ˈrāməs-\ *n, usu cap R* [after Henry Charles *Ramos*, 19th–20th cent. Am. bartender] **:** a mixed drink consisting of gin, cream, white of egg, lemon and lime juice, sugar, and orange-flower water shaken vigorously, strained, and served often with the addition of a little soda water in a tall glass

**ra·mous** \ˈrāməs\ *adj* [L *ramosus*] **1 :** RAMOSE **2 :** of, relating to, or resembling branches

**¹ramp** \ˈramp, ˈraa(ə)mp, ˈraimp\ *vb* -ED/-ING/-S [ME *rampen*, fr. OF *ramper*, to climb, crawl, rear, of Gmc origin; akin to MD & MLG *ramp* cramp, MHG *rampf* cramp, OHG *rimpfan* to wrinkle — more at RUMPLE] *vi* **1 a :** to be rampant or in the posture of a beast rampant in heraldry **b (1) :** to stand or advance with forelegs or with arms raised as if in menace, anger, or excitement **(2) :** to move or act furiously **:** RAGE, STORM ⟨would ~ and rage and hop about like a veritable Sioux —Norman Douglas⟩ **c** *chiefly dial* **:** to rush about esp. in a boisterous excited manner **2 :** to crawl or move along the ground ⟨a boa does not ~ about the jungle —*Current History*⟩ **3 a (1) :** CLIMB **(2) :** to creep up — used esp. of plants ⟨grew here as roses should be allowed to grow — untamed . . . *~ing* over the rocks —Douglas Carruthers⟩ **b** *chiefly dial* **:** to grow rapidly **4 :** to rise or fall to a higher or lower level **~** *vt* **1 :** to bend so as to fit to a ramp (as in a stair rail) ⟨gracefully *~ed* mahogany handrail —H.S.Morrison⟩ **2 :** to furnish with a ramp ⟨the auditorium was *~ed* to better visual efficiency —Al Hine⟩

**²ramp** \"\ *n* -s **:** the act of ramping; *esp* **:** a rearing or advancing in a threatening or warlike posture ⟨in the roar and the ~ of the southern gale —Hamlin Garland⟩

**³ramp** \"\ *n* -s [F *rampe*, fr. *ramper*] **1 a :** the perpendicular distance between the springing lines of a rampant arch **b :** a sloping member other than a purely constructional one (as a continuous parapet to a staircase) **2 :** a short bend, slope, or curve usu. in the vertical plane where a handrail or coping changes its direction; *esp* **:** a vertical curve in a handrail, concave, or top **:** EASING **3 :** a sloping way: as **a :** a sloping floor or walk leading from one level to another — see BASTION illustration **b :** a platform and incline from which logs are loaded **c :** an inclined roadway connecting two thoroughfares (as in an interchange) or serving as a means of access to or exit from a bridge, a tunnel, or a parking area ⟨inclined *~s* at each end of the pontoon bridge —C.R.Ege⟩ **4 :** a contrivance (as of blocks or wedges of wood) laid parallel in a roadway for passing traffic over lines of hose **5 a :** APRON 8c(1) **b :** the stairway by which passengers enter the main door of an airplane **6 :** a wedge-shaped block forming a base for a front sight of a firearm **7 a :** a thrust fault having a relatively high angle of dip **b :** RAMP VALLEY **c :** an accumulation of snow forming an inclined plane between land or land ice and sea or shelf ice

ramp 5b

**⁴ramp** \"\ *n* -s [ME *rampe*, perh. fr. *rampen* to ramp, rage — more at ¹RAMP] **:** a bold woman

**⁵ramp** \"\ *n* -s [in sense 1, by shortening; in sense 2, back-formation fr. *ramps*, alter. of *rams*, fr. ME, fr. OE *hramsa* — more at RAMSON] **1 :** RAMPION **2 :** any of several plants of the genus *Allium*; *esp* **:** RAMSON

**⁶ramp** \ˈramp\ *vt* -ED/-ING/-S [origin unknown] **1** *Brit* **:** ROB **2** *Brit* **:** to swindle from

**⁷ramp** \"\ *n* -s *Brit* **:** a confidence game **:** HOAX, SWINDLE ⟨the whole thing was a moneymaking ~ —Nicholas Monsarrat⟩

**¹ram·page** \(ˈ)ramˈpāj, (ˈ)raam- *sometimes* -ˌpij *or* -ˌpēj\ *vb* -ED/-ING/-S [fr. Sc, prob. irreg. fr. ¹*ramp*] *vi* **:** to go on a rampage **:** act, rush, or storm wildly or excitedly ⟨go *rampaging* over the western prairies —Elinor Wylie⟩ **~** *vt* **:** to rush or storm in or about ⟨the peculiarly stirring timbres of thin brass . . . which can ~ a man's soul —Whitney Balliett⟩

**²ram·page** \ˈ=,pāj *sometimes* -ˌpij *or* -ˌpēj\ *n* -s **:** violent, riotous, or reckless action or behavior **:** a state of being turbulently active, wildly agitated, or destructive ⟨the river going on a ~ —N.M.Clark⟩ ⟨~ of wanton killings —Vicki Baum⟩

**ram·pa·geous** *also* **ram·pa·gious** \(ˈ)ramˈpājəs, (ˈ)raam-\ *adj* **:** displaying violence or recklessness **:** often destructive **:** being out of control **:** UNRULY ⟨seamen who are wild and ~ —Kenneth Roberts⟩ ⟨vegetation is startlingly — almost overwhelmingly ~ —Hamilton Basso⟩

**ram·pa·geous·ly** *adv* **:** in a rampageous manner ⟨the lobsters . . . were ~ lively when they reached me —*New Yorker*⟩

**ram·pa·geous·ness** *n* -ES **:** the quality or state of being rampageous ⟨his ~ on finding himself in a frontier township after months of hard and dangerous work —*Times Lit. Supp.*⟩

**rampaging** *adj* **:** wildly storming **:** TURBULENT, VIOLENT ⟨safe from the ~ surf —*Springfield (Mass.) Union*⟩ ⟨~ self-pity —David Driscoll⟩

**ram·pal·lian** *also* **ram·pal·lion** \ramˈpalyən\ *n* -s [origin unknown] **:** a good-for-nothing scoundrel **:** WRETCH

**ram·pan·cy** \ˈrampənsē\ *n* -ES **:** the quality or state of being rampant **:** excessive exuberance **:** EXTRAVAGANCE

**ram·pant** \ˈrampənt, ˈraam- *also* -m,pant *or* -m,paa(ə)nt\ *adj* [ME *rampaunt*, fr. MF *rampant*, pres. part. of *ramper* to climb, crawl, rear — more at RAMP] **1 a :** rearing upon the hind legs with forelegs or forepaws extended **b** *of a heraldic beast* **:** reared up, standing on one hind foot with one foreleg raised above the other, and seen in profile **2 :** characterized by fierceness or high spirits ⟨below was the bull, ~, slobbering froth —Francis Birtles⟩ ⟨the long crow of a ~ cock —William Sansom⟩ **3 :** marked by the absence of check or restraint **:** UNBRIDLED ⟨the crime wave ~ here in recent months —T.W. Arnold⟩ ⟨rumor ran ~ . . . the other day —Harvey Breit⟩ **4 :** threatening or extravagant in action, bearing, or manner **:** displaying aggression or violence ⟨her wrath, feral and ~, utterly possessed her —W.H.Wright⟩ **5 :** having one impost or abutment higher than the other ⟨a ~ arch⟩ **6 a :** extremely profuse in growth **:** RANK ⟨~ beds of yellow flowers on the lawn —Janet Flanner⟩ **b :** used extravagantly **:** very much in evidence ⟨pleats . . . are ~ in skirts for daytime —Lois Long⟩

**ram·pant·ly** *adv* **:** in a rampant manner

**¹ram·part** \ˈram,pärt, ˈraam-, -pət, -mpə(r)t, *usu* -d·+V\ *n* -s [MF *rampart, rempart*, fr. *ramparer, remparer* to fortify, strengthen, fr. *re-* + *emparer* to defend, protect, seize, fr. OProv *antparar, amparar*, fr. (assumed) VL *anteparare* — more at AMPARO] **1 :** a broad embankment or mound of earth raised as a fortification about a place and usu. surmounted by a parapet **2 :** something that fortifies, defends, or secures against attack or intrusion **:** a protective barrier **:** BULWARK ⟨our villages . . . are often surrounded by these great *~s* of trees —Anne D. Sedgwick⟩ ⟨the great ~ of mountains loomed before them⟩ **3 :** a ridge like a wall of unconsolidated rock fragments, earth, or other debris: as **a :** ice pushed up along a lakeshore **b :** snow at the foot of a talus slope **c :** a shingle ridge formed along a beach by strong waves and currents

**²rampart** \"\ *vt* -ED/-ING/-S **:** to surround or protect with or as if with a rampart ⟨glittering dells proudly *~ed* with rocks —S.T.Coleridge⟩

**ramped** *past of* RAMP

**ram·per** \ˈrampə(r)\ *n* -s [by alter.] *dial* **:** LAMPREY

**ram·phas·ti·dae** \ramˈfastə,dē\ *n pl, cap* [NL, fr. *Ramphastos*, type genus + *-idae*] **:** a family of birds (order Piciformes) consisting of the toucans

**ram·phas·ti·des** \-ēz\ *n pl, cap* [NL, fr. *Ramphastos* + *-ides*] *in some esp. former classifications* **:** a suborder of birds coextensive with the family Ramphastidae

**ram·phas·tos** \-ˈfa,stäs\ *n, cap* [NL, irreg. fr. Gk *rhamphos* curved beak + *astos* citizen, fr. *asty* city; akin to Skt *vasati* he remains, dwells — more at RHAMPH-, WAS] **:** a genus (the type of the family Ramphastidae) comprising various typical toucans

**ramphoid** *var of* RHAMPHOID

**ram·pick** \ˈram,pik\ *dial var of* RAMPIKE

**ram·pike** \-pīk\ *n* [origin unknown] **:** a dead tree **:** a pointed stump or partly-burned tree **:** a tree broken off by the wind leaving a splintered end to the trunk

**ramping** *pres part of* RAMP

**ram·pi·on** \ˈrampēən\ *n* -s [prob. modif. of MF *raiponce*, fr. OIt *raponzo*, prob. fr. *rapa*, *rapo* turnip, fr. L *rapa, rapum* rape, turnip — more at RAPE] **:** a European bellflower (*Campanula rapunculus*) having an edible tuberous root used with the leaves as a salad

**¹ram·pire** \ˈram,pī(ə)r\ *n* -s [MF *rampar, rempart, rampart* — more at RAMPART] **:** RAMPART

**²rampire** \"\ *vt* -ED/-ING/-S [MF *remparer, ramparer* — more at RAMPART] *archaic* **:** to fortify, strengthen, secure, or enclose with or as if with a rampart

**ramp·man** \ˈrampmən\ *n, pl* **rampmen** [³*ramp* + *man*] **:** a sawmill worker who unloads logs from truck or conveyor to deck

**ram pressure** *n* **:** the difference between the observed scoop pressure in the inlet air system of an airplane engine and the atmospheric pressure

**ramps** *pl of* RAMP, *pres 3d sing of* RAMP

**ram·pur** \ˈräm,pu̇(ə)r\ *adj, usu cap* [fr. *Rampur*, India] **:** of or from the city of Rampur, India **:** of the kind or style prevalent in Rampur

**ramp valley** *n* [³*ramp*] **:** a fault trough bounded laterally by faults that dip away from the valley axis and underlaid by a depressed block that is supposed to have been forced down by lateral pressure

**ramrace** \ˈ=,=\ *n* [¹*ram* (animal) + *race*] *chiefly Scot* **:** a headlong rush **:** a short hard run

**ram rocket** [²*ram*] *n* **:** a rocket propelled by a ramjet engine

**¹ramrod** \ˈ=,=\ *n* [²*ram* + *rod*] **1 :** a rod used in ramming home the charge in a muzzle-loading firearm **2 :** a strict disciplinarian; *esp* **:** the foreman of a ranch

**²ramrod** \"\ *vt* **:** to exert discipline and authority on ⟨he was *ramrodding* the whole outfit⟩

**³ramrod** \"\ *adj* **:** very straight and unbending **:** characterized by rigidity, severity, or stiffness **:** INFLEXIBLE ⟨in awe of the ~ characteristics of the elders —J.H.Raleigh⟩ ⟨the ~ rote of a Prussian drillmaster —Al Hine⟩

**¹rams** *pl of* RAM, *pres 3d sing of* RAM

**²rams** \ˈrämz\ *n* -ES [G *rams, rammes, ramsch*, rams, ramsch — more at RAMSCH] **:** a card game similar to loo

**ram·sack** \ˈram,sak\ *dial var of* RANSACK

**ram·say·ite** \ˈramzē,īt\ *n* -s [Sir Andrew C. *Ramsay* †1891 Brit. geologist + E *-ite*] **:** a mineral $Na_2Ti_2Si_2O_9$ consisting of a silicate of titanium and sodium

**rams·bot·tom safety valve** \ˈramz,bäd·əm-\ *n, usu cap R* [after John *Ramsbottom*, 19th cent. Brit. mechanical engineer] **:** a safety valve used esp. on locomotives in which two valves are pressed down by a single spring attached to a crosspiece prolonged to form a hand lever by which the valves may be eased up to test their adjustment

**ramsch** \ˈräm(p)sh\ *n* -ES [G, fr. F dial. *ramser* to collect, ramass, alter. of *ramasser* — more at RAMASS] **:** a game in which the jacks alone are trumps and the object is to lose tricks

**ram schooner** *n* **:** a schooner with pole masts but no topmasts

**rams·dell·ite** \ˈramz,de,līt\ *n* -s [Lewis S. *Ramsdell* *b*1895 Am. mineralogist + E *-ite*] **:** a mineral consisting of manganese dioxide that is polymorphous with pyrolusite

**rams·den eyepiece** \ˈramzdən-\ *n, usu cap R* [after Jesse *Ramsden* †1800 Eng. instrument maker] **:** a nearly achromatic optical system of two lenses used as a magnifying glass or as an eyepiece in transits or telescopes fitted with micrometer wires **:** a positive eyepiece

**¹ram·shackle** \ˈram,shakəl, ˈraam-\ *adj* [short for earlier *ramshackled*, alter. of *ransackled*, fr. past part. of obs. *ransackle* to ransack, freq. of *ransack*] **1 :** appearing as if ready to collapse **:** DILAPIDATED, RICKETY ⟨once imposing though now ~ roof —Ellen Glasgow⟩ ⟨mounted on a ~ horse —W.F. Starkie⟩ ⟨a dirty ~ pier —George Santayana⟩ **2 :** having little moral sense **:** DISSIPATED, UNRULY ⟨worrying about the ~ morality of . . . adolescents —John McCarten⟩ ⟨I may be getting ~ —H.G.Wells⟩ **3 :** carelessly or loosely constructed ⟨the plot is innocent and ~ —Wolcott Gibbs⟩ ⟨the book is a ~ affair —J.A.Michener⟩

**²ramshackle** \"\ *n* **:** a ramshackle thing ⟨here in the faded ~ —Carl Sandburg⟩

**ram·shack·le·ness** *n* -ES **:** the quality or state of being ramshackle

**ram·shack·ly** \-klē\ *adj* [¹*ramshackle* + *-y*] **:** RAMSHACKLE ⟨~ booths displaying souvenirs —Joseph Mitchell⟩

**ram's-head** \ˈ=,=\ *also* **ram's-head lady's slipper** *n, pl* **ram's-heads :** an orchid (*Cypripedium arietinum*) of northern No. America having a brownish green flower with a red-and-white veiny lip suggestive of a ram's head

**ram's head** *n* **:** a carved or sculptured decoration found in Greek and Roman art and revived as a decorative motive esp. in 18th century furniture

**ram's horn** *n* **1 :** a box with holes in the sides in which fish are washed **2 a :** a cat's claw (*Acacia greggii*) **b :** UNICORN PLANT **3 :** a crane attachment consisting of two hooks forged into one in a manner suggesting the shape of a ram's horns **4 :** SHOFAR

ram's horn 3

**ramshorn** \ˈ=,=\ *also* **ramshorn snail** *n* **:** a snail of the genus *Planorbis* often used as a scavenger in aquariums

**ramshorn crab** *n* **:** a small Australian spider crab (*Noxia aries*) with divergent rostral spines and very slender legs

**ram·son** \ˈramzən, -msən\ *n* -s [ME *ramsyn*, fr. OE *hramsan*, pl. of *hramsa*; akin to MLG *ramese*, *remese* ramson, OHG *ramusia*, Sw, Dan & Norw *rams* ramson, MIr *crim* garlic, Gk *kremyon, kromyon*, a kind of onion, Lith *kermušė* wild garlic] **1 :** a broad-leaved garlic (*Allium ursinum*) common in European gardens **2 :** the bulbous root of the ramson used esp. in salads — usu. used in pl.

**¹ram·stam** \ˈram,stam\ *adj* [prob. by redupl. & alter. fr. ¹*ram*] *Scot* **:** HEADSTRONG, RECKLESS

**²ramstam** \"\ *adv, Scot* **:** HEADLONG

**ramstead** *var of* RANSTEAD

**ram through** *vt* **:** to force the passage or acceptance of usu. over considerable opposition ⟨*rammed through* his law —*Time*⟩ ⟨*rammed through* the bitterly opposed nomination —*New Republic*⟩ ⟨legislation *rammed through* by a bare majority of left-wing fellow travelers —T.R.Ybarra⟩

**ram·til** \ˈram,til\ *n* -s [Hindi *rāmtil*, fr. Skt *Rāma* Rama, Hindu epic hero + *tila* sesamum] **:** a tropical African herb (*Guizotia abyssinica*) of the family Compositae widely cultivated in India for its seeds — see NIGER SEED

**ram·u·lar** \ˈramyələ(r)\ *adj* [L *ramulus* small branch + E *-ar* — more at RAMULUS] **:** of or relating to a branch ⟨~ trace⟩

**ram·u·lar·ia** \,ramyəˈla(a)rēə\ *n, cap* [NL, fr. L *ramulus* + NL *-aria*] **:** a genus of imperfect fungi (family Moniliaceae) having oblong to cylindrical hyaline septate conidia often borne in chains

**ram·u·lif·er·ous** \,ramyəˈlif(ə)rəs\ *adj* [*ramulus* + *-iferous*] **:** bearing ramuli

**ram·u·lose** \ˈ==,lōs\ *or* **ram·u·lous** \-ləs\ *adj* [L *ramulosus*, fr. *ramulus* + *-osus* -ose, -ous] **:** having many small branches

**ram·u·lus** \-ləs\ *n, pl* **ramu·li** \-yə,lī\ [L, dim. of *ramus* branch] **:** a small branch **:** BRANCHLET

**ra·mus** \ˈrāməs\ *n, pl* **ra·mi** \-ā,mī\ [NL, fr. L, branch of a tree — more at RAMIFY] **:** a projecting part or elongated process **:** RAMIFICATION: as **a :** the posterior more or less vertical part of the lower jaw on each side which articulates with the skull; *also* **:** the entire right or left half of the jaw — used when the jaw has no plainly distinguishable vertical part **b :** one of the branches of the pubis or ischium **c :** either of the two branches of the incus in the mastax of a rotifer **d :** a branch of a nerve ⟨the dorsal and ventral *rami* of the spinal nerve roots⟩ — compare RAMUS COMMUNICANS **e :** a barb of a feather

**ramus com·mu·ni·cans** \-kəˈmyünə,kanz\ *n, pl* **rami communican·tes** \-=,==ˈkan·,tēz\ [NL, communicating ramus] **:** one of the bundles of nerve fibers connecting a sympathetic ganglion with a spinal nerve and being divided into white rami communicantes consisting of preganglionic fibers and gray rami communicantes consisting of postganglionic fibers

**ra·mus·cule** \rəˈmə,skyül\ *n* -s [NL *ramus* + L *-culus*, dim. suffix] **:** a small ramus

**ra·mu·si** \rəˈmüsē\ *also* **ra·moo·sii** \-ē,ē\ *n, pl* **ramusi** *or* **ramusis** *also* **ramoosii** *or* **ramoosiis** *usu cap* **:** one of a pre-Aryan people in northwestern India

**¹ran** [ME, fr. OE & ON *rann*] *past of* RUN

**²ran** \ˈran\ *n* -s [origin unknown] **:** a hank of twine

**¹ra·na** \ˈränə\ *n* -s [Hindi *rānā*, fr. Skt *rājan* — more at RICH] **:** an Indian prince ⟨the ~ of Koti . . . rode in a sedan chair, as befitted the ruler of the Indian state —*Time*⟩

**²ra·na** \ˈrānə\ *n, cap* [NL, fr. L, frog, prob. of imit. origin] **:** a nearly cosmopolitan genus of frogs that is the type of the family Ranidae

**ra·na·les** \rəˈnā(,)lēz\ *n pl, cap* [NL, irreg. fr. *Ranunculus* + *-ales*] **:** a large order of dicotyledonous herbs, shrubs, and trees including the Ranunculaceae, Berberidaceae, Magnoliaceae, Annonaceae, and Lauraceae and being distinguished in general by flowers with spirally arranged parts, numerous stamens, and an apocarpous gynoecium

**ra·na·li·an** \rəˈnālēən\ *also* **ra·nal** \ˈrānᵊl\ *adj* [*ranalian* fr. NL *Ranales* + E *-ian*; *ranal* fr. NL *Ranales*] **:** relating to or belonging to the order Ranales

**ran·a·tra** \ˈranə·trə\ *n, cap* [NL] **:** a genus of elongate very slender bugs (family Nepidae) with long slender legs the first pair of which is fitted for seizing prey in the manner of a mantis

**rancel** *vi* **rancelled; rancelled; rancelling; rancels** [of Scand origin; akin to Icel *reynsla* experience, trial & Norw *røynsla* experience, fr. ON *reyna* to experience, examine, search, causative-denominative *raun* attempt, trial, experience; akin to Gk *ereunan* to seek, search for, *ereuna* inquiry, search] *obs Scot* **:** to search thoroughly **:** RANSACK

**ran·cel·man** \ˈran(t)sᵊlmən\ *n, pl* **rancelmen** *Scot* **:** a constable with the duty of searching for stolen or missing goods

**ranc·er** \ˈran(t)sə(r)\ *n* -s [prob. fr. Sc *rance, ranse* bar, stick (perh. fr. F dial. *rance* bar, peg, rung, fr. L *ramic-*, *ramex* staff, fr. L *ramus* branch) + *-er* — more at RAMIFY] **:** REAMER

**¹ranch** \ˈranch, ˈraa(ə)nch, ˈrainch, ˈrănch\ *vt* -ED/-ING/-ES [ME *ranschen, ranchen*, alter. of *rasen, racen* — more at RASE] *archaic* **:** SCRATCH, TEAR

**²ranch** \"\ *n* -ES [MexSp *rancho* small ranch, fr. Sp, camp, temporary habitation, hut & Sp dial. (Andalusia), small farm, fr. OSp *ranchar(se), ranchear(se)* to take up quarters, be billeted, fr. MF *(se) ranger* to take up a position, be quartered, fr. *ranger* to set in a row, place, station — more at RANGE] **1 :** an establishment for the grazing and rearing of horses, cattle, or sheep that usu. includes the buildings occupied by the owner and employees with the adjacent barns and corrals **2 :** a farm of any size usu. devoted to the raising of one particular specialty ⟨poultry ~⟩ ⟨wheat ~⟩ ⟨mink ~⟩ **3 :** DUDE RANCH

**³ranch** \"\ *vb* -ED/-ING/-ES *vi* **:** to live or work on a ranch **:** engage in the business of a rancher **~** *vt* **1 :** to work as a rancher on ⟨settlers who ~ the dry uplands —Elspeth Huxley⟩ **2 :** to raise on a ranch ⟨*~es* cattle —*Time*⟩ **3 :** to breed and care for (fur-bearing animals) on or as if on a ranch; *esp* **:** to care for animals belonging to another on shares or for a fee ⟨do not offer to ~ animals for the purchaser for an indefinite period of time —*Nat'l Fur News*⟩

**⁴ranch** \"\ *adj, of furs* **:** coming from animals bred and raised in captivity — compare WILD

**ranche** \ˈranch\ *n* -s [F, bar, peg, rung, fr. a dial. word (Normandy or Picardy) derived fr. L *ramic-*, *ramex* staff — more at RANCER] **:** a stroke in pin pool that leaves only the center pin standing and thereby wins the game

**ranch·er** \ˈranchə(r), ˈraan-, ˈrain-, ˈrăn-\ *n* -s [MexSp *ranchero*, fr. *rancho* small ranch + *-ero* -er — more at RANCH] **1 :** one who owns, operates, or is employed on a ranch — called also *ranchero, ranchman* **2 :** one who ranches a particular kind of animal ⟨a mink ~⟩ ⟨wise *~s* . . . naturally look for . . . qualities in selecting their fox and mink feed —*Amer. Fur Breeder*⟩

**ran·che·ria** \,ranchəˈrēə\ *n* -s [MexSp *ranchería*, fr. *ranchero* + Sp *-ia* -y (fr. L *-ia*)] **1 :** a dwelling place of a ranchero **2 :** a small settlement often consisting of huts occupied esp. by Amerindians or Mexicans ⟨it was among these *~s* . . . that the missions found their most fertile field for labor —F.M. & Marie Keesing⟩

**ran·che·ro** \ranˈche(,)rō, raan-\ *n* -s [MexSp] **:** RANCHER

**ranch house** *n* **1 :** the main dwelling house on a ranch **2 :** a one-story dwelling typically having an open plan and a low-pitched roof

ranch house 2

**ranchland** \'=,=\ *n* **:** land suitable for ranching

**ranch·man** \'=mən\ *n, pl* **ranch·men :** RANCHER

**ranch mink** *n* **:** mink scientifically bred and raised for fur production

**ran·cho** \'ran(,)chō, 'raan-, 'rän-\ *n* -s [MexSp, small ranch — more at RANCH] **:** RANCH

**ranchwoman** \'=,==\ *n, pl* **ranchwomen :** a woman who operates or lives on a ranch

**ran·cid** \'ran(t)səd, 'raan-, 'rain-\ *adj* [L *rancidus* fr. *rancēre* to be rancid, stink] **1 :** having a rank smell or taste usu. from chemical change or decomposition **:** affecting the senses disagreeably or unpleasantly ⟨~ butter⟩ ⟨the wet ~ smells of a basement —Ben Hecht⟩ **2 :** showing an obnoxious quality **:** ODIOUS, ROTTEN ⟨a ~ little psychopath who murdered a number of people —Bernard De Voto⟩ — **ran·cid·ly** *adv* — **ran·cid·ness** *n* -ES

**ran·cid·i·fi·ca·tion** \ran,sidəfə'kāshən\ *n* -s **:** the chemical change that produces rancidity

**ran·cid·i·fy** \ran'sidə,fī\ *vb* -ED/-ING/-ES [*rancid* + *-ify*] *vt* **:** to make rancid ~ *vi* **:** to become rancid

**ran·cid·i·ty** \ran'sidəd-ē, raan-, -ətē, -i\ *n* -ES **:** the quality or state of being rancid **:** a rancid odor or flavor

**ran·cio** \'rän(t)sē,ō\ *adj* [Sp, rancid, stale, old, rancio, fr. L *rancidus* rancid — more at RANCID] **:** of, relating to, or constituting the nutty flavor peculiar to some fortified wines (as sherry and Madeira)

**ran·cor** \'raŋkə(r), 'raiŋ-\ *n* -s *see -or in Explan Notes* [ME *rancour*, fr. MF *ranceur*, fr. LL *rancor* rancidity, grudge, rancor, fr. L *rancēre* to be rancid, stink + *-or*] **:** vehement hatred or ill will **:** intense malignity or spite **:** deep-seated enmity **:** inveterate malevolence ⟨hopelessly involved . . . in the political ~s of the times —E.M.Coulter⟩ ⟨essential that we consider . . . without ~ —Chester Bowles⟩ **syn** see ENMITY

**ran·cored** \-(r)d\ *adj* **:** infected by rancor **:** made rancorous ⟨voice, ~ by a deep-seated . . . malignity —Beatrice Levin⟩

**ran·cor·ous** \-k(ə)rəs\ *adj* **:** full of rancor **:** evincing or caused by rancor **:** deeply malevolent **:** MALIGNANT ⟨preserve . . . from ~ envy of the rich —Aldous Huxley⟩ ⟨a ~ man, as petty and cruel as he was dictatorial —C.H.Grandgent⟩ — **ran·cor·ous·ly** *adv*

[1]**rand** \'rand\ *n* -s [ME, fr. OE *rand, rond;* akin to MD & MLG *rant* edge, rim, OHG edging, rim of a shield, shield, ON *rönd* rim, shield, OE *rima* rim — more at RIM] **1** *dial chiefly Eng* **:** an unplowed edge of a field **:** BORDER **2** *dial* **:** the coarse grass growing on the edge **3** *Africa* **:** a long low stony ridge **4 :** a beveled U-shaped strip usu. of leather put on a shoe before the lifts of the heel **5 :** a course of simple weaving in basketmaking with one osier rod at a time often of thin material used to fill in — see BASKET illustration

[2]**rand** \"\ *vt* -ED/-ING/-S **1 :** to cut into rands or strips **2 :** to fit with rands (as in the manufacture of shoes)

**ran·dall grass** \'randᵊl-\ *n* [fr. the name *Randall*] **1 :** MEADOW FESCUE **2 :** PERENNIAL RYEGRASS

**ran·dall·ite** \'randᵊl,īt\ *n* -s *usu cap* [Benjamin *Randall* †1808 Am. religious leader + E *-ite*] **:** one of a group of Freewill Baptists organized in the northern part of the U. S. in 1787

[1]**ran·dan** \'ran,dan, =ˈ=\ *n* -s [origin unknown] *dial* **:** boisterous noisy conduct **:** RAMPAGE, SPREE

[2]**randan** \"\ *n* -s [origin unknown] **1 :** a boat propelled by three rowers of whom the middle rower pulls two short oars while bow and stroke pull one oar each **2 :** the style used to row a randan

**ran·dan·nite** \ran'da,nīt\ *n* -s [modif. of F *randanite*, fr. *Randan*, Dept. Puy-de-Dôme, France + F *-ite*] **1 :** a variety of diatomaceous earth **2 :** an earthy form of opal

**R and C** *abbr* rail and canal

**R and CC** *abbr* riot and civil commotion

[1]**ran·dem** \'randəm\ *adv* [prob. blend of [2]*random* and *tandem*] **:** with three horses harnessed to a vehicle one behind another

[2]**randem** \"\ *n* -s **:** a team or vehicle driven randem

**rand·er** \'randə(r)\ *n* -s **:** a worker who trims or bevels the edges of shoe soles or welts

**ran·dia** \'randēə\ *n, cap* [NL, fr. Isaac *Rand* †1743 Eng. botanist + NL *-ia*] **:** a large genus of tropical shrubs and trees (family Rubiaceae) having white or yellow solitary or clustered flowers and a many-seeded berry — see BOX BRIER

**randie** *chiefly Scot var of* [1]RANDY

**randies** *pl of* RANDY

**rand·ing** \'randiŋ\ *n* -s **1 a :** the act of making a rand **b :** the material for making a rand **2 :** the act or process of making and applying rands for shoes

**rand·kluft** \'ränt,klüft\ *n* -s [G, fr. *rand* rim (fr. OHG *rant*) + *kluft* crevice, fr. OHG, gap, tongs — more at RAND, CLEFT] **:** a chasm formed when ice recedes from a mountainside or breaks away from stationary ice

**R and L** *abbr* rail and lake

**ran·dle tree** \'randᵊl-\ *var of* RANNEL TREE

**R and O** *abbr* rail and ocean

[1]**ran·dom** \'randəm, 'raan-\ *n* -s [ME *randoun, raundon, randon*, fr. MF *randon* (as in *de randon, a randon* with impetuosity), fr. OF, fr. *randir* to run, gallop, of Gmc origin; akin to G dial. (Bavarian & Alemannic) *rand* run, running, fr. stem of OHG *rinnan* to run — more at RUN] **1** *obs* **:** FORCE, IMPETUOSITY **2 :** a haphazard course **:** chance progress **3** *obs* **a :** the range of a gun or projectile **b :** the elevation given to a gun **4 :** [3]BANK 3b — **at random** *adv* **1 :** without definite aim, direction, rule, or method **:** with no specific goal or purpose in view ⟨upon the table soiled dishes were piled *at random* —William Faulkner⟩ ⟨worn cow paths led through *at random* —Christopher Rand⟩ **2** *obs* **:** without restraint or attention **:** at liberty ⟨to be left *at random*⟩

[2]**random** \"\ *adv* **:** in a random manner **:** at random — usu. used in combination ⟨*random*-jointed⟩

[3]**random** \"\ *adj* **1 :** lacking or seeming to lack a regular plan, purpose, or pattern ⟨~ thoughts laid hold of him —George Meredith⟩ ⟨a ~ assortment of vases, ivory elephants and other . . . ornaments —Robert Shaplen⟩ ⟨the tail end of the conference was becoming frayed and ~ —Christopher Rand⟩ ⟨~ brick and timber panels —*Amer. Guide Series: Conn.*⟩ ⟨~ widths⟩ **2 a :** marked by absence of bias **:** chosen at random ⟨a true ~ sample of the whole list —Daniel Melcher & Nancy Larrick⟩ ⟨placing a finger on a ~ passage —Charlton Laird⟩ **b :** involving or resulting from randomization **c :** having the same probability of occurring as every other member of a set ⟨~ numbers⟩

**syn** HAPHAZARD, HIT-OR-MISS, DESULTORY, CHANCE, CHANCY, CASUAL, HAPPY-GO-LUCKY: RANDOM stresses lack of definite aim, fixed goal, regular procedure, or predictable incidence ⟨a *random* collection of literary and archeological odds and ends —Aldous Huxley⟩ ⟨the clerks become tired and bored and start making *random* mistakes —Martin Gardner⟩ ⟨a kitten's *random* play with a spool or ball⟩ That which is HAPHAZARD is done according to chance or whim without regularity or order and with careless disregard for ultimate fitness or efficiency. HIT-OR-MISS further stresses lack of aim, care, plan, or system ⟨all his shop training had given him a profound prejudice against inexact work, experimental work, *hit-or-miss* work —C.S.Forester⟩ DESULTORY stresses lack of regularity or steadiness and suggests an erratic performance marked by false starts, lapses, breaks, shifts, or inconsistencies ⟨medieval warfare was often of the nature of a mild adventure . . . the fighting was generally sporadic and *desultory* —Edwin Benson⟩ ⟨a little Latin and Greek and much outdoor life, with a *desultory* education got from vagrant books —V.L. Parrington⟩ CHANCE stresses complete lack of design, intent, plan, or prearrangement ⟨he had never before given Cuba, under Spanish rule, a thought, but at a *chance* sentence it dominated him completely —Joseph Hergesheimer⟩ It suggests lack of plan, reason, forethought in connection with persons encountered or objects found or discovered in various places ⟨his temper grew uncertain and he found it increasingly difficult to welcome *chance* visitors with his usual affability —Robert Graves⟩ ⟨snatching a *chance* piece of billiard chalk from his pocket, he ran it across the hall floor —G.K.Chesterton⟩ In reference to things and situations CHANCY suggests uncertainty of outcome through dependence on chance and hence implies risk or hazard ⟨despite recent advances in geophysics, oil drilling is still a *chancy* business —H.T.Kane⟩ CASUAL suggests lack of intentness or purpose ⟨his jottings are by no means *casual* —*Listener*⟩ HAPPY-GO-LUCKY suggests carefree, insouciant lack of forethought or plan or cheerful, indifferent acceptance of what ensues ⟨a funny little *happy-go-lucky*, native-managed railway —Rudyard Kipling⟩ ⟨the old *happy-go-lucky* methods of production —Bernard Pares⟩

**random bond** *n* **:** a bond in stonemasonry in which the stones are laid at random and not in regular courses

**random error** *n* **:** a statistical error that is wholly due to chance and does not recur — opposed to *systematic error*

**ran·dom·iza·tion** \,randəmə'zāshən\ *n* -s **1 :** controlled distribution usu. of given tests, factors, samplings, treatments, or units so as to simulate a random or chance distribution and yield unbiased data from which a generalized conclusion can be drawn **2 :** a random process used in a statistical experiment to reduce or eliminate interference by variables other than those being studied

**ran·dom·ize** \'randə,mīz\ *vt* -ED/-ING/-S [[3]*random* + *-ize*] **:** to distribute by or use randomization on

**randomized block** *n* **:** an experimental design (as in horticulture) in which different treatments are distributed in random order within a block or plot

**random line** *also* **random traverse** *n* **:** a trial surveying line avoiding obstacles between stations

**ran·dom·ly** *adv* **:** in a random manner

**ran·dom·ness** *n* -ES **:** the quality or state of being random

**random noise** *n* **:** a usu. electric or acoustic signal that consists of equal amounts of all frequencies

**random walk** *n* **:** the preferential drift in one direction of an ensemble of particles otherwise in random motion (as of the heat-agitated molecules of a flowing gas)

[1]**ran·dori** \rän'dōrē\ *n* -s [Jap, lit., free practice] **:** free practice between two judo experts

[2]**randori** \"\ *vi* -ED/-ING/-S **:** to practice judo informally

**R and R** *abbr* rest and recreation

**rands** *pl of* RAND, *pres 3d sing of* RAND

**R and W** *abbr* rail and water

[1]**randy** \'randē, -di\ *adj* [prob. fr. obs. E *rand* to rant, rave (fr. obs. D *randen, ranten*) + E *-y*] **1** *chiefly Scot* **:** having a coarse manner **:** loud-spoken **2 :** LUSTFUL, LECHEROUS

[2]**randy** \"\ *n* -ES **1** *chiefly Scot* **:** a rough-mannered beggar **2** *chiefly Scot* **:** a scolding or dissolute woman

[3]**randy** \"\ *n* -ES *dial Brit* **:** a noisy festivity **:** CAROUSAL ⟨the next ~ we come to . . . is to be a wedding —Mary Webb⟩ ⟨a rattling good ~ with fiddles and bassviols —Thomas Hardy⟩

**ranee** *var of* RANI

**ra·nel·la** \rə'nelə\ *n* [NL, fr. L *rana* frog + NL *-ella* — more at RANA] **1** *cap* **:** a genus of marine snails related to *Triton* having a thick shell usu. with two lateral varices continuous over all the whorls **2** -s **:** any snail of the genus *Ranella*

**ra·ney nickel** \'rānē-\ *n, usu cap R* [after Murray *Raney* *b*1885 Am. engineer and manufacturer] **:** a finely divided nickel in the form of a pyrophoric powder or crystals or a suspension (as in alcohol) that is prepared from an alloy of equal parts of nickel and aluminum by dissolving the aluminum in warm sodium hydroxide solution and rinsing thoroughly and that is used as a catalyst for the hydrogenation of various organic compounds

**rang** [ME, alter. (prob. influenced by [1]*sang*) of *ringde*, fr. OE *hringde*] *past of* RING

**ranga·ti·ra** \,räŋə'tirə\ *n* -s [Maori] **1 :** a Maori chief **:** a Maori of rank, authority, or distinction **2** *NewZeal* **:** a leading citizen **:** MAGISTRATE

**rang·doo·dles** \'raŋ,düdᵊlz\ *n pl* [prob. alter. of *roodles*] **:** roodles in draw poker

[1]**range** \'rānj\ *n* -s *often attrib* [ME, fr. MF, fr. OF *renge*, fr. *renc, reng* line, place, row — more at RANK] **1 a :** a row or rank usu. of people or animals ⟨the first ~ of soldiers⟩ ⟨pupils in a ~⟩ **b :** a series of things in a line: as (1) **:** a line of buildings or sections of a building ⟨in a ~ of buildings near the house was a dairy and meat store —H.V.Morton⟩ ⟨a big nursery over which was a ~ of attics —David Garnett⟩ (2) **:** a row or course of masonry with the horizontal joints continuous (3) **:** a series of double-faced sections of shelves in a stack abutting one another and usu. terminating in aisles at each end (4) **:** a greenhouse establishment often having several houses that may be connected **2 a :** a grate let down when required over an open fire to support cooking utensils **b :** a cooking apparatus enclosing controlled heat (as from wood, coal, gas, electricity) and having a flat top with solid plates or open racks to hold utensils over flames or coils and an oven and sometimes also a storage space for utensils or a second oven **3 a :** something that may be ranged over **:** place or room for excursion **b :** an open region over which cattle, sheep, or other livestock may roam and feed **:** pasturage esp. when unenclosed ⟨low-lying valley bottoms . . . providing meager amounts of winter ~ —T.R.Weir⟩ **c :** the region throughout which a kind of organism or ecological community naturally lives or occurs ⟨the elk ~ in the Rocky mountain area —T.W.Daniels⟩ ⟨this snail thrived and spread . . ., its ~ being directly increased —Joyce Allan⟩ **4 a :** the act of ranging about or of roving **:** EXCURSION, RAMBLE ⟨taking the dogs for a ~⟩ **b :** freedom to range **:** opportunity to roam about ⟨giving the horses free ~⟩ **5 a** (1) **:** the horizontal distance to which a shot or other projectile is or may be propelled ⟨the gun has a ~ of six miles⟩ (2) **:** the horizontal distance of the target or thing aimed at from a weapon (3) **:** a place where shooting (as with bows, guns, or missiles) is practiced **b :** the maximum distance an airplane or other vehicle (as a tank) can travel without refueling — compare RADIUS 4d **c :** the average distance radioactive or other projected particles of a given type will penetrate a given medium before their velocity is reduced to less than a detectable value **6 :** an aggregate of individuals in one order **:** a social class ⟨in the lower ~s of the council —F.M.Stenton⟩ ⟨at the lowest ~ the family, at the uppermost the state —B.N.Cardozo⟩ **7 a :** a large cleat in the waist of a sailing ship for handling lines **b :** a length of slack cable ranged along the deck preparatory to letting go the anchor **8 a :** the space or extent included, covered, or used ⟨the ~ of printed documents . . . is enormous —Robert Walcott⟩ ⟨a faith worldwide in its ~ and power —Norman Goodall⟩ **b :** a field of operation **:** an area actively occupied or used ⟨lanterns at night to attract fish within ~ of net or spear —*Lamp*⟩ ⟨building a nest within ~ of the house⟩ **c :** the scope or span usu. of activity, experience, or knowledge ⟨a technical vocabulary a little outside my ~ —Wolcott Gibbs⟩ ⟨men defy classification because of the ~ and diversity of their interests —Dumas Malone⟩ **d :** COMPASS 1d **9 :** a direction line **:** DIRECTION ⟨the buoys in ~ with the pier⟩ **10 a** (1) **:** a series or chain of mountain peaks considered as forming one connected system **:** a ridge of mountains ⟨from the summit they could see ~ after ~ of mountains⟩ (2) **:** mountainous country — often used in pl. **b :** a mineral belt; *esp* **:** an iron-bearing formation **11 a :** a sequence, series, or scale between limits ⟨a wide ~ of patterns⟩ ⟨a ~ of possible solutions —W.S.Campbell⟩ **b :** the limits of a series **:** the distance or extent between possible extremes ⟨spring tides . . . have a greater ~ —C.F.Chapman⟩ **12 a** (1) **:** a strip of leather cut from a butt or hide (2) **:** the lie or line of the upper edge of the counter in a top boot (3) **:** the cutting of a butt or side of sole leather into strips **b :** a part of a hide **13 :** one of the north-south rows of a township in a U. S. public-land survey that are numbered east and west from the principal meridian of the survey **14 a :** a set of points lying on a line (as on the axis of an independent variable at which a function is defined) **b :** the difference between the least and greatest values of the attribute or variable of a frequency distribution **15 :** the class of admissible values of a variable **16 :** a gage for determining the thickness of glass **17 :** a group of shipping ports within an area for which the same rates are charged **18 :** RADIO RANGE

range 2b

**syn** GAMUT, REACH, RADIUS, COMPASS, SWEEP, SCOPE, ORBIT, HORIZON, KEN, PURVIEW: RANGE is the general term indicating the extent of one's perception or the extent of powers, capacities, or possibilities ⟨safe, well out of the *range* of the pursuers⟩ ⟨a beautiful voice with a wide *range* between the high and the low tones —Havelock Ellis⟩ ⟨a creative writer can do his best only with what lies within the *range* and character of his deepest sympathies —Willa Cather⟩ ⟨the whole *range* of Greek political life —G.L.Dickinson⟩ GAMUT suggests a graduated series running from one possible extreme to another ⟨types of light each occupying its particular place in that far-reaching roster or *gamut* which is called the spectrum —K.K.Darrow⟩ REACH suggests an extent of perception, knowledge, ability, or activity attained to or experienced by or as if by stretching out ⟨moving step by step toward the widest generalizations within his *reach* —L.J.Henderson⟩ ⟨out of *reach* of the first invading forces⟩ ⟨anything like sustained reasoning was beyond his *reach* —Leslie Stephen⟩ RADIUS suggests an area, usu. circular, of activity, implied by a known or determined center ⟨the town's history has been the history of coal; within a *radius* of five miles are twelve large mines of coal —*Amer. Guide Series: Pa.*⟩ COMPASS indicates an extent, sometimes more limited than that suggested by RANGE, of perception, knowledge, or activity; it is likely to connote a bounding circumference ⟨the powers expressly granted to the government . . . are to be contracted . . . into the narrowest possible *compass* —John Marshall⟩ ⟨here we get in very small *compass* . . . as many different reminders of the continuity of the country . . . as you will find anywhere —S.P.B.Mais⟩ SWEEP suggests extent, often circular or arc-shaped, of motion or activity, which latter notion it more strongly suggests than the preceding terms ⟨the boldness and *sweep* of Webster's original scheme appear plainly —Kemp Malone⟩ ⟨in the *sweep* of their universal robbery, they showed at least no discrimination between native and foreign victims —Osbert Sitwell⟩ SCOPE is applicable to an area of activity, an area predetermined and limited, but an area of free choice within the set limits ⟨its *scope* was widened by the legislature to include other departments —*Amer. Guide Series: Texas*⟩ ⟨the infinite *scope* for personal initiative in business —G.B.Shaw⟩ ORBIT suggests a range of activity or influence, often circumscribed and bounded, within which forces work toward accustoming, integrating, absorbing ⟨communities . . . outside the *orbit* of modernity —Walter Lippmann⟩ ⟨the war as a gigantic cosmic drama, embracing every quarter of the globe and the whole *orbit* of man's life —John Buchan⟩ HORIZON suggests an area, perhaps arc-shaped or semicircular, of knowledge, interest, perception; it may suggest the new or the potential or envisioned ⟨science has provided a new frontier with unlimited *horizons* —A.H.Compton⟩ ⟨possibilities he hadn't known were upon its *horizon* —Mary Austin⟩ KEN indicates range of perception or cognizance ⟨they seemed trivial at the time they came into his *ken* —W.A.White⟩ ⟨the bulk of his known reading, until the great Italians swam into his *ken*, was French —J.L.Lowes⟩ PURVIEW may indicate either range of perception or knowledge or range of authority or competence ⟨the inclusion of dependent areas within the *purview* of Point Four —Rupert Emerson⟩ ⟨the problem of ethnic variation falls very definitely within the *purview* of the social life of man —M.F.A.Montagu⟩

[2]**range** \"\ *vb* -ED/-ING/-S [ME *raungen, rangen*, fr. MF *ranger* to set in a row, place, station, fr. OF *rengier*, fr. *renc, reng* line, place, row — more at RANK] *vt* **1 a :** to set in a row **:** place in a regular line **:** dispose in the proper order ⟨half a dozen straight-backed chairs are *ranged* in front of the desk —Philip Hamburger⟩ ⟨the women, *ranged* along the north side, wore their usual dress —Oliver LaFarge⟩ **b :** to place among others in a given position or situation ⟨*ranged* himself with the reform movement —Charles Moore⟩ ⟨came and *ranged* yourself beside me —T.B.Costain⟩ **2 a :** to rove over or through **:** ROAM ⟨took his fine new rifle and *ranged* the woods —S.H.Holbrook⟩ **b :** to cause to pass over ⟨*ranged* his eyes over the scene before him⟩ **3 :** to dispose in a classified or systematic order **:** place in a class, rank, or category ⟨~ plants in genera⟩ **4 :** to sail or pass along or about usu. in a direction parallel to or near ⟨had been out the night before, *ranging* the enemy coast —Irwin Shaw⟩ **5 :** to arrange (an anchor cable) on deck **6** *chiefly Brit* **:** ALIGN; *specif* **:** to place (a line of type) so that one end is flush with the end of a preceding or following line **7 :** to graze or pasture (livestock) on or as if on a range ⟨on the uplands thousands of head of cattle are *ranged* each year —*Spokane (Wash.) Spokesman-Rev.*⟩ **8 :** to determine the elevation necessary for (a gun) to propel a projectile to a given distance **:** give (a gun) such elevation ~ *vi* **1 a** (1) **:** to roam here and there **:** rove at large ⟨the custom . . . to ~ through the town on the last night of carnival —P.L.Fermor⟩ ⟨*ranged* like a grey moose . . . guiding himself by the sun —Van Wyck Brooks⟩ ⟨*ranging* around remote parts of England —Max Beerbohm⟩ (2) **:** to move out or about freely **:** survey esp. with the mind ⟨has *ranged* among the masterpieces of past and present art —William Barrett⟩ ⟨talk *ranged* widely, even in aesthetics —H.S.Canby⟩ ⟨likes to ~ over current issues —*Newsweek*⟩ **b :** to move over an area so as to explore it more or less thoroughly ⟨*ranging* about in search of some promising spot upon which to pitch the . . . tent —F.V.W. Mason⟩ ⟨the beagle will not ~ too far afield of the hunter —*Time*⟩ **2 :** to take a position ⟨*ranged* with the great pillars and supporters of our art —Joshua Reynolds⟩ **3** *archaic* **:** to be fickle or inconstant ⟨given to ~ —Lord Byron⟩ **4 a :** to correspond in direction or line **b** *chiefly Brit* **:** ALIGN ⟨these two type faces, although of the same size, do not ~ well⟩ **c :** to have or extend in a particular direction **:** run in a line ⟨the fence ~s with the street⟩ **5 a :** to have range **:** be capable of projecting or to admit of being projected ⟨the gun ~s over three miles⟩ or to admit of being projected ⟨the gun ~s over three miles⟩ **b :** to obtain the range of an object by firing alternately over and short of it altering the elevation after each shot until a hit is made **6 :** to change or differ within limits ⟨its products ~ from carpet tacks to pig iron —*Amer. Guide Series: N. Y.*⟩ ⟨discounts ~ from 20% to 40% —Nathan Kelne⟩ **7** *of an organism* **:** to live or occur in or be native to an indicated district or region ⟨the hardy ring-necked pheasant . . . ~s over all but the most northern areas —*Amer. Guide Series: Minn.*⟩ **8 :** to obtain the range of an object by means of a range finder

**range angle** *n* **:** the angle formed between a vertical line and the line of sight to an aiming point at the instant of release of an aerial bomb — called also *dropping angle, sighting angle*

**range bracket** *n* **:** BRACKET 5a(1)

**range-bred** \'=,=\ *adj* **:** bred and reared on the range **:** accustomed to the open country

**range crane fly** *n* **:** a grayish brown crane fly (*Tipula simplex*) with a wingless female and a pale brown burrowing larva that emerges from the ground at night or on dull days to feed on green vegetation and is sometimes very destructive to grasslands and grain crops in the southwestern U. S.

**ranged** *adj* [fr. past part. of [2]*range*] **:** arranged in line, in ranks, or according to a system ⟨a kitchen gleaming with ~ coppers —Anne D. Sedgwick⟩ ⟨the hierarchically ~ members of the staff —Lyman Bryson⟩

**ranged rubble** *n* **:** masonry in which the quarry stones are roughly dressed to an almost uniform height

**range finder** *n* **1 :** an instrument used to determine the distance of an object and usu. constructed to give a rapid mechanical solution of a triangle having the target at its apex and the range finder at one corner of its base **2 :** TACHYMETER **3 :** a camera attachment for measuring by optical means the distance between the camera and an object

**range-finding** \'=,==\ *n* **1 :** the determination of the range to a target by adjusting fire on it **2 :** the determination of a range by means of a range finder at which to start adjustment on a target

**rangeland** \'=,=\ *n* **:** land used or suitable for range ⟨brush-covered ~s sweep to distant horizons —*Amer. Guide Series: Texas*⟩

**range·ley lake trout** \'rānjlē-\ *n, usu cap R* [fr. *Rangeley lakes*, chain of lakes in western Maine] **:** OQUASSA

**range light** *n* **1 :** either of two or more lights on shore placed to guide a ship by keeping it in line (as through a channel) **2 a range lights** *pl* **:** two white lights in the same vertical plane as the keel with one at least fifteen feet higher than and horizontally distant from the other that may be carried by a steamer under way to indicate her course **b :** the after of these two lights

**range masonry** *n* **:** RANGEWORK

**range of accommodation :** the range through which accommodation is able so to adjust the optical system of the eye that an image falls in sharp focus on the retina **:** the distance between the near point and the far point of the eye

**range officer** *n* **:** one who is in charge of a firearms range and of firing on the range

**range oil** *n* **:** a high-boiling petroleum distillate for burning in the wick of an oil-burning kitchen range; *esp* **:** the least volatile portion of the kerosine fraction

**range paralysis** *n* **:** NEUROLYMPHOMATOSIS

**range pole** *also* **ranging pole** *n* **:** a straight pole or rod sometimes jointed, usu. painted in one-foot bands of alternate colors of red and white, and used for sighting points and lines in surveying — called also *flagpole*

**rang·er** \ˈrānjə(r)\ *n* -s [ME *raunger,* fr. *raungen, rangen* to range + *-er* — more at RANGE] **1 a :** the keeper of a British royal park or forest; *esp* **:** a royal officer formerly appointed to walk through the forest, recover beasts that had strayed, watch the deer, and prevent trespasses **b :** FOREST RANGER **2** *archaic* **:** one who wanders **:** ROVER **3 :** an animal that ranges: as **a :** a dog that covers the course fully in search of game **b :** HARBOR SEAL **c :** a meat animal marketed directly from the range without being fattened on grain **4 a :** one usu. of a body of troops or organized armed men who range over a region for its protection **b :** an officer of a county who is responsible for taking charge of and protecting an area against stray animals **c :** a soldier specially trained in close-range fighting and raiding tactics — compare COMMANDO **5 :** a senior member of the Girl Guide movement in Britain, Canada, and various other countries — compare SENIOR GIRL SCOUT

**range rake** *n* **:** a device that is used in harbor-defense gunnery for determining the range deviations of shots from a target and that consists essentially of two arms in the form of a T along whose cross member pegs are placed at regular intervals

**rang·er·ship** \-(r),ship\ *n* **:** the position of ranger of a park or forest

**ranges** *pl of* RANGE, *pres 3d sing of* RANGE

**range shelter** *n* **:** a small open usu. movable shelter for growing fowls on range

**range table** *n* **:** a large table made up of a set of identical small tables placed side by side

**rang·ette** \(ˈ)rānˈjet\ *n* -s [ˈ*range* + *-ette*] **:** a portable cooking apparatus consisting of a top with one or more burners for gas or electricity but having no oven; *also* **:** a very small range with an oven

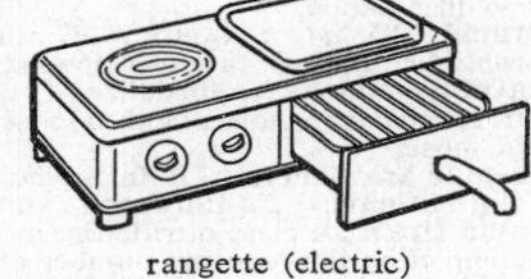

rangette (electric)

**rangework** \ˈ=,=\ *n* **:** ashlar laid in horizontal courses of even height **:** COURSED ASHLAR — called also *range masonry;* compare BROKEN ASHLAR

**ran·gi·fer** \ˈranjəfə(r)\ *n, cap* [NL, fr. ML, reindeer, prob. modif. of MF *rangier,* fr. ON *hreindȳri* — more at REINDEER] **:** a genus consisting of the domestic and wild reindeer and caribous

**ran·gif·er·ine** \ranˈjifə,rīn\ *adj* [NL *Rangifer* + E *-ine*] **:** of or relating to the genus *Rangifer*

**rang·i·ness** \ˈrānjēnəs\ *n* -ES **:** the quality or state of being rangy ⟨the dark blue jacket . . . was much too skimpy for a man of his ~ —Alan Masters⟩ ⟨a ~, a freewheeling robustness, an engaging lustiness of style and expression here —V.P.Hass⟩

**ranging** *pres part of* RANGE

**ranging bond** *n* **:** a chain bond formed by strips of wood projecting slightly from the face to provide a nailing surface

**ran·gi·o·ra** \,raŋgēˈōrə\ *n* -s [Maori] **:** a New Zealand shrub or small tree (*Brachyglottis repanda*) of the family Compositae having stout branches and lower leaf surfaces densely covered with white tomentum and small heads of flowers crowded in terminal clusters

**rang·khol** \rāŋˈkōl\ *n* -s *usu cap* **:** one of a Kuki people of eastern Assam

**ran·gle** \ˈraŋgəl\ *n* -s [origin unknown] **:** bits of gravel fed to hawks

**¹ran·goon** \(ˈ)ranˈgün, -aŋ,-\ *adj, usu cap* [fr. *Rangoon,* Burma] **:** of or from Rangoon, the capital of Burma **:** of the kind or style prevalent in Rangoon

**²rangoon** \"\ *n* -s *often cap* **:** SHERRY 2

**rangoon creeper** *n, usu cap R* **:** a woody vine (*Quisqualis indica*) that is native to Burma, Malaysia, and the Pacific islands and that is grown in tropical regions for its showy flowers

**rang·pur** \ˈrəŋ,pu̇(ə)r, =ˈ=\ *or* **rangpur lime** *n* -s [fr. *Rangpur,* town and region in East Bengal, Pakistan] **:** any of various mandarin oranges with sour highly acid fruits

**rangy** *also* **rangey** \ˈrānjē, -ji\ *adj, sometimes* **rangier;** *sometimes* **rangiest** [¹*range* & ²*range* + *-y*] **1 :** having room for ranging **:** OPEN, SPACIOUS ⟨our vast, unpeopled, ~ country —E.A.Weeks⟩ **2 :** having ranges **:** MOUNTAINOUS **3 :** inclined, able, or apt to range or rove about often for considerable distances **4** *of an animal* **a :** of large proportions **:** being long-limbed and long-bodied ⟨big ~ cattle, strong enough to climb over the hills to market —Russell Lord⟩ **b :** giving an appearance of slenderness ⟨a horse to be fast must be long and ~ —C.W.Gay⟩ — compare COBBY, CHUFFY **5** *of a person* **:** being long-legged and slender ⟨~ kilted soldiers stalking along the streets —A.W.Long⟩ **6 :** having great range or scope ⟨these ~ considerations rise immediately out of reading —Richard Sullivan⟩

**ra·ni** *or* **ra·nee** \(ˈ)räˈnē\ *n* -s [Hindi *rānī,* fr. Skt *rājñī,* fem. of *rājan* king — more at ROYAL] **:** a Hindu queen **:** a rajah's wife **:** a reigning Indian princess

**rani-** *comb form* [L *rana* — more at RANA] **:** frog ⟨*raniform*⟩

**¹ran·id** \ˈranəd\ *adj* [NL *Ranidae*] **:** of or relating to the Ranidae

**²ranid** \"\ *n* -s **:** a frog of the family Ranidae

**ran·i·dae** \ˈranə,dē\ *n pl, cap* [NL, fr. *Rana,* type genus + *-idae*] **:** a large family of frogs (suborder Diplasiocoela) distinguished by slightly dilated transverse sacral processes and comprising the typical frogs — see RANA

**ra·ni·khet disease** \ˈrānə,ket-\ *n, usu cap R* [fr. *Ranikhet,* town in northern India] **:** NEWCASTLE DISEASE

**ra·ni·na** \rəˈnīnə\ *n, cap* [NL, fr. L *rana* frog + NL *-ina* — more at RANA] **:** the type genus of Raninidae comprising typical frog crabs — **ra·nin·i·an** \-ˈninēən\ *adj or n*

**ra·nine** \ˈrā,nīn\ *adj* [L *rana* frog + E *-ine*] **1 :** of or relating to frogs **2 :** of or relating to the region beneath the tip of the tongue; *specif* **:** constituting the branch of the lingual artery supplying this region or the corresponding vein which is a tributary of the facial vein

**ranine artery** *n* **:** the terminal part of the lingual artery supplying the tip of the tongue

**ra·nin·i·dae** \rəˈninə,dē\ *n pl, cap* [NL, fr. *Ranina,* type genus + *-idae*] **:** a family of atypical elongated crabs (tribe Brachyura) that have existed since at least Cretaceous time and comprise the frog crabs

**¹rank** \ˈraŋk, ˈraiŋk\ *adj, often* -ER/-EST [ME, fr. OE *ranc* overbearing, strong, brave, mature, ostentatious; akin to MD & MLG *ranc* tall and thin, slender, ON *rakkr* straight, slender, bold, OE *riht* right — more at RIGHT] **1** *chiefly dial* **a :** STRONG, MIGHTY, POWERFUL **b :** HEADLONG, VIOLENT **2 a :** luxuriant or vigorous in growth **:** grown to immoderate height **:** grown coarse ⟨~ weeds⟩ ⟨seven ears of corn came up upon one stalk, ~ and good —Gen 41:5 (AV)⟩ ⟨among the forms of ~ plant life common in the hot humidity . . . were great tree ferns —R.W.Murray⟩ **b :** covered with a vigorous growth esp. of vegetation **:** producing luxuriantly **:** excessively rich and fertile ⟨its garden was . . . ~, too thickly crowded with trees and bushes and plants —Rebecca West⟩ **3 :** offensively gross or coarse **:** INDECENT, FOUL ⟨objected to his ~ language⟩ **4** *obs* **:** grown too large **:** GROSS, SWOLLEN **5** *chiefly dial* **a :** crowded together **b :** NUMEROUS **6 a :** conspicuously or shockingly poor, stupid, or wrong ⟨must lecture him on his ~ disloyalty —David Walden⟩ **b :** COMPLETE — used as an intensive ⟨that is . . . the opinion of a ~ outsider —G.W.Johnson⟩ ⟨most of the actors were not big names, but ~ beginners —Dean Jennings⟩ **7** *archaic* **a :** filled with lust **b :** RUTTISH ⟨the ewes, being ~, in the end of autumn turned to the rams —Shak.⟩ **8 :** offending with or as if with a strong rancid odor or taste **:** having a heavy offensive smell ⟨wreathed in smoke from a ~ cigar —Ralph Watson⟩ ⟨the heat seemed to purify the ~ air —Willa Cather⟩ **9 :** marked by putridity **:** CORRUPT, FESTERING ⟨the ~ wounds of the dying men⟩ **10 :** unreasonably high in amount **:** EXCESSIVE ⟨a ~ modus⟩ ⟨a ~ rate of interest⟩ **11 :** projecting to an unusual extent beyond a surface **syn** see FLAGRANT

RANKS OF THE UNITED STATES ARMED FORCES

| ARMY | MARINES | NAVY | AIR FORCE | COAST GUARD |
|---|---|---|---|---|
| general of the army | | fleet admiral | general of the air force | |
| general | general | admiral | general | admiral *or* commandant |
| lieutenant general | lieutenant general | vice admiral | lieutenant general | vice admiral |
| major general | major general | rear admiral | major general | rear admiral |
| brigadier general | brigadier general | commodore | brigadier general | commodore |
| colonel | colonel | captain | colonel | captain |
| lieutenant colonel | lieutenant colonel | commander | lieutenant colonel | commander |
| major | major | lieutenant commander | major | lieutenant commander |
| captain | captain | lieutenant | captain | lieutenant |
| first lieutenant | first lieutenant | lieutenant, j.g. | first lieutenant | lieutenant, j.g. |
| second lieutenant | second lieutenant | ensign | second lieutenant | ensign |
| chief warrant officer, W-4 | chief warrant officer, W-4 | chief warrant officer, W-4 | chief warrant officer, W-4 | chief warrant officer, W-4 |
| chief warrant officer, W-3 | chief warrant officer, W-3 | warrant officer, W-3 | chief warrant officer, W-3 | warrant officer, W-3 |
| chief warrant officer, W-2 | chief warrant officer, W-2 | warrant officer, W-2 | chief warrant officer, W-2 | warrant officer, W-2 |
| warrant officer, W-1 | warrant officer, W-1 | warrant officer, W-1 | warrant officer, W-1 | warrant officer, W-1 |
| sergeant major of the army | sergeant major of the marine corps | master chief petty officer of the navy | chief master sergeant of the air force | master chief petty officer of the coast guard |
| command sergeant major | sergeant major *or* master gunnery sergeant | master chief petty officer | chief master sergeant | master chief petty officer |
| first sergeant *or* master sergeant | first sergeant *or* master sergeant | senior chief petty officer | senior master sergeant | senior chief petty officer |
| platoon sergeant *or* sergeant first class *or* specialist 7 | gunnery sergeant | chief petty officer | master sergeant | chief petty officer |
| staff sergeant *or* specialist 6 | staff sergeant | petty officer first class | technical sergeant | petty officer first class |
| sergeant *or* specialist 5 | sergeant | petty officer second class | staff sergeant | petty officer second class |
| corporal *or* specialist 4 | corporal | petty officer third class | sergeant | petty officer third class |
| private first class | lance corporal | seaman | airman first class | seaman |
| private, E-2 | private first class | seaman apprentice | airman | seaman apprentice |
| private, E-1 | private | seaman recruit | airman basic | seaman recruit |

**²rank** \"\ *adv* **:** RANKLY

**³rank** \"\ *n* -s [MF *renc, ranc, reng, rang* line, place, row, rank, of Gmc origin; akin to OHG *hring* ring, circle, circle of warriors, meeting — more at RING] **1 a :** a straight row or line **:** RANGE, SERIES ⟨a ~ of marble pillars —Sax Rohmer⟩ ⟨~s of parcel lockers —Lewis Mumford⟩ ⟨great pines, whose ~s climbed to the mountaintops —Agnes M. Cleaveland⟩ **b :** a series or set of organ pipes of the same construction and quality having one pipe for each digital **c** *Brit* **:** STAND 6 ⟨a taxi at the ~ just at the end of the street —Katherine Mansfield⟩ **2 :** a row of people ⟨the men and women . . . were standing in two separate ~s —Ivor Jones⟩ **3 :** an orderly arrangement **:** ARRAY, FORMATION ⟨the company break ~s —Lafcadio Hearn⟩ **4 a :** a line of soldiers ranged side by side in close order ⟨armored ~s of men-at-arms—John Reed⟩—compare FILE **b ranks** *pl* **:** ARMED FORCES **:** ARMY **c ranks** *pl* **:** the body of enlisted men ⟨he rose from the ~s⟩ **5 :** an aggregate of individuals classed together **:** a division of the social order — usu. used in pl. ⟨excluded from the ~s of organized labor —Oscar Handlin⟩ ⟨would consider any opportunity . . . provided it is in your executive ~s —*Phoenix Flame*⟩ ⟨keep the ~s of fire fighters thin —Richard Ginder⟩ **6 :** a row of squares extending horizontally across a chessboard ⟨each player's pieces are placed on his first ~ and his pawns on his second ~⟩ **7 a :** a position or order in relation to others in a group **:** relative standing ⟨occupied a particularly high ~ among the dramas —Matthew Arnold⟩ ⟨declining to consider him a novelist of the first ~ —Granville Hicks⟩ **b :** a degree or position of dignity, eminence, or excellence **:** DISTINCTION ⟨soon took ~ as a leading attorney —J.D.Hicks⟩ **c :** high social position or standing ⟨many of the institutions . . . maintained and emphasized the privileges of ~ —Abram Kardiner⟩ ⟨his distinction lay in office, not in ~ —John Buchan⟩ **d :** a faculty position usu. in an institution of higher learning ⟨visiting lecturer in psychology . . . with ~ of full professor —W.H.Hale⟩ **8 :** a grade of official standing: as **a :** a grade in the armed forces **b :** a title of nobility **c :** a diplomatic or high government position ⟨appointed with the ~ of ambassador⟩ ⟨office of cabinet ~⟩ **9 a :** the standing of words in their mutual relations as qualified and qualifying terms **b :** the functioning of a word, word group, or clause as substantive, adjective, or adverb **10 :** the order according to some statistical characteristic **11 :** one of the classes or varieties of coal arranged in a series extending from lignite through bituminous to anthracite that indicates its thermal properties

**⁴rank** \"\ *vb* -ED/-ING/-S *vt* **1 :** to arrange usu. in lines **:** draw up in a regular formation ⟨gazed lazily out a window above the ~*ed* heads —William Faulkner⟩ ⟨the battalion, perfectly ~*ed,* listened to the citation⟩ **2 :** to arrange in a row or pattern **:** place in order ⟨the hills ~*ed* with apple trees —John Dos Passos⟩ ⟨the ranch and chuck wagons were ~*ed* out of the weather —Luke Short⟩ ⟨carefully ~*ed* the little figurines along the mantlepiece⟩ **3 :** to determine the relative position or merit of **:** CLASSIFY, IDENTIFY, RATE ⟨seldom given to ~*ing* the concerns of others as high as his own —M.C.Bauer⟩ ⟨were asked to ~ the instructor —W.C.Allee⟩ ⟨a population of 205,000 ~*s* the city third —Howell Walker⟩ **4 :** to place properly or in order of priority among the claimants upon a bankrupt estate according to Scots law **5 :** to take precedence of **:** OUTRANK ⟨the chairman ~*s* all other officers —A.J.Liebling⟩ ⟨did not know who ~*ed* whom in the new . . . setup —*Newsweek*⟩ **6** *Scot* **:** to get ready — usu. used with *out* **~** *vi* **1 :** to form or move in ranks **:** take a place in a rank **2 :** to become ranged in order or graded esp. according to rank or merit **:** have a place or grade in an ascending series ⟨English ~*s* as the most important and essential subject in the curriculum of our public schools —*Education Digest*⟩ ⟨the artisan . . . ~*s* no doubt lower than the professional man —G.L.Dickinson⟩ ⟨the profession of religion . . . ~*s* above all the other professions —Virginia Woolf⟩ **3 :** to have a place among the list of claims or claimants upon a bankrupt estate **4 :** to have the highest rank **:** be senior **:** be supremely eminent ⟨ordered by the ~*ing* head of the provincial government —Marjory S. Douglas⟩

**rank and file** *n* **1 :** the enlisted men of an armed force (as privates and corporals) whose normal position is in the ranks of a formation ⟨most of their *rank and file* . . . had heavy shields bound with iron and a long cutting sword —Tom Wintringham⟩ **2 a :** the individuals who constitute the body of an organization, society, or nation ⟨the *rank and file* was made up of brawling adventure lovers —Julian Dana⟩ ⟨the inner circle of leaders had forced the program, rather than the *rank and file* —F.L.Paxson⟩ ⟨bring the government . . . into more intimate relations with the *rank and file* —F.A.Ogg & Harold Zink⟩ **b :** the general membership of a union ⟨when irresponsible labor leaders . . . entice away the *rank and file* from the legislation they desire —A.M.Schlesinger b.1917⟩

**rank-and-filer** \ˌ==ˈfīlə(r)\ *n* [*rank and file* + *-er*] **:** one that belongs to the rank and file ⟨still basically a *rank-and-filer* —C.Y.Harrison⟩

**rank badge** *n* **:** one of the Girl Scout badges designating rank (as for first class, second class)

**rank correlation** *n* **:** a measure of correlation depending on rank

**rank-difference coefficient of correlation :** the correlation coefficient applied to the rank numbers of two sets of variables

rank badge, second class

**¹ranker** *comparative of* RANK

**²rank·er** \ˈraŋkə(r)\ *n* -s [in sense 1, fr. ⁴*rank* + *-er;* in sense 2, fr. ³*rank* + *-er*] **1 :** one that ranks or draws up in line **2 :** one who serves in the ranks of the armed forces; *esp* **:** a commissioned officer promoted from the ranks

**rankest** *superlative of* RANK

**ran·ket** \ˈraŋkət\ *n* -s [G *rackett, rankett*] **1 :** RACKETT **2 :** a reed organ pipe of 16-foot or 8-foot pitch producing a smothered tone

**rank indigo** *n* **:** indigo derived from the leaves of an East Indian woody vine (*Marsdenia tinctoria*)

**ran·kine** \ˈraŋkən\ *adj, usu cap* [after William J. M. *Rankine* †1872 Scot. engineer and physicist] **:** being, according to, or relating to an absolute-temperature scale on which the unit of measurement equals a Fahrenheit degree and according to which the freezing point of water is 491.69° and the boiling point 671.69°

**rankine cycle** *n, usu cap R* **:** an ideal reversible heat-engine cycle approximated by the operating cycle of an actual steam engine

**ranking bar** *n* **:** a handbarrow used by lumbermen

**ranking jumper** *n* **:** an all-wood sled used by lumbermen for hauling tanbark

**ranking member** *n* **1 :** the congressional member next to the chairman in order of seniority **2 :** the senior in rank or service who becomes chairman of a committee or court-martial

**ran·kin·ite** \ˈraŋkə,nīt\ *n* -s [George A. *Rankin* †1963 Am. chemist + E *-ite*] **:** a mineral $Ca_3Si_2O_7$ consisting of a rare calcium silicate

**¹ran·kle** \ˈraŋkəl, ˈraiŋ-\ *vb* **rankled; rankled; rankling** \-k(ə)liŋ\ **rankles** [ME *ranclen,* fr. MF *rancler,* fr. OF *draoncler, raoncler, rancler,* fr. *draoncle, drancle, raoncle, rancle* festering sore, fr. (assumed) VL *dracunculus,* fr. L, small serpent, dim. of *draco* serpent, dragon — more at DRAGON] *vi* **1 a :** to become inflamed or infected **:** FESTER **b** *obs* **:** to inflict a painful wound **2 a :** to produce or continue to produce an effect resembling a festering sore ⟨much hatred still ~*s* —H.L. Matthews⟩ **b :** to continue to cause anger, irritation, or bitter often malignant feelings ⟨this escapade *rankled* longer in his mind —Leonard Bacon⟩ ⟨has long *rankled* as an act of injustice —Clement Attlee⟩ **3 :** to become inflamed with anger **:** chafe in vexation ⟨the prophets . . . who ~ under defeat —J.G.Fletcher⟩ **~** *vt* **1 :** to cause to fester **2 :** to cause irritation or bitter feelings in **:** make angry **:** INFLAME ⟨paying . . . above the market price which *rankled* him —J.H.Wheelwright⟩

**²rankle** \"\ *n* -s **:** an emotion that rankles

**rankling** *adj* **:** festering within the mind **:** producing angry often malignant feelings **:** insidiously irritating or annoying ⟨a ~ word —R.M.Coates⟩ ⟨dull ~ anger —Rudyard Kipling⟩ ⟨a ~ sentiment of injustice —A.L.Guérard⟩ — **rank·ling·ly** *adv*

**rank·ly** *adv* [ME, fr. OE *ranclīce* boldly, ostentatiously, fr. *ranc* overbearing, strong, brave + *-līce* -ly — more at RANK] **:** in a rank manner

**rank·ness** *n* -ES [ME *ranknesse,* fr. *rank* + *-nesse* -ness] **:** the quality or state of being rank

**rank of a determinant :** the rank of the matrix of the determinant

**rank of a matrix :** the order of the nonzero determinant of highest order that may be formed from the elements of a matrix by selecting arbitrarily an equal number of rows and columns from it

**rank order** *n* **:** arrangement according to rank

**ranks** *pl of* RANK, *pres 3d sing of* RANK

**rann** \ˈran\ *n* -s [IrGael] *Irish* **:** a stanza esp. of a song ⟨known . . . for his stinging ~*s* —Padraic Colum⟩

**ran·nel tree** \ˈranᵊl-\ *or* **rannel bean** *n* [*rannel* prob. of Scand origin; akin to Norw dial. *randatre* rannel tree, fr. *rand* edge, space above a fireplace (fr. ON *rand-, rönd* rim, shield) — more at RAND] *dial Brit* **:** a bar to support pothooks over an open fireplace

**¹ran·ny** \ˈranī\ *n* -ES [prob. modif. of L *araneus* (*mus*), fr. *araneus* of a spider (fr. *aranea* spider) + *mus* mouse — more at ARACHN-] *dial Eng* **:** SHREW 1

**²ran·ny** \ˈranē\ *n* -ES [origin unknown] **:** a poor quality calf of mongrel breeding

**rans** *pl of* RAN

**¹ran·sack** \ˈranˌsak, ˈraan-\ *vt* -ED/-ING/-S [ME *ransaken,* fr. ON *rannsaka,* fr. *rann* house + *-saka* (akin to ON *sækja* to seek) — more at REST, SEEK] **1 :** to look very thoroughly and zealously through **:** search often forcefully or roughly **:** RUMMAGE ⟨~*ed* the kitchen for candles —Dorothy Sayers⟩ **2 :** to subject to close investigation or study **:** examine critically and carefully ⟨with the true persistence of a scholar has ~*ed* all the authorities —T.G.Bergin⟩ ⟨~*ed* literature and the dictionary for the unusual word —J.G.Southworth⟩ **3 :** to remove wealth or valuables from **:** PLUNDER ⟨~*ed* the premises⟩ **syn** see SEEK

**²ransack** \"\ *n* -s *archaic* **:** the act of ransacking

**ran·sack·er** \-kə(r)\ *n* -s **:** one that ransacks

**ran·sack·le** \ˈran,sakəl\ *vt* -ED/-ING/-S [freq. of *ransack*] *archaic* **:** RANSACK

**ransel** *var of* RANCEL

**¹ran·som** \ˈran(t)səm, ˈraan-, ˈrain-\ *n* -s [ME *raunsoun, ransoun,* fr. OF *reançon, rançon,* fr. L *redemption-, redemptio* redemption, ransom — more at REDEMPTION] **1 :** the money, price, or consideration paid or demanded for the redemption of a captured person : a payment that releases from captivity **2 :** the act of ransoming : the redeeming or releasing of a captive by a payment esp. of money **3 :** something paid in medieval times for the pardon of an offense in lieu of corporal punishment : FINE

**[2]ransom** \"\ *vt* -ED/-ING/-S [ME *raunsounen, ransounen,* fr. OF *reançonner, rançonner,* fr. *reançon, rançon,* n.] **1 :** to deliver esp. from sin or its penalty ⟨He lives, triumphant o'er the grave, . . . my ~*ed* soul to keep and save —Charles Wesley⟩ **2** *archaic* **:** to atone for : EXPIATE **3 :** to redeem usu. from captivity, slavery, or punishment by paying a price : buy out of bondage ⟨an escaped slave . . . he was ~*ed* by two Englishwomen —*Amer. Guide Series: Md.*⟩ **4 :** to exact a ransom for or from : hold or offer for ransom : oppress by exacting ransoms or fines **syn** see RESCUE

**ran·som·able** \-məbəl\ *adj* **:** capable of being ransomed ⟨during the Crusades . . . the search for ~ prisoners became so intense —*N.Y.Times*⟩

**ransom bill** *also* **ransom bond** *n* **:** a contract valid by the law of nations given in time of war for the ransom of property esp. when captured at sea and a safe-conduct for it to a friendly destination

**ran·som·er** \-mə(r)\ *n* -S **:** one that ransoms or redeems; *specif* **:** a hostage for the ransom of a captured vessel under a ransom bill

**ran·som·ite** \'ran(t)sə,mīt\ *n* -S [Frederick L. *Ransome* †1935 Am. mining geologist + E *-ite*] **:** a mineral $Cu(Fe,Al)_2(SO_4)_4.7H_2O$ consisting of hydrous sulfate of copper, iron, and aluminum

**ran·som·less** \'ran(t)səmləs\ *adj* **:** free from or lacking ransom

**ransom theory** *n* **:** a patristic theory of the atonement: on the cross Christ gave his finite soul as a ransom to the devil for the souls of sinful humanity over which he had acquired rights by the fall; hell could not hold a soul without sin; and in the resurrection divine love triumphed once and for all over sin and death — compare SATISFACTION THEORY

**ran·stead** \'ran,sted\ *or* **ram·stead** \-am,-\ *n* -S [prob. after *Ranstead,* 18th cent. American born in Wales] **:** an erect perennial Old World toadflax (*Linaria vulgaris*) that bears racemes of pale yellow to citron yellow flowers with coppery markings and is naturalized in No. America where it is sometimes a troublesome weed

**[1]rant** \'rant, -aa(ə)nt,-aint\ *vb* -ED/-ING/-S [obs. D *ranten, randen*] *vi* **1** *archaic* **:** to have a noisy good time with dancing, singing, and drinking : CAROUSE, REVEL **2 :** to talk noisily, excitedly, often extravagantly : declaim in bombastic fashion ⟨~ and rave in loud voices —Priscilla Hughes⟩ **3 :** to scold vehemently : be in a rage : RAIL ⟨~*ed* at the boy who paid no attention⟩ ~ *vt* **:** to speak in an extravagant grandiose fashion : declaim noisily ⟨the actor who ~*s* Shakespeare —H.E. Clurman⟩

**[2]rant** \"\ *n* -S **1 a :** ostentatious speech or utterance : discourse that is often wildly excessive and unrestrained ⟨going to yell out the customary ~ which he kept for big occasions —Bruce Marshall⟩ ⟨the depth of feeling without ~ —Walter Hampden⟩ **b :** extravagant often flowery language or sentiment usu. empty of meaning ⟨sometimes mere ~, the book has genuine depths —Edgar Johnson⟩ **2** *dial Brit* **a :** a rousing good time : SPREE **b :** a gay song or dance tune **3 :** the act of ranting : a ranting state **syn** see BOMBAST

**ran–tan** \'ran·,tan\ *n* -S [imit.] **1 :** a knocking, banging, or pounding noise ⟨no rest for Niagara, but perpetual ~ on those limestone rocks —H.D.Thoreau⟩ **2 :** riotous conduct : SPREE

**ran·tan·ker·ous** \(')ran·¦taŋk(ə)rəs, -aan·¦taŋ-\ *adj* [by alter.] **:** CANTANKEROUS

**rant·er** \'rantə(r), -aan-,-ain-\ *n* -S **1 :** one that rants; *esp* **:** a noisy bombastic speaker **2** *usu cap* **a :** a member of a 17th century pantheistic, antinomian, and highly individualistic religious group in England **b :** a member of the Primitive Methodists who seceded from the Wesleyan Methodists as being deficient in fervor and zeal — usu. used in derision and in allusion to the loud tones of their preaching and responses

**ranter–go–round** \'==(,)=,=\ *n* **:** a round game in which each player is dealt a card face down which in some circumstances he may pass to the player on his left for exchange, the object being to win the pool by showing the lowest card at the table

**rant·er·ism** \-tə,rizəm\ *n* -S *usu cap* **:** the practice or tenets of the Ranters

**rant·ing·ly** *adv* [fr. *ranting,* pres. part. of *rant* + *-ly*] **:** in a ranting manner

**[1]rant·i·pole** \-tē,pōl -tə,-\ *n* -S [prob. fr. *ranty* + *pole,* alter. of *poll* (head)] **:** a wild reckless sometimes quarrelsome person

**[2]rantipole** \"\ *adj* **:** characterized by a wild unruly manner or attitude : RAKISH ⟨~ laughter —J.B.Cabell⟩

**[3]rantipole** \"\ *vi* -ED/-ING/-S **:** to act like a rantipole

**rant·ism** \-n·,tizəm\ *n* -S *usu cap, obs* **:** RANTERISM

**ran·tree** \'rän·(,)trē\ *Scot var of* ROWAN TREE

**ran·tum–scan·tum** \¦rantəm¦skantəm\ *adj* [irreg. fr. [1]*rant*] **:** CARELESS, DISORDERLY

**ranty** \'ranti\ *adj* [[1]*rant* + *-y*] *dial Brit* **:** EXCITED, RIOTOUS

**ran·u·la** \'ranyələ\ *n* -S [NL, fr. L, little frog, little swelling on the tongue of cattle, dim. of *rana* frog — more at RANA] **:** a cyst formed under the tongue by obstruction of the duct of a sublingual or submaxillary gland or any mucous gland

**ra·nun·cu·la·ce·ae** \rə,nəŋkyə'lāsē,ē\ *n pl, cap* [NL, fr. *Ranunculus,* type genus + *-aceae*] **:** a large family of plants (order Ranales) distinguished by colorless acrid juice, usu. alternate leaves, and regular or irregular polypetalous or apetalous flowers with hypogynous stamens — see RANUNCULUS

**ra·nun·cu·la·ceous** \=¦==¦lāshəs\ *adj* [NL *Ranunculaceae* + E *-ous*] **:** of or relating to the Ranunculaceae

**ra·nun·cu·la·les** \=,=='lā(,)lēz\ [NL, fr. *Ranunculus* + *-ales*] *syn of* RANALES

**ra·nun·cu·lus** \='==ləs\ *n* [NL, fr. L, any of several species of Ranunculus, lit., small frog, dim. of *rana* frog] **1** *cap* **:** a large and widely distributed genus (the type of the family Ranunculaceae) of herbs that have simple or variously lobed leaves and mostly yellow flowers with five deciduous sepals and five nectariferous petals followed by numerous flattened achenes borne in a head or spike — see BUTTERCUP **2** *pl* **ranunculus·es** \-ləsəz\ *or* **ranuncu·li** \-,lī\ **:** any plant of the genus *Ranunculus*

**ran·vier's node** \(')rän¦vyāz-\ *n, usu cap R* **:** NODE OF RANVIER

**ran·za·nia** \ran'zānēə, -nyə\ *n, cap* [NL, fr. C. A. *Ranzani* †1841 Ital. naturalist + NL *-ia*] **:** a genus of marine sunfishes (family Molidae) with slightly elongated bodies

**ranz des vaches** \rän(s)dāvåsh\ *n* [F dial. (Switzerland), lit., rows of cows; prob. intended as trans. (influence of G *reihen* rows) of G dial. (Switzerland) *kuhreihen, kuhreigen*] **:** a melody sung by Swiss herdsmen or played on the alpenhorn to call cattle

**ra·ob** \'rā,äb\ *n* -S *often cap* [*ra*diosonde *ob*servation] **:** a meteorological observation made by means of a radiosonde

**ra·ou·lia** \rā'ülēə\ *n* [NL, fr. Étienne F. L. *Raoul* †1852 French surgeon + NL *-ia*] **1** *cap* **:** a genus of large white hoary caespitose cushion plants (family Compositae) that are natives chiefly of New Zealand uplands and have small solitary flower heads resembling those of *Helichrysum* — see SHEEP PLANT **2** -S **:** any plant of the genus *Raoulia*

**ra·oult's law** \rä'ülz-\ *n, usu cap R* [after François M. *Raoult* †1901 French chemist] **:** a law in physical chemistry: the fraction by which the vapor pressure of a liquid is lowered when a small amount of a substance that is nonvolatile, not dissociable, and usu. not a high polymer is dissolved in it is equal to the mole fraction of the solute — compare IDEAL SOLUTION

**raoult's method** *n, usu cap R* [after F. M. *Raoult*] **:** a method of determining the molecular weight of a dissolved substance by the extent to which it depresses the freezing point of the solvent

**RAP** *abbr* **1** regimental aid post **2** rupees, annas, pies

**[1]rap** \'rap\ *n* -S [ME *rappe,* prob. of imit. origin] **1 a :** a quick sharp blow ⟨got a ~ on the knuckles from the teacher's stick⟩ **b :** a sharp knock ⟨heard a ~ on the door⟩ **2 a :** a sharp rebuke ⟨got a hard ~ from his boss for the blunder⟩ **b :** an adverse criticism ⟨annoyed by her ~*s* at his slowness⟩ **3 a** (1) **:** the legal responsibility for and consequences of a criminal act ⟨accused of trying to take the ~ for his fellow officers —*Springfield* (*Mass.*) *Union*⟩ (2) **:** a criminal charge ⟨in court to face a forgery ~⟩ (3) **:** a prison sentence ⟨sent up for a 30 year ~⟩ **b :** the blame for or adverse consequences of an action ⟨scapegoats . . . who took the ~ and kept their mouths shut —Percy Winner⟩ **4** *slang* **:** an identification of one charged with a crime

**[2]rap** \"\ *vb* **rapped; rapped; rapping; raps** [ME *rappen,* prob. of imit. origin] *vt* **1 :** to strike with a quick smart blow ⟨~ struggling rioters with nightsticks⟩ ⟨*rapped* a double off the left-field wall —W.G.Smith⟩ **:** strike a rap with ⟨~*s* his pipe on the ashtray⟩ **2 :** to utter suddenly and forcibly — usu. used with *out* ⟨~*s* out a series of curt commands⟩ **3** *slang* **:** to swear or testify to esp. falsely **4 a :** to cause to be or come by rapping ⟨~ the occupants awake⟩ ⟨~ the meeting to order⟩ **b :** to communicate (a message) by knocks ⟨says the spirit ~*s* out an answer to the medium's question⟩ **5 :** to censure severely : criticize sharply ⟨criticism . . . *rapping* the pretensions of semi-intellectuals —B.R.Redman⟩ **6** *slang* **:** to arrest, hold, or sentence on a criminal charge ⟨had been . . . *rapped* with one-to-ten years at the state reformatory —Bunque Mooney⟩ ~ *vi* **1 :** to strike a person or thing with a quick sharp blow or succession of blows ⟨~*s* on wood for good luck⟩ **2 :** to make a short sharp sound or a succession of such sounds ⟨clatter of hoofs *rapped* sharply from the walls —Zane Grey⟩

**[3]rap** \"\ *vt* **rapped** *also* **rapt; rapped** *also* **rapt; rapping; raps** [back-formation fr. [1]*rapt*] **1** *obs* **:** to snatch and steal : GRAB **2 a :** to snatch away : to seize and hurry off **b :** to carry upward (as by supernatural force) ⟨it *rapt* us from red gulphs of war —P.B.Shelley⟩ **3 :** to transport out of oneself : affect with ecstasy or rapture — **rap and rend 1 :** to seize and steal **2 :** to get together by fair means or foul : procure at any cost ⟨make and mend, or *rap and rend,* for me —Robert Browning⟩

**[4]rap** \"\ *n* -S [perh. fr. [1]*rap*] **1 a :** a counterfeit halfpenny in circulation in Ireland early in the 18th century **b :** a coin of trifling value **2 :** the least bit ⟨don't care a ~⟩

**ra·pa·cious** \rə'pāshəs\ *adj* [L *rapac-, rapax* rapacious, (fr. *rapere* to seize and carry off, snatch away) + *-ious* — more at RAPID] **1 :** excessively grasping or covetous : given to seizing or extorting what is coveted ⟨~ invaders⟩ **2 :** subsisting on prey : PREDACIOUS ⟨the ~ wolf⟩ **3 :** RAVENOUS ⟨a ~ appetite⟩ **syn** see VORACIOUS

**ra·pa·cious·ly** *adv* **:** in a rapacious manner

**ra·pa·cious·ness** *n* -ES **:** the quality or state of being rapacious

**ra·pac·i·ty** \rə'pasəd·ē, -paas-, -sətē, -i\ *n* -ES [MF *rapacité,* fr. L *rapacitat-, rapacitas,* fr. *rapac-, rapax* rapacious + *-itat-, -itas* -ity — more at RAPACIOUS] **1 :** RAPACIOUSNESS **2 :** a rapacious act or appetite **syn** see CUPIDITY

**ra·pa·ki·vi** \¦räpə'kēvē\ *n* -S [Finn, fr. *rapa* dregs, mud, gravel + *kivi* stone, rock] **:** a coarse red granite quarried in Finland having curious ovoid ringed feldspars composed of central cores of orthoclase surrounded by a shell of oligoclase and being much used for building in northern Russia

**rap·a·nea** \,rapə'nēə\ *n, cap* [NL] **:** a genus of chiefly tropical trees or shrubs (family Theophrastaceae) having mostly shining leathery leaves and small flowers with stamens adnate to the corolla lobes

**ra·pa·te·a·ce·ae** \rə,pād·ē'āsē,ē\ *n pl, cap* [NL, fr. *Rapatea,* type genus (prob. fr. a native name in Guiana) + *-aceae*] **:** a family of So. American herbs (order Xyridales) somewhat resembling members of the family Juncaceae and having a greenish perianth in two series, six anthers, and numerous capitate flowers subtended by two foliaceous bracts — **ra·pa·te·a·ceous** \=¦==¦āshəs\ *adj*

**[1]rape** \'rāp\ *n* -S [ME, fr. OE *rāp,* lit., rope; prob. fr. such districts being marked out by stakes and ropes — more at ROPE] **:** one of six divisions of the county of Sussex, England, intermediate between a hundred and a shire

**[2]rape** \"\ *n* -S [ME, fr. L *rapa, rapum* turnip, rape; akin to MD *roeve* turnip, rape, MLG *röve,* OHG *rāba & ruoba, ruoppa* turnip, rape, ON *rōfa* hard part of a tail, Gk *rhapys, rhaphys* turnip, Lith *ropė*] **1** *obs* **:** TURNIP **2 :** an annual herb (*Brassica napus*) of European origin but known only as a cultigen that differs from the cabbage in its deeply lobed leaves which are not hairy like those of the turnip and is widely grown in the Old World as a forage crop for sheep and in the U. S. chiefly as a forage crop for hogs and sheep, as a cover crop in orchards, or for its seeds which yield rape oil and are a food for birds

**[3]rape** \"\ *vt* -ED/-ING/-S [ME *rapen,* fr. L *rapere* — more at RAPID] **1** *archaic* **:** to seize and take away by force : PLUNDER, DESPOIL **2 :** to commit rape upon **3** *archaic* **:** to make rapt (as with delight) : TRANSPORT

**[4]rape** \"\ *n* -S [ME, fr. *rapen*] **1 :** the act or an instance of robbing or despoiling : violent seizure ⟨the ~ of the city by the invading soldiers⟩ ⟨the ~ of the region's forests⟩ **2 :** the act of carrying away a person by force ⟨the ~ of the Sabine women⟩ **3 a :** illicit sexual intercourse without the consent of the woman and effected by force, duress, intimidation, or deception as to the nature of the act — see STATUTORY RAPE **b :** sexual aggression other than by a man toward a woman **4 :** an outrageous violation (as of a fundamental principle or institution) ⟨trials that have been criticized as a ~ of justice —Hal Foust⟩ ⟨a judicial ~ of the Constitution —H.E.Talmadge⟩

**[5]rape** \"\ *n* -S [F *râpe* grape stalk, prob. of Gmc origin; akin to OHG *raspōn* to scrape together, collect — more at RASP] **1 :** the pomace of grapes left after expression of the juice or must and used for filtering (as in vinegar making) — often used in pl. **2 :** a filter consisting of a large cask with a false bottom and containing rape or some other filtering material

**[6]rape** \"\ *dial var of* ROPE

**rape butterfly** *n* [[2]*rape*] **:** a cabbage butterfly (*Pieris napi*) occurring in Europe and No. America

**rape cake** *n* [[2]*rape*] **:** the residue from rapeseed that remains after the oil is expressed and is used as cattle feed or ground to rapeseed meal

**rap·ee** \(')rā¦pē\ *n* -S [[3]*rape* + *-ee*] **:** the victim of a rape

**rape oil** *n* [[2]*rape*] **:** a light yellow to brown fatty nondrying or semidrying oil obtained from rapeseed and turnip seed and used chiefly as a lubricant, illuminant, and food — compare COLZA OIL

**rap·er** \'rāpə(r)\ *n* -S [[3]*rape* + *-er*] **:** one that rapes : RAPIST

**rapeseed** \'=,=\ *n* [[2]*rape* + *seed*] **:** the seed of rape

**rapeseed meal** *n* **:** ground rape cake

**[1]rap full** *adj* [prob. fr. [3]*rap*] **1 :** sailing with sails filled and almost close-hauled **2** *of sails* **:** being full and drawing steadily

**[2]rap full** *n* **:** a state of having the sails full of wind ⟨with a *rap full* she would heel more —H.A.Calahan⟩

**raph·a·el·esque** *or* **raf·fa·el·esque** \¦rafēə¦lesk, ¦rāf-\ *adj, usu cap* [*Raphael* or *Raffael* (*Raffaello Santi* or *Sanzio*) †1520 Ital. painter + E *-esque*] **:** done in or resembling the style of the painter Raphael

**raph·a·el·ism** \'==ə,lizəm\ *n* -S *usu cap* [*Raphael* + E *-ism*] **:** the artistic principles, method, or style of the painter Raphael

**[1]raph·a·el·ite** \-,līt\ *n* -S *usu cap* [*Raphael* + E *-ite*] **:** one who advocates or adopts Raphaelism

**[2]raphaelite** \"\ *n* -S **:** VANADIFEROUS ASPHALTUM

**raph·a·nus** \'rafənəs\ *n, cap* [NL, fr. L, radish, fr. Gk *raphanos;* akin to Gk *rhapys, rhaphys* turnip — more at RAPE] **:** a genus of Eurasian herbs (family Cruciferae) characterized by the torulose pods containing globose seeds in a single row — see JOINTED CHARLOCK, RADISH

**ra·phe** *or* **rha·phe** \'rāfē\ *n* -S [NL, fr. Gk *rhaphē* seam, suture of the skull, fr. *rhaptein* to sew together, stitch — more at WRAP] **1 :** the seamlike union of the two lateral halves of a part or organ (as of the tongue, perineum, scrotum) having externally a ridge or furrow, and internally usu. a fibrous connective tissue septum **2 a :** the part of the funiculus of an anatropous ovule adnate to the integument, forming a ridge along the body of the ovule, and providing a diagnostic character in various seeds (as those of *Sarracenia*) **b :** the median line or slit of a valve of a diatom **c :** the suture between the two mericarps of the fruit of an umbelliferous plant

**ra·phia** \'rāfēə\ *n* [NL, fr. E *raffia*] **1** *cap* **:** a genus of pinnate-leaved palms native to Africa and So. America with short stout trunks, very large spiny leaves, spicate inflorescences often six feet in length, and spongy fruit containing a single hard seed — see JUPATI, RAFFIA PALM **2** -S **:** RAFFIA 1

**raphia wax** *n* **:** RAFFIA WAX

**raph·i·dae** \'rafə,dē\ *n pl, cap* [NL, fr. *Raphus,* type genus + *-idae*] **:** a family of extinct flightless birds (order Columbiformes) related to the pigeons and comprising the dodos and solitaires

**ra·phide** \'rāfəd, -,fid\ *n* -S [back-formation fr. *raphides,* pl., fr. NL, irreg. fr. Gk *rhaphid-, rhaphis* needle, fr. *rhaptein* to sew together — more at WRAP] **:** one of the needle-shaped crystals irritating to mucous membrane and usu. consisting of calcium oxalate that occur in bundles or sheaflike groups as metabolic by-products of plant cells, are found most abundantly in stems, leaves, and roots of herbs and in the bark of trees, and are discharged when moistened — see CRYSTAL SAND

**[1]ra·phid·i·an** \rə'fidēən\ *or* **ra·phid·i·id** \rə'fidēəd\ *adj* [*raphidian* fr. NL *Raphidium* + E *-an; raphidiid* fr. NL *Raphidiidae*] **:** of or relating to the Raphidiidae

**[2]raphidian** \"\ *or* **raphidiid** \"\ *n* -S **:** an insect of the family Raphidiidae

**raph·i·dif·er·ous** \¦rafə¦dif(ə)rəs\ *adj* [*raphide* + *-iferous*] **:** bearing or containing raphides

**raph·i·di·idae** \,=='dīə,dē\ *n pl, cap* [NL, fr. *Raphidium,* type genus (irreg. fr. Gk *rhaphid-, rhaphis* needle + NL *-ium*) + *-idae* — more at RAPHIDE] **:** a family of predatory insects (suborder Raphidiodea) remarkable for their long prothorax and elongate setiform ovipositor

**ra·phid·i·o·dea** \rə,fidē'ōdēə\ *n pl, cap* [NL, fr. *Raphidium* + *-odea*] **:** a small suborder of Neuroptera that comprises the snake flies, includes the family Raphidiidae and a few related insects, and is often considered an independent order or replaced by Megaloptera

**raph·i·ol·e·pis** \,rafē'äləpəs\ *n, cap* [NL, irreg. fr. Gk *rhaphis* needle + NL *-o-* + *-lepis*] **:** a small genus of ornamental Asiatic shrubs (family Rosaceae) grown for their evergreen, glossy, alternate leaves and rather showy white or pink flowers in racemes or panicles — see INDIAN HAWTHORN, JAPANESE HAWTHORN

**ra·phus** \'rāfəs\ *n, cap* [NL] **:** the type genus of Raphidae — see DODO

**[1]rap·id** \'rapəd\ *adj, often* **rapider;** *often* **rapidest** [L *rapidus* seizing, tearing, hurrying, rapid, fr. *rapere* to seize, rob, kidnap, ravish; akin to OE *refsan, repsan* to reprove, blame, OS *respian* to reprove, OHG *refsen* to punish, ON *refsa* to punish, Gk *ereptesthai* to feed on, Lith ap*rėpti* to seize; basic meaning: to seize, grasp] **1 :** marked by a notably high rate of motion, activity, succession, or occurrence : requiring notably little time : not slow or retarded ⟨a ~ stream⟩ ⟨a ~ train⟩ ⟨a ~ journey⟩ ⟨~ movement⟩ ⟨racquets, most delightfully ~ of games —H.W.Nevinson⟩ **2 :** marked by abrupt action or decision without delay or hesitation ⟨a train of thought made ~ by the stimulus of cupidity —George Eliot⟩ ⟨the ~ assurance of one who needs not to inquire about tastes and appetites —Arnold Bennett⟩ **3 :** permissive of or conducive to action in less than normal or ordinary time ⟨~ growth⟩ **4 :** FAST 5d **syn** see FAST

**[2]rapid** \"\ *n, pl* **rapids** *but sing or pl in constr* **:** a part of a river where the current moves with great swiftness and where the surface is usu. broken by obstructions but has no actual waterfall or cascade ⟨a shallow ~ —P.B.Shelley⟩ ⟨shoot the ~*s* in a canoe⟩

**[3]rapid** \"\ *adv* **:** RAPIDLY — usu. used in combination ⟨a *rapid*-firing gun⟩ ⟨a *rapid*-flowing stream⟩

**ra·pi·da·men·te** \,räpēdä'men·(,)tā\ *adv* [It, fr. *rapido* rapid, fr. L *rapidus* — more at RAPID] **:** RAPIDLY — used as a direction in music

**ra·pide** \ra'pēd\ *n* -S [F, fr. *rapide,* adj., rapid, fr. L *rapidus* — more at RAPID] **:** a European express train

**rapid fire** *n* **:** a class of rifle fire in which a time limit is set for completing the required number of shots

**rapid–fire** \¦==¦=\ *adj* [*rapid fire*] **1 :** firing or adapted for firing shots in rapid succession **2 :** proceeding with or characterized by rapidity, liveliness, or sharpness ⟨a *rapid-fire* cross-examination⟩

**rapid–fire gun** *n* **:** CASE GUN

**rapid–fire mount** *n* **:** a mount permitting easy and quick elevation or depression and training of a gun and fitted with a device for taking up the recoil

**ra·pid·i·ty** \rə'pidəd·ē, ra'-, -dətē, -i\ *n* -ES [L *rapiditas,* fr. *rapidus* rapid + *-itas* -ity — more at RAPID] **:** the quality or state of being rapid : SWIFTNESS, CELERITY, VELOCITY ⟨the ~ of a current⟩

**rap·id·ly** *adv* **:** in a rapid manner : at a rapid rate

**rap·id·ness** *n* -ES **:** the quality or state of being rapid : RAPIDITY

**ra·pi·do** \'räpē,dō\ *n* -S [It (fr. *rapido,* adj., rapid, fr. L *rapidus*) & Sp *rápido,* fr. *rápido,* adj., rapid, fr. L *rapidus* — more at RAPID] **:** an express train of Italy, Spain, or Latin America

**rapid plant bug** *n* **:** a No. American mirid bug (*Adelphocoris rapidus*) that is a serious pest on cotton, alfalfa, and other crops

**rapid transit** *n* **1 :** local passenger transportation in or near cities by methods of conveyance (as subway, elevated railway) more rapid than the ordinary ones **2 :** chess play with a limit of a few (as ten) seconds per move — called also *lightning chess*

**ra·pier** \'rāpēə(r), -pyə(r)\ *n* -S [MF (*espee*) *rapiere*] **:** a straight two-edged sword esp. of the 16th and 17th centuries with a narrow pointed blade used chiefly for thrusting and heavier than the 18th century smallsword

rapier

**rap·ine** \'rapən\ *n* -S [ME *rapyne,* fr. L *rapina,* fr. *rapere* to seize, rob, kidnap, ravish + *-ina* (fr. fem. of *-inus* -ine) — more at RAPID] **:** the seizing and carrying away of things by force : SPOLIATION, PILLAGE, PLUNDER

**raping** *pres part of* RAPE

**rap·ist** \'rāpəst\ *n* -S [[4]*rape* + *-ist*] **:** one who commits rape

**[1]rap·loch** \'rapləḵ\ *adj* [origin unknown] *Scot* **:** COARSE, ROUGH

**[2]raploch** \"\ *n* -S *Scot* **:** homespun woolen cloth

**rap·pa·ree** \,rapə'rē\ *n* -S [IrGael *rāpaire, ropaire* short pike, rapparee] **1 :** an Irish irregular soldier or freebooter esp. of the 17th century **2 :** PLUNDERER, VAGABOND

**rapped** *past of* RAP

**rap·pee** \ra'pē\ *n* -S [F (*tabac*) *râpé,* lit., grated tobacco, fr. *tabac* tobacco + *râpé,* past part. of *râper* to grate, fr. (assumed) MF *rasper* — more at RASP] **:** a moist pungent snuff made from dark rank tobacco leaves

**[1]rap·pel** \ra'pel, rə'-\ *n* -S [F, lit., recall, summons, fr. OF *rapel,* fr. *rapeler* to call again, recall, summon, fr. *re-* + *apeler* to summon, appeal, accuse — more at APPEAL] **1** *archaic* **:** the drum call to arms **2 :** descent of a precipitous cliff by means of a double rope passed under one thigh, diagonally across the body, and over the opposite shoulder

**[2]rappel** \"\ *vi* **rappelled; rappelled; rappelling; rappels :** to make a rappel ⟨*rappelling* down a cliff⟩

**rap·pen** \'räpən\ *n, pl* **rappen** [G, fr. *rappe, rappen* raven, crow, black horse (with jocular reference to the eagle on the first rappen), fr. MHG *rappe;* akin to OHG *hraban* raven — more at RAVEN] **:** a small Swiss coin; *specif* **:** the Swiss centime

**[1]rap·per** \'rapə(r)\ *n* -S [[2]*rap* + *-er*] **1 :** one that raps; *specif* **:** the knocker of a door **2 a** *archaic* **:** a whopping oath or curse ⟨if you can swear such ~*s* —John Dryden⟩ **b** *dial* **:** a barefaced lie

**[2]rapper** \"\ *n* -S [prob. by folk etymology fr. *rapier*] **:** a short flat flexible steel sword made with a handle at each end and used in English folk dancing

**rapping** *pres part of* RAP

**rap·pi·ni** \ra'pēnē\ *n pl* [It *rapini,* pl. of *rapino* small turnip, dim. of *rapo* turnip, fr. L *rapum* turnip, rape — more at RAPE] **:** small turnip plants pulled from the soil prior to the development of the fleshy root and marketed in bunches or in bulk for use as greens

**rapp·ist** \'rapəst\ *or* **rapp·ite** \-,pīt\ *n* -S *usu cap* [George (Johann Georg) *Rapp* †1847 Am. religious leader born in Germany + E *-ist* or *-ite*] **:** HARMONITE

**rap poker** *n* **:** KNOCK POKER

**rap·port** \ra'pō(ə)r, rə'-, -ȯ(ə)r, -ōə, -ȯ(ə) *sometimes* "+t *or* (*before a vowel*) d·\ *n* -S [F, relation, connection, ratio, rapport, fr. *rapporter* to bring back, yield, produce, refer, ascribe, report, fr. OF *raporter* to bring back, fr. *re-* + *aporter* to bring — more at APPORT] **1 :** RELATION; *esp* **:** relation characterized by harmony, conformity, accord, or affinity ⟨bring one into closer ~ with his environment⟩ — compare

EN RAPPORT **2 :** confidence of a subject in the operator (as in hypnotism, psychotherapy, mental testing) with willingness to cooperate

**rap·por·tage** \ˌra,pȯrˈtäzh\ *n* -S [F, fr. *rapporter* + *-age*] **:** REPORTAGE 2

**rap·por·teur** \-ˈtər(·)\ *n* -S [F, fr. *rapporter* + *-eur* -or] **:** an official charged with drawing up and presenting reports (as from a parliamentary commission to the main body)

**rap·proche·ment** \ˌra,prōshˈmäⁿ *also* ˈrä,- *or* ˈra,- *or* -rȯsh- *or* ˌ==ˈ= *sometimes* -mänt; *sometimes* raˈ=,= *or* ra,=ˈ=\ *n* -S [F, fr. *rapprocher* to bring together (fr. MF, fr. *re-* + *approcher* to approach, bring near, fr. OF *aprochier*) + *-ment* — more at APPROACH] **:** the act or fact of coming or being drawn near or together **:** establishment or a state of cordial relations ⟨the gradual ~ between the papacy and Austria —Wilfrid Ward⟩

**raps** *pl of* RAP, *pres 3d sing of* RAP

**rap·scal·lion** \rapˈskalyən\ *n* -S [alter. of *rascallion*] **:** RASCAL, NE'ER-DO-WELL **syn** see VILLAIN

**rap·scal·lion·ly** *adj* **:** good for nothing **:** RASCALLY

**rap·son's slide** \ˈrapsənz-\ *n, usu cap R* [fr. the name *Rapson*] **:** a device that consists of a crosshead capable of moving in fixed guides and having a pivoted block with a hole in it through which passes a lever hinged at a fixed point outside and that is used as a differential gear for a ship's rudder

**¹rapt** \ˈrapt\ *adj* [ME, fr. L *raptus*, past part. of *rapere* to seize, rob, kidnap, ravish — more at RAPID] **1 :** lifted (as by supernatural force) and carried up or away **:** transported in spirit or to another place ⟨~ into future times, the bard began —Alexander Pope⟩ **2 :** transported with emotion (as love, delight) **:** ENRAPTURED ⟨the ~ exaltation of the devotee —J.A. Symonds⟩ **3 :** wholly absorbed or engrossed (as in feeling, meditation, or special interests) ⟨~ in secret studies —Shak.⟩ **4** *obs* **:** ABDUCTED, RAPED — **rapt·ly** *adv* — **rapt·ness** *n* -ES

**²rapt** \ˈ"\ *n* -S [L *raptus* action of seizing, robbing, kidnapping, or ravishing, fr. *raptus*, past part. of *rapere*] **:** a violent or sudden transporting; *also* **:** an ecstatic state **:** RAPTURE

**³rapt** *vt* -ED/-ING/-S [L *raptus*, past part.] *obs* **:** to carry away by force **:** TRANSPORT, RAVISH

**⁴rapt** *past of* RAP

**rap·ta·to·ri·al** \ˌraptəˈtōrēəl, -tȯr-\ *adj* [alter. (influenced by L *raptatus*, past part. of *raptare* to seize and carry off, ravage, plunder, fr. *raptus*, past part. of *rapere*) of *raptorial*] **:** PREDACIOUS

**rap·tor** \ˈraptər, -,tȯ(ə)r\ *n* -S [L, one that robs, plunders, kidnaps, or ravishes, fr. *raptus* (past part. of *rapere* to seize, rob, kidnap, ravish) + *-or* — more at RAPID] **1** *obs* **:** one that rapes **2** *also* **rap·tore** \-,tō(ə)r\ [NL *Raptores*] **:** a bird of the order Raptores **:** bird of prey

**¹rap·to·res** \rapˈtōr(,)ēz\ *n pl, cap* [NL, fr. L, pl. of *raptor*] *in former classifications* **:** an order of birds comprising Falconiformes and Strigiformes of current usage and including all the birds of prey

**²raptores** \ˈ"\ [NL, fr. L, pl. of *raptor*] *syn of* FALCONIFORMES

**rap·to·ri·al** \(ˈ)rapˈtōrēəl, -tȯr-\ *adj* [*raptor* + *-ial*] **1 :** living on prey **2 :** adapted to seize prey **3 :** of or relating to the Raptores

**rap·ture** \ˈrapchə(r)\ *n* -S [L *raptus* (past part. of *rapere*) + E *-ure*] **1** *archaic* **a :** the act of seizing and carrying off with force **:** forcible capture **:** ABDUCTION **b :** RAPE 3a **2** *archaic* **:** the act of carrying or being carried along **:** force of onward movement **3 a :** a carrying of a person to heaven **b :** Christ's raising up of his true church and its members to a realm above the earth where the whole company will enjoy celestial bliss with its Lord **4 a :** the state of being carried out of oneself **:** spiritual or emotional ecstasy **:** possession by an overwhelming emotion (as joy, love) **b :** an experience of this sort ⟨the ~*s* of the deep hazardous to divers are caused by nitrogen narcosis⟩ **5 :** a spasm or fit of emotion **:** PAROXYSM **6 :** an expression or manifestation of ecstasy or passionate feeling **:** RHAPSODY **7 :** a mystical phenomenon in which the soul is borne out of itself and exalted to a knowledge of divine things **syn** see ECSTASY

**²rapture** \ˈ"\ *vt* -ED/-ING/-S **:** to transport with rapture (as of joy) **:** ENRAPTURE

**rap·ture·less** \chə(r)ləs\ *adj* **:** feeling or expressing no rapture

**rap·tur·ize** \-chə,rīz\ *vi* -ED/-ING/-S [¹*rapture* + *-ize*] **:** to indulge in rapture

**rap·tur·ous** \-chərəs\ *adj* **:** feeling, expressing, or marked by rapture **:** ECSTATIC ⟨~ crowds⟩ ⟨~ applause⟩ ⟨a ~ moment⟩ — **rap·tur·ous·ly** *adv* — **rap·tur·ous·ness** *n* -ES

**rap·tus** \ˈraptəs\ *n* -ES [NL, fr. L, action of seizing, fr. *raptus*, past part. of *rapere*] **1 :** a state of spiritual rapture marked by anesthesia **2 :** a state of intense mental or emotional excitement ⟨the unpredictable ~ of the poet⟩ **3 :** a pathological paroxysm of activity giving vent to impulse or tension (as in an act of violence)

**raquet organ** *n* **:** one of a series of racket-shaped or T-shaped structures found on the last pair of legs of a solpugid and regarded as sense organs

**rara avis** \ˌra(a)rəˈāvəs, ˌrärəˈäwəs\ *n, pl* **rara avises** \-əsəz\ *or* **ra·rae aves** \ˌrä,rīˈä,wās\ [L, rare bird] **:** a rare person or thing **:** RARITY ⟨that *rara avis* of politics, a disinterested man —*Atlantic*⟩

**¹rare** \ˈra(a)(ə)r, ˈre|, |ə\ *adj* **rarer**; **rarest** [alter. (influenced by ²*rare*) of earlier *rere*, fr. ME, fr. OE *hrēre* boiled lightly; akin to OE & OS *hrōr* busy, active, strong, OE *hrēran* to stir — more at CRATER] **:** cooked to a slight degree ⟨~ roast beef⟩

**²rare** \ˈ"\ *adj* **rarer**; **rarest** [ME, fr. L *rarus*; perh. akin to L *rete* net — more at RETINA] **1 :** characterized by wide separation of component particles **:** THIN ⟨the ~ air of the mountain top⟩ — compare DENSE **2 a :** marked by unusual quality, merit, appeal, or capacity to please **:** DISTINCTIVE, EXCELLENT ⟨what is so ~ as a day in June —J.R.Lowell⟩ **b :** superlative or extreme in its kind **:** FINE, GREAT, REAL ⟨he'll make a ~ fuss —Eden Phillpots⟩ **3 :** seldom occurring or appearing **:** widely separated in space or time **:** few and far between **:** UNUSUAL, UNCOMMON, INFREQUENT ⟨~ patches of green in the desert —Emma Hawkridge⟩ ⟨in back country where automobiles from other parts are ~ —Cornelius Weygandt⟩; *specif* **:** belonging to a small group or class ⟨argon is a ~ gas⟩ **4 :** valued for its scarcity or exceptional character ⟨a ~ book⟩ **syn** see CHOICE, THIN

**³rare** \ˈ"\ *adj & adv* [prob. alter. of *rathe*] *chiefly dial* **:** EARLY

**⁴rare** \ˈ"\ *chiefly dial var of* REAR

**⁵rare** \ˈ"\ *chiefly dial var of* ROAR

**rare bird** *n* [trans. of L *rara avis*] **:** RARA AVIS

**rare·bit** \ˈra(a)(ə)rbət, ˈre|, |əb-, *usu* -əd·+V\ *n* -S [(*Welsh*) *rarebit*] **:** WELSH RABBIT

**rare earth** *n* **1 :** any of a group of very similar oxides of metals or a mixture of such oxides that occur together often associated with thorium in widely distributed but relatively scarce minerals (as monazite, bastnaesite, xenotime, gadolinite) and that are separated only with difficulty (as by fractional crystallization or by ion exchange) **2** *or* **rare-earth element** *or* **rare-earth metal :** any of the series of metallic elements whose oxides are the rare earths, which include the fourteen elements following lanthanum through lutetium with atomic numbers 58 through 71, usu. lanthanum itself, and according to some yttrium and even scandium, which are chiefly trivalent, and which except for lanthanum, lutetium, yttrium, and scandium form paramagnetic salts in many cases colored — symbol *RE*; compare CERIUM METAL, LANTHANIDE, PERIODIC TABLE, YTTRIUM METAL; ELEMENT table

**rar·ee-show** \ˈra(a)rē-, ˈrerē-\ *n* [²*rare* + *-ee*] **1 :** a show carried about in a box **:** PEEP SHOW **2 :** a cheap street show **:** CARNIVAL

**rar·e·fac·tion** \ˌra(a)rəˈfakshən, ˌrer-\ *n* -S [F or ML; F *raréfaction*, fr. MF *rarefaction*, fr. ML *rarefaction-*, *rarefactio*, fr. L *rarefactus* (past part. of *rarefacere* to rarefy) + *-ion-*, *-io* -ion — more at RAREFY] **1 :** the act or process of rarefying **2 :** the quality or state of being rarefied ⟨~ of bone⟩ **3 a :** state or region of minimum pressure in a medium traversed by compression waves (as sound waves) — compare CONDENSATION 4b — **rar·e·fac·tion·al** \-shənᵊl, -shnəl\ *adj*

**rar·e·fac·tive** \-ktiv\ *adj* [prob. fr. F *raréfactif*, fr. MF *rarefactif*, fr. L *rarefactus* + MF *-if* -ive] **:** producing or marked by rarefaction

**rar·e·fi·able** \ˌra(a)rəˈfīəbəl, ˌrer-\ *adj* **:** capable of being rarefied

**rarefied** *adj* [fr. past part. of *rarefy*] **1 :** of, belonging to, or interesting to a select group **:** ESOTERIC, ABSTRUSE ⟨the ~ realm of first editions —John Mason Brown⟩ ⟨~ aristocrats⟩ **2 :** very high ⟨former colonels and majors, newly promoted to ~ rank —*Newsweek*⟩

**rar·e·fi·er** \ˈ==,fī(ə)r\ *n* -S **:** one that rarefies

**rar·e·fy** *also* **rar·i·fy** \-rə,fī\ *vb* -ED/-ING/-ES [*rarefy* fr. ME *rarefien*, fr. MF *rarefier*, modif. (influenced by *-fier* -fy) of L *rarefacere*, irreg. fr. *rarus* + *facere* to make, do; *rarify* fr. ME *rarifien*, fr. ML *rarificare*, fr. L *rarus* + *-ificare* -ify — more at RARE, DO] *vt* **1 :** to make rare, thin, porous, or less dense **:** expand or enlarge without adding any new portion of matter to — opposed to *condense* ⟨the expansive power of moisture *rarified* by heat —T.B.Macaulay⟩ **2 :** to make more spiritual, refined, tenuous, or abstruse ⟨their wits are refined and *rarefied* —Ben Jonson⟩ ~ *vi* **:** to become less dense or gross **:** become rare **syn** see THIN

**rarefying osteitis** *n* **:** OSTEOPOROSIS

**rare gas** *n* **:** INERT GAS 2

**rare·ly** *adv* **1** *obs* **:** not thickly, not densely, not compactly **2 :** not often **:** SELDOM ⟨sometimes it is of clay, ~ of gold, most commonly of porcelain —Lafcadio Hearn⟩ **3 :** with rare skill **:** BEAUTIFULLY, EXCELLENTLY ⟨played so ~ on the flageolet —Sir Walter Scott⟩ **4 :** in an exceptional degree **:** EXTREMELY, UNUSUALLY ⟨she was ~ beautiful⟩

**rare·ness** *n* -ES **:** the quality or state of being rare **:** RARITY

**rarer** *comparative of* RARE

**¹rareripe** \(ˈ)=ˈ=\ *adj* [³*rare* + *ripe*] **:** early ripe **:** ripe before others or earlier than usual

**²rareripe** \ˈ"\ *n* -S **1 :** an early ripening fruit or vegetable **2** *dial* **:** GREEN ONION

**rarest** *superlative of* RARE

**raring** *adj* [fr. pres. part. of ⁴*rare*] **:** full of enthusiasm or eagerness — usu. used with an infinitive ⟨all set and ~ to go⟩

**rar·i·o·ra** \ˌra(a)rēˈōrə\ *n pl* [NL, fr. L, neut. pl. of *rarior*, comp. of *rarus* rare — more at RARE] **:** rare collectors' items (as books) ⟨a place in ~ —A.E.Norman⟩

**rar·ish** \ˈra(a)rish, ˈrer-\ *adj* [¹*rare* + *-ish*] **:** somewhat rare

**rar·i·ty** \ˈra(a)rəd·ē, ˈrer-, -rətē, -i\ *n* -ES [L *raritas*, fr. *rarus* rare + *-itas* -ity — more at RARE] **1 a :** the quality or state of being rare ⟨relish the ~ of his wit⟩ **b :** the fact of being rare **:** INFREQUENCY, SCARCITY ⟨occurs only twice or three times, or with extreme ~ —Joshua Whatmough⟩ **2 :** something rare

**¹ra·ro·i·an** \ˌrärəˈwēən\ *adj, usu cap* [*Raroia*, island in the Tuamotu archipelago in the southern Pacific + E *-an*] **:** of or relating to the island of Raroia

**²raroian** \ˈ"\ *n* -S *cap* **:** a native or inhabitant of Raroia Island

**¹rar·o·ton·gan** \ˌrarəˈtäŋgən\ *adj, usu cap* [*Rarotonga*, chief island of the Cook islands in the southern Pacific + E *-an*] **:** of or relating to the island or language of Rarotonga

**²rarotongan** \ˈ"\ *n* -S *cap* **1 :** a native or inhabitant of Rarotonga **2 :** the Polynesian language of the Rarotongan people

**¹ras** \ˈräs\ *n* -ES [Ar *raʼs* lit., head] **1 :** CAPE, HEADLAND **2 :** an Ethiopian prince or feudal overlord; *also* **:** the ruler of an Ethiopian province **3 :** a local Italian Fascist boss orig. acting as a despot in his area

**²ras** \ˈrəs, ˈräs\ *also* **ra·sa** \-sə\ *n, pl* **rasas** [native name in India] **:** a Manipuri dance drama enacting the legend of the deity Krishna and his consort Radha

**ra·sa·ma·la** \ˌrasəˈmälə\ *n* -S [Malay (*kayu*) *raksamala*, (*kayu*) *raʼsamala*, fr. *kayu* tree + *raksamala*, *raʼsamala*, a kind of fragrance, fr. Skt *surasa* sweet + *mālā* garland] **:** a southern Asiatic timber tree (*Altingia excelsa*) of the family Hamamelidaceae yielding a fragrant resin

**ras·bo·ra** \razˈbōrə, ˈrazbərə\ *n* [NL, fr. a native name in the East Indies] **1** *cap* **:** a genus of tiny brilliantly colored freshwater fishes (family Cyprinidae) of which several forms are often kept in the tropical aquarium **2** -S **:** any fish of the genus *Rasbora*

**ras·ca·cio** \räˈskä(,)syō\ *n* -S [Sp *rascacio*, *rescacio*, fr. Prov *rascasso*, fr. fem. of *rascàs* mangy, rough, wrinkled, fr. *rasco* ringworm, fr. *rascà* to scratch, scrape, fr. (assumed) VL *rasicare* — more at RASH] **1 :** a variegated spinose scorpion fish (*Scorpaena plumieri*) of the western Atlantic from Cape Cod to Brazil **2 :** any of various scorpion fishes

**¹ras·cal** \ˈraskəl, ˈraas-, *chiefly Brit* ˈrȧs-\ *n* -S [ME *rascaile*, *rascaille*, prob. fr. ONF *rasque* mud, ordure] **1 a** *obs* **:** the lowest class of an army or populace **:** RABBLE **b** *archaic* **:** a member of the rabble ⟨he was rich and I was still a ~ —Robert Frost⟩ **2** *obs* **a :** the inferior and ill-conditioned animals in a herd of deer **b :** a deer of this kind **3 a :** a mean, unprincipled, or dishonest person **:** ROGUE ⟨believed that dishonesty in public office . . . was more dangerous than incompetence, and he rode past the blatherskites to get at the ~*s* —James Thurber⟩ **b :** a person often of a pleasingly mischievous nature ⟨nostalgic sketches of many lovable ~*s* —*Linguaphone Mag.*⟩ ⟨the Yankee . . . was already established as a comic ~ —Bergen Evans⟩ **syn** see VILLAIN

**²rascal** \ˈ"\ *adj* [ME *rascayl*, fr. *rascaile*, *rascaille*, n.] **:** of, forming, or befitting the rabble **:** LOW, MEAN, BASE ⟨~ fiddler —Shak.⟩ ⟨the ~ many —Edmund Spenser⟩ ⟨a battered ~ guard —Vachel Lindsay⟩

**ras·cal·dom** \-dəm\ *n* -S **:** the whole body of rascals

**ras·cal·i·ty** \raˈskaləd·ē, -lətē, -i, *chiefly Brit* rȧˈ-\ *n* -ES **1 :** the rascals forming a group or class **:** RABBLE **2 a :** the character or actions of a rascal **:** KNAVERY ⟨more evidence of ~ and selfishness than disinterested benevolence —Daniel Aaron⟩ **b :** a rascally act ⟨political *rascalities*⟩

**ras·cal·lion** \raˈskalyən\ *n* -S [¹*rascal* + *-ion* (as in *cullion*)] **:** RAPSCALLION

**¹ras·cal·ly** \ˈrask(ə)lē, ˈraas-, -li, *chiefly Brit* ˈrȧs-\ *adj* [¹*rascal* + *-ly*] **1** *obs* **:** of or relating to the rabble **2 :** of or characteristic of a rascal **:** meanly tricky or dishonest **:** MEAN, BASE, WORTHLESS ⟨notorious for their quarrelsome and ~ proclivities —Jack London⟩ ⟨our ~ porter is fallen fast asleep —Jonathan Swift⟩

**²rascally** \ˈ"\ *adv* **:** in a rascally fashion

**ras·cal·ry** \-kəlrē, -ri\ *n* -ES **:** RASCALITY

**ras·casse** \raˈskas\ *n* -S [F, fr. Prov *rascasso* rascacio — more at RASCACIO] **:** RASCACIO 2

**ra·sce·ta** \rəˈsēd·ə\ *n pl* [ML *raseta*, fr. Ar *rāḥah* palm of the hand] **:** transverse creases of the skin on the palmar surface of the wrist

**ra·scette** \raˈset\ *n* -S [F, fr. ML *raseta*] **:** a line crossing the wrist below the palm of the hand that is sometimes held by palmists to provide additional indication of a strong or weak constitution — called also *bracelet*; see PALMISTRY illustration

**ra·schel knitting** \(ˈ)räˈshel-\ *n* [fr. *Raschel* (*machine*), a kind of loom, fr. G *Raschelmaschine*, after *Rachel* (Elisa R. Félix) †1858 Fr. actress] **:** warp knitting resembling tricot but usu. coarser and with openwork patterns

**ra·schig ring** \ˈräshəg-\ *n, usu cap 1st R* [fr. the name *Raschig*] **:** a small hollow cylinder having a length about equal to the diameter, made usu. of metal, carbon, or ceramic material, and used as packing material for chemical towers

**¹rase** *vt* [ME *rasen*, alter. of *racen* — more at ³RACE] *obs* **:** PLUCK, PULL, SNATCH

**²rase** \ˈrāz\ *vb* -ED/-ING/-S [ME *rasen*, fr. MF *raser*, fr. (assumed) VL *rasare*, fr. L *rasus*, past part. of *radere* to scrape, shave — more at RAT] *vt* **1 a** *obs* **:** to slash, tear, or scratch with something sharp **b :** to form by carving or engraving **:** INCISE **2 a :** to rub, scrape, or scratch out or off **:** ERASE **b** *obs* **:** alter by erasing **3 :** RAZE 1 ~ *vi* **:** to make an incised mark

**rased** *adj, heraldry* **:** ERASED

**ras·er** \ˈrāzə(r)\ *n* -S **:** one that rases

**ras·gā·do** \räsˈgä(,)dō\ *n* -S [Sp, lit., tear, rip, fr. past part. of *rasgar* to tear, rip, alter. (influenced by *rascar* to scratch, fr. — assumed — VL *rasicare*) of *resgar*, fr. L *resecare* to cut loose, cut off, fr. *re-* + *secare* to cut — more at RASH, SAW] **:** the arpeggio effect produced by sweeping the strings with the thumb in guitar playing

**¹rash** \ˈrash, -aa(ə)sh, -aish\ *adj* -ER/-EST [ME (northern dial.) *rasch* active, quick, eager, prob. fr. MD or MLG; akin to OHG *rasc* fast, hurried, strong, clever, ON *röskr* brave, vigorous, and perh. to OE *ræd*, *ræth* quick, OHG *rado* quickly, Goth *rathizo* easier] **1** *chiefly dial* **:** full of life and vigor **:** ENERGETIC **2 :** characterized by or proceeding from lack of deliberation or caution **:** acting, done, or expressed with undue haste or disregard for consequences **:** imprudently involving or incurring risk **:** PRECIPITATE ⟨in Elizabethan drama the critic is ~ who will assert boldly that any play is by a single hand —T.S.Eliot⟩ ⟨given to ~ generalization from inadequate data —V.L.Parrington⟩ ⟨do something ~ that he will forever repent —George Meredith⟩ **3** *obs* **:** working quickly and strongly **:** quickly effective ⟨do this . . . with no ~ potion but with a lingering dram —Shak.⟩ **4** *obs* **:** PRESSING, URGENT ⟨my matter is so ~ —Shak.⟩ **syn** see ADVENTUROUS

**²rash** \ˈ"\ *adv* [ME (northern dial.) *rasshe* swiftly, vigorously, fr. *rasch*, adj.] *archaic* **:** RASHLY

**³rash** \ˈ"\ *n* -ES [modif. of MF *ras*, fr. OIt *raso*, fr. *raso*, adj., smooth, fr. L *rasus*, past part. of *radere* to scrape, shave — more at RAT] **:** an English clothing fabric of the 16th, 17th, and 18th centuries made of silk or wool or silk and wool

**⁴rash** \ˈ"\ *n* -ES [obs. F *rache* scurf, fr. OF *rasche*, *rache*, fr. OF *raschier* to scratch (attested only in the meaning "to spit"), fr. (assumed) VL *rasicare*, fr. L *rasus*, past part. of *radere* to scrape, shave — more at RAT] **1 a :** an eruption on the body typically with little or no elevation **:** EXANTHEM **b :** a large number of instances or manifestations in the same period ⟨the ~ of archaeological forgeries that had broken out all over town —John Kobler⟩ ⟨fiesta week is also a ~ of lavish parties —Ray Duncan⟩ **2 :** coal so mixed with waste as to be unsalable **:** dirty coal

**⁵rash** \ˈ"\ *dial var of* RUSH

**¹rash·er** \ˈrashə(r), ˈraash-, ˈraish-\ *n* -S [perh. fr. obs. *rash* to cut, slash (fr. ME *rashen*, prob. alter. of *rasen*) + *-er* — more at RASE] **:** a thin slice of bacon or ham broiled or fried; *also* **:** a portion (as of bacon) consisting of several slices ⟨eggs with a ~ of bacon⟩

**²rasher** \ˈ"\ *n* -S [perh. modif. of Sp *rescacio*, *rascacio* rascacis — more at RASCACIO] **:** a large brick-red or vermilion rockfish (*Sebastodes miniatus*) of the Pacific coast from Vancouver Island to southern California

**rash·ing** \-shiŋ, -shēŋ\ *n* -S [perh. fr. E dial. *rash* brittle + *-ing* — more at ¹RASH] **:** soft flaky rock or clay immediately beneath a coal seam that is readily mixed with the coal in mining

**rash·ly** *adv* **:** in a rash manner

**rash·ness** *n* -ES **:** the quality or state of being rash

**rasing** *pres part of* RASE

**rasing iron** *n* **:** a caulker's tool for cleaning out seams before recaulking — compare RAVEHOOK

**ras·kol·nik** \rəˈskȯlnik\ *n, pl* **raskolniks** \-ks\ *or* **raskol·ni·ki** \-nəkē\ *usu cap* [Russ *raskol'nik*, fr. *raskol* schism (fr. *raz-*, prefix denoting separation — fr. OSlav — + *-kol*, fr. *kolot'* to separate, divide) + *-nik*, n. suffix denoting a person engaged in or connected with something specified; akin to Lith *kalti* to beat, forge — more at HALT (lame)] **:** a dissenter from the Russian Orthodox Church and member of one of the several groups (as the Doukhobors, Khlysty) developing from the schism of the 17th century in protest against liturgical reforms — called also *Old Believer*, *Old Ritualist*

**rason** *var of* RHASON

**rasophore** *var of* RHASOPHORE

**ra·so·res** \rəˈsōr(,)ēz\ *n pl, cap* [NL, fr. LL, pl. of *rasor* one that scrapes, fr. L *rasus* (past part. of *radere* to scrape, shave) + *-or* — more at RAT] *in former classifications* **:** an order of birds comprising the Gallinae and the Columbae or coextensive with Gallinae

**ra·so·ri·al** \-ˈsōrēəl, -sȯr-\ *adj* [NL *Rasores* + E *-ial*] **1** *of a bird* **:** habitually scratching the ground in search of food **2 :** of or relating to the Rasores **:** GALLINACEOUS

**ra·sor·ite** \ˈrāzə,rīt\ *n* -S [C. M. *Rasor*, 20th cent. Am. engineer + E *-ite*] **:** KERNITE

**¹rasp** \ˈrasp, -aa(ə)-, -ai-, -ȧ-\ *vb* -ED/-ING/-S [ME *raspen*, fr. (assumed) MF *rasper* (whence *raper*), of Gmc origin; akin to OHG *raspōn* to scrape together, collect; akin to OE *gehrespan* to tear, OFris *hrespa* to tear, OHG *hrespan* to pluck, and perh. to OE *hreppan* to touch — more at RAFFLE] *vt* **1 :** to rub or grate with something rough or harsh ⟨a cataract that ~*s* away the rock⟩; *specif* **:** to abrade with a rasp ⟨~ off any irregularities or sharp corners⟩ **2 :** to grate harshly upon **:** serve as an irritant to ⟨some sounds ~ the ear⟩ ⟨remarks that ~ the nerves⟩ **3 :** to utter in an irritated or grating tone ⟨~ out a denial⟩ ~ *vi* **1 :** to grate or scrape something **2 :** to produce or move while producing a grating sound ⟨the chalk ~*ed* across the blackboard⟩

**²rasp** \ˈ"\ *n* -S [MF *raspe*, fr. OF, fr. (assumed) *rasper*] **1 :** a coarse file on which the cutting prominences are distinct points raised by the oblique stroke of a sharp punch instead of lines raised by a chisel (as on the true file) — called also *rasp-cut file* **2 :** a machine or contrivance used for rasping or grating **3 :** an act or effect of rasping **:** a rasping sound, sensation, or effect ⟨the ~ of a cricket⟩; *specif* **:** an unpleasant quality imparted to the voice by excessive tightness of the muscles of the larynx and pharynx ⟨some voices have the hail-fellow ~ of the western plains —R.M.Hodesh⟩ **4 a :** a roughened surface (as in the stridulating organ of an insect) **b :** TOOTH, DENTICLE ⟨lamprey eels . . . with row upon row of horny ~*s* in place of teeth —Robert Kane⟩

rasp 1

**³rasp** \ˈ"\ *n* -S [short for earlier *raspis*, of unknown origin] *chiefly dial* **:** RASPBERRY

**ras·pa** \ˈräspə\ *n* -S [MexSp, fr. Sp *raspar* to scrape, of Gmc origin; akin to OHG *raspōn* to scrape together, collect — more at RASP] **:** a modern Mexican couple dance consisting of an alternate shuffling of the feet forward and backward and ending with a polka pivot

**ras·pa·dor** \ˌräspəˈdō(ə)r\ *n* -S [Sp, fr. *raspado* (past part. of *raspar* to scrape) + *-or*] **:** a crude machine for decorticating or scraping fiber of henequen or sisal

**ras·pa·to·ry** \ˈraspə,tōrē\ *n* -ES [ML *raspatorium*, fr. *raspatus* (past part. of *raspare* to rasp, of Gmc origin; akin to OHG *raspōn* to scrape together, collect) + L *-orium* -ory — more at RASP] **:** a file or rasp used (as for scraping bone) in surgery

**rasp-bar cylinder** \ˈ=,=-\ *n* **:** a thresher or combine cylinder with coarse rasps instead of teeth bolted to the cylinder bars

**rasp·ber·ry** \ˈraz,berē, ˈrȧ|, -,b(ə)rē, -ri *sometimes* |s(,)b- — *see* BERRY\ *n* [³*rasp* + *berry*] **1 a :** any of various usu. black or red sweet juicy edible berries that technically are aggregate fruits consisting of numerous small drupes crowded upon a fleshy receptacle from which they are easily separated when ripe and that are usu. rounder and smaller than the closely related blackberries **b :** any of various plants of the genus *Rubus* that bear raspberries and include various cultivated forms derived chiefly from a common European raspberry (*Rubus idaeus*), an American red raspberry (*R. strigosus*), and the blackcap **2 a :** a variable color averaging a dark purplish red that is bluer and paler than pansy purple, lighter and stronger than raisin, and bluer, lighter, and stronger than Bokhara or dahlia purple (sense 1) **b :** a dark red that is bluer, lighter, and stronger than average garnet or average wine and bluer and paler than cranberry **3 a :** a sound of contempt or derision made by trilling the extended tongue between the protruded lips **b :** something resembling a raspberry in expressing dislike, disapproval, or derision

**raspberry beetle** *n* **:** a small brownish beetle (*Byturus unicolor*) whose adults feed on the buds and whose larvae feed on the fruits of raspberries

**raspberry bug** *n* **:** a very small nearly black negro bug (*Corimelaena pulicaria*) that infests the raspberry, strawberry, and blackberry giving them a very disagreeable flavor

**raspberry cane borer** *n* **:** a slender black and yellow longicorn beetle (*Oberea bimaculata*) having a larva that is a borer in the canes of raspberries, blackberries, and sometimes roses

**raspberry cane maggot** *n* **:** the larva of a small fly (*Pegomya rubivora*) of the family Anthomyiidae that mines in the shoots of the raspberry and blackberry

**raspberry curl** *n* **:** LEAF CURL c

**raspberry fruit worm** *n* **:** the larva of either of two dermestid beetles (*Byturus bakeri* or *B. rubi*) that bores into the fruit of raspberries

**raspberry glacé** *n* **:** a grayish purplish red that is redder, lighter, and stronger than average rose plum or Aztec maroon and redder and deeper than tourmaline pink

**raspberry jamwood** *n* **:** the very hard lustrous wood of an Australian tree (*Acacia acuminata*) having a fragrance suggestive of raspberry jam
**rasp·ber·ry·like** \-,līk\ *adj* **:** resembling the raspberry
**raspberry mosaic** *n* **:** any of several virus diseases affecting raspberries and sometimes other cane fruits and causing leaf mottling and yellowing
**raspberry red** *n* **:** a moderate red that is yellower and lighter than cerise, claret (sense 3a), Harvard crimson (sense 1), or Turkey red and yellower, lighter, and very slightly less strong than average strawberry (sense 2a) — called also *jacqueminot*
**raspberry root borer** *n* **:** the larva of a large clearwing moth (*Bembecia marginata*) of the family Aegeriidae that bores in the roots and canes of the raspberry and blackberry
**raspberry root rot** *n* **:** a very destructive rot of the crowns of raspberry bushes in Australia and New Zealand caused by an agaric (*Hypholoma fasciculare*)
**raspberry rose** *n* **:** a variable color averaging a moderate purplish red that is bluer and deeper than average rose, redder and deeper than violine pink, paler and slightly redder than magenta rose, and bluer and paler than fuchsia rose
**raspberry sawfly** *n* **:** a small black sawfly (*Monophadnoides geniculatus*) with reddish abdomen the spiny greenish larva of which eats the leaves of the raspberry and blackberry
**raspberry streak** *n* **:** BLUESTEM 2b
**raspberry wine** *n* **:** a dark purplish red that is bluer and duller than redgrape or pansy purple, darker and slightly bluer than raisin, and bluer and paler than Bokhara
**raspberry yellows** *n pl but sing or pl in constr* **:** RASPBERRY MOSAIC
**rasp–cut file** \'=,=-\ *n* **:** RASP
**rasped** *adj* **1** *of a book cover* **:** having the sharp angles removed but not beveled **2** *of a book edge* **:** uncut but roughened with a coarse rasp to imitate a deckle edge
**rasp·er** \'raspə(r), -aa(ə)-,-ai-,-á-\ *n* -s **:** one that rasps: as **a :** an instrument or machine for rasping (as a file for removing the black surface from a burnt loaf of bread, a grater for beetroot or potatoes, a sawmill for reducing dyewoods to powder) **b :** one that smooths something (as of metal or wood) with a rasp **c :** a rasping fence
**rasp house** *n* **:** a house of correction formerly in use (as in Holland, Germany) whose prisoners rasped wood to powder for dyeing
**¹rasping** *n* -s [fr. gerund of ¹*rasp*] **:** a particle or piece separated by rasping ⟨~*s* of logwood⟩
**²rasping** *adj* [fr. pres. part. of ¹*rasp*] **1 :** GRATING, HARSH, IRRITATING ⟨a ~ sound⟩ ⟨a ~ smell⟩ ⟨~ inconveniences⟩ **2** *hunting* **a :** high or difficult to leap ⟨a ~ ditch⟩ ⟨a ~ fence⟩ **b :** very fast ⟨a ~ pace⟩ — **rasp·ing·ly** *adv* — **rasp·ing·ness** *n* -ES
**rasp·ish** \-pish, -pēsh\ *adj* [¹*rasp* + *-ish*] **:** IRRITABLE, RASPING
**rasp·ite** \'ra,spīt, 'rä,-\ *n* -s [G *raspit*, fr. Charles *Rasp*, 19th cent. Australian prospector + G *-it* -ite] **:** a mineral $PbWO_4$ consisting of lead tungstate occurring in yellow monoclinic crystals (hardness 2.5)
**rasp leaf** *n* [²*rasp*] **:** a virus disease of cherry characterized by the development of elongated outgrowths from the lower leaf surfaces and depressed lighter green areas on the upper leaf surfaces
**rasps** *pres 3d sing of* RASP, *pl of* RASP
**raspy** \'raspē, -aa(ə)-,-ai-,-á-, -pi\ *adj* -ER/-EST [¹*rasp* + *-y*] **1 a :** resembling the sound made by a rasp **:** GRATING, HARSH ⟨talks with a ~ New England twang —*New Yorker*⟩ **b :** having a rough texture ⟨pulled the ~ army blanket about my shoulders —Herbert Gold⟩ **2 :** RASPISH, IRRITABLE ⟨they were all ~ from lack of sleep —Ira Wolfert⟩
**rasse** \'rasə, 'ras\ *n* -s [Jav *rasé*] **:** a grizzled black-marked semiarboreal civet (*Viverricula malaccensis* or *V. indica*) that is related to but is smaller than the common civet, is native to China and the East Indies, and furnishes a perfume prized by the Javanese — called also *lesser civet*
**ras·sen·kreis** \'räsᵊn,krīs\ *n, pl* **rassenkrei·se** \-īzə\ *usu cap* [G, fr. *rasse* race + *kreis* circle, cycle] **:** a polytypic species esp. when exhibiting a pattern of geographical replacement of one type by another
**ras sham·ra** \'räs'shamrə\ *adj, usu cap R & S* [fr. *Ras Shamra*, Syria] **1 :** of or from the village of Ras Shamra, Syria, site of the ancient city of Ugarit **2 :** of or being the alphabetical cuneiform script of Ugaritic discovered on a collection of clay tablets excavated at Ras Shamra between 1929 and 1936 **:** UGARITIC
**ras·ta·couère** *or* **ras·ta·quouère** \¦rastə¦kwe(ə)r\ *n, pl* **rastacouères** *or* **rastaquouères** \-(z)\ [F, fr. AmerSp *arrastracuero*, fr. Sp *arrastra* he drags (3d sing. pres. ind. of *arrastrar* to drag) + *cuero* skin, hide, fr. L *corium* — more at ARRASTRA, CUIRASS] **:** a foreign parvenu
**ra·stel·lus** \rə'steləs\ *n* -ES [NL, fr. L, small rake, mattock, dim. of *rastrum* rake, mattock] **:** a toothed structure like a rake on the basal segment of the chelicera of many burrowing spiders that is of use in digging
**ras·ter** \'rastə(r)\ *n* -s [G, fr. L *raster, rastrum* rake, mattock, fr. *radere* to scrape, rake, shave — more at RAT] **:** the area upon which the image is reproduced in the cathode-ray tube of a television set
**ras·tik** *or* **ras·tick** \'rastək\ *n* -s [Turk *rastik*, fr. Per *rāsukht*] **:** any of various hair dyes: as **a :** a paste made formerly from nutgalls roasted with copper and iron filings and oil **b :** a mixture containing pyrogallol and a metallic salt (as ferrous sulfate)
**ra·sure** \'rāzhə(r)\ *n* -s [MF, fr. L *rasura*, fr. *rasus* (past part. of *radere* to scrape, shave) + *-ura* -ure — more at RAT] **:** the act of rasing, scraping, or erasing **:** ERASURE, OBLITERATION
**¹rat** \'rat, *usu* -ad·+V\ *n* -s [ME, fr. OE *ræt*; akin to OS *ratta* rat, MLG *rotte*, MD *ratte*, OHG *ratta, rato, ratza* rat, *rāzi* wild, sharp to the taste, L *rodere* to gnaw, *radere* to scrape, shave, W *rhathell* rasp; basic meaning: to scrape, gnaw] **1 a :** any of numerous rodents (family Muridae) of *Rattus* and related genera that differ from the murid mice by their usu. considerably larger size and by features of the teeth and other structures and that include forms (as the brown rat, the black rat, and the roof rat) which live in and about human habitations and in ships, have become naturalized by commerce in most parts of the world, and are destructive pests consuming or destroying vast quantities of food and other goods and acting as vectors of various diseases (as bubonic plague) **b :** any of various other rodents of similar size and appearance — used often in combination ⟨muskrat⟩ ⟨spiny ~⟩ **2 a :** one who deserts his party, friends, or associates (as in adversity or for selfish ends) **b (1) :** a printer who works for less than the established or prevailing rate of pay **(2) :** SCAB 4b **c :** a despicable or contemptible person **:** LOUSE, HEEL ⟨hoodlums, shysters, and assorted ~*s* —Stanley Walker⟩; *esp* **:** INFORMER 3, STOOL PIGEON **3 :** a pad with tapering ends over which a woman's hair is arranged for an illusion of greater quantity **4 :** an olive gray that is deeper and slightly greener than the color mouse, deeper than nutria, and redder and deeper than stone gray
**²rat** \"\ *vb* **ratted; ratted; ratting; rats** *vi* **1 :** to desert one's party or associates for personal advantage ⟨incurred the reproach of having *ratted*, solely by his inability to follow the friends of his early days —Thomas De Quincey⟩ **2 :** to catch rats; *esp* **:** to hunt rats with a dog **3 :** to work as a rat **:** SCAB; *specif* **:** to work as a printer for less than the established or customary rate of pay **4 :** to act as an informer or stool pigeon **:** SQUEAL ⟨*ratting* on the men they live with —J.M. Murtagh & Sara Harris⟩ ~ *vt* **1 :** to employ scabs or strikebreakers in (an industry) **2 :** to give (hair) the effect of greater quantity by use of a rat or style of combing — **rat on :** to go back on (as an agreement or statement) **:** welsh on **:** RECANT ⟨*ratted on* her debts —Ellery Sedgwick⟩ ⟨*ratting on* a private confession written to him fourteen years ago —William Empson⟩
**³rat** \"\ *vt* **ratted; ratted; ratting; rats** [prob. euphemism for ¹*rot*] **:** DAMN, CONFOUND, DRAT — used as a mild oath ⟨~ me if it was not a meritorious action —Henry Fielding⟩
**ra·ta** \'räd·ə\ *n* -s [Maori] **1 :** a tree of the genus *Metrosideros*; *esp* **:** either of two New Zealand timber trees (*M. robusta* and *M. lucida*) **2 :** the hard dark red wood of a rata tree used by the Maoris for paddles and war clubs **3 :** POLYNESIAN CHESTNUT

**rat·abil·i·ty** *or* **rate·abil·i·ty** \,rād·ə'biləd·ē, ,rātə'-, -lətē, -i\ *n* **:** the quality or state of being ratable
**rat·able** *or* **rate·able** \'==bəl\ *adj* [*rate* + *-able*] **1 :** capable of being rated or estimated ⟨~ taking of gas —W.F.Cloud⟩ **2 :** made or reckoned according to a proportionate rate **:** PROPORTIONAL ⟨a ~ distribution of an estate⟩ **3** *Brit* **:** TAXABLE ⟨the ~ value of property⟩ ⟨the analysis of ~ values —*Country Life*⟩
**rat·ably** *or* **rate·ably** \-blē, -bli\ *adv* **:** in a ratable manner **:** PROPORTIONATELY ⟨distribute the net proceeds . . . among the shareholders ~ —T.J.Grayson⟩
**rat·a·fia** \,rad·ə'fēə\ *n* -s [F] **1 :** a liqueur made by infusion and usu. not distilled, flavored with plum, peach, and apricot kernels and bitter almonds, and supplied with a base of brandy and fruit juices **2 :** a small sweet biscuit made from almond paste
**ratama** *var of* RETAMA
**ratan** *var of* RATTAN
**ra·ta·na church** \rə'tänə-\ *n, cap R&C* [after Wiremu Tahupotiki *Ratana*, 20th cent. New Zealand religious leader] **:** a Christian sect organized in New Zealand about 1925 that emphasizes faith healing and the agency of angels
**rat·a·plan** \,rad·ə'plan, -aa(ə)n\ *n* -s [F, of imit. origin] **:** the rhythmic sound of beating (as from a drum or the hoofs of a galloping horse) ⟨the ~ of machine guns —H.W.Baldwin⟩
**rat–a–tat** \¦rad·ə¦tat, -atə¦-, *usu* -tad·+V\ *or* **rat–a–tat–tat** \¦==¦=¦=\ *n* -s [imit.] **:** a sound of sharp, repeated knocking or tapping ⟨a peremptory *rat-a-tat* on the door⟩
**ra·ta·touille** \rätätüy\ *n* -s [F, fr. *touiller* to stir, fr. L *tudiculare*, fr. *tudes* hammer, fr. the root of *tundere* to beat — more at STUTTER] **:** a stew made of eggplant, tomatoes, green peppers, squash, and sometimes meat and seasoned with garlic and other condiments
**ratbag** \'=,=\ *n, Austral* **:** an odd or disagreeable person
**rat bandicoot** *n* **:** any of numerous small ratlike bandicoots that are related to the rabbit bandicoots but have shorter ears and hindlegs
**rat–bite fever** \'=,=-\ *n* **:** either of two febrile diseases of man commonly transmitted by the bite of a rat or other animal vector: **a :** a septicemia marked by irregular relapsing fever, rashes, muscular pain and arthritis, and great weakness and caused by a microorganism (*Streptobacillus moniliformis* or *Haverhillia multiformis*) that is included among the typical bacteria or regarded as an actinomycete **b :** a disease that is marked by sharp elevation of temperature, swelling of lymph glands, eruption, recurrent inflammation of the bite wound, and muscular pains in the part where the bite wound occurred and that is caused by a bacterium (*Spirillum minus*) — called also *sodoku*
**ratcatcher** \'=,==\ *n* **1 :** a person or animal employed in exterminating rats **2** *chiefly Brit* **:** informal hunting dress; *esp* **:** a tweed jacket with tan breeches
**¹ratch** *var of* RACH
**²ratch** \'rach\ *n* -ES [origin unknown] *chiefly dial* **:** a blaze on an animal's face
**³ratch** \"\ *vi* -ED/-ING/-ES [back-formation fr. *raught*, after E *caught*: *catch*] *chiefly dial* **:** STRETCH, REND
**⁴ratch** \"\ *n* -ES **:** the distance between nip of back and front drafting rolls in spinning
**⁵ratch** \"\ *n* -ES [G *ratsche, rätsche* clapper, rattle, ratchet, fr. *ratschen, rätschen* to rattle, fr. MHG *ratzen*; akin to MHG *razzeln* to rattle — more at RATTLE] **1 :** RATCHET 1 **2 :** a notched bar with which a pawl or click works to prevent reversal of motion
**⁶ratch** \"\ *vt* -ED/-ING/-ES **1 :** to cut gear teeth on (a wheel) **2 :** to turn (as a tool) by or as if by a ratchet and pawl
**rat cheese** *also* **rat–trap cheese** *n* **:** STORE CHEESE
**¹ratch·et** *or* **rach·et** \'rachət, *usu* -əd·+V\ *n* -s [alter. (influenced by ⁵*ratch*) of earlier *rochet*, fr. F, alter. of MF *rocquet* head of a lance, of Gmc origin; akin to OHG *rocko, roccho* distaff — more at ROCK (distaff)] **1 :** a pawl, click, or detent for holding or propelling a ratchet wheel **2 :** a mechanism that consists of a bar or wheel having inclined teeth into which a pawl drops so that motion can be imparted to the wheel or bar or can be governed or prevented and that is used in a hand tool (as a carpenter's brace or screwdriver) to allow effective motion in one direction only; *specif* **:** a mechanism on a typewriter roll for governing the vertical spacing of the lines **3 :** a tool with a toothed blade used to turn the toothed wheels that clamp and release patent blocks or bases in printing
**²ratchet** \"\ *vb* **ratchetted; ratchetted; ratchetting; ratchets** *vi* **:** to move or operate by a ratchet ~ *vt* **:** to furnish (as a machine or tool) with a ratchet
**ratchet brace** *n* **1 :** a carpenter's bitbrace that has a ratchet-driven chuck and is used in close quarters where complete revolutions of the handle are impossible **2 :** a lever that has a ratchet-driven chuck at one end and is used for drilling holes in metal by hand
**ratchet coupling** *n* **:** a shaft coupling having a ratchet and pawl or a similar device whereby the driven member may be turned in one direction only by the driving member and may also overrun the driving member
**ratchet crank** *n* **:** a crank mounted on but not keyed to a shaft which it moves intermittently through a ratchet wheel and pawl
**ratchet drill** *n* **:** a hand drill in which the drill holder is revolved intermittently by a lever through a ratchet wheel and pawl
**ratchet jack** *n* **:** a jack raised or lowered by means of a pawl and ratchet
**ratchet screwdriver** *n* **:** a screwdriver that is operated by the reciprocating motion of the handle and that usu. has a removable screwdriver bit
**ratchet stop** *n* **:** a device for limiting the motion of machinery in one direction that consists of a ratchet wheel or bar and a pawl which acts as a positive stop or controls the motion through a friction brake
**ratchet thread** *n* **:** BUTTRESS THREAD
**ratchet tooth** *n* **:** a gear tooth one side of which is radial and the other inclined so that a pawl will catch on the former and slide over the latter
**ratchet wheel** *n* **1 :** a notched or toothed wheel either held in position or turned by an engaging detent, pawl, or click **2 :** the retaining wheel over the mainspring arbor of a timepiece
**ratchet wrench** *n* **:** a wrench in which torque is applied in one direction only by means of a ratchet
**ratch·ety** \'rachəd·ē, -chətē, -i\ *adj* **:** resembling the operation of a ratchet **:** JERKY, IRREGULAR, CREAKY
**rat chinchilla** *n* **:** ABROCOME
**ratching** *n* -s [fr. gerund of ³*ratch*] **:** extra draft due to excess speed of the mule carriage over the roller delivery in spinning
**rat–claw foot** \'=,=-\ *n* **:** a claw-and-ball foot on a piece of furniture having the claws very sharp and thin

ratchet wheel: *1* wheel, *2* reciprocating lever, *3* click, pawl, or ratchet for communicating motion, *4* pawl for preventing backward motion

**¹rate** \'rāt, *usu* -ād·+V\ *vb* -ED/-ING/-S [ME *raten*, perh. of Scand origin; akin to Sw *rata* to find fault, blame, despise, ON *hrata* to fall, stagger — more at CARDINAL] *vt* **1 :** to rebuke (as a person or a hunting dog) angrily or violently **:** SCOLD, UPBRAID ⟨shall have you soundly *rated* and dismissed —Rex Ingamells⟩ ⟨the proper words for *rating* foxhounds —C.E. Hare⟩ **2** *obs* **:** to drive away (a person or dog) by scolding ⟨*rated* mine uncle from the council board —Shak.⟩ ~ *vi* **:** to voice angry reprimands — usu. used with *at* ⟨like her none the less for *rating* at her —Alfred Tennyson⟩ **syn** see SCOLD
**²rate** \"\ *n* -s [ME, fr. MF, fr. ML *rata*, fr. L (*pro*) *rata* (*parte*) according to a fixed proportion, fr. *pro* for, according to + *rata* calculated, fixed (fem. of *ratus*, fr. past part. of *reri* to reckon, calculate) + *parte*, abl. of *pars* part — more at REASON] **1 a :** reckoned value **:** VALUATION ⟨stones whose ~*s* are . . . as fancy values them —Shak.⟩ ⟨appraised him at a low ~⟩ **b** *obs* **:** ESTIMATION ⟨wise men . . . in the ordinary ~ and esteem of the world —Daniel Defoe⟩ **2** *obs* **:** a fixed or established portion or measure **:** QUANTITY ⟨brought every man his present . . . a ~ year by year —2 Chron 9:24 (AV)⟩ **3 a :** a fixed relation (as of quantity, amount, or degree) between two things **:** RATIO ⟨~ of exchange⟩ **b :** a charge, payment, or price fixed according to a ratio, scale, or standard ⟨hotel ~*s*⟩ ⟨the publisher's usual ~ for short stories⟩ ⟨drapery fabrics bought at the ~ of a dollar a yard⟩ ⟨sold at cut ~*s*⟩: as **(1) :** a charge per unit of a public-service commodity (as electricity, gas, water) ⟨an electric ~ of 7 cents per kilowatt-hour⟩ **(2) :** a price or charge per unit of freight or passenger service (as cents per hundred pounds or dollars per ton, per car, per passenger-mile); *specif* **:** a common carrier charge shown on an official published tariff on file with a governmental regulatory agency **(3) :** the price charged an advertiser per unit of publication space or of radio or television time **(4) :** a unit charge or ratio used by the government for assessing taxes on property **(5)** *Brit* **:** a local tax — usu. used in pl. ⟨parish ~*s*⟩ **4 a :** quantity, amount, or degree of something measured per unit of something else (as time) ⟨at the ~ of 60 miles an hour⟩ ⟨a birth ~ of 40 per thousand of population⟩ ⟨~ of progress over the past century⟩ ⟨the ~ of corporate profits⟩ ⟨~ of depreciation⟩ **b :** amount of payment or charge based on some other amount ⟨~ of interest per annum⟩ ⟨~ of commission per bond sold⟩: as **(1) :** the wage paid on an incentive or time basis for a particular job **(2) :** the amount of premium per unit of insurance or exposure **5 a** *archaic* **:** relative behavior or manner **:** STYLE, FASHION — usu. used with *after* ⟨I proceed much after the old ~ —William Cowper⟩ **b :** relative condition or quality **:** RANK, KIND ⟨I am a spirit of no common ~ —Shak.⟩ **6 a :** the order or class to which a warship belongs determined according to a specified criterion (as size or armament) ⟨a ship of the first ~⟩ **b :** the class of a merchant ship for marine insurance determined by its relative safety as a risk (as A 1, A 2) **c :** the relative standing or grade of a sailor; *specif* **:** the rank of an enlisted man (as in the U. S. Navy) within a specified rating ⟨the ~ of radarman third class⟩ **7 :** the gain or loss in the running of a timepiece within a specified unit of time ⟨daily ~⟩ ⟨hourly ~⟩ — **at any rate** *adv* **1** *obs* **:** at any price **2 :** in any case **:** at least ⟨art . . . perhaps immature but *at any rate* virile —Alan McCulloch⟩ — **at this rate** *or* **at that rate** *adv* **:** under such conditions **:** this being so ⟨*at this rate*, he won't be elected⟩
**³rate** \"\ *vb* -ED/-ING/-S [ME *raten*, fr. *rate*, n.] *vt* **1** *obs* **:** to allot (a share) to ⟨had not *rated* him his part —Shak.⟩ **2 :** CONSIDER, REGARD ⟨*rated* an excellent golfer⟩ ⟨*rated* the highest office in the state⟩ **3 a :** to set an estimate on **:** APPRAISE, VALUE ⟨copper is *rated* . . . above its real value —Adam Smith⟩ ⟨buyers . . . ~ black broadcloth high for fall —*Women's Wear Daily*⟩ **b** *chiefly Brit* **:** to assess the value of (property) for taxing purposes **c** *archaic* **:** to calculate the total ⟨then must we ~ the cost —Shak.⟩ **d :** to determine or assign the relative rank or class of (as a ship or a seaman) **e :** to evaluate with reference to specific traits or given standards **:** GRADE ⟨~ the way the . . . companies treat their dealers —S.L.Payne⟩ ⟨each job was *rated* on a five-point scale —Mildred Mitchell⟩ **f :** to estimate the normal capacity or power of ⟨current flowing at the *rated* capacity —*Cannon Catalog*⟩ ⟨flooring system is *rated* to withstand a . . . fire and water test —*Amer. Builder*⟩ **4 :** to fix the amount of premium to be charged per unit of insurance or exposure on (a particular risk) **5 a :** to adjust (a timepiece) to a given rate of going (as by altering the effective length of the pendulum) **:** REGULATE **b :** to find the gain or loss of (a timepiece) in a given unit of time **c :** to pace or restrain (as a horse or oneself) in a race in order to conserve energy for the finish ⟨*rated* the 4-year-old . . . colt perfectly —F.M.Blunk⟩ **6 :** to have a right to **:** DESERVE ⟨most . . . do not ~ so much remembrance —*Harper's*⟩ ⟨sufficient appeal to ~ a network show —Charles Miller⟩ ~ *vi* **:** to be of consequence **:** RANK, COUNT ⟨human ingenuity was to ~ . . . as a vital national resource —*Steelways*⟩; *specif* **:** to enjoy a status of special privilege or consideration ⟨I never did ~ with him —Bess A. Garner⟩ **syn** DESERVE, ESTIMATE
**⁴rate** \"\ *dial Eng var of* RET
**rateable** *var of* RATABLE
**rate base** *n* **:** the valuation of a property that is used by a commission or court to determine the reasonableness of rates or taxes on it
**rate basis** *n* **:** the combination of factors that constitute the formula used in making a rate
**rate bill** *n* **:** a school fee collected from each pupil by American schools in the 18th and early 19th centuries
**rate–buster** \'=,==\ *n* **:** a pieceworker who produces to the utmost of his ability despite opposition by his fellows who fear that his high earnings may cause a reduction in the piece rate
**rated horsepower** *n* **:** the maximum power an airplane engine can develop without failure when operated continuously or for a specified long period under specified conditions
**rated load** *n* **:** the load a machine is designed to carry as usu. stated on the nameplate in appropriate power units (as of horsepower for motors and engines or of kilovolt amperes for alternating-current generators)
**rate–gene** \'=,=\ *n* **:** a gene controlling the speed at which a developmental process occurs and therefore indirectly the relative effectiveness of that process in competition with various others occurring at the same time
**ra·tel** \'rād·ᵊl, 'räd-\ *n* -s [Afrik, lit., rattle, fr. MD *ratele, ratel*; fr. its cry — more at RATTLE] **:** any of several powerful nocturnal carnivorous mammals of the genus *Mellivora* resembling the badger and having the pelt ashy gray above and black beneath (as the southern African *M. capensis* and the Indian *M. indica*)
**rate meter** *n* **:** an instrument that indicates the counting rate of an electronic counter — compare ²COUNTER e
**rate–of–climb indicator** *n* **:** a standard flight instrument that indicates the rate of ascent or descent of an airplane
**rate of exchange :** the amount of one currency that will buy a given amount of another
**rate of interest :** the percentage usu. on an annual basis that is paid by the borrower to the lender for a loan of money — compare INTEREST 3a
**rate of return :** the ratio of net railway operating income to the value of the property in common carrier use including allowance for working capital
**rate–of–rise thermostat** \¦==¦=-\ *n* **:** a thermostat that operates when the rate of increase of temperature exceeds a predetermined amount
**ratepayer** \'=,==\ *n, Brit* **:** TAXPAYER
**rat·er** \'rād·ə(r), -ātə-\ *n* -s [³*rate* + *-er*] **1 :** one that rates **:** a person who scores, estimates, or determines a rating (as of examination papers, merit of employees, or premium on property insurance) **2 :** a person or thing (as a ship) of a certain rating or class — usu. used in combination ⟨a *first-rater*⟩
**rate range** *n* **:** a series of rates of pay for the same job running from a stated minimum to a stated maximum
**rates** *pres 3d sing of* RATE, *pl of* RATE
**rate setter** *n* **:** a person charged with determining the proper rate of pay for a job esp. on an incentive rate basis
**rate up** *vt* **:** to class with risks paying a higher rate of premium in order to offset additional risk
**ratfish** \'=,=\ *n* **:** ²CHIMAERA 2; *esp* **:** a silvery iridescent white-spotted chimaera (*Hydrolagus colliei*) of cold deep waters of the Pacific coast of No. America
**rat flea** *n* **:** any of various fleas that occur on rats; *esp* **:** either of two fleas (*Nosopsyllus fasciatus* and *Xenopsylla cheopis*) that are carriers of bubonic plague
**rat goose** *n* **:** BRANT
**rat guard** *n* **:** one of the circular sheet metal shields fastened to the mooring lines of a vessel to prevent rats from boarding or leaving it
**rath** \'räth, 'rä\ *n* -s [IrGael *rāth*] **:** a usu. circular earthwork serving as stronghold and residence of an ancient Irish chief ⟨fairy denizens of ~ and hill —O.S.J.Gogarty⟩
**rat hare** *n* **:** PIKA
**¹rathe** \'rāth\ *adv* [ME, rapidly, fr. OE *hrathe, hræthe*; akin to MD *rade* rapidly, OHG *rado*; derivative fr. the stem of OE *hræd* rapid, fast] *chiefly dial* **:** early in the day, season, or period ⟨~ she rose —Alfred Tennyson⟩
**²rathe** \"\ *or* **rath** \'rath\ *adj* [ME, quick, rapid, fast, fr. OE *hræth*, alter. (influenced by *hrathe, hræthe*, adv.) of *hræd*; akin to MD & MLG *rat* quick, rapid, fast, OHG *hrad, rad*, ON *hrathr*, and perh. MIr *crothaim* I shake, Lith *kresti* to shake] *chiefly dial* **:** early in the day, the season, or year **:** done, com-

ing, or ready before others of its class or before the usual time or season; *specif* **:** early-blooming or early-bearing ⟨bring the ~ primrose that forsaken dies —John Milton⟩ ⟨the ~ wheat —W.E.Henley⟩ — **rathe·ness** *n* -ES

**¹rath·er** \'rat͟hə(r), ÷'rət͟h- *also* 'rät͟h- *or* 'ret͟h- *or* 'rāt͟h-\ *adv* [ME, fr. OE *hrathor*, comp. of *hrathe, hræthe* rapidly, quickly] **1** *dial chiefly Eng* **:** more quickly **:** EARLIER, BEFORE **2 :** with better reason or more propriety ⟨pity ~ than despise —Shak.⟩ **3 :** more readily or willingly **:** PREFERABLY ⟨my soul chooseth . . . death ~ than my life —Job 7:15 (AV)⟩ ⟨would ~ starve than pick the garbage dump —Erskine Caldwell⟩ — often used as an interjection to express decided affirmation ⟨"Do you smoke?" "*Rather!*" —J.D.Beresford⟩ **4 :** more properly or truly **:** more correctly speaking ⟨~ like a dream than an assurance —Shak.⟩ ⟨their inspiration or, ~, their idol⟩ **5 :** to the contrary **:** INSTEAD ⟨was no better but ~ grew worse —Mk 5:26 (RSV)⟩ ⟨no longer a traveler's nightmare, ~ his joy —Wyn Roberts⟩ **6 :** in some degree **:** SOMEWHAT, QUITE ⟨it's ~ cold⟩ ⟨a ~ unusual gesture⟩ ⟨~ a boring play⟩ ⟨shaped ~ like an onion⟩ ⟨~ on the childish side⟩ ⟨cost ten thousand or ~ more⟩ ⟨~ doubted the truth of the remark⟩ — **the rather 1** *obs* **:** the more quickly **:** the sooner ⟨asleep (whereto *the rather* shall his day's hard journey soundly invite him) —Shak.⟩ **2 :** the more so **:** all the more **:** ESPECIALLY ⟨you are come to me in happy time *the rather* for I have some sport in hand —Shak.⟩ ⟨all *the rather*⟩

**²rather** \"\ *verbal auxiliary* **:** prefer to — not often in formal use ⟨I ~ sleep than eat⟩

**¹ratheripe** \(ˈ)=ˌ=\ *also* **rathripe** \(ˈ)=ˌ=\ *adj* [¹*rathe* + *ripe*] *chiefly dial* **:** RARERIPE, PRECOCIOUS

**²ratheripe** \"\ *n, chiefly dial* **:** RARERIPE

**rath·er·ish** *pronunc at* RATHER + ish\ *adv* [¹*rather* + *-ish*] **:** SOMEWHAT, FAIRLY ⟨a ~ handsome fellow⟩

**rath·er·ly** *adv* [¹*rather* + *-ly*] *dial Brit* **:** RATHER, SOMEWHAT ⟨his deep voice that was like a mellow bell and trembled ~ —Hall Caine⟩

**rath·ite** \'rä,tīt, -,thīt\ *n* -S [G *rathit*, fr. G. vom *Rath* †1888 Ger. mineralogist + G *-it* -ite] **:** a mineral $Pb_{13}As_{18}S_{40}$ consisting of a lead arsenic sulfide occurring in dark gray metallic orthorhombic crystals (hardness 3, sp. gr. 5.4)

**rath·ke's pouch** \'rätkəz-\ *also* **rathke's pocket** *n, usu cap R* [after Martin H. *Rathke* †1860 Ger. anatomist] **:** a pouch of ectoderm that grows out from the upper surface of the embryonic stomodaeum and gives rise to the anterior lobe of the pituitary body

**rathole** \'=,=\ *n* **1 a :** a rat's burrow **b :** a hole gnawed by a rat **2 a :** a narrow opening, tunnel, or passageway **b :** a cramped space (as for storage or living quarters); *esp* **:** one that is oppressive or filthy ⟨cooped up in a ~ like this —Jack Ward⟩ **3 :** a seemingly bottomless or unfillable hole ⟨his last pile of money . . . went down the ~ when he tried to save an old friend from bankruptcy —Stanley Walker⟩

**raths·kel·ler** \'rät,skelə(r), 'rat,s-, 'rát,s-, 'rath,s-, 'raath-\ *n* -S [G *ratskeller* (formerly spelled *rathskeller*) restaurant in the basement of a town hall, fr. *rat* council (fr. MHG *rāt* advice, supply, council, fr. OHG *rāt* advice, supply) + *keller* cellar, basement, fr. OHG *kellāri*, fr. L *cellarium* — more at READ, CELLAR] **:** a restaurant located usu. below the street level and patterned after the cellar or basement of a German city hall where beer or wine is sold

**ra·tib·i·da** \rə'tibədə\ *n, cap* [NL] **:** a genus of perennial No. American composite herbs that are sometimes cultivated for their showy flower heads

**rat·i·cide** \'rad·ə,sīd\ *n* -S [¹*rat* + *-i-* + *-cide*] **:** a substance (as red squill) for killing rats

**rat·i·fi·ca·tion** \,rad·əfə'kāshən, -atə-\ *n* -S [ME, fr. MF or ML; MF, fr. ML *ratification-, ratificatio*, fr. *ratificatus* (past part. of *ratificare* to ratify) + L *-ion-, -io* -ion — more at RATIFY] **:** the act or process of ratifying **:** CONFIRMATION, SANCTION ⟨proposed . . . ~ of treaties by a simple majority of both houses of Congress —Vera M. Dean⟩

**rat·i·fi·ca·tion·ist** \-sh(ə)nəst\ *n* -S **:** an advocate of ratification (as of a treaty or contract)

**rat·i·fi·er** \'==,fī(ə)r\ *n* -S **:** one that ratifies

**rat·i·fy** \'rad·ə,fī, -atə-\ *vt* -ED/-ING/-ES [ME *ratifien*, fr. MF *ratifier*, fr. ML *ratificare*, fr. L *ratus* calculated, fixed, determined + *-ificare* -ify — more at RATE] **1 :** to approve and sanction esp. formally (as the act of an agent or servant) **:** make (as a treaty) valid or legally operative **:** CONFIRM ⟨~ the nomination⟩ ⟨~ the contract⟩ ⟨can by . . . refusal to ~ the adopted amendment prevent its coming into force —Herbert Weinschel⟩ ⟨~*ing* his precocious habit of smoking —Arnold Bennett⟩ **2 :** to confirm the truth of **:** VERIFY ⟨time had *ratified* the soundness of the idea⟩ ⟨merely ~*ing* a tradition —E.R. Bentley⟩

**rat·i·ha·bi·tion** \,rad·ēhə'bishən\ *n* -S [LL *ratihabition-, ratihabitio*, fr. L *ratus* fixed, determined + LL *habition-, habitio* act of having, fr. L *habitus* (past part. of *habēre* to move) + *-ion-, -io* -ion — more at RATE, GIVE] **:** RATIFICATION, SANCTION

**ra·ti·né** \rat°n'ā\ *or* **ra·tine** \", ra'tēn\ *n* -S [F *ratiné*, fr. past part. of *ratiner* to frieze, fr. *ratine* ratteen] **1** *also* **ratiné yarn :** a nubby ply yarn of various fibers made by twisting under tension a thick and a thin yarn **2 :** a rough bulky fabric often of cotton but also of other fibers that is usu. woven loosely in plain weave from ratiné yarns and is used for dresses, suits, and coats — called also *sponge cloth*

**¹rating** *n* -S [fr. gerund of ¹*rate*] **:** SCOLDING, REBUKE ⟨gave him a severe ~⟩

**²rating** *n* -S [fr. gerund of ³*rate*] **1 :** a classification according to grade **:** RANK: as **a :** the relative standing of a sailor in a ship's company ⟨had the ~ of boatswain's mate⟩ **b :** an assignment in an occupational group (as in the U.S. Navy) within which a petty officer holds a rate ⟨a petty officer with a ~ of radarman⟩ **c :** a specialist classification in the armed forces (as pilot, parachutist, gunner) **2** *chiefly Brit* **:** a naval enlisted man ⟨two officers and ten ~*s* aboard each vessel —*Manchester Guardian Weekly*⟩ **3 a :** a relative estimate or evaluation (as of status, achievement, or appeal) **:** STANDING, MARK ⟨his ~ was high⟩ ⟨the good academic ~ of the school⟩ ⟨a high ~ for honesty in government —J.A.Morris b. 1904⟩ ⟨had the highest ~ in the examination⟩ **b :** an estimate of the credit and responsibility of an individual or business concern **c :** estimation of an individual's traits and qualities (as interests, abilities, attitudes, or personality) by his indicated preferences on a scale of items **d :** an estimate of the percentage of the public listening to or viewing a particular radio or television program ⟨was Mr. Television himself . . . had a ~ of twenty-eight —Pete Martin⟩ **4 :** a stated operating limit of a machine expressible in power units (as in horsepower of a motor, kilowatts of a direct-current generator, or kilovolt amperes of an alternator) or in characteristics (as speed, voltage, or frequency) — compare DUTY 5b

**rating badge** *n* **:** a distinctive mark of a petty officer (as in the U.S. Navy) that consists of an eagle, one, two, or three chevrons, an arc for a chief, and a specialty mark and that is worn between shoulder and elbow formerly on the right by members of the seaman branch and on the left by others but from 1948 on the left by all branches

rating badge of a chief radioman

**rating flume** *n* **:** a flume of known capacities at different depths and velocities that is used for the measurement of large flows of irrigation water

**rating nut** *n* **:** a milled nut under a pendulum bob for varying the effective pendulum length in rating a clock

**ra·tio** \'rā,shō, -shē,ō\ *n* -S [L, reason, computation, reasoning — more at REASON] **1 a :** the real ground or nature of a thing esp. as determined by its relation to other things **:** RATIONALE — compare PYTHAGOREANISM, REASON **b :** the understanding or reason in Scholasticism that has the capacity to think discursively and make abstractions — compare INTELLECT **2 a :** the quotient of one quantity divided by another **b :** the fixed or approximate relation of one thing to another or between two or more things (as in number, quantity, or degree) **:** RATE, PROPORTION ⟨the ~ between births and deaths⟩ ⟨the 10:1 student-teacher ~ of the school⟩ ⟨the ~ between stock prices, earnings, and dividends —*Time*⟩ ⟨combining . . . in such ~ understanding of technics and of human rights —Roger Burlingame⟩; *specif* **:** specified proportion of ingredients (as in plant foods or fertilizers) ⟨tomatoes were grown outdoors with . . . use of widely different nutrient ~*s* —*Experiment Station Record*⟩ **c :** the expression of the relative values of gold and silver as determined by the currency laws of a country — called also *coinage ratio* **3** *archaic* **:** RATION, PORTION ⟨furnished the . . invaders with a ~ of biscuit and wine —Archibald Duncan⟩

**ratio arm** *n* **:** a branch of an electrical bridge circuit — compare WHEATSTONE BRIDGE

**ratio chart** *n* **:** a chart employing the Cartesian coordinate system in which the points on a curve are determined by measuring time as the independent variable along one axis and the logarithms of the values of the corresponding dependent variables along the other

**rati·oci·nate** \,rad·ē'ōsᵊn,āt, -ashē-, -atē-, -ē'äs-, *usu* -ād·+V\ *vi* -ED/-ING/-S [L *ratiocinatus*, past part. of *ratiocinari* to reckon, deliberate, consider, fr. *ratio* reason, computation, reasoning] **:** to reason discursively or according to a logical process

**rati·oci·na·tion** \,==,=='āshən\ *n* -S [MF or L; MF, fr. L *ratiocination-, ratiocinatio*, fr. *ratiocinatus* + *-ion-, -io* -ion] **1 a :** the process of exact thinking **:** REASONING ⟨pure ~, where the intellect works cold and aloof in dry light —J.L.Lowes⟩ **b :** a specific train of thought or piece of reasoning ⟨~*s* on conscience and conventional morality —M.S.Day⟩ **2** *archaic* **a :** the faculty of reason **b :** the habit of reasoning

**rati·oci·na·tive** \,==ˈ==,ād·iv\ *adj* [L *ratiocinativus*, fr. *ratiocinatus* + *-ivus* -ive] **1 :** of or relating to ratiocination ⟨~ powers⟩ ⟨stimulate one's ~ faculties —Max Beerbohm⟩ **2 :** marked by or devoted to ratiocination ⟨assume a dogmatic rather than a ~ attitude —*Scientific Monthly*⟩ ⟨our educational system . . . not basically ~ —C.W.Shumaker⟩

**rati·oci·na·tor** \-,ād·ə(r)\ *n* -S [L, fr. *ratiocinatus* + *-or*] **:** REASONER

**rati·oci·na·to·ry** \-s°nə,tōrē, -ȯrē, -ri\ *adj* **:** RATIOCINATIVE

**ra·tio cog·no·scen·di** \'räd·ē,ō,kōgnə'sken(,)dē\ *n, pl* **rati·o·nes cognoscendi** \,räd·ē'ō(,)nā,skōg-\ [L] **:** the ground of knowledge **:** something through or by means of which a thing is known

**ratio de·ci·den·di** \-,desə'den(,)dē\ *n, pl* **rationes decidendi** [L] **:** the reason or ground for a judicial decision

**ratio es·sen·di** \-e'sen(,)dē\ *n, pl* **rationes essendi** [ML] **:** the cause or ground of the existence of a thing

**ra·ti·om·e·ter** \,rāshē'äməd·ə(r)\ *n* [*ratio* + *-meter*] **:** a device for making a succession of photographic exposures to obtain the filter ratios of color-sensitive materials under given conditions of work

**ratiomotor** \'=(=),=,==\ *n* **:** a motor integral with a speed-reducing gear

**¹ra·tion** \'rashən, 'rāsh-\ *n* -S [F, fr. L *ration-, ratio* reason, computation, reasoning — more at REASON] **1** *archaic* **:** RATIO **2 a :** the food allowance of one person or one animal for one day; *specif* **:** a fixed daily food allowance provided for the subsistence of a soldier or sailor — compare FIELD RATION, K RATION **b rations** *pl* **:** FOOD, PROVISIONS ⟨cooked two days' ~*s* —G.R.Stewart⟩ ⟨issued ~*s* to the needy —*Amer. Guide Series: Fla.*⟩ **3 :** a share esp. as determined by supply **:** allotted or permitted amount ⟨a reduction of the wartime meat ~⟩ ⟨saved up their gas ~ to go on a short motor trip —MacKinlay Kantor⟩ ⟨pouring the whiskey, a neat two fingers, obviously a ~ —Margery Allingham⟩

**²ration** \"\ *vt* **rationed; rationed; rationing** \-sh(ə)niŋ\ **rations :** to supply with rations **:** put on rations ⟨~ the inhabitants of a besieged city⟩ ⟨the Food Administration did not ~ the people —Will Irwin⟩ **2 a :** to distribute as rations **:** allot in rations ⟨~ sugar during the emergency⟩ ⟨~*ed* out beef, pork, and flour, often to hundreds —*Amer. Guide Series: Minn.*⟩ **b :** to distribute or divide (as commodities in short supply) in an equitable manner or so as to achieve a particular object (as maximum production of particular items) — compare DIRECT CONTROL **c :** to use or indulge in sparingly ⟨an official communiqué in which words were strictly ~*ed* —*Time*⟩ **syn** see APPORTION

**¹ra·tio·nal** \'rashnəl, -shnəl, 'raash-, 'raish-\ *adj* [ME *racional*, fr. L *rationalis*, fr. *ration-, ratio* reason, computation, reasoning + *-alis* -al] **1 :** having reason or understanding **:** REASONING ⟨~ creature⟩ ⟨a ~ being⟩ ⟨embryo had a vegetable life, then an animal life, and finally a ~ life —S.F.Mason⟩ **2 a :** of, relating to, or based upon reason ⟨provide a literary as well as a ~ education —G.K.Chalmers⟩ ⟨~ analysis of the problem —R.C.Doty⟩ **b :** using medical treatments based on reason or general principles — used esp. of an ancient school of physicians; opposed to *empirical* **3 :** involving only multiplication, division, addition, and subtraction and only a finite number of times **:** not involving a surd or indicated but not extractable root ⟨3 and 2+⅗ are ~ expressions⟩ **4 a :** agreeable to reason **:** INTELLIGENT, SENSIBLE ⟨gives a quite ~ explanation of the passage —*Modern Language Notes*⟩ ⟨a ~ . . . world trade policy —*Nation's Business*⟩ ⟨the advantages of a ~ orthography —C.H.Grandgent⟩ **b :** RATIONALISTIC **5 :** capable of being measured in terms of the mora in Greek and Latin prosody **:** having the normal ratio between arsis and thesis

**syn** REASONABLE: RATIONAL usu. implies a latent or active power to make logical inferences and draw conclusions that enable one to understand the world about him and relate such knowledge to the attainment of ends, often, in this use, opposed to *emotional* or *animal;* in application to policies, projects, or acts, RATIONAL implies satisfactory to the reason or chiefly actuated by reason ⟨the triumph of the *rational* over the emotional side of man⟩ ⟨his was a mind so purely *rational* that it had long since demanded and received absolute divorce from his naturally impetuous heart —Elinor Wylie⟩ ⟨the *rational*, the intelligent, the orderly processes of behavior —Lewis Mumford⟩ ⟨we may seek to change another person's convictions in a *rational* manner either by bringing to his notice evidence that he did not previously know about or by inducing in him a process of *rational* inference —R.H.Thouless⟩ REASONABLE usu. carries a much weaker implication of the power to reason in general or of guidance by conclusions drawn by the reasoning power, rather applying to actions or decisions or choices that are practical, sensible, just, or fair ⟨the longing to achieve is more emotional than *reasonable* —H.S.Canby⟩ ⟨no English author has given an ampler and more *reasonable* interpretation of life —W.S.Maugham⟩ ⟨the amount of uncompleted work is relatively small and can be completed within a *reasonable* period of time —*Loyola Univ. Bull.*⟩ ⟨the heifers and cows may be expected to give a *reasonable* milk yield —Allan Fraser⟩ ⟨contributions must be *reasonable* in amount —C.M.Winslow⟩

**²rational** \"\ *n* -S **:** something rational: as **a** *archaic* **:** a rational creature; *esp* **:** a human being ⟨not as ~*s*, but as animals —Thomas Paine⟩ **b :** a rational expression in mathematics ⟨consider the set of all ~*s*, excluding zero —Harry Lass⟩ **c :** RATIONALE ⟨the decided shift in production ~ —*Dun's Rev.*⟩

**ra·tio·nale** \,rashə'nal *sometimes* -näl *or* -nál *or* ,==ˈ=ē *or* ,=='nālē *or* -li\ *n* -S [L, neut. of *rationalis* rational — more at RATIONAL] **1 :** an explanation or exposition of controlling principles (as of an opinion, belief, practice, or phenomenon) ⟨the ~ of the decision in the case —J.D.Johnson⟩ ⟨the most popular ~ of religious behavior —J.D.Hart⟩ ⟨a ~ of present practice in probation and parole —*Columbia Univ. Press Books*⟩ ⟨a ~ of retail prices —C.G.Burke⟩ **2 :** the underlying reason **:** rational basis **:** JUSTIFICATION, GROUND ⟨the ~ of the law —Walter Adams⟩ ⟨a plausible . . . ~ for conformity —W.H.Whyte⟩ ⟨no ~ underlying the new therapeutic approach can be offered at this early stage —*Jour. Amer. Med. Assoc.*⟩

**rational fraction** *n* **:** a fraction of which both numerator and denominator are rational numbers or are polynomials

**rational function** *n* **1 :** POLYNOMIAL **2 :** the quotient of two polynomials

**rational horizon** *n* **:** HORIZON 1b(1), 1b(2)

**ra·tio·nal·ism** \'rashənᵊl,izəm, -shnə,li-, 'raash-, 'raish-\ *n* -S **1 :** reliance on reason as the basis for establishment of religious truth ⟨outbreaks of ~ . . . manifested themselves in heretical movements —S.H.Cross⟩ **2 a :** a theory that reason is in itself a source of knowledge superior to and independent of sense perceptions — contrasted with *sensationalism* **b :** a theory that philosophical knowledge may be arrived at by deduction from a priori concepts or necessary ideas **:** APRIORISM — compare INTUITIONISM; contrasted with *empiricism* **c :** elaboration and development of theories (as in pure mathematics) by reasoning alone without testing them by experience **d :** a view that an appeal to reason and experience rather than to the nonrational (as emotion, intuition, faith, revelation, or authority) is to be employed as the fundamental criterion in the solution of problems **3 :** the technical and practical approach to architectural design as opposed to the traditional **:** FUNCTIONALISM

**¹ra·tio·nal·ist** \-shənᵊləst, -shnəl-\ *n* -S [¹*rational* + *-ist*] **:** an advocate of rationalism

**²rationalist** \"\ *adj* **:** RATIONALISTIC ⟨ruthless suppression of ~ opinion —Kingsley Martin⟩

**ra·tio·nal·is·tic** \¦rashənᵊl¦istik, -shnə¦l-, 'raash-, ¦raish-, -tēk\ *adj* **1 :** of, relating to, or in accordance with the principles of rationalism ⟨~ philosophies⟩ ⟨a ~ theory⟩ ⟨all ~ argument from axiomatic principles —J.H.Randall⟩ **2 :** marked by or having a tendency toward rationalism ⟨~ liberalism⟩ ⟨the possibility of viewing thinkers as predominantly either ~ or mystic —M.R.Cohen⟩ — **ra·tio·nal·is·ti·cal·ly** \-tək(ə)lē, -tēk-, -li\ *adv*

**ra·tio·nal·i·ty** \,rashə'naləd·ē, ,raash-, ,raish-, -lətē, -i\ *n* -ES [LL *rationalitas*, fr. L *rationalis* rational + *-itas* -ity — more at RATIONAL] **1 :** the quality or state of being rational ⟨man's ~ is not a higher faculty . . . imposed upon his animal nature —Grace De Laguna⟩ **2 :** acceptability to reason **:** REASONABLENESS ⟨gives a ~ . . . and a justification to the universe —J.W.Krutch⟩ ⟨the social ~ that . . . alone can save us —A.L. Locke⟩ **3 :** something (as an opinion, belief, or practice) that is rational — usu. used in pl ⟨a race . . . between the *rationalities* of technology and the irrationalities of style —Lewis Mumford⟩

**ra·tio·nal·iza·tion** \,rashənᵊlə'zāshən, -shnələ-, ,raash-, ,raish-, -ᵊl,ī'-, -nə,lī'-\ *n* -S **:** the act, process, or result of rationalizing: as **a :** substitution of a rational for a supernatural explanation ⟨by giving the Bible a poetic . . . interpretation . . . in short, by ~ —*Humanist*⟩ **b :** an account or ordering in conformity with reason or rational principles ⟨offering this ~ of a people —Kay Boyle⟩ ⟨a ~ of . . . customs procedures —*N. Y. Times*⟩ ⟨this process of ~ in . . . biological thinking —P.S.Hudson⟩ **c :** the organization of a business or industry upon scientific principles of management and simplified procedures to obtain greater efficiency of operation **d :** the provision of plausible reasons to explain to oneself or others behavior for which one's real motives are different and unknown or unconscious ⟨the reasons most commonly given for anti-Semitism . . . are ~*s* of prejudices —*Harper's*⟩

**ra·tio·nal·ize** \'rashənᵊl,īz, -shnə,līz, 'raash-, 'raish-\ *vb* -ED/-ING/-S [¹*rational* + *-ize*] *vt* **1 :** to free (a mathematical equation) from irrational expressions **2 a :** to make conformable (as an attitude or belief) with rational principles **:** give a rational explanation of ⟨~ one's attitude to life⟩ ⟨chauvinists ~ race prejudice⟩ ⟨labored . . . to ~ history into a science —H.S.Commager⟩ **b :** to substitute a natural for a supernatural explanation of ⟨~ the Greek myths⟩ — often used with *away* ⟨~ away all miracles⟩ **3 :** to attribute (one's actions) to rational and creditable motives without adequate analysis of the true and esp. unconscious motives ⟨easy for men of principle to ~ lapses from high standards where the cause seems to them good —J.A.R.Pimlott⟩ **4 :** to apply the principles of scientific management to (a factory, industrial process, or industry) ⟨*rationalizing* the supply lines so as to eliminate duplicate hauling —*Fortune*⟩ ~ *vi* **:** to provide plausible but untrue reasons or motives for a course of conduct ⟨urged him to stop *rationalizing* and admit he acted selfishly⟩ **syn** see EXPLAIN

**ra·tio·nal·ly** \-nᵊlē, -nəlē, -li\ *adv* **:** in a rational manner: as **a :** in accordance with reason **:** REASONABLY, SENSIBLY ⟨conditions . . . required for living ~ —Herbert Read⟩ **b :** with respect to reason ⟨training and direction would make them . . . ~ competent beings —G.P.Musselman⟩

**ra·tio·nal·ness** *n* -ES **:** RATIONALITY 1

**rational number** *n* **:** an integer or the quotient of two integers (as ⅔)

**rationals** *pl of* RATIONAL

**rational soul** *n* **:** the soul that in the scholastic tradition has independent existence apart from the body and that is the characteristic animating principle of human life as distinguished from animal or vegetable life — compare ANIMAL SOUL, VEGETABLE SOUL

**rationed** *past of* RATION

**ra·ti·o·ne do·mi·ci·lii** \,räd·ē'ō(,)nā,dȯmə'kilē,ē\ *adv* [L] **:** by reason of domicile

**ratione rei si·tae** \-,rā,ē'si,tī\ *adv* [L] **:** by reason of the situs of the thing

**rationes cognoscendi** *pl of* RATIO COGNOSCENDI

**rationes decidendi** *pl of* RATIO DECIDENDI

**rationes essendi** *pl of* RATIO ESSENDI

**rationing** *n* -S [fr. gerund of ²*ration*] **:** the act or process of distributing commodities as rations ⟨~ device⟩ ⟨~ system⟩ ⟨moved promptly to eliminate ~ on gasoline, fuel oil —H.S. Truman⟩

**rations** *pl of* RATION, *pres 3d sing of* RATION

**ratio of a geometric progression :** the constant quantity by which each term in a geometric progression is multiplied to produce the succeeding one

**ratio of expansion :** the ratio of the volume of steam in an engine cylinder or turbine when the piston is at the end of the stroke to the volume at cut-off

**ratio of similitude :** the ratio between any two corresponding linear extents (as line segments) in two similar figures

**ratios** *pl of* RATIO

**ra·ti·tae** \rə'tīd·,ē\ *n pl, cap* [NL, fr. L, fem. pl. of *ratitus* marked with the figure of a raft, fr. *ratis* raft; perh. akin to L *rete* net — more at RETINA] *in some classifications* **:** a superordinal group of birds comprising forms with small or rudimentary wings, no pygostyle, and no keel to the breastbone that are nonetheless evidently descended from birds with the power of flight, including the ostriches, rheas, cassowaries and emus, elephant birds, moas, and kiwis, and usu. constituting a primary subdivision of the subclass Neornithes

**¹rat·ite** \'ra,tīt\ *adj* [NL *Ratitae*] **1 :** having a flat unkeeled breastbone — compare CARINATE **2 :** of or relating to the Ratitae

**²ratite** \"\ *n* -S **:** a bird with a flat breastbone **:** one of the Ratitae

**rat·i·tous** \'rad·əd·əs\ *adj* [NL *Ratitae* + E *-ous*] **:** RATITE

**rat kangaroo** *n* **:** any of various small Australian and Tasmanian kangaroos of *Bettongia, Potorous*, and closely related genera that are no larger than a rabbit and have persistent canine teeth and a long and often prehensile tail

**ratlike** \'=,=\ *adj* **1 :** of, relating to, or characteristic of a rat ⟨a ~ tail⟩ **2 :** resembling a rat in appearance or behavior ⟨a ~ slippery little man with sharp features and small beady eyes⟩

**rat·line** *also* **rat·lin** *or* **rat·ling** \'ratlən\ *n* -S [origin unknown] **1** *or* **ratline stuff :** small, usu. 3-stranded, tarred rope used for cross ropes on ship's shrouds **2 :** one of the small transverse ropes attached to the shrouds of a ship and forming the steps of a rope ladder — see SHIP illustration

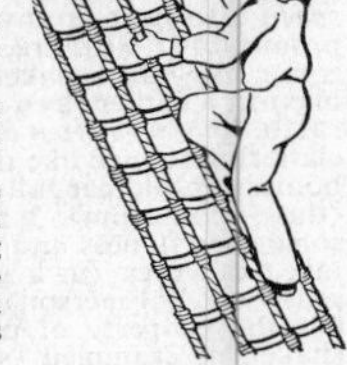
ratlines and shrouds

**rat louse** *n* **:** a sucking louse (*Polyplax spinulosa*) that is a widely distributed parasite of rats

**rat mite** *n* **:** a widely distributed mite (*Bdellonyssus bacoti*) formerly limited to warm regions but rapidly spreading into more temperate areas that sometimes causes severe dermatitis in man and is a vector of epidemic typhus particularly in the Orient

**rat mole** *n* **:** MOLE RAT

**RATO** \'räd·(,)ō\ *abbr, often not cap* **:** rocket-assisted takeoff

**¹ra·toon** \ra'tün\ *n* -S [Sp *retoño* sprout, shoot, fr. *retoñar* to sprout, shoot a second time, fr. *re-* + *otoñar* to grow in the autumn, fr. *otoño* autumn, fr. L *autumnus*] **1 :** a stalk or shoot arising from the root or crown of a perennial plant:

as **a** : a sugarcane sucker arising from the base of a harvested plant **b** : one of the suckers arising below the developing pineapple fruit and used to produce a second crop **c** : a shoot of the third generation after planting of a banana plant **d** : Jamaica ginger of inferior quality consisting of small fibrous offsets of the rhizome **2** *or* **ratoon crop** : a crop (as of cotton or pineapples) produced by or on ratoon growth

**²ratoon** \"\ *vb* -ED/-ING/-S [Sp *retoñar*] *vi* : to sprout or spring up from the root ⟨some cottons ~ freely⟩ ⟨sugarcane ~*ing* from the root of the previous year's planting⟩ ~ *vt* : to grow or produce (a crop) from or on ratoons ⟨~ a pineapple field⟩

**ra·toon·er** \-nə(r)\ *n* -S : a plant that propagates by ratooning

**rato unit** *n* : JATO UNIT

**rat-poison plant** \ˈ=,==-\ *n* : SCARLET HAMELIA

**¹ratproof** \ˈ=,=\ *adj* [¹*rat* + *proof*] : proof against rats ⟨~ construction⟩ ⟨a ~ warehouse⟩

**²ratproof** \"\ *vt* : to make (as a building or ship) secure against the entry of rats

**rat race** *n* : a violent, confused, and usu. competitive activity or rush; *esp* : one that is meaningless or profitless : VICIOUS CIRCLE ⟨life was a *rat race* . . . no time for gracious living or warm family feeling —Frances G. Patton⟩ ⟨caught in the *rat race*, they may still work hard —Henry Hazlitt⟩

**rat rhyme** *n* **1** *chiefly Scot* : a scrap of nonsense or doggerel verse **2** *chiefly Scot* : RIGMAROLE

**¹rats** *pl of* RAT, *pres 3d sing of* RAT

**²rats** \ˈrats\ *interj* [fr. pl. of ¹rat] — used to express disappointment, disgust, or scoffing incredulity

**ratsbane** \ˈ=,=\ *n* -S **1** : ARSENIC TRIOXIDE **2** : any of various plants that are or are supposed to be poisonous to rats: as **a** : a West African shrub (*Dichapetalum toxicarium*) with extremely poisonous seeds — called also *African ratsbane* **b** : a No. American rattlesnake plantain (*Goodyera pubescens*) **c** : SPOTTED WINTERGREEN **d** : CHERVIL 1

**rat snake** *n* : any of numerous rat-eating colubrid snakes: as **a** : any member of a common Indian genus (*Ptyas*) of snakes that enter buildings in pursuit of their prey **b** : any member of a No. American genus (*Elaphe*) of large constricting snakes that include the widely known pilot black snake and the chicken snake

**rat's-tail fescue** \ˈ=,=-\ *n* : RATTAIL FESCUE

**rat-stripper** \ˈ=,==\ *n* : MOUNTAIN LOVER 1

**¹rattail** \ˈ=,=\ *n* [¹*rat* + *tail*] : something suggestive of a rat's tail: as **a** (1) : a horse's tail having little or no hair (2) : a horse with such a tail (3) : MULE **b** (1) *also* **rattail fish** *or* **rattail grenadier** : GRENADIER 2 (2) : ²CHIMAERA **c** (1) : any of several plants (as a plantain or various grasses) having elongated terete spikes (2) : any of several grasses having slender cylindrical flower spikes

**²rattail** \"\ *adj* : round, slender, and tapering : resembling a rat's tail

**rattail cactus** *n* : a commonly cultivated tropical American cactus (*Aporocactus flagelliformis*) having slender creeping stems and very showy crimson flowers three inches long that bloom for several days

**rat-tailed** \(ˈ)=ˈ=\ *adj* : having a long tapering tail like that of a rat ⟨a *rat-tailed* horse⟩

**rat-tailed larva** *or* **rat-tailed maggot** *n* : the larva of a syrphid fly of *Eristalis* or related genera that is remarkable for the long telescopic tubular tail with spiracles at the tip through which air is brought down from above the mud or putrefying matter in which the larva lives

**rat-tailed radish** *n* : a radish (*Raphanus sativus caudatus* or *R. caudatus*) that has an inedible root and is grown for its long slender edible pods

**rat-tailed serpent** *n* : FER-DE-LANCE

**rat-tailed shrew** *n* : MUSK SHREW 1

**rattail fescue** *n* : a slender European grass (*Festuca myuros*) naturalized as a weed in the eastern U.S.

**rattail file** *n* : a small round file

**rattail hinge** \ˈ=,=-\ *n* : a pintle type hinge in which the pin is extended so that it can be fastened to the casing of a door

**rattail spoon** *n* : a form of spoon developed in the later 17th century with a thin pointed tongue on the bottom of the bowl to reinforce the joint of bowl and handle

**¹rat·tan** *also* **ra·tan** \raˈtan, rəˈ-, -aa(ə)n, ˈra,t-\ *or* **rattan palm** *or* **ro·tan** \rōˈt-\ *n* -S [Malay *rotan*] **1** : any of several climbing palms (esp. of the genera *Calamus* and *Daemonothops*) remarkable for the great length attained by their stems **2** : a portion of the very tough stem of a rattan palm used esp. for walking sticks, wickerwork, chairs, seats of chairs, cords, and cordage — see CALAMUS 4, MALACCA CANE **3** : a rattan cane or switch ⟨whipping on the open hand with a thin ~ —R.M.Lovett⟩

rattail hinge

**²rat·tan** \raˈtan, rəˈ-, -aa(ə)n\ *vt* **rattaned** *or* **rattanned**; **rattaning** *or* **rattanning**; **rattans** **1** : to provide or strengthen with rattan **2** : to punish by striking with a rattan ⟨the schoolmaster ~*ing* a young culprit⟩

**³rat·tan** *or* **rat·ten** \ˈratᵊn\ *var of* RATTON

**rattan vine** *n* : SUPPLEJACK 1a

**rat-tat** \(ˈ)ra(t)ˈtat, *usu* -tad+V\ *also* **rat-tat-tat** \ˌrad·əˈtat, *usu* -tad·+V\ *or* **rat·tat·too** \ˌ==ˈtü\ *n* -S [imit.] : RAT-A-TAT

**ratted** *past of* RAT

**rat·teen** \raˈtēn\ *n* -S [F *ratine*] *archaic* : any of various coarse woolen fabrics (as frieze, baize, drugget)

**rat·ter** \ˈrad·ə(r), -atə-\ *n* -S [¹*rat* + *-er*] : RATCATCHER; *specif* : a rat-catching dog or cat

**ratti** *var of* RUTTEE

**rattier** *comparative of* RATTY

**rattiest** *superlative of* RATTY

**ratting** *pres part of* RAT

**rat·tish** \ˈrad·ish, -atish, -ēsh\ *adj* [¹*rat* + *-ish*] : resembling or having the characteristics of a rat ⟨a fellow with a ~ look⟩

**¹rat·tle** \ˈrad·ᵊl, -atᵊl\ *vb* **rattled**; **rattled**; **rattling** \-d·ᵊliŋ, -t(ᵊ)l-\ **rattles** [ME *ratelen*; akin to OE *hratele*, a plant, MD *ratelen* to rattle, *ratele*, *ratel* rattle, MHG *razzeln*, *razzen* to rage, rattle, ON *hrata* to fall, stagger — more at CARDINAL] *vi* **1** : to make, cause, or emit a rapid succession of short sharp noises or of similarly discontinuous sounds (as through shaking or recurrent collisions of hard bodies) : CLATTER ⟨the windows ~ in the wind⟩ ⟨a diamondback rattlesnake . . . slow to coil or ~ unless angered —Marjory S. Douglas⟩ **2** : to make a rattle in the throat **3** : to chatter incessantly and aimlessly ⟨she *rattled* on for an hour⟩ ⟨walked over the grounds . . . *rattling*, chatting —George Meredith⟩ **4** : to move or proceed with a clatter or rattle : drive or ride clatteringly ⟨a wagon *rattling* through the streets⟩ ⟨we *rattled* along briskly⟩ ~ *vt* **1** : to say, perform, or affect in a brisk lively fashion esp. with a rattle or clatter ⟨the gale *rattled* the tiles from the roof⟩ — often used with *off* ⟨guides . . . ~ off the history of atomic energy —Daniel Lang⟩ **2** : to cause (something) to make a rattling sound ⟨*rattling* their mess kits impatiently⟩ **3** *archaic* : to rail at : SCOLD ⟨for this he has been *rattled* —Thomas Gray⟩ **4** : to shake up : ROUSE ⟨*rattling* us up at this hour of the night —Walter Macken⟩; *specif* : to beat (a cover) for game **5** : to disturb the composure of : AGITATE, DISCONCERT ⟨~ a player⟩ ⟨hecklers trying to ~ the speaker⟩ **6** : to test or tumble (as metal castings) in a rattler **syn** see EMBARRASS

**²rattle** \"\ *n* -S *often attrib* **1 a** : a rapid succession of sharp clattering sounds like those made by repeated collision of hard bodies ⟨an old car full of knocks and ~*s*⟩ ⟨the ~ of musketry⟩ ⟨the ~ of a drum⟩ **b** : RACKET ⟨cannot bear a place without some cheerfulness and ~ —Samuel Johnson⟩ **c** : noisy rapid talk : CHATTER ⟨in a good deal of ~ . . . a grain or two of sense —R.W.Emerson⟩ ⟨a light ~ of small talk —E.G.Lowry⟩ **d** : the property of paper that causes it to be noisy when shaken or crumpled ⟨starch . . . imparts snap and ~ to the sheet —F.H.Norris⟩ **2 a** : a child's toy that rattles when shaken and that consists usu. of a case containing loose pellets **b** : a noisemaker with a tongue that plays on the teeth of a ratchet wheel when revolved formerly used by watchmen and now by merrymakers — called also *watchman's rattle* **c** : a dance instrument (as a receptacle with noise-making contents or a stick with clashing objects) that is rhythmically shaken during various dances (as of American Indians) : IDIOPHONE **d** : a tiresome or frivolous chatterer : senseless talker ⟨from the point of view of an artless, affectionate ~ —Mary Bailey⟩ **3 a** : a plant of the genus *Rhinanthus*; *esp* : an annual herb (*R. crista-galli*) of the north temperate zone with showy yellow purple-spotted flowers that is partially parasitic on grasses and other plants and that has seeds which rattle in the inflated capsule when ripe — called also *yellow rattle* **b** : a European lousewort (*Pedicularis palustris*) — called also *red rattle* **4 a** : the sound-producing organ on a rattlesnake's tail **b** : one of the constituent segments of this organ **5** : the noise in the throat caused by air passing through mucus; *specif* : that heard at the approach of death — compare RALE **6** : a movement of brushing forward and striking back with the ball of the foot in dancing

**³rattle** \"\ *vt* **rattled**; **rattled**; **rattling** \-d·ᵊliŋ, -t(ᵊ)l-\ **rattles** [back-formation fr. ²*rattling*] : to furnish (a ship's shrouds) with ratlines : fasten ratlines on — often used with *down* ⟨~ down the rigging⟩

**rattle about** *vi* : to rattle around

**rattle around** *vi* : to have or give the impression of being tumbled about (as by living in too spacious quarters or holding a post one cannot fill) ⟨gave him a suite of offices to *rattle around* in but nothing to do⟩

**rattlebag** \ˈ==,=\ *n* **1** : a rattle in the form of a bag **2 a** *usu* **rattlebags** *pl but sing or pl in constr* : BLADDER CAMPION 1 **b** : RATTLE 3a

**rattlebones** \ˈ==,=\ *n pl* **1** : ¹BONE 5a **2** *usu sing in constr* : a lean and bony person or animal

**rattlebox** \ˈ==,=\ *n* **1** : a rattle in the shape of a box **2 a** : RATTLE 3a **b** : a plant of the genus *Crotalaria*; *esp* : an American annual herb (*C. sagittalis*) the ripe seeds of which rattle in the inflated pod **c** : SILVER BELL **d** : BLADDER CAMPION 1 **e** : SEEDBOX 2

**rattlebrain** \ˈ==,=\ *n* : a rattlebrained person : an empty-headed chatterer

**rattlebrained** \ˌ==ˈ=\ *adj* : marked by giddiness : EMPTY-HEADED ⟨a ~ youngster —Sinclair Lewis⟩ ⟨his ~ . . . crackpot ideas —Ellen Glasgow⟩

**rattlebush** \ˈ==,=\ *n* **1** : a rattlebox (*Crotalaria sagittalis*) **2** : INDIGO BROOM

**rattlehead** \ˈ==,=\ *n* : RATTLEBRAIN ⟨his idea of a mighty pretty girl was a ~ —W.A.White⟩

**rattleheaded** \ˌ==ˈ==\ *adj* : RATTLEBRAINED

**rattlemouse** *n, obs* : ³BAT

**rattlepate** \ˈ==,=\ *n* : RATTLEBRAIN

**rattlepated** \ˌ==ˈ==\ *adj* : RATTLEBRAINED ⟨how ~ I am! I've forgotten what I came for —Glenway Wescott⟩

**rattlepod** \ˈ==,=\ *n* : SEEDBOX 2

**rat·tler** \ˈratlə(r), -adᵊl-, -atᵊl-\ *n* -S [ME *rateler*, fr. *ratelen* to rattle + *-er* — more at RATTLE] **1** : one that rattles: as **a** : RATTLE 2b **b** : a vehicle (as an automobile, trolley car, or railway car) that rattles; *specif* : a freight train ⟨grab fast ~*s* for the West —Thomas Wolfe⟩ **2** : something extraordinarily good of its kind : a fine specimen (as of a horse, storm, blow, game, or book) ⟨a ~ of a storm⟩ **3 a** : RATTLESNAKE **b** : RATTLE 4 — usu. used in pl. ⟨a rattlesnake rattling his ~*s* —Ernest Hemingway⟩ **4 a** : a revolving drum in which paving bricks are rotated with a charge of cast iron to test their abrasive resistance **b** : a device for shaking out the cores from small castings : TUMBLING BARREL **c** : a device for finishing materials (as metal, concrete blocks, or bricks) consisting of a closed receptacle in which the material to be finished is shaken up with blocks of metal or abrasive **5** : RATTLEBRAIN

**rattleroot** \ˈ==,=\ *n* : a bugbane (*Cimicifuga racemosa*)

**rattlertree** \ˈ==,=\ *n* : WHITE POPLAR 1a

**rattles** *pres 3d sing of* RATTLE, *pl of* RATTLE

**rattlesnake** \ˈ==,=\ *n* : any of numerous New World pit vipers that have a series of horny interlocking joints at the end of the tail which make a sharp rattling sound when vibrated, that comprise two genera of which one (*Sistrurus*) contains small snakes (as the massasaugas and ground rattlesnakes) having the head covered with symmetrical plates and the other (*Crotalus*) contains usu. larger snakes that have scales instead of headplates, are rather thick-bodied, large-headed snakes of sluggish disposition which seldom bite unless startled or pursuing prey, and occur across most of America from southern Canada to Argentina — see CANEBRAKE RATTLER, DIAMONDBACK RATTLESNAKE, PRAIRIE RATTLESNAKE, SIDEWINDER, TIMBER RATTLESNAKE, WESTERN DIAMOND RATTLESNAKE

**rattlesnake-bite** \ˈ==,=,=\ *n* : TALL MEADOW RUE

**rattlesnake fern** *n* **1** : any of several American grape ferns (esp. *Botrychium virginianum*) with clustered sporangia resembling a snake's rattles **2** : CHAIN FERN

**rattlesnake flag** *n* : any of several flags bearing a rattlesnake and usu. the motto "Don't Tread On Me" in use by the colonies at the outbreak of the American Revolution

**rattlesnake grass** *n* : a showy American grass (*Glyceria canadensis*) with an ample panicle of rather large ovate spikelets whose shape suggests a snake's rattle

**rattlesnake herb** *n* : BANEBERRY

**rattlesnake master** *or* **rattlesnake's master** *n* : any of various plants held to cure the bite of a rattlesnake: as **a** : any of various button snakeroots of the genera *Liatris* or *Eryngium* **b** : FALSE ALOE 1

**rattlesnake pilot** *n* : COPPERHEAD 1a

**rattlesnake plantain** *n* : an orchid of the genus *Goodyera*

**rattlesnake root** *n* : any of various plants formerly believed to be distasteful to rattlesnakes or effective against their venom: as **a** : a lion's foot of the genus *Prenanthes* — called also *cankerweed*; compare GALL OF THE EARTH **b** : SENEGA ROOT 1 **c** : a bugbane (*Cimicifuga racemosa*)

**rattlesnake violet** *n* : DOGTOOTH VIOLET

**rattlesnake weed** *n* **1** : a hawkweed (*Hieracium venosum*) with purple-veined leaves **2** : BUTTON SNAKEROOT **3** : a weedy herb (*Daucus pusillus*) of the western U.S. having short involucral bracts and bristly fruit — called also *bristly carrot* **4** : RATTLEBOX 2b **5** : RATTLESNAKE PLANTAIN

**rattle-top** \ˈ==,=\ *n* : a bugbane (*Cimicifuga racemosa*)

**¹rattletrap** \ˈ==,=\ *n* [¹*rattle* + *trap*] **1** : a small showy article of little value : GEWGAW, KNICKKNACK — usu. used in pl. ⟨a mantelpiece covered with ~*s*⟩ **2** : something rattling or rickety (as a vehicle) ⟨my car . . . an old ~ —Ida A.R.Wylie⟩ ⟨~ of a typewriter —J.G.Jones⟩

**²rattletrap** \"\ *adj* : RAMSHACKLE, RICKETY ⟨a ~ car⟩ ⟨the ~ desk in the lobby —Donald Windham⟩

**rat·tle·ty-bang** \ˌrad·ᵊlˈdē;=ˈ=\ *n* [irreg. fr. ¹*rattle* + *bang*] : a loud rattling and banging sound ⟨the ~ in the barn had . . . ceased —G.A.Chamberlain⟩

**rattleweed** \ˈ==,=\ *n* [²*rattle* + *weed*] **1** : any of various leguminous plants esp. of the genera *Astragalus*, *Phaca*, and *Oxytropis* **2** : BLADDER CAMPION 1 **3** : BUGBANE **4** : RATTLEBOX 2b

**¹rattling** *adj* [ME *rateling*, fr. pres. part. of *ratelen* to rattle — more at RATTLE] **1** : that rattles ⟨a ~ cough⟩ ⟨the harness . . . thrown with a ~ crash on the floor —Sherwood Anderson⟩ **2** : marked by liveliness and quickness (as in speech or action) : BRISK, SPRIGHTLY ⟨a ~ breeze⟩ ⟨move at a ~ pace⟩ ⟨her energy . . . and ~ independent tongue —Mary McCarthy⟩ **3** : extraordinarily good : SPLENDID ⟨played a ~ game —*Sunday Independent* (*Dublin*)⟩ ⟨bought ~ outfits —O.Henry⟩ — **rat·tling·ly** *adv*

**²rattling** *adv* : EXTREMELY ⟨a ~ good story⟩

**³rattling** *var of* RATLINE

**rat·tly** \ˈrad·ᵊlē, -at(ᵊ)lē, -lī\ *adj* [¹*rattle* + *-y*] : having a tendency to rattle : making a rattling sound ⟨a little boy . . . with his ~ red wagon —Florence Butler⟩

**¹rat·ton** \ˈratᵊn\ *n* -S [ME *ratoun*, fr. MF *raton* small rat, fr. OF, dim. of *rat*, prob. of Gmc origin; akin to OS *ratta* rat — more at RAT] *chiefly dial*

**²ratton** *also* **rattoon** *var of* RATOON

**rattrap** \ˈ=,=\ *n* **1** : a trap for rats **2** : a dirty ramshackle structure ⟨~ that passed for a jail —Pat Brennan⟩ **3** : a situation of hopeless doom ⟨troops surrounded and caught in a ~ with the river at their backs⟩

**rat-trap cheese** *var of* RAT CHEESE

**rattrap pedal** *n* : a pedal (as for a bicycle or tricycle) made with toothed edges in order to prevent slipping of the shoe

**rat·tus** \ˈrad·əs\ *n, cap* [NL, fr. E ¹*rat*] : a genus of rodents (family Muridae) that comprises the common rats and is distinguished from the closely related *Mus* by bevel-edged upper incisors and comparatively large second and third molars

**rat·ty** \ˈrad·ē, -atē, -ī\ *adj* -ER/-EST [¹*rat* + *-y*] **1 a** : infested with rats ⟨live on one floor of a ~ tenement —Joseph Mitchell⟩ **b** : rat-eaten in appearance : SHABBY, UNKEMPT ⟨~ and ragged —P.H.Lowrey⟩ ⟨a ~ brown overcoat —John Lardner⟩ ⟨a long ~ moustache —Eve Langley⟩ **c** : of, relating to, or characteristic of a rat ⟨like a terrier who smells something . . . ~ —E.F.Benson⟩ ⟨said in his ~ voice —Floyd Dell⟩ **2 a** : having a low, despicable, or treacherous character : MEANSPIRITED ⟨mean as a snake . . . forever taking up with ~ people — Frances G. Patton⟩ **b** : having an irritable or irascible disposition : ILL-TEMPERED, NASTY ⟨that ~ genius whose words . . . were thunder and lightning —Geoffrey Grigson⟩

**ra·tu·fa** \rəˈtüfə, rəˈtyü-\ *n, cap* [NL] : a genus of rodents (family Sciuridae) comprising the Asiatic giant squirrels

**rat unit** *n* : a bioassay unit consisting of the amount of a material (as a vitamin) that under standardized conditions is just sufficient to produce a specified response in all or a designated proportion of a group of experimental rats

**rat·wa** \ˈratwə\ *n* -S [Nepali *ratuvā*] : a muntjac (*Muntiacus muntjak*)

**rau·cid** \ˈrȯsəd\ *adj* [L *raucus* + E *-id* (as in *rancid*)] : RAUCOUS

**rau·ci·ty** \-səd·ē, -ətē, -ī\ *n* -ES [L *raucitas*, fr. *raucus* hoarse + *-itas* -ity] : the quality or state of being raucous

**rau·cle** \ˈrákəl\ *Scot var of* RACKLE

**rau·cous** \ˈrȯkəs\ *adj* [L *raucus* hoarse; akin to L *ravus* hoarse — more at RUMOR] **1** : disagreeably harsh or strident : HOARSE ⟨a ~ voice⟩ **2** : boisterously disorderly **syn** see LOUD

**rau·cous·ly** *adv* : in a raucous manner

**rau·cous·ness** *n* -ES : the quality or state of being raucous

**raught** [ME *raughte* (past), *raught* (past part.), fr. OE *rǣhte* (past), *geræht* (past part.) — more at REACH] *dial chiefly Brit past of* REACH

**¹rauk** \ˈrōk\ *vb* -ED/-ING/-S [prob. alter. of ²*rake*] **1** *dial Brit* : SCRATCH **2** *dial Eng* : POKE, STIR

**²rauk** *var of* ROKE

**rau·li** \(ˈ)rau̇ˈlē\ *also* **rauli beech** *n* -S [AmerSp *rauli, reuli*, fr. Mapuche *ruylin, ruili*] : a large Chilean timber tree (*Nothofagus procera*) yielding a coarse lumber that is used esp. for cooperage

**raun** \ˈrȯn\ *n* -S [ME *rawne*, of Scand origin; akin to ON *hrogn* roe — more at ROE] : ROE, SPAWN; *also* : a female fish (as a herring or salmon)

**raunchy** \ˈrȯnchē, ˈräu-, ˈrän-, -chi\ *adj, sometimes* -ER/-EST [origin unknown] : falling below a usual or normal standard: as **a** : SLOVENLY, UNKEMPT ⟨refuses to serve such ~ people as motorcyclists —*Newsweek*⟩ **b** : LEWD, VULGAR ⟨merry musings of that ~ old Wife of Bath —A.H.Weiler⟩

**raunge** *obs var of* RANGE

**rau·po** \ˈrau̇(,)pō\ *n* -S [*Maori*] : a common cattail (*Typha angustifolia*) used esp. in New Zealand for thatching

**rau·ra·ci** *also* **rau·ri·ci** \ˈrȯrə,sī\ *n pl, usu cap* [L] : an ancient people of Gaul west of the Rhine and near Basel

**rau·ri·ki** \ˈrau̇rə(,)kē\ *n* -S [Maori, fr. *rau* leaf + *riki* small] *NewZeal* : SOW THISTLE

**rausch·pfei·fe** \ˈrau̇sh,(p)fīfə\ *n* -S [G, fr. *rausch* reed + *pfeife* pipe] : a 2-rank mixture stop in a pipe organ speaking at 2 and 1⅓ foot pitches

**rausch·quin·te** \-,kuintə\ *n* -S [G, fr. *rausch* reed + *quinte* fifth (in music)] : a 2-rank mixture stop in a pipe organ speaking at 2⅔ and 2 foot pitches

**rau·vite** \ˈrō,vīt, ˈrau̇,v-\ *n* -S [fr. the symbols *Ra* + *U* + *V* + E *-ite*] : a mineral $CaU_2V_{12}O_{36}.20H_2O$ that is a hydrous oxide of calcium, uranium, and vanadium

**rau·wol·fia** \rau̇ˈwu̇lfēə, rȯˈw-, -wȯl-\ *n* [NL, fr. Leonhard *Rauwolf* †1596 Ger. botanist + NL *-ia*] **1 a** *cap* : a large pantropical genus of somewhat poisonous trees and shrubs (family Apocynaceae) having verticillate leaves and small cymose flowers with a salver-shaped corolla and bicarpellary ovary and yielding emetic and purgative substances and in the case of an Indian form (*R. serpentina*) an alkaloidal root extract used in the treatment of hypertension and some mental disorders **b** -S : any plant of the genus *Rauwolfia* **2** -S : the medicinal extract that is obtained from the root of the Indian rauwolfia

**¹rav·age** \ˈravij, -vēj\ *n* -S [F, fr. MF, fr. *ravir* to ravish + *-age* — more at RAVISH] **1** : an act or operation of ravaging : a violently destructive action or agency ⟨complete a victory with ~⟩ ⟨secure from ~ by fire⟩ **2** : havoc or damage resulting from ravaging : violently destructive effect : RUIN, DEVASTATION ⟨repair the ~ wrought by war⟩ ⟨the ~ of time⟩

**²ravage** \", *esp in pres part* -vəj\ *vb* -ED/-ING/-S [F *ravager*, fr. MF, fr. *ravage*] *vt* : to lay waste to : subject to depredations : work havoc or devastation upon : PLUNDER ~ *vi* : to commit ravages — **rav·ag·er** \-jə(r)\ *n* -S

**syn** DEVASTATE, WASTE, SACK, PILLAGE, DESPOIL, SPOLIATE: RAVAGE implies violent severe depredation, wasting, and destruction, often cumulative, so that restoration is impossible or unlikely ⟨a forest area *ravaged* by fire⟩ ⟨four major disasters had *ravaged* the country in the interval; the great smallpox epidemic, the great rinderpest outbreak, an intense drought with consequent famine and a devastating locust invasion —L.S.B.Leakey⟩ ⟨the cities of the Main were *ravaged*, citizens were tortured, robbed, murdered, women were ravished, churches looted while the bells tolled horror —Marjory S. Douglas⟩ DEVASTATE may stress the ruin and desolation ensuing from ravaging, demolishing, burning, and eradicating ⟨*devastating* conflicts such as those which destroyed Greek, Roman, and Saracen civilization, which drenched Europe in blood —M.R.Cohen⟩ ⟨the city was a *devastated* waste of smoldering embers: seventeen thousand four hundred and fifty people were homeless —*Amer. Guide Series: Mass.*⟩ ⟨if an atom or hydrogen bomb should be dropped on an American city, the *devastated* community would not be expected to confront the emergency unaided —Felix Morley⟩ WASTE, often a close synonym for DEVASTATE, may on the other hand apply to situations in which damage and desolation are accomplished more slowly and less dramatically and definitively ⟨with four legions, seized their cattle, *wasted* their country —J.A.Froude⟩ ⟨his fingers *wasted* by illness —Winston Churchill⟩ SACK may apply to the acts of a victorious invader in stripping a captured area of everything of value; it may suggest large-scale or complete burglarizing and looting ⟨the retreating Federals *sacked* and burned as they went, leaving scarcely a cabin in their wake —*Amer. Guide Series: La.*⟩ ⟨after De Soto helped Pizarro *sack* Peru —*Amer. Guide Series: Fla.*⟩ ⟨summer cottages *sacked* by the gang⟩ PILLAGE, often interchangeable with SACK, may suggest somewhat less ruthless and general devastation and slightly more selectivity in plundering ⟨their goods and chattels are *pillaged*, or filched for worthless money —Sir Winston Churchill⟩ DESPOIL usu. applies to the ransacking, looting, or expropriation of valuables, often of a particular building or specific place ⟨the same Roman raid that had *despoiled* his home and enslaved him at twenty had likewise brought disaster to their neighbors —L.C. Douglas⟩ SPOLIATE is a legalistic synonym for DESPOIL, often applicable to destruction visited on a neutral, noncombatant, or victim of piracy ⟨from the ages, from the barbarians, the land has been burnt and *spoliated* —Richard Llewellyn⟩

**¹rave** \ˈrāv\ *vb* -ED/-ING/-S [ME *raven*, prob. fr. MF *resver, raver, rever* to wander, be delirious] *vi* **1 a** *obs* : to be or seem to be mad or delirious **b** : to talk irrationally in or as if in delirium **c** : to declaim wildly, passionately, or boisterously ⟨in vain may heroes fight, and patriots ~ —Alexander Pope⟩ **2** : to move or advance with violence or in wild agitation : STORM, RAGE — used esp. of a natural phenomenon ⟨'tis dark: the iced gusts still ~ and beat —John Keats⟩ **3** : to be unduly loud or rapturous in one's praise : talk with excessive enthusiasm ⟨~ about her beauty⟩ ⟨*raved* over the baby⟩ ~ *vt* : to utter in madness or frenzy : pour forth wildly

**²rave** \"\ *n* -S *often attrib* **1** : an act or instance of raving **2 a** : INFATUATION, CRUSH **b** : an extravagantly commendatory critique : BLURB; *esp* : an excessively favorable dramatic criticism ⟨~ reviews of the new show⟩

**³rave** \"\ *n* -S [alter. of *rathe*, fr. ME] : one of the upper side pieces of the frame of the body of a wagon or sleigh

**ravehook** \'=,=\ n [prob. fr. obs. *rave* to pull (fr. ME *raven*) + *hook*] : a hooked tool for enlarging or clearing seams (as of a boat) to receive oakum or other caulking material

ravehook

**1ravel** \'ravəl\ vb **raveled** or **ravelled; raveled** or **ravelled; raveling** or **ravelling** \-v(ə)liŋ\ **ravels** [D *rafelen*, fr. *rafel* loose thread; akin to OHG *ravo*, *rāvo* beam, rafter, OE *rǣfter* — more at RAFTER] *vt* **1 a** : to let fall into a tangled mass (as the threads of a fabric after pulling it apart) **b** : to make intricate : ENTANGLE, INVOLVE **2** : to separate or undo the texture of : UNRAVEL, UNTWIST, UNWIND, UNWEAVE — often used with *out* or sometimes with *off* **3** : to undo the intricacies of : make plain ~ *vi* **1** *obs* **a** : to become entangled or confused **b** : to make investigation or search **2** : to become untwisted, unwoven, or unwound : FRAY; *also* : to become disentangled : become cleared of intricacy — often used with *out* **3** : to crumble or break up — used of the surface of a roadway when the road metal is no longer bonded and loose pieces are scattered about **4** : to fracture and partly cave : SLOUGH — used of ground about a mining drill hole

**2ravel** \"\ n -s : an act or result of raveling: as **a** : something (as a mass or situation) that is tangled : SNARL **b** : something raveled out, torn, or frayed : a loose thread : RAVELING

**3ra·vel** \'rāvəl\ n -s [origin unknown] *Scot* : RAILING ⟨a wooden stair ~⟩

**4ravel** \'ravəl\ n -s [3*rave* + -*el*] : RADDLE 3

**rav·el·er** or **rav·el·ler** \-v(ə)lə(r)\ n -s : one that ravels

**rave·lin** \'ravlən\ n -s [MF, fr. OIt *ravellino*, alter. of *rivellino*, dim. of *riva* bank, fr. L *ripa* — more at RIVE] : a detached work formerly used in fortifications and consisting of two embankments forming a salient angle in front of the curtain of the fortified position

**rav·el·ing** or **rav·el·ling** \'rav(ə)liŋ, -lən\ n -s : something that is raveled out; *esp* : a thread that is detached from a fabric

**rav·el·ly** \-v(ə)lē, -li\ *adj* : raveled or likely to ravel

**rav·el·ment** \'ravəlmənt\ n -s : RAVEL, TANGLE

**1ra·ven** \'rāvən\ n -s [ME *raven, reven*, fr. OE *hræfn*; akin to MD & MLG *raven*, OHG *hraban*, ON *hrafn*, L *corvus* raven, *cornix* crow, *crepare* to crack, creak, break, Gk *korax* raven, and perh. to Skt *krpate* he laments, implores] **1 a** : a large glossy-black bird (*Corvus corax*) that is widely distributed in northern parts of the northern hemisphere but now largely extinct in the eastern U.S., occurs in many local races, is omnivorous and somewhat predacious and noted for intelligent and mischievous behavior, and differs from the closely related common crow chiefly in its greater size and in having the feathers of the throat narrow and pointed **b** : any of several other usu. large and glossy-black birds of the genus *Corvus* or family Corvidae; *esp* : a somewhat predacious Australian bird (*C. coronoides*) — called also *Australian raven* **2** : a figure of a raven (as on a standard or coat of arms)

**2raven** \"\ *adj* : of the color or glossy sheen of the raven : of the color raven black ⟨~ curls⟩ ⟨~ darkness⟩

**3raven** *var of* RAVIN

**4rav·en** *also* **rav·in** \'ravən\ *vb* **ravened; ravened; ravening** \-v(ə)niŋ\ **ravens** [MF *raviner* to rush forward, take by force, ravish, fr. *ravine* rapine, impetuosity, rush — more at RAVINE] *vt* **1** *obs* : to obtain or seize by violence **2** : to devour eagerly or greedily : consume wholly ⟨like rats that ~ down their proper bane —Shak.⟩ ~ *vi* **1** : to prey or plunder with rapacity : prowl after or devour prey : feed greedily : be or become ravenous or consuming ⟨shall ~ as a wolf —Gen 49:27 (AV)⟩

**rav·e·na·la** \,ravə'nälə\ n [NL, fr. a native name in Madagascar] **1** *cap* : a genus of tropical woody plants (family Musaceae) having tall trunks, oblong distichous very long-stalked leaves, and large flowers with three sepals and three petals followed by woody 3-valved capsules — see TRAVELER'S-TREE **2** -s : any plant of the genus *Ravenala*

**raven black** n : a black approximating to violet in hue

**raven cockatoo** n : a black cockatoo of the genus *Calyptorhynchus*

**rav·e·nel·ia** \,ravə'nēlēə, -lyə\ n, *cap* [NL, fr. Henry W. *Ravenel* †1887 Am. botanist + NL -*ia*] : a genus of rust fungi (family Pucciniaceae) having the teliospores united into a head on a compound pedicel and being mostly parasites of leguminous plants

**rav·en·er** \'rav(ə)nə(r)\ n -s [ME *ravaynour, ravener*, fr. MF *ravineor*, fr. *raviner* to rush forward, take by force, ravish + -*eor* -or — more at RAVEN] **1** : one that ravens, plunders, or ravishes : ROBBER, RAVISHER **2** : a ravenous person or animal : GLUTTON

**raven gray** n : a dark gray approximating to violet in hue

**1ravening** *adj* [fr. pres. part. of 4*raven*] **1** : greedily devouring : RAPACIOUS, PREYING **2** : MAD, RABID **syn** see VORACIOUS

**2ravening** n -s [fr. gerund of 4*raven*] **1** : RAVIN **2** *obs* : RABIES

**ra·ven·ling** \'rāvənliŋ, -lēŋ\ n -s [1*raven* + -*ling*] : a young raven

**ra·ven·na grass** \rə'venə-\ n, *usu cap R* [fr. *Ravenna*, province and commune in northern Italy] : a grass (*Erianthus ravennae*) that is often cultivated for its long white-ribbed leaves and large plumes resembling those of pampas grass — called also *plume grass, wool grass*

**rav·en·ous** \'rav(ə)nəs\ *adj* [ME *rauynous* rushing, impetuous, rapacious, fr. MF *ravineus*, fr. *raviner* + -*eus* -ous] **1** : RAPACIOUS; *esp* : devouring with voracious eagerness ⟨nations ~ as wolves⟩ **2** : urgently eager for food : craving for satisfaction or gratification ⟨~ appetite⟩ ⟨a ~ boy⟩ ⟨this ~ desire⟩ **syn** see VORACIOUS

**rav·en·ous·ly** *adv* : in a ravenous manner : to a ravenous degree ⟨~ hungry⟩

**rav·en·ous·ness** n -ES : the quality or state of being ravenous

**ra·ven·ry** \'rāvənrē\ n -ES [1*raven* + -*ry*] : a place where ravens nest

**ravens** *pl of* RAVEN, *pres 3d sing of* RAVEN

**rav·en·sa·ra** \,ravən'sārə\ n, *cap* [NL, fr. Malagasy *ravendsara*, *ravin'tsara*, a tree of the genus Ravensara, lit., good leaf] : a genus of Madagascan trees (family Lauraceae) having trimerous flowers and lobed seeds — see CLOVE NUTMEG

**rav·er** \'rāvə(r)\ n -s [ME, fr. *raven* to rave + -*er* — more at RAVE] : one that raves

**rav·ery** \-v(ə)rē\ n -ES [ME *ravery*, fr. MF *resverie, reverie, raverie* — more at REVERIE] : a fit of madness or passion : RAVING, DELIRIUM

**raves** *pres 3d sing of* RAVE, *pl of* RAVE

**ra·vi·gote** \rȧvēgȯt\ n -s [F, fr. *ravigoter* to revive, refresh, alter. of *ravigorer*, fr. MF, fr. *ra-* (fr. L *re-*) + *vigueur* vigor — more at VIGOR] : a sauce or dressing colored green with spinach puree and seasoned with vinegar and a mixture of herbs (as chervil, tarragon, chives, capers)

**1rav·in** *also* **rav·en** \'ravən\ n -s [ME *ravin, ravine*, fr. MF *ravine* — more at RAVINE] **1** : RAPINE, RAPACITY **2 a** : an act or habit of preying or of devouring : PREDACITY, PREDATISM **b** : something seized or devoured as prey ⟨red in tooth and claw with ~ —Alfred Tennyson⟩

**2ravin** *adj* [ME, fr. *ravin, ravine*, n.] *obs* : RAVENOUS

**3ravin** *var of* RAVEN

**rav·i·nat·ed** \'ravə,nād·əd\ *adj* [2*ravine* + -*ate* + -*ed*] : having or broken by ravines ⟨~ hills⟩

**1ra·vine** \rə'vēn\ n -s [F, mountain torrent, ravine, fr. OF, rapine, rush, impetuosity, rush of water, fr. L *rapina* rapine — more at RAPINE] : a small narrow steep-sided valley that is larger than a gully and smaller than a canyon and is usu. worn down by running water : GORGE, GULCH

**2ravine** \"\ *vt* -ED/-ING/-s : to mark or score with or as if with ravines ⟨a badly *ravined* road⟩

**rav·ined** \'ravənd\ *adj* [1*ravin* + -*ed*] *obs* : RAVENOUS

**ravine deer** or **ravine buck** n : FOUR-HORNED ANTELOPE

**ra·viney** \rə'vēnē\ *adj* [2*ravine* + -*y*] : full of or marked by ravines

**1rav·ing** \'rāviŋ, -vēŋ\ n -s [ME, fr. gerund of *raven* to rave — more at RAVE] : irrational, incoherent, wild, or extravagant utterance or declamation; *also* : an utterance of such character — usu. used in pl.

**2raving** *adj* [ME, fr. pres. part. of *raven* to rave] **1** : talking wildly or irrationally ⟨a ~ lunatic⟩ **2** : worth raving about : notable of its kind : SUPERLATIVE ⟨a ~ beauty⟩

**3raving** or **ravingly** *adv* : in a raving manner : to such a degree as to cause or deserve raving ⟨~ mad⟩

**rav·i·o·li** \,ravē'ōlē, -li\ n -s [It *ravioli, ravioli*, fr. It dial. (southern Italy), pl. of *raviuolo, raviolo*, lit., little turnip, dim. of *rava* turnip, fr. L *rapa* — more at RAPE] : alimentary paste made in little shells or cases and stuffed (as with cheese, spinach, or meat)

**rav·ish** \'ravish, -vēsh, *esp in pres part* -vəsh\ *vb* -ED/-ING/-ES [ME *ravisshen*, fr. MF *raviss-*, extended stem of *ravir*, fr. (assumed) VL *rapire*, alter. of L *rapere* to seize, rob, kidnap, ravish — more at RAPID] *vt* **1 a** : to seize and carry away by violence : snatch by force ⟨this hand shall ~ thy pretended right —John Dryden⟩ **b (1)** : to remove from one place or state to another (as from earth to heaven); *esp* : to transport spiritually **(2)** : to transport with emotion and esp. with joy or delight ⟨~*ed* by Rome's beauty⟩ **c (1)** *obs* : to carry (a woman) away forcibly or unlawfully : ABDUCT **(2)** : to commit rape upon (a woman) : VIOLATE **2** : PLUNDER, ROB, DESPOIL **3** *obs* **a** : to alter in state, belief, or other quality — used with *from* or *to* **b** : CORRUPT ~ *vi* : to transport one with emotion

**rav·ished·ly** \-shtlē\ *adv* : in a ravished manner : as if ravished

**rav·ish·er** \-shə(r)\ n -s [ME *ravissher*, fr. *ravisshen* + -*er*] : one that ravishes

**rav·ish·ing** \'ravishiŋ, -vēsh-\ *adj* [ME *ravisshing*, fr. pres. part. of *ravisshen*] : outstandingly attractive, pleasing, or striking — **rav·ish·ing·ly** *adv*

**rav·ish·ment** \-mənt\ n -s [MF *ravissement*, fr. *raviss-* (stem of *ravir*) + -*ment*] **1** : an act or the means or effect of ravishing **2** : the condition of being ravished; *usu* : TRANSPORT, RAPTURE, ECSTASY

**rav·i·son** \'ravəsən\ n -s [F, modif. (influenced by *rave* turnip, rape, fr. L *rapa*) of G dial. *rübesan*, fr. G *rübe* rape (fr. OHG *ruoba*) + G dial. *san* seed, fr. OHG *sāmo*; akin to OS *sāmo* seed, OHG *sājen* to sow — more at RAPE, SOW] : rapeseed of an inferior quality

**ravison oil** n : a fatty oil similar to rape oil obtained from ravison in the Black sea region

**1raw** \'rȯ\ *adj* -ER/-EST [ME, fr. OE *hrēaw, hrǣw*; akin to OHG *hrō* raw, ON *hrār* raw, L *cruor* blood, *crudus* raw, Gk *kreas* flesh, Skt *kravis* raw flesh] **1** : not subjected to heat in the course of preparation as food : not cooked ⟨lived on ~ grains and fruits⟩ ⟨a ~ egg⟩ ⟨likes his steak nearly ~⟩ **2 a** : being in or nearly in the natural state : little changed by art or technical processes : UNWROUGHT, UNPROCESSED, CRUDE 1 ⟨~ textile fibers⟩ ⟨~ starch⟩ ⟨~ linseed oil⟩; *also* : not diluted or blended ⟨~ spirits⟩ **b** : unprepared or imperfectly prepared for use or enjoyment : lacking a normal or usual finish : UNDRESSED ⟨left the edges ~⟩ ⟨~ wooden shacks⟩ **c** : not presented in polished and finished form : UNDIGESTED, UNCORRECTED, UNEDITED ⟨a ~ draft of a thesis⟩ ⟨~ statistics⟩ **d** : lacking the usual guard : UNBOUND ⟨a shoe with ~ eyelets⟩ ⟨a ~ buttonhole⟩ **e** : UNCULTIVATED, UNIMPROVED ⟨~ land awaiting the builder⟩ **f** *of photographic film* : UNEXPOSED **3 a (1)** : having the skin removed so that the underlying tissues are exposed : severely chafed or galled ⟨a ~ wound⟩ **(2)** : sore from or as if from being galled ⟨a ~ irritated throat⟩ **(3)** : looking as if galled : RAWBONED **b** : lacking a natural covering ⟨a ~ eroded slope⟩ **c** : lacking clothing : NAKED ⟨liked to swim ~⟩ **4 a** : lacking in experience or understanding : serving in a new and unfamiliar role : untrained and unskilled and of problematical worth : GREEN ⟨a civilizing influence for me as for other ~ youths —R.M. Lovett⟩ ⟨~ servant girls⟩: as **(1)** *obs* : UNRIPE, IMMATURE **(2)** : new to military life ⟨an army of ~ recruits⟩ **b** : lacking in amenities and refinements since newly developed, occupied, or established and elemental, direct, primitive, and unrestrained ⟨in the West of the ~ and exciting days before the coming of the automobile —Seth Agnew⟩ ⟨creating a new world in a ~ continental mass⟩ **c** : starkly new and entirely unmellowed ⟨endless new buildings, ~ and just finished —*New Yorker*⟩ **d (1)** : lacking in refinement or graciousness : deficient in savoir faire or elegance : CRUDE 5 **(2)** *slang* : COARSE, INDELICATE, VULGAR ⟨a ~ remark⟩ **5** : disagreeably damp or cold : chilly and disagreeable : BLEAK ⟨a ~ wind⟩ ⟨~ winter days⟩ **6** *of a ceramic glaze mixture* : having no soluble ingredients and not requiring fritting **syn** see RUDE

**2raw** \"\ *vt* -ED/-ING/-s [ME *rawen*, fr. *raw*, adj.] : to cause to become raw

**3raw** \"\ n -s **1** : a raw, sore, or galled place : a sensitive spot **2** : someone or something raw, uncultivated, or unprocessed — usu. used in pl. of commercial products (as sugar or oysters) ⟨bought 100 tons of ~*s*⟩ — **in the raw** : in the natural or crude state : with the true nature or character exposed : NAKED ⟨life *in the raw*⟩ ⟨always slept *in the raw*⟩

**4raw** \"\ *chiefly Scot var of* ROW

**ra·wal·pin·di** \,rȯwəl'pindē\ *adj, usu cap* [fr. *Rawalpindi*, Pakistan] : of or from the city of Rawalpindi, Pakistan : of the kind or style prevalent in Rawalpindi

**rawbone** \(')=;=\ *adj, archaic* : RAWBONED

**rawboned** \(')=;=\ *adj* : having little flesh : gaunt to such a degree that the prominent bones seem to press on the skin **syn** see LEAN

**rawbones** \'=,=\ n *pl but sing or pl in constr* : a rawboned individual : SKELETON

**raw deal** n : unfair treatment : an act of injustice ⟨the boss gave him a *raw deal*⟩

**raw edge** n : an unfinished, rough, or undecorated edge (as at the top of a piece of hollow ware or at the margin of a piece of textile) — compare SELVAGE

**raw file** n : a file of uncoordinated and unevaluated data (as on a person or project)

**rawhead** \'=,=\ n : HOBGOBLIN, SPECTER — see BLOODYBONES

**1rawhide** \'=,=\ n [1*raw* + *hide*] **1** : untanned cattle skin that is made into leather by dehairing, liming, stuffing, and other processes **2** : a whip of untanned hide that is twisted, braided, or rolled

**2rawhide** \"\ *vt* **1** : to whip or drive with or as if with a rawhide **2** : to carry (as ore) in a hide sack

**raw·hid·er** \-də(r)\ n **1** : one that rawhides: as **a** : a miner who rawhides ore; *broadly* : a small-scale miner : PROSPECTOR **b** : a harsh taskmaster (as a domineering executive) **2** : a user of rawhide: as **a** : a border pioneer of the southwestern U.S. **b** : one that puts a protective leather covering on wooden artificial limbs

**ra·win** \'rā(,)win\ n -s [*radar* + *wind*] : a wind sounding of the atmosphere made by tracking a balloon with radar

**ra·win·sonde** \-,sänd\ n -s [*rawin* + radio*sonde*] : a radiosonde that is tracked by a radio direction-finding device to determine the velocity of winds aloft

**raw·ish** \'rȯish, -ēsh\ *adj* [1*raw* + -*ish*] : somewhat raw — **raw·ish·ness** n -ES

**Rawl** \'rȯl\ *trademark* — used for a fiber expansion insert used to fasten screws in masonry

**raw·ly** *adv* : in a raw manner : so as to be raw

**raw material** n : material available, suitable, or required for manufacture, development, training, or other finishing process but not yet so used

**raw milk** n : milk that has not been pasteurized

**rawn** \'rȯn\ *dial Eng var of* ROWEN

**raw·ness** n -ES [ME *rawnesse*, fr. *raw* + -*nesse* -ness] : the quality or state of being raw

**raw oil** n : untreated oil; *specif* : linseed oil that has not been heated or treated with driers

**raw–pack method** \'=;=-\ n : COLD-PACK METHOD 1

**raw score** n : an individual's actual achievement (as on a test) usu. expressed numerically and uncorrected for relative position (as in regard to age) in the reference population

**raw sienna** n **1** : sienna that has not been calcined — compare BURNT SIENNA 1 **2** : a brownish orange to light brown that is yellower than sorrel or tawny and yellower and darker than caramel — called also *Italian earth, Italian ocher, Mexican red, terra sienna*

**raw silk** n **1** : reeled silk before the gum is removed **2** : a woven or knitted fabric of spun silk

**raw stock** n **1** : BODY PAPER **2** : raw film

**raw sugar** n : the product of sugar manufacture before refining that consists of pale yellow to brown sugar crystals covered with a film of syrup

**raw umber** n **1** : umber that has not been calcined — compare BURNT UMBER 1 **2** : a moderate to dark yellowish brown — called also *Cyprus earth, partridge, Roman umber, Sicilian umber, Turkey umber, umber*

**raw water** n **1** : water that has not been purified ⟨for *raw water*, there's the Mississippi river at your factory door —*Time*⟩ **2** : water that has not been distilled (as for use in making ice)

**rax** \'raks\ *vb* [ME (northern dial.) *raxen*, fr. OE *raxan*; akin to OE *reccan* to stretch — more at RACK] *vi, chiefly Scot* : to stretch oneself (as on awaking); *also* : to become longer : ELONGATE ~ *vt, chiefly Scot* : to stretch or strain (oneself) toward or after; *also* : PASS, HAND

**1ray** \'rā\ n -s [ME *raye*, fr. MF *raie*, fr. L *raia*] : any of numerous elasmobranch fishes of the order Hypotremata and esp. of the suborder Batoidea having the body dorsoventrally flattened often to an extreme degree with the mouth and gill clefts on the lower and the eyes on the upper surface, the pectoral fins usu. enormously developed and continuous along the margin of the head and body, the pelvic fins of moderate size, the anal fin absent, and typically a slender whiplike caudal process often with venomous spines, being adapted for life on the sea bottom, and feeding chiefly on mollusks which they crush with blunt flattened pavement teeth; *sometimes* : any of the typical rays as distinguished from the skates and the more sharklike members of the order — see ELECTRIC RAY, GUITARFISH, STINGRAY; compare SAWFISH

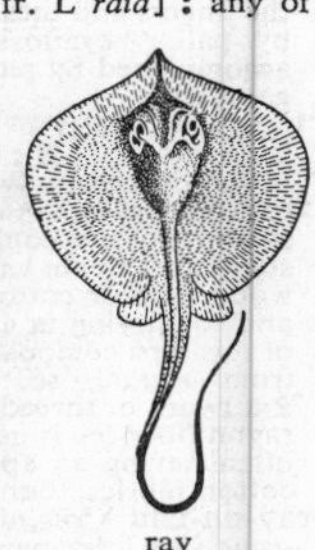

ray

**2ray** \"\ n -s [ME, fr. MF *rai*, fr. L *radius* staff, rod, spoke, radius, ray, beam; perh. akin to L *radix* root — more at ROOT] **1 a** : one of the lines of light that appear to radiate from a bright or luminous object **b** : a beam of light or other radiant energy of small cross section or infinitesimal cross section **c** : a geometrical line normal to the wave front in which radiation (as heat or light) is propagated **d** : a stream of material particles all traveling in the same line (as in radioactive phenomena); *also* : a single particle of such a stream ⟨an alpha ~⟩ **e** : a specific or limited portion of the total radiation ⟨the red ~⟩ **2** *obs* : a glance of the eye : SIGHT, VISION, PERCEPTION — see VISUAL RAY **3 a** : light cast by or in a ray or rays : RADIANCE ⟨glimmering by the lantern's dim ~⟩ **b** : moral or intellectual light or a gleam of such light **4** : a thin line suggesting a ray: **a** : any of a group of lines or processes diverging from a common center like the radii of a circle **b** : any of a system of lines passing through a point and regarded as extending indefinitely in both directions : HALF LINE **c** : any of the bright whitish lines seen on the moon near full and appearing to radiate from lunar craters **5** : any of various parts or structures (as of organisms) that are felt to resemble rays of light: as **a (1)** : any of the nearly parallel or somewhat divergent bony or cartilaginous or horny rods that extend and support the membrane in the fin of a fish and are ordinarily slender bony rods supported at their bases by parts of the internal skeleton and usu. transversely segmented into many short segments near their outer end which is often also longitudinally cleft so that the ray is soft and flexible but are stiff and unsegmented forming definite spines **(2)** : any of the radiating divisions of the body of an echinoderm with all its included parts; *also* : an arm of a crinoid or starfish **(3)** : any of the longitudinal veins of an insect's wing **b (1)** : RAY FLOWER **(2)** : a branch or flower stalk of an umbel **(3)** : a radially oriented band of parenchymatous tissue in the stele of a vascular plant usu. functioning as a storage tissue and in the radial transport of nutrients — see MEDULLARY RAY, VASCULAR RAY **6** : a representation of a ray of light : a bright strip, bar, or band **7** : a small or unsubstantial amount : PARTICLE, TRACE ⟨saw the merest ~ of hope⟩

**3ray** \"\ *vb* -ED/-ING/-s *vi* **1** : to shine or shine out with or as if with rays : emit rays; *also* : to issue as rays **2** : to issue or extend like the radii of a circle : RADIATE ⟨the little town ~*ed* out into leafy lanes —Anne D. Sedgwick⟩ ~ *vt* **1** : to send forth or emit in rays ⟨eyes that ~ out intelligence —Thomas Carlyle⟩ **2** : to furnish or mark with rays, radiating lines, or stripes **3 a** : to brighten or illuminate (as one's face or darkness) with rays of light **b** : to expose to rays (as X rays, radiations from radium, or ultraviolet light) : IRRADIATE

**4ray** \"\ n -s [ME *raye*, fr. AF (*drap de*) *raye*, lit., striped cloth; *raye* fr. OF *raie, roie* stripe, furrow, of Celt origin; akin to Gaulish *rica* furrow, W *rhych*; akin to OE *furh* furrow — more at FURROW] : a striped woolen cloth used from the 13th to the 16th centuries

**5ray** \"\ *vt* -ED/-ING/-s [ME *rayen*, short for *arayen, arrayen* — more at ARRAY] **1** *obs* : to form in order or array : EQUIP, ARRANGE; *also* : to deal with or dispose of **2** *dial chiefly Eng* : ARRAY, DRESS **3** *obs* : to make dirty : SOIL

**6ray** n -s [ME, short for *aray, array* — more at ARRAY] **1** *obs* : ARRAY, ORDER, ARRANGEMENT; *also* : a line or rank (as of soldiers) **2** *obs* : DRESS, RAIMENT

**7ray** \'rā\ *chiefly Scot var of* RYE

**8ray** \"\ *var of* RE

**ra·ya** or **ra·yah** \'rīə\ n -s [Turk *rāiyye*, fr. Ar *ra'īyah* flock, herd] : a subject Christian peasant under the Ottoman empire

**ray blight** n : a disease of chrysanthemums caused by a fungus (esp. *Ascochyta chrysanthemi*) that produces a rapid blighting of the ray flowers and often also blind or one-sided flower heads

**rayed** *adj* **1** : having rays — often used in combination ⟨spiny-*rayed* fishes⟩ **2** : having ray flowers

**ray·er** \'rāə(r)\ n -s [3*ray* + -*er*] : one that gives a swirl or radial finish to watch parts on a specially adjusted lathe

**ray filter** n : COLOR FILTER

**ray flower** or **ray floret** n **1** : one of the flowers with strap-shaped corolla occupying the margin of the head in composite plants that also have disk flowers (as aster, goldenrod, daisy, and sunflower) or making up the entire head when disk flowers are lacking (as in chicory) — see COMPOSITE illustration **2** : one of the usu. larger flowers at the margin of the umbel in some plants of the family Umbelliferae

**ray fungus** n : ACTINOMYCETE

**ray grass** n : PERENNIAL RYEGRASS

**ray gun** n : a hypothetical future weapon releasing deadly or stunning rays of unknown nature

**ray initial** n : a cell in the cambium that gives rise to cells of the rays [sense 5b (3)] — compare FUSIFORM INITIAL

**ray·leigh disk** \'rālē-, -li-\ n, *usu cap R* [after Baron John W. S. *Rayleigh* †1919 Eng. physicist] : a thin circular disk of mica or aluminum that when suspended in a beam of sound tends to set itself at right angles to the direction of propagation and by the angle assumed gives a measure of the sound intensity

**rayleigh equation** n, *usu cap R* [after Baron John W. S. *Rayleigh*] : an equation expressing the proportions in which red and green must be mixed to appear to match a given yellow in a test for anomalous color vision

**rayleigh–jeans law** \-'jēnz-\ n, *usu cap R&J* [after Baron J. W. S. *Rayleigh* and Sir James Hapwood *Jeans* †1946 Eng. physicist] : an approximation in respect to thermal radiation: the emissive power of a blackbody at absolute temperature T and at a given wavelength $\lambda$ is directly proportional to T and inversely proportional to $\lambda^4$ — compare PLANCK RADIATION LAW

**rayleigh scattering** n, *usu cap R* [after Baron John W. S. *Rayleigh*] : scattering of light by particles small enough to render the effect selective so that different colors are deflected through different angles — compare TYNDALL EFFECT

**rayleigh wave** n, *usu cap R* [after Baron John W. S. *Rayleigh*] : an elastic wave confined to the surface layers of a solid medium; *specif* : an elastic wave traveling along the surface of the earth with the plane of vibration coincident with the plane of propagation that is observed esp. in seismic disturbances

**ray·less** \'rāləs\ *adj* **:** having no rays: as **a :** DARK, BLIND **b :** having no raylike parts; *specif* **:** lacking ray flowers **c :** emitting no rays ⟨a ~ sun⟩ **d :** admitting no rays ⟨in ~ caverns dim —Lewis Morris⟩

**rayless chamomile** *n* **:** PINEAPPLE WEED

**rayless goldenrod** *n* **:** any of several plants of *Haplopappus* and related genera some of which (esp. *H. heterophyllus* and *H. fruticosus*) produce trembles in cattle — see CHRYSOTHAMNUS

**ray·less·ness** *n* -ES **:** the quality or state of being rayless

**ray·let** \'rālət\ *n* -S **:** a small ray

**raylike** \'=,=\ *adj* **:** resembling a ray esp. in having a slender elongated tapering form

**ray–liver oil** *n* [1*ray*] **:** a fish-liver oil from rays

**ray·naud's disease** \(')rā¦nōz-\ *n, usu cap R* [after Maurice *Raynaud* †1881 French physician] **:** a vascular disorder marked by recurrent spasm of the capillaries and esp. those of the fingers and toes and during exposure to cold, characterized by pallor, cyanosis and redness in succession, commonly accompanied by pain, and in severe cases progressing to local gangrene

1**rayon** \(')rā¦(y)ōn\ *n* -S [MF, fr. *rai* ray — more at RAY] **1 :** RAY, BEAM **2 :** RADIUS ⟨the ~ of a cannon's fire⟩ **3 :** a postal district in Switzerland

2**ray·on** \'rā,än\ *n* -S *often attrib* [irreg. fr. 2*ray*] **1 a :** a fine smooth hygroscopic textile fiber made in filament and staple form from various solutions of modified cellulose (as of wood pulp or cotton linters) by extruding through spinnerets and solidifying in a chemical bath or in warm air **b :** a fiber of this type composed of regenerated cellulose — distinguished from *acetate;* see CUPRAMMONIUM RAYON, VISCOSE RAYON **2 a :** yarn or thread made from continuous or staple lengths of rayon fiber ⟨~ is used in tire cords⟩ **b :** fabric made of rayon often having an appearance similar to that of silk, linen, or cotton fabrics ⟨butcher linen is a ~⟩ — see SPUN RAYON

**ray·on·ism** \'rāə,nizəm\ *n* -S [F *rayonisme,* fr. *rayon* ray + *-isme* -ism] **:** a painting style initiated in Russia in 1911 by Michael Larionov in which natural appearances are depicted as semiabstractions of radiating rays of light

**ray·on·nant** \'rāənənt\ *adj* [F, fr. pres. part. of *rayonner* to radiate, fr. MF, fr. *rayon* ray — more at RAYON] **1 :** depicted with rays darting forth — used esp. in heraldry ⟨a sun ~⟩ **2 :** characterized by the use of radiating lines (as in window tracery) — used of a French Gothic architectural style of the 14th century

**ray parenchyma** *n* [2*ray*] **:** the horizontal and usu. radially arranged parenchyma that constitutes all or most of a plant ray — compare PHLOEM PARENCHYMA, WOOD PARENCHYMA

**rays** *pl of* RAY, *pres 3d sing of* RAY

**ray's woodsia** \'rāz-\ *n, usu cap R* [fr. the name *Ray*] **:** RUSTY WOODSIA

**ray tracheid** *n* [2*ray*] **:** any of various chiefly marginal tracheids in the vascular rays of some gymnosperms that have bordered pits and lack living contents but resemble typical ray cells in position and shape

1**raze** \'rāz\ *vt* -ED/-ING/-S [alter. of *rase*] **1 :** to overthrow from the foundation **:** lay level with the ground **:** DESTROY **2 a :** to scrape, cut, or shave off **b** *obs* **:** ERASE, EFFACE, OBLITERATE **3 a** *archaic* **:** CUT, SCRATCH **b** *archaic* **:** to scrape, graze, or wound slightly **syn** see DESTROY

2**raze** \"\ *n* -S *obs* **:** an act or the result of razing **:** CUT, SCRAPE

1**ra·zee** \rā'zē\ *n* -S [F (*vaisseau*) *rasé,* fr. *vaisseau* ship + *rasé,* past part. of *raser* to rase, raze — more at RASE] **1 :** a wooden ship having its upper deck cut away and thus reduced to the next lower rate or to an intermediate class (as a seventy-four cut down to a frigate) **2 :** something (as a chest) subjected to razeeing

2**razee** \"\ *vt* **razeed; razeed; razeeing; razees 1 :** to convert (a ship) to a razee **2 :** to make less, prune, or abridge by or as if by cutting off or retrenching parts ⟨men *razeed* by poverty⟩

**raz·er** \'rāzə(r)\ *n* -S **:** one that razes

**razmataz** *var of* RAZZMATAZZ

**ra·zon** \'rā,zän\ *or* **razon bomb** *n* -S [blend of *range* and *azon* bomb] **:** an aerial bomb that can be guided to the right or left and controlled in range by radio means — compare AZON

1**ra·zor** \'rāzə(r)\ *n* -S *often attrib* [ME *rasour,* fr. OF *raseor,* fr. *raser* to rase, shave + *-eor* -or — more at RASE] **1 :** a keen-edged cutting instrument made with the cutting blade and handle in one (as a straight razor) or with the cutting blade inserted into a holder (as a safety razor or electric razor) and used chiefly for shaving or cutting the hair **2 :** RAZOR CLAM **3 :** OCKHAM'S RAZOR

razors: *1* straight, *2* safety

2**razor** \"\ *vt* -ED/-ING/-S **:** to shave or cut with or as if with a razor ⟨a closely ~*ed* beard⟩

**ra·zor·able** \-rəbəl\ *adj* [2*razor* + *-able*] *obs* **:** ready or suitable for shaving

**razorback** \'==,=\ *n* **1 :** RORQUAL **2** *or* **razorback hog** *or* **razor–backed hog :** a thin-bodied long-legged hog chiefly of the southeastern U.S. that is the half-wild mongrel descendant of improved breeds **3 :** a sharp narrow back or ridge (as of a range of hills) ⟨ridges and ~s rise precipitously from deep valleys —Lowell Thomas⟩ **4 :** a laborer who loads and unloads the cars of a traveling circus **:** ROUSTABOUT ⟨the audience at rehearsal included all the . . . ~s —T.W.Duncan⟩

**razorback buffalo fish** *n* **:** SMALLMOUTH BUFFALO

**razor–backed** \¦==¦=\ *or* **razorback** \¦==¦=\ *adj* **:** having a sharp narrow back ⟨a *razor-backed* horse⟩

**razorback sucker** *n* **:** HUMPBACK SUCKER

**razorbill** \'==,=\ *n* **1** *or* **razor–billed auk :** an auk (*Alca torda*) of the American and European coasts and islands of the northern No. Atlantic that is about 16 inches long with the plumage black above and white below and has a compressed sharp-edged black bill crossed by a white band **2 :** SKIMMER 3

**razor–billed** \¦==¦=\ *or* **razorbill** \¦==¦=\ *adj* **:** having a razor-shaped bill

**razor–billed curassow** *n* **:** any of several So. American curassows of the genus *Mitu* having a short laterally compressed bill with a knob on the culmen

**razor clam** *n* **:** any of numerous marine bivalve mollusks (family Solenidae) having a long narrow curved thin shell

**razor–edge** \'==,=\ *n* **:** an edge comparable to a razor's edge (as in fineness, sharpness, hazardous possibilities) ⟨an appetite whetted to a ~⟩

**razor fish** *n* **1 a :** any of several small wrasses (genus *Xyrichthys*); *esp* **:** a fish (*X. psittacus*) marked with bright red and blue and found esp. in the Mediterranean and West Indies **b** *southern Africa* **:** a common heavily armored shrimpfish (*Aeoliscus punctulatus*) that is found in the Indian ocean **2 :** RAZOR CLAM

**razor grass** *n* **:** a West Indian climbing sedge (*Scleria scindens*) with very rough triangular stems and leaves

**razor–grinder** \'==,==\ *n, Brit* **:** GOATSUCKER

**ra·zor·less** \'==ləs\ *adj* **:** lacking a razor

**razor saw** *n* **:** a narrow saw used in excavating limestone

**razor–sharp** \¦==¦=\ *adj* **:** very sharp **:** notably keen ⟨a *razor-sharp* wit⟩

**razor shell** *n* **1 :** RAZOR CLAM; *also* **:** its shell **2 :** PEN SHELL

**razor stone** *n* **:** NOVACULITE

**razor strop** *n* **:** STROP b

1**razz** \'raz, -aa(ə)z\ *n* -ES [short for *razzberry,* alter. of *raspberry*] *slang* **:** RASPBERRY 3

2**razz** \"\ *vt* -ED/-ING/-ES **:** to tease and banter at **:** RIDICULE ⟨~*ed* me over my friend⟩ ⟨the fans who sit in the bleachers and ~ the visiting outfielders⟩

**raz·zia** \'razēə\ *n* -S [F, fr. colloq. Ar *ghazyah* (Ar *ghazwah, ghazāh*)] **:** a plundering and destructive incursion **:** FORAY, RAID

**raz·zle** \'razəl\ *n* -S [by shortening] **:** RAZZLE-DAZZLE 1

**razzle–dazzle** \¦==¦==\ *n* [irreg. redupl. of *dazzle*] **1 :** a state of confusion, hilarity, or disorder; *esp* **:** SPREE **2 :** something that induces or is intended to induce a state of confusion: as **a :** a swiftly revolving undulating carrousel without seats **b :** complex maneuvers (as in a competitive sport) designed to confuse the opponent ⟨complaining about the lack of much *razzle-dazzle* in modern football⟩ **c :** a loud, fast-moving, and often cheap atmosphere or exhibition ⟨the *razzle-dazzle* of the circus⟩ ⟨a sideshow of dancing girls and other *razzle-dazzle* —*Time*⟩

**razz·ma·tazz** *also* **raz·ma·taz** \¦razmə¦taz, ¦raaz-, -taa(ə)z\ *n* -ES [by alter.] **:** RAZZLE-DAZZLE

**rb** *abbr* ruble

**RB** *abbr* **1** rifle brigade **2** right back **3** right fullback

**Rb** *symbol* rubidium

**RBC** *abbr* red blood cells; red blood count

**RBH** *abbr* regimental beachhead

**RBI** *abbr or n* -S **:** a run batted in

**rbl** *abbr* ruble

**RC** \'är¦sē\ *abbr or n* -S Roman Catholic

**RC** *abbr* **1** recruiting center **2** rehabilitation center **3** reinforced concrete **4** relief claim **5** release clause **6** remote control **7** reply coupon **8** *often not cap* resistance-capacitance **9** right center

**rcd** *abbr* **1** received **2** record

**RCG** *abbr, often not cap* reverberation-controlled gain

**RCL** *abbr* ruling case law

**RCM** *abbr* **1** radar countermeasure **2** regimental court-martial

**rcn** *abbr* reconnaissance

**r color** *n* **:** an acoustic effect of a simultaneously articulated \r\ imparted to a vowel by retroflexion or bunching of the tongue — **r–colored** \'=,==\ *adj*

**rcpt** *abbr* receipt

**rct** *abbr* **1** receipt **2** recruit

**RCT** *abbr* regimental combat team

**rctg** *abbr* recruiting

**rcvr** *abbr* receiver

**rd** *abbr* **1** red **2** reduce; reduced; reduction **3** road **4** rod **5** rood **6** round **7** rutherford

**-rd** *symbol* — used after the figure 3 to indicate the ordinal number *third* or any ordinal number ending with *third* ⟨June 3rd⟩ ⟨43rd St.⟩; compare -D, -ND

**RD** *abbr* **1** reaction of degeneration **2** refer to drawer **3** regional director **4** right defense **5** *often not cap* rix dollar **6** *often not cap* running days **7** rural dean **8** rural delivery **9** rural district

**RDA** *abbr, often not cap* recommended dietary allowance

**RdAc** *symbol* radioactinium

**RDC** *abbr* **1** rail diesel car **2** running-down clause **3** rural district council

**RDF** *abbr* radio direction finder

**rdg** *abbr* **1** reading **2** reducing **3** ridge

**rdm** *abbr* **1** radarman **2** random

**rdo** *abbr* radio

**RdTh** *symbol* radiothorium

**rdv** *abbr* rendezvous

**RDX** \¦är(,)dē¦eks\ *n* -ES [code name, prob. fr. *R*esearch *D*epartment e*x*plosive] **:** CYCLONITE

**RDY** *abbr* royal dockyard

1**re** *or* **ray** \'rā\ *n* -S [ML *re,* fr. L *re*sonare to resound, a word sung to this note in a medieval hymn to St. John the Baptist] **1 :** the second tone of the diatonic scale in solmization **2 :** the tone *D* in the fixed-do system

2**re** \'rā, 'rē\ *prep* [L, abl of *res* thing, affair, matter — more at REAL] **:** with regard to **:** REGARDING **:** in the matter of **:** on the subject of **:** CONCERNING **:** IN RE ⟨their remarks ~ the new building were most interesting⟩ ⟨~ your letter of last month⟩

**re–** *prefix* [ME, fr. OF, fr L *re-, red-*] **1 :** again **:** anew ⟨*re*do⟩ ⟨*re*tell⟩ — usu. joined to the second element by a hyphen when (1) the word (as *re-create*) would otherwise be confused with another word (as *recreate*) of different meaning, or (2) the word (as *re-recover*) has a second element beginning with *re-,* or (3) the second element begins with a capital letter (as *re-Christianization*) **2 :** back **:** backward ⟨*re*call⟩

**re** *abbr* **1** reference **2** rupee

**RE** *abbr* **1** rate of exchange **2** real estate **3** red edges **4** repayable to either **5** *often not cap* reticuloendothelial **6** right end **7** right eye **8** right excellent **9** rural electrification

**RE** *symbol* rare earth (sense 2)

**Re** *symbol* rhenium

**'re** \(ə)r, ə\ *vb* [by contr.] **:** ARE ⟨what'*re* you doing⟩ ⟨these '*re* right⟩

**rea** *var of* REUS

**re·able** \(')rē+\ *vt* -ED/-ING/-S [*re-* + *able*] *chiefly Brit* **:** REHABILITATE — **re·able·ment** \(')rē¦ābəlmənt\ *n* -S

**re·absorb** \¦rē+\ *vb* [*re-* + *absorb*] *vt* **:** to absorb again; RESORB 2 ~ *vi* **:** RESORB

**re·absorption** \"+\ *n* [*re-* + *absorption*] **:** the act, process, or condition of absorbing again or of being absorbed again

**re·accept** \"+\ *vt* [*re-* + *accept*] **:** to accept again — **re·acceptance** \"+\ *n*

**re·access** \(¦)rē+\ *n* [*re-* + *access*] **:** renewed access **:** RETURN ⟨a ~ of fever⟩

**re·accession** \¦rē+\ *n* [*re-* + *accession*] **:** renewed accession ⟨~ to power⟩

**re·acclimatization** \"+\ *n* [*re-* + *acclimatization*] **:** the act or process of reacclimatizing or condition of being reacclimatized ⟨the patient's ~ to society —*Digest of Neurology & Psychiatry*⟩

**re·acclimatize** \"+\ *vt* [*re-* + *acclimatize*] **:** to acclimatize again ⟨~ their children and themselves to the different rhythms of urban life —*N. Y. Times*⟩

**re·accommodate** \¦rē+\ *vt* [*re-* + *accommodate*] **:** to accommodate again

**re·accommodation** \"+\ *n* [*re-* + *accommodation*] **:** renewed accommodation

**re·accounting** \"+\ *n* [*re-* + *accounting*] **:** retroactive accounting

**re·accredit** \"+\ *vt* [*re-* + *accredit*] **:** to accredit again ⟨~ their envoys —*N. Y. Times*⟩

**re·accreditation** \"+\ *n* [*re-* + *accreditation*] **:** renewed accreditation

**re·acetylation** \"+\ *n* [*re-* + *acetylation*] **:** renewed acetylation

1**reach** \'rēch\ *vb* **reached** \'rēcht\ *or dial* **retch** \'rech\ *or dial chiefly Brit* **raught** \'rȯ(k)t\ *or dial chiefly Brit* **rought** \"\ **reached** *or dial chiefly Brit* **raught** *or dial chiefly Brit* **rought; reaching; reaches** [ME *rechen* (past *raughte, rechede,* past part. *raught, yraught, reched, yreched*), fr. OE *rǣcan* (past *rǣhte,* past part. *gerǣht*); akin to OHG *reichen* to reach, ON *reik* parting of the hair, Lith *ráižytis* to stretch oneself repeatedly] *vt* **1 a** (1) **:** to stretch out **:** EXTEND ⟨~*ed* out his hand to her⟩ (2) **:** to put forth ⟨a tree that ~*es* its branches over the wall⟩ **b :** THRUST ⟨~*ed* his sword up and touched the mark⟩ **c** *archaic* (1) **:** to strike, hit, or touch with a weapon (2) **:** to aim or deliver (a blow) by stretching out the hand **:** DEAL ⟨a sudden punch which he ~*ed* at the nose of his lordship —Henry Brooke⟩ **2 a** *obs* **:** to get possession of esp. by or as if by seizing and making off with ⟨the hand of death hath *raught* him —Shak.⟩ **b** (1) **:** to succeed in touching or grasping by or as if by stretching out the hand or some other part of the body or some other object ⟨the shelf was too high for the little boy to ~ it⟩ ⟨probed about in the darkness with his foot and at last ~*ed* the bottom step⟩ ⟨could not ~ the bullet with the probe⟩ (2) *archaic* **:** SNATCH (3) **:** to pick up and draw toward one **:** TAKE ⟨~*ed* a cup from the shelf⟩ ⟨~*ed* down his hat⟩ **c** (1) **:** to stretch out as far as **:** extend to ⟨by evening the shadow of the tree ~*ed* the wall⟩ (2) **:** to arrive at **:** get up to or as far as **:** come to ⟨can ~ the gate by following this path⟩ ⟨your letter has ~*ed* me⟩ ⟨her voice was not strong enough to ~ everyone in the auditorium⟩ ⟨has ~*ed* middle age⟩ **:** go as far as ⟨has ~*ed* a new height of absurdity⟩ ⟨a book that has now ~*ed* its third edition⟩ **:** ATTAIN ⟨spent his whole life trying to ~ happiness⟩ ⟨think we can ~ an understanding by further discussion⟩ (3) **:** to penetrate to ⟨a telescope that ~*es* remote points in space⟩ ⟨the news ~*ed* every part of the world⟩ (4) **:** to succeed in getting or obtaining **:** ACQUIRE ⟨~*ing* a profound knowledge of the subject⟩ **d** (1) **:** to stretch out to and affect **:** COVER, EMBRACE ⟨a situation that the law certainly ~*es*⟩ (2) **:** to get into contact with (as intellectually or emotionally) and so influence ⟨was not sure how she could ~ a person with a background like that⟩ **:** make an impression on (3) **:** to get in touch with (as by correspondence, publication) **:** communicate with ⟨~*ed* him by phone at the office⟩ ⟨you can ~ me by addressing your letters to New York⟩ ⟨could ~ a vast audience with such a magazine⟩ **3** *dial chiefly Eng* **:** to cause (as a piece of leather) to be stretched **4 :** to take hold of and give **:** PASS **:** hand over ⟨~ me the catsup⟩ **5** *archaic* **:** to succeed in understanding **:** COMPREHEND ⟨some double sense that I ~ not —P.B.Shelley⟩ ~ *vi* **1 a :** to make a stretch (as in proceeding to grasp, touch, strike) in some direction with or as if with one's hand or some other part of the body **:** stretch out ⟨~*ed* for some money⟩ ⟨stood on tiptoe and ~*ed* toward the book on the top shelf⟩ ⟨~*ed* for the stone with his foot⟩ **b** (1) **:** to make a stretch of a particular length or extent ⟨does not dare to ~ after fame⟩ (2) **:** to strain after something **:** make efforts ⟨~*ing* above our nature does no good —John Dryden⟩ **2 a :** to undergo continuous extension **:** become drawn out **:** PROJECT, EXTEND ⟨his land ~*es* to the river⟩ ⟨power that ~*es* to every corner of the country⟩ **b :** to get up to or as far as something **:** arrive at something **:** come to something **:** PENETRATE, CARRY ⟨the forest stretched as far as the eye could ~⟩ **3** *dial chiefly Brit* **:** to become stretched **:** undergo stretching **4 :** to sail on a reach

**syn** GAIN, COMPASS, ACHIEVE, ATTAIN: REACH may be used in reference to any goal, point, or end arrived at ⟨our team *reached* the finals⟩ ⟨the wheat crop *reached* 500,000 tons⟩ ⟨the automobile *reached* a speed of 120 miles per hour⟩ ⟨the life boat *reached* land in the morning⟩ ⟨Pictured Rocks, where the coloration *reaches* its greatest intensity —*Amer. Guide Series: Mich.*⟩ GAIN often but not always implies coming to a desired goal, vantage point, or advantage through effort or struggle ⟨to *gain* the championship⟩ ⟨*gaining* the presidency⟩ ⟨*gaining* distinction by his research⟩ ⟨*gaining* prestige⟩ ⟨*gaining* success in his field⟩ ⟨he *gained* the confidence of the mountain people by his understanding and sympathetic approach —F.T. Persons⟩ COMPASS may suggest gaining an end as by skillful resolution, crafty encirclement, circumvention, or extension ⟨*compassing* almost equally with verse man's thought however sublime, his emotion however profound —A.T.Quiller-Couch⟩ ⟨he certainly managed to *compass* the hardest thing that a man who has drunk heavily can do. He took his peg and wine at dinner; but he never drank alone, and never let what he drank have the least hold on him —Rudyard Kipling⟩ ACHIEVE may imply skill, courage, persistence, or endurance in struggle or quest ⟨in twenty-five years of unremitting toil, he had *achieved* a distinguished position —R.J.Wickenden⟩ ⟨man will want consciously and desperately to *achieve* the consolation and create the beauty we have always called literature —C.F. Strauch⟩ ATTAIN sometimes suggests a reaching to the extreme, the difficult, the unusual ⟨an object, in its own nature so really and undeniably good, as to be the compensation of a great deal of thought in the *compassing,* and a great deal of trouble in the *attaining* —J.H.Newman⟩ ⟨men had *attained* the stratosphere —Waldemar Kaempffert⟩ ⟨its refinement of detail and subtle proportions, which *attain* an almost monumental quality —*Amer. Guide Series: Maine*⟩

2**reach** \"\ *n* -ES **1 a** (1) **:** the action or an act of reaching ⟨made a ~ for the nearest one⟩ (2) **:** a single movement **:** an individual part of a progression or journey ⟨arriving at the post after three ~*es*⟩ **b** (1) **:** the particular distance or extent of reaching ⟨if the shelf is lowered, a long ~ won't be necessary⟩ (2) **:** the particular distance over which or the extent to which one can reach ⟨has a remarkable ~⟩ ⟨this is within your ~⟩ **c :** power of comprehension or range of knowledge or thought ⟨a mind of vast ~⟩ **2 a :** a continuous unbroken stretch or expanse: as (1) **:** an extended portion of water or land (2) **:** a straight portion of a stream or river (3) **:** a level stretch of water between locks in a canal (4) **:** an arm of the sea extending up into the land (5) **:** PROMONTORY **b :** a limited distance **:** a measured part ⟨the narrow stairwell turned back upon itself in a succession of niggard ~*es* —William Faulkner⟩ **3** *obs* **:** DESIGN, SCHEME, PLAN **4 a :** a bearing shaft or a coupling pole; *esp* **:** the pole or rod joining the hind axle to the forward bolster of a wagon **b :** the sum of the hoist and the minimum distance between the hooks of a pulley tackle **c :** the length of the threaded portion of a bolt or spark plug **5 :** the tack sailed by a ship with the wind coming just forward of the beam or with the wind directly abeam or abaft the beam **syn** see RANGE

3**reach** \"\ *vb* -ED/-ING/-ES [prob. fr. (assumed) ME *rechen,* fr. OE *hrǣcan;* akin to OE *hrāca* phlegm from the throat, ON *hrāki* spittle, *hrækja* to hawk, spit, Lith *krėgėti* to grunt, L *crepare* to crack, creak, break — more at RAVEN] **1** *dial chiefly Eng* **a :** SPIT **b :** HAWK **2** *dial chiefly Eng* **a :** VOMIT **b :** RETCH

**reach·able** \-chəbəl\ *adj* **:** capable of being reached ⟨all these cities are ~ in a few hours —*N. Y. Times*⟩

**reached** *past of* REACH

**reach·er** \'rēchə(r)\ *n* -S [1*reach* + *-er*] **:** HANDER-IN

**reacher–in** \¦==¦=\ *n, pl* **reacher–ins** *also* **reachers–in** [fr. the phrase *reach in* + *-er*] **:** HANDER-IN

**reaches** *pres 3d sing of* REACH, *pl of* REACH

1**reaching** *n* -S [ME *rechynge,* fr. OE *rǣcing,* fr. *rǣcan* to reach + *-ing* (suffix forming nouns from verbs)] **:** the action of one that reaches for something or an instance of grasping or seeking to grasp ⟨incomplete, abstracted ~*s* for the meaning of things —Walter Lippmann⟩

2**reaching** *adj* [fr. pres. part. of 1*reach*] **:** that reaches out, forward, or into something; *esp* **:** deeply penetrating ⟨the views of the lord deputy, somewhat more ~ than their own, startled them —Robert Browning⟩

**reaching jib** *or* **reaching sail** *n* **:** BALLOON SAIL

**reaching post** *n* **:** the post at the lower end of a rope walk

**reach·less** \'rēchləs\ *adj* **:** that cannot be reached **:** not within reach ⟨~ heights⟩

**reach–me–down** \'==,=\ *adj or n, chiefly Brit* **:** HAND-ME-DOWN

**reach rod** *n* **:** a rod with a double eye at each end for communicating the motion of the reversing lever of a link motion to the lifting shaft

**reachy** \'rēchē\ *adj* -ER/-EST [2*reach* + *-y*] **1 :** marked by notable extension ⟨a long, ~ trot —C.W.Gay⟩ **2 :** marked by notable length of neck and body ⟨~ poultry⟩

**re·acknowledge** \¦rē+\ *vt* [*re-* + *acknowledge*] **:** to acknowledge again

**re·acquaint** \"+\ *vt* [*re-* + *acquaint*] **:** to make acquainted again

**re·acquire** \"+\ *vt* [*re-* + *acquire*] **:** to acquire again

**re·acquisition** \(¦)rē+\ *n* [*re-* + *acquisition*] **:** renewed acquisition

**re·act** \rē+\ *vb* -ED/-ING/-S [NL *reactus,* past part. of *reagere,* fr. L *re-* + *agere* to drive, act — more at AGENT] *vi* **1 :** to exert a reciprocal or counteracting force or influence — often used with *on* or *upon* ⟨exhausting work must ~ on human character —Samuel Van Valkenburg & Ellsworth Huntington⟩ **2 :** to respond in a particular way to a particular treatment, situation, or other stimulus ⟨~*ed* with instinctive indignation —J.P.Frank⟩ — often used with *to* ⟨was not sure how the patient would ~ to the drug⟩ **3 :** to act in opposition to some force or influence — usu. used with *against* ⟨~*ed* against the threat of dictatorship —*New School for Social Research Bull.*⟩ ⟨~*ing* against mass ideologies —Henry Hewes⟩ **4 :** to move in or tend toward a reverse direction **:** return to or toward a prior condition ⟨public opinion wavered briefly but soon ~*ed* in his favor⟩ ⟨stock prices ~*ed* strongly after a brief drop⟩ **5 :** to undergo chemical reaction ~ *vt* **:** to cause to react; *specif* **:** to bring about a chemical reaction in ⟨produces ethyl chloride by ~*ing* chlorine with waste —*Lamp*⟩ **syn** see ACT

**re–act** \(¦)rē+\ *vt* [*re-* + *act*] **:** to act or perform a second time ⟨in his imagination he *re-acted* the scene —Aldous Huxley⟩

**re·ac·tance** \rē'aktən(t)s\ *n* -S [ISV *react* + *-ance*] **1 :** the part of the impedance of an alternating-current circuit that is due either to capacitance or inductance or to both and that is expressed in ohms **2 :** ACOUSTIC REACTANCE

**reactance coil** *n* **:** REACTOR 3

**reactance drop** *n* **:** the voltage drop in a circuit due to the current traversing the reactance

**reactance tube** *n* **:** an electron tube that by a variation of its operating voltage can give the effect of a variation of reactance across its electrodes or across a network connected to its electrodes

**1re·ac·tant** \-nt\ *n* -s [*react* + *-ant*, n. suffix] **1 :** a chemically reacting substance **2 :** an initial factor in a chemical reaction — opposed to *resultant*
**2reactant** \"\ *adj* [*react* + *-ant*, adj. suffix] **1 :** of, relating to, or marked by reactance **2** [*1reactant*] **:** of or relating to a reactant
**re·action** \rē+\ *n* -s [NL *reaction-, reactio*, fr. *reactus* (past part. of *reagere* to react) + L *-ion-, -io* -ion — more at REACT] **1 a :** exertion of reciprocal or counteracting force or influence ⟨the ~ between an individual and his environment⟩ **b :** action in opposition to some force or influence ⟨~ against dictatorship⟩ **c :** movement in or tendency toward a reverse direction **:** return to a prior condition ⟨a strong ~ in stock prices⟩ **d :** a tendency toward or movement in support of a former esp. outmoded or repressive political or social condition, policy, or form of government ⟨mixture of sober conservatism, timid standpattism, and angry ~ —Clinton Rossiter⟩ **2 a :** a particular response to a particular treatment, situation, or other stimulus ⟨watched her ~ to the news⟩ **b :** bodily response to or activity aroused by a stimulus: (1) **:** motor response (as muscular movement or secretion) to stimulation (2) **:** the whole sensorimotor process comprising intellectual and emotional elements as well as pure motor response **:** total response of an organism to a stimulus **c** (1) **:** an action induced by vital resistance to some other action ⟨inflammatory ~ to bacterial infection⟩; *esp* **:** the specific result (as hemolysis, local inflammation, or a rise in bodily temperature) characteristically evoked in cells or tissues or in vitro by a foreign substance and used in various serological tests to determine specific sensitivities or the presence of particular infection ⟨the tuberculin ~⟩ ⟨the precipitin ~⟩ ⟨allergic ~*s*⟩ (2) **:** depression or exhaustion of vital force consequent on overexertion or overstimulation (3) **:** heightened activity and overaction succeeding depression or shock (4) **:** a psychosis, psychoneurosis, or other mental or emotional disorder forming an individual's response to his life situation ⟨an anxiety ~⟩ ⟨a schizophrenic ~⟩ **3 :** the force that a body subjected to the action of a force from another body exerts in the opposite direction **4 a** (1) **:** chemical transformation or change **:** the reversible or irreversible interaction of molecules, atoms, ions, or radicals to form one or more new substances ⟨the ~ of acid with base⟩ ⟨the ~ of hydrogen with oxygen gives water⟩ ⟨endothermic and exothermic ~*s*⟩ — see EQUATION 2b, ORDER OF A REACTION; compare CATALYSIS, DECOMPOSITION, POLYMERIZATION, SUBSTITUTION, SYNTHESIS (2) **:** the state resulting from such a reaction ⟨an alkaline ~⟩ **b :** a process involving change in atomic nuclei (as the disintegration of uranium 239 into neptunium and an electron or the union of heavy-hydrogen nuclei to form helium nuclei) — called also *nuclear reaction*; compare CHAIN REACTION, FISSION, FUSION, SPALLATION **5 :** the effect of organisms upon their habitat — compare COACTION **6 :** the degree of acidity or alkalinity of soil
**re·ac·tion·al** \rē'akshən°l, -kshnəl\ *adj* [ISV *reaction* + *-al*] **:** of, relating to, or marked by reaction ⟨a ~ rise in temperature⟩ — **re·ac·tion·al·ly** \-°lē, -əlē\ *adv*
**re·ac·tion·ar·i·ness** \rē'akshə,nerēnəs, -rin-, ...\ *n* -ES **:** REACTIONISM
**re·ac·tion·arism** \-ˌnə,rizəm\ *n* -s [*1reactionary* + *-ism*] **:** REACTIONISM
**re·ac·tion·arist** \-ˌrəst\ *n* -s [*1reactionary* + *-ist*] **:** REACTIONARY
**1re·ac·tion·ary** \rē'akshə,nerē, -eri\ *adj* [F *réactionnaire*, fr. *réaction* reaction (fr. NL *reaction-, reactio*) + *-aire* -ary] **:** relating to, marked by, or favoring reaction (as toward a former political order) **syn** see CONSERVATIVE
**2reactionary** \"\ *n* -ES **:** one that is reactionary
**re·ac·tion·ary·ism** \-,izəm\ *n* -s [*1reactionary* + *-ism*] **:** the quality or state of being reactionary **:** REACTIONISM
**reaction engine** *n* **:** an engine that develops thrust by expelling a jet of fluid or a stream of particles
**reaction formation** *n* **:** an attitude, trait, or behavioral tendency that substitutes for or conceals a diametrically opposed repressed impulse
**re·ac·tion·ism** \-shə,nizəm\ *n* -s [*reaction* + *-ism*] **:** the quality or state of being reactionary
**1re·ac·tion·ist** \-sh(ə)nəst\ *n* -s [*reaction* + *-ist*] **:** REACTIONARY
**2reactionist** \"\ *adj* **:** REACTIONARY
**reaction kinetics** *n pl but sing or pl in constr* **:** a branch of chemistry that deals with the rate of chemical reactions, with factors influencing such rates, and with applications of rate studies to elucidate the mechanism of reactions — compare ORDER OF A REACTION
**reaction motor** *n* **:** REACTION ENGINE
**reaction propulsion** *n* **:** propulsion produced by a reaction engine
**reaction rim** *also* **reaction border** *n* **:** a zone of one or more species of mineral surrounding a larger crystal of another kind and representing reaction between a solidified mineral and the surrounding liquid magma — compare RESORPTION BORDER
**reaction ring** *n* **:** a heavy internal cast-iron flange set in cement and used to resist the thrust of the jacks when sinking a shaft by a process in which a continuous casing is forced downward as the excavation progresses
**reactions** *pl of* REACTION
**reaction time** *n* **:** the time elapsing between the beginning of the application of a stimulus and the beginning of an organism's reaction to it — compare LATENT PERIOD, PRESENTATION TIME
**reaction turbine** *n* **:** a turbine with rotating blades curved and arranged so as to develop torque from gradual decrease of steam pressure from inlet to exhaust — compare IMPULSE TURBINE
**reaction type** *n* **:** PHENOTYPE
**reaction wood** *n* **:** wood (as compression wood, tension wood) that develops abnormally by reason of varying factors (as atypical gravitational pull)
**re·activate** \(')rē+\ *vb* [*re-* + *activate*] *vt* **:** to activate again **:** cause to be again active or more active **:** restore to a state of activity or greater activity **:** make again operational and effective **:** REVIVE, REVIVIFY: as **a** (1) **:** to restore (as a military unit) to an active state (as from a state of disorganization or deactivation) (2) **:** to cause (as an industrial plant, a society, a program, a commission) to function again after a suspension of activity ⟨*reactivated* the factory as soon as the strike was over⟩ **b :** to cause (as a repressed complex) to reappear in consciousness or behavior ⟨persecution feelings *reactivated* by new social failures⟩ **c :** to cause (a quiescent disease) to become active again in an individual ⟨tuberculosis that was *reactivated* by fatigue⟩ **d :** to restore complement to (an inactivated serum) by addition of fresh normal serum **e :** to restore ability of (an electron tube) to emit electrons copiously from a cathode **f :** to make (as a catalyst or an adsorbent) active again ~ *vi* **:** to become active again
**re·activation** \(ˌ)rē+\ *n* [*reactivate* + *-ion*] **:** the act or process of reactivating or condition of being reactivated
**re·activator** \(')rē+\ *n* [*reactivate* + *-or*] **:** one that reactivates: as **a :** a substance that restores the reactivity of another substance **b :** ACTIFIER
**re·active** \rē+\ *adj* [prob. fr. (assumed) NL *reactivus*, fr. NL *reactus* (past part. of *reagere* to react) + L *-ivus* -ive — more at REACT] **1 a :** of, relating to, or marked by reaction ⟨~ symptoms⟩ ⟨a ~ process⟩ **b :** of, relating to, or marked by reactance **2 a :** readily responsive to stimulus ⟨the skin of the geriatric is less ~ than that of younger persons —Louis Tuft⟩ **b :** occurring as a result of stress or emotional upset ⟨~ depression⟩ — **re·actively** \"+\ *adv* — **re·activeness** \"+\ *n*
**reactive coil** *n* **:** REACTOR 3
**reactive component** *n* **1 :** the component of an alternating current that has a phase difference of 90° with the electromotive force **2 :** the component of the voltage across the circuit that is in quadrature with the current and that produces no power in an alternating current circuit — called also *wattless component*
**reactive factor** *n* **:** a factor that is constituted by the ratio of the reactive volt-amperes to the apparent power in an alternating-current circuit and that is equal to the sine of the angular phase difference between voltage and current
**reactive load** *n* **:** a load which is carried by an alternating current generating station or system in which the current and voltage are out of phase and which is measured in volt-amperes or kilovolt-amperes
**reactive power** *n* **:** REACTIVE VOLT-AMPERES
**reactive volt-amperes** *n pl* **:** the product of the effective voltage and effective current in an alternating-current circuit and the sine of the angular phase difference between them
**re·activity** \(ˌ)rē+\ *n* [ISV *reactive* + *-ity*] **1 :** the quality or state of being reactive **2 :** the rate of nuclear disintegration in a reactor
**re·ac·to·log·i·cal** \rē¦aktə¦läjəkəl\ *adj* **:** of or relating to reactology
**re·ac·tol·o·gist** \(ˌ)rē,ak'täləjəst\ *n* -s **:** a specialist in reactology
**re·ac·tol·o·gy** \-jē\ *n* -ES [*reaction* + *-o-* + *-logy*] **:** the scientific study of psychological reactions — compare REFLEXOLOGY
**re·actor** \rē+\ *n* -s [ISV *react* + *-or*] **1 :** one that reacts: as **a :** a chemical reagent **b** (1) **:** the subject reacting to a stimulus in a psychological experiment (2) **:** the subject reacting positively to a foreign substance (as in a test for disease) ⟨tuberculous cattle are ~*s* to tuberculin⟩ **2 :** an organism that produces reaction in its environment **3 :** a coil, winding, or conductor of small resistance and large inductance used in an alternating-current circuit to impede or throttle the current or to change its phase **4 a :** a piece of equipment in which a chemical reaction is carried out esp. on an industrial scale ⟨batch and continuous ~*s*⟩ **b :** an apparatus in which a chain reaction of fissionable material is initiated and controlled (as for generation of heat for power or for production of plutonium from uranium) — called also *atomic furnace, atomic pile, nuclear reactor, pile*
**re·actualization** \(ˌ)rē+\ *n* **:** the act of reactualizing or condition of being reactualized
**re·actualize** \(')rē+\ *vt* [*re-* + *actualize*] **:** to actualize again
**re·actuate** \"+\ *vt* [*re-* + *actuate*] **:** to actuate again
**1read** \'rēd\ *vb* **read** \'red\ **read** \"\ **reading** \'rēdiŋ, -dēŋ\ **reads** \'rēdz\ [ME *reden* to read, advise, interpret, govern, fr. OE *rǣdan*; akin to OE *rǣd* advice, counsel, council, OHG *rātan* to advise, *rāt* advice, supply, ON *rātha* to advise, interpret, govern, *rāth* advice, management, Goth *garedan* to take into consideration, Skt *rādhnoti, rādhyati* he succeeds, prepares, accomplishes, Gk *arariskein* to fit — more at ARM] *vt* **1 a** (1) **:** to look at or otherwise scan (as letters or other symbols representing words or sentences) with mental formulation of the words or sentences represented ⟨~*ing* books⟩ ⟨~*ing* inscriptions⟩ (2) **:** to study the movements of (as lips) or the formation of (as smoke signals) or the manipulation of (as signaling flags) with mental formulation of the communication expressed ⟨can ~ lips⟩ (3) **:** to form with the lips or utter aloud (such mental formulations) ⟨~ the text clearly⟩ (4) **:** to understand the meaning and grasp the full sense of (such mental formulations) either with or without vocal reproduction ⟨students that can really ~ the classics⟩ **b** (1) **:** to see or find in printed or written form or in some similar form ⟨~ that the marriage would take place soon⟩ (2) **:** to learn from what one has seen or found in such form ⟨had ~ that the mineral was rare⟩ **c :** to deliver aloud by or as if by reading: as (1) **:** to cause another to become acquainted with the contents of (as something written or printed) ⟨please ~ me the letter⟩ ⟨~ them a story⟩ (2) *obs* **:** to give instruction in ⟨~ Euclid to some of his disciples —John Davies †1693⟩ (3) **:** to submit (a proposed measure) to a legislative assembly by reading all or part of (4) **:** to speak the lines of (as a character in a play) or deliver the text of (as a selection by a particular writer) and interpret (as by intonation, gesture) ⟨~*s* the part with conviction⟩ ⟨~*s* Shakespeare with moving simplicity⟩ **d** (1) **:** to go over or become acquainted with or get through the contents of (as a book, magazine, newspaper, letter) by reading **:** PERUSE ⟨~*ing* the evening newspapers⟩ ⟨haven't yet ~ the novel⟩ (2) **:** to make a special study of (as by reading books and attending lectures) **:** apply oneself to the study of by following an organized course in ⟨~ law but later chose journalism —E.E.Allen⟩ **e :** to read books or other printed or written material in (a particular language) ⟨is learning to ~ Danish⟩; *esp* **:** to have such knowledge of (a particular language) as to be able to read with full understanding ⟨~*s* German, French, and Italian⟩ ⟨~*s* Spanish but can't speak it⟩ **f :** to observe and note the indications of (as a thermometer or other graduated instrument) ⟨is ~*ing* the meter⟩ **g** (1) **:** to check or edit (copy) to be set in type (2) **:** to check (proof) for discrepancies between proof and copy **h** (1) **:** to receive (a message) over a communication system (2) **:** to be able to understand (as a transmitted message) ⟨~ you loud and clear⟩ (3) **:** COMPREHEND, JUDGE ⟨sister . . . I ~ you all wrong —C.B.Kelland⟩ **i** *of a computer* **:** to scan and register or reproduce: (1) **:** to transfer (data fed in) to an internal medium (as magnetic tape, cards) for storage or computation (2) **:** to transfer (stored or computed data) to an external reproducing medium **2 a :** to study and advance an interpretation of the meaning or significance of (as a riddle, dream, omen, the palms of the hands) **b :** to make known (as the future) beforehand **:** FORETELL, PREDICT, FORESEE ⟨says she can ~ your fortune⟩ **3 a** (1) **:** to find revealed (as in the face or look of a person) ⟨~ dismay in her countenance⟩ (2) **:** to penetrate into (as the thoughts, mind of another) ⟨claims he can ~ your thoughts⟩ **b :** to learn the nature of (as another's character, feelings) by close observation of outward signs ⟨~ him like a book⟩ **4 a :** to attribute a particular meaning or interpretation to (something read) **:** take in a particular way **:** put a particular construction on **:** infer as being meant ⟨asked him how he ~ the passage⟩ **b :** to adopt a particular view of under a particular aspect or insight ⟨can ~ the situation in two ways⟩ **c :** to cause (as a particular often wrong idea) to be introduced into something being read or considered ⟨~*ing* false implications into the book⟩ **5 a :** to have or give (as a particular form of a word, phrase, or similar element) in a particular passage, text, or version ⟨in this copy the text ~*s* *hurry* rather than *harry*⟩ **b :** to cause (such an element) to be substituted in a particular passage, text, or version ⟨told him to ~ *hurry* for *harry*⟩ **6 :** to record and show **:** INDICATE ⟨the thermometer ~*s* zero⟩ **7 a :** to transfer (a pattern) in jacquard weaving to a set of cards by the perforation of each card with a punch **b :** to set up (a loom) for such a patterned fabric **8 :** to interpret and perform (a musical passage or composition) ⟨~*s* Bach with astonishing insight⟩ ~ *vi* **1 a :** to read something ⟨looks as though he's ~*ing*⟩ **b :** to apply oneself or devote oneself to reading books or other printed or written material ⟨likes to ~⟩ **c** (1) **:** to learn something by reading books or other printed or written material ⟨is ~*ing* up on space rockets⟩ (2) **:** to devote oneself to the special study of something (as by reading books and attending lectures) ⟨~ in classics and passed the honors examination —*Current Biog.*⟩ **2 a** (1) **:** to give a particular meaning, piece of information, or instruction when read ⟨the book ~*s* in only one unmistakable way⟩ (2) **:** to produce a particular impression when read ⟨was not sure how the letter would ~ to her⟩ **b** (1) **:** to have particular qualities (as of style, organization) that affect comprehension or enjoyment ⟨a book that ~*s* well⟩ (2) **:** to have particular qualities that favor comprehension and enjoyment ⟨gifted at writing magazine articles that ~⟩ **3 :** to consist of or be drawn up in certain words, phrases, or other similar elements ⟨a passage that ~*s* differently in the older versions⟩ — **read a lecture** *also* **read a lesson :** to reprimand severely — **read the riot act 1 :** to order (as a mob) to disperse **2 a :** to issue a peremptory order or warning to cease doing something **b :** to protest vehemently **:** express great objection **c :** to reprimand severely
**2read** \'rēd\ *n* -s *chiefly Brit* **:** an act or period of reading ⟨thought I would have a ~ in it presently —Rose Macaulay⟩
**3read** *or* **reed** \'rēd\ *n* -s [ME *rede*, fr. OE *rēada*] **:** ABOMASUM
**4read** \'red\ *adj* [fr. past part. of *1read*] **:** instructed by or informed through reading **:** LEARNED ⟨far better ~ than most —B.J.Hendrick⟩ ⟨is widely ~ in contemporary literature⟩
**read·abil·i·ty** \,rēdə'biləd·ē\ *n* **:** the quality or state of being readable ⟨traces our history with skill and ~ —R.L.Duffus⟩ ⟨the physical ~ of the book is poor because of its heavy, close typography —Robert Halsband⟩ ⟨testing the ~ of prose by measuring the length of sentences —F.L.Mott⟩ ⟨improvement in the ~ of newspaper writing —Bruce Westley⟩
**read·able** \'rēdəbəl\ *adj* **1 :** that can be read with ease: **a :** LEGIBLE ⟨~ handwriting⟩ **b :** pleasing, interesting, or offering no great difficulty to the reader ⟨a ~ novel⟩ ⟨a ~ treatise on physics⟩ **c** *of a map* **:** clear in detail and the significance of symbols **2 :** that can be read throughout ⟨a novel, ~ at a sitting⟩
**read·able·ness** *n* -ES **:** READABILITY
**read·ably** \-blē\ *adv* **:** in a readable manner **:** in such a way as to be readable
**re·adapt** \¦rē+\ *vb* [*re-* + *adapt*] *vt* **:** to adapt again ~ *vi* **:** to become adapted again
**re·adaptability** \"+\ *n* **:** the quality or state of being readaptable
**re·adaptable** \"+\ *adj* **:** capable of being adapted again
**re·adaptation** \(ˌ)rē+\ *n* **:** renewed adaptation
**re·address** \"+\ *vt* [*re-* + *address*] **:** to address again; *esp* **:** to put a new address on ⟨~*ed* and forwarded the letter⟩
**read·er** \'rēdə(r)\ *n* -s [ME *redere*, fr. OE *rǣdere*, fr. *rǣdan* to read + *-ere* -er] **1 :** one that reads: as **a** (1) **:** one that is able to read ⟨a slow ~⟩ ⟨a good ~⟩ (2) **:** one that applies himself to reading ⟨a room set aside for ~*s*⟩ (3) **:** one devoted to reading **:** one fond of reading ⟨is a great ~⟩ **b :** one that is appointed to read to others: as (1) **:** one appointed to read aloud during meals (as in a monastery or convent) (2) **:** LECTOR 1 (3) **:** one chosen to read aloud selected material in a Christian Science church or society **c** (1) **:** PROOFREADER (2) **:** one that reads and evaluates manuscripts (as for possible publication or for use as material in producing a motion picture or play) (3) **:** one that reads esp. newspapers and other periodical literature and indicates items to be marked, copied, abstracted, or clipped as having special interest or value to some individual or group **d :** one that reads and records the indications of meters or similar gauges (as for a public utilities company) **e :** one that assists a professor or other teacher by reading and marking the papers of students enrolled in a class **2** *Brit* **:** one who reads lectures or expounds subjects to students: **a :** a lecturer on law in the Inns of Court — used as an honorary title **b :** a university teacher chosen as a specialist in a particular field and ranking lower than a professor **3 a :** READING GLASS **b :** a device for projecting a readable image of a transparency on a self-contained or separate screen **c :** a unit (as of a computer) that scans material recorded (as on punched cards, magnetic tape) for storage or computation **4 a :** a book for instruction and practice in reading ⟨a third-grade ~⟩ **b :** a book containing selections for reading esp. for beginners in a subject ⟨a citizenship ~⟩ ⟨a French ~⟩ **c :** ANTHOLOGY ⟨a G.B. Shaw ~⟩ **5 a :** READING NOTICE **b :** a card (as in a window display) that carries a sale price, caption, or similar information **6 :** a playing card marked on the back so that it can be identified (as by a gambler, conjurer) — compare STAMP **7 :** a worker who records a textile design (as in string or in numbers) that he reads from a card
**read·er·ship** \-,ship\ *n* **1 a :** the quality or state of being a reader ⟨subscribers and purchasers on most levels of ~ —F.L.Mott⟩ **b :** the office, position, or profession of being a reader; *esp, Brit* **:** the position of a university teacher ranking lower than a professor ⟨there are new chairs and ~*s* in almost every British university —M.M.Postan⟩ **2 a :** the total mass of individuals actually reading or estimated to read something (as a book, magazine, newspaper, advertisement) ⟨increasing the ~ of a magazine⟩ — distinguished from *circulation* 5 **b :** a particular class of readers ⟨will appeal to an intelligent ~⟩
**re·adhere** \¦rē+\ *vi* [*re-* + *adhere*] **:** to adhere again
**re·adhesion** \"+\ *n* [*re-* + *adhesion*] **:** the action of readhering
**readied** *past of* READY
**readies** *pres 3d sing of* READY, *pl of* READY
**readier** *comparative of* READY
**readiest** *superlative of* READY
**read·i·ly** \'red°lē, -°li, -dl-, -dəl-\ *adv* [ME *redily*, fr. *redy* ready + *-ly*] **:** in a ready manner **:** with readiness: as **a :** with prompt willingness **:** without hesitating, quibbling, or delaying **:** with alacrity **:** WILLINGLY ⟨~ accepted my help —Nora Waln⟩ **b :** with fairly quick efficiency **:** without needless loss of time **:** reasonably fast **:** SPEEDILY ⟨information can when needed be ~ acquired by consulting appropriate books —J.B.Conant⟩ **c :** with a fair degree of ease **:** without much difficulty **:** with facility **:** EASILY ⟨ideas that a layman could ~ understand if plainly expressed —E.S.McCartney⟩
**read in** *vt* **:** to cause (oneself) to enter formally upon a new benefice in the Church of England after appointment by public reading of a set of accepted doctrinal statements and by assenting to the statements ~ *vi* **:** to enter formally upon a new benefice in the Church of England by reading oneself in
**read·i·ness** \'redēnəs, -din-\ *n* -ES [ME *redinesse*, fr. *redy* ready + *-nesse* -ness] **:** the quality or state of being ready: as **a :** prompt willingness **:** ALACRITY ⟨~ to welcome more co-operative relations —*Current Biog.*⟩ ⟨~ to continue discussions —*Wall Street Jour.*⟩ **b :** fairly quick efficiency **:** reasonable speed ⟨acquired ~ and accuracy in writing —J.S. Reeves⟩ **c :** EASE, FACILITY ⟨a happy ~ of conversation —Jane Austen⟩ **d :** a state of preparation ⟨putting them in ~ —H.E.Scudder⟩ ⟨gauging the child's ~ to begin reading⟩
**1read·ing** \'rēdiŋ, -dēŋ\ *n* -s [ME *redinge*, fr. OE *rǣding*, fr. *rǣdan* to read + *-ing* (suffix forming nouns from verbs)] **1 a :** material designed to be read **:** matter for reading ⟨chose the ~ for the great books course⟩; *esp* **:** a particular selection of such material designed to be read at one time or as a unit ⟨~*s* from contemporary fiction⟩ **b** (1) **:** the material read (as in a particular field) by an individual ⟨were discriminating in their ~⟩ ⟨thought he had seen the word somewhere in his ~⟩ (2) **:** the extent to which an individual has read ⟨a person of vast ~⟩ **2 a :** the particular form (as a variation in spelling, style, syntax, choice of vocabulary) used in a particular edition or other source of material designed to be read **:** a particular version ⟨found an interesting ~ of the same passage in one of the older manuscripts⟩ ⟨the generally accepted ~⟩ **b :** an indication of particular data made by an instrument ⟨examined the ~ of the thermometer⟩ **3 a :** a particular interpretation of something observed, studied, or experienced ⟨new ~*s* of the history —James Martineau⟩ **b :** a particular performance and interpretation of something (as the lines of a play, the score of a musical composition) ⟨a sensitive ~ of the principal role⟩ ⟨a knowledgeable ~ of the symphony⟩
**2reading** \"\ *adj* **1 :** of or relating to reading ⟨a ~ list⟩ or readers ⟨formed a small ~ group⟩ **2 a :** designed or used for reading ⟨a ~ lamp⟩ ⟨a ~ desk⟩ **b :** set aside for reading ⟨a ~ room⟩
**3read·ing** \'rediŋ, -dēŋ\ *adj, usu cap* [fr. *Reading*, county borough in southern England] **1 :** of or from the county borough of Reading, England **:** of the kind or style prevalent in Reading **2** [fr. *Reading*, city in southeast Pennsylvania] **:** of or from the city of Reading, Pa. **:** of the kind or style prevalent in Reading
**reading chair** *n* **:** a chair with a narrow back, high short arms, a small slanted shelf attached to the top of the back, and a seat designed for straddling and for permitting one to sit facing the shelf

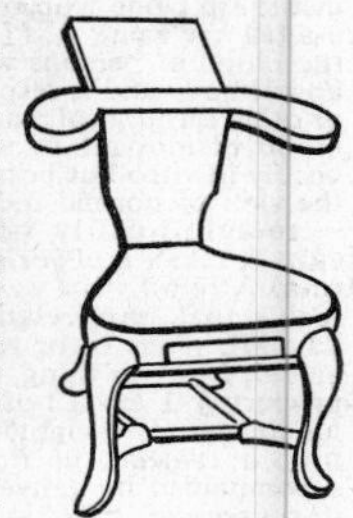
reading chair

**reading clerk** *n* **:** a clerk in a legislative assembly whose principal duty is the reading of bills or other formal documents to the assembly
**reading desk** *n* **:** a desk with a sloping top used to support a book in a convenient position for a reader standing before it
**reading glass** *n* **:** a large magnifying lens that is usu. attached to a handle and that is used to facilitate reading (as of fine print) or examination (as of map details)
**reading man** *n* **:** one who by choice does much reading; *esp, chiefly Brit* **:** a university student devoted often excessively to reading and study
**reading matter** *n* **:** the regular contents (as news, features) of a newspaper or other periodical exclusive of the advertising

**reading notice** *n* **:** an advertisement in a newspaper or other periodical that is set up to have the appearance of regular reading matter but is usu. labeled inconspicuously and in fine print as an advertisement

**re·adjourn** \¦rē+\ *vb* [F *réajourner*, fr. MF *reajourner*, fr. *re-* + *ajourner* to adjourn] *vt* **:** to adjourn again **~** *vi* **:** to become adjourned again

**re·adjust** \"+\ *vb* [*re-* + *adjust*] *vt* **:** to adjust again; *esp* **:** to modify (the terms of a corporation's debts and sometimes preferred stocks) by voluntary action so as to meet new conditions and take advantage of new opportunities **~** *vi* **:** to become readjusted

**re·adjustable** \"+\ *adj* **:** capable of being readjusted

**re·adjustment** \"+\ *n* **:** the act of readjusting or state of being readjusted

**re·administer** \"+\ *vt* [*re-* + *administer*] **:** to administer again

**re·admission** \"+\ *n* [*re-* + *admission*] **:** the act of readmitting

**re·admit** \"+\ *vt* [*re-* + *admit*] **:** to admit again

**re·admittance** \"+\ *n* **:** READMISSION

**re·adopt** \"+\ *vt* [*re-* + *adopt*] **:** to adopt again

**re·adoption** \"+\ *n* [*re-* + *adoption*] **:** the act or process of readopting or state of being readopted

**re·adorn** \"+\ *vt* [*re-* + *adorn*] **:** to adorn again

**read out** *vt* **1 :** to read aloud **2 :** to expel (as from a political party or other organization) by or as if by a public reading of notice of dismissal ⟨threatened to have him *read out* of the party⟩

**readout** \'=,=\ *n* -s [*read out*] **1 :** the act of reading out **2 :** a device that displays in digits data computed or registered

**reads** *pres 3d sing of* READ, *pl of* READ

1**re·advance** \(¦)rē+\ *vb* [*re-* + *advance*] *vt* **:** to advance again **~** *vi* **1 :** to go forward again **2** *of a glacier* **:** to advance again after having retreated from a position occupied in an earlier advance

2**readvance** \"\ *n* -s **:** the action of readvancing

**re·advent** \"+\ *n* [*re-* + *advent*] **:** a renewed advent

1**ready** \'redē, -di\ *adj, usu* -ER/-EST [ME *redy;* akin to OE *rǣde* ready, OHG *reiti*, ON *greithr* ready, Goth *garaiths* ordered, Gk *arariskein* to fit — more at ARM] **1 a** (1) **:** prepared for something about to be done or experienced ⟨are ~ to see their father⟩ ⟨is ~ to hear the news⟩ (2) **:** prepared for immediate movement or action ⟨the troops are ~ to march⟩ **b :** equipped or supplied with what is needed for some action or event ⟨are ~ for the trip⟩ **c :** fitted, arranged, or placed for immediate use ⟨a room is now ~ for you⟩ ⟨dinner is ~⟩ **2 a** (1) **:** prepared in mind or disposition so as to be willing and not reluctant **:** not hesitant **:** INCLINED, DISPOSED ⟨are ~ to die for their country⟩ (2) **:** brought into or being in such a state as to be likely to do something indicated **:** immediately liable **:** on the verge of something ⟨seemed ~ to cry⟩ ⟨the house looks as though it's ~ to fall down⟩ **b :** spontaneously prompt **:** not slow ⟨always has a ~ answer for any difficulty that may arise⟩ ⟨with a ~ smile on her lips⟩ **3 :** quick in some indicated action or perception in such a way as to be notably dexterous, adroit, or skilled ⟨a ~ wit⟩ ⟨a ~ worker⟩ **4 :** that is immediately available or at hand **:** that can be had or used at once ⟨~ assets⟩ ⟨~ cash⟩ ⟨had a gun ~⟩ **syn** see QUICK

2**ready** \"\ *adv, usu* -ER/-EST [ME *redy*, fr. *redy*, adj.] *archaic* **:** READILY

3**ready** \"\ *vt* -ED/-ING/-ES [ME *redien*, fr. *redy*, adj.] **:** to cause to be ready **:** PREPARE ⟨~*ing* themselves for battle⟩ **syn** see PREPARE

4**ready** \"\ *n* -ES [1*ready*] **1 :** money on hand **:** ready cash ⟨was well supplied with the ~⟩ **2 :** the state of being ready; *esp* **:** preparation of a gun (as by loading, cocking, and holding in readiness) for immediate aiming and firing ⟨had their rifles at the ~⟩ **3 :** a left-handed strand formed by twisting together a number of right-handed yarns of which three go to form a plain-laid rope

**ready box** *n* **:** a box placed near a gun (as on a ship) to hold ammunition kept ready for immediate use

1**ready-made** \¦==¦=\ *adj* **1 a :** made and finished in such a way as to be ready for immediate sale or use with few or no alterations **:** ready for general sale or use rather than prepared according to individual specifications ⟨a *ready-made* suit⟩ — opposed to *made-to-order* **b :** of, relating to, or dealing in what is ready-made ⟨a *ready-made* clothier⟩ **2 :** lacking individual distinctiveness **:** not original **:** COMMONPLACE, STOCK ⟨a banal play full of *ready-made* situations⟩

2**ready-made** \"\ *n, pl* **ready-mades** *or* **ready-made :** something that is ready-made

1**ready-mix** \¦==¦=\ *n* [1*ready* + *mix*] **:** a combination of ingredients commercially mixed and prepared so as to be sold or delivered in a form requiring the addition of few or no further ingredients before use: as **a :** MIX 2a **b :** a concrete or mortar manufactured for sale or delivery in a plastic state **c :** a paint mixed and ready for use

2**ready-mix** \"\ *or* **ready-mixed** \¦==¦=\ *adj* [*ready-mix* fr. 1*ready-mix; ready-mixed* fr. 1*ready* + *mixed*] **:** consisting of a ready-mix ⟨*ready-mixed* concrete⟩

**ready money** *n* [ME *redy monay*] **:** money on hand or quickly available; *esp* **:** money held ready for payment or actually paid at the time of a transaction

**readyprint** \'==,=\ *n* **:** newsprint sold in newspaper-size sheets on the inside pages of which feature material and advertisements have already been printed at the time of sale

**ready reckoner** *n* **:** RECKONER 2

**ready room** *n* **:** a room or compartment (as of an aircraft carrier) in which plane pilots are briefed and in which they await takeoff orders

1**ready-to-wear** *also* **ready-for-wear** \¦===¦=\ *adj* **:** READY-MADE ⟨*ready-to-wear* clothing⟩

2**ready-to-wear** \"\ *n, pl* **ready-to-wears** *or* **ready-to-wear :** something ready-made; *esp* **:** a ready-made garment or suit

**ready-witted** \¦==¦==\ *adj* **:** quick in intelligence and perception **:** SHARP

**reae** *pl of* REA

**re·aeration** \(¦)rē+\ *n* [*re-* + *aeration*] **:** renewed aeration

**re·affirm** \¦rē+\ *vt* [*re-* + *affirm*] **:** to affirm again esp. so as to strengthen or confirm ⟨~*ed* certain fundamental principles —Vera M. Dean⟩

**re·affirmance** \"+\ *n* [*re-* + *affirmance*] **:** REAFFIRMATION

**re·affirmation** \(¦)rē+\ *n* **:** the act of reaffirming or condition of being reaffirmed

**re·afforest** \¦rē+\ *vt* [*re-* + *afforest*] *chiefly Brit* **:** REFOREST

**re·afforestation** \(¦)rē+\ *n, chiefly Brit* **:** REFORESTATION

**re·agency** \rē+\ *n* [fr. *react*, after E *act: agency*] **:** reactive power or operation

**re·agent** \"+\ *n* [NL *reagent-*, *reagens*, pres. part. of *reagere* to react — more at REACT] **1 :** a substance used for various purposes (as in detecting, examining, or measuring other substances, in preparing material, in developing photographs) because it takes part in one or more chemical reactions or biological processes **2 :** the subject of a psychological experiment; *esp* **:** one who reacts to a stimulus

**re·agin** \rē'ājən\ *n* -s [ISV *reagent* + *-in*] **1 :** a substance in the blood of persons with syphilis that is sometimes held to be an antibody and is responsible for positive Wassermann, Kahn, or other serological reactions for syphilis **2 :** an antibody in the blood of individuals with atopic allergy that does not react visibly in vitro but possesses the power of passively sensitizing the skin of normal individuals — **re·agin·ic** \¦rēə¦jinik\ *adj* — **re·agin·i·cal·ly** \-nək(ə)lē\ *adv*

**reaks** \'rēks\ *n pl* [origin unknown] *chiefly Scot* **:** PRANKS

1**re·al** \'rē(ə)l, 'riəl *sometimes* 'ril\ *adj, often* -ER/-EST [ME, real, actual, of or relating to things (in law), fr. MF, fr. ML & LL; ML *realis* of or relating to things (in law), fr. LL, real, actual, fr. L *res* thing, fact + *-alis* -al; akin to Skt *rai* wealth, property] **1** *law* **a :** of or relating to things themselves or to a jus in rem ⟨a ~ right⟩ ⟨~ privileges⟩ — opposed to *personal* **b** *of a contract in Roman & civil law* **:** existing, made, or accompanied by delivery of the object concerned — opposed to *consensual* **c :** of or relating to things (as lands, tenements) that are fixed, permanent, or immovable; *specif* **:** of or relating to real estate ⟨~ property⟩ **2 a :** that is precisely what its name implies **:** not merely so called **:** truly possessing the essence of what it is called: as (1) **:** AUTHENTIC, GENUINE ⟨was made of ~ gold⟩ (2) **:** not merely apparent **:** ACTUAL, TRUE ⟨discovered the ~ reason⟩ (3) **:** not artificial or counterfeit ⟨a bouquet of ~ flowers⟩ **:** NATURAL (4) **:** not illusory **:** INDUBITABLE, UNQUESTIONABLE ⟨at last found ~ happiness⟩ (5) **:** free from affectation or pretense ⟨had a ~ interest in what was happening⟩ ⟨is a ~ friend⟩ **b :** actually existing, occurring, or present in fact **:** corresponding to actuality ⟨a story from ~ life⟩ **c** (1) **:** having an objective independent existence ⟨could hardly believe that what she saw was ~ and not a hallucination⟩ (2) **:** relating to, based on, or concerned with individual objectively existent things in the physical world ⟨~ propositions —J.H.Newman⟩ **d** (1) **:** that is neither derivative nor dependent **:** necessarily existent **:** not contingent **:** ABSOLUTE ⟨the concept of a ~ being as opposed to an accidental being⟩ (2) **:** that is fundamental, intrinsic, and ultimate **:** not nominal or relative ⟨~ essences —J.S.Mill⟩ **e :** having no imaginary part ⟨a ~ quantity⟩ **f :** not merely verbal or formal **:** SIGNIFICANT ⟨a ~ statement⟩ **g** *of a name* **:** not assumed by oneself nor applied to oneself by others in place of one's original name ⟨refused to give her ~ name⟩ **h** *of wages or income* **:** measured by actual purchasing power ⟨though the salary might seem a reasonable one, its ~ value is small⟩ **3 :** exact as regards repetition of musical intervals in transposition ⟨a ~ fugue⟩ — compare TONAL **4** *of lace* **:** HANDMADE 1

**syn** ACTUAL, TRUE: these words are here considered only in their general uses and not in uses philosophical, aesthetic, or critical. So considered, they are often interchangeable. REAL may stress genuineness, especially identity or correspondence between appearance and essence ⟨a *real* diamond⟩ ⟨*real* people who had actually lived around here and who had been part of some *real* event —Dorothy Barclay⟩ ⟨the difference between *real* and sham enjoyment —G.B.Shaw⟩ ⟨*real* intelligence must recognize its own limitations —M.R.Cohen⟩ ACTUAL stresses the fact of existence, of fidelity to the existent, as opposed to the nonexistent, hypothetical, abstract, or conjectural ⟨the possible way — I am far from asserting it was the *actual* way —Havelock Ellis⟩ ⟨a cultural — perhaps, for some, impossible — ideal and not the *actual* pattern of behavior, even in our own society —Weston La Barre⟩ ⟨most men are potential autocrats, the strong and capable may become *actual* autocrats —V.L. Parrington⟩ TRUE states or implies conformity to the real or actual, esp. as indicating or implying a standard, norm, or type ⟨a *true* poet —A.T.Quiller-Couch⟩ ⟨in the seventh and eighth centuries there were no *true* kings of England —Kemp Malone⟩ ⟨of the three waterways surrounding Manhattan, only the Hudson River is a *true* river —*Amer. Guide Series: N.Y.City*⟩

2**real** \"\ *n* -s **:** something real: **a :** a particular reality; *esp* **:** a mathematical real quantity **b :** reality in general — used with *the* ⟨the ~ as contrasted with what is ideal⟩

3**real** \"\ *adv* **:** VERY ⟨was ~ glad to see her⟩ — not often in formal use

4**re·al** \rā'äl, rē'-\ *n, pl* **reals** \-lz\ *or* **re·ales** \rā'ä(,)lās\ *or* **reis** \'rās(h), -āz\ *see numbered senses* [Sp, fr. *real*, adj., royal, fr. L *regalis* — more at ROYAL] **1** *or* **ri·al** \rē'-\ *pl reals or reales or* **rials** *or* **ri·a·les a :** the chief former monetary unit of Spain — compare PIECE OF EIGHT **b :** an old silver coin representing one real **2** *pl reals or reis* [Pg, fr. *real*, adj., royal, fr. L *regalis*] **a :** a Portuguese monetary unit before 1911 which became so depreciated that it was usu. quoted in milreis **b :** a monetary unit of Brazil before 1942

**real account** *n* **:** any one of the asset, liability, or net worth accounts — compare MIXED ACCOUNT, NOMINAL ACCOUNT

**real action** *n* **1 :** a local legal action founded on seisin or possession in which title is placed in issue and which aims at establishing title to a particular piece or part of real estate and at recovering the piece or part of real estate — compare LOCAL ACTION, PERSONAL ACTION, TRANSITORY ACTION **2** *Roman & civil law* **:** an action which aims at recovering a movable or immovable subject of property or at establishing a property interest therein

**real attribute** *n, logic* **:** an attribute inherent in the substance of the thing rather than merely involved in the thought of it

**real bigamy** *n* **:** BIGAMY 2a

**real burden** *n, Scots law* **:** a duty of the grantee or owner of specific land to pay the grantor or another at stated times a fixed sum of money that is charged upon the land and its succeeding owners and that is apparent from the public record of the grant

**real cost** *n* **:** cost as measured by the physical labor and materials consumed in production

**real covenant** *n* **:** a legal covenant affecting real property or requiring its conveyance; *esp* **:** a covenant that runs with the land — compare PERSONAL COVENANT

**real definition** *n* **:** a statement of the nature or essence of a thing — contrasted with *nominal definition*

**realer** *comparative of* REAL

**real essence** *n, Lockeanism* **:** the objectively real resemblance of constitution that may underlie a group of individuals to which a general name has been given — contrasted with *nominal essence*

**realest** *superlative of* REAL

**real estate** *n* **1 :** lands, tenements, or hereditaments that on the owner's death pass to his heir or devisee rather than to his administrator or executor **2 a** (1) **:** land and its permanently affixed buildings or other structures together with its improvements and its natural assets (as minerals, crops, waters) and with the inclusion of corporeal rights or incorporeal rights that follow ownership of the land and with the interests in such rights (2) **:** a freehold estate either in possession or in remainder in such real estate **b** *in some statutes* **:** leasehold estates, ordinary personalty, or equitable interests

**real fallacy** *n* **:** MATERIAL FALLACY

**re·al·gar** \rē'al,gär, -,gər\ *n* -s [ME, fr. ML, fr. Catal, fr. Ar *rahj al-ghār* powder of the mine] **:** an orange-red mineral $As_4S_4$ or AsS that consists of arsenic sulfide and that occurs in monoclinic crystals or in granular or compact form, has a resinous luster, and burns with a bluish flame giving off arsenical and sulfurous fumes while burning (hardness 1.5–2, sp. gr. 3.56) — see ARSENIC DISULFIDE

**realgar orange** *n* **:** DUTCH ORANGE

**realgar yellow** *n* **:** ORPIMENT 2

**re·al·gym·na·si·um** \rā¦äl(,)gim¦näzēəm\ *n, pl* **realgymnasiums** \-ēəmz\ *or* **realgymna·sia** \-ēə\ [G, fr. *real* objective, practical (fr. LL *realis* real, actual) + *gymnasium*] **:** a German secondary school that prepares students for the university, that offers Latin but no Greek, and that typically emphasizes sciences and modern languages — compare GYMNASIUM

**re·a·lia** \rē'ālēə, -rā'äl-\ *n pl* [LL, neut. pl. of *realis* real, actual] **1** *philos* **:** real things **:** REALITIES **2 :** objects or activities used by a teacher to relate classroom teaching to real life; *esp* **:** things (as costumes, tools, objects of worship) relating to the daily living of peoples studied in geography or language classes

**real idealism** *n* **:** IDEAL REALISM

**re·align** *also* **re·aline** \¦rē+\ *vt* [*re-* + *align, aline*] **:** to align again; *esp* **:** to make new divisions or groupings of according to other lines of cleavage ⟨~ American political parties⟩

**re·aligner** *also* **re·aliner** \"+\ *n* **:** one that realigns

**re·alignment** *also* **re·alinement** \"+\ *n* [*re-* + *alignment, alinement*] **:** the act of realigning or condition of being realigned

**real image** *n* **:** an optical image formed of real foci

**real injury** *n* **1** *civil & Scots law* **:** an intentional injury inflicted by an unlawful act and affecting the person, honor, or dignity of another **2** *Scots law* **:** misappropriation of another's coat of arms

**re·al·ise** *like* REALIZE\ *chiefly Brit var of* REALIZE

**re·al·ism** \'rēə,lizəm, 'riə- *also* 'rē,l- *sometimes* 'ri,l-\ *n* -s [G *realismus* philosophical realism, fr. LL *realis* real, actual + G *-ismus* -ism — more at REAL] **1 :** preoccupation with fact or reality **:** objective procedure not influenced by idealism, speculation, or sentimentalism **:** disposition to think and act objectively and unemotionally and to reject what is impractical or visionary **2 a :** a doctrine in philosophy that universals exist outside the mind **:** the conception that what a general or abstract term names is an independent and unitary reality or essence: (1) **:** the doctrine that universals exist prior to things — called also *Platonic realism* (2) **:** the doctrine that universals exist in things — called also *Aristotelian realism* **b :** the philosophical conception that objects of sense perception or sometimes of cognition in general are real in their own right and exist independently of their being known or related to mind — called also *epistemological realism;* compare IDEALISM, PHENOMENALISM **c :** a doctrine or theory in sociology that holds that a human collectivity, group, or institution has a reality apart from the individual members comprising it — contrasted with *nominalism* **3 a :** the theory or practice in art and literature of fidelity to nature or to real life and to accurate representation without idealization of the most typical views, details, and surroundings of the subject ⟨photographic ~ or naturalism in the realm of art —John Somerville⟩ — opposed to *idealism* **b :** excessive minuteness of detail or preoccupation with trivial, sordid, or squalid subjects in art and literature ⟨a fearless ~ that exploited until then forbidden subject matter —J.W.Aldridge⟩ **4 :** a conception of the science of law and of the administration of justice that sees significance in the unique elements of particular cases, judges rules by their consequences, and emphasizes the nonlogical and irrational factors in decision

1**re·al·ist** \-,ləst\ *n* -s [F *réaliste*, fr. MF *realiste*, fr. *real* real, actual + *-iste* -ist — more at REAL] **:** an adherent or advocate of realism **:** one that is influenced by or acts in accordance with the principles of realism

2**realist** \"\ *adj* **:** of or relating to realists or realism **:** REALISTIC

**re·al·is·tic** \¦rēə¦listik, ¦riə-, -tēk\ *adj* **:** of, relating to, or marked by realism ⟨a ~ novel⟩ ⟨a ~ attitude⟩ **:** facing reality squarely **:** not impractical or visionary ⟨~ planning⟩ — **re·al·is·ti·cal·ly** \-tək(ə)lē, -tēk-, -li\ *adv*

**re·al·i·ty** \rē'aləd·ē, -lətē, -i\ *n* -ES [ML *realitat-*, *realitas*, fr. LL *realis* real, actual + *-itat-*, *-itas* -ity] **1 :** the quality or state of being real ⟨remove the vagueness from history and give it ~ —G.W.Curtis⟩ ⟨doubted the ~ of what was alleged⟩ **2 a** (1) **:** something that is real ⟨the *realities* of life⟩ ⟨what was his dream is now a ~⟩ (2) **:** the aggregate of real things ⟨trying to escape from ~⟩ **b** (1) **:** the actual nature or constitution of something ⟨had read about love but was amazed by its ~⟩ (2) **:** the actual state of things ⟨had evaded the issue but at last told her of the ~⟩ **c** (1) **:** what actually exists **:** what has objective existence **:** what is not a mere idea **:** what is not imaginary, fictitious, or pretended (2) **:** what exists necessarily **:** what is neither derivative nor dependent **3** *obs* **:** sincere devotion or loyalty to some individual — **in reality** *adv* **:** in actual fact

**reality principle** *n* **:** the tendency for man to defer immediate instinctual gratification so as to achieve longer-range goals or so as to meet the demands of physical environment, reference group, or other form of external pressure — compare PLEASURE PRINCIPLE

**reality testing** *n* **:** a function of the ego in which acts are explored and their outcomes determined so that the individual will be aware of these consequences when the stimulus to act in a given fashion recurs

**re·al·iz·abil·i·ty** \,rēə,līzə'biləd·ē, ,riə-, -lətē, -i\ *n* **:** the quality or state of being realizable

**re·al·iz·able** \'==,=zəbəl, ,=='===\ *adj* [F *réalisable*, fr. *réaliser* to realize + *-able*] **:** capable of being realized

**re·al·iz·ably** \-blē,-bli\ *adv* **:** in a realizable manner

**re·al·iza·tion** \,rē(ə)lə'zāshən, ,riəl-, -,lī'z- *sometimes* ,ri(,)l-\ *n* -s [F *réalisation*, fr. MF *realisation*, fr. *realiser* to realize + *-ation*] **1 a :** the action of realizing or condition of being realized **b** *philos* **:** the act or process of becoming real **2 :** something realized

**realization and liquidation account** *n* **:** an account or statement used in settling or winding up a business or estate to show the results of the disposition of assets and the liquidation of the debts

**re·al·ize** \'rēə,līz, 'riə,l- *also* 'rē,l- *sometimes* 'ri,l-\ *vb* -ED/-ING/-S *see -ize in Explan Notes* [F *réaliser*, fr. MF *realiser*, fr. *real* real, actual + *-iser* -ize — more at REAL] *vt* **1 a** (1) **:** to make real **:** change from what is imaginary or fictitious into what is actual **:** bring into concrete existence **:** ACCOMPLISH ⟨*realizing* a long-cherished wish⟩ ⟨*realized* the project at last⟩ (2) **:** to bring from potentiality into actuality **:** ACTUALIZE **b** (1) **:** to cause to seem real **:** make appear real ⟨a stage set that *realized* the atmosphere of a colonial town perfectly⟩ (2) **:** to present or bring before the mind with vividness and clarity ⟨a picture that recalled to her and *realized* scenes of her early childhood⟩ **2 a** (1) **:** to convert into actual money ⟨*realized* assets⟩ (2) **:** to bring by sale or investment ⟨*realized* a good price on the sale of his house⟩ **b :** to acquire as an actual possession **:** obtain as the result of plans and efforts **:** GAIN ⟨*realized* a large profit on the deal⟩ **3 :** to conceive vividly as real **:** be fully aware of **:** understand clearly ⟨*realized* the risk he was taking⟩ ⟨*realized* that everything depended on the move⟩ ⟨hardly *realized* what was happening⟩ **4 :** to write out or play at sight on a keyboard instrument the full harmony as indicated by a figured bass with or without elaborate ornamentation **~** *vi* **1 :** to convert an intangible right or property into real property **2 :** to convert tangible property into money **syn** see THINK

**re·al·iz·er** *pronunc at* REALIZE +ə(r)\ *n* -s **:** one that realizes

**realizing** *adj* **:** marked by keen awareness (as of the meaning or implications of something) ⟨a more ~ sense . . . of the true meaning of German conquest —B.K.Sandwell⟩ — **re·al·iz·ing·ly** *adv*

**re·allege** \¦rē+\ *vt* [*re-* + *allege*] **:** to allege again

**re·alliance** \"+\ *n* [*re-* + *alliance*] **:** renewed alliance

**re·allocate** \(')rē+\ *vt* [*re-* + *allocate*] **:** to allocate again

**re·allocation** \(¦)rē+\ *n* [*re-* + *allocation*] **:** the act of reallocating or state of being reallocated

**re·allot** \¦rē+\ *vt* [*re-* + *allot*] **:** to allot again

**re·allotment** \"+\ *n* **:** renewed allotment

**re·al·ly** \'rē(ə)lē, 'ri(ə)-, -li\ *adv* [ME *rialliche*, fr. *rial*, *real* real, actual + *-liche* -ly] **1 a :** in actual fact **:** in reality **:** ACTUALLY ⟨didn't ~ mean what she said⟩ ⟨was ~ the best thing that could have happened⟩ **b :** UNQUESTIONABLY, TRULY ⟨was a ~ beautiful morning⟩ **2 :** INDEED ⟨well ~, you needn't have said that⟩

**re-ally** \(¦)rē+\ *vt* [ME *realyen* to rally, fr. MF *realier*, *ralier* — more at RALLY] **:** to ally again

**realm** \'relm, 'reùm\ *n* -s [ME *realme*, *reaume*, fr. OF *reialme*, *realme*, *reaume*, modif. (influenced by OF *reial* royal, fr. L *regalis*) of L *regimen* rule, government — more at REGIMEN, ROYAL] **1 :** KINGDOM **2 a :** REGION, TERRITORY ⟨seized power throughout the whole ~⟩ **b :** SPHERE, DOMAIN, RANGE ⟨within the ~ of possibility⟩ **3 :** any of several major biogeographic divisions: as **a :** a primary marine faunal division **b :** a primary terrestrial division consisting of one or more regions **c :** a division coordinate with a biogeographic region

**re·al·ness** *n* -ES **:** the quality or state of being real **:** REALITY ⟨began to feel a ~ in life again —Adria Langley⟩

**real number** *n* **:** a number in which there is no imaginary part

**real party in interest 1 :** the party entitled to the benefits or proceeds of a cause of action (as an assignee or subrogee) as distinguished from the person ordinarily entitled to maintain the action **2 :** the party primarily responsible for a liability or obligation

**re·al·po·li·tik** \rā¦äl,pōlē¦tēk\ *n* -s [G, fr. *real* objective, practical (fr LL *realis* real, actual) + *politik* politics, fr. F *politique*, fr. LL *politice*, fr. Gk *politikē*, fr. fem. of *politikos* political — more at POLITIC] **:** practical politics **:** politics based on practical and material factors, on political realities, or on the realities of national interest and power esp. as distinguished from theoretical, ethical, or moralistic objectives **:** politics considered as an end in itself rather than as a means to objectives — compare MACHTPOLITIK, POWER POLITICS

**re·al·po·li·ti·ker** \-,pō¦lēd·əkə(r)\ *n* -s [G, fr. *real* + *politiker* politician, fr. *politik* + *-er*] **:** one that believes in, advocates, or practices realpolitik

**real presence** *n, often cap R&P* **:** the doctrine that Christ is actually present in the Eucharist ⟨a comparison of Roman Catholic, Lutheran, and Anglican interpretations of *real presence*⟩ — compare CONSUBSTANTIATION, TRANSUBSTANTIATION

**real representative** *n* **:** the representative (as the heir, devisee, or sometimes an executor or administrator) for a deceased person with regard to the person's real estate

**reals** *pl of* REAL

**re·al·schu·le** \rā'äl,shülə\ *n, pl* **realschu·len** \-lən\ [G, fr. *real* objective, practical (fr. LL *realis* real, actual) + *schule* school, fr. OHG *scuola*, fr. L *schola* — more at REAL, SCHOOL] **:** a German secondary school that includes in its curriculum modern languages, mathematics, science, practical arts, and commercial subjects and that teaches no classics and is not designed to prepare students for the university — compare GYMNASIUM

**real servitude** *n, civil law* **:** a praedial servitude or right over one tract of real estate in favor of another

**real subject** *n* **:** LOGICAL SUBJECT

**re·alter** \(ˈ)rē+\ *vt* [*re-* + *alter*] **:** to alter again

**Re·al·tor** \ˈrē(ə)ltər, ˈriəl-, -ˌtȯ(ə)r *sometimes* rēˈal(ˌ)- *or substand* rēˈaləd·ər *or* ˈrēləd·ər\ *service mark* — used for a real estate agent who is a member of the National Association of Real Estate Boards

**real treaty** *n* **:** a treaty relating only to the subject matter of a compact — compare PERSONAL TREATY

**re·al·ty** \ˈrē(ə)ltē, ˈriəl-, -ti\ *n* -ES [¹*real* + *-ty*] **:** REAL ESTATE

**real variable** *n* **1 :** a mathematical variable whose values are real **2 :** FREE VARIABLE

**real yellow wood** *n* **:** any of certain podocarps of the southern part of Africa; *esp* **:** a large tree (*Podocarpus latifolius*) of the southern part of Africa

¹**ream** \ˈrēm, ˈrām\ *n* -S [ME *rem* cream, froth, fr. OE *rēam* cream; akin to MLG *rōm*, *rōme* cream, MHG *roum*, Icel *rjōmi* cream, Av *raoγna-* butter] **1** *dial chiefly Brit* **:** CREAM **2** *dial chiefly Brit* **:** froth or foam on top of a liquid

²**ream** \"\ *vb* -ED/-ING/-S [ME *remen*, fr. *rem*, n.] *vi, dial chiefly Brit* **:** FROTH, FOAM ~ *vt, dial chiefly Brit* **:** to skim cream or foam from

³**ream** \"\ *vb* -ED/-ING/-S [ME *remen*, perh. fr. OE *-rǣman* to raise (in *ārǣman* to raise) — more at ROAM] *dial chiefly Eng* **:** STRETCH

⁴**ream** \ˈrēm\ *n* -S [ME *rem*, *reme*, fr. MF *raime*, fr. Ar *rizmah*, lit., bundle] **1 :** a quantity of paper in lots that vary in the number of sheets included: **a :** a lot of 480 sheets of paper **:** 20 quires **b :** a lot of 472 sheets of drawing paper or handmade paper **c :** 500 sheets of book paper or of newsprint **d :** PRINTER'S REAM **2 :** a great amount (as of something printed) — usu. used in pl. ⟨wrote ~*s* on the subject⟩

⁵**ream** \"\ *vt* -ED/-ING/-S [perh. fr. (assumed) ME (dial.) *remen* to open up, clear, fr. OE (dial.) *rēman* to open up, clear, extend; akin to OE *rȳman* to open up, clear, extend, OHG *rūmen* to vacate, make room, ON *rȳma*; causative fr. the root of OE *rūm* spacious — more at ROOM] **1 a :** to widen the opening of (a hole) **:** bevel out **:** COUNTERSINK **b :** to enlarge or dress out (a hole) with a reamer **:** enlarge the bore of (as a gun) in this way **c :** to remove (a defective part) by reaming — often used with *out* **2 :** to open (the seams of a ship's planking) for the purpose of caulking them **3 a :** to press out (fruit juice) with a reamer **b :** to press out the juice of (as an orange or similar fruit) with a reamer **4 :** CHEAT, VICTIMIZE ⟨in the capacity of storekeepers or handymen, cheerfully ~ them at every opportunity —A.C.Spectorsky⟩

**ream·age** \ˈrēmij\ *n* -S **:** the number of reams in a lot of paper

**re·amend** \ˌrē+\ *vt* [*re-* + *amend*] **:** to amend again

¹**ream·er** \ˈrēmə(r)\ *n* -S [⁵*ream* + *-er*] **:** one that reams: as **a** (1) **:** a rotating finishing tool with straight or spiral cutting edges used to enlarge or shape a hole (2) **:** a drilling tool for enlarging a bored well or for making the borehole circular when the drill has failed to do so (3) **:** a chisel for cutting two V-shaped grooves from a round blasthole in the line of the desired rift (4) **:** an instrument used in dentistry to enlarge a hole in a tooth preparatory to filling the hole **b :** a fruit squeezer with a ridged and pointed dome projecting from the hollowed center of a plate **c :** a worker who enlarges or shapes holes or smooths a bore with a reamer

reamers a(1)

²**reamer** \"\ *vt* -ED/-ING/-S **:** to use a reamer on

**re·amination** \(ˌ)rē+\ *n* [*re-* + *amination*] **:** TRANSAMINATION

**reaming** *n* -S [fr. gerund of ⁵*ream*] **:** SCORING

**ream out** *vt* [⁵*ream*] *slang* **:** to reprimand severely

**re·amputation** \(ˌ)rē+\ *n* [*re-* + *amputation*] **:** the second of two amputations performed upon the same member

**re·analysis** \ˌrē+\ *n* [*re-* + *analysis*] **:** renewed analysis

**re·analyze** \(ˈ)rē+\ *vt* [*re-* + *analyze*] **:** to analyze again

**re·anchor** \"+\ *vb* [*re-* + *anchor*] *vt* **:** to anchor again ~ *vi* **:** to become anchored again

¹**re·animate** \"+\ *vb* [*re-* + *animate*, v.] *vt* **:** to animate again ~ *vi* **:** to become reanimated

²**re·animate** \"+\ *adj* [*re-* + *animate*, adj.] **:** REANIMATED

**re·animation** \(ˌ)rē+\ *n* **:** the action of reanimating or state of being reanimated

**re·anneal** \ˌrē+\ *vt* [*re-* + *anneal*] **:** to anneal again

**re·annex** \(ˌ)rē+\ *vt* [ME *reannexen*, fr. MF *reannexer*, fr. *re-* + *annexer* to annex] **:** to annex again

**re·annexation** \"+\ *n* **:** the act of reannexing or state of being reannexed

¹**reap** \ˈrēp\ *vb* -ED/-ING/-S [ME *repen*, *ripen*, fr. OE *reopan*, *rīpan*; akin to MD *repen*, *reipen* to hackle, card, Norw *ripa* to scratch, OE *rāw* row — more at ROW] *vt* **1 a** (1) **:** to cut (as grain) with a sickle, scythe, or reaping machine ⟨~*ed* the rye in that part of the field⟩ (2) **:** to clear (as a field) of a crop by so cutting **b :** to gather or obtain by so cutting; *esp* **:** HARVEST ⟨has ~*ed* all his crops⟩ **2 :** to gather, obtain, or win as the fulfillment, reward, or other recompense of effort, labor, or some other action ⟨~ lasting benefits⟩ ~ *vi* **:** to reap something **:** gather a harvest **:** gain or receive a return or requital ⟨they that sow in tears shall ~ in joy —Ps 126:5 (AV)⟩

**syn** REAP, GLEAN, GATHER, GARNER, and HARVEST may mean, in common, to do the work or a given part of the work of collecting ripened crops. REAP applies to the cutting down and usu. collecting of ripened grain; in extension, it may suggest a return or requital ⟨*reap* early wheat for market⟩ ⟨the lucky artisan producing something they could use would *reap* a fortune —R.A.Billington⟩ GLEAN applies to the stripping of a field or vine that has already been gone over once, extending in meaning to any picking up of valuable bits from here and there, esp. what has been left or missed ⟨*glean* in the fields after the reapers have gone⟩ ⟨assembled a multitude of facts *gleaned* from many and varied sources —*Amer. Guide Series: Wash.*⟩ ⟨she had *gleaned* all the information the library contained —Robertson Davies⟩ ⟨data *gleaned* from the questionnaire —Estelle C. Terry⟩ GATHER, the most general of these, applies to the collecting or bringing together of all the produce of the farm, plantation, or garden; in extension, it can apply to any similar amassing or accumulating ⟨the fruit is *gathered* in late July and August —*Amer. Guide Series: Tenn.*⟩ ⟨workers who *gathered* rubber —P.E.James⟩ ⟨she had traveled by safari to *gather* her material —*Current Biog.*⟩ ⟨the multitude of pitfalls in the *gathering*, writing, and processing of the news —F.L.Mott⟩ ⟨mail is *gathered* and distributed by electrically operated conveyors —*Amer. Guide Series: Minn.*⟩ GARNER implies the storing of produce, esp. grain; in extension, it can apply to any laying away as of a store ⟨more harvest than one man can *garner* —Pearl Buck⟩ ⟨a skilled picker may *garner* 100 quarts —*Amer. Guide Series: Ark.*⟩ ⟨wisdom *garnered* through the years —W.F.Hambly⟩ ⟨these short pieces *garnered* from a magazine catering to the masculine taste —Lisle Bell⟩ HARVEST, the general term, may imply any or all of these processes, extending in meaning to apply to any gathering together or husbanding ⟨the *harvesting* of cranberries —E.B.Garside⟩ ⟨the *harvesting* of shellfish —*Amer. Guide Series: Conn.*⟩ ⟨busy *harvesting* your crop of furs —*Nat'l Fur News*⟩ ⟨he had sown pain and *harvested* regret —Maurice Samuel⟩

²**reap** \", ˈrip\ *n* -S [ME *repe*, fr. OE *reopa*; akin to OE *reopan*, *rīpan*, v.] *dial chiefly Eng* **:** a handful or unbound sheaf of grain

³**reap** \"\ *vt* -ED/-ING/-S [alter. of *rip*] *chiefly dial* **:** to bring (as a subject, a person) into conversation — often used with *up*

⁴**reap** \ˈrēp\ *dial Eng var of* ROPE

**reap·er** \ˈrēpə(r)\ *n* -S [ME *repere*, fr. OE *rīpere*, fr. *reopan*, *rīpan* to reap + *-ere* -er] **:** one that reaps: as **a :** HARVESTER **b :** a machine that cuts a crop and drops it in unbound gavels

**reaper-binder** \ˈ==ˌ=ˌ=\ *n* **:** BINDER 4b

**reaper-thresher** \ˈ==ˌ=ˌ=\ *n* **:** COMBINE 3

**reaping** *pres part of* REAP

**reaping hook** *or* **reap hook** *n* **:** a hand implement with a hook-shaped blade used in reaping **:** SICKLE

**reaping machine** *n* **:** a machine used in reaping grain and typically equipped with a raking device that bends the grain against the cutter bar with power taken from a ground wheel — compare BINDER 4b, COMBINE 3

**re·apparel** \ˌrē+\ *vt* [*re-* + *apparel*] **:** to apparel again

**re·apparition** \(ˌ)rē+\ *n* [*re-* + *apparition*] **:** REAPPEARANCE

**re·appeal** \ˌrē+\ *vb* [*re-* + *appeal*] *vt* **:** to appeal again ~ *vi* **1 :** to resort to a further appeal **2 :** to arouse again a particular interest or attraction

**re·appear** \"+\ *vi* [*re-* + *appear*] **:** to appear again

**re·appearance** \"+\ *n* **:** the act of reappearing **:** a second or fresh appearance

**re·application** \(ˌ)rē+\ *n* [*re-* + *application*] **:** a second or fresh application

**re·applier** \ˌrē+\ *n* **:** one that reapplies

**re·apply** \"+\ *vb* [*re-* + *apply*] *vt* **:** to apply again ~ *vi* **:** to engage in or undergo reapplication

**re·appoint** \"+\ *vt* [*re-* + *appoint*] **:** to appoint again

**re·appointment** \"+\ *n* **:** a second or fresh appointment

**re·apportion** \"+\ *vt* [*re-* + *apportion*] **:** to apportion again

**re·apportionment** \"+\ *n* **:** the act of reapportioning or state of being reapportioned

**re·appraisal** \"+\ *n* [*re-* + *appraisal*] **:** a second or fresh appraisal **:** REVALUATION ⟨if reforms do emerge from whatever agonizing ~ is now to be attempted —H.S.Commager⟩

**re·appraise** \"\ *vt* [*re-* + *appraise*] **:** to appraise again **:** make a new valuation of **:** REVALUATE

**re·appraisement** \"+\ *n* **:** REAPPRAISAL

**re·apprehend** \ˌrē+\ *vt* [*re-* + *apprehend*] **:** to apprehend again

**re·approach** \ˌrē+\ *vi* [*re-* + *approach*] **:** to approach again

**re·appropriate** \"+\ *vt* [*re-* + *appropriate*] **:** to appropriate again

**re·appropriation** \"+\ *n* **:** the act of reappropriating

**reaps** *pres 3d sing of* REAP, *pl of* REAP

**reaptd** *abbr* reappointed

¹**rear** \ˈri(ə)r, -iə\ *vb* -ED/-ING/-S [ME *reren*, fr. OE *rǣran*; akin to OHG *rēren* to cause to fall, ON *reisa* to raise, Goth *urraisjan* to arouse, raise, lift up; causative fr. the root of OE *rīsan* to rise — more at RISE] *vt* **1 a :** to erect by building **:** CONSTRUCT ⟨~*ed* a huge pagan temple⟩ **b** *obs* **:** to bring into being **:** PRODUCE, ORIGINATE **2 a** (1) **:** to lift up to an erect position **:** set up on end **:** raise upright ⟨~*ed* a flagpole in front of the building⟩ ⟨~*ing* heavy marble columns⟩ (2) **:** to lift upward esp. so as to hold aloft or so as to cause to project far upward **:** ELEVATE, RAISE ⟨a castle that ~*s* its towers into the sky⟩ **b** *dial chiefly Eng* (1) **:** to rouse from bed or sleep (2) **:** to drive (game) from cover **c** *dial chiefly Eng* **:** to stir up to action **:** AROUSE **3 a** (1) **:** to breed and raise (an animal) for use or market (2) **:** to bring up (a person) by fostering, nourishing, and instructing ⟨was ~*ed* in a fine family⟩ **b :** to cause (as plants, produce) to grow **4 :** to cause (a horse) to rise up on the hind legs ~ *vi* **1 a :** to rise up to an erect position **:** rise high **:** TOWER ⟨a steeple ~*ing* far into the sky⟩ **b** *of a horse* **:** to rise up on the hind legs **2** *dial* **:** to come into sight **:** APPEAR **syn** see BUILD, LIFT

²**rear** *vt* -ED/-ING/-S [ME *reren*, of unknown origin] *obs* **:** to slice up (as a roasted fowl) **:** CARVE

³**rear** \ˈri(ə)r, -iə\ *dial var of* ¹RARE

⁴**rear** \"\ *n* -S [prob. fr. *rear-* (in such terms as *rear guard*)] **1 :** the back part of something **:** hindmost part: as **a :** the unit (as of an army) or area farthest from the enemy **b :** the part of something that is located opposite to its front ⟨the ~ of a store⟩ ⟨the ~ of a house⟩ ⟨the ~ of a bookcase⟩ **c :** BUTTOCKS ⟨got kicked in the ~⟩ **2 :** the space or position behind or at the back ⟨moved to the ~⟩

⁵**rear** \"\ *adj* **:** being at the back or in the hindmost part **:** HINDMOST ⟨the ~ rank of a company⟩

⁶**rear** \"\ *adv* **:** toward or from the rear — used chiefly in combination ⟨a *rear*-driven car⟩

**rear admiral** *n* **:** a commissioned naval officer ranking just below a vice admiral and above a captain — abbr. *Rear Adm, R.A.*

**rear arch** *also* **rere-arch** \ˈri(ə)ˌrärch\ *n* **:** an inner arch of an opening (as for a door or window) that differs in size or form from the external arch of the opening

**rear commodore** *n* **:** an officer of a yacht club who ranks lower than a vice-commodore

**rear echelon** *n* **:** an element of a military headquarters or unit located at a considerable distance from the front and concerned esp. with administrative and supply duties — compare FORWARD ECHELON

rear arch

**rear end** *n* **1 :** the back part, division, or section of something ⟨crashed into the *rear end* of the train⟩ **2 :** BUTTOCKS

**rear-fanged** \ˈ=ˌ=\ *adj* **:** BACK-FANGED

**rear guard** *n* [ME *reregarde*, fr. MF, fr. OF *reregarde*, *rereguarde*, fr. *rere*, *riere* backward, behind (fr. L *retro*) + *garde*, *guarde* guard — more at RETRO-, GUARD] **:** a military detachment detailed to bring up and protect the rear of a main body or force

**rearguard action** *n* **1 :** a defensive or delaying fight engaged in by a rear guard (as in covering the retreat of an army or the evacuation of a besieged garrison) **2 :** an effort put forth by means of preventive or delaying measures or tactics and usu. against great odds in defense of a threatened existing order or situation or in opposition to a proposed new departure ⟨to be something of a brake, to perform a *rearguard action*, if you will, on inflationary trends —D.V.Brown⟩ ⟨dissipate their influence in relatively ineffective *rearguard actions* designed to prevent particular regulatory measures —H.R.Bowen⟩

**re·argue** \(ˈ)rē+\ *vt* [*re-* + *argue*] **:** to argue again

**re·argument** \"+\ *n* **:** a second or fresh argument

**rearhorse** \ˈ=ˌ=\ *n* [¹*rear* + *horse*; fr. the way it rears up when disturbed] **:** MANTIS

**re·arise** \ˌrē+\ *vi* [*re-* + *arise*] **:** to arise again

**re·arm** \(ˈ)rē+\ *vb* [*re-* + *arm*] *vt* **:** to arm again: as **a :** to equip (as a disarmed nation) with military materiel **b :** to equip with new or better weapons ~ *vi* **:** to become armed again

**re·armament** \"+\ *n* [*re-* + *armament*] **:** the act of rearming or state of being rearmed

**rear·most** \ˈri(ə)rˌmōst, -iəˌm-\ *adj* **:** farthest in the rear **:** LAST

**rearmouse** *var of* REREMOUSE

**re·arousal** \ˌrē+\ *n* **:** a second or fresh arousal

**re·arouse** \"+\ *vt* [*re-* + *arouse*] **:** to arouse again

**rear projection** *n* **:** the projection of a motion or still picture upon a large translucent screen from the rear to serve as a background for performances of motion-picture actors being photographed in front of the screen

**re·arrange** \ˌrē+\ *vb* [*re-* + *arrange*] *vt* **:** to arrange again ~ *vi* **:** to undergo chemical rearrangement

**re·arrangement** \"+\ *n* **1 :** the act of rearranging or state of being rearranged **2 :** a shifting of the atoms or groups in the molecule of a compound to form an isomeric compound **:** ISOMERIZATION

**re·arranger** \"+\ *n* **:** one that rearranges

**re·array** \"+\ *vt* [*re-* + *array*] **:** to array again

¹**re·arrest** \"+\ *vt* [*re-* + *arrest*] **:** to arrest again

²**re·arrest** \"+\ *n* **:** a second or fresh arrest

**rears** *pres 3d sing of* REAR, *pl of* REAR

**rear sight** *n* **:** the sight nearest the breech of a firearm

**rear vassal** *n* [trans. of F *arrière-vassal*] **:** a vassal's vassal

¹**rear vault** *n* [⁵*rear* + *vault* (arched structure); trans. of F *arrière-voussure*] **:** a deep arch used where a wall is very thick and the window recess becomes a vaulted area

²**rear vault** *n* [⁵*rear* + *vault* (leap)] **:** a vault in which the body is raised sideward to either right or left and then rotated a quarter turn outward so that the back of the body passes over the apparatus used

**rearview mirror** \ˈ=ˌ=-\ *or* **rear-vision mirror** \ˈ=ˌ==-\ *n* **:** a mirror installed (as in an automobile) and designed to give a view of the area behind a vehicle

¹**rear·ward** \ˈri(ə)rˌwȯrd, -iəˌwȯ(ə)d\ *n* -S [ME *rerewarde*, fr. AF; akin to OF *reregarde*, *rereguarde* rear guard — more at REAR GUARD] **:** REAR; *esp* **:** the rear division of an army or fleet

²**rear·ward** \-ˌwə(r)d\ *adj* [⁴*rear* + *-ward*, adj. suffix] **1 :** located at, near, or toward the rear ⟨the ~ section of the store⟩ **2 :** directed toward the rear **:** BACKWARD ⟨bumping it shut with a ~ motion —Gertrude Schweitzer⟩ — **rear·ward·ness** *n* -ES

³**rearward** \"\ *also* **rear·wards** \-dz\ *adv* [⁴*rear* + *-ward*, *wards*, adv. suffix] **:** at, near, or toward the rear **:** BACKWARD ⟨gazing ~ out the window —*Monsanto Mag.*⟩ ⟨lobbed the football ~ to one of the halfbacks⟩

**rear·ward·ly** *adv* [²*rearward* + *-ly*] **:** REARWARD

**re·ascend** \ˌrē+\ *vb* [ME *reascenden*, fr. *re-* + *ascenden* to ascend] *vt* **:** to ascend (as stairs) again ~ *vi* **:** to go up again

**re·ascendancy** \"+\ *n* [*reascendant* + *-cy*] **:** renewed ascendancy

**re·ascendant** \"+\ *adj* [*re-* + *ascendant*] **:** again ascendant

**re·ascension** \"+\ *n* [*re-* + *ascension*] **:** a second ascension

**re·ascent** \"+\ *n* [*re-* + *ascent*] **:** a second or fresh ascent

**re·ascertain** \(ˌ)rē+\ *vt* [*re-* + *ascertain*] **:** to ascertain again

**re·ascertainment** \"+\ *n* **:** the act of reascertaining

**re·ask** \(ˈ)rē+\ *vb* [*re-* + *ask*] *vt* **:** to ask again ~ *vi* **:** to make a new inquiry or petition

¹**reas·on** \ˈrezᵊn\ *n* -S [alter. of ME *rasen*, fr. OE *ræsn*; akin to Goth *razn* house — more at RANSACK] **:** a horizontal timber over a row of posts or puncheons supporting a beam

²**rea·son** \ˈrēzᵊn\ *n* -S [ME *resoun*, fr. OF *raison*, fr. L *ration-*, *ratio* reason, computation, reasoning; akin to OFris *rethe* speech, proof, OHG *redia* account, Goth *rathjo* account, number, *garathjan* to count, L *reri* to calculate, believe, think, Gk *arariskein* to fit — more at ARM] **1 a :** an expression or statement offered as an explanation of a belief or assertion or as a justification of an act or procedure ⟨gave ~*s* that were quite satisfactory⟩ **b :** a consideration, motive, or judgment inducing or confirming a belief, influencing the will, or leading to an action or course of action **:** a rational ground or motive ⟨will mention a ~ for this situation⟩ ⟨the ~ that this is so should now be clear⟩ ⟨a good ~ to act as you do⟩ ⟨does not know the ~ why⟩ **c :** a sufficient ground of explanation or of logical defense; *esp* **:** a general principle, law, or warranted presumption that supports a conclusion, explains a fact, or validates a course of conduct ⟨brilliantly outlined the ~*s* that supported his client's action⟩ **d :** the thing that makes some fact intelligible **:** CAUSE ⟨the ~ for the tides lies in the gravitational pull of the moon and the sun⟩ **e :** a sane or sound view or consideration ⟨that's a ~ that you should keep in mind⟩ **2 a** (1) **:** the power of comprehending, inferring, or thinking esp. in orderly, sensible, rational ways ⟨was afraid that his ~ might be deranged⟩ ⟨must use ~ to solve this problem⟩ **:** the ability to trace out the implications of a combination of facts or suppositions ⟨a ~ that is far beyond her years⟩ (2) **:** proper exercise of the intellective faculty in accordance with right judgment **:** right use of the mind **:** right thinking ⟨attempted to bring her to ~⟩ (3) **:** a sane or sound mind marked by the right use of the intellective faculty **:** reasonableness and sanity of the mind ⟨was afraid she would lose her ~⟩ **b** (1) **:** a distinct cognitive faculty coordinate with perception and understanding **:** human intelligence or intellect (2) **:** the sum of the intellectual powers (3) **:** universal or general rationality of all minds viewed as a whole (4) **:** mind or intelligence viewed as a rational soul pervading the whole of nature or of the universe **c :** NOUS, NOESIS ⟨a transcendent ideal that only ~ beyond experience can conceive —John Dewey⟩ **d** *Aristotelianism* (1) **:** the function of the soul that is pure actuality, operates on the material furnished by passive reason, is immaterial and imperishable, and enjoys impersonal immortality — called also *active reason*, *creative reason* (2) **:** the function of the soul which operates with sensuous images and in which concepts are merely potential so that they need to be formed by active reason — called also *passive reason* (3) **:** PRACTICAL REASON **e** *Scholasticism* (1) **:** INTELLECT (2) **:** RATIO **f** *Kantianism & German idealism* **:** the highest faculty of the mind esp. when conceived of as the faculty of framing general conceptions or of directly apprehending universals — distinguished from *understanding* **3** *logic* **:** PREMISE; *esp* **:** MINOR PREMISE **4 a** *archaic* **:** equitable or honorable treatment that affords satisfaction and that is prompted by the demands of either propriety or justice **b** *archaic* **:** a formal accounting **c** *obs* **:** a reasonable amount or degree

**syn** REASON, GROUND, ARGUMENT, PROOF can mean, in common, a point or set of related points offered or offerable in support of something disputed. REASON can indicate any motive, consideration, or inducement offered in explanation or defense of a practice, action, opinion, or belief ⟨the family side of the house is used for cooking, and for this *reason* visitors are invited to sit at the other end —Wilfred Thesiger⟩ ⟨for various *reasons*, the times and his own health included —J.C.Archer⟩ ⟨present illogical but forceful *reasons* for refusing an invitation —Emily Post⟩ GROUND and GROUNDS are often used interchangeably with REASON and REASONS but tend to apply to evidence, facts, data, reasoning used in defense rather than to motives or considerations, often suggesting a more solid support than REASON ⟨a *ground* for apprehension that is not unjustified —D.W. Brogan⟩ ⟨belittles the effectiveness of several provisions on the *ground* they are not new —*Wall Street Jour.*⟩ ⟨the future as we see it offers no *grounds* for easy optimism —*Current Biog.*⟩ ⟨objects to the statement on *grounds* that it reflects upon him personally —*Monsanto Mag.*⟩ ARGUMENT stresses the intent to convince or persuade, implying the use of evidence or reasoning in support of a contention or enhancement of the persuasive effect ⟨hear the *arguments* for and against pacifism⟩ ⟨a good *argument* can be made for the position that economic integration is very difficult if it is tackled on its own side alone —Dean Acheson⟩ ⟨this book is an inquiry into the proper limitations upon freedom of speech, and is in no way an *argument* that any one should be allowed to say whatever he wants anywhere and at any time —Zechariah Chafee⟩ ⟨one of the commonest of all evasions; the *argument* which is not an argument but an appeal to the emotions —Virginia Woolf⟩ ⟨the best *argument* against vegetarianism is the Eskimos —Rudolf Flesch & A.H.Lass⟩ PROOF implies conclusive logical demonstration but has come to mean any piece of evidence (as a fact or document), any testimony or argument that evokes a feeling of certainty in those who are to be convinced ⟨Euclid, the author of the Elements, who gave irrefutable *proofs* of the looser demonstrations of his predecessors —Benjamin Farrington⟩ ⟨that he did not break under the terrible strain seems *proof* enough that he was sent by Providence to lead America to freedom —F.V.W.Mason⟩ ⟨laughter is supposed to be our affair and optimism a *proof* of our youth and our resilience —John Mason Brown⟩ ⟨left the house with a ton of conjecture, though without a grain of *proof* —Thomas Hardy⟩

**syn** UNDERSTANDING, INTUITION: REASON centers attention on the faculty for order, sense, and rationality in thought, inference, and conclusion about perceptions ⟨the maintenance of *reason* — the establishment of criteria, by which ideas are tested empirically and in logic —Dorothy Thompson⟩ ⟨*reason* is logic; its principle is consistency; it requires that conclusions shall contain nothing not already given in their premises —H.M. Kallen⟩ UNDERSTANDING may sometimes widen the scope of REASON to include both most thought processes leading to comprehension and also the resultant state of knowledge ⟨*understanding* is the entire power of perceiving and conceiving, exclusive of the sensibility; the power of dealing with the impressions of sense, and composing them into wholes —S.T. Coleridge⟩ ⟨philosophy is said to begin in wonder and end in *understanding* —John Dewey⟩ INTUITION stresses quick knowledge or comprehension without orderly reason, thought, or cogitation ⟨all this . . . I saw, not discursively, or by effort, or by succession, but by one flash of horrid simultaneous *intuition* —Thomas De Quincey⟩ ⟨do we not really trust these faint lights of *intuition*, because they are lights, more than *reason*, which is often too slow a councillor? —G.W.Russell⟩ Used in connection with 19th century literary and philosophic notions, UNDERSTANDING often suggests the cold analytical order usually associated with REASON and REASON in turn suggests the spontaneity of INTUITION ⟨the *understanding* was the faculty that observed, inferred, argued, drew conclusions . . . the cold, external, practical notion of life . . . The *reason* was the faculty of intuition, warm, perceptive, immediate that represented the mind of young New England —Van Wyck Brooks⟩

**syn** see in addition CAUSE

— **in reason** *adv* **:** with reason **:** JUSTIFIABLY, RIGHTLY ⟨cannot *in reason* doubt that this must be done⟩ — **within reason** *adv* **:** within reasonable limits ⟨drinks and relaxes *within reason*⟩ — **with reason** *adv* **:** with good cause **:** JUSTIFIABLY ⟨have chosen to do so *with reason*⟩

³**reason** \"\ *vb* **reasoned; reasoned; reasoning** \-z(ᵊ)niŋ\ **reasons** [ME *resonen*, fr. MF *raisonner* to discuss, reason, fr. OF, fr. *raison*, n. — more at ²REASON] *vi* **1 :** to use the faculty of reason so as to arrive at conclusions **:** THINK ⟨is able to ~ brilliantly⟩ **2 a** *obs* **:** to take part in a conversation, discussion, or argument with another **b :** to talk or discourse persuasively with another so as to influence, modify, or change the other's actions or opinions ⟨is someone you simply can't ~ with⟩ ~ *vt* **1** *archaic* **a :** DISCUSS, ARGUE ⟨am in no humor to ~ that point —Maria Edgeworth⟩ **b** (1) **:** to analyze by the use of reason (as in critically examining or in seeking out inferences or conclusions) (2) **:** to justify or support with reasons ⟨this boy . . . does ~ our petition —Shak.⟩ **2 :** to persuade, influence, or otherwise prevail on by the use of reason ⟨~*ed* myself out of the instincts and rules by which one mostly surrounds oneself —W.B.Yeats⟩ ⟨~*ed* her into believing what he said⟩ **3 :** to discover, formulate, or conclude by the use of reason — usu. used with *out* ⟨~ out a plan⟩ ⟨the steadiness of a ~*ed* conviction —A.L.Guérard⟩ **syn** see THINK

**rea·son·abil·i·ty** \ˌrēz(ᵊ)nə'biləd·ē\ *n* **:** the quality or state of being reasonable **:** REASONABLENESS

¹**rea·son·able** \'rēz(ᵊ)nəbəl\ *adj* [ME *resonable*, fr. OF *raisonnable*, fr. L *rationabilis*, fr. *ration-, ratio* reason + *-abilis* -able — more at REASON] **1 a :** being in agreement with right thinking or right judgment **:** not conflicting with reason **:** not absurd **:** not ridiculous ⟨a ~ conviction⟩ ⟨a ~ theory⟩ **b :** being or remaining within the bounds of reason **:** not extreme **:** not excessive ⟨a ~ request⟩ ⟨a ~ hope of succeeding⟩ ⟨spent a ~ amount of time in relaxation⟩ ⟨is of a ~ size⟩ **c :** MODERATE: as (1) **:** not demanding too much ⟨a ~ boss⟩ (2) **:** not expensive ⟨fresh vegetables are now ~⟩ (3) **:** that allows a fair profit ⟨sold the material at a ~ rate⟩ **2 a :** having the faculty of reason **:** RATIONAL ⟨a ~ being⟩ **b :** possessing good sound judgment **:** well balanced **:** SENSIBLE ⟨can rely on the judgment of a ~ man⟩ **syn** see RATIONAL

²**reasonable** \"\ *adv* [ME *resonable*, fr. *resonable*, adj.] *chiefly dial* **:** REASONABLY ⟨can do it ~ well⟩

**reasonable care** *n* **:** DUE CARE

**reasonable doubt** *n* **:** solid doubt about the actual guilt of a defendant that arises or remains after careful and impartial examination of all evidence

**rea·son·able·ness** *n* -ES **:** the quality or state of being reasonable **:** REASONABILITY

**reasonable part** *n* **:** the portion of his estate that a decedent could not under Old English law will away from his widow and children — compare DEAD'S PART, JUS RELICTAE, LEGITIM

**rea·son·ably** \-blē, -bli\ *adv* [ME *resonably*, fr. *resonable*, adj. + *-ly*] **1 :** in a reasonable manner ⟨acted quite ~⟩ **2 :** to a fairly sufficient extent ⟨a book that is ~ good⟩

**reasoned** *adj* **1 :** based on or marked by reasoning ⟨material for a ~ verdict —John Buchan⟩ **2 :** provided with or marked by the detailed listing or mention of reasons ⟨by means of a ~ amendment —T.E.May⟩

**rea·son·er** \'rēz(ᵊ)nə(r)\ *n* -S **:** one that reasons

**reasoning** *n* -S [ME *resoninge*, fr. gerund of *resonen* to reason] **1 :** the use of reason; *esp* **:** the drawing of inferences or conclusions through the use of reason — compare APPREHENSION **2 :** a particular instance of the use of reason; *esp* **:** a particular argument ⟨seems to me that this ~ is altogether sound⟩

**rea·son·less** \'rēzᵊnləs\ *adj* [ME *resonles*, fr. *reson, resoun* reason + *-les* -less] **1 a :** not having the faculty of reason ⟨a ~ brute⟩ **b :** not marked by the use of reason **:** devoid of common sense **:** SENSELESS ⟨a ~ hostility⟩ **2 :** not based on or supported by reasons ⟨an apparently arbitrary and ~ change⟩ — **rea·son·less·ly** *adv* — **rea·son·less·ness** *n* -ES

**reason of state** [trans. of F *raison d'état*] **:** a motive for governmental action based on alleged needs or requirements of a political state regardless of possible transgressions of the rights or the moral codes of individual persons

**reasons** *pl of* REASON, *pres 3d sing of* REASON

**re·assail** \ˌrē+\ *vt* [*re-* + *assail*] **:** to assail again

**re·assault** \"+\ *vt* [*re-* + *assault*] **:** to assault again

**re·assay** \"+\ *vb* [*re-* + *assay*] *vi* **:** to make a new attempt ~ *vt* **:** to assay again

**re·assemblage** \"+\ *n* [*re-* + *assemblage*] **:** a new assemblage

**re·assemble** \"+\ *vb* [*re-* + *assemble*] *vt* **:** to bring or put together again ~ *vi* **:** to come together again

**re·assembly** \"+\ *n* [*re-* + *assembly*] **:** a second or fresh assembly

**re·assent** \"+\ *vi* [*re-* + *assent*] **:** to assent again

**re·assert** \"+\ *vt* [*re-* + *assert*] **:** to assert again

**re·assertion** \"+\ *n* **:** a second or fresh assertion

**re·assertor** \"+\ *n* **:** one that reasserts

**re·assess** \"+\ *vt* [*re-* + *assess*] **:** to assess again

**re·assessment** \"+\ *n* [*re-* + *assessment*] **:** a second or fresh assessment

**re·assign** \"+\ *vt* [*re-* + *assign*] **:** to assign again

**re·assignment** \"+\ *n* **:** the act of reassigning or state of being reassigned

**re·associate** \ˌrē+\ *vb* [*re-* + *associate*] *vt* **:** to bring into association again ~ *vi* **:** to become reassociated

**re·association** \"+\ *n* **1 :** the act of reassociating or state of being reassociated **2 :** the restoration of lost memories and behavior patterns — opposed to *dissociation*

**re·associative** \"+\ *adj* **:** of, relating to, or marked by reassociation

**re·assort** \"+\ *vb* [*re-* + *assort*] *vt* **:** to assort again ~ *vi* **:** to become assorted again **:** separate anew ⟨the genes ~ during meiosis⟩

**re·assortment** \"+\ *n* **:** the action of reassorting or state of being reassorted

**re·assume** \"+\ *vt* [ML *reassumere*, fr. L *re-* + *assumere* to assume] **:** to assume again **:** take up once more **:** adopt again ⟨*reassumed* the place she had held before⟩

**re·assumption** \"+\ *n* [*re-* + *assumption*] **:** the act of reassuming or state of being reassumed

**re·assurance** \"+\ *n* **1 :** the action of reassuring or state of being reassured ⟨a timid man in constant need of ~⟩ **2 :** REINSURANCE

**re·assure** \"+\ *vt* [*re-* + *assure*] **1 :** to assure anew **2 :** REINSURE — **re·assurement** \"+\ *n* -S — **re·assurer** \"+\ *n*

**reassured** *adj* **1 :** having confidence restored **:** freed from fear or anxiety **2 a :** having renewed insurance **b :** having insurance covered by being placed with another insurance company

**re·assuredly** \"+\ *adv* **:** by way of reassurance

**reassuring** *adj* **:** restoring or intended to restore confidence ⟨a very ~ remark⟩ — **re·as·sur·ing·ly** *adv*

**reas·ti·ness** \'rēstinės, 'rās-, 'ras-\ *n* -ES *dial chiefly Eng* **:** RANCIDITY

**reas·ty** \-ti\ *adj* -ER/-EST [ME *resty*, fr. OF *resté* left over, past part. of *rester* to remain — more at REST] *dial chiefly Eng* **:** RANCID

**re·ata** \rē'ad·ə, -'ä-\ *n* -S [AmerSp, lariat, lasso — more at LARIAT] **:** LARIAT

**re·attach** \ˌrē+\ *vb* [*re-* + *attach*] *vi* **:** to become attached anew ⟨the parasite ~*es* to the host⟩ ~ *vt* **:** to attach again

**re·attachment** \"+\ *n* [*re-* + *attachment*] **:** the act of reattaching or state of being reattached

**re·attack** \"+\ *vb* [*re-* + *attack*] *vt* **:** to attack again ~ *vi* **:** to make a new attack

**re·attain** \"+\ *vt* [*re-* + *attain*] **:** to attain again

**re·attainment** \"+\ *n* **:** the act of reattaining or state of being reattained

¹**re·attempt** \"+\ *vb* [*re-* + *attempt*] *vt* **:** to attempt again ~ *vi* **:** to make a new attempt

²**reattempt** \"\ *n* **:** a new attempt

**re·attire** \ˌrē+\ *vt* [*re-* + *attire*] **:** to attire again

**re·auction** \(ˈ)rē+\ *vt* [*re-* + *auction*] **:** to auction again

**re·audit** \(ˈ)rē+\ *vt* [*re-* + *audit*] **:** to audit again

**re·audition** \ˌrē+\ *vt* [*re-* + *audition*] **:** to audition again

**re·au·mur** \ˌrāō'myu̇(ə)r, -āō'm-, -ˌmər\ *adj, usu cap* [after René Antoine Ferchault de *Réaumur* †1757 Fr. physicist who formulated the Reaumur scale] **:** relating or conforming to a thermometric scale on which under standard atmospheric pressure the boiling point of water is at 80 degrees above the zero of the scale and the freezing point is at zero — abbr. *R*

**re·authenticate** \ˌrē+\ *vt* [*re-* + *authenticate*] **:** to authenticate again

**re·authentication** \"+\ *n* [*re-* + *authentication*] **:** the act of reauthenticating or state of being reauthenticated

**re·authorize** \(ˈ)rē+\ *vt* [*re-* + *authorize*] **:** to authorize again

¹**reave** \'rēv\ *vb* **reaved** \-vd\ *or* **reft** \'reft\ *or archaic* **raft** \'raft\ **reaved** *or* **reft** *or archaic* **raft; reaving; reaves** [ME *reven*, fr. OE *rēafian*; akin to OHG *roubōn* to rob, ON *raufa* to break up, open, Goth *biraubon* to rob, strip, L *rumpere* to break, burst, Skt *ropayati* he breaks off, ON *rögg* tuft, shagginess — more at RUG] *vi, archaic* **:** to take something away by or as if by stealth or force **:** PILLAGE, PLUNDER, ROB ~ *vt, archaic* **:** to take away by or as if by stealth or force: as **a :** ROB, DESPOIL ⟨of what enjoyments thou hast *reft* us —Robert Burns⟩ **b** (1) **:** to deprive one of ⟨~ his life —Edmund Spenser⟩ (2) **:** SEIZE ⟨thy father . . . *reft* from my dead lord a field with violence —Alfred Tennyson⟩ **c :** to carry or tear away **:** REMOVE ⟨who hath *reft* . . . my dearest pledge —John Milton⟩

²**reave** \"\ *vb* **reaved** \-vd\ *or* **reft** \'reft\ **reaved** *or* **reft; reaving; reaves** [ME *reven*, prob. modif. (influenced by ME *reven* to take away by or as if by stealth or force, rob, despoil) of ON *rīfa* to rive, tear — more at RIVE] *archaic* **:** BURST, TEAR, SPLIT

**rea·vel** \'rāvəl\ *chiefly Scot var of* RAVEL

**reav·er** *or* **riev·er** \'rēvə(r)\ *n* -S [ME *revere*, fr. OE *rēafere*, fr. *rēafian* to take away by or as if by stealth or force, rob, despoil + *-ere* -er] **:** one that takes away by or as if by stealth or force

**re·awake** \ˌrē+\ *vb* [*re-* + *awake*] *vt* **:** to awake again ~ *vi* **:** to become reawaked

**re·awaken** \"+\ *vb* [*re-* + *awaken*] *vt* **:** to awaken again ~ *vi* **:** to become reawakened

**re·awakenment** \"+\ *n* **:** the act of reawakening or state of being reawakened

**re·aware** \"+\ *adj* [*re-* + *aware*] **:** again aware **:** freshly aware

¹**reb** \'reb\ *n* -S [short for *rebel*] **:** JOHNNY REB

²**reb** \"\ *n* -S *usu cap* [Yiddish, fr. Heb *rabbī* my master, rabbi — more at RABBI] **:** RABBI, MISTER — used as a complimentary title

**re·bab** \rə'bäb\ *n* -S [Ar *rebāb*] **:** a medieval Arabic bowed musical instrument having from one to three strings, shaped typically like a small lute, and now used in gamelan orchestras

rebab

**re·back** \(ˈ)rē+\ *vt* [*re-* + *back*] **1 :** to reshape the backbone of (a book) after casing or covering **2 a :** to add a new backbone to (a book) without entirely rebinding **b :** to support the backbone of (a book) with new material

**re·banking** \"+\ *n* [*re-* + *banking*, fr. gerund of ²*bank*] **:** a malfunction in a watch caused by excessive balance motion that makes the roller jewel strike outside the fork horns and renders the escapement inoperative — distinguished from *overbanking*

**re·baptism** \"+\ *n* [*re-* + *baptism*] **:** a second baptism

**re·baptismal** \(ˌ)rē+\ *adj* [*rebaptism* + *-al*] **:** of or relating to a second baptism

**re·baptize** \"+\ *vt* [LL *rebaptizare*, fr. *re-* + *baptizare* to baptize] **:** to baptize again or a second time; *also* **:** to name or christen again

**re·baptizer** \"+\ *n* **:** one that rebaptizes

**re·bar·ba·tive** \rē'bärbəd·iv, -bäb-\ *adj* [F *rébarbatif*, fr. MF *rebarber* to be repellent (fr. *re-* + *barbe* beard, fr. L *barba*) + *-atif* -ative — more at BEARD] **:** serving or tending to repel or irritate **:** CRABBED, REPELLENT ⟨the impression given by these letters is not so much ~ as infinitely pathetic —*New Statesman & Nation*⟩

¹**re·bate** \'rē,bāt, ≈'≈, *usu* -ād·+V\ *vb* -ED/-ING/-S [ME *rebaten*, fr. MF *rabattre* to beat down again, turn back down, reduce, fr. OF, fr. *re-* + *abattre* to beat down, fr. *a-* (fr. L *ad-*) + *battre* to beat, fr. L *battuere, battere* — more at BAT] *vt* **1 :** to reduce the force, effect, intensity, or activity of **:** DIMINISH, LESSEN **2 :** to reduce the sharpness or edge of **:** make dull **:** BLUNT ⟨~ and blunt his natural edge —Shak.⟩ **3** *heraldry* **:** to remove a part of (a charge) **b :** to remove part of a charge from (an escutcheon) **4 a :** to make a rebate of ⟨*rebated* over a hundred dollars in interest⟩ **b :** to give a rebate to ⟨secretly *rebated* a few large shippers of freight⟩ ~ *vi* **:** to give or make a practice of giving rebates ⟨disliked *rebating* but accepted it as a necessary evil to . . . stay in business —D.L. Kemmerer⟩

²**rebate** \"\ *n* -S [F *rabat*, fr. MF *rabattre*] **:** ABATEMENT, REPAYMENT: as **a :** a return of a portion of the interest on a loan for payment of the loan before its due date **b :** a retroactive abatement, credit, discount, or refund (as from a wholesaler to a retailer) usu. as consideration for a specified volume of business **c :** a portion of an insurance premium returned directly or indirectly to the policyholder by an agent or broker from commissions received either as an inducement to purchase insurance or to gain a competitive advantage over another agent or broker in selling insurance

³**rebate** *var of* RABBET

**re·bate·ment** \rē'bātmənt\ *n* -S [MF, fr. *rebatre* to reduce (fr. OF, fr. *re-* + *battre, batre* to beat) + *-ment* — more at REBATE] **:** ABATEMENT 2

**re·bat·er** \rē'bād·ə(r), ≈'≈≈\ *n* -S **:** one that rebates

**re·ba·to** \rə'bäd·(ˌ)ō\ *n* -S [modif. of MF *rabat* — more at RABAT] **:** RABATO

**reb·be** \'rebə\ *n* -S [Yiddish, fr. Heb *rabbī* rabbi] **1 :** a teacher of Hebrew esp. in a heder **2 :** a rabbi or Jewish spiritual leader esp. of the Hasidic sect

**reb·betz·in** *or* **reb·bitz·in** \-bətsən\ *n* -S [Yiddish, fem. of *rebbe*] **:** the wife of a rabbi

**re·beamer** \(ˈ)rē+\ *n* [*re-* + ¹*beam* + *-er*] **:** a textile worker who winds cloth and yarn from one beam to another

**re·bec** *or* **re·beck** \'rē,bek\ *n* -S [MF *rebec*, alter. (perh. influenced by *bec* beak) of OF *rebebe*, fr. OProv *rebeb*, fr. Ar *rebāb* rebab — more at BEAK] **:** a bowed musical instrument derived from the rebab and having a pear-shaped body, a slender neck, and usu. three strings ⟨the jocund ~*s* sound —John Milton⟩

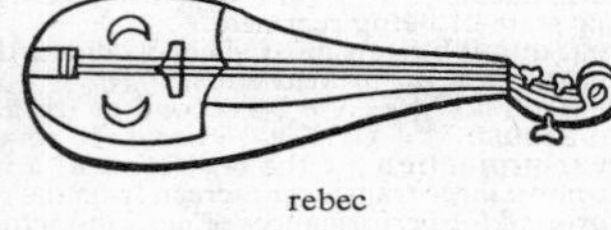

rebec

¹**reb·el** \'rebəl\ *adj* [ME, fr. OF *rebelle*, fr. L *rebellis*, fr. *re-* + *bellum* war, fr. OL *duellum* — more at DUEL] **1 a :** opposing or taking arms against the government or ruler of a country ⟨the ~ general⟩ ⟨the ~ lord⟩ ⟨his ~ son⟩ **b :** of, relating to, or belonging to rebels ⟨the ~ army⟩ ⟨the ~ camp⟩ **2 :** DISOBEDIENT, REBELLIOUS ⟨fonder of alliterative rhythm, and now ~ to strict metrical ways —George Saintsbury⟩

²**rebel** \"\ *n* -S [ME, fr. MF *rebelle*, fr. OF *rebelle*, adj.] **1 :** one who opposes authority or restraint **:** one who breaks with established custom or tradition ⟨a ~ against the conventions of education —Allen Johnson⟩ ⟨a ~ priding himself on his unorthodoxy —Anthony West⟩ **2 :** one who participates in a rebellion ⟨forsook peaceful methods of reform and became a real ~ —*Amer. Guide Series: R. I.*⟩ ⟨cities that were faithful have gone under to ~*s* —Gilbert Parker⟩

³**re·bel** \rə'bel, rē'-\ *vi* **rebelled; rebelled; rebelling; rebels** [ME *rebellen*, fr. MF *rebeller*, fr. L *rebellare* to make war again, rebel, fr. *re-* + *bellare* to make war, fr. *bellum* war] **1 a :** to oppose or disobey one in authority or control ⟨*rebelled* against the leaders of his party and voted with the opposition⟩ **b :** to renounce and resist by force the authority of the ruler or government to which one owes allegiance ⟨*rebelled* and raised an army to overthrow the king⟩ ⟨*rebelled* against the national government and declared their autonomy⟩ **2 a :** to put up a fight **:** show opposition ⟨*rebelled* against the industrialized urban life about him —W.P.Clancy⟩ ⟨*rebelled* at the routine of a clerk's work —J.E.Ferris⟩ **b :** to feel or exhibit anger or revulsion ⟨*rebelled* at the injustice of his situation and cursed his fate⟩ ⟨his senses *rebelled* at the sights and smells of the town⟩

**reb·el·dom** \'rebəldəm\ *n* -S [²*rebel* + *-dom*] **:** an area controlled by rebels

**re·bel·ler** \rə'belə(r), rē'-\ *n* -S [ME, fr. *rebellen* to rebel + *-er*] **:** REBEL

**re·bel·lion** \-lyən\ *n* -S [ME, fr. MF, fr. L *rebellion-, rebellio*, fr. *rebellare* to rebel + *-ion-, -io* -ion] **1 :** open opposition to a person or thing in a position of authority or dominance ⟨continuing the ~ started by the beboppers —Whitney Balliett⟩ ⟨a moral ~ against the oppression of everyday pettiness and misery —A.H.Pekelis⟩ **2 a :** open defiance of or armed resistance to the authority of an established government ⟨gross ~ and detested treason —Shak.⟩ **b** *often cap* **:** an instance of such defiance or resistance ⟨a taxpayers' ~⟩ ⟨the Great *Rebellion*⟩ ⟨the Whiskey *Rebellion*⟩ **3** *Scots law* **:** disobedience of a legal command or summons resulting in actual outlawry or later in certain penalties

**syn** REVOLUTION, UPRISING, REVOLT, INSURRECTION, MUTINY, PUTSCH: REBELLION commonly indicates open armed resistance to government of such strength as to constitute a formidable problem to the authorities ⟨the term *rebellion* is applied to an insurrection of large extent, and is usu. a war between the legitimate government of a country and portions or provinces of the same who seek to throw off their allegiance to it and set up a government of their own —*Instructions for Govt. of U. S. Armies*⟩ REVOLUTION usu. applies to a successful rebellion accomplishing the overthrow of a government or the permanent nullifying of its sovereign authority in the territory in question, sometimes with concomitant sweeping economic and social changes ⟨distinguish between *revolutions* affecting a change in a whole way of life, including religion, economics, and manners, as well as politics, and *revolutions* changing the form of government —C.J.Friedrich⟩ UPRISING may refer to a localized rebellion that flares into sudden, spontaneous, militant activity designed to overthrow authority ⟨an Indian *uprising* drove him and his family from home, but on its suppression they returned —W.J.Ghent⟩ ⟨an *uprising* now viewed as the real beginning of Ireland's "War of Independence" —*Current Biog.*⟩ REVOLT may apply to a rebellion or uprising against legitimate authority by those owing it allegiance but refusing to accept its dictates ⟨a premature *revolt*, of some 200 native soldiers . . . had resulted in the deaths of their officers and in lusty shouts for independence —C.A.Buss⟩ INSURRECTION may suggest more truculent intransigeance and surging activity and less organized purpose than REVOLT ⟨the new government was harassed by internal controversies and by assassinations, disorders, and *insurrections* —*Collier's Yr. Bk.*⟩ MUTINY applies to a determined localized insurrection and insubordination against maritime, naval, or military authority ⟨*mutiny* imports collective insubordination and necessarily includes some combination of two or more persons in resisting lawful military authority —*U. S. Manual for Courts-Martial*⟩ PUTSCH suggests a revolt, turbulent demonstration, or planned attempt at a coup to seize a governmental administration ⟨a *putsch* to take control of the government —A.L.Funk⟩

**re·bel·lious** \-yəs\ *adj* [ME, fr. ML *rebelliosus*, fr. L *rebellio* rebellion + *-osus* -ous] **1 a :** given to or engaged in rebellion against constituted authority ⟨~ troops⟩ ⟨a ~ politician⟩ ⟨a ~ student⟩ **b :** of, relating to, or characteristic of a rebel or rebellion ⟨~ actions⟩ ⟨~ speeches⟩ ⟨~ times⟩ **c :** resisting control **:** hostile to authority or tradition ⟨the early twentieth century was increasingly raucous, ~, and ribald —H.F. Mooney⟩ **2 :** resisting treatment or management **:** REFRACTORY, UNYIELDING ⟨eczema of long standing or which is ~ to treatment —H.G.Armstrong⟩ ⟨bend his head and crash with his full weight into ~ circumstances —Francis Hackett⟩ **syn** see INSUBORDINATE

**re·bel·lious·ly** *adv* **:** in a rebellious manner

**re·bel·lious·ness** *n* -ES **:** the quality or state of being rebellious

**reb·el·ly** \'rebəlē\ *adj* [²*rebel* + *-y*] **:** REBELLIOUS ⟨the ~ spirit of the century —Sean O'Faolain⟩

**rebels** *pl of* REBEL, *pres 3d sing of* REBEL

**rebel yell** *n* **:** a prolonged high-pitched yell traditionally given by Confederate soldiers in the U. S. Civil War

¹**re·bid** \(ˈ)rē+\ *vb* [*re-* + *bid*] *vt* **:** to bid (one's previously bid suit) again in bridge ~ *vi* **:** to bid again in the auction of a bridge deal

²**re·bid** \'rē+,≈\ *n* **:** a bid by a bridge player who has previously bid

**re·biddable** \(ˈ)rē+\ *adj* **:** capable of being rebid **:** long or strong enough to warrant a rebid even if not supported by one's partner ⟨a ~ suit⟩

**re·billing** \"+\ *n* [*re-* + *billing*] **:** the issuing of a new waybill at a junction point

¹**re·bind** \"+\ *vt* [*re-* + *bind*] **:** to bind anew or again; *esp* **:** to put a new binding on (a book)

²**re·bind** \'rē+,≈\ *n* **:** a rebound book

**re·birth** \(ˈ)rē+\ *n* [*re-* + *birth*] **1 a :** a new or second birth **:** METEMPSYCHOSIS ⟨the individual continues his pilgrimage through various ~*s* —R.N.Dandekar⟩ **b :** spiritual regeneration ⟨a bench in the front of the church to which all sinners and those in the struggle of ~ were invited —J.C.Brauer⟩ ⟨a novel of death and ~ of a spiritual purging and regeneration —M.D.Geismar⟩ **2 :** RENAISSANCE, REVIVAL ⟨the greatest achievement of modern science has been the ~ of the historical sense —Benjamin Farrington⟩ ⟨the ~ of the nationalist movement —M.S.Handler⟩

**re·blo·chon** \ˌreblə'shōⁿ\ *n* -S [F] **:** a soft French whole-milk cheese of delicate flavor

**reb·o·ant** \'rebəwənt\ *adj* [L *reboant-, reboans*, pres. part. of *reboare* to resound, fr. *re-* + *boare* to cry aloud, roar, fr. Gk *boan* to cry aloud, shout, of imit. origin] **:** REVERBERATING ⟨gave out a joyous howl, ~ with the sounds of conquest —Adria Langley⟩

**reb·o·a·tion** \-ə'wāshən\ *n* -S [L *reboatus* (past part. of *reboare*) + E *-ion*] **:** a loud reverberation ⟨the deep-mouthed ~ of a ship's horn seems to have lost itself in the fog —*Atlantic*⟩

**re·boil** \(ˈ)rē+\ *vt* [ME *reboilen*, fr. MF *rebouillir*, fr. *re-* + *bouillir, boillir* to boil] **:** to boil again; *specif* **:** to boil (as distilled water) again in order to remove occluded air and gases

**re·boil·er** \"+ə(r)\ *n* [*reboil* + *-er*] **:** a piece of equipment (as one with steam coils) for supplying additional heat esp. to the lower part of a fractionating column

**re·boise** \rə'bȯiz, rəb'wäz\ *vt* -ED/-ING/-S [F *reboiser*, fr. *re-* + *bois* wood, forest — more at BOISERIE] **:** REFOREST — **re·boise·ment** \-mənt\ *n* -S

**re·bo·le·ra** \ˌrebə'lerə\ *n* -S [Sp] **:** a pass ending a series of veronicas in bullfighting in which one end of the cape is released and swung in a graceful arc around the bullfighter's waist

**re·bop** \'rē,bäp\ *n* [imit.] **:** ³BOP

**re·born** \(ˈ)rē+\ *adj* [*re-* + *born*] **:** born again **:** having or experiencing a rebirth **:** REGENERATED, REVIVED ⟨thus men could be ~ and become sons of God —K.S.Latourette⟩ ⟨old states were ~ and new ones created —Samuel Van Valkenburg & Ellsworth Huntington⟩

**rebosa** *or* **reboso** *var of* REBOZO

**re·bo·te** \rə'bōd·ē\ *n* -S [Sp, bounce, rebound, fr. *rebotar* to rebound, fr. *re-* + *botar* to hurl, thrust, fr. OF *boter* to butt — more at BUTT] **1 :** the rear wall of a jai alai court **2 :** a shot played off the rebote

**re·bou·lia** \rə'büləə\ *n, cap* [NL, fr. H. P. I. *Reboul* †1839 French naturalist + NL *-ia*] **:** a genus of liverworts (family Marchantiaceae) that are widely distributed on rocks and soil and are distinguished by a conspicuous pseudoperianth split into fringy lanceolate lobes

¹**re·bound** \(ˈ)rē+\ *vb* [ME *rebounden*, fr. MF *rebondir*, fr. OF, fr. *re-* + *bondir* to bound — more at BOUND] *vi* **1 :** to spring back on collision or impact with another body ⟨a lattice or diffraction grating from which the electrons would ~ —*Current Biog.*⟩ **b :** to recover from or react to a setback or frustration ⟨~*ed* less quickly from disappointment —Ellen Glasgow⟩ ⟨was supposed to fall in love with someone else quickly . . . but she herself had ~*ed* differently —G.R.Stewart⟩ **2 :** to bound back as if upon impact **:** LEAP, SPRING ⟨released

from the downward pull, the submerged crustal material would ~ upward —A.E.Benfield⟩ **3 :** REECHO ⟨such a resounding whack that the echoes *~ed* from the mountains forty miles away —Darrell Berrigan⟩ **~** *vt* **1 :** to cause to spring back **:** RETURN **2 :** to make resound **:** REECHO

**syn** REVERBERATE, RECOIL, RESILE, REPERCUSS: REBOUND indicates a resilient springing, bouncing, or hurtling back after or as if after some collision, impact, or other forcible contact ⟨a ball *rebounding* from the wall⟩ ⟨literature is *rebounding* again from the scientific-classical pole to the poetic-romantic one —Edmund Wilson⟩ REVERBERATE is used of waves or rays that bound back or are forced back, reflected, or deflected; it is most typically used of sound and suggests loud reechoing ⟨the explosion *reverberated* between a series of low ridges, sounding like some giant's bowling ball —F.V.W.Mason⟩ ⟨its acoustics are magnificent: the merest mumble *reverberates* like the solemn voice of judgment —Green Peyton⟩ ⟨she presents even simple subjects with a perceptiveness that makes them *reverberate* in the mind —Babette Deutsch⟩ RECOIL applies to a springing or flying back, commonly in consequence of a release of pressure or stretching, to or against a point of origin, or in retreat, receding, or shrinking in apprehension or revulsion ⟨a spring *recoiling* to its natural position⟩ ⟨military commentators *recoiled* from the spectacle as if it were too loathsome for remark —S.L.A.Marshall⟩ RESILE may apply to a resilient but not abrupt drawing back to a former position ⟨the rubber attachments *resiling* at the normal temperatures⟩ ⟨apprehensive about the agreement and trying to *resile* to his former unattached position⟩ REPERCUSS, now notably less common than the noun *repercussion*, implies the return of something moving ahead with or as if with great force back to or toward the starting point ⟨sickness produces an abnormally sensitive emotional state in almost everyone, and in many cases the emotional state *repercusses*, as it were, on the organic disease —F.W.Peabody⟩

2**rebound** \"\ *n* **1 a :** the action of rebounding **:** a springing back after impact or the sudden release of pressure **:** RECOIL, RESILIENCE ⟨the reflection of light was just a ~ of the light particles from an elastic surface —S.F.Mason⟩ ⟨the origin of nationalism in Asia was in the nature of a ~ from the European imperialism of the last century —B.R.Sen⟩ **b :** an upward leap or movement **:** RECOVERY ⟨strength in selected issues . . . ushered in a sharp ~ in prices —J.G.Forrest⟩ **2 :** something that is reverberated **:** ECHO ⟨such *~s* our inward ear catches sometimes from afar —William Wordsworth⟩ **3 a :** a basketball or hockey puck that rebounds (as from a backboard or sideboard) ⟨grabbed the ~ and sank a basket⟩ **b :** an instance of securing possession of a rebounding basketball ⟨leads the league in *~s*⟩ **4 :** an immediate and spontaneous reaction to a setback, frustration, or intellectual or emotional crisis ⟨is also on the ~, not from ennui but from a dead lover —*Time*⟩ ⟨caught the middle class on the ~, and received perhaps a million votes which in subsequent elections it failed to hold —*Times Lit. Supp.*⟩

**rebound clip** *n* **:** a clip surrounding the back and one or two other leaves of a leaf spring and usu. rigidly fastened to the shortest to distribute the load during rebounds

**re·bounder** \"+\ *n* [2*rebound* + *-er*] **:** a basketball player skilled at getting possession of rebounds ⟨the top ~ on the team⟩

**re·bo·zo** \rā'bō(,)sō, rə̇'-\ *also* **re·bo·sa** \-‚sə\ *or* **re·bo·so** \-(,)sō\ *or* **ri·bo·so** \rə̇'-\ *n* -S [Sp *rebozo* shawl, fr. *rebozar* to muffle, fr. *re-* + *bozo* mouth, lips, fr. (assumed) VL *bucceum*, fr. L *bucca* cheek — more at POCK] **:** a long scarf made of any of various plain or embroidered fabrics often fringed on the ends and worn chiefly by Mexican women ⟨all decently shawled in long black *~s* —Gertrude Diamant⟩

**re·breather** \(')rē+\ *n* [*re-* + *breathe* + *-er*] **:** an apparatus with face mask and gas supply forming a closed system from which one can breathe as long as the concentrations of oxygen and carbon dioxide remain within tolerable limits

1**re·broadcast** \"+\ *vt* [*re-* + *broadcast*] **1 :** to broadcast simultaneously (a radio or television program or signals being received from another source) **2 :** to repeat (a radio or television broadcast) at a later time usu. by transcription

2**rebroadcast** \"\ *n* **:** something that is broadcast again; *specif* **:** a usu. transcribed repetition of a radio or television program

**rebs** *pl of* REB

1**re·buff** \rə̇'bəf, rē'-\ *vt* -ED/-ING/-S [MF *rebuffer*, fr. It *ribuffare*, to reprimand, fr. *ribuffo* reprimand] **1 :** to refuse or repulse without ceremony **:** give a sharp check to **:** SNUB ⟨mix only with the right people and ~ invitations from those we didn't like —H.E.Salisbury⟩ **2 :** to drive or beat back ⟨thunder and drenching flood ~ the winds —Robert Bridges †1930⟩ ⟨*~ed* the enemy attack⟩

2**rebuff** \", 'rē,-\ *n* -S [MF *rebuffe*, fr. It *ribuffo* reprimand] **1 :** an abrupt or unceremonious rejection of an offer or advance **:** SNUB ⟨the task was uncongenial to one sensitive to *~s*, but he succeeded in raising the outside amount necessary —H.K.Rowe⟩ **2 :** a sharp setback **:** REPULSE ⟨four costly *~s* of a tiny outpost detachment —F.V.W.Mason⟩ ⟨the reader who picks it up as casually as he would a common novel is headed for a ~ that will set him back upon his heels —B.R.Redman⟩

1**re·build** \(')rē+\ *vb* [*re-* + *build*] *vt* **1 a :** to make extensive repairs to including the replacement of missing or defective parts **:** RECONSTRUCT ⟨~ a vacuum cleaner⟩ **b :** to restore to a previous state or condition **:** RE-CREATE ⟨was struggling to ~ values for stockholders —L.M.Hughes⟩ ⟨~ inventories⟩ ⟨~ grazing resources⟩ **2 :** to make extensive changes in **:** REMODEL ⟨individuals should ~ their lives, so that social morality as a whole may be strengthened —D.R.Weimer⟩ **~** *vi* **:** to build again or anew ⟨bought the house with the intention of *~ing*⟩ **syn** see MEND

2**re·build** \'rē+,-\ *n* **:** something that is rebuilt ⟨many soldiers prefer the *~s*, because they are pliable and easier on the feet —*Newsweek*⟩

**re·builder** \(')=+\ *n* **:** one that rebuilds

**re·built** \"+\ *adj* [fr. past part. of 1*rebuild*] **:** disassembled and reconstructed with the addition of new parts ⟨a ~ typewriter⟩

**re·buk·able** \rə̇'byükəbəl, rē'-\ *adj* [1*rebuke* + *-able*] **:** meriting rebuke ⟨~ and worthy shameful check —Shak.⟩

1**re·buke** \-'byük\ *vt* -ED/-ING/-S [ME *rebuken*, fr. ONF *rebuker*, fr. *re-* + *-buker* (perh. fr. MHG *būsch* cudgel) — more at BOAST] **1 a :** to criticize sharply **:** censure severely **:** REPRIMAND ⟨their children where they could be watched and *rebuked* if they became restless —J.H.Cutler⟩ ⟨*rebuked* abuse of the uniform for commercial purposes —Dixon Wecter⟩ **b :** to serve as a rebuke to ⟨his industry *~s* me⟩ **2 :** to turn back or keep down **:** CHECK, REPULSE ⟨whose courtiers vowed he could ~ the waves —Thomas Wood †1950⟩ ⟨the mountaineering willow, sharply *rebuked* by drying winds, rises no higher than an inch —Andrew Young⟩ **syn** see REPROVE

2**rebuke** \"\ *n* -S [ME, fr. *rebuken* to rebuke] **:** an expression of strong disapproval **:** REPRIMAND, REPROOF ⟨clambering on the divan with muddy shoes brought sharp parental ~ —Lucius Garvin⟩ ⟨dreading a ~ . . . by venturing to dance —Jane Austen⟩

**re·buke·ful** \-fəl\ *adj* [2*rebuke* + *-ful*] **:** serving to or disposed to rebuke — **re·buke·ful·ly** \-fəlē\ *adv*

**re·buk·er** \-kə(r)\ *n* -S [ME, fr. *rebuken* to rebuke + *-er*] **:** one that rebukes ⟨able to recall that no one was more mischievous than their ~ in his own youth —A.D.Rees⟩

**re·buk·ing·ly** *adv* [*rebuking* (pres. part. of 1*rebuke*) + *-ly*] **:** in a rebuking manner

**re·burial** \(')rē+\ *n* [*re-* + *burial*] **:** an act or instance of reburying

**re·bury** \"+\ *vt* [*re-* + *bury*] **:** to bury again

1**re·bus** \'rēbəs\ *n* -ES [L, by things (abl. pl. of *res* thing) — more at REAL] **1 :** a representation of words or syllables by pictures of objects or by symbols whose names resemble the intended words or syllables in sound; *also* **:** a riddle made up wholly or in part of such pictures or symbols ⟨*ICURYY4 me* is a ~ for *I see you are too wise for me*⟩ **2 :** a badge that suggests the name of the person to whom it belongs — compare CANTING 2

2**rebus** \"\ *vt* **rebused; rebused; rebusing; rebuses :** to mark with or indicate by a rebus ⟨Abbot Islip's . . . name is *~ed* as an eye and the slip of a tree with the hand apparently of a slipping man hanging to it —Edward Clodd⟩

**rebus sic stan·ti·bus** \-(,)sik'stantəbəs\ *adv* [NL, lit., things continuing thus] **:** so long as conditions have not substantially changed ⟨a doctrine in international law that treaties are binding only *rebus sic stantibus*⟩

**re·but** \rə̇'bət, rē'-, *usu* -əd·+V\ *vb* **rebutted; rebutted; rebutting; rebuts** [ME *rebuten*, fr. OF *reboter*, fr. *re-* + *boter* to butt, thrust — more at BUTT] *vt* **1 a :** to drive or beat back **:** REPULSE ⟨this mare . . . took no interest in the horse and . . . she did not ~ him either —Henry Wynmalen⟩ **b :** to check the advance or influence of **:** REPEL ⟨luckily a few pictures in the house to ~ a despairing mood —Sacheverell Sitwell⟩ **2 a :** to contradict, meet, or oppose by formal legal argument, plea, or countervailing proof ⟨where evidence is offered to ~ presumption against suicide, presumption disappears —*Detroit Law Jour.*⟩ **b :** to expose the falsity of **:** CONTRADICT, REFUTE ⟨~ my contention that something cannot be done by doing it —F.H.Cleobury⟩ ⟨in her first sentence she *~s* the long-accepted dictum that Africa is a continent without a history —D.H.Jones⟩ **~** *vi* **:** to make or put in an answer or counter proof (as to a plaintiff's surrejoinder) **:** make a rebuttal **syn** see DISPROVE

**re·bute** \rə̇'büt, -bœt, -byüt\ *n* -S [ME, fr. *rebuten* to rebut] *Scot* **:** REBUFF

**re·but·ment** \rə̇'bətmənt, rē'-\ *n* -S [1*rebut* + *-ment*] **:** REBUTTAL

**re·but·table** \-bəd·əbəl\ *adj* **:** capable of being rebutted

**rebuttable presumption** *n* **:** a presumption that may be rebutted by other legal evidence — compare PRESUMPTION OF LAW

**re·but·tal** \rə̇'bəd·ᵊl, rē'-, -ətᵊl\ *n* -S [1*rebut* + *-al*] **:** the act of rebutting; *specif* **:** the giving of evidence in a legal suit to destroy the effect of evidence introduced by the other side in the same suit

1**re·but·ter** \-əd·ə(r), -ətə-\ *n* -S [AF *rebuter*, fr. OF *reboter*, *rebouter* to rebut] **:** the answer of a defendant in matter of fact to a plaintiff's surrejoinder

2**rebutter** \"\ *n* -S [1*rebut* + *-er*] **:** something that rebuts or refutes **:** REFUTATION

**rec** \'rek\ *adj* [by shortening] **:** RECREATION ⟨~ hall⟩ ⟨~ activities⟩

**rec** *abbr* **1** receipt **2** receive; receiver **3** receptacle **4** reception **5** recipe **6** reclamation **7** recommended **8** record; recorded; recorder; recording **9** recovery

**re·cal·ci·trance** \rə̇'kalsə·trən(t)s, rē'-\ *or* **re·cal·ci·tran·cy** \-nsē, -si\ *n, pl* **recalcitrances** *or* **recalcitrancies** [*recalcitrance* fr. *recalcitrant*, after such pairs as E *obedient: obedience; recalcitrancy* fr. *recalcitrant* + *-cy*] **:** the state of being recalcitrant **:** obstinate noncompliance **:** stubborn opposition ⟨in the best reformed society elements of selfish ~ will remain —J.A.Hobson⟩ ⟨a wayward, contrary, ungovernable element in human nature — an element akin to the ~ of our cousins the camel, mule, and goat —A.J.Toynbee⟩

1**re·cal·ci·trant** \-nt\ *adj* [LL *recalcitrant-*, *recalcitrans*, fr. pres. part. of *recalcitrare* to be stubbornly disobedient, fr. L, to kick back, fr. *re-* + *calcitrare* to kick, fr. *calc-*, *calx* heel — more at CALK] **1 :** obstinately defiant of authority or restraint **:** stubbornly disobedient ⟨~ and dangerous heretics and obstructionists —G.L.Kline⟩ ⟨a ~ child⟩ ⟨call forth the forces of the Union to coerce ~ states —S.E.Morison & H.S.Commager⟩ **2 a :** difficult or impossible to handle or operate **:** UNMANAGEABLE ⟨the materials in these fields are more complex and more ~ than the simpler and more readily measurable phenomena of the languages —Mortimer Graves⟩ ⟨the car had a ~ gearshift lever —M.M.Musselman⟩ **b :** not responsive to treatment ⟨many of these patients were suffering from ~ forms of the disease —*Jour. Amer. Med. Assoc.*⟩ **c :** RESISTANT — usu. used with *to* ⟨this subject is ~ both to observation and to experiment —G.G.Simpson⟩ ⟨nothing perhaps is more ~ to logical systematization than local custom —G.H.Sabine⟩ **syn** see UNRULY

2**recalcitrant** \"\ *n* -S **:** one who is recalcitrant

**re·cal·ci·trate** \-sə·,trāt, *usu* -ād·+V\ *vi* -ED/-ING/-S [L *recalcitratus*, past part. of *recalcitrare* to kick back] **1 :** to kick back **2 :** to protest or resist vigorously **:** show stubborn opposition

**re·cal·ci·tra·tion** \=,=='trāshən\ *n* -S [*recalcitrate* + *-ion*] **:** a kicking back or against something **:** OPPOSITION, REPUGNANCE, REFRACTORINESS

**re·calculate** \(')rē+\ *vt* [*re-* + *calculate*] **:** to calculate or estimate again esp. in order to discover the source of an error or formulate new conclusions ⟨*recalculated* their data and tried to explain the unexpected force of the big blast —*Time*⟩ ⟨requires that the United States ~ our own risks and reconsider the possible alternatives —Herbert Hoover⟩

**re·calculation** \¦rē+\ *n* **:** an act or process of recalculating

**re·ca·les·cence** \,rēkə'lesᵊn(t)s\ *n* -S [L *recalescere* to grow warm again (fr. *re-* + *calescere* to grow warm, incho. of *calēre* to be warm) + E *-ence* — more at LEE] **:** the increase in temperature when the rate of heat liberation during transformation exceeds the rate of heat dissipation while cooling metal through a transformation range — compare DECALESCENCE

**re·ca·les·cent** \¦==¦lesᵊnt\ *adj* [prob. back-formation fr. *recalescence*] **:** of, relating to, or marked by recalescence

1**re·call** \rə̇'kȯl, rē'-\ *vt* [*re-* + *call*] **1 a :** to call back **:** summon or cause to return ⟨was *~ed* from abroad to report to the government⟩ ⟨was *~ed* to active service⟩ ⟨other automotive divisions will ~ their hourly workers —*Sacramento (Calif.) Bee*⟩ ⟨is thought that his soul has quitted his body and must be *~ed* —J.G.Frazer⟩ **b :** to call or bring back the thought or memory of ⟨the sight of the streets thronged with buyers . . . *~ed* to me the purpose of my journey —James Joyce⟩ ⟨knowledge of an event or fact which the sign *~s* —Edward Clodd⟩ **c :** to remind one of **:** exhibit a resemblance to ⟨look with suspicion upon anything that might savor of economic exploitation or ~ old imperialist ideas —Arthur Rucker⟩ ⟨the rectangular, four-story mass of unusually high proportions *~s* numerous courthouse designs of the period —*Amer. Guide Series: N.Y.*⟩ **d :** RECOLLECT ⟨seem always to ~ him in his brown velvet smock —Osbert Sitwell⟩ ⟨*~ing* the emotions and events and spectacles which have come to a man with the years —P.E.More⟩ **2 :** to annul by taking back ⟨past sentence may not be *~ed* —Shak.⟩ **3 :** to cause to exist again **:** RESTORE ⟨beauty . . . whose season was, and cannot be *~ed* —William Wordsworth⟩ **4 :** to bring back to consciousness or awareness **:** REVIVE ⟨trying to ~ her stunned senses —George Meredith⟩ ⟨stared and *~ed* himself and was ashamed —Pearl Buck⟩ **syn** see REMEMBER, REVOKE

2**re·call** \'rē,kȯl, rə̇'k-, rē'k-\ *n* **1 a :** the act or an instance of calling back **:** a summons to return from or to a position, situation, or place ⟨the ~ of an ambassador from his post⟩ ⟨the ~ of a reserve officer to active duty⟩ ⟨announced the ~ of 500 workers after a 2-week layoff⟩ **b** (1) **:** a signal (as a bugle call) summoning soldiers back (as to ranks or camp) or indicating the end of a drill or work period (2) **:** a signal calling a boat back to a ship **c :** the right or procedure by which a legislative, judicial, or executive official may be removed from office before the end of his term by a vote of the people to be taken on the filing of a petition signed by a required number (as 25 percent) of qualified voters ⟨nearly one third of the states allow the ~ to be used by all cities —J.E.Pate⟩ ⟨~ election⟩ **2 :** remembrance of what has been previously learned or experienced **:** REPRODUCTION, REVIVAL — compare RECOGNITION ⟨mere ~ of past memories without integrating them in terms of current reality is ineffective —M.H.Erickson⟩ ⟨could remember strange streets, bays, oceans, harbors, countrysides with almost total visual ~ —Henry Wallace⟩ **3 :** the act of revoking or the possibility of being revoked ⟨the war is completed — the price is paid — the title is settled beyond ~ —Walt Whitman⟩ ⟨this is a matter past ~ —Robert Browning⟩

**re·call·able** \rə̇'kȯləbəl\ *adj* **:** capable of being recalled

**recall dose** *n* **:** BOOSTER 10a

**re·call·ment** \-lmənt\ *n* -S [1*recall* + *-ment*] **:** RECALL

**ré·ca·mier** \,rākə'myā\ *n* -S *often cap* [after Mme. J. F. J. A. *Récamier* †1849 Fr. society beauty and wit] **:** a moderate pink to strong yellowish pink

**re·cant** \rə̇'kant, rē'-, -kaa(ə)nt\ *vb* -ED/-ING/-S [L *recantare*, fr. *re-* + *cantare* to sing — more at CHANT] *vt* **1 a :** to withdraw or repudiate (a statement or belief) formally and publicly ⟨~ all opinions which differed from those proclaimed by the central leadership —P.E.Mosely⟩ **b :** to make renunciation of (a course of action) ⟨didn't show up . . . to ~ his sins —*Time*⟩ **2 :** RETRACT, REVOKE ⟨do this or else I do ~ the pardon —Shak.⟩ **~** *vi* **:** to take back or disavow an opinion, declaration, or course of action **:** make an open confession of error ⟨never hesitates to ~ whenever the progress of his thinking has brought about what he considers an improvement upon his former views —André Martinet⟩ **syn** see ABJURE

**re·can·ta·tion** \,rē,kan·'tāshən, -kaan-\ *n* -S [*recant* + *-ation*] **:** the act or an instance of recanting **:** public confession of error **:** RETRACTION ⟨*~s* among those who had opposed him —Waldemar Kaempffert⟩

**re·cant·er** \rə̇'kantə(r)\ *n* -S **:** one that recants

1**re·cap** \(')rē¦kap\ *vt* [*re-* + *cap*] **1 :** to cap again **:** put a new cap on **2 :** to cement, mold, and vulcanize a strip of camelback upon the buffed and roughened surface of the tread of (a worn pneumatic tire) — distinguished from *retread*

2**recap** \'rē,kap\ *n* **:** a recapped tire

3**recap** \"\ *vt* [by shortening] **:** RECAPITULATE

4**recap** \"\ *n* [by shortening] **:** RECAPITULATION

**re·cap·i·tal·iza·tion** \¦rē,kapəd·ᵊlə̇¦zāshən\ *n* [*recapitalize* + *-ation*] **:** a revision of the capital structure of a corporation commonly effected by amendment of the charter or merger with a subsidiary

**re·capitalize** \(')rē+\ *vt* [*re-* + *capitalize*] **:** to capitalize again **:** change the capital structure of

**re·ca·pit·u·late** \,rēkə'pichə,lāt, *usu* -ād·+V\ *vb* [LL *recapitulatus*, past part. of *recapitulare* to sum up, restate by heads, fr. L *re-* + LL *capitulare* (fr. *capitulum* division of a book, heading) — more at CHAPTER] *vt* **1 a :** to repeat the principal points of **:** restate briefly **:** give a summary of ⟨~ . . . the whole situation as I see it —J.C.Powys⟩ ⟨a host of writers have attempted to define addiction and there is no point in *recapitulating* here the history of those attempts —D.W.Maurer & V.H.Vogel⟩ **b :** to repeat the principal stages or phases of ⟨adopted the theory that the child *~s* primitive experience —H.J.Muller⟩ ⟨the individual organism *~s* the history of its race —S.F.Mason⟩ **2 :** UNITE ⟨to ~ ourselves, to assemble and muster ourselves —John Donne⟩ **~** *vi* **:** to sum up **:** go back over an argument or discussion ⟨now that I ~ he was correct with less than one percent error —*New Republic*⟩

**re·ca·pit·u·la·tion** \,==,=='lāshən\ *n* [ME *recapitulacion*, fr. MF or LL; MF *recapitulation*, fr. LL *recapitulation-*, *recapitulatio*, fr. *recapitulatus* + *-ion-*, *-io* -ion] **1 a :** the act of recapitulating **:** a summing up ⟨the third and very important contribution to a successful daytime serial is the announcer's ~ of what went on yesterday —Goodman Ace⟩ **b :** the process by which according to Irenaeus the Logos passed through all phases of human experience thus reversing the evil caused by sin and winning complete salvation for man **2 :** the supposed repetition in the development of the individual of its phylogenetic history — see RECAPITULATION THEORY **3 :** the third section of a musical movement in sonata form consisting of a usu. modified repetition of the exposition and typically followed by a coda

**re·ca·pit·u·la·tion·ist** \-sh(ə)nə̇st\ *n* -S **:** one who accepts the recapitulation theory

**recapitulation theory** *n* **:** a theory in biology: an organism passes through successive stages resembling the series of ancestral types from which it has descended so that the ontogeny of the individual is a recapitulation of the phylogeny of its group — compare BIOGENESIS 2, PALINGENESIS, VON BAER'S LAW

**re·ca·pit·u·la·tive** \,=='pichə,lād·|iv, -āt|, |ēv *also* |əv\ *adj* [*recapitulate* + *-ive*] **:** of, relating to, or characterized by recapitulation — **re·ca·pit·u·la·tive·ly** \|ə̇vlē\ *adv*

**re·ca·pit·u·la·to·ry** \,=='pichələ,tōrē, -tȯr-, -ri\ *adj* [*recapitulate* + *-ory*] **:** of, relating to, or marked by recapitulation ⟨the apparent ~ relationship between growth stages and adults —G.F.Elliott⟩

**re·cap·pa·ble** \(')rē¦kapəbəl\ *adj* [3*recap* + *-able*] **:** capable of being recapped

**re·cap·per** \-pə(r)\ *n* **:** one that recaps

**re·cap·tion** \rə̇'kapshən\ *n* [*re-* + L *caption-*, *captio* act of taking, seizing — more at CAPTION] **:** the act of retaking; *specif* **:** the peaceable retaking of one's own goods, chattels, wife, or children from one who has taken and wrongfully detains them

**re·cap·tor** \-ptə(r)\ *n* [*re-* + L *captus* (past part. of *capere* to take, capture) + E *-or* — more at HEAVE] **1 :** one that recaptures; *specif* **:** one that takes a prize at sea that had been previously taken **2 :** one that recovers (something) by recaption

1**re·capture** \(')rē+\ *n* [*re-* + *capture*, n.] **1 a** (1) **:** the act of retaking or the fact of being retaken **:** RECOVERY ⟨the ~ of three fourths of the lake shore, which had fallen completely into private ownership —Harland Bartholomew⟩ ⟨the development of new markets and ~ of former markets —W.M.Blair⟩ (2) **:** the retaking of a prize or goods usu. thereby under international law devesting the property acquired in captured booty or prize — compare POSTLIMINIUM **b :** a governmental seizure under law of earnings or profits beyond a fixed amount **c :** a capture that completes an even exchange in chess **2 :** something that is captured again

2**recapture** \"\ *vt* [*re-* + *capture*, vb.] **1 a :** to capture again ⟨*recaptured* the hill they had lost the day before⟩ ⟨informal history that *~s* much of the flavor of a composite society —W.H.Stephenson⟩ **b :** to experience again **:** RECOVER ⟨by no effort of the imagination could she ~ the ecstasy —Ellen Glasgow⟩ ⟨~ the past⟩ **2 :** to take by law or through negotiations under law (a portion of earnings or profits above a fixed amount) — **re·cap·tur·er** \"+ə(r)\ *n* -S

**re·carbonize** \"+\ *vt* [*re-* + *carbonize*] **:** to carbonize again

**re·carburization** \(¦)rē+\ *n* **:** the process of recarburizing

**re·carburize** \(')rē+\ *vt* [*re-* + *carburize*] **:** to carburize again

**re·car·bu·riz·er** \(')rē¦kärbyə,rīzə(r)\ *n* [*recarburize* + *-er*] **:** a recarburizing agent (as spiegeleisen or anthracite coal)

**re·case** \(')rē+\ *vt* [*re-* + *case*] **:** to put the original or another cover on (a book separated from its cover) without changing the construction of the leaves

1**re·cast** \(')rē'kast, -kaa(ə)st, -kaist, -kȧst\ *vb* [*re-* + *cast*] *vt* **1 :** to throw again; *esp* **:** to make a second cast of (a fishline) **2 a :** to put into a mold again **:** REMOLD ⟨many hypothetical questions can be ~ into a factual mold —S.L.Payne⟩ **b :** to give a different form or quality to **:** REFASHION, REMODEL ⟨we have only to alter slightly, not to ~, the standards by which we have judged —Virginia Woolf⟩ ⟨all our notions of relative velocity must be ~ —A.N.Whitehead⟩ ⟨~ the poem⟩ **3 :** to compute again **:** RECALCULATE ⟨descended to the store cellars, *~ing* the inventory of their supplies —A.J.Cronin⟩ **4 :** to provide a new set of performers for ⟨the opera has been almost completely ~⟩ **~** *vi* **:** to cast a second time; *esp* **:** to make a second cast in fishing — **re·cast·er** \-tə(r)\ *n*

2**recast** \'=,=\ *n* **1 :** the act or an instance of recasting **2 :** a product of recasting **:** a new form of something

**rec·ce** \'rekē\ *also* **rec·co** \-e(,)kō\ *or* **rec·cy** \-ekē\ *n, pl* **recces** *also* **reccos** *or* **reccies** [by shortening and alter.] **:** RECONNAISSANCE ⟨rain . . . prevented a plane ~ of the blocked river —*Jour. of the Royal Central Asian Society*⟩

**recd** *abbr* received

1**re·cede** \rə̇'sēd, rē'-\ *vi* [L *recedere* to go back, withdraw, fr. *re-* + *cedere* to go — more at CEDE] **1** *archaic* **:** DIFFER, VARY — usu. used with *from* **2 :** to go away **:** DEPART ⟨watched the August days ~ —Francis Russell⟩ ⟨had drooped in his chair after dinner, and the accumulation of ninety years had *receded* abruptly into history —Victoria Sackville-West⟩ **3 a :** to move back or away **:** fall or draw back to a more distant line or position **:** WITHDRAW ⟨the tide, having risen to its highest, was *receding* —Arnold Bennett⟩ ⟨a hairline *receding* almost visibly —Leslie Waller⟩ ⟨far too self-willed to ~ from a position —Thomas Hardy⟩ **b** (1) **:** to extend farther back **:** lie more remote ⟨south of the town the river not only spreads out, but the hills ~ —Sherwood Anderson⟩ (2) **:** to slant backward ⟨a *receding* forehead⟩ **4 a :** to withdraw wholly (as from an agreement or promise) ⟨once he had given his word, he could not ~⟩ ⟨*receded* from the bargain he had made⟩ **b :** to deviate in some degree (as from a principle, belief, position) ⟨a height of devotion to human liberties from which she has never *receded* —F.A.Ogg & Harold Zink⟩ ⟨define a position from which he never *receded* —Stanislaus Joyce⟩ **c :** to withdraw opposition to an amendment passed by the other house of a bicameral legislature **5 a :** to grow less : CONTRACT, DIMINISH, SHRINK ⟨some feared that employment might ~ to as few as 14,000 employees —*N.Y. Times*⟩ ⟨colleges will ~ in their public importance —R.W.Emerson⟩ **b :** to fall to a lower level : DECLINE ⟨demand in general eased and prices *receded* for practically all types of skins —*Farmer's Weekly (So. Africa)*⟩ **6** *of a color* **:** to seem to go away from the viewer ⟨light colors ~⟩ — contrasted with *advance*

**syn** RETREAT, RETROGRADE, RETRACT, BACK: RECEDE is applied to withdrawing or going backward, sometimes slowly and gradually, from some fixed or definite forward or high point or position ⟨the flood waters *receded*⟩ ⟨the frontier soon *receded* before the ax and plow —*Amer. Guide Series: Texas*⟩ ⟨west coast lay opinion *receded* somewhat from its previous intransigent attitude —*Americana Annual*⟩ RETREAT often applies to a drawing back or withdrawing induced by uncertainty, danger, fear, or superior opposing force or other agency exciting pressure ⟨the outnumbered troops *retreated* before the enemy⟩ ⟨have been forced to *retreat*, for the earliest tabulations produced patterns too complex to be handled or understood —W.O.Aydelotte⟩ ⟨educational theory and practice have *retreated* into cultural parochialism —Douglas Bush⟩ RETROGRADE applies to movement backward in contrast to expected forward movement, to reversion or going backward rather than progressing ⟨where one man advances, hundreds *retrograde* —T.L.Peacock⟩ ⟨he had progressed, and he could never, by any possibility, afford to *retrograde* —P.B.Kyne⟩ RETRACT indicates a drawing backward or inward from an outer, exposed, prominent, or more apparent position ⟨a cat *retracting* its claws⟩ ⟨*retracted* the platoons on the left flank⟩ BACK may refer to any backward or reversed motion or, esp. with *down*, to a receding or retreating ⟨*back* a car⟩ ⟨water *backing* up in the pipes⟩ ⟨*back* down and accept defeat⟩

**²re·cede** \(')rē+\ *vt* [*re-* + *cede*] **:** to cede back : grant or yield again to a former possessor

**re·ced·ence** \rə'sēdᵊn(t)s\ *n* -s [¹*recede* + *-ence*] **:** RECESSION

**re·ced·er** \rə'sēdə(r)\ *n* -s **:** one that recedes; *specif* **:** a device in a sawmill for making the knees of the headblocks recede a sufficient distance to take on another log when the last board of the previous log has dropped

**receding color** *n* **:** any of various colors (as greens, blues, violets, and their variations) that tend to appear farther from the eye than other colors lying in the same plane

**¹re·ceipt** \rə'sēt, rē'-, *usu* -ēd·+V\ *n* -s [ME *receite*, fr. ONF, fr. ML *recepta* (sing.), prob. fr. L *recepta*, neut. pl. of *receptus*, past part. of *recipere* to receive, take] **1 a :** RECIPE ⟨a very special kind of mince pie she had been trying a new ~ on —Esther Forbes⟩ ⟨a perfect man, as the baronet trusted to make this one son of his, after a ~ of his own —George Meredith⟩ **b :** something that serves as a cure or remedy ⟨the newest ~ for avoiding calumny —R.B.Sheridan⟩ **2 a** *obs* **:** a place for receiving or storing something : RECEPTACLE **b :** a place at which money is officially received : a revenue office esp. formerly in England ⟨a man . . . sitting at the ~ of custom —Mt 9:9 (AV)⟩ **3 :** the act or process of receiving ⟨in ~ of a salary which he had earned —O.S.J.Gogarty⟩ ⟨ports equipped for the ~ of large vessels —L.D.Stamp⟩ **4 :** something (as food, goods, money) that is received — usu. used in pl. ⟨ranks about tenth in the United States in volume of fresh fruit and vegetable ~*s* —*Calif. Agric. Bull.*⟩ ⟨improve the harbor to accommodate larger raw material ~*s* —*Steel Facts*⟩ ⟨took the day's ~*s* to the bank's night depository —J.C. Furnas⟩ **5 :** a writing acknowledging the taking or receiving of goods or money delivered or paid ⟨could offer only poor paper money or ~*s* to pay for it —F.V.W.Mason⟩ ⟨paid the bill in cash and was given a ~⟩

**²receipt** \"\ *vb* -ED/-ING/-S *vt* **1 :** to give a receipt for or acknowledge the receipt of ⟨the radio officer ~*ed* the message and took a copy of it up to the bridge —R.F.Mirvish⟩ **2 :** to mark paid ⟨had paid by check, and the ~*ed* bill had been returned to him on the following day —F.W.Crofts⟩ ~ *vi* **:** to give a receipt — used with *for* ⟨an officer of the receiving side would ~ for each lot —*Newsweek*⟩

**receipt book** *n* **1 :** a book containing recipes **2 :** a book containing forms to be used in giving receipts for payment of money

**re·ceipt·or** \-sēd·ə(r)\ *n* -s [²*receipt* + *-or*] **:** one that receipts for property taken by a sheriff and agrees to return it upon demand

**re·ceiv·abil·i·ty** \rə,sēvə'biləd·ē\ *n* **:** the quality or state of being receivable

**re·ceiv·able** \rə'sēvəbəl, rē'-\ *adj* [*receive* + *-able*] **1 :** capable of being received ⟨a broadcast ~ over a wide area⟩; *specif* **:** legally admissible or acceptable ⟨~ testimony⟩ ⟨~ evidence⟩ ⟨~ certificates⟩ **2 :** subject to a call or claim for payment ⟨accounts ~⟩ ⟨notes ~⟩

**re·ceiv·ables** \-lz\ *n pl* **:** accounts, accepted bills, or notes created in the course of business that are due from others or will become due at an assignable date ⟨retail department stores, where the ~ are high in volume —R.M.Trueblood & R.M.Cyert⟩

**re·ceiv·al** \rə'sēvəl\ *n* -s [*receive* + *-al*] **:** RECEIPT 3

**re·ceive** \rə'sēv, rē'-\ *vb* -ED/-ING/-S [ME *receiven*, fr. ONF *receivre*, fr. L *recipere* to take back, take, accept, receive, fr. *re-* + *-cipere* (fr. *capere* to take) — more at HEAVE] *vt* **1 a** (1) **:** to take possession or delivery of ⟨~ a gift⟩ ⟨~ a letter⟩ (2) **:** to knowingly accept (stolen goods) ⟨suspected of *receiving* the stolen jewels⟩ **b :** to give attention to : listen to ⟨~ his confession⟩ ⟨refused to ~ advice from his friends⟩ **2 a :** to take in : act as a receptacle or container for ⟨a great interior lake *received* this young giant among rivers —Tom Marvel⟩ **b :** to take in through the mind or senses ⟨any young, active mind that was ready to ~ ideas —M.R.Cohen⟩ ⟨at an age when he was most ready to ~ new impressions⟩ **c :** CONTAIN, HOLD ⟨too small to ~ the burnt offering —1 Kings 8:64 (RSV)⟩ **3 a :** to give accommodation, protection, or refuge to : HARBOR ⟨go back to a husband who was still ready to ~ her —*Atlantic*⟩ **b** *of a female mammal* **:** ACCEPT 8 **4 a :** to admit or accept in some character or capacity ⟨*received* him as a colleague⟩ ⟨would not ~ her as his son's wife⟩ **b :** to admit to a place, faith, group, or condition ⟨they were *received* both at the tribal fire and at the trading post —*Amer. Guide Series: Minn.*⟩ ⟨having shortly before abandoned his skepticism and been *received* into the Catholic faith —H.W. H.Knott⟩ **5 a :** to welcome on arrival : GREET ⟨the small lady who *received* them at his house —William Black⟩ **b :** to give a formal and official welcome to ⟨shall ~ ambassadors and other public ministers —*U.S. Constitution*⟩ **c :** to greet or react to in a specified manner ⟨began his first concert tour, on which he was well *received* —*Current Biog.*⟩ ⟨the academic world *received* it with hostility —Max Lerner⟩ **6 a :** to acquiesce in or submit to : endure willingly ⟨couldn't unquestioningly ~ acceptance by these white patients —F.A.Perry⟩ **b :** to support the weight or pressure of : BEAR ⟨~*s* the weight of the world on his shoulders⟩ **c :** to take (a mark or impression) from the weight or pressure of something ⟨the ground was too hard to ~ a footprint⟩ ⟨his tenderer cheek ~*s* her soft hand's print —Shak.⟩ **d :** to undergo the impact of or interrupt the course of : CATCH, INTERCEPT ⟨get their full share of light, *receiving* the cooler level rays of the rising and setting sun —Andrew Young⟩ ⟨available to ~ the discharge of such emotions —R.M.Weaver⟩ **7 a :** to come into possession of : ACQUIRE ⟨*received* his early education in the public schools⟩ ⟨*received* his medical training abroad⟩ **b :** to meet with : EXPERIENCE ⟨a book that has never *received* the attention it deserves⟩ ⟨has *received* love and understanding from those around him⟩ **c :** to be exposed or subjected to : SUFFER ⟨*received* the royal displeasure on one occasion —Harvey Graham⟩ **d :** to be hurt or damaged by (a specified blow or injury) ⟨*received* a mortal wound⟩ ⟨*received* a broken nose⟩ **e :** to be placed under the burden, charge, or constraint of : be made subject to ⟨*received* a heavy sentence from the judge⟩ ⟨*received* written orders from the commanding general⟩ ⟨*received* a subpoena⟩ **8 a :** to partake of (the eucharistic sacrament) **b :** to take in at the mouth ⟨for fear of opening my lips and *receiving* the bad air —Shak.⟩ ⟨~ nourishment⟩ **9 a :** to accept as true or valid : recognize as authoritative : BELIEVE ⟨attacked *received* theological and philosophical opinion on the nature of the universe —*Brit. Book News*⟩ ⟨the material theory of heat, the idea of caloric, which was generally *received* until the 1850's —S.F.Mason⟩ **b :** to admit as evidence ⟨no objection to the ice pick being *received* in evidence —Erle Stanley Gardner⟩ ~ *vi* **1 :** to be a recipient ⟨more blessed to give than to ~ —Acts 20:35 (AV)⟩ **2 :** to take the eucharistic sacrament : take Communion **3 :** to be at home to visitors ⟨she ~*s* on Tuesdays⟩ **4 :** to catch pitched balls in a baseball game ⟨worked hard on his *receiving* —Lou Boudreau⟩ **5 :** to convert incoming radio waves into perceptible signals

**syn** ACCEPT, ADMIT, TAKE: although RECEIVE can sometimes suggest a positive welcoming or recognition ⟨*receive* the group with open arms⟩ ⟨the work has been *received* with enthusiasm —*Current Biog.*⟩ it usu. implies that something comes or is allowed to come into one's presence, possession, group, consciousness, or substance while one is passive ⟨*receive* military instruction⟩ ⟨*receive* a gift⟩ ⟨be *received* into the church⟩ ACCEPT adds to this the notion of positive acquiescence or consent even though tacit ⟨*accept* a gift⟩ ⟨*accept* an appointment⟩ ⟨*accept* an apology⟩ ⟨*accept* a new member into a club⟩ ADMIT suggests permission given or sufferance granted to come or enter ⟨*admit* an ambassador into one's presence⟩ ⟨*admit* new members into a club⟩ ⟨a door wide enough to *admit* a small car⟩ TAKE carries the notion of accepting or, more commonly, of making no positive protest against receiving, often of almost welcoming on principle, something offered, conferred, or inflicted ⟨*take* a plate when it is passed to you⟩ ⟨*take* advice in good spirit⟩ ⟨*take* a good deal of punishment before protesting⟩

**received pronunciation** *n, usu cap R & P* **:** the pronunciation of Received Standard

**received standard** *n, usu cap R&S* **:** the form of English spoken at the English public schools, at the universities of Oxford and Cambridge, at the English court, and by many educated Englishmen elsewhere

**re·ceiv·er** \-və(r)\ *n* -s [ME *receyvour*, *receivere*, fr. (assumed) ONF *receivour*, fr. *receivre* to receive + *-our* -er] **1 :** one that receives ⟨the sense of touch, not ordinarily a ~ of information originating at a distance —F.A.Geldard⟩ ⟨threw a long forward pass into the arms of a waiting ~⟩ **2 :** one that receives on behalf of others: as **a :** a person appointed to receive money due : TREASURER **b** (1) **:** a person appointed usu. by a court of equity jurisdiction to receive and conserve property that is the subject of litigation, to administer it under the supervision of the court as its agent, and to apply, manage, and dispose of it in accordance with the orders and decrees of the court until the final determination of the litigation (2) **:** a person appointed under a statute by an administrative public officer to wind up the affairs of a business (as a bank, railroad, or insurance company) involving a public interest in case of dissolution or insolvency or to manage under the direction of a court a corporation financially embarrassed during a period of reorganization in an effort to avoid bankruptcy (3) **:** a person appointed by a court under British statute to receive the income of those incompetent to manage their affairs (4) **:** a person appointed by a court under British statute to conserve the property of an alleged bankrupt until it can be determined whether he is a bankrupt (5) **:** a person appointed under British statute by a mortgagee or other holder of security in accordance with the terms of the mortgage or security agreement to take possession of the security and apply it in satisfaction of the indebtedness in accordance with the statute and agreement **3 :** one who knowingly takes or buys stolen goods from a thief : FENCE 4a **4 :** something that acts as a receptacle or container: as **a :** the bell jar of an air pump **b :** a vessel used to store a product (as steam or air) for later use **c** (1) **:** the metal frame in which the action of a firearm is fitted and to which the breech end of the barrel is attached (2) **:** the main body of the lock in a breech mechanism **d** (1) **:** a vessel or tube for use esp. with a condenser or retort to collect and sometimes to condense the product of distillation (2) **:** a vessel to receive and contain gases **5 :** one that receives electric currents or waves: as **a :** RECEIVING SET **b :** the portion of a telegraphic or telephonic apparatus by which the electric currents or waves are converted into visible or audible signals

**receiver general** *n, pl* **receivers general** [ME *receyvour general*, fr. *receyvour* receiver + *general*, adj.] **:** a public officer in general charge of receipts ⟨*receiver general* of Massachusetts⟩

**receiver ring** *n* **:** the threaded ringlike portion of the forward end of the receiver of a rifle into which the breech end of the barrel is fitted

**receiver's certificate** *n* **:** a promise to repay to a lender a definite sum loaned and an acknowledgment thereof made by a receiver under order of court to obtain funds for the preservation of the assets held by him (as for operating a railroad) and often made by the court a first lien upon the receivership assets

**re·ceiv·er·ship** \-(r),ship\ *n* [ME *receyvourship*, fr. *receyvour* + *-ship*] **1 :** the office or function of a receiver appointed by a court or under a statute **2 :** the state or condition of being in the hands of a receiver ⟨put a corporation into ~⟩

**receives** *pres 3d sing of* RECEIVE

**receiving** *pres part of* RECEIVE

**receiving barn** *n* **:** a supervised barn into which racehorses are checked several hours before saddling to prevent their being doped

**receiving blanket** *n* **:** a small lightweight blanket used to wrap an infant (as after bathing)

**receiving clerk** *n* **:** one who takes charge of the receipt of goods shipped to a business concern

**receiving gauge** *n* **:** a gauge that has an inside measuring surface for testing the size and contour of a male part

**receiving order** *n, Brit* **:** an order made by a bankruptcy court appointing a receiver for a bankrupt's estate

**receiving set** *n* **:** an apparatus for receiving radio or television signals and broadcasts

**receiving ship** *n* **:** a usu. obsolete or unseaworthy ship moored at a navy yard and used for new recruits or men in transit between stations

**receiving yard** *n* **:** a railroad yard where freight trains are received — compare CLASSIFICATION YARD, DEPARTURE TRACK

**re·cen·cy** \'rēsᵊnsē, -nsi\ *n* -ES [fr. *recent* + *-cy*] **:** the quality or state of being recent ⟨the eagerness of the people for ~ in their news —F.L.Mott⟩

**re·cense** \rə'sen(t)s, rē'-\ *vt* -ED/-ING/-S [L *recensēre* to review, revise] **:** to make a recension of

**re·cen·sion** \-nchən\ *n* -s [L *recension-*, *recensio*, fr. *recensēre* to review, revise (fr. *re-* + *censēre* to assess, tax, estimate) + *-ion-*, *-io* -ion — more at CENSOR] **1 :** REVIEW, SURVEY ⟨some 30 pages are devoted in each issue to a review of reviews on philosophy and theology . . . this ~ may prove of special use —*Times Lit. Supp.*⟩ **2 a :** a revising of a text (as of an ancient author) by an editor; *esp* **:** critical revision with intent to establish a definitive text ⟨did pioneer work in the ~ of newly discovered manuscripts⟩ **b :** a version of a text established by critical revision ⟨has come down to us in various ~*s* —R.L. Ramsay⟩ **3 :** a revised form of something ⟨started a vogue for sophisticated ~*s* of ancient myths —Paul Pickrel⟩

**re·cent** \'rēsᵊnt\ *adj, sometimes* -ER/-EST [MF or L; MF *recent*, fr. L *recent-*, *recens* fresh, recent; akin to Gk *kainos* new, Skt *kanīna* young] **1 a :** of or belonging to the present period or the very near past ⟨a ~ alumni⟩ ⟨~ leaders⟩ ⟨the ~ election⟩ ⟨the ~ storm⟩ **b :** having lately come into existence : just made or formed : NEW ⟨~ buds on the peach trees⟩ ⟨pride ourselves on our ~ transcontinental highways —R.W.Murray⟩ ⟨almost before the ~ ink is dry —John Keats⟩ **c :** newly arrived ⟨~ from the roar of foreign foam —A.C.Swinburne⟩ **2 :** of or belonging to a period of time relatively near : not remote ⟨in more ~ times the Romans formed a great camp here —J.K.Jerome⟩ ⟨is only of ~ origin, and was wholly unknown in old times —Herman Melville⟩ **3** *usu cap* **:** of or relating to the present or existing epoch which is dated from the close of the Pleistocene : DILUVIAL 3, HOLOCENE — see GEOLOGIC TIME table — **re·cent·ly** *adv* — **re·cent·ness** *n* -ES

**re·cept** \'rē,sept\ *n* -s [*re-* + *-cept* (as in *concept*, *percept*)] **:** a mental image or idea formed by repeated exposure to a particular stimulus or class of stimuli

**re·cep·ta·cle** \rə'septəkəl, rē'-, -tēk-\ *n* -s [L *receptaculum*, fr. *receptare* (iterative of *recipere* to receive) + *-culum*, suffix denoting an instrument — more at RECEIVE] **1 :** one that receives and contains something : CONTAINER, REPOSITORY ⟨a metal ~ to catch the sap —Hamilton Basso⟩ ⟨the poet's mind is in fact a ~ for seizing and storing up numberless feelings —T.S.Eliot⟩ **2 :** a place of shelter ⟨palatial gloomy chambers for parade . . . never constructed as ~*s* —Robert Browning⟩ **3 a :** an intercellular cavity containing oil, resin, or other secretion products **b :** the end of the flower stalk upon which the floral organs are borne and which is often somewhat enlarged (as in the composites) — called also *torus* **c :** an organized often stalked structure in a cryptogamous plant containing reproductive bodies : a modified branch bearing sporangia: as (1) **:** a swollen tip of a thallus branch of a seaweed (as of the genus *Fucus*) (2) **:** any of various envelopes or structures supporting the fructification of a fungus (3) **:** an umbrella-shaped outgrowth of the thallus of various liverworts (as of the genus *Marchantia*) that bears the sex organs : CUPULE (4) **:** PLACENTA 2b **4 :** a permanently mounted female electrical fitting that contains the live parts of the circuit

**re·cep·tac·u·lar** \¦rē,sep¦takyələ(r)\ *adj* [NL *receptaculum* + E *-ar*] **:** of, relating to, or developing from the receptacle of a plant

**re·cep·ta·cu·li·da** \rə,septə'kyüləda\ *n pl, cap* [NL, fr. *receptaculum* + *-ida*] **:** a class of calcareous fossils of uncertain systematic relations — see RECEPTACULITIDAE

**re·cep·tac·u·li·tes** \,rēsep,takyə'līd·(,)ēz\ *n, cap* [NL, fr. *receptaculum* + *-ites*] **:** a genus (the type of the family Receptaculitidae) of Ordovician and Devonian calcareous fossils consisting of closely spaced plates or pillars that form a globose or discoidal mass — see SUNFLOWER CORAL

**re·cep·tac·u·li·tid** \-d·əd\ *n* -s [NL *Receptaculidae*] **:** a fossil of the family Receptaculitidae

**re·cep·tac·u·lit·i·dae** \,==,=='lid·ə,dē\ *n pl, cap* [NL, fr. *Receptaculites*, type genus + *-idae*] **:** a family of calcareous fossils sometimes placed in the Hyalospongiae but usu. set apart as the class Receptaculida — see RECEPTACULITES

**re·cep·tac·u·lum** \,rē,sep'takyələm\ *n, pl* **receptacu·la** \-lə\ [NL, fr. L — more at RECEPTACLE] **:** RECEPTACLE 3

**receptaculum chy·li** \-'kī,lī\ *n* [NL, lit., receptacle of the chyle] **:** CISTERNA CHYLI

**re·cep·ti·bil·i·ty** \rə,septə'biləd·ē\ *n* -ES **:** the quality or state of being receptible

**re·cep·ti·ble** \rə'septəbəl, rē'-\ *adj* [LL *receptibilis* recoverable, fr. L *receptus* + *-ibilis* -ible] **:** capable of receiving or of being received

**re·cep·tion** \rə'sepshən, rē'-\ *n* -s [ME *recepcion*, fr. MF or L; MF *reception*, fr. L *reception-*, *receptio*, fr. *receptus* (past part. of *recipere* to take back, receive) + *-ion-*, *-io* -ion — more at RECEIVE] **1 :** the act or action of receiving in place or position ⟨the native soil . . . is boxed out for the ~ of the pavement —John Kemp⟩ ⟨clearing away a space at the top for the ~ of a small piece of butter —T.L.Peacock⟩ **2 :** the act or action of taking possession or getting : RECEIPT ⟨the ~ of significant amounts of American capital —A.B.Lans⟩ **3 a :** the act or action of taking in or giving shelter to : HARBORING ⟨make ready for the ~ of ten thousand sheep —Rachel Henning⟩ ⟨the ~ of outlaws —F.M.Stenton⟩ **b :** the state or fact of being admitted or given shelter : ADMISSION ⟨my ~ into grace —John Milton⟩ ⟨his ~ into the church⟩ **4 a :** REACTION, RESPONSE ⟨met with an unfriendly ~ from the critics⟩ ⟨the play received a mixed ~⟩ **b :** the act or action of giving assent, approval, or recognition ⟨a world ready for the ~ of new ideas⟩ ⟨~ of a point of view other than their own —J.D.Adams⟩ **5 a :** the act of greeting or welcoming ⟨gave a cordial ~ to her guest⟩ ⟨received an enthusiastic ~ from the crowds lining the streets⟩ **b :** a social gathering often for the purpose of extending a ceremonious or formal welcome ⟨an afternoon ~ for the new members of the staff⟩ **6 a :** mental apprehension ⟨has very weak powers of ~ and is slow to understand anything⟩ **b :** the process by which a stimulus affects a sensory end organ by means of real but usu. minute and transitory physical or chemical alteration of the end organ **7 :** the receiving of a radio or television broadcast ⟨a fringe area where ~ is poor⟩

**reception center** *n* **:** a place where persons (as agricultural workers or military recruits) are assembled and processed

**re·cep·tion·ism** \-shə,nizəm\ *n* -s [*reception* + *-ism*] **:** the view that in the Communion the bread and wine remain as such but that with them the faithful communicant receives the body and blood of Christ

**re·cep·tion·ist** \-shənəst\ *n* -s [*reception* + *-ist*] **1 :** one who believes in the doctrine of receptionism **2 :** one who is employed in a business or professional establishment to greet and help visitors, business callers, or patients

**reception room** *n* **:** a room for the formal reception of visitors (as in a place of business or an institution)

**re·cep·tive** \rə'septiv, rē'-, -tēv *also* -təv\ *adj* [ML *receptivus*, fr. L *receptus* (past part. of *recipere* to take back, receive) + L *-ivus* -ive — more at RECEIVE] **1 a :** able or inclined to receive; *specif* **:** open to ideas, impressions, or suggestions ⟨incredulous where they should be ~ —Bertrand Russell⟩ ⟨made ~ by education at its best —E.T.Cone⟩ **b :** characterized by passive dependency and a need to receive or accept **2 a** *of a sensory end organ* **:** fit to receive and transmit stimuli **b :** of or relating to sense organs or the reception of stimuli : SENSORY **3** *of a female mammal* **:** willing to accept a male — **re·cep·tive·ly** \-tə̇vlē, -li\ *adv* — **re·cep·tive·ness** \-tivnə̇s, -tēv- *also* -təv-\ *n* -ES

**receptive hypha** *n* **:** a haploid hyphal thread that develops from an aecial primordium in many heterothallic rust fungi, that protrudes from a pycnium, and that is joined by a pycniospore to establish a diploid mycelium prior to aeciospore formation

**receptive spot** *n* **:** the colorless spot in an egg or oosphere at which a male gamete or sperm enters

**re·cep·tiv·i·ty** \(,)rē,sep'tivəd·ē, rə,s-, -ətē, -i\ *n* -ES [*receptive* + *-ity*] **:** the quality or state of being receptive; *specif* **:** the power or capacity of receiving impressions : SENSIBILITY ⟨her active intellectual ~ —Havelock Ellis⟩ ⟨heighten the spectator's ~ to the theme —Michael Kitson⟩

**re·cep·tor** \rə'septə(r), rē'-\ *n* -s [ME *receptour*, fr. MF, fr. L *receptor*, fr. *receptus* (past part. of *recipere* to receive) + *-or*] **1 :** one that receives: as **a :** a part of the body (as a cell, group of cells, complex organ) that is esp. sensitive to alteration of some environmental factor (as light or sound waves, temperature, pressure), that undergoes specific stimulation when exposed to such alteration, and that transmits impulses arising from such stimulation to the central nervous system : SENSE ORGAN — distinguished from *effector* **b :** a body or surface sensitive to radiation : a surface illuminated in making a color test **c :** STOCK 5b(1) **d :** the part of a stall shower that receives and drains away the water **2 :** the chemical groups or groupings of an antigen or hapten that combine specifically with the corresponding groups of antibody : chemical groups of a cell that combine esp. with antibodies or viruses

**recepts** *pl of* RECEPT

**re·cep·tu·al** \rə'sepchəwəl\ *adj* [fr *recept*, after such pairs as E *concept: conceptual*] **:** of or relating to recepts — **re·cep·tu·al·ly** \-wəlē\ *adv*

**re·cer·ce·lée** \rə,sərsə'lā\ *adj* [obs. F, fr. OF, fem. of past part. of *recerceler* to curl back, fr. OF *re-* + *cerceler* to circle, curl, fr. *cercle*, *cercel* circle — more at CIRCLE] *of a cross* **:** having the ends of the arms divided and curled back on each side like rams' horns — compare MOLINE

**¹re·cess** \'rē,ses, rə'ses, rē'ses\ *n* -ES [L *recessus*, fr. *recessus*, past part. of *recedere* to withdraw, recede — more at RECEDE] **1 :** the action of receding : RECESSION ⟨the ~ of the tides⟩ **2 a** (1) **:** a hidden or retired place ⟨the ~*es* of the echoing mountains —John Muir †1914⟩ ⟨took from some ~ in his crumpled clothing a copper coin —Pearl Buck⟩ (2) **:** an inner or concealed part of something ⟨sought to lay bare the ~*es* of the soul —R.W.Southern⟩ ⟨explore the hidden ~*es* of the mind —C.B.Tinker⟩ ⟨illuminating the ~*es* of American politics —*Times Lit. Supp.*⟩ **b :** a secret hiding place or retreat ⟨there I lay close covered o'er in my ~ —Robert Browning⟩ **3 a :** an indentation in a straight line or in a surface bounded by a line conceived of as straight : CLEFT ⟨a large ~ in the steep, rocky bank —*Amer. Guide Series: Maine*⟩ **b :** ALCOVE ⟨lazily reading in an armchair in the pleasant ~ where the books are —Rachel Henning⟩ **c :** a cleft in a living body **:** SINUS **4 a :** a suspension of business or procedure (as of a legislative body, court, school) for a comparatively short time **:** a usu. brief vacation period ⟨most members of Congress took advantage of the Easter ~ to go back to their home districts —*Springfield (Mass.) Union*⟩ ⟨the justices adjourned for their summer ~ —*N.Y.Times*⟩ ⟨~ from December 21 to January 4 inclusive —*Official Register of Harvard Univ.*⟩ **b :** a period lasting from 10 minutes to an hour that intervenes between the class or study periods of a school day and is used for rest, play, or lunch **5** [ML *recessus*, fr. L, act of receding, going away; fr. the practice of writing up the decrees before the members of the diet departed] **:** a decree or ordinance of a diet of the Holy Roman Empire or the Hanseatic League ⟨the Frankfort ~⟩

**²recess** \"\ *vb* -ED/-ING/-ES *vt* **1 :** to put into a recess **:** conceal or seclude in a recess **:** set back ⟨~*ed* lighting fixtures⟩ ⟨in the school auditorium are four ~*ed* mural panels —*Amer. Guide Series: Mich.*⟩ **2 :** to make a recess in ⟨~*ed* type⟩ **3 :** to interrupt the course or sitting of for a comparatively short period ⟨~*ed* contract negotiations until this week —*Newsweek*⟩ ⟨can ~ the Senate when its work is done —*Time*⟩ ~ *vi* **:** to take a recess ⟨the court will now ~ for lunch⟩

**recess appointment** *n* **:** an appointment made by a president of the U.S. under his constitutional powers to fill vacancies when the Senate is not in session subject to later confirmation by the Senate

**recess bed** *n* **:** a bed so constructed that it may be folded and stood or hung vertically in a recess or closet when not in use — compare DOOR BED

**recessed arch** *n* [fr. past part. of *²recess*] **:** an arch set within another to correspond with splayed jambs of a doorway

**recess engraving** *n* [*¹recess*] **:** intaglio engraving

**re·cess·er** \-sə(r)\ *n* -S **:** one that recesses; *specif* **:** a worker who recesses watch dials to make track for the second hand

**¹re·ces·sion** \rə'seshən, rē'-\ *n* -S [L *recession-, recessio,* fr. *recessus* (past part. of *recedere* to recede) + *-ion-, -io* -ion — more at RECEDE] **1 a :** the act or action of receding **:** RETREAT ⟨the shy ~ of a votary of love taking the veil —Rebecca West⟩ ⟨the ~ of optimism —R.H.Bainton⟩ **b :** the appearance or effect of receding ⟨flatten his figures by reducing their rounds and ~*s* to roughly the same plane —R.M.Coates⟩ **c :** a return procession (as of clergy and choir after a service) **2 :** the receding or diminishing of a natural feature or the process by which such movement occurs: as **a :** the upstream retreat of a waterfall **b :** the retreat of an eroded escarpment **c :** the melting back of a glacier **d :** the landward movement of a shoreline undergoing erosion **e :** the withdrawal of a body of water exposing formerly submerged areas to the air **3 :** a period of reduced general economic activity marked by a decline in employment, profits, production, and sales that is not as severe or as prolonged as a depression

**²re·cession** \(')rē+\ *n* [*re-* + *cession*] **:** the act of ceding back **:** RESTORATION ⟨the ~ of conquered territory⟩

**¹re·ces·sion·al** \rə'seshənᵊl, rē'-, -shnəl\ *adj* [*recession* + *-al*] **:** of or relating to a retirement or withdrawal

**²recessional** \"\ *n* -S **1 :** RECESSIONAL HYMN **2 :** a musical piece played at the end of a play, performance, or service while the audience or congregation is leaving

**recessional hymn** *n* [*¹recessional*] **:** a hymn sung during the recession of the clergy and choir from the chancel to the robing room

**recessional moraine** *n* **:** a moraine left by a glacier during a temporary halt in the retreat of the ice

**re·ces·sion·ary** \rə'seshə,nerē\ *adj* [*recession* + *-ary*] **:** RECESSIVE

**¹re·ces·sive** \rə'sesiv, rē'-, -sēv *also* -səv\ *adj* [L *recessus* (past part. of *recedere* to recede) + E *-ive*] **1 a :** tending to go back **:** RECEDING ⟨the mental apparatus of a considerable percentage of the population tends to be disorganized, becoming ~ —P.A. Sorokin⟩ **b :** RETIRING, WITHDRAWN ⟨a lonely ~ savant who could hardly bear to raise his voice in the classroom —*Harper's*⟩ **2** *of an allele* **:** being subordinate to a contrasting allele in manifestation — opposed to *dominant;* compare MENDEL'S LAW — **re·ces·sive·ly** \-sə̇vlē\ *adv* — **re·ces·sive·ness** \-sivnə̇s\ *n* -ES

**²recessive** \"\ *n* -S **1 :** a recessive character or factor **2 :** an organism possessing one or more recessive characters

**recessive accent** *n* **:** an accent typically falling on the first syllable of a word (as in English words of Old English origin) or as far from the end of a word as the accentual habits of the language permit (as in Latin or in some classes of Greek words)

**recess-print** \'=,='=\ *vt* [*recess* + *print*] **:** to print by an intaglio-engraved die or plate ⟨a *recess-printed* stamp⟩

**re·ces·sus** \rə'sesəs\ *n* -ES [NL, fr. L, recession, retired place — more at RECESS] **:** ¹RECESS 3c

**rech·ab·ite** \'rekə,bīt\ *n* -S *usu cap* [LL *Rechabitae* (pl.), fr. Heb *Rēkhābh* Rechab, ancestor of the family (Jer 35:2) + L *-ita* -ite] **1 :** a member of a family group in ancient Israel that lived in tents rather than in houses and abstained from drinking wine **2 :** an abstainer from intoxicating drinks; *esp* **:** a member of a benefit society founded in England in 1835 and dedicated to total abstinence **3 :** one who lives in tents

**rech·a·bit·ism** \-,bīd·,izəm, -ī,tiz-\ *n* -S *usu cap* **:** the practice of a Rechabite

**re·channel** \(')rē+\ *vt* [*re-* + *channel*] **:** to direct into a different channel ⟨the impact of such persons . . . diverts or ~*s* the tide of history —A.B.Miller⟩

**¹re·charge** \"+\ *vb* [*re-* + *charge*] *vi* **:** to make a new attack ⟨the bull *recharged* as the pase natural finished —Ernest Hemingway⟩ ~ *vt* **:** to charge again **:** put a new charge in ⟨~ a battery⟩ ⟨refreshes and ~*s* your morals, remodels and revivifies your intellect —R.P.Blackmur⟩

**²recharge** \"\ *n* **1 :** the act of recharging ⟨raise basin water levels above sea levels by direct ~ —F.B.Laverty⟩ **2 :** a new load ⟨clean off a small area next to the hot coals and cover it with a small ~ of nut coal —*Newsweek*⟩

**¹ré·chauf·fé** \,rā(,)shō¦fā\ *n* -S [F, fr. *réchauffé* warmed over] **1 :** a dish of food that has been warmed over ⟨a ~ of lamb⟩ **2 :** something that is served up again **:** REHASH ⟨the crudest, clumsiest ~ of an old dreary melodrama —*Sydney (Australia) Bull.*⟩

**²réchauffé** \"\ *adj* [F, past part. of *réchauffer* to warm again, fr. *ré-* re- + *chauffer* to warm, fr. MF *chaufer* — more at CHAFE] **1 :** warmed over ⟨chicken ~⟩ **2 :** worked over **:** REHASHED ⟨two hundred pages of reasonably fresh material and six hundred that are merely ~ —*Nation*⟩

**re·cheat** \rə'chēt\ *also* **re·chate** \-chāt\ *n* -S [ME *rechate,* fr. *rechaten* to blow the recheat, fr. MF *rachater, racheter* to assemble, rally, fr. *re-* + *achater, acheter* to acquire, fr. (assumed) VL *accaptare,* fr. L *ac-* + *captare* to seek to obtain, intens. of *capere* to take, receive — more at HEAVE] **:** a hunting call sounded on a horn to assemble the hounds

**re·check** \(')rē+\ *vb* [*re-* + *check*] **:** to check again

**re·cher·ché** *also* **re·cher·che** \rə¦sher¦shā\ *adj* [F, fr. past part. of *rechercher* to seek out — more at RESEARCH] **1 a :** sought out with care ⟨the exhibition consists of a ~ choice of the finest productions of their archaic arts ever discovered —Janet Flanner⟩ **b :** EXOTIC, RARE ⟨feel cheated of the ~ experiences we have come to expect —*New Republic*⟩ ⟨discusses all manner of words — common, ~, and slang —*New Yorker*⟩ **c :** FARFETCHED, PRECIOUS ⟨his inner monologues and their ~ highbrow references —Anthony Green⟩ **2 :** lavishly elegant and refined **:** CHOICE, EXQUISITE ⟨we are not accustomed to seeing this type of book in such a ~ format —F.O.Brenner⟩ **syn** see CHOICE

**re·chew** \(')rē+\ *vb* [*re-* + *chew*] **:** to chew again

**re·christen** \(')rē+\ *vt* [*re-* + *christen*] **:** to christen again **:** change the name of ⟨the Curb finally acknowledged the fact that it was no longer on the sidewalk and ~*ed* itself the American Stock Exchange —John Brooks⟩

**re·ci·bien·do** \,rāsē¦byen(,)dō\ *adv* [Sp, lit., receiving, fr. L *recipiendum,* gerund of *recipere* to receive — more at RECEIVE] *of a bullfighter* **:** in a stance with feet motionless to receive the bull's charge

**re·cid·i·vate** \rə'sidə,vāt, rē'-, *usu* -ād·+V\ *vi* -ED/-ING/-S [ML *recidivatus,* past part. of *recidivare* to fall back, relapse, fr. L *recidivus* falling back, recurring — more at RECIDIVOUS] **:** to fall back **:** RELAPSE ⟨those who ~ are characteristically minor offenders —P.W.Tappan⟩

**re·cid·i·va·tion** \=,==''vāshən\ *n* -S [ML *recidivation-, recidivatio,* fr. *recidivatus* + *-ion-, -io* -ion] **:** RECIDIVISM

**re·cid·i·vism** \='==,vizəm\ *n* -S [fr. *recidivist,* after such pairs as E *purist: purism*] **:** a tendency to relapse into a previous condition or mode of behavior ⟨a study of ~ in mental patients⟩; *specif* **:** repeated relapse into criminal or delinquent habits ⟨unemployment of discharged prisoners is at the root of much of the ~ that is overcrowding the prisons —*Survey Midmonthly*⟩

**re·cid·i·vist** \-,və̇st\ *n* -S [F *récidiviste,* fr. *récidiver* to recidivate (fr. ML *recidivare*) + *-iste* -ist] **:** one who relapses or has suffered a relapse ⟨some of the patients admitted are new cases, others are ~*s*⟩; *specif* **:** one who persists in crime **:** an habitual criminal **:** REPEATER ⟨the casual offender expiates his offense in the company of defectives and ~*s* —B.N.Cardozo⟩

**re·cid·i·vous** \-vəs\ *adj* [L *recidivus,* fr. *recidere* to fall back, recur (fr. *re-* + *cadere* to fall) + *-ivus* -ive — more at CHANCE] **:** tending to relapse or having relapsed

**re·ci·fe** \rə'sēfə\ *adj, usu cap* [fr. *Recife,* city of eastern Brazil] **:** of or from the city of Recife, Brazil **:** of the kind or style prevalent in Recife

**recip** *abbr* reciprocal; reciprocate; reciprocity

**rec·i·pe** \'resə(,)pē\ *n* -S [L, take, imper. of *recipere* to take, receive — more at RECEIVE] **1 :** a formula for compounding a medicine or remedy **:** PRESCRIPTION ⟨some of his ~*s* are printed in pharmacopoeias of today —Norman Douglas⟩ **2 a :** a set of instructions for making something; *esp* **:** a formula for compounding something from various ingredients ⟨many hundreds of different ~*s* are used in making steel, and each ingredient is measured to a fraction of one percent —*Hot-Metal Magic*⟩ **b :** a formula for cooking or preparing something to be eaten or drunk **:** a list of ingredients and a statement of the procedure to be followed in making an item of food or drink ⟨a ~ for salad dressing⟩ ⟨a ~ for a new cocktail⟩ **3 :** a method or procedure for doing or attaining something ⟨attempts to extract from science the ~ for all human activities —Peggy Erskine⟩ ⟨presents a four-page ~ for organizing and conducting a meeting —W.A.L.Johnson⟩ ⟨a ~ for success⟩ ⟨reading good books . . . is the ~ for those who would learn to read —M.J.Adler⟩

**¹re·cipher** \(')rē+\ *vt* [*re-* + *cipher*] **:** to encipher (a message in code) for added security

**²recipher** \"\ *n* **:** a reciphered message

**re·cip·i·ence** \rə'sipēən(t)s, rē'-\ *or* **re·cip·i·en·cy** \-nsē, -si\ *n, pl* **recipiences** *or* **recipiencies** [*recipience* fr. *¹recipient,* after such pairs as E *benevolent: benevolence; recipiency* fr. *¹recipient* + *-cy*] **:** RECEPTIVITY

**¹re·cip·i·ent** \-nt\ *adj* [L *recipient-, recipiens,* pres. part. of *recipere* to receive — more at RECEIVE] **:** serving to receive or capable of receiving ⟨elements of the invading and ~ cultures have been blended —G.R.Willey⟩

**²recipient** \"\ *n* -S **:** one that receives **:** RECEIVER ⟨two choices open to the unfortunate ~ of homemade cookies —J.P. O'Neill⟩ ⟨the ~ of honorary degrees —*Current Biog.*⟩

**¹re·cip·ro·cal** \rə'siprəkəl, rē'-\ *adj* [L *reciprocus* returning the same way, alternating (fr. — assumed — *recus* backward — fr. *re-* — + — assumed — *procus* forward, fr. *pro-* ¹pro-) + E *-al*] **1 a :** inversely related **:** OPPOSITE ⟨each flexor muscle which contracts has its ~ extensor muscle which operates in the reverse direction —A.E.Wier⟩ **b :** of, constituting, or resulting from paired crosses in which the form that supplies the male parent of the first cross supplies the female parent of the second cross and vice versa ⟨a cross between a black Leghorn male and a white Leghorn female and one between a white Leghorn male and a black Leghorn female are ~ crosses⟩ **2 a :** mutually existing **:** shared, felt, or shown by both sides ⟨two congenial spirits united . . . by mutual confidence and ~ virtues —T.L.Peacock⟩ ⟨~ love⟩ ⟨~ understanding⟩ **b :** expressive of mutual action or relationship — used of verbs and esp. of compound pronouns; compare RECIPROCAL PRONOUNS **3 :** serving to reciprocate **:** consisting of or functioning as a return in kind ⟨an unselfish friend who helped him without expecting any ~ benefit⟩ **4 a :** corresponding to each other **:** being equivalent or complementary ⟨agreed to extend ~ privileges to each other's citizens⟩ ⟨~ cultural missions⟩ ⟨the public and private systems engage in ~ services —Albert Lepawsky⟩ **b :** marked by or based upon reciprocity ⟨~ trade agreements⟩

**syn** MUTUAL, COMMON: RECIPROCAL describes an equivalence, balance, equal counteraction, equal return, or equal sharing ⟨not a mere cooperation of distinct forces, but an extremely powerful *reciprocal* action, each in turn firing the other and fired by it —C.E.Montague⟩ ⟨the connection between law and political theory has not been one-sided; it has been completely *reciprocal* —Huntington Cairns⟩ MUTUAL is likely to apply to feelings or actions shared by two, indicating either an accompanying reciprocity, equality, or interreaction or simply stressing the fact of a common experience or emotion ⟨a devoted attachment and *mutual* admiration between aunt and niece —George Eliot⟩ ⟨*mutual* obligation — on the part of the lord to protect his vassal against the violence of others, and on the vassal's part to make good the homage pledged by him —H.O. Taylor⟩ ⟨sometimes mingles poetry and propaganda to their *mutual* disaster —J.L.Lowes⟩ COMMON conveys no suggestion of reciprocity between two parties or agencies; instead it indicates the fact of joint participation or possession among any number ⟨death and other incidents of our *common* fate —M.R. Cohen⟩ ⟨generally agreed that all men belong to the same species, that all were probably derived from the same ancestral stock, and that all share in a *common* patrimony —M.F.A. Montagu⟩ ⟨looked at each other for one instant, as if each had in mind those few moments during which a certain moonlit scene was *common* to both —Thomas Hardy⟩

**²reciprocal** \"\ *n* -S **1 :** something that reciprocates or has a reciprocal relationship to something else; *esp* **:** a reciprocal term, expression, or concept ⟨freedom — or its ~, the control of human behavior —B.F.Skinner⟩ ⟨corruption is a ~ to generation —Francis Bacon⟩ **2 :** a number that when multiplied by a given number gives one ⟨$\frac{4}{3}$ is the ~ of $\frac{3}{4}$⟩ ⟨$\frac{1}{9}$ is the ~ of 9⟩ **3 :** RECIPROCAL EXCHANGE

**reciprocal alphabet** *n* **:** a substitution alphabet in which cipher and plaintext equivalents are reciprocal (as when $A_p = X_c$ and $X_p = A_c$)

**reciprocal demand** *n* **:** the demand of two persons or communities for one another's products

**reciprocal diagram** *n* **:** the force diagram for a framed structure — see BOW'S NOTATION

**reciprocal exchange** *n* **:** an unincorporated association of companies or individuals set up to permit its members to take out reciprocal insurance

**reciprocal insurance** *n* **:** a plan of insurance by which each member of a reciprocal exchange acting through an attorney-in-fact becomes an insurer of and is insured by every other member — called also *interinsurance*

**re·cip·ro·cal·i·ty** \=,=='kalәd·ē, -lәtē, -i\ *n* -ES [*¹reciprocal* + *-ity*] **:** RECIPROCITY

**re·cip·ro·cal·ly** \='==k(ə)lē, -li\ *adv* [*¹reciprocal* + *-ly*] **1 :** INVERSELY ⟨wavelength and frequency are, of course, related ~ —F.A.Geldard⟩ **2 :** MUTUALLY ⟨the ultimate goals of the various negotiators are not ~ exclusive —W.R.Frye⟩ **3 :** in return ⟨he trusted his friend and his friend ~ trusted him⟩ **4 :** CONVERSELY

**reciprocally proportional** *adj* **:** INVERSELY PROPORTIONAL

**reciprocal pronoun** *n* **:** a pronoun (as *each other*) that is used to denote a mutual action or cross relationship between the members comprised in a plural subject (as in *A and B like each other;* that is, *A likes B and B likes A*)

**reciprocal quantities** *n pl* **:** two quantities whose product is 1

**reciprocal ratio** *n* **:** INVERSE RATIO

**reciprocal switching** *n* **:** an interchange of inbound and outbound carload freight among railroads in which the cars are switched by one railroad to or from the siding of another under a regular switching charge that is usu. absorbed by the carrier receiving the line-haul

**reciprocal translocation** *n* **:** exchange of parts between nonhomologous chromosomes

**reciprocal wills** *n pl* **:** MUTUAL WILLS

**re·cip·ro·cate** \rə'siprə,kāt, rē'-, *usu* -ād·+V\ *vb* -ED/-ING/-S [L *reciprocatus,* past part. of *reciprocare* to move back and forth, to reciprocate, fr. *reciprocus* alternating — more at RECIPROCAL] *vt* **1 :** to give and take reciprocally **:** exchange mutually **:** INTERCHANGE ⟨the two countries *reciprocated* pledges of friendship⟩ **2 :** to cause to move in alternate directions **3 :** to return in kind or degree **:** respond in like measure to **:** REPAY ⟨~ the compliments just paid them —J.G.Cozzens⟩ ⟨is peevish and sensitive when his advances are not *reciprocated* —G.B.Shaw⟩ ~ *vi* **1 :** to make a return for something done, given, or said ⟨hope in a few days to ~ for your verses by sending you a few remarks —O.W.Holmes †1935⟩ **2 :** to move forward and backward alternately usu. in a straight line ⟨a tiny knife *reciprocating* rapidly up and down —J.V.A.Long⟩ **3 :** to be equivalent or correspondent

**syn** RECIPROCATE, RETALIATE, REQUITE, and RETURN can mean to give back usu. in kind or in quantity. RECIPROCATE can imply a mutual, equivalent or roughly equivalent, exchange or a paying back of what one has received ⟨the love of Lavinia for the hero, most correctly *reciprocated* by him —H.O.Taylor⟩ ⟨touched his friend's glass lightly and *reciprocated* the former toast —James Joyce⟩ ⟨a man for whom he has an intense and growing dislike, which the other *reciprocated* —*Times Lit. Supp.*⟩ ⟨bringing their rude gifts of mussels and wild seeds, which were always *reciprocated* with beads and some of our food —Francisco Palou⟩ RETALIATE usu. implies a paying back in exact kind, often vengefully ⟨considers the possibility of revenge, of *retaliating* on those who have injured him —J.W. Krutch⟩ ⟨our need to protect ourselves from military attack and to *retaliate* in case an enemy dared to attack us —Mary Gregoire⟩ ⟨*retaliate,* blow for blow⟩ REQUITE can imply simply a paying back usu. reciprocally, but also often implies a paying back according to what one considers the merits of the case ⟨*requite* a friend's love⟩ ⟨face every danger rather than *requite* with ingratitude and treachery the devoted attachment of the Western peasantry —T.B.Macaulay⟩ ⟨hospitality should be *requited* in kind —Agnes M. Miall⟩ ⟨*requited* their hospitality by robbing them of much of their supplies —*Amer. Guide Series: Maine*⟩ RETURN usu. implies only a giving back in return ⟨*return* a social call⟩ ⟨*return* good for evil⟩

**reciprocating** *adj* [fr. pres. part. of *reciprocate*] **1 :** characterized by alternation in movement **:** moving to-and-fro ⟨a ~ piston⟩ **2 :** having parts characterized by alternation in movement; *specif* **:** having a reciprocating piston ⟨a ~ engine⟩

**reciprocating conveyor** *n* **:** a vibrating trough conveyor

**reciprocating drill** *n* **:** PISTON DRILL

**reciprocating proposition** *n* **:** a proposition in logic that asserts an interchangeable relationship between subject and predicate

**re·cip·ro·ca·tion** \rə,siprə'kāshən, rē'-\ *n* -S [L *reciprocation-, reciprocatio,* fr. *reciprocatus* (past part. of *reciprocare* to reciprocate) + *-ion-, -io* -ion] **1 a :** a mutual exchange ⟨the ~ of courtesies between the two families⟩ **b :** a return in kind or of like value ⟨the ~ of hatreds must produce a greater hatred —Stuart Hampshire⟩ **2** *archaic* **:** the quality or state of being harmonious **:** CORRESPONDENCE **3 :** an alternating motion, action, or succession **:** ALTERNATION ⟨the reciprocating action continues with the dropper in action lowering two needles at each ~ —W.E.Shinn⟩

**re·cip·ro·ca·tive** \='==,kād·iv, -,kəd·-\ *adj* [*reciprocate* + *-ive*] **:** characterized by reciprocation or serving to reciprocate

**re·cip·ro·ca·tor** \-,kād·ə(r)\ *n* -S [*reciprocate* + *-or*] **:** one that reciprocates

**re·cip·ro·ca·to·ry** \-,kə,tōrē, -tȯr-, -ri, *chiefly Brit* =;==¦kātəri *or* -ā·tri\ *adj* [*reciprocate* + *-ory*] **:** RECIPROCATING

**rec·i·proc·i·ty** \,resə'präsəd·ē, -sətē, -i\ *n* -ES [L *reciprocus* reciprocal + E *-ity*] **1 :** the quality or state of being reciprocal **:** mutual dependence, action, or influence **:** GIVE-AND-TAKE, MUTUALITY ⟨a deep ~ of sympathy and strength between lovers —Mary Webb⟩ ⟨a ~ of influence between a writer and his public —*College English*⟩ **2 a :** a mutual exchange of trade or other concessions or privileges (as reduction of tariff rates and liberalization of quota and exchange restrictions) between two countries **b :** a mutual exchange of courtesies between two states or institutions; *specif* **:** a recognition by each state or institution of the validity of licenses or privileges granted by the other to its citizens or members

**reciprocity law** *n* **:** a statement in photography: a constant density is obtained on a photographic material if the product of the intensity of light and the time for which it acts is a constant

**re·circulate** \(')rē+\ *vt* [*re-* + *circulate*] **:** to circulate again

**re·ci·sion** \rə'sizhən, rē'-\ *n* -S [MF, alter. (influenced by *recision* act of cutting back, fr. L *recision-, recisio,* fr. *recisus* — past part. of *recidere* to cut back, lop off, fr. *re-* + *caedere* to cut — + *-ion-, -io* -ion) of *rescision,* fr. L *rescission-, rescissio* — more at CONCISE, RESCISSION] **:** the act or action of rescinding **:** CANCELLATION ⟨no criticism or ~ of its doctrinal contents was expressed or implied by such withdrawal —Theodore Graebner⟩

**ré·cit** \rā'sē\ *n* -S [F, narrative, account, fr. MF *reciter* to narrate, tell — more at RECITE] **:** a brief novel usu. with a simple narrative line

**recit** *abbr* recitative

**re·cit·al** \rə'sīd·ᵊl, rē'-, -sītᵊl\ *n* -S [*recite* + *-al*] **1 :** the formal statement or setting forth of some relevant matter of fact in a deed or legal document (as to explain the reasons for a transaction, to evidence the existence of facts, or to introduce a positive allegation in pleading) **2 a :** a particularized account **:** ENUMERATION ⟨too much a ~ of details —H.S.Ellis⟩ **b :** something that is told or related **:** DISCOURSE, STORY ⟨listened to this ~ with a mixture of awe and skepticism —Hallam Tennyson⟩ **3 a :** a reading or repetition from memory of some piece of writing ⟨gave a ~ of his own poems before a large and attentive audience⟩ **b (1) :** a homogeneous program of vocal or instrumental music usu. by a single performer or by a soloist with an accompanist ⟨a piano ~⟩ ⟨a song ~⟩ — distinguished from *concert* **(2) :** an exhibition concert given by music pupils **c (1) :** a public performance given by a dancer **(2) :** a dance concert; *esp* **:** an exhibition concert given by dance pupils

**re·cit·al·ist** \-ᵊlə̇st\ *n* -S [*recital* + *-ist*] **:** one who gives recitals ⟨a lieder ~ —Abraham Veinus⟩

**re·ci·tan·do** \,rāchē'tän·(,)dō\ *adv (or adj)* [It, fr. L *recitandum,* gerund of *recitare* to recite] **:** in reciting style **:** DECLAMATORY — used as a direction in music

**rec·i·ta·tif** \,res(ə)tə¦tēf\ *n* -S [F, fr. It *recitativo*] **:** RECITATIVE

**rec·i·ta·tion** \,resə'tāshən\ *n* -S [MF or L; MF *recitation,* fr. L *recitation-, recitatio,* fr. *recitatus* (past part. of *recitare* to recite) + *-ion-, -io* -ion] **1 :** the act of enumeration **:** DETAILING ⟨explanation in this type of philosophy consists of a ~ of relevant events —L.A.White⟩ **2 :** the act or an instance of reading or repeating aloud esp. before an audience ⟨a ~ of the rosary at 8 P.M. Sunday —*Springfield (Mass.) Daily News*⟩ ⟨the program consisted usually of a serious play, followed by songs, ~*s,* tableaux —*Amer. Guide Series: Ind.*⟩ **3 a :** a school exercise in which students in a class or course reply orally to questions on subject matter previously taught or assigned ⟨poor ~*s* in history⟩ **b :** a regularly scheduled class period or course session ⟨only ten ~*s* a week⟩

**rec·i·ta·tion·ist** \-sh(ə)nə̇st\ *n* -S [*recitation* + *-ist*] **:** ELOCUTIONIST

**¹rec·i·ta·tive** \,res(ə)tə¦tēv\ *adj* [It *recitativo,* n.] **:** of, relating to, or having the characteristics of recitative — distinguished from *ariose*

**²recitative** \"\ *n* -S [It *recitativo,* fr. *recitare* to recite (fr. L) + *-ivo* -ive] **1 a :** a vocal passage, part, or performance in which a singer delivers a narrative text (as in opera or oratorio) in a declamatory and rhetorical manner and which is characterized by freedom from strict form in its tonal and metrical structure and by speechlike recitation instead of flowing melody **b :** a composition intended to be sung as a recitative — compare ARIA **c :** a passage of instrumental music in the style of a recitative **2 :** RECITATION ⟨a long, leisurely ~ about curates at teas —Anne Fremantle⟩

**rec·i·ta·ti·vo** \,resəd·ə'tē(,)vō\ *n, pl* **recitati·vi** \-(,)vē\ *or* **recitativos** [It] **:** RECITATIVE

**re·cite** \rə'sīt, rē'-, *usu* -īd·+V\ *vb* [ME *reciten,* fr. MF or L; MF *reciter* to narrate, recite, fr. L *recitare* to read aloud, repeat from memory, recite, fr. *re-* + *citare* to call, cite — more at CITE] *vt* **1 :** to state formally in a deed or legal document ⟨all representations and agreements required by this section shall be *recited* in the instrument of transfer —*U. S. Code*⟩ **2 :** to repeat from memory or read aloud esp. before an audience ⟨still sing the folksongs and ~ the charms of their childhood

—*Amer. Guide Series: Minn.*⟩ ⟨*recited* ballads in public —W.P. Eaton⟩ ⟨*recited* his poems from manuscript⟩ **3 a :** to give a detailed narration of **:** relate in full ⟨the other gabblers who ~ dull anecdotes, in fullest detail, of relatives and friends unknown to the hearer —Sophie Kerr⟩ **b :** to list in detail **:** set out **:** ENUMERATE ⟨*recited* with indignation . . . a catalog of illegalities and atrocities —F.L.Paxson⟩ **4 :** to repeat or answer questions about (a school assignment or lesson) ⟨could only ~ what they had copied from the blackboard —*Americas*⟩ ~ *vi* **1 :** to repeat or read aloud esp. before an audience something memorized or prepared ⟨who ~*s* aloud with a dramatic art that she has made her own —H.V.Gregory⟩ **2 :** to reply to a teacher's question on a lesson or assignment ⟨the teacher called on him to ~⟩ **syn** see RELATE

**re·cit·er** \-d·ə(r), -tə-\ *n* **:** one that recites

**reciting note** *n* [fr. *reciting*, gerund of *recite*] **:** a musical note on which a varying number of syllables are uttered in chanting as distinguished from a note that receives but one syllable

[1]**reck** \'rek\ *vb* -ED/-ING/-S [ME *recchen, recken* to be concerned, take heed, fr. OE *reccan, rēcan;* akin to OHG *ruohhen* to take heed, ON *rækja*] *vi* **1 a :** to be apprehensive or fearful — usu. used with *of* ⟨little ~*ing* of the dangers I was running —Claud Cockburn⟩ **b :** to take heed or thought **:** take account **:** be aware **:** CONSIDER, DEEM — usu. used with *of* ⟨the language ~*ed* of their decrees as little as the advancing ocean did of those of Canute —R.C.Trench⟩ ⟨content with the plaudits of the hour, and ~*ing* little of the morrow —B.N. Cardozo⟩ **c :** to become concerned **:** CARE ⟨little we ~*ed* . . . we had a holiday spirit —Stephen Graham⟩ **2 :** to be of account or interest **:** MATTER ⟨it ~*s* little to think of that now . . . what he has done cannot be effaced —R.A.T.G.Cecil⟩ ~ *vt* **1 :** to care for **:** take account of **:** REGARD ⟨lay in a bed of musk and tenderness, nor ~*ed* no risk —Henry Treece⟩ **2 :** to matter to **:** CONCERN ⟨what ~*s* it them —John Milton⟩

[2]**reck** \"\ *chiefly dial var of* RICK

**reckan** *var of* RACKAN

**reck·less** \'rekləs\ *adj* [ME *recheles, reckeles*, fr. OE *recceléas, rēceléas*, fr. (assumed) *recce, rēce* care, heed (akin to *reccan, rēcan* to give heed) + *-lēas* -less — more at RECK] **1 a :** lacking in caution **:** deliberately courting danger **:** FOOLHARDY, RASH ⟨brave and daring but never foolishly ~ —J.L.Hodson⟩ ⟨a band of brigands, outlawed by government, strong in discipline, furious from penury, ~ by habit —J.L.Motley⟩ **b :** CARELESS, NEGLECTFUL, THOUGHTLESS — often used with *of* ⟨lives on his nervous energy, ~ of consequences —Rose Macaulay⟩ ⟨if a man were to fire a machine gun at a crowd, ~ whether he killed anyone or not —Edward Jenks⟩ **2 a :** marked by a lack of caution **:** HEEDLESS, RASH ⟨gold in the men's purses meant heavy drinking and ~ gambling —Robert Graves⟩ ⟨~ audacity came to be considered courage —Derek Patmore⟩ **b :** marked by a lack of foresight or consideration **:** IMPROVIDENT, NEGLIGENT ⟨devastated by forest fires and ~ lumbering —*Amer. Guide Series: Pa.*⟩ ⟨replace the ~ mining habits of the earlier period with a thrifty and conservative use of the natural environment —Lewis Mumford⟩ **c :** IRRESPONSIBLE, WILD ⟨~ in its charges⟩ ⟨a check on ~ generalizations and the vagaries of impressionism —C.I.Glicksberg⟩ **syn** see ADVENTUROUS

**reckless driving** *n* **:** driving that evidences a deliberate or culpably negligent disregard of life and property and creates an unreasonable risk of harm to others

**reck·less·ly** *adv* [ME *rechelesly*, fr. OE *recceléaslīce*, fr. *recceléas* reckless + *-līce* -ly] **:** in a reckless manner

**reck·less·ness** *n* -ES [ME *rechelesnes*, fr. OE *rēceléasnes*, fr. *rēceléas* reckless + *-nes* -ness] **:** the quality or state of being reckless

**reck·ling** \'reklən, -liŋ\ *n* -S [origin unknown] **1** *dial Eng* **:** the weakest or smallest one of a litter, brood, or family **:** RUNT **2** *dial Eng* **:** WEAKLING

**reck·ling·hausen** \'rekliŋ,haùzən\ *adj, usu cap* [fr. *Recklinghausen*, city of northwest Germany] **:** of or from the city of Recklinghausen, Germany **:** of the kind or style prevalent in Recklinghausen

**recklinghausen's disease** *n, usu cap R* [after F. D. von *Recklinghausen* †1910 Ger. pathologist] **:** NEUROFIBROMATOSIS

**reck·on** \'rekən\ *vb* **reckoned; reckoned; reckoning** \-k(ə)niŋ\ **reckons** [ME *rekenen, rikenen*, fr. OE *-recenian* (as in *gerecenian* to recount, narrate); akin to MD *rekenen* to reckon, OHG *rehhanōn*, OE *reccan* to give heed — more at RECK] *vt* **1 :** to go over one by one **:** ENUMERATE — used with *up* or *over* ⟨would need several pages merely to ~ up the names⟩ ⟨~*ing* her wrongs over vividly —George Meredith⟩ **2 a :** COUNT ⟨I have not art to ~ my groans —Shak.⟩ **b :** to arrive at or estimate by calculation **:** COMPUTE ⟨in ~*ing* the height, allow for a thick mat or excelsior cushion underfoot —Emily Holt⟩ ⟨stood gazing about, trying to ~ the size of the cave —Willa Cather⟩ **c :** to calculate or determine by reference to a fixed point or basis ⟨the existence of the U. S. is ~*ed* from the Declaration of Independence⟩ ⟨the society is matrilineal and all blood relations and personal loyalties are ~*ed* on the blood ties —Abram Kardiner⟩ **3 a :** to regard or think of as **:** ACCOUNT, CONSIDER ⟨the artist is ~*ed* a freak —Clive Bell⟩ ⟨taught men to ~ virtue of more moment than security —W.F. Hambly⟩ **b :** to include as part of a total or classification **:** CLASS, PLACE ⟨has commonly been ~*ed* an American philosopher —*Americana Annual*⟩ ⟨many anthropologists have accordingly ~*ed* them as an early Caucasoid offshoot —A.L. Kroeber⟩ **c :** ATTRIBUTE, ASSIGN — used with *to* ⟨despite his astonishing anticipations of the painting of the end of the nineteenth century, it seems better to ~ him to the old school —F.J.Mather⟩ **d :** to evaluate the character or worth of **:** SUM — used with *up* ⟨sitting opposite the boys in church, and ~*ing* them up with her keen eyes —Samuel Butler †1902⟩ **4 a :** to conclude on the basis of a calculation or estimation ⟨~ that we lost a fifth of the oats through sprouting —*Country Life*⟩ ⟨~*s* that his phone rings on an average three times a day —*N. Y. Herald Tribune*⟩ **b** *chiefly dial* **:** to be of the impression or opinion that **:** SUPPOSE, THINK ⟨been doing this work for six years and we ~ we know something about it —C.D. Lewis⟩ ~ *vi* **1 :** to settle accounts or claims — usu. used with *with* ⟨after a long time the lord of those servants cometh, and ~*eth* with them —Mt 25:19 (AV)⟩ **2 :** to make a calculation **:** COMPUTE ⟨seemed to ~ in her mind —H.G.Wells⟩ ⟨~*ed*, and put his money on his newfound fellow clerk —Winston Churchill⟩ **3** *chiefly dial* **a :** EXPECT, INTEND **b :** CLAIM, PRETEND **4 a :** ESTIMATE, JUDGE ⟨thoroughly nice people, as the world ~*s* —Mary Ross⟩ **b** *chiefly dial* **:** SUPPOSE, THINK ⟨it's faith, I ~, that's kept her goin' —Ellen Glasgow⟩ **5 :** to place reliance **:** COUNT, DEPEND — used with *on* or *upon* ⟨~ on your promise to aid me —George Meredith⟩ ⟨do not ~ upon it with certainty —Rachel Henning⟩ **syn** see CALCULATE, CONSIDER, RELY — **reckon with :** to take into account ⟨it had to *reckon with* a challenging current of popular contradiction —Herbert Feis⟩ ⟨a man to be *reckoned with*⟩ — **reckon without :** to leave out of account **:** IGNORE ⟨*reckoned without* chemistry and man's ingenuity when he predicted that man sooner or later faced starvation —*Monsanto Mag.*⟩

**reck·on·able** \-k(ə)nəbəl\ *adj* **:** capable of being reckoned ⟨an occupation which seemed to them idleness because it made no ~ profits —H.S.Canby⟩

**reck·on·er** \-k(ə)nə(r)\ *n* -S [ME *rikenere*, fr. *rikenen* to reckon + *-ere* -er] **1 :** one that reckons **2 :** an aid to reckoning; *esp* **:** a book of tables — called also *ready reckoner*

**reck·on·ing** \-k(ə)niŋ, -nēŋ\ *n* -S [ME *rekening*, fr. gerund of *rekenen* to reckon] **1 a :** the act or an instance of computing or calculating ⟨the ~*s* of local, solar, and sidereal time —*Times Lit. Supp.*⟩ **b :** a method of calculating ⟨a need felt for a more precise time ~ —A.L.Kroeber⟩ **c :** a calculation or statement of money owed **:** ACCOUNT, BILL ⟨an old beggar who could not pay his ~ —Virginia Woolf⟩ **d :** the result of a process of calculating **:** COMPUTATION ⟨more than 10 percent off in his ~⟩ ⟨experiments verified the correctness of his ~⟩ **e** (1) **:** the calculation of a ship's position from astronomical observations or from dead reckoning; *also* **:** dead reckoning as opposed to observation (2) **:** the position of a ship determined by reckoning **2 :** the act or an instance of settling accounts ⟨would demonstrate their loyalty by postponing a ~ of their grievances —Oscar Handlin⟩ **3 :** the act of accounting for one's conduct or the fact of being called to account ⟨if the cause be not good, the king himself hath a heavy ~ to make —Shak.⟩ ⟨a time of ~⟩ ⟨a bitter ~⟩ — see DAY OF RECKONING **4 :** the act or an instance of judging **:** a summing up **:** APPRAISAL ⟨when the final ~ of this composer's complete works is made —Arthur Berger⟩ ⟨its people have lived under the system for more than a generation . . . a ~ can now be taken —Nathaniel Peffer⟩

**recks** *pres 3d sing of* RECK

[1]**re·claim** \rə̇'klām, rē'-\ *vb* [ME *reclamen, reclaimen*, fr. OF *reclamer* to appeal to, call back, fr. L *reclamare* to cry out against, call for, fr. *re-* + *clamare* to cry out, call — more at CLAIM] *vt* **1** *obs* **:** to call back (as a hawk to the wrist) **:** RECALL **2 a :** to recall from wrong or improper conduct **:** amend the behavior or character of **:** REFORM ⟨~*ed* him from a life of drunkenness⟩ ⟨~ the wicked⟩ **b :** to make obedient **:** SUBDUE, TAME ⟨my heart is wondrous light, since this same wayward girl is so ~*ed* —Shak.⟩ **3 a :** to rescue from an undesirable or unhealthy state **:** bring to a state of literacy, culture, or health ⟨an effort to ~ the illiterates who would otherwise be excellent material for the armed forces —*Amer. Library Assoc. Bull.*⟩ ⟨work done in ~*ing* diseased and debilitated horses —Charles Murray⟩ **b :** to rescue from a wild or uncultivated state **:** make fit for cultivation or use ⟨filled in valleys, diverted creeks and ~*ed* swamps —G.R.Gilbert⟩ ⟨the most arid area in the country ~*ed* from the desert by irrigation —*Amer. Guide Series: Calif.*⟩ **4 a :** to obtain from a waste product or by-product **:** RECOVER ⟨~ wool fibers from textile wastes⟩ **b :** to recover the useful material from ⟨~ scraps⟩ ~ *vi* **1 :** to cry out **:** OBJECT, PROTEST ⟨his opponents loudly ~*ed* against his attempt to shut off debate⟩ **2** *Scots law* **:** to appeal from a judgment of the lord ordinary of the Court of Session to the Inner House **3 :** to demand surrender of a person or thing belonging to one state and found to be irregularly under the control of another state or its citizens **syn** see RESCUE

[2]**reclaim** \"\ *n* [ME, fr. OF, appeal, recall, fr. *reclamer*] **1 :** a reclaiming or state of being reclaimed ⟨past hope of all ~ —Ben Jonson⟩ **2 :** something that is reclaimed; *esp* **:** RECLAIMED RUBBER

**re–claim** \(')rē+\ *vt* [*re-* + *claim*] **1 :** to claim back **:** demand the return of as a right **:** attempt to recover possession of ⟨returned from the war and *re-claimed* his factory job —J.N. Bell⟩ **2 :** regain possession of ⟨the tall young pines which slowly but surely are *re-claiming* the land a former generation toiled to clear —Corey Ford⟩

**re·claim·able** \-məbəl\ *adj* **:** capable of being reclaimed

**re·claim·ant** \-mənt\ *n* -S [[1]*reclaim* + *-ant* (n)] **:** one who reclaims

**reclaimed rubber** *n* **:** rubber recovered from vulcanized scrap rubber (as by grinding old tires and treating with alkali, oils, and plasticizers), often mixed with crude rubber for compounding, and used chiefly in mechanical rubber goods

**re·claim·er** \-mə(r)\ *n* **:** one that reclaims ⟨oil ~*s* are used to clarify used lubricants⟩; *esp* **:** WARMER 1b

**rec·la·ma·tion** \,rekla'māshən\ *n* -S [MF, fr. L *reclamation-, reclamatio*, fr. *reclamatus* (past part. of *reclamare* to cry out against) + *-ion-, -io* -ion — more at RECLAIM] **1 :** the act of making a claim or protest ⟨~*s* of disappointed investors —R.E.Cameron⟩ **2 :** the act or process of reforming or rehabilitating ⟨an agency devoted to the ~ of delinquents⟩ ⟨its ministry of ~ to down-and-out men —Sidney Lovett⟩ **3 :** the act or process of restoring to cultivation or use ⟨land ~⟩ ⟨a large-scale ~ project⟩

**reclamation disease** *n* **:** a copper-deficiency disease of many crops and esp. of cereals occurring chiefly on newly reclaimed peat land and characterized by chlorotic leaf tips and failure to set seed

**reclamation district** *n* **:** a district created by legislation for the purpose of reclaiming swamp, marshy, or desert lands and making them suitable for cultivation and usu. given the power to levy assessments or issue bonds

**ré·clame** \rā'klàm\ *n* -S [F, advertising, publicity, fr. *réclamer* to claim, appeal, fr. OF *reclamer* to appeal, call back — more at RECLAIM] **1 :** public attention or acclaim not necessarily based on or proportionate to real value or achievement **:** PUBLICITY, VOGUE ⟨wrote pungent articles which enjoyed immense ~ —F.A.Swinnerton⟩ ⟨modern artists have become respectable and can even attach ~ to the organization that uses them —Ian McCallum⟩ **2 :** a gift or passion for publicity **:** SHOWMANSHIP ⟨his energy, his experimental verve, his ~ —Herbert Read⟩ ⟨that innocent ~ of his, that irresistible passion for the limelight —Van Wyck Brooks⟩

**re·clean** \(')rē+\ *vt* [*re-* + *clean*] **:** to clean again

**re·clin·able** \rə̇'klīnəbəl, rē'-\ *adj* **:** able to be reclined

**rec·li·nate** \'reklə,nāt, -,nət\ *also* **rec·li·nat·ed** \-,nād·əd\ *adj* [L *reclinatus*, past part. of *reclinare* to recline] **:** bent downward so that the apex is below the base — used esp. of a stem or leaf

**rec·li·na·tion** \,==='nāshən\ *n* -S [LL *reclination-, reclinatio*, fr. L *reclinatus* + *-ion-, -io*, -ion] **:** the act of reclining or the state of being reclined

**re·cline** \rə̇'klīn, rē'-\ *vb* -ED/-ING/-S [ME *reclinen*, fr. MF or L; MF *recliner*, fr. L *reclinare*, fr. *re-* + *clinare* to bend, lean — more at LEAN] *vt* **:** to cause or permit to incline backward **:** place in a recumbent position **:** LEAN, REST ⟨~*s* her head on a pillow⟩ ⟨*reclined* the seat a little —Henry LaCossitt⟩ ~ *vi* **1 :** to lean or incline backward ⟨was *reclining* against the mantelpiece in a strained counterfeit of perfect ease —Scott Fitzgerald⟩ **2 :** to lie in a recumbent position — usu. used with *on* ⟨on a sofa with two cylindrical pillows *reclined* a . . . pretty woman —Thomas Hardy⟩

**reclined** *adj* [fr. past part. of *recline*] **:** in a reclining position; *specif* **:** RECLINATE

**re·clin·er** \-nə(r)\ *n* -S **:** one that reclines; *specif* **:** a reclining dial or plane

**reclining** *adj* [fr. pres. part. of *recline*] **1 a :** bending or curving gradually back from the perpendicular **b :** RECUMBENT **2** [fr. gerund of *recline*] **:** suitable for reclining in ⟨a ~ chair⟩

**reclining–chair car** *n* **:** CHAIR CAR 1

**re·closer** \(')rē+\ *n* [*re-* + *closer*] **:** a switch or circuit breaker that establishes an electrical circuit again manually, remotely, or automatically after an interruption of service

**re·closure** \"+\ *n* [*re-* + *closure*] **:** establishment of an interrupted electrical circuit again by the closing of a switch or circuit breaker

[1]**rec·luse** \'re,klüs, -rə̇'k-, rē'k-, -üz\ *adj* [ME *reclus, recluse*, fr. OF *reclus*, lit., shut up, fr. LL *reclusus*, past part. of *recludere* to shut up, fr. L *re-* + *claudere* to shut, close — more at CLOSE] **1 a :** removed from society **:** shut up **:** CLOISTERED ⟨wondered who the ~ reader previously occupying the house could have been —F.N.Souza⟩ **b :** avoiding others **:** SOLITARY ⟨this bird . . . is shy and ~, affecting remote marshes —John Burroughs⟩ **2 :** characterized by solitariness or retirement from society ⟨a ~ existence⟩ **3 :** REMOTE, SECLUDED ⟨a barren and ~ region⟩ — **rec·luse·ly** *adv* — **rec·luse·ness** *n* -ES

[2]**recluse** \"\ *n* -S [ME *reclus, recluse*, fr. MF *reclus*, fr. *reclus* shut up] **1 :** a person who lives in seclusion; *specif* **:** INCLUSE **2 :** one who leads a retired or solitary life ⟨the quiet doings of an old would-be ~ —O.W.Holmes †1935⟩

[3]**recluse** *vt* -ED/-ING/-S [ME *reclusen*, fr. LL *reclusus*, past part. of *recludere*] *obs* **:** to shut up **:** SECLUDE

**re·clu·sion** \rə̇'klüzhən, rē'-\ *n* -S [ME, fr. ML *reclusion-, reclusio*, fr. LL *reclusus* + L *-ion-, -io* -ion] **:** the state of being shut up or removed from society

**re·clu·sive** \rə̇'klüs|iv, 'rē,k-, |ēv *also* -üz| *or* |əv\ *adj* [[3]*recluse* + *-ive*] **1 :** marked by seclusion or retirement **:** SOLITARY ⟨a vast difference between an acceptable social attitude and an asocial or ~ attitude —A.T.Weaver⟩ ⟨sit under the ~ calm of the acacia tree —H.E.Bates⟩ **2 :** seeking solitude **:** retiring from society ⟨said to be broken down in health and mind, to be ~, melancholy —Joyce Cary⟩

**recm** *abbr* recommend· recommended

**re·coal** \(')rē+\ *vb* [*re-* + *coal*] *vt* **:** to load with a fresh supply of coal ⟨~*ing* a ship⟩ ~ *vi* **:** to take on a fresh supply of coal ⟨traveled without ~*ing*⟩

**re·coat** \"+\ *vt* [*re-* + *coat*] **:** to coat again

**re·coat·a·bil·i·ty** \(¦)=,kōd·ə'biləd·ē\ *n* [*recoat* + *-ability*] **:** a quality in a paint that makes the paint esp. adapted to being applied in a coat over which one or more additional coats can be satisfactorily applied

**re·cock** \(')rē+\ *vb* [*re-* + *cock*] *vt* **:** to cock again ⟨~*ed* the gun⟩ ~ *vi* **:** to cock a firearm again

**recoct** *vt* -ED/-ING/-S [L *recoctus*, past part. of *recoquere* to cook again, fr. *re-* + *coquere* to cook — more at COOK] *obs* **:** to cook or boil a second time

**re·code** \(')rē+\ *vt* **:** to code again

**re·codification** \(¦)rē+\ *n* [fr. *recodify*, after E *codify: codification*] **:** the action of recodifying or state of being recodified

**re·codify** \(')rē+\ *vt* [*re-* + *codify*] **:** to codify again

**re·cogitate** \(')rē+\ *vi* [L *recogitatus*, past part. of *recogitare* to think over again, fr. *re-* + *cogitare* to cogitate] **:** to think over again

**rec·og·ni·tion** \,rekə̇g'nishən, -kēg'n- *sometimes* -kə'-\ *n* -S [L *recognition-, recognitio*, fr. *recognitus* (past part. of *recognoscere* to recognize, examine, investigate) + *-ion-, -io*, -ion — more at RECOGNIZE] **1 :** the action of recognizing or state of being recognized: as **a :** formal acknowledgment (as of a fact or claim): (1) **:** an expression of reception of the sovereign by the people at a coronation (2) **:** a formal acknowledgment of the de facto existence of a government of a country or of the independence of an insurgent or rebelling community or province that allows the establishment of relations but does not imply the de jure acknowledgment of the government recognized (3) **:** formal acknowledgment of a union by an employer in its capacity as the official representative of or bargaining agent for an employee group or bargaining unit **b :** acceptance of an individual as being entitled to consideration or attention ⟨~ by the chair of one rising to speak in a meeting⟩ **c :** acknowledgment of something done or given esp. by making some return ⟨a gift in ~ of a service⟩ **d :** perception of identity as already known in fact or by description ⟨~ of a former friend⟩ ⟨~ of a genuine diamond⟩ ⟨escaped ~⟩ **e :** discernment of the character, status, or class of something ⟨~ of a principle involved⟩ **f :** the form of memory that consists in knowing or feeling that a present object has been met before — compare RECALL **g :** an incident or solution of plot in tragedy in which the main character recognizes his own or some other character's true identity or discovers the true nature of his own situation **h :** identification of friendly and enemy planes and ships **2 :** special notice or attention ⟨a writer who has received much ~⟩ **3 a :** a form of inquest by jury existing under the early Norman kings **b** *Scots law* **:** the act of a feudal superior in recognoscing lands from a tenant esp. for unauthorized alienation

**re–cognition** \¦rē+\ *n* [*re-* + *cognition*] **:** a second cognition **:** a knowing usu. without conscious identification of something that has been known before — **re–cognitional** \"+\ *adj*

**recognition mark** *n* **:** a distinctive usu. conspicuous marking of an animal (as the white tail of an antelope) supposed to serve as a signal to other animals of the same kind

**recognition panel** *n* **:** a distinctively colored piece of cloth used to mark the position of friendly ground forces and serving as a visual aid to pilots coming in to fire on nearby enemy troops or to drop supplies or reinforcements

**re·cog·ni·tive** \rə̇'kägnəd·iv\ *adj* [L *recognitus* (past part. of *recognoscere* to recognize) + E *-ive*] **:** of, relating to, or marked by recognition

**re·cog·ni·tor** \-nəd·ə(r)\ *n* -S [ML, fr. L *recognitus* (past part. of *recognoscere* to know again, examine, investigate) + *-or* — more at RECOGNIZE] **:** one of a jury impaneled on an assize to hold a recognition in England in the period following the Norman Conquest

**re·cog·ni·to·ry** \-nə,tōrē\ *adj* [L *recognitus* + E *-ory*] **:** of, relating to, or marked by recognition

**rec·og·niz·abil·i·ty** \¦rekə̇g,nīzə¦biləd·ē, -kēg,n- *sometimes* -kə,n- *or* -lətē, -i\ *n* **:** the quality or state of being recognizable

**rec·og·niz·able** \'==,nīzəbəl, ,=='===\ *adj* **:** capable of being recognized

**rec·og·niz·ably** \-blē, -bli\ *adv* **:** in a recognizable manner

**re·cog·ni·zance** \rə̇'kägnəzən(t)s, rē'- *sometimes* -känə-\ *n* -S [alter. (influenced by *recognize*) of ME *reconissaunce*, fr. MF *reconoissance, reconissance* recognition, fr. *reconois-* (stem of *reconoistre* to recognize) + *-ance*] **1 a** (1) **:** an obligation of record entered into before a court of record or before a magistrate duly authorized that makes the performance of some act (as appearing in court, keeping the peace, paying a debt) the condition of nonforfeiture and that is witnessed by the record only — compare BOND 5a(1) (2) **:** the sum liable to forfeiture upon such an obligation **b :** a simple personal obligation or undertaking entered into before a magistrate and having no money penalty attached ⟨on his own ~⟩ **2** *archaic* **:** RECOGNITION **3** *archaic* **:** TOKEN, PLEDGE

**re·cog·ni·zant** \-zənt\ *adj* [*recognize* + *-ant*] *archaic* **:** recognizing or acknowledging something — usu. used with *of* ⟨~ of merit — Elinor Wylie⟩

**re–cognize** \(')rē+\ *vt* [*re-* + *cognize*] **:** to cognize again

**rec·og·nize** \'rekə̇g,nīz, -kēg,n- *also* ÷ -kə,n-\ *vb* -ED/-ING/-S *see -ize in Explan Notes* [modif. (influenced by L *recognoscere* & E *-ize*) of MF *reconoiss-* (stem of *reconoistre*, fr. L *recognoscere* to know again, recognize, examine, investigate, fr. *re-* + *cognoscere* to know) — more at COGNITION] *vt* **1** *obs* **a :** to admit the fact, truth, or validity of **b :** REVISE, CORRECT **2 a :** to recall knowledge of **:** make out as or perceive to be something previously known ⟨*recognized* her long lost brother⟩ ⟨*recognized* the word when they heard it again⟩ ⟨*recognized* something familiar about the place⟩ **b :** to perceive clearly **:** be fully aware of **:** REALIZE ⟨*recognized* that this sort of thing had to stop sometime⟩ **3 :** to acknowledge formally: as **a :** to admit as being of a particular status ⟨*recognized* as the legitimate representative⟩ **b :** to admit as being ruler or sovereign ⟨*recognized* him as king⟩ **c :** to admit as being one entitled to be heard (as in a meeting) **:** give the floor to **d** (1) **:** to acknowledge the de facto existence of (as a government in a state) (2) **:** to acknowledge the independence of (as a community or body that has thrown off the sovereignty of a state to which it was subject) and treat as independent or as otherwise effective **4 :** to acknowledge in some definite way **:** take notice of: as **a :** to acknowledge with a show of approval or appreciation ⟨*recognizing* with gratitude what had been done⟩ **b :** to acknowledge acquaintance with ⟨refused to ~ him when he walked into the room⟩ **c :** to admit the fact or existence of ⟨*recognized* the obligation⟩ **5 :** to bind by a recognizance ~ *vi* **:** to enter into an obligation of record before a tribunal

**rec·og·nized·ly** \¦==¦nīz(ə̇)dlē, -li\ *adv* [*recognized* (fr. past part. of *recognize*) + *-ly*] **:** in a way that is recognized or acknowledged or that allows or compels recognition **:** ADMITTEDLY ⟨is ~ superior in this sort of work⟩

**re·cog·ni·zee** \rə̇¦kä(g)nə¦zē\ *n* -S [*recognize* + *-ee*] **:** the person in whose favor a recognizance is made

**rec·og·niz·er** \'rekə̇g,nīzə(r), -kēg,n- *sometimes* -kə,n-\ *n* -S [*recognize* + *-er*] **:** one that recognizes

**rec·og·niz·ing·ly** *adv* [*recognizing* (pres. part. of *recognize*) + *-ly*] **:** with recognition ⟨looked at him ~⟩

**re·cog·ni·zor** \rə̇¦kä(g)nə¦zȯ(ə)r\ *n* -S [*recognize* + *-or*] **:** one that enters into a recognizance

**re·cog·nosce** \¦rē,käg¦näs\ *vb* -ED/-ING/-S [L *recognoscere* to recognize] *vt, Scots law* **:** to resume the possession of (lands granted to a tenant) esp. for unauthorized alienation ~ *vi, Scots law, of lands* **:** to return to the superior by recognition

[1]**re·coil** \rə̇'kȯil, rē'-, *esp before pause or consonant* -ȯiəl\ *vb* -ED/-ING/-S [ME *reculen, recoilen*, fr. OF *reculer*, fr. *re-* + *cul* backside, fr. L *culus* — more at CULET] *vt, obs* **:** to force back **:** cause to retreat or withdraw ~ *vi* **1 a :** to fall or draw back under the impact of force or pressure **:** undergo a forcing backward ⟨the troops ~*ed* before the savage onslaught of the enemy⟩; *esp* **:** to reel back ⟨~*ed* under the heavy blows⟩ **b :** to shrink back esp. with a sudden movement (as in horror, fear, disgust) **:** move suddenly backward or away ⟨opened the door and ~*ed* in terror⟩ **2** *archaic* **:** to withdraw oneself (as into solitude) **:** go away or apart **:** RETIRE ⟨~*ed* into the wilderness —William Wordsworth⟩ **3 a :** to spring back **:** REBOUND: as (1) **:** to fly back (as of a released spring) into an uncompressed position (2) **:** to kick back (as of a gun being fired) **b :** to return suddenly to or as if to a source or starting point ⟨their hatred ~*ed* on themselves⟩ **4** *obs* **:** DEGENERATE

**syn** SHRINK, FLINCH, WINCE, BLENCH, QUAIL: RECOIL may indicate a drawing back, starting back, or swerving backward through fear, shock, or disgust; it may indicate an inner drawing back with emotion ⟨she makes a gesture as if to touch him.

He *recoils* impatiently —G.B.Shaw⟩ ⟨he had so great a dread of snakes that he instinctively *recoiled* at the sight of one —T.B.Costain⟩ SHRINK indicates an instinctive recoil through sensitiveness, scrupulousness, or cowardice ⟨when it came to telling the truth about himself he *shrank* from the task with all the horror of a well-bred English gentleman —Virginia Woolf⟩ ⟨a nervous avoidance of crowds, a *shrinking* from any change in her secluded manner of living —Ellen Glasgow⟩ ⟨to *shrink* from responsibility is to invite social and economic insecurity —H.G.Armstrong⟩ FLINCH involves a recoiling, retreating, or evading when one cannot muster up resolution to face the frightening, painful, or revolting ⟨all retreat was cut off, and he looked his fate in the face without *flinching* —John Burroughs⟩ ⟨he raised the head that lay in the dust with cautious strength, fearing that any touch might only be so much more needless pain. But there was no appearance of *flinching* —W.F.De Morgan⟩ ⟨did not *flinch* from the contemplation of the violent aggression —J.H.Plumb⟩ WINCE applies to an involuntary starting back or away caused by sensitiveness, dread, fear, or pain ⟨to bring a beaten and degraded look into a man's face, rend manhood out of him in fear, is a sight that makes decent men *wince* in pain; for it is an outrage on the decency of life, an offense to natural religion, a violation of the human sanctities —G.D.Brown⟩ ⟨her eyes *winced* for a moment as if she had become suddenly afraid —Liam O'Flaherty⟩ ⟨he *winced* as though she had uttered blasphemy —W.J.Locke⟩ BLENCH may refer especially to fainthearted fearful flinching ⟨she had not been prepared for an attack in flank, and *blenched* before it —Maurice Hewlett⟩ ⟨though his death seemed near he did not *blench* —John Masefield⟩ QUAIL implies cowering and shrinking in fright, consternation, or defeated dejection ⟨despite his professions of sanity and reason, had an inexplicable, invincible horror of death; he *quailed* at the mere mention of the black phantom —Norman Douglas⟩ ⟨I am never known to *quail* at the fury of a gale —W.S.Gilbert⟩ **syn** see in addition REBOUND

²**recoil** \", ˈ=,=\ *n* -S **1 a :** the action of recoiling; *esp* **:** the kickback of a gun upon being fired **b :** the condition of having recoiled; *specif* **:** REACTION ⟨the ~ from formalism is skepticism —F.W.Robertson⟩ **2 :** the extent to which something (as a gun, spring) recoils

**re-coil** \(ˈ)rē+\ *vb* [*re-* + *coil*] *vt* **:** to coil again **~** *vi* **:** to become coiled again

**recoil click** *n* **:** a pawl in a timepiece that recoils slightly after each winding and that is designed to prevent excessively tight coiling of the mainspring

**recoil cylinder** *n* **:** a fixed cylinder into which a piston attached to a gun that is to be fired is forced by the recoil of the gun on firing and which is so designed (as by the use of a hydraulic system or pneumatic system) as to lessen or altogether check the recoil or counterrecoil of the gun

**recoil escapement** *n* **:** ANCHOR ESCAPEMENT

**re·coil·less** \-lləs\ *adj* [²*recoil* + *-less*] **:** having a minimum of recoil ⟨a ~ gun⟩

**re·coil·ment** \-lmənt\ *n* -S [¹*recoil* + *-ment*] *archaic* **:** RECOIL

**recoil–operated** \(ˈ)=ˈ=ˌ=ˈ==,==\ *adj* [²*recoil* + *operated*, past part. of *operate*] *of a firearm* **:** having an action that functions by the movement of parts in recoil

**recoil pad** *n* **:** a soft rubber pad fitted to the butt of a rifle or shotgun for absorbing part of the shock of recoil

**recoil spring** *n* **:** a spring used to cushion the shock of a recoiling gun or other mechanism

**re·coin** \(ˈ)rē+\ *vt* [*re-* + *coin*] **:** to coin again; *specif* **:** to melt down (old or worn coin) and make into new coin

**re·coinage** \"+\ *n* [*re-* + *coinage*] **1 :** the action or process of recoining **2 :** coinage produced by recoining

**re-collect** \ˌrē+\ *vb* [partly fr. L *recollectus*, past part. of *recolligere* to gather again, fr. *re-* + *colligere* to collect; partly fr. *re-* + *collect* — more at COLLECT] *vt* **1 a :** to gather together again ⟨*re-collecting* the frightened chicks⟩ **b :** to get back again **:** RECOVER ⟨*re-collected* his courage⟩ **c :** to pull (oneself) together **:** recover control over (oneself) **:** COMPOSE ⟨was briefly flurried but then *re-collected* herself⟩ **2** *obs* **:** RECALL ⟨can also ~ you from . . . desperation —John Donne⟩ **~** *vi* **:** REASSEMBLE ⟨found the people gradually *re-collecting* in the town square⟩

**rec·ol·lect** \ˌrekəˈlekt\ *vb* -ED/-ING/-S [ML *recollectus*, fr. past part. of *recolligere* to recall to mind, fr. L, to gather again] *vt* **1 a :** to recall the knowledge of **:** call to mind ⟨~*ed* having seen her somewhere⟩ **b :** to recall something forgotten to (oneself) ⟨~*ed* himself just in time and addressed her by name⟩ **2 :** to cause (as oneself, one's mind) to be absorbed in thought, meditation, or contemplation ⟨could not ~ herself in church⟩ **~** *vi* **:** to call something to mind **:** remember something **:** have a recollection **syn** see REMEMBER

**recollected** *adj* [fr. past part. of *recollect*] **1 :** COMPOSED, CALM ⟨not sufficiently ~ to discuss the matter⟩ ⟨cool and ~ at all times⟩ **2 :** marked by or given to recollection ⟨a ~ nun⟩ **3 :** recalled to memory ⟨~ happiness⟩ — **rec·ol·lect·ed·ly** *adv* — **rec·ol·lect·ed·ness** *n* -ES

**re-collection** \ˌrē+\ *n* [*re-collect* + *-ion*] **:** the action of re-collecting **:** a gathering together again

**rec·ol·lec·tion** \ˌrekəˈlekshən\ *n* -S [F *récollection*, fr. ML *recollection-, recollectio*, fr. *recollectus* (past part. of *recolligere* to recollect) + L *-ion-, -io* -ion] **1 :** quiet tranquillity of mind and self-possession; *esp* **:** religious composure **2 a** (1) **:** the action of recalling to the mind **:** REMEMBRANCE (2) **:** the power of recalling to the mind **:** MEMORY **b :** what is recalled to the mind ⟨happy ~*s*⟩ **syn** see MEMORY

**rec·ol·lec·tive** \ˌrekəˈlektiv\ *adj* [*recollect* + *-ive*] **1 :** of or relating to recollection **:** RECOLLECTED **2 :** having the power of recollecting — **rec·ol·lec·tive·ly** \-tə̇vlē\ *adv* — **rec·ol·lec·tive·ness** \-tivnə̇s\ *n* -ES

**rec·ol·let** \ˌrekəˈlet, rākōlā\ *n* -S [CanF *récollet*, fr. F, member of a branch of the Franciscan order, fr. ML *recollectus*, lit., recollected, fr. past part. of *recolligere* to recollect; fr. the resemblance of the bird's crest to the friar's hood] **:** CEDAR WAXWING

**re·colonization** \(ˌ)rē+\ *n* [*recolonize* + *-ation*] **:** the action of recolonizing or state of being recolonized

**re·colonize** \(ˈ)rē+\ *vt* [*re-* + *colonize*] **:** to colonize again

**re·color** \(ˈ)rē+\ *vt* [*re-* + *color*] **:** to color again

**re·comb** \(ˈ)rē+\ *vt* [*re-* + *comb*] **:** to comb again

**re·com·bi·nant** \rēˈkämbənənt\ *n* -S [*recombination* + *-ant*] *biol* **:** an individual exhibiting recombination

**re·combination** \(ˌ)rē+\ *n* [*re-* + *combination*] **1 a :** the formation of new combinations of genes in fertilization **b :** the formation of new combinations of linked genes (as by crossing over) resulting in new heritable characters or new combinations of such characters **2 :** the union of a positive and a negative ion to form a neutral atom or molecule — **re·combinational** \"+\ *adj*

**re·combine** \ˌrē+\ *vb* [*re-* + *combine*] **:** to combine again

**recombined milk** *n* [*re-* + *combined*] **:** milk made by combining cream, butterfat, or milk fat and water with nonfat dry milk solids — compare RECONSTITUTED MILK

**re·comfort** \rə̇+\ *vt* [ME *recomforten*, fr. MF *reconforter*, fr. OF, fr. *re-* + *conforter* to comfort] **1** *archaic* **:** COMFORT, CONSOLE **2** *archaic* **:** REFRESH, STRENGTHEN

**re·commence** \ˌrē+\ *vb* [ME *recommencen*, fr. MF *recommencer*, fr. OF, fr. *re-* + *commencer* to commence] *vi* **:** to undergo a new beginning **:** start up again **:** commence again **~** *vt* **:** to cause to begin again **:** RENEW

**re·commencement** \"+\ *n* [*re-* + *commencement*] **:** a second or fresh commencement

**re·com·menc·er** \-(t)sə(r)\ *n* [*recommence* + *-er*] **:** one that recommences

¹**rec·om·mend** \ˌrekəˈmend, ˈ==,=\ *vb* -ED/-ING/-S [ME *recommenden*, fr. ML *recommendare*, fr. L *re-* + *commendare* to commend] *vt* **1 a** *obs* **:** PRAISE **b** (1) **:** to mention or introduce as being worthy of acceptance, use, or trial ⟨~*ed* the medicine⟩ (2) **:** to make a commendatory statement about as being fit or worthy (as for a job) ⟨~*ed* him highly⟩ (3) **:** to bring forward as being fit or worthy **:** present with approval **:** indicate as being one's choice for something or as otherwise having one's approval or support **:** offer or suggest as favored by oneself ⟨~*ed* several people to the governor for appointment⟩ ⟨~*ed* the book for leisure reading⟩ ⟨asked the waitress which item she would ~⟩ **2 :** ENTRUST, COMMIT, CONSIGN ⟨~*ed* them with confidence to her care⟩ ⟨~*ed* his soul to God⟩ ⟨~*ed* the case to the courts —Irving Brant⟩ **3 :** to make acceptable **:** attract favor to ⟨had other points to ~ it —Archibald Marshall⟩ **4 :** ADVISE, COUNSEL ⟨asked him what he would ~ doing⟩ **~** *vi* **:** to recommend something **:** make a recommendation ⟨a committee with power only to ~⟩

²**recommend** \"\ *n* -S *chiefly Brit* **:** RECOMMENDATION ⟨would get you a ~ —D.H.Lawrence⟩

**rec·om·mend·able** \-dəbəl\ *adj* [ME, fr. *recommenden* + *-able*] **1 :** that can be recommended **:** deserving recommendation ⟨a highly ~ novel⟩ **2 :** that is to be advised **:** PRUDENT, ADVISABLE ⟨it is ~ to keep apart large and small minorities —Yakov Malkiel⟩

**rec·om·men·da·tion** \ˌrekəmənˈdāshən, -ˌmenˈ-\ *n* -S [ME *recommendacion*, fr. ML *recommendation-, recommendatio*, fr. *recommendatus* (past part. of *recommendare* to recommend) + *-ion-, -io* -ion] **1 :** the action of recommending or condition of having been recommended **2 a :** a letter or some similar piece of writing indicating commendation ⟨had several good ~*s* with him when he applied for the job⟩ **b :** a statement expressing commendation ⟨could not get a ~ from him⟩ or giving advice or counsel ⟨followed his ~*s*⟩ **3 :** something that makes acceptable or pleasing ⟨a personality like that is already a big ~⟩

**rec·om·mend·a·to·ry** \ˌ==ˈmendəˌtōrē, -tȯr-, -ri\ *adj* [ML *recommendatus* + E *-ory*] **1 :** serving to commend or to attract favorable attention ⟨a ~ letter⟩ ⟨~ features⟩ **2 :** made or being in the form of a recommendation **:** ADVISORY ⟨~ legislation⟩

¹**re·commission** \ˌrē+\ *vt* [*re-* + *commission*] **:** to commission again

²**recommission** \"\ *n* **1 :** the action of recommissioning or state of being recommissioned **2 :** RECOMMITMENT

**re·commit** \"+\ *vt* [*re-* + *commit*] **1 a :** to refer (as a bill) again to a committee ⟨voted to ~ the bill for further study —*N.Y. Times*⟩ **b :** to entrust or consign again ⟨was *recommitted* into her keeping⟩ **2 :** to commit (as an offense, error) again ⟨*recommitted* the same offense⟩

**re·commitment** \"+\ *also* **re·committal** \"+\ *n* [*recommit* + *-ment, -al*] **:** the action of recommitting or state of being recommitted

**re·communicate** \"+\ *vb* [*re-* + *communicate*] *vt* **:** to communicate again **~** *vi* **:** to enter into communication again **:** hold fresh or further communication

**re·compare** \"+\ *vt* [*re-* + *compare*] **:** to compare again

**re·comparison** \"+\ *n* [*re-* + *comparison*] **:** a second or fresh comparison

**rec·om·pence** \ˈrekəmˌpen(t)s\ *archaic var of* RECOMPENSE

**re·com·pen·sa·ble** \ˌ==ˈpen(t)səbəl\ *adj* [¹*recompense* + *-able*] **:** capable of being recompensed

**re·compensation** \(ˌ)rē+\ *n* [ME *recompensacion*, fr. MF, fr. LL *recompensation-, recompensatio*, fr. *recompensatus* (past part. of *recompensare* to recompense) + *-ion-, -io* -ion] **1** *obs* **:** RECOMPENSE **2** *Scots law* **:** a plaintiff's plea of a counterclaim made to meet a defendant's counterclaim in an action for debt

¹**rec·om·pense** \ˈrekəmˌpen(t)s\ *vb* -ED/-ING/-S [ME *recompensen*, fr. MF *recompenser*, fr. LL *recompensare*, fr. L *re-* + *compensare* to compensate] *vt* **1 a :** to give compensation to **:** REQUITE, REMUNERATE, COMPENSATE ⟨*recompensed* him for his losses⟩ ⟨were *recompensed* for our efforts⟩ **b :** to give an equivalent for **:** make up for by or as if by atoning for or requiting **:** pay for ⟨agreed to ~ all losses⟩ ⟨a pleasure that *recompensed* our trouble⟩ **2 :** to return in kind **:** reciprocate by or as if by rewarding or avenging **:** pay back ⟨*recompensed* the deed —William Cowper⟩ **~** *vi* **:** to repay something **:** make amends **:** make requital **syn** see PAY

²**recompense** \"\ *n* -S [ME, fr. MF, fr. *recompenser* to recompense] **1 :** the action or fact of recompensing **2 :** an equivalent or a return for something done, suffered, or given **:** a repayment made (as by way of satisfaction, restitution, retribution) **:** COMPENSATION ⟨offered in ~ for his injuries⟩

**rec·om·pens·er** \-n(t)sə(r)\ *n* -S **:** one that recompenses

**rec·om·pen·sive** \-siv\ *adj* [¹*recompense* + *-ive*] **:** that recompenses

**re·compete** \ˌrē+\ *vi* [*re-* + *compete*] **:** to compete again

**re·compile** \"+\ *vt* [*re-* + *compile*] **:** to compile again

**re·complete** \"+\ *vt* [*re-* + *complete*] **:** to make complete again

**re·completion** \"+\ *n* [*recomplete* + *-ion*] **:** the action of recompleting or state of being recompleted

**re·complicate** \(ˈ)rē+\ *vt* [*re-* + *complicate*] **:** to complicate again

**re·complication** \(ˌ)rē+\ *n* [*recomplicate* + *-ion*] **:** the action of recomplicating or state of being recomplicated

**re·comply** \ˌrē+\ *vi* [*re-* + *comply*] **:** to comply again

**re·compose** \"+\ *vb* [*re-* + *compose*] *vt* **1 :** to compose again **:** form anew **:** RECOMBINE, REARRANGE ⟨shifting colors that constantly ~ themselves⟩ **2 :** to restore to composure ⟨*recomposed* his spirits⟩ **~** *vi* **:** to become recomposed

**re·composition** \(ˌ)rē+\ *n* [fr. *recompose*, after E *compose: composition*] **:** the action of recomposing or state of being recomposed

**re·compound** \ˌrē+\ *vt* [*re-* + *compound*] **:** to compound again

**re·compress** \"+\ *vt* [*re-* + *compress*] **:** to compress again **:** subject again to compression

**re·compression** \"+\ *n* [*recompress* + *-ion*] **:** the action of recompressing or state of being recompressed

**re·computation** \(ˌ)rē+\ *n* [*recompute* + *-ation*] **:** the action of recomputing or state of being recomputed

**re·compute** \ˌrē+\ *vt* [*re-* + *compute*] **:** to compute again

**re·con** \rə̇ˈkän, rēˈ-\ *n* -S [by shortening] **:** RECONNAISSANCE

**re·conceive** \ˌrē+\ *vt* [*re-* + *conceive*] **:** to conceive again

**re·concentrate** \(ˈ)rē+\ *vb* [*re-* + *concentrate*] *vt* **:** to concentrate again **:** subject to reconcentration **~** *vi* **:** to become reconcentrated

**re·concentration** \(ˌ)rē+\ *n* [*reconcentrate* + *-ion*] **:** the action of reconcentrating or state of being reconcentrated; *esp* **:** the action or policy of concentrating the rural population in or about towns for convenience in political or military administration (as in Cuba during the revolution of 1895–98)

**re·conception** \ˌrē+\ *n* [*re-* + *conception*] **:** the action of reconceiving or state of being reconceived

**re·conceptualization** \"+\ *n* [*re-* + *conceptualization*] **:** a second or fresh conceptualization

**re·conceptualize** \"+\ *vt* [*re-* + *conceptualize*] **:** to conceptualize again

**rec·on·cil·abil·i·ty** \ˌrekənˌsīləˈbilədē, -lətē, -i\ *n* **:** the quality or state of being reconcilable

**rec·on·cil·able** \ˈrekənˌsīləbəl, ˌ==ˈ===\ *adj* **:** capable of being reconciled — **rec·on·cil·able·ness** *n* -ES

**rec·on·cil·ably** \-blē, -bli\ *adv* **:** in a reconcilable manner

**rec·on·cile** \ˈrekənˌsīl, ˌ==ˈ=\ *vb* -ED/-ING/-S [ME *reconcilen*, fr. MF or L; MF *reconcilier*, fr. L *reconciliare*, fr. *re-* + *conciliare* to conciliate] *vt* **1 a** (1) **:** to restore to friendship, compatibility, or harmony ⟨*reconciled* the two quarreling factions⟩ (2) **:** to restore (one under ecclesiastical interdict or excommunication) to communion (3) **:** to restore (as a desecrated church or cemetery) to sacred use esp. by reconsecration **b :** ADJUST, SETTLE ⟨*reconciling* differences⟩ **2 a :** to make consistent or congruous **:** HARMONIZE ⟨*reconciled* their ideals with practical reality⟩ **b :** to obtain agreement between (two financial records) by accounting for all outstanding items ⟨~ a checkbook with a bank statement⟩ **3 :** to cause to submit to or accept **:** bring into acquiescence with ⟨*reconciled* to hardship⟩ **~** *vi* **:** to become reconciled **syn** see ADAPT

**rec·on·cile·less** \ˈ==ˌsīlləs\ *adj* [*reconcile* + *-less*] *archaic* **:** IRRECONCILABLE

**rec·on·cile·ment** \-lmənt\ *n* -S [*reconcile* + *-ment*] **:** RECONCILIATION

**rec·on·cil·er** *also* **rec·on·ci·lor** \ˈrekənˌsīlə(r)\ *n* -S [*reconcile* + *-er, -or*] **:** one that reconciles

**rec·on·cil·i·ate** \ˌrekənˈsilēˌāt\ *vt* [L *reconciliatus*, past part. of *reconciliare* to reconcile] **:** RECONCILE

**rec·on·cil·i·a·tion** \ˌ==ˌ==ˈāshən\ *n* -S [ME *reconciliacion*, fr. MF or L; MF *reconciliation*, fr. L *reconciliation-, reconciliatio*, fr. *reconciliatus* + *-ion-, -io* -ion] **:** the action of reconciling or state of being reconciled

**rec·on·cil·i·a·tor** \ˈ==ˌ==ˌād·ə(r)\ *n* -S [L, fr. *reconciliatus* + *-or*] **:** RECONCILER

**rec·on·cil·ia·to·ry** \ˌ==ˈsilyəˌtōrē, -lēə-, -tȯr-, -ri\ *adj* [L *reconciliatus* + E *-ory*] **:** serving or tending to reconcile

**reconciling** *adj* [fr. pres. part. of *reconcile*] **:** that reconciles — **rec·on·cil·ing·ly** *adv*

**re·condemn** \ˌrē+\ *vt* [*re-* + *condemn*] **:** to condemn again

**re·condemnation** \(ˌ)rē+\ *n* [*recondemn* + *-ation*] **:** the action of recondemning or state of being recondemned

**re·condensation** \"+\ *n* [*recondense* + *-ation*] **:** the action of recondensing or state of being recondensed

**re·condense** \ˌrē+\ *vb* [*re-* + *condense*] *vt* **:** to condense again **~** *vi* **:** to become condensed again

**recon·dite** \ˈrekənˌdīt, rə̇ˈkän-, rēˈk-, *usu* -īd·+V\ *adj* [L *reconditus*, fr. past part. of *recondere* to put up again, lay up, conceal, fr. *re-* + *condere* to bring together, store up — more at CONDITE] **1** *archaic* **:** hidden away or otherwise concealed so as not to be seen ⟨produced some ~ flasks of wine —T.L.Peacock⟩ **2 a :** very difficult to understand and beyond the reach of ordinary comprehension and knowledge **:** DEEP ⟨found the subject somewhat too ~⟩ **b** (1) **:** consisting of, relating to, or dealing with what is uncommon, abstruse, or profound ⟨spent his life in ~ studies⟩ (2) **:** unknown or little known except to a specialist ⟨the ~ literature of ancient India⟩ **c :** OBSCURE ⟨~ mysteries⟩

**recon·dite·ly** *adv* **:** in a recondite manner

**recon·dite·ness** *n* -ES **:** the quality or state of being recondite

**re·condition** \ˌrē+\ *vt* [*re-* + *condition*] **1 :** to restore to a good condition (as by repairing, replacing parts, beautifying) ⟨a ~*ed* car⟩ **2 :** REFORM ⟨~*ing* her emotional attitudes⟩

**re·conduct** \ˌrē+\ *vt* [L *reconductus*, past part. of *reconducere* to lead back, fr. *re-* + *conducere* to conduct] **:** to conduct back

**re·conduction** \"+\ *n* [*reconduct* + *-ion*] **1 :** the action of reconducting or state of being reconducted **2** [F *reconduction*, fr. L *reconductus* (past. part. of *reconducere* to lead back, lease again, fr. *re-* + *conducere* to conduct, hire, lease) + F *-ion*] *civil law* **:** a renewal of a lease **:** RELOCATION

**re·confer** \"+\ *vt* [*re-* + *confer*] **:** to confer again

**re·confess** \"+\ *vb* [*re-* + *confess*] *vt* **:** to confess again **~** *vi* **:** to make another or a new confession

**re·confide** \"+\ *vt* [*re-* + *confide*] **:** to confide again

**re·confine** \"+\ *vt* [*re-* + *confine*] **:** to confine again

**re·confirm** \"+\ *vt* [*re-* + *confirm*] **:** to confirm again; *esp* **:** to confirm again the reservation of (a seat on a particular plane flight)

**re·confirmation** \(ˌ)rē+\ *n* [*reconfirm* + *-ation*] **:** the action of reconfirming or state of being reconfirmed

**re·confiscate** \(ˈ)rē+\ *vt* [*re-* + *confiscate*] **:** to confiscate again

**re·confiscation** \(ˌ)rē+\ *n* [*reconfiscate* + *-ion*] **:** the action of reconfiscating or state of being reconfiscated

**re·congeal** \ˌrē+\ *vb* [*re-* + *congeal*] **:** to congeal again

**re·con·nais·sance** *also* **re·con·nois·sance** \rēˈkänəzən(t)s, rə̇ˈ-, -əsən-\ *n* -S *often attrib* [F *reconnaissance* recognition, exploration, fr. obs. *reconnoissance*, fr. MF *reconoissance* — more at RECOGNIZANCE] **1 :** an exploratory or preliminary survey, inspection, or examination made to gain information: as **a :** an exploratory military survey (as by aircraft or by the probes of small land units) of enemy territory and of enemy installations, movements, activities, and strength **b :** aerial photographing of activity (as shipping) or installations in friendly, enemy, or neutral areas **c** (1) **:** an engineering survey of a region (as in preparing for triangulation of the region) designed esp. to yield information about its general natural features (2) **:** a geological survey of a region **2** *or* **reconnaissance car :** a fast military car used for reconnaissance and typically provided with light armor, machine guns, and a two-way radio

**reconnaissance in force :** an attack by a large force for the purpose of discovering the position and strength of an enemy

**re·connect** \ˌrē+\ *vt* [*re-* + *connect*] **:** to connect again

¹**recon·noi·ter** *also* **recon·noi·tre** \ˌrekəˈnȯid·ə(r), ˌrēk-, -ȯitə-\ *vb* **reconnoitered** *also* **reconnoitred**; **reconnoitered** *also* **reconnoitred**; **reconnoitering** *also* **reconnoitring** \-ȯid·əriŋ, -ȯi·triŋ\ **reconnoiters** *also* **reconnoitres** [obs. F *reconnoître*, fr. MF *reconoistre* — more at RECOGNIZE] *vt* **1 :** to make an exploratory or preliminary survey, inspection, or examination of **:** make a reconnaissance of ⟨~*ing* enemy territory⟩ **2** *obs* **:** RECALL, REMEMBER **~** *vi* **:** to make a reconnaissance

²**reconnoiter** *also* **reconnoitre** \"\ *n* -S **:** RECONNAISSANCE

**recon·noi·ter·er** \-ȯid·ərə(r), -ȯi·trə-\ *also* **recon·noi·trer** \-trə(r)\ *n* -S **:** one that reconnoiters

**recon·noi·ter·ing·ly** *adv* [*reconnoitering* (pres. part. of ¹*reconnoiter*) + *-ly*] **:** in such a way as to reconnoiter

**re·conquer** \(ˈ)rē+\ *vt* [*re-* + *conquer*] **:** to conquer again; *esp* **:** recover by conquest

**re·conquest** \"+\ *n* [*re-* + *conquest*] **:** a second or new conquest of something previously conquered; *esp* **:** recovery of something by conquest

**re·consecrate** \(ˈ)rē+\ *vt* [*re-* + *consecrate*] **:** to consecrate again

**re·consecration** \(ˌ)rē+\ *n* [*reconsecrate* + *-ion*] **:** the action of reconsecrating or state of being reconsecrated

**re·consider** \ˌrē+\ *vb* [*re-* + *consider*] *vt* **:** to consider again: as **a :** to think over, discuss, or debate (as a plan, decision) esp. with a view to changing or reversing ⟨an opportunity to ~ my decision, so painfully arrived at —R.M.Lovett⟩ **b :** to take up again (as a motion or vote previously acted on) in a meeting (as a legislative assembly) ⟨asked the house to ~ the measure⟩ **~** *vi* **:** to consider something again **:** engage in reconsideration ⟨asked him to ~ before taking such a step⟩

**re·consideration** \"+\ *n* [*reconsider* + *-ation*] **:** the action of reconsidering or state of being reconsidered

**re·consign** \"+\ *vt* [*re-* + *consign*] **:** to consign again or anew

**re·consignment** \"+\ *n* [*reconsign* + *-ment*] **:** the action of reconsigning or state of being reconsigned; *esp* **:** a change (as in consignee, destination, route) in the original billing of goods in transit

**re·console** \"+\ *vt* [*re-* + *console*] **:** to console again

**re·consolidate** \"+\ *vb* [*re-* + *consolidate*] *vt* **:** to consolidate again **~** *vi* **:** to become reconsolidated

**re·consolidation** \"+\ *n* [*re-* + *consolidation*] **:** the action of reconsolidating or state of being reconsolidated **:** a second or fresh consolidation

¹**re·constituent** \"+\ *adj* [*re-* + *constituent*] **:** that reconstitutes; *esp* **:** serving to build up new tissue to replace that wasted by disease or other factors ⟨a ~ tonic⟩

²**reconstituent** \"\ *n* **:** something that is reconstituent

**re·constitute** \(ˈ)rē+\ *vt* [*re-* + *constitute*] **1 :** to build up again by putting back together the original parts or elements **:** RECONSTRUCT, RE-FORM ⟨~ a fragmentary text⟩; *esp* **:** to restore the constitution of (as a concentrated juice) by adding water **2 :** to build up again in a somewhat new or different form **:** REORGANIZE ⟨~ a bankrupt company⟩ ⟨~ an armored division⟩

**reconstituted milk** *n* [fr. past part. of *reconstitute*] **:** milk reconstituted by combining dry whole milk solids with the appropriate amount of water; *also* **:** milk made by adding water to evaporated milk —compare RECOMBINED MILK

**re·constitution** \(ˌ)rē+\ *n* [*re-* + *constitution*] **1 :** the action of reconstituting or state of being reconstituted **2 :** regeneration of an organic form by reorganization of existent tissue without blastema formation

**re·construct** \ˌrē+\ *vt* [*re-* + *construct*] **:** to construct again: as **a** (1) **:** to build again **:** REBUILD ⟨~*ing* destroyed railroads⟩ (2) **:** to make over **:** REPAIR ⟨~*ed* the highways that needed it⟩ **b :** to subject (an organ or part of the body) to surgery so as to correct a defect in or to reform **c** (1) **:** RECONSTITUTE ⟨~*ed* lemon juice⟩ (2) **:** REORGANIZE, REESTABLISH ⟨~*ing* society during the postwar period⟩ (3) **:** REHABILITATE ⟨~*ing* a twisted personality⟩ **d** (1) **:** to put together again **:** REASSEMBLE ⟨~*ing* a ruined pagan temple⟩ (2) **:** to restore or mount (a sheet of postage stamps) in the original form or in a replica of the original form (3) **:** to form (as a gem) by fusing together particles derived from one or more natural stones of the kind desired ⟨a ~*ed* ruby⟩ **e :** to build up again mentally (as from available evidence) **:** form a concept of **:** REEVOKE, RE-CREATE ⟨~*ing* the culture of a lost civilization⟩ **f :** to win over, make conform, or reconcile to a new or different order ⟨refuses to be ~*ed* by events —Carl Van Doren⟩

**re·constructible** \"+\ *adj* **:** capable of being reconstructed
**re·construction** \"+\ *n* [*re-* + *construction*] **1 a :** the action of reconstructing or state of being reconstructed **b** *often cap* **:** the reorganization and reestablishment in the Union during a period (1867–1877) following the American Civil War of those states that had seceded **2 :** something reconstructed: as **a :** a model or replica of something **b :** something reassembled (as from parts) into its original form or appearance
**re·constructional** \"+\ *adj* [*reconstruction* + *-al*] **:** of or relating to reconstruction
**re·con·struc·tion·ary** \ˌrēkənzˈtrəkshəˌnerē, -kənˈstr-\ *adj* [*reconstruction* + *-ary*] **:** RECONSTRUCTIONAL
**re·constructionism** \ˌrē+\ *n* [*reconstruction* + *-ism*] **:** adherence to or advocacy of reconstruction; *specif, often cap* **:** a movement in 20th century American Judaism influenced by Conservative Judaism and by pragmatism that advocates a creative adjustment of Jewish life to contemporary conditions by stressing the cultivation of traditions and folkways shared by all Jews as a basis for reconstructing historic Judaism into a religious civilization that would transcend denominationalism and ensure the unity and survival of the Jewish people
**re·constructionist** \"+\ *n* [*reconstruction* + *-ist*] **1 :** an adherent or advocate of reconstruction **2** *often cap* **:** an adherent or advocate of reconstructionism
**re·constructive** \"+\ *adj* [*reconstruct* + *-ive*] **:** relating to, marked by, or aimed at reconstruction ⟨~ penology⟩ — **re·constructively** \"+\ *adv*
**reconstructive surgery** *n* **:** surgery that aims at restoring function or normal appearance by remaking defective organs or parts ⟨*reconstructive surgery* of the femoral head⟩
**re·constructor** \"+\ *n* [*reconstruct* + *-or*] **:** one that reconstructs
**re·construe** \"+\ *vt* [*re-* + *construe*] **:** to construe again
**re·consult** \"+\ *vb* [*re-* + *consult*] *vt* **:** to consult again ~ *vi* **:** to engage in a second or fresh consultation
**re·consultation** \(ˌ)rē+\ *n* [*re-* + *consultation*] **:** a second or fresh consultation
**re·contact** \(ˈ)rē+\ *vt* [*re-* + *contact*] **:** to contact again
**re·contaminate** \ˌrē+\ *vt* [*re-* + *contaminate*] **:** to contaminate again
**re·contamination** \"+\ *n* [*recontaminate* + *-ion*] **:** the action of recontaminating or state of being recontaminated
**re·contemplate** \(ˈ)rē+\ *vt* [*re-* + *contemplate*] **:** to contemplate again
**re·contemplation** \(ˌ)rē+\ *n* [*recontemplate* + *-ion*] **:** the action of recontemplating or state of being recontemplated
**re·continue** \ˌrē+\ *vb* [*re-* + *continue*] *vt* **:** to continue again ~ *vi* **:** to proceed again
**¹re·contract** \(ˈ)rē+, ˌrē+\ *vb* [*re-* + *contract*, v.] *vt* **:** to contract again ~ *vi* **1 :** to make a new contract **2 :** to undergo a new contraction
**²re·contract** \(ˈ)rē+\ *n* [*re-* + *contract*, n.] **:** a new contract
**re·contraction** \ˌrē+\ *n* [*re-* + *contraction*] **:** a new contraction
**¹re·control** \"+\ *vt* [*re-* + *control*] **:** to subject (as prices, rents) to new control
**²recontrol** \"\ *n* **:** the action of recontrolling or state of being recontrolled
**re·convalesce** \(ˌ)rē+\ *vi* [*re-* + *convalesce*] **:** to undergo reconvalescence
**re·convalescence** \"+\ *n* [*re-* + *convalescence*] **1 :** renewed convalescence **2 :** complete convalescence
**re·convalescent** \"+\ *adj* [*re-* + *convalescent*] **:** of or relating to reconvalescence
**re·convene** \ˌrē+\ *vb* [*re-* + *convene*] *vi* **:** to convene again **:** assemble once more in a meeting ~ *vt* **:** to cause to convene again
**re·convention** \"+\ *n* [MF, fr. *re-* + *convention* agreement between two parties — more at CONVENTION] **:** a cross action by a defendant against a plaintiff before the same judge **:** COUNTERCLAIM
**re·converge** \"+\ *vi* [*re-* + *converge*] **:** to converge again
**re·conversion** \"+\ *n* [*re-* + *conversion*] **1 :** a second or fresh conversion **2 :** conversion back to a previous state: as **a :** change back to a previous state of belief or other conviction **b :** change back to a previous complex of qualities **c :** change (as of industry) from a wartime basis to a peacetime basis
**re·convert** \"+\ *vb* [*re-* + *convert*] *vt* **:** to cause to undergo reconversion **:** cause to change back ~ *vi* **:** to undergo reconversion **:** become changed back
**re·convertible** \"+\ *adj* [*reconvert* + *-ible*] **:** capable of being reconverted
**re·convey** \"+\ *vt* [*re-* + *convey*] **1 :** to convey back (as to a previous place or position) **2 :** to restore (as an estate) to a previous owner
**re·conveyance** \"+\ *n* [*reconvey* + *-ance*] **:** the action of reconveying or state of being reconveyed
**re·convict** \"+\ *vt* [*re-* + *convict*] **:** to convict again
**re·conviction** \"+\ *n* [*re-* + *conviction*] **:** a second or fresh conviction
**re·convince** \"+\ *vt* [*re-* + *convince*] **:** to convince again
**re·convocation** \(ˌ)rē+\ *n* [*re-* + *convocation*] **:** the action of reconvoking or state of being reconvoked
**re·convoke** \ˌrē+\ *vt* [*re-* + *convoke*] **:** to convoke again
**re·cook** \(ˈ)rē+\ *vt* [*re-* + *cook*] **:** to cook again
**re·cool** \"+\ *vt* [*re-* + *cool*] **:** to cool again
**re·cooper** \"+\ *vt* [*re-* + *cooper*] **:** to repair faults in (as barrels, casks, crates)
**re·copper** \"+\ *vt* [*re-* + *copper*] **:** to copper again
**re·copy** \"+\ *vt* [*re-* + *copy*] **:** to copy again
**¹re·cord** \rəˈkȯ(ə)rd, rēˈ-, -ȯ(ə)d\ *vb* -ED/-ING/-S [ME *recorden* to recall, recite, set down in writing, fr. OF *recorder*, fr. L *recordari* to call to mind, remember, fr. *re-* + *cord-, cor* heart, mind — more at HEART] *vt* **1 a** *obs* **:** RECALL, REMEMBER **b** *archaic* **:** SING, WARBLE ⟨hear the lark ~ her hymns —Edward Fairfax⟩ **2 a** (1) **:** to set down in writing **:** make a written account or note of **:** furnish written evidence of **:** put into written form ⟨a people that carefully ~*ed* their history⟩ ⟨~*ed* her impressions in a series of books⟩ ⟨~*ed* the sounds heard in phonetic symbols⟩ (2) **:** to make or have made an authentic official copy of (as a deed, mortgage, lease) and deposit or have deposited esp. as in an office designated by law (3) **:** to cause to be noted officially in or as if in writing ⟨~*ing* and tallying the votes⟩ ⟨~*ed* the proceedings of the court⟩ **b** (1) **:** to make an objective lasting indication of in some mechanical or automatic way **:** register permanently by mechanical means ⟨studied the intensity of the earthquake as it had been ~*ed* by the seismograph⟩ (2) *of an instrument* **:** to point out (data) at a particular time or under particular circumstances on or as if on a scale **:** show in this way ⟨noticed that at that moment the thermometer ~*ed* 90°⟩ **c :** to give evidence of ⟨the extent of the explosion is ~*ed* on the charred tree trunks of the surrounding area⟩ **3 a :** to cause (sound, visual images) to be transferred to and registered on something (as a phonograph disc, magnetic tape) by mechanical usu. electronic means in such a way that the thing so transferred and registered can (as by the use of a phonograph, tape recorder) be subsequently reproduced **b :** to register in this way a performance of (as an orchestra, singer, actor) or rendition or playing of (as a piece of music, an instrument) ~ *vi* **1 a :** to record something ⟨spent the whole day ~ing⟩ **b :** to admit of being recorded ⟨a voice that ~*s* beautifully⟩ **2** *archaic* **:** SING, WARBLE
**²rec·ord** \ˈrekə(r)d, -kȯ(ə)d\ *n* -S [ME, fr. MF, fr. *recorder* to record] **1 a :** the state or fact of being recorded **b :** something (as a monument) on which a record has been made **c** (1) **:** evidence, knowledge, or information remaining in permanent form (as a relic, inscription, document) ⟨the ~ of an extinct people⟩ (2) **:** an account in writing or print (as in a document) or in some other permanent form (as on a monument) intended to perpetuate a knowledge of acts or events **2 :** something that serves to record: as **a** (1) **:** a piece of writing that recounts or attests to something ⟨a ~ of the early history of a nation⟩ (2) **:** an official contemporaneous document recording the acts of some public body or public officer ⟨a ~ of city ordinances⟩ (3) **:** an authentic official copy of a document entered in a book or deposited in the keeping of some officer designated by law — compare CONVEYANCE 2b (4) **:** an official contemporaneous memorandum stating the proceedings of a court of justice (5) **:** an official copy of the legal papers used in a case and of memoranda of the proceedings of the court **b :** something that is known or can be learned or has been recorded: as (1) **:** an officially or sometimes nonofficially attested top performance or achievement (as in a competitive sport) ⟨a high jump that broke the ~⟩ (2) **:** cumulative data usu. consisting of written systematically arranged notes relating to an individual's or group's activities, abilities, accomplishments, or physical or moral qualities in a particular area (as school, business) ⟨a child with a good school ~⟩ ⟨carefully kept health ~*s*⟩ (3) **:** a body of known, recorded, or available facts about something **:** the sum of something done or achieved or the body of data known, recorded, or available about something ⟨looked at the ~ of the candidate⟩ ⟨had a long criminal ~⟩ ⟨a brilliant ~ as an executive⟩ **3 :** something to which sound has been transferred by mechanical usu. electronic means and so registered as to be capable of subsequent reproduction by a specially designed instrument; *specif* **:** a disc with a spiral groove carrying recorded sound — **off the record** *adv* (*or adj*) **:** not for quotation (as by the press) or publication as something official or authoritative ⟨spoke *off the record*⟩ ⟨my remarks are *off the record*⟩ — **of record 1 :** appearing on the record of a court in connection with a particular case, judgment, or other proceeding ⟨the attorney *of record*⟩ **2 :** documented or otherwise attested ⟨a reversal of opinion that is *of record*⟩ — **on record** *adv* **1 :** in the position of having publicly declared oneself ⟨go *on record* as opposing tax increases⟩ **2 :** in the status of being known, published, or documented ⟨the judge's opinion is *on record*⟩
**³record** \"\ *adj* **:** of, relating to, or consisting of something (as a performance, occurrence, condition) that goes beyond or is extraordinary among others of its kind ⟨a ~ run⟩ ⟨~ prices⟩ ⟨~ heat⟩
**re·cord·able** \rəˈkȯ(ə)rdəbəl, rēˈ-, -ȯ(ə)d-\ *adj* **:** suitable for recording or capable of being recorded ⟨~ music⟩ ⟨~ underground explosions⟩ ⟨~ aspects of African life —*Geog. Jour.*⟩
**record agent** *n* [²*record*] **:** RECORDING AGENT
**re·cord·ant** \rəˈkȯrdᵊnt, -ȯ(ə)d-\ *adj* [¹*record* + *-ant*] *archaic* **:** RECORDATIVE
**rec·or·da·tion** \ˌrekə(r)ˈdāshən\ *n* -S [ME *recordacion*, fr. MF or L; MF *recordation*, fr. L *recordation-, recordatio*, fr. *recordatus* (past part. of *recordari* to remember) + *-ion-, -io* -ion — more at RECORD] **1** *obs* **:** REMEMBRANCE, RECOLLECTION **2 :** the action or process of setting down in writing a record (as of transactions, data, events) ⟨~ of property acquired⟩ ⟨careful fieldwork, with meticulous ~ —E.K.Reed⟩ ⟨~ of past events —*Atlantic*⟩
**re·cor·da·tive** \rəˈkȯrdəd·iv\ *adj* [MF *recordatif*, fr. LL *recordativus*, fr. L *recordatus* + *-ivus* -ive] *archaic* **:** bearing or containing a record **:** evoking a memory or reminiscence of something **:** COMMEMORATIVE
**record-breaking** \ˈ==ˌ==\ *adj* [²*record* + *breaking*, pres. part. of *break*] **:** that surpasses some previously established record ⟨a *record-breaking* high jump⟩ ⟨*record-breaking* production⟩ ⟨a *record-breaking* crowd⟩
**record changer** *n* **:** a phonograph attachment that automatically places in position and plays successively each one of a stack of records
**re·cord·er** \rəˈkȯrdər, rēˈ-, -ȯ(ə)də\ *n* -S [ME, partly fr. *recorden* to record + *-er*, partly fr. AF *recordour* a magistrate, fr. *recorder* to record (fr. L *recordari*) + *-our* -or] **1 :** one that records: as **a** (1) **:** one whose official duty it is to make a record of writings or transactions (2) **:** a surveying party's noteman (3) **:** one that inspects and records the progress of construction work **b :** a machine, instrument, or device that records (as sound, visual images) for subsequent reproduction **2 a :** the chief judicial magistrate of some British cities and boroughs having now only criminal jurisdiction **b :** a judge with criminal jurisdiction of first instance and sometimes also a magistrate's civil jurisdiction in a municipality **3 a :** a fipple flute with eight finger holes — called also *English flute* **b :** a pipe-organ stop similar in tone quality to the recorder **:** BLOCKFLÖTE 2

recorder 3a

**re·cord·er·ship** \-ˌship\ *n* [*recorder* + *-ship*] **:** the office or term of office of a recorder
**recording** *n* -S [fr. gerund of ¹*record*] **1 a :** the process of recording something esp. sound ⟨the ~ took place at the studio⟩ **b :** a period or session of recording something ⟨said several ~*s* would be necessary⟩ **2 a :** what is recorded (as on a phonograph record, magnetic tape) ⟨analyzed the ~⟩ **b :** a phonograph record, magnetic tape, or some other thing (as a film, wire, one of the perforated rolls played by a player piano) on which sound or visual images have been recorded for subsequent reproduction ⟨has a collection of unusual ~*s*⟩
**recording agent** *n* [fr. pres. part. of ¹*record*] **:** a local insurance agent empowered to commit the companies represented and to issue policies in their behalf
**recording head** *also* **record head** *n* **:** a device used in the recording of sound for transforming electrical energy into a magnetic record or into a groove undulation on a disc
**recording meter** *n* **:** an instrument usu. driven by clockwork and containing a chart upon which a record of variations (as in current, pressure) is made
**re·cord·ist** \rəˈkȯrdəst, rēˈ-, -ȯ(ə)d-\ *n* -S [¹*record* + *-ist*] **:** one who records (as sound on film)
**rec·ord·less** \ˈrekə(r)dləs\ *adj* [²*record* + *-less*] **:** lacking a recorded history ⟨the student of ~ primitive peoples —Margaret Hodgen⟩
**record-of-performance** *also* **record-of-production** \ˈ===-ˈ==\ *adj* **1 :** based on or used for determining the relative productivity of a domestic animal under standardized conditions ⟨*record-of-performance* tests⟩ ⟨a *record-of-performance* rating⟩ **2 :** attaining an acceptable level of productivity on a record-of-performance test ⟨a *record-of-production* sire⟩ ⟨*record-of-performance* hens⟩
**record player** *n* [²*record*] **:** an instrument for reproducing the recorded sound of a phonograph record; *esp* **:** such an instrument using an electric pickup whose output is fed into one or more audio amplifiers and loudspeakers
**records** *pres 3d sing of* RECORD, *pl of* RECORD
**re·cork** \(ˈ)rē+\ *vt* [*re-* + *cork*] **:** to cork again
**re·correct** \ˌrē+\ *vt* [*re-* + *correct*] **:** to correct again
**re·corrupt** \"+\ *vt* [*re-* + *corrupt*] **:** to corrupt again
**re·cor·te** \rāˈkȯr(ˌ)dā\ *n* -S [Sp, fr. *recortar* to cut off, trim, fr. *re-* + *cortar* to cut — more at CORTADERIA] **:** a cape movement executed after a series of Veronicas to cut short a bull's charge, turn him, and place him for the picadors
**¹re·count** \rəˈkau̇nt, rēˈ-\ *vt* [ME *recounten*, fr. MF *reconter*, fr. *re-* + *conter* to count, relate — more at COUNT] **1 :** to give a detailed account of **:** tell the particulars of **:** NARRATE ⟨~*s* his adventures with admirable restraint —Lynn Groh⟩ **2 :** to go over, call to mind, or mention one by one ⟨~*ing* all their victories⟩ **3** *obs* **:** REGARD, CONSIDER **syn** see RELATE
**²re·count** \(ˈ)rē+\ *vb* [*re-* + *count*, v.] *vt* **:** to count over again ~ *vi* **:** to make a new count
**³recount** \"\ *n* [*re-* + *count*, n.] **:** a second or fresh count ⟨a ~ of election votes⟩
**re·count·al** \rəˈkau̇ntᵊl, rēˈ-\ *n* -S [¹*recount* + *-al*] **:** a detailed account **:** NARRATION, RECITAL
**re·coup** \(ˈ)rēˈküp, rəˈ-\ *vb* -ED/-ING/-S [F *recouper* to cut back, fr. OF, fr. *re-* + *couper* to cut — more at COPE] *vt* **1** *law* **:** to keep back rightfully a part of so as to diminish a sum due **:** DEDUCT; *specif* **:** to abate or reduce (a claim sued on) by setting up in defense some act or fact growing out of the matters constituting the cause or ground of the action brought **2 a :** to make good (as expenses, losses) ⟨this is largely ~*ed* to states from taxes —John Kemp⟩ **:** make up for ⟨~*ed* their losses⟩ **b :** to compensate (as oneself) for something (as expenses, losses) **:** REIMBURSE, INDEMNIFY ⟨in order to ~ himself for this outlay —G.G.Coulton⟩ **3 :** to get back **:** REGAIN ⟨an attempt to ~ his fortunes —W.J.Ghent⟩ ⟨try to ~ their strength —Gordon Harrison⟩ ⟨so as to ~ without interruption the hour of sleep they had lost —*N.Y. Times*⟩ ~ *vi* **:** to regain, make good, or make up for something lost ⟨needed time to ~⟩ **syn** see RECOVER
**re·couple** \(ˈ)rē+\ *vt* [*re-* + *couple* (v.)] **:** to couple again
**re·coup·ment** \rēˈküpmənt, rəˈ-\ *n* -S [*recoup* + *-ment*] **1 :** the action of recouping or state of being recouped **2 :** something recouped — compare COUNTERCLAIM, SETOFF
**¹re·course** \ˈrēˌkō(ə)rs, -ȯ(ə)rs, -ōəs, ˈ=ˈ=\ *n* [ME *recours*, fr. MF, fr. LL *recursus*, fr. L, act of running back, fr. *recursus*, past part. of *recurrere* to run back — more at RECUR] **1 a :** a turning to someone or something in search of help, support, protection, or safety ⟨had ~ to his brother⟩ ⟨does not hesitate to have ~ to religion —J.G.Frazer⟩ ⟨handle their own difficulties without ~ to outside help —G.P.Wibberley⟩ **b :** someone or something that can be turned to for help, support, protection, or safety **:** a source of help or strength **:** RESORT ⟨was afraid no ~ was left⟩ **2** *obs* **a :** a movement or flow in one direction or another **b :** a periodical recurrence of something **c :** repeated visiting **:** habitual resort **d :** admittance to someone or something **:** ACCESS **3 :** the right to demand payment; *specif* **:** the right to demand payment from the one that makes out or endorses a negotiable instrument (as a check) — used chiefly in the phrase *without recourse* placed after the endorsement of a negotiable instrument to protect the endorser from liability to the endorsee and subsequent holders
**²recourse** *vi, obs* **:** to have recourse **:** RESORT
**¹re·cov·er** \rəˈkəvə(r), rēˈ-\ *vb* **recovered; recovered; recovering** \-v(ə)riŋ\ **recovers** [ME *recoveren*, fr. MF *recoverer*, fr. L *recuperare*; akin to L *recipere* to take back, receive — more at RECEIVE] *vt* **1 :** to get or win back ⟨sat down to ~ his breath⟩ ⟨died without ~*ing* consciousness⟩ ⟨answered as soon as he could ~ his voice⟩ ⟨~ the pioneering spirit of their ancestors⟩ **2** *archaic* **:** to get well from (as an injury, a sickness) **3 a :** to bring (oneself) back to normal balance or self-possession ⟨stumbled and ~*ed* himself⟩ **b** *archaic* **:** RESCUE, DELIVER ⟨that they may ~ themselves out of the snare of the devil —2 Tim 2:26 (AV)⟩ **4 a :** to make good the loss, injury, or cost of **:** make up for ⟨~ increased costs through higher prices⟩ ⟨hoped to ~ his gambling losses with a big coup⟩ **b :** to gain by legal process ⟨~ damages and costs in a libel suit⟩ ⟨~ title to a disputed property⟩ ⟨~ judgment against a defendant⟩ **5** *archaic* **:** to gain by motion or effort **:** REACH **6** *archaic* **:** RESTORE, CURE, HEAL ⟨from death to life thou might'st him yet ~ —Michael Drayton⟩ ⟨she hath ~*ed* the king and undone me —Shak.⟩ **7 :** to find again ⟨~ a lost scent⟩ ⟨~ the trail of a fugitive⟩ **8 a :** to obtain from an ore, a waste product, or a by-product ⟨~ gold from ore with cyanide⟩ **b :** to save from loss and restore to usefulness **:** RECLAIM ⟨~ land from the sea⟩ **c :** to bring out or bring to light after neglect, burial, obscurity ⟨~ the lost secrets of ancient glassblowers⟩ ⟨~ the key of a cryptographic message⟩ ⟨~ petroleum from deep deposits⟩ ~ *vi* **1 a :** to regain health after sickness **:** become well ⟨~*ing* from a bout of pneumonia⟩ ⟨patients on the southern side of a hospital ~ faster than those on the northern side —Herbert Spencer⟩ **b :** to regain a former or normal state (as of vigor, self-control, consciousness) ⟨when she had ~*ed* from the first shock of the news⟩ ⟨the cotton industry was ~*ing* after a slump during the war⟩ **2 :** to regain a position of guard or readiness ⟨~ after a lunge in fencing⟩ ⟨~ for the next rowing stroke⟩ **3 :** to obtain a final judgment in one's favor **:** to succeed in a lawsuit or proceeding **4** *obs* **:** to make one's way back **:** RETURN
**syn** RECOVER, REGAIN, RETRIEVE, RECOUP, and RECRUIT can mean to get back what has been let go or lost. RECOVER, the most comprehensive, can apply to anything lost and got back in any way ⟨*recover* a lost wallet⟩ ⟨*recover* one's sanity⟩ ⟨*recover* one's balance⟩ ⟨*recover* one's position in a firm⟩ REGAIN, often interchangeable with RECOVER, implies more strongly a winning back ⟨*regain* one's health⟩ ⟨*regain* one's liberty after a long imprisonment⟩ ⟨*regain* one's rights as a citizen⟩ ⟨*regain* popularity⟩ RETRIEVE implies a recovering or regaining after some effort ⟨*retrieve* a lost fortune⟩ ⟨*retrieve* one's position lost through ill fortune⟩ although the verb can have as its object such a word as *loss, error, failure,* or *disaster*, with which it then implies a reparation or a setting right ⟨*retrieve* an error in addition⟩ ⟨*retrieve* a bad financial disaster by careful investment⟩ RECOUP, a legal term implying a fair deduction as of part of a claim of a successful plaintiff in a law suit, in common use implies recovery or retrieval, usu. in equivalent rather than identical form, of something lost ⟨*recoup* gambling losses by more careful play⟩ ⟨*recoup* by some good hard work the money lost in bad investments⟩ RECRUIT in this context can imply a regaining, by fresh additions or a replenishment of the supply, of what has been lost ⟨*recruit* a new battalion for the foot army⟩ ⟨the present difficulty of *recruiting* staff in the accountancy profession —*Accountancy*⟩ ⟨I fed and watered my horse and *recruited* my own energies with roast beef —W. H. Hudson †1922⟩ In extension it has come to apply to any acquiring as of members or a supply ⟨a fair-sized audience can be *recruited* —Sidney Kaufman⟩ ⟨hundreds of thousands of Americans who had never worked before . . . were *recruited* for war production —Dorothy Jones⟩ ⟨*recruit* a staff for a new restaurant⟩
**²recover** \"\ *n* -S [ME *recovere*, fr. MF *recovre*, fr. *recoverer* to recover] **:** RECOVERY 3
**re-cover** \(ˈ)rē+\ *vt* [ME *recoveren*, fr. *re-* + *coveren* to cover] **:** to cover again **:** provide with a new covering ⟨*re-cover* an upholstered couch⟩ ⟨*re-cover* a lampshade⟩
**re·cov·er·able** \rəˈkəv(ə)rəbəl, rēˈ-\ *adj* [ME, fr. *recoveren* to recover + *-able*] **:** capable of being recovered ⟨~ truth of a past event⟩ or of recovering ⟨~ action at law⟩ — **re·cov·er·able·ness** *n* -ES
**re·cov·er·ance** \-v(ə)rən(t)s\ *n* -ES [ME, fr. MF *recovrance*, fr. OF, fr. *recoverer* to recover + *-ance*] *archaic* **:** RECOVERY
**recovered** *adj* [ME, fr. past part. of *recoveren* to recover] **:** no longer sick **:** CURED, WELL ⟨when the ~ patient tries to remember what occurred during his delirium —Norman Cameron⟩ ⟨appears to be entirely ~⟩
**re·cov·er·ee** \rəˌkəvəˈrē, rēˌk-\ *n* -S [¹*recover* + *-ee*] **:** the person against whom a judgment is obtained in common recovery
**re·cov·er·er** \rəˈkəv(ə)rə(r), rēˈ-\ *n* -S [ME, fr. *recoveren* to recover + *-er*] **:** one that recovers
**recovering** *pres part of* RECOVER
**re·cov·er·or** \rəˌkəvəˈrȯ(ə)r, rēˌ-, -rȯə, ˈ=ˈ==ˌrə(r)\ *n* -S [¹*recover* + *-or*] **:** the demandant in a common recovery after judgment in his favor
**recovers** *pres 3d sing of* RECOVER, *pl of* RECOVER
**re·cov·ery** \rəˈkəv(ə)rē, rēˈ-, -ri\ *n* -ES [ME, perh. fr. MF *recovree*, fr. *recoverer* to recover + *-ee* -y] **1** *obs* **:** means of restoration **:** CURE, REMEDY **2 a :** the obtaining in a suit at law of a right to something by a verdict, decree, or judgment of court **b :** COMMON RECOVERY **3 a :** the action of regaining an upright position after curtseying **b :** a movement sequence in dance technique for rising after a fall **c :** the action of regaining the position of guard after making an attack in fencing or sparring **d :** the action following the completion of a rowing stroke in which the blade is raised and feathered and readied for the next stroke **e :** a golf stroke played from the rough or a trap to the green or fairway **4 :** the act of regaining or returning toward a normal or usual state ⟨~ from a heart attack⟩ ⟨~ from childbirth⟩ ⟨~ in the bond market⟩ **5 :** a period of economic upturn following a depression **6 a :** the recovering of useful material from spent products or waste ⟨~ of solvents used for dry cleaning⟩ ⟨~ of aluminum from loose scrap⟩ **b :** the amount of metal or valuable substance obtained in a process of ore treatment expressed sometimes as a percentage of the metal orig. in the ore **7 :** removal of residual stress from cold worked metal by low-temperature annealing
**recovery furnace** *n* **:** ¹SMELTER
**recovery oven** *n* **:** BY-PRODUCT OVEN
**recovery room** *n* **:** a hospital room which is equipped with apparatus for meeting postoperative emergencies and in which surgical patients are kept during the immediate postoperative period for care and recovery from anesthesia
**recp** *abbr* reception
**recpst** *abbr* receptionist
**recpt** *abbr* receipt
**recr** *abbr* receiver
**re·crat·er** \(ˈ)rēˈkrātə(r)\ *n* -S [*re-* + *crate* + *-er*] *Brit* **:** a machine for loading bottles or cans into shipping cases — compare DECRATER

**rec·re·ance** \ˈrekrēən(t)s\ *n* -s [fr. ¹*recreant*, after such pairs as E *assistant: assistance*] : RECREANCY

**rec·re·an·cy** \-nsē, -si\ *n* -ES [¹*recreant* + *-cy*] : the quality or state of being recreant : shameful cowardice : PERFIDY

¹**rec·re·ant** \-nt\ *adj* [ME, fr. MF, fr. pres. part. of *recroire to* renounce one's cause in a trial by battle, to surrender, fr. OF, fr. *re-* + *croire* to believe, fr. L *credere* — more at CREED] **1** : crying for mercy esp. in the trial of battle : yielding in a cowardly manner : CRAVEN **2** : unfaithful to one's duty or allegiance : APOSTATE, FALSE ⟨those responsible for teaching the common folk were ~ to their task —I.M.Price⟩ **syn** see COWARDLY

²**recreant** \"\ *n* -s [ME, fr. MF, fr. *recreant*, adj.] **1** : one that yields cravenly in combat : a cowardly wretch **2** : one that is unfaithful : BETRAYER, DESERTER

**rec·re·ate** \ˈrekrēˌāt, *usu* -ād·+V\ *vb* [L *recreatus*, past part. of *recreare*, to create anew, restore, refresh, fr. *re-* + *creare* to create] *vt* **1 a** : to cheer by giving consolation or encouragement **b** : to renew or enliven (as the spirits) through the influence of pleasant surroundings **2** : to refresh after wearying toil or anxiety usu. by change or diversion ⟨might not choose to ~ themselves on a scenic railway —*Blackwood's*⟩ ⟨I charge you not to hunt or ~ yourselves on that sacred day —R.S.Monahan⟩ **3** : to give fresh life to : restore the strength of : REVIVE ⟨my soul stood at that gate to ~ itself with bliss —A.T.Quiller-Couch⟩ ~ *vi* : to take recreation ⟨all nuns of the same community dress alike, eat alike, and ~ alike —Sister Marian Elizabeth⟩ **syn** see AMUSE

**re-create** \ˌrē+\ *vt* [*re-* + *create*] : to create again ⟨*re-create* the boom of the old frontier on a small scale —W.P.Webb⟩ : form anew esp. in the imagination : recollect and reform in the mind ⟨his mind, which *re-creates* the cosmos out of a grain of sand —L.J.Halle⟩

¹**rec·re·a·tion** \ˌrekrēˈāshən\ *n* -s [ME *recreacion*, fr. MF *recreation*, fr. L *recreation-*, *recreatio* restoral to health, fr. *recreatus* (past part. of *recreare* to restore, refresh) + *-ion-*, *-io* -ion] **1 a** : the act of recreating or the state of being recreated : refreshment of the strength and spirits after toil : DIVERSION, PLAY ⟨to sit in the sun . . . is one of my country ~s —L.P.Smith⟩ ⟨obvious that there is little time for ~ —J.M.Mogey⟩ ⟨I . . . consider intervals of ~ and amusement as desirable for everybody —Jane Austen⟩ **b** : a means of getting diversion or entertainment ⟨his ~ is gardening —*Current Biog.*⟩ **2** *obs* : one that provides recreation or amusement ⟨if I do not gull him . . . and make him a common ~ —Shak.⟩

²**recreation** \"\ *adj* : RECREATIONAL; *esp* : equipped so as to provide diversions or amusements ⟨has introduced winter ~ facilities —*Amer. Guide Series: Pa.*⟩

**re-creation** \ˌrē+\ *n* [*re-* + *creation*] : the act of creating over again : RENEWAL ⟨our watchful care for their interests, for the *re-creation* of their industries —Ernest Bevin⟩ ⟨not merely playacting but the *re-creation* of a great story —R.M. Hodesh⟩

**rec·re·a·tion·al** \ˌrekrēˈāshənᵊl, -shnəl\ *adj* : of or relating to recreation ⟨a ~ area with cinder track, tennis courts, and practice fields —*Amer. Guide Series: Oreg.*⟩ ⟨reading matter which is at once ~ and mentally activating —A.C.Ward⟩

**recreational therapist** *n* : one trained in or engaged in the practice of recreational therapy

**recreational therapy** *n* : therapy by means of recreational activities engaged in by the patient — compare OCCUPATIONAL THERAPY

**rec·re·a·tion·ist** \ˌrekrēˈāsh(ə)nəst\ *n* -s [*recreation* + *-ist*] : one who takes or seeks recreation esp. in the open

**recreation room** *n* **1** : a room (as a playroom or rumpus room) furnished and reserved for relaxation and recreation **2** : a public room (as in a hospital) for recreational and social activities

**rec·re·a·tive** \ˈrekrēˌād·iv, -ātiv, -ēv *also* -əv\ *adj* [*recreate* + *-ive*] : tending to recreate : giving pleasure and enjoyment : DIVERTING ⟨some activities are ~ and amusing because of their contrast with work —John Dewey⟩

**re-creative** \ˌrē+\ *adj* [*re-create* + *-ive*] : able to create again ⟨constantly grew in insight and *re-creative* power —C.M.Smith⟩

**re-creator** \"+\ *n* [*re-create* + *-or*] : one that creates again ⟨known as the *re-creator* of the Hebrew language —*Springfield (Mass.) Union*⟩

**rec·re·a·tor** \ˈrekrēˌād·ə(r), -ātə-\ *n* -s [*recreate* + *-or*] : one that recreates ⟨from the standpoint of the ~, most recreation is intensely purposeful —George Hjelte⟩

**rec·re·a·to·ry** \-ēəˌtōrē, -tȯr-, -ri\ *adj* [*recreate* + *-ory*] : RECREATIONAL ⟨the students return to their fourth-grade room for . . . ~ reading —Roul Tunley⟩

**re·credential** \ˌrē+\ *n* [*re-* + *credential*] : a letter of appreciation given to a diplomatic envoy on his permanently leaving a post by the head of the state to which he has been accredited — compare LETTER OF CREDENCE

**rec·re·ment** \ˈrekrəmənt\ *n* -s [MF or L; MF *recrement*, fr. L *recrementum*, fr. *re-* + *cre-* (stem of *cernere* to separate, sift) + *-mentum* -ment — more at CERTAIN] : superfluous matter separated from that which is useful : DROSS, SCORIA ⟨the ~ of ore⟩

**rec·re·men·ti·tious** \ˌ==mənˈtishəs, -ˌmen-\ *adj* [*recrement* + *-itious*] : of, relating to, consisting of, or of the nature of recrement or dross : SUPERFLUOUS

**re·crim·i·nate** \rəˈkriməˌnāt, rē'-, *usu* -ād·+V\ *vb* [ML *recriminatus*, past part. of *recriminare*, fr. L *re-* + *criminare*, *criminari* to accuse — more at CRIMINATE] *vi* : to make a counter accusation : charge back a fault or crime upon an accuser ⟨in the moment's mortification however, I *recriminated* —W.J.Locke⟩ ~ *vt* **1** : to make a charge against (an accuser) in return **2** : to return (as a charge) in bitter retort ⟨*recriminated*, "You've made the same mistake yourself"⟩

**re·crim·i·na·tion** \=ˌ==ˈnāshən\ *n* [ML *recrimination-*, *recriminatio*, fr. *recriminatus* (past part. of *recriminare* to recriminate) + *-ion-*, *-io* -ion] **1** : the act of recriminating : an accusation brought by the accused against the accuser : a counter accusation ⟨work so often demands . . . that we refrain from ~s that won't mend the situation —Alan Gregg⟩ **2** : a counter accusation barring a divorce esp. where the plaintiff is also guilty of conduct constituting cause for divorce

**re·crim·i·na·tive** \=ˈkriməˌnā|d·|iv, -m(ə)nə|, |t|, |ēv *also* |əv\ *adj* [*recriminate* + *-ive*] : RECRIMINATORY

**re·crim·i·na·tor** \-ˌnād·ə(r)\ *n* [*recriminate* + *-or*] : one that recriminates

**re·crim·i·na·to·ry** \-ˌnəˌtōrē, -tȯr-, -ri\ *adj* [*recriminate* + *-ory*] : having the character or nature of recrimination : RECRIMINATING ⟨a ~ defence⟩ ⟨approval of the tense ~ speeches was expressed —Jean Lyon⟩

**re·cross** \(ˈ)rē+\ *vb* [*re-* + *cross*] *vi* : to cross again ⟨his legs crossing, uncrossing, ~*ing* —A.T.Quiller-Couch⟩ ~ *vt* : to traverse again ⟨watching the man in overalls ~ the floor —William Faulkner⟩

**re·cru·desce** \ˌrēkrüˈdes\ *vi* -ED/-ING/-S [L *recrudescere* — more at RECRUDESCENT] : to become recrudescent : break out again : renew activity ⟨the general influence . . . which is liable every now and then to ~ in his absence —Edmund Gurney⟩

**re·cru·des·cence** \-sᵊn(t)s\ *n* -s [L *recrudescere* + E *-ence*] : the state of being recrudescent: as **a** : a return or revival (as of an undesirable condition or ill-advised idea) after a period of abatement or inactivity : RENEWAL ⟨a marked ~ of nationalist slogans and propaganda —E.J.Salter⟩ ⟨confident of its ability to handle any ~ of aggression from neighboring states —John Hersey⟩ **b** : increased severity of a disease after a remission, or recurrence after a brief intermission — compare RELAPSE

**re·cru·des·cen·cy** \-nsē, -si\ *n* -ES [L *recrudescere* + E *-ency*] : RECRUDESCENCE

**re·cru·des·cent** \ˌ==ˈdesᵊnt\ *adj* [L *recrudescent-*, *recrudescens*, pres. part. of *recrudescere* to become raw again, fr. *re-* + *crudescere* to become hard or raw, fr. *crudus* raw — more at RAW] : breaking out again : renewing disease or dangerous activity after abatement, suppression, or cessation ⟨a ~ typhus⟩ ⟨a ~ discontent among the factory workers⟩

¹**re·cruit** \rəˈkrüt, rē'- *also* ˈrē,-, *usu* -üd·+V\ *n* -s [F *recrute*, *recrue*, lit., regrowth, fresh growth, fr. *recru*, past part. of *recroître* to grow up again, fr. L *recrescere*, fr. *re-* + *crescere* to grow — more at CRESCENT] **1 a** : a renewal of strength : a return to a previously satisfactory condition **b** : a means of recovery **2 a** *obs* : a number of people added to or replacing a group **b** : a fresh or additional supply **3 a** *obs* : a newly raised or additional body of soldiery **b** *obs* : a strengthening or increase of an army by reinforcements or new levies **4 a** (1) : a fresh levy : REINFORCEMENTS —usu. used in pl. (2) : a newly enlisted or drafted member of the armed services; *specif* : an enlistee or draftee of the lowest grade in the army **b** : a newcomer to a field of activity ⟨accommodate more ~s on farms —*Atlantic*⟩ ⟨find among these men good ~s for our faculties —F.N.Robinson⟩

²**recruit** \"\ *vb* -ED/-ING/-S [F *recruter*, fr. *recrute*, *recrue* recruit] *vt* **1 a** (1) : to strengthen or supply (as an army, a military organization) with fresh or additional members : to reinforce, fill up, or make up by enlistment of personnel : MUSTER, RAISE ⟨when a nation must suddenly ~ a maximal armed force —Leonard Carmichael⟩ ⟨~ a regiment⟩ (2) : to enlist as a member of an armed service ⟨~*ed* 300 men in two days⟩ **b** : to increase or maintain the number of : build up : fill up ⟨America having ~*ed* her population largely from foreign immigrants —Katharine E. Caffrey⟩ ⟨the party was ~*ed* chiefly from among the farmers⟩ **c** : to hire or otherwise obtain to perform services (as on a work force or for an organization) : secure the services of ⟨came to look for her husband who was ~*ed* for the mines —Alan Paton⟩ ⟨done an admirable job in ~*ing* research staffs —Harold Zink⟩ ⟨our big job was to ~ youths for future teachers —*Education Digest*⟩ ⟨busy ~*ing* volunteer social workers⟩ **2** : to provide with what is needed (as with fresh supplies, material, efforts) to correct or prevent depletion, exhaustion, or waste : add to : REPAIR, REPLENISH ⟨it was from gifts bestowed upon him . . . that he ~*ed* his finances —Charles Dickens⟩ **3** : to restore the vigor or health of : invigorate anew ⟨detach him . . . till he ~s his strength —Walt Whitman⟩ ⟨come down here . . . to ~ yourself after an excess of work —G.B.Shaw⟩ ~ *vi* **1 a** : to raise or enlist or attempt to raise or enlist new soldiers ⟨both armies ~*ed* easily⟩ ⟨the army is not ~*ing* at present⟩ **b** : to raise or seek to raise new supplies of men for service and work forces **2** : to recover what has been lost or spent (as strength or health) : RECUPERATE **syn** see RECOVER

**re·cruit·al** \rəˈkrüd·ᵊl, rē'-, -ütᵊnl\ *n* -s [²*recruit* + *-al*] : a new supply

**re·cruit·er** \-üd·ə(r), -tə(r)\ *n* -s [²*recruit* + *-er*] **1** : an extra member of the British parliament chosen to increase the number esp. during an emergency (as the Civil War) **2** : one that recruits ⟨a navy ~⟩ ⟨~s from 600 companies are on the nation's college and university campuses —*Fortune*⟩

¹**recruiting** *adj* [fr. pres. part. of ²*recruit*] : having military or personnel recruiting as a duty or purpose ⟨a ~ officer⟩ ⟨we have encountered high-powered ~ programs —R.S.Bogue⟩ ⟨the employment department is in a position to begin its ~ activities —*Labor Problems in America*⟩

²**recruiting** *n* -s [fr. gerund of ²*recruit*] : the raising of recruits (as for the armed forces, a labor force, a volunteer agency)

**recruiting ground** *n* [²*recruiting*] : a place for obtaining, enlisting, or supplying recruits : a source of supply ⟨the *recruiting ground* for young politicians —Lytton Strachey⟩

**re·cruit·ment** \rəˈkrütmənt, rē'-\ *n* -s [²*recruit* + *-ment*] **1** : REINFORCEMENT ⟨would guarantee the ~ of this group from the most promising young men of the land —J.B.Conant⟩ **2** : the act or process of recruiting: as **a** : the recruiting of men for an army **b** : an act of offering inducement to qualified personnel to enter a particular job or profession ⟨a ~ of teachers which shall bring to the profession . . . men and women of right minds —K.I.Brown⟩ **3** : an increment to a natural population (as that resulting from increased survival over a period of time) **4** : the increase in intensity of a reflex when the initiating stimulus is prolonged without alteration of intensity due to the activation of increasing numbers of motoneurons — compare FACILITATION **5** : an abnormally rapid increase in the sensation of loudness with increasing sound intensity that occurs in deafness of neural origin and esp. in neural deafness of the aged in which soft sounds may be completely inaudible while louder sounds are distressingly loud

**re·crusher** \(ˈ)rē+\ *n* [*re-* + *crusher*] : a rock crusher for producing fine aggregate for concrete by crushing again material which has already been crushed

**re·crystallization** \(ˌ)rē+\ *n* [*recrystallize* + *-ation*] : the act or process of recrystallizing: as **a** : replacement of the distorted grain structure of a cold-worked metal by a new strain-free grain structure during annealing **b** : the regeneration of rock fabric producing coarser texture and eliminating impurities ⟨limestone transformed by ~ to marble⟩

**recrystallize** *vb* [*re-* + *crystallize*] *vt* : to crystallize again or repeatedly ~ *vi* : to become crystallized again

**rect** \ˈrekt\ *n* -s [L *rectus* straight, right — more at RIGHT] : an element analogous to a right line in a geometrical system

**rect** *abbr* **1** receipt **2** rectangle **3** rectified; rectifier **4** rector; rectory

¹**rect-** *or* **recti-** *comb form* [L *rectus* — more at RIGHT] : straight, right ⟨*recti*lineal⟩ ⟨*rect*angular⟩

²**rect-** *or* **recto-** *comb form* [NL *rectum*] **1** : rectum ⟨*recto*cele⟩ **2** : rectal and ⟨*recto*abdominal⟩

**recta** *pl of* RECTUM

**rec·tag·o·nal** \(ˈ)rekˈtagənᵊl, -taig-\ *adj* [irreg. fr. ¹*rect-* + *-gon* + *-al*] : RECTANGULAR

**rec·tal** \ˈrektᵊl\ *adj* [²*rect-* + *-al*] : of, relating to, affecting, or located near the rectum — **rec·tal·ly** \-tᵊlē, -li\ *adv*

**rectal valve** *n* : any of three or four crescentic folds projecting into the cavity of the rectum

**rec·tan·gle** \ˈrekˌtaŋgəl, -taiŋ-\ *n* [ML *rectangulus* having a right angle, fr. L *rectus* right + *angulus* angle — more at RIGHT, ANGLE] : a parallelogram all of whose angles are right angles — see AREA table

**rec·tan·gled** \-gəld\ *adj* [*rectangle* + *-ed*] : RECTANGULAR

**rec·tan·gu·lar** \(ˈ)rekˈtaŋgyələ(r), -taiŋ-\ *adj* [ML *rectangulus* having a right angle + E *-ar*] **1** : having a flat surface shaped like a rectangle **2** : forming a right angle : crossing, lying, or meeting at a right angle ⟨~ directions⟩ ⟨~ course⟩

rectangles

**rectangular coordinate** *n* : either of two Cartesian coordinates which have two or three dimensions and in which the axes are mutually at right angles

**rectangular drainage pattern** *n* : the drainage pattern of streams that make many right-angle bends

**rectangular hyperbola** *n* : EQUILATERAL HYPERBOLA

**rec·tan·gu·lar·i·ty** \(ˌ)rekˌtaŋgyəˈlarəd·ē, -taiŋ-, -lətē, -i *also* -ler-\ *n* -ES [*rectangular* + *-ity*] : the quality or state of being rectangular : rigidity of form

**rec·tan·gu·lar·ly** *adv* : in a rectangular manner

**rectangular parallelepiped** *n* : a parallelepiped whose dihedral angles are right angles

**rec·tan·gu·lom·e·ter** \ˌ==ˌ==ˈlämәd·ə(r)\ *n* [*rectangular* + *-o-* + *-meter*] : an instrument used for testing right angles

**recti** *pl of* RECTUS

**recti-** — see RECT-

**rec·ti·fi·able** \ˈrektəˌfīəbəl, ˌ==ˈ===\ *adj* : capable of being rectified ⟨a ~ curve⟩

**rec·ti·fi·ca·tion** \ˌ==fəˈkāshən\ *n* -s [LL *rectification-*, *rectificatio*, fr. *rectificatus* (past part. of *rectificare* to rectify) + *-ion-*, *-io* -ion] **1** : the act or process of making or setting right (as by correcting an error or amending a fault) ⟨mistakes needing ~⟩ ⟨interpreted this to mean the ~ of its own grievances —Harry Hansen⟩ **2** : the determination of a straight line equal in length to a portion of a curve : the determination of the length of a given curve or of a portion of it **3** : the conversion of alternating to direct current **4** : a new alignment to correct a deviation (as of a river channel or bank) **5** : a procedure for correcting the distortions in perspective caused by the tilt of a camera during exposure by printing the negative with a compensating tilt so that vertical and horizontal lines in the reproduction have the same appearance as in the original scene **6** : a process by which distilled spirits are blended together or substantially changed by the addition usu. of spirits, flavoring, or coloring material — **rectification of a globe** : the adjustment of a globe (as for latitude) preparatory to solution of a proposed problem

**rec·ti·fi·ca·tor** \ˈrektəfəˌkād·ə(r)\ *n* -s [LL *rectificatus* + E *-or*] : RECTIFIER

**rectified** *adj* [fr. past part. of *rectify*] : having unusual color markings : showing variegation caused by a virus — used of flowers esp. tulips

**rectified spirit** *n* : alcohol purified or concentrated by redistillation

**rec·ti·fi·er** \ˈrektəˌfī(ə)r, -īə\ *n* -s **1** : one that rectifies **2 a** : one who blends different whiskeys or who mixes whiskey with distilled water and alcohol to obtain a desired proof **b** : a part of a distilling apparatus in which the more volatile portions are separated by evaporation and condensation; *esp* : COLUMN 3d **3** : a device (as a vacuum tube) for converting alternating current into direct current **4** : a part of a gas refrigerating apparatus in which the water vapor is condensed from the ammonia vapor

**rectifier instrument** *n* : an instrument used for measuring alternating currents and consisting of a rectifier in conjunction with a direct-current meter whose reading gives the value of the rectified alternating current

**rec·ti·fy** \ˈrektəˌfī\ *vt* -ED/-ING/-S [ME *rectifien*, fr. MF *rectifier*, fr. ML *rectificare*, fr. L *rectus* straight, right + *-ificare* -ify — more at RIGHT] **1 a** : to make or set right (as a faulty position or state) : REMEDY ⟨a situation that can be *rectified* only by . . . evidence with which we can relate the past to the present —A.H.Shroeder⟩ **b** : to make good (as a mistake or omission) : AMEND ⟨and would do your best to ~ the mischief —George Meredith⟩ ⟨mistakes can be *rectified* by care and industry —Bertrand Russell⟩ **2 a** : to restore to a healthy state ⟨set about cutting down the contracted hoofs and ~*ing* the horny pad —Gerald Beaumont⟩ **b** : to restore to a condition previously considered desirable ⟨the increase would not ~ unbalanced world trade —*Time*⟩ **3 a** : to reform from erroneous or evil ways ⟨must ~ his life if he would be saved⟩ **b** *obs* : to free from mistaken ideas or errors ⟨a man has frequent opportunities of . . . ~*ing* the prejudiced —Joseph Addison⟩ **4** : to purify esp. by repeated or fractional distillation sometimes with the addition of flavoring substances **5** : to correct by removing errors or mistakes ⟨it is important to ~ the opinion —Curt Stern⟩ ⟨compile a better set of astronomical tables, ~ the calendar —H.J.J.Winter⟩ **6 a** : to set right by adjustment or calculation **b** : to determine the length of (an arc of a curve) **7** : to bring into line : STRAIGHTEN ⟨~*ing* the guttering after that gale in the spring —Adrian Bell⟩ **8** : to make (an alternating current) unidirectional **syn** see CORRECT

**rec·ti·grade** \-ˌgrād\ *adj* [¹*rect-* + *-grade*] : moving or proceeding in a straight line or course

**rec·ti·lineal** \ˈrektə+\ *adj* [LL *rectilineus* + E *-al*] : RECTILINEAR

**rec·ti·linear** \"+\ *adj* [LL *rectilineus* (fr. L *rectus* straight + *linea* line) + E *-ar* — more at RIGHT, LINE] **1** : moving in a straight line : having an undeviating direction : forming a straight line **2 a** : characterized by straight lines **b** : lying in a straight line : formed or bounded by straight lines **3** : PERPENDICULAR 5

**rectilinear coordinate** *n* : RECTANGULAR COORDINATE

**rectilinear lens** *n* : a lens specially corrected for distortion so that straight lines are reproduced accurately even on the margins of the pictures

**rectilinear motion** *n* : a linear motion in which the direction of the velocity remains constant and the path is a straight line

**rec·tion** \ˈrekshən\ *n* -s [L *rection-*, *rectio*, fr. *rectus* (past part. of *regere* to rule) + *-ion-*, *-io* -ion — more at RIGHT] : GOVERNMENT 5a

**rec·ti·pe·tal·i·ty** \ˌrektəpəˈtaləd·ē\ *n* -ES [¹*rect-* + *-petal* + *-ity*] : the tendency of growing plant organs to grow in a straight line

**rec·ti·rostral** \ˈrektə+\ *adj* [*rect-* + L *rostrum* beak + E *-al* — more at ROSTRUM] : having a straight beak

**rec·ti·tude** \ˈrektəˌtüd, -əˌtyüd\ *n* -s [ME, fr. MF, fr. LL *rectitudin-*, *rectitudo*, fr. L *rectus* straight, right + *-i-* + *-tudin-*, *-tudo* -tude — more at RIGHT] **1 a** : the quality or state of being straight : STRAIGHTNESS ⟨the young pines bent by the snow . . . regain their natural ~ —Van Wyck Brooks⟩ **b** : a straight line **2** : strict observance of standards of integrity and honesty : adherence to a high moral code : intrepid virtue : RIGHTEOUSNESS ⟨the absolute truth of his speech and the ~ of his behavior —R.W.Emerson⟩ **3** : correctness of judgment or procedure esp. in the field of intellectual or artistic activity ⟨was . . . convinced of the ~ of his musical ideas —Charles O'Connell⟩

**rec·ti·tu·di·nous** \ˌ==ˈtüdənəs, -ˈtyü-\ *adj* [LL *rectitudin-*, *rectitudo* rectitude + E *-ous*] : piously self-righteous — **rec·ti·tu·di·nous·ly** *adv*

¹**rec·to** \ˈrek(ˌ)tō\ *n* -s [ML (*breve de*) *recto*] : WRIT OF RIGHT

²**recto** \"\ *n* -s [NL *recto* (*folio*), the page being straight, i.e. unturned] **1** : the side of a leaf (as of a manuscript) that is to be read first — contrasted with *verso* **2** : a right-hand page (as of a book) usu. carrying an odd page number **3** : the front cover esp. the outside front cover of a book; *also* : the corresponding part of a book jacket

**recto-** — see RECT-

**rec·to·cele** \ˈrektəˌsēl\ *n* -s [ISV ²*rect-* + *-cele*] : a bulging of the rectum into the vagina

**rec·to·coccygeus** \ˈrektō+\ *n* [NL, fr. ²*rect-* + *coccyg-*, *coccyx* coccyx + L *-eus* -eous] : a band of smooth muscle extending from the coccyx to the posterior wall of the rectum and serving to retract and elevate the rectum

**rec·tor** \ˈrektə(r)\ *n* -s [L, fr. *rectus* (past part. of *regere* to rule, govern) + *-or*; in senses 3 & 4, fr. ML *rector* ecclesiastical director, parish priest, director of a university, fr. L, governor, ruler — more at RIGHT] **1** *obs* **a** : a governor or ruler usu. of a country **b** *cap* : God as ruler of the world **2** : one that directs : LEADER **3 a** : a clergyman of the Church of England who has the charge and care of a parish and owns the tithes from it : the clergyman of a parish where the tithes are not impropriate **b** : a clergyman of the Protestant Episcopal Church elected by the vestrymen who is the spiritual head and legally the presiding officer of a parish **c** *Roman Catholicism* : the head priest of a church or other religious institution **4** : the head of a university, school, or other teaching institution: as **a** : LORD RECTOR **b** : the master of a college at some English universities **c** : the head of one of the 17 departments into which the French educational system is divided **d** : the head of a German elementary or secondary school

**rec·tor·al** \-t(ə)rəl\ *adj* [*rector* + *-al*] : RECTORIAL; *specif* : of or relating to God as governor or ruler of men

**rec·tor·ate** \-t(ə)rət, *usu* -əd·+V\ *n* -s [ML *rectoratus*, fr. L *rector* + *-atus* -ate] : the office, rank, station, or term of a rector

**rec·tor·ess** \-rəs\ *n* -ES [*rector* + *-ess*] : the wife of a rector

**rec·to·ri·al** \(ˈ)rekˈtōrēəl, -tȯr-\ *adj* [*rector* + *-ial*] : of or relating to a rector, a rectory, or a rectorate

**rec·tor·ship** \ˈrektə(r)ˌship\ *n* [*rector* + *-ship*] **1** : the office of a governor or ruler **2** : the office of rector esp. of a university or of a parish

**rec·to·ry** \ˈrekt(ə)rē, -ri\ *n* -ES [MF or ML; MF *rectorie*, fr. ML *rectoria* office of a governor, fr. fem. of *rectorius* of a governor, fr. L *rector* governor, rector] **1 a** : a benefice held by a rector : the province of a rector : a parish church, parsonage, or spiritual living with all its rights, tithes, and glebes **b** : a rector's residence : PARSONAGE **2** *obs* : RECTORSHIP

**rec·to·scope** \ˈrektəˌskōp\ *n* [ISV *rect-* + *-scope*] : PROCTOSCOPE

**rec·to·sigmoid** \ˈrek(ˌ)tō+\ *n* [*rect-* + *sigmoid*] : the distal part of the sigmoid flexure and the proximal part of the rectum

**rec·to·sigmoidoscope** \"+\ *n* [*rectosigmoid* + *-o-* + *-scope*] : SIGMOIDOSCOPE — **rec·to·sigmoidoscopic** \"+\ *adj* — **rec·to·sigmoidoscopy** \"+\ *n* -ES

**rec·to·vesical fascia** \"+-\ *n* [*rect-* + L *vesica* bladder + E *-al* — more at VENTER] : a membrane derived from the pelvic fascia and investing the rectum, bladder, and adjacent parts

**rectress** *n* -ES [*rector* + *-ess*] *obs* : a woman that rules

**rec·trix** \ˈrektriks\ *n, pl* **rectri·ces** \rekˈtrī(ˌ)sēz\ [L, fem. of *rector* — more at RECTOR] **1** : RECTRESS **2** [NL, fr. L] : any of the quill feathers of the tail of a bird that are important in controlling the direction of flight — usu. used in pl.

**rects** *pl of* RECT

**rec·tum** \ˈrektəm\ *n, pl* **rectums** \-mz\ *or* **rec·ta** \-tə\ [NL, fr. *rectum intestinum*, lit., straight intestine] : the terminal part of the intestine being in man the part of the large intestine of somewhat variable length but usu. about eight inches from the sigmoid flexure to the anus

**rec·tus** \ˈrektəs\ *n, pl* **rec·ti** \-ˌtī\ [NL, fr. *rectus musculus*, lit., straight muscle] **1** : any of several straight muscles (as the rectus abdominis or the rectus femoris) **2** *or* **rectus ocu·li** \-ˈäkyəˌlī\ [NL, lit., rectus of the eye] : any of four muscles of the eyeball that arise from the borders of the optic foramen and running forward are inserted into the sclerotic coat of the eyeball and that are distinguished according to position as the superior, inferior, lateral (or external), and medial (or internal) recti

**rectus ab·do·mi·nis** \-abˈdämənəs\ *n* [NL, lit., rectus of the abdomen] : a long flat muscle on either side of the linea alba extending along the whole length of the front of the abdomen, arising from the pubic crest and symphysis, and being inserted into the cartilages of the fifth, sixth, and seventh ribs

**rectus fe·mo·ris** \-femərəs\ *n* [NL, lit., rectus of the thigh] : a division of the quadriceps muscle lying in the anterior middle region of the thigh, arising from the ilium by two heads, and inserted into the tuberosity of the tibia by a narrow flattened tendon

**rectus in cu·ria** \-inˈkyu̇rēə\ *adj (or adv)* [NL] : upright in the court : free from charge or impeachment : competent to participate in litigation and entitled to the benefit of law — see LEGALIS HOMO

**re·cuay** \rāˈkwī\ *adj, usu cap* [fr. *Recuay*, town in northern Peru] : of or belonging to a cultural period in northern Peru characterized by houses of two or three stories below ground, stone carving of felines in high relief and seated figures in the round, and pottery in a great variety of shapes

**recule** *obs var of* RECOIL

**re·cumb** \rəˈkəm\ *vi* -ED/-ING/-S [L *recumbere* — more at RECUMBENT] : LEAN, RECLINE

**re·cum·bence** \rəˈkəmbən(t)s, rēˈ-\ *n* -S [fr. L *recumbent-, recumbens* recumbent, after such pairs as L *excellent-, excellens* excellent: E *excellence*] : RECUMBENCY

**re·cum·ben·cy** \-nsē, -si\ *n* -ES [L *recumbent-, recumbens* + E *-cy*] **1** : the state of leaning, resting, or reclining : a recumbent position : REPOSE **2** : a reliance or dependence upon something

[1]**re·cum·bent** \-nt\ *n* -S [L *recumbent-, recumbens*, pres. part. of *recumbere*] : one that is recumbent

[2]**recumbent** \ˈ"\ *adj* [L *recumbent-, recumbens*, pres. part. of *recumbere* to lie back, lie down, recline, fr. *re-* + *-cumbere* to lie down (akin to L *cubare* to lie down) — more at HIP] **1 a** : suggestive of repose : LEANING, RESTING ⟨comfortably ~ against a fallen tree⟩ **b** : having a horizontal position : lying down ⟨the horse who was now ~ with one of my legs under him —Siegfried Sassoon⟩ ⟨the pulse may be as rapid in the ~ as in the standing posture —F.A.Faught⟩ **c** : representing a person lying down **2** *biol* : of or relating to structures which tend to rest upon the surface from which they extend **syn** see PRONE

**recumbent anticline** *n* : an overturned anticline having its axial plane more nearly horizontal than vertical

**re·cum·ben·ti·bus** \ˌrekəmˈbentəbəs\ *n* -ES [ME, fr. L *recumbent-, recumbens* + *-ibus*, dat. or abl. pl. ending] : a knockdown blow ⟨the advantage of inflicting upon an assailant a ~ —J.R.Newman⟩

**re·cu·per·a·bil·i·ty** \rəˌk(y)üp(ə)rəˈbiləd·ē\ *n* [L *recuperare* + E *-ability*] : the power of recuperation

**re·cu·per·ate** \rəˈk(y)üpəˌrāt, rēˈ-, *usu* -ād·+V\ *vb* -ED/-ING/-S [L *recuperatus*, past part. of *recuperare* to recover — more at RECOVER] *vt* : to get back : RECOVER, REGAIN ⟨*recuperating* health and strength after pneumonia⟩ ~ *vi* **1** : to recover health or strength : CONVALESCE ⟨the animals . . . would not ~ until they got water —Willa Cather⟩ **2** : to recover from pecuniary loss

**re·cu·per·a·tion** \=,=pəˈrāshən\ *n* -S [L *recuperation-, recuperatio*, fr. *recuperatus* + *-ion-, -io* -ion] **1** : recovery esp. of something lost; *specif* : restoration to health or strength **2** *biol* : reappearance of the property of competence at a late stage of development (as in blastema formation) **3** : the heating of incoming gases in a furnace by passing them through flues adjacent to the exhaust flues ⟨in ~ some of the heat from the flue gases is transferred to the air supply⟩

**re·cu·per·a·tive** \rəˈk(y)üpə,rād·|iv, -p(ə)rəl, |t|, |ēv *also* |əv\ *adj* [LL *recuperativus* recoverable, fr. *recuperatus* + L *-ivus* -ive] **1** : of or relating to recuperation : tending to recovery : RESTORATIVE : having the power of recuperating ⟨~ powers⟩ ⟨strongly ~ remedies⟩ **2** : having a recuperator ⟨a ~ furnace⟩ — **re·cu·per·a·tive·ness** *n* -ES

**re·cu·per·a·tor** \-ˌrād·ə(r)\ *n* -S *see sense 2* [L, lit., recoverer, fr. *recuperatus* + *-or*] **1** : one that recuperates **2** *also pl* **recuperato·res** \=,=pərəˈtōr(ˌ)ēz\ : a judge in ancient Rome orig. appointed to hear cases involving foreigners **3** REGENERATOR 4 **4** : a device for returning a gun into the firing position after recoil

**re·cu·per·a·to·ry** \rəˈk(y)üp(ə)rəˌtōrē, rēˈ-, -tȯr-, -ri\ *adj* [L *recuperatorius*, fr. *recuperatus* + *-orius* -ory] : of or relating to recuperation or to a recuperator

**re·cur** \R rəˈkər, rēˈ-, + V -kər-; -R -kə̄, + *suffixal vowel* -kər- *also* -kər, + *vowel in a word following without pause* -kər- *or* -kə̄ *also* -kər\ *vi* **recurred**; **recurred**; **recurring**; **recurs** [ME *recurren*, fr. L *recurrere* to run back, return, fr. *re-* + *currere* to run — more at CURRENT] **1** : to return to a place or status ⟨may elect to ~ to his nationality of parentage —W.E.Hall⟩ **2** : to have recourse : go for help : RESORT ⟨the dire necessity of *recurring* to arms in the face of . . . stubborn and stupid refusal to govern otherwise —Salvador de Madariaga⟩ **3** : to go back in thought or discourse ⟨in his conversations here he *recurred* to the plan he had outlined —C.G.Bowers⟩ **4** : to come up again for consideration : confront one again ⟨a problem which has *recurred* to this day —G.G.Weigend⟩ ⟨knew the difficulties would only ~⟩ **5** : to come again to mind : return vividly to the memory ⟨he had forgotten it . . . but it *recurred* to him now —Archibald Marshall⟩ **6** : to happen, take place, or appear again : occur again usu. after a stated interval or according to some regular rule ⟨would the occasion ever ~ —Van Wyck Brooks⟩ ⟨by the light of each *recurring* full moon —G.W.Johnson⟩ **7** : to repeat itself usu. indefinitely in fixed periods of figures (as of a decimal)

**recure** *vt* [ME *recuren*, fr. L *recurare*, fr. *re-* + *curare* to take care of, heal — more at CURE] **1 a** *obs* : to restore to health : CURE **b** *obs* : to bring back to a better state or condition **2 a** *obs* : to make whole : HEAL ⟨thy death's wound which he who comes thy Savior shall ~ —John Milton⟩ **b** *obs* : to provide a remedy for : REPAIR **3** [ME *recuren*, alter. (influenced by *recuren* to restore to health) of *recouren*, contr. of *recoveren* to recover] *obs* : to get back : RECOVER

**re·cur·rence** \rəˈkər·ən(t)s, rēˈ- *also* -kərə-\ *n* -S [*recur* + *-ence*] **1** : a periodic or frequent returning : REAPPEARANCE ⟨~s of faith and resignation and simple joy —James Joyce⟩ **2** : RECOURSE, RESORT ⟨the treaty should eliminate further ~ to armed action⟩ **3** : the act or fact of recurring : the state of being recurrent ⟨the main ~s of life are too insistent to escape . . . notice —A.N.Whitehead⟩ **4** *bot* : repetition of the same type **5 a** : return of symptoms of a disease after a remission **b** : reappearance of a tumor after previous removal

**recurrence formula** *n* : a formula expressing any term of a sequence or series after a stated term as a function of preceding terms

**re·cur·rent** \-nt\ *adj* [L *recurrent-, recurrens*, pres. part. of *recurrere* to run back, recur — more at RECUR] **1 a** : running or turning back in a direction opposite to its former course — used of various nerves and branches of vessels in the arms and legs ⟨the radial ~ artery⟩ ⟨the ~ laryngeal nerve⟩ **b** *of a veinlet* : returning toward the main rib **2** : returning from time to time : appearing or coming periodically : happening again and again ⟨food is the urgent and ~ need of individuals and of society —Ellen Semple⟩ ⟨investigate the ~ . . . strike situation —*Current Biog.*⟩ ⟨an endlessly ~ set of problems —I.A.Richards⟩ **3** : reappearing at other than the first geologic horizon ⟨a ~ fauna⟩

**recurrent fever** *n* : RELAPSING FEVER

**re·cur·rent·ly** *adv* : in a recurrent manner ⟨the problem has been around ~ for a long time —*Time*⟩

**recurrent nova** *n* : a variable star that at intervals usu. of several decades undergoes outbursts similar to that of a nova and declines in brightness

**recurring** *adj* [fr. pres. part. of *recur*] : coming or happening again ⟨a ~ need for solitude and silence —Havelock Ellis⟩ — **re·cur·ring·ly** *adv*

**recurring decimal** *n* : a repeating decimal

**re·cur·sion** \rəˈkər|zhən, rēˈ-, -kə̄|, -kəi|, *chiefly Brit* |shən\ *n* -S [LL *recursion-, recursio*, fr. *recursus* (past part. of *recurrere* to run back, return) + *-ion-, -io* -ion — more at RECUR] : RETURN

**re·cur·sive definition** \rəˈkər|s|iv, rē-, (ˈ)rē|ˈk-, -kə̄|, -kəi|, |z|, |ēv *also* |əv-\ *n* [[2]*recursion* + *-ive*] : a definition of a function permitting values of the function to be calculated systematically in a finite number of steps; *esp* : a mathematical definition in which the first case is given and the nth case is defined in terms of one or more previous cases and esp. the immediately preceding one ⟨a ~ of the factorial is given by 0! = 1 and (n + 1)! = (n + 1) · n!⟩

[1]**re·cur·vate** \rəˈkərˌvāt, ˈrēkər,-\ *vb* -ED/-ING/-S [L *recurvatus*, past part. of *recurvare*, fr. *re-* + *curvare* to curve — more at CURVE] *vt* : to cause to bend backwards ~ *vi* : to curve back — **re·curvation** \ˌrē+\ *n*

[2]**re·cur·vate** \rəˈkərˌvāt, (ˈ)rē|kərvət\ *adj* [L *recurvatus*] : RECURVED

**re·curved** \(ˈ)rē+\ *adj* [*re-* + *curved*] : curved backward or inward — compare DECURVED

**re·cur·vi·ros·tra** \rəˌkərvəˈrästrə\ *n, cap* [NL, fr. L *recurvus* curved back (fr. *re-* + *curvus* curved) + *-i-* + *rostrum* beak — more at CROWN, ROSTRUM] : a genus (the type of the family Recurvirostridae) of birds consisting of the avocets

**re·cur·vi·ros·tral** \=¦==+\ *adj* [L *recurvus* + *-i-* + *rostrum* + E *-al*] : having the beak bent upward

**recu·sance** \ˈrekyəzən(t)s, rəˈkyüzᵊn(t)s\ *n* -S [fr. *recusant*, after such pairs as E *assistant: assistance*] : RECUSANCY

**recu·san·cy** \-nsē, -si\ *n* -ES [*recusant* + *-cy*] **1** : the quality or state of being recusant : refusal to accept or obey constituted authority : NONCONFORMITY ⟨for there is in her . . . a ~, a stubborn antipathy to the disciplining —R.B.Heilman⟩ **2** : the refusal esp. of Roman Catholics to attend the services of the Church of England constituting a statutory offense punishable by fines and disabilities until the late 18th century

[1]**recu·sant** \-nt\ *n* -S [L *recusant-, recusans*, pres. part. of *recusare* to object to, refuse, fr. *re-* + *-cusare* (fr. *causari* to give a reason, plead, fr. *causa* cause, reason) — more at CAUSE] **1 a** : a person (as a Roman Catholic) refusing to attend the services of the Church of England **b** : one that dissents : NONCONFORMIST ⟨a secular ~ who favored what he called the liberal divinities of Greece —R.L.Cook⟩ **2** : one who refuses to comply with some regulation or to conform to some general practice or opinion

[2]**recusant** \ˈ"\ *adj* [L *recusant-, recusans* refusing] **1** : refusing to attend the services of the Church of England **2** : refusing to submit to authority : DISSENTIENT ⟨the ~ electors returned . . . and cooperated in electing a new Senate —Mary W. Williams⟩

**re·cu·sa·tion** \ˌrekyəˈzāshən\ *n* -S [MF or L; MF *recusation*, fr. L *recusation-, recusatio* refusal, fr. *recusatus* (past part. of *recusare* to refuse) + *-ion-, -io* -ion] *civil & canon law* : REFUSAL, OBJECTION, EXCEPTION; *esp* : a plea challenging a judge for alleged interest, partiality, or other incompetency

**re·cu·sa·tor** \rəˈkyüzəd·ə(r)\ *n* -S [L *recusatus* + E *-or*] *Scots law* : a recusation to a judge

**re·cuse** \rəˈkyüz\ *vt* -ED/-ING/-S [ME *recusen*, fr. MF *recuser*, fr. L *recusare* to refuse — more at RECUSANT] *civil and canon law* : REFUSE, REJECT: as **a** : to challenge or except to (a judge) as interested or otherwise incompetent **b** : to disqualify (oneself) as judge in a particular case

**re·cut** \(ˈ)rē+\ *vt* [*re-* + *cut* (v)] : to cut again

[1]**re·cycle** \(ˈ)rē+\ *vt* [*re-* + *cycle*] : to pass again through a cycle of changes or treatment ⟨an industrial plant . . . ~s cooling water through cooling towers as many as 50 times —J.R. Whitaker & E.A.Ackerman⟩; *esp* : to feed back continuously in a laboratory or industrial operation or process for further treatment

[2]**recycle** \ˈ"\ *n* : a fraction of a product that is recycled

[1]**red** \ˈred\ *adj* **redder**; **reddest** [ME *read, reed, red*, fr. OE *rēad*; akin to OE *rēod* red, OHG *rōt*, ON *rauthr* & *rjōthr*, Goth *rauths*, L *ruber* & *rufus*, Gk *erythros* red, Skt *rohita* red, reddish, *rudhira* red, bloody] **1 a** : of the color red ⟨~ rose⟩ ⟨as ~ as a ruby⟩ **b** : lit by or as if by fire ⟨no matter how scarlet the sunset, those ~ hills never became vermilion —Willa Cather⟩ **2 a** (1) : dyed with red ⟨the ~ hat of a cardinal⟩ (2) : producing a red color ⟨logwood used for ~ dyes⟩ **b** : having red as a distinguishing color ⟨captain of the ~ team⟩ **3 a** (1) : flushed esp. with anger or embarrassment ⟨plain from his ~ face that the insult had struck home⟩ ⟨turned uncomfortably ~ when called upon to speak⟩ (2) : RUDDY, FLORID ⟨the large ~ health that uncivilized women admire —Walter Bagehot⟩ (3) : of a coppery hue ⟨~ skin of the American Indian⟩ **b** *of the eyes* (1) : naturally red (2) : reddened by inflammation : BLOODSHOT ⟨eyes ~ from weeping⟩ **c** *of hair or the coat of an animal* : being somewhere in the color range between carrot red and russet or bay ⟨a flaming thatch of ~ hair⟩ ⟨~ setter⟩ ⟨~ roan⟩ **d** : tinged with red : REDDISH ⟨flat sandy country . . . the ~ heart of Australia —Myrtle R. White⟩ **4 a** : stained or covered with blood ⟨waving our ~ weapons o'er our heads —Shak.⟩ **b** : full of or colored with blood ⟨good ~ beef⟩ **5** : heated to redness : GLOWING ⟨~ slag from a blast furnace⟩ ⟨~ lava flowing from a volcano⟩ **6 a** : characterized by wrath or violence : CHOLERIC, BLOODY ⟨convulsed with ~ rage —Hudson Strode⟩ ⟨the ~ rules of tooth and claw —P.B.Sears⟩ **b** : of an extreme or profligate nature : FLAGRANT, WANTON ⟨the ~ waste of his youth —Thomas Wolfe⟩ ⟨is she really so . . . ~ as she is painted —W.J.Locke⟩ **7** [fr. the flag used by revolutionaries] **a** : inciting or endorsing sweeping social or political reform esp. by the use of force : REVOLUTIONARY, RADICAL — compare WHITE 8 **b** *often cap* : COMMUNIST ⟨fighting ~ guerrillas in the Malayan forests —J.M.Flagler⟩ **c** *often cap* : of or relating to the U.S.S.R. or its allies or satellites : lying within or emanating from the Soviet orbit ⟨each *Red* worker must be politically educated . . . in Marxist-Leninist terms —O.O.Trullinger⟩ ⟨building up the German ~ army —R.E.M.Morris⟩ ⟨Kremlin is pouring a torrent of ~ books and newspapers into India —F.C.Laubach⟩ **8** [so called fr. the bookkeeping practice of entering debit items in red ink] : failing to show a profit ⟨haven't had a ~ month in the past year —R.J.Schrick⟩

[2]**red** \ˈ"\ *n* -S [ME *read, reed, red*, fr. *read, reed, red*, adj.] **1 a** : a color whose hue resembles that of blood or of the ruby or is that of the long-wave extreme of the visible spectrum **b** : the one of the four psychologically primary hues that is evoked in the normal observer under normal conditions by radiant energy from the long-wave extreme of the visible spectrum combined with a very small amount of radiant energy from the shortwave extreme **c** : one of the six psychologically primary object colors **2 a** : red clothing or cloth ⟨lady in ~⟩ **b** : one that uses red as a distinguishing color; *specif* : a member of an athletic team having red insignia ⟨Cincinnati *Reds*⟩ **3 a** : one that is of a red or reddish color: as (1) : RED WINE ⟨killed another bottle of California ~ —A.R.Foff⟩ (2) : RED CENT ⟨not another cent to waste, not another . . . ~ —P.E. Green⟩ (3) : the red ball in billiards (4) : an animal with a reddish coat ⟨pressed his pony, a small, nervous ~ —W.V.T. Clark⟩ **b** : an American Indian : REDSKIN ⟨risking himself on a wearied horse in a country alive with ~s —S.H.Adams⟩ **4 a** : a pigment or dye that colors red ⟨~ can be made from the cochineal insect —Helen Coates⟩; *specif* : ROUGE ⟨plenty of powder, and a little ~ too —Willa Cather⟩ **b** : a shade or tint of red ⟨the ~s in the petrified woods of Arizona —*Buick Mag.*⟩ **c** : an incandescent glow ⟨the ~ of his cigar like a small, fiery flower between his fingers —Josephine Johnson⟩ **d reds** *pl* : insoluble red substances yielded by vegetable tanning materials (as phlobaphenes) and deposited on the surface of the leather **5 a** : one who advocates or is thought to advocate or endorse the violent overthrow of an existing social or political order : SUBVERSIVE, REVOLUTIONARY ⟨leftists called themselves liberals, and their opponents called them ~s —Upton Sinclair⟩ ⟨rank-and-file German Social Democrats, whom they classify as ~s —*Atlantic*⟩ — compare [10]PINK 3, RED REPUBLICAN **b** *usu cap* : COMMUNIST ⟨in Kremlin protocol he now takes precedence . . . over all European satellite *Reds* —E.P. Snow⟩ ⟨*Reds* reject . . . all hope of real reforms without a revolution —Jacob Spolansky⟩ **c** : COMMUNISM, RADICALISM ⟨lesser forms of internationalism . . . have a distinctly lighter tinge of ~ —*New Freeman*⟩ **6 a** : the red circle of an archery target that is next to the gold **b** : a shot that hits such a circle **7** [so called fr. the bookkeeping practice of entering debit items in red ink] : the condition of showing a loss — usu. used with *the* ⟨a moneymaking scheme for getting the organization out of the ~⟩; opposed to *black* **8** : RED ALERT

[3]**red** \ˈ"\ *vb* **redded**; **redded**; **redding**; **reds** [ME *readen*, fr. *read, reed, red*, adj.] *chiefly dial* : REDDEN

**red** *abbr* **1** redactor **2** reduce; reduced; reducer; reducing **3** reduction

**re·dact** \rəˈdakt, rēˈ-\ *vt* -ED/-ING/-S [L *redactus*, past part. of *redigere* to drive, lead, or bring back, get together, collect, arrange, reduce, fr. *red-* re- + *-igere* (fr. *agere* to drive, lead, act, do) — more at AGENT] **1** *obs* : to lower in condition or quality : REDUCE ⟨being a little prodigal in his spending, ~*ed* his estate to a weak point —Robert Monro⟩ **2** [back-formation fr. *redaction*] **a** : to put in writing : make a draft of : COMPOSE, FRAME ⟨council of ministers . . . engaged in ~*ing* the two proclamations —W.G.Clark⟩ **b** : to select or adapt for publication : EDIT, REVISE ⟨historical accounts ~*ed* for the modern reader⟩

**re·dac·tion** \-kshən\ *n* -S [F *rédaction*, fr. LL *redaction-, redactio* action of bringing back, gathering together, reduction, fr. L *redactus* + *-ion-, -io* -ion] **1 a** : an act or instance of preparing for publication : EXPOSITION, REVISION ⟨deciding that your search for material is completed, you turn to its ~ —André Morize⟩ **b** : an act or instance of putting into a different written form : ADAPTATION, TRANSLATION ⟨a novel which seems as though it were the ~ of a play —W.T.Scott⟩ ⟨English ~s of earlier French romances⟩ **2** : a work that has been redacted : EDITION, VERSION ⟨it may be expedient to edit the various ~s separately —L.P.G.Peckham⟩ — **re·dac·tion·al** \-nᵊl\ *adj*

**re·dac·tor** \-ktə(r)\ *n* -S [G & F; G *redakteur*, fr. F *rédacteur*, fr. L *redactus* + F *-eur* -or] : one that redacts; *esp* : EDITOR

**red admiral** *n* : a showy butterfly (*Vanessa atalanta*) common in both Europe and America having the front wings crossed by a broad orange-red band and larvae that feed on nettles — compare WHITE ADMIRAL

**red alder** *n* **1** : an alder (*Alnus rubra*) of the Pacific coast of No. America **2** : the hard red wood of the red alder tree much used for furniture

**red-alder family** *n* : CUNONIACEAE

**red alert** *n* : the final stage of alert in which attack by enemy aircraft appears to be imminent; *also* : the signal for this ⟨at the sound of the *red alert* pedestrians must take shelter⟩ — compare BLUE ALERT, WHITE ALERT, YELLOW ALERT

**red alga** *n* : an alga (division Rhodophyta) having predominantly red pigmentation

**red alpine campion** *n* : ALPINE CAMPION

**red amaranth** *n* **1** : THORNY AMARANTH **2** : PRINCE'S-FEATHER 1

**re·dan** \rəˈdan\ *n* -S [F, alter. of *redent*, fr. *re-* + *dent* tooth, fr. L *dent-, dens* — more at TOOTH] : a fortification having two parapets forming a salient angle, an unfortified entrance usu. protected by its location (as on the bank of a stream, at the head of a bridge, or in advance of a strong line), and often a connection (as by curtains) with other such fortifications as a simple form of fieldwork

**red ant** *n* : any of various reddish ants: as **a** : PHARAOH ANT **b** : the sanguinary ant or any of several rather large closely related ants of Europe and America that make hills in open ground

**red antimony** *n* : KERMESITE

**red ape** *n* : ORANGUTAN

**red archangel** *n* : a Eurasian annual weedy herb (*Lamium purpureum*) naturalized in No. America and having purplish red flowers in axillary clusters — called also *red dead nettle*

**re·dar·gue** \rəˈdärˌgyü\ *vt* -ED/-ING/-S [ME *redarguen*, fr. L *redarguere*, fr. *red-* re- + *arguere* to accuse, assert, make clear — more at ARGENT] *archaic* : to confute by argument : DISPROVE

**red·ar·gu·tion** \ˌredärˈgyüshən\ *n* -S [MF, fr. LL *redargution-, redargutio*, fr. L *redargutus* (past part. of *redarguere*) + *-ion-, -io* -ion] *archaic* : REFUTATION

**red arsenic** *n* : REALGAR

**red arsenic glass** *n* : ARSENIC DISULFIDE

**red ash** *n* **1 a** : an American ash (*Fraxinus pennsylvanica*) with densely velvety tomentose branchlets and petioles and lower leaf surfaces pubescent — called also *downy ash*; see GREEN ASH **b** : an Australian tree (*Alphitonia excelsa*) of the family Rhamnaceae with hard wood **c** : an Australian tree (*Orites excelsa*) of the family Proteaceae **2** : the wood of a red ash tree

**redback** \ˈ=,=\ *n* **1** : a non-interest-bearing treasury note issued in 1838 by the Republic of Texas **2** : RED-BACKED SANDPIPER

**red-backed cutworm** \ˈ=,=-\ *n* : a cutworm that is the larva of a noctuid moth (*Euxoa ochrogaster*), that is a serious pest on wheat, barley, rye, sugar beets and other plants in Canada and northern U. S., and that feeds both above and below ground

**red-backed lemming** *n* : GRAY LEMMING

**red-backed mouse** *n* : any of many small short-tailed voles of the genus *Clethrionomys* of northern and mountainous parts of Europe, Asia, and America

**red-backed parrot** *n* : a small long-tailed green parrot (*Psephotus haematonotus*) of New So. Wales, Victoria, and So. Australia having a red patch on the lower portion of the back — called also *grassie*; compare GRASS PARROT

**red-backed saki** *n* : an active untamable rufous-tinged So. American monkey (*Pithecia chiropotes*) — compare SAKI

**red-backed salamander** *n* : a common salamander (*Plethodon cinereus*) of eastern No. America; *also* : a related salamander (*P. vehiculum*) of the Pacific coast

**red-backed sandpiper** *n* : a widely distributed rather small sandpiper (*Erolia alpina*) that is typically cinnamon to rusty brown above, often variously streaked or marked with black (as on the abdomen), and largely white below, has a long and downcurved bill, breeds in northern or arctic regions, and winters chiefly in the southern U.S. and around the Mediterranean — called also *dunlin*

**red-backed shrike** *n* : a European shrike (*Lanius collurio*)

**redback spider** *n* : a theridiid spider (*Latrodectus hasselti*) that is closely related to the American black widow and prob. identical with the katipo, has a venom which produces neurotoxic symptoms in man, and occurs in Australia, New Zealand, and the major islands of the East Indies — called also *red-streaked spider*

**red bag** *n* : prolapse and eversion of the vagina esp. in a ewe

**red-bait** \ˈred,bāt\ *vb, often cap R* [back-formation fr. *red-baiter* & *red-baiting*, n.] *vi* : to engage in red-baiting ⟨indignantly pointed out that he had never *Red-baited* in his life —W.E.Shelton⟩ ~ *vt* : to subject to red-baiting ⟨you will be *red-baited* almost beyond endurance —Henry Wallace⟩

**red-baiter** \ˈ=,==\ *n, often cap R* [[2]*red* + *baiter*] : one that red-baits ⟨do not intend to let the smear tactics of professional *red-baiters* produce in me a silly timidity in saying what I think to be the truth —*Nation's Schools*⟩

**red-baiting** \ˈ=,==\ *n, often cap R* [[2]*red* + *baiting*] : the act of baiting or harassing as a red often in a malicious or irresponsible manner ⟨the increase of *red-baiting* within the country in order to stifle even liberal dissent —Joseph Barnes⟩

[1]**red ball** *adj* [so called fr. the red mark painted on freight cars requiring expeditious movement] : having top priority : URGENT — used of freight or a carrier moving top priority freight ⟨*red ball* train⟩ ⟨*red ball* express⟩

[2]**red ball** *n* : HOTSHOT 1a

**red-banded leaf roller** \ˈ=,==-\ *n* : a leaf roller that is the larva of a small grayish brown moth (*Argyrotaenia velutinana*) and that has become a serious orchard pest in the northeastern U.S.

**red–banded thrips** *n* **:** a chiefly tropical thrips (*Selenothrips rubrocinctus*) that is extremely destructive to cacao and in Florida is sometimes a pest of avocado and mango — called also *cacao thrips*

**red baneberry** *n* **:** a No. American perennial herb (*Actaea rubra*) with ternately compound leaves, small white flowers in terminal racemes, and bright red oval berries — called also *redberry*

**red bark** *n* **:** a reddish bark obtained from a cinchona tree (*Cinchona succirubra*) and its hybrids containing quinine and used esp. in the manufacture of a bitter tonic — compare CINCHONA 3

**red bartsia** *n* **:** a European annual herb (*Odontites serotina*) of the family Scrophulariaceae that is naturalized in northeastern No. America, and that has oblong-lanceolate remotely serrate leaves and rose-red flowers in elongated spikes

**red bass** *n* **1 :** CHANNEL BASS **2** *Austral* **:** any of several snappers (family Lutjanidae); *esp* **:** a common food fish (*Lutjanus coatesi*) of tropical coral reefs and kelp beds

**red bat** *n* **:** a No. American bat (*Lasiurus borealis*) varying in color from rusty red to reddish gray and having the interfemoral membrane densely hairy

**red bay** *n* **:** a small tree (*Persea borbonia*) of the southern U. S. having dark red heartwood

**red bean** *n* **:** an Australian tree (*Dysoxylum muelleri*) of the family Meliaceae whose timber resembles rosewood — called also *pencil cedar*

**red bear** *n* **:** a heavily furred often reddish bear (*Ursus arctos isabellinus*) of the Himalayan mountains

**red bearberry** *n* **:** BEARBERRY 1

**red beds** *n pl* **:** sedimentary strata predominantly red in color and composed largely of sandstone and shale

**red beech** *n* **1 :** AMERICAN BEECH **2 :** an Australian timber tree (*Tarrietia trifoliolata*) of the family Sterculiaceae **3 :** RED BIRCH 3

**red bell** *n* **:** a columbine (*Aquilegia canadensis*)

**red–bellied snake** \ˈ=,==-\ *n* **1 :** any of several American colubrid snakes with coral or reddish ventral surfaces: as **a :** WESTERN RING-NECKED SNAKE **b :** a woodland snake (*Storeria occipitomaculata*) of the Mississippi valley and southeast to Florida **2 :** an Australian elapid snake (*Pseudelaps squamulosus*) that is brown or blackish above and salmon-red below and is venomous but not dangerous to man

**red–bellied snipe** *n* **:** DOWITCHER

**red–bellied squirrel** *n* **:** any of numerous arboreal squirrels (genus *Callosciurus*) of southeastern Asia; *esp* **:** a squirrel (*C. erythraeus*) having reddish underparts and a greenish gray or reddish back more or less marked with black

**red–bellied terrapin** *or* **red–bellied turtle** *n* **:** a terrapin (*Pseudemys rubriventris*) of the tributaries of Chesapeake Bay having more or less red on the plastron and carapace and reaching a length of about 18 inches — called also *redbelly, red fender*

**red–bellied woodpecker** *n* **:** a woodpecker (*Melanerpes carolinus* or *Centurus carolinus*) of the eastern U. S. having a scarlet head and nape, barred black-and-white back, and grayish underparts tinged with red

**redbelly** \ˈ=,==\ *n* **1 a :** a pumpkinseed (*Lepomis gibbosus*) **b :** a European char (*Salvelinus salvelinus*) **c :** RED GROUPER **2 :** RED-BELLIED TERRAPIN

**redbelly dace** *or* **red–bellied dace** *n* **:** either of two small No. American cyprinid fishes (*Chrosomus eos* and *C. erythrogaster*) that are widely but irregularly distributed from the Hudson Bay drainage to New Brunswick and southward and westward to New Mexico, are dusky greenish black above with a creamy or pale yellow stripe along each side bounded by narrower black stripes, the belly deep red and the fins golden more-or-less marked with black and red, and esteemed in Europe as aquarium fishes

**red benjamin** *n* **:** a birthroot (*Trillium erectum*)

**red–berried elder** \ˈ=,==-\ *n* **:** a common No. American shrub (*Sambucus pubens*) with pointed cymes of small whitish flowers and bright scarlet fruit

**red·berry** \ˈred- — *see* BERRY\ *n* **1 :** any of several Australian shrubs of the genus *Rhagodia* having red berries **2 a :** RED BANEBERRY **b :** a ginseng (*Panax quinquefolium*) of No. America **c :** a spiny evergreen California shrub (*Rhamnus crocea*) with minute flowers and bright red berries

**redberry disease** *n* **:** a disease of blackberries caused by a gall mite (*Aceria essigi* or *Eriophyes essigi*) that feeds on the young fruit and causes it to become hard and bright red

**red betty** *n* [*betty* fr. the name *Betty*] **:** CARDINAL FLOWER

**redbill** \ˈ=,=\ *n* **1 :** an oyster catcher (*Haematopus unicolor*) of New Zealand **2 :** the common black-and-white long-tailed whydah (*Vidua macroura*) of Africa **3 :** an African waxbill (*Estrilda astrild*)

**red–billed mud hen** \ˈ=,=-\ *n* **:** FLORIDA GALLINULE

**red–billed pigeon** *n* **:** a large pigeon (*Columba flavirostris*) that occurs from extreme southern Texas southward into Nicaragua, is highly esteemed as a game bird, has much reddish purple on head, breast, and lesser wing coverts, grayish brown greater coverts and remiges, and the rest of the body bluish gray, and is distinguished by a reddish bill tipped with bright yellow — called also *blue rock*

**red–billed teal** *n* **:** a southern African duck (*Anas erythrorhyncha*)

**red–billed tropic bird** *n* **:** a tropic bird (*Phaëton aethereus*)

**red birch** *n* **1 :** RIVER BIRCH 1 **2 :** the heartwood lumber of the yellow birch (*Betula lutea*) and of the sweet birch (*Betula lenta*) **3 a :** a valuable New Zealand timber tree (*Nothofagus fusca*) — called also *clinker beech, red beech* **b :** the hard wood of this tree

**redbird** \ˈ=,=\ *n* **1 :** CARDINAL **2 a :** SUMMER TANAGER **b :** SCARLET TANAGER **3 :** the European bullfinch

**redbird cactus** *or* **redbird flower** *n* **:** a jewbush (*Pedilanthus tithymaloides*)

**red bird of paradise :** a bird of paradise (*Uranornis rubra*) with red lateral plumes in the male

**red–bird's–eye** *n* **1 :** HERB ROBERT **2 :** RED CAMPION

**red–blind** \ˈ=,=\ *adj* **:** affected with red blindness

**red blindness** *n* **:** color blindness in which red is not perceived as such **:** PROTANOPIA

**red blood cell** *or* **red blood corpuscle** *n* **:** one of the cells responsible for the red color of vertebrate blood **:** ERYTHROCYTE

**red–blooded** \ˈ=ˈ==\ *adj* **:** full of spirit and vigor **:** LUSTY, ENERGETIC ⟨a *red-blooded* American⟩ ⟨a *red-blooded* adventure story⟩

**red blotch** *n* **:** ADUSTIOSIS

**red board** *n* **:** a railroad stop signal — called also *red eye*

**red body** *n* **:** a mass of capillaries on the inner wall of the air bladder of various teleost fishes thought to control the diffusion and absorption of the gases contained in the air bladder

**red bole** *n* **:** BOLE 3

**red bone** *n, usu cap R&B* **1 :** one of a group of people of mixed white, Indian, and Negro ancestry esp. in Louisiana — often used disparagingly **2 :** CROATAN

**redbone** \ˈ=,=\ *n* **:** a moderate-sized speedy dark red or red and tan American hound used esp. for hunting coon and sometimes considered a distinct breed

**red book** *n, usu cap R&B* **:** an official British register bound in red; *esp* **:** a 19th century British peerage or court guide

**red box** *n* **1 :** any of several Australian eucalypts; *esp* **:** a gum tree (*Eucalyptus polyanthemos*) **2 :** an Australian timber tree (*Tristania conferta*)

**red brass** *n* **1 :** brass having a reddish tint due to a high copper content **:** GUINEA GOLD **2 :** COMPOSITION METAL

**redbreast** \ˈ=,=\ *n* [ME *redbrest*, fr. [1]*red* + *brest* breast] **1 a :** ROBIN **b :** [3]KNOT **2** *or* **red–breasted bream :** a sunfish (*Lepomis auritus*) of the eastern and southern U. S. having the belly largely orange-red

**red–breasted goose** \ˈ=,==-\ *n* **:** a Siberian goose (*Branta ruficollis*) that is chiefly black-and-white with a chestnut breast

**red–breasted merganser** *n* **:** a widely distributed merganser (*Mergus serrator*) of Europe and America having in the male a reddish breast band separated from the green head by a conspicuous white collar

**red–breasted nuthatch** *n* **:** a nuthatch (*Sitta canadensis*) of coniferous forests having the upper parts bluish gray and black and the underparts white and reddish

**red–breasted rail** *n* **:** VIRGINIA RAIL

**red–breasted sandpiper** *or* **red–breasted plover** *n* **:** [3]KNOT

**red–breasted sapsucker** *n* **:** a sapsucker (*Sphyrapicus varius ruber*) of western No. America

**red–breasted snipe** *n* **:** DOWITCHER

**red–brown butt rot** *n* **:** a destructive butt and root rot of various conifers caused by a pore fungus (*Polyporus schweinitzii*)

**red–brown rot** *n* **:** a fungous decay of conifers and various deciduous plants caused by a pore fungus (*Fomes pinicola*)

**redbrush** \ˈ=,=\ *n* **:** either of two No. American cornels with red or reddish purple twigs: **a :** SILKY CORNEL **b :** RED OSIER 2

**red bryony** *n* **:** a bryony (*Bryonia dioica*)

**redbuck** \ˈ=,=\ *n, pl* **redbuck** *or* **redbucks :** IMPALA

**red buckeye** *n* **:** a shrubby buckeye (*Aesculus pavia*) of the southern U. S.

**redbud** \ˈ=,=\ *n* **:** an American tree of the genus *Cercis*; *esp* **:** a tree (*C. canadensis*) of eastern No. America that resembles but is usu. smaller than the common Eurasian Judas tree and has pale rosy pink or occasionally white flowers appearing before the leaves expand

**red buffalo** *n* **:** a small reddish tropical African buffalo that constitutes a race (*Bubalus caffer nana*) of the Cape buffalo

**red bug** *n* **:** any of various red insects: as **a** *South & Midland* **:** CHIGGER 2 **b :** any of several red mirid bugs that live on apple trees **c :** COTTON STAINER

**red campion** *n* **:** a biennial European catchfly (*Lychnis dioica*) having red or pink flowers — called also *red bird's-eye*

**redcap** \ˈ=,=\ *n* **1 :** one that wears a red cap: as **a :** a baggage porter at a transportation terminal (as a railroad station) **b** *Brit* **:** MILITARY POLICEMAN **2** *dial Eng* **:** GOLDFINCH 1 **3** *usu cap* **a :** an old English breed of medium-sized domestic fowls resembling Old English Game fowls but distinguished by a very large full rose comb **b :** a bird of this breed

**red carabeen** *also* **red carrobean** *n* **:** any of several Australian trees; *specif* **:** a large tree (*Geissois bentanii*) of the family Cunoniaceae having reddish brown hard heavy wood that is used in flooring and paneling

**red cardinal** *n* **:** CARDINAL FLOWER

**red carp** *n* **:** GOLDFISH 1a

**red–carpet** \ˈ=ˈ==\ *adj* [so called fr. the traditional laying down of a red carpet for important guests to walk upon] **:** marked by the formal ceremonial courtesy accorded persons of rank or importance ⟨the *red-carpet* treatment given visiting dignitaries⟩

**red cedar** *n* **1 a :** an American juniper (*Juniperus virginiana*) found commonly east of the Rocky mountains and having dark green closely imbricated needle-shaped leaves — called also *eastern red cedar*; see TREE illustration **b :** the fragrant close-grained red wood of this tree **c :** any of several related trees of the genus *Juniperus* **2 a :** CANOE CEDAR **b :** the strong durable wood of this tree **c :** INCENSE CEDAR **d :** SPANISH CEDAR **3** *Austral* **a :** TOON **b :** FLINDOSA

**red cell** *or* **red corpuscle** *n* **:** a red blood cell **:** ERYTHROCYTE

**red cent** *n* **1 :** CENT 1b; *specif* **:** a large copper U.S. cent of the series coined 1793–1857 **2 :** a trivial amount **:** PENNY, WHIT

**red chalk** *n* **:** BOLE 3

**red char** *n* **:** a common European char (*Salvelinus alpinus*)

**red charcoal** *n* **:** a substance intermediate between wood and ordinary charcoal made by heating wood to about 300° C

**red chickweed** *n* **:** SCARLET PIMPERNEL

**red chokeberry** *n* **:** a common swamp shrub (*Aronia arbutifolia*) of the eastern U. S. with terminal cymes of pearly white flowers and bright red long-persistent fruit

**red clay** *n* **1 :** clay that usu. owes its reddish color to oxide of iron **2 :** a slowly accumulating abysmal deposit covering some 55,000,000 square miles of the deepest parts of the ocean bottom and consisting of the insoluble residual material of volcanic and meteoritic or cosmic dust mingled with nodules of manganese oxide, crystals of the zeolite phillipsite, sharks' teeth, the siliceous tests of Radiolaria, and other resistant organic debris

**red clover** *n* **:** a Eurasian clover (*Trifolium pratense*) naturalized in America, cultivated as a hay, forage, and cover crop, and having globose heads of reddish purple flowers

**red cluster pepper** *n* **:** a rather small compact pepper (*Capsicum frutescens fasciculatum*) that has narrow clustered leaves and is sometimes cultivated for its slender elongated brilliant red and extremely pungent fruits

**redcoat** \ˈ=,=\ *n, often cap* **:** a member of the British armed forces in America during the Revolutionary War

**red coat** *n* **:** BEDBUG 1a

**red coati** *n* **:** a coati (*Nasua rufa*) of So. America

**red cobalt** *n* **:** ERYTHRITE

**red cock** *n* **:** the male of the red grouse

**red cod** *n* **1 :** a gadid food fish (*Physiculus bachus*) of Australia and New Zealand that is reddish gray above and pink beneath but quickly becomes red when removed from the water **2 :** RED ROCK COD

**red coffee borer** *n* **:** TEA BORER

**red copper ore** *n* **:** CUPRITE

**red coral** *n* **:** an alcyonarian (*Corallium nobile* syn. *C. rubrum*) of the Mediterranean and adjacent parts of the Atlantic that forms branching shrubby colonies sometimes about a foot high and has in the axis of the stems and branches a hard stony skeleton of a delicate red or pink color used for ornaments and jewelry; *also* **:** a related coral of the Indian ocean

**red core** *n, chiefly Brit* **:** RED STELE

**red cotton bug** *n* **:** a pyrrhocorid bug (*Dysdercus cingulatus*) that causes great damage to cotton in parts of Asia

**red cotton tree** *n* **:** a tree (*Bombax malabaricum*) of India having striking red fleshy flowers borne while the leaves are off the tree

**red count** *n* **:** a blood count of the red blood cells

**red crab** *n* **:** a dark red edible crab (*Cancer productus*) widely distributed in shallow water from Alaska to Mexico

**red crescent** *adj, usu cap R&C* **:** of or relating to the Muslim equivalent of the International Red Cross

**red–crested pochard** \ˈ=,==-\ *n* **:** an Old World duck (*Netta rufina*) having in the male a chestnut head with a large crest, a red bill and feet, and a white speculum

[1]**red cross** *n, usu cap R&C* **:** a red Greek cross on a white ground adopted by the Geneva convention of 1864 as the emblem to identify noncombat installations, vehicles, and personnel ministering to the sick and wounded in war and now used as the emblem of the International Red Cross and its affiliates not only in war but in disaster relief and other humanitarian services — called also *Geneva cross*

[2]**red cross** *adj, usu cap R&C* [fr. the *Red Cross*, an international humanitarian organization] **:** of or relating to the International Red Cross or its affiliates — compare RED CRESCENT

**red crossbill** *n* **:** a common crossbill (*Loxia curvirostra*) of the northern hemisphere being in the male vermilion with dark brown wings and tail

**red crowberry** *n* **1 :** a low heathlike subantarctic shrub (*Empetrum rubrum*) bearing red berries and forming a main constituent of peat deposits in some areas **2 :** the edible red berry of red crowberry

**red curlew** *n* **1 :** SCARLET IBIS **2 :** MARBLED GODWIT

**red currant** *n* **1 a :** any of various red-fruited currants: as (1) **:** any of numerous cultivated currants derived from either of two natural species (*Ribes sativum* and *R. rubrum*) (2) **:** WILD RED CURRANT 1 **b :** WILD RED CURRANT 2 **2 :** GOYA

**red cypress** *n* **1 :** a bald cypress (*Taxodium distichum*) **2 :** the wood of bald cypress

[1]**redd** \ˈred\ *vt* [ME *redden*, fr. OE *hreddan*; akin to OFris *hredda* to save, OS *riddian*, OHG *hretten*, *retten* to save, free, and prob. to OE *hræd* quick, rapid, fast — more at RATHE] *chiefly dial* **:** to make free (as from trouble or from another person) **:** DELIVER, RESCUE

[2]**redd** \ˈ"\ *vb* **redded** *or* **redd; redded** *or* **redd; redding; redds** [ME *redden*, prob. alter. (influenced by *redden* to save, free) of *ridden* to rid — more at RID] *vt* **1** *archaic* **a :** to clear (a passage) out **:** OPEN, UNBLOCK **b :** UNRAVEL, DISENTANGLE **c :** to take (as combatants) apart **d :** to put an end to (a controversy) **:** compose (a difference) **2** *chiefly dial* **a :** to set in order **:** clear of debris **:** NEATEN, SMARTEN — usu. used with *up* or *out* ⟨~ up the bedrooms, get fresh flowers, dust —Jessamyn West⟩ ⟨~ out the cabin —Conrad Richter⟩ **b :** to straighten out **:** ARRANGE, SETTLE — usu. used with *up* ⟨~ up the affairs of Europe —John Buchan⟩ **3** *Midland* **:** COMB ⟨~ the hair⟩ **~** *vi, chiefly dial* **:** to make things tidy — usu. used with *up* ⟨stay and ~ up . . . I want to leave things nice —B.A.Williams⟩

[3]**redd** \ˈ"\ *n* -s [ME *red*, fr. *redden*, v.] **1** *chiefly Scot* **:** an act of redding **2** *chiefly Scot* **:** LITTER, REFUSE

[4]**redd** \ˈ"\ *adj* [fr. past part. of [2]*redd*] *chiefly Scot* **:** cleared for a new occupant ⟨leaves my premises void and ~ —Sir Walter Scott⟩

[5]**redd** \ˈ"\ *n* -s [origin unknown] **1 :** the spawn of a fish **2 :** the spawning ground or nest of various fishes (as the salmon and trout)

**red dagga** *n* **:** [1]DAGGA 2

**red daisy** *n* **:** ORANGE HAWKWEED

**red dane** *or* **red danish** *n* **1** *usu cap R&D* **:** a Danish breed of highly productive usu. solid red dairy cattle that are very popular in northern Europe **2** *often cap R & usu cap D* **:** an animal of the Red Dane breed

**red dead nettle** *n* **:** RED ARCHANGEL

**red deal** *n* **:** the wood of Scotch pine

**redded** *past of* RED

**red deer** *n* **1 :** the common stag (*Cervus elaphus*) of temperate Europe and Asia similar to but smaller than the wapiti **2 :** the Virginia deer in its summer coat

**red·den** \ˈredᵊn\ *vb* **reddened; reddened; reddening** \-d(ᵊ)niŋ\ **reddens** [[1]*red* + *-en*] *vt* **:** to make red or reddish ⟨blood ~*s* the bandage⟩ **~** *vi* **1 :** to become suffused with red **:** BLUSH ⟨the lawyer's face ~*s* with annoyance —Stuart Chase⟩ **2 :** to turn red or reddish in color ⟨the long sunlight ~*ed* slowly in the little room —Mary Deasy⟩

**red·den·do** \rəˈden(,)dō, reˈ-\ *n* -s [L, abl. of *reddendum*; fr. its being the first word in such clauses] *Scots law* **1 :** a clause in a charter specifying the particular duty or service due from a vassal to his superior **2 :** the duty specified in a reddendo

**red·den·dum** \-ndəm\ *n, pl* **redden·da** \-ndə\ [L, neut. of *reddendus*, gerundive of *reddere* to give back, hand over, yield, grant — more at RENDER] **:** a clause in a deed usu. following the tenendum by which some new thing (as rent) is reserved out of what had been granted before

**redder** *comparative of* RED

**red desert soil** *n* **:** any of a group of zonal soils of warm-temperate and tropical deserts that have light reddish brown friable soil over a reddish brown or dull red heavy horizon which grades into an accumulation of calcium carbonate and that supports more or less scanty desert-shrub vegetation

**reddest** *superlative of* RED

**red·di** \ˈredē\ *n, pl* **reddi** *or* **reddis** *usu cap* **1 :** a Munda-speaking migratory agricultural people of central India situated along the Godavari river in southeast Hyderabad, representing an ancient pre-Dravidian agricultural group of the Deccan plateau **2 :** a member of the Reddi people

**red diarrhea** *or* **red dysentery** *n* **:** bloody diarrhea of calves; *esp* **:** coccidiosis caused by a microscopic animal parasite (*Eimeria zurnii*)

**red·ding** \ˈrediŋ\ *n* -s [ME *reding*, fr. *read, reed, red* red + *-ing* — more at RED] *chiefly dial* **:** RED OCHER 1

**red·ding·ite** \ˈrediŋ,īt\ *n* -s [*Redding*, Conn. + E *-ite*] **:** a mineral $Mn_3(PO_4)_2.3H_2O$ consisting of a pinkish or yellowish white orthorhombic hydrous manganese phosphate isomorphous with phosphoferrite

**red·dish** \ˈredish, -dēsh\ *adj* [ME *redische*, fr. *read, reed, red* red + *-ische, -ish* -ish] **:** tinged with red

**reddish-brown lateritic soil** *n* **:** any of a group of zonal soils developed under humid tropical forest vegetation that have granular dark reddish brown surface soils underlain by reddish friable clay B-horizons and red reticulately mottled lateritic parent material

**reddish chestnut soil** *n* **:** any of a group of zonal soils developed under mixed grass with some shrubs in a warm-temperate semiarid climate that have dark brown surface soils tinted pinkish or reddish and up to 2 feet thick underlain by heavier reddish brown soil on grayish or pinkish lime accumulations

**reddish egret** *n* **:** a medium-sized heron (*Dichromanassa rufescens*) of Central America, the Gulf states, and the West Indies that is usu. slate colored with rufous head and neck and black legs but has forms in which the entire plumage is white

**red·dish·ness** *n* -ES **:** the quality or state of being reddish

**reddish prairie soil** *n* **:** any of a group of zonal soils developed under tall grass in a warm-temperate humid to subhumid climate that have dark reddish brown somewhat acid surface soils which grade to the parent material through slightly heavier reddish soils

**red·di·tion** \rəˈdishən\ *n* -s [ME *reddicion*, fr. MF *reddition* act of rendering, fr. LL *reddition-, redditio*, fr. L *redditus* (past part. of *reddere* to give back, hand over, yield, grant) + *-ion-, -io* -ion — more at RENDER] **1** *archaic* **:** RESTITUTION, SURRENDER **2** *obs* **a :** ELUCIDATION **b :** the application of a comparison **c :** the clause that contains such application

**reddle** *var of* RUDDLE

**red·dock** \ˈredək\ *dial Eng var of* RUDDOCK 1

**red dog** *n* **1** [so called fr. the red ink endorsement] **:** unreliable paper money issued by wildcat banks in the U.S. prior to the establishment of the national banking system **2** [so called fr. the fact that such flour was once packed in bags with a red dog on the front] **:** the lowest grade of flour; *specif* **:** a dark flour containing aleurone, little wheat flour, and bran particles obtained as a by-product of flour milling and used as an animal feed **3 :** a card game in which each player contributes to a pool and then in turn bets that he holds in his hand a card of the same suit and of higher rank than the top card of the stock — called also *high-card pool* **4 :** DHOLE **5 :** reddish ashes derived from burning piles of rejected coal and used esp. for paving in mine areas **6 :** a rush by the linebackers on the passer in football

**red–dog** \ˈ=ˈ=\ *vb* [fr. the noun phrase *red dog*] *vt* **:** to rush (the passer) in football **~** *vi* **:** to rush the passer in football

**red dogwood** *n* **1 :** a common and often cultivated European shrub (*Cornus sanguinea*) with white flowers in dense cymes and bright red twigs **2 :** RED OSIER 2

**red drum** *n* **:** CHANNEL BASS

**redds** *pres 3d sing of* REDD, *pl of* REDD

**redd–up** \ˈ=,=\ *adj* [fr. past part. of *redd up*] *chiefly dial* **:** redded up **:** TIDIED

**red duster** *n* **:** RED ENSIGN

**red dwarf** *n* **:** a star at the lower end of the main sequence in the spectrum-luminosity diagram having low surface temperature and small intrinsic luminosity, mass, and size

[1]**rede** \ˈrēd\ *vt* [ME *reden* to read, advise, interpret, govern, guess — more at READ] **1** *dial Brit* **a :** to arrive at by conjecture **:** GUESS, SURMISE **b :** PREDICT **2** *dial* **:** to give counsel to **:** ADVISE, WARN ⟨I ~ you not to stay here when I am gone —J.H.Wheelwright⟩ **3** *dial* **:** to put a construction upon **:** INTERPRET, EXPLAIN ⟨found the riddle . . . not possible to ~ —C.G.Harper⟩

[2]**rede** \ˈ"\ *n* -s [ME *reed, red, rede*, fr. OE *rǣd* advice, counsel, council — more at READ] **1** *chiefly dial* **:** COUNSEL, ADVICE ⟨my ~ is this, that we to gain . . . bliss, risk dying —William Morris⟩ **2** *archaic* **a :** an explanatory statement or interpretation **:** ACCOUNT, STORY ⟨read your ~ to me then boldly —Richard Brathwaite⟩ **b :** a proverbial saying **:** ADAGE, MAXIM

**redear** \ˈ=,=\ *also* **redear sunfish** *n* -s **:** a common sunfish (*Lepomis microlophus*) of the southern and eastern U.S. resembling the bluegill but somewhat darker above and paler beneath and with the back part of the gill cover bright orange-red — called also *shellcracker*

**red earth** *n* **:** hard red deep clays of tropical climates that are usu. leached and low in combined silica

**re·decorate** \(ˈ)rē+\ *vb* [*re-* + *decorate*] *vt* **:** to freshen or change in appearance **:** REFURBISH, RENOVATE; *esp* **:** to paint or paper (as the interior of a building) **~** *vi* **:** to freshen or change a decorative scheme; *esp* **:** to paint or paper walls and woodwork ⟨under the terms of the lease, the landlord is required to ~ every three years⟩

**re·decoration** \(ˌ)rē+\ *n* **:** an act or instance of redecorating

**re·decussate** \(ˈ)rē, ˈrē+\ *vi* [*re-* + *decussate*] *of nerve fibers* **:** to cross again

**re·dedicate** \(ˈ)rē+\ *vt* [*re-* + *dedicate*] **:** to dedicate again ⟨repair and ~ a gutted church⟩

**re·dedication** \(ˌ)rē+\ *n* **:** an act or instance of rededicating

**re·deem** \rə'dēm, rē'-\ *vb* -ED/-ING/-S [ME *redemen*, modif. (perh. influenced by *demen* to judge, deem) of MF *redimer*, fr. L *redimere*, fr. *red-* re- + *-imere* (fr. *emere* to take, buy, acquire); akin to OIr *arfoem* to take, Lith *imti* to take, OSlav *imǫ* I take away, Hitt *u-emijami* I grasp, find] *vt* **1 a :** to buy back : REPURCHASE ⟨if a man sell a dwelling house in a walled city, then he may ~ it within a whole year after —Lev 25:29 (RSV)⟩ **b :** to get or win back ⟨~*ed* his championship status by winning the return bout⟩ **2 a :** to liberate (as from slavery or captivity) by paying a price : RANSOM ⟨a parley to decide the terms for ~*ing* captured warriors⟩ **b** (1) **:** to free by force : LIBERATE ⟨the ~*ed* land of France —*N.Y. Times*⟩ (2) **:** to extricate from or help to surmount (a detrimental influence or circumstance) ⟨~*s* life from futility and meaninglessness —J.H.Hallowell⟩ **c :** to release from blame or debt : CLEAR, JUSTIFY ⟨a yearly tribute . . . ~*ed* the borough from all claims —E.A.Freeman⟩ ⟨eager . . . to ~ himself by furthering the national interest —Oscar Handlin⟩ **d** [modif. of LL *redimere*, fr. L] **:** to absolve from the bondage of sin ⟨Christ hath ~*ed* us from the curse of the law —Gal 3:13 (AV)⟩ ⟨God has demonstrated His love for human souls by ~*ing* them through a supreme act of self-sacrifice —A.J. Toynbee⟩ **e :** to change from worse to better : PURIFY, REFORM ⟨our civilization cannot survive materially unless it be ~*ed* spiritually —Woodrow Wilson⟩ ⟨your auditors are hardened sinners, not easily ~*ed* —B.N.Cardozo⟩ **f :** to put back into proper condition : REPAIR, RESTORE ⟨~*ing* cocoa plantations which have been neglected in recent years —*N.Y. Times*⟩ **g** *archaic* **:** to recover from a state of submersion : RECLAIM ⟨considerable spaces were ~*ed* from the original ocean and converted into dry land —Charles Lyell⟩ **3 a :** to repossess upon fulfillment of an obligation; *specif* **:** to free (property) from a lien or encumbrance and regain absolute title by payment of an amount secured thereby or by performing the condition securing the same **b** (1) **:** to remove the obligation of by payment ⟨the U. S. Treasury ~*s* war bonds upon demand⟩ (2) **:** to convert into cash ⟨stockholders who want to ~ their stock —*Time*⟩ **c** (1) **:** to make good (a promise or pledge) : FULFILL ⟨graver peril arose, and Washington ~*ed* his promise to stand by the army —H.E.Scudder⟩ (2) **:** to convert into actuality : REALIZE ⟨looked to the north with a childlike trust which . . . has not been ~*ed* by the event —W.L.Sperry⟩ **4 a :** to atone for or cleanse : EXPIATE, PURGE ⟨~ an error⟩ ⟨a tireless attempt to make the twentieth century ~ this tragedy of the nineteenth —Anne Fremantle⟩ ⟨~ themselves by means of frank confessions —Q.K.Y. Huang⟩ **b** (1) **:** to cancel out the detrimental effect of : make up for : COMPENSATE, OFFSET ⟨a plain pale face ~*ed* by very beautiful eyes —Elizabeth Goudge⟩ ⟨style and malicious epigram . . . ~ much that is tedious —L.O.Coxe⟩ (2) **:** to make worth while : give merit to : RETRIEVE ⟨a resynthesis . . . might ~ the whole undertaking —R.M.Weaver⟩ **c** *obs* **:** to be accepted in exchange for ⟨would some part of my young years might but ~ the passage of your age —Shak.⟩ **5 :** to make profitable use of (time) ⟨worked . . . with indefatigable energy, ~*ing* the time —J.F.Clarke⟩ ~ *vi* **1 :** DELIVER, SAVE ⟨is my hand shortened, that it cannot ~ —Isa 50:2 (RSV)⟩ **2 :** to buy back property : regain title by purchase ⟨rights . . . must be exercised within forty years from the time at which the proprietor is allowed to ~ —William Bell⟩ **syn** see RESCUE

**re·deem·abil·i·ty** \rə,dēmə'biləd-ē\ *n* **:** capability of being redeemed

**re·deem·able** \rə'dēməbəl, rē'-\ *adj* **:** capable of being redeemed: as **a :** recoverable upon payment of a price or fulfillment of a condition ⟨~ goods in a pawn shop⟩ **b :** convertible into cash at the request of the holder ⟨~ stocks and bonds⟩ **c :** susceptible to improvement or reform or esp. to spiritual redemption ⟨~ sinner⟩ — **re·deem·ably** \-blē\ *adv*

**re·deem·er** \-mə(r)\ *n* -S [ME *redemer*, fr. *redemen* to redeem + *-er* — more at REDEEM] **:** one that redeems ⟨has been called the ~ of his people⟩

**redeeming** *adj* **:** serving to offset or compensate for a defect ⟨a cynical man with a ~ sense of humor⟩ ⟨the ~ feature of the plan is its simplicity⟩

**re·deem·less** \-mləs\ *adj, archaic* **:** admitting of no improvement or recovery ⟨change his pleasure into wretched and ~ misery —Henry Chettle⟩

**re·define** \¦rē+\ *vt* [*re-* + *define*] **:** to define (a concept) again; *esp* **:** REFORMULATE ⟨business men must ~, liberalize capitalism —*Magazine Intelligence*⟩ ⟨to deal with the problem effectively, we must ~ our terms⟩

**re·definition** \(¦)rē+\ *n* [*re-* + *definition*] **:** an act or instance of redefining ⟨asking for . . . a ~ of the objectives of the liberal college —B.F.Wright⟩ ⟨such terms as *liberal* call for periodic ~⟩

**red eft** *n* **:** a brick red terrestrial form of a common No. American newt (*Triturus viridescens*)

**red elder** *n* **:** CRANBERRY TREE

**re·deliver** \¦rē+\ *vt* [*re-* + *deliver*] **1** *archaic* **a :** to give back : RETURN **b :** to set free : LIBERATE **2 a** *obs* **:** to report the answer of ⟨shall I ~ you e'en so —Shak.⟩ **b** *archaic* **:** to utter again : REPEAT

**re·delivery** \"+\ *n* **:** an act or instance of redelivering; *esp* **:** RESTITUTION

**red elm** *n* **1 :** any of several American elms having reddish wood: as **a :** SLIPPERY ELM **b :** WINGED ELM **c :** SEPTEMBER ELM **2 :** the wood of a red elm tree

**red els** \-'elz\ *n, pl* **red elses** [part trans. of Afrik *rooie-els*, fr. *rooie* red + *els* alder, fr. MHG *else*; akin to OHG *elira*, *erila* alder — more at ALDER] **:** a southern African shrub or small tree (*Cunonia capensis*) having bark that yields tannin

**re·demand** \¦rē+\ *vt* [*re-* + *demand*] **:** to demand again — **re·de·mand·able** \"+əbəl\ *adj*

**re·demp·ti·ble** \rə'dem(p)təbəl\ *adj* [*redemption* + *-ible*] **:** REDEEMABLE

**re·demp·tion** \rə'dem(p)shən, rē'-\ *n* -S [ME *redempcioun*, fr. MF *redemption*, fr. LL & L; LL *redemption-, redemptio* redemption from sin, fr. L, act of buying back or redeeming, ransom, fr. *redemptus* (past part. of *redimere* to redeem) + *-ion-, -io* -ion — more at REDEEM] **1 a :** deliverance from the bondage of sin : spiritual salvation ⟨man's damnation and God's ~ —J.C.Brauer⟩ **b :** expiation of guilt or wrong : EXONERATION, ATONEMENT ⟨disgrace . . . from which there could never be ~ —Thomas Wolfe⟩ **2 a :** emancipation or liberation through payment of a price : RANSOM ⟨modes of ~ and manumission —*Notes & Queries on Anthropology*⟩ **b :** PIDYON HABEN **3 a :** an act or instance of repairing or restoring : RECLAMATION ⟨the ~ of chronically polluted areas —R.M.Paul⟩ **b :** an act or instance of bettering : IMPROVEMENT ⟨the ~ of society through science —Mary Austin⟩; *esp* : REFORM ⟨the defective or recidivist, whose ~ is hopeless —B.N.Cardozo⟩ **c :** release from a detrimental influence or circumstance ⟨the aim of life is ~ from the wheel of rebirth —F.B.Artz⟩ **4 a :** the removal of an obligation by payment ⟨~ of a promissory note⟩ ⟨~ of the unused portion of a railroad ticket⟩ **b :** the regaining of property by satisfaction of an obligation; *specif* **:** the process of regaining absolute legal title by paying off a defeasible title — **re·demp·tion·al** \-shənᵊl\ *adj*

**re·demp·tion·er** \-nə(r)\ *n* -S **1 :** an emigrant from Europe to America in the 18th and 19th centuries obtaining passage by becoming an indentured servant at the disposal of the shipowner or master for a specified length of time **2 :** one redeeming himself or his property (as from servitude or debt)

**re·demp·tion·ist** \-nəst\ *n* -S *cap* **:** TRINITARIAN 1

**re·demp·tive** \-(p)tiv, -tēv *also* -təv\ *adj* [*redemption* + *-ive*] **:** of, relating to, or bringing about redemption ⟨a detailed ~ theory about life —E.K.Brown⟩ ⟨the ~ love of the Gospels —W.B.Stein⟩

**re·demp·tor** \-tə(r)\ *n* -S [ME *redemptour*, fr. LL *redemptor*, fr. L, contractor, fr. *redemptus* (past part. of *redimere* to redeem, contract) + *-or* — more at REDEEM] **:** REDEEMER

**re·demp·to·ri·al** \¦rē,dem(p)¦tōrēəl\ *adj* [*redemptory* + *-al*] **:** REDEMPTIVE

**re·demp·tor·ist** \rə'dem(p)tərəst, rē'-\ *n* -S *cap* [F *rédemptoriste*, fr. LL *redemptor* + F *-iste* -ist] **:** a member of the Roman Catholic Congregation of the Most Holy Redeemer founded in Naples in 1732 by St. Alphonsus Liguori and devoted to preaching to the poor

**re·demp·to·ry** \-rē, -ri\ *adj* [*redemption* + *-ory*] **:** REDEMPTIVE

**re·demp·tress** \-trəs\ *n* -ES [*redemptor* + *-ess*] **:** REDEMPTRIX

**re·demp·trix** \-riks\ *n, pl* **redempti·ces** \-rə,sēz\ [LL, fem. of *redemptor*] **:** a female redeemer

**red ensign** *n* **:** an ensign with a red field borne by British merchantmen — called also *red duster*

**re·deploy** \¦rē+\ *vb* [*re-* + *deploy*] *vt* **:** to transfer (military forces or equipment) from one area or fighting front to another ⟨forces which recently attacked the Allied beachhead . . . have now been ~*ed* to the southwest —*Army-Navy-Air Force Jour.*⟩ ⟨the first plane to be ~*ed* —*N.Y. Times*⟩ ~ *vi* **:** to carry out a redeployment ⟨aiding the Army to ~ —H.S. Truman⟩

**re·de·ploy·ment** \"+mənt\ *n* **:** a relocation or reassignment of men or equipment ⟨~ of United States forces from western Europe to the Far East —E.L.Erickson⟩ ⟨large-scale ~ of labor —Thomas Balogh⟩ ⟨the Soviet Union's mammoth ~ of industry into the Ural Mountains —*Newsweek*⟩

**¹re·deposit** \¦rē+\ *vt* [*re-* + *deposit*] **:** to deposit again ⟨~*ed* interest⟩ ⟨manganese ore . . . dissolved and ~*ed* in the form of concretions —*Jour. of Geol.*⟩

**²redeposit** \"\ *n* **:** something that is deposited again ⟨the ~ is made up of the exact amount refunded —*Your Retirement System*⟩

**re·deposition** \(¦)rē+\ *n* [*re-* + *deposition*] **:** formation into a new accumulation ⟨clearly a product of solution and ~ in a highly porous rock —*Jour. of Geol.*⟩

**redes** *pl of* REDE

**re·descend** \¦rē+\ *vb* [*re-* + *descend*] **:** to descend again

**¹re·design** \"+\ *vt* [*re-* + *design*] **:** to revise in appearance, function, or content ⟨~ a tool⟩ ⟨~ a curriculum⟩

**²redesign** \"\ *n* **:** a revision or act of revising in design ⟨a ~ of the existing product label —*Modern Packaging*⟩ ⟨called in . . . to go over the blueprints and advise in the ~ and rebuilding of the fireplaces —*New Yorker*⟩

**re·determination** \¦rē+\ *n* **:** an act or instance of fixing again or confirming ⟨administrative procedures . . . in the ~ of prices —*Jour. of Accountancy*⟩ ⟨undertook the ~ of the atomic weights —William Ramsay⟩

**re·determine** \"+\ *vt* [*re-* + *determine*] **:** to fix again : REESTABLISH, CONFIRM ⟨~ the orbit of a comet⟩ ⟨~ the boiling point of liquid hydrogen⟩

**re·develop** \"+\ *vt* [*re-* + *develop*] **1 :** to develop again : REDESIGN, REBUILD ⟨~ a slum area⟩ **2 a :** to reverse the tones of (a photographic image) — compare REVERSAL 2 **b :** to make (a developed image) more intense **c :** to tone (a developed image) by bleaching and sulfiding — **re·de·vel·op·er** \"+ə(r)\ *n*

**re·de·vel·op·ment** \"+mənt\ *n* **:** the act or process of redeveloping; *esp* **:** the renovation of a blighted area ⟨urban ~⟩

**redevelopment company** *n* **:** a public or private body corporate organized to encourage the economic development of a particular area by loaning capital to business enterprises willing to locate in that area or by leasing or selling real estate owned by it to such enterprises

**redeye** \'=,=\ *n* **1 :** any of several fishes with more or less reddish eyes: as **a :** RUDD **b :** ROCK BASS 1 **c** (1) **:** SMALLMOUTH BLACK BASS (2) **:** REDEYE BLACK BASS **d :** WARMOUTH **2 :** COPPERHEAD 1a

**red-eye** \'=,=\ *n* **1 :** cheap whiskey **2 a :** RED-EYED VIREO **b :** a large black Australian cicada (*Psaltoda moerens*) **3 a :** CATSUP 1 **b** *or* **red-eye gravy :** gravy made with catsup or tomato sauce

**red eye** *n* **:** RED BOARD

**redeye black bass** *n* **:** a black bass (*Micropterus coosae*) of the southeastern U.S. in most respects resembling a smallmouth black bass but usu. considered a distinct species — called also *redeye*

**red-eyed** \'=¦=\ *adj* **1 a :** having red eyes **b :** having a red ring around the eye **2 :** having the eyes reddened or inflamed ⟨as from weeping⟩

**red-eyed pochard** *n* **:** a pochard (*Aythya ferina*) — called also *redhead*

**red-eyed vireo** *n* **:** a common vireo (*Vireo olivaceus*) of northeastern No. America having a grayish green back, white underparts, and the iris red — called also *red-eye*

**red-faced** \'=¦=\ *adj* **:** having a red face; *esp* **:** flushed with anger or embarrassment — **red-fac·ed·ly** \(')=¦fāsədlē, -stl-, -li\ *adv*

**red factor** *n* **:** a canary carrying some proportion of black-hooded red siskin blood and used in breeding to increase reddish tones in the plumage of the offspring

**red feather** *adj, usu cap R&F* [so called fr. the red feather symbolic of the United Fund, a charitable organization in the U.S.] **:** of, relating to, or supported by contributions to a community chest ⟨*Red Feather* agency⟩

**red feed** *n* **:** small red marine surface-swimming copepod crustaceans that are a leading food of some commercial fishes — called also *red seed*

**red fender** *n* **:** RED-BELLIED TERRAPIN

**red fescue** *n* **:** a perennial pasture and turf grass (*Festuca rubra*) of Europe and America with creeping rootstocks, erect culms, and reddish spikelets

**red fever** *n* **:** SWINE ERYSIPELAS

**red-figure** \'=¦==\ *or* **red-figured** \'=¦=\ *adj* **:** of, belonging to, or constituting a style of vase painting developed in Athens at the end of the 6th century B.C. in which the outer surfaces of the ware are covered in black except for the decorative figures and other elements which show as exposed areas of the red body clay and which are drawn chiefly from mythology in a style distinguished by convincing representation and graceful line ⟨*red-figure* vase⟩ ⟨*red-figure* ware⟩ — compare BLACK-FIGURE, POLYCHROME

**redfin** \'=,=\ *n* **:** any of various fishes with more or less red fins: as **a :** the common shiner (*Notropis cornutus*) the male of which has bright red fins in the breeding season **b** *also* **redfin shiner :** a similar and closely related fish (*N. umbratilis*) esp. abundant in sluggish prairie streams of central No. America **c :** REDHORSE

**redfin pickerel** *n* **:** a small but gamy pickerel (*Esox americanus*) of the Atlantic coastal states that is dusky green with curved black bars on the sides — called also *barred pickerel*

**red fir** *n* **1 a :** any of several western American firs of the genus *Abies:* as (1) **:** NOBLE FIR (2) **:** CALIFORNIA RED FIR (3) **:** AMABILIS FIR **b :** the wood of a red fir tree **2 :** DOUGLAS FIR **3 :** NORWAY SPRUCE **4 :** SCOTCH PINE

**red fire** *n* **:** a composition usu. containing a strontium or lithium salt that burns with a bright red light for use in pyrotechny and signaling

**redfish** \'=,=\ *n, pl* **redfish** *or* **redfishes :** any of various more or less reddish fishes: as **a** (1) **:** BLUEBACK SALMON (2) *Brit* **:** the male salmon in spawning condition **b :** ROSEFISH **c :** a sheepshead (*Pimelometopon pulcher*) **d :** CHANNEL BASS **e :** a red phase of the coney (*Cephalopholis fulvus*)

**red flannel hash** *n* **:** hash made from corned beef, beets, potatoes, and other leftover vegetables and turned red according to the quantity of beets

**red flannels** *n pl* **:** winter underwear; *esp* **:** red long johns

**red flour beetle** *n* **:** a reddish brown beetle (*Tribolium castaneum*) that feeds on grain, cereals, stored fruits and other products

**red-footed booby** \'=¦==-\ *also* **redfoot** \'=,=\ *n, pl* **red-footed boobies** *also* **redfoots :** a booby (*Sula piscator*) of the coasts of Central America and southern No. America

**red-footed falcon** *n* **:** a small chiefly lead-colored European falcon (*Falco vespertinus*) with bright reddish orange bill, eye patches and legs — called also *red-legged falcon*

**red for lake** *n, usu cap R&L* **:** LAKE RED

**red fox** *n* **:** a fox with bright orange red to dusky reddish brown fur that is usu. considered to constitute a single circumpolar species (*Vulpes vulpes*) with several subspecies and that exhibits a marked tendency to deviation from the typical coloring — see BLACK FOX, CROSS FOX, SILVER FOX

**red giant** *n* **:** a star of low surface temperature and absolute magnitude about zero having many times the sun's diameter

**red ginger** *n* **:** an ornamental ginger (*Alpinia purpurata*) native to islands of the western Pacific

**red gland** *n* **:** a red body covered with glandular epithelium in the air bladder of various teleost fishes

**red goatfish** *n* **:** a small usu. brilliant but highly variable red mullet (*Upeneus maculatus*) of the tropical western Atlantic and the West Indies

**red goosefoot** *n* **:** a common Eurasian annual weed (*Chenopodium rubrum*) naturalized in No. America — called also *French spinach*

**red grain beetle** *n* **:** SQUARE-NECKED GRAIN BEETLE

**redgrape** \'=,=\ *n* **:** a dark purplish red that is bluer and duller than pansy purple, redder and stronger than raisin, bluer, lighter, and stronger than Bokhara, and bluer and deeper than Indian purple

**red grape** *n* **:** MISSOURI GRAPE

**red grass** *n* **:** a southern African grass (*Themeda triandra*) used for pasture and forage — called also *red oat*

**red-green blindness** \'=¦=-\ *n* **:** dichromatism in which the spectrum is seen in tones of yellow and blue — see DALTONISM, DEUTERANOPIA, PROTANOPIA

**red groper** *n* **:** a groper (sense 2) of the red color phase

**red grouper** *n* **:** a common marine food fish (*Epinephelus morio*) of the Atlantic coast from Virginia southward reaching a length of three feet and with age acquiring a flesh-red color — called also *negre, red snapper;* compare SNAPPER 3b

**red grouse** *n* **:** a ptarmigan (*Lagopus scoticus*) of the British Isles, closely related to the willow ptarmigan but not turning white in winter as related birds do — called also *moorbird, moorfowl, moor game*

**¹red gum** *n* [by folk etymology fr. *redgound*, fr. ME *red-gownd*, fr. *read, reed, red* red + *gound, gownd* pus, fr. OE *gund* — more at RED, GROUNDSEL] **:** STROPHULUS

**²red gum** *n* [¹*red* + *gum*] **1 a** (1) **:** any of several Australian trees of the genus *Eucalyptus* (esp. *E. camaldulensis, E. amygdalina*, and *E. calophylla*) (2) **:** the timber of one of these trees **b :** EUCALYPTUS GUM **c :** red acaroid resin **2 :** SWEET GUM 1b

**red gurnard** *n* **1 :** a European gurnard (*Trigla cuculus*) that is chiefly red in color **2 :** an Australian fish (*Chelidonichthys kumu*) that is related to the European red gurnard

**red hand** *n, usu cap R&H* **:** a heraldic hand that is erect, open, and couped at the wrist — called also *Badge of Ulster*

**red-handed** \'=¦==\ *adv (or adj)* [so called fr. the idea of a murderer caught with the blood of his victim on his hands] **:** in the act of committing or exhibiting evidence of having committed a crime or misdeed : with the mainour ⟨surprised the murderer *red-handed* in the study —Erle Stanley Gardner⟩ ⟨caught *red-handed* with a hand in the cookie jar⟩ ⟨have a preacher catch us *red-handed* in the act of sinning —Frederick Way⟩

**red-hard** \'=¦=\ *adj* **:** hard when red-hot — used esp. of high-speed steel — **red-hard·ness** *n*

**red-harden** \'=¦==\ *vt* **:** to make (metal) red-hard

**red hare** *n* **:** ROCK HARE

**red hartebeest** *n* **:** CAPE HARTEBEEST

**red hat** *n* **:** CARDINAL'S HAT

**red haw** *n* **:** any of several American hawthorns: as **a :** a spiny shrub or small tree (*Crataegus coccinea*) **b :** a red-fruited hawthorn (*C. mollis*) with foliage and inflorescence copiously tomentose — called also *downy haw*

**red hawk** *n* **:** a hawk in its first year

**redhead** \'=,=\ *n* **1 a :** a person having red hair **b :** a member of a group distinguished by red headgear **c** *usu cap* **:** KIZILBASH 3 **2 a :** RED-EYED POCHARD **b :** an American duck (*Aythya americana*) that is similar to the European pochard and highly esteemed as a game bird and that is also related to the canvasback but has in the male a brighter rufous head and a shorter bill **3 a :** REDHEADED WOODPECKER **b :** HOUSE FINCH

**redheaded** \'=¦==\ *adj* **1 :** having red hair or a red head **2 a :** EXCITABLE, IMPETUOUS **b :** HOT-TEMPERED — **red-head·ed·ly** *adv*

**redheaded fungus** *also* **redheaded scale fungus** *n* **:** any of various ascomycetous fungi (genus *Sphaerostilbe*) that are parasitic on scale insects; *esp* **:** a fungus (*S. aurantiicola*)

**redheaded linnet** *n* **:** HOUSE FINCH

**redheaded lizard** *n* **:** BLUE-TAILED SKINK

**red-head·ed·ness** *n* -ES **1 :** the quality or state of having red hair or a red head ⟨~ runs in the family⟩ **2 :** the quality or state of being excitable : IMPETUOSITY, TEMPER

**red-headed pine sawfly** *n* **:** a sawfly (*Neodiprion lecontei*) that feeds in the larval stage on various pines in the eastern U.S.

**redheaded woodpecker** *n* **:** a rather large woodpecker (*Melanerpes erythrocephalus*) widely but irregularly distributed in No. America having in the adult white underparts and wing patches with back, tail, and the rest of the wings black and a red head and neck — called also *redhead*

**redhead-grass** \'=,=,=\ *n* **:** a very common submerged pondweed (*Potamogeton perfoliatus*) with broad clasping or perfoliate leaves and a terminal spike of greenish apetalous flowers

**red heart** *n* **:** incipient decay in lumber indicated by a dark red discoloration not found in sound wood; *specif* **:** RED ROT 2b

**redheart** \'=,=\ *n* **:** a California straggling shrub or small tree (*Ceanothus spinosus*) having dark red wood and blue-gray to white flowers and being used as an ornamental

**redheart hickory** *n* **:** SHAGBARK HICKORY

**red heat** *n* **:** a temperature at which a substance glows red

**red heath** *n* **1 :** a heather (*Calluna vulgaris*) **2 :** a New Zealand shrub (*Dracophyllum recurvum*) of the family Epacridaceae resembling a heath and having small red flowers **3** *or* **red heather :** either of two low growing alpine heaths (*Phyllodoce empetriformis* and *P. bremeri*) having rose-colored flowers

**red hematite** *n* **:** HEMATITE

**red herring** *n* [ME] **1 :** a herring cured by heavy salting and slow smoking to a dark brown color — compare ²KIPPER; see *neither fish nor fowl* at ¹FISH **2** [so called fr. the traditional practice of dragging a red herring across a trail to destroy the scent] **:** a diversion intended to distract attention from the real issue ⟨there are many false issues, straw men, and *red herrings* —H.W.Baldwin⟩ ⟨the nominal subject of imaginative art . . . is nearly always a *red herring* —*Times Lit. Supp.*⟩ **3 :** a preliminary prospectus for a new security with a warning notice in red on each page that sale will begin only when the registration statement is effective ⟨a *red herring* . . . is sent to the dealers for their information —B.E.Shultz⟩

**red·hi·bi·tion** \,red(h)ə'bishən\ *n* -S [F *rédhibition*, fr. L *redhibition-, redhibitio*, fr. *redhibitus* (past part. of *redhibēre* to take back, give back, fr. *red-* re- + *-hibēre*, fr. *habēre* to hold, have) + *-ion-, -io* -ion — more at GIVE] *civil law* **:** an annulment of the sale of an article and return of it to the seller because of some material defect

**red·hib·i·to·ry** \red'hibə,tōrē\ *adj* **:** of or relating to redhibition

**red hickory** *n* **1 :** MOCKERNUT **2 :** a pignut (*Carya glabra*)

**red hind** *n* **1 :** a grouper (*Epinephelus guttatus*) ranging from the Carolinas to Brazil having red spots, being variably colored but usu. light gray, tannish yellow, or whitish, and being important as a food fish in Cuba — called also *cabrilla* **2 :** GRAYSBY

**red honeysuckle** *n* **:** an Australian shrub (*Banksia serrata*) often cultivated for its beautiful rusty foliage and thick spikes of red flowers

**redhorse** \'=,=\ *or* **redhorse sucker** *n* **1 :** any of numerous large suckers of the genera *Moxostoma* and *Placopharynx* of No. American rivers and lakes having in the male red fins esp. in the breeding season — called also *redfin* **2 :** CHANNEL BASS

**red horse chestnut** *n* **:** a much cultivated ornamental tree (*Aesculus carnea*) of hybrid origin resembling the common horse chestnut but having red flowers

**¹red-hot** \'=¦=\ *adj* [¹*red* + *hot*] **1 :** glowing with heat ⟨*red-hot* iron⟩ **2 a :** exhibiting or characterized by intense emotion : BURNING, FURIOUS ⟨*red-hot* abolitionist⟩ ⟨*red-hot* political campaign⟩ ⟨*red-hot* passion⟩ **b :** full of scandal : JUICY, TORRID ⟨*red-hot* story of a secret love affair⟩ **c** (1) **:** full of energy or enthusiasm : VIGOROUS, PEPPY ⟨*red-hot* line drive⟩ ⟨*red-hot* jazz band⟩ (2) : arousing enthusiasm : currently extolled ⟨a *red-hot* favorite to win the derby⟩ **3** : of or relating to the immediate present : up-to-the-minute : FRESH, RECENT ⟨*red-hot* news⟩ ⟨*red-hot* data⟩

²**red-hot** \ˈ=,=\ *n* **1** : one that exhibits intense emotion or partisanship **2 a** : HOT DOG **b** : a small red candy strongly flavored with cinnamon

**red hot cattail** *n* : CHENILLE

**red-hot poker** *n* : POKER PLANT

**red-humped caterpillar** \ˈ=,=-\ *n* : a variably but predominantly black and yellow striped gregarious caterpillar with the head and dorsally humped fourth body segment bright red that is the larva of a notodontid moth (*Schizura concinna*) and is an important pest on various deciduous trees in No. America

**re·dia** \ˈrēdēə\ *n, pl* **redi·ae** \-dē,ē\ [NL, fr. Francesco *Redi* †1698? Ital. naturalist + NL *-ia*] : a larva produced within the sporocyst of many trematodes that in turn either produces another generation of rediae or develops into a cercaria — compare ¹FLUKE 2 — **re·di·al** \-dēəl\ *adj*

**redid** *past of* REDO

**re·differentiation** \(ˌ)rē+\ *n* [*re-* + *differentiation*] : the act, process, or result of developing additional new characteristics

**re·diffusion** \"+\ *n* [*re-* + *diffusion*] *chiefly Brit* : an act or instance of broadcasting or rebroadcasting a radio or television program

**re·digest** \"+\ *vt* [*re-* + *digest*] : to digest again — **re·digestion** \"+\ *n*

**red indian** *n* **1** *usu cap R & I* : AMERICAN INDIAN **2** *usu cap I* : an Indian paintbrush (*Castilleja coccinea*)

**red indian paint** *n, usu cap I* : BLOODROOT 1

**red·in·gote** \ˈrediŋ,gōt\ *n* -s [F, modif. of E *riding coat*] : a fitted outer garment: as **a** (1) : a double-breasted coat with wide flat cuffs and collar worn by men in the 18th century (2) : a late 19th century chesterfield **b** (1) : a woman's lightweight coat usu. cut in princess style, belted, and open at the front to show the skirt of the dress (2) : a coatdress with a front gore of a contrasting material

redingote b(2)

**red·ing·ton·ite** \ˈrediŋtə,nīt\ *n* -s [*Redington* mercury mine, Napa county, Calif. + E *-ite*] : a mineral approximately $(Fe,Mg,Ni)(Cr,Al)_2(SO_4)_4.22H_2O$ consisting of a hydrous sulfate of iron, magnesium, nickel, chromium, and aluminum that is possibly a chromium halotrichite

**red ink** *n* **1** : red-colored ink used esp. in financial statements to indicate a loss **2 a** : a business loss : DEFICIT **b** : the condition of showing a loss ⟨the company was going into *red ink*⟩

**red-ink** \ˈ=ˈ=\ *vt* [*red ink*] : to mark with or print in red ink

**red inkberry** *or* **red-ink plant** *n* : POKEWEED

¹**re·din·te·grate** \rəˈdintə,grāt, rē-, re'-\ *vt* [ME *redintegraten*, fr. L *redintegratus*, past part. of *redintegrare*, fr. *red-* re- + *integrare* to make complete — more at INTEGRATE] **1** *archaic* : to put back together : REPAIR, REUNITE **2** *archaic* : to restore to integrity or soundness : REESTABLISH, REINSTATE

²**redintegrate** \"\ *adj* [L *redintegratus*, past part.] *archaic* : REDINTEGRATED

**re·din·te·gra·tion** \=,==ˈgrāshən\ *n* -s [ME *redyntegracyon*, fr. L *redintegration-*, *redintegratio*, fr. *redintegratus* + *-ion-*, *-io* -ion] **1** *archaic* : restoration to a former state **2 a** : revival of the whole of a previous mental state when a phase of it recurs **b** : arousal of any response by a part of the complex of stimuli that orig. aroused that response

**re·din·te·gra·tive** \=ˈ==,grād·iv\ *adj* : of or relating to redintegration

**re·dip** \(ˈ)rēˈdip\ *vb* [*re-* + *dip*] : to dip again

**re·dip·per** \-pə(r)\ *n* : one that redips; *esp* : a worker who gives tin plate a protective coating by dipping it into a terne= mixture bath as it comes from the tinning machine

**re·direct** \ˌrē+\ *vt* [*re-* + *direct*, v.] **1 a** : to change the course of : channel in a new direction ⟨the policeman ~*s* him⟩ ⟨~*ing* attitudes . . . toward acceptable life standards —M.E. Alexander⟩ ⟨in an emergency ~ the scientist from basic research to applied research —M.H.Trytten⟩ **b** : READDRESS ⟨~*ed* the letter⟩ **2** : to change the direction of (as a flux) in a definite manner — **re·directive** \"+\ *adj*

**redirect examination** *n* [*re-* + *direct*, adj.] : the examination of a witness by the party calling him after the cross-examination to clarify matters brought out on the cross-examination

**re·direction** \"+\ *n* : an act or instance of redirecting

**red ironbark** *n* : any of several Australian eucalypts (as *Eucalyptus sideroxylon*) with white to pink or red flowers — called also *mugga*

**red iron ore** *n* : HEMATITE

**red ironwood** *n* **1** : a small tree (*Reynosia septentrionalis*) of the family Rhamnaceae of the Bahamas and southern Florida with persistent usu. opposite leaves and an edible drupe — called also *Darling plum* **2** : a closely related Cuban tree (*Reynosia latifolia*)

¹**re·dis·count** \(ˈ)rēˈdi,skau̇nt *also* ˌrēdəˈs-\ *vt* [*re-* + *discount* (v.)] : to discount again (as commercial paper) ⟨a Federal Reserve Bank may also ~ any bill drawn by a bank —Alexander Wall⟩ — **re·dis·count·able** \-təbəl\ *adj*

²**rediscount** \"\ *n* [*re-* + *discount* (n.)] : the act or process of rediscounting or the negotiable paper involved in such a transaction

**rediscount rate** *n* : the discount rate charged by Federal Reserve banks for rediscounting commercial paper for member banks or making secured advances to them on their own notes

**re·discover** \ˌrē+\ *vt* [*re-* + *discover*] **1 a** : to find again ⟨~*ed* the island of Madeira —H.W. Van Loon⟩ **b** : to arrive at independently or try to recapture by analysis (a technique or concept already discovered or once employed) ⟨~*ing* the methods of the Greek sculptors —Herbert Read⟩ **2 a** : to bring to light again ⟨the original Hittites, recently ~*ed* by excavation and decipherment —*advt*⟩ **b** : to take new interest in or create fresh appreciation for (one fallen into low esteem) ⟨Americans . . . have ~*ed* their frontier painters —Bernard Smith⟩ **c** : to make new use of (a neglected asset) ⟨~*ed* the Slavonic sources of their culture —Oscar Handlin⟩ — **re·discovery** \"+\ *n*

**re·dispose** \"+\ *vt* [*re-* + *dispose*] : REDEPLOY — **re·disposition** \(ˌ)rē+\ *n*

**re·disseise** *or* **re·disseize** \(ˌ)rē+\ *vt* [*re-* + *disseise* or *disseize*] : to disseise anew — **re·disseisor** *or* **re·disseizor** \"+\ *n*

**re·disseisin** *or* **re·disseizin** \"+\ *n* [*re-* + *disseisin* or *disseizin*] : a disseisin by one previously adjudged to have disseised the same person of the same estate

**re·dissoluble** \ˌrē+\ *adj* [*re-* + *dissoluble*] : capable of dissolving or being dissolved more than once

**re·dissolution** \(ˌ)rē+\ *n* [*re-* + *dissolution*] : an act or process of dissolving again

**re·dissolve** \ˌrē+\ *vb* [*re-* + *dissolve*] **1** : to dissolve again or repeatedly **2** : to disperse again

**re·distill** \"+\ *vt* [*re-* + *distill*] : to distill again or repeatedly — **re·distillation** \(ˌ)rē+\ *n*

**re·distribute** \ˌrē+\ *vt* [*re-* + *distribute*] **1** : to alter the distribution of : apportion again : REALLOCATE, REASSIGN ⟨~ land⟩ ⟨~ income⟩ **2** : to spread to other areas : DISSEMINATE ⟨mountains turn . . . the upper air currents and ~ their moisture —*Amer. Guide Series: Tenn.*⟩ — **re·distribution** \(ˌ)rē+\ *n*

**re·distributive** \ˌrē+\ *adj* : tending to redistribute ⟨public finance is ~ when it makes real incomes less unequal by manipulating taxes —K.E.Knorr⟩

**re·district** \(ˈ)rē+\ *vt* [*re-* + *district*] : to organize into new territorial esp. political divisions

**red·i·vi·vus** \,redəˈvīvəs\ *adj* [LL (influenced in meaning by L *vivere* to live), fr. L, renovated, restored, perh. fr. *reduvia*, *redivia* hangnail, exuviae (fr. *red-* re- + *-uvia*, *-ivia*, fr. *-uere* to put on) + *-ivus* -ive — more at QUICK, EXUVIAE] : brought back to life : living again : REBORN ⟨a case of the phoenix ~ —*Fortune*⟩

**red ivory** *n* : a southern African buckthorn (*Rhamnus zeheri*) with hard heavy red even grained wood esp. suitable for decorative work and turnery

**re·djang** *also* **re·jang** \rāˈzhaŋ\ *n, pl* **redjang** *or* **redjangs** *usu cap* [native name in southern Sumatra] **1** : an Indonesian people of southern Sumatra **2** : a member of the Redjang people

**red jasmine** *or* **red jessamine** *n* **1** : a frangipani (*Plumeria rubra*) widely cultivated in warm regions for its very large leaves and large terminal cymes of pink, red, or purple richly fragrant flowers **2** : CYPRESS VINE

**red-jointed fiddler crab** \ˈ=,=-\ *n* : a brackish marsh fiddler crab (*Uca minax*) of the eastern coast of No. America

**red juniper** *n* : RED CEDAR

**red kangaroo** *n* : a large kangaroo (*Macropus rufus*) of the plains and tablelands of So. Australia — compare BLUE DOE

**red kauri** *n* **1** : KAURI 1 **2** : a tree (*Agathis lanceolata*) of New Zealand having glossy leaves and scaly reddish brown bark

**red lac** *n* : JAPANESE WAX TREE

**red larch** *n* : a tamarack (*Larix laricina*)

**red larkspur** *n* : a perennial herb (*Delphinium nudicaule*) of the Pacific coast often cultivated for its reddish yellow flowers

**red-lattice** \ˈ=ˈ==\ *adj* [so called fr. the red latticework formerly common in windows of alehouses] *obs* : of or relating to an alehouse ⟨your *red-lattice* phrases —Shak.⟩

**red lauan** *n* **1 a** : a valuable Philippine timber tree (*Shorea teysmanniana* **b** : the hard heavy red wood of the red lauan tree often sold as Philippine mahogany **2** : TANGUILE

**red laurel** *n* : CATAWBA RHODODENDRON

**red laver** *n* : any of several common purple seaweeds of the genus *Porphyra* (esp. *P. laciniata* and *P. vulgaris*) the fronds of which are eaten in Europe either stewed or pickled

**red lead** *n* **1** : an orange-red to brick-red lead oxide $Pb_3O_4$ that is prepared by heating lead monoxide in the presence of air, that when produced commercially may contain litharge and other impurities, and that is used chiefly in storage= battery plates, in glass and ceramics, and as a paint pigment (as for protecting metals from corrosion) — called also *minium* **2** : FIERY RED **3** *slang* : CATSUP

**red-lead** \ˈredˈled\ *vt* [*red lead*] : to paint with red lead

**red-lead·er** \-də(r)\ *n* [*red-lead* + *-er*] : a worker who paints exposed metal surfaces with red lead

**red lead ore** *n* : CROCOITE

**red-lead putty** *n* : a mixture of red and white lead and boiled linseed oil used as a lute in pipe fitting

**red leaf** *n* **1** : a smartweed (*Polygonum hydropiper*) **2** : any of several plant diseases characterized by reddening of the foliage: as **a** : a nonparasitic disease of oats of uncertain cause **b** : a disease of the pear and grape caused by nutritional disturbances producing dark red or purplish red discoloration of the leaves **3** : a high grade of Burley tobacco comprised of leaves from near the top of the stalk

**red leaf blight** *n* : a disease of cotton characterized by red or reddish brown foliage and reduced vigor and believed to be related to a shortage of potash

**red leaf spot** *n* : a disease of the cranberry caused by a fungus (*Exobasidium vaccinii*)

**redleg** \ˈ=,=\ *n* **1 a** : REDSHANK **b** : TURNSTONE **c** : RED= LEGGED PARTRIDGE **d** *Wales* : PURPLE SANDPIPER **2** : a bacterial disease of frogs that is esp. destructive when numbers of them are kept together **3 a** *usu cap* [so called fr. the red leggings worn] : a guerrilla raider of pro-secessionist territory esp. in Missouri during the Civil War — compare BUSHWHACKER c **b** *often cap* [so called fr. the red piping formerly worn on the legs by U. S. artillerymen] : ARTILLERYMAN

**red-legged crow** \ˈ=,=(=)-\ *n* : CHOUGH

**red-legged earth mite** *n* : a mite (*Halotydeus destructor*) that is an important pest of clover and other crops in parts of Australia

**red-legged falcon** *n* : RED-FOOTED FALCON

**red-legged grasshopper** *also* **red-legged locust** *n* : a very widely distributed and sometimes highly destructive small No. American grasshopper (*Melanoplus femur-rubrum*) with red hind legs

**red-legged ham beetle** *n* : a small cosmopolitan bluish green iridescent beetle (*Necrobia rufipes*) with the legs and the bases of the antennae reddish that feeds on animal products and cereal grains and that is often a pest around warehouses and ships

**red-legged kittiwake** *n* : a kittiwake (*Rissa brevirostris*) of the north Pacific having red legs and a red bill — compare PACIFIC KITTIWAKE

**red-legged partridge** *n* **1** : a common western European partridge (*Alectoris rufa*) having bright red legs and bill **2** : a partridge of the genus *Alectoris* having distinctly red legs — called also *redleg*

**red-legged plover** *n* : TURNSTONE

**red-legged snipe** *n* : REDSHANK

**red-letter** \ˈ=ˈ==\ *adj* **1** : employing red letters to call attention to something of special significance ⟨*red-letter* Bible⟩ **2** [so called fr. the practice of marking holy days in red letters in church calendars] : of special significance : HAPPY, MEMORABLE ⟨*red-letter* day⟩ ⟨the testimonial dinner was a *red-letter* occasion⟩

**red light** *n* **1 a** : a warning signal ⟨four times the *red light* on the instrument board blinked —*Time*⟩; *esp* : a red traffic signal ⟨at a *red light* a snarl of traffic waited —Thomas Savage⟩ **b** : a cautionary sign : DETERRENT ⟨the bill is a *red light* to labor, warning of what may lie ahead —*New Republic*⟩ **2** : a game in which players run toward a goal while the player who is it with his back to them counts ten and whips around on the phrase "red light" when any player he catches in motion must return to the starting line

**red-light district** *n* [so called fr. the traditional practice of employing red lights to indicate houses of prostitution] : a district in which houses of prostitution are frequent

**red lily** *n* **1 a** : WOOD LILY **1 b** : WESTERN RED LILY **c** : SOUTHERN RED LILY **2** *West Indies* : BARBADOS LILY

**redline** \ˈ=,=\ *vt* **1** : to cross off (an item) from a list (as a military payroll) **2 a** : GROUND ⟨~ an airplane⟩ **b** : to indicate the maximum safe speed of (an airplane)

**red liquor** *n* **1 a** : the mother liquor left in the evaporation of the solution obtained by leaching black ash in the Leblanc process **b** : the mother liquor obtained in the recrystallization of tartar **2** *also* **red mordant** : a solution consisting essentially of an aluminum acetate used in making red color lakes and as a mordant esp. in dyeing red

**red lobelia** *n* : CARDINAL FLOWER

**red locust** *n* **1** : an African insect (*Nomadacris septemfasciata*) that often forms migratory swarms in southern Africa **2 a** : an American tree (*Robinia pseudacacia*) with strong and durable wood **b** : CLAMMY LOCUST

**red louse** *n* **1** : CHIGGER **2** : a small reddish biting louse (*Bovicola bovis*) that infests the skin of cattle feeding chiefly on hair and skin debris — compare BLUE LOUSE

**red·ly** *adv* : in a red manner : with red color : FLAMINGLY, RUDDILY ⟨the forge belched ~ at the sky —Adria Langley⟩

**red maggot** *n* : the larva of the wheat midge

**red mahogany** *n* **1 a** (1) : an Australian eucalypt (*Eucalyptus resinifera*) that yields a dark-colored kino (2) : the hard deep red commercially valuable wood of this tree **b** : an African mahogany (*Khaya nyasica*) **2** : a variable color averaging a dark reddish brown

**red maids** *n pl but sing or pl in constr* : an annual branching herb (*Calandrinia menziesii*) of the Pacific coast of No. America cultivated for its crimson flowers

**red man** *n* **1** : AMERICAN INDIAN **2** *usu cap R & M* : a member of one of the major benevolent and fraternal orders

**red manganese oxide** *n* : MANGANESE TETROXIDE

**red mange** *n* : DEMODECTIC MANGE

**red mangrove** *n* **1 a** : a true mangrove having red wood; *esp* : an African tree (*Rhizophora mangle*) **b** : the wood of the African red mangrove tree **2** : any of several trees of the genus *Bruguiera* (family Rhizophoraceae) of Australia and Polynesia **3** : LOOKING-GLASS PLANT

**redman's orchard** \ˈ=,=-\ *n, West* : a grove or stand of a piñon (*Pinus monophylla*)

**red maple** *n* : any of several American maples distinguished by crimson flowers produced before the leaves in very early spring; *esp* : a common tree (*Acer rubrum*) of the eastern and central U.S. that grows chiefly on moist soils, has reddish twigs and somewhat pubescent leaves, and yields a lighter and softer wood than the sugar maple — called also *swamp maple*

**red mass** *n, often cap R & M* : a votive mass of the Holy Spirit celebrated in red vestments esp. at the opening of courts and congresses

**red meat** *n* **1** : meat (as beef or lamb) that in its raw and uncured state is distinctly red **2** : meat from one of the larger domestic mammals as distinguished from poultry or fish

**red mite** *n* : any of several mites having a red color: as **a** : CHIGGER **b** : EUROPEAN RED MITE **c** : CHICKEN MITE **d** *Austral* : CLOVER MITE

**red mombin** *n* : SPANISH PLUM

**red monkey** *n* **1** : the patas or a related monkey **2** : TOQUE MACAQUE

**redmouth** \ˈ=,=\ *n* **1** : any of several grunts having the inside of the mouth red or pink **2** : a common buffalo fish (*Ictiobus cyprinella*)

**redmouthed buffalo fish** \ˈ=,=-\ *n* : REDMOUTH 2

**red-mouthed grunt** \ˈ=,=-\ *or* **redmouth grunt** *n* : REDMOUTH

**red mud** *n* **1** : a marine offshore deposit deriving its yellow= brown to red-brown color from iron oxide ⟨*red mud* . . . is most prevalent in the Yellow sea and off the coasts of Brazil —F.C.Lane⟩ — compare BLUE MUD **2** : a residue high in iron oxide resulting from purification of alumina in the Bayer process

**red mulberry** *n* **1** : a No. American forest tree (*Morus rubra*) with soft weak but durable wood — called also *black mulberry* **2** : the dark purple edible fruit of the red mulberry tree

**red mullet** *n* **1** : a mullet of the family Mullidae — distinguished from *gray mullet* **2** : a redhorse (*Moxostoma macrolepidotum*) of the streams of the eastern U. S. from Delaware to No. Carolina

**red mustard** *n* : BLACK MUSTARD

**red-neck** \ˈ=,=\ *n* : one belonging to or identified with the rural laboring class of the South — usu. used disparagingly

**red-necked cane borer** \ˈ=,=-\ *n* : the larva of a buprestid beetle (*Agrilus ruficollis*) that bores into the canes of raspberry and blackberry producing swellings or galls

**red-necked gazelle** *n* : ADDRA

**red-necked grebe** *n* : either of two grebes: **a** : a European grebe (*Colymbus grisegena*) **b** : HOLBOELL'S GREBE

**red-necked nightjar** *n* : a nightjar (*Caprimulgus ruficollis*) of southwestern Europe and northern Africa

**red-necked phalarope** *n* : NORTHERN PHALAROPE

**red·ness** \ˈrednəs\ *n* -ES [ME *rednesse*, fr. *read*, *reed*, *red* red + *-nesse* -ness — more at RED] : the quality or state of being red or red-hot

**red node** *n* : a virus disease of beans characterized by reddish discoloration at the nodes

**red nucleus** *n* : a nucleus of gray matter in the tegmentum of the midbrain on each side of the middle line that receives fibers from the cerebellum of the opposite side by way of the superior cerebellar peduncle and gives rise to fibers of the rubrospinal tract of the opposite side

¹**re·do** \(ˈ)rē+\ *vt* [*re-* + *do*] **1 a** : to execute again : do over : REPRODUCE, RESTYLE **b** : REDACT ⟨Broadway successes *redone* on radio or television —J.C.Bushman⟩ **2** : REDECORATE ⟨~ the kitchen in yellow⟩

²**re·do** \ˈrē,dü\ *n* -s **1** : REPETITION, RESTYLING ⟨no pleasanter prospect than a ~ of our South American trek —D.B.Shields⟩ **2** : REDACTION

**red oak** *n* **1** : any of numerous American oaks having four stamens in each floret, acorns that require two years to mature and that have the inner surface of the shell lined with woolly hairs, the acorn cap covered with thin scales, and leaf veins that usu. run beyond the margin of the leaf to form bristles: as **a** : a large symmetrical oak (*Quercus borealis* or *Q. rubra*) that has large leaves with triangular spiny tipped lobes and medium-weight coarse-grained wood less durable than white oak and that is widely distributed in eastern No. America with the exception of the southern coastal region and piedmont — called also *northern red oak* **b** : a large round-topped oak (*Q. falcata* or *Q. rubra*) that has thin leaves with deeply sinuate lobes and wood similar to the northern red oak and that is widely distributed in eastern No. America from New Jersey to Illinois and southward — called also *southern red oak, Spanish oak, turkey oak* **2** : the wood of red oak

**red oat** *n* **1** : an oat (*Avena byzantina*) with red hulls esp. adapted to warm climates **2** : RED GRASS

¹**red ocher** *n* [¹*red* + *ocher*] **1** : a red earthy and often impure hematite used as a pigment **2** : BOLE 3

²**red ocher** *adj, usu cap R&O* : of or relating to a phase of the Woodland pattern characterized by beautifully made leaf-shaped projectile points, crude pottery, copper implements, and burials covered with red ocher

**red oil** *n* **1** : any of various oils that are red often because they are impure: as **a** : commercial oleic acid containing other fatty acids (as linoleic, palmitic, or stearic acid) **b** : a domestic remedy for bruises made by macerating the tops of the common St.-John's-wort in olive oil **2** : a lubricating oil produced from petroleum in various ways

**red·o·lence** \ˈredᵊlən(t)s\ *n* -s [ME, fr. MF, fr. *redolent*] : the quality or state of being redolent : SCENT, AROMA **syn** see FRAGRANCE

**red·o·lent** \-nt\ *adj* [ME, fr. MF, fr. L *redolent-*, *redolens*, pres. part. of *redolēre* to emit a scent, smell like, fr. *red-* re- + *olēre* to smell — more at ODOR] **1 a** : exuding fragrance : AROMATIC ⟨the pinewoods were more ~ —Jean Stafford⟩ **b** : RICH, DISTINCTIVE — used of an odor ⟨the ancient ~ odor of plowed land —Norman Mailer⟩ **2 a** : full of fragrance : SCENTED, SMELLING — used with *of* or *with* ⟨air . . . ~ of seaweed —Nancy Hale⟩ ⟨a corridor ~ of floor wax —Joseph Wechsberg⟩ ⟨~ with homegrown apples —*Nat'l Geographic*⟩ ⟨air . . . ~ with the fumes of beer and whiskey —Herbert Asbury⟩ **b** : conveying an aura : tending to suggest : EVOCATIVE, REMINISCENT ⟨cannot forbear to close on this ~ literary note —Wilder Hobson⟩ — usu. used with *of* or *with* ⟨every page here is ~ of . . . fine scholarship —Walter Pach⟩ ⟨a perfect day . . . ~ with the charm of late autumn —Gerald Beaumont⟩ ⟨conversation . . . ~ with profanity —P.A.Rollins⟩

**red·o·lent·ly** *adv* : in a redolent manner

**re·domesticate** \ˌrē+\ *vt* [*re-* + *domesticate*] : to domesticate again

**re·don·di·lla** \,rādōnˈdēlyə\ *n* -s [Sp, dim. of *redonda* district, province, pastureland, fr. fem. of *redondo* round, fr. L *rotundus* — more at ROUND] : a Spanish verse form consisting of a quatrain of octosyllabic lines with varying rhyme scheme

**re·doppe** \rəˈdäp\ *n* -s [F, fr. It *raddoppio*, lit., redoubling, fr. *raddoppiare* to double, redouble, fr. *rad-* (fr. *re-* — fr. L *re-* — + *ad-*, fr. L) + *doppiare* to double, fr. L *duplare* — more at DOUBLE] : a show-ring movement in which a horse gallops in circles whose diameter never exceeds ten feet

**red orache** *n* : an annual weed (*Atriplex rosea*) native to the Old World but established in parts of No. America and having fruiting bracteoles with dark veinlets — called also *red scale*

**red orpiment** *n* : REALGAR

**redos** *pl of* REDO

**red osier** *n* **1** : any of several willows with reddish twigs that are used for basketry; *esp* : PURPLE WILLOW **2** *also* **red osier dogwood** : a common No. American shrub (*Cornus stolonifera*) with reddish purple twigs, white flowers, and globose blue or whitish fruit — called also *kinnikinnick, redbrush, red dogwood* **3** : SILKY CORNEL

¹**re·double** \(ˈ)rē+\ *vb* [*re-* + *double*, v.] *vt* **1** : to make twice as great in size or amount : renew more vigorously : DOUBLE, INTENSIFY ⟨*redoubled* attacks⟩ ⟨the German radio *redoubled* its frenzied screaming —S.L.A.Marshall⟩ **2 a** *obs* : to echo back ⟨their moans the vales *redoubled* —John Milton⟩ **b** *archaic* : to repeat a second time : DUPLICATE

⟨the negative . . . should be once expressed in a simple sentence; but we generally find it *redoubled* in old English —John Stoddart⟩ ~ *vi* **1 :** to become twice as great or greatly intensified ⟨the wails *redoubled* —Josephine Pinckney⟩ **2** *archaic* **:** RESOUND ⟨peal upon peal *redoubling* all around —William Cowper⟩ **3 :** to double again ⟨the noise doubles and *redoubles*⟩ ⟨the mountain path doubles and *redoubles* upon itself⟩ **4 :** to double an opponent's double in bridge

**²redouble** \"\ *n* **1 :** an act or instance of redoubling; *specif* **:** a bridge call permissible only when the last previous call other than a pass was a double by an opponent and having the effect of doubling the scoring values established by the double for tricks and penalties — compare AUCTION BRIDGE, CONTRACT BRIDGE **2 :** any attack excepting the straight thrust made when a fencing opponent closes the original line of attack but does not riposte

**re·dou·ble·ment** \"+mənt\ *n* [F, fr. MF, fr. *redoubler* to redouble (fr. *re-* + *doubler* to double) + *-ment* — more at DOUBLE] *archaic* **:** an act or instance of redoubling

**¹re·doubt** \rə'daůt, rē'-, *usu* -aůd.+V\ *vt* [ME *redouten,* fr. MF *redouter,* fr. *re-* + *douter* to doubt, fear — more at DOUBT] *archaic* **:** to regard with awe or dismay **:** DREAD, FEAR

**²redoubt** \"\ *n* [F *redoute,* fr. It *ridotto,* fr. ML *reductus* secret place, fr. L, withdrawn, fr. past part. of *reducere* to lead or bring back, withdraw — more at REDUCE] **1 a** *obs* **:** a small separate work inside a fortification — compare RAVELIN **b :** a small usu. temporary enclosed defensive work used esp. in fortifying a hilltop or pass ⟨saw that Bunker Hill had been crowned in the night by a strong ~ —Mabel Swan⟩ **c :** a defended position or protective barrier ⟨encircling the Ruhr and reducing the south German ~ —W.H.Hale⟩ ⟨surrounded by a ~ of lawbooks —R.L.Neuberger⟩ **2 :** a secure retreat **:** STRONGHOLD ⟨the missionary's final ~, faith —Jerome Ellison⟩

**re·doubt·able** \-aůd·əbəl, -aůtəb-\ *adj* [ME *redoutable,* fr. MF, fr. *redouter* + *-able*] **1 a :** causing fear or alarm **:** FORMIDABLE ⟨a tougher and more ~ adversary than the heel-clicking, jackbooted fanatic —G.H.Johnston⟩ ⟨~ gains made by the Communist Party —Max Ascoli⟩ **b :** inspiring awe or reverence **:** AUGUST, EMINENT ⟨that ~ scholar of Spain's golden age —Carol Bache⟩ **2 :** DOUGHTY, ILLUSTRIOUS ⟨a nimble-witted . . . guest, as ~ with a clue as he is at a press conference —*N.Y. Herald Tribune*⟩ ⟨born . . . of the ~ flour-milling family —*New Yorker*⟩

**re·doubt·ably** \-blē, -li\ *adv* **:** in a redoubtable manner

**re·doubt·ed** \-aůd·əd\ *adj* [ME, fr. past part. of *redouten, redoubten* to redoubt — more at REDOUBT] *archaic* **:** REDOUBTABLE

**re·dound** \rə'daůnd, rē'-\ *vi* -ED/-ING/-S [ME *redounden,* fr. MF *redonder,* fr. L *redundare* to overflow, be in excess, fr. *red-* re- + *undare* to billow, overflow — more at UNDULATE] **1** *archaic* **a :** to become swollen **:** surge up **:** BILLOW ⟨waves ~*ing* roar —Alexander Pope⟩ **b :** to be excessive in quantity **:** PREDOMINATE, OVERFLOW ⟨for every dram of honey therein found, a pound of gall doth over it ~ —Edmund Spenser⟩ **2 a :** to have an effect for good or ill **:** CONDUCE ⟨their efforts . . . will ~ to the general good —Lucius Garvin⟩ **b :** to be a contributing factor to repute ⟨will always ~ to his honor and self-sacrifice —Aidan Mulloy⟩ ⟨what he does ~*s* to the credit of geology —K.K.Darrow⟩ **3 a :** to become transferred or added **:** ACCRUE ⟨every value he creates ultimately ~*s* to himself, his neighbor and his country —A.R.Williams⟩ **b** *obs* **:** to issue forth ⟨sacred lore . . . from her sweet lips did ~ —Edmund Spenser⟩ **4 :** to become deflected backward **:** REBOUND, REFLECT ⟨the child's behavior ~*s* on the mother⟩

**red out** *vi* **:** to experience a redout — compare BLACK OUT, GRAY OUT

**redout** \'ˌ=,=\ *n* -S [*red out*] **:** a condition in which blood is driven to the head as a result of centripetal acceleration that causes severe headache and reddening of the field of vision — compare BLACKOUT, GRAYOUT

**red·o·wa** \'redəwə, -dəvə\ *n* -S [F & G; F *rédowa,* fr. G *redowa,* fr. Czech *rejdovák,* fr. *rejdovati* to steer around, drive, whirl around] **:** either of two popular Bohemian ballroom dances of the 19th century: **a :** a dance in triple time resembling a waltz **b :** a dance in ¾ time resembling a polka

**red owl** *n* **:** an American screech owl in its red phase

**re·dox** \'rē,däks\ *n* -ES [*reduction* + *oxidation*] **:** OXIDATION-REDUCTION

**red oxide** *also* **red oxide of iron** *n* **:** ferric oxide esp. when used as a pigment

**red oxide of zinc :** ZINCITE

**redox potential** *n* **:** OXIDATION-REDUCTION POTENTIAL

**red-pencil** \'ˌ=ˈ==\ *vt* **:** to censor, correct, or revise with or as if with a red pencil ⟨much of the truth about the . . . peace talks has been *red-penciled* —R.C.Miller⟩ ⟨*red-penciling* the program down to this figure —*Newsweek*⟩ — compare BLUE-PENCIL

**red pepper** *n* **:** CAYENNE PEPPER; *esp* **:** a pepper fruit that is red at maturity

**red perch** *n* **:** YELLOW PERCH

**red periwinkle** *n* **:** ¹PERIWINKLE 1c

**red phalarope** *n* **:** a phalarope (*Phalaropus fulicarius*) breeding in the arctic regions of the Old and New Worlds and often occurring in large flocks far out at sea

**red phosphorus** *n* **:** the element phosphorus in its red allotropic form

**red pimpernel** *n* **:** SCARLET PIMPERNEL

**red pine** *n* **1 a :** a No. American pine (*Pinus resinosa*) having reddish bark **b :** the hard but not durable wood of the No. American red pine tree consisting chiefly of sapwood — called also *Canadian red pine* **c :** PONDEROSA PINE **d :** DOUGLAS FIR **2 a :** an Australian cypress pine (*Callitris calcarata*) **b :** the timber of the Australian cypress pine **3 a :** RIMU **b :** a black pine (*Podocarpus spicata*) of New Zealand

**red plum** *n* **1 :** a red-fruited plum; *specif* **:** either of two American wild plums (*Prunus americana* and *P. nigra*) **2 :** a variable color averaging a dark purplish red that is bluer and duller than pansy purple or raisin, bluer and paler than Bokhara or dahlia purple (sense 1), and bluer and less strong than redgrape

**red podzolic soil** *n* **:** any of a group of zonal soils developed in a warm-temperate moist climate under deciduous or mixed forests that have thin organic and organic-mineral layers overlying a yellowish brown leached layer resting on an illuvial red horizon — called also *red soil*

**redpole** \'ˌ=,=\ *n* [by folk etymology] **:** REDPOLL 1

**redpoll** \'ˌ=,=\ *n* **1** *or* **redpoll linnet :** any of several small finches (genus *Carduelis* or *Acanthis*) of northern Europe, Asia, and America which are similar in size and habits to the siskins and in which the males usu. have a red or rosy crown and streaked back and sides: as **a :** a common bird (*C. flammea*) distinguished by a rosy breast and rump — compare HORNEMANN'S REDPOLL **b :** LINNET 1 **2** *also* **redpoll warbler :** a palm warbler (*Dendroica palmarum*) — compare YELLOW PALM WARBLER

**red poll** *also* **red polled** *n* **1** *usu cap R&P* **:** a British breed of large hornless fast-growing long-lived dual-purpose cattle that are red with a little white on switch and belly **2** *often cap R&P* **:** an animal of the Red Poll breed

**red pop** *n, South* **:** the male painted bunting (*Passerina ciris*)

**red poppy** *n* **:** CORN POPPY

**red porgy** *n* **:** PORGY 1a

**red precipitate** *n* **:** red mercuric oxide

**red prussiate of potash :** POTASSIUM FERRICYANIDE

**red puccoon** *n* **:** BLOODROOT 1

**red quebracho** *n* **:** QUEBRACHO 1b

**¹re·draft** \(ˈ)rē+\ *n* [*re-* + *draft,* n.] **1 :** a draft on the maker or endorsers of a bill of exchange dishonored by the drawee for the amount of the bill and the protest fee and other charges **2 :** a modified draft **:** REVISION

**²redraft** \"\ *vt* [*re-* + *draft,* v.] **:** to prepare a revised copy or a new version of

**red rag** *n* [so called fr. the tradition that a red rag incites a bull to rage] **:** something that incites to anger or vexation ⟨the jibe was a *red rag* goading him to violence⟩

**red raspberry** *n* **1 :** a raspberry plant with red fruit: as **a :** a European bramble (*Rubus idaeus*) with red or sometimes yellow fruit **b :** a No. American bramble (*R. strigosus*) with red fruit **c :** any of various cultivated raspberry plants that have red fruit and have been derived from the European or American red raspberry by selection or breeding **2 :** the fruit of a red raspberry

**red rat snake** *n* **:** CORN SNAKE

**red rattle** *n* **:** RATTLE 3b

**red rattlesnake** *n* **:** a reddish diamondback rattlesnake (*Crotalus ruber*) of the extreme southwestern U.S. and adjacent Mexico

**re·draw** \(ˈ)rē+\ *vb* [*re-* + *draw*] *vi* **:** to issue a new bill of exchange to cover a protested one ~ *vt* **1 :** to draw again **2 :** to take out or select by lot again **3 :** to delineate again or in another way **4 :** REVISE **5 :** to extrude or shape again **6 :** REWIND

**re·draw·er** \"+(ə)r\ *n* **:** one that redraws; *specif* **:** WINDER

**red republican** *n* **1** *usu cap both Rs* **:** an extreme Republican of the French Revolution **2 :** an extreme radical in political reform — compare RED 5a

**¹re·dress** \rə'dres, rē'-\ *vt* [ME *redressen,* fr. MF *redresser,* fr. OF *redrecier,* fr. *re-* + *drecier* to make straight — more at DRESS] **1** *obs* **a :** to make vertical again ⟨~ a leaning wall —Earl of Shaftesbury †1713⟩ **b :** to put back into good condition physically or spiritually **:** REPAIR ⟨rise God . . . this wicked earth ~ —John Milton⟩ **2 a** (1) **:** to set (a wrong) right **:** REMEDY ⟨looked to charity, not to legislation, to ~ social wrongs —W.R.Inge⟩ (2) **:** to make up for **:** COMPENSATE ⟨what they lacked in apparatus they ~*ed* in understanding —C.F.Mullett⟩ **b :** to remove the cause of (a grievance or complaint) ⟨had not the slightest intention of listening to the grievances of the colonies with a desire to ~ them —H.E. Scudder⟩ ⟨committee has ~*ed* these medievalisms and submitted its draft bill —Harvey Breit⟩ **c :** to exact reparation for **:** AVENGE ⟨must such wrongs either be ignored or ~*ed* in hot blood —R.H.Jackson⟩ **3** *archaic* **a :** to requite (a person) for a wrong or loss **b :** HEAL **4 a :** to eliminate the faults of **:** impart renewed stability to **:** RECTIFY ⟨more divided about how to ~ the economy than they are about . . . ratification —*New Statesman & Nation*⟩ **b :** to neutralize the effect of **:** COUNTERACT, OFFSET ⟨another broadcast may ~ whatever imbalances the first creates —Gilbert Seldes⟩ **c :** to return (an airplane) to normal flying position **:** flatten out **syn** see CORRECT

**²re·dress** \", 'rē,dres\ *n* -ES [ME *redresse,* fr. AF *redresse, redresce,* fr. OF *redrecier*] **1 a :** relief from distress ⟨suicide . . . is a common method of seeking ~ —K.E.Read⟩ **b** *obs* **:** removal of faults **:** REFORMATION, IMPROVEMENT ⟨too long have we driven off the applying of our ~ —Joseph Hall⟩ **c :** the means or possibility of seeking a remedy ⟨there is no ~ whatever, since the accused may not be tried twice for the same offense —Curtis Bok⟩ **2 :** compensation for a wrong or loss **:** REPARATION ⟨discharged officials could seek . . . ~ by appeal —*New Statesman & Nation*⟩ **3 a :** an act or instance of redressing ⟨petition the government for a ~ of grievances —*U.S. Constitution*⟩ **b :** CORRECTION, RETRIBUTION ⟨can be prosecuted for dangerous driving, while the pedestrian can walk dangerously without the slightest fear of ~ —*Brit. Automobile Racing Club Gazette*⟩

**³re·dress** \(ˈ)rē+\ *vt* [*re-* + *dress*] **:** to dress again; *esp* **:** to put through a finishing process again ⟨~ leather before dyeing⟩ ⟨~ tools that show signs of wear⟩

**re·dress·er** \rə'dresə(r)\ *n* [ME *redressere,* fr. *redressen* + *-ere* -er] **:** one that redresses

**re·dress·ment** \-smənt\ *n* -S **:** REDRESS

**red ribbon** *n* **:** a red ribbon usu. with appropriate words or markings that is awarded the second-place winner in a competition

**red rice** *n* **1 :** a Chinese vegetable dye used in food products — called also *ang-khak* **2 :** a wild rice (*Oryza rufipogon*) with a red husk and pinkish white seed that is considered an objectionable weed in the rice fields of the southern U.S. but that has grain which is comparable to common rice in nutritive value

**re·dri·er** \(ˈ)rē,drī(ə)r\ *n* [*redry* + *-er*] **:** a device for drying panels of plywood after they are glued

**red ring** *n* **:** a disease of tomatoes caused by a plant bug (*Cyrtopeltis varians*) and characterized by reddish brown marks around the stems and petioles

**red ring disease** *n* **:** a disease of the coconut palm caused by an eelworm (*Aphelenchoides cocophilus*) in which a cross section of the trunk shows a red ring

**red river hog** *n* **:** PAINTED PIG

**red river maple** *n, usu cap both Rs* [fr. the *Red river* in Kentucky or the *Red river* in Tennessee] **:** BOX ELDER

**red-roan** \'ˌ=ˈ=\ *adj* **:** of a roan color produced by mingling of bay and white hairs

**red robin** *n* **1 :** SCARLET TANAGER **2** *dial Eng* **:** HERB ROBERT **3 :** INDIA RED

**red rock** *n* **:** RED BEDS

**red rock cod** *n* **1 :** any of numerous pinkish or red rockfishes (genus *Sebastodes*) of considerable importance as market fishes along the Pacific coast of No. America — called also *red cod* **2 :** a fish (*Scorpaena cruenta*) of southern Australia, Tasmania, and New Zealand related to the American red rock cods

**red rockfish** *n* **1 :** a large rockfish (*Sebastodes ruberrimus*) of the Pacific coast of No. America that is crimson above fading to yellowish pink on the sides and is a highly esteemed food fish — called also *red snapper* **2 :** a red color phase of a large common grouper (*Mycteroperca venenosa* or *Trisotropis venenosa*) of the tropical western Atlantic and the West Indies — called also *rock grouper*

**red rock trout** *n* **:** a greenling (*Hexagrammos superciliosus*)

**red rod** *n* **:** SILKY CORNEL

**red roe** *n* **:** CORAL 3a

**red roman** *n* **:** ROMAN 6

**red roncador** *n* **1 :** BLACK CROAKER **2 :** SPOTFIN CROAKER

**redroot** \'ˌ=,=\ *n* **1 :** a perennial herb (*Lachnanthes tinctoria*) of the eastern U.S. having sword-shaped leaves, cymose woolly flowers, and a red root that is sometimes used as the source of a dye **2 :** a plant of the genus *Ceanothus; esp* **:** NEW JERSEY TEA **3 :** BLOODROOT 1 **4 :** a gromwell (*Lithospermum officinale*) **5 :** ALKANET 1a **6** *or* **redroot pigweed :** PIGWEED **a 7 :** a West Indian and Central American shrub (*Morinda roioc*) with white flowers **8 :** PINKROOT

**red rot** *n* **1 :** a common sundew (*Drosera rotundifolia*) **2 a :** either of two diseases of sugarcane: (1) **:** a destructive disease caused by a fungus (*Physalospora tucumanensis*) characterized by red patches within the canes and found also on sorgo (2) **:** a rot of the leaf sheaths caused by a fungus (*Sclerotium rolfsii*) **b :** a wood decay of various conifers and deciduous trees caused by various pore fungi — called also *red heart* **c :** ADUSTIOSIS

**red rover** *n* **:** a game in which two teams line up facing each other, a challenged player rushes the opposition's line in an effort to break through their joined hands, and upon failure to do so becomes one of their number

**red rust** *n* **1 a :** the uredinial stage of a rust (as of a cereal grass) **b :** the diseased condition produced by such fungi **2 :** an infestation of plants by red spiders **3 a :** a disease of the leaves or twigs of tropical or subtropical plants (as tea and citrus) characterized by a rusty appearance and caused by a parasitic green alga (*Cephaleuros virescens*) of the family Trentepohliaceae — called also *algal disease* **b :** the alga producing red rust of tea

**reds** *pl of* RED, *pres 3d sing of* RED

**red sable** *n* **:** KOLINSKY 1b

**red sage** *n* **1 :** a tropical shrub (*Lantana camara*) with flat clusters of small tubular flowers that open yellow or pink but change to scarlet or orange — called also *wild sage* **2 :** any of various plants of the genus *Kochia* (esp. *K. americana*)

**red salamander** *n* **1 :** any of several salamanders (genus *Pseudotriton*) of the eastern U.S. exclusive of New England **2 :** a Pacific coast salamander (*Ensatina eschscholtzii eschscholtzii*) related to the eastern red salamander

**red salmon** *n* **:** SOCKEYE SALMON

**red sandalwood** *n* **1 a** *or* **red sanders** *or* **red sanderswood** *or* **red saunders :** a tree (*Pterocarpus santalinus*) of India and the East Indies **b :** the hard durable fragrant timber of this tree that is much prized for cabinetwork — called also *ruby wood* **c :** the dark red heartwood of red sandalwood used as a dyewood and for coloring tinctures and other liquid preparations **2 :** an East Indian tree (*Adenanthera pavonina*) much cultivated for ornament — called also *bead tree, Barbados pride, coralwood;* see CIRCASSIAN SEED

**red sandpiper** *n* **:** the knot in summer plumage

**red scale** *n* **1 :** a red or reddish scale: as **a :** CALIFORNIA RED SCALE **b :** FLORIDA RED SCALE **2 :** RED ORACHE

**red seaweed** *n* **:** RED ALGA; *specif* **:** a red alga of the genus *Polysiphonia*

**red seed** *n* **:** RED FEED

**red-seeded dandelion** \'ˌ=,==-\ *n* **:** a European perennial dandelion (*Taraxacum laevigatum*) naturalized in No. America and having narrow leaf lobes and sulphur yellow flowers

**red-shafted** \'ˌ=ˈ==\ *adj* **:** having the shaft of the quills red

**red-shafted flicker** *n* **:** a flicker (*Colaptes cafer collaris*) of the western U.S. differing from the common eastern flicker in lacking the red nape patch and in having the undersurface of the wings and tail reddish and in the male a red stripe on the side of the throat

**redshank** \'ˌ=,=\ *n* **1 :** a common Old World limicoline bird (*Tringa totanus*) having the legs and feet pale red — called also *redleg, red-legged snipe;* compare SPOTTED REDSHANK **2 :** a Celtic inhabitant of the Scottish Highlands or of Ireland; *esp* **:** HIGHLANDER — often used disparagingly **3 a :** REDROOT 2 **b :** any of various persicaries with red stem bases (as *Polygonum persicaria* and *P. hydropiper*)

**red shift** *n* **:** a displacement of a spectrum toward longer wavelengths: as **a :** such a displacement in the spectrum of a celestial body usu. caused by the Doppler shift that results from a recession relative to the observer **b :** a shift in the spectrum of galaxies outside the local group that is interpreted as a Doppler shift, increases in proportion to distance, and constitutes evidence for belief in the expanding universe

**redshirt** \'ˌ=ˈ=\ *n* **:** a member of an organization having a red shirt as a distinctive part of its dress or uniform; *esp* **:** a member of the revolutionary forces of Giuseppe Garibaldi

**red-short** \'ˌ=ˈ=\ *adj* [by folk etymology fr. Sw *rödskört,* neut. of *rödskör,* fr. *röd* red (fr. OSw *röther*) + *skör* brittle, fr. OSw *skör, skyr;* akin to ON *rauthr* red and ON *skera* to cut — more at RED, SHEAR] *of metal* **:** brittle when red-hot — compare COLD-SHORT, HOT-SHORT

**red-short·ness** *n* **:** the quality or state of being red-short

**red-shouldered hawk** \'ˌ=,==-\ *n* **:** a common hawk (*Buteo lineatus*) of eastern No. America that is slightly smaller than the red-tailed hawk and has reddish rufous lesser wing coverts in the adult — called also *hen hawk*

**red shrew** *n* **:** a musk shrew (*Crocidura flavescens*)

**red shrimp** *n* **:** BRAZILIAN SHRIMP

**redside dace** \'ˌ=,==-\ *also* **red-sided dace** \'ˌ=,==-\ *n* **:** a small freshwater cyprinid fish (*Clinostomus elongatus*) of central and eastern No. America having in the male in the breeding season a red band along each side

**red silk cotton** *n* **:** SIMAL

**red silky oak** *n* **:** a beefwood (*Stenocarpus salignus*)

**red silver fir** *n* **:** AMABILIS FIR

**red silver ore** *n* **1 :** PYRARGYRITE **2 :** PROUSTITE

**red sindhi** *n* **1** *usu cap R&S* **:** an Indian breed of rather small red humped dairy cattle extensively used for crossbreeding with European stock in tropical areas **2** *often cap R&S* **:** an animal of the Red Sindhi breed

**red siskin** *n* **:** a finch (*Carduelis cucullata*) of northern So. America that is scarlet with black head, wings, and tail, is often kept as a cage bird, and is the wild parent of the red factor canary

**redskin** \'ˌ=,=\ *n* **:** a No. American Indian

**red snapper** *n* **:** any of various reddish fishes: as **a :** any of several snappers; *esp* **:** a large chiefly rose-red form (*Lutjanus aya*) that ranges from Long Island to Brazil, is abundant in the Gulf of Mexico and on banks off the Florida coast, and is an important food fish **b** (1) **:** RED ROCKFISH (2) **:** RASHER **c :** RED GROUPER **d** *Austral* **:** a fish of the family Berycidae; *esp* **:** a silvery blood-red fish (*Trachichthodes girardi*) much prized as a food fish

**red snow** *n* **1 :** snow colored by various airborne dusts or by the growth of various algae (as the flagellate *Chlamydomonas nivalis*) that contain red pigment and live in the upper layer of snow in arctic and alpine regions **2 :** an alga causing red snow

**red soil** *n* **:** RED PODZOLIC SOIL

**red sorrel** *n* **1 :** ROSELLE **2 :** SHEEP SORREL

**red spider** *also* **red spider mite** *n* **:** any of the small web-spinning mites of the family Tetranychidae that are pests attacking forage and crop plants and in some areas seriously damaging fruit trees by piercing the leaves with their mouthparts and draining out the cellular material near the puncture

**red spider crab** *n* **:** CORAL CRAB 1

**red spirit** *n* **:** a tin spirit used in dyeing red

**red-spotted purple** \'ˌ=,==-\ *n* **:** a butterfly with red spots on the underwing surfaces that constitutes a variety of and generally resembles the banded purple

**red spruce** *n* **:** a coniferous tree (*Picea rubens*) of eastern No. America having deeply furrowed brown or purplish bark and in two rows short-stalked blunt dark green needles which are lighter beneath and being the chief lumber spruce of the area and important as a source of pulp wood — called also *eastern spruce, yellow spruce*

**red squill** *n* **:** a squill that is a red-rooted form of the European squill (*Urginea maritima*) and that has a reddish brown bulb used chiefly in rat poison

**red squirrel** *n* **1 :** a common and widely distributed No. American squirrel (*Tamiasciurus hudsonicus* or *Sciurus hudsonicus*) much smaller than the gray squirrel and having the upper parts chiefly red — called also *chickaree, mountain boomer* **2 :** the native English squirrel (*Sciurus vulgaris leucourus* or *S. leucourus*)

**red stain** *n* **:** a reddish discoloration of the wood of trees esp. as caused in jack pine by fungi of the genera *Fomes* and *Stereum*

**red-stalk aster** *n* **:** COCASH

**red star** *n* **:** a star of spectral type M, N, R, or S having a very low surface temperature and a red color

**redstart** \'ˌ=,=\ *n* [¹*red* + obs. E *start* tail, fr. ME *stert* — more at START] **1 :** a small European singing bird (*Phoenicurus phoenicurus*) related to the redbreast, bluethroat, and nightingale and having a white forehead, black face and throat, and bright chestnut breast and tail — called also *redtail;* compare AMERICAN REDSTART **2 :** any of various Asiatic or European birds of the genus *Phoenicurus* (as the black redstart *P. ochruros* syn. *P. titys* of Europe)

**red steenbras** *n* **:** a southern African fish (*Dentex rupestris*) resembling a snapper and reaching a weight of 50 to 60 pounds — compare WHITE STEENBRAS

**red stele** *n* **:** a fatal root-rotting disease of strawberries caused by a fungus (*Phytophthora fragariae*) and characterized by dwarfing and sudden wilting of the plants and by reddening of the steles of affected roots — called also *red core*

**red-stem filaree** *also* **red-stemmed filaree** \'ˌ=,==-\ *n* **:** ALFILARIA

**red stopper** *n* **:** a small tree (*Eugenia rhombea*) of southern Florida and the West Indies having white flowers and orange or blackish fruit

**red-streaked spider** \'ˌ=,==-\ *or* **red striped spider** *n* **:** REDBACK SPIDER

**red stringybark** *n* **:** an Australian tree (*Eucalyptus macrorrhyncha*) with light brown moderately hard wood

**red stripe** *n* **:** any of several diseases of plants marked by reddish stripes or streaks: as **a :** a decay of timber caused by a pore fungus (*Polyporus vaporarius*) and characterized by red or brown streaks **b :** a disease of sugarcane caused by a bacterium (*Xanthomonas rubrilineans*) and characterized by long narrow dark red streaks on the leaves of young plants and later invasion of the vascular system with occasional top rotting

**red stuff** *n* **:** a polishing agent consisting of rouge or crocus

**red stumpnose** *n* **:** a southern African sea bream (*Chrysoblephus gibbiceps*) — compare WHITE STUMPNOSE

**red sumac** *n* **:** SMOOTH SUMAC

**red sunflower** *n* **:** PURPLE CONEFLOWER

**red suture** *n* **:** a virus disease of peaches marked by a premature reddish coloration that is evident first in the suture

**redtab** \'ˌ=,=\ *n* [so called fr. the red tabs on the collar] **:** a high-ranking officer in the British army

**red tai** *n* **:** a brilliant crimson Pacific porgy (*Pagrus major* or *Chrysophrys major*) that is a favorite food fish of Japan and is commonly figured as a symbol of the Japanese fish god
**redtail** \ˈ=,=\ *n* **1 a :** RED-TAILED HAWK **b :** REDSTART 1 **2 :** BRAZILIAN SHRIMP
**red–tailed hawk** \ˈ=,=-\ *n* **:** a widely distributed New World buteonine hawk (*Buteo jamaicensis*); *esp* **:** a common rodent-eating hawk (*Buteo jamaicensis borealis*) of eastern No. America that is mottled dusky above and white tinged with buff and streaked dusky below and has a rather short typically rufous tail — called also *redtail*; see HARLAN'S HAWK, KRIDER'S HAWK
**red–tailed tropic bird** *n* **:** a tropic bird (*Phaëton rubricauda*)
**red tail snapper** *n* **:** LANE SNAPPER
**red tape** *n* [so called fr. the red tape formerly used to tie up legal documents in England] **:** bureaucratic procedure esp. as characterized by mechanical adherence to regulations, needless duplication of records, and the compilation of an excessive amount of extraneous information resulting in prolonged delay or inaction
**red–tape·ism** *or* **red–tap·ism** \ˈredˈtā,pizəm\ *n* -s **:** insistence on or preoccupation with red tape
**red tassel flower** *n* **:** a prairie clover (*Petalostemon purpureus*) of central No. America with linear leaflets and purplish flowers
**red thread** *n* **:** a disease of turf grasses caused by a fungus (*Corticium juciforme*) and characterized esp. by reddish stromata on or in the pinkish web of hyphal threads
**red three–awn** *n* **:** a needlegrass (*Aristida longiseta*)
**redthroat** \ˈ=,=\ *n* **:** a small Australian singing bird (*Pyrrholaemus brunneus*) having the upper parts brown and the center of the throat rufous
**red–throated loon** *or* **red–throated diver** \ˈ=,==-\ *n* **:** a small loon (*Gavia stellata*) with a thin and uptilted bill and a reddish throat patch
**redthroat trout** *n* **:** CUTTHROAT TROUT
**red tick** *n* **:** a common African tick (*Rhipicephalus evertsi*) that transmits various protozoan and spirochete diseases to cattle
**red tide** *n* **:** seawater discolored by the presence of large numbers of dinoflagellates (esp. of the genera *Peridinium* and *Gymnodinium*) in a density fatal to many forms of marine life — called also *red water*
**red tiercel** *n* **:** an immature male peregrine falcon
**red titi** *n* **:** LEATHERWOOD 1b
**red tobacco** *n* **:** leaves of air-cured or flue-cured tobacco having a reddish color
**red–toothed shrew** \ˈ=,=-\ *n* **:** a shrew of the genus *Sorex* — compare WHITE-TOOTHED SHREW
**redtop** \ˈ=,=\ *also* **redtop grass** *n* **1 :** any of various grasses of the genus *Agrostis*; *esp* **:** an important pasture forage and lawn grass (*A. alba*) of eastern No. America having reddish panicles — called also *bonnet grass* **2 :** BLUEJOINT 1 **3 :** NATAL GRASS
**red tourlourou** *n* -s **:** BLACK CRAB
**red tree mouse** *n* **:** a large lemming mouse (*Phenacomys longicaudus*) of a bright reddish cinnamon color with a long hairy black tail and whitish underparts
**red trillium** *n* **:** any of several wakerobins of the genus *Trillium* with red or dark purple flowers (esp. *T. sessile* and *T. erectum*)
**red truffle** *n* **:** a hard-skinned puffball (*Melanogaster variegatus*)
**red tulip oak** *n* **:** an Australian tree (*Tarrietia argyrodendron*) of the family Sterculiaceae with variegated pink to reddish brown wood
**red turnip beetle** *n* **:** a leaf beetle (*Entomoscelis americana*) that does severe damage to cruciferous garden crops in western No. America
**red turpentine beetle** *n* **:** a rather large reddish bark beetle (*Dendroctonus valens*) that attacks the basal part of various pines throughout most of No. America
**re·duce** \rəˈd(y)üs, rēˈ-\ *vb* -ED/-ING/-S [ME *reducen* to lead back, bring back, draw together, fr. L *reducere*, fr. *re-* + *ducere* to lead — more at TOW] *vt* **1 a :** to draw together or cause to converge **:** CONDENSE, CONSOLIDATE ⟨for the sake of brevity I ~ all their questions to one —Arnold Isenberg⟩ ⟨all springs ~ their currents to my eyes —*Shak.*⟩ **b** (1) **:** to diminish in size, amount, extent, or number **:** make smaller **:** LESSEN, SHRINK ⟨the highway, here *reduced* to a street —G.R. Stewart⟩ ⟨~ excise rates on automobiles —*Wall Street Jour.*⟩ ⟨abolition of aggressive weapons would . . . ~ the likelihood of aggressive war —R.L.Buell⟩ ⟨a safety campaign to ~ forest fires⟩ ⟨a diet to ~ weight⟩ (2) **:** to decrease the volume and concentrate the flavor of (as a gravy) by boiling off excess liquid (3) **:** to concentrate or decrease the volume of (as crude petroleum) by removing light hydrocarbons by distillation ⟨the residue or topped crude oil is further *reduced* —W.L.Nelson & A.P.Buthod⟩ **c :** to narrow down **:** CONFINE, LIMIT, RESTRICT ⟨when we know more about the capacities of man, we do not ~ them, but expand them —A.H.Compton⟩ ⟨the Indians were *reduced* to a small fragment of their former domain —E.M.Coulter⟩ **d :** to make shorter or divest of nonessentials **:** ABRIDGE, CURTAIL ⟨great body of religious lyrics . . . skillfully *reduced* and edited —H.S.Bennett⟩ ⟨double ax-head occurring among the hieroglyphic forms *reduced* to a linear outline —Edward Clodd⟩ **2** *archaic* **a :** to lead back **:** cause to return ⟨~ the Protestants within the pale of the Romish Church —Nicholas Tindal⟩ **b :** to restore to righteousness **:** SAVE ⟨if any of these erring men may be *reduced*, I have my end —John Milton⟩ **3 a** *obs* **:** REDIRECT ⟨with these words ~ they thoughts that roam —William Austin⟩ **b** *obs* **:** to bring back ⟨~, replant our bishop president —Edward Dering⟩ **c :** to bring to a specified state or condition by guidance or leadership ⟨his task was to ~ to order the economic and political chaos following war —W.L.Fleming⟩ **4** *archaic* **a :** to cause to recur ⟨traitors . . . that would ~ these bloody days again —*Shak.*⟩ **b :** to restore to a former condition ⟨~ them to their former shape —Jonathan Swift⟩ **5 a** (1) **:** to force to capitulate **:** bring under control **:** SUBDUE, SUBJUGATE ⟨after a long siege he *reduced* Alexandria —*Encyc. Americana*⟩ ⟨a pioneer . . . *reducing* the savage wilderness for civilization —D.B.Davis⟩ ⟨about thirty years ago the aboriginal tribes of the interior were *reduced* —E.P.Hanson⟩ (2) **:** to wipe out (an enemy position) **:** ELIMINATE, DEMOLISH ⟨~ a salient⟩ ⟨~ a machine gun nest⟩ **b :** to make captive or hand over ⟨helped ~ the New Amsterdam Dutch to English control —R.P.Stearns⟩ **c** (1) **:** to put under obligation **:** MAKE, COMPEL ⟨one passage so painful that he was *reduced* to explain it by the arts of . . . wizards —G.G.Coulton⟩ (2) **:** to force to resort ⟨were *reduced* to the knee holds and body clings detested by all mountaineers —D.L.Busk⟩ (3) **:** to cause to succumb ⟨a scene that had *reduced* his wife to tears —Scott Fitzgerald⟩ ⟨his exaggerated stories had *reduced* the patrons to openmouthed credulity —*Amer. Guide Series: Pa.*⟩ **d** *obs* **:** to make more temperate **:** OVERCOME ⟨it was necessary . . . their tempers be *reduced* by my kindness —Daniel Defoe⟩ **e :** to cause to revert to one's possession by exercising a legal claim **6 a :** to assign to or describe in terms of some fundamental classification ⟨attempt to ~ life, mind, and spirit to the quantitative categories of physics, chemistry, and mathematics —W.R.Inge⟩ **b :** to bring to a systematic form or character — used with *to* ⟨system of nature, which it is the business of science to study and ~ to laws —C.H.Whiteley⟩ **c :** to endow with a definite shape ⟨the idea . . . was *reduced* to exact form —Graham Wallas⟩ **d :** to transfer to or as if to paper — used with *to* ⟨~ to writing his notions regarding the ideal bird dog —W.F.Brown b.1903⟩ **7 a :** to put back (as a herniated mass) into place **b :** to restore (as elevated blood pressure) to a normal condition **c :** to set (as a fracture) by restoring misplaced parts to a normal position **8 a** *chiefly Scots law* **:** RESCIND, ANNUL **b :** to lower in grade or rank **:** DEMOTE ⟨*reduced* from cruiser command to an inconspicuous post in the merchant marine because of . . . political differences —Lee Rogow⟩ **9 a :** to lower in condition or status **:** DEBASE, DOWNGRADE ⟨at storekeeping he was a failure, and . . . was soon *reduced* to poverty —H.E. Starr⟩ ⟨an old Crusader . . . *reduced* to menial work —T.B. Costain⟩ ⟨historical reporting . . . ~*s* the novel to a news supplement —Allen Tate⟩ **b :** to be driven by poverty or deficiency ⟨*reduced* to going about the . . . villages soliciting alms —J.G.Frazer⟩ ⟨radicals . . . who used to speak of Russia as a land of hope are now *reduced* to saying that it is no worse than any other country —Zechariah Chafee⟩ **c :** to make physically weak ⟨my father was so *reduced*, that I . . . made a bed for him on the deck —Charles Dickens⟩ **d :** to diminish in strength or density ⟨rising sun quickly *reduced* the fog⟩: as (1) **:** to dilute (as a paint) with a thinner (2) **:** to extend (as a pigment) with an inert extender or pigment (3) **:** to make (a photographic negative) less dense **e :** to diminish in value ⟨stocks have been *reduced* to a low level —*Collier's Yr. Bk.*⟩ **10 a** (1) **:** to change the denominations of without changing the value ⟨~ days and hours to minutes⟩ (2) **:** to change the form of (an arithmetical expression) without changing the value ⟨~ fractions to a common denominator⟩ (3) **:** to construct a geometrical figure similar to but smaller than (a given figure) **b :** to transpose from one form into another **:** CONVERT, TRANSLATE ⟨given . . . credit for *reducing* time to space —N.E.Nelson⟩ ⟨~ disputes about ideas and values to factual, sociological terms —Cushing Strout⟩ ⟨~ government regulations to plain language⟩ **c** (1) **:** to change (an expression) from a form that is given to another that is equivalent but considered to be more fundamental or important ⟨*reducing* all sentential connectives to the stroke function⟩ (2) **:** to change (a syllogism) to a mood in the first figure **11 a :** to break down (as by crushing, grinding, or burning) **:** cause to disintegrate **:** PULVERIZE ⟨breaker rolls . . . ~ the wheat kernels to middlings —*Amer. Guide Series: Minn.*⟩ ⟨tree stumps left on a clearing . . . are *reduced* by swarms of ants —C.D.Forde⟩ ⟨a recent earthquake *reduced* the cathedral of Cuzco almost to a heap of rubble —Angélica Mendoza⟩ **b** *archaic* **:** to cause (a military unit) to disperse **:** DISBAND **c :** to separate into commercially usable elements ⟨~ trees to lumber⟩ ⟨~ pilchards into oil and meal⟩ **d :** to treat (garbage) so as to recover grease and other products **12 a :** to bring to the metallic state by removal of nonmetallic elements ⟨iron ores are *reduced* to metallic iron⟩ ⟨metals are *reduced* from their ores⟩ — compare SMELT **b :** DEOXIDIZE ⟨~ anthraquinone to anthracene⟩ **c :** to combine with or subject to the action of hydrogen **:** HYDROGENATE ⟨acetaldehyde is *reduced* to alcohol in the final step of alcoholic fermentation⟩ **d :** to change (a compound) by decreasing the proportion of the electronegative part ⟨~ mercuric chloride to mercurous chloride⟩ **:** change (an element or ion) from a higher to a lower oxidation state ⟨in electrolysis, ferric ions are *reduced* to ferrous ions at the cathode —Farrington Daniels & R.A.Alberty⟩ **:** add one or more electrons to (an atom or ion or molecule) ⟨~ ionic copper to metallic copper⟩ — opposed to *oxidize* **13 :** to transform to actuality ⟨faces the task of *reducing* theory to a course of instruction —J.R. Butler⟩ **14 a** (1) **:** to use an unstressed vowel (as \ə\) or no vowel at all instead of (a stressed vowel) (2) **:** to make such alteration in (a syllable) **b :** to cause the loss of a member from (a series of consonants or vowels) **~** *vi* **1 a :** to become diminished or lessened; *esp* **:** to lose weight by dieting ⟨no more, thanks, I'm *reducing*⟩ **b :** to become concentrated ⟨let the stock ~, strain . . . and keep hot —Roger Angell⟩ **c :** to undergo meiosis **d :** to become consolidated ⟨the number 53, which is composed of 5 and 3, *reduces* to the primate number 8 —W.B.Gibson⟩ **2 :** to become converted or equated ⟨romanticism and classicism . . . ~ in the end to differences of psychological type —Herbert Read⟩ **3 :** to become weakened or diluted ⟨poster paints ~ with water⟩ **4 :** to undergo processing esp. for commercial purposes ⟨canneries send a stink of *reducing* fish into the air —John Steinbeck⟩ **syn** see CONQUER, DECREASE
**re·duce·able** \-səbəl\ *adj, archaic* **:** REDUCIBLE
**re·duced** \-st\ *adj* **1 a :** made smaller ⟨a ~ illustration⟩ **b :** imperfect in form or function or lacking parts **:** DWARFED, VESTIGIAL **2 :** WEAKENED, IMPOVERISHED ⟨his poor ~ body —Charles Dickens⟩
**reduced hematin** *n* **:** HEME 1
**reduced iron** *n* **:** finely divided iron prepared by a chemical process (as by heating ferric oxide at a dull red heat in hydrogen) and used as a tonic
**reduced oil** *n* **:** petroleum freed from volatile and suspended matter
**reduced rate contribution clause** *n* **:** AVERAGE CLAUSE 1
**reducement** *n* -s **1** *obs* **:** restoration to righteousness **2** *obs* **:** SUBJUGATION **3** *obs* **:** DIMINUTION
**re·duc·er** \-sə(r)\ *n* -s **1 :** one that reduces **2 a :** one that condenses or consolidates **b :** one that makes smaller or less: as (1) **:** REDUCING COUPLING (2) **:** REDUCING VALVE (3) **:** a hydraulic device that lowers pressure and increases movement used to transmit the load from the hydraulic support of the lower shackle to the lever weighing apparatus in some kinds of heavy testing machines (4) **:** SHELL REDUCER **3 :** one that weakens or dilutes: as **a :** REDUCING AGENT; *specif* **:** one used in photographic development **b :** a chemical solution for reducing the density of a silver image in photography **c :** a paint thinner **d :** a vessel or apparatus in which chemical reduction is carried out **:** REDUCTOR **e :** a worker who adds thinners to paint or varnish to obtain the proper consistency **4 :** one that processes esp. for commercial use ⟨a ~ of iron ore⟩
**reducer sleeve** *n* **:** TAPER REDUCER SLEEVE
**reduces** *pres 3d sing of* REDUCE
**re·duc·ibil·i·ty** \rə,d(y)üsəˈbiləd·ē, rē,-, -lətē, -i\ *n* -ES **:** the quality or state of being reducible
**re·duc·ible** \rəˈd(y)üsəbəl, rēˈ-\ *adj* [*reduce* + *-ible*] **:** capable of being reduced ⟨~ to a set of principles of human nature —Edmund Wilson⟩
**reducible polynomial** *n* **:** a polynomial expressible as the product of two or more polynomials of lower degree
**re·duc·ibly** \-blē, -li\ *adv* **:** in a reducible manner
[1]**re·duc·ing** \-siŋ, -sēŋ\ *n* -s [ME, fr. gerund of *reducen* to reduce — more at REDUCE] **:** REDUCTION
[2]**reducing** \"\ *adj* [fr. pres. part. of *reduce*] **:** causing or facilitating reduction
**reducing agent** *n* **:** a substance that reduces; *esp* **:** a substance (as hydrogen, sodium, or hydroquinone) that donates electrons or a share in its electrons to another substance — called also *reducer, reductant;* compare OXIDIZING AGENT
**reducing coupling** *n* **:** a coupling for joining a pipe to another of smaller diameter
**reducing flame** *n* **:** a flame or part of a flame (as the inner cone of a gas flame) having partially burned gas and being capable of extracting oxygen from various metallic oxides placed within it
**reducing furnace** *n* **:** a furnace for reducing ores
**reducing glass** *n* **:** a diverging lens or convex mirror giving a virtual image of reduced size of an object
**reducing press** *n* **:** a punch press for redrawing metal articles (as cartridge shells)
**reducing sugar** *n* **:** a sugar that is capable of reducing a mild oxidizing agent (as Fehling solution) ⟨glucose, maltose, and lactose are *reducing sugars* but sucrose and methyl glucoside are not⟩ — compare BENEDICT'S TEST
**reducing turbine** *n* **:** a steam turbine that is used as a reducing valve to perform useful work in the process of pressure reduction
**reducing valve** *n* **:** an automatic valve that reduces pressure (as of steam entering a pipe from a boiler)
**re·duct** \rəˈdəkt\ *vt* -ED/-ING/-S [L *reductus*, past part. of *reducere* — more at REDUCE] **1 :** REDUCE **2** *dial* **:** DEDUCT ⟨you can ~ it from my wages —A.E.Coppard⟩
**re·duc·tant** \rəˈdəktənt\ *n* -s [*reduction* + *-ant*] **:** REDUCING AGENT — compare OXIDANT
**re·duc·tase** \-k,tās, -āz\ *n* -s [*reduction* + *-ase*] **:** an enzyme that catalyzes reduction — compare DEHYDROGENASE
**reductase test** *n* **:** a test for the bacterial content esp. of milk and milk products in which methylene blue is added and the time determined for decolorization of the dye by the reducing action of the bacteria
**re·duc·tic acid** \-ktik-\ *n* [*reduction* + *-ic*] **:** a crystalline enolic ketone $C_5H_6O_3$ that has properties both of an acid and a strong reducing agent in alkaline solution and is formed by the action of dilute sulfuric acid on various carbohydrates at high temperature or synthetically from cyclopentanone; 2,3-dihydroxy-2-cyclopenten-one
**re·duc·tio** \rəˈdəkshē,ō, rēˈ-; räˈdüktē,ō\ *n, pl* **reducti·o·nes** \=,==ˈō,nēz; =,==ˈō,nās\ [LL — more at REDUCTION] **:** an act or process of reducing — used as the first term in phrases relating to disproof of a proposition by arguing it to an obviously false conclusion ⟨~ ad impossibile⟩; compare AD ABSURDUM
**re·duc·tion** \rəˈdəkshən, rēˈ-\ *n* -s [ME *reduccion*, fr. MF *reduction*, fr. LL & L; LL *reduction-, reductio* reduction (in a syllogism), fr. L, action of leading or bringing back, restoration, fr. *reductus* (past part. of *reducere* to lead back, bring back, draw together) + *-ion-, -io* -ion — more at REDUCE] **1** *obs* **:** REDEMPTION, RESTORATION ⟨~ of the soul —Theophilus Gale⟩ ⟨~ of Christ from the dead —John Owen⟩ **2 a** (1) **:** domination by force **:** CONQUEST, SUBJUGATION (2) **:** elimination of a defended enemy position **b** (1) **:** the act or process of resettlement (as by Spanish missionaries) of So. American Indians in villages or compounds for purposes of acculturation or control (2) **:** a village or compound so established **3 a** (1) **:** the conversion of numbers into units of the same denomination (2) **:** the reducing of an algebraic equation to its simplest terms (3) **:** the determination of the true position of a celestial object by correcting observational data for known errors (4) **:** the substitution for a meteorological reading of a value computed from it so as to bring all to a common basis (as pressures to sea level values) **b :** an act or instance of reproducing in a smaller size ⟨~*s* — scaled down from life size —J.C.Furnas⟩ **4 a :** the act or process of reducing a syllogistic argument to the first figure — compare DIRECT REDUCTION, INDIRECT REDUCTION **b** (1) **:** the classification or description (as of a set of terms or phenomena) in terms of what are regarded as simpler or more fundamental concepts ⟨~ of the complex problems of intergroup relations to attitude formation —J.R.Kantor⟩; *specif* **:** the process of explaining the terms of a science on the basis of and deducing its laws from those of another ⟨the ~ of chemical to physical laws —C.H.Whiteley⟩ (2) **:** analysis of a psychological motive into its instinctive elements **c :** the act or process of investing with definite form ⟨behavioral responses which are in process of ~ to habitual terms —Ralph Linton⟩ ⟨the ~ of generalization to particular fact —Jonathan Daniels⟩ **5 :** the replacement or realignment of a body part in normal position or restoration of a bodily condition to normal **6 a :** the process of reducing by chemical or electrochemical means ⟨the ~, or deoxidation, of the iron ore is brought about by carbon monoxide produced by the combustion of the coke —J.H.Bateman⟩ ⟨the photographic process depends upon . . . the ~ of silver ion to metallic silver by a developing solution —C.E.K.Mees⟩ **b :** treatment under reducing conditions by exclusion of air to a point below that needed for complete combustion of fuel gases (as in a pottery kiln) ⟨~ produces various color effects in pottery⟩ **7 a** (1) **:** a decrease in size, amount, extent, or number **:** DIMINUTION; *specif* **:** the psychological diminishment of emotion through activity or adjustment (2) **:** SUBTRACTION ⟨arrangements can be made for premiums to be paid by ~ from salary —*Irish Digest*⟩ **b :** MEIOSIS; *specif* **:** production of the gametic chromosome number in the first meiotic division **c :** limitation in scope **:** RESTRICTION ⟨whether the ~ of *existence* to *human existence* does not seriously . . . restrict the domain of philosophy —J.E. Smith⟩ **8 a :** demotion in rank **b :** lowering in condition or status **:** DEGRADATION ⟨~ of living to an animal business of . . . survival —Fred Majdalany⟩ ⟨~ to absurdity is a common device by which teachers demonstrate the essential fallacy of a proposal —Alexander Laing⟩ **9 a :** transformation into objective form or reality ⟨~ of a novel to words on paper⟩ ⟨~ of the device to practice —Ruth Riddell⟩ **b :** transformation into a new or different form **:** ADAPTATION, TRANSLATION ⟨~ of a metaphor⟩ ⟨every art involves a system of ~ —Stuart Gilbert⟩ **c :** a musical arrangement; *esp* **:** a piano score or part arranged or reduced from an orchestral score **10 :** an act or instance of breaking down **:** DISINTEGRATION, PROCESSING ⟨~ of land surfaces . . . to low plains —O.D. Von Engeln⟩ ⟨~ of . . . pine by lumbering, turpentining, and fire —*Amer. Guide Series: N.C.*⟩ ⟨~ of fish and fish waste to . . . oil —*Commercial Fisheries Rev.*⟩; *specif* **:** the gradual crushing of grain in milling by passing it repeatedly through break rolls **11 :** an act or instance of reducing phonetically
**re·duc·tion·al** \-nᵊl\ *adj* **:** of, relating to, or characterized by reduction
**reduction crusher** *n* **:** a crusher for reducing particle sizes of coal, rock, or ore
**reduction division** *n* **:** the first meiotic division
**reduction gear** *n* **:** a pair or combination of gears to reduce the input speed (as of a marine turbine) to a lower output speed (as of a ship's propeller)
**reduction–improbation** \=ˈ==,==ˈ==\ *n, Scots law* **:** a rescissory action for setting aside a writing or a part of it in which the summons provides that if the document is not produced it will be judged false or forged
**re·duc·tion·ism** \rəˈdəksha,nizəm, rēˈ-\ *n* -s **:** a procedure or theory of reducing complex data or phenomena to simple terms; *esp* **:** OVERSIMPLIFICATION ⟨materialism and idealism have been criticized as ~*s*⟩ ⟨the phenomenalistic ~ according to which statements about objects or the physical world can be translated into statements about sense-data or immediate experience⟩
**re·duc·tion·ist** \-_nəst\ *n* -s **:** an advocate of reduction or reductionism
**re·duc·tion·is·tic** \=ˈ==ˈnistik\ *adj* **:** REDUCTIVE
**reduction potential** *n* **:** the potential at which reduction occurs at the cathode in an electrochemical cell — compare OXIDATION-REDUCTION POTENTIAL
**reduction roll** *n* **:** a roller for decreasing the thickness of ductile material
[1]**re·duc·tive** \rəˈdəktiv, rēˈ-, -tēv *also* -təv\ *adj* [*reduction* + *-ive*] **1 :** of, relating to, characterized by, or causing diminution or curtailment **:** REDUCING ⟨their views of life were . . . ~ and depreciatory —R.H.Rovere⟩; *esp* **:** of or relating to psychological reduction (as of emotional tension) **2 :** of, relating to, or advocating analytical reduction or reductionism **:** REDUCTIONISTIC ⟨the attempt to squeeze these data, with all their variegated content, into the limited perspectives of one science . . . must always lead to ~ distortion —J.D.Wild⟩ **3 :** of or relating to conversion or processing into another form — **re·duc·tive·ly** \-təvlē\ *adv*
[2]**reductive** \"\ *n* -s **:** a reductive agent
**re·duc·tone** \-k,tōn\ *n* -s [*reduction* + *-one*] **:** any of a class of reducing enediol aldehydes or ketones RC(OH)=C(OH)-COR; *esp* **:** a crystalline osone $HOCH_2COCHO$ or a tautomer [as HOCH=C(OH)CHO] that is a strong reducing agent in alkaline solution and is obtained from glucose by alkaline degradation or from dihydroxy-acetone by oxidation; hydroxy-pyruvaldehyde ⟨ascorbic acids . . . may be considered as ~*s* —W.W.Pigman & R.M.Goepp †1946⟩
**re·duc·tor** \-ktə(r)\ *n* -s [*reduction* + *-or*] **:** an apparatus for carrying out chemical reduction (as of a ferric salt to a ferrous salt) — compare JONES REDUCTOR
**re·duc·to·ri·al** \,rē,dəkˈtōrēəl\ *adj* **:** REDUCTIVE
**reducts** *pres 3d sing of* REDUCT
**re·dun·ca** \rəˈdəŋkə\ *n, cap* [NL, fr. L, fem. of *reduncus* bent backward, fr. *red-* re- + *uncus* bent, curved; akin to L *uncus* hook — more at ANGLE] **:** a genus of antelopes consisting of the reedbucks — **re·dun·cine** \-dən(t),sīn\ *adj*
**re·dun·dan·cy** \rəˈdəndənsē, rēˈ-, -si\ *also* **re·dun·dance** \-n(t)s\ *n, pl* **redundancies** *also* **redundances** [L *redundantia*, fr. *redundant-, redundans* + *-ia* -y] **1 :** the quality or state of being redundant **:** SUPERFLUITY ⟨dread of economic ~ that drove terrified mill hands to wreck Arkwright's spinning jenny —*Times Lit. Supp.*⟩ **2 a :** a lavish or excessive supply **:** PROFUSION, OVERABUNDANCE ⟨a ~ of jewelry and a scarcity of clothing —Alan Moorehead⟩ ⟨a magnificent ~ of beard —Elinor Wylie⟩ **b :** a nonessential appendage **c :** surplusage in a legal pleading **3 a :** superfluous repetition or verbosity **:** PROLIXITY, TAUTOLOGY ⟨the . . . florid ~ of Italian prose —Havelock Ellis⟩ **b :** an act or instance of needless repetition ⟨*redundancies* result . . . when the writer fails to perceive tne scope of a word —Bruce Westley⟩ **4 :** the part of a communication that can be eliminated without loss of essential information; *specif* **:** the number arrived at by subtracting from one the ratio of the actual information content of a communication to the maximum information content and expressed as a percentage
**re·dun·dant** \-nt\ *adj* [L *redundant-, redundans*, pres. part.

of *redundare* to overflow, be in excess — more at REDOUND] **1 a :** exceeding what is necessary or normal **:** SUPERFLUOUS, SURPLUS ⟨older areas, plants and occupations are becoming ~ and obsolete —Solomon Barkin⟩ ⟨so many books on heraldry . . . that yet another might be thought ~ —*Times Lit. Supp.*⟩ ⟨a ~ secretion of bile⟩; *specif* **:** PLEONASTIC ⟨at the risk of being ~, I return to my original proposition —J.B.Conant⟩ ⟨use a ~ personal pronoun for emphasis —*New Republic*⟩ **b :** characterized by or containing an excess ⟨the skin . . . was ~ and lay too loosely on her fingers —Jean Stafford⟩; *specif* **:** IMMATERIAL 3b ⟨the court may order stricken from any pleading . . . any ~, immaterial, impertinent, or scandalous matter —*U.S. Code*⟩ **2 :** characterized by abundance **:** PROFUSE, LAVISH ⟨skirts became somewhat shorter and less ~ —G.M. Trevelyan⟩ **3 :** expanding beyond ordinary bounds **:** SWELLING, OVERFLOWING ⟨a gradual spilling over of the ~ population —Ellen Semple⟩ **syn** see WORDY

**re·dun·dant·ly** *adv* **:** in a redundant manner

**redundant member** *n* **:** a member in a framed structure that is not actually necessary for support

**redundant verb** *n* **:** a verb that has alternative forms (as for the past tense)

**¹re·du·pli·cate** \(ˈ)rē¦d(y)üplə,kāt, rəˈd-, *usu* -ād.+V\ *vt* [LL *reduplicatus*, past part. of *reduplicare*, fr. L *re-* + *duplicare* to double — more at DUPLICATE] **1 :** to make or perform again **:** COPY, REITERATE ⟨mechanism . . . capable of being *reduplicated* almost without limit —George Iles⟩ ⟨*reduplicating* oaths on different altars —H.C.Lea⟩ **2 :** to repeat all or part of (a radical word element) **:** form (a word) by reduplication

**²re·du·pli·cate** \-ləkət, -lə,kāt, *usu* -d.+V\ *adj* [LL *reduplicatus*, past part.] **1 :** REDUPLICATED **2 :** valvate with the margins curved outwardly

**re·du·pli·cat·ed** \-lə,kād.əd\ *adj* **1** *archaic* **:** DOUBLED, REITERATED **2 :** having radical elements repeated **:** formed by reduplication

**re·du·pli·ca·tion** \(¦)rē,d(y)üpləˈkāshən, rə,-\ *n* [LL *reduplication-, reduplicatio*, fr. *reduplicatus* + L *-ion-, -io* -ion] **1 :** an act or instance of doubling or reiterating **:** DUPLICATION, REPLICA **2 a :** repetition of a radical element or a part of it occurring usu. at the beginning of a word, often accompanied by change of the radical vowel, found in many languages, and in some Indo-European languages being grammatically functional esp. in the formation of the perfect and present tenses (as in Sanskrit *dadāmi* "I give", Sanskrit *dadarśe* "I have seen", Latin *poposci* "I have demanded", Gothic *lailot* "I have let") **b** (1) **:** a word or form produced by reduplication (2) **:** the repeated element in such a word or form (as *po-* in Latin *poposci*) **3 :** ANADIPLOSIS

**¹re·du·pli·ca·tive** \(ˈ)rē¦d(y)üplə,kād.iv, rəˈd-\ *adj* [¹*reduplicate* + *-ive*] **:** of, relating to, or formed by reduplication — **re·du·pli·ca·tive·ly** \-d.əvlē\ *adv*

**²reduplicative** \"\ *n* -S **:** ITERATIVE

**re·du·pli·ca·ture** \-ləkə,chü(ə)r\ *n* -S **:** a part folded back on itself

**¹re·du·vi·id** \rəˈd(y)üvēəd\ *adj* [NL *Reduviidae*] **:** of or relating to the Reduviidae

**²reduviid** \"\ *n* -S **:** a bug of the family Reduviidae

**re·du·vi·idae** \,rejəˈvīə,dē\ *n pl, cap* [NL, fr. *Reduvius*, type genus + *-idae*] **:** a very large and widely distributed family of bloodsucking hemipterous insects comprising the assassin bugs and having a short 3-jointed proboscis that is curved back under the head when at rest and 3-jointed tarsi — see TRIATOMA

**re·du·vi·us** \rəˈd(y)üvēəs\ *n, cap* [NL, fr. L *reduvia, redivia* hangnail, exuviae — more at REDIVIVUS] **:** the type genus of Reduviidae

**red valerian** *n* **:** a European herb (*Centranthus ruber*) with small crimson or white spurred flowers — called also *French honeysuckle*

**red vitriol** *n* **1 :** BIEBERITE **2 :** COLCOTHAR

**red·ward** \ˈredwə(r)d\ *adv* (*or adj*) **:** toward the red end of the spectrum

**¹redware** \ˈ⸗,⸗\ *n* [¹*red* + *ware* (seaweed)] **:** a large brown edible seaweed (*Laminaria digitata*)

**²redware** \"\ *n* [¹*red* + *ware* (pottery)] **:** pottery made from low-firing clay containing much iron oxide

**red-wat** \ˈre,dwät\ *adj* [¹*red* + *wat*, Sc var. of *wet*] *Scot* **:** wet with blood **:** BLOODSTAINED, BLOODY

**red water** *n* **1 :** any of certain diseases of cattle characterized by hematuria: as **a :** a babesiasis (as Texas fever) in which hemoglobin liberated by destruction of red blood cells appears in the urine **b :** a chronic disease affecting cattle esp. at the end of winter attributed to oxalic acid in the forage and marked by escape of blood into the urine from lesions in the bladder **c :** EAST COAST FEVER **d :** an acute febrile septicemia that is caused by a bacterium (*Clostridium hemolyticum*), is marked by hemoglobinuria and sometimes by intestinal hemorrhages, and less commonly affects horses, sheep, and swine **e :** bovine leptospirosis **2 :** any of various diseases of other animals of which hematuria is a prominent symptom **3 a :** water that is colored red (as by iron compounds) **b :** RED TIDE

**red-wat-shod** \ˈ⸗,⸗\ *adj* [*red-wat* + *shod*] *Scot* **:** having bloodstained shoes **:** wading in blood

**redweed** \ˈ⸗,⸗\ *n* **1** *dial Eng* **:** CORN POPPY **2 :** POKEWEED

**red whelk** *n* **:** an edible European whelk (*Neptunea antiqua*) with a slightly ridged yellowish or reddish shell — called also *buckie*

**red whortleberry** *n* **:** any of various cranberries; *esp* **:** MOUNTAIN CRANBERRY

**red willow** *n* **1 :** any of several willows (as a sandbar willow) with reddish or purplish twigs; *esp* **:** PURPLE WILLOW **2 a :** SILKY CORNEL **b :** RED OSIER 2

**red wine** *n* **:** a wine with a predominantly red color derived during fermentation from the natural pigment in the skins of red or otherwise dark-colored grapes — compare ROSÉ, WHITE WINE

**redwing** \ˈ⸗,⸗\ *n* **1** *or* **red-winged thrush** \ˈ⸗,⸗-\ **:** a European thrush (*Turdus musicus* syn. *T. iliacus*) having the underwing coverts red **2 :** REDWING BLACKBIRD **3 :** a southern African francolin (*Francolinus levaillanti*) **4 :** GADWALL

**redwing blackbird** *or* **red-winged blackbird** *n* **:** a bird (*Agelaius phoeniceus*) of the family Icteridae which is widely distributed in No. America, breeds in swampy places, and collects in the fall in large flocks for migration and whose adult male is black with a patch of bright scarlet bordered behind with white or buff on the wing coverts while the female and the young of both sexes are brown with dusky streaks —called also *maizebird, maizer*

**red wolf** *n* **1 :** MANED WOLF **2 :** a member of any of several races of a small wolf (*Canis niger*) of the southeastern U.S. that survives chiefly in Texas and has reddish hairs interspersed with black and the short hairs shading from yellow to red

**¹redwood** \ˈ⸗,⸗\ *adj* [¹*red* + *wood* (mad)] *Scot* **:** stark mad **:** FURIOUS

**²redwood** \ˈ⸗,⸗\ *n* [¹*red* + *wood* (growth of trees)] **1 :** a wood yielding a red dye: as **a :** BRAZILWOOD **b :** CAMWOOD **c :** SAPPANWOOD **d :** LIMA WOOD **e :** BARWOOD **2 :** a tree that yields a red dyewood or that produces wood of a red or reddish color: as **a :** RED SANDALWOOD **b :** AMBOYNA 1 **c :** ROHUN **d :** any of various So. American trees of the genera *Caesalpinia* and *Erythroxylon* **e :** MAHOGANY **f :** SCOTCH PINE **g :** CORNELIAN CHERRY **h :** an Asiatic buckthorn (*Rhamnus erythroxylon*) **i :** a tree (*Melhania erythroxylon*) of the family Sterculiaceae of St. Helena **j :** an African tree (*Ochna arborea*) with reddish wood **k :** FALSE LOGWOOD **l :** a snakebark (*Colubrina ferruginosa*) of the West Indies **3 a :** a commercially important coniferous timber tree (*Sequoia sempervirens*) of California found only on the Coast Range often reaching a height of 300 feet **b :** the brownish red light wood of the California redwood tree that takes a fine polish and is much used commercially **4 :** a variable color averaging a moderate reddish brown that is lighter and stronger than mahogany, yellower, lighter, and stronger than roan, and lighter, stronger, and very slightly redder than oxblood

**red worm** *n* **1 :** BLOODWORM; *esp* **:** a small reddish aquatic oligochaete worm (genus *Tubifex*) that is often fed to aquarium fish **2 a :** GAPEWORM **b :** PALISADE WORM

**redworm disease** \ˈ⸗,⸗-\ *n* **:** strongylosis of horses

**red zinc ore** *n* **:** ZINCITE

**¹ree** \ˈrē, ˈrā\ *vt* [ME *reien*] *dial Eng* **:** SIFT

**²ree** \ˈrē, ˈrā\ *adj* [origin unknown] *chiefly Scot* **:** IRRATIONAL, BEFUDDLED

**³ree** \ˈrē\ *n* -S *usu cap* **:** ARIKARA

**reebok** *var of* RHEBOK

**reech** \ˈrēch\ *dial var of* REEK

**re·echo** \(ˈ)rē+\ *vi* **:** to repeat or return an echo **:** echo again or repeatedly ⟨the words . . . ~ through the book —Eila Campbell⟩ **:** REVERBERATE, RESOUND ⟨thunder ~*ed* through the valley⟩ ⟨the house ~*ed* with laughter⟩ **~** *vt* **:** to send (an echo) back **:** cause an echo of to return

**reechy** \ˈrēchē\ *adj* -ER/-EST [ME *rechy*, fr. *rech*, *rek* reek + *-y* — more at REEK] **1** *archaic* **:** having a strong odor **:** RANCID **2** *archaic* **:** blackened by smoke

**¹reed** \ˈrēd\ *n* -S *often attrib* [ME *rede*, *reod*, fr. OE *hrēod*; akin to MD *ried*, *riet* reed, OS *hriod*, OHG *hriot*, *riot* reed, Lith *krutėti* to stir, move, Toch A *kru* reed] **1 a :** any of various tall grasses with slender often jointed stems: as (1) **:** DITCH REED (2) **:** GIANT REED 1 **b :** a stem of such a grass **c :** a person or thing too weak to rely on **:** one easily swayed or overcome **2 a :** a growth or mass of reeds **:** reeds for thatching or for plastering on **b :** reeds as a material **c** *dial Eng* **:** straw prepared for thatching **d :** the strong fibrous core of rattan used in basket weaving **3 :** ARROW **4 :** a musical instrument made of the hollow joint of a plant (as of reed or cane) with a mouthpiece and finger holes **:** PIPE ⟨heard the shepherd's ~ —Sir Walter Scott⟩ **5 :** an ancient Hebrew unit of length equal to 6 cubits or about 10.25 feet ⟨the foundations . . . measured a full ~ of six long cubits —Ezek 41:8 (RSV)⟩ **6 a :** a thin elastic tongue of cane, wood, or metal fastened at one end to the mouthpiece of a musical instrument (as the clarinet or the organ reed pipe) or to a reed block or other fixture over an air opening (as in the reed organ or accordion) and set in vibration by the breath or other air current **b :** the immediate mechanism (as the beak of a clarinet) surrounding and comprising the reed proper **c :** a reed instrument ⟨the ~*s* of an orchestra⟩ **d :** REED STOP **7 a** (1) **:** a device on a loom that resembles a comb and is attached to the lay, set with a series of flat parallel wires called dents, and used to space the warp yarns evenly and to beat up the filling (2) **:** the fineness of cloth as determined by the number of dents and therefore of threads per inch of the reed **b :** a comb of boxwood or other hard material for pressing down the weft of tapestry **8 a :** REEDING 1 a **b :** one of a series of corrugations on the edge of a coin

**²reed** \"\ *vt* -ED/-ING/-S [ME *reden*, fr. *rede* reed] **1 a :** to cover with reed or thatch **b :** to prepare (as straw) for use in thatching **2 :** to decorate with reeds or reeding ⟨the foot posts are deeply ~*ed* —*Antiques*⟩ **3 :** to draw (yarns) through the reed of a loom ⟨~ the warp⟩ **4 :** to make corrugations on (the edge of a coin)

**³reed** \"\ *var of* REDE

**⁴reed** \"\ *var of* READ

**reed-back** \ˈ⸗,⸗\ *adj, of a chair* **:** having a back of vertical and flat or curved and narrow balusters often with a connecting member at the center

**redbed** \ˈ⸗,⸗\ *n* **:** a bed of reeds

**reed bent** *or* **reed bent grass** **1 :** a grass of the genus *Calamagrostis* **2 :** a perennial grass (*Arctagrostis arundinacea*) of northern No. America and Asia

**reedbird** \ˈ⸗,⸗\ *n* **1 :** BOBOLINK — used esp. of this bird when flocking in reedy marshes in fall and winter **2 :** any of several small Asiatic timaliine birds of the genera *Schoenicola* and *Laticilla* **3 :** SEDGE WARBLER

**reed·buck** \ˈrēd,bək\ *n, pl* **reedbuck** *also* **reedbucks** [trans. of Afrik *rietbok*] **:** any of several African antelopes (as the bohor, nagor, reitbok) that are related to the waterbuck and kobs but smaller, constitute the genus *Redunca*, and are of a brownish fawn color with horned males and hornless females

**reed bunting** *n* **1 :** a European bunting (*Emberiza schoeniclus*) frequenting marshy places and having the face and head chiefly black, the wings and back chestnut, and the underparts white — called also *reed sparrow* **2 :** BEARDED TIT

**reed canary grass** *n* **:** a perennial grass (*Phalaris arundinaceae*) occurring commonly in marshy meadows and ditches of Europe and No. America, used in some areas for forage, and having broad leaves and narrow dense panicles — called also *lady's-laces*

**reede** *obs var of* REED

**reed·en** \ˈrēdᵊn\ *adj* [ME, fr. ¹*reed* + *-en*] **:** made or consisting of reed

**reed·er** \-də(r)\ *n* -S [ME *redare*, fr. *reden* to reed + *-are* -er] **1 :** one that reeds: as **a :** one that thatches with reeds **b :** a textile worker who replaces the broken reeds of a loom or draws the warp threads through the reeds **c :** a worker who tapes a reed or wire on sweatband leathers **2 :** a reed-covered frame to protect drying china clay

**reed fescue** *n* **:** a tall robust fescue that is usu. considered a variety (*Festuca elatior arundinacea*) of meadow fescue

**reedfish** \ˈ⸗,⸗\ *n* **:** a long slender West African freshwater fish (*Erpetoichthys calabaricus* or *Calamoichthys calabaricus*) that lacks pelvic fins, in many respects resembles an eel, and is closely related to the bichir — see CLADISTIA

**reed grass** *n* **1 :** any of various reeds or reedy grasses: as **a :** a tall perennial grass of the genus *Calamagrostis* sometimes used for hay; *esp* **:** an Australian grass (*C. quadriseta* or *Deyeuxia quadriseta*) **b :** a grass of the genus *Arundo*; *esp* **:** GIANT REED 1 **c :** WOOD GRASS 1 **d :** a grass of the genus *Phragmites*; *esp* **:** DITCH REED **2 :** BUR REED

**reed green** *n* **:** a light yellow green that is yellower and duller than glass green and yellower and less strong than sky green

**reed horn** *n* **:** a lighthouse and lightship sound signal obtained by vibrating a steel reed with compressed air

**reedier** *comparative of* REEDY

**reediest** *superlative of* REEDY

**re·edification** \(¦)rē+\ *n* [ME *reedification*, fr. MF or LL; MF *reedification*, fr. LL *reaedification-*, *reaedificatio*, fr. *reaedificatus* (past part. of *reaedificare* to rebuild) + L *-ion-*, *-io* -ion] **:** the act or process of rebuilding

**re·edify** \(ˈ)rē+\ *vt* [ME *reedifien*, fr. MF *reedifier*, fr. LL *reaedificare*, fr. L *re-* + *aedificare* to build — more at EDIFY] **:** REBUILD

**reed·i·ly** \ˈrēdᵊlē, -dəlē, -li\ *adv* **:** with a reedy quality

**reed·i·ness** \-dēnəs, -din-\ *n* -ES **:** the quality or state of being reedy

**reed·ing** \ˈrēdiŋ\ *n* -S [fr. gerund of ²*reed*] **1 a :** a small convex molding — called also *reed*; compare FLUTING; see MOLDING illustration **b :** decoration by series of parallel reeds (as on chair legs or table legs) **2 :** corrugations on the edge of a coin

**reed·less** \ˈrēdləs\ *adj* **1 :** having no reed **2** *of a pipe-organ stop* **:** lacking a reed but producing a reedlike tone

**reedlike** \ˈ⸗,⸗\ *adj* **:** resembling a reed (as in slender form or upright growth) or that of a reed ⟨a ~ grass⟩ ⟨a ~ tone⟩

**reed·ling** \ˈrēdliŋ\ *n* -S [¹*reed* + *-ling*] **:** BEARDED TIT

**reed mace** *n* **:** CATTAIL

**reed mark** *n* **:** a warp mark in cloth caused by defective reeds or a faulty setting of the loom or yarns

**reed meadow grass** *n* **:** a pasture grass (*Glyceria grandis*) found in moist places throughout No. America

**reed organ** *n* **:** a keyboard wind instrument (as the harmonium, American organ) in which the wind acts on a set of free metal reeds

**reed pheasant** *n* **:** BEARDED TIT

**reed pipe** *n* **1 :** a musical instrument made of a reed **:** PIPE **2 :** a pipe of a pipe organ producing its musical tone by vibration of a beating reed in a current of air — compare FLUE PIPE

**reeds** *pl of* REED, *pres 3d sing of* REED

**reed-shade** \ˈ⸗,⸗\ *n* **:** a shade constructed of reeds for the protection of plants in hot locations

**reed sparrow** *n* [ME *rede sparowe*, fr. *rede* reed + *sparowe* sparrow — more at REED, SPARROW] **:** REED BUNTING

**reed stop** *n* **:** a set of reed pipes in a pipe organ controlled by a single stop knob and constructed to be generally imitative of some orchestral instrument

**reed thrush** *n* **:** GREAT REED WARBLER

**re·educate** \(ˈ)rē+\ *vt* [*re-* + *educate*] **1 :** to train the physically disabled in the use of muscles in new functions or of prosthetic appliances in old functions in an effort to replace or restore lost competence ⟨~ the amputee⟩ **2 :** to cause to develop new attitudes or habits replacing others held to be undesirable or unsatisfactory usu. as the result of faulty training ⟨~ a delinquent⟩

**re·education** \(¦)rē+\ *n* [*reeducate* + *-ion*] **:** the act or process of reeducating **:** rehabilitative training ⟨~ for youthful offenders aimed at their restoration to society⟩

**re·educative** \(ˈ)rē+\ *adj* [*reeducate* + *-ive*] **:** having the purpose or power to reeducate

**reed vole** *n* **:** a large long-tailed Chinese vole (*Microtus fortis*) in color resembling the Norway rat

**reed warbler** *n* **:** a small chiefly European warbler (*Acrocephalus scirpaceus*) that is brown above and buffy white below, is often mistaken for the marsh warbler, and is usu. seen about reedbeds and other marshy areas; *broadly* **:** any of various birds of the genus *Acrocephalus* (as a great reed warbler or a marsh warbler)

**reed wolf** *n* **:** a jackal that inhabits reed beds of the Danube valley

**reedwork** \ˈ⸗,⸗\ *n* [¹*reed* + *work*] **:** the reed stops of a pipe organ — compare FLUEWORK

**reed wren** *n* **1 :** a reed warbler (*Acrocephalus scirpaceus*) **2 :** LONG-BILLED MARSH WREN

**reedy** \ˈrēdē, -di\ *adj* -ER/-EST [ME, fr. ¹*reed* + *-y*] **1 :** abounding in or covered with reeds ⟨~ marshes⟩ **2 :** made of or resembling reeds **:** long and slender like a reed ⟨thin ~ arms⟩ **:** FRAIL, WEAK **3 :** having the tone quality of a reed instrument ⟨~ music⟩ ⟨~ singing⟩ **4 :** showing reed marks ⟨~ cloth⟩

**reed yellow** *n* **:** CHALCEDONY YELLOW

**¹reef** \ˈrēf\ *n* -S [ME *riff*, fr. ON *rif*; prob. akin to OE *rāw* row — more at ROW] **1 :** a part of a sail that is taken in or let out by means of the reef points in order to regulate the size of the sail **:** a strip of sail set off by a reef band **2 :** the reduction in area of a sail by reefing

**²reef** \"\ *vb* -ED/-ING/-S *vt* **1 a :** to reduce the area of (a sail) by rolling or folding a portion at the head (as of a square sail) or at the foot (as of a fore-and-aft sail) and securing to the yard or spar with reef points **b :** to lower or bring inboard (a spar) wholly or partially ⟨~ the topmast⟩ **2 :** to move the floats of (a paddle wheel) toward the center so that they will not dip so deeply **3 :** to roll or fold up in the manner of a sail ⟨~ a parachute⟩ **~** *vi* **1 :** to reduce a sail by taking in a reef **2** *slang* **:** to pick a pocket esp. by drawing up the lining — **reef one's sails :** to reduce the scope of one's activities **:** curtail one's efforts **:** withdraw in part

**³reef** \"\ *n* -S [earlier *riff*, fr. D *rif*, prob. of Scand origin; akin to ON *rif* reef of a sail] **1 a** (1) **:** a chain or range of rocks or ridge of sand lying at or near the surface of the water; *esp* **:** one where there is not more than six fathoms at low water — see BARRIER REEF, CORAL REEF, FRINGING REEF, SAND REEF; compare BANK, SHOAL (2) **:** a hazardous obstruction to the achievement of an objective ⟨many stars in the entertainment world helped themselves over early financial ~*s* by working in the . . . store —W.F.Longgood⟩ **b :** a sedimentary rock or part thereof composed almost or exclusively of the remains of reef-building organisms **:** BIOHERM **2 a :** a deposit of ore **:** VEIN, LODE **b :** the barren rock and shale surrounding the diamondiferous rock in the diamond mines of southern Africa **3 :** REEF SPONGE

**⁴reef** \"\ *n* -S [ME *ref*, *reof* rough, scabby, fr. OE *hrēof* rough, scabby, leprous — more at DANDRUFF] *dial Brit* **:** an eruption on the skin **:** ITCH

**reef·able** \ˈrēfəbəl\ *adj* **:** that can be reefed

**reef band** *n* **:** a piece of canvas sewed across a sail to strengthen it at the eyelet holes for reef points

**reef bass** *n* **:** CHANNEL BASS

**reef crab** *n* **:** a small Australian crab (*Ozius truncatus*) that is a great nuisance in reef netting because of its entering the nets in great numbers and cutting them to escape

**reef cringle** *n* **:** one of the cringles on the leech of a sail at the end of a reef band through which a rope passes binding the edge of a reefed sail to the yard or spar

**¹reef·er** \ˈrēfə(r)\ *n* -S **1 a :** one that reefs **b :** MIDSHIPMAN **2 a :** a close-fitting usu. double-breasted jacket or short coat of thick cloth **b :** a woman's usu. princess style single-breasted or double-breasted coat with a collar

**²reefer** \"\ *n* [*reef* to roll up (i.e., a cigarette) + *-er*, n. suffix] **:** a cigarette containing the dried leaves and flowers of marijuana

**³ree·fer** \"\ *n* -S [by shortening & alter.] **1 :** REFRIGERATOR **2 :** a refrigerator car, truck, trailer, or ship

**reef goose** *n* **:** CANADA GOOSE

**reef heron** *n* **:** a white or slaty-blue heron (*Demigretta sacra*) of the coasts of southern Asia, Australia, and Oceania

**reef jig** *or* **reef jigger** *n* **:** a light tackle on a yard for stretching the reef band before reefing

**reef knoll** *n* **:** a mass of coralline limestone within a sedimentary series **:** a fossil coral or algal reef

**reef knot** *n* **:** a square knot used in tying reef points

**reef-knot** \ˈ⸗,⸗\ *vt* **:** to make a reef knot in

reef knot

**reef line** *n* **:** REEF POINT

**reef netting** *n* **:** fishing with a net suspended between two boats anchored off a reef

**reef pendant** *n* **:** a short rope passed or fixed through a reef cringle and used to fasten the clew to the boom or the leach to the reef tackle in reefing a sail

**reef point** *also* **reefing point** *n* **:** one of the pieces of small rope passing through the eyelet holes of a reef band and used in reefing the sail — called also *point*; see SAIL illustration

**reefs** *pl of* REEF, *pres 3d sing of* REEF

**reef sponge** *n* **:** a soft close-grained fine-textured West Indian commercial sponge (*Spongia obliqua*)

**reef tackle** *n* **:** a tackle by which the reef cringles of a square sail are hauled up and out to the yardarm to give slack for reefing — see SAIL illustration

**reefy** \ˈrēfē\ *adj* -ER/-EST [³*reef* + *-y*] **1 :** full of reefs or rocks **2 :** containing sedimentary material resembling that of a sedimentary reef

**reeing** *pres part of* REE

**¹reek** \ˈrēk\ *n* -S [ME *rek*, *reke*, fr. OE *rēc*; akin to OFris *rēk* smoke, OS *rōk*, OHG *rouh*, ON *reykr*, OE *rēocan* to reek] **1** *chiefly dial* **:** SMOKE **2 :** VAPOR, MIST, FOG ⟨the wettest imaginable blanket of sea ~ enveloped us —Osbert Sitwell⟩ **3 :** a strong or disagreeable fume or odor ⟨exuded the sharp, spiced ~ of tobacco —A.W.Turnbull⟩ ⟨the overpowering ~ of sewage⟩

**²reek** \"\ *vb* -ED/-ING/-S [ME *reken*, fr. OE *rēocan*; akin to OFris *rēka* to smoke, OHG *rouhhan* to smoke, smoke up, ON *rjūka* to smoke, steam] *vi* **1 :** to emit smoke or vapor ⟨a marsh ~*ing* in the sun⟩ **2 a :** to give off or become permeated with a strong often offensive odor ⟨horses that ~ with sweat⟩ ⟨a restaurant that ~*s* of garlic⟩ **b :** to give a strong impression of some constituent quality or feature **:** show permeation with a dominant quality or feature ⟨a mean building which ~*ed* of poverty —D.G.Gerahty⟩ ⟨historical best sellers ~ with sentiment —A.L.Guérard⟩ **3 :** EMANATE, ISSUE, RISE, FUME ⟨smoke which still away did ~ . . . from that eternal pyre —John Keats⟩ ⟨an atmosphere . . . which ~*ed* up from decayed trees —E.A.Poe⟩ **~** *vt* **1 :** to subject to the action of smoke or vapor **2 :** to give off as or as if a reek **:** EXHALE, EXUDE, VENT ⟨his manner ~*s* prosperity⟩ **syn** see EMIT

**³reek** \"\ *vt* -ED/-ING/-S [origin unknown] *Scot* **:** EQUIP, OUTFIT

**⁴reek** \"\ *n* -S [prob. alter. of ¹*rick*] *dial Brit* **:** HEAP, PILE

**⁵reek** \"\ *vt* -ED/-ING/-S *dial Brit* **:** to pile up **:** HEAP

**⁶reek** \"\ *Scot var of* REACH

**reek·er** \ˈrēkə(r)\ *n* -S **:** one that reeks

**reek·ing·ly** *adv* **:** in a reeking manner **:** with a reek

**reeky** \ˈrēkē\ *adj* -ER/-EST [ME *reky*, fr. *rek* reek + *-y*] **:** emitting or permeated with a reek **:** REEKING ⟨~ fen —Sir Walter Scott⟩

**¹reel** \ˈrēl, *esp before pause or consonant* ˈrēəl\ *n* -S *often attrib* [ME, fr. OE *hrēol*; akin to ON *hræll* weaver's sley, Latvian *krekls* shirt, Gk *krekein* to weave] **1 a :** a revolving device used in winding yarn or thread into hanks or skeins and in winding raw silk from cocoons and consisting usu. of a light frame with radial arms on a central axle **b :** any of various revolving devices (as a flanged cylinder) for winding up or paying out something flexible (as rope, wire, strip metal or plastic, hose) ⟨lamps that pull down from overhead tension ~*s*⟩ ⟨a surveyor's ~ containing a tape measure⟩ ⟨a garden hose ~ on wheels⟩ ⟨an industrial ~ for feeding coiled steel stock to a punch press⟩ **c** (1) **:** a flanged metal cylinder and crank attached to the butt of a fishing rod for winding up or letting out line (2) *chiefly Brit* **:** a spool or bobbin of wood to hold sewing thread ⟨a cotton ~⟩ (3) **:** a shaft or drum on which the full-width sheet coming from a papermaking machine is wound (4) **:** a flanged spool on which image-bearing motion-picture film or signal-bearing tape or wire is wound ⟨a standard ~ of 35 mm. film containing 1000 or 2000 feet⟩ **d :** a reel with its contents **:** the amount on a reel ⟨steel rope in ~*s* of 1800 feet⟩: as (1) WEB; *specif* **:** the part of a web in process of manufacture that has passed the driers of a paper machine (2) **:** a strip of image-bearing motion picture film (3) **:** a roll of postage stamps for use in a dispenser **2 a :** a rotating conveyer used in dyeing **b :** a frame carrying the bolting cloth or mesh wire screen used to sift ground grain (as wheat, corn) or to grade and size hulled rice **c :** the upright revolving wheel in a reel oven consisting of connected pairs of radial arms from which the trays holding the baking pans are suspended **d :** a revolving set of bars that feed grain stalks through a harvester **e :** the spiral blading of a lawn mower **f :** a clothes dryer consisting of lines on a frame of usu. radial arms revolving on a vertical pole **3 :** a humming noise like that made by a moving reel ⟨a kingfisher . . . with his loud clicking ~ —John Burroughs⟩ — **off the reel** *adv* **1 :** in straight succession **:** without interruption ⟨can sell 20 percent more cars right *off the reel* —*Time*⟩ **2 :** without hesitation **:** as if reeled off **:** DIRECTLY ⟨write his impressions *off the reel*⟩

**²reel** \"\ *vb* -ED/-ING/-S [ME *reelen, relen,* fr. ¹*reel*] *vt* **1 a :** to wind (as yarn, thread, fishline) upon a reel **b :** to unwind (silk) from a cocoon onto a reel **c :** to roll up (as postage stamps) into a pack **2 :** to draw by reeling a line ⟨~ a fish in⟩ **3 :** to straighten (as pipe, rail, rod) by passing above two rolls and under a third ~ *vi* **:** to wind on a reel

**³reel** \"\ *vb* -ED/-ING/-S [ME *relen,* prob. fr. ¹*reel*] *vi* **1 :** to turn or move round and round **:** WHIRL: **a** *of the eyes* **:** to roll with dizziness or excitement **b :** to be giddy **:** be in a whirl ⟨her head ~*ed* under the blow —Kathleen Freeman⟩ ⟨feats of heroism . . . so stupendous and so numerous that the mind ~*s* absorbing them —Douglas Stewart⟩ **2 :** to behave in a violent disorderly manner **:** run riot ⟨the ~*ing* days of faction fights —Sean O'Faolain⟩ **3 :** to waver or fall back from a blow ⟨~*s* under the impact⟩ ⟨a fierce attack that sent the enemy ~*ing*⟩ **:** RECOIL ⟨~*ed* back in horror⟩ **4 a :** to sway unsteadily on one's feet (as from dizziness or intoxication) ⟨~ down the street⟩ ⟨having no strap to hold to, she ~*ed* and staggered and pitched with every sudden start or jerking stop of the car —Clara Morris⟩ **b :** to move with great irregularity and unsteadiness (as of a ship in a storm, a building in an earthquake) **5** *dial* **:** to twist one's foot in walking ~ *vt* **1 :** to cause to reel ⟨~ his partner in a dance⟩ **2** *obs* **:** to cause (as a stone) to roll **3** *obs* **:** to stagger through (a street)

**⁴reel** \"\ *n* -S **1 :** a reeling motion **2 :** TUMULT **3 reels** *pl, obs* **:** REVELS

**⁵reel** \"\ *n* -S **1 a :** a lively dance of the Scottish Highlanders marked by circular figures and performed with gliding movements **b :** music for or having the rhythm of this dance in moderately quick duple time **2 :** VIRGINIA REEL **3** *dial* **:** a dance song

**⁶reel** \"\ *vi* -ED/-ING/-S **:** to dance a reel

**⁷reel** \"\ *n* -S [prob. fr. ³*reel*] **:** a paver's hammer of from 5 to 7 pounds in weight having rectangular ends and used for finishing small paving blocks

**reel·able** \'rēləbəl\ *adj* **:** capable of being wound on a reel

**re·elect** \ˌrē+\ *vt* [*re-* + *elect*] **:** to elect for another term in office — **re·election** \"+\ *n*

**reeled** \'rē(ə)ld\ *adj* **1 :** wound on a reel ⟨partly ~ cocoons⟩ **2 :** disposed in a zigzag line **:** STAGGERED ⟨~ rivet holes⟩

**reeled silk** *n* **:** high quality raw silk reeled in one continuous filament from the cocoon directly into a skein — compare SPUN SILK

**reel·er** \'rēlə(r)\ *n* -S **1 :** one that reels or works with a reel: as **a :** a worker who reels (as thread or yarn) by hand or by machine **b :** an instrument or machine for reeling **c :** a leather worker who uses a beam machine to transfer hides from one vat of solution to another **2 :** a motion picture having a given number of reels ⟨a two-*reeler*⟩

**reel foot** *n, Scot* **:** CLUBFOOT

**re·eligibility** \(ˌ)rē+\ *n* **:** the quality or state of being reeligible

**re·eligible** \(ˈ)rē+\ *adj* **:** capable of being reelected or reappointed to office

**reeling** *pres part of* REEL

**reeling hammer** *n* **:** ⁷REEL

**reel·ing·ly** *adv* **:** in a reeling manner **:** with a reeling motion

**reel off** *vt* [²*reel*] **:** to tell or recite fluently ⟨*reeled* off the story of his life⟩ ⟨*reeled* the figures *off* without hesitation⟩

**reel oven** *n* **:** an oven with a revolving wheel equipped with suspended trays holding food (as meat or bread) in the process of baking that is adjusted to bake the contents in one revolution of the wheel and is automatically controlled to stop when a tray is level with the loading door

**¹reel·rall** \'rēl,ral, -ˌrȧ\ *n* -S [prob. redupl. of ⁴*reel*] *Scot* **:** DISTURBANCE, FUSS

**²reelrall** \"\ *adv, dial Brit* **:** TOPSY-TURVY

**reels** *pl of* REEL, *pres 3d sing of* REEL

**reel seat** *n* **:** the part of a fishing rod butt upon which the reel is mounted

**re·embodiment** \ˌrē+\ *n* **1 :** the act or process of reembodying **2 :** a person or thing that reembodies another

**re·embody** \"+\ *vt* **:** to embody again or anew **:** put in or into a new form **:** RESHAPE, REINCORPORATE, REORGANIZE

**re·emerge** \"+\ *vi* **:** to emerge again after concealment, retirement, suppression, quiescence — **re·emergence** \"+\ *n* — **re·emergent** \"+\ *adj*

**reem·ing beetle** \'rēmiŋ-\ *n* [*reeming* fr. (assumed) ME (dial.) *reming,* pres. part. of *remen* to open up, clear — more at REAM] **:** the largest mallet used by a calker

**reeming iron** *n* **:** a chisel for reaming the seams of planks in calking ships

**re·emission** \ˌrē+\ *n* [*re-* + *emission*] **:** an act or process of emitting anew

**re·emphasis** \(ˈ)rē+\ *n* **:** an act or instance of reemphasizing

**re·emphasize** \"+\ *vt* **:** to emphasize again or anew; *specif* **:** to declare one's continued faith in (as a questioned doctrine)

**re·employ** \ˌrē+\ *vt* **:** to hire back ⟨workers were ~*ed* after the layoff⟩ — **re·employment** \"+\ *n*

**reen** \'rēn, 'rān\ *var of* RHINE

**re·enact** \ˌrē+\ *vt* [*re-* + *enact*] **1 :** to enact (as a law) again **2 :** to act or perform again ⟨the actor will ~ the role he made famous⟩ ⟨taken to the scene shortly after he confessed to ~ the crime —*Springfield (Mass.) Daily News*⟩ ⟨a land rush that ~*ed* on a minor scale scenes associated with the opening of the Cherokee Strip —*Amer. Guide Series: Ark.*⟩ — **re·enactment** \"+\ *n*

**re·enforce** \"+\ *var of* REINFORCE

**re·engrave** \"+\ *vt* [*re-* + *engrave*] **:** to cut decorative lines or patterns into (an etched halftone plate)

**reengraving** *n* [*re-* + *engraving*] **:** a reengraved plate

**re·enlist** \ˌrē+\ *vb* **:** to enlist again ⟨found civilian life too hard and ~*ed* in the army⟩ ⟨~ the same volunteer help⟩

**re·enlistment** \"+\ *n* **1 :** the act of reenlisting **2 :** the term served in consequence of reenlisting **3 :** a person who has reenlisted

**re·enter** \(ˈ)rē+\ *vb* [ME *reentren* fr. *re-* + *entren* to enter — more at ENTER] *vt* **1 :** to enter again **2 :** to cut (as engraved lines on a plate of metal) deeper ~ *vi* **:** to enter again

**reentering angle** *or* **reentrant angle** *n* **:** an angle pointing inward; *specif* **:** an angle in a line of troops or of fortifications with its apex turned away from the enemy — opposed to *salient angle*

**reentering order of battle :** a formation of attacking or rarely defending forces in lines converging away from the enemy that is feasible only when both flanks are protected against being turned or when they overlap the enemy's lines

**re·entrance** \(ˈ)rē+\ *n* **1 :** REENTRY **2** *also* **re·en·tran·cy** \(ˈ)≈ˈen·trənsē\ -ES **:** the quality or state of being reentrant **3 :** REENTERING ANGLE

**¹re·entrant** \(ˈ)rē+\ *adj* **1 :** directed inward **2 :** having its ends closed on itself ⟨~ armature winding⟩

**²reentrant** \"\ *n* **1 :** one that reenters or is reentrant **2 a :** REENTERING ANGLE ⟨a ~ in a fortification⟩ **b :** an indentation between two salients in a horizontal plane ⟨a ~ in a coastline⟩

**re·entry** \(ˈ)rē+\ *n* [ME *reentre,* fr. *re-* + *entre* entry — more at ENTRY] **1 :** a retaking possession; *esp* **:** entry by a lessor or grantor on premises leased or granted in exercise of a right reserved on the tenant's failure to perform the covenants or conditions of the lease, grant, or other conveyance **2 :** a second or new entry ⟨a ~ into public life⟩ ⟨granted a ~ permit by the consulate⟩ **3 a :** a regaining of the right to lead by winning a trick in bridge **b :** a playing card that will win a trick in the hand of a player who has previously had the right to lead **4 :** a double impression on a line-engraved stamp produced in the transfer of the design to the printing plate; *also* **:** DOUBLE TRANSFER **5 :** the action of reentering the earth's atmosphere after traveling into space — used of a missile or vehicle ⟨a nose cone, or ~ body, that would not burn up like a meteor when it plunged back into the atmosphere —Clay Blair⟩

**ree·per** \'rēpə(r)\ *n* -S [Marathi *rīp*] **:** a strip of wood used in India as a batten or a lath

**re·equip** \ˌrē+\ *vt* [*re-* + *equip*] **:** to equip again

**rees** *pres 3d sing of* REE, *pl of* REE

**ree·shle** \'rēshəl\ *or* **ree·sle** \'rēsəl\ *chiefly Scot var of* RUSTLE

**¹reest** \'rēst, 'rāst\ *adj* [ME *reest, rest,* alter. of *resty* — more at REASTY] *dial* **:** REASTY

**²reest** \'rēst\ *vt* -ED/-ING/-S [origin unknown] *Scot* **:** to cure (as meat) by smoking

**³reest** \"\ *vi* -ED/-ING/-S [prob. short for E dial. (Sc) *arreest* to arrest, fr. ME (Sc) *arreisten,* fr. MF *arester* — more at ARREST] *chiefly Scot, of a horse* **:** BALK

**⁴reest** \"\ *dial var of* REST

**re·establish** \ˌrē+\ *vt* [*re-* + *establish*] **1 :** to establish again in or to a former place, position, or state **:** set up, fix, or confirm again **:** RESTORE ⟨~ the air base closed after the war⟩ ⟨a campaign to ~ orthodoxy in the school⟩ **2 :** to establish anew in a different place, position, or state **:** REFOUND, RESETTLE ⟨~ the flooded town on a higher site⟩ ⟨~ the refugees uprooted by war in new homes⟩ — **re·establishment** \"+\ *n*

**re·esterification** \ˌrē+\ *n* [*re-* + *esterification*] **:** TRANSESTERIFICATION

**rees·ty** \'rēsti, 'rās-\ *var of* REASTY

**reet** \'rēt\ *chiefly dial var of* RIGHT

**re·etch** \(ˈ)rē+\ *vt* **:** to etch again (as a lithographic stone in continuation of a partial etching) **:** touch up (a plate) with a brush dipped in acid — **re·etcher** \"+\ *n*

**re·evaluate** \ˌrē+\ *vt* [*re-* + *evaluate*] **:** to evaluate again ⟨forcing one to reexamine and ~ its merits —R.H.Popkin⟩

**re·evaluation** \"+\ *n* [*re-* + *evaluation*] **:** the act or result of evaluating again ⟨remarks . . . meant to stimulate a ~ of present-day procedure —*Long Island Med. Jour.*⟩

**re·evaporation** \"+\ *n* **:** evaporation a second time; *specif* **:** evaporation in a steam engine of the moisture from condensation due to the steam temperature falling below that of the cylinder walls in expansion

**¹reeve** \'rēv\ *n* -S [ME *reve, ireve,* fr. OE *gerēfa,* fr. *ge-* (perfective, associative, and collective prefix) + *-rēfa* (fr. OE *-rōf* number, array); akin to OHG *ruova* number, array — more at CO-] **1 :** a local administrative agent of the king in Anglo-Saxon times having a position and function similar to that of the bailiff under the Norman kings ⟨away from court, the king's estates were managed by resident ~*s*, who also collected the dues which the king's subjects owed —R.F.Treharne⟩ — see PORTREEVE; compare SHERIFF **2 :** an officer on a medieval English manor orig. chosen by the villeins to represent their interests but later becoming the lord's agent associated with the bailiff and responsible for maintaining order and overseeing the discharge of feudal obligations (as rents) **3 a :** the chief magistrate of a town; *specif* **:** the president of the council in rural municipalities and in some villages in central and western Canada **b :** an official charged with the enforcement of local regulations in various English and American communities ⟨field ~⟩ ⟨deer ~⟩ — see HOGREEVE; compare WARDEN

**²reeve** \"\ *vb* **rove** \'rōv\ *or* **reeved; rove** *or* **reeved; reeving; reeves** [origin unknown] *vt* **1 a :** to pass (as the end of a rope) through a hole or opening in a block, thimble, cleat, ringbolt, cringle, or similar device **b :** to fasten by passing through a hole or around something — usu. used with *on, about, to, around, over* ⟨they *rove* a rope over the yard⟩ **c :** to pass a rope through ⟨~ a block⟩ **2 :** to pass cautiously through **:** THREAD ⟨the ship *reeved* the shoals⟩ ~ *vi, of a rope* **:** to pass through a block or similar device ⟨two strong lines *reeving* through ringbolts on the deck head —Peter Heaton⟩

**³reeve** \"\ *n* -S [prob. alter. of *ruff*] **:** the female of the ruff

**reeve·land** *also* **reve·land** \'rēv,land\ *n* [OE *gerēfland,* fr. *gerēfa* reeve + *land* — more at LAND] **:** land having reverted to the king and not being granted to tenants but placed in charge of a reeve

**reeves's pheasant** \'rēvz(əz)-\ *n, usu cap R* [prob. after the name *Reeves*] **:** a pheasant (*Syrmaticus reevesii*) native to China having in the male plumage that is largely buffy with dark edgings on the feathers, black collar, white nape and throat, and black belly and having a white head with a dark facial band and a very long tail

**reeving line bend** *n* **:** a bend for joining two lines without making a bulky knot so that they will reeve through an opening

**re·evoke** \ˌrē+\ *vt* **:** to evoke again; *specif* **:** to recall to life or to the imagination

**ree wheatgrass** \'rē-\ *n* [*ree* prob. fr. ³*ree*] **:** INTERMEDIATE WHEATGRASS

**re·examination** \"+\ *n* **:** a second or new examination; *esp* **:** an examination made by a party calling a witness after and upon matters arising out of the cross-examination **:** REDIRECT EXAMINATION

**re·examine** \"+\ *vt* **:** to subject to reexamination — **re·examiner** \"+\ *n*

**re·exchange** \"+\ *n* **1 :** a renewed or second exchange **2 a :** the process by which is recovered the expense chargeable on a bill of exchange or draft which has been dishonored in a foreign country and returned to the country in which it was made or endorsed to be there taken up **b :** the draft so drawn or the expense or percentage included in it

**¹re·export** \(ˌ)rē+\ *vt* **:** to export again (something imported) — **re·exportation** \"+\ *n* — **re·exporter** \"+\ *n*

**²re·export** \(ˈ)rē+\ *n* **1 :** the act of reexporting **2 :** a reexported commodity

**re·extent** \ˌrē+\ *n* **:** a second extent or execution made in old English law on complaint that a former one was wrong

**¹ref** \'ref\ *n* -S [short for *referee*] **:** the referee of a game or sport

**²ref** \"\ *vb* **reffed; reffed; reffing; refs :** REFEREE

**ref** *abbr* **1** referee **2** reference **3** referred **4** refinery; refining **5** reformation; reformed; reformer **6** refrain **7** refrigeration; refrigerator **8** refunding

**re·face** \(ˈ)rē+\ *vt* [*re-* + *face*] **1 :** to supply with a new front **:** renew the front or appearance of ⟨~ a church⟩ **2 :** to renew a faced surface on (as the end of a cylindrical piece) by recutting or regrinding

**refacimento** *var of* RIFACIMENTO

**refaction** *n* -S [F *réfaction* rebate, repairs, fr. *refaire* to remake, do over again, repair, after such pairs as F *satisfaire* to satisfy (fr. L *satisfacere*): *satisfaction* (fr. L *satisfaction-, satisfactio*)] *obs* **:** RECOMPENSE

**re·fait** \rə'fā\ *n* -S [F, fr. *refait,* past part. of *refaire* to remake, do over again, repair, deal (cards) over again, fr. OF, to remake, do over again, repair, fr. *re-* + *faire* to make, do, fr. L *facere* — more at DO] **:** a drawn or inconclusive game or coup in the game of trente-et-quarante requiring a new deal or turn to effect a decision

**re·fall** \(ˈ)rē+\ *vi* [*re-* + *fall*] *archaic* **:** to fall again **:** fall repeatedly

**re·fashion** \(ˈ)rē+\ *vt* [*re-* + *fashion*] **:** to make again **:** make over **:** ALTER ⟨spiritual enthusiasm which ~*ed* the forms of religious devotion in the twelfth century —R.W.Southern⟩ — **re·fashioner** \"+\ *n*

**re·fasten** \"+\ *vt* [*re-* + *fasten*] **:** to fasten again ⟨nervously unfastening and ~*ing* her glove⟩

**refd** *abbr* **1** referred **2** reformed

**re·fect** \rə'fekt, rē'-\ *vt* -ED/-ING/-S [L *refectus,* past part. of *reficere* to remake, renew, restore] *archaic* **:** to restore after hunger or fatigue **:** refresh with food or drink

**re·fect·ed** \-təd\ *adj* [fr. *refection,* after such pairs as E *correction: corrected*] **:** in a state of refection ⟨~ rats⟩

**re·fec·tion** \rə'fekshən, rē'-\ *n* -S [ME *refeccioun,* fr. MF *refection,* fr. L *refection-, refectio* refreshment, repairing, fr. *refectus* (past part. of *reficere* to remake, renew, restore, fr. *re-* + *facere* to make, do) + *-ion-, -io* -ion] **1 :** refreshment of mind, spirit, or body esp. after hunger or fatigue **:** NOURISHMENT, RELIEF **2 a :** the taking of refreshment **:** satisfaction of hunger and thirst **b :** food and drink **:** REPAST **3 a :** the eating of feces esp. by the animal producing them **b :** spontaneous recovery of vitamin-depleted animals on a high starch diet presumably resulting from consumption of feces enriched with vitamins synthesized by intestinal bacteria

**re·fec·tion·er** \-sh(ə)nə(r)\ *n* -S **:** REFECTORIAN

**refection sunday** *n, usu cap R&S* [prob. so called because the gospel for the day relates the miracle of feeding the five thousand (Jn 6: 1-14)] **:** MID-LENT SUNDAY

**re·fec·tive** \-tiv\ *adj* [*refect* + *-ive*] **1 :** REFRESHING, RESTORING **2 :** designed to induce refection ⟨a ~ diet⟩

**re·fec·to·rar·i·an** \rə,fektə'ra(a)rēən\ *n* -S [ML *refectorarius* refectorian (fr. LL *refectorium* refectory + L *-arius* -ary) + E *-an*] **:** REFECTORIAN

**re·fec·to·rer** \rə'fektərə(r)\ *n* -S [*refectory* + *-er*] **:** REFECTORIAN

**re·fec·to·ri·al** \ˌrē,fek'tōrēəl\ *adj* [*refectory* + *-al*] **:** of, relating to, or used for refection

**re·fec·to·ri·an** \ˌrē,fek'tōrēən\ *n* -S [*refectory* + *-an*] **:** one in charge of a refectory or of refections — called also *refectioner*

**re·fec·to·ry** \rə'fekt(ə)rē, rē'f-\ *n* -ES [LL *refectorium,* fr. L *refectus* (past part. of *reficere* to remake, renew, restore) + *-orium* -ory] **:** a dining hall; *esp* **:** a dining hall in a monastery, convent, or religious college

**refectory table** *n* **:** a long narrow table with heavy legs and long heavy stretcher

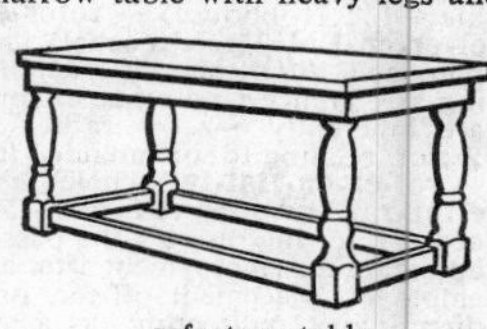
refectory table

**refel** *vt* **refelled; refelled; refelling; refels** [L *refellere* to refute, disprove, fr. *re-* + *fallere* to deceive — more at FAIL] **1** *obs* **:** REFUTE, DISPROVE, DISCREDIT **2** *obs* **:** REJECT, REPULSE

**re·fer** *R* rə'fər, rē'f-, + *vowel* -fər·; -*R* -fō, + *suffixal vowel* -fər· *also* -fōr, + *vowel in a following word* -fər· *or* -fō *also* -fōr\ *vb* **referred; referred; referring; refers** [ME *referren, referen,* fr. L *referre,* lit., to carry back, fr. *re-* + *ferre* to carry — more at BEAR] *vt* **1 a :** to think of, regard, or classify under a subsuming principle or with a general group **:** explain in terms of a general cause ⟨the Anthocerotes cannot certainly be *referred* to this common stock —D.H.Campbell⟩ ⟨*referred* the dearth to the Civil War —Katharine F. Gerould⟩ **b :** to allot to a particular place, stage, or period ⟨legend *refers* the tying of knots in strings to about 2800 B.C. —Edward Clodd⟩ **c :** to regard as coming from or localized in a certain portion of the body or of space ⟨visual sensations are *referred* to external space⟩ ⟨the pain of appendicitis may be *referred* to any region of the abdomen —*Encyc. Americana*⟩ **2 a :** to send or direct for treatment, aid, information, decision ⟨~ a student to a dictionary⟩ ⟨~ a bill to a committee⟩ ⟨~ a patient to a specialist⟩ **b :** to direct for testimony or guaranty as to one's character or ability ⟨~ an office to a former employer⟩ **3** *obs* **:** to reserve for subsequent discussion **:** DEFER **4** *obs* **:** to submit or entrust (oneself) for aid or advice ~ *vi* **1** *obs* **:** RECUR, RETURN **2 a :** to have relation or logical or factual connection **:** POINT, RELATE ⟨the superscript numerals ~ to notes at the foot of the page⟩ ⟨red pepper may ~ to cayenne —J.W. Parry⟩ **b :** to direct attention **:** ALLUDE ⟨his remarks *referred* only indirectly to the opposing party⟩ ⟨for *referring* to these familiar facts the excuse is made —Herbert Spencer⟩ **3 :** to have recourse **:** APPLY, APPEAL ⟨pausing frequently in his speech to ~ to his notes⟩ ⟨*referred* to his watch and hurried away⟩ **syn** see ASCRIBE

**refer·able** \'ref(ə)rəbəl, rə'fər·əb- rē'f- *also* -'fōrəb-\ *adj* [*refer* + *-able*] **:** capable of being considered in relation to something else **:** ASSIGNABLE, ASCRIBABLE ⟨decide to which of these motives such extraordinary scenes were ~ —Charles Dickens⟩ ⟨in head injuries . . . persistent symptoms ~ to trauma should be carefully considered —H.G.Armstrong⟩ ⟨such differences are ~ to the particular environments within which the members of various societies are reared —Ralph Linton⟩

**¹ref·er·ee** \ˌrefəˈrē, (ˈ)reˈfrē\ *n* -S [*refer* + *-ee*] **1 :** one to whom a thing is referred: as **a :** a person to whom a matter (as a private bill) is referred by parliament to examine and report upon **b** (1) **:** a person orig. in equity practice a master to whom a matter in dispute has been referred that he may settle it (2) **:** an attorney at law appointed to act as an officer of the court in determining or reporting on an issue referred to him in a pending proceeding or suit with or without the consent of the parties — distinguished from *arbitrator* (3) **:** a qualified person appointed by a judge in a juvenile or domestic relations case to investigate and report the facts and often to make recommendations **2 :** an official in a sports contest usu. having final authority for administering the game — compare UMPIRE **3** *Brit* **:** REFERENCE 5a

**²referee** \"\ *vb* **refereed; refereed; refereeing; referees** *vt* **1 :** to administer (as a match, a game) as referee **2 :** to arbitrate (a dispute) as a judge or third party ~ *vi* **:** to act as referee ⟨the teacher . . . ~*ing* in the rain on Saturday morning —*Scots Mag.*⟩

**¹ref·er·ence** \'refərn(t)s, -f(ə)rən-\ *n* -S [*refer* + *-ence*] **1 :** the act of referring ⟨~ to a map will make the position clear⟩ or consulting ⟨~ to an almanac⟩ ⟨items arranged alphabetically for ease of ~⟩ ⟨a manual designed for ready ~⟩ ⟨the report was filed for future ~⟩ **2 :** the act of referring a matter in dispute to a referee **3 :** the capability or character of alluding to or bearing on or directing attention to something **:** RELATION, RESPECT ⟨with ~ to his suggestion⟩ ⟨in ~ to your letter of the 14th⟩ **4 :** something that refers to something else: as **a :** ALLUSION, MENTION ⟨omitted all ~ to his prison record⟩ ⟨the play is full of ~*s* to contemporary events⟩ **b :** a specific direction of the attention **:** a sign or indication referring a reader to another passage or book ⟨a list of ~*s* is appended⟩ **c :** consultation of sources of information ⟨books more suitable for ~ than for reading⟩ ⟨volumes for ready ~⟩ **d :** TAB 1a(4) **5 :** one that is referred to or consulted: as **a :** a person of whom inquiries can be made as to the character or capacity of another **b :** a written statement of the qualifications of a person seeking employment or appointment given by his previous employer or by someone familiar with his character, ability, experience, or training **:** RECOMMENDATION ⟨three ~*s* must accompany each application⟩ **c :** a book or a passage in a work to which a reader is referred **d :** DENOTATION, MEANING **6 :** the direction of others' attention or behavior to one's self ⟨delusions of ~⟩ — see IDEAS OF REFERENCE

**²reference** \"\ *vt* -ED/-ING/-S **1 :** to supply with references ⟨the work is fully *referenced*⟩ **2 :** to put in a form (as a table, list) adapted to easy reference

**³reference** \"\ *adj* **:** used or usable for reference **:** taken or laid down as standard for measuring, reckoning, or constructing ⟨~ point⟩ ⟨~ plane⟩; *specif* **:** of known potency and used as a standard in the biological assay of a sample of the same drug of unknown strength

**reference book** *n* **1 :** a book (as a dictionary, encyclopedia, atlas) intended primarily for consultation rather than for consecutive reading **2 :** a library book that may be used on the premises but may not be taken out

**reference frame** *n* **:** FRAME OF REFERENCE

**reference gage** *n* **:** MASTER GAGE

**reference group** *n, sociol* : a group toward whose interests, attitudes, and values the individual is oriented
**reference library** *n* **1** : a collection of books often about a particular subject useful for consultation ⟨a *reference library* of science⟩ **2** : a library the books of which may be used on the premises but may not be taken out
**reference line** *n* : an arbitrary fixed line (as an x-axis or a polar axis) from which coordinates of a point are computed
**reference mark** *n* : a conventional mark (as *, †, ‡, §, ‖, ¶, ☞) or a superior figure or letter placed in a text for directing attention to a footnote or a key on the same or another page — see respectively ASTERISK, DAGGER, DOUBLE DAGGER, SECTION, PARALLEL, PARAGRAPH, INDEX
**ref·er·en·dal** \ˌrefəˈrendᵊl\ *adj* [*referend*um + *-al*] : REFERENDARY
**¹ref·er·en·da·ry** \ˌrefəˈrendərē\ *n* -ES [LL *referendarius*, fr. L *referendus* to be referred (gerundive of *referre* to refer) + *-arius* -ary] **1** : an official at various imperial, papal, and royal courts charged with investigative or advisory duties — used as a title **2** : REFEREE, ARBITRATOR **3** *obs* : one who furnishes news : REPORTER
**²referendary** \ˌ≈≈ˈ≈≈≈\ *adj* [*referend*um + *-ary*] : of or relating to a referendum
**ref·er·en·dum** \ˌrefəˈrendəm\ *n, pl* **referen·da** \-də\ *or* **referendums** \-dəmz\ [L, neut. of *referendus* to be referred, gerundive of *referre* to refer — more at REFER] **1 a** : the principle or practice of submitting to popular vote a measure passed upon or proposed by a legislative body or by popular initiative **b** : a vote on a measure so submitted **c** : a similar practice or method for ascertaining the will of members of an organized group (as a union, club, faculty) : POLL **2** : a diplomatic agent's note asking his government for instructions
**¹ref·er·ent** \rəˈfərənt, ˈref(ə)rənt\ *n* -S [L *referent-, referens*, pres. part. of *referre*] **1** : someone that is referred to or consulted **2 a** : a word or a term that refers to another **b** *logic* : the term (as *a* in the proposition *a* has the relation R to *b*) from which a relation proceeds : the first term of a relation (as *a* in R*a*, *b*, *c*) — compare RELATUM **3** : that which is denoted or named by an expression or a statement : a spatiotemporal object or event to which a term, sign, or symbol refers : the object of a reference
**²referent** \"\ *adj* [L *referent-, referens*, pres. part. of *referre*] : that refers : having reference ⟨judgments ~ to the entirety of life —L.T.Hobhouse⟩ — **refer·ent·ly** *adv*
**ref·er·en·tial** \ˌrefəˈrenchəl\ *adj* [fr. ¹*reference*, after such pairs as E *difference: differential*] **1** : containing or constituting a reference : pointing to something out of itself ⟨symbols are inherently ~⟩ ⟨~ rather than emotive use of words⟩ **2** : of, relating to, or intended for reference ⟨notes for ~ use⟩ — **ref·er·en·tial·ly** \-chəlē\ *adv*
**re·fer·ral** \rəˈfərəl, rēˈf- *also* -fərəl\ *n* -S [*refer* + *-al*] **1** : the act of referring: as **a** : the passing along or forwarding of an applicant for employment after an initial interview to a selected employer, placement officer, or bureau **b** : the process of directing or redirecting (as a medical case, a patient) to an appropriate specialist or agency for definitive treatment **2 a** : one that is referred ⟨50 percent of its ~*s* are turned down at the plant —*Survey Graphic*⟩ **b** : an instance or case of referring ⟨need to make ~*s* to family agencies more frequently —Bernard Kogon⟩
**referred** *past of* REFER
**referred pain** *n* : a pain subjectively localized in one region though due to irritation in another region
**re·fer·rer** \rəˈfərə(r), rēˈf-, -R *also* -fərə(r\ *n* -S [*refer* + *-er*] : one that refers
**re·fer·ri·ble** \rəˈfər·əbəl, rēˈf- *also* -fərəb-\ *adj* [*refer* + *-able*] : REFERABLE
**referring** *pres part of* REFER
**refers** *pres 3d sing of* REFER
**reff** *abbr* references
**reffed** *past of* REF
**reffing** *pres part of* REF
**ref·fo** \ˈre(ˌ)fō\ *n* -S [*ref-* (fr. *refugee*) + *-o*] *Austral* : a refugee from Europe
**refg** *abbr* refrigerating; refrigerator
**re·fight** \(ˈ)rē+\ *vt* [*re-* + *fight*] : to fight over again (as in imagination) ⟨spent every Saturday ~*ing* the Revolution — visiting homes, battlefields, museums, forts —Dorothy Barclay⟩
**re·figure** \"+\ *vt* [*re-* + *figure*] : to figure again
**¹re·fill** \"+\ *vb* [*re-* + *fill*] *vt* : to fill again : REPLENISH ~ *vi* : to become filled again
**²re·fill** \ˈrē+ˌ-\ *n* **1** : a commercial product designed to fill again a container with its appropriate contents ⟨~ for a vanity case⟩ ⟨a loose-leaf notebook ~⟩ **2** *med* : a replacement in a cavity of removed liquid or other material or a substitution (as of gas) for such material ⟨pneumothorax ~⟩ **3** : a prescription compounded and dispensed for the second time without an order from the physician **4** : a second serving of food or drink
**re·fill·able** \(ˈ)rēˈfiləbəl\ *adj* : capable of being refilled ⟨~ prescription⟩ ⟨~ notebook⟩
**re·film** \(ˈ)rē+\ *vt* [*re-* + *film*] : to film again
**re·filter** \(ˈ)rē+\ *vt* [*re-* + *filter*] : to filter again
**re·finance** \(ˈ)rē+\ *vt* [*re-* + *finance*] : to renew or reorganize the financing of : provide capital for afresh : provide for (an outstanding indebtedness) by making another loan or a larger loan on fresh terms
**re·find** \(ˈ)rē+\ *vt* [*re-* + *find*] : to find again : REDISCOVER, RECOVER
**¹re·fine** \rəˈfīn, rēˈf-\ *vb* -ED/-ING/-S [*re-* + *fine* (to refine)] *vt* **1** : to reduce to a fine, unmixed, or pure state : separate from extraneous matter : free from dross or alloy ⟨~ silver⟩ : free or cleanse from impurities ⟨~ sugar⟩ **2 a** (1) : to give a final mechanical treatment to (paper stock) so as to put in the best possible condition for the grade of paper being made (2) : to prepare (pulp screenings) for manufacture into coarse paper **b** : to treat (pig iron) in the refinery furnace so as to remove the silicon and other unwanted elements **c** : to manufacture (petroleum products) by distilling crude petroleum and purifying the resulting successive distillates **d** : to subject (raw sugar) to a series of processes (as defecation or carbonation, filtration through bone black or activated carbon, and crystallization) to produce white sugar **3** : to free (as the mind or soul) from moral imperfection, grossness, dullness, earthiness : SPIRITUALIZE, ELEVATE ⟨tried in sharp tribulation and *refined* by faith and faithful works —John Milton⟩ **4** : to improve or perfect by pruning, polishing, or rarefying ⟨~ a poetic style⟩ ⟨the imagination cannot escape from the literal but at best can only ~ it —Bernard DeVoto⟩ **5** : to attenuate or reduce in vigor, intensity, vitality by pruning, polishing, or purifying ⟨much of the really nutritive material actually was *refined* out of the foods —W.H.Camp⟩ **6** : to increase or heighten the discriminatory power of : SUBTILIZE ⟨~ a method of analysis⟩ ⟨spent . . . years patiently *refining* the crude statistics of economic change —*Times Lit. Supp.*⟩ **7** : to free from what is coarse, vulgar, uncouth : cause to become fastidious, elegant, cultivated ⟨sent to a finishing school to ~ her taste and manners⟩ ~ *vi* **1** : to become pure or perfected : become free or freer from what is extraneous or crude or debasing **2** : to make improvement by adding or introducing subtleties or distinctions — used with *on* or *upon* ⟨the earlier science had only *refined* upon the ordinary notions of ordinary people —A.N.Whitehead⟩
**²refine** *adj, obs* : REFINED
**re·fined** \-nd\ *adj* **1** : free from impurities ⟨to gild ~ gold, to paint the lily —Shak.⟩ **2** : FASTIDIOUS, CULTIVATED, HIGHBRED ⟨she spoke in a painfully ~ accent⟩ ⟨sensitive, ~ face⟩ ⟨belief that the function of music is to cause a ~ sort of sensuous pleasure —Susanne K. Langer⟩ **3** : marked by subtlety of discrimination or precision of method or technique : carried to a fine point : PRECISE, EXACT ⟨drawn out with that ~ analysis of terms which I always find a waste of time —H.J.Laski⟩ ⟨men learned the necessity of exact measurement and ~ calculations —J.H.Randall⟩ — **re·fined·ly** \-n(ə)dlē\ *adv* — **re·fined·ness** \-nədnəs, -n(d)nəs\ *n* -ES
**refined madder** *n* : FLOWERS OF MADDER
**refined wool fat** *n* : LANOLIN b
**re·fine·ment** \rəˈfīnmənt, rēˈf-\ *n* -S **1** : the action or process of refining ⟨~ of metals⟩ ⟨~ of torture⟩ ⟨~ of measuring techniques⟩ **2** : the quality or state of being refined : CULTIVATION, ELEGANCE, POLISH ⟨always comparing immigrant vitality with native ~ —M.D.Geismar⟩ ⟨sniffed with exquisite ~ —Elinor Wylie⟩ **3 a** : something that is the product or outcome of a refining process or that conduces to refining : a refined feature or method ⟨pursued the delicate art of suggestion to its furthest ~*s* —Maurice Bowra⟩ **b** : subtlety in reasoning ⟨~*s* of logic⟩ ⟨~ is what characterizes our intellectualist philosophies —William James⟩ **c** : a contrivance, device, or feature intended to improve or perfect ⟨introduce ~*s* into a machine⟩ ⟨this ~ will increase the cost of the automobile⟩ **d** : a slight departure from mechanical exactness or uniformity of line intended to enhance the beauty of a building or overcome undesirable optical effects
**re·fin·er** \-īnə(r)\ *n* -S : one that refines: as **a** : one whose work is refining a specified thing ⟨lard ~⟩ ⟨oil ~⟩ **b** : a machine that gives the final mechanical treatment to paper stock
**re·fin·er·man** \-mən, -ˌman\ *n, pl* **refinermen** : a millman who refines reclaimed rubber
**refiners' sirup** *n* : the residual liquid product obtained in the process of refining raw sugars
**re·fin·ery** \rəˈfīn(ə)rē, rēˈf-, -)ri\ *n* -ES : a building and equipment for refining or purifying metals, oil, or sugar; *specif* : a furnace with a shallow hearth for refining pig iron to wrought iron or to iron suitable for puddling
**re·finger** \(ˈ)rē+\ *vt* [*re-* + *finger*] : to alter or replace the fingering of (a musical passage)
**refining** *n* -S : the action or process of removing impurities from a crude or impure material: as **a** *of metals* : subjection to high heat or other purification methods (as electrolysis or treatment with chemicals) ⟨fire ~ of copper⟩ — compare PARTING **b** *of glass* : FINING 1b **c** *of sugar* : processing in a series of steps ending with crystallization **d** *of petroleum* : fractional distillation usu. followed by other processing (as cracking)
**refining engine** *n* : REFINER b
**re·finish** \(ˈ)rē+\ *vt* [*re-* + *finish*] : to give (as furniture) a new surface
**re·finisher** \"+\ *n* : one that refinishes furniture
**¹re·fit** \(ˈ)rē+\ *vb* [*re-* + *fit*] *vt* : to prepare for use again : fit out or supply again : restore after damage or decay ⟨~ a ship⟩ ~ *vi* : to get refitted : obtain repairs or fresh supplies or equipment ⟨the fleet returned to ~⟩
**²re·fit** \ˈrē+ˌ-, ≈ˈ≈\ *n* : a refitting or fitting out again : a repairing of damages or replacing of what is worn or useless; *esp* : a refitting and renovating of a ship ⟨assisting with ~*s* of other submarines as they came and went —E.L.Beach⟩
**re·fit·ment** \(ˈ)rēˈfitmənt\ *n* : REFIT
**re·fix** \(ˈ)rē+\ *vt* [*re-* + *fix*] : to fix again : set up again : attach again or in a new place
**re·fixture** \"+\ *vt* [*re-* + *fixture*] : to renew or replace the fixtures of (as a store, an office)
**refl** *abbr* **1** reflection; reflective; reflectively; reflector **2** reflex; reflexive
**re·flash** \(ˈ)rē+\ *n* [*re-* + *flash*] : a rekindling and bursting into flame ⟨prevent possible ~ by cooling the hot surface and any glowing material —*Training Manual for Auxiliary Firemen*⟩
**re·flate** \rəˈflāt, rēˈf-\ *vb* -ED/-ING/-S [back-formation fr. *reflation*] *vi* : to expand again the quantity of currency and credit after a period of deflation ~ *vt* : to expand again the amount of (currency and credit)
**re·fla·tion** \-āshən\ *n* -S [*re-* + *-flation* (as in *inflation*)] : restoration of deflated prices to a desirable level by the use of monetary powers
**¹re·flect** \rəˈflekt, rēˈf-\ *vb* -ED/-ING/-S [ME *reflecten*, fr. L *reflectere*, fr. *re-* + *flectere* to bend, turn] *vt* **1** *archaic* : to turn into or away from a certain course : turn aside : DEFLECT, DIVERT **2 a** : to turn, throw, or bend off or backward at an angle ⟨light ~*ed* from the moon⟩ ⟨heat ~*ed* by the light surface⟩ **b** : to cast back : cause to rebound or reverberate : to project out ⟨his internal stresses ~*ed* a dry bitterness upon the world —H.G.Wells⟩ ⟨new music . . . ~*s* just as much emotion as any other kind of music —Aaron Copland⟩ **3 a** : to bend or fold back : impart a backward curve, bend, or fold to : make retrorse in form ⟨petals ~*ed* at the tops⟩ **b** : to push or lay aside (as tissue, an organ) during surgery in order to gain access to the part to be operated on **4** : to give back or exhibit as an image, likeness, or outline : reproduce or show as a mirror does ⟨the trees on the shore line were ~*ed* in the clear water⟩ ⟨dignity was ~*ed* in her vivid blue eyes —Ellen Glasgow⟩ ⟨this body, with full power to enact laws, more truly ~*ed* the popular will —*Amer. Guide Series: Pa.*⟩ **5** : to bring or cast as a result : bring about as an attribute, characterization, designation ⟨his attitude would ~ little credit on his political judgment —W.H.Chamberlin⟩ **6** : to make manifest or apparent as a likely cause, plausible conditioning factor, fitting background element, or concomitant : SHOW ⟨the influence of the lumbering period is ~*ed* in Bay City's many large frame dwellings —*Amer. Guide Series: Mich.*⟩ ⟨the pulse generally ~*s* the condition of the heart —Morris Fishbein⟩ ⟨the structure of the compound sentence often ~*s* a simple artlessness —R.M.Weaver⟩ **7** : to remember with thoughtful consideration : come to recollect, realize, or consider in a course of thought — used with a following clause ⟨Blake's poetry . . . told me that he must be an Irishman before ever I ~*ed* that his name was Irish —A.T.Quiller-Couch⟩ ~ *vi* **1** *obs* **a** : to become turned or thrown back : REBOUND ⟨the sun darts forth his rays at right angles which ~ back upon themselves —Nathanael Carpenter⟩ **b** : to cast light : SHINE ⟨whose virtues will, I hope, ~ on Rome, as Titan's rays on earth —Shak.⟩ **2** : to throw back light or sound : return rays, beams, or waves **3** : to think and consider esp. after the immediate event : think quietly and calmly : RECONSIDER ⟨~ on the role of philosophy in a liberal civilization —M.R.Cohen⟩ **4** *obs* : to bounce back : spring back after impact : RECOIL **5 a** : to tend to bring reproach : cast or bring censure, discredit, reproach, doubt, or suspicion ⟨the investigation ~*s* on the integrity of the officials involved⟩ ⟨did not ~ on the general's character in his speech⟩ **b** : to have a bearing or influence ⟨the steel strike naturally ~*ed* in the sale of plastics⟩ **6** : to become mirrored : produce a mirrored image ⟨clouds ~*ing* on the lake⟩ **syn** see THINK — **reflect in a plane** : to construct a figure each of whose points *P′* is related with a corresponding point *P* of a given figure in such a way that the line joining *P* and *P′* is bisected perpendicularly by the plane
**²reflect** *n* -S *obs* : REFLECTION
**re·flec·tance** \-tən(t)s\ *n* -S : the fraction of the total luminous flux incident upon a surface that is reflected and that varies according to the wave-length distribution of the incident light — called also *reflection coefficient, reflection factor*; compare ALBEDO
**reflected** *adj* [ME, fr. past part. of *reflecten* to reflect] **1** : bent or sent back : MIRRORED; *specif* : derived through the reflection of waves or rays ⟨~ heat⟩ ⟨~ color⟩ **2** : coming indirectly or from a source other than oneself or itself : received from another ⟨enjoying the ~ glory of his famous brother⟩ **3** : turned back upon itself ⟨a sea shell with a ~ lip⟩ — **re·flect·ed·ly** *adv* — **re·flect·ed·ness** *n* -ES
**reflected impedance** *n* : a part of the impedance of an electric circuit that is due to the influence of another coupled circuit
**reflecterize** *var of* REFLECTORIZE
**reflecting** *adj* : that reflects or causes reflection: as **a** : having some contrivance or apparatus to reflect light or heat ⟨~ microscope⟩ ⟨~ projector⟩ ⟨~ oven⟩ **b** : THOUGHTFUL ⟨in our less ~ moments we are apt to claim a very intimate acquaintance with matter —James Jeans⟩ — **re·flect·ing·ly** *adv*
**reflecting galvanometer** *n* : a galvanometer in which the deflections of the needle or coil are read by means of a mirror attached to it that reflects a ray of light or the image of a scale
**reflecting telescope** *n* : REFLECTOR 4
**re·flec·tion** \rəˈflekshən, rēˈf-\ *n* -S [ME, alter. (influenced by *reflecten* to reflect) of *reflexion*, fr. MF, fr. LL *reflexion-, reflexio* action of bending back, fr. L *reflexus* (past part. of *reflectere* to reflect, bend back) + *-ion-, -io* -ion] **1** : the partial or complete return of a wave motion (as of light or sound) from a surface that it encounters into the medium that it originally traversed and in a manner that is usu. diffuse or irregular — compare SPECULAR REFLECTION **2** : the production of an image by or as if by a mirror ⟨the eye sees not itself but by ~ —Shak.⟩ ⟨the officers were a ~ of their men, more restrained —John Steinbeck⟩ **3 a** : the action of bending or folding back **b** : a reflected part ⟨the mesentery is a ~ of the peritoneum⟩ : FOLD **4** : something produced by reflecting: **a** : reflected light or heat **b** : reflected brilliance (as of wit) or warmth (as of emotion) ⟨joy is only the ~ of what is sought, a will-o'-the wisp —Gouverneur Paulding⟩ **c** : an image given back by a reflecting surface : a reflected counterpart **d** : an effect produced by an influence ⟨~*s* of ancient Celtic legend in Italian literature⟩ **5** : reproach cast or brought to bear : CENSURE, BLAME, IMPUTATION ⟨the ~*s* on certain named persons' chastity and honesty —*Geog. Jour.*⟩ **6** : a thought, idea, or opinion formed or a remark made as a result of meditation ⟨random ~*s* and essays by one of our finest stylists —Orville Prescott⟩ **7 a** : consideration of some subject matter, idea, or purpose often with a view to understanding or accepting it or seeing it in its right relations ⟨as . . . walking gave him a better chance for ~, the prospect slowly brightened —John Buchan⟩ **b** : introspective contemplation of the contents or qualities of one's own thoughts or remembered experiences ⟨~ can be practiced on every experience —Edmund Husserl⟩ **8** *obs* : turning back : RETURN **9** *obs* : RELATION, CONNECTION **10** *obs* : RECOLLECTION
**re·flec·tion·al** \-shənᵊl,-shnəl\ *adj* : relating to or caused by reflection
**reflection coefficient** *n* : REFLECTANCE
**reflection factor** *n* : REFLECTANCE
**reflection grating** *n* : a diffraction grating whose lines are ruled on a mirror surface
**reflection plane** *n* : a mirror plane of symmetry of a crystal
**reflection twin** *n* : a twin crystal in which the individuals are so related that one is a mirror image of the other — compare ROTATION TWIN
**re·flec·tive** \rəˈflektiv, rēˈf-, -tēv *also* -təv\ *adj* **1** : capable of throwing back light, images, sound waves : REFLECTING ⟨~ surfaces⟩ ⟨~ insulation⟩ **2** : marked by reflection : concerned with ideas or with introspective pondering : THOUGHTFUL, DELIBERATIVE ⟨~ reading of history⟩ ⟨~ temperament⟩ **3** : of, relating to, or caused by reflection ⟨~ glare of the beach⟩ ⟨poise and swoop of a gull's flight casts in addition a ~ beauty on its animal structure —Lewis Mumford⟩ **4** : REFLEXIVE ⟨~ verb⟩ — **re·flec·tive·ly** \-tivlē, -li\ *adv* — **re·flec·tive·ness** \-tivnəs, -tēv- *also* -təv-\ *n* -ES
**reflective judgment** *n, Kantianism* : a judgment that proceeds from given particulars to the discovery of a general concept or universal principle under which the particulars may be subsumed — contrasted with *determinative judgment*
**re·flec·tiv·i·ty** \(ˌ)rēˌflekˈtivəd·ē, rəˌf-\ *n* -ES **1** : ability to reflect beams or rays : reflective power ⟨the high ~ of snow fields⟩ **2** : REFLECTANCE
**re·flec·tom·e·ter** \-ˈtäməd·ə(r)\ *n* [¹*reflect* + *-o-* + *-meter*] : a photometric or electronic device for measuring the reflectances of light or other radiant energy
**re·flec·tor** \rəˈflektə(r), rēˈf-\ *n* -S [¹*reflect* + *-or*] **1** *obs* **a** : one that meditates or considers **b** : one that casts reflections : CRITIC **2** : a polished body or surface for reflecting light or other radiation: as **a** : a device used to modify the distribution of light from an illuminant, to shade the source, to direct the beams, and to produce artistic effect **b** : a highly polished curved usu. parabolic metal piece for reflecting the light forward in a head lamp **c** : a bowl-shaped device commonly of polished metal placed behind lamps to increase the amount of light reaching a scene to be photographed **d** : a panel (as of wallboard covered with metallic foil) used to reflect light onto the subject (as in portraiture or motion pictures) **e** : a utensil designed to reflect heat from an open fire and used in baking **f** : a device for reflecting sound toward an audience **3** : a portion of an antenna array that serves to reverse the direction of part of the radio waves sent out from the radiating portion and is often used to improve the directional quality of the antenna **4** : a telescope in which the principal focusing element is a mirror usu. of spherical or paraboloidal shape **5** : a part of a nuclear reactor that reflects neutrons back toward the reactor core
**re·flec·tor·ize** *or* **re·flect·er·ize** \-təˌrīz\ *vt* -ED/-ING/-S [*reflectorize* fr. *reflector* + *-ize*; *reflecterize* alter. (influenced by *-er*) of *reflectorize*] **1** : to prepare (a surface) so as to make reflecting **2** : to provide with reflectors ⟨~ a road sign⟩ ⟨~ a curved margin of a highway⟩
**reflects** *pres 3d sing of* REFLECT, *pl of* REFLECT
**re·flesher** \(ˈ)rē+\ *n* [*re-* + *flesher*] : a leather worker who removes from hides any flesh left by the fleshing machine operator
**re·flet** \rəˈflā, rēˈf-\ *n* -S [F, modif. (influenced by L *reflectere*) of It *riflesso*, fr. *riflesso*, adj., reflected, fr. L *reflexus*, past part. of *reflectere* to reflect] : special brilliance of surface : metallic luster esp. on ceramic ware ⟨gold ~ of majolica ware⟩
**¹re·flex** \ˈreˌfleks *sometimes* rəˈf- *or* rēˈf-\ *n* -ES [L *reflexus*, past part. of *reflectere* to reflect] **1** : reflected heat, light, or color; *specif* : light represented as reflected from an illuminated surface to one in shade (as in a painting) **2 a** : a mirrored image ⟨like the ~ of the moon seen in a wave —P.B.Shelley⟩ **b** : a copy that reflects an original in essential features or peculiar characteristics ⟨to make legislation a ~ of the popular will —W.E.H.Lecky⟩ **3 a** *obs* : considered thought or statement **b** *obs* : a glancing reference : ALLUSION **4 a** *or* **reflex act** : an act (as a movement) performed automatically and without conscious volition in consequence of a nervous impulse transmitted inward by afferent fibers from a receptor to a nerve center and commonly through adjustor neurones outward by efferent fibers to an effector (as a muscle or gland) **b** *or* **reflex action** : the whole process comprising reception, transmission, and reaction that culminates in such an act **c reflexes** *pl* : the power of acting or responding with adequate speed ⟨his strength and the agility in his legs were gone and his ~*es* no longer as they had been —Ernest Hemingway⟩ ⟨his ~*es* are gone . . . I will never okay him to fight again —*Time*⟩ **d** : an automatic or strongly habitual and predictable way of thinking or behaving ⟨to obscure emotion was becoming for him a natural ~ —Truman Capote⟩ ⟨the dangers of this wholesale conditioning of human mental ~*es* —*New Republic*⟩ **5 a** : a phonemic, grammatical, or vocabulary element as found in a language in a form determined by development from an earlier stage of the language **b** : a cognate element
**²reflex** \"\ *adj* [L *reflexus*, past part. of *reflectere*] **1** : bent, turned, or directed back : reversed in direction or course : REFLECTED ⟨~ current in a river⟩ ⟨stem with ~ leaves⟩ **2** : directed back upon the mind or its operations : INTROSPECTIVE **3** : produced in reaction, in resistance, or in return ⟨monetary deflation is the ~ consequence of undue inflation⟩ **4** *of an angle* : greater than two and less than four right angles : being between 180° and 360° — see ANGLE illustration **5 a** : of, relating to, or produced by stimulus without necessarily the intervention of consciousness ⟨~ contraction of the iris⟩ **b** : relating to, marked by, connected with, or constituting a reflex ⟨~ center⟩ **6** : having an amplifier tube functioning simultaneously as both a radio-frequency and an audio-frequency amplifier by leading the current through a tube both before and after detection ⟨~ receiving set⟩ **7** : relating to the reproduction of print or other graphic matter by means of a contact printing method in which light transmitted through light-sensitive material is reflected back onto the material from the matter to be reproduced ⟨~ paper⟩ ⟨~ copying⟩
**reflex arc** *n* : the complete nervous path that is involved in a reflex
**reflex camera** *n* : a camera in which the image formed by the lens is reflected by a mirror onto a ground-glass screen for focusing and composition
**re·flexed** \-kst\ *adj* [ME *reflexid*, fr. L *reflexus* (past part. of *reflectere*) + *-id*, *-ed* -ed] **1** *obs* : thrown back : caused or

produced by reflection **2 :** bent or curved backward or downward ⟨~ petals⟩ ⟨~ leaves⟩

**reflexed bow** *n* **:** a bow whose limbs curve away from the string side when unbraced

**re·flex·i·bil·i·ty** \rə̇ˌfleksə'bilədē, (ˌ)rēˌf-\ *n* -ES **:** the quality or state of being reflexible

**re·flex·i·ble** \rə̇'fleksəbəl, rē'f-\ *adj* [L *reflexus* (past part. of *reflectere*) + E *-able*] **:** capable of being reflected

**re·flex·ion** *Brit var of* REFLECTION 1

**re·flex·ism** \'rēˌflekˌsizəm *sometimes* rə̇'f- *or* rē'f-\ *n* -S **:** the limitation of psychological research to the study of reflexes

**¹re·flex·ive** \rə̇'fleksiv, rē'f-, -sēv *also* -səv\ *adj* [ML *reflexivus* reflected, turned back, fr. L *reflexus* (past part. of *reflectere* to reflect) + *-ivus* -ive] **1 :** capable of bending back **2 a :** directed or turned back upon itself **:** INTROSPECTIVE — used of a mental act **b :** marked by or capable of reflection **:** REFLECTIVE **3** *logic, of a relation* **:** existing between an entity and itself ⟨identity is a ~ relation⟩ ⟨all members of a class are in ~ relation with one another⟩ **4 :** of, relating to, or constituting an action (as in "the witness perjured himself" or "I bethought myself") that is directed back upon the agent or the grammatical subject **5 :** relating to or consisting of a reflex or reflexes ⟨the nervous process which forms the basis of all ~ actions —A.L.Schniermann⟩ — **re·flex·ive·ly** \-səvlē, -li\ *adv* — **re·flex·ive·ness** \-sivnəs, -sēv- *also* -səv-\ *n* -ES

**²reflexive** \"\ *n* -S **:** a reflexive pronoun or verb

**reflexive pronoun** *n* **:** a pronoun referring to the subject of the sentence, clause, or verbal phrase in which it stands; *specif* **:** a personal pronoun compounded with *-self*

**re·flex·iv·i·ty** \(ˌ)rēˌflek'sivədē, rə̇ˌf-\ *n* -ES **:** the quality or state of being reflexive

**re·flex·ly** *adv* **:** in a reflex manner ⟨~ induced contractions⟩ **:** by means of reflexes ⟨~ contracting the iris⟩

**re·flex·ness** *n* -ES **:** the quality or state of being reflex

**re·flexo·gen·ic** \rə̇ˌfleksə'jenik\ *or* **re·flex·og·e·nous** \ˌrēˌflek'säjənəs\ *adj* [¹*reflex* + *-o-* + *-genic* or *-genous*] **1 :** causing reflexes; *esp* **:** being the point of origin of reflexes ⟨a ~ zone⟩ **2 :** originating reflexly ⟨~ components of respiration⟩

**re·flexo·log·ic** \rə̇ˌfleksə'läjik\ *adj* **:** relating to reflexology — **re·flexo·log·i·cal·ly** \-jək(ə)lē\ *adv*

**re·flex·ol·o·gist** \ˌrēˌflek'säləjəst\ *n* -S **:** one who interprets behavior as consisting of reflexes

**re·flex·ol·o·gy** \-jē\ *n* -ES [ISV ¹*reflex* + *-o-* + *-logy*; orig. formed as Russ *refleksologiya*] **1 :** the study and interpretation of behavior in terms of simple and complex reflexes **2 :** the reflex component of the function of a body part or system or of a particular kind of activity ⟨the ~ of locomotion⟩

**re·float** \(')rē+\ *vt* [*re-* + *float*] **:** to set afloat again ⟨~ a grounded ship⟩

**re·florescence** \ˌrē+\ *n* [L *reflorescere* to blossom again (fr. *re-* + *florescere* to begin to bloom) + E *-ence* — more at FLORESCENCE] **:** a renewed blossoming

**re·florescent** \"+\ *adj* [L *reflorescent-, reflorescens*, pres. part. of *reflorescere* to blossom again] **:** flowering again

**re·flourish** \(')rē+\ *vi* [ME *reflorissen*, fr. *re-* + *florissen, florisshen* to flourish] **:** to flourish again

**¹re·flow** \(')rē+\ *vi* [ME *reflowen*, fr. *re-* + *flowen* to flow] **1 :** to flow back **:** EBB **2 :** to flow in again **:** FLOOD ⟨universal deluge . . . that ebbs but to ~ —Lord Byron⟩

**²re·flow** \'rē+ˌ-\ *n* **1 :** REFLUX, EBB **2 :** renewed flowing or flooding

**re·flower** \(')rē+\ *vi* [*re-* + *flower*] **:** to blossom or flourish anew

**ref·lu·ence** \'reˌflüən(t)s, -ˌfləwən-\ *n* -S [L *refluere* to flow back (fr. *re-* + *fluere* to flow) + E *-ence* — more at FLUID] **:** refluent action **:** REFLUX

**ref·lu·ent** \-nt\ *adj* [L *refluent-, refluens*, pres. part. of *refluere* to flow back] **:** flowing back ⟨~ blood in the veins⟩ **:** EBBING, SUBSIDING ⟨~ tides⟩

**¹re·flux** \'rēˌfləks\ *n* [ME, fr. ML *refluxus*, fr. L *re-* + *fluxus* flow — more at FLUX] **1 a :** a flowing back **:** REFLUENCE ⟨the flux and ~ of the tides⟩ ⟨the fluxes and ~*es* of the mind when agitated by the great and simple affection —William Wordsworth⟩ **b :** a process of refluxing or the condition of being refluxed **2 :** a reflux apparatus; *esp* **:** REFLUX CONDENSER **3 :** the liquid condensed from the vapors in a refluxing operation

**²reflux** \"\ *adj* **1 :** of or relating to reflux **:** RETURNING, EBBING **2 :** admitting or controlling reflux ⟨~ tower in an oil field⟩

**³reflux** \"\ *vt* -ED/-ING/-ES **:** to cause to flow back or return; *esp* **:** to heat (as under a reflux condenser) so that the vapors formed condense to a liquid that flows back to be heated again

**reflux condenser** *n* **:** a condenser usu. placed upright so that the condensed vapors flow back into the distilling flask and continued boiling of easily volatile substances is possible with little loss from evaporation

**reflux valve** *n* **:** a back-pressure valve

**re·fly** \(')rē+\ *vb* [*re-* + *fly*] *vi* **:** to fly again **:** fly back ~ *vt* **1 :** to travel or cover (a course) again in flight **2 :** to transport again or back in flight

**re·focil·late** \rē'fäsəˌlāt, -fōs-\ *vt* -ED/-ING/-S [LL *refocillatus, refocilatus*, past part. of *refocillare, refocilare* to warm into life again, fr. L *re-* + *focilare, foculare* to revive or refresh by warmth, fr. *foculum* chafing dish, brazier, fr. *fovēre* to warm, keep warm — more at DAY] **:** REFRESH, REVIVE ⟨*refocillating* their spirits with whiskey and soda⟩ — **re·focil·la·tion** \(ˌ)ˌ==ˈlāshən\ *n* -S

**re·focus** \(')rē+\ *vb* [*re-* + *focus*] **:** to focus again

**re·fold** \"+\ *vt* [*re-* + *fold*] **:** to fold again **:** return to a folded state

**re·fold·er** \"ə(r)\ *n* **:** one that inspects and refolds garments

**re·foot** \(')rē+\ *vt* [*re-* + *foot*] **:** to provide (as a stocking, a pillar) with a new foot

**re·ford** \"+\ *vt* [*re-* + *ford*] **:** to ford again

**re·forest** \"+\ *vt* [*re-* + *forest*] **:** to renew forest cover on (denuded land) by natural seeding or artificial planting — **re·forestation** \(ˌ)rē+\ *n*

**re·forge** \(')rē+\ *vt* [ME *reforgen*, fr. MF *reforgier*, fr. *re-* + *forgier* to forge] **:** to forge again or anew **:** fashion or fabricate anew **:** make over ⟨*reforging* of the raw materials into a new and valid film form —Arthur Knight⟩

**¹re·form** \rə̇'fȯ(ə)rm, rē'f-, -ō(ə)m\ *vb* [ME *reformen*, fr. MF *reformer*, fr. OF, fr. L *reformare*, fr. *re-* + *formare* to form, fr. *forma* form — more at FORM] *vt* **1** *obs* **:** RESTORE, RENEW **2 a :** to restore to a former good state **:** bring from bad to good ⟨hopes that Congress may, somehow, ~ itself —T.H. Eliot⟩ **b :** to amend or improve by change of form or by removal of faults or abuses ⟨the fact is that the world does not care to be ~*ed* —S.M.Crothers⟩ ⟨need for ~*ing* news writing in order to make it more readable —F.L.Mott⟩ **c :** to put or change into a new and improved form or condition ⟨his ambition to ~ the map of the world —Benjamin Farrington⟩ **3 :** to put an end to (an evil) by enforcing or introducing a better method or course of action or behavior ⟨~ the abuses of political patronage⟩ **4 :** to induce or cause to abandon an evil manner of living and follow a good one **:** change from worse to better ⟨attempts to ~ the criminal⟩ ⟨~ a drunkard⟩ **5** *obs* **:** CENSURE, REPROVE **6** *obs* **:** to improve by cutting **:** PRUNE ⟨labor to ~ yon flowery arbors —John Milton⟩ **7 a :** to correct the errors in **:** EMEND ⟨~ the calendar⟩ **b :** to rectify (as an error in a legal instrument) in accordance with the real intention of the parties to a transaction **8 a** *obs* **:** to form (a military unit) into a new organization (as by reduction in number) **b** *obs* **:** DISBAND **c :** RE-FORM **9 a :** to subject (hydrocarbon oils or gases) to reforming **b :** to produce by reforming ⟨~*ed* gasoline⟩ ⟨~*ed* refinery oil gas⟩ ~ *vi* **:** to change for the better **:** amend or correct one's character or habits ⟨if given more time, I think the Church would have ~*ed* from within —A.N.Whitehead⟩ **syn** see CORRECT

**²reform** \"\ *n* -S [prob. fr. F *réforme*, fr. *réformer* to reform, fr. OF *reformer*] **1 a :** amendment of what is defective, vicious, corrupt, or depraved ⟨~ of the law courts⟩ ⟨a school for ~ of young criminals⟩ **b :** a removal or correction of an abuse, a wrong, or errors ⟨calendar ~⟩ ⟨~ of election procedures⟩ **2** *usu cap* **:** REFORMATION 2 **3** *usu cap* **:** REFORM JUDAISM

**³reform** \"\ *adj* **:** relating to or favoring reform ⟨~ movement⟩ ⟨~ bill⟩ ⟨~ candidate⟩

**re-form** \(')rē¦f-\ *vb* [*re-* + *form*] *vt* **:** to form again ⟨the Mexicans *re-formed* their lines and came on again and again —*Amer. Guide Series: Texas*⟩ ⟨the cartel has recently been *re-formed*⟩ ~ *vi* **:** to take form again ⟨clouds were dissolving and *re-forming*⟩ **:** come together again in a formation ⟨escaped . . . by an epic retreat . . . later to *re-form* and become the spearhead of the Allied offensive —*Atlantic*⟩

**re·form·abil·i·ty** \rə̇ˌfȯ(r)mə'bilədē, (ˌ)rēˌf-\ *n* **:** the capability of being reformed ⟨question of the ~ of alcoholics⟩

**re·form·able** \=ˈ=məbəl\ *adj* [ME *reformabyll*, fr. *reformen* to reform + *-abyll*, *-able* -able] **:** capable of being reformed ⟨a ~ type of criminal offender⟩

**reformade** *n* -S [by alter.] *obs* **:** REFORMADO

**ref·or·ma·do** \ˌrefə(r)'mä(ˌ)dō, -mā(-\ *n, pl* **reformados** *or* **reformadoes** [Sp, fr. *reformado*, past part. of *reformar* to reform, reorganize, fr. L *reformare* to reform] **1 a :** an officer deprived of command by the reorganization or disbandment of his troops but retaining rank and receiving full or half pay **b :** a volunteer serving without a commission but with an officer's rank **2** *obs* **:** a reformed person **3** *obs* **:** a supporter of reform

**ref·or·ma·tion** \ˌrefə(r)'māshən\ *n* -S [ME *reformacion*, fr. MF *reformation*, fr. L *reformation-, reformatio*, fr. *reformatus* (past part. of *reformare* to reform) + *-ion-, -io* -ion] **1 :** the act of reforming or state of being reformed: as **a** *obs* **:** RESTORATION, REESTABLISHMENT **b :** improvement in form or condition ⟨urging a radical ~ of society⟩ **c :** amendment of moral behavior ⟨satire lashes vice into ~ —John Dryden⟩ **d :** correction or improvement of what is faulty, defective, inefficient, or objectionable ⟨~ of the postal service⟩ **e :** the correction by a court of equity of errors and mistakes in or arising out of the execution of a written instrument to make the instrument conform to the real intention of the parties thereto **2** *usu cap* **:** a 16th century religious movement aimed at correcting real or assumed abuses in the Roman Catholic Church and marked ultimately by rejection of the supremacy of the pope, rejection or modification of much of Roman Catholic doctrine, and establishment of the Protestant churches

**re-formation** \ˌrē(ˌ)fō(r)'māshən\ *n* [*re-* + *formation*] **:** a shaping or forming again or anew ⟨*re-formation* of a granitic magma⟩ ⟨*re-formation* of a regiment⟩

**ref·or·ma·tion·al** \ˌrefə(r)¦māshən³l, -shnəl\ *adj* **:** of or relating to reformation ⟨~ zeal⟩

**re·for·ma·tive** \rə̇'fȯ(r)mədiv, rē'f-, -mətiv\ *adj* [¹*reform* + *-ative*] **:** tending or disposed to reform ⟨~ and rehabilitative agencies⟩ ⟨the puritan conscience of the middle class was rousing itself for a final ~ fling —Roy Lewis & Angus Maude⟩ — **re·for·ma·tive·ly** \-əvlē, -li\ *adv* — **re·for·ma·tive·ness** \-ivnəs\ *n* -ES

**¹re·for·ma·to·ry** \-məˌtōrē, -tȯr-, -ri\ *adj* [¹*reform* + *-atory*] **:** intended for reformation **:** REFORMATIVE ⟨~ measures⟩

**²reformatory** \"\ *n* -ES **:** a penal institution to which young or first offenders or women are committed and in which repressive and punitive measures are held to be subordinated to training in industry and exercise of the physical, mental, and moral faculties — compare TRAINING SCHOOL 2

**¹reformed** *adj* **1 :** restored to purity or excellence **:** AMENDED, IMPROVED, CORRECTED ⟨~ calendar⟩ **2** *usu cap* **a :** of or relating to the whole body of Protestant Christianity stemming from the Reformation **:** PROTESTANT ⟨*Reformed* theological doctrines⟩ **b :** of or relating to a Protestant church other than Lutheran formed in various European continental countries — used in official titles of several churches ⟨Dutch *Reformed*⟩ ⟨Christian *Reformed* Church⟩ **3 :** observing a religious discipline more strictly conformable to the original rule or set of directives — used of a branch or congregation of a religious order ⟨the ~ Benedictines of that era⟩ **4** *obs, of an officer* **:** left without a command and retired on half or full pay **5** *usu cap* **:** of or relating to Reform Judaism

**²reformed** *n, pl* **reformed** *usu cap* **:** a member of a Protestant church; *esp* **:** a member of a Reformed church

**reformed spelling** *n* **:** any of several methods of spelling English words that use letters with more phonetic consistency than conventional English spelling and usu. discard some of the silent letters (as in *thoro* for *thorough*, *markt* for *marked*, *laps* for *lapse*)

**re·form·er** \rə̇'fȯrmər, rē'f-, -ō(ə)mə(r\ *n* -S **1 :** one that effects or tries to effect a reformation or amendment **:** one that works for or urges reform ⟨once the moralist, the religionist, or the puritan ~ becomes the censor of art —Hunter Mead⟩ **2** *usu cap* **:** a leader of the Reformation in the 16th century ⟨this is not what the *Reformers* meant by faith —B.E.Meland⟩ **3 :** an advocate or promoter of political reform: **a :** an advocate or promoter of parliamentary reform; *esp* **:** a participator in the reform movement in Great Britain in 1831–32 **b** *usu cap* **:** a member of a reform party (as in Canada or New Zealand) **4 :** an apparatus for reforming hydrocarbon materials (as naphtha or natural gas) ⟨catalytic ~⟩

**reforming** *n* -S [fr. gerund of ¹*reform*] **:** cracking of various hydrocarbon oils or gases to form specialized products: as **a :** cracking of petroleum naphtha or straight-run gasoline of low octane number usu. to form gasoline containing lighter constituents and having a higher octane number — compare HYDROFORMING **b :** cracking of natural gas or other hydrocarbon gases often in the presence of steam to reduce the heating value or to produce hydrogen

**re·form·ing·ly** *adv* [*reforming* (pres. part. of ¹*reform*) + *-ly*] **:** in a reforming manner **:** so as to reform

**re·form·ism** \-ˌmizəm\ *n* -S [ISV ¹*reform* + *-ism*] **:** a doctrine or policy or movement of reform ⟨moral ~⟩ ⟨economic ~⟩

**¹re·form·ist** \-ˌməst\ *n* -S [¹*reform* + *-ist*] **1 a :** REFORMER **b :** one that advocates gradual rather than revolutionary change **2 :** a member of a reformed branch or congregation of a religious group

**²reformist** \"\ *or* **re·form·is·tic** \=ˌ=ˈmistik\ *adj* **:** relating or belonging to a policy or movement of reform ⟨~ elements in the labor movement⟩ ⟨~ views⟩

**reform jew** *n, usu cap R&J* **:** an adherent of Reform Judaism

**reform judaism** *n, cap R&J* **:** a development of Judaism that began in Germany in the early part of the 19th century and is marked by an effort to promote faith in God through a rationalization of belief according to the truths of modern sciences, by an acceptance of the doctrine of ethical monotheism and a rejection of the legal authority of the Talmud, by a simplification of many ritual and ceremonial observances, and by the affirmation of the essentially religious rather than national character of Judaism — called also *Liberal Judaism*; compare CONSERVATIVE JUDAISM, ORTHODOX JUDAISM

**reforms** *pres 3d sing of* REFORM, *pl of* REFORM

**reform school** *n* **:** a reformatory for boys or girls

**re·formulate** \(')rē+\ *vt* [*re-* + *formulate*] **:** to formulate again; *esp* **:** to formulate in a different way — **re·formulation** \(ˌ)rē+\ *n*

**re·fortify** \(')rē+\ *vt* [*re-* + *fortify*] **:** to fortify again or afresh

**¹re·found** \"+\ *vt* [*re-* + *found* (to establish)] **:** to establish again

**²refound** \"\ *past of* REFIND

**³refound** \"\ *vt* [*re-* + *found* (to cast)] **:** to cast again ⟨~ type⟩

**re·founder** \(')rē+\ *n* [³*refound* + *-er*] **:** one that founds again ⟨~ of a monastery⟩

**refr** *abbr* **1** refraction **2** refrigerate; refrigerating; refrigeration

**¹re·fract** \rə̇'frakt, rē'f-\ *vt* -ED/-ING/-S [L *refractus*, past part. of *refringere* to refract, break off, fr. *re-* + *frangere* to break — more at BREAK] **1** *obs* **:** REFLECT **2** *obs* **:** to break up **:** DIVIDE **3 :** to subject (rays of light) to refraction **4 :** to determine the refracting power of or abnormality of refraction in (as an eye or a lens)

**²refract** *adj* [L *refractus*, past part. of *refringere*] *obs* **:** REFRACTED

**re·frac·ta·ry** \rə̇'fraktərē, rē'f-, -təri\ *adj* [L *refractarius*, fr. *refractus* (past part. of *refringere* to refract, break off) + *-arius* -ary] **:** REFRACTORY

**re·fract·ed** \-təd\ *adj* [fr. past part. of ¹*refract*] **:** bent backward angularly as if half-broken ⟨~ stem⟩ ⟨~ spines⟩

**re·frac·tile** \-t³l\ *adj* **:** capable of refracting **:** REFRACTIVE ⟨~ cells⟩ — **re·frac·til·i·ty** \=ˌ=ˈtiləd·ē\ *n* -ES

**refracting angle** *n* **:** the dihedral angle (as of a prism) included between the planes of the two sides through which the refracted beam passes — compare REFRACTION ANGLE

**refracting system** *n* **:** REFRACTIVE SYSTEM

**refracting telescope** *n* **:** REFRACTOR

**re·frac·tion** \rə̇'frakshən, rē'f-\ *n* -S [LL *refraction-, refractio*, fr. L *refractus* (past part. of *refringere*) + *-ion-, -io* -ion] **1 :** the action of refracting or the state of being refracted: as **a :** the deflection from a straight path undergone by a light ray or a wave of energy in passing obliquely from one medium (as air) into another (as water, glass) in which its velocity is different **b** *obs* **:** REFLECTION, REBOUND **c** *obs* **:** a breaking up **d :** the change in the apparent position of a celestial body that is due to the bending of the light rays emanating from it as they pass through the earth's atmosphere; *also* **:** the correction to be applied to the apparent position of a body because of this bending **2** *obs* **:** reduction of a bill **:** REBATE **3 a :** the refractive power of the eye **b :** the act or technique of determining ocular refraction and identifying abnormalities as a basis for the prescription of corrective lenses **4 :** the action of distorting an image by viewing through a medium ⟨looking at the world . . . observing it without the ~ of moral judgment —Janet Flanner⟩

**refraction angle** *n* **1 :** the difference between the geometrical and observed altitude of a celestial body that is produced by atmospheric refraction **2 :** ANGLE OF REFRACTION

**re·fractionate** \(')rē+\ *vt* [*re-* + *fractionate*] **:** to fractionate again (as by distillation) — **re·fractionation** \(ˌ)rē+\ *n*

**refraction circle** *n* **:** an instrument with a graduated circle for measuring deviations due to refraction

**re·frac·tion·ist** \rə̇'fraksh(ə)nəst, rē'f-\ *n* -S **:** one skilled in the practical application of the laws of refraction esp. to the determination of errors of refraction in the eye

**re·frac·tive** \-ktiv, -ktēv *also* -ktəv\ *adj* **1 :** having power to refract ⟨~ lens⟩ **2 :** relating to or due to refraction ⟨~ phenomena⟩ ⟨~ dispersion of light⟩ — **re·frac·tive·ly** \-təvlē, -li\ *adv* — **re·frac·tive·ness** \-tivnəs, -tēv- *also* -təv-\ *n* -ES

**refractive index** *n* **:** INDEX OF REFRACTION

**refractive power** *n* **:** the ability of a substance to refract light expressed quantitatively by either its index of refraction or its refractivity

**refractive system** *n* **:** an optical system in which lenses instead of mirrors are used for focusing light, forming an image, or changing the path of a beam of light by refraction; *specif* **:** a mode of lighting in lighthouses by a central lamp surrounded by a combination of lenses — called also *refracting system*

**re·frac·tiv·i·ty** \rə̇ˌfrak'tivədē, (ˌ)rēˌf-, -vətē, -i\ *n* -ES **:** REFRACTIVE POWER; *specif* **:** the index of refraction minus one — compare SPECIFIC REFRACTIVITY

**re·frac·tom·e·ter** \-'tämədə(r)\ *n* [ISV *refraction* + *-o-* + *-meter*] **:** an instrument for measuring indices of refraction

**re·frac·to·met·ric** \rə̇ˌfraktə¦me·trik, rē'f-\ *adj* **:** of or relating to refractometry

**re·frac·tom·e·try** \rə̇ˌfrak'tämə·trē, (ˌ)rēˌf-\ *n* -ES [ISV *refraction* + *-o-* + *-metry*] **:** the art or process of measuring indices of refraction **:** the use of the refractometer

**re·frac·tor** \rə̇'fraktə(r), rē'f-\ *n* -S **:** something that refracts light rays; *specif* **:** a telescope in which the principal focusing element is a lens that is usu. an achromat with crown glass and flint glass components

**re·frac·to·ri·ly** \-kt(ə)rəlē, -li\ *adv* **:** in a refractory manner

**re·frac·to·ri·ness** \-rēnəs, -rin-\ *n* -ES **:** the quality or state of being refractory: as **a :** the ability of a material to resist a high temperature **b :** the insensitivity to further immediate stimulation that develops in nervous or other irritable tissue as a result of intense or prolonged stimulation

**¹re·frac·to·ry** \rə̇'frakt(ə)rē, rē'f-, -)ri\ *adj* [alter. (influenced by *-ory*) of *refractary*] **1 :** resisting control or authority **:** STUBBORN, UNMANAGEABLE, PERVERSE ⟨to persuade her ~ daughter to agree to the propriety of what she was going to do —Anthony Trollope⟩ ⟨bold attempts to reduce ~ material to poetic treatment —F.B.Millett⟩ ⟨the boy was solitary and ~ to all education save that of wide and desultory reading —F.J.Mather⟩ **2 a :** resistant to treatment or cure ⟨a ~ fulminating lesion⟩ **b :** unresponsive to stimulus ⟨the ~ period of a muscle fiber⟩ **c :** resistant or not responding to an infectious agent **:** IMMUNE, INSUSCEPTIBLE ⟨after recovery the animals were completely ~ to reinfection⟩ **3 :** resisting treatment under ordinary or various extraordinary conditions **:** difficult to fuse, corrode, reduce, or draw out ⟨~ ore⟩ ⟨~ metals⟩; *esp* **:** capable of enduring or resisting high temperature ⟨~ clays⟩ ⟨~ brick⟩ ⟨~ mortar⟩ **syn** see UNRULY

**²refractory** \"\ *n* -ES **1** *obs* **:** a refractory person **2 :** a refractory material: as **a :** any of various nonmetallic ceramic substances that are characterized esp. by their suitability for use as structural materials at high temperatures usu. in contact with metals, slags, glass, or other corrosive materials (as in furnaces, crucibles, or saggers), that are classified chemically as acid (as silica and fireclay), basic (as magnesite and dolomite), or neutral (as high-alumina refractories, carbon, and silicon carbide), and that are produced in the form of brick and other shapes, finely ground cementing materials, castable concretes, plastics, and granular materials in bulk **b :** a substance resistant to corrosion by chemical agents and used esp. in chemical plants and laboratories

**refractory clay** *n* **:** FIRECLAY

**refractory period** *or* **refractory phase** *n* **:** the brief period immediately following the response of a muscle, nerve, or other irritable element before it recovers its capacity to make a second response

**refractory rock** *n* **:** a naturally occurring rock material that has refractory qualities and is used in the form of blocks for lining certain types of furnaces

**refractory ware** *n* **:** clayware so composed as to resist a high temperature and suitable for saggers, crucibles, blocks and pots for glass furnaces, blast-furnace linings, and heating elements

**refracts** *pres 3d sing of* REFRACT

**¹re·frain** \rə̇'frān, rē'f-\ *vb* -ED/-ING/-S [ME *refreynen*, fr. MF *refraindre* to restrain, moderate, echo, fr. OF, alter. (influenced by *fraindre* to break, fr. L *frangere*) of *refreindre*, fr. L *refringere* to refract, break off — more at REFRACT] *vt* **1** *archaic* **:** to hold back **:** put a restraint upon **:** CURB, GOVERN, RESTRAIN **2** *obs* **:** to abstain from **:** give up **:** AVOID, SHUN ~ *vi* **:** to keep oneself from doing, feeling, or indulging in something **:** hold aloof **:** FORBEAR, ABSTAIN ⟨had an impulse to speak, but on second thought ~*ed*⟩ ⟨promised to obey our laws, support our government and ~ from treachery —Kenneth Roberts⟩ ⟨carefully ~*s* from setting too great a store by miracle and prophecy —*Times Lit. Supp.*⟩

**syn** ABSTAIN, FORBEAR: REFRAIN is more suitable than ABSTAIN or FORBEAR to indicate checking or inhibiting an inclination or impulse, especially a momentary or passing one ⟨no tolerable parent could *refrain* from praising a child when it first walks and when it first says an intelligible word —Bertrand Russell⟩ ⟨I have since tried, not very successfully, to *refrain* from muttering proudly when the brighter young minds among contemporaries are mentioned: "Former student of mine!" —Irwin Edman⟩ ABSTAIN is applicable to deliberate self-denial, renunciation, or nonparticipation on principle ⟨the early Christians avoided contact with the State, *abstained* from the responsibilities of office, and were even reluctant to serve in the army —J.E.E.Dalberg-Acton⟩ ⟨in time of war it was incumbent upon all wives who were left behind to live chaste lives, to make offerings to the gods, and to *abstain* from cutting their hair —J.G.Frazer⟩ FORBEAR may apply to instances of restraining, checking, or withholding motivated by self-restraint, patience, stoicism, compassion, or clemency ⟨her prudent mother, occupied by the same ideas, *forbore* to invite him to sit by herself —Jane Austen⟩ ⟨he was not a seaman but a merchant who could not *forbear* the fun of setting sail with his merchandise —*Times Lit. Supp.*⟩

**²refrain** \"\ *n* -S [ME *refreyn*, fr. MF *refrain*, fr. *refraindre* to restrain, moderate, echo] **:** a phrase or verse which recurs regularly esp. at the end of each stanza or division of a poem or song **:** BURDEN, CHORUS; *also* **:** the musical setting of such a phrase or verse

**refraination** *n* -S [by alter. (influenced by ¹*refrain*)] *obs* **:** REFRENATION

**re·frain·ment** \rə̇'frānmənt, rē'f-\ *n* -S **:** the act of refraining **:** ABSTINENCE

**re·frame** \(')rē+\ *vt* [*re-* + *frame*] **:** to frame or construct again or afresh **:** put in or provide with a new frame ⟨~ a statement⟩ ⟨~ a picture⟩

**refranation** *n* -s [by alter.] *obs* : REFRENATION
**re·fran·gent** \rə'franjənt, rē'f-\ *adj* [*refrang-* (as in *refrangible*) + *-ent*] : REFRACTING
**re·fran·gi·bil·i·ty** \=,=jə'biləd-ē\ *n* -ES : the quality or state of being refrangible
**re·fran·gi·ble** \='==bəl\ *adj* [fr. ¹*refract*, after L *fractus* (past part. of *frangere* to break): ML *frangibilis* frangible, breakable — more at BREAK, FRANGIBLE] : capable of being refracted ⟨a prism divides the differently ~ rays of sunlight⟩ — **re·fran·gi·ble·ness** *n*
**re·freeze** \(')rē+\ *vb* [*re-* + *freeze*] *vt* : to freeze again after thawing ~ *vi* : to become frozen again
**ref·re·na·tion** \,refrə'nāshən\ *n* -s [ME *refrenacion*, fr. L *refrenation-, refrenatio*, fr. *refrenatus* (past part. of *refrenare* to restrain, fr. *re-* + *frenare* to bridle, restrain, fr. *frenum* bridle) + *-ion-, -io* -ion — more at FRENUM] **1** *obs* : the act of restraining or refraining **2** : the failure of an expected planetary aspect to occur because one of the planets becomes retrograde
**re·fresh** \rə'fresh, rē'f-\ *vb* [ME *refresshen*, fr. MF *refreschir, refreschier*, fr. OF, fr. *re-* + *freis* fresh (fem. *fresche*) — more at FRESH] *vt* **1** : to restore strength and animation to (as through food or rest) : relieve from fatigue or depression : REVIVE, REINVIGORATE ⟨rode many hours, but a brief rest and change of position ~*ed* him —Oliver La Farge⟩ ⟨~*ed* himself with a cold shower and rubdown⟩ : CHEER ⟨~*ing* himself with a little tobacco —Winston Churchill⟩ ⟨it ~*es* me to find a woman so charmingly direct, so completely feminine —Louis Bromfield⟩ **2** : to freshen up (as by cleaning, trimming) : RENOVATE **3 a** : to restore or maintain by renewing supply : REPLENISH ⟨English middle classes . . . continually renewed and ~*ed* themselves from the countryside —Roy Lewis & Angus Maude⟩ ⟨the steward ~*ed* our glasses —A.J.Liebling⟩ ⟨supply ship ~*ed* the attacking submarines⟩ **b** : QUICKEN ⟨let me ~ your memory of the events with this letter⟩ **4** : to make fresh by wetting or cooling; *specif* : to restore water to (dehydrated food) ~ *vi* **1** : to become fresh again : REVIVE **2** : to refresh oneself : take refreshment **3** : to lay in fresh provisions ⟨harbors where ships can ~⟩
**re·fresh·ant** \-shənt\ *n* -s : something that invigorates or reanimates : REFRESHER ⟨caffeine is a real stimulant and ~ —*Arthur Little's Industrial Bull.*⟩
**re·fresh·en** \(')rē¦freshən\ *vt* [*re-* + *freshen*] : make fresh again : REFRESH, RENOVATE ⟨~*ing* of old disciplines —W.H. Whyte⟩
**re·fresh·er** \rə'freshə(r), rē'f-\ *n* -s [ME *refressher*, fr. *refresshen* to refresh + *-er*] **1 a** : something (as a drink) that refreshes or revives ⟨stopped in the bar for a quick ~⟩ **b** : something that makes fresh or vivid again : REMINDER **c** : something that provides review or additional instruction after a period of inactivity or gives instruction designed to keep one abreast of developments in scholarly investigation or new professional techniques and developments ⟨for those who need a simple ~ on the basic science involved in atomic energy —Alfred Friendly⟩ ⟨the serviceman is called to London for a ~ course whenever a new machine is marketed —Bryan Morgan⟩ **2 a** *Brit* : an extra fee paid to counsel in a case adjourned from one term to another or unusually protracted ⟨my retainer is reasonable, my ~*s* modest —Hervey Allen⟩ **b** *Austral* : an extra fee paid counsel for each day of trial beyond the first five hours
**re·fresh·ful** \-shfəl\ *adj* : full of power to refresh : REFRESHING — **re·fresh·ful·ly** \-fəlē\ *adv*
**refreshing** *adj* **1** : giving new life or vigor : STIMULATING ⟨the complicated challenge of the world he was facing had been ~ —Victor Canning⟩ : HEARTENING ⟨a letter from you this morning was ~ beyond words —H.J.Laski⟩ **2** : giving an unexpected pleasant or agreeable sensation : providing relief from boredom : contrasting with what is commonplace or hackneyed ⟨a new and ~ informality⟩ ⟨has the ~ good sense to say favorable things about his own work —M.W. Fishwick⟩ — **re·fresh·ing·ly** *adv* — **re·fresh·ing·ness** *n* -ES
**re·fresh·ment** \rə'freshmənt, rē'f-\ *n* -s [ME *refresshement*, fr. MF *refreschement*, fr. *refreschier* to refresh + *-ment*] **1** : the act of refreshing or state of being refreshed: **a** : spiritual restoration : reanimation of the soul ⟨often turned for guidance, inspiration, and ~ to the masters of his boyhood —B.R.Redman⟩ **b** : restoration of strength, spirit, vigor, or liveliness esp. after fatigue or depression ⟨walking . . . for the ~ of the frosty air —Charles Dickens⟩ **2 a** : something (as food, drink) that refreshes : means of restoration or reanimation **b refreshments** *pl* : a light meal : LUNCH ⟨serve ~*s* at a card party⟩ ⟨a booth for ~*s* was set up on the fairgrounds⟩
**refreshment sunday** *n, usu cap R&S* [prob. so called because the gospel for the day relates the miracle of feeding the five thousand (Jn 6:1–14)] : MID-LENT SUNDAY
**¹re·frig·er·ant** \rə'frij(ə)rənt, rē'f-\ *adj* [MF or L; MF, fr. L *refrigerant-, refrigerans*, pres. part. of *refrigerare*] : COOLING ⟨~ latitudes⟩ : allaying heat or fever ⟨~ medicines⟩ : REFRESHING
**²refrigerant** \"\ *n* -s : a refrigerant agent or agency: as **a** : a medicine or an application for allaying fever or its symptoms **b** : a substance (as ice, ammonia, carbon dioxide) used in refrigeration
**¹refrigerate** *adj* [ME, fr. L *refrigeratus*, past part. of *refrigerare*] **1** *obs* : REFRIGERATED **2** *obs* : REFRIGERANT
**²re·frig·er·ate** \-jə,rāt, *usu* -ād·+V\ *vb* -ED/-ING/-S [L *refrigeratus*, past part. of *refrigerare*, fr. *re-* + *frigerare* to make cool, fr. *frigor-, frigus* coolness, frost, cold — more at FRIGID] *vt* **1** : to cause to become cool : make or keep cold or cool; *specif* : to freeze or chill (food) for preservation **2** : to extract heat from (as a body, a substance) by lowering the temperature of the body and by keeping its temperature below that of its surroundings ~ *vi* : to become cool or cold
**refrigerating engine** *or* **refrigerating machine** *n* : an apparatus working in a reversed heat-engine cycle for utilizing mechanical energy (as by compressing and expanding ammonia gas) to extract heat from a substance (as circulating brine) — compare BRAYTON CYCLE
**re·frig·er·a·tion** \rə,frijə'rāshən, rē,f-\ *n* -s [ME *refrygeracion*, fr. L *refrigeration-, refrigeratio* coolness, cooling, fr. *refrigeratus* (past part. of *refrigerare*) + *-ion-, -io* -ion] : the action or process of refrigerating: as **a** : the cooling or freezing of food or perishables for storage — see ELECTRIC REFRIGERATION, MECHANICAL REFRIGERATION **b** : a deliberate lowering of the temperature of the body or of a part (as a leg) for therapeutic purposes or to facilitate surgery — compare HYPOTHERMIA
**re·frig·er·a·tive** \='==,rād·iv\ *adj* [MF *refrigeratif*, fr. LL *refrigerativus*, fr. L *refrigeratus* (past part. of *refrigerare* to refrigerate) + *-ivus* -ive] : tending to cool : allaying heat : COOLING
**re·frig·er·a·tor** \-,rād-ə(r), -ātə-\ *n* -s : something that refrigerates or keeps cool: **a** : a cabinet or room for keeping food or other articles cool **b** : an apparatus for rapidly cooling heated liquids or vapors in a distilling process : CONDENSER 2 f
**refrigerator car** *n* : a freight car constructed and used primarily as a refrigerator in transporting fresh meats, fruits, vegetables and usu. also adaptable by the installation of heating units for transporting commodities that must be protected from cold
**refrigerator van** *n, Brit* : REFRIGERATOR CAR

refrigerator a

**¹re·frig·er·a·to·ry** \rə'frij(ə)rə,tōrē, rē'f-, -tȯr-, -ri\ *n* -ES [²*refrigerate* + *-ory*] : something that cools or refrigerates: **a** : an apparatus (as in a still) for condensing vapors **b** : the chamber or tank in which ice is formed in an ice machine **c** : a place of cooling or getting cooled
**²refrigeratory** \"\ *adj* [L *refrigeratorius*, fr. *refrigeratus* (past part. of *refrigerare*) + *-orius* -ory] : REFRIGERATIVE
**re·frin·gen·cy** \rə'frinjənsē\ *also* **re·frin·gence** \-jən(t)s\ *n, pl* **refringencies** *also* **refringences** [*refringency* fr. *refringent* + *-cy*; *refringence* ISV, fr. *refringent*, after such pairs as E *evident: evidence*] : REFRACTIVITY
**re·frin·gent** \-jənt\ *adj* [L *refringent-, refringens*, pres. part. of *refringere* to refract, break off — more at REFRACT] : REFRACTIVE, REFRACTING — compare BIREFRINGENT
**re·front** \(')rē+\ *vt* [*re-* + *front*] : to change or renew the front of ⟨~ a house⟩
**refs** *pl of* REF, *pres 3d sing of* REF
**¹reft** *past of* REAVE
**²reft** \'reft\ *n* -s [alter. (prob. influenced by *cleft*) of *rift*] : CLEFT, FISSURE
**re·fuel** \(')rē+\ *vb* [*re-* + *fuel*] *vt* : to provide with fresh fuel : replenish the fuel supply of ~ *vi* : to take on a fresh fuel supply
**¹ref·uge** \'re(,)fyüj, *esp before a syllable-increasing suffix* -,fyəj\ *n* -s [ME, fr. MF, fr. L *refugium*, fr. *refugere* to run away, avoid, escape, fr. *re-* + *fugere* to run away, flee — more at FUGITIVE] **1** : shelter or protection from danger or distress ⟨seek ~ in flight⟩ ⟨take ~ in the home of a friend⟩ ⟨a house of ~⟩ **2 a** : a home for those who are destitute, homeless, or in disgrace **b** : a sanctuary for birds or wild animals **c** : a mountain hut or cabin erected to serve as sleeping quarters for mountaineers **d** : a safety zone for pedestrians crossing a street in heavy traffic : SAFETY ISLAND **3** : a means of resort for help in difficulty : RESOURCE ⟨patriotism is the last ~ of a scoundrel —Samuel Johnson⟩ ⟨the ivory tower . . . as a place of ~ from unpleasant reality —H.N.Russell⟩
**²refuge** \"\ *vb* -ED/-ING/-S *vt* : to give refuge to ~ *vi* : to seek or take refuge
**³ref·uge** \", 'refij\ *n* [by alter.] *chiefly dial* : ³REFUSE
**¹ref·u·gee** \'refyə,jē, -efyü,j-, ,==''=\ *n* -s [F *réfugié*, past part. of *réfugier* to put in a place of safety (*se réfugier* to take refuge), fr. L *refugium* refuge] **1** : one that flees to a place of safety; *esp* : one who flees to a foreign country or power to escape danger or persecution in his own country or habitual residence because of his race, religion, or political beliefs **2** : one who flees from justice : FUGITIVE **3** : COWBOY 2a
**²refugee** \"\ *vi* **refugeed; refugeed; refugeeing; refugees** : to flee as a refugee
**³refugee** \"\ *adj* **1** : that is a refugee ⟨~ slaves⟩ **2** : that has taken flight from unfavorable investment conditions or from invading armies to carry on in another country ⟨~ capital⟩ ⟨~ government⟩
**ref·u·gee·ism** \-ē,izəm\ *n* -s : the state of being a refugee
**re·fu·gi·um** \rə'fyüjēəm, rē'f-\ *n, pl* **refu·gia** \-ēə\ [L, refuge — more at REFUGE] : an area of relatively unaltered climate that is inhabited by plants and animals during a period of continental climatic change (as a glaciation) and remains as a center of relic forms from which a new dispersion and speciation may take place after climatic readjustment
**re·ful·gence** \rə'fəljən(t)s, rē'f-\ *also* **re·ful·gen·cy** \-nsē, -nsi\ *n, pl* **refulgences** *also* **refulgencies** [L *refulgentia*, fr. *refulgent-, refulgens* (pres. part. of *refulgēre*) + *-ia* -y] : the quality or state of being refulgent : BRILLIANCE, SPLENDOR, RADIANCE ⟨came into the ~ of the headlights —Kay Boyle⟩
**re·ful·gent** \-nt\ *adj* [L *refulgent-, refulgens*, pres. part. of *refulgēre* to shine brightly, glitter, fr. *re-* + *fulgēre* to shine, flash — more at FULGENT] : giving out a bright light : richly radiant ⟨~ sunset⟩ : SHINING, BRILLIANT ⟨in arms . . . of golden panoply, ~ host —John Milton⟩ **syn** see BRIGHT
**¹re·fund** \rə'fənd, (')rē¦f-\ *vt* -ED/-ING/-S [ME *refunden*, fr. MF & L; MF *refonder, refunder* to reimburse, fr. L *refundere* to pour back, give or put back, fr. *re-* + *fundere* to pour — more at FOUND] **1 a** *obs* : to pour back **b** : to give or put back **2** : to return (money) in restitution, repayment, or balancing of accounts ⟨~ the price of a defective article⟩ ⟨~ the excess on a tax⟩ **3** : REPAY, REIMBURSE
**²re·fund** \'rē,fənd *sometimes* rə'f- *or* rē'f-\ *n* -s **1** : the act of refunding **2** : a sum that is paid back : REPAYMENT
**³re·fund** \(')rē¦fənd\ *vt* [*re-* + *fund*] : to fund again or anew; *specif* : to borrow usu. by the sale of bonds in order to pay off an existing loan with the proceeds ⟨~ a debt⟩ ⟨~ a mortgage⟩
**re·fund·able** \rə'fəndəbəl, rē'f-\ *adj* [¹*refund* + *-able*] : capable of being refunded ⟨overpayment of a tax is ~ at the end of the year⟩ ⟨~ deposit⟩
**refund annuity** *n* : an annuity payable until annuitant's death when if total payments have not equalled all or a stated part of the purchase price the difference is paid to the annuitant's estate or to a designated beneficiary
**refunding bond** *n* [*refunding* fr. gerund of ³*refund*] : a bond issued to pay off an outstanding issue
**re·furbish** \(')rē+\ *vt* [*re-* + *furbish*] : to brighten or freshen up : to make as if new : RENOVATE ⟨~ an old house⟩ ⟨~ an antique table⟩ ⟨~ an old legend⟩
**re·fur·bish·ment** \"+mənt\ *n* -s : the act or result of refurbishing : RENEWAL ⟨various kinds of adjustments and ~*s* of beliefs —W.W.Howells⟩ ⟨spring ~ of houses⟩
**re·furl** \(')rē+\ *vt* [*re-* + *furl*] : to furl again
**re·furnish** \"+\ *vt* [*re-* + *furnish*] : to furnish anew; *specif* : TOPWORK
**re·fus·able** \rə'fyüzəbəl, rē'f-\ *adj* [¹*refuse* + *-able*] **1** : capable of being refused : admitting of refusal **2** *obs* : meriting refusal or rejection
**re·fus·al** \-zəl\ *n* -s [ME *refusell*, fr. *refusen* to refuse + *-ell, -aille* -al] **1** : the act of refusing or denying : rejection of something demanded, solicited, or offered for acceptance ⟨~ to answer questions⟩ ⟨her ~ of all marriage proposals⟩ ⟨the horse was disqualified by his ~ at the first fence⟩ **2** : the opportunity or right of refusing or taking before others : the choice of refusing or taking (as a purchase) ⟨promised to give him the first ~ of my house⟩ **3** *obs* : one that has been refused or rejected **4 a** : stoppage of a driven bolt or pile because of resistance greater than the driving force **b** : the point of such stoppage **c** : the distance a pile sinks under a single blow **d** : the total distance a pile sinks under a volley of blows
**¹re·fuse** \rə'fyüz, rē'f-\ *vb* -ED/-ING/-S [ME *refusen*, fr. MF *refuser*, fr. OF, fr. (assumed) VL *refusare*, fr. L *refusus*, past part. of *refundere* to pour back, give or put back — more at REFUND] *vt* **1** *obs* : AVOID, SHUN **2** : to decline to accept : REJECT ⟨~ an office⟩ ⟨~ a gift⟩ ⟨~ advice⟩; *specif* : to decline to have as husband **3 a** : to show or express a positive unwillingness to do or comply with (as something asked, demanded, expected) — used with a following infinitive ⟨*refused* to answer the question⟩ ⟨motor *refused* to start⟩ **b** : DENY ⟨*refused* to give his permission⟩ ⟨has never *refused* his help before⟩ ⟨was *refused* entrance at the club door⟩ **4** *obs* : to give up : RENOUNCE ⟨still ~ this world, to do their Father's will —John Bunyan⟩ ⟨deny thy father and ~ thy name —Shak.⟩ **5** *of a horse* : to decline to jump or leap over (as a fence or ditch) **6** : to fail to follow with a card from (the suit led) because of not having one **7** : to bend back or keep back (as the flank of one's defensive position) ~ *vi* **1** : to withhold acceptance, compliance, or permission ⟨that the King had offered him the Garter, but that he had asked permission to ~ —Valentine Heywood⟩ **2** *of a horse* : to decline to jump **3** : to fail to follow suit in a card game **syn** see DECLINE — **refuse stays** *of a ship* : to fail to go about : miss stays
**²refuse** \"\ *n* -s *dial chiefly Eng* : REFUSAL
**³ref·use** \'re,fyüs, -üz\ *n* -s [ME, fr. MF *refus* refusal, rejection, fr. OF, fr. *refuser* to refuse] **1** : the worthless or useless part of something : LEAVINGS, DREGS, DROSS ⟨~ from silver mining⟩ ⟨sugar cane ~⟩ ⟨propertyless gentlemen . . . have to be content nowadays with the ~ of middle class employment —G.B.Shaw⟩ **2** : RUBBISH, TRASH, GARBAGE
**syn** WASTE, RUBBISH, TRASH, DEBRIS, GARBAGE, OFFAL: REFUSE applies to any matter or materials rejected as useless and fit only to be thrown out or away ⟨there was a huge stinking heap of week-old *refuse* . . . old clothes, sad boots with calloused heels, and hats that were just misshapen basins of felt; old books and magazines, stained with tea leaves and the sodden heterogeneous mass of household garbage —Ruth Park⟩ WASTE is also comprehensive; it may indicate that unused or rejected in one operation but possible for use in another capacity or under different circumstances ⟨mechanics using cotton *waste* to clean their hands⟩ ⟨*waste* in lumbering, the parts of trees that could be used but are not⟩ ⟨barnyard *wastes*⟩ ⟨tea *waste* — slack bushes, waste leaf, and crushed sugarcane leaf and pulp —Eve Langley⟩ RUBBISH now is likely to indicate a heterogeneous accumulation of worn-out, used-up, broken, rejected, or worthless materials or things ⟨*rubbish*. This material includes the household and business wastes that are not classified as garbage or ashes. It includes paper, rags, excelsior and other packing, wood, glass, crockery, and metals —V.M.Ehlers & E.W.Steel⟩ TRASH in general use has about the same suggestion as RUBBISH; it may refer to a somewhat lighter welter of discarded material and may be less likely to suggest separate objects and more likely to suggest a crumpled mass ⟨cleaning the old newspapers, rags, tin cans and other *trash* out of the cellar⟩ DEBRIS is likely to indicate broken fragments of bricks, rocks, walls, or buildings ⟨cleaning up the *debris* after the fire⟩ ⟨the *debris* left after mining operations⟩ GARBAGE now usu. indicates animal or vegetable refuse from the processes of shipping, preparing, and serving food ⟨egg shells, orange peels, coffee grounds and the rest of the *garbage* after breakfast⟩ OFFAL may refer to anything cut off or allowed to fall off in processing (as animal entrails or feet or fish heads or chicken heads); it may suggest the offensive but does not always do so, since such meat offal as hearts and livers may be sought for eating ⟨"*Offal!*" she gasped. "Take that carrion out" —Kenneth Roberts⟩
**⁴refuse** \"\ *adj* [ME, fr. *refuse*, n.] : thrown aside or left as worthless or of no value : REFUSED, REJECTED, WORTHLESS, USELESS ⟨~ land⟩ ⟨~ wood⟩
**¹re-fuse** \(')rē¦fyüz\ *vt* [*re-* + *fuse* (to melt)] : to melt again
**²re-fuse** \"\ *vt* [*re-* + *fuse* (to equip with a fuse)] : to replace a fuse in
**re·fus·er** \rə'fyüzə(r), rē'f-\ *n* -s [ME, fr. *refusen* to refuse + *-er*] **1** : one that refuses ⟨that horse has become a chronic ~⟩ **2** : RECUSANT
**re·fus·ible** \(')rē¦fyüzəbəl\ *adj* [²*re-fuse* + *-able*] : capable of renewal with a new fuse ⟨~ plug in a safety valve⟩
**re·fu·sion** \rə'fyüzhən, rē'f-\ *n* -s [F *réfusion* act of giving or putting back, fr. LL *refusion-, refusio* restitution, overflowing, fr. L *refusus* (past part. of *refundere* to pour back, give or put back) + *-ion-, -io* -ion] : the act of pouring back : REINFUSION
**re-fusion** \(')rē¦fyüzhən\ *n* [*re-* + *fusion*] : a second or fresh melting ⟨~ of rocks⟩
**re·fut·abil·i·ty** \rə,fyüd·ə'biləd-ē, rē,fyü|, ,refyə|, |tə'-, -lətē, -i\ *n* : capability of being refuted
**re·fut·able** \rə'fyü|d·əbəl, rē'fyü|, 'refyə|, |təb-\ *adj* [LL *refutabilis*, fr. L *refutare* to refute + *-abilis* -able] : capable of being refuted — **re·fut·ably** \-blē,-bli\ *adv*
**re·fut·al** \rə'fyüd·ᵊl, rē'f-, -üt ᵊl\ *n* -s : REFUTATION
**ref·u·ta·tion** \,refyə'tāshən\ *n* -s [L *refutation-, refutatio*, fr. *refutatus* (past part. of *refutare* to refute) + *-ion-, -io* -ion] : the act or process of refuting : proof of falsehood or error : overthrowing by argument or proof : DISPROOF, CONFUTATION ⟨some of his blunders seem rather to deserve a flogging than a ~ —T.B.Macaulay⟩
**re·fut·ative** \rə'fyüd·əd·iv, rē'f-, -ütətiv\ *adj* [fr. *refutation*, after such pairs as E *negation: negative*] : tending to refute : relating to refutation ⟨~ force of his argument⟩
**re·fut·ato·ry** \-üd·ə,tōrē, -ütə-, -tȯr-, -ri\ *adj* [LL *refutatorius*, fr. L *refutatus* (past part. of *refutare*) + *-orius* -ory] : REFUTATIVE
**re·fute** \rə'fyüt, rē'f-, *usu* -üd·+V\ *vt* -ED/-ING/-S [L *refutare* to check, drive back, refute, fr. *re-* + *-futare* to beat — more at BEAT] : to overthrow by argument, evidence, or proof : prove to be false or erroneous : CONFUTE ⟨~ arguments⟩ ⟨~ testimony⟩ ⟨*refuted* the charge of laziness by working hard⟩ **syn** see DISPROVE
**re·fut·er** \-üd·ə(r), -ütə-\ *n* -s : one that refutes something
**reg** \'reg\ *n* -s [of Hamitic origin; akin to Amharic *'ərāgā* rise, ascend] : ²ERG
**reg** *abbr* **1** regent **2** regiment **3** [L *regina*] queen **4** region **5** register; registered **6** registrar; registry **7** regius **8** regular; regularly **9** regulate; regulation; regulator
**¹re·gain** \(')rē+\ *vt* [*re-* + *gain*] **1** : to gain anew : get again : RECOVER ⟨~ health⟩ ⟨~*ed* his position in society⟩ **2** : to get back to : reach again ⟨~ the shore⟩ **syn** see RECOVER
**²regain** \"\ *n* **1** : an act or instance of regaining **2** : an amount regained; *specif* : the percentage based on the bone-dry weight of materials of moisture that a textile material absorbs in a standard atmosphere
**re·gain·er** \-nə(r)\ *n* : one that regains something
**re·gain·ment** \-mənt\ *n* -s : an act or instance of regaining ⟨waiting for her ~ of composure⟩
**¹regal** *n* -s [ME, kingdom, royal jewel, fr. MF *regale* kingdom, royal garment, fr. OF, fem. of (assumed) OF *regal* royal, regal (whence MF *regal*), fr. L *regalis*] *obs* : something relating or belonging to royalty: as **a** : a royal jewel ⟨the ~ of France⟩ **b** : a regal privilege **c** : a chalice used in the Communion at English coronations
**²re·gal** \'rēgəl\ *adj* [ME, fr. MF or L; MF, fr. L *regalis* royal, regal — more at ROYAL] **1** : of, relating to, suitable to, or like a king **2** : of notable excellence or magnificence : STATELY, SPLENDID
**³regal** \"\ *n* -s [MF *regale*, perh. fr. fem. of *regal* royal, regal] : a small portable organ of the 16th and 17th centuries having orig. reed pipes only but later incorporating flue pipes and having keys played with one hand while the bellows are worked with the other
**¹re·ga·le** \rə'gālē, rē'-\ *n, pl* **re·ga·lia** \-lyə, -lēə\ [ML, royal prerogative, royal ornament, fr. L, neut. of *regalis* royal, regal] **1 a** : the right, power, or privilege of a king : royal prerogative — usu. used in pl. **b** [F & ML; F *régale*, fr. ML *regale*, fr. L, neut. of *regalis*] : a right or prerogative of enjoying the revenues of vacant sees and abbacies and of presenting to benefices dependent on them claimed by rulers in the middle ages **2** *regalia pl* **a** : the emblems, symbols, or paraphernalia (as crown, scepter, or standard) indicative of royal state **b** : decorations, insignia, or special costume indicative of an office or of membership in a group (as a social or fraternal order) ⟨the lord mayor in full *regalia*⟩ **3** *regalia pl* : costume devoted to a particular situation or use : special costume : FINERY ⟨unrecognizable in his Sunday *regalia*⟩
**²re·gale** \rə'gāl, rē'-, *esp before pause or consonant* -āəl\ *vb* -ED/-ING/-S [F *régaler*, fr. MF *regaler*, fr. *regale, rigalle*, n.] *vt* **1 a** : to entertain (as a person) sumptuously or agreeably : feast with delicacies ⟨*regaled* her guests with the best of everything⟩ **b** : to indulge, refresh, or renew (oneself) with food or drink and esp. with delicacies ⟨*regaling* himself with a vast platter of chitterlings⟩ **c** : to serve as a delicacy for : REFRESH ⟨good ale to ~ our throats⟩ **2** : to offer pleasant entertainment to (as the senses) : give pleasure or amusement to : affect pleasurably ⟨a sight that ~*s* the eye⟩ ⟨*regaled* the meeting with the tale of the committee's troubles⟩ ~ *vi* : to feast oneself : FEED ⟨*regaling* on dewberries —George Meredith⟩ **syn** see PLEASE
**³regale** \"\ *n* -s [F *régal*, fr. MF *regale, rigalle*, fr. *re-* + *gale* pleasure, merrymaking — more at GALLANT] **1 a** : a choice or sumptuous repast : FEAST **b** : a ration or treat of food or drink **2** : REGALEMENT
**reg·a·lec·i·dae** \,regə'lesə,dē\ *n pl, cap* [NL, fr. *Regalecus*, type genus + *-idae*] : a family of large marine fishes (order Allotriognathi) constituted by the oarfishes
**re·gal·e·cus** \rə'galəkəs\ *n, cap* [NL (intended as trans. of Norw *sildekonge* oarfish, fr. *sild* herring + *konge* king), fr. L *reg-, rex* king + *allec* fish pickle — more at ROYAL] : the type and sole genus of the family Regalecidae
**re·gale·ment** \rə'gā(ə)lmənt, rē'-\ *n* -s **1** : an act of regaling **2** : something that regales : ENTERTAINMENT, REFRESHMENT
**re·gal·er** \-ālə(r)\ *n* -s : one that regales
**regal fern** *n* : ROYAL FERN
**regal fritillary** *n* : a common fritillary butterfly (*Speyeria idalia*) of the eastern U. S.
**¹regalia** *pl of* REGALE
**²regalia** *or* **regalio** *obs var of* REGALO
**³re·ga·lia** \rə'gālyə, -lēə, ,rägə'lēə\ *n* -s [AmerSp *regalia*, fr. Sp, royal prerogative, fr. ML *regalia*, pl. of *regale* royal prerogative] : a cigar of large size and superior quality; *also* : the size in which such cigars are classed
**re·ga·lian** \rə'gālyən, rē'-, -lēən\ *adj* [F *régalien*, fr. L *regalis* royal, regal + F *-en* -an (fr. L *-anus*)] : of or belonging to a royal ruler : REGAL, SOVEREIGN ⟨~ rights⟩
**re·gal·ism** \'rēgə,lizəm\ *n* -s : the doctrine of royal supremacy esp. in church affairs

**re·gal·ist** \-ləst\ *n* -s **:** an advocate of regalism

**re·gal·i·ty** \rəˈgaləd·ē, rēˈ-, -lətē, -i\ *n* -ES [ME *regalite*, fr. MF & ML; MF *regalité*, fr. ML *regalitat-, regalitas*, fr. L *regalis* royal, regal + *-tat-, -tas* -ty] **1 a :** sovereign right or privilege **:** sovereign jurisdiction or prerogative **b regalities** *pl* **:** REGALIA **2 :** a country or territory subject to royal jurisdiction or to such jurisdiction in the hands of a subject **3 :** a royal grant under former English or Scots law permitting a lord of a particular territory to exercise jurisdiction similar in civil matters to that of a sheriff and with more extensive jurisdiction to hear criminal cases — see LORD OF REGALITY

**re·gal lily** \ˈrēgəl-\ *also* **re·ga·le lily** \rəˈgälē-\ *n* [*regal lily* fr. ²*regal* + *lily*; *regale lily* fr. NL *regale* (specific epithet of *Lilium regale*) (fr. L, neut. of *regalis* royal, regal) + E *lily*] **:** a widely cultivated garden lily (*Lilium regale*) of western China grown for its showy flowers that are white and yellow inside but streaked or flushed with pink or light lilac purple on the outer surface of the petals

**re·gal·ly** \ˈrēgəlē, -li\ *adv* [ME *regaliche*, fr. ²*regal* + *-liche* -ly] **:** in a regal manner **:** so as to be or appear regal

**regal moth** *n* **:** a large showy American moth (*Citheronia regalis*) having the forewings olive spotted with yellow and heavily veined with red and the hind wings orange-red spotted with yellow — see HICKORY HORNED DEVIL

**re·gal·ness** *n* -ES **:** the quality or state of being regal

**re·ga·lo** \rəˈgä(ˌ)lō, -gä(ˌ)-, -ga(ˌ)-\ *n* -S [Sp, fr. MF *regale* feast — more at REGALE] *archaic* **:** GIFT, BONUS, TREAT; *esp* **:** an offering of superior food or drink

**regal purple** *n* **:** ROYAL PURPLE 2

**regals** *pl of* REGAL

**regalty** *n* -ES [ME *regalte*, prob. modif. of MF *regalité*] *obs* **:** REGALITY

**re·galvanize** \(ˈ)rē+\ *vt* [*re-* + *galvanize*] **:** to restore vitality or activity to as if by galvanizing

**regal water** *n* [trans. of NL *aqua regia*] *archaic* **:** AQUA REGIA

¹**re·gard** \rəˈgärd, rēˈ-, -gȧd\ *n* -S [ME, fr. MF *regard, regart*, fr. OF, fr. *regarder*, v.] **1** *archaic* **:** ASPECT, APPEARANCE, MIEN **2 a :** attention of the mind with a feeling of interest **:** attention or respect as shown in action or conduct **:** CONSIDERATION, HEED, CONCERN **b :** LOOK, GLANCE, GAZE ⟨fixed on him his magisterial ~⟩ **c :** inspection of a forest by officials under old English law to learn if any trespasses have been committed **:** the right or office of such inspection; *also* **:** a district under the jurisdiction of such an official **3 a :** the worth or estimation in which something is held ⟨a man of small ~⟩ **b** (1) **:** a feeling of blended approval, appreciation, respect, liking, and affection usu. based on attractive characteristics of the object ⟨their ardor and their faithful endurance of all the hardships have won them the ~ of their British comrades —Sir Winston Churchill⟩ (2) **:** friendly greetings implying such a feeling — usu. used in pl. ⟨give them our ~*s*⟩ **c :** an evidence of affection or kindly feeling **:** a protective interest based on esteem **:** CARE ⟨a man with any ~ for his health⟩ **4 :** something that is considered as a ground of action or opinion **:** CONSIDERATION, MOTIVE **5 :** an aspect to be taken into consideration or significant to the matter in question **:** RELATION, RESPECT ⟨knowing nothing of the divine will in our ~⟩ ⟨considered with some ~ for its effect on my health⟩ ⟨in ~ to internal policy —M.R.Cohen⟩ ⟨in doubt in ~ to its aims —J.H.Robinson †1936⟩ ⟨no melodramatics with ~ to art —J.C.Powys⟩ ⟨this agreement, with ~ to which there was an express understanding —Ellen Wilkinson⟩ **6** *obs* **:** INTENTION **syn** RESPECT, ESTEEM, ADMIRATION: REGARD is the least connotative in this group and is often accompanied by a modifier like *high* to indicate a favorable feeling ⟨a pilot held in high *regard*⟩ REGARD may be used to suggest friendly feelings without impulse to emulation or closer relationship ⟨gave her their affection in full measure . . . with a manly *regard*, in which there was nothing akin to what is distinctively called love —Nathaniel Hawthorne⟩ RESPECT may add to REGARD implications of deference to or veneration of on the part of an inferior or junior. It may suggest that the feeling implied is justly due ⟨an important form of rewards and punishments for young children, and also for older boys and girls if conferred by a person who inspires *respect* —Bertrand Russell⟩ It may suggest deference to rank with or without implications of accompanying liking ⟨the *respect* which he felt for her high rank, and his veneration for her as his patroness —Jane Austen⟩ ⟨but nobody really liked her: malignity commands *respect*, not liking —Robert Graves⟩ ESTEEM may suggest more genuine feeling than RESPECT; it may connote warmth of feeling or conviction of a worthiness to be emulated ⟨if Stephen did disclose himself to him, it would be a signal mark of *esteem* —Archibald Marshall⟩ ⟨expressing my *esteem* for his character —Edmund Burke⟩ ADMIRATION is a strong term suggesting pleasure, delight, and wonder, often with impulse to emulate or possess; it stresses feeling, sometimes, although certainly not always, implying a subordination of thoughtful judgment ⟨his own romantic *admiration* of Mary, Queen of Scots —S.M.Crothers⟩ ⟨should not hold up military conquerors to *admiration* —Bertrand Russell⟩ ⟨in proportion to his *admiration* for his father —George Meredith⟩ REGARD stresses the fact of feeling, RESPECT due feeling suitably expressed, ESTEEM genuine warm and lasting feeling, and ADMIRATION strong feeling with less suggestion of judicious analysis.
— **in regard of** *prep* **1** *archaic* **:** in comparison with **2 :** in respect to **:** as to **3** *obs* **:** on account of **:** because of **4** *obs* **:** out of consideration or respect for

²**regard** \"\ *vb* -ED/-ING/-S [ME *regarden*, fr. MF *regarder, reguarder* to regard, look at, fr. OF, fr. *re-* + *garder, guarder* to guard — more at GUARD] *vt* **1 a :** to pay attention to **:** notice or remark particularly ⟨don't ~ this very seriously⟩ **b** *obs* **:** to look after **:** take care of or for **2 a** *obs* **:** to treat (a thing) as something of peculiar value, sanctity, or worth **b :** to have care for **:** heed in conduct or practice **:** have respect for (as a person) **:** show respect or consideration for ⟨each must ~ the rights of all⟩ **c :** to hold (one) in high esteem **:** care for **3 a :** to keep in view **:** look at **:** gaze upon ⟨your niece ~*s* me with an eye of favor —Shak.⟩ **b** *obs* **:** to face toward **4 :** to take into consideration or account **:** take account of ⟨neither ~*ing* that she is my child nor fearing me as if I were her father —Shak.⟩ **5 :** to have relation to or bearing upon **:** relate to **:** touch on ⟨your argument does not ~ the question⟩ **6 :** to look at from a particular point of view **:** think of **:** CONSIDER, EVALUATE, JUDGE — usu. used with *as* ⟨~*ed* their chief as a brave soldier and a resourceful leader⟩ ⟨he ~*ed* no task as too humble for him to undertake —Aldous Huxley⟩ ~ *vi* **1 :** to look attentively **:** GAZE **2** *obs* **:** to take heed or pains **3 :** to pay attention **:** HEED **syn** see CONSIDER

**re·gard·able** \-dəbəl\ *adj* **:** fit for or deserving of notice

**re·gar·dant** \rəˈgärdᵊnt, -gȧd-\ *adj* [ME, fr. MF *regardant, reguardant*, pres. part. of *regarder, reguarder* to look at] **1 :** annexed to a particular manor whoever owned it — used of a medieval English villein; compare *in gross* at ²GROSS **2** *also* **re·guar·dant** \"\ **a :** GUARDANT **b :** looking backward over the shoulder — used of a heraldic representation of an animal

**regarded** *past of* REGARD

**re·gard·er** \rəˈgärdər, rēˈ-, -gȧdə(r\ *n* -S [²*regard* + *-er*; trans. of AF *regardour*] **1 :** an officer having the right and duty under Old English law to inspect the royal forests and ascertain the presence or absence of trespasses or violations of the law **2 :** one that regards

**re·gard·ful** \-ˈ-fəl\ *adj* **1 :** HEEDFUL, OBSERVANT **2 :** full or expressive of regard or respect **:** RESPECTFUL — **re·gard·ful·ly** \-fəlē, -li\ *adv* — **re·gard·ful·ness** *n* -ES

**regarding** *prep* **:** with respect to **:** CONCERNING

¹**re·gard·less** \-ˈ-ləs\ *adj* **1 :** having no regard **:** HEEDLESS, CARELESS ⟨crushing the bloom with ~ tread⟩ **2** *archaic* **:** not meriting regard — **re·gard·less·ly** *adv* — **re·gard·less·ness** *n* -ES

²**regardless** \"\ *adv* **:** without regard to impeding elements (as of prudence, expense, or effort) ⟨everything's been done ~ —James Montgomery⟩ ⟨insisted we have dinner ~⟩

**regardless of** *prep* **:** without taking into account **:** in spite of ⟨*regardless of* our mistakes⟩

**regards** *pl of* REGARD, *pres 3d sing of* REGARD

**re·gather** \(ˈ)rē+\ *vb* [*re-* + *gather*] *vt* **:** to gather anew **:** bring together once more **:** REUNITE **:** RECRUIT ⟨~*ing* our forces⟩ ~ *vi* **:** to come together anew **:** become whole again ⟨storm clouds ~*ing* over the hills⟩ ⟨the crowd ~*ed* after the storm⟩

**re·gat·ta** \rəˈgad·ə, rēˈ-, -gatə, -gäd·ə, -gätə\ *n* -S [It *regatta*, *regata*, fr. It (Venetian dial.)] **1 a :** a gondola race in Venice **b :** a rowing, speedboat, or sailing race; *esp* **:** an organized series of such races **2 :** a strong twilled English cotton fabric for clothing usu. with colored stripes or checks **3 :** LIBERTY 6

**regd** *abbr* registered

**re·gear** \(ˈ)rē+\ *vt* [*re-* + *gear*] **:** to alter so as to be suitable for a new purpose or condition ⟨~*ing* the national economy for war⟩

**re·ge·late** \ˈrējəˌlāt, ˌ-ˈ-\ *vi* [back-formation fr. *regelation*] **:** to freeze together again **:** undergo regelation

**re·gelation** \ˌrē+\ *n* [*re-* + *gelation* (freezing)] **:** the refreezing of water derived from the melting of ice under pressure when the pressure is relieved

**re·gel's privet** \ˈrāgəlz-\ *or* **regel privet** *n* [prob. after Edward August von *Regel* †1892 Ger. botanist in Russia] **:** a deciduous Asiatic shrub (*Ligustrum obtusifolium regelianum*) with horizontally spreading branches and pubescent branchlets and leaves that is used as a hedge plant and is notably tolerant of shade and soil

**re·gence** \ˈrējən(t)s\ *adj* [F *Régence* belonging to or characteristic of the regency of Philippe II, Duc d'Orléans †1723 regent of France 1715–23 during the minority of Louis XV, fr. *régence*, n., regency, fr. MF *regence* rule, fr. ML *regentia* regency, rule] **:** of, relating to, or being furniture or a furniture style characteristic of the regency of the Duke of Orleans, prevalent between about 1680 and 1725, and marked by a gradual transition from the earlier severely angular and massive to the delicate curvatures of Louis XV style

¹**re·gen·cy** \-nsē, -si\ *n* -ES [ME *regencie*, fr. ML *regentia*, fr. *regent-, regens* ruler, regent + L *-ia* -y — more at REGENT] **1 a :** the office, jurisdiction, or dominion of a regent or vicarious ruler or of a body of regents **b** *archaic* **:** the office or position of ruler **:** royal office or state **:** RULE **2 :** a territory governed by a regent or regency **3 a** *obs* **:** a governing body of various cities or states **b :** a body of men entrusted with vicarious government ⟨a ~ constituted during a king's minority⟩ **4 :** a period during which a regent or body of regents governs

²**regency** \"\ *adj, often cap* [¹*regency*; fr. the regency of George, Prince of Wales (afterwards George IV †1830 King of Great Britain and Ireland) during the period (1811–20) when his father George III was still alive but permanently deranged] **:** of, relating to, typical of, or adapted from early 19th century England, its customs, or its styles ⟨a ~ poem⟩ ⟨~ furniture⟩ ⟨~ dress⟩

**re·gen·er·a·ble** \(ˈ)rēˈjen(ə)rəbəl, rəˈ-\ *adj* [³*regenerate* + *-able*] **:** capable of being regenerated

**re·gen·er·a·cy** \-n(ə)rəsē\ *n* -ES [¹*regenerate* + *-cy*] **:** the quality or state of being regenerated

**re·gen·er·ant** \-n(ə)rənt\ *n* -S [³*regenerate* + *-ant*] **:** a regenerating agent

¹**re·gen·er·ate** \-n(ə)rət, *usu* -əd·+V\ *adj* [ME *regenerat*, fr. L *regeneratus*, past part. of *regenerare* to regenerate, fr. *re-* + *generare* to beget — more at GENERATE] **1 :** formed or created again **2 :** spiritually reborn or converted **:** having undergone regeneration; *specif* **:** having become a Christian **3 :** restored to a better, higher, or more worthy state ⟨~ by redemption from error or decay⟩

²**regenerate** \"\ *n* -S **:** a regenerated thing or person: as **a :** an individual who is spiritually reborn **b** (1) **:** an organism that has undergone regeneration (2) **:** a regenerated body part or structure

³**regenerate** \-nəˌrāt, *usu* -ād·+V\ *vb* [L *regeneratus*, past part. of *regenerare*] *vi* **1 :** to become formed again **:** become shaped anew **2 :** to become regenerate **:** REFORM **3 :** to undergo regeneration ~ *vt* **1 a :** to cause to be spiritually born again **:** subject to spiritual regeneration **b :** to make a radical change for the better in **:** reform completely ⟨forces that will ~ society⟩ **2 a :** to generate or produce anew **:** REPRODUCE, RE-CREATE, REVIVE ⟨~ hatred⟩; *esp* **:** to replace (a body part) by a new growth of tissue ⟨lizards that ~ lost tails⟩ **b** (1) **:** to form (a compound) again chemically from a derivative (2) **:** to produce again from a modified form by chemical treatment in a form changed physically but usu. not to a great extent chemically from the original raw material ⟨*regenerated* fibers⟩ **3 :** to reestablish on a new and usu. better basis **4 :** to restore (a material) to original strength (as by adding salt to a brine that has been weakened by the absorption of atmospheric moisture) or to restore original properties to (a material) **5 :** to increase the amplification of (an electron current) by causing a part of the power in the output circuit to act upon the input circuit by means of electron tubes

**regenerated cellulose** *n* **:** cellulose obtained in a changed form by sulfuric acid or other chemical treatment of an extruded coagulated solution (as of viscose or cuprammonium solution) or a stretched acetate fiber ⟨*regenerated cellulose* and acetate fibers⟩ — see CELLOPHANE, ²RAYON 1b

**re·gen·er·ate·ly** *adv* **:** in a regenerate manner **:** as if regenerated

**re·gen·er·ate·ness** *n* -ES **:** the quality or state of being regenerate

**re·gen·er·a·tion** \(ˌ)rēˌjenəˈrāshən, rəˌ-\ *n* [ME *regeneracioun*, fr. MF & LL; MF *regeneration*, fr. LL *regeneration-, regeneratio*, fr. L *regeneratus* (past part. of *regenerare*) + *-ion-, -io* -ion] **1 :** an act of regenerating or the condition of being regenerated **2 :** spiritual rebirth **:** spiritual renewal, re-creation, or revival **:** a radical spiritual transformation in which the center of one's life is shifted under the action of a divine agency (as the Holy Spirit) from a self-centered ultimate concern to a God-centered ultimate concern **3 :** the renewal, regrowth, or restoration of a body or a bodily part, tissue, or substance after injury or as a normal bodily process ⟨~ of a plant from a cutting⟩ ⟨~ of a lost claw by a lobster⟩ ⟨continual ~ of epithelial cells⟩ ⟨~ of the contractile substance of muscle after exercise⟩ — compare REGULATION **4 a :** the process by which part of the power in the output circuit of an amplifying device is caused to act upon the input circuit so as to increase the amplification **:** FEEDBACK **b :** the utilization by special devices of heat or other products that would ordinarily be lost — see REGENERATOR 4

**re·gen·er·a·tive** \rēˈjenəˌrād·|iv, rəˈ-, -n(ə)rə|, |t|, |ēv\ *adj* [ME, fr. ML *regenerativus*, fr. L *regeneratus* (past part. of *regenerare*) + *-ivus* -ive] **1 :** of, relating to, marked by, or using regeneration **:** tending to regenerate ⟨~ influences⟩ ⟨a ~ furnace⟩ ⟨the ~ phase of the cycle⟩ **2 :** constituting or relating to the returning of energy to a supply system (as when a descending motor-driven hoist returns energy to the line by acting as a generator); *specif* **:** relating to a method of amplification with electron tubes in which a part of the power in the output circuit acts upon the input circuit to increase the amplification — **re·gen·er·a·tive·ly** \|əvlē, -li\ *adv*

**regenerative braking** *n* **:** electric braking in which electrical energy that is produced by the motor is transferred to the supply line

**regenerative cooling** *n* **:** a cryogenic method in which the rapid expansion of a portion of a gas to be liquefied is utilized to lower the temperature of the remainder

**regenerative cycle** *n* **:** a cycle in a steam engine using heat that would ordinarily be lost: as **a :** a multiple-expansion steam-engine cycle in which the receivers are used as successive feed-water heaters **b :** a steam-turbine cycle in which the condensate or feed water is heated to a temperature that is much higher than that corresponding to saturation at the exhaust pressure by means of steam that has been bled from the turbine at points intermediate between the throttle and exhaust

**regenerative furnace** *n* **:** a gas-burning furnace equipped with a regenerator

**regenerative motor** *n* **:** a jet or rocket motor in which the incoming combustion air is heated by passage through the motor cooling jacket

**re·gen·er·a·tor** \rēˈjenəˌrād·ə(r), -ātə-\ *n* [LL, fr. L *regeneratus* (past part. of *regenerare* to regenerate) + *-or*] **1 :** one that regenerates **2 :** a heavy swinging counterpoise or other balancing device for a mine pump rod to permit a higher engine speed **3 :** a hypothetical body (as used with a reversible engine operating on a Stirling cycle) that stores heat from the working substance of an engine so that each part of the body and the contiguous gas or vapor have the same temperature, each increment of heat is maintained at the temperature at which it was received, and the stored heat is returned to the working substance by the reversal of the process **4 :** a device used esp. with hot-air engines or gas-burning furnaces in which the incoming air or gas is heated by contact with masses (as of iron, brick) previously heated by the outgoing hot air or gas or by being passed through a pipe or pipes heated by a flow of the hot air or gas escaping in the opposite direction — compare HEAT EXCHANGER

**re·gen·er·a·trix** \-ˌ-ˈ-rā·(ˌ)triks\ *n* [NL, fem. of LL *regenerator* — more at -TRIX] **:** a female regenerator ⟨regarded herself as fit to be the ~ of the world —Mortimer Collins⟩

**re·genesis** \(ˈ)rē+\ *n* [*re-* + *genesis*] **:** new birth **:** RENEWAL

**re·gens·burg** \ˈrāgənzˌbərg, -bōg, -bəig; -gənsˌbu̇r|g, -u̇ə|, |k\ *adj, usu cap* [fr. *Regensburg*, city in southern Germany] **:** of or from the city of Regensburg, Germany **:** of the kind or style prevalent in Regensburg

¹**re·gent** \ˈrējənt\ *adj* [ME, fr. ML *regent-, regens*, fr. L, pres. part. of *regere* to rule — more at RIGHT] **1** *archaic* **:** functioning as a presiding officer over academic debates and disputations — used postpositively of a master of arts of less than five years standing at Oxford or Cambridge universities **2** [²*regent*] **:** exercising vicarious authority **:** acting as a regent (as of a country) **3** [L *regent-, regens*, pres. part. of *regere*] *archaic* **:** RULING, GOVERNING, REGNANT

²**regent** \"\ *n* -S [ME, fr. MF or ML; MF, ruler, regent, fr. ML *regent-, regens*, fr. L, pres. part. of *regere* to rule] **1 a** *archaic* **:** something that rules or governs **:** a ruling authority or principle **b :** one who rules or reigns **:** GOVERNOR, RULER **2 :** one invested with vicarious authority **:** one who governs a kingdom in the minority, absence, or disability of the sovereign: as **a :** a member of a former governing body of some European cities **b :** a native official in the former Dutch administration of Java through whom a resident and his assistants carry out the details of the government of a residency **3 a** (1) **:** a regent master of arts (2) **:** an instructor in a Scottish college in charge of students through the entire course **:** PROFESSOR **b** *obs* **:** the headmaster of a school **c :** a member of an academic or cultural governing board (as of a state university) **4** *or* **regent pump :** a woman's pump having a circular vamp and a quarter unbroken at the heel

**regent bird** *n* [so called in honor of George, Prince of Wales (afterward George IV †1830 King of Great Britain and Ireland), regent during the period (1811-20) when his father George III was still alive but permanently deranged] **:** a showy Australian bowerbird (*Sericulus chrysocephalus*) that in the male has the head, neck, and large patches on the wings bright golden yellow and the rest of the plumage deep velvety black

**regent honey eater** *n* [*regent* (as in *regent bird*) + *honey eater*] **:** FLYING COACHMAN

**regent parrot** *n* [*regent* (as in *regent bird*) + *parrot*] **:** a predominantly yellowish green Australian parrot (*Polytelis anthopeplus*) with dark bluish green outer and black under tail feathers and dark red markings on the wings

**re·gent·ship** \ˈ-ˌ-ˌship\ *n* **:** the office or state of a regent

**re·germinate** \(ˈ)rē+\ *vi* [*re-* + *germinate*] **:** to grow or develop anew **:** REGENERATE — **re·germination** \(ˌ)rē+\ *n*

**reges** *pl of* REX

**reg·ga** \ˈregə\ *n, pl* **regga** *or* **reggas** *usu cap* **:** a member of a Bantu-speaking people northwest of Lake Tanganyika

**reg·gia·no** \reˈjä(ˌ)nō\ *also* **reggiano cheese** *n* -S *usu cap R* [It *reggiano*, fr. *reggiano*, adj., of or from the city of Reggio nell'Emilia, Italy] **:** a high quality Parmesan cheese that is usu. aged for several years before use

**reg·gio** \ˈre(ˌ)jō\ *also* **reg·gian** \-jən\ *adj, usu cap* [*reggio* fr. *Reggio* di Calabria, city in southern Italy; *reggian* fr. It *reggiano*, fr. *Reggio* di Calabria + It *-ano* -an (fr. L *-anus*)] **1 :** of or from the city of Reggio di Calabria, Italy **:** of the kind or style prevalent in Reggio di Calabria **2** [*reggio* fr. *Reggio* nell'Emilia, city in northern Italy; *reggian* fr. It *reggiano*, fr. *Reggio* nell'Emilia + It *-ano* -an (fr. L *-anus*)] **:** of or from the city of Reggio nell'Emilia, Italy **:** of the kind or style prevalent in Reggio nell'Emilia

**regia dona** *pl of* REGIUM DONUM

**reg·i·ci·dal** \ˌrejəˈsīdᵊl\ *adj* **:** relating to regicide or a regicide **:** constituting or disposed to regicide

**reg·i·cide** \ˈrejəˌsīd\ *n* -S [prob. fr. (assumed) NL *regicida*, fr. L *regi-* (fr. *reg-, rex* king) + *-cida* -cide — more at ROYAL] **1 :** one who kills, murders, or shares overt responsibility (as by acting as judge or executioner) for the death of a king esp. to whom he is naturally subject **2** [prob. fr. (assumed) NL *regicidium*, fr. L *regi-* (fr. *reg-, rex* king) + *-cidium* -cide] **:** the killing or murder of a king

**reg·i·cid·ism** \-ˌ-dizəm\ *n* -S **:** the practice of regicide

**re·gi·dor** \ˌrāhēˈthō(ə)r\ *n, pl* **regido·res** \-ō(ˌ)rās\ [Sp, fr. *regir* to rule, fr. L *regere*] **:** one of a body of officers charged with the government of a Spanish or Latin American municipality and corresponding to the English alderman

**re·gie** \rāˈzhē, ˈ-ˌ-\ *n* -S [F *régie*, fr. MF *regie* government, jurisdiction, fr. *regir* to rule, fr. L *regere*] **1 a :** a government monopoly (as on tobacco or salt) used chiefly as a means of taxation **b :** tobacco or tobacco products bought or supplied by agents of such a monopoly ⟨a ~ cigarette⟩ **2 :** direct management of public finance or public works by agents of the government for government account as distinguished from a system under which such public business is done under contract **3 :** the system of collecting taxes by officials who have either no interest or a very small interest in the proceeds as distinguished from the system of farming them out

**re·gild** \(ˈ)rē+\ *vt* [*re-* + *gild*] **:** to gild anew **:** BRIGHTEN, FRESHEN ⟨~*ing* his renown with new triumphs⟩

**re·gime** *also* **ré·gime** \rāˈzhēm, rəˈ-, reˈ- *sometimes* -ˈjēm\ *n* -S [F *régime*, fr. L *regimin-, regimen*] **1 a :** REGIMEN 1 **b :** a regular pattern of occurrence or action (as of seasonal rainfall) **2 a :** a method of ruling or management **:** a manner of administration **b :** a form of government or administration ⟨totalitarian ~⟩; *specif* **:** a governmental or social system ⟨Nazi ~⟩ **c :** the period during which a regime prevails **3 :** the condition of a river with respect to the rate of its flow as measured by the volume of water passing different cross sections in a given time **4 :** a fruiting cluster of the African oil palm

**regime dotal** *n* [F *régime dotal*, lit., dotal system of management] **:** the right and power of a husband under civil law to administer during his life his wife's dotal property under the rules of law safeguarding its return upon the dissolution of the marriage by death or other cause

**reg·i·men** \ˈrejəmən, -ˌmen\ *n* -S [ME, fr. L *regimin-, regimen* rule, government, fr. *regere* to rule — more at RIGHT] **1 a :** a systematic plan (as of diet, therapeutic and sanitary measures, and medication) designed to improve and maintain the health of a patient or to control a particular ailment **b :** a regulation or treatment intended to benefit by gradual operation **2 :** GOVERNING, GOVERNMENT, RULE, ADMINISTRATION **3 :** GOVERNMENT 5a **4 :** the characteristic behavior or orderly procedure of a natural phenomenon or process (as of a river or a glacier)

¹**reg·i·ment** \ˈrejəmənt *sometimes* -jm-\ *n* -S [ME, fr. MF, fr. LL *regimentum*, fr. L *regere* to rule + *-mentum* -ment] **1 a :** governmental rule **b** *obs* **:** REGIMEN 2, REGIME 2a **2** *obs* **a :** RULERSHIP, GOVERNORSHIP; *also* **:** the period of a particular reign **b :** GOVERNANCE, MANAGEMENT, GUIDANCE **c :** a region or district governed **3 :** a body of soldiers commanded by a colonel and consisting of a variable number of companies, troops, or batteries: as **a :** a parent military organization that may include many battalions or other units which rarely serve together but share a common history, traditions, uniforms, and other matters **b :** a military unit composed basically of a headquarters and two or more battalions — compare GROUP **4 a** *obs* **:** a group (as of dogs, birds, devils) forming a particular class or kind **b** *chiefly dial* **:** a large quantity ⟨a ~ of company for Sunday dinner⟩ ⟨put up a ~ of peaches last summer⟩

²**regiment** \-jəˌment, -j(ə)mənt — *see* ²-MENT\ *vt* -ED/-ING/-S **1 a :** to form (military personnel) into a regiment **b :** to place in or assign to a regiment **2 a :** to organize into groups, classes, or other units esp. for the sake of central regulation or control ⟨~ the industries of a country⟩ **b :** to subject to systematization or rigid discipline **:** reduce to strict order or uniformity ⟨an education that ~*s* children⟩

¹**reg·i·men·tal** \ˌrejəˈmentᵊl\ *adj* **1 :** belonging to, used by, or concerning a regiment ⟨~ officers⟩ ⟨~ supplies⟩ **2 :** serving to regiment **:** tending to regimentation

²**regimental** \"\ *n* -s **1 a :** the uniform worn by the officers and soldiers of a regiment **:** military dress — usu. used in pl. **b regimentals** *pl* **:** special clothing required for a particular activity **2 :** a grayish purplish blue that is redder and duller than Wedgwood (sense 2b) or average delft and redder and lighter than average navy blue — called also *Persian blue*

**regimental color** *also* **regimental flag** *or* **regimental standard** *n* **:** a flag, ensign, or pennant usu. bearing symbols associated with the regiment by which it is carried as a mark of identification ⟨for many years . . . state flags continued to be carried as *regimental colors* —Leslie Thomas⟩

**regimental combat team** *n* **:** a tactical organization usu. formed by attaching artillery, engineers, or other special details to an infantry regiment for a particular mission

**reg·i·men·tal·ly** \-ᵊlē, -ᵊli\ *adv* **:** in a regimental manner **:** by regiment

**reg·i·men·ta·ry** \-tərē\ *adj* **:** involving or tending toward regimentation

**reg·i·men·ta·tion** \ˌrejəmənˈtāshən, -ˌmen·ˈ-\ *n* -s **:** the act or process of regimenting; *esp* **:** reduction to strict order or uniformity

**re·gim·i·nal** \rəˈjimənᵊl\ *adj* [L *regimin-, regimen* rule, government + E *-al* — more at REGIMEN] **:** of, relating to, or constituting regimen ⟨~ rules⟩

¹**re·gi·na** \rəˈjīnə, rēˈ-, -jēnə\ *n, pl* **regi·nae** \-jī(ˌ)nē, -jēˌnī\ [L, fem. of *reg-, rex* king — more at ROYAL] **:** QUEEN

²**re·gi·na** \rəˈjīnə, rēˈ-\ *adj, usu cap* [fr. *Regina*, capital of Saskatchewan, province in western Canada] **:** of or from Regina, the capital of Saskatchewan **:** of the kind or style prevalent in Regina

**re·gi·nal** \-ˈjīnᵊl, -jēn-\ *adj* [MF or ML; MF, fr. ML *reginalis*, fr. L *regina* + *-alis* -al] **:** of or relating to a queen **:** QUEENLY

**re·gion** \ˈrējən\ *n* -s [ME *regioun*, fr. MF *region* territory, region, fr. L *region-, regio* direction, territory, region, fr. *regere* to guide, rule + *-ion-, -io* -ion — more at RIGHT] **1 a** *obs* **:** REALM, KINGDOM **b :** an administrative area, division, or district (as in Rome under Augustus or in Soviet Russia) **2 a :** a major indefinite division of inanimate creation ⟨in the dark ~*s* of the night sky⟩ ⟨the aquatic ~*s* of the earth⟩ **b :** a sphere (as of activity or interest) subject to expressed or implied forces ⟨the abstract ~ of higher mathematics⟩ **:** FIELD 2a **3 :** a particular part of the world or universe (as natural waters, the sky, a particular galaxy): as **a :** a large tract of land **:** one of the large districts or quarters into which a space or surface is conceived of as divided; *broadly* **:** an indefinite area of land (as a country, province, district, or tract) ⟨there are few unknown ~*s* left on earth⟩ **b :** a broad geographical area containing a population whose members possess sufficient historical, cultural, economic, and social homogeneity to distinguish them from others ⟨the ~ of the Southwest in the U. S.⟩ **c** (1) **:** a major area of the world that is to some degree isolated by climatic or physical barriers and that supports a characteristic fauna differing both qualitatively and quantitatively from that of other regions ⟨faunal overlap of the Ethiopian and Oriental ~*s*⟩ (2) **:** an area often with distinct natural boundaries that is characterized by the prevalence of one or more vegetational climax types or by a mosaic of such types ⟨the oak-chestnut ~ of the deciduous forest formation of eastern No. America⟩ **4 a :** one of the major subdivisions into which the body or one of its parts may logically be divided ⟨the nine ~*s* of the abdomen⟩ **b :** an indefinite area surrounding a specified body part ⟨a pain in the heart ~⟩ **c :** space occupied by something **:** part in question, engaged, occupied, or under discussion ⟨the ~ of highest concentration⟩ **5 :** one of the portions or zones into which the atmosphere is divided according to height or the sea according to depth ⟨the dark abyssal ~ of the sea⟩ **6 :** a mathematical aggregate consisting of the totality of all values of an aggregate of continuous variables each varying over an interval

**re·gion·al** \-jənᵊl, -jnəl\ *adj* [L *regionalis*, fr. *region-, regio* + *-alis* -al] **1 a :** of or relating esp. to a geographical region ⟨allowing local needs to take precedence over ~⟩ **b :** of, relating to, or located in the peripheral parts of a district as distinguished from its central or major part **:** PROVINCIAL ⟨what items should properly be ~ and what central —*Brit. Book News*⟩ ⟨transactions on all ~ exchanges (those exchanges located outside New York City) —*Los Angeles (Calif.) Times*⟩ ⟨a ~ turn of speech⟩ **2 a :** of or relating to a region of a country **:** SECTIONAL, LOCAL ⟨~ governments⟩ **b :** of, relating to, or affecting a particular bodily region **:** LOCALIZED ⟨~ enteritis⟩ **3 :** marked by or having an effect of regionalism ⟨~ art⟩ — **re·gion·al·ly** \-ᵊlē, -əlē, -lī\ *adv*

**regional anatomy** *n* **:** a branch of anatomy dealing with regions and levels of the body esp. with reference to diagnosis and treatment of disease or injury

**regional anesthesia** *n* **:** anesthesia of a region of the body accomplished by a series of encircling injections of an anesthetic — compare BLOCK ANESTHESIA

**regional climax** *n* **:** CLIMAX 4

**regional ileitis** *n* **:** ileitis that involves the distal portion of the ileum, sometimes spreads to the colon, and is characterized by diarrhea, cramping, loss of appetite and weight with local abscesses and scarring which produce a thickened, indurated, inelastic, and stenosed intestine

**re·gion·al·ism** \ˈrējənᵊlˌizəm, -jnəˌli-\ *n* -s [ISV *regional* + *-ism*] **1 a :** consciousness of and loyalty to a distinct sub-national or supra-national area usu. characterized by a common culture, background, or interests **b :** development of a political or social system based on one or more such areas **2 :** the theory or practice of selecting a particular locale or region for subject matter and stressing its characteristic aspects in art or literature **3 :** a peculiarity (as of speech) that predominates or persists in a particular geographic area **4 :** the study of regional societies as distinct geographical and sociocultural complexes esp. in their relationship to other regions and to the composite national societies of which they form a part

**re·gion·al·ist** \-ˌləst\ *n* -s [ISV *regional* + *-ist*] **:** an advocate or practitioner of regionalism

**re·gion·al·is·tic** \ˌrējənᵊlˈistik, -jnəˈli-\ *also* **regionalist** *adj* **:** of or relating to regionalism

**re·gion·al·i·ty** \ˌrējəˈnalədē\ *n* -ES **:** arrangement or ordering in regions ⟨~ in embryonic differentiation⟩

**re·gion·al·iza·tion** \ˌrējənᵊləˈzāshən, -jnələˈz-, -ᵊlˌīz-, -əˌlīˈz-\ *n* -s **:** an act or instance of regionalizing

**re·gion·al·ize** \ˈrējənᵊlˌīz, -jnəˌlīz\ *vt* -ED/-ING/-S **:** to divide into regions or administrative districts **:** arrange regionally

**regional library** *n* **:** a public library system serving and supported by several contiguous counties usu. in the same state

**regional metamorphism** *n* **:** geological metamorphism involving a wide area

**regional servant** *n* **:** one of six major leaders of the Jehovah's Witnesses who is responsible for one of six geographical areas of the U.S.

**re·gion·ary** \ˈrējəˌnerē\ *adj* [LL *regionarius*, fr. L *region-, regio* + *-arius* -ary] **:** REGIONAL

**re·gioned** \ˈrējənd\ *adj* **:** divided into regions **:** occupying a particular region

**regions** *pl of* REGION

**ré·gis·seur** \R, rāzhēˈsər, + V -ˈsər·; -R -ˈsə̄, + *vowel in a word following without pause* -ˈsər· *or* -ˈsə̄ *also* -ˈsər\ *n* -s [F *régisseur*, fr. *régiss-* (stem of *régir* to direct, rule, fr. L *regere* to guide, rule) + *-eur* -or — more at RIGHT] **:** DIRECTOR 1c; *sometimes* **:** STAGE MANAGER

¹**reg·is·ter** \ˈrejəstə(r)\ *n* -s [ME *registre*, fr. MF, fr. OF, fr. ML *registrum*, alter. of LL *regesta* (pl.) list, register, fr. L, neut. pl. of *regestus*, past part. of *regerere* to bring back, transcribe, fr. *re-* + *gerere* to bear, wage, cherish — more at CAST] **1 :** a written record containing regular entries of items or details **:** an official or formal enumeration, description, or record of particulars **:** a memorial record ⟨a municipal ~ of births, marriages, and deaths⟩ **2 a :** a book or system of public records ⟨a ~ of births⟩ ⟨a ~ of patents⟩ **b :** the records of landed property under Scots law — called also *register of sasines* **c :** a record containing the names of seamen of a district or country or a list and description of the merchant vessels belonging to a port, district, or country **d :** the formal record maintained by a corporation of names and addresses of holders of its registered securities **e :** a roster of individuals qualified or available for some particular end or service ⟨a civil service ~⟩ ⟨the medical ~⟩ ⟨an employment ~⟩ **3 :** a list of signatures printed in some early books for the guidance of the binder **4 :** an entry in a register ⟨could find no ~ of her death⟩ **5 a :** a set of pipes of the same quality in a pipe organ **:** STOP **b** (1) **:** the compass or range of a human voice (2) **:** the series of musical tones of like quality within the compass of a voice that are produced by a particular adjustment of the vocal cords **c :** the compass of a musical instrument; *also* **:** a special portion of the compass (as a series of tones similarly produced and of the same quality) ⟨the ~ of the clarinet⟩ **6 :** a lid, stopper, or sliding plate in a furnace, stove, or other heating device for regulating the admission of air to the fuel; *also* **:** an arrangement containing dampers or shutters (as in the floor or wall of a room or passage or in a chimney) for admitting or excluding heated air or for regulating ventilation **7 :** REGISTRATION, REGISTRY ⟨a port of ~⟩ **8 a :** something that registers or records: as (1) **:** a device for registering automatically a cumulative number (as of persons admitted, fares taken) (2) **:** the part of a gas, water, or electric meter that consists of the mechanism and dials for indicating the total quantity consumed (3) **:** a contrivance for automatically noting the performance of a machine or the rapidity of a process **b :** a number or amount registered by such a device **9 a :** exact correspondence in position of a page with its counterpart on the other side of a leaf or sheet ⟨the printed matter on both sides of the sheet was in perfect ~ —W.T.Berry⟩ **b :** exact placement (as of the successive impressions that make a multicolor illustration or of folds or creases) ⟨knife folders sometimes have creasings and foldings out of ~ on 32-page signatures —*Book Production*⟩ **c :** complete or virtual agreement with respect to position (as in the component images in a three-color photograph) **10 :** a certificate signed by the commissioner of navigation and issued by the customs collector of a port to the owner of a ship engaged in foreign trade that sets forth the description, name, ownership, and other identifying data of the ship and serves as evidence of nationality and as a muniment of title **11 :** a telegraphic recorder **12 :** a piece of registered mail **13 :** a range or row esp. when one of a series ⟨the upper ~ of a design in fresco⟩ **14 :** a condition of being in correct alignment or in proper relative position

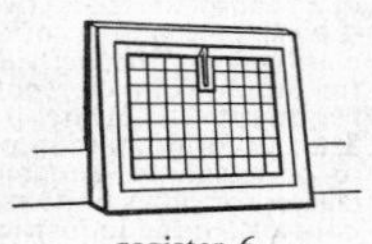
register 6

²**register** \"\ *vb* **registered; registered; registering** \-t(ə)riŋ\ **registers** [ME *registeren, registren*, fr. MF *registrer*, fr. OF, fr. ML *registrare*, fr. *registrum*, n.] *vt* **1 a :** to record formally and exactly **:** make an accurate entry of in a formal record **b :** to make or secure an official entry of in a register ⟨~*ed* the birth of his child⟩ ⟨~ a car⟩ **c :** to enroll formally as a voter ⟨a time set for ~*ing* new voters⟩ **d :** to record automatically **:** INDICATE **e :** to enter (a security) in the name of the owner in a formal record ⟨a ~*ed* security, bearing the name of its owner on its face, is transferable only on written assignment of the owner of record and actual surrender of the certificate⟩ **f :** to engage or assist in the formal enrollment of in a school or course ⟨spent the morning ~*ing* graduate students⟩ **2 a :** to make correspond exactly **:** adjust so as to secure correspondence **b :** to superimpose (two or more images) exactly (as in photographic printing or projection) **c :** to place or adjust (as a form, paper, or a cut) to print in register **3 a :** to record (a piece of mail) in the post office of mailing and at each successive point of transmission guaranteeing special care in delivery or for a fee above the minimum guaranteeing indemnity in case of loss, rifling, or damage **b :** to have (a piece of mail) registered **4 :** to convey an impression of ⟨his whole bearing ~*ed* intense fear⟩; *esp* **:** to convey (as a piece of information, a mood, or awareness of a situation) by expression and bodily movements without the use of words — used esp. of actors in motion pictures ~ *vi* **1 :** to enroll one's name in a register ⟨~*ed* at the hotel⟩: as **a :** to enroll one's name in a list of voters — compare REGISTRATION 5 **b :** to enroll oneself as a student in a school or course ⟨planned to ~ for the second semester⟩ **2 a :** to correspond exactly **:** fit correctly in relative position **:** be in correct alignment one with another ⟨the holes for the bolts ~ perfectly⟩ **b** *of printed matter* **:** to be in register **c :** to adjust gunfire (as by artillery) on a visible point which preferably can be located on a map in order to permit prompt shifts to other visible targets or to secure data for corrections in firing on targets located on the map but not visible **3 a :** to manipulate organ registers **b** *of an actor* **:** to convey (as by bodily movement or facial expression) an emotion, information, or other matter without the use of words **4 :** to make an impression ⟨the name simply didn't ~ with me⟩

³**register** \"\ *n* -s [prob. alter. of *registrer*] **:** one who registers or records **:** REGISTRAR, RECORDER; *esp* **:** a public officer charged with recording specific documents, transactions, or events or with keeping them in a public office ⟨a ~ of deeds⟩ ⟨~ of probate⟩

**registerable** *var of* REGISTRABLE

**registered** *adj* **1 a :** having the owner's name entered in a register ⟨a ~ security⟩ **b :** recorded as the owner of a security ⟨~ holders of a stock⟩ **2 :** recorded on the basis of pedigree, possession of breed characteristics, or both in the studbook of a recognized breed association ⟨a ~ Holstein⟩ ⟨a ~ Percheron⟩ **3 a :** qualified formally or officially (as by passage of an examination or licensing) to perform a specified function or practice a specified skill or function **b :** qualified officially to vote ⟨as a ~ Democrat he maintains his legal residence in New Mexico —*Current Biog.*⟩

**registered bond** *n* **:** a bond registered in the name of the holder on the books of the company and issued with the name of the holder written on the bond certificate

**registered envelope** *or* **registration envelope** *n, Brit* **:** a government-stamped envelope for use in sending a registered letter

**registered mail** *n* **:** mail recorded in the post office of mailing and at each successive point of transmission so as to guarantee special care in delivery or for a fee above the minimum to guarantee indemnity in case of loss, rifling, or damage — compare CERTIFIED MAIL

**registered mail insurance** *n* **:** insurance against loss due to the theft or destruction of property that is sent by registered mail

**registered nurse** *n* **:** a graduate trained nurse who has been licensed by a state authority (as a board of nursing examiners) after successfully passing examinations for registration

**registered representative** *n* **:** an employee of a brokerage house authorized (as by the New York Stock Exchange) to obtain orders from customers for a commission — compare CUSTOMER'S BROKER

**registered seed** *n* **:** seed or seed stock (as of potatoes) that is produced from foundation stock and is used for the production of additional registered seed or of commercial certified seed

**registered tonnage** *n* **:** REGISTER TONNAGE

**reg·is·ter·er** \ˈrejəst(ə)rə(r)\ *n* -s [²*register* + *-er*] **:** one that registers **:** REGISTRAR

**registering** *pres part of* REGISTER

**registering thermometer** *n* **:** a thermometer that indicates the maximum or the minimum temperature or both between settings and is commonly of the liquid-in-glass type

**register office** *n* **:** an office (as an employment office) where a register or record is kept

**register of sasines :** REGISTER 2b

**registers** *pl of* REGISTER, *pres 3d sing of* REGISTER

**reg·is·ter·ship** \ˈ-ˌ-ˌship\ *n* [³*register* + *-ship*] **:** REGISTRARSHIP

**register tonnage** *n* **:** the gross tonnage of a ship less deductions (as of space actually occupied by engines and crew) and consisting of the part actually available for commercial use (as in the transport of freight or passengers)

**reg·is·tra·bil·i·ty** \ˌrejəstrəˈbilədē\ *n* **:** the quality or state of being registrable

**reg·is·tra·ble** \ˈrejəstrəbəl\ *also* **reg·is·ter·able** \-st(ə)rəbəl\ *adj* [¹*register* + *-able*] **:** capable of being registered **:** subject to registration

**reg·is·trant** \ˈrejəstrənt\ *n* -s [¹*register* + *-ant*] **:** one who registers; *esp* **:** one who by virtue of securing an official registration obtains a specific right or title of possession and use (as to a trademark)

**reg·is·trar** \ˈrejəˌsträr, -strä(r, ˌ-ˈ-\ *n* -s [alter. (prob. influenced by ML *registrarius*) of *registrer*] **1 :** one who registers **:** an official recorder or keeper of records ⟨a ~ of voters⟩ ⟨a ~ of a diocese⟩: as **a :** an officer of an educational institution charged with registering students, keeping academic records, issuing official information (as catalogs and bulletins), corresponding with candidates for admission, and evaluating their credentials **b :** an agent of a corporation (as a bank or trust company) appointed to keep account of and to authenticate issues of stocks and bonds **c :** an admitting officer at a hospital **d :** a guard at the entrance to a national forest who tells people of the forest laws and who keeps records of hunters and the game they bring out **2 :** a registering contrivance **:** REGISTER 8 **3** *Brit* **:** RESIDENT 4a

**registrar-general** *n, pl* **registrars-general :** the head of a general register office

**reg·is·trar·ship** \-ˌship\ *n* **:** the office or dignity of a registrar

**reg·is·trary** \ˈrejəstrərī\ *n* -ES [ML *registrarius*, fr. *registrum* register + L *-arius* -ary — more at REGISTER] **:** REGISTRAR

¹**registrate** *adj* [ME (Sc) *registrat*, fr. ML *registratus*, past part. of *registrare* to register] *obs* **:** REGISTERED

²**reg·is·trate** \ˈrejəˌstrāt, *usu* -ād·+V\ *vb* -ED/-ING/-S [ML *registratus*, past part. of *registrare*] *vt, obs* **:** REGISTER ~ *vi* **:** to select and adjust pipe organ stops

**reg·is·tra·tion** \ˌ-ˌ-ˈstrāshən\ *n* -s [MF or ML; MF, fr. ML *registration-, registratio*, fr. *registratus* (past part. of *registrare* to register) + L *-ion-, -io* -ion — more at REGISTER] **1 :** an act or the fact of registering ⟨completed ~ for a course of study⟩ ⟨the office will be open for the ~ of the unemployed⟩ **2 :** something registered (as a name or fact) **:** an entry in a register ⟨search for a particular ~⟩ **3 :** the number of individuals registered **:** ENROLLMENT ⟨a course with a large ~⟩ **4 a :** the art or act of registrating **b :** the combination of stops selected for the performing of a particular musical composition on an organ **5 :** an act whereby a person by appearing publicly before the proper officials gives oath about matters (as citizenship, age, residence) required of a qualified voter and signs a register to afford proof of his right to vote at a caucus, primary, or election **6 :** the act of bringing together (as two or more images in color photography or in animation motion picture photography) in complete agreement with respect to position **7 :** REGISTER 9 **8 :** a document certifying an act of registering ⟨carried his automobile ~ in his wallet⟩

**reg·is·tra·tion·al** \ˌ-ˌ-ˈstrāshənᵊl, -shnəl\ *adj* **:** of or relating to registration

**registration area** *n* **:** the part of the U.S. having a public registration of births or deaths that meets the standards set by the Census Bureau and including more than 95 percent of the population of the U.S.

**registration statement** *n* **:** a comprehensive statement required to be filed (as with the Securities and Exchange Commission) by all issuers of securities in the U.S. except those specifically exempted

**reg·is·trer** \ˈrejəstrə(r)\ *n* -s [ME *registrer, registrere*, modif. (influenced by ME *-er, -ere* -er) of MF *registreur*, fr. *registrer* to register + *-eur* -or — more at REGISTER] **1** *obs* **:** REGISTRAR **2** [²*register* + *-er*] **:** a registering device

**reg·is·try** \-strē, -ri\ *n* -ES [²*register* + *-ry*] **1 :** an act of registering **:** ENROLLMENT, REGISTRATION **2 a :** the condition or fact of being entered in a register ⟨a certificate of ~⟩; *specif* **:** the particular nationality of a ship as evidenced by such an entry **:** FLAG **b :** a certificate of registry of a ship ⟨ships of Greek ~⟩ **3 :** the place where a register is kept **:** a place of registration **:** REGISTER OFFICE **4 :** an official record book or an entry in one

**re·gi·um do·num** \ˌrējēəm ˈdōnəm\ *n, pl* **re·gia do·na** \-jēə ˈdōnə\ [NL, royal gift] **:** a former annual grant of public money in England for the Presbyterian clergy in Ireland

**re·gius professor** \ˈrēj(ē)əs-\ *n* [NL, royal professor] **:** a holder of a professorship founded by royal bounty or dependent on royal patronage at the older British universities

**re·give** \(ˈ)rē+\ *vt* [*re-* + *give*] **:** to give again **:** RESTORE

**regl** *abbr* regimental

**re·glaze** \(ˈ)rē+\ *vt* [*re-* + *glaze*] **:** to provide (as windows) with new glass **:** replace damaged or lost glass of

**regle** *vt* [MF *regler*, fr. LL *regulare* to regulate — more at REGULATE] *obs* **:** RULE, GOVERN

**reglement** *n* -s [MF, fr. *regler* + *-ment*] *obs* **:** REGULATION

**reg·le·men·ta·ry** \ˌregləˈmentərē, -n·trē\ *adj* [F *réglementaire*, fr. *règlement* regulation (fr. MF *reglement*) + *-aire* -ary] **:** of, relating to, or involving regulations

**reg·let** *also* **rig·let** \ˈreglət, *chiefly Brit* ˈrig-\ *n* -s [F *réglet* reglet, straightedge, fr. MF *reglet* straightedge, fr. *regle* straightedge, rule (fr. L *regula*) + *-et* — more at RULE] **1 :** a flat narrow molding used in architecture chiefly to separate parts or members of compartments or panels or doubled, turned, and interlaced to form knots, frets, or other ornaments or to cover joints between boards **:** FILLET, BATTEN **2 a :** a strip of wood less than type high and ranging in thickness from 3 point to 24 point or more used as spacing material in the makeup and lockup of type — compare FURNITURE, ⁴LEAD 2e **b :** reglets or material for them

**re·glow** \(ˈ)rē+\ *vi* [*re-* + *glow*] **:** to glow again or anew

**re·glue** \"+\ *vt* [*re-* + *glue*] **:** to make fast, whole, or secure again with glue ⟨~ a loose cover⟩

**reg·nal** \ˈregnəl\ *adj* [ML *regnalis*, fr. L *regnum* kingly government, rule, reign, kingdom + *-alis* -al — more at REIGN] **:** of or relating to a reign, kingdom, or king — **reg·nal·ly** \-nəlē, -li\ *adv*

**regnal year** *n* **:** a year of a sovereign's reign dating from the moment or anniversary of the moment of accession ⟨the first *regnal year* of George V was from May 6, 1910 to May 5, 1911⟩ — used esp. in the citation of laws

**reg·nan·cy** \ˈregnənsē, -si\ *n* -ES [*regnant* + *-cy*] **:** the quality or state of being regnant **:** SOVEREIGNTY, RULE

**reg·nant** \-nənt\ *adj* [L *regnant-, regnans*, pres. part. of *regnare* to reign — more at REIGN] **1 :** exercising rule or authority **:** REIGNING ⟨a queen ~⟩ **2 a :** having the chief power **:** exercising sway **:** DOMINANT ⟨filled with a ~ determination to defend herself —Gilbert Parker⟩ **b :** of common or widespread occurrence **:** PREVALENT ⟨the vices ~ —Jonathan Swift⟩

**re·gnault's formula** \rənˈyōz-\ *n, usu cap R* [after Henri V. *Regnault* †1878 Fr. chemist and physicist] **:** an empirical formula giving the specific enthalpy of steam at any centigrade temperature in calories per gram **:** $H = 606.5 + 0.305\ t$

**regnault's law** *n, usu cap R* **:** a statement in physics: the specific heat of a gas at constant pressure is the same whatever the pressure

**reg·num** \ˈregnəm\ *n, pl* **reg·na** \-nə\ [L] **1 a :** DOMINION, RULE **b :** tenure of power **2 :** any of the major divisions of animal, plant, and nonliving things into which natural objects fall **:** KINGDOM 6

**reg·o·lith** \ˈregəˌlith\ *n* -s [Gk *rhēgos* blanket + E *-lith*; akin to Gk *rhezein* to dye — more at RAGA] **:** MANTLEROCK

**re·gorge** \(ˈ)rē+\ *vb* [F *regorger*, fr. MF, fr. *re-* + *gorger* to gorge — more at GORGE] *vt* **1 :** to vomit up or out **:** throw back **:** DISGORGE **2** [*re-* + *gorge*] **:** to swallow again **:** swallow or suck back ⟨tides at highest mark *regorge* the flood —John Dryden⟩ ~ *vi* **:** to gush again **:** be thrown back

**reg·o·sol** \ˈregəˌsäl, -ˌsȯl\ *n* -s [*rego-* (as in *regolith*) + L *solum* ground, soil — more at SOLE] **:** an azonal soil consisting chiefly of soft and imperfectly consolidated material (as sand or recent volcanic ash), exhibiting little or no pedological development, and having no clearcut and specific morphology

**regr** *abbr* registrar

**re·grade** \(ˈ)rē+\ *vt* [*re-* + *grade*] **1 :** to provide (as a road or slope) with a new grade **2 :** to assign to a new category or grade ⟨*regrading* stored apples⟩; *often* **:** to regroup (students) for purposes of more effective instruction

¹**re·grant** \"+\ *vt* [*re-* + *grant*] **:** to grant back or again ⟨the charter was not ~*ed*⟩

²**regrant** \"\ *n* **:** a granting again (as back to a former proprietor or by way of renewal of a grant)

**re·grasp** \"+\ *vt* [*re-* + *grasp*] **:** to take again into one's grasp **:** seize hold of anew ⟨seeking to ~ lost liberties⟩
**re·grass** \"+\ *vt* [*re-* + *grass*] **:** to plant again with grass **:** cause grass to grow on (as barren or cutover land)
**¹re·grate** \rə'grāt, rē'-\ *archaic Scot var of* REGRET
**²regrate** \"\ *vt* -ED/-ING/-S [ME *regraten*, fr. MF *regrater*, fr. *regratier* regrater] **1 :** to buy up (necessities of life) at a market or fair with the intention of reselling in or near the same place at a profit — compare ENGROSS **2 :** to sell or dispose of (commodities bought in regrating) usu. at retail
**³regrate** \"\ *vt* -ED/-ING/-S [F *regratter*, fr. *re-* + *gratter* to scratch, scrape, fr. MF *grater* — more at GRATE] **:** to remove the outer surface of (masonry) so as to freshen in appearance
**re·grat·er** *also* **re·gra·tor** \-ād·ə(r)\ *n* -S [*regrater* fr. ME *regrater, regratere*, fr. MF *regratier*, fr. OF; *regrator* fr. ME *regratour*, fr. AF, alter. (influenced by AF *-our* -or, fr. OF *-eor*, *-eur*) of MF *regratier;* akin to OSp *regatero* regrater, OIt *rigattiere*] **1 a** *chiefly Brit* **:** one that regrates supplies or necessities **b** *dial* **:** a middleman who travels about the country buying up farm produce for market **2** *chiefly Brit* **:** one that gets the profits or credits due to another esp. by irregular means
**re·grede** \rə'grēd\ *vi* -ED/-ING/-S [L *regredi* to go back] *astron* **:** to go back **:** RETROGRADE
**¹re·greet** \(')rē+\ *vt* [*re-* + *greet*] **1** *obs* **:** to greet again **2** *archaic* **:** to return the salutation of **:** offer a greeting to
**²regreet** *n* **1** *obs* **:** a greeting in return **:** a return salutation **2 regreets** *pl, obs* **:** a message or words of greeting **:** GREETINGS
**¹re·gress** \'rē,gres\ *n* -ES [ME *regresse*, fr. L *regressus*, fr. *regressus*, past part. of *regredi* to go back, fr. *re-* + *gradi* to step, go — more at GRADE] **1 :** an act or the privilege of going or coming back **:** WITHDRAWAL, EGRESS ⟨free ingress and ~ for ships⟩: as **a :** the right or power of falling back on another as primarily liable **:** RECOURSE **b :** reentry or right of reentry (as upon lands redeemed from forfeiture or default or upon a vacated benefice) **2 :** RETROGRESSION, RETROGRADATION **3 :** the act of reasoning backward (as from effect to cause)
**²re·gress** \rə'gres, rē'-\ *vb* -ED/-ING/-ES [L *regressus*, past part. of *regredi* to go back] *vi* **:** to make or undergo regress **:** be subject to or exhibit regression **:** RETROGRADE; *often* **:** to tend to approach or revert to a mean ~ *vt* **:** to induce a state of psychological regression in (as by hypnosis or suggestion)
**re·gres·sion** \ₑ'greshən\ *n* -S [L *regression-, regressio*, fr. *regressus* (past part. of *regredi* to go back) + *-ion-, -io* -ion] **1 a :** an act or the fact of regressing **:** REGRESS, RETROGRESSION, REVERSION **b :** a hypothetical reversal of direction in a biological evolutionary process that is sometimes invoked to explain the extinction of the graptolites and similar paleontologic phenomena **2 :** a trend or shift toward a mean or toward a lower or less perfect state (as of function or differentiation): as **a :** apparent trend of offspring in respect to heritable characters away from specializations exhibited by their parents and toward the mean development characteristic of their biotype **b :** the fact that in associated or correlated pairs on selecting one member with a given value for its character the second has on the average a less value and regresses toward the value for the mean of all members of the class **c :** a gradual spontaneous diminution or fading of a latent or developed photographic image **d** (1) **:** progressive decline (as in size, severity, or intensity) of a manifestation of disease ⟨marked ~ of a tumor often follows radiation⟩ ⟨~ of symptoms followed the climax⟩ (2) **:** gradual loss of specific differentiation and function by a body part esp. as a physiological change accompanying aging ⟨menopausal ~ of the ovaries⟩ **e** (1) **:** reversion in behavior, thinking, attitudes, or identifications to an earlier mental or behavioral level or to an earlier stage of psychosexual development in response to organismic stress or to suggestion — compare FIXATION (2) **:** gradual loss of memories and acquired skills (as in old age) in which the order of development is reversed so that the most recent memories are lost first and the earliest acquisitions are the last to go **3 :** retrograde motion esp. of an astronomical orbital characteristic ⟨~ of the moon's nodes⟩
**regression coefficient** *n* **:** a coefficient in a regression equation **:** the slope of the regression line
**regression curve** *n* **:** a curve that best fits particular data according to some principle (as the principle of least squares)
**regression equation** *n* **:** the equation of a regression curve
**regression line** *n* **:** a regression curve that is a straight line
**re·gres·sive** \rə'gresiv, rē'-, -sēv *also* -səv\ *adj* **1 :** that regresses or tends to regress **:** RETROGRESSIVE **2 :** characterized by or derived from reasoning backward (as from effect to cause or from observed facts to a principle) **3 :** constituting or relating to a technique of micrological staining in which the stain is applied to excess and the excess later removed in order to enhance the specificity of the staining **4 a :** of, relating to, typical of, or tending to produce regression ⟨~ tissue changes⟩ **b :** being, characterized by, or developing in the course of an evolutionary process involving increasing simplification of bodily structure **5 :** having the nature of the first of two sounds dependent on the nature of the second ⟨~ assimilation⟩ **6 :** decreasing in rate as the base increases — used of taxation and methods of apportioning taxes **7 :** DEGRESSIVE b — **re·gres·sive·ly** \-səvlē, -li\ *adv* — **re·gres·sive·ness** \-sivnəs, -sēv- *also* -səv-\ *n* -ES
**regressive sorites** *n* **:** a sorites in which the order of the premises is reversed
**re·gres·siv·i·ty** \,rē,gre'sivəd·ē\ *n* -ES **:** the quality or state of being regressive **:** tendency toward regression
**re·gres·sor** \rə'gresə(r), rē'-\ *n* -S **:** one that regresses or is regressing
**re·gres·sus** \-səs\ *n* -ES [L — more at REGRESS] **:** REGRESS
**¹re·gret** \rə'gret, rē'-, *usu* -ed·+V\ *vb* **regretted; regretted; regretting; regrets** [ME *regretten*, fr. MF *regreter, regrater*, fr. OF, fr. *re-* + *-greter, -grater* (of Scand origin; akin to ON *grāta* to weep) — more at GREET] *vt* **1 :** to remember with sorrow or grief **:** mourn the loss or death of **:** miss poignantly ⟨that fair lady whom thou dost ~ —P.B.Shelley⟩ **2 :** to have dissatisfaction, misgivings, or distress of mind concerning **:** be keenly sorry for ⟨~ one's mistakes⟩ ⟨~ my inability to be present⟩ ~ *vi* **:** to experience regret
**²regret** \"\ *n* -S [MF, fr. OF, lamentation, fr. *regreter, regrater*, v.] **1 :** sorrow aroused by circumstances beyond one's control or power to repair **:** grief or pain tinged with disappointment, dissatisfaction, longing, remorse, or comparable emotion ⟨a scene that awakens ~⟩ ⟨keen ~ for past deeds⟩ **2 a :** an expression of sorrow, disappointment, or other distressing emotion ⟨weary him with vain ~s⟩ **b regrets** *pl* **:** a note politely declining an invitation ⟨send ~s⟩ **syn** see SORROW
**re·gret·ful** \ₑ'ₑfəl\ *adj* **:** full of regret **:** indulging in regrets **:** REPINING — **re·gret·ful·ly** \-fəlē, -li\ *adv* — **re·gret·ful·ness** \-lnəs\ *n* -ES
**re·gret·less** \ₑ'ₑləs\ *adj* **:** feeling no regret **:** free from regrets
**re·gret·ta·ble** *also* **re·gret·able** \rə'gred·əbəl, rē'-, -etəb-\ *adj* **:** admitting of, deserving, or demanding regret — **re·gret·ta·ble·ness** \-bəlnəs\ *n* -ES — **re·gret·ta·bly** \-blē, -li\ *adv*
**re·gret·ter** \ₑ'gred·ə(r), -etə-\ *n* -S **:** one that regrets
**re·gret·ting·ly** *adv* **:** in a regretting manner **:** with regret
**re·grind** \(')rē+\ *vt* [*re-* + *grind*] **:** to grind anew **:** to reshape or refit by grinding ⟨had his valves *reground*⟩
**re·group** \"+\ *vb* [*re-* + *group*] *vt* **:** to form into a new group ⟨~*ed* the products to make a better display⟩; *esp* **:** to alter the tactical formation of (a military force) usu. preparatory to beginning a new phase of an operation ~ *vi* **:** to form a new group (as in altering the tactical formation of a military force) — **re·groupment** \"+\ *n*
**re·grow** \"+\ *vb* [*re-* + *grow*] *vt* **:** to grow (as a missing part) anew ⟨many lower vertebrates can ~ lost limbs or tails⟩ ~ *vi* **:** to grow again **:** continue to grow after interruption or injury ⟨forests ~ but slowly after a severe fire⟩
**re·growth** \"+\ *n* [*re-* + *growth*] **:** a product of regrowing; *esp* **:** the vegetation that appears after denudation of land (as by clearing, burning, or excessive grazing)
**regs** *pl of* REG
**regt** *abbr* **1** regent **2** regiment
**regtl** *abbr* regimental
**reguardant** *var of* REGARDANT
**¹re·guer·don** \rə'gərdᵊn\ *vt* [ME *reguerdonen*, fr. MF *reguerdoner*, fr. OF *reguerdoner, reguerredoner*, fr. *re-* + *guerdoner, guerredoner* to reward — more at GUERDON] *archaic* **:** REWARD
**²reguerdon** \"\ *n* [ME *reguerdoun*, fr. MF *reguerdon*, fr. OF, fr. *reguerdoner, reguerredoner*, v.] *archaic* **:** REWARD
**reg·u·la** \'regyələ\ *n, pl* **reg·u·lae** \-,lē\ [L *regula* straightedge, rule] **1 :** an architectural band or fillet esp. when one of a series beneath the taenia in a Doric architrave of which each corresponds to a triglyph above and has a row of six guttae on its lower side **2 :** RULE ⟨the authoritative ~ for community life⟩
**reg·u·la·ble** \'regyələbəl\ *adj* [*regul*ate + *-able*] **:** capable of being regulated
**reg·u·lant** \-lənt\ *n* -S [*regul*ate + *-ant*] **:** a substance or agent that regulates something (as plant growth)
**¹reg·u·lar** \'regyələ(r), ÷ -g(ə)l-\ *adj* [ME *reguler*, fr. MF, fr. LL *regularis* canonical, regular, containing a set of rules, fr. L, of or belonging to a bar, fr. *regula* straightedge, rule + *-aris* -ar — more at RULE] **1 :** belonging to a Christian monastic order or community **:** living under or relating to a monastic rule ⟨the ~ clergy⟩ — opposed to *secular* **2 a :** formed, built, arranged, or ordered according to some established rule, law, principle, or type **:** harmonious in form, structure, or arrangement **:** SYMMETRICAL ⟨~ verse⟩ ⟨a man with ~ features⟩ ⟨a disciplined ~ landscape⟩ **b** (1) **:** both equilateral and equiangular ⟨a ~ polygon⟩ (2) **:** having faces that are congruent regular polygons and all the polyhedral angles congruent ⟨a ~ polyhedron⟩ **c** *of a flower* **:** having the members of each whorl symmetrical with respect to form **:** ACTINOMORPHIC — compare IRREGULAR **d :** having or constituting an isometric system ⟨~ crystals⟩ **3 a :** steady or uniform in course, practice, or occurrence **:** not subject to unexplained or irrational variation **:** steadily pursued **:** ORDERLY, METHODICAL ⟨~ habits⟩ **b** (1) **:** returning, recurring, or received at stated, fixed, or uniform intervals ⟨a ~ income⟩ ⟨in the ~ course of events⟩ (2) **:** functioning at proper intervals — used esp. of the bowels **4 a :** constituted, selected, conducted, made, or otherwise handled in conformity with established or prescribed usages, rules, or discipline ⟨a ~ meeting⟩ ⟨a ~ election⟩ **b :** NORMAL, STANDARD, CORRECT: as (1) **:** undeviating in conformance to a standard set (as by convention, established authority, or a particular group) (2) **:** being such without any doubt **:** THOROUGH, COMPLETE, UNMITIGATED ⟨a ~ scoundrel⟩ (3) *slang* **:** like other good fellows in views and ways **c** (1) **:** conforming to the normal or usual manner of inflection ⟨~ English nouns take *-s* or *-es* plurals⟩ (2) **:** WEAK 8a **d** *of a postage stamp* **:** issued without restriction for the payment of all types of postage ⟨the list included stamps of the ~ issue as well as airmails, special deliveries, and commemoratives⟩ **5 a :** of, relating to, or constituting the regular army of a state ⟨a ~ soldier⟩ **b :** constituting or made up of individuals properly recognized as legitimate combatants in war **6** *usu cap* **:** of, relating to, or belonging to the Regular Baptists **7 :** of, relating to, or being a transaction on a stock exchange requiring delivery of the securities involved on the third full business day after purchase
**syn** NORMAL, TYPICAL, NATURAL: REGULAR may imply conformity to a prescribed rule, standard, or established pattern ⟨a *regular* meeting of the society⟩ ⟨following the *regular* procedure of the legislature⟩ ⟨their action was made *regular* and legal —J.R.Green⟩ NORMAL suggests falling within the limits of a norm ⟨if a boy has abnormal mental powers in some direction, combined with poor physique and great nervousness, he may be quite incapable of fitting into a crowd of *normal* boys —Bertrand Russell⟩ ⟨her intensity, which would leave no emotion on a *normal* plane, irritated the youth into a frenzy —D.H.Lawrence⟩ TYPICAL applies to whatever shows to a marked degree characters or characteristics of a type, class, or group, sometimes to the exclusion of distinctive individual characteristics ⟨peculiar to himself, not *typical* of Greek ideas —G.L.Dickinson⟩ ⟨until twenty years ago a *typical* English country town with wide High Street, narrow Market Street, picturesque Market Square, two ancient hostelries, fine old church, gabled almshouses —Compton Mackenzie⟩ ⟨what he had to do was to give plot and accurate delineation of character to the winds, make his personages *typical* rather than individual —Richard Garnett †1906⟩ NATURAL describes whatever conforms with its nature, kind, or essence ⟨the *natural* love of a mother for her child⟩ ⟨water as the *natural* environment of a fish⟩ These words are often interchangeable and are often used together ⟨a mode of thinking, a distinctive type of reaction, gets itself established, in the course of a complex historical development, as typical, as *normal* —Edward Sapir⟩
**²regular** \"\ *n* -S **1 :** a member of a Christian monastic order or community following a rule **:** one of the regular clergy ⟨controversy between the seculars and the ~*s*⟩ **2 :** a soldier in a regular army — usu. used in pl. **3 a :** one (as a customer or contributor) that is regular esp. in pursuing a fixed or recurrent routine **b :** one that can be trusted or depended upon with assurance **c :** a player on an athletic team who usu. starts every game **4 :** a clothing size designed to fit the person of average height
**³regular** \"\ *adv, chiefly dial* **:** REGULARLY
**⁴regular** \"\ *adj* [NL *Regularia* & NL *Regulares*] **:** of or relating to the Regularia or Regulares
**regular army** *n* **:** a permanently organized body constituting the army of a state and being often identical with the standing army that is maintained by a federal government
**regular baptist** *n, usu cap R&B* **1 :** a member of a moderately Calvinistic Baptist sect that is found chiefly in the southern U.S., represents the original English Baptists before the division into Particular and General Baptists, and observes close communion and foot washing **2 :** a Baptist who belongs to the General Association of Regular Baptist Churches formed in 1932 by churches which had withdrawn from the Northern Baptist Convention
**regular canon** *n, sometimes cap R&C* **:** CANON REGULAR
**regular canoness** *n* **:** a canoness bound by a vow of poverty and following a strict religious rule
**regular clerk** *n* **:** CLERK REGULAR
**regular clerk of st. paul** *usu cap R&C&S&P* [after *St. Paul ab* A.D. 67 Christian apostle to the Gentiles] **:** a member of a Roman Catholic congregation founded in 1530 in Milan — called also *Barnabite*
**regular deposit** *n* **:** SPECIAL DEPOSIT
**reg·u·lar·es** \,regyə'la(a)(,)rēz\ *n pl, cap* [NL, fr. LL, pl. of *regularis* regular] *in former classifications* **:** an order or other group comprising all symmetrical Blastoidea
**¹reg·u·lar·ia** \,ₑₑ'la(a)rēə\ *n pl, cap* [NL, fr. LL, neut. pl. of *regularis* regular] *in some classifications* **:** a division of Echinoidea including the ordinary sea urchins that have a more or less globular symmetrical shell with 20 meridional rows of plates and the mouth and anus at opposite poles
**²regularia** \"\ [NL, fr. LL, neut. pl. of *regularis* regular] *syn of* REGULARES
**reg·u·lar·i·ty** \,regyə'larəd·ē, -rətē, -i *also* -ler-\ *n* -ES [F *régularité*, fr. MF *regularité*, fr. LL *regularis* regular + MF *-té* -ty] **1 :** the quality or state of being regular ⟨~ of outline⟩ ⟨~ of habits⟩ **2 :** something that is regular
**regularity theory** *n* **:** a view held by Humeans: an event may be the cause of another event without there being a necessary connection between the two
**reg·u·lar·iza·tion** \,regyələrə'zāshən, -,rī'z-\ *n* -S **:** the act or an instance of regularizing ⟨his ~ of their informal marriage⟩
**reg·u·lar·ize** \'ₑₑₑ,rīz\ *vt* -ED/-ING/-S *see -ize in Explan Notes* **:** to make regular (as by conformance to law, rules, or custom) **:** make steady or uniform
**reg·u·lar·iz·er** \-,rīzə(r)\ *n* -S **:** one that regularizes
**regular lay** *n* **:** MEDIUM LAY
**regular–lay rope** *n* **:** a wire rope having the wires in the strands twisted in directions opposite to the strands in the rope
**regular lot** *n* **:** a number or amount regularly intended when the number or amount is not specified; *esp* **:** a standard unit of trade (as on an exchange) of a commodity or stock
**reg·u·lar·ly** \'regyələ(r)lē ÷ -gyə(r)l, ÷ -g(ə)lə(r)l, |i\ *adv* **:** in a regular, orderly, lawful, or methodical way **:** SYMMETRICALLY, CORRECTLY, PROPERLY
**regular ode** *n* **:** an ode that is divided into sections each having a strophe and an antistrophe of identical and an epode of contrasting form
**regular peloria** *n* **:** peloria in which symmetry is attained by decrease in number of normally irregular parts — compare IRREGULAR PELORIA
**regular pyramid** *n* **:** a pyramid whose base is a regular polygon and whose vertex is on the perpendicular to the base through its center
**regular reflection** *n* **:** reflection such that the angle of reflection of the light is equal to the angle of incidence and on the opposite side of the normal to the point of incidence
**regulars** *pl of* REGULAR
**regular sequence** *n* **:** a sequence possessing a limit **:** a convergent sequence
**regular solid** *n* **:** any of five regular polyhedrons **:** a regular tetrahedron, hexahedron, octahedron, dodecahedron, or icosahedron
**regular year** *n* **:** a common year of 354 days or a leap year of 384 days in the Jewish calendar — see YEAR table
**reg·u·lat·able** \'regyə,lād·əbəl, -lātə-, ,ₑₑ'ₑₑₑ\ *adj* **:** capable of being regulated
**reg·u·late** \'ₑₑ,lāt, *usu* -ād·+V\ *vb* -ED/-ING/-S [LL *regulatus*, past part. of *regulare*, fr. L *regula* straightedge, rule — more at RULE] *vt* **1 :** to govern or direct according to rule ⟨laws which ~ the succession of seasons⟩; *usu* **:** to bring under the control of law or constituted authority **:** make regulations for or concerning ⟨~ the industries of a country⟩ **2 a :** to reduce to order, method, or uniformity **:** REGULARIZE ⟨~ one's habits⟩ **b** *obs* **:** DISCIPLINE **3 :** to fix the time, amount, degree, or rate of (as by adjusting, rectifying) ⟨~ the pressure of a tire⟩; *also* **:** to adjust so as to work accurately or regularly ⟨~ a clock⟩ ~ *vi* **:** to make regulations
**regulated company** *n* **:** a mercantile association holding by government charter exclusive trading rights with specified lands and combining freedom for the individual to trade on his own capital with regulations limiting trade in order to keep up prices
**regulating box** *n* **:** a rheostat for regulating the electric current passing through the field-magnet coils (as of a dynamo)
**regulating station** *n* **:** a military command agency that controls all movements of personnel and supplies into and out of a given area
**¹reg·u·la·tion** \,ₑₑ'lāshən\ *n* -S [*regulate* + *-ion*] **1 :** an act of regulating or the condition of being regulated ⟨the ~ of her mind⟩ ⟨business suffering from undue ~⟩ **2 a :** an authoritative rule or principle dealing with details of procedure; *esp* **:** one intended to promote safety and efficiency (as in a school or factory) **b :** a rule or order having the force of law issued by an executive authority of a government usu. under power granted by a constitution or delegated by legislation: as (1) **:** a piece of subordinate legislation issued by a British administrative unit under the authority and subject to the veto of parliament — compare PROVISIONAL ORDER, STATUTORY ORDER (2) **:** one issued by the president of the U.S. or by an authorized subordinate — called also *executive order* (3) **:** an administrative order issued by an executive department or a regulatory commission of the U.S. government to apply and supplement broad congressional legislative enactments **3 :** the percentage variation in some characteristic quantity (as voltage) as a machine or apparatus becomes loaded; *also* **:** the ratio of deviation of such a quantity at rated load to its normal value at no load **4 a :** redistribution of material (as in an embryo) to restore a damaged or lost part independent of new tissue growth — compare REGENERATION **b :** the mechanism by which an early embryo maintains essentially normal development in the face of abnormal conditions **c :** DETERMINATION **syn** see LAW
**²regulation** \ₑ;ₑₑ;ₑₑ\ *adj* **:** prescribed by or being in accord with regulations ⟨the ~ cap of a nurse⟩; *broadly* **:** USUAL, CUSTOMARY ⟨the ~ accompaniments of a Thanksgiving dinner⟩
**¹reg·u·la·tive** \'ₑₑ,lād·iv, -,lə|, |t|, |ēv *also* |əv\ *adj* **1 :** tending to regulate **:** having regulation as an aim ⟨a ~ statute⟩ **2 a :** directing or regulating in the manner of a rule to be followed or an end to be attained — compare REGULATIVE PRINCIPLE **b :** constituting in Kantianism the ideas of reason (as First Cause) that arise in the mind because ideal knowledge requires the conception of the totality of conditions for anything given as conditioned — contrasted with *constitutive* **3 :** capable of regulation **:** involving progressive determination and restriction of initially totipotent material — used of a developing zygote or its state; compare MOSAIC
**²regulative** \"\ *n* -S **:** something (as a principle or enactment) that has regulative force
**reg·u·la·tive·ly** \|əvlē, -li\ *adv* **:** in a regulative manner **:** so as to be regulative
**regulative principle** *n* **:** a rule or principle of procedure: as **a** *archaic* **:** the principle underlying syllogistic inference or in accordance with which any particular inference is drawn **b :** a rule of procedure to which there is no alternative if the desired end is to be secured although it cannot itself assure attainment
**reg·u·la·tor** \'ₑₑ,lād·ə(r), -lātə-\ *n* -S **:** one that regulates: as **a** (1) **:** one of a board of seven appointed by King James II in 1687 with powers to appoint and remove officers and freemen at their discretion for the purpose of influencing the election of members of Parliament (2) *usu cap* **:** a member of any of various associations of the poorer people in No. Carolina existing from 1767 to 1771, formed to resist official extortion, refusing to pay taxes, and committing many deeds of violence (3) **:** a member of any of various bands or volunteer committees in the U.S. formed in newly occupied or settled regions before the establishment of local government to preserve order, prevent crime, and administer justice **b** (1) **:** a person who regulates mechanisms (as clocks) or conditions (as of traffic) (2) **:** a worker who hangs or bolts up ship plates on the frame of a ship **c** (1) **:** an automatic device for maintaining the current, voltage, speed, or other characteristic of a machine, transformer, or comparable device at a specified value or for adjusting these quantities at will (2) **:** a lever or index in a watch for altering the effective length of the hairspring to make the watch go faster or slower (3) **:** a standard clock used for timing watches and clocks — compare ASTRONOMICAL CLOCK (4) **:** GOVERNOR 4b (5) **:** a sliding door for controlling ventilation in a mine (6) **:** a balance valve for controlling the admission of steam to the steam chest in a locomotive (7) **:** a reducing valve or steamₑ pressure regulating device (8) *Brit* **:** a throttle on a locomotive **d** (1) **:** a substance added in a reaction to regulate the amount of another substance formed (2) **:** GROWTH REGULATOR (3) **:** PLANT REGULATOR
**regulator pin** *n* **:** either of two short upright thin cylindrical pins that are fitted in a watch regulator bearing or banking the hairspring in such a manner that moving the regulator into a position in which the pins touch the hairspring closer to its center shortens the spring and causes the watch to run faster
**reg·u·la·to·ry** \'ₑₑlə,tōrē, -tȯr-, -ri\ *adj* **1 :** of or relating to regulation **:** making or concerned with the making of regulations **:** REGULATIVE ⟨~ measures⟩ ⟨a local ~ body⟩ **2 :** subject to regulation ⟨~ products that are considered dangerous and may be shipped only under stipulated conditions of packaging, labeling, and handling⟩
**¹reg·u·line** \'regyə,līn, -,lən\ *adj* [prob. fr. (assumed) NL *regulinus*, fr. ML *regulus* + L *-inus* -ine] **:** of, relating to, or being a regulus ⟨~ silver⟩ ⟨a ~ deposit⟩
**²reguline** \-,lən, -,līn\ *n* -S **:** a smooth coherent electrodeposit of metal
**reg·u·lus** \'regyələs\ *n* [ML, metallic antimony, fr. L, petty king, fr. *reg-, rex* king + *-ulus* — more at ROYAL] **1** *pl* **reguluses** \-ləsəz\ *or* **reg·u·li** \-,lī\ **a :** the more or less impure button, globule, or mass of metal or metallic substance formed beneath the slag in smelting and reducing ores ⟨~ of antimony⟩ **b :** the metal of such a mass **:** coarse metal **:** MATTE **2** *pl* **reguluses** *or* **reguli** [L] **:** a petty king **:** a ruler of little power or consequence **3 a** *pl* **reguluses** *or* **reguli** [LL, fr. L] **:** KINGLET **b** *cap* [NL, fr. LL] **:** a genus (the type of the family Regulidae) of passerine birds consisting of the kinglets **4** *pl* **reguluses** *or* **reguli** [LL, fr. L] **:** a mythical Nubian snake supposed to kill its victim by its hiss — compare BASILISK, COCKATRICE

**re·gur** \'regər, 'rāg-\ *n* -s *sometimes cap* [Hindi *regar*] **:** a rich black loam of India similar to the Russian chernozem

**re·gurge** \rə'gərj, rē'-, -gəj,-gəij\ *vb* [by shortening & alter.] **:** REGURGITATE

**re·gur·gi·tant** \-jəd·ənt, -ətənt *also* -t°nt\ *adj* [ML *regurgitant-, regurgitans*, pres. part. of *regurgitare*] **:** throwing or flowing back **:** REGURGITATING

**re·gur·gi·tate** \-jə,tāt, *usu* -ād·+V\ *vb* -ED/-ING/-S [ML *regurgitatus*, past part. of *regurgitare*, fr. L *re-* + LL *gurgitare* to engulf — more at GURGITATION] *vi* **:** to become thrown or poured back **:** gush, rush, or surge back ~ *vt* **:** to throw, cast, or pour back or out again (as from a cavity)

**re·gur·gi·ta·tion** \(')rē,gərjə'tāshən, -gəj-,-gəij-, rə,⸗⸗'⸗⸗\ *n* [ML *regurgitation-, regurgitatio*, fr. *regurgitatus* (past part. of *regurgitare*) + L *-ion-, -io* -ion] **:** an act of flowing, pouring, or gushing back or out again; *specif* **:** reversal of the natural direction in which the current or contents flow through a tube or cavity of the body (as the casting up of incompletely digested food by some birds feeding their young or the backward flow of blood through a defective heart valve) ⟨mitral ~⟩ — **re·gur·gi·ta·tion·al** \-shən°l, -shnəl\ *adj*

**reh** \'rā\ *n* -s [Hindi *rēh*] **:** a mixture of soluble sodium salts appearing as an efflorescence on the ground in arid or semiarid regions in India

**re·ha·bil·i·tant** \,rē(h)ə'bilətənt *sometimes* ,rēha'b-\ *n* -s [*rehabilitate* + *-ant*] **:** a disabled person undergoing rehabilitation

**re·ha·bil·i·tate** \-lə,tāt, *usu* -ād·+V\ *vt* -ED/-ING/-S [ML *rehabilitatus*, past part. of *rehabilitare*, fr. L *re-* + LL *habilitare* to habilitate — more at HABILITATE] **1 a :** to restore (as a delinquent) by a formal act or declaration to a former right, rank, or privilege lost or forfeited **:** invest or clothe again with some right, authority, or dignity **:** restore to a former capacity **:** qualify again **:** REINSTATE ⟨the judges . . . were *rehabilitated* by the payment of a fine —William Stubbs⟩ **b :** to restore to good repute by vindicating **:** clear of unjust or unfounded charges **:** reestablish the good name of ⟨a campaign to ~ the memory of . . . England's wickedest king —*N.Y. Times*⟩ ⟨wish to ~ this country in the eyes of those nations whose good opinion we value —Edith Summerskill⟩ **2 a :** to put on a proper basis or into a previous good state **:** restore (as something damaged or decayed) to a state of efficiency and good management ⟨~ . . . forests that once supplied a large share of the country's timber —*Amer. Guide Series: Minn.*⟩ ⟨~ wastelands⟩ ⟨~ slum areas⟩ **b :** to restore to a condition of health or normal activity by a process of medical rehabilitation ⟨~ a person after he has lost his sight —*Current Biog.*⟩ **c :** to restore to a useful and constructive place in society through social rehabilitation ⟨nuns who attempt to ~ a prostitute —Curtis Harrington⟩ **d :** to restore to a state of solvency or efficiency ⟨~ a company financially⟩ ⟨~ equipment⟩

**re·ha·bil·i·ta·tion** \,⸗⸗,⸗⸗'tāshən\ *n* -s *often attrib* [ML *rehabilitation-, rehabilitatio*, fr. *rehabilitatus* (past part. of *rehabilitare* to rehabilitate) + L *-ion-, -io* -ion] **1 :** the action or process of rehabilitating or of being rehabilitated: as **a :** the reestablishment of the reputation or standing of a person **:** the vindication of one's character **b :** the physical restoration of a sick or disabled person by therapeutic measures and reeducation to participation in the activities of a normal life within the limitations of his physical disability ⟨the ~ of patients with a lower extremity amputation —*Jour. Amer. Med. Assoc.*⟩ ⟨~ after coronary occlusion⟩ **c :** the process of restoring an individual (as a convict, mental patient, or disaster victim) to a useful and constructive place in society through some form of vocational, correctional, or therapeutic retraining or through relief, financial aid, or other reconstructive measure **d :** the restoration of something damaged or deteriorated to a prior good condition **:** improvement to a higher level or greater value ⟨the ~ of devastated libraries —*Amer. Library Assoc. Bull.*⟩ ⟨the ~ of the power of Britain —R.H.Gabriel⟩ ⟨~ of buildings in a slum area⟩ **2 :** the result of rehabilitating **:** the state of being rehabilitated ⟨the ultimate aim of any antituberculosis program is the ~ of the patient —*Jour. Amer. Med. Assoc.*⟩ ⟨this inmate's . . . struggle toward ~ —*Saturday Rev.*⟩

**re·ha·bil·i·ta·tive** \,⸗⸗'⸗⸗,tād·|iv, - āt|, |ēv *also* |əv\ *adj* [*rehabilitate* + *-ive*] **:** of, relating to, or designed to accomplish rehabilitation ⟨from a penal to a ~ philosophy —J.B.Costello⟩ ⟨~ treatment⟩

**re·ha·bil·i·tee** \,⸗⸗,⸗⸗'tē\ *n* -s [*rehabilitate* + *-ee*] **:** one who is in the process of being rehabilitated ⟨this form of therapy fitted . . . our ~s' needs —M.C.Bettis⟩

**re·hair** \(')rē+\ *vt* [*re-* + *hair*] **:** to attach new hair to (a bow of a musical instrument)

**re·hallow** \"+\ *vt* [*re-* + *hallow*] **:** to hallow again ⟨though it is sullied . . . your august coldness shall ~ it —Gordon Bottomley⟩

**re·hammer** \"+\ *vt* [*re-* + *hammer*] **:** to hammer again

**re·handle** \"+\ *vt* [*re-* + *handle*] **:** to handle again ⟨~ tobacco before using⟩; *esp* **:** to give a new and different treatment to (as a subject or theme) ⟨*rehandled* the legend⟩

**re·hang** \"+\ *vt* [*re-* + *hang*] **:** to hang again esp. in a new and different way ⟨~ the portraits in the gallery⟩ ⟨take off the dust covers and ~ the curtains⟩

**re·harmonize** \"+\ *vt* [*re-* + *harmonize*] **:** to harmonize again or anew; *specif* **:** to provide (as a melody or musical passage) with a different harmony

**¹re·hash** \"+\ *vt* [*re-* + *hash*] **:** to hash over again **:** present or use again in another form without real change or improvement in substance **:** restate (as old arguments) in new language ⟨~*ed* the previous night's ball —Lillian Ross⟩ ⟨does more than ~ an old tale —T.H.Williams⟩ ⟨~*ed* all their old propaganda charges —*N.Y. Times*⟩

**²re·hash** \'rē+,- ⸗'⸗\ *n* **1 :** a product of rehashing **:** something presented in a new form without change of substance ⟨the text . . . is simply a dull ~ of the operatic plots —John Haverstick⟩ ⟨popular ~*es* of history and legend are many —T.F.Reddaway⟩ ⟨a ~ of stale ideas hurriedly dashed off —J.F.McComas⟩ **2 :** the action or process of rehashing ⟨in the course of the long ~ of old arguments —A.H. Vandenberg †1951⟩

**rehave** *vt* [ME *rehaven*, fr. *re-* + *haven* to have] *obs* **:** to have or get again **:** REGAIN

**re·hear** \(')rē+\ *vt* [back-formation fr. *rehearing*] **:** to hear judicially again or anew ⟨the Interstate Commerce Commission . . . proceeded to ~ the matters appertaining to that application —*McLean v. Keith*⟩

**re·hearing** \(')rē+\ *n* [*re-* + *hearing*] **:** a second or new hearing (as of a trial or an argument on appeal) by the same tribunal and upon the pleadings and depositions already in the case

**re·hears·al** \rə'hərsəl, rē'h-, -həs-,-həis-\ *n* -s [ME *rehersaille*, fr. *rehersen* to rehearse + *-aille* -al] **1 :** the action of rehearsing ⟨a series of blackout ~s —Winifred Bambrick⟩ ⟨require a ~ of the whole of American history —H.S.Commager⟩ ⟨seemed like a ~ of her own life, terrible in its vividness —Sherwood Anderson⟩ **2 :** a private recital, performance, or practice session held in preparation for a public appearance ⟨much confusion at the ~⟩

**re·hearse** \-s\ *vb* -ED/-ING/-S [ME *rehersen, rehercen*, fr. MF *rehercier* to repeat, to harrow over again, fr. *re-* + *hercier* to harrow, fr. *herce* harrow — more at HEARSE] *vt* **1 a :** to repeat or say again (as something already said or heard) ⟨the term is duly *rehearsed* in most of the history books —S.L.Faison⟩ ⟨no need to ~ here in detail the familiar story —F.L.Allen⟩ **b :** to recite or repeat aloud in a formal manner **:** say or tell over *usu.* from beginning to end ⟨as if she had been in the dock she *rehearsed* her poor tale —Maurice Hewlett⟩ **2** *archaic* **:** to present an account of **:** describe at length **:** NARRATE, RECOUNT, RELATE, TELL ⟨~s to a youth . . . the checkered story of her life —J.L.Lowes⟩ **3 :** to recount in order **:** mention one by one or one after another **:** ENUMERATE ⟨an address which *rehearsed* the wrongs suffered by the army —H.E.Scudder⟩ ⟨~ the multitude of things produced by . . . savages and peasants —John Dewey⟩ **4 a :** to practice or go through (as a play, scene, or part) in private in preparation for a more formal and public presentation **:** recite or repeat (as lines) in such a practice ⟨*rehearsed* the shooting of a rural story —Andrew Buchanan⟩ ⟨while his grandfather *rehearsed* campaign speeches —*Current Biog.*⟩ ⟨familiar symphonies . . . rarely get *rehearsed* —Virgil Thomson⟩ **b :** to train, instruct, or make proficient by rehearsal ⟨staff members have been *rehearsed* for the gala opening —*Springfield (Mass.) Union*⟩ ⟨~s the orchestra three times for each of his programs —Virgil Thomson⟩ **5 :** to perform or practice as if in a rehearsal ⟨the kitten ~s the kind of actions the cat employs in catching its prey —John Dewey⟩ ⟨the Pacific Fleet will ~ . . . a mission they might be called to perform —*N.Y. Times*⟩ ~ *vi* **:** to recite something esp. for practice **:** engage in a rehearsal ⟨dominant actors who *rehearsed* in submissive roles —Helen H. Nowlis⟩ **syn** see RELATE

**re·hears·er** \-sə(r)\ *n* -s **:** one that rehearses; *specif* **:** a person who conducts rehearsals of an orchestra

**¹re·heat** \(')rē+\ *vt* [*re-* + *heat*] **:** to heat again

**²re·heat** \'rē+,- ⸗'⸗\ *n* **1 :** a device (as an afterburner) used to recover heat for improved efficiency of a jet engine **2 :** AFTERBURNING 2

**re·heater** \(')rē+\ *n* [*re-* + *heater*] **:** one that reheats: as **a :** a furnaceman who reheats metal **b :** a receiver furnished with means for heating the steam in a compound engine or turbine **c :** an apparatus for reheating compressed air before use to prevent excessively low temperatures due to expansion

**reheating furnace** *n* **:** a furnace used in steel making in which bars are reheated before being rolled

**reh·fuss tube** \'rāfəs-\ *n*, *usu cap R* [after Martin E. *Rehfuss* *b*1887 Am. physician] **:** a flexible tube fitted with a slotted endpiece at the end that passes into the stomach and a syringe at the upper end and used esp. for withdrawing gastric juice for gastric analyses

**re·ho·bo·am** \,rēə'bōəm *sometimes* ,rēhə-\ *n* -s *usu cap* [after *Rehoboam fl ab* 925 B.C. son of King Solomon and first king of the southern kingdom of Judah, fr. Heb *Rĕhabh'ām*, lit., the nation is enlarged] **:** an oversize wine bottle holding about five quarts ⟨a *Rehoboam* of champagne⟩

**re·ho·both** \'rēə,bōth, rə'hōbəth\ *also* **re·he·both** \'rēə,bōth\ *n* -s *usu cap* [prob. after *Rehoboth*, site where Isaac dug a well for which the herdsmen of Abimelech did not fight and that he named (Gen 26:22), fr. Heb *Rĕḥōbhōth*, lit., wide spaces] **:** a member of a community or company of peoples in southwestern Africa of mixed European and native and esp. Hottentot and Herero origin

**re·house** \(')rē¦hau̇z\ *vt* [*re-* + *house*] **:** to establish in a new or different housing unit of a better quality ⟨get rid of slums and ~ slum dwellers —Catherine Bauer⟩ ⟨county boroughs . . . must ~ a large surplus population outside their own areas —*Economist*⟩

**rehs** *pl of* REH

**re·hy·drat·able** \¦rē,hī¦drād·əbəl, rē'hī,dr-\ *adj* **:** capable of being rehydrated ⟨~ rice⟩

**re·hydrate** \(')rē+\ *vt* [*re-* + *hydrate*] **:** to hydrate again: as **a :** to restore moisture to (dehydrated foods) **b :** to restore body fluid lost in dehydration to ⟨~ the patient⟩

**re·hydration** \¦rē+\ *n* [*re-* + *hydration*] **:** the action or process of rehydrating

**re·hypothecation** \¦rē+\ *n* [*re-* + *hypothecation*] **:** the action of a broker who pledges with a bank or other lender securities already left on deposit with him by a customer as a pledge for their purchase on margin

**rei** *pl of* REUS

**reichert-meissl number** *or* **reichert-meissl value** \'rīkə(r)t, 'mīsəl-\ *n*, *usu cap R&M* [after Karl *Reichert* and E. *Meissl*, 19th cent. Ger. chemists] **:** a Reichert value expressed as the milliliters of tenth-normal alkali required to neutralize the acids obtained from five grams of fat by a specified method of saponification and distillation

**reichert value** *or* **reichert number** *n*, *usu cap R* [after Karl *Reichert*, 19th cent. Ger. chemist] **:** a value that indicates the content in butter or other fat of the water-soluble volatile fatty acids (as butyric acid, caproic acid, caprylic acid); *esp* **:** REICHERT-MEISSL NUMBER

**reichs·mark** \'rīks+,-\ *n*, *pl* **reichsmarks** *also* **reichsmark** *sometimes cap* [G, fr. *reichs* (gen. of *reich* empire, realm, fr. OHG *rīhhi*) + *mark* — more at RICH, MARK] **:** the German mark from 1925 to 1948

**reichs·pfennig** \"+,-\ *n*, *pl* **reichspfennigs** *also* **reichspfennige** *sometimes cap* [G, fr. *reichs* (gen. of *reich* realm) + *pfennig* — more at PFENNIG] **1 :** the German pfennig from 1925 to 1948 equal to ¹⁄₁₀₀ reichsmark **2 :** a coin representing one reichspfennig

**reichs·taler** \"+,-\ *n* -s *often cap* [G, fr. *reichs* (gen. of *reich* realm) + *taler* — more at TALER] **:** the old German taler of legal weight and fineness as distinguished from one of the many local varieties — called also *speciestaler*

**reid** \'rēd\ *Scot var of* RED

**reif** \'rēf\ *n* -s [ME (Sc) *ref, reif*, fr. OE *rēaf*; akin to OHG *roubōn* to rob — more at REAVE] *chiefly Scot* **:** ROBBERY, PLUNDER ⟨keep the house frae ~ and wear —Sir Walter Scott⟩

**re·ifi·ca·tion** \,rēəfə'kāshən\ *n* -s [L *res* thing + E *-i-* + *-fication* — more at REAL] **:** the process or result of reifying **:** HYPOSTATIZATION ⟨~s of idealized abstractions —Joseph Katz⟩

**re·ify** \'rēə,fī\ *vt* -ED/-ING/-ES [L *res* + E *-ify*] **:** to regard (as an abstraction, a mental construction) as a thing **:** convert mentally into something concrete or objective **:** give definite content and form to **:** MATERIALIZE ⟨~*ing* both space and time⟩ ⟨a culture can be *reified* into a body of traditions —M.J. Herskovits⟩

**¹reign** \'rān\ *n* -s [ME *rein, regne*, fr. OF *reigne, regne*, fr. L *regnum* reign, fr. *reg-, rex* king — more at ROYAL] **1 a :** royal authority **:** the power or rule of a monarch **:** SOVEREIGNTY ⟨crown prince . . . assumed active ~ from his father —*Current Biog.*⟩ ⟨under the ~ of the Stuart kings⟩ **b :** the dominion, sway, or influence of one resembling or held to resemble a monarch ⟨the ~ of the . . . Puritan ministers was stern and intolerant —W.L.Sperry⟩ ⟨the full ~ of egotism as the ideal behind action —S.L.A.Marshall⟩ ⟨assuring the ~ of justice for all —*Loyola Univ. Bull.*⟩ **2** *archaic* **:** the territory or sphere that is reigned over **:** EMPIRE, KINGDOM, REALM ⟨the pole, Nature's remotest ~ —P.B.Shelley⟩ **3 :** the period of time during which someone (as a monarch) or something reigns ⟨the 20th year of the queen's ~⟩ ⟨at the beginning of his ~ as president of the college⟩ ⟨the ~ of Sanskrit . . . was longer than that of Greek and Latin —*Times Lit. Supp.*⟩

**²reign** \"\ *vi* -ED/-ING/-S [ME *reignen, regnen*, fr. OF *regner*, fr. L *regnare*, fr. *regnum* reign] **1 a :** to possess or exercise sovereign power **:** hold supreme authority in a state **:** govern as king, emperor, or other royal ruler **:** hold supreme power and dignity in a kingdom or empire **:** GOVERN, RULE ⟨Holy City . . . where Christ, the Lamb, doth ~ —W.R.Bowie⟩ **b :** to hold office as chief of state (as in a kingdom) without exercising more than minimal powers of making and executing governmental policy **:** have limited or nominal sovereignty ⟨the queen . . . ~s but does not rule —*Brit. Parliament*⟩ ⟨an Arab sultan ~s but British administrators . . . rule —Orville Prescott⟩ ⟨the royal governor both ~*ed* and ruled —D.W. Brogan⟩ ⟨will be the constitutional head of his country and will be above party and politics, an arbitrator and conciliator. He will not govern but will ~ —*N.Y. Times*⟩ **2 :** to exercise authority or hold sway in the manner of a monarch ⟨the archbishop . . . ~s as supreme moral authority on this island —George Weller⟩ ⟨in the countryside . . . the priest ~s most completely —Paul Blanshard⟩ ⟨the campus queen ~*ed* over the weekend festivities⟩ **3 :** to be predominant or prevalent **:** PREDOMINATE, PREVAIL ⟨these forests have ~*ed* supreme for countless millennia —W.H.Hodge⟩ ⟨commotion . . . ~*ed* through the house —E.J.Simmons⟩ ⟨a complete silence still ~*ed* inside —T.B.Costain⟩

**reign of terror** [fr. *Reign of Terror*, a period of the French Revolution that was conspicuous for the mass executions of political suspects] **1 :** a state characterized by conditions (as violence, threats of violence, or actions as injurious as physical violence) that produce terror among the people involved ⟨created a *reign of terror* throughout . . . the state —*Amer. Guide Series: Oreg.*⟩ ⟨no overt *reign of terror* among our intellectuals —W.G.Carleton⟩ **2 :** a period of time during which such conditions prevail ⟨gave ordinary prisoners some measure of confidence that the *reign of terror* . . . was finished —*N.Y. Herald Tribune*⟩

**¹rei·hen·grä·ber** \'rīən,grābə(r)\ *n pl*, *usu cap* [G, lit., graves in rows, fr. *reihen* (pl. of *reihe* row, fr. MHG *rīhe* line) + *gräber*, pl. of *grab* grave, fr. OHG; fr. their being arranged in rows — more at GRAVE] **:** long barrows that are found in southern Germany

**²reihengräber** \"\ *n pl*, *usu cap* **:** the prehistoric prob. Teutonic people that are buried in the Reihengräber

**re·illumine** \¦rē+\ *vt* [*re-* + *illumine*] **:** to illumine again

**re·im·burs·able** \¦rēəm¦bərsəbəl, -bəs-,-bəis-\ *adj* [*reimburse* + *-able*] **:** REPAYABLE ⟨~ indebtedness⟩ ⟨replacement of . . . equipment on a ~ basis —*U.S.Code*⟩

**re·im·burse** \-s\ *vt* -ED/-ING/-S [*re-* + obs. E *imburse* to pocket money, make rich, pay, fr. MF *embourser* to pocket money, fr. OF *em-* en- + *borser* to get money — more at DISBURSE] **1 :** to pay back (an equivalent for something taken, lost, or expended) to someone **:** REPAY ⟨costs shall be . . . *reimbursed* from such funds —*U.S. Code*⟩ **2 :** to make restoration or payment of an equivalent to (as a person) **:** INDEMNIFY ⟨~ government employees for travel expenses⟩ **syn** see PAY

**re·im·burse·ment** \,⸗⸗'⸗mənt\ *n* -s [prob. fr. F *remboursement*, fr. MF, fr. *rembourser* to reimburse (fr. *re-* + *embourser* to pocket money) + *-ment*] **:** the action of reimbursing **:** REPAYMENT ⟨make direct ~s to private corporations for federal income taxes —*New Republic*⟩ ⟨~ for out-of-pocket expenditures⟩

**reimer–tiemann reaction** \'rīmə(r)¦tēmən-, -ē,män-\ *n*, *usu cap R & T* [after Karl *Reimer* 19th cent. Ger. chemist and Ferdinand *Tiemann* †1899 Ger. chemist] **:** either of two similar chemical reactions: **a :** a reaction for producing phenolic aldehydes by the action of chloroform and caustic alkali on phenols **b :** a reaction for producing phenolic acids from carbon tetrachloride, alkali, and phenols

**re·impose** \¦rē+\ *vt* [*re-* + *impose*] **:** to impose again ⟨~ recently relaxed . . . restrictions —*Current Biog.*⟩ ⟨duties are to be *reimposed* for a further ten years —*Contemporary Rev.*⟩ ⟨*reimposing* the ban on parking⟩

**re·imposition** \(¦)rē+\ *n* [*re-* + *imposition*] **:** the action of reimposing ⟨~ of installment credit controls —*Wall Street Jour.*⟩ ⟨~ of taxes⟩

**re·impression** \¦rē+\ *n* [*re-* + *impression*] **:** a second or repeated impression (as of a book) without change **:** a reprint as distinguished from a new edition

**reims** *also* **rheims** \'rēmz, *F* raaⁿs\ *adj*, *usu cap* [fr. *Reims* (*Rheims*), France] **:** of or from the city of Reims, France **:** of the kind or style prevalent in Reims **:** RHEMISH

**¹rein** \'rān\ *n* -s [ME *rene, reine*, fr. MF *rene, resne*, fr. (assumed) VL *retina*, fr. L *retinere* to hold back — more at RETAIN] **1 :** a line (as a leather strap) which is fastened to a bit on each side and through which a rider or driver exerts pressure on the bit for governing or guiding an animal (as a horse) ⟨use of the ~ . . . to lead the horse's head and neck to the right —Harry Disston⟩ — usu. used in pl. ⟨seize the ~s from the grasp of the slumbering coachman —Thomas De Quincey⟩ — see BRIDLE illustration **2 :** something held to resemble the rein of a horse: as **a :** a restraining influence **:** CURB, CHECK ⟨let their eyes move without ~ —John Milton⟩ ⟨regulation . . . imposes ~s on consumer credit —John Elliott⟩ ⟨hold him under a tight ~ in his youth —R.A.Hall b. 1911⟩ **b :** the controlling or guiding power **:** position of command ⟨the ~s of government . . . have been handed to men of one party —A.N.Holcombe⟩ ⟨without the ~s of patronage . . . the forces of party organization lack guidance —Gladwin Hill⟩ **3 :** the part of a horse on which the reins exert leverage ⟨a horse with a good ~ has a well-sloped shoulder, rather long neck, and well-set head⟩ — **give rein to :** to give freedom, unlimited scope, or full course to ⟨*gave* full *rein to* his mingled exasperation and boredom —S.H.Adams⟩ ⟨the military forces *given free rein to* quell the rebellion —Virginia Valentine⟩ ⟨*giving free rein to* his commanding general⟩

**²rein** \"\ *vb* -ED/-ING/-S [ME *reinen*, fr. *reine* rein] *vt* **1** *obs* **:** to fasten or tie up (as a horse) to something by means of reins ⟨alight thy steed and ~ his proud head to the saddlebow —Shak.⟩ **2** *archaic* **:** to provide with a rein ⟨~*ed* with gold his foaming steeds —Alexander Pope⟩ **3 a :** to check or stop and hold by a pull at the reins **:** pull up by means of reins ⟨cowboys ~*ed* their sweating ponies to a halt —J.C.MacDonald⟩ — often used with *back, in*, or *up* ⟨the squire . . . ~*ed* in his horse —T.B.Costain⟩ **b :** to put a check or restraint upon as if by the use of reins — often used with *in* or *up* ⟨unable to ~ in his impatience any longer —Vicki Baum⟩ ⟨~ the tongue⟩ ⟨tries hard to ~ in his imagination —Kendall Smith⟩ **4 a :** to control, direct, or turn with the reins ⟨~ a horse to the left⟩ ⟨they ~*ed* their horses through the chaparral —*Underworld Detective*⟩ **b :** to guide, manage, or govern as if by the use of reins ⟨~*ed* our conversation round to . . . future prospects —Joseph Furphy⟩ ~ *vi* **1** *archaic* **:** to submit or yield to the use of reins ⟨will bear you easily and ~s well —Shak.⟩ **2 :** to move or pull in or as if in response to tightened reins — usu. used with *back, in, up* **3 :** to stop or slow up one's horse or oneself by or as if by pulling the reins — often used with *back, in*, or *up* ⟨cavalrymen ~*ed* up⟩ ⟨~*ed* in to a jog⟩ ⟨~ back and take your places —J.H.Wheelwright⟩

**³rein** \"\ *n* -s [Norw, fr. ON *hreinn* — more at REINDEER] **:** REINDEER

**rei·na** \'rānə\ *n* -s [Sp, queen, fr. L *regina*, fem. of *reg-, rex* king — more at ROYAL] **:** a California rockfish (*Sebastodes elongatus*)

**¹re·incarnate** \(¦)rē+\ *vt* [*re-* + *incarnate*] **:** to incarnate again or anew — compare TRANSMIGRATE

**²re·incarnate** \"+\ *adj* [*re-* + *incarnate*, adj.] **:** incarnate again

**re·incarnation** \"+\ *n* [*re-* + *incarnation*] **1 a :** the action of reincarnating or the state of being reincarnated **b :** rebirth in new bodies or forms of life; *esp* **:** a rebirth of a soul in a new human body **2 :** a belief (as in metempsychosis and transmigration) that the souls of the dead successively return to earth in new forms or bodies **3 :** one that has been reincarnated **:** a fresh embodiment of someone or something ⟨a lively ~ of the busy . . . colonial capital —*Amer. Guide Series: Va.*⟩

**re·in·car·na·tion·ist** \"əst\ *n* -s [*reincarnation* + *-ist*] **:** a believer in reincarnation

**re·incorporate** \¦rē+\ *vt* [trans. of F *reincorporer*] **:** to incorporate again

**¹rein·deer** \'rān+,-\ *n*, *pl* **reindeer** *also* **reindeers** [ME *reindere*, fr. ON *hreinn* reindeer (prob. akin to ON *horn* horn) + ME *dere* deer — more at HORN, DEER] **:** any of several deers of the genus *Rangifer* that inhabit the northern parts of Europe, Asia, and America, have large crescentic hooves with very large dewclaws, antlers present in both sexes with those of the male long, sweeping, often somewhat palmate at the ends, and with broad greatly developed brow antlers and with those of the female much smaller and simpler, and are often domesticated and used esp. in Lapland for drawing sleds and as a source of food — compare CARIBOU, ELK, MOOSE

European reindeer

**²reindeer** \"\ *adj*, *usu cap* **:** of, belonging to, or constituting a Paleolithic period in central Europe when reindeer were esp. numerous **:** MAGDALENIAN

**reindeer moss** *or* **reindeer lichen** *n* **:** any fruticose lichen of the genus *Cladonia*; *esp* **:** a gray erect tufted and much-branched lichen (*C. rangiferina*) that is found in extensive patches on the ground in arctic and even in north temperate regions and forms a large part of the food of reindeer and caribou in the

far north (as in Lapland) and is sometimes eaten by man — called also *arctic moss*
**reindeer pest** *or* **reindeer plague** *n* : an enzootic highly fatal malignant edema of reindeer characterized by excitement, lack of appetite, staggering gait, difficult respiration, and edematous swellings
**rei·nec·kate** \ˈrīnə,kāt\ *n* -s *sometimes cap* [*reinecke* + *-ate*] : a salt of reinecke acid
**rei·nec·ke acid** \ˈrīnəkə-, -kē-\ *n, usu cap R* [after A. *Reinecke*, 19th cent. Ger. chemist] : the monobasic acid $HCr(NH_3)_2(SCN)_4$ of which Reinecke salt is the ammonium salt
**reinecke salt** *n, usu cap R* [after A. *Reinecke*, 19th cent. Ger. chemist] : a red crystalline coordination complex $NH_4[Cr(NH_3)_2(SCN)_4].H_2O$ that is formed by adding ammonium dichromate to hot ammonium thiocyanate and that with heavy-metal ions and with organic bases, alkaloids, and basic antibiotics gives precipitates useful in separations and characterizations
**re·infection** \ˌrē+\ *n* [*re-* + *infection*] : an additional infection following recovery from or superimposed on a previous infection of the same type ⟨reactivation of a lesion which has become temporarily arrested is not in the pathologic sense a "~" but rather . . . delayed progression —F.D.Gunn⟩
¹**re·inforce** *also* **re·enforce** \ˌrē+\ *vb* -ED/-ING/-S [*reinforce* fr. *re-* + *inforce*, alter. of *enforce*; *reenforce* fr. *re-* + *enforce*] *vt* **1 a** : to strengthen with additional force, assistance, material, or support : make stronger or more pronounced ⟨walls . . . *reinforced* with mud —*Amer. Guide Series: Minn.*⟩ ⟨details piled upon details ~ the picture —Emory Ross⟩ ⟨~ the elbows of a jacket⟩ ⟨the atmosphere *reinforced* by candle fumes was stifling —Ronald Storrs⟩ **b** : to strengthen (a military or naval force) with additional units ⟨~ the regular troops —Manfred Nathan⟩ ⟨the Englishman . . . was *reinforced* by three other ships of the line —*U.S. Naval Inst. Proceedings*⟩ **c** : to strengthen or increase (a group or number) by fresh additions ⟨the faculty . . . was *reinforced* from the ranks of its students —R.M.Lovett⟩ ⟨the reformers were *reinforced* in the assembly —B.K.Sandwell⟩ ⟨trout eggs can be treated by the same solution provided it is *reinforced* after each lot —*Transactions of the Amer. Fisheries Society*⟩ **d** : to make more forcible, cogent, or convincing ⟨movements we make with face, head, hands, feet to ~ our words —Stuart Chase⟩ ⟨~ an argument⟩ **e** : to make greater (as by the provision of fresh force or additional units) ⟨~ the collections on government . . . science, and technology —L.H.Evans⟩ ⟨~ their own productivity by the creation of . . . marvelous machinery —R.W.Emerson⟩ **2** *obs* : to renew or repeat with fresh force **3** *obs* : to enforce again ⟨~ . . . the laws against the conventicles —Andrew Marvell⟩ **4** : to increase the likelihood of (a response) by a reward ~ *vi* : to seek or get reinforcements **syn** see STRENGTHEN
²**re·inforce** \"\ *n* -s : something that reinforces or strengthens; *specif* : the metal band placed over the chamber and rear part of the bore of a gun — see CANNON illustration
**reinforced bow** *n* : a bow backed with sinew — called also *sinew-backed bow*
**reinforced concrete** *n* : concrete in which metal (as steel) in the form of rods, bars, or meshwork is embedded in such a manner that the two materials act together in resisting forces — called also *ferroconcrete*
**re·inforcement** \ˌrē+\ *n* -s [*reinforce* + *-ment*] **1** *obs* **a** : fresh or renewed assault ⟨with a sudden ~ struck . . . like a planet —Shak.⟩ **2 a** : the action of reinforcing or the state of being reinforced : augmentation of strength or force ⟨willow mattresses used for ~ of caving banks —*Amer. Guide Series: La.*⟩ ⟨his task is the factual ~ of Christian theology by ethnology —Rodney Needham⟩ ⟨heavy ~ of credit supplies . . . had taken place —*Financial Times* (*London*)⟩ **b** : the strengthening of the response to one stimulus by the concurrent action of another stimulus (as a reward) — compare RECRUITMENT **3** *archaic* : the action of enforcing again or anew **4** : something that reinforces: as **a** : an additional unit (as of troops or ships) to augment the strength of an army, fleet, or other military force ⟨received . . . a ~ of 30,000 men —Thomas Lediard⟩ — often used in pl. ⟨without ~s he would not be able to maintain his position —*U.S. Naval Inst. Proceedings*⟩ **b** : an additional supply or contribution ⟨great ~s of sympathy —Walter Pater⟩ **c** : something designed to provide additional strength (as in a weak area) ⟨leather ~s on the jacket and trouser pockets —*N.Y. Times*⟩ ⟨gummed ~s . . . prevent paper from tearing —J.R.Gregg⟩
**re·inforcer** \"+\ *n* -s [*reinforce* + *-er*] : one that reinforces
**reinforcing** *n* -s [fr. gerund of ¹*reinforce*] : REINFORCEMENT 4c
**reinforcing agent** *n* : a substance (as carbon black or other pigment) used esp. in compounding rubber to improve the physical properties (as resilience, toughness, and tensile strength)
**re·inform** \ˌrē+\ *vt* [*re-* + *inform*] : to form anew : invest again with form ⟨~ features and attributes that have long been laid . . . in the quiet of the grave —R.L.Stevenson⟩
**reining** *pres part of* REIN
**rein·less** \ˈrānləs\ *adj* [¹*rein* + *-less*] **1** : having no reins : ungoverned by reins ⟨~ steeds⟩ **2** : lacking control or guidance : UNCHECKED, UNRESTRAINED ⟨the ~ play of the imagination —John Ruskin⟩
**rein orchis** \ˈrān-\ *n* [*rein* prob. back-formation fr. *reins*; fr. the kidney-shaped lip in some species] : any of several orchids of *Habenaria* or a related genus usu. with a kidney-shaped lip to the flower
¹**reins** \ˈrānz\ *n pl* [ME *reins*, fr. MF & L; MF *reins*, fr. L *renes*] **1** : KIDNEYS ⟨cleaveth my ~ asunder —Job 16:13 (AV)⟩ **2** : the region of the kidneys : LOINS ⟨girdled about the ~ with a curse —A.C.Swinburne⟩ **3** : the seat of the feelings, affections, or passions ⟨my ~ also instruct me —Ps 16:7 (AV)⟩ ⟨searcheth the ~ and hearts —Rev 2:23 (AV)⟩ **4** : the parts of a vault between the crown and the spring or abutment including the filling behind the vault shell
²**reins** *pl of* REIN, *pres 3d sing of* REIN
**re·insert** \ˌrē+\ *vt* [*re-* + *insert*] : to insert again ⟨~ a letter in an envelope⟩
**reins·man** \ˈrānzmən\ *n, pl* **reinsmen** [*reins* (gen. of ¹*rein*) + *man*] : a person skilled in handling reins; *specif* : a skillful jockey or harness driver ⟨30-year-old ~ . . . won the two major driving titles —*N.Y. Times*⟩
**re·instate** \ˌrē+\ *vt* [*re-* + *instate*] **1** : to instate again : place again (as in possession or in a former position) ⟨*reinstated* in British favor —*Amer. Guide Series: Fla.*⟩ ⟨*reinstated* in his former government and university posts —*Current Biog.*⟩ ⟨able to ~ law and order —Michael Blundell⟩ ⟨~ an insurance policy⟩ **2** : to restore to a proper condition : replace in an original or equivalent state ⟨the broken glass hacked out and *reinstated* —Samuel Butler †1902⟩
**re·instatement** \"+\ *n* [*reinstate* + *-ment*] **1 a** : the action of reinstating (as in a post or position formerly held but relinquished) ⟨~ of the postmaster⟩ ⟨~ to amateur status of a tennis star turned professional⟩ **b** : the action of replacing or restoring the effectiveness of (as something damaged, worn out, or lapsed) ⟨the cost of ~ may exceed the market value of the whole farm —*Country Life*⟩; *esp* : the action of restoring an insurance policy to its previous status or amount after it has been reduced by the payment of a claim or allowed to lapse **2** : the state or condition of being reinstated ⟨his ~ in popular favor quickly followed⟩
**re·in·sta·tion** \ˌrēənzˈtāshən, -ənˈst-\ *n* -s [*reinstate* + *-ion*] : REINSTATEMENT ⟨his ~ in the service —George Meredith⟩
**re·insurance** \ˌrē+\ *n* [*re-* + *insurance*] **1** : an insurance by another insurer of all or a part of a risk previously assumed by the direct-writing company **2** : the amount assumed in reinsurance **3** : the action of reinsuring — see EXCESS-LOSS REINSURANCE, EXCESS REINSURANCE, FACULTATIVE REINSURANCE, FLAT REINSURANCE, TREATY REINSURANCE
**reinsurance reserve** *n* : RESERVE 6b(2)
**re·insure** \"+\ *vb* [*re-* + *insure*] *vt* **1** : to insure again by transferring to another insurance company the liability in whole or in part assumed by the direct-writing company : transfer (the whole or part of a risk) to another company **2** : to insure again by assuming the liability in whole or in part of an insurance company which is already covering the risk : assume (the whole or part of a risk) in reinsurance ~ *vi* : to provide increased insurance ⟨tried to ~ against invasion by making concessions to the enemy⟩ ⟨~ by hanging on to regions important . . . for supply or defense —*Economist*⟩
**re·insurer** \"+\ *n* [*reinsure* + *-er*] : one that reinsures
**re·integrate** \(ˈ)rē+\ *vt* [ML *reintegratus*, past part. of *reintegrare* to renew, reinstate, fr. L *re-* + *integrare* to integrate — more at INTEGRATE] **1** *archaic* : REINSTATE 1 ⟨all . . . should be *reintegrated* in their former possessions —Edward Herbert⟩ **2** : to cause or bring about the reintegration of: as **a** : to integrate again into an entity ⟨if . . . her economy is not *reintegrated* into the European and world economy —Heinz Eulau⟩ **b** : to restore to unity after disintegration ⟨magical practices . . . ~ the individual and organize society —A.L.Kroeber⟩
**re·integration** \(ˌ)rē+\ *n* [ML *reintegration-, reintegratio*, fr. *reintegratus* (past part. of *reintegrare* to reinstate) + L *-ion-, -io* -ion] : repeated or renewed integration ⟨the ~ of veterans into an expanding civilian economy —H.S.Truman⟩
**re·integrative** \(ˈ)rē+\ *adj* [*reintegrate* + *-ive*] **1** : tending to reintegrate ⟨~ phenomena⟩ **2** : favoring or implementing reintegration ⟨~ trends⟩
**re·interpret** \ˌrē+\ *vt* [*re-* + *interpret*] : to interpret again; *specif* : to give a new or different interpretation to ⟨patterns which the lapse of time has ~*ed* beyond recognition —Edward Sapir⟩ ⟨the New Testament . . . needs constantly to be ~*ed* for each succeeding generation —Walter Murdoch⟩
**re·interpretation** \"+\ *n* [*re-* + *interpretation*] : the action of reinterpreting or the state of being reinterpreted ⟨~ of borrowed behavior patterns —Ralph Linton⟩ ⟨the scholarly revaluation and ~ of form —*Yale Rev.*⟩
**re·inthrone** \ˌrē+\ *vt* [*re-* + *inthrone*, alter. of *enthrone*] *archaic* : to enthrone again
**re·introduce** \(ˌ)rē+\ *vt* [*re-* + *introduce*] : to introduce again
**re·invasion** \ˌrē+\ *n* [*re* + *invasion*] : a second or another invasion
**re·invest** \"+\ *vb* [*re-* + *invest*] *vt* **1** : to invest again or anew ⟨great poetry . . . searches how to ~ words with meaning —C.S.Kilby⟩ **2 a** : to invest (as the income or repaid capital from old investments) in the purchase of additional securities **b** : to invest (as a part of earnings) in a business rather than making a distribution of dividends or profits ~ *vi* : to make a reinvestment ⟨before you ~, weigh the alternatives carefully⟩
**re·investiture** \"+\ *n* [*re-* + *investiture*] : the action of reinvesting or the state of being reinvested : REINSTATEMENT ⟨~ in their prerogatives —J.P.Peters⟩
**re·investment** \"+\ *n* [*re-* + *investment*] : the action of reinvesting or the state of being reinvested : a second or repeated investment
**re·invigorate** \"+\ *vt* [*re-* + *invigorate*] : to give renewed or fresh vigor to ⟨studies designed to ~ the humanities —W.H. Whyte⟩
**re·invigoration** \"+\ *n* [*re-* + *invigoration*] : the action of reinvigorating or the state of being reinvigorated ⟨his strong ~ of the forces of democracy —F.R.Dulles⟩
**rein·wardt·ia** \rīnˈwärd·ēə, rān-\ *n, cap* [NL, fr. Caspar G. C. *Reinwardt* †1854 Du. botanist + NL *-ia*] : a small genus of East Indian undershrubs (family Linaceae) having alternate and rather large leaves and yellow flowers with fugacious petals
¹**reis** *pl of* REAL
²**reis** *var of* RAIS
**reis·ner work** \ˈrīz|nə(r)-, -īs|\ *n* [after *Reisner*, 17th cent. Ger. cabinetmaker] : wooden inlaid work of different colors
**reiss·ner's fiber** \ˈrīsnə(r)z-\ *n, usu cap R* [after Ernst *Reissner* †1878 Ger. anatomist] : a band of fibers arising from the roof of the midbrain in many vertebrates, passing along the aqueduct and fourth ventricle to enter the central canal of the spinal cord, ending in the regions of the spinal nerves, being esp. large in fishes, and probably taking part in visual reflexes or regulating flexion of the body
**reissner's membrane** *n, usu cap R* [after Ernst *Reissner* †1878 Ger. anatomist] : a thin cellular membrane separating the vestibular and cochlear canals of the inner ear
¹**re·issue** \(ˈ)rē+\ *vb* [*re-* + *issue*] *vi* : to come forth again ⟨it ~s into the ocean at the northerly end of the gulf —Thomas Jefferson⟩ ~ *vt* : to issue again; *esp* : to cause to appear or become available after a period of absence or unavailability ⟨~ a film⟩ ⟨~ a book⟩ ⟨~ a stamp⟩
²**reissue** \"\ *n* [*re-* + *issue*, n.] **1** : a second or repeated issue (as of a publication) with change only in price or form ⟨a ~ in one volume of the two-volume . . . edition —Harvey Breit⟩ ⟨~ of a recording long unavailable⟩ ⟨~ of a postage stamp⟩ **2** : a postage stamp (as of an earlier time no longer available) that has been reissued for postal use — compare REPRINT
**reist** \ˈrēst\ *var of* REEST
**reister** *n* -s [MF *reistre*, fr. G *reiter* rider] *obs* : REITER
**reit·bok** *also* **reit·boc** \ˈrēt,bäk\ *or* **reit·buck** \-,bək\ *or* **riet·bok** *or* **riet·boc** *n, pl* **reitbok** *or* **reitboks** [Afrik *rietbok*, fr. D *riet* reed (fr. MD) + *bok* buck, fr. MD *bok, boc*; akin to OE *buc* buck — more at REED, BUCK] : any of several reedbucks (esp. *Redunca arundinum*) of southern Africa having a bushy tail and in the male small ringed horns that curve forward
**rei·ter** \ˈrīd·ə(r)\ *n* -s [G, lit., rider, fr. MHG *rīter*, fr. OHG *ritāri*, fr. *rītan* to ride + *-āri* -er — more at RIDE] : a German cavalry soldier esp. of the 16th and 17th centuries
**re·it·er·ant** \rēˈid·ərənt, -itər-\ *adj* [L *reiterant-, reiterans*, pres. part. of *reiterare* to repeat] : iterant to an increased degree ⟨a meaningless ~ jangle of noise —Julian Maclaren-Ross⟩ ⟨~ cry⟩
¹**re·it·er·ate** \-rət\ *adj* [ME *reiteraten*, fr. L *reiteratus*, past part. of *reiterare* to repeat, fr. *re-* + *iterare* to iterate — more at ITERATE] : REITERATED, REPEATED ⟨in ~ refrain —Frances Bushnell⟩
²**re·it·er·ate** \rēˈid·ə,rāt, -itə-, *usu* -ād-+V\ *vt* -ED/-ING/-S [ME reitterate, fr. L *reiteratus*, past part. of *reiterare* to repeat] **1** : to say or do over again or repeatedly : repeat often or continually sometimes with a wearying effect ⟨information . . . *reiterated* day after day by every organ of publicity —John Dewey⟩ ⟨the sharp *reiterated* strokes of a woodpecker —J.C. Powys⟩ ⟨on a fence built around the mill he *reiterated* his warning against anyone attempting entrance —*Amer. Guide Series: Minn.*⟩ **2** *obs* : to repeat the application or use of (as a medicine) **syn** see REPEAT
**re·it·er·at·ed·ly** \≈ˈ≈≈,≈≈≈, ≈,≈≈ˈ≈≈≈\ *adv* : in a reiterated or repeated manner : REPEATEDLY
**re·it·er·a·tion** \(ˌ)rē,idəˈrāshən, -itə-\ *n* -s [ML *reiteration-, reiteratio*, fr. L *reiteratus* (past part.) + *-ion-, -io* -ion] **1** : the action of reiterating : REPETITION ⟨development by ~ of short simple motifs —Henry Cowell⟩ ⟨the poem is concluded with a ~ of the initial idea —C.S.Kilby⟩ **2** *archaic* **a** : a form printed on the reverse side of a sheet already printed on one side **b** : the action of printing a reiteration : PERFECTING **c** : matter printed by reiteration
**re·it·er·a·tive** \≈ˈ≈≈,rād·iv, -,rəd-\ *adj* [¹*reiterate* + *-ive*] : exhibiting or marked by reiteration ⟨~ imagery⟩
**re·it·er·a·tive·ly** \-ə̇vlē\ *adv* : in a reiterative manner
**rei·ter's disease** \ˈrīd·ə(r)z-\ *also* **reiter's syndrome** *n, usu cap R* [after Hans *Reiter* b1881 Ger. physician] : a disease of unknown cause characterized by arthritis, conjunctivitis, and urethritis
**rei·thro·don·to·mys** \ˌrīthrəˈdäntə,mis\ *n, cap* [NL, fr. *reithr-* (fr. Gk *rheithron* that which flows, stream, fr. *rhein* to flow) + *odont-* + *-mys* — more at STREAM] : a genus of cricetid rodents comprising the harvest mice
**reive** \ˈrēv\ *vb* -ED/-ING/-S [ME (Sc) *reifen*, fr. OE *rēafian* to rob, despoil — more at REAVE] *Scot* : RAID
**reiv·er** \ˈrēvər\ *n* -s [ME (Sc) *reiffar*, fr. OE *rēafere*, fr. *rēafian* to rob + *-ere* -er] *Scot* : RAIDER ⟨a hiding place of stolen cattle in the days of the Border ~s —Janet MacPherson⟩ ⟨defense against sea ~s —D.G.Duff⟩
**reiz·ianum** \ˌrītsēˈanəm, -ˈän-,-ˈān-\ *n* -s [NL, fr. F. W. *Reiz* †1790 Ger. metrist + NL *-anum* (fr. L *-ianus* -ian)] **1** : an acephalous pherecratic (as ⏓ – ⏑ ⏑ – ⏓) **2** : a combination of an anapest or sometimes an iambus or a trochee with a bacchius
**re·ja** \ˈrā(,)hä\ *n* -s [Sp] : a grille or screen made usu. of wrought or cast metal and used in Spanish architecture to protect a window in a house or to enclose a chapel or a tomb in a church
**re·jane green** \rāˈzhän-\ *n, often cap R* [prob. after Gabrielle Charlotte *Réjane* †1920 Fr. actress] : a moderate yellowish green that is greener and paler than tarragon and yellower and paler than malachite green
**rejang** *usu cap, var of* REDJANG
**rejd** *abbr* rejoined
¹**re·ject** \rəˈjekt, rēˈj-\ *vt* -ED/-ING/-S [ME *rejecten*, fr. L *rejectus*, past part. of L *reicere, rejicere*, fr. *re-* + *-icere, -jicere* (fr. *jacere* to throw) — more at JET] **1** : to refuse to acknowledge, adopt, believe, acquiesce in, receive, or submit to : decline to accept : REFUSE ⟨considered a proposition fairly and ~*ed* it —Willa Cather⟩ ⟨~ a diplomatic note⟩ ⟨~ a claim⟩ **2** *obs* : to cast off (as a person) : FORSAKE **3** : to refuse to have, use, or take for some purpose : cast or throw away as useless, unsatisfactory, or worthless : DISCARD ⟨several publishers ~*ed* the manuscript —*Amer. Guide Series: N.Y.*⟩ ⟨memory . . . ~s what has not interested and impressed it —Laurence Binyon⟩ ⟨~*ed* by the recruiting station —O.S.J. Gogarty⟩ **4 a** : to refuse to hear, receive, or admit : REBUFF, REPEL ⟨parents who ~ the child —A.L.Porterfield⟩ ⟨underprivileged people who feel basically ~*ed* by society —Frank Fremont-Smith⟩ **b** : to refuse (a person) as lover or spouse ⟨~*ed* by her lover —J.T.Farrell⟩ **5** : to refuse to grant, consider, or accede to ⟨the demand was at once ~*ed* by the baronage —J.R.Green⟩ **6 a** : to throw or cast back : REPULSE **b** *obs* : to cut off (as a person) from something ⟨the young men were . . . ~*ed* from any hopes of the kingdom —William Whiston⟩ **7** : to spew out (as from the mouth or stomach) : EJECT **syn** see DECLINE
²**re·ject** \ˈrē,jekt *sometimes* rəˈj- *or* rēˈj-\ *n* -s : one that is or has been rejected: as **a** : one rejected as not wanted, unsatisfactory, or not fulfilling standard requirements ⟨good eggs found in the ~s by recandling —*Experiment Station Record*⟩ ⟨how often the deepest convictions of one generation are the ~s of the next —Learned Hand⟩ **b** : a partly chipped stone once started as an implement and then rejected **c** : a person rejected as unfit for military service ⟨army culls, physical or mental ~s from overseas duty —Taliaferro Boatwright⟩
**re·ject·able** \rəˈjektəbəl, rēˈj-\ *adj* : capable of being rejected : suitable for rejection
**re·ject·age** \-tij\ *n* -s [¹*reject* + *-age*] : rejected material or objects ⟨from examination of large quantities of ~ —*Popular Science Monthly*⟩
**re·jec·ta·men·ta** \rə,jektəˈmentə, (ˌ)rē,j-\ *n pl* [NL, pl. of *rejectamentum*, fr. L *rejectare* (freq. of *rejicere* to reject) + *-mentum* -ment] : things rejected : a quantity of rejects : RUBBISH, REFUSE, WRACK
**rejectaneous** *adj* [L *rejectaneus*, fr. *rejectus* (past part. of *rejicere* to reject) + *-aneus* (as in *subterraneus* subterranean)] *obs* : deserving rejection : REJECTABLE ⟨profane, ~, and reprobate people —Isaac Barrow⟩
**reject back** *n* : a back veneer (as of a table top) concealed from view and having specified allowable imperfections or open joints
**re·ject·ee** \rə,jekˈtē, rēˌj-, ˌrē,j-\ *n* -s [¹*reject* + *-ee*] : one that is or has been rejected; *specif* : REJECT c ⟨selective service ~s⟩
**re·ject·er** \rəˈjektə(r), rēˈj-\ *n* -s : one that rejects
**re·jec·tion** \-kshən\ *n* -s [MF or L; MF *rejection*, fr. L *rejection-, rejectio*, fr. *rejectus* (past part. of *rejicere* to reject) + *-ion-, -io* -ion] **1** : the action of rejecting or the state of being rejected ⟨an intellectual ~ of liberalism —Raymond Walters b. 1912⟩ ⟨~ of the atypical child by the . . . group —G.S.Speer⟩ ⟨criminal behavior is sometimes ~ of existing institutions —H.A.Murray & C.K.Kluckhohn⟩ **2** : something rejected
**rejection slip** *n* : a printed slip enclosed with a rejected manuscript returned by an editor (as of a magazine) to an author or his agent
**rejectitious** *adj* [¹*reject* + *-itious*] *obs* : deserving or requiring rejection : REJECTABLE ⟨persons spurious and ~ —Edward Waterhouse⟩
**re·jec·tive** \rəˈjektiv, rēˈj-\ *adj* : rejecting or tending to reject ⟨~ or overcritical attitudes of disappointed parents —Rudolf Hirschberg⟩
**re·jec·tor** \-tə(r)\ *n* -s **1** : REJECTER **2** : a circuit that combines inductance and capacitance in parallel so as to offer high impedance to a given impressed frequency and to resonate to all other frequencies — compare ACCEPTOR, FILTER, WAVE TRAP
**re·jigger** \(ˈ)rē+\ *vt* [*re-* + *jigger*] : to alter or rearrange again : manipulate in a new or different way ⟨executives ~ their organization charts —*Management Rev.*⟩ ⟨the government ~*ed* price ceilings on various pork cuts —*Chicago Daily Drovers Jour.*⟩
**re·joice** \rəˈjȯis, rēˈj-\ *vb* -ED/-ING/-S [ME *rejoicen, rejoisen*, fr. MF *rejoiss-*, extended stem of *rejoir* to rejoice, fr. *re-* + *joir* to rejoice, fr. L *gaudēre* — more at JOY] *vt* : to give joy to : make joyful : GLADDEN ⟨this book will ~ his many admirers —*advt*⟩ ⟨my enforced silence *rejoiced* me all the more —Kay Boyle⟩ ⟨a letter from you *rejoiced* my heart —H.J.Laski⟩ ⟨dispelled the clouds and *rejoiced* the optimists —S.B.Fay⟩ ~ *vi* : to feel joy or great delight : experience gladness or pleasurable satisfaction ⟨*rejoiced* that the Fates had agreed —George Meredith⟩ ⟨a layman can only ~ at the legal subtlety —Robert Lekachman⟩ ⟨truly *rejoiced* to be preserved —Jane Austen⟩ **syn** see PLEASE — **rejoice in** : HAVE, OWN, POSSESS ⟨it *rejoices* in the name of pigweed —Rachel Henning⟩ ⟨the mountains *rejoice in* an average annual rainfall of thirty inches —Oliver La Farge⟩
**re·joice·ful** \-sfəl\ *adv* : JOYFUL ⟨makes the season . . . ~ —*N. Y. Herald Tribune*⟩
**re·joice·ment** \-smənt\ *n* -s : REJOICING ⟨a golden festival of ~ was taking place —Jack Kerouac⟩
**re·joic·er** \-sə(r)\ *n* -s : one that rejoices
**rejoicing** *n* -s [ME *rejoising*, fr. gerund of *rejoisen* to rejoice] **1 a** : the action of one that rejoices : the feeling and expression of joy ⟨sounds of ~ from the distant camp —T.B.Macaulay⟩ **b** : an instance, occasion, or expression of joy : FESTIVITY **2** *obs* : something that causes one to rejoice : an occasion of joy or gladness ⟨thy testimonies . . . are the ~ of my heart —Ps 119:111 (AV)⟩
**rejoicing in the law** *or* **rejoicing of the law** *or* **rejoicing over the law** [trans. of Heb *simḥāth tōrah*] *usu cap R&L* : SIMHATH TORAH
**re·joic·ing·ly** *adv* : in a rejoicing manner : with joy or exultation ⟨a fact to be thankfully and ~ accepted —A.C.Swinburne⟩
**re·join** \rəˈjȯin, rēˈj-, *in vt senses 1 & 2* (ˈ)rēˈj-\ *vb* [ME *rejoinen* to answer to a legal charge, join one's own plea to that of the plaintiff, fr. MF *rejoin-*, stem of *rejoindre* to rejoin, fr. *re-* + *joindre* to join, fr. OF — more at JOIN] *vi* : to make a reply to a legal charge or pleading; *esp* : to answer the replication of the plaintiff ~ *vt* **1** : to join (as two things together or one with another) again : reunite after a separation ⟨~ the broken pieces⟩ ⟨the road ~s the highway two miles east⟩ **2** : to join (as a person or group) again ⟨~*ed* his regiment⟩ ⟨~*ed* the Republican party⟩ **3** : to say in answer or as a rejoinder : state in reply **syn** see ANSWER
**re·join·der** \rəˈjȯində(r), rēˈj-\ *n* -s [ME *rejoiner*, fr. MF *rejoindre* to rejoin (taken as n.)] **1** : the defendant's answer to the plaintiff's replication **2** : REPLY; *specif* : an answer to a reply ⟨her remarks . . . met with no ~ —Owen Wister⟩ ⟨drew the sharpest ~s in the panel discussion which ensued —H.W. Sams⟩ ⟨a statement in ~⟩
**re·join·dure** \-d(y)ə(r)\ *n* -s [F *rejoindre* to rejoin + E *-ure*] *obs* : a joining again : REUNION ⟨rudely beguiles our lips of all ~ —Shak.⟩
**re·joint** \(ˈ)rē+\ *vt* -ED/-ING/-S [*re-* + *joint*] **1** : to reunite the joints of : join or unite anew **2** : to fill up the joints of (as stones in buildings when the mortar has been dislodged)
**re·jon** \rāˈhōn\ *n* -s [Sp *rejón*, fr. *rejo* iron nail, sharp point, fr. *reja* plowshare, fr. L *regula* iron bar, straight piece of wood, ruler — more at RULE] : a short barbed spear used by the rejoneador in bullfighting
**re·jo·ne·a·dor** \ˌrā,hōnēəˈdȯ(ə)r, -ēəˈthȯ-\ *n* -s [Sp, fr. *rejón*] : the mounted man who thrusts a rejon into the shoulder muscles of the bull in bullfighting
**re·jo·neo** \ˌrāhōˈnā(ˌ)ō\ *n* -s [Sp, fr. *rejón*] : the art of bullfighting from on horseback with a short barbed spear
**re·judge** \(ˈ)rē+\ *vt* [*re-* + *judge*] : to judge again : deliver a new judgment upon : REEXAMINE, REVIEW

**re·junction** \"+\ *n* [*re-* + *junction*] **:** REUNION ⟨where burnt bodies went . . . to await ~ to their souls —Bruce Marshall⟩

**re·ju·ve·nate** \rə̇'jüvə,nāt, rē'j-, *usu* -ād·+V\ *vb* -ED/-ING/-S [*re-* + L *juvenis* young person + E *-ate*] *vt* **1 a :** to make young or youthful again **:** restore to youth **:** impart renewed vitality to **:** REINVIGORATE ⟨the fruit . . . ~*s* even the most decrepit old men —Robert Graves⟩ ⟨~ and reorganize . . . economic and social life —A.R.Williams⟩ **b :** to restore to a condition resembling an original or new state ⟨fenders . . . that can be *rejuvenated* and kept —*Buick Mag.*⟩ ⟨~ four tired chairs —*McCall's Needlework*⟩ **2 :** to restore to a more youthful condition; *specif* **:** to restore sexual vigor in (as by hormones or an operation) **3 a :** to stimulate (as by uplift) to renewed erosive activity — used of streams **b :** to develop youthful features of topography in (an area previously worn down nearly to base level) ⟨recently *rejuvenated* glaciated mountains —R.L.Ives⟩ ~ *vi* **1 :** to cause or bring about rejuvenation ⟨creams that ~ as you sleep —Lois Long⟩ ⟨nothing ~*s* like being on the offensive —Mollie Panter-Downes⟩ **2 :** to undergo rejuvenation ⟨her novices continued to ~ till their mental outlook was almost that of eight-year-olds —*Times Lit. Supp.*⟩

**re·ju·ve·na·tion** \rə̇,jüvə'nāshən, (,)rē,j-\ *n* -s **1 :** the action of rejuvenating or the state of being rejuvenated **:** restoration of youthful vigor ⟨~ of streams⟩ ⟨schemes for the ~ of the drama —Arnold Bennett⟩ ⟨poured half a billion dollars into Italy's post-war ~ —A.H.Vandenberg †1951⟩ **2 :** the restoration of vigor to a tree by pruning, spraying, soil treatment, or other means

**re·ju·ve·na·tor** \=ˈ==,nād·ə(r), -ātə-\ *n* -s **:** one that rejuvenates

**re·ju·ve·nes·cence** \rə̇,jüvə'nesᵊn(t)s, (,)rē,j-\ *n* -s [ML *rejuvenescere* to become young again (fr. L *re-* + *juvenescere* to become young, fr. *juvenis* young person) + E *-ence*] **1 a :** a renewal of youth **:** a restoration of physical, mental, or spiritual youthfulness **:** REJUVENATION 1 ⟨secure a new lease of life and of his divine energies —E.O.James⟩ **2 :** reinvigoration of an individual or strain esp. when following and dependent on some change in its vital behavior (as associated with zoospore formation in various lower algae or held to follow conjugation in some protozoans)

**re·ju·ve·nes·cen·cy** \-ᵊnsē\ *n* -ES [ML *rejuvenescere* + E *-ency*] *archaic* **:** REJUVENESCENCE

**re·ju·ve·nes·cent** \rə̇;jüvə;nesᵊnt, (ˌ)rē;j-\ *adj* [*rejuvenescence* + *-ent*] **:** becoming or causing to become rejuvenated **:** becoming youthful again **:** growing young **:** REJUVENATING

**re·ju·ve·nize** \=ˈ==,nīz\ *vt* -ED/-ING/-S [*re-* + L *juvenis* young person + E *-ize*] **:** REJUVENATE

**rekh·ta** \'rektə\ *or* **rekh·ti** \-tē\ *n* -s [Hindi *rekhta*, fr. Per] **:** a very highly persianized form of Urdu used in Urdu poetry

**re·ki** \'rākē\ *n, pl* **reki** *or* **rekis** *usu cap* **1 :** a group of nomadic peoples in the deserts of Baluchistan **2 :** a member of the Reki peoples

**¹re·kindle** \(')rē+\ *vt* **:** to kindle again **:** arouse again ⟨*rekindled* the ancient flame of Indian religion —*Amer. Guide Series: Ind.*⟩ ⟨the timely arrival . . . *rekindled* hope —R.A. Billington⟩ ~ *vi* **:** to ignite anew ⟨in the event that the fire ~*s* —*Fire Manual (Mass.)*⟩

**²rekindle** \"\ *n* [fr. gerund of ¹*rekindle*] **:** an instance of rekindling (as of a fire) **:** a fire believed to be extinguished that starts up again

**re·knit** \(')rē+\ *vt* [*re-* + *knit*] **:** to knit up or together again **:** REFASTEN ⟨~ the severed integrations of peace —Edmond Taylor⟩

**rel** \'rel\ *n* -s [*rel*uctance] **:** a unit of reluctance equal to one ampere turn per maxwell

**rel** *abbr* **1** related; relating; relative; relatively **2** relay **3** release; released **4** relief; relieve; relieved; relieving **5** religion **6** [L *reliquae*] relics

**relaid** *past of* RELAY

**re·lamp** \(')rē+\ *vt* [*re-* + *lamp* (n.)] **:** to replace the incandescent units of (as a light fixture)

**¹re·lapse** \rə̇'laps, rē'-, 'rē,l-\ *n* [L *relapsus*, past part. of *relabi* to slide back, sink back, relapse, fr. *re-* + *labi* to slide, glide, fall — more at SLEEP] **1 :** the act or fact of backsliding, becoming worse, or subsiding ⟨~ into barbarism⟩ ⟨~ of the stock market⟩ **2 :** a recurrence of illness; *esp* **:** recurrence of symptoms of a disease after a prolonged abatement — compare RECRUDESCENCE

**²re·lapse** \rə̇'laps, rē'-\ *vi* [L *relapsus*, past part. of *relabi*] **1 :** to slip or fall back into a former state (as of illness, vice) after a change for the better ⟨he *relapsed* when allowed out of bed⟩ ⟨reformed drunkards often ~⟩ **2 :** SINK, SUBSIDE, LAPSE ⟨*relapsed* into obscurity⟩ **3** *obs* **:** to fall away **:** WITHDRAW ⟨~ into silence⟩ **4 :** to fall back into paganism, evil, error, heresy, or unbelief **:** BACKSLIDE

**³re·lapse** \"\ *n* [L *relapsus*, past part. of *relabi*] **:** one who has relapsed **:** BACKSLIDER

**re·laps·er** \-sə(r)\ *n* **:** one that relapses

**relapsing fever** *n* **:** any of several forms of an acute epidemic infectious disease marked by sudden recurring paroxysms of high fever lasting from five to seven days, articular and muscular pains, and sudden crisis and caused by a spirochete (genus *Borrelia*) transmitted by the bites of lice and ticks and found in the circulating blood

**re·last·er** \(')rē'lastə(r)\ *n* [*re-* + *last* + *-er*] **:** a worker who puts shoes on a finishing last after the sole has been sewed to the upper

**relata** *pl of* RELATUM

**re·lat·abil·i·ty** \rə̇,lād·ə'biləd·ē\ *n* **:** the quality or state of being relatable

**re·lat·able** \rə̇'lād·əbəl\ *adj* [¹*relate* + *-able*] **:** that may be related

**¹re·late** \rə̇'lāt, rē'-, *usu* -ād·+V\ *vb* -ED/-ING/-S [L *relatus* (suppletive past part. of *referre* to carry back, refer, relate), fr. *re-* + *latus*, suppletive past part. of *ferre* to carry — more at REFER, TOLERATE] *vt* **1 a :** to give an account of **:** TELL ⟨tradition ~*s* that he once rode horseback all the way to Washington —*Amer. Guide Series: N. C.*⟩ **b** *archaic* **:** SAY, ASSERT, REPUTE **2 :** to show or establish a logical or causal connection between ⟨seeks to ~ poverty and crime⟩ ⟨~ the flow of individual consciousness to large political and social contours —Warren Beck⟩ ⟨utterly unable to ~ these two events⟩ ~ *vi* **1 :** to apply or take effect retroactively ⟨a will upon approval ~*s* back to the date of testator's death⟩ **2** *obs* **:** to give an account or report ⟨I might ~ of thousands —John Milton⟩ **3 :** to be in relationship **:** have reference ⟨public acts that ~ to crime prevention⟩ ⟨most of the lecture *related* to the causes of common ailments⟩ **4** *of a person* **:** to have meaningful social relationships **:** interact realistically ⟨a boy with a long history of emotional maladjustment and inability to ~ well to people —Edwin Powers & Helen Witmer⟩

**syn** RELATE, REHEARSE, RECITE, RECOUNT, NARRATE, DESCRIBE, STATE, and REPORT can all mean to tell orally or in writing the details or circumstances of a situation or combination of events. RELATE implies the giving of an account, usu. detailed or orderly, of something one has experienced ⟨*related* how it screamed, how it followed him in the brush, how he took to his boat, how its eyes gleamed from the shore —John Burroughs⟩ REHEARSE usu. suggests a repetition, a summary, a retold account, or a going over as in one's mind ⟨these defects arise out of the difficulties which have been *rehearsed* in these opening pages —*Orient Bk. World*⟩ ⟨in the interval . . . I *rehearsed* a great many ways of meeting him —Mary Austin⟩ RECITE and the more common RECOUNT imply a particularity, often enumeration, of detail, RECOUNT often implying a retelling ⟨would be asked to fill out a questionnaire *reciting* what the condition of the lot was, the view of the lot, the orientation of the lot, the size of their family, their needs, what they wanted to achieve —J.W.Rouse⟩ ⟨a review that merely *recited* the contents of a book —Raymond Walters b.1912⟩ ⟨often *recounts* the conversations with which they filled the long, hot days of driving —L.P.Smith⟩ ⟨*recounted* the story he had heard from the soldier —Hanama Tasaki⟩ NARRATE suggests a chronological account often with the use of devices of literary narration as plot or movement toward a climax ⟨this is not the place to *narrate* the achievements of the Canadian forces in that tremendous struggle —B.K.Sandwell⟩ ⟨it *narrates* the story of the shepherd Aminta and his love for the shepherdess Silvia —R.A.Hall b.1911⟩ DESCRIBE emphasizes details which provide a picture or a representation to other than visual senses ⟨bitter sea and glowing light, bright clear air, dry as dry, — that *describes* the place —Richard Jefferies⟩ ⟨a woman to be *described* as stout or thin, as jolly or crabbed, but always mature —Joseph Conrad⟩ ⟨the water, rich in iron and sulphur, is *described* as similar to that of the Vichy springs in France —*Amer. Guide Series: Minn.*⟩ STATE suggests definiteness of detail and economy of presentation ⟨*state* the case rather than render an opinion⟩ ⟨*state* facts, then explain them⟩ REPORT implies a recounting, esp. factual, for the information of others, as the readers of a newspaper ⟨the human tedium which the skilled novelist suggests without *reporting* in grim detail —*Time*⟩ ⟨newspapers are already *reporting* the ravages of dysentery —Justina Hill⟩ ⟨similar practices . . . are *reported* from other parts of the world —J.G.Frazer⟩ **syn** see in addition JOIN

**²relate** \"\ *n* -s [L *relatus*, suppletive past part. of *referre*] **:** something related to something else; *esp* **:** the first term in a relationship — compare CORRELATE

**related** *adj* [fr. past part. of ¹*relate*] **1 :** having relationship **:** connected by reason of an established or discoverable relation ⟨painting and the ~ arts⟩ ⟨including the ~ species of quartz⟩ ⟨chemistry and ~ sciences⟩ ⟨church-*related* colleges⟩ **2 :** allied by kindred; *esp* **:** connected by consanguinity ⟨persons ~ in the first degree⟩ **3 :** having similar properties **:** belonging to the same family of chemical elements ⟨cobalt, iron, and nickel are ~ elements⟩ **4 :** having a close harmonic connection — used of tones, chords, or tonalities — **re·lat·ed·ly** *adv*

**related key** *n* **:** a key having important tones in common with another key and hence admitting of ready modulation; *esp* **:** a key whose tonic chord is a triad of tones in the original key (as, for C major, the keys F major, G major, A minor, D minor, and E minor)

**re·lat·ed·ness** *n* -ES **1 :** the state or character of being related **2 :** a particular manner of being related or of being constituted by relations; *esp* **:** the manner of being related which characterizes a type of reality or level of existence ⟨the specific ~ of the organic⟩ ⟨relativity means ~ and not mere chaos or anarchy —N.E.Nelson⟩

**re·lat·er** \rə̇'lād·ə(r)\ *n* -s **:** one that relates; *esp* **:** NARRATOR

**relates** *pres 3d sing of* RELATE, *pl of* RELATE

**relating** *pres part of* RELATE

**re·la·tion** \rə̇'lāshən, rē'-\ *n* -s [ME *relacioun*, fr. MF *relation*, fr. L *relation-*, *relatio*, fr. *relatus* (suppletive past part. of *referre* to carry back, refer, relate) + *-ion-*, *-io* -ion — more at RELATE] **1 :** the act of telling or recounting **:** RECITAL, ACCOUNT, NARRATION ⟨was the hero of the affair according to his own ~⟩ ⟨tedious ~ of circumstantial details⟩ **2 :** an extended account or report ⟨the Jesuit ~*s* of missionary work in the New World⟩ **3 :** an aspect or quality (as resemblance, direction, difference) that can be predicated only of two or more things taken together **:** something perceived or discovered by observing or thinking about two or more things at the same time **:** CONNECTION ⟨discovered a ~ between dreams and waking actions⟩ ⟨the ~*s* between the objects in the picture are all wrong⟩ **4 :** the referring of an act to a prior date as the time of its taking effect **:** the giving force or operation to an act or proceeding as of some previous date or time by the fiction that it had happened or begun at that time **5 a** (1) **:** a person connected by consanguinity or affinity **:** KINSMAN, KINSWOMAN, RELATIVE (2) **:** a person who in case of intestacy would be legally entitled to a share of the property of the intestate under the statute of distributions in force in the jurisdiction in question — compare CONSANGUINITY **b** *dial* **:** RELATIVES **c :** relationship by consanguinity or affinity **:** KINSHIP **6 :** REFERENCE, RESPECT — used esp. in the phrase *in relation to* ⟨had a lot to say in ~ to that affair⟩ ⟨stingy only in ~ to his family⟩ **7 a :** the mode in which one thing or entity stands to another, itself, or others ⟨the ~ of father to son, parent to children⟩ or in which two or more entities stand to one another ⟨the ~ of members of the same community⟩ **b :** a logical bond; *specif* **:** a dyadic or polyadic predicate or propositional function — compare ASYMMETRIC, INTRANSITIVE, IRREFLEXIVE, ONE-ONE, REFLEXIVE, SYMMETRICAL, TRANSITIVE **8 a :** the state of being mutually or reciprocally interested (as in social or commercial matters) **b relations** *pl* **:** DEALINGS, AFFAIRS ⟨the foreign ~*s* of a country⟩ **:** INTERCOURSE ⟨broke off all ~*s* with him and his family⟩ **:** sexual union ⟨charged with having ~*s* with a woman not his wife⟩

**re·la·tion·al** \-shənᵊl, -shnəl\ *adj* **1 :** of or relating to kinship ⟨~ duties⟩ **2 :** characterized by or constituted by relations ⟨~ nature of space⟩ ⟨the form of propositions we classify as ~ is expressed as a function of two or more arguments —Alice Ambrose & Morris Lazerowitz⟩ ⟨~ anatomy⟩ ⟨~ plant morphology⟩ **3 :** having the function chiefly of indicating a relation of syntax ⟨~ words⟩ — distinguished from *notional*

**re·la·tion·ary** \-shə,nerē\ *adj* **:** RELATIONAL

**re·la·tion·ism** \-,nizəm\ *n* -s **1 :** RELATIVITY 2c **2 :** a doctrine holding that relations exist as real entities **3 :** a theory holding that any ideological perspective or system is conditioned by its sociocultural context

**re·la·tion·ist** \-sh(ə)nə̇st\ *n* -s **:** one who supports or follows a doctrine of relationism

**re·la·tion·less** \-shənlə̇s\ *adj* **:** not related **:** not having relations

**re·la·tion·ship** \-n,ship\ *n* **1 :** the state or character of being related or interrelated **:** a connection by way of relation ⟨show the ~ between two things⟩ ⟨this text's ~ to that is obvious but difficult to account for⟩ ⟨study language ~*s*⟩ **2 :** KINSHIP, CONSANGUINITY, AFFINITY ⟨claimed a ~ with the deceased⟩; *also* **:** a specific instance or type of this ⟨a list of family ~*s*⟩ **3 :** a state of affairs existing between those having relations or dealings; ⟨improve church ~*s*⟩ ⟨a psychologist's study of the mother-child ~⟩ ⟨a good doctor-patient ~⟩

**rel·a·ti·val** \,relə;tīvəl\ *adj* [¹*relative* + *-al*] **:** relating to or resembling a relative pronoun or other relative word ⟨~ construction⟩ ⟨~ use of *that*⟩

**¹rel·a·tive** \'reləd·iv, -ətiv\ *n* -s [ME, fr. MF *relatif* (adj.) or LL *relativus* (adj.)] **1 :** a word (as a relative pronoun) referring grammatically to an antecedent **2 :** a thing having a relation to or connection with or necessary dependence upon another thing **:** a being or object posited by virtue of its relations — opposed to *absolute* **3 a :** a person connected with another by blood or affinity; *esp* **:** one allied by blood **:** RELATION, KINSMAN ⟨gifts to friends and ~*s*⟩ **b :** an animal or plant related to another by common descent ⟨teosinte, corn's closest ~ —P.C. Mangelsdorf⟩ **4 :** a relative term ⟨using the ~*s father* and *son* instead of the absolutes *man* and *boy*⟩ **5 :** one of two or more related chemical substances: as **a :** one of a group of chemical compounds derived from a common parent **b :** one of a series of isomeric compounds **6 :** a statistical figure obtained by taking the value of a variable (as a price, a production total) for one time or place, dividing it by the value of the same variable for another time and place, and multiplying by 100

**²relative** \"\ *adj* [MF or LL; MF *relatif*, fr. LL *relativus*, fr. L *relatus* (suppletive past part. of *referre* to carry back, refer, relate) + *-ivus* -ive — more at RELATE] **1 :** referring to an antecedent **:** introducing a subordinate clause qualifying an expressed or implied antecedent ⟨a ~ connective⟩; *also* **:** introduced by a connective referring to an expressed or implied antecedent — see RELATIVE ADJECTIVE, RELATIVE ADVERB, RELATIVE CLAUSE, RELATIVE PRONOUN **2 a** *archaic* **:** having mutual relation with each other **:** RELATED, CORRESPONDING ⟨several different yet ~ designs —Nathaniel Hawthorne⟩ **b :** correlating with a right or duty of another **:** CORRESPONDING ⟨~ rights of husband and wife⟩ **3 :** having relation, reference, or application **:** PERTAINING, RELEVANT, PERTINENT ⟨matters ~ to maintenance of international peace —Vera M. Dean⟩ **4 :** arising from relation **:** resulting from or existing in connection with or reference to something else **:** not absolute or independent **:** COMPARATIVE — distinguished from *positive* ⟨~ velocity⟩ ⟨~ value of dollars and pounds⟩ ⟨~ isolation of life in the country⟩ **5 :** having the same key signature — used of major and minor keys and scales ⟨G major and E minor are ~ keys⟩ **6 :** expressed as the ratio of the specified quantity to the total magnitude or to the mean of all the quantities involved ⟨~ constant error in measuring⟩ ⟨~ probable error⟩

**relative adjective** *n* **:** a pronominal adjective that introduces a clause qualifying an antecedent (as *which* in "our next meeting will be on Monday, at which time a new chairman will be elected") or a clause functioning as a substantive (as *which* in "I do not know which course I should follow")

**relative advantage** *n* **:** COMPARATIVE ADVANTAGE

**relative adverb** *n* **:** an adverb that introduces a clause qualifying an antecedent (as *when* in *the season when roses bloom; where* in *entered the room where they were sitting;* and *why* in *the reason why he did it*)

**relative aperture** *n* **:** a measure of the angle of the cone of light rays from an object that traverse an optical system; *specif* **:** the effective aperture of a camera lens expressed as a fraction of its focal length with the symbol *f* being used instead of 1 as the numerator or expressed as the ratio of the effective aperture to the focal length ⟨a lens having an effective aperture that is 1/4.5 of its focal length has a *relative aperture* of f/4.5 or 1:4.5⟩

**relative bearing** *n* **:** a bearing relative to the heading of a ship or airplane

**relative clause** *n* **1 :** an adjective clause introduced by a relative pronoun expressed or suppressed, relative adjective, or relative adverb and having either a purely descriptive force (as in *John, who often tells fibs*) or a limiting one (as in *boys who tell fibs*) **2 :** a substantive clause introduced by an indefinite relative (as in *he belittles whatever his sister tries to do*)

**relative error** *n* **:** the ratio of an error in a measured or calculated quantity to the magnitude of that quantity

**relative frequency** *n* **:** the ratio of the frequency of a particular event in a statistical experiment to the total frequency

**relative fugacity** *n* **:** ACTIVITY 6b

**relative humidity** *n* **:** the ratio of absolute humidity to the maximum possible density of water vapor in the air at the same temperature

**relative impediment** *n* **:** an impediment that forbids marriage only with certain persons (as close relations)

**relative inclinometer** *n* **:** an inclinometer that shows the attitude of an airplane with reference to apparent gravity — compare TURN INDICATOR

**relative index of refraction :** the ratio of the velocity of light in two different media

**relative-in-law** \'====,=\ *n, pl* **relatives-in-law :** a connection by marriage **:** a relative of one's spouse

**relative location** *n* **:** the marking and arrangement of library books with relation to each other and not to particular shelves

**rel·a·tive·ly** \'reləd·əvlē, -ətə-, -li\ *adv* **:** in a relative manner **:** in relation or respect to something else **:** not absolutely ⟨foreign policy . . . determined by ~ small but strongly organized groups —Vera M. Dean⟩

**relative motion** *n* **1 :** motion as observed from or referred to some material system constituting a frame of reference (as two adjacent walls and floor of a room) — see RELATIVITY 3 **2 :** the motion of one body with respect to another regarded as fixed — compare RELATIVE VELOCITY

**rel·a·tive·ness** \-d·ivnə̇s, -tiv-\ *n* -ES **:** the quality or state of being relative **:** RELATIVITY

**relative nullity** *n* **:** nullity existing only in favor of particular persons

**relative personal equation** *n* **:** the deviation between values obtained by different observers — compare ABSOLUTE PERSONAL EQUATION

**relative pitch** *n* **1 :** the pitch of a musical tone as determined by its position in a scale — distinguished from *absolute pitch* **2 :** the ability to recognize or produce a musical tone at its correct pitch according to its relative position in a scale ⟨she has good *relative pitch*⟩

**relative pronoun** *n* **1 :** a pronoun (as *who, which, that*) that introduces a clause modifying an antecedent (as in *the man who would be king*) **2 :** an indefinite relative (as *who, whoever, what, whatever*) that introduces a clause functioning as a substantive (as in *order what you like* or *invite whomever you please*)

**relative rank** *n* **1 :** the rank in a service or branch of the armed services other than an officer's own which corresponds with the rank held by him — distinguished from *lineal rank* **2 :** comparative rank according to date of commission among officers holding the same grade

**relative refractive index** *n* **:** RELATIVE INDEX OF REFRACTION

**relatives** *pl of* RELATIVE

**relative term** *n* **:** a term (as *father, predecessor, employee*) which names either a relationship or an object as standing in a certain relation — compare ABSOLUTE 9a

**relative velocity** *n* **:** the vector difference between the velocities of two bodies **:** the velocity of a body with respect to another regarded as being at rest — compare RELATIVE MOTION

**relative wind** *n* **:** the motion of the air relative to a body in it usu. determined so as to exclude disturbance at the surfaces of the body

**rel·a·tiv·ism** \'reləd·ə,vizəm, -ətə,-\ *n* -s [ISV ²*relative* + *-ism*] **1 :** a doctrine of relationism or of relativity: as **a :** a theory that knowledge is relative to the limited nature of the mind and the conditions of knowing and hence not true to the nature of independent reality and that holds that absolutely true knowledge is impossible because of the limitations and variability of sense perceptions or that reality as it is in itself cannot be known by mind whose modes of thinking and perception are essentially subjective or that thinking and perception seize relations of one thing to another only and not the intrinsic nature of an object and hence are merely symbolic — called also *epistemological relativism* **b :** a view that theories of what is right and good are relative in that ethical truths depend upon the individuals and groups holding them so that what is considered right and good by one person or group may be considered wrong and bad by another — called also *ethical relativism* **2 :** RELATIVITY

**rel·a·tiv·ist** \-,və̇st\ *n* -s [ISV ²*relative* + *-ist*] **:** a believer in, or advocate of relativity, relativism, or the theory of relativity

**rel·a·tiv·is·tic** \;===;vistik\ *adj* **1 :** of, relating to, or characterized by relativity or relativism; *specif* **:** tending to regard human nature and values as subject to changing sociocultural or conditions rather than as absolute or universal **2 :** of or relating to the physical theory of relativity — **rel·a·tiv·is·ti·cal·ly** \-stə̇k(ə)lē\ *adv*

**rel·a·tiv·i·ty** \,relə'tivəd·ē, -ətē, -i\ *n* -ES [prob. fr. F *relativité*, fr. *relatif* relative + *-ité* -ity — more at RELATIVE] **1 :** the quality or state of being relative **:** relativeness ⟨~ of means to ends⟩ **2 :** the fact or condition of being relative as opposed to absolute or independent **:** the state of being dependent for existence or determined in nature, value, or some other quality by relation to something else: as **a :** the quality of variability arising from necessary connection with or reference to something contingent ⟨the ~ of beauty to taste or of rights to law⟩ **b :** the mutual dependence or concomitant variability of two or more related things **c :** dependence on the subjective nature of man or upon limitations and peculiar character of individuals ⟨the ~ of knowledge⟩ **3 a :** the study of the relative motion of bodies and of the associated phenomena **b :** a theory formulated by Albert Einstein and leading to the assertion of the equivalence of mass and energy and of the increase of the mass of a body with increased velocity and based on the two postulates that if two systems are in relative motion with uniform linear velocity it is impossible for observers in either system by observation and measurement of phenomena in the other to learn more about the motion than the fact that it is relative motion and that measurements of the velocity of light in either system regardless of the position of the source of light always give the same numerical value — called also *special theory of relativity* **c :** an extension of the theory to include a discussion of gravitation and related phenomena — called also *general theory of relativity* **4 :** a theory of culture which holds that societal systems of value, ethical standards, and social norms must be understood as inevitably related to their specific cultural context of historical development and which questions the extension of moral judgments arising out of a single tradition to another culture

**rel·a·tiv·iza·tion** \,relad·ivə'zāshən\ *n* -s **:** the act or result of making relative or regarding as relative rather than absolute ⟨assert again the dignity of human action against modern historical contemplation and ~ —Hannah Arendt⟩ ⟨~ of space and time determinations⟩

**rel·a·tiv·ize** \'reləd·i,vīz\ vt -ED/-ING/-S [²relative + -ize] **1** : to make relative : reduce from absoluteness to relativity : treat as contingent or limited to particular conditions **2 a** : to describe (a physical process) in relativistic terms **b** : to modify (an equation or formula) to accord with relativity theory

**re·la·tor** \rə'lād·ə(r)\ n -s [L, fr. *relatus* (suppletive past part. of *referre* to carry back, refer, relate) + -*or* — more at RELATE] **1** : one that relates : RELATER, NARRATOR ⟨~ of folk tales⟩ **2** : a private person at whose relation or in whose behalf an information in the nature of a quo warranto or mandamus is filed

**re·la·trix** \-ā·triks\ n -ES [LL, fem. of L *relator*] : a female relator

**re·la·tum** \rə'lād·əm\ n, pl **rela·ta** \-d·ə\ [NL, fr. L, neut. of *relatus*] : a thing or term related : one of a group of related things : CORRELATIVE; *specif* : one of the terms to which a logical relation proceeds : the second or one of the succeeding terms of a relation — compare REFERENT 2b

¹**re·lax** \rə'laks, rē'-\ vb -ED/-ING/-ES [ME *relaxen*, fr. L *relaxare*, fr. *re-* + *laxare* to loosen, slacken, fr. *laxus* loose — more at SLACK] vt **1** *obs* : to make less close in structure, texture, or formation : lessen the density or compactness of **2** : to make less tense or rigid : lessen the tension or pressure of : SLACKEN ⟨alternately contracting and ~*ing* his muscles⟩ ⟨pain forced him to ~ his grip⟩ ⟨after a mile of hard driving he ~*ed* the pace⟩ ⟨unsafe to ~ our vigilance for an instant⟩ **3** : to make less severe or strict : lessen the stringency, austerity, or harshness of ⟨~*es* its rigid immigration laws for all members of learned professions —*Report: (Canadian) Royal Commission on Nat'l Development*⟩ ⟨wartime is well known to ~ conventions —C.W.Cunnington⟩ **4** : to make soft or enervated : deprive of energy, zeal, strength of purpose ⟨this ~*ing* of his critical faculties —Steven Marcus⟩ **5** : to relieve from nervous tension : cause to unbend in manner or behavior ⟨a shampoo soothed and ~*ed* him⟩ **6** : to relieve from constipation ⟨~ a horse's bowels by putting him on wet bran⟩ ~ vi **1** : to become lax, weak, or loose : REST ⟨lay back and let his eyes and mind ~⟩ **2** : to abate in intensity : let up ⟨set up a standard of perfection which seldom permitted him to ~ —Edward Ryerson⟩ **3 a** *of a muscle or muscle fiber* : to become inactive and lengthen **b** *of yarn* : to shrink to original length after release of stress **4** : to cast off social restraint, nervous tension, or attitude of anxiety or suspicion ⟨found it hard to ~ in the presence of his social inferiors⟩ ⟨the country ~*es* into its habitual tolerance of free expression —H.L.Smith b.1906⟩ **5** : to seek rest or recreation : escape from pressure of duty or responsibility ⟨~ at the seashore⟩ ⟨is ushered into a private anteroom to ~ before addressing the convention⟩

²**relax** n -ES **1** *obs* : RELAXATION **2** *obs* : DIARRHEA

¹**re·lax·ant** \-sənt\ adj [L *relaxant-, relaxans*, pres. part. of *relaxare*] : of, relating to, or producing relaxation ⟨~ effect of a drug⟩

²**relaxant** \"\ n -s **1** : a drug that relaxes; *specif* : one that relieves tension of smooth or striated muscle — compare PARALYTIC 2 **2** : LAXATIVE

**relaxate** vb -ED/-ING/-S [L *relaxatus*, past part. of *relaxare*] *obs* : RELAX, RELEASE

**re·lax·a·tion** \(,)rē,lak'sāshən, rə,-\ n -s [MF or L; MF, fr. L *relaxation-, relaxatio*, fr. *relaxatus* (past part. of *relaxare* to relax) + -*ion-*, -*io* -ion — more at RELAX] **1** : the act or fact of relaxing or of being relaxed ⟨~ of the muscles⟩ ⟨the ~ of discipline⟩ ⟨~ of a law⟩ **2** : an abatement or remission of a penalty or payment ⟨ask for ~ in war reparations⟩ ⟨a ~ of a fine⟩ **3** : a relaxing or recreative state, activity, or pastime; DIVERSION, RECREATION ⟨play golf as a ~⟩ ⟨seek ~ in the country⟩ **4** *Scots law* : release from or cancellation of legal restriction or penalty; *esp* : release from a penalty (as outlawry) judicially imposed **5** : the lengthening that characterizes inactive muscle fibers or muscles **6** : the adjustment of a system to a state of equilibrium following the abrupt removal of some influence (as a magnetic force, a high temperature) **syn** see REST

**relaxation oscillation** n : a mechanical, electric, or acoustic oscillation (as of a road scraper, wires singing in wind) that consists of a build-up of displacement followed by sudden release of the displaced system

**relaxation oscillator** n : an electric oscillator by which are produced rapid surges due to the alternate charging and discharging of a condenser, the discharges being initiated by a thyratron when the condenser voltage reaches a certain value

**relaxation time** n **1** : the time required for an exponentially decreasing variable (as the amplitude of a damped oscillation) to drop from an initial value to 1/*e* or 0.368 of that value (where *e* is the base of natural logarithms) **2** : the period required for the attainment of statistical equipartition of energy (as of motion) within the Milky Way galaxy, any other galaxy, groups of galaxies, clusters, stars or any selected group of similar celestial bodies **3** : the time required for a viscous substance to recover from shearing stress after flow has ceased

**re·lax·a·tive** \rə'laksəd·iv\ adj [*relaxation* + -*ive*] : that relaxes or tends to relax ⟨light, ~ reading⟩

**re·lax·a·to·ry** \-sə,tōrē\ adj [*relaxation* + -*ory*] : RELAXATIVE

**re·laxed** \rə'lakst, rē'-\ adj **1** : not strict, nor exact, nor severe : lacking in precision or stringency ⟨~ rules of procedure⟩ ⟨~ restrictions on imports⟩ ⟨person of somewhat ~ morals⟩ **2** : set at rest or at ease ⟨found him in one of his rare ~ moments smoking a pipe⟩ **3** : easy of manner : free from stiffness : INFORMAL, EASYGOING ⟨~ style of comedy⟩ ⟨a characteristic poem of his . . . the record of a moment of ~ and undirected consciousness —F.R.Leavis⟩ — **re·laxed·ly** \-sədlē, -stlē, -li\ adv — **re·laxed·ness** \-sədnəs, -s(t)nəs\ n -ES

**re·lax·er** \-sə(r)\ n -s : one that relaxes ⟨music is often an excellent ~⟩

**re·lax·in** \-sən\ n -s [¹*relax* + -*in*] : a sex hormone that is apparently a neutral polypeptide, that is produced by the corpus luteum, and that facilitates childbirth by causing relaxation of the pubic symphysis

**re·lax·om·e·ter** \(,)rē,lak'sämǝd·ə(r)\ n [¹*relax* + -*o-* + -*meter*] : an instrument for measuring relaxation times in the study of anelastic stress relaxation in plastic or viscous substances

¹**re·lay** \'rē,lā\ n -s [ME, fr. MF *relais*, fr. *relaier*] **1** : a supply arranged beforehand for successive relief: as **a** : a supply of hunting horses or dogs kept in readiness at certain places to continue the pursuit of game if it comes that way **b** : a supply of horses placed at stations to be ready to relieve others so that a traveler may proceed without delay; *also* : the post or station at which the fresh supply is obtained **c** : a number of men who relieve others in carrying on some work : a relief gang ⟨working in ~s around the clock⟩ **2 a** : RELAY RACE **b** : one of the legs or divisions of a relay race **c relays** *pl* : a track meet featuring relay races **3** : an electromagnetic device for remote or automatic control that is actuated by a variation in conditions of an electric circuit and that operates in turn other devices (as switches, circuit breakers) in the same or a different circuit **4** : SERVOMOTOR **5** : the act of passing along (a message, a signal, a ball) by stages; *also* : one of such stages ⟨the shortstop's ~ from center field was too late to catch the runner at the plate⟩ **6** : an arrangement by which water is pumped through two or more pumping engines in order to increase the pressure in a fire hose **7** : a bundle of relayed mail **8** : RADIO RELAY

²**relay** \", rə'lā, rē'-\ vb -ED/-ING/-S [ME *relayen*, fr. MF *relaier*, fr. OF, fr. *re-* + *laier* to leave — more at DELAY] vt **1 a** : to place or dispose in relays **b** : to provide with relays **c** : to divide up (mail) into bundles each of which is to be placed in a storage box along a carrier's route to be picked up by him **2** : to pass along by relays ⟨news was ~*ed* to distant points⟩ ⟨promised to ~ my message⟩ **3** : to control or operate (as a circuit, a switch) by a relay **4** : to pump (water) through two or more pumping engines in order to increase the pressure in a fire hose ~ vi **1** : to obtain a fresh relay ⟨gained time by ~*ing* at each town⟩ **2** : to operate the contacts of a relay

³**re·lay** \(')rē+\ vt [*re-* + ¹*lay*] : to lay again ⟨the flagstones will have to be taken up and relaid⟩ ⟨~*ing* several miles of track⟩

**relay broadcast** n : REBROADCAST

**relay governor** n : a speed regulator (as a waterwheel governor) embodying the relay principle

**relay nucleus** n : a nucleus of the brain that serves primarily to relay stimuli from lower receptor centers to coordinating cortical centers

**relay race** n : a race between teams of two or more contestants with each team member covering a specified portion of the entire course — see MEDLEY RELAY

**relay rail** n : worn rail that is suitable for relaying in sidings and guardrails

**relay station** n : RADIO RELAY

**reld** *abbr* relieved

**re·learn** \(')rē+\ vt [*re-* + *learn*] : to learn again what has been partly or completely forgotten or lost

**re·leas·abil·i·ty** *also* **re·leas·ibil·i·ty** \rə,lēsə'biləd·ē\ n -ES : the quality or state of being releasable

**re·leas·able** *also* **re·leas·ible** \rə'lēsəbəl\ adj [¹*release* + -*able* or -*ible*] : capable of being released; *esp* : PUBLISHABLE — **re·leas·ably** \-blē\ adv

¹**re·lease** \rə'lēs, rē'-\ vt -ED/-ING/-S [ME *relesen, relessen*, fr. OF *relessier, relaissier*, fr. L *relaxare* to loosen, relax — more at RELAX] **1** *obs* : to loosen or remove the force or effect of : ALLEVIATE **2** : to set free from restraint, confinement, or servitude : set at liberty : let go ⟨~ a bent bow⟩ ⟨ordered all prisoners *released*⟩ ⟨~ a caged bird⟩ ⟨treated as an inferior himself and he has to ~ his frustrations somewhere —Darrell Berrigan⟩ **3** : to relieve from something that confines, burdens, or oppresses ⟨waiting for death to ~ him from his agony⟩ ⟨asked her to ~ him from his promise⟩ **4** : to give up (a claim, title, right) in favor of another : SURRENDER, RELINQUISH, RESIGN, QUIT ⟨~ a claim to property⟩ ⟨~ all claims or demands regarding personal injury⟩ ⟨~ a reserved seat in a plane flight⟩ **5** : to give permission for the publication, performance, exhibition, or sale of (as a film, news article, phonograph record) on but not before a specified date **6 a** *obs* : to grant remission of (a debt, tax) **b** : MITIGATE **syn** see FREE

²**release** \"\ n -s [ME *reles*, fr. MF *reles, relais*, fr. OF, fr. *relessier, relaissier*] **1 a** : relief or deliverance from sorrow, suffering, or trouble ⟨unconsciousness brought a merciful ~ from his pain⟩ **b** : salvation or spiritual liberation from all earthly bondage and temporal contingencies : MOKSHA **2 a** : discharge from obligation or responsibility (as a debt, penalty, or claim) : a giving up (as of a right or claim) : RELINQUISHMENT **b** : an act or instrument by which a legal right is discharged : QUITCLAIM; *specif* : a conveyance of a man's right in lands or tenements to another having an estate in possession — compare ACQUITTANCE **3 a** : the act of liberating or freeing : discharge from restraint ⟨awaiting ~ from jail⟩ ⟨sudden ~ of free oxygen caused the explosion⟩ ⟨~ of homing pigeons⟩ ⟨~ of gas from a balloon⟩ **b** : the mode of holding and loosing an arrow in shooting with a bow — compare MEDITERRANEAN RELEASE, MONGOLIAN RELEASE, PRIMARY RELEASE **c** : the act or manner of concluding a musical tone or phrase — compare ATTACK **d** : the act or manner of ending a sound : the movement of one or more vocal organs in quitting the position for a speech sound **e** : a relaxation of the muscles after contraction in dancing **4** : an instrument formally discharging from restraint or custody **5 a** : the act of permitting a working fluid (as steam) to escape from the cylinder at the end of the working stroke **b** : the point in the cycle of operations or on the corresponding indicator diagram at which this act occurs **c** : the period during exhaust from the point of escape to where the pressure of the exhausting fluid is sensibly that of the condenser or of the outside air **6 a** : the state of being liberated or freed ⟨the long summer ~ from school⟩ **b** : a freeing (as of a young forest tree) from the competing effects of taller overshadowing vegetation ⟨a statistical analysis of the value of ~ cuttings⟩ ⟨the time of ~ is apparent in cross section because of the sudden increase in growth increment —E. Lucy Braun⟩ **7** : a device adapted to hold and later release a mechanism as required: as **a** : a catch on a motor-starting rheostat that automatically releases the rheostat arm and so stops the motor in case of a break in the field circuit **b** : the catch on an electromagnetic circuit breaker for a motor which acts in case of an overload **c** : a device for releasing the cocked shutter of a camera during picture taking **8 a** : the act of permitting performance or publication **b** : the matter released; *esp* : a statement prepared for the press by a public figure, a government agency, an organization **c** : a printed card conveying information and instructions to be used with a block-signaling system at intermediate sidings or at offices lacking telegraphic stations **9** : the usu. contrasting middle portion of a popular song

**re-lease** \(')rē+\ vt [*re-* + *lease*] : to lease again : grant a new lease of

**released rate** n : a transportation rate reduced as a result of partial release of a carrier (as a railroad) from liability

**released time** n : a time set aside for dismissing children from public school once a week to receive religious instruction in the faith of their parents

**released valuation** n : a value lower than the usual commercial value of a commodity agreed upon by carriers and shippers to obtain a released rate and reduced carrier liability — compare AGREED VALUATION

**re·leas·ee** \rə,lē'sē\ n -s [¹*release* + -*ee*] : one to whom a release is given

**re·lease·ment** \rə'lēsmənt\ n -s **1** *archaic* : the act of releasing or fact of being released **2** *obs* : RELAXATION

**release print** n : a positive print of a motion picture used for exhibition

**re·leas·er** \-sə(r)\ n -s : one that releases; *specif* : a stimulus that esp. in lower organisms serves as the initiator of complex reflex behavior ⟨exposure to changing day length may be a ~ for nidification in many migratory birds⟩

**release therapy** n : psychiatric therapy in which the patient acts out his inner conflicts

**releasible** *var of* RELEASABLE

**re·lea·sor** \-sə(r)\ n -s [¹*release* + -*or*] : one that gives a release

**re·lec·tion** \rə'lekshən\ n -s [LL *relection-, relectio*, fr. L *relectus* (past part. of *relegere* to read again, fr. *re-* + *legere* to gather, select, read) + -*ion-*, -*io* -ion — more at LEGEND] **1** *obs* : REREADING **2** *obs* : a revised reading : EMENDATION

**rel·e·ga·ble** \'reləgəbəl\ adj [*relegate* + -*able*] : that may be relegated

**rel·e·gate** \'relə,gāt, *usu* -ād·+V\ vt -ED/-ING/-S [L *relegatus*, past part. of *relegare*, fr. *re-* + *legare* to send with a commission or charge — more at LEGATE] **1 a** : to send into exile : BANISH **b** : to put out of sight or mind : consign to insignificance or oblivion ⟨~ this sofa to the trash heap⟩ ⟨details *relegated* to the footnotes⟩ **c** : DEGRADE, DEMOTE ⟨in the oldest Neolithic settlements . . . hunting has been *relegated* to a secondary role —V.G.Childe⟩ ⟨the living tongues are *relegated* to a lower plane than Greek and Latin —C.H.Grandgent⟩ **2** : to consign by classifying or appraising ⟨muscular atrophies . . . are not properly *relegated* to the group of neuromuscular disorders —W.A.D.Anderson⟩ ⟨no wrong is done to a great and influential work by *relegating* it to rhetoric, to philosophy —René Wellek & Austin Warren⟩ **3** : to submit or refer for decision, judgment, or execution ⟨smaller companies can ~ the job of planning to a semiclerical level —E.J.Mann⟩ ⟨much of the work was *relegated* to special committees⟩ **syn** see COMMIT

**rel·e·ga·tion** \,==ˈgāshən\ n -s [L *relegation-, relegatio*, fr. *relegatus* + -*ion-*, -*io* -ion] **1** *Roman law* : a mild banishment not entailing loss of property or civil rights — compare DEPORTATION **2** : the act of relegating or state of being relegated : REMOVAL, BANISHMENT **3** : ASSIGNMENT, DELEGATION ⟨~ of minor decisions to his subordinates⟩

¹**re·lent** \rə'lent, rē'-\ vb -ED/-ING/-S [ME *relenten*, perh. fr. *re-* + L *lentus* flexible, slow — more at LITHE] vi **1** *obs* : MELT, LIQUEFY **2** : to become less severe, harsh, or strict : become mollified, compassionate, or forgiving ⟨when a second appeal, couched in more urgent terms, was dispatched to him, he ~*ed* —Bennett Cerf⟩ **3** : to let up : SLACKEN ⟨the wind blast would have to ~ . . . nothing like that could keep on and on —G.W. Brace⟩ ~ vt **1** *obs* : cause to be less harsh or severe : SOFTEN, MOLLIFY **2** *obs* : SLACKEN, ABATE ⟨oftentimes he would ~ his pace —Edmund Spenser⟩ **3** *obs* : to give up ⟨no discouragement shall make him once ~ his . . . intent to be a pilgrim —John Bunyan⟩ **4** *obs* : REPENT, REGRET **syn** see YIELD

²**relent** \"\ n -s *archaic* : an act of relenting, yielding, or slackening

**re·lent·ing·ly** adv : with relentment : MERCIFULLY

**re·lent·less** \-tləs\ adj : that cannot or does not relent or give way to appeals or to pity : mercilessly hard or harsh : immovably stern or persistent ⟨~ avenger⟩ ⟨~ pursuer⟩ ⟨~ judge⟩ ⟨~ and unsparing criticism⟩ — **re·lent·less·ly** adv — **re·lent·less·ness** n -ES

**re·lent·ment** \-tmənt\ n -s : an act of relenting

**re·les·see** \rə,le'sē\ n [by alter. (influence of *lessee*)] : RELEASEE

**re·les·sor** \-sȯ(ə)r\ n [by alter. (influence of *lessor*)] : RELEASOR

**re·let** \(')rē+\ vt [*re-* + *let*] : to let again : renew the lease of

**re·letter** \"+\ vt [*re-* + *letter*] **1** : to renew the lettering of **2** : to change the lettering of

**rel·e·vance** \'reləvən(t)s\ *also* **rel·e·van·cy** \-nsē, -si, *substand* 'revələn-\ n, pl **relevances** *also* **relevancies** : relation to the matter at hand : PERTINENCE ⟨a scholar's activities should have ~ to the immediate future of our civilization —J.B.Conant⟩

**rel·e·vant** \-nt\ adj [ML *relevant-, relevans*, fr. L, pres. part. of L *relevare* to raise up, lift up — more at RELIEVE] **1** : bearing upon or properly applying to the matter at hand : affording evidence tending to prove or disprove the matters at issue or under discussion : PERTINENT ⟨began work on the problem by reading all the ~ literature⟩ ⟨~ testimony⟩ **2** : CORRESPONDENT, PROPORTIONAL, COMMENSURATE ⟨the human concepts of one inch in length, and one second in time . . . are purely ~ to human life —A.N.Whitehead⟩ **3** *Scots law* : VALID, SUFFICIENT ⟨~ defense⟩

**syn** RELEVANT, GERMANE, MATERIAL, PERTINENT, APPOSITE, APPLICABLE, APROPOS can signify, in common, having a relation to or a bearing upon a matter in hand or upon present circumstances. A thing is RELEVANT when it has a connection, esp. a logical connection, with a matter under consideration ⟨nor shall any amendment not germane or *relevant* to the subject matter contained in the bill be received —*U.S.Code*⟩ ⟨what the cartman is saying is *relevant* to his case —John Hersey⟩ ⟨had thoroughly familiarized himself with all the knowledge *relevant* to his new duties —Benjamin Farrington⟩ GERMANE is interchangeable with RELEVANT but usu. adds to it the idea of unquestionable closeness and fitness or appropriateness of relationship as in spirit, tone, or quality ⟨almost every fact — religious, social, political, economic — was, somehow or other, *germane* to the war or the peace —Katharine F. Gerould⟩ ⟨the fierce aversions and the passionate cravings which are *germane* to the hermit life —H.O.Taylor⟩ A thing is MATERIAL when it has so close a relationship with a case in hand that it cannot be dispensed with without serious alteration of the case ⟨the motion is supported by an affidavit showing that the evidence is *material* —B.F.Tucker⟩ ⟨information *material* to the solution of a problem⟩ PERTINENT is interchangeable with RELEVANT, although it often stresses a more decisive or significant relationship, characterizing what not only bears upon but also contributes materially to the understanding or solution as of a problem or matter in hand ⟨had something *pertinent* to say about every horse that was brought out —Gerald Beaumont⟩ ⟨relatively few studies *pertinent* to the transplantation of lung tissue have been made —C.A.Hardin & C.F.Kittle⟩ ⟨deal in a specific kind of emotional conflict for *pertinent* dramatic ends —Irving Kolodin⟩ APPOSITE usu. applies to what is relevant and germane to the point of felicitousness ⟨*apposite* quotations from the classics came easily to his pen to grace the pellucid flow of his English —V.L.Parrington⟩ ⟨his sermons . . . are replete with *apposite* arguments and quotations from the Latin classics in support of the teachings of Christianity —G.C.Sellery⟩ A thing is APPLICABLE when it can be brought to bear upon or be used fittingly in reference to a matter in hand ⟨beauty in this broad sense is *applicable* to widely differing artistic achievements —C.W.H.Johnson⟩ ⟨this assumption is not *applicable* to many economic problems —Robert Dorfman⟩ A thing is APROPOS when it is opportunely appropriate ⟨once asked him, *apropos* of his liberal politics . . . what ideal of society he would approve —George Santayana⟩ ⟨she stays glued to her easel, creating futuristic pictures *apropos* of which the author observes, "She had a moderate talent for painting" —S.J. Perelman⟩

**rel·e·vant·ly** adv : with relevance

**relevate** vt -ED/-ING/-S [L *relevatus*, past part. of *relevare* — more at RELIEVE] *obs* : RAISE, RELIEVE; *esp* : to restore to good spirits

**re·le·vé** \,reləˈvā\ n -s [F, lit., raised, fr. past part. of *relever* to raise — more at RELIEVE] : a rise to the toes from the flat foot in ballet dancing

**re·li·abil·i·ty** \rə,līə'biləd·ē, rē,-, -ətē, -i\ n : the quality or state of being reliable; *specif* : the extent to which an experiment, test, or measuring procedure yields the same result on repeated trials

**reliability coefficient** n : a measure of the accuracy of a test or measuring instrument obtained by measuring the same individuals twice and computing the correlation of the two sets of measures

**re·li·able** \rə'līəbəl, rē'-\ adj [*rely* + -*able*] : suitable or fit to be relied on ⟨~ witness⟩ ⟨~ history⟩ : worthy of dependence or reliance : of proven consistency in producing satisfactory results ⟨~ recipe⟩ ⟨~ remedy⟩; *specif* : giving the same results on successive trials ⟨~ intelligence test⟩ ⟨~ measuring device⟩

**syn** DEPENDABLE, TRUSTWORTHY, TRUSTY, TRIED: RELIABLE describes what can be counted on or trusted in to do as expected or to be truthful ⟨a *reliable* employee⟩ ⟨*reliable* guards at the gates⟩ ⟨*reliable* on duty, but a wild, desperate fellow off the deck of his ship —A. Conan Doyle⟩ ⟨a *reliable* machine⟩ ⟨*reliable* testimony⟩ DEPENDABLE is a close synonym for RELIABLE and may indicate a steady predictability or trustworthiness or reliability worthy of fullest confidence ⟨a *dependable* workman⟩ ⟨*dependable* amounts of rainfall⟩ ⟨a *dependable* hard-working physician⟩ ⟨the most *dependable* of our allies⟩ TRUSTWORTHY indicates meriting confidence for proved soundness, integrity, veracity, judgment, or ability ⟨after considerable deliberation on the part of the captain and mate, four of the seamen were pitched upon as the most *trustworthy* —Herman Melville⟩ ⟨his careful use of sources makes him the first *trustworthy* American historian —*Amer. Guide Series: Mass.*⟩ TRUSTY implies that the person or thing described has been tested and found dependable ⟨*trusty* servants who have been with us for some time —A.Conan Doyle⟩ TRIED likewise stresses proved dependability ⟨the men who fought there were the *tried* fighters, the hammered, the weather-beaten, the very hard-dying men —S.V.Benét⟩

**re·li·able·ness** n -ES : RELIABILITY

**re·li·ably** \-blē, -li\ adv : in a reliable manner : with certainty

**re·li·ance** \rə'līən(t)s, rē'-\ n -s [*rely* + -*ance*] **1** : the act of relying ⟨~ on income tax revenues to carry government costs⟩ **2** : the condition or attitude of one who relies : DEPENDENCE, CONFIDENCE ⟨~ on promises⟩ **3** : something or someone relied upon : MAINSTAY ⟨long a main ~ of the administration in foreign affairs⟩ **syn** see TRUST

**re·li·ant** \-nt\ adj [back-formation fr. *reliance*] **1** : having reliance on something or someone ⟨~ on sleeping pills⟩ ⟨~ on her brother for news of the family⟩ **2** : DEPENDENT, TRUSTING — **re·li·ant·ly** adv

**rel·ic** \'relik, -lēk\ n -s [ME *relik, relike*, fr. OF *relique*, fr. ML *reliquia*, back-formation fr. LL *reliquiae*, pl., remains of a martyr, fr. L, remains, leavings, remains of a deceased person, fr. *relinquere* to leave behind — more at RELINQUISH] **1 a** : an object (as a bone, an article of clothing or of personal use) kept in esteem and veneration because of its association with a saint or martyr **b** : something that serves as a remembrance of a person, place, or event : SOUVENIR, MEMENTO ⟨snapshots and other ~s of her youth⟩ **2 relics** *pl* : REMAINS, CORPSE ⟨sacred earth where his dear ~s lie —William Wordsworth⟩ **3** : something that is left behind after decay, disintegration, or disappearance (as of a structure, a race, a nation) : a surviving ruin or specimen or remnant ⟨~s of ancient cities⟩ ⟨the chimney . . . may be a ~ of the earlier building —*Amer. Guide Series: Conn.*⟩ ⟨residual landforms many of which are capped by isolated ~s of once continuous dolerite sills —Arthur Holmes⟩ **4 :** a trace of some past or outmoded practice, custom, or belief **:** SURVIVAL, VESTIGE ⟨the prison . . . is an anachronistic ~ of medieval concepts of crime and punishment —R.S.Banay⟩ **5 :** RELICT 4 **6 :** RELICT 5 **7 :** a term, form, or pronunciation once common over a wide area but now occurring only in a usu. isolated place

**relic area** *n* **:** a region that retains characteristic speech features from an earlier stage of a language which have been lost or have undergone greater change in other regions — compare FOCAL AREA, GRADED AREA

**rel·i·cary** \ˈreləˌkerē\ *n* -ES [Sp *relicario*, fr. ML *reliquiarium* — more at RELIQUARY] **:** RELIQUARY

**¹rel·ict** \ˈrelikt, -lēkt\ *n* -S [in sense 1, fr. L *relictum*, neut. of *relictus*, past part. of *relinquere* to leave behind; in sense 2, fr. L *relicta*, neut. pl. of *relictus*; in sense 3, fr. LL *relicta*, fr. L, fem. of *relictus*; in senses 4 & 5, fr. ²*relict* — more at RELINQUISH] **1** *obs* **:** RELIC 1a **2 relicts** *pl*, *archaic* **:** RELIC 2 **3 :** WIDOW ⟨the ~ of a famous general⟩ ⟨a banker's wife who behaved as if she had been his ~ —George Meredith⟩ **4 :** a persistent remnant of an otherwise extinct flora or fauna or kind of organism ⟨various Australian cycads are probably Carboniferous ~s⟩ ⟨the metasequoia is a ~ of a once abundant genus⟩ **5 :** a relict relief feature or rock ⟨older view that the Scandinavian mountain range is simply a ~ of the higher ancient Caledonian range —*Jour. of Geol.*⟩

**²re·lict** \rəˈlikt, rēˈ-\ *adj* [L *relictus*, past part. of *relinquere*] **1** *obs* **:** left behind by death; *specif* **:** WIDOWED **2** *also* **relic a :** remaining after other parts have been removed or have disappeared **:** RESIDUAL ⟨~ lake⟩ ⟨~ mountain⟩ ⟨~ quartz⟩ **b :** left behind in a process of change ⟨~ sulfides in a partly oxidized ore body⟩ **3** *also* **relic :** surviving as a remnant of a vanishing race, type, or species **:** belonging to an otherwise extinct class or kind ⟨such ~ animals as the opossum —Weston La Barre⟩

**re·lict·ed** \-təd\ *adj* **:** RELICT 2

**re·lic·tion** \-kshən\ *n* -S [L *reliction-*, *relictio* act of leaving behind, fr. *relictus* (past part. of *relinquere*) + *-ion-*, *-io* -ion] **:** the gradual withdrawal of the water in the sea, a lake, or a stream leaving permanently exposed and uncovered land whose title then vests in the abutting owner of adjacent land; *also* **:** the land so left uncovered — compare ACCRETION

**relied** *past of* RELY

**¹re·lief** \rəˈlēf, rēˈ-\ *n* -S [ME *relefe*, *releve*, *relief*, fr. MF *relief*, fr. OF, fr. *relever* to raise again, relieve — more at RELIEVE] **1 a :** a fine or money composition (as a year's rent or a fixed sum) formerly paid by the heir of a deceased tenant to his lord for the privilege of taking up the landed estate which on strict feudal principles had escheated — distinguished from *heriot* **b :** an acknowledgment made by the heir of his vassal tenure of a lord as a condition of being received or had as a vassal **2 :** removal or lightening of something oppressive, burdensome, painful, dangerous, or distressing ⟨expressing his secret fears gave him great ~⟩ ⟨it was a ~ to take off his tight shoes⟩: **a :** aid in the form of money or necessities for the indigent, aged, or handicapped ⟨public ~⟩ ⟨work ~⟩ ⟨disaster ~⟩ **b** *obs* **:** FEEDING, SUSTENANCE **c :** military assistance in or rescue from a position of extreme difficulty or encirclement ⟨sent to the ~ of a besieged city⟩ **d :** diversion or amusement serving to ease or relax the mind ⟨have no ~ but in passing their afternoons in visits . . . and their evenings at cards —Jonathan Swift⟩ **e :** means of breaking or avoiding monotony, tedium, or prolonged straining of attention ⟨the appearance on the horizon of even the swagman's silhouette may be a welcome ~ —William Power⟩ **3 :** release from a post or from the performance of duty by the intervention of others, by discharge, or by relay ⟨~ of a sentry⟩ ⟨the ~ of the commanding general was to be expected⟩ **4 a :** one that relieves from performance of duty by taking the place of another ⟨explained their duties and equipment to their ~s —G.J.Dufek⟩ **:** RELAY, REPLACEMENT ⟨send up a ~ to consolidate the position —Bill Mauldin⟩ **b :** SCRUB 3b(2) **5 a :** legal remedy or redress **b** *Scots law* **:** release from an obligation or contribution from a joint obligor for his proportionate share of liability **6** [F; trans. of It *rilievo*, fr. *rilevare* to raise, fr. L *relevare* — more at RELIEVE] **a :** a mode of sculpture in which forms and figures are distinguished (as by modeling of soft material, hammering of thin malleable material, or cutting away the surface in a hard material) from a surrounding plane surface — compare INTAGLIO, *in the round* at ROUND; see BAS-RELIEF, FLAT RELIEF, MEZZO-RELIEVO, SUNK RELIEF **b :** sculpture or a sculptural form executed in this mode ⟨a stone ~ above the arch⟩ **c :** projecting detail, ornament, or figures in sculpture ⟨the sharp edges of the ~ cannot stand the test of time⟩ **7 a :** the suggestion in pictorial art of spatial dimensions and relations communicated by the arrangement of lines, colors, or shadings **b :** vividness or sharpness of outline due to contrast (as of color or shading) ⟨a roof in bold ~ against the sky⟩ **8 :** the difference of level between the highest part of a fortification works and the bottom of the ditch or trench **9 :** the elevations or inequalities of a land surface **:** the difference in elevation between the hilltops or summits and the lowlands of a region **10 :** the character of the surface of a mineral section as observed under the microscope **11 a :** a passage in a tailstock center for the facing or parting tool made by cutting away one side of the center so that the tool may be advanced to or almost to the center of the work **b :** a slight modification in the dimension of a part of a machine to secure clearance **c :** the lessening of excessive pressure (as of a tool, a moving part, a confined gas) **d :** CLEARANCE 2e

**²relief** \"\ *adj* **1 :** providing relief from distress, pressure, strain, congestion ⟨~ measures during a famine⟩ ⟨~ highway⟩ **2 :** characterized by surface inequalities **3 :** of or used in letterpress ⟨~ form⟩ ⟨~ plate⟩ ⟨~ engraving⟩

**³relief** \"\ *adj*, *usu cap* [fr. the *Relief* Church, founded in 1761 in Scotland by Thomas Gillespie †1774 Scottish clergyman and his followers] **:** of or relating to the Relief Church that was founded to provide relief from the evils of patronage and that joined in 1847 with the United Secession to form the United Presbyterian Church (of Scotland)

**re·lief·er** \-fə(r)\ *n* -S [¹*relief* + *-er*] **1 :** RELIEF PITCHER **2 :** one who receives public relief

**relief frame** *n* **:** a frame or ring interposed between the back of a slide valve and the inside of the steam-chest cover in some large engines to prevent access of the steam to the greater part of the valve thereby relieving the pressure on the valve and materially reducing friction

**relief map** *n* **:** a map representing topographic relief by contour lines, hachures, coloring, shading, or similar graphic means

**relief model** *n* **:** a three-dimensional scale model of a part of the earth's surface

**relief pitcher** *n* **:** a baseball pitcher who takes over for another during a game; *esp* **:** one who is regularly held in readiness for relief

**relief printing** *n* **:** LETTERPRESS 1a

**relief process** *n* **:** a process for making subtractive color prints that employs photographic images of varying thickness in a material (as gelatin) that may contain a pigment or may be dyed to show variations in optical density in proportion to thickness

**relief valve** *n* **:** a valve for the escape of steam or fluid under excessive pressure

**relief well** *n* **:** a vertical drain used for the drainage of a deep pervious stratum to relieve waterlogging of the surface soil

**re·li·er** \rəˈlī(ə)r\ *n* -S [*rely* + *-er*] **:** one that relies

**relies** *pres 3d sing of* RELY

**re·liev·able** \rəˈlēvəbəl\ *adj* **:** capable of being relieved ⟨~ wrongs⟩

**re·lieve** \rəˈlēv, rēˈ-\ *vb* -ED/-ING/-S [ME *releven*, fr. MF *relever* to lift up, raise, relieve, fr. L *relevare*, fr. *re-* + *levare* to raise — more at LEVER] *vt* **1 :** to free from a burden, evil, pain, or distress **:** give ease, comfort, or consolation to ⟨knowing the truth will ~ anxious parents⟩ **:** give aid, help, or succor to **:** RESCUE, DELIVER ⟨~ a besieged city⟩ ⟨a society for *relieving* the poor⟩ **2 a :** to bring about the removal or alleviation of **:** make less burdensome or afflicting **:** MITIGATE, LESSEN, ALLEVIATE ⟨strenuous efforts to ~ the food shortage⟩ ⟨frequently smokes to ~ nervous tension⟩ ⟨no words can ~ her sorrow⟩ **b :** to remove something from the possession of **:** ROB, DEPRIVE ⟨crooks . . . eager to ~ the Texas cowboys of their pay —E.V.Buckholder⟩ **3 a :** to release from a post, station, or duty ⟨asked to be *relieved* of command of the army⟩ ⟨he was *relieved* of further responsibility for the program⟩ **b :** to take the place of **:** take over from ⟨sent to ~ the gate sentry⟩ **:** SUCCEED ⟨tulips bloom . . . to be *relieved* by roses when their time is up —E.O.Hauser⟩ ⟨*relieved* the operator for lunch and a smoke⟩ **4 :** to set free from an obligation, condition, or restriction **5 :** to acquire or take (a feudal estate) by paying or rendering a relief **6 :** to ease of an imposition, burden, wrong, or oppression by judicial or legislative interposition **:** RIGHT ⟨a zoning law cannot constitutionally ~ land . . . from lawful restrictions affecting its use, imposed by convenants —*Amer. Jurisprudence*⟩ **7 :** to remove or lessen the monotony of by contrast or variety ⟨brown hills *relieved* by patches of green⟩ **8 a :** to give prominence or conspicuousness to **:** set off by contrast **:** give sharp outline to ⟨her tall figure *relieved* against the blue sky —Sir Walter Scott⟩ **b :** to raise (as figures, letters) in relief **9 :** to supply with food, munitions, stores ⟨~ a lighthouse by ship⟩ ⟨~ an arctic weather station⟩ **10 a :** to furnish (as a cutting tool) with a relief angle **b :** to free from tightness in relative movement **c :** to cut away a small amount of material from a part of (a machine) to obtain clearance **11 :** to empty the bladder or bowels of (oneself) ⟨children are likely to ~ themselves on any street —*Time*⟩ ~ *vi* **1 :** to bring or give relief **2 :** to stand out in relief **3 :** to clear one from a legal obligation, condition, or restriction ⟨a *relieving* clause⟩

**syn** ALLEVIATE, LIGHTEN, ASSUAGE, MITIGATE, ALLAY: RELIEVE indicates a lifting, perhaps temporary, of a burden, pain, or anxiety, so that it is no longer quite oppressive ⟨particularly zealous in taking steps to control the fire and *relieve* the suffering it entailed —Donald Milner⟩ ⟨a sex offender, deeply guilty over his past acts and *relieved* by analysis of the neurotic demands that had prompted them —Walter Goodman⟩ ALLEVIATE indicates a temporary lightening of pain, distress, or difficulty, and may contrast with *cure* or *eliminate* ⟨no dentists to care for them; not even any oil of cloves to *alleviate* the ache —C.C.Furnas⟩ ⟨activation of the Parking Authority in order to help *alleviate* New York's chronic traffic problem —*Current Biog.*⟩ LIGHTEN may suggest a cheering, buoying up, or refreshing abatement of depression or oppression ⟨forever grumblingly attempting to *lighten* their sufferings —Kenneth Roberts⟩ ⟨his experience in copyreading and criticizing other people's efforts at expression ought to *lighten* the task of the editor to whom he eventually submits something —R.L.Greene⟩ ASSUAGE suggests a moderating of pain, vexation, or sorrow by soothing, softening, or mollifying ⟨the fugitive breezes, the life-giving zephyrs that *assuage* the torment of the summer heat —Stuart Cloete⟩ ⟨grief that Professor Abbott did not live to enjoy the fame he had earned is *assuaged* by the knowledge that he survived to complete his great work —Godfrey Davies⟩ MITIGATE also suggests moderating, by any means, or countering the force or intensity of something painful ⟨*mitigate* the barbarity of criminal law —W.R.Inge⟩ ⟨group friction and conflict are generally *mitigated* when people realize their common interests —M.R.Cohen⟩ ⟨the torment of his thirst *mitigated* a trifle by a drenching in the brine —C.G.D.Roberts⟩ ALLAY applies to any effective calming, soothing, quieting, or pacifying ⟨the approach of winter *allayed* the fear of Indian raids —G.R.Stewart⟩ ⟨the president, in a TV chat intended to *allay* the country's fears —W.L.Miller⟩ ⟨something must be done to *allay* growing public discontent and to still the disagreements —*New Statesman & Nation*⟩

**re·lieved** \-vd\ *adj* **:** experiencing or showing relief esp. from anxiety or pent-up emotion ⟨answered presently in a ~ tone⟩ ⟨greatly ~ or disappointed . . . to find that there is little or no sensation of speed —H.G.Armstrong⟩ — **re·lieved·ly** \-vədlē, -vd-, -li\ *adv*

**re·liev·er** \-və(r)\ *n* -S **:** one that relieves: **a :** any of various mechanical devices for relieving strain **b :** something that relieves pain or distress **c :** RELIEF PITCHER

**relieving arch** *n* **:** an arch built over a lintel to relieve or distribute the weight of the wall above — called also *discharging arch*

relieving arch

**relieving officer** *n*, *Brit* **:** an official administering public relief

**relieving tackle** *n* **1 :** a temporary tackle rigged to a ship's tiller during gales or in battle to assist or replace the steering gear **2 :** a tackle to a careened ship to prevent her from going over entirely and to assist in righting her

**¹re·lie·vo** \rēˈlē(ˌ)vō; relˈyā(-, -ye(-\ *n* -S [It *rilievo* — more at RELIEF] **:** RELIEF 6

**²re·lie·vo** \rəˈlē(ˌ)vō\ *n* -S [prob. fr. *relieve* + *-o*] **:** a game in which members of one team are given time to hide, then are sought by those of the other team who try to capture them, take them to a place of confinement, and keep them from being released by their teammates — called also *ring-a-lievo*

**rel·i·gate** \ˈreləˌgāt\ *vb* -ED/-ING/-S [L *religatus*, past part. of *religare* to tie back, tie up, tie fast — more at RELY] **:** to bind together **:** CONSTRAIN — **rel·i·ga·tion** \ˌ==ˈgāshən\ *n* -S

**re·light** \(ˈ)rē+\ *vt* [*re-* + *light*] **:** to light again

**re·lig·i·fy** \rəˈlijəˌfī\ *vt* -ED/-ING/-ES [*religious* + *-fy*] **:** to make religious in form, content, appearance, or function

**religio-** *comb form* [*religion*] **:** religion ⟨*religio*centric⟩ **:** religious and ⟨*religio*philosophical⟩

**re·li·gio·ethical** \-ˌlijē(ˌ)ō+\ *adj* [*religio-* + *ethical*] **:** religious and ethical

**re·li·gion** \rəˈlijən, rēˈ-\ *n* -S [ME *religioun*, fr. L *religion-*, *religio* reverence, piety, religion, prob. fr. *religare* to tie back, tie up, tie fast + *-ion-*, *-io* -ion — more at RELY] **1 :** the personal commitment to and serving of God or a god with worshipful devotion, conduct in accord with divine commands esp. as found in accepted sacred writings or declared by authoritative teachers, a way of life recognized as incumbent on true believers, and typically the relating of oneself to an organized body of believers ⟨ministers of ~⟩ **2 :** the state of a religious ⟨retire into ~⟩ ⟨the nun died in her thirtieth year of ~⟩ **3 a :** one of the systems of faith and worship **:** a religious faith ⟨monotheistic ~s⟩ ⟨tolerant of all ~s⟩ ⟨forbidding discrimination because of race, color, or ~⟩ **b :** the body of institutionalized expressions of sacred beliefs, observances, and social practices found within a given cultural context ⟨the ~ of this primitive people⟩ **4 :** the profession or practice of religious beliefs **:** religious observances ⟨the kernel of his practical ~ was that it was respectable, and beneficial to one's business, to be seen going to services —Sinclair Lewis⟩ **5** *archaic* **:** scrupulous conformity **:** CONSCIENTIOUSNESS, FIDELITY **6 a :** a personal awareness or conviction of the existence of a supreme being or of supernatural powers or influences controlling one's own, humanity's, or all nature's destiny ⟨only man appears to be capable of ~⟩ **b :** the access of such an awareness or conviction accompanied by or arousing reverence, gratitude, humility, the will to obey and serve **:** religious experience or insight ⟨in middle life he suddenly got ~⟩ **7 a :** a cause, principle, system of tenets held with ardor, devotion, conscientiousness, and faith **:** a value held to be of supreme importance ⟨by making democracy our ~ and by practicing as well as preaching its doctrines —W.O.Douglas⟩ ⟨Marxism was his ~⟩ ⟨he has made a ~ of pleasure, and it is a brave thing to do these days —Gerald Sykes⟩ **b :** a quality, condition, custom, or thing inspiring zealous devotion, conscientious maintenance, and cherishing ⟨a ~ with him to preserve in good condition all that had lapsed from his mother's hands —Thomas Hardy⟩

**syn** FAITH, CHURCH, CREED, COMMUNION, DENOMINATION, SECT, CULT, PERSUASION: RELIGION is a general term esp. applicable to the great revelations and the larger subdivisions among their believers ⟨the Christian *religion*⟩ ⟨the Roman Catholic or Methodist *religion*⟩ FAITH is applicable to any formulated and established major religious group; it may or may not suggest ardent, complete acceptance ⟨the Muhammadan *faith*⟩ ⟨the Mormon *faith*⟩ ⟨men of all *faiths*⟩ CHURCH is likely to stress the existence of an established formal organization and procedure; it may suggest a Christian rather than non-Christian context ⟨the Orthodox *Church*⟩ ⟨the Presbyterian *Church*⟩ CREED differs from FAITH in more strongly suggesting formal doctrinal expression of what is believed — accord on the basis of doctrinal assent — but is applicable to most religious groups ⟨men of the Lutheran *creed*⟩ ⟨the *creed* of Hebraism⟩ COMMUNION may suggest accord on liturgical or sacramental practice and earnest, close fellowship in worship; it is applicable to both larger and smaller groups. DENOMINATION is likely to suggest a smaller section called by a distinctive name of a larger group ⟨various Protestant *denominations*⟩ SECT now indicates a smaller group which has split off from a larger through discontent with some matter of doctrine or observance ⟨the Uniat *sect*⟩ ⟨a *sect* composed of the followers of John Huss⟩ CULT suggests a small group holding to unusual, grotesque, or secret spurious notions and rituals ⟨forbade the practice of certain eastern *cults*, and expelled from Rome Greek and Asiatic magicians —John Buchan⟩ PERSUASION may suggest conviction arising from evangelism or exhortation; often it is more or less interchangeable with FAITH ⟨chapel goers, people of Wesleyan *persuasion*⟩

**¹religionary** *n* -ES [*religion* + *-ary* (n. suffix)] *obs* **:** one whose vocation is religion

**²re·li·gion·ary** \-jəˌnerē\ *adj* [*religion* + *-ary* (adj. suffix)] **:** RELIGIOUS

**re·li·gion·er** \-jənə(r)\ *n* -S **:** RELIGIONIST

**re·li·gion·ism** \-jəˌnizəm\ *n* -S **:** strict practice of or devotion to religion; *also* **:** exaggerated religious zealotry

**re·li·gion·ist** \-nəst\ *n* -S **:** one earnestly devoted or attached to a religion **:** a religious zealot — **re·li·gion·is·tic** \=ˌ==ˈnistik\ *adj*

**re·li·gion·ize** \=ˈ==ˌnīz\ *vt* -ED/-ING/-S **:** to make religious **:** imbue with religious principles **:** bring into conformity with religious standards **:** interpret or understand (a thing) from a religious framework ⟨~ our politics⟩ ⟨~ death⟩

**re·li·gion·less** \rəˈlijənləs\ *adj* **:** lacking religion

**religions** *pl of* RELIGION

**re·li·gio·political** \-ˌlijē(ˌ)ō+\ *adj* [*religio-* + *political*] **:** religious and political

**re·li·gi·ose** \rəˌlijēˈōs\ *adj* [*religion* + *-ose*] **:** excessively or obtrusively or sentimentally religious ⟨a leader of a ~ nationalism —Percy Winner⟩ ⟨modern advertising methods will not long need to lack leaders who can use the ~, fanatical technique —*English Jour.*⟩

**re·li·gi·os·i·ty** \rəˌlijēˈäsədˌē, rēˌ-, -ətē, -i\ *n* -ES [ME *religiosite*, fr. L *religiositas* religiousness, fr. *religiosus* religious + *-itas* -ity] **:** intense, excessive, or affected religiousness ⟨~ of the converted worldling and intellectual —Douglas Bush⟩ ⟨it was precisely sadness and ~ and grandiloquence that first attracted me in poetry —George Santayana⟩

**re·li·gi·o·so** \rəˌlijēˈō(ˌ)sō\ *adj* (or *adv*) [It, religious, fr. L *religiosus*] **:** religious in style and feeling — used as a direction in music

**¹re·li·gious** \rəˈlijəs, rēˈ-\ *adj* [ME, fr. OF *religieus*, fr. L *religiosus*, fr. *religio* religion + *-osus* -ous — more at RELIGION] **1 :** relating to that which is acknowledged as ultimate reality **:** manifesting devotion to and reflecting the nature of the divine or that which one holds to be of ultimate importance **:** exemplifying the influence of religion **:** PIOUS, GODLY ⟨a ~ purpose⟩ ⟨a ~ man⟩ ⟨~ attitude⟩ **2 :** committed, dedicated, or consecrated to the service of the divine **:** set apart to religion ⟨a Buddhist monk of a ~ order⟩ ⟨the ~ life of a nun⟩ ⟨~ offerings⟩ **3 :** of or relating to religion **:** concerned with religion **:** teaching or setting forth religion ⟨~ liberty⟩ ⟨a ~ duty⟩ ⟨a ~ poet⟩; *also* **:** SACRED, HOLY ⟨a ~ book⟩ ⟨~ rites⟩ **4 a :** scrupulously and conscientiously faithful ⟨~ in his observance of rules of health⟩ **b :** FERVENT, ZEALOUS **syn** see DEVOUT

**²religious** \"\ *n*, *pl* **religious** [ME, fr. OF *religieus*, fr. *religieus*, adj.] **:** one (as a monk or nun) who is bound by vows, sequestered from secular concerns, and devoted to a life of piety

**religious education** *n* **1 :** instruction in religion as a subject of general education **2 :** instruction in the principles of a particular religious faith

**religious house** *n* **:** CONVENT, MONASTERY

**religious humanism** *n* **:** a modern American movement composed chiefly of nontheistic humanists and humanist churches and dedicated to achieving the ethical goals of religion without beliefs and rites resting upon supernaturalism

**re·li·gious·ly** *adv* [ME, fr. *religious* + *-ly*] **:** in a religious manner **:** FAITHFULLY, CONSCIENTIOUSLY ⟨clock which my father ~ wound each Sunday morning —Della Lutes⟩ ⟨kept his diary ~⟩ **:** in favor of religion ⟨she was ~ inclined⟩

**religious naturalism** *n* **:** PROCESS PHILOSOPHY

**re·li·gious·ness** *n* -ES [ME *religiousnesse*, fr. *religious* + *-nesse* -ness] **:** the quality or state of being religious **:** RELIGIOSITY

**religious of the cenacle** *usu cap R&C* **:** a member of the Roman Catholic Society of Our Lady of the Cenacle, a congregation of nuns established in France in 1826 and devoted esp. to directing retreats for women

**religious of the sacred heart** *usu cap R&S&H* **:** a member of the Roman Catholic Society of the Sacred Heart, a religious community of women founded in France in 1800 and devoted to the education of girls

**re·line** \(ˈ)rē+\ *vt* [*re-* + *line*] **1 :** to put new or fresh lines on **2 :** to put a new lining in ⟨~ brakes⟩

**re·lin·quent** \rəˈliŋkwənt\ *adj* [L *relinquent-*, *relinquens*, pres. part. of *relinquere*] **:** RELINQUISHING

**re·lin·quish** \rəˈliŋkwish, rēˈ-, -ink-, -wēsh, *esp in pres part* -wəsh\ *vb* -ED/-ING/-ES [ME *relinquisshen*, fr. MF *relinquiss-*, lengthened stem of *relinquir*, fr. L *relinquere*, lit., to leave behind, fr. *re-* + *linquere* to leave — more at LOAN] *vt* **1 a** *obs* **:** FORSAKE **b :** to withdraw or retreat from **:** ABANDON ⟨the shores they have ~*ed* shrink to . . . remoteness —George Meredith⟩ **2 a :** to desist from **:** leave off **:** cease from considering, practising, exercising, or cherishing ⟨~*ing* the law, Webster resumed teaching —H.E.Scudder⟩ ⟨the . . . scheme had been deferred, not ~*ed* —Jane Austen⟩ **b :** to assent to withdrawal, dropping, or cessation of **:** give up **:** RENOUNCE ⟨his concealment from herself of the name he had ~*ed* —Charles Dickens⟩ ⟨refused to ~ his claim to the inheritance⟩ ⟨~*ed* all hope of finding survivors⟩ **3 a :** to let go of physically **:** stop holding **:** RELEASE ⟨~*ed* his grip on his armchair⟩ **b :** to give over possession or control of **:** YIELD, SURRENDER ⟨the ambition which incites a man to seize power seldom allows him to ~ it —*Times Lit. Supp.*⟩ ~ *vi*, *obs* **:** to go away **:** DISAPPEAR, VANISH

**syn** LEAVE, ABANDON, WAIVE, RESIGN, CEDE, YIELD, SURRENDER: RELINQUISH, a word wide in meaning, as the preceding definitions indicate, usu. does not suggest forceful action or strong feeling in dropping, desisting, renouncing; it sometimes suggests regret at giving up or delay in the process ⟨and your system . . . have courage to cast the dream of it out of you; *relinquish* an impossible project —George Meredith⟩ ⟨did not lightly *relinquish* his hope of victory —*Amer. Guide Series: Ind.*⟩ ⟨it cost him a few struggles to *relinquish* her —Jane Austen⟩ LEAVE may connote more peremptory and definite action than RELINQUISH ⟨"he has *left* me," Sophia interrupted him in her weak and fatigued voice —Arnold Bennett⟩ ⟨always carries his mouth open, a practice which, it is prophesied, he will soon *leave* off in this land of flies —Rachel Henning⟩ ABANDON may stress finality and completeness in giving up, esp. before dangers, hostile advances, encroachments that cannot be checked, or against the claims of duty or loyalty ⟨the stations were withdrawn . . . and northern Texas *abandoned* to the savages —R.A.Billington⟩ ⟨*abandoning* wife and children, home and business, and renouncing normal morality and humanity —G.B.Shaw⟩ WAIVE may suggest either temporary or permanent forgoing; it often connotes a voluntary, complaisant giving up of something in the interests of conciliation or convenience ⟨from that time onward the office rule was *waived* —E.H.Collis⟩ RESIGN may suggest either a formal and definite giving up or relinquishing or a wistful, stoic, or confiding yielding or acceptance without struggle ⟨Britain rightly refused to budge from the position that it would not *resign* its trusteeship —*Nation*⟩ ⟨these saintly self-deniers, these *resigned* sufferers, who would not strive nor cry —Matthew Arnold⟩ CEDE suggests giving up or granting formally by or as if by treaty, negotiation, or arbitration holdings, either willingly or under duress and compulsion, but always peacefully ⟨strongly urging the states to *cede* these lands to the United States —R.B.Taney⟩ ⟨the Dutch were forced to *cede* New Amsterdam —Stringfellow Barr⟩ YIELD may suggest a giving up through diplomatic concession but is more likely to connote submitting and giving over to superior force ⟨he already saw that his friend and employer was a man who knew no moderation in his requests and impulses and he *yielded* gracefully —Thomas Hardy⟩ ⟨after a spirited contest lasting three quarters of a century, theocratic Puritanism *yielded* to ecclesiastical democracy —V.L.Parrington⟩ SURRENDER is likely to indicate giving up under compulsion to superior forces, esp. after resistance or preparation for or show of resistance ⟨Fort Orange *surrendered* to the English —A.C.Flick⟩

**re·lin·quish·ment** \-shmənt\ *n* -s **1 :** the act of relinquishing **:** a giving up **:** SURRENDER, RENUNCIATION **2 :** a piece of relinquished or abandoned land

**¹rel·i·quary** \'relə,kwerē, -ri\ *n* -ES [F *reliquaire*, fr. ML *reliquiarium*, fr. *reliquia* relic + L *-arium* -ary — more at RELIC] **:** a casket, shrine, or container for keeping or exhibiting relics

**²reliquary** \"\ *adj* [ML *reliquia* relic + E *-ary*] **:** of, relating to, or serving as relics ⟨~ case⟩ ⟨the general tendency . . . was towards a circular form for devotional and ~ pendants —Joan Evans⟩

**rel·ique** \'relik, rə'lēk\ *archaic var of* RELIC

**re·liq·ui·ae** \rə'likwə,ē\ *n pl* [L — more at RELIC] **:** remains of the dead **:** organic remains **:** RELICS

**re·liq·ui·al** \-wēəl\ *adj* [L *reliquiae* remains + E *-al*] **:** RELICT 3

**re·liq·ui·an** \-ən\ *adj* [L *reliquiae* + E *-an*] **:** being or resembling a relic **:** RELIQUARY

**rel·i·quism** \'relə,kwizəm\ *n* -s [*relic* + *-ism*] **:** practice of keeping or venerating relics

**¹rel·ish** \'relish, -lēsh\ *n* -ES [alter. of ME *reles* taste, aftertaste, odor, scent, fr. OF *reles, relais* something left behind, release — more at RELEASE] **1 :** characteristic flavor; *esp* **:** pleasing or zestful flavor **:** TANG, SAVOR ⟨now I have better things to write of — things that have some ~ of good in them —Irving Bacheller⟩ **2 :** a quantity just sufficient to flavor or characterize **:** TRACE, DASH ⟨your lordship . . . hath yet some smack of age in you . . . some ~ of the saltness of time —Shak.⟩ **3** *obs* **:** power to discern and appreciate; *often* **:** personal taste **:** LIKING **4 a :** enjoyment of or delight in something that satisfies one's tastes, inclinations, desires **:** GRATIFICATION ⟨men have a keener ~ for privileges and honors than for equality —Réne Sédillot⟩ ⟨with the ~ of a child digging into a dish of ice cream⟩ **b :** APPETITE, STOMACH, INCLINATION ⟨a studious boy with little ~ for sports⟩ **5 a :** something served to add a zestful flavor to a plain dish **:** CONDIMENT ⟨horseradish sauce is a favorite ~ with boiled beef⟩; *esp* **:** a savory pickled or preserved food prepared from mixed chopped vegetables or fruits and usu. served with meat ⟨corn ~⟩ ⟨beet ~⟩ ⟨pickle ~⟩ **b :** APPETIZER, HORS D'OEUVRE **syn** see TASTE

**²relish** \", *esp in pres part* -ləsh\ *vb* -ED/-ING/-ES *vt* **1 :** to add a relish, flavor, or zest to **:** serve as a condiment to ⟨a savory bit that served to ~ wine —John Dryden⟩ **2 :** to be pleased or gratified by **:** approve of **:** ENJOY ⟨~*ed* the relaxed attentiveness and technical aplomb of the instrumentalists —Herbert Weinstock⟩ ⟨could not expect them to ~ the prospect of a cut in salary⟩ **3 a :** to eat or drink with pleasure **:** like the taste of ⟨so hungry that he will ~ plain food⟩ **b :** to delight in **:** take keen pleasure in ⟨bargains . . . with a fruit vendor, both of them laughing and ~*ing* the process and each other —Roger Angell⟩ **4 :** to appreciate with taste and discernment ⟨a people trained by oratory to ~ virtuosity of speech —H.M.Reynolds⟩ ⟨~*es* literature with his palate as well as with his brain —Henri Peyre⟩ **5** *obs* **:** to have a savor or suggestion of **:** smack of ~ *vi* **:** to have a characteristic or pleasing taste ⟨find ways in which the soldiers' food could be made more ~*ing* —*Current Biog.*⟩ ⟨his style ~*es* perhaps too much of the schoolroom⟩ **syn** see LIKE

**³relish** \"\ *n* -ES [perh. fr. ¹*relish*] **:** a grace or embellishment in early English music

**⁴relish** \"\ *vt, obs* **:** to sing with embellishments **:** WARBLE ⟨~ a love song, like a robin redbreast —Shak.⟩

**⁵relish** \"\ *n* -ES [F *relais*] **:** the projection or shoulder at the side of or around a tenon — compare MORTISE

**⁶relish** \"\ *vt* **:** to cut or shape the shoulder on (a tenon)

**rel·ish·able** \-shəbəl\ *adj* **:** capable of being relished **:** TASTY ⟨~ to readers hungry for spiritual fare —H.M.Robinson⟩

**relishing** *adj* [fr. pres. part. of ²*relish*] **:** that relishes or gives a relish **syn** see PALATABLE

**re·live** \(')rē+\ *vb* [*re-* + *live*] *vt* **1** *obs* **:** to recall to life **:** REVIVE **2 :** to live over again **:** experience again imaginatively ⟨*reliving* his battle experiences⟩ ~ *vi* **:** to return to life **:** live again

**re·lle·no** \ral'yā(,)nō\ *n* -s [Sp, fr. *rellenar* to refill, stuff, fr. *re-* (fr. L) + *llenar* to fill, fr. *lleno* full, fr. L *plenus* — more at FULL] **:** stuffed pepper

**rel·ly·an** \'relēən\ *adj, usu cap* [James *Relly* †1778 British theologian who organized a Universalist congregation in London soon after 1750 + E *-an*] **:** of or relating to the theologian Relly or to a short-lived minority group of Universalists named after him — **rel·ly·an·ism** \-ə,nizəm\ *n* -s *usu cap* — **rel·ly·an·ite** \-nīt\ *n* -s *usu cap*

**¹re·load** \(')rē¦lōd\ *vt* [*re-* + *load*] **:** to load again: as **a :** to put fresh ammunition into after firing ⟨~ a shotgun⟩ **b :** to load (a cartridge) by hand ⟨a ~*ing* tool⟩

**²reload** \'=,=\ *n* **:** the act or result of reloading: as **a :** a gun cartridge loaded by hand **b :** worthless securities or real estate sold to a person who has already bought

**re·load·er** \-də(r)\ *n* **:** one that reloads; *esp* **:** a salesman skilled in selling reloads of securities or property

**re·lo·cat·able** \¦rēlō¦kād·əbəl\ *adj* **:** capable of being relocated ⟨~ partitions⟩

**re·lo·cate** \(')rē¦lō,kāt, ¦rēlō'kāt, *usu* -ād.+V\ *vt* [*re-* + *locate*] **:** to locate or allocate again **:** establish or lay out in a new place ⟨~ families forced out by floods⟩ ⟨~ the roadbed of a washed-out railroad line⟩

**re·lo·ca·tion** \,rēlō'kāshən\ *n* [*re* + *location*] **1** *Roman, civil, & Scots law* **:** renewal of a lease — see TACIT RELOCATION **2** [*relocate* + *-ion*] **:** removal and establishment in a new place ⟨~ of war refugees⟩

**re·lo·ca·tor** \(')rē¦lō,kād·ə(r), ¦rēlō¦k-\ *n* **:** one that relocates: as **a :** an instrument used in seacoast fortifications for obtaining the range and position of a target from the range and position as determined with respect to the end of the base line **b :** one that relocates an abandoned or forfeited mining claim

**re·lu·cence** \rə'lüsᵊn(t)s, rē- *also* rəl'yü *or* rēl-\ *n* -s **:** the quality of being relucent **:** BRIGHTNESS

**re·lu·cent** \-nt\ *adj* [L *relucent-, relucens*, pres. part. of *relucēre* to shine back, fr. *re-* + *lucēre* to shine — more at LIGHT] **:** reflecting light **:** RADIANT, REFULGENT, SHINING ⟨large, dark, ~ eyes set well apart —Compton Mackenzie⟩

**re·luct** \rə'ləkt, rē-\ *vi* -ED/-ING/-S [L *reluctari*] **1 :** to make a determined resistance **:** STRUGGLE **2 :** to feel or show repugnance or reluctance **:** REVOLT ⟨many readers . . . ~ at works containing dialect —L.P.Smith⟩

**re·luc·tance** \-tən(t)s\ *n* -s [L *reluctari* + E *-ance*] **1** *obs* **:** the act of struggling against or opposing **:** OPPOSITION **2 :** the quality or state of being reluctant **:** UNWILLINGNESS, AVERSION, REPUGNANCE ⟨obeyed with ~⟩ ⟨showed a ~ to accept charity⟩ **3 :** a quantity in a magnetic circuit analogous to the resistance of an electric circuit or conductor; *specif* **:** the ratio of the magnetic potential difference to the corresponding flux — compare PERMEANCE

**reluctance cartridge** *n* **:** a device for converting phonograph-record groove undulations into an electrical voltage by electromagnetic means

**re·luc·tan·cy** \-nsē, -si\ *n* -ES [L *reluctari* + E *-ancy*] **1 a :** a mental conflict **b :** OPPOSITION, RESISTANCE **c :** REGRET ⟨memories bring regrets and *reluctancies* of the spirit —Victor Canning⟩ **2 :** DISINCLINATION, RELUCTANCE, REPUGNANCE ⟨~ to testify in court⟩

**re·luc·tant** \-nt\ *adj* [L *reluctant-, reluctans*, pres. part. of *reluctari* to struggle against, oppose, resist, be reluctant, fr. *re-* + *luctari* to struggle, wrestle — more at LOCK] **1 :** offering opposition **:** RESISTING **2 :** hesitant from or as if from dislike, doubt, fear, or scruple **:** AVERSE, UNWILLING ⟨~ to charge a dead man with an offense from which he could not clear himself —Edith Wharton⟩ ⟨persuaded him into ~ consent⟩ ⟨trying to scratch a living from ~ soil⟩ **syn** see DISINCLINED

**re·luc·tant·ly** *adv* **:** with reluctance **:** UNWILLINGLY, GRUDGINGLY

**re·luc·tate** \rə'lək,tāt\ *vb* -ED/-ING/-S [L *reluctatus*, past part. of *reluctari*] *vi* **:** to show reluctance **:** RELUCT ~ *vt* **:** to struggle against **:** REPUDIATE, REPEL

**rel·uc·ta·tion** \,reləkˈtāshən, ,rē,lək'-\ *n* -s [LL *reluctation-, reluctatio*, fr. L *reluctatus* + *-ion-, -io* -ion] **:** RELUCTANCE, RELUCTANCY

**rel·uc·tiv·i·ty** \-'tivəd·ē\ *n* -ES [*reluctance* + *-ivity* (as in *conductivity*)] **:** the reciprocal of magnetic permeability

**re·lume** \rə'lüm, rē- *also* rəl'yüm *or* rēl-\ *vt* -ED/-ING/-S [irreg. fr. LL *reluminare*] **:** to light or light up again **:** RELUMINE, REKINDLE ⟨jets of affection which ~ a young world for me —R.W.Emerson⟩ ⟨then shall be no lamp *relumed* in heaven —Rupert Brooke⟩

**re·lu·mine** \-mən\ *vt* -ED/-ING/-S [LL *reluminare*, fr. L *re-* + *luminare* to light up — more at ILLUMINATE] **:** RELUME

**re·ly** \rə'lī, rē-\ *vb* **relied; relied; relying; relies** [ME *relien*, fr. MF *relier* to connect, fasten together, repair, rally, fr. L *religare* to tie back, tie up, tie fast, fr. *re-* + *ligare* to tie — more at LIGATURE] *vt* **1** *obs* **:** to gather together (as soldiers) **:** RALLY **2** *obs* **:** BASE, REST, REPOSE ~ *vi* **1** *obs* **:** HOLD, CLEAVE, BELONG — used with *to* **2** *obs* **:** CONSIST, SUBSIST — used with *in* **3** *obs* **:** LEAN, REST — used with *on* or *upon* **4 :** to have confidence **:** have a feeling of security **:** place faith without reservation **:** TRUST — used with *on, upon*, or sometimes *in* ⟨~ on his own wits⟩ ⟨can this rope be *relied* upon⟩ ⟨*relied* on the letter reaching you in time⟩ **:** expect with confidence or certainty ⟨dangerous to ~ on higher market prices⟩ **5 :** to find support **:** DEPEND ⟨~ on a well for all their water needs⟩ ⟨~ on foreign sources of rubber⟩

**syn** COUNT (*on*), RECKON (*on*), BANK (*on*), TRUST, DEPEND (*on*): RELY, COUNT, RECKON, and BANK are about equal in force and are often interchangeable. RELY may connote an objectivity of judgment based on previous experience with whatever is in question ⟨that unskilled copyists cannot be *relied* on in matters of punctuation, line structure —Van Wyck Brooks⟩ COUNT (*on*) may suggest a situation involving calculation or computation ⟨a special sum set apart . . . in addition to her pin money; *on* that she may absolutely *count* —Edith Wharton⟩ RECKON (*on*) likewise connotes calculating or planning. In affirmative situations it is common in reference to the known or determined as of one nature or another ⟨the king scarcely knew *on* what members of his cabinet he could *reckon* —T.B.Macaulay⟩ BANK (*on*), which is the least formal in this series, may carry connotations from the noun *bank* (meaning "financial institution") and suggest the certainty of money in a bank. BANK (*on*) is wide in its use in applying to persons, things, facts, and ideas, and to either their general existence as such or their utility and benefit to the speaker ⟨today, as hitherto, we *bank on* war —J.H. Holmes⟩ ⟨you can *bank on* Jeeves —P.G.Wodehouse⟩ TRUST may or may not suggest more complete belief or confidence in on the basis of faith rather than empirical fact ⟨let us to Providence *trust* —A.H.Clough⟩ ⟨better not *trust* her instinct —George Meredith⟩ ⟨*trusting* to common sense as well as Allah —Aldous Huxley⟩ DEPEND (*on*) may suggest weakness or lack of forethought, invention, or self-sufficiency. It may apply to situations in which no alternate recourse or measure has been planned ⟨he was always getting himself into crusades, or feuds, or love, or debt, and *depended on* the woman to get him out —Henry Adams⟩

**rem** \'rem\ *n, pl* **rem** *or* **rems** [roentgen equivalent *man*] **:** the dosage of any ionizing radiation that will cause the same amount of biological injury to human tissue as one roentgen of X-ray or gamma-ray dosage — compare REP

**rem** *abbr* **1** remain; remainder **2** remark **3** remit; remitted; remittance **4** remove

**remade** *past of* REMAKE

**remade milk** *n* **:** RECONSTITUTED MILK

**¹re·main** \rə'mān, rē-\ *vb* -ED/-ING/-S [ME *remainen*, fr. MF *remanoir, remaindre*, fr. L *remanēre* to stay behind, be left, fr. *re-* + *manēre* to stay, remain — more at MANSION] *vi* **1 a :** to be a part not destroyed, taken away, or used up **:** be still extant, present, or available **:** be left when the rest is gone ⟨ruins . . . of the officers' quarters ~ —*Amer. Guide Series: Texas*⟩ ⟨the pulpy . . . substance ~*ing* after the juice is ground from sugarcane —*Amer. Guide Series: La.*⟩ ⟨in the two weeks that ~*ed* to us —Kenneth Roberts⟩ **b :** to be something yet to be shown, done, or treated ⟨how it will work ~*s* to be seen⟩ ⟨looked around to see what work ~*ed*⟩ ⟨it ~*s* to add that the author has read very widely in the subject —C.E.Bazell⟩ **2 a :** to stay in the same place or with the same person or group ⟨will ~ in town for two days⟩ ⟨the matter ~*ed* with Congress —A.G.Larke⟩; *specif* **:** to stay behind while others withdraw ⟨asked the student to ~ after school⟩ **b** *obs* **:** RESIDE, DWELL **3 :** to continue unchanged in form, condition, status, or quantity **:** continue to be ⟨the pact was to ~ in force for 50 years —*Americana Annual*⟩ **:** STAND ⟨population ~*s* at around eight hundred —Fred Zimmer⟩ ⟨stir well and let the mixture ~ until morning⟩ ⟨a lubricant that ~*s* liquid at low temperatures⟩ ⟨~ silent rather than sounding off —Stuart Chase⟩ ⟨~*s* primarily a livestock state —*Amer. Guide Series: Nev.*⟩ **4** *of land* **:** to stay or continue for the benefit of another than the grantor ⟨after life estate the land still ~*ed* for the grantor's children⟩ — see REMAINDER 1a ~ *vt, obs* **:** AWAIT **syn** see STAY

**²remain** \"\ *n* -s [ME, fr. MF, fr. *remaindre* to remain — more at ¹REMAIN] **1** *obs* **:** the state of remaining **:** STAY ⟨my here ~ in England —Shak.⟩ **2 :** a remaining part or trace — usu. used in pl. ⟨the crumpled ~*s* of stone chimneys —Frederick Nebel⟩ ⟨repacked the ~*s* of the supper —C.S. Forester⟩ ⟨fossil ~*s* of prehistoric animals —*Amer. Guide Series: Minn.*⟩ ⟨a female of advanced years with the ~*s* of irresistible beauty —G.B.Shaw⟩ **3 remains** *pl* **:** the works of a writer who has died; *esp* **:** writings left unpublished by a writer at his death ⟨edited his dead friend's literary ~*s*⟩ **4 remains** *pl* **:** a dead body ⟨the custom of filing past the open casket to view the ~*s*⟩ ⟨secondary burials sometimes comprise masses of bone with the ~*s* of several individuals —G.R. Willey⟩

**¹re·main·der** \-də(r)\ *n* -s [ME, fr. AF, fr. MF *remaindre* to remain] **1 a :** an estate (as land) in expectancy that becomes an estate in possession upon the determination of a particular prior estate created at the same time and by the same instrument ⟨if land be conveyed to A for life, and on his death to B, A's life interest is a particular estate and B's interest is a ~⟩ — distinguished from *reversion* **b :** the right to succeed to a title or dignity upon the death of the holder ⟨the earl marshalship was granted anew . . . with many specific ~*s* —J.H.Round⟩; *specif* **:** the right of succession to a peerage assigned to a specified person or line of descent in default of male issue in the direct line ⟨living members in ~ to the title —*Burke's Peerage*⟩ **2 a :** a remaining group, part, or trace **:** REST ⟨half of whom are transported by regular bus service . . . and the ~ by private conveyances —H.W.H.King⟩ ⟨for the second year's work, and throughout the ~ of his course —*Bull. of Meharry Med. Coll.*⟩ **b :** the number left after subtraction or deduction; *specif* **:** the undivided part less or lower in degree than the divisor left after division **c** *obs* **:** a person remaining out of a number **3 a :** a book belonging to or forming a supply sold at a reduced price by the publisher after sales have become unprofitable ⟨guess that a half of all fiction books . . . and a quarter of the nonfiction end up as ~*s* —*N.Y. Times Bk. Rev.*⟩ **b :** a stamp of an unsold post office supply of a demonetized issue — usu. used in pl.

**²remainder** \"\ *adj* **1 :** not taken, used, or gone **:** LEFTOVER, REMAINING ⟨as dry as the ~ biscuit after a voyage —Shak.⟩ **2 :** of, forming, or selling remainders ⟨a ~ counter⟩ ⟨~ prices⟩

**³remainder** \"\ *vb* **remaindered; remaindered; remaindering** \-d(ə)riŋ\ **remainders** *vt* **1 :** to sell the unsold copies of (a publication) at a lowered price **2 :** to sell usu. at a discount the remaining supply of (a demonetized postage stamp) to collectors or dealers ~ *vi* **:** to sell remainders

**remainder binding** *n* **:** an inferior binding put (as by a jobber) on remainders sold unbound by the publisher

**remainder cancellation** *n* **:** a cancellation on a remainder stamp making it invalid for postal use and available as a philatelic item

**re·main·der·man** \=ˈ==mən\ *n, pl* **remaindermen** [*remainder* + *man*] **:** one who holds or is entitled to a legal remainder

**remainder theorem** *n* **:** a theorem in algebra: if $f(x)$ is a polynomial in $x$ then the remainder on dividing $f(x)$ by $x-a$ is $f(a)$

**¹re·make** \(')rē+\ *vt* [*re-* + *make*] **:** to give a different form to **:** TRANSFORM ⟨eastern Germany . . . is being *remade* according to the Soviet image —*Americana Annual*⟩ **:** REVISE ⟨~ their plans for the weekend —Josephine Y. Case⟩ — **re·maker** \"+\ *n*

**²remake** \'=,=\ *n* **:** a refilmed version of a previously made motion picture

**re·mak's fiber** \'rā,mäks-\ *n, usu cap R* [after Robert *Remak* †1865 Ger. physician, its discoverer] **:** an unmyelinated peripheral nerve fiber serving to conduct impulses that arise in pain receptors

**re·man** \(')rē+\ *vt* [*re-* + *man*] **1 :** to man (as a ship or gun) again or anew **2 :** to imbue with courage or manliness again

**re·man·ci·pate** \rə'man(t)sə,pāt\ *vt* [L *remancipatus*, past part. of *remancipare* to remancipate, fr. *re-* + *mancipare* to deliver as property, transfer — more at MANCIPATE] *Roman law* **:** to reconvey (a person or thing) by mancipation to the mancipant or to a third person — **re·man·ci·pa·tion** \=,==-'pāshən\ *n*

**¹re·mand** \rə'mand, rē-, -maa(ə)nd, -mänd\ *vt* -ED/-ING/-S [ME *remaunden*, fr. MF *remander*, fr. LL *remandare* to send back word, fr. L *re-* + *mandare* to hand over, order, send word — more at MANDATE] **1 :** to cause to go back to a place (as by an authoritative command) **:** order back **:** consign again **2 :** to return (a case) from one court to another esp. lower court or from a court to an administrative agency **3 :** to send (a person charged with a crime) back into custody by court order (as pending trial) ⟨the judge discharges him or ~*s* him⟩ **:** to turn (a prisoner) over for continued detention ⟨she temporarily ~*ed* him to . . . New York's detention home for boys —Marjorie Rittwagen⟩ ⟨those . . . in need of further treatment are usually ~*ed* to state or private institutions —S.R.Cutolo⟩

**²remand** \"\ *n* -s **:** the act of remanding or state of being remanded **:** an order to remand an accused person ⟨a prisoner appearing on ~⟩ **:** detention under an order to remand ⟨use ~ for studying the child's background and attitude⟩

**remand center** *n* **:** a British institution to which the court may commit for temporary detention juvenile offenders too unruly or depraved for a remand home

**remand home** *n* **:** a British institution to which juvenile offenders may be committed by the court for temporary detention **:** DETENTION HOME ⟨children from 8 to 16 sent to *remand homes* for periods up to one month⟩ — compare BORSTAL

**rem·a·nence** \'remənən(t)s\ *n* -s [²*remanent*, after such pairs as E *excellent: excellence*] **1 :** the property of being residual or enduring **2 :** the magnetic induction remaining in a magnetized substance when the external magnetizing force has become zero — compare COERCIVE FORCE

**¹remanent** *n* -s [L *remanent-, remanens*, pres. part. of *remanēre* to be left, remain — more at REMAIN] *obs* **:** REMAINDER, REMNANT, RESIDUE

**²rem·a·nent** \-nənt\ *adj* [ME, fr. L *remanent-, remanens*] **1** *obs* **:** PERMANENT, LASTING, ENDURING **2 :** left after the rest has been used, removed, done **:** REMAINING, RESIDUAL ⟨~ sugar in new wine⟩ **3** *chiefly Scot* **:** SUPPLEMENTARY, FURTHER **4 :** of, relating to, or characterized by magnetic remanence

**remanent magnetism** *n* **:** RESIDUAL MAGNETISM

**rem·a·net** \'remə,net, *usu* -ed·+V\ *n* -s [L, it is left, remains, 3rd sing. pres. indic. of *remanēre* to be left, remain] **:** something remaining; *specif* **:** a case or proceeding the hearing of which is postponed

**re·ma·nié** \rə,mān'yā\ *n* -s [F, past part. of *remanier* to rework, rehandle, fr. *re-* + *manier* to handle, fr. OF, fr. *main* hand, fr. L *manus* — more at MANUAL] **:** a part or fragment (as a pebble or fossil) of an older formation incorporated in a younger deposit **:** RELICT, RESIDUAL

**¹re·manufacture** \(¦)rē+\ *n* [*re-* + *manufacture*, n.] **:** the process of remanufacturing ⟨paper . . . for ~ into shell wrappings —*Literary Digest*⟩

**²remanufacture** \"\ *vt* [*re-* + *manufacture*, v.] **:** to manufacture (used or scrap material) into a new product ⟨~ calculating machines⟩ ⟨~ the refuse of cotton and woolen yarn⟩

**re·margin** \(')rē+\ *vb* [*re-* + *margin*] *vt* **1 :** to put a fresh margin on (the leaves of a book) **2 :** to make good the margin on ⟨~ a loan⟩ ~ *vi* **:** to replenish or add to an existing margin (as one decreased by a change in prices)

**re·mark** \rə'märk, rē-, -mák\ *vb* [F *remarquer*, fr. MF, fr. *re-* + *marquer* to mark — more at MARQUE] *vt* **1** *obs* **a :** to mark in a notable manner **:** distinguish clearly ⟨his manacles ~ him; there he sits —John Milton⟩ **b :** to direct attention to **:** point out **2 :** to take notice of **:** OBSERVE, PERCEIVE, NOTE ⟨a passer-by would have ~*ed* an elderly shopkeeper bent apparently on a day in the country —John Buchan⟩ ⟨~*ed* no stiffness in her speech, but thought she spoke in music —William Black⟩ **3 :** to express as an observation or comment in speech or writing **:** STATE, SAY — usu. used with a direct or indirect quotation ⟨"Nice day!" he ~*ed*⟩ ⟨a metropolitan newspaper ~*ed* that no one today hopes for progress —Robert Bierstedt⟩ ~ *vi* **:** to make an observation or comment — used with *on* or *upon* ⟨~*ed* on the prosperous look of the countryside⟩ **syn** see SEE

**²remark** \"\ *n* [F *remarque*, fr. MF, fr. *remarquer* to remark] **1** *obs* **:** the quality or state of deserving special consideration **:** IMPORTANCE **2 :** the act of remarking **:** NOTICE, OBSERVATION **3 a :** the expression in speech or writing of something remarked or noticed **:** the mention of that which deserves attention or notice ⟨worthy of special ~ in a social history —G.M. Trevelyan⟩ **b :** a casual expression of an opinion or judgment ⟨began to pass ~*s* at the new guy —Harvey Granite⟩ **4** *obs* **a :** a notable sign or characteristic **:** an indicative mark **b :** TOKEN, INDICATION **c :** something noteworthy

**re·mark·abil·i·ty** \=,=kə'bilәd·ē, -lәtē, -i\ *n* **:** the quality or state of being remarkable

**¹re·mark·able** \=ˈ=kəbəl\ *adj* [F *remarquable*, fr. *remarquer* to remark + *-able*] **1 a :** worthy of being or likely to be noticed **b :** UNCOMMON, EXTRAORDINARY ⟨~ for his generosity⟩ ⟨the ~ features of a place⟩ ⟨~ beauty⟩ **2** *obs* **:** that can be seen or observed **:** DISCERNIBLE **syn** see NOTICEABLE

**²remarkable** \"\ *n* -ES *archaic* **:** a remarkable thing or occurrence

**re·mark·able·ness** *n* -ES **:** the quality or state of being remarkable

**re·mark·ably** \-kəblē, -li\ *adv* **:** in a remarkable manner or to a remarkable degree **:** UNUSUALLY, EXTRAORDINARILY ⟨~ tall trees⟩ ⟨~ few fences⟩

**re·mark·ed·ly** \-kədlē, -li\ *adv* [*remarked* (past part. of ¹*remark*) + *-ly*] **:** MARKEDLY, NOTABLY ⟨the megalithic relics . . . have ~ constant features —Lancelot Hogben⟩

**re·mark·er** \rə'märkər, rē-, -mákə(r)\ *n* -s **:** one that remarks

**re·marque** *also* **re·mark** \rə'märk, rē-, -mák\ *n* -s [F *remarque* remark — more at REMARK] **1 :** a drawn, etched, or incised scribble or sketch done on the margin of a plate or stone and removed before the regular printing **2 :** REMARQUE PROOF

**remarque proof** *n* **:** a proof taken before remarques have been removed

**re·marriage** \(')rē+\ *n* [*re-* + *marriage*] **:** an act or instance of remarrying **:** the state of being remarried ⟨lost the inheritance by ~⟩

**re·marry** \"+\ *vb* [*re-* + *marry*] **:** to marry again ⟨were *remarried* in a religious ceremony after the civil marriage⟩ ⟨the mothers . . . had *remarried* soulless loafers who treated the children's pensions as a life income —*Sydney (Australia) Bull.*⟩ ⟨~ his divorced wife after a reconciliation⟩ ⟨waited a year after his wife's death before he *remarried*⟩

**re·match** \'rē,mach\ *n* [*re-* + *match*] **:** a second match between the same two sports contestants or teams **:** a return match

**re·ma·te** \rā'mätā\ *n* -s [Sp, lit., end (fr. its usually being the last of a series of pases), fr. *rematar* to finish off, end, fr. *re-* (fr. L) + *matar* to kill, perh. fr. L *mattus* stupid, drunk — more at MAT] **:** a whirling pase used by a matador to fix the position of the bull

**rem·a·zol dye** \'remə,zōl-, -zōl-\ *n, usu cap R* [origin unknown] **:** any of several fiber-reactive dyes — see DYE table I

**rem·ba·ran·ga** \,rembə'raŋgə\ *n, pl* **rembaranga** *or* **rembarangas** *usu cap* **1 :** an aboriginal people of central Arnhem-land, Australia **2 :** a member of the Rembaranga people

**rem·brandt** \'rem,brant\ *n* -s *often cap* [after *Rembrandt* van Rijn †1669 Dutch painter] **:** a dark grayish brown that is very slightly yellower and paler than Liberia and slightly less strong than average chocolate brown

**rem·brandt·esque** \,rem,brant·¦esk, -n·¦te-\ *adj, usu cap* [*Rembrandt* van Rijn + E *-esque*] **:** resembling the style or manner of the Dutch painter Rembrandt (as in his use of strongly contrasted light and shade) ⟨*Rembrandtesque* setting for the moving throng of figures —Mrs Humphry Ward⟩

**rem·brandt·ish** \'rem,brantish\ *adj, usu cap* [*Rembrandt* van Rijn + E *-ish*] **:** REMBRANDTESQUE

**rem·brandt·ism** \-nt·,izəm, -n,ti-\ *n* -s *usu cap* [*Rembrandt* van Rijn + E *-ism*] **:** Rembrandtesque style

**rembrandt's madder** *n, often cap R* [after *Rembrandt* van Rijn] **:** ANTIQUE RED

**rembrandt tulip** *n, usu cap R* **:** any of various Darwin tulips with blotched or mottled coloring that result from color breaks

**re·mede** *or* **re·mead** \rə'mēd\ *n* [ME, fr. MF, fr. L *remedium* remedy] *chiefly Scot* **:** REMEDY, REDRESS

**re·me·di·able** \rə'mēdēəbəl, rē'-\ *adj* [ME, fr. MF, fr. L *remediabilis*, fr. *remediare* to remedy + *-abilis* -able] **:** capable of being remedied ⟨not a crime but only a ~ blunder —T.E. Ennis⟩ ⟨children with ~ defects in vision⟩ — **re·me·di·a·ble·ness** *n* -ES — **re·me·di·a·bly** \-blē, -li\ *adv*

**re·me·di·al** \-dēəl\ *adj* [LL *remedialis*, fr. L *remedium* remedy + *-alis* -al] **1 :** affording a remedy **:** intended for a remedy or for the removal or abatement of a disease or of an evil ⟨~ surgery⟩ ⟨~ legislation⟩ — compare DECLARATORY **2 :** concerned with the correction of faulty study habits, the improvement of skills imperfectly learned, and the raising of a pupil's general competence ⟨~ reading⟩ ⟨~ instruction⟩ — **re·me·di·al·ly** \-əlē, -li\ *adv*

**remedial loan society** *n* **:** a bank or other financial institution that lends small sums to needy borrowers at a relatively moderate rate of interest

**remedial right** *n* **:** a right (as of self-defense) arising on a violation of and for the protection of a substantive right

**remediate** *adj* [L *remedium* remedy + E *-ate*] *obs* **:** REMEDIAL

**re·me·di·a·tion** \rə,mēdē'āshən\ *n* -s [L *remediation-*, *remediatio*, fr. *remediatus* (past part. of *remediare* to remedy) + *-ion-*, *-io* -ion] **:** the act or process of remedying ⟨~ of reading difficulties⟩

**rem·e·di·less** \'remədēləs, -dəl-\ *adj* [ME *remedilesse*, fr. [1]*remedy* + *-lesse* -less] **1 a** *obs* **:** lacking hope of assistance or relief **:** being beyond help **b :** having no legal remedy **2 :** not admitting of remedy **:** IRREMEDIABLE, IRREPARABLE — **rem·e·di·less·ly** *adv* — **rem·e·di·less·ness** *n* -ES

[1]**rem·e·dy** \-dē, -di\ *n* -ES [ME *remedie*, fr. AF, fr. L *remedium* fr. *remederi* to heal again, cure, fr. *re-* + *mederi* to heal — more at MEDICAL] **1 :** something that relieves or cures a disease **:** a medicine or application that serves or helps to terminate disease and restore health **2 :** something that corrects or counteracts an evil **:** CORRECTIVE, COUNTERACTIVE, REPARATION ⟨whose simple ~ for discontent was the wall and the firing-squad —H.J.Laski⟩ **3 :** TOLERANCE 3a **4 :** the legal means to recover a right or to prevent or obtain redress for a wrong **:** the relief (as damages, restitution, specific performance, an injunction) that may be given by a court for a wrong **5 :** a half-holiday in an English school

**syn** CURE, MEDICINE, MEDICAMENT, MEDICATION, SPECIFIC, PHYSIC: REMEDY applies to a substance or treatment that is known or regarded as effective in bringing about recovery or restoration of health or the normal functioning of the body ⟨patent medicines and cold *remedies*⟩ ⟨a toothache *remedy*⟩ ⟨much has been written on the subject of fear and many inspirational and emotional *remedies* have been suggested —W.J. Reilly⟩ ⟨a homely *remedy* is to rub a moist cake of carbolic soap over the skin —F.D.Smith & Barbara Wilcox⟩ ⟨psychoanalysis as a *remedy* for mental ills⟩ CURE, more positive than REMEDY in implying complete recovery or restoration of health, is a common term to designate anything advocated as being or thought to be conducive to complete recovery ⟨no known specific *cure* for tuberculosis —*Therapeutic Notes*⟩ ⟨the climate was advertised during the eighties as a *cure* for tuberculosis —*Amer. Guide Series: Minn.*⟩ ⟨reaching into the medicine cabinet for a *cure* for the baby —W.J.Reilly⟩ ⟨all current surgical intervention in mental disease is not proposed as a *cure* —*Collier's Yr. Bk.*⟩ MEDICINE is the ordinary term for any substance or preparation taken internally in treating a disturbance of the normal functions of the body ⟨most *medicines* are alleviative in their action and not definitely curative —A.C. Morrison⟩ ⟨the witch doctor is there to give them some magic *medicine* to drink —J.G.Frazer⟩ MEDICAMENT or MEDICATION are general terms esp. used by doctors and pharmacists for all medicinal substances and preparations whether taken internally or applied externally ⟨doctors admit that they can do more for their patients now that they do not have to worry about the size of their bills and the cost of *medicaments* —*New Statesman & Nation*⟩ ⟨made the rounds of her five patients with a *medicament* of her own — a quart of Grandfather's best bonded bourbon —J.A.Maxwell⟩ ⟨prescribe several kinds of *medication* hoping to hit on a cure⟩ SPECIFIC is applied to something, usu. a drug, known to be effective in curing a specific disease ⟨various rheumatism *specifics* containing cinchophen, found to have notably injurious effects on the liver —*Encyc. Americana*⟩ PHYSIC is the archaic equivalent of MEDICINE ⟨this first revolt against authority took the form of refusing *physic* when he was ill —Agnes Repplier⟩; in modern use it has specialized to become synonymous with *purgative* or *cathartic*.

[2]**remedy** \"\ *vt* -ED/-ING/-ES [ME *remedien* to provide remedy for, fr. MF *remedier*, fr. L *remediare*, fr. L *remedium*] **1** *obs* **:** to give legal redress to **:** render justice to **2 :** to provide or serve as a remedy for **:** RELIEVE, REPAIR ⟨certain mental blocks can be *remedied* —Stuart Chase⟩ ⟨some defect in total mobilization to be *remedied* in time —H.W.Neuberg⟩ **syn** see CORRECT, CURE

**re·meid** \rə'mēd\ *var of* REMEDE

[1]**re·melt** \(')rē¦melt\ *vt* [*re-* + *melt*] **:** to melt (as a metal) again

[2]**remelt** \'=,=\ *n* **:** something remelted (as a metal) or to be remelted (as sugar)

**re·mem·ber** \rə'membə(r), rē'-\ *vb* **remembered; remembered; remembering** \-b(ə)riŋ\ **remembers** [ME *remembren*, fr. MF *remembrer*, fr. LL *rememorari*, fr. *re-* + *memorari* to be mindful of, fr. L *memor* mindful — more at MEMORY] *vt* **1 :** to have (a notion or idea) come into the mind again as previously perceived, known, or felt **:** have a renewed apprehension of **:** bring to mind again **:** think of again ⟨~ events of one's childhood⟩ ⟨racked his brain to ~ the name⟩ **2** *archaic* **a :** to take thought of ⟨now, I ~ me, I'm married —William Congreve⟩ **b :** to put in mind **:** bring to recollect ⟨~*ing* them the truth of what they themselves know —John Milton⟩ **3 :** to hold in memory with some feeling or intention **:** keep the recollection of: as **a :** to keep in mind so as to bestow attention or consideration upon **:** be continually thoughtful or regardful of ⟨~ one's friends at Christmas⟩ ⟨~ the Sabbath day to keep it holy —Exod 20:8 (RSV)⟩ **b** (1) **:** to keep in mind as deserving a reward (2) **:** REWARD ⟨was ~*ed* in the will⟩ **4 :** to hold or bear in mind **:** retain in the memory ⟨~ the dates until after the examination⟩ **5 a :** to recall to the mind of another **b :** to convey greetings from ⟨~ me to your father when you get home⟩ **6 :** MENTION, RECORD, COMMEMORATE ⟨tradition and history have not ~*ed* their names —V.L.Parrington⟩ ~ *vi* **1 :** to exercise or have the power of memory ⟨some ~ better than others⟩ ⟨give him time to ~⟩ **2 :** to have a recollection or remembrance ⟨ask your grandmother about it — she'll ~⟩ — sometimes used with *of* ⟨you'll find conditions very different to what you ~ of —Henry Green⟩

**syn** RECOLLECT, RECALL, REMIND, REMINISCE, BETHINK, MIND: REMEMBER may indicate an effortless or unwilled permitting of something held in one's memory to occupy one's attention, vividly or not ⟨when people talked about things they could *remember* Matey always wondered which kind of *remembering* they meant — the kind that was just a sort of knowing how something in the past had happened or the other kind when suddenly everything seemed to be happening all over again —Dorothy C. Fisher⟩ RECOLLECT may differ from REMEMBER in involving a bringing back, sometimes with conscious effort, of something of which one has not thought for a time ⟨I can *recollect* my reply to the postscript, but not the whole letter —W.F.DeMorgan⟩ ⟨I had begun by making simple notes after our various conversations on the ship, so that I shouldn't forget details; later, as certain aspects of the thing began to grip me, I had the urge to do more, to fashion the written and *recollected* fragments into a single narrative —James Hilton⟩ Used of persons, RECALL may suggest a process whereby the mind is summoned to bring back in toto rather than slowly reassembling; used of things, it indicates evoking or calling forth a memory ⟨"had you any conversation with the prisoner on that passage across the Channel?" "Yes, sir." "*Recall* it." In the midst of a profound stillness, she faintly began —Charles Dickens⟩ ⟨that tree always awakened pleasant memories, *recalling* a garden in the South of France where he used to visit young cousins —Willa Cather⟩ REMIND suggests the evoking of something forgotten or hard to think of again, sometimes by way of admonition; when used reflexively of persons it indicates a conscious jogging of memory ⟨the young soldier was *reminded* by his sister of their childhood hideout —*Amer. Guide Series: La.*⟩ ⟨the drone of the remorse-mongers as they *remind* him that he is partially to blame —E.M.Forster⟩ ⟨might *remind* ourselves that criticism is as inevitable as breathing —T.S.Eliot⟩ REMINISCE may imply a casual, unguided, and perhaps nostalgic consideration of the past ⟨cut me short to *reminisce* of his schoolmates —Hervey Allen⟩ ⟨listening to papa *reminisce* how he had gone around Thanksgiving Day as a boy —Betty Smith⟩ BETHINK applies to thinking back and recollecting with reflection ⟨he *bethought* him of certain meals his mother had cooked at home —Stephen Crane⟩ MIND, close in meaning and suggestion to RECOLLECT, often seems dialectal or quaint in suggestion ⟨I can *mind* her well as a nursing mother — a comely woman in her day —A.T.Quiller-Couch⟩

**re·mem·ber·able** \-b(ə)rəbəl\ *adj* [*remember* + *-able*] **:** capable of being remembered **:** MEMORABLE ⟨describe our feelings in ~ words —Aldous Huxley⟩

**re·mem·ber·er** \-b(ə)rə(r)\ *n* -s [*remember* + *-er*] **:** one that remembers ⟨the forgetter . . . has fewer facts but many more ideas than the ~ —Odell Shepard⟩

**re·mem·ber·ing·ly** *adv* [*remembering* (pres. part. of *remember*) + *-ly*] **:** in a remembering manner

**re·mem·brance** \rə'membrən(t)s, rē'- *also* -bər-\ *n* -s [ME, fr. MF, fr. *remembrer* to remember + *-ance*] **1 :** the state of bearing in mind ⟨Roman soldiers . . . keep the Jews in ~ of their provincial status —L.C.Douglas⟩ **2 a :** the ability to remember **:** the function of memory **:** present consciousness of past experience ⟨paints largely from ~, from a wealth of rich experiences —Henry Miller⟩ **b :** the period over which one's memory extends **:** the reach of personal knowledge **3 :** an act of recalling to mind ⟨put in a fresh rage by the ~ of their past offenses⟩ **4 :** a memory of a person, thing, or event ⟨how the rest of the night was passed . . . I have only the dimmest ~ —John Burroughs⟩ **5 a :** something that serves to keep in or bring to mind **:** REMINDER, SOUVENIR ⟨the wreck of the armor-plated vessel . . . is a ~ of the war —*Saturday Rev.*⟩ **b :** an act or thing evoking or honoring the memory of a person or event **:** COMMEMORATION, MEMORIAL ⟨the sabbath is to be kept in ~ of the deliverance from Egypt —G.E.Wright⟩ ⟨in lieu of flowers ~*s* may be made —*N. Y. Herald Tribune*⟩ **c :** a greeting or gift recalling or expressing friendship or affection ⟨give my ~*s* to them⟩ ⟨shopping for some little ~ to send her friend at Christmas⟩ **syn** see MEMORY

**remembrance day** *n, usu cap R&D, Brit* **:** ARMISTICE DAY

**re·mem·branc·er** \-nsə(r)\ *n* -s [ME, fr. AF, fr. MF *remembrance* + AF *-er*] **1** *usu cap* **:** any of several officials of the Court of Exchequer in England having orig. the duty of bringing various matters to the attention of the proper persons — see KING'S REMEMBRANCER, QUEEN'S REMEMBRANCER **2** *usu cap* **:** an official of the City of London who represents that corporation before parliamentary committees and at council and treasury boards — called also *City Remembrancer* **3 :** a person who brings things to the mind of another **:** one that reminds **4 :** a thing that serves to bring to or keep in mind **:** REMINDER, MEMENTO, MEMORIAL

**re·mem·o·rate** \rə'memə,rāt\ *vi* -ED/-ING/-S [LL *rememoratus*, past part. of *rememorari* to remember — more at REMEMBER] *obs* **:** REMIND, REMEMBER — **re·mem·o·ra·tion** \=,==¦rāshən\ *n* -s *archaic*

**remercy** *vt* [ME *remercien*, fr. MF *remercier*, fr. *re-* + *mercier* to thank, fr. *merci* favor, mercy, thanks — more at MERCY] *obs* **:** THANK

**re·mex** \'rē,meks\ *n, pl* **rem·i·ges** \'remə,jēz\ [NL *remig-*, *remex*, fr. L, oarsman, fr. *remus* oar + *-ig-* (fr. *agere* to drive) — more at ROW, AGENT] **:** a primary or secondary quill feather of the wing of a bird

**re·mi** \'rē,mī\ *n pl, usu cap* [L] **:** an ancient people in Gaul forming a division of the Belgae and allied to Caesar in the campaign of 57 B.C.

**remi-** *comb form* [L, fr. *remus* oar — more at ROW] **:** oar ⟨*remi*form⟩ ⟨*remi*ped⟩

**rem·i·cle** \'reməkəl\ *n* -s [NL *remiculum*, irreg. dim. of *remex*] **:** a small remex

**re·mig·i·al** \rə'mijēəl\ *adj* [NL *remig-*, *remex* + E *-ial*] **1 :** of or relating to the remiges **2** [NL *remigium* + E *-al*] **:** of or relating to a remigium

**re·mig·i·um** \-ēəm\ *n* -s [NL, fr. L, oarage, fr. *remig-*, *remex* oarsman — more at REMEX] **:** the anterior rigid part of the wing of an insect that is acted on by the muscles and is the chief effector of flight

**rem·i·grant** \'reməgrənt\ *n* [L *remigrant-*, *remigrans*, pres. part. of *remigrare*] **:** a migrant who returns; *specif* **:** an aphid of the winged generation that returns to its former host

**re·migrate** \(')rē+\ *vi* [L *remigratus*, past part. of *remigrare* to remigrate, fr. *re-* + *migrare* to migrate — more at MIGRATE] **:** to migrate again or back — **re·migration** \(¦)rē+\ *n*

**re·mij·ia** \rə'mijēə\ *n, cap* [NL, fr. *Remijo*, 19th cent. surgeon + NL *-ia*] **:** a genus of tropical So. American shrubs and trees (family Rubiaceae) having leaves with large stipules and racemes of small white woolly flowers — see CUPREA BARK

**re·militarization** \(¦)rē+\ *n* [*re-* + *militarization*] **1 :** the act or process of remilitarizing **2 :** the state of being remilitarized

**re·militarize** \(')rē+\ *vt* [*re-* + *militarize*] **:** to equip again with military forces and defenses

**re·mind** \rə'mīnd, rē'-\ *vt* [*re-* + *mind*] **1** *obs* **:** to recall to mind **2 :** to put (one) in mind of something **:** cause to remember ⟨~ him to stop for groceries⟩ ⟨a man whose appearance ~*ed* her of her father⟩ **syn** see REMEMBER

**re·mind·er** \-də(r)\ *n* -s [*remind* + *-er*] **:** one that reminds: as **a :** something that reminds by association ⟨areas of rubble that stand as grim ~*s* of the war⟩ ⟨occasional sawmills, ~*s* of the once-active lumber industry —*Amer. Guide Series: Maine*⟩ **b :** a device designed to prompt or aid the memory ⟨tied a string around his finger as a ~⟩

**re·mind·ful** \-dfəl\ *adj* [*remind* + *-ful*] **1 :** MINDFUL, REGARDFUL **2 :** tending to remind **:** SUGGESTIVE, EVOCATIVE ⟨the river's scarred sides . . . are ever ~ of the destruction its floodwaters have wrought —*Amer. Guide Series: Texas*⟩

**re·mind·ing·ly** *adv* [*reminding* (pres. part. of *remind*) + *-ly*] **:** in a reminding way

**rem·i·nisce** \,remə'nis\ *vb* -ED/-ING/-S [back-formation fr. *reminiscence*] *vi* **:** to indulge in reminiscence ⟨got to *reminiscing* about the old days —F.D.Roosevelt⟩ ~ *vt* **:** to write or say in reminiscence **syn** see REMEMBER

**rem·i·nis·cence** \-s°n(t)s\ *n* -s [MF or LL; MF *reminiscence*, fr. LL *reminiscentia* (trans. of Gk *anamnēsis*, lit., recollection, remembrance), fr. L *reminiscent-*, *reminiscens* + *-ia* — more at REMINISCENT] **1 :** the apprehension of a form (as an idea) as if it had been known in a previous existence **2 a :** the recall to mind of a long-forgotten experience or fact **b :** the process or practice of thinking or telling about past experiences ⟨after another quarter of an hour of ~ they had got around to the things that had happened to each of them since they had last met —Mary Austin⟩ **3 a :** a remembered experience **b :** an oral or written account of a memorable experience ⟨the ~ of his trip into the family vault . . . borders on the macabre —F.E.Coenen⟩ — often used in pl. ⟨published the ~*s* of the old settler⟩ **4 :** something (as a phrase, custom, feature) so suggestive of something else as to be regarded as an unconscious repetition, imitation, or survival **5 :** improvement of the memory for an experience despite the lapse of time since that experience **syn** see MEMORY

[1]**rem·i·nis·cent** \¦==¦nis°nt\ *adj* [L *reminiscent-*, *reminiscens*, pres. part. of *reminisci* to recall to mind, remember, fr. *re-* + *-minisci* (fr. the root of *ment-*, *mens* mind) — more at MIND] **1 :** of the character of or relating to reminiscence; *also* **:** having or marked by reminiscence of something previously known or experienced ⟨some other state of existence of which we have been previously conscious and are now ~ —William Hamilton †1856⟩ **2 :** given to or indulging in reminiscences **:** characterized by reminiscing **:** abounding in reminiscences ⟨~ old men⟩ ⟨a ~ mood⟩ ⟨a ~ essay⟩ **3 :** that reminds one of something previously seen or known **:** SUGGESTIVE ⟨dignity and elegance ~ of powdered ladies and gentlemen of the eighteenth century —*Amer. Guide Series: N.H.*⟩

[2]**reminiscent** \"\ *n* -s **:** a relater of reminiscences

**rem·i·nis·cen·tial** \¦remənə¦senchəl\ *adj* [LL *reminiscentia* reminiscence + E *-al*] **:** REMINISCENT ⟨the chatty, anecdotal, ~ record of persons and places —Leon Edel⟩ — **rem·i·nis·cen·tial·ly** \-chəlē\ *adv*

**rem·i·nis·cent·ly** *adv* **:** in a reminiscent manner ⟨talked ~ of his early struggles⟩

**rem·i·nis·cer** \,remə'nisə(r)\ *n* -s **:** one that reminisces

**rem·i·nis·ce·re sunday** \¦remə¦nisərē-\ *n, usu cap R&S* [L *reminiscere* remember, imper. of *reminisci*; fr. the first word of the Introit for the day — more at REMINISCENT] **:** the second Sunday in Lent

**rem·i·nis·cing·ly** *adv* [*reminiscing* (pres. part. of *reminisce*) + *-ly*] **:** REMINISCENTLY

**re·mint** \(')rē+\ *vt* [*re-* + *mint*] **:** to mint (an old coin) again **:** RECOIN; *also* **:** to resume the minting of (an obsolete coin)

[1]**rem·i·ped** \'remə,ped\ *n* -s [F *rémipède*, fr. L *remiped-*, *remipes* oar-footed, fr. *remi-* + *ped-*, *pes* foot — more at FOOT] **:** a crustacean or insect with feet or legs used as oars

[2]**remiped** \"\ *adj, of a crustacean or insect* **:** having feet or legs that are used as oars

[1]**re·mise** \rə'mīz, rē'-\ *n* -s [ME, fr. MF, fr. *remis* (past part. of *remettre* to put back, fr. L *remittere* to send back), fr. L *remissus*, past part. of *remittere* — more at REMIT] **1** *archaic* **:** a legal surrender or release (as of a claim) **2** *obs* **:** a remittance of money **3 a :** a carriage house **b :** a livery carriage superior to a hackney **4 :** the second of two fencing thrusts delivered on the same lunge (as on failure of the opponent to riposte)

[2]**remise** \"\ *vb* -ED/-ING/-S [ME *remisen*, partly fr. MF *remis*, past part. of *remettre* to put back, partly fr. [1]*remise*] *vt* **1** *obs* **:** to send or put back **:** REPLACE, RETURN **2 :** to give, grant, or release a claim to **:** make over or surrender by deed ~ *vi* **:** to make a remise in fencing

**re·miss** \rə'mis, rē'-\ *adj* [ME, fr. L *remissus* slack, loose, fr. past part. of *remittere* to let go back, relax — more at REMIT] **1** *obs* **a :** LIQUEFIED, DISSOLVED **b :** DILUTED, FAINT, PALE **2 :** negligent in the performance of one's work, duty, or duties **:** CARELESS, INATTENTIVE, SLACK ⟨a ~ correspondent⟩ ⟨~ in paying one's bills⟩ **3 a :** manifesting lack of energy or care or due strictness **:** unduly lenient **:** LAZY, LANGUID ⟨in one's ~ hours⟩ ⟨~ discipline⟩ **b :** showing neglect or inattention **:** negligently performed **:** LAX ⟨the service in this hotel is very ~⟩ **4** *obs* **:** GENTLE, MILD, MODERATE, RELAXED **syn** see NEGLIGENT

**re·miss·ibil·i·ty** \rə,misə'bilədē\ *or* **re·miss·ible·ness** *n* -ES [*remissible* + *-ity*, *-ness*] **:** the quality or state of being remissible

**re·miss·ible** \rə'misəbəl\ *adj* [MF or LL; MF *remissible*, fr. LL *remissibilis*, fr. L *remissus* (past part. of *remittere* to remit) + *-ibilis* -ible] **:** that may be forgiven ⟨~ sins⟩ — **re·miss·ibly** \-blē\ *adv*

**re·mis·sion** \rə'mishən, rē'-\ *n* -s [ME, fr. OF, fr. L *remission-*, *remissio*, fr. *remissus* (past part. of *remittere* to remit) + *-ion-*, *-io* -ion] **:** the act of remitting: as **a :** the act of pardoning sin or offense **:** FORGIVENESS ⟨~ of his sins through the sacrament of penance⟩ **b** (1) **:** cancellation or relinquishment of the whole or a part of a financial obligation ⟨tax ~*s*⟩ (2) **:** the voluntary release of a debt or claim to a debtor or person liable by a creditor or claimant having legal capacity to alienate **c :** pardon granted (as by the British parliament) for a legal offense **d** (1) **:** relief from a forfeiture or penalty (as by the surrender by the government to a former owner of property forfeited for violation of revenue laws) (2) **:** the act or procedure of so restoring property or of so remitting a penalty **e :** a temporary abatement of the symptoms of a disease — distinguished from *intermission*

**remission thursday** *n, usu cap R&T* **:** MAUNDY THURSDAY

**re·mis·sive** \rə'misiv\ *adj* [ML *remissivus*, fr. L *remissus* + *-ivus* -ive] **1** *obs* **:** REMISS **2 :** granting or bringing about remission or pardon **3 :** causing or permitting abatement **4 :** marked by diminution or abatement — **re·mis·sive·ly** \-səvlē\ *adv* — **re·mis·sive·ness** \-sivnəs\ *n* -ES

**re·miss·ly** *adv* **:** in a remiss manner

**re·miss·ness** *n* -ES **:** the quality or state of being remiss

[1]**re·mit** \rə'mit, rē'-, *usu* -id·+V\ *vb* **remitted; remitted; remitting; remits** [ME *remitten*, fr. L *remittere* to let go back, send back, relax, give up, forgive, fr. *re-* + *mittere* to let go, send — more at SMITE] *vt* **1 a** (1) **:** to release one from the guilt or penalty of **:** PARDON, FORGIVE ⟨held that God had granted to . . . the apostles and through them to the priests the power to ~ sins —K.S.Latourette⟩ (2) *obs* **:** to set free (as a prisoner) **:** RELEASE **b :** to refrain from exacting (as a payment) ⟨the rents of the husbandman and other taxes were *remitted* —James Mill⟩ **c :** to cancel or refrain from inflicting (a penalty) ⟨in sentences involving loss of pay and confinement, the loss of pay is frequently *remitted* —*Naval Orientation*⟩ **d :** to give relief from (suffering) ⟨grace that turned staleness sweet, peace that *remitted* pain —Edmund Wilson⟩ **2 a :** to lay aside (a mood or disposition) partly or wholly **b** *obs* **:** to give up (a right or possession) **:** SURRENDER, RESIGN **c :** to desist from (an activity) **d :** to let (as attention, diligence) slacken **:** MITIGATE, RELAX **3 a :** to submit or refer (something) for consideration, judgment, decision or action esp. to one in authority ⟨~ the question to a special committee⟩; *specif* **:** REMAND 2 **b :** REMAND 3 **c :** to refer (a person) for information or help (as to a book or person) **d :** to refer, assign, or allot to **4 :** to restore or consign to a former status or condition; *specif* **:** to restore to a former and more valid title **5 :** to put off **:** POSTPONE, DEFER ⟨~ consideration of the matter until the next session⟩ **6 :** to send (money) to a person or place (as in payment of a demand, account, draft) ~ *vi* **1 a :** to abate in force or intensity **:** MODERATE **b** *of a disease or abnormality* **:** to abate symptoms for a period **:** be remittent or go into a remission **2 :** to send money (as in payment) ⟨please ~ promptly by check or money order⟩ **syn** see SEND

[2]**remit** \"\ *n* -s **:** an act of remitting or a matter, cause, or proceeding remitted to another person or authority for consideration or judgment

**re·mit·ment** \-itmənt\ *n* -s [*remit* + *-ment*] **1 :** an act of remitting **2 :** a sum of money remitted

**re·mit·ta·ble** \-idəbəl\ *adj* [*remit* + *-able*] **:** that may be remitted

**re·mit·tal** \-d°l\ *n* -s [*remit* + *-al*] **:** REMISSION

**re·mit·tance** \rə'mit°n(t)s, rē'-\ *n* -s [*remit* + *-ance*] **1 a :** a sum of money sent to another person or place **b :** an instrument by which money is remitted **2 :** transmittal of money (as to a distant place)

**remittance man** *n* **:** a person living on a remittance; *esp* **:** one living away from the British Isles but subsisting chiefly on remittances from home

**re·mit·tee** \rə¦mi¦tē\ *n* -s [*remit* + *-ee*] **:** one to whom a remittance is sent

[1]**re·mit·tent** \rə'mit°nt, rē'-\ *adj* [L *remittent-*, *remittens*, pres. part. of *remittere* to remit] *of a disease* **:** characterized by

alternating periods of abatement and of increase of symptoms ⟨a ~ fever⟩ — **re·mit·tent·ly** *adv*

**[2]remittent** \"\ *n* -s **:** a remittent fever

**[1]re·mit·ter** \-id·ə(r), -itə-\ *n* -s [*remit* + *-er* (as in *cesser*)] **1 :** the principle or operation of law by which a person who obtains possession of property under a defective title is placed in the same legal position as if he had entered under some prior and more valid title which he also holds **2 :** an act remitting a person to a former status or a cause to another court

**[2]remitter** \"\ *n* -s [*remit* + *-er*, agent suffix] **:** one that remits; *specif* **:** one that sends a remittance

**re·mit·ti·tur** \rə'mid·əd·ə(r)\ *n* -s [L, it is sent back, remitted, 3d sing. pres. indic. pass. of *remittere* to send back, remit] **1 a :** a remission to a defendant by a plaintiff of the portion of a verdict for damages considered excessive by trial or appellate court **b :** the formal agreement or stipulation of the plaintiff waiving or releasing his right to receive such portion representing the excessive damages **c :** the direction or order of the court approving such stipulation and judgment for the reasonable portion of damages or ordering a new trial unless such remission is made by the plaintiff **2 :** a sending back from an appellate or superior to a trial or inferior court of a case and its record for further proceedings (as additional findings of fact) or for entry of a final judgment in accordance with instructions or the decision of the appellate or superior court

**re·mix** \(')rē+\ *vb* [*re-* + *mix*] **:** to mix again

**[1]rem·nant** \'remnənt\ *n* -s [ME, contr. of *remenant*, fr. MF, fr. pres. part. of *remenoir, remanoir* to be left, remain — more at REMAIN] **1 :** a usu. small part, member, or trace remaining ⟨her rather sweet expression . . . was the only ~ of a former prettiness —Osbert Sitwell⟩ ⟨occasional erosion ~*s* stand above the general land surface —P.G.Worcester⟩ **:** REMAINDER, REST ⟨more at ease during the ~ of the London season —G.B.Shaw⟩ ⟨the ship came up and the ~ on the boat were saved —B.N.Cardozo⟩ **:** SURVIVOR — often used in pl. ⟨the ~*s* of a camp group that had suffered misfortune —C.D. Forde⟩ ⟨the crumbled ~*s* of a business section —*Amer. Guide Series: Oregon*⟩ **2 :** an unsold or unused end of piece goods **3** *often cap* **:** a minority of Israel preserved by God from the calamities visited upon the wicked to become the nucleus of a new and holy community

**[2]remnant** \"\ *adj* [modif. (influenced by [1]*remnant*) of MF *remenant*, pres. part. of *remenoir* to be left] **:** yet left **:** REMAINING ⟨always thereafter . . . would carry in his heart some ~ feeling of disgrace —Bernard DeVoto⟩

**rem·nant·al** \(')rem¦nantᵊl\ *adj* **:** of the nature of a remnant

**re·mod·el** \(')rē¦mädᵊl\ *vt* [*re-* + *model*] **:** to model anew **:** RECONSTRUCT **syn** see MEND

**re·mod·el·er** *or* **re·mod·el·ler** \-d(ᵊ)lə(r)\ *n* **:** one that remodels

**remolade** *var of* REMOULADE

**re·mold** \(')rē+\ *vt* [*re-* + *mold*] **:** to mold again ⟨~*ing* the world to the heart's desire —H.J.Muller⟩

**re·monetization** \(¦)rē+\ *n* [*remonetize* + *-ation*] **:** the act of remonetizing

**re·monetize** \(')rē+\ *vt* [*re-* + *monetize*] **:** to restore to use as legal tender ⟨~ silver⟩

**re·mon·strance** \rə'män(t)strən(t)s, rē'-\ *n* -s [MF, fr. *remonstrer* to remonstrate (fr. ML *remonstrare*) + *-ance* — more at REMONSTRATE] **1 a** *archaic* **:** a written or spoken representation or demonstration of a matter **b :** an earnest presentation of reasons in opposition to something; *specif* **:** a document formally stating points of opposition or grievance **2** *archaic* **:** a demonstration or manifestation of a fact or quality **:** PROOF, EVIDENCE **3 :** an act or instance of remonstrating **:** EXPOSTULATION ⟨a plan that provoked violent ~⟩ ⟨the vociferous ~*s* of a football team's supporters when a doubtful offside has been awarded —E.A.Armstrong⟩ **4 :** MONSTRANCE

**remonstrancer** *n* -s *often cap* [*remonstrance* + *-er*] *obs* **:** REMONSTRANT 1

**[1]re·mon·strant** \-ənt\ *n* -s [ML *remonstrant-, remonstrans*, fr. pres. part. of *remonstrare* to remonstrate] **1 :** one who remonstrates; *specif, usu cap* **:** one of 46 ministers of Arminian views who in 1610 addressed a remonstrance to the States General of Holland and West Friesland containing five articles which set forth their differences from the strict Calvinists and which were condemned by the Synod of Dort in 1619 when the remonstrating ministers were removed from their ministry — compare ARMINIANISM **2** *usu cap* **:** a member of a small Arminian sect in Holland deriving from the Remonstrants of 1610

**[2]remonstrant** \"\ *adj* [in sense 1, fr. [1]*remonstrant*; in sense 2, fr. ML *remonstrant-, remonstrans*, pres. part. of *remonstrare*] **1** *usu cap* **:** of or relating to the Remonstrants **2 :** vigorously objecting or opposing **:** making a protest **:** REMONSTRATING ⟨a quality urgent, piercingly ~ in those quacks —Owen Wister⟩

**re·mon·strant·ly** *adv* **:** in a remonstrant manner

**re·mon·strate** \rə'män(t)strāt, rē'- *sometimes* 'remənz,t- *or* 'remən,st-, *usu* -ād·+V\ *vb* -ED/-ING/-S [ML *remonstratus*, past part. of *remonstrare* to point out, demonstrate, fr. L *re-* + *monstrare* to show — more at MUSTER] *vt* **1** *obs* **:** to point out **:** DEMONSTRATE **2** *obs* **:** to call attention to (as a fault, wrong, or aggrieving condition) by way of censure, complaint, or protest **3 :** to say or plead in protest, reproof, or opposition **~** *vi* **:** to present and urge reasons in opposition (as to an act, measure, or proceedings) **:** EXPOSTULATE ⟨~ with a person regarding his habits⟩ **syn** see OBJECT

**re·mon·strat·ing·ly** *adv* [*remonstrating* (pres. part. of *remonstrate*) + *-ly*] **:** in a remonstrating way

**re·mon·stra·tion** \,rē,män'strāshən, ,remənz't-, ,remən'st-\ *n* -s [ME, fr. MF or ML; MF *remonstration*, fr. ML *remonstration-, remonstratio*, fr. *remonstratus* + L *-ion-, -io* -ion] **:** the act or an instance of remonstrating **:** PROTEST

**re·mon·stra·tive** \rə'män(t)strəd·iv\ *adj* [*remonstrate* + *-ive*] **:** having the character of a remonstrance **:** expressing a remonstrance — **re·mon·stra·tive·ly** \-d·əvlē\ *adv*

**re·mon·stra·tor** \-(t),strād·ə(r)\ *n* -s [*remonstrate* + *-or*] **:** one that remonstrates

**re·mon·stra·to·ry** \-(t)strə,tōrē\ *adj* [*remonstrate* + *-ory*] **:** REMONSTRANT

**[1]re·mon·tant** \rə'mänt'nt, rē'- -tənt\ *adj* [F, lit., rising again, fr. pres. part. of *remonter* to remount] **:** flowering again ⟨~ roses⟩ ⟨a ~ plant⟩

**[2]remontant** \"\ *n* -s **:** a hybrid perpetual rose

**rem·on·toir** *or* **rem·on·toire** \¦remən-¦twär\ *n* -s [F *remontoir* device for winding clocks, fr. *remonter* to remount, rewind — more at REMOUNT] **:** a device to give a uniform impulse to a pendulum or balance

**rem·o·ra** \'remərə\ *n* [L, delay, echeneid (fr. its supposed ability to delay ships), fr. *remorari* to delay, fr. *re-* + *morari* to delay — more at MORATORY] **1 a** -s **:** any of several highly specialized fishes constituting *Echeneis* and various related genera (order Discocephali), having the anterior dorsal fin converted into an oval transversely lamellate suctorial disc on the top of the head, by means of which they adhere firmly to sharks and other large fishes and to ships but are able to let go at will, and being distributed throughout tropical and warm temperate seas — called also *shark sucker, sucking fish* **b** *cap* **:** an important genus of such fishes **2** -s **:** something that holds back or delays **:** CLOG, DRAG — **rem·o·rid** \-rəd\ *adj*

**re·mord** \rə'mȯ(ə)rd\ *vt* [ME *remorden* to afflict with remorse, fr. MF *remordre*, fr. L *remordēre* to bite again, vex — more at REMORSE] *archaic* **:** AFFLICT

**re·morse** \rə'mȯ(ə)rs, rē', -ȯ(ə)s\ *n* -s [ME *remors, remorse*, fr. MF *remors*, fr. ML *remorsus*, fr. L, act of biting again, fr. *remorsus*, past part. of *remordēre* to bite again, vex, fr. *re-* + *mordēre* to bite — more at SMART] **1 a :** a gnawing distress arising from a sense of guilt for past wrongs (as injuries done to others) **:** SELF-REPROACH ⟨knew ~ for sermon times spent in daydreams —Rose Macaulay⟩ ⟨felt a twinge of ~ for having been so brusque⟩ **b :** an attack of remorse **2** *obs* **:** sympathetic sorrow **:** COMPASSION **3** *obs* **:** a lessening or break in a process or action **4** *obs* **:** a solemn obligation **syn** see PENITENCE

**re·morse·ful** \-sfəl\ *adj* [*remorse* + *-ful*] **1 :** springing from or characterized by remorse ⟨a ~ confession⟩ **2** *obs* **:** COMPASSIONATE — **re·morse·ful·ly** \-fəlē, -li\ *adv* — **re·morse·ful·ness** *n* -ES

**re·morse·less** \-sləs\ *adj* [*remorse* + *-less*] **1 :** being without remorse **:** PITILESS, MERCILESS ⟨a monster of . . . ~ cruelty —Leslie Stephen⟩ **2 :** continuing without lessening or break **:** RELENTLESS ⟨the drive of technology was so ~ that younger economists . . . turned from philosophy to research —C.A. & Mary Beard⟩ — **re·morse·less·ly** *adv* — **re·morse·less·ness** *n* -ES

**[1]re·mote** \rə'mōt, rē'-, *usu* -ōd·+V\ *adj, often* -ER/-EST [L *remotus*, fr. past part. of *removēre* to move back, move away — more at REMOVE] **1 a :** separated by intervals greater than usual **:** far apart **b :** not extending the full distance from the margin of the pileus to the stipe ⟨a mushroom with a ~ veil⟩ **2 :** far removed in space, time, relation, or likeness **:** not near or immediate **:** FAR, DISTANT ⟨the church was too ~ for a walking bridal party —Thomas Hardy⟩ ⟨from ~ antiquity up to modern times —S.F.Mason⟩ ⟨work to which ~ generations may look back with pride —Benjamin Farrington⟩ ⟨fourth cousins and *remoter* relatives⟩ **:** DIVERGENT ⟨nations as ~ in culture and civilization as Poland and China, . . . Czechoslovakia and Morocco —H.A.Rusk⟩ ⟨fantastically unreal and utterly ~ from the slightest vestige of truth —John Russell b.1872⟩ **:** SEPARATED, ABSTRACTED ⟨the ideas of an ether, of waves in it . . . are ~ from ordinary experience —A. N.Whitehead⟩ **3 :** located out of the way **:** SECLUDED ⟨the Coast Guard Service renders invaluable aid to natives living along the ~ seacoast —G.A.Parks⟩ ⟨the ~ atmosphere of these retired wold villages —*Brit. Book News*⟩ **4 a :** not proximate or acting directly **:** not primary **b :** not arising from the effect of that which is primary or proximate in its action ⟨~ damages⟩ — compare CONSEQUENTIAL **5 :** small in degree **:** SLIGHT ⟨if one solves the economic difficulties, the danger of war becomes ~ —F.D.Smith & Barbara Wilcox⟩ ⟨hasn't the *remotest* notion what time it is⟩ **6 :** distant in manner **:** ALOOF, INACCESSIBLE ⟨they can be cold or warm, ~ or friendly —John Mason Brown⟩ **7 a :** arising elsewhere than from the part of the body that makes a movement — opposed to *resident* **b :** not present to the senses at the moment

**[2]remote** \"\ *n* -s **1 :** one that is remote **2 :** a radio or television program or portion of a program (as sports and news events) originating outside the studio

**[3]remote** \"\ *adv, often* -ER/-EST **:** at a distance

**remote control** *n* **:** control (as by a switch or switchboard or by a radio signal) of operation from a point at some distance removed

**remoted** *adj* [L *remotus* + E *-ed*] *obs* **:** REMOTE

**remote indication** *n* **:** transfer and repetition (as by telemetering) of information from one point to another more or less remote

**re·mote·ly** *adv, sometimes* -ER/-EST **:** in a remote manner or to a remote extent ⟨a sphinx who smiles ~⟩ ⟨every man she had ever known closely or ~ —Ellen Glasgow⟩ **:** at or from a distance ⟨processes controlled ~ by the tiny brain —W.E. Swinton⟩ **:** DISTANTLY

**remote matter** *n* **:** MATTER OF A SYLLOGISM 2

**re·mote·ness** *n* -ES **:** the quality or state of being remote

**re·mo·tion** \rə'mōshən\ *n* -s [ME *remocion, remosion*, fr. L *remotion-, remotio* removal, fr. *remotus* (past part. of *removēre* to remove) + *-ion-, -io* -ion — more at REMOVE] **1 :** the quality or state of being remote **:** REMOTENESS **2 a :** the act of removing **:** REMOVAL **b** *obs* **:** DEPARTURE **3** [MF, fr. L *remotion-, remotio* removal] **:** the process of reaching or defining a conception by the successive elimination of what is extraneous

**re·mo·tive** \-ōd·iv\ *adj* [L *remotus* (past part. of *removēre* to remove) + E *-ive*] **1 :** REMOVING **2 :** REMOVABLE

**remotive proposition** *n* **:** PRIVATIVE PROPOSITION; *esp* **:** one that asserts the absence of something to be of the essence of the subject

**re·mou·lade** *also* **re·mo·lade** \,rāmə'läd\ *n* -s [F *rémolade, rémoulade*, fr. F dial. *rémola, rémolat* horseradish (modif. of L *armoracea, armoracium*) + F *-ade*] **:** a pungent sauce or dressing resembling mayonnaise but usu. made with cooked egg yolks and often with savory herbs or condiments

**[1]re·mount** \(')rē+\ *vb* [ME *remounten*, partly fr. *re-* + *mounten* to mount, partly fr. MF *remonter* to remount, fr. *re-* + *monter* to mount — more at MOUNT] *vt* **1 :** to mount (something) again ⟨~ this map on the other wall⟩ ⟨reaching the mouth of the stream, they ~*ed* it to its source⟩ **2 :** to furnish remounts to ⟨the regiment must be ~*ed*⟩ **~** *vi* **1 :** to mount again ⟨~ at once and ride back⟩ **2 :** to go back (as during a study) to a point or period

**[2]re·mount** \'rē+,-, ≈'≈\ *n* **1 :** a fresh horse to replace one no longer available (as by reason of fatigue, disablement, loss, or age); *specif* **:** a green or incompletely trained cavalry horse **2 :** a group, stud, or supply of remounts

**[3]remount** \"\ *adj* [[2]*remount*] **:** of or relating to a remount

**re·mov·abil·i·ty** \rə,müvə'biləd·ē, rē,-, -lətē, -i\ *n* **:** the quality or state of being removable

**re·mov·able** \rə'müvəbəl, rē'-\ *adj* [[1]*remove* + *-able*] **:** capable of being removed, displaced, transferred, dismissed, or eradicated ⟨~ partition⟩ ⟨a ~ bed⟩ ⟨a headman appointed and ~ by the mayor —G.M.Harris⟩ — **re·mov·able·ness** *n* -ES — **re·mov·ably** \-blē\ *adv*

**removable truck-type switchboard** *n* **:** a switchboard in which the instruments and main control equipment are mounted upon a removable structure that runs on guide rails

**re·mov·al** \rə'müvəl, rē'-\ *n* -s [*remove* + *-al*] **:** the act of removing or fact of being removed ⟨surgical ~ of the growth⟩ **:** dismissal from office **:** shift of location **:** change of residence

**removal of causes 1 :** the taking of pending cases from a state to a federal court because of diversity of citizenship or because of federal question **2 a :** the transfer of a case from one federal court to another **b :** the transfer of a case from one to another court within the same state for original hearing or trial — compare APPEAL, REVIEW

**[1]re·move** \rə'müv, rē'-\ *vb* [ME *removen, remeven*, fr. OF *remouvoir, removoir*, fr. L *removēre*, fr. *re-* + *movēre* to move — more at MOVE] *vt* **1 :** to change or shift the location, position, station, or residence of (as in order to reestablish) **:** SHIFT, TRANSFER — usu. used with *to* and specified place ⟨~ the troops to the front⟩ ⟨~ the family to the seashore⟩; *specif* **:** to transfer (a pending case) for original hearing or trial from one court to another in the same or another jurisdiction — compare REMOVAL OF CAUSES **2 :** to move by lifting, pushing aside, or taking away or off **:** put aside, apart, or elsewhere ⟨~*s* his hat in the house⟩ ⟨~ a book from a shelf to examine it⟩ **3 :** to force (one) to leave a place or to go away: as **a :** to dismiss from office **b :** ASSASSINATE **c :** to take away by death **4 :** to get rid of as though by moving **:** ERADICATE, ELIMINATE ⟨~ the causes of poverty⟩ **~** *vi* **1 :** to change location, station, or residence ⟨~ from their town house to the country⟩ **2 :** to go away **:** DISAPPEAR, DEPART **3 :** to be capable of being removed ⟨a bottle cap that ~*s* easily⟩ **syn** see MOVE

**[2]remove** \"\ *n* -s **1 a :** REMOVAL; *specif* **:** the transfer of one's business or of one's domestic belongings from one location or dwelling house to another **:** MOVE **b** *archaic* **:** the act of removing a horse's shoe to dress the hoof **c** *Brit* **:** a change of dishes during a meal **d** *Brit* **:** promotion of a pupil to the next form **2 a :** a distance (as a space, time, or divergence of state) separating one person or thing from another **:** distance apart or away ⟨at a short ~ upon the same platform was an officer —Ambrose Bierce⟩ ⟨her poems . . . work best at a slight ~ from the personal —Richard Wilbur⟩ **b** (1) **:** a degree distant (as in derivation or relationship) **:** a grade or stage of separation from the immediate or direct **:** a step apart or away ⟨such a popular song . . . simply repeats, at many ~*s*, a motif of the conventional behavior of the courtly lover —R.A.Hall b.1911⟩ ⟨a primary and intense experience . . . which men at best know only at second ~ —M.F.A. Montagu⟩ — compare FIRSTHAND (2) **:** a degree of lineal consanguinity **:** a generation removed ⟨only at one ~ from the villager —G.M.Trevelyan⟩ ⟨the sixteen sire lines . . . of these famous racehorses at the fourth ~ —Dennis Craig⟩ **3** *obs* **:** ABSENCE **4 :** an intermediate form between two others in an English school

**removed** *adj* [fr. past part. of [1]*remove*] **1 a :** distant in degree of relationship **b** *of a cousin* **:** belonging to a generation separated from the propositus by a given degree of lineal consanguinity **:** of a younger or older generation — used in law only of cousins of a younger generation ⟨a second cousin's child is a second cousin once ~⟩ ⟨a first cousin's grandchild is a first cousin twice ~⟩ **2 :** separate or remote (as in space, time, or character) from something **:** DISTANT, AWAY, OFF ⟨with peace as far ~ as it had been at the time of his election —F.L.Paxson⟩ ⟨considerations entirely ~ from politics⟩ — **re·moved·ly** \-vədlē, -vd-\ *adv* — **re·moved·ness** \-vədnəs, -v(d)n-\ *n* -ES

**re·move·ment** \-vmənt\ *n* -s [[1]*remove* + *-ment*] **:** REMOVAL

**[1]re·mov·er** \-və(r)\ *n* -s [*remove* + *-er*, agent suffix] **1 :** one that removes something: as **a** *Brit* **:** MOVER a(4) **b :** a solvent or chemical used in removing a substance (as from a surface) ⟨paint and varnish ~⟩ ⟨rust ~⟩ ⟨dye ~⟩ ⟨hair ~⟩ **2** *obs* **:** a changeable or unsettled person

**[2]remover** \"\ *n* -s [[1]*remove* + *-er* (as in *cesser*)] **:** transfer of a proceeding from one tribunal to another

**rem·scheid** \'rem,shīt\ *adj, usu cap* [fr. *Remscheid*, city of northwestern Germany] **:** of or from the city of Remscheid, Germany **:** of the kind or style prevalent in Remscheid

**rem·sen cooler** \'remzən-\ *n, usu cap R* [prob. fr. the proper name *Remsen*] **:** a cooler the base of which is gin

**re·mu·da** \rə'müdə\ *n* -s [AmSp, relay, shift of horses or oxen, fr. Sp, exchange, fr. *remudar* to exchange, fr. *re-* + *mudar* to change, fr. L *mutare* — more at MISS] **:** the herd of saddle horses from which are chosen those to be used for the day by the ranch hands **:** a relay of remounts

**re·mu·ner·a·ble** \rə'myün(ə)rəbəl\ *adj* [ML *remunerabilis*, fr. L *remunerare* to reward + *-abilis*] **:** admitting or worthy of remuneration — **re·mu·ner·a·bly** \-blē\ *adv*

**re·mu·ner·ate** \rə'myünə,rāt, rē'-, *usu* -ād·+V\ *vt* -ED/-ING/-S [L *remuneratus*, past part. of *remunerare* to recompense, reward, fr. *re-* + *munerare* to give, present, fr. *muner-, munus* gift — more at MEAN] **1 :** to pay an equivalent for (as a service, loss, expense) **2 :** to pay an equivalent to (a person) for a service, loss, or expense **:** RECOMPENSE, COMPENSATE **syn** see PAY

**re·mu·ner·a·tion** \≈,≈≈'rāshən\ *n* -s [ME *remuneracion*, fr. MF or L; MF *remuneration*, fr. L *remuneration-, remuneratio*, fr. *remuneratus* + *-ion-, -io* -ion] **1 :** an act or fact of remunerating **2 :** something that remunerates **:** RECOMPENSE, PAY

**re·mu·ner·a·tive** \rə'myünə,rād·|iv, rē'-, -n(ə)rə|, |t|, |ēv *also* |əv\ *adj* [*remunerate* + *-ive*] **1 :** serving to remunerate **:** REWARDING ⟨~ justice⟩ **2 :** affording remuneration **:** PROFITABLE, GAINFUL ⟨a ~ business⟩ ⟨a ~ salary⟩ — **re·mu·ner·a·tive·ly** \|əvlē\ *adv* — **re·mu·ner·a·tive·ness** \|ivnəs\ *n* -ES

**re·mu·ner·a·tor** \-nə,rād·ə(r)\ *n* -s [LL, fr. L *remuneratus* (past part. of *remunerare* to remunerate) + *-or*] **:** one that remunerates

**re·mu·ner·a·to·ry** \-nərə,tōrē\ *adj* [*remunerate* + *-ory*] **:** REMUNERATIVE

**remuneratory sanction** *n* **:** a sanction in the form of a reward withheld for failure to comply with the law

**re·murmur** \(')rē+\ *vb* [L *remurmurare*, fr. *re-* + *murmurare* to murmur] *vi* **:** to murmur repeatedly **~** *vt* **:** to repeat, echo, utter again, or reply in murmurs

**[1]ren·ais·sance** \¦renə¦sän(t)s *also* -¦zä- *sometimes* -äⁿs *or* -äⁿn(t)s, *chiefly Brit* rə'nāsᵊn-\ *n* -s [F, fr. MF, rebirth, fr. *renais-* (stem of *renaistre* to be born again, fr. L *renasci*, fr. *re-* + *nasci* to be born) + *-ance* — more at NATION] **1** *often cap* **a :** enthusiastic and vigorous activity along literary, artistic, and cultural lines distinguished by a revival of interest in the past, by an increasing pursuit of learning, and by an imaginative response to broader horizons generally ⟨conceptions of the nature of the *Renaissance* —W.K.Ferguson⟩ ⟨the transcendental movement that marked the full flowering of the New England ~ —V.L.Parrington⟩ **b :** the period of such a revival ⟨the *Renaissance* of the eighth and ninth centuries —Kemp Malone⟩ ⟨that second *Renaissance*, the Victorian Age —Edwin Benson⟩ ⟨the period conventionally known as the *Renaissance* —David Daiches⟩ **2** *usu cap* **:** the neoclassic style of art prevailing during the Renaissance period **3 :** a return of youthful vigor, freshness, zest, or productivity **:** a renewal of life or interest in some aspect of it **:** REBIRTH ⟨a postwar ~ —Granville Hicks⟩ ⟨grand opera . . . is currently enjoying a ~ —Joseph Wechsberg⟩ ⟨the biggest tennis ~ ever known in this country —*Holiday*⟩

**[2]renaissance** \"\ *adj* **1 :** of or relating to a renaissance **2** *usu cap* **:** of, relating to, or typical or suggestive of the transitional movement in Europe between medieval and modern times beginning in the 14th century in Italy, lasting into the 17th century, and marked by a humanistic revival of classical influence expressed in a flowering of the arts and literature and by the beginnings of modern science ⟨*Renaissance* painting⟩ ⟨the *Renaissance* ideal of the universal man —*Horizon*⟩

**renaissance architecture** *n, usu cap R* **:** the style of building and decoration that arose in the early 15th century in Italy based on the study and adaptation of the Roman classic orders and design and that spread later through western Europe succeeding the Gothic style

**renaissance furniture** *n, usu cap R* **:** a style of furniture developed early in the Renaissance distinguished in its national types but in general of oak or walnut richly carved, massive and palatial in structure, and classical in decorative motifs

**renaissance lace** *n, usu cap R* **:** a lace of braid or tape used for curtains and dresses **:** GUIPURE — called also *Battenberg lace*

**ren·ais·sant** \-nt\ *adj, usu cap* [back-formation fr. [1]*renaissance*] **:** of or relating to the Renaissance

**re·nal** \'rēnᵊl\ *adj* [F or LL; F *rénal*, fr. LL *renalis*, fr. L *renes* (pl.) kidneys + *-alis* -al] **:** of, relating to, or involving the kidneys **:** located in the region of the kidneys **:** NEPHRIC

**renal artery** *n* **:** any of the branches of the abdominal aorta that supply the kidneys being in man one to each kidney, arising immediately below the origin of the superior mesenteric artery, dividing into four or five branches which enter the hilum of the kidney, and giving off smaller branches to the ureter, adrenal gland, and adjoining structures

**renal calculus** *n* **:** a calculus in the kidney — called also *kidney stone*

**renal cast** *n* **:** a cast of a renal tubule consisting of granular, hyaline, albuminoid, or other material formed in and discharged from the kidney in renal disease

**renal clearance** *n* **:** CLEARANCE 2g

**renal colic** *n* **:** the severe pain produced by the passage of a calculus from the kidney through the ureter

**renal corpuscle** *n* **:** MALPIGHIAN CORPUSCLE

**renal glycosuria** *or* **renal diabetes** *n* **:** excretion of glucose associated with increased permeability of the kidneys without increased sugar concentration in the blood

**renal papilla** *n* **:** one of the eminences projecting into the pelvis of a vertebrate kidney through which the collecting tubules discharge

**renal plexus** *n* **:** the sympathetic plexus supplying the kidney

**renal portal vein** *n* **1 :** one of the portal veins carrying blood from some of the posterior parts of the body to the kidneys in most lower vertebrates and including typically two trunks formed one for each kidney by the bifurcation of the caudal vein but enlarged or largely replaced by branches from the hind limbs in many of the higher forms **2 :** either of a pair of veins in birds that originate like the renal portal veins of lower forms but pass through the corresponding kidney and enter the femoral vein without breaking into capillaries in the kidney

**renal splanchnic nerve** *n* **:** either of a pair of sympathetic nerves that arise from the lower ganglia of the sympathetic chain and end in the renal plexus and the lower part of the solar plexus

**renal threshold** *n* **:** the concentration level up to which a substance (as glucose) in the blood is prevented from passing through the kidneys into the urine

**renal vein** *n* **:** any of the veins that return the blood from the kidneys to the vena cava being in man one from each kidney and lying in front of the renal arteries

**re·name** \(')rē+\ *vt* [*re-* + *name*] **:** to name again or anew

**re·nan·i·an** \rə'nanēən\ *adj, usu cap* [Joseph Ernest *Renan* †1892 Fr. philologist and historian + E *-ian*] **:** of or relating to the French philologist and historian Ernest Renan or resembling his thought or style

**re·nard·ite** \rə'när,dīt\ *n* -s [F, fr. Alphonse François *Renard* †1903 Belg. geologist + F *-ite*] **:** a mineral $Pb(UO_2)_4(PO_4)_2$-

$(OH)_4.7H_2O$ consisting of a hydrous basic lead and uranyl phosphate

**re·nas·cence** \rə'nas°n(t)s, rē'-, -naas-, -nais-\ *n* -s *often cap* [alter. (influenced by *renascent*) of *renaissance*] : RENAISSANCE ⟨blossomed into new freedom, an artistic ~, of eager and elaborate experimentation —Marjory S. Douglas⟩

**re·nas·cent** \-°nt\ *adj* [fr. L *renascent-, renascens*, pres. part. of *renasci* to be born again — more at RENAISSANCE] : springing or rising again into being or vigor : being born again or reproduced ⟨~ paganism⟩

**re·na·tur·a·tion** \(')rē,nāchə'rāshən\ *n* -s [*renature* + *-ation*] : the process of renaturing ⟨denaturation and ~ of proteins⟩

**re·nature** \(')rē+\ *vt* [*re-* + *nature*] : to restore (as denatured material) to its original nature ⟨silk fibroin is the first protein to be completely *renatured* after denaturation —J.W.McBain⟩

**ren·con·tre** \ren'käntə(r)\ *or* **ren·coun·ter** \-kaůn-\ *n* -s [*rencounter* fr. MF *rencontre* chance or hostile meeting, fr. *rencontrer* to rencounter; *rencontre* fr. F, fr. MF] **1** : a hostile meeting between forces or individuals : COMBAT, ACTION, DUEL **2** : a personal contest (as in debate or repartee) ⟨a lively ~ of two famous wits⟩ **3** : a casual meeting with a person or thing ⟨a lucky ~ with a friend⟩ **4** *archaic* : a sudden meeting or collision of two bodies

**ren·coun·ter** \-kaůn-\ *vb* [MF *rencontrer*, fr. *re-* + *encontrer* to encounter, fr. OF — more at ENCOUNTER] *vt* **1** *obs* **a** : to meet in hostility : encounter in combat or fight **b** : to meet forcibly : collide with **2** : to meet (as a friend) casually ~ *vi* : to come together in rencontre

**rend** \'rend\ *vb* **rent** \-nt\ *also* **rended; rent** *also* **rended; rending; rends** [ME *renden*, fr. OE *rendan*; akin to OFris *renda* to tear, rend, Skt *randhra* split, opening, hole] *vt* **1** : to pull violently from a person or thing : remove from place by violence : tear out or away : WRENCH, WREST ⟨glaciers may . . . ~ boulders from their beds —G.W.Tyrrell⟩ ⟨~ manhood out of him in fear —G.D.Brown⟩ **2 a** : to split or tear apart or in pieces by violence : CLEAVE ⟨saw lightning ~ a tree⟩ : DISMEMBER ⟨many a carcass they left . . . for the horny-nibbed raven to ~ —Alfred Tennyson⟩ **b** : to convert straight-grained wood into (laths) by splitting **3** : to tear (the hair or clothing) as a sign of anger, grief, or despair ⟨foam, fling myself flat, ~ my clothes to shreds —Robert Browning⟩ **4** : to affect as if tearing or splitting: as **a** : to lacerate (as the heart) with painful feelings ⟨look in his face . . . and ~ him with her scorn —Ellen Glasgow⟩ **b** : to pierce with sound ⟨suddenly this dead stillness was *rent* by a shot —Zane Grey⟩ **c** : to divide (as a nation) into parties : DISINTEGRATE ⟨a long dispute over where it should be built *rent* the community —*Amer. Guide Series: Va.*⟩ ~ *vi* **1** : to perform an act of tearing or splitting ⟨a time to ~ and a time to sew —Eccles 3:7 (RSV)⟩ **2** : to become torn or split ⟨made of rotten black cloth . . . or else it would not have *rent* —Edmund Hickeringill⟩ **syn** see TEAR

[1]**ren·der** \'rendə(r)\ *vb* **rendered; rendered; rendering** \-d(ə)riŋ\ **renders** [ME *rendren*, fr. MF *rendre* to give back, deliver, yield, cause to become, fr. (assumed) VL *rendere*, alter. (influenced by L *prendere* to take, contr. of *praehendere*) of L *reddere*, partly fr. *red-* re- + *dare* to give, partly fr. *red-* + *-dere* to put — more at PREHENSILE, DATE, DO] *vt* **1** *obs* : to say over : RECITE, REPEAT **2 a** : to melt down : extract or clarify by melting : TRY ⟨~ lard, oil, or wax⟩ **b** : to treat so as to extract the fat ⟨~ garbage⟩ **3 a** : to hand over to another (as the intended recipient) : DELIVER, TRANSMIT ⟨his father left him gold . . . which was not ~*ed* to him —Alfred Tennyson⟩ **b** : to give up : SURRENDER, YIELD ⟨~ one's life for a cause⟩ ⟨a term . . . so sacrosanct that the material goods of this life must be mysteriously ~*ed* up for it —R.M.Weaver⟩ **c** : to furnish for consideration, approval, or information ⟨~*ed* a report to . . . Congress concerning plant disposal —D.D.Eisenhower⟩ ⟨~ an annual account to the court of his trusteeship⟩ as (1) : to send (a bill) to a customer ⟨~ accounts at the first of the month⟩ (2) : to hand down (a legal judgment) : give as a verdict ⟨in the Federal District Court . . . a verdict of $1,295 and costs was ~*ed* against them —*Amer. Guide Series: Mich.*⟩ **d** *archaic* : to present (oneself) at a place ⟨the most distant members . . . may probably ~ themselves at Philadelphia in fifteen to twenty days —Benjamin Franklin⟩ **4 a** (1) : to give in reward or retribution ⟨~ them their due reward —Ps 28:4 (RSV)⟩ ⟨see that none ~ evil for evil —1 Thess 5:15 (AV)⟩ (2) : to give (thanks) for something received ⟨thanksgiving . . . we ~ to God for you —1 Thess 3:9 (RSV)⟩ (3) *archaic* : to give reward or retribution for : REQUITE ⟨~ every man his righteousness —1 Sam 26:23 (AV)⟩ **b** (1) : to give back : REPAY, RESTORE ⟨~ to the earth the bodies of the dead⟩ (2) : to cause (an image or sound) to return : REFLECT, ECHO ⟨the heart's echoes ~ no song when the spirit is mute —P.B.Shelley⟩ **c** : to give (as rent, honor) in acknowledgment of dependence or obligation : give (something due) to another : PAY ⟨the serf . . . might enjoy his land so long as he ~*ed* three days' work in the week to his lord —G.G.Coulton⟩ ⟨the failure of those living to . . . ~ due respect to its memory —*Amer. Guide Series: Del.*⟩ **d** : to do (a service) for another ⟨thanked them for the service they had ~*ed* him⟩ : give (as help) to another ⟨having ~*ed* at least five years of service as such an officer —*U.S. Code*⟩ ⟨stand by and ~ help if help be needed —Rafael Sabatini⟩ ⟨the protection they ~ in winter against the cold winds from the interior —Samuel Van Valkenburg & Ellsworth Huntington⟩ **5** *obs* : to give out : EMIT ⟨cedar, which ~*s* a fine fragrancy —Samuel Gale⟩ **6 a** : to put into a state ⟨a novelist of more meager talents . . . would ~ this sugary situation into pure hokum —Martin Levin⟩ **b** (1) : to cause to be or become : MAKE ⟨enough rainfall in the average year to ~ irrigation unnecessary —P.E.James⟩ ⟨the building of the railroad . . . ~*ed* a road of even less importance —G.R.Stewart⟩ ⟨this literalness . . . ~*s* it a fine introduction to twelve-tone music —Arthur Berger⟩ (2) : to cause something to have : IMPART ⟨the college is one of the great social institutions which ~*s* form and continuity to American culture —*Encyc. Americana*⟩ **c** (1) : to put into artistic or verbal form : reproduce or represent by artistic or verbal means (as music, painting, writing) : execute in an artistic or verbal medium : DEPICT, EXPRESS ⟨music has set itself to ~*ing* the modern mood —Irving Babbitt⟩ ⟨a society painter must ~ a likeness of his subject —Arnold Isenberg⟩ ⟨the problem of ~*ing* every unique sensation, never merely pointing, naming, summarizing —H.J.Muller⟩ ⟨aimed at ~*ing* its meaning in an English that would not become dated —*Current Biog.*⟩ (2) *obs* : to describe or represent as having a given character or being in a given condition : give out to be ⟨I have heard him speak of that same brother, and he did ~ him the most unnatural that lived amongst men —Shak.⟩ (3) : to give an interpretation or performance of (an artistic work or element or dramatic role) ⟨called upon to ~ duets at every stop —*Current Biog.*⟩ (4) : to produce a copy or version of ⟨the documents are ~*ed* in their original French —Robert Lawrence⟩ (5) : to execute the motions of (as a salute) ⟨a . . . major appeared before us to ~ a meticulous salute —*Infantry Jour.*⟩ **d** : to put into another language or into other words : TRANSLATE ⟨every document . . . must be ~*ed* into several languages —R.H.Jackson⟩ : REWORD ⟨a famous sea song now ~*ed* down for landsmen's hearing —Gavin Douglas⟩ **7** : to direct the execution of (as justice) : ADMINISTER ⟨in ancient Ireland it was either the local king or the high king . . . who ~*ed* justice —E.D.Chapple & C.S.Coon⟩ **8** : to apply a coat of plaster or cement directly to ⟨buildings should be made as ratproof as possible by ~*ing* the walls with cement —F.D.Smith & Barbara Wilcox⟩ **9 a** : to cause (a rope) to pass or run through a block or loop (as by slackening it off) **b** : to coil (a rope) so as to ensure kink-free redelivery when wanted **10** *chiefly Brit* : to apply a medium (as ink, crayon, ink wash) to (a drawing) so as to bring out form and modeling ~ *vi* **1** : to give recompense ⟨for he will ~ to every man according to his works —Rom 2:6 (RSV)⟩ **2** : to pass or run smoothly (as through a block or off a coil) **3** : to extract fat, oil, or wax by melting (as in boiling water, steam, benzine) **4** *chiefly Brit* : to finish a perspective drawing so as to bring out form and modeling

[2]**render** \"\ *n* -s **1** *obs* : SURRENDER **2** : a return in kind, services, or money due from a tenant to his superior in feudal England ⟨the normal ~ due to a lord from a ten-hide estate —F.M.Stenton⟩ **3** *archaic* : the act of rendering an account or statement **4** : a coat of plaster or cement applied directly on a wall

[3]**rend·er** \"\ *n* -s [*rend* + *-er*] : one that rends

**ren·der·able** \-d(ə)rəbəl\ *adj* [[1]*render* + *-able*] : capable of being rendered

**ren·der·er** \-rə(r)\ *n* -s [[1]*render* + *-er*] : one that renders; *specif* : one that operates a rendering plant

**rendering** *n* -s [fr. gerund of [1]*render*] **1** : a work forming a presentation, expression, or interpretation (as of an idea, theme, or part) : RENDITION, VERSION: as **a** : TRANSLATION **b** : a finished perspective drawing of a proposed building or product : VISUALIZATION ⟨nicely colored ~*s* of buildings on the drawing boards . . . from a huge cement plant to a modest church —A.W.Baum⟩ **c** : a rendered illustration of an object of art ⟨made ~*s* of Spanish colonial arts in New Mexico for the *Index of American Design* —*Southwest Review*⟩ **2 a** : a coat of plaster laid directly on brickwork or stonework **b** *Brit* : the finish coat of mortar on a concrete floor or roof on which tiles are laid **c** : the finish application of a material on a wall usu. for decorative purposes

**rendering plant** *n* : a plant that converts packing house waste, kitchen grease, and livestock carcasses into industrial fats and oils (as tallow for soap) and various other products (as fertilizer)

**rendering works** *n pl but sing or pl in constr* : RENDERING PLANT

**renderset** \'==,=\ *or* **render-and-set** \',===',=\ *adj* [[1]*render* + *set*] : consisting of two coats of plaster

[1]**ren·dez·vous** \'rändə,vü, -dē,-, -dā,-\ *n, pl* **rendezvous** \-üz\ [MF, fr. the phrase *rendez vous* present yourselves, fr. *rendez* (2d pl. imper. of *rendre* to render, deliver) + *vous* you, fr. L *vos*; akin to Gk *hymeis* you, Skt *vas*, OSlav *vy*] **1 a** : a place appointed for assembling or meeting ⟨met him at the ~ agreed on the night before⟩; *specif* : a place appointed for the assembly of troops, ships, or airplanes before or after an operation ⟨the belated arrival of this division at the ~ —*Amer. Guide Series: Fla.*⟩ ⟨there were three ports of . . . ~, any one of which the whaling fleet might make at the end of a season to transship the catch to the schooner tenders —H.A. Chippendale⟩ **b** : a place to which people customarily come in numbers : a place of popular resort : HAUNT ⟨Lower City Park, a favorite ~ for anglers seeking small panfish —*Amer. Guide Series: Mich.*⟩ **c** : a place used (as by a band of outlaws or pirates) as a headquarters to work out of **2 a** : a meeting at an appointed place and time ⟨blue-jacketed sailors hurry to some long-anticipated ~ —*Amer. Guide Series: Va.*⟩ ⟨~ was made with a tanker and escort and . . . the ships of the task group refueled —Martin Dibner⟩ **b** : an agreement to meet each other or with another person or thing ⟨kept their ~⟩ ⟨I have a long-delayed ~ with the city beneath the sea —H.E.Rieseberg⟩ **c** : an annual gathering of fur trappers for trade and fun **3** *obs* : RETREAT, REFUGE **4** *obs* : a gathering or assemblage of persons or things **syn** see ENGAGEMENT

[2]**rendezvous** \"\ *vb* **rendezvoused; rendezvoused** \-üd\ **rendezvousing** \-üiŋ\ **rendezvouses** \-üz\ *vi* **1** : to come together at a place; *esp* : to meet or assemble by appointment ⟨all the cars ~ each night at prearranged destinations —*Ford Times*⟩ **2** *obs* : to mobilize one's forces ~ *vt* : to bring together at a rendezvous ⟨decided to ~ two fleets . . . and to decoy U.S. ships away with a third fleet —*Newsweek*⟩

**rend·ible** \'rendəbəl\ *adj* [*rend* + *-ible*] : capable of being rent

**rending** *pres part of* REND

**ren·di·tion** \ren'dishən\ *n* -s [obs. F, fr. MF, alter. (influenced by *rendre* to render) of *reddition* — more at REDDITION] **1** : the act or result of rendering ⟨timely and adequate ~ of medical care —*Jour. Amer. Med. Assoc.*⟩ : INTERPRETATION ⟨his sensitive ~ gave the lyrics a haunting and dramatic quality⟩ : TRANSLATION ⟨the first ~ of the work into English⟩ : PERFORMANCE ⟨the whole ~ lasted only a minute⟩ : EXPRESSION ⟨read it . . . for its pleasing ~ of a state of mind —David Daiches⟩ **2** : EXTRADITION 1

**ren·dle·wood** \'ren(d)°l,wůd\ *n* [perh. fr. *rend*] *dial Eng* : wood (as oak) with the bark off

**rendrock** \'=,=\ *n* [*rend* + *rock*] : a dynamite used in blasting and consisting of nitroglycerin, potassium nitrate, wood pulp, and paraffin or pitch

**rends** *pres 3d sing of* REND

**ren·du** \rän(,)dü\ *n* -s [F, rendering, fr. past part. of *rendre* to render, fr. MF — more at RENDER] : an artistically finished architectural drawing representing a design problem

**ren·dzi·na** \ren'jēnə\ *n* -s [Pol, rich limy soil] : an intrazonal group of dark grayish-brown soils developed in humid to subhumid grassy regions from soft calcareous marl or chalk and having brown friable upper layer and grayish or yellowish underlayers

**re·neague** \rə'nēg\ *dial Brit var of* RENEGE

**re·ne·al·mia** \,renē'almēə\ *n, cap* [NL, fr. Paul de *Reneaulme* †1624 Fr. botanist + NL *-ia*] *in some classifications* : a genus of tropical American and African herbs (family Zingiberaceae) having leafy or naked stems and racemose showy flowers

[1]**ren·e·gade** \'renə,gād, -nē,-\ *n* -s [Sp *renegado*, fr. ML *renegatus*, fr. past part. of *renegare* to deny, fr. L *re-* + *negare* to deny — more at NEGATION] **1** : a person who leaves one religious faith for another : a religious apostate **2** : a deserter from one cause, principle, party, or allegiance to another often hostile one : TURNCOAT, TRAITOR ⟨venom the ~ can summon up against his former beliefs and associates —*New Yorker*⟩ **3** : an individual who rejects the restraints of law or convention

[2]**renegade** \"\ *vi* -ED/-ING/-S : to become a renegade

[3]**renegade** \"\ *adj* : that is a renegade; *specif* : having deserted a cause, principle, or allegiance for a hostile one : TRAITOROUS, APOSTATE ⟨better to be . . . an honest animal than a ~ human being —Eleanor Dark⟩

**ren·e·ga·do** \,renə'gā(,)dō, -gā(-\ *n* -ES [Sp — more at RENEGADE] : RENEGADE

**renegate** *n* -s [ML *renegatus* — more at RENEGADE] *obs* : RENEGADE

[1]**re·nege** \rə'nig, rē'- *also* -neg *sometimes* -nēg *or* -näg\ *vb* -ED/-ING/-S [ML *renegare* — more at RENEGADE] *vt* **1** : DENY, RENOUNCE, DESERT, RETRACT **2** : REFUSE, DECLINE ~ *vi* **1** *obs* : to make a denial **2** : REVOKE 2 **3** : to break one's word : go back on a promise ⟨I'll wed him, and I'll not ~ —J.M.Synge⟩ ⟨both had *reneged* on paying off the loan —*Time*⟩ **4** : to reverse a stand or plan : back out : back down ⟨can do this without *reneging* on our traditions of due legal procedure —*New Republic*⟩

[2]**renege** \"\ *n* -s : REVOKE 2

**re·neg·er** \-gə(r)\ *n* -s : one that reneges

**re·negotiable** \,rē+\ *adj* [*renegotiate* + *-able*] : that can be renegotiated : subject to renegotiation ⟨a sale becomes ~ if the purchaser, or some subsequent purchaser, uses the material or article in the performance of a ~ contract —*Jour. of Accountancy*⟩

**re·negotiate** \"+\ *vb* [*re-* + *negotiate*] *vt* : to negotiate anew; *specif* : to determine under statutory procedure the existence and amount of excessive profits on (a government defense contract or subcontract or the price stipulated) in order to eliminate or to obtain a refund of such profits ~ *vi* : to adjust a defense contract price in order to eliminate or recover excessive profits — **re·negotiation** \"+\ *n* — **re·negotiator** \"+\ *n*

**re·nerve** \(')rē+\ *vt* [*re-* + *nerve*] : to nerve again : REINVIGORATE

**re·nest** \"+\ *vi* [*re-* + *nest*] : to nest again after the failure, disturbance, or destruction of the first nesting

**ren·ette** \(')re¦net\ *n* -s [L *renes* kidneys + E *-ette*] : a specialized excretory cell in some nematode worms

**re·new** \rə'n(y)ü, rē'-\ *vb* -ED/-ING/-S [ME *renewen*, fr. *re-* + *new*] *vt* **1** : to make new again : restore to freshness, perfection, or vigor ⟨steams . . . to ~ felt, suede, velvet —*Sears, Roebuck Cat.*⟩; *also* : to gain again as new : RESUME ⟨~ his strength⟩ **2** : to make new spiritually : REGENERATE ⟨be ye transformed by the ~*ing* of your mind —Rom 12:2 (AV)⟩ **3** : to restore to existence : REESTABLISH, RECREATE, REBUILD ⟨~ the old splendor of a palace⟩ : REVIVE, RESUSCITATE ⟨~ the sentiments of youth⟩ **4** : to go over again : make or do again : REPEAT ⟨~ a motion⟩ **5** : to begin again : RECOMMENCE, RESUME ⟨felt reluctant to rise and ~ my ramble —W.H.Hudson †1922⟩ **6** : to restore to fullness or sufficiency : REPLACE ⟨twisting the knob that ~*ed* the film —Arthur Gordon⟩ ⟨~ water in a tank⟩ ⟨~ one's equipment⟩ **7 a** : to grant or obtain an extension of : continue in force for a fresh period ⟨~ a lease⟩ **b** : to grant or obtain an extension of the loan of ⟨~*ed* the library book for another two weeks⟩ ~ *vi* **1** : to become new or as new : grow again : REVIVE **2** : to begin again : RESUME ⟨their friendship ~*ed*⟩ **3** : to make a renewal (as of a lease) **4** *obs* : to come back (as to a fresh attack) — **re·new·abil·i·ty** \rə,n(y)üə'biləd·ē\ *n* -ES — **re·new·able** \rə'n(y)üəbəl\ *adj* — **re·new·ably** \-blē\ *adv*

**renewable fuse** *n* [*renew* + *-able*] : a cartridge fuse permitting the replacement of a burned-out link

**re·new·al** \rə'n(y)üəl, rē'-, -(y)ůəl *also* -ül\ *n* -s [*renew* + *-al*] **1** : the act or process of renewing ⟨a ~ of the copyright by the publisher⟩ : REPETITION ⟨the 15th ~ of the . . . winter carnival —*Springfield (Mass.) Union*⟩ **2** : the quality or state of being renewed **3** : something renewed; *specif* : an expiring agreement (as a library loan or a subscription to a periodical) renewed for an additional period **4** : something used for renewing; *specif* : an expenditure that betters (as by prolonging useful lives, increasing output) existing fixed assets and is usu. capitalized in the accounts — usu. used in pl; compare REPAIR, REPLACEMENT **5** : a forbearance from enforcing an obligation (as on commercial paper) in virtue of an agreement by which the obligee relinquishes his right of action for a definite period or until a specified date

**renewed bark** *n* [fr. past part. of *renew*] : the new growth appearing on a cinchona under mossed bark — compare NATURAL BARK

**re·newed·ly** \-üədlē, -üd-\ *adv* [*renewed* + *-ly*] : in a renewed manner : ANEW

**re·newed·ness** \-dnəs\ *n* -ES : the quality or state of being renewed

**re·new·er** \-üə(r)\ *n* -s [ME, fr. *renewen* to renew + *-er*] : one that renews

**ren·frew·shire** \'ren,frü,shi(ə)r, -shiə, -,shə(r)\ *or* **ren·frew** \-ü\ *adj, usu cap* [fr. *Renfrewshire*, county of southwestern Scotland] : of or from the county of Renfrew, Scotland : of the kind or style prevalent in Renfrew

**ren·gas** \'reŋ,gäs\ *n* -ES [Malay *rĕngas*] : BLACK-VARNISH TREE

**reng·ma** \'reŋmə\ *n, pl* **rengma** *or* **rengmas** *usu cap* **1** : a Naga people inhabiting the Mikir hills of Assam **2** : a member of the Rengma people

**ren·gue** \'reŋgā\ *n* -s [AmerSp] : a coarse piña cloth made in the Philippines

**ren·gue·ra** \ren'gerə\ *n* -s [AmerSp, lameness, fr. *rengo* lame, fr. Sp *renco*, prob. of Gmc origin; akin to OE *wrencan* to twist — more at WRENCH] *Peru* : swayback of sheep

**reni-** *comb form* [L *renes* kidneys] **1** : kidney ⟨*reni*form⟩ ⟨*reni*puncture⟩ **2** : nephridial and ⟨*reni*cardiac⟩ ⟨*reni*pericardial⟩

**re·ni·fleur** \,renə'flər\ *n* -s [F, sniffer, fr. *renifler* to sniff (fr. MF, fr. OF *re-* + *nifler* to sniff, prob. of imit. origin) + *-eur* -er] : one who receives sexual gratification from smells (as of urine)

**ren·i·form** \'renə,fòrm, 'rēn-, -ō(ə)m\ *adj* [NL, fr. *reni-* + *-formis* -form] : resembling a mammalian kidney in shape : NEPHROID; *specif* : bean-shaped in outline ⟨a ~ leaf⟩ ⟨a ~ table⟩ — see LEAF illustration

**re·nig** \rə'nig, rē'-\ *vi* **renigged; renigged; renigging; renigs** [alter. of *renege*] : RENEGE

**re·nil·la** \rə'nilə\ *n* [NL, fr. L *renes* kidneys + NL *-illa*] **1** *cap* : a genus (the type of the family Renillidae) comprising the sea pansies **2** -s : SEA PANSY

[1]**re·nil·lid** \-ləd\ *adj* [NL *Renillidae*] : of or relating to the Renillidae

[2]**renillid** \"\ *n* -s : a coelenterate of the family Renillidae

**re·nil·li·dae** \-lə,dē\ *n pl, cap* [NL, fr. *Renilla*, type genus, + *-idae*] : a family of colonial alcyonarians (order Pennatulacea) having a circular or reniform rachis with the polyps dorsal

**re·nin** \'rēnən\ *n* -s [L *renes* kidneys + ISV *-in*] : a proteolytic enzyme that is found in kidney and that hydrolyzes hypertensinogen to hypertensin

**reni·portal** \,renə, ¦renə+\ *adj* [*reni-* + *portal*] : renal portal

**ren·i·ten·cy** \'renəd·ənsē, rə'nīt°nsē\ *also* **ren·i·tence** \'renəd·ən(t)s, rə'nīt°n(t)s\ *n, pl* **renitencies** *also* **renitences** [*renitency* fr. LL *renitentia*, fr. L *renitent-, renitens* + *-ia* -y; *renitence* fr. F *rénitence*, fr. MF, fr. LL *renitentia*] : the quality or state of being renitent : RESISTANCE, OPPOSITION, RELUCTANCE

**ren·i·tent** \'renəd·ənt, rə'nīt°nt\ *adj* [F or L; F *rénitent* fr. L *renitent-, renitens*, pres. part. of *reniti* to struggle against, fr. *re-* + *niti* to lean, push, strive — more at NISUS] **1** : resisting pressure or the effect of it : acting against impulse by elastic force **2** : resisting constraint or compulsion : persistently opposed : RECALCITRANT ⟨the Italians . . . have a traditional way of being subtly and stubbornly ~ to any government —Eric Mettler⟩

**rennes** \'ren\ *adj, usu cap* [fr. *Rennes*, city of northwest France] : of or from the city of Rennes, France : of the kind or style prevalent in Rennes

[1]**ren·net** \'renət, *usu* -əd·+V\ *n* -s [ME, fr. (assumed) *rennen* to cause to coagulate (fr. OE *gerennan*, fr. *ge-* together + — assumed — *rennan* to cause to run — akin to OHG *rennen* to cause to run, ON *renna*, Goth *urrannjan*; all fr. a prehistoric causative of the verb represented by OE *rinnan* to run) + *-et* — more at CO-, RUN] **1 a** : the contents of the stomach of an unweaned calf or other animal **b** : the lining membrane of the stomach (as the fourth stomach of ruminants) used for curdling milk; *also* : a preparation of the stomach of animals that is used for this purpose **c** : RENNIN **d** *or* **rennet bag** *or* **rennet stomach** : ABOMASUM **2** : something used to curdle milk ⟨vegetable ~⟩

[2]**rennet** \"\ *vt* -ED/-ING/-S : to add rennet to (milk) in cheese making to promote formation of curd

**rennet casein** *n* : CASEIN C

**ren·nin** \-nən\ *n* -s [*rennet* + *-in*] : a crystallizable enzyme that coagulates milk, that occurs esp. with pepsin in the gastric juice of young animals and is obtained as a yellowish powder, grains, or scales usu. by extraction of the mucous membrane of the fourth stomach of calves, and that is used chiefly in making cheese, junkets, and casein for plastics — called also *chymosin*

**reno-** *comb form* [L *renes* kidneys] **1** : kidney ⟨*reno*graphy⟩ **2** : renal and ⟨*reno*cutaneous⟩ ⟨*reno*gastric⟩ ⟨*reno*intestinal⟩ ⟨*reno*pulmonary⟩

**re·nominate** \(')rē+\ *vt* [*re-* + *nominate*] : to nominate again or anew esp. for a term of office in immediate succession — **re·nomination** \(,)rē+\ *n*

**ren·o·trophic** \¦renə·¦träfik, ¦rēn-\ *adj* [*reno-* + *-trophic*] : tending to induce enlargement of the kidney ⟨~ hormonal agents⟩

**ren·o·trop·ic** \-äpik\ *adj* [*reno-* + *-tropic*] **1** : RENOTROPHIC **2** : specifically attracted to kidney tissue ⟨~ infective agents⟩

[1]**re·nounce** \rə'naůn(t)s, rē'-\ *vb* -ED/-ING/-S [ME *renouncen*, fr. MF *renoncer*, fr. L *renuntiare* to report back, retract, renounce, fr. *re-* + *nuntiare* to report, fr. *nuntius* message, messenger — more at NUNCIO] *vt* **1** *obs* : ANNOUNCE, DECLARE, PROCLAIM **2** : to make known one's abandonment of the ownership of : give up, abandon, or resign usu. formally (something possessed) ⟨~ a title⟩ ⟨~ a claim⟩ **3** : to give up or abandon (something practiced, professed, intended) ⟨~ his errors⟩ ⟨~ faith⟩ ⟨~ a purpose⟩ ⟨~ the use of nuclear weapons⟩ **4** : to refuse further to follow, obey, or recognize : cast off : DISCLAIM, REPUDIATE ⟨~ one's son⟩ ⟨~ the authority of the church⟩ **5 a** : REVOKE *vt* 2 **b** : REFUSE *vt* 6 ~ *vi* **1** : to make a renunciation **2 a** : REVOKE *vi* 2 **b** : REFUSE *vi* 3 **3** : to abandon, decline, or resign formally some legal right or trust (as citizenship) **syn** see ABJURE

[2]**renounce** \"\ *n* -s [F *renonce*, fr. *renoncer* to renounce] **1** : failure to follow suit when able to do so **2** : a failure to follow suit

**re·nounce·able** \-səbəl\ *adj* : that can be renounced

**re·nounce·ment** \-smənt\ *n* -s [MF *renoncement*, fr. *renoncer* to renounce + *-ment*] : RENUNCIATION

**re·nounc·er** \-sə(r)\ *n* -s : one that renounces

**ren·o·vate** \'renə,vāt, *usu* -ād·+V\ *vb* -ED/-ING/-S [L *renovatus*, past part. of *renovare* to renovate, fr. *re-* + *novare* to make new, fr. *novus* new — more at NEW] *vt* **1** : to restore to life, vigor, or activity : REVIVE, REGENERATE **2** : to restore to a former state (as of freshness, soundness, purity, or newness of appearance) : make over : RENEW ⟨~ a house⟩ **3 a** : to prune (old shrubs or trees) so that the old wood is subsequently replaced by new growth **b** : to invigorate (old lawns, fields, or pastures) by fertilization or cultivation ~ *vi* : to become renewed : REVIVE

**renovated butter** *n* [fr. past part. of *renovate*] : PROCESS BUTTER

**ren·o·vat·ing·ly** *adv* [*renovating* (pres. part. of *renovate*) + *-ly*] : in a renovating manner

**ren·o·va·tion** \ˌ==ˈvāshən\ *n* [ME *renovacion*, fr. MF or L; MF *renovation*, fr. L *renovation-, renovatio*, fr. *renovatus* (past part. of *renovare* to renew) + *-ion-, -io* -ion — more at RENOVATE] **1** : the act or process of renovating : making over : REVIVAL **2** : the state of being renovated

**ren·o·va·tion·ist** \-sh(ə)nəst\ *n* -s [*renovation* + *-ist*] : an advocate of renovation (as of a government)

**ren·o·va·tor** \ˈ==ˌvād·ə(r), -ātə-\ *n* [LL, fr. L *renovatus* + *-or*] **1** : one that renovates (as worn or damaged articles) **2** : a nozzle attachment for the suction pipe of a vacuum cleaner

**¹re·nown** \rəˈnau̇n, rē'-\ *n* -s [ME *renoun*, fr. MF *renon*, fr. OF, fr. *renomer* to celebrate, fr. *re-* + *nomer* to name, fr. L *nominare*, fr. *nomin-, nomen* name — more at NAME] **1** : the state of being widely acclaimed and highly honored (as for signal achievement) ⟨poet of great ~⟩ ⟨the increasing ~ of the university⟩ ⟨win ~ by a deed of heroism⟩ **2** *obs* **a** : REPORT, RUMOR; *also* : good report **b** : REPUTATION; *also* : NOTORIETY **3** : something renowned (as a deed) **syn** see FAME

**²renown** \"\ *vt* -ED/-ING/-S [MF *renommer*, fr. OF *renomer*] : to give renown to : make renowned

**re·nowned** \-nd\ *adj* [ME *renouned*, fr. past part. of *renoun* to renown] : having renown : CELEBRATED ⟨one of the most ~ shrines on the continent⟩ — **re·nowned·ly** \-nədlē, -nd-\ *adv* — **re·nowned·ness** \-nədnəs, -n(d)n-\ *n* -ES

**re·nown·er** \-nə(r)\ *n* -s [*renown* + *-er*] : one that gives renown

**rens·se·laer·ite** \ˈren(t)sələˌrīt, ˌren(t)səˈliˌrīt\ *n* -s [Stephen Van *Rensselaer* †1839 Am. army officer and politician + E *-ite*] : a soft compact talc that is an altered pyroxene and is often worked in a lathe into articles (as inkstands)

**¹rent** \ˈrent\ *n* -s *often attrib* [ME *rente*, fr. OF, income from a property, fr. (assumed) VL *rendita*, fr. fem. of past part. of (assumed) *rendere* to yield — more at RENDER] **1** *also* **rents** *pl, chiefly dial* : a piece of property that the owner allows another to use in exchange for a payment in services, kind, or money : a rented property; *esp* : an apartment or house that rents **2** *obs* **a** : REVENUE, INCOME **b** : TRIBUTE, TAX, TOLL **3 a** : a return made by a tenant or occupant of land or corporeal hereditaments to the owner for the possession and use thereof : a fixed periodical profit in money, provisions, chattels, or services issuing out of lands and tenements in payment for use; *esp* : a pecuniary sum agreed upon between a tenant and his landlord and paid at fixed intervals by the tenant to the landlord for the use of land or its appendages ⟨~ for a house⟩ **b** : the amount paid by a hirer or lessee of personal property (as farming stock, machinery) to the owner for the use thereof under whether confined with rent for land or not **c** : a royalty under a mineral lease **d** : compensation for use and occupation of real estate not arising out of a lease in writing **4 a** : the portion of the income of an economy (as of a nation) attributable to land as a factor of production in addition to capital and labor : the income of landowners as a class — compare PROFIT, WAGE **b** : the income earned by a unit of production (as a market garden, a repairman) beyond the minimum required to make employment in such production worth while by meeting costs and at least equaling other possible employments in returns : the difference between the actual return from a commodity or service and the supply price : ECONOMIC RENT **c** : income or gain that is a differential return (as the excess of personal earnings of a producer of rare ability over those of an average producer) or as a surplus above costs ⟨entrepreneur's ~ denotes the profits of an ably managed . . . enterprise, conceived of as a differential above the return secured by a marginal undertaking which is barely able to meet its costs —A.A.Young⟩ — see CONSUMER'S SURPLUS, PRODUCER'S SURPLUS — **for rent** : available for use or service in return for payment : to let ⟨a house *for rent*⟩ : for hire ⟨costumes *for rent*⟩

**²rent** \"\ *vb* -ED/-ING/-S [ME *renten*, fr. *rente* rent] *vt* **1** *obs* : to give revenues or an endowment to : ENDOW **2** : to take and hold under an agreement to pay rent : pay rent for ⟨the tenant ~s the house by the month under a one-year lease⟩ **3** : to grant the possession and enjoyment of for rent : hire out : LET ⟨the owner ~s the house at a reasonable figure⟩ ~ *vi* **1** : to be for rent ⟨the largest apartment ~s for $800 a year⟩ **2 a** : to obtain the possession and use of a place or article for rent ⟨~s from the family in the other apartment⟩ **b** : to allow the possession and use of property for rent ⟨~s to families with children⟩

**³rent** *past of* REND

**⁴rent** \ˈrent\ *vb* [ME *renten*, alter. (influenced by *³rent*) of *renden* to rend] *dial chiefly Eng* : REND, TEAR

**⁵rent** \"\ *n* -s **1** : an opening (as a tear in cloth, a cleft in the earth, a gorge, a crack in wood) made by or as if by rending **2** : a split in a party or organized group : SCHISM **3** : an act or an instance of rending **syn** see BREACH

**rent·abil·i·ty** \ˌrentəˈbiləd·ē\ *n* : the quality or state of being rentable

**rent·able** \-təbəl\ *adj* [²*rent* + *-able*] : that can be rented

**rent·age** \ˈrentij\ *n* -s [¹*rent* + *-age*] : RENT, RENTAL

**¹rent·al** \-tᵊl\ *n* -s [ME, fr. ML *rentale*, fr. ME *rente* rent + L *-ale*, neut. of *-alis* -al] **1** : RENT-ROLL **2** : an amount paid or collected as rent : income from rent ⟨collected the most ~ of the city's apartment house owners⟩ : return (as a sum of money) given or received as rent : the amount of rent ⟨the average ~ (including gas, electricity, heat, and janitor service) is $8.08 per month for each room —*Amer. Guide Series: N.J.*⟩ **3** *Scots law, obs* : a tack usu. for life for a low customary rent granted to kindly tenants **4** : a property (as an apartment, automobile, dinner jacket) that is given for use in return for payment : something rented ⟨moved to a cheaper ~⟩ **5** : an act of renting ⟨~s are made only to . . . established film societies —*Saturday Rev.*⟩ **6** : a business that rents something

**²rental** \"\ *adj* **1** : of or relating to rent ⟨~ charges⟩ **2** : that can be or has been rented ⟨~ housing⟩ ⟨a ~ car⟩ ⟨~ books⟩ **3** : dealing in rental property ⟨a ~ agency⟩

**rental collection** *n* : a collection of books in an otherwise free library (as in a college) that may be borrowed at a daily fee

**rentaler** *or* **rentaller** *n* -s [¹*rental* + *-er*] *obs* : KINDLY TENANT

**rental library** *n* : a commercially operated library (as in a store) that lends books at a usu. fixed charge per book per day ⟨a drug store with a *rental library* serviced by a concession company⟩ — called also *lending library*

**rental value insurance** *n* : insurance against loss to the occupant of the rental value of described premises because of specified damage to such premises

**rent charge** *n, pl* **rents charge** [¹*rent*] **1** : a periodical payment made a charge on land by reservation in a conveyance of land for life or in fee simple or granted by deed and expressly giving to the holder who has no reversionary interest in the land the right of distress for arrears — compare RENT SECK **2** *Brit* : an annual sum charged on land or payable out of the income of land to which attaches a statutory power of distress for arrears

**rent charger** *n* : the owner of a rent charge

**rent control** *n* : government regulation of the amount charged as rent for housing and often also of eviction

**rente** \ˈränt\ *n* -s [F, income, rent, fr. OF — more at RENT] **1** : annual income under French law on property forever alienated of the same type as the English rents charge, rents seck, and annuities **2 a** : interest payable by the government of France and some other European countries on the consolidated debt **b** : a government security yielding rente

**ren·ten·mark** \ˈrentᵊnˌmärk\ *n, sometimes cap* [G, fr. *rente* income (fr. OF) + *mark* — more at RENT, MARK] : a temporary German monetary unit used for bank notes issued in 1923 to stabilize currency, made equivalent to one billion inflated imperial marks, and superseded by the reichsmark

**¹rent·er** \ˈrentə(r)\ *n* -s [ME, fr. *renten* to enjoy the possession of for rent + *-er*] : one that rents: as **a** : the lessee or tenant of lands, tenements, or other property **b** *chiefly Brit* : a motion-picture distributor

**²ren·ter** \"\ *vt* -ED/-ING/-S [F *rentrer*, alter. (influenced by *rentrer* to enter again, fr. OF, fr. *re-* + *entrer* to enter) of MF *rentraire*, fr. *re-* + *entraire* to draw in, fr. OF, fr. *en-* in- (fr. L *in-*) + *traire* to draw, fr. L *trahere* — more at ENTER, DRAW] : to fine-draw rents in cloth

**³rent·er** \"\ *n* -s [⁴*rent* + *-er*] : CHIPPER d

**ren·tier** \ˈrän·(ˌ)tyā\ *n* -s [F, fr. OF, fr. *rente* + *-ier* -er] **1** : one who owns rentes **2** : a person who receives a fixed income (as from land, stocks, bonds) : one who lives on income from investments

**renting** *pres part of* RENT

**rent insurance** *n* [¹*rent*] : insurance against loss to a landlord because of suspension of rents resulting from specified damage to rented premises

**¹rent·less** \ˈrentləs\ *adj* [¹*rent* + *-less*] **1** *obs* : not yielding rent **2** : rent free **3** : UNRENTABLE

**²rentless** \"\ *adj* [⁵*rent* + *-less*] : not torn

**rent of assize** [¹*rent*] : a fixed rent paid by freeholders or ancient copyholders of an English manor

**rent party** *n* : a party to which admission is charged with the profits going to pay the host's rent

**rent resolute** *n, Old Eng law* : crown rents from lands formerly in possession of now dissolved religious bodies

**rent-roll** \ˈ=ˌ=\ *n* [¹*rent* + *roll*] : a register of rents including the names of tenants and the amounts due; *also* : the total income indicated by such a register

**rents** *pl of* RENT, *pres 3d sing of* RENT

**rent seck** *n, pl* **rents seck** [ME *rent sek*, fr. AF *rente seque*, lit., dry rent] : a rent reserved or granted like a rent charge orig. not having the right of distress but in England having a power of distress annexed in 1730

**rent service** *n* [¹*rent*] : rent reserved out of land held by fealty or other corporeal service and under the common law having attached the right of distress

**rents, issues, and profits** *n pl* : the total wealth or profit either gross or net after the satisfaction of reasonable expenses arising from the ownership or possession of property

**rent table** *n* : a round or polygonal table made during the second half of the 18th century in England with small drawers often labeled with the days of the week and possibly used for a simple filing system for rent collecting

rent table

**re·number** \(ˈ)rē+\ *vt* [ME *renombren*, fr. *re-* + *nombren* to number] : to number again (as with different numbers) ⟨~ the street⟩ ⟨~ pages 15 to 34⟩

**¹re·nun·ci·ant** \rəˈnən(t)sēənt\ *n* -s [L *renuntiant-, renuntians*, pres. part. of *renuntiare* to renounce — more at RENOUNCE] : one who renounces (as the world)

**²renunciant** \"\ *adj* [L *renuntiant-, renuntians*] : RENUNCIATIVE

**re·nun·ci·a·tion** \rəˌnən(t)sēˈāshən, rē-, *sometimes* -ˌnənchē-\ *n* -s [ME, fr. L *renuntiation-, renuntiatio*, fr. *renuntiatus* (past part. of *renuntiare* to renounce) + *-ion-, -io*, -ion — more at RENOUNCE] **1** : the act or practice of renouncing : SACRIFICE, REJECTION, REPUDIATION ⟨the ~ of a title⟩ ⟨a ~ of ambitions⟩ ⟨made a ~ of his chairmanship⟩; *specif* : ascetic self-denial ⟨a life of complete ~ . . . as a nun —C.C.Cregan⟩ **2** *Brit* : a legal document by which a person appointed in a will to be its executor or a person preferentially entitled to administer the estate of an intestate renounces his right

**re·nun·ci·a·tive** \=ˈ==ˌād·iv\ *adj* [L *renuntiatus* + E *-ive*] : marked by or expressive of renunciation

**re·nun·ci·a·to·ry** \=ˈ=əˌtōrē\ *adj* [L *renuntiatus* + E *-ory*] : of or relating to renunciation : RENUNCIATIVE

**¹ren·verse** \renˈvərs\ *vt* -ED/-ING/-S [MF *renverser*, fr. *re-* + *enverser* to invert, fr. OF, fr. *envers* upside down, fr. L *inversus* — more at INVERSE] *archaic* : to turn back : REVERSE, OVERTURN, OVERTHROW

**²ren·ver·sé** \ˌränˌverˈsā\ *adj* [F, lit., turned back, fr. past part. of *renverser* to turn back, fr. MF] : consisting of or accompanied by a bending of the head and body from the waist while turning in ballet : REVERSED ⟨a ~ movement⟩

**ren·verse·ment** \renˈvərsmənt\ *n* -s [F, reversal, inversion, fr. MF, fr. *renverser* to turn back, turn over + *-ment* — more at RENVERSE] : an airplane maneuver consisting of a half-roll followed by a half-loop

**ren·voi** \renˈvȯi\ *n* -s [F, act of sending back, reference, fr. MF, fr. *renvoyer* to send back, fr. OF, fr. *re-* + *envoyer*, *envoier* to send — more at ENVOY] **1** : the return by a government of an alien to his own country **2** : the reference of a matter involving a conflict of jurisdiction in private international law to the law or courts of a jurisdiction other than the local jurisdiction involved

**re·occupy** \(ˈ)rē+\ *vt* [*re-* + *occupy*] : to occupy again

**re·occur** \ˌrē+\ *vi* [*re-* + *occur*] : to occur again

**re·occurrence** \"+\ *n* [*re-* + *occurrence*] : a second or another occurrence

**re·odorization** \(ˌ)rē+\ *n* : the act or process of reodorizing or the state of being reodorized

**re·odorize** \(ˈ)rē+\ *vt* [*re-* + *odorize*] : to change the odor of — compare DEODORIZE

**re·open** \(ˈ)rē+\ *vb* [*re-* + *open*] *vt* **1** : to open again ⟨~*ed* his eyes⟩ ⟨~*ed* the school⟩ **2 a** : to take up again : RESUME ⟨the right to ~ discussion of matters affecting international peace —Vera M. Dean⟩ **b** : to resume the discussion or consideration of (a closed matter) ⟨~ the contract to discuss wages —*Wall Street Jour.*⟩ **c** : to try or hear (a legal suit or action) anew esp. for the purpose of hearing new evidence **3** : to begin again ⟨~ fire⟩ ⟨~ hostilities⟩ ~ *vi* **1** : to open again; *specif* : to resume operations after an interruption or suspension ⟨the store ~*ed* after a one-week shutdown⟩

**re·opener** \"+\ *n* : REOPENING CLAUSE

**reopening clause** *n* : a clause in a collective bargaining contract providing for a reconsideration of an issue (as wages) during the life of the contract

**¹re·order** \(ˈ)rē+\ *vb* [*re-* + *order*] *vt* **1** : to order again or anew : arrange in a different way : REORGANIZE ⟨our greatest opportunity to ~ our city patterns —Charles Abrams⟩ **2** : to give a reorder for ⟨~*ed* two dozen blouses of the same style⟩ ~ *vi* : to place a reorder ⟨when I sell these, I'll ~⟩

**²reorder** \"\ *n* : an order for the same goods previously ordered from a particular firm or supplier

**re·ordination** \(ˌ)rē+\ *n* [LL *reordination-, reordinatio*, fr. *reordinatus* (past part. of *reordinare* to ordain again, fr. L *re-* + LL *ordinare* to ordain) + L *-ion-, -io* -ion — more at ORDAIN] : a second or repeated ordination

**re·organization** \"+\ *n* **1** : the act of reorganizing or the state of being reorganized ⟨a thorough-going ~ of our entire body of subject-matter along new lines —*School & Society*⟩ **2 a** : the rehabilitation of the finances of a business concern under procedures prescribed by federal bankruptcy legislation **b** : any of various procedures (as recapitalizations or mergers) that affect the tax structure of a corporation under federal income tax legislation **3** : the alteration of the existing structure of governmental units (as bureaus or legislative committees) and the lines of control and authority between them usu. to promote greater efficiency and responsibility

**re·organize** \(ˈ)rē+\ *vb* [*re-* + *organize*] *vt* : to organize again or anew : change the organization of ⟨~ the department to increase efficiency⟩ ~ *vi* : to effect a reorganization ⟨with the option then to continue, suspend, or ~ —W.Z.Ripley⟩ — **re·organizer** \"+\ *n*

**re·orient** \"+\ *vt* [*re-* + *orient*] : to orient again or anew : change the orientation of ⟨suggests that American institutions of higher learning ~ their programs to include professional or vocational training for all —H.J.Carman⟩

**re·orientate** \"+\ *vt* [*re-* + *orientate*] : REORIENT

**re·orientation** \(ˌ)rē+\ *n* [*re-* + *orientation*] : a changed orientation ⟨a ~ of attitudes toward this part of the world —Robert Trumbull⟩

**¹rep** \ˈrep\ *n* -s [short for *reputation*] *slang* : REPUTATION; *esp* : status in a group (as a street gang)

**²rep** \"\ *n* -s [prob. short for ³*reprobate*] : a person given to immoral behavior

**³rep** *or* **repp** \ˈrep\ *n* -s [modif. of F *reps*, modif. of E *ribs*, pl. of ¹*rib*] : a clothing and upholstery fabric in plain weave with prominent rounded crosswise ribs that is usu. made by alternating fine and coarse yarns or by the slacking and tensioning of yarns and that is woven from various fibers singly or in combination

**⁴rep** \"\ *n* -s [short for ²*representative*] : REPRESENTATIVE; *specif* : a cowboy who rides in a roundup as the representative of a particular ranch ⟨a ~ from each ranch in the area would see that everything was done fair and square —S.E.Fletcher⟩

**⁵rep** \"\ *vi* **repped; repped; repping; reps** : to act as a rep in a roundup ⟨inquired what brand we were *repping* for —Emma Yates⟩

**⁶rep** \"\ *n* -s [by shortening] : REPERTORY

**⁷rep** \"\ *or* **rep unit** *n, pl* **rep** *or* **reps** [*rep* fr. roentgen equivalent physical] : the dosage of any ionizing radiation that will develop the same amount of energy upon absorption in human tissues as one roentgen of X-ray or gamma-ray dosage — compare REM

**rep** *abbr* **1** repair **2** repeat **3** report; reported; reporter **4** republic; republican

**re·pack** \(ˈ)rē+\ *vt* [ME *repakken*, fr. *re-* + *pakken* to pack] : to pack again or anew; *specif* : to put into a different container ⟨~*ed* tomatoes⟩

**re·package** \"+\ *vt* [*re-* + *package*] : to package again or anew; *specif* : to put into a more efficient or attractive form

**¹re·paint** \"+\ *vt* [*re-* + *paint*] : to paint again or anew ⟨figures of the past whom I should like to ~ for this generation —H.J.Laski⟩ ⟨~ the house⟩; *specif* : to paint over (part of a picture) ⟨the painting turned up again heavily ~*ed* —*Time*⟩

**²re·paint** \ˈrē+ˌ, =ˈ=\ *n* **1** : the fact of having been repainted ⟨is marred by a clumsy ~⟩ **2** : something repainted

**¹re·pair** \rəˈpa(a)(ə)r, rēˈp-, -pe|, |ə\ *vi* -ED/-ING/-S [ME *repairen*, fr. MF *repairer, repairier* to return, go back to one's own country, dwell, fr. OF *repairier*, fr. LL *repatriare* to go back to one's own country, fr. L *re-* + LL *-patriare* (fr. L *patria* native country) — more at EXPATRIATE] **1 a** : to betake oneself : GO ⟨summoned me to ~ immediately to the lobby —Horace Sutton⟩ **b** : to go habitually : RESORT ⟨sacred trees to which they ~ at various times, but especially before harvest —J.G.Frazer⟩ **c** : to go to a specified place for a specified purpose ⟨~ to the second-floor cafe to drink tea and coffee —C.S.Coon⟩ ⟨~*ing* to their villages in the rainy season to plant their plots —R.H.Lowie⟩ **d** : to go for the purpose of assembling : RALLY ⟨raise a standard to which the wise and honest can ~ —George Washington⟩ ⟨a standard of ethical professional conduct to which all architects of good will might ~ —G.B.Cummings⟩ **2** *obs* : RETURN ⟨all to Athens back again ~ —Shak.⟩

**²repair** \"\ *n* -s [ME *repair, repaire*, fr. MF *repaire* return, dwelling, fr. OF, fr. *repairier*, v.] **1** : the act or fact of repairing to a place : RESORT ⟨as the day gets warm, ~ is had to the shade of a tree —James Stevenson-Hamilton⟩ **2** *chiefly Scot* : a concourse esp. of people : FLOCKING **3** : a place of resort : HAUNT ⟨this house became a ~ for rising politicians⟩

**³repair** \"\ *vb* -ED/-ING/-S [ME *repairen, reparen*, fr. MF *reparer*, fr. L *reparare*, fr. *re-* + *parare* to prepare — more at PARE] *vt* **1 a** : to restore by replacing a part or putting together what is torn or broken : FIX, MEND ⟨so neatly ~*ed* that he could see no trace of the once familiar rents —T.B.Costain⟩ ⟨~ a house⟩ ⟨~ a shoe⟩ **b** : to restore to a sound or healthy state : RENEW, REVIVIFY ⟨~ his strength⟩ ⟨resume his law practice in order to ~ his private fortune —E.M.Coulter⟩ ⟨~ the tissues of the body⟩ **2** : to make good : REMEDY ⟨the material and moral damage took long to ~ —Jacquetta & Christopher Hawkes⟩ ⟨~ the lack of early education —E.H. Collis⟩ ⟨with his ignominious failure —Bernard DeVoto⟩ **3** : to make up for : compensate for ⟨~ an insult⟩ ⟨~ an injustice⟩ ~ *vi* : to make repairs **syn** see MEND

**⁴repair** \"\ *n* -s **1 a** : the act or process of repairing : restoration to a state of soundness, efficiency, or health ⟨the boat was beyond ~⟩ ⟨a thorough ~ of the crazy fabric of human nature —T.L.Peacock⟩ **b** : an instance or result of repairing ⟨the coat needed only a simple ~⟩ ⟨made a few ~s to the stairs where some boards had come loose⟩ ⟨the ~ to the rug was evident to the eye⟩ **c** : the replacement of destroyed cells or tissues by new formations **2 a** : relative condition with respect to soundness or need of repairing ⟨the car is in reasonably good ~⟩ ⟨the building is in poor ~⟩ **b** : the state of being in good or sound condition ⟨the house is in ~⟩ ⟨the house is out of ~⟩ ⟨his judgment was in constant ~ —F.A.Swinnerton⟩ **3 repairs** *pl* : the portion of maintenance charges expended to keep fixed assets in adequate and efficient operating condition and recorded on the books as expense — contrasted with *renewal* and *replacement*

**re·pair·able** \-pa(a)rəbəl, -per-\ *adj* : capable of being repaired

**re·pair·er** \-pa(a)rə(r), -perə-\ *n* -s : one that repairs; *specif* : one whose occupation is to make repairs ⟨shoe ~⟩ ⟨watch ~⟩

**re·pair·man** \-pa(a)rmən, -per-\ *n, pl* **repairmen** : one who repairs; *specif* : one whose occupation is to make repairs or readjustments in a mechanism ⟨a typewriter ~⟩ ⟨a radio ~⟩

**repair ship** *n* : a naval auxiliary vessel fitted with shops for the handling of repairs to naval vessels

**repair shop** *n* : an establishment where repairs are made ⟨a small *repair shop* that mends all sorts of items⟩

**re·pand** \rəˈpand, rēˈp-\ *adj* [L *repandus* bent backward, turned up, fr. *re-* + *pandus* bent; akin to ON *fattr* bent backward and perh. to L *pandere* to spread — more at FATHOM] *of a leaf* : having a slightly undulating margin

**rep·a·ra·ble** \ˈrep(ə)rəbəl *also* ÷ *like* REPAIRABLE\ *adj* [L *reparabilis*, fr. *reparare* to repair + *-bilis* -able] **1** : capable of being mended or put into sound condition : REPAIRABLE ⟨when inspected parts are found defective but ~ —G.J.Stegemerten⟩ **2** : capable of being remedied or made good ⟨~ damage⟩

**rep·a·ra·tion** \ˌrepəˈrāshən\ *n* -s [ME *reparacioun*, fr. MF *reparation*, fr. LL *reparation-, reparatio*, fr. L *reparatus* (past part. of *reparare* to repair) + *-ion-, -io* -ion — more at REPAIR] **1 a** : the act or process of mending or restoring : a repairing or keeping in repair ⟨the ~ of wasted tissue⟩ ⟨a church in need of constant ~⟩ **b reparations** *pl* : REPAIRS **2 a** : the act of making amends, offering expiation, or giving satisfaction for a wrong or injury ⟨the treatment may consist of ~ to and propitiation of the offended spirit —*Notes & Queries on Anthropology*⟩ **b** : something done or given as amends or satisfaction ⟨was educated in France at royal expense as ~ for the death of his father —H.C.Nixon⟩ **3** : the payment of damages : INDEMNIFICATION; *specif* : compensation in money or in materials (as commodities or capital equipment) payable by a defeated nation as war indemnity for direct damages to or expenditures sustained by another nation as a result of hostilities with the defeated nation — usu. used in pl. ⟨extract maximum ~s by dismantling and transferring plants —Karl Loewenstein⟩

**re·par·a·tive** \rəˈparəd·iv, rēˈp-\ *adj* [LL *reparativus*, fr. L *reparatus* (past part. of *reparare*) + *-ivus* -ive] **1** : of, relating to, or effecting repair **2** : serving to make amends ⟨does a fine ~ job for several neglected poets —George Dillon⟩

**re·par·a·to·ry** \-arəˌtōrē\ *adj* [fr. *reparative*, after such pairs as E *preparative: preparatory*] : REPARATIVE

**¹rep·ar·tee** \ˌrepə(r)ˈtē, -ˌpärˈt-, -ˌpäˈt-, -ˈtā\ *n* -s [F *repartie*, fr. *repartir* to retort, fr. MF, fr. *re-* + *partir* to divide, go away — more at PART] **1 a** : a quick and witty reply : a clever retort ⟨won the applause of the audience with his ~ to a heckler⟩ **b** : a succession of clever retorts ⟨beneath the surface of ~ and mock seriousness —R.M.Weaver⟩ ⟨the constant ~ is artificial and wearying⟩ **2** : adroitness and cleverness in reply : quickness and sharpness in retort ⟨was noted for his ~ and impromptu wit⟩ **3** : the uttering of clever retorts ⟨her skill at ~ has made her many enemies⟩ **syn** see WIT

**²repartee** \"\ *vi* **reparteed; reparteed; reparteeing; repartees** : to make or be able to make clever retorts

**re·par·ti·mi·en·to** \rəˌpärd·əmēˈen·(ˌ)tō, ˌrāˌpärd·əmˈyen·-\ *n* -s [AmerSp, fr. Sp, distribution, fr. *repartir* to distribute (fr. *re-* — fr. L — + *partir* to divide, fr. L *partire, partiri*) + *-miento* -ment (fr. L *-mentum*) — more at PART] : a grant or distribution formerly made to Spanish colonists or establishments in America; *esp* **:** a grant of Indian forced labor (as for use in agriculture, in mining, or in construction) — compare ENCOMIENDA

**re·partition** \ˌrē+, *in sense 1* ¦rē *or* ˌre+\ *n* [prob. fr. Sp *repartición*, fr. *repartir* to distribute, after Sp *partir* to divide: *partición* division (fr. L *partition-, partitio* division, partition)] **1 :** DISTRIBUTION ⟨the relative ~ of land and water is very different from what prevails on the earth —*Popular Science Monthly*⟩ **2 :** a second or additional partition ⟨the ~ of the country⟩

**re·pass** \(ˈ)rē+\ *vb* [ME *repassen*, fr. MF *repasser*, fr. OF, fr. *re-* + *passer* to pass] *vi* **:** to pass again esp. in the opposite direction **:** RETURN ⟨they pass and they ~ with pallid eyes —Robert Browning⟩ **~** *vt* **1 a :** to cross again in returning ⟨~ the desert⟩ ⟨~ the ocean⟩ **b :** to pass through, over, or by again ⟨~ the gate⟩ ⟨~ the road⟩ ⟨~ the house⟩ **2 :** to cause to pass again ⟨~ the needle through the cloth⟩ **3** [*re-* + *pass*] **:** to adopt again ⟨~*ed* the bill over the presidential veto⟩ ⟨~*ed* the resolution⟩

**re·passage** \"+\ *n* [ME, fr. MF, fr. *repasser* + *-age*] **:** the act or privilege of repassing **:** passage back or freedom to repass ⟨granted them passage and ~ through his territory⟩

**¹re·past** \rəˈpast, rēˈp-, -paa(ə)st,-paist,-påst *also* ˈrē,p-\ *n* -s [ME, fr. MF, food, fr. OF, fr. *repaistre* to give a meal to, feed (fr. *re-* + *paistre* to feed, fr. L *pascere*), after OF *paistre* to feed: *past* food, meal (fr. L *pastus*, past part. of *pascere* to feed — more at FOOD] **1 :** something that is taken as food ⟨crow is hardly a palatable ~ for the average citizen —*Phoenix Flame*⟩; *specif* **:** a supply of food and drink served as a meal ⟨a delicious ~ of simple but perfectly cooked food⟩ **2 a :** the act of taking food ⟨if, before ~, it shall please you to gratify the table with a grace —Shak.⟩ **b :** the time or occasion of eating a meal ⟨preferred to be alone during his evening ~⟩

**²repast** \"\ *vb* -ED/-ING/-S [ME *repasten*, fr. *repast*, n.] *vt*, *obs* **:** to supply food to **:** FEED ⟨~ them with my blood —Shak.⟩ **~** *vi* **:** to take food **:** FEAST — usu. used with *on* or *upon*

**repastination** *n* -s [L *repastination-, repastinatio*, fr. *repastinatus* (past part. of *repastinare* to dig again, fr. *re-* + *pastinare* to dig and trench in preparation for the planting of vines, fr. *pastinum* 2-pronged dibble) + *-ion-, -io* -ion] *obs* **:** the act of digging over again ⟨this continual motion, ~, and turning of the mold with the spade —John Evelyn⟩

**re·patri·a·ble** \rēˈpā·trēəbəl *also* -pa-\ *adj* [¹*repatriate* + *-able*] **:** capable of being repatriated

**¹re·patri·ate** \(ˈ)ˌ≈ˌ≈,āt, *usu* -ˌād·+V\ *vt* -ED/-ING/-S [LL *repatriatus*, past part. of *repatriare* to go back to one's own country — more at REPAIR] **1 :** to restore or return to one's country of origin, allegiance, or citizenship ⟨*repatriated* prisoners of war as quickly as they could be processed⟩ **2 :** to restore to the country of origin ⟨has at the moment no dollars to remit any profits or ~ any capital —*Time*⟩

**²re·patri·ate** \-ˌə̇t, -ˌa¦t, *usu* ¦d·+V\ *n* -s **:** one who is repatriated

**re·patri·a·tion** \(ˌ)≈ˌ≈'āshən\ *n* -s [ML *repatriation-, repatriatio*, fr. LL *repatriatus* (past part. of *repatriare*) + L *-ion-, -io* -ion] **:** the act of repatriating or the state of being repatriated

**¹re·pay** \(ˈ)rē¦pā, rə¦pā\ *vb* [*re-* + *pay*] *vt* **1 a :** to pay back **:** REFUND ⟨~ the investment in the first year of operation —R.E.Cross⟩ **b :** to give or inflict in return or requital ⟨evil pursueth sinners; but to the righteous good shall be *repaid* —Prov 13:21 (AV)⟩ ⟨~ her scorn for scorn —John Keats⟩ **2 :** to make a return payment to **:** COMPENSATE, REQUITE ⟨if the traveller would only leave the boat and wander inland, he would be *repaid* by the revelation of marvellous beauties of Nature —Anthony Trollope⟩ **3 :** to make requital for **:** RECOMPENSE ⟨a friendly act that was later *repaid* with treachery —*Amer. Guide Series: Maine*⟩ ⟨a society which will well ~ intensive study —W.H.Goodenough⟩ **~** *vi* **:** to make return payment or requital ⟨loans are judged on . . . the ability of the borrower to ~ —*Collier's Yr. Bk.*⟩ **syn** see PAY

**²repay** \"\ *n* **:** REPAYMENT

**re·pay·able** \≈'≈əbəl\ *adj* **:** subject to repayment

**repaying** *adj* **:** PROFITABLE, REWARDING ⟨the necessary, ~ effort to acquire command of the realities masked by musical terminology —*N.Y.Herald Tribune Bk. Rev.*⟩

**re·pay·ment** \rəˈpāmənt, rēˈp-\ *n* [ME, fr. *re-* + *payment*] **1 :** the act or an instance of paying back **:** REIMBURSEMENT ⟨was unable to make ~ of the loan at the time specified⟩ **2 :** REQUITAL ⟨this ingratitude was a poor ~ for his sacrifices⟩

**¹re·peal** \rəˈpēl, rēˈp-, *esp before pause or consonant* -ēəl\ *vt* -ED/-ING/-S [ME *repelen*, fr. MF *repeler, rapeler*, fr. OF, fr. *re-* + *apeler* to appeal, call — more at APPEAL] **1 :** to rescind or revoke (as a sentence or law) from operation or effect **:** ABROGATE, ANNUL ⟨pledged that laws forbidding strikes for the duration of the rebellion would be ~*ed* —*Current Biog.*⟩ **2 :** to give up **:** ABANDON, RENOUNCE ⟨all past forgiveness it ~*ed* —William Wordsworth⟩ **3 a** *obs* **:** to summon to return **:** recall from exile ⟨I here forget all former griefs, cancel all grudge, ~ thee home again —Shak.⟩ **b** *obs* **:** to bring back or attempt to bring back **:** restore or seek to restore ⟨she ~*s* him for her body's lust —Shak.⟩ **syn** see REVOKE

**²repeal** \"\ *n* -s [MF *rapel*, fr. OF, fr. *repeler, rapeler*, v.] **1** *obs* **:** RECALL; *esp* **:** a summoning back from exile ⟨rash in the ~ —Shak.⟩ **2 :** the act or an instance of repealing **:** ABROGATION, REVOCATION ⟨the ~ of a law⟩ ⟨the ~ of the 18th amendment to the U.S. Constitution⟩ ⟨the ~ of a too hasty resolution⟩

**re·peal·able** \-ēləbəl\ *adj* **:** capable of being repealed

**re·peal·er** \-ēlə(r)\ *n* -s **1 :** one that repeals; *specif* **:** a legislative act that abrogates an earlier act **2 a :** one who seeks a repeal **b** *usu cap* **:** a supporter of a political campaign initiated about 1830 to repeal the Articles of Union between Great Britain and Ireland

**re·peal·ist** \-ēləst\ *n* -s **:** one who advocates repeal (as of some specific legislative measure)

**¹re·peat** \rəˈpēt, rēˈp-, *usu* -ēd· +V\ *vb* -ED/-ING/-S [ME *repeten*, fr. MF *repeter*, fr. L *repetere* to repeat, go back to, fr. *re-* + *petere* to go to or toward — more at FEATHER] *vt* **1 a :** to say or state again **:** REITERATE ⟨~*ed* his command⟩ ⟨~*ed* his question⟩ **b :** to say over from memory **:** RECITE ⟨remember the rest of her lesson, and ~ correctly all those verses —Robert Browning⟩ **c :** to say after another ⟨~ the following words after me⟩ **d :** to make public **:** relate to others **:** DIVULGE ⟨I will not ~ your words . . . outside this cloister; because the consequences to you would certainly be fatal —Henry Adams⟩ ⟨the child ~*s* everything he hears⟩ **2 a :** to make, do, or perform again ⟨~*ed* his earlier protests⟩ ⟨was sent on a similar errand and ~*ed* the theft —Edward Clodd⟩ ⟨for several years this annual fete was ~*ed* —*Amer. Guide Series: Minn.*⟩ **b :** to make appear again **:** cause to recur **:** PRESENT, SHOW, REPRODUCE ⟨two end pavilions ~ the dominant motif of the central pavilion —*Amer. Guide Series: Minn.*⟩ ⟨a game that ~*ed* the pattern of many previous ones between the same teams⟩ ⟨a program ~*ed* on tape⟩ **c :** to go through or experience again ⟨expected to ~ the years of practical banishment endured by his father —W.C.Ford⟩; *specif* **:** to take (a grade or course in school or college) again esp. to make up a failure ⟨had to ~ the fourth grade⟩ ⟨~*ed* English composition⟩ **3 :** to express or present (oneself) again in the same words, terms, or form as before ⟨history sometimes seems to ~ itself⟩ ⟨a writer who ~*s* himself shamelessly⟩ ⟨wrote innumerable songs without ever ~*ing* himself⟩ **~** *vi* **1 :** to say, do, or accomplish something again ⟨there were, to ~ and to conclude, three saving accidents —R.P.Blackmur⟩ ⟨is favored to ~ as batting champion⟩: as **a :** to vote illegally more than once in a particular election ⟨registration of voters is designed to eliminate ~*ing*⟩ **b** *of a timepiece* **:** to strike again the last hour and sometimes the last half hour, quarter hour, or minute if so adjusted **2** *of food* **:** to seem to rise in the gullet **:** give one its taste again ⟨boiled onions always ~ on me⟩

**syn** ITERATE, REITERATE, INGEMINATE: REPEAT is a general term centering attention on the fact of uttering, saying, or presenting again one or a number of times. ITERATE and REITERATE may stress the fact of frequent repetitive utterance ⟨the bird in the dusk *iterating* . . . his one phrase —C.P.Aiken⟩ ⟨*reiterated* the words until her voice died away in a mumble —Gertrude Atherton⟩ INGEMINATE may indicate a single repetition, a saying twice ⟨comes . . . with his olive branch *ingeminating* peace —*Pall Mall Gazette*⟩ **syn** see in addition QUOTE

**²re·peat** \", ˈrē,p-\ *n* -s *often attrib* **1 :** the act of repeating ⟨bloom usu. from the latter part of June to the end of July, with an occasional ~ late in August —*New Yorker*⟩ **2 :** something that is repeated **:** REPETITION: as **a** (1) **:** a musical passage to be repeated in performance (2) **:** a sign consisting typically of a vertical series of two or four dots that are placed before and after or often only at the end of a passage to be repeated **b :** a repeated pattern in a textile design **c :** a reorder of merchandise **d :** a repeated telegraph message **e :** a rebroadcast of a radio or television program **3 :** the number of threads necessary to make the basic unit of a weave

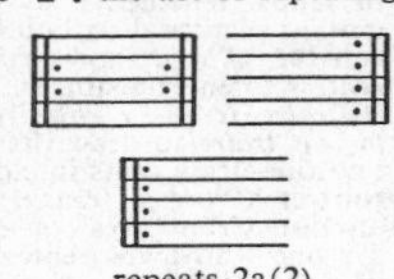

repeats 2a(2)

**re·peat·abil·i·ty** \rəˌpēd·əˈbilədē, rē,p-, -pētə-, -lətē, -i\ *n* **:** the quality or state of being repeatable

**re·peat·able** \≈'≈≈bəl\ *adj* **:** capable of being repeated or fit to be repeated

**repeated** *adj* **1 :** renewed or recurring again and again **:** CONSTANT, FREQUENT ⟨~ absences⟩ ⟨~ mistakes⟩ ⟨~ changes of plan⟩ **2 :** said, done, or presented again ⟨an often ~ excuse⟩ ⟨an eloquently ~ speech⟩ ⟨an easily ~ pattern⟩ — **re·peat·ed·ly** *adv*

**repeated twinning** *n* **:** twinning in which more than two simple crystals are involved

**re·peat·er** \rəˈpēd·ə(r), rēˈp-, -pētə-\ *n* -s **:** one that repeats: as **a :** one who relates or recites ⟨a ~ of old stories and ballads⟩ **b :** a watch or clock with a striking mechanism that upon pressure of a spring will indicate the time in hours and quarters or sometimes minutes **c :** a rifle or shotgun having a magazine that holds a number of cartridges that are loaded shot by shot into the firing chamber by the operation of the action of the piece **d** (1) **:** an arrangement for receiving signals from one telegraph line and retransmitting corresponding signals into another line (2) **:** a vacuum-tube or electronic amplifier inserted at proper intervals in long-distance telephone or television transmission lines and capable of delivering to the line an amplified copy of the received message **e :** RECIDIVIST **f :** one who votes again in an election **:** FLOATER 3a **g :** a pennant used to repeat a flag above it in signal hoist so that no two flags in one hoist are the same **h :** a gyrocompass device having a compass card and lubber's line and receiving electrically the indications from the master compass — called also *gyro repeater* **i :** a performer (as an animal or athlete) who duplicates or repeats a feat **j :** a member of a theatrical audience who has attended a previous performance of the same production **k :** a student enrolled in a grade, class, or course for the second or a subsequent time **l :** a trough-shaped semicircular horizontal guide in a rolling mill to deflect the rod from one pass into the next

**repeating** *pres part of* REPEAT

**repeating back** *n* **:** an arrangement of parts for a camera permitting the exposure through suitable color filters of three-color separation negatives in rapid succession

**repeating coil** *n* **:** a transformer used in a telephone system to associate two circuits

**repeating decimal** *n* **:** a decimal in which after a certain point a particular digit or sequence of digits repeats itself indefinitely

**repeating firearm** *n* **:** a firearm having a magazine or a revolving cylinder holding several rounds and an action that makes possible rapid firing of successive shots

**repeating watch** *n* **:** REPEATER b

**repeat key** *n* **1 :** a key on a business machine that when depressed allows a calculating operation set up on the machine to be repeated indefinitely **2 :** a key on an electric typewriter that continues to operate as long as the key is depressed

**repeat order** *n* **:** REORDER

**repeats** *pres 3d sing of* REPEAT, *pl of* REPEAT

**re·pe·chage** \rəpəˈshäzh\ *n* -s [F *repêchage* second chance, supplementary examination for a candidate that has previously failed, fr. *repêcher* to rescue, fish out (fr. *re-* + *pêcher* to fish, fr. L *piscari*, fr. *piscis* fish) + *-age* — more at FISH] **:** a second-chance trial heat (as in olympic rowing) in which losers in the first round of competition are given another chance to qualify for the semifinals

**re·pel** \rəˈpel, rēˈp-\ *vb* **repelled; repelled; repelling; repels** [ME *repellen*, fr. L *repellere*, fr. *re-* + *pellere* to drive — more at FELT] *vt* **1 a :** to drive back **:** beat off **:** REPULSE ⟨~ the enemy⟩ ⟨execute the laws of the Union, suppress insurrections, and ~ invasions —*U.S.Constitution*⟩ ⟨~ onslaughts by starveling barbarians —V.G.Childe⟩ **b :** to fight against **:** RESIST ⟨cannot claim the assistance of the law in *repelling* the trade competition of rivals —C.A.Cooke⟩ **c :** to keep in check **:** REPRESS ⟨~ the temptation to take the easy way out⟩ **d :** to reverse the advance or movement of ⟨the rocks ~ the waves⟩ **2 :** to turn away **:** refuse to receive or credit **:** REJECT ⟨*repelled* the suggestion when it was made to him and opposed it wherever he decently could —J.C.Fitzpatrick⟩ ⟨*repelled* the insinuation⟩ **3 a :** to drive away **:** DISCOURAGE ⟨foul words and frowns must not ~ a lover —Shak.⟩ ⟨concerned about the effect his actions will have in attracting or *repelling* votes —E. N.Griswold⟩ **b :** to be incapable of adhering to, mixing with, taking up, or holding ⟨a fabric that ~*s* moisture⟩ ⟨oil ~*s* water⟩ **c :** to force away or apart or tend to do so by mutual action at a distance ⟨two like electric charges ~ one another⟩ **4 :** to cause aversion in **:** DISGUST ⟨a tendency toward suspicion and sarcasm that *repelled* people —W.A.Swanberg⟩ ⟨their cold intelligence, their stereotyped, unremitting industry ~ me —L.P.Smith⟩ **~** *vi* **:** to cause aversion **:** exercise repulsion ⟨so malodorous as to be more calculated to ~ than to invite —*Irish Digest*⟩ ⟨when a picture of little merit attracts or a recognized masterpiece ~*s* —C.W.H.Johnson⟩

**re·pel·lence** *also* **re·pel·lance** \-lən(t)s\ *n* -s [fr. ¹*repellent, repellant*, after such pairs as E *evident: evidence* and such pairs as E *abundant: abundance*] **:** REPELLENCY

**re·pel·len·cy** *also* **re·pel·lan·cy** \-nsē,-nsi\ *n* -ES [¹*repellent, repellant* + *-cy*] **:** the quality or capacity of repelling **:** REPULSION ⟨has none of the ~ of textbooks —*New Yorker*⟩ ⟨the attraction or ~ of the odor —*Jour. of Economic Entomology*⟩

**¹re·pel·lent** *also* **re·pel·lant** \-nt\ *adj* [*repellent* fr. L *repellent-, repellens*, pres. part. of *repellere* to repel; *repellant* alter. (influenced by *-ant*, adj. suffix) of *repellent*] **1 :** serving or tending to drive away or ward off ⟨put forth her hands with an involuntary ~ gesture —Nathaniel Hawthorne⟩ — often used in combination ⟨a mosquito-*repellent* spray⟩ ⟨a water-*repellent* coat⟩ **2 :** arousing aversion or disgust **:** REPUGNANT ⟨his peculiar and ~ characteristic was the fantastic manner in which he was deformed —P.I.Wellman⟩ ⟨finds the paintings mostly meaningless and ~ —Havelock Ellis⟩ **syn** see HATEFUL

**²repellent** *also* **repellant** \"\ *n* -s [*repellent* fr. ¹*repellent; repellant* alter. (influenced by *-ant*, n. suffix) of *repellent*] **:** something that repels: as **a :** a substance obnoxious to insects and employed to prevent their attacks **:** INSECTIFUGE **b :** a solution used (as on fabrics) to resist absorption of a liquid (as water or ink)

**re·pel·lent·ly** *adv* **:** in a repellent manner

**re·pel·ler** \-lə(r)\ *n* -s **:** one that repels

**re·pel·ling·ly** *adv* **:** in a repelling manner ⟨made no sign of greeting but looked at him ~⟩

**¹re·pent** \rəˈpent, rēˈp-\ *vb* -ED/-ING/-S [ME *repenten*, fr. OF *repentir*, fr. *re-* + *pentir* to be sorry, fr. L *paenitēre* to be sorry, cause to be sorry — more at PENITENT] *vi* **1 :** to turn from sin out of penitence for past wrongdoings, abandon sinful or unworthy purposes and values, and dedicate oneself to the amendment of one's life ⟨unless you ~ you will all likewise perish —Lk 13:3 (RSV)⟩ **2 a :** to feel regret or contrition for what one has done or omitted to do ⟨marry in haste and ~ at leisure⟩ — often used with *of* ⟨~*ed* of his decision to give up the study of medicine⟩ **b :** to change one's mind about something one has done or said ⟨begins with a sweeping condemnation of his opponent's views, but later ~*s* somewhat and finds some good in them⟩ ⟨take him up on his promise before he ~*s*⟩ **~** *vt* **1 :** to cause (one or oneself) to feel regret or contrition for a past action, course of conduct, or decision ⟨it ~*ed* the Lord that he had made man on the earth —Gen 6:6 (AV)⟩ ⟨it ~*ed* me of my boldness —Grant Allen⟩ **2 a :** to feel sorrow or regret for **:** be dissatisfied or regretful about ⟨he ~*ed* his marriage and suffered from it —George Eliot⟩ ⟨~*ed* her rashness⟩ ⟨~*ed* his bargain⟩ **b :** to feel repentance for **:** do penance for ⟨~ his sins⟩ ⟨~ the evil of his ways⟩

**²re·pent** \ˈrēpənt\ *adj* [L *repent-, repens*, pres. part. of *repere* to creep — more at REPTILE] **:** CREEPING, PROSTRATE

**re·pent·ance** \rəˈpentᵊn(t)s, rēˈp-, -entən-\ *n* -s [ME *repentaunce*, fr. MF *repentance*, fr. OF, fr. *repentant*, after such pairs as OF *abundant: abundance*] **:** the act or process of repenting; *specif* **:** contrition for one's sins together with the dedication of oneself to the abandonment of unworthy purposes and values and to the amendment of one's life ⟨there's no ~ in the grave —Isaac Watts⟩ **syn** see PENITENCE

**¹re·pent·ant** \-ᵊnt,-ənt\ *adj* [ME *repentaunt*, fr. OF *repentant*, pres. part. of *repentir* to repent] **1 :** experiencing repentance **:** PENITENT ⟨the ~ little prodigal —W.M.Thackeray⟩ **2 :** expressing or showing repentance ⟨~ tears⟩ — **re·pent·ant·ly** *adv*

**²repentant** \"\ *n* -s *archaic* **:** PENITENT

**re·pent·er** \-entə(r)\ *n* -s **:** one that repents

**re·pent·ing·ly** *adv* **:** in a repenting manner **:** REPENTANTLY

**re·people** \(ˈ)rē+\ *vt* [MF *repeupler*, fr. OF *repuepler*, fr. *re-* + *puepler* to people] **1 :** to people anew **2 :** RESTOCK

**re·percolation** \(ˌ)rē+\ *n* [*re-* + *percolation*] **:** percolation again or anew; *specif* **:** the process of repeatedly percolating the same menstruum through fresh material

**reper·cuss** \ˌrēpə(r)¦kəs *also* ˌrep-\ *vt* -ED/-ING/-ES [L *repercussus*, past part. of *repercutere*, fr. *re-* + *percutere* to beat, strike — more at PERCUSSION] **:** to drive or reflect back **syn** see REBOUND

**reper·cus·sion** \ˌ≈≈'kəshən\ *n* [L *repercussion-, repercussio*, fr. *repercussus* (past part. of *repercutere*) + *-ion-, -io* -ion] **1 a** *archaic* **:** a driving or forcing back of one thing by another or the state of being driven back **:** RECOIL, REPULSE **b :** REFLECTION, REVERBERATION ⟨if the sun's glory were not endlessly caught, splintered and thrown back by atmospheric ~*s* —Thomas De Quincey⟩ **2 a :** an impact, action, or effect given or exerted in return **:** a reciprocal action or effect ⟨caught up in the ~*s* of the movement —Stuart Cloete⟩ **b :** a widespread, indirect, or unforeseen effect of an act, action, or event ⟨this drastic depletion must have ~*s* elsewhere and play a part in lowering the country's water table —*Farmer's Weekly (So. Africa)*⟩ ⟨the accelerated rate of mobility produced complex social ~*s* —Oscar Handlin⟩ **3 a :** the dominant in a Gregorian chant **b :** the reentrance of a fugue subject and answer after the development or after an episode **4 :** BALLOTTEMENT

**reper·cus·sive** \¦≈≈'kəsiv\ *adj* [ME *repercussif* serving to drive away, prob. fr. (assumed) ML *repercussivus*, fr. L *repercussus* (past part. of *repercutere*) + *-ivus* -ive] **1 a :** REVERBERATING ⟨the ~ banjoes and sobbing saxophones —Carl Sandburg⟩ **b :** thrown back **:** REFLECTED, REVERBERATED ⟨rages loud the ~ roar —James Thomson †1748⟩ **2 :** serving to throw back a sound ⟨a ~ cave⟩

**re·perforator** \ˌrē+\ *n* [*re-* + *perforator*] **:** a device that receives a message and perforates a tape that can then be used to retransmit the message

**rep·er·toire** *R* ˈrepə(r)·ˌtwär *sometimes* -wȯ(ə)r; *-R* -pə-ˌtwȧ(r *sometimes* -wȯə(r *or* -wȯ(r\ *n* -s [F *répertoire* repertory, repertoire, fr. LL *repertorium* repertory] **1 a :** a list or supply of dramas, operas, pieces, or parts that a company or a person has thoroughly rehearsed and is prepared to perform ⟨a fine pianist but with a very limited ~⟩ **b :** a supply of skills, devices, or expedients possessed by a person or necessary to him in his occupation **:** BAG OF TRICKS, STOCK-IN-TRADE ⟨essential to the ~ of the right halfback —Josephine Lees⟩ ⟨had a small but dependable ~ of jokes designed to amuse the young —Frank Sullivan⟩ ⟨blackmail, seduction and plain old-fashioned lying . . . are all part of her ~ —*Theatre Arts*⟩ **c :** the dishes available at a particular restaurant or in a particular place ⟨both serve good inexpensive food, though their ~ is small —Frederic Morton⟩ **2 a :** the complete list or supply of dramas, operas, or musical works available for performance ⟨our modern orchestral ~⟩ **b :** the complete list or supply of skills, devices, methods, or ingredients used in a particular field, occupation, or practice ⟨has done almost everything in the ~ of modern criticism —S.E.Hyman⟩ ⟨tracer methodology already is well established in the biochemical ~ —M.D. Kamen⟩

**rep·er·to·ri·al** \¦repə(r)¦tōrēəl, -tȯr-\ *adj* **:** of or relating to a repertory

**rep·er·to·ri·um** \ˌ≈≈'≈≈əm\ *n, pl* **reperto·ria** \-ēə\ [LL, repertory] **:** REPOSITORY ⟨constitute *repertoria* of source material —Joshua Whatmough⟩

**rep·er·to·ry** *R* ˈrepə(r),tōrē, -tȯr-, -ri, *-R* -pə,t-\ *n* -ES [LL *repertorium*, fr. L *repertus* (past part. of *reperire* to find, find out, acquire, fr. *re-* + *parere, parire* to bring forth, produce) + *-orium* -ory — more at PARE] **1 :** an ordered list, index, or catalog **2 :** a place where something may be found **:** REPOSITORY ⟨suggests the shop of a country job printer — until a closer look takes in the type ~ —*Printing & Graphic Arts*⟩ **3 :** REPERTOIRE ⟨whose ~ of dialects and characters is large —*Current Biog.*⟩ ⟨the violin ~⟩ ⟨has introduced the whole ~ of the supposed feats of mesmerism —Edmund Wilson⟩

**repertory theater** *also* **repertory** *n* **:** a theater housing a company that presents year after year a number of different productions during a season either successively or alternately

**repet** *abbr* [L *repetatur*] let it be repeated — used as a direction in medical prescriptions

**rep·e·tend** \ˈrepə,tend, ˌ≈≈'≈\ *n* -s [L *repetendum* something to be repeated, neut. of *repetendus*, gerundive of *repetere* to repeat] **:** a repeated or recurrent sound, cadence, word, or phrase or one that is to be repeated for conformity to a pattern; *specif* **:** REFRAIN ⟨in the deepening music of the vowels, in subtle and haunting ~*s* —*Atlantic*⟩

**re·pe·ti·teur** \ˌrā,pād·əˈtər(·), -ped-·-\ *n* -s [F *répétiteur* singing coach, tutor, fr. L *repetitus* (past part. of *repetere* to repeat) + F *-eur* -or] **:** a singing coach; *esp* **:** one who coaches singers in operatic roles

**rep·e·ti·tion** \ˌrepəˈtishən\ *n* -s [L *repetition-, repetitio*, fr. *repetitus* (past part. of *repetere* to repeat) + *-ion-, -io* -ion — more at REPEAT] **1 a :** the act or an instance of repeating something that one has already said or done ⟨she heard again that he was a widower and a grandfather but there seemed to be design in his ~ —Lenard Kaufman⟩ ⟨no more than two ~*s* of the same course will be allowed to any student —*Loyola Univ. Bull.*⟩ **b :** the act of repeating or saying something over in order to learn it **:** REHEARSAL **c :** the act of reciting something learned ⟨listened with delight to her ~*s* of her favorite passages —T.L.Peacock⟩ **d :** MENTION, RECITAL ⟨yawning at the ~ of delights which she saw no likelihood of sharing —Jane Austen⟩ **2** *Scots law* **:** a demand for restitution or repayment; *broadly* **:** RESTITUTION, RECOVERY, RESTORATION **3 a :** the fact of occurring, appearing, or being repeated again ⟨wait a long time for a ~ of this feat⟩ ⟨the design consists of a ~ of the same geometrical figure⟩ **b :** COPY, REPRODUCTION ⟨when Greek art, even in Roman copies, was the only indisputable art, except for some Renaissance ~*s* —Roger Fry⟩ **c :** spore germination in various fungi in which a spore is produced at the end of a stalk arising from another spore and in turn often germinates in the same way **4 :** the ability of a musical instrument to respond to the repeated striking of the same key in rapid succession ⟨an organ defective in ~⟩ ⟨a piano with excellent ~⟩

**rep·e·ti·tion·al** \¦≈≈'tishənᵊl, -shnəl\ *adj* **:** REPETITIOUS ⟨something deadening and ~ has been happening to even the best modernist art —Janet Flanner⟩

**repetition compulsion** *n* **:** an irresistible tendency to repeat an emotional experience or to return to a previous psychological state

**rep·e·ti·tious** \¦repə¦tishəs\ *adj* [fr. *repetition*, after such pairs as E *ambition: ambitious*] **1 :** marked by repetition **:** containing frequent repetitions **:** tediously repeating ⟨the tiresome ~ analyses . . . which sometimes make him so exasperating to read —Edmund Wilson⟩ **2 :** repeating the same process or action again and again ⟨the industrial revolution has freed man's hands from much dull and ~ work —Bryan Morgan⟩ — **repetitiously** *adv* — **repetitiousness** *n* -ES

**re·pet·i·tive** \rəˈped·əd·iv, rēˈp-, -etətiv\ *adj* [fr. *repetition*, after such pairs as E *action: active*] **1 :** containing repetition

: REPEATING ⟨~ combinations of the symbols for one and ten —Lancelot Hogben⟩ **2 :** REPETITIOUS ⟨the vast deluge of ~ verbiage found in legal documents —W.H.Wright⟩ ⟨a ~ job that might drive you or me crazy —Stuart Chase⟩ — **re·pet·i·tive·ly** \-ə̇vlē, -li\ *adv* — **re·pet·i·tive·ness** \-ivnə̇s\ *n* -ES

**re·pha·im** \ˈrefēə̇m, rə̇ˈfāə̇m\ *n pl, usu cap* [Heb *rěphāʾīm*] **:** ancient giants reported in the Old Testament to have flourished in Canaan and its vicinity prior to the Hebrews

**re·phonemicize** \ˌrē+\ *vt* [*re-* + *phonemicize*] **:** to transcribe (a phoneme) or all amenable phonemes of (a language) with multiple symbols that are more accurately descriptive than single symbols of the phonetic makeup involved — **re·phonemicization** \"+\ *n*

**1re·photograph** \(ˈ)rē+\ *vt* [*re-* + *photograph*] **:** to photograph (a scene or object) again **:** RETAKE ⟨no unusual experience to find myself ~*ing* a group of trees⟩

**2rephotograph** \"\ *n* **1 :** a photographing again of a scene or object **:** RETAKE **2 :** a picture resulting from rephotographing

**re·phrase** \(ˈ)rē+\ *vt* [*re-* + *phrase*] **:** to phrase anew or in a new form

**1re·pine** \rə̇ˈpīn, rēˈp-\ *vb* -ED/-ING/-S [*re-* + *pine* (to languish)] *vi* **1 :** to feel or express dejection or discontent **:** COMPLAIN, FRET ⟨we may regret but not ~ at the disappearance of much of interest and value as the result of progress —Edwin Benson⟩ ⟨courage, when misfortune comes, to bear without *repining* the ruin of our hopes —Bertrand Russell⟩ **2 :** to wish discontentedly ⟨~ for an unwritten masterpiece —T.S.Eliot⟩ ~ *vt, archaic* **:** to complain or fret about **syn** see COMPLAIN

**2repine** \"\ *n* -S **:** DISCONTENT

**re·pin·er** \-nə(r)\ *n* -S **:** one that repines

**re·pin·ing·ly** *adv* **:** COMPLAININGLY

**re·pique** *or* **re·pic** \rə̇ˈpēk\ *n* -S [F *repic*, fr. *repiquer* to prick again, fr. MF, fr. *re-* + *piquer* to prick — more at PIKE] **:** the making of 30 or more points in combinations alone before an opponent in the game of piquet scores; *also* **:** a bonus of 60 points given for this

**repl** *abbr* replace; replacement

**repla** *pl of* REPLUM

**re·place** \rə̇ˈplās, rēˈp-\ *vt* [*re-* + *place*] **1 :** to place again **:** restore to a former place, position, or condition ⟨*replaced* the card in the file⟩ ⟨*replaced* the king on the throne⟩ **2 :** to take the place of **:** serve as a substitute for or successor of **:** SUCCEED, SUPPLANT ⟨the saw and sawmill rapidly *replaced* the ax —*Amer. Guide Series: Mich.*⟩ ⟨the dried wood . . . has long been *replaced* by steel and concrete —T.H.Matthews⟩ **3 :** to put in place of **:** provide a substitute or successor for ⟨necessary to ~ all the machinery in the plant⟩ **4 :** to fill the place of **:** supply an equivalent for ⟨a broken toy should not be immediately *replaced* —Bertrand Russell⟩ ⟨promised to ~ the money he had stolen⟩

**syn** DISPLACE, SUPPLANT, SUPERSEDE: REPLACE implies supplying a substitute or equivalent for someone or something, often something lost, worn out, broken, dismissed, destroyed, or otherwise no longer usable ⟨Doe *replacing* Roe in the line-up⟩ ⟨nor would I admit that the human actor can be *replaced* by a marionette —T.S.Eliot⟩ ⟨an old bridge *replaced* by a new one⟩ DISPLACE implies an ousting, dislodging, putting out, discharging, or crowding out, preceding a replacing ⟨prehistoric Siouan tribes have been *displaced* almost entirely by Indians of Algonquian stock —*Amer. Guide Series: Minn.*⟩ ⟨when large-scale commercial farms *displaced* the old peasant holdings —Oscar Handlin⟩ ⟨since machinery has *displaced* manual labor —Karl Meyer⟩ ⟨in this realm of science symbols first *displace* words —T.H.Savory⟩ SUPPLANT is now likely to indicate an uprooting and eradication followed by a replacing or displacing by something newer, better, more modern or effective ⟨horse cars *supplanted* by trolleys⟩ ⟨rock fireplaces *supplanted* those of sapling and mud construction —*Amer. Guide Series: Tenn.*⟩ ⟨a valuable means of *supplanting* editorial guesswork with facts —F.L.Mott⟩ ⟨a secure national government *supplanting* the provisional one⟩ SUPERSEDE is rarely without suggestions of replacement by something better or newer ⟨the old-fashioned fishing luggers with their varicolored sails have been *superseded* by motorboats —*Amer. Guide Series: La.*⟩ ⟨frame houses soon *superseded* the original log ones —*Amer. Guide Series: N.C.*⟩ ⟨that is the worst of erudition — that the next scholar sucks the few drops of honey that you have accumulated, sets right your blunders, and you are *superseded* —A.C.Benson⟩

**re·place·abil·i·ty** \=,=əˈbiləd·ē\ *n* **:** the quality or state of being replaceable

**re·place·able** \=ˈ=əbəl\ *adj* **:** capable of being replaced ⟨a cheap, standardized, and ~ product —Lewis Mumford⟩

**replaced crystal** *n* **:** PSEUDOMORPH

**re·place·ment** \=ˈ=mənt\ *n* -S **1 :** the act of replacing or the state of being replaced **:** SUBSTITUTION ⟨the problem of blood loss and its ~ is ever present in this type of surgery —*Jour. Amer. Med. Assoc.*⟩: as **a :** the removal of an edge or an angle of a crystal by one or more faces **b :** substitution of one substance in a rock fabric for another by solution and redeposition **2 :** something that replaces **:** SUBSTITUTE: as **a :** an individual available for assignment to a military unit to replace a loss or complete a quota **b :** a new fixed asset or portion of an asset that takes the place of a discarded one **c :** an artificial substitute for a lost or amputated body part **:** PROSTHESIS

**replacement cost** *n* **:** the current cost of replacing a fixed asset with a new one of equal effectiveness

**replacement depot** *n* **:** a military installation usu. in a theater of operations where replacements are assembled and then assigned to fill vacancies in military units

**replacement set** *n* **:** a set of elements any one of which may be used to replace a given variable or placeholder in a mathematical phrase or sentence — compare DOMAIN

**replacement therapy** *n* **:** therapy involving the supplying of something (as nutrients or blood) lacking from or lost to the system

**replacement vein** *also* **replacement deposit** *n* **:** SUBSTITUTION VEIN

**re·plac·er** \-sə(r)\ *n* **:** one that replaces; *specif* **:** RERAILER

**replaces** *pres 3d sing of* REPLACE

**replacing** *pres part of* REPLACE

**re·pla·cive** \-siv\ *n* -S [*replace* + *-ive*] **:** a difference of phonemes in the word stem of two or more grammatically distinct forms ⟨the vowel of *feet* as compared with that of *foot* displays a ~ plural form instead of the usual suffix *-s*⟩

**1re·plant** \(ˈ)rē+\ *vt* [*re-* + *plant*] **1 a :** to plant again or anew ⟨~ a tree⟩ ⟨~ a bulb⟩ **b :** RESETTLE ⟨move people out of submarginal and blighted areas and ~ them in communities which have a resource base —Stuart Chase⟩ **2 :** to provide with new plants ⟨~ the flower bed⟩

**2re·plant** \ˈrē+,-, =ˈ=\ *n* **:** something planted again or anew; *specif* **:** a plant used to fill a vacancy in a row or planting esp. after a first or initial planting

**re·plantation** \ˌrē+\ *n* **1 :** a new or second planting **2 :** the implantation of a drawn tooth in its socket

**re·plate** \ˈrē+,-\ *n* [*re-* + *plate*, v.] **:** a printing of an edition of a newspaper or periodical in which new material is inserted by an alteration or resetting of a plate

**1re·play** \(ˈ)rē+\ *vt* [*re-* + *play*] **:** to play again or over ⟨acted the part more effectively each time he ~*ed* it⟩ ⟨ruled that the entire game would have to be ~*ed*⟩

**2re·play** \ˈrē+,-, =ˈ=\ *n* **:** something that is replayed

**replay duplicate** *n* **:** a game of duplicate whist or bridge in which two pairs compete and in which the boards are played twice with each pair holding the same hands on the second play that its opponents held before

**re·plead** \(ˈ)rē+\ *vt* [*re-* + *plead*] **:** to plead again; *specif* **:** to file a new legal pleading appropriate under the circumstances (as after a demurrer has been overruled)

**re·plead·er** \"ə(r)\ *n* [*replead* + *-er* (as in *cesser*)] **1 :** a second legal pleading or course of pleadings **2 :** the right of pleading again even after trial or verdict

**re·pledge** \(ˈ)rē+\ *vt* [MF *replegier* to become surety for, fr. OF, fr. *re-* + *plegier* to guarantee, become surety for — more at PLEDGE] *Scots law* **:** to remove from the jurisdiction of another court to one's own

**re·ple·gi·ate** \rə̇ˈplējē,āt\ *vt* [ML *replegiatus*, past part. of *replegiare*. fr. OF *replegier*] **:** REPLEDGE

**re·plen·ish** \rə̇ˈplenish, rēˈp-, *esp in pres part* -nəsh\ *vb* [ME *replenisshen*, *replenissen*, fr. MF *repleniss-*, stem of *replenir* to fill, supply abundantly, fr. OF, fr. *re-* + *-plenir* (fr. *plein* full, fr. L *plenus*) — more at FULL] *vt* **1 a :** to fill with persons or animals **:** people or stock ⟨be fruitful and multiply and ~ the earth —Gen 1:28 (AV)⟩ **b** *archaic* **:** to supply fully **:** equip completely **:** PERFECT ⟨his hive had so long been ~*ed* with honey —William Wordsworth⟩ ⟨the most ~*ed* villain in the world —Shak.⟩ **c :** to fill with some quality or source of inspiration or power **:** provide with intellectual or spiritual sustenance **:** NOURISH ⟨the American mind should cease to ~ itself with the mighty wonders of Europe —Van Wyck Brooks⟩ **d :** to fill completely **:** occupy or pervade all parts of ⟨their vacant heart ~*ed* with a child —Robert Browning⟩ ⟨she saw the blood his cheeks ~ —Shak.⟩ **2 a :** to fill up again ⟨she kept his glass ~*ed* —Charles Dickens⟩ ⟨the heavy demands for his legal services that promised to ~ his exchequer —A.C. Cole⟩ ⟨remains below the surface until he needs to ~ his lungs with another gulp —John Tassos⟩ **b :** to build up again **:** RENEW, RESTORE ⟨he ~*ed* the fire and drew up close to it —T.B. Costain⟩ ⟨the plants are still growing, and ~*ing* their food reserves —*Farm Jour.*⟩ ⟨the supply of oil will have ~*ed* itself —*Amer. Guide Series: Pa.*⟩ **c :** to supply again **:** REFIT ⟨finds it cheaper and faster to ~ its ships while under way —George Weller⟩ **d :** to make good **:** REPLACE ⟨how fast have the shipyards . . . been able to ~ these losses —*Fortune*⟩ **3 :** to add replenisher to (as a photographic developer or fixing bath) ~ *vi* **:** to become full **:** fill up again

**re·plen·ish·er** \-shə(r)\ *n* -S **:** one that replenishes ⟨enormous deposits of marl or bog lime, a valuable soil ~ —*Amer. Guide Series: Minn.*⟩; *specif* **:** a chemical solution added to a photographic working solution (as a developer or fixing bath) for restoring or maintaining chemical activity

**re·plen·ish·ment** \-shmənt\ *n* -S **1 :** something that replenishes **:** a new supply ⟨organizations accustomed to recruit new members from among the new immigrants were now cut off from ~*s* —Oscar Handlin⟩ **2 :** the act or process of replenishing or the state of being replenished ⟨propagates cutthroat trout, chiefly for the ~ of mountain streams —*Amer. Guide Series: Oregon*⟩ ⟨promised him rest and ~ —Winifred Bambrick⟩

**1re·plete** \rə̇ˈplēt, rēˈp-, *usu* -lēd·+V\ *adj* [ME *repleet*, fr. MF & L; MF *replet*, fr. L *repletus*, past part. of *replēre* to fill up, fr. *re-* + *plēre* to fill — more at FULL] **1 a :** fully or abundantly provided **:** well supplied ⟨the race itself is ~ with thrills, sometimes with spills —*Amer. Guide Series: Ind.*⟩ ⟨~ with hard and book-learned words, impressively sonorous —R.W.Southern⟩ **b :** fully or richly charged, imbued, or impregnated ⟨a warmly affectionate book, ~ with both human and religious value —Frances Witherspoon⟩ ⟨a life ~ with charm —P.E.More⟩ **2 a :** FILLED ⟨a thin limestone bed ~ with characteristic echinoids —*Science*⟩ **b :** abundantly fed **:** GORGED, SURFEITED ⟨could not face the thought of being ~ in a starving world —A.L.Guérard⟩ **c :** filled out **:** FAT, STOUT ⟨richly and healthily ~, though with less of his substance in stature; a frankly fat gentleman —Henry James †1916⟩ **3 :** COMPLETE, FULL ⟨the text is too ~ to be used in abbreviated survey or cultural courses —*Rev. of Scientific Instruments*⟩

**2replete** \"\ *vt* -ED/-ING/-S [ME *repleten*, fr. L *repletus*, past part. of *replēre* to fill up] **1 :** to fill to satiety **:** STUFF ⟨fat with *repleted* appetite —Charles Dickens⟩ **2 :** REPLENISH ⟨mostly stolen . . . later *repleted* —Eleanor Clark⟩

**3replete** \"\ *n* -S [1*replete*] **:** a worker ant capable of greatly distending its abdomen and serving as a reservoir of liquid food for the rest of the colony — called also *plerergate;* compare HONEY ANT

**re·plete·ness** *n* -ES **:** the quality or state of being replete

**re·ple·tion** \-ēshən\ *n* -S [ME *replecioun* surfeit, condition of being filled up, fr. MF & LL; MF *repletion* surfeit, fr. LL *repletion-*, *repletio* completion, fr. L *repletus* (past part. of *replēre* to fill up) + *-ion-*, *-io* -ion] **1 a :** the act of overeating or the state of being overfed **:** SURFEIT ⟨made sick by ~⟩ ⟨eat to ~⟩ **b :** fullness of blood **:** PLETHORA **2 :** the condition of being filled up or overcrowded ⟨a hall filled to ~⟩ **3 :** fulfillment of a need or desire **:** SATISFACTION ⟨the peace and spiritual ~ of the evening's rest —R.L.Stevenson⟩

**re·ple·tive** \-ēd·iv\ *adj* [LL *repletivus* complementary, fr. L *repletus* (past part. of *replēre*) + *-ivus* -ive] **:** serving or tending to make replete **:** FILLING

**re·plevi·able** \rə̇ˈplevēəbəl, rēˈp-\ *adj* **:** capable of being replevied

**1re·plev·in** \-və̇n\ *n* -S [ME, fr. AF *replevine*, fr. *replevir* to give security, fr. OF, to give security for, fr. *re-* + *plevir* to pledge, fr. (assumed) LL *plebere* — more at PLEDGE] **1 a :** the return to or recovery by a person of goods or chattels claimed to be wrongfully taken or detained upon the person's giving security to try the matter in court and return the goods if defeated in the action **b :** the writ by or the common-law action in which goods and chattels are replevied **2 :** the act of bailing a person or the bail given

**2replevin** \"\ *vt* -ED/-ING/-S **:** REPLEVY

**replevin bond** *n* **:** a bond required of a plaintiff in a replevin action to indemnify the defendant or the court officer seizing the property in the defendant's possession and transferring it to the plaintiff in the event the plaintiff loses his case

**re·plev·i·sa·ble** \-vəsəbəl\ *adj* [AF *replevisable*, *replevissable*, fr. OF *repleviss-* (stem of *replevir*) + *-able*] **:** REPLEVIABLE

**re·plev·i·sor** \-sər, -ˌsȯ(ə)r\ *n* -S [*replevis-* (as in *replevisable*) + *-or*] **:** the plaintiff in a replevin action

**1re·plevy** \-vē\ *n* -ES [ME, fr. AF *replevir*, v.] **:** REPLEVIN

**2replevy** \"\ *vb* -ED/-ING/-ES [AF *replevir*] *vt* **1** *archaic* **:** to bail or admit to bail **2 :** to take or get back by a writ for replevin ~ *vi* **:** to recover goods by replevin

**re·pli·ant** \rə̇ˈplīənt, rēˈp-\ *n* -S [1*reply* + *-ant*] **:** one who makes replication

**rep·li·ca** \ˈreplə̇kə, -lēkə\ *n* -S [It, repetition, fr. *replicare* to repeat, fr. LL, fr. L, to fold back — more at REPLY] **1 :** a reproduction, facsimile, or copy (as of a picture or statue) done by the maker of the original or under his direction **2 :** a facsimile of an original work of art **3 :** COPY, DUPLICATE ⟨a legislative body which would not be merely a ~ of the lower house —R.M.Dawson⟩ ⟨bored by their conversation, which was the ~ of a conversation he had heard a thousand times before —Victoria Sackville-West⟩

**replica grating** *n* **:** a diffraction grating formed by molding a film (as of collodion) on a ruled grating

**1rep·li·cate** \ˈreplə,kāt\ *vt* -ED/-ING/-S [LL *replicatus*, past part. of *replicare* to reply, repeat, fr. L, to fold back] **1 :** to give as an answer **:** REPLY **2 :** DUPLICATE, REPEAT ⟨the sequence of elementary responses necessary in the act of *replicating* the outline of the triangle —D.M.MacKay⟩ ⟨~ a statistical experiment⟩ ⟨*replicated* row plantings⟩ **3** [L *replicatus*, past part. of *replicare*] **:** to fold or bend back ⟨a *replicated* leaf⟩

**2rep·li·cate** \-lə̇kə̇t\ *n* -S [LL *replicatus*, past part. of *replicare* to repeat] **1 :** a repeated musical tone one or more octaves above or below a given tone **2 :** an experiment or procedure that repeats another done at the same time

**3replicate** \"\ *adj* [L *replicatus*, past part. of *replicare* to fold back] **1 :** folded over or backward **:** folded back upon itself **2** [LL *replicatus*, past part. of *replicare* to repeat, fr. L, to fold back] **:** MANIFOLD, REPEATED ⟨~ samples of 10 gm. were used for determining total nitrogen —*Jour. of Agric. Research*⟩

**re·plic·a·tile** \rə̇ˈplikə,tīl, rēˈp-, -kəd·ᵊl, -kə(,)til\ *adj* [1*replicate* + *-ile*] **:** capable of being folded back on itself ⟨~ wings of an insect⟩

**rep·li·ca·tion** \ˌrepləˈkāshən\ *n* -S [ME *replicacioun*, fr. MF *replication*, fr. LL *replication-*, *replicatio*, fr. L, action of folding back, fr. *replicatus* (past part. of *replicare* to fold back) + *-ion-*, *-io* -ion] **1 a :** ANSWER, REPLY ⟨what ~ should be made by the son of a king —Shak.⟩ **b** (1) **:** an answer to a reply **:** REJOINDER ⟨by way of ~ to your answer —O.W.Holmes †1935⟩ (2) **:** a plaintiff's or complainant's reply in matters of fact to a defendant's plea, answer, or counterclaim (3) *Roman law* **:** a plaintiff's reply to a defendant's exceptio **2 :** ECHO, REVERBERATION ⟨trembled underneath her banks to hear the ~ of your sounds made in her concave shores —Shak.⟩ **3 a :** COPY, REPRODUCTION ⟨a home conceived as a ~ of a medieval castle⟩ **b :** the act or action of reproducing ⟨half=plate and addressing machine methods of ~ —*Library Science Abstracts*⟩ **4 :** repetition of an experiment or procedure at the same time and place; *esp* **:** a systematic or random repetition of agricultural test rows or plats to reduce error (as due to variation in soil)

**re·pli·er** \rə̇ˈplī(ə)r, rēˈp-, -īə\ *n* -S **:** one that replies

**rep·lum** \ˈrepləm\ *n, pl* **rep·la** \-lə\ [L, part of a door (prob. bolt for covering the gap in a folding door), fr. *replēre* to fill up — more at REPLETE] **:** a thin false dissepiment separating the two valves of some fruits (as siliques and some legumes) from which the valves fall away at maturity

**re·plume** \(ˈ)rē+\ *vt* [*re-* + *plume*] **:** to plume anew **:** PREEN

**1re·ply** \rə̇ˈplī, rēˈp-\ *vb* -ED/-ING/-ES [ME *replien* (influenced in meaning by LL *replicare* to reply, fr. L, to fold back), fr. MF *replier* to fold again, fr. L *replicare* to fold back, fr. *re-* + *plicare* to fold — more at PLY] *vi* **1 a :** to respond in words or writing **:** ANSWER ⟨*replied* to the speech with a few words of thanks⟩ ⟨received your letter a week ago but have waited to ~⟩ **b :** ECHO, RESOUND **c :** to answer a defendant's original plea or response **2 :** to do something in response ⟨the ship *replied* to the flagship's signal⟩; *specif* **:** to return an attack or gunfire ⟨poured broadside after broadside into the forts, which *replied* continuously —*Amer. Guide Series: La.*⟩ ⟨~*ing* with rifles and bayonets —*Newsweek*⟩ ~ *vt* **:** to give as an answer ⟨*replied* not a word⟩ ⟨did not know what to ~⟩ **syn** see ANSWER

**2reply** \"\ *n* -ES **1 :** something that is said, written, or done in answer or response ⟨made a long-winded ~ to the teacher's question⟩ ⟨a letter in ~ to a request for a loan⟩ ⟨only three or four of the train guard had been able to fire a ~ —F.V.W. Mason⟩ **2 :** REPLICATION 1b(2)

**reply brief** *n* **:** a brief required by some courts of a party to a legal action in answer to points of law raised in an opponent's brief but not in his own

**reply card** *n* **1** *or* **reply postal card :** DOUBLE POSTAL CARD **2 :** any card for use in mailing a reply that is provided by the one who requests the reply and who sometimes offers to pay the postage for the reply

**reply coupon** *n* **:** a coupon sold by a post office in one country and exchangeable in another country for a stamp to be used on a letter of reply

**reply envelope** *n* **:** BUSINESS REPLY ENVELOPE

**reply–paid postcard** *n* **:** DOUBLE POSTAL CARD

**reply–paid telegram** *n* **:** a telegram to which a reply is prepaid by the sender

**re·pone** \rə̇ˈpōn, rēˈp-\ *vt* -ED/-ING/-S [L *reponere* to put back — more at REPOSIT] **1** *Scots law* **:** to restore (as a minister) to former standing or office **2** *Scots law* **:** to restore (as a defaulting party in an action) to former legal status in order to try the action again **:** REHABILITATE

**1re·port** \rə̇ˈpō(ə)r|t, rēˈp-, -pȯ(ə)r|, -pōə|, -pȯ(ə)| *sometimes* ˈrē,p-; *usu* |d·+V\ *n* -S [ME, fr. MF, statement, account, fr. OF, fr. *reporter*, v.] **1 a :** common talk or an account spread by common talk **:** a story or statement casually repeated and generally believed **:** RUMOR ⟨denies the common ~ that he ghosted the whole document —Bruce Bliven b.1889⟩ **b :** FAME, REPUTATION ⟨evil ~ beset him early and pursued him throughout his active life —S.H.Adams⟩ ⟨member, 27, well experienced all branches, and of good ~ —*Veterinary Record*⟩ **2 a :** something that gives information **:** a usu. detailed account or statement ⟨a weather ~⟩ ⟨an intelligence ~⟩ ⟨a news ~⟩ ⟨a stock market ~⟩ **b :** NOTIFICATION ⟨the health authorities had received no new ~*s* of typhoid cases for 24 hours⟩ **c** (1) **:** an account or statement of the facts of a legal case heard and of the decision and opinion of the court or quasi-judicial administrative agency determining the case (2) **:** a written submission of a question of law (as by a lower court) to an appellate court for review before final decision is entered **d :** a record of the speeches and remarks delivered and the actions taken during a meeting or session (as of a convention) esp. as formally published ⟨a ~ of the proceedings of the nominating convention⟩ **3 :** an explosive noise ⟨the roar of airplane engines and the sharp ~*s* of opening parachutes filled the skies —O.N.Bradley⟩ ⟨the ~ of a gun served to scare some hundreds more —C.L.Barrett⟩ **4 a :** a usu. formal and sometimes official statement giving the conclusions and recommendations of a person or group authorized or delegated to consider a proposal ⟨the committee made an unfavorable ~ on the bill⟩ **b :** a usu. formal account of the results of an investigation given by a person or group authorized or delegated to make the investigation ⟨an audit ~⟩ ⟨after exhaustive study the committee made its ~ on the causes of the accident⟩ ⟨the committee presented its ~ on the teaching of science in the high schools⟩ **c :** an analysis of operations and progress and a statement of future plans made at stated intervals by an administrator or executive to his superiors or those to whom he is responsible ⟨gave his departmental ~ to the president of the company⟩ ⟨the board of directors issued its annual ~ to the stockholders⟩ **d :** a statement of a student's academic record for a particular period often including also an evaluation of his rate of progress — **on report :** required to appear before one's commanding officer to answer for an infraction of regulations **:** subject to disciplinary action ⟨perhaps he could put somebody *on report*, get him some extra duty —K.M.Dodson⟩

**2report** \=ˈ=\ *vb* -ED/-ING/-S [ME *reporten*, fr. MF *reporter* to report, carry back, fr. OF, fr. L *reportare*, fr. *re-* + *portare* to carry — more at FARE] *vt* **1 a :** to give an account of **:** NARRATE, RELATE, TELL ⟨fiction should confine itself solely to ~*ing* emotion and behavior —Bernard De Voto⟩ ⟨it was ~*ed* that she exercised great political influence over her husband —Martha T. Stephenson⟩ **b :** to describe as being in a specified state or condition ⟨a servant came to the door and ~*ed* her asleep —Sherwood Anderson⟩ ⟨~*ed* him much improved⟩ **2 a :** to serve as carrier of (a message) ⟨the ambassador ~*ed* the president's answer to his government⟩ **b :** to relate the words or sense of (something said) ⟨what she confessed I must ~ —Shak.⟩ ⟨~ what he actually did say —Benjamin Farrington⟩ **c** (1) **:** to make a written record or summary of ⟨~ a speech⟩ ⟨~ a trial⟩ (2) **:** to make a shorthand record of ⟨most radio speakers talk too fast, and trying to ~ them is often discouraging —C.I.Blanchard & C.E.Zoubek⟩ **d** (1) **:** to watch for and write about the newsworthy aspects or developments of **:** COVER ⟨a newsman assigned to ~ the trial⟩ ⟨a foreign correspondent ~*ing* events in the Far East⟩ (2) **:** to prepare or present an account of for radio or television broadcast ⟨~*s* the news every evening at seven⟩ ⟨the excited enthusiastic voice of a commentator ~*ing* a baseball game —Maritta Wolff⟩ **3 a** (1) **:** to give a formal or official account or statement of **:** state formally ⟨the treasurer ~*ed* a balance of ten dollars⟩ ⟨the company ~*ed* a sales total of over a million dollars for the month⟩ (2) **:** to return or present (a matter officially referred for consideration) with conclusions or recommendations; *specif* **:** report out **b :** to announce or relate as the result of a special search, examination, or investigation ⟨~*ed* the discovery of new diamond mines⟩ ⟨~*ed* no sign of disease⟩ ⟨~*ed* new evidence bearing on the authorship of the play⟩ **c :** to announce the presence, arrival, or sighting of ⟨~*ed* himself present⟩ ⟨while waiting for the tower to ~ the general's plane —J.G.Cozzens⟩ ⟨~*ed* land straight ahead⟩ **d :** to make known to the proper authorities **:** give notification of ⟨~ a fire⟩ ⟨~ an accident⟩ ⟨~ a case of diphtheria⟩ **e :** to make a charge of misconduct against ⟨the stationmaster all but threatened to ~ me —Walter de la Mare⟩ ⟨~*ed* the abusive student to the principal⟩ ~ *vi* **1 a :** to give an account of someone or something **:** TELL ⟨he did not simply ~: he criticized and reflected —Ilse Lind⟩ **b :** to give an account of oneself **:** make one's whereabouts or activities known to someone ⟨promised to ~ by letter⟩ ⟨hasn't ~*ed* for days⟩ **c :** to present oneself ⟨~ for duty⟩ ⟨~ to the commanding officer⟩ ⟨the children will ~ for class each day whether the school is open or not —*New Republic*⟩ — often used with *in* or *back* ⟨~*ed* in every morning⟩ ⟨time to ~ back for work⟩ **2 :** to make, issue, or submit a report **:** present a formal statement or account ⟨the committee will ~ at twelve o'clock⟩ ⟨the inspector has not yet ~*ed* on the condition of the mine⟩ **3 :** to act in the capacity of a reporter **:** furnish news reports ⟨~*ing* for a living⟩ **syn** see RELATE

**re·port·able** \=ˈ=əbəl\ *adj* **1 :** admitting of or meriting a report ⟨ten years of research that produced no ~ results⟩ **2 :** required by law to be reported ⟨~ income⟩

**re·port·age** \=ˈ=ij, -ēj, *esp for 2* ˌrepərˈtäzh *or* -ˌpȯr- *or* -täzh\ *n* -S [F, fr. *reporter*, n., news reporter (fr. E) + *-age*] **1 a :** the act or process of reporting news ⟨in which he described some of the new skills in ~ required to carry out such an assignment —*Time*⟩ **b** : a news story ⟨their front pages are usu. divided between local scandals and romantic ~*s* —*Atlantic*⟩ **c** : DOCUMENTATION ⟨the superiority of pictures over the written word as a means of ~ —*Coming Events in Britain*⟩ **2** : writing intended to give a factual and detailed account of directly observed or carefully documented events and scenes ⟨seem to be saying that straightforward ~ is the only branch of literature that matters —George Orwell⟩

**report card** *n* : a report on a student that is periodically submitted by a school to the student's parents or guardian

**re·port·ed·ly** \-ˈ=ədlē, -li\ *adv* : according to report : REPUTEDLY ⟨has ~ made many anonymous benefactions to hospitals —*Current Biog.*⟩

**re·port·er** \-ˈ=ə(r)\ *n* -s [alter. (influenced by *-er*) of ME *reportour*, fr. MF *reporteur*, fr. *reporter* to report + *-eur* -or] : one that reports ⟨a ~ of spiritual and physical reality —H.S. Canby⟩ ⟨ask him to continue being a ~ and judge of what is new in the arts —Malcolm Cowley⟩: as **a** : an officer or person who makes authorized statements of law proceedings and decisions or of legislative debates **b** : one who makes a shorthand record of a speech or proceeding; *specif* : COURT REPORTER **c** (1) : one who is employed by a newspaper or magazine to gather and write news for publication ⟨a sports ~⟩ ⟨a financial ~⟩ ⟨a society ~⟩ (2) : one who reports news events on a radio or television program : COMMENTATOR **d** *archaic* : PISTOL

**reporting pay** *n* : a payment made to a worker who reports for work without having previously been told that no work is available — called also *call-in pay*

**repor·to·ri·al** \ˌrepə(r)ˈtōrēəl, -tȯr- *also* ˌrēp- *or* -ˌpōr- *or* -ˌpȯr-\ *adj* [irreg. (influenced by *-or*) fr. *reporter* + *-ial*] **1** : of, relating to, or characteristic of a reporter ⟨a long ~ career⟩ ⟨~ curiosity⟩ ⟨~ skills⟩ **2** : of, resembling, or characteristic of a report ⟨a ~ book⟩ ⟨~ prose⟩ ⟨it is too topical, too transitory, too ~ —C.P.Aiken⟩ — **repor·to·ri·al·ly** \-ēəlē, -li\ *adv*

**report out** *vt, of a legislative committee* : to return (a bill) after consideration and often with revisions to a legislative body for debate and vote ⟨on the fifteen-man body there are eight sure votes for *reporting* the measure *out* —*Newsweek*⟩

**reports** *pl of* REPORT, *pres 3d sing of* REPORT

**report stage** *n* : the stage in the British legislative process that occurs prior to the third reading and that involves the receipt by the legislative body of the report of the committee to which the bill has been assigned, consideration of amendments made in committee, and usu. discussion esp. of details and amendment — compare LEGISLATION 1

**reposal** *n* -s *obs* : the act of reposing ⟨the ~ of any trust, virtue, or worth in thee —Shak.⟩

**¹re·pose** \rəˈpōz, rēˈp-\ *vt* -ED/-ING/-S [ME *reposen* to replace, put back, irreg. (influenced by such verbs as ME *deposen* to depose) fr. L *reponere* (perfect stem *repos-*) — more at REPOSIT] **1** *archaic* : to put away or set down : DEPOSIT **2** : to place (as confidence or trust) : SET — usu. used with *in* ⟨~ full confidence in their leader —T.B.Macaulay⟩ ⟨the complete trust *reposed* in him and his policies —*Newsweek*⟩ **3** : to place for control, management, or use ⟨~*s* the judicial power in a supreme court —*Amer. Guide Series: La.*⟩

**²repose** \"\ *vb* -ED/-ING/-S [ME *reposen*, fr. MF *reposer*, fr. OF, fr. LL *repausare*, fr. L *re-* + LL *pausare* to stop, rest — more at PAUSE] *vt* **1 a** : to lay at rest : place in a restful or resting position : REST ⟨upon that cottage bench *reposed* his limbs —William Wordsworth⟩ **b** : to give rest to : refresh by rest ⟨enter in the castle and there ~ you for the night —Shak.⟩ **2** : to cause to be calm or quiet : COMPOSE ⟨extraordinarily difficult to ~ a man whose leg troubled him, whose war troubled him, whose bank troubled him and whose wife troubled him —Francis Hackett⟩ ~ *vi* **1 a** : to lie at rest ⟨during the hot afternoon, the entire town ~*s*⟩ **b** : to lie dead ⟨*reposing* in state⟩ **c** : to remain still or concealed : lie quiet or hidden ⟨under the soil . . . there ~ vastly greater quantities of raw materials —F.C.James⟩ ⟨the existence of similar sunken lands now *reposing* on the bottom of the Pacific —J.F. McComas⟩ **2** : to take rest : cease from activity, exertion, or movement ⟨she did not ~; she could not . . . she sat thinking —Arnold Bennett⟩ **3** *archaic* : to rest in confidence : RELY ⟨upon whose faith and honor I ~ —Shak.⟩ **4** : to rest for support : LIE — usu. used with *on* or *upon* ⟨cutting generous portions with a huge knife from the loaf *reposing* on a round wooden base —Sidney Lovett⟩ ⟨medieval justice *reposed* so greatly on the system of fines —G.G.Coulton⟩

**³repose** \"\ *n* -s [MF *repos*, fr. OF, fr. *reposer*, v.] **1 a** : a state of resting after exertion or strain : temporary mental or physical inactivity used to restore vigor; *esp* : rest in sleep ⟨a little feast that would make other men heavy and desirous of ~ —Willa Cather⟩ ⟨earned one's night's ~ —H.A.Overstreet⟩ **b** : relief from excitement, danger, or difficulty : restful change : RELAXATION ⟨where at last he could find warmth and the brief, treacherous ~ of dissipation —J.T.Soby⟩ **2 a** : a place or state of rest; *esp* : eternal or heavenly rest ⟨to pray for the ~ of a soul⟩ **b** : freedom from something that disturbs or excites : CALM, PEACE, TRANQUILLITY ⟨the unfailing ~ of the bayou —*Christian Science Monitor*⟩ ⟨induce a sense of ~ and contentment —S.P.B.Mais⟩ **c** : a harmony in the disposition of parts and colors that is restful to the eye ⟨his painting was criticized as lacking ~⟩ **3 a** : QUIESCENCE ⟨the volcano was in ~⟩ **b** : cessation or absence of activity, movement, or animation ⟨his face in ~ is grave and thoughtful —R.C.Doty⟩ ⟨~ again freezes the burning features of his face —C.L.Sulzberger⟩ **4** : composure of manner : quiet dignity : EASINESS, POISE **syn** see REST

**re·pose·ful** \-fəl\ *adj* : full of repose : QUIET, RESTFUL ⟨a graveled alley vaulted with fine straight green oaks, which seemed marvellously cool and ~ —Edmund Wilson⟩ **syn** see COMFORTABLE

**re·pose·ful·ly** \-fəlē, -li\ *adv* : in a reposeful manner : RESTFULLY

**re·pose·ful·ness** \-fəlnəs\ *n* -ES : the quality or state of being reposeful : RESTFULNESS

**reposing room** *n* : a room (as in a funeral home) used for the viewing of the deceased by mourners

**re·pos·it** \rəˈpäzət, rēˈp-\ *vt* [L *repositus*, past part. of *reponere* to replace, put back, fr. *re-* + *ponere* to put, place — more at POSITION] **1** : to lay away : DEPOSIT, STORE ⟨buried sedimentary rocks which have entrapped the water in which the rocks were originally ~*ed* —*Westralian Farmers Co-op Gazette*⟩ **2** : to put back in place : REPLACE ⟨he ~*ed* the stomach in the abdomen —John Kobler⟩

**¹repo·si·tion** \ˌrēpəˈzishən, ˌrep-\ *n* [LL *reposition-*, *repositio*, fr. L *repositus* (past part. of *reponere*) + *-ion-*, *-io* -ion] **1** : the act of repositing or the state of being reposited **2** *Scot* : restoration to a position, possession, or office : REINSTATEMENT

**²re·po·si·tion** \ˌrēpəˈzishən\ *vt* [*re-* + *position*] : to change the position of ⟨a malposition of the lower jaw . . . may be assumed and the jaw temporarily ~*ed* —H.G.Armstrong⟩ ⟨advise the receiver pilot to ~ his craft —*Ethyl News*⟩

**¹re·pos·i·to·ry** \rəˈpäzəˌtōrē, rēˈp-, -tȯr-, -ri\ *n* -ES [L *repositorium*, fr. *repositus* (past part. of *reponere*) + *-orium* -ory] **1** : a place, room, or container where something is deposited or stored : DEPOSITORY ⟨the child's desk . . . as a ~ for his music papers and other oddments —Marcia Davenport⟩: as **a** : a building or room for the exhibition of a collection (as of works of art) : MUSEUM ⟨a single museum serves not only as local ~ for cultural monuments but also as a community center —Lincoln Kirstein⟩ **b** : a burial vault **c** : a place where something is kept or shown for sale : a warehouse, store, or showroom ⟨now had an office and a clerk and they had a ~ . . . for their finished work —Ben Riker⟩ **d** : a side altar or niche in a Roman Catholic church where the consecrated Host is deposited from Maundy Thursday until Good Friday — called also *altar of repose* **2** : one that contains or stores something nonmaterial : STOREHOUSE ⟨although well written and attractively printed, is little more than a ~ of linguistic superstitions —R.A.Hall *b*.1911⟩ ⟨theoretically the mob is the ~ of all political wisdom and virtue —H.L.Mencken⟩ **3** : a place or region richly supplied with some natural resource ⟨the ~ of fabulous oil resources —A.E.Stevenson *b*.1900⟩ **4** : a person to whom something is confided or entrusted ⟨he had been an entranced ~ of many secrets —John Buchan⟩

**²repository** \"\ *adj, of a drug* : designed to act over a prolonged period : slowly absorbed : DEPOT ⟨~ penicillin⟩

**re·possess** \ˌrē+\ *vt* [*re-* + *possess*] **1 a** : to possess again : regain possession of ⟨~*ed* her vanity bag —Christopher Morley⟩ ⟨a young playwright, seeking a way to ~ the great classical tradition of comedy —William Becker⟩ **b** : to resume possession of (an item purchased on installment) in default of the payment of installments due ⟨~*ed* the car⟩ ⟨~*ed* the sofa⟩ **2** *Scot* : REINSTATE ⟨for the purpose of ~*ing* his uncle again in the lodge —Sir Walter Scott⟩ **3** : to restore to possession : put in possession again ⟨theology has ~*ed* itself of a good conscience and a sense of authority —A.N.Wilder⟩ — **re·possessor** \"+\ *n*

**re·possession** \"+\ *n* : the act or state of possessing again : RECOVERY; *specif* : the act of resuming possession of property when the purchaser fails to keep up payments on it

**repost** *var of* RIPOSTE

**re·pot** \(ˈ)rē+\ *vt* [*re-* + *pot*] : to transfer a plant from one pot to another usu. with the addition of fresh soil

**re·pous·sage** \rəˈpüˌsäzh\ *n* -s [F, fr. *repousser* + *-age*] **1** : the art or process of hammering out or pressing thin metal from the reverse side **2** : the hammering out of an etching and photoengraving plate from behind to level up any part that has been worked into a depression

**¹re·pous·sé** \-ˈsā\ *adj* [F, past part. of *repousser* to press back, thrust back, fr. MF, fr. *re-* + *pousser* to push, thrust, fr. OF *poulser* — more at PUSH] **1** *of metal work* **a** : shaped or ornamented with patterns in relief made by hammering or pressing on the reverse side ⟨~ work⟩ ⟨a silver dish with a ~ rim⟩ **b** : formed in relief ⟨a ~ pattern⟩ **2** : resembling or giving the effect of repoussé work ⟨an elongated box bag of crushed silver or gold kid stitched in a ~ design —Marion Miller⟩

**²repoussé** \"\ *n* -s : repoussé work

**repp** *var of* REP

**rep·pe chemistry** \ˈrepə-\ *n, usu cap R* [after Walter *Reppe b*1892 Ger. chemist] : a branch esp. of industrial chemistry that is based on reactions of acetylene under pressure and also of the products so obtained and that includes vinylation, ethynylation, polymerization to cyclic compounds, and carbonylation

**repped** \ˈrept\ *adj* [³*rep* + *-ed*] : resembling rep : having a ribbed surface ⟨~ paper⟩

**repping** *pres part of* REP

**rep·ple dep·ple** \ˈrepəlˈdepəl\ *n* [by shortening & alter.] *slang* : REPLACEMENT DEPOT

**repr** *abbr* **1** repair **2** represent; representative; represented; representing **3** reprint; reprinted

**rep·re·hend** \ˌreprəˈhend, -prēˈ-\ *vt* -ED/-ING/-S [ME *reprehenden*, fr. L *reprehendere* to hold back, seize, reprehend, fr. *re-* + *prehendere* to grasp, seize — more at PREHENSILE] : to voice disapproval of esp. after judgment : find fault with usu. with sternness and as a rebuke : BLAME, CENSURE, CHIDE, REPRIMAND, REPROVE ⟨~ not the imperfection of others —George Washington⟩ ⟨I severely ~*ed* him on this occasion —Samuel Richardson⟩ **syn** see CRITICIZE

**reprehender** *n* -s *obs* : one that voices disapproval

**rep·re·hen·si·bil·i·ty** \ˌreprəˌhen(t)səˈbiləd-ē\ *n* -ES : the quality or state of being reprehensible

**rep·re·hen·si·ble** \-en(t)səbəl\ *adj* [ME, fr. LL *reprehensibilis*, fr. L *reprehensus* (past part. of *reprehendere*) + *-ibilis* -able] : worthy of or deserving reprehension : BLAMABLE, CENSURABLE, CULPABLE, REPROVABLE ⟨to capitalize on his ignorance is morally ~ —Nicholas Samstag⟩ ⟨it is my ~ nature to welcome excitement —Carl Van Doren⟩ ⟨when a work of art excites . . . ~ passions —Samuel Alexander⟩

**rep·re·hen·si·bly** \-blē, -bli\ *adv* : in a reprehensible manner or degree ⟨those laws . . . were in his judgment ~ lenient —T.B.Macaulay⟩

**rep·re·hen·sion** \ˌ==ˈhenchən\ *n* -s [ME *reprehensioun*, fr. MF or L; MF *reprehension*, fr. L *reprehension-*, *reprehensio*, fr. *reprehensus* (past part. of *reprehendere*) + *-ion-*, *-io* -ion] **1** : the act of reprehending : REPROOF ⟨if they are corrupt, they merit . . . blame and ~ —Edmund Burke⟩ ⟨lifted no voice in ~ of his corrupt deals —S.H.Adams⟩ **2** *archaic* : an instance of reprehending ⟨his writings contained . . . severe ~*s* —Thomas Brown⟩

**rep·re·hen·sive** \ˌ==ˈhen(t)siv, -sēv *also* -səv\ *adj* [fr. *reprehension*, after such pairs as E *apprehension*: *apprehensive*] : serving to reprehend : conveying reprehension or reproof ⟨~ aspects and unfortunate results of unwarranted charges —*New Republic*⟩ — **rep·re·hen·sive·ly** \-səvlē, -li\ *adv*

**rep·re·hen·so·ry** \-n(t)s(ə)rē\ *adj* [fr. *reprehension*, after such pairs as E *commendation*: *commendatory*] *archaic* : REPREHENSIVE ⟨no reason for making any ~ complaint —Samuel Johnson⟩

**rep·re·sent** \ˌreprəˈzent, -prēˈz-, *in rapid speech often* ÷ -pəˈz, *chiefly in substand speech* -pərˈz-\ *vb* -ED/-ING/-S [ME *representen*, fr. MF *representer*, fr. L *repraesentare*, fr. *re-* + *praesentare* to present — more at PRESENT] *vt* **1** : to bring clearly before the mind : cause to be known, felt, or apprehended : present esp. by description **2** : to serve as a sign or symbol of **3** : to portray by pictorial, plastic, or musical art : DELINEATE, DEPICT **4** *archaic* : to make manifest : DISPLAY, EXHIBIT, SHOW **5** : to exhibit by delineation, depiction, or portrayal — used esp. of a work of art **6** : to present by means of something standing in the place of : serve as the counterpart or image of : TYPIFY **7** : to exhibit dramatically: **a** : to produce on the stage **b** : to act the part or role of : personate in acting or on the stage **8 a** : to supply the place, perform the duties, exercise the rights, or receive the share of : take the place of in some respect : fill the place of for some purpose : substitute in some capacity for : act the part of, in the place of, or for (as another person) usu. by legal right **b** : to serve (as in a legislative body) by delegated or deputed authority usu. resulting from election ⟨the state was ~*ed* in Congress by two Republicans⟩ **9** : to describe as having a specified character or quality **10** : to set forth or place before someone (as by statement, account, or discourse) : exhibit (a fact) to another mind in language : give one's own impressions and judgment of : state with advocacy or with the design of affecting action or judgment : point out by way of protest or remonstrance **11** : to serve as a specimen, example, or instance of **12 a** : to form an image or representation of in the mind **b** (1) : to apprehend (an object) by means of an idea (2) : to recall in memory (an object of previous experience) **13** : to correspond to in kind ~ *vi* : to make representations against something : present objections : PROTEST

**syn** REPRESENT, DEPICT, PORTRAY, DELINEATE, PICTURE, and LIMN can mean to present an image or lifelike imitation of, as in art. REPRESENT implies a placing before the mind as if real or as if living, as by a picture, description, or piece of sculpture ⟨the statue *represented* the great man as even more heroic than he was in fact⟩ ⟨the stage setting *represents* a hotel lobby⟩ ⟨seemed to think that music could *represent* physical objects and literary or historical events —*New Republic*⟩ DEPICT suggests specifically a graphic representation ⟨*depicted* hill-country scenes in woodcuts and etchings —*Amer. Guide Series: Ark.*⟩ ⟨miniature tapestries that *depict* quaint eighteenth-century scenes —Horace Sutton⟩ ⟨action can tell a story, display all the most vivid relations between men, and *depict* every kind of human emotion, without the aid of a word —O.W. Holmes †1935⟩ PORTRAY suggests specifically a detailed representation as of a character by means of a portrait ⟨a picture vividly *portraying* the passion of Joan of Arc⟩ ⟨in literature are portrayed all human passions, desires, and aspirations —C.W.Eliot⟩ DELINEATE, suggesting a line drawing, stresses a care for accuracy of detail and fullness of outline ⟨his brush did its work with a steady and sure stroke that indicated command of his materials. He could *delineate* whatever he elected with technical skill —Richard Jefferies⟩ ⟨various clinical studies which fairly well *delineated* the usefulness of this drug —R.R.Tompsett & Walsh McDermott⟩ ⟨those who perform on the screen have to *delineate* character and to display the emotions —P.W.Tell⟩ PICTURE suggests perhaps more pictorial quality or definiteness of representation ⟨on the walls were *pictured* buffalo and reindeer⟩ ⟨the writer is a master of vivid illustrations from nature and history, of rhythmical period or terse antithesis, of emotional appeal and concrete *picturing* of facts —*Encyc. Americana*⟩ ⟨*picture* things as they were in the golden thirteenth century —G.G.Coulton⟩ LIMN is chiefly a literary equivalent of DEPICT or DELINEATE ⟨prosecution *limned* a somewhat different picture —*Newsweek*⟩ ⟨his talent for dialogue as a means for *limning* character —Margaret Hexter⟩ ⟨the life of the community is drawn in detail and the sorrows and sacrifices *limned* with deep compassion —Mary L. Dunn⟩

**re-present** \ˌrē + *pronunc at verb* PRESENT\ *vt* [*re-* + *present*] : to present again, anew, or through the medium of art

**rep·re·sent·able** *pronunc at* REPRESENT + əbəl\ *adj* : capable of being represented

**rep·re·sen·ta·men** \ˌreprəˌzenˈtāmən, -prēˌz-, -ˌzən-\ *n, pl* **represen·tam·i·na** \-tamənə\ [fr. *representation*, after such pairs as L *putation-*, *putatio* act of pruning (fr. *putatus* — past part. of *putare* to cut, prune — + *-ion-*, *-io* -ion): *putamen* that which falls off in pruning — more at PUTAMEN] : the product as distinguished from the act of philosophical representation — compare REPRESENTATION 1e

**rep·re·sent·ant** \ˌreprəˈzentᵊnt, -prēˈ-, -zentənt\ *n* -s [F *représentant*, fr. MF *representant*, fr. *representant*, pres. part. of *representer* to represent] : one that represents another : REPRESENTATIVE ⟨the greatest literary ~ of the revolution —*Nineteenth Century & After*⟩

**rep·re·sen·ta·tion** \ˌreprəˌzenˈtāshən, -prēˌz-, -zən-, *in rapid speech often* ÷ -pə(ˌ)z-, *chiefly in substand speech* -pər(ˌ)z-\ *n* -s [ME *representacion*, fr. MF *representation*, fr. L *repraesentation-*, *repraesentatio*, fr. *repraesentatus* (past part. of *repraesentare* to represent) + *-ion-*, *-io* -ion] **1** : one that represents or is represented: as **a** : a likeness, picture, model, or other reproduction ⟨~*s* in pottery of frogs and turtles —*Times Lit. Supp.*⟩ ⟨an allegorical ~ . . . decorates the main pediment —*Amer. Guide Series: Mich.*⟩ **b** (1) : a statement or account esp. made to convey a particular view or impression of something with the intention of influencing opinion or action ⟨his ~*s* . . . influenced the president to investigate —*Amer. Guide Series: Minn.*⟩ ⟨making no false ~*s* to me —Thomas Hardy⟩ ⟨defendant's ~*s* that said automobile was new —*Southeastern Reporter*⟩ (2) : a statement of fact incidental or collateral to a contract made orally or in writing and on the faith of which the contract is entered into — compare ¹AFFIRMATIVE 3b, PROMISSORY, WARRANTY ⟨written ~*s* obtained from officials of the client —R.S.Johns⟩ ⟨the contract of sale contains a ~ by the purchaser —*U.S.Code*⟩ **c** : a dramatic production or performance ⟨a theatrical ~⟩ **d** (1) : a usu. formal and serious statement (as of facts, reasons, or arguments) made against something or to effect a change ⟨the colonial secretary made ~*s* on behalf of the Uitlanders —Ethel Drus⟩ (2) : a usu. formal protest : EXPOSTULATION, REMONSTRANCE ⟨the tenants had decided not to pay the increase until they had made ~*s* to the Native Affairs Department —H.S.Warner⟩ **e** (1) : an image or idea formed by the mind (2) : an idea that is the direct object of thought and the mental counterpart or transcript of the object known by means of it **2** : the act or action of representing or the state of being represented: as **a** : the action of representing (as by portrayal or delineation) in a visible image or form ⟨a strict ~ of nature would require that it curve —Hunter Mead⟩ ⟨entrance of light rays into the eye and their final ~ in the brain —F.A.Geldard⟩ ⟨an exponent of ~ rather than abstraction in art⟩ **b** : the action of setting forth or placing before another (as by a statement, account, or discourse) esp. with a view to affecting action ⟨the ~ of student opinion to the administration —*Seton Hall Univ. Bull.*⟩ ⟨yielding to the artful ~ of ambitious hypocrites —Sir Walter Scott⟩ **c** (1) : the action or fact of one person standing for another so as to have to a greater or less extent the rights and obligations of the person represented; *specif* : the relation of an heir to his predecessor when both the rights and obligations of the predecessor devolve upon the heir (as in Roman and Scots law) (2) : the substitution of an individual or class of individuals in place of a person (as when a child or children take the share of an estate that would have fallen to a deceased parent) **d** (1) : the action of representing or the fact of being represented in a legislative body ⟨~ of territory . . . rather than of population —G.A.Graham⟩ ⟨raise the issue of Chinese ~ —*New Statesman & Nation*⟩ ⟨the ancient world knew nothing of the device of ~ —Woodrow Wilson⟩ (2) : the action or fact of being represented in some other grouping, body, or aggregation ⟨in . . . such universities and colleges there is no ~ of any non-West European culture —*Amer. Council of Learned Soc. Newsletter*⟩ ⟨~ of classic issues in the collection⟩ **e** (1) : the action or process by which the mind forms an image or idea of an object (2) : recurrent as opposed to simple presentation **3** : the whole body of persons representing a constituency ⟨when vacancies happen in the ~ of any state in the Senate —*U. S. Constitution*⟩ ⟨chosen head of the U. S. ~ —*Current Biog.*⟩ ⟨small ~ from the Baltic states —Henry Giniger⟩

**re-presentation** \(ˌ)rē + *pronunc at* PRESENTATION\ *n* [*re-present* + *-ation*] : a presentation again or anew ⟨the revision and *re-presentation* of established favorite titles —Louise S. Bechtel⟩ ⟨a *re-presentation* of facts previously stated⟩

**rep·re·sen·ta·tion·al** \ˌ==(ˌ)= *as in* REPRESENTATION + ˈtāshənᵊl *or* -shnəl\ *adj* **1** : of, based upon, or of the nature of representation ⟨~ art⟩ ⟨~ powers⟩ ⟨~ office⟩ **2** : of, relating to, or supporting representationalism ⟨~ school⟩ ⟨~ theory⟩

**rep·re·sen·ta·tion·al·ism** \ˌ==(ˌ)=ˈtāshənᵊlˌizəm, -shnəˌli-\ *n* -s **1** *also* **rep·re·sen·ta·tion·ism** \-shəˌnizəm\ : the philosophical doctrine asserting that the immediate or direct object of knowledge is an idea in the mind distinct from the external or independent object which is the occasion of perception and holding sometimes that the idea is a mental counterpart or true copy of the external object and sometimes that the idea is a modification of the consciousness determined in part by the nature of the independent object and in part by the nature or limitations of the mind **2** : REPRESENTATIVE ART ⟨unorthodox ~ in his work —J.J.Sweeney⟩ ⟨~ is better left to the action film —Delmore Schwartz⟩

**rep·re·sen·ta·tion·al·ist** \-shənᵊləst, -shnəl-\ *n* -s : one that practices or advocates representative art — compare ABSTRACTIONIST 2

**rep·re·sen·ta·tion·ist** \-sh(ə)nəst\ *n* -s : an adherent of philosophical representationalism

**¹rep·re·sent·a·tive** \ˌreprəˈzentəd·iv, -prēˈz-, -tətiv, *in rapid speech often* ÷ -pəˈz-, *chiefly in substand speech* -pərˈz-\ *adj* [ME, fr. MF or ML; MF *representatif*, fr. ML *repraesentativus*, fr. L *repraesentatus* (past part. of *repraesentare* to represent) + *-ivus* -ive] **1** : serving to represent, portray, or typify : characterized by representation ⟨a painting ~ of a battle⟩ **2** : standing for or in the place of another : acting for another or others : constituting the agent for another esp. through delegated authority **3** : of, based upon, or constituting a form of government in which the many are represented by persons chosen from among them usu. by election ⟨~ government⟩ ⟨~ democracy⟩ ⟨development of the ~ system⟩ **4** : serving as a characteristic example : illustrative of a class : conveying an idea of others of the kind : TYPICAL ⟨a ~ modern play⟩ ⟨a ~ romantic poem⟩ **5 a** : having the character of a mental representation — compare REPRESENTATION 1e **b** : of or relating to the doctrine of representationalism ⟨the ~ theory of knowledge⟩

**²representative** \"\ *n* -s **1 a** : one that stands for a number or class (as of persons or things) : one that in some way corresponds to, replaces, or is equivalent to someone or something else : SAMPLE, SPECIMEN ⟨many ~*s* of the Protozoa —R.E.Coker⟩ ⟨the student body includes ~*s* of 36 states —*Amer. Guide Series: N.C.*⟩ ⟨where distinctly different biological ~*s* are found —*Amer. Guide Series: Minn.*⟩ **b** : a typical embodiment of some quality or abstract concept : TYPE ⟨the most authoritative ~ . . . of the ideal of priestly stewardship —V.L.Parrington⟩ ⟨of the Semitic family Arabic is the chief living ~ —A.L.Kroeber⟩ ⟨the sole ~ . . . of the feelings and the knowledge of the middle ages —H.T.Buckle⟩ **2** *obs* : a representative body or assembly ⟨debate in the grand ~ of the kingdom —Nathaniel Bacon⟩ **3** : one that represents another or others in a special capacity: as **a** (1) : one that represents a constituency as a member of a legislative or other governing body ⟨the people exercises this sovereignty . . . through the votes of its ~*s* —D.W.S.Lidderdale⟩ ⟨committee . . . to which no ~ of an Arab state had been named —*U. N. Bull.*⟩ ⟨summoned ~*s* of the shires and the boroughs to parliament⟩ (2) : a member of the House of Representatives of the U.S. Congress (3) : a member of a house of representatives in a state legislature **b** (1) : one that represents another as agent, deputy, substitute, or delegate usu. being invested with the authority of the principal (2) : one appointed to represent a sovereign or government abroad ⟨the permanent ~ of Canada to the North Atlantic Council —*Current Biog.*⟩ ⟨served as ~ of the president of the U.S. in conferences with the allies⟩ **c** : one who legally represents or stands in the place of a deceased person : LEGAL REPRESENTATIVE a, PERSONAL REPRESENTATIVE **d** : one that in some respect stands for or in the place of another ⟨money is only a commodious ~ of the commodities which may be purchased with it —Joseph Priestley⟩ **e** : one that represents a business organization : SALESMAN ⟨local ~ of an insurance company⟩ **f** : one that represents another as successor or heir : one representing a line or tradition ⟨the last ~ of one of the founding families⟩ ⟨do not know if his large family has left any ~s today —*Notes & Queries*⟩

**representative art** *n* : art that is concerned with the representation of reality and esp. the characteristic or verisimilar representation of nature or life ⟨the earliest works of art from the caves of Europe are not only realistic, but meritoriously *representative art* —Clark Wissler⟩

**representative-at-large** *n, pl* **representatives-at-large** \ˌ==-ˈ===ˈ=\ : CONGRESSMAN-AT-LARGE

**representative democracy** *n* : DEMOCRACY 1b(2)

**representative firm** *n* : a model firm not necessarily in existence which as an abstract construction is used to illustrate the operations of a market as a whole

**representative fraction** *n* : a map scale in which figures representing units (as centimeters, inches, or feet) are expressed in the form of the fraction 1/*x* (as 1/250,000) or of the ratio 1:*x* to indicate that one unit on the map represents *x* units (as 250,000 centimeters) on the earth's surface

**representative legislature** *n* : a British colonial legislature in which at least one half of the members are elected by the people of the colony — compare LEGISLATIVE COUNCIL 2

**rep·re·sent·a·tive·ly** \-əvlē, -li\ *adv* [ME *representatyfliche*, fr. *representatyf, representative* representative + *-liche* -ly] : in a representative manner

**representative money** *n* : paper money backed by an equal amount of gold or silver coin or bullion held by a government

**rep·re·sent·a·tive·ness** \-ivnəs\ *n* -ES **1** : the quality or state of being representative ⟨his ~ as an American⟩ **2** : the characteristic of a specific scientific experiment that makes it an adequate sample of the general case

**representative peer** *n* : a peer chosen to represent other peers in the House of Lords: **a** : one of 16 Scottish peers elected as their representatives for the duration of a single parliament by persons holding Scottish peerages only **b** : one of 28 Irish peers elected as their representatives for life by persons holding Irish peerages only

**representative sampling** *n* : sampling in which the relative sizes of sub-population samples are chosen equal to the relative sizes of the sub-populations

**representative theory** *n* : REPRESENTATIONALISM 1

**representative town meeting** *n* : a town meeting in which a usu. small number of representatives previously elected by the townspeople vote and transact business although other residents may attend and often are allowed to speak

**representator** *n* -S [LL *repraesentator*, fr. L *repraesentatus* (past part. of *repraesentare* to represent) + *-or*] *obs* : REPRESENTER

**represented** *past of* REPRESENT

**representee** *n, obs* : a parliamentary representative

**rep·re·sent·er** \ˌ==ˈzentə(r)\ *n* -S : one that represents (as by exhibition, acting, or presentation)

**representing** *pres part of* REPRESENT

**rep·re·sent·ment** \ˌ==ˈzentmənt\ *n, archaic* : REPRESENTATION ⟨the presentments of sense or the ~s of memory —E.R. Conder⟩ ⟨expect to prevail . . . by a bare ~ of the unreasonableness of their actions —Henry Dodwell⟩

**representor** *n* -S *obs* : REPRESENTATIVE

**represents** *pres 3d sing of* REPRESENT

**¹re·press** \rəˈpres, rēˈp-\ *vb* -ED/-ING/-ES [ME *repressen*, fr. L *repressus*, past part. of *reprimere* to check, repress — more at REPRIMAND] *vt* **1** : to check by or as if by pressure : keep or hold in check : restrain from spreading, increasing, or doing harm : CONTROL, CURB ⟨obstruction of justice . . . is sternly ~ed —Edward Jenks⟩ ⟨developed psychic interests . . . but then these were ~ed by her parents —A.G.N.Flew⟩ ⟨law tended to foster rather than ~ grammar —H.O.Taylor⟩ ⟨~ bleeding⟩ **2** : to keep down or under by self-control : restrain oneself from expression (as by showing, feeling, or uttering) of : keep under control ⟨could not ~ a smile at the comical figure —Ellen Glasgow⟩ ⟨~ed the temptation to talk about it —Kathleen Freeman⟩ ⟨a remarkable ability to ~ his home worries while on the job —W.H.Whyte⟩ **3 a** : to reduce to subjection or quietness : put down by force : SUBDUE ⟨a hopeless undertaking . . . to try to ~ such powerful subjects —H.T.Buckle⟩ **b** : to suppress by exercising force : put down : QUELL ⟨the royal commissioners sent to ~ the tumult —J.R.Green⟩ **4** : to prevent the natural or normal expression, activity, or development of : cause repression of or in ⟨chill penury ~ed their noble rage —Thomas Gray⟩ ⟨natural instinct ~ed by a perpetual stern control —Havelock Ellis⟩ **5** : to exclude from consciousness : subject to repression ⟨new experiential material . . . ~ed in one of the personality to the level of the unconscious —H.W.Dunham⟩ ⟨~ conflicts⟩ ~ *vi* : to cause or bring about repression : take repressive action ⟨the dominant minority's will to ~ —A.J.Toynbee⟩ ⟨taboos against the gentler emotion force him to ~ —Howard Griffin⟩

**²re·press** \ˈrēˌpres\ *n* : a machine for re-pressing brick

**re–press** \(ˈ)rēˌpres\ *vt* [*re-* + *press*] : to press again ⟨~ bricks in a mold after coming from the brick machine and before burning in kiln⟩ ⟨was ~ed into government service —Whitney Balliett⟩ ⟨~ a record⟩

**repressed** *adj* **1 a** : subjected to repression ⟨a ~ child⟩ ⟨~ ambition⟩ **b** : characterized by restraint ⟨the ~ delicacy of its general design —*Amer. Guide Series: Conn.*⟩ **2** : affected by repression ⟨infantile anxiety based on ~ phantasies —Christine Olden⟩ ⟨~ hostilities and guilt reactions —Louise Heathers⟩

**repressed inflation** *n* : a condition in which direct economic controls (as price and wage controls and rationing) are utilized to prevent inflation without removing the underlying inflationary pressures

**re·press·er** \rəˈpresə(r), rēˈp-\ *n* -S [ME, fr. *repressen* to repress + *-er*] : one that represses

**repressing** *n* -S [fr. gerund of ²*repress*] : a phonograph record by one other than the original manufacturer or under a different label than that originally used when first released ⟨concertos . . . now available in domestic ~s —C.M.Smith⟩

**re·pres·sion** \rəˈpreshən, rēˈp-\ *n* -S [ME *repressioun* ability to repress, fr. ML *repression-, repressio*, fr. LL, suppression, fr. L *repressus* (past part. of *reprimere* to check, repress) + *-ion-, -io* -ion] **1 a** : the action of repressing or the state of being repressed ⟨relentless ~ of all Christian sects —R.H. Jackson⟩ ⟨auxiliary units dealing with vice ~ —F.A.Ogg & P.O.Ray⟩ ⟨~ of unpopular opinions⟩ **b** : an instance of repressing ⟨religious wars and the ~s which followed —G.C. Sellery⟩ ⟨racial ~s are more harmful to well-being —Charles Abrams⟩ **2 a** : a process or mechanism of ego defense whereby wishes or impulses that are incapable of fulfillment are kept from or made inaccessible to consciousness except in disguised form (as conversion in neurosis or sublimation or symbolization in normality) **b** : an idea, memory, or experience that has been extruded from consciousness into the unconscious — contrasted with *suppression;* compare MECHANISM OF DEFENSE

**re·pres·sive** \-esiv,-esəv *also* -esəv\ *adj* [ML *repressivus*, fr. L *repressus* (past part. of *reprimere* to check, repress) + *-ivus* -ive] : having power or tending to repress : causing or intended to cause repression ⟨~ measures⟩ ⟨~ taxation⟩ ⟨~ policy⟩

**re·pres·sive·ness** *n* -ES : the quality or state of being repressive ⟨a ~ natural to the man —G.D.Brown⟩

**re·pres·sor** \-sə(r)\ *n* -S [L, fr. *repressus* (past part. of *reprimere*) + *-or*] : one that represses

**re·pressure** \(ˈ)rē+\ *vt* [*re-* + *pressure*] : to raise the pressure of (an oil-bearing formation) by pumping in air or gas with the object of forcing out additional oil

**re·price** \(ˈ)rē+\ *vt* [*re-* + *price*] : to give a new price to : fix a new price schedule for ⟨stock that does not move may be *repriced* —*Dry Goods Economist*⟩ ⟨give the government authority to ~ any orders —Helen Fuller⟩

**re·priev·al** \rəˈprēvəl, rēˈp-\ *n* -S *archaic* : REPRIEVE ⟨~s and prolongings of this present life —Robert Leighton⟩ ⟨brought no ~ from anguish —Robert Southey⟩

**¹re·prieve** \rəˈprēv, rēˈp-\ *vt* -ED/-ING/-S [alter. (perh. influenced by obs. E *repreve* to reprove, fr. ME *repreven*) of earlier *repry*, perh. fr. MF *repris*, past part. of *reprendre* to take back — more at REPRISE, REPROVE] **1** *obs* : to put off (as something evil) : DELAY, POSTPONE ⟨since we cannot death ~ —Katherine Philips⟩ **2** : to delay the punishment of (as a condemned prisoner) : suspend the execution of sentence on : RESPITE **3** : to give relief or deliverance to for a time : preserve temporarily ⟨whose hard hand *reprieved* the empire from its fate —Robert Browning⟩

**²reprieve** \"\ *n* -S **1 a** : the act of reprieving or the state of being reprieved **b** : a formal temporary suspension of the execution of a sentence ⟨the president . . . shall have power to grant ~s and pardons for offenses against the United States —*U.S. Constitution*⟩; *esp* : a remission or commutation of a capital sentence **c** : something resembling such a formal suspension : a respite from a decision or penalty ⟨unless there is an eleventh-hour ~ the . . . elevated will cease operating at midnight —*N.Y. Times*⟩ **2** : an order or warrant for a formal suspension (as of a capital sentence) ⟨a messenger was dispatched with a ~ —*Amer. Guide Series: Conn.*⟩ **3** : a respite or temporary escape (as from death, pain, or trouble) ⟨the first relief over the ~ from a railway strike —*Blackwood's*⟩

**¹rep·ri·mand** \ˈreprəˌmand, -maa(ə)nd,-månd\ *n* -S [F *réprimande*, alter. of MF *reprimende*, fr. L *reprimenda*, fem. of *reprimendus* that is to be checked or repressed, gerundive of *reprimere* to check, repress, fr. *re-* + *-primere* (fr. *premere* to press) — more at PRESS] : a severe or formal reproof : a sharp rebuke : CENSURE; *esp* : one given with authority

**²reprimand** \", ˌ==ˈ=\ *vt* -ED/-ING/-S [F *réprimander*, fr. *réprimande*, n.] : to reprove severely : chide for a fault : censure formally and esp. with authority : REPREHEND ⟨had done something naughty and knew that she was going to be ~ed —I.V.Morris⟩ ⟨this member was found guilty . . . and voted by the House to be ~ed —D.G.Hitchner⟩ ⟨the court can ~ them . . . in the event of negligence —F.W.Crofts⟩ **syn** see REPROVE

**¹re·print** \(ˈ)rē+\ *vt* [*re-* + *print*] : to print again : make a reprint of

**²re·print** \ˈrē+,- *also* =ˈ=\ *n* **1 a** (1) : a subsequent printing of a book already published having the identical text of the previous printing (2) : such a printing with cheaper paper and binding and put out by a different publisher **b** : a second or new impression of printed matter **c** : an article or extract issued separately after being first published as part of a collection or in a periodical : OFFPRINT **d** : printed text used as copy for something to be typeset **e** (1) : matter (as in a periodical) that has appeared in print before (2) : a later printing of material published in more than one edition of the same newspaper; *esp* : matter in one day's early edition printed in a late edition of the previous day **2 a** : a government or private reprinting of a postage stamp no longer current usu. on different paper or in a different color or perforation from the first printing and esp. for other than postal use — compare REISSUE **b** : a stamp so reprinted **3** : REPRESSING

**re·print·er** \(ˈ)rē+\ *n* : one that publishes a reprint

**re·pri·sal** \rəˈprīzəl, rēˈp-\ *n* -S [ME *reprisail*, fr. MF *reprisaille*, modif. (influenced by MF *repris*, past part. of *reprendre* to take back) of OIt *ripresaglia*, fr. *ripreso* (past part. of *riprendere* to take back, recapture, fr. L *reprehendere* to hold back, seize, reprehend, recover) + *-aglia* -al (fr. L *-alia*, neut. pl. of *-alis* -al)] **1 a** : the act or practice in international law of resorting to force short of war (as by embargo, sequestration, forcible seizure, retortion, or retaliatory acts of the nature of those complained of) to procure redress of grievances **b** : an instance of such action **2** *obs* : PRIZE ⟨this rich ~ is so nigh and yet not ours —Shak.⟩ **3** : the regaining of something (as by recapture) **4** : something (as an amount or sum of money) given or paid in restitution : COMPENSATION — usu. used in pl. **5** : an action of retaliation (as for injury or attack)

**¹re·prise** \rəˈprīz, rēˈp-, *in senses 6 & 7* rəˈprēz\ *n* -S [ME, fr. MF, reprise, action of taking back, fr. OF, action of taking back, fr. fem. of *repris*, past part. of *reprendre* to take back, fr. L *reprehendere* to hold back, seize, reprehend, recover — more at REPREHEND] **1** : a deduction or charge (as rent charge, rent seck, pensions, or annuities) to be made yearly out of a manor or estate — usu. used in pl. ⟨the clear yearly value above all ~s of the rectory —*Stat. 1 & 2 William IV*⟩ **2** *archit* : a return in an internal angle **3** *archaic* : REPRISAL 4 ⟨by exchanging an apartment . . . he might well have got a ~ of several million francs —Carleton Lake⟩ **4** *obs* : a retaliatory act : REPRISAL **5 a** : a recurrence, renewal, or resumption of an action : a separate or repeated occurrence ⟨were plunged . . . not once or twice but in frequent ~s —George MacKenzie⟩ **b** : a renewal of attack following a return to guard in fencing **6 a** : the second section of pieces in binary form in 17th century French music **b** : a musical repetition: (1) : the repetition of the exposition preceding the development (2) : RECAPITULATION **c** : something resembling or held to resemble a reprise in a musical score : a subsequent and identical performance : REPETITION

**²re·prise** \-īz, *in sense 3* -ēz\ *vt* -ED/-ING/-S [ME *reprisen* to begin again, fr. MF *repris*, past part. of *reprendre* to take back] **1** *archaic* : to take back; *esp* : recover by force ⟨might ~ the arms . . . forfeited —George Chapman⟩ **2** *archaic* : COMPENSATE **3** : to repeat the performance of ⟨~ a song⟩

**re·pris·ti·nate** \(ˈ)rēˈpristəˌnāt\ *vt* -ED/-ING/-S [*re-* + *pristine* + *-ate*] : to restore to an original state or condition : REVIVE ⟨~ the cosmic order as of before the Fall —H.M.Rosenthal⟩

**re·pris·ti·na·tion** \(ˌ)rēˌpristəˈnāshən\ *n* -S : the act or action of restoring to a pristine state or condition : renewal of purity : RESTORATION ⟨~ of the American Idea as a fighting faith in freedom —H.M.Kallen⟩

**re·privatization** \(ˌ)rē+\ *n* -S [*re-* + *private* + *-ization*] : the act or action of privatizing again : restoration to private ownership or control (as after nationalization) ⟨the ~ of the subways is . . . to be desired —Henry Hazlitt⟩

**¹re·proach** \rəˈprōch, rēˈp-\ *n* -ES [ME *reproche*, fr. MF, fr. OF, fr. *reprochier*, v.] **1 a** : a source of disgrace or shame : a cause of blame or censure : an occasion of discredit : something (as a fact, matter, feature, or quality) producing disgrace or blame ⟨make us see in our whole prison system a ~ —B.N. Cardozo⟩ ⟨made their calling a ~ and a hissing —A.M. Young⟩ **b** : the quality or state (as disgrace, shame, blame, discredit, or opprobrium) so incurred ⟨these rare exceptions did not take away the ~ which lay on the whole body —T.B. Macaulay⟩ **2** : the act or action of reproaching sometimes sternly or abusively and sometimes mildly and gently as an upbraiding ⟨a term of ~⟩ ⟨was above ~⟩ ⟨turned a look of keen ~ on him —George Eliot⟩ ⟨the abstainers are not regarded with ~ —Freeman Lincoln⟩ **3** : an expression of censure, disapproval, or rebuke ⟨raged at . . . him with contradictory ~es —Joseph Conrad⟩ ⟨answer . . . letters sadly and patiently and with no ~es —Margaret Deland⟩ ⟨her greeting was a playful ~ —Willa Cather⟩ **4** *obs* : one subjected to censure or scorn : an object of contempt ⟨we are become a ~ to our neighbors —Ps 79:4 (AV)⟩ **5 reproaches** *pl, usu cap* : a series of antiphons that are made up of sentences represented as addressed by Christ to his people to remind them of his services to mankind and their ingratitude and are individually followed by the Trisagion sung as a respond and that constitute a service or part of a service on Good Friday in the Roman Catholic and some Anglican churches

**²reproach** \"\ *vt* -ED/-ING/-ES [MF *reprocher*, fr. OF *reprochier*, fr. (assumed) VL *repropiare*, fr. L *re-* + LL *-propiare* (as in *appropiare* to approach) — more at APPROACH] **1** : to cast up to someone as deserving reproach : bring up as a fault or demerit : allude to as blameworthy : make a matter of reproach — usu. used with *to* or *against* ⟨his conscience ~ed him nothing —Andre Ambron⟩ ⟨the mere fact . . . should not be ~ed against them —*London Daily News*⟩ **2** : to utter a reproach to: **a** : to upbraid, censure, or tax with something blameworthy or reprehensible esp. through hurt disappointment or chagrin : rebuke strongly or sternly : SCOLD ⟨I should like to . . . ~ her for being false —George Meredith⟩ **b** : to chide gently or in a friendly spirit often in an appeal for amendment : reprove constructively and helpfully : express disappointment and disapproval to ⟨she was very glad to see me and ~ed me for giving her no notice of my coming —Jane Austen⟩ **3** : to bring into discredit : constitute a cause of reproach to ⟨you might ~ your life —Shak.⟩ **4** : to cast reproach, blame, or discredit on ⟨the triviality with which we often ~ the remarks of the chorus —Matthew Arnold⟩ **syn** see REPROVE

**re·proach·able** \-chəbəl\ *adj* [ME *reprochable*, fr. OF, fr. *reprochier* + *-able*] *archaic* : deserving reproach : CENSURABLE ⟨conduct . . . in the highest degree ~ —George Keate⟩

**re·proach·er** \-chə(r)\ *n* -S : one that reproaches

**re·proach·ful** \-chfəl\ *adj* **1** : full of reproach or reproaches : expressing censure or rebuke ⟨~ words⟩ ⟨a ~ glance⟩ **2** *archaic* : involving or incurring reproach, shame, or censure : BLAMEWORTHY, DISGRACEFUL, SHAMEFUL ⟨a most ~ death —Samuel Parker †1688⟩

**re·proach·ful·ly** \-fəlē, -li\ *adv* **1** : in a reproachful manner ⟨my hostess was annoyed . . . and looked at me ~ —Maude Hutchins⟩ **2** *obs* : in a shameful or disgraceful manner ⟨publicly and ~ executed —Edward Hyde⟩

**re·proach·ful·ness** \-fəlnəs\ *n* -ES : the quality or state of being reproachful

**re·proach·ing·ly** *adv* : REPROACHFULLY ⟨seemed to look at him ~ —Charlotte Smith⟩

**rep·ro·ba·cy** \ˈreprəbəsē\ *n* -ES [²*reprobate* + *-cy*] : the quality or state of being reprobate ⟨committed defiantly, in open ~ —J.A.Symonds⟩

**rep·ro·bance** \-bən(t)s\ *n* -S [²*reprobate* + *-ance*] *archaic* : REPROBATION ⟨fallen to ~ —A.C.Swinburne⟩

**¹rep·ro·bate** \-ˌbāt, *usu* -ād·+V\ *vt* -ED/-ING/-S [ME *reprobaten*, fr. LL *reprobatus*, past part. of *reprobare* to disapprove, condemn — more at REPROVE] **1** : to disapprove of : reject as unworthy or evil : censure strongly and forcefully : CONDEMN, DISCOUNTENANCE ⟨*reprobated* the decoration of churches with images —G.G.Coulton⟩ ⟨such sentiments . . . are now severely *reprobated* —Walter Moberly⟩ ⟨she genuinely *reprobated* . . . disorderliness —Margery Sharp⟩ **2** : to reject from Himself : foreordain to damnation : EXCLUDE — used of God **3** : to refuse to accept : REJECT ⟨every scheme . . . recommended by one of them was *reprobated* by the other —T.B.Macaulay⟩ **4** : to reject (as an instrument or deed) as not binding on account of forgery, perjury, or reliance upon incompetent evidence : take exception to : put away : DISALLOW — compare APPROBATE 1b **syn** see CRITICIZE

**²rep·ro·bate** \" *sometimes* -ˌbət *or* +V -bəd·\ *adj* [LL *reprobatus*, past part. of *reprobare*] **1** *archaic* : rejected as not enduring proof or trial : inferior in purity or fineness when compared to a standard : CONDEMNED, WORTHLESS **2 a** : condemned or rejected by God's decree : lost in sin **b** : morally abandoned : lost to all sense of religious or moral obligation : DEPRAVED, UNPRINCIPLED **3** : expressing or involving reprobation ⟨the ~ sense of a word⟩ **4** : of, relating to, or having the characteristics of a reprobate : CORRUPT ⟨~ conduct⟩

**³reprobate** \"\ *n* -S **1** : one rejected or foreordained to condemnation by God : one not of the elect : one fallen from grace : a lost soul **2 a** : a depraved, vicious, or unprincipled person : one whose character is utterly bad : SCOUNDREL **b** : one held to resemble such a scoundrel : SCAMP

**rep·ro·ba·tion** \ˌreprəˈbāshən\ *n* -S [ME *reprobacion* action of raising objections, fr. LL *reprobation-, reprobatio* rejection by God's decree, fr. *reprobatus* (past part. of *reprobare*) + L *-ion-, -io* -ion] : the act of reprobating or the state of being reprobated: as **a** : the act of raising legal exceptions or objections — compare REPROBATOR **b** : rejection by God's decree : predestination or foreordination to eternal damnation ⟨the election, ~, and fatality of Calvinism are rejected —F.S.Mead⟩ — compare ELECTION 1d, PRETERITION 4 **c** *archaic* : rejection as inferior or spurious : condemnation as worthless ⟨a brand of ~ on clipped poetry and false coin —John Dryden⟩ **d** : severe disapproval : CENSURE, REPROOF ⟨the result of this almost universal ~ . . . was his ruin —G.C.Sellery⟩ ⟨first to fix a mark of ~ upon the African slave trade —R.B.Taney⟩ ⟨the shaken head of moral ~ —S.H.Adams⟩

**rep·ro·ba·tive** \ˈreprəˌbād·iv\ *adj* [¹*reprobate* + *-ive*] : expressing or conveying reprobation ⟨employed language more stern and ~ —Isaac Taylor⟩ ⟨the curious ~ force . . . acquired by the term —R.M.Weaver⟩

**rep·ro·ba·tor** \-ād·ə(r)\ *n* [¹*reprobate* + *-or*] : a onetime proceeding in Scots law to disqualify or reject a witness

**rep·ro·ba·to·ry** \ˈreprəbəˌtōrē\ *adj* [¹*reprobate* + *-ory*] : REPROBATIVE ⟨wagged a ~ head —Marguerite Steen⟩

**re·processed** \(ˈ)rē+\ *adj* [*re-* + *processed* (past part. of *process*)] *of wool fibers* : obtained from finished but unused wool products (as mill ends and clippings from wholesale clothing manufacture) and remade into merchandise — compare REUSED

**re·pro·duce** \ˌrēprəˈd(y)üs *sometimes* ˌrep-\ *vb* [*re-* + *produce*] *vt* : to produce again: as **a** : to produce again by generation : cause the existence of (something of the same class, kind, or nature as another thing) ⟨~ a rose⟩ ⟨an animal which can ~ a lost part⟩ **b** : to cause to exist again or anew ⟨~ water from steam⟩ **c** : to cause to be or seem to be repeated : bring about again : REPEAT ⟨actors *reproduced* the sound of running horses by pounding . . . pillows —*Amer. Guide Series: N.Y.*⟩ **d** : to bring forward, present, or exhibit again ⟨letter from which I ~ a few characteristic passages —Havelock Ellis⟩ ⟨~ a play⟩ **e** : to make an image, copy, or other representation of : copy by a different process or method than that orig. employed : PORTRAY ⟨~ a face on canvas⟩ ⟨~ an oil painting by color lithography⟩ **f** : to cause to exist in the mind or imagination : create again mentally : represent clearly to the mind **g** : to revive mentally : have a mental image of : RECITE, REMEMBER **h** : to translate (a recording) into sound or into an electrical voltage ~ *vi* **1** : to turn out in a specified way in reproduction ⟨the original will ~ clearly in a . . . photocopy —*Dun's Rev.*⟩ **2** : to reproduce its kind : produce offspring : multiply by generation ⟨the young couples did not ~ freely —Willa Cather⟩

**re·pro·duc·er** \-sə(r)\ *n* : one that reproduces: as **a** : a device (as a record player, magnetic-recorder playback, or a photoelectric amplifier for cinema sound tracks) for utilizing recordings to produce an electrical voltage that may be amplified and usu. reproduced as sound ⟨disc ~⟩ ⟨film ~⟩ ⟨tape ~⟩ **b** : a device in a manograph for reproducing the engine stroke on a reduced scale

**re·pro·duc·ibil·i·ty** \ˌ==ˌd(y)üsəˈbiləd·ē, -lətē, -i\ *n* -ES : capability of being reproduced ⟨a product giving excellent ~ on the spectrograph —*Economic Geology*⟩ ⟨~ of results in successive tests —F.A.Geldard⟩

**re·pro·duc·ible** \ˌ==ˈd(y)üsəbəl\ *adj* : capable of being reproduced : permitting reproduction ⟨astonishingly ~ results can be obtained —S.E.Luria⟩

**reproducing characteristic** *n* : a relation between system amplification change and frequency in tape, disc, or film record reproduction necessary to compensate for record and recording characteristics

**reproducing head** *n* : a device for utilizing a tape or disc recording to produce an electrical voltage that is usu. amplified and used to produce sound

**reproducing tube** *or* **reproduction tube** *n* : the cathode ray tube in which the image is reproduced in television

**re·pro·duc·tion** \ˌ==ˈdəkshən\ *n* -S [fr. *reproduce*, after E *produce: production*] **1** : the act or process of reproducing: as **a** : the act of forming, creating, or bringing into existence again ⟨the squire interposed his authority towards the ~ of peace —T.L.Peacock⟩ ⟨~ of capital⟩ ⟨sound ~⟩ **b** : REGENERATION **c** : the process by which plants and animals give rise to offspring that fundamentally consists of the segregation of a portion of the parental body and its subsequent growth and differentiation into a new individual, that in its simpler forms is asexual or vegetative and involves the multiplication of a single parent by building, fission, or the formation of specialized bodies (as tubers, corms, or gemmules) any of which normally grows and differentiates into a new living unit genetically identical with the parent, that may also be sexual involving union of gametes of two parents in fertilization to form a new individual combining genetic characters from each parent although in various modifications offspring may be produced by a single parent in an essentially sexual manner, and that among the higher plants and in many invertebrate animals is characterized by sexual generations alternating with asexual in a characteristic pattern so that long-continued vegetative reproduction without genetic recombination is the exception rather than the rule — compare CLONE, HERMAPHRODITE, PARTHENOGENESIS **d** : a revival of what has been previously learned or experienced : RECALL **e** : the process of producing a representation in another form or medium (as a copy or likeness) **2** : something reproduced: as **a** : a representation in another form or medium ⟨printed ~s of the great masters⟩ : COPY, LIKENESS, COUNTERPART, RECONSTRUCTION ⟨to make a ~ of the Elizabethan theater⟩ **b** : an exact copy : REPLICA **c** : an imprint, impression, engraving, etching, woodcut, cast, or statuette of a work of art subject to copyright after being published if embracing artistic elements apart from the original **d** : young seedling trees in a forest ⟨fires . . . killed all small ~ and larger trees —*Ecology*⟩ **3** : the capacity of plants and animals to give rise to offspring

**reproduction cost** *n* : PHYSICAL VALUE

**reproduction factor** *or* **reproduction constant** *n* : MULTIPLICATION FACTOR

**re·pro·duc·tion·ist** \ˌ==ˈdəksh(ə)nəst\ *n* : one who makes reproductions or copies

1**re·pro·duc·tive** \ˌ==ˈdəktiv, -tēv *also* -təv\ *adj* [fr. *reproduce*, after E *produce: productive*] : of, relating to, or capable of reproduction : tending to reproduce : resembling, employed in, or effecting reproduction ⟨~ organs⟩ ⟨~ industries⟩ ⟨records and other ~ devices⟩ — compare VEGETATIVE — **re·pro·duc·tive·ness** *n* -ES

2**reproductive** \"\ *n* **1** : an individual engaging in reproduction : an actual or potential parent **2** : a member of the termite caste that subserves the reproductive function of the colony — compare SOLDIER, WORKER

**reproductive imagination** *n* : IMAGINATION 1

**re·pro·duc·tive·ly** \-təvlē, -li\ *adv* : in respect to reproduction : in reproductive terms ⟨amphibians . . . were still ~ bound to the water —Weston La Barre⟩

**reproductive potential** *n* : the relative capacity of a species to reproduce itself under optimum conditions

**re·pro·duc·tiv·i·ty** \ˌ==ˌdəkˈtivəd·ē, -vətē, -i\ *n* [ISV 1*reproductive* + *-ity*] : the state of or capacity for being reproductive

**repromission** *n* -S [ME, fr. L *repromission-, repromissio*, fr. *repromissus* (past part. of *repromittere* to promise in return, fr. *re-* + *promittere* to promise) + *-ion-, -io* -ion — more at PROMISE] *obs* : a promise made in return

**re·proof** \rəˈprüf, rēˈp-\ *n* [ME *reprof, repref, reprove, repreve*, fr. MF *reprove, repreuve*, fr. OF, fr. *reprover* to reprove] **1** : censure for a fault : an expression of censure or blame : REBUKE, REPRIMAND ⟨the latter action is almost like a ~ to the players —Warwick Braithwaite⟩ ⟨pained by the severity of his father's ~ —Jane Austen⟩ ⟨highly sensitive . . . and cannot bear ~ —Robert Littell⟩ **2** *archaic* : DISPROOF, REFUTATION ⟨in . . . . ~ and conviction of Roman errors —Jeremy Taylor⟩

**re·pro proof** \ˈrē(ˌ)prō\ *or* **repro** *or* **reproduction proof** *n* -S [*repro* short for *reproduction*] : a clean sharp proof made esp. from a letterpress printing surface to serve as photographic copy for a printing plate (as for letterpress, offset, or gravure)

**reprovable** *adj* [ME, fr. MF *reprouvable*, fr. *reprouver, reprover* to reprove + *-able*] *obs* : deserving reproof or censure : BLAMEWORTHY, REPREHENSIBLE

**re·prove** \rəˈprüv, rēˈp-\ *vb* [ME *reproven, repreven*, fr. MF *reprouver, reprover* (3d pers. sing. pres. indic. *repreuve*), fr. OF, fr. LL *reprobare* to disapprove, condemn, fr. L *re-* + *probare* to test, prove — more at PROVE] *vt* **1** : to chide as blameworthy : administer a rebuke to : call attention to remissness in often in a kindly or gentle way : seek to correct esp. by mild rebuke, suasion, or implication ⟨embarrassed to hear the children *reproved* in this way —Victoria Sackville-West⟩ **2** : to express disapproval of (as conduct, actions, or beliefs) : indicate disapprobation of esp. by contrast or implication : CENSURE, CONDEMN ⟨it is not for me to ~ popular taste —D.W.Brogan⟩ **3** *obs* : to prove (as an idea or statement) to be false or erroneous : DISPROVE, REFUTE ⟨~ my allegation, if you can —Shak.⟩ **4** *obs* : CONVINCE, CONVICT ⟨will ~ the world of sin and of righteousness —Jn 16:8 (AV)⟩ ~ *vi* : to express rebuke or reproof ⟨came . . . to ~ and exhort —Mary E. Braddon⟩

**syn** REBUKE, REPRIMAND, REPROACH, CHIDE, ADMONISH: REPROVE indicates an expression of disapproval made without harshness and with mild and kindly urging of betterment ⟨a light to guide, a rod to check the erring, and *reprove* —William Wordsworth⟩ REBUKE indicates a sharper and more severe expression of disapproval, designed to rebuff and check shortly or sharply ⟨must *rebuke* this drunkenness of triumph —P.B.Shelley⟩ REPRIMAND may indicate a severe, formal or official rebuke ⟨in *reprimanding* an officer —T.B.Macaulay⟩ REPROACH indicates upbraiding faultfinding often arising from vexed disappointment of hopes or expectations ⟨bitterly *reproach* him in your own heart and seriously think that he has behaved very badly to you —Oscar Wilde⟩ CHIDE is likely to indicate mild pointing out of errors, esp. venial ones, and lightly scolding for them ⟨there stood he *chiding* dilatory grooms —Robert Browning⟩ ADMONISH indicates earnest sympathetic or friendly warning, counsel, or exhortation; the notion of reproving for a fault is not stressed ⟨wife who "told a lie, not a pernicious lie, but unadvisedly" was simply *admonished* —Agnes Repplier⟩ ⟨softly *admonished* the child⟩

**re·prov·er** \-və(r)\ *n* -S [ME *reprovere*, fr. *reproven* to reprove + *-ere* -er] : one that reproves

**re·prov·ing·ly** *adv* : in a reproving manner ⟨looks at me ~ —Willa Cather⟩

**reps** *pl of* REP

**rept** *abbr* **1** receipt **2** report

1**rep·tant** \ˈreptənt\ *adj* [L *reptant-, reptans*, pres. part. of *reptare* to creep, fr. *reptus*, past part. of *repere* to creep] : REPENT

2**reptant** \"\ *n* -S [NL *Reptantia*] : a member of the Reptantia

**rep·tan·tia** \repˈtanch(ē)ə, -ntēə\ *n pl, cap* [NL, fr. L, neut. pl. of *reptant-, reptans*, pres. part. of *reptare* to creep] : a suborder of decapod crustaceans comprising lobsters, crabs, hermit crabs, and related forms and having no stylocerite, the abdomen well developed to greatly reduced and frequently depressed but never laterally compressed, the rostrum reduced or absent and usu. depressed if present, and the second antennal scale reduced or absent

**rep·ta·to·ri·al** \ˌreptəˈtōrēəl\ *or* **rep·ta·to·ry** \ˈ==ˌtōrē\ *adj* [*reptatorial* fr. *reptatory* + *-al; reptatory* prob. fr. (assumed) NL *reptatorius*, fr. L *reptatus* (past part. of *reptare* to creep) + *-orius* -ory] : REPTANT

**reptd** *abbr* **1** reported **2** reprinted

1**rep·tile** \ˈrept^əl, -ˌtīl\ *n* -S [ME *reptil*, fr. MF or LL; MF *reptile* (fem.), irreg. fr. LL *reptile* (neut.), fr. neut. of *reptilis*, adj., reptant, fr. L *reptus* (past part. of *repere* to creep) + *-ilis* -ile; akin to OHG *reba* tendril, Lith *rėplioti* to creep] **1** : an animal that crawls or moves (as a snake) on its belly or (as a lizard) on small short legs **2 a** : a vertebrate of the order Reptilia **b** : AMPHIBIAN 1b — not used technically **3** : one held to resemble a reptile : a person having a low, groveling, mean, repulsive, or despicable character

2**reptile** \"\ *adj* [LL *reptilis*] **1** : moving on the belly or on small and short legs : CREEPING, REPTANT **2** : having characteristics associated with a reptile : GROVELING, DESPICABLE, LOW, MALIGNANT, MEAN ⟨a false ~ prudence, the result not of caution but of fear —Edmund Burke⟩ ⟨~ press⟩ **3** : of, of the nature of, or relating to a reptile, reptiles, or the Reptilia

**rep·tile·like** \-t^əl,(l)īk\ *adj* : resembling a reptile

**rep·til·ia** \repˈtilēə, -lyə\ *n pl, cap* [NL, fr. LL, pl. of *reptile*] : a class of Vertebrata comprising air-breathing animals that have lungs but never gills, usu. a three-chambered heart, two aortic arches from which the systemic arteries arise, a bony skeleton in which the skull articulates with the vertebral column by a single occipital condyle, the vertebrae gastrocentral, and the compound mandible articulate with the skull through a quadrate bone, that lack hair or feathers and have the skin more or less covered with horny epidermal plates or scales and relatively free from glands, that are known since the Carboniferous and as the dominant form of life in the Mesozoic, and that are represented in the recent fauna by the snakes and lizards, the turtles, the loricates, and the aberrant tuatara — see COTYLOSAURIA, LORICATA, MESOSAURIA, PELYCOSAURIA, PTEROSAURIA, RHYNCHOCEPHALIA, SQUAMATA, TESTUDINATA, THERAPSIDA

1**rep·til·ian** \(ˈ)repˈtilēən, -lyən\ *adj* [NL *Reptilia* + E *-an*, adj. suffix] **1 a** : resembling or having the characteristics of the Reptilia or a reptile ⟨his light green ~ eye —Jean Stafford⟩ **b** : held to resemble a reptile in nature or character : MEAN ⟨a ~ villain —Theodore Dreiser⟩ **2** : of or relating to the Reptilia or a reptile ⟨a ~ skull⟩

2**reptilian** \"\ *n* -S [NL *Reptilia* + E *-an*, n. suffix] : one of the Reptilia : REPTILE 2

**reptilian age** *n* : the Mesozoic era during which reptiles were the dominant form of life

**rep·ti·loid** \ˈreptəˌlȯid\ *adj* [1*reptile* + *-oid*] : resembling a reptile

1**re·pub·lic** \rəˈpəblik, rēˈp-, -lēk\ *n* -S [F *république*, fr. MF *republique*, fr. L *respublica, res publica*, fr. *res* thing, fact, matter + *publica*, fem. of *publicus* public — more at REAL, PUBLIC] **1** *obs* : COMMONWEAL, STATE **2 a** (1) : a government characterized by having a chief of state who is not a monarch and who in modern times is usu. a president (2) : a political unit (as a nation or state) having such a form of government ⟨the ~ of England, Scotland, and Ireland under Oliver Cromwell —E.E.Reynolds⟩ ⟨the ~s of South America have been the happy hunting ground of dictators —L.A.Mills⟩ ⟨the ancient Roman ~⟩ **b** (1) : a government in which supreme power resides in a body of citizens entitled to vote and is exercised by elected officers and representatives responsible to them and governing according to law : REPRESENTATIVE DEMOCRACY (2) : a political unit (as a nation or state) having such a form of government ⟨pledge allegiance to the flag of the United States of America and to the ~ for which it stands —Francis Bellamy⟩ ⟨the German people . . . by creating a federal ~ resting upon a democratic constitution —*U.S.Code*⟩ **c** : a usu. specified republican government of a political unit ⟨France's ~s are numbered . . . consecutively —*Times Lit. Supp.*⟩ ⟨the Fourth *Republic*⟩ **3 a** : a community of beings that resembles in organization a political republic and is usu. characterized by a general equality among members ⟨a curious ~ of industrious hornets —M.G.J.deCrèvecoeur⟩ **b** : a body of persons freely engaged in a specified activity ⟨the ~ of art⟩ ⟨the ~ of letters⟩ **4** : an organization modeled after a junior republic ⟨establish a boys' ~ in this state —*Springfield* (*Mass.*) *Daily News*⟩ **5** : a constituent political and territorial unit of the U.S.S.R. and Yugoslavia ⟨our visits to four of the ~s of Yugoslavia —G.E.Shipler⟩ ⟨the Ukraine and the other ~s within the U.S.S.R. —Bogdan Raditsa⟩

2**republic** *also* **republical** *adj* [*republic* fr. 1*republic; republical* fr. 1*republic* + *-al*] *obs* : REPUBLICAN 1 ⟨the ~ cities . . . of Greece —Roger Boyle⟩ ⟨devoted to the . . . *republical* party —Edward Hyde⟩

1**re·pub·li·can** \rəˈpəbləkən, rēˈp-, -lēk-\ *adj* [modif. (influenced by E *-an*, adj. suffix) of F *républicain*, fr. MF *republicain*, fr. *republique*] **1 a** : of, relating to, or having the characteristics of a republic : having the form or based on the principles of a republic ⟨the United States shall guarantee to every state in this union a ~ form of government —*U.S.Constitution*⟩ ⟨the success of ~ institutions in So. American countries —John Dewey⟩ **b** : favoring, supporting, or advocating a republic ⟨so little ~ and so much aristocratic sentiment —Philip Marsh⟩ ⟨a ~ party⟩ **c** : held to belong to or be appropriate for one living in or supporting a republic ⟨our ~ and artistic simplicity —Nathaniel Hawthorne⟩ ⟨a ~ indifference to the majesty of office —H.S.G.Saunders⟩ **2** *usu cap* **a** : of, relating to, or constituting the Democratic-Republican party **b** : of, relating to, or constituting one of the two major political parties in the U.S. evolving in the mid-19th century from the Whigs, Free-Soilers, and Democrats primarily for the purpose of opposing the extension of slavery and becoming usu. associated with business, financial, and some agricultural interests and with favoring a restricted governmental role in social and economic life — compare DEMOCRATIC 2, LIBERAL REPUBLICAN, NATIONAL REPUBLICAN **3** : living, nesting, or breeding in large flocks or communities

2**republican** \"\ *n* -S **1** : one that favors or supports a republican form of government **2** *usu cap* **a** : a member of a political party advocating republicanism **b** : a member of the Democratic-Republican party **c** : a member of the Republican party of the U.S.

**re·pub·li·can·ism** \-kəˌnizəm\ *n* -S [1*republican* + *-ism*] **1** : adherence to or sympathy for a republican form of government : republican practices or spirit : attachment to republican principles or institutions ⟨~, driven underground by the era of reaction, was kept alive —*Times Lit. Supp.*⟩ ⟨such popular democratic sentiment came forth as ~ —Alfredo Mendizábal Villalbo⟩ **2** : a republican form of government : the principles or theory of republican government ⟨maintenance of ~ in Latin America —Alexander Marchant⟩ ⟨~ in the seventeenth century was . . . an aristocratic doctrine —G.H.Sabine⟩ **3** *usu cap* **a** : the principles, policy, or practices of the Republican party of the U.S. ⟨the leading theorist of modern *Republicanism* —Stewart Alsop⟩ **b** : the Republican party or its members ⟨a rousing battle between midwest *Republicanism* and Democratic liberalism —*N.Y.Times*⟩

**re·pub·li·can·ize** \-ˌnīz\ *vt* -ED/-ING/-S [F *républicaniser*, fr. *républicain* republican + *-iser* -ize] **1** : to make republican in character, form, or principle : change (as a state) into a republic ⟨the first public measure which tended . . . to ~ France —William Taylor †1836⟩ **2** : to alter or reorganize on republican principles ⟨took France at least thirty years . . . to ~ its civil service —Arnold Brecht⟩

**republican marriage** *n, usu cap R* [trans. of F *mariage républicain*] : a method of execution practiced during the French Revolution consisting of binding a man and woman together and throwing them into the water — compare NOYADE

**republican pawnee** *n, usu cap R&P* : KITKEHAHKI

**republican swallow** *n* : CLIFF SWALLOW

**re·publication** \(ˌ)rē+\ *n* [*re-* + *publication*] **1** : the act or action of republishing or the state of being republished : a new or second publication (as of a will, code, religion, literary work, or law) ⟨two novels . . . that highly deserve ~ —*N.Y. Herald Tribune Bk. Rev.*⟩ ⟨~ of a former will revokes one of a later date —William Blackstone⟩ **2** : something (as a book) that has been republished : a fresh publication (as of a literary work)

**republic day** *n, usu cap R&D* : a day established as a holiday in various countries to commemorate the foundation of a republic

**re·publish** \(ˈ)rē+\ *vt* [*re-* + *publish*] : to publish again or anew: as **a** : to publish a reprint of (as a book or statement) **b** : to execute (a will) anew ⟨subsequent to the purchase . . . the devisor ~*ed* his will —William Blackstone⟩

**re·publisher** \"+\ *n* : one that republishes

**re·pub·lo·crat** *also* **re·pub·li·crat** \rəˈpəbləˌkrat, -rēˈp-\ *n* -S *usu cap* [*republocrat* fr. 2*republican* + *democrat*; *republicrat* blend of 2*republican* and *democrat*] : a member of the Democratic party esp. in the southern states who supports to a large extent the policy and measures of the Republican party ⟨if the Democratic convention appeases the Southern *Republocrats* —Bruce Bliven b.1889⟩ — compare DIXIECRAT

1**re·pu·di·ate** \rəˈpyüdēˌāt, rēˈp-, *usu* -ād·+V\ *vt* -ED/-ING/-S [L *repudiatus*, past part. of *repudiare* to cast off, reject, divorce, fr. *repudium* casting off, divorce, fr. *re-* + *-pudium* (perh. akin to L *pudēre* to be ashamed) — more at PUDIC] **1** : to divorce, put away, or discard (a wife) : separate formally from (a woman to whom one is betrothed or married) **2** : to cast off : refuse to have anything to do with : DISOWN, RENOUNCE **3 a** : to refuse to accept as having rightful authority or obligation : reject as unauthorized or as having no binding force ⟨~ a contract⟩ ⟨~ a will⟩ **b** : to refuse approval or belief to : reject as untrue or unjust ⟨~ a charge⟩ **4** : to refuse to acknowledge or to pay ⟨~ a debt⟩ **syn** see DECLINE, DISCLAIM

2**repudiate** *adj* [L *repudiatus*, past part. of *repudiare*] *obs* : REPUDIATED : DIVORCED

**re·pu·di·a·tion** \=ˌ==ˈāshən\ *n* -S [L *repudiation-, repudiatio*, fr. *repudiatus* (past part. of *repudiare*) + *-ion-, -io* -ion] : the action of repudiating or the state of being repudiated: as **a** : divorce or legal separation from a woman **b** : the action of refusing to be bound by the terms of a contract (as in refusing to acknowledge or pay a debt); *specif* : such an action on the part of public authorities against whom no claim can be enforced ⟨~ of the state debt⟩ ⟨~ is bad for credit —Stringfellow Barr⟩ **c** : the action in canon law of refusing a benefice **d** : the act or action of rejecting or refusing to accept something ⟨resulted in the magistrate's ~ by both parties —*Current Biog.*⟩ ⟨the ~ of a great tradition —J.L.Lowes⟩ ⟨expressed his ~ of this counsel —G.B.Shaw⟩

**re·pu·di·a·tion·ist** \-sh(ə)nəst\ *n* -S : one that favors repudiation esp. of a public debt

**re·pu·di·a·tor** \=ˈ==ˌād·ə(r), -ˌātə-\ *n* -S [LL, fr. L *repudiatus* (past part. of *repudiare*) + *-or*] : one that repudiates or advocates repudiation (as of a public debt)

**re·pugn** \rəˈpyün, rēˈp-\ *vb* -ED/-ING/-S [ME *repugnen*, fr. MF & L; MF *repugner*, fr. L *repugnare*] *vi, archaic* : to make resistance : offer opposition, objection, or resistance : fight against someone : strive against something : OBJECT, OPPOSE, RESIST ~ *vt* **1** *obs* : to be contrary to, inconsistent with, or opposed to **2** : to contend against : OPPOSE, REFUTE, REJECT, REPEL ⟨stubbornly he did ~ the truth —Shak.⟩

**re·pug·nance** \rəˈpəgnən(t)s, rēˈp-\ *n* -S [ME *repugnaunce*, fr. MF *repugnance*, fr. L *repugnantia*] **1 a** : the quality or fact of being opposed and esp. reciprocally opposed : contradictory opposition or disagreement (as of ideas, opinions, or statements) : INCOMPATIBILITY, INCONGRUITY, INCONSISTENCY ⟨no inconsistency or natural ~ between this poetical and religious faith in the same mind —William Hazlitt⟩ **b** : an instance of such contradiction or inconsistency ⟨preparing the draft . . . seeing that it is free from errors or ~s —James Bryce⟩ **2** : deep-rooted antagonism : settled aversion : strong dislike, distaste, or antipathy ⟨the ~ which vulgarity inspires —Albert Dasnoy⟩ ⟨her instinctive dignity and ~ to any show of emotion —George Eliot⟩ ⟨her ~ toward the political philosophy of the Fascist states —Maurice Halperin⟩

**re·pug·nan·cy** \-gnənsē, -si\ *n* -ES [L *repugnantia*, fr. *repugnant-, repugnans* (pres. part. of *repugnare*) + *-ia* -y] **1** : REPUGNANCE 1 ⟨local legislation is void for ~ to the terms of the mandate —Martin Wight⟩; *specif* : a contradiction or inconsistency between sections of a legal instrument ⟨risks of ~ being discovered between the text . . . and the explanatory matter —T.E.May⟩ **2 a** : opposition or resistance (as of feeling) usu. based upon aversion or antipathy **b** : REPUGNANCE 2

**re·pug·nant** \-gnənt\ *adj* [ME *repugnaunt*, fr. MF *repugnant*, fr. L *repugnant-, repugnans*, pres. part. of *repugnare* to resist, fr. *re-* + *pugnare* to fight — more at PUGNACIOUS] **1** : characterized by opposition and esp. contradictory opposition : INCOMPATIBLE, INCONSISTENT, OPPOSED ⟨where there are ~ provisions in a statute the one last in order shall . . . govern —Roscoe Pound⟩ ⟨the statute . . . is ~ to the Constitution —C.P.Curtis⟩ ⟨such procedure was ~ to fair employment practices —Dwight Macdonald⟩ **2** *archaic* : disposed to fight against something : making or offering resistance : HOSTILE ⟨tempering the ~ mass —P.B.Shelley⟩ **3** : distasteful to a high degree : exciting distaste or aversion : LOATHSOME, OBJECTIONABLE, REPULSIVE ⟨unclean and ~ food —Willa Cather⟩ ⟨one custom ~ to nature —G.G.Coulton⟩ ⟨found the idea thoroughly ~ to him⟩ **syn** see HATEFUL, OFFENSIVE

**repugnant condition** *n* : a condition given no effect because inconsistent with and contrary to the quality and nature of an estate previously granted or an obligation already imposed in a deed : an insensible condition

**re·pug·nant·ly** *adv* : in a repugnant manner

**re·pug·na·to·ri·al** \rəˌpəgnəˈtōrēəl, rēˌp-\ *adj* [L *repugnatorius* repugnatorial (fr. *repugnatus* — past part. of *repugnare* — + *-orius* -ory) + E *-al*] : serving to repel enemies ⟨the ~ pores of millipedes⟩

**repugnatorial gland** *n* : a gland of some insects that by emitting an offensive secretion or vapor serves to repel enemies — called also DEFENSIVE GLAND

**re·pullulate** \(ˈ)rē+\ *vi* -ED/-ING/-S [L *repullulatus*, past part. of *repullulare*, fr. *re-* + *pullulare* to sprout — more at PULLULATE] *archaic* : to bud or sprout again ⟨whose branches . . . are withered, never to ~ again —Eliza Nathan⟩

**re·pullulation** \(ˌ)rē+\ *n, archaic* : the action of budding or sprouting again : the state of having budded or sprouted again ⟨the ~ of the pure love —Henry More⟩

**re·pulp** \(ˈ)rē +\ *vt* [*re-* + *pulp*] : to pulp again

1**re·pulse** \rəˈpəls, rēˈp- *also* -lts\ *vt* -ED/-ING/-S [L *repulsus*, past part. of *repellere* to repel — more at REPEL] **1** : to drive or beat back (as an assault or an enemy) : repel usu. by force of arms ⟨police charging the plant gates were *repulsed* at every attempt —*Amer. Guide Series: Mich.*⟩ ⟨*repulsed* an Indian attack here —*Amer. Guide Series: Tenn.*⟩ **2** : to repel by discourtesy, coldness, or denial : REBUFF, REFUSE, REJECT ⟨*repulsed* every attempt . . . at conversation —Jane Austen⟩ ⟨she had learned to . . . ~ advances that were disagreeable —Ellen Glasgow⟩ ⟨repudiate and ~ any suggestion that we are making a questionable compromise —Sir Winston Churchill⟩ **3** : to cause a feeling of repulsion in : DISGUST ⟨*repulsed* by the sight of . . . green flies feeding upon the putrefying flesh of a crocodile —Bernice Matlowsky⟩ ⟨*repulsed* by his own weakness —Carson McCullers⟩

2**repulse** \"\ *n* -S [in sense 1, fr. L *repulsa*, fr. fem. of *repulsus*, past part. of *repellere*; in other senses, fr. L *repulsus* action of driving back, fr. *repulsus*, past part. of *repellere*] **1** : refusal of a request or suit : DENIAL, REBUFF, REJECTION ⟨court ~ from her husband —Thomas Hardy⟩ ⟨reap nothing but ~ and hate —John Milton⟩ **2** : the action of repelling (as an assailant or a hostile force) or the fact of being repelled in hostile encounter **3** *archaic* : the action of forcing or driving back : the state of being forcing or driven back — opposed to *impulse* ⟨what a most powerful suction that ~ will create —George Semple⟩

**re·pul·sion** \rəˈpəlshən, rēˈp-\ *n* -S [MF, fr. ML *repulsion-, repulsio*, fr. LL, refutation, fr. L *repulsus* (past part. of *repellere*) + *-ion-, -io* -ion] **1** : the action of repulsing or the state of being repulsed : the action of driving off, back, or away : the state of being driven off, back, or away ⟨the ~ of the Spanish army —Alexander Ranken⟩ ⟨magnetic attraction and ~⟩ **2** : a force (as between like electric charges, like magnetic poles, or antiparallel electric currents) tending to produce separation **3** : a feeling of aversion : strong dislike : REPUGNANCE ⟨towards whom . . . she felt strong physical ~ —T.S.Eliot⟩ ⟨voice tinged with fastidious ~ —Agatha Christie⟩ **4** : the tendency of particular genetic characters to be inherited separately presumably because of linkage of dominant genes that control expression of one character and recessive genes of another — compare COUPLING

**repulsion-induction motor** *n* : an alternating current motor with both a commutated and squirrel-cage rotor winding

**repulsion motor** *n* : an alternating current motor with a stator winding and a rotor winding with the latter short-circuited by a commutator and jumper

**re·pul·sive** \rəˈpəlsiv, rēˈp-, -sēv *also* -səv\ *adj* **1** : tending to repel or reject (as by denial or coldness of manner) : having or motivated by an intention to reject (as advances) : COLD, FORBIDDING ⟨his reserve may be a little ~ —Jane Austen⟩ ⟨her manner became daily colder and more ~ —Emily Eden⟩ **2** : serving to repulse : able to repel : characterized by repulsion ⟨~ of his might the weapon stood —Alexander Pope⟩ ⟨two bodies endowed with a ~ power —Tobias Smollett⟩ ⟨~ force⟩ **3** : repellent to the mind : arousing aversion or disgust : DISGUSTING ⟨contracted a ~ disease —V.G.Heiser⟩ ⟨the most ~ character in recent novels —John Farrelly⟩ ⟨the idea . . . was utterly ~ to her —J.C.Powys⟩ **syn** see OFFENSIVE

**re·pul·sive·ly** *adv* : in a repulsive or repelling manner

**re·pul·sive·ness** *n* -ES : the quality or state of being repulsive ⟨the moral ~ of the race theory —A.J.Toynbee⟩

**rep unit** *var of* REP

1**re·purchase** \(ˈ)rē+\ *vt* [*re-* + *purchase*] : to buy back or again : regain by purchase : REDEEM ⟨~ the family estate —*Quarterly Rev.*⟩

2**repurchase** \"\ *n* : the action of repurchasing ⟨an option of ~⟩

**repurchase agreement** *n* **1** : a contract giving the seller the right to repurchase property sold on specified terms; *specif* : one giving a dealer the right to repurchase government securities sold to Federal Reserve banks **2 :** a contract that requires a dealer to buy back a durable good (as an automobile) on which payments have been defaulted to the finance company

**repure** *vt* [*re-* + *pure*] *obs* **:** to make pure again ⟨nor state nor honor can ~ dishonored sheets —William Barksted⟩

**rep·u·ta·bil·i·ty** \ˌrepyəd·ə'biləd·ē, -pyətə-, -lətē, -i, *chiefly in substand speech* -pə-\ *n* **:** the quality or state of being reputable ⟨conspicuous consumption . . . is a means of ~ to the gentleman of leisure —Thorstein Veblen⟩

**rep·u·ta·ble** \'⸗⸗⸗ˌbəl\ *adj* [1*repute* + *-able*] **1 :** enjoying good repute **:** of excellent reputation **:** held in esteem **:** ESTIMABLE, RESPECTABLE ⟨quite a ~ scientist in his day —Benjamin Farrington⟩ ⟨the most ~ newspaper of a hundred years ago —H.L.Smith b.1906⟩ ⟨~ conduct⟩ **2 :** employed widely or sanctioned by good writers ⟨~ use is the use of no single writer —Barrett Wendell⟩ ⟨not . . . ~ speech at all but jargon —A.T.Quiller-Couch⟩

**rep·u·ta·bly** \-blē,-bli\ *adv* **:** in a reputable manner

**rep·u·ta·tion** \ˌrepyə'tāshən, *chiefly in substand speech* -pə-\ *n* -S [ME *reputacioun*, fr. L *reputation-*, *reputatio* consideration, fr. *reputatus* (past part. of *reputare*) + *-ion-*, *-io* -ion] **1 :** the fact of being highly esteemed **:** the condition of being regarded as worthy or meritorious **:** public esteem either attained or in the process of attainment **:** good name **:** high regard **:** CELEBRITY, DISTINCTION, NOTE ⟨native artists . . . made their ~*s* abroad —*Amer. Guide Series: Mich.*⟩ ⟨a younger illustrator who is gaining a ~ —*Amer. Guide Series: Ark.*⟩ ⟨a man of ~⟩ **2 :** the estimation in which one is generally held **:** the character commonly imputed to one as distinct from real or inherent character ⟨a task of some difficulty to disentangle him from his ~ —T.S.Eliot⟩ ⟨cases which hold that evidence about the ~ of the accused is inadmissable —F.W.Lacey⟩ ⟨a good ~⟩ **3 a :** the honor or credit belonging to one **:** one's good name **:** one's place in public esteem or regard ⟨save the ~*s* of several ladies —Mary W. Montagu⟩ **b :** a particular good name ⟨laughs at the ~*s* she has torn —William Cowper⟩ **4 :** a particular character in popular estimation or ascription — used with *of* ⟨had the ~ of being a hard worker⟩ **syn** see FAME

**re·pu·ta·tive** \rə̇'pyüd·əd·iv, rē'p-\ *adj* [1*repute* + *-ative*] *archaic* **:** PUTATIVE

**re·pu·ta·tive·ly** \-ə̇vlē\ *adv*, *archaic* **:** by repute **:** PUTATIVELY ⟨have this . . . ~ by divine appointment —Cotton Mather⟩

**1re·pute** \rə̇'pyüt, rē'p-, *usu* -üd·+V\ *vb* -ED/-ING/-S [ME *reputen*, fr. MF *reputer*, fr. L *reputare* to compute, think over, fr. *re-* + *putare* to consider, think — more at PAVE] *vt* **:** to hold in thought **:** ACCOUNT, ESTEEM, THINK ⟨Negroes were *reputed* the good workers —Oscar Handlin⟩ ⟨men and women who are *reputed* moral —Samuel Butler †1902⟩ ⟨she is *reputed* to make nocturnal visits to the guest room —*Amer. Guide Series: La.*⟩ **~** *vi*, *obs* **:** to hold an appraising opinion; *esp* **:** to hold a high opinion ⟨you should ~ highly . . . of your own endowments —Ben Jonson⟩

**2repute** \"\ *n* -S **1** *obs* **:** OPINION, ESTIMATION, JUDGMENT ⟨their judgment and ~ of thee is true —William Tomlinson⟩ **2 :** the character or status commonly ascribed to one **:** the popular opinion of one **:** reputation of a specified kind ⟨a large farmer of good ~ —Thomas Hardy⟩ ⟨the popular ~ of . . . later empresses —John Buchan⟩ ⟨a work held in high ~⟩ **3** *obs* **:** POSITION, RANK, STATUS ⟨these cardinals have the ~ of princes —James Howell⟩ **4 :** the state of being widely and favorably known, spoken of, or esteemed **:** DISTINCTION, HONOR ⟨the gentleman was of ~ in Paris —Charles Dickens⟩ ⟨only a general of ~ could get recruits —John Buchan⟩ ⟨won him a deserved ~ —Irving Kolodin⟩ **5** *obs* **:** the reputation of having or being something ⟨who had then the ~ of an honest man —Donald Mackay⟩ **6 :** the reputation of a particular person or thing ⟨jeopardizing the company's ~⟩ ⟨threats to the ~ of an honest man⟩ **syn** see FAME

**reputed** *adj* **1 :** held in repute and esp. high repute **:** having a good repute **:** held in estimation **:** REPUTABLE 1 ⟨a member of a ~ legal firm —Edith Wharton⟩ ⟨selected from ~ vineyards —*Farmer's Weekly* (*So. Africa*)⟩ **2 :** according to reputation or popular belief **:** supposed, thought, or reckoned to be the thing specified **:** generally accepted **:** PUTATIVE ⟨the ~ father of the child⟩ — compare REPUTED MANOR

**re·put·ed·ly** *adv* **:** by repute **:** in common estimation **:** according to reputation or general belief ⟨fishes with ~ poisonous flesh —R.E.Coker⟩ ⟨small, conservative, and ~ aristocratic town —Helen Martin⟩

**reputed manor** *n* **:** a manor that has lost its manorial status by the lack of some necessary adjunct (as the absence of a court baron)

**reputed quart** *n*, *Brit* **:** an amount about equal to a quart **:** ⅙ gallon

**re·pute·less** \-ütlə̇s\ *adj*, *obs* **:** devoid of good repute **:** INGLORIOUS ⟨left me in ~ banishment —Shak.⟩

**req** *abbr* **1** request **2** require; required **3** requisition

**reqmt** *abbr* requirement

**re·queen** \(')rē+\ *vt* [*re-* + *queen*] **:** to replace an old queen of (a hive of bees) with a young one of the same season's raising

**1re·quest** \rə̇'kwest, rē'k-\ *n* -S [ME *requeste*, fr. MF, fr. OF, fr. (assumed) VL *requaesita*, fr. fem. of (assumed) VL *requaesitus*, past part. of (assumed) VL *requaerere* to need, seek for, inquire after — more at REQUIRE] **1 :** the act of asking for something (as an object, a favor, or some action desired) **:** an expression of a desire or wish **:** ENTREATY, PETITION ⟨I will marry her, sir, at your ~ —Shak.⟩ ⟨let me renew my ~ that you would repeat the tale —Benjamin Jowett⟩ **2 a :** an instance of asking for something **:** an expressed desire ⟨~*s* for murals . . . are more numerous —*Amer. Guide Series: Minn.*⟩ ⟨staff personnel answer individual ~*s* for specific information —*U.S. Atomic Energy Commission*⟩ **b :** a document or other writing embodying such an expressed desire **:** PETITION ⟨first⸗class mail bearing the sender's return ~ —*U.S. Post Office Manual*⟩ **3 :** the thing that is asked for **:** the matter or subject of the asking ⟨his own bank has refused him . . . because his ~ exceeds its legal limit —*Nation's Business*⟩ ⟨turned down the growers' ~ for a . . . council —*Farmer's Weekly* (*So. Africa*)⟩ ⟨granted a ~⟩ **4 :** the condition or fact of being requested ⟨the pamphlet . . . is available on ~ —*Official Register of Harvard Univ.*⟩ ⟨tickets will be available only upon ~⟩ **5 :** the state of being asked for or held in such estimation as to be sought after **:** DEMAND ⟨his scientific knowledge . . . brought him otherwise into moderate ~ —Charles Dickens⟩ ⟨much in ~ as an after-dinner speaker⟩ ⟨a book in great ~⟩ — **by request** *or* **at request** *adv* **:** in compliance with or in response to a request ⟨the bills were introduced *by request*⟩

**2request** \"\ *vt* -ED/-ING/-S [MF *requester*, fr. OF, fr. *requeste*, n.] **1 a :** to ask (as a person or an organization) to do something ⟨the essay I am ~*ed* to write —Ellen Glasgow⟩ ⟨I ~ you to give my poor host freedom —Shak.⟩ ⟨~*ed* the Parliament to act —*Current Biog.*⟩ **b :** to ask (as a person or an organization) for something ⟨~ the board for an opinion⟩ **2 :** to ask for permission or opportunity (to do something) **:** express a wish or desire (to do something) ⟨he . . . ~*s* to be excused from the ungrateful task —G.S.Faber⟩ ⟨we had ~*ed* to sleep in the straw-loft —G.J.Cayley⟩ **3** *obs* **:** to ask (a person) to come or go to something or someplace ⟨I was ~*ed* to supper last night —Ben Jonson⟩ **4 :** to ask for ⟨~*ed* a brief delay —Vera M. Dean⟩ ⟨officials ~*ed* the area for Indian families —*Amer. Guide Series: Minn.*⟩ ⟨~*ed* that seven physicians withdraw from the . . . organization —*Current Biog.*⟩ **syn** see ASK

**re·quest·er** \-tə(r)\ *n* -S **:** one that requests something

**request note** *n* **:** a legal request directed to an English revenue officer for permission to remove goods subject to excise

**1requi·em** \'rekwēəm *also* 'rāk- *or* 'rēk- *sometimes* -ēˌem\ *n* -S [ME, fr. L *requiem* (first word of the introit of the requiem mass), accus. of *requies* rest, fr. *re-* + *quies* rest, quiet — more at WHILE] **1** *or* **requiem mass** *sometimes cap R* **:** a mass for the repose of one or more departed souls commonly sung at funerals and on All Souls' Day **2** *obs* **:** an invitation to rest or repose **3 a :** a dirge or other solemn chant for the repose of the dead **b :** something resembling or held to resemble such a dirge or chant ⟨the book, then, is a ~ . . . for the old life of laissez-faire —Albert Hubbell⟩ **4** *archaic* **:** a state or time of repose **:** PEACE, QUIET, REST ⟨in his presence alone is to be found the ~ of their troubled souls —George Walker⟩ **5** *usu cap* **a** (1) **:** a musical setting of the mass for the dead including the Requiem, Kyrie, several stanzas of the hymn Dies Irae, the Domine Jesu Christe, Sanctus, Benedictus, Agnus Dei, and the Lux Aeterna (2) **:** a piece of like character on other words from Scripture or elsewhere **b :** a grand musical service or hymn in honor of the dead

**2requiem** \"\ *or* **requiem shark** *n* -S [obs. F *requiem*, alter. (influenced by F *requiem* requiem mass, fr. L) of F *requin*] **:** REQUIN

**re·qui·es·cat** \ˌrekwē'eˌskät, -kat\ *n* -S [L, may he (or she) rest, 3d pers. sing. pres. subj. of *requiescere* to rest, fr. *re-* + *quiescere* to be quiet, fr. *quies* rest, quiet] **:** a prayer for the repose of a dead person

**req·ui·es·cence** \ˌrekwē'esᵊn(t)s\ *n* -S [L *requiescere* + E *-ence*] **:** REPOSE ⟨retire to silence and ~ —N.W.Wraxall⟩

**re·quin** \rə'kan\ *also* **requin shark** *n* -S [F *requin*] **:** a voracious shark of the family Carcharhinidae (as a cub shark or sometimes the man-eater)

**re·quir·able** \rə̇'kwīrəbəl, rē'k-\ *adj* **:** capable of being required **:** REQUISITE

**1re·quire** \-ī(ə)r, -īə\ *vb* -ED/-ING/-S [ME *requeren*, *requiren*, fr. MF *requerre* (3d pers. sing. pres. indic. *requiert*), fr. (assumed) VL *requaerere* to need, seek for, inquire after, alter. (influenced by L *quaerere* to seek, ask) of L *requirere*, fr. *re-* = *-quirere* (fr. *quaerere*)] *vt* **1** *obs* **:** to ask, request, or desire (a person) to do something ⟨in humblest manner I ~ your Highness that it shall please you to declare —Shak.⟩ ⟨when he was *required*, he . . . put forth his tongue —2 Mach 7:10 (NCE)⟩ **2 a :** to ask for authoritatively or imperatively **:** claim by right and authority **:** insist upon usu. with certainty or urgency **:** DEMAND, EXACT ⟨this night your soul is *required* of you —Lk 12:20 (RSV)⟩ ⟨informed . . . that his lord *required* to speak with him —Sir Walter Scott⟩ **b** *archaic* **:** to ask for as a favor **:** REQUEST ⟨they go commission'd to ~ a peace —John Dryden⟩ **3 a :** to call for as suitable or appropriate in a particular case **:** need for some end or purpose ⟨contributions to American art ~ more detailed treatment —*Amer. Guide Series: Minn.*⟩ **b :** to demand as necessary or essential (as on general principles or in order to comply with or satisfy some regulation) **:** make indispensable ⟨the inference . . . is not absolutely *required* by the facts —Edward Sapir⟩ ⟨no religious test shall ever be *required* as a qualification —*U.S. Constitution*⟩ **c :** to demand as a necessary help or aid **:** need as an essential **:** stand in urgent need of **:** NEED, WANT ⟨growing children ~ more food⟩ **4** *archaic* **:** to search for as needed or wanted **:** seek after ⟨the brave chiefs . . . wandering o'er the camp, *required* their lord —Alexander Pope⟩ **5 :** to impose a compulsion or command upon (as a person) to do something **:** demand of (one) that something be done or some action taken **:** enjoin, command, or authoritatively insist (that someone do something) ⟨a farmer will be *required* to comply with all acreage allotments —*Nation's Business*⟩ **6 :** to feel or be under the necessity of (doing or being something specified) — used with a following infinitive ⟨one does not ~ to be a specialist —Elizabeth Bowen⟩ ⟨a candidate ~*s* to hold a . . . certificate —*Achievement in the Gold Coast*⟩ **~** *vi* **1** *archaic* **:** to make request or demand **:** ASK ⟨they must . . . ~ of Heaven with upward eyes for all that they desire —John Keats⟩ **2** *archaic* **:** to be necessary or requisite **syn** see DEMAND, LACK

**2require** \"\ *n* -S *archaic* **:** REQUIREMENT

**re·quire·ment** \-ī(ə)rmənt, -īəm-\ *n* -S **:** something required: **a :** something that is wanted or needed **:** NECESSITY ⟨production was not sufficient to satisfy both civilian and governmental ~*s* for automobiles⟩ ⟨permit agriculturalists to buy their ~*s* upon favorable conditions —*Nineteenth Century*⟩ **b :** something called for or demanded **:** a requisite or essential condition **:** a required quality, course, or kind of training ⟨two ~*s* are necessary . . . for a material to rate as an insulation —P.D.Close⟩ ⟨compel the school board to revoke the oath ~ —David Clinton⟩ ⟨the doctoral student must satisfy the language ~ —H.R.Bowen⟩ ⟨fulfill the ~*s* for college entrance⟩

**re·quir·er** \-īrə(r)\ *n* -S *archaic* **:** one that requires ⟨Christ . . . a ~ of mercy —E.B.Pusey⟩

**1req·ui·site** \'rekwəzə̇t, *usu* -ə̇d·+V\ *adj* [ME, fr. L *requisitus*, past part. of *requirere* to need, seek for, inquire after] **:** required by the nature of things or by circumstances or by the end in view **:** ESSENTIAL, INDISPENSABLE, NECESSARY ⟨the ~ quorum of forty members was not present —R.L.Schuyler⟩ ⟨food ~ for the journey —P.A.Rollins⟩ ⟨lacked the skill ~ for delicate execution —H.O.Taylor⟩ **syn** see NEEDFUL

**2requisite** \"\ *n* -S **:** something that is required or necessary **:** an indispensable or essential thing or quality ⟨neither of these ~*s* for an heuristic work . . . is fulfilled —L.C.Feldstein⟩ ⟨intellectual freedom . . . is the prime ~ for a free people —*Science*⟩ ⟨the first ~ in the storyteller's art is to tell a story —W.S.Maugham⟩

**req·ui·site·ness** *n* -ES **:** the quality or state of being requisite **:** NECESSITY ⟨proof of the ~ of attending to the customs of the East —Thomas Harmer⟩

**1req·ui·si·tion** \ˌrekwə'zishən\ *n* -S [MF or ML; MF, fr. ML *requisition-*, *requisitio*, fr. L, examination, fr. *requisitus* (past part. of *requirere*) + *-ion-*, *-io* -ion] **1 a** *archaic* **:** the act of requesting or requiring **b** *archaic* **:** a request or demand made by a person **c :** a necessary condition **:** REQUIREMENT ⟨~*s* of a position⟩ ⟨~ of a science⟩ **2 a :** the act of formally requiring or calling upon someone to perform some action **b :** a formal demand in civil and Scots law for the performance of an obligation; *esp* **:** one made through a notary **c :** a formal demand made by one international jurisdiction (as a nation) upon another for the surrender or extradition of a fugitive from justice ⟨the prisoner . . . had been arrested in England on the ~ of the Swiss Government —*In Re Castioni*⟩ — compare EXTRADITION **3 a :** the act of requiring something to be furnished **b :** a demand or application made usu. with authority: as (1) **:** a demand made by military authorities upon civilians (as the people of an invaded country) for supplies, labor, shelter, or other military needs — compare CONTRIBUTION 1 (2) **:** a written request for something (as materials, supplies, or personnel) authorized but not made available automatically ⟨sent a ~ to the purchasing department⟩ ⟨a ~ for clothing⟩ **4 :** the state of being demanded or called for **:** the condition of being put into service or use — used with *in* or *into* ⟨every sort of vehicle is put in ~ —Tyrone Power †1841⟩ ⟨the hangman . . . was in constant ~ —Charles Dickens⟩

**2requisition** \"\ *vt* **requisitioned; requisitioned; requisitioning** \-sh(ə)niŋ\ **requisitions :** to make a requisition for **:** demand or call for with authority **:** require to be furnished ⟨officers have been authorized . . . to ~ billeting facilities —H.S.Truman⟩ ⟨during the war most of the hotels were ~*ed* —S.P.B.Mais⟩ ⟨~ equipment from the supply officer⟩

**req·ui·si·tion·ist** \-sh(ə)nə̇st\ *also* **req·ui·si·tion·er** \-nə(r)\ *n* -S [*requisitionist* fr. 1*requisition* + *-ist*; *requisitioner* fr. 2*requisition* + *-er*] **:** one that makes or signs a requisition

**re·quis·i·to·ri·al** \rə̇ˌkwizəˈtōrēəl, rēˌk-\ *adj* [1*requisitory* + *-al*] **:** making requisition **:** expressing a request **:** REQUISITORY ⟨letters ~ came into use —Manfred Nathan⟩

**1re·quis·i·to·ry** \⸗'⸗⸗ˌtōrē\ *adj* [ME *requisitorie*, fr. ML *requisitorius*, fr. L *requisitus* (past part. of *requirere* to need, seek for, inquire after) + *-orius* -ory — more at REQUIRE] **:** containing or constituting a requisition **:** making a requisition ⟨a ~ letter⟩

**2requisitory** \"\ *n* -ES [modif. (influenced by 1*requisitory*) of F *réquisitoire*, fr. MF *requisitoire*, fr. *requisitoire*, adj., requisitory, fr. ML *requisitorius*] **:** the formal demand made in French law by the public prosecutor for the punishment of an accused person on the charges stated

**re·quit·al** \rə̇'kwīd·ᵊl, rē'k-, -ītᵊl\ *n* -S **1 :** the act or action of requiting or the state of being requited **:** return or repayment for something (as a service, an injury) ⟨to receive benefits as long as there is hope of ~ —Thomas Hobbes⟩ ⟨in ~ of those well-intended offices —Samuel Johnson⟩ ⟨the distribution of good rather than . . . the ~ of evil —Lucius Garvin⟩ **2 :** something that requites **:** something given in return, compensation, or retaliation ⟨an ungrateful ~ of the unquestioned services of the company —H.H.Wilson⟩

**re·quite** \-īt, *usu* -īd·+V\ *vt* -ED/-ING/-S [*re-* + obs. E *quite* to set free, discharge, repay, fr. ME *quiten* — more at QUIT] **1 a :** to make return for (as a kindness, service, benefit) **:** REPAY, REWARD ⟨cards left without a visit are *requited* by cards similarly left —Agnes M. Miall⟩ ⟨whose patronage is happily *requited* with . . . ritual slaughter —John Marks⟩ **b :** to make retaliation for (as a wrong or an injury) **:** AVENGE ⟨thought . . . incumbent on a man to ~ injuries —Henry Sidgwick⟩ **2** *archaic* **:** to give, pay, or do in return **:** make return of ⟨~ like for like —J.C.Geikie⟩ **3 :** to make return to (as a person, a community) for a benefit or service ⟨you will ~ me . . . by the sight of your ardor for what is noble —A.T. Quiller-Couch⟩ or for an injury ⟨~ a traitor with death⟩ **4** *obs* **:** to take the place of **:** compensate or make up for ⟨deserves that short delight, the nauseous qualms of . . . travel to ~ —John Dryden⟩ **syn** see RECIPROCATE

**re·quit·er** \rə̇'kwīd·ə(r), -ītə-\ *n* -S **:** one that requites something ⟨ungrateful ~ of the kindness of such friends —*American*⟩

**re·radiate** \(')rē+\ *vt* [*re-* + *radiate*] **:** to radiate again or anew

**re·radiation** \(ˌ)rē+\ *n* [*re-* + *radiation*] **:** radiation again or anew; *specif* **:** radiation emitted by a body or system as a result of its absorbing radiation incident on it ⟨the intensity of the sun's radiation . . . not dissipated by ~ —*Experiment Station Record*⟩

**re·rail** \(')rē+\ *vt* [*re-* + *-rail* (as in *derail*)] **:** to replace (as a railway engine) on the rails

**re·rail·er** \(')rēˌrālə(r)\ *n* -S **:** a device for putting derailed cars or locomotives back on the rails

**1rerd** *or* **rerde** \'re(ə)rd\ *n* -S [ME, fr. OE *reord* voice, speech; akin to OHG *rarta* modulation, ON *rödd* voice, Goth *razda* tongue, speech, Skt *rasati* he roars, yells] *dial* **:** a noisy cry **:** DIN, CLAMOR, ROAR

**2rerd** \"\ *vi* -ED/-ING/-S [ME *rerden* to roar, speak, fr. OE *reordian* to speak, fr. *reord*, n.] *dial* **:** to make a noise **:** cry out **:** ROAR

**rere-** *comb form* [ME, fr. MF *rere*, *riere* backward, behind, fr. L *retro* — more at RETRO-] **:** subsequent **:** rear ⟨*rere*-banquet⟩

**rere-account** \'ri(ə)r+⸗ˌ⸗\ *n* [ME *rereaccompt*, fr. *rere-* + *acount*, *accompt* account] *archaic* **:** a subsequent or later accounting

**re·read** \(')rē+\ *vt* [*re-* + *read*] **:** to read again or anew

**rere-arch** *var of* REAR ARCH

**rere-banquet** *n*, *obs* **:** a repast taken after the noon or evening meal

**rere·brace** \'ri(ə)rˌbrās\ *n* [ME, fr. *rere-* + *brace* armor esp. for the arm — more at BRACE] **:** plate armor for the upper part of the arm

**re·record** \ˌrē+\ *vt* [*re-* + *record*] **:** to record again or anew; *specif* **:** to transfer (sound records) electrically from one or more films, magnetic recordings, or discs to other films, tapes, or discs

**rere-dorter** \'ri(ə)r+ˌ-\ *n* [ME *rere-dortour*, fr. *rere-* + *dorter*, *dortour* dorter] **:** a latrine situated at the rear of a medieval convent or monastery

**rere·dos** \'rerəˌdäs *also* 'rirəˌd- *sometimes* 'ri(ə)rˌd- *or* 'riəˌd-\ *n* -ES [ME, modif. of AF *areredos*, fr. MF *arere*, *arrere* behind, backward + *dos* back, fr. L *dorsum* — more at ARREAR] **1 a :** a screen or partition wall usu. ornamental and of wood or stone located behind an altar ⟨a high altar with a vast late Gothic ~ —Nikolaus Pevsner⟩ **b :** CHOIR SCREEN **2** *obs* **:** a wall drapery back of an altar **3 :** the back of a fireplace or in some ancient halls of an open hearth immediately under the louver in the center of the hall **4 :** BRAZIER ⟨no suggestion of fire in the ~ —T.B.Costain⟩

**rerefief** \'ri(ə)r+ˌ-\ *n* [MF *rerefief*, *rierefief*, *rierefié*, fr. OF, fr. *rere*, *riere* backward, behind + *fief*, *fié* fief, fee — more at FEE] **:** ARRIERE FEE

**rere·mouse** \'ri(ə)r+ˌ-\ *n*, *pl* **rere·mice** [ME *reremous*, fr. OE *hrēremūs*, prob. fr. *hrēran* to move, stir + *mūs* mouse — more at CRATER, MOUSE] *archaic* **:** BAT

**rere·supper** \'ri(ə)r+ˌ-\ *n* [ME *reresoper*, fr. AF *rere super*, fr. OF *rere*, *riere* + *soper*, *super* supper] **:** a late or second supper ⟨trestles still stood from last night's ~ —T.B.Costain⟩

**rere·ward** \'ri(ə)rˌwȯrd, 'riəˌwȯ(ə)d\ *n* [ME *rerewarde*, fr. AF, fr. OF *rere* backward, behind + ONF *warde* guard; akin to OF *garde*, *guarde* guard — more at RETRO-, GUARD] *obs* **:** REAR GUARD ⟨the Lord will go before you; and the God of Israel will be your ~ —Isa 52:12 (AV)⟩

**re·roll** \(')rē+\ *vt* [*re-* + *roll*] **:** to roll again or anew

**re·roller** \"+\ *n* **:** one that rolls again or anew: as **a :** a textile worker who winds cloth from large rolls onto separate tubes **b :** a worker who repairs defective cigars

**1re·run** \(')rē+\ *vt* [*re-* + *run*] **:** to run again or anew

**2re·run** \'rē+ˌ-, ⸗'⸗\ *n* **1 :** the act or action of running something again or anew; *esp* **:** the presentation of a motion picture or television film after its first run — compare REISSUE **2 :** an instance of running something again or anew **:** a subsequent identical presentation **3 :** a film presented in a rerun

**1res** *pl of* RE

**2res** \'rās, 'rēz\ *n*, *pl* **res** \"\ [L — more at REAL] **:** THING; *usu* **:** a particular thing **:** MATTER, POINT, SUBJECT — used esp. in various chiefly legal phrases

**res** *abbr* **1** resawed **2** research **3** reserve **4** residence; residency; resident; residential **5** residue **6** resigned **7** resistance **8** resistor **9** resolution **10** resort

**RES** *abbr* reticuloendothelial system

**re·saca** \rə̇'sakə\ *n* -S [AmSp, fr. Sp *resacar* to draw back, fr. *re-* re- (fr. L) + *sacar* to draw, take out, perh. fr. L *saccus* sack — more at SACK] *Southwest* **:** the dry channel or the former often marshy course of a stream

**res·acetophenone** \(ˌ)rez+\ *n* [ISV *res*orcinol + *acetophenone*] **:** a crystalline phenolic ketone $(HO)_2C_6H_3COCH_3$ made from resorcinol, acetic acid, and zinc chloride; 2,4⸗dihydroxy-acetophenone

**res ad·ju·di·ca·ta** \'rāˌsädˌyüdə'käd·ə, ˌrēzəˌjüdə'kād·ə\ *n* [LL] **:** RES JUDICATA

**resai** *var of* REZAI

**re·sail** \(')rē+\ *vb* [*re-* + *sail*] *vt* **:** to sail (as a race or course) again **~** *vi* **:** to sail back or again ⟨planned to ~ about sundown⟩

**re·sak** \rə̇'sak\ *n* -S [fr. native name in Malaysia] **:** durable hard heavy Malaysian wood from trees of the family Dipterocarpaceae and esp. of the genus *Shorea*

**re·salable** \(')rē+\ *adj* [*re-* + *salable*] **:** fit for resale **:** that may be sold again usu. to the next link in a chain of distribution

**re·sale** \'rē+ˌ-, ⸗'⸗\ *n* [*re-* + *sale*] **1 :** the act of selling again usu. to the next link in a chain of distribution ⟨the wholesaler lives by ~ to the retailer⟩ **2 a :** a sale at second hand **b :** an additional sale to the same buyer

**resale price** *n* **1 :** a price at which an article is resold by a business concern that buys it for resale **2 a :** a price suggested (as by a producer) as proper to be charged on resale of an article usu. to the ultimate consumer **b :** a stipulated price under the various state price maintenance laws at which a branded article must be resold as agreed with the brand owner or a minimum price below which such article cannot be lawfully resold

**re·salutation** \(ˌ)rē+\ *n* [L *resalutation-*, *resalutatio*, fr. *resalutatus* (past part. of *resalutare* to greet in return) + *-ion-*, *-io* -ion] **:** the giving of a salutation in response to one given

**re·salute** \ˌrē+\ *vt* [ME *resaluten* to salute in return, fr. L *resalutare*, fr. *re-* + *salutare* to salute] **:** to salute in return or anew

**1re·saw** \(')rē+\ *vt* [*re-* + *saw*] **:** to saw over again; *specif* **:** to saw into boards or dimension lumber

**2re·saw** \'rē+ˌ-, ⸗'⸗\ *n* **:** a machine for resawing lumber — compare HEADSAW

**re·sawer** \(')rē+\ *n* [1*resaw* + *-er*] **:** RESAWYER

**re·sawyer** \"+\ *n* [fr. 1*resaw*, after E *saw*: *sawyer*] **:** one that resaws something; *esp* **:** an operator of a resaw

**re·say** \"+\ *vt* [*re-* + *say*] **1 :** to say in answer **:** REPLY **2 :** to say again **:** REPEAT

**res·azurin** \(')reˌzazhərə̇n\ *n* -S [ISV *res*orcinol + *azure* + *-in*] **:** a blue crystalline dye $C_{12}H_7NO_4$ of the phenoxazine class made by the action of nitrous acid on resorcinol and used chiefly as an oxidation-reduction indicator in the resazurin test for bacteria

**resazurin test** *n* **:** a test of the keeping quality of milk based on the speed with which a standard quantity of the dye resazurin is reduced by a sample of milk

**re·scale** \(')rē+\ *vt* [*re-* + *scale*] **:** to plan, establish, or formulate on a new and usu. smaller scale ⟨*rescaling* our living to conform to our budget⟩

**re·scind** \rə'sind, rē's-\ *vt* -ED/-ING/-S [L *rescindere* to cut loose, annul, fr. *re-* + *scindere* to cut, split — more at SCHISM] **1** : to do away with : take away : REMOVE ⟨~ this needless outlay⟩ **2 a** : to take back : ANNUL, CANCEL ⟨refused to ~ his harsh order⟩ **b** : to abrogate (a contract) by tendering back or restoring to the opposite party what one has received from him (as in cases of fraud, duress, mistake, or minority) **3** : to vacate or make void (as an act) by the enacting or a superior authority : REPEAL ⟨~ a law⟩ ⟨~ a judgment⟩ **syn** see REVOKE

**re·scind·able** \-dəbəl\ *adj* : capable of being rescinded

**re·scind·er** \-də(r)\ *n* -S : one that rescinds something

**re·scind·ment** \-in(d)mənt\ *n* -S [*rescind* + *-ment*] : an act of withdrawing : ABROGATION, ANNULMENT, CANCELLATION

**re·scis·si·ble** \-isəbəl, -izə-\ *adj* [L *rescissus* + E *-ible*] : capable of being rescinded

**re·scis·sion** \-izhən, -ish-\ *n* -S [LL *rescission-, rescissio* annulment, fr. L *rescissus* (past part. of *rescindere* to rescind) + *-ion-, -io* -ion] **1** *obs* : an act of cutting off **2** : an act of rescinding, annulling, or vacating or of cancelling or abrogating (as by restoring to another party to a contract or transaction what one has received from him)

**re·scis·so·ry** \-isərē, -izə-\ *adj* [LL *rescissorius*, fr. L *rescissus* + *-orius* -ory] : relating to, tending to, or having the effect of rescission : REVOKING ⟨a ~ action⟩

**res co·gi·tans** \(')rās'kōgə,tän(t)s, (')rēz'käjə,tanz\ *n* [NL] : a thinking thing (as the mind or soul)

**res com·mu·nes** \ˌräskə'mü,nās, ˌrēzkə'myü(ˌ)nēz\ *n pl* [LL, lit., common things] *Roman & civil law* : things owned by no one and subject to use by all : things (as light, air, the sea, running water) incapable of entire exclusive appropriation

**re·score** \(')rē+\ *vt* [*re-* + *score*] : to score again or anew; *specif* : to arrange (a musical ensemble instrumental composition) for a different combination of instruments

**res cor·po·ra·les** \ˌrā,skò(r)pə'rā,lās, 'rēz,kò(r)pə'rā(ˌ)lēz\ *n pl* [L] *Roman & civil law* : corporeal or tangible things or those perceptible to the senses

**rescounter** *n* [It *riscontro*, fr. *riscontrare* to check an account, fr. *ri-* re- (fr. L *re-*) + *scontrare* to meet, fr. L *ex-* out of + *contra* opposite, against — more at EX-, COUNTER] *obs* : settlement of accounts

**res·cous** \'reskəs\ *n* -ES [ME *rescous, rescus*, fr. MF *rescousse*, fr. OF, fr. *rescourre* to rescue — more at RESCUE] : RESCUE 2

**re·scramble** \(')rē+\ *vt* [*re-* + *scramble*] : to rearrange in a scrambled or disorderly fashion

**re·screen** \"+\ *vt* [*re-* + *screen*] : to screen anew; *esp* : to assort once more often according to more liberal specifications

**re·scribe** \"+\ *vt* -ED/-ING/-S [L *rescribere*, fr. *re-* + *scribere* to write — more at SCRIBE] **1** *obs* : to write in reply **2** : to write over again : REWRITE

**re·script** \'rē,skript\ *n* [L *rescriptum*, fr. neut. of *rescriptus*, past part. of *rescribere* to write in reply] **1 a** : a written answer of a Roman emperor or of a sovereign or a pope to an inquiry upon some matter of law or state **b** *Roman Catholicism* : an official written reply from the Holy See or an ordinary answering a private petition or a question covering a particular case **c** : a written message of the Japanese emperor carrying both temporal and religious authority and defining the position of the state **2** : an official or authoritative order, decree, or formal announcement **3 a** : an act of rewriting **b** : something that is rewritten : REWRITING

**re·scrip·tion** \rə'skripshən, rē's-\ *n* -S [MF or LL; MF fr. LL *rescription-, rescriptio*, fr. L *rescriptus* + *-ion-, -io* -ion] **1** *obs* **a** : RESCRIPT, REWRITING **b** : a reply in writing **2** : a promissory note or warrant formerly issued by a government

**re·scrip·tive** \-ptiv\ *adj* [*rescript* + *-ive*] : relating to or serving for a rescript; *also* : DECIDING, SETTLING — **re·scrip·tive·ly** \-ptəvlē\ *adv*

**res·cu·able** \'reskyəwəbəl, -(ˌ)skyüəb-\ *adj* [*rescue* + *-able*] : that may be rescued

**¹res·cue** \'re(ˌ)skyü\ *vb* **rescued; rescued; rescuing** \-ˌskyəwiŋ, -(ˌ)skyüiŋ\ **rescues** [ME *rescuen, rescowen*, fr. MF *rescourre*, fr. OF, fr. *re-* + *escourre* to shake out, wrest away, fr. L *excutere*, fr. *ex-* + *-cutere* (fr. *quatere* to shake) — more at QUASH] *vt* **1 a** : to free from confinement, violence, danger, or evil : liberate from actual restraint : SAVE, DELIVER ⟨~ a prisoner of war from the enemy⟩ ⟨*rescued* a drowning child⟩ **b** : to take forcibly from the custody of the law **2** : to recover by force: as **a** : to deliver (as a place besieged) by force of arms **b** : to effect a rescue of (a prize) **3** : to bid over a bid by (one's partner or oneself) in a card game on the assumption that the previous bid would entail a serious penalty ~ *vi* : to bring about deliverance

**syn** DELIVER, REDEEM, RANSOM, RECLAIM, SAVE : RESCUE indicates freeing from capture, assault, evil, death, or destruction by ready prompt action ⟨*rescuing* a soldier from the enemy⟩ ⟨*rescuing* the guards held as hostages⟩ ⟨the seamen *rescued* from the lost ship⟩ ⟨*rescue* his nation from defeat⟩ DELIVER signifies setting free from confinement, suffering, tribulation, embarrassment, or vexation ⟨*delivered* the prisoners from the Bastille⟩ ⟨*deliver* us from evil —Mt 6:13 (RSV)⟩ ⟨the population of Russia had only just been *delivered*, nominally at least, from serfdom —Havelock Ellis⟩ REDEEM applies to releasing from captivity, retribution, sequestration, or deterioration by some necessary expenditure ⟨let me *redeem* my brothers both from death —Shak.⟩ ⟨the labored for eighty years, *redeeming* them to Christianity from their magical and bloodthirsty practices —Norman Douglas⟩ ⟨a plot of land *redeemed* from the heath, and after long and laborious years brought into cultivation —Thomas Hardy⟩ RANSOM usu. applies specifically to buying a captive out of his captivity ⟨*ransom* a child held by kidnappers⟩ ⟨back in Quebec with a number of Iroquois captives whom he had *ransomed* —J.J. Wynne⟩ RECLAIM indicates a bringing back or returning to a former sound, good, or valuable condition of something that has undergone error, degenerating, waste, neglect, or abandonment ⟨the priest labored zealously to *reclaim* those of the redmen that had listened to Baptist teachings —Louise P. Kellogg⟩ ⟨I fear he is not to be *reclaimed*; there is scarcely a hope that anything in his character or fortunes is reparable now —Charles Dickens⟩ ⟨a large-scale program of *reclaiming* land and of bringing new land into cultivation —H.S.Truman⟩ SAVE is a general term that can be used in place of any of the preceding; it may imply a freeing from danger, evil, or trial and a maintaining or preserving for continued existence, security, use, or service ⟨*saved* a tired swimmer from drowning⟩ ⟨firemen *saving* the rear wing of the house⟩

**²rescue** \"\ *n* -S [ME *rescue, rescowe*, fr. *rescuen, rescowen* to rescue] **1** : an act of rescuing : deliverance or aid in delivering from restraint, violence, or danger ⟨three ~s to his credit⟩ ⟨come to their ~⟩ **2 a** : the forcible taking of a person or goods from the custody of the law (as in retaking or taking away against law of things lawfully distrained or in the forcible liberation of a person from an arrest or imprisonment) **b** (1) : the retaking of a prize by those captured with it resulting in the restoration of the property to the owner by the effect of the right of postliminium — compare RECAPTURE (2) : succor rendered by the arrival of outside help before the succored party is entirely overcome

**rescue breathing** *n* [²*rescue*] : MOUTH-TO-MOUTH METHOD

**rescue buoy** *n* : BREECHES BUOY

**rescued** *past of* RESCUE

**res·cue grass** \'re(ˌ)skyü- *or* **rescue brome** *n* [prob. alter. of *fescue grass*] : a tall American bromegrass (*Bromus catharticus*) that somewhat resembles chess and is cultivated for hay and forage in the southern U.S. and other mild regions

**res·cue·less** \'re(ˌ)skyüləs, -ˌskyəl-\ *adj* : lacking rescue

**rescue mission** *n* : a city mission established to help persons esp. of low income who are unable to help themselves and are in desperate need of moral and spiritual rehabilitation

**res·cu·er** \-ˌskyəwə(r), -(ˌ)skyüə(-\ *n* -S : one that rescues

**rescues** *pres 3d sing of* RESCUE, *pl of* RESCUE

**rescuing** *pres part of* RESCUE

**res do·mi·nans** \(')rās'dōmə,nän(t)s, (')rēz'dämə,nanz\ *n* [NL] : the dominant property or tenement entitled to enjoy a servitude

**¹re·seal** \(')rē+\ *vt* [*re-* + *seal*] : to seal again or anew

**²re·seal** \"\ *adj* : designed to be resealed ⟨~ jars⟩

**¹re·search** \rə'sərch, 'rē's-, 'rē,s-, -səch, -səich\ *n* [MF *recerche*, fr. *recercher* to research] **1** : careful or diligent search : a close searching ⟨~*es* after hidden treasure⟩ **2 a** : studious inquiry or examination; *esp* : critical and exhaustive investigation or experimentation having for its aim the discovery of new facts and their correct interpretation, the revision of accepted conclusions, theories, or laws in the light of newly discovered facts, or the practical applications of such new or revised conclusions, theories, or laws ⟨gave his time to ~⟩ **b** (1) : a particular investigation of such a character : a piece of research (2) : a presentation (as an article or book) incorporating the findings of a particular research **3** : capacity for or inclination to research ⟨a scholar of great ~⟩ **syn** see INQUIRY

**²research** \"\ *vb* [MF *recercher* to research, seek out, fr. OF, fr. *re-* + *cercher* to search — more at SEARCH] *vt* : to search or investigate exhaustively : make researches into ~ *vi* : to make researches or investigations

**re-search** \(')rē'sərch, -səch, -səich\ *vt* [*re-* + *search*] : to search again or anew ⟨decided to *re-search* the chest for the lost letters⟩

**researched** *adj* [fr. past part. of ²*research*] : based on thorough investigation of pertinent data ⟨a carefully ~ study⟩ ⟨a show with accurate obviously ~ costumes⟩

**re·search·er** *pronunc at* ¹RESEARCH +ə(r)\ *n* [²*research* + *-er*] : one that researches : a person who devotes himself to research

**re-search·er** *pronunc at* RE-SEARCH +ə(r)\ *n* [*re-search* + *-er*] : a worker who cleans tobacco a second time to remove dirt and stems

**re·search·ful** *pronunc at* ¹RESEARCH + fəl\ *adj* [¹*research* + *-ful*] : making researches or evincing research : SCHOLARLY

**re·search·ist** \"+əst\ *n* -S [¹*research* + *-ist*] : one engaged in research : RESEARCHER

**research professor** *n* [¹*research*] : a professor in a college or university who is free to devote his whole time to research

**re·seat** \(')rē+\ *vt* [*re-* + *seat*] **1** : to seat or set again ⟨had his valves ~*ed*⟩ **2** : to fit with a new seat ⟨the chair needs to be ~*ed*⟩ or equip with new seats ⟨~ a theater⟩

**re·seau** \rā'zō, rə'-\ *n, pl* **reseaus** \-ōz\ *or* **re·seaux** \-ō(z)\ [F *réseau*, fr. OF *resel*, dim. of *rais, rois* net, fr. L *retis, rete* — more at RETINA] : NETWORK: as **a** : a system of lines forming small squares of standard size that is photographed by a separate exposure on the same plate with star images (as to facilitate measurements or detect changes of the film) **b** : a net ground or foundation in lace **c** : a screen with minute elements of three colors in a regular geometric pattern used for taking and viewing additive color photographs **d** : a group of meteorological stations under common direction or cooperating in some common purpose

**re·secrete** \ˌrē+\ *vt* [*re-* + *secrete*] : to secrete again or anew

**re·sect** \rə'sekt, rē's-\ *vt* -ED/-ING/-S [L *resectus*, past part. of *resecare* to cut off, fr. *re-* + *secare* to cut — more at SAW] **1** *obs* : to cut or pare off, away, or out : EXCISE **2** : to perform the surgical operation of resection on

**re·sect·abil·i·ty** \ˌ=ˌsektə'bilədē\ *n* [*resectable* + *-ity*] : the condition of being resectable — compare OPERABILITY

**re·sect·able** \=ˈsektəbəl\ *adj* : capable of being resected : suitable for resection ⟨~ cancer⟩ — compare OPERABLE

**re·sec·tion** \=ˈsekshən\ *n* [L *resection-, resectio*, fr. *resectus* (past part. of *resecare* to cut off) + *-ion-, -io* -ion — more at RESECT] **1** *obs* : an act of cutting or paring off **2** : the surgical removal of part of an organ or structure ⟨gastric ~⟩ ⟨~ of the lower bowel⟩ — sometimes distinguished from *excision* **3** : a method in surveying by which one determines a position on a map after it has been properly oriented by drawing lines from two or more distant objects through their plotted positions on the map

**re·sec·tion·al** \-shənᵊl,-shnəl\ *adj* [*resection* + *-al*] : of or relating to resection

**re·sec·to·scope** \=ˈsektəˌskōp\ *n* [*resection* + *-o-* + *-scope*] : an instrument consisting of a tubular fenestrated sheath with a sliding knife within it that is used for surgery within cavities (as of the prostate through the urethra)

**re·se·da** \rə'sēdə, rē's-\ *n* [NL, fr. L, a plant used to reduce tumors] **1 a** *cap* : a genus of Old World herbs (family Resedaceae) having racemose flowers with cleft petals, numerous stamens, and an urn-shaped horned capsule opening at the summit — see DYER'S ROCKET, MIGNONETTE 1 **b** -S : any plant of the genus *Reseda* **2** *or* **reseda green** -S **a** : a variable color averaging a grayish green that is yellower and darker than average bayberry, yellower, lighter, and stronger than slate green, and yellower and slightly lighter than average blue spruce (sense 2a) — called also *mignonette* **b** : a light olive that is greener and less strong than citrine and darker than grape green **c** *of textiles* : a grayish to dark grayish green

**res·e·da·ce·ae** \ˌresə'dāsē,ē\ *n pl, cap* [NL, fr. *Reseda*, type genus + *-aceae*] : a family of mainly Mediterranean herbs (order Parietales) having alternate or fascicled leaves, glandular stipules, and racemose irregular flowers and including several that are cultivated as ornamentals — compare MIGNONETTE — **res·e·da·ceous** \ˌresə'dāshəs\ *adj*

**re·see** \(')rē+\ *vt* [*re-* + *see*] : to see again or anew

**re·seed** \"+\ *vb* [*re-* + *seed*] *vt* **1** : to sow seed on again or anew ⟨had to ~ the lower land⟩ **2** : to maintain (itself) by self-sown seed ⟨some plants will ~ themselves indefinitely⟩ ~ *vi* : to maintain itself by self-sown seed

**re·seize** \"+\ *vt* [MF *resaisir*, fr. OF, fr. *re-* + *saisir* to seize — more at SEIZE] **1** *or* **re·seise** \"+\ : to put into possession or seizin again : reinvest with seisin — used with *of, in*, and sometimes *with* **2** : to seize again or anew

**¹re·seiz·er** *or* **re·seis·er** \(')rē'sēzə(r)\ *n* -S [*reseize* + *-er* (as in *cesser*)] : resumption of possession by a feudal lord after a tenant's default

**²reseizer** \"\ *n* [*reseize* + *-er*, agent suffix] : one that seizes again

**re·seizure** \(')rē+\ *n* [*re-* + *seizure*] : the action or an act of reseizing

**re·select** \ˌrē+\ *vt* [*re-* + *select*] : to select again or anew; *esp* : to select among (the progeny of a selected breeding population) for individuals exhibiting to best advantage a desired quality

**re·sell** \(')rē+\ *vb* [*re-* + *sell*] : to sell again

**re·sem·blance** \rə'zembləns(t)s, rē'z-\ *n* -S [ME, fr. AF, fr. OF *resembler* to resemble + *-ance*] **1** *obs* **a** : a thing or person resembling or suggesting another **b** : SYMBOL **c** : SIMILE, COMPARISON **2** : the quality or state of resembling : LIKENESS, SIMILITUDE, SIMILARITY; *also* : a point of likeness ⟨there is no ~ between the two⟩ ⟨family ~⟩ **3** : REPRESENTATION, IMAGE **4** *archaic* : characteristic appearance of nature : outward aspect or manifestation : SEMBLANCE **5** *obs* **a** : DEMONSTRATION **b** : PROBABILITY

**re·sem·blant** \-nt\ *adj* [ME, fr. MF, pres. part. of *resembler* to resemble] **1** : manifesting or characterized by resemblance **2** : dealing with resemblances or representations of things

**re·sem·ble** \rə'zembəl, rē'z-\ *vb* **resembled; resembled; resembling** \-b(ə)liŋ\ **resembles** [ME *resemblen*, fr. MF *resembler*, fr. OF, fr. *re-* + *sembler* to be like, seem, fr. L *similare, simulare* to copy, imitate, fr. *similis* like, resembling — more at SIMILAR] *vt* **1** : to be like or similar to : bear the similitude of in appearance or qualities ⟨these brothers ~ each other⟩ **2** *archaic* : to represent as like : LIKEN, COMPARE **3** *obs* : to make a likeness or image of : REPRESENT, PORTRAY, DEPICT; *also* : SYMBOLIZE **4** : to cause to be like : make like ~ *vi* **1** *obs* : to seem in outward show : APPEAR **2** : to have a resemblance : bear a likeness **3** : to be alike : resemble each other

**re·sem·bler** \-b(ə)lə(r)\ *n* -S : one that resembles

**resemblingly** *adv* [*resembling* (fr. pres. part. of *resemble*) + *-ly*] *obs* : in a resembling manner : so as to resemble

**re·seminate** \(')rē+\ *vt* [L *reseminatus*, past part. of *reseminare* to sow again, fr. *re-* + *seminare* to sow, fr. *semin-, semen* seed — more at SEMEN] : to produce again by or as if by means of seed

**re·send** \(')rē+\ *vt* [*re-* + *send*] **1 a** : to send again or anew **b** : to send back **2** : to send on (a telegraphic message) by means of a repeater

**res·ene** \'re,zēn\ *n* -S [ISV *resin* + *-ene*] : any of various mixtures of neutral alkali-resistant compounds that are found in rosin and other natural resins and that contain carbon, hydrogen, and oxygen — not used systematically

**re·sensitize** \(')rē+\ *vt* [*re-* + *sensitize*] : to render sensitive (as to light, an allergen) again or anew

**re·sent** \rə'zent, rē'z-\ *vt* -ED/-ING/-S [F *ressentir*, fr. OF *resentir, ressentir*, fr. *re-* + *sentir* to feel, fr. L *sentire* — more at SENSE] **1** *obs* : to be sensible of: as **a** : to receive with satisfaction, appreciation, pleasure, or similar response; *also* : to remember gratefully **b** : to feel (oneself) affected by sorrow, pain, or distress **c** : to take (something) well or ill **2** : to feel, express, or exhibit indignant displeasure at ⟨~ undue familiarity⟩ **3** *archaic* : to have the quality of : SUGGEST

**re·sent·ful** \-ntfəl\ *adj* **1** : full of resentment or inclined to resent **2** : caused or marked by resentment — **re·sent·ful·ly** \-fəlē, -li\ *adv* — **re·sent·ful·ness** *n* -ES

**resentiment** *n* -S [MF — more at RESENTMENT] *obs* : RESENTMENT

**re·sent·ing·ly** *adv* [*resenting* (fr. pres. part. of *resent*) + *-ly*] : in a resenting manner : with resentment

**resentive** *adj* [*resent* + *-ive*] *obs* : that resents or tends to resent

**re·sent·ment** \rə'zentmənt, rē'z-\ *n* -S [F *ressentiment, ressentiment*, fr. MF, fr. *resentir, ressentir* to resent (fr. OF) + *-ment*] **1** : a feeling of indignant displeasure because of something regarded as a wrong, insult, or other injury : UMBRAGE **2 a** *obs* : a state of feeling an emotion or sentiment or a sensation (as of smell); *sometimes* : a keenly felt emotion : a sharp sense, perception, or realization **b** *archaic* : a specific emotion or expression of an emotion (as appreciation, interest, good will) **syn** see OFFENSE

**re·se·quent** \(')rē'sēkwənt, 'rēsək-\ *adj* [*re-* + *-sequent* (as in *consequent, subsequent*)] **1** : of, relating to, or being a stream that flows down the dip of underlying formations in the same direction as an original consequent stream but developed later and generally tributary to a subsequent stream **2** : of, relating to, or being a fault-line scarp that faces in the same direction as an initial fault scarp but is due to differential erosion rather than to crustal movement

**reserate** *vt* -ED/-ING/-S [L *reseratus*, past part. of *reserare* to unlock, unbar, fr. *re-* + *sera* bar, bolt] *obs* : UNLOCK, OPEN

**re·ser·pic acid** \rə'sərpik-, rē'-, -'zə-\ *n* [ISV *reserpine* + *-ic*] : a pentacyclic acid $C_{21}H_{27}N_2O_3COOH$ obtained by hydrolysis of reserpine and derived from both harmine and isoquinoline

**reser·pine** \rə'sərpən, rē'-, -'zər-, -ˌpēn; 'resər,pēn, 'rezə-\ *n* -S [G *reserpin*, fr. *reserp-* (prob. irreg. fr. NL *Rauwolfia serpentina*, fr. *Rauwolfia* + *serpentina*, fr. LL, fem. of *serpentinus* serpentine) + G *-in* -ine] : a crystalline pentacyclic sedative hypotensive alkaloid $C_{33}H_{40}N_2O_9$ that is extracted esp. from the root of shrubs of the genus *Rauwolfia* (as *R. serpentina*) and is used in the treatment of hypertension and various mental diseases and tension states

**re·serv·able** \rə'zərvəbəl, rē'z-, -zɔv-,-zəiv-\ *adj* : that may be reserved

**res·er·va·tion** \R ˌrezər'vāshən *or sometimes* -zə'v- *by r-dissimilation*, -R -zə'v-\ *n* -S [ME *reservacioun*, fr. MF *reservation*, fr. *reserver* to reserve + *-ation*] **1** : an act of reserving something (as for a particular use or the use of a particular person or group) ⟨~ of rights by the states⟩: as **a** *Christian relig* (1) : retention of tithes (2) : retention of the right of nomination to a vacant benefice (3) : retention of the power of absolution in particular cases (4) : retention of a portion of the eucharistic elements for adoration by those worshiping at the church or for the administration of communion to the sick **b** (1) : the act or fact of a grantor's reserving some new thing out of the thing granted and not in esse as such before; *also* : the right or interest so reserved or the clause by which it is reserved — distinguished from *exception* (2) : EXCEPTION 4b, PROVISO **c** (1) *obs* : a keeping concealed of something pertinent : a holding back (2) : the setting of limiting conditions or withholding from complete exposition ⟨answered without ~⟩ **d** : an engaging in advance of some accommodation or service ⟨the ~ of a hotel room⟩; *also* : a promise, guarantee, or record of such engagement ⟨it is advisable to telegraph for ~*s*⟩ **2** : something that is reserved: as **a** (1) : a limiting condition : LIMITATION ⟨agreed with several ~*s* to their plan⟩ (2) *obs* : something kept hidden : a deceptively expressed statement (as an answer) **b** (1) : a tract of public land set aside for a particular purpose (as schools, forest, or the use of Indians) (2) : an area in which hunting is not permitted; *esp* : one set aside as a secure breeding place for game birds or mammals **syn** see CONDITION — **off the reservation** : free from the usual restraints and controls

**res·er·va·tion·ist** \-sh(ə)nəst\ *n* -S [*reservation* + *-ist*] : one who has or makes reservations

**re·serv·ato·ry** \rə'zərvə,tōrē\ *n* -ES [ML *reservatorium*, fr. L *reservatus* (past part. of *reservare* to reserve) + *-orium* -ory] *archaic* : a place (as a cupboard or reservoir) in which things are kept

**¹re·serve** \rə'zərv, rē'z-, -zɔv,-zəiv\ *vb* [ME *reserven*, fr. MF *reserver*, fr. L *reservare* to keep back, save up, fr. *re-* + *servare* to save, protect, keep — more at CONSERVE] *vt* **1 a** : to keep in store for future or special use : hold or keep in reserve **b** (1) : to retain power of absolution of to oneself — used of a religious superior (as the pope, a bishop) (2) : to set apart (a case) for such action on the part of a superior (3) : to retain or set aside (a portion of the consecrated elements) at the time of a celebration of the Eucharist for future use (as for communion of the sick) **c** : to keep back : retain or hold over to a future time or place : fail to deliver, make over, or disclose at once : defer the discussion or determination of **d** : to make legal reservation of : withhold from the operation of a grant, agreement, or release **2 a** : to keep or leave safe, sound, or intact : SPARE, SAVE **b** *obs* : to keep unaltered or free from decay **c** : to continue to have or show **d** : to retain particular areas (as in porcelain) in the same color as the original surface **3 a** : to set aside or apart — usu. used with *for* or *to* ⟨*reserved*, and destined to eternal woe —John Milton⟩ **b** : to have set aside (as for one's use) ⟨~ seats at the opera⟩ **4** *archaic* : to make an exception of or in favor of : EXCEPT **5** *obs* : to keep from being known to others ~ *vi, obs* : to continue to be (as in existence or a specified condition) : REMAIN **syn** see KEEP

**²reserve** \"\ *n* -S [F *réserve*, fr. MF, fr. *reserver* to reserve] **1** : something that is reserved : something kept back or held available (as for future use) : STORE, STOCK **2** : something reserved or set aside for a particular purpose, use, or reason (as a tree in a part of a wood that is to be felled or a part of a lode): as **a** (1) : a military force intended to be withheld temporarily from action for use by a commander when he desires to commit it to influence decisively the course of an engagement — usu. used in pl.; compare SUPPORT (2) : forces not in the field for any reason but available (3) : the military forces of a country not part of the regular services or in the U.S. of the National Guard; *also* : a member of these forces : RESERVIST **b** : a tract (as of public land) set apart for a particular purpose : RESERVATION ⟨forest ~s⟩ **c** : a distinction in an exhibition that indicates that the recipient will get a prize if another should be disqualified **d** : an area left the natural color of the background or original surface color **3** : an act of reserving : EXCEPTION, RESTRICTION, QUALIFICATION — usu. used with reference to adherence to a principle, belief, or standard ⟨a mental ~⟩ **4 a** : self-restraint, closeness, or caution in one's words and bearing toward others : self-control in expression (as of one's thoughts, feelings, plans) : lack of effusiveness or sometimes of cordiality **b** : forbearance from making a full explanation, complete disclosure, or free expression of one's mind (as in casuistry or religious instruction) : intentional withholding or suppression of truth when it is regarded as inconvenient to disclose it (as from people who are regarded as unable to understand it or receive it with benefit) **5** *archaic* : a case of withholding information or knowledge; *also* : a piece of information not fully disclosed : SECRET **6** : money or its equivalent kept in hand or set apart usu. to meet a specified liability or anticipated liabilities: as **a** (1) : uninvested cash kept on hand by a bank (2) : such cash together with deposits in a central depository (as a Federal Reserve bank or the Bank of England) — see LEGAL RESERVE **b** (1) : the portion of an insurance company's assets set aside for some special purpose as evidenced by showing the reserve as a liability on the books (2) : the amount of funds or assets calculated on net premiums to be necessary for a life insurance company to have at any given time to enable it with interest and premiums paid as they shall accrue to meet all claims on the insurance then in force as they would mature according to the particular mortality table accepted **:** the theoretical difference between the present value of the total insurance and the present value of the future premiums on the insurance constituting the amount for which another insurance company could afford to take over the insurance and often regarded as a reinsurance fund — called also *reinsurance reserve;* see CATASTROPHE RESERVE, INITIAL RESERVE, INSURANCE RESERVE, INVESTMENT RESERVE, LEGAL RESERVE, LOSS RESERVE, MEAN RESERVE, TERMINAL RESERVE, UNEARNED PREMIUM RESERVE **c :** RESERVE ACCOUNT **d** (1) **:** the portion of the earnings of a corporation set aside for a specific purpose such as to meet future losses or contingent liabilities — compare SURPLUS (2) **:** a deduction from the book value of an asset to bring its valuation into line with current market conditions or possible future losses ⟨a ~ against losses on bank loans⟩ ⟨a ~ for depreciation of securities of an investment company⟩ — called also *valuation reserve* **e :** the liquid resources (as gold and foreign exchanges) of a nation for meeting international payments **7 a :** RESIST 2a **b :** the capacity of a solution to neutralize alkali or acid when its reaction is shifted from one hydrogen-ion concentration to another; *esp* **:** the capacity of blood or bacteriological media to react with acid or alkali within predetermined and usu. physiological limits of hydrogen-ion concentration — compare BUFFER 4a, BUFFER SOLUTION **c :** a preparation used on an object in electroplating to fix the limits of the deposit **8 :** SUBSTITUTE — **in reserve** *adv* **:** held back for other or future use **:** still available ⟨had other arguments *in reserve*⟩ ⟨kept *in reserve*⟩ — **without reserve** *adv* **1 :** freely and openly **:** so as to give complete information ⟨answered *without reserve*⟩ **2 :** without qualification, condition, or restriction; *usu* **:** without a fixed minimum price or other restriction to sale

**³reserve** \"\ *adj* **:** constituting or having the form or function of a reserve ⟨a ~ supply⟩ ⟨~ strength⟩

**re–serve** \(ˈ)rē+\ *vt* [*re-* + *serve*] **:** to serve again or anew ⟨*re-served* the warrant⟩

**reserve account** *n* [*³reserve*] **1 :** a valuation account that shows the estimated or actual decline in value of an asset and is always subtracted on a balance sheet from the related asset account to show net value ⟨a *reserve account* for depreciation⟩ ⟨*reserve accounts* for bad debts⟩ ⟨*reserve account* to reduce investments to market value⟩ — called also *allowance account, provision account, valuation account* **2 :** an account that shows an accrued usu. estimated liability ⟨*reserve account* for income taxes⟩ **3 :** an account that shows profits or surplus segregated or appropriated for a particular purpose ⟨*reserve account* for contingencies⟩ ⟨*reserve account* for replacement of fixed assets⟩

**reserve air** *n* **:** SUPPLEMENTAL AIR

**reserve bank** *n* [*²reserve*] **1 :** any of 12 Federal Reserve banks in the U.S. **2 :** a central bank holding reserves of other banks ⟨the South African *Reserve Bank*⟩

**reserve buoyancy** *n* [*³reserve*] **:** the volume of a ship above the water plane that can be made watertight and thus increase the ship's buoyancy — called also *reserve of buoyancy*

**reserve capacity** *n* **:** installed equipment (as in an electric power plant) that is in excess of that required to carry peak load

**reserve card** *n* [*¹reserve*] **:** a postal card notifying a library patron that a book he was previously unable to consult or borrow is now available

**reserve city** *n* [*²reserve*] **:** a city of the U.S. designated by the Board of Governors of the Federal Reserve system in which member banks of the system are required to maintain higher legal reserves than in other areas — compare CENTRAL RESERVE CITY, COUNTRY BANK

**re·served** \-vd\ *adj* [fr. past part. of *¹reserve*] **1 :** marked by a disposition to be restrained in words and actions: as **a :** checking free expression of knowledge or ideas through caution **:** not open, communicative, or candid ⟨habitually was ~ in speech, withholding her opinion —Victoria Sackville-West⟩ **b :** checking easy free conversation or activity through formality, stiffness, or other inhibition **:** not spontaneous, natural, or hearty ⟨a certain vulgar gusto in his movement that divided him from the ~, watchful rest of the family —D.H.Lawrence⟩ **2 :** kept or set apart or aside for future or special use or for an exigency **3 :** left of the same color as the background or as the original color of the surface of the material **syn** see SILENT

**reserved book** *n* **:** a book (as in a college library) used for students' required or collateral reading in courses and segregated from the general collections

**reserved list** *n* **:** a list of officers in the British navy retired from active service on half pay but available to be called upon to serve in time of war or emergency

**re·serv·ed·ly** \-vədlē, -li\ *adv* **:** in a reserved manner **:** with reserve

**re·serv·ed·ness** \-dnəs\ *n* -ES **:** the quality or state of being reserved

**reserved power** *n* **:** a political power reserved by a constitution or similar constituent instrument to the exclusive jurisdiction of a specified political authority (as a state or executive) usu. held to constitute the original source of powers undergoing allocation and distinguished from those delegated to other authority ⟨some *reserved powers* in the U.S. federal system belong to the states⟩ ⟨the *reserved powers* at the disposal of a British colonial governor⟩ — compare IMPLIED POWER, RESIDUAL POWER

**re·serve·less** \-vləs\ *adj* **:** lacking reserve or a reserve

**reserve of buoyancy** [*²reserve*] **:** RESERVE BUOYANCY

**reserve officer** *n* [*²reserve*] **:** an officer in a military reserve

**reserve price** *n* [*³reserve*] **:** a price announced at an auction as the least that will be entertained — compare BY-BIDDER

**reserver** *n* -s *obs* **:** one that reserves; *esp* **:** RESERVOIR

**reserve ratio** *n* [*²reserve*] **:** the ratio of the cash reserves of a bank to liabilities; *esp* **:** the ratio of gold certificates to combined deposit liabilities and outstanding Federal Reserve notes of the Federal Reserve banks

**reserve ration** *n* [*³reserve*] **:** a ration consisting of concentrated foods packed in a sealed container for use only in emergency

**reserves** *pres 3d sing of* RESERVE, *pl of* RESERVE

**reserving** *pres part of* RESERVE

**re·serv·ist** \-vəst\ *n* -s [*²reserve* + *-ist*] **:** a member of the reserves of the armed forces

**¹res·er·voir** *R* ˈrezəv,wär (-zəv- *by r-dissimilation*), -zə,vȯ(ə)r *also* -zərv,w- *or* -zər,v- *or* -v,wȯ(ə)r *or* ÷ -,vȯi *sometimes* -,vär *or by r-dissimilation* -v,wä *or* -,vȯ *or* -,vä; *-R* -zəv,wä(r, -,vȯ(ə) *also* -v,wȯ(ə) *or* ÷ -,vȯi *sometimes* -,vä(r\ *n* -s [F *réservoir,* fr. MF, fr. *reserver* to reserve + *-oir* -ory] **1 :** a place where something is kept in store: as **a :** a place where water is collected and kept in quantity for use when wanted; *esp* **:** an artificial lake in which water is impounded for domestic and industrial use, irrigation, hydroelectric power, flood control, or other purposes **b :** a part of an apparatus in which a liquid is held ⟨the ~ of an oil lamp⟩ **c :** a tank on the back of an old-fashioned kitchen range in which water is kept hot by escaped heat from the oven **2 a :** a space (as an enlargement of a vessel or the cavity of a glandular acinus) in which a body fluid or other product is stored ⟨oil ~s on a leaf⟩ **b :** the enlarged posterior portion of the gullet of some flagellates **3 :** an extra supply **:** RESERVE, STORE **4 a :** a body of rock sufficiently porous to permit the accumulation of water, petroleum, or natural gas **b :** the gathering ground where snow collects to form a glacier **:** the area covered by the névé **c :** a space within the earth occupied by molten rock or magma **5 :** STORAGE BELLOWS **6 a** *also* **reservoir host :** an organism in which a parasite that is pathogenic for some other species lives and multiplies without damaging its host; *broadly* **:** a noneconomic organism within which a pathogen of economic or medical importance flourishes without regard to its pathogenicity for the reservoir ⟨rats are ~s of plague⟩ ⟨*reservoir hosts* are important in the epidemiology of virus diseases⟩ **b :** a colony or group of organisms (as noxious animals) that persists when the general population of the species declines and serves as a breeding nucleus ⟨small ~ populations missed by control operations⟩

**²reservoir** \"\ *vt* -ED/-ING/-S **1 :** to provide with a reservoir **2 :** to collect, store, or keep in or as if in a reservoir

**reservoir rock** *n* **:** a permeable rock that contains oil or gas in appreciable quantity

**¹re·set** \rəˈset\ *n* -s [ME *recet, resset,* fr. OF *recet,* fr. L *receptus* retreat, retirement, place of refuge, fr. *receptus,* past part. of *recipere* to take back, receive — more at RECEIVE] **1** *obs* **:** an opportunity or right of refuge or shelter **:** SUCCOR, HELP; *also* **:** a place of refuge or shelter **:** ABODE, RESORT **2** *obs* **:** one who shelters another **3** *Scots law* **a :** the receiving of goods obtained by theft, robbery, swindling, or embezzlement with intent to deprive the owner of them by one knowing the goods to have been so obtained **b** *obs* **:** the harboring of an outlaw

**²reset** \"\ *vt* [ME *recetten, resetten,* fr. OF *recetter,* fr. L *receptare,* freq. of *recipere* to receive] **1** *chiefly Scot* **:** to give shelter to **:** WELCOME **2** *Scots law* **:** to receive and secrete (stolen goods)

**³re·set** \(ˈ)rē+\ *vt* [*re-* + *set*] **:** to set again or afresh ⟨~ type⟩ ⟨~ a diamond⟩ ⟨~ a field with tomato plants⟩

**⁴re·set** \ˈrē+,-, ≈ˈ≈\ *n* **1 :** something that is reset: as **a :** matter set up in print again **b :** REPLANT **2 :** an act of resetting **3 :** something used in resetting: as **a :** a device for releasing the brakes of a train after they have been applied by automatic train control **b :** a device for restoring a contact or pointer to its normal or prior position

**re·settable** \"+\ *adj* [*³reset* + *-able*] **:** capable of being reset

**¹re·set·ter** \rəˈsetər\ *n* [ME *recettor, ressettour,* fr. MF *recetteur,* fr. OF *recetter* to give shelter to + *-eur* -or] **1** *obs* **:** one that harbors or assists criminals **2** *chiefly Scot* **:** a receiver of stolen goods

**²re·setter** \(ˈ)rē+\ *n* [*³reset* + *-er*] **1 :** one that resets something (as type) **2 :** a leather worker who smooths and stretches hides by applying tallow and rubbing with a dull blade

**resetter–out** \(ˈ)≈ˈ≈≈-≈\ *n* **:** a leather worker who improves the grain of and removes the moisture from leather by stretching with a dull blade

**re·settle** \(ˈ)rē+\ *vb* [*re-* + *settle*] *vt* **:** to settle again or anew; *esp* **:** to settle (people) in a new place or a new way of life ~ *vi* **:** to become settled again or anew (as after disturbance or upheaval) — **re·settlement** \"+\ *n*

**re·sew** \"+\ *vb* [*re-* + *sew*] **:** to sew again

**res ex·ten·sa** \ˌrā,sekˈsten(t)sə, ˌrēzik-\ *n, pl* **res exten·sae** \-n,sī, -n,sē\ [NL] **:** an extended thing or substance **:** material substance — compare CARTESIANISM

**res ges·tae** \(ˈ)rāsˈge,stī, (ˈ)rēzˈje,stē\ *n pl* [L] **:** things done **:** TRANSACTIONS, DEEDS, EXPLOITS; *esp* **:** the facts that form the environment of a litigated issue **:** the things or matters and spontaneous oral statements accompanying and incident to a transaction or event and admissible in evidence as illustrating or explaining it

**¹resh** \ˈrāsh\ *n* -ES [Heb *rēsh,* lit., head] **1 :** the 20th letter of the Hebrew alphabet — symbol ר; see ALPHABET table **2 :** the letter of the Phoenician alphabet or of any of various other Semitic alphabets corresponding to Hebrew resh

**²resh** \ˈresh\ *dial var of* RUSH

**re·shape** \(ˈ)rē+\ *vb* [*re-* + *shape*] *vt* **:** to give a new form or orientation to ⟨*reshaping* the nation's foreign policy⟩ ~ *vi* **:** to take on a new form

**re·shaper** \"+\ *n* **:** one that reshapes something; *esp* **:** a worker who does the final blocking of hats

**re·shearer** \"+\ *n* [*re-* + *shearer*] **:** a worker who shears steel sheets to specified sizes

**re·shelve** \"+\ *vt* [*re-* + *shelve*] **:** to restore (as books) to a shelf

**re·ship** \"+\ *vb* [*re-* + *ship*] *vt* **:** to ship again: as **a :** to put on board of a ship a second time **:** transfer to another ship ⟨~ bonded merchandise⟩ **b :** to put in place or set up again ~ *vi* **:** to embark on a ship again or anew; *esp* **:** to sign again or anew for service on a ship

**re·shipment** \"+\ *n* [*reship* + *-ment*] **1 :** an act of reshipping **2 :** something that is reshipped

**re·shipper** \"+\ *n* [*reship* + *-er*] **1 :** one that re hips **2 :** a container used for reshipping; *usu* **:** a case or box used to ship empty unit containers (as glass jars) and reused for the subsequent shipping of the filled containers

**re·show** \"+\ *vt* [*re-* + *show*] **:** to show again or anew; *specif* **:** to show (a motion picture) on a second or later run

**resht** \ˈresht\ *adj, usu cap* [fr. *Resht,* city of northwest Iran] **:** of or from the city of Resht, Iran **:** of the kind or style prevalent in Resht

**¹re·shuffle** \(ˈ)rē+\ *vt* [*re-* + *shuffle*] **1 :** to shuffle (cards) again **2 :** to reorganize (as a cabinet or a political alignment) usu. by reordering of forces without other major changes (as of personnel)

**²reshuffle** \"\ *n* **:** an act or a result of reshuffling

**res·i·ance** \ˈrezēən(t)s\ *also* **res·i·an·cy** \-nsē\ *n, pl* **resiances** *also* **resiancies** [*resiance* fr. MF *reseance,* fr. *reseoir* to reside (fr. L *residēre*) + *-ance; resiancy* fr. *resiant* + *-cy*] *archaic* **:** ABODE, RESIDENCE

**¹res·i·ant** \-nt\ *n* -s [ME *resceant,* fr. MF *reseant,* fr. *reseant,* adj.] *archaic* **:** RESIDENT

**²resiant** \"\ *adj* [ME *reseant,* fr. MF, fr. OF, fr. pres. part. of *reseoir* to reside, fr. L *residēre*] *archaic* **:** abiding in a place **:** RESIDENT

**¹re·side** \rəˈzīd, rēˈz-\ *vi* -ED/-ING/-S [ME *residen,* fr. MF or L; MF *resider,* fr. L *residēre* to sit back, remain, abide, fr. *re-* + *sedēre* to sit — more at SIT] **1** *obs* **:** to settle oneself or a thing in a place **:** be stationed **:** REMAIN, STAY **2 a :** to be in residence as the incumbent of a benefice or an office **b :** to dwell permanently or continuously **:** have a settled abode for a time **:** have one's residence or domicile **3 :** to have an abiding place **:** be present as an element or inhere as a quality **:** be vested as a right — usu. used with *in* ⟨the power of decision ~s in the electorate⟩

**syn** LIVE, DWELL, SOJOURN, LODGE, STAY, PUT (*up*), STOP: RESIDE, despite the fact that it is somewhat formal, may be the preferred term for expressing the idea that a person keeps or returns to a particular dwelling place as his fixed, settled, or legal abode ⟨all persons born or naturalized in the United States, and subject to the jurisdiction thereof, are citizens of the United States and of the State wherein they *reside* —*U.S. Constitution*⟩ LIVE is the more general word for indicating that one has one's home in a place, often with special reference especially to hours away from work ⟨those who *lived* apart in temples —Agnes Repplier⟩ ⟨he works in New York but *lives* in New Jersey⟩ ⟨officially *residing* in Pennsylvania but *living* most of the time in Washington⟩ ⟨*living* in an old farmhouse⟩ DWELL is a somewhat elevated or bookish synonym for LIVE in this sense ⟨a young Indian girl whose people *dwelt* on the west side of the gorge —Ted Sumner⟩ ⟨in far-flung crown colonies and other dependencies *dwell* millions of people for whom political authority requires to be expressed in terms of tangible, visible personality —F.A.Ogg & Harold Zink⟩ SOJOURN is used in connection with a temporary habitation held for a limited or uncertain time ⟨artists who *sojourned* for a time amidst the western scene —*Amer. Guide Series: Oregon*⟩ LODGE applies to having sleeping and general living accommodations at a place, sometimes implying that meals are taken elsewhere ⟨*lodging* at the inn nearby⟩ ⟨a house in the Outer Bailey where you may *lodge* until morning —J.H. Wheelwright⟩ STAY is now perhaps the most usual common equivalent for SOJOURN; it may be used in reference to paid quarters, as in a hotel, or to visits with friends or relatives ⟨*stay* and eat at middle-class British hotels —Richard Joseph⟩ ⟨*staying* in the country in a house where . . . was also a guest —W.S.Maugham⟩ PUT (*up*) is a colloquial equivalent for STAY ⟨*put up* at a motel⟩ STOP is commonly used to indicate breaking a trip or journey and staying for a period ⟨*stop* at a hotel⟩ ⟨*stop* in Chicago for the night⟩

**²reside** *vi* [L *residere* to sink back, fr. *re-* + *sidere* to sit down, settle, sink; akin to L *sedēre* to sit] *obs* **:** SINK, SUBSIDE, SETTLE

**res·i·dence** \ˈrez(ə)dən(t)s, -zədᵊn-, *sometimes* -zə,den- *or chiefly substand South* ,≈≈ˈden(t)s\ *n* -s [ME, fr. MF, fr. ML *residentia,* fr. L *resident-, residens* (pres. part. of *residēre* to reside, abide) + *-ia* -y] **1 a :** the act or fact of abiding or dwelling in a place for some time **:** an act of making one's home in a place ⟨a center of fashionable ~⟩ ⟨where scepter'd angels held their ~ —John Milton⟩ **b :** the act or fact of living or regularly staying at or in some place either in or as a qualification for the discharge of a duty or the enjoyment of a benefit ⟨the governor was in ~⟩ **c :** the presence of an incumbent in his benefice **2 a** (1) **:** the place where one actually lives or has his home as distinguished from his technical domicile (2) **:** a temporary or permanent dwelling place, abode, or habitation to which one intends to return as distinguished from a place of temporary sojourn or transient visit (3) **:** a domiciliary place of abode **b** (1) **:** the place of the principal office of a corporation or business concern designated in its articles of incorporation or originally registered in accordance with law (2) **:** a place of doing business or maintaining an office of a corporation or business concern that is registered in accordance with law — used in some statutes (3) **:** a place in which in fact business is being done, an office is being maintained, or lawful powers or rights are being exercised by a corporation or business concern — used in broad statutory interpretations **c :** the place where something is permanently established **:** a seat or center of something (as power or prerogative) **3** *obs* **:** continuance or insistence in action **4 a :** a building used as a home **:** DWELLING; *esp* **:** a house of superior or pretentious character **b :** housing or a unit of housing provided for students and administered by a department of an educational institution; *also* **:** the department administering such residence **5 a :** the period or duration of one's abode in a place ⟨after a ~ of some 30 years⟩ **b :** the period during which one is actively engaged in academic duties or study or research at a college or university

**²residence** *n* -s [*²reside* + *-ence*] **1** *obs* **:** matter that falls or settles to the bottom of liquors **:** SEDIMENT; *also* **:** RESIDUUM **2** *obs* **:** depositing of sediment **:** SETTLING

**res·i·denc·er** \ˈrez(ə)dənsə(r), -zədᵊns- *sometimes* -zə,den(t)s-\ *n* -s [ME, residentiary (adj.), fr. AF, fr. ML *residentiarius* — more at RESIDENTIARY] **1** *obs* **:** a clergyman in residence **2 :** a resident representative or minister

**res·i·den·cia** \,rezəˈden(t)sēə, -)thēə\ *n* -s [Sp, lit., residence, fr. ML *residentia*] **:** a court or inquiry held in Spanish countries for a period of 70 days by a specially commissioned judge to examine into the conduct of a retiring high official (as a viceroy, captain general, governor)

**res·i·den·cy** \ˈrez(ə)dənsē, -zədᵊns-, -si *sometimes* -zə,den(t)s-\ *n* -ES [*resident* + *-cy*] **1 :** place of residence **:** DWELLING **2 a :** the official residence of a resident diplomatic agent or governor **b :** a territory in a protected state in which the powers of the protecting state are executed by a resident agent; *specif* **:** such an administrative division in parts of the East Indies (as formerly in India or Java) **3 :** a period of advanced medical training and education that normally follows graduation from medical school and completion of an internship and that consists of supervised practice of a specialty in a hospital and in its outpatient department and instruction from specialists on the hospital staff

**¹res·i·dent** \-nt, *chiefly substand South* ,rezəˈdent\ *adj* [ME, fr. L *resident-, residens,* pres. part. of *residēre* to reside] **1 :** dwelling or having an abode for a continued length of time **:** being in residence **:** RESIDING ⟨while ~ at college⟩ ⟨a ~ landowner⟩ **2 :** PRESENT, INHERENT ⟨energy ~ in matter⟩ **3 a** *obs* **:** not moving **:** FIXED, STABLE, RESTING **b :** not migratory **4 :** appertaining directly to a moving part of the body ⟨~ sensations⟩ — opposed to *remote* **5 :** involving, requiring, or taken during residence at an educational institution ⟨degree requirements include a year of ~ study⟩

**²resident** \"\ *n* -s **1 :** one who resides in a place **:** one who dwells in a place for a period of some duration — often distinguished from *inhabitant* **2 a :** a diplomatic agent residing at a foreign court or seat of government; *esp* **:** MINISTER RESIDENT 1 **b :** the governor of a residency **3 :** an ecclesiastical incumbent who is in residence **4 a :** a physician serving a residency usu. in preparation for independent practice in a specialty — compare HOUSE PHYSICIAN, INTERN **b :** a graduate student or postgraduate who resides in an educational institution to assist in its administration, pursue his own further studies, or gain practical experience

**resident buyer** *n* [*¹resident*] **:** a market representative located in a central market area and acting as buyer and consultant to one or more retailers in a line (as women's clothing) subject to much variation and rapid change

**resident commissioner** *n* **1 :** a representative of a dependency in the U.S. House of Representatives having the right to speak but not to vote **2 :** an administrator in a colony or possession who is the resident representative of the British government

**res·i·dent·er** \ˈrezə,dentə(r), ,≈≈ˈ≈≈\ *n* -s [*²resident* + *-er*] *chiefly dial* **:** RESIDENT, INHABITANT

**resident–general** \ˌ≈(≈)(,)≈ˌ≈(≈)≈\ *n, pl* **residents–general** *or* **resident–generals** [F *résident général,* fr. *résident* resident (fr. L *resident-, residens*) + *général* general, fr. L *generalis*] **:** a political resident of high rank; *specif* **:** one serving as the principal administrative officer in a French North African territory

**res·i·den·tial** \ˌrezəˌdenchəl *sometimes* (ˈ)rezˌd-\ *adj* [fr. *¹residence,* after such pairs as E *essence: essential*] **1 a :** used, serving, or designed as a residence or for occupation by residents ⟨a ~ hotel⟩ **b** (1) **:** providing and administering living accommodations for students ⟨a ~ college⟩ (2) **:** requiring or involving attendance of classes on a campus ⟨~ study⟩ ⟨a ~ course⟩ **2 :** adapted or restricted to or occupied by residences ⟨a ~ quarter⟩ **3 :** of, relating to, or connected with residence or residences ⟨~ trade⟩ ⟨a ~ zone⟩ ⟨~ construction⟩ — **res·i·den·ti·al·i·ty** \,rezə,denchēˈaləd·ē, -lətē, -i\ *n* -ES — **res·i·den·tial·ly** \ˌrezəˌdench(ə)lē, -li *sometimes* (ˈ)rezˌd-\ *adv*

**¹res·i·den·ti·ary** \,rezəˈdenchē,erē, -chərē\ *n* -ES [ML *residentiarius,* fr. *residentia* residence + *-arius* -ary] **1 :** an ecclesiastic who is or who is obliged to be in residence for a certain time **2 :** one who is resident **:** RESIDENT

**²residentiary** \"\ *adj* [ML *residentiarius,* fr. *residentia* residence + *-arius* -ary] **1 :** having residence **:** RESIDING, RESIDENT ⟨a ~ guardian⟩; *specif* **:** under ecclesiastical obligation to be in residence for a certain time (as at a cathedral) ⟨a canon ~⟩ **2 :** RESIDENTIAL

**res·i·den·ti·ary·ship** \-,ship\ *n* [*¹residentiary* + *-ship*] **:** the position or state of an ecclesiastical residentiary

**res·i·dent·ship** *pronunc at* ¹RESIDENT + ,ship\ *n* [*²resident* + *-ship*] **:** the position or state of a resident

**re·sid·er** \rəˈzīdə(r), rēˈz-\ *n* -s [*¹reside* + *-er*] **:** one that resides **:** RESIDENT

**resides** *pres 3d sing of* RESIDE

**residing** *pres part of* RESIDE

**residua** *pl of* RESIDUUM

**¹re·sid·u·al** \rəˈzij(ə)wəl, rēˈz-, -jəl\ *adj* [L *residuum* residue + E *-al*] **1 :** of, relating to, or constituting a residue **:** remaining after a part is taken **:** left as a residuum **2 :** relating to or like a residue or remainder ⟨~ analysis⟩ ⟨a ~ quantity⟩ **3 :** remaining in a body cavity after maximum normal expulsion has occurred ⟨~ urine⟩ — compare RESIDUAL AIR **4 a :** leaving a residue that remains effective for some time after application ⟨~ insecticides⟩ **b :** of or relating to a residual insecticide ⟨a ~ spray⟩

**²residual** \"\ *n* -s **:** REMAINDER, RESIDUUM: as **a** (1) **:** a binomial expression with one negative term (2) **:** the difference of the results obtained by observation and by computation from a formula (3) **:** the difference between the mean of several observations and any one of them **b :** a product or substance remaining over (as at the end of a chemical process, distillation, extraction) ⟨the various ~s of metabolic activity⟩ **c** (1) **:** an internal aftereffect of experience or activity that influences later behavior **:** a memory trace ⟨the ~s of past training⟩ (2) **:** the disability (as a scar or a limp) remaining after satisfactory recovery from a disease or operation

**residual affinity** *n* [*¹residual*] **:** RESIDUAL VALENCE

**residual air** *n* **:** the volume of air still remaining in the lungs after the most forcible expiration possible and amounting usu. to 60 to 100 cubic inches — compare SUPPLEMENTAL AIR

**residual charge** *n* **:** a comparatively feeble charge that appears on a condenser whose dielectric is not homogeneous a short time after being discharged — compare ABSORPTION 3

**residual claimant theory** *n* **:** a theory in economics: wages are a residual after the distributive shares of other factors of production are determined

**residual dextrin** *n* : LIMIT DEXTRIN

**residual error** *n* : the difference between a group of values observed and their arithmetical mean

**residual estate** *n* : RESIDUARY ESTATE

**re·sid·u·al·ly** \-əlē, -əli\ *adv* [¹*residual* + *-ly*] : as a residue : in a residual manner

**residual magnetism** *or* **residual induction** *n* : magnetization remaining in a magnetized body no longer under external magnetic influence : the magnetism of a permanent magnet

**residual phenomena** *n pl* : the phenomena that remain to be explained after the effects of known causes are subtracted — compare METHOD OF RESIDUES

**residual placer** *n* : a placer deposit consisting of decomposed rock or residual portions of such rock and lying at the locality of origin

**residual power** *n* : power held to remain at the disposal of a governmental authority (as an executive or the central government of a federation) after an enumeration or delegation of specified powers to other authorities ⟨the *residual power* of the Dominion could not be employed . . . except in the case of extraordinary national emergency —Alexander Brady⟩ — compare RESERVED POWER

**residual product** *n* : BY-PRODUCT ⟨coke and coal tar from gasworks are *residual products*⟩

**residual ray** *n* : any of the infrared rays that remain in a beam of thermal radiation after a series of reflections from a crystal

**residual soil** *n* : soil formed in situ by rock decay and left as a residue after the leaching out of the more soluble products

**residual sound** *n* : echoing sound audible in a place after the source has become silent : REVERBERATION

**residual stress** *n* : a stress that exists within a solid body though no external stress-producing forces are acting and that is due to some inequality of previous treatment of adjacent parts ⟨poorly annealed glass may be highly unstable because of *residual stresses* and shatter from a slight shock⟩ — compare RUPERT'S DROP

**residual valence** *n* : unemployed valence; *esp* : combining power that is not utilized when the elements combine to form simple molecules and so leads to such phenomena as association and hydration — compare HYDROGEN BOND

¹**re·sid·u·ary** \rə'zijə,werē, rē'z-, -jər|, |i\ *adj* [L *residuum* residue + E *-ary*] : of, relating to, consisting of, or constituting a residue, residuum, or remainder ⟨the ~ part of an estate⟩

²**residuary** \"\ *n* -ES : a residuary legatee

**residuary clause** *n* [¹*residuary*] : the part of a testator's will in which the residue of his estate is disposed of to one or more persons — compare BEQUEATH 1a

**residuary estate** *n* : the residue of a testator's estate

**residuary legacy** *n* : a legacy that includes all of a testator's estate not specifically distributed in other legacies or in charges against the estate

**residuary legatee** *n* : a legatee inheriting a testator's residuary estate

**res·i·due** \'rezə,d(y)ü\ *n* -S [ME, fr. MF *residu*, fr. L *residuum*, fr. neut. of *residuus* left over, remaining, fr. *residēre* to sit back, remain — more at RESIDE] : something that remains after a part is taken, separated, removed, or designated : REMNANT, REMAINDER, REST: as **a** : the part of a testator's estate or of any part thereof remaining after the satisfaction of all debts, charges of administration, statutory allowances for support of a widow and children, and previous devises and bequests **b** *obs* : REMAINDER 2b **c** : the part of a molecule that remains after the removal of a portion of its constituents : an atom or group regarded as a portion of a molecule : UNIT ⟨fatty acid ~*s* in fats⟩ ⟨like starch they [glycogens] are based upon maltose ~*s*, and like amylopectin . . . the branches contain less than half as many maltose units —J.W.McBain⟩ — compare RADICAL **d** : GRUFFS

**re·sid·u·ous** \rə'zij(ə)wəs, rē'z-\ *adj* [L *residuus* — more at RESIDUE] *archaic* : REMAINING, RESIDUAL

**re·sid·u·um** \-j(ə)wəm\ *n, pl* **resid·ua** \-wə\ *also* **residuums** [L — more at RESIDUE] : something that remains behind (as after charges are met or a process completed): as **a** : RESIDUE a **b** : a residual product (as from the distillation of crude petroleum) : DEPOSIT, SEDIMENT **c** : RESIDUAL c

**re·sign** \rə'zīn, rē'z-\ *vb* -ED/-ING/-S [ME *resignen*, fr. MF *resigner*, fr. L *resignare* to unseal, cancel, resign, fr. *re-* + *signare* to mark, sign, seal — more at SIGN] *vt* **1** *obs* : to refrain from : give over or desist from **2** : to give up deliberately : renounce by a considered or formal act : RELINQUISH ⟨the publisher did not hesitate to ~ all claims to the copyright on these terms —Jane Austen⟩ ⟨~*ing* all his rights in the property⟩ ⟨tempted to ~ the search —*Times Lit. Supp.*⟩ **3 a** : to give over or consign (as to the care or possession of another) : let go into another's possession or control, often submissively or confidingly : RELEGATE, COMMIT ⟨she loves me all that she can, and her ways to my ways ~ —Edna S.V. Millay⟩ ⟨~*ed* the child to the care of an aunt⟩ **b** : to give (oneself) over unresistingly, typically to effects of an indicated dominance, control, or influence, with stoic acceptance, calm resignation, or confidence ⟨we must ~ ourselves to such epidemics of human pugnacity and egotism —G.B.Shaw⟩ ⟨had ~*ed* himself to playing a minor role⟩ ~ *vi* **1 a** : to give up, relinquish, or forswear one's office, rank, membership, post, or charge esp. formally and definitely — often used with *from* ⟨~*ed* from the club⟩ or with *as* ⟨~ as chairman⟩ **b** *obs* : ABDICATE **2** : to accept something as inevitable : SUBMIT — usu. used with *to* ⟨we must ~ to our fate⟩ **syn** see RELINQUISH

**re–sign** \(')rē¦sīn\ *vt* [*re-* + *sign*] : to sign again : affix one's signature to a second time

**re·sig·na·tary** \rə'zignə,terē\ *n* -ES [F *résignataire*, fr. L *resignatus* + F *-aire* -ary] : one in whose favor a resignation is made

**res·ig·na·tion** \,rez|əg'nāshən, |ēg- *sometimes* -es|\ *n* -S [ME, fr. MF, fr. ML *resignation-, resignatio*, fr. L *resignatus* (past part. of *resignare* to resign) + *-ion-, -io* -ion] **1 a** : the act or fact of resigning something (as a claim, possession, office) : SURRENDER **b** : a formal notification of relinquishment (as of an office, a position) ⟨wrote out his ~ the same day⟩ **2** : the quality or state of being resigned : SUBMISSION, ACQUIESCENCE; *esp* : quiet and patient submissiveness (as to the rule or will of another) **3** : the formal return by a vassal of a fee to the superior from whom it was held under former Scots law **syn** see PATIENCE

**resignation bond** *n* : a bond given by a beneficed clergyman of the Church of England to secure resignation of his benefice on some contingency

**res·ig·na·tion·ism** \-shə,nizəm\ *n* -S [*resignation* + *-ism*] : resignation as a mood, pose, or form of emotional indulgence

**res·ig·na·tion·ist** \-sh(ə)nəst\ *n* -S [*resignation* + *-ist*] : a person (as a writer) devoted to or exhibiting resignationism

**re·signed** \-zīnd\ *adj* [fr. past part. of *resign*] **1 a** : given up : SURRENDERED ⟨a ~ post⟩ **b** : having resigned from office ⟨the ~ vice president⟩ **2** : being resigned to something : characterized by resignation : SUBMISSIVE, ACQUIESCENT — **re·sign·ed·ly** \-nədlē, -li\ *adv* — **re·sign·ed·ness** \-nədnəs\ *n* -ES

**re·sign·ee** \rə'zī¦nē, rē¦z-\ *n* -S [*resign* + *-ee*] **1** : one to whom or in whose favor something is resigned **2** : a person who resigns from something (as a job)

**re·sign·er** \-'zīnə(r)\ *n* [*resign* + *-er*] : one that resigns; *specif* : one that resigns a fee under Scots law — compare RESIGNATION 3

**re·sign·ful** \-nfəl\ *adj* [*resign* + *-ful*] : full of or expressive of resignation

**re·sign·ment** \-nmənt\ *n* -S [ME *resignement*, fr. *resignen* to resign + *-ment*] : the act of resigning : RESIGNATION

**resigns** *pres 3d sing of* RESIGN

**re·sile** \rə'zīl, rē'z-, *esp before pause or consonant* -īəl\ *vi* -ED/-ING/-S [MF & LL; MF *resilir* to withdraw from an agreement, fr. LL *resilire* to withdraw, fr. L to jump back, rebound — more at RESILIENT] : to draw back : RECOIL, RETRACT, RETREAT, RECEDE; *esp* : to return to a prior or original position ⟨~ from an agreement⟩ ⟨give a tube time to ~ after being stretched⟩ **syn** see REBOUND

**resilia** *pl of* RESILIUM

**re·sil·i·ate** \-zilē,āt\ *vt* -ED/-ING/-S [F *résilier* (alter. of MF *resilir* to withdraw from an agreement) + E *-ate* — more at RESILE] : CANCEL

**re·sil·ience** \rə'zilyən(t)s, -lēən-\ *n* -S [L *resilire* to rebound + E *-ence*] **1 a** : an act of springing back : REBOUND, RECOIL, ELASTICITY **b** : capability of a strained body to recover its size and shape after deformation, esp. when the strain is caused by compressive stresses — called also *elastic resilience* **2** : the recoverable potential energy of an elastic solid body or structure due to its having been subjected to stress not exceeding the elastic limit

**re·sil·ien·cy** \-nsē,-nsi\ *n* -ES [*resilient* + *-cy*] : the property of being resilient : RESILIENCE 1

**re·sil·ient** \-nt\ *adj* [L *resilient-, resiliens*, pres. part. of *resilire* to jump back, rebound, fr. *re-* + *salire* to jump, leap — more at SALLY] : returning freely to a previous position, shape, or condition: as **a** : moving swiftly back : RECOILING **b** : capable of withstanding shock without permanent deformation or rupture ⟨~ bodies⟩ **c** : SPRINGY ⟨a ~ turf⟩ **d** : looking backward **e** : tending to regain strength or high spirits after weakness or depression : BUOYANT **syn** see ELASTIC, FLEXIBLE

**resilient escapement** *n* : a lever escapement in a timepiece having yielding banking pins designed to resist sudden shock

**re·sil·ient·ly** *adv* : in a resilient manner : with resilience

**re·sil·i·fer** \-ləfə(r)\ *n* -S [NL *resilium* + E *-fer*] : a spoon-shaped process on the hinge plate of some bivalve mollusks (as members of the genus *Mactra*) supporting the resilium

**re·sil·i·om·e·ter** \-,zilē'ämәd·ә(r)\ *n* [*resilience* + *-o-* + *-meter*] : an instrument for testing resilience

**resilition** *n* -S [fr. *resilient*, after such pairs as E *ebullient: ebullition*] *obs* : RESILIENCE

**re·sil·i·um** \rə'zilēəm, rē'z-\ *n, pl* **resil·ia** \-lēə\ [NL, fr. L *resilire* to rebound — more at RESILIENT] : the internal part of the hinge ligament of a bivalve shell resembling in consistency and often described as cartilage but being in fact chitinous

**re·silver** \(')rē+\ *vt* [*re-* + *silver*] : to silver again or anew ⟨~ an old mirror⟩

¹**res·in** \'rez^ən\ *n* -S [ME, fr. MF *resine*, fr. L *resina*, fr. Gk *rhētinē* resin of the pine] **1 a** : any of various hard brittle solid to soft semisolid amorphous fusible flammable substances (as amber, copals, dammars, mastic, guaiacum) that are usu. transparent or translucent and yellowish to brown in color with a characteristic luster, that are formed esp. in plant secretions and are obtained as exudates of recent or fossil origin (as from tropical trees or pine or fir trees) or as extracts of plants, that contain usu. resin acids and their esters and are soluble in ether and other organic solvents but not in water, that are electrical nonconductors, and that are used chiefly in varnishes, printing inks, plastics, and sizes, in medicine, and as incense ⟨the spirit soluble ~*s* are in general of the soft variety, while the oil soluble are usually hard —*Natural Resins Handbook*⟩ — called also *natural resin;* compare BALSAM, FOSSIL RESIN, GUM, GUM RESIN, LAC, MINERAL RESIN, OLEORESIN, PITCH **b** : ROSIN **c** : a solid pharmaceutical preparation consisting chiefly of the resinous principles of a drug or drugs usu. extracted by solvents (as by alcohol followed by precipitation with water) or by driving off the essential oil from an oleoresin ⟨~ of jalap⟩ ⟨~ of podophyllum⟩ **2 a** : any of a large class of synthetic products (as alkyd resins or phenolic resins) usu. of high molecular weight that have some of the physical properties of natural resins but typically are very different chemically, that may be thermoplastic or thermosetting, that are made by polymerization or condensation, and that are used chiefly as plastics or the essential ingredients of plastics, in varnishes and other coatings, in adhesives, and in ion exchange ⟨when the ~ itself is capable of being shaped into a finished article without a plasticizer, as polystyrene, the terms resin and plastic are interchangeable for that material —G.M.Kline⟩ ⟨in industrial terminology the unfabricated material is sometimes called a ~ and the fabricated article a plastic —L.F. & Mary Fieser⟩ — called also *synthetic resin;* compare ION-EXCHANGE RESIN, SYNTHETIC RUBBER **b** : any of various resinlike products made from a natural resin (as rosin) or a natural high polymer (as cellulose or rubber) by chemical modification

²**resin** \"\ *vt* -ED/-ING/-S : to treat (as by rubbing or coating) with resin : apply resin to

**re·si·na** \rə'zīnə\ *n* -S [L — more at RESIN] : RESIN 1a

**res·in·a·ceous** \¦rez^ən¦āshəs\ *adj* [L *resinaceus*, fr. *resina* resin + *-aceus* -aceous] : RESINIFEROUS, RESINOUS

**resin acid** *n* : any of the acids (as abietic acid or pimaric acid) found free or in the form of esters in rosin, other natural resins, and tall oil and used chiefly in the form of salts (as sodium resinate or metallic soaps)

**resin alcohol** *n* : any of the alcohols found in the form of esters in natural resins

¹**res·in·ate** \'rez(ə)nət, -z^ən,āt\ *n* -S [*resin* + *-ate*, n. suffix] : a salt or ester of a resin acid, of a mixture of such acids, or of rosin

²**res·in·ate** \-z^ən,āt\ *vt* [*resin* + *-ate*, v. suffix] : to impregnate or flavor with resin

**resinback** \'ˌˌ,ˌ\ *n* : a circus horse used in bareback riding, vaulting, and tumbling acts

**resin bee** *n* : a solitary bee (genus *Anthidium*) that uses resin as cement in constructing its nest

**resinbush** \'ˌˌ,ˌ\ *n* **1** : a low southern African shrub (*Euryops athanasiae*) of the family Compositae having smooth pinnately parted leaves and abounding in resin **2** : a much-branched tropical African shrub (*Heeria insignis*) of the family Anacardiaceae having narrowly oblong leaves usu. in groups of three and with a silvery lower surface, small whitish flowers, black oval fruit, and very resinous sap

**resin canal** *or* **resin duct** *n* : a tubular intercellular space in gymnosperms and some angiosperms that occurs either normally or in response to injury, is formed either by dissolution of cells or by splitting of the walls of adjacent layers of cells, and is lined with epithelial cells which secrete resin

**resin cell** *n* : a plant cell that secretes or stores resin

**resin cerate** *n* : BASILICON OINTMENT 2

**res in·cor·po·ra·les** *n pl* \'ra,sin,kȯ(r)pə'rä,lās, 'rē,zin,kȯ(r)pə'rā(,)lēz\ [L] : incorporeal things — used esp. in Roman and civil law

**resin emulsion paint** *n* : a paint either ready-mixed or in paste form having as its binder or nonvolatile vehicle an emulsion of synthetic and generally alkyd resin

**res·in·er** \'rez(^ə)nə(r)\ *n* -S [²*resin* + *-er*] **1** : one that resins something **2** [¹*resin* + *-er*] : one that collects resin from trees

**re·sing** \(')rē+\ *vt* [*re-* + *sing*] : to sing again or anew

**resin gnat** *or* **resin midge** *n* [¹*resin*] : any of various small two-winged flies (genus *Retinodiplosis*) with larvae that injure pine trees by causing an exudation of resin in which they live

**res·in·ic** \(')re¦zinik\ *adj* [¹*resin* + *-ic*] : of, relating to, or obtained from resin ⟨~ acids⟩

**res·in·if·er·ous** \¦rez^ən¦if(ə)rəs\ *adj* [¹*resin* + *-iferous*] : secreting or bearing resin ⟨~ vessels⟩

**re·sin·i·fi·ca·tion** \re,zinəfə'kāshən\ *n* -S [F *résinification*, fr. *résinifier* to resinify, after such pairs as F *gratifier* to gratify: *gratification*] : the action or process of resinifying ⟨~ takes place in the stumps of the fallen trees —E.L.Kropa⟩

**res·in·i·fy** \re'zinə,fī\ *vb* -ED/-ING/-ES [F *résinifier*, fr. *résine* resin + *-ifier* -ify] *vt* : to convert into or treat with resin ~ *vi* **1** : to change into or become resin **2** : to form a gummy material — used of an oil evaporating to such a residue

**resining** *pres part of* RESIN

**res·in·ize** \'rez^ən,īz\ *vt* -ED/-ING/-S [¹*resin* + *-ize*] : to treat with resin : apply resin to

**resinlike** \'ˌˌ,ˌ\ *adj* [¹*resin* + *like*] : resembling resin esp. in properties or texture

**resino-** *comb form* [L *resina* resin] **1** : resin ⟨*resinography*⟩ ⟨*resinogenous*⟩ **2** : resinous and ⟨*resinoextractive*⟩ ⟨*resinovitreous*⟩

**res·in·og·e·nous** \¦rez^ən¦äjənəs\ *adj* [*resino-* + *-genous*] : RESINIFEROUS

**res·in·og·ra·phy** \,rez^ən'ägrəfē\ *n* -ES [*resino-* + *-graphy*] : the micrography of polished or etched surfaces of resins or plastics

¹**res·in·oid** \'rez^ən,ȯid\ *adj* [¹*resin* + *-oid*] : somewhat like resin : more or less resinous

²**resinoid** \"\ *n* -S **1** : a resinoid substance; *esp* : a thermosetting synthetic resin either before or after curing ⟨~ bonds for abrasives⟩ **2** *pharmacy* **a** : any of a class of resinlike preparations introduced by the eclectics and made by pouring a concentrated alcoholic extract of a drug into cold water and separating and drying the precipitate formed **b** : GUM RESIN **c** : any of various flower essences used in the perfume industry

**resin oil** *n* : an oil distilled from resin; *esp* : ROSIN OIL

**res·in·ol** \'rez^ən,ȯl, -,ōl\ *n* -S [ISV ¹*resin* + *-ol*] : any of various alcohols found as esters in resins

**resin opal** *n* : opal with a resinous appearance

**res·in·osis** \,rez^ən'ōsəs\ *n, pl* **resino·ses** \-ō,sēz\ [NL, fr. L *resina* resin + NL *-osis*] : an excessive outflow of resin from coniferous plants usu. resulting from injury or disease

**res·in·ous** \'rez(^ə)nəs\ *adj* [L *resinosus*, fr. *resina* resin + *-osus* -ous] **1** : of, relating to, containing, like, or obtained from resin ⟨~ exudates⟩ ⟨~ products⟩ **2** : of or relating to a luster of certain minerals and rocks (as sphalerite, pitchstone) that on fractured surfaces have the appearance of resin

**res·in·ous·ly** *adv* : in a resinous manner : so as to be resinous

**res·in·ous·ness** *n* -ES : the quality or state of being resinous

**resin plant** *n* : INCIENSO

**resins** *pl of* RESIN, *pres 3d sing of* RESIN

**resin soap** *n* **1** : soap made from resin as well as fat and containing sodium or potassium resinates; *esp* : ROSIN SOAP **2** : a soapy substance formed from a resin (as rosin) and alkali, composed essentially of sodium or potassium resinates, and used esp. in sizing paper or as an insecticide

**resin spirit** *n* : ROSIN SPIRIT

**res in·tegra** \rā'sintəgrə, ,rās^ən'tegrə, rē'zi-, ,rēz^ən-\ *n* [L, lit., thing untouched] : a case or a question that has not been examined or passed upon — used chiefly in law and diplomacy

**res in·ter ali·os ac·ta** \'rā,sintə,rälē,ō'saktə\ *n* [LL, lit., thing done among others] : the act of a person who is a stranger to the matter under adjudication

**resinweed** \'ˌˌ,ˌ\ *n* [¹*resin* + *weed*] : ROSINWEED

**res·iny** \'rez(^ə)nē, -ni\ *adj* [*resin* + *-y*] : RESINOUS 1

**res·i·pis·cence** \,resə'pis^ən(t)s\ *n* -S [LL *resipiscentia*, fr. L *resipiscent-, resipiscens* (pres. part. of *resipiscere* to recover one's senses, fr. *re-* + *-spiscere*, fr. *sapere* to taste, have sense, be wise) + *-ia* -y — more at SAGE] : change of mind or heart : REFORMATION; *often* : return to a sane, sound, or correct view or position

**res ip·sa lo·qui·tur** \'rā,sipsə'lōkwə,tü(ə)r\ *n* [L, the thing speaks for itself] : a case in which mere proof that an accident took place is sufficient under the circumstances to warrant an inference that it was caused by defendant's negligence unless otherwise explained

¹**re·sist** \rə'zist, rē'z-\ *vb* -ED/-ING/-S [ME *resisten*, fr. MF or L; MF *resister*, fr. L *resistere*, fr. *re-* + *sistere* to take a stand, cause to stand; akin to L *stare* to stand — more at STAND] *vt* **1** : to withstand the force or the effect of : be able to repel or ward off ⟨armor that ~*s* all weapons⟩ ⟨a constitution that ~*s* disease⟩ ⟨metal that ~*s* acid⟩ **2** : to exert oneself to counteract or defeat : strive against : OPPOSE ⟨~ the enemy valiantly⟩ ⟨~*ing* arrest⟩ ⟨~*ed* temptation⟩ ⟨~ the lowering of moral standards⟩ **3** *obs* : to be distasteful to ~ *vi* : to exert force in opposition ⟨it can overrule him, yes, but he must somehow ~ —H.D.Thoreau⟩ **syn** see CONTEST

²**resist** \"\ *n* -S **1** *obs* : RESISTANCE **2** : something (as a coating) that resists or prevents a particular action: as **a** : a substance (as a paste) used in textile printing to prevent either by mechanical or chemical means or both the fixing of a color or mordant on parts of the fabric ⟨additions of inert substances to chemical ~*s* . . . are often useful —Ellis Clayton⟩ **b** : a substance applied to a surface to render it nonconducting during electroplating and thus prevent deposition **c** : a protective acid-proof coating on the printing area of a photoengraving undergoing etching — called also *acid resist*

³**resist** \"\ *adj* [²*resist*] : decorated by or involving decoration by a process in which blank areas of design are made by coating ceramic materials with washable resist before applying glaze, luster, or other finish ⟨a pink and bronze ~ jug⟩ ⟨a ~ technique⟩

**re·sist·ance** \rə'zistən(t)s, rē'z-\ *n* -S [ME, fr. MF *resistence* resistance, fr. LL *resistentia*, fr. L *resistent-, resistens*, (pres. part. of *resistere* to resist) + *-ia* -y] **1** : the act or an instance of resisting : passive or active opposition; *also* : a means or method of resisting ⟨unfold to us some warlike ~ —Shak.⟩ **2** : power or capacity to resist; *esp* : the inherent ability of an animal or plant body to resist untoward circumstances (as disease, toxic agents, or infection) — compare IMMUNITY, SUSCEPTIBILITY **3** : an opposing force : a force tending to prevent motion or other action : a retarding force ⟨the ~ of the air to a body passing through it⟩ ⟨good ~ to wear⟩ ⟨grade ~ of a railroad⟩ **4 a** : the property of a body whereby it opposes and limits the passage through it of a steady electric current — see OHM'S LAW; compare ACOUSTIC RESISTANCE **b** : a source of resistance; *specif* : RESISTOR **5** : the retardation of a boat passing through the water due to (1) the friction between its wetted surface and the water, (2) the making of eddies or dead water, or (3) the formation of waves — called also respectively (1) *frictional resistance, skin resistance,* (2) *eddy resistance,* (3) *wave resistance* **6** : a mechanism of ego defense wherein a psychoanalysis patient rejects, denies, or otherwise opposes therapeutic efforts by the analyst — compare MECHANISM OF DEFENSE **7** *often cap* : an organized underground movement of a conquered country made up of groups of fighters engaged in sabotage and secret operations to thwart, waylay, and otherwise wear down occupation forces and often also in punishing collaborators among fellow countrymen — often used with *the* ⟨a former member of the French ~⟩

**resistance box** *n* : an instrument for measuring and comparing electrical resistances

**resistance coil** *n* : a coil of wire introduced into an electrical circuit to provide resistance

**resistance derivatives** *n pl* : quantities expressing the variation of the forces and moments on aircraft due to disturbance of steady motion

**resistance drop** *n* : the voltage drop in an electrical circuit due to the current traversing a nonreactive resistor — see IMPEDANCE DROP, REACTANCE DROP

**resistance furnace** *n* : an electric furnace in which heat is obtained from the energy loss of a resistor

**resistance heating** *n* : heating by means of energy produced by the passing of electric current through resistance units

**resistance point** *n* : a point at which a trend meets with opposing or nullifying forces; *esp* : the price at which a security on a declining market tends to stabilize or reverse its downward trend

**resistance thermometer** *n* : a thermometer utilizing a wire as the thermoelectric element and indicating variations in temperature by corresponding changes of the electrical resistance of the wire

**resistance welding** *n* : a form of electric pressure welding in which the necessary heat is produced by a flow of current through the parts to be welded and sufficient pressure to make the weld is applied simultaneously with the flow of current — compare BUTT WELDING, PERCUSSIVE WELDING, SEAM WELDING, SPOT WELDING

¹**re·sist·ant** *also* **re·sist·ent** \-stənt\ *adj* [*resistant* fr. MF *resistent, resistant*, fr. L *resistent-, resistens*, pres. part. of *resistere* to exist; *resistent* fr. L *resistent-, resistens*] : making or having powers of resistance : RESISTING ⟨a constitution ~ to disease⟩ — often used in combination ⟨corrosion-*resistant* materials⟩

²**resistant** \"\ *n* -S : one that resists : RESISTER

**re·sist·ant·ly** *adv* : in a resistant manner : so as to resist

**resist–dye** *vt* [²*resist*] **1** : to print (a fabric) by repeatedly putting a resist on different parts of the pattern and placing the fabric in successive dye baths — compare BATIK **2** : to cross-dye (fabric) by weaving with an undyed yarn and a dyed yarn that will resist further dyeing of the completed fabric

**resisted** *past of* RESIST

**re·sist·er** \-stə(r)\ *n* -S [ME, fr. *resisten* to resist + *-er*] : one that resists

**re·sist·ful** \-stfəl\ *adj* [*resist* + *-ful*] : inclined to resistance : making much resistance

**re·sist·ibil·i·ty** \-,zistə'bilәd·ē\ *n* -ES **1** : the quality or state of being resistible ⟨the ~ of divine grace⟩ **2** : ability to resist : power of resistance ⟨the ~ of granite to erosion⟩

**re·sist·ible** \-'zistəbəl\ *adj* [¹*resist* + *-ible*] : capable of being resisted, withstood, opposed, or frustrated ⟨a ~ attack⟩ ⟨such ~ temptations⟩ — **re·sist·ible·ness** \-bəlnəs\ *n* -ES — **re·sist·ibly** \-blē,-bli\ *adv*

**resisting** *pres part of* RESIST

**re·sist·ing·ly** *adv* : in a resisting manner : so as to resist

**re·sist·ive** \-stiv\ *adj* [*resist* + *-ive*] : tending to resist : disposed to resistance : RESISTANT ⟨fire-*resistive* materials⟩; *esp* : exhibiting or relating to electrical resistance — **re·sist·ive·ly** \-təvlē\ *adv* — **re·sist·ive·ness** \-tivnəs\ *n* -ES

**re·sis·tiv·i·ty** \rə,zis'tivəd·ē, (,)rē,z-\ *n* -ES [*resistive* + *-ity*] **1** : capacity for resisting : RESISTANCE ⟨high chemical ~⟩ **2 a** : a characteristic of a given substance upon which depends the electrical resistance of a body of that substance **b** : the longitudinal electrical resistance of a uniform rod of unit length and unit cross-sectional area — called also *specific resistance*

**re·sist·less** \-'zistləs\ *adj* [[1]*resist* + *-less*] **1** : incapable of being resisted **2** : having no power to resist : making no opposition — **re·sist·less·ly** *adv* — **re·sist·less·ness** *n* -ES

**re·sis·tor** \-istə(r)\ *n* -S [*resist* + *-or*] : a device possessing electrical resistance used in an electric circuit for protection, operation, or current control

**resist printing** *n* [[2]*resist*] : a method of printing textiles by roller printing a pattern in resist paste on a white fabric, placing the fabric in a dye bath, and subsequently removing the resist to leave a white pattern on a colored ground

**resists** *pres 3d sing of* RESIST, *pl of* RESIST

**res·ite** \'re,zīt\ *n* -S [ISV [1]*resin* + *-ite*; prob. orig. formed as G *resit*] : an infusible insoluble resin formed as the final cured stage in the alkaline condensation of a phenol and an aldehyde to a phenolic resin — called also *C-stage resin*; compare RESITOL, RESOL

**re-site** \(')rē+\ *vt* [*re-* + *site*] : to place on another site

**res·i·tol** \'rezə,tōl, -tōl\ *n* -S [prob. fr. [1]*resite* + *resol*] : a thermoplastic resin that is insoluble in alkali, that is formed as the second resin stage in the alkaline condensation of a phenol and an aldehyde to a phenolic resin, and that is used chiefly in molding powders and as an adhesive for wood — called also *B-stage resin*; compare RESITE, RESOL

**re-sitting** \(')rē+\ *n* [*re-* + *sitting*] : a sitting (as of a legislature) for a second time : another sitting

**re-size** \(')rē+\ *vt* [*re-* + *size*] : to shape again to size : bring again to a correct size after deformation ⟨~ a cartridge shell by driving it with a mallet into a hardened steel die⟩

**re·sizer** \"+\ *n* -S [*resize* + *-er*] : one that resizes: as **a** : a die for resizing shells **b** : a die through which a bullet purposely made a trifle larger than standard size is forced to bring it to a correct final shape and size

**res ju·di·ca·ta** \'rās,yüdə'kād·ə, 'rēz,jüdə'kād·ə\ *n* [L] : a thing or matter that has been finally decided on its merits (as between the parties) by a court having jurisdiction of the subject of the litigation and of the defendant if the judgment is a personal one against him and that cannot be litigated again between the same parties — called also *former adjudication*

**re-slant** \(')rē+\ *vt* [*re-* + *slant*] : to slant again or anew; *specif* : to orient in accord with a new outlook

**res man·ci·pi** \(')rā'smaŋkə,pē, (')rēz'man(t)sə,pī\ *n pl* [L, lit., things of mancipium] : property subject under Roman law to transfer by the formal ceremony of mancipation

**res mo·bi·les** \-'smōbə,lās, -z'mōbə,lēz\ *n pl* [L] *civil law* : movable things

**re-smooth** \(')rē¦smüth\ *vt* [*re-* + *smooth*] : to make smooth anew

**res·na·tron** \'reznə,trän\ *n* -S [*resonator* + *-tron*] : a high-power wide-frequency electron tube used esp. in World War II to jam enemy radar

**res nec man·ci·pi** \'rā,snek'maŋkə,pē, 'rēz,nek'man(t)sə,pī\ *n pl* [L, lit., things not of mancipium] : things other than res mancipi

**res nul·li·us** \,rāsnə'lēəs, rā'snulē-; ,rēznə'līəs, rēz'nəlēəs\ *n* [LL, lit., thing of no one] **1** : a thing belonging to no one whether because never appropriated (as a wild animal) or because abandoned by its owner but acquirable by appropriation **2** : property not subject to private ownership under Roman law

**re-socialization** \(;)rē+\ *n* [*re-* + *socialization*] : readjustment of an individual (as a psychotic, a physically handicapped person) to life in society : REHABILITATION

**re-sod** \(')rē+\ *vt* [*re-* + *sod*] : to cause to become covered anew with sod (as by seeding with grass)

**re-soil** \"+\ *vt* [*re-* + *soil*] **1** : to make dirty again **2** : to cover anew with soil ⟨~*ing* a terrace⟩

**reso·jet engine** \'rezō,jet-\ *n* [*resonance* + *jet* + *engine*] : a jet engine consisting essentially of a continuously open air inlet, a diffuser, a combustion chamber, and an exhaust nozzle, having fuel admitted continuously, and having resonance established within the engine so that there is a pulsating thrust produced by the intermittent flow of hot gases

**res·ol** *or* **res·ole** \'re,zōl, -zōl\ *n* -S [ISV [1]*resin* + *-ol*; prob. orig. formed as G *resol* (pl. *resole*)] : a fusible resin soluble in alkali and alcohol that is formed as the first resin stage in the alkaline condensation of a phenol and an aldehyde to a phenolic resin, that consists essentially of a mixture of phenol alcohols, and that is used chiefly in laminating and impregnating paper and fabrics — called also *A-stage resin*; compare RESITE, RESITOL

**re-sole** \(')rē+\ *vt* [*re-* + *sole*] : to put a new sole on (as a shoe)

[1]**re·sol·u·ble** \rə'zälyəbəl, rē'zäl-, 'rezəl-\ *adj* [LL *resolubilis*, fr. L *resolvere* to resolve + *-bilis* capable of (being acted upon)] : admitting of being resolved

[2]**re-sol·u·ble** \(')rē¦sälyəbəl\ *adj* [*re-* + *soluble*] : capable of being redissolved

[1]**res·o·lute** \'rezə,lüt *also* -əl,yül *sometimes* -zələ|; *usu* |d·+V\ *adj, sometimes* -ER/-EST [L *resolutus*, past part. of *resolvere* to resolve] **1** *obs* : PAID **2** *obs* : DECIDED, POSITIVE **3** : having or characterized by a decided purpose : DETERMINED, RESOLVED ⟨stood ~ against the enemy⟩ ⟨~ for peace⟩; *also* : BOLD, FIRM, STEADY ⟨a ~ man⟩ ⟨this ~ purpose⟩ **syn** see FAITHFUL

[2]**resolute** \"\ *n* -S [in sense 1 fr. L *resolutum*, neut. of *resolutus*, past part. of *resolvere* to resolve, pay; in sense 2 fr. [1]*resolute*] **1** *obs* : PAYMENT **2** : one who is resolute or daring

[3]**res·o·lute** \'rezə,lü| *also* -əl,yü|\ *vi* -ED/-ING/-S [back-formation fr. *resolution*] : to draw up, pass, or express a resolution

**res·o·lute·ly** \'rezə,lütlē, -tli *also* -əl,yüt- *or* ,==ˈ== *sometimes* 'rezələt-\ *adv* : in a resolute manner : with resolution

**res·o·lute·ness** \'==(,)=nəs, ,=='=\ *n* -ES : the quality or state of being resolute

**res·o·lu·tion** \,rezə'lüshən *also* -zəl'yü-\ *n* -S [ME, fr. MF or L; MF *resolution*, fr. L *resolution-, resolutio*, fr. *resolutus* (past part. of *resolvere* to resolve) + *-ion-, -io* -ion] **1** : the act or process of reducing to simpler form: as **a** : the act of analyzing or converting a complex notion into simpler ones or into its elements **b** : the act of solving **c** : the act of determining **d** : the passing of a musical voice part from a dissonant to a consonant tone or the progression of a chord from dissonance to consonance — see SUSPENSION illustration **e** : the act of separating a chemical compound into its elements or a mixture into its component parts; *specif* : separation of a racemic compound or mixture into its two components **f** (1) : the division of a prosodic element into its component parts (as the components of a long syllable in ancient Greek and Latin verse into two short syllables) (2) : the substitution in Greek or Latin prosody of two short syllables for a long syllable **g** : the analysis of a vector into two or more vectors of which it is the sum; *esp* : the finding of the components of a vector (as a force) in specified directions **h** : the act, process, or capability of rendering distinguishable the individual parts of an object, closely adjacent optical images (as with a microscope) or sources of light (as with a telescope), nearly identical wavelengths of light (as with a spectrograph), particles of nearly the same energy, particles of nearly the same mass (as with a mass spectrograph), or events occurring at nearly the same time (as with a nuclear radiation detector) **2 a** *archaic* : the dissipation of unhealthy matter (as of humors or a contagium) from the body **b** *archaic* : weakening or relaxation of control of a bodily part **c** : the subsidence of inflammation; *specif* : the solution and enzymic digestion of lung exudates in pneumonia and their absorption by the blood resulting in restoration of a normal aerated condition to the lung — compare CONSOLIDATION, ORGANIZATION **3** : a result of resolution : something that is resolved: as **a** : something separated into its component parts or reduced to a simpler form (as by dissolution or melting); *also* : conversion into liquid **b** : something that is determined upon : settled determination; *also* : firmness or constancy of resolve **c** (1) *archaic* : a decisive or clarifying statement or verdict (2) : a formal expression of opinion, will, or intent by an official body or assembled group ⟨the committee sent a ~ of sympathy⟩; *also* : a declaration submitted to an assembly for adoption — see CONCURRENT RESOLUTION, JOINT RESOLUTION **d** : the consonant tone or consonance in which a musical dissonance is resolved **e** : a product of prosodic resolution ⟨two short syllables forming the ~ of a long⟩ **f** (1) : the precision with which a television picture is or can be reproduced usu. measured in terms of the number of lines that can be distinguished in a picture (2) : the minimum separation at which two targets can be distinguished by radar **4 a** : the quality of mind or spirit admitting or productive of resolution (as of problems) : decision of character : RESOLUTENESS **b** *obs* : firmness in opinion : assured knowledge : CERTAINTY **5** : the point in a play or other work of literature at which the chief dramatic complication is worked out **syn** see COURAGE

**re-solution** \¦rēsə'lüshən *also* -səl¦yü-\ *n* [*re-* + *solution*] : the act of solving or dissolving again

**res·o·lu·tion·ary** \,rezə'lüshə,nerē *also* -zəl'yü-\ *adj* [*resolution* + *-ary*] : involving resolution

**res·o·lu·tion·er** \-sh(ə)nə(r)\ *n* -S [*resolution* + *-er*] **1** : one that makes a resolution or joins with others in a declaration **2** *usu cap* : one of a party among the Covenanters favoring the resolution of 1650 that all persons not professed enemies to the Covenant or excommunicated should be allowed to serve in the army — compare PROTESTER

**res·o·lu·tion·ist** \-nəst\ *n* -S [*resolution* + *-ist*] : RESOLUTIONER

[1]**re·sol·u·tive** \rə'zälyəd·iv, 'rezə,lüd·-\ *adj* [ME, fr. MF *resolutif*, fr. ML *resolutivus*, fr. L *resolutus* (past part. of *resolvere* to resolve) + *-ivus* -ive] **1** : serving to dissolve or relax : designed to dissolve ⟨a ~ medical application⟩ **2** : operating to resolve or annul ⟨a ~ condition in an agreement⟩ **3** : ANALYTICAL, EXPLICATIVE — used chiefly in formal logic

[2]**resolutive** \"\ *n* -S [ME, fr. MF *resolutif*, fr. *resolutif*, adj.] *archaic* : RESOLVENT

**re·sol·u·to·ry** \rə'zälyə,tōrē, 'rezələ,tōrē, ¦rezə¦lüd·ərē\ *adj* [LL *resolutorius*, fr. L *resolutus* + *-orius* -ory] **1** *obs* : serving to explain **2** : RESOLUTIVE

**resolutory condition** *n* : a condition that under civil and Scots law upon fulfillment terminates a contract and entitles the parties to be restored to the status quo

**re·solv·abil·i·ty** \rə,zälvə'biləd·ē, rē,z-, -zȯlv-, -lətē, -i *also* -zä(ù)v- *or* -zȯv-\ *n* : the quality or state of being resolvable

**re·solv·able** *also* **re·solv·ible** *adj* \-vəbəl\ : capable of being resolved ⟨a ~ quarrel⟩; *esp* : capable of optical resolution ⟨a ~ image⟩ ⟨~ stars⟩ — **re·solv·able·ness** *n* -ES

**re·solv·an·cy** \vənsē\ *n* -ES [[1]*resolve* + *-ancy*] : the state of being resolved

[1]**re·solve** \rə'zälv, rē'z-, -zȯlv *also* -zä(ù)v *or* -zȯv\ *vb* [L *resolvere* to unloose, dissolve, break up, pay back, fr. *re-* + *solvere* to loosen, release, pay — more at SOLVE] *vt* **1** *obs* : DISSOLVE, MELT ⟨O, that this too too solid flesh would melt, thaw, and ~ itself into a dew —Shak.⟩ **2** : to separate or break up : change or convert by disintegration : reduce by or as if by analysis — used with *into* or formerly with *in* ⟨the prism *resolved* the light into a play of color⟩ ⟨winter will ~ the sods into mellow loam⟩ ⟨*resolving* the nation into warring factions⟩ ⟨~ the problem into simple elements⟩ **3** : to cause to disintegrate : break into bits or separate into constituent elements ⟨fall plowing allows winter to ~ the clods⟩: as **a** : to perform the operations required and solve (a mathematical equation) **b** : to distinguish between or render independently visible adjacent parts of ⟨~ the lines of a spectrum⟩ ⟨~ a galaxy into its stars and nebulas⟩ **c** : to split up (as a force or velocity) into two or more components esp. in assigned directions : find a component of in a given direction usu. with the assumption of one other component in a direction at right angles ⟨*resolved* force *AB* along *AC*⟩ **d** : to separate (a racemic compound or mixture) into two components — opposed to *racemize* **4 a** : to cause (as inflammation, pain) to dissipate : cause resolution of **b** *obs* (1) : to make weak or slack : RELAX (2) : to cause to become lax (as in conduct) **5 a** *archaic* : to free (as a person) from doubt or uncertainty : make certain or assured : INFORM, CONVINCE **b** : to take away (as a doubt or impediment) : clear up : DISPEL ⟨gradually *resolved* his doubts⟩ **c** : to find an answer to : make clear or certain : SOLVE, UNRIDDLE ⟨~ a problem⟩ **6 a** : to bring oneself or another to (as a course of action) : DECIDE ⟨having *resolved* his fate⟩ — usu. used with a following clause ⟨we *resolved* that we must part⟩ or infinitive ⟨if you ~ to go⟩ **b** : to reach a decision about : SETTLE ⟨determined to ~ all disputed points⟩ **7 a** : to express (as an opinion or determination) by resolution and vote : declare or decide by a formal vote — used with a following clause ⟨the house *resolved* that no money should be appropriated⟩ or infinitive ⟨*resolved* to censure the speaker⟩ **b** : to change or convert (itself) by resolution or formal vote ⟨the house *resolved* itself into a committee⟩ **8** : to make (as one or more voice parts or the total musical harmony) progress from a dissonance into a consonance **9** : to work out the resolution of (as a play) ~ *vi* **1** *archaic* : to become fluid : MELT, DISSOLVE **2** : to become separated into its component parts or elements : DISINTEGRATE; *also* : to become reduced by or as if by dissolving or analysis ⟨physiological processes ultimately ~ into the integration of matter and the dissipation of motion —James Ward⟩ **3** : to undergo resolution — used esp. of a disease or inflammation **4** : to form a purpose or resolution; *esp* : to determine after reflection ⟨~ on a better course of life⟩ **5** *obs* **a** : to become of opinion : become convinced **b** : CONSULT, DELIBERATE **6** *archaic* : to determine to start or leave — used with *for* **7** : to progress from a dissonance to a consonance — used of a voice part or of the total musical harmony **8** : to become void : LAPSE **syn** see ANALYZE, DECIDE, SOLVE

[2]**resolve** \"\ *n* -S **1** : something that has been resolved : RESOLUTION **2** : resolute quality : fixity of purpose **3** : a legal or official determination; *esp* : a legislative declaration : a formal resolution **4** *obs* : an act of resolving or expounding

**re·solv·ed·ly** \-vədlē\ *adv* : in a resolved manner : RESOLUTELY

**re·solv·ed·ness** \-dnəs\ *n* -ES : the quality or state of being resolved

**resolved rhyme** *n* : rhyme exhibiting resolution

[1]**re·solv·ent** \-vənt\ *adj* [L *resolvent-, resolvens*, pres. part. of *resolvere* to resolve] : having power to resolve : causing solution : SOLVENT ⟨a ~ drug⟩

[2]**resolvent** \"\ *n* **1** : an agent that has power to disperse inflammatory or other lesions : something that aids the absorption of effused products **2** : something that can cause solution : SOLVENT **3** : a means of solving something (as a problem)

**re·solv·er** \-və(r)\ *n* -S [[1]*resolve* + *-er*] : one that resolves

**re·solv·ible** \-vəbəl\ *var of* RESOLVABLE

**resolving power** *n* [fr. gerund of [1]*resolve*] **1** : the ability of an optical system to form distinguishable images of objects separated by small angular distances **2** : the ability of a photographic film or plate to reproduce the fine detail of an optical image commonly evaluated in lines per millimeter **3** : the ability of observing equipment to give evidence of the existence and nature of celestial objects of very small angular dimensions depending esp. on the wavelength of the received radiation and being least for longest wavelengths

**resolving time** *n* : the shortest time interval between pulses in a nuclear counter that will permit them to be separately detected — compare DEAD TIME

**res·o·nance** \'rez(ᵊ)nən(t)s\ *n* -S *often attrib* [MF, fr. L *resonantia* echo, fr. *resonant-, resonans*, pres. part. of *resonare* to echo, resound — more at RESOUND] **1 a** : the quality or state of being resonant **b** (1) : a vibration of large amplitude in a mechanical or electrical system caused by a relatively small periodic stimulus of the same or nearly the same period as the natural vibration period of the system (as when a child in a swing is given pushes with the natural frequency of the swing, when an organ pipe responds to a tuned reed, or when a radio receiving circuit is tuned to a broadcast frequency) (2) : the state of adjustment that produces resonance in a mechanical or electrical system ⟨a violin string in ~ with a vibrating tuning fork⟩ ⟨two circuits in ~ with each other⟩ **2 a** : the intensification and enriching of a musical tone by supplementary vibration that is either sympathetically or mechanically induced **b** : a quality imparted to voiced sounds by the resonance-chamber action of mouth and pharynx configurations and in some cases of the nostrils in addition **3** : the sound elicited on percussion of the chest **4** : the complex of internal bodily processes that occur in emotional states : RAPPORT, EMPATHY **5** : a phenomenon that is shown by a molecule, ion, or radical to which two or more structures differing only in the distribution of electrons can be assigned, that is detected by shortened atomic distances and by lessened heats of hydrogenation or combustion over those expected from comparable structures not exhibiting this phenomenon, and that gives rise to a general stabilization of the structure because of the several orbital paths that the electrons may take among the atoms concerned ⟨~ is usually responsible for the deep color of certain organic compounds —J.A.Leermakers & Arnold Weissberger⟩ — called also *mesomerism*; compare HYPERCONJUGATION, TAUTOMERISM

**resonance absorption** *n* **1** : the absorption of electromagnetic energy at a frequency such that the photon energy is equal to a quantum excitation energy of the absorbing system **2** : the abnormally strong absorption by atomic nuclei of neutrons having certain definite energies

**resonance acceleration** *n* : an imparting of high speeds to electric particles by periodically varying the accelerating electric field so as to give a fresh impulse at the beginning of each successive segment of the path — compare CYCLOTRON

**resonance band** *n* : a frequency region in a sound spectrum that has relatively great intensity

**resonance curve** *n* : a curve whose abscissas are frequencies lying near to and on both sides of the natural frequency of a vibrating system and whose ordinates are the corresponding amplitudes of the near-resonant vibrations

**resonance hybrid** *n* : a compound, molecule, ion, or radical exhibiting resonance and having a structure represented in the written form as the average of two or more structural formulas separated each from the next by a double-headed arrow ⟨the *resonance hybrid* of carbon dioxide is represented by $^{-}O—C{\equiv}O^{+}\longleftrightarrow O{=}C{=}O\longleftrightarrow {}^{+}O{\equiv}C—O^{-}$⟩

$$CH_3C\begin{matrix}\diagup\!\!\!\!=O\\ \diagdown O^-\end{matrix} \longleftrightarrow CH_3C\begin{matrix}\diagup O^-\\ \diagdown\!\!\!\!=O\end{matrix}$$

resonance hybrid of the acetate ion

**resonance pipe** *n* : a pipe in a musical instrument (as an organ) for increasing its sonority

**resonance potential** *n* : the energy in volts required to remove an electron from a normal orbit to the next nearest orbit

**resonance radiation** *n* : radiation emitted by atoms or molecules excited by radiation of the same wavelength and constituting one type of fluorescence

**resonance spectrum** *n* : a spectrum of resonance radiation

**resonance theory** *n* **1** : a theory of hearing: different sections of the basilar membrane of the organ of Corti are tuned to different vibration rates and set up sympathetic vibrations that stimulate sensory nerve endings when the cochlear endolymph is vibrating at a corresponding frequency **2** : a theory in physiology: different forms of excitation arise in the central nervous system, are transmitted diffusely to the endorgans, but are individually capable of effectively stimulating only those muscles or other motor organs that are responsive to their particular frequency

[1]**res·o·nant** \-z(ᵊ)nənt\ *adj* [L *resonant-, resonans*, pres. part. of *resonare* to resound — more at RESOUND] **1** : continuing or capable of continuing to sound : able to resound : echoing back ⟨a harsh ~ boom⟩ **2 a** : capable of inducing resonance in sound : tending to reinforce or cause prolongation of sound ⟨violins of fine ~ wood⟩ **b** : relating to or exhibiting resonance : adjusted so as to respond to vibrations of a given frequency **3 a** : intensified and enriched by or as if by resonance : having a resounding quality ⟨a ~ voice⟩ ⟨the ~ beauty of his prose⟩ **b** : marked by or suggestive of the loud, oratorical, or grandiloquent ⟨a new and more ~ sort of headline, the streamer —H.G.Wells⟩ **c** *of colors* : producing mutual enhancement by contrast ⟨richer impasto and more ~ color —*Nat'l Gallery of Art*⟩ **4** : characterized by phonetic resonance : being a phonetic resonant

**syn** RESOUNDING, RINGING, VIBRANT, SONOROUS, OROTUND: RESONANT may indicate the full effect of the possibilities of vibration or the ready reactive effect of similar stimuli ⟨the beating small drums — a hollow *resonant* sound —C.B. Nordhoff & J.N.Hall⟩ ⟨the connotative words . . . have a quality and tone which is *resonant* in combination as though a tuning fork had been struck —R.L.Cook⟩ It may suggest clear and lasting carrying power and consequent force, intensity, or effect ⟨it was *resonant* with feeling and through long centuries gave voice to emotions —H.O.Taylor⟩ RESOUNDING adds the notion of echoing, reechoing, or reverberating as vibrations are thrown back ⟨the sound of a great underground river, flowing through a *resounding* cavern —Willa Cather⟩ Through the suggestion of repetition to make clear and unequivocal, it may connote the certain, positive, unreserved, and convincing ⟨the queen of Egypt was not ill-pleased by the Parthian failure, since a *resounding* success would have made Antony independent of her —John Buchan⟩ RINGING may be associated with bell-like sounds, ample and full, made without external or contrived vibrating devices ⟨a perfect ecstasy of song — clear, *ringing*, copious —John Burroughs⟩ Used of speech or composition, it connotes the clear, vigorous, and fervent ⟨his *ringing* appeal for independence . . . was followed in December by another shrill cry to the people, rallying them to the patriot side —C.A. & Mary Beard⟩ VIBRANT calls attention to attendant vibrations and overtones in actualizing sound, but, unlike the preceding words, does not imply their reflection, continuation, or amplification ⟨the speaker paused a moment, his low *vibrant* tones faltering into silence —Israel Zangwill⟩ ⟨a deep strong voice, more musical than any merely human voice, richer, warmer, more *vibrant* with love and yearning and compassion —Aldous Huxley⟩ In other uses it connotes keen sensitivity, pleasing or invigorating awareness or aliveness ⟨Latin verses that were freed from the dead rules of quantity, and were already *vibrant* with a vital feeling for accent and rhyme —H.O.Taylor⟩ ⟨there was something *vibrant* and clean about the sense of conviction and affirmation that was rising within us as the challenge crystallized —Norman Cousins⟩ SONOROUS is likely to suggest fullness or loudness of sound without much suggestion of vibration or timbre ⟨the deep, *sonorous* voice of the red-bearded Duke, which boomed out like a dinner gong —A. Conan Doyle⟩ Applied to speeches and writing it suggests the imposing or high-flown ⟨here all day long rolled forth, in *sonorous* Latin, the interminable periods of episcopal oratory —Lytton Strachey⟩ ⟨a *sonorous* declaimer . . . he went out of his way to invite majestic effects —V.L.Parrington⟩ OROTUND, etymologically suggesting maximum opening of the mouth, likewise connotes full sound ⟨to be sung to the tune of Yankee Doodle, yet in a slower, more *orotund* fashion —Vachel Lindsay⟩ Applied to style of composition or delivery it may indicate the pompous or bombastic ⟨the phrase needs be fitly *orotund* —J.B.Cabell & A.J.Hanna⟩

[2]**resonant** \"\ *n* -S **1 a** : a sound characterized by resonance : a resonant sound **b** *phonetics* : a sound in whose production there is neither friction nor complete stoppage and whose sole acoustic effect is the product of vocal cord vibration and its resonance : a vowel or one of the sounds \m, n, ŋ, l, r, y, w\ in English — compare OBSTRUENT **2** : a resonant body

**resonant cavity** *n* [[1]*resonant*] : CAVITY RESONATOR

**resonant frequency** *or* **resonance frequency** *n* : a frequency capable of exciting a resonance maximum in a given body or system

**res·o·nant·ly** *adv* : in a resonant manner : with resonance

**res·o·nate** \'rezᵊn,āt, *usu* -ād·+V\ *vb* -ED/-ING/-S [L *resonatus*, past part. of *resonare* to resound — more at RESOUND] *vi* **1** : to produce or exhibit resonance : vibrate sympathetically (as with some source of sound or electric oscillations) ⟨the geometry of the *resonating* ions —K.J.Brunings & A.H.Corwin⟩ **2** : to respond as if by resonance : REECHO ⟨a boy reared in a minister's home may all his life ~ . . . to moral dogmas —C.W. Shumaker⟩ ~ *vt* : to subject to resonating : make resonant

**res·o·na·tor** \-ād·ə(r), -ātə-\ *n* -S [*resonate* + *-or*] **1** : something that resounds or resonates: as **a** : a hollow acoustic vessel with two openings one of which is to be held to the ear and the other directed toward a source of sound which may be intensified in certain frequencies by the resonance of the enclosed air **b** : an electric circuit in which are incorporated inductance and capacitance so connected that a periodic electromotive force of suitable frequency causes the circuit to resonate with electric oscillations of maximum amplitude **c** : CAVITY RESONATOR **d** : a device (as the piano soundboard, the body of a stringed instrument) for increasing the power or beauty of tone of a musical instrument by sympathetic vibration **e** : any of the pharynx, mouth, or nose cavities that serve to reinforce tones in the formation of speech sounds **f** : an open box for containing a telegraph sounder and designed to concentrate and amplify the sound **2** : a small auxiliary muffler behind the regular muffler in the exhaust system of an automobile

**re·sorb** \rə'sȯ(ə)rb, (')rē'-, -'zȯ-\ *vb* -ED/-ING/-S [L *resorbēre*, fr. *re-* + *sorbēre* to suck up, swallow — more at ABSORB] *vt* **1** : to swallow or suck in again : take up again **2** *of a living organism* : to lyse and assimilate (the substance of a differentiated structure previously produced by the body) ⟨~*ed* the fetuses⟩ ~ *vi* : to undergo resorption ⟨the injected protein ~*s* after some days⟩

**re·sorb·ent** \-bənt\ *adj* [L *resorbent-*, *resorbens*, pres. part. of *resorbēre*] : swallowing or sucking in again : REABSORBING

**res·orcin** \rə̇z, (')rez+\ *n* -S [ISV *res-* (fr. L *resina* resin) + *orcin*] : RESORCINOL — not used systematically

**resorcin brown** *n*, *often cap R&B* : an acid dye — see DYE table I (under *Acid Orange 24*)

**resorcin dark brown** *n*, *often cap R&D&B* : an acid dye — see DYE table I (under *Acid Brown 14*)

**res·orcinol** \"+\ *n* -S [ISV *resorcin* + *-ol*] : a sweetish crystalline phenol $C_6H_4(OH)_2$ that turns pink in air, that is obtained from various resins (as galbanum or asafetida) or tannins by degradation but is usu. made by fusion of *meta*-benzene-disulfonic acid with sodium hydroxide, and that is used chiefly in making dyes, pharmaceuticals, phenolic resins esp. for adhesives, and rubber products and in medicine in the treatment of skin diseases; *meta*-dihydroxy-benzene

**res·or·cyl·ic acid** \ˌreˌzȯrˈsilik-\ *n* [ISV *resorc*in + *-yl* + *-ic*] : any of three isomeric crystalline acids $C_6H_3(OH)_2COOH$ that are both carboxyl derivatives of resorcinol and dihydroxy derivatives of benzoic acid; *esp* : the crystalline beta or 2,4-dihydroxy derivative used chiefly in making dyes, pharmaceuticals, and fine chemicals

**re·sorp·tion** \rə'sȯrpshən, -'zȯ-, (')rēˈ-\ *n* -S [L *resorpt*us (past part. of *resorbēre* to resorb) + E *-ion*] : the act or process of resorbing : REABSORPTION ⟨the ~ of a tooth root⟩

**resorption border** *or* **resorption rim** *n* : one of a series of borders of one or more minerals around a central larger crystal representing recrystallizations of material dissolved by a molten magma from previously crystallized minerals — called also *corrosion border;* compare REACTION RIM

**re·sorp·tive** \-ptiv\ *adj* [L *resorpt*us + E *-ive*] : relating to or caused by resorption : tending to cause resorption : capable of being resorbed

**[1]re·sort** \rə'zȯ(ə)r|t, rē'z-, -ȯ(ə)| *sometimes* -'sȯ-; *usu* |d·+V\ *n* -S [ME, fr. MF, resource, jurisdiction to which one has recourse, fr. *resortir* to resort] **1 a** : something to which or someone to whom one looks for help : a source of aid or refuge : RESOURCE, EXPEDIENT ⟨an appeal to his uncle seemed his last ~⟩ **b** : an act of going to or making application (as in seeking aid) : RECOURSE ⟨have ~ to force⟩ **2 a** : frequent, habitual, or general going or repairing to or visiting ⟨a place of popular ~⟩ **b** : persons who frequent a place : ASSEMBLAGE, COMPANY, THRONG **c** (1) : a place to which one betakes himself or persons go habitually : a place of frequent assembly : HAUNT (2) : a popular place of entertainment or recreation **3** *obs* **a** : frequenting in numbers : CONCOURSE **b** : a going of one person with others or to a place **4** *obs* **a** : a mechanical spring **b** : motive power : CAUSE, SOURCE **syn** see RESOURCE

**[2]resort** \"\ *vb* -ED/-ING/-S [ME *resorten*, fr. MF *resortir* to come out again, rebound, recoil, resort, fr. OF, fr. *re-* + *sortir* to escape] *vi* **1** : to have recourse (as to a source of aid or for a purpose) : to seek aid, relief, or advantage ⟨~*ed* to a trick⟩ ⟨knew no one to whom he could ~ for help⟩ **2** : to betake oneself : REPAIR; *esp* : to go frequently, customarily, or usually **3** *obs* : to fall back : REVERT, RETURN **4** *obs* : to direct one's attention : TURN ~ *vt*, *obs* : VISIT

**re-sort** \(')rēˈsȯ(ə)r|, -ȯ(ə)|\ *vt* [*re-* + *sort*] : to separate again : classify anew

**re·sort·er** *pronunc at* [1]RESORT +ə(r)\ *n* -S [[1]*resort* + *-er*] : a frequenter of a resort or resorts

**re-sort·er** *pronunc at* RE-SORT +ə(r)\ *n* [*re-sort* + *-er*] : one that re-sorts

**res·o·ru·fin** \ˌrezō'rüfə̇n\ *n* -S [ISV *reso*rcin + L *ruf*us red + ISV *-in* — more at RED] : a red-brown crystalline dye $C_{12}H_7NO_3$ of the phenoxazine class that gives fluorescent red or pink solutions, that is formed by the action of nitrosylsulfuric acid on resorcinol or by reduction of resazurin, and that on reduction yields a colorless dihydro derivative

**[1]re·sound** \rə̇'zau̇nd, rē'z- *sometimes* -'sau̇-\ *vb* [ME *resounen*, fr. MF *resoner*, fr. L *resonare* to sound again, echo, resound, fr. *re-* + *sonare* to sound — more at SOUND] *vi* **1** : to become filled with sound : RING, ECHO, REVERBERATE ⟨the earth ~*ed* with his praise⟩ **2** : to produce an echoing sound ⟨through the dell his horn ~*s* —Sir Walter Scott⟩ **3** : to become proclaimed or renowned ⟨a name to ~ for ages —Alfred Tennyson⟩ ~ *vt* **1** : to proclaim (as someone's praises or virtues) : celebrate in music, song, or story : extol loudly or widely **2** : to cause (a sound) to be repeated : REECHO **3** : to sound or utter in full resonant tones

**[2]resound** \"\ *n* : something that resounds (as an echo)

**re-sound** \(')rēˈsau̇nd\ *vb* [*re-* + *sound*] *vt* : to sound (as a horn) again or anew ~ *vi* : to sound again or anew

**resounding** *adj* [ME *resouning*, fr. pres. part. of *resounen* to resound] **1 a** : producing or characterized by resonant sound : echoing or awakening echoes : RESONATING ⟨a ~ harp⟩ ⟨a ~ hall⟩ **b** : giving an effect of resonance through repetition or multiplication ⟨~ cries⟩ **2 a** : sounding inflated or orotund : excessively sonorous or unduly impressive ⟨"Princess Patricia Pattipam of Patagonia", a ~ name for a slipper-chewing puppy⟩ **b** : admitting or designed to admit of no equivocation or doubt : FORCEFUL, EMPHATIC, UNEQUIVOCAL ⟨a ~ denial⟩ ⟨a ~ success⟩ **syn** see RESONANT

**re·sound·ing·ly** *adv* : in a resounding manner : so as to resound ⟨a voice rang out ~⟩

**re·source** \'rēˌs|ō(ə)rs, rə̇'s|, rē's|, |ȯ(ə)rs, |ōəs, |ȯ(ə)s *also* -ˌz| *or* -'z|\ *n* -S [F *ressource*, fr. OF *ressourse* relief, resource, fr. *resourdre* to rise again, relieve, fr. L *resurgere* to rise again — more at RESURRECTION] **1 a** : a new or a reserve source of supply or support : a fresh or additional stock or store available at need : something in reserve or ready if needed ⟨exhausted every ~⟩ ⟨open up new ~*s* to an impoverished culture⟩ **b resources** *pl* : available means (as of a country or business) : computable wealth (as in money, property, products) : immediate and possible sources of revenue ⟨rich natural ~*s*⟩ ⟨the book value of a company's ~*s*⟩ **2** : something to which one has recourse in difficulty : means of resort in exigency : EXPEDIENT, STRATAGEM ⟨her usual ~ was confession⟩ **3** : possibility of relief or recovery — usu. used in negative construction ⟨lost without ~⟩ **4** : a means of spending or utilizing one's leisure time ⟨Boston at that time offered few healthy ~*s* for boys or men —Henry Adams⟩ **5** : capability of or skill in meeting a situation : ability to rise to an occasion : RESOURCEFULNESS **6** : an accounting asset — usu. used in pl.

**syn** RESORT, EXPEDIENT, SHIFT, MAKESHIFT, STOPGAP, SUBSTITUTE, SURROGATE: RESOURCE may refer to any asset or means benefiting or assisting one, often to an additional, new, previously unused, or reserve asset ⟨the nursing mother feeds the newborn from the *resources* of her own vitality —H.M.Parshley⟩ ⟨almost the only *resource* upon which people can depend for a living appears to be fish and other animals —Samuel Van Valkenburg & Ellsworth Huntington⟩ ⟨in their relative inexperience of the variety of humans and of human beliefs, they all tend to turn inward upon their own limited *resources:* the primitive to his sacred tribalism, the child to his narcissistic self and body, and the psychotic to the inward resources of his autistic thinking —Weston La Barre⟩ RESORT in this sense is now uncommon except in the phrases *last resort* and *to have resort to*, in which it is close synonym to RESOURCE ⟨brotherhood was invoked more wholeheartedly, as the last *resort* against nihilist desperation —Ignazio Silone⟩ ⟨except in revolutionary unions, the strike is used only as a last *resort* —G.S.Watkins⟩ EXPEDIENT may apply to any continuance, means, or plan for solution of a particular immediate problem, especially to one not commonly or customarily used ⟨if all fears arise from suggestion, they can be prevented by the simple *expedient* of not showing fear or aversion before a child —Bertrand Russell⟩ ⟨but is not this a desperate *expedient*, a last refuge likely to appeal only to the leaders of a lost cause —J.W.Krutch⟩ ⟨as the war endures, this spirit replaces the aims with which the war was begun by *expedients* forced on the rulers by the character of the gigantic conflict itself —D.W.Brogan⟩ SHIFT may refer to a temporary or tentative expedient, admittedly imperfect; in reference to plans and stratagems it may suggest dubiousness or trickery ⟨most people who were brought into intimate contact with the two-roomed cottage, not always perhaps including the inhabitants, who had grown up amidst the *shifts* they enforced, heartily condemned them —G.E.Fussell⟩ MAKESHIFT usu. designates that which is frankly temporary and inferior and either adopted through urgent need or countenanced through indifference and carelessness ⟨the premises . . . being only a *makeshift* until the works . . . should be finished —F.W.Crofts⟩ ⟨like all attempts to pigeonhole human emotions, these classifications are, of course, *makeshifts*. They have no scientific value whatsoever —H.W.Van Loon⟩ STOPGAP refers to something used or employed momentarily or temporarily as an emergency measure ⟨both vigilantes and mass meeting were looked upon as temporary *stopgaps*, to be disbanded as soon as governmental machinery was provided by the United States —R.A.Billington⟩ SUBSTITUTE indicates anything which replaces a thing or article originally or customarily used; it does not necessarily connote anything about merit or cause ⟨peat as a coal *substitute*⟩ ⟨a *substitute* for milk itself could be manufactured from the soya bean —V.G.Heiser⟩ ⟨this mock king who held office for eight days every year was a *substitute* for the king himself —J.G.Frazer⟩ SURROGATE is a more learned word for SUBSTITUTE, often used of synthetic products or of replacement figures in psychological and sociological analyses ⟨that is why slang is so insidious and so pervasive; it too is a facile *surrogate* for thought —J.L.Lowes⟩ ⟨his accounts are full, informed, trustworthy, but he does not pretend to the depersonalized objectivity that too often serves as a *surrogate* for authority in such writing —Howard M. Jones⟩ ⟨usually each child thus receives his turn to act as parent-*surrogate* to a younger child —Allison Davis⟩

**re·source·ful** \='=fəl *also* '=ˌ=fəl\ *adj* [*resource* + *-ful*] **1** : characterized by resource in the meeting of situations : fertile in devising ways and means **2** : having great resources richly endowed (as with natural products) — **re·source·ful·ly** \-fəlē, -li\ *adv* — **re·source·ful·ness** *n* -ES

**re·source·less** \'=ˌ=lə̇s, ='=lə̇s\ *adj* : lacking or deficient in resources — **re·source·less·ness** *n* -ES

**resources** *pl of* RESOURCE

**re·sow** \(')rē+\ *vt* [*re-* + *sow*] : to sow (as land or seed) again or anew

**resp** *abbr* **1** respective; respectively **2** respiration; respiratory **3** respondent

**re·spar** \(')rē+\ *vt* [*re-* + *spar*] : to install new spars (as in a ship's rigging)

**re·speak** \"+\ *vb* [*re-* + *speak*] *vt* : ECHO, RESOUND ~ *vi* : to speak further : make additional utterance

**[1]re·spect** \rə̇'spekt, rē's-\ *n* -S [ME, fr. L *respectus* act of looking back, regard, consideration, fr. *respectus*, past part. of *respicere* to look back — more at [2]RESPECT] **1 a** : a relation to or concern with something usu. specified ⟨the final questions had ~ to her financial situation⟩ **b** : a relation or reference to a particular thing or situation : RELEVANCE ⟨remarks having ~ to an earlier plan⟩ **c** *obs* : ASPECT **2 a** : an act of noticing with attention : the giving of particular attention to : CONSIDERATION ⟨having ~ to the views of another⟩ **b** *obs* : HEED, CARE, CIRCUMSPECTION **c respects** *pl*, *obs* : attention to diverse matters **3 a** : high or special regard : deferential regard (as from a servant to his master) : ESTEEM ⟨a great ~ for his judgment⟩ — often used in negative construction ⟨having no ~ for class distinctions⟩ **b** : the quality or state of being esteemed : HONOR ⟨a man generally held in high ~⟩ **c** *obs* : STANDING, REPUTATION **d respects** *pl* (1) *obs* : COURTESIES (2) : expressions of respect or deference ⟨paid his ~*s*⟩ **4** *obs* : CONSIDERATION, MOTIVE, INTEREST **5 a** *obs* : COMPARISON — used chiefly in the phrase *in respect* **b** : a point regarded : PARTICULAR, DETAIL ⟨in all ~*s* perfect⟩ **syn** see REGARD — **in respect** *or* **in respect that** *archaic* : seeing that : SINCE — **in respect of** *prep* **1** : as to : as regards : insofar as concerns : with respect to **2** *archaic* : in consideration of : on account of — **in respect to** *prep* : in relation to : with regard to : as respects — **with respect to** *prep* : as regards : insofar as concerns : with reference to ⟨*with respect to* your last letter⟩

**[2]respect** \"\ *vb* -ED/-ING/-S [L *respectus*, past part. of *respicere* to look back, look back at, regard, have respect for, fr. *re-* + *specere* to look — more at SPY] *vt* **1** *obs* : RESPITE, POSTPONE, NEGLECT **2 a** *obs* (1) : CONSIDER, DEEM, HEED (2) : to look for : ANTICIPATE (3) : to look toward or at : front upon or toward (4) : to look upon **b** : to be depicted facing (as one another) — used of heraldic figures **3 a** : to consider worthy of esteem : regard or treat with respect ⟨loved and ~*ed* his parents⟩ : ESTEEM, VALUE **b** : to refrain from obtruding upon or interfering with ⟨~ a person's privacy⟩ **4** : to have regard or reference to : relate to : be concerned with ⟨the treaty ~*s* our commerce⟩ ~ *vi* : LOOK, FRONT, FACE — usu. used in heraldry — **as respects** : as regards : with regard to : as to ⟨perfectly tolerant except *as respects* his personal honor⟩ — **respect the person** **1** : to consider a case or question with reference to the person involved and one's bias for or against him **2** *archaic* : to have regard for the quality (as of rank, station, outward aspect) of a person

**re·spect·abil·i·ty** \-ˌspektə'biləd·ē, -lətē, -i\ *n* **1 a** : the quality or state of being respectable **b** : the status of being respectable : CONSEQUENCE **2 a** : a respectable person : respectable persons ⟨the ~ of the town⟩ **b** : a respectable convention : DECENCY ⟨those little *respectabilities* that make group life bearable⟩

**re·spect·abi·lize** \='==_bəˌlīz\ *vt* -ED/-ING/-S [*respectable* + *-ize*] : to make respectable : give an apparent respectability to

**[1]re·spect·able** \rə̇'spektəbəl, rē's-\ *adj* [[2]*respect* + *-able*] **1** : worthy of note : having claims to consideration : of consequence ⟨everything relating to bulls is popular and ~ in Thebes —P.B.Shelley⟩ **2** : worthy of esteem or deference : ESTIMABLE, RESPECTED ⟨a highly ~ authority⟩ **3 a** : decent in behavior or character : morally estimable ⟨a ~ innkeeper⟩ **b** : exhibiting respect for the decencies or proprieties : conventionally correct in conduct ⟨many persons find it easier to be good than ~⟩ **4** : being such to a significant degree : TOLERABLE: as **a** : fair in size or quantity ⟨a ~ amount⟩ ⟨a ~ volume of work⟩ **b** : moderately good : pleasing but not exceptional ⟨a house with a ~ view⟩ ⟨a ~ performance⟩ **5** : decent in appearance or standing : PRESENTABLE ⟨a ~ coat⟩ ⟨a ~ address⟩ — **re·spect·able·ness** \-nə̇s\ *n* -ES — **re·spect·ably** \-blē,-bli\ *adv*

**[2]respectable** \"\ *n* -S : a respectable person

**re·spect·ant** \-ktənt\ *adj* [L *respectant-*, *respectans*, pres. part. of *respectare* to look back, look back at — more at RESPITE] **1** : depicted upright and facing one another — used of heraldic representations of fishes and mammals; compare AFFRONTÉ, COMBATANT **2** : looking back

**re·spect·er** \-ktə(r)\ *n* -S [[2]*respect* + *-er*] : one that respects esp. unduly or to the point of partiality — usu. used in negative constructions ⟨death is no ~ of preachers⟩ ⟨wombats are no ~*s* of fences or crops —Bill Beatty⟩

**re·spect·ful** \-ktfəl, *in rapid speech* -kfəl\ *adj* [[1]*respect* + *-ful*] : full of respect: as **a** *obs* : HEEDFUL, CAREFUL — usu. used with *of* **b** *obs* : deserving or receiving respect **c** : marked or characterized by respect : showing deference ⟨~ deportment⟩ ⟨a ~ glance⟩ — **re·spect·ful·ly** \-fəlē, -li\ *adv* — **re·spect·ful·ness** *n* -ES

**respecting** *prep* [fr. pres. part. of [2]*respect*] **1** : in view of : CONSIDERING ⟨~ what a rancorous mind he bears —Shak.⟩ **2** : with regard or relation to : REGARDING, CONCERNING ⟨~ his conduct there is but one opinion⟩

**re·spec·tive** \rə̇'spektiv, rē's-, -tēv *also* -təv\ *adj* [partly fr. ML *respectivus* having respect to, fr. L *respectus* (past part. of *respicere* to look back at) + *-ivus* -ive; partly fr. [2]*respect* + *-ive* — more at RESPECT] **1 a** *obs* : noticing with attention : REGARDFUL, ATTENTIVE **b** *archaic* : CAREFUL, HEEDFUL **2** *obs* : rendering respect : COURTEOUS **3** *obs* **a** : having reference : RELATED, CORRESPONDENT **b** : RELATIVE **4** *obs* : fitted to awaken respect : RESPECTABLE **5** *obs* **a** : regardful of particular persons or things **b** : PARTIAL, DISCRIMINATIVE **6** : proper or relating to particular persons or things each to each : PARTICULAR, SEVERAL ⟨their ~ homes⟩ ⟨assembling the ~ parts according to the diagram⟩

**re·spec·tive·ly** \-tə̇vlē, -li\ *adv* : in a respective manner : so as to be respective; *usu* : as relating to each : in particular : each to each : each in the order given ⟨two philosophers who stressed ~ deductive and empirical aspects of science⟩ ⟨when the daughters were 12, 10, and 7 years old ~⟩

**re·spec·tive·ness** \-tivnə̇s, -tēv- *also* -təv-\ *n* -ES : the quality or state of being respective

**re·spect·less** \-ktlə̇s\ *adj* : not having or not showing respect : CARELESS, DISRESPECTFUL

**respectlessly** *adv* [*respectless* + *-ly*] *obs* : without respect

**respects** *pl of* RESPECT, *pres 3d sing of* RESPECT

**respectuous** *adj* [MF *respectueux*, fr. L *respectus* respect + F *-eux* -ous] *obs* : deserving or showing respect

**respectworthy** \='=ˌ==\ *adj* : worthy of respect

**re·spell** \(')rē+\ *vt* [*re-* + *spell*] : to spell again, anew, or in another way; *esp* : to spell out according to a phonetic system ⟨words ~*ed* to show the pronunciation⟩

**re·spin** \"+\ *vt* [*re-* + *spin*] : to spin again or anew

**res·pi·ra·bil·i·ty** \ˌresp(ə)rə'biləd·ē, rə̇ˌspīr-, rēˌspīr-\ *n* : the quality or state of being respirable

**res·pi·ra·ble** \'resp(ə)rəbəl, rə̇'spīr-,rē'spīr-\ *adj* [F or LL; F *respirable*, fr. LL *respirabilis*, fr. L *respirare* to respire + *-abilis* -able] **1** : suitable for being breathed : adapted for respiration ⟨a ~ atmosphere⟩ **2** : capable of respiration ⟨~ beings⟩ — **res·pi·ra·ble·ness** *n* -ES

**res·pi·rat·ing** \'respəˌrād·iŋ\ *adj* [fr. *respiration*, after such pairs as E *inspiration: inspirating*, pres. part. of *inspirate*] : functioning in respiration ⟨~ muscles⟩

**res·pi·ra·tion** \ˌrespə'rāshən\ *n* -S [ME *respiracioun*, fr. L *respiration-*, *respiratio*, fr. *respiratus* (past part. of *respirare* to breathe) + *-ion-*, *-io* -ion — more at RESPIRE] **1 a** : the placing of air or dissolved gases in intimate contact with the circulating medium (as blood) of a multicellular organism whether by breathing, diffusion through gills or body surface, or other means ⟨most fishes use gills in ~⟩ **b** : a single complete act of breathing ⟨30 ~*s* per minute⟩ **2** : the physical and chemical processes by which an organism supplies its cells and tissues with the oxygen needed for metabolism and relieves them of the carbon dioxide formed in energy-producing reactions and which typically involve osmotic exchange between regions of greater and lesser concentration, mechanical transport in a fluid medium (as blood), and chemical storage by mean of carriers (as hemoglobin) or buffers **3** : any of various energy-yielding oxidative reactions in living matter that typically involve transfer of oxygen and production of carbon dioxide and water as end products — called also *cellular respiration;* compare FERMENTATION

**res·pi·ra·tion·al** \ˈ==ˈrāshənᵊl, -shnəl\ *adj* : of or relating to respiration : RESPIRATORY ⟨~ disorders⟩

**respiration calorimeter** *n* : an apparatus for measuring the gaseous exchange between a man or lower animal and the surrounding atmosphere with particular reference to the oxygen consumed and carbon dioxide eliminated and simultaneously the quantity of energy given out in the form of heat and work in order to determine the relation of these factors to the food and drink consumed and to body activity

**res·pi·ra·tor** \'respəˌrād·ə(r), -ātə- *sometimes* -ˌsprā-\ *n* -S [L *respirat*us (past part. of *respirare* to breathe) + E *-or* — more at RESPIRE] **1** : a device (as a gas mask) for protecting the respiratory tract (as against irritating and poisonous gases, fumes, smoke, dusts) with or without equipment supplying oxygen or air ⟨filter ~*s* provide protection against any particulate matter, either solid, mist, or spray in an atmosphere containing a sufficient amount of oxygen —F.A. Van Atta⟩ ⟨air line ~*s*⟩ **2** : a device for maintaining artificial respiration ⟨chest and tank ~*s*⟩ — compare CUIRASS 4b, IRON LUNG

**res·pi·ra·to·ri·um** \ˌrespərə'tōrēəm, rə̇ˌspīr-\ *n*, *pl* **respi·rato·ria** \-ēə\ [NL, fr. LL, neut. of *respiratorius*] : a tracheal gill (as of a dipterous larva)

**res·pi·ra·to·ry** \'resp(ə)rəˌtōrē, ÷'respəˌt- (*by* r-*dissimilation*), -tȯr-, -ri *also* rə̇'spīrəˌ- *or* rē'spīrəˌ- *sometimes* (')reˈspīrəˌ-\ *adj* [LL *respiratorius*, fr. L *respiratus* (past part. of *respirare* to breathe) + *-orius* -ory — more at RESPIRE] : of or relating to respiration ⟨~ function⟩ : serving for or functioning in respiration ⟨~ organs⟩ ⟨~ nerves⟩

**respiratory center** *n* : a region in the medulla oblongata that regulates respiratory movements

**respiratory enzyme** *n* : an enzyme (as an oxidase, dehydrogenase, or catalase) associated with the processes of cellular respiration; *esp* : CYTOCHROME OXIDASE

**respiratory leaf** *or* **respiratory leaflet** *n* : one of the laminae of a book lung

**respiratory nerve** *n* : any of four nerves supplying the muscles of respiration and comprising two internally located phrenic nerves and two externally located posterior thoracic nerves

**respiratory pigment** *n* : any of various conjugated proteins that function in the transfer of oxygen in cellular respiration and that are permanently colored (as hemoglobin), alternate between a colored and a colorless phase (as hemocyanin) depending on their degree of oxygenation, or are permanently colorless (as the pigment of a few marine mollusks)

**respiratory plate** *n* : a flattened expansion of the body wall of an insect larva or other aquatic invertebrate that serves as a gill

**respiratory quotient** *also* **respiratory ratio** *n* : a ratio indicating the relation of the volume of carbon dioxide given off in respiration to that of the oxygen consumed and having a value near 1 when the organism is burning chiefly carbohydrates, near 0.7 when chiefly fats, and near 0.8 when chiefly proteins but sometimes exceeding 1 when carbohydrates are being changed to fats for storage — abbr. *RQ*

**respiratory system** *n* : a system of organs subserving the function of respiration and in air-breathing vertebrates consisting typically of the lungs and their nervous and circulatory supply, the channels by which these are continuous with the outer air, various supportive and protective structures, and usu. the muscles and skeletal structures concerned with emptying and filling the lungs

**respiratory tree** *n* **1** : an internal arborescent usu. paired tubular appendage of the cloaca of some holothurians that is considered to be an organ of respiration **2** : the trachea, bronchi, and bronchioles

**respiratory trumpet** *n* : either of the two trumpet-shaped projections that bear the thoracic spiracles in the pupae of mosquitoes and midges

**re·spire** \rə̇'spī(ə)r, rē's-, -īə\ *vb* -ED/-ING/-S [ME *respiren*, fr. MF & L; MF *respirer* to revive, fr. L *respirare* to blow back, breathe, breathe again, recover breath, fr. *re-* + *spirare* to blow, breathe — more at SPIRIT] *vi* **1** : to have or enjoy a breathing space or respite : REVIVE; *also* : to recover hope or courage **2** *obs, of the wind* : BLOW **3 a** : BREATHE; *specif* : to inhale air into the lungs and exhale it from them successively in carrying on the gaseous exchange of the blood **b** : to engage in or perform respiration **4** *of a cell or tissue* : to take up oxygen and produce carbon dioxide through oxidation ~ *vt* **1** : to breathe (as air) in and out : inspire and expire **2** : to give off as or as if an exhalation : EXHALE

**re·spirit** \(')rē+\ *vt* [*re-* + *spirit*] : to put new spirit or courage in

**res·pi·rom·e·ter** \ˌrespə'rämәd·ə(r)\ *n* [L *respir*are to breathe + E *-o-* + *-meter*] **1** : an instrument for studying the character and extent of respiration **2** : a diver's headdress having a receptacle for compressed oxygen for replenishing the oxygen in the expired air after its harmful ingredients have been chemically removed

**res·pi·rom·e·try** \-mə·trē\ *n* -ES [L *respirare* + E *-o-* + *-metry*] : the study of respiration (as cellular respiration) by means of a respirometer

**1res·pite** \'respə̇t *sometimes* 're,spīt *or* rə̇'spīt *or* rē'spīt; *usu* |d.+V\ *n* -s [ME *respit*, fr. OF, fr. ML *respectus*, fr. L, act of looking back — more at RESPECT] **1** : a putting off of that which was appointed : extension of time : POSTPONEMENT, DELAY: as **a** : temporary suspension of the execution of a capital offender : REPRIEVE **b** : a delay of appearance at court granted to a jury **2** : temporary intermission of labor or of any process or operation : interval of rest **3** *obs* : delay in acting **4** *obs* : LEISURE, OPPORTUNITY **5** : one that is reprieved

**2respite** \"\ *vb* -ED/-ING/-S [ME *respiten*, fr. MF *respiter*, fr. ML *respectare* to respect, delay, respite, fr. L, to look back repeatedly, wait for, respect, freq. of *respicere* to look back — more at RESPECT] *vt* **1** : to give or grant a respite to: as **a** : to delay or postpone : put off **b** : to keep back from execution : REPRIEVE **2** *archaic* : to desist from : FORBEAR, SUSPEND **3 a** : to suspend temporarily the necessity for meeting (as an obligation) or paying (a penalty) **b** *obs* : to relieve by a pause or interval of rest **4** *obs* : PROLONG ~ *vi, archaic* : to take a respite : REST

**res·pite·less** \-tlə̇s\ *adj* : having no respite

**re·splend** \rə̇'splend, rē's-\ *vi* -ED/-ING/-S [ME *resplenden*, fr. L *resplendēre* — more at RESPLENDENT] : to shine resplendently : be resplendent ⟨natural moral values ~ among all other values —Dietrich von Hildebrand⟩

**re·splen·dence** \-dən(t)s\ *n* -s [ME, fr. LL *resplendentia*, fr. L *resplendent-, resplendens* + *-ia* -y] : the quality or state of being resplendent : brilliant luster : SPLENDOR

**re·splen·den·cy** \-dənsē, -si\ *n* -ES [LL *resplendentia*] **1** : RESPLENDENCE **2** : a resplendent thing (as a garment) ⟨her folds and *resplendencies* —H.L.Davis⟩

**re·splen·dent** \-dənt\ *adj* [L *resplendent-, resplendens*, pres. part. of *resplendēre* to shine back, fr. *re-* + *splendēre* to shine — more at SPLENDID] : shining brilliantly : LUSTROUS **syn** see SPLENDID

**re·splen·dent·ly** *adv* : in a resplendent manner : with resplendence

**1re·spond** \rə̇'spänd, rē's-\ *n* -s [ME, fr. MF *respondre* to respond] **1** : something sung or said after or in reply to the officiant in a liturgy : a response to or as if to a versicle : RESPONSORY **2** : an engaged pillar supporting an arch or closing a colonnade of arcade ⟨the nave arcade will be of nine pillars and two ~*s*⟩; *also* : a corbel so used or a pilaster that backs up a free column **3** : ANSWER, REPLY

**2respond** \"\ *vb* -ED/-ING/-S [MF *respondre* to answer, correspond, fr. L *respondēre* to promise in return, answer, correspond, fr. *re-* + *spondēre* to promise — more at SPOUSE] *vi* **1** *archaic* : to correspond to or accord with something **2** : to say something in return : make an answer ⟨~*ed* negatively to the question⟩: as **a** : to make a respond or response in a liturgy **b** (1) : to make a bid in bridge based wholly or partly on strength promised by a previous bid by one's partner (2) : to bid as directed by a forcing bid made by one's partner **3** : to show some reaction to a force or stimulus ⟨the pupil of the eye ~*s* to change of light intensity⟩ : react in response ⟨a horse ~*ing* to kindly treatment⟩ ⟨~*ed* with rage to the insult⟩ ⟨the abscess ~*ed* well to heat treatment⟩; *often* : to react favorably in response ⟨is at last ~*ing* to medication⟩ **4** : to render satisfaction : be answerable ~ *vt, archaic* : to answer to : correspond to **syn** see ANSWER

**re·spon·de** \-n,dē\ *n* -s [L, 2nd sing. imper. of *respondēre* to respond] *Scots law* : an entry formerly made in a book of record in chancery of a nonentry or relief duty payable by an heir taking a precept from chancery; *also* : the amount of the duties in such an entry

**re·spon·de·at ouster** \-,dēət-\ *n* [L *respondeat* let him make answer (3d sing. pres. subj. of *respondēre* to respond) + AF *ouster, oustre* further, beyond, alter. of OF *outre*, fr. L *ultra* — more at ULTERIOR] : a judgment or order used upon denial of a dilatory plea to direct the party who made it to plead to the merits

**respondeat superior** *n* [ML, let the superior give answer] : the responsibility of a principal for his agent's acts ⟨the power of control is the test of liability under the doctrine of *respondeat superior* —J.D.Johnson⟩

**re·spon·dence** \rə̇'spändən(t)s, rē's-\ *also* **re·spon·den·cy** \-dənsē\ *n, pl* **respondences** *also* **respondencies** [L *respondēre* to answer, correspond + E *-ence, -ency*] : the act of responding : the quality or state of being respondent : ANSWERING, RESPONSE; *also* : CORRESPONDENCE, AGREEMENT

**1re·spon·dent** \-dənt\ *n* -s [L *respondent-, respondens*, pres. part. of *respondēre* to answer, correspond — more at RESPOND] : one that responds (as with a reply): as **a** : one that maintains a thesis in reply — distinguished from *opponent* **b** (1) : one that answers in various legal proceedings that are usu. not according to the course of the common law (as in equity, admiralty, ecclesiastical, or statutory cases) (2) : the prevailing party in the lower court — distinguished from *appellant*

**2respondent** \"\ *adj* [L *respondent-, respondens*] **1** *obs* : serving to correspond **2** : making response : ANSWERING, RESPONSIVE; *esp* : being a defendant or respondent at law

**re·spon·den·tia** \,rē,spän'dench(ē)ə\ *n* -s [NL, fr. L *respondent-, respondens* + *-ia* -y; fr. the fact that it is only a personal obligation on the borrower who is bound to answer the contract] : a loan upon goods laden on a ship conditioned to be repaid with maritime interest only in the event of the safe arrival of some part of the goods — compare BOTTOMRY

**re·spond·er** \rə̇'spändə(r), rē's-\ *n* -s : one that responds: **a** : a person that responds (as to a question, a bid, a kindness) **b** : something that reacts responsively: as (1) : the main charge of an explosive that requires an initiator to set it off (2) : the part of a transponder that transmits a radio signal

**responsa** *pl of* RESPONSUM

**1responsal** *adj* [ME *responsaill*, fr. ML *responsalis* of a reply, answerable, fr. L *responsum* reply + *-alis* -al — more at RESPONSE] **1** *obs* : ANSWERABLE, RESPONSIBLE **2** *obs* : RESPONSIVE

**2re·spon·sal** \rə̇'spän(t)səl, rē's-\ *n* -s **1** [ME, fr. ML *responsalis* of a reply] **a** *obs* : REPLY, ANSWER **b** *archaic* : a respond in a liturgy **2** [ML *responsalis*, fr. *responsalis* of a reply] *obs* : the respondent in a disputation **3** : RESPONSALIS

**re·spon·sa·lis** \-,spän'sälə̇s\ *n, pl* **responsa·les** \-'sä(,)lās\ [LL *responsalis* (trans. of LGk *apokrisiarios*), fr. L *responsum* reply + *-alis* -al — more at RESPONSE] : one who gives answers as the representative of an ecclesiastic : APOCRISIARIUS

**re·spon·sa pru·den·ti·um** \-sə(,)prü'dentēəm, -dench(ē)əm\ *n pl* [LL] : the responses or opinions of eminent lawyers or professional jurists on legal questions addressed to them — compare OBITER DICTUM

**re·spon·sa·ry** \-n(t)sərē\ *n* -ES [*response* + *-ary*] : RESPONSORY, RESPONSE

**re·sponse** \rə̇'spän(t)s, rē's-\ *n* -s [ME & L; ME *respounse*, fr. MF *respons*, fr. L *responsum* reply, fr. neut. of *responsus*, past part. of *respondēre* to answer — more at RESPOND] **1** : an act or action of responding (as by an answer) : a responsive or corresponding act or feeling : a responding to a motive force or situation : REACTION ⟨the sensitive and wistful ~ of a poet to the gentler phase of beauty —*Amer. Guide Series: Minn.*⟩ ⟨the ~ of a wire to the flow of electric current⟩: as **a** : a liturgical answer in the form of a verse, sentence, phrase, or word sung or said by the people or choir after or in reply to the officiant at a religious service and often indicated in liturgical books by R or ℟ : RESPOND, RESPONSORY; *also* : an anthem sung after or during a lection **b** : a supernatural answer (as by an oracle) **c** (1) : ANSWER 5 (2) : the chorus or refrain of a folk song or rhyme **d** : reply to an objection in formal disputation **e** (1) : activity or inhibition of previous activity of an organism or of any of its parts resulting from stimulation ⟨a motor ~⟩ ⟨a native ~⟩ (2) : such activity or inhibition existing in a covariant relationship with drive, cue, and reinforcement **f** : the output of a transducer or detecting device resulting from a given input; *specif* : the voltage output of a microphone per unit amplitude of sound pressure at the diaphragm — compare RESPONSE CURVE **g** : a bridge bid made by a player who responds **2** : a half pier or pillar that supports an arch

**response curve** *n* : a curve graphically exhibiting the magnitude of the response of a sensitive device to a varying stimulus (as of a microphone to sounds of varying intensity)

**re·sponse·less** \-slə̇s\ *adj* [*response* + *-less*] : making no response : UNRESPONSIVE

**re·spons·er** \-sə(r)\ *n* -s [*response* + *-er*] : RESPONDER

**re·spon·si·bil·i·ty** \rə̇,spän(t)sə'bilədē, rē,s-, -lətē, -i\ *n* -ES **1** : the quality or state of being responsible: as **a** : moral, legal, or mental accountability ⟨assume the ~ for another's debt⟩ ⟨prove the ~ of the accused⟩ ⟨a person completely lacking in ~⟩ **b** : RELIABILITY, TRUSTWORTHINESS; *sometimes* : ability to pay ⟨the ~ of one seeking a loan⟩ **2** : something for which anyone is responsible or accountable ⟨leadership carries great *responsibilities*⟩ ⟨sought relief from his ~⟩ ⟨a ~ he had never asked for⟩

**1re·spon·si·ble** \-'spän(t)səbəl\ *adj, sometimes* -ER/-EST [L *responsus* (past part. of *respondēre* to answer, correspond) + E *-ible* — more at RESPOND] **1** *obs* : CORRESPONDENT, ACCORDANT **2 a** : likely to be called upon to answer ⟨a man is ~ for his acts⟩ **b** : answerable as the primary cause, motive, or agent whether of evil or good : creditable or chargeable with the result — used with *for* ⟨~ for her injury⟩ ⟨a committee ~ for assembling supplies⟩ **c** : liable or subject to legal review or in case of fault to penalties ⟨a guardian is ~ to the court for his conduct in office⟩ **3 a** : able to respond or answer for one's conduct and obligations : trustworthy in respect to financial or other matters ⟨a ~ citizen⟩ **b** : of decent appearance : PRESENTABLE **c** (1) : having the character of a free moral agent : capable of determining one's own acts (2) : capable of being deterred by consideration of sanctions or consequences **4** : involving responsibility : involving a degree of accountability ⟨a ~ office⟩ **5** : politically answerable (as to a legislature or an electorate); *esp* : required to submit to the electorate if defeated by the legislature — used esp. of the British cabinet

**syn** ANSWERABLE, ACCOUNTABLE, AMENABLE, LIABLE: RESPONSIBLE may differ from ANSWERABLE and ACCOUNTABLE in centering attention on a formal organizational role, function, duty, or trust ⟨while held *responsible* for the bank's operations, the president has powers considered largely nominal —*Current Biog.*⟩ ⟨chief of personnel for the *New York Herald Tribune*, where she is also *responsible* for special editorial work in the field of industrial relations —*Current Biog.*⟩ ANSWERABLE is likely to be used in situations involving moral or legal obligation or duty under judgment ⟨we must take heed, however, that we do not load their memory with infamy which of right belongs to their master. For the treaty of Dover the King himself is chiefly *answerable* —T.B.Macaulay⟩ ⟨there was something ineradicably corrupt inside her for which her father was not *answerable* —E.K.Brown⟩ ACCOUNTABLE may be used in situations involving imminence of retribution for unfulfilled trust or violated obligation ⟨the president is invested with certain important political powers, in the exercise of which he is to use his own discretion, and is *accountable* only to his country in his political character and to his own conscience —John Marshall⟩ AMENABLE may indicate the fact of subjection to review, judgment, or control by a higher agency ⟨certain boats are sometimes not *amenable* to the rules of the right-of-way. A naval boat, for instance, on official business, may demand and take the right-of-way —H.A. Calahan⟩ ⟨scholar and teacher alike ranked as clerks, free from lay responsibilities or the control of civil tribunals, and *amenable* only to the rule of the bishop and the sentence of his spiritual courts —J.R.Green⟩ LIABLE may indicate the fact of being legally answerable without making further indication or implication ⟨judgment in cases of impeachment shall not extend further than to removal from office, and disqualification to hold and enjoy any office of honor, trust, or profit under the United States; but the party convicted shall, nevertheless, be *liable* and subject to indictment, trial, judgment, and punishment, according to law —*U. S. Constitution*⟩

**2responsible** \"\ *n* -s : one that accepts responsibility; *esp* : an actor prepared to fill various important roles as occasion demands

**re·spon·si·ble·ness** *n* -ES : the quality or state of being responsible

**re·spon·si·bly** \-blē,-bli\ *adv* : in a responsible manner : so as to exhibit responsibility

**re·spon·sion** \-nchən\ *n* -s [ME, fr. MF or ML; MF *responsion* answer, sum to be paid, fr. ML *responsion-, responsio*, fr. L, answer, fr. *responsus* (past part. of *respondēre* to answer) + *-ion-, -io* -ion — more at RESPOND] **1** *obs* : a sum required to be paid; *esp* : an annual payment required of a member of a military order of knighthood **2 a** : an act of answering : ANSWER, RESPONSE **b responsions** *pl* : the first examination taken by a candidate for the B.A. degree at Oxford University and required for matriculation — called also *smalls;* compare PREVIOUS EXAMINATION

**re·spon·sive** \-n(t)siv, -sēv *also* -səv\ *adj* [MF or LL; MF *responsif*, fr. LL *responsivus*, fr. L *responsus* + *-ivus* -ive] **1** : giving or serving as an answer : constituting a response or made in response to something ⟨a ~ glance⟩ ⟨prairie fires sprang up ~ to the draught⟩ **2** *obs* : CORRESPONDENT, CORRESPONDING **3** : readily inclined to respond or react appropriately or sympathetically to influences, suggestions, impressions : SENSITIVE : not dull, apathetic, unreceptive, impassive, or unaffected ⟨sensitive to atmospheric conditions, ~ to every varying shift of wind and weather —J.C.Powys⟩ ⟨efforts . . . to keep government in America ~ to the will of the people —V.L.Parrington⟩ **4** : involving the use of responses ⟨~ worship⟩ **syn** see TENDER

**re·spon·sive·ly** \-səvlē, -li\ *adv* : in a responsive manner

**re·spon·sive·ness** \-sivnə̇s, -sēv- *also* -səv-\ *n* -ES [*responsive* + *-ness*] : the quality or state of responding or being responsive; *esp* : the rapidity with which a member (as an instrument pointer) comes to rest after a change of any kind

**responsive reading** *n* : textual matter read aloud as part of a religious service or exercise in which a verse or sentence by the leader is followed by a verse or sentence by the congregation; *also* : a liturgical form or process in which leader and congregation read passages aloud alternatively

**re·spon·siv·i·ty** \rə̇,spän'sivədē, (,)rē,s-\ *n* -ES [*responsive* + *-ity*] : RESPONSIVENESS

**re·spon·sor** \rə̇'spän(t)sə(r), rē's-\ *n* -s [L, one that answers, fr. *responsus* + *-or*] : the receiver component of an interrogator

**1re·spon·so·ri·al** \rə̇,spän¦sōrēəl, (,)rē¦s-\ *adj* [*1responsory* + *-al*] : relating to or consisting of responses : ANTIPHONAL

**2responsorial** \"\ *n* -s [ML *responsoriale*, fr. LL *responsorium* responsory + L *-ale* (neut. of *-alis* -al)] : a book of religious responsories

**1re·spon·so·ry** \rə̇'spän(t)sərē, rē's-, -ri\ *n* -ES [ME, fr. LL *responsorium*, fr. L *responsus* (past part. of *respondēre* to answer) + *-orium* -ory — more at RESPOND] : a liturgical response; *esp* : an anthem that is sung or said after or during a lection

**2responsory** *adj* [ML *responsorius*, fr. L *responsus* + *-orius* -ory] *obs* : relating to or constituting an answer : ANSWERING, RESPONSIVE

**re·spon·sum** \rə̇'spän(t)səm, rē's-\ *n, pl* **respon·sa** \-)sə\ [NL, fr. L, reply, formal opinion of a jurisconsult — more at RESPONSE] : a written decision from a rabbinical authority in response to a submitted question or problem

**re·spool·er** \(')rē+\ *n* [*re-* + *spooler*] : a worker who winds yarn from one spool to another

**re·spot** \"+\ *vt* [*re-* + *spot*] : to replace (as a tenpin) precisely in position

**re·spray** \"+\ *vt* [*re-* + *spray*] : to spray (as fruit trees) an additional time ⟨had to ~ the orchard because of rain⟩

**re·spring** \"+\ *vb* [*re-* + *spring*] *vi* : to spring up again ~ *vt* : to equip with new springs ⟨had the chair *resprung*⟩

**res pu·bli·ca** \rā'spübləkä\ *n, pl* **res publi·cae** \-,kī\ [L — more at REPUBLIC] : COMMONWEAL, COMMONWEALTH, STATE, REPUBLIC

**res publicae** *n pl* [LL, public things] : things (as the sea, navigable waters, and highways) that are construed under Roman and civil law as owned by no one but subject to use by the public

**re·spue** \rə̇'spyü\ *vt* [L *respuere* to spit back, fr. *re-* + *spuere* to spit — more at SPEW] : to reject vigorously

**ressala** *var of* RISALA

**ressaldar** *var of* RISALDAR

**res·sault·ed** \rə̇'sȯltə̇d, (')rē¦s-\ *adj* [F *ressault, ressaut* projection (fr. It *risalto*, fr. *risaltare* to spring back, project, fr. *ri-* re- — fr. L *re-* — + *saltare* to leap, fr. L) + E *-ed* — more at SALTANT] : having projections from the plane of a wall or surface

**res ser·vi·ens** \'rās'servē,en(t)s, 'rēz'sərvē,enz\ *n* [NL] : a servient property or tenement subject to a servitude

**1rest** \'rest\ *n* -s [ME, fr. OE *ræst, rest* rest, bed; akin to OHG

rests 5a(2)

*rasta* rest, a measure of distance between two resting places, ON *rōst* a measure of distance, mile, Goth *rasta* mile, OE *rōw* rest, calm, OHG *ruowa*, ON *rō*, Gk *erōē* rest, respite, and perh. to OE *ærn, ren* house, OFris *-ern*, ON *rann*, Goth *razn*] **1** : refreshment or repose of body or mind due to more or less complete cessation of activity esp. to sleep ⟨eight hours of ~ a night⟩ ⟨for this I had deprived myself of ~ and health —Mary W. Shelley⟩ **2 a** (1) : cessation or temporary interruption of motion, exertion, or labor : freedom from activity or labor ⟨~ from hard physical effort⟩ ⟨a ten-minute ~ period⟩ ⟨for the purpose of drawing a line between such bodily motions and ~*s* —O.W.Holmes †1935⟩ (2) : a bodily state (as that attained by a fasting individual lying supine) characterized by minimal functional and metabolic activities ⟨the patient must have complete ~⟩ (3) : a position on any gymnastic apparatus in which the body is supported wholly or mainly by the hands or arms, the elbows are above the point of support, and the center of gravity is below the shoulders **b** : absence or cessation of motion as a physical phenomenon : continuance in the same place ⟨a body will continue in a state of ~ unless acted upon⟩ **c** : the repose of death ⟨went to his final ~⟩ **3** : a place where one may rest or abide: as **a** : a permanent or transitory lodging place ⟨found their ~ in the shelter of a wayside tree⟩ ⟨whether that luxurious roadside ~ is a hotel or motel —Frances W. Browin⟩ **b** : a halting place or breathing spot (as a landing between flights of a stair) ⟨a steep trail with little ~*s* chipped out of the rock⟩ **c** : an establishment for the accommodation of a particular group or class (as when out of work or off duty) ⟨a sailors' ~⟩ **4** : freedom from anything that fatigues, disturbs, or troubles : peace of mind or spirit ⟨there was ~ now, not disquietude, in the knowledge —Ellen Glasgow⟩ **5 a** (1) : a rhythmic silence in music or in one of its parts (2) : a character that stands for such silence ⟨half ~⟩ ⟨quarter ~⟩ **b** : a brief pause in reading : CAESURA **6** : something on which anything rests or leans or may rest or lean for support ⟨chin ~ for a violin or viola⟩ ⟨a rail serving as a ~ for the feet⟩: as **a** : a support for a gun when firing **b** : a part in a lathe or similar machine that supports the cutting tool or steadies the work **c** *Brit* : BRIDGE 3e **d** : the part of a partial denture that rests on an abutment tooth, distributes stresses, and holds the clasp in position **e** : a sand-filled pillow or similar firm but moldable cushion used to raise or support a portion of the body during surgery ⟨kidney ~⟩ **7** : renewed vigor

**syn** REST, RELAXATION, LEISURE, REPOSE, EASE, COMFORT: of these closely related terms the first three — REST, RELAXATION, and LEISURE — stress the condition of being free from labor or from the tension or necessity of effort; the second three — REPOSE, EASE, and COMFORT — stress more the frame of mind or condition of body incident to such a condition. REST, the most general of the terms, emphasizes primarily the fact of cessation or intermission of activity, esp. fatiguing activity or effortful movement, although it also usu. indicates the consequent relief, refreshment, or reinvigoration ⟨night came and with it but little *rest* —Thomas Hardy⟩ ⟨to enjoy a *rest* from struggling —Leslie Rees⟩ RELAXATION emphasizes the release of the muscular or spiritual tension necessary to work or worry; it may be identical with REST or achieved in it so that in some uses it has come to be synonymous with *recreation* ⟨throughout the hours of busiest work and closest application, as well as in the preceding and following moments of leisure and occasional intervals of *relaxation* —W.C.Brownell⟩ ⟨the active amusements and *relaxations* of life can only rest certain of our faculties —John Galsworthy⟩ LEISURE is rather the time exempt from labor as well as the freedom from the necessity of effort; it usu., but not necessarily, implies rest or relaxation, and frequently indicates the unhurriedness of life incident to such a sense of freedom ⟨he who knows how to employ rationally any amount of *leisure* that may fall to his lot —Norman Douglas⟩ ⟨the absence of worry and anxiety about oneself . . . has always been assumed to be a prerequisite condition of *leisure* —R.A.Beals & Leon Brody⟩ ⟨the capacity for civilized enjoyment, for *leisure* and laughter —Bertrand Russell⟩ REPOSE usu. indicates a rest distinguished by physical or mental tranquillity, a freedom from any agitation or disturbance as in peaceful sleep, and has therefore developed to indicate such tranquillity or freedom itself or the appearance of it ⟨a certain woodenness when her face was in *repose* —Scott Fitzgerald⟩ ⟨the pleasant *repose* of the upper valley villages —*Amer. Guide Series: Vt.*⟩ ⟨a langorous *repose* in keeping with the season —Elinor Wylie⟩ EASE indicates a physical or mental condition from which tension, anxiety, effort, or pain have been removed; it may carry a range of meanings from a pleasant release from pain to a rather luxurious absence of all physical or mental effort; by extension from this it has come to signify a relaxed effortlessness in movement, conduct, or accomplishment ⟨a mild sedative brought a certain *ease*⟩ ⟨to live in *ease* and comfort⟩ ⟨the *ease* which he displayed in the conduct of practical affairs —Arnold Bennett⟩ ⟨*ease* and strength, effort and weakness, go together —G.B.Shaw⟩ COMFORT indicates essentially the physical or mental state induced by relief from what disturbs or troubles, but more widely indicates a state not only in which all things that disturb or pain are absent but in which usu. there is a positive physical if passive pleasure. COMFORT stresses more than EASE does the physical pleasurableness of the state and in usu. implying an outside agency which induces the state it has come to signify the thing or things that bring such relief or pleasure ⟨every word brought *comfort* rather than grief —Virginia D. Dawson & Betty D. Wilson⟩ ⟨it was a great *comfort* to me to get back home alive⟩ ⟨if it went on long there would be no *comfort* in the home for anybody —Stuart Cloete⟩ ⟨he is a layman which will be a *comfort* to those of his readers who have not had a scientific training —*London Calling*⟩

**at rest 1** : resting or reposing esp. in sleep or death ⟨after so long a sickness it was merciful that she was finally *at rest* and in her grave⟩ **2** : QUIESCENT, MOTIONLESS ⟨the center of buoyancy of a floating body which is *at rest* —*Water & Sewage Control Engineering*⟩ ⟨no small child is ever really *at rest*⟩ **3** : free of anxieties : CALM ⟨set your mind *at rest*⟩

**2rest** \"\ *vb* -ED/-ING/-S [ME *resten*, fr. OE *ræstan, restan;* akin to OE *ræst* rest] *vi* **1 a** : to take or get repose by lying down; *esp* : to get refreshment of body by sleep **b** : to be in the repose of death : be dead or in the grave **c** : SLEEP, SLUMBER **2** : to cease from action or motion : desist from labor or exertion ⟨planned to ~ during her vacation⟩ **3** : to be free from whatever wearies or disturbs : be quiet or still : remain the same or in the same place **4** : to have place : sit or lie fixed or supported : SETTLE ⟨a column ~*s* on its pedestal⟩ ⟨one wing of the army ~*ed* on the hills⟩ **5 a** : to remain confident : put trust **b** : to lean in confidence : repose without anxiety : TRUST, RELY ⟨~ secure on his word⟩ **c** : to become based or founded : have a use as a foundation — usu. used with *on* or *upon* ⟨the verdict ~*ed* on several sound precedents⟩ ⟨a charge ~*ing* upon one man's unsupported statement⟩ **6 a** *obs* : to become vested **b** *obs* : CONSIST **c** : to remain or lie for action or accomplishment ⟨the maintenance of peace ~*s* with him alone⟩ **7** *of farmland* : to remain idle or uncropped **8** : to bring to an end voluntarily the introduction of evidence in a law case and thereby lose the right to introduce fresh evidence except in rebuttal ~ *vt* **1 a :** to give rest or repose to **:** refresh by repose **:** lay or place at rest **:** allow to remain inactive, quiet, or undisturbed ⟨~*ed* his horse before starting up the grade⟩ ⟨you should ~ your eyes from so much reading⟩ **b :** to permit (as soldiers in ranks) to move, talk, and smoke while keeping one foot in place ⟨~*ed* his men between the drill exercises⟩ **2 :** to set (as oneself) at rest ⟨~ yourself before the fire⟩ — often used formerly in greetings ⟨God ~ you merry, Sir —Shak.⟩ **3 :** to place or lay on a support **:** support on or with something ⟨~ the book against the lamp⟩ ⟨~*ed* his gouty foot on a cushion⟩ **4 a :** to cause to be firmly fixed **:** GROUND ⟨was ~*ing* all his hopes on his son⟩ ⟨~*ed* her case on this argument⟩ **b :** to desist voluntarily from presenting evidence pertinent to (a case at law) **5 :** to allow (land) to remain idle **syn** see BASE — **rest with :** to be the prerogative or province of ⟨any further investigation *rests with* the supervisor⟩

**³rest** \"\ *n* -s [ME, short for *arest* — more at ARREST] **1** *obs* **:** a checking or halting by or as if by arrest; *specif* **:** legal arrest **2 :** a projection from or attachment on the side of the breastplate of medieval armor intended to support the butt of the lance **3 :** CLARION 5

**⁴rest** \"\ *vt* [ME *resten*, short for *aresten* — more at ARREST] *chiefly dial* **:** ARREST

**⁵rest** \"\ *n* -s [ME, fr. MF *reste*, fr. *rester* to remain, rest] **1 :** something that remains over: as **a rests** *pl* **:** REMAINS, RELICS **b** (1) *obs* **:** an amount still unpaid **:** a balance due (2) *Brit* **:** a reserve (as of a bank) consisting of profits remaining undivided after payment of dividends **:** SURPLUS **c :** the part remaining after removal of a part in fact or contemplation **:** all that is left **:** REMAINDER, RESIDUE — used with *the* ⟨if you will take the baby we can care for the ~⟩ ⟨used the ~ of the butter at breakfast⟩ **d :** a mass of surviving embryonic cells or of cells misplaced in development ⟨some neoplasms probably always arise from embryonic ~*s*⟩ ⟨adrenal *rests* in the kidney⟩ **2 :** a series of repeated returns (as in a game of tennis) **:** a spell of uninterrupted returning — compare RALLY

**⁶rest** \"\ *vi* -ED/-ING/-S [ME *resten*, fr. MF *rester* to remain, be left over, fr. L *restare* to stand back, stop behind, be left over, fr. *re-* + *stare* to stand — more at STAND] **1** *obs* **:** to remain unpaid **2 :** to be left over **:** remain after something is taken away **:** continue to exist

**rest** *abbr* restored

**re·staff** \(ˈ)rē+\ *vt* [*re-* + *staff*] **:** to provide with a new staff ⟨had to ~ the entire hotel⟩

**re·stage** \"+\ *vt* [*re-* + *stage*] **:** to present again or anew on the stage; *esp* **:** to present (as a play) with a new setting

**re·stain** \"+\ *vt* [*re-* + *stain*] **:** to stain again or anew; *esp* **:** to re-treat with a stain ⟨destaining and ~*ing* histological slides⟩

**rest and residue** *or* **rest, residue, and remainder** *n* [⁵*rest*] **:** the residuary estate of a testator

**re·start** \(ˈ)rē+\ *vb* [*re-* + *start*] *vt* **1 :** to start again or anew ⟨~*ed* his car⟩ **2 :** to resume (as an activity) after interruption ~ *vi* **:** to commence once more **:** resume operation

**re·starter** \"+\ *n* [*restart* + *-er*] **:** one that restarts; *esp* **:** a device for automatically restarting an apparatus or mechanism (as a phonograph)

**re·state** \"+\ *vt* [*re-* + *state*] **:** to state again or in a new form — **re·statement** \"+\ *n*

**re·staur** *or* **re·stor** \rə'stȯ(ə)r\ *n* -s [*restaur* fr. F, alter. (influenced by *restaurer* to restore) of OF *restor* restoration, reparation; *restor*, alter. (influenced by *restore*) of *restaur* — more at RESTAURANT, RESTORE, n.] **1 :** the legal recourse that insurers have against each other according to the date of their insurance **2 :** the recourse of an insurer against the master of a ship if loss occurs through his negligence; *also* **:** the recourse of one against a guarantor or against one under obligation to indemnify

**res·tau·rant** \'rest(ə)rənt, -stə,ränt *also* -,stränt *or* -,stərnt\ *n* -s [F, food that restores, restaurant, fr. pres. part. of *restaurer* to restore, fr. L *restaurare* — more at RESTORE] **:** an establishment where refreshments or meals may be procured by the public **:** a public eating house

**restaurant car** *n, Brit* **:** DINING CAR

**res·tau·rant·er** \-ntə(r)\ *n* -s [*restaurant* + *-er*] **:** RESTAURATEUR

**res·tau·ra·teur** \;restə|rə¦tər(·), |,rä¦-, -¦tü(ə)r\ *also* **res·tau·ran·teur** \|,rän·¦t- *also* |,ran-\ *n* -s [*restaurateur* fr. F, fr. LL *restaurator* restorer, fr. L *restauratus* (past part. of *restaurare* to restore) + *-or*; *restauranteur*, modif. (influenced by *restaurant*) of F *restaurateur* — more at RESTORE] **:** the operator or proprietor of a restaurant

**¹res·tau·ra·tion** \,restə'rāshən, -e,stȯ'r-\ *archaic var of* RESTORATION

**²res·tau·ra·tion** \restȯräsyōⁿ\ *n* -s [F, lit., restoral, restoration, fr. MF — more at RESTORATION] **:** RESTAURANT; *also* **:** the purveying of food (as by a restaurant)

**res·tau·ra·tor** \'restə,rād·ə(r)\ *n* -s [LL] *archaic* **:** RESTORER

**res·tau·ra·trice** \;restərə¦trēs\ *n* -s [F, fr. LL *restauratric-, restauratrix*, fem. of *restaurator* restorer — more at RESTAURATEUR] **:** a woman who operates or owns a restaurant

**¹restbalk** \'=,=\ *n* [¹*rest* + *balk*] **:** a ridge of land between furrows

**²restbalk** \"\ *vt* **:** to leave restbalks in (land) in ploughing

**rest cure** *n* [¹*rest*] **:** treatment of disease (as neurasthenia or tuberculosis) by rest and isolation in a good hygienic environment

**rest day** *n* **:** a day which is set aside for rest or on which one departs from a normal or usual routine: as **a** (1) **:** SABBATH (2) **:** a day of equivalent religious import in religions other than Judaism and Christianity **b :** a day that is not a workday **c :** any of the days sometimes introduced into an open season on which hunting is not permitted

**rested** *past of* REST

**re·steel** \(ˈ)rē+\ *vt* [*re-* + *steel*] **:** to equip with or as if with new steel ⟨~*ed* himself to meet the challenge⟩

**re·stem** \"+\ *vt* [*re-* + *stem*] **:** to stem again ⟨a ship *restemming* its way⟩

**rest·er** \'restə(r)\ *n* -s **:** one that rests

**rest·ful** \'restfəl\ *adj, sometimes* **restfuller** \-fələ(r)\ *sometimes* **restfullest** \-fələst\ [ME, fr. ¹*rest* + *-ful*] **1 :** marked by, affording, or suggesting rest and repose **:** offering freedom from toil, agitation, or effort ⟨something so beautiful and ~ about his method . . . so free from that fretful haste, that vehement striving —J.K.Jerome⟩ **2 :** enjoying rest **:** being at ease **:** RELAXED, TRANQUIL, PLACID ⟨as if no . . . circumstances could put her for long together out of temper . . . her lips were full and ~ —Samuel Butler †1902⟩ **syn** see COMFORTABLE

**rest·ful·ly** \-fəlē, -li\ *adv* [ME, fr. *restful* + *-ly*] **:** in a restful manner or style **:** so as to be restful

**rest·ful·ness** *n* -ES [ME *restfulnes*, fr. *restful* + *-nes* -ness] **:** the quality or state of being restful

**restharrow** \'=,=(,)=\ *n* [⁴*rest* + *harrow*] **:** a plant of the genus *Ononis*; *esp* **:** a European woody herb (*O. repens*) with pink flowers, unifoliolate leaves, and long tough roots

**rest home** *n* [¹*rest*] **:** an establishment for the care and housing of persons (as the aged, convalescents) that need special attention or services

**rest house** *n* **1 :** a house or building for the rest and shelter of travelers; *specif* **:** a dak bungalow **2 :** a resort facility (as a boarding house) featuring a quiet relaxing life and simple wholesome food and appealing esp. to a clientele seeking rest and relaxation

**restie** *obs var of* RESTY

**restier** *comparative of* RESTY

**restiest** *superlative of* RESTY

**res·tiff** *or* **res·tif** \'restəf\ *adj* [ME *restife, restiffe* — more at RESTIVE] **:** RESTIVE 1c

**res·ti·form body** \'restə,fȯrm-\ *n* [L *restis* rope, cord + E *-form* — more at RUSH] **:** either of a pair of prominent bands of nerve fibers on the dorsal surface of the medulla oblongata that form part of the lateral boundaries of the fourth ventricle and are continued upward as the inferior peduncles of the cerebellum

**re·stimulate** \(ˈ)rē+\ *vt* [*re-* + *stimulate*] **:** to reactivate by stimulation

**resting** *adj* [ME, fr. pres. part. of *resten* to rest, repose] **1 :** not in growing condition **:** not physiologically active **:** DORMANT, QUIESCENT ⟨a ~ lily bulb⟩ ⟨~ nerve cells⟩; *also* **:** of, relating to, or marked by dormancy ⟨a ~ period⟩ ⟨~ stages⟩ **2 :** not undergoing or marked by mitosis or other form of division though otherwise physiologically active ⟨a ~ stage⟩

**resting cell** *n* **1 :** RESTING SPORE **2 :** a living cell with a resting nucleus

**resting egg** *n* **:** WINTER EGG

**resting nucleus** *n* **:** a cell nucleus when not undergoing reproduction (as by mitosis)

**resting-place** \'==,=\ *n* [ME, fr. *resting* (gerund of *resten* to rest, repose) + *place*] **1 :** a place where rest may be taken **2 :** the place where a dead person is laid **3 :** a landing in a staircase **:** HALFPACE, QUARTERPACE

**resting spore** *n* [*resting*] **:** a spore (as many zygospores) that remains dormant for a period before germination and is usu. invested with a thickened cell wall to withstand adverse conditions (as of desiccation, heat, or cold) — see CHLAMYDOSPORE

**resting wandering cell** *n* **:** a fixed histiocyte of the loose connective tissue of the body

**res·tio** \'restē,ō\ *n, cap* [NL, fr. L, maker of rope, fr. *restis* rope, cord — more at RUSH] **:** a large genus of leafless southern African and Australian herbs (family Restionaceae) having one-celled anthers and many-flowered spikelets with imbricated glumes — see CORDLEAF, ROPE GRASS

**res·ti·o·na·ce·ae** \,restēə'nāsē,ē\ *n pl, cap* [NL, fr. *Restion-, Restio*, type genus + *-aceae*] **:** a family of monocotyledonous herbs (order Xyridales) that resemble rushes and have either no leaves or tiny sheathing ones and glumaceous panicled flowers — **res·ti·o·na·ceous** \;===¦nāshəs\ *adj*

**re·stipulation** \(;)rē+\ *n* [*re-* + *stipulation*] **:** an act of stipulating anew **:** RESTATEMENT

**res·ti·tute** \'restə,tüt, -stə·,tyüt\ *vb* -ED/-ING/-S [L *restitutus*, past part. of *restituere* to restore — more at RESTITUTION] *vt* **1 :** to restore to a former state or position **:** REHABILITATE **2 :** to give back **:** REFUND ~ *vi* **:** to become restored, rehabilitated, or refunded **:** undergo restitution

**res·ti·tu·tio in in·te·grum** \,restə'tüd·ē,ōi'nintəgrəm, -,ō-(,)inin·'teg-\ *n* [LL] *Roman & civil law* **:** restoration to a whole or uninjured condition **:** restoration to the status quo ante

**res·ti·tu·tion** \,restə'tüshən, -stə·'tyü-\ *n* -s [ME, fr. OF, fr. L *restitution-, restitutio*, fr. *restitutus* (past part. of *restituere* to set up again, restore, fr. *re-* + *-stituere* — fr. *statuere*, to set up) + *-ion-, -io* -ion — more at STATUTE] **1 :** an act of restoring or a condition of being restored: as **a :** restoration of something to its rightful owner **:** the making good of or giving an equivalent for some injury (as a loss of or damage to property) **b :** the final restoration of all things and persons to harmony with God's will **c :** restoration of a person to a former position or status; *also* **:** the condition of one so restored **:** REINSTATEMENT **d :** restoration of a thing or institution to its original state or form **e** *Brit* **:** restoration of conjugal rights **f :** a return to or recovery of a former physical state ⟨the ~ of an elastic body⟩ — compare COEFFICIENT OF RESTITUTION **2 :** something intended to cause or serving to cause restoration of a previous state: as **a** (1) *Brit* **:** a legal action to compel resumption of cohabitation between a husband and wife who have separated that is now used only as preliminary to divorce (2) **:** an action based upon equitable principles to recover money or property that in good conscience belongs to the plaintiff or to prevent a defendant from being unjustly enriched at the expense of the plaintiff (3) **:** an action to restore the parties to a transaction that is being rescinded or avoided to the respective positions they occupied prior to entering into the transaction **b :** a movement of rotation that usu. occurs in childbirth after the head has been delivered and that causes it to point toward the side to which it was directed at the beginning of labor

**res·ti·tu·tion·ism** \-shə,nizəm\ *n* -s [*restitution* + *-ism*] **:** RESTORATIONISM

**res·ti·tu·tion·ist** \-sh(ə)nəst\ *n* -s *often cap* [*restitution* + *-ist*] **:** one who holds some form of religious doctrine based on the belief that everything is ultimately to be restored to its pristine form and purity **:** RESTORATIONIST

**restitution nucleus** *n* **:** a cell nucleus that contains a diploid or double number of chromosomes and that results typically from failure of completion of a division in mitosis

**res·ti·tu·tive** \'restə,tüd·iv, -stə·,tyü-\ *adj* [ML *restitutivus*, fr. L *restitutus* (past part. of *restituere* to restore) + *-ivus* -ive — more at RESTITUTION] **:** constituting or tending toward restitution

**res·ti·tu·to·ry** \;restə¦tüd·ərē, -stə·¦tyü-; rə'stichə,tōrē\ *adj* [LL *restitutorius*, fr. L *restitutus* + *-orius* -ory] **:** of, relating to, or aiming at restitution

**res·tive** \'restiv, -tēv *also* -təv\ *adj* [ME *restife, restiffe* stationary (of animals), refusing to go forward, resisting control, fr. MF *restif*, (fr. *rester* to remain, stop behind) + *-if* -ive — more at REST] **1** *archaic* **a :** disposed to rest **:** INACTIVE, SLUGGISH **b :** standing firm **:** unwilling to yield or adjust **:** PERSISTENT, STUBBORN, INFLEXIBLE **c :** stubbornly resisting control or guidance **:** obstinate in refusal **:** BALKY **2 a** *of a horse* **:** high-spirited and unwilling to submit to discipline or to stand at ease **:** FRACTIOUS **b :** marked by uneasiness and lack of quietness or attentive interest **:** FIDGETY ⟨a ~ crowd⟩ **syn** see CONTRARY

**res·tive·ly** \-tivlē, -li\ *adv* **:** in a restive manner

**res·tive·ness** \-tivnəs, -tēv- *also* -təv-\ *n* -ES **:** the quality or state of being restive

**rest·less** \'restləs, *in rapid speech* -sl-\ *adj* [ME *restles*, fr. ¹*rest* + *-les* -less] **1 a :** deprived of rest or sleep **:** finding no rest **:** UNEASY ⟨the patient was ~ from pain⟩ **b :** not affording rest **:** UNRESTFUL ⟨a ~ night⟩ **2 a :** continuing without end **:** UNCEASING ⟨~ change⟩ **b :** moving or operating continuously **:** UNQUIET ⟨the ~ sea⟩ **3 :** characterized by or manifesting unrest esp. of mind **:** lacking in repose **:** averse to inaction; *also* **:** CHANGEFUL, UNSETTLED, DISCONTENTED

**restless cavy** *n* **:** APEREA

**restless flycatcher** *n* **:** a small flycatcher (*Seisura inquieta*) of Australia that is steely blue above and white below and has the habit of hovering with the body arched and wings quivering

**rest·less·ly** *adv* **:** in a restless manner

**rest·less·ness** *n* -ES **:** the quality or state of being restless

**rest mass** *n* [¹*rest*] **:** the mass of a body exclusive of additional mass acquired by the body when in motion according to the theory of relativity

**re·stock** \(ˈ)rē+\ *vt* [*re-* + *stock*] **:** to stock again **:** provide new stock for ⟨~*ing* a forest with seedlings⟩ ⟨~*ed* the stream with trout⟩

**restor** *var of* RESTAUR

**re·stor·able** \rə'stōrəbəl, -rē's-, -tȯr-\ *adj* [¹*restore* + *-able*] **:** fit for restoring or reclaiming; *esp* **:** capable of being rehabilitated ⟨~ prisoners⟩

**re·stor·al** \-ōrəl,-ȯrəl\ *n* -s [¹*restore* + *-al*] **:** RESTORATION

**¹res·to·ra·tion** \,restə'rāshən\ *n* -s [alter. (influenced by ¹*restore*) of ME *restauracion*, fr. MF or LL; MF *restauration*, fr. LL *restauration-, restauratio*, fr. L *restauratus* (past part. of *restaurare* to restore) + *-ion-, -io-* -ion — more at RESTORE] **1 :** an act of restoring or the condition or fact of being restored: as **a :** a bringing back to or putting back into a former position or condition **:** REINSTATEMENT, RENEWAL, REESTABLISHMENT ⟨the ~ of peace⟩ ⟨the ~ of the monarchy⟩ ⟨behold the different climes agree rejoicing in thy ~ —John Dryden⟩ **b :** a putting back into consciousness or health **:** recovery of health or strength ⟨~ from sickness⟩ **c :** the ultimate bringing of the whole universe including all men into harmony with the will of God — called also *final restoration* **d :** the act of giving back something to one deprived of it **:** RESTITUTION **e :** a putting back into an unimpaired or much improved condition ⟨the ~ of a painting⟩ **f :** the act or fact of replacing missing teeth or crowns or associated structures; *also* **:** the replacement (as a denture) used **g :** the reinstatement of the amount or penalty of a fidelity bond (as by a special payment) **2 :** something that is restored; *specif* **:** a representation of the original form (as of a fossil animal or of a building) **3 :** the process of putting a building back into nearly or quite the original form; *also* **:** the making of drawings or models or both designed to show the conceived original form of a building (as a ruin)

**²restoration** \;==¦=\ *adj, usu cap* **:** of, relating to, or constituting a period in English history often held to coincide with the reign of Charles II but sometimes considered to extend from his accession to that of Queen Anne ⟨*Restoration* drama⟩

**res·to·ra·tion·er** \,restə'rāsh(ə)nə(r)\ *n* -s [*restoration* + *-er*] **:** RESTORATIONIST

**res·to·ra·tion·ism** \-shə,nizəm\ *n* -s [*restauration* + *-ism*] **:** the belief or doctrines of the restorationists

**res·to·ra·tion·ist** \-sh(ə)nəst\ *n* -s [*restauration* + *-ist*] **1 :** one who believes in a temporary future punishment and a final restoration of all to the favor and presence of God **2 :** one who makes restorations of buildings

**restoration style** *n, usu cap R* **:** an English style esp. of furniture and architecture characteristic of the period of the restoration of Charles II

**¹re·stor·ative** \rə'stōrəd·iv, -tȯr-\ *adj* [ME *restoratif*, alter. (influenced by ¹*restore*) of *restauratif*, fr. MF, fr. L *restauratus* (past part. of *restaurare* to restore) + MF *-if* -ive — more at RESTORE] **:** of or relating to restoration **:** having power to restore — **re·stor·ative·ly** *adv* — **re·stor·ative·ness** *n* -ES

**²restorative** \"\ *n* -s [ME *restoratif*, fr. *restoratif*, adj.] **:** something (as a food or medicine) that serves to restore esp. a person to consciousness or rapidly to normal vigor

**res·to·ra·tor** \'restə,rād·ə(r)\ *n* -s [modif. (influenced by E ¹*restore*) of F *restaurateur* — more at RESTAURATEUR] *archaic* **:** RESTAURATEUR; *also* **:** RESTAURANT

**¹re·store** \rə'stō(ə)r, rē's-, -tȯ(ə)r, -tōə, -tȯ(ə)\ *vb* -ED/-ING/-S [ME *restoren*, fr. OF *restorer*, fr. L *restaurare* to put back into an original state, renew, fr. *re-* + *-staurare* (fr. *instaurare* to renew, restore, perform) — more at STORE] *vt* **1 :** to give back (as something lost or taken away) **:** make restitution of **:** RETURN ⟨*restored* the lost child to its parents⟩ **2 :** to put or bring back (as into existence or use) ⟨~ harmony among foes⟩ ⟨*restored* a city-manager plan of government⟩ **3 :** to bring back or to put back into a former or original state **:** RENEW: as **a :** REBUILD, RECONSTRUCT **b** (1) **:** to put back into or replace in a former state of favor or grace **:** deliver from the consequences of sin (2) **:** to reinstate in a former position or office **c :** to bring back to a healthy state **:** cause to recover ⟨and his hand was *restored* whole as the other —Mk 3:5 (AV)⟩ **d :** to make calm or tranquil in mind **e** (1) **:** to bring back from a state of injury or decay or from a changed condition (as by repairing or retouching) **:** RENOVATE ⟨~ a painting⟩ (2) **:** to repair and alter (a building) with the aim of putting back into the original form ⟨~ a cathedral⟩ **f :** to form a picture or model of the original form of (as something lost or mutilated) **:** represent or reproduce in the original form ⟨~ ancient ruins⟩ **g :** to place in a text as conjecturally the original reading **4 :** to bring (as a person) back to some former state ⟨*restored* the child to health⟩ **:** put again in possession of something ⟨~ the king to his throne⟩ **5 a** *obs* **:** to make amends or compensation for **b** *Scots law* **:** to give or make restitution to **c** *archaic* **:** to make good the loss or damage due to **d :** to put back into (a processed food) the original nutritive value by adding elements lost in processing or equivalents of such elements **6 a :** to put (itself) back into the original position or form ⟨an elastic body automatically ~*s* itself after deformation⟩ **b :** to bring (as steel damaged by overheating) back to normal condition **c :** to put back into a former or proper position ⟨*restored* the book to the shelf⟩ ~ *vi* **1** *obs* **:** RECOVER, REVIVE **2 :** to restore a person or thing — **restore in blood :** to readmit to rights (as of a title or inheritance) forfeited under English law by attainder either of the person himself or of his ancestors — compare CORRUPTION OF BLOOD

**²restore** *n* -s [ME, fr. MF *restor*, fr. OF, fr. *restorer* to restore] *obs* **:** RESTORATION

**restorement** *n* -s [ME, fr. MF, fr. OF, fr. *restorer* to restore + *-ment*] *obs* **:** RESTORATION

**re·stor·er** \rə'stōrə(r), rē's-, -tȯr-\ *n* -s [¹*restore* + *-er*] **:** one that restores or makes restorations

**restoring force** *or* **restoring torque** *n* [fr. pres. part. of ¹*restore*] **:** any one of the forces or torques that tend to restore a system or parts thereof to equilibrium after displacement

**restoring moment** *n* **:** RIGHTING MOMENT

**restoritie** *or* **restority** *n, pl* **restorities** [by alter.] *obs* **:** RESTORATIVE

**re·stow** \(ˈ)rē¦stō\ *vt* [*re-* + *stow*] **:** to stow (as freight) again or anew — **re·stow·al** \-ōəl\ *n* -s

**rest period** *n* [¹*rest*] **1 :** a period when the internal condition of a wood plant is unfavorable for the growth of buds even though external conditions are favorable **2 :** a period (as during winter or in a dry season) when bulbous plants lose their foliage and mature their bulbs

**restr** *abbr* restaurant

**re·straighten** \(ˈ)rē+\ *vt* [*re-* + *straighten*] **:** to straighten again or anew ⟨bent to ~ the seams of her hose⟩

**re·strain** \rə'strān, rē's-\ *vb* -ED/-ING/-S [ME *restreynen, restraynen*, fr. MF *restreindre, restraindre*, fr. L *restringere* to draw back tight, restrain, restrict, fr. *re-* + *stringere* to draw tight — more at STRAIN] *vt* **1 a :** to hold (as a person) back from some action, procedure, or course **:** prevent from doing something (as by physical or moral force or social pressure) ⟨~*ing* her charges . . . from overt acts of violence —C.H. Grandgent⟩ **b :** to limit or restrict to or in respect to a particular action or course **:** keep within bounds or under control ⟨~*ing* state banks which were inclined to do unsound business —*Dict. of Amer. Biog.*⟩ **2 a :** to moderate or limit the force, effect, development, or full exercise of **:** prevent or rule out excesses or extremes of ⟨~*ing* lax management⟩ **b :** to keep from being manifested or performed **:** REPRESS ⟨could hardly ~ her astonishment from being visible —Jane Austen⟩ **3** *obs* **:** to draw back (as a rein) tightly **4 a :** to deprive of liberty **:** place under arrest or restraint **b :** to deprive (as of liberty) by restraint **:** abridge the freedom of — used with *of* **5** *obs* **:** FORBEAR, FORBID ~ *vi* **1** *archaic* **:** REFRAIN **2 :** to restrain a person or thing

**syn** CHECK, CURB, BRIDLE, SNAFFLE, INHIBIT: RESTRAIN is a general term suggesting use of force, pressure, or strenuous persuasion to hold back a person or thing from a course or action or to prevent the action itself ⟨Delaware, in commissioning its delegates, *restrained* them from assenting to any change in the "rule of suffrage" —E.K.Alden⟩ ⟨one wants to produce in the child the same respect for the garden that *restrains* the grown-ups from picking wantonly —Bertrand Russell⟩ RESTRAIN may also be used with any moderating action, any action that prevents extremes ⟨a law of 17 B.C. gave a legal position to slaves informally manumitted . . . but drastically *restrained* their power to acquire and bequeath property —John Buchan⟩ CHECK indicates a restraining of a course, activity, impetus, or effect; its suggestions may rest on uses of the word in horsemanship, chess, or military affairs ⟨if you, my dear father, will not take the trouble of *checking* her exuberant spirits . . . she will soon be beyond the reach of amendment —Jane Austen⟩ ⟨the ambition of churchmen to shine in worldly contests is disciplined and *checked* by the broader interests of the church —Henry Adams⟩ CURB, BRIDLE, and SNAFFLE likewise carry suggestions from horsemanship, CURB indicating drastic and quick checking, BRIDLE indicating a steady, continued guiding, controlling, holding from excess, and SNAFFLE indicating a light curbing ⟨control of money, bills, and the right of electing the councillors *curbed* somewhat the Governor's immense power —*Amer. Guide Series: Mass.*⟩ ⟨endowed . . . with zest, with abundance, with romping blood. She had never been *bridled* in mind or body —Francis Hackett⟩ ⟨whose potential violence of feeling is *bridled* by good form —*N.Y. Herald Tribune Bk. Rev.*⟩ INHIBIT, largely psychological or scientific in its suggestions, is likely to bring into consideration repressive or curbing effects of custom, morality, precept, or conscience ⟨the inherent immorality of the acts has become as strong an *inhibiting* factor as the fear of punishment —T.L.Karsten & J.H.Mathias⟩ ⟨a more and more courageous, a less and less *inhibited* medium of expression —F.B.Millett⟩

**re·strain·able** \-nəbəl\ *adj* **:** capable of being or subject to being restrained

**re·strain·ably** \-blē\ *adv* **:** in a restrainable manner

**re·strained** \-nd\ *adj* [fr. past part. of *restrain*] **:** marked by or manifesting restraint (as in art) **:** devoid of excess or extravagance **:** DISCIPLINED — **re·strain·ed·ly** \-n(ə)dlē, -li\ *adv* — **re·strain·ed·ness** \-nədnəs, -n(d)nəs\ *n* -ES

**restrained beam** *n* **:** a beam built in at the supports **:** an encastre beam

**re·strain·er** \-nə(r)\ *n* -s **:** one that restrains; *esp* **:** a chemical (as potassium bromide) used to retard the action of a photographic developer esp. on unexposed silver salts

**restraining** *adj* [fr. pres. part. of *restrain*] **:** used for restraining : designed to restrain (as from a course of action) — see RESTRAINING ORDER — **re·strain·ing·ly** *adv*

**restraining order** *n* : a preliminary legal order sometimes issued to keep a situation unchanged pending decision upon an application for an injunction

**re·straint** \rə'strānt, rē's-\ *n* -S [ME, fr. MF *restrainte*, fr. fem. of *restraint*, past part. of *restraindre* to restrain — more at RESTRAIN] **1 a** : an act of restraining, hindering, checking, or holding back from some activity or expression ⟨to act upon his own choice and judgment free from ~s . . . imposed by the arbitrary will of other human beings —John Dewey⟩ **b** : a means, force, or agency that restrains, checks free activity, or otherwise controls ⟨if a woman has no inclination to do what is wrong, being secured from it is no ~ to her —James Boswell⟩ ⟨the ~s of an academic habit —Irwin Edman⟩ **c** : the condition of being restrained, checked, or controlled : deprivation of liberty : CONFINEMENT ⟨absolute liberty is absence of ~ —Henry Adams⟩ ⟨facilities for the accommodation and ~ of so large a number of frenzied patients —V.G. Heiser⟩ **2** : a check on free commercial or business activity : EMBARGO ⟨production being hindered by governmental ~s⟩ **3** : a check or control over free, easy, or unruly expression : CONSTRAINT : reserved expression avoiding extravagance or excess : stiffness and lack of easy naturalness and liveliness ⟨a ~ which kept them mutually silent on the subject —Jane Austen⟩ ⟨so much ~ of feeling, so much impersonality, so much coldness —Manny Farber⟩ ⟨designed with . . . ~ without overemphasis of decoration —*Amer. Guide Series: Del.*⟩ **syn** see FORCE

**restraint of marriage** : a condition attached to a gift or bequest or in a contract that nullifies the grant if the donee or grantee marries and is usu. void if general and unlimited in scope

**restraint of princes** *archaic* : EMBARGO

**restraint of trade** : an attempt or intent to eliminate or stifle competition, to effect a monopoly, to maintain prices artificially, or otherwise to hamper or obstruct the course of trade and commerce as it would be if left to the control of natural and economic forces

**re·strengthen** \(')rē+\ *vt* [*re-* + *strengthen*] : to make strong again (as by recruiting or reinforcing) : impart new strength to

**re·stress** \"+\ *vt* [*re-* + *stress*] : to subject to phonetic stress (as a form or vowel that originated by loss of stress) and in so doing produce a stressed form different from the original stressed form ⟨\,frăm\ *from* yielded \,frəm\, which by ~*ing* yields \,frəm\⟩

**re·strict** \rə'strikt, rē's-\ *vt* -ED/-ING/-S [L *restrictus*, past part. of *restringere* to restrain, restrict — more at RESTRAIN] **1** : to set bounds or limits to : hold within bounds: as **a** : to check free activity, motion, progress, or departure of : RESTRAIN ⟨intellectual snobbery which has tended to ~ men and women from an understanding of religion —A.H. Compton⟩; *also* : HAMPER, DIMINISH **b** : to check, bound, or decrease the range, scope, or incidence of : set what is to be included or embraced by : bar or carefully govern addition or increment to ⟨countries where literacy was largely ~*ed* to the upper classes —Helen Sullivan⟩ **2** : to place (land) under restrictions as to use (as by zoning ordinances) **syn** see LIMIT

**restricted** *adj* [fr. past part. of *restrict*] : subject or subjected to restriction: as **a** : limited to the use of particular classes of people or specifically excluding others (as members of a class or ethnic group felt to be inferior) ⟨a ~ residential area⟩ ⟨~ hotels⟩ **b** : not given a security classification but not for general circulation or release ⟨a ~ publication⟩ — used officially by the U.S. prior to Nov. 1953; see RESTRICTED DATA — **re·strict·ed·ly** *adv* — **re·strict·ed·ness** *n* -ES

**restricted area** *n* : an area from which military personnel are excluded for reasons of security or safety unless specially authorized : an off limits area

**restricted data** *n pl* : all data concerning the design, manufacture, and utilization of atomic weapons, the production of special nuclear material, or the use of special nuclear material in the production of energy but not including data declassified by the proper lawful authority

**re·stric·tion** \-kshən\ *n* -S [ME *restriccioun*, fr. LL *restriction-*, *restrictio* limitation, fr. L *restrictus* (past part. of *restringere* to restrict) + *-ion-*, *-io* -ion — more at RESTRAIN] **1** : something that restricts : QUALIFICATION: as **a** : a regulation that restricts or restrains ⟨new ~s for hunters⟩ **b** : a limitation placed on the use or enjoyment of real or other property; *esp* : an encumbrance on land restricting the uses to which it may be put **c** : a limitation that is imposed upon a class or ethnic group and that excludes its members from a fairly competitive use and enjoyment of the facilities of a community (as housing, employment, or education) **d** : limitation of the opening two or three moves in a game of checkers to one series chosen by lot from an accepted list **2** : an act of restricting or the condition of being restricted : confinement within bounds ⟨undue ~ of children⟩ **3** : a tacit or expressed qualification : RESERVATION ⟨a mental ~⟩ **4** : TIGHTENING, CONSTRICTION

**re·stric·tion·ary** \-shə,nerē\ *adj* [*restriction* + *-ary*] : RESTRICTIVE

**re·stric·tion·ism** \-,nizəm\ *n* -S [*restriction* + *-ism*] : a policy or philosophy advocating restriction or restrictions: as **a** : a policy or practice of trade restraints (as by internal restrictive practices or by import restrictions) : a monopolistic policy **b** (1) : a policy of labor resistance to mechanization and automation based on a desire to increase the number of available jobs (2) : a policy of curtailing the individual worker's output to make the job last longer

**¹re·stric·tion·ist** \-sh(ə)nəst\ *n* -S [*restriction* + *-ist*] : an advocate of restriction or restrictionism

**²restrictionist** \"\ *adj* : of, relating to, or concerned with restrictionism or restrictionists ⟨~ opinions⟩ ⟨a ~ policy⟩

**¹re·stric·tive** \rə'striktiv, rē's-, -ktēv *also* -ktəv\ *adj* [ME, fr. MF *restrictif*, serving to restrict, astringent, fr. L *restrictus* (past part. of *restringere* to restrict) + MF *-if* -ive — more at RESTRAIN] **1** *obs* : ASTRINGENT, BINDING, STYPTIC **2** : serving or tending to restrict : conveying restrictions ⟨a ~ tariff⟩ ⟨~ regulations⟩ ⟨a ~ railroad signal⟩ **3** : expressing a limitation of the reference of the term qualified ⟨a ~ adjective⟩ ⟨~ phrases⟩ — see RESTRICTIVE CLAUSE **4** : prohibiting further negotiation or giving authority to deal with an instrument as directed but not to transfer ownership ⟨a ~ endorsement of a negotiable instrument⟩ — **re·stric·tive·ly** \-təvlē, -li\ *adv* — **re·stric·tive·ness** \-tivnəs, -tēv- *also* -təv-\ *n* -ES

**²restrictive** \"\ *n* -S : a restrictive term or expression

**restrictive clause** *n* : an adjective clause so closely attached to its noun as to be essential to the definiteness of the noun's meaning (as *who succeeded* in "the boy who succeeded had worked hard") — called also *determinative clause*

**restrictive covenant** *n* : an agreement generally running with the land and restricting the free use of land (as to particular purposes or to occupancy by members of a particular ethnic group)

**restrictive endorsement** *n* : an endorsement transferring commercial paper for a particular purpose (as for deposit or collection or payment to a named person only) thereby indicating negotiability is to cease — compare SPECIAL ENDORSEMENT

**restricts** *pres 3d sing of* RESTRICT

**¹re·strike** \(')rē+\ *vb* [¹*re-* + *strike*] *vt* : to strike again or anew ~ *vi* : to strike again or anew

**²re·strike** \'rē+,-ˌ=ˌ=\ *n* **1** : a coin or medal struck from an original die at some time after the original issue and usu. esp. for collectors **2** : an impression made from a surface that has already been printed from; *typically* : a new print made from an old woodcut, lithographic stone, or metal engraving **3** : a coin struck on another coin

**re·string** \(')rē+\ *vt* [*re-* + *string*] : to fit (as a violin, a tennis racket) with new strings

**re·stringe** \rə'strinj\ *vt* -ED/-ING/-S [L *restringere* to draw back tight, restrict — more at RESTRAIN] **1** *obs* : to make costive : BIND **2** *archaic* : CONFINE, RESTRICT

**re·strin·gen·cy** \-njənsē\ *n* -ES [¹*restringent* + *-cy*] : the quality or state of being restringent

**¹re·strin·gent** \-jənt\ *adj* [L *restringent-*, *restringens*, pres. part. of *restringere* to draw back tight, restrict — more at RESTRAIN] *archaic* : BINDING, ASTRINGENT, STYPTIC

**²restringent** \"\ *n* -S *archaic* : something (as a word or a medication) with restringent properties

**rest room** *n* [¹*rest*] : a room or suite of rooms in a public or semipublic building or a business establishment provided with lavatory, toilet, and other facilities for clients', visitors', or employees' rest or comfort

**re·structure** \(')rē+\ *vt* [*re-* + *structure*] : to give a new structure or organization to

**rests** *pl of* REST, *pres 3d sing of* REST

**re·study** \(')rē+\ *vt* [*re-* + *study*] : to study again or anew : make a new appraisal or evaluation of ⟨had to ~ the whole program in terms of recent developments in technique⟩

**re·stuff** \"+\ *vt* [*re-* + *stuff*] : to provide with a new stuffing ⟨~*ed* the old cushions⟩

**rest up** *vi* [²*rest*] : to get a complete rest : rest oneself thoroughly

**rest·ward** \'restwə(r)d\ *also* **rest·wards** \-dz\ *adv* [¹*rest* + *-ward*] : toward rest or a resting place

**res·ty** \'restē\ *adj* -ER/-EST [alter. of *restive*] **1** : SLUGGISH, INDOLENT **2** *chiefly dial* : RESTIVE

**re·style** \(')rē+\ *vt* [*re-* + *style*] : REFASHION: **a** : to make in a new style **b** : to design or set a new style for

**re·subject** \,rē+\ *vt* [*re-* + *subject*] : to bring again into subjection — **re·subjection** \"+\ *n*

**re·sublime** \"+\ *vt* [*re-* + *sublime*] : to sublime again ⟨*resublimed* iodine⟩

**re·submission** \"+\ *n* [*re-* + *submission*] : an act of resubmitting

**re·submit** \"+\ *vt* [*re-* + *submit*] : to offer (as a question for popular vote) again or anew

**re·sue** \rə'sü\ *vt* -ED/-ING/-S [origin unknown] : to mine (a very narrow vein) by first stoping the rock wall on one side and then removing the ore

**¹re·sult** \rə'zəlt, rē'z-\ *vi* -ED/-ING/-S [ME *resulten*, fr. ML *resultare*, fr. L, to leap back, spring back, fr. *re-* + *-sultare* (fr. *saltare* to leap) — more at SALTANT] **1** : to proceed, spring, or arise as a consequence, effect, or conclusion : come out or have an issue : TERMINATE, END — used with *from* or *in* ⟨this measure will ~ in good⟩ ⟨an injury ~*ing* from a fall⟩ **2** *archaic* : to leap or spring back : REBOUND, RECOIL **3** *law* **a** : REVERT ⟨the estate will ~ to him⟩ **b** *archaic* : DEVOLVE — used with *to*

**²result** \"\ *n* -S **1** : a decision or resolution of a deliberative or legislative body **2** : something that results as a consequence, effect, issue, or conclusion ⟨suffer from the ~s of war⟩ ⟨the causes and ~s of sleeping sickness⟩; *sometimes* : beneficial or tangible effect : FRUIT ⟨an inquiry without ~⟩ ⟨get ~s from a new treatment⟩ **3** : something obtained, achieved, or brought about by calculation, investigation, or similar activity (as an answer to a problem or knowledge gained by scientific inquiry) ⟨he added the long column of figures and offered the ~⟩ ⟨his thesis was the ~ of his study⟩ **4 results** *pl* : a synoptic publication of the outcome of related competitive events ⟨the race ~s are on the back page⟩ ⟨have you seen the football ~s⟩ **syn** see EFFECT — **in result** *adv* : as a result ⟨the dam broke and *in result* the land was flooded⟩

**re·sult·ance** \-tᵊn(t)s, -tən-\ *also* **re·sult·an·cy** \-nsē\ *n*, *pl* **resultances** *also* **resultancies** [¹*result* + *-ance*, *-ancy*] **1** *obs* : a combined result : AGGREGATE, GIST **2** *obs* : EMANATION, REFLECTION **3** *obs* : the fact or character of being resultant **4** : RESULT, OUTCOME

**¹re·sult·ant** \-nt\ *adj* [ML *resultant-*, *resultans*, pres. part. of *resultare* to result] : being derived from or consequent upon something else : having the character of a result or consequence : RESULTING ⟨a ~ force⟩ ⟨~ measures⟩

**²resultant** \"\ *n* -S [partly fr. ¹*resultant*, partly fr. F *résultante*, fr. fem. of *résultant* resultant (adj.), fr. ML *resultant-*, *resultans*] : something that results or constitutes a result : a resulting quality, character, condition, or product : OUTCOME: as **a** (1) : a mathematical vector sum (2) : the single vector that is equivalent to a given set of vectors (as of forces or velocities) and is usu. the sum of these vectors (3) : ELIMINANT **b** (1) : COMBINATION TONE (2) *also* **resultant base** : ACOUSTIC BASS **c** : an effective force that results from the cooperation and antagonism of varied individual forces : a product or mean of conflicting and cooperating elements ⟨life in a democracy is . . . the ~ of millions of individual decisions —A.A.Berle⟩ ⟨social adjustment of an individual is the ~ of two complementary forces —L.E. Rosenzweig⟩ **d** : a substance formed in a chemical reaction : PRODUCT — opposed to *reactant*

**re·sult·ant·ly** *adv* [¹*resultant* + *-ly*] : so as to be resultant : in the manner of a resultant

**re·sult·ative** \-ltəd·iv\ *adj* [¹*result* + *-ative*] : RESULTANT; *esp* : expressive of result ⟨German *ergreifen* is a ~ verb⟩

**re·sult·ful** \-ltfəl\ *adj* [²*result* + *-ful*] : bearing or full of results : FRUITFUL ⟨a ~ investigation⟩ ⟨passed ~ hours in the library⟩ — **re·sult·ful·ly** \-fəlē\ *adv*

**re·sult·ing·ly** *adv* [*resulting* + *-ly*] : as a result

**resulting trust** *n* : a trust based upon the presumed intentions of the parties as inferred from all the circumstances that the one holding legal title to trust property holds it for the benefit of the other — compare CONSTRUCTIVE TRUST, EXPRESS TRUST

**resulting use** *n* : a use raised in a court of equity in favor of a grantor or donor transferring property to uses when failing to declare the use for a particular person or when a use declared has come to an end or cannot possibly vest and no other person is designated to enjoy it

**re·sult·less** \-ltləs\ *adj* [²*result* + *-less*] : productive of no result : INEFFECTIVE — **re·sult·less·ly** *adv* — **re·sult·less·ness** *n* -ES

**results** *pres 3d sing of* RESULT, *pl of* RESULT

**re·sum·able** \rə'züməbəl, rē'z-\ *adj* : capable of being resumed : fit to be resumed

**¹re·sume** \-m\ *vb* -ED/-ING/-S [ME *resumen*, fr. MF or L; MF *resumer* fr. L *resumere* to take up again, take back, resume, fr. *re-* + *sumere* to take up, take, fr. *sub-* under, up + *emere* to take — more at REDEEM] *vt* **1** : to assume or take again : put on anew : REOCCUPY ⟨*resumed* his old habits⟩ ⟨~ her place in society⟩ ⟨*resumed* our coats and hats⟩ **2** : to enter upon or begin again : take up after interruption ⟨sat down and *resumed* her work⟩ ⟨~ reading where you left off⟩ **3** : to take back to oneself ⟨on default the grantor does not automatically ~ title⟩ **4** : to take or pick up again : go back to using **5** : to make repetition of (as a sentence); *also* : REITERATE, SUMMARIZE, EPITOMIZE ~ *vi* **1** : to take possession again **2** : to recommence something (as a discourse, work, business) interrupted : go on again after an interruption

**²ré·su·mé** \,rez|ə|,mā *also* |rā| *or* |(,)ü|mā *sometimes* |zh|\ *n* -S [F, fr. past part. of *résumer* to recapitulate, sum up, fr. MF, to resume] : a summing up : a condensed statement : ABRIDGMENT, SUMMARY; *specif* : a brief account of one's education and professional experience

**³résumé** \"\ *vt* -ED/-ING/-S : SUMMARIZE

**re·sum·er** \rə'züm, rē'z-\ *n* -S : one that resumes

**re·summon** \(')rē+\ *vt* [*re-* + *summon*] : to summon again or anew

**re·summons** \"+\ *n* [ME *resommons*, fr. AF *resomons*, fr. past part. of *resomondre*, *resemondre* to resummon, fr. OF *re-* + *semondre* to summon — more at SUMMON] : a summons to a party or witness already once summonsed : another summons issued in a case after the original

**re·sump·tion** \rə'zəm(p)shən, rē'- *sometimes* -'sə-\ *n* -S [ME fr. MF or LL; MF *resomption* act of resuming, fr. LL *resumption-*, *resumptio*, fr. L *resumptus* (past part. of *resumere* to resume) + *-ion-*, *-io* -ion] **1 a** : the taking again by the crown or other authority of lands or tenements previously granted (as on the ground of false suggestions or other error) **b** : the taking back or recovery of something previously given up or lost ⟨a ~ of power by the opposition⟩ **2 a** : the act or fact of taking up again : RECOMMENCEMENT ⟨the ~ of her duties after the holiday⟩ **b** : a return to payment in specie ⟨~ seems unlikely in the U. S. under present conditions⟩

**re·sump·tive** \-m(p)tiv\ *adj* [L *resumptus* + E *-ive*] **1** : constituting a résumé : SUMMARIZING **2** : tending toward or indicative of resumption — **re·sump·tive·ly** \-təvlē\ *adv*

**res uni·ver·si·ta·tis** \'rā,sünə,versə'tād·əs, 'rē,zünə,vərsə'tād-\ *n pl* [L] : things belonging under Roman or civil law to a society, corporation, university, or other community or public or private group for the use of the group and not the constituent members thereof

**re·su·pi·nate** *also* **re·su·pi·nat·ed** \(')rē+\ *adj* [L *resupinatus*, past part. of *resupinare* to bend back to a supine position, fr. *re-* + *supinus* supine] **1** : inverted in position : appearing by a twist of the axis to be upside down or reversed ⟨many orchids have ~ flowers⟩ **2** : having or being a fruiting body that forms a hyphal mat on the substrate with the hymenium at the periphery or over the whole surface ⟨a ~ fungus⟩

**re·su·pi·na·tion** \(,)rē+\ *n* [L *resupinatus* + E *-ion*] **1** : the act of lying on the back or the position of one so lying **2** : a turning or twisting (as of a flower) to an inverted or apparently upside-down position; *also* : a resupinate condition

**re·su·pine** \"+\ *adj* [L *resupinus*, fr. *resupinare*] : SUPINE

**¹re·supply** \,rē+\ *vt* [*re-* + *supply*] : to supply again : provide anew with supplies; *esp* : to provide (a military force in action) with replacement or supplementary matériel

**²resupply** \"\ *n* : an act or system of resupplying

**re·surface** \(')rē+\ *vb* [*re-* + *surface*] *vt* : to provide with a new or fresh surface: as **a** : to dress the surface of anew ⟨~ a tool⟩ **b** : to renew the surface pavement of ⟨~ a street⟩ ~ *vi*, *of a submarine* : to come again to the surface of the water

**¹re·surge** \rə'sərj, rē's-\ *vi* [L *resurgere* — more at RESURRECTION] : to rise again : become resurrected ⟨the *resurging* of nationalism⟩

**²re·surge** \(')rē+\ *vi* [*re-* + *surge*] : to surge back or to and fro ⟨as the battle ~s⟩

**re·sur·gence** \rə'sərjən(t)s, rē's-, -səj-, -səij-\ *n* -S [fr. ²*resurgent*, after such pairs as E *excellent*: *excellence*] : a rising again into life, activity, or prominence ⟨a ~ of religious feeling⟩

**re·sur·gen·cy** \-nsē, -nsi\ *n* -ES [²*resurgent* + *-cy*] : the quality or state of being resurgent : RESURGENCE

**¹re·sur·gent** \-nt\ *n* -S [L *resurgent-*, *resurgens*, pres. part. of *resurgere*] : one that experiences resurgence

**²resurgent** \"\ *adj* [L *resurgent-*, *resurgens*, pres. part. of *resurgere* to rise again — more at RESURRECTION] **1** : rising again from an inferior state (as death, torpor, decadence) to a superior state ⟨~ life of spring —W.P.Smith⟩ **2** : tending to produce resurgence ⟨nationalism is a powerful, even a ~ force —*New Republic*⟩

**resurgent water** *n* : water that having once been at the surface of the earth has supposedly been incorporated in molten magma and again reached the surface by expulsion

**res·ur·rect** \,rezə'rekt\ *vb* -ED/-ING/-S [back-formation fr. *resurrection*] *vt* **1 a** : to raise from the dead : restore to life **b** : to bring to view again (something forgotten or lost) **2** : to disinter or exhume (a body) in the character of a resurrectionist **3** : to bring again (a feature buried beneath sedimentary deposits) to the surface by erosion ⟨~*ed* peneplain⟩ ~ *vi* : to become risen again from the dead

**¹res·ur·rec·tion** \,rezə'rekshən\ *n* -S [ME, fr. LL *resurrection-*, *resurrectio* act of rising from the dead, Easter festival, fr. *resurrectus* (past part. of *resurgere* to rise from the dead, fr. L, to rise again, fr. *re-* + *surgere* to rise) + L *-ion-*, *-io* -ion — more at SURGE] **1 a** *usu cap* : a service or festival (as Easter) commemorating the rising of Jesus Christ from the dead ⟨*Resurrection* services at the cathedral⟩ **b** *often cap* : the rising again to life of all the human dead before the final judgment that is predicted in Christian religions ⟨there will be a ~ of both the just and the unjust —Acts 24:15 (RSV)⟩ **c** : the state of one risen from the dead ⟨for in the ~ they neither marry nor are given in marriage —Mt 22:30 (RSV)⟩ **d** *usu cap* : a representation of Christ's resurrection (as in art or drama) **2** : the act or fact of rising again from an inferior state (as death, decay, disuse) into a superior : RESURGENCE, REVIVAL **3** : an agent, cause, or exemplar of a rising of the dead ⟨I am the ~ and the life —Jn 11:25 (RSV)⟩ **4** *Christian Science* : spiritualization of thought : material belief yielding to spiritual understanding

**²resurrection** \ˌ=ˌ=ˈ=ˌ=\ *vt* -ED/-ING/-S [¹*resurrection*] : RESURRECT

**res·ur·rec·tion·al** \,rezə'rekshənᵊl, -shnəl\ *adj* : of or relating to resurrection

**res·ur·rec·tion·ary** \,rezə'rekshə,nerē\ *adj* [¹*resurrection* + *-ary*] : constituting resurrection; *also* : of or relating to resurrectionism

**resurrection body** *n* : man's body as restored by resurrection

**res·ur·rec·tion·er** \,rezə'reksh(ə)nə(r)\ *n* -S [²*resurrection* + *-er*] : RESURRECTIONIST 1

**resurrection fern** *n* [¹*resurrection*] : GRAY POLYPODY

**res·ur·rec·tion·ism** \,rezə'rekshə,nizəm\ *n* -S [¹*resurrection* + *-ism*] : the practice of body snatchers

**res·ur·rec·tion·ist** \-sh(ə)nəst\ *n* -S [¹*resurrection* + *-ist*] **1** : a stealer of dead bodies : BODY SNATCHER **2** : one who resurrects (as by restoring, reviving, or reemploying) **3** : one who believes in the resurrection of the body

**res·ur·rec·tion·ize** \-shə,nīz\ *vt* -ED/-ING/-S [¹*resurrection* + *-ize*] : RESURRECT

**resurrection man** *n* [¹*resurrection*] : BODY SNATCHER

**resurrection plant** *n* **1** : any of several club mosses of the genus *Selaginella* (as *S. convoluta* and *S. lepidophylla*) that close up when dry but expand again when moistened **2** : ROSE OF JERICHO **3** : a fig marigold (*Mesembryanthemum tripolium*)

**resurrection woman** *n* : a body snatcher who is a woman

**res·ur·rec·tive** \,rezə'rektiv\ *adj* [LL *resurrectus* (past part. of *resurgere* to rise from the dead) + E *-ive* — more at RESURRECTION] : of, relating to, or causing resurrection

**res·ur·rec·tor** \-tə(r)\ *n* -S [*resurrect* + *-or*] : one that resurrects ⟨a ~ of things past⟩

**resurrects** *pres 3d sing of* RESURRECT

**re·surrender** \,rē+\ *vt* [*re-* + *surrender*] : to yield anew

**¹re·survey** \(,)rē+\ *vt* [*re-* + *survey*] : to survey again or anew; *esp* : to recheck the boundaries of by surveying

**²resurvey** \"+\ *n* [*re-* + *survey*] : a second or fresh survey ⟨made a ~ of 15th century Irish writings⟩

**re·sus·ci·ta·ble** \rə'səsəd·əbəl, rē's-\ *adj* [L *resuscitare* to revive + E *-able*] : capable of resuscitation — **re·sus·ci·ta·bly** \-blē, -bli\ *adv*

**re·sus·ci·tate** \-'səsə,tāt, *usu* -ād·+V\ *vb* -ED/-ING/-S [L *resuscitatus*, past part. of *resuscitare* to stir up again, revive, fr. *re-* + *suscitare* to stir up, rouse, fr. *sus-* up (var. of *sub-*) + *citare* to put in motion, stir — more at CITE] *vt* **1** : to revive from apparent death or from unconsciousness ⟨*resuscitating* a nearly drowned person by artificial respiration⟩ **2** : to restore from a state of desuetude or decay ⟨withered plants *resuscitated* by rain⟩ ⟨plans to ~ the liberal party⟩ ~ *vi* : to come to : regain vigor or vitality : REVIVE

**re·sus·ci·ta·tion** \rə,səsə'tāshən, (,)rē,s-\ *n* -S [LL *resuscitation-*, *resuscitatio*, fr. L *resuscitatus* + *-ion-*, *-io* -ion] : an act of resuscitating or the state of being resuscitated : RESTORATION, REVIVAL, RENEWAL ⟨~ by means of artificial respiration or cardiac massage⟩

**re·sus·ci·ta·tive** \-ˌ=ˌ=,tād·iv\ *adj* [*resuscitate* + *-ive*] : tending to resuscitate : REVIVING, REVIVIFYING ⟨lifeguards were taught the basic ~ methods⟩

**re·sus·ci·ta·tor** \-ād·ə(r)\ *n* -S [*resuscitate* + *-or*] : one that resuscitates; *specif* : an apparatus that delivers oxygen or a mixture of oxygen and carbon dioxide to and induces a renewal of respiration in the asphyxiated

**re·swear** \(')rē+\ *vt* [*re-* + *swear*] : to swear to or cause to swear anew or again

**re·symbolization** \(,)rē+\ *n* [*re-* + *symbolization*] : symbolization again or anew; *specif* : a mental transformation either for better or for worse consisting in the finding of new meanings and new forms of expression for one's thoughts and desires

**re·symbolize** \(')rē+\ *vt* [*re-* + *symbolize*] : to provide with new symbols : symbolize anew

**re·synthesis** \"+\ *n* [*re-* + *synthesis*] : a reuniting usu. in a new combination of parts or elements that have been separated (as by prior analysis)

**re·synthesize** \"+\ *vt* [*re-* + *synthesize*] : to synthesize again : subject to resynthesis : practice resynthesis upon

**¹ret** \'ret, *usu* -ed·+V\ *vb* **retted**; **retted**; **retting**; **rets** [ME *reten*, fr. MD *reten*, *reeten*] *vt* **1** : to soak or expose (as flax or hemp) to moisture in order to promote the loosening of the fiber from the woody tissue by bacterial action; *also* : to treat chemically for loosening of the fiber from the woody tissue **2** : to rot or injure by exposure to moisture ~ *vi* : to become retted : undergo loosening of the fiber from the woody tissue after soaking ⟨it finally ~s, and the black inner fiber . . . can be gathered up and baled —Thomas Barbour⟩

**²ret** \"\ *n* -s : RETTING ⟨dew-*ret*⟩ ⟨water-*ret*⟩

**ret** *abbr* **1** retain; retainer; retaining **2** retard **3** retired **4** return; returned

**re·ta·ble** \rə'tābəl, rē'-\ *n* -s [F, fr. Sp *retablo*, modif. of Catal *retaula*, fr. *rea*- backward, behind (fr. L *retro*-) + *taula* table, fr. L *tabula* tablet, board] : a raised shelf or ledge behind an altar on which are placed the altar cross, the altar lights, and vases of flowers; *also* : an elaborate framework rising behind the altar and enclosing a panel decorated with painting, sculpture, or mosaic — compare PREDELLA

**re·ta·blo** \rā'tä(,)blō\ *n* -s [Sp, retable] **1** : a votive offering made in the form of a religious picture typically portraying Christian saints, painted on a panel, and hung in a church or chapel esp. in Spain and Mexico **2** : REREDOS 1

**¹re·tail** \'rē,tāl; *in sense 2* rə't- *or* rē't-, *esp before pause or consonant* -āəl\ *vb* -ED/-ING/-S [ME *retailen*, fr. MF *retaillier* to cut off, diminish, divide into pieces, fr. OF, fr. *re*- + *taillier* to cut — more at TAILOR] *vt* **1** : to sell in small quantities (as the single yard, pound, gallon) : to sell directly to the ultimate consumer ⟨~ cloth⟩ ⟨~ groceries⟩ **2** : to relate in detail or to one person after another : tell again or again and again ⟨~ a conversation⟩ ⟨~ gossip⟩ ⟨~ a story⟩ ~ *vi* : to sell at retail ⟨~*s* a book that ~*s* for $10⟩

**²re·tail** \'rē,tāl\ *n* -s [ME, fr. MF, cut, piece, fr. OF, fr. *retaillier* to cut off; influenced in meaning by ME *retailen* to retail] : the sale of commodities or goods in small quantities to ultimate consumers — opposed to WHOLESALE — **at retail** *adv* : at a price customarily asked by a retailer : RETAIL ⟨sold *at retail*⟩

**³retail** \"\ *adj* : of, relating to, or engaged in the sale of commodities at retail ⟨~ trade⟩ ⟨~ merchant⟩ ⟨~ business⟩ ⟨~ selling⟩ ⟨~ price⟩

**⁴retail** \"\ *adv* : in small quantities : from a retailer ⟨a blend costing five cents more a pound ~ —W.H.Ukers⟩ ⟨cartridge sells ~ for less —E.T.Canby⟩

**retail credit** *n* : CONSUMER CREDIT

**re·tail·er** \-lə(r)\ *n* -s [ME, fr. *retailen* to retail + -*er*] : one that retails something ⟨a ~ of gossip⟩; *specif* : a merchant middleman who sells goods mainly to ultimate consumers

**re·tail·ing** \-liŋ\ *n* -s [ME, fr. gerund of *retailen* to retail] : the activities involved in the selling of goods to ultimate consumers for personal or household consumption : selling at retail

**re·tail·ment** \-lmənt\ *n* -s [¹*retail* + -*ment*] : act of retailing ⟨~ of the news⟩

**retail store** *n* : a place of business usu. owned and operated by a retailer but sometimes owned and operated by a manufacturer or by someone other than a retailer in which merchandise is sold primarily to ultimate consumers

**re·tain** \rə'tān, rē'-\ *vb* -ED/-ING/-S [ME *reteinen*, *retainen*, fr. MF *retenir*, fr. OF, fr. L *retinēre*, fr. *re*- + -*tinēre* (fr. *tenēre* to hold) — more at THIN] *vt* **1** *obs* : RESTRAIN, PREVENT **2 a** : to hold or continue to hold in possession or use : continue to have, use, recognize, or accept : maintain in one's keeping ⟨a person does not always ~ his human form or qualities —Frederica de Laguna⟩ ⟨some of the terms are ~*ed* today because of constant use —R.L.Whistler⟩ ⟨~*ed* his seat on the bench of the Supreme Court —T.P.Abernethy⟩ **b** : to keep in pay or in one's service ⟨was ~*ed* to make a survey of operations of the agency —*Current Biog.*⟩ ⟨~*s* the clinic to examine all its employees —Stuart Chase⟩; *specif* : to employ (a lawyer) by paying a preliminary fee that secures a prior claim upon services in case of need **c** : to keep in mind or memory : REMEMBER ⟨each of the principals in his way has ~*ed* the imprint of a hideous scene —Sylvia Berkman⟩ **3** : to hold secure or intact (as in a fixed place or condition) : prevent escape, loss, leakage, or detachment of ⟨the habit of chewing betel leaf and ~*ing* the cud against the mucous lining of the cheek —*N.Y. Times Mag.*⟩ ⟨available water which could be . . . ~*ed* by small dams —F.J.R.Rodd⟩ ⟨modern mammals . . . ~*ed* the egg within the body after fertilization —Weston La Barre⟩ ~ *vi*, *obs* : to serve as a retainer : BELONG, PERTAIN **syn** see KEEP

**retained income** *n* : EARNED SURPLUS

**retained object** *n* : an object in a passive construction that is identical with the direct or indirect object in the corresponding active construction ⟨*me* in *a book was given me* and *book* in *I was given a book* are *retained objects*⟩

**¹re·tain·er** \-nə(r)\ *n* -s [ME *reteiner*, prob. fr. MF *retenir* to retain (vb. taken as n.)] **1 a** : the act of withholding what one has in his hands by virtue of some right (as where a creditor pays his own claim out of the debtor's property that has come into his hands as representative of the debtor) **b** (1) : the act of a client by which he engages the services of a lawyer, counselor, or adviser (2) : the document expressing such engagement or the authority so conferred **c** : a fee paid to a lawyer to maintain a cause or to a professional adviser for advice or for a claim upon his services in case of need — called also *retaining fee*; see GENERAL RETAINER **2** : engagement for a position or job : EMPLOYMENT

**²retainer** \"\ *n* -s [*retain* + -*er*] **1** : one that retains : MAINTAINER **2** : one that is retained : a person attached or owing service to a household : one that serves a person of high position or rank : DEPENDENT, SERVANT ⟨an old family ~⟩ ⟨civil affairs were belatedly put into the hands of native ~*s* of the French —R.H.Rovere⟩ ⟨recruited from the landowning class and their ~*s* —*Amer. Scholar*⟩; *broadly* : EMPLOYEE ⟨old civil service ~*s*⟩ **3** : a civilian employee of a military camp or unit ⟨~*s* and persons accompanying or serving with the armies of the United States in the field —*U.S. Manual for Courts-Martial*⟩ **4** : any of various devices used for holding something: as **a** : a cage or frame for keeping the balls or rollers in a ball or roller bearing properly spaced **b** : a rebound clip in a leaf spring **c** : a pressure valve on a railroad car for retaining part of the brake cylinder pressure to aid in slowing the train on a long grade while increasing the brake pipe pressure to recharge the auxiliary reservoirs **d** : the part of a bridge or other dental replacement by which it is made fast to adjacent natural teeth

**retaining fee** *n* : RETAINER 1c

**retaining wall** *n* : a wall built to resist lateral pressure other than wind pressure; *esp* : one to prevent an earth slide — compare BREAST WALL

**¹re·take** \(')rē+\ *vt* **retook; retaken; retaking; retakes** [ME *retaken*, fr. *re*- + *taken* to take — more at TAKE] **1** : to take or receive again : take back **2** : to take from a captor : RECAPTURE **3** : REPHOTOGRAPH ⟨~ a motion-picture scene⟩

**²retake** \'rē+,-\ *n* -s **1** : a rephotographing of a scene or object ⟨~ of a scene in a motion picture⟩ **2** : a picture made by rephotographing

**re·taker** \(')rē+\ *n* -s : one that retakes

**re·tal·i·ate** \rə'talē,āt, rē'-, *usu* -ād+V\ *vb* [LL *retaliatus*, past part. of *retaliare* to retaliate, fr. L *re*- + -*taliare* (akin to *talio* talion) — more at TALION] *vt* **1** : to return the like for : repay or requite in kind (as an injury) **2** : to put or inflict in return ⟨~ a wrong⟩ ⟨~ a charge upon the accuser⟩ ~ *vi* : to return like for like : make requital; *esp* : to return evil for evil ⟨terrorist violence erupts in Algeria and Morocco — troops ~ quickly —Henry Giniger⟩ ⟨schoolmates quick to recognize a victim who would never ~ —Geoffrey Gorer⟩ ⟨the judicial process . . . permits society to ~ against the transgressor —Walter Goodman⟩ ⟨one person stands as the butt of the other's wit, and though he can ~ he must not take offense —*Notes & Queries on Anthropology*⟩ ⟨easy for anyone of moderate genius, and some erudition, who was desirous of ~*ing* upon those authors, to compose a work with this title —H.W.Church⟩ **syn** see RECIPROCATE

**re·tal·i·a·tion** \=,==ˈāshən\ *n* -s [L *retaliatus* (past part. of *retaliare* to retaliate) + E -*ion*] : an act of retaliating : REQUITAL; *esp* : return of evil for evil ⟨sanguinary ~ on the part of a rejected office seeker —W.A.Swanberg⟩ ⟨~ by revenge or blood feud on a collective scale —*Notes & Queries on Anthropology*⟩ ⟨~ against aggression at places of our own choosing —Arthur Krock⟩

**re·tal·i·a·tive** \=ˈ==,ād·iv\ *adj* : RETALIATORY

**re·tal·i·a·tor** \-d·ə(r)\ *n* -s : one that retaliates

**re·tal·ia·to·ry** \rə'talyə,tōrē, rē'-, -lēə,-, -tōr-, -ri, ÷-lə,-\ *adj* : tending to, involving, or having the nature of retaliation ⟨from ~ political revenge the transition was easy to pillage and wholesale murder —J.A.Froude⟩ ⟨deterrent force of our ~ air power —Dean Acheson⟩ ⟨the ~ sanction of blood revenge on the part of animal ghosts —W.H.Gilbert⟩

**retaliatory tariff** *n* : a tariff imposed as a means of coercing a foreign government and intended to compel the grant of reciprocity privileges

**¹re·ta·ma** \rə'tämə, rē'-, -tamə\ [NL, fr. Sp, shrub of the genus *Genista*, fr. Ar *ratam* retem] *syn of* GENISTA

**²retama** \"\ *also* **ra·ta·ma** \"\ *n* -s **1 a** : JERUSALEM THORN 2 **b** : PALOVERDE **2** [AmerSp, *retama*, fr. Sp, canary broom] : any of several yellow-flowered tropical American shrubs of the genus *Cassia*

**¹re·tan** \'rē+,-\ *adj* [*re*- + *tan*] : produced by a combination of two different tanning methods ⟨~ leather uppers⟩

**²retan** \"\ *n* -s : retan leather — compare CHROME RETAN

**¹re·tard** \rə'tärd, rē'-, -tād\ *vb* -ED/-ING/-S [L *retardare*, fr. *re*- + *tardare* to make slow, to delay, fr. *tardus* slow — more at TARDY] *vt* **1** : to make slow or slower : delay or impede the progress, course, or event of : slow up by preventing or hindering advance or accomplishment : keep back ⟨the rate of downcutting in the section of the channel upstream from the gap was ~*ed* —*Jour. of Geol.*⟩ ⟨frequent wars, lack of roads and railroads, and bad government long combined to ~ this area —Samuel Van Valkenburg & Ellsworth Huntington⟩ ⟨language is at one and the same time helping and ~*ing* us in our exploration of experience —Edward Sapir⟩ ⟨mental evolution has perhaps ~*ed* the progress of physical changes —W.R.Inge⟩ **2** : to delay academic progress by failure to promote (a pupil) **3** : to restrain (a plant) from growing **4** : to readjust the timing of (an ignition spark) so that ignition occurs later with reference to top dead center in the piston stroke ⟨with a ~*ed* spark and a late explosion, the combustion or burning of the charge of gas is not complete —A.L.Dyke⟩ ~ *vi* : to become delayed : undergo retardation **syn** see DELAY

**²retard** \"\ *n* -s [F, fr. MF *retarder* to retard, fr. L *retardare*] **1** : delay through being retarded : RETARDATION ⟨a ~ was needed in one passage of the *Te Deum* —*Time*⟩ **2** : a device for retarding an automotive ignition spark — **in retard** *archaic* : in the rear : BEHIND — usu. used with *of*

**re·tard·ance** \-dᵊn(t)s\ *n* -s [MF, fr. *retarder* to retard + -*ance*] : RETARDATION

**re·tard·an·cy** \-nsē\ *n* -ES [¹*retard* + -*ancy*] : the quality or capacity of retarding ⟨a paint having fire ~⟩

**¹re·tard·ant** *also* **re·tard·ent** \-nt\ *adj* [¹*retard* + -*ant* or -*ent*] : serving or tending to retard ⟨a flame-*retardant* paint⟩ ⟨rust-*retardant* coatings⟩

**²retardant** \"\ *n* -s : something that is retardant : RETARDER ⟨a fire ~⟩ ⟨a rust ~⟩

**¹retardate** *vt* -ED/-ING/-S [L *retardatus*, past part. of *retardare* to retard] *obs* : RETARD

**²re·tard·ate** \rə'tär,dāt\ *n* -s [L *retardatus*, past part.] : one who is mentally retarded; *esp* : a pupil who is retarded in school

**re·tar·da·tion** \,rē,tär'dāshən, -tȧ'-\ *n* -s [ME *retardacioun*, fr. MF *retardation*, fr. L *retardation-*, *retardatio*, fr. *retardatus* (past part.) + -*ion-*, -*io* -ion] **1** : the action or an instance of retarding ⟨the amount of ~ obtained by the braking system of a vehicle —*Principles of Automotive Vehicles*⟩ — opposed to *acceleration* **2** : the extent to which anything is retarded : the amount of retarding or delay ⟨the percent ~ in speed of reading —M.A.Tinker⟩ **3 a** : a musical suspension; *esp* : one that resolves upward **b** : a slackening of the tempo **4 a** : an abnormal slowness of thought or action **b** : slowness or limitation in development or progress **c** : the act or process of falling behind the norm for one's age **d** : the amount of such falling behind ⟨a ~ of two years in intelligence⟩ **5** : backwardness in progress through school as a result of nonpromotion

**retardation of the tide** **1** : LUNITIDAL INTERVAL **2** : RETARD OF THE TIDE **3** : LAG OF THE TIDE

**re·tard·a·tive** \rə'tärdəd·iv\ *adj* [¹*retardate* + -*ive*] : relating to, expressing, or tending to cause retardation

**re·tard·a·to·ry** \-də,tōrē, -tōr-, -ri\ *adj* [¹*retardate* + -*ory*] : RETARDING, RETARDATIVE

**retarded** *adj* [fr. past part. of ¹*retard*] : slow or limited in intellectual development, in emotional development, or in academic progress ⟨physically precocious, mentally ~, overripe and immature at the same time —Arthur Koestler⟩ ⟨~ children are frequently subjected to tasks which they cannot possibly understand or perform —Elise Martens⟩

**retarded depression** *n* : a depression marked by slowness of thought and action; *specif* : the depressed phase of manic-depressive psychosis — contrasted with AGITATED DEPRESSION

**re·tard·er** \rə'tärdər, rē'-, -tȧdə(r\ *n* -s [¹*retard* + -*er*] : one that retards: as **a** : a substance that when added to a cement or to gypsum plaster prolongs the setting time **b** : RESTRAINER **c** : a power-operated braking device placed in the classification tracks of hump yards to control the speed of moving railroad cars **d** : a substance added in small proportion to a rubber compound for retarding vulcanization

**retarding** *pres part of* RETARD

**re·tard·ing·ly** *adv* : in a retarding manner

**re·tard·ment** \-dmənt\ *n* -s [F *retardement*, fr. MF, fr. *retarder* to retard + -*ment* — more at RETARD] : an act of retarding : RETARDATION

**retard of the tide** : the interval between the moon's transit at which a tide originates and advent of the tide itself which is not principally due to the transit immediately preceding but to a transit which has occurred some time before — compare LUNITIDAL INTERVAL

**re·taste** \(')rē+\ *vt* [*re*- + *taste*] : to taste again

**¹retch** \'rech, *chiefly Brit* 'rēch\ *vb* -ED/-ING/-ES [alter. of ³*reach*] *vi* : to make an effort to vomit : strain to vomit ~ *vt* : to throw up : VOMIT

**²retch** \"\ *n* -ES : an act or instance of retching

**³retch** *dial var of* REACH

**⁴retch** \"\ *dial past of* REACH

**retd** *abbr* **1** retained **2** retired **3** returned

**re·te** \'rēd·ē, 'rētē\ *n*, *pl* **re·tia** \'rēshēə, 'rēd·ēə, 'rētēə\ [ME *riet*, fr. L *rete* net — more at RETINA] **1** : a circular plate with many holes used on the astrolabe to indicate the positions of the principal fixed stars **2** [NL, fr. L, net] **a** : NET, NETWORK; *esp* : a plexus of blood vessels or nerves **b** : an anatomical part resembling or including a network; *specif* : MALPIGHIAN LAYER

**rete cord** *n* : one of the strands of cells that grow from the region of the mesonephros into the developing gonad of the vertebrate embryo

**retel** *abbr* referring to telegram

**re·tell** \(')rē+\ *vt* **retold; retold; retelling; retells** [*re*- + *tell*] **1** : to count again **2** : to tell in another form ⟨simple as these myths are, they are *retold* with dignity and understanding —Irene Smith⟩

**retelling** *n* -s [fr. gerund of *retell*] : a new version of an old story ⟨a charming ~ of the great Greek, Roman and Norse myths —Bennett Cerf⟩

**re·tem** \'rē,tem\ *also* **rae·tam** \-tam\ *n* -s [Ar *ratam*] : a desert shrub (*Retama raetam*) that constitutes the juniper of the Old Testament, that has tiny white flowers, and that is found in Syria and Arabia

**rete mi·rab·i·le** \-mə'rabə,lē\ *n*, *pl* **retia mir·a·bil·ia** \-,mirə'bilēə\ [NL, fr. L, wonderful net] : a small but dense network of blood vessels formed by the breaking up of a larger vessel into branches that usu. reunite into one trunk and believed esp. important as an oxygen-storing mechanism in aquatic mammals

**re·temper** \(')rē+\ *vt* [*re*- + *temper*] : to mix (concrete or mortar) again with or without additional water after initial set has taken place

**retene** \'re,tēn, 'rē,-\ *n* -s [Gk *rhētinē* resin] : a crystalline hydrocarbon $C_{18}H_{18}$ isolated esp. from pine tar, rosin oil, and various fossil resins but usu. prepared from abietic acid and related compounds by dehydrogenation; 1-methyl-7-isopropyl-phenanthrene

**re·tent** \rə'tent\ *n* -s [L *retentum*, neut. of *retentus*] : something that is retained esp. in the mind

**re·ten·tion** \rə'tenchən, rē'-\ *n* -s [ME *retencioun*, fr. L *retention-*, *retentio*, fr. *retentus* (past part. of *retinēre* to retain) + -*ion-*, -*io* -ion — more at RETAIN] **1 a** : the act of retaining or state of being retained **b** : continuance in use (as of a name or custom) ⟨specific African cultures came to predominate, and recognizable ~*s* of these customs are present —M.J.Herskovits⟩ **c** : abnormal retaining in a canal, reservoir, or tissue of the body of a fluid or secretion which is to be voided ⟨~ of urine⟩ ⟨~ of bile⟩ **d** (1) : a retaining or an ability to retain things in mind : MEMORY ⟨recall, recognition, and relearning are the three experimental tests of ~ —R.S.Woodworth⟩ (2) : the preservation of aftereffects of experience and learning so that recall or recognition is possible or that relearning is easier than the learning of new material **e** : a keeping in one's own possession or control ⟨the ~ by the railways of about 3,500 trucks—Alzada Comstock⟩ ⟨her ~ of the world figure skating title —*Current Biog.*⟩ ⟨the ~ of part of the medical personnel taken prisoner —J.S.Pictet⟩ **f** (1) : a retaining or holding fixed in some place, position, or condition ⟨~ is the fixation of a removable partial denture in the mouth in such a manner that . . . it may be inserted and retained with sufficient firmness —*Rev. of Dentistry*⟩ (2) : state of being kept in place **2** : power or capacity of retaining : RETENTIVENESS ⟨shape, crease, and pleat-*retention* are not obtainable with any of the natural fibers —J.B.Goldberg⟩ ⟨good initial color and color ~, are properties that can be attained by alkyds —H.E.Hillman⟩ **3** : something that is retained ⟨the amount of precipitation that falls on an area but does not run off is the ~⟩ **4** : a possessory lien **5** : the portion of the insurance on a particular risk not reinsured or ceded by the originating insurer

**re·ten·tion·ist** \-chənəst\ *n* -s : one who advocates the retention of something (as territory or a policy)

**¹re·ten·tive** \rə'tentiv, rē'-, -tēv *also* -təv\ *adj* [ME *retentif*, *retentive*, fr. MF & ML; MF *retentif*, fr. ML *retentivus*, fr. L *retentus* (past part.) + -*ivus* -ive] : tending to retain : having the power, property, or capacity of retaining ⟨soils ~ of moisture⟩: as **a** : retaining knowledge : having a good memory : TENACIOUS ⟨a ~ memory⟩ ⟨a ~ mind⟩ ⟨a ~ person⟩ **b** : PARSIMONIOUS **c** : holding in place or custody : preventive of escape : RESTRAINING **d** : RESTRAINED, RETICENT — **re·ten·tive·ly** \-təvlē, -li\ *adv* — **re·ten·tive·ness** \-tivnəs, -tēv- *also* -təv-\ *n* -ES

**²retentive** \"\ *n* -s : something that retains or confines : RESTRAINT

**re·ten·tiv·i·ty** \,rē,ten'tivəd·ē, -ətē, -i\ *n* -ES : the power of retaining : retentive force ⟨moisture ~⟩; *specif* : the capacity for retaining magnetism after the action of the magnetizing force has ceased measured by the ratio of the residual magnetism to the maximum previously attained

**re·ten·tor** \rə'tentə(r)\ *n* -s [L, one that holds back, fr. *retentus* (past part. of *retinēre* to hold back, retain) + -*or*] : a muscle that serves to retain a part in place esp. when retracted

**rete peg** *n* : any of the inwardly directed prolongations of the Malpighian layer of the epidermis that intermesh with the dermal papillae of the skin

**re·test** \'rē+,-\ *n* [*re*- + *test*] : a repeated test

**rete testis** *n*, *pl* **retia testium** [NL, lit., network of the testis] : the network of tubules in the mediastinum of the testis

**ret·ger·site** \'retgə(r),sīt\ *n* -s [Jan Willem *Retgers* †1896 Du. chemical crystallographer + E -*ite*] : a mineral $NiSO_4.6H_2O$ consisting of hydrous nickel sulfate

**re·think** \(')rē+\ *vb* [*re*- + *think*] : to think again : RECONSIDER

**re·throne** \"+\ *vt* -ED/-ING/-S [*re*- + *throne*] : to enthrone again

**retia** *pl of* RETE

**re·ti·al** \'rēshēəl\ *adj* [NL *rete* + E -*al*] : of or relating to a rete

**re·ti·ar·i·us** \,rēshē'a(a)rēəs\ *n*, *pl* **retiar·ii** \-rē,ī\ [L, fr. *rete* net + -*arius* -ary — more at RETINA] : a Roman gladiator armed with a net and a trident

**re·ti·ary** \'rēshē,erē\ *adj* [L *retiarius* one armed with a net, retiarius] **1** : armed with a net **2** : skillful to entangle

**ret·i·cel·la** \,redə'chelə\ *also* **reticel·lo** \-che(,)lō\ *n* -s [*reticella* fr. It, little net, dim. of *rete* net, fr. L; *reticello* alter. (prob. influenced by *cello*) of *reticella*] : an early needlepoint lace derived from cutwork and drawnwork and made by buttonholing geometric patterns on or over a fabric foundation and cutting away the foundation

**ret·i·cence** \'red·əsən(t)s, -etəs-\ *n* -s [F *réticence*, fr. L *reticentia*, fr. *reticent-*, *reticens* (pres. part. of *reticēre* to keep silent) + -*ia* -y] **1** : the quality or state or an instance of being reticent : restraint in speaking or communicating : RESERVE ⟨people who speak their minds and their souls without ~ —Gerald Bullett⟩ ⟨difference between stony ~ and a torrent of impulsive unbosoming —W.S.Gilbert⟩ ⟨after the death of a writer certain ~*s* need no longer be observed —Leon Edel⟩ ⟨a man of few ~*s*, the disc jockey must rank among the most thoroughly overt —C.W.Morton⟩ **2** : restraint in behavior, expression, or performance ⟨the value of ~ in art —Thomas Wood †1950⟩ ⟨accompaniment in duo-piano playing requires even more ~ than is necessary in accompanying a voice or another instrument —A.E.Wier⟩ ⟨family was Quaker-like in its emotional ~ —H.S.Canby⟩

**ret·i·cen·cy** \-nsē, -si\ *n* -ES [L *reticentia*] : RETICENCE

**ret·i·cent** \-nt\ *adj* [L *reticent-*, *reticens*, pres. part. of *reticēre* to keep silent, fr. *re*- + -*ticēre* (fr. *tacēre* to be silent) — more at TACIT] **1** : inclined to keep silent or uncommunicative : given to reserve in speech ⟨particularly ~ about their knowledge — Irving Kristol⟩ ⟨though ~ about his personal history, on other matters he was garrulous —W.J.Ghent⟩ ⟨~ of his opinions —D.C.Peattie⟩ ⟨~ persons who are afraid to express themselves in a company —F.H.Allport⟩ **2** : restrained in expression, presentation, or appearance ⟨magnificently ~ study of a housewife —Roger Manvell⟩ ⟨the room has an aspect of ~ dignity—A.N.Whitehead⟩ ⟨art is thoughtful, ~, and stern, being composed of black and gray striations —*Saturday Rev.*⟩ **syn** see SILENT

**ret·i·cent·ly** *adv* : in a reticent manner

**ret·i·cle** \'red·|ēkəl, -et|, |ēk-\ *n* -s [L *reticulum* little net, reticulum] : a system of lines, dots, cross hairs, or wires in the focus of the eyepiece of an optical instrument (as a gunsight, microscope, telescope, or transit) used typically for estimating speed or distance, for measuring or counting, or as a centering or aiming device

**reticul-** *or* **reticulo-** *also* **reticuli-** *comb form* [L, fr. *reticulum*] **1** : a reticulum ⟨*reticulo*cyte⟩ **2** : the reticulum ⟨*reticul*itis⟩ **3** : reticulose and ⟨*reticulo*ramose⟩ ⟨*reticulo*venose⟩

**reticula** *pl of* RETICULUM

**re·tic·u·lar** \rə'tikyələ(r), rē'-\ *adj* [NL *reticularis*, fr. L *reticulum* little net, reticulum + -*aris* -ar — more at RETICULE] **1** : resembling a net in appearance or structure : RETICULATED, RETICULATE; *specif* : of or relating to a reticulum : taking on the form of or being a reticulum **2** : resembling a net in operation or effect : INTRICATE

**reticular cartilage** *n* : ELASTIC CARTILAGE

**reticular cell** *n* : RETICULUM CELL; *esp* : one that gives rise to blood cells

**reticular formation** *n* : nervous tissue within the brain made up of intermingled neuropil and medullated fibers

**reticular layer** *n* : the deeper layer of the dermis formed of interlacing fasciculi of white fibrous tissue

**re·tic·u·lar·ly** *adv* : in a reticular manner

**reticular theory** *n* : a theory in cytology: protoplasm consists essentially of a reticulum of more solid consistency containing a more fluid substance and suspended granules in its interstices

**¹re·tic·u·late** \rə'tikyələt, rē'-, -yə,lāt, *usu* -d·+V\ *adj* [L *reticulatus*, fr. *reticulum* little net + -*atus* -ate] **1** : resembling network : having the form or appearance of a net : NETTED; *specif* : having veins, fibers, or lines crossing like the threads or fibers of a network ⟨a ~ leaf⟩ ⟨a ~ wing⟩ **2** : covered with small polygonal scales — used of the tarsus of a bird **3** : involving repeated intercrossing between a number of lines; *specif* : of or relating to evolutionary change dependent on complex recombination of genes from varied strains of a diversified interbreeding population ⟨~ evolution⟩ — compare POLYPLOID COMPLEX

**²re·tic·u·late** \-yə,lāt, *usu* -ād+V\ *vb* -ED/-ING/-S [back-formation fr. *reticulated*] *vt* **1 a** : to divide, mark, or construct so as to resemble or form network **b** : to distribute (as electricity, water, or goods) by means of a network **c** : to form a reticulation in (a photographic material) ⟨~ gelatin⟩

⟨~ a print⟩ **2 :** to provide or construct with a reticle **~** *vi* **:** to become reticulated

**re·tic·u·lat·ed** \-ād·əd, -ātəd\ *adj* [L *reticulatus* reticulated + E *-ed*] **1 :** RETICULATE **2 a :** having lines or roads intercrossed **:** forming or formed like a network or a web ⟨~ canals⟩ ⟨a ~ system of transportation⟩ **:** pierced or open in a pattern resembling a net ⟨a ~ pottery jar⟩ **b :** constructed or faced with diamond-shaped stones or square stones placed diagonally ⟨~ masonry⟩

**reticulated glass** *n* **:** ornamental ware made from glass in which one set of white or colored lines seems to meet and interlace with another set

**reticulated python** *n* **:** a very large python (*Python reticulatus*) of southeastern Asia that is usu. considered the largest of recent snakes

**reticulated tracery** *n* **:** NET TRACERY

**re·tic·u·late·ly** *adv* **:** in a reticulate manner

**re·tic·u·la·tion** \=ˌ==ˈlāshən\ *n* -s [¹*reticulate* + *-ion*] **1 :** reticulated formation or appearance **:** NETWORK; *also* **:** something reticulated (as a system of transportation) **2 :** a network of corrugations produced accidentally or intentionally by a treatment producing rapid expansion and shrinkage of the swollen photographic gelatin and displacement of the image particles in processing

**reticulato-** *comb form* [L *reticulatus* reticulated (fr. *reticulum* + *-atus* -ate) + E *-o-*] **:** reticulately ⟨*reticulato*coalescent⟩ ⟨*reticulato*granulate⟩ ⟨*reticulato*ramose⟩ ⟨*reticulato*venose⟩

**ret·i·cule** \ˈred·əˌkyül, -etə-\ *n* -s [F *réticule*, fr. L *reticulum* little net, network, dim. of *rete* net — more at RETINA] **1 :** RETICLE **2 :** a woman's small drawstring bag used as a pocketbook, workbag, or carryall

**re·tic·u·lin** \rəˈtikyələn\ *n* -s [ISV *reticul-* + *-in*] **:** a protein substance similar to collagen and held to be a constituent of reticular tissue

**re·tic·u·li·termes** \rəˈtikyələ+\ *n, cap* [NL, fr. *reticul-* + *Termes*] **:** a widely distributed genus of termites that includes several forms common in the U.S.

**re·tic·u·li·tis** \rəˈtikyəˈlīd·əs\ *n* -ES [NL, fr. *reticul-* + *-itis*] **:** inflammation of the reticulum of a ruminant

**reticulo-** — see RETICUL-

**re·tic·u·lo·cyte** \rəˈtikyəlōˌsīt\ *n* -s [ISV *reticul-* + *-cyte*] **:** a young red blood cell that contains a fine basophilic reticulum representing the remains of the nucleus and is present in small numbers in normal blood and greatly increased following hemorrhage or other conditions in which many red cells are lost or destroyed — **re·tic·u·lo·cyt·ic** \=ˌ===ˈsid·ik\ *adj*

**re·tic·u·lo·cy·to·sis** \=ˌ===ˌsīˈtōsəs\ *n, pl* **reticulocyto·ses** \-ōˌsēz\ [NL, fr. ISV *reticulocyte* + NL *-osis*] **:** increase in the number of reticulocytes in the blood typically following hemorrhage or accompanying hemolytic anemia and representing an attempt of the system to restore the blood balance by hastening the maturation of red blood cells

**re·tic·u·lo·endothelial** \rəˈtikyəlō+\ *adj* [*reticul-* + *endothelial*] **:** of, relating to, or being the reticuloendothelial system

**reticuloendothelial system** *n* **:** a diffuse system of cells arising from mesenchyme, including reticulum cells and endothelial cells of capillaries and various other ducts and cavities, comprising all the phagocytic cells of the body except the circulating leukocytes; functioning to rid the body of debris, and according to some authorities being the ultimate source of all blood cells and playing a major role in hemoglobin conservation and synthesis

**re·tic·u·lo·en·do·the·li·o·sis** \rəˌtikyəlōˌendōˌthēlēˈōsəs\ *or* **re·tic·u·lo·sis** \rəˌtikyəˈlōsəs\ *n, pl* **reticuloendothelio·ses** \-ōˌsēz\ *or* **reticulo·ses** \-ˈlōˌsēz\ [*reticuloendotheliosis* fr. NL, fr. *reticuloendothelium* + *-osis; reticulosis* fr. NL, fr. *reticul-* + *-osis*] **:** an abnormal state characterized by proliferation of reticuloendothelial cells or their derivatives and their collection in bone and soft tissue (as Gaucher's disease, Hand-Schüller-Christian disease, or Niemann-Pick disease) **:** EOSINOPHILIC GRANULOMA

**re·tic·u·lo·endothelium** \rəˈtikyəlō+\ *n* [NL, fr. *reticul-* + *endothelium*] **:** the cells of the reticuloendothelial system regarded as a tissue

**re·tic·u·lo·sarcoma** \"+\ *n* [NL, fr. *reticul-* + *sarcoma*] **:** a sarcoma derived from reticulum cells

**re·tic·u·lose** \rəˈtikyəˌlōs, rēˈ-\ *adj* [*reticul-* + *-ose*] **:** RETICULATE 1

**re·tic·u·lum** \-yələm\ *n, pl* **reticu·la** \-lə\ [NL, fr. L, little net, network — more at RETICULE] **1 :** the second stomach of a ruminant in which folds of the mucous membrane form hexagonal cells — called also *honeycomb stomach;* see TRIPE **2 :** a netlike structure **:** NETWORK: as **a :** interstitial tissue composed of reticulum cells **b :** the network often visible in fixed protoplasm both of the cell body and nucleus of many cells and according to the reticular theory regarded as an essential structural part of the protoplasm

**reticulum cell** *n* **:** one of the branched anastomosing cells of the reticuloendothelial system that form an intricate interstitial network ramifying through other tissues and organs and being esp. abundant in perivascular connective tissue

**ret·i·form** \ˈre|d·əˌfȯrm, ˈrē|, |tə-, -ô(ə)m\ *adj* [NL *retiformis*, fr. L *rete* net + *-iformis* -iform] **:** composed of crossing lines and interstices **:** RETICULAR, NETLIKE; *specif* **:** being the connective tissue cells of the framework of the lymphatic glands

**re·timber** \(ˈ)rē+\ *vt* [*re-* + *timber*] **:** to furnish with new timber **:** to plant with timber again

**¹retin-** *or* **retini-** *also* **retina-** *comb form* [NL, fr. Gk *rhētinē* resin] **:** resin ⟨*Retinispora*⟩ ⟨*retinoid*⟩ ⟨*retinalite*⟩

**²retin-** *or* **retino-** *comb form* [fr. *retina*] **:** retina ⟨*retinitis*⟩ ⟨*retinoscope*⟩

**ret·i·na** \ˈretᵊnə *sometimes* -tnə\ *n, pl* **retinas** \-əz\ *or* **reti·nae** \-ᵊnˌē\ [ME *rethina*, fr. ML *retina*, prob. fr. L *rete* net; akin to Gk *erēmos* desolate, lonely, Lith *rėtis* sieve, OSlav *oriti* to loosen, Skt *ṛte* without, except; basic meaning: loose] **:** the sensory membrane that lines most of the large posterior chamber of the vertebrate eye, receives the image formed by the lens, is the immediate instrument of vision, is connected to the brain by the optic nerve, and consists essentially of supporting and protective structures, nervous elements, and sensory end organs arranged in several layers of which the sensory layer composed of small rodlike bodies interspersed with shorter conical bodies both of which are the specialized terminal parts of neuroepithelial cells is one of the outermost — see CONE, FOVEA, MACULA LUTEA, ROD

**ret·i·nac·u·lar** \ˌretᵊnˈakyələ(r)\ *adj* [NL *retinaculum* + E *-ar*] **:** relating to or resembling a retinaculum

**ret·i·nac·u·late** \-yələt, -yəˌlāt\ *adj* [NL *retinaculum* + E *-ate*] **:** having a retinaculum

**ret·i·nac·u·lum** \ˌ==ˈnakyələm\ *n, pl* **retinacu·la** \-lə\ [NL, fr. L, that which holds or binds, band, fr. *retinēre* to hold back, retain — more at RETAIN] **1 a :** a small structure on the forewings of many moths and butterflies that catches and holds the frenulum **b :** a small organ on the underside of the abdomen of a springtail that articulates with the apex of the springtail **c :** a connecting or retaining band **:** FRENUM **2 a :** any of the small glands or bodies resembling glands at the base of the stalk of a pollinium **b :** the hooklike funicle of a seed of a plant of the family Acanthaceae

**ret·i·nal** \ˈretᵊnəl *sometimes* -tnəl\ *adj* [²*retin-* + *-al*] **:** of, relating to, involving, or being a retina

**re·tin·a·lite** \rəˈtinᵊlˌīt\ *n* -s [¹*retin-* + *-lite*] **:** a massive variety of serpentine of a honey-yellow or greenish color and a waxy or resinous luster

**retinal purple** *n* **:** VISUAL PURPLE

**retinal rivalry** *n* **:** the oscillating perception of first one then the other of two visual stimuli which differ radically in color or form when they are presented simultaneously to congruent areas of both eyes

**ret·in·as·phalt** \ˌretᵊnˈaˌsfȯlt\ *or* **ret·in·as·phal·tum** \ˌ==-ˌaˈsfaltəm\ *n* [*retinasphalt* fr. NL *retinasphaltum; retinasphaltum* fr. NL, fr. Gk *rhētinē* resin + NL *asphaltum* asphalt — more at ASPHALT] **:** a fossil resin usu. found with lignite

**ret·i·nene** \ˈretᵊnˌēn\ *n* -s [²*retin-* + *-ene*] **:** either of two carotenoid pigments that are aldehydes corresponding to the two vitamin A alcohols from which they are formed reversibly by oxidation: **a :** a light yellow crystalline compound $C_{19}H_{27}CHO$ related to vitamin $A_1$ and formed from rhodopsin or iodopsin by the action of light — called also *retinene₁* **b :** an orange-red crystalline compound $C_{19}H_{25}CHO$ related to vitamin $A_2$ and formed from porphyropsin by the action of light — called also *retinene₂*

**¹ret·i·nis·po·ra** \ˌretᵊnˈispərə\ [NL, fr. ¹*retin-* + *-spora*] *syn of* CHAMAECYPARIS

**²retinispora** \"\ *or* **ret·i·nos·po·ra** \-ˈäs-\ *n* -s [NL] **1 :** any of various Japanese ornamental dwarf shrubs of the genus *Chamaecyparis* that resemble cypresses; *esp* **:** any of several shrubs that are horticultural varieties derived from the sawara cypress or the sun tree **2 :** any of several shrubs of the genus *Thuja* that retain the needlelike juvenile foliage permanently and are propagated by cuttings or grafting

**ret·i·nite** \ˈretᵊnˌīt\ *n* -s [F *rétinite*, fr. *rétin-* ¹*retin-* + *-ite*] **:** a fossil resin of variable composition

**ret·i·ni·tis** \ˌretᵊnˈīd·əs\ *n, pl* **reti·nit·i·des** \-ˈid·əˌdēz\ [NL, fr. ²*retin-* + *-itis*] **:** inflammation of the retina

**retino-** — see RETIN-

**ret·i·no·blas·to·ma** \ˌretᵊnōˌblaˈstōmə\ *n* [NL, fr. ²*retin-* + *blast-* + *-oma*] **:** a malignant tumor of the retina derived from retinal germ cells and believed to be hereditary

**ret·i·no·cho·roid·i·tis** \ˌretᵊnōˌkōrˌȯiˈdīd·əs\ *n* [NL, fr. ²*retin-* + *choroid* + *-itis*] **:** inflammation of the retina and the choroid

**ret·i·noid** \ˈretᵊnˌȯid\ *adj* [¹*retin-* + *-oid*] **:** resembling a resin

**ret·i·no·pap·il·li·tis** \ˌretᵊnōˌpapəˈlīd·əs\ *n* [NL, fr. ²*retin-* + *papilla* + *-itis*] **:** inflammation of both the retina and the optic papilla

**ret·i·nop·a·thy** \ˌretᵊnˈäpəthē\ *n* -ES [²*retin-* + *-pathy*] **:** a noninflammatory disease of the retina ⟨hypertensive ~⟩ ⟨diabetic ~⟩

**ret·i·noph·o·ral** \ˌ==ˈäfərəl\ *adj* [*retinophore* + *-al*] **:** of or relating to a retinophore

**ret·i·no·phore** \ˈretᵊnəˌfō(ə)r\ *n* -s [²*retin-* + *-phore*] **:** one of a group of cells enclosing a crystalline cone in the distal portion of an ommatidium

**ret·i·no·scope** \-ˌskōp\ *n* [²*retin-* + *-scope*] **:** an apparatus for viewing the retina; *specif* **:** an apparatus for retinoscopy

**ret·i·no·scop·ic** \ˌ===ˈskäpik\ *adj* [*retinoscopy* + *-ic*] **:** relating to or made by means of retinoscopy ⟨a ~ study⟩ — **ret·i·no·scop·i·cal·ly** \-pək(ə)lē\ *adv*

**ret·i·nos·co·py** \ˌretᵊnˈäskəpē\ *n* -ES [²*retin-* + *-scopy*] **:** observation of the retina of the eye; *specif* **:** a method of determining the state of refraction of the eye by illuminating the retina with a mirror and observing the direction of movement of the retinal illumination and adjacent shadow when the mirror is turned — called also *skiascopy*

**ret·i·nos·po·ra** \ˌretᵊnˈäspərə\ [NL, alter. of *Retinispora*] *syn of* CHAMAECYPARIS

**ret·i·nue** \ˈretᵊnˌ(y)ü\ *n* -s [ME *retenue*, fr. MF, fr. fem. of *retenu*, past part. of *retenir* to retain — more at RETAIN] **:** the body of retainers who follow a prince or other distinguished person **:** a train of attendants **:** SUITE ⟨the largest ~ ever to accompany a candidate for the vice-presidency —R.H.Rovere⟩ ⟨a ~ of slave-servants —J.R.Perkins⟩ ⟨a school for a devoted ~ of students —Stuart MacClintock⟩ ⟨there were two assisting priests, and a ~ of altar boys —Mary Deasy⟩

**re·tin·u·la** \rəˈtinyələ\ *n, pl* **retinu·lae** \-yəˌlē\ [NL, dim. of *retina*, fr. ML — more at RETINA] **:** the neural receptor of a single facet of an arthropodan compound eye — **re·tin·u·lar** \-yələ(r)\ *adj*

**ret·i·nule** \ˈretᵊnˌyül\ *n* -s [NL *retinula*] **:** RETINULA

**re·tir·a·cy** \rəˈtīrəsē\ *n* -ES [fr. ¹*retire*, after such pairs as E *conspire: conspiracy*] **1 :** RETIREMENT, SECLUSION **2 :** sufficient means or property to make possible retirement from business

**ret·i·rade** \ˌred·əˈräd\ *n* -s [F, fr. It *ritirata* retreat, fr. fem. of *ritirato*, past part. of *ritirare* to retreat, withdraw, fr. *ri-* re- (fr. L *re-*) + *tirare* to draw, pull, shoot — more at TIRADE] **:** a fortification retrenchment usu. of two faces making a reentering angle

**re·tir·al** \rəˈtīrəl\ *n* -s [¹*retire* + *-al*] **:** an act of retiring: as **a :** RETREAT, WITHDRAWAL **b** *Brit* **:** RETIREMENT ⟨headmaster must be approaching the ~ age —*Scots Mag.*⟩ ⟨rumor about my ~ —Harry Lauder⟩ ⟨~ from a directorship⟩

**re·tir·ant** \-rənt\ *n* -s [¹*retire* + *-ant*] **:** RETIREE

**¹re·tire** \rəˈtī(ə)r, rēˈ-, -īə\ *vb* -ED/-ING/-s [MF *retirer*, fr. *re-* + *tirer* to draw, pull, fr. OF — more at TIRADE] *vi* **1 a :** to withdraw from action or danger **:** RETREAT ⟨the raiders *retired* by this route —H.L.Merillat⟩ ⟨ordered his command to ~ —*Amer. Guide Series: La.*⟩ **b :** to give ground in fencing **:** take a step back **c :** to cease batting in cricket and leave the field (as when dismissed or injured) **2 :** to withdraw, go away, or betake onself esp. for the sake of privacy, seclusion, or protection **:** go into retreat ⟨the men usually remain at table or ~ to the library —June Platt⟩ ⟨the alligator is generally considered as disposed to ~ from man —*Encyc. Americana*⟩ ⟨~ to the nearest wineshop —Norman Douglas⟩ ⟨*retired* to comb his hair —John Pudney⟩ ⟨*retired* to a cloister —H.O. Taylor⟩ **3 :** to move, fall, or bend back **:** recede or appear to recede ⟨*retired* a few yards —William Black⟩ ⟨plants and animals . . . closely followed the *retiring* ice —John Muir †1914⟩ **4 :** to withdraw from office, public station, business, occupation, or active duty ⟨~ from the diplomatic service⟩ ⟨~ from the editorship⟩ ⟨~ as a soldier⟩ ⟨~ from the sea⟩ **5 :** to go to bed ⟨perhaps she was tired and would like to ~ —P.B.Kyne⟩ **~** *vt* **1 a :** WITHDRAW **b :** to march (a military force) away from the enemy esp. in order to avoid decisive combat **2 :** to draw or pull back ⟨~ a needle⟩ **3** *obs* **:** to remove or bring by or as if by leading **4 a :** to withdraw from circulation or from the market **:** take up or pay **:** RECALL, REDEEM ⟨the bonds would be *retired* inside the Treasury's walls —G.B.Robinson⟩ ⟨unwanted currency is returned to the Federal Reserve banks where it is either *retired* or held for future demand —J.A.Leavitt & C.O.Hanson⟩ ⟨~ a loan⟩ ⟨~ a bond⟩ ⟨~ stock⟩ ⟨~ indebtedness⟩ ⟨~ a note⟩ **b :** to withdraw from usual use or service ⟨~ this poor land from agriculture and plant extensive forests —*Amer. Guide Series: Ind.*⟩ ⟨worn-out equipment was *retired* from service —*Yrbk. of Railroad Information*⟩ **5 a :** to cause to retire ⟨any employee who has served at least 15 years is automatically *retired* at the end of the month in which he reaches age 70 —*Your Retirement System*⟩ ⟨once a man is put on a committee, he stays on it . . . until the voters ~ him —Bruce Catton⟩ **b :** to release from active duty and place on the retired list ⟨~ a military officer⟩ **6 :** to put out (a batter or side) in baseball or cricket **syn** see GO

**²retire** \"\ *n* -s **:** RETIREMENT, WITHDRAWAL; *also* **:** a place to which one retires

**³re·ti·ré** \rəˌtēˈrā\ *n* -s [F, past part. of *retirer* to retire, fr. MF] **:** a ballet movement in which the foot of one leg is brought to the knee of the other

**retired** *adj* [fr. past part. of ¹*retire*] **1 :** SECLUDED, SEQUESTERED ⟨a ~ life⟩ ⟨a ~ village⟩ ⟨a ~ path⟩ **2 :** withdrawn into oneself **:** RESERVED **3** *obs* **a :** PRIVATE, SECRET ⟨~ thoughts⟩ **b :** ABSTRUSE, RECONDITE **4 :** withdrawn from active duty or business ⟨a ~ officer⟩ ⟨a ~ physician⟩ **5 :** received by or due to a person on a retired status ⟨~ pay⟩ ⟨~ pension⟩ — **re·tired·ly** *adv* — **re·tired·ness** *n* -ES

**retired list** *n* **:** a list of officers or enlisted men who by reason of age, length of service, failure of promotion, or physical disability are relieved from active military service and retired with reduced pay

**re·tir·ee** \rəˌtīˈrē\ *n* -s [¹*retire* + *-ee*] **:** one who retires from his vocation

**re·tire·ment** \rəˈtī(ə)rmənt, rēˈ-, -ˈtīəm-\ *n* -s [MF, fr. *retirer* to retire + *-ment*] **1 :** an act of retiring or state of being retired: as **a :** a falling back ⟨~ of an army⟩ **b :** a withdrawing into seclusion or retreat **c :** withdrawal from office, active service, or business **d :** secluded condition or state **:** withdrawal from society or publicity **:** PRIVACY; *also* **:** a time or occasion of this **2 :** a place of seclusion or privacy **:** a place to which one withdraws or retreats **:** a private abode **:** RETREAT

**retirement annuity** *n* **:** accumulation of net premiums and interest used to purchase a life annuity at the time annuitant reaches specified retirement date

**retirement income insurance** *n* **:** a policy providing a death benefit should the insured die before reaching a stated age or a life income should he survive to that age

**retirement plan** *n* **:** a systematic arrangement established by an employer for guaranteeing an income to employees upon retirement according to definitely established rules with or without employee contributions but usu. funded — compare PENSION PLAN

**re·tir·er** \-īrə(r)\ *n* -s [¹*retire* + *-er*] **:** one that retires

**retiring** *adj* **:** RESERVED, SHY **:** not forward or obtrusive ⟨a ~ man⟩ ⟨~ manners⟩ ⟨~ disposition⟩ ⟨~ habits⟩ — **re·tir·ing·ly** *adv* — **re·tir·ing·ness** *n* -ES

**retnr** *abbr* retainer

**retold** *past of* RETELL

**ret·o·na·tion wave** \ˌretᵊnˈāshən-\ *n* [*retonation* fr. *re-* + *-tonation* (as in *detonation*)] **:** a compressional wave propagated backward from the starting point of an explosion wave in a gaseous mixture

**retook** *past of* RETAKE

**re·tool** \(ˈ)rē+\ *vt* [*re-* + *tool*] **1 :** to reequip (as a factory or an industry) with tools (as dies and punches) for manufacturing ⟨~ an aircraft plant to build prefabricated houses⟩ ⟨~ an industry for armaments work⟩ ⟨~ a nation to war production —*Nat'l Geographic*⟩ **2 :** REORGANIZE ⟨~*ing* of our academic structure —Mortimer Graves⟩ ⟨period of economic and social ~*ing* —Vera M. Dean⟩

**re·tor·sio fac·ti** \rəˈtȯ(r)shēˌōˈfakˌtī\ *n, pl* **retorsiones facti** [NL] **:** the infliction of retaliatory injuries by one nation on another equal to those it has suffered

**ré·tor·sion de droit** \rātȯrsyōⁿdədrwä\ *n, pl* **rétorsions de droit** [F] **:** lawful retaliation or reprisal in international law

**¹re·tort** \rəˈtȯ(ə)r|t, rēˈ-, -ô(ə)|, *usu* |d·+V\ *vb* -ED/-ING/-s [L *retortus*, past part. of *retorquēre* to turn back, bend back, retort, fr. *re-* + *torquēre* to bend, twist — more at TORTURE] *vt* **1 :** to toss, cast, or hurl back **:** RETURN, REPAY ⟨~ an accusation⟩ ⟨~ a wrong⟩ ⟨~ a censure⟩ ⟨~ an incivility⟩ **2 :** to make a like reply to **:** answer in kind **:** say in reply ⟨will ~ the question . . . by another question —Sir Winston Churchill⟩ ⟨triumph on being able to ~ . . . the comfort of having a daughter well married —Jane Austen⟩ ⟨"it is false," he ~*ed*⟩ **3 :** to answer or meet (as an argument) by a counter argument of a like kind **4 a** *obs* **:** to throw back (as a spear) **:** REVERBERATE ⟨~ sound⟩ **:** REFLECT ⟨~ heat⟩ **b :** to turn, twist, or curve back ⟨our driver's head was ~*ed* to harangue the back seat —Christopher Morley⟩ **~** *vi* **1** *obs* **:** to turn or spring back **:** RECOIL **2 :** to make retort **:** return an argument or charge ⟨I ~ upon the ethnologists —A.T.Quiller-Couch⟩ ⟨~*ed* upon the teasers, without stammering —Arnold Bennett⟩ **3 :** RETALIATE ⟨~*ed* with worse revenge of his own sort —Arthur Morrison⟩ ⟨there exists in the animals the impulse to ~ upon offenders —Samuel Alexander⟩ **syn** see ANSWER

**²retort** \"\ *n* -s **1 :** a quick sharp witty cutting or severe reply; *esp* **:** one that turns the first speaker's statement or argument against him or counters it ⟨make some quick ~ that silenced her tormenters —T.S.Eliot⟩ ⟨wrote an article in the *Standard* (as a ~ to my criticism of her) —Arnold Bennett⟩ **2 :** the act or practice of making retorts ⟨the ~ courteous —Shak.⟩

**³retort** \"\ *n* -s [MF *retorte*, fr. ML *retorta*, fr. fem. of L *retortus*, past part. of *retorquēre* to bend back; fr. its bent shape] **1 :** a vessel in which substances are subjected to distillation or decomposition by heat and which may be made in various forms and of various materials for different uses: as **a :** a bulb of glass or metal with a curved or slanting beak to enter a receiver for general chemical operations **b :** a long semicylinder now usu. of fireclay or silica for the manufacture of coal gas **2 :** MAGAZINE 5b

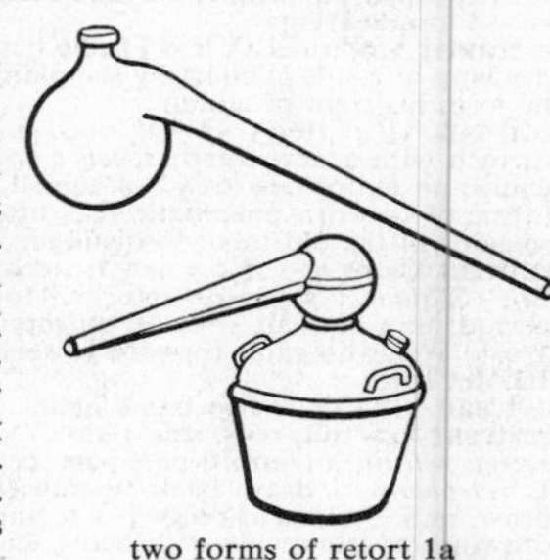

two forms of retort 1a

**⁴retort** \"\ *vt* -ED/-ING/-s **1 :** to treat (as oil shale) by heating in a retort **2 :** AUTOCLAVE ⟨~ canned food⟩

**re·tort·er** \|d·ə(r)\ *n* -s **:** one that retorts

**re·tor·tion** \rəˈtȯrshən, rēˈ-, -tȯ(ə)sh-\ *n* -s [ML *retortion-, retortio*, fr. L *retortus* (past part.) + *-ion-, -io* -ion] **1 :** an act of retorting **:** a turning, twisting, bending, or throwing back **:** REFLECTION **2** *obs* **:** ²RETORT **3** *or* **re·tor·sion** \"\ **:** RETALIATION — used chiefly of acts by which an aggrieved state treats the subjects of another state giving provocation in a manner similar to that in which the subjects of the state using retortion are treated by the state giving provocation

**retort stand** *n* **:** a stand for holding a retort — compare RING STAND

**re·toss** \(ˈ)rē+\ *vt* [*re-* + *toss*] **:** to toss back or again

**¹re·touch** \(ˈ)rēˈtəch\ *vb* [F *retoucher*, fr. MF, fr. *re-* + *toucher* to touch — more at TOUCH] *vt* **1 :** to touch again or rework in order to improve **:** amend by retouches **:** touch up ⟨~ a picture⟩ ⟨~ a written record⟩ ⟨~ makeup⟩ **2 :** to alter (a photographic negative or print or an engraving plate) so as to produce a more desirable appearance (as by disguising physical defects of the subject or of the photographic material) **3 :** to color (new growth of hair) to match previously dyed, tinted, or bleached hair **~** *vi* **:** to make or give retouches

**²retouch** \ˈ=ˌ=, =ˈ=\ *n* **1 :** the act, process, or an instance of retouching; *specif* **:** the retouching of a new growth of hair **2 :** a retouched detail or part

**re·touch·er** \-chə(r)\ *n* -s **:** one that retouches

**¹re·tour** \rəˈtü(ə)r\ *n* [ME, fr. MF, fr. *retourner* to return — more at RETURN] **1** *chiefly Scot* **:** RETURN **2** *Scots law* **a :** the return made to the court of chancery on a brieve of inquest with the jury's verdict thereon **b :** a copy or extract of such return

**²retour** \"\ *vt, Scots law* **:** to make a retour of

**re·tour·able** \-rəbəl\ *adj* [²*retour* + *-able*] *Scots law* **:** RETURNABLE

**¹re·trace** \(ˈ)rēˈtrās\ *vt* [F *retracer*, fr. MF *retracier*, fr. *re-* + *tracier* to trace — more at TRACE] **:** to trace again or back: as **a :** to trace the origin or early history of by going back over previous steps ⟨~ one's family line⟩ **b :** to go over again with the eyes **:** reinspect closely **c :** to go over again in memory **:** RECALL **d :** to go back upon (as one's steps) **:** go over again usu. in a reverse direction ⟨decided to ~ his course⟩ **e :** to trace over again or renew the outline of ⟨~ a drawing⟩ ⟨~ letters⟩

**²retrace** \ˈ=ˌ=, =ˈ=\ *n* **:** the return of the electron beam to the starting point in a cathode ray tube after completion of all or a part of the scanning process **:** FLYBACK

**re·trace·ment** \-smənt\ *n* -s **:** an act or result of retracing ⟨~ of the outline made it sharper⟩

**re·track** \(ˈ)rē+\ *vt* [*re-* + *track*] **:** to track or trace again

**re·tract** \rəˈtrakt, rēˈ-\ *vb* -ED/-ING/-s [ME *retracten*, fr. L *retractus*, past part. of *retrahere* to draw back, withdraw — more at RETREAT] *vt* **1 a :** to draw or pull back or in ⟨a cat can ~ its claws⟩ ⟨flipped out its wings and ~*ed* them again —E.A.Armstrong⟩ ⟨throwing out and ~*ing* their left fists —G.B.Shaw⟩ **b (1) :** to move (the tongue) further back **(2) :** BACK 3b **2** *obs* **:** to draw or bring (a person) back **b :** to hold back **:** PREVENT, RESTRAIN **c :** to take away **:** REMOVE **3** [MF *retracter*, fr. L *retractare* to pull back, withdraw, retract, freq. of *retrahere* to draw back] **:** to take back (as an accusation or promise) **:** RECALL, RECANT, DISAVOW ⟨~ the wish as brutal —Thomas Hardy⟩ ⟨~ everything we had previously said —L.L.Snyder⟩ ⟨a confession she later ~*ed* —Robert Parris⟩ ⟨refused to ~ his previous naturalism —*Americana Annual*⟩ **~** *vi* **1 :** to draw back **:** undergo retraction ⟨beds automatically ~ into the walls —*Current Biog.*⟩ ⟨watched the boat ~ from the beach —K.M.Dodson⟩ ⟨she did not ~ in horror; but laughed —Elizabeth Taylor⟩ **2 :** to withdraw, recant, or disavow something (as an accusation, statement, opinion) ⟨was tarred, feathered, and carried several miles in a cart, but refused to ~ —E.K.Alden⟩ **syn** see ABJURE, RECEDE

**re·tract·able** \-ktəbəl\ *adj* **:** capable of being retracted ⟨~ wheels⟩ ⟨a ~ landing gear⟩

**re·trac·ta·tion** \ˌrē,trakˈtāshən\ *n* -s [L *retractation-, retractatio*, fr. *retractatus* (past part. of *retractare* to retract) + *-ion-, -io* -ion] **:** RETRACTION, RECANTATION

**retracted** *adj* [fr. past part. of *retract*] **:** drawn, pulled, or moved back **:** WITHDRAWN, RECANTED

**re·trac·tile** \rəˈtrakt³l\ *adj* [*retract* + *-ile*] **:** capable of, or exhibiting retraction **:** capable of being drawn back or in ⟨the claws of a cat are ~⟩ ⟨a ~ spring⟩ — compare PROTRACTILE — **re·trac·til·i·ty** \ˌrē,trakˈtiləd·ē\ *n* -ES

**re·trac·tion** \rəˈtrakshən, rē-ˈ-\ *n* -s [ME *retracciou*n, fr. MF *retraction*, fr. L *retraction-, retractio* hesitation, refusal, fr. *retractus* (past part. of *retrahere* to draw back) + *-ion-, -io* -ion] **1 :** an act of withdrawing a declaration, accusation, promise **:** RECANTATION, REVOCATION, RECALL; *also* **:** a statement made by one retracting ⟨a ~ of a charge or decree⟩ ⟨insist upon a ~⟩ **2 :** an act of retracting or drawing back or in **:** a state of being retracted **:** ability to retract ⟨the ~ of claws⟩ ⟨the ~ of rubber . . . the property which causes rubber to return to its original shape —*Science*⟩ ⟨~ of the oceans from the polar areas —*Jour. of Geol.*⟩ ⟨fear of life and ~ from its exigencies and challenges —John Dewey⟩ ⟨print a ~ of errors —Lister Hill⟩

**re·trac·tor** \-ktə(r)\ *n* -s **:** one that retracts: as **a :** a surgical

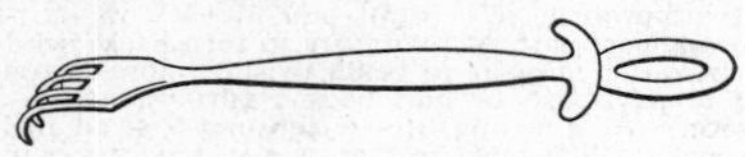

retractor a

instrument for holding tissues away from the field of operation **b :** a muscle that draws in an organ or part — opposed to *protractor*

**re·trad** \ˈrē,trad, ˈre-,-\ *adv* [L *retro* backward + E *-ad* — more at RETRO-] **:** BACKWARD, POSTERIORLY

**re·tra·hent** \ˈre·trəhənt\ *adj* [L *retrahent-, retrahens*, pres. part. of *retrahere* to withdraw — more at RETREAT] **:** that retracts ⟨~ muscles⟩

**retraict** *n* -s [MF, alter. of *retrait* retreat] *obs* **:** RETREAT

**re·train** \(ˈ)rē¦trān\ *vb* [*re-* + *train*] *vt* **:** to train again ⟨~ a muscle⟩ ⟨~ men⟩ ~ *vi* **:** to become trained again ⟨vocational ~*ing*⟩ ⟨a reemployment, ~*ing*, and rehabilitation program for returning veterans —*Current Biog.*⟩

**re·tral** \ˈrē·trəl\ *adj* [L *retro* backward + E *-al* — more at RETRO-] **1 :** situated at or toward the back **:** POSTERIOR **2 :** BACKWARD, RETROGRADE — **re·tral·ly** \-lē\ *adv*

**re·transmission** \¦rē+\ *n* [*re-* + *transmission*] **:** transmission back or again

**re·transmit** \(ˌ)rē+\ *vt* [*re-* + *transmit*] **:** to transmit back or again

**re·traverse** \¦rē+\ *vt* [*re-* + *traverse*] **:** to traverse again ⟨caves whose cunning twists and turns no one could possibly ~ —Florette Henri⟩

**re·trax·it** \rəˈtraksət\ *n* -s [L, he has withdrawn] **:** the withdrawing of a suit in court by the plaintiff personally by which he loses his right of action

**[1]retread** \(ˈ)rē¦tred\ *vt* -ED/-ING/-S [*re-* + *tread*, n.] **:** to furnish with a new tread; *specif* **:** to cement, mold, and vulcanize an entire new tread of camelback upon the bare cord fabric of (a worn pneumatic tire) after the buffing off of the remains of the old tread — distinguished from *recap*

**[2]retread** \ˈ=,=\ *n* -s **1 :** a new tread on a tire **2 :** a retreaded tire **3** *slang* **:** a person returned to military service after a period as a civilian ⟨~*s* — officers or veterans of the last World War who came forward to serve their country again —J.J.McCloy⟩

**re-tread** \(ˈ)=¦=\ *vt* **:** to tread again

**[1]re·treat** \rəˈtrēt, rē-ˈ-, *usu* -ēd·+V\ *n* -s [ME *retret*, fr. MF *retret, retrait*, fr. *retrait*, past part. of *retraire* to withdraw, fr. L *retrahere* to draw back, withdraw, fr. *re-* + *trahere* to draw, pull — more at DRAW] **1 a :** an act of retiring or withdrawing (as from what is difficult, dangerous, or disagreeable or as into privacy from business, public life, or society) **:** the process of receding ⟨this ~ from reality characterizes much of our thinking about social and criminal problems —D.W. Maurer & V.H.Vogel⟩ ⟨the squalor of the medieval village had long been in ~ before the homely dignity and comfort of the rural middle class —G.M.Trevelyan⟩ ⟨an escape from the world of men, a refusal to accept the responsibility of social and adult life, a ~ into the egocentric —*Times Lit. Supp.*⟩ ⟨the ~ of the forest —*Amer. Guide Series: Minn.*⟩ ⟨the final ice ~ during the Ice Age —W.J.Miller⟩ **b** (1) **:** the withdrawal esp. when forced of troops from the presence of an enemy or from ground occupied to ground farther from the enemy or from an advanced position (2) **:** a signal for retreating or retiring (3) **:** a signal given by bugle with or without drums at the beginning of the flag-lowering ceremony at a military installation (4) **:** the flag-lowering ceremony at a military installation that may constitute part of the ceremony of evening parade **2 a :** a place to which someone retires **:** a place of seclusion, privacy, safety, or resort **:** a retired abode **:** hiding place **:** REFUGE ⟨quiet city that is becoming a ~ for writers and artists —R.F.Warner⟩ ⟨three acres for a country ~ —Green Peyton⟩ ⟨regard the hut as a ~ and a camp rather than a home —H.S.Canby⟩ **b :** ASYLUM ⟨a charitable ~ for down-and-outs —Van Wyck Brooks⟩ ⟨the provincial house and novitiate . . . is a ~ for aged or invalid members —*Amer. Guide Series: Md.*⟩ **3 :** recessed work **:** a retired part **:** RETIREMENT, RECESS ⟨a facade in ~⟩ **4 :** a special period of group withdrawal to a place of seclusion for the purpose of deepening the spiritual life of participants through such means as prayer, meditation, study, and instruction under a director ⟨priests and religious usually make a retreat every year for a week or eight days —Cyprian Emanuel⟩ **5 :** the extent to which an aeronautical structure (as an airplane wing tip) or similar structure recedes

**[2]retreat** \"\ *vb* -ED/-ING/-S [ME *retreten*, fr. *retret* retreat] *vi* **1 :** to make a retreat **:** retire from a position or place **:** WITHDRAW ⟨the army ~*ed*⟩ ⟨stared after the ~*ing* cab —G.B.Shaw⟩ ⟨labor determined not to ~ from the position it had attained —Oscar Handlin⟩ ⟨became despondent, and ~*ed* within herself —*Jour. of Child Psychiatry*⟩ ⟨as though a glacier had just ~*ed* —Walter Bernstein⟩ ⟨a ~*ing* chin⟩ **2 :** to slope backward — used of an airplane wing tip ~ *vt* **:** to draw or lead back **:** WITHDRAW, REMOVE ⟨~*ing* his chair with intense disgust —George Meredith⟩ ⟨no hurt ~*s* us from this calm —Genevieve Taggard⟩; *specif* **:** to move (a piece) back in chess **syn** see RECEDE

**re-treat** \(ˈ)rē+\ *vt* **:** to treat again **:** RECONSIDER

**re·treat·al** \rəˈtrēd·³l\ *adj* **:** of or relating to retreat

**re·treat·ant** \-ēt³nt\ *n* -s **:** one who is on a religious retreat

**re·treat·ism** \-ēd·,izəm\ *n* -s **:** the attitude of being resigned to abandonment of an original goal or the means of attaining it (as in political or cultural matters)

**re·treatment** \(ˈ)rē+\ *n* **:** further treatment

**re·tree** \rəˈtrē\ *or* **retree paper** *n* -s [*retree* prob. fr. F *retrait* withdrawal, retreat, fr. MF] **:** paper that is imperfect or slightly damaged (as by dirty stains, specks, or pinholes occurring in the process of manufacture) ⟨packages of ~ are often marked *R* in the U.S. and *XX* in Great Britain⟩ — compare CASSIE PAPER

**re·trench** \rəˈtrench, rē-ˈ-\ *vb* [obs. F *retrencher* (now *retrancher*), fr. MF *retrenchier*, fr. *re-* + *trenchier* to trench — more at TRENCH] *vt* **1** *obs* **a :** to cut short **:** REPRESS **b :** to cut off **:** INTERCEPT **2 :** to cut down **:** LESSEN, REDUCE, CURTAIL ⟨must expect to have her pay ~*ed* —Mary W. Montagu⟩ ⟨a long speech . . . but I could be glad you would ~ it —Thomas Gray⟩ ⟨the gentry, compelled to ~ their expenses —T.B. Macaulay⟩ **3 :** to cut out **:** EXCISE, OMIT ⟨~ a paragraph⟩ **4 :** to cut off **:** pare away **:** do away with **:** REMOVE **5 :** to furnish with a retrenchment in fortifying ~ *vi* **:** to make retrenchments or reductions; *specif* **:** to cut down living expenses **:** ECONOMIZE ⟨the lords are ~*ing* visibly —Nancy Mitford⟩ **syn** see SHORTEN

**re·trench·ment** \-chmənt\ *n* -s [MF, fr. *retrenchier* + *-ment*] **1 :** an act or process of retrenching **:** REDUCTION, CURTAILMENT, EXCISION **:** cutting down of expenses ⟨~ of their way of living — Willa Cather⟩ ⟨~ both in public expenditures and international commitments —Max Ascoli⟩ **2 :** a defense work (as a simple traverse or parapet and ditch) constructed within another to prolong the defense when the enemy has gained the outer work

**retrg** *abbr* retracting

**re·trial** \(ˈ)rē+\ *n* [*re-* + *trial*] **:** a second trial, experiment, or test **:** a second judicial trial (as of an accused person)

**re·trib·ute** \rəˈtri,byüt, ˈre·trə,-\ *vb* -ED/-ING/-S [L *retributus*, past part. of *retribuere* to retribute] *vt* **:** to pay back **:** give in return **:** REQUITE ~ *vi*, *obs* **:** to make requital

**ret·ri·bu·tion** \ˌre·trəˈbyüshən\ *n* -s [ME *retribucioun*, fr. MF *retribution*, fr. LL *retribution-, retributio*, fr. L *retributus* (past part. of *retribuere* to retribute, fr. *re-* + *tribuere* to bestow) + *-ion-, -io* -ion — more at TRIBUTE] **1 :** RECOMPENSE, RETURN, REWARD ⟨denied just ~ for their services⟩ **2 :** the dispensing or receiving of reward or punishment according to the deserts of the individual esp. in the hereafter ⟨interpret justice in terms of ~ —Lucius Garvin⟩ ⟨by a whimsical ~, his own novels have passed for pantomimes —Richard Garnett †1906⟩; *specif* **:** LAST JUDGMENT ⟨the day of ~⟩ **3 a :** something given or exacted in recompense **b :** PUNISHMENT ⟨a visitation of divine ~ in the form of elemental phenomena —*Amer. Guide Series: Texas*⟩ ⟨knew the ~ in store for them if they misbehaved —*Time*⟩; *esp* **:** condign punishment in the hereafter

**re·trib·u·tive** \rəˈtribyəd·iv, rē-ˈ-, -ətiv\ *adj* [*retribute* + *-ive*] **:** of, relating to, or having the nature of retribution **:** involving condign punishment ⟨his ultimate fate of ~ assassination —*Times Lit. Supp.*⟩ ⟨~ murderer —Warren Ramsey⟩ ⟨the righteousness of God is both ~ and forgiving —*Lutheran Quarterly*⟩ ⟨~ punishment is the essential of medieval justice —M.R.Cohen⟩ — **re·trib·u·tive·ly** \-əd·əvlē, -ətəv-, -li\ *adv*

**retributive justice** *n* **:** justice concerned with punishing or rewarding an individual

**re·trib·u·tor** \-əd·ə(r)\ *n* -s [LL, fr. L *retributus* (past part.) + *-or*] **:** one that exacts or pays retribution

**re·trib·u·to·ry** \-yə,tōrē, -tór-, -ri\ *adj* [L *retributus* (past part.) + E *-ory*] **:** involving, causing, or characterized by retribution **:** RETRIBUTIVE ⟨in that era of ~ religion —*Times Lit. Supp.*⟩

**re-tried** *past of* RE-TRY

**re-tries** *pres 3d sing of* RE-TRY

**re·triev·able** \rəˈtrēvəbəl, rē-ˈ-\ *adj* **:** capable of being retrieved **:** admitting of retrieval

**re·triev·al** \-vəl\ *n* -s **1 :** an act or process of retrieving ⟨the application of punched-card machines for the organization and ~ of information —*Amer. Documentation*⟩ ⟨any ~ of his error became more and more difficult —George Eliot⟩ **2 :** possibility of being retrieved or of recovering ⟨beyond ~⟩

**[1]re·trieve** \rəˈtrēv, rē-ˈ-\ *vb* -ED/-ING/-S [ME *retreven, retriven*, modif. of MF *retrover, retrouver* to find again, fr. *re-* + *trouver* to find, prob. fr. (assumed) VL *tropare* to compose — more at TROUBADOUR] *vt* **1 a** *obs* **:** to discover again (game once sprung); *esp* **:** to flush (partridges) a second time **b :** to discover and bring in (killed or wounded game) **2 :** to call to mind again (as by study or an effort of memory) **:** find again ⟨memory withdrew further, *retrieved* the visit of two summers ago —George Green⟩ ⟨a gesture *retrieved* from long ago —*New Yorker*⟩ **3 :** REGAIN, REPOSSESS ⟨*retrieved* his fortune —H.E.Scudder⟩ ⟨go back to the box and ~ the letter —Elizabeth M. Roberts⟩ ⟨*retrieved* his position of preeminence —*Current Biog.*⟩ **4 a** *obs* **:** to bring back **:** make return **:** RECALL **b :** to reel in **:** draw back ⟨allowing the fly to sink beneath the surface of the water before *retrieving* it —Alexander MacDonald⟩ **c :** to get possession of **:** RESCUE, SALVAGE ⟨Greek sculpture *retrieved* from the ruins of Roman Carthage —A.J. Liebling⟩ ⟨built his shanty from lumber *retrieved* from steamboat disasters —*Amer. Guide Series: Ark.*⟩ **d :** to successfully return (a ball or shuttlecock that is difficult to reach) **5 :** RESTORE, REVIVE ⟨wrote . . . to ~ the heroic past —Van Wyck Brooks⟩ ⟨*retrieved* himself by deciding to become a lawyer —C.R.Williams⟩ **6 :** to remedy the evil consequences of **:** make good **:** REPAIR, CORRECT ⟨third edition . . . ~*s* many of the faults of the second —F.L.Pick & G.N.Knight⟩ ⟨the defeat was *retrieved* —Jacquetta & Christopher Hawkes⟩ ⟨*retrieving* the fundamental error of underestimating the skill of the enemy general —*New Republic*⟩ ⟨~ the situation⟩ ~ *vi* **1 :** to bring in game; *also* **:** to bring back an object thrown by a person ⟨teach a dog to ~⟩ **2** *obs* **:** RECUPERATE **3 :** to reel or draw in a fishing line ⟨allow the lure to sink close to the bottom, then give a sharp jerk and ~ for a few feet —*Fishing Tackle Cat.*⟩ **syn** see RECOVER

**[2]retrieve** \"\ *n* -s **1** *obs* **:** the rediscovery or second flushing of game (as birds once sprung) **2 :** RETRIEVAL ⟨surface . . . baits always float upon the surface of the water and remain there during the ~ —*Fishing Tackle Cat.*⟩ **3 :** the successful return of a ball that is difficult to reach or control (as in tennis or volleyball)

**re·trieve·less** \-vləs\ *adj* **:** IRRETRIEVABLE

**re·trieve·ment** \-vmənt\ *n* -s **:** RETRIEVAL

**re·triev·er** \-və(r)\ *n* -s [ME *retriver*, fr. *retriven* to retrieve + *-er*] **1 :** a dog used or trained primarily for retrieving game; *usu* **:** a dog of any of several strains or breeds of vigorous active medium-sized dogs with heavy water resistant coats developed by crossbreeding and noted for ability to retrieve — see CHESAPEAKE BAY RETRIEVER, CURLY-COATED RETRIEVER, GOLDEN RETRIEVER, LABRADOR RETRIEVER **2 :** one that retrieves ⟨the most dogged ~ tennis has seen —*Time*⟩ ⟨~ of foreign orders and degrees —H.G.Wells⟩ **3 :** TROLLEY RETRIEVER

**retrim** \(ˈ)rē+\ *vt* [*re-* + *trim*] **:** to trim again or anew

**retro-** *prefix* [ME, fr. L, fr. *retro*, adv., backward, back, behind, fr. *re-* back, again + *-tro* (as in *intro* inwardly) — more at RE-, INTRO-] **1 a :** backward **:** back **:** retroverse ⟨*retro*mingent⟩ ⟨*retro*-rocket⟩ ⟨*retro*serrate⟩ **b :** back in time **:** past ⟨*retro*dict⟩ ⟨*retro*cognition⟩ **2 a :** situated behind ⟨*retro*choir⟩ **b :** situated behind a (specified) part ⟨*retro*auricular⟩ ⟨*retro*pubic⟩ **3 :** contrary to the usual or natural course **:** retrograde ⟨*retro*infection⟩

**ret·ro·act** \¦re·trō +, *sometimes* ¦rē·trō+\ *vi* [*retro-* + *act*] **:** REACT

**ret·ro·action** \"+\ *n* [*retroactive* + *-ion*] **1 :** retroactive or retrospective operation (as of a law or tax) **2** [*retro-* + *action*] **:** a reciprocal action **:** REACTION

**ret·ro·active** \"+\ *adj* [F *retroactif*, fr. L *retroactus* (past part. of *retroagere* to turn back, drive back, fr. *retro-* + *agere* to drive, act) + F *-if* -ive — more at AGENT] **:** having relation or reference to or efficacy in a prior time: as **a :** operative, binding, and taking effect prior to enactment, promulgation or imposition ⟨the ~ effect of the Redemption⟩ ⟨~ decree⟩ ⟨~ tax⟩ **b :** consisting of an increase in wages effective as of an earlier date ⟨~ pay⟩ — **ret·ro·actively** \"+\ *adv*

**retroactive inhibition** *n* **:** obliteration of the results of learning by immediately subsequent activity

**retroactive law** *or* **retroactive statute** *n* **:** a law that operates to make criminal or punishable or in any way expressly affects an act done prior to the passing of the law — compare EX POST FACTO LAW

**ret·ro·activity** \"+\ *n* **1 :** the quality or state of being retroactive **2 :** the capacity of a bacterial agent in biological warfare to react upon the user

**ret·ro·bulbar** \"+\ *adj* [ISV *retro-* + *bulbar*] **:** situated behind a bulbar structure; *specif* **:** being behind the eyeball

**ret·ro·caval** \"+\ *adj* [*retro-* + *caval*] **:** situated behind the vena cava

**ret·ro·cecal** *or* **ret·ro·caecal** \"+\ *adj* [*retro-* + *cecal, caecal*] **:** situated behind the cecum ⟨the vermiform appendix is considered ~ when directed upward behind the cecum⟩

**ret·ro·cede** \ˌre·trəˈsēd *sometimes* ˌrē·t-\ *vb* [L *retrocedere*, fr. *retro-* + *cedere* to go — more at CEDE] *vi* **:** to go back **:** RECEDE ~ *vt* [F *rétrocéder*, fr. ML *retrocedere*, fr. L, to go back] **1 :** to cede back (a territory or jurisdiction) ⟨there is hereby *retroceded* to the state of New Mexico the exclusive jurisdiction heretofore acquired from the state of New Mexico by the United States —*U.S.Code*⟩ **2 :** to reassign (all or a part of a risk) to another reinsurer

**ret·ro·ced·ence** \-d³n(t)s\ *n* -s **:** RETROCESSION

**[1]ret·ro·ces·sion** \-ˈseshən\ *n* -s [LL *retrocession-, retrocessio*, fr. L *retrocessus* (past part. of *retrocedere* to go back, go backward) + *-ion-, -io* -ion] **1 :** the act or process of retroceding **:** RETROGRESSION **2 :** an instance of retrocession

**[2]retrocession** \"\ *n* [*retro-* + *cession*] **1 a** *Scots law* **:** the assignment by an assignee of a right to the cedent **b :** the return of a title to property to its former or its true owner **:** the confirmation of the original title in its true owner **2** [F *rétrocession*, fr. ML *retrocession-, retrocessio* retreat, fr. LL, act of going back] **:** the act of ceding back ⟨a ~ of jurisdiction over a territory⟩ **3 a :** a process of reassigning or ceding by a reinsurer to another insurance company all or a part of the risks assumed **b :** the amount reassigned or ceded

**ret·ro·ces·sion·al** \-shən³l\ *n* -s [[1]*retrocession* + *-al*] **:** RECESSIONAL

**ret·ro·ces·sive** \¦==¦sesiv\ *adj* [L *retrocessus* (past part. of *retrocedere* to go backward) + E *-ive*] **:** RETROGRADE

**ret·ro·choir** \ˈre·trō+,-, *sometimes* ˈrē·trō+,-\ *n* [*retro-* + *choir*] **1 :** the space left in a church behind the high altar or choir enclosure sometimes used as a chapel and occas. containing a second choir enclosure **2 :** the space beyond the line of the eastern face of the altar in an apsidal church

**ret·ro·cognition** \¦re·trō+, *sometimes* ¦rē·trō+\ *n* [*retro-* + *cognition*] **:** direct or extrasensory perception of past events

**ret·ro·cognitive** \"+\ *adj* [*retro-* + *cognitive*] **:** of, relating to, or having the characteristics of retrocognition

**ret·ro·dict** \ˌre·trəˈdikt *sometimes* ˌrē·t-\ *vt* -ED/-ING/-S [*retro-* + *-dict* (as in *predict*)] **:** to infer (a past state of affairs) from present observational data ⟨future and past eclipses . . . can be predicted and ~*ed* equally successfully —Maurice Cranston & J.W.N.Watkins⟩ — **ret·ro·dic·tion** \-kshən\ *n* — **ret·ro·dic·tive** \¦==¦diktiv\ *adj*

**ret·ro·displacement** \¦re·trō+, *sometimes* ¦rē·trō+\ *n* [*retro-* + *displacement*] **:** displacement backwards of an organ of the body

**ret·ro·duc·tion** \ˌre·trəˈdəkshən *sometimes* ˌrē·t-\ *n* -s [*retro-* + *-duction* (as in *abduction, induction*)] **:** ABDUCTION 3b

**ret·ro·duc·tive** \¦==¦dəktiv\ *adj* [*retroduction* + *-ive*] **:** of or relating to retroduction

**ret·ro·fec·tion** \ˌ==ˈfekshən\ *n* -s [*retro-* + in*fection*] **:** infection with pinworms in which the eggs hatch on the anal skin and mucosa and the larvae migrate up the bowel to the cecum where they mature

**ret·ro·fit** \ˈre·trō+,-, *sometimes* ˈrē·trō+,-\ *n* [*retro-* + *fit*] **:** a modification of equipment or an airplane to include changes made in later production models

**ret·ro·flex** \ˈre·trə,fleks *sometimes* ˈrē·t-\ *or* **ret·ro·flexed** \-st\ *adj* [*retroflex* ISV, fr. NL *retroflexus* bent backward, fr. *retro-* + L *flexus*, past part. of *flectere* to bend; *retroflexed* fr. NL *retroflexus* bent backward + E *-ed*] **1 :** turned or bent abruptly backward **:** REFLEXED **2 a :** articulated with or involving the participation of the tongue tip curled up and back until its under surface touches the hard palate — used esp. of various consonants in Asiatic-Indian languages **b** *of a vowel* **:** articulated with or involving the participation of the tongue tip raised and retracted toward the hard palate

**ret·ro·flex·ion** *or* **ret·ro·flec·tion** \ˌ==ˈflekshən\ *n* [prob. fr. (assumed) NL *retroflexion-, retroflexio*, fr. NL *retroflexus* bent backward + L *-ion-, -io* -ion] **1 :** the act or process of bending back **2 :** the state of being bent back; *specif* **:** the bending back of the body of the uterus upon the cervix which is little if at all out of its normal axis — compare RETROVERSION **3** [*retroflex* + *-ion*] **:** retroflex articulation

**retrog** *abbr* retrogression; retrogressive

**ret·ro·gra·da·tion** \ˌre·trōgrāˈdāshən *sometimes* ˌrē·t-\ *n* [LL *retrogradation-, retrogradatio*, fr. L *retrogradare* to retrograde (fr. *retrogradus* retrograde) + *-ation-, -atio* -ation] **:** the act or process of retrograding: as **a :** REGRESSION 3 **b :** a step-by-step reexamination of an investigation or argument backward from the conclusion to the first fact or premise **c :** a backward movement **:** RETREAT ⟨the ~ of a coastline⟩ **d :** RETROGRESSION 2 **e :** reversal of a fluid colloidal solution to an insoluble or gelled state on standing or on cooking — used esp. of starch solutions

**ret·ro·gra·da·to·ry** \¦==¦grādə,tōrē\ *adj* [*retrogradation* + *-ory*] **:** causing retrogradation

**[1]ret·ro·grade** \ˈre·trə,grād *sometimes* ˈrē·t-\ *adj* [ME, fr. L *retrogradus*, fr. *retro-* + *gradus* step — more at GRADE] **1 a** *of a celestial body* **:** having a direction contrary to that of the general motion of similar bodies **:** exhibiting regression **b :** moving, directed, or tending in a backward direction **:** contrary to the previous direction **:** RETREATING ⟨fight a ~ action —A.E.Younger⟩ ⟨a ~ step⟩ ⟨~ telescope⟩ **c** (1) **:** contrary to the normal order **:** INVERSE, INVERTED ⟨a ~ order of enumeration⟩; *specif* **:** written from right to left ⟨a ~ alphabet⟩ (2) **:** repeated backward ⟨a ~ melody in a contrapuntal composition⟩ ⟨~ imitation⟩ **2 :** tending towards or resulting in a worse state ⟨a ~ people⟩ ⟨~ ideas⟩ ⟨a ~ measure⟩ **3** *archaic* **:** OPPOSED, CONTRADICTORY ⟨it is most ~ to our desires —Shak.⟩ **4 :** characterized by retrogression **5 :** effective for a period immediately prior to a shock or seizure ⟨~ amnesia⟩

**[2]retrograde** \"\ *n* **1 :** one that degenerates **2 :** RETROGRESSION

**[3]retrograde** \"\ *adv* **:** BACKWARD, REVERSELY

**[4]retrograde** \"\ *vb* [L *retrogradi*, fr. *retro-* + *gradi* to step, go — more at GRADE] *vt*, *archaic* **:** to turn back **:** REVERSE ⟨events . . . which seem to retard or ~ the civility of ages —R.W.Emerson⟩ ~ *vi* **1** *of a celestial body* **:** to move in a direction contrary to the normal: as **a :** to move opposite to the general eastward movement in the solar system **:** move westward on the sky **b :** to move backward in an orbit **:** turn and move actually or apparently for a while in the direction opposite to its own usual direction **2 a :** to recede over the path of a previous advance **:** RETREAT ⟨a glacier ~*s*⟩ ⟨the army ~*s* from the front⟩ **b :** to go back over (as a narrative or argument) **:** RECAPITULATE **3 :** to decline from a better to a worse condition **:** fall back from a higher to a lower state of development ⟨~ in intelligence⟩ ⟨manufacturing *retrograding* to a cottage industry⟩ **syn** see RECEDE

**ret·ro·grade·ly** *adv* **:** in a retrograde manner

**retrograde pyelogram** *n* **:** a roentgenogram of the kidney made after injection of opaque material through the ureter — compare PYELOGRAPHY

**[1]ret·ro·gress** \ˈre·trə,gres *sometimes* ˈrē·t-\ *n* -ES [LL *retrogressus*, fr. L, past part. of *retrogradi* to retrogress] **:** retrogression

**[2]retrogress** \¦==¦=\ *vb* -ED/-ING/-ES [L *retrogressus*, past part. of *retrogradi* to retrogress] *vi* **:** to move backward **:** revert to an earlier state or condition ~ *vt* **:** REGRESS

**ret·ro·gres·sion** \ˌ==ˈgreshən\ *n* -s [L *retrogressus* (past part.) + E *-ion*] **1 :** REGRESSION 3 **2 :** a reversal in development or condition: as **a :** a passing from a higher to a lower or from a more to a less specialized state or type of organization or structure in the course of the development of an organism **b :** subsidence or decline of symptoms or manifestations of a disease **c :** retrograde imitation in contrapuntal music

**ret·ro·gres·sive** \¦==¦gresiv, -sēv *also* -səv\ *adj* [L *retrogressus* (past part.) + E *-ive*] **:** characterized by or tending to retrogression **:** RETROGRADE: as **a :** going or directed backwards ⟨the senses represent to us the course of the planets as now progressive, now retrogressive —L.W.Beck⟩ **b :** declining from a better to a worse state **c :** passing from a higher to a lower organization ⟨~ metamorphosis⟩ — **ret·ro·gres·sive·ly** \-səvlē, -li\ *adv*

**ret·ro·hypophyseal** \¦re·trō+, *sometimes* ¦rē·trō+\ *adj* [*retro-* + *hypophyseal*] **:** POSTPITUITARY

**ret·ro·infection** \"+\ *n* [*retro-* + *infection*] **:** infection contrary to the usual course; *specif* **:** infection communicated to a mother by her fetus

**ret·ro·ject** \ˈre·trə,jekt *sometimes* ˈrē·t-\ *vt* -ED/-ING/-S [*retro-* + *-ject* (as in *project*)] **:** to project into the past ⟨~ an hallucination into one's childhood⟩ — **ret·ro·jec·tion** \ˌ==ˈjekshən\ *n* -s

**ret·ro·len·tal** \¦==¦lent³l\ *adj* [*retro-* + NL *lent-, lens* lens + E *-al* — more at LENS] **1 :** situated or occurring behind a lens **2 :** of or involving the parts of the eye behind the lens

**retrolental fibroplasia** *n* **:** a disease of the retina in premature infants of low birth weight characterized by the presence of an opaque fibrous membrane behind the lens of the eye

**ret·ro·lenticular** \ˌre·trō+, *sometimes* ¦rē·trō+\ *adj* [*retro-* + *lenticular*] **:** situated behind the lens of the eye

**ret·ro·lingual** \"+\ *adj* [*retro-* + *lingual*] **:** situated behind or near the base of the tongue ⟨~ salivary glands⟩

**¹ret·ro·min·gent** \ˌre·trə'minjənt *sometimes* ˌrē·t-\ *n* -s [*retro-* + L *mingent-, mingens,* pres. part. of *mingere* to urinate — more at MIXEN] **:** an animal that urinates backward

**²ret·ro·min·gent** \ˌ⁼⁼'⁼⁼\ *adj* **:** urinating backward ⟨the male cat is a ~ animal⟩ — **ret·ro·min·gent·ly** *adv*

**ret·ro·molar** \ˌre·trō+, *sometimes* ¦rē·trō+\ *adj* [*retro-* + *molar*] **:** distal to the last molar

**ret·ro·ne·cine** \ˌre·trō'nēˌsēn, -sən *sometimes* ˌrē·t-\ *n* -s [*retrorsine* + *senecionine*] **:** a crystalline amino dihydroxy bicyclic alcohol $C_8H_{13}NO_2$ derived from pyrrole and formed by hydrolysis of various alkaloids (as senecionine or monocrotaline)

**ret·ro–ocular** \ˌre·trō+, *sometimes* ¦rē·trō+\ *adj* **:** situated behind the eye **:** RETROBULBAR

**retro–operative** \"+\ *adj* **:** RETROACTIVE

**ret·ro·peritoneal** \"+\ *adj* [*retro-* + *peritoneal*] **:** situated behind the peritoneum — **ret·ro·per·i·to·ne·al·ly** *adv*

**ret·ro·pubic** \"+\ *adj* [*retro-* + *pubic*] **1 :** situated behind the pubis **2 :** constituting a pad of fat behind the pubic symphysis

**ret·ro·pul·sion** \ˌre·trə'pəlshən *sometimes* ˌrē·t-\ *n* [ISV *retro-* + *pulsion*] **:** a disorder of locomotion attending paralysis agitans that is marked by a tendency to walk backwards

**ret·ro·reflective** \ˌre·trō+, *sometimes* ¦rē·trō+\ *adj* [*retro-* + *reflective*] **:** REFLECTIVE

**ret·ro–rocket** \"+\ *n* **:** an auxiliary rocket or jet engine on a rocket or artificial satellite that thrusts in a direction opposite to or at an oblique angle to the motion of the vehicle in order to decelerate it for a landing upon a celestial body

**re·trorse** \rə̇'trȯ(ə)rs\ *adj* [L *retrorsus,* contr. of *retroversus* retroverse — more at RETROVERSION] **:** bent backward or downward — compare ANTRORSE, EXTRORSE, INTRORSE — **re·trorse·ly** *adv*

**re·tror·sine** \rə̇'trȯrˌsēn, -sə̇n\ *n* -s [NL *retrorsus* (specific epithet of *Senecio retrorsus*) (fr. L, bent backwards) + E *-ine*] **:** a poisonous crystalline alkaloid $C_{18}H_{25}NO_6$ found in various plants of the genus *Senecio* (as *S. retrorsus*)

**ret·ro·serrate** \¦re·trō+, *sometimes* ¦rē·trō+\ *adj* [*retro-* + *serrate*] **:** having retrorse teeth or barbs ⟨a ~ leaf⟩

**ret·ro·serrulate** \"+\ *adj* [*retro-* + *serrulate*] **:** having minute retrorse teeth or barbs ⟨~ spicules⟩

**¹ret·ro·spect** \'re·trəˌspekt *sometimes* 'rē·t-\ *n* -s [L *retrospectus,* past part. of *retrospicere* to look back at, fr. *retro-* + *specere* to look at, see — more at SPY] **1** *archaic* **:** reference to or regard of a precedent or authority ⟨we may introduce a song without ~ to the old comedy —W.S.Landor⟩ **2 :** a review of or meditation upon past events ⟨the essence of memory, the vital, tangible ~ —William Beebe⟩ ⟨feel that wise historical ~ as well as the decent opinion of mankind will confirm it —S.F.Bemis⟩ ⟨the new chapter starts with a ~⟩ ⟨accomplished results that in ~ pleased him —W.C.Ford⟩ ⟨shivered in ~ when I thought of that afternoon meeting in that freezing hall —Anna L. Strong⟩

**²retrospect** \"\ *adj* **:** retrospective

**³retrospect** \"\ *vb* -ED/-ING/-S [L *retrospectus,* past part. of *retrospicere* to look back at] *vi* **1 :** to practice retrospection ⟨able to ~ at fairly long distances backward —*Vancouver (Canada) Morning Star*⟩ **2 :** to refer back **:** REFLECT ⟨it may be useful to ~ to an early period —Alexander Hamilton⟩ ~ *vt* **:** to go back over in thought **:** consider or think of with reference to the past ⟨~*ed* the faces and minds of grown people —Samuel Richardson⟩

**ret·ro·spec·tion** \ˌ⁼⁼'spekshən\ *n* -s [L *retrospectus* (past part. of *retrospicere*) + E *-ion*] **1** *archaic* **:** reference or allusion to a past event **2 a :** the act or process of surveying the past ⟨he lives in anticipation, not in ~⟩ **b :** an instance of retrospection **3 :** observation of mental processes through primal memory immediately after their occurrence

**¹ret·ro·spec·tive** \ˌ⁼⁼'spektiv, -tēv *also* -təv\ *adj* [L *retrospectus* (past part. of *retrospicere*) + E *-ive*] **1 :** contemplative of or relative to past events **:** characterized by, given to, or indulging in retrospection ⟨a ~ exhibit of an artist's work⟩ ⟨after the decline of interest in nature ancient culture became introspective and ~ —John Dewey⟩ ⟨~ self-justification⟩ ⟨~ octogenarian⟩ **2 :** affecting things past **:** RETROACTIVE — compare EX POST FACTO **3** *of a view* **:** that is in the direction of the rear (as of a house) — **ret·ro·spec·tive·ly** \-tə̇vlē, -li\ *adv*

**²retrospective** \"\ *n* -s **:** a generally comprehensive exhibition showing the work of an artist over a span of years ⟨the big ~ of his works at the Museum of Modern Art —R.M.Coates⟩

**retrospective rate** *n* **:** an insurance premium rate computed for a particular risk at the close of the period of coverage by adding the expense constant and the actual losses incurred with the final rate being subject to an agreed maximum

**ret·ro·stal·sis** \ˌre·trə'stȯlsə̇s, -stal- *sometimes* ˌrē·t-\ *n, pl* **retrostal·ses** \-ˌsēz\ [NL, fr. *retro-* + *peristalsis*] **:** backward motion of the intestines **:** reversed peristalsis

**ret·ro·stal·tic** \¦⁼⁼'stȯltik, -stal-\ *adj* [*retro-* + *-staltic* (as in *peristaltic*)] **:** of or relating to retrostalsis

**¹ret·rous·sage** \ˌre·trə'säzh\ *n* -s [F, act of tucking up, turning up, fr. *retrousser* to tuck up, turn up + *-age*] **:** the wiping of an inked engraved plate with a cloth so as to draw up a slight amount of ink to the edges of the filled lines and soften the definition of the lines when printed

**²retroussage** \"\ *vt* -ED/-ING/-S **:** to treat (an engraved plate) by retroussage

**ret·rous·sé** *also* **ret·rous·sée** \ˌre·trə'sā\ *adj* [retroussé fr. F, fr. past part. of *retrousser* to turn up, tuck up, fr. MF, fr. *re-* + *trousser* to tuck up, truss up; *retroussée* fr. F, fem. of *retroussé* — more at TRUSS] **:** turned up ⟨a ~ nose⟩

**ret·ro·vaccination** \ˌre·trō+, *sometimes* ¦rē·trō+\ *n* [*retro-* + *vaccination*] **:** vaccination in which smallpox virus from human vesicles is used as seed virus in producing smallpox vaccine in cattle

**ret·ro·verse** \ˌre·trə¦vərs *sometimes* ¦rē·t-\ *adj* [L *retroversus*] **:** turned backward **:** REVERSED

**ret·ro·ver·sion** \ˌ⁼⁼'vərzhən, -vȯzh-, -vəizh-\ *n* [L *retroversus* turned backward (fr. *retro-* + *versus* toward, in the direction of — fr. *versus,* past part. of *vertere* to turn) + E *-ion* — more at WORTH] **1 a :** the act or process of turning back **b :** regression to a lower stage of development ⟨these political and moral ~*s,* the totalitarian states —Max Eastman⟩ **c :** translation into the original language **2 :** the bending backward of the uterus and cervix out of the normal axis so that the fundus points toward the sacrum and the cervix toward the pubic symphysis — compare RETROFLEXION

**ret·ro·vert·ed** \¦⁼⁼¦vərd·əd\ *adj* [fr. past part. of obs. E *retrovert* to turn back, fr. E *retro-* + L *vertere* to turn] **:** turned back **:** REVERTED ⟨~ uterus⟩

**re·trude** \rə̇'trüd\ *vt* -ED/-ING/-S [L *retrudere* to thrust backward] **:** to produce retrusion of

**re·tru·sion** \-üzhən\ *n* -s [L *retrusus* (past part. of *retrudere* to thrust backward, fr. *re-* + *trudere* to thrust) + E *-ion* — more at THREAT] **1 :** a condition in which a tooth or the jaw is posterior to its proper occlusal position **2 :** the act of moving a tooth posteriorly

**re·tru·sive** \-üsiv\ *adj* [*retrusion* + *-ive*] **:** marked by retrusion

**re·try** \(ˈ)rē+\ *vt* **:** to try again ⟨*re-try* on the same charges persons who had already faced trial —Tom Fitzsimmons⟩

**rets** *pres 3d sing of* RET

**ret·si·na** *also* **ret·zi·na** \'retsənə\ *n* -s [NGk *retsina,* perh. fr. It *resina* resin, fr. L] **:** resin-flavored wine of Greek origin

**retted** *past of* RET

**ret·ter** \'red·ə(r)\ *n* -s [¹*ret* + *-er*] **:** one that rets

**ret·tery** *also* **ret·tory** \-ərē\ *n* -ES [¹*ret* + *-ery* or *-ory*] **:** a place or establishment where flax is retted

**retting** *pres part of* RET

**re·tube** \(ˈ)rē+\ *vt* [*re-* + *tube*] **:** to equip (as a gun or a boiler) with a new tube ⟨~ a larger gun to 4.7 in. caliber —*Mech. Engineering*⟩

**re·tund** \rə̇'tənd\ *vt* -ED/-ING/-S [L *retundere,* fr. *re-* + *tundere* to beat — more at STUTTER] *archaic* **:** to beat or drive back **:** make impotent or ineffective **:** BLUNT, REFUTE ⟨~ the edge of a sword⟩

**¹re·turn** \rə̇'tərn, rē'-, -tə̄n, -təin\ *vb* -ED/-ING/-S [ME *retournen, retornen,* fr. MF *retourner, retorner,* fr. *re-* + *torner* to turn — more at TURN] *vi* **1 a :** to go back or come back again (as to a place, person, or condition) ⟨~*s* to his home⟩ ⟨to the mainland —R.W.Hatch⟩ ⟨~*ing* to his former associates⟩ ⟨consciousness ~*s* quickly —H.G.Armstrong⟩ ⟨the same themes ~*ing* later in the movement⟩ **b :** to go back in thought or practice **:** REVERT 1 ⟨now, to ~ to my story⟩ ⟨her mind ~*ed* to her early youth —Ellen Glasgow⟩ ⟨~*s* to a . . . representational mode of painting —Herbert Read⟩ **2 :** to pass back to an earlier possessor **:** REVERT 2 ⟨now shall the kingdom ~ to the house of David —1 Kings 12:26 (AV)⟩ **3 :** to speak or write in answer **:** REPLY, RETORT ⟨"very well," ~*ed* the reviewer . . . "that's the way I see the book" —Edward Bok⟩ ~ *vt* **1 a :** to give (an official account or report) to a superior (as by a list or statement) ⟨~ the names of all residents of the ward⟩ ⟨~ a list of jurors⟩ **b :** to elect (a candidate) as attested by official report or returns ⟨~*ing* a Labor candidate, the first ever elected in that constituency⟩ **c :** to bring back (as a writ or verdict) to an office or tribunal ⟨~ a verdict of not guilty⟩ ⟨grand jury ~*ed* 214 indictments —P.M.Angle⟩ **2 a :** to bring, send, or put (a person or thing) back to or in a former position ⟨~ the lever to the first position⟩ ⟨~*ed* his handkerchief to his pocket⟩ ⟨~ your swords to their scabbards⟩ ⟨the pilot ~*ed* his attention to the controls —Joseph Wechsberg⟩ **b :** to restore to a former or to a normal state ⟨~*ing* the mansion to the way it looked when erected —Betty Pepis⟩ ⟨these lands will be ~*ed* to forest —*Amer. Guide Series: Conn.*⟩ **3 a :** to send back upon **:** VISIT — usu. used with *on* or *upon* ⟨the Lord shall ~ thy wickedness upon thine own head —1 Kings 2:44 (AV)⟩ **b** *obs* **:** to retort (as an accusation) upon ⟨recollecting what he had said . . . I ~*ed* it back upon him —Daniel Defoe⟩ **4 :** to bring in or produce (as earnings or profit) **:** YIELD ⟨subscription concerts barely ~*ed* the musicians a living wage —*Amer. Guide Series: Mich.*⟩ **5 a :** to give or perform (something) in return **:** REPAY ⟨~ good for evil⟩ ⟨~ a courtesy call⟩ ⟨the devotion it was not in her nature to ~ —Naomi Lewis⟩ ⟨~ thanks for the repast —T.B.Macaulay⟩ **b :** to give back (as a greeting) ⟨~ an answer⟩ ⟨~*ed* his greeting with a friendly smile⟩ **c :** to give (something) back to the owner ⟨a man who would even ~ a borrowed umbrella —R.W.Emerson⟩ **d :** REFLECT ⟨~ an echo⟩ **6 :** to cause (as a wall or molding) to continue in a different direction esp. at a right angle **7 :** to lead (a specified suit or specified card of a suit) in response to one's partner's earlier lead ⟨~*ing* a seven of spades to partner's spade lead⟩ **8 a :** to play back (as a ball) to an opponent (as in tennis) ⟨found his service difficult to ~⟩ **b :** to throw back (as a fielded ball in baseball or cricket) ⟨~*ed* the ball from deep centerfield to the first baseman⟩ **c :** to hit (a bowled ball in cricket) back to the bowler **syn** see RECIPROCATE

**²return** \"\ *n* -s [ME *retourn, retorn,* fr. *retournen, retornen* to return] **1 a :** the act of coming back to or from a place or condition ⟨his ~ to civilian life⟩ ⟨on their ~ from a long trip⟩ ⟨the ~ of health⟩ ⟨a ~ to nationalism⟩ ⟨the ~ of the blood pressure to normal —H.G.Armstrong⟩ **b :** a regular or frequent returning to the same place or condition **:** RECURRENCE ⟨the ~ of the seasons⟩ ⟨the ~ of the tide⟩ ⟨wished him on his birthday many happy ~*s* of the day⟩ ⟨sorry to hear you had a ~ of your rheumatism —Walt Whitman⟩ **c :** REVERSION ⟨~*s* to a childhood form of functioning —H.A.Overstreet⟩ **d :** RESTORATION ⟨the ~ of the monarchy after a generation⟩ **2 a** (1) **:** the delivery of a legal order (as a writ, precept, or execution) to the proper officer or court (2) **:** the endorsed certificate of an official stating what he has done in or about the execution of such a legal order ⟨required to make a ~ of his proceedings in the matter⟩ (3) **:** the sending back of a commission with the certificate of the commissioners (4) **:** RETURN DAY **b :** an account or formal report (as of an action performed or a duty discharged or of facts or statistics) ⟨a ~ of government revenue and expenditure⟩ ⟨census ~*s*⟩; *esp* **:** a set of tabulated statistics prepared for general information — usu. used in pl. **c** (1) **:** a report of the results of balloting — usu. used in pl. ⟨election ~*s*⟩ (2) **:** an official declaration of the election of a candidate ⟨each house shall be the judge of the elections, ~*s,* and qualifications of its own members —*U.S. Constitution*⟩ (3) *chiefly Brit* **:** ELECTION ⟨his ~ to parliament on his first try for public office⟩ **d :** an official report or statement submitted by a military officer to his superior; *esp* **:** one accounting for personnel, property, or supplies **e** (1) **:** a formal document executed in accordance with law on a required form showing taxable income, allowable deductions and exemptions, and the computation of the tax due ⟨income tax ~*s*⟩ — called also *tax return* (2) **:** a list of taxable property **3 a :** the continuation in a different direction and usu. at a right angle of the face or of any member of a building (as a colonnade or molding) or of a molding or group of moldings (as in the mitering of a picture frame at the corners) **:** the short wall at an angle to a longer wall ⟨a facade of 60 feet east has a ~ of 20 feet north⟩ **b :** one of the two flats on the sides of a stage that are fastened at right angles to the downstage ends of the set and run parallel to the footlights and that both mask the backstage and complete the set **c :** a turn, bend, or winding (as in a line, rod, stream, mining gallery, or military trench) back to or toward itself **d :** a short branch track (as in a mining gallery) to hold returning trucks as others pass on the main track **e :** a means (as a channel, pipe, or duct) for conveying something (as steam, water, or gas) back to its source or starting point; *specif* **:** the conductor that conveys an electric current to the source after its energy is utilized **f :** AIRWAY 1 **g :** the track on which a bowling ball is returned from the pit to the bowler **4 a :** a quantity of goods, consignment, or cargo coming back in exchange for goods sent out as a mercantile venture **b :** the value of or profit from such venture ⟨enterprises which . . . yield their promoters a handsome ~ —R.E.Cameron⟩ **c** (1) **:** the profit from labor, investment, or business **:** income or profit in relation to its source **:** YIELD ⟨had a good cash ~ from his writings⟩ — often used in pl. ⟨box-office ~*s*⟩ (2) **returns** *pl* **:** RESULTS ⟨showing ~*s* from his long hours of study⟩ **d :** the rate of profit in a process of production per unit of cost — compare LAW OF CONSTANT RETURN, LAW OF DIMINISHING RETURNS **5 a :** the act of returning something to a former place, condition, or ownership **:** RESTITUTION ⟨arranged for the ~ of the toppled statue to its pedestal⟩ ⟨demands the ~ of the property to its rightful owner⟩ **b :** something returned: as (1) **:** a paper calling for payment (as a check or draft) returned by a bank to the clearinghouse (as the London Bankers' Clearing House) because of lack of funds, insufficient endorsement or other defect (2) **returns** *pl* **:** unsold books, periodicals, or newspapers returned to publishers for cash or credit (3) **returns** *pl* **:** mail received as the result of an advertising appeal (as by mail, radio, or television) ⟨the ~*s* on the mailing were running about 3%⟩ **c returns** *pl* (1) **:** refuse tobacco made up of fragments and siftings (2) **:** tobacco prepared by returning shag for recutting **6 a :** something given to repay or reciprocate **:** REQUITAL ⟨gives all and expects no ~ —Eden Phillpotts⟩ ⟨making some ~ to society for the educational opportunities one has enjoyed —*Bull. of Bates Coll.*⟩ **b :** ANSWER, RETORT ⟨when he criticizes, can . . . be sure of a responsive ~ —Fred Rodell⟩ **c :** a lead in a suit previously led by one's partner (as in bridge) **d :** an answering or retaliatory play: as (1) **:** the act of returning a ball to an opponent (as in tennis, badminton, handball, or cricket) ⟨his ~ of service was a strong backhand drive⟩ (2) **:** a counterthrust in fencing **:** RIPOSTE (3) **:** the runback of the ball after a kick by the other team in football **7** *chiefly Brit* **:** a round-trip ticket

**³return** \"\ *adj* **1 a :** having or formed by a return or change of direction ⟨a ~ facade⟩ **b :** turned back **:** doubled upon itself ⟨a ~ flue⟩ **2 :** played, delivered, or given in return ⟨a ~ game⟩ ⟨a ~ blow⟩ ⟨a ~ courtesy⟩ **3 :** used or taken on returning or on a trip back ⟨a ~ cargo⟩ ⟨the ~ road has been blocked —Gail Kennedy⟩ **4 :** returning or permitting return ⟨a ~ current⟩ ⟨a ~ valve⟩ **5 :** of, relating to, causing, or permitting a return to a place or condition **:** RECURRING ⟨~ orders⟩ ⟨a ~ bout with tuberculosis —E.P.Snow⟩

**re·turn·abil·i·ty** \rə̇ˌtərnə'biləd·ē\ *n* [*returnable* + *-ity*] **:** the quality or state of being returnable

**re·turn·able** \rə̇'tərnəbəl, -tə̄n-, -təin-\ *adj* [ME *retournable, retornable,* fr. *retournen, retornen* to return + *-able* — more at RETURN] **1 :** legally required to be returned, delivered, or argued at a specified time or place ⟨a writ ~ at the next court session⟩ ⟨a verdict ~ to the court⟩ ⟨an interlocutory matter ~ on the date indicated⟩ **2 a :** capable of being returned (as for reuse) ⟨~ bottles⟩ **b :** permitted to be returned ⟨~ fees⟩ ⟨a ~ deposit⟩ ⟨the merchandise is not ~⟩ **3 :** able to return ⟨a source of . . . short-term power could make the military glider a ~ weapon —G.E.Pendray⟩

**returnable container** *n* **:** a heavy-duty drum or shipping case or box that can be used for several trips **:** a glass container (as a milk bottle) that can be returned for cleaning and refilling

**return address** *n* **:** an address at which shipped or mailed articles may be returned to the sender

**return ball** *n* **:** a child's ball held by an elastic string so that it returns to the hand or cup from which it is thrown

**return bead** *n* **:** a bead molding that is nearly a complete circle in section

**return bend** *n* **:** a bend (as in a pipe fitting) that alters the direction of its center line 180 degrees

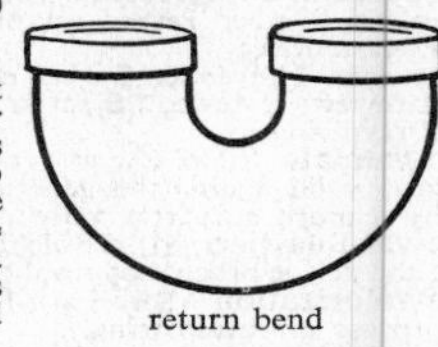
return bend

**return block** *n* **:** SNATCH BLOCK

**return card** *n* **1 :** a card sent out by an advertiser with other printed matter to be filled in (as with an order) and returned to the sender **2 :** sender's name and address in the upper left-hand corner of the face of a piece of mail for assuring its return if undeliverable — called also *corner card*

**return–cocked bead** \⁼'⁼,⁼-\ *n* **:** a bead that projects from an angle and is not flanked by quirks — compare COCK BEAD, QUIRK BEAD

**return connecting rod** *n* **:** a connecting rod having its crankpin end on the same side of the crosshead as the engine cylinder

**return crease** *n* **:** a line at each end of and at right angles to the bowling crease in cricket

**return day** *n* **:** a day when a return is to be made: as **a :** a day on which the defendant in an action or proceeding is to appear in court and answer the writ or other mandate which is to be then returned **b :** a day fixed for the return of all writs issued subsequent to the next prior return day **c :** a day fixed by law for canvassing election returns

**returned** *past of* RETURN

**returned shipment rate** *n* **:** a reduced railroad rate on containers returned empty

**re·turn·ee** \rə̇ˌtər¦nē\ *n* -s [¹*return* + *-ee*] **:** one that has returned (as from a sojourn abroad or from exile or imprisonment); *esp* **:** a person who has served overseas and been returned (as for leave, reassignment, or discharge) to the continental U.S.

**return envelope** *n* **:** a usu. stamped and self-addressed envelope enclosed with a mailed communication for the requested reply

**re·turner** \(ˈ)rē+\ *n* [*re-* + *turner*] **:** one that helps fasten metal bands around bales of cotton by turning ends of bands under the bales as they come through the press

**return game** *or* **return match** *n* **1 :** a second game or match (as of tennis or bridge) played by the same contestants to give the loser of the first a chance to recoup the loss **2 :** the second of a pair of games (as of basketball) scheduled between two teams for the same season often in a home-and-home series

**returning** *pres part of* RETURN

**returning board** *n* **:** an official body (as a state commission or a court) designated by law to canvass election returns

**returning officer** *n* **:** an English government official (as a mayor or sheriff) designated to receive nominations and to conduct and report on elections

**re·turn·less** \rə̇'tərnlə̇s\ *adj* **:** allowing no return from or way out of **:** INESCAPABLE ⟨an almost ~ depth of misery and crime —*Blackwood's*⟩

**return piece** *n* **:** one of the two wings connected to an interior setting that turn off the stage back of each side of the proscenium opening

**return postage** *n* **:** postage enclosed in a letter for the expected reply

**return receipt** *n* **:** a postal receipt sent back to the sender of a piece of insured or registered mail on payment of a special fee that shows to whom and at what time the mail was delivered

**returns** *pres 3d sing of* RETURN, *pl of* RETURN

**return shock** *n* **:** an electric shock that follows electric discharge from a cloud and is due to the sudden release of electricity induced on bodies on the earth by the charge of the cloud

**return ticket** *n, chiefly Brit* **:** a round-trip ticket

**return trace** *n* **:** RETRACE

**return trap** *n* **:** a trap in a return pipe

**return trip** *n, chiefly Brit* **:** ROUND TRIP

**return wall** *n* **:** a wall that makes a decided angle with and is approximately the same height as an outer wall of a building and that is distinguished from a partition or a low wall carrying a partition

**re·tuse** \rə̇'tüs, rə̇t'yüs\ *adj* [L *retusus,* past part. of *retundere* to beat back, to dull — more at RETUND] **:** having the apex rounded or obtuse with a slight notch ⟨a ~ leaf⟩ — compare EMARGINATE, OBCORDATE

**ret·zian** \'retsēən\ *n* -s [Sw, fr. Anders Jahan *Retzius* †1821 Swed. botanist] **:** a mineral consisting of a basic arsenate of manganese, calcium, and the yttrium earths occurring in brown orthorhombic crystals

**retzina** *var of* RETSINA

**ret·zi·us's vein** \'retsēəs(əz)-\ *n, usu cap R* [after Anders Adolf *Retzius* †1860 Swed. anatomist and anthropologist] **:** any of various veins in the dorsal part of the abdomen forming anastomoses between the inferior vena cava and the superior and inferior mesenteric veins

**reu·ben·ite** \'rübəˌnīt\ *n* -s *usu cap* [*Reuben,* oldest son of Jacob and ancestor of the tribe (fr. LL *Ruben,* fr. Heb *R'ūbhēn*) + E *-ite*] **:** a member of the Hebrew tribe of Reuben

**re·une** \rē'yün\ *vi* -ED/-ING/-S [back-formation fr. *reunion*] **:** to hold a reunion (as of college alumni) ⟨two dinners will be held for each class . . . *reuning* this summer —*Dartmouth Alumni Mag.*⟩

**re·unification** \(¦)rē+\ *n* [*re-* + *unification*] **:** the act or process of reunifying ⟨advocating ~ of the divided country⟩

**re·unify** \(ˈ)rē+\ *vt* [*re-* + *unify*] **:** to restore the unity or integrity of (as a divided country)

**re·union** \(ˈ)rē¦yünyən\ *n* [*re-* + *union*] **1 :** a union formed again after separation or discord ⟨a ~ of the dissident sect with its parent body⟩ **2 a :** a meeting of persons long separated ⟨the lovers' ~ after the war⟩ ⟨a family ~⟩ **b :** an assembly of persons associated by former membership in a group (as a college class) ⟨alumni ~*s* on the campus during commencement week⟩ ⟨a regimental ~⟩ **c :** a social gathering held at a more or less customary time and place **:** GET-TOGETHER ⟨the moments of their weekly ~ —Joseph Conrad⟩

**re·un·ion·ist** \-ənə̇st\ *n* **:** an advocate of reunion (as of sects or parties) — **re·un·ion·is·tic** \(¦)rē¦yünyə¦nistik\ *adj*

**re·u·nit·able** \¦rēyü¦nīd·əbəl\ *adj* [*reunite* + *-able*] **:** capable of being reunited ⟨separated but ~ forces⟩

**re·unite** \¦rē+\ *vb* [ML *reunitus,* past part. of *reunire* to reunite, fr. L *re-* + LL *unire* to unite — more at UNITE] *vt* **:** to bring together again or unite (persons or things) after a separation ⟨the beach patrols *reunited* parents and their lost children⟩ ⟨both *reunited* in the splendid tomb —Henry Riddell⟩ ~ *vi* **:** to come together or unite again **:** REJOIN ⟨will manage . . . sooner or later to ~ under one color —A.J. Toynbee⟩

**re·u·ni·tion** \ˌrēyü'nishən\ *n* [ML *reunitus* (past part.) + E *-ion*] **:** the act or process of reuniting; *esp* **:** the reassembling of an organism from its separated constituent parts or cells ⟨~ may be observed to occur experimentally with various sponges⟩

**re–up** \(ˈ)rē+\ *vi, slang* **:** REENLIST ⟨refusing in droves to *re-up* —*Time*⟩

**re·us** \'rēəs\ *also* **rea** \-ēə\ *n, pl* **rei** \-ēˌī\ *also* **re·ae** \-ēˌē\ [*reus* fr. L; *rea* fr. L, fem. of *reus;* perh. akin to L *res* thing, fact — more at REAL] *Roman, civil, & canon law* **:** DEFENDANT 2 — opposed to *actor*

**re·us·able** \(ˈ)rē¦yüzəbəl\ *adj* [[1]*reuse* + *-able*] : capable of being used again or repeatedly ⟨a new 55-gallon ~ drum . . . suitable for shipping oils —*Scientific Monthly*⟩

**[1]re·use** \(ˈ)rē+\ *vt* [*re-* + *use* (v.)] : to use again : to use (as a container) again or repeatedly ⟨the oil-saturated water is *reused* —R.N.Shreve⟩

**[2]re·use** \"+\ *n* [*re-* + *use* (n.)] : repeated use ⟨waste paper is pulped for ~ —*Chem. Abstracts*⟩

**reused** *adj, of wool fibers* : obtained from finished wool products used by the ultimate consumer, sanitized, and remade into merchandise — compare REPROCESSED

**[1]rev** \ˈrev\ *n* -s [short for *revolution*] : a revolution of a motor ⟨300 ~*s* per minute⟩

**[2]rev** \"\ *vb* **revved**; **revved**; **revving**; **revs** *or* **revvs** *vt* : to step up the number of revolutions per minute of (a motor) ⟨*revving* the engine and slamming the clutch in —Richard McCloskey⟩ — often used with *up* ⟨three people *revving* up motor-bikes —*London Calling*⟩ ~ *vi, of a motor* : to operate at an increased speed of revolution — usu. used with *up* ⟨a bomber *revved* up on the hangar apron —*General Electric Rev.*⟩

**rev** *abbr* **1** revenue **2** *often cap* reverend **3** reverse; reversed **4** review; reviewed **5** revise; revised; revision **6** revolution **7** revolving

**re·validate** \(ˈ)rē+\ *vt* [*re-* + *validate*] : to make (as a law) valid again ⟨the general assembly . . . may ~ the law by a mere majority vote —*Amer. Guide Series: Conn.*⟩

**re·val·i·da·tion** \(ˌ)rē͵valə¦dāshən\ *n* [*revalidate* + *-ion*] : the act or process of revalidating

**re·valorization** \(ˌ)rē+\ *n* [*re-* + *valorization*] : the act or process of revalorizing

**re·valorize** \(ˈ)rē¦valə͵rīz\ *vt* [back-formation fr. *revalorization*] : to change the valuation of (as assets or currency) following an inflation ⟨~ assets on a balance sheet⟩ ⟨~ the treasury's gold stock⟩

**re·val·u·ate** \(ˈ)rē¦valyə͵wāt, *usu* -ād·+V\ *vt* [back-formation fr. *revaluation*] : to valuate (as currency) again : make a new or different evaluation of ⟨*revaluated* on a par with the U.S. dollar⟩ ⟨*revaluating* great . . . works of fiction —J.T.Farrell⟩

**re·valuation** \(ˌ)rē+\ *n* [*re-* + *valuation*] **1** : a revised or new valuation or estimate : REAPPRAISAL ⟨this ~ of primitive art —Herbert Read⟩ **2** : the act or process of revaluating ⟨the ~ of property⟩

**re·value** \(ˈ)rē+\ *vt* [*re-* + *value*] : to value (as currency) again or afresh : make a second or new valuation or appraisal of : REAPPRAISE ⟨prepared, if necessary, to ~ the dollar —Leon Halden⟩ ⟨*revalued* everything in his house according to the measure of response it drew from her —Scott Fitzgerald⟩

**re·vamp** \"+\ *vt* [*re-* + *vamp*] : to vamp again or anew: as **a** : to put in repair (as an old house) : RENOVATE, RECONSTRUCT ⟨~*ed* cherry wood showcases —*Jewelers' Circular-Keystone*⟩ ⟨~*ing* old cars⟩ **b** : to revise (as a play) by bringing up to date or by fitting to a new need ⟨a story a hundred years old, ~*ed* every few years —Edward Bok⟩ ⟨~ much of what was heretofore believed true —*Science News Letter*⟩

**re·vanche** \rəˈvänch\ *n* -s [F, fr. MF, alter. of *revenche*, *revenge* revenge — more at REVENGE] : REVENGE; *esp* : the policy of a government intent on the recovery of lost territory

**[1]re·vanch·ist** \-chəst\ *adj* : of, relating to, or marked by a policy of revanche

**[2]revanchist** \"\ *n* -s : one who advocates a policy of revanche

**revd** *abbr, often cap* reverend

**[1]re·veal** \rəˈvēl, rēˈ-\ *vt* -ED/-ING/-S [ME *revelen*, fr. MF *reveler*, fr. L *revelare* to reveal, unveil, fr. *re-* + *velare* to veil, fr. *velum* veil] **1** : to communicate or make known by superhuman means or agency : disclose or make manifest through divine inspiration (as in a vision) **2** : to make (something secret or hidden) publicly known : DIVULGE ⟨~ a confidence⟩ ⟨~*ed* his plans for the nation⟩ **3** : to open up to view : show plainly or clearly : DISPLAY ⟨the rising curtain ~*ed* a street scene⟩ ⟨the painting ~*s* the painter⟩ ⟨the dress ~*ed* nearly everything⟩

**syn** DISCOVER, DISCLOSE, DIVULGE, TELL, BETRAY, BEWRAY: REVEAL indicates a making known or setting forth sometimes comparable to unveiling; it may apply to supernatural or inspired revelation, to simple disclosure, or to indication by signs, symptoms, or similar evidence ⟨laws divine deduced by reason or to faith *revealed* —William Wordsworth⟩ ⟨the artist, the man of genius, raises this veil and *reveals* nature to us —Havelock Ellis⟩ ⟨he *revealed* his gift for patient diplomacy —John Buchan⟩ ⟨conversation *revealed* a persistent, if muted, snobbery —Francis King⟩ DISCOVER indicates a making known or showing by or as if by uncovering; it is commonly used in connection with matters kept secret and not previously known ⟨a test which we may apply to all figure painters—a test which will often *discover* the secret of unsatisfactory design —Laurence Binyon⟩ DISCLOSE is more common than DISCOVER to indicate these notions ⟨the stress of passion often *discloses* an aspect of the personality completely ignored till then by its closest intimates —Joseph Conrad⟩ ⟨did not *disclose* his objective —Willa Cather⟩ DIVULGE indicates disclosing, often with a degree of publicity or with a suggestion of impropriety or breach of confidence, real or implied ⟨knew of the conspiracy and did not *divulge* it —Hilaire Belloc⟩ ⟨the prefaces written for it . . . *divulged* the closest workshop secrets that any novelist has yet confided to nonnovelists —C.E.Montague⟩ TELL may simply indicate giving necessary or helpful information ⟨kiss and *tell*⟩ ⟨*tell* him the news⟩ BETRAY is stronger than DIVULGE in centering attention on breaches of confidence and than REVEAL when outward signs or indications are involuntary ⟨letters that would *betray* the conspiracy he had entered into —Sherwood Anderson⟩ ⟨the deep fondness of her heart *betrayed* itself by a faint smile —Anne D. Sedgwick⟩ BEWRAY is an archaic synonym for REVEAL or BETRAY ⟨silence in love *bewrays* more woe than words —Walter Raleigh⟩

**[2]reveal** \"\ *n* -s : REVELATION, DISCLOSURE

**[3]reveal** \"\ *n* -s [alter. (influenced by [2]*reveal*) of earlier *revale*, fr. ME *revalen*, v., to lower, bring down, fr. MF *revaler*, fr. *re-* + *-valer* (fr. *val* valley) — more at VALE] **1** : the side of an opening (as for a window or doorway) between a doorframe or window frame and the outer surface of a wall; *also* : the whole thickness of the wall where the opening is not filled (as with a door) : JAMB **2** : the border surrounding a window of an automobile

**re·veal·able** \-ləbəl\ *adj* : capable of being revealed : fit for revealing

**re·vealed·ly** \-ēlədlē, -ld-\ *adv* : in a revealed manner : with or as if with revelation

**revealed religion** *n* : religion based on revelation — compare NATURAL RELIGION

**revealed theology** *n* : theology based on and attainable from revelation only

**re·veal·er** \-ˈvēlə(r)\ *n* -s : one that reveals

**re·veal·ing·ly** *adv* : in a revealing manner : so as to reveal

**re·veal·ing·ness** *n* -ES : the quality or state of being revealing

**re·veal·ment** \-lmənt\ *n* -s : an act or instance of revealing : REVELATION

**re·vegetate** \(ˈ)rē+\ *vt* [*re-* + *vegetate*] : to provide anew with vegetation; *esp* : to provide a new vegetative cover for (land previously stripped of vegetation) — **re·vegetation** \(ˌ)rē+\ *n*

**rev·e·hent** \ˈrevəhənt, rəˈvē(h)ə-\ *adj* [L *revehent-*, *revehens*, pres. part. of *revehere* to carry back, fr. *re-* + *vehere* to carry — more at WAY] : carrying back ⟨~ veins⟩

**[1]reveil** *vt* [alter. (influenced by *veil*) of [1]*reveal*] *obs* : to make known : DISCLOSE

**[2]reveil** \(ˈ)rē+\ *vt* [*re-* + *veil*] : to cover again or conceal with or as if with a veil

**rev·eil·le** \ˈrevəlē, -li, *Brit* rəˈvali *or* -veli\ *n* -s [modif. of F *réveillez*, imper. pl. of *réveiller* to awaken, arouse, fr. MF *reveiller*, fr. *re-* + *eveiller* to rouse, watch, fr. OF *esveillier*, fr. (assumed) VL *exvigilare*, fr. L *evigilare*, fr. *e-* + *vigilare* to wake, watch, fr. *vigil* awake, watchful — more at VIGIL] **1 a** (1) : a signal usu. sounded by bugle at about sunrise summoning soldiers or sailors to the day's duties (2) : a military formation held after the sounding of such a signal **b** : a signal to arise or commence **2** : a time of arising or commencing

**reveille gun** *n* : a firing of a gun immediately preceding the first note of reveille or sometimes the first note of a march that immediately precedes reveille

**ré·veil·lon** \͵rāvāˈyōⁿ\ *n* -s [F, fr. MF *reveillon*, fr. *reveiller* to awaken, arouse] : a festive supper commonly eaten in France following Christmas midnight mass

**[1]rev·el** \ˈrevəl\ *vi* **reveled** *or* **revelled**; **reveled** *or* **revelled**; **reveling** *or* **revelling** \-v(ə)liŋ\ **revels** [ME *revelen*, fr. MF *reveler* to rebel, make noise, be merry, fr. L *rebellare* to rebel, make war again — more at REBEL] **1** : to be festive in a riotous or noisy manner : indulge or take part in a revel ⟨they ~*ed* the night away⟩ **2** : to take great or intense delight or satisfaction — used with *in* ⟨~*ing* in pride⟩ ⟨~*ed* in her unhappiness —Agnes Repplier⟩

**[2]revel** \"\ *n* -s [ME, fr. MF, rebellion, disorder, feast, fr. *reveler* to rebel, be merry] **1** : MERRYMAKING, REVELRY, CAROUSING, CONVIVIALITY ⟨he fishes, drinks, and wastes the lamps of night in ~ —Shak.⟩ **2 a** : a merry or noisy celebration (as of a feast or wedding) **b revels** *pl* : the entertainment (as dances, games, pageants, and masques) provided at a revel **3** *dial Eng* : a parish festival **4 revels** *pl* : REVELS OFFICE — used with *the*

**[3]revel** *vt* [L *revellere* — more at REVULSION] *obs* : to draw back : WITHDRAW

**rev·el·a·bil·i·ty** \͵revələˈbilədˑē\ *n* [L *revelare* to reveal + E *-ability*] : the quality or state of being revealable

**reveland** *var of* REEVELAND

**rev·e·la·tion** \͵revəˈlāshən\ *n* -s [ME *revelacioun*, fr. MF *revelation*, fr. LL *revelation-*, *revelatio*, fr. L *revelatus* (past part. of *revelare* to reveal, unveil) + *-ion-*, *-io* -ion — more at REVEAL] **1 a** : an act of revealing or communicating divine truth; *esp* : God's disclosure or manifestation of himself or of his will to man ⟨the ~ to the Jews assembled around Mount Sinai⟩ **b** : something that is revealed by God to man **c** : something that contains or serves to communicate revelation or that purports to do so ⟨the *Revelations* of Bartholomew⟩ **2 a** : an act of revealing or opening to view : the disclosing or discovering to others of what was before unknown to them **b** : something that is revealed : DISCLOSURE **3** : something that tends (as by its unexpectedness, excellence, charm, or worth) to create surprise ⟨her alert keenness was a ~⟩ ⟨the ease of handling of the new machine was a ~ to me⟩

**rev·e·la·tion·al** \¦==¦lāshənᵊl\ *adj* : of or relating to revelation ⟨prophets who claim divine inspiration for their message . . . as a ~ religion —E.A.Nida⟩

**rev·e·la·tion·ist** \͵==ˈlāshənəst\ *n* -s **1** : one who makes a revelation **2** : one who accepts revelation as a religious principle; *esp* : one who holds that knowledge of God or ultimate reality has its basis in and can be attained only from revelation

**re·vel·a·tive** \rəˈveladˑiv, rēˈ-; ˈrevə͵lādˑ-\ *adj* [L *revelatus* (past part. of *revelare* to reveal) + E *-ive*] : REVEALING

**rev·e·la·tor** \ˈrevə͵lādˑə(r)\ *n* -s [LL, fr. L *revelatus* (past part.) + *-or*] : REVEALER; *esp* : one that reveals the will of God

**re·vel·a·to·ry** \rəˈvelə͵tōrē, rēˈ-; ˈrevəl-\ *adj* [L *revelatus* (past part.) + E *-ory*] : relating to or having the nature of revelation; *usu* : serving to disclose something (as character or conditions) ⟨~ glimpses of their home life⟩ ⟨a ~ account⟩

**rev·el·er** *or* **rev·el·ler** \ˈrev(ə)lə(r)\ *n* -s [alter. (influenced by *-er*) of ME *revelour*, fr. *revelen* to revel + *-our* -or — more at REVEL] : one that revels

**[1]re·vel·lent** \rəˈvelənt\ *n* -s [L *revellent-*, *revellens*, pres. part. of *revellere* to draw back, pull away — more at REVULSION] : a revulsive agent (as a medicine)

**[2]revellent** \"\ *adj* [L *revellent-*, *revellens*] : causing revulsion : REVULSIVE

**revelling** *pres part of* REVEL

**re·vel·ly** \rəˈvelē\ *n* -ES [F *réveillez* — more at REVEILLE] *chiefly dial* : REVEILLE

**rev·el·ment** \ˈrevəlmənt\ *n* -s [[1]*revel* + *-ment*] : an act of reveling : REVELRY

**rev·el·rous** \-lrəs\ *adj* [*revelry* + *-ous*] : marked by or full of revelry ⟨a ~ night⟩

**revelrout** \ˈ==͵=\ *n* [[2]*revel* + *rout*] **1** *obs* : REVELRY, CAROUSAL; *also* : REVEL **2** *archaic* : a troop of revelers

**rev·el·ry** \ˈrevəlrē, -ri\ *n* -ES [ME *revelrie*, fr. *revelen* to revel + *-rie* -ry — more at REVEL] : an act of reveling : boisterous merrymaking

**revels** *pres 3d sing of* REVEL, *pl of* REVEL

**revels office** *n, usu cap R&O* : a former office in the English royal household of which the master of the revels was head and which had charge of court entertainment

**[1]rev·e·nant** \ˈrevənənt, ¦revə¦näⁿ\ *n* -s [F, fr. pres. part. of *revenir* to come back, fr. MF — more at REVENUE] : one that returns: as **a** : the ghost of a dead person : SPECTER, WRAITH ⟨a lovely woman's wistful ~, surviving in disembodied beauty —John Bennett⟩ **b** : one who returns to a former place after prolonged absence ⟨our ~ from a hundred years ago —K.K. Darrow⟩ **c** : a person having qualities characteristic of another age or time as if returned therefrom ⟨a ~ from Regency times⟩

**[2]revenant** \"\ *adj* [F, pres. part. of *revenir* to come back] **1** : coming back : RECURRING ⟨a ~ spirit⟩ **2** : of, relating to, or typical of a revenant ⟨~ shrieks⟩

**re·ven·di·cate** \rəˈvendə͵kāt\ *vt* -ED/-ING/-S [back-formation fr. *revendication*] **1** : to recover by a formal demand for restoration **2 a** : to bring action under civil law to enforce rights in specific property whether corporeal or incorporeal or movable or immovable **b** : to proceed to recover goods sold for which the price has not been paid when vendee becomes insolvent and goods are in the same condition — compare STOPPAGE IN TRANSITU

**re·ven·di·ca·tion** \=͵==ˈkāshən\ *n* -s [F, fr. MF, prob. fr. *revendiquer* to revendicate (fr. *re-* + *vendiquer* to lay claim to something, fr. L *vindicare*) + *-ation* — more at VENGEANCE] : an act or instance of revendicating

**[1]re·venge** \rəˈvenj, rēˈ-\ *vb* -ED/-ING/-S [ME *revengen*, fr. MF *revengier*, *revenchier*, fr. OF, fr. *re-* + *vengier*, *venchier* to avenge — more at VENGEANCE] *vt* **1** : to inflict harm or injury in return for (as an injury or insult) : exact satisfaction for under a sense of injury ⟨~ his father's murder⟩ ⟨the gods are just, and will ~ our cause —John Dryden⟩ **2** : to avenge or seek vengeance for a wrong done (oneself or another) ⟨~ oneself on one's enemies⟩ **3** *obs* : PUNISH ~ *vi* : to take vengeance — usu. used with *upon* **syn** see AVENGE

**[2]revenge** \"\ *n* -s [MF *revenge*, *revenche*, fr. *revengier*, *revenchier* to revenge] **1** : the disposition or desire to seek vengeance ⟨a prey to ~⟩; *also* : the gratification of such a desire ⟨determined to have his ~⟩ **2** : an act or instance of revenging or returning evil for evil : vindictive retaliation ⟨a terrible ~⟩ **3** *obs* **a** : AVENGING ⟨none would strike a stroke in his ~ —Shak.⟩ **b** : PUNISHMENT **4** : an opportunity of getting satisfaction or retrieving oneself (as by a return match) ⟨give one his ~⟩

**re·venge·ful** \-jfəl\ *adj* : full of or prone to revenge : desirous of vengeance ⟨a harsh ~ spirit⟩ **syn** see VINDICTIVE

**re·venge·ful·ly** \-fəlē\ *adv* : in a revengeful manner

**re·venge·ful·ness** *n* -ES : the quality or state of being revengeful : VINDICTIVENESS

**re·venge·less** \-jləs\ *adj* **1** : free from revengefulness : lacking in vindictiveness **2** *obs* : UNREVENGED

**re·venge·ment** \-jmənt\ *n* -s : REVENGE

**re·veng·er** \-jə(r)\ *n* -s : one that revenges : AVENGER

**re·veng·ing·ly** *adv* : in a revenging manner

**re·vent** \(ˈ)rē+\ *vt* [*re-* + *vent*] : to fit with a new vent ⟨~*ed* the plumbing⟩

**rev·e·nue** \ˈrevə͵n(y)ü\ *n* -s *often attrib* [ME, fr. MF, fr. fem. of *revenu*, past part. of *revenir* to come back, fr. L *revenire*, fr. *re-* + *venire* to come — more at COME] **1 a** *obs* : the return from landed property or other source of income — used with *of* **b** : the income that comes back from an investment (as in real or personal property) : the annual or periodical rents, profits, interest, or issues of any species of real or personal property; *often* : investment income as distinguished from salary, wages, or donations **c** : the annual or periodical yield of taxes, excises, customs, duties, and other sources of income that a nation, state, or municipality collects and receives into the treasury for public use : public income of whatever kind **2** : an item of income : the total income produced by a given source ⟨a property expected to yield an annual ~ of 10,000 dollars⟩ **3 a** : a government department concerned with the collection of the national revenue **b** : REVENUE STAMP

**revenue account** *n* : INCOME ACCOUNT 1

**revenue act** *or* **revenue law** *n* : a statute imposing a tax to defray the expenses of government; *esp* : a federal revenue act making a major change in existing tax law

**revenue bond** *n* : a bond issued by a public agency authorized to build, acquire, or improve a revenue-producing property and payable solely out of revenue derived from such property

**revenue cutter** *n* : an armed government vessel employed esp. to enforce revenue laws and prevent smuggling

**rev·e·nued** \-üd\ *adj* : provided with a revenue

**revenue expenditure** *n* : an expenditure allocable to and chargeable against revenue — contrasted with *capital expenditure*

**rev·e·nu·er** \-(y)üə(r), -(y)u̇(ə)r, -(y)u̇ə\ *n* -s : a revenue officer or cutter ⟨a fast ~⟩

**revenue stamp** *n* : a stamp for use as evidence of payment of a tax (as on a package of cigarettes, a proprietary article, a lease, or a mortgage) — called also *fiscal stamp*

**revenue tariff** *n* : a tariff intended wholly or primarily to produce public revenue — compare PROTECTIVE TARIFF

**re·ver** \rəˈver\ *n* -s [F *revers* — more at REVERS] : REVERS

**re·ver·able** \rəˈvirəbəl\ *adj* [[1]*revere* + *-able*] : meriting reverence

**[1]re·verb** \rəˈvərb\ *vb* [L *reverberare*] : REVERBERATE

**[2]reverb** \"\ *n* -s [by shortening] : REVERBERATION

**re·ver·ba·to·ry** \rəˈvərbə͵tōrē, rēˈ-, -vəb-, -vəib-\ *adj* [by contr.] : REVERBERATORY

**re·ver·ber·ance** \-b(ə)rən(t)s\ *n* -s : the quality or state of being reverberant

**re·ver·ber·ant** \-nt\ *adj* [L *reverberant-*, *reverberans*, pres. part. of *reverberare* to reverberate] : tending to reverberate : marked by reverberation : RESONANT ⟨~ rooms⟩ ⟨~ voices⟩ ⟨sound of the waves, made weirdly hollow and ~ by the fog —Jack London⟩ — **re·ver·ber·ant·ly** *adv*

**[1]re·ver·ber·ate** \rəˈvərbə͵rāt, rēˈ-, -vəb-, -vəib-, *usu* -ād·+V\ *vb* -ED/-ING/-S [L *reverberatus*, past part. of *reverberare* to strike back, cause to rebound, fr. *re-* + *verberare* to lash, whip, beat, fr. *verber* rod — more at VERVAIN] *vt* **1** : to return or send back : force or drive back: as **a** : REPEL **b** : ECHO **c** : REFLECT ⟨a mirror *reverberating* the glaring light⟩; *esp* : to drive from one side to another (as flame in a furnace) **2** : to subject to the action of a reverberatory furnace : fuse by reverberated heat ~ *vi* **1** : to become driven or sent back : become reflected (as from a surface) ⟨warmth *reverberating* from the sunny court⟩ **2** : to continue or become repeated in or as if in a series of echoes ⟨his call *reverberated* from the hills⟩ **3** : to be forced to strike or go — used with *upon* or *over* ⟨so arranged that the flames ~ upon the charge of ore⟩ ⟨*reverberating* over the surface to be heated⟩ **syn** see REBOUND

**[2]re·ver·ber·ate** \-bərət, -bə͵rāt\ *adj* [L *reverberatus*, past part. of *reverberare*] : REVERBERATED, REVERBERATING, REVERBERANT, REFLECTED ⟨~ sound⟩

**re·ver·ber·a·tion** \=͵==ˈrāshən\ *n* -s [ME *reverberacioun*, fr. MF *reverberation*, fr. ML *reverberation-*, *reverberatio*, fr. L *reverberatus* (past part.) + *-ion-*, *-io* -ion] **1 a** *obs* : the fact of being sent forcibly back (as by or after impact) **b** : a reflecting of something (as light or heat); *also* : the repetitive effect or impact resulting from such reflecting **2** *obs* : the reflecting action of some medium or body **3** : an act of reverberating ⟨the ~ of voices in the narrow corridor⟩: as **a** : an act of reflecting radiation (as sound, heat, or light); *also* : the reflected condition of such radiation **b** : subjection to the action of a reverberatory furnace **4** : something that is reverberated: as **a** : a sound persisting because of repeated reflections after the source has been cut off — distinguished from *echo*; compare RESIDUAL SOUND **b** : a reflected light or color

**reverberation time** *n* : the time that it takes a sound made in a room to diminish to one millionth of its original intensity

**re·ver·ber·a·tive** \=ˈ==͵rā|dˑ|iv, -b(ə)rə|, |t|, |ēv *also* |əv\ *adj* [[1]*reverberate* + *-ive*] : constituting reverberation : tending to reverberate : REFLECTIVE ⟨the ~ light of the beach outside —R.M.Coates⟩

**re·ver·ber·a·tor** \-bə͵rādˑə(r)\ *n* -s [[1]*reverberate* + *-or*] : something (as a reflector) that produces reverberation

**[1]re·ver·ber·a·to·ry** \rəˈvərb(ə)rə͵tōrē, rēˈ-, -vəb-, -vəib-, -bə͵-, -tȯr-, -ri\ *adj* [[1]*reverberate* + *-ory*] : acting by reverberation : forced back or diverted onto material under treatment ⟨a ~ fire⟩ ⟨~ heat⟩

**[2]reverberatory** \"\ *n* -ES : a furnace or kiln in which heat is radiated from the roof onto the material (as cast iron or copper ore) treated

**re·ver·brate** \rəˈvər͵brāt\ *adj* [contr. of [2]*reverberate*] : REVERBERATING, RESOUNDING, ECHOING ⟨~ hills⟩

**re·ver·di** *or* **re·ver·die** \rəˈverdē\ *n* -s [OF *reverdie*, lit., foliage, verdure, fr. *reverdier*, *reverdoier* to grow green again, fr. *re-* + *verdier*, *verdoier* to grow green — more at VERDANT] : an old French song signalizing the return of spring

**[1]re·vere** \rəˈvi(ə)r, rēˈ-, -iə\ *vt* -ED/-ING/-S [L *reverērī*, fr. *re-* + *verērī* to respect, revere, fear — more at WARY] : to regard with reverence or profound respect and affection : practice an affectionate deference toward : show love and honor to ⟨whom he rather *revered* as his father than treated as his partner —Joseph Addison⟩

**syn** REVERENCE, VENERATE, WORSHIP, ADORE: one REVERES, usu. with tenderness and deference, persons or often institutions, or their accomplishments or attributes, entitled to respect and honor, or objects closely associated with or symbolic of such people or institutions ⟨academic idols which they, in their turn, had been taught to *revere* —Joanne Wheeler⟩ ⟨*revere* past national glories, almost to the point of worship —T.H. Fielding⟩ ⟨*revered* for the wisdom of his counsels and the nobility of his character —Theodore Collier⟩ REVERENCE, applying more often to things than persons, suggests more the fact of holding in high respect and with a certain self-abnegation, esp. a respecting of things commonly respected or regarded as inviolable ⟨brought up to love and *reverence* her mother —Margaret Deland⟩ ⟨pledged to *reverence* the name of God —F.B.Steck⟩ VENERATE applies commonly to persons or things regarded as holy, sacred, or sacrosanct because of character, associations, or age ⟨those who *venerate* . . . Dante and Shakespeare and Milton —Havelock Ellis⟩ ⟨*venerate* and obey natural law —W.R.Inge⟩ ⟨revered him as much as he *venerated* her —Osbert Sitwell⟩ One commonly WORSHIPS a divine being when one pays homage by word or ceremonial, but more broadly one WORSHIPS anyone or anything to whom he attributes an esp. exalted character or before whom he abases himself in great respect or adoration ⟨*worship* God each Sunday⟩ ⟨*worship* the flag of one's country⟩ ⟨the grave of a famous hunter, where they *worship* his spirit —J.G.Frazer⟩ ⟨the unwavering *worship* of a good dog for his master —Elizabeth Goudge⟩ ADORE is often used in the sense of WORSHIP in its application to a divine being although suggesting a more personal emotion; but commonly and much more generally it applies to any extremely great and usu. unquestioning love, however manifest ⟨his staff *adored* him, his men worshiped him —W.A.White⟩ ⟨music that he *adored* —Marcia Davenport⟩ ⟨still *adores* baseball and never expects to tire of it⟩

**[2]revere** \"\ *n* -s [alter. of *rever*] : REVERS

**rev·er·ee** \͵revəˈrā\ *n* -s [prob. fr. F *révérée*, fem. past part. of *révérer* to revere, fr. L *reverērī*] : MINIATURE PINK

**[1]rev·er·ence** \ˈrevərn(t)s *also* -v(ə)rən-\ *n* -s [ME, fr. OF, fr. L *reverentia*, fr. *reverent-*, *reverens* (pres. part. of *reverērī* to revere) + *-ia* -y — more at REVERE] **1 a** : honor or respect felt or manifested : deference duly paid or expressed ⟨a seemly ~ may be paid to power —William Wordsworth⟩ **b** : profound respect mingled with love and awe (as for a holy or exalted being or place or thing) ⟨pray with ~⟩ — often used with *in* ⟨a child reared in ~ of his parents⟩ **2 a** : a gesture of respect (as an obeisance, bow, or curtsy) ⟨made a slight ~ in passing⟩ **b** : a deep bow performed in a court dance or ballet **3 a** : the character or state of being revered or honored : exalted position ⟨remembering the ~ of the place in which he stood⟩ ⟨attained great ~ among the citizens⟩ **b** : something held in reverence : an object of honor and respect ⟨one's private ~*s*⟩ **4** : CLERGYMAN — used as a respectful form of address (as in the phrases *his Reverence, saving your reverence*) **syn** see HONOR

2**reverence** \"\ *vt* -ED/-ING/-S [ME, fr. *reverence*, n.] **:** to regard or treat with reverence, respect, honor, or veneration **:** show reverence to or respect for **:** esteem highly ⟨~ the gods⟩ ⟨those who ~ the laws of their country⟩ ⟨truly *reverenced* honest effort⟩ **syn** see REVERE

**rev·er·enc·er** \-nsə(r)\ *n* -S **:** one that reverences

1**rev·er·end** \'revərnd *also* -v(ə)rən-\ *adj, sometimes* -ER/-EST [ME, fr. MF, fr. L *reverendus*, gerundive of *reverērī* to revere] **1 :** worthy of reverence **:** entitled to respect or honor (as on account of age or position) **:** inspiring reverence **:** REVERED ⟨these ~ halls⟩ ⟨my ~ father⟩ — often used in respectful address ⟨you may trust my aim, ~ sir⟩ **2** *obs* **:** SACRED, HOLY **3 :** REVERENT ⟨experienced a ~ awe at the sight⟩ **4 a :** of, relating to, or characteristic of the clergy **b** *usu cap* **:** belonging to the clergy **:** being a clergyman — used in a form of address usu. preceded by *the*, followed by a title or a full name, and sometimes qualified by an honorific ⟨the *Reverend* Dr. Doe⟩; abbr. *Rev.* ⟨*Rev.* John Doe⟩; compare MOST REVEREND, RIGHT REVEREND, VERY REVEREND **5** *chiefly Midland* **:** STRONG, POTENT, UNDILUTED ⟨a ~ whiskey⟩

2**reverend** \"\ *n* -S **:** a member of the clergy **:** MINISTER, PRIEST, PASTOR ⟨churches don't hire ~s, they hire families —Monte Linkletter⟩ ⟨saw the ~ walking down the road⟩ ⟨good morning, *Reverend*⟩

**reverendly** *adv* [ME, fr. 1*reverend* + *-ly*] **1** *obs* **:** REVERENTLY **2** *obs* **:** in a manner to inspire reverence

**rev·er·end·ship** \-n(d),ship\ *n* **:** the condition of being a clergyman

**rev·er·ent** \'revərnt *also* -v(ə)rən-\ *adj* [in sense 1, fr. ME, alter. (influenced by L *reverent-, reverens*) of MF *reverend*; in sense 2, fr. ME, fr. L *reverent-, reverens*, pres. part. of *reverērī* to revere — more at REVERE] **1** *obs* **:** REVEREND 1, 4 **2 :** disposed to revere **:** expressing or characterized by reverence or veneration **:** very or profoundly respectful ⟨~ disciples⟩ ⟨~ conduct⟩ **3 :** REVEREND 5 — **rev·er·ent·ly** *adv* — **rev·er·ent·ness** *n* -ES

**rev·er·en·tial** \¦revə¦renchəl\ *adj* **1 :** proceeding from or expressing reverence **:** having a reverent quality ⟨~ awe⟩ **2 :** inspiring reverence **:** VENERABLE ⟨a ~ judge with a long white beard⟩ — **rev·er·en·ti·al·i·ty** \,==,renche'aləd·ē\ *n* -ES — **rev·er·en·tial·ly** \¦==¦renchəlē, -li\ *adv* — **rev·er·en·tial·ness** *n* -ES

**re·ver·er** \rə'virə(r)\ *n* -S **:** one that reveres

**reveres** *pres 3d sing of* REVERE, *pl of* REVERE

**rev·er·ie** *or* **rev·ery** \'rev(ə)rē, -ri\ *n, pl* **reveries** [F *rêverie*, fr. MF *resverie, raverie, reverie* delirium, rage, revelry, fr. *resver, raver, rever* to wander, be delirious + *-erie* -ery] **1 :** an extravagant or fanciful product of the mind **:** a theory or notion marked by strangeness or impracticality **:** a purely visionary or theoretical concept ⟨the scheme was pure ~⟩ **2 a :** the condition of being lost in thought or abstracted musing ⟨passed the day in ~ before the fire⟩ **b :** a sequence of thoughts or images not purposively directed ⟨had a ~ about the children's future⟩

**re·verification** \(¦)rē+\ *n* [*re-* + *verification*] **:** a new or second act of verifying

**re·verify** \(')rē+\ *vt* [*re-* + *verify*] **:** to verify again or anew **:** RECHECK

**revering** *pres part of* REVERE

**rev·er·ist** \'revərə̇st\ *n* -S **:** one who indulges in reveries

**re·vers** *n, pl* **revers** \rə'vi(ə)r, rē'-, \|ə *also* -ve\| *or* -va(a)\|\ [F, lit., reverse, fr. MF] **1 :** a wide turned-back or applied facing that is usu. one of a pair along the front edges of a garment (as a coat or dress), sometimes includes a continuous section for a collar, and often extends to the hemline **2 :** a lapel on women's garments

**re·ver·sal** \-səl\ *n* -S [ME, fr. *reversen* to reverse + *-al*] **1 :** an act or the process of reversing: as **a :** a change or overthrowing of some legal proceeding or judgment ⟨the ~ of an attainder⟩ **b :** the causing to move or face in an opposite direction or to appear in an inverted position ⟨the ~ of a rotation⟩ ⟨the ~ of objects by a lens⟩ **c :** a method of testing or determining the collimation (as of a transit) by inverting the telescope in its supports **d :** INVERSION 2c **e :** an act or instance of going from the defensive position to the position of advantage in amateur wrestling — compare TAKEDOWN **2 a :** a conversion in whole or part of a photographic positive into a negative or vice versa **b :** SOLARIZATION

**reversal process** *n* **:** a photographic process in which the reverse of the image formed by direct development is obtained (as by destroying the primary developed negative image with a bleach and developing the residual silver halide to form the reversed image)

1**re·verse** \rə'vərs, rē'-, -və̄s, -vəis\ *adj* [ME *revers*, fr. MF, fr. L *reversus*, past part. of *revertere* to turn back — more at REVERT] **1 a :** turned back **:** opposite or contrary to one another or to a thing specified ⟨came back in the ~ order⟩ **b :** having the back presented to the observer or opponent — opposed to *obverse* **2** *obs* **:** BACKHANDED ⟨a ~ blow⟩ ⟨~ thrust⟩ **3 :** relating to, facing, or commanding the rear of a military force **4 :** acting or operating in opposite or contrary fashion esp. to what is usual **5 :** effecting reverse movement or operation ⟨a ~ gear⟩ **6 a** (1) **:** so made that the part of a print normally black is white and vice versa ⟨a ~ photoengraving⟩ (2) **:** FLOPPED **b :** constituting a mirror image ⟨the ~ symbols ☞ and ☜⟩ ⟨a ~ positive image⟩

2**reverse** \"\ *vb* -ED/-ING/-S [ME *reversen*, fr. MF *reverser*, fr. LL *reversare* to turn round, freq. of L *revertere* to turn back] *vt* **1** *obs* **:** to cause to return **2** *obs* **:** OVERTHROW, SUBVERT **3 :** to turn completely about in position or direction **:** change to the opposite as regards position **:** TRANSPOSE ⟨a picture *reversed* in reproduction⟩ **4 :** to turn upside down **:** INVERT ⟨*reversing* his glass as a signal that he would drink no more⟩ **5 :** ANNUL: as **a :** to overthrow (a legal decision) by a contrary decision **:** make void (as for error) ⟨the higher court may ~ the judgment⟩ **b :** to take an opposite stand from that formerly held by (oneself) — usu. used with *about* or *over* ⟨*reversed* himself about the superiority of mother's cooking⟩ **c :** to change to the contrary in character or trend ⟨~ a policy⟩ **6 :** to cause to go or move in the opposite direction ⟨~ the flow of a stream⟩; *esp* **:** to cause (as an engine or machine) to perform its revolutions or action in the opposite direction **7 a :** to use (as a tool) or do (as an experiment) in the opposite way **b :** to produce by or use in reverse printing ⟨*reversed* plates⟩ ⟨*reversing* lettering into a color panel⟩ ~ *vi* **1** *obs* **a :** to draw or move back **:** turn away **:** RECOIL **b :** to fall down **:** turn over **c :** RETURN **2 :** to alter or revoke a decision (as on a point of law) **3 :** to turn or move in the opposite direction (as in waltzing) **:** become reversed **4 :** to put a mechanism (as an engine or a machine) in reverse **5 :** to make a reverse bid in bridge **syn** see REVOKE

3**reverse** \"\ *n* -S [ME *revers*, fr. MF, fr. *revers*, adj.] **1 :** something that is directly opposite or contrary to something else **:** CONTRARY, OPPOSITE ⟨hoped for a sunny day but the fact was just the ~⟩ — often followed by *of* or *to* ⟨the ~ of good luck⟩ **2** *obs* **:** a backhanded thrust, cut, or stroke (as with a sword) **3 :** an act or instance of reversing: as **a :** a turning completely about (as in dancing) **:** a complete change or reversal ⟨an unexpected ~ of plans⟩ **b :** a change from better to worse **:** MISFORTUNE, CHECK, DEFEAT — often used in pl. ⟨meet with heavy ~s⟩ **4 a :** matter that appears or is presented when something is reverted or is turned or viewed oppositely to the position or direction in which it is ordinarily seen ⟨the ~ of a leaf⟩ **b :** the side of a coin, token, medal, seal, or currency note that is considered the back **c :** the back of a book leaf **:** VERSO **d :** an inverted utterance (as a phrase or sentence) **e :** something (as a negative or lettering) produced by or used in reverse printing **5 :** the rear of a military force **6 a :** a gear that reverses something; *also* **:** the mechanical train brought into play when such a gear is used ⟨something out of order in the ~⟩ ⟨put the transmission in ~⟩ (2) **:** movement or course in reverse **b :** a turn or fold made in bandaging by which the direction of the bandage is changed **c :** an offensive play in football in which a back moving in one direction passes or hands the ball to a player moving in the opposite direction **7 :** REVERSE BID **syn** see CONVERSE — **in reverse** *adv* **:** in an opposite manner or direction **:** BACK, BACKWARD

4**reverse** \"\ *adv* [ME *revers*, fr. *revers*, adj.] **:** so as to oppose **:** REVERSELY ⟨acted ~ to his own best interests⟩

**reverse arms** *n* **:** a position of a soldier in which a rifle is held between the right elbow and the body at an angle of 45 degrees with the barrel downward and the muzzle down and to the rear

**reverse bar** *n* **:** a portion or section of a reverse frame in a ship; *also* **:** REVERSE FRAME

**reverse bearing** *n* **:** a bearing in surveying resulting from a backsight

**reverse bid** *n* **:** a bridge rebid in a suit higher in rank than a suit previously bid by the same player made at a level of two or higher and usu. requiring a strong hand

**reverse casehardening** *n* **:** a condition in wood resulting from excessive steaming (as in an attempt to correct casehardening) and characterized by the surface layers being under tension and the inner layers under compression

**reverse circulation** *n* **:** flow in a direction opposite to the normal

**reverse current** *n* **:** flow of direct electric current in a reverse direction or of alternating current in phase opposition to normal

**reverse-current circuit breaker** *n* **:** a circuit breaker that opens the circuit controlled upon the reversal of the direction of the flow of power

**reverse curve** *n* **:** an S-shaped curve (as in a railway line or a highway) made by joining two simple curves turning in opposite directions; *broadly* **:** a stretch formed of two oppositely turning simple curves joined by a tangent

**reversed** *adj* [fr. past part. of 2*reverse*] **1 :** turned backward or the contrary way **:** turned side for side or end for end: as **a :** RESUPINATE **b :** SINISTRAL — used esp. of a univalve shell **c :** INVERTED 1c **d :** exhibiting sexual behavior characteristic of the opposite sex **2 :** having the edges turned back to give the appearance of greater thickness — used of sheet-metal work **3 :** set aside **:** ANNULLED, VACATED ⟨a ~ decision⟩ — **re·versed·ly** \-sədlē, -stlē, -li\ *adv*

**reversed calf** *n* **:** calf leather finished on flesh side by light buffing and used flesh side out (as for shoes)

**reversed collar** *n* **:** CLERICAL COLLAR

**reversed foot** *n* **:** a foot in which the prevailing cadence of a metrical series or of an adjacent foot is reversed or inverted by exchanging the positions of stressed and unstressed or long and short elements ⟨a trochee in an iambic series is a *reversed foot*⟩ — compare INVERSION

**reverse discard** *n* **:** a discard or play in bridge or whist of two or more losing cards in some order other than that conventionally expected by one's partner as a signal — compare ECHO, HIGH-LOW

**reverse dive** *n* **:** one of several competitive dives in which the body rotates backward around a transverse axis from a front takeoff — compare BACK DIVE, FRONT DIVE, INWARD DIVE, TWIST DIVE

**reversed line** *also* **reversed spectrum line** *n* **:** a strong line in an emission spectrum that has a dark line down its middle due to absorption by the colder vapor which surrounds the central luminous vapor

**reverse english** *n, usu cap E* **1** *or* **reverse side :** English imparted to a cue ball causing it to rebound at a more obtuse angle and at a slower speed — compare RUNNING ENGLISH **2 :** something that is an apparent contradiction or inverted application ⟨putting *reverse English* on one's words —Richard Wilbur⟩

**reverse fault** *n* **:** a geological fault in which the hanging wall appears to have been pushed up along the footwall

**reverse flush** *vt* **:** to circulate water or a cleansing fluid through (the cooling system of an automobile) in reverse of the normal circulation to dislodge an accumulation of sludge

**reverse frame** *n* **:** a part of the frame of a steel ship formed by an angle iron placed opposite the frame proper but with its flanges reversed in direction from those forming the frame — see SHIP illustration

**reverse graft** *n* **:** a plant graft in which the scion is inserted in an inverted position usu. in order to develop a dwarf plant

**reverse half nelson** *n* **:** a half nelson applied (as from a cross-body ride) with the arm under the opponent's opposite rather than corresponding arm — see GUILLOTINE 7

**reverse hydrant** *n* **:** a hydrant through which water is pumped into a main from another source

**reverse indention** *n* **:** HANGING INDENTION

**reverse index** *n* **:** a list (as an index or glossary) in which items are arranged alphabetically under their final element

**reverse keys** *n pl* **:** an arrangement of keys or wedges resembling a stonemason's plug and feather used for forcing apart two pieces previously fastened by a key or cotter

**re·verse·ly** *adv* **:** in an opposite way **:** so as to be reversed

**re·verse·ment** \rə'vərsmənt\ *n* -S **:** REVERSAL; *esp* **:** a flight maneuver consisting of a half-roll and a half-loop performed in that order

**reverse of the medal :** an opposite and usu. less favorable aspect of an affair or question

**reverse painting** *n* **:** the art or method of painting on the back of a glass panel in which the details are done first so that the finished work may be seen correctly from the opposite side; *also* **:** an example of such painting

**reverse perspective** *n* **:** visual perspective (as in Byzantine painting and medieval illumination) characterized by divergence of parallel lines and diminution of objects toward the observer — compare LINEAR PERSPECTIVE

**reverse-phase relay** *n* **:** a phase-rotation relay applied to protect electric motors against damage by reversal of phase sequence

**reverse pitch** *n* **:** propeller blade pitch in which the thrust produced is opposite to that normally obtained

**re·vers·er** \-sər\ *n* -S **1 :** one that reverses ⟨a signal ~⟩: as **a :** a device for reversing an electric current or polarity **b :** a switching device for interchanging electrical circuits to reverse the direction of motor rotation **2** *Scots law* **a :** REVERSIONER **b :** MORTGAGOR; *also* **:** one granting a wadset of his land

**reverses** *pres 3d sing of* REVERSE, *pl of* REVERSE

**reverse slope** *n* **:** a slope that descends away (as from an enemy force) esp. when marked by a hill or ridge

**reverse spelling** *n* **:** an unphonetic and unetymological spelling imitating the same spelling in words where it is etymological but no longer phonetic (as *limb* from *lim*, compare *lamb*, where *b* is etymological; *delight* from *delit*, compare *light; Swanage* from *Swanwich* \'swänij\ compare *savage*)

**reverse taper** *n* **:** a planform configuration in which the chord of the wing of an airplane increases with distance outboard from the root

**reverse turn** *n* **1 :** IMMELMANN TURN **2 a :** counterclockwise rotation **b :** a counterclockwise turn in dancing

**re·ver·si** \rə'vərsē\ *n* -S [F, fr. obs. F *reversin*, modif. (influenced by F *revers* reverse, fr. MF) of It *rovescina*, fr. *rovescio*, adj., reverse, inside out, fr. *rovesciare* to reverse, turn inside out, fr. (assumed) VL *reversiare*, fr. LL *reversare* to turn round; fr. the fact that the game is won by losing — more at REVERSE] **1 :** a card game in which the player who makes the fewest points and takes the fewest tricks wins **2 :** a game for two which is played on a checkerboard with 64 pieces having one color on one side and another on the other and in which if a player can so place his men as to enclose one of the opponent's he may reverse it and use it as one of his own

**re·vers·ibil·i·ty** \rə,vərsə'biləd·ē, rē,-, -vəs-, -vəis-, -lətē, -i\ *n* -S **:** the quality or state of being reversible

**reversibility principle** *n* **:** a principle in optics: if light travels from a point *A* to a point *B* over a particular path, it can travel over the same path from *B* to *A*

1**re·vers·ible** \=ˈ=səbəl\ *adj* [2*reverse* + *-ible*] **:** capable of being reversed or of reversing ⟨a chair with a ~ back⟩ ⟨a ~ judgment⟩: as **a :** capable of going through a series of actions (as movements or changes) in either direction backward or forward ⟨a ~ chemical reaction⟩ — see REVERSIBLE PROCESS **b** (1) **:** having two finished usable sides often with different patterns or colors ⟨~ fabric⟩ ⟨~ panels⟩ — compare DAMASK 1 (2) **:** made to be worn with either side out and often with a different fabric on each side ⟨~ overcoat⟩ ⟨~ jacket⟩ **c :** capable of being corrected **:** not permanent or irrevocable ⟨~ hypertension⟩ — **re·vers·ible·ness** *n* -ES — **re·versibly** \-blē, -li\ *adv*

2**reversible** \"\ *n* -S **:** a reversible cloth

**reversible cell** *or* **reversible element** *n* **:** an electrical cell the chemical action in which can be reversed by passing through it a current opposite in direction to that generated by the cell ⟨a storage cell is a *reversible cell*⟩

**reversible colloid** *n* **:** a colloid that can be precipitated as a gel and then again dispersed as a sol

**reversible disc plow** *n* **:** a disc plow having the disc reversible so that the soil can be thrown in the same direction regardless of the direction of travel

**reversible electrode** *n* **:** a metallic electrode that will dissolve when a current is passed from it into a solution and that will have plated on it metal from the solution when the current is passed in the reverse direction

**reversible error** *n* **:** error justifying the vacating of a judgment or decree, sustaining an exception or appeal, or remanding a case for new trial or hearing

**reversible lock** *n* **:** a lock that may be applied to a door opening in either direction or hinged to either jamb

**reversible-pitch propeller** *n* **:** a propeller whose blade pitch may be adjusted to produce thrust in a direction opposite to that normally obtained

**reversible process** *n* **:** an ideal process or series of changes of a system which is in complete equilibrium at each stage such that when the process is reversed each of the changes both internal and external is reversed but with the amount of transferred energy unaltered

**reversible reaction** *n* **:** a reaction that takes place in either direction according to conditions (as the formation of hydriodic acid by union of hydrogen and iodine or its decomposition into these elements) — compare EQUILIBRIUM 1b

**re·versify** \(')rē+\ *vt* [*re-* + *versify*] **:** to formulate anew in verse

**reversing** *pres part of* REVERSE

**reversing eyepiece** *n* **:** an eyepiece (as of a telescope) equipped with a prism or mirror to interchange opposite sides of the field and give a mirror image — compare REVERSING PRISM

**reversing layer** *n* **:** the lowest layers of the sun's chromosphere which are perhaps a few hundred miles in depth and in which occurs the absorption that produces most of the dark lines in the solar spectrum; *also* **:** a corresponding region in the atmosphere of a star

**reversing link** *n* **:** the slotted link of a link motion

**re·vers·ing·ly** *adv* **:** so as to reverse **:** in a reversing manner

**reversing prism** *n* **:** a right-angled prism that reverses in one coordinate the images of objects viewed through it by total reflection — compare PORRO PRISM

**reversing switch** *n* **:** an electric switch that has four terminals capable of being connected in pairs in two different ways so as to reverse the direction of current flow

**reversing thermometer** *n* **:** a thermometer for registering temperature in deep water by means of the breaking of a column of mercury when the thermometer inverts at a specified depth

**re·ver·sion** \rə'vərzhən, rē'-, -vəs\, -vəi\ *also* \shən\ *n* -S [ME, fr. MF, fr. L *reversion-, reversio* act of turning back, fr. *reversus* (past part. of *revertere* to turn back) + *-ion-, -io* -ion — more at REVERT] **1 a** (1) **:** the returning of an estate upon its termination to its former owner or his successor in interest (2) **:** the part of a simple estate remaining in its owner after he has granted therefrom a lesser particular estate (as the future reversionary interest when a term for years, a life estate, a fee tail, or a contingent remainder) that will upon the termination of the lesser estate automatically return to the possession of the owner **b :** the right of redemption under Scots law from wadset existing during the time allowed for the payment of the debt secured thereby **c :** a future interest in property left in a grantor or his successor in interest that is not subject to a condition precedent **2 a** *archaic* **:** the residue of food or drink left over (as from a meal) **:** SCRAPS, LEFTOVERS **b** *obs* **:** a small amount or number **:** REMAINDER, REMNANT **3 :** the right of succession or of future possession or enjoyment (as of an office or of material or immaterial goods) **4 :** an act or instance of returning (as to a former condition or faith) **:** RECONVERSION: as **a :** the act of reverting an algebraic series **b :** a return toward some ancestral type or condition **:** the reappearance of an ancestral character **:** ATAVISM **5 :** an act or instance of turning the opposite way or the state of being so turned ⟨the breeze underwent an abrupt ~⟩ **6 :** a product of reversion: as **a :** an organism with an atavistic character **:** THROWBACK **b :** a reversionary annuity **c :** a virus disease of black currants transmitted by a gall mite and characterized by narrow rugose leaves, abnormally elongated and partially or completely sterile flowers, and degeneration of the plant as a whole

**re·ver·sion·able** \-nəbəl\ *adj* **:** capable of reversion

**re·ver·sion·al** \|zhən'l, |zhnəl, |sh-\ *adj* **:** of, relating to, or constituting a reversion **:** REVERSIONARY — **re·ver·sion·al·ly** \-°lē, -əlē, -i\ *adv*

**re·ver·sion·ary** \|zhə,nerē, |sh-, -ri\ *adj* **:** of, relating to, constituting, or involving a reversion and esp. a legal reversion to be enjoyed in succession or after the termination of a particular estate ⟨a ~ interest⟩

**reversionary annuity** *n* **:** an annuity payable to some person upon another becoming for any reason unable to receive it and usu. equivalent to a survivorship annuity

**reversion duty** *n, chiefly Brit* **:** a duty levied on a lessor at the termination of a long lease based on increase of property valuation during the period of the lease

**re·ver·sion·er** \|zh(ə)nə(r), |sh-\ *n* -S **:** one that has or is entitled to a reversion; *broadly* **:** someone having a vested right to a future estate

**re·ver·sion·ist** \-nəst\ *n* -S **1 :** REVERSIONER **2 :** an advocate of reversion to some previous state (as of political affiliation)

**reversion to type :** REVERSION 4b

**reversis** *pl of* REVERSI

**re·ver·sive** \rə'vərsiv\ *adj* [2*reverse* + *-ive*] **:** relating to or marked by reversion **:** tending to reverse or revert

**re·verso** \rə+\ *n* [*re-* + *verso*] **:** VERSO

1**re·vert** \rə'vər\|t, rē'-, -vā\|, -vəi\|, *usu* \|d·+V\ *vb* -ED/-ING/-S [ME *reverten*, fr. MF *revertir*, fr. OF, fr. L *revertere* to turn back, fr. *re-* + *vertere* to turn — more at WORTH] *vi* **1 :** to come or go back (as to a place, person, condition, or topic) ⟨a people that ~*ed* to savagery⟩ **2 :** to return to the proprietor or his heirs or assigns after the termination of a particular estate or reversion granted by him **3 :** to undergo reversion **:** return toward some ancestral type **4 :** to return to a former chemical state — used esp. of solubilized phosphoric acid or phosphate in fertilizer that becomes insoluble again **5 :** to develop an off-flavor — used esp. of a fat or a fatty oil ~ *vt* **1** *obs* **a :** to cause to return to; *esp* **:** RESTORE **b :** to turn, force, or throw back **c :** REVOKE, REVERSE, ANNUL **2 :** to turn to the contrary **:** REVERSE, INVERT **3 :** to turn (as the eyes) or direct back or to the rear **4 :** to cause (as phosphates) to revert — **revert a series :** to so treat an infinite algebraic series (as $y=a+bx+cx^2+$etc.) as to find $x$ in a series in powers of $y$

2**revert** \"\ *n* -S **:** one that reverts or is reverted; *esp* **:** one that returns to a former faith

3**revert** \"\ *adj* **:** REVERTED

**reverted** *adj* **:** turned or curled back or the wrong way ⟨a ~ leaf⟩ **:** directed back ⟨with eyes ~⟩ **:** REVERSED; *also* **:** affected with reversion ⟨a ~ culture of bacteria⟩ ⟨~ black currants⟩

**reverted train** *n* **:** an epicyclic train in which the first and last wheels revolve on the same axis so that when these two wheels are nearly equal a very slow relative rotation is secured

1**re·vert·er** \|d·ə(r)\ *n* -S [ME, fr. AF *reverter* to return (taken as a n.), fr. OF *revertir* to return, revert] **1 :** REVERSION **2 a :** a possibility of reversion of an estate in land ⟨land subject to a ~⟩

2**reverter** \"\ *n* -S [1*revert* + *-er*] **:** one that reverts

**re·vert·ible** \|d·əbəl\ *adj* [ME, fr. *reverten* to revert + *-ible*] **:** that may revert or be reverted

**re·ver·tive** \|d·iv\ *adj* **:** reverting or tending to revert **:** RETURNING

**revery** *var of* REVERIE

**re·vest** \rə'vest, rē'-\ *vb* -ED/-ING/-S [ME *revesten*, fr. OF *revestir*, fr. LL *revestire* to clothe again, fr. L *re-* + *vestire* to clothe, fr. *vestis* garment — more at WEAR] *vt* **1 a** *obs* **:** to clothe in clerical vestments **:** ROBE **b** *obs* **:** to clothe (as oneself) anew **:** dress with fresh or different garments **c :** to put on (as a costume) again **:** RESUME **2 :** to vest again **:** REIN-

STATE, REINVEST ⟨~ a king in his kingdom⟩ ⟨lands ~*ed* in a former owner⟩ ~ *vi* : to take effect or vest again (as of a title) : revert to a former owner ⟨the title ~*ed* in A⟩

**re·ves·ti·ary** \-tē,erē\ *n* -ES [ME *revestiarie*, fr. MF] : VESTRY

**re·ves·try** \-trē\ *n* [ME, modif. (influenced by *vestrie* vestry) of MF *revestiarie*, fr. ML *revestiarium*, fr. *re-* + *vestiarium* vestry — more at VESTRY] : a place for the vesting of priests : VESTRY

**re·vet** \rə'vet, rē'-, *usu* -ed·+V\ *vt* **revetted; revetted; revetting; revets** [F *revêtir*, lit., to clothe again, dress up, dress, fr. OF *revestir*] : to face (as an embankment) with a revetment

**re·vête** \rə'vet\ *vt* -ED/-ING/-S [F *revêtir*] : REVET

**re·vête·ment** \rə'vetmäⁿ\ *n* -S [F, fr. MF *revestement*, fr. OF *revestir* to clothe again + *-ment*] : REVETMENT

**re·vet·ment** \rə'vetmənt, rē'-\ *n* -S [F *revêtement*] **1** : a facing of stone, concrete, fascines, or other material to sustain an embankment **2** : EMBANKMENT; *esp* : a bank or barricade (as of earth or sandbags) built up to provide shelter (as for planes, magazines, or personnel) against bomb splinters, strafing, or overrun of landing space

**re·victual** \(')rē+\ *vb* [*re-* + *victual*] *vt* : to supply (as an army) with a fresh stock of provisions ~ *vi* : to obtain fresh stocks of provisions — **re·victual·ment** \"+mənt\ *n* -S

**1re·vie** \(')rē¦vī\ *vb* -ED/-ING/-S [MF *renvier*, fr. *re-* + *envier* to challenge, vie — more at VIE] *vt* : to meet a wager on (as the taking of a trick in a card game) with a higher wager ~ *vi* **1** *obs* : to exceed an adversary's wager **2** *obs* : to make a retort : bandy words

**2revie** *n* -S [MF *renvi*, fr. *re-* + *envi* challenge, vie, fr. *envier*] *obs* : a higher wager (as in a card game) than an adversary's

**1re·view** \rə'vyü, rē'-\ *n* [MF *revue*, fr. fem. of *revu*, past part. of *revoir* to look over, fr. *re-* + *voir* to look, see — more at VIEW] **1** : a looking over or examination with a view to amendment or improvement : REVISION ⟨an author's ~ of his works⟩ **2** : an inspection (as of troops under arms or of a naval force) by a high officer (as for the purpose of ascertaining the state of discipline and equipment); *specif* : a march past a reviewing officer usu. following an inspection **3** : a general survey or view (as of the events of a period) ⟨take a ~ of the war⟩ ⟨pass one's life in ~⟩ **4** : an act of inspecting or examining : REVIEWING **5** : judicial reexamination (as of the proceedings of a lower tribunal by a higher) **6 a** : an explanatory and critical account of an artistic production or performance (as a book, play, exhibition, or concert) usu. in a periodical : CRITICISM, CRITIQUE **b** : a periodical containing primarily critical articles **7 a** : a second or repeated view : REEXAMINATION **b** : a retrospective view or survey (as of one's life) **c** (1) : renewed study (as at the end of a course or before an examination) of material previously studied (2) : an exercise designed to facilitate such study **8** : REVUE

**2review** \", *in senses 1&2* (')rē¦vyü\ *vb* [*re-* + *view*] *vt* **1** *archaic* : to view or see again **2** : to examine again : make a second or additional inspection of : study anew ⟨the officers viewed and ~*ed* the fortifications⟩ **3** [1*review*] **a** : to take a view of : examine with consideration or attention : SURVEY ⟨on ~*ing* all the circumstances⟩ **b** : to look back on : take a retrospective view of **4** : to reexamine judicially ⟨a higher court may ~ the proceedings and judgments of a lower one⟩ **5** : to go over or examine critically or deliberately: as **a** *obs* : to subject to revision (as a manuscript before printing or a book for a new edition) **b** : to go over with critical examination in order to discover excellences or defects; *also* : to give a critical examination of ⟨~ a new novel⟩ **6** : to make a formal or official examination of the state of (as troops) : hold a review of ⟨~ a regiment⟩ **7** : to recapitulate (previous calls in the auction of the current deal) in a bridge game ~ *vi* : to make a review ⟨~*ing* for a test⟩; *usu* : to write reviews : be a reviewer

**re·view·abil·i·ty** \rə,vyüə'biləd·ē\ *n* : the quality or state of being reviewable

**re·view·able** \rə'vyüəbəl\ *adj* : subject to review : capable of being reviewed

**re·view·al** \-üəl\ *n* -S **1** : an act of reviewing : REVISION **2** : a literary review : CRITICISM

**re·view·er** \rə'vyüə(r), rē'-, -yü(ə)r, -yüə\ *n* : one that reviews or reexamines: as **a** : one that examines publications critically and writes his opinion of them for publication : a professional critic of books : a review writer **b** *obs* : REVISER **c** *obs* : one that looks back **d** : a clerk that examines insurance applications to see whether they are properly filled out and whether they introduce suitable risks

**reviewing authority** *n* : one having authority to review some decision; *esp* : a military commander to whom the record of a court-martial trial is submitted for review and approval

**re·view·less** \-yüləs\ *adj* : receiving or meriting no review ⟨~ paperbacks⟩

**re·vig·or·ate** \rə'vigə,rāt\ *vt* -ED/-ING/-S [ML *revigoratus*, past part. of *revigorare* to make strong again, fr. L *re-* + LL *vigorare* to make strong, fr. L *vigor* strength — more at VIGOR] : REINVIGORATE

**1re·vile** \rə'vīl, rē'-, *esp before pause or consonant* -īəl\ *vb* -ED/-ING/-S [ME *revilen*, fr. MF *reviler* to despise, regard as vile, fr. *re-* + *-viler* (fr. *vil* vile) — more at VILE] *vt* : to subject to verbal abuse : address or assail with opprobrious language : rail at ~ *vi* : to use contemptuous or opprobrious language : RAIL **syn** see SCOLD

**2revile** *n* -S *obs* : a reviling remark or speech; *also* : REVILING

**re·vile·ment** \-lmənt\ *n* -S : an act or instance or the practice of reviling

**re·vil·er** \-lə(r)\ *n* -S : one that reviles

**re·vil·ing·ly** *adv* : in a reviling manner

**re·vindicate** \(')rē+\ *vt* [*re-* + *vindicate*] : to vindicate again; *esp* : to demand and take back — **re·vindication** \(¦)rē+\ *n*

**rev·i·res·cence** \,revə'res³n(t)s\ *n* -S : the condition or fact of being virescent

**rev·i·res·cent** \¦==¦res³nt\ *adj* [L *revirescent-, revirescens*, pres. part. of *revirescere* to grow green again, fr. *re-* + *virescere* to grow green — more at VIRESCENT] : growing fresh or young again : REVIVING

**re·vis·abil·i·ty** \rə,vīzə'biləd·ē\ *n* : the quality or state of being revisable

**re·vis·able** \rə'vīzəbəl\ *adj* : capable of being revised : subject to or meriting revision ⟨a ~ estimate⟩

**re·vis·al** \-zəl\ *n* -S : an act of revising : REVISION ⟨the ~ of a manuscript⟩

**1re·vise** \rə'vīz, rē'-\ *vb* -ED/-ING/-S [MF *reviser*, fr. L *revisere* to look back, look again, freq. of *revidēre* to see again, fr. *re-* + *vidēre* to see — more at WIT] *vi* **1** *obs* : to look again, often, or back : look in retrospect : REFLECT **2** : to make a revision : be engaged in revision (as of a manuscript) ~ *vt* **1** : to look at or over again for the purpose of correcting or improving : go or read over to correct errors or make improvements ⟨~ a manuscript⟩ **2 a** : to make a new, amended, improved, or up-to-date version of : subject to revision ⟨~ a dictionary⟩ ⟨*revised* the game laws⟩ **b** : to provide with a new taxonomic arrangement ⟨*revising* the alpine ferns⟩ **syn** see CORRECT

**2revise** \"\ *n* -S **1** : an act of revising : REVIEW, REVISION, REEXAMINATION **2** : a printing proof taken from matter that incorporates changes marked in a previous proof **3** : a revised form

**revised edition** *n* : an edition (as of a book) incorporating major revisions by the author or an editor and often supplementary matter designed to bring it up to date — compare REISSUE, REPRINT

**re·vis·er** \-zə(r)\ *n* -S : one that revises something (as printer's proofs)

**re·vis·ible** \-zəbəl\ *adj* [1*revise* + *-ible*] : REVISABLE

**re·vi·sion** \rə'vizhən, rē'-\ *n* -S [F, fr. LL *revision-, revisio* fact of seeing again, fr. L *revisus* (past part. of *revidēre* to see again) + *-ion-, -io* -ion] **1** : an act of revising : reexamination or careful reading over for correction or improvement ⟨the ~ of a book⟩ **b** : something made by revising : a revised form or version **2** : a seeing again

**re·vi·sion·ary** \-zhə,nerē, -ri\ *also* **re·vi·sion·al** \-zhən³l, -zhnəl\ *adj* : of, relating to, or made up of revision

**re·vi·sion·ism** \-zhə,nizəm\ *n* -S **1** : advocacy of revision (as of an original doctrine or treaty) : the theory or practice of a revisionist **2** : a movement among socialists to modify Marxian socialism esp. so as to be evolutionary rather than revolutionary in spirit

**1re·vi·sion·ist** \-zh(ə)nəst\ *n* -S [*revision* + *-ist*] **1** : an advocate of revision (as of a court decision or an accepted attitude or point of view) **2** : REVISER **3** : an advocate of revisionism

**2revisionist** \"\ *adj* : advocating revision or revisionism; *esp* : seeking to reanalyze and re-present historical data in light of subsequent knowledge

**1re·visit** \(')rē+\ *vt* [*re-* + *visit* (v.)] **1** *obs* : to inspect or check anew : REEXAMINE **2** : to visit again : return to

**2revisit** \"\ *n* [*re-* + *visit* (n.)] : a second or subsequent visit

**re·vis·i·tant** \(')rē¦vizət³nt\ *adj or n* [1*revisit* + *-ant*] : REVISITING

**re·vis·i·ta·tion** \(¦)rē,vizə¦tāshən\ *n* [1*revisit* + *-ation*] : an act of revisiting

**re·vi·sor** \rə'vīzə(r), rē'-\ *n* -S [1*revise* + *-or*] : REVISER

**re·vi·so·ry** \-z(ə)rē, -ri\ *adj* [1*revise* + *-ory*] : having the power or purpose to revise : making or intended to make revision ⟨~ body⟩ ⟨a ~ function⟩

**re·visualize** \(')rē+\ *vt* [*re-* + *visualize*] : to bring again into view esp. as a mental image

**re·vi·tal·iza·tion** \(¦)rē,vīd·³lə¦zāshən\ *n* [*revitalize* + *-ation*] **1** : an act or instance of revitalizing **2** : something that is revitalized

**re·vitalize** \(')rē+\ *vt* [*re-* + *vitalize*] : to impart new life or vigor to : restore to a vigorous active state — **re·vitalizer** \"+\ *n*

**re·viv·abil·i·ty** \rə,vīvə'biləd·ē\ *n* : the quality or state of being revivable

**re·viv·able** \rə'vīvəbəl\ *adj* [*revive* + *-able*] : capable of being revived; *usu* : not wholly or permanently lifeless — **re·viv·ably** \-blē\ *adv*

**re·viv·al** \rə'vīvəl, rē'-\ *n* -S [*revive* + *-al*] **1** : an act or instance of reviving or the state of being revived : RESTORATION: as **a** : renewed attention to something (as to letters, a technique, or a custom) ⟨a ~ of the old independent spirit⟩ ⟨enjoyed the ~ of costume parties that season⟩ **b** : renewed performance of or interest in the drama and literature : a new presentation or publication (as of a play or book) **c** : a period of religious awakening : renewed interest in religion ⟨plans of the American Baptists to promote a nationwide ~ this year⟩; *also* : an evangelistic meeting or a series of evangelistic meetings often characterized by emotional excitement **d** (1) : reanimation from a state of languor or depression — used esp. of the health, spirits, or similar qualities (2) : restoration to consciousness or life **e** : renewed pursuit or cultivation or flourishing state of something (as commerce, arts, agriculture) ⟨a ~ of weaving⟩ **f** : renewed prevalence of something (as a practice or a fashion); *esp* : the reappearance of Gothic forms in 19th century architecture **2** : restoration of force, validity, or effect (as to a legal judgment) ⟨the ~ of a debt barred by limitation⟩ ⟨the ~ of a revoked will⟩ **3** : RECALL 2

**re·viv·al·ism** \-ə,lizəm\ *n* -S **1** : the spirit or kind of religion or the methods characteristic of religious revivals **2** : a tendency or desire to revive or restore

**re·viv·al·ist** \-ləst\ *n* -S **1** : a clergyman or layman who promotes religious revivals : an advocate of or participator in religious revivals; *specif* : a clergyman (as an evangelist) without a particular charge who goes about to promote revivals **2** : a reviver or restorer of something disused (as an earlier architectural or literary style) — **re·viv·al·is·tic** \=¦==¦listik\ *adj*

**re·vive** \rə'vīv, rē'-\ *vb* -ED/-ING/-S [ME *reviven*, fr. MF *revivre*, fr. L *revivere* to live again, fr. *re-* + *vivere* to live — more at QUICK] *vi* **1** : to return to consciousness or life : recover life, vigor, or strength : become reanimated or reinvigorated : become active, operative, valid, or flourishing again ⟨hope *revived* in him⟩ ⟨the drooping plants *revived* in the rain⟩ **2** : to recover the metallic state — used esp. of a metal ~ *vt* **1** : to restore to consciousness or life : REANIMATE, REVITALIZE **2** : to raise from languor, depression, or discouragement : bring into action after a suspension : make active, operative, valid, or flourishing again : REINVIGORATE **3** : to raise from a state of neglect or disuse : bring back (as into currency, use, performance) ⟨~ a play⟩ **4** : to renew in the mind or memory : bring to recollection : recall attention to ⟨*reviving* the scene in his mind⟩ **5 a** : to reduce or restore (as a metal after calcination) to the metallic state **b** : REVIVIFY **6** : REJUVENATE 3

**re·vive·ment** \-īvmənt\ *n* -S **1** *archaic* : REVIVAL **2** *obs* : a reviving influence : a cause of revival

**1re·viv·er** \-īvə(r)\ *n* -S : one that revives: as **a** : STIMULANT **b** : a preparation for restoring finish **c** : one that restores to use, reestablishes, or reintroduces something **d** : a renovator of old or outworn things (as buildings or clothes)

**2reviver** *n* -S *obs* : REVIVAL, REESTABLISHMENT

**re·viv·i·ca·tion** \(,)rē,vivə'kāshən\ *substand var of* REVIVIFICATION

**re·vivification** \(¦)rē+\ *n* [LL *revivification-, revivificatio*, fr. *revivificatus* (past part. of *revivificare* to restore to life) + *-ion-, -io* -ion] **1** : renewal or restoration of life : an act of recalling or restoring or the state of being recalled from death or apparent death or torpidity to life **2** : the process of chemically reviving (as a metal) or revivifying (as char) **3** : REVIVAL, RENEWAL, REINVIGORATION

**re·viv·i·fi·er** \(')rē¦vivə,fī(ə)r, rə'v-\ *n* [*revivify* + *-er*] : one that revivifies : REVIVER

**re·viv·i·fy** \-,fī\ *vb* [F *révivifier*, fr. LL *revivificare* to restore to life, fr. L *re-* + LL *vivificare* to make alive, vivify — more at VIVIFY] *vt* : to impart new life to : cause to revive: as **a** : REANIMATE, REINVIGORATE **b** : to restore to life : RESUSCITATE **c** (1) : REVIVE 5a (2) : to restore to a chemically active state : REACTIVATE ~ *vi* : REVIVE

**reviving** *adj* **1** : regaining an active state **2** : RESUSCITATIVE **3** : RENEWING — **re·viv·ing·ly** *adv*

**rev·i·vis·cence** \,revə'vis³n(t)s\ *also* **rev·i·vis·cen·cy** \-³nsē\ *or* **rev·i·ves·cence** \-'ves³n(t)s\ *or* **rev·i·ves·cen·cy** \-³nsē\ *n, pl* **reviviscences** *also* **reviviscencies** [*reviviscence, reviviscency* fr. L *reviviscere* to revive + E *-ence* or *-ency*; *revivescence, revivescency* alter. (influence of *-escence*) of *reviviscence, reviviscency*] : an act of reviving or the condition of being revived : renewal of life : restoration to life, vigor, or activity

**rev·i·vis·cent** \-'vis³nt\ *adj* [L *reviviscent-, reviviscens, revivescent-, revivescens*, pres. part. of *reviviscere, revivescere* to come to life again, fr. *re-* + *viviscere, vivescere* to come to life, incho. of *vivere* to live — more at QUICK] : able or disposed to revive : causing revival

**re·vi·vor** \rə'vīvə(r)\ *n* -S [alter. (influenced by *-or*) of 2*reviver*] : revival under English law of a suit that is abated

**rev·o·ca·bil·i·ty** \,revəkə'biləd·ē, -lətē, -i *also* ÷rə,vōk- *or* ÷rē,-\ *n* : the quality or state of being revocable

**rev·o·ca·ble** \'revəkəbəl *also* ÷rə'vōk- *or* ÷rē'-\ *adj* [ME, fr. MF, fr. L *revocabilis*, fr. *revocare* to call back, revoke + *-abilis* -able] : capable of being revoked — **rev·o·ca·ble·ness** *n* -ES — **rev·o·ca·bly** \-blē, -li\ *adv*

**rev·o·ca·tion** \,revə'kāshən, ,rē(,)vō'-\ *n* [ME *revocacioun*, fr. MF *revocation*, fr. L *revocation-, revocatio*, fr. *revocatus* (past part. of *revocare* to revoke) + *-ion-, -io* -ion] **1** *archaic* : an act of recalling or calling back or the condition of being recalled **2** : an act of revoking : the act by which one having the right annuls something previously done, a power or authority given, or a license, gift, or benefit conferred : REPEAL, REVERSAL, WITHDRAWAL ⟨the ~ of an edict⟩ ⟨subject to ~ of a license⟩ **3** *obs* : RECANTATION, RETRACTION

**rev·o·ca·tive** \'revə,kād·iv, rə'väkəd·-\ *adj* [L *revocatus* (past part.) + E *-ive*] : able or serving to revoke : REVOKING

**rev·o·ca·to·ry** \'revəkə,tōrē, rə'väk-\ *adj* [ME, fr. LL *revocatorius*, fr. L *revocatus* (past part. of *revocare* to revoke) + *-orius* -ory] : of or relating to revocation : tending to or involving revocation : REVOKING, RECALLING

**revoice** \(')rē+\ *vt* [*re-* + *voice*] **1** : to voice again : ECHO **2 a** : to refurnish with a voice **b** : to adjust (as an organ pipe) in tone

**re·vok·able** \rə'vōkəbəl\ *adj* [*revoke* + *-able*] : REVOCABLE

**1re·voke** \rə'vōk, rē'-\ *vb* -ED/-ING/-S [ME *revoken*, fr. MF *revoquer*, fr. L *revocare*, fr. *re-* + *vocare* to call — more at VOICE] *vt* **1** : to bring or call back: as **a** *obs* : RESTRAIN, CHECK, PREVENT **b** : to call or summon back **c** : to call back to mind or memory **d** *obs* : to restore to use or operation : REVIVE **2** : to annul by recalling or taking back (as something granted by a special act) : RESCIND, CANCEL, REPEAL ⟨~ a will⟩ ⟨~ a privilege⟩ **3** *obs* : WITHDRAW: as **a** : RECANT, RETRACT **b** : to take back : REASSUME, RECOVER **c** : to draw back ~ *vi* **1** : to make revocation **2** : to fail to follow suit when able in a card game in violation of the rule of the game : RENEGE

**syn** REVERSE, REPEAL, RESCIND, RECALL: REVOKE indicates an annulling or abrogating, esp. of something given or assigned, with formality or not ⟨*revoke* a license⟩ ⟨*revoke* a grant⟩ ⟨his power of attorney . . . has never been *revoked* —Hamilton Basso⟩ REVERSE may be a close synonym for REVOKE, esp. in indicating decision directly opposed to that previously made; it is often used of a higher agency or instrumentality acting on a lower ⟨the plate umpire *reversing* his decision after conferring with the others⟩ ⟨the superior court *reversing* the decision of the lower court⟩ REPEAL is likely to be used in reference to formal abrogation by constituted authority ⟨the legislature *repealed* the unpopular law the next year⟩ ⟨the eighteenth article of amendment to the Constitution of the United States is hereby *repealed* —*U.S. Constitution*⟩ RESCIND applies to abolishing, abrogating, or making void, sometimes with suggestions of summary or definitive procedure ⟨one body of customs after another was swept away; ordinances were overhauled or *rescinded* —F.A. Ogg & Harold Zink⟩ ⟨the legislature refused to function until martial law was *rescinded* —*Current Biog.*⟩ RECALL in this sense indicates a calling back, suspending, or abrogating, either finally as erroneous or ill-advised or tentatively for deliberation ⟨would have done anything to *recall* the word, as soon as it was out of his mouth —Margaret Kennedy⟩ ⟨*recall* a bridge bid⟩ ⟨*recall* a stringent edict⟩

**2revoke** \"\ *n* -S **1** : ANNULLING, CANCELLATION; *also* : RECALL **2** : an act or instance of revoking in a card game

**revokement** *n* -S *obs* : REVOCATION

**re·vok·er** \-kə(r)\ *n* -S : one that revokes

**re·vok·ing·ly** *adv* : in a revoking manner : so as to revoke

**revol** *abbr* revolution

**re·volatilize** \(')rē+\ *vt* [*re-* + *volatilize*] : to volatilize again or anew

**1re·volt** \rə'vōlt, rē'- *sometimes* -vȯlt\ *vb* -ED/-ING/-S [MF *revolter*, fr. OIt *rivoltare* to turn over, overthrow, fr. (assumed) VL *revolvitare*, freq. of L *revolvere* to roll back, revolve — more at REVOLVE] *vi* **1** : to renounce allegiance or subjection : desert (as a party, leader, or formerly a religion) for another : go over to another : turn away from a party, leader, or duty **2 a** : to be disgusted, shocked, or grossly offended : feel disgust or nausea : turn or rise in disgust or repugnance — used with *at* or *against* ⟨the stomach ~*s* at such food⟩ ⟨his nature ~*s* against such treatment⟩ **b** : to turn away or shrink with disgust or loathing — usu. used with *from* ⟨~*ing* from such a scene of carnage⟩ ~ *vt* **1** *obs* : to cause to turn back **2** : to cause to turn away or shrink with disgust or abhorrence : affect with disgust or loathing : NAUSEATE ⟨such acts ~ the conscience⟩ ⟨is ~*ed* by the indecency of hanging —R.G.G.Price⟩

**2revolt** \"\ *n* -S [MF *revolte*, fr. *revolter* to revolt] **1** : a casting off of allegiance : an uprising against legitimate authority : a renunciation of allegiance and subjection (as to a government) : INSURRECTION ⟨the ~ of a province⟩; *also* : the act of revolting **2** : a movement or expression of vigorous dissent or refusal to accept ⟨iconoclasm is a ~ against image worship⟩ **3** : a change of party or opinion ⟨transitory parties rising in ~ against rigid old guard conservatism⟩ **syn** see REBELLION

**3revolt** \"\ *n* : REVOLTER

**re·volt·er** \-tə(r)\ *n* -S : one that revolts : REBEL

**re·volt·ing** *adj* : giving rise to disgust or shock : strongly offensive : NAUSEATING ⟨~ cant about the duty of obedience —Henry Adams⟩ **syn** see OFFENSIVE

**re·volt·ing·ly** *adv* : in a revolting manner : so as to be revolting ⟨~ sordid details⟩

**re·volt·ress** \-l·trəs\ *n* -ES [*revolter* + *-ess*] : a female revolter

**re·vo·lu·ble** \'revəlyəbəl, rə'väl-\ *adj* [L *revolubilis*, fr. *revolvere* to revolve + *-ibilis* -ible] : capable of revolving : REVOLVABLE, ROTATING — **rev·o·lu·bly** \-blē\ *adv*

**1rev·o·lute** \'revə,lüt, -əl,yüt, *usu* -üd·+V\ *adj* [L *revolutus*, past part. of *revolvere* to revolve] : rolled backward or downward ⟨a leaf with ~ margins⟩ — compare CONVOLUTE, INVOLUTE

**2revolute** \"\ *vi* -ED/-ING/-S [back-formation fr. 1*revolution*] : to make or undergo revolution

**rev·o·lut·ed** \-üd·əd\ *adj* [L *revolutus* (past part. of *revolvere* to revolve) + E *-ed*] : REVOLUTE

**1rev·o·lu·tion** \,revə'lüshən *also* -əl'yü-\ *n* -S [ME *revolucioun*, fr. MF *revolution*, fr. LL *revolution-, revolutio*, fr. L *revolutus* (past part. of *revolvere* to roll back, revolve) + *-ion-, -io* -ion — more at REVOLVE] **1 a** (1) : the act of a celestial body of going around in an orbit or elliptic course; *also* : apparent movement of such a body around the earth — usu. distinguished from *rotation* (2) : the time taken by a celestial body to make a complete round in its orbit (3) : the rotation of a celestial body on its axis — not used technically **b** : completion of a course (as of years); *also* : the period made by the regular succession of a measure of time or by a succession of similar events **c** *obs* : CYCLE, EPOCH **d** *archaic* : RECURRENCE, REPETITION **e** (1) : a progressive motion of a body around a center or axis such that any line of the body remains throughout parallel to its initial position to which it returns on completing the circuit (2) : motion of any figure about a center or axis in which each point of the figure traces a circular arc of the same angular size about its projection on the axis as center ⟨the ~ of a right-angled triangle about one of its legs generates a cone⟩ (3) : ROTATION 1b ⟨a bell rings for each ~ of the hectograph⟩ **2** : alteration or change in some matter or respect: as **a** : a sudden, radical, or complete change ⟨a ~ in thought⟩ : a basic reorientation and reorganization ⟨a ~ in technology⟩ **b** : a fundamental change in political organization or in a government or constitution : the overthrow or renunciation of one government or ruler and the substitution of another by the governed **c** : profound crustal movement involving mountain-making and other physical changes on a continent-wide or world-wide scale; *also* : the interval of time during which such a movement occurs **3 a** *archaic* : a turning over in the mind or in discussion : PONDERING, CONSIDERATION **b** *obs* : a winding or curving form or course : TWIST, BEND **syn** see REBELLION

**2revolution** \"\ *vt* -ED/-ING/-S : REVOLUTIONIZE

**rev·o·lu·tion·al** \¦revə¦lüshən³l, -shnəl *also* -əl¦yü-\ *adj* : REVOLUTIONARY — **rev·o·lu·tion·al·ly** \-³lē, -əlē, -i\ *adv*

**rev·o·lu·tion·ar·i·ly** \¦==¦==shə¦nerəlē\ *adv* : in a revolutionary manner : so as to be revolutionary

**rev·o·lu·tion·ar·i·ness** \,==¦==,nerēnəs\ *n* -ES : the quality or state of being revolutionary

**1rev·o·lu·tion·ary** \¦revə¦lüshə,nerē, -ri *also* -əl¦yü-\ *adj* [1*revolution* + *-ary*] **1** : of, relating to, or having the nature of a revolution ⟨a ~ war⟩ ⟨a ~ party⟩ **2** : tending to, promoting, or involving revolution ⟨~ motion⟩ ⟨a ~ speech⟩ ⟨~ improvements in technique⟩; *often* : RADICAL, EXTREMIST ⟨a ~ outlook⟩ **3** *usu cap* : of or relating to the American Revolution or to the period in which it occurred ⟨*Revolutionary* history⟩ ⟨*Revolutionary* costume⟩

**2revolutionary** \"\ *n* -ES : REVOLUTIONIST

**revolution counter** *n* : a mechanism tallying the elapsed revolutions of a piece of apparatus and often indicating as well the instantaneous rotational speed

**rev·o·lu·tion·eer·ing** \,==¦==shə'niriŋ\ *n* -S [1*revolution* + *-eering* (as in *engineering*)] : the promoting or conducting of revolutions

**rev·o·lu·tion·er** \,==¦==sh(ə)nə(r)\ *n* -S : one that supports or is engaged in a revolution : REVOLUTIONIST

**rev·o·lu·tion·ism** \-shə,nizəm\ *n* -S : revolutionary acts or practices : revolutionary doctrines or principles : advocacy of such doctrines or principles

**1rev·o·lu·tion·ist** \-sh(ə)nəst\ *n* -S [1*revolution* + *-ist*] : one engaged in a revolution : a favorer of revolution : one who advocates revolutionary doctrines or principles

**²revolutionist** \¦==¦=(=)=\ *adj* **:** of or relating to revolution or revolutionists ⟨~ doctrines⟩

**rev·o·lu·tion·ize** \,==ˈ=shə,nīz\ *vb* -ED/-ING/-S *see -ize in Explan Notes* [¹*revolution* + *-ize*] *vt* **1 :** to change fundamentally or overthrow completely the established government of **2 :** to make revolutionary **:** imbue with revolutionary doctrines or principles **3 :** to change completely or fundamentally ~ *vi* **:** to undergo revolution

**rev·o·lu·tion·iz·er** \-zə(r)\ *n* -S **:** one that revolutionizes ⟨~ of heavy industry⟩

**re·volv·able** \rəˈvälvəbəl\ *adj* **:** capable of being revolved — **re·volv·ably** \-blē\ *adv*

**¹re·volve** \rəˈvälv, rēˈ-, -ˈvȯlv *also* -ˈvä(ů)v *or* -ˈvȯv\ *vb* -ED/-ING/-S [ME *revolven*, fr. L *revolvere* to roll back, fr. *re-* + *volvere* to roll — more at VOLUBLE] *vt* **1** *obs* **:** to turn (the eyes or sight) back or around **2 :** to consider or meditate upon at length or repeatedly considering various aspects and phases (as in seeking a solution or reaching a decision) ⟨*revolving* a scheme to get a pension for his brother⟩ ⟨*revolved* the story in his mind as he waited⟩ **3** *obs* **:** to turn or bring back **:** RESTORE **4** *archaic* **:** to skim or search through (as a book) **:** turn the pages of; *also* **:** to read through **:** STUDY **5** *obs* **:** to wrap up **:** BIND **6 a :** to cause to go around in an orbit **b :** to cause to turn around on or as if on an axis **:** ROTATE ~ *vi* **1 a** *obs* **:** RETURN **b :** to come around again **:** RECUR **2 a :** to meditate on something **:** consider deliberately **:** PONDER ⟨with thoughts *revolving* upon his holiday plans⟩ **b :** to be a source or cause of meditation ⟨the idea continued to ~ in his mind⟩ **3 a :** to move in a curved path around a center or axis ⟨the planets ~ around the sun⟩ — compare REVOLUTION 1e(1) **b :** to turn or roll around on or as if on an axis like a wheel **:** ROTATE — compare REVOLUTION 1e(2) **4 :** to come to a center or focal point **:** PIVOT ⟨the whole household ~s about the baby⟩ **syn** see CONSIDER, TURN

**²revolve** \"\ *n* -S **:** an act or instance of revolving **:** REVOLUTION

**re·volve·ment** \-vmənt\ *n* -S **:** an act of revolving or the condition of being revolved ⟨the periodic ~ of funds⟩

**re·vol·ven·cy** \-vənsē\ *n* -ES **:** a capacity or tendency to revolve

**re·volv·er** \-və(r)\ *n* -S [¹*revolve* + *-er*] **1 :** a handgun having a cylinder of several chambers that are brought successively into line with the barrel and discharged with the same hammer — compare PISTOL **2 :** the particular indeterminate form assumed by the three-point problem in surveying or navigating when the point of observation falls on a circle through the three fixed points **3 :** one that revolves; *esp* **:** a revolving device

**re·volv·ered** \-(r)d\ *adj* **:** bearing a revolver

**revolving** *adj* **1 :** that revolves or rotates or recurs ⟨grief returns with the ~ year —P.B.Shelley⟩; *esp* **:** recurrently available ⟨scrap metal is our one great ~ industrial resource —*Canadian Purchasor*⟩ — see REVOLVING CREDIT, REVOLVING FUND **2** *of a firearm* **:** having a cylinder or a series of barrels that turn about a common longitudinal axis — **re·volv·ing·ly** *adv*

**revolving credit** *n* **:** a credit which may be used repeatedly up to the limit specified after partial or total repayments have been made

**revolving die holder** *n* **:** a releasing die head

**revolving door** *n* **:** an outer door (as of a public building) consisting of two or more flaps revolving together on a common vertical axis within a cylindrical vestibule and having the flaps so constructed or arranged as to prevent the direct passage of air through the vestibule

revolving door

**revolving field alternator** *n* **:** an alternator operating by stationary conductors and rotating field magnets

**revolving fund** *n* **:** a fund set up for specified purposes with the proviso that repayments to the fund may be used again for these purposes ⟨a *revolving fund* to make loans to disabled veterans going into business ventures⟩

**revolving letter of credit :** a letter of credit authorizing drafts up to a specified amount and permitting additional drafts to be drawn up to the amount of accepted drafts previously paid off

**revolving light** *n* **:** FLASHLIGHT a(2)

**revolving plug** *n* **:** the rotating part of a cylinder lock **:** the part into which the key is inserted

**revolving storm** *n* **:** CYCLONE

**re·vomit** \(ˈ)rē+\ *vt* [*re-* + *vomit*] **:** to vomit up **:** vomit forth again

**re·vote** \"+\ *vt* [*re-* + *vote*] **:** to regrant by voting

**revs** *pl of* REV, *pres 3d sing of* REV

**re·vue** \rəˈvyü, rēˈ-\ *n* -S [F, fr. MF, review — more at REVIEW] **:** a light theatrical entertainment consisting of brief items (as sketches, songs, monologues) in which recent events and esp. plays of the past year are satirically reviewed **:** a medley of songs, tableaux vivants, and chorus dances with light skits

**re·vu·ist** \-üəst\ *n* -S [F *revuiste*, fr. *revue* + *-iste* -ist] **:** a writer of revues

**re·vulsed** \rəˈvəlst\ *adj* [L *revulsus* (past part. of *revellere* to draw back) + E *-ed*] **:** affected with or having undergone revulsion

**re·vul·sion** \rəˈvəlshən, rēˈ- *sometimes* -lzh-\ *n* -S [L *revulsion-*, *revulsio* act of pulling away, fr. *revulsus* (past part. of *revellere* to pull away, fr. *re-* + *vellere* to pull, pluck) + *-ion-*, *-io* -ion — more at VULNERABLE] **1 :** an act or technique of turning or diverting a disease or blood from a diseased region in one part of the body to another (as by counterirritation) **2 :** a strong pulling or drawing back or away **:** WITHDRAWAL ⟨public ~ from such political cynicism⟩ **3 a :** a sudden or strong reaction, reversion, or change ⟨a ~ of mood⟩ **b :** a sense or mood of utter distaste or repugnance **:** REPULSION ⟨met his advances with ~⟩ ⟨a scene of utmost ~⟩

**re·vul·sion·ary** \-ə,nerē\ *adj* **:** of, relating to, or constituting a revulsion

**¹re·vul·sive** \rəˈvəlsiv, rēˈ-, -sēv *also* -səv\ *adj* [L *revulsus* (past part.) + E *-ive*] **:** causing or tending to revulsion — **re·vul·sive·ly** \-səvlē, -li\ *adv*

**²revulsive** \"\ *n* -S **:** something that causes revulsion

**revved** *past of* REV

**revving** *pres part of* REV

**revvs** *pres 3d sing of* REV

**rew** \ˈrü\ *chiefly dial var of* RUE

**re·wake** \(ˈ)rē+\ *or* **re·waken** \"+\ *vb* [*re-* + *wake* or *waken*] *vt* **:** to waken again or anew ~ *vi* **:** to become once more awake (~ to her opportunity⟩

**¹re·ward** \rəˈwȯ(ə)rd, rēˈ-, -ȯ(ə)d\ *vb* -ED/-ING/-S [ME *rewarden*, fr. ONF *rewarder* to reward, regard, look at, fr. *re-* + *warder* to watch over, guard, of Gmc origin; akin to OHG *wartēn* to watch, take care — more at WARD] *vt* **1** *obs* **a :** to give or assign to as due **:** recompense or requite with **b :** to give (as a hawk or hound) a share or particular part of prey usu. when taken **2 :** to make a return or give a reward to (as a person) or for (as a service or accomplishment) ⟨~*ing* his friends and repaying his enemies⟩ ⟨~ small personal services generously⟩ ~ *vi* **:** to give rewards **:** make requital

**²reward** \"\ *n* -S [ME, fr. ONF, fr. *rewarder* to reward] **1 :** something that is given in return for good or evil done or received ⟨one of our fine old members . . . who passed to his ~ —R.T.Smith⟩ and esp. that is offered or given for some service or attainment (as a prize for excellence in studies, a sum of money for the return of something lost or for the capture of a criminal) **:** RECOMPENSE, REQUITAL ⟨thy great misdeeds have met a due ~ —John Dryden⟩ **2** *obs* **a :** ¹QUARRY 1a **b :** REMUNERATION; *esp* **:** extra pay **c :** an extra supply of food **:** an extra dish **3 :** compensation for services **:** a sum of money paid or taken for doing or forbearing to do some act (as for furnishing information leading to the arrest and conviction of criminals or for restoring lost property) **4 :** PROFIT

**re·ward·able** \-dəbəl\ *adj* **:** subject to or meriting reward — **re·ward·able·ness** *n* -ES

**re·ward·ed·ly** \-dədlē\ *adv* **:** in a rewarded manner

**re·ward·er** \-də(r)\ *n* -S [ME, fr. *rewarden* to reward + *-er*] **:** one that rewards

**re·ward·ful** \-dfəl\ *adj* **:** offering or productive of reward ⟨~ pursuits⟩ — **re·ward·ful·ness** *n* -ES

**rewarding** *adj* **1 :** valuable and pleasing **:** yielding or likely to yield a reward ⟨reading is a ~ pastime⟩ ⟨a most ~ meeting⟩ **2 :** offered by way of reward **:** serving as or suitable for a reward ⟨a warmly ~ smile of thanks⟩ — **re·ward·ing·ly** *adv*

**re·ward·less** \-dləs\ *adj* **:** receiving no reward

**re·warehouse** \(ˈ)rē+\ *vt* [*re-* + *warehouse*] **:** to return to a warehouse **:** store anew under warehouse conditions

**re·wa·re·wa** \ˈrewəˈrewə\ *n* -S [Maori] **1 :** a slender New Zealand tree (*Knightia excelsa*) resembling the Lombardy poplar in habit but yielding a valuable timber **2 :** the strong heavy mottled red wood of the rewa-rewa — called also *New Zealand honeysuckle*

**re·warm** \(ˈ)rē+\ *vt* [*re-* + *warm*] **:** to make warm again

**re·warper** \"+\ *n* [*re-* + *warper*] **:** a textile worker who rewinds yarn from the warp beam for dyeing

**rewash** \"+\ *vt* [*re-* + *wash*] **:** to wash anew or again and again ⟨waves ~ and undermine the cliffs⟩ ⟨~*ing* mine tailings for color⟩

**re·water** \"+\ *vt* [*re-* + *water*] **:** to provide anew with water ⟨rains ~*ing* the hills⟩

**re·waybill** \"+\ *vt* [*re-* + *waybill*] **:** to provide (as freight at a junction point) with a new waybill

**re·weaken** \"+\ *vb* [*re-* + *weaken*] *vt* **:** to cause to become weak again ⟨wind had ~*ed* the timbers⟩ ~ *vi* **:** to become weak again **:** yield anew to weakness ⟨afraid she would ~ and agree to go⟩

**re·weave** \"+\ *vt* [*re-* + *weave*] **:** to make whole by or as if by weaving

**re·wed** \"+\ *vb* [*re-* + *wed*] **:** REMARRY

**re·weigh** \"+\ *vt* [*re-* + *weigh*] **:** to weigh again or anew — **re·weigher** \"+\ *n*

**re·weld** \"+\ *vt* [*re-* + *weld*] **:** to reunite or make secure by or as if by welding

**re·wet** \"+\ *vt* [*re-* + *wet*] **:** to make wet again

**re·win** \"+\ *vt* [*re-* + *win*] **:** REGAIN

**¹re·wind** \"+\ *vt* [*re-* + *wind*] **:** to wind again ⟨~ yarn⟩; *esp* **:** to reverse the winding of (a motion-picture film, magnetic tape, or wire) on a reel usu. so as to place the beginning on the outside of the roll

**²re·wind** \ˈrē+,-, =ˈ=\ *n* **1 :** something that has been rewound **2 :** an act of rewinding **3 :** a device for rewinding something; *esp* **:** a mechanism for rewinding motion-picture film consisting of a mounted reel or roll hub rotated manually or by an electric motor

**re·winder** \(ˈ)rē+\ *n* **:** one that rewinds something: as **a :** an operator of a machine for rewinding yarn, cloth, paper **b** [*re-* + *winder*] (1) **:** REWIND 3 (2) **:** a machine that takes paper from a reel and winds it onto a core and usu. slits and trims the edges at the same time

**re·wir·able** \(ˈ)rē¦wīrəbəl\ *adj* **:** capable of being rewired ⟨a ~ electric fixture⟩

**re·wire** \(ˈ)rē+\ *vt* [*re-* + *wire*] **1 :** to wire (as a house, a cable, an electric machine) anew **2 :** to telegraph (as a message) or telegraph to (as a person) in return

**re·wood** \"+\ *vt* [*re-* + *wood*] **:** REFOREST

**re·word** \"+\ *vt* [*re-* + *word*] **1 :** to put into words again **:** repeat in the same words **2 :** to alter the wording of **:** restate in other words ⟨~ a message⟩

**re·work** \"+\ *vt* [*re-* + *work*] **:** to work again or anew ⟨decided to ~ the old mine⟩: as **a :** to reorganize and revise ⟨~*ing* an old legend in a contemporary scene⟩ **b :** to reprocess (used, imperfect, or discarded material) for further use ⟨~ condemned butter⟩ **c :** to subject again after a lapse of time to the action of a geologic agent ⟨sediment . . . has been ~*ed* and redeposited —G.L.Knight⟩

**re·workable** \"+\ *adj* **:** fit to be reworked ⟨~ scrap⟩

**reworked wool** *n* **:** wool that has been used and is subsequently reprocessed for further use — compare SHODDY

**re·wound** \"+\ *vt* [*re-* + *wound*] **:** to wound again or afresh

**¹re·write** \"+\ *vb* [*re-* + *write*] *vt* **1 :** to write in reply **:** answer in writing **2 :** to make a revision or recast of (as a paragraph, story, or article): as **a :** to put (material supplied to a newspaper or periodical by a collector or contributor) into form for publication **b :** to alter (previously published material) for use in another publication ~ *vi* **:** to revise or recast something previously written ⟨an author usu. spends a good deal of time *rewriting*⟩: as **a :** to rewrite material supplied to a newspaper or periodical by a collector or contributor **b :** to alter previously published material for use in another publication

**²re·write** \ˈrē+,-\ *n* -S **:** a piece of writing (as an article or news story) constructed by rewriting ⟨a complete ~ of the first draft of a novel⟩

**rewrite man** *n* **:** a newspaperman who specializes in rewriting

**re·writer** \(ˈ)rē¦rīd·ə(r), -ītə-\ *n* [¹*rewrite* + *-er*] **:** one that rewrites; *specif* **:** REWRITE MAN

**¹rex** *n pl* [origin unknown] *obs* **:** PRANKS — used in the phrase *to play rex*

**²rex** \ˈreks\ *n, pl* **re·ges** \ˈrē,jēz\ [L, king — more at ROYAL] **1 :** KING **2** *usu cap* **:** the presiding masquer in a Mardi Gras festival or parade (as at New Orleans)

**³rex** \"\ *n, pl* **rexes** *or* **rex** [NL, fr. L, king] **1 :** a genetic variation esp. of the domestic rabbit and various rodents which behaves as a simple recessive and in which the guard hairs are shorter than the undercoat or entirely lacking **2 :** an animal or fur exhibiting the rex characteristic

**⁴rex** \"\ *vt* -ED/-ING/-ES **:** to breed (as rabbits) selectively for the establishment of the rex variation

**rex begonia** *n* **:** any of various rhizomatous begonias derived from an East Indian species (*Begonia rex*) and having variegated heavily-veined rough-textured leaves, thick hairy stems, and usu. insignificant flowers

**rex·ine** \ˈrek,sīn\ *n* -S [²*rex* + *-ine*] *Brit* **:** a strong coated cloth usu. imitating leather and used esp. for bookbinding

**rex·ist** \ˈreksəst\ *n* -S *usu cap* [F *rexiste*, fr. *rex-* (fr. *Christus Rex*, title of a publication issued by founders of the party) + *-iste* -ist] **:** a member of a Belgian fascist political party established in 1935

**rey** \ˈrā\ *n, pl* **re·yes** \ˈrā,(y)ās\ [Sp, fr. L *reg-, rex*] **:** KING

**rey·kja·vik** \ˈrākyə,vēk, -vik\ *adj, usu cap* [fr. *Reykjavik*, Iceland] **:** of or from Reykjavik, the capital of Iceland **:** of the kind or style prevalent in Reykjavik

**reyn** \ˈrān\ *chiefly Scots var of* REIN

**rey·nard** \(ˈ)rā¦närd, ˈre,n-, -nåd, ˈrānə(r)d, ˈrenə(r)d\ *n* -S *often cap* [ME *Renard*, fox who is the hero of the French medieval beast epic *Roman de Renart*, fr. MF *Renart, Renard, Regnard*] **:** FOX

**reyn·olds number** \ˈrenᵊldz-\ *n, usu cap R* [after Osborne *Reynolds* †1912 Eng. physicist] **:** an abstract number characteristic of the flow of a fluid in a pipe or past an obstruction used esp. in the testing of scale models of airplanes in a wind tunnel **:** the ratio of the product of the density of the fluid, the flow velocity, and a characteristic linear dimension of the body under observation to the coefficient of absolute viscosity

**re·youth** \(ˈ)rē+\ *vt* -ED/-ING/-S [*re-* + *youth*] **:** to make (as oneself) young again

**re·zai** *or* **re·sai** \rəˈzäē\ *n* -S [Hindi *razāī*, fr. Per] **:** a cotton-filled coverlet or mattress of India

**rez·ban·yite** \ˈrez'ban,yīt\ *n* -S [G *rezbanyit*, fr. *Rézbánya*, Hungary (now *Băiţa*, Romania) + G *-it* -ite] **:** a mineral $Pb_3Cu_2Bi_{10}S_{19}$ consisting of lead, copper, and bismuth sulfide and occurring in metallic-gray granular masses (sp. gr. 6.1–6.4)

**rez-de-chaus·sée** \,rāchōˈsā\ *n* -S [F, lit., level of the street] **:** the ground story of a building whether on a level with the street or slightly above it — used esp. of a building on the continent of Europe

**re·zone** \(ˈ)rē+\ *vt* [*re-* + *zone*] **:** to zone anew **:** alter the zoning of ⟨~ a street⟩

**rf** *abbr* **1** refunding **2** rinforzando **3** roof

**RF** *abbr* **1** *often not cap* radio frequency **2** range finder **3** rapid fire **4** reducing flame **5** representative fraction **6** reserve force **7** rheumatic fever **8** right field **9** right foot **10** right forward **11** right front **12** rough finish

**RFB** *abbr* right fullback

**RFC** *abbr* radio-frequency choke

**RFD** *abbr* rural free delivery

**rfg** *abbr* **1** refunding **2** roofing

**RFG** *abbr* rapid-fire gun

**rfl** *abbr* refuel

**rfn** *abbr* rifleman

**rfr** *abbr* roofer

**rf station** *n, usu cap R&F* [Radio Frequency] **:** a radio beacon that transmits radio signals equally in all directions

**rfz** *abbr* rinforzando

**RG** *abbr* **1** red-green **2** *often not cap* reduction gear **3** right guard **4** rolled gold

**rgr** *abbr* ringer

**rgt** *abbr* regiment

**rh** *usu cap R, var of* RH FACTOR

**rH** *symbol* the negative logarithm of the pressure in atmospheres of hydrogen gas that would exist at an electrode in equilibrium with an oxidation-reduction system and that serves as a measure of the state of oxidation-reduction of the system ⟨where linear relationships hold ~ is of importance and care should be taken to restrict its use only to such systems —H.T.S.Britton⟩ — compare PH

**RH** *abbr* **1** *often not cap* relative humidity **2** right halfback **3** right hand **4** Rockwell hardness **5** roundhouse **6** Royal Highness

**Rh** *symbol* rhodium

**rhabd** \ˈrabd\ *n* -S [NL *rhabdus*] **:** RHABDUS

**rhabd-** *or* **rhabdo-** *comb form* [LGk, fr. Gk, fr. *rhabdos* rod — more at VERVAIN] **1 :** rod **:** stick ⟨*rhabdo*nema⟩ **2 :** rodlike structure ⟨*rhabdo*lith⟩ ⟨*rhabdo*some⟩

**rhab·di·on** \ˈrabdē,än\ *n* -S [NL, fr. Gk, little rod, dim. of *rhabdos* rod] **:** any of the sclerotized segments making up the lining of the buccal cavity of a nematode worm

**rhab·dite** \ˈrab,dīt\ *n* -S [*rhabd-* + *-ite*] **1 :** one of the minute, smooth, rodlike or fusiform structures produced in the cells of the epidermis or in cells sunk within the underlying parenchyma of many turbellarians and a few trematodes and discharged in great numbers in the mucous secretions of these animals **2 :** one of the paired appendages that unite to form the ovipositor in some insects

**¹rhab·ditid** \(ˈ)rab¦did·əd, -¦did·əd\ *adj* [NL *Rhabditidae*] **:** of or relating to the Rhabditidae or Rhabditida

**²rhabditid** \"\ *n* -S **:** a rhabditid worm

**rhab·dit·i·da** \rabˈdid·ədə\ *n pl, cap* [NL, fr. *Rhabditis* + *-ida*] **:** a large order of Aphasmidia comprising free-living and parasitic nematode worms having the esophagus more or less clearly divided into three regions, usu. three or six lips, and the musculature meromyarian or polymyarian

**rhab·dit·i·dae** \-id·ə,dē\ *n pl, cap* [NL, fr. *Rhabditis*, type genus + *-idae*] **:** a large family of nematode worms that with related forms comprises a superfamily of the order Rhabditida

**rhab·dit·i·form** \-id·ə,fȯrm\ *adj* [NL *Rhabditis* + E *-iform*] **:** RHABDITOID

**rhab·di·tis** \rabˈdēd·əs\ *n, cap* [NL, fr. Gk *rhabdos* rod] **:** a genus (the type of the family Rhabditidae) of minute nematode worms having the esophagus clearly divided into three regions, dwelling in soil and organic debris, and occas. behaving as facultative parasites

**rhab·di·toid** \ˈrabdə,tȯid\ *adj* [NL *Rhabditis* + E *-oid*] **1 :** resembling or related to the genus *Rhabditis* **2** *of a larval nematode* **:** having the esophagus functional and with an enlarged pharyngeal bulb like that of a rhabditid

**rhab·di·um** \ˈrabdēəm\ *n, pl* **rhab·dia** \-ēə\ [NL, fr. Gk *rhabdion*, dim. of *rhabdos* rod] **:** a striated muscle fiber

**rhab·do·car·pon** \,rabdōˈkär,pän\ *or* **rhab·do·car·pum** \-,pəm\ [NL, fr. *rhabd-* + *-carpon, -carpum* (fr. Gk *karpos* fruit) — more at HARVEST] *syn of* RHABDOCARPUS

**rhab·do·car·pus** \-,pəs\ *n, cap* [NL, fr. *rhabd-* + *-carpus*] **:** a form genus of Paleozoic fossil plants based on seeds and now known to belong for the most part to the genus *Cordaites*

**rhab·do·coel** *or* **rhab·do·coele** \ˈrabdə,sēl\ *adj* [NL *Rhabdocoela*] **:** of or relating to the order Rhabdocoela

**rhab·do·coe·la** \,rabdəˈsēlə\ *n pl, cap* [NL, fr. *rhabd-* + *-coela -coele*] **:** an order of Turbellaria comprising small marine, freshwater, or rarely terrestrial flatworms with simple unbranched intestine — **rhab·do·coe·lan** \¦==¦=lən\ *adj or n* — **rhab·do·coe·lid** \-ləd\ *or* **rhab·do·coe·lous** \-ləs\ *adj*

**rhab·do·coele** \ˈrabdə,sēl\ *n* -S [NL *Rhabdocoela*] **:** a flatworm of the order Rhabdocoela

**¹rhab·do·coe·li·da** \,rabdəˈsēlədə\ *n pl, cap* [NL, fr. *Rhabdocoela* + *-ida*] *in former classifications* **:** an order or other division of Turbellaria including the Alloiocoela, the Rhabdocoela, and sometimes the Acoela — **rhab·do·coe·li·dan** \¦==¦=ləd·ᵊn\ *adj or n*

**²rhabdocoelida** \"\ [NL, fr. *rhabd-* + *coel-* + *-ida*] *syn of* RHABDOCOELA

**¹rhab·doid** \ˈrab,dȯid\ *adj* [NL *rhabdoides*, fr. Gk *rhabdoeidēs* like a rod, striped, fr. *rhabd-* + *-oeidēs* -oid — more at RHABD-] **1 :** shaped like a rod **2 :** RHABDOIDAL

**²rhabdoid** \"\ *n* -S **:** a rhabdite or similar body in the integument of a flatworm

**³rhabdoid** \"\ *n* -S **:** a rod-shaped protoplasmic body in the sensitive cells of leaves of various plants of the family Droseraceae — **rhab·doi·dal** \(ˈ)rab¦dȯidᵊl\ *adj*

**rhab·do·lith** \ˈrabdə,lith\ *n* -S [ISV *rhabd-* + *-lith*] **:** a minute calcareous rodlike structure found both at the surface and on the bottom of the ocean

**rhab·dom** \ˈrab,däm, -dəm\ *or* **rhab·dome** \-,dōm\ *n* -S [LGk *rhabdōma* bundle of rods, fr. Gk *rhabdos* rod] **:** one of the minute rodlike structures in the retinulae in the compound eyes of arthropods — **rhab·do·mal** \(ˈ)=¦dōməl, ˈ=,dəm-\ *adj*

**rhab·do·man·cer** \ˈrabdə,man(t)sə(r)\ *n* -S [*rhabdomancy* + *-er*] **:** one who practices rhabdomancy

**rhab·do·man·cy** \-sē\ *n* -ES [LGk *rhabdomanteia*, fr. Gk *rhabd-* (fr. *rhabdos* rod) + *manteia* divination — more at VERVAIN, -MANCY] **:** divination by rods or wands

**rhab·do·mere** \ˈrabdə,mi(ə)r\ *n* -S [*rhabdom* + *-mere*] **:** a division of a rhabdom

**rhab·dom·o·nas** \rabˈdämənəs, -,nas\ *n, cap* [NL, fr. *rhabd-* + *-monas*] **:** a genus of motile, elongated, often spindle-shaped sulfur bacteria (family Thiorhodaceae) usu. rose-red in color

**rhab·do·myoma** \,rab(,)dō+\ *n* [NL, fr. *rhabd-* + *myoma*] **:** a benign tumor composed of striated muscle fibers

**rhab·do·myosarcoma** \"+\ *n* [NL, fr. *rhabd-* + *my-* + *sarcoma*] **:** a malignant rhabdomyoma

**rhab·doph·a·ga** \rabˈdäfəgə\ *n, cap* [NL, fr. *rhabd-* + *-phaga*] **:** a widely distributed genus of gall midges

**rhab·do·phane** \ˈrabdə,fān\ *n* -S [G *rhabdophan*, fr. *rhabd-* + *-phan* -phane] **:** a brown, pinkish, or yellowish white hydrous phosphate (Ce, Y, La, etc.,)$(PO_4).H_2O$ of cerium, yttrium, and rare-earth elements occurring massive

**rhab·doph·a·nite** \rabˈdäfə,nīt\ *n* -S [G *rhabdophan* + E *-ite*] **:** RHABDOPHANE

**rhab·doph·o·ra** \rabˈdäfərə\ [NL, fr. *rhabd-* + *-phora*] *syn of* GRAPTOLITOIDEA

**rhab·doph·o·ran** \-fərən\ *n* -S **:** GRAPTOLITE

**rhab·do·pleu·ra** \,rabdəˈplürə\ *n, cap* [NL, fr. *rhabd-* + Gk *pleura* side, rib — more at PLEURISY] **:** a widely distributed genus of marine compound animals having two tentacle-bearing arms and usu. classed as hemichordates in the order Pterobranchia

**rhab·do·pod** \ˈrabdə,päd\ *n* -S [*rhabd-* + *-pod*] **:** one of the rodlike styles of the males of many insects

**rhab·do·some** \ˈrabdə,sōm\ *n* -S [*rhabd-* + *-some*] **:** a colonial graptolite derived from a single individual

**rhabds** *pl of* RHABD

**rhab·dus** \ˈrabdəs\ *n* -ES [NL, fr. Gk *rhabdos* rod — more at VERVAIN] **:** a simple uniaxial sponge spicule

**rhachi-** *or* **rhachio-** — see RACHI-

**rha·chi·a·nec·tes** \,rākēəˈnek(,)tēz\ *n, cap* [NL, fr. Gk *rhachia* surf, beach + NL *-nectes*] **:** a genus of whalebone whales comprising solely the gray whale

**rhach·i·tome** \ˈrakə,tōm\ *n* -S [NL *Rhachitomi*] **:** an amphibian of the order Rhachitomi

**rha·chit·o·mi** \rəˈkid·ə,mī, raˈk-\ *n pl, cap* [NL, fr. *rachi-* + *-tomi* (fr. Gk *tomos* cut, slice) — more at TOME] : an order of Labyrinthodontia including most of the larger Permian amphibians and comprising forms having rhachitomous vertebrae, relatively stocky salamandriform bodies, and in some cases external gills

**rha·chit·o·mous** *also* **ra·chit·o·mous** \rəˈkid·əməs, (ˈ)raˌk-\ *adj* [*rachi-* + *-tomous*] : being, having, or relating to vertebrae with centra of which the parts remain separate, an intercentrum wedge-shaped and ventral, and separate pleurocentra above and behind the intercentra

**rhaco·mit·ri·um** \ˌrakōˈmi·trēəm, ˌrāk-\ *n, cap* [NL, fr. Gk *rhakos* ragged garment + *mitrion*, dim. of *mitra* headband — more at MITER] : a genus of acrocarpous mosses (family Grimmiaceae) growing chiefly on sandstone rocks and having often hair-pointed leaves and sinuous leaf cells

**rha·coph·o·rus** \rəˈkäfərəs, raˈk-\ [NL, fr. Gk *rhakos* ragged garment + NL *-phorus*] *syn of* POLYPEDATES

**rhad·a·man·thine** \ˌradəˈman(t)thən, -an,thīn\ *adj, often cap* [*Rhadamanthus*, one of the judges in the lower world + E *-ine*] : of, relating to, or characteristic of Rhadamanthus; *esp* : rigorously just ⟨a ~ judgment —A.C.Benson⟩ ⟨morals to become less ~ —*Times Lit. Supp.*⟩

**rhad·a·man·thus** \-an(t)thəs\ *n* -ES *usu cap* [after *Rhadamanthus*, son of Zeus and Europa in Greek mythology who for his exemplary justice was made one of the judges of souls in the lower world, fr. L, fr. Gk *Rhadamanthos, Rhadamanthys*] : an extremely strict judge

[1]**rhae·tian** *also* **rhe·tian** \ˈrēsh(ē)ən\ *n* -S *cap* [L *rhaetus* rhaetian + E *-an*] **1** : a native or inhabitant of ancient Rhaetia **2** : RHAETO-ROMANIC

[2]**rhaetian** *also* **rhetian** \"\ *adj, usu cap* [L *Rhaetia*, ancient Roman province south of the Danube river corresponding with Tirol and the Grisons (fr. *Rhaeti* Rhaetians + *-ia* -y) + E *-an*] **1** : of or relating to ancient Rhaetia **2** : of or relating to the people of ancient Rhaetia

**rhae·tic** \ˈrēd·ik\ *n, cap* [L *rhaeticus* of Rhaetia, fr. *Rhaetia* + *-icus* -ic] **1** : an ancient language of Rhaetia of unknown relationship **2** : RHAETO-ROMANIC

**rhaeto-romanic** *or* **rhaeto-romance** *or* **rhaeto-romansh** *or* **rheto-romance** *or* **rheto-romansh** \ˌrēd·(ˌ)ō+\ *n, cap both Rs* [*rhaeto-, rheto-* (fr. L *rhaetus* Rhaetian) + *romanic* or *romance* or *romansh*; trans. of G *rätoromanisch*] : a Romance language of eastern Switzerland, northeastern Italy, and adjacent parts of Austria — see FRIULIAN, ROMANSH

**rhag·a·des** \ˈragə,dēz\ *n pl* [L, fr. Gk, pl. of *rhagas* rent, chink, fissure on the skin; akin to Gk *rhēgnynai* to break, OSlav *rězati* to cut, slaughter] : linear cracks or fissures in the skin, occurring esp. at the angles of the mouth or about the anus

**rha·gad·i·form** \rəˈgadə,fȯrm\ *adj* [Gk *rhagad-, rhagas* fissure + E *-iform*] : having or characterized by cracks or fissures ⟨~ eczema⟩

**rha·gio·crine cell** \ˈrājēə,krin-, -rīn-,-rēn-\ *n* [*rhagiocrine* ISV *rhagio-* (fr. Gk *rhagion*, dim. of *rhag-, rhax* berry, grape) + *-crine* (fr. Gk *krinein* to separate) — more at RAISIN, CERTAIN] : HISTIOCYTE

[1]**rhag·i·o·nid** \ˈrajēə,nid\ *adj* [NL *Rhagionidae*] : of or relating to the Rhagionidae

[2]**rhagionid** \"\ *n* -S : an insect of the family Rhagionidae

**rhag·i·on·i·dae** \ˌrajēˈänə,dē\ *n pl, cap* [NL, fr. *Rhagion-, Rhagio*, type genus (fr. Gk *rhagion*, a spider, dim. of *rhag-, rhax* malmignatte, grape, berry) + *-idae*] : a widely distributed family of predaceous two-winged flies having usu. a tapering body, long slender legs, and sometimes a conspicuous downward-projecting proboscis

**rha·go·dia** \rəˈgōdēə\ *n, cap* [NL, fr. Gk *rhagōdēs* like grapes (fr. *rhag-, rhax* grape + *-ōdēs* -ode) + NL *-ia*] : a genus of Australian shrubs or herbs (family Chenopodiaceae) with small greenish spicate or panicled flowers succeeded by fleshy berries

**rhag·o·le·tis** \ˌragəˈlēd·əs\ *n, cap* [NL, irreg. fr. Gk *rhag-, rhax* malmignatte] : a genus of trypetid flies containing many whose larvae feed on fruits and berries — see APPLE MAGGOT, CHERRY FRUIT FLY

**rhagon** \ˈrā,gän, ˈra,-\ *n* -S [NL, fr. Gk *rhag-, rhax* grape, berry] **1** : LEUCON **2** : a sponge or sponge larva of leuconoid structure in which the flagellated chambers are few in number and often adjoin the paragaster — **rhagonoid** *adj or n*

**rhamn-** *comb form* [ISV, fr. NL *Rhamnus*] : buckthorn : rhamnose ⟨*rhamn*itol⟩

**rham·na·ce·ae** \ramˈnāsē,ē\ *n pl, cap* [NL, fr. *Rhamnus*, type genus + *-aceae*] : a widely distributed family (order Rhamnales) of thorny shrubs and trees having undivided stipulate leaves and cymose flowers with the stamens opposite the petals and a superior ovary that becomes a 3-celled capsule or a drupe — **rham·na·ceous** \(ˈ)ramˈnāshəs\ *adj*

**rham·na·les** \ramˈnā(ˌ)lēz\ *n pl, cap* [NL, fr. *Rhamnus* + *-ales*] : an order of dicotyledonous woody plants in which the stamens are equal in number with the sepals and alternate with them and the ovary is surrounded by a disk

**rham·na·zin** \ˈramnəzən, ramˈnazᵊn\ *n* -S [*rhamn-* + *-azin* (fr. *azine*)] : a pale yellow crystalline dye $C_{17}H_{14}O_7$ occurring as a glycoside esp. in Persian berries; a dimethyl ether of quercetin

**rham·ne·tin** \ˈramnətən\ *n* -S [ISV *rhamn-* + *-etin* (as in *quercetin*)] : a yellow crystalline dye $C_{16}H_{12}O_7$ that is obtained by hydrolysis of xanthorhamnin from Persian berries and is a methyl ether of quercetin

**rham·ni·nose** \-nōs *also* -nōz\ *n* -S [ISV *rhamn-* + *-in* + *-ose*] : a crystalline reducing trisaccharide sugar $C_{18}H_{32}O_{14}$ obtained by hydrolysis of xanthorhamnin and on further hydrolysis yielding rhamnose and galactose

**rham·ni·tol** \ˈramnə,tōl, -tȯl\ *n* -S [*rhamn-* + *-itol*] : a crystalline pentahydroxy alcohol $C_6H_9(OH)_5$ obtained by reducing rhamnose

**rham·nonic acid** \(ˈ)ramˈnänik-, -ˈnōnik\ *n* [ISV *rhamn-* + *-onic*] : an acid $CH_3(CHOH)_4COOH$ obtained by oxidation of rhamnose

**rham·nose** \ˈram,nōs *also* -ōz\ *n* -S [ISV *rhamn-* + *-ose*] : a crystalline aldose sugar $CH_3(CHOH)_4CHO$ obtained in the common dextrorotatory L form usu. by hydrolysis of xanthorhamnin, quercitrin, and other rhamnosides; 6-deoxy-mannose — compare GLUCOSE

**rham·no·side** \ˈramnə,sīd\ *n* -S [*rhamnose* + *-ide*] : a glycoside (as xanthorhamnin, quercitrin, frangulin, hesperidin) that yields rhamnose on hydrolysis

**rham·nus** \ˈramnəs\ *n, cap* [NL, fr. Gk *rhamnos* buckthorn — more at VERVAIN] : a genus (the type of the family Rhamnaceae) of trees and shrubs having strongly pinnately veined leaves, small perfect or polygamous flowers with the ovary free from the disk, and a fruit that is an oblong or globular drupe with two to four stones — compare RHAMNALES; see BUCKTHORN, LOKAO

**rhamph-** *or* **rhampho-** *comb form* [Gk, fr. *rhamphos*; akin to Gk *rhabdos* rod — more at VERVAIN] : beak : crooked beak ⟨*Rhampho*charus⟩ ⟨*rhamph*oid⟩

**ram·phas·ti·dae** \ramˈfastə,dē\ [NL, fr. *Rhamphastos* + *-idae*] *syn of* RAMPHASTIDAE

**rhamphastos** [NL — more at RAMPHASTOS] *syn of* RAMPHASTOS

**rham·phoid** *also* **ram·phoid** \ˈram,fȯid\ *adj* [*rhamph-* + *-oid*] : shaped like a beak ⟨~ cusp⟩

[1]**rham·pho·rhyn·chid** \ˌram(p)fəˈriŋkəd\ *adj* [NL *Rhamphorynchidae*] : of or relating to the genus *Rhamphorhynchus* or the family Rhamphorhynchidae

[2]**rhamphorhynchid** \"\ *n* -S : a rhamphorhynchid pterosaur

**rham·pho·rhyn·choid** \ˌ==ˈ=ˌkȯid\ *adj* [NL *Rhamphorhynchus* + E *-oid*] : resembling or related to the genus *Rhamphorhynchus*

**rham·pho·rhyn·chus** \ˌ==ˈ=ˌkəs\ *n, cap* [NL, fr. *rhamph-* + *-rhynchus*] : a genus (the type of the family Rhamphorhynchidae) of pterosaurs having an elongated tail supporting a leathery expansion at the tip and slender forwardly directed teeth

**rham·pho·the·ca** \ˌram(p)fəˈthēkə\ *n* -S [NL, fr. *rhamph-* + *theca*] : the horny sheath composed of modified scales of a bird's bill

**rh antigen** *n, usu cap R* : RH FACTOR

**rhap** *abbr* rhapsody

**rhaphe** *var of* RAPHE

**rha·pon·tic** \rəˈpäntik\ *n* [NL *rhaponticum*, fr. *rha ponticum* pontic rhubarb, fr. LL *rha* rhubarb + L *ponticum*, neut. of *ponticus* pontic — more at RHUBARB, PONTIC] **1** *archaic* : either of two European knapweeds (*Centaurea centaurium* and *C. rhaponticum*) **2** *archaic* **a** : a rhubarb (*Rheum rhaponticum*) **b** : the root of this plant used in pharmacy

**rha·pon·ti·gen·in** \ˌrə,päntəˈjenən\ *n* -S [ISV *rhapontin* + *-genin*] : a crystalline phenol $C_{15}H_{14}O_4$ derived from stilbene and obtained by hydrolysis of rhapontin

**rha·pon·tin** \rəˈpäntᵊn\ *or* **rha·pon·ti·cin** \-təsən\ *n* -S [ISV *rhapontic* + *-in*] : a crystalline glucoside $C_{21}H_{24}O_9$ found in rhubarb

**rhap·sode** \ˈrap,sōd\ *n* -S [F, fr. Gk *rhapsōidos* — more at RHAPSODY] : RHAPSODIST

**rhapsoder** *n* -S [*rhapsody* + *-er*] *obs* : a collector of literary pieces

**rhap·sod·ic** \(ˈ)rapˈsädik, -dēk\ *adj* [Gk *rhapsōidikos*, fr. *rhapsōidos* rhapsodist + *-ikos* -ic] **1 a** : characteristic or suggestive of a rhapsody : having the form or manner of a rhapsody ⟨the first movement . . . is loose and ~ in form —Douglas Watt⟩ ⟨a ~ gypsy air —Sara R. Watson⟩ **b** : given to expression or composition in the form or manner of the rhapsody ⟨a ~ composer whose music is fed on the most outspoken type of romantic fervor —Nicolas Slonimsky⟩ **2** : extravagantly emotional : RAPTUROUS ⟨the ~ quality of the program notes —Robert Lawrence⟩ ⟨the most laudatory, if not downright ~, adjectives —Bernard Kalb⟩ ⟨a terrible bliss of self-love, a ~ egotism —Peggy Bennett⟩ ⟨sent ~ greetings —Sidney Wallach⟩ **3** : of or relating to the recitation of rhapsodies ⟨the ~ exhibitions of ancient Greek festivals⟩

**rhap·sod·i·cal** \-dəkəl, -dēk-\ *adj* [Gk *rhapsōidikos* rhapsodic + E *-al*] **1** *archaic* : of a disconnected or fragmentary style ⟨the reader of this ~ work —Laurence Sterne⟩ **2** : RHAPSODIC

**rhap·sod·i·cal·ly** \-dək(ə)lē, -dēk-, -li\ *adv* : in a rhapsodic manner : RAPTUROUSLY

**rhap·so·dist** \ˈrapsədəst\ *n* -S [[1]*rhapsody* + *-ist*] **1** *obs* : ANTHOLOGIST **2** : one who recites a rhapsody; *esp* : a professional reciter of epic poems (as of Homer) **3** : one who recites or sings poems for a livelihood **4** : one who writes or speaks rhapsodically ⟨any ~ of motorcars —Edmund Wilson⟩ — **rhap·so·dis·tic** \ˌ==ˈdistik, -tēk\ *adj*

**rhap·so·dize** \ˈrapsə,dīz\ *vb* -ED/-ING/-S [[1]*rhapsody* + *-ize*] *vt* **1** *archaic* : to patch together (as stories) : make a medley of ⟨*rhapsodizing* all these affairs —Laurence Sterne⟩ **2** : to utter or recite as or in the manner of a rhapsody ~ *vi* : to indulge in rhapsody : utter rhapsodies ⟨~ about a new book⟩ ⟨heard friends ~ about a dinner —*Harper's Bazaar*⟩

[1]**rhap·so·dy** \ˈrapsədē, -di\ *n* -ES [L *rhapsodia*, fr. Gk *rhapsōidia*, fr. *rhapsōidos* rhapsodist (fr. *rhaptein* to sew, stitch together + *ōidē* ode, song) + *-ia* -y; akin to Gk *rhepein* to bend, incline, *rhapis* rod, ON *orf, orb* handle of a scythe, OHG *worf* handle of a scythe, Lith *verpti* to spin, and prob. to L *repens* sudden — more at ODE] **1** : a recitation or song of a rhapsodist : a portion of an epic poem (as a book of the *Iliad* or *Odyssey*) adapted for recitation **2** *archaic* : a literary work consisting of disconnected pieces; *also* : a miscellaneous collection or disconnected series : MEDLEY, JUMBLE ⟨a ~ of words —Shak.⟩ **3 a** : an ecstatic or highly emotional utterance or literary work : effusively incoherent and extravagant discourse ⟨a speech that bordered upon ~⟩ ⟨recite a long ~ to the joys of viewing America from a caboose —R.P.Cooke⟩ ⟨the novel ends in a kind of meditative ~ —Mark Schorer⟩ **b** : RAPTURE, ECSTASY ⟨reading poetry often seems a state of ~ in which rhyme and meter and sound stir the mind as wine and dance stir the body —Virginia Woolf⟩ **4** : an instrumental composition that is irregular in form like an improvisation or free fantasia **syn** see BOMBAST

[2]**rhapsody** \"\ *vb* -ED/-ING/-ES : RHAPSODIZE

**rha·son** *or* **ra·son** \ˈrä,sȯn\ *n* -S [MGk *rhason*, a napless woolen cloth, rhason, perh. fr. L *rasus*, past part. of *radere* to scrape, scratch, shave — more at RAT] *Eastern Church* **1** : an ecclesiastical garment resembling the cassock **2** : a long loose cloak worn over the rhason — called also *exorhason*

**rhas·o·phore** *or* **ras·o·phore** \ˈrazə,fō(ə)r\ *n* -S [MGk *rhasophoros* fr. *rhason* + Gk *-phoros* -phore] *Eastern Church* : a member of a monastic order who has not yet passed through the novitiate : NOVICE

**rhat·a·ny** \ˈratᵊnē\ *n* -ES [Sp *ratania* & Pg *ratânhia*, fr. Quechua *ratánya*] **1** : the dried root of either of two American shrubs (*Krameria triandra* and *K. argentea*) that is used as an astringent — see PARÁ RHATANY, PERUVIAN RHATANY **2** : a plant that yields rhatany

**rha·thy·mia** \rəˈthīmēə\ *n* -S [Gk, fr. *rhathymos* lighthearted, easy-tempered, carefree (fr. *rha* easy, ready + *thymos* spirit, mind, courage) + *-ia* -y — more at FUME] : the state of being carefree : LIGHT-HEARTEDNESS

**RHB** *abbr* right halfback

**rhd** *abbr* railhead

**rhe** \ˈrē\ *n* -S [Gk *rhein* to flow — more at STREAM] : the cgs unit of fluidity : the reciprocal of poise

[1]**rhea** \ˈrēə\ *n* [NL, prob. fr. *Rhea*, mother of Zeus and other gods in Greek mythology, fr. L, fr. Gk] **1** *cap* : a genus of large tall flightless So. American birds (order Rheiformes) that resemble but are smaller than the African ostrich, have three toes, a fully feathered head and neck, an undeveloped tail, and pale gray to brownish feathers that droop over the rump and back **2** -S : any bird of the genus *Rhea* or broadly of the order Rheiformes comprising as surviving forms only a larger bird (*R. americana*) ranging from Brazil to Patagonia and a smaller (*Pterocnemia pennata*) from the highlands of Peru to the Straits of Magellan — called also *nandu*

[2]**rhea** \ˈrēˈä\ *n* -S [Assamese *rihā*] : CHINA GRASS

**rhe·a·dine** *or* **rhoe·a·dine** \ˈrēə,dēn, -dᵊn\ *n* -S [ISV *rhead-, rhoead-* (fr. NL *rhoead-, rhoeas* — specific epithet of the corn poppy *Papaver rhoeas* — fr. Gk *rhoiad-, rhoias* corn poppy) + *-ine*] : a nonpoisonous crystalline alkaloid $C_{21}H_{21}NO_6$ found in various poppies (as the corn poppy)

**rhe·bok** *or* **ree·bok** \ˈrē,bäk\ *n, pl* **rhebok** *or* **rheboks** [Afrik *reebok*, fr. MD *reeboc* male of the roe deer, fr. *ree* roe deer + *boc* buck; akin to OE *rā* roe deer and to OE *buc* buck — more at ROE, BUCK] : a southern African antelope (*Pelea capreolus*) nearly as large as the fallow deer but having the form and habits of the chamois and being light gray with short upright horns

**rhe·buck** \ˈrē,bək\ *n, pl* **rhebuck** *or* **rhebucks** [part trans. of Afrik *reebok*] : RHEBOK

**rheg·nop·teri** \regˈnäptə,rī\ [NL, fr. Gk *rhēgnynai* to break, break loose, burst forth + *pteron* wing, feather — more at RHAGADES, FEATHER] *syn of* POLYNEMOIDEA

**rhe·ic acid** \ˈrēik-\ *n* [*rheic* fr. *rhe-* (fr. NL *Rheum*) + *-ic*] : CHRYSOPHANIC ACID

**rhe·idae** \ˈrēə,dē\ *n pl, cap* [NL, fr. *Rhea*, type genus + *-idae*] : a family of birds coextensive with the order Rheiformes

**rhe·ifor·mes** \ˌrēəˈfȯr(ˌ)mēz\ *n pl, cap* [NL, fr. *Rhea* + *-iformes*] : an order of birds that are intermediate in some respects between the ostriches and the emus and cassowaries and that comprise the recent and extinct rheas

**rheims** *usu cap, var of* REIMS

**rhe·in** \ˈrēən\ *n* -S [ISV *rhe-* (fr. NL *Rheum*) + *-in*] : a yellow crystalline acid $C_{15}H_8O_6$ occurring esp. in rhubarb and senna leaves; 4,5-dihydroxy-2-anthraquinone-carboxylic acid

**rhe·mish** \ˈrēmish\ *adj, usu cap* [*Rheims* (*Reims*), city in northeastern France + E *-ish*] : REIMS

**rhenish** \ˈrenish, ˈrēn-, -nēsh\ *adj, usu cap* [L *Rhenus* Rhine, river in western Europe flowing from Switzerland through Germany and the Netherlands into the North Sea + E *-ish*] : of or relating to the river Rhine or the region on or near it esp. in Germany ⟨*Rhenish* wine⟩ ⟨*Rhenish* Confederation⟩

**rhenish architecture** *n, usu cap R* : the German Romanesque architecture of the Rhine valley combining native elements with others derived from Byzantine and esp. Lombard architecture

**rhe·ni·um** \ˈrēnēəm\ *n* -S [NL, fr. L *Rhenus* Rhine river + NL *-ium*] : a rare heavy polyvalent metallic element that resembles manganese chemically, that occurs esp. in molybdenite, gadolinite, columbite, or platinum ores, that is obtained either as a black or grayish powder by ignition in hydrogen usu. of a perrhenate or as a silver-white hard metal (as by sintering the powder), and that is usu. used in catalysts for dehydrogenation and in thermocouples — symbol *Re;* see ELEMENT table

**rheo-** *comb form* [Gk *rheos* anything flowing, stream, fr. *rhein* to flow — more at STREAM] : flow : current ⟨*rheo*taxis⟩ ⟨*rheo*stat⟩

**rheo** *abbr* rheostat

**rheo·base** \ˈrēō+,-\ *n* [ISV *rheo-* + *base*] : the minimal electrical current required to excite a tissue (as nerve or muscle) given indefinitely long time during which the current is applied — compare CHRONAXIE — **rheo·basic** \ˌrēō+\ *adj*

**rhe·o·log·i·cal** \ˌrēəˈläjəkəl\ *also* **rhe·o·log·ic** \-jik\ *adj* [*rheology* + *-ical* or *-ic*] : of or relating to rheology or to the phenomena of flowing matter ⟨the fundamental ~ properties of metals —*Technical News Bull.*⟩ ⟨~ properties of cheddar cheese —*Biol. Abstracts*⟩ — **rhe·o·log·i·cal·ly** \-jək(ə)lē\ *adv*

**rhe·ol·o·gist** \rēˈäləjəst\ *n* -S [*rheology* + *-ist*] : a specialist in rheology

**rhe·ol·o·gy** \-jē\ *n* -ES [ISV *rheo-* + *-logy*] : a science dealing with the deformation and flow of matter

**rhe·om·e·ter** \rēˈämәd·ə(r)\ *n* [ISV *rheo-* + *-meter*] : an instrument for measuring the flow of viscous substances — **rheo·met·ric** \ˌrēəˈme·trik\ *adj* — **rhe·om·e·try** \rēˈämə·trē\ *n* -ES

**rheo·mor·phic** \ˌrēəˈmȯrfik\ *adj* [*rheomorphism* + *-ic*] : of or relating to rheomorphism

**rheo·mor·phism** \ˌrēəˈmȯr,fizəm\ *n* -S [*rheo-* + *-morphism*] : metamorphism in which flow of the solid rock fabric is conspicuous

**rheo·pexy** \ˈrēə,peksē\ *n* -ES [*rheo-* + *-pexy*] : the accelerated gelation of a thixotropic sol brought about by jarring the containing vessel, by slow stirring, or by pouring

**rheo·phile** \ˈrēə,fīl\ *also* **rheo·phil** \-,fil\ *adj* [ISV *rheo-* + *-phile, -phil*] : preferring or living in flowing water ⟨~ fauna⟩

**rhe·oph·i·lous** \(ˈ)rēˈäfələs\ *adj* [*rheo-* + *-philous*] : RHEOPHILE

**rheo·plankton** \ˌrēō+\ *n* [*rheo-* + *plankton*] : plankton of running waters (as of rivers)

**rhe·o·stat** \ˈrēə,stat, *usu* -ad·+V\ *n* -S [*rheo-* + *-stat*] : a resistor for regulating a current by means of variable resistances — compare RESISTANCE BOX — **rhe·o·stat·ic** \ˌ==ˈstad·ik, -atˌ|ēk\ *adj*

**rheo·tac·tic** \ˌrēəˈtaktik\ *adj* [*rheo-* + *-tactic*] : relating to or exhibiting rheotaxis ⟨~ response⟩

**rheo·taxis** \ˌrēəˈtaksəs\ *n, pl* **rheotaxes** [NL, fr. *rheo-* + *-taxis*] : a taxis in which mechanical stimulation by a stream of fluid (as water) is the directive factor

**rheo·trope** \ˈrēə,trōp\ *n* -S [ISV *rheo-* + *-trope*] : a commutator for reversing a current

**rheo·trop·ic** \ˌrēəˈträpik\ *adj* [*rheotropism* + *-ic*] : relating to or exhibiting rheotropism

**rhe·ot·ro·pism** \rēˈä·trə,pizəm\ *n* [ISV *rheo-* + *tropism*] : a tropism in which mechanical stimulation by a stream of fluid (as water) is the orienting factor ⟨many motile animals . . . exhibit either positive or negative ~ —P.S.Welch⟩

**rhes** *pl of* RHE

**rhe·sus factor** *or* **rhesus antigen** \ˈrēsəs-\ *n* : RH FACTOR

**rhesus monkey** *or* **rhesus** *also* **rhesus macaque** *n* -ES [*rhesus* fr. NL] : a pale brown Indian monkey (*Macaca mulata*) of active and playful disposition often kept in zoological gardens and much used in medical research

**rhetian** *usu cap, var of* RHAETIAN

**rhetor** \ˈrēd·ə(r), ˈred·ə-\ *n* -S [ME *rethor*, modif. of L *rhetor*, fr. Gk *rhētōr*] : RHETORICIAN 1

**rhet·o·ric** \ˈred·ərik, -etə-\ *n* -S [ME *rethorik*, fr. MF *rethorique*, modif. of L *rhetorica*, fr. Gk *rhētorikē*, fr. fem. of *rhētorikos* rhetorical, oratorical, fr. *rhētor-, rhētōr* orator + *-ikos* -ic — more at WORD] **1** : the art of expressive speech or discourse; *specif* : **a** : the study of principles and rules of composition formulated by ancient critics (as Aristotle and Quintilian) and interpreted by classical scholars for application to discourse in the vernacular **b** : the art or practice of writing or speaking as means of communication or persuasion often with special concern for literary effect ⟨freshman composition is a course in ~ —H.C.Bowersox⟩ ⟨the cultivation of grammar and ~ —John Dewey⟩ **2 a** : skill in the effective use of speech : ELOQUENCE **b** (1) : artificial elegance of language : discourse without conviction or earnest feeling (2) : inflated language : VERBOSITY, BOMBAST ⟨that passage, sir, is not empty ~ —Virginia Woolf⟩ ⟨the enemy of ~ and every kind of artifice and virtuosity —Philip Rahv⟩ ⟨the mocking ~ upon a tombstone —J.C.Powys⟩ **c** : style of language ⟨his ~ would not have been commended at Cambridge⟩ ⟨large, and sometimes loose, exalted simplicities of his ~ —*Times Lit. Supp.*⟩ **3 a** : verbal communication : DISCOURSE, SPEECH ⟨the temptation to establish peace by ~ —W. W. Van Kirk⟩ ⟨a ~ of fantastic slang —Edmund Wilson⟩ **b** : the verbal content of a composition (as a poem) or a body of literature ⟨the deep hold that the symbols of free speech and other civil liberties have in the American ~ —Max Lerner⟩ **c** : the verbal elements employed in or characteristic of discourse relating to a particular subject or area ⟨made effective use of the ~ of liberalism —Sidney Hook⟩ **4** : persuasive or moving power ⟨mastery of expressive musical ~ —Carl Parrish & J.F.Ohl⟩ ⟨sweet, silent ~ of persuading eyes —Samuel Daniel⟩ **5** : a treatise on rhetoric; *esp* : a textbook on literary composition ⟨the authors of freshman ~*s* —C.W.Shumaker⟩

**rhe·tor·i·cal** \rəˈtȯrəkəl, -tär-, -rēk-\ *also* **rhe·tor·ic** \rəˈtȯrik, -tär-, -rēk\ *adj* [*rhetorical* fr. ME, fr. L *rhetoricus* rhetorical (fr. Gk *rhētorikos*) + E *-al*; *rhetoric* fr. ME *rethorick*, fr. MF *rethorique*, modif. of L *rhetoricus*] **1 a** : of, relating to, or concerned with rhetoric ⟨accepted two or three verbal and ~ changes that I suggested —W.A.White⟩ ⟨make science, in part, at least, a subject for ~ discourse —*Quarterly Journ. of Speech*⟩ ⟨the ~ sin of the meaningless variation —Lewis Mumford⟩ **b** : employed for rhetorical effect ⟨don't remember a single decorative or ~ word in his first ten cantos —Ezra Pound⟩ — often used without regard to some actual condition or circumstance qualifying or negating the literal significance of the statement ⟨must have known that he was acting too late to stay the legislators' stampede to vote and adjourn, so his message was partly ~ —*New Republic*⟩ ⟨the offer was ~, with no certainty . . . that the money would be paid at all —T.E. Lawrence⟩ ⟨an essentially ~ charge —Rupert Emerson⟩ **2 a** : given to rhetoric : emphasizing style often at the expense of thought : GRANDILOQUENT, BOMBASTIC ⟨wrote long ~ speeches like operatic solos, regarding my plays as musical performances —E.R.Bentley⟩ ⟨an essay on friendship, high-flown, ~ —H.S.Canby⟩ ⟨flamboyant and ~ tastes, which produced the most beautiful architecture of the past —Stephen Spender⟩ **b** : employing or relating to speech or oratory esp. in contradistinction to other modes of communication or contest ⟨the actual thought of a real war, not a ~ one —Vincent Sheean⟩ ⟨has finally repudiated color caste — at the ~ level —Carey McWilliams⟩

**rhetorical accent** *n* : ACCENT 6c

**rhe·tor·i·cal·ly** \-rək(ə)lē, -rēk-, -li\ *adv* : with respect to rhetoric : for rhetorical effect : in a rhetorical manner ⟨aim has been to punctuate as lightly as possible, and ~ rather than grammatically —J.R.Sutherland⟩ ⟨threw up her hands and asked ~ what was going to happen to them now —Louis Auchincloss⟩

**rhe·tor·i·cal·ness** \-rəkəlnəs, -rēk-\ *n* -ES : the condition of being rhetorical

**rhetorical question** *n* : a question not intended to elicit an answer but asked for rhetorical effect often with an assumption that only one answer is possible (as in "Who does not love his country?")

**rhetorical syllogism** *n* : a truncated syllogism that is persuasive but not necessarily valid

**rhe·tor·i·cate** \-rə,kāt\ *vi* -ED/-ING/-S *archaic* [*rhetoric* + *-ate*] : to use rhetorical language

**rhet·o·ri·cian** \ˌred·əˈrishən, -etə-\ *n* -S [ME *rethoricien*, fr. MF, fr. *rethorique* rhetoric + *-ien* -ian] **1 a** : a master or teacher of rhetoric (as in ancient Greece and Rome) : one concerned with rhetoric ⟨he was a ~ and cared little for give-and-take —Jean Stafford⟩ **b** : ORATOR ⟨the only university whose ~*s* have twice won the . . . tournament, outtalking all opponents in that oratorical round robin —T.D.Durrance⟩ **2 a** : an eloquent writer or speaker ⟨a great ~, a master of telling phrases and emphatic effects —Maurice Bowra⟩ **b** : one who writes or speaks in an inflated or bombastic style ⟨seen, too often, to have been but a pompous ~ —W.S.Maugham⟩

**rhet·o·rize** \'red·ə,rīz\ *vi* -ED/-ING/-S [ML *rhetorizare* to play the orator, fr. Gk *rhētorizein* to be an orator, fr. *rhētor-, rhētōr* orator + *-izein* -ize] *archaic* : to use rhetorical language

**rheto-romance** *or* **rheto-romansh** *usu cap both Rs, var of* RHAETO-ROMANIC

¹**rheum** \'rüm, 'rům\ *n* -S [ME *reume*, fr. MF, fr. L *rheuma*, fr. Gk — more at RHEUMATISM] **1 a** : a watery discharge from the mucous membranes esp. of the eyes or nose **b** : a condition marked by such discharge (as a cold or catarrh) **2** *archaic* : TEARS ⟨indisposed by a very great ~ —John Evelyn⟩

²**rhe·um** \'rēəm\ *n, cap* [NL, fr. Gk *rhēon* rhubarb — more at RHUBARB] : a genus of Asiatic herbs (family Polygonaceae) with large leaves, loose stipular sheaths, and small flowers in ample paniculate racemes, the perianth 6-parted, the fruit 3-winged — see RHUBARB

¹**rheu·mat·ic** \(')rü¦mad·|ik, -at|, |ēk *also* (')rů¦m- *or* rə'm-\ *adj* [ME *rewmatik*, fr. L *rheumaticus* troubled with rheum, fr. Gk *rheumatikos* subject to rheum or flux, fr. *rheumat-, rheuma* rheum, flux + *-ikos* -ic] **1** *obs* : derived from or being rheum : full of rheum : suffering from rheum : tending to cause rheum **2 a** : of, relating to, or characteristic of rheumatism : attending or caused by rheumatism ⟨~ pain⟩ **b** : affected with rheumatism ⟨a ~ joint⟩ — **rheu·mat·i·cal·ly** \|ək(ə)lē, |ēk-, -li\ *adv*

²**rheumatic** \", *in sense 2* -iks,-ēks, 'rümə,tiks *also* 'růmə-\ *n* -S **1** : one affected with rheumatism **2 rheu·matics** *pl, dial* : RHEUMATISM — often used with *the*

**rheu·mat·i·cal** \(')rü¦mad·|əkəl, -at|, |ēk- *also* (')rů¦m- *or* rə'm-\ *archaic var of* RHEUMATIC

**rheumatic disease** *n* : any of several diseases (as rheumatoid arthritis, rheumatic fever, fibrositis) characterized by inflammation and pain in muscles or joints from various causes

**rheumatic fever** *n* : an acute often recurrent disease occurring chiefly in children and young adults and characterized by fever, inflammation, pain, and swelling in and around the joints, inflammatory involvement of the pericardium and valves of the heart, and often the formation of small nodules chiefly in the subcutaneous tissues and the heart

**rheumatic heart disease** *n* : active or inactive disease of the heart resulting from rheumatic fever and characterized by inflammatory changes in the myocardium or scarring of the valves that reduce the functional capacity of the heart

**rheu·mat·icky** \(')rü¦mad·əkē, -atə-, -ki *also* rə'm-; 'rümə,tik- *also* 'rům-\ *adj* [²*rheumatic* + *-y*] : RHEUMATIC

**rheu·ma·tism** \'rümə,tizəm *also* 'rům-\ *n* -S [L *rheumatismus* rheum, fr. Gk *rheumatismos*, fr. *rheumatizesthai* to suffer from a flux, fr. *rheumat-, rheuma* flux, rheum; akin to Gk *rhein* to flow — more at STREAM] **1** : any of numerous conditions characterized by inflammation or pain in muscles, joints, or fibrous tissue ⟨muscular ~⟩ **2** : RHEUMATOID ARTHRITIS

**rheumatism root** *n* **1** : TWINLEAF **2** : SPOTTED WINTERGREEN

**rheumatism weed** *n* : any of several chiefly So. American plants used esp. formerly in folk medicine for pain or inflammation in the joints: as **a** : PIPSISSEWA **b** : either of two common dogbanes (*Apocynum cannabinum* and *A. androsaemifolium*)

**rheu·ma·tiz** \'⸗⸗,tiz\ *n* -ES [by shortening & alter.] *chiefly dial* : RHEUMATISM

¹**rheu·ma·toid** \-,tȯid\ *adj* [ISV *rheumatism* + *-oid*; orig. formed as F *rhumatoïde*] : characteristic of or affected with rheumatoid arthritis

²**rheumatoid** \"\ *n* -S : one affected with rheumatoid arthritis

**rheumatoid arthritis** *n* : a constitutional disease of unknown cause characterized by inflammation and swelling of joint structures and marked by a chronic progressive course ending in complete stiffening of one or more joints, permanent disability, and invalidism — compare DEGENERATIVE ARTHRITIS

**rheumatoid spondylitis** *n* : rheumatoid arthritis of the spine

**rheu·ma·tol·o·gist** \,rümə'täləjəst *also* ,rům-\ *n* -S [*rheumatology* + *-ist*] : a specialist in rheumatic diseases

**rheu·ma·tol·o·gy** \-jē\ *n* -ES [ISV *rheumatism* + *-o-* + *-logy*] : a branch of medicine dealing with rheumatic diseases

**rheumed** \'rümd, 'růmd\ *adj* [¹*rheum* + *-ed*] : RHEUMY

**rheum·i·ly** \'rüməlē, 'rům-\ *adv* : in a rheumy manner

**rheums** *pl of* RHEUM

**rheumy** \-mē\ *adj* [¹*rheum* + *-y*] **1** : consisting of or full of rheum ⟨his blinking and ~ eyes—Margery Sharp⟩ **2** : affected with or subject to catarrh or rheumatism : RHEUMATIC ⟨falsetto voice, ~ with age and grief —Ellen Glasgow⟩ **3** : causing or tending to cause catarrh or rheumatism ⟨~ mists of winter —*Architect & Building News*⟩

**rhex·ia** \'reksēə\ *n* [NL, fr. L, a plant] **1** *cap* : a small genus of herbs (family Melastomaceae) having 3-nerved leaves and red or yellow flowers with 4 petals and 8 equal anthers — see DEER GRASS **2** -S : any plant of the genus *Rhexia*

**rhex·is** \'reksəs\ *n, pl* **rhex·es** \-k,sēz\ [NL, fr. Gk *rhēxis* act of breaking, fr. *rhēgnynai* to break — more at RHAGADES] : RUPTURE ⟨~ of a blood vessel⟩ ⟨~ of an organ⟩

**rh factor** *also* **rh** \'ä'rāch-, ä'(r)äch-\ *n, usu cap R* [*rhesus* monkey (in which it was first detected)] : a substance or one of a group of substances that is present in the red blood cells of a large majority of persons and in those of other higher animals, is prob. an agglutinogen, is inherited according to Mendelian principles, and is capable of inducing intense antigenic reaction under suitable circumstances (as in repeated transfusion of Rh-positive blood to an Rh-negative person) — called also *Rh antigen, rhesus factor*; compare HR FACTOR

**RHI** *abbr* range-height indicator

**rhig·o·lene** \'rigə,lēn, -lən\ *n* -S [Gk *rhigos* cold + E *-ol* + *-ene* — more at FRIGID] : a petroleum product intermediate between cymogene and gasoline containing chiefly pentanes and used formerly in medicine as a local anesthetic

**rhin-** *or* **rhino-** *comb form* [NL, fr. Gk, fr. *rhin-, rhis* nose; perh. akin to Skt *sara* flowing, Gk *oros* whey — more at SERUM] **1 a** : nose ⟨*rhin*itis⟩ ⟨*rhino*logy⟩ **b** : nose and ⟨*rhino*laryngology⟩ ⟨*rhino*pharyngitis⟩ **2 a** : nasal ⟨*rhino*lith⟩ ⟨*rhino*caul⟩ **b** : nasal and ⟨*rhino*pharyngeal⟩

**rhi·na** \'rīnə\ [NL, fr. L, a shark, fr. Gk *rhinē*, a shark, file, rasp — more at WRITE] *syn of* SQUATINA

**-rhi·na** \"\ *n comb form* [NL, fr. Gk *rhin-, rhis* nose] : one or ones having (such) a nose — in taxonomic names in zoology ⟨*Amphirhina*⟩ ⟨Phyllo*rhina*⟩

**rhi·nal** \'rīn°l\ *adj* [*rhin-* + *-al*] : of or relating to the nose : NASAL, NARIAL

¹**rhi·nan·tha·ce·ae** \,rī,nan'thāsē,ē\ *n pl, cap* [NL, fr. *Rhinanthus*, type genus + *-aceae*] *in some esp former classifications* : a family of dicotyledonous plants that includes those figworts having the lower lip or lateral lobes of the corolla external in the bud

²**rhinanthaceae** \"\ *syn of* SCROPHULARIACEAE

**rhi·nan·thus** \rī'nan(t)thəs\ *n, cap* [NL, fr. *rhin-* + *-anthus*] : a small genus of partially parasitic herbs (family Scrophulariaceae) that have an inflated 4-toothed calyx, bilabiate corolla, four unequal stamens, and winged seeds — see RATTLE

**rhi·nar·i·um** \rī'na(a)rēəm\ *n, pl* **rhinar·ia** \-ēə\ [NL, fr. Gk *rhin-, rhis* nose + NL *-arium*] **1** : the lower part of the clypeus in some insects (as dragonflies) **2** : the hairless area of roughened skin at the tip of the snout of a mammal

**rhinc·odon** \'riŋkə,dän\ *n, cap* [NL, fr. *rhinc-* (irreg. fr. L *rhina*, a shark) + *-odon*] : a genus of elasmobranch fishes that contains only the whale shark and is now usu. isolated in a separate family though formerly often included in Orectolobidae

**rhine** \'rēn\ *n* -S [earlier *royne*, prob. alter. of ME *rune* watercourse, fr. OE *ryne* course, flow, watercourse; akin to OFris *rene* flow; derivative fr. the root of E ¹*run*] *dial chiefly Eng* : a drainage ditch : RUNNEL

**-rhine** — see -RRHINE

**rhine·grave** \'rīn,grāv\ *n* [MD *rijngrave*, fr. *Rijn* Rhine river + *grave* count — more at BURGRAVE] : a count who has possessions bordering the Rhine

**rhine·land·er** \'rīn,landə(r), -,lan-\ *n* -S *cap* [G *rheinländer*, fr. *Rheinland* Rhineland, part of Germany west of the Rhine river] **1 a** : a native or inhabitant of the part of Germany west of the Rhine river **b** : a native or inhabitant of the Rhine province of Prussia **2** : a native speaker of one of the Rhenish dialects of the German language — compare BAVARIAN, SWABIAN, WESTPHALIAN

**rhin·encephalic** \(¦)rīn+\ *also* **rhin·encephalous** \¦rīn+\ *adj* [*rhinencephalic* fr. F *rhinencephalique*, fr. NL *rhinencephalon* + F *-ique* -ic; *rhinencephalous* fr. NL *rhinencephalon* + E *-ous*] : of or relating to the rhinencephalon

**rhin·encephalon** \¦rīn+\ *n, pl* **rhinencephala** [NL, fr. *rhin-* + *encephalon*] : the anterior inferior part of the forebrain that is chiefly concerned with olfaction

**rhi·ne·odon** \'rīnēə,dän, rī'n-\ [NL, fr. L *rhina*, a shark + *-odon* — more at RHINA] *syn of* RHINCODON

**rhine·stone** \'rīnz,tōn, -īn,st-\ *n* [*Rhine*, river in western Europe + E *stone*; trans. of F *caillou du Rhin*] : a colorless imitation stone of high luster made of glass, paste, or gem quartz

**rhine·stoned** \-ōnd\ *adj* : set with or as if with rhinestones

**rhin·eura** \rī'n(y)ůrə\ *n, cap* [NL, fr. *rhin-* + Gk *eurys* broad — more at EURY-] : a genus of limbless burrowing lizards (family Amphisbaenidae) that includes solely the thunderworm

**rhine wine** \'rīn-\ *n, usu cap R* [*rhine* fr. *Rhine*, river in western Europe flowing from Switzerland through Germany and the Netherlands into the North sea] **1** : a wine that is produced in the valley of the Rhine; *esp* : one that is light-bodied, dry, and white and that averages 7 to 10 percent ethyl alcohol by volume **2** : a wine that is similar to the white wine of the Rhine but is produced elsewhere (as in California or New York state)

**rhin·i·on** \'rinē,än\ *n* -S [NL, fr. Gk, dim. of *rhin-, rhis* nose — more at RHIN-] : a point at the lower end of the median suture joining the nasal bones — see CRANIOMETRY illustration

**rhi·ni·tis** \rī'nīd·əs\ *n, pl* **rhinit·i·des** \-'nid·ə,dēz\ [NL, fr. *rhin-* + *-itis*] **1** : inflammation of the mucous membrane of the nose from infectious, allergic, or other causes: as **a** : COMMON COLD **b** : CORYZA b **2** : bullnose of swine

¹**rhi·no** \'rī(,)nō\ *n, pl* **rhino** [origin unknown] : MONEY, CASH

²**rhino** \"\ *n, pl* **rhino** *or* **rhinos** [by shortening] : RHINOCEROS

³**rhino** \"\ *or* **rhino ferry** *n* -S : a pontoon or group of pontoons propelled by outboard motor and used esp. by a naval force during landing operations for transportation of vehicles, docking facilities, and other functions

**rhino-** — see RHIN-

**rhi·no·bat·i·dae** \,rīnō'bad·ə,dē\ *n pl, cap* [NL, fr. *Rhinobatos*, type genus + *-idae*] : a family of viviparous elasmobranch fishes of warm seas comprising the guitarfishes, fiddlers, and related forms that are included among the rays but somewhat approach the sharks in the long narrow body and the possession of a tail fin

**rhi·nob·a·tos** \rī'näbəd·əs\ *n, cap* [NL, fr. Gk, a fish, perh. of the genus *Rhinobatos*, fr. *rhinē*, a shark, file, rasp + *batos* skate (fish) — more at WRITE] : a genus (the type of the family Rhinobatidae) of viviparous elasmobranch fishes

**rhi·nob·a·tus** \"\ [NL, fr. Gk *rhinobatos*] *syn of* RHINOBATOS

**rhi·no·cer·i·cal** \¦rīnə¦serəkəl\ *adj* [prob. fr. ¹*rhino* + *-cer* (as in *rhinoceros*) + *-ical*] *archaic* : full of money : RICH

**rhi·noc·er·ine** \rī'näsə,rīn, -sərən\ *or* **rhi·noc·er·oid** \-sə,rȯid\ *adj* [*rhinoceros* + *-ine* or *-oid*] : RHINOCEROTIC

**rhinoceroid** \"\ *n* -S [NL *Rhinoceros* + E *-oid*] : RHINOCEROTID

**rhi·noc·er·os** \rī'näs(ə)rəs\ *n* [ME *rinoceros*, fr. L *rhinocerot-*, *rhinoceros*, fr. Gk *rhinokerōt-, rhinokerōs*, fr. *rhin-, rhis* nose + *-kerōt-, -kerōs* (fr. *keras* horn) — more at RHIN-, HORN] **1** *pl* **rhi·noceroses** \-rəsəz\ *or* **rhinoceros** \-rəs\ *or* **rhi·noc·eri** \-äsə,rī\ *also* **rhinoc·er·o·tes** \(,)rī,näsə'rōd·(,)ēz\ : any of various large powerful herbivorous thick-skinned perissodactyl mammals of the family Rhinocerotidae that have one or two heavy upright horns on the snout or that in some extinct genera are hornless — see BLACK RHINOCEROS, WHITE RHINOCEROS, WOOLLY RHINOCEROS **2** *cap* [NL, fr. L] : a genus (the type of the family Rhinocerotidae) that contains the Indian and Malayan rhinoceroses

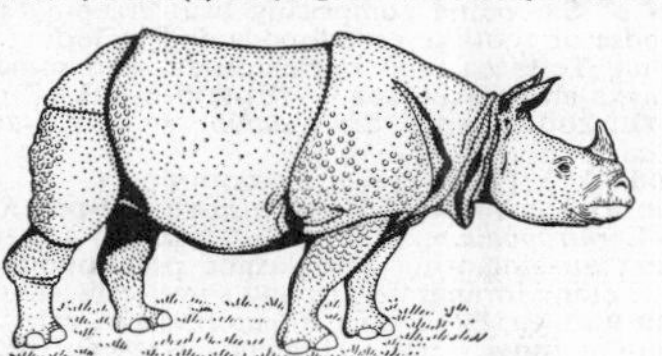

Indian rhinoceros

**rhinoceros auklet** *n* : an auklet (*Cerorhinca monocerata*) of the northern Pacific that has a deciduous horn on the bill

**rhinoceros beetle** *n* : any of various chiefly tropical very large beetles of *Dynastes* and closely related genera having projecting horns on thorax and head and large larvae that bore in living or decaying plant tissue and are sometimes eaten by man; *esp* : a lustrous greenish gray dark spotted beetle (*Dynastes tityus*) of tropical America and southeastern U.S.

**rhinoceros bird** *n* **1** : OXPECKER **2** : RHINOCEROS HORNBILL

**rhinoceros hornbill** *n* : any of various hornbills; *esp* : a hornbill (*Buceros rhinoceros*) of the Malay peninsula and islands of Indonesia having a casque on the bill that is very large and turned up in front

**rhinoceros viper** *n* : a heavy-bodied brightly-colored West African viper (*Bitis nasicornis*) with a pair of hornlike outgrowths on the snout — called also *river jack*

**rhi·noc·er·ot** \rī'näsə,rät\ *n* -S [L *rhinocerot-, rhinoceros*] *archaic* : RHINOCEROS

**rhi·noc·er·ot·ic** \(¦)rī¦näsə¦räd·ik\ *adj* [LL *rhinoceroticus*, fr. L *rhinocerot-, rhinoceros* + *-icus* -ic] : of, relating to, or resembling a rhinoceros

¹**rhi·noc·er·o·tid** \-sə¦rōd·id\ *adj* [NL *Rhinocerotidae*] : of or relating to the Rhinocerotidae

²**rhinocerotid** \"\ *n* -S : a mammal of the family Rhinocerotidae : RHINOCEROS

**rhi·noc·er·oti·dae** \(,)rī,näsə'räd·ə,dē, -'rōd-\ *n pl, cap* [NL, fr. *Rhinocerot-, Rhinoceros*, type genus + *-idae*] : a family of mammals that contains all the true rhinoceroses and that is often considered to constitute together with extinct related forms a distinct superfamily of Perissodactyla

**rhi·noc·er·oti·form** \(¦)⸗¦⸗¦⸗⸗,fȯrm\ *adj* [L *rhinocerot-, rhinoceros* + E *-iform*] : resembling a rhinoceros

**rhi·noc·er·o·tine** \rī'näsərə,tīn\ *adj* [L *rhinocerot-, rhinoceros* + E *-ine*] : RHINOCEROTIC

**rhi·noc·er·o·toid** \-,tȯid\ *adj* [L *rhinocerot-, rhinoceros* + E *-oid*] : RHINOCEROTIC

**rhi·no·cryp·ti·dae** \,rīnə'kriptə,dē\ *n pl, cap* [NL, fr. Rhinocrypta, type genus (fr. *rhin-* + *-crypta*, fr. Gk *kryptos* hidden) + *-idae* — more at CRYPT] : a family of So. American birds closely related to Furnariidae — see TAPACOLO

**rhino ferry** *var of* RHINO

**rhi·no·gen·ic** \¦rīnə¦jenik\ *or* **rhi·nog·e·nous** \(')rī¦näjənəs\ *adj* [*rhin-* + *-genic* or *-genous*] : originating in or transmitted by way of the nose ⟨~ meningitis⟩

**rhi·no·la·lia** \,rīnə'lālēə, -ālyə\ *n* -S [*rhin-* + *-lalia*] : nasal tone in speech esp. when caused by excessive closure or openness of the posterior nares

**rhi·no·laryngology** \¦rī(,)nō+\ *n* [*rhin-* + *laryng-* + *-logy*] : a branch of medical science that deals with the nose and larynx and their diseases

**rhi·no·laryngoscope** \"+\ *n* [*rhin-* + *laryng-* + *-scope*] : a scope fitted with mirrors and a lighting system used for examination of the nose and larynx — **rhi·no·laryngoscopic** \"+\ *adj*

**rhi·no·lith** \'rīnə,lith\ *n* -S [ISV *rhin-* + *-lith*] : a concretion formed within the cavities of the nose — **rhi·no·lith·ic** \¦⸗⸗¦lithik\ *adj*

**rhi·no·log·ic** \¦⸗⸗¦läjik\ *or* **rhi·no·log·i·cal** \-jəkəl\ *adj* [*rhinology* + *-ic* or *-ical*] : of or relating to the nose

**rhi·nol·o·gist** \rī'näləjəst\ *n* -S [*rhinology* + *-ist*] : a physician who specializes in rhinology

**rhi·nol·o·gy** \-jē\ *n* -S [*rhin-* + *-logy*] : a branch of medical science that deals with the nose and its diseases

**rhi·nol·o·phid** \rī'näləfəd\ *n* -S [NL *Rhinolophidae*] : a leaf-nosed bat of the family Rhinolophidae

**rhi·no·loph·i·dae** \,rīnə'läfə,dē\ *n pl, cap* [NL, fr. *Rhinolophus*, type genus (fr. *rhin-* + Gk *lophos* crest) + *-idae*] : a family of Old World leaf-nosed bats that includes many common horseshoe bats

¹**rhi·nol·o·phine** \rī'nälə,fīn, -,fən\ *adj* [NL *Rhinolophina* (syn. of *Rhinolophidae*), fr. *Rhinolophus* + *-ina*] : of or relating to the family Rhinolophidae

²**rhinolophine** \"\ *n* -S : a bat of the family Rhinolophidae

**rhi·no·nic·ter·is** \,rīnō'niktərəs\ *n, cap* [NL, fr. *rhin-* + Gk *nykteris* bat — more at NYCTERIS] : a genus of Australian bats related to *Hipposideros* and including solely the orange horseshoe bat

**rhi·no·nys·si·dae** \-'nisə,dē\ *n pl, cap* [NL, fr. *Rhinonyssus*, type genus (fr. *rhin-* + Gk *nyssein* to prick, sting) + *-idae* — more at NUMEN] : a widely distributed family of mites that are parasitic in the nasal passages of birds

**rhi·no·pharyngitis** \¦rī(,)nō+\ *n* [NL, fr. *rhin-* + *pharyngitis*] : inflammation of the mucous membrane of the nose and pharynx

**rhi·no·pharynx** \"+\ *n* [NL, fr. *rhin-* + *pharynx*] : NASOPHARYNX

**rhi·noph·i·dae** \rī'näfə,dē\ [NL, fr. *Rhinophid-, Rhinophis* + *-idae*] *syn of* UROPELTIDAE

**rhi·no·phis** \'rīnəfəs\ *n, cap* [NL, fr. *rhin-* + *-ophis*] : a genus of shieldtail snakes of the family Uropeltidae

**rhi·no·pho·nia** \,rīnə'fōnēə\ *n* -S [NL, fr. *rhin-* + *-phonia*] : marked nasal resonance

**rhi·no·phore** \'rīnə,fō(ə)r\ *n* -S [*rhin-* + *-phore*] : one of the two tentacles that are considered to be olfactory organs on the back of the head or neck of a mollusk of the order Opisthobranchia

**rhi·no·phyma** \¦rīnə+\ *n* [NL, fr. *rhin-* + *phyma*] : a nodular swelling and congestion of the nose in an advanced stage of acne rosacea

**rhi·no·plas·tic** \¦rīnə¦plastik\ *adj* [*rhin-* + *-plastic*] : of or relating to rhinoplasty

**rhi·no·plas·ty** \'⸗⸗,plastē\ *n* -ES [ISV *rhin-* + *-plasty*] : plastic surgery of the nose

**rhi·no·po·ma** \,rīnə'pōmə\ *n, cap* [NL, fr. *rhin-* + Gk *pōma* lid, cover; akin to OE *fōdder* case, sheath — more at FUR] : a genus (coextensive with the family Rhinopomatidae) of insectivorous bats comprising the mouse-tailed bats

**rhi·nop·tera** \rī'näpt(ə)rə\ *n, cap* [NL, fr. *rhin-* + *-ptera*] : a genus of rays comprising the cow-nosed rays and being sometimes placed in a separate family but usu. included among the Myliobatidae

**rhi·nor·rha·gia** \,rīnə'rāj(ē)ə\ *n* -S [NL, fr. *rhin-* + *-rrhagia*] : NOSEBLEED

**rhi·nor·rhea** *or* **rhi·nor·rhoea** \-'rēə\ *n* -S [NL, fr. *rhin-* + *-rrhea, -rrhoea*] : excessive mucous secretion from the nose

**rhinos** *pl of* RHINO

**rhi·no·scleroma** \¦rī(,)nō+\ *n, pl* **rhinoscleromata** [NL, fr. *rhin-* + *scleroma*] : a chronic inflammatory disease of the nasopharyngeal mucosa that is characterized by the formation of granulomas and by dense induration of the tissues and nodular deformity

**rhi·no·scope** \'rīnə,skōp\ *n* [ISV *rhin-* + *-scope*] : an instrument for examining the cavities and passages of the nose

**rhi·no·scop·ic** \¦⸗⸗¦skäpik\ *adj* [ISV *rhinoscopy* + *-ic*] : of or relating to rhinoscopy

**rhi·nos·co·py** \rī'näskəpē\ *n* -ES [ISV *rhin-* + *-scopy*] : examination of the nasal cavity and passages (as by means of a speculum or laryngoscopic mirror introduced into the pharynx)

**rhi·no·spo·rid·i·o·sis** \¦rī(,)nōspə,ridē'ōsəs\ *n, pl* **rhinosporidio·ses** \-dē'ō,sēz\ [NL, fr. *Rhinosporidium* + *-osis*] : a fungous disease of the external mucous membranes (as of the nose) that is characterized by the formation of pinkish red, friable, sessile, or pedunculate polyps and is believed to be caused by a microparasite (*Rhinosporidium seeberi*)

**rhi·no·sporidium** \¦rī(,)nō+\ *n* [NL, fr. *rhin-* + *sporidium*] **1** *cap* : a genus of microparasites that are associated with some types of nasal polyps in man and in horses and that are sometimes regarded as chytrids related to the Olpidiaceae but are now often held to be protozoans possibly related to the Sarcosporidia **2** *pl* **rhinosporidia** : a microparasite of the genus *Rhinosporidium*

**rhi·no·ter·mit·i·dae** \¦rī(,)nō(,)tər'mid·ə,dē\ *n pl, cap* [NL, fr. *Rhinotermit-, Rhinotermes*, type genus (fr. *rhin-* + *Termit-, Termes*) + *-idae*] : a large and widely distributed family of termites that occur in temperate, subtropical, and tropical regions

**rhi·no·theca** \¦rīnə+\ *n, pl* **rhinothecae** [NL, fr. *rhin-* + *theca*] : the sheath of the upper mandible of a bird — **rhi·no·thecal** \"+\ *adj*

**-rhi·nus** \'rīnəs\ *n comb form* [NL, fr. Gk *rhin-, rhis* nose — more at RHIN-] : one having (such) a nose — in generic names in zoology ⟨*Megarhinus*⟩

**rhipi-** *comb form* [NL, fr. Gk *rhipid-, rhipis* fan] : RHIPID-

**rhipi·ceph·a·lus** \,ripə'sefələs\ *n, cap* [NL, fr. *rhipi-* + *-cephalus*] : a large and widely distributed genus of ixodid ticks that are parasitic on many mammals and some birds and include vectors of serious diseases (as Rocky Mountain spotted fever and east coast fever)

**rhipid-** *or* **rhipido-** *comb form* [NL, fr. Gk, fr. *rhipid-, rhipis* fan; akin to Gk *rhip-, rhips* wickerwork, *rhiptein* to throw, OHG *rîban* to grate, rub, turn, twist, MD *wriven* to rub, twist; basic meaning: turning] : fan — chiefly in taxonomic names ⟨*Rhipid*istia⟩ ⟨*Rhipido*glossa⟩

**rhip·i·date** \'ripə,dāt\ *adj* [*rhipid-* + *-ate*] : FAN-SHAPED

**rhi·pid·i·a·ce·ae** \rə,pidē'āsē,ē\ *n pl, cap* [NL, fr. *Rhipidium*, type genus + *-aceae*] : a family of phycomycetous fungi (order Leptomitales) that have the thallus differentiated into holdfast, basal cell, and hyphal branches

**rhip·i·dist** \'ripədəst\ *n* -S [NL *Rhipidistia*] : a fish or fossil of the order Rhipidistia

**rhip·i·dis·tia** \,ripə'distēə\ *n pl, cap* [NL, fr. *rhipid-* + Gk *histia*, pl. of *histion* sail; akin to Gk *histanai* to cause to stand — more at STAND] : an order of extinct crossopterygian fishes that have the basal bones of the median fins united into one mass — see HOLOPTYCHIIDAE, OSTEOLEPIDAE — **rhip·i·dis·ti·an** \¦⸗⸗¦distēən\ *adj or n* — **rhip·i·dis·tid** \-təd\ *adj or n*

**rhi·pid·i·um** \-'pidēəm\ *n* -S [NL, fr. Gk *rhipidion* small bellows, dim. of *rhipid-, rhipis* fan] : a fan-shaped cymose inflorescence (as in some sedges) in which the branches lie in the same plane and are suppressed alternately on each side

**rhip·i·do·glos·sa** \,ripədō'gläsə, -lȯsə\ *n pl, cap* [NL, fr. *rhipid-* + *-glossa*] : a suborder of Aspidobranchia that comprises gastropod mollusks (as the abalones, the top shells, and the keyhole limpets) having a long radula with teeth that are long and hooklike in each transverse row and with indefinitely numerous marginal teeth becoming smaller toward the edges — see HELICINA — **rhip·i·do·glos·sal** \-səl\ *adj* — **rhip·i·do·glos·sate** \-sət, -,sāt\ *adj*

**rhip·i·dop·tera** \,ripə'däpt(ə)rə\ [NL, fr. *rhipid-* + *-ptera*] *syn of* STREPSIPTERA

**rhip·i·dop·ter·ous** \¦⸗⸗¦däpt(ə)rəs\ *adj* [NL *Rhipidoptera* + E *-ous*] : STREPSIPTERAL

¹**rhi·piph·o·rid** \rə'pifərəd\ *adj* [NL *Rhipiphoridae*] : of or relating to the Rhipiphoridae

²**rhipiphorid** \"\ *n* -S : a beetle of the family Rhipiphoridae

**rhip·i·phor·i·dae** \,ripə'fȯrə,dē\ *n pl, cap* [NL, fr. *Rhipiphorus*, type genus (fr. *rhipi-* + *-phorus*) + *-idae*] : a family of small beetles that are parasitic on wasps and other insects, have a pointed abdomen, and undergo hypermetamorphosis

**rhi·pip·tera** \rə'pipt(ə)rə\ [NL, fr. *rhipi-* + *-ptera*] *syn of* STREPSIPTERA

**rhi·pip·ter·ous** \-(ə)rəs\ *adj* [NL *Rhipiptera* + E *-ous*] : STREPSIPTERAL

**rhip·sa·lis** \rip'sāləs\ *n, cap* [NL, fr. Gk *rhip-, rhips* wickerwork + L *-alis* -al — more at RHIPID-] : a genus consisting of chiefly tropical American unarmed cacti that have fleshy mostly cylindrical stems of very diverse habit and small flowers with 6 to 10 petals followed by a berrylike fruit and are often epiphytes with pendent branches — see MISTLETOE CACTUS

**rhip·to·glos·sa** \,riptə'gläsə, -lȯsə\ *n pl, cap* [NL, fr. Gk *rhiptos* thrown (fr. *rhiptein* to throw) + NL *-glossa* — more at RHIPID-] : a division of reptiles often considered a superfamily of Lacertilia that comprises the Old World chameleons

**rhiz-** *or* **rhizo-** *comb form* [NL, fr. Gk, fr. *rhiza* — more at ROOT] : root ⟨*rhiz*anthous⟩ ⟨*Rhizo*mys⟩ ⟨*rhizo*philous⟩

**-rhi·za** *or* **-r·rhi·za** \'rīzə\ *n comb form, pl* **-rhi·zae** \-(,)zē\ *or* **-rhizas** *or* **-r·rhi·zae** *or* **-rrhizas** [NL, fr. Gk *rhiza* root] **1 :** root : part resembling or connected with a root ⟨coleo*rhiza*⟩ ⟨mycor*rhiza*⟩ **2 :** plant having (such) a root — in genus names in botany ⟨Balsamo*rrhiza*⟩

**rhi·zan·thous** \(')rī¦zan(t)thəs\ *adj* [ISV *rhiz-* + *-anthous*] **:** producing flowers apparently directly from the root

**rhiz·autoicous** \¦rīz+\ *adj* [*rhiz-* + *autoicous*] **:** having the antheridia on a branch connected by rhizoids to the archegonial branch — used of mosses; compare CLADAUTOICOUS

**rhi·zid·i·a·ce·ae** \rə,zidē'āsē,ē\ *n pl, cap* [NL, fr. *Rhizidium*, type genus (fr. *rhiz-* + *-idium*) + *-aceae*] **:** a family of fungi (order Chytridiales) that are mostly ectoparasites on various algae and that have a plant body with a globose fertile portion and a vegetative portion of tapering rhizoidal branches

**¹rhi·zi·na** \rə'zīnə, -zēnə\ *n, cap* [NL, fr. *rhiz-* + *-ina*] **:** a genus of ascomycetous fungi (family Pezizaceae) that form flat ascocarps with rootlike outgrowths

**²rhizina** \"\ *also* **rhi·zine** \'rī,zīn, -,zᵊn\ *n* -s [NL *rhizina*, fr. *rhiz-* + *-ina* -ine] **:** RHIZOID — **rhi·zi·nous** \rə'zīnəs, -'zēn-; 'rīzᵊn-\ *adj*

**rhi·zo·bi·a·ce·ae** \(,)rī,zōbē'āsē,ē\ *n pl, cap* [NL, fr. *Rhizobium*, type genus + *-aceae*] **:** a small family of rod-shaped or irregular usu. flagellated and gram-negative aerobic bacteria (order Eubacteriales) that includes saprophytes, important nitrogen-fixing symbionts of plants, and some plant pathogens — see AGROBACTERIUM, RHIZOBIUM

**rhi·zo·bi·um** \rī'zōbēəm\ *n* [NL, fr. *rhiz-* + *-bium*] **1** *cap* **:** the type genus of Rhizobiaceae comprising small heterotrophic soil bacteria capable of forming symbiotic nodules on the roots of leguminous plants and of there becoming bacteroids that fix atmospheric nitrogen **2** *pl* **rhizo·bia** \-ēə\ *often cap* **:** any bacterium of the genus *Rhizobium*

**rhi·zo·caline** \¦rī(,)zō+\ *n* [*rhiz-* + *caline*] **:** a hormone or hormonelike factor distinct from auxin that is held to play a role in the formation of plant roots — compare CAULOCALINE

**rhi·zo·car·pous** \,rīzō¦kärpəs\ *or* **rhi·zo·car·pic** \-pik\ *adj* [*rhizocarpous* fr. *rhiz-* + *-carpous*; *rhizocarpic* ISV *rhiz-* + *-carpic*] **1 :** having perennial underground parts but annual stems and foliage — used of perennial herbs **2 :** producing hypogeal cleistogamous flowers

**rhi·zo·caul** \'rīzə,kȯl\ *or* **rhi·zo·cau·lus** \,==¦kȯləs\ *n, pl* **rhizocauls** \'==,kȯlz\ *or* **rhizocau·li** \,=='kō,lī\ [NL *rhizocaulus*, fr. *rhiz-* + Gk *kaulos* stalk — more at COLE] **:** HYDRORHIZA

**rhi·zo·ceph·a·la** \,rīzō'sefələ\ *n pl, cap* [NL, fr. *rhiz-* + *-cephala*] **:** an order of Cirripedia comprising extremely degenerate forms that live as parasites on crabs and hermit crabs, are hermaphroditic though complementary males occur, when young pass through stages similar to those of a developing barnacle, and afterward attach themselves to suitable hosts where after a complex series of changes they become limbless unsegmented tumid sacs attached by a short peduncle from which rootlike processes penetrate to all parts of the host and absorb its juices — see PELTOGASTER, SACCULINA

**rhi·zo·ceph·a·lan** \-lən\ *or* **rhi·zo·ceph·a·lid** \-ləd\ *n* -s [NL *Rhizocephala* + E *-an* or *-id*] **:** a crustacean of the order Rhizocephala

**rhi·zo·ceph·a·lous** \¦==¦==ləs\ *adj* [NL *Rhizocephala* + E *-ous*] **:** of or relating to the Rhizocephala

**rhi·zo·chlor·i·da·les** \,rīzō,klōrə'dā(,)lēz\ *n pl, cap* [NL, fr. *Rhizochlorid-*, *Rhizochloris*, genus of yellow-green algae (fr. *rhiz-* + L *Chlorid-*, *Chloris*, goddess of flowers) + *-ales* — more at CHLORIS] **:** an order of yellow-green algae (class Xanthophyceae) that have the vegetative cells permanently amoeboid, are naked or partially surrounded by an envelope, and are often joined in groups by cytoplasmic bridges — see RHIZOCHRYSIDALES

**rhi·zo·chrys·i·da·les** \-,krisə'dā(,)lēz\ *n pl, cap* [NL, fr. *Rhizochrysid-*, *Rhizochrysis*, genus of yellow-green algae (fr. *rhiz-* + Gk *chrysid-*, *chrysis* vessel of gold) + *-ales* — more at CHRYSIS] **:** an order of yellow-green algae (class Xanthophyceae) that have the vegetable cells either amoeboid or with temporary flagellated stages but in other respects resemble the Rhizochloridales

**rhi·zoc·to·nia** \,rī,zäk'tōnēə\ *n* [NL, fr. *rhiz-* + Gk *ktonos* murder + NL *-ia* — more at -CTONUS] **1** *cap* **:** a form genus of imperfect fungi (order Mycelia Sterilia) that formerly included numerous fungi which since the discovery of their perfect stages have been placed in other genera (as *Corticium* and *Pellicularia*) **2** -s **:** any fungus now or formerly belonging to the form genus *Rhizoctonia*

**rhizoctonia disease** *also* **rhizoctonia** *n* -s [NL *Rhizoctonia*] **1 :** a disease caused by fungi of *Rhizoctonia* or closely related genera **2 :** a disease of potatoes caused by a fungus (*Pellicularia filamentosa* syn. *Rhizoctonia solani*) and characterized esp. by black scurfy spots on the tubers — called also *little potato, rosette, russet scab, stem canker;* compare DAMPING-OFF

**rhi·zoc·to·ni·ose** \-ē,ōs *also* -ōz\ *n* -s [NL *Rhizoctonia* + E *-ose*] **:** RHIZOCTONIA DISEASE 1

**rhi·zo·dermis** \¦rīzō+\ *n* -ES [ISV *rhiz-* + *-dermis*] **:** EPIBLEM

**rhi·zo·din·i·a·les** \,rīzō,dinē'ā(,)lēz\ *n pl, cap* [NL, prob. fr. *rhiz-* + *dini-* (fr. Gk *deinos* terrible) + *-ales* — more at DIRE] **:** an order of colorless marine algae (class Dinophyceae) having the vegetative cells naked and amoeboid

**rhi·zo·gen** \'rīzəjən, -,jen\ *adj* [ISV *rhiz-* + *-gen*] **:** RHIZOGENIC

**rhi·zo·genesis** \,rīzə+\ *n* [NL, fr. *rhiz-* + *genesis*] **:** root development

**rhi·zo·gen·ic** \¦rīzə¦jenik\ *or* **rhi·zo·ge·net·ic** \-jə¦ned·ik\ *or* **rhi·zog·e·nous** \(')rī¦zäjənəs\ *adj* [*rhiz-* + *-genic* or *-genetic* or *-genous*] **:** producing roots — used of the tissue of the pericycle in the roots of seed plants that gives rise to rootlets endogenously

**rhi·zog·ly·phus** \rī'zägləfəs\ *n, cap* [NL, fr. *rhiz-* + Gk *glyphē* carved work — more at GLYPH] **:** a widely distributed genus of mites including some that are injurious to winter wheat and rye and to lily and other bulbs — see BULB MITE

**rhi·zo·graph** \'rīzə,graf, -rȧf\ *n* [*rhiz-* + *-graph*] **:** a device to trace the movement of roots in the soil

**¹rhi·zoid** \'rī,zȯid\ *adj* [ISV *rhiz-* + *-oid*] **:** resembling a root

**²rhizoid** \"\ *n* -s [*rhiz-* + *-oid*] **:** a rootlike structure: as **a :** one of the slender unicellular or multicellular filaments that attach the gametophyte of a fern, moss, or liverwort to the substrate and that function as absorptive organs **b :** a similar process in a thallophyte that often forms a specially differentiated basal holdfast — called also *rhizina* **c :** any of various processes of animals (as those by which a rhizocephalan attaches to its host) — **rhi·zoi·dal** \(')rī¦zȯidᵊl\ *adj*

**rhi·zo·ma** \rī'zōmə\ *n, pl* **rhizoma·ta** \-məd·ə\ [NL] **:** RHIZOME

**rhi·zo·mas·ti·gi·na** \¦rī(,)zō,mastə'jīnə\ *n pl, cap* [NL, fr. *Rhizomastig-*, *Rhizomastix*, genus of protozoa (fr. *rhiz-* + Gk *mastig-*, *mastix* whip, scourge) + *-ina* — more at MASTIG-] **:** an order of Zoomastigina that comprises protozoans which have both flagella and pseudopods and which chiefly are obscure soil or water organisms though a few are commensals and one (*Histomonas meleagris*) causes the serious blackhead of turkeys and other fowl

**rhi·zo·mat·ic** \¦rīzə¦mad·ik\ *adj* [ISV *rhizomat-* (fr. NL *rhizomat-*, *rhizoma*) + *-ic*] **:** of, relating to, or resembling a rhizome

**rhi·zom·a·tous** \(')rī¦zämədəs, -zōm-\ *adj* [ISV *rhizomat-* (fr. NL *rhizomat-*, *rhizoma*) + *-ous*] **:** having the characteristics of or resembling a rhizome

**rhizomatous begonia** *n* **:** any of a group of begonias that have prominent horizontal or creeping shaggy stems or rhizomes — compare FIBROUS-ROOTED BEGONIA, TUBEROUS BEGONIA

**rhi·zome** \'rī,zōm\ *n* -s [NL *rhizoma*, fr. Gk *rhizōma* mass of roots (of a tree), stem, race, fr. *rhizoun* to cause to strike root, fr. *rhiza* root — more at ROOT] **1 :** a more or less elongate stem or branch of a plant that is often thickened or tuber-shaped as a result of deposits of reserve food material, is usu. horizontal and underground, produces shoots above and roots below, and is distinguished from a true root in possessing buds, nodes, and usu. scalelike leaves — called also *rootstalk;* compare BULB 1, CORM **2 :** STOLON 2

**rhi·zomic** \-zōmik, -zäm-\ *adj* [*rhizome* + *-ic*] **:** of, relating to, or made up of rhizomes

**rhi·zo·morph** \'rīzə,mȯrf\ *n* [NL *rhizomorpha*, fr. *rhiz-* + *-morpha*, fem. sing. of *-morphus* -morphous] **1 :** an aggregation of fungous threads intertwining like the strands of a rope that frequently resembles a root and is characteristic of many basidiomycetes (as *Armillaria mellea*) **2** [*rhiz-* + *-morph*] **:** the lower part of the short cormoid axis from which the true roots develop in members of the genus *Isoetes* and various other lower vascular plants — **rhi·zo·mor·phic** \¦==¦mȯrfik\ *adj*

**rhi·zo·mor·phoid** \¦==¦mȯr,fȯid\ *adj* [*rhiz-* + *morph-* + *-oid*] **:** RHIZOMORPHOUS

**rhi·zo·mor·phous** \-,fəs\ *adj* [ISV *rhiz-* + *-morphous*] **:** having the form of a root

**rhi·zo·mycelial** \¦rī(,)zō+\ *adj* [NL *rhizomycelium* + E *-al*] **:** of, relating to, or resembling a rhizomycelium

**rhi·zo·mycelium** \"+\ *n, pl* **rhizomycelia** [NL, fr. *rhiz-* + *mycelium*] **:** an aggregation of gradually attenuated hyphal branches (as in the fungi of the family Cladochytriaceae) having fertile regions developed at various points

**¹rhi·zo·my·id** \¦rīzō¦mīəd\ *adj* [NL *Rhizomyidae*] **:** of or relating to the Rhizomyidae

**²rhizomyid** \"\ *n* -s **:** a rodent of the family Rhizomyidae

**rhi·zo·my·i·dae** \,rīzō'mīə,dē\ *n pl, cap* [NL, fr. *Rhizomys*, type genus + *-idae*] **:** a family of Asiatic and African fossorial rodents that are related to but somewhat more specialized than the common murid rodents — see RHIZOMYS

**rhi·zo·mys** \'==,mis\ *n, cap* [NL, fr. *rhiz-* + *-mys*] **:** the type genus of Rhizomyidae comprising the oriental bamboo rats

**rhi·zo·per·tha** \,rīzō'pərthə\ *n, cap* [NL, fr. *rhiz-* + Gk *perthein* to plunder, sack; perh. akin to Gk *pherein* to carry — more at BEAR] **:** a genus of minute beetles (family Bostrychidae) that feed on grain and other seeds

**rhi·zoph·o·ra** \rī'zäfərə\ *n, cap* [NL, fr. *rhiz-* + *-phora*] **:** a small genus (the type of the family Rhizophoraceae) of tropical trees and shrubs that have tetramerous flowers and a partly inferior ovary forming a fleshy berry — see MANGROVE

**rhi·zopho·ra·ce·ae** \rī,zäfə'rāsē,ē, ,rīzəf-\ *n pl, cap* [NL, fr. *Rhizophora*, type genus + *-aceae*] **:** a family of trees and shrubs (order Myrtales) that usu. form dense jungles along tropical seacoasts and that have opposite coriaceous leaves, flowers with valvate calyx and 2- to 6-celled ovary, and seeds that germinate while the fruit is still attached — compare MANGROVE — **rhi·zopho·ra·ceous** \¦=¦==¦rāshəs, ¦===-\ *adj*

**rhi·zo·phore** \'rīzə,fō(ə)r\ *n* -s [ISV *rhiz-* + *-phore*] **:** one of the downward-growing leafless dichotomous shoots in club mosses of the genus *Selaginella* that bear tufts of adventitious roots at the apex

**rhi·zo·plane** \-,plān\ *n* [*rhiz-* + *plane*] **:** the external surface of roots together with closely adhering soil particles and debris ⟨the ~ forms a particular subdivision of a rhizosphere⟩

**rhi·zo·plast** \-,plast\ *n* -s [ISV *rhiz-* + *-plast*] **:** a fibril that connects the blepharoplast with the nucleus in flagellated cells or organisms

**¹rhi·zo·pod** \-,päd\ *adj* [NL *Rhizopoda*] **:** of or relating to the Rhizopoda

**²rhizopod** \"\ *n* -s **:** a protozoan of the subclass Rhizopoda

**¹rhi·zop·o·da** \rī'zäpədə\ *n pl, cap* [NL, fr. *rhiz-* + *-poda*] **:** a subclass of Sarcodina comprising usu. creeping protozoans with lobose or rootlike pseudopods and including the orders Amoebina, Testacea, and Foraminifera, and sometimes also Proteomyxa and Mycetozoa — **rhi·zop·o·dal** \(')rī¦zäpədᵊl\ *adj* — **rhi·zop·o·dan** \-dᵊn\ *adj or n* — **rhi·zop·o·dous** \-dəs\ *adj*

**²rhizopoda** \"\ [NL] *syn of* SARCODINA

**rhi·zo·po·di·um** \,rīzə'pōdēəm\ *also* **rhi·zo·pod** \'rīzə,päd\ *n* -s [NL *rhizopodium*, fr. *rhiz-* + *-podium*] **:** a filamentous branching anastomosing ectoplasmic pseudopodium that is typical of many foraminiferans and some testaceans

**rhi·zo·po·gon** \,rīzə'pō,gän\ *n, cap* [NL, fr. *rhiz-* + *-pogon*] **:** a genus of fungi (family Hymenogastraceae) that produce subterranean sporophores resembling tubers with 2-spored to 8-spored basidia in a compact gleba of irregular chambers

**rhi·zop·ter·in** \rī'zäptərən\ *n* -s [*rhiz-* + *pterin*] **:** a pale yellow crystalline aldehydo amino acid $C_{15}H_{12}N_6O_4$ obtained in the fumaric acid fermentation by a black mold (*Rhizopus nigricans*) that promotes the growth of several streptococci **:** a formyl derivative of pteroic acid

**rhi·zo·pus** \'rīzəpəs\ *n, cap* [NL, fr. *rhiz-* + *-pus*] **:** a genus of fungi (family Mucoraceae) that have columellate hemispherical aerial sporangia formed in fascicles anchored to the substrate and tufts of rhizoids or root hyphae connected by stolons — see BREAD MOLD, ²LEAK 3, RING ROT; compare MUCOR, SOFT ROT

**rhi·zo·sphere** \'rīzə+,-\ *n* [ISV *rhiz-* + *sphere*] **:** soil that surrounds and is influenced by the roots of a plant — see RHIZOSPHERE EFFECT

**rhizosphere effect** *n* **:** the enhancement of the growth of a soil microorganism resulting from physical and chemical alteration of the soil and the contribution of excretions and organic debris of roots within a rhizosphere

**rhi·zos·to·mae** \rī'zästə,mē\ *n pl, cap* [NL, fr. *Rhizostoma*, genus of jellyfishes, fr. *rhiz-* + *-stoma*] **:** an order of Scyphozoa comprising jellyfishes that are related to the Semaeostomeae but are distinguished from them by fused oral lobes, by numerous small mouths replacing the primary mouth, and by the absence of tentacles and including various large jellyfishes that are dried and used as food in China and Japan — **rhi·zo·stoma·tous** \¦rīzə¦stōməd·əs, -täm-\ *adj* — **rhi·zo·stome** \'rīzə,stōm\ *n* -s — **rhi·zos·to·mous** \(')rī¦zästəməs\ *adj*

**rhi·zo·sto·ma·ta** \,rīzə'stōməd·ə\ [NL, fr. *rhiz-* + *-stomata*] *syn of* RHIZOSTOMAE

**rhi·zo·ta** \rī'zōd·ə\ *n pl, cap* [NL, irreg. fr. Gk *rhizoun* to cause to strike root — more at RHIZOME] *in some classifications* **:** an order of rotifers that when adult are attached by the truncated end of the tail — **rhi·zote** \'rī,zōt\ *adj* — **rhi·zotic** \(')rī¦zōd·ik, -zäd-\ *adj*

**rhi·zot·o·my** \rī'zäd·əmē\ *n* -ES [ISV *rhiz-* + *-tomy*] **:** the operation of cutting the anterior or posterior spinal nerve roots for therapeutic purposes

**rhm** \'rəm\ *n* -s [*r*oentgen per *h*our at one *m*eter] **:** a unit of gamma-ray source intensity equal to the intensity of a source that delivers one roentgen of gamma-ray dosage per hour at a distance of one meter

**rh-negative** *adj, usu cap R* **:** lacking Rh factor in the red blood cells

**rho** \'rō\ *n* -s [Gk *rhō*, of Sem origin; akin to Heb *rēsh*] **:** the 17th letter of the Greek alphabet — symbol P or ρ; see ALPHABET table

**rhod-** *or* **rhodo-** *comb form* [NL, fr. L, fr. Gk, fr. *rhodon* rose — more at ROSE] **:** rose **:** red ⟨*rhod*ium⟩ ⟨*rhodo*plast⟩

**rho·damine** \'rōdə,mēn, -,mən; rō'damən\ *n, often cap* [ISV *rhod-* + *amine*] **:** any of a group of yellowish red to blue fluorescent xanthene dyes: as **a** *or* **rhodamine B :** a brilliant bluish red basic dye made usu. by fusing *meta*-diethyl-aminophenol with phthalic anhydride and used chiefly in coloring paper, lacquers, and stains, in making organic pigments esp. for printing inks, and as a biological stain — see DYE table I (under *Basic Violet 10, Pigment Violet 1,* and *Solvent Red 49*) **b** *or* **rhodamine 6G :** a brilliant yellowish red basic dye made similarly from *meta*-ethyl-aminophenol and phthalic anhydride and used similarly — see DYE table I (under *Basic Red 1* and *Pigment Red 81*)

**rho·danate** \'rōdᵊn,āt, rō'danət\ *n* -s [*rhodan-* (in *rhodanic acid*) + *-ate*] **:** THIOCYANATE — not used systematically

**rho·da·nese** \'rōdᵊn,ēz, -ēs\ *n* -s [prob. irreg. fr. *rhodanic* (in *rhodanic acid*)] **:** a crystallizable enzyme that catalyzes the conversion of cyanide and thiosulfate or thiosulfonate to thiocyanate and sulfite and that occurs in animal tissues and bacteria

**rho·dan·ic acid** \(')rō¦danik-\ *n* [*rhodanic* ISV *rhodan-* (modif. of Gk *rhodon* rose) + *-ic*] **1 :** THIOCYANIC ACID — not used systematically **2 :** RHODANINE

**rho·da·nide** \'rōdᵊn,īd, rō'danəd\ *n* -s [ISV *rhodan-* (in *rhodanic acid*) + *-ide*] **:** THIOCYANATE — not used systematically

**rho·danine** \'rōdᵊn,ēn, rō'danən\ *n* -s [ISV *rhodan-* (in *rhodanic acid*) + *-ine*] **:** a pale yellow crystalline acidic derivative $C_3H_3NOS_2$ of thiazole that is formed by reaction of sodium chloroacetate, ammonia, and carbon disulfide or from ammonium thiocyanate and that condenses with aldehydes and many ketones to give colored products

**¹rho·dan·the** \rō'dan(t)thē\ [NL, fr. *rhod-* + Gk *anthos* flower — more at ANTHOLOGY] *syn of* HELIPTERUM

**²rhodanthe** \"\ *n* -s **:** an Australian annual everlasting (*Helipterum manglesii*) having nodding flower heads with scarious involucral bracts

**rhode is·land** \(')rō¦dīlənd, *before a consonant often* -n\ *adj, usu cap R&I* [fr. *Rhode Island*, northeastern state of the U. S., prob. modif. (influenced by D *Rood Eiland* Rhode Island, lit., red island, fr. *rood* red — fr. MD *root* — + *eiland* island — fr. MD *eilant*) of *Rhodes*, island of the eastern Mediterranean + E *island;* akin to OHG *rōt* red and to OFris *eiland* island; prob. fr. the belief that it was the size of the isle of Rhodes and that its Atlantic coast had a red appearance — more at RED, ISLAND] **:** of or from the state of Rhode Island **:** of the kind or style prevalent in Rhode Island

**rhode island bent** *n, usu cap R&I* **:** a lawn grass (*Agrostis tenuis*) of eastern No. America with very slender culms

**rhode is·land·er** \rō'dīləndə(r)\ *n, cap R&I* [*Rhode Island*, state of the U. S. + E *-er*] **:** a native or resident of the state of Rhode Island

**rhode island red** *n* [so called fr. its being bred first in Rhode Island] **1** *usu cap both Rs & I* **:** a leading American breed of general-purpose domestic fowls having a long heavy body, smooth yellow or reddish legs, rich brownish red plumage, and single or rose comb **2** *usu cap 1st R&I & often cap 2d R* **:** a bird of the Rhode Island Red breed

**rhode island white** *n* **1** *usu cap R&I&W* **:** an American breed of domestic fowls resembling Rhode Island reds but having pure white plumage **2** *usu cap R&I & often cap W* **:** a bird of the Rhode Island White breed

**rho·de·ose** \'rōdē,ōs *also* -,ōz\ *n* -s [Gk *rhodeos* of roses, rosy, fr. *rhodon* rose] **:** FUCOSE

**rhodes grass** \'rōdz-\ *n, usu cap R* [after Cecil J. *Rhodes* †1902 Eng. statesman and financier in So. Africa] **:** a perennial grass (*Chloris gayana*) native to southern Africa and introduced into the U. S. that is cultivated as a forage grass esp. in dry regions

**rhodes-grass scale** *n, usu cap R* **:** a mealybug (*Antonina graminis*) that is a serious pest on grass in the southern U. S.

**rho·de·sia** \rō'dēzh(ē)ə\ *adj, usu cap* [fr. *Rhodesia*, region in southern Africa] **:** of or from the region of Rhodesia **:** of the kind or style prevalent in Rhodesia

**¹rho·de·sian** \(')rō¦dēzh(ē)ən\ *adj, usu cap* [*Rhodesia* + E *-an*] **1 :** of, relating to, or characteristic of Rhodesia **2 :** of, relating to, or characteristic of the people of Rhodesia

**²rhodesian** \"\ *n* -s *cap* **:** a native or inhabitant of Rhodesia

**rhodesian mahogany** *n, usu cap R* **:** either of two African trees: **a :** POD MAHOGANY **b :** a southern African leguminous timber tree (*Copaifera coleosperma*) with very hard reddish wood used esp. for high-grade flooring

**rhodesian man** *n, usu cap R* [so called fr. the fact that remains of the type were found in Northern Rhodesia] **:** an extinct primitive African man (*Homo rhodesiensis* or *Africanthropus rhodesiensis*) of doubtful age and obscure affinities having long bones of modern type and prob. upright posture and a skull with very prominent brow ridges and large face but thoroughly human palate and dentition and a simple but relatively large brain — compare BOSKOP MAN

**rhodesian ridgeback** *n* **1** *usu cap both Rs* **:** an African breed of powerful long-bodied hunting dogs of uncertain ancestry having a dense harsh short coat in some shade of tan with a characteristic ridge or crest of reversed hair along the spine **2** *usu cap 1st R & often cap 2d R* **:** a dog of the Rhodesian Ridgeback breed used in its native area esp. for hunting the larger cats (as leopards or lions)

**rhodesian teak** *n, usu cap R* **:** a southern African leguminous timber tree (*Baikiaea plurijuga*) with very hard moderately heavy reddish brown wood that is highly resistant to insect attack and is used esp. for railroad ties and block flooring

**rho·de·soid** \rō'dē,zȯid\ *adj, usu cap* [*rhodesian* (in *rhodesian man*) + *-oid*] **:** resembling or having the characteristics of Rhodesian man

**rhodes scholar** \'rōdz'(s)kälə(r), -d'sk-\ *n, usu cap R* [after Cecil J. *Rhodes* †1902] **:** a holder of a Rhodes scholarship

**rhodes scholarship** *n, usu cap R* [after Cecil J. *Rhodes* †1902 Eng. statesman and financier in South Africa] **:** one of numerous scholarships founded under the will of Cecil J. Rhodes that are tenable at Oxford University for a term of two or three years and are distributed among candidates from the British Commonwealth, the U. S., and Germany

**rhodes·wood** \'rōdz,wu̇d\ *n* [prob. trans. of F *bois de Rhodes*] **:** a torchwood (*Amyris balsamifera*)

**¹rho·di·an** \'rōdēən\ *adj, usu cap* [L *rhodius* Rhodian (fr. *Rhodos, Rhodus* Rhodes, fr. Gk *Rhodos*) + E *-an*, adj. suffix] **1 :** of, relating to, or characteristic of Rhodes, an island of the eastern Mediterranean **2 :** of, relating to, or characteristic of the people of Rhodes

**²rhodian** \"\ *n* -s *cap* [L *rhodius*, adj., Rhodian + E *-an*, n. suffix] **:** a native or inhabitant of Rhodes

**rho·din** \'rōdᵊn\ *also* **rho·dine** \", -,dēn\ *n* -s [ISV *rhod-* + *-in*, *-ine*] **:** any of several derivatives of chlorophyll b that are formyl derivatives of the chlorins

**rho·di·nal** \'rōdᵊn,al\ *n* -s [ISV *rhodin-* (as in *rhodinol*) + *-al*] **:** levorotatory citronellol

**rho·di·nol** \'rōdᵊn,ōl, -,ōl\ *n* -s [ISV *rhodin-* (fr. L *rhodinus* made from roses, fr. Gk *rhodinos*, fr. *rhodon* rose) + *-ol* — more at ROSE] **1 :** a liquid obtained usu. from geranium oil or rose oil, consisting essentially of citronellol and geraniol, and used in perfumes esp. of the rose type **2 :** levorotatory citronellol

**rho·dite** \'rō,dīt\ *n* -s [NL *rhodium* + E *-ite*] **:** a mineral consisting of a native alloy of rhodium and gold

**rho·di·um** \'rōdēəm\ *n* -s [NL, fr. *rhod-* + *-ium*] **:** a bright white hard ductile metallic element that is one of the platinum metals, that is chiefly trivalent and is resistant to attack by acids and other corrosive agents at ordinary temperatures, that occurs esp. in platinum ores, and that is used chiefly in alloys with platinum (as for catalysts, thermocouples, or spinnerets for rayon) and in plating for reflectors, electrical contacts, or jewelry — symbol *Rh;* see ELEMENT table

**rhodium oil** *n* [*rhodium* (*wood*) + *oil*] **1 :** a thick yellowish essential oil with roselike odor obtained from rhodium wood — called also *rosewood oil* **2 :** a commercial mixture containing rose oil

**rhodium wood** *n* [part trans. of NL *lignum rhodium*, fr. L *lignum* wood + NL *rhodium*, neut. of *rhodius* of the rose, fr. Gk *rhodon* rose] **:** the fragrant wood of the root and stem of either of two shrubs (*Convolvulus scoparius* and *C. virgatus*) native to the island of Teneriffe

**rhodi·zite** \'rōdə,zīt, 'räd-\ *n* -s [G *rhodizit*, fr. Gk *rhodizein* to be rose-red (fr. *rhodon* rose + *-izein* -ize) + G *-it* -ite; fr. its reddening effect on the blowpipe flame] **:** a mineral $NaKLiAl_4Be_3B_{10}O_{27}$ consisting of a borate of aluminum, beryllium, lithium, potassium, and sodium occurring in white isometric crystals (hardness 8, sp. gr. 3.4)

**rho·di·zon·ic acid** \¦rōdə¦zänik-\ *n* [G *rhodizon-* (in *rhodizonsäure* rhodizonic acid, fr. Gk *rhodizein* to be rose-red + G *säure* acid) + E *-ic*] **:** a cyclic acid $C_6H_2O_6$ known in an unstable colored enediol form and a colorless more stable tautomeric form but obtained usu. in the form of a colored salt (as the red disodium salt by passing carbon monoxide into a solution of sodium in liquid ammonia)

**rhod·ni·us** \'rädnēəs\ *n, cap* [NL, prob. irreg. fr. Gk *rhodon* rose; fr. the pink body fluid] **:** a genus of reduviid bugs including some that are intermediate hosts of the trypanosome causing Chagas' disease

**rhodo-** — see RHOD-

**rho·do·bac·te·ri·a·ce·ae** \¦rō(,)dō(,)bak,tirē'āsē,ē\ *n pl, cap* [NL, fr. *Rhodobacterium*, type genus (fr. *rhod-* + *Bacterium*) + *-aceae*] *in some classifications* **:** a family of Thiobacteriales coextensive with Rhodobacteriinae

**rho·do·bac·te·ri·a·les** \-ē(,)lēz\ *n pl, cap* [NL, fr. *Rhodobacterium* + *-ales*] *in some classifications* **:** an order of bacteria coextensive with Rhodobacteriinae

**rho·do·bac·te·ri·inae** \-rē'ī(,)nē\ *n pl, cap* \-rē'ī(,)nē\ [NL, fr. *Rhodobacterium* + *-inae*] **:** a suborder of Pseudomonadales comprising bacteria that contain bacteriochlorophyll or a related green pigment and carry on a form of photosynthesis not resulting in release of free oxygen but requiring extraneous oxidizable material (as hydrogen, reduced sulfur compounds, or alcohols) which is dehydrogenated with concurrent reduction of carbon dioxide to form water as a metabolic end product

**rho·do·chro·site** \ˌrōdəˈkrōˌsīt, rōˈdäkrəˌs-\ *n* -s [G *rhodochrosit,* fr. *rhod-* + Gk *chrōsis* coloring (fr. *chrōs, chroos* color, skin) + G *-it* -ite — more at CHROMATIC] **:** a characteristically rose red mineral $MnCO_3$ consisting essentially of manganese carbonate that is isomorphous with calcite and siderite and commonly occurs massive with rhombohedral cleavage like calcite (hardness 3.5–4.5, sp. gr. 3.45–3.60)

**rho·do·den·dron** \ˌrōdəˈdendrən\ *n* [NL, fr. L, fr. Gk, fr. *rhodon* rose + *dendron* tree — more at ROSE, DENDR-] **1** *cap* **:** a genus of shrubs or trees (family Ericaceae) that are native to the cooler regions of the northern hemisphere and are cultivated widely and that have alternate short-petioled often leathery leaves scattered or in clusters at the branch ends and flowers in terminal umbellate racemes **2** -s **:** any of various plants of the genus *Rhododendron* with persistent leathery leaves and campanulate flowers — compare AZALEA

**rho·do·lite** \ˈrōdᵊlˌīt\ *n* -s [*rhod-* + *-lite*] **:** a pink or purple garnet intermediate between pyrope and almandite that is used as a gem

**rho·do·me·la·ce·ae** \ˌrōˌdäməˈlāsēˌē\ *n pl, cap* [NL, fr. *Rhodomela,* type genus (fr. *rhod-* + Gk *melas* black) + *-aceae* — more at MULLET] **:** a large family of filamentous red algae (order Rhodymeniales) characterized by a much-branched thallus in which the main axis and branches consist of a polysiphonic arrangement of filaments — **rho·dom·e·la·ceous** \ˌ≈ˌ≈ˈlāshəs\ *adj*

**rho·do·microbium** \ˈrō(ˌ)dō+\ *n, cap* [NL, fr. *rhod-* + *microbium*] **:** a genus of reddish nitrogen-fixing soil bacteria (family Hyphomicrobiaceae)

**rhodomontade** *var of* RODOMONTADE

**rho·do·nite** \ˈrōdᵊnˌīt\ *n* -s [G *rhodonit,* fr. Gk *rhodon* rose + G *-it* -ite] **:** a pale red triclinic mineral $MnSiO_3$ consisting essentially of manganese silicate that commonly occurs massive and is used as an ornamental stone esp. in Russia (hardness 5.5–6.5, sp. gr. 3.40–3.68) — called also *manganese spar*

**rhodonite pink** *n* **:** a dark purplish pink that is redder and less strong than clover pink or Persian lilac

**rhod·o·pe** \ˈrädə(ˌ)pē\ *n, cap* [NL, prob. fr. Gk *Rhodopē,* nymph of a Thracian well] **:** a genus of minute marine animals that resemble planarians but are commonly regarded as degenerate nudibranch mollusks because of the structure of their nervous system

**rho·do·phy·ce·ae** \ˌrōdəˈfīsēˌē\ *n pl, cap* [NL, fr. *rhod-* + *-phyceae*] **:** a class of chiefly marine multicellular algae (division Rhodophyta) comprising algae in which red phycoerythrin and sometimes blue phycocyanin mask the chlorophyll, in which no motile form or stage exists, and in which there is a well-marked and often complex alternation of generations — compare RED ALGA — **rho·do·phyce·ous** \ˌ≈≈ˈfīsēəs, -ˈfis-\ *adj*

**rho·doph·y·ta** \rōˈdäfəd·ə\ *n pl, cap* [NL, fr. *rhod-* + *-phyta*] **:** a division or other category of lower plants coextensive with the class Rhodophyceae

**rho·do·plast** \ˈrōdəˌplast\ *n* -s [ISV *rhod-* + *-plast*] **:** one of the reddish chromatophores occurring in the red algae — compare PHAEOPLAST

**rho·dop·sin** \rōˈdäpsən\ *n* -s [ISV *rhod-* + *ops-* (fr. Gk *opsis* sight) + *-in* — more at -OPSIS] **:** a brilliant red photosensitive pigment in the retinal rods of marine fishes and most higher vertebrates that is important in vision in dim light and that is quickly bleached by light to a mixture of opsin and the retinene related to vitamin $A_1$ and is regenerated in the dark — called also *visual purple;* compare OPTOGRAM, PORPHYROPSIN

**rho·do·ra** \rəˈdōrə\ *n* [NL, fr. L, a plant] **1** *cap* **:** a genus closely related to *Rhododendron* and comprising shrubs that are found in Canada and New England and have delicate pink flowers produced before or with the leaves in the spring **2** -s **:** any plant of the genus *Rhodora*

**rho·do·sper·me·ae** \ˌrōdəˈspərmēˌē\ [NL, fr. *rhod-* + *-spermeae*] *syn of* RHODOPHYCEAE

**rho·do·sper·min** \-mən\ *n* [ISV *rhod-* + *sperm-* + *-in*] **:** PHYCOERYTHRIN

**rho·do·sper·mous** \ˌ≈≈ˈspərməs\ *adj* [*rhod-* + *-spermous*] **:** RHODOPHYCEOUS

**rho·do·spirillum** \ˈrō(ˌ)dō+\ *n, cap* [NL, fr. *rhod-* + *Spirillum*] **:** a genus of spiral actively motile bacteria (family Athiorhodaceae) that live in mud and stagnant water and are held to fix atmospheric nitrogen

**rho·do·ty·pos** \ˌrōdəˈtīpəs\ *n, cap* [NL, fr. *rhod-* + Gk *typos* model — more at TYPE] **:** a genus of Japanese shrubs (family Rosaceae) having solitary white tetramerous flowers and shining black persistent drupelets — see JETBEAD

**rho·dy·me·nia** \ˌrōdəˈmēnēə\ *n, cap* [NL, fr. *rhod-* + Gk *hymēn* membrane + NL *-ia* — more at HYMEN] **:** a genus of red algae (the type of the family Rhodymeniaceae) having a thallus that consists of numerous leaflike divisions — see DULSE

**rho·dy·me·ni·a·ce·ae** \ˌrōdəˌmēnēˈāsēˌē\ *n pl, cap* [NL, fr. *Rhodymenia,* type genus + *-aceae*] **:** a family of red algae (order Rhodymeniales) — **rho·dy·me·ni·a·ceous** \ˌrōdəˌmēnēˈāshəs\ *adj*

**rho·dy·me·ni·a·les** \ˌrōdəˌmēnēˈā(ˌ)lēz\ *n pl, cap* [NL, fr. *Rhodymenia* + *-ales*] **:** an order of red algae (subclass Florideae) that resemble those of the order Ceramiales but are distinguished by having the auxiliary cell formed prior to fertilization

**rhoe·ada·les** \ˌrēəˈdā(ˌ)lēz\ *n pl, cap* [NL, fr. Gk *rhoiad-, rhoias* corn poppy + NL *-ales*] **:** an order of dicotyledonous plants including the families Papaveraceae, Fumariaceae, and Cruciferae and having regular or irregular cyclic flowers with hypogynous stamens and a superior compound ovary

**rhoeadine** *var of* RHEADINE

**rhoeo** \ˈrē(ˌ)ō\ *n, cap* [NL] **:** a monotypic genus of herbs (family Commelinaceae) — see OYSTER PLANT 3

**rhomb** \ˈräm(b)\ *n* -s [MF *rhombe,* fr. L *rhombus,* fr. Gk *rhombos* rhombus, spinning top, magic wheel; akin to Gk *rhembein* to whirl — more at VERVAIN] **1 :** RHOMBUS **2** *obs* **:** CIRCLE, WHEEL **3 :** RHOMBOHEDRON

**rhomb-** *or* **rhombo-** *comb form* [MF, fr. L, fr. Gk, fr. *rhombos* rhomb] **1 :** rhomb ⟨*rhomb*encephalon⟩ ⟨*rhombo*hedron⟩ **2 :** rhombic and ⟨*rhombo*quadratic⟩ ⟨*rhombo*vate⟩

**rhomb·encephalon** \ˈräm,b+\ *n, pl* **rhombencephala** [NL, fr. *rhomb-* + *encephalon*] **:** the parts of the definitive vertebrate brain that develop from the embryonic hindbrain; *sometimes* **:** HINDBRAIN 1a

**rhombi** *pl of* RHOMBUS

**¹rhom·bic** \ˈrämbik\ *adj* [*rhomb-* + *-ic*] **1 :** having the form of a rhombus **2 :** ORTHORHOMBIC

**²rhombic** \"\ *or* **rhombic antenna** *also* **rhombic aerial** *n* -s **:** an aerial antenna with pronounced directional characteristics

**rhombic sulfur** *n* **:** the familiar yellow orthorhombic crystalline form of sulfur of density 2.07 that changes to the monoclinic form at 95.5° C

**rhom·bi·form** \ˈrämbəˌfȯrm\ *adj* [*rhomb-* + *-iform*] **1 :** RHOMBIC **2 :** RHOMBOID

**rhom·bo·clase** \ˈrämbəˌklās, -āz\ *n* -s [Hung *rhomboklas,* fr. *rhomb-* + *-klas* -clase] **:** a mineral $HFe(SO_4)_2.4H_2O$ consisting of a hydrous acid ferric sulfate and occurring in colorless rhombic plates with basal cleavage

**rhom·bo·gan·oid** \ˌrämbōˈgaˌnȯid\ *n* [NL *Rhomboganoidei*] **:** HOLOSTEAN

**rhom·bo·ga·noi·dei** \ˌräm(ˌ)bōgəˈnȯidēˌī\ *n pl, cap* [NL, fr. *rhomb-* + *Ganoidei*] *in some classifications* **:** an order or other group coextensive with Holostei in its narrowest scope

**rhom·bo·gen** \ˈrämbəjən, -ˌjen\ *or* **rhom·bo·gene** \-ˌjēn\ *n* -s [*rhomb-* + *-gen, -gene*] **:** the form of a mesozoan of the order Dicyemida that occurs in the sexually mature host, arises from a final generation of nematogens, and gives rise to free-swimming ciliated larvae — compare INFUSORIGEN — **rhom·bo·gen·ic** \ˌrämbəˈjenik\ *adj* — **rhom·bog·e·nous** \(ˈ)rämˈbäjənəs\ *adj*

**rhom·bo·he·dral** \ˌrämbōˈhēdrəl *sometimes chiefly Brit* -ˈhed-\ *adj* [NL *rhombohedron* + E *-al*] **1 :** relating to or having the form of a rhombohedron or a form derivable from a rhombohedron **2 :** of or relating to the rhombohedral system — **rhom·bo·he·dral·ly** \-drəlē\ *adv*

**rhombohedral iron ore** *n* **1 :** HEMATITE **2 :** ²SIDERITE

**rhombohedral system** *n* **:** a crystal system characterized by three equal and interchangeable axes at equal angles to each other and usu. classed as a division of the hexagonal system — compare TETRAGONAL SYSTEM

**rhom·bo·he·dric** \-drik\ *adj* [ISV *rhombohedr-* (fr. NL *rhombohedron*) + *-ic;* orig. formed as F *rhombohédrique*] **:** RHOMBOHEDRAL

**rhom·bo·he·dron** \-drən *sometimes* -ˌdrän\ *n, pl* **rhombohedrons** \-drənz\ *or* **rhombohe·dra** \-drə\ [NL, fr. *rhomb-* + *-hedron*] **:** a parallelepiped whose faces are rhombuses

**¹rhom·boid** \ˈrämˌbȯid\ *n* -s [MF *rhomboïde,* fr. L *rhomboides,* fr. Gk *rhomboeidēs* rhombus-shaped, rhomboidal, fr. *rhombos* rhomb + *-oeidēs* -oid — more at RHOMB] **:** a parallelogram in which the angles are oblique and adjacent sides are unequal

rhomboid

**²rhomboid** \"\ *adj* [*rhomb-* + *-oid*] **1 :** shaped somewhat like a rhombus **2 :** RHOMBOIDAL

**rhom·boi·dal** \(ˈ)rämˈbȯidᵊl\ *adj* [¹*rhomboid* + *-al*] **:** shaped somewhat like a rhomboid

**rhom·boi·des** \rämˈbȯi(ˌ)dēz\ *n* [L] **1** *archaic* **:** RHOMBOID **2** *archaic* **:** RHOMBOIDEUS

**rhom·boi·de·us** \rämˈbȯidēəs\ *n, pl* **rhomboi·dei** \-ēˌī\ [NL, lit., rhomb-like, fr. L *rhomboides* + *-eus* -eous] **:** either of two muscles that lie beneath the trapezius muscle and connect the spinous processes of various vertebrae with the medial border of the scapula: **a** *or* **rhomboideus minor :** a muscle arising from part of the ligamentum nuchae and the last cervical and first thoracic vertebrae **b** *or* **rhomboideus major :** a muscle arising from the four or five upper thoracic vertebrae and the supraspinous ligament

**rhomboid fossa** *n* **:** the floor of the fourth ventricle of the brain

**rhom·boid·ly** *adv* [²*rhomboid* + *-ly*] **:** in a rhomboid form

**rhom·bo·zoa** \ˌrämbəˈzōə\ [NL, fr. *rhomb-* + *-zoa*] *syn of* MESOZOA

**rhombs** *pl of* RHOMB

**rhomb spar** *n* **:** dolomite esp. in rhombohedral crystals

**rhom·bus** \ˈrämbəs\ *n, pl* **rhombuses** \-bəsəz\ *or* **rhom·bi** \-ˌbī\ [L — more at RHOMB] **:** an equilateral parallelogram

rhombus

**rhon·chi·al** \ˈräŋkēəl\ *adj* [LL *rhonchus* + E *-ial*] **1 :** of or relating to a rhonchus **2 :** due to rhonchi

**rhon·chus** \-ŋkəs\ *n, pl* **rhon·chi** \-nˌkī, -ŋ,-, -ˌkē\ [LL, act of snoring, fr. Gk *rhonchos, rhonkos* snoring, wheezing — more at RHYNCH-] **:** a whistling or snoring sound heard on auscultation of the chest when the air channels are partly obstructed — compare RALE

**rhon·dda** \ˈrändə, -nthə\ *adj, usu cap* [fr. *Rhondda,* Wales] **:** of or from the urban district of Rhondda **:** of the kind prevalent in Rhondda

**rhopal-** *or* **rhopalo-** *comb form* [LL, fr. Gk, fr. *rhopalon*] **:** club ⟨*Rhopal*ocera⟩ ⟨*Rhopal*ura⟩ — in taxonomic names in zoology

**¹rho·pal·ic** *or* **ro·pal·ic** \(ˈ)rōˈpalik\ *adj* [LL *rhopalicus,* fr. Gk, *rhopalikos* rhopalic, like a club (i.e., thicker toward the end), fr. *rhopalon* club + *-ikos* -ic; perh. akin to Gk *rhabdos* rod — more at VERVAIN] **:** having each succeeding unit in a prosodic series larger or longer than the preceding one: **a :** having each successive word in a line or verse longer by one syllable than its predecessor **b :** having successive lines of a stanza increasing in length by the addition of one element (as a syllable or metrical foot)

**²rhopalic** \"\ *n* -s **:** a rhopalic line, verse, or stanza

**rho·pa·li·oid** \rōˈpalēˌȯid\ *n* -s [NL *rhopalium* + E *-oid*] **:** an organ of some scyphozoans that resembles a rhopalium

**rho·pa·lism** \ˈrōpəˌlizəm\ *n* -s [¹*rhopalic* + *-ism*] **1 :** the quality or state of being rhopalic **2 :** the use or production of rhopalic forms **3 :** an instance of rhopalic form in verse

**rho·pa·li·um** \rōˈpālēəm\ *n, pl* **rhopa·lia** \-ēə\ [NL, fr. Gk *rhopalion,* dim. of *rhopalon* club] **:** one of the marginal sensory bodies of a discomedusan

**rho·pa·loc·era** \ˌrōpəˈläsərə\ *n pl, cap* [NL, fr. *rhopal-* + *-cera*] **:** a division of Lepidoptera consisting of the butterflies — compare HETEROCERA — **rho·pa·loc·er·al** \ˌrōpəˈläsərəl\ *adj* — **rho·pa·loc·er·ous** \-sərəs\ *adj*

**rho·pa·lo·cer·cous** \ˌrōpəlōˈsərkəs\ *adj* [*rhopal-* + *-cercous* (fr. Gk *kerkos* tail)] *of a cercaria* **:** having a tail as wide as or wider than the body

**rho·pa·lo·si·phum** \-ˈsīfəm\ *n, cap* [NL, prob. fr. *rhopal-* + Gk *siphōn* tube, pipe — more at SIPHON] **:** a widely distributed genus of aphids including several that attack numerous crop plants and some that are vectors of plant viruses — see APPLE GRAIN APHID, CORN LEAF APHID

**rho·pa·lu·ra** \ˌrōpəˈlu̇rə\ *n, cap* [NL, fr. *rhopal-* + *-ura*] **:** the chief genus of Orthonectida

**rhos** *pl of* RHO

**rho·ta·cism** \ˈrōd·əˌsizəm\ *also* **rho·ta·cis·mus** \ˌ≈≈ˈsizməs\ *or* **ro·ta·cism** \ˈ≈≈ˌsizəm\ *n* -s [NL *rhotacismus,* MGk *rhōtakizein* to make too much or wrong use of the letter rho or *r* (fr. *rhō* rho) + L *-ismus* -ism — more at RHO] **1 :** a defective pronunciation of *r; esp* **:** substitution of some other sound for that of *r* **2 :** the change of the sound \z\ to \r\ esp. common between vowels (as in forlo*r*n [lose] or Latin gene*r*is [Sanskrit janasas])

**rho·ta·cize** \-ˌsīz\ *vi* -ED/-ING/-S [MGk *rhōtakizein*] **:** to undergo or produce rhotacism

**rh-positive** *adj, usu cap R* **:** containing Rh factor in the red blood cells

**RHQ** *abbr* regimental headquarters

**RHS** *abbr, often not cap* right-hand side

**rhu·barb** \ˈrüˌbärb, -ˌbäb\ *n* -s [ME *rubarbe,* fr. MF *rubarbe, reubarbe,* prob. fr. ML *reubarbum,* alter. of *reubarbarum,* prob. alter. of *rha barbarum* barbarian rhubarb, fr. LL *rha* rhubarb (fr. Gk *rha, rhēon,* perh. fr. *Rha* Volga river) + L *barbarum,* neut. of *barbarus* barbarous, barbarian — more at BARBAROUS] **1 :** a plant of the genus *Rheum* (as *R. rhaponticum, R. officinale,* or *R. palmatum*) having large leaves with thick succulent petioles that are often eaten as a sauce, in pies, or in preserves **2 :** the dried rhizome and roots of any of several herbs of the genus *Rheum* (as *R. officinale* and *R. palmatum*) grown in China and Tibet and used as a purgative and stomachic bitter **3 :** CITRINE 1 **4 :** a heated dispute or controversy **:** ROW ⟨election was no hotter than the ~ which followed it —*News of Orange County (Hillsboro, N.C.)*⟩; *specif* **:** a dispute on the field during a baseball game ⟨beanball throwing, deliberately manufactured ~*s* and umpire baiting —John Durant⟩ **5** *chiefly dial* **:** an aerial strafing mission against targets of opportunity ⟨when a fighter pilot flies low over France, strafing whatever he finds — trains, troops, airdromes — he is on a ~ —*Time*⟩ **6** *slang* **:** an out-of-the-way sparsely populated countrified area ⟨the slick chick from the deep ~ —W.M.Swann⟩

**rhum** \ˈrəm, ˈrōm\ *n* -s [F, fr. E *rum* — more at RUM] **:** RUM

**rhumb** \ˈrəm(b)\ *n* -s [earlier *rumb,* fr. OSp *rumbo* or MF *rumb,* prob. modif. (influenced by L *rhombus* rhomb) of MD *ruum, rume* space, room, hold (of a ship); akin to OHG *rūm* space, room — more at RHOMB, ROOM] **1 :** RHUMB LINE **2 :** one of the points of the mariner's compass — compare COMPASS CARD

**rhum·ba** \ˈrəmbə, ˈru̇m-, ˈrüm-\ *var of* RUMBA

**rhum·ba·tron** \-bəˌträn\ *n* -s [*rhumba* + *-tron;* fr. the rhythmic oscillation of the waves inside it] **:** the buncher and catcher singly or in combination in a klystron

**rhumb line** \ˈrəmˌlīn\ *n* **:** a line on the surface of the earth that makes equal oblique angles with all meridians, that is a spiral coiling round the poles but never reaching them, and that is the path of a ship sailing always oblique to the meridian in the direction of one and the same point of the compass ⟨the only projection on which the *rhumb line* on the earth is reduced to a straight line on the map is the Mercator projection —C.H. Deetz⟩ — called also *loxodrome, loxodromic curve*

**rhu·punt** \ˈrēˌpint\ *n* -s [W] **:** a Welsh verse composed of three, four, or five four-syllable sections linked by cynghanedd and rhyme, the first three sections made to rhyme with each other and the fourth section to rhyme with the fourth of the next verse, and the whole written as a single line or divided into as many lines as it has rhyming sections

**rhus** \ˈrəs, ˈrüs\ *n* [NL, fr. L, sumac, fr. Gk *rhous*] **1** *cap* **:** a genus of shrubs and trees (family Anacardiaceae) native to temperate and warm regions having simple or pinnate leaves and small polygamous flowers in panicles with persistent calyx and one-ovuled ovary that produces a small one-seeded drupe — see POISON IVY, POISON OAK, STAGHORN SUMAC **2** *pl* **rhuses** *or* **rhus :** any plant of the genus *Rhus*

**rhus dermatitis** *n* **:** dermatitis caused by contact with various plants of the genus *Rhus* and esp. with the common poison ivy (*R. toxicodendron*)

**rhus gla·bra** \-ˈglābrə, -ˈläb-\ *n* [NL, lit., bald rhus] **:** the dried ripe fruit of the smooth sumac used as an astringent, in gargles, and as a refrigerant

**rhu·sio·path·ia** \ˌrüzēōˈpathēə\ *n* -s [NL, prob. fr. Gk *rhysos* shriveled, wrinkled + NL *-pathia* — more at RHYSSA] **:** SWINE ERYSIPELAS

**rhy·ac·o·lite** \rīˈakəˌlīt\ *n* -s [G *ryakolith,* fr. *ryako-* (fr. Gk *rhyak-, rhyax* stream, stream of lava) + *-lith* -lite; akin to Gk *rhein* to flow — more at STREAM] **:** SANIDINE

**rhy·aco·phil·i·dae** \(ˌ)rīˌakōˈfiləˌdē, ˌrīəkōˈf-\ *n pl, cap* [NL, fr. *Rhyacophila,* type genus (fr. Gk *rhyak-, rhyax* stream + NL *-phila*) + *-idae*] **:** a large and widely distributed family of caddis flies

**¹rhyme** *or* **rime** \ˈrīm\ *n* -s [*rhyme* alter. (influenced by L *rhythmus* rhythm) of *rime; rime* fr. ME *rime, ryme,* fr. OF *rime,* prob. modif. (influenced by OHG *rīm* number, series) of L *rhythmus* rhythm — more at RITE, RHYTHM] **1 a :** correspondence in terminal sounds of two or more words, lines of verse, or other units of composition or utterance: as (1) *also* **rhyme proper :** correspondence of the last accented vowels and all succeeding sounds in two lines or units esp. (as in English verse) when the sounds preceding the last accented vowel are different in the two rhyming units (2) **:** ASSONANCE 2 b (3) **:** CONSONANCE 2 d **b :** one of two or more words thus corresponding in sound ⟨*fall, appall, haul,* and *awl* are approved ~*s*⟩ ⟨there were no more ~*s* for *sky* —Lord Dunsany⟩ **c :** correspondence of other than terminal word sounds: as (1) **:** BEGINNING RHYME (2) **:** ALLITERATION (3) **:** INTERNAL RHYME **d :** RHYME SCHEME **2 a** (1) **:** rhyming verse ⟨some love of yours has writ to you in ~ —Shak.⟩ (2) **:** POETRY ⟨there is no such thing as a dialect for ~, or a language for verse —John Ruskin⟩ ⟨in the style of folk ~ —H.W.Wells⟩ ⟨writers of pleasant ~*s* —*Australasian*⟩ **b :** a composition in verse that rhymes ⟨my passionate ~ —W.B. Yeats⟩ ⟨as an extraordinary English doggerel ~ —J.M. Synge⟩ **3 :** RHYTHM, MEASURE ⟨gay broad leaves shone and swung in ~ —John Galsworthy⟩

**²rhyme** *or* **rime** \"\ *vb* **rhymed** *or* **rimed; rhymed** *or* **rimed; rhyming** *or* **riming; rhymes** *or* **rimes** [*rhyme* alter. (influenced by ¹*rhyme*) of *rime; rime* fr. ME *rimen, rymen,* fr. OF *rimer,* fr. *rime* rhyme] *vi* **1 :** to make rhymes **:** compose rhyming verse ⟨talked nothing but blank verse for the rest of the afternoon, except once or twice when she *rhymed* —J.B.S. Haldane⟩ ⟨how vilely doth this cynic ~ —Shak.⟩ **2 a** *of a word or verse* **:** to end in syllables that rhyme **:** form a rhyme ⟨the middle line of each terzina, or triplet, ~*s* with the first and third lines of the next —J.A.Macy⟩ **b** *of a word or syllable* **:** to be a rhyme ⟨since stressed can ~ with unstressed syllables the number of possible full rhymes in English is greatly extended —G.S.Fraser⟩ ⟨*cover* ~*s* with *lover*⟩ **3 :** to be in accord **:** HARMONIZE ⟨the sun, the banners, the rose leaves, the young children . . . ~ with the new joy and innocence to be achieved —George Santayana⟩ ~ *vt* **1 a :** to relate or praise in rhyming verse ⟨~*s* the struggles of the first settlers —Katharine L. Bates⟩ **b :** to put into rhyme ⟨if I could have the wish I ~ —H.A.Blood⟩ **c :** to compose (verse) in rhyme ⟨I *rhymed* out poetry in my youth —Donagh MacDonagh⟩ **d :** to cause to rhyme **:** use as rhyme ⟨*sleight* is *rhymed* with *counterfeit* as well as *height* —*Notes & Queries*⟩ **2 :** to drive or bring to a particular state or condition by rhyming or a rhyme ⟨pretty friendship 'tis to ~ your friends to death before their time —A.E.Housman⟩

**rhyme·less** \ˈrīmləs\ *adj* **:** lacking rhyme **:** UNRHYMED

**rhyme or reason** *n* [trans. of F *(sans) rime ni raison* (without) rhyme or reason] **:** GOOD SENSE, REASON, REASONABLENESS ⟨the order of entries is utterly without *rhyme or reason* —*Saturday Rev.*⟩

**rhym·er** *or* **rim·er** \ˈrīmə(r)\ *n* -s [*rhymer* alter. (influenced by ¹*rhyme*) of *rimer; rimer* alter. (influenced by *-er*) of ME *rymor,* fr. MF *rimeur,* fr. OF, fr. *rime* rhyme + *-eur* -or] **:** one that makes rhymes **:** VERSIFIER; *specif* **:** a mediocre poet

**rhyme royal** *n, pl* **rhyme royals :** a stanza of seven lines in iambic pentameter in which the first and third, the second, fourth, and fifth, and the sixth and seventh lines rhyme — compare BALLADE ROYAL, CHANT ROYAL, SEPTET

**rhyme scheme** *n* **:** the arrangement of rhymes in a stanza or a poem

**rhyme·ster** *or* **rime·ster** \ˈrīmztə(r), -m(p)st-\ *n* -s [*rhymester* alter. (influenced by ¹*rhyme*) of *rimester; rimester* fr. *rime,* n. + *-ster*] **:** an inferior poet **:** a maker of poor verse ⟨contended with the easy vernacular solution of the ~ —W.F. DeMorgan⟩

**rhyme-tag** \ˈ≈ˌ≈\ *n* **:** a word or phrase used primarily to produce a rhyme

**rhyming dictionary** *n* **:** a dictionary that groups rhyme words under the rhymes they form

**rhyming slang** *n* **:** slang in which a word whose meaning is intended is replaced by a word or phrase that rhymes with it (as *jimmygrant* for *immigrant*) or by part of a rhyming phrase (as *turtles* for *turtle doves* for *gloves*)

**rhym·ist** \ˈrīməst\ *n* -s [²*rhyme* + *-ist*] **:** POET; *esp* **:** one that uses rhymes

**rhynch-** *or* **rhyncho-** *comb form* [NL, fr. Gk, fr. *rhynchos* snout, bill, beak; prob. akin to Gk *rhonchos, rhonkos* snoring, wheezing, *rhenchein, rhenkein* to snore, snort, OIr *srennim* I snore] **:** snout — chiefly in taxonomic names in zoology

**rhyn·chob·del·lae** \ˌriŋˌkäbˈde(ˌ)lē\ [NL, fr. *rhynch-* + *-bdellae*] *syn of* RHYNCHOBDELLIDA

**¹rhyn·chob·del·lid** \ˌ≈ˌ≈ˈ≈ləd\ *adj* [NL *Rhynchobdellida*] **:** of or relating to the Rhynchobdellida

**²rhynchobdellid** \"\ *n* -s **:** a leech of the order Rhynchobdellida

**rhyn·chob·del·li·da** \ˌ≈ˌ≈ˈ≈lədə\ *n pl, cap* [NL, fr. *rhynch-* + Gk *bdella* leech + NL *-ida*] **:** an order of leeches with an exsertile proboscis, without jaws, and with colorless blood

**rhyn·cho·ceph** \ˈriŋkəˌsef\ *n* -s [NL *Rhynchocephalia*] **:** a reptile of the order Rhynchocephalia

**rhyn·cho·ceph·a·la** \ˌriŋkōˈsefələ\ *or* **rhyn·cho·ceph·a·li** \-ˌlī\ [NL, fr. *rhynch-* + *-cephala* or *-cephali*] *syn of* RHYNCHOCEPHALIA

**rhyn·cho·ce·pha·lia** \ˌriŋ(ˌ)kōsəˈfālyə, -ālēə\ *n pl, cap* [NL, fr. *rhynch-* + *cephal-* + *-ia*] **:** an order of Reptilia that comprises forms resembling lizards but having biconcave vertebrae, immovable quadrate bones, and other peculiar osteological characters and that includes *Sphenodon* and numerous fossil genera — compare TUATARA — **rhyn·cho·ce·pha·lian** \ˌ≈(ˌ)≈≈ˈfālyən, -lēən\ *adj or n* — **rhyn·cho·ce·phal·ic** \-ˈfalik\ *adj* — **rhyn·cho·ceph·a·lous** \ˌ≈(ˌ)≈ˈsefələs\ *adj*

**rhyn·cho·coel** *also* **rhyn·cho·coele** \ˈriŋkōˌsēl\ *or* **rhyn·cho·coelom** *or* **rhyn·cho·coelome** \ˈriŋkō+\ *n* -s [*rhynch-* + *-coel, -coele* or *coelom, coelome*] **:** a tubular cavity that holds the introverted proboscis of a nemertean worm and is sometimes considered homologous with the coelom

**rhyn·cho·coe·la** \ˌ≈≈ˈsēlə\ [NL, fr. *rhynch-* + *-coela* -coele] *syn of* NEMERTEA

**rhyn·cho·coe·lic** \ˌ≈≈ˈsēlik\ *or* **rhyn·cho·coe·lous** \-ləs\ *adj* [NL *Rhynchocoela* + E *-ic* or *-ous*] **:** NEMERTEAN

**rhyn·cho·lite** \ˈriŋkəˌlīt\ *n* -s [*rhynch-* + *-lite*] **:** the calcified tip of a jaw of a Triassic nautiloid cephalopod

**rhyn·cho·nel·la** \ˌriŋkəˈnelə\ *n, cap* [NL, fr. *rhynchon-* (irreg. fr. Gk *rhynchos* snout) + *-ella*] **:** a genus (the type of the family Rhynchonellidae) of articulate brachiopods having a sharply beaked ridged shell with the dorsal valve convex and the ventral more or less flattened — **rhyn·cho·nel·lid** \-ləd\ *n* -s — **rhyn·cho·nel·loid** \ˌ≈≈ˈ≈ˌlȯid\ *adj or n*

**rhyn·cho·nel·li·dae** \ˌ≈≈ˈ≈ləˌdē\ *n pl, cap* [NL, fr. *Rhynchonella,* type genus + *-idae*] **:** a family of articulate brachiopods that is known from the Ordovician to the Recent and is usu. placed in a distinct suborder or superfamily of Telotremata but is sometimes considered to form a separate order

**rhyn·choph·o·ra** \riŋ'käfərə\ *n pl, cap* [NL, fr. *rhynch-* (fr. Gk. fr. *rhynchos* snout) + *-phora* — more at RHYNCH-] **:** a large and economically important group of beetles consisting of the weevils that usu. have the head more or less prolonged in front to form a snout — **rhyn·choph·o·ran** \(ˈ)=ˌ==rən\ *adj or n* — **rhyn·cho·phore** \'riŋkəˌfō(ə)r\ *n* -s

**rhyn·choph·o·rous** \(ˈ)riŋ'käfərəs\ *adj* [*rhynch-* + *-phorous*] **1 :** having a beak **2** [NL *Rhynchophora* + E *-ous*] **:** of or relating to the Rhynchophora

**rhyn·cho·sia** \riŋ'kōzh(ē)ə\ *n, cap* [NL, fr. Gk *rhynchos* snout + NL *-ia;* fr. the shape of the pod] **:** a large genus of chiefly tropical often twining plants (family Leguminosae) with trifoliolate stipulate leaves and racemose yellow flowers

**rhyn·chos·po·ra** \riŋ'käspərə\ *n, cap* [NL, fr. *rhynch-* + *-spora*] **:** a genus of widely distributed sedges (family Cyperaceae) having leafy culms, clustered spikelets, a perianth usu. of barbed bristles, and an achene crowned by the persistent style base

**rhyn·cho·ta** \riŋ'kōd·ə\ [NL, fr. Gk *rhynchos* snout] *syn of* HEMIPTERA

**¹rhyn·chote** \'riŋˌkōt\ *or* **rhyn·cho·tal** \(ˈ)riŋ'kōd·əl\ *or* **rhyn·cho·tous** \-d·əs\ *adj* [*rhynchote* fr. NL *Rhynchota; rhynchotal, rhynchotous* fr. NL *Rhynchota* + E *-al* or *-ous*] **:** of or relating to the Hemiptera

**²rhynchote** \"\ *n* -s [NL *Rhynchota*] **:** HEMIPTERON, BUG

**-rhyn·chus** \'riŋkəs\ *n comb form* [NL, fr. Gk *rhynchos* — more at RHYNCH-] **:** one having a snout, bill, or beak of a (specified) kind — in generic names in zoology ⟨*Calyptorhynchus*⟩

**rhyn·cos·to·mi** \riŋ'kästəˌmī\ [NL, fr. *rhync-* (fr. Gk *rhynchos* snout) + *-stomi*] *syn of* ACARINA

**rhy·nia** \'rīnēə\ *n* [NL, fr. *Rhynie*, Scotland, where the fossil plant was discovered + *-ia*] **1** *cap* **:** a genus (the type of the family Rhyniaceae) of small leafless dichotomously branching fossil plants with terminal sporangia, a primitive stele, and smooth branching rhizomes — compare HORNEOPHYTON **2** -s **:** any plant or fossil of *Rhynia* or a closely related genus

**rhy·ni·a·ce·ae** \ˌrīnē'āsēˌē\ *n pl, cap* [NL, fr. *Rhynia*, type genus + *-aceae*] **:** a family of Paleozoic plants (order Psilophytales) known chiefly from the genera *Rhynia* and *Horneophyton*

**rhy·noch·e·ti** \rī'näkəˌtē\ *n pl, cap* [NL, fr. *Rhynochetos, Rhinochetus*, genus of kagus, fr. *rhyn-, rhin-* (fr. Gk *rhin-, rhis* nose) + *-ochetos, -ochetus* (fr. Gk *ochetos* channel, duct, means of carriage); akin to Gk *ochos* carriage — more at RHIN-, WAY] **:** a suborder of Gruiformes comprising the kagus

**rhyns·bur·ger** \'rīnzˌbərgə(r)\ *n* -s *usu cap* [D *rijnsburger*, fr. *Rijnsburg* Rhynsburg, village near Leiden in the southwestern Netherlands where the Collegiants first held independent services] **:** COLLEGIANT

**rhyo·dacite** \ˌrīō+\ *n* [*rhyolite* + *dacite*] **:** a rock intermediate between rhyolite and dacite that is the extrusive equivalent of granodiorite

**rhy·o·lite** \'rīəˌlīt\ *n* -s [G *ryolith*, fr. *rhyo-* (irreg. fr. Gk *rhyak-, rhyax* stream of lava) + *-lith* -lite — more at RHYACOLITE] **:** a very acid volcanic rock that consists typically of phenocrysts of quartz, sanidine, and sometimes oligoclase embedded in a groundmass of minute crystals usu. mixed with glass and is the lava form of granite — **rhy·o·lit·ic** \ˌrīə'lid·ik\ *adj*

**rhyo·tax·it·ic texture** \ˌrī(ˌ)ōˌtak'sid·ik-\ *n* [*rhyotaxitic* modif. (influenced by *-ic*) of G *rhyotaxitisch*, fr. *rhyo-* (in *rhyolith* rhyolite) + *taxitisch* taxitic, fr. *taxit* taxite + *-isch* -ish — more at TAXITE] **:** FLUIDAL TEXTURE

**rhypa·rog·ra·pher** \ˌripə'rägrəfə(r), ˌrip-\ *n* -s [Gk *rhyparographos* painting sordid subjects + E *-er*] **:** a painter who practices rhyparography

**rhypa·ro·graph·ic** \ˌ;==ˌrō;grafik\ *adj* [F *rhyparographique*, fr. Gk *rhyparographos* + F *-ique* -ic] **:** of or relating to rhyparography

**rhypa·rog·ra·phy** \ˌ==ˈrägrəfē\ *n* -ES [Gk *rhyparographos* painting sordid subjects (fr. *rhyparos* filthy, dirty + *-graphos* writing, painting — fr. *graphein* to write —) + E *-y* — more at CARVE] **1 :** the painting or literary depiction of mean, unworthy, or sordid subjects **2 :** the painting of genre or still-life pictures

**rhys·sa** \'risə\ *n, cap* [NL, fr. Gk *rhyssos, rhysos* shriveled, wrinkled; akin to Gk *rhytid-, rhytis* wrinkle — more at RHYTIDOME] **:** a genus of ichneumon flies parasitic on the larvae of wood-boring insects

**¹rhythm** \'rith̲əm\ *n* -s [MF & L; MF *rhythme*, fr. ⁴L *rhythmus*, fr. Gk *rhythmos* measure, rhythm, measured motion; akin to Gk *rhein* to flow — more at STREAM] **1** *obs* **:** RHYME **2 a :** an ordered recurrent alternation of strong and weak elements in the flow of sound and silence in speech including the grouping of weaker elements around stronger, the distribution and relative disposition of strong and weak elements, and the general quantitative relations of these elements and their combinations **b :** a particular example or form of rhythm ⟨the ~ of Homeric verse⟩ ⟨Sapphic ~⟩ ⟨iambic ~⟩ **3 a :** the forward movement of music **:** the temporal pattern produced by the grouping and balancing of varying stresses and tone lengths in relation to an underlying steady and persisting succession of beats **:** the aspect of music comprising all the elements (as accent, meter, time, tempo) that relate to forward movement as contrasted with pitch sequence or tone combination **b :** a symmetrical and regularly recurrent grouping of tones according to accent and time value ⟨rumba ~⟩ **c :** a particular typical accent pattern that groups the beats of a composition or movement into measures ⟨six-eight ~⟩ **d** *or* **rhythm section :** the group of instruments (as in a dance or jazz band) that supplies the rhythm ⟨the sound of the cornet . . . is a very stirring sound indeed, especially when accompanied by clarinet, trombone, and ~ —Wilder Hobson⟩ — see RHYTHM BAND **4 a :** the regular recurrence of similar features in a literary, musical, or artistic composition ⟨the effect of a pitched or a flat roof or a dome, the ~ of projections and recessions —Nikolaus Pevsner⟩ — compare PROPORTION, SYMMETRY **b :** an ordered sequence of harmonious or related compositional elements **5 a :** harmonious or orderly movement, fluctuation, or variation with recurrences of action or situation at fairly regular intervals ⟨investigators, concentrating on recurrent processes, have been able to demonstrate the existence of many ~s with a definite temporal sequence of phases repeated again and again —P.A. Sorokin⟩ ⟨the discipline of the factory hooter . . . had to be accepted by a people used to the entirely different ~s of country life —Roy Lewis & Angus Maude⟩ **b :** a segment of a rhythm ⟨the rising ~ of border incidents —*Atlantic*⟩ **6 : a :** regularly recurrent quantitative change in a variable biological process: as **a :** the pattern of recurrence of the cardiac cycle ⟨an irregular ~ marked by dropped systoles⟩ **b :** the recurring pattern of physical and functional changes associated with the mammalian and esp. human sexual cycle — see RHYTHM METHOD **7 a :** a patterned succession of various combinations in long and short time divisions of impulse and release in dancing that is usu. regularly recurrent in folk and simple art dances and often irregular and complex in modern dance when representative of erratic moods and their correlated movements **b :** easy muscular coordination (as in running, swimming, skating) **8 :** the repetition in a literary work at varying intervals and in an altered form or under changed circumstances of phrase, incident, character type, or symbol **9 :** the effect created by the elements in a play, motion picture, or novel that relate to the temporal development of the action (as the length and diversity of scenes, language, lighting, and the timing of the actors; *specif* **:** a sense of emotional intensity or of logical development in the plot of a motion picture produced by the use of montage ⟨a series of alternate long and short scenes securing a quicker ~ —Herbert Read⟩ ⟨even as the emotional ~ catches hold, the mood is continually jolted by meaningless digressions —*Time*⟩

**syn** CADENCE, METER: RHYTHM is wider in its use than CADENCE or METER. It is applicable to sound in poetry and music and also to any recurrent sound, movement, arrangement, or condition in virtually any sphere. Sometimes the word connotes little more than regular alternation ⟨the alternating *rhythm* of conquest and rebellion, repression and reprisal —Lewis Mumford⟩ ⟨a mysterious *rhythm* of elation and depression —Cyril Connolly⟩ Often it suggests subtlety and variation in recurrence ⟨prose *rhythm* should not have a conspicuous movement of sound —Allen Tate⟩ ⟨the shaking of the house was periodic but without rhythm —Christopher La Farge⟩ Often it suggests a recurrence pattern too varied to be easily grasped ⟨the wavering, lovely *rhythms* of the sea —Rose Macaulay⟩ ⟨a *rhythm*, even though not reducible to law, is manifest in the history of supreme court adjudication —Felix Frankfurter⟩ CADENCE is used mostly in relation to sound or to coordinated motion and is mainly applicable to shorter phrases or series. While RHYTHM stresses orderly recurrence with possible variety, CADENCE stresses variety in ordered sequence, often with falling or rising effects ⟨the song of the ruby-crowned wren, or kinglet — the same liquid bubble and *cadence* which characterize the wren songs generally . . . beginning in a fine, round, needlelike note, and rising into a full sustained warble —John Burroughs⟩ It may suggest the quite subtle or affective ⟨leaves in the mind of the sensitive reader an intangible residuum of pleasure; a *cadence*, a quality of voice that is exclusively the writer's own —Willa Cather⟩ METER applies almost entirely to more mechanical and more obvious poetic measures ⟨iambic pentameter is the most common *meter* in English poetry⟩

**²rhythm** *vb, obs* **:** RHYME

**rhyth·mal** \'rith̲məl\ *adj* **:** RHYTHMIC

**rhythm band** *n* **:** a band usu. composed of school children in the lowest grades who play simple percussion instruments (as rhythm sticks, sleigh bells, cymbals, or tambourines) to learn fundamentals of coordination and music

**rhythmed** \'rith̲əmd\ *adj* [fr. past part. of ²*rhythm*] **:** RHYTHMIC ⟨the scenes open with a kind of ~ dialogue which gradually rises into song —W.P.Eaton⟩

**rhyth·mic** \'rith̲mik, -mēk *sometimes* -th-\ *adj* [LL *rhythmicus*, fr. Gk *rhythmikos*, fr. *rhythmos* rhythm + *-ikos* -ic — more at RHYTHM] **:** marked by or moving in pronounced rhythm **:** regularly recurrent **:** CADENCED ⟨the ~ chiming of church bells —John Galsworthy⟩

**rhyth·mi·cal** \-məkəl, -mēk-\ *adj* [LL *rhythmicus* + E *-al*] **1** *obs* **:** RHYMING, RHYMED **2 :** RHYTHMIC ⟨~ prose⟩ **3 :** of, relating to, or involving rhythm ⟨~ skill ⟨~ systems⟩

**rhythmical accent** *n* **:** ACCENT 6d

**rhyth·mi·cal·ly** \-k(ə)lē, -li\ *adv* **1 :** in a rhythmic manner **2 :** with regard to rhythm

**rhyth·mic·i·ty** \rith̲'misəd·ē, -setē, -i\ *n* -ES [*rhythmic* + *-ity*] **:** the state of being rhythmic or of responding rhythmically

**rhythmic precipitation** *n* **:** the process of forming Liesegang rings

**rhyth·mics** \'rith̲miks, -mēks *sometimes* -th-\ *n pl but usu sing in constr, also* **rhyth·mic** \-k\ [*rhythmics* fr. ¹*rhythm* + *-ics; rhythmic* fr. LL *rhythmicus* rhythmical] **1 :** the science or theory of rhythms **2 :** rhythmical system

**rhyth·mist** \'rith̲(ə)məst\ *n* -s **:** one who studies, produces, or has a feeling for rhythm

**rhyth·miz·able** \'rith̲(ə)ˌmīzəbəl\ *adj* [*rhythmize* + *-able*] **:** capable of being rhythmized

**rhyth·mi·za·tion** \ˌrith̲(ə)mə'zāshən, -th̲əˌmī'z-\ *n* -s [*rhythmize* + *-ation*] **:** the organization of a series of events or processes into a rhythmic whole ⟨~ transforms walking into marching, prancing into dancing —Susanne K. Langer⟩

**rhyth·mize** \'rith̲(ə)ˌmīz\ *vt* -ED/-ING/-S [¹*rhythm* + *-ize*] **:** to make rhythmic

**rhythm·less** \'rith̲əmləs\ *adj* **:** devoid of rhythm

**rhythm method** *n* **:** a method of birth control involving continence during the period of the sexual cycle in which ovulation is most likely to occur — compare SAFE PERIOD

**rhyth·mol·o·gist** \rith̲'mäləjəst\ *n* -s [Gk *rhythmos* rhythm + E *-log* + *-ist*] **:** a specialist in rhythm

**rhyth·mo·poe·ia** *or* **rhyth·mo·pe·ia** \ˌrith̲mə'pē(y)ə\ *n* -s [LL *rhythmopoeia* making of rhythm, fr. Gk *rhythmopoiia*, fr. *rhythmos* rhythm + *-poiia* making (fr. *poiein* to make) — more at RHYTHM, POET] **:** rhythmic composition or art

**rhythms** *pl of* RHYTHM

**rhythm section** *n* **:** RHYTHM 3d

**rhythm stick** *n* **:** one of a pair of plain or notched wood sticks that are struck or rubbed together to produce various percussive sounds and used esp. by young children in rhythm bands

**rhyth·mus** \'rith̲məs\ *n, pl* **rhyth·mi** \-ˌmī\ [L — more at RHYTHM] **:** RHYTHM

**rhy·tid·odon** \rə'tidəˌdän\ [NL, fr. Gk *rhytid-, rhytis* wrinkle + NL *-odon*] *syn of* RUTIODON

**rhyt·i·dome** \'rid·əˌdōm\ *n* -s [prob. fr. (assumed) NL *rhytidoma*, fr. Gk *rhytidōma* wrinkle, fr. *rhytidoun* to wrinkle, fr. *rhytid-, rhytis* wrinkle; perh. akin to Gk *eryein* to drag, draw, L *rudent-, rudens* ship's rope] **:** the part of the bark external to the last formed periderm — called also *scale bark, shell bark*

**¹rhy·ti·na** \rə'tīnə, -tēnə\ [NL, fr. *rhyt-* (fr. Gk *rhytis* wrinkle) + *-ina*] *syn of* HYDRODAMALIS

**²rhytina** \"\ *n* -s **:** STELLER'S SEA COW

**rhy·tis·ma** \rə'tizmə, rī't-\ *n, cap* [NL, fr. Gk *rhytisma* patch] **:** a genus of fungi (family Phacidiaceae) forming black stromata — see TAR SPOT

**rhy·ton** \'rīˌtän\ *n* -s [Gk *rhyton*, neut. of *rhytos* flowing; akin to Gk *rhein* to flow — more at STREAM] **:** an ancient Greek drinking horn of pottery usu. having a base in the form of the head of an animal, woman, or mythological creature

**¹ri** *var of* RIG

**²ri** \'rē\ *n, pl* **ri** [Jap, fr. Chin *li³*] **:** a Japanese unit of distance equal to about 2.44 miles

**RI** *abbr* **1** refractive index **2** reinsurance **3** repulsion induction

**ria** \'rēə\ *n* -s [Sp *ría*, fr. *río* river — more at RIO] **:** a long narrow inlet that gradually gets shallower inward and that is caused by submergence of the lower part of a narrow river valley **:** CREEK

**ri·al** \'rīəl\ *adj* [ME, fr. MF *rial, real, royal* — more at ROYAL] *archaic Scot* **:** ROYAL, MAGNIFICENT

**²rial** *var of* RYAL

**³rial** *var of* REAL

**⁴rial** *var of* RIYAL

**⁵ri·al** \rē'(y)ȯl, -ˌäl\ *n* -s [Per, fr. Ar *riyāl* riyal] **1 a :** the basic monetary unit of Iran — see MONEY table **b :** a coin representing the rial **2 a :** a Sudanese monetary unit equal to ¹⁄₁₀ pound **b :** a coin representing one rial

**ri·al·to** \rē'al(ˌ)tō\ *n* -s [fr. *Rialto*, island and district on the Grand Canal, Venice, Italy in which the exchange was situated] **1 :** an exchange or market place **2 :** the theater district of a town

**ri·ant** \'rīənt\ *adj* [MF, pres. part. of *rier* to laugh, fr. L *ridēre* — more at RIDICULOUS] **:** pleasingly mirthful or gay ⟨a ~ landscape⟩ — **ri·ant·ly** *adv*

**ri·ata** \rē'ad·ə, -'ä-\ *n* -s [modif. of AmerSp *reata* — more at LARIAT] **:** LARIAT

**¹rib** \'rib\ *n* -s [ME *rib, ribbe*, fr. OE *rib, ribb;* akin to OHG *rippi* rib, ON *rif*, OSlav *rebro*, Gk *erephein* to roof over] **1 a :** one of the paired curved bony or partly cartilaginous rods that stiffen the lateral walls of the body of most vertebrates and protect the viscera, that are usu. movably articulated with the spinal column at the dorsal end and sometimes connected also at the ventral end with the sternum by costal cartilages morphologically considered unossified segments, that occur in mammals exclusively or almost exclusively in the thoracic region, and that form in man normally 12 pairs — see FALSE RIB, TRUE RIB; COW illustration **b :** one of the swimming bands of a ctenophore **c :** a cut of meat including a rib ⟨~ roast⟩ — see BEEF illustration, LAMB illustration **d** [so called fr. the biblical account of Eve's creation from Adam's rib, Gen 2:21–22] **:** WIFE **2 :** an elongated elevation running the length of an object: as **a** (1) **:** the quill of a feather (2) **:** a vein of an insect's wing (3) **:** one of the primary veins of a leaf **b** (1) **:** a strip of land lying between furrows (2) **:** STRATUM, DIKE *specif* **:** a small ridge on a steep mountainside **c** *chiefly Scot* **:** a bar of a gate **d** (1) **:** one of the vertical ridges formed in knitting by ribbing and containing one or more wales (2) **:** one of the horizontal or vertical ridges in a woven fabric that are in a close regular pattern and made by the use of coarser yarns in the warp or weft **e** (1) **:** a ridge, fin, or wing (as on a plate, cylinder, or beam) used to strengthen, stiffen, or dissipate heat (2) **:** a metal strip running the length or most of the length of a shoulder weapon (as a shotgun) or of a handgun (as a target pistol) and designed to facilitate alignment of the sights or to bring the sighting plane into prominence **f :** RAISED BAND **3 :** an object designed to provide lateral, longitudinal, or horizontal support: as **a :** a framing timber in a house or other similar building **b** (1) **:** a transverse member of the frame of a ship that runs from keel to deck and carries the planking or plating (2) **:** a light fore-and-aft member in the wing of an airplane that supports the fabric covering or metal skin and that determines the form of the wing section **c :** a stiff strip (as of metal) supporting the fabric in an umbrella **d :** one of a number of parallel members supporting a bridge **e** (1) **:** one of the quadrantal or otherwise curved members of the framing for a dome (2) **:** an arched longitudinal frame of timber or one of a set of such frames parallel and equidistant supporting the transverse laggings and with them forming the centering of an arch (3) **:** one of the arches in Romanesque and Gothic vaulting meeting and crossing one another and dividing the whole vaulted space into triangles (4) **:** a projecting band in a vault or arched ceiling **f** (1) **:** solid coal on the side of a gallery or solid ore in a vein (2) **:** an elongated pillar of ore or coal left as a support in a mine **4 :** an object so curved as to resemble a human rib: as **a :** a curved side connecting the top and back of a musical instrument of the violin class **b :** a piece of thin wood or slate used in ceramic work that is cut to the shape of the section or profile of a cup and that is employed in smoothing the inner surface of the clay

**²rib** \"\ *vt* **ribbed; ribbed; ribbing; ribs 1 :** to furnish, strengthen, or enclose with or as if with ribs ⟨~ a vessel⟩ ⟨~ a structure⟩ **2 :** to form (vertical ridges) in knitting by alternating knit and purl stitches in a regular pattern

**³rib** \"\ *n* -s [IrGael *ribe, ruibe*] *Irish* **:** a single hair **:** BRISTLE

**⁴rib** \"\ *vt* **ribbed; ribbed; ribbing; ribs** [prob. fr. ¹*rib;* fr. the tickling of one's ribs to cause laughter] **:** to poke fun at **:** KID ⟨players *ribbing* an umpire⟩

**⁵rib** \"\ *n* -s **1 :** JOKE ⟨always enjoying a ~ on someone else⟩ **2 :** PARODY ⟨an uproarious ~ of a Western⟩

**rib-** *or* **ribo-** *comb form* [*ribose*] **1 :** related to ribose ⟨*rib*itol⟩ ⟨*ribo*flavin⟩ **2** *ribo-, usu ital* **:** having the stereochemical arrangement of atoms or groups found in ribose ⟨D-*ribo*-3-hexulose⟩

**¹rib·ald** \'ribəld *also* 'riˌbōld *or* ÷'rīˌbōld *or* ÷'rībəld\ *n* -s [ME *ribald, ribaud*, fr. OF *ribauld, ribaut* wanton, rascal, fr. *riber* to be wanton, of Gmc origin; akin to OHG *rīban* to be wanton, lit., to turn, twist, rub — more at RHIPID-] **1 a :** a retainer employed in a feudal household in the meanest positions and in the field as an irregular soldier **b :** ROGUE, RASCAL **2 :** a person coarse or lewd in appearance, speech, writing, or thought

**²ribald** \"\ *adj* **1 :** marked by coarseness and indecency **:** OFFENSIVE **2 :** characterized by broad indecent humor ⟨a ~ tale⟩ **:** capable of, displaying, or suggesting rough convivial wit ⟨a ~ mind⟩ ⟨a ~ company⟩ **syn** see COARSE

**rib·ald·ly** *adv* [²*ribald* + *-ly*] **:** in a ribald manner ⟨stayed only to hoot ~ at the delegates —W.A.White⟩

**rib·al·drous** \-drəs\ *adj* [*ribaldry* + *-ous*] *archaic* **:** RIBALD

**rib·al·dry** \-drē, -dri\ *n* -ES [ME *ribaldrie, ribaudrie*, fr. MF *ribaulderie, ribauderie*, fr. OF, fr. *ribauld* ribald + *-erie* -ery] **1** *obs* **:** lewd or licentious acts **:** DEBAUCHERY **2 a :** ribald quality, nature, or element ⟨the ~ in an author's works⟩ ⟨the lusty ~ of peasant humor —*Times Lit. Supp.*⟩ **b :** ribald language, jesting, or wit ⟨the ~ of a stag party⟩

**rib·and** *also* **rib·band** \'ribən(d)\ *n* -s [ME *riband, ribband*, alter. (prob. influenced by ¹*band*) of *riban* ribbon — more at RIBBON] **1 :** a ribbon used esp. as a decoration **2 :** RIBBON 2a

**ri·bat** \rə'bät\ *n* -s [Ar *ribāṭ* station, inn, religious house] **:** an Islamic monastery

**¹rib·band** \'ri(b)ˌban(d), -ibən(d)\ *n* [¹*rib* + *band*] **1 a :** a long narrow strip or bar used in shipbuilding that is bent and bolted longitudinally to the frames to hold them in position **b :** a timber secured along the ground ways in shipbuilding to keep the sliding ways from spreading to the side **2 :** a scantling, spar, or plank used in construction work (as in making a corduroy road or a pontoon bridge)

**²ribband** \"\ *vt* -ED/-ING/-S **:** to provide, secure, or fasten with a riband

**ribbed** \'ribd\ *adj* [¹*rib* + *-ed*] **:** furnished, marked, or strengthened with a rib ⟨a ~ structure⟩ ⟨~ land⟩ ⟨a ~ sweater⟩

**ribbed-knit** *var of* RIB-KNIT

**ribbed vault** *n* **:** a vault in which solid ribs carry the vaulted surface

**¹rib·ber** \'ribə(r)\ *n* -s [²*rib* + *-er*] **:** one that ribs: as **a :** one that builds or installs ribs in construction work **b :** a knitting machine that produces ribbed fabrics or that makes ribbing for cuffs, waistbands, or similar pieces of clothing

**²ribber** \"\ *n* -s [⁴*rib* + *-er*] **:** one that mocks or teases

**ribbier** *comparative of* RIBBY

**ribbiest** *superlative of* RIBBY

**¹rib·bing** \'ribiŋ, -bēŋ\ *n* -s [¹*rib* + *-ing*] **:** a pattern, system, or structure composed of ribs: as **a** (1) **:** a framework (as of a building or ship) made up chiefly of ribs (2) **:** the ribwork in vaulting **b :** the veins of a leaf **c :** a strip of ribbed fabric (as a semielastic band of ribs used as a close-fitting edge finish on sweaters, socks, and mittens) **d :** a part of an artificial fly wound over the body material and often added to simulate the stripes on a natural insect — see FLY illustration

**²ribbing** \"\ *n* -s [fr. gerund of ⁴*rib*] **:** an act of teasing or mocking

**rib·bok** \'riˌbäk\ *n, pl* **ribbok** *or* **ribboks** [by alter.] **:** RHEBOK

**¹rib·bon** \'ribən *also* -bᵊm\ *n* -s *often attrib* [ME *riban*, fr. MF *riban, ruban*, prob. fr. a Gmc compound whose first element is akin to OE *ring* and whose second element is akin to ME *band*] **1 a :** a flat or tubular narrow fabric (as of silk, rayon, nylon, cotton, tinsel) closely woven in various constructions (as in velvet, satin, taffeta, or grosgrain) and used for trimmings, decorations, or knitting **b :** a narrow fabric (as of paper or textile fibers pasted on tape) used chiefly for tying packages **c :** a piece of usu. multicolored ribbon that serves as a decoration (as for military service) or that is worn in place of a medal represented by its colors ⟨campaign ~⟩ ⟨service ~⟩ **d :** a strip of imprinted red, blue, white, or yellow satin often attached to a button or badge and given in recognition of winning one of the first three or four places in competition (as at a horse show, livestock show) **2 :** a long narrow strip resembling or suggestive of a ribbon: as **a :** a single bendlet that surmounts the other heraldic bearings and is borne as a difference mark **b :** a board framed into the studs to support the ceiling or floor joists **c :** a straight or crumpled varicolored stripe across slate that shows the location of the original bedding **d** (1) **:** RADULA (2) **:** an egg case (as of a mollusk) when produced in a long string **e** (1) **:** a strip of inked fabric (as in a typewriter) on which the type faces strike and which prints the type characters on a sheet below (2) **:** a continuous roll of paper that regulates casting in the monotype **f** (1) **:** the form in which molten glass is taken from the furnace in the manufacture of some types of glass (2) **:** a pressed and flattened sliver ready for spinning **g :** a bookmark consisting of a length of material often attached by one end to the top headband of the book **3 ribbons** *pl* **:** REINS **4 :** FRAGMENT, PIECE, SHRED — usu. pl. ⟨torn to ~s⟩ **5 :** RIBBAND

**²ribbon** \"\ *vt* **ribboned** \-bənd, -bᵊmd\ **ribboned** \"\ **ribboning** \-b(ə)niŋ\ **ribbons** \-bənz, -bᵊmz\ **1 a :** to adorn or mark out with or as if with a ribbon ⟨gaily ~*ed* schoolgirls⟩ **b :** to divide into ribbons ⟨~ material for bandages⟩ **2 :** to rip to shreds ⟨a flag ~*ed* by the wind⟩

**ribbonback** \'==ˌ=\ *adj* **:** having a back with open slats carved to represent intertwined ribbons ⟨a ~ chair⟩

**ribbon bed** *n* **:** a flower bed in which the plants are set in parallel lines or rows with one kind to a row

**ribbon brake** *n* **:** BAND BRAKE

**ribbon bush** *n* **:** CENTIPEDE PLANT

**ribbon candy** *n* **:** a thin brittle usu. colored sugar candy made in the form of a ribbon folded back and forth upon itself and bought esp. at Christmastime

**ribbon conveyor** *n* **:** a spiral continuous conveyor having an open space between the shaft and the ribbon flight so that damp or sticky material cannot build up around the shaft

**ribbon copy** *n* **:** a copy (as of a document) made by the typewriter ribbon **:** ORIGINAL — compare CARBON COPY
**ribbon development** *or* **ribbon building** *n* **:** a system of buildings built side by side or adjoining that follow in succession along a road ⟨the drear *ribbon developments* of British industrial areas⟩ — called also *string development*
**rib·bon·er** \ˈribənə(r)\ *n* -s [¹*ribbon* + *-er*] **:** one that produces, processes, or handles ribbon; *specif* **:** one that inserts ribbon or tape into a tubing or beading on garments
**ribbon fern** *n* **1 :** a fern of the genus *Vittaria* having grasslike fronds **2 :** a commonly cultivated Asiatic fern (*Pteris serrulata*) naturalized in tropical America **3 :** an Australian adder's-tongue (*Ophioglossum pendulum*)
**ribbon figure** *or* **ribbon grain** *or* **ribbon stripe** *n* **1 :** ²ROE 2 **2 :** a banded figure fundamentally similar to roe but having the dark marks elongated to extend the length of the piece
**ribbonfish** \ˈ=,=\ *n* **1 :** any of various elongate greatly compressed marine fishes: as **a :** DEALFISH **b :** any of numerous elongated fishes constituting the family Cepolidae — called also *bandfish* **c :** OARFISH **d :** CUTLASS FISH **2 :** any of several fishes of the genus *Equetus* (family Sciaenidae) having striping usu. in gray and black
**ribbon grass** *n* **:** a reed canary grass (*Phalaris arundinacea picta*) grown for its white-striped leaves — called also *gardener's-garters, lady's-laces, painted grass*
**ribbon gum** *n* **:** an Australian eucalypt (*Eucalyptus viminalis*) with long slender leaves; *also* **:** any of several closely related trees (as the peppermint gum)
**rib·bon·ism** \ˈribə,nizəm\ *n* -s *usu cap* **:** the principles or practices of Ribbonmen
**ribbon jasper** *n* **:** jasper having stripes (as of red and green)
**ribbon lightning** *n* **:** a more or less continuous lightning discharge over an appreciable time producing a picture in the shape of a ribbon in a rotating camera
**ribbonlike** \ˈ==,=\ *adj* **:** resembling a ribbon
**ribbon loom** *n* **:** a narrow fabric loom usu. wide enough to weave forty or more pieces at one time
**rib·bon·man** \-,man\ *n, pl* **ribbonmen** *usu cap* [¹*ribbon* + *man;* fr. the green ribbon worn as a badge by members of the society] **:** a member of a Roman Catholic secret society founded in Ireland in 1808 in opposition to the landlord class
**ribbon microphone** *n* **:** a dynamic microphone in which the pick-up device is a thin metallic ribbon
**ribbon movement** *n* **:** the mechanism for moving the ribbon of a typewriter
**ribbon park** *n* **:** an extended area a few hundred feet wide landscaped like a park through which a highway winds
**ribbon reverse** *n* **:** a mechanism on a typewriter that works both automatically and manually to reverse the direction of travel of the ribbon
**ribbon rock** *n* **:** vein rock usu. quartz banded with stripes of darker mineral
**ribbons** *pl of* RIBBON, *pres 3d sing of* RIBBON
**ribbon saw** *n* **:** BAND SAW
**ribbon seal** *n* **:** a No. Pacific seal (*Histriophoca fasciata* or *Phoca fasciata*) of which the adult male is broadly banded with brown and yellowish white
**ribbon snake** *n* **:** a common No. American garter snake (*Thamnophis saurita*) found chiefly in wet places that is slender and striped with bright yellow and dark brown
**ribbon structure** *n* **:** a structure common in quartz veins consisting of narrow layers of quartz separated by thin dark seams of altered wall rock
**ribbon tree** *n* **:** a New Zealand tree (*Plagianthus betulinus*) from whose inner bark a strong fiber resembling flax is obtained — see NEW ZEALAND COTTON
**ribbon vibrator** *n* **:** a device behind the printing point indicator of a typewriter that carries the ribbon and raises it into printing position each time a character key is struck
**ribbon windows** *n pl* **:** a series of windows set side by side to form a continuous band horizontally across a facade
**ribbonwood** \ˈ==,=\ *n* **1 :** a New Zealand shrub or small tree (*Hoheria populnea*) of the family Malvaceae having bark that is used for cordage and a profusion of small snow-white flowers in close axillary clusters — called also *houhere* **2 :** RIBBON TREE **3** *West* **:** a small tree or shrub (*Adenostoma sparsifolium*) related to the chamiso
**ribbon worm** *n* **:** NEMERTINE
**ribbony** \ˈribənē\ *adj* [¹*ribbon* + *-y*] **:** of, adorned with, or like ribbon

ribbon windows

**rib·by** \ˈribē\ *adj* -ER/-EST [¹*rib* + *-y*] **:** showing or characterized by ribs ⟨~ fabric⟩
**rib cage** *n* **:** the bony enclosing wall of the chest consisting chiefly of the ribs and their connectives — called also *thoracic cage*
**ribe** \ˈrīb\ *n* -s [origin unknown] *dial* **:** a scrawny or thin person or animal
**ri·bes** \ˈrī(,)bēz\ *n, cap* [NL, fr. ML, currant, fr. Ar *ribās* rhubarb] **:** a genus of shrubs (family Saxifragaceae) having small racemose variously colored flowers with four or five scalelike petals, four or five stamens, two styles, a wholly inferior ovary, and a pulpy few-seeded to many-seeded berry that disarticulates from its pedicel — see CURRANT 2
**rib eye** *n* **:** the large piece of meat that lies along the outer side of the rib (as of a steer) and is a continuation of the longissimus dorsi muscle
**rib-faced deer** \ˈ=,=-\ *n* [¹*rib* + *faced*] **:** a muntjac (*Muntiacus muntjak*)
**ribgrass** \ˈ=,=\ *n* **:** ¹PLANTAIN; *usu* **:** an Old World plantain (*Plantago lanceolata*) with long narrow ribbed leaves that is now generally established in temperate regions — called also *buckhorn, English plantain, ribwort*
**ri·bi·tol** \ˈrībə,tōl, -,tȯl\ *n* -s [*rib-* + *-itol*] **:** ADONITOL
**ri·bi·tyl** \-,til\ *n* -s [*ribitol* + *-yl*] **:** the univalent radical $HOCH_2(CHOH)_3CH_2$— formed by removal of one of the terminal hydroxyl groups of adonitol
**rib-knit** *also* **ribbed-knit** \ˈrib(d),nit\ *n* **1 :** a knitting with a ribbed pattern **2 :** a fabric or a piece of fabric knitted with a ribbed pattern ⟨a dress with collars and cuffs of *rib-knit*⟩
**rib lath** *n* **:** metal lath with ribs at intervals to increase its rigidity
**rib·less** \ˈribləs\ *adj* **:** having no ribs or no visible ribs
**rib·let** \-lət\ *n* -s [¹*rib* + *-let*] **:** one of the rib ends in the strip of breast of lamb or veal cut from the rack — see LAMB illustration
**riblike** \ˈ=,=\ *adj* **:** resembling a rib
**rib meristem** *n* **:** a meristem in which cell divisions occur chiefly in one plane at right angles to the longitudinal axis and give rise to vertical rows or columns of cells — called also *file meristem;* compare MASS MERISTEM, PLATE MERISTEM
**ribo-** — see RIB-
**ri·bo·fla·vin** \,rībəˈflāvən, ˈ==,==\ *also* **ri·bo·fla·vine** \",-,vēn\ *n* [ISV *rib-* + *flavin*] **:** a yellow fluorescent crystalline flavin pigment $C_{17}H_{20}N_4O_6$ derived from ribose that is a growth-promoting member of the vitamin B complex occurring both free (as in milk) and combined as nucleotides and flavoprotein enzymes (as in liver, green leafy vegetables, yeast, anaerobic fermentation bacteria), that is made synthetically or by fermentation, and that is used in nutrition (as in vitamin preparations, enriching flour and bread, and poultry feed) and in medicine (as in treating lesions of the tongue, lips, and face) — called also *lactoflavin, vitamin $B_2$, vitamin G;* see ARIBOFLAVINOSIS 1
**riboflavin phosphate** *n* **:** a yellow crystalline mono-phosphoric ester $C_{17}H_{21}N_4O_9P$ of riboflavin that is a coenzyme of several flavoprotein enzymes — called also *flavin mononucleotide, riboflavin 5'-phosphate;* compare FLAVIN ADENINE DINUCLEOTIDE
**ri·bon·ic acid** \(ˈ)rīˈbänik-\ *n* [part trans. of G *ribonsäure,* fr. *ribon* (alter. by transposition of letters of *arabinose*) + *säure* acid] **:** an acid $HOCH_2(CHOH)_3COOH$ obtained by oxidation of ribose
**ri·bo·nu·cle·ase** \,rībōˈn(y)ükle,ās, -āz\ *n* -s [*ribonucleic* + *-ase*] **:** a crystalline enzyme found esp. in the pancreas that acts on ribonucleic acid by catalyzing its hydrolysis only to nucleotides and also by catalyzing the transfer but not liberation of phosphate groups from the nucleotides
**ri·bo·nu·cle·ate** \-ēət, -ē,āt\ *n* [*ribonucleic* + *-ate*] **:** a salt of a ribonucleic acid
**ri·bo·nu·cle·ic acid** \ˌrībō¦n(y)ü¦klēik-\ *n* [*rib-* + *nucleic*] **:** any of various nucleic acids that yield ribose as one product of hydrolysis, that are found in cytoplasm and some nuclei, and that are associated with the control of cellular chemical activities — abbr. *RNA;* called also *yeast nucleic acid;* compare DEOXYRIBONUCLEIC ACID
**ri·bo·nu·cleo·protein** \ˌrībō¦n(y)üklēō+\ *n* [*ribonucleic* + *-o-* + *protein*] **:** a nucleoprotein that yields a ribonucleic acid on hydrolysis
**ri·bose** \ˈrī,bōs *also* -ōz\ *n* -s [ISV *ribonic* + *-ose*] **:** a crystalline aldose sugar of the pentose class $C_5H_{10}O_5$ found esp. as the D-form as a constituent of many nucleosides (as adenosine, cytidine, guanosine) and obtained usu. from ribonucleic acid by hydrolysis or from altrose by degradation
**ri·bo·side** \ˈrībə,sīd, -,səd\ *n* -s **:** a glycoside that yields ribose on hydrolysis
**riboso** *var of* REBOZO
**ri·bo·syl** \ˈrībə,sil\ *n* -s [*rib-* + glyco*syl*] **:** a glycosyl radical $C_5H_9O_4$ derived from ribose
**ribroast** \ˈ=,=\ *vt* [¹*rib* + *roast,* v.] *archaic* **:** THRASH
**rib roast** *n* [¹*rib* + *roast,* n.] **:** a cut of meat containing the rib eye with rib or with rib removed — see BEEF illustration
**ribs** *pl of* RIB, *pres 3d sing of* RIB
**rib stitch** *n* **:** a ribbed knitting pattern — see ²RIB 2
**ri·buck** \ˈrī,bək\ *adj* [origin unknown] *slang Austral* **:** FIRST-RATE, GENUINE — often used interjectionally
**ri·bu·lose** \ˈribyə,lōs *also* -ōz\ *n* -s [*rib-* + *-ulose*] **:** a ketose $C_5H_{10}O_5$ that is formed from ribose or arabinose during epimerization and that plays a role in carbohydrate metabolism
**rib-vault** \ˈ=,=\ *n* **:** RIBBED VAULT
**ribwork** \ˈ=,=\ *n* **:** a ribbed structure, arrangement, or pattern
**ribwort** \ˈ=,=\ *or* **ribwort plantain** *n* **:** a ribgrass (*Plantago lanceolata*)
**ri·car·di·an** \rəˈkärdēən\ *adj, usu cap* [David *Ricardo* †1823 Eng. economist + E *-ian*] **:** of or relating to the English political economist Ricardo or to his theory of rent as an economic surplus
**ric·cia** \ˈrichēə\ *n, cap* [NL, fr. P.F.*Ricci* 18th cent. Ital. nobleman + NL *-ia*] **:** a genus (the type of the family Ricciaceae) of floating liverwort resembling duckweed and characterized by a dichotomously branched thallus which may be floating, submerged, or rooted on damp soil
**ric·ci·a·ce·ae** \,richēˈāsē,ē\ *n pl, cap* [NL, fr. *Riccia,* type genus + *-aceae*] **:** a family comprising fleshy and typically rosette-forming liverworts that are nearly cosmopolitan in distribution and being usu. included in Marchantiales but sometimes isolated in a separate order — see RICCIA
**ric·cio·car·pus** \,richēōˈkärpəs\ *n, cap* [NL, fr. *Riccia* + *-o-* + *-carpus*] **:** a genus of liverworts closely resembling and often included in *Riccia* but distinguished by the arrangement of archegonia and antheridia along the median groove of the gametophyte
**ric·co's law** \ˈri(,)kōz-\ *n, usu cap R* [after *Ricco,* its formulator] **:** a statement in physiology: when a light source of a given size and intensity is just capable of producing visual sensation reduction of either size or intensity will make it invisible
**¹rice** \ˈrīs\ *n* -s [ME *ris, rise,* fr. OE *hrīs;* akin to OHG & ON *hrīs* twig — more at CREST] **1** *chiefly dial* **:** TWIG, BRANCH **2** *chiefly dial* **:** BRUSHWOOD
**²rice** \"\ *n, pl* **rice** [ME *rys, ryce,* fr. OF *ris,* fr. It *riso,* fr. Gk *oryzon, oryza,* of non-IE origin; akin to the source of Skt *vrīhi* rice] **:** an annual cereal grass (*Oryza sativa*) widely cultivated in warm climates for its seed that is used for human food, for its hulls and other by-products that are used to feed livestock, and for its straw that is used in making paper
**³rice** \"\ *vt* -ED/-ING/-S [²*rice*] **:** to put through a ricer
**⁴rice** \"\ *adj* **1 :** consisting of, containing, or concerned with rice **2 :** made from nubby seedlike yarns ⟨~ fabrics⟩ **3 :** finished to resemble rice paper
**rice bean** *n* [²*rice*] **:** an annual half-twining bean (*Phaseolus calcaratus*) adapted to about the same area as the cowpea and cultivated for its seed to a limited extent in Asia and the East Indies
**ricebird** \ˈ=,=\ *n* **1 :** any of several small birds common in rice fields: as **a :** JAVA SPARROW **b :** BOBOLINK **c :** YELLOW-BREASTED BUNTING **d :** FLORIDA GALLINULE **2** *usu cap* **:** SOUTH CAROLINIAN — used as a nickname
**rice body** *n* **:** a smooth glistening ovoid particle like a grain of rice in joints and the sheaths of tendons and bursae occurring as a result of chronic inflammation — usu. used in pl.
**rice borer** *n* **:** any of several small caterpillars that are the larvae of pyralidid moths and that feed on rice plants
**rice bowl** *n* **:** an area (as southeast Asia) that produces large quantities of rice
**rice bran** *n* **:** a product obtained by milling rice consisting of the seed coat, a fraction of the grain removed in milling, the germ, and broken grains, and used as a stock feed and medicinally as a source of thiamine
**rice bug** *n* **:** an unpleasant smelling coreid bug (*Leptocorixa varicornis*) that is injurious to rice in India and the Far East — called also *rice sapper*
**rice bunting** *n* **:** BOBOLINK
**rice christian** *n, usu cap C* **:** a convert to Christianity who accepts baptism not on the basis of personal conviction but out of a desire for food, medical services, or other benefits
**rice coal** *n* **:** anthracite coal of a small size **:** number 2 buckwheat coal — see ANTHRACITE table
**rice cut-grass** *n* **:** a rough-leaved marsh grass (*Leersia oryzoides*) of eastern No. America having grains that somewhat resemble those of rice
**rice drier** *n* **:** an installation employing a series of tempering bins and blasts of heated air to dry and cure newly threshed rice
**rice-field eel** *n* **:** any of several small dark-colored eel-shaped Asiatic and East Indian fishes (family Synbranchidae) common in ditches and flooded rice fields from China to India
**rice-field mouse** *or* **rice-field rat** *n* **:** RICE RAT
**rice-field rail** *n* **:** SORA
**rice-field tire** *n* **:** a large rubber tire with deep lugs on the tread used on self-propelled machines working in wet rice fields
**rice flower** *n* **:** any of several commonly cultivated shrubs of the genus *Pimelea* whose small unopened flower buds suggest grains of rice
**rice glue** *n* **:** a cement made by boiling ground rice in soft water and used somewhat like papier-mâché to make various molded articles (as statuary)
**rice grain** *n* **:** the granular structure of the sun's surface or photosphere when observed in white light
**rice-grain decoration** *n* **:** ceramic decoration consisting of translucent spots produced by piercing the greenware before firing and allowing glaze to fill the openings
**ricegrass** \ˈ=,=\ *n* **1 :** a stoloniferous marsh grass (*Leersia hexandra*) of tropical America cultivated (as in the Philippines and southern Africa) for green forage **2 :** a European spartina (*Spartina townsendi*) used as a fodder and soil-binding plant **3 :** any of several grasses of the genus *Oryzopsis* (esp. *O. oryzoides*)
**rice grub** *n* **:** the larva of any of several beetles injurious to the rice plant in the southern U.S.
**rice hen** *n* **:** FLORIDA GALLINULE
**rice meal** *n* **:** the ground by-product of rice milling consisting of rice bran, polishings, and some rice flour and used chiefly as a feedstuff for livestock
**rice paddy** *n* **:** PADDY 2
**rice paper** *n* [so called fr. its resemblance to paper made from rice straw] **:** a thin delicate material resembling paper made by cutting the pith of the rice-paper tree into one roll or sheet and flattening under pressure
**rice-paper tree** *or* **rice-paper plant** *n* **:** a small Asiatic tree or shrub (*Tetrapanax papyriferum*) of the family Araliaceae widely cultivated in China and Japan and having large leaves with five to seven lobes, small white flowers, and stems with pith from which rice paper is made
**rice polish** *also* **rice dust** *n* **:** a finely powdered material obtained in milling white rice consisting of the inner bran layer with a little of the starchy interior that is rubbed off the kernels and used as a source of thiamin, riboflavin, and niacin and as stock feed
**rice polishings** *n pl* **:** the inner bran layer of rice that is rubbed off in milling
**rice powder** *n* **:** a face powder derived from rice
**ric·er** \ˈrīsə(r)\ *n* -s [³*rice* + *-er*] **:** a kitchen utensil designed for pressing cooked soft vegetables or uncooked soft foods through a perforated container so that the resulting product emerges as strings about the diameter of a grain of rice
**rice rail** *n* [²*rice*] **:** SORA
**rice rat** *or* **rice mouse** *n* **:** any of various cricetid rats (genus *Oryzomys*) abundant in moist or swampy areas from New Jersey to Venezuela; *esp* **:** a rodent (*O. palustris*) of the southeastern U.S. that greatly resembles the Norway rat

ricer

**ri·cer·car** \,rēcherˈkär\ *or* **ri·cer·ca·re** \-ä(,)rā\ *n, pl* **ricercars** \-ärz\ *or* **ricercari** \-ä(,)rē\ [It, fr. *ricercare* to seek again, seek out, fr. *ri-* re- (fr. L *re-*) + *cercare* to seek (fr. LL *circare* to go about, traverse); fr. the disguising of the subjects by various alterations — more at SEARCH] **1 :** a contrapuntal instrumental composition analogous to the motet in vocal music usu. consisting in the 16th century of a series of fugal expositions on different subjects and in the 17th century developing into the true fugue on a single subject **2 :** a learned and elaborate fugue esp. in the 18th century
**ri·cer·ca·ta** \-äd·ə\ *n* -s [It, fr. fem. of *ricercato,* past part. of *ricercare*] **:** RICERCAR
**rice root** *n* [²*rice*] **1** *also* **rice-root grass :** BROOMROOT **2** *also* **rice-root lily :** CHECKERED LILY
**rices** *pl of* RICE, *pres 3d sing of* RICE
**rice sapper** *n* **:** RICE BUG
**rice shell** *n* **:** any of numerous small white olive shells of *Olivella* or related genera
**rice stalk borer** *n* **:** a rice borer that is the larva of a moth (*Chilo plejadellus*)
**rice stinkbug :** a pentatomid bug (*Oebalus pugnax*) that feeds on developing rice grains in the southern U.S.
**rice tenrec** *n* **:** a tenrec of the genus *Oryzorictes*
**rice water** *n* **:** a drink chiefly for invalids made by boiling a small quantity of rice in water
**rice-water stool** *n* **:** a watery stool containing white flecks of mucus, epithelial cells, and bacteria and discharged from the bowels in Asiatic cholera and other severe forms of diarrhea
**rice water weevil** *n* **:** a weevil (*Lissorhoptrus oryzophilus*) that feeds as a larva on the roots of the rice plant when under water and as an adult on the rice leaves
**rice weevil** *n* **1 :** a small weevil (*Sitophilus oryzae*) destructive esp. of stored rice, wheat, flour, and biscuit — called also *black weevil* **2 :** RICE WATER WEEVIL
**ric·ey** \ˈrīsē\ *adj;* **riceyer; riceyest** [²*rice* + *-y*] **:** of or resembling rice ⟨~ texture⟩ ⟨~ color⟩
**¹rich** \ˈrich\ *adj* -ER/-EST [ME *riche,* fr. OE *rīce;* akin to OHG *rīhhi* rich, ON *rīkr,* Goth *reiks* mighty, ruler, OE *rīce* kingdom, realm, rule, OHG *rīhhi,* ON *rīki,* Goth *reiki;* all fr. prehistoric Gmc borrowings fr. Celt words whose root is represented by OIr *rī* (gen. *rīg*) king — more at ROYAL] **1** *obs* **:** possessed of great temporal power **:** MIGHTY **2 :** possessing or controlling great wealth **:** WEALTHY ⟨~ bankers⟩ **3 a :** possessed of high intrinsic or estimated value ⟨~ jewels⟩ ⟨the best uranium, that is to say the ~*est* rock in the world —J.D.Hillaby⟩ **b :** abounding in natural wealth (as ore, water, productive soil) — often used with *in* ⟨a kingdom ~ in forests and mines and lush pastureland⟩ **4 a** (1) **:** burdened with every luxury **:** SUMPTUOUS ⟨a ~ banquet⟩ (2) **:** gorgeously and pleasingly showy ⟨~ garments⟩ **:** splendidly costly ⟨~ tapestries⟩ (3) **:** magnificently impressive **:** gorgeously replete with pomp and ceremony ⟨a ~ military funeral⟩ **b** (1) **:** elaborately adorned **:** sumptuously ornamented ⟨a ~ altar⟩ (2) **:** fabricated from the best material and with the best skill and care ⟨~ furnishing⟩ ⟨~ interior decorations⟩ **5 a** (1) *of color* **:** vivid but pleasing; *specif* **:** of high or very high saturation and commonly of low lightness ⟨a ~ red⟩ (2) **:** warmly and pleasingly colorful ⟨a ~ landscape⟩ ⟨a ~ sunset⟩ **b :** full and mellow in tone and quality ⟨a ~ voice⟩ ⟨~ music⟩ **c** (1) **:** possessed of strong pleasant fragrance ⟨~ perfume⟩ (2) **:** pleasantly pungent ⟨a ~ barnyard odor⟩ **6 a :** ABUNDANT, PLENTIFUL — often used with *in* ⟨a mixture ~ in lime⟩ or postposed and hyphenated ⟨an iron-*rich* soil⟩ ⟨manganese-*rich* ore⟩ **b :** producing abundantly or yielding large returns **:** PRODUCTIVE ⟨a ~ mine⟩ ⟨~ farmland⟩ **7 a :** abundantly supplied with plant nutrients ⟨~ soil⟩ **b :** abounding in resinous heartwood ⟨~ stumps⟩ **c :** containing a large proportion of cementing material ⟨~ mortar⟩ ⟨~ concrete⟩ ⟨~ plaster⟩ **d :** containing a pronounced complement of fat or fatty substances ⟨turkey, pork, and other ~ meats⟩ ⟨~ eggnogs⟩ **e :** high in the combustible component — used esp. of a fuel mixture for an internal-combustion engine ⟨the ~ mixtures are generally used at high power output —*Aircraft Power Plants*⟩ — opposed to *lean* **8 a :** high in entertainment ⟨a ~ first act⟩ **:** strongly amusing ⟨~ humor⟩ **b :** pregnant with meaning, import, or significance ⟨~ words⟩ ⟨~ allusions⟩ **c :** LUSH ⟨~ foliage⟩ ⟨~ meadows⟩ **9 :** containing coarse, shocking, or scurrilous expressions ⟨~ abuse⟩ **10 :** pure or very nearly pure ⟨~ lime⟩ **11 :** PLASTIC — used in ceramics of clay

**syn** WEALTHY, AFFLUENT, OPULENT: applied to persons and to groups, RICH and WEALTHY are often interchangeable in indicating possession of considerable wealth ⟨was indeed *rich,* according to the standards of the Square; nay, *wealthy* —Arnold Bennett⟩ RICH may occasionally apply to greater possession than WEALTHY ⟨a *wealthy* but not a *rich* man —*Times Lit. Supp.*⟩ but it is more likely to be used in extended senses than WEALTHY ⟨lived alone, poor in worldly goods to the verge of distress, but *rich* beyond avarice in his vast and unique collection of snow-crystal pictures —W.J.Humphreys⟩ WEALTHY may suggest along with the fact of ownership its established, accustomed, or lasting enjoyment ⟨many of the *wealthy* supporters of the drama in Providence bought boxes by the season and were served wines and sherbets between the acts —*Amer. Guide Series: R.I.*⟩ AFFLUENT often is interchangeable with WEALTHY but may suggest a comfortably increasing wealth ⟨ride in larger and larger cars so that we may seem more *affluent* than we actually are —J.D.Adams⟩ OPULENT, applied less often to persons than to things, may suggest extreme wealth attended with lavish, luxuriant, or splendid expenditure ⟨an *opulent* frock of gold brocade —Jean Stafford⟩ ⟨an *opulent* blue mink coat —*Time*⟩ ⟨an *opulent* and glittering eastern throne —John Buchan⟩

**²rich** \"\ *n, pl* **rich** *or* **riches** \ˈrichəz\ **1** *pl rich* **:** a rich person ⟨the ~ has many friends —Prov 14:20 (RSV)⟩ — usu. used collectively ⟨respected by both ~ and poor⟩ ⟨the ~ all belong to the same clubs here⟩ **2** *riches pl* [ME (sing. or pl.), fr. *richesse* richness, wealth, fr. OF, fr. *riche* rich, of Gmc origin; akin to OE *rīce* rich — more at RICH] **:** something that makes one rich **:** rich possessions **:** abundant means **:** WEALTH ⟨spiritual ~*es*⟩ ⟨what care I in ~*es* to wallow —Robert Burns⟩
**¹ri·char·dia** \rəˈchärdēə\ *n, cap* [NL, fr. *Richard* Richardson †1741 Eng. physician and botanist + NL *-ia*] **:** a small genus of tropical American hairy herbs (family Rubiaceae) with inconspicuous flowers in dense heads and an ovary of two to four cells — see MEXICAN CLOVER
**²ri·char·dia** \rəˈshärdēə\ [NL, fr. L.C.M.*Richard* †1821, Fr. botanist + NL *-ia*] *syn of* ZANTEDESCHIA
**rich·ard miles** \,richə(r)dˈmī(ə)lz\ *n, usu cap R&M* [fr. the name *Richard Miles*] **:** a party to legal proceedings whose true name is unknown; *esp* **:** the fourth such party when four are unknown — compare JOHN DOE, JOHN STILES, RICHARD ROE
**richard roe** \-ˈrō\ *n, usu cap both Rs* [fr. the name *Richard Roe*] **:** a party to legal proceedings whose true name is unknown; *esp* **:** the second such party when two are unknown — compare JOHN DOE, JOHN STILES, RICHARD MILES

**rich·ard·so·nia** \\,richə(r)d'sōnēə\\ [NL, fr. Richard *Richardson* †1741 Eng. botanist + NL *-ia*] *syn of* RICHARDIA

**rich·ard·so·ni·an** \\¦==¦=nēən\\ *adj, usu cap* [Samuel *Richardson* †1761 Eng. novelist + E *-ian*] : of or relating to the English novelist Richardson or to the sentimental or psychological fiction he produced

**rich·ard·son's grouse** \\'richə(r)dsənz-\\ *n, usu cap R* [after Sir John *Richardson* †1865 Scot. naturalist] : a northern dusky grouse (*Dendragapus obscurus richardsonii*)

**richardson's jaeger** *n, usu cap R* [after Sir John *Richardson*] : PARASITIC JAEGER

**richardson's owl** *n, usu cap R* [after Sir John *Richardson*] : a small gray white-speckled owl (*Aegolius funereus richardsoni*) of the boreal forests of No. America

**rich·ards's indicator** \\'richə(r)dz(əz)-\\ *n, usu cap R* [after Charles B. *Richards* †1919 Am. engineer, its inventor] : a steam-engine indicator using a straight-line reducing motion between the working piston and the recording stylus or pencil which makes it suitable for use on high-speed engines

**richard's weed** *n* [after *Richard* Richardson †1741 Eng. physician and botanist] : MEXICAN CLOVER

**rich·ea** \\'rishēə\\ *n, cap* [NL, fr. Col. A. *Riche* †1791 Fr. naturalist] : a genus of chiefly Tasmanian and usu. evergreen shrubs or trees (family Epacridaceae) with elongated sheathing leaves often in terminal tufts that resemble those of the ti

**ri·chell·ite** \\rə'she,līt\\ *n* -s [F *richellite*, fr. *Richelle*, near Visé, Liége prov., Belgium + F *-ite*] : a mineral $Ca_3Fe_{10}(PO_4)_8(OH,F)_{12}.nH_2O(?)$ consisting of a basic hydrous fluophosphate of iron and calcium in yellow masses

**rich·en** \\'richən\\ *vt* -ED/-ING/-S [¹*rich* + *-en*] : to make rich or richer ⟨~ a mixture⟩ ⟨he used a privately furnished slush fund to ~ himself —R.C.Ruark⟩

**richer** *comparative of* RICH

**rich·esse** \\'ri,ches, rə'ch-\\ *n* -s [ME — more at RICH] : RICHNESS

**richest** *superlative of* RICH

**rich·ling** \\'richliŋ\\ *n* -s [¹*rich* + *-ling*] : a rich youth

**rich·ly** *adv* [ME *richely*, fr. OE *rīclīce*, fr. *rīce* rich + *-līce* -ly] **1** : in a rich manner **2** : in full measure : FULLY, AMPLY ⟨~ deserving of praise⟩

**rich·mond** \\'richmənd\\ *adj, usu cap* **1** [fr. *Richmond*, capital of Virginia] : of or from Richmond, the capital of Virginia ⟨a *Richmond* historical site⟩ : of the kind or style prevalent in Richmond **2** [fr. *Richmond*, borough of New York City, N.Y.] : of or from the borough of Richmond, New York, N.Y. ⟨*Richmond* officials⟩ : of the kind or style prevalent in Richmond

**rich·mon·de·na** \\,richmən'dēnə\\ *n, cap* [NL, irreg. fr. Charles W. *Richmond* †1932 Am. ornithologist] : a genus of birds (family Fringillidae) consisting of the cardinals

**rich·mond·er** \\'richməndə(r)\\ *n* -s *cap* [*Richmond*, capital of Virginia + E *-er*] : a native or resident of Richmond, Virginia

**rich·ness** *n* -ES [ME *richenesse*, fr. *riche* rich + *-nesse* -ness] : the quality or state of being rich ⟨the ~ of a country⟩ ⟨~ of allusion⟩

**rich oil** *n* : an absorbent oil rich in gasoline (as used in the manufacture of natural gasoline)

**rich-pine** \\'=,=\\ *n* [¹*rich*] *chiefly Midland* : KINDLING WOOD

**rich rhyme** *n* [trans. of F *rime riche*] : RIME RICHE

**richt** \\'rikt\\ *Scot var of* RIGHT

**rich·ter·ite** \\'riktə,rīt\\ *n* -s [G *richterit*, fr. Theodor *Richter* †1898 Ger. metallurgical chemist + G *-it* -ite] : a mineral $(Na,K)_2(Mg,Mn,Ca)_6Si_8O_{22}(OH)_2$ that is a variety of amphibole containing as bases sodium, magnesium, manganese, potassium, and calcium

**richweed** \\'=,=\\ *n* [¹*rich* + *weed*] **1** : a plant of the genus *Pilea* — called also *clearweed* **2** : RAGWEED 2 a **3** : WHITE SNAKEROOT **4** : HORSE BALM 1

**ricin** \\'rīsᵊn, 'ris-\\ *n* -s [L *ricinus* castor-oil plant] : an amorphous and violently poisonous protein in the castor bean

**ricin·elaidic acid** \\¦rīsᵊn, ¦risᵊn+. . .-\\ *n* [*ricinoleic* + *elaidic*] : a crystalline unsaturated hydroxy fatty acid $HOC_{17}H_{32}COOH$ obtained from ricinoleic acid; the trans isomer of ricinoleic acid

**ricing** *pres part of* RICE

**ri·cin·i·dae** \\rə'sinə,dē, rī's-\\ *n pl, cap* [NL, fr. *Ricinus*, type genus (fr. L *ricinus* tick, louse) + *-idae*] : a large family of biting lice that includes numerous parasites of land and water birds

**ric·i·nine** \\'risᵊn,ēn, -ᵊnən\\ *n* -s [L *ricinus* castor-oil plant + E *-ine*] : a crystalline compound $C_8H_8N_2O_2$ derived from pyridone and obtained from castor beans

**ricin·ole·ate** \\,==='ōlēət, -ē,āt\\ *n* [*ricinoleic* + *-ate*] : a salt or ester of ricinoleic acid

**ricin·oleic acid** \\¦==+. . .-\\ *n* [L *ricinus* castor-oil plant + E *oleic*] : an oily unsaturated hydroxy fatty acid $HOC_{17}H_{32}COOH$ that is found in castor oil in the form of a glyceride and that readily polymerizes on heating; 12-hydroxy-oleic acid

**ricin·ole·in** \\,=='ōlēən\\ *n* [*ricinoleic* + *-in*] : an ester of glycerol and ricinoleic acid; *esp* : the tri-ricinoleate $C_3H_5(C_{18}H_{33}O_3)_3$ constituting the chief component of castor oil

**ric·i·nu·lei** \\,risᵊn'(y)ülē,ī\\ *n pl, cap* [NL, pl. dim. of L *ricinus* tick] : a small order of Arachnida comprising living and fossil forms with an oval hard body bearing a large movable hood that folds down in front over the mouthparts — **ric·i·nu·le·id** \\-ēəd\\ *n or adj*

**ric·i·nus** \\'risᵊnəs\\ *n* [NL, fr. L, tick, castor-oil plant (perh. fr. the resemblance of its seed to a tick)] **1** *cap* : a genus of plants (family Euphorbiaceae) having large palmate leaves and monoecious flowers with very numerous stamens — see CASTOR-OIL PLANT **2** -ES : any plant of the genus *Ricinus*

**ricinus oil** *n* [NL *Ricinus*] : CASTOR OIL

¹**rick** \\'rik\\ *n* -s [ME *reke, reek*, fr. OE *hrēac*; akin to ON *hraukr* rick, and perh. to OE *hrycg* ridge — more at RIDGE] **1** : an elongated stack or pile (as of grain, straw, or hay) in the open air and often protected from wet with thatching **2** : a pile of cordwood, stave bolts, or other material split from short logs; *specif* : a cord eight feet long by four feet high and of a width equal to the length of one stick **3** : a framework of wood or metal used in a warehouse to hold barrels of whiskey during the aging period

²**rick** \\"\\ *vt* -ED/-ING/-S : to heap up (as hay) in ricks : pile up

³**rick** \\"\\ *vt* -ED/-ING/-S [perh. fr. ME *wrikken* to move unsteadily] *chiefly Brit* : WRENCH, SPRAIN

⁴**rick** \\"\\ *n* -s *chiefly Brit* : SPRAIN

**rick·ard·ite** \\'rikə(r),dīt\\ *n* -s [Thomas A. *Rickard* †1953 Am. mining engineer + E *-ite*] : a mineral $Cu_4Te_3$ consisting of a copper telluride and occurring in deep metallic purple masses

¹**rick·er** \\'rikə(r)\\ *n* -s [origin unknown] : POLE, SPAR

²**ricker** \\"\\ *n* -s [²*rick* + *-er*] : one that ricks; *specif* : one that places barrels of whiskey in ricks

**rick·et·i·ly** \\'rikəd·ᵊlē\\ *adv* [*rickety* + *-ly*] : in a rickety manner

**rick·et·i·ness** \\-ədēnəs, -ətin-\\ *n* -ES : the quality or state of being rickety

**rick·ets** \\'rikəts\\ *n pl but sing in constr* [origin unknown] **1** : a nutritional disturbance affecting the young of animals and man characterized by defective nutrition of the entire body and esp. faulty ossification of bone due to defective deposition and utilization of minerals (as calcium and phosphorus) owing to inadequate exposure to sunlight or deficient intake of vitamin D **2** : OSTEOMALACIA

**rick·etts·emia** \\,rikət'sēmēə\\ *n* -s [NL, fr. *Rickettsia* + *-emia*] : the abnormal presence of rickettsiae in the blood

**rick·ett·sia** \\rə'ketsēə\\ *n* [NL, fr. Howard T. *Ricketts* †1910 Am. pathologist + NL *-ia*] **1** *cap* : the type genus of Rickettsiaceae comprising pleomorphic rod-shaped nonfilterable microorganisms that live intracellularly in biting arthropods and when transmitted to man by the bite of an arthropod host cause a number of serious diseases (as Rocky Mountain spotted fever and typhus) **2** *pl* **rickettsi·ae** \\-sē,ē\\ *or* **rickettsias** *also* **rickettsia** *sometimes cap* : any member of the genus *Rickettsia* or the family Rickettsiaceae

**rickettsia body** *n, sometimes cap R* : RICKETTSIA 2

**rick·ett·si·a·ce·ae** \\rə,ketsē'āsē,ē, (,)ri,k-\\ *n pl, cap* [NL, fr. *Rickettsia*, type genus + *-aceae*] : a family of microorganisms (order Rickettsiales) resembling bacteria and being typically inhabitants of arthropod tissues but capable in some cases of causing serious disease in man and other vertebrates — compare COWDRIA, RICKETTSIA

**rick·ett·si·al** \\rə'ketsēəl, (')ri¦k-\\ *adj* [NL *Rickettsia* + E *-al*] : of, relating to, or caused by rickettsiae ⟨a ~ disease⟩ ⟨~ vaccines⟩

**rick·ett·si·a·les** \\rə,ketsē'ā(,)lēz, (,)ri,k-\\ *n pl, cap* [NL, fr. *Rickettsia* + *-ales*] : an order of small pleomorphic gram-negative microorganisms of uncertain biological position that are obligate parasites living in vertebrates or in arthropods which often serve as vectors of those parasitic in vertebrates — see BARTONELLACEAE, RICKETTSIACEAE; compare CHLAMYDIACEAE

**rickettsialpox** \\(,)=¦===¦=\\ *n* [*rickettsial* + *pox*] : a disease characterized by fever, chills, headache, backache, and a spotty rash and caused by a rickettsia (*Rickettsia akari*) thought to be transmitted to man by the bite of a mite living on mice

**rick·ett·si·o·sis** \\rə,ketsē'ōsəs, (,)ri,k-\\ *n, pl* **rickettsio·ses** \\-ō,sēz\\ [NL *Rickettsia* + *-osis*] : a disease caused by a rickettsia ⟨a mild ~⟩

**rick·ett·sio·stat·ic** \\rə¦ketsēō¦stad·ik\\ *adj* [NL *Rickettsia* + *-o-* + Gk *statikos* causing to stand — more at STATIC] : growth-inhibiting for rickettsiae

**rick·ety** \\'rikəd·ē, -ət¦, ¦i\\ *adj* [*rickets* + *-y*] **1** : affected with rickets : RACHITIC **2 a** : feeble in the joints : TOTTERING ⟨a ~ old man⟩ **b** : SHAKY, UNSOUND ⟨a ~ building⟩

**rick·ey** \\'rikē, -ki\\ *n* -s [prob. fr. the name *Rickey*] **1** : a long drink consisting of a spirituous liquor, lime juice, sugar, and soda water and served with ice cubes and the peel of the used lime in the glass ⟨gin ~⟩ **2** : a nonalcoholic carbonated drink usu. containing lime juice or orange juice

¹**rick·le** \\'rikəl\\ *n* -s [perh. of Scand origin; akin to Norw dial *rikl, rukl* small heap of stones] **1** *dial Brit* : a small stack : loose heap : PILE ⟨a ~ of stones⟩ **2** *dial Brit* : something loosely put together; *specif* : a lanky loose-jointed person

²**rickle** \\"\\ *vt* -ED/-ING/-S *dial Brit* : to make into a pile

**rick·ma·tic** \\'rikmə,tik\\ *n* -s [origin unknown] *chiefly Scot* : CONCERN, BUSINESS ⟨the whole ~ was a wreck⟩

**rick·rack** *or* **ric·rac** \\'ri,krak\\ *n* -s [redupl. of ⁴*rack*] : a flat braid usu. of cotton or rayon woven under tension to form small even zigzags and used as a decorative trimming or an openwork insertion on clothing

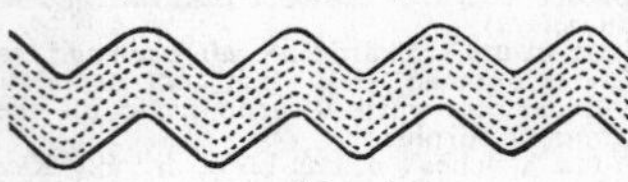

rickrack

**ricks** *pl of* RICK, *pres 3d sing of* RICK

**rick·sha** *or* **rick·shaw** \\'rik(,)shȯ\\ *n* -s [by shortening & contr.] : JINRIKISHA

**rickstand** \\'=,=\\ *n* [¹*rick* + *stand*] : a flooring or frame for a rick

**rickyard** \\'=,=\\ *n* [¹*rick* + *yard*] : the part of a farm in which hay or fodder is ricked or stacked : STACKYARD

¹**ric·o·chet** \\'rikə,shā, ¦==¦=, *chiefly Brit* -shet\\ *n* -s [F] **1 a** : a glancing rebound or skipping (as of a projectile along the ground when a gun is fired at a low angle of elevation or of a flat stone thrown along the surface of water); *also* : an object that ricochets **2** : a bounding or thrown staccato played or to be played in one bow stroke (as on the down bow) — used as a musical direction for bowed stringed instruments

²**ricochet** \\"\\ *vi* **ricocheted** \\-ād\\ *or* **ricochetted** \\-etəd\\ **ricocheted** *or* **ricochetted**; **ricocheting** \\-āiŋ\\ *or* **ricochetting** \\-etiŋ\\ **ricochets** **1** : to skip with a glancing rebound or series of rebounds ⟨a ~*ing* bullet⟩ **2** : to move, fly, or strike in the manner of a ricochet

**ricochet fire** *n* : fire in which the projectile glances from a surface after impact

**ric·o·let·ta·ite** \\,rikə'led·ə,īt\\ *n* -s [*Ricoletta*, locality in Tirol + E *-ite*] : an igneous rock that is a basic granogabbro composed of anorthite, some orthoclase, and pyroxene with accessory biotite, olivine, and magnetite

**ri·cot·ta** \\rē'kȯd·ə, -ȯt(,)tä\\ *n* -s [It, fr. L *recocta*, fem. of *recoctus*, past part. of *recoquere* to cook again, boil again, fr. *re-* + *coquere* to cook — more at COOK] : cottage cheese made of skim milk by repeated slow boiling

**ric·tal** \\'riktᵊl\\ *adj* [NL *rictus* + E *-al*] : of or relating to the rictus

**ric·tus** \\-təs\\ *n, pl* **rictus** *or* **rictuses** [NL, fr. L, open mouth, fr. *rictus*, past part. of *ringi* to open the mouth, show the teeth; akin to OSlav *regnǫti* to gape, and perh. to OE *wrencan* to twist — more at WRENCH] **1** : the gape of the mouth of a bird **2 a** : the mouth orifice **b** : a gaping grin or grimace ⟨a face frozen in a ~ of terror⟩

¹**rid** \\'rid, *dial* 'red\\ *vb* **rid** *also* **ridded**; **rid** *also* **ridded**; **ridding**; **rids** [ME *ruden, rudden, ridden*, fr. ON *rythja*; akin to OE *āryddan* to plunder, OHG *riutan* to clear land, Av *raoiδya-* to prepare for cultivation, L *ruere* to dig up — more at RUIN] *vt* **1** *archaic* **a** : to clear or free (as land) of obstructions, waste, or encumbrances **b** : to clear away : clean up **2 a** *archaic* : to set free : DELIVER — often used with *of* or *from* **b** : to make (someone or something) free : RELIEVE — often used in the phrase *be rid of* or *get rid of* ⟨succeeded in getting ~ of a huge billboard —Edward Bok⟩ ⟨was glad to ~ herself of the burden —C.S.Forester⟩ ⟨the desire of emancipated persons to be ~ of all sense of further obligation to the Puritan tradition —W.L.Sperry⟩ **3** : to take away : clear off : REMOVE **4** *chiefly dial* : to get through (work) : DISPATCH **5** *dial* : ²REDD **~** *vi, chiefly dial* : to become dispatched

**syn** CLEAR, UNBURDEN, DISABUSE, PURGE: RID is a rather general term but is likely to refer to concrete or specific matters which are burdensome or pestiferous ⟨England had in the meantime *ridded* herself of the Stuarts, worried along under the Hanoverians —Agnes Repplier⟩ ⟨a lazy man's expedient for *ridding* himself of the trouble of thinking and deciding —B.N.Cardozo⟩ CLEAR is likely to be used to refer to tangible matters which obstruct progress, clutter an area, or block vision ⟨wars which . . . enabled the United States first to *clear* its own territory of foreign troops —S.F.Bemis⟩ ⟨rose from the food she had barely tasted and began to *clear* the table —Ellen Glasgow⟩ and may be used also in relation to ideas that hinder progress ⟨of service to his fellow Methodists in *clearing* away obstructions to modern thinking —H.K. Rowe⟩ UNBURDEN is likely to indicate freeing oneself from something taxing or something distressing the mind or spirit, in the latter situation often by confessing, revealing, frankly discussing ⟨insisted that he *unburden* himself of most of the 80 chores that go with the job of majority leader —*Time*⟩ ⟨conquers his own submissiveness and *unburdens* himself, before his domineering wife, of all the accumulated resentment and dislike of years —S.M.Fitzgerald⟩ DISABUSE is likely to refer to freeing the mind from an erroneous notion or an attitude or feeling making clear straightforward thought difficult ⟨if men are now sufficiently enlightened to *disabuse* themselves of artifice, hypocrisy, and superstition —John Adams⟩ ⟨neither familiarity with the history and institutions of Old World nations nor contact with them during two wars *disabused* the average American of his feeling of superiority —H.S.Commager⟩ PURGE may refer to cleansing out of or purification from that which is impure or alien or extrinsic ⟨*purged* of all its unorthodox views —G.B.Shaw⟩ ⟨the room had never quite been *purged* of the bad taste of preceding generations —Edmund Wilson⟩ In political matters it may suggest ruthless elimination ⟨the dictator has *purged* academic faculties of every savant suspected of being opposed to his regime —Howard M. Jones⟩

²**rid** [ME *riden* (past pl. & past part.), fr. OE *ridon* (past pl.), *geriden* (past part.)] *chiefly dial past of* RIDE

³**rid** \\'rid\\ *dial var of* ⁵REDD

⁴**rid** \\"\\ *dial var of* REDE

**rid·abil·i·ty** \\,rīdə'biləd·ē, -lətē, -i\\ *n* : the quality or state of being ridable

**rid·able** *or* **ride·able** \\'rīdəbəl\\ *adj* [¹*ride* + *-able*] **1** : capable of being ridden (as a horse) : fit for riding **2** : fit to be ridden over (as a road or ford) — **ridably** *adv*

**rid·dance** \\'ridᵊn(t)s\\ *n* -s [¹*rid* + *-ance*] **1** : an act of ridding, freeing, or cleaning : CLEARANCE ⟨the experiments showed high rates of kill with some of them showing 100 percent ~ —J.B.Robson⟩ **2** *obs* : progress with a task : dispatch of work **3** : DELIVERANCE, RELIEF — often used in the phrase *good riddance* ⟨if it's gone, it's gone — and good ~ too —Weston LaBarre⟩

**rid·del** *also* **rid·dle** \\'ridᵊl\\ *n* -s [ME *ridel, riddel*, perh. fr. *riddil* riddle (sieve)] : a church curtain : one of the side curtains of an altar

**ridden** [ME *riden*, fr. OE *geriden*] *past part of* RIDE

¹**rid·der** \\'ridə(r)\\ *n* -s [ME, fr. OE *hrider, hridder* — more at *riddle* (sieve)] *chiefly Eng* : a sieve esp. for sifting grain

²**ridder** \\"\\ *n* -s [¹*rid* + *-er*] : one that rids

**rid·ding** \\'ridᵊn\\ *n* -s [fr. gerund of ¹*rid*] *dial Eng* : a clearing in the woods — used esp. in place names

¹**rid·dle** \\'ridᵊl\\ *n* -s [ME *redels, redel, ridel*, fr. OE *rǣdels, rǣdelse* opinion, conjecture, riddle; akin to MHG *rätsel* riddle, OE *rǣdan* to advise, interpret — more at READ] **1** : a mystifying, misleading, or puzzling question posed as a problem to be solved or guessed often as a game : CONUNDRUM, ENIGMA **2** : something or someone difficult to understand : a problematical event, situation, or person : MYSTERY ⟨the eternal ~ of nominalism and realism —B.N.Cardozo⟩ ⟨will help the scientist to solve one of the many ~*s* of cancer —Waldemar Kaempffert⟩ **syn** see MYSTERY

²**riddle** \\"\\ *vb* **riddled**; **riddled**; **riddling** \\-d(ᵊ)liŋ\\ **riddles** *vt* **1** : to find the solution of : EXPLAIN, INTERPRET **2** : to create or set a riddle for : MYSTIFY, PERPLEX, PUZZLE **~** *vi* : to speak in or propound riddles

³**riddle** \\"\\ *n* -s [ME *riddil*, fr. OE *hriddel*, alter. of *hrider*, *hridder* — more at CERTAIN] **1** : a coarse sieve: as **a** : a sieve for grading potatoes **b** : a device for sifting coal **c** : a sieve for panning gold **d** : a sieve for sand used in a foundry **e** : a strainer kept in motion to sift middlings in flour milling **2** *archaic* : a compartmented case or container or its contents; *esp* : a 13-bottle case of wine **3** *archaic* : a board set with zigzag pins between which wire is drawn to straighten it

riddle 1d

⁴**riddle** \\"\\ *vb* -ED/-ING/-S [ME *ridlen, riddlen*, fr. *riddil* sieve] *vt* **1** : to separate (as grain from the chaff) with a riddle : pass through or as if through a riddle : SCREEN, SIFT ⟨*riddled* the coal to grade it by size⟩ **2 a** : to fill (something or someone) as full of holes as a sieve : puncture often and thoroughly ⟨he stood up, *riddled* them with fire and flopped down again — Dave Richardson⟩ ⟨*riddled* the ship with a broadside⟩ ⟨it had become badly *riddled* by termites —*Amer. Guide Series: La.*⟩ **b** : CORRUPT, DEBASE, PERMEATE ⟨the graft that ~s virtually every metropolitan police force —August Heckscher⟩ ⟨the administration of the church was *riddled* with abuses — Stringfellow Barr⟩ ⟨its lawns *riddled* with weeds —Bernard Kalb⟩ **~** *vi* : to use a riddle : sift through : PENETRATE, PIERCE ⟨cold winds ~ through the thin walls⟩

**riddle and shears** *n pl but sing in constr* [³*riddle*] *dial Brit* : SIEVE AND SHEARS

**riddle canon** *n* [¹*riddle*] : a musical canon esp. popular in the 15th and 16th centuries in which the entrances of the successive parts were indicated by monograms, symbols, or other cabalistic devices — called also *enigma canon*

**rid·dle·me·ree** \\¦ridᵊlmə¦rē\\ *n* -s [by shortening and alter. fr. the phrase *riddle my riddle*] *archaic* : RIGMAROLE

¹**rid·dler** \\'rid(ᵊ)lə(r)\\ *n* -s [²*riddle* + *-er*] : one that propounds, speaks in, or tries to solve riddles

²**riddler** \\"\\ *n* -s [⁴*riddle* + *-er*] : a worker who sifts with a riddle: as **a** : one who screens cut tobacco to remove coarse pieces **b** : one who cleans metal parts by shaking them in a riddle to remove loose chips

¹**riddling** *n* -s [fr. gerund of ²*riddle*] : a posing of or play with riddles

²**riddling** *adj* [fr. pres. part. of ²*riddle*] **1** : speaking in riddles : containing or presenting riddles : EQUIVOCAL, ENIGMATIC ⟨the hero's own language is often ~ —Maynard Mack⟩ **2** : riddle-solving : DIVINING — **rid·dling·ly** *adv*

³**riddling** *n* -s [fr. gerund of ⁴*riddle*] **1** : the act of sifting : SCREENING **2 riddlings** *pl* : coarse material left in a riddle after shaking : SIFTINGS

¹**ride** \\'rīd\\ *vb* **rode** \\'rōd\\ *or chiefly dial* **rid** \\'rid\\ *or* **rade** \\'rād\\ **rid·den** \\'ridᵊn\\ *or chiefly dial* **rid** *or* **rode**; **riding** \\'rīdiŋ\\ **rides** [ME *riden*, fr. OE *rīdan* to ride, travel, swing; akin to OHG *rītan* to ride, ON *rītha* to ride, travel, swing, OIr *rīadaim* I ride, travel, Gaulish *rēda* wagon] *vi* **1 a** : to sit and be carried on the back of an animal (as a horse) that one directs and controls **b** : to participate in a raid or military or vigilante action of mounted men **c** : to travel or become conveyed by a vehicle (as a carriage, an automobile, or a railroad train) : become carried (as in a litter or on men's shoulders) **2** : to seem to move or become borne along by an intangible agency : become sustained, supported, or forwarded ⟨*rode* on the wave of popularity⟩ **3** : to seem to float : FLOAT: as **a** : LIE, REST ⟨the squadron *rode* safely at anchor⟩ **b** : to sail, skim, or become driven over the water ⟨the little boat *rode* lightly before a breeze⟩ **c** : to move like a floating object ⟨a full moon *rode* in the night sky⟩ **4** : to become supported at rest or in motion on an axle, pivot, or other bearing point or surface ⟨the lever carries two studs, both of which ~ in the cam —William Landon & George Hafferkamp⟩ **5** *of a male animal* : to mount in copulation **6** : to move with a rider : GO ⟨a big powerful car that ~*s* smoothly and quietly⟩ **7** *archaic* : PROJECT **8** : to take its course : continue without interference ⟨let it ~⟩ **9** : to be contingent : DEPEND ⟨his party's hopes seemed to ~ on his renomination⟩ **10** : to climb up on the body : bunch up in folds or ridges ⟨my skirt had *ridden* up above my knees, the way a tight skirt will —S.A.Offit⟩ **11 a** : to become bet ⟨his money is *riding* on the favorite⟩ **b** : to remain as a bet — used of an original bet or stake plus accumulated winnings ⟨he let his winnings ~⟩ **12** : to improvise variations freely on a jazz theme **~** *vt* **1 a** : to sit and be carried on while directing and controlling ⟨a jockey who had *ridden* many a winner⟩ ⟨*rode* a bicycle daily to a ripe age⟩ **b** : to move with or be carried by like a rider ⟨*rode* the waves with an experienced swimmer's ease⟩ ⟨bad news ~*s* the lightning —Irving Stone⟩ **2 a** : to traverse (as a route or distance) on horseback or by vehicle ⟨*rode* a mail route daily for years⟩ ⟨abolishing the requirement that supreme court judges ~ circuit —C.B.Swisher⟩ ⟨*rode* hundreds of miles⟩ **b** : to ride a horse in ⟨~ a winning race⟩ **3 a** : to endure without great damage : SURVIVE, LAST ⟨a large sailing vessel . . . *riding* the storm —*Western Mail*⟩ — usu. used with *out* ⟨*rode* out the gale in safety —R.H.Dana⟩ ⟨can ~ out the current adjustment without having to make drastic price revisions —*Newsweek*⟩ **b** : to move with (something fluctuating or dangerous) so as to emerge unharmed : SURMOUNT, SURVIVE ⟨~ an adverse situation⟩ ⟨were now trying to ~ the devastating postwar slump in agriculture —Roy Lewis & Angus Maude⟩ **4** : to traverse on horseback in order to inspect or maintain ⟨~ fence⟩ **5** : to mount in or as if in copulation — used of a male animal **6 a** : to sit on as a rider does a horse : domineer over : OBSESS, OPPRESS ⟨only a man, *ridden* by anxiety and impotence, by desire and guilt —L.A.Fiedler⟩ ⟨was *ridden* by a veritable devil —E.P.Hanson⟩ **b** (1) : to harass persistently (as by carping criticism, ridicule, or abuse) : subject to pertinacious or concerted annoyance, irritation, or distress ⟨the officers in that tropic outpost *rode* the artist mercilessly⟩ (2) : TEASE, RIB, BANTER **7 a** : to convey like a rider : give a ride to ⟨*rode* the youngster on his back⟩ ⟨exposed him and *rode* him out of town on a rail⟩ **b** : to convey in a vehicle ⟨*rode* a shipment of castings back to the plant in the truck on his return trip⟩ **c** *archaic* : to keep (a ship) anchored or moored **8** : to project over : OVERLAP, OVERRIDE **9** : to urge (a racehorse) to the limit **10** : to aim too long at (a moving target) thereby losing coordination and proper lead and making a miss more likely **11** : to manipulate (a log drive) while standing on floating logs **12** : to recoil from or give with (a landing punch or blow) in order to soften the impact **13** : to legally charge (an opponent who has possession of the ball) in lacrosse **14** : to improvise variations on (a jazz theme) at will **syn** see BAIT — **ride a hobby** : to pursue a favorite topic

or activity — **ride and tie** *archaic* **:** to share a single horse with someone by taking turns in riding and walking, each rider leaving the horse tied at the end of his ride for the use of the man following on foot — **ride circuit :** to hold court in the various towns where court may be lawfully held in a judicial circuit under laws requiring the judge to travel for that purpose — **ride for a fall :** to court danger **:** behave recklessly — **ride herd on :** to look out for **:** keep in check **:** OVERSEE, POLICE ⟨here comes an officer to *ride herd on* us —Erle Stanley Gardner⟩ — **ride roughshod over :** to put down ruthlessly **:** SUPPRESS, TRAMPLE ⟨*rode roughshod over* one opponent after another⟩ — **ride rusty** *archaic* **:** to grow obstinate or refractory — **ride the brake** *or* **ride the clutch :** to keep in partial engagement by resting a foot continuously on the pedal with resultant unnecessary mechanical wear — **ride the gain :** to control the output of sound reproducing equipment manually to prevent blasting at high volume — **ride the line :** to ride around the edges of a herd of cattle to round up strays — **ride the marches** *archaic* **:** to ride along boundaries to inspect or reaffirm them — **ride the rods :** to ride the truss rods beneath a railroad car as a hobo — **ride the vents :** to prepare a submarine to submerge — **ride to hounds :** to chase a fox on horseback with hounds

[2]**ride** \"\ *n* -s **1 :** an act of riding **:** an excursion, journey, or trip on horseback or by vehicle ⟨the train ~ was long⟩ ⟨came back refreshed from a ~ in the woods⟩ **2 :** a road or way where one may ride ⟨the district affords many beautiful ~s⟩; *esp* **:** a lane cut in a forest **3 :** any of various mechanical devices provided for customers of an amusement park or carnival to ride on — compare FERRIS WHEEL, MERRY-GO-ROUND, WHIP 14 **4 a :** a trip on which gangsters take a victim in order to murder him ⟨this case has the earmarks of a ~ —Jack Heise⟩ — usu. used in the phrase *take for a ride* **b :** DECEPTION, VICTIMIZATION ⟨she is giving him a ~, isn't she —Ernest Hemingway⟩ — usu. used in the phrase *take for a ride* **5 :** any of various positions in which a wrestler is astride or above a prone opponent — compare CROSS-BODY RIDE **6 :** public attention **:** NOTICE ⟨the newspapers gave the case a big ~⟩ **7 :** the qualities of comfort and smooth travel provided to an operator or passenger by a vehicle

[3]**ride** \"\ *n* -s [perh. fr. [1]*ride*] *chiefly dial* **:** the strap of a hinge

**rideable** *var of* RIDABLE

**rideal-walker test** \rə'dē(ə)l'wȯkə(r)-\ *n, usu cap R&W* [after Samuel *Rideal* †1929 & J.T.A.*Walker* Eng. chemists] **:** a test for determining the phenol coefficient esp. of a disinfectant

**ri·deau** \rə'dō\ *n* -s [F, fr. MF, lit., curtain; perh. fr. ME *ridel, riddel* curtain — more at RIDDEL] **:** a small ridge or mound of earth **:** ground slightly elevated

**ride down** *vt* **1 :** to tread under one's horse's feet **:** OVERTHROW, TRAMPLE **2 :** to bear down on (as a halyard when hoisting a sail)

**ri·dent** \'rīdᵊnt\ *adj* [L rident-, ridens, pres. part. of *ridēre* to laugh — more at RIDICULOUS] *archaic* **:** broadly smiling **:** LAUGHING

**ride off** *vt* **1 :** to ride so as to deflect (an opposing polo player) **2 :** RIDE OUT 1

**rideoff** \'=,=\ *n* -s [*ride off*] **:** an act or instance of riding alongside a polo opponent and pushing him away from the line of the ball to prevent his hitting it

**ride out** *vt* **1 :** to cut out or separate by riding ⟨*rode* the bull *out* of the herd⟩ **2 :** to urge (a racehorse) to the limit

**rid·er** \'rīdə(r)\ *n* -s [ME, fr. OE *rīdere*, fr. *rīdan* to ride + *-ere* -er] **1 :** one that rides horseback: as **a :** *archaic* **:** a mounted highwayman, freebooter, or moss-trooper **b :** COWBOY 3a **c :** a circus performer who rides horses **d :** a mounted agent employed on a plantation — compare DITCH RIDER **e :** JOCKEY **2 :** one that rides a vehicle ⟨train ~⟩ ⟨motorcycle ~⟩ **3 a** [trans. of D *rijder*] **:** a Dutch ryder **b :** a Scotch gold coin issued by James III and his successor **4 a :** an addition or amendment to a manuscript, printer's proof, or other document often attached on a separate piece of paper **:** ALLONGE, ANNEX, CODICIL **b :** something added as an extra to a seemingly completed statement or act **c** *Brit* **:** a recommendation by a jury appended to its verdict **d :** a clause appended to a legislative bill to secure an object usu. entirely distinct from that of the bill itself ⟨wantonly violates the Constitution in attaching legislative ~s to appropriation bills —*New Republic*⟩ **5 :** something used to overlie or cover another (as an upper tier of casks, a turn of a rope, or a tree placed on a wall) **6 a :** a rail laid slanting in the forks of the cross stakes at the corner of a worm fence as a reinforcement **b :** a small movable adjusting weight on the beam of a balance resembling the weight on a steelyard **c :** a pipe above and parallel to a main pipe into which part of the flow is diverted over a considerable distance and from which the flow is redirected into the main **7** *archaic* **:** TRAVELING SALESMAN **8 a :** the top raker of a set of raking shores **b :** the strap of a hinge **9 :** ENDORSEMENT 2 b **10 a :** a thin parallel coal seam or mineral vein overlying a larger seam or vein **b :** the country rock between them **c :** a body of barren or country rock occurring as a horse within a vein **11 :** a vibrating steel roller that rests on and rotates in contact with a form roller to augment the distribution of printing ink **12 :** a man who rides on a freight car which is being switched over the hump of a railroad classification yard in order to set the brakes and stop the car at the proper point **13 :** an extra rib timber set in between the frames of a wooden ship **14 :** a logger who drives a horse or mule to haul rigging equipment back to the woods after each log has been skidded to the yard or landing

**rid·ered** \'rīdə(r)d\ *adj* [*rider* + *-ed*] **:** having riders across the stakes — used of a fence

**rider embolus** *n* **:** SADDLE EMBOLUS

**rid·er·ess** \'rīdərəs\ *n* -ES [*rider* + *-ess*] **:** a female rider

**rider keelson** *n* **:** a line of timber or plates fastened to the top of a ship's keelson

**rid·er·less** \'rīdə(r)ləs\ *adj* **:** having no rider

**rider plate** *n* **:** a continuous horizontal flat plate connected to the top of a ship's vertical keel

**rider's bone** *n* **:** a bony deposit in the muscles of the upper and inner part of the thigh due to pressure and chronic irritation that are caused by the saddle in riding — called also *cavalry bone*

**ride up** *vi* **:** to work up on the person **:** climb up — used of clothing ⟨a girdle that won't *ride up*⟩

[1]**ridge** \'rij\ *n* -s [ME *rigge*, fr. OE *hrycg*; akin to OHG *hrukki* back, spine, mountain ridge, ON *hryggr* back, spine, mountain ridge, L *cruc-, crux* stake used for punishment, cross, Skt *kruñcati* it curves, L *curvus* curved — more at CROWN] **1 a** *obs* **:** the back or backbone of a man or an animal **b :** the projecting or elevated part of the back along the line of the backbone **c :** an elevated body part projecting from a surface ⟨the urogenital ~⟩ **2 a :** a range of hills or mountains or the upper part of such a range **:** an extended elevation between valleys **b :** an elongate elevation on an ocean bottom **3 :** a top or upper part esp. when long and narrow **:** CREST **4 a :** a raised line or strip (as of ground thrown up by a plow between furrows) **b :** BEACH RIDGE **c :** a small raised line on the surface of metal, cloth, or bone **5 a :** the line of intersection at the top between the opposite slopes or sides of a roof **b :** a shingle, tile, or slate adjacent to the ridge of a roof **c :** the horizontal beam to which the upper ends of the rafters of a roof are fixed **:** RIDGEPOLE **d :** the internal angle of a vault **6 :** either of the two projections of a bound book parallel to the joint and formed by the bend put in the sections in the backing operation — called also *shoulder* **7 :** a wedge-shaped extension of a high-pressure area — opposed to *trough* **8 :** the upper part of the narrow posterior end of the body of a whale **9 :** the raised knitting pattern formed by garter stitch made by two rows of knit stitch

[2]**ridge** \"\ *vb* -ED/-ING/-S *vt* **1 :** to form into a ridge **:** furnish or mark with ridges **2 a :** to plow alternate strips in by turning the furrow onto an unplowed strip **b :** to throw soil toward (a crop row) from both sides ⟨*ridged* his corn⟩ **c :** to spade or plow (ground) into alternate ridges and troughs ⟨if low lands must be used for the bean crop, they should be *ridged* —E.V.Wilcox⟩ ~ *vi* **:** to form into or become marked with ridges **:** extend in ridges ⟨the land ~s northward⟩ ⟨the sea ~s under the wind⟩

**ridgeband** \'=,=\ *n* [[1]*ridge* + *band*] *dial Brit* **:** the part of a harness that passes over the saddle and supports the shafts of a cart

**ridge beech** *n* **:** a common beech (*Fagus grandifolia*) of No. America

**ridgeboard** \'=,=\ *n* **:** RIDGEPOLE 1

**ridgebone** \'=,=\ *n* [ME *riggebone*, fr. OE *hrycgbān*, fr. *hrycg* ridge + *bān* bone] *archaic* **:** BACKBONE

**ridge buster** *n* **:** a cultivator equipped with disks for tearing down ridges and filling the furrows

**ridgecap** \'=,=\ *n* **:** a wood or metal covering placed over the ridge of a roof

**ridged** \'rijd\ *adj* [[1]*ridge* + *-ed*] **:** having a ridge **:** RIDGY

**ridge fillet** *n* **1 :** a ridge between flutes of a column or other depressions **2 :** a main runner for molten metal

**ridge harrow** *n* **:** a harrow hinged longitudinally so as to run partly on the side of a ridge

**ridg·el** \rijəl\ *n* -s [perh. fr. [1]*ridge*] **:** RIDGELING

**ridge-let** \'rijlət\ *n* -s [[1]*ridge* + *-let*] **:** a small ridge

**ridgelike** \'=,=\ *adj* **:** resembling a ridge

**ridgeline** \'=,=\ *n* **:** a line marking or following a ridge top

**ridge·ling** *or* **ridg·ling** \'rijliŋ\ *n* -s [perh. fr. [1]*ridge* + *-ling*; fr. the supposed remaining of the undescended testes near the animal's back] **1 :** a male animal having one or both testes undescended; *esp* **:** a horse exhibiting such abnormality and being typically male in conformation and behavior but sterile when the condition is bilateral **2 :** an imperfectly castrated male animal — compare HALF-CASTRATE

**ridge plow** *n* **:** [2]LISTER 1

**ridgepole** \'=,=\ *n* **1 :** the highest horizontal timber in a roof and the receiver of the upper ends of the rafters — see ROOF illustration **2 :** the horizontal pole at the top of a tent

[1]**ridg·er** \'rijə(r)\ *n* -s [[1]*ridge* + *-er*] *dial Brit* **:** RIDGEBAND

[2]**ridger** *n* -s [[2]*ridge* + *-er*] **:** one that ridges: as **a :** [2]LISTER 1 **b :** LISTER CULTIVATOR **c :** an implement for making levees in the check system of irrigation

**ridge rib** *n* **:** a rib marking the ridge of a vault

**ridge roll** *n* **:** a metal, tile, or wood strip rounded at the top and used as finishing for the ridge of a roof

**ridge roof** *n* **:** GABLE ROOF

**ridgerope** \'=,=\ *n* [[1]*ridge* + *rope*] **1 :** a lifeline alongside the bowsprit of a ship **2 :** a rope just above and parallel to a ship's rail **3 a :** the backbone of a ship's awning **b :** a rope along a ship's side to which the side of an awning is made fast **c :** a rope forming the backbone or ridgepole of a tent

**ridge runner** *n, chiefly Midland* **:** a mountain farmer **:** HILLBILLY, HICK

**ridges** *pl of* RIDGE, *pres 3d sing of* RIDGE

**ridge stone** *n* **1 :** a stone for the margin of a well or shaft **2 :** APEX STONE

**ridge tile** *n* **:** an often decorative tile of bent or curved section used in covering the ridge of a roof — compare HIP TILE

**ridgetop** \'=,=\ *n* **:** the crest of a ridge

**ridgetree** \'=,=\ *n, archaic* **:** RIDGEPOLE

**ridgeway** \'=,=\ *n* **:** a road following the ridge of a hill or of a range of hills ⟨on road and on ~, on sea and on land —J.M.Synge⟩

**ridging** *n* -s [fr. gerund of [2]*ridge*] **1 a :** the making of a ridge **b :** the throwing of soil toward a crop row from both sides ⟨the ~ of potatoes⟩ ⟨the ~ of sugarcane⟩ **2 :** the material of which the ridge of a roof is made or with which it is covered

**ridging plow** *n* **:** [2]LISTER 1

**ridgy** \'rijē\ *adj* -ER/-EST [[1]*ridge* + *-y*] **:** having ridges **:** rising in a ridge

[1]**rid·i·cule** \'ridə,kyül, -dē,k-\ *n* -s [F or L; F *ridicule* fr. L *ridiculum* laughing matter, jest — more at RIDICULOUS] **1** *archaic* **:** something or someone absurd or laughable **2 :** the arousing of laughter, mockery, or scorn at someone or something **:** the casting of an absurd or derisive light on a person or thing ⟨my early work was written in secret to escape ~ —Ellen Glasgow⟩ **3** *archaic* **:** the quality or state of being laughable **:** RIDICULOUSNESS ⟨gave an air of ~ to his greatest actions —Oliver Goldsmith⟩

[2]**ridicule** \"\ *vt* -ED/-ING/-S **:** to subject to ridicule or mockery **:** make fun of **:** DERIDE ⟨death and disease ~ man's petty arrogance —Harriet Zinnes⟩ ⟨pointed a moral or *ridiculed* his opponents —*Amer. Guide Series: La.*⟩

**syn** RIDICULE, DERIDE, MOCK, TAUNT, TWIT, and RALLY agree in meaning to make someone or something the object of laughter. RIDICULE implies the belittling, often malicious, of the person or thing ridiculed ⟨gouge, expose, and *ridicule* the stupidity of human beings —Edwin Edwards⟩ ⟨the man who wants to preserve his personal identity is *ridiculed* as an eccentric or resented as a snob —S.J.Harris⟩ DERIDE implies bitterness against or contempt for the person or thing derided ⟨took his revenge on the fate that had made him sad by fiercely *deriding* everything —Aldous Huxley⟩ ⟨books were likely to be *derided* or ignored by the critics —E.A.Davidson⟩ MOCK stresses the scorn, often ironic, of the person mocking ⟨anger seized her at the suspicion that he was *mocking* them —Ellen Glasgow⟩ ⟨now taking on one expression and then another, in imitation of various people he was *mocking* —D.H.Lawrence⟩ TAUNT implies mockery and suggests jeeringly provoking insults ⟨*taunt* a boy into a fight⟩ ⟨the mill foreman so *taunted* the workers, so belabored them and told them that they dared not quit —Sinclair Lewis⟩ TWIT formerly implied taunts or throwing something up to someone, but now, like RALLY, implies a bantering, good-humored teasing or mockery, though sometimes coming close to taunting ⟨the absence of ideas with which Matthew Arnold *twits* them —W.R.Inge⟩ ⟨*twit* Victorian manners and morals —*Time*⟩ ⟨all the charming witticisms of English lecturers who *twitted* us about our standardization and materialism —Eric Sevareid⟩ ⟨he loved his mistress . . . no one dared . . . *rally* him on his weakness —G.B.Shaw⟩ ⟨it would be amusing to *rally* her friend . . . for neglecting his wife —Edith Sitwell⟩

[3]**ridicule** \", -kəl\ *n* -s [F, alter. of *réticule* — more at RETICULE] *chiefly dial* **:** RETICULE 2

**rid·i·cul·er** \-,kyülə(r)\ *n* -s [[2]*ridicule* + *-er*] **:** one that engages in ridicule

**ri·dic·u·los·i·ty** \rə,dikyə'läsəd·ē\ *n* -ES [L *ridiculosus* + E *-ity*] **1 :** the quality or state of being ridiculous **:** RIDICULOUSNESS **2 :** something ridiculous

**ri·dic·u·lous** \rə'dikyələs, *chiefly in substand speech* -k(ə)ləs\ *adj* [L *ridiculosus* or *ridiculus*; *ridiculosus* fr. *ridiculum* laughing matter, jest (fr. neut. of *ridiculus* laughable, ridiculous) + *-osus* -ous; *ridiculus* fr. *ridēre* to laugh; akin to Skt *vrīdate* he is ashamed] **1 :** fit or likely to excite ridicule **:** unworthy of serious consideration **:** ABSURD, COMICAL, FUNNY, LAUGHABLE, PREPOSTEROUS ⟨here surely is the world's record in the domain of the ~ and the contemptible —Sir Winston Churchill⟩ ⟨to be made ~ before her increased his humiliation —W.S. Maugham⟩ **2** *dial* **:** violating decency or moral sense **:** INDECENT, OUTRAGEOUS, SCANDALOUS **syn** see LAUGHABLE

**ri·dic·u·lous·ly** *adv* **:** in a ridiculous manner **:** ABSURDLY, LAUGHABLY ⟨was ~ absent-minded, and many stories circulated regarding her peculiarities —H.E.Starr⟩

**ri·dic·u·lous·ness** *n* -ES **:** the quality or state of being ridiculous **:** LAUGHABLENESS

[1]**ri·ding** \'rīdiŋ, -dēŋ\ *n* -s [ME *riding, rithing*, by simplification of *-th th-, -t th-* in (assumed) *north thriding, east thriding, west thriding*, fr. (assumed) OE *thriding, thrithing* (whence ML *treding, trehinga*), fr. ON *thrithjungr* third part, fr. *thrithi* third + *-ungr* -ing — more at THIRD, -ING (one of a kind)] **1 :** one of the three administrative jurisdictions into which Yorkshire, England, is divided ⟨East *Riding*⟩ ⟨West *Riding*⟩ ⟨North *Riding*⟩ **2 :** an administrative jurisdiction or electoral district in an English county other than Yorkshire or in one of the British dominions (as New Zealand or Canada)

[2]**rid·ing** \"\ *n* -s [ME, fr. gerund of *riden* to ride] **1 :** the action of one that rides **:** a trip or journey made by a rider on horseback or in a vehicle **2** *chiefly Brit* **a :** a festival or pageant marked by a procession **b :** SHIVAREE, SKIMMINGTON **3** *archaic* **:** an avenue or lane cut in a wood esp. as a place for riding **4 :** ANCHORAGE **5 :** OVERLAP 1 a **6 :** the harassment of someone who has made himself unpopular, conspicuous, or offensive ⟨the Old Man's favorite often takes a hard ~ for this good reason —J.G.Cozzens⟩

[3]**rid·ing** \"\ *adj* **1 :** used for riding on ⟨a ~ horse⟩ **2 a :** used for riding or when riding **:** devoted to riding ⟨a ~ whip⟩ ⟨a ~ academy⟩ **b :** worn when riding **3 :** operated or driven by a rider ⟨a ~ plow⟩ ⟨a ~ cultivator⟩

[4]**rid·ing** \'ridᵊn\ *var of* RIDDING

**riding bitts** *n pl* [[3]*riding*] **:** massive bitts formerly used to secure the anchor cables of a ship riding at anchor

**riding boot** *n* **:** a leather boot esp. for horseback riding; *specif* **:** TOP BOOT — compare COWBOY BOOT, JODHPUR 2

**riding breeches** *n pl* **:** breeches made wide through the lower thighs and with tight-fitting calf-length legs and worn for horseback riding

riding breeches

**riding buckler** *n, naut* **:** a buckler with a hole for the passage of a cable

**riding chair** *n, archaic* **:** [1]CHAIR 3 b

**riding chock** *n* **:** a chock often fitted with a pawl and used to relieve the strain of an anchor cable on a windlass **:** CABLE STOPPER

**riding habit** *n* **:** an outfit for horseback riding; *esp* **:** a woman's outfit including jacket with breeches for riding astride or with a skirt for riding sidesaddle

**riding hood** *n* **:** an enveloping hood or hooded cloak worn for riding and as an outdoor wrap by women and children

**riding interest** *n* **:** a creditor's interest resting upon the share of a claimant in multiplepoinding or other action under Scots law

**riding light** *n* [[3]*riding*] **:** ANCHOR LIGHT

**ridingman** *n, pl* **ridingmen** [*riding*, pres. part. of [1]*ride*] **:** a man bound by feudal law to do service on horseback as an escort or messenger but not to do military service

**riding master** *n* [[3]*riding*] **:** an instructor in horsemanship

**riding rhyme** *n* **:** a rhymed couplet in iambic pentameter (as used by Chaucer and Lydgate) **:** an early form of heroic couplet

**riding roller** *n* [*riding*, pres. part. of [1]*ride*] **:** RIDER 11

**riding sail** *n* [[3]*riding*] **:** a triangular sail sometimes set usu. on the aftermast to keep a vessel head to wind when riding at anchor

**riding whip** *or* **riding crop** *n* **:** a short whip used by horsemen

**rid·ley** \'ridlē\ *n* -s [prob. fr. the name *Ridley*] **:** a marine turtle (*Caretta kempii* or *Lepidochelys kempii*) of the family Cheloniidae found off the Atlantic coast of the U.S. — called also *bastard turtle*

**ri·dot·to** \rə'däd·(,)ō, -'dȯd·-\ *n* -s [It, retreat, place of entertainment, redoubt — more at REDOUBT] **1 :** a public entertainment consisting of music and dancing often in masquerade introduced from Italy and very popular in England in the 18th century **2 :** an arrangement or abridgment of a musical composition from the full score

**rids** *pres 3d sing of* RID

**ridy-horse** \'rīdē,=\ *n* [alter. of *riding horse*] *Midland* **:** SEESAW, TEETER

**RIE** *abbr, often not cap* retirement income endowment

**rie·beck·ite** \'rē,be,kīt\ *n* -s [G *riebeckit*, fr. Emil *Riebeck* †1885 Ger. explorer + G *-it* -ite] **:** a black monoclinic amphibole $Na_2Fe_5Si_8O_{22}(OH)_2$ containing much iron and sodium

**rief** \'rēf\ *var of* REIF

**rief·ler clock** \'rēflə(r)-\ *n, cap R* [after Siegmund *Riefler* †1912 Ger. engineer] **:** a high-precision standard clock having a pin escapement and a partially free mercurial pendulum

**rie·gel** \'rēgəl\ *n* -s [G, lit., crossbar] **:** a low transverse rock ridge on the floor of a glaciated valley commonly situated at the down-valley end of a flat

**riel** \'rē(ə)l\ *n* -s [origin unknown] **:** the basic monetary unit of Cambodia from 1954 divided into 100 sen — see MONEY table

**riem** \'rēm\ *n* -s [Afrik, strap, belt, fr. MD *rieme* — more at RIM] *Africa* **:** a pliable strip usu. of rawhide **:** THONG

**rie·man·ni·an** \(')rē¦mänēən, -man-\ *adj, usu cap* [G.F.B. *Riemann* †1866 Ger. mathematician + E *-ian*] **:** relating to or discovered by the German mathematician Riemann

**riemannian geometry** *n, usu cap R* **:** a non-Euclidian geometry one of whose assumptions is that if two opposite sides of a quadrilateral are equal and make right angles with a third side, the fourth side makes equal obtuse angles with the first two sides

**riem·pie** \'rempē\ *n* -s [Afrik *riempje* thong, dim. of *riem* strap, belt — more at RIEM] *southern Africa* **:** a rawhide strip used esp. as webbing in making furniture seats ⟨dozing in her wide *riempie*-bottomed chair —Stuart Cloete⟩

**ries·ling** \'rēzliŋ, -ēsl-, -lēŋ\ *n* -s *usu cap* [G] **:** a dry white table wine resembling Rhine wine

**rietbok** *or* **rietboc** *var of* REITBOK

**riever** *var of* REAVER

**RIF** \'rif\ *n* -s [reduction *in force*] **1 :** a process of reduction of personnel (as of a government organization) esp. for reasons of economy — compare [9]RIFF **2 :** the act of dismissing a person esp. from government employment for reasons of economy; *also* **:** a notice of such dismissal

**ri·fa·ci·men·to** \(,)rē,fächē'men·(,)tō\ *or* **re·fa·ci·men·to** \rā,f-\ *n, pl* **rifacimen·ti** \-tē\ *or* **rifacimentos** *or* **refaci·men·ti** *or* **refacimentos** [It *rifacimento*, fr. *rifaci-* (stem of *rifare* to make over, fr. *ri-* re- — fr. L *re-* — + *facere, fare* to make, do, fr. L *facere*) + *-mento* -ment (fr. L *-mentum*) — more at DO] **:** a recasting or adaptation esp. of a literary work or musical composition

[1]**rife** \'rīf\ *adj* -ER/-EST [ME *rif, rive, ryfe*, fr. OE *rȳfe*; akin to MLG *rīve* abundant, ON *rīfr* munificent, abundant] **1 a :** existing generally **:** PREVALENT ⟨similar magical practices were ~ in antiquity —J.G.Frazer⟩ ⟨speculation was ~ as to a possible alliance —*Americana Annual*⟩ ⟨manipulation in the stock was ~ —Harold Wincott⟩ ⟨disease and starvation were ~ —*Collier's Yr. Bk.*⟩ **b :** commonly reported **:** CURRENT ⟨rumors of overwhelming evidence to convict him were ~ —George Meredith⟩ ⟨legends were ~ of its extraordinary wealth —John Buchan⟩ **c :** frequently heard or used ⟨what's the adage ~ in man's mouth —Robert Browning⟩ **2 a :** ABUNDANT, PLENTIFUL, NUMEROUS ⟨a considerable poet himself in days when poets were ~ —O.S.J.Gogarty⟩ ⟨genius . . . is nearly extinct, and talent is unprecedentedly ~ —G.D.Painter⟩ ⟨berets are ~ here —Lois Long⟩ **b :** RANK, STRONG ⟨in the deep jungle . . . everything was damp and ~ and hot —Norman Mailer⟩ ⟨when issues are hotly contested and prejudices are ~ —F.L. Mott⟩ **3 :** ABOUNDING, REPLETE — usu. used with *with* ⟨the district is ~ with legends —Richard Joseph⟩ ⟨the science of animal behavior is ~ with controversy —*Scientific American Reader*⟩ **4** *dial* **:** QUICK, READY, INCLINED ⟨could see that Katty's eyes were ~ for mischief —Daniel Corkery⟩ **syn** see PREVAILING

[2]**rife** \"\ *adv* -ER/-EST [ME *rif, rife*, fr. *rif, rife* rife, adj.] **:** RIFELY ⟨weeds grew ~ in the vacant lots⟩

**rife·ly** *adv* [ME *rively*, fr. *rive* rife + *-ly*] **:** in a rife manner

**rife·ness** *n* -ES [ME *ryfenes*, fr. *ryfe* rife + *-nes* -ness] **:** the quality or state of being rife ⟨appalling ~ of the terrain —Norman Mailer⟩

[1]**riff** \'rif\ *n* -s [D *rif* — more at REEF] *dial* **:** REEF ⟨giant rays frequent the tidal ~s —Hodding Carter & Anthony Ragusin⟩ ⟨Long *Riff*, Virgin Islands⟩

[2]**riff** *n* -s [back-formation fr. *midriff*] *obs* **:** DIAPHRAGM

[3]**riff** *also* **rif** \'rif\ *n, pl* **riffs** \-fs\ *or* **riffi** \-fē\ *or* **riff** *cap* [fr. Er *Rif*, coastal area of northern Morocco] **:** a Berber of Er Rif, a hilly coastal region of northern Morocco — called also *Riffian*

[4]**riff** \'rif\ *n* -s [short for [1]*riffle*] *dial* **:** RIFFLE, RIPPLE ⟨beyond the breakers or in the ~s at the inlet —E.A.Weeks⟩

[5]**riff** \"\ *vb* -ED/-ING/-S [short for [2]*riffle*] **:** RIFFLE, SKIM ⟨~ through the pages of a book⟩ ⟨~ through items on a bargain counter⟩

[6]**riff** \"\ *n* -s [prob. by shortening and alter. fr. *refrain*] **:** a short rhythmic jazz figure repeated without melodic development and often serving as background of a solo improvisation; *also* **:** a piece constructed on such a repeated figure

[7]**riff** \"\ *vi* -ED/-ING/-S **:** to perform or make use of riffs esp. in jazz

[8]**riff** \"\ *n* -s [origin unknown] **:** a tap dance step of foot swing and ball-heel or heel-ball impact in any direction

[9]**riff** *also* **rif** \"\ *vt* **riffed; riffed; riffing; riffs** *also* **rifs**

[*RIF*] **:** to discharge esp. from government service for reasons of economy

**riff·ian** \'rifēən\ *n* -s *cap* [Er *Rif*, coastal area of northern Morocco + E *-ian*] **:** RIFF

**¹rif·fle** \'rifəl\ *n* -s [perh. alter. (influenced by *ripple*) of *ruffle*] **1 a :** a shallow extending across the bed of a stream over which the water flows swiftly so that the surface of the water is broken in waves ⟨passed a very bad ~ of rocks in the evening —G.R.Clark⟩; *also* **:** any expanse of shallow bottom causing broken water ⟨channel into the port was hard to navigate due to reef patches and ~ —Michael Rosene⟩ **b :** a stretch of water flowing over a riffle ⟨fish the ~*s;* cast in swift white water —Richard Salmon⟩ **c :** a wave of a riffle ⟨white-topped ~*s* racing past their heads out in midstream —H.L. Davis⟩ **2 a :** a small wave or succession of small waves **:** RIPPLE ⟨a ~ of laughter passed among them —Virginia A. Oakes⟩ ⟨flats and slow swells, breaking here and there into ~*s* of rounded foothills —Russell Lord⟩ **b :** a patch of ripples or small waves (as caused by a light breeze) on an otherwise calm or unbroken surface of water ⟨the march of ~*s* across the water marked the approach of the breeze —R.J.Smith⟩ ⟨could see a little ~ of dark coming along where the morning northerly was making up —G.W.Brace⟩ ⟨a ~ caused by a school of fish⟩ **3** [*²riffle*] **a :** the act or process of shuffling (as cards) ⟨the dealer merely manipulated the ~ so that a disproportionate number of splits appeared —C.B.Davis⟩; *specif* **:** RIFFLE-SHUFFLE **b :** the sound made while doing this ⟨heard the stiff ~ of cards —Wallace Stegner⟩

**²riffle** \"\ *vb* **riffled; riffled; riffling** \-f(ə)liŋ\ **riffles** *vi* **1 :** to form a riffle **:** flow over a riffle **:** move in riffles ⟨a fish nosed the surface . . . and the water *riffled* and lay quiet again —A.B.Guthrie⟩ ⟨*riffling* brooks⟩ ⟨our flags *riffling* in the breeze —Shelby Foote⟩ **2 :** to engage in turning or mixing lightly or hastily (as in cursory search of something) **:** RUN, SKIM — usu. used with *through* ⟨*riffled* through hundreds of letters and cards —M.L.Bach⟩ ⟨~ through one's files⟩ ⟨~ through a manuscript⟩ ⟨watched a child ~ through the gifts under a tree —*New Yorker*⟩ ~ *vt* **1 a :** to ruffle slightly **:** form undulations in **:** RIPPLE ⟨flag *riffled* by the breeze⟩ ⟨fish-*riffled* sloughs —*Ford Times*⟩ **b :** to produce as riffles ⟨choppy waves, *riffled* by the wind —Wyman Richardson⟩ **2 a :** to stir or shift lightly or hastily (as in cursory search of something) **:** leaf through (as a book) rapidly or hastily ⟨*riffled* my field guidebook —D.C.Peattie⟩ ⟨~ the papers on the desk top⟩ **b :** to leaf or thumb (a stack of pieces of paper) by holding in one hand and sliding the thumb of the other hand along the edge so as to release sheets successively from the pressure of the thumb or by holding against a flat surface and thumbing similarly by lifting one side or corner with the thumb of the same hand ⟨would ~ the cards . . . then deal —C.B.Davis⟩ ⟨*riffling* the cards with his white hands —Grace Metalious⟩ ⟨~ the bills⟩ **c :** to shuffle (playing cards) by separating the deck into two parts that are laid flat on the table, elevating a corner or side of each part of the pack slightly, and thumbing in such a manner that the two parts are intermixed and then sliding the entire pack together **d :** to manipulate (a stack of objects) idly between the fingers of one hand or of both hands ⟨fingers of his right hand, rapidly *riffling* a little pile of chips —Richard Donovan & H.M.Greenspun⟩ ⟨the sheriff *riffled* his coins —H.L.Davis⟩

**³riffle** \"\ *n* -s [prob. fr. *¹riffle*] **1 a** (1) **:** any of various contrivances (as blocks, rails, poles, or iron bars often combined with sacking, matting, or hides with the hair up) laid on the bottom of a sluice or launder to make a series of grooves or interstices to catch and retain a mineral (as gold) (2) **:** a groove or interstice so formed **b** *or* **riffle bar :** a bar or cleat in a riffle, table, cradle, or similar gold-washing apparatus **2** *also* **riffle block a** (1) **:** a cleat or bar fastened to an inclined surface (as of a Wilfley table) to catch and hold mineral grains (2) **:** the groove formed by two such parallel cleats or bars **b :** one of a series of cleats or bars used (as in a trough) to separate foreign matter from any material (as paper pulp) suspended in flowing water **3 :** a device for dividing ground ore or other material (as in sampling) consisting usu. of an even number of narrow sloping troughs of equal width with adjacent troughs discharging in opposite directions or of a series of parallel troughs separated by gaps of the same width as the troughs **4 :** a transverse board in a fishway to check the flow of the current and afford a resting pool for ascending fish

**⁴riffle** \"\ *vt* -ED/-ING/-S **1 :** to run (a material) through a riffle or over a series of riffles ⟨~ ground ore in sampling⟩ ⟨~ pulp in paper manufacture⟩ **2 :** to run the point of the trowel along the center of a spread of (mortar) in bricklaying

**riffle file** *n* [back-formation fr. *¹riffler*] **:** RIFFLER

**rif·fle·man** \-mən\ *n, pl* **rifflemen** [*³riffle* + *man*] **:** a worker who scoops gold particles from behind the riffles of gold-washing apparatus

**¹rif·fler** \'rif(ə)lə(r)\ *n* -s [modif. of F *rifloir*, fr. MF, fr. *rifler*

riffler

to file + *-oir* -ory — more at RIFLE] **:** a small file with ends curved to various shapes used for working in depressions (as in die sinking)

**²riffler** \"\ *n* -s [*⁴riffle* + *-er*] **:** a trough used in papermaking containing upright partitions that slow the flow of pulp and permit heavy irregular particles to drop out

**riffler man** *n* [*²riffler*] **:** a worker who uses a riffler to remove impurities from pulp stock

**riffle-shuffle** \'=,==\ *n* [*¹riffle* + *shuffle*] **:** the act or process of shuffling playing cards by first separating the pack into two parts

**¹riff·raff** \'ri,fraf, -raa(ə)f, -raif\ *n* [ME *riffe raffe*, fr. *rif and raf* every single one, fr. MF *rif et raf* completely, fr. *rifler* to plunder + *raffe* act of sweeping — more at RIFLE, RAFFLE] **1 a :** persons of the lowest or most disreputable class ⟨beachcombers, adventurers, rough traders, and general ~ —Ellen La Motte⟩; *broadly* **:** any group of persons looked upon as common, disreputable, or very unconventional ⟨all the ~ for miles around have been using my garden as if it were their own —P.G.Wodehouse⟩ ⟨painters, authors, and other vagrant ~ who frequented the premises —Norman Douglas⟩ **b :** the lowest or most disreputable element of the populace **:** RABBLE, MOB, CANAILLE ⟨the ~ might sack the town —*Harper's*⟩ **c :** one of the riffraff **:** a disreputable person ⟨will not have some ~ . . . trailing about with us —Elizabeth Janeway⟩ **2 :** REFUSE, RUBBISH, TRASH ⟨waistcoats of dirty damask, legs of velvet breeches—in a word, all the cast-off ~ of centuries —W.W.Story⟩ ⟨had once actually said that pigeons were mere ~ —Sean O'Faolain⟩

**²riffraff** \"\ *adj* **:** composed of, belonging to, or characteristic of the rabble **:** DISREPUTABLE, TRASHY, WORTHLESS ⟨a score of ~ gunslingers, barroom brawlers —*New Yorker*⟩ ⟨~ opinions⟩ ⟨a ~ army⟩ ⟨row of ~ dwellings —Booth Tarkington⟩

**riffs** *pl of* RIFF, *pres 3d sing of* RIFF

**¹ri·fle** \'rīfəl\ *vb* **rifled; rifled; rifling** \-f(ə)liŋ\ **rifles** [ME *riflen*, fr. MF *rifler* to scratch, file, plunder, fr. OF, of Gmc origin; akin to obs. D *riffelen* to scrape, groove, MD *riven* to rake — more at RIVEL] *vt* **1 :** to ransack and rob or plunder **:** pillage thoroughly **:** despoil completely ⟨his mail was repeatedly *rifled* —William MacDonald⟩ ⟨not only dug deep into local archives but *rifled* the memories of farmers —*Newsweek*⟩ **2 :** to steal and carry away **:** snatch away **:** carry off ⟨till time shall ~ every youthful grace —Alexander Pope⟩ ~ *vi* **:** to engage in ransacking and pillaging ⟨*rifling* through her desk in a desperate search for writing materials —Brand Blanshard⟩ **syn** see ROB

**²rifle** \"\ *n* -s [ME, fr. ONF, perh. fr. OF *rifler* to scratch, file] **1 :** a strip of wood covered with emery or similar material and used for sharpening scythes **2** *Brit* **:** a bent stick fastened at the butt of a scythe and serving to lay the mowed grain in rows

**³rifle** \"\ *vt* **rifled; rifled; rifling** \-f(ə)liŋ\ **rifles :** to whet with a rifle ⟨*rifling* scythes and filing hoes —William Humphrey⟩

**⁴rifle** \"\ *vt* **rifled; rifled; rifling** \-f(ə)liŋ\ **rifles** [F *rifler* to scratch, file, fr. MF] **:** to cut spiral grooves into the bore of (as a firearm or piece of ordnance) ⟨*rifled* arms⟩ ⟨*rifled* pipe⟩

**⁵rifle** \"\ *n* -s **1** *archaic* **:** one of the spiral grooves in the bore

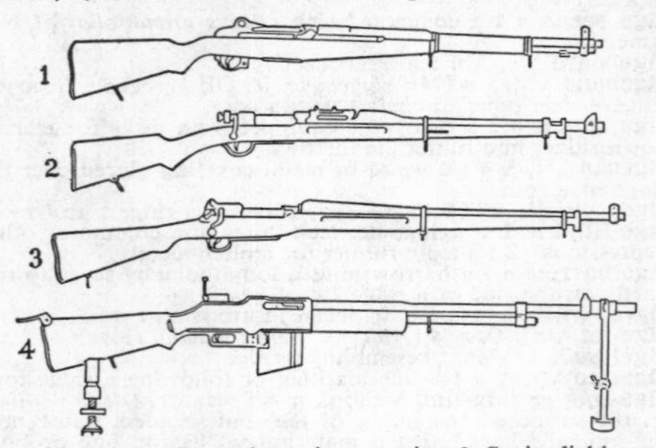


rifles 2: *1* Garand semiautomatic, *2* Springfield, *3* Enfield, *4* Browning automatic

of a rifled firearm **2 a :** a firearm having a rifled bore and intended to be fired from the shoulder — see CARBINE; compare MUSKET, PISTOL, SHOTGUN **b :** a rifled artillery piece ⟨startling crack of a single great fourteen-inch ~, carefully aimed —K.M. Dodson⟩ **3 a :** RIFLEMAN ⟨attended captain of a Maryland company of ~*s* —*Amer. Guide Series: Md.*⟩ **b rifles** *pl* **:** a body of soldiers armed with rifles ⟨the 6th Gurkha *Rifles*⟩ **4** *or* **rifle green :** a dark grayish olive green to black **5 :** a mobile lighting unit with a spirally ribbed parabolic reflector throwing a narrow beam that is used esp. in television and motion-picture making

**⁶rifle** \"\ *vt* **rifled; rifled; rifling** \-f(ə)liŋ\ **rifles** [*⁵rifle*] **:** to hit or throw (a ball) with great force ⟨*rifled* a single to center field⟩

**rifle bar** *n* [*⁵rifle*] **:** a rifled steel bar used for rotating drill steel in a machine drill

**riflebird** \'==,=\ *n* [*⁵rifle;* fr. the sound of its cry] **:** any of several birds of paradise of *Ptiloris* or a related genus; *esp* **:** a bird of paradise (*P. paradisea*) of New So. Wales and Queensland the male of which is chiefly velvety black with greenish and purplish iridescence on the head, underparts, and middle tail feathers

**rifle drill** *n* **:** a drill designed to create long straight holes of small diameter (as for a rifle)

**rifled slug** *n* [fr. past part. of *⁴rifle*] **:** a shotgun projectile having a round nose, a hollow base, and sides cut with a series of oblique grooves that increase the accuracy of the projectile by causing it to rotate as it passes through the smooth bore of the shotgun

**rifle frock** *n* [*⁵rifle*] *archaic* **:** a rifleman's tunic

**rifle grenade** *n* **:** a grenade projected from a launching device attached to the muzzle of a rifle or carbine and requiring a special cartridge

**rifle gun** *n* **:** RIFLE; *esp* **:** a muzzle-loading rifle

**ri·fle·man** \'rīfəlmən\ *n, pl* **riflemen 1 :** a soldier armed with a rifle **2 :** one skilled in shooting with a rifle — **ri·fle·man·ship** \-,ship\ *n*

**rifleman bird** *n* [so called fr. the resemblance of its plumage to the uniform of the early British volunteer rifle corps] **1 :** RIFLEBIRD **2 :** a small passerine bird (*Acanthisitta chloris*) of New Zealand with green-and-bronze plumage

**rifle pit** *n* **:** a short trench or excavation with a parapet of earth in front to shelter one or more riflemen

**¹ri·fler** \'rīf(ə)lə(r)\ *n* -s [ME *riffler, rifeler*, fr. *riflen* to rifle, plunder + *-er*] **:** one that rifles **:** ROBBER

**²rifler** \"\ *n* -s [*⁴rifle* + *-er*] **:** one that grooves rifling by machine

**ri·fle·ry** \'rīfəlrē\ *n* -ES [*⁵rifle* + *-ry*] **1 :** rifle shots ⟨storm of ~ cracked and rattled among the northern foothills —Richard Dehan⟩ **2 :** rifle shooting; *esp* **:** the practice of shooting with a rifle at a target

**rifles** *pres 3d sing of* RIFLE, *pl of* RIFLE

**rifle salute** *n* [*⁵rifle*] **:** a position in the manual of arms in which the disengaged hand extended is brought across the body touching the rear of the receiver of the rifle when held at shoulder arms or near its muzzle when held at order or trail arms

**ri·fle·scope** \'rīfəlz,kōp, -l,sk-\ *n* [*⁵rifle* + *-scope*] **:** a telescopic sight for a rifle

**rifleshot** \'==,=\ *n* **:** one who shoots a rifle skillfully

**rifle tie** *n* **:** a tie with the pith of the tree at or near the center of the ends

**rifle whiskey** *n* **:** inferior or cheap whiskey

**rifling** *n* -s [fr. gerund of *⁴rifle*] **1 :** the act or process of making spiral grooves (as in a gun barrel) **2 a :** a system of spiral grooves cut in the surface of the bore of a gun leaving intervening lands that cut into the projectile when fired or into a metal band secured to it and rotate it about its longer axis **b :** a system of spiral grooves (as in a pipe or drill core)

rifle salute

**¹rift** \'rift\ *n* -s [ME, of Scand origin; akin to ON *ript* breach of contract, *rīfa* to rive, Dan & Norw *rift* rent, fissure — more at RIVE] **1 a :** an opening made by cracking or splitting **:** FISSURE, CREVASSE ⟨a ~ in the ice⟩ ⟨spring that gushes from a ~ in a red sandstone bluff —*Amer. Guide Series: Texas*⟩ ⟨widened lattice intervals are evidently ~*s* in the crystal lattice, produced initially by plastic deformation —*Science*⟩; *broadly* **:** any crack or flaw caused by stress or conflict — often used of minute or immaterial things ⟨little ~ within the lute —Alfred Tennyson⟩ ⟨first split Western man's acts from his ideals, for only by such a ~ in his mind could he hold on to these mutually destroying beliefs —Lillian Smith⟩ **b** (1) **:** a normal fault; *esp* **:** one along which movement has occurred in comparatively recent geologic time (2) **:** a depression or valley along the trace of a fault or fault zone — compare RIFT VALLEY **2 :** an open space **:** a clear interval ⟨glimpsed occasionally through ~*s* in the dense foliage —*Amer. Guide Series: Pa.*⟩ ⟨high ~*s* of blue, white-cloud-dappled sky —Flora Thompson⟩ ⟨had one of those ~*s* of lucidity in which I saw him whole and limited —Mary Austin⟩ **3 :** wood split or cut radially from the log ⟨~ flooring⟩ **4 :** the direction of easiest splitting esp. of a granite — used esp. by quarrymen **5 :** a divergence (as of interests or beliefs) resulting in disagreement or dispute ⟨this little ~ it was that had widened to a now considerable breach —H.G.Wells⟩ ⟨a growing ~ and an atmosphere of suspicion between the two parties —*Farmer's Weekly (So. Africa)*⟩ ⟨developments in the industrial crisis which reveal significant ~*s* among his own supporters —*New Statesman & Nation*⟩ **syn** see BREACH

**²rift** \"\ *vb* -ED/-ING/-S [ME *riften*, of Scand origin; akin to ON *ripta* to break a contract, *ript* breach of contract] *vt* **1 a :** CLEAVE, RIVE, SPLIT, DIVIDE ⟨mica ~*ed* into sheets⟩ ⟨the mist is ~*ed* and we can look straight at the words —R.P.Warren⟩ **b :** to saw (wood) radially from the log so as to have the annual rings perpendicular or nearly so to the face **2 :** to penetrate by or as if by cleaving ⟨the intellect is a cleaver; it discerns and ~*s* its way into the secret of things —H.D.Thoreau⟩ ~ *vi* **1 :** to burst open **:** SPLIT ⟨the clouds ~*ed*⟩ **2 :** to form a rift in the earth's crust ⟨sedimentary deposits surviving the denudation following the ~*ing* —*E. African Agric. Jour.*⟩

**³rift** \"\ *vi* -ED/-ING/-S [ME *riften*, fr. ON *rypta*; prob. akin to Skt *rauti* he roars — more at RUMOR] *chiefly dial* **:** to belch or break wind

**⁴rift** \"\ *n* -s [prob. alter. of *¹riff*] **:** a shallow or rocky place in a stream forming either a ford or a rapid ⟨trout waters, where the ~*s* and pools harbor flashing rainbows —G.P.Manning⟩

**⁵rift** \"\ *adj* [by shortening] **:** RIFT-SAWED ⟨~ fir⟩ ⟨~ laths⟩

**rift crack** *n* [*¹rift*] **:** HEART SHAKE

**rift·er** \'riftə(r)\ *n* -s [*¹rift* + *-er*] **:** a crack in sea ice **:** an open space in a floe

**rift grain** *n* [*¹rift*] **:** edge grain of quarter-sawed or rift-sawed boards with the annual rings nearly perpendicular to the surface

**rift·less** \'riftləs\ *adj* **:** having no rift

**rift saw** *n* [*²rift* + *saw*] **:** a saw for rifting timber (as into boards and laths); *esp* **:** a circular saw having four or more toothed projecting arms for sawing cants into flooring strips

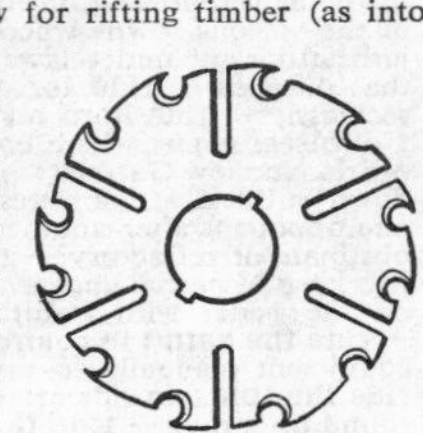

rift saw

**rift-sawed** *or* **rift-sawn** \'=,=\ *adj* [*¹rift* + *sawed* or *sawn*] **1 :** sawed radially from the log so as to have the annual rings perpendicular or nearly so to the face **2 :** QUARTERSAWED

**rift valley** *n* [*¹rift*] **:** an elongated valley formed by the depression of a block of the earth's crust between two faults or fault zones of approximately parallel strike **:** a graben having surface expression

**rift valley fever** \'=,==-\ *n, usu cap R&V* [fr. *Rift Valley*, western Kenya, Africa] **:** a virus disease of east African sheep and sometimes cattle characterized by fever and destructive hepatitis and occasionally transmitted to man in a much-attenuated form

**¹rig** \'rig\ *n* -s [ME *ryg*, of Scand origin; akin to ON *hregg* storm, Faroese *reiggj* powerful movement, Icel *hrægja* to rain slowly, Dan *ræg* frost] *dial Eng* **:** a high wind **:** STORM

**²rig** \"\ *n* -s [ME (northern dial.), back, ridge, fr. OE *hrycg* — more at RIDGE] **1** *chiefly Scot* **:** RIDGE **2** *chiefly Brit* **:** RIDGELING **3 :** a measure of land in Scotland ⟨will buy me ~*s* o'land —Robert Burns⟩

**³rig** \"\ *vb* **rigged; rigged; rigging; rigs** [ME *riggen*, prob. of Scand origin; akin to Norw *rigga* to bind, wrap up, Sw *rigga* (*på*) to harness (up)] *vt* **1 a :** to fit out (as a ship) with the necessary tackle **:** fit the shrouds, stays, and braces of (as a ship) to their respective masts and spars **:** make (as a ship) ready for sea **b :** to fit shrouds, stays, or similar devices to (as a mast or spar) ⟨~ the mainmast⟩ **2 :** to fit out or provide with clothes **:** CLOTHE, DRESS ⟨*rigged* him in moccasins —H.L. Davis⟩ — usu. used with *out* ⟨~ him out in garments like the British noblemen wore —F.B.Gipson⟩ ⟨she was *rigged* out in Victorian style —Ellery Queen⟩ **3 a :** to furnish with apparatus or gear **:** provide with equipment **:** fit up **:** EQUIP ⟨some of the craft are *rigged* for dredging —H.M.Parshley⟩ ⟨crushing stone *rigged* with an ox yoke and pole —*Amer. Guide Series: Conn.*⟩ **b :** to fit out in some way ⟨why the book should have been *rigged* out as a liturgy —*Times Lit. Supp.*⟩ **4 a :** to put into proper position or condition for use **:** set up in working order **:** ADJUST, FIX ⟨*rigged* the tarpaulins over stakes —Rex Ingamells⟩ ⟨alarm clocks are *rigged* to turn on radios —Gladwin Hill⟩ ⟨*rigged* up a Christmas tree in the town hall —W.A. White⟩ **b :** to move (as a boom on a sailing vessel) in a desired direction or to the proper position ⟨~ in a boom⟩ ⟨~ out a boom⟩ **5 :** to fit up as a makeshift **:** set up as an expedient ⟨~ jury masts⟩ — often used with *out* or *up* ⟨*rigged* up an affair . . . to take the place of a bed —D.B.Putnam⟩ ⟨*rigged* up a temporary shelter⟩ **6 :** to assemble, adjust, and align the component parts including the control surfaces of (an airplane) to assure satisfactory flight-handling characteristics ~ *vi, obs* **:** to become or get rigged — used of a ship

**⁴rig** \"\ *n* -s **1 :** the distinctive shape, number, and arrangement of sails and masts differentiating types of vessels without reference to the hull ⟨schooner ~⟩ ⟨ship ~⟩ — compare ⁵BARK 2, ¹BRIG, CATBOAT, HERMAPHRODITE BRIG, KETCH, KNOCKABOUT 3, LUGGER, SCHOONER, SLOOP, YAWL; see FORE-AND-AFT RIG, SQUARE RIG **2 :** TURNOUT, EQUIPAGE; *esp* **:** a carriage with its horse **3 :** DRESS 2; *esp* **:** clothing designed for a special purpose or worn as a distinctive costume ⟨dressed in festive ~ —Mollie Panter-Downes⟩ ⟨an English judge in full ~ —F.J.Warburg⟩ ⟨boats' crews should be correctly . . . dressed in the ~ ordered —*Manual of Seamanship*⟩ **4 :** tackle, apparatus, or machinery fitted up for a specified purpose: as **a** (1) **:** a derrick complete with enginehouse and other equipment necessary for operation that is used for boring and afterwards pumping an oil well (2) **:** an oil derrick (3) **:** a similar apparatus used for other types of drilling (as pile-driving or drilling for water) **b** (1) **:** a cultivator gang composed of a combination of beam, shank, and shovels (2) **:** such a combination in a cultivator **c :** a thresher with a tractor and other equipment **:** a threshing outfit **d :** a fisherman's terminal tackle or gear **e :** FIRE ENGINE **f :** a trailer truck **:** a tractor-trailer **:** a tractor hitched to a trailer **g** (1) **:** the complete station of an amateur radio operator (2) **:** a high fidelity sound system **5** *West* **:** SADDLE

**⁵rig** \"\ *vi* **rigged; rigged; rigging; rigs** [perh. by shortening & alter. fr. *wriggle*] **1** *chiefly dial* **:** to romp and wriggle about **2** *chiefly dial* **:** to behave lewdly

**⁶rig** \"\ *n* -s *dial Eng* **:** a wanton immoral woman

**⁷rig** \"\ *n* -s [origin unknown] **1** *chiefly Brit* **:** the action of ridiculing **:** BANTER, RIDICULE, SPORT **2 a** *chiefly Brit* **:** a fraudulent or cheating trick **:** SWINDLE **b :** manipulation of prices to a desired level in a securities or commodity market by artificial means (as a corner) **3** *chiefly Brit* **:** a wanton or mischievous act **:** PRANK

**⁸rig** \"\ *vt* **rigged; rigged; rigging; rigs 1** *dial Eng* **:** to play tricks on **:** FOOL, HOAX **2 a :** to arrange or manage esp. by deceptive means **:** manipulate in an underhanded manner **:** achieve or carry out by fraudulent means **:** control by dishonest means ⟨attempt to ~ the scales —*Adelaide S. A. Sunday Mail*⟩ ⟨~ an election⟩ ⟨~ the stock market⟩ **b :** to fix in advance to secure or show a desired result ⟨dealers had combined to ~ the auction price very low —James Higgins & Gordon Donald⟩ ⟨~ a quiz by furnishing the contestants with answers⟩ ⟨~ prices⟩

**⁹rig** *or* **ri** \'rē\ *n* -s [IrGael *rī* (gen. *rīogh, rīgh*, dat. *rīgh*), fr. OIr, (gen., dat., & acc. *rīg*) — more at ROYAL] **:** an ancient Irish king

**ri·ga** \'rēgə\ *adj, usu cap* [fr. *Riga*, Latvia] **:** of or from Riga, the capital of Latvia **:** of the kind or style prevalent in Riga

**rig·a·doon** \¦rigə¦dün\ *or* **ri·gau·don** \rēgōdōⁿ\ *n, pl* **rigadoons** \-ünz\ *or* **rigaudons** \-ōⁿ\ [F *rigaudon, rigodon*, perh. fr. the name *Rigaud*] **1 :** a lively dance performed with a jumping step and popular in the 17th and 18th centuries **2 :** the music for the rigadoon usu. in spirited duple or quadruple time

**riga fir** *or* **riga pine** *n, usu cap R* **:** SCOTCH PINE

**rig·a·ma·jig** \'rig(ə)mə,jig\ *n* -s [alter. (influenced by *⁴rig*) of *thingumajig*] **:** something the name of which is unknown or not remembered **:** THINGUMBOB ⟨the ~ they keep track of the rooms on —Sinclair Lewis⟩

**rigamarole** *var of* RIGMAROLE

**rig-and-fur** \¦rigən¦fər\ *adj* [*²rig*] *chiefly Scot* **:** ridged and furrowed **:** RIBBED ⟨*rig-and-fur* stockings⟩

**rig·a·ree** \'rigə,rē, ,==¦=\ *n* -s [origin unknown] **:** ornamentation on glass (as of early wine decanters) consisting of narrow applied bands forming parallel ribs

**rigation** *n* -s [L *rigation-, rigatio*, fr. *rigatus* (past part. of *rigare* to water) + *-ion-, -io* -ion — more at RAIN] *obs* **:** IRRIGATION

**ri·ga·to·ni** \,rigə'tōnē\ *n, pl* **rigatoni** [It, pl., fr. *rigato*, past part. of *rigare* to draw a line, make a furrow, make fluting, fr. *riga* line, of Gmc origin; akin to OHG *riga* line — more at ROW] **:** hollow alimentary paste made in short curved fluted pieces

**rigged** *past of* RIG

**rig·ger** \'rigə(r)\ *n* -s [*³rig* + *-er*] **1 :** one that rigs: as **a :** one whose occupation is fitting the rigging of ships **b :** one that manipulates something (as the stock market or an auction) usu. by dishonest means **c :** one who installs or operates the rigging involved in skidding logs from a forest with a power-drawn cable **d :** one of a crew of men who build oil and gas well rigs — called also *climber* **e :** one who assists in the installation and repair of underground electric cables **f :** one who assembles the parts of awnings that are to be hung **g :** a netmaker who sews the outer edges of netting to ropes **h :** one employed in assembling and aligning aircraft or parachutes **i :** one that works with rigging or similar equipment or tends a rigging machine ⟨crane ~*s*⟩ ⟨scaffold ~*s*⟩ **j :** one that rigs a racing shell **2 :** a band pulley or drum

**3** : a long slender and pointed sable brush used in painting pictures **4** : a ship of a specified rig ⟨square-*rigger*⟩ **5** : OUTRIGGER 1 **6** : a scaffold erected in building operations to protect passersby from falling objects

**rigger's screw** *n* : RIGGING SCREW 1

**¹rig·ging** \'rigən, -giŋ\ *n* -s [ME (northern dial.), fr. *rig* back, ridge + *-ing* — more at RIG (ridge)] **1** *chiefly Scot* : the ridge or roof of a building **2** *chiefly Scot* : the back of an animal or human being

**²rig·ging** \-giŋ\ *n* -s [fr. gerund of ³*rig*] **1 a** : the ropes, chains, and other lines used aboard a vessel esp. in working sail and supporting masts and spars — see RUNNING RIGGING, STANDING RIGGING; SHIP illustration **b** : a similar network of ropes or wires used for support and manipulation (as in scaffolding or in theater scenery) **2** : CLOTHING 1 a ⟨the tall old woman in the dark ~ —Sir Walter Scott⟩ **3** : the exterior leather trappings of a saddle — see STOCK SADDLE illustration **4** : the cables, blocks, and other equipment used in power skidding and hauling logs **5** : the system of cords and wires that distribute the load of an aerostat over the envelope **6** : the network of thongs used to attach a snowshoe to the foot **7** : pattern and related equipment for making a mold in founding

rigging 6

**rigging loft** *n* **1** : a loft in which rigging is prepared for use on ships **2** : an open floor of beams over the stage and under the roof of a theater from which the scenery is raised and lowered

**rigging screw** *n* **1** : a screw clamp or vise for bending rope around a thimble for splicing or seizing **2** *Brit* : TURNBUCKLE

**rig·gish** \'rigish\ *adj* [⁶*rig* + *-ish*] *chiefly dial* : WANTON ⟨~ embraces —C.E.Montague⟩

**rig·got** \'rigət\ *n* -s [fr. obs. F *rigot*, fr. MF, prob. alter. of *rigole* drain, irrigation ditch, canal — more at RIGOLET] *dial Eng* : a surface drain, esp. for rain water : GUTTER

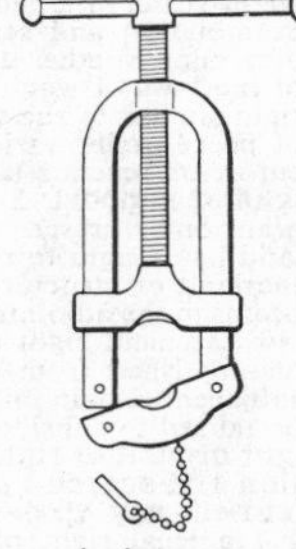
rigging screw

**riggs' disease** \'rigz-\ *n, usu cap R* [after John M. *Riggs* †1885 Am. dentist] : PERIODONTITIS

**righi-leduc effect** \¦rēgēlə¦dük-, ¦ri\ *n, usu cap R&L* [after Augusto *Righi* †1920 Ital. physicist and Sylvestre Anatole *Leduc*, 20th cent. Fr. physicist] : a transverse temperature gradient observed in a metal when the metal is in a magnetic field whose lines of force are perpendicular to the heat flux — called also *Leduc effect*

**¹right** \'rīt, *usu* -īd·+V\ *adj, sometimes* -ER/-EST [ME *riht, right*, fr. OE *riht;* akin to OHG *reht* right, ON *rēttr*, Goth *raihts* right, L *rectus* straight, right, *regere* to lead straight, guide, rule, *rogare* to ask, Gk *oregein* to stretch out, *oreklos* stretched out, upright, Skt *ṛjyati, ṛñjati* he stretches, hastens, *raji* straightening up, straight; basic meaning: straight] **1** : disposed to do what is just or good : RIGHTEOUS, UPRIGHT ⟨a God of faithfulness . . . just and ~ is he —Deut 32:4 (RSV)⟩ ⟨the ~ soul, high and true and pure —W.L.Sullivan⟩ ⟨a ~ conscience⟩ ⟨a ~ man⟩ **2 a** : being in accordance with what is just, good, or proper ⟨conflicting notions of ~ conduct —B.N.Cardozo⟩ ⟨teach young girls ~ behavior when faced with . . . temptations —*London Calling*⟩ ⟨it is ~ that we should do this⟩ ⟨religious teachings as to what is ~ and what is wrong⟩ ⟨doing something he thought not quite ~⟩ **b** : held to be in accordance with justice, morality, and goodness usu. because approved by a person or group ⟨asserted that he was on the ~ side of the controversy⟩ ⟨of course the ~ cause and the ~ men won —*Times Lit. Supp.*⟩ **3 a** : agreeable to a standard or principle : FIT, SUITABLE ⟨educating by a ~ use of pleasure —Benjamin Jowett⟩ ⟨the perfectioning of our countrymen in . . . the ~ use of their native language —Samuel Foote⟩ **b** : agreeing with or conforming to facts : characterized by strict accordance with fact or truth : devoid of error or fault : CORRECT, EXACT ⟨a ~ description of our sport —Shak.⟩ ⟨the answer to a sum is either ~ or wrong —Bertrand Russell⟩ **c** : leading in the proper direction or toward a desired objective ⟨took the ~ road⟩ ⟨set out in the ~ direction⟩ ⟨the ~ way to salvation⟩ **4** : satisfying the requirements of necessity, propriety, or suitability : APPROPRIATE, FITTING ⟨the ~ man for the job —B.R. Redman⟩ ⟨knew that he said the ~ thing —Elizabeth Goudge⟩ ⟨marry when she has found the ~ chap —Robert Reid⟩ ⟨an audience that . . . applauded at the ~ moments —Joseph Wechsberg⟩ **5** *obs* : having proper title or right : LAWFUL, RIGHTFUL ⟨they slew their ~ king —Thomas Becon⟩ ⟨he has a great estate, only the ~ owner keeps him out —Jonathan Swift⟩ **6** : devoid of bends or curves : STRAIGHT ⟨a ~ line⟩ ⟨streets made very broad and ~ —Richard Tomson⟩ **7 a** : justly entitled to the name : having the true character of : ACTUAL, GENUINE, REAL ⟨manifested themselves to be ~ barbarians —John Milton⟩ ⟨a ~ woman⟩ ⟨a spillway rather than a ~ river —H.S.Canby⟩ ⟨~ deer⟩ — compare RIGHT WHALE **b** : having a genuine rather than a counterfeit or spurious character ⟨an ounce of ~ Virginia tobacco —Richard Steele⟩ ⟨wainscoted with ~ wainscot —John Entick⟩ **8** : properly relating or attached to one ⟨give it its ~ name⟩ **9** : characterized by normality : SANE, SOUND ⟨offers no man in his ~ mind could resist —Bennett Cerf⟩ ⟨no rancher in his ~ senses goes into business on borrowed capital —Green Peyton⟩ **10 a** (1) : of, relating to, or constituting the hand that in most persons is stronger, the side of the body on which it is located, or the parts of that side of the body ⟨her ~ foot⟩ ⟨the ~ side of a human body⟩ ⟨delivered a ~ hook to the jaw⟩ (2) : of, relating to, or constituting a similarly located part of another object **b** : located on, designed for, or used on that side of the body ⟨the ~ pocket of a shirt⟩ ⟨a ~ glove⟩ **c** : located on an observer's right or directed as his right hand would point ⟨the ~ side of a house⟩ ⟨took the ~ fork in the road⟩ **d** : located on the right of an observer facing in the same direction as the object involved ⟨stage ~⟩ ⟨the ~ wing of an army⟩ ⟨the ~ bank of a river⟩ **11** : erect from a base : having its axis perpendicular to the base : upright rather than oblique — compare RIGHT ANGLE, RIGHT SPHERE **12** : of, relating to, or constituting the side of something that is usu. held to be the principal one or the one naturally or by design turned up, outward, or toward one or the one that is most finished or polished ⟨turn your socks ~ side out⟩ ⟨the ~ side of a piece of velvet⟩ ⟨in the ditch beside the road, ~ side up . . . rested a new coupe —Scott Fitzgerald⟩ **13** : held to presage good luck or good spirits during the day ⟨got up on the ~ side of the bed⟩ ⟨get the project started off on the ~ foot⟩ **14** : acting, thinking, or judging in accordance with truth or the facts (as of a case) : correct in opinion, judgment, or procedure : stating truth ⟨he was ~ in refusing the offer⟩ ⟨time proved him ~⟩ ⟨~ you are, sir⟩ **15 a** : mentally normal or sound : SANE ⟨not ~ in his head⟩ ⟨not ~ in her mind⟩ **b** : well in physical health : being in good health and spirits : being in good physical condition : SOUND, WELL ⟨the patient doesn't look quite ~ yet⟩ ⟨a few days' rest would put him ~ —Max Peacock⟩ **16** : being in a proper or satisfactory state : being in good order ⟨everything will come out ~ in the end⟩ ⟨get something ~⟩ ⟨that will make it ~⟩ ⟨hunches which turned out ~ —A.G.N.Flew⟩ **17** : being in a correct or properly directed state ⟨we'll set the world ~ —Eden Phillpotts⟩ ⟨the readiness . . . to put things ~ —*London Calling*⟩ ⟨proceeded to set him ~⟩ **18** : most favorable, convenient, or desired : ADVANTAGEOUS, PREFERABLE ⟨I'm still on the ~ side of 50 —Alan Villiers⟩ ⟨get on the ~ side of the law —Hugo Wall⟩ ⟨the ~ side of the tracks⟩ **19** *often cap* : of, adhering to, or constituted by the Right esp. in politics — compare RIGHT WING **20 a** : producing or likely to produce a winning roll or series of rolls in craps and other dice games ⟨the dice are ~ tonight⟩ ⟨bet he's ~⟩ **b** : hopeful that a roll or series of rolls on which a bet is placed in craps and other dice games will result in a natural or a point made ⟨a ~ bet⟩ ⟨a ~ bettor⟩ **21** : socially acceptable, prominent, or correct ⟨did not know the ~ people except in a business way —J.P.Marquand⟩ ⟨a ~ school⟩ ⟨belongs to the ~ clubs —H.N.Maclean⟩ **22 a** : ALL RIGHT 3 ⟨a ~ guy⟩ **b** : held by criminals to be trustworthy and sympathetic or made safe through bribery ⟨a ~ official⟩ ⟨in ~ territory⟩ **syn** see CORRECT

**²right** \"\ *n* -s [ME *riht, right*, fr. OE *riht* (akin to OS & OHG *reht*, OFris *riucht*), fr. *riht*, adj.] **1** : an ethical or moral quality that constitutes the ideal of moral propriety and involves various attributes (as adherence to duty, obedience to lawful authority, whether divine or human, and freedom from guilt) : something morally just or consonant with the light of nature : the straight course **2** : something to which one has a just claim: as **a** : the power or privilege to which one is justly entitled (as upon principles of morality, religion, law, or custom) ⟨held their lands by ~ of the sword —Kemp Malone⟩ ⟨might, not ~ . . . put her in the position she occupied —J.H.Blunt⟩ ⟨accorded of grace and not of ~⟩ ⟨primacy by ~ of merit⟩ **b** : a power, privilege, or condition of existence to which one has a natural claim of enjoyment or possession ⟨the ~s of the people⟩ ⟨~ of liberty⟩ — see NATURAL RIGHT **c** : a power, privilege, or immunity vested in one (as by authority or social custom) **d** (1) : a power or privilege vested in a person by the law to demand action or forbearance at the hands of another : a legally enforceable claim against another that the other will do or will not do a given act : a capacity or privilege the enjoyment of which is secured to a person by law — see ABSOLUTE RIGHT, REMEDIAL RIGHT, SUBSTANTIVE RIGHT; compare PERSON OF INCIDENCE, PERSON OF INHERENCE (2) : a claim recognized and delimited by law for the purpose of securing it (3) : the aggregate of the capacities, powers, liberties, and privileges by which a claim is secured (4) : the capacity to assert a legally recognized claim (5) : the interest or share that one has in a piece of property (6) : a claim or title to property or a possession — often used in pl. ⟨bought land and water ~s here —*Amer. Guide Series: Md.*⟩ ⟨leased some mineral ~s —*Lamp*⟩ ⟨his ~s to the throne⟩ (7) **rights** *pl* : the property interest possessed under common law, copyright law, or custom and agreement in an intangible thing esp. of a literary and artistic nature ⟨sold the film ~s of the novel for $50,000 —Arnold Bennett⟩ ⟨promised me the Australian ~s of his play —Mrs. Patrick Campbell⟩ ⟨publishing ~s under a contract⟩ **e** : a power, privilege, or immunity vested in an animal or group of animals (as by custom) ⟨grazing ~s of a herd of antelope⟩ **3 a** : something that justly accrues or falls to one : something that one may properly claim : one's due ⟨claim your ~s⟩ ⟨honor and admiration are her ~s —John Fletcher⟩ **b** *archaic* : an estate, dominion, or other territory belonging to one; *esp* : the piece of land allocated by a colonial New England town to an individual settler **4** : just or equitable treatment : righteous action : fairness in decision : JUSTICE ⟨in ~ to his majesty and the service —Thomas Hale⟩ ⟨had fortune done him ~ —John Dryden⟩ **5 a** : the cause of truth or justice; *esp* : a cause alleged to be true or just by the party supporting it **b** : the person, party, or cause that maintains what is right **6 a** : the right hand ⟨sneaked his ~ home to the jaw —Donn Byrne⟩ **b** (1) : the location or direction lying on the right side of one's body ⟨on our ~ was a large house⟩ (2) : a similar location or direction with respect to another object ⟨as you look at the . . . flag, its ~ is on your own left —*Boy Scout Handbook*⟩ **c** : the part of something (as the wing of an army, the stage of a theater, or the portion of a line of men) that is on the right side of an observer facing in the direction it faces **d** : the road (as of a pair diverging from a point) lying to one's right ⟨take the ~ at the fork⟩ **e** : RIGHT FIELD ⟨sent a nice single to ~ —*Springfield (Mass.) Republican*⟩ **7** : one of the principal tines of a stag's antler (as a brow antler, bay antler, or royal antler) — usu. used in pl. **8** : the true account or correct interpretation of something (as a story, matter, or dispute) ⟨could not . . . learn the very ~ of it —Henry Fielding⟩ — usu. used in pl. ⟨have never heard the ~s of that story —Frederick Marryat⟩ **9** : the quality or state of being factually correct : consonance with fact : truthfulness of statement : freedom from error or falsehood : adherence to truth or fact : CORRECTNESS ⟨some mixture of ~ and wrong in their reasoning —Edmund Burke⟩ **10** : the member of a pair situated or used on the right side: as **a** : a shoe or other article of footwear for the right foot **b** : a glove or other article of apparel for the right hand **11** *often cap* **a** : the part of a legislative chamber located to the right of the presiding officer and usu. occupied in continental European and other countries having a similar political pattern by members professing a more conservative or rightist position on political issues than other members ⟨loud applause from benches of the ~⟩ ⟨the ~ is occupied by a neo-Fascist group⟩ — compare CENTER 3 c, LEFT 3 a **b** : the members of a legislative body occupying such seats as a result of their political views **12 a** (1) *usu cap* : individuals or groups sometimes professing views characterized by opposition to change in the established political, social, and economic order and favoring the preservation of traditional attitudes and practices and sometimes advocating the establishment of an authoritarian political order by revolution or other forceful means ⟨a sweeping victory for the conservative *Right* —F.A.Magruder⟩ ⟨brickbats from the extreme *Right* —Al Hine⟩ — compare AUTHORITARIAN, CONSERVATIVE, FASCIST, LEFT 4 a, NAZI, REACTIONARY, TRADITIONALIST (2) : a group or party in another organization that favors conservative, traditional, or sometimes authoritarian attitudes and policies ⟨the ~ in a labor union⟩ ⟨left and ~ in the literary world⟩ **b** *often cap* : the symbolic position occupied by persons professing such views : a conservative or rightist as distinguished from a radical position ⟨drove the Government to the ~⟩ ⟨people ranging from center to extreme ~ —*Harper's*⟩ **13** : a blow (as given by a boxer) with the right fist ⟨a hard ~ to the jaw —*Amer. Guide Series: N.Y.*⟩ **14 a** : a privilege given stockholders of a corporation to subscribe pro rata to a new issue of securities generally at a price below that prevailing in the market ⟨the prospective offering of ~s to . . . railroad stockholders —*N.Y. Times*⟩ **b** : the negotiable certificate evidencing such privilege — usu. used in pl. **15** *dial* **a** : DUTY, OBLIGATION ⟨you have a ~ to behave better⟩ **b** : likely reason or excuse ⟨a ~ to fall in if you skate on thin ice⟩

**syn** RIGHT, PREROGATIVE, PRIVILEGE, PERQUISITE, APPANAGE, BIRTHRIGHT can signify, in common, something to which one has a just or legal claim. RIGHT, the most inclusive, can designate anything, as a power, condition of existence, or possession to which one is entitled by nature, legal or moral law, a grant, or purchase ⟨the *right* to life, liberty, and the pursuit of happiness⟩ ⟨the *right* to freedom of speech⟩ ⟨the *right* to property⟩ ⟨the *right* to command⟩ ⟨the *right* to respect⟩ PREROGATIVE is a right by reason of one's sex, rank, office, character giving precedence, superiority, or advantage over others ⟨entitled to the full *prerogative* of his office —F.M. Stenton⟩ ⟨it may at times exercise the *prerogative* of art by a deliberate use of vague language or imagery —C.S.Kilby⟩ ⟨endurance and stamina in the last analysis are the *prerogatives* of the male —Gerald Beaumont⟩ PRIVILEGE is a special right granted as a favor or concession or belonging to one as a prerogative ⟨the installment buyer must usually pay extra for the *privilege* of deferring payment for what he has bought —J.A.Leavitt & C.O.Hanson⟩ ⟨a propertied class struggling for its *privileges* which it honestly deems to be its rights —W.A.White⟩ ⟨took over all the chartered rights and *privileges* of the existing power companies —*Amer. Guide Series: Maine*⟩ PERQUISITE signifies something, usu. money or something of value, to which one is entitled, esp. by custom, in addition to one's regular salary or wages ⟨the petty graft and favoritism which are normal *perquisites* of machine rule —Green Peyton⟩ ⟨salary is generally supplemented by a rent-and-rate-free house, fuel, and sometimes other *perquisites* —*Auctioneering, Estate Agency & Land Agency*⟩ ⟨shipwrecks and their jetsam are treated as an age-old *perquisite* of the native —*Times Lit. Supp.*⟩ APPANAGE denotes anything to which one has a claim through custom, tradition, or natural necessity but sometimes extends to signify merely an appurtenance ⟨armaments at one's own discretion must be regarded as no longer an *appanage* of nationhood —W.H.B.Beveridge⟩ ⟨fashion at Court and their acquired prestige as a token of power and dignity made gloves an *appanage* of the ruling classes —Anny Varron⟩ ⟨whose literary work had become a mere *appanage* of his domestic life —Van Wyck Brooks⟩ BIRTHRIGHT is a right to which one is entitled by reason of one's birth or the appurtenances of it, as the fact that one is a man, or a citizen of a particular country, descendant of a given family line ⟨the poetic imagination that was his Elizabethan *birthright* —V.L.Parrington⟩ ⟨free public education was the *birthright* of every child —*Proposals for Public Education*⟩ ⟨a group which regarded creative painting as its special *birthright* —Rosamund Frost⟩ ⟨if the college holds to its *birthright* and remains committed as a matter of purpose to serious concern with the issues of conscience —J.S.Dickey⟩

**— by rights** *adv* : with reason or justice : PROPERLY, RIGHTLY ⟨I should not *by rights* have told you —H.R.Haggard⟩ ⟨which is *by rights* the job of a trained psychologist —J.P.Warburg⟩ **— in one's own right** : by title vested in oneself rather than through the ownership or title of another : by virtue of qualifications or properties belonging to someone or something ⟨a life peeress *in her own right* —*N.Y. Times*⟩ ⟨a man of letters *in his own right* —*Amer. Guide Series: N.H.*⟩ ⟨an excellent novel *in its own right* —B.R.Redman⟩ **— in right of** : through right or title derived from or belonging to ⟨claiming the dukedom *in right of* his wife —J.M.Jephson & L.A.Reeve⟩ **— in the right** : with justice, reason, or fact on one's side : RIGHT, CORRECT ⟨in the disagreement he was *in the right*⟩ **— in the right of** : by title vested in the person specified rather than through the ownership or title of another **— of right** **1** : as an absolute right not depending on discretion or favor ⟨asserting that all land belongs *of right* to the Crown —*Times Lit. Supp.*⟩ ⟨the provision, as *of right*, of an income —J.F.Golay⟩ **2** : legally or morally demandable : properly exactable ⟨bail in misdemeanors is *of right*⟩ **— right now** *adv* : at once : IMMEDIATELY, INSTANTANEOUSLY ⟨came alive *right now* —Ross Santee⟩ **— to rights** *adv* **1** : in order : into a proper condition ⟨put things *to rights*⟩ ⟨set matters *to rights*⟩ ⟨set the rooms *to rights* —Agnes S. Turnbull⟩ **2 a** *chiefly dial* : at once : without delay : DIRECTLY, STRAIGHTWAY ⟨ordered him to be carried *to rights* to the tower —Thomas Tryon⟩ **b** *obs* : COMPLETELY, ALTOGETHER ⟨the hulk . . . sunk *to rights* —Jonathan Swift⟩

**³right** \"\ *adv* [ME *riht, right*, fr. OE *rihte*, fr. *riht*, adj.] **1** : in conformity with the standard of justice and duty : in accordance with righteousness : according to right : in harmony with the moral standard of actions : RIGHTEOUSLY, UPRIGHTLY ⟨live ~⟩ ⟨act ~⟩ **2** : EXACTLY, PRECISELY, JUST, ALTOGETHER ⟨~ where you are⟩ ⟨~ at his fingertips⟩ ⟨~ here and now⟩ ⟨~ outside the door⟩ **3 a** : in a suitable, proper, fitting, or desired manner : in the required or necessary way : DULY, WELL ⟨my boys . . . dress ~ —Jack Kramer⟩ ⟨with strict discipline instructed ~ —Wentworth Dillon⟩ ⟨you counsel ~ —Oliver Goldsmith⟩ ⟨hold your pen ~⟩ **b** : in a fortunate, desirable, or satisfactory way ⟨everything will come out ~⟩ **4 a** : in a straight line or direct course : DIRECTLY, STRAIGHT ⟨I'm going ~ home⟩ ⟨his tea came ~ from China⟩ ⟨I'll come ~ back⟩ **b** *archaic* : in the proper course ⟨directed them that went ~ —Ecclus 49:9 (AV)⟩ **5** : according to fact or truth : ACCURATELY, CORRECTLY, TRULY ⟨tell a story ~⟩ ⟨estimate a distance ~⟩ ⟨guess ~⟩ ⟨she couldn't believe she had heard ~ —Virgie Roger⟩ **6 a** : all the way ⟨first . . . to take his ship ~ round the world —A.L.Rowse⟩ ⟨windows coming ~ down to the floor —Sacheverell Sitwell⟩ ⟨cut it back . . . ~ back —Audrey Barker⟩ ⟨~ through the hot summer⟩ **b** : COMPLETELY ⟨get ~ away from any such historical basis —Christopher Hawkes⟩ ⟨streamlined square-root ~ out of the curriculum —Bice Clemow⟩ ⟨running ~ out of soap —Elizabeth Bowen⟩ ⟨blurted the words ~ out⟩ **7 a** : IMMEDIATELY ⟨~ after his marriage —Janet Flanner⟩ ⟨~ after an early breakfast —W.A. White⟩ **b** : without delay : very soon : almost at once ⟨I'll be ~ with you —Scott Fitzgerald⟩ ⟨go ~ out of the business course here and get jobs —Hannah Lees⟩ **8** : in a great degree : EXTREMELY, VERY ⟨knew ~ well what was happening —W.A.White⟩ ⟨~ graciously he smiled on us —E.C.Stedman⟩ ⟨it's ~ pleasant sitting here —Ellen Glasgow⟩ — see RIGHT HONORABLE, RIGHT REVEREND, RIGHT WORSHIPFUL **9** : on or to the right ⟨he looked neither ~ nor left —Sir Walter Scott⟩ ⟨the local elections showed that the country was moving ~⟩ **10** : on the shooter or the dice to win ⟨consistently bets ~⟩

**⁴right** \"\ *vb* -ED/-ING/-S [ME *rihten, righten*, fr. OE *rihtan;* akin to OHG *rihten* to straighten, make right, rule, regulate, ON *rētta* to straighten, make right, adjust, Goth *garaihtjan* to guide; causative-denominative fr. the root of E ¹*right*] *vt* **1 a** : to do justice to : make reparation to : relieve from wrong : restore rights to : assert or regain the rights of : redress the injuries of ⟨so just is God to ~ the innocent —Shak.⟩ ⟨the injured person would be . . . coming back to ~ himself —Leslie Stephen⟩ **b** : to set right : JUSTIFY, VINDICATE ⟨felt the need to ~ himself at court⟩ **2 a** : to make right (something that has been wrong) : bring into accordance with truth : make correct or exact ⟨~ the stupidities in our immigration laws —*New Republic*⟩ ⟨false habits which must be consciously ~*ed* —J.M. Barzun⟩ **b** : to correctly inform or otherwise set right (as a person) ⟨endeavor to ~ the public mind⟩ **3** : AVENGE ⟨~ all wrongs⟩ **4 a** : to restore to the proper state or condition : put right : ADJUST ⟨~ all matters to our satisfaction⟩ **b** *chiefly dial* : to set in order : clear from a disorderly condition : REPAIR — often used with *up* ⟨air the beds and ~ the room —St. John Honeywood⟩ ⟨the old fence . . . was ~*ed* up to keep creatures out —George Washington⟩ **5 a** : to bring (as a ship or conveyance) back into the proper, normal, or natural position : restore to an upright or vertical position ⟨the room ~*ed* itself —Agnes S. Turnbull⟩ ⟨~ a capsized boat⟩ ⟨in the hope that things will ~ themselves —Bernard De Voto⟩ **b** : to bring (oneself) back to one's balance or footing : recover the balance, equilibrium, or footing of (oneself) ⟨tripped but ~*ed* himself⟩ ~ *vi* : to reassume the proper position : recover the natural position : become upright ⟨the ship slowly ~*ed* again⟩ **— right the helm** : to put the helm in line with the keel

**⁵right** \"\ *n* -s [by alter.] *archaic* : RITE

**right-about** \'‗‗‚‗\ *n* -s [fr. *(to the) right about!*] **1** : the position arrived at by turning directly about by the right or sometimes by the left so as to face in the opposite direction : the quarter directly opposite — usu. used with *to* ⟨the officer is . . . not to face his guard to the *right-about* —*Army Regulations & Ordinances*⟩ ⟨the fox took the opportunity to swing to the *right-about* —E.P.Elmhirst⟩ **2** : RIGHT-ABOUT-FACE

**¹right-about-face** \¦‗‗‚‗¦‗\ *vi* [fr. the imper. phrase *right about face*] **1** : to execute a right-about-face **2** : to turn to the right-about esp. as a military maneuver

**²right-about-face** \"\ *n* : a complete reversal of attitude, point of view, or policy ⟨another change in the party line, pretty nearly a *right-about-face* —Upton Sinclair⟩

**right along** *adv* : without cessation ⟨worked *right along*⟩ ⟨busy *right along* with court work —O.W.Holmes †1935⟩

**¹right and left** *adv* **1** : on or toward the right and the left : toward the right and then the left ⟨dodged *right and left*⟩ **2** : on both or all sides : in both or all directions ⟨troops looting *right and left* —A.N.Dragnich⟩ ⟨social events . . . have been rained out *right and left* —*Springfield (Mass.) Daily News*⟩

**²right and left** *n* : a dance figure in which the men and the women winding in and out in opposite directions clasp right and left hands alternately as they pass one another

**right-and-left** \¦‗‗¦‗\ *adj* **1 a** : of or relating to the right and the left **b** : designed for right and left feet or for right and left hands **2** : of, relating to, or constituting a screw, pipe coupling, coupling, turnbuckle, or sleeve nut formed with right-handed threads at one end and left-handed threads at the other

**right angle** *n* [ME *riht angle*] : the angle bounded by two radii that intercept a quarter of a circle : an angle formed by two lines perpendicular to each other — see ANGLE illustration **— at right angles** *adv* : in a perpendicular direction : in a direction perpendicular to something ⟨the teeth are filed straight across the saw *at right angles* to the blade —*U. S. War Dept. Technical Manual*⟩ ⟨set in a plane *at right angles* to the table —*Machinery & Tools*⟩

**right-angle** \(ˈ)≈¦≈≈\ *vb* [*right angle*] *vt* **:** to bend, direct, or locate at a right angle ⟨white benches were *right-angled* to every doorstep —Anna Cunningham⟩ ~ *vi* **:** to proceed at a right angle ⟨the car . . . *right-angled* sharply north —J.D. Salinger⟩

**right-angle clamp** *n* **:** a clamp whose clamping face and supporting arm make a right angle

**right-angled** *also* **right-angle** \(ˈ)≈¦≈≈\ *adj* **1 :** containing or forming a right angle ⟨*right-angled* triangle⟩ ⟨*right-angle* streets⟩ ⟨*right-angled* change of course —P.H.Taylor⟩ — see TRIANGLE illustration **2 :** characterized by right angles ⟨this most *right-angled* of cities —J.L.Motley⟩

**right-angle gauge** *n* **:** TRY SQUARE

**right-angular** \(ˈ)≈¦≈≈\ *adj* **:** forming a right angle or right angles ⟨*right-angular* bends⟩ ⟨*right-angular* fences⟩

**right ascension** *n* **:** one of the equator coordinates of a heavenly body; *specif* **:** the arc of the celestial equator between the vernal equinox and the point where the hour circle through the given body intersects the equator reckoned eastward commonly in terms of the corresponding interval of sidereal time in hours, minutes, and seconds

**right at** *adv* [ME] *dial* **:** APPROXIMATELY ⟨fetch *right at* three hundred dollars apiece —H.L.Davis⟩

**right away** *adv* **:** without delay or hesitation **:** at once **:** IMMEDIATELY, STRAIGHTWAY ⟨said he couldn't do the job *right away* —H.B.Hough⟩ ⟨sign you on *right away* —H.A.Chippendale⟩

**right azygous vein** *n* **:** the azygous vein on the right side of the vertebral column

**right-bank** \ˈ≈¦≈\ *vb* **:** to bank to the right — used esp. of an airplane or a bird in flight

**right bower** *n* **:** the jack of trumps (as in euchre and five hundred)

**right boy** *n, usu cap R* **:** a member of a secret association formed in Ireland in the late 18th century principally to obtain redress of agrarian grievances

**right-center** \ˈ≈¦≈\ *n, often cap R&C* **:** a political group or an organized party belonging to the Center but closely associated with the Right in policies and practice — compare LEFT-CENTER

**right circular cone** *or* **right cone** *n* **:** CONE 2a

**right cylinder** *or* **right-circular cylinder** *n* **:** a cylinder whose side is perpendicular to its base

**¹right-down** \ˈ≈¦≈\ *adj* [³*right* + *down*] **:** characterized by genuineness or thoroughness **:** COMPLETE, THOROUGH ⟨a real *right-down* New York trotter —T.C.Haliburton⟩ ⟨many *right-down* vices —Richard Free⟩

**²right-down** \"\ *adv* **:** without reserve or limitation **:** POSITIVELY, THOROUGHLY, VERY ⟨a regular *right-down* bad 'un —Charles Dickens⟩

**righted** *past of* RIGHT

**right·en** \ˈrīt³n\ *vt* -ED/-ING/-S [¹*right* + *-en*] **:** to restore to the original or proper condition **:** set right **:** STRAIGHTEN ⟨the agility to ~ himself at once —Robert Rankin⟩ ⟨old confusions which his reason must ~ —H.B.Alexander⟩

**righ·teous** \ˈrīchəs\ *adj* [alter. (influenced by *-eous*) of earlier *rightwise, rightuous*, fr. ME *rightwise, rightwos*, fr. OE *rihtwīs*, fr. *riht*, n., right + *wīs* wise — more at RIGHT, WISE] **1 :** doing that which is right **:** acting rightly or justly **:** conforming to the standard of the divine or the moral law **:** free from guilt or sin **:** JUST, UPRIGHT, VIRTUOUS ⟨the gift of God Almighty makes a man essentially ~ —Walter Lowrie⟩ ⟨he who is ~ in the treatment of his slaves —Benjamin Jowett⟩ **2 a :** according with that which is right **:** characterized by uprightness or justice **:** morally right or justifiable **:** free from wrong **:** EQUITABLE ⟨the ~ authority of God's chosen rulers —V.L.Parrington⟩ ⟨fearless in his ~ cause —John Milton⟩ **b :** arising from an outraged sense of justice, morality, or fair play ⟨~ indignation⟩ ⟨~ wrath⟩ **c :** characterized by or expressing satisfaction based on a belief in the correctness or moral uprightness of something (as an action) ⟨meets the resultant gossip . . . with a ~ indifference to either its unfairness or his share in it —*Harper's Bazaar*⟩ **syn** see MORAL

**righ·teous·ly** *adv* [alter. of earlier *rightwisely*, fr. ME, fr. OE *rihtwīslīce*, fr. *rihtwīs* + *-līce* -ly] **:** in a righteous manner ⟨~ indignant with anything so vague —Havelock Ellis⟩ ⟨acting ~ in separating husband and wife —George Meredith⟩

**righ·teous·ness** *n* -ES [alter. of earlier *rightwiseness*, fr. ME *rightwisenes*, fr. OE *rihtwīsnes*, fr. *rihtwīs* + *-nes* -ness] **1 :** the quality or state of being righteous **:** conformity to the divine or the moral law **:** RECTITUDE, UPRIGHTNESS ⟨walking before thee in holiness and ~ all our days —*Bk. of Com. Prayer*⟩ ⟨belief that ~ lies on the side of . . . property —H.L.Matthews⟩ **2** *obs* **:** a righteous act, deed, or quality **:** righteous conduct ⟨all our ~*es* are as filthy rags —Isa 64 : 6 (AV)⟩ **3 :** the quality or state of being rightful or just ⟨the ~ of one's claim⟩ **4 :** the state of acceptance with God **:** a right relationship to God **:** JUSTIFICATION

**¹righter** *comparative of* RIGHT

**²right·er** \ˈrīd·ə(r), -ītə-\ *n* -S **:** one that sets right **:** one that does justice or redresses wrong ⟨a ~ of wrongs⟩

**rightest** *superlative of* RIGHT

**right-eyed** \ˈ≈¦≈\ *adj* **1 :** having the right eye dominant **2 :** using the right eye rather than the left esp. in sighting

**right face** *n* [fr. the imper. phrase *right, face*] **:** an act of turning 90 degrees to the right from the halted position of attention as a military maneuver — often used as a command; compare ABOUT-FACE, LEFT FACE

**right field** *n* **1 :** the part of the baseball outfield to the right facing from the plate **2 :** the station of the right fielder

**right fielder** *n* [*right field* + *-er*] **:** the player defending right field in baseball or softball — see BASEBALL illustration

**right·ful** \ˈrītfəl\ *adj* [ME *rihtful, rightful*, fr. *riht, right*, n., right + *-ful* — more at RIGHT] **1** *archaic* **:** disposed to do right **:** RIGHTEOUS, UPRIGHT ⟨most ~ judge —Shak.⟩ **2 :** conforming to what is right, just, or moral **:** thoroughly fair **:** EQUITABLE ⟨a ~ cause⟩ **3 :** having a right or just claim according to established laws **:** being or holding by right **:** LEGITIMATE ⟨~ owner⟩ ⟨~ king⟩ ⟨~ heir⟩ **4 :** having an appropriate character or status **:** FITTING, PROPER ⟨proceeded in the ~ order —F.W.Robertson⟩ ⟨grimy colliery villages having no ~ place in a rural landscape —L.D.Stamp⟩ ⟨~ objectives⟩ **5 :** held by right **:** possessed by just claim **:** LEGAL ⟨~ share⟩ ⟨~ inheritance⟩ ⟨~ authority⟩ **syn** see DUE

**right·ful·ly** \-f(ə)lē, -li\ *adv* [ME *rihtfulli, rightfully*, fr. *rihtful, rightful* + *-ly*] **1 :** in accordance with right or justice **:** FAIRLY, JUSTLY ⟨no man can ~ be condemned without reference to some definite law —S.T.Coleridge⟩ **2 :** in a correct or proper manner **:** RIGHTLY ⟨those things which we dread . . . so ~ —*Key Reporter*⟩

**right·ful·ness** \-fəlnəs\ *n* -ES [ME *rihtfulnes, rightfulnes*, fr. *rihtful, rightful* + *-nes* -ness] **1 :** the quality or state of being right **:** the justness or equity of something **:** accordance with right and justice ⟨feeling the ~ of the world —Willard Luce⟩

**right hand** *n* [ME, fr. OE *riht hond, riht hand*] **1 a :** the hand on a person's right side **b :** the hand of greeting, welcome, or friendship **c :** a reliable or indispensable person **:** a useful or efficient helper ⟨indispensable as the *right hand* and instrument of the gods —George Grote⟩ **2 a :** the right side **:** the direction toward the right **b :** a place of honor or precedence ⟨sitteth on the *right hand* of God —*Bk. of Com. Prayer*⟩

**right-hand** \ˈ≈¦≈\ *adj* [*right hand*] **1 :** situated on the right **:** nearer the right hand than the left ⟨*right-hand* room⟩ ⟨*right-hand* side of the road⟩ ⟨the *right-hand* upper vest pocket —Sinclair Lewis⟩ **2 a :** of, using, or performed with the right hand ⟨*right-hand* blow⟩ ⟨*right-hand* dexterity⟩ **b :** designed for or used on the right hand ⟨a *right-hand* glove⟩ **3 :** chiefly relied on **:** almost indispensable — compare RIGHT-HAND MAN 2 **4 :** having, operating in, or delivering power in a right-handed direction ⟨a *right-hand* motor⟩ ⟨*right-hand* engine revolution⟩ **5 a** *of a door* **:** opening to the right away from one **b** *of a hinge* **:** fitting or designed to fit a right-hand or right-hand reverse bevel door **c** *of a lock* (1) **:** fitting or designed to fit on a right-hand or right-hand reverse bevel door or on a left-hand reverse bevel door if both sides of the lock operate (2) **:** throwing or designed to throw right **6 a** *of a turning tool* **:** designed to cut to the right **b** *of a thread chaser* **:** designed to cut a right-hand screw thread **c** *of a milling cutter* **:** designed to rotate counterclockwise **7** *of a rope* **:** RIGHT-LAID **8 a :** of or relating to a division of non-Brahmanical castes in southern India engaging in social and ceremonial rivalry with the left-hand castes **b :** of or relating to a division of Shaktism marked by public Vedic and puranic rites

**right-hand convention** *n* **:** RIGHT-HANDED SCREW CONVENTION

**¹right-handed** \ˈ≈¦≈≈\ *adj* [ME *right handed*, fr. *right hand* + *-ed*] **1 :** having the right hand more apt or usable than the left **:** preferring the right hand ⟨a *right-handed* pitcher⟩ **2 a :** of, belonging to, or designed for the right hand ⟨a *right-handed* glove⟩ ⟨a *right-handed* implement⟩ **b :** done or made with or as if with the right hand ⟨a *right-handed* stroke⟩ ⟨a *right-handed* blow⟩ **3 :** having the same direction or course as the movement of the hands of a watch viewed from in front **:** CLOCKWISE — used of a twist, rotary motion, or spiral curve as viewed from a given direction with respect to the axis of rotation ⟨a *right-handed* propeller⟩ **4 :** dextrally spiral ⟨most univalve shells are *right-handed*⟩ **5** *of a rope* **:** RIGHT-LAID **6 :** RIGHT-HAND ⟨*right-handed* door⟩ **7 a :** having a crystal structure that has a mirror-image relationship to another enantiomorphous structure regarded as left-handed in which the same compound can crystallize ⟨*right-handed* quartz⟩ **b :** having crystal faces that result from and may be used to characterize such a structure **c :** DEXTROROTATORY — **right-handed·ly** *adv* — **right-handed·ness** *n*

**²right-handed** \"\ *adv* **:** with the right hand **:** in a right-handed manner ⟨throws and bats *right-handed*⟩

**right-handed rope** *or* **right-hand rope** *n* **1 :** a right-laid rope in which the strands are formed of yarns with left-handed twist **:** a plain-laid rope — compare LEFT-HANDED ROPE **2 :** any right-laid rope

**right-handed screw** *n* **:** a screw the threads of which (as of a common wood screw) wind spirally in such a direction that the screw advances away from the observer when turned with a right-handed rotation in a fixed nut

**right-handed screw convention** *n* **:** a convention in mathematics: if linear motion is produced perpendicular to a plane by a rotation in the plane in a given direction, the direction of the linear motion will be that of the usual motion along its axis of a right-handed screw with axis perpendicular to the plane and with the given direction of rotation in a resisting medium

**right-hand·er** \ˈ≈¦≈ə(r)\ *n* [*right hand* + *-er*] **1 :** a blow struck with the right hand **2 :** a right-handed person

**right-hand lady** *n* **:** the woman of the couple to a man's right in a square dance set — compare CORNER LADY, OPPOSITE LADY, PARTNER

**right-hand man** *n* **1** *obs* **:** a soldier holding a position of responsibility or command on the right of a troop of horse **2 :** a valuable assistant upon whom one is accustomed to rely

**right hand of fellowship :** a handclasp with the right hand given in some Christian communions in token of the fellowship of the church at occasional ceremonies (as a formal public welcome of new members by the pastor of a congregation or as the installation or ordination of a minister)

**right-hand regular lock** *n* **:** a right-hand lock for a door that opens inward

**right-hand reverse bevel** *adj, of a cupboard or closet door* **:** opening to the right toward one

**right-hand reverse lock** *n* **:** a right-hand lock for a door that opens outward

**right-hand rule** *n* **:** a rule in electricity: if the thumb, the forefinger, and the middle finger of the right hand are bent at right angles to one another with the thumb pointed in the direction of motion of a conductor relative to a magnetic field and the forefinger in the direction of the field, then the middle finger will point in the direction of the induced electromotive force — compare THUMB-AND-FINGER RULE

**right-hand screw thread** *n* **:** a screw thread whose helix moves downward when the screw is inserted vertically from above in a fixed mating thread and turned clockwise

**right-hand·wise** \ˈ≈¦≈,≈\ *adv* **:** CLOCKWISE

**right heart** *n* **:** the right auricle and ventricle **:** the half of the heart by which blood is passed through the pulmonary circulation

**right heir** *n* **1 :** an heir at law by blood **2 :** the particular heir granted or devised an estate tail as distinguished from the heirs in general

**right helicoid** *n* **:** a helicoid with generating line perpendicular to its axis

**right honorable** — used as a courtesy title or an official title for earls, viscounts, and barons, for peers' sons and daughters having courtesy titles, and for various high governmental officials (as members of the Privy Council)

**righting** *pres part of* RIGHT

**righting moment** *n* **:** a moment that tends to restore an airplane or a naval vessel to its previous attitude after any small rotational displacement — called also *restoring moment*

**right·ism** \ˈrīd·,izəm, -ī,ti-\ *n* -S *sometimes cap* [²*right* + *-ism*] **1 :** the principles and views of the Right; *also* **:** the movement embodying these principles **2 :** advocacy of or adherence to the doctrines of the Right

**¹right·ist** \ˈrīd·əst, -ītə-\ *n* -S *often cap* [²*right* + *-ist*] **1 :** a member of a group (as a political party) belonging to the Right **2 :** one that believes in or advocates principles associated with the Right

**²rightist** \"\ *adj, often cap* **1 :** of, relating to, or favoring the Right or a group belonging to the Right **2 :** favoring, characterized by, or based upon the principles of the Right

**right-laid** \ˈ≈¦≈\ *adj, of rope* **:** formed of strands twisted together counterclockwise

**righ·tle** \ˈrīt³l\ *vt* -ED/-ING/-S [¹*right* + *-le*] *dial Eng* **:** to put right **:** set in order **:** MEND

**right·less** \ˈrītləs\ *adj* **:** deprived of rights **:** without rights

**right·less·ness** *n* -ES **:** the quality or state of being rightless ⟨the serf's ~ as regards his lord —Frederick Pollock & F.W. Maitland⟩

**right·ly** *adv* [ME *rihtly, rightly*, fr. OE *rihtlīce*, fr. *rihtlīc* right, proper, fr. *riht* right + *-lic* -ly — more at RIGHT] **1 :** according to justice or equity **:** in conformity with the divine will or moral rectitude **:** in accordance with right conduct **:** FAIRLY, JUSTLY ⟨wondering if he did quite ~ in supporting the Fascists —*Hibbert Jour.*⟩ **2 :** in the right or proper manner **:** APPROPRIATELY, FITLY ⟨~ proud of its ancient buildings —John Durant⟩ ⟨being ~ cast for the role —Warwick Braithwaite⟩ ⟨the courts are ~ reluctant to thrust themselves into the administrative process —H.S.Commager⟩ **3 :** according to truth or fact **:** ACCURATELY, CORRECTLY, EXACTLY ⟨could ~ identify her if we . . . meet —Hartley Howard⟩ ⟨advised ~ or wrongly by his colleagues —Ed Nellor⟩

**right lymphatic duct** *n* **:** a short vessel discharging into the right subclavian vein, the lymph from the right side of the head, neck, and thorax, the right arm, right lung, right side of the heart, and convex surface of the liver

**right-minded** \ˈ≈¦≈≈\ *adj* **:** having a right or honest mind **:** possessing a mind disposed or inclined toward what is right **:** purposing well ⟨that respect for law which every *right-minded* citizen ought to have —Bertrand Russell⟩

**right-mind·ed·ness** *n* **:** the quality or state of being right-minded ⟨confidence in the *right-mindedness* of his fellow men —J.R.Lowell⟩

**right·most** \ˈrīt,mōst\ *adj* **:** farthest on the right

**right·ness** *n* -ES [ME *rihtnes, rightnes*, fr. OE *rihtnes*, fr. *riht* right + *-nes* -ness] **1 :** the quality or state of being right (as in character or conduct) **:** moral rectitude **:** INTEGRITY **2 :** factual correctness **:** ACCURACY, TRUTH **3 :** the quality or state of being appropriate **:** FITNESS, SUITABILITY

**righto** \ˈrī(,)tō, (ˈ)≈¦≈\ *interj* [¹*right* + *-o*] *chiefly Brit* — used to express cheerful concurrence, assent, or understanding

**right of action 1 :** a right to begin and prosecute an action in the courts (as for the purpose of enforcing a right or redressing a wrong) **2 :** CHOSE IN ACTION 1

**right of approach :** the right of a man-of-war to approach and in time of war to board and inspect a merchant ship at sea in order to ascertain her nationality without interfering with her voyage

**right of assembly :** the principle of popular government often constitutionally guaranteed that it is the right of the people peaceably to assemble for any purpose not expressly prohibited by law — compare UNLAWFUL ASSEMBLY

**right of asylum :** the right of receiving protection at a place (as the residence of a sovereign or an ambassador or a foreign state) recognized by custom or treaty

**right of common :** ²COMMON 4

**right of confrontation :** the right of one accused of a crime to hear the witnesses testify against him and to cross-examine them

**right of drip :** an easement or servitude existing only as acquired by grant or prescription that gives one the right to have the water running or dripping from his house fall on the land of his neighbor

**right of emption** *or* **right of sole emption :** the right formerly exercised by the English Crown of buying commodities at its need or for its use at such price or on such terms of payment as circumstances might warrant

**right of entry 1 a :** the legal right of taking or resuming possession of real estate in a peaceable manner **b :** POWER OF TERMINATION **c :** a legal right to enter upon land in the possession of another for a special purpose (as of an owner to show land to a prospective purchaser or of a landlord to make repairs) without being guilty of a trespass **2 :** the right of an alien to enter a nation, state, or other political jurisdiction for some special purpose (as of a journalist to report or of a student to study)

**right off** *adv* **:** right away ⟨the catalog copy caught our eye *right off* —Harvey Breit⟩ ⟨three things should be said *right off* —R.E.Lauterbach⟩

**right of privacy :** the qualified legal right of a person to have reasonable privacy in not having his private affairs made known or his likeness exhibited to the public having regard to his habits, mode of living, and occupation

**right of redemption :** the legal right to regain ownership of property that one has formerly enjoyed by freeing it from a debt, charge, or lien, (as by paying to the creditor what is due to release the secured property) — compare EQUITY OF REDEMPTION

**right of search 1 :** the right of a belligerent to stop a merchant vessel of a neutral state on the high seas and make such examination and search as may be reasonably necessary to determine whether it has become liable to capture by violation of the laws of war (as by carrying contraband goods) **2 :** a right similar to the wartime right of search that arises in time of peace under various circumstances (as for the purpose of enforcing revenue law or preventing piracy)

**right of support 1 :** the easement or servitude acquired by grant or by prescription by which an owner of a structure on land has a right to rest or support it in whole or in part upon the land or structure of an adjoining owner (as by inserting beams in the adjoining wall on the boundary) **2 :** the common law easement right of an owner of land to have his soil (as distinguished from the structures thereon) both lateral and subjacent remain in its natural condition without being moved or caused to subside without his consent

**right of visit** *or* **right of visit and search** *or* **right of visitation and search :** RIGHT OF SEARCH

**right-of-way** \ˌ≈≈ˈ≈\ *n, pl* **rights-of-way** *or* **right-of-ways 1 :** a legal right of passage over another person's ground — compare EASEMENT, SERVITUDE **2 :** the area or way over which a right-of-way exists: as **a :** a path or thoroughfare which one may lawfully use (as in crossing the property of another) **:** one established by persons exercising the right to pass over the property of another **b :** the strip of land devoted to or over which is built a public road ⟨miles of *right-of-way* at the sides of improved highways —A.W.Wells⟩ **c :** the land occupied by a railroad for its tracks, yards, and buildings but esp. for its main line **d :** the land used by a public utility (as for an electric power transmission line or a natural gas pipeline) **3 :** a precedence in passing accorded to one vehicle (as an automobile, an airplane, a railroad train, or a boat) over another either by custom, by decision of an appropriate officer (as a train dispatcher), by municipal ordinance, or by statute **4 :** the customary or legal right of traffic to take precedence over any other traffic (as from a certain direction) ⟨usu. street or road traffic in the U.S. has the *right-of-way* over all intercepting traffic except that approaching on the right-hand side and over all following traffic⟩ ⟨a sailing vessel ordinarily has the *right-of-way* over a steam or motor ship⟩ **5 :** the right to take precedence over others (as in speaking, acting, or being brought to the attention of a person or group) **:** permission or opportunity to proceed usu. in precedence over others ⟨if the rules committee refuses to give a bill *right-of-way* —Harold Zink⟩ ⟨the generals were given the *right-of-way* where they should have been checked —J.T.Shotwell⟩

**right out** *adv, obs* **:** OUTRIGHT ⟨swears he will . . . be a boy *right out* —Shak.⟩

**right reverend** — used as a courtesy title for various high ecclesiastical officials (as Anglican bishops, some Roman Catholic abbots and abbesses, vicars general, prothonotaries apostolic and domestic prelates, the moderator of the Church of Scotland)

**right rudder** *n* **:** a position of a ship's rudder that will turn the ship to the right — often used as a command

**rights** *pl of* RIGHT, *pres 3d sing of* RIGHT

**right sailing** *n* **:** the movement of a vessel when it sails on one of the four cardinal points so as to alter either its latitude or longitude but not both

**right section** *n* **:** a cross section (as of a cylinder)

**right shoulder arms** *n* [fr. the imper. phrase *right shoulder, arms*] **:** a position in the manual of arms in which the rifle is held in the right hand with the barrel resting against the right shoulder and the muzzle inclined to the rear — often used as a command; compare LEFT SHOULDER ARMS

right shoulder arms

**right side** *n* **1 :** WIRE SIDE **2 :** FELT SIDE

**¹right smart** *adj* [³*right* + *smart*] *chiefly Midland* **:** CONSIDERABLE, LARGE ⟨a *right smart* distance⟩

**²right smart** *n, South & Midland* **:** a large amount, number, or quantity **:** a good deal ⟨suffered a *right smart* with a misery in his side —Elizabeth M. Roberts⟩ ⟨she'll leave him a *right smart* when she passes on —Lonnie Coleman⟩

**³right smart** *adv, South & Midland* **:** CONSIDERABLY, VERY ⟨the hill there . . . is *right smart* steeper than the side we were on —Alder Jernigan⟩

**rights on** *adv* **:** with the rights attached to or accruing to the security mentioned — used esp. of stock sold or bought with the value of rights included in the price

**right sphere** *n* **1 :** a sphere so placed that a meridian is parallel to the horizon or plane of projection **2 :** the celestial sphere as seen from all stations on the equator where all bodies rise and set at right angles to the horizon

**¹right stage** *n* **:** the half of a theatrical stage to the right of an actor facing the audience

**²right stage** *adv (or adj)* [¹*right stage*] **:** toward or on the half of a theatrical stage to the right of an actor facing the audience ⟨exit *right stage*⟩ — compare DOWNSTAGE, LEFT STAGE, UPSTAGE

**right triangle** *n* **:** a triangle having a right angle

**right·ward** \ˈrītwə(r)d\ *also* **right·wards** \-dz\ *adv (or adj)* [¹*right* + *-ward, -wards*] **:** toward or on the right ⟨looked ~ across the cliffs —*Listener*⟩ ⟨signs of . . . a ~ turn in politics —*Newsweek*⟩

**right whale** *n* **:** a large whalebone whale of the family Balaenidae having no dorsal fin, the baleen very long, the head enormous and about one third the total length, the throat unfurrowed, and the small eye situated near the angle of the mouth: as **a :** GREENLAND WHALE **b:** SOUTHERN RIGHT WHALE

**right whale porpoise** *n* **:** a porpoise of the genus *Lissodelphis*

**right wing** *n* **1 :** the division of a group (as a political party) that believes in or advocates rightist principles and practices ⟨the *right wing* of the Republican party⟩ ⟨member of the fascist *right wing*⟩ — compare LEFT WING **2 :** RIGHT 12 ⟨the *right wing* in British politics⟩

**right-wing** \ˈ≈¦≈\ *adj* [*right wing*] **:** of, adhering to, or favoring the Right ⟨in most European countries the Liberals today are a *right-wing* party —A.M.Schlesinger b.1917⟩ ⟨a *right-wing* majority in the legislative elections —Lionel Durand & Calvin Tomkins⟩ ⟨*right-wing* views⟩

**right-wing·er** \'⸗ˌwiŋə(r)\ *n* -s **1 :** a member of a right wing **2 :** RIGHTIST

**right worshipful** — used as a title of honor for various British municipal officials (as mayors, sheriffs, aldermen)

**rig·id** \'rijəd\ *adj* [MF or L; MF *rigide,* fr. L *rigidus,* fr. *rigēre* to be stiff; perh. akin to L *regere* to lead straight, guide, rule — more at RIGHT] **1 a :** very firm rather than pliant in composition or structure **:** lacking or devoid of flexibility **:** inflexible in nature **:** HARD ⟨metals are not perfectly ~ but elastic — Charles Babbage⟩ ⟨a ~ totalitarian system —Harrison Smith⟩ ⟨~ governmental controls⟩ **b :** stiff and unyielding in appearance ⟨his face was ~ with pain⟩ **2 a :** inflexibly fixed or set in opinion **:** scrupulously exact with respect to opinions or observances ⟨~ on points of theology —G.R.Crone⟩ ⟨a ~ Catholic⟩ **b :** strictly observed **:** characterized by scrupulous exactness in observance ⟨~ principles of honesty⟩ ⟨~ adherence to rules⟩ ⟨condemns the ~ observance of artistic conventions —Laurence Binyon⟩ **3 :** rigorous or harsh in character **:** inflexible rather than lax or indulgent **:** SEVERE ⟨~ inquiry⟩ ⟨a ~ schoolmaster⟩ ⟨~ treatment⟩ **4 :** precise and accurate in procedure **:** exact in method **:** characterized by an undeviating adherence to strict accuracy ⟨~ control of chemical composition and processing methods —*Steel*⟩ **5 a :** having the gas containers enclosed within compartments of a fixed fabric-covered framework or hull that carries cabins, gondolas, and motors ⟨a ~ airship⟩ **b :** having the outer shape maintained by a fixed framework **6 :** of, relating to, or constituting a branch of dynamics in which the bodies whose motions are considered are treated as being absolutely invariable in shape and size under the application of force

**syn** RIGOROUS, STRICT, STRINGENT: RIGID may suggest stiff, uncompromising or unbending inflexibility ⟨a *rigid* system, faithfully administered, would be better than a slatternly compromise —A.C.Benson⟩ ⟨The Mosaic conception of morality as a code of *rigid* and inflexible rules, arbitrarily ordained, and to be blindly obeyed —Havelock Ellis⟩ RIGOROUS suggests a harsh, severe, inflexible exaction or imposition unabated or unmitigated and entailing hardship and difficulty ⟨the king, therefore, although far from clement, was not extremely *rigorous.* He refused the object of the appeal, but he did not put the envoys to death —J.L.Motley⟩ ⟨to stay in the harsh, cruel, cold climate and endure the cramped and *rigorous* life of the struggling back-country settlement —B.K.Sandwell⟩ ⟨a time-table almost as *rigorous* as that of the locomotive engineer —Lewis Mumford⟩ STRICT implies tight conformity ruling out deviation, looseness, laxity, latitude, or mitigation ⟨*strict* enforcement of the speed laws⟩ ⟨ritual is not easy compliance with usage; it is *strict* compliance with detailed and punctilious rule —W.G.Sumner⟩ STRINGENT suggests severe, tight restriction, constriction, or limitation that checks, curbs, circumscribes, or coerces ⟨he bound me in the most *stringent* terms to say no further word to himself, his methods, or his successes —A. Conan Doyle⟩ ⟨the law was so *stringent* that magazines containing patent medicine advertising could not be shipped into the Philippines unless the formulae were published —V.G.Heiser⟩ ⟨the legal terms of his bondage became more *stringent,* the possibility of emancipation narrower, and the regulation of the emancipated more restrictive —Oscar Handlin⟩ **syn** see in addition STIFF

**rigid conduit** *n* **:** firm thick-wall metallic conduit for electric wiring — compare THIN-WALL CONDUIT

**rigid constitution** *n* **:** a constitution that is difficult or slow to change usu. because of a prescribed process of amendment that is detailed and lengthy in execution

**ri·gid·i·fi·ca·tion** \rəˌjidəfə'kāshən\ *n* -s **:** the action of rigidifying or the state of being rigidified ⟨an increasing ~ of policy —G.D.H.Cole⟩

**ri·gid·i·fy** \rə'⸗⸗ˌfī\ *vb* -ED/-ING/-ES [*rigid* + *-ify*] *vt* **:** to make rigid ⟨this historical conception has been *rigidified* by the Stalinists —J.T.Farrell⟩ ~ *vi* **:** to become rigid ⟨relations that ~ into fixed patterns⟩

**ri·gid·i·ty** \rə'jidədē, -ədē, -i\ *n* -ES [L *rigiditas,* fr. *rigidus* rigid + *-itas* -ity — more at RIGID] **1 :** the quality or state of being rigid: as **a :** the quality or state of resisting change of form **:** want of pliability **:** HARDNESS ⟨the ~ of armor —V.H.S. Mercier⟩ ⟨that perfect state of flux between ~ and liquefaction —C.J.Phillips⟩ ⟨the distinctions . . . had lost much of their ~ —Douglas Bush⟩ ⟨wage ~⟩ ⟨emotional ~⟩ **b :** stiffness of appearance, manner, opinion, or conduct ⟨there had come into his face a ~ —John Galsworthy⟩ **c :** abnormal stiffness of muscle (as over a site of inflammation or from systemic disease) ⟨~ of abdominal wall in peritonitis⟩ ⟨nuchal ~⟩ **d :** the quality or state of being strict or severe **:** HARSHNESS, INFLEXIBILITY **e :** the quality or state of being fixed in position — used esp. of a movable object **2 :** an instance of being rigid **:** someone or something that is rigid (as in form or conduct) ⟨the *rigidities* of small-town life —*Times Lit. Supp.*⟩ ⟨create *rigidities* in the economic system —H.G.Johnson⟩ ⟨new *rigidities* of thought —C.J.Rolo⟩ **3 :** the amount of resistance of a body to change of form **4** *or* **rigidity modulus :** SHEAR MODULUS

**rig·id·ly** *adv* **:** in a rigid manner **:** with rigidity **:** STIFFLY, SEVERELY, STRICTLY ⟨a ~ suspended, electrically operated car —*Amer. Guide Series: Minn.*⟩ ⟨a ~ stratified society —Ralph Linton⟩ ⟨restricting ~ the exchange of information —Raymond Daniell⟩

**rig·id·ness** *n* -ES **:** the quality or state of being rigid **:** RIGIDITY

**rig irons** *n pl* [⁴*rig*] **:** the hardware with nails excluded necessary to complete an oil-well drilling rig

**riglet** *var of* REGLET

**rig·ling** \'riglən, -liŋ\ *n* -s [²*rig* + *-ling*] *chiefly Scot* **:** RIDGELING

**rig·ma·ree** \'rigməˌrē\ *n* -s [NL *Reg. Maria,* abbr. for *Regina Maria* Queen Mary that appeared on coins struck during the reign of Mary Stuart †1587 Queen of Scots] **1** *chiefly Scot* **:** a small coin **2** *chiefly Scot* **:** TRIFLE

¹**rig·ma·role** *or* **rig·a·ma·role** \'rig(ə)məˌrōl *sometimes* -ˌrō\ *n* -s [alter. of *ragman roll*] **1 :** a succession of confused, meaningless, or foolish statements **:** prolix and rambling or incoherent talk ⟨a snarling violent ~ . . . kept on coming from him —Claud Cockburn⟩ ⟨never heard such a ~ —George Meredith⟩ **2 :** a complex and ritualistic procedure that is characterized more by form than genuine meaning ⟨the odd procedures and mysterious ~*s* of industrial laboratories —John McCarten⟩ ⟨the whole academic ~ of scales and exercises was unnecessary —Winthrop Sargeant⟩

²**rigmarole** \"\ *also* **rig·ma·rol·ish** \-ōlish\ *adj* **:** consisting of or marked by rigmarole ⟨babbling its indistinct ~ story —Edmund Wilson⟩ ⟨read some long *rigmarolish* old records —Samuel Lover⟩

**rig·o·let** \ˌrigə¦let\ *n* -s [AmerF (Mississippi Valley), dim. of F *rigole* drain, irrigation ditch, canal, fr. OF *regol*] *South* **:** a small stream **:** CREEK, RIVULET

**rig·or** \'rigə(r), *in sense 2* " *or chiefly Brit* 'rīˌgȯ(ə)(r *or* -īgə(r\ *n* -s *see -or in Explan Notes* [ME *rigour,* fr. MF *rigueur,* fr. L *rigor* stiffness, hardness, inflexibility, fr. *rigēre* to be stiff + *-or* — more at RIGID] **1 a** (1) **:** often harsh inflexibility in opinion, temper, or judgment **:** SEVERITY, STERNNESS ⟨the moral ~ . . . which prohibits . . . such innocent pleasures as . . . dancing at the crossroads —H.M.Reynolds⟩ (2) **:** the quality of being unyielding or inflexible **:** exactingness without allowance, deviation, or indulgence **:** STRICTNESS ⟨juries are the device by which the ~ of the law is modified —C.E.Wyzanski⟩ (3) **:** strictness or severity of life **:** AUSTERITY **b :** an act or instance of strictness, severity, harshness, oppression, or cruelty ⟨the humanist must recognize the normality, the practical necessity of the very ~*s* he is trying to soften —H.J.Muller⟩ **2 :** a chill or chilliness, with contraction of muscle and convulsive shuddering or tremor (as in the chill preceding a fever) **3 :** a condition that makes life difficult, challenging, or uncomfortable; *esp* **:** extremity of cold ⟨the ~*s* of a northern winter⟩ ⟨did not intend to let the ~*s* of a strange land frighten her away —Green Peyton⟩ **4 :** strict precision **:** EXACTNESS ⟨built upon systems of postulates by means of theorems developed with logical ~ —Joshua Whatmough⟩ **5 a** *obs* **:** the quality or state of being rigid **:** RIGIDITY, STIFFNESS **b :** a state of rigidity in organs, tissues, or cells during which they are incapable of responding to stimuli and which is induced by factors arising in the organism (as accumulation of toxic substances) or impinging on the organism from without (as excessive but not immediately lethal temperature) — see RIGOR MORTIS **syn** see DIFFICULTY

**rig·or·ism** \'rigəˌrizəm\ *n* -s [F *rigorisme,* fr. L *rigor* + F *-isme* -ism] **1 :** rigidity in principle or practice: as **a :** austerity of life **b :** strictness in ethical principles — usu. used of ascetic ethics **2 :** a system of moral theology holding that when doubt exists as to whether a law of Roman Catholicism is binding in a particular case the law must always be obeyed

¹**rig·or·ist** \-gərəst\ *n* -s [F *rigoriste,* fr. L *rigor* + F *-iste* -ist] **1 :** one who is strict in adherence to or enforcement of rules, standards, laws, or principles **2 :** one who professes rigorism

²**rigorist** \"\ *or* **rig·or·is·tic** \ˌrigə¦ristik\ *adj* **1 :** rigid in principles or actions **:** STRICT **2 :** of or relating to the doctrine of rigorism

**rig·or mor·tis** \ˌrigər'mȯr|d·əs, |təs, -gə'mȯ(ə)|, *chiefly Brit* ¦rīˌgȯ(ə)'m- *or* ˌrīgə'm-\ *n* [L, stiffness of death] **:** rigidity of muscles after death depending in time of onset and duration upon variable factors in the body and in the environment

**rig·or·ous** \'rig(ə)rəs\ *adj* [ME, fr. ML *rigorosus,* fr. L *rigor* + *-osus* -ous] **1 a :** manifesting, exercising, or favoring rigor **:** allowing no abatement or mitigation **:** inflexibly strict **:** INEXORABLE ⟨liquor smuggling . . . has been another problem . . . to vex governments seeking to maintain a ~ policy of liquor control —D.W.McConnell⟩ **b :** extremely or excessively strict **:** HARSH, STERN ⟨a ~ academy where the girls wore uniforms, were forbidden to correspond with male contemporaries . . . and were not given diplomas until they passed college entrance examinations —Robert Rice⟩ ⟨juries are now ~, now indulgent —F.A.Ogg & Harold Zink⟩ **2 :** marked by extremes of temperature or climate, barrenness of comforts or necessities, or other strenuous challenging obstacles ⟨the life was ~, conditions primitive —*Amer. Guide Series: Texas*⟩ ⟨a combination of high altitudes, ~ climate, poor drainage and thin soils giving rise to poor land —G.P.Wibberley⟩ **3 :** scrupulously accurate **:** EXACT, PRECISE ⟨the reader, missing . . . poets whom he expected to find, may complain that my criterion of significance is too ~ —F.R.Leavis⟩ **syn** see RIGID

**rig·or·ous·ly** *adv* [ME, fr. *rigorous* + *-ly*] **:** in a rigorous manner **:** with rigor

**rig·or·ous·ness** *n* -ES **:** the quality or state of being rigorous

**rig-out** \'⸗ˌ⸗\ *n* -s [fr. *rig out,* v.] *Brit* **:** a suit of clothes **:** OUTFIT

**rigs** *pl of* RIG, *pres 3d sing of* RIG

**rigs·by** \'rigzbi\ *n* -ES [⁶*rig* + *-sby* (as in the name *Crosby*)] *dial Eng* **:** a rough or loose woman

**rigs·da·ler** \'rigzˌdälə(r)\ *n* -s [Dan, fr. *rig* kingdom, realm (fr. ON *rīki*) + *daler* — more at RICH] **:** an old Danish dollar coin similar to the German reichstaler

**rig up** *vt* **:** to assemble or improvise (as equipment)

**rijder** *var of* RYDER

**rijks·daal·der** \'rīksˌdäl(d)ə(r)\ *n* -s [D, alter. of *rijksdaler,* fr. *rijk* kingdom, realm (fr. MD *rike, rijc*) + *daler* taler; akin to OHG *rīhhi* kingdom, realm — more at RICH, DOLLAR] **1 :** an old Dutch dollar similar to the German reichstaler **2 :** the modern Dutch 2½ guilder piece

**rijst·ta·fel** \'rīˌstäfəl\ *n* -s [D, fr. *rijst* rice (fr. MD *rijs,* fr. MF *ris*) + *tafel* table, fr. MD *tavele, tafele,* fr. (assumed) VL *tavola,* fr. L *tabula* tablet — more at RICE, TABLE] **:** an Indonesian midday meal consisting chiefly of rice to which are added small portions of a wide variety of meats and vegetables, fish, chicken, fruit, eggs, curries, pickles, and condiments

**ri·ker mount** \ˌrīkə(r)-\ *n, usu cap R* [after Albert Joyce *Riker* b1894 Am. botanist] **:** a flat pasteboard container having a glass cover, containing cotton wool, and used for mounting a specimen (as a plant or insect)

**rik·i·sha** *or* **rik·sha** *or* **rik·shaw** \'rik(ˌ)shȯ\ *n* -s [short for *jinrikisha, jinriksha, jinrikshaw*] **:** JINRIKISHA

**riks·da·ler** \'riksˌdälə(r)\ *n* -s [Sw, fr. *rike* kingdom, realm (fr. ON *rīki*) + *daler* — more at RICH] **:** an old Swedish dollar serving as the basic monetary unit of Sweden from the 16th century to 1878

**riks·mål** *or* **riks·maal** \'rikˌsmȯl\ *n* -s *often cap* [Norw *riksmål* (formerly spelled *riksmaal*), fr. *rik* kingdom, realm + *māl* speech, fr. ON *māl* — more at MAIL] **:** a literary form of Norwegian developed by the gradual reform of written Danish in conformity to Norwegian usage — compare LANDSMÅL

**ril·a·wa** \'riləˌwä\ *n* -s [Sinhalese *rilavā*] **:** TOQUE MACAQUE

**rile** \'rīl, *esp before pause or consonant* -īəl\ *vt* -ED/-ING/-S [alter. of ¹*roil*] **1 :** ¹ROIL 1 ⟨a shower would quickly ~ many streams with the runoff from dirt roads —Christopher Rand⟩ **2 :** to make angry **:** arouse resentment in ⟨in our complex world of overorganization, we cannot get at the people who ~ us —T.V.Smith⟩ **syn** see IRRITATE

**ril·ey** *also* **rily** \'rīlē\ *adj* **1 :** TURBID, ROILED **2 :** ANGRY, IRRITATED

¹**rill** \'ril\ *n* -s [D *ril* or LG *rille* furrow, channel made by a small stream, rill; akin to Fris *ril* narrow passage, narrow path, OE *rīth, rithe* brook, stream, OS *rīth* gushing brook, MLG *rīde* brook, and prob. to OE *rīsan* to rise — more at RISE] **1 a :** a very small brook **:** RIVULET, STREAMLET **b :** a small depression or channel eroded by a rill **2 :** a transient runnel in which the water of a wave returns to the sea or a lake after breaking on a beach

²**rill** \"\ *vi* -ED/-ING/-S **:** to run in a small stream **:** flow like a rill

³**rill** \"\ *adj* **:** GROOVE

⁴**rill** \'ril\ *or* **rille** \", 'rilə\ *n* -s [G *rille,* lit., furrow, channel made by a small stream, fr. LG] **:** one of several long, narrow telescopic valleys on the surface of the moon

**rill·et** \'rilət\ *n* -s [¹*rill* + *-et*] **:** a little rill

**ril·lett** *or* **ril·lette** \rə'let\ *n* -s [F *rillette,* dim. of *rille* piece of pork, fr. MF, dial. var. of *reille* board, plank, lath, fr. L *regula* rule, straightedge — more at RULE] **:** highly seasoned potted pork

**rillstone** \'⸗ˌ⸗\ *n* [¹*rill* + *stone;* intended as trans. of G *rillenstein,* fr. *rille* furrow + *stein* stone] **:** VENTIFACT

**rill stope** *n* **:** an overhand stope in which the back is carried up like a series of inverted steps

¹**rim** \'rim\ *n* -s [ME *rime, rim,* fr. OE *rima;* akin to OFris *rim* edge, ON *rimi* strip of land, rim fence rail, Goth *rimis* quietness, OIr *forim-* to set, put, Gk *ērema* gently, softly, slowly, Lith *remti* to support, Skt *ramate* he stands still, rests; basic meaning: to rest, support] **1 a :** the outer often curved or circular edge or border of something **:** BRIM, LIP, MARGIN ⟨~ of a coin⟩ ⟨~ of a tabletop⟩ ⟨~ of a bowl⟩ ⟨~ of a cup⟩ ⟨~ of an ocean⟩ ⟨hayricks on the ~ of a field —Gladys B. Stern⟩ ⟨each sheet written to the ~ in Swift's crabbed little hand —Virginia Woolf⟩ ⟨a glow along the ~ of the hills —Lord Dunsany⟩ **b :** BRINK ⟨close to the ~ of world war —M.W.Straight⟩; *specif* **:** RIMROCK 2 ⟨~ of a plateau⟩ ⟨north ~ of the canyon⟩ **2 a :** the outer circular part of a wheel joined to the hub usu. by spokes **b :** a removable outer metal band on an automobile wheel to which the tire is attached **3 a :** a raised or projecting outer edge or border ⟨~ of a plate⟩ ⟨inside ~ of a turntable⟩ **b :** something applied as a border ⟨licking the ~ of milk from her upper lip —Nicholas Monsarrat⟩ **4 :** FRAME 3m(1) — compare HORN-RIMMED **5 :** the outer edge of a usu. horseshoe-shaped copydesk where the copyreaders as distinguished from the copy editor sit ⟨from the ~ to the slot to the city editor to the reporter —Bruce Westley⟩ ⟨because he couldn't write a headline to fit the allotted space, he persuaded a fellow ~ man to do it for him —*Newsweek*⟩ —compare SLOT **syn** see BORDER

rim 2b

²**rim** \"\ *vb* **rimmed; rimmed; rimming; rims** *vt* **1 :** to furnish with a rim **:** serve as a rim for **:** BORDER, ENCLOSE ⟨*rimmed* the outline of another letter in gold —Gordon Webber⟩ ⟨a balcony *rimming* the second floor —Morris Gilbert⟩ ⟨high mountains which *rimmed* the region —R.A. Billington⟩ ⟨nails *rimmed* black with grease —Kay Boyle⟩ **2** *of a ball* **:** to run around the rim of ⟨a putt that *rimmed* the cup⟩ ~ *vi* **:** to form or show a rim, edge, or border ⟨opened the door. The yellow light from inside *rimmed* about her —R.J.Hogan⟩ ⟨till *rimmed* into the east the risen sun —Walter de la Mare⟩ ⟨the biotite . . . does not ~ or interfinger with hornblende —*Economic Geology*⟩

³**rim** \"\ *n* -s [ME *reme, rime, rim* membrane, fr. OE *rēama, rēoma* membrane, ligament; akin to OS & OHG *riomo* strap, MD *rieme,* MLG *rēme*] *archaic* **:** PERITONEUM

**ri·ma** \'rīmə\ *n, pl* **ri·mae** \-īˌmē\ [NL, fr. L, slit, fissure, crack — more at ROW] **1 :** a long narrow aperture **:** CLEFT, FISSURE **2** *also* **rima glot·ti·dis** \-'glädədəs\ [*rima glottidis,* NL, lit., rima of the glottis] **:** the passage in the glottis between the true vocal cords — **ri·mal** \-īməl\ *adj*

**ri·mas** \'rēməs\ *n* -ES [Tag] *Philippines* **:** BREADFRUIT

**ri·mate** \'rīˌmāt\ *adj* [L *rima* + E *-ate*] **:** having fissures **:** FISSURED

**ri·ma·tion** \rī'māshən\ *n* -s [NL *rima* + E *-ation*] **:** RIMA

**rim·base** \'rimˌbās\ *n* **1 :** the mass of metal connecting a trunnion with the trunnion band or the body of a cannon — see CANNON illustration **2 :** the shoulder of the stock of a firearm on which the breech of the barrel rests

**rim blight** *n* **:** a disease of tea caused by a fungus of the genus *Cladosporium* and characterized by yellowing of the leaf margins followed by browning

**rim-bound** \'⸗¦⸗\ *adj* **:** having the tips and margins of the leaves curved downward (as in tobacco suffering from potash hunger)

**rim clutch** *n* **:** a friction clutch having for one of the friction contacting members a cylindrical rim that is gripped (as by lever action, fitted ring segments, or shoes) on both cylindrical surfaces

**rim-drive** \'⸗ˌ⸗\ *n* **:** a method of driving a disc recorder or phonograph turntable by frictional contact between a motor shaft and the rim of the turntable and often by interposing a rubber-covered wheel between shaft and turntable

¹**rime** \'rīm\ *n* -s [ME *rim,* fr. OE *hrīm;* akin to OS *hrīpo* frost, OHG *hrīffo, riffo,* MHG *rīm,* ON *hrīm, hrīmi* frost, Latvian *kreims* cream, Lith *krēna*] **1** *or* **rime frost :** FROST 1c(1) **2 :** an accumulation of granular ice tufts on the windward sides of exposed objects slightly resembling hoarfrost but formed only from undercooled fog or cloud and always built out directly against the wind **3 :** CRUST, INCRUSTATION ⟨~ of snow —D.C.Peattie⟩ ⟨dust settled down . . . making a gray ~ on eyebrows, nose —Thomas Wood †1950⟩ ⟨a ~ of alkali on flatland⟩

²**rime** \"\ *vt* -ED/-ING/-S **:** to cover with or as if with rime ⟨hedgerows were *rimed* and stiff with frost —William Faulkner⟩ ⟨age had *rimed* his beard —Kay Rogers⟩ ⟨wagons *rimed* with clay —Hamilton Basso⟩

³**rime** *var of* RHYME

⁴**rime** \'rīm\ *n* -s [L *rima* — more at ROW] **:** CHINK, CRACK, FISSURE

⁵**rime** \"\ *dial chiefly Eng var of* REAM

**rime couée** \ˌremkü'ā\ *n, pl* **rimes couées** \"\ [F] **:** TAIL RHYME

**rime·less** \'rīmləs\ *adj* **:** being without rime **:** FROSTLESS

**rime riche** \rēm'rēsh\ *n, pl* **rimes riches** \"\ [F, lit., rich rhyme] **:** a rhyme produced by agreement in sound not only of the last accented vowel and any succeeding sounds but also of the consonant preceding this rhyming vowel ⟨in English, *church spire* and *aspire* would be *rimes riches*⟩ — called also *identical rhyme;* distinguished from *rime suffisante*

**rime suf·fi·sante** \ˌrēmˌsüfē'zäⁿt\ *n, pl* **rimes suffisantes** \"\ [F, lit., sufficient rhyme] **:** end rhyme produced by agreement in sound of an accented final vowel and following final consonant or consonants if any ⟨in English, *dip* and *ship, flee* and *see* are *rimes suffisantes*⟩ — distinguished from *rime riche*

¹**rimfire** \'⸗ˌ⸗\ *adj* [¹*rim* + *fire* (v.)] **1** *of a cartridge* **:** having the percussion compound in a rim surrounding the base — distinguished from *center-fire* **2 :** designed for or adapted to the use of rimfire cartridges ⟨~ rifle⟩

²**rimfire** \"\ *n* [¹*rim* + *fire* (n.)] **:** the burning of the leaf margins (as in tobacco) caused by potash hunger

**rim·land** \'rimˌland, -ˌlaa(ə)nd, -ˌlənd\ *n* **:** a region on the periphery of the heartland

**rim·less** \'rimləs\ *adj* **1 :** lacking a rim or frame ⟨wearing ~ glasses⟩ **2** *of a cartridge case* **:** having a rim diameter equal to or less than that of the body of the case

**rim lighting** *n* **:** BACKLIGHTING

**rim lock** *or* **rim latch** *n* **:** a lock or latch made to be fastened to the face of a door — compare MORTISE LOCK

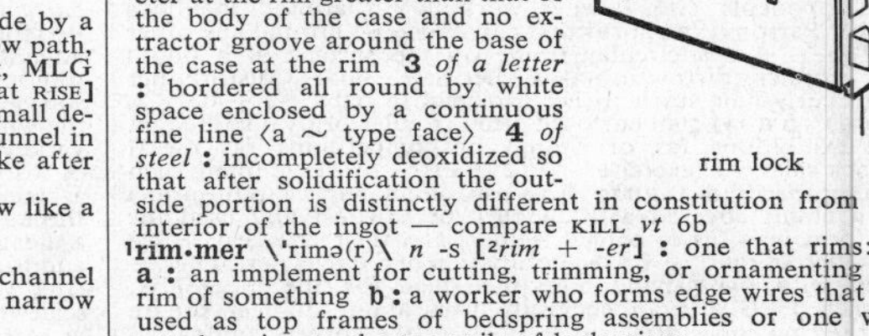

rim lock

**rimmed** \¦rimd\ *adj* [¹*rim* + *-ed*] **1 :** having a rim — usu. used in combination ⟨gold-*rimmed*⟩ ⟨narrow-*rimmed*⟩ ⟨red-*rimmed*⟩ **2** *of a cartridge case* **:** having a diameter at the rim greater than that of the body of the case and no extractor groove around the base of the case at the rim **3** *of a letter* **:** bordered all round by white space enclosed by a continuous fine line ⟨a ~ type face⟩ **4** *of steel* **:** incompletely deoxidized so that after solidification the outside portion is distinctly different in constitution from the interior of the ingot — compare KILL *vt* 6b

¹**rim·mer** \'rimə(r)\ *n* -s [²*rim* + *-er*] **:** one that rims: as **a :** an implement for cutting, trimming, or ornamenting the rim of something **b :** a worker who forms edge wires that are used as top frames of bedspring assemblies or one who attaches rims to the top edges of bedsprings

²**rimmer** \"\ *n* -s [⁵*rim* + *-er*] **:** REAMER

**rimming** *pres part of* RIM

**rim of sa·nio** \-'sänēˌō\ *usu cap S* [after Carl *Sanio,* 19th cent. botanist] **:** CRASSULA

**ri·mose** \(')rī¦mōs\ *or* **ri·mous** \'rīməs\ *adj* [L *rimosus,* fr. *rima* slit, crack, fissure + *-osus,* -ose, -ous — more at ROW] **:** having numerous clefts, cracks, or fissures ⟨the ~ bark of a tree⟩ — **ri·mose·ly** *adv* — **ri·mos·i·ty** \rī'mäsədē\ *n* -ES

¹**rim·ple** \'rimpəl\ *n* -s [ME, fr. OE *hrympel* — more at RUMPLE] **:** FOLD, WRINKLE, RUMPLE, RIPPLE

²**rimple** \"\ *vb* -ED/-ING/-S **:** RUMPLE, WRINKLE, RIPPLE

**rimp·tion** \'rim(p)shən\ *n* -s [origin unknown] *South & Midland* **:** ABUNDANCE, LOT — usu. used in pl. ⟨~*s* of food⟩

¹**rimrock** \'⸗ˌ⸗\ *n* [¹*rim* + *rock*] **1 :** a top stratum or overlying strata of resistant rock of a plateau outcropping to form a more or less vertical face (as in the wall of a canyon) ⟨mesas topped with ~ —Agnes M. Cleaveland⟩ — compare ¹CAP 2a(3) **2 :** the edge or face of an outcropping of rimrock ⟨stopping the car on the high ~, we looked down —Frank Waters⟩ ⟨a high flat mesa, with ~*s* all around —Will James⟩

²**rimrock** \"\ *vt, West* **:** to destroy (as a flock of sheep) by driving over a cliff

**rims** *pl of* RIM, *pres 3d sing of* RIM

**rim saw** *n* **:** a disk saw having the teeth on a separate ring

**rim·stone** \'rimzˌtōn, -mˌst-\ *n* **:** a calcareous deposit formed as a ring around an overflowing basin (as of a mineral hot spring)

**ri·mu** \'rē(ˌ)mü\ *n* -s [Maori] **1 :** a tall New Zealand timber tree (*Dacrydium cupressinum*) with a small head, drooping terminal branches covered with tiny keeled linear leaves, and an ovoid terminal nut with a fleshy red receptacle **2 :** the wood of the rimu tree used for furniture and general construction — called also *imou pine, red pine*

**rim·u·la** \'rimyələ\ *n, pl* **rimu·lae** \-yəˌlē\ [NL, dim. of *rima*] **:** a small fissure (as in the brain or spinal cord)

**rim·u·lose** \-yəˌlōs\ *adj* [NL *rimula* + E *-ose*] **:** having small chinks or fissures

**ri·mur** \'rēmə(r)\ *n pl* [ON *rīmur,* pl. of *rīma,* fr. *rīm* rhyme, fr. MLG, fr. OF *rime* — more at RHYME] **:** a complex form of versified saga or treatment of episodes from the sagas popular in Iceland from the 15th century

**rimy** \'rīmē\ *adj* -ER/-EST [fr. (assumed) ME, fr. OE *hrīmig,* fr. *hrīm* frost + *-ig* -y — more at RIME] **:** covered with rime **:** FROSTY

¹**rin** \'rin\ *chiefly Scot var of* RUN

²**rin** \"\ *n, pl* **rin** [Jap] **1 :** a Japanese monetary unit equal to ¹⁄₁₀ sen **2 :** a coin representing one rin

**rin·ceau** \raⁿ'sō\ *n, pl* **rin·ceaux** \-ō(z)\ [F, fr. MF *rainsel* branch, fr. (assumed) VL *ramuscellus,* alter. of LL *ramusculus* small branch, dim. of *ramus* branch — more at RAMIFY] **:** an ornamental motif consisting essentially of a sinuous and branching scroll elaborated with leaves and other natural forms (as derived from the acanthus)

**rin·con** \riŋ'kōn\ *n, pl* **rincons** \-ōnz\ *or* **rinco·nes** \-ō,nās\ [Sp *rincón*, lit., corner, nook, alter. of *recón*, *rencón*, fr. Ar dial. (Spain) *rukun* (Ar *rukn*)] **1** *Southwest* **:** a small secluded valley **2** *Southwest* **:** an alcove or angular recess in a cliff **3** *Southwest* **:** a bend in a river

**¹rind** \'rīnd, *dial or before consonant or pause* 'rīn\ *n* -s [ME *rind, rinde*, fr. OE; akin to MD *rinde, rende & runde* bark, OS *rinda*, OHG *rinda, rinta* bark, G dial (Hesse) *runde* scab, Norw *rind* strip, OE *rendan* to rend — more at REND] **1 :** BARK, CORTEX ⟨~ of a tree⟩ **2 a :** PEEL ⟨watermelon ~⟩ ⟨grated lemon ~⟩ **b :** a piece of peel **:** PEELING ⟨grapefruit ~*s*⟩ **3 a :** an outer layer or covering **:** CRUST, SKIN ⟨~ of cheese⟩ ⟨~ of ham⟩ ⟨atmosphere, the earth's invisible ~ —Waldemar Kaempffert⟩ ⟨dreams that lie hidden beneath the ~ of the commonplace —H.A.Overstreet⟩ **b :** a piece of skin or other outer layer ⟨bacon ~*s*⟩ **4 :** a strip of cloth under the leather grip of a golf club

**²rind** \"\ *vt* -ED/-ING/-s **:** to remove the rind of **:** BARK

**³rind** *or* **rynd** \'rīnd, 'rind\ *n* -s [ME *rynd;* akin to MD *rijn* millrind, MLG *rin, ryn*] **:** MILLRIND 1

**⁴rind** \"\ *vt* -ED/-ING/-s [alter. of earlier *rend*, fr. ME *renden*, fr. MF *rendre* to render — more at RENDER] *dial Brit* **:** RENDER ⟨~ tallow⟩ ⟨~ butter⟩

**⁵rind** \'rīn(d)\ *n* -s [alter. of ¹*rime*] *dial chiefly Brit* **:** FROST 1c(1)

**rind disease** *n* **:** a disease of sugarcane formerly thought to be caused by a fungus (*Melanconium sacchari*) that is now known to be an accompaniment of other diseases (as red rot) and characterized by dark bluish shrunken wrinkled lesions on the stems

**rind·ed** \ˌrīndəd\ *adj* [¹*rind* + *-ed*] **:** having a rind — usu. used in combination ⟨smooth-*rinded*⟩ ⟨green-*rinded*⟩

**rin·der·pest** \'rində(r),pest\ *n* [G, fr. *rinder* (pl. of *rind* head of cattle, fr. OHG *hrind, rind*) + *pest*, fr. L *pestis* — more at RUNT] **:** an acute highly infectious febrile disease of cattle and less often of sheep, goats, and wild game animals caused by a filterable virus and producing diphtheritic inflammation of the mucous membranes and esp. of the intestines — called also *cattle plague*

**rind gall** *n* **:** a defect in timber caused by the growth of annual layers of wood over a bruise in the bark

**rind graft** *n* **:** BARK GRAFT

**rin·dle** \'rindᵊl, -nᵊl\ *n* -s [alter. of earlier *rinel* — more at RUNNEL] *dial chiefly Eng* **:** RUNNEL

**rind·less** \'rīn(d)ləs\ *adj* **:** lacking a rind ⟨~ cheese⟩

**rindy** \-ndē\ *adj* [¹*rind* + *-y*] **:** having a rind or skin

**rin·for·zan·do** \ˌrēnfȯrˈtsän(ˌ)dō\ *adj (or adv)* [It, reinforcing, strengthening, verbal of *rinforzare* to reinforce, strengthen, fr. *ri-* re- (fr. L *re-*) + *inforzare* to enforce, strengthen, fr. OIt, fr. MF *enforcier* — more at ENFORCE] **:** played with a sudden increase of force — used as a direction in music usu. for special emphasis of a note, chord, or short phrase; abbr. *rf* or *rfz;* compare SFORZANDO

**rin·for·za·to** \-ädˌ(ˌ)ō\ *adj (or adv)* [It, past part. of *rinforzare*] **:** RINFORZANDO

**¹ring** \'riŋ\ *n* -s *often attrib* [ME, fr. OE *hring;* akin to OFris, OS, & OHG *hring* ring, ON *hringr*, Crimean Goth *rinck, ringo* ring, Umbrian *krenkatrum* belt, OSlav *krogŭ* circle, L *curvus* curved — more at CROWN] **1 a :** a circular or curved band (as of metal, wood, fabric, or plastic) used for holding, connecting, hanging, or pulling ⟨curtain ~⟩ ⟨key ~⟩ ⟨towel ~⟩ ⟨the ~ of a drawer pull⟩ ⟨the ~ of an anchor⟩ **b :** one of the small iron circles used in making chain mail **c :** a usu. circular band of metal or other material used for packing or sealing ⟨rubber ~*s* for sealing fruit jars⟩; *specif* **:** PISTON RING **2 a :** a circlet of metal or other material often set with a gem that is worn on the finger as an ornament, token, or amulet or for use as a seal ⟨diamond ~⟩ ⟨fraternal ~⟩ — see ENGAGEMENT RING, SIGNET RING, WEDDING RING; compare ¹BAND 6e **b :** a circlet of metal or other material worn as an ornament on any part of the body (as the arm, ankle, toe) — compare EARRING **3 :** the rim or border of a circular object ⟨the ~ of the horizon⟩ **4 a :** any circular or continuous round line, figure, or object ⟨coffee cup ~*s* on a table⟩ ⟨dog with a ~ of white around his neck —F.B.Gipson⟩ ⟨smoke ~*s*⟩ ⟨~ of scum in a washbasin⟩ **b :** an encircling arrangement (as of persons, things, or material) ⟨a ~ of suburbs⟩ ⟨a ~ of encircling hills —G.H.Reed b.1887⟩ ⟨surrounded by a wide ~ of suspicion —Bradford Smith⟩ **c :** a circular or spiral course ⟨run in ~*s*⟩ — often used figuratively in the pl. with *around* and often with *run* to characterize a performance that easily or greatly surpasses that of a competitor ⟨the mayoral candidate ran ~*s* around his opponent⟩ ⟨was always working ~*s* around the boys —R.P.Parsons⟩ ⟨a chorus that can dance ~*s* around any other —*Time*⟩ **d :** a circular ripple on the surface of a liquid **e :** RINGLET ⟨distracting ~*s* of her hair —Mary Austin⟩ ⟨her light curly hair stuck to her forehead in baby ~*s* —Mary J. Ward⟩ **5 a** (1) **:** an enclosed often circular or oval space esp. for exhibitions (as of riding) or competitions (as races) ⟨stock sales ~⟩ ⟨exercise ~⟩ (2) **:** a structure containing such a ring; *specif* **:** BULLRING **b :** a usu. circular space in the arena of a circus covered with tanbark or sawdust and used for performances (as of animal trainers and their charges) — see THREE-RING CIRCUS **c :** the occupation of a circus performer — used with *the* ⟨abandoning the stage for the ~ —T.W. Duncan⟩ **6 a :** an enclosure usu. about 20 feet square marked by ropes attached to posts at the corners and raised on a platform in which boxers or wrestlers contest; *also* **:** this enclosure together with its supporting platform — see PRIZE RING **b :** PRIZEFIGHTING ⟨fought a few professional bouts only to decide against continuing in the ~ —*Current Biog.*⟩ ⟨end of his ~ career⟩ **7 :** a cut made into or through the bark and around the trunk or a limb of a tree **8 :** one of the ridges increasing in number with age that encircle the horns of cattle **9 :** one of three concentric bands usu. believed to be composed of meteoric fragments revolving around the planet Saturn **10 rings** *pl* **:** the cage at masthead for lookout (as on a whaling vessel) — compare CROW'S NEST **11 a :** ANNULUS 5 **b :** GROWTH RING **12 a :** an enclosure or space devoted to betting at a horse race **b :** those who bet in a ring; *esp* **:** the bookmakers of a ring **13 a :** an archivolt made up of a half ring of voussoirs **b :** a parallel course of half bricks or other small voussoirs forming a rowlock arch **c :** an encircling architectural element (as a corridor or a series of rooms) **14 a :** an exclusive combination of persons for a selfish and often corrupt purpose (as to control the market, distribute offices, or obtain contracts) ⟨not a member of the inner party ~ —*Times Lit. Supp.*⟩ ⟨had the courage to tackle price ~*s* —Seamus Brady⟩ ⟨organized ~*s* stealing cars —*Springfield (Mass.) Union*⟩ ⟨innocent women were frequently framed by a ~ consisting of police officers, stool pigeons, bondsmen and lawyers —Morris Ploscowe⟩ **b :** a temporary group of persons working cooperatively **:** POOL ⟨organization of spray ~*s* where a group of growers uses one spraying outfit —*Experiment Station Record*⟩ **15 a :** a series of buyers and sellers in a produce exchange in which each buyer is the seller in the same amount of the same goods to another buyer so that the entire series of transactions can be settled by ringing out **b :** ¹PIT 1b(9) **16 :** the field of a political contest **:** RACE ⟨threw his hat into the presidential ~⟩ **17 :** a circle drawn around a marginal marking on a proof to indicate that the change ordered is not in correction of a printer's error, that the circled writing is a query to the author, or that a circled arabic numeral or abbreviation is to be spelled out **18 a :** SPINNING RING **b :** RING SPINNER **19 :** food in the shape of a circle: as **a :** cooked food folded in a circle ⟨noodle ~⟩ ⟨~ cake⟩ **b :** a long sausage tied together at the ends ⟨Polish ~⟩ **20 :** WATER RING **21 :** a circle of worked stitches used to form patterns in tatting **22 :** an arrangement of atoms represented in formulas or models in a cyclic manner or as a closed chain and commonly consisting of five or six atoms although smaller and also much larger rings are known ⟨carbocyclic and heterocyclic ~*s*⟩ — called also *cycle;* compare BENZENE RING, NUCLEUS 2j, OPEN CHAIN, STRUCTURAL FORMULA **23** *chiefly Brit* **:** a band attached (as to the leg of a bird) to identify **24 :** a pair of meiotic chromosomes associated end-to-end due to the formation of terminal chiasmata at both ends of the pair **25 :** one of a pair of heavy usu. leather covered metal circles suspended from the ceiling or a crossbar and used for gymnastic exercise **26 :** a round disk of rattan or metal with intertwined thongs used to prevent a ski pole from sinking into the snow **27** *Austral* **:** ²RINGER 4 **28 :** an aggregate in which addition is commutative, the product of two elements is unique, and multiplication is distributive with respect to addition and associative

**²ring** \"\ *vb* -ED/-ING/-s [ME *ringen*, fr. *ring*, n.] *vt* **1 :** to place or form a ring entirely or nearly around **:** station or take position around in a ring or cordon **:** mark by drawing a ring around **:** ENCIRCLE ⟨~*ed* on three sides by mountains —*Amer. Guide Series: N.H.*⟩ ⟨a guard was set that he might not flee — a score of bayonets ~*ed* the tree —Rudyard Kipling⟩ ⟨a name that has ~*ed* the world —*advt*⟩ **2 :** to place a ring on **:** provide with a ring: as **a :** to put a ring in the nose or around the neck in order to subdue, check, or shackle ⟨hogs ~*ed* to prevent rooting⟩ **b** *chiefly Brit* **:** to place a ring around the leg of (a bird or animal) to classify or identify **:** BAND **3 :** to wheel around **:** run or ride around encircling (as to prevent straying or escape) **:** move in a circle ⟨eagles sailing round and round them like sheep dogs ~*ing* a flock —Francis Ratcliffe⟩ ⟨herders ~*ing* cattle⟩ **4 :** GIRDLE 3 **5 :** to throw a ring over (the mark) in a game where rings or other curved objects (as horseshoes) are tossed at a standing or projecting mark **6 :** to exhibit or exercise in a ring **:** introduce into a ring (as at a dog or horse show or a circus) **7 :** to settle (a contract) by ringing out **8 :** to enter (as a horse or dog) in a contest as a ringer **~** *vi* **1 a :** to move in a ring **b :** to rise in the air spirally **2 :** to form or take the shape of a ring **syn** see SURROUND — **ring an anchor :** to haul the anchor up until its ring is at the hawsehole or cathead — usu. used with *up*

**³ring** \"\ *vb* **rang** \'raŋ, -aiŋ\ *also* **rung** \'rəŋ\ **rung; ring·ing; rings** [ME *ringen*, fr. OE *hringan;* akin to MD *ringen* to ring, ON *hringja* to ring, *hrang* noise, din, Toch B *krańko* cock, Lith *krañkti* to croak, Skt *kruñ* curlew, and perh. to OE *hræfn* raven — more at RAVEN] *vi* **1 :** to sound clearly and resonantly ⟨the ~*ing* of many bells⟩ ⟨the doorbell *rang*⟩ ⟨dense porcelaneous ware usually high fired enough to ~ —W.E. Cox⟩ ⟨weird ~*ing* voices of veeries —W.P.Smith⟩ **2 :** to sound loudly and sonorously ⟨cheers *rang* out⟩ ⟨his voice *rang* with indignation⟩ ⟨the trumpet *rang*⟩ ⟨oaths *rang* across the stable yard —Margaret Kennedy⟩ **3 a :** to be filled with a ringing or reverberating sound **:** RESOUND, ECHO ⟨woods *rang* with the sound of the ax⟩ **b :** to have the sensation of being filled with a humming sound ⟨his ears *rang*⟩ **4 :** to cause something to ring (as in giving a summons) ⟨~ for breakfast⟩ **5 :** to engage in bell ringing or making music with bells **6 a :** to become filled with talk or report ⟨newspapers *rang* with the unknown author's story —W.E.Smith⟩ ⟨the world *rang* with his fame⟩ ⟨their letters ~ with sincere praise —*advt*⟩ **b :** to cause much talk **:** have great renown ⟨his deeds *rang* through the country⟩ **c :** to sound repetitiously **:** DIN ⟨their praises *rang* in our ears⟩ ⟨a tune that ~*s* in one's memory⟩ **7 :** to have a particular sound or character expressive of some quality ⟨a spirited story that ~*s* true in all its incidental details —Frances Gaither⟩ ⟨piece of empty heroics, which must ~ false from the screen —Lee Rogow⟩ ⟨a well-meant effort *rang* hollow —S.L.A.Marshall⟩ ⟨his heroine . . . is a little too sensitive to ~ true —James Yaffe⟩ **8** *chiefly Brit* **:** to place a telephone call **:** TELEPHONE — usu. used with *up* or *through* **~** *vt* **1 :** to cause (a metallic body) to sound esp. by striking ⟨the soldier *rang* each dollar against his bayonet to test the purity of the coin —Nora Waln⟩; *specif* **:** to sound (a church bell) with a full swing from a mouth-up position — compare CHIME, CLOCK **2 :** to make (a sound) by or as if by ringing a bell ⟨the shard-borne beetle, with his drowsy hums, hath *rung* night's yawning peal —Shak.⟩ **3 :** to announce or proclaim by or as if by ringing **:** usher in or out by ringing a bell ⟨~ an alarm⟩ ⟨~ in the new year, ~ out the old⟩ **4 :** to repeat often, loudly, or earnestly ⟨~ denunciations⟩ ⟨~ the praises of a compatriot⟩ **5 a :** to summon esp. by bell **b** *chiefly Brit* **:** TELEPHONE — usu. used with *up* **6 :** to cause (a machine or device) to register **:** ring up ⟨~ a cash register⟩ ⟨~ a time clock⟩ ⟨~ a sale⟩ — **ring a bell :** to arouse a response **:** strike a sympathetic chord **:** call out recognition **:** stir a memory ⟨his remarks on federal aid and increased taxes *rang a bell* —J.A.Morris b.1904⟩ ⟨have a sense of the ridiculous which *rings a bell* with us —Henry Baerlein⟩ ⟨if the name *rings no bell* in your mind —Howard Nemerov⟩ — **ring down the curtain 1 a :** to give the signal for lowering the curtain in a theater or auditorium **b :** to lower the curtain in a theater or auditorium **2 :** to conclude a performance or action ⟨this sorry episode *rang down the curtain* on what was planned to be a spectacular adventure⟩ — **ring the bell :** to be convincing or successful ⟨this last advantage *rang the bell* with bankers —*Newsweek*⟩ ⟨good title, a good blurb, army lingo; it *rang the bell* —R.A.Robinson⟩ — **ring the changes** *or* **ring changes :** to run through the whole range of possible variations **:** reiterate in exhaustive variety of expression ⟨*rings the changes* on possible meanings of words —David Daiches⟩ ⟨clever at *ringing the changes* with a black frock and a white one —Frances Towers⟩ — **ring up the curtain 1 a :** to give the signal for raising the curtain in a theater or auditorium **b :** to raise the curtain in a theater or auditorium **2 :** to begin a performance or action

**⁴ring** \"\ *n* -s **1 :** a set of church bells; *esp* **:** one tuned in scale for change ringing **2 :** a clear resonant sound made by or resembling that made by vibrating metals ⟨the ~ of a bell⟩ ⟨the ~ of hammer upon anvil —Elizabeth Goudge⟩ ⟨each ~ of the telephone filled me with dread —Ralph Ellison⟩ ⟨the ~ of laughter⟩ **3 :** resonant tone (as in response to plucking or striking) **:** SONORITY ⟨the ~ of a glass goblet⟩ ⟨the ~ of a porcelain dish⟩ ⟨the ~ of a coin⟩ ⟨a voice of ~ and warmth —Irving Kolodin⟩ **4 :** a loud sound **:** a sound continued, repeated, or reverberated ⟨hear the ~ in your ears of wind from the solitude of mountain heights —Alicita & Warren Hamilton⟩ **5 :** a sound or character (as of speech or writing) expressive of some particular quality ⟨a ~ of ardent sincerity in his voice —G.G.Carter⟩ ⟨strange circumlocutions that . . . still have the ~ of natural speech —Arthur Knight⟩ ⟨such generalizations have the ~ of plausibility —Alexander Gerschenkron⟩ ⟨scheme has a fantastic ~ about it —O.S. Nock⟩ **6 a :** the act or an instance of sounding a bell or similar device **b :** the act or an instance of summoning (as by a bell or buzzer) **c :** a telephone call — often used with *give*

**⁵ring** \"\ *Scot var of* REIGN

**ring-a-lievo** \ˌriŋəˈlē(ˌ)vō\ *or* **ring-a-levio** \-ēvē,ō\ *n* -s [alter. of *ring relievo*] **:** ²RELIEVO

**ring-a-rosy** \ˈriŋəˈrōzē\ *n* -ES **:** RING-AROUND-A-ROSY

**ring-around-a-rosy** *or* **ring-around-the-rosy** \ˈ=ˌ==ˈ==\ *n* -ES **:** a children's singing game in which the players dance around in a circle and at a given signal squat

**rin·gas** \'riŋgəs\ *n* -ES [Malay *rĕngas*] **:** BLACK-VARNISH TREE

**rin·ga·tu** \ˌriŋəˈtü\ *n* -s *cap* [Maori, fr. *ringa* hand + *tu* to stand] **:** a semi-Christian Maori sect in New Zealand that was a milder development from an antichristian cult evolved by the Maoris when fighting against the English

**ring auger** *n* **:** an auger turned by a bar inserted in a ring or eye at the upper end of the shank

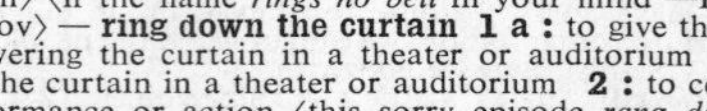

ring auger

**ringbark** \'=ˌ=\ *vt* **:** ²GIRDLE 3

**ring-barked** \'=ˌ=\ *adj* **:** having the periderm in more or less complete concentric layers often with the bark shedding in sheets (as in birch trees) ⟨a herd . . . grazing among the *ringbarked* trees on the slope above —Francis Ratcliffe⟩

**ringbarker** \'=ˌ==\ *n* **:** a large gregarious Australian phasmid (*Podocanthus wilkinsoni*) that defoliates eucalyptus and some other trees

**ringbill** \'=ˌ=\ *n* **:** RING-NECKED DUCK

**ring-billed duck** *or* **ring-billed blackhead** *or* **ring-billed bluebill** \'=ˌ=-\ *n* **:** RING-NECKED DUCK

**ring-billed gull** *n* **:** a rather small American gull (*Larus delawarensis*) having when adult a black band on the bill

**ring binder** *n* **:** a loose-leaf binder in which split metal rings attached to a metal back hold the perforated leaves

**ringbird** \'=ˌ=\ *n* **:** REED BUNTING

**ring blackbird** *n* **:** RING OUZEL

**ringbolt** \'=ˌ=\ *n* **:** an eyebolt with a ring through its eye

**ringbone** \'=ˌ=\ *n* **:** an exostosis on the pastern bones of the horse usu. producing lameness — compare SIDEBONE — **ring·boned** \'=ˌ=\ *adj*

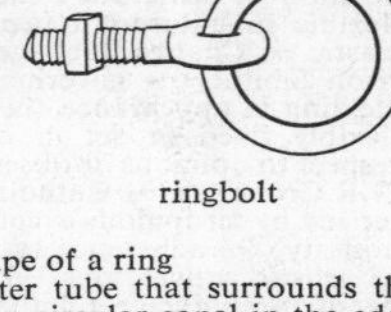

ringbolt

**ring boot** *n* **:** a rubber ring placed around the fetlock of a horse to prevent injury from brushing, cutting, or interfering

**ring budding** *n* **:** ANNULAR BUDDING

**ring bunting** *n* **:** REED BUNTING

**ring buoy** *n* **:** a life buoy in the shape of a ring

**ring canal** *n* **1 :** the circular water tube that surrounds the esophagus of echinoderms **2 :** the circular canal in the edge of the umbrella of a jellyfish that links the radial canals

**ring carrier** *n, obs* **:** GO-BETWEEN

**ring cell** *n* **:** one of the cells in the annulus of a fern

**ring-chain isomerism** *n* **:** isomerism between a cyclic and an open-chain form esp. when the two forms are tautomeric

**ring closure** *n* **:** a chemical reaction in which an open chain of atoms is closed to form a ring **:** CYCLIZATION

**ring clutch** *n* **:** RIM CLUTCH

**ring complex** *n* **:** an occurrence of diverse igneous rocks characterized by approximately circular outcropping of a dike rock

**ring compound** *n* **:** a cyclic compound containing one or more rings in the molecule

**ring cowrie** *n* **:** a cowrie (*Cypraea annulus*)

**ringcraft** \'=ˌ=\ *n* **:** the tactics, strategy, and skill of a boxer

**ring dance** *n* **:** ROUND DANCE 1

**ring dial** *n* **:** a small portable dial in the shape of a cylindrical ring for determining time

**ring dike** *n* **:** a dike of igneous rock having an arcuate outcrop that if fully developed is elliptical or circular in plan

**ring disease** *n* **1 :** RING ROT 2b **2 :** BROWN ROT 1c

**ring dollar** *n* **:** HOLEY DOLLAR

**ring dotterel** *also* **ringed dotterel** *n* **:** a European ring plover

**ringdove** \'=ˌ=\ *n* **1 :** a common European pigeon (*Columba palumbus*) larger than the stock dove or rock pigeon and having on each side of the neck a whitish patch and the wing edged with white **2 :** a small dove (*Streptopelia risoria*) of southeastern Europe and much of Asia that is related to the common turtledove, is often kept as a cage bird, and is buffy with a black collar

**ring dropper** *n* **:** a sharper who pretends to have found a ring dropped by himself and fraudulently tries to induce one to buy it

**ring dropping** *n* **:** a method of swindling practiced by ring droppers

**ringed** *adj* **1 :** encircled or marked with or as if with a ring **:** forming or shaped like a ring **:** composed or formed of rings **:** ANNULAR **2 :** wearing a wedding ring **:** lawfully wedded ⟨a ~ wife —Alfred Tennyson⟩

**ringed perch** *var of* RING PERCH

**ringed plover** *var of* RING PLOVER

**ringed seal** *n* **:** a seal (*Phoca hispida*) of northern waters having ringlike white spots on the body

**ringed snake** *or* **ring snake** *n* **1 :** a harmless European colubrid snake (*Natrix natrix*) common in England **2 :** RING-NECKED SNAKE

**ringed worm** *n* **:** ANNELID

**ring·elnat·ter** \'riŋəl,näd·ə(r)\ *n* -s [G, fr. *ringel* small ring (dim. of *ring*, fr. OHG *hring*) + *natter* adder, fr. OHG *nātara* — more at RING, ADDER] **:** RINGED SNAKE 1

**rin·gent** \'rinjənt\ *adj* [L *ringent-, ringens*, pres. part. of *ringi* to open the mouth, show the teeth — more at RICTUS] **1 :** having the lips widely separated and gaping like an open mouth ⟨~ corolla⟩ **2 :** gaping irregularly ⟨the ~ valves of various bivalves⟩

**¹ring·er** \'riŋə(r)\ *n* -s [ME, fr. *ringen* to ring (a bell) + *-er* — more at RING] **1 :** one that sounds esp. by ringing; *specif* **:** BELL RINGER **2 :** a device providing electric current for operating telephone bells **3 a :** one that enters a competition under false representations esp. as to identity or past performances; *esp* **:** a horse entered fraudulently in a race under a false name to obtain better odds in the betting **b :** one that strongly resembles another — often used with *dead* ⟨a man who is a dead ~ for the senator⟩

**²ringer** \"\ *n* -s [²*ring* + *-er*] **1 :** one that encircles or puts a ring around (something): as **a :** one who puts rings or bands on articles (as on bottles or cigars) **b :** one that rings trees; *specif* **:** a fitter who prepares logs for peeling by cutting through the bark **c :** a quoit or horseshoe that lodges so as to surround the peg; *also* **:** the throw by which it is so lodged **2 :** a billiard ball encircled with a distinguishing band of color (as usu. any of those numbered from nine to fifteen) **3 :** a game of marbles in which marbles are placed in a cross in the center of a ring marked on the ground and players try to knock them out of the ring **4** *Austral* **a :** SHEEPSHEARER; *esp* **:** a very fast and competent one **b :** STOCKMAN, COWBOY

**ring·er's solution** \'riŋə(r)z-\ *or* **ringer solution** *also* **ringer's fluid** *or* **ringer fluid** *n, usu cap R* [after Sydney *Ringer* †1910 Eng. physician] **:** a balanced aqueous solution of the chlorides of sodium, potassium, and calcium, sodium bicarbonate, and sodium dihydrogen phosphate used in physiological experiments to provide a medium essentially isotonic to many animal tissues esp. of poikilothermic vertebrates — compare PHYSIOLOGICAL SALINE

**ring fence** *n* **:** a fence that encircles a large area or a whole estate within one enclosure

**ring-fence** \'=ˌ=\ *vt* [*ring fence*] **:** to enclose in or as if in a ring fence

**ring finger** *n* **:** the third finger of the left hand on which engagement and wedding rings are placed; *also* **:** the corresponding finger of the right hand

**ring formula** *n* **:** a structural formula containing one or more rings

**ring frame** *n* **:** RING SPINNER

**ring gage** *n* **1 :** an external gage in the form of a cylindrical ring or washer often provided with a bushing of hardened steel **2 a :** a tapered stick with graduated markings for measuring finger rings **b :** a set of ring blanks for determining the size of ring worn by an individual

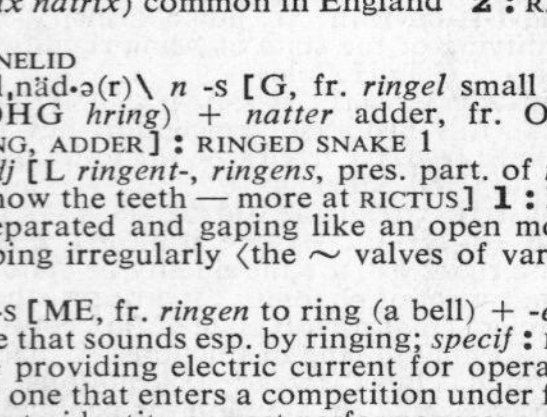

ring gages 2

**ring gear** *n* **:** a gear cut on a ring-shaped rim; *specif* **:** the large gear in the differential of an automobile that is driven by the propeller shaft pinion and transmits the power through the differential to the live axle

**ring gland** *n* **:** an endocrine organ of various two-winged flies that lies about the aorta and is apparently concerned with the initiation of metamorphosis

**ring grass** *also* **ring muhly** *n* **:** a No. American perennial muhly (*Muhlenbergia torreyana*) having scaly rhizomes and a slender cylindrical panicle of purplish spikelets

**ring growth** *n* **:** the tendency of various plants (as grasses) to grow in rings — compare FAIRY RING

**ring·hals** \'riŋ,hals\ *also* **rin·kals** \'riŋ,kals\ *n* -ES [Afrik *rinkals* (formerly spelled *ringhals*), fr. *ring* (fr. MD *rinc*) + *hals* neck, fr. MD; akin to OHG *hring* ring and to OHG *hals* neck — more at RING, COLLAR] **:** a venomous African elapid snake (*Haemachates haemachatus*) that is closely related to the true cobras but has keeled scales and that seldom strikes but spits or sprays its venom aiming at the eyes of its victim where the poison causes intense pain and possible blindness — called also *spitting snake*

**ring head** *n* **:** a magnetic head in which the magnetic core is ring-shaped and contains one or more very short air gaps and in which the magnetic tape or wire is in contact with or close proximity to the outer surface of the ring and bridges one of these gaps

**ringier** *comparative of* RINGY

**ringiest** *superlative of* RINGY

**ring in** *vt* **1 :** to cause (a bell) to take part in the changes in change ringing **2 :** to introduce unwelcomely, surreptitiously, or fraudulently **:** FOIST ⟨*ring in* a horse in a race under a false name⟩ ⟨*ring in* marked cards on one's opponents⟩ **~** *vi* **:** to register one's arrival by ringing a time clock **:** begin work

**ring·i·ness** \'riŋēnəs\ *n* -ES **:** the state of being ringy; *specif* **:** the state of having the annual rings of wood easily separable — compare RING SHAKE

**¹ring·ing** \'riŋiŋ, 'riŋēŋ\ *n* -s [ME, fr. gerund of *ringen* to ring — more at RING (make sounds)] **1 :** the sounding of a bell or other sonorous body **2 :** a sound of ringing or a sensation like that caused by the sound of ringing ⟨a ~ in the ears⟩

**²ringing** \"\ *adj* [ME, fr. pres. part. of *ringen* to ring] **1 :** sounding like a bell **:** clear and full in tone **:** SONOROUS, OROTUND, RESOUNDING ⟨her beautiful, ~, honest voice —Havelock Ellis⟩ ⟨gave me a ~ crack on the head —Vincent McHugh⟩ **2 :** vigorously unequivocal **:** DECISIVE, FERVID ⟨find some opportunity of sealing this document by a ~ declaration —*Economist*⟩ ⟨a ~ appeal⟩ **syn** see RESONANT

**³ringing** \"\ *n* -s [ME, fr. gerund of *ringen* to ring — more at RING (make a ring)] **1 :** the act or result of putting a ring on or about something **2 :** the state of being encircled or marked by a ring

**ringing engine** *n* **:** a simple form of pile driver in which the pile hammer is lifted by men pulling on ropes

**ringing loft** *n* **:** a floor for bell ringers in the tower of a church

**ring·ing·ly** *adv* [*²ringing* + *-ly*] **:** in a ringing manner ⟨~ denounced the proposal⟩

**ring·ing·ness** *n* -ES **:** the quality of being ringing

**ring joint** *n* **:** the joint between the proximal and middle phalanges of a finger

**ring·le** \'riŋəl\ *n* -s [*¹ring* + *-le*] **1** *dial Eng* **:** a metal ring; *esp* **:** one placed in an animal's nose **2** *obs* **:** CIRCLE

**ring·lead** \'riŋ,lēd\ *vb* [back-formation fr. *ringleader*] *vt* **:** to act as ringleader to **~** *vi* **:** to act as ringleader

**ringleader** \'=,==\ *n* [*¹ring* (group) + *leader*] **:** a leader of a group of individuals engaged esp. in violation of law or an improper enterprise ⟨one of the ~s of the abortive revolution —Ethel Drus⟩ ⟨vengeful murder of the mutiny's bloodthirsty ~ —F.R.Dulles⟩

**ringle-eyed** \'==,ēd\ *adj, Scot* **:** WALLEYED

**ring·less** \'riŋləs\ *adj* **:** lacking a ring **:** being without rings ⟨~ knitting⟩

**¹ring·let** \-lət, *usu* -əd.+V\ *n* -s [*¹ring* + *-let*] **1** *archaic* **a :** a small ring **:** a small circle **b :** FAIRY RING **2 :** CURL; *esp* **:** a long curl of hair **3 :** any of various butterflies belonging to *Coenonympha, Erebia,* and closely related genera of the family Satyridae

**²ringlet** \"\ *vt* **ringleted** *also* **ringletted; ringleted** *also* **ringletted; ringleting** *also* **ringletting; ringlets :** to form in ringlets ⟨each head tenderly is ~*ed* —James Stephens⟩ ⟨the bay was ~*ed* with rain —James Daugherty⟩

**ringleted** *also* **ringletted** *adj* [*¹ringlet* + *-ed*] **:** having ringlets **:** worn in ringlets ⟨bearded and ~ men —*Time*⟩ ⟨~ locks⟩

**ringlike** \'=,=\ *adj* **:** resembling a ring in form ⟨~ spots⟩

**ring lock** *n* **:** a combination lock in which a series of grooved rings surrounding the bolt must be arranged so as to bring their grooves in line before the bolt can be shot

**ringlock nail** \'=,=-\ *n* **:** a nail with annular grooving for better holding power

ring-lock nail

**ring lubrication** *n* **:** lubrication of a shaft bearing by means of a ring riding on the shaft in rotation and bringing up oil from a well into which it dips

**ring·man** \'riŋmən\ *n, pl* **ringmen :** ¹BOXER

**ringmaster** \'=,==\ *n* **1 :** one in charge of the performance of trained horses in a ring (as of a circus) **2 :** EQUESTRIAN DIRECTOR

**ring money** *n* **:** annular pieces of metal used as money among primitive peoples

**ring muscle** *n* **:** ORBICULARIS

**ringneck** \'=,=\ *n* **:** a ring-necked bird or animal (as a ring plover, a ring-necked duck, or a ring-necked pheasant)

**ring-necked** \'=;'=\ *or* **ring-neck** \'=,=\ *adj* **:** having a ring of color about the neck

**ring-necked duck** *n* **:** an American scaup duck (*Aythya collaris*) the male of which has the head, neck, and breast black, a narrow chestnut ring encircling the neck, the sides vermiculated with black, and the belly mostly white

**ring-necked lizard** *n* **:** COLLARED LIZARD

**ring-necked parrakeet** *n* **:** a medium-sized parrakeet (*Psittacula krameri*) found from western Africa to the Red sea and in India that is green with a rose-colored collar and reddish bill and is often kept as a pet

**ring-necked pheasant** *n* **:** a pheasant that is a Chinese variety (*Phasianus colchicus torquatus*) of the common Old World pheasant distinguished by a white neck ring; *broadly* **:** any of various pheasants widely introduced in temperate regions as game birds that are varieties of or hybrids between varieties of the common pheasant

**ring-necked plover** *n* **:** RING PLOVER

**ring-necked snake** *also* **ringneck snake** *n* **:** any of numerous small smooth colubrid snakes having a yellowish ring about the neck and constituting a genus (*Diadophis*) with representatives in all parts of the U. S.

**ring necrosis** *n* **:** a browning of the vascular ring in stems or tubers (as that characteristic of fusarium wilt and a form of necrosis of the potato caused by frost)

**ring nematode** *n* **:** a nematode worm of a genus (*Criconemoides*) of the family Criconematidae having cuticle divided into annuli that give an effect of pseudosegmentation, being soil-dwelling, and feeding on roots and possibly causing winter injury of the peach

**ring net** *n* **:** a fishing net somewhat resembling a purse seine used esp. in the European herring fishery — **ring-netter** \'=,==\ *n*

**ring off** *vi* **1** *chiefly Brit* **:** to terminate a telephone call **:** HANG UP **2** *chiefly Brit* **:** to stop talking

**ring of saturn** *usu cap R&S* [after *Saturn*, Roman god connected with the sowing of seed, fr. L *Saturnus*] **:** a small line forming a semicircle around the base of the finger of Saturn and usu. held by palmists to indicate a lack of stability or purpose and often failure in life

**ring of sol·o·mon** \-'sälәmәn\ *usu cap R&S* [after *Solomon*, †*ab*933 B.C. king of Israel noted for his wisdom] **:** a small line forming a semicircle around the base of the finger of Jupiter and usu. held by palmists to indicate a love of and possible proficiency in occult studies

**ring-oil** \'riŋ,ȯil\ *vt* [back-formation fr. *ring oiler*] **:** to oil (a bearing) by conveying the oil to the point to be lubricated by means of a ring that rests upon and turns with the journal and dips into a reservoir containing the lubricant

**ring oiler** *n* **:** a ring-oiling device

**¹ring out** *vi* [*²ring*] **:** to settle or close a transaction (as in futures) in a produce exchange by forming into a series a number of buyers and sellers in which the first and the last deal with each other to complete the ring and all settle by paying differences

**²ring out** *vi* [*³ring*] **:** to register one's departure from work by ringing a time clock

**ring ouzel** *n* **:** a thrush (*Turdus torquatus*) that is related to the European blackbird and the American robin, is black with a white bar across the breast, and breeds in mountainous regions of northern Europe and migrates to Africa — called also *ring blackbird, ring thrush*

**ring parrakeet** *or* **ring parrot** *n* **:** any of several Old World chiefly green parrakeets having a red ring around the neck (as *Psittacula krameri* found in India and Africa and *P. alexandri* of Java)

**ring perch** *or* **ringed perch** *n* **:** YELLOW PERCH

**ring pin** *n* **:** a pin whose head is in the form of a ring for receiving a label

**ring plain** *n* **:** a lunar crater of exceptional diameter with relatively smooth interior

**ring plover** *or* **ringed plover** *n* **:** any of various small plovers of the widely distributed genus *Charadrius* (as the common European species *C. hiaticula* and the American semipalmated, piping, and killdeer plovers) having the upper part chiefly brownish or buffy and the underparts white and a black breast band or collar

**ring-porous** \'=;==\ *adj* **:** having vessels more numerous and usu. larger in cross section in the springwood with a resulting more or less distinct line between the springwood and the wood of the previous season — used of woody stems and roots (as of oaks); compare DIFFUSE-POROUS

**ring relievo** *n* **:** ²RELIEVO

**ring road** *n, chiefly Brit* **:** BELT HIGHWAY

**ring-roll mill** *n* **:** a crusher or pulverizer in which the material is squeezed by rolling between rings

**ring rope** *n* **1 :** a rope rove through sheaves in the cathead and the ring of an anchor to haul the latter close up under the former **2 :** a rope for bending a cable to an anchor

**ring rot** *n* **1 :** decay in a log following closely the annual rings **2 a :** a disease of sweet potatoes caused by a fungus (*Rhizopus stolonifer*) in which the roots are girdled by bands of dry rot **b :** a disease of potatoes caused by a bacterium (*Corynebacterium sepedonicum*) and characterized by browning of the ring of vascular bundles — called also *ring disease* **c :** BROWN ROT 1c

**rings** *pl of* RING, *pres 3d sing of* RING

**ring screw** *n* **:** a screw having a ring formed on its end (as for attaching chain or rope)

**ring seal** *n* **:** an engraved gem or precious stone set in a ring and used as a seal

**ring settlement** *n* **:** a settlement made in a produce exchange by ringing out

**ring shake** *n* **:** a defect in timber consisting of shrinkage and separation of the annual rings — called also *cup shake;* compare HEART SHAKE

**ring shout** *n* **:** a dance of African origin done by Negro slaves and revivalists in which all form a circle and shuffle counterclockwise usu. with much shouting

**¹ringside** \'=,=\ *n* [*¹ring* + *side*] **:** the area just outside a ring esp. in which a contest (as boxing or racing) occurs; *broadly* **:** a place from which one may have a close view (as of a show)

**²ringside** \"\ *adj* **:** at or from the ringside ⟨a ~ table in a nightclub⟩ ⟨shiny-topped ~ clientele —T.H.Fielding⟩

**³ringside** \"\ *adv* **:** at the ringside ⟨sit ~ at a hockey game⟩

**ring·sid·er** \'riŋ,sīdə(r)\ *n* -s [*¹ringside* + *-er*] **:** one that watches a performance (as a boxing or wrestling match) at or near ringside

**ring sight** *n* **:** a gunsight having a ring or series of concentric rings through which one sights

**ring-silicate** \'=,==(,)=\ *n* **:** CYCLOSILICATE

**ring snake** *var of* RINGED SNAKE

**ring spinner** *n* **:** a machine for spinning in which the twist given to the yarn by a revolving bobbin is regulated by a small metal loop sliding on a ring around the bobbin — called also *ring frame*

**ring spinning** *n* **:** a method of spinning employing a ring spinner

**ring spot** *n* **1 :** a lesion of plant tissue consisting of yellowish, purplish, or necrotic, often concentric rings **2 :** any plant disease of which ring spots are the characteristic lesion: as **a :** a virus disease of tobacco and related plants producing chlorotic rings on the leaves **b :** a disease of sugarcane caused by a fungus (*Leptosphaeria sacchari*) and characterized by purplish bordered spots **c :** a disease of the lower leaves of cauliflower and related crucifers caused by a fungus (*Mycosphaerella brassicicola*) **d :** an anthracnose of lettuce caused by a fungus (*Marssonina panathoniana*) **e :** FROGEYE a(1) **f :** FAIRY RING SPOT

**ring stand** *n* **:** a stand (as of iron) consisting of a long upright rod attached to a heavy rectangular base and used with rings and clamps fastened to the rod to support laboratory apparatus (as distilling flasks, retorts, condensers)

**ring·ster** \'riŋztə(r), -ŋ(k)st-\ *n* -s [*¹ring* + *-ster*] **:** a member of an esp. political or price-fixing ring

**ring stick** *n* **:** RING GAGE 2

**ring stone** *n* **:** a voussoir showing on the face of the wall

**ring stopper** *n* **1** *archaic* **:** a cathead stopper **2 :** a chain passing under and around the shank of an anchor near the ring and made fast to the releasing tumbler in securing an anchor on the billboard

**ringstraked** \'=,=\ *adj, archaic* **:** marked with circular stripes ⟨removed that day the he-goats that were ~ and spotted —Gen 30:35 (AV)⟩

**ring system** *n* **:** the structure typical of a cyclic chemical compound and consisting of one or more rings (as fused rings) ⟨five- and six-membered *ring systems*⟩ — compare SKELETON

**ringtail** \'=,=\ *n* **1 a** *dial Eng* **:** the female or immature hen harrier **b :** an immature golden eagle **c :** HUDSONIAN GODWIT **2 a :** CACOMISTLE **b :** RING-TAILED OPOSSUM **c :** RACCOON **3 :** a studding sail set on the gaff of a fore-and-aft sail abaft the leech **4** *or* **ringtail monkey** *also* **ring-tailed monkey :** CAPUCHIN

**ring-tailed** \'=;'=\ *adj* **1 :** having a tail marked with rings of differing colors **2 :** having a tail carried in the form of a circle ⟨a *ring-tailed* dog⟩

**ring-tailed cat** *n* **:** CACOMISTLE

**ring-tailed eagle** *n* **:** an immature golden eagle

**ring-tailed lemur** *n* **:** MADAGASCAR CAT

**ring-tailed marlin** *or* **ringtail marlin** *n* **:** HUDSONIAN GODWIT

**ring-tailed opossum** *n* **:** any of several relatively small herbivorous arboreal marsupials (genus *Pseudocheirus*) common in much of Australia and in New Guinea and having strongly prehensile tails

**ring-tailed roarer** *n* **:** an imaginary animal

**ring-tail perch** *n* **:** YELLOW PERCH

**ringtaw** \'=,=\ *n* **:** a game of marbles in which marbles are placed in a circle on the ground and shot at from a line about two yards distant with the object of knocking them out of the circle

**ring tennis** *n* **:** DECK TENNIS

**ring test** *n* **:** a test for antigens or antibodies in which a layer of diluted material suspected of containing antigen is placed over a column of known antiserum in a small test tube or a layer of diluted known antigen is placed over serum suspected of containing antibodies and is then examined for a positive reaction signaled by formation of a thin plane or ring of precipitate

**ring thrush** *n* **:** RING OUZEL

**ringtoss** \'=,=\ *n* **:** a game the object of which is to toss a ring so that it will fall over an upright stick

**ring traveler** *n* **:** TRAVELER 5

**ring up** *vt* [*³ring*] **1 :** to total and record esp. by means of a cash register ⟨the groceries were *rung up*⟩ ⟨*ring up* a sale⟩ **2 :** RECORD ⟨below the margin *rung up* in the last election⟩ ⟨highest figure so far *rung up* elsewhere is $50 million —J.N. Wallace⟩ ⟨*rang up* social triumphs —*Sat. Eve. Post*⟩

**ringwalk** \'=,=\ *n, archaic* **:** a walk made by hunters around a wood or other covert

**ringwall** \'=,=\ *n* **:** a wall that encircles an area

**ring watch** *n* **:** a very small timepiece set in a case mounted on a finger ring

**ring willow** *n* **:** a weeping willow (*Salix babylonica crispa*) with folded and spirally curved leaves

**ring winding** *n* **:** armature winding in which the wire is wound round the outer and inner surfaces alternately of an annular or cylindrical core — distinguished from *drum winding*

**ringworm** \'=,=\ *n* [ME, fr. *ring* + *worm*] **1 :** any of several contagious diseases of the skin, hair, or nails of man and domestic animals caused by fungi esp. of the genera *Trichophyton* and *Microsporum* and characterized on the skin by ring-shaped discolored patches covered with vesicles and scales **2 :** MILLIPEDE

**ringworm bush** *or* **ringworm cassia** *n* **:** a tropical American shrub (*Cassia alata*) whose leaves yield a juice used as a cure for ringworm and poisonous bites

**ringy** \'riŋē\ *adj* -ER/-EST **:** resembling or suggesting a ring

**¹rink** \'riŋk\ *n* -s [ME (Sc dial.) *renk, rinc* area in which a combat or contest takes place, fr. MF *renc, ranc, reng, rang* line, place, row, rank — more at RANK] **1 a :** a smooth level extent of ice marked off for curling or ice hockey — see CURLING illustration, ICE HOCKEY illustration **b :** an enclosed sheet of ice usu. artificial and under cover for ice-skating; *also* **:** a building containing such a rink **c :** a covered enclosure for roller-skating **2 :** a division of a bowling green 19 to 21 feet in width and running the length of the green and large enough for a match **3 a :** a team of four players in a game of bowls or curling **b :** a game of bowls or curling played by four players on each side

**²rink** \"\ *vi* -ED/-ING/-S **:** to skate at a rink

**rin·ka·fad·da** \'riŋkə'fäthə\ *also* **rin·ka** \'riŋkə\ *n* -s [IrGael *rince fada,* fr. *rince* dance + *fada* long] **:** an Irish dance resembling the Virginia reel

**rinkals** *var of* RINGHALS

**rink·ite** \'riŋ,kīt\ *n* -s [G *rinkit,* fr. Hinrich J. *Rink* †1893 Dan. explorer + G *-it* -ite] **:** a mineral $Na(Ca,Ce)_2(Ti,Ce)(SiO_4)_2F$ consisting chiefly of a yellowish crystalline silicate of cerium

**rink·man** \'riŋkmən\ *n, pl* **rinkmen :** one who takes care of a skating rink and assists and instructs skaters

**rin·ko·lite** \'riŋkə,līt\ *n* -s [Russ *rinkolit,* alter. of *rinkit* rinkite, fr. G] **:** a strontian variety of rinkite

**rink·tum dit·ty** \'riŋktəm'did·ē\ *n* [origin unknown] **:** a mixture of tomato sauce, onion, cheese, egg, and seasonings served on toast

**rin·man's green** *or* **rin·mann's green** \'rinmənz-\ *n, usu cap R* [after Sven *Rinman* †1792 Swedish mineralogist] **:** COBALT GREEN 1

**rin·ne·ite** \'rinē,īt\ *n* -s [G *rinneit,* fr. W. B. *Rinne* †1933 Ger. mineralogist + G *-it* -ite] **:** a mineral $NaK_3FeCl_6$ consisting of a chloride of iron, potassium, and sodium and occurring in colorless, pink, violet, or yellow granular masses (hardness 3, sp. gr. 2.3)

**rin·ne·mann's green** \'rin(ə)mənz-\ *n, usu cap R* [after Sven *Rinman* †1792 Swedish mineralogist] **:** COBALT GREEN 2

**rin·ner** \'rinə(r)\ *dial Brit var of* RUNNER

**rins·abil·i·ty** *or* **rins·ibil·i·ty** \,rin(t)sə'bilәd·ē\ *n* -ES **:** capability of being rinsed

**rins·able** *or* **rins·ible** \'rin(t)səbəl\ *adj* **:** capable of being rinsed

**¹rinse** \'rin(t)s, *dial* 'rench *or* 'ren(t)s *or* 'rinch\ *vb* -ED/-ING/-S [ME *rincen,* fr. MF *rincer,* fr. OF *recincier,* fr. (assumed) VL *recentiare,* fr. L *recent-, recens* fresh, young, recent — more at RECENT] *vt* **1 :** to cleanse by the introduction of water or other liquid ⟨~ a bottle⟩ — often used with *out* ⟨~ out the mouth⟩ **2 a :** to cleanse by dipping into water **:** cleanse (as from the soap used in washing) by agitating in clear water or by pouring clear water over ⟨~ clothes⟩ ⟨~ the hands⟩ **b :** to treat (the hair) with a rinse **3 :** to remove (dirt or impurities) by washing lightly or in water only **4 :** to cleanse (a surface) by the application of any suitable substance ⟨*rinsed* his hands in snow —W.V.T.Clark⟩ ⟨counters were *rinsed* with a very dilute solution of lacquer in amyl acetate —*Physical Rev.*⟩ **~** *vi* **:** to be removable by the use of water ⟨a soap that ~s easily⟩

**²rinse** \"\ *n* -s **1 a :** the act or process of rinsing **b :** DOUCHE **2 a :** water or other liquid used for rinsing **b** (1) **:** any of various cosmetic solutions that remove soap, bring out highlights of the hair's color, or temporarily tint the hair another color (2) **:** an application of such a solution

**rins·er** \"+ə(r)\ *n* -s **1 :** one that rinses **2 :** a utensil used to hold water for rinsing

**rinsing** *n* -s [fr. gerund of *¹rinse*] **1 :** water that has been used for rinsing — usu. used in pl. **2 :** the last dregs **:** RESIDUE — usu. used in pl. ⟨the ~s of an unwashed wineglass —O.W. Holmes †1894⟩

**¹rio** \'rē(,)ō\ *adj, usu cap* [fr. *Rio,* nickname for *Rio de Janeiro,* Brazil] **:** RIO DE JANEIRO

**²rio** \"\ *n* -s *usu cap* [fr. *Rio,* nickname for *Rio de Janeiro*] **:** a Brazilian coffee

**rio de ja·nei·ro** \'rē(,)ō,dā|zhə'ne(,)rō, -dē|, |jə'-, -'ni(,)-\ *adj, usu cap R&J* [fr. *Rio de Janeiro,* Brazil] **:** of or from the city of Rio de Janeiro, Brazil **:** of the kind or style prevalent in Rio de Janeiro

**ri·o·din·i·dae** \,rīə'dinə,dē\ *n pl, cap* [NL, fr. *Riodina,* type genus + *-idae*] **:** a family of small or medium-sized often brightly colored butterflies having metallic spots on the wings and the first pair of legs reduced in the males and occurring mostly in the New World tropics

**rio grande disease** \'rē|(,)ō'grand-, -aand-, -dē-, -di- *sometimes* 'rī| *or* |ə'-\ *n, usu cap R&G* [fr. the *Rio Grande,* river in the southwestern U.S.] **:** a disease of lettuce of unknown cause first reported from the Rio Grande valley and causing the older leaves to become reddish esp. on the tips while the younger central ones blanch and do not grow to normal size

**rio ipecac** *n, usu cap R* **:** IPECAC 2a

**rio pie·dras** *or* **rio pie·dras** \'rē(,)ō'pyādrəs\ *adj, usu cap R&P* [fr. *Río Piedras,* Puerto Rico] **:** of or from the city of Río Piedras, Puerto Rico **:** of the kind or style prevalent in Río Piedras

**¹ri·ot** \'rīət, *usu* -əd.+V\ *n* -s *often attrib* [ME *riot, riote,* fr. OF *riot, rihot, riote, rihote* quarrel, dispute, fr. *ruihoter, rihoter, rioter* to quarrel, dispute, perh. fr. *ruire* to roar, fr. L *rugire* — more at BRUIT] **1** *archaic* **a :** profligate or wanton behavior **:** DEBAUCHERY, EXCESS, EXTRAVAGANCE **b :** unrestrained revelry or merrymaking **c :** noise, uproar, or disturbance made by revelers **2 :** an assemblage of three or more persons in a public place for the purpose of accomplishing by concerted action and in a turbulent and disorderly manner a common purpose irrespective of the lawfulness of the purpose **3 :** a hunting dog's following of the scent of an animal the hunter does not want **4 :** a random or disorderly profusion esp. of color ⟨a rhythmic ~ of color —*Amer. Guide Series: Oregon*⟩ **5 :** something or someone wildly amusing **:** a cause or occasion of mirth or hilarity ⟨her latest hat is a ~⟩ **syn** see BRAWL

**²riot** \"\ *vb* -ED/-ING/-S [ME *rioten,* fr. *riote, riot,* n.] *vi* **1 :** to indulge in revelry or wantonness **:** practice license or excess **2** *archaic* **:** to take great pleasure — used with *in* or *upon* **3 :** to create or engage in a disturbance or tumult; *specif* **:** to disturb the peace by a riot **4** *of a hound* **:** to follow the scent of an animal which it is not intended to hunt **~** *vt* **1 :** to waste or spend recklessly ⟨would hardly care to see him ~*ing* away her whole property —Leslie Ford⟩ **2 :** ATTACK, DESPOIL

**riot act** *n* [fr. the *Riot Act,* an English law of 1715 that provided for the dispersal of gatherings disturbing the peace] **:** a vigorous reproof, reprimand, or warning **:** DRESSING DOWN — used in the phrase *read the riot act* ⟨read me the *riot act* for what I'd done —J.B.Benefield⟩

**ri·ot·er** \'rīəd·ə(r), -ətə-\ *n* -s [ME *rioter,* alter. of *riotour,* fr. *rioten* + *-our* -or] **:** one that riots: as **a** *archaic* **:** a profligate liver **:** REVELER, ROISTERER **b :** one that creates or takes part in a disturbance, tumult, or riot

**riot gun** *n* **:** a small arm used to disperse rioters rather than to inflict serious injury or death; *esp* **:** a short-barreled shotgun

**ri·ot·ing·ly** *adj* **:** RIOTOUSLY

**riotise** *n* -s [*¹riot* + obs. *-ise* -ice (fr. ME *-ice, -ise*)] *obs* **:** LICENTIOUSNESS, EXCESS, REVELRY

**ri·ot·ous** \'rīəd·əs, -ətəs\ *adj* [ME, fr. *riote, riot* debauchery, riot + *-ous* — more at RIOT] **1 a :** practicing or marked by license or excess **:** PROFLIGATE, WANTON **b :** ABUNDANT, EXUBERANT, PROFUSE ⟨a ~ display of color⟩ ⟨~ slapstick⟩ **2 :** of the nature of a riot **:** marked by public uproar and disturbance **:** participating in riot **:** TURBULENT, SEDITIOUS

**ri·ot·ous·ly** *adv* **:** in a riotous manner

**ri·ot·ous·ness** *n* -ES **:** the quality, state, or habit of being riotous

**ri·ot·ry** \'rīətrē\ *n* -ES [*²riot* + *-ry*] **1** *archaic* **:** RIOTING **2** *archaic* **:** rioting persons

**¹rip** \'rip\ *n* -s [ME *rippe, ripp,* fr. ON *hrip;* akin to OHG *href* carrying basket, Latvian *kribas,* pl., wicker bottom of a sled, and perh. to L *curvus* curved — more at CROWN] **1** *dial* **:** a wicker basket (as for fish) **2** *dial* **:** a coop for fowl

**²rip** \"\ *vb* **ripped; ripped; ripping; rips** [prob. fr. Flem *rippen* to rip, strip off roughly; prob. akin to MD *reppen, rippen* to set in motion, pull, touch, MLG *reppen* to touch, move, OE *hreppan, hrepian* to touch — more at RAFFLE] *vt* **1 a :** to cut or tear apart **:** split open **:** slash off ⟨machinery commenced *ripping* up the earth —G.S.Perry⟩ ⟨something the dogface hopefully *ripped* open with anxious hands only to discover a can —J.P.O'Neill⟩ ⟨its passage *ripped* away the crown of the arch, and immediately the whole bridge collapsed —O.S. Nock⟩ **b** : to saw or split (wood) with the grain **c** *dial Brit* : to remove and replace (tiles) on a roof **d** : to cut, break, ravel, take out, or undo (stitches) in sewing : separate (as a garment) into its parts **2 a** : to slash or slit with or as if with a sharp blade ⟨*ripped* up his waistcoat to feel if he was not wounded —Daniel Defoe⟩ **b** *archaic* : to tear open (an old sore or grievance) **3** *archaic* : to recall to notice or reopen (as a closed issue or an unpleasant business) **4** : to utter violently (as an oath) : burst out with : spit out ⟨*ripped* out vituperation, cursing, and blasphemy⟩ ~ *vi* **1** : to pull or tear apart : REND ⟨the strain was too great; the sleeve *ripped* away from the coat⟩ **2** : to move unchecked : proceed without restraint : rush headlong ⟨a smart convertible coupe came *ripping* up the short steep drive —Christopher Morley⟩ **3** : to burst out with violent or profane utterance — usu. used with *out* ⟨*ripped* out with an oath⟩ **syn** see TEAR — **rip into** : to tear into like a buzz saw : ATTACK ⟨*ripped into* his antagonist with fury⟩ — **rip up the back** : to assail with hostile comment esp. behind the victim's back : BACK-BITE

**3rip** \"\ *n* -s **1** : a rent made by ripping : a torn place : a gap left by a seam giving way : TEAR **2** : a cut of wood along the grain (as by a ripsaw) **3** *dial Brit* : RUSH, SPEED

**4rip** \'rip\ *Scot var of* 2REAP

**5rip** \"\ *n* -s [perh. fr. 3*rip*] **1** : a body of water made rough by the meeting of opposing tides or currents : TIDE RIP **2** : a current roughened by passing over an irregular bottom — used esp. of tidal currents and sometimes of currents in rivers; compare UNDERTOW

**6rip** \"\ *n* -s [perh. alter. of 2*rep*] **1** : a worn-out worthless horse ⟨left the spavin-legged old ~ standing there —Bruce Siberts⟩ **2** : a reckless or dissolute person : LIBERTINE, RAKE ⟨his elder brother was a bit of a ~ —Ngaio Marsh⟩

**rip** *abbr* **1** ripieno **2** ripped

**RIP** *abbr* **1** [L *requiescat in pace*] may he (she) rest in peace **2** [L *requiescant in pace*] may they rest in peace

**1ri·par·i·an** \rə'perēən, (')rī¦p-, -pa(a)r-,-pār-\ *also* **ri·par·i·al** \-ēəl\ *adj* [L *riparius* riparian + E *-an* or *-al* — more at RIVER] **1** : of or relating to or living or located on the bank of a watercourse (as a river or stream) or sometimes a lake ⟨~ vegetation⟩ ⟨~ states⟩ ⟨~ scenery⟩ **2** : LITTORAL

**2riparian** \"\ *n* -s : one that lives or has property on the bank of a river

**riparian right** *n* : the right of one owning riparian land to have access to and use of the shore and water — compare LITTORAL RIGHT, WATER RIGHT

**ri·par·i·ous** \-ēəs\ *adj* [L *riparius*] : RIPARIAN

**rip cord** *n* **1** : a cord by which the gasbag of a balloon may be ripped open for a limited distance to release the gas quickly and so cause immediate descent **2** : a cord or wire pulled manually or automatically in making a descent to release the pilot parachute which lifts the main parachute out of its container ready to open **3 a** : a cord inserted longitudinally in a sheathed electric cable for use in ripping the sheath at the ends for easier removal (as in making connections) **b** : an electric cord consisting of two individually insulated wires readily separable by ripping usu. for a short distance to make a connection

**rip current** *n* [5*rip*] : a strong surface current flowing outward from a shore — called also *riptide*

**1ripe** \'rīp\ *adj* -ER/-EST [ME, fr. OE *rīpe*; akin to OS *rīpi* ripe, MD *ripe*, OHG *rīfi*; derivative fr. the root of E *reap*] **1** : fully grown and developed : MATURE: as **a** : ready for reaping or harvesting ⟨~ grain⟩ ⟨a ~ field⟩ **b** *of fruit* (1) : having mature seed (2) : fully developed and so usable as food **c** : mature enough for use as cuttings — used of stems or other plant parts **d** *of timber or a forest* : ready to be cut **e** : free from budding cells — used of a yeast **2** : having the full development and powers of maturity: as **a** : having full mental and physical maturity **b** : having mature knowledge, understanding, or judgment : CONSUMMATE, PERFECTED ⟨a ~ scholar⟩ ⟨~ wisdom⟩ **c** : stemming from thorough consideration or reflection : based on full deliberation ⟨they deal with many subjects and are characterized by ~ reflection and consummate mastery of style —*Encyc. Americana*⟩ **3** : marked by maturity or fullness of time: as **a** : exhibiting full mental or physical powers ⟨a ~ time of life⟩ ⟨a ~ age⟩ **b** : of advanced years : LATE ⟨lived to the ~ age of 90⟩ **c** : fully arrived : SUITABLE ⟨the time seemed ~ to proceed to . . . evangelization —Kemp Malone⟩ **4** : ready for some action or purpose : fully prepared for some use or object : fit for consummation ⟨a state of affairs ~ for axis exploitation —H.M.Sachar⟩ ⟨the classical type of monopoly capitalism ~ for public ownership —*New Statesman & Nation*⟩ ⟨here is a mixed-up character, ~ for the analyst —Lucy Crockett⟩ **5** : brought by aging to full flavor or to the height of desirability as food or drink : MELLOW ⟨~ cheese⟩ ⟨a ~ port⟩ ⟨~ venison⟩ **6** : ready to discharge : MATURED — used of an abscess or boil **7** *archaic* : DRUNK — used in the phrase *reeling ripe* **8** : ruddy, plump, or full like ripened fruit ⟨the invitation of ~ young lips⟩ **9** : due or ready for action, trial, or payment (as a lawsuit or a claim) **10** : sufficiently developed to be removed by surgery — used of a cataract in the eye **11 a** : ready to be discharged — used of eggs **b** : containing ripe eggs or spermatozoa — used of fish; compare GREEN

**2ripe** \"\ *vb* -ED/-ING/-S [ME *ripen*, fr. OE *rīpian*, fr. *rīpe* ripe] *chiefly dial* : RIPEN, MATURE

**3ripe** \"\ *vb* -ED/-ING/-S [ME *ripen*, fr. OE *rȳpan*; akin to OHG *roufen* to pluck, ON *ruppa*, *rupla*, Goth *raupjan* to pluck, ON *rögg* tuft of hair — more at RUG] *vt* **1** *chiefly Scot* **a** : to make a thorough search of **b** : to subject to thorough examination or investigation **2** *chiefly Scot* : to steal from : ROB **3** *chiefly Scot* : to clear of something that obstructs : clean out **4** *chiefly Scot* : to break up or remove stones from (rough ground) ~ *vi*, *chiefly Scot* : to make a search

**4ripe** \"\ *chiefly dial var of* REAP

**5ripe** \"\ *n* -s [ME, fr. L *ripa* — more at RIVER] *archaic* : RIVERBANK, SEASHORE

**ripe·ly** *adv* [ME, fr. *ripe* + *-ly*] **1** *obs* : with mature deliberation **2** : in a ripe manner : with mature or developed appearance : AMPLY

**rip·en** \'rīpən, -pᵊm\ *vb* **ripened** \-pənd,-pᵊmd\ **ripened** \"\ **ripening** \-p(ə)niŋ\ **ripens** \-pənz,-pᵊmz\ [1*ripe* + *-en*] *vi* **1** : to grow ripe : become mature (as of grain, fruit, or a microorganism) **2** : to approach or come to full development : arrive at completeness or perfection : become fit for use, for action, or for an appropriate purpose **3** : to become ready to discharge — used of an abscess or boil **4** *of a photographic emulsion* : to increase in average grain size as a result of physical treatment (as prolonged heating) or in sensitivity as a result of chemical treatment ~ *vt* **1** : to make ripe ⟨the grower may . . . ~ the fruit in transit or on arrival by means of ethylene —G.L.Jenkins & W.H.Hartung⟩ ⟨time had ~*ed* his life and mellowed its fruits —Van Wyck Brooks⟩ **2** : to bring to maturity, completeness, or perfection : cause full development of : fit or prepare for some use or purpose: as **a** : to sour (cream) by bacterial action as a prelude to churning for butter to reduce fat loss and improve the flavor of the finished product **b** : to age or cure (cheese) to develop characteristic flavor, odor, body, texture, and color **c** : to improve flavor and tenderness of (beef or game) through the action of enzymes in the meat during a period of refrigeration **3** : to cause to become ready to discharge — used of an abscess or boil **syn** see MATURE

**rip·en·er** \'rīp(ə)nə(r)\ *n* -s : one that ripens

**ripe·ness** \'rīpnəs\ *n* -ES [ME *ripenes*, fr. OE *rīpnes*, fr. *rīpe* ripe + *-nes* -ness — more at RIPE] : the quality or state of being ripe : MATURITY, COMPLETENESS, PERFECTION

**riper** *comparative of* RIPE

**ripe rot** *n* : decay of ripe fruit caused by a fungus; *esp* : BITTER ROT 1

**ripest** *superlative of* RIPE

**ripgut** \'ₛ,ₛ\ *or* **ripgut grass** *n* [2*rip* + *gut*] : a troublesome weedy European grass (*Bromus rigidus*) adventive in California

**ri·pic·o·lous** \rə'pikələs, (')rī¦p-\ *adj* [fr. L *ripa* river bank + E *-i-* + *-colous*] : RIPARIAN

**ri·pid·o·lite** \rə'pidᵊl,īt, rī'p-\ *n* -s [G *ripidolith*, irreg. fr. *rhipid-* + *-lith* -lite] : a mineral $(Mg,Fe)_9Al_6Si_5O_{20}(OH)_{16}$ consisting of a basic magnesium iron aluminum silicate of the chlorite group

**ri·pie·nist** \rəp'yānəst\ *n* -s [2*ripieno* + *-ist*] : one that plays a ripieno

**1ri·pie·no** \-ā(,)nō\ *adj* [It, filled up, stuffed, supplementary, fr. *ri-* re- (fr. L *re-*) + *pieno* full, fr. L *plenus* — more at FULL] **1** : of or relating to a musical instrument or performer serving solely to swell the mass of an orchestra : SUPPLEMENTARY **2** : TUTTI

**2ripieno** \"\ *n*, *pl* **ripie·ni** \-ā(,)nē\ *or* **ripienos** [It, fr. *ripieno*, adj.] : a supplementary musical instrument or performer or the group playing the ripieno part — compare CONCERTINO

**1ri·poste** *also* **re·post** \rə'pōst, rē'p-\ *n* -s [F *riposte*, alter. of *risposte*, fr. It *risposta*, lit., answer — more at RISPOSTA] **1** : a fencer's quick return thrust following a successful parry **2** : a retaliatory verbal sally : RETORT ⟨the critic's ~ might be that most of these stories are machine-made too —Harrison Smith⟩ **3** : a retaliatory maneuver or measure : COUNTERATTACK ⟨the raid upriver was a successful ~ to the enemy's earlier attack⟩

**2riposte** *also* **repost** \"\ *vb* -ED/-ING/-S [F *riposter*, fr. *riposte*] *vi* **1** : to make a riposte in fencing **2** : to deliver a verbal counterthrust : make a telling retort ⟨the two men argued and *riposted* —Janet Flanner⟩ **3** : to deliver a counterblow or counterattack ⟨the general evaded pursuit and *riposted*⟩ ~ *vt* : to deliver (a verbal counterthrust) in reply : RETORT

**rip panel** *n* : a strip in the upper part of the fabric of a balloon or semirigid or nonrigid airship which is torn off when immediate deflation is desired

**ripped** *past of* RIP

**1rip·per** \'ripə(r)\ *n* -s [2*rip* + *-er*] **1** : a worker who rips: as **a** : one who opens seams to prepare them for resewing **b** : an operator of a ripsaw or variety saw **c** : a member of a fish-dressing gang who opens the belly of fish and removes the viscera **2** : a tool, device, or machine that rips: as **a** : a long bar or thin steel blade used to remove damaged roofing slates and notched for drawing nails **b** : a device for opening stitched seams in cloth **c** : RIPSAW **d** : a machine with revolvable knives for cutting millboard **e** : a road machine to break up worn or disintegrated pavement **f** : a subsoiler or chisel implement that loosens surface soil and subsoil **3** : any of the larger blocks on which the first few drawings are effected in wiredrawing **4 a** : an excellent example or instance of a kind : HUMDINGER ⟨a ~ American musical comedy in the highest gear —*Newsweek*⟩ **b** : a wild or reckless person **5** *chiefly NewEng* : 1BOBSLED 2 **6** : a madman or criminal who slashes his victims with a knife

**2ripper** \"\ *adj* : designed to make drastic changes in a governmental agency for purely partisan purposes ⟨~ legislation⟩ ⟨~ bill⟩ ⟨~ amendment⟩

**rip·pet** *or* **rip·pit** \'ripət\ *n* -s [origin unknown] *dial* : a noisy quarrel : FUSS, UPROAR

**rip·pi·er** *or* **rip·i·er** \'ripēə(r)\ *n* -s [1*rip* + *-ier*] *archaic* : a fish peddler

**rip·ping** \'ripiŋ, -pēŋ\ *adj* [prob. fr. pres. part. of 2*rip*] : GRAND, SWELL ⟨also some ~ letters from you —O.W.Holmes †1935⟩

**ripping bar** *n* : a steel bar having one end formed into a ripping chisel and the other end shaped like a gooseneck with a claw for pulling nails

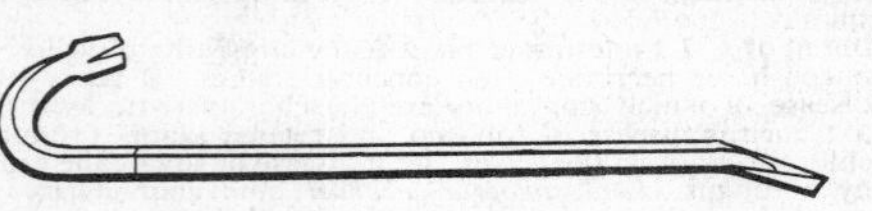

ripping bar

**ripping chisel** *n* : a long slender chisel sometimes with a slightly bent and cleft cutting end used for cleaning mortises or for heavy prying

**ripping cord** *n* : RIP CORD 1

**ripping iron** *n* : RAVEHOOK

**rip·ping·ly** *adv* : SPLENDIDLY

**ripping panel** *or* **ripping strip** *n* : RIP PANEL

**ripping punch** *n* : a tool with a rectangular point used in a punching machine for crosscutting metal plates

**ripping saw** *n* : RIPSAW

**ripping size** *n* : the size of rough wood stock required for the production of a finished product

**1rip·ple** \'ripəl\ *vt* -ED/-ING/-S [ME *riplen*; akin to MD *repelen* & *repen* to ripple, MLG *rēpelen*, MHG *reffen* to ripple, OHG *riffilōn* to saw] **1** : to remove (seeds) from flax or hemp with a ripple **2** : to draw (flax) through a ripple

**2ripple** \"\ *n* -s [ME *repylle*, *ryppyll*; akin to MLG *rēpel* ripple, OHG *riffila* saw, *riffilōn* to saw — more at 1RIPPLE] : a large instrument like a comb for removing seeds and other matter from flax or hemp

**3ripple** \"\ *vi* -ED/-ING/-S [ME *riplen*, of Scand origin; akin to Norw *ripla* & *ripa* to scratch, Sw *repa* — more at REAP] *dial Brit* : to scratch slightly

**4ripple** \"\ *n* -s *dial Brit* : a slight cut : SCRATCH

**5ripple** \"\ *vb* **rippled**; **rippled**; **rippling** \-p(ə)liŋ\ **ripples** [perh. fr. 2*rip* + *-le*] *vi* **1 a** : to become fretted or lightly ruffled on the surface (as water) : become covered with or form in small waves or undulations ⟨a blue river *rippled* into the bay —Israel Zangwill⟩ ⟨the ripened cornfields *rippled* up to the doorsteps of the cottages —Flora Thompson⟩ ⟨his lean, sun-bronzed upper body *rippled* all over with long, graceful muscle —Frank Yerby⟩ **b** : to flow in small waves ⟨the brook *rippled* onward below her⟩ **c** : to fall in soft undulating folds or wavy lines ⟨the cloth *rippled* to the floor⟩ **2** : to flow with a light rise and fall of sound or inflection ⟨laughter *rippled* over the audience⟩ **3** : to move with an undulating motion or so as to cause ripples ⟨the canoe *rippled* through the water⟩ **4** : to run irregularly through a crowd, group, or population ⟨had watched discontent ~ through the seaports and back country —Oscar Handlin⟩ ~ *vt* **1** : to stir up small waves on (water) : move or disturb lightly ⟨a moderate breeze was *rippling* the lagoon —Ernest Beaglehole⟩ **2** : to impart a wavy motion or appearance to ⟨began to stretch and ~ his muscles —*Time*⟩ **3** : to utter or play with a slight rise and fall of sound : make a light rapid cadence or melody of ⟨*rippling* a boogiewoogie beat on the piano —Noel Houston⟩

**6ripple** \"\ *n* -s **1 a** : a shallow stretch of running water in a stream roughened or broken by rocky or uneven bottom **b** (1) : the fretting or ruffling of the surface of water (as by wind) (2) : a small wave **c** : a small wave propagated by both surface tension and gravity — distinguished from *gravity wave* **2** : something resembling or suggesting a ripple of water: as **a** : RIPPLE MARK 2 **b** : a soft fold (as in a full skirt) or a wavy outline (as in a hat brim) **c** : CHATTER MARK 1 **d** : a sound like that of rippling water ⟨a ~ of laughter⟩ ⟨a ~ of conversation⟩ **3** : 1RIFFLE 1 **4** : a slight fluctuation in the intensity of an otherwise steady electrical current

**ripple fire** *n* : the discharge of rockets in quick succession

**ripple grass** *n* : a ribgrass (*Plantago lanceolata*)

**ripple index** *n* : the horizontal distance from crest to crest divided by the vertical distance from crest to trough of the ripples on a ripple-marked surface

**rip·ple·less** \'ripəl(l)əs\ *adj* : having no ripples : GLASSY, SMOOTH

**ripple mark** *n* **1 a** : the undulating surface of a ridge or trough produced in incoherent granular material (as loose sand) by wind, currents of water, or the agitation of waves **b** : one of the ridges on such a surface **2** : a striation across the grain of wood esp. on the tangential surface caused by storied cambial and other cells — **ripple–marked** \'ₛₛ,ₛ\ *adj*

**rip·pler** \'rip(ə)lə(r)\ *n* -s : one that ripples; *esp* : 2RIPPLE

**rip·plet** \'rip(ə)lət\ *n* -s : a small ripple

**ripple voltage** *n* : the alternating component of unidirectional voltage from a rectifier or generator

**ripple weld** *n* : a weld having a rippled surface

**ripple–weld** \'ₛₛ,ₛ\ *vt* [*ripple weld*] : to unite by means of a ripple weld

**rip·pling·ly** *adv* : in a rippling manner : WAVILY

**rip·ply** \'rip(ə)lē, -li\ *adj* [5*ripple* + *-y*] **1** : having ripples ⟨~ water⟩ **2** : resembling the sound of rippling water

**rip·pon** \'ripən\ *n* -s [fr. *Rippon* (Ripon), Yorkshire, England] *archaic* : a horseman's spur

**1rip·rap** \'ri,prap\ *n* [fr. obs. *riprap* sound of rapping, redupl. of 1*rap*] **1** : a foundation or sustaining wall of stones thrown together without order (as in deep water, on a soft bottom, or on an embankment slope to prevent erosion) **2** : stone used for riprap

**2riprap** \"\ *vt* : to form a riprap in or upon : strengthen or support with a riprap ⟨*riprapped* the breakwater with stone⟩

**riprapping** *n* -s : a riprap foundation or wall

**rip–roaring** \'ri,prōriŋ, -prȯr-\ *adj* [alter. of *rip-roarious*] : noisily excited or exciting : HILARIOUS

**rip–roarious** \(')ri¦prōrēəs, -prȯr-\ *adj* [2*rip* + *-roarious* (as in *uproarious*)] : HILARIOUS

**rips** *pl of* RIP, *pres 3d sing of* RIP

**ripsack** \'ₛ,ₛ\ *n* [2*rip* + *sack*] : GRAY WHALE

**1ripsaw** \'ₛ,ₛ\ *n* [2*rip* + *saw*] : a coarse-toothed saw for cutting wood in the direction of the grain — compare CROSSCUT SAW

**2ripsaw** \"\ *vt* : to saw (wood) in the direction of the grain

**rip·sawyer** \'rip+,-\ *n* [2*ripsaw* + *-yer* (as in *sawyer*)] : a worker who uses a ripsaw

**ripsnorter** \'ₛ¦ₛₛ\ *n* [2*rip* + *snorter*] **1** : a violently energetic or noisily outspoken person : someone using slambang methods ⟨that venerable old ~ defended the right of the clergy to drive fast horses —Phil Stong⟩ **2** : something extreme : HUMDINGER ⟨yesterday's performance was a ~ for gaiety, vigor, and general run-around —Virgil Thomson⟩ — compare SNORTER — **ripsnorting** \'ₛ¦ₛₛ\ *adj*

**riptide** \'ₛ,ₛ\ *n* [5*rip* + *tide*] **1** : RIP CURRENT **2** : a situation in which confused overwhelming forces play on someone : a destructive vortex ⟨creators and culture heroes who crack up in a ~ of alcohol —Richard Chase⟩

**rip track** *n* : a siding on which railroad cars are given minor repairs

**1rip·u·ar·i·an** \¦ripyə¦werēən, -wa(a)r-,-wār-\ *adj*, *usu cap* [ML *Ripuarius* Ripuarian + E *-an*] : of or relating to a group of Franks settling in the 4th century on both banks of the Rhine near the present city of Cologne

**2ripuarian** \"\ *n* -s *cap* : a Ripuarian Frank

**rip van win·kle** \,rip,van'wiŋkəl\ *n* -s *usu cap R&V&W* [after *Rip Van Winkle*, fictional ne'er-do-well in the Catskill mountains of N.Y. state in colonial days who slept for 20 years, as portrayed in a story of *The Sketch Book* (1820) by Washington Irving †1859 Am. writer] : someone not alert to current conditions ⟨some *Rip Van Winkle* in an obscure corner . . . who has read nothing for four years —*Manchester Guardian Weekly*⟩

**rir·o·ri·ro** \,rirə'rē(,)rō\ *n* -s [Maori] : GRAY WARBLER

**ri·sa·la** *or* **res·sa·la** \rə'sälə\ *n* -s [Hindi *risāla* troop, fr. Per, fr. Ar *risālah* mission] : a troop of irregular cavalry in the Anglo-Indian army

**ri·sal·dar** *or* **ris·sal·dar** \rə'säl,där, 'risəl,-\ *or* **res·sal·dar** \rə'säl,där, 'resəl,-\ *n* -s [Hindi *risāldār*, fr. Per *risāladār*, fr. *risāla* + *-dār* holder — more at BHUMIDAR] : a native commander of a risala in the Anglo-Indian army

**risco** *n* -s [It *risco*, *risico*, *rischio*] *obs* : RISK, VENTURE

**1rise** \'rīz\ *vb* **rose** \'rōz\ *or archaic* **rise** *or dial* **riz** \'riz\ **ris·en** \'rizᵊn\ *or dial* **riz**; **ris·ing** \'rīziŋ\ **ris·es** \'rīzəz\ [ME *risen*, fr. OE *rīsan*; akin to OHG *rīsan* to rise, climb, fall, ON *rīsa* to rise, Goth *urreisan* to get up, L *oriri* to rise, *rivus* brook, stream, Gk *ornynai* to urge on, cause to rise, *oros* mountain, Skt *arṇa* wave, *ṛṣva* high, *raya* stream, Hitt *arāi* he rises] *vi* **1 a** : to assume an upright or standing position : get up from lying, kneeling, or sitting **b** : to get up from sleep or from one's bed **c** : to get back on one's feet after a fall **d** : to regain standing after a lapse, disgrace, or failure **e** (1) : to stand erect (as of a terrified person's hair) (2) : to resume an upright position (as of flattened grass or grain) **2** : to come back to life : return from death or the grave ⟨witnesses who ate and drank with him after he *rose* from the dead —Acts 10:41 (RSV)⟩ **3 a** : to go to war : take up arms : launch an attack : make insurrection ⟨the people of Boston *rose* and seized all of the Dominion officers who could be found —Viola F. Barnes⟩ — usu. used with *against* ⟨the Lord will cause your enemies who ~ against you to be defeated before you —Deut. 28:7 (RSV)⟩ **b** *obs* (1) : to break camp (2) : to withdraw a besieging force **4 a** *obs* : to show respect : DEFER — used with *up* **b** : to respond warmly : show enthusiasm : APPLAUD, CHEER — usu. used with *to* ⟨the audience *rose* to his verve and wit⟩ **5** : to end a session : ADJOURN ⟨when the committee *rose* on Friday the clerk had read through section 203 —*Congressional Record*⟩ **6 a** : to move up from the horizon : climb the skies : come up ⟨a pale sun *rose* in lowering skies⟩ — opposed to *set* **b** : to come in view (as of a ship at sea) above the horizon or to appear larger on nearer approach **7 a** : to ascend into the air : move upward ⟨smoke *rose* quietly from cottage chimneys all through the valley below⟩ **b** : to grow taller : increase in height ⟨~ to heights unusual for other trees⟩ **8** : to swell in size or volume : reach a higher level ⟨the river *rose* rapidly with the heavy rains⟩ ⟨becomes an island each time the tide *rises*⟩ ⟨a blister *rose* at the burn⟩ ⟨bread dough *rises*⟩ **9** : to extend upward : grow in process of construction : incline or reach above other objects ⟨at a little distance above him *rose* a small butte —Oliver La Farge⟩ ⟨octagonal towers ~ a story higher than the main body of the structure —*Amer. Guide Series: Texas*⟩ ⟨a meeting place or assembly hall will ~ —Sidonie M. Gruenberg⟩ ⟨between the valleys of the gorge ~ miniature mountain peaks —*Amer. Guide Series: La.*⟩ **10 a** : to become lifted up or raised : swell with joy : increase in cheer, hope, or courage : become elated ⟨spirits *rose* as the danger passed⟩ **b** : to increase in fervor : grow heated or ardent : INTENSIFY ⟨members of his staff watched indignation ~ in him —Stewart Cockburn⟩ **11** : to move aloft : become lifted higher : go up : SOAR ⟨the curtain *rose* on a lovely set⟩ ⟨birds *rose* all around in alarm⟩ **12 a** : to come up to the surface (as of the water or the ground) ⟨a diver *rose* near him in the water⟩ ⟨the spring ~*s* cool and fresh from great depths⟩ **b** : to move up through the water to take food or bait ⟨trout were *rising* hungrily⟩ **13** *of locked-up printing type* **a** : LIFT **b** : to work up **14 a** : to attain a higher level : gain in vigor, clarity, grace, or effectiveness ⟨his painting *rose* to a fresh expressiveness and revealed a shrewder, gentler insight⟩ ⟨*rose* to heights of passionate eloquence⟩ **b** : to increase in quantity or number ⟨funds available for investment *rose* sharply —R.P.Edmunds⟩ ⟨cotton acreage *rose* over 50 percent —*Americana Annual*⟩ **c** : to advance in rank, position, or esteem ⟨*rose* to the rank of brigadier general of cavalry when still in his twenties —J.H.Easterby⟩ **d** : to increase in price : grow dearer ⟨the cost of paper *rose*⟩ **e** : to become higher in pitch or louder ⟨her voice *rose* then in a shrill crescendo⟩ **15 a** : to grow stronger or more resolute ⟨his courage *rose* as difficulties multiplied about him⟩ **b** : to increase in force or rate of speed ⟨the wind *rose* rapidly⟩ ⟨storms *rose* often to wild fury⟩ **16** : to take place : HAPPEN, OCCUR ⟨then *rose* a little circumstance that was to have far-reaching results⟩ **17 a** : to attain existence : come on the scene : become born : APPEAR ⟨search and you will see that no prophet is to ~ from Galilee —Jn 7:52 (RSV)⟩ ⟨great regimes *rose*, based upon the irrational and negative in man's nature —M.W.Straight⟩ **b** *archaic* : to spring up : GROW — used of a plant **18** : to follow as a consequence : become derived : ORIGINATE, RESULT ⟨wars had *risen* out of incidents more trivial —L.C.Douglas⟩ **19** : to gain currency : CIRCULATE ⟨a rumor *rose* in city hall circles that the mayor would resign⟩ **20 a** : to have source or origin : SPRING ⟨the river ~*s* in the foothills⟩ **b** : to have a beginning ⟨great nations ~ and fall⟩ **21** : to exert oneself to meet a challenge or provocation : show oneself equal to a demand or test : prove adequate — usu. used with *to* ⟨their ministerial leaders *rose* ably to the occasion with consummate theological arguments —*Amer. Guide Series: Conn.*⟩ **22** : to become raised (as of a vowel) ~ *vt* **1** : to cause to rise; *esp* : to lure (a fish) to rise **2** *chiefly dial* : to make higher : INCREASE — used of price **3** *archaic* : to reach the top of : SURMOUNT

**syn** RISE, ARISE, ASCEND, MOUNT, SOAR, TOWER, ROCKET, LEVITATE, SURGE can mean, in common, to move or come up from a lower to a higher level. RISE is the most general, interchangeable with all the others ⟨the fountain *rose* to a 6-foot spout⟩ ⟨she felt the color *rising* in her face —Anne D. Sedgwick⟩ ⟨the building *rose* a story at a time⟩ ⟨the balloon *rose* into the heavens⟩ ⟨the table *rose* from the floor and seemed to poise in midair⟩ ⟨the wave *rose* and crashed against the cliff⟩ It is usu. used in some idioms that refer to getting up from a lying, sitting, or kneeling position ⟨awake and *rise* at dawn⟩ ⟨*rise* from a chair⟩ or to objects as the sun, moon, or a mountain that seem to get up or lift themselves in this way ⟨the moon rose at 10:35 in the evening⟩ ⟨stairways *rising* diagonally across the porch —*Amer. Guide Series: La.*⟩ ⟨cliffs around the bay *rise* steep from the waters —Leonard Lyons⟩ or to a fluid under the influence of a natural force ⟨the mercury *rose* steadily until the temperature was over 100 degrees⟩ ⟨in the flood the river *rose* five feet⟩ ARISE is narrower in application and is used to indicate literal movement upward usu. to getting up after a sleep; in figurative applications it is more synonymous with *appear* or *come into existence* ⟨an apparition *arose* before us⟩ ⟨city after city *arose* —R.W. Murray⟩ ⟨an eager babbling *arose* from the shore —Kenneth Roberts⟩ ⟨a haze of dust *arose* —Melvin Van den Bark⟩ ASCEND and MOUNT carry a strong idea of continuous, progressive upward movement ⟨*ascend* a mountain⟩ ⟨*mount* a long flight of stairs⟩ ⟨the smoke rose and *ascended* to the treetops⟩ ⟨after the initial rise the temperature *mounted* steadily⟩ ⟨*ascend* a stream in a canoe⟩ ⟨as the road *mounted*, the air became sharper —Joseph Wechsberg⟩ SOAR, always suggesting the straight upward flight of a bird, therefore indicates continuous, usu. swift ascent to high altitudes, literal or figurative ⟨the flight of hawks is impressive . . . *soaring* in intricate spirals —*Amer. Guide Series: Pa.*⟩ ⟨snowy mountains *soaring* into the sky twelve and thirteen thousand feet —John Muir †1914⟩ ⟨food items, the prices of which may *soar* or plummet —Carey Longmire⟩ TOWER usu. applies to things that attain conspicuous height through growth or building up, connoting extension to a height considerably above neighboring objects ⟨peaks that *tower* in the distance —Laurence Binyon⟩ ⟨surrounded by mountains which *tower* thousands of feet higher —Tom Marvel⟩ ⟨great chimneys *tower* above its roof —*Amer. Guide Series: Md.*⟩ ⟨the great men *tower* over the young making their authority manifest in the land —H.J.Laski⟩ ROCKET suggests the startlingly swift speed, usu. upward, of a projectile ⟨teal *rocketed* over the treetops —*New Yorker*⟩ ⟨prices have *rocketed* sky-high —Patrick Kent⟩ LEVITATE implies a force that causes something to rise through actual or induced buoyancy, usu., however, being associated with spiritualistic practices and illusory risings of a person or thing ⟨had once *levitated* himself three feet from the ground by a simple act of the will —Katherine A. Porter⟩ ⟨in other experiments . . . with *levitated* tables —H.H.U.Cross⟩ SURGE, often with *up*, suggests the heaving upward or forward of a large wave ⟨water forced in by the ocean waves would *surge* up through it and trickle down the mountains —*Amer. Guide Series: Oregon*⟩ ⟨strong emotions *surged* through him as he strode on —O.E. Rølvaag⟩ **syn** see in addition SPRING

**²rise** \"\ *sometimes* -īs\ *n* -S **1 :** an act of rising or a state of being risen: as **a :** a movement upward **:** an ascent to a higher plane **b :** the emergence of the sun or some other celestial body above the horizon **c** *obs* (1) **:** a leap upward esp. from a running start (2) **:** a place providing a takeoff point for such a leap **d :** the upward movement of a fish to seize food or bait **e** (1) **:** an increase in the pitch of sound or an upward change of key ⟨a ~ of a tone or semitone⟩ (2) **:** a rising-pitch intonation in speech — compare ²FALL 3d **f** (1) **:** the reaching of a higher level by an increase of quantity or bulk (2) **:** the amount or height of such an increase ⟨the ~ of the river was six feet⟩ **g :** the distance from the firing line to the traps in trapshooting **2 :** BEGINNING, DERIVATION, ORIGIN, SOURCE, START ⟨with the ~ of tin mining in more recent years, the community has once again regained its position of importance —P.E.James⟩ **3 :** the distance or elevation of one point above another: as **a :** the height of an arch from base to apex **b :** the height of a step in a staircase measured from one tread to the next **4 :** an increase in amount, number, or volume: as **a :** an increase in the loudness of the voice ⟨the ordinary ~*s* and falls of the voice —Francis Bacon⟩ **b** *chiefly Brit* **:** an increase in wages or salary ⟨five shillings a week ~ from the first of January —Victoria Sackville-West⟩ **c :** an increase in price, value, rate, or sum ⟨the corn shortage that followed land expropriation caused a ~ in corn prices —Virginia Prewett⟩ ⟨it had no concomitant provision for a tax ~ —J.C.Ingraham⟩ ⟨a general ~ in the cost of living —C.L.Guthrie⟩ ⟨a walkout, a fare ~ — or both — appeared inevitable —*N.Y. World-Telegram*⟩ **d :** the difference in diameter between two points on a log **:** TAPER **5 a :** an upward slope **:** INCLINE ⟨hopes for a ~ in the road —*Amer. Guide Series: Fla.*⟩ ⟨a ~ in the ocean bottom⟩ **b :** a spot higher than the surrounding ground **:** HILLTOP ⟨the road breaks suddenly over a ~ —*Amer. Guide Series: Wash.*⟩ **6 :** ²RAISE 4 **7 :** an irritated or retaliatory response to provocation **:** an angry reaction **:** RETORT ⟨got a ~ out of him⟩ **8 :** the vertical displacement of the center of gravity of a seaplane float or hull from an arbitrary reference level **9 a :** the distance from the crotch to the waistline on pants **b :** the distance above the waistline on skirts

**³rise** \"\ *chiefly dial var of* ¹RICE

**rise and fall** *n* **:** the vertical up and down movement of the tide resulting from but not necessarily coincident with its flow and ebb

**rise and shine** *vi* **:** to get out of bed — often used as a command

**risen** [ME, fr. OE] *past part of* RISE

**rise of floor :** DEAD RISE

**ris·er** \'rīzə(r)\ *n* -S [ME, fr. *risen* to rise + *-er* — more at RISE] **1 :** one that rises: as **a :** one that gets up from sleep ⟨birds are early ~*s*⟩ **b :** INSURGENT **c :** a part in a machine that operates by rising **2 a :** the upright member between two stair treads — compare OPEN RISER **b :** an upright face (as of a platform or veranda) suggesting a stair riser **c :** a topographic feature resembling a stair riser (as a steep slope between terraces of different altitude or between flat parts of a stepped glaciated valley floor) **3 :** ²RAISE 4 **4 a :** FEEDHEAD **b :** a channel or head in a foundry mold (as to permit escape of air) **5 :** a block on which a printing plate (as a stereotype or electrotype) is mounted **6 :** a device or structure used to increase elevation: as **a :** one of two members placed below a seat to raise it **b :** any of various movable platforms for stage use on which performers are placed for better visibility ⟨portable ~*s* adequate for a full orchestra⟩ **7 a :** a vertical supply or return pipe for steam, water, or gas **b :** a vertical wire connecting two floors in the electric wiring system of a building **8 :** a raised or marked spot where the warp passes over the weft or over the filling in a weaving pattern — compare SINKER 8 **9 :** one of four straps by which a parachutist's harness is attached to the parachute — see PARACHUTE illustration

**riser plate** *n* **:** a plate used with a railroad gage or tie plate to raise and support a point rail above the base of the rail and maintain minimum gage

**rises** *pres 3d sing of* RISE, *pl of* RISE

**rishi** *also* **rsi** \'rishē\ *n* -S [Skt *ṛṣi*; akin to Skt *rasa* juice, fluid — more at RORIC] **:** a holy Hindu sage, saint, or inspired poet

**ris·i·bil·i·ty** \ˌrizə'bilәd·ē, -lәtē, -i\ *n* -ES [LL *risibilitas*, fr. *risibilis* + L *-itas* -ity] **1 :** the ability or inclination to laugh **:** alertness or sensitiveness to the ridiculous, incongruous, or absurd — often used in pl. ⟨our *risibilities* support us as we skim over the surface of a deep issue —J.A.Pike⟩ **2 :** LAUGHTER, MERRIMENT ⟨excites much ~ by being tossed in a blanket —Wilmot Harrison⟩

**ris·i·ble** \'rizәbәl\ *adj* [LL *risibilis*, fr. L *risus* (past part. of *ridēre* to laugh) + *-ibilis* -ible — more at RIDICULOUS] **1 :** capable of laughing **:** disposed to laugh ⟨heaven is not for pallid saints but raging and ~ men —Christopher Morley⟩ **2 :** arousing, exciting, or provoking laughter **:** FUNNY, RIDICULOUS ⟨~ courtroom antics —Robert Hatch⟩ ⟨my salary is ~ —W.J. Locke⟩ **3 :** associated with, relating to, or used in laughter ⟨~ muscles⟩ ⟨something would be said to touch his ~ faculties —W.H.Hudson †1922⟩ **syn** see LAUGHABLE

**ris·i·bles** \-lz\ *n pl* **:** sense of the ridiculous **:** SENSE OF HUMOR ⟨an article which tickled my ~ immensely —Vinnie Hicks⟩

**¹rising** *n* -S [ME, action of rising, fr. gerund of *risen* to rise — more at RISE] **1** *chiefly dial* **:** a pathological excrescence **:** a puffing up **:** BOIL, PUSTULE **2** *chiefly dial* **:** a leavening agent (as yeast) used to make dough rise **3 :** ²RAISE 4 **4 a :** a narrow strake to support the thwarts of a boat **b :** fore-and-aft bearers to support a deck

**²rising** *adj* [fr. pres. part. of ¹*rise*] **1** *heraldry* **:** having the wings opening as if for flight **2 a** *of an animal's age* **:** slightly less than a specified number of years — distinguished from *off* **b :** approaching a stated age ⟨he was ~ 45⟩ — **3** *chiefly Midland* **:** more than **:** EXCEEDING — often used with *of* **4 :** passing from a less vigorous to a more vigorous physical condition **:** IMPROVING — used esp. of domestic livestock; compare FALLING

**rising diphthong** *n* **:** a diphthong in which the final vowel element is more prominent than the beginning element (as the \yä\ in \'yät\ *yacht*) — compare FALLING DIPHTHONG, ²GLIDE 3b

**rising hinge** *n* **:** a door hinge designed so that the door is lifted a little when opened

rising hinge

**rising line** *n* **:** a line drawn in the plan of a ship to show the heights of the floors

**rising rhythm** *n* **:** a rhythm in which the stresses regularly fall on the last syllable of each foot (as in iambic or anapestic lines) — opposed to *falling rhythm;* compare CADENCE 5, UNDULATING CADENCE

**rising seat** *n* **:** one of the tiered seats facing the congregation in a Friends' meetinghouse that are occupied by the elders

**rising timbers** *n pl* **:** the floor timbers in the forward or afterparts of a wooden ship inclined up from the rest of the deck

**rising vote** *n* **:** a vote in which the voters on each side rise in turn to be counted — compare DIVISION, VOICE VOTE

**rising wood** *n* **1 :** timber used to fill in at the junctions of a wooden ship's keelson with the stem and stern posts **2 :** the upper timber of a wooden ship's keel when composed of two timbers

**¹risk** \'risk, *dial* 'resk\ *n* -S [F *risque*, fr. It *risco, risico, rischio*] **1 :** the possibility of loss, injury, disadvantage, or destruction **:** CONTINGENCY, DANGER, PERIL, THREAT ⟨the infinite care and ~ which are involved in the dangerous mission of bomb disposal —E.A.Weeks⟩ ⟨foreign ships and planes refused to run the ~ of attack —*Collier's Yr. Bk.*⟩ **2 :** someone or something that creates or suggests a hazard or adverse chance **:** a dangerous element or factor — often used with qualifiers to indicate the degree or kind of hazard ⟨the wife who didn't fix her husband a good breakfast . . . wasn't a good ~ —W.H.Whyte⟩ ⟨must be kept clean and free from fire ~*s* —Peter Heaton⟩ ⟨a poor ~ for surgery⟩ **3 a** (1) **:** the chance of loss or the perils to the subject matter of insurance covered by a contract (2) **:** the degree of probability of such loss **b :** AMOUNT AT RISK **c :** a person or thing judged as a (specified) hazard to an insurer ⟨a poor ~ for insurance⟩ **d :** an insurance hazard from a (specified) cause or source ⟨war ~⟩ ⟨disaster ~⟩ **4 :** the product of the amount that may be lost and the probability of losing it — compare EXPECTATION 6b **syn** see DANGER

**²risk** \"\ *vb* -ED/-ING/-S [F *risquer*, fr. It *riscare, risicare, rischiare*, fr. *risco, risico, rischio*] *vt* **1 :** to expose to hazard or danger ⟨wasn't going to ~ his neck —Barnaby Conrad⟩ ⟨father and son were ready to ~ their futures on the book business alone —A.E.Peterson⟩ **2 :** to incur the risk or danger of **:** venture upon ⟨these privateers ~*ed* being hung as pirates —*Amer. Guide Series: N. H.*⟩ **~** *vi* **:** to take risks **syn** see VENTURE

**³risk** \'risk\ *vi* -ED/-ING/-S [prob. of imit. origin] *Scot* **:** to make a crackling or grating sound

**risk capital** *n* **:** VENTURE CAPITAL

**risk·er** \'riskә(r), *dial* 'res-\ *n* -S **:** one that risks

**risk·ful** \-kfәl\ *adj* **:** RISKY — **risk·ful·ness** *n* -ES

**risk·i·ly** \'riskәlē, -li\ *adv* **:** in a risky manner **:** HAZARDOUSLY

**risk·i·ness** \-kēnәs, -kin-\ *n* -ES **:** the quality or state of being risky **:** CHANCINESS

**risk·less** \-klәs\ *adj* **:** having no danger **:** free of adverse chance **:** CERTAIN, SAFE ⟨relatively ~ financial arrangements —Albert Lepawsky⟩ ⟨the return on ~ investments is not sufficiently attractive —John Ryan⟩

**risk premium** *n* **:** NET PREMIUM

**risky** \-kē, -ki\ *adj*, *usu* -ER/-EST [¹*risk* + *-y*] **1 :** attended with risk or danger **:** HAZARDOUS ⟨pretty ~ going out there in the tide and in the fog —D.B.Putnam⟩ **2 :** danger-loving **:** BOLD, DARING, VENTURESOME ⟨those are ~ captives —Alexander Forbes⟩ **3** [modif. of F *risqué* — more at RISQUÉ] **:** RISQUÉ ⟨~ anecdotes were discouraged —Gamaliel Bradford⟩ ⟨she had on the *riskiest* dress she'd bought —Ring Lardner⟩ **syn** see DANGEROUS

**ris·ley act** \'rizlē-\ *n*, *usu cap R* [after the *Risley* family, 19th cent. circus trio consisting of Richard *Risley* Carlisle †1874 Am. gymnast and circus performer and his two sons] **:** a circus act in which an acrobat lying on his back juggles barrels or fellow acrobats with his feet

**ri·so·lu·to** \ˌrēsә'lü(ˌ)tō, -ēzә-\ *adv (or adj)* [It, resolute, fr. L *resolutus* — more at RESOLUTE] **:** resolutely and with marked accent — used as a direction in music

**ri·sor·gi·men·to** \(ˌ)rēˌsȯ(r)jә'men·(ˌ)tō\ *n* -S [It, fr. *risorgere* to rise again (fr. L *resurgere*) + *-i-* + *-mento* -ment (fr. L *-mentum*) — more at RESURRECTION] **:** a time of renewal or renaissance **:** REVIVAL ⟨a ~ of culture —R.P.Casey⟩ ⟨an industrial and agricultural ~ —B.A.Javits⟩ ⟨men of the *Risorgimento* who made Italy a free nation —*Times Lit. Supp.*⟩

**ri·so·ri·us** \rә'sōrēәs, rī'-, -'zō-\ *n, pl* **riso·rii** \-ē,ī\ [NL, fr. L *risus* (past part. of *ridēre* to laugh) + *-orius* -ory — more at RIDICULOUS] **:** a narrow band of muscle fibers arising from the fascia over the masseter muscle and inserted into the tissues at the corner of the mouth

**ri·sot·to** \rә'sȯd·(ˌ)ō, -'z|, |äd-\ *or* **ri·zot·to** \-'z|\ *n* -S [It *risotto*] **:** rice cooked in meat stock and seasoned in any of various ways (as with butter and cheese or with wine and saffron)

**¹risp** \'risp\ *vb* [ME *rispen*, fr. ON *rispa* to scratch; akin to G *rispeln* to scrape together, LG *rispe* hackle, and perh. to Norw *ripa* to scratch — more at REAP] *Scot* **:** RASP, SCRATCH

**²risp** \"\ *n* -S [origin unknown] *dial chiefly Eng* **:** a stem or stalk of a plant

**ri·spet·to** \rә'sped·(ˌ)ō\ *n* -S [It, lit., respect, fr. L *respectus* — more at RESPECT] **:** an Italian verse stanza of from 6 to 10 lines with rhymes

**ri·spos·ta** \rә'spȯstә\ *n* -S [It, lit., answer, fr. fem. of *risposto*, past part. of *rispondere* to answer, fr. L *respondēre* to answer, respond — more at RESPOND] **:** the answer in a musical fugue or the consequent in a canon

**ris·qué** \rә'skā, (')ri¦s-\ *adj* [F, fr. past part. of *risquer* to risk — more at RISK] **:** verging on impropriety or indecency **:** DARING, OFF-COLOR ⟨a ~ story⟩

**¹riss** \'ris\ *n* -ES *usu cap* [fr. the *Riss* river, tributary of the Danube in southwestern Germany] **:** the third stage of Pleistocene glaciation in Europe

**²riss** \"\ *or* **riss·ian** \-sēәn\ *adj, usu cap* **:** of or relating to the Riss glaciation

**rissaldar** *var of* RISALDAR

**ris·soa** \'risәwә, rә'sōә\ *n, cap* [NL, after Giovanni A. *Risso* †1845 Ital. naturalist] **:** a genus (the type of the family Rissoidae) of small brackish-water snails having an acuminate often finely sculptured shell with a corneous operculum

**¹ris·soid** \'risәwȯid, -ˌsȯid\ *or* **ris·soid·e·an** \ˌrisә¦widēәn, rә'sȯid-\ *adj* [*rissoid* fr. NL *Rissoidae; rissoidean* fr. NL *Rissoidae* + E *-an*] **:** of or relating to the Rissoidae

**²rissoid** \"\ *n* -S **:** a snail of the family Rissoidae

**ris·soi·dae** \rә'sōә,dē, -sȯi(ˌ)dē\ *n pl, cap* [NL, fr. *Rissoa*, type genus + *-idae*] **:** a large family of marine and freshwater snails (suborder Taenioglossa) with a long snout, ciliated tentacles, and eyes on small prominences at the base of the tentacles — see RISSOA

**¹ris·sole** \rә'sōl, 'ri,s-\ *n* -S [F, fr. MF *roissole*, fr. (assumed) VL *russeola*, fr. L *russeus* reddish, fr. *russus* red — more at RUSSET] **:** minced meat or fish covered with pastry and fried in deep fat

**²ris·so·lé** \'risәlē, ¦==¦lā\ *adj* [F, fr. past part. of *rissoler* to brown by frying in deep fat, fr. *rissole*] **:** browned by frying in deep fat ⟨~ potatoes⟩

**ris·som** \'risәm, 'rizәm\ *n* -S [ME *risom*, of Scand origin; akin to Sw dial. *resma, resme* ear of oats, Norw *risla* bush, treetop, ear of grain; akin to OHG *hrīs* twig — more at CREST] **1** *chiefly dial* **:** an ear or stalk of grain **:** STRAW 2 **2** *chiefly dial* **:** a tiny bit **:** PARTICLE

**riss-würm** \'ri's¦wәrm, ¦wu̇(ә)rm, ¦vi(ә)rm, *G* ¦vʏrm\ *n* -S *usu cap R&W* [fr. the *Riss* river, a tributary of the Danube in southwestern Germany, and the *Würm*, a small stream of southern Bavaria, Germany] **:** the third interglacial interval during the Pleistocene glaciation of Europe

**ri·sus sar·do·ni·cus** \ˌrēsә(s),sär'dänәkәs, ¦rīs-\ *n* [NL, lit., sardonic laugh] **:** a facial expression characterized by raised eyebrows and grinning distortion of the face resulting from spasm of facial muscles esp. in tetanus

**rit** \'rit\ *vt* [ME *ritten;* akin to OHG *rizzōn, rizzen* to scratch, tear; derivative fr. the stem of OE *wrītan* to scratch (on something), write — more at WRITE] *dial Brit* **:** to scratch or cut esp. with a sharp instrument

**rit** *abbr* ritardando

**RIT** *abbr* refining in transit

**rita** *also* **rta** \'rid·ә\ *n* -S [Skt *ṛta*, fr. *ṛta* fit, right, true — more at ARTICLE] **:** the cosmic-moral principle of order that in Vedic tradition establishes regularity and righteousness in the world

**ri·tard** \rә'tärd, 'rē,t-\ *n* -S [by shortening] **:** RITARDANDO

**¹ri·tar·dan·do** \ˌrē,tär'dän(ˌ)dō, -dan-\ *adv (or adj)* [It, fr. L *retardandum*, gerund of *retardare* to retard — more at RETARD] **:** with a gradual slackening in tempo **:** RALLENTANDO — used as a direction in music

**²ritardando** \"\ *n* -S **1 :** a movement or passage in gradually slackening tempo **2 :** a gradually slackening tempo

**¹rite** \'rīt, *usu* -īd·+V\ *n* -S [ME, fr. L *ritus;* akin to OE *rīm* number, OHG, series, number, ON, calculation, OIr, number, Gk *arithmos* number, *arariskein* to fit — more at ARM] **1 a :** a prescribed form or manner governing the words or actions of a ceremony esp. of considerable religious, courtly, social, or tribal significance ⟨the introduction into a particular ~ of features not sanctioned by the texts —L.P.Smith⟩ **b** *often cap* **:** LITURGY; *esp* **:** one of the historical forms of the eucharistic service ⟨Charlemagne introduced the Roman ~ throughout his territories⟩ **2 :** a ceremonial act or action or series of such acts esp. in established religious usage, in tribal custom, or occas. in bizarre practices or unduly formalized conduct in ordinary life ⟨~ of baptism⟩ ⟨~*s* of a fraternal organization⟩ ⟨at puberty, initiation ~*s* are held —*African Abstracts*⟩ ⟨woman engaged in the ~*s* of good grooming —Agnes Rogers⟩ ⟨making an apologetic ~ of pulling up his trousers and stuffing in his shirt —Richard Llewellyn⟩ — see RITE OF INTENSIFICATION, RITE OF PASSAGE **3** *sometimes cap* **:** a division of the Christian church as determined by liturgy ⟨Eastern Orthodox of the Byzantine ~⟩ ⟨Protestants of the Anglican ~⟩ — see LATIN RITE **syn** see FORM

**²ri·te** \'rīd·ē, -ī,tē\ *adv (or adj)* [NL, fr. L, in accordance with religious usage, fitly, aptly; akin to L *ritus* rite] **:** with a pass — used as a mark of undistinguished achievement in the academic requirements for graduation

**rite de pas·sage** \ˌrētdәpә'säzh\ [F] **:** RITE OF PASSAGE

**rite·less** \'rītlәs\ *adj* **:** lacking a rite **:** devoid of ceremony

**rite·less·ness** *n* -ES **:** the state of being riteless

**ritely** *adv, obs* **:** according to rite or ritual **:** DULY

**riten** *abbr* ritenuto

**ri·te·nen·te** \ˌrēd·ә'nentē, -en·(ˌ)tā\ *adv (or adj)* [It, fr. L *retinent-, retinens*, pres. part. of *retinēre* to hold back, detain, restrain, retain — more at RETAIN] **:** RITARDANDO — used as a direction in music

**ri·te·nu·to** \ˌrēd·ә'nü(ˌ)tō\ *adj* [It, past part. of *ritenere* to hold back, detain, restrain, retain, fr. L *retinēre*] **:** held back in tempo — used as a direction in music usu. indicating an abrupt slowing down

**rite of intensification :** a ritualistic procedure associated with periodic events or seasonal crises affecting a societal group as a whole

**rite of passage :** a ritualistic procedure associated with a nonperiodic crisis or a transitional change of status for an individual (as initiation, marriage, illness, or death)

**rithe** \'rīth\ *n* -S [ME, fr. OE *rith, rīthe* — more at RILL] *dial Eng* **:** a small stream **:** RUNNEL, RIVULET ⟨in the channels and ~*s* of Colchester Harbor —Alan Moore⟩

**rit·ling** \'ritlәn\ *var of* RECKLING

**ri·tor·nel·lo** \ˌrid·әr'ne(ˌ)lō, ˌri,tȯr'n- *or* **ri·tor·nelle** *or* **ri·tor·nel** \¦=(ˌ)=¦nel\ *n, pl* **ritornelli** *or* **ritornellos** *or* **ritornelles** *or* **ritornels** [It *ritornello*, dim. of *ritorno* return, fr. *ritornare* to return, fr. *ri-* re- (fr. L *re-*) + *tornare* to turn, return, fr. L, to turn in a lathe — more at TURN] **1 a :** a short instrumental passage in a vocal musical composition often consisting of a burden or refrain **b :** an instrumental interlude between the parts of an opera **2 :** a tutti passage in a concerto **3 :** the last two lines of a 14th century madrigal serving as a concluding passage or section

**¹ritsch·li·an** \'richlēәn\ *adj, usu cap* [Albrecht *Ritschl* †1889 Ger. theologian + E *-ian*] **:** of, relating to, or in accordance with the theological principles of Ritschl who rejected the metaphysical development of theology emphasizing its ethical-social content and held that religious judgments are judgments of value and that Christian theology should rest mainly on an appreciation of the inner life of Christ

**²ritschlian** \"\ *n* -S *usu cap* **:** an advocate of Ritschlian views

**ritsch·li·an·ism** \-ēә,nizәm\ *n* -S *usu cap* **:** Ritschlian theological views and principles

**ri·tsu** \'rit(ˌ)sü, 'rēt-\ *n* -S [Jap, lit., law, moral law] **:** a Hinayana Buddhist school founded in Japan in A.D. 754

**rit·ter** \'rid·ә(r)\ *n, pl* **ritter** *or* **ritters** [G, fr. MHG *riter*, fr. MD *riddere, ridder* horseman, knight, prob. alter. (influenced by an assumed n. akin to OE *ridda* horseman, fr. the stem of *rīdan* to ride) of *ridere, rider*, fr. *riden* to ride + *-ere*, *-er* -er; akin to OE *rīdan* to ride — more at RIDE] **:** KNIGHT; *specif* **:** a member of one of the lowest orders of German or Austrian nobility

**ritt·master** *or* **rit·master** \'rit+,-\ *n* [part trans. of G *rittmeister*, fr. *ritt* troop of horsemen (fr. *reiten* to ride, fr. OHG *rītan*) + *meister* master — more at RIDE] *archaic* **:** a captain of cavalry

**¹rit·u·al** \'rich(ә)wәl, -chәl\ *adj* [L *ritualis*, fr. *ritus* rite + *-alis* -al — more at RITE] **:** of, relating to, or employed in rites or a ritual **:** forming a ritual **:** CEREMONIAL ⟨a ~ dance of Haiti —Nicolas Slonimsky⟩ ⟨the kind of material and the kind of knot have great ~ importance —N.F.Busch⟩ ⟨relatives and most ardent disciples, paying their ~ calls —*Time*⟩ ⟨our favorite ~ phrases —James Blish⟩ ⟨sedate little colonial tribe, with its ~ tea parties and tennis parties —Nadine Gordimer⟩

**²ritual** \"\ *n* -S **1 :** the forms of conducting a devotional service esp. as established by tradition or by sacerdotal prescription **:** the prescribed order and words of a religious ceremony ⟨the rain ~ is simple —M.A.Jaspan⟩ ⟨thus the religion becomes more and more of an empty ~ —C.W.Thayer⟩ **2 a :** a code or system of rites (as of a fraternal society) ⟨the opposition party is compelled by parliamentary ~ to vote no —V.O.Key⟩ **b :** any practice done or regularly repeated in a set precise manner so as to satisfy one's sense of fitness and often felt to have a symbolic or quasi-symbolic significance ⟨busy among her pots and pans, making a ~ of her household duties —W.S.Maugham⟩ ⟨essential to reach a cave round the next headland where she would sit down facing the sea before she thought about anything — thus making a little ~ against despair —Audrey Barker⟩ **3 a :** a book containing the rites or ceremonial forms to be observed by an organization (as a church or fraternal society) **b :** the verbal formulas of ritual **4 :** an act of ritual ⟨to take your girl to the flicks on Saturday night is a ~ —John Berger⟩ ⟨the neurotic is isolated by his very ~*s* —David Riesman⟩ ⟨the elaborate ~*s* of present-day medicine —*Jour. Amer. Med. Assoc.*⟩ **syn** see FORM

**rit·u·al·ism** \-ә,lizәm\ *n* -S **1 :** a conducting of religious worship according to a ritual **:** the use of ritual **2 :** adherence to or observance of a ritual or ritualistic forms; *often* **:** excessive devotion to prescribed ritual forms in worship **3 :** the study of ritual and its use

**rit·u·al·ist** \-әlәst\ *n* -S **1 :** one skilled in or attached to a ritual **:** one who studies ritual **2 a :** one who advocates or practices the increased use of religious ritual esp. to an extent often deemed excessive by others **b** *usu cap* **:** a member of the High Church party in the Anglican communion **3 :** one rigidly conforming to established procedures or institutional norms ⟨the syndrome of the social ~ —R.K.Merton⟩ ⟨like a trout fisherman he is a fanatical ~ —Bernard DeVoto⟩

**rit·u·al·is·tic** \ˌrich(ə)wəˈlistik, -chəˈl-, -tēk\ *adj* **1 :** of, in accordance with, or characterized by the use of ritual ⟨~ work of a lodge⟩ **2 :** stressing the use of ritual forms **:** adhering to or devoted to ritualism ⟨a feudal or ~ society —Michael Polanyi⟩ — **rit·u·al·is·ti·cal·ly** \-tək(ə)lē, -tēk-, -li\ *adv*

**rit·u·al·i·ty** \(ˌ)rich(ə)ˈwalədē\ *n* -ES **:** ritual quality **:** RITUALISM ⟨openings, seasons, closings, all accomplished with majestic ~ —Arnold Gifford⟩

**rit·u·al·iza·tion** \ˌrich(ə)wələˈzāshən, -chəl-, -ˌlīˈz-\ *n* -S **:** the act of ritualizing **:** the condition of being ritualized

**rit·u·al·ize** \ˈ⸗(⸗)⸗ˌlīz\ *vb* -ED/-ING/-S *see -ize in Explan Notes*, *vi* **:** to practice ritualism ~ *vt* **1 :** to make a ritual of ⟨the *ritualized* spectacle of a bullfight —Wallace Stegner⟩ **2 :** to impose a ritual upon ⟨a highly *ritualized* society —Ernest Beaglehole⟩

**rit·u·al·less** \ˈrich(ə)wəl(l)əs, -chəl-\ *adj* **:** devoid of ritual **:** lacking a ritual

**rit·u·al·ly** \-chəlē, -ch(ə)wəlē, -li\ *adv* **:** by rites or by a particular rite **:** by or according to a ritual **:** as a ritual

**ritual murder** *n* **:** the sacrificial slaying of a human as a propitiatory offering to a deity

**rit·wan** \ˈritwən\ *n, pl* **ritwan** *or* **ritwans** *usu cap* **1 :** a language stock of northern California comprising Wiyot and Yurok and possibly related to Algonquian — see WEITSPEKAN, WISHOSKAN **2 a :** the peoples speaking Ritwan languages **b :** a member of any such peoples

**¹ritz** \ˈrits\ *vt* -ED/-ING/-ES [fr. the *Ritz* hotels] *slang* **:** to behave superciliously toward **:** SNUB

**²ritz** \"\ *n* -ES [fr. the *Ritz* hotels] *slang* **:** ostentatious display — used in the phrase *put on the ritz*

**ritz·i·ly** \-tsəlē, -li\ *adv* **:** in a ritzy manner

**ritz·i·ness** \-tsēnəs, -tsin-\ *n* -ES **:** the condition of being ritzy **:** OSTENTATION

**ritzy** \-sē, -si\ *adj* -ER/-EST [*Ritz* hotels (esp. the *Ritz-Carlton* in New York City) founded by César *Ritz* †1918 Swiss entrepreneur + E *-y*] **1 :** ostentatiously smart in appearance or manner **:** ULTRAFASHIONABLE ⟨winter visitors pay $30 a night at ~ hotels —*Nat'l Geographic*⟩ **2 :** HAUGHTY, SNOBBISH

**rivage** \ˈrivij, ˈriv-\ *n* -S [ME, fr. MF, fr. *rive* bank, shore (fr. L *ripa*) + *-age* — more at RIVE] **1** *archaic* **:** SHORE, COAST, BANK **2** *old Eng law* **:** a duty paid to the crown for the passage of ships on various rivers

**ri·vage green** \rəˈväzh-\ *n* **:** a moderate yellow green to light yellowish green

**¹ri·val** \ˈrīvəl\ *n* -S [MF or L; MF, fr. L *rivalis* one having water rights to the same stream as another, rival in love, fr. *rivalis*, adj., of a brook or stream, fr. *rivus* brook, stream + *-alis* -al — more at RISE] **1 a :** one of two or more striving for what only one can possess ⟨~*s* for the throne⟩ **b :** one striving for competitive advantage ⟨~*s* in business⟩ **2** *obs* **:** ASSOCIATE, COMPANION ⟨the ~*s* of my watch —Shak.⟩ **3 :** one that equals another in the possession of desired qualities or aptitudes **:** PEER ⟨fir is a ~ of pine⟩ ⟨was easily Carson's ~ as a pistol shot —Willa Cather⟩

**²rival** \"\ *adj* **:** having the same pretensions or claims **:** COMPETING, CONTESTING ⟨problem of the ~ claims of sense and reason —Benjamin Farrington⟩ ⟨a world where ~ propagandists are perpetually blazing falsehoods at us —Bertrand Russell⟩ ⟨tried to make myself persona grata to ~ factions —V.G.Heiser⟩ ⟨~ labor unions⟩

**³rival** \"\ *vb* **rivaled** *or* **rivalled**; **rivaled** *or* **rivalled**; **rivaling** *or* **rivalling** \-v(ə)liŋ\ **rivals** *vi* **1 :** to act as a rival **:** COMPETE ⟨friends ~*ing* in good deeds⟩ ~ *vt* **1 :** to be in competition with **:** strive to gain some object in opposition to **2 :** to strive to equal or excel **:** EMULATE **3 :** to possess qualities or aptitudes that equal (those of another) ⟨such ancient glass as we have in our parish churches ~*s* any in the world —Ivor Bulmer-Thomas⟩ ⟨growing rich in a boom that ~*ed* the Yukon gold rush —*Amer. Guide Series: Mich.*⟩ **syn** see MATCH

**ri·val·i·ty** \rīˈvalədē\ *n* -ES [L *rivalitas*, fr. *rivalis* rival + *-itas* -ity — more at RIVAL] **:** RIVALRY

**ri·val·ize** \ˈrīvəˌlīz\ *vi* -ED/-ING/-S **:** to act as a rival ⟨her urge to ~ with menfolk in the things of the mind —Frank Budgen⟩

**ri·val·less** \-vəl(l)əs\ *adj* **:** being without a rival

**ri·val·rous** \-vəlrəs\ *adj* [*rivalry* + *-ous*] **:** given to rivalry **:** COMPETITIVE ⟨ascendant, expansive, and ~ students —F.H. Allport⟩ ⟨one of the leading families has shown a ~ attitude toward the others —M.C.Yang⟩ — **ri·val·rous·ness** *n* -ES

**ri·val·ry** \ˈrīvəlrē, -lri\ *n* -ES [¹*rival* + *-ry*] **1 :** the act of rivaling **:** the state of being a rival **:** COMPETITION ⟨sibling ~ in our society —Weston LaBarre⟩ ⟨~ and even antagonism between the two nations —Edward Shils⟩ ⟨excitable subjects are prone to overstimulation through ~ —F.H.Allport⟩ **2 :** an instance of rivalry ⟨public reaction to the *rivalries* of the court factions —Evelyn G. Cruickshanks⟩ **3 :** RETINAL RIVALRY

**ri·val·ship** \-l,ship\ *n* -S **:** RIVALRY

**¹rive** \ˈrīv\ *vb* **rived** \ˈrīvd\ *also* **rove** \ˈrōv\ **riv·en** \ˈrivən\ *also* **rived** \ˈrīvd\ **riv·ing** \ˈrīviŋ\ **rives** \ˈrīvz\ [ME *riven*, fr. ON *rīfa*; akin to OFris *rīva* to tear, rend, L *ripa* bank, shore, Gk *ereipein* to dash down, tear down, OE *rāw* row — more at ROW] *vt* **1 a :** to wrench open or tear apart or to pieces ⟨great gray masses of cloud, *riven* by the hurricane —William Black⟩ **b :** to split or break up by or as if by a sharp instrument **:** CLEAVE, SEVER ⟨new highways *riving* the green —Donald Davidson⟩ **c :** to break or crack by or as if by a shock or impact **:** BURST ⟨*riven* pinnacles of stone gnawed by the waves into bizarre shapes —Norman Douglas⟩ **d :** PIERCE ⟨not dug by the hand of man, these tunnels, but *riven* by nature —I.L.Idriess⟩ **e** (1) **:** to divide into many pieces or factions **:** SHATTER ⟨were *riven* with fears and alarms about subversion at home —Reinhold Niebuhr⟩ ⟨the union is *riven* with discord —Earl Brown⟩ ⟨bellows of triumph ~ the night —H.H.Martin⟩ (2) **:** FRACTURE ⟨a country so often *riven* by earthquakes —G.B.Sansom⟩ ⟨detrital beds . . . *riven* by a series of faults —*Amer. Guide Series: Md.*⟩; *specif* **:** to crack or break up by the alternate freezing and thawing of water contained in fissures ⟨where massive rock . . . is exposed in polar regions and on high mountain summits, frost *riving* is the dominant weathering process —O. D. Von Engeln⟩ ⟨brecciated bedrock, perhaps largely frost-*riven* —*Jour. of Geol.*⟩ **2 a :** to wrench or tear away ⟨cloak *riven* from his back⟩ — often used with *off* or *away* ⟨bark of the trunk was *riven* off⟩ ⟨a few stout heaves *rived* off the upper part of the lid —Harvey Graham⟩ **b :** to pull or tear down or out ⟨storms . . . that ~ the trunks of tallest cedars down —Thomas Otway⟩ **c :** to split off ⟨huge rocks, *riven* by frost action from the side of the mountain —*Amer. Guide Series: N. H.*⟩ **3 :** to affect (as the heart or soul) with painful thoughts **:** stir by strong emotion ⟨all thoughts to ~ the heart are here —A.E.Housman⟩ ⟨his soul does not appear to have been *riven* by a consciousness of sin —H.O.Taylor⟩ ⟨a sudden craving *rived* him to be working again —Richard Llewellyn⟩ ⟨was plainly *riven* by anger —T.R.Fyvel⟩ **4 :** to make or form (as laths or boards) by splitting ⟨hand-*riven* shingles⟩ ⟨*rived* staves⟩ — often used with *out* ⟨went to work on those old cypress logs, sawing, chopping, hewing, and *riving* out boards to cover the house —Marjory S. Douglas⟩ **5** *Scot* **:** PLOW 1 ~ *vi* **1 :** to become split **:** CRACK ⟨the oak . . . *riving* and splitting round about the passage of the bullet —Thomas Fuller⟩ **2 :** to break esp. with sorrow **:** BURST ⟨he prays you as his heart would ~ . . . to save his dear son's soul alive —D.G.Rossetti⟩ **syn** see TEAR

**²rive** \ˈrīv\ *n* -S **1** *dial Eng* **:** PULL, TUG **2** *dial Eng* **:** CLEFT, RENT

**¹riv·el** \ˈrivəl\ *vb* **riveled** *or* **rivelled**; **riveled** *or* **rivelled**; **riveling** *or* **rivelling** \-v(ə)liŋ\ **rivels** [ME *rivelen*, fr. OE *gerifilian*; akin to LG *riffel* furrow, MD *riven* to rake, *rive* rake, OFris *rive* rake, ON *hrīfa* to rake, and prob. to OE *sceran* to cut, shear — more at SHEAR] **:** WRINKLE, SHRIVEL

**²rivel** \"\ *n* -S **:** WRINKLE

**¹riv·er** \ˈrivə(r)\ *n* -S *often attrib* [ME *rivere*, *river*, fr. OF *rivere*, *riviere* riverbank, land along a river, river, fr. (assumed) VL *riparia*, fr. L, fem. of *riparius* riparian, fr. *ripa* bank, shore + *-arius* -ary — more at RIVE] **1 a :** a natural surface stream of water of considerable volume and permanent or seasonal flow ⟨~ channel⟩ ⟨~ gravel⟩ ⟨~ engineer⟩ — compare BROOK, CREEK **b :** WATERCOURSE ⟨dry ~⟩ ⟨underground ~⟩ **c :** ESTUARY, TIDAL RIVER ⟨York *River*, Va.⟩ ⟨Neponset *River*, Mass.⟩; *also* **:** INLET, STRAIT ⟨East *River*, N.Y.⟩ ⟨Sakonnet *River*, R.I.⟩ ⟨Indian *River*, Fla.⟩ **2 a :** something resembling a river ⟨~ of ice⟩ ⟨~ of air⟩ ⟨~*s* of lava glow an angry red —*Read Mag.*⟩ ⟨the enormous oceanic ~ of the Gulf Stream —Marjory S. Douglas⟩ ⟨costumes . . . made a rippling, many-colored ~ of the street —H.A.Sinclair⟩ ⟨the never-failing ~ of student life —J.B.Conant⟩ **b rivers** *pl* **:** copious flow **:** large or overwhelming quantities **:** OUTPOURING ⟨~*s* of birds pouring against the sunset back to the rookeries —Marjory S. Douglas⟩ ⟨rain, pouring down through the blackness in solid ~*s* —C.S.Forester⟩ ⟨~*s* of print that gushed forth about her —Mollie Panter-Downes⟩ ⟨drank ~*s* of coffee⟩ **3 :** a pure-white diamond of very high grade occas. with a prismatic blue radiance **4 :** a white typically irregular streak or area running through several lines of close-set printed matter and caused by a series of wide spaces that appear to form a continuous line — called also *channel*, *gutter*, *staircase* — **down the river** *adv (or adj)* **:** into a less desirable situation than formerly **:** in an abandoned and inconsiderate manner **:** with damage to prestige, reputation, or status — used with *sell* — **up the river** *adv (or adj)* **:** to or in prison ⟨takes the rap and goes *up the river* —Nigel Balchin⟩

**²riv·er** \ˈrīvə(r)\ *n* -S [ME, one that rives, fr. *riven* to rive + *-er* — more at RIVE] **:** one that rives; *specif* **:** a worker who splits blocks of wood with a froe to make pickets, posts, or rails

**¹riv·er·ain** \ˈrivəˌrān, ˌ⸗⸗ˈ⸗\ *adj* [F, fr. MF *riverain*, fr. *rivere*, *riviere* river — more at RIVER] **:** relating to a riverbank **:** situated or dwelling near or on a river **:** RIPARIAN ⟨wooded ~ districts —Cuthbert Christy⟩ ⟨~ tribes⟩ ⟨an immemorial ~ right —Eliot Gregory⟩

**²riverain** \"\ *n* -S [F, fr. *riverain*, adj.] **:** a district situated beside a river

**river ash** *n* **:** RED ASH 1a

**riverbank** \ˈ⸗⸗ˌ⸗\ *n* **:** the bank of a river

**riverbank grape** *n* **:** a wild grape (*Vitis riparia*) abundant along riverbanks in the eastern U.S. and characterized by high climbing stems and acid blackish fruit

**riverbank willow** *n* **:** SANDBAR WILLOW a

**river basin** *n* **:** BASIN 3d

**riverbed** \ˈ⸗⸗ˌ⸗\ *n* **:** the channel occupied or formerly occupied by a river

**river birch** *n* **1 :** an American birch (*Betula nigra*) having reddish brown bark and growing in swamps and river bottoms throughout the eastern U.S. **2 :** the hard close-grained brownish wood of the river birch tree **3 :** SWEET BIRCH

**river blackfish** *n* **:** a medium-sized food fish (*Gadopsis marmoratus*) of the Murray river system of Australia noted for its rich oily flesh

**river black oak** *n* **:** an Australian beefwood (*Casuarina suberosa*)

**river blue** *n* **:** a grayish blue to moderate greenish blue

**riverboat** \ˈ⸗⸗ˌ⸗\ *n* **:** a boat (as a towboat, a barge, a shallow-draft passenger boat, or a rowboat) used on or plying a river

**riv·er·boat·man** \-mən\ *n, pl* **riverboatmen 1 :** the navigator of a riverboat **2 :** one employed on a riverboat

**river bottom** *n* **:** low-lying land along a river

**river bottom disease** *n* **:** INFECTIOUS ANEMIA

**river brethren** *n pl, usu cap R&B* [fr. the Susquehanna *river*, near which the denomination was formed] **:** members of a body of Christians formed about 1770 in Pennsylvania among Swiss and German immigrants, resembling the Mennonites in doctrines and practices, and now divided into the Brethren in Christ, the Yorker Brethren, and the United Zion Church

**river bulrush** *or* **river club rush** *n* **:** a stout perennial herb (*Scirpus fluviatilis*) with numerous spikelets in a large terminal umbel

**riverbush** \ˈ⸗⸗ˌ⸗\ *n* **:** BUTTONBUSH

**river carpsucker** *n* **:** a carpsucker (*Carpiodes carpio*)

**river chub** *n* **:** HORNYHEAD CHUB

**river coal** *n* **:** coal dredged from riverbeds downstream from mining areas whence it has been washed

**river cottonwood** *n* **:** SWAMP COTTONWOOD

**river crab** *n* **1 :** a freshwater crab of the family Potamonidae; *esp* **:** a common crab (*Potamon fluviatile*) of flowing waters of southern Europe **2 :** a Central American grapsid crab (*Platychirograpsus typicus*) living in burrows along riverbanks

**rivercraft** \ˈ⸗⸗ˌ⸗\ *n* **:** RIVERBOAT

**river crawfish** *n* **:** a crayfish living chiefly in rivers; *esp* **:** a small white crayfish (*Cambarus blandingi*) of the southeastern U.S.

**river cress** *n* **:** LAKE CRESS

**river deer** *n* **:** a small deer (*Hydropotes inermis*) of the river marshes in southern China the males of which have no antlers but are provided with tusklike canine teeth

**river dog** *n* **:** HELLBENDER 1a

**river dolphin** *n* **:** any of several So. American and Asiatic long-snouted dolphins (family Platanistidae) of medium size that are chiefly confined to freshwater

**river driver** *n* **:** one who drives logs on a river

**river duck** *n* **:** any of various rather small ducks chiefly of the genus *Anas* that typically nest and live about freshwater and usu. feed by dabbling

**riv·ered** \ˈrivə(r)d\ *adj* [¹*river* + *-ed*] **:** supplied with rivers ⟨such dew as only ~ lands beget —Eileen Duggan⟩

**riveret** *n* -S [MF *riverete*, dim. of *rivere*, *riviere* river — more at RIVER] *obs* **:** RIVULET

**riverfront** \ˈ⸗⸗ˌ⸗\ *n* **:** the land or area along a river; *esp* **:** an area (as in a city) devoted to business done on the river

**river-god** \ˈ⸗⸗ˌ⸗\ *n* **:** a deity supposed to preside over a river as its tutelary divinity

**river grape** *n* **:** CHICKEN GRAPE

**river grass** *n* **:** TEXAS MILLET

**river gum** *n* **:** an often somewhat crooked and irregular Australian red gum (*Eucalyptus rostrata* or *E. camaldulensis*) that grows chiefly along rivers, has lanceolate leaves, and yields a durable reddish lumber used in heavy construction

**riverhead** \ˈ⸗⸗ˌ⸗\ *n* **:** the source of a river

**river hog** *n* **:** any of several stream-frequenting African wild hogs constituting the genus *Koiropotamus* — compare BUSHPIG, PAINTED PIG

**river horse** *n* **:** HIPPOPOTAMUS

**riv·er·ine** \ˈrivəˌrīn\ *adj* [¹*river* + *-ine*] **1 :** of, relating to, formed by, or resembling a river ⟨~ traffic⟩ ⟨~ gold-bearing deposits⟩ **2 :** living or situated on the banks of a river ⟨~ villages⟩ ⟨elephant feeding in the ~ thickets —*African Wild Life*⟩

**river jack** *n* **:** RHINOCEROS VIPER

**river lamprey** *n* **:** a river-dwelling lamprey; *esp* **:** LAMPERN

**riv·er·less** \ˈrivə(r)ləs\ *adj* **:** lacking a river

**riv·er·let** \ˈrivə(r)lət\ *n* -S [¹*river* + *-let*] **:** a little river

**riverlike** \ˈ⸗⸗ˌ⸗\ *adj* **:** resembling a river

**river limpet** *n* **:** FRESHWATER LIMPET

**river locust** *n* **:** a false indigo (*Amorpha fruticosa*)

**riv·er·ly** \ˈrivə(r)lē\ *adj* **:** RIVERINE ⟨rivers . . . go about their ~ business of flowing into the seas —*Lamp*⟩

**riv·er·man** \-)mən\ *n, pl* **rivermen 1 :** one who lives and works on or along a river **2 :** RIVER DRIVER **3 a :** a deckhand on a riverboat

**river mangrove** *n* **:** an Old World tropical tree (*Aegiceras majus*) of the family Myrsinaceae having the habit of a mangrove

**river maple** *n* **:** SILVER MAPLE

**river mussel** *n* **:** MUSSEL 2

**river novel** *n* [trans. of F *roman-fleuve*] **:** ROMAN-FLEUVE

**river oak** *n, Austral* **:** SHE-OAK

**river pear** *n* **:** ANCHOVY PEAR

**river peppermint** *n* **:** a medium-sized fast-growing peppermint gum (*Eucalyptus lindleyana*) that grows chiefly along water-courses

**river perch** *n* **:** YELLOW PERCH

**river pine** *n* **:** JERSEY PINE

**river pink** *n* **:** PINXTER FLOWER

**river poplar** *n* **:** BALSAM POPLAR

**river prawn** *n* **:** a large edible freshwater prawn (*Palaemon australis*) common in Australian rivers where it may reach a length of a foot or more — called also *long-clawed prawn*

**river rat** *n* **1 :** RIVERMAN 1 **2 :** one who spends his leisure time on or along a river

**river red gum** *n* **:** RIVER GUM

**river rock** *n* **:** a dark variety of phosphate rock obtained from stream beds

**rivers** *pl of* RIVER

**river shad** *n* **:** a shad that spawns in one of the streams of the Mississippi drainage and is prob. identical with the common American shad (*Alosa sapidissima*) but is sometimes considered a distinct species (*A. chrysochloris*)

**river shark** *n* **:** a small but ferocious shark (*Carcharinus lamia*) of tropical coastal waters and rivers

**rivershed** \ˈ⸗⸗ˌ⸗\ *n* **:** the watershed of a river

**river shrew** *n* **:** OTTER SHREW

**river shrimp** *n* **:** a common commercial freshwater shrimp (*Macrobrachium ohionis*) of the southeastern U.S.

**riverside** \ˈ⸗⸗ˌ⸗\ *n* [ME, fr. *river* + *side*] **:** the side or bank of a river **:** RIVERFRONT ⟨the ~*s* had been only partly drained —D.R.Macgregor⟩

**riverside grape** *n* **1 :** CHICKEN GRAPE **2 :** RIVERBANK GRAPE

**riverside tobacco** *n* **:** WILD TOBACCO 3

**river tern** *n* **:** a tern (*Sterna aurantia*) of India that frequents rivers

**river terrace** *n* **:** STREAM TERRACE

**river trout** *n* **1 :** a small brownish green trout that is a variety of the European brown trout **2 :** WALLEYE 4

**riv·er·ward** \ˈrivə(r)wə(r)d\ *or* **riv·er·wards** \-dz\ *adv (or adj)* [¹*river* + *-ward*, *-wards*] **:** toward a river ⟨door on the ~ side —D.C.Peattie⟩

**riverwash** \ˈ⸗⸗ˌ⸗\ *n* **:** soil material transported and deposited by streams

**riverway** \ˈ⸗⸗ˌ⸗\ *n* **:** a river used to convey traffic ⟨battled up the ~*s* of the unhappy land —John Craig⟩

**riverweed** \ˈ⸗⸗ˌ⸗\ *n* **:** a plant of the genus *Podostemon*

**riverweed family** *n* **:** PODOSTEMONACEAE

**riv·ery** \ˈriv(ə)rē, -)ri\ *adj* **1 :** having many streams of water ⟨amid the thresh of weirs in the ~ lands —Louis Golding⟩ **2 :** of, relating to, or resembling a river ⟨a ~ field spread out below —W.B.Yeats⟩ ⟨~ pleasures —*Times Lit. Supp.*⟩

**rives** *pres 3d sing of* RIVE, *pl of* RIVE

**¹riv·et** \ˈrivət, *usu* -əd·+V\ *n* -S [ME *ryvette*, *revette*, fr. MF *river* to be attached] **:** a headed pin or bolt of some malleable material (as wrought iron, mild steel, or copper) used for uniting two or more pieces by passing the shank through a hole in each piece and then beating or pressing down the plain end so as to make a second head

rivets: *1* steeple-head, *2* button-head, *3* countersunk, *4* conehead

**²rivet** \"\ *vt* **riveted** *also* **rivetted**; **riveted** *also* **rivetted**; **riveting** *also* **rivetting**; **rivets** [ME *rivetten*, *reveten*, fr. *ryvette*, *revette*, n.] **1 :** to fasten with or as if with rivets ⟨~ two pieces of iron⟩ ⟨copper ~*ing* for pants —*Fortnight*⟩ ⟨could not drink tea from ~*ed* china —Elizabeth Taylor⟩ **2 :** to upset the end or point of (as a metallic pin, rod, or bolt) by beating or pressing so as to form a head **:** PEEN **3 :** to fasten firmly **:** make firm, strong, or immovable **:** fix closely (as the eye, gaze, or mind) ⟨made abundant gifts to ~ this fealty —Bernard DeVoto⟩ ⟨stood ~*ed* to the earth . . . in the fascination of that dreaded gaze —Sheridan Le Fanu⟩ ⟨reporters' attention was temporarily ~*ed* on some pelicans —Percy Sillitoe⟩ **4 :** to attract and hold engrossingly (as the attention) ⟨another part of the room soon ~*ed* her gaze —Thomas Hardy⟩

**rivet buster** *n* **:** a tool that resembles a chisel and is used for knocking off rivet heads

**riv·et·er** *also* **riv·et·ter** \-əd·ə(r), -ətə-\ *n* -S **1 :** a worker who inserts and upsets rivets by hand or by machine **2 :** a riveting machine

**rivet forge** *or* **riveting forge** *also* **rivet hearth** *n* **:** a forge for heating rivets

**rivet heater** *n* **1 :** RIVET FORGE **2 :** a worker who heats rivets in a rivet forge

**rivet hole** *n* **:** the drilled or punched hole in which a rivet is to be inserted

**riveting** *n* -S [¹*rivet* + *-ing*] **1 :** the act of one who rivets **2 :** the work of a riveter **3 :** a set of rivets

**riveting die** *n* **:** SETTING PUNCH

**riveting hammer** *n* **:** a hammer usu. with a feat face and cross peen used for driving rivets and beating metal

**riveting stake** *n* **:** a block of steel used in watchmaking that is pierced with holes for the reception of arbors so that the pinion or collet to be riveted finds a resting place round the edge of a suitable hole

**rivet knob** *or* **riveting knob** *n* **:** SETTING PUNCH

**riv·et·less** \-ətləs\ *adj* **:** made without rivets

**rivet line** *n* **:** a line through the centers of a row of rivets

**rivet pitch** *n* **:** the distance between the centers of adjacent rivets that hold together the parts of a built member

**rivet set** *or* **riveting set** *n* **:** SETTING PUNCH

**rivet snap** *n* **:** SNAP 11a

**rivet weld** *n* **:** a weld having the form of a countersunk-head rivet and serving as a rivet

**rivet wheat** *n* **:** POULARD WHEAT

**ri·vi·era** \ˌrivēˈerə, rəvˈye-, ˌrēvˈye-\ *n* -S *often cap* [fr. the *Riviera*, region much frequented as a resort area on the Mediterranean in southeastern France and northwestern Italy] **:** a coastline much frequented as a resort area and usu. having a mild climate ⟨the Cornish *Riviera*⟩ ⟨other men were living riotously on ~*s* —Clare & Harris Wofford⟩

**ri·vi·ère** \ˌrivēˈe(ə)r, rəvˈye-, ˌrēvˈye-\ *n* -S [F, lit., river, fr. OF *rivere*, *riviere* riverbank, land along a river, river — more at RIVER] **:** a necklace of diamonds or other precious stones

**ri·vi·na** \rəˈvīnə, -vēnə\ *n, cap* [NL, after August Q. *Rivinus* (Bachmann) †1723 Ger. botanist and physiologist] **:** a small genus of tropical American herbs (family Phytolaccaceae) having small racemose pink flowers succeeded by flattened red berries — see BLOODBERRY

**riving** *pres part of* RIVE

**riving knife** *n* **:** FROE

**riving machine** *n* **:** a machine for splitting wood (as for making staves or shingles)

**rivo** *interj* [prob. modif. of Sp *arriba* up, up with (often used in interjectional phrases), fr. *a* to (fr. L *ad*) + *riba* slope, embankment, fr. L *ripa* bank, shore — more at AT, RIVE] *obs* — used as an encouragement to drink and be merry

**riv·ol·ta·sia** \ˌrivəlˈtāzh(ē)ə\ *n, cap* [NL] **:** a genus of mites that occur on the skin and feathers of birds

**riv·u·lar·ia** \ˌrivyəˈla(a)rēə\ *n, cap* [NL, fr. L *rivulus* rivulet + NL *-aria* — more at RIVULET] **:** a genus (the type of the family Rivulariaceae) of blue-green algae with radially arranged filaments exhibiting false branching and forming spherical to irregular somewhat gelatinous colonies

**riv·u·lar·i·a·ce·ae** \ˌ⸗⸗ˌ⸗⸗ˈāsēˌē\ *n pl, cap* [NL, fr. *Rivularia*, type genus + *-aceae*] **:** a family of freshwater blue-green algae (order Hormogonales) consisting of slender gradually attenuated or hair-tipped filaments usu. growing in tufts attached to the substrate and frequently mucilaginous — see CALOTHRIX, RIVULARIA — **riv·u·lar·i·a·ceous** \ˌ⸗⸗ˌ⸗⸗ˈāshəs\ *adj*

**riv·u·let** \ˈrivyələt, *usu* -əd·+V\ *n* -S [modif. (influenced by L *rivulus* rivulet) of It *rivoletto*, dim. of *rivolo*, fr. L *rivulus*, dim. of *rivus* brook, stream — more at RISE] **:** a small stream **:** BROOK, RUNNEL, STREAMLET ⟨rills running down the steepest slopes develop into ~*s* —C.A.Cotton⟩ ⟨~*s* of melted snow coursing along the ruts —F.V.W.Mason⟩ ⟨~*s* of perspiration ran down their flushed cheeks —Kenneth Roberts⟩

**riv·u·lose** \ˈrivyəˌlōs\ *adj* [L *rivulus* rivulet + E *-ose*] **:** marked with irregular, narrow, sinuous, or crooked lines ⟨a ~ thallus⟩

**riv·u·lus** \-ləs\ *n, cap* [NL, fr. L, rivulet — more at RIVULET] **:** a large genus of brightly colored but often sluggish So. and Central American killifishes several species of which are sometimes kept in a tropical aquarium

**rix** \ˈriks\ *dial var of* ¹RUSH 1a

**rix·da·ler** \ˈriksˌdälə(r)\ *n* [fr. obs. D *rijksdaler* — more at RIJKSDAALER] **:** RIJKSDAALER

**rix-dollar** \"\ *n* [part trans. of obs. D *rijksdaler*] **1 :** any of various old dollar coins of Germany, the Netherlands, or Scandinavia **:** REICHSTALER, RIGSDALER, RIKSDALER, RIJKSDAALDER **2 :** any of several silver coins formerly issued by England for colonies (as Ceylon, Cape Colony) **3 :** RIJKSDAALDER 2
**rixy** \'riksī\ *n, pl* **rix·ies** [origin unknown] *dial Eng* **:** TERN
**ri·yadh** \rē'(y)äd\ *adj, usu cap* [fr. *Riyadh*, Saudi Arabia] **:** of or from Riyadh, a capital of Saudi Arabia **:** of the kind or style prevalent in Riyadh
**ri·yal** *or* **ri·al** \rē'(y)ōl, -)äl\ *n, pl* **riyal** *or* **riyals** *or* **rial** *or* **rials** [Ar *riyāl*, fr. Sp *real* — more at REAL (coin)] **1 :** a silver coin of Saudi Arabia equivalent to $\frac{1}{10}$ pound sterling when first issued in 1928 — see MONEY table **2 :** MARIA THERESA DOLLAR **3 :** a coin of Iraq equivalent to $\frac{1}{5}$ dinar
**riz** *dial past of* RISE
**ri·zal day** \rə'zäl-, rē'säl-\ *n, usu cap R&D* [after José *Rizal* †1896 Philippine patriot] **:** December 30, observed as a legal holiday in the Philippines in commemoration of the death of the Filipino patriot José Rizal in 1896
**rizotto** *var of* RISOTTO
**¹riz·zar** \'rizər\ *n* -S [prob. fr. obs. F *ressoré* dried in the sun] *Scot* **:** RED CURRANT
**²rizzar** \"\ *n* -S [prob. fr. obs. F *ressoré* dried in the sun] **1** *Scot* **:** the act or process of drying or curing in the sun **2** *Scot* **:** a dry haddock cured in the sun
**³rizzar** \"\ *vt* -ED/-ING/-S *Scot* **:** to dry or cure (fish) in the sun
**riz·zom** *var of* RISSOM
**RJ** *abbr* road junction
**rk** *abbr* rock
**RK** *abbr* run of kiln
**rkt** *abbr* rocket
**RKVA** *abbr, often not cap* reactive kilovolt-ampere
**rky** *abbr* rocky
**RL** *abbr* **1** radiolocation **2** *often not cap* random lengths **3** reduced level **4** rhumb line **5** right line **6** rocket launcher
**RL and R** *abbr* rail, lake, and rail
**r-less** \'ärləs, 'äl-\ *adj, of a dialect of English* **:** having with varying regularity as the speech counterpart of a prepausal or preconsonantal orthographic *r* the sound \ə\ or greater duration or nothing at all instead of the retroflex sound of some dialects
**RLF** *abbr* retrolental fibroplasia
**RLO** *abbr* returned letter office
**rls** *abbr* release
**rly** *abbr* railway
**rm** *abbr* **1** ream **2** room
**RM** *abbr* **1** radioman **2** reichsmark **3** resident magistrate **4** royal mail
**r-meter** \'är,mēd·ər\ *n* **:** an instrument or device for measuring the intensity of X rays or gamma radiation
**RMI** *abbr* radio magnetic indicator
**r month** *n, usu cap R* [so called fr. the fact that the letter *r* appears in the name of each month] **:** one of the months from September to April during which oysters are traditionally in season in the northern hemisphere
**RMS** *abbr* **1** railway mail service **2** *often not cap* root-mean-square **3** royal mail ship; royal mail steamer
**rmt** *abbr* remount
**RN** *abbr* **1** registered nurse **2** Reynolds number
**Rn** *symbol* radon
**RNA** *abbr or n* -S ribonucleic acid
**rnd** *abbr* round
**rng** *abbr* range
**rnwy** *abbr* runway
**ro** \'rō\ *n* -S *usu cap* [coined 1906 by Edward P. Foster †1937 Am. clergyman] **:** an artificial language intended to be international that rejects all existing words and roots and is based on analysis and classification of ideas — **ro·ist** \'rōəst\ *n* -S *usu cap*
**ro** *abbr* **1** recto **2** road **3** roan **4** rood **5** [F *rouble*] ruble
**RO** *abbr* **1** radar operator **2** receiving office **3** reconnaissance officer **4** recruiting officer **5** regimental order **6** royal observatory **7** royal octavo
**¹roach** \'rōch\ *n* -ES [ME *roche*, fr. OF, rock, fr. (assumed) VL *rocca* — more at ROCK] **1** *dial Eng* **:** a stony hill **:** ROCK **2 :** gravelly or stony soil **:** refuse stone
**²roach** \"\ *n, pl* **roach** *also* **roaches** [ME *roche*, fr. MF, fr. OF, of unknown origin] **1 a :** a silver-white European freshwater cyprinid fish (*Rutilus rutilus*) with a greenish back **b :** any of various other cyprinid fishes (as the No. American golden shiner) **2 :** any of several American freshwater sunfishes (family Centrarchidae) **3 :** SPOT 7
**³roach** \"\ *vt* -ED/-ING/-ES [origin unknown] **1 :** to cause to arch; *specif* **:** to brush (the hair) in a roach — often used with *up* **2 :** to cut off (as a horse's mane) so the part left stands upright **3 :** to cut (a sail) with a roach
**⁴roach** \"\ *n* -ES **1 :** a curved cut in the edge of a sail and esp. in the leech or foot to prevent chafing or to secure a better fit **2 :** a roll of hair brushed straight back from the forehead or occas. the side of the head **3 :** a sheet of water thrown upwards behind the float of a seaplane
**⁵roach** \"\ *n* -ES [short for *cockroach*] **1 :** COCKROACH **2 :** the butt of a marijuana cigarette
**roachback** \'ˌ=ˌ=\ *n* [³*roach* + *back*, n.] *West* **:** GRIZZLY BEAR
**roach back** \'=ˌ=\ *n* [³*roach* + *back*, n.] **:** an arched back
**¹road** \'rōd\ *n* -S [ME *rood*, *rode*, fr. OE *rād* ride, riding, journey; akin to MD *rede* ride, manner of riding, ON *reith* vehicle, riding; derivative fr. the root of OE *rīdan* to ride — more at RIDE] **1** *obs* **a** (1) **:** the act of riding on a horse (2) **:** a journey on horseback **b :** an armed hostile incursion on horseback against a person or place **:** FORAY, RAID **2 :** a place less sheltered or enclosed than a harbor where ships may ride at anchor — often used in pl. ⟨shipping lying in the ~*s* — Mary Johnston⟩ ⟨Hampton *Roads*, Virginia⟩; called also *roadstead* **3 a :** an open way or public passage for vehicles, persons, and animals **:** a track for travel or transportation to and fro serving as a means of communication between two places usu. having distinguishing names **b :** a public way outside of an urban district **:** HIGHWAY — contrasted with *street* **c :** the part of a thoroughfare over which vehicular traffic moves **:** the space between curbs **:** ROADWAY **d :** a vehicular way for local traffic: as (1) **:** a private way (2) **:** one that is unpaved (3) **:** one located in a rural area **e :** STREET, AVENUE — used esp. in arterial street names **4 a :** a route followed on a journey **:** WAY, PATH ⟨get out of my ~⟩ ⟨knew that the Arkansas river, with its tributaries . . . was the ~ to the southwest —*Amer. Guide Series: Ark.*⟩ **b :** the course or route to an end, conclusion, or circumstance ⟨the path of promotion lay through the schools rather than along the ~ of military service —R.W.Southern⟩ **5 :** public highways ⟨take to the ~⟩ **6 :** RAILROAD, RAILWAY **7 :** GANGWAY 4 **8 :** the places and routes frequented on a tour (as of a theatrical troupe or a sports team) ⟨community theater attempted to fill the need which the professional ~ either failed to meet or failed to find —W.C.Glackin⟩ — **for the road** *adv* **:** as a friendly gesture of farewell ⟨gave me a final glass *for the road* —T.H.White b.1906⟩ ⟨gave the passenger ship one more blast *for the road* —R.F.Mirvish⟩ — **on the road** *adv (or adj)* **1 :** away from home usu. in regular travel on business esp. as a traveling salesman **2 :** in transit through a circuit of scheduled performances or games in several centers ⟨a brief stage career *on the road*, in summer stock, and on Broadway —*Current Biog.*⟩ ⟨the team is *on the road*⟩ — **over the road** *adv* **:** to prison
**²road** *vt* -ED/-ING/-S **1** *of a dog* **:** to track (a game bird) by the foot scent **2 :** to put or drive onto or carry on a road
**road·abil·i·ty** \ˌrōdə'biləd-ē, -lətē, -i\ *n* [¹*road* + *-ability*] **:** the qualities (as steadiness, flexibility in speed, and balance) that are desirable in an automobile on the road
**road·able** \'rōdəbəl\ *adj* [¹*road* + *-able*] **1 :** capable of being driven along roads like an automobile usu. under power delivered to one or more wheels **2** *of an airplane* **:** capable of being transformed into an automobile by removal or folding of wings and tail
**road actor** *n* **:** a performer in a company playing only on the road
**road agent** *n* **:** a highwayman esp. on stage routes
**road band** *n* **:** a steel rim attached to steel tractor wheels to prevent damage to the road by the lugs on the tractor wheels
**roadbed** \'=ˌ=\ *n* **1 a :** the bed or foundation of a railroad on which the ties, rails, and ballast rest **b :** the ballast or the upper surface of the ballast on which the ties rest **2 a :** the earth foundation of a highway or street, graded and prepared for paving or surfacing **b :** the part of the surface of a highway or street traveled by vehicles
**¹roadblock** \'=ˌ=\ *n* **1 a :** a barricade (as of concrete, logs, boards, sandbags, barbed wire) often with traps or mines for holding up an enemy's advance at a point on the road covered by heavy fire from shelter **b :** a road barricade set up esp. by law enforcement officers **c :** an obstruction in a road caused by wrecked vehicles, fallen trees, landslides, or debris **2 :** a fact, condition, or countermeasure that blocks progress along a course or that prevents accomplishment of an objective ⟨the hope that something could be done to remove the ~ of the filibuster —P.H.Douglas⟩
**²roadblock** \"\ *vt* -ED/-ING/-S **:** to put a roadblock in the way of
**roadbook** \"\ *n* **:** a guidebook esp. devoted to routes and distances
**road brand** *n* **:** a lightly burned brand marked upon all the cattle of a herd driven beyond a county line when the herd is composed of cattle from various owners
**road breaker** *n* **:** a powered tool to break up road pavements
**road builder** *n* **:** one that builds roads
**road cart** *n* **:** a light 2-wheeled vehicle often with a back
**road coach** *n* **:** the stagecoach as revived in England during the last half of the 19th century
**road commissioner** *n* **:** a local or county official who supervises the construction of roads
**road donkey** *n* **:** a stationary donkey engine mounted on a sled for dragging logs along a skid road by a cable wound on a drum
**road drag** *n* **:** a drag for smoothing dirt roads with an unpacked surface
**road·ed** \'rōdəd\ *adj* **:** provided with roads
**road engine** *n* **:** a locomotive used in line-haul service — compare SWITCH ENGINE
**road·eo** \'rōdē,ō\ *n* -S [blend of ¹*road* and *rodeo*, n.] **:** a contest featuring events that test driving skill esp. of professional truck drivers
**road·er** \'rōdə(r)\ *n* -S **1 :** a craft anchored in a roadstead **2 :** ROADSTER 1 **3 :** ROAD DONKEY
**road freight conductor** *n* **:** a railroad employee who takes charge of the makeup for freight trains and the removal of freight at destinations
**road game** *n* **:** a sports contest (as a baseball or basketball game) played while a team is on the road; *broadly* **:** a game played at an opponent's field, court, or stadium
**road gang** *n* **:** a crew of men building or working on a road
**road goose** *n, Brit* **:** a brant (*Branta bernicla*)
**road grade** *n* **:** the level and gradient of a roadway determined along the center line
**road grader** *or* **road machine** *also* **road scraper** *n* **:** a wheeled device having a long inclined vertically adjustable steel blade used to throw earth and other surface material from the side to the center of a road
**road hack** *n* **:** a fast trotting horse for saddle or harness use
**road harrow** *n* **:** a harrow designed to reshape a disturbed surface of a gravel-covered or stone-covered road
**roadhead** \'=ˌ=\ *n* **:** the end of a road: as **a :** one where men and goods must continue on foot or on animals ⟨heroic bands of soldiers labor . . . to keep the trucks moving through to the ~, where mules or porters will take over the traffic —G.H. Johnston⟩ **b :** the farthest point reached by a road under construction
**road hog** *n* **:** a driver esp. of an automotive vehicle who selfishly obstructs others using the road esp. by occupying part of another's traffic lane
**road horse** *n* **:** a driving or carriage horse for use on a road
**roadhouse** \'=ˌ=\ *n* **1 a :** an inn furnishing meals and lodging to travelers **b :** an often rudely constructed hotel or lodge in Alaska and northern Canada **2 :** an inn or tavern usu. located outside city limits and set up for serving liquor and usu. meals, for dancing, and often for gambling
**road·ing** \'rōdiŋ\ *n* -S **:** highway construction and maintenance
**road·less** \-dləs\ *adj* **1 :** having no roads **2 :** legally barred to the construction of permanent roads but open to temporary roads (as for logging or driving cattle) — **road·less·ness** *n* -ES
**roadmaker** \'=ˌ==\ *n* **:** one that makes roads
**road making** *n* **:** the process or technique of constructing roads
**road·man** \'rōd,man, -_mən\ *n, pl* **roadmen 1 a :** one who works at the building and repairing of roads and esp. of logging roads **b :** one who makes, repairs, or keeps clean the roads of a mine **2 a :** PEDDLER, CANVASSER, TRAVELING SALESMAN **b :** one who manages the sales and distribution of a newspaper within a specific county district
**road map** *n* **:** a map showing roads esp. for automobile travel
**roadmaster** \'=ˌ==\ *n* **1 :** a railroad maintenance official in charge of a division of from 50 to 150 miles of roadway **2 :** a public overseer of repairs of roads
**road mender** *n* **:** one that repairs roads
**road metal** *n* **:** broken stone or cinders used in making and repairing roads or ballasting railroads
**road mix** *n* **:** a mixture of aggregate and bituminous binder rolled down to provide a road surface
**road monkey** *n* **:** a man who inspects and repairs a logging road
**roadnet** \'=ˌ=\ *n* **:** the system of roads within an area
**road oil** *n* **:** oil (as from asphalt-base petroleum) put on roads to lay the dust and act as a waterproof binder
**road pen** *n* **:** a special pen with two points used by map makers

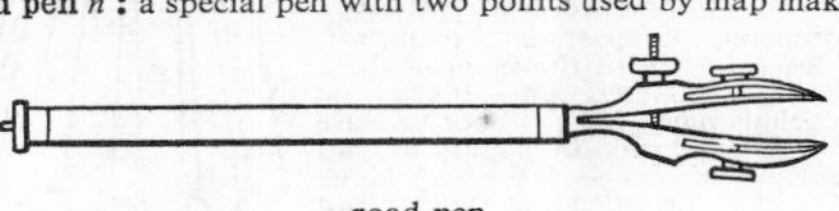

road pen

in representing roads
**road ripper** *n* **:** SCARIFIER
**road roller** *n* **:** one that rolls roadways; *specif* **:** a machine equipped with heavy wide smooth rollers for compacting roads and pavements
**roadrunner** \'=ˌ==\ *n* **1 :** a bird (*Geococcyx californianus*) of largely terrestrial habits that resembles a cuckoo and is noted for running with great speed and that ranges from California to Mexico and eastward to Texas — called also *chaparral bird* **2 :** a Mexican bird (*Geococcyx velox*) similar and closely related to the roadrunner
**roads** *pl of* ROAD, *pres 3d sing of* ROAD
**road shock** *n* **:** the sensation experienced at the steering wheel of a vehicle traveling over a rough pavement
**road show** *n* **1 :** a theatrical performance given by a troupe on tour **2 :** a special engagement of a new motion picture usu. at advanced prices
**road-show** \'=ˌ=\ *vt* [*road show*] **:** to present (a motion picture) as a road show
**¹roadside** \'=ˌ=\ *n* **:** the strip of land adjoining a road **:** the side of a road
**²roadside** \"\ *adj* **:** situated at the side of a road; *specif* **:** located along a highway and accessible to motorists ⟨~ café⟩ ⟨~ table⟩
**roadside thistle** *n* **1 :** BULL THISTLE **2 :** TALL THISTLE
**road sign** *n* **:** a sign bearing information about a road
**roads·man** \'rōdzmən\ *n, pl* **roadsmen** [*road's* (gen. of ¹*road*) + *man*] **:** ROADMAN 1
**road·stead** \'rōdz,ted, -ōd,st-\ *n* **:** ROAD 2
**road·ster** \'rōdztə(r), -dst-\ *n* -S **1 a :** ROAD HORSE **b :** a utility saddle horse of the hackney type — distinguished from *hunter* and *charger* **2 a :** HIGHWAYMAN **b :** TRAMP **3 a** *Brit* **:** a sturdy bicycle adapted for ordinary use on common roads **b :** a light carriage **:** BUGGY **c :** an automobile with an open body having one cross seat and a luggage compartment in the rear or sometimes a rumble seat
**roadstone** \'=ˌ=\ *n* **:** stone for making roads
**¹road test** *n* **:** a test of a vehicle or driver under practical operating conditions on the road
**²road test** *vt* **:** to administer a road test on or to
**road wagon** *n* **:** a wagon for use on common roads; *esp* **:** BUGGY
**roadway** \'=ˌ=\ *n* **1 a :** the strip of land through which a road is constructed and which is physically altered **b :** ROAD; *specif* **:** the part of a road over which the vehicular traffic travels **2 :** the right of way of a railroad with tracks, structures, and appurtenances necessary for the operation of trains **3 :** the part of a bridge used by vehicles
**road wheel** *n* **:** a vehicular wheel that holds to the track or road but on which no driving power is exerted
**roadwork** \'=ˌ=\ *n* **:** work done on a road; *specif* **:** conditioning exercise in preparation for an athletic contest (as a boxing match or track event) consisting mainly of long runs in the open country
**roadworthiness** \'=ˌ===\ *n* **:** the quality or state of being roadworthy
**roadworthy** \'=ˌ==\ *adj* **:** fit for or for use on the road
**¹roam** \'rōm\ *vb* -ED/-ING/-S [ME *romen*; perh. akin to OE *arǣman* to raise, ON *reimt* haunted, OE *rīsan* to rise — more at RISE] *vi* **1 a :** to go from place to place without a specific purpose or direction **:** ROVE, WANDER ⟨while various bands had moved to their reservations . . . they showed an increasing tendency to ~ —*Amer. Guide Series: Minn.*⟩ **b :** to travel purposefully throughout a wide area unhindered ⟨a mobile and elusive floating air base that can ~ at will over three-quarters of the globe —R.A.Ofstie⟩ **2** *obs* **:** to direct one's course **:** GO, PROCEED **3 :** to contemplate a wide range of thoughts or memories ⟨scientists have more to do . . . than to allow their imaginations to ~ at large —Joan Younger⟩ ~ *vt* **:** to range over **:** wander about ⟨cattle and sheep ~ hillside meadows —*Amer. Guide Series: N.C.*⟩ ⟨~*ing* the streets⟩ ⟨his imagination ~*ed* a continent —H.S.Commager⟩
**²roam** \"\ *n* -S **:** an act of roaming **:** WANDERING, RAMBLE
**ro·a·mai·na** \ˌrōə'mīnə\ *n, pl* **roamaina** *or* **roamainas** *usu cap* **1 a :** a people of Ecuador and northern Peru of uncertain linguistic affiliation **b :** a member of the Roamaina people **2 :** the language of the Roamaina people
**roam·er** \'rōmə(r)\ *n* -S [ME *romere*, fr. *romen* to roam + *-ere* -er] **:** one that roams
**roaming** *adj* **:** that roams
**¹roan** \'rōn *sometimes* -ōən\ *adj* [MF, fr. OSp *roano*, prob. irreg. fr. Goth *rauths* red — more at RED] **1** *of an animal's coat* **:** having the base color (as black, red, gray, or brown) muted and lightened by a liberal admixture of white hairs — compare BLUE-ROAN, RED-ROAN, STRAWBERRY ROAN **2 :** of the color roan **3** [²*roan*] **:** made of roan ⟨~ binding⟩
**²roan** \"\ *n* -S **1 a :** an animal (as a horse) with a roan coat — usu. used of a red roan when unqualified; see BLUE-ROAN **b :** ROAN ANTELOPE **2 a :** the color of a roan horse — used esp. when the base color is red **b :** a moderate reddish brown that is redder and slightly lighter and stronger than mahogany, redder, less strong, and slightly lighter than oxblood, and redder and paler than Tuscan red **3 :** a sheepskin used esp. for bookbinding generally made from skins that are tanned with sumac and colored and finished to imitate morocco — distinguished from *basil*
**roan antelope** *n* **:** a southern African antelope (*Hippotragus equinus*) slightly larger and lighter-colored than the sable antelope
**ro·a·noke** \'rō(ə),nōk\ *n* -S [fr. *rawranoke* shell money (in some Algonquian language of Virginia), prob. fr. *rarenawok* smoothed shells, fr. *rar* to smooth, rub] **:** WAMPUM
**roanoke bell** *n, usu cap R* [fr. *Roanoke*, city in west central Virginia] **:** VIRGINIA COWSLIP
**¹roar** \'rō(ə)r, 'rȯ(ə)r, -ōə, -ȯ(ə)\ *vb* -ED/-ING/-S [ME *roren*, fr. OE *rārian*; akin to MD *reren* to roar, OHG *rērēn* to bleat, Skt *rāyati* he barks] *vi* **1 a :** to utter or emit a full loud heavy prolonged sound ⟨the lions ~*ed*⟩ ⟨the little brass cannon ~*ed* again and again —*Amer. Guide Series: Tex.*⟩ **b :** to sing or shout with full force ⟨the lumbermen had their own songs, ~*ed* in the forests and in mill-town saloons —*Amer. Guide Series: Mich.*⟩ **2 a :** to make or emit a loud mixed confused sound (as background reverberation or rumbling) ⟨a city that normally grumbles and screeches and ~*s* —I.J.C.Brown⟩ **b :** to laugh out loudly and continuously with fullest enjoyment ⟨the audience ~*ing* at the pantomime⟩ **3 a :** to be boisterous **:** act or proceed in a riotous turbulent disorderly way ⟨desperadoes from the hills regularly ~*ed* in to take over the town —R.A.Billington⟩ **b :** to show surprising or extravagant activity or noise ⟨around which all this controversy ~*s* —A.H.Vandenberg †1951⟩ **c :** to proceed or rush with great speed, activity, or impetus and with great noise or commotion ⟨rivers ~*ed* in the abandoned channels of the glaciers —John Muir †1914⟩ ⟨get a good view of the express as she ~*ed* through —O.S.Nock⟩ **4 :** to make a loud noise in breathing (as horses afflicted with roaring) ~ *vt* **1 :** to utter or proclaim with a roar ⟨~*ing* names . . . like a railway porter shouting out a list of stations —Robert Lynd⟩ ⟨delegates to the union's . . . convention ~*ed* approval of a resolution —Mary K. Hammond⟩ ⟨~ defiance⟩ **2 :** to bring into a specified state by roaring ⟨the river ~*ed* him to sleep⟩ **3 :** to cause to roar ⟨pressed on the accelerator, savagely ~*ing* the engine —Russell Thacher⟩
**syn** HOWL, ULULATE, BELLOW, BAWL, BLUSTER, CLAMOR, VOCIFERATE: ROAR suggests the full loud reverberating sound made by lions or the booming sea or by persons in rage or boisterous merriment ⟨far away guns *roar* —Virginia Woolf⟩ ⟨the harsh north wind . . . *roared* in the piazzas —Osbert Sitwell⟩ ⟨*roared* the blacksmith, his face black with rage —T.B.Costain⟩ HOWL indicates a higher, less reverberant sound often suggesting the doleful or agonized or the sounds of unrestrained laughter ⟨frequent *howling* of jackals and hyenas —James Stevenson-Hamilton⟩ ⟨how the wind does *howl* —J.C.Powys⟩ ⟨*roared* at his subject . . . *howled* at . . . inconsistencies —Martin Gardner⟩ ULULATE is a literary synonym for HOWL but may suggest mournful protraction and rhythmical delivery ⟨an *ululating* baritone mushy with pumped-up pity —E.B.White⟩ BELLOW suggests the loud, abrupt, hollow sound made typically by bulls or any similar loud, reverberating sound ⟨most of them were drunk. They went *bellowing* through the town —Kenneth Roberts⟩ BAWL suggests a somewhat lighter, less reverberant, unmodulated sound made typically by calves ⟨a woman *bawling* abuse from the door of an inn —C.E.Montague⟩ ⟨the old judge was in the hall *bawling* hasty orders —Sheridan Le Fanu⟩ BLUSTER suggests the turbulent noisiness of gusts of wind; it often suggests swaggering and noisy threats or protests ⟨expressed her opinion gently but firmly, while he *blustered* for a time and then gave in —Sherwood Anderson⟩ ⟨swagger and *bluster* and take the limelight —Margaret Mead⟩ CLAMOR suggests sustained, mixed and confused noisy outcry as from a number of agitated persons ⟨half-starved men and women *clamoring* for food —Kenneth Roberts⟩ ⟨easy . . . for critics . . . to *clamor* for action —Sir Winston Churchill⟩ VOCIFERATE suggests loud vehement insistence in speaking ⟨was not willing to break off his talk; so he continued to *vociferate* his remarks —James Boswell⟩
**²roar** \"\ *n* -S [ME *rore*, fr. *roren*, v.] **:** the sound of roaring: **a :** the deep loud cry of some wild beasts ⟨the ~ of a lion⟩ **b :** a loud deep cry of emotion (as pain or anger) **c :** a loud continuous confused sound ⟨the ominous, steady ~ of airplane engines —Erle Stanley Gardner⟩ ⟨a ~ of conversation coming from the bar —Claud Cockburn⟩ ⟨able to make his thin whistling rise above the ~ of the stream —T.B.Costain⟩ **d :** a boisterous outcry or shouting ⟨a ~ of laughter⟩
**roar·er** \'rōrə(r), 'rȯr-\ *n* -S **:** one that roars: as **a** *obs* **:** a riotous swaggering disorderly person **:** BULLY **b :** a horse subject to roaring **c :** a person having esp. in his own opinion remarkable abilities (as of fighting or rafting) **d :** GUSHER; *esp* **:** a noisy gassy oil well
**¹roaring** *n* -S [ME *roringe*, *roring*, fr. OE *rārung*, fr. *rārian* to roar + *-ung* -ing] **1 a :** a loud deep prolonged sound (as an utterance or cry of an animal or of a person in distress, anger or mirth) **b :** a loud indistinct steady sound (as of wind, waves, or a crowd) **2 :** noisy respiration in a horse caused by paralysis of the left recurrent laryngeal nerve and atrophy of the muscles of the arytenoid cartilage on that side, occurring only during exercise, and constituting an unsoundness in the horse — compare GRUNTING, THICK WIND
**²roaring** *adj* [ME *roring*, alter. (influenced by *roringe*, *roring*, n.) of *rorende*, pres. part. of *roren* to roar] **1 :** making or characterized by a noise like a roar **:** LOUD ⟨~ applause⟩

**2 :** RIOTOUS, DISORDERLY **3 :** marked by prosperity or bustle esp. of a temporary nature **:** THRIVING, BOOMING ⟨overnight the sleepy post became a ~ construction camp —Tom Marvel⟩ ⟨doing a ~ trade⟩ — **roar·ing·ly** *adv*

**³roaring** *adv* **:** EXTREMELY — used in the phrase *roaring drunk*

**roaring boy** *or* **roaring lad** *n* **:** a noisy bullying street roisterer of Elizabethan and Jacobean England intimidating passersby (as if to commit robbery) — called also *circling boy*

**roaring forties** *n pl* **:** either of two stormy tracts of ocean between 40 degrees and 50 degrees latitude north or south

**roaring meg** \-ˈmeg\ *n, usu cap M* [fr. *Meg,* nickname fr. the name *Margaret*] *obs* **:** CANNON

**¹roast** \ˈrōst\ *vb* -ED/-ING/-S [ME *rosten,* fr. OF *rostir,* of Gmc origin; akin to MD *roosten* to roast, OHG *rōsten* (both derivatives fr. a noun represented by MD *roost* gridiron, grill, OHG *rōst*)] *vt* **1 a :** to cook by exposure to radiant heat before a fire or in an oven open toward the fire and having reflecting surfaces within — distinguished from *bake* ⟨~ meat on a spit⟩ **b :** to cook in an oven by dry heat **c :** to cook by surrounding with hot embers, ashes, sand, or stones ⟨~ a potato in ashes⟩ **d :** to dry and parch by exposure to heat ⟨~ coffee⟩ ⟨~ chestnuts⟩ **2 :** to heat (inorganic material) with access of air and without fusing in order to effect useful physical changes: as **a :** to expel volatile matter **b :** to effect oxidation **c :** to remove sulfur from sulfide ores — compare CALCINE **3 a :** to heat to excess ⟨after supper, when the sun no longer ~*ed* the valley —Oliver La Farge⟩ **b** *obs* **:** to cause to be hot with fury **4 :** to ridicule or criticize severely ⟨the critics ~*ed* the elaborately staged work —*Newsweek*⟩ ~ *vi* **1 :** to cook meat, fish, or vegetables by heat (as before a fire or in an oven) **2 :** to undergo the process of being roasted or of getting heated as if being roasted

**²roast** \"\ *n* -S [in sense 1, fr. ME *rost,* fr. MF, fr. OF, fr. *rostir,* v.; in other senses, fr. ¹*roast*] **1 :** a piece of meat which has been roasted or is suitable for being roasted; *esp* **:** a roast of beef ⟨pork ~⟩ — see BEEF illustration **2 :** a party or social gathering at which the main food is prepared by roasting before an open fire or in hot ashes or sand ⟨corn ~⟩ ⟨wienie ~⟩ **3 :** an act or process of roasting; *specif* **:** severe banter, ridicule, or criticism **4 :** a class or variety of roasted coffee as determined by length of roasting or extent of change during that process

**³roast** \"\ *adj* [ME *rost,* past part. of *rosten,* v.] **:** ROASTED ⟨~ beef⟩

**roast·er** \-tə(r)\ *n* -S [ME *roostare,* fr. *roosten, rosten* to roast + *-er, -ere, -are* -er] **1 :** one that roasts something (as meat, coffee, cacao beans, or nuts) **2 :** a machine or contrivance for roasting: as **a :** a device for roasting coffee or peanuts **b :** a pan for roasting meat **c :** a furnace for roasting ore **3 :** something adapted to roasting esp. whole: as **a :** a sucking pig **b :** a young domestic fowl for table use weighing more than four pounds **c :** any animal (as a rabbit) suitable for roasting **4 :** BURNER 1a(2) **5 :** SCORCHER 1b

**roasting** *adv* **:** to a roasting degree ⟨~ hot meat⟩

**roasting ear** *n* **1 :** an ear of sweet corn roasted or suitable for roasting usu. in the husk in hot ashes, before an open fire, or in an oven **2** *often* ˈrōsᵊn,i(ə)r, -ō,sni(ə)r, -iə\ *chiefly South & Midland* **:** an ear of sweet corn boiled or steamed after removal of the husk or suitable for boiling or steaming ⟨picked an armful of *roasting ears* in the garden⟩ **:** an ear of corn on the cob

**roasting jack** *n* **:** a device for turning a spit on which meat is roasted or barbecued

**roast·ing·ly** *adv* **:** in a roasting manner

**roast set** *n* **:** CARVING SET

**roast sintering** *n* **:** BLAST ROASTING

**roat** *or* **roate** *obs var of* ROTE

**¹rob** \ˈräb\ *vb* **robbed; robbed; robbing; robs** [ME *robben,* fr. OF *rober,* of Gmc origin; akin to OHG *roubōn* to rob — more at REAVE] *vt* **1 a** (1) **:** to take something away from (a person) by force **:** steal from ⟨~s me of that which not enriches him —Shak.⟩ ⟨*robbed* the messenger as he left the bank⟩ (2) **:** to take personal property from (the person or presence of another) feloniously and by violence or threat of violence **b** (1) **:** to remove valuables without right from (a place) ⟨~ a safe⟩ ⟨where the coyotes gathered most often they had *robbed* the henhouse —Jean Stafford⟩ (2) **:** to take the contents of (a receptacle) ⟨~ a hive of honey⟩ ⟨raising, *robbing,* baiting, and lowering the traps —Ronald Sercombe⟩ **c :** to take away as loot **:** STEAL ⟨contrive to ~ the honey and subvert the hive —John Dryden⟩ **2 a :** to deprive of something due, expected, or desired ⟨speechless death, which ~s my tongue from breathing native breath —Shak.⟩ ⟨racketeering rings that were *robbing* guileless citizens —J.A.Morris b. 1904⟩ ⟨not ready to agree that air power had changed the principles of warfare or *robbed* sea power of its sovereign values —S.L.A.Marshall⟩ **b :** to withhold unjustly or injuriously from a person or thing ⟨concave surfaces are troublesome in that they tend to focus sound in some spots and ~ sound energy from others —J.F.Nickerson⟩ **c :** to deprive (an opponent) of a hit or run in baseball by a spectacular play **3 :** to exchange a less valuable card in one's hand for (another card) **4 a :** to mine coal or ore without provision for the preservation of (a mine): as (1) **:** to take out pillars of coal or ore from (a mine) as a final operation before the abandonment of the mine (2) **:** to take out the richer and more accessible ores from (a mine) leaving valuable material behind while destroying the mine **b :** to mine (coal or ore) without provision for the preservation of the mine ~ *vi* **:** to take without right or permission and usu. by violence something belonging to another **:** commit robbery

**syn** PLUNDER, RIFLE, LOOT, THIEVE, BURGLARIZE: ROB indicates the taking of another's property either by such felonious methods as violence, intimidation, or fraud, or, by extension, by any unjust procedure ⟨to *rob* a bank⟩ ⟨to *rob* one's partners by embezzlement⟩ ⟨*robbed* of his good name by slander⟩ PLUNDER suggests despoiling and robbing in force, as by gangs, bandits, or soldiery, or on a massive scale ⟨a band of Tories who were escaping after *plundering* the home of a patriotic resident —*Amer. Guide Series: Conn.*⟩ ⟨went to prison for his activities as head of a ring which *plundered* at least $75,000,000 from the city —Paul Blanshard⟩ RIFLE suggests a ransacking or more or less complete despoliation, sometimes done systematically ⟨a boat presently came alongside with a gang of desperadoes, who boarded her, and *rifled* her of everything valuable —Francis Parkman⟩ ⟨tomb was *rifled* by the sexton after her burial for the sake of her jewelry which had been buried with her —S.P.B.Mais⟩ LOOT may add suggestions of extreme reprehensibility, as in situations involving barbarism, desperation, or colossal venality; sometimes it applies to pillaging by undisciplined soldiery or by mobs ⟨*looting* the bodies of those killed in the wreck⟩ ⟨a group of officials *looting* the state treasury⟩ THIEVE may imply stealthy taking of another's possessions, often habitual or accustomed ⟨thousands of these people have, since the liberation, become almost nomads, wandering about, *thieving* for their food —Ernest Bevin⟩ BURGLARIZE technically implies a breaking and entering of premises, often with notable force ⟨the house had been *burglarized*⟩ ⟨*burglarizing* fur storage lofts⟩

— **rob the cradle :** to select as a companion or spouse a person much younger than oneself

**²rob** \"\ *n* -S [MF, fr. Ar *rubb*] **:** the thickened juice of ripe fruit obtained by evaporation of the juice over a fire till it has the consistency of a syrup and afterward sometimes mixed with honey or sugar

**ROB** *abbr, often not cap* remain on board; remaining on board

**ro·ba·lo** \rōˈbä(,)lō\ *n, pl* **robalos** *or* **ro·balo** [Sp *róbalo, robalo,* prob. modif. of (assumed) Sp *lobaro,* irreg. fr. Sp *lobo* wolf, fr. L *lupus* — more at WOLF] **:** SNOOK 1a

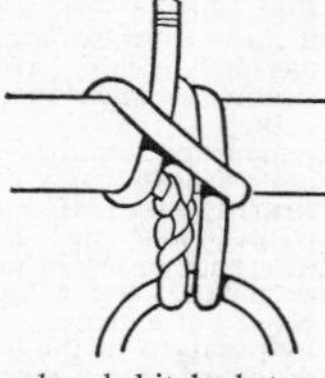
roband hitched to a ring and tied around a spar

**roband** \ˈrōbən, ˈräb-, -bənd\ *also* **rob·bin** \ˈräbən\ *or* **rope·band** \ˈrōp,ban(d)\ *n* -S [*roband* prob. fr. (assumed) ME *roband,* prob. fr. MD *rabant,* fr. *ra* sail yard + *bant* band, hoop (akin to OHG *bant* fetter); *robbin* fr. ME *robyn,* prob. alter. (influenced by *Robin,* nickname fr. the name *Robert*) of (assumed) ME *roband; ropeband* by folk etymology fr. *roband;* MD *ra* sail yard akin to MHG *rahe* pole, sail yard, ON *rā* sail yard, Lith *rėklės* wooden frame for drying or smoking foods — more at BAND] **:** a small piece of spun yarn or marline used to fasten the head of a sail to a spar

**rob·ber** \ˈräbə(r)\ *n* -S *often attrib* [ME *robbere, robbour,* fr. OF *robere, robeor,* fr. *roben* to rob + *-ere, -eor* -er] **:** one that robs: as **a :** one that commits the crime of robbery **b** *or* **robber bee :** a honeybee worker that steals honey from a colony not its own **c :** a miner who rips out the supporting pillars of coal after the regular mining has been done

**robber ant** *n* **:** any of various slave-making ants (as *Formica sanguinea* and *Polyergus rufescens*)

**robber baron** *n* **1 :** a medieval lord subsisting by robbing, holding for ransom, or exorbitantly taxing travelers through his domain **2 :** an American capitalist of the latter part of the 19th century grown wealthy through exploitation of natural resources, governmental influence, or low wage scales

**robber crab** *n* **1 :** PURSE CRAB **2 :** HERMIT CRAB

**robber fly** *n* **:** any of numerous often large predaceous flies of the family Asilidae that usu. are covered with coarse bristly hair and have a slender body and long legs but sometimes closely resemble the bumblebees and that as larvae prey upon other insect larvae and as adults prey upon other insects

**robber frog** *n* **:** any of several frogs of the genus *Eleutherodactylus* with a call like the bark of a dog that are chiefly native to Central America though one species extends into extreme southern Texas

**robber gull** *n* **:** JAEGER 3

**robbers' roost** *n* **:** an outlaw hideout esp. in the western U. S.

**rob·bery** \ˈräb(ə)rē, -)ri\ *n* -ES [ME *robberie,* fr. OF *roberie,* fr. *rober* to rob + *-erie* -ery] **:** the act or practice of robbing; *specif* **:** a larceny from the person or immediate presence of another by violence or threat of violence — compare MIXED LARCENY, THEFT

**robbery insurance** *n* **:** insurance against loss by theft of property from the person or immediate presence of the possessor

**robbia work** *n, usu cap R* **:** DELLA ROBBIA WARE

**rob·bin** *Brit var of* ROBIN

**robbing** *pres part of* ROB

**¹robe** \ˈrōb\ *n* -S [ME, fr. OF, robe, booty, of Gmc origin; akin to OE *rēaf* garment, armor, booty, OHG *roub* booty, *roubōn* to rob — more at REAVE] **1 a :** a long loose outer garment cut in flowing lines and used for ordinary wear by men and women during the middle ages and in modern times esp. in Asian and African countries ⟨supply purple ~s for the courtiers —Connop Thirlwall⟩ ⟨the Indians wove their own heavy cotton ~s —C.B.Hitchcock⟩ **b :** a similar garment often of special or elegant style and material used for state, ceremonial, and official occasions or as a symbol of office or profession ⟨the Sovereign has . . . been invested with the Royal *Robe* of cloth of gold in which he is crowned —L.E. Fanner⟩ ⟨the judge was already rising and arranging his ~s —Frances P. Keyes⟩ **c :** a usu. loose wraparound garment of varying length for informal wear esp. at home (as a bathrobe or dressing gown) ⟨found him . . . wearing a natty red lounging ~ and white pajamas —*New Yorker*⟩ ⟨the girls . . . have beach ~s and hats —Bernard De Voto⟩ **2 :** something resembling or suggesting a long loose enveloping garment ⟨a vast and fruitful land . . . clad with a ~ of plants —Russell Lord⟩ ⟨the glorious congregation of peaks . . . in their ~s of snow and light—John Muir †1914⟩ ⟨shed your ~ of sanctity —Rafael Sabatini⟩ **3 :** the legal profession — usu. used with preceding *the* ⟨the cadets of many of our good families follow the ~ as a profession —W.M.Thackeray⟩ **4 a :** a covering for the lower body made from pelts finished with the fur on the top side and often a lining of fabric on the underside that resembles a blanket and is used while driving or at outdoor events — see BUFFALO ROBE, LAP ROBE **b :** a similar covering of fabric ⟨warm woolen auto ~s⟩ **5 :** WARDROBE ⟨double-door cedar ~s —*advt*⟩

**²robe** \"\ *vb* -ED/-ING/-S [ME *roben,* fr. *robe,* n.] *vt* **1 :** to clothe or invest with a robe ⟨helped to ~ him in . . . a quilted robe of scarlet silk —Nora Waln⟩ ⟨bathers must immediately ~ themselves upon leaving the water —*Time*⟩ **2 :** to dress or cover as if with a robe ⟨~s himself in moonlight —John Foster⟩ ⟨love *robed* her in a blush —T.T.Lynch⟩ ~ *vi* **:** to put on a robe ⟨in the early morning, he *robed* . . . and drove abroad —Mary Lindsay⟩

**robe de cham·bre** \rōbdəshäⁿbr(ᵊ), -b(rə)\ *n, pl* **robes de chambre** \"\ [F] **:** DRESSING GOWN

**robe de nuit** \-dənwʸē\ *n, pl* **robes de nuit** \"\ [F] **:** NIGHTGOWN

**robe de style** \-dəstēl\ *n, pl* **robes de style** \"\ [F] **:** a usu. long formal gown with a tight bodice and a bouffant skirt

robe de style

**robe·less** \ˈrōbləs\ *adj* **:** lacking a robe

**ro·ben·hau·si·an** \ˌrōbənˈhaůzēən\ *adj, usu cap* [*Robenhausen,* locality in northeast central Switzerland where evidences of such a culture have been found + E *-an*] **:** of or relating to a stage of Neolithic culture characterized by lake dwellings, polished stone tools, agriculture, weaving, and domestic animals

**rob·er** \ˈrōbə(r)\ *n* -S **:** one that robes

**rob·erds·man** \ˈräbə(r)dzmən\ *n, pl* **roberdsmen** *usu cap* [ME *roberdesman, robertesman,* prob. fr. *Robertes* (gen. of the name *Robert,* prob. considered an appropriate fictitious name for a robber because of the similarity in sound to ME *robbere* robber) + ME *man*] **:** one of a class of vagabond thieves and robbers in 14th century England

**rob·ert of lin·coln** \ˌräbərd·ə(v)-ˈliŋkən\ *usu cap R&L* [alter. (influenced by the name *Robert* and by E *of*) of obs. E *Bob-o-Lincoln* — more at BOBOLINK] **:** BOBOLINK

**ro·ber·val's balance** \ˈrōbə(r),vōlz-\ *n, usu cap R* [after Gilles Personne de *Roberval* †1675 Fr. mathematician] **:** a balance in which the pans are fixed to the prolonged vertical sides of a jointed parallelogram whose two other sides are pivoted in their midpoints to a vertical post

**robes·pierr·ist** \ˈrōb,spirəst, -bz,pyer-\ *n* -S *usu cap* [F *robespierriste,* fr. Maxmilien F. M. I. de *Robespierre* †1794 Fr. revolutionist + F *-iste* -ist] **:** a follower or supporter of Robespierre

**ro·bi·ga·lia** \ˌrōbəˈgālēə\ *n* -S *usu cap* [L, fr. *Robigus,* Roman god associated with wheat blight] **:** an ancient Roman festival celebrated April 25 including a procession and the sacrifice of a dog to the god Robigus to avert blight from the fields

**rob·in** \ˈräbən *sometimes* -bᵊm\ *n* -S [in sense 1, short for *robin redbreast;* in other senses, fr. *Robin,* nickname fr. the name *Robert*] **1 a :** a small European thrush (*Erithacus rubecola*) resembling a warbler and having a brownish olive back and yellowish red throat and breast — called also *redbreast* **b :** any of various Old World songbirds (as members of the genera *Petroica, Melanodryas, Saxicola,* and *Saxicoloides*) that are related to or resemble in size, color, or habits the European robin — compare WOOD ROBIN **c :** a large No. American thrush (*Turdus migratorius*) with olivaceous gray upper parts, blackish head and tail, black and whitish streaked throat, and chiefly dull reddish breast and underparts that often nests in orchard or shade trees close to human habitations and lays pale greenish blue eggs **d :** any of various other American birds — usu. used in combination ⟨golden ~⟩; compare TOWHEE, VARIED THRUSH **e** *Jamaica* **:** GREEN TODY **2** *dial Eng* **:** any of various plants: as **a :** RAGGED ROBIN **b :** RED CAMPION **c :** HERB ROBERT **3 :** SEA ROBIN

**robin accentor** *n* **:** a small Asiatic songbird (*Prunella rubeculoides*) somewhat resembling the European robin in color

**robin chat** *n* **:** any of various African thrushes of *Cossypha* and closely related genera that are slaty blue with orange breasts

**robin dipper** *n* **:** BUFFLEHEAD

**rob·in·et** \ˈräbənət\ *n* -S [ME, short for *robinet redbrest,* fr. *Robinet* (dim. of *Robin,* nickname fr. the name *Robert*) + ME *redbrest* redbreast] **1 a** *dial Eng* **:** ROBIN **b :** CHAFFINCH **2** [fr. *Robinet,* dim. of *Robin,* nickname fr. the name *Robert*] **:** a light cannon of the 16th century throwing a projectile weighing about half a pound

**robi·ne·tin** \ˌrōbəˈnētᵊn, ˌräb-\ *n* -S [*robin-* (fr. NL *Robinia*) + *-et-* + *-in*] **:** a yellow crystalline flavone pigment $C_{15}H_{10}O_7$ obtained esp. from the stem wood of a locust (*Robinia pseudoacacia*)

**rob·ing** \ˈrōbiŋ\ *n* -S [ME, fr. gerund of *roben* to robe] **1 :** ROBE 1 **2** *also* **rob·in** \-bən\ **:** a band or flounce for trimming a robe or gown

**robing room** *n* **:** a small room in a church where robes or ecclesiastical vestments are put on before a service

**rob·in hood** \ˌräbənˈhůd, *sometimes* -bᵊmˌ-\ *n, usu cap R&H* [*Robin Hood,* legendary Eng. outlaw, hero of a cycle of ballads, first mentioned *ab*1377] **1 :** a person or group whose acts lie partly or wholly outside accepted standards of legality, morality, or propriety; *esp* **:** one that robs the wealthy to aid the needy ⟨a kind of primitive and rather unscrupulous *Robin Hood* — taking from the rich to give to the poor and keeping undisclosed amounts for itself —J. Halero Ferguson⟩ **2 :** a spectacular hero ⟨interstellar *Robin Hoods* . . . on rocket-motor bikes and space-sphere junkets —T.H.Robsjohn-Gibbings⟩

**robin hood's barn** *n, usu cap R&H* **:** a long circuitous route ⟨tortuous meanderings around *Robin Hood's barn* —H.P. Fairchild⟩

**ro·bin·ia** \rōˈbinēə\ *n* [NL, fr. Jean *Robin* †1629 Fr. botanist + NL *-ia*] **1** *cap* **:** a genus of No. American trees and shrubs (family Leguminosae) having showy racemose pink or white flowers — see BRISTLY LOCUST, CLAMMY LOCUST, LOCUST **2** -S **:** any plant of the genus *Robinia*

**robi·nin** \ˈrōbənən, ˈräb-\ *n* -S [*robin-* (fr. NL *Robinia*) + *-in*] **:** a yellow crystalline glycoside $C_{33}H_{40}O_{19}$ derived from kaempferol and found in the flowers of a locust (*Robinia pseudoacacia*)

**robi·nose** \-ˌnōs *also* -ōz\ *n* -S [*robin-* (fr. NL *Robinia*) + *-ose*] **:** a trisaccharide sugar $C_{18}H_{32}O_{14}$ obtained from robinin by hydrolysis and yielding one part of galactose and two of rhamnose on hydrolysis

**robin redbreast** *n* [ME *robin redbrest,* fr. *Robin* (nickname fr. the name *Robert*) + ME *redbrest* redbreast] **1 :** ROBIN 1a **2 :** ROBIN 1c

**robin runaway** *n* **1 :** DEWDROP **2 :** GROUND IVY 1

**robins** *pl of* ROBIN

**robin sandpiper** *or* **robin snipe** *n* **1 :** *also* **robin breast :** ³KNOT **2 :** DOWITCHER

**robin's egg** *n* **:** a grayish blue that is greener and paler than electric or copenhagen, lighter, stronger, and slightly greener than Gobelin, and greener and lighter than old china — compare ROBIN'S-EGG BLUE

**robin's-egg blue** *n* **1 :** a variable color averaging a light greenish blue that is bluer and paler than average turquoise (sense 2a) or average turquoise blue and bluer and deeper than average aqua blue — compare ROBIN'S EGG **2 :** a light bluish green that is greener and duller than average aqua green (sense 1) and greener and paler than average turquoise green — called also *bird's-egg green, eggshell blue*

**robin snow** *n, chiefly New Eng* **:** a light snowfall after the return of the first robin

**rob·in·son·ade** \ˌräbənsəˈnād, ˌrōbənzōˈnädə\ *n, pl* **robinson·ades** \-ādz\ *also* **robinson·aden** \-ˈädᵊn\ *often cap* [G *robinsonade,* fr. *Robinson Crusoe,* sailor who survives by great resourcefulness when marooned on a desert island in the fictional prose narrative *Robinson Crusoe* (1719) by Daniel Defoe †1731 Eng. journalist and novelist] **:** a fictitious narrative of often fantastic adventures in real or imaginary distant places; *esp* **:** a story of the adventures of a person marooned on a desert island ⟨the *Robinsonade* in world literature —E.G. Gudde⟩

**robinson crusoe** *n, usu cap R&C* **:** CRUSOE

**rob·in·son·ite** \ˈräbənsəˌnīt *also probably by n-dissimilation* ÷-bəs-\ *n* -S [Stephen C. *Robinson* b1911 Canadian geologist + E *-ite*] **:** a mineral $Pb_7Sb_{12}S_{25}$ consisting of a sulfide of lead and antimony that is found in Pershing county, Nev.

**robin's plantain** *n* **:** a common perennial herb (*Erigeron pulchellus*) of eastern No. America having flower heads with violet purple rays

**rob·i·son ester** \ˈräbəsən-\ *n, usu cap R* [after Robert *Robison* †1941 Eng. biochemist] **:** GLUCOSE PHOSPHATE b

**ro·ble** \ˈrō(,)blā, -ōbəl\ *n* -S [AmerSp, fr. Sp, oak, fr. L *robur* — more at ROBUST] **1 :** any of several oaks of California and Mexico: as **a :** CALIFORNIA WHITE OAK **b :** CANYON LIVE OAK **2 :** any of several hard-timbered tropical American trees: as **a :** a quira (*Platymiscium polystachyum*) **b :** any of various trees of the genera *Catalpa, Tabebuia,* and *Tecoma* **c :** UMBU-RANA **3 :** a So. American tree of the genus *Nothofagus* (as *N. obliqua* or *N. dombeyi*)

**ro·bomb** \ˈrō+,-\ *n* [blend fr. *robot bomb*] **:** ROBOT BOMB

**¹robo·rant** \ˈräbərənt, ˈrōb-\ *n* -S [L *roborant-, roborans,* pres. part. of *roborare* to strengthen] **:** an invigorating drug **:** TONIC

**²roborant** \"\ *adj* [L *roborant-, roborans,* pres. part. of *roborare*] **:** STRENGTHENING

**roborate** *vt* [ME *roboraten,* fr. L *roboratus,* past part. of *roborare* to strengthen, confirm, fr. *robor-, robur* strength — more at ROBUST] **1** *obs* **:** RATIFY, CORROBORATE **2** *obs* **:** STRENGTHEN — **roboration** *n* -S

**ro·bot** \ˈrō,bät, -bət, *usu* -äd- *or* -əd- +V; *sometimes* -(,)bō *or* -,bət *or* (+V) -,bəd-\ *n* -S *often attrib* [Czech, fr. *robota* work, compulsory service; akin to OSlav *rabota* servitude, OE *earfothe* hardship, labor, OHG *arabeit* trouble, distress, ON *erfithi* toil, distress, Goth *arbaiths* labor, L *orbus* orphaned, bereft — more at ORPHAN] **1 a :** a machine in the form of a human being that performs the mechanical functions of a human being but lacks emotions and sensitivity ⟨electronically controlled ~s with hands, eyebrows, and bodies that move —*Time*⟩ ⟨a world of men and women — not of cast iron ~s —*Spectator*⟩ — compare AUTOMATON, GOLEM **b :** an automatic apparatus or device that performs functions ordinarily ascribed to human beings or operates with what appears to be almost human intelligence; *esp* **:** such an apparatus that is started by means of radiant energy or sound waves ⟨a ~ mechanism that steers a cultivator precisely along a row of crops —*Newsweek*⟩ ⟨a ~ taking pictures at intervals⟩ **c** (1) **:** a mechanism that operates without human assistance; *esp* **:** one that is guided by automatic controls ⟨automatic percolator ~⟩ ⟨~ airplane⟩ ⟨~ factory⟩ (2) *southern Africa* **:** TRAFFIC SIGNAL (3) **:** ROBOT BOMB **2 :** an efficient, insensitive, and often brutalized person ⟨social ~s, taking whatever is brought to us, always grateful —Gilbert Seldes⟩ ⟨the average worker who has functioned from adolescence as a ~ —Henry Miller⟩

**robot bomb** *n* **:** a small pilotless jet-propelled airplane that is steered by a gyroscopic device, that is heavily loaded with explosives, and that descends as an aerial bomb — called also *buzz bomb, flying bomb, robomb, V-1*

**ro·bot·ism** \ˈ=(,)=,izəm\ *n* -S **:** machinelike behavior in a human being

**ro·bot·iza·tion** \ˌ=(,)=əˈzāshən, -ˌīˈz-\ *n* -S **1 :** the act or process of turning a human being into a robot **2 :** AUTOMATION

**ro·bot·ize** \ˈ=(,)=,īz\ *vt* -ED/-ING/-S **1 :** to make automatic ⟨chemical process plants so highly *robotized* that their complex operations are controlled by one or two operators at a push-button panel —Gerard Piel⟩ **2 :** to turn (a human being) into a robot

**rob roy** \ˈräˈbrȯi\ *n, usu cap both Rs* [prob. fr. *Rob Roy,* nickname of Robert Macgregor †1734 Scot. freebooter] **:** a cocktail consisting of Scotch whisky, sweet vermouth, and bitters stirred with ice, strained, and served garnished with a maraschino cherry

**robs** *pres 3d sing of* ROB, *pl of* ROB

**ro·bur** \ˈrōbə(r)\ *n* -S [L, oak] **:** ENGLISH OAK

**ro·bust** \rōˈbəst, ˈrō,bəst *also* ˈrō̇b-\ *adj, often* -ER/-EST [L *robustus* oaken, hard, strong, fr. *robor-, robur* oak, strength; perh. akin to L *ruber* red — more at RED] **1 a :** having or exhibiting strength or vigorous health **:** POWERFUL, MUSCULAR, VIGOROUS ⟨a new land, full of ~ people —Green Peyton⟩ ⟨a hearty, ~ man in his middle sixties —Jule Mannix⟩ **b :** firm and assured in purpose, opinion, or outlook ⟨this embodied moral healthiness, this ~ sayer of Yea and Nay . . . this genuine man —W.L.Sullivan⟩ ⟨the ~ skepticism of science —M.R.Cohen⟩ ⟨a faith so ~ as to outlive shock upon shock of disillusion —Irving Babbitt⟩ **c :** exceptionally sound **:** FLOURISHING ⟨men and women of ~ health and keen intelligence —W.R.Inge⟩ ⟨protected by history, by geography and . . . by its ~ liberal tradition —A.M.Schlesinger b. 1917⟩ **d :** strongly formed or constructed **:** STURDY ⟨~ flowering plants such as veratrum, larkspur, lupine —John Muir †1914⟩ ⟨the furniture is structurally as ~ as the society it served —John Gloag⟩ ⟨sex in any race is shown by the general proportion of the bones . . . the male frame being more ~ and the bones . . . more rugged —R.W.Murray⟩ **2 :** ROUGH, RUDE ⟨appease their hunger with pemmican and their spirits with roistering songs and ~ stories —*Amer. Guide Series: Minn.*⟩ **3 :** requiring strength or vigor ⟨the physical weakling . . . of little material value to the group in the ~ economy of the hunters —R.W. Murray⟩ **4 :** FULL-BODIED, STRONG ⟨splendidly ~ soups and stews —*New Yorker*⟩ ⟨~ coffee⟩ **syn** see HEALTHY

**ro·bus·ta coffee** \rō'bəstə-\ *n* [NL *robusta* (specific epithet of *Coffea robusta*, syn. of *Coffea canephora*), fr. L, fem. of *robustus*] **1 :** a coffee (*Coffea canephora*) that is indigenous to Central Africa but grown in Java and elsewhere and has high resistance to coffee rust **2 a :** the seed of robusta coffee **b :** coffee brewed from the seed of robusta coffee

**ro·bus·tic·i·ty** \(,)rō,bə'stisəd·ē, ,rō b-\ *n* -ES [obs. E *robustic* robust (fr. E *robust* + *-ic*) + E *-ity*] **:** ROBUSTNESS

**ro·bus·tious** \(')rō¦bəschəs, rə'b-\ *adj* **1 :** ROBUST, STOUT, HEALTHY **2 :** rudely vigorous **:** BOISTEROUS, ROUGH ⟨a likeable fellow, direct and ~ —S.H.Adams⟩ ⟨~ times when broadcloth in politics had gone out of fashion and homespun had come in —V.L.Parrington⟩ — **ro·bus·tious·ly** *adv* — **ro·bus·tious·ness** *n* -ES

**ro·bust·ly** *adv* **:** in a robust manner

**ro·bust·ness** \rō'bəs(t)nəs, 'rō,b- *also* 'rō b-\ *n* -ES **:** the quality or state of being robust

**ro·bus·tu·ous** \(')rō¦bəsch(əw)əs\ *adj* [*robust* + *-uous* (as in *contemptuous*)] **:** ROBUSTIOUS

**roc** \'räk\ *n* -S [Ar *rukhkh*] **1 :** a legendary bird of great size and strength believed to inhabit the Indian ocean area — compare SIMURGH **2 :** an aerial bomb with a television apparatus for transmitting information used to guide the bomb by remote radio control to the target

**ROC** *abbr* reserve officer candidate

**ro·caille** \rō'kī, rä'-\ *n* -S [F, fr. *roc* rock, fr. MF, irreg. fr. *roche* rock, fr. (assumed) VL *rocca* — more at ROCK] **1 :** a style of ornamentation developed in the 18th century and characterized by forms derived from the artificial rockwork and pierced shellwork of the period **2 :** ROCOCO

**roc·am·bole** *or* **roc·om·bole** \'räkəm,bōl\ *n* -S [F *rocambole*] **:** a European leek (*Allium scorodoprasum*) often cultivated like the shallot and similarly used

**roc·cel·la** \rō'chelə\ *n, cap* [NL, fr. It, archil (plant), alter. of *oricello*] **:** a genus (the type of the family Roccellaceae) of chiefly maritime rock-inhabiting lichens that have a fruticulose or pendulous thallus and include some (esp. *Roccella tinctoria*) which are the chief sources of the dye archil and some which furnish litmus — compare LECANORA, PERTUSARIA — **roc·cel·line** \-elən, -e,līn\ *adj*

**roc·cel·lic acid** \rō'chelik-\ *n* [*roccellic* ISV *roccell-* (fr. NL *Roccella*) + *-ic*] **:** a crystalline dicarboxylic acid $C_{17}H_{32}O_4$ derived from succinic acid and found in various lichens (as *Roccella tinctoria*)

**roc·cus** \'räkəs\ *n, cap* [NL, perh. irreg. fr. E *rockfish*] **:** a genus of fishes (family Serranidae) including the common marine striped bass

**roch** \'räk\ *Scot var of* ROUGH

**roch·dale principles** \'räch,dāl-\ *n pl, usu cap R* [fr. *Rochdale*, city in northwest England where such cooperative marketing was begun in 1844] **:** a system of cooperative marketing in which no credit is given and all profits are distributed among the customers

**roche** \'rōch\ *n* -S [obs. E *roche* stony hill, rock, fr. ME — more at ROACH] *dial Eng* **:** any of various rocks, stones, or geological strata

**ro·chea** \'rōshēə\ *n, cap* [NL, fr. François Dela-*Roche* †1813 Swiss botanist] **:** a small genus of southern African fleshy undershrubs (family Crassulaceae) with showy cymose salver-shaped flowers of various colors

**roche limit** \'rȯsh-, 'rōsh-\ *or* **roche's limit** \-shəz-\ *n, usu cap R* [after E. A. *Roche* †1883 Fr. mathematician] **:** the distance between a planet's center and its satellite within which the satellite cannot approach without suffering disruption; *specif* **:** the distance 2.44 times the planet's radius from its center when the planet and the satellite are of the same density

**ro·chelle powders** \(')rō¦shel-\ *n pl, usu cap R* [fr. La *Rochelle*, city in western France] **:** SEIDLITZ POWDERS

**rochelle salt** *n, usu cap R* **:** a crystalline salt $KNaC_4H_4O_6 \cdot 4H_2O$ that has a cooling saline taste, that is a mild purgative, and that is used also esp. in the silvering of mirrors and in piezoelectric devices — often used in pl.; called also *potassium sodium tartrate, Seignette salt*

**roche mou·ton·née** \¦rȯsh,müt°n'ā, ¦rōsh-\ *n, pl* **roches moutonnées** \-ā(z)\ [F, lit., fleecy rock] **:** an elongate rounded ice-sculptured knob or hillock of bedrock

**roch·es·ter** \'rächəstə(r), -,ches-\ *adj, usu cap* [fr. *Rochester*, city in western New York] **:** of or from the city of Rochester, N.Y. ⟨the *Rochester* business district⟩ **:** of the kind or style prevalent in Rochester

**roch·es·te·ri·an** \,rächə'stirēən, -,che's-\ *n* -S *cap* [*Rochester* (any of several cities including one in southeast England and one in western New York) + E *-an*] **:** a native or resident of Rochester, esp. Rochester, New York

[1]**roch·et** \'rächət\ *n* -S [ME *rochet*, *roget*, *ruget*, fr. MF *rouget*, fr. OF, fr. *rouge* red + *-et* — more at ROUGE] **:** RED GURNARD

[2]**rochet** \"\ *n* -S [ME, fr. MF, fr. OF, fr. (assumed) OF *roc* coat (of Gmc origin; akin to OHG *roc* coat) + OF *-et* — more at FROCK] **1 :** a close-fitting white ecclesiastical vestment resembling a surplice usu. with long close sleeves but sometimes winged or sleeveless that is worn esp. by bishops and privileged prelates in some ceremonies **2** *archaic* **:** a loose smock or cloak worn as an outer garment

**ro·chet·ta** \rō'ked·ə\ *n* -S [It *rocchetta*, dim. of *rocca* rock, fr. (assumed) VL *rocca* — more at ROCK] *archaic* **:** POLVERINE

**ro·chon prism** \(')rō¦shōⁿ-\ *n, usu cap R* [after Alexis M. *Rochon* †1817 Fr. astronomer and optician] **:** a polarizing prism consisting of two equal prisms of calcite or other doubly refracting material cut so that the optic axis of one of the prisms is parallel to its refracting edge, the axis of the other is perpendicular to its refracting edge, and the directions of the optic axes make angles of 90 degrees with each other

[1]**rock** \'räk\ *vb* -ED/-ING/-S [ME *rokken*, fr. OE *roccian*; akin to OHG *rucken* to cause to move, shift, ON *rykkja* to jerk] *vt* **1 a :** to move (as a child) back and forth in or as if in a cradle **b :** to bring into or maintain in a state of rest, sleep, or serenity by gentle motion to and fro ⟨~*ing* the child on her breast⟩ **c :** to wash (placer gravel) in a cradle **d :** to prepare the surface of (a mezzotint plate) by the use of a cradle **2 a :** to cause (as a cradle) to sway gently backward and forward ⟨a warning sea bell ~*ed* by rising waves —J.C.Powys⟩ ⟨the languid spring breeze ~*ed* the little green bombshells of maple sprays —*New Republic*⟩ **b** (1) **:** to cause to shake violently ⟨when artillery maneuvers are held . . . the quiet countryside is shattered and ~*ed* by the roaring thunder of the big guns —*Amer. Guide Series: Vt.*⟩ ⟨she began to cry, great sobs that ~*ed* her —Robert Lowry⟩ (2) **:** to daze with a vigorous blow ⟨three smashing right crosses that ~*ed* him —Nat Fleischer⟩ (3) **:** to astonish or disturb esp. by upsetting cherished opinions or customary ways of life ⟨~*ing* the solid beliefs they had never dreamed of questioning —Virginia D. Dawson & Betty D. Wilson⟩ ⟨the news of the coming degree had ~*ed* the household with surprise —Agnes S. Turnbull⟩ **c** (1) **:** to dislodge (something stuck or wedged) by rhythmic back and forth movement ⟨set up on your towline and we'll ~ her out of here —K.M. Dodson⟩ (2) **:** to move clumsily first from one side and then from the other ⟨~*ed* his shoulders up the stairs —Scott Fitzgerald⟩ ⟨~*ed* the box across the platform⟩ (3) **:** to move (airplane wings) up and down usu. as a signal ⟨~*ed* my wings to let the landing signal officer know that I needed to land at once —D.A.Bryla⟩ **d :** to move (a vehicle or animal) at a steady fairly rapid pace ⟨~*ing* my mule right along but riding him as easy as I could —Jackson Burgess⟩ **~** *vi* **1 a :** to move violently backward and forward under impact **:** REEL, TOTTER ⟨the tower ~*ed* under the impact of the hurricane⟩ **b** (1) **:** to move gently and rhythmically back and forth ⟨~*ing* on the balls of his feet —Richard Llewellyn⟩ ⟨the speedometer was ~*ing* between sixty and sixty-five —Charley Robertson⟩ ⟨a low, steady breeze drove the little waves ~*ing* to the shore —John Burroughs⟩ (2) **:** to sit and move back and forth in a rocking chair ⟨~*ed* all day on her veranda —Laura Krey⟩ **c :** to sway gently under outside impact ⟨boats ~*ing* on the yellow river —W.G.Hardy⟩ **2 a :** to react with intense emotion ⟨the continent ~*ed* with surprise —*Woman*⟩ ⟨the audience was ~*ing* with laughter —H.J.Laski⟩ **b :** to seem to sway as if in response to human illness or emotion ⟨felt a blow against the back of his head, saw the walls of the house ~*ing* in sick blackness, and slid out on the hot steps —Josephine Johnson⟩ ⟨the room with its portions of shells ~*ed* more frequently with laughter than with explosives —*N.Y. Times Bk. Rev.*⟩ **3 a :** to move forward at a steady rhythmic pace ⟨the chuffing doubleheaders of the narrow-gage ~*ed* cautiously along the tracks —Helen Rich⟩ **b :** to move forward at high speeds ⟨~*ed* around town at furious speeds —R.L.Taylor⟩ **4 :** to sing, play music, or dance in a quick lively tempo — **rock the boat :** to do something that disturbs the equilibrium of a project ⟨trips should not be timed to *rock the boat* in countries where elections are being held —*Reporter*⟩ **syn** see SHAKE

[2]**rock** \"\ *n* -S **:** a rocking movement; *specif* **:** a change of balance in a step dance from one foot to the other with feet crossed

[3]**rock** \"\ *n* -S [ME *roc*, *rokke*, fr. MD *rocke*; akin to OHG *rocko* distaff, ON *rokkr* distaff, OHG *roc* coat — more at FROCK] **1 :** DISTAFF; *esp* **:** one with wool or flax on it **2 :** the wool or flax on a distaff

[4]**rock** \"\ *n* -S *often attrib* [ME *rokke*, fr. ONF *roque*, fr. (assumed) VL *rocca*, prob. of non-IE origin] **1 a :** a usu. bare cliff, promontory, peak, or hill that is one mass ⟨the ~ of Gibraltar⟩ **b :** a mass of stone lying at or near the surface of the water ⟨scattered ~*s* with 3¾–6 fathoms . . . of water over them —*U. S. Coast Pilot: West Indies*⟩ ⟨a reef, with four ~*s* showing above water —*U. S. Coast Pilot: West Indies*⟩ **c :** a barren islet **d :** a jagged rocky coastline esp. when a source of danger to shipping — often used in pl. ⟨the schooner was driven onto the ~*s*⟩ **2 a :** extremely hard dense stone ⟨hewn out of adamant ~ —Edmund Spenser⟩ **b** (1) **:** a large concreted mass of stony material **:** a large fixed stone (2) **:** stony material broken from such a mass **c** (1) **:** consolidated or unconsolidated solid mineral matter composed of one or usu. two or more minerals or partly of organic origin (as coal) that occurs naturally in large quantities or forms a considerable part of the earth's crust ⟨granite, sand, gravel, clay, and glacial ice are ~*s*⟩ (2) **:** a particular mass or kind of such material within the earth's surface (3) **:** an often jagged fragment of rock ranging in size from a boulder to a pebble ⟨chunkin' ~*s* at my granddaddy —Stetson Kennedy⟩ (4) **:** ore as mined; *esp* **:** Lake Superior copper ore **3 a** (1) **:** something that resembles a rock in firmness **:** FOUNDATION, SUPPORT ⟨the concept of a law that is independent of any sovereign, which cannot be repealed . . . is the ~ on which our society rests —Herbert Agar⟩ (2) **:** something that serves as a defense or refuge ⟨the Lord is my ~, and my fortress —2 Sam 22:2 (RSV)⟩ (3) **:** something that threatens or causes a disaster or wreck — often used in pl. ⟨the university, so near the ~*s* in preceding years, had become one of the best-rounded educational institutions in the country —*Current Biog.*⟩ ⟨our political parties must never flounder on the ~*s* of moral equivocation —A.E.Stevenson †1965⟩ **b :** a small island that is a place of confinement or of dangerous or monotonous duty ⟨three divisions of Marines . . . on the hottest ~ of them all —L.M.Uris⟩ **4 :** STRIPED BASS a **5 a** (1) **:** a hard stick candy with color running through and variously flavored (as with peppermint, clove, or anise) (2) **:** ROCK CANDY 1 **b** *or* **rock cake :** a cookie that is made of firm dough dropped from a spoon to a cookie sheet and that when baked retains an uneven form and contour **6 a :** a piece of money; *esp* **:** a dollar bill **b rocks** *pl* **:** MONEY ⟨a pocket full of ~*s*⟩ **7 :** PLYMOUTH ROCK **8** *slang* **a :** GEM **b :** DIAMOND **9 :** a mass consisting of lime soap obtained in a process for saponifying fats by heating them with lime and water under pressure **10 :** a stupid mistake **:** BONER ⟨pulled a ~ . . . in right field —Casey Stengel⟩ **11 :** ROCK 'N' ROLL — **of the old rock :** of proved and seasoned excellence — used esp. of a gem — **on the rocks** *adv* (*or adj*) **1 a :** in or into a state of destruction or wreckage ⟨lived together six years and had one daughter before the marriage went *on the rocks* —F.B.Gipson⟩ **b :** in or into a state of bankruptcy or destitution ⟨in a brief space of time the company went *on the rocks* —*Amer. Guide Series: La.*⟩ **2 :** on ice cubes ⟨bourbon *on the rocks*⟩

[5]**rock** \"\ *vt* -ED/-ING/-S **:** to throw stones at

**rock·a·by** *or* **rock·a·bye** \'räkə,bī\ *v imper* [[1]*rock* + *-aby*, *-abye* (as in *hushaby*, *hush-a-bye*)] **:** HUSHABY

**rock·a·hom·i·ny** \,räkə'hämənē\ *n* [perh. fr. *rokahamĕn* (in some Algonquian language of Virginia)] *obs* **:** parched corn finely ground

**rock along** *vi* **:** to continue steadily and easily along the same path ⟨an industry that . . . would *rock along* quietly from one decade to the next —*New Yorker*⟩

**rock and roll** *var of* ROCK 'N' ROLL

**rock and rye** *n* **:** an American rye whiskey flavored with orange, lemon, and occas. pineapple and cherry

**rock arm** *n* **:** ROCKER ARM

**rock asphalt** *n* **:** ASPHALT ROCK

**rock·a·way** \'räkə,wā\ *n* -S [perh. fr. *Rockaway*, town in northern New Jersey where carriages were made] **1 :** a light low American four-wheel carriage with a fixed top and open sides that may be covered by waterproof curtains **2 :** a heavy carriage enclosed at sides and rear with a door on each side

**rock badger** *n* **:** [2]HYRAX

**rock barnacle** *n* **:** ACORN BARNACLE

**rock basin** *n* **:** a depression in solid rock often resulting from ice erosion in mountain regions and usu. containing small lakes

**rock bass** *n* **1 :** a sunfish (*Ambloplites rupestris*) that is widely distributed in eastern No. America west of the Alleghenies and esp. the upper Mississippi valley and Great Lakes region that is a good food fish though little esteemed as food — called also *rock sunfish* **2 a :** STRIPED BASS a **b :** any of several sea basses (genus *Paralabrax*) that are widely distributed along the California and adjoining Mexican coast — called also *cabrilla*

**rock beauty** *n* **:** a European alpine perennial herb (*Draba pyrenaica*) having fragrant lilac purple flowers

**rock·bell** \'räk,bel\ *n* **:** COLUMBINE 1a

**rock·ber·ry** \'räk- — *see* BERRY\ *n* **1 :** BEARBERRY 1 **2 a :** CROWBERRY 1a **b :** RED CROWBERRY 1

**rockbird** \'=,=\ *n* **1 :** a seabird (as a murre) that breeds in rocky cliffs **2 :** COCK OF THE ROCK **3 :** PURPLE SANDPIPER

**rock bit** *n* **:** a hardened drill for making holes in hard rock

**rock borer** *n* **:** any of several marine bivalve mollusks (as various members of the genera *Petricola*, *Pholas*, and *Lithophaga*) that bore holes in rock

**rock-boring isopod** \'=,==-\ *n* **:** a marine isopod (*Sphaeroma pentodon*) of the Pacific Coast of No. America that burrows into stone or wood by biting off pieces with its powerful mandibles

**rock bottom** *n* **:** the absolute bottom, foundation, or core ⟨all human beings . . . are, at *rock bottom*, psychologically primitive —Edward Sapir⟩

**rock-bottom** \'=¦==\ *adj* [*rock bottom*] **:** the very lowest ⟨a ~ price⟩

**rockbound** \'=,=\ *adj* **1 :** fringed, surrounded, or covered with rocks **:** ROCKY ⟨a stern and ~ coast —Felicia D. Hemans⟩ ⟨as desolate a stretch of ~ desert as may be found —*Geog. Jour.*⟩ **2 :** stern, rigid, and unyielding in character, doctrine, or moral views ⟨breaks through the barrier of ~ custom —F.C.Laubach⟩ ⟨a square, hulking man who . . . believed with all his ~ soul —P.B.Martin⟩

**rock brake** *n* **:** any of several ferns that grow chiefly on or among rocks: as **a :** CLIFF BRAKE **b :** a fern of the genus *Cryptogamma* **c :** POLYPODY

**rock breaker** *n* **:** STONE CRUSHER

**rock·bridge·ite** \'räk,bri,jīt\ *n* -S [*Rockbridge* County, west central Virginia, its locality + E *-ite*] **:** a mineral ($Fe^{II}Fe_4^{III}(PO_4)_3(OH)_5$) consisting of a basic phosphate of iron isomorphous with frondelite

**rock-built** \'=,=\ *adj* **:** made of or built on rock

**rock burst** *n* **:** a violent expulsion of rock from the walls of a mine opening caused by heavy pressure on brittle rocks in deep mines where mining has deprived the rock of support on one side — compare BUMP

**rock cake** *n* **:** ROCK 5b

**rock candy** *n* **1 :** boiled sugar crystallized in large masses on lightweight string and used esp. in rock and rye **2 :** ROCK 5a(1)

**rock catchfly** *n* **:** a wild pink (*Silene caroliniana*)

**rock cavy** *n* **:** MOCO

**rock cedar** *n* **:** a juniper (*Juniperus mexicana*) of the southwestern U.S. and Mexico that closely resembles the red cedar and has valuable wood used for ties and telegraph poles — called also *mountain cedar*

**rock chestnut oak** *n* **:** a common chestnut oak (*Quercus prinus*)

**rock chute** *n* **:** ROCK HOLE

**rock-climber** \'=,==\ *n* **:** one that engages in rock-climbing

**rock-climbing** \'=,==\ *n* **:** mountain climbing up difficult rocky faces

**rock club moss** *n* **:** FESTOON PINE

**rock cock** *n* **:** COCK OF THE ROCK

**rock cockle** *n* **:** any of several comparatively small edible clams (family Veneridae) of the Pacific coast of No. America that have thick rounded ridged shells resembling those of the cockles

**rock cod** *n* **1 :** ROCKFISH **2 :** any of several groupers of the genus *Epinephelus; esp* **:** BLACK ROCK COD **3 :** a cod that is a variety of the true cod

**rock cork** *n* **:** MOUNTAIN CORK

**rock cornish** *n, usu cap R&C* **:** a crossbred domestic fowl produced by breeding Cornish and White Rock fowls and used esp. for the production of small well-fleshed roasters

**rock crab** *n* **:** any of several crabs inhabiting rocky shores: as **a :** a crab (*Cancer irroratus*) of the east coast of No. America **b :** a crab (*Cancer antennarius*) of the Pacific coast **c :** SALLY LIGHTFOOT **d :** an Australian crab (*Nectocarcinus integrifrons*)

**rockcraft** \'=,=\ *n* **1 a :** the art of building with rock **b :** skill in rockcraft **2 :** skill in climbing over rocks and ledges

**rock cranberry** *n* **:** MOUNTAIN CRANBERRY

**rock cress** *n* **:** any of several rock-loving cresses (as members of the genus *Arabis*)

**rockcrusher** \'=,==\ *n* **1 :** STONE CRUSHER **2 :** a very strong hand of cards held by one player

**rock crystal** *n* **:** transparent quartz **:** CRYSTAL 2

**rock dash** *n* **:** a stucco finish in which crushed rock or pebbles are embedded in the stucco base

**rock dassie** *n* **:** KLIPDASSIE

**rock day** *n, usu cap R&D* [[3]*rock*; fr. the resumption of domestic duties after the Christmas holidays] **:** the day after Epiphany

**rock dove** *n* **:** ROCK PIGEON 1

**rock drill** *n* **:** a machine (as a hammer drill or piston drill) for making holes in rock

**rock dust** *n* **:** pulverulent rock (as shale or limestone) used in rock-dusting — called also *stone dust*

**rock-dust** \'=,=\ *vt* [*rock dust*] **:** to spread or distribute rock dust in (coal mine workings) to reduce the explosion hazard

**rocked** *past of* ROCK

**rock eel** *n* **1 :** GUNNEL **2 :** a blackish green blenny (*Xiphister mucosus*) common in the intertidal zone from Alaska to southern California

**rock elm** *n* **1 a :** a tall widely distributed elm (*Ulmus thomasii*) of eastern No. America that has broadly obovate leaves narrowing abruptly to a point, grayish deeply fissured bark, and light brown wood **b :** the strong tough durable springy wood of the rock elm **2 :** SLIPPERY ELM **3 :** AMERICAN ELM

[1]**rock·er** \'räkə(r)\ *n* -S [ME *rokkere*, fr. *rokken* to rock + *-ere* -er] **1** *archaic* **:** one that rocks a cradle **2 a :** either of two curving pieces of wood or metal on which an object (as a cradle or chair) rocks **b :** any of various objects that rock upon rockers: as (1) **:** CRADLE 1a (2) **:** ROCKING CHAIR (3) **:** an infant's toy having a seat placed between side pieces that are usu. constructed to resemble an animal **c :** any of various objects having the form of a rocker or with parts resembling a rocker: as (1) **:** ROCKER PANEL (2) **:** a skate with a curved blade (3) **:** a curved dentate blade used in mezzotint to roughen the surface of the plate (4) **:** a boat with a rockered keel (5) **:** one of the curved stripes under the three chevrons that indicate the grade of a sergeant (as in the U.S. Army and Marine Corps) **3 :** any of various devices that work with a rocking motion: as **a :** CRADLE 3a **b** *or* **rocker pit** *or* **rocker vat :** a vat equipped with frames on which hides are hung and which rock continuously in order to keep the hides in motion **c** (1) **:** a lever (as in some link motions and gas-engine gears) that is pivoted at or near its center and operates with an up-and-down motion (2) **:** ROCKSHAFT **d :** an adjustable brush holder for a dynamo or motor **e :** a steel or cast-iron pedestal supporting the end of a truss or girder and permitting rotation and horizontal movement caused by expansion and contraction **f :** ROCKING BAR **4 :** a miner or engraver that uses a rocker **5 :** a three-lobed school skating figure performed on either edge and either forward or backward in which the skater executes a turn at each junction of the three lobes in the direction of the natural rotation of the curve being skated and remains on the same edge throughout — compare [5]COUNTER 11 — **off one's rocker :** in a state of insanity or confusion ⟨went *off her rocker*, and had to be put away in a mental home —Mervyn Wall⟩

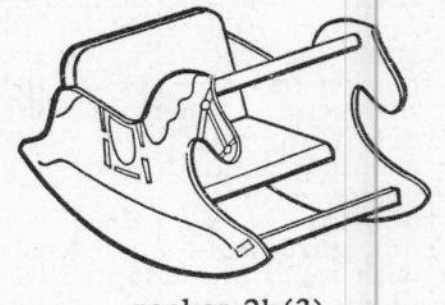

rocker 2b(3)

[2]**rocker** \"\ *vt* -ED/-ING/-S **:** to build (as a boat keel) with a camber like a rocker

[3]**rocker** \"\ *n* -S [[4]*rock* + *-er*] **:** ROCK PIGEON

**rocker arm** *n* **:** a center-pivoted lever to push an automotive engine valve down when the camshaft pushes the lift rod against the other end of the lever

**rocker bent** *n* **:** a bent supporting a bridge span hinged at one or both ends to provide for expansion and contraction of the span

**rocker cam** *n* **:** a cam (as on a rockshaft) with a rocking or reciprocating movement

**rocker keel** *n* **:** a rockered keel

**rocker panel** *n* **:** the portion of the body paneling of a vehicle that is situated below the doorsills of the passenger compartment

**rocker shaft** *n* **:** ROCKSHAFT

**rocker-stamp** \'==,=\ *vt* **:** to impress a continuous design on (pottery) with an implement rocked at successive points

**rock·ery** \'räkərē, -əri\ *n* -ES [[4]*rock* + *-ery*] **:** ROCK GARDEN

[1]**rock·et** \'räkət, *usu* -əd·+V\ *n* -S [ME *roket*, fr. ONF *roquet*, fr. (assumed) OF *roc* coat + OF *-et* — more at ROCHET] *chiefly dial* **:** ROCHET

[2]**rocket** \"\ *n* -S [MF *roquette*, fr. OIt *rochetta*, *ruchetta*, dim. of *ruca* garden rocket, fr. L *eruca* — more at ERUCA] **1 :** GARDEN ROCKET 1 **2 a :** a plant of the genus *Hesperis; esp* **:** DAME'S VIOLET **b :** any of several plants resembling dame's violet

[3]**rocket** *n* -S *often attrib* [It *rocchetta* rocket, small distaff, dim. of *rocca* distaff, of Gmc origin; akin to OHG *rocko* distaff — more at ROCK] **1 :** a firework consisting of a cylindrical case partly filled with a combustible composition (as potassium nitrate, charcoal, and sulfur), fastened to a guiding stick, projected through the air by gases liberated when the charge is ignited by a fuse, and used for pyrotechnic display (as stars, gold or silver rain, floral designs) and for signaling **2 :** an incendiary weapon consisting of a tailpiece, fuse and powder charge, and a round-nosed hollow warhead filled with pitch, powder, tallow, and potassium nitrate and fired upward at about 45 degrees through a metal pipe in a wooden chute leading to a square hole in the side of a ship ⟨the ~*s*' red glare —F.S.Key⟩ **3 :** a device consisting of a case containing a combustible composition projected through the air by reac-

tion from the rearward discharge of gases liberated by combustion and used as an incendiary or explosive missile or as a propelling unit (as for a lifesaving line or a whaling harpoon) **4** *also* **rocket engine** *or* **rocket motor :** a jet engine that operates on the same principle as the firework rocket, that consists essentially of a combustion chamber and an exhaust nozzle, that carries either liquid or solid propellants which provide the fuel and oxygen needed for combustion and thus make the engine independent of the oxygen of the air, and that is used esp. for the propulsion of a missile (as a bomb or shell) or a vehicle (as an airplane or automobile) **5 :** a rocket-propelled bomb, missile, or other projectile **6** *chiefly Brit* **:** REBUKE

4**rocket** \"\ *vb* -ED/-ING/-S *vt* **1 :** to attack with rockets ⟨bombing, strafing and ~*ing* enemy frontline troops and rear-area supply lines —*N.Y.Times*⟩ **2 :** to convey by means of a rocket ⟨~ a satellite into orbit⟩ **3 :** to bring into prominence ⟨coal . . . suddenly ~*ed* this railroad flag stop . . . into industrial importance —*Amer. Guide Series: Va.*⟩ ~ *vi* **1 :** to rise straight up and swiftly when flushed — used esp. of pheasants **2 a :** to rise up swiftly, spectacularly, and with force ⟨~*ed* to stardom almost overnight —*Time*⟩ **b :** to travel rapidly ⟨the salesmen . . . piled back into their cars and ~*ed* off to the next live account —Richard Bissell⟩ ⟨faster and faster the tons of marble ~ down the valley —Judson Philips⟩ **syn** see RISE

**rocket bomb** *n* **1 :** an aerial bomb designed for release at low altitude and equipped with a rocket apparatus for giving it added momentum **2 :** a rocket-propelled bomb launched from the ground

**rocket candytuft** *n* **:** a European candytuft (*Iberis amara*) having large and full flower clusters

**rocket cress** *n* **:** a winter cress (*Barbarea vulgaris*)

**rock·e·teer** \¦räkə¦ti(ə)r, -iə\ *n* -S **1 :** one who fires, pilots, or rides in a rocket **2 :** a scientist who specializes in rocketry; *specif* **:** a designer of rockets

**rock·et·er** \ˈräkəd·ə(r), -ətə-\ *n* -S **1 :** a game bird that rockets **2 :** ROCKETEER

**rocket larkspur** *n* **:** a commonly cultivated annual larkspur (*Delphinium ajacis*) of southern Europe with showy blue or sometimes violet or pinkish flowers

**rocket launcher** *n* **:** a launcher consisting of a tube or cluster of tubes (as a three-tube unit placed on the underside of an airplane wing) for firing rocket shells — see BAZOOKA

**rocket plane** *n* **:** an airplane propelled by rockets or armed with rocket launchers

**rocket-propelled** \¦===¦=\ *adj* **:** propelled by a rocket engine

**rocket propulsion** *n* **:** propulsion by means of a rocket engine

**rock·et·ry** \ˈräkətrē, -tri\ *n* -ES **:** the study of, experimentation with, or use of rockets

**rocket salad** *n* **:** GARDEN ROCKET 1

**rocket ship** *n* **1 :** a rocket-propelled ship **2 :** a small warship equipped with rocket launchers **3 :** a rocket-propelled craft capable of navigation beyond the earth's atmosphere

**rocket sled** *n* **:** a rocket-propelled sled on a rail

**rock face** *n* **1 :** a weather-worn quarry face **2 :** FACE 7c

**rock-faced** \ˈ=¦=\ *adj* **:** having a face of or resembling rock

**rock falcon** *n* **1** *or* **rock hawk :** MERLIN **2 :** PEREGRINE FALCON

**rockfall** \ˈ=,=\ *n* **:** a mass of falling or fallen rocks — compare ROCKSLIDE

**rock fastener** *n* **:** an interlocking seal formed by looped ends of wire binding a wood box

**rock fence** *n, chiefly South* **:** STONE WALL 1

**rock fern** *n* **:** any of various ferns that grow chiefly on or among rocks: as **a :** EVERGREEN WOOD FERN 1 **b :** a finely divided tropical Asiatic and Australasian fern (*Cheilanthes tennifolia*) that has been implicated in Australia in an acute intoxication of cattle **c :** any of several chiefly tropical ferns of the genus *Asplenium*

**rock-fill** \ˈ=,=\ *adj* [4*rock* + *fill*, n.] **:** composed of large rock or stone loosely placed ⟨*rock-fill* dam⟩

**rockfish** \ˈ=,=\ *n* **:** any of various fishes that live among rocks or on rocky bottoms: as **a :** any of several fishes of the family Scorpaenidae including the black rockfish, the cabezone, the priestfish, and the red rockfish that are all valuable market fishes — see GOPHER 4 **b :** STRIPED BASS a **c :** any of several groupers **d :** GREENLING 1a

**rock flour** *n* **:** finely powdered rock material produced by grinding action (as of a glacier on its bed) — called also *glacial meal*

**rockfoil** \ˈ=,=\ *n* [4*rock* + *foil* (leaf)] **:** SAXIFRAGE

**rock garden** *n* **:** a garden laid out among rocks or decorated with rocks and adapted for the growth of particular kinds of plants (as alpines) — compare ALPINE GARDEN

**rock gas** *n* **:** NATURAL GAS

**rock geranium** *n* **:** ALUMROOT 1

**rock glacier** *n* **:** a rock stream having the general appearance of a valley glacier

**rock goat** *n* **:** IBEX

**rock goldenrod** *n* **:** a perennial goldenrod (*Solidago pumila*) of western No. America having tufted basal leaves, a very short stem, and yellow flower heads

**rock goose** *n* **:** KELP GOOSE

**rock grouper** *n* **:** RED ROCKFISH 2

**rock grouse** *n* **1 :** ROCK PTARMIGAN **2 :** SANDGROUSE

**rock guenon** *n* **:** PATAS

**rock gypsum** *n* **:** massive coarsely crystalline to fine-grained gypsum

**rockhair** \ˈ=,=\ *n* **:** a slender rock-inhabiting tufted lichen (*Alectoria jubata*) used in dyeing

**rock hare** *n* **:** any of several very fleet short-eared usu. reddish hares (genus *Pronolagus*) of southern Africa — called also *red hare*

**rock hind** *n* **:** any of various spotted groupers commonly found about rocky coasts or reefs; *esp* **:** a common small form (*Epinephelus adscensionis*) of the tropical Atlantic and Mediterranean typically grayish green with red or red-brown spots and white blotches — compare HIND

**rock hole** *n* **:** a raise in a coal mine driven from a gangway or breast to an overlying coal seam — called also *rock chute*

**rock hopper** *n* **:** any of several small penguins (genus *Eudyptes*) of the Falkland Islands, New Zealand, and antarctic waters that have a short thick bill and a yellow crest — called also *crested penguin*

**rock hound** *n* **1 :** GEOLOGIST; *esp* **:** one who searches for oil **2 :** one who hunts and collects gemstones or minerals as a hobby

**rock hyrax** *n* **:** a hyrax that frequents barren rocky areas: **a :** KLIPDASSIE **b :** SYRIAN HYRAX

**rockier** *comparative of* ROCKY

**rockies** *pl of* ROCKY

**rockiest** *superlative of* ROCKY

**rock·i·ness** \ˈräkēnəs, -kin-\ *n* -ES **:** the quality or state of being rocky

1**rock·ing** \ˈräkiŋ, -kēŋ\ *adj* [ME *rokkinge*, pres. part. of *rokken* to rock] **1 a :** having a swaying, rolling, or back-and-forth movement **b :** used for rocking **2 :** held up by a horizontal quarter circle — see BRAND illustration

2**rock·ing** \ˈräkən, -kiŋ\ *n* -S [3*rock* + *-ing*] *Scot* **:** an evening gathering; *esp* **:** a spinning party

**rocking bar** *n* **1 :** a bascule-shaped plate in a watch that contains the winding wheels and rocks them alternately to engage first the winding and then the hand setting mechanism **2 :** a device in an alarm clock or watch that engages the time and alarm mainsprings

**rocking bed** *n* **:** a powered bed that uses gravity as an artificial respirator by raising a person's head above the feet so that the weight of the abdominal organs stretches the diaphragm and raising the feet above the head so that the weight of the organs compresses the diaphragm

**rocking cam** *n* **:** ROCKER CAM

**rocking chair** *n* **:** a chair mounted on rockers

**rocking furnace** *n* **:** an often electrically heated horizontal cylindrical melting furnace rolling back and forth in a usu. geared cradle

**rock·ing·ham ware** \ˈräkiŋ,ham-, -ŋəm-\ *n, usu cap R* [after Charles Watson-Wentworth, Marquis of *Rockingham* †1782 Eng. statesman on whose estate it was originally made] **1 :** a white earthenware covered with brown glaze of varying shades **2 :** a very brilliantly gilded and painted bone china

**rocking horse** *n* **:** a toy consisting of a figure of a horse mounted on rockers or on a mechanism permitting rocking on which a child may sit and rock — called also *hobbyhorse*

rocking horse

**rock·ing·ly** *adv* **:** in a rocking manner

**rocking pier** *n* **:** a bridge pier hinged so as to allow a slight longitudinal motion of the bridge when the latter expands or contracts

**rocking rhythm** *n* **:** UNDULATING CADENCE

**rocking shaft** *n* **:** ROCKSHAFT

**rocking stone** *n* **:** an often large stone so balanced upon its foundation that it can be rocked or slightly moved with little force

**rocking tool** *n* **:** ROCKER 2c(3)

**rocking valve** *or* **rocking slide valve** *n* **:** a steam engine valve consisting of a disk or cylindrical piece with the necessary openings that oscillates or revolves on its seat

**rock jasmine** *n* **:** a plant of the genus *Androsace*

**rock kangaroo** *n* **:** ROCK WALLABY

**rock kelp** *n* **:** ROCKWEED

**rock lark** *n* **:** ROCK PIPIT

**rock larkspur** *n* **:** DWARF LARKSPUR

**rock·lay** \ˈrä,klā\ *chiefly Scot var of* ROQUELAURE

**rock leather** *n* **:** MOUNTAIN LEATHER

**rock·less** \ˈräkləs\ *adj* **:** lacking rocks

**rock·let** \-lət\ *n* -S **:** a small rock

**rock lever** *or* **rocking lever** *n* **:** a hinged lever that works with a rocking movement **:** an equalizing bar for draft animals hinged by a knuckle joint

**rocklike** \ˈ=,=\ *adj* **:** resembling a rock esp. in hardness

**rock lily** *n* **1 :** a tropical American club moss (*Selaginella convoluta*) that grows in dense tufts **2 :** an Australian orchid (*Dendrobium speciosum*) having large green pseudobulbs and dense racemes of creamy white flowers that is usu. found growing on rocks **3 :** any of several rock-loving herbs: as **a :** COLUMBINE **b :** PASQUEFLOWER

**rock·ling** \ˈräkliŋ\ *n, pl* **rocklings** *also* **rockling** [4*rock* + *ling*] **1 :** any of several small rather elongate marine cods (family Gadidae); *esp* **:** a fish (*Gadus mustela* or *Motella mustela*) that is common in tide pools along European coasts and has four barbels on the snout and one beneath the chin — called also *five-bearded rockling* **2 :** an Australian and New Zealand fish (genus *Genypterus*) of the family Ophidiidae

**rock lobster** *n* **1 :** SPINY LOBSTER **2 :** the flesh of the Cape crawfish esp. when canned or frozen for use as food

**rock louse** *n* **:** a small innocuous Australian isopod (*Deto marina*) living under rocks along the seashore

**rock madwort** *n* **:** BASKET-OF-GOLD

**rock·man** \ˈräkmən, -,man\ *n, pl* **rockmen 1 :** a worker who removes rocks or ledges by blasting **2 :** a worker in a mine: **a** *Brit* **:** a miner who gets out slate rock in a slate mine **b :** SLATEMAN **3 :** a jackhammer operator **4 :** TOWERMAN d

**rock manakin** *n* **:** COCK OF THE ROCK

**rock maple** *n* **:** a sugar maple (*Acer saccharum*)

**rock martin** *n* **:** ROCK SWALLOW

**rock mat** *n* **:** any of several evergreen prostrate subshrubs constituting a genus (*Petrophytum*) of the family Rosaceae

**rock melon** *n* **:** CANTALOUPE

**rock milk** *n* **:** AGARIC MINERAL

**rock moss** *n* **1 :** a rock-loving lichen **2 :** WIDOW'S-CROSS

**rock mouse** *n* **:** a small southern African murid rodent (*Petromyscus collinus*) living in rocky areas

**rock 'n' roll** *or* **rock and roll** \¦räkən¦rōl\ *n* **1 :** jazz characterized by a strong beat and much repetition of simple phrases often with both blues and folk song elements **2 :** an improvisatory style of popular dancing associated with rock 'n' roll music

**rock oak** *n* **:** any of several American oaks: as **a :** BASKET OAK **b :** CHESTNUT OAK C **c :** BLUE OAK

**rock oil** *n* [trans. of ML *petroleum*] **:** PETROLEUM

**rock·oon** \(ˈ)rä¦kün\ *n* -S [3*rock*et + ball*oon*] **:** a small rocket carried to a high altitude by a balloon and then fired

**rock opossum** *n* **:** a rock wallaby (*Petrogale xanthopus*)

**rock ouzel** *n* **:** RING OUZEL

**rock oyster** *n* **:** any of various oysters or other bivalves occurring attached to rocks: **a :** a mollusk of the genus *Hinnites* represented on the west coast of No. America by a large flattened bivalve (*H. giganteus*) **b :** a mollusk of *Chama* or related genera **c :** JINGLE SHELL

**rock painting** *n* **:** a painting on rock (as a cave wall, cliff, or boulder) made by primitive peoples

**rock parrakeet** *or* **rock parrot** *n* **:** a small chiefly greenish Australian parrakeet (*Neophema petrophila*) that nests in holes in cliffs

**rock partridge** *n* **:** a partridge (*Alectoris graeca*) having many varieties widely distributed in southern and eastern Asia and about the Mediterranean esp. in dry uplands — compare CHUKAR, GREEK PARTRIDGE, RED-LEGGED PARTRIDGE

**rock phosphate** *n* **:** phosphate rock used as a fertilizer

**rock pigeon** *n* **1 :** a bluish gray wild pigeon (*Columba livia*) with a purplish breast, white rump, and dark wing bars that is found chiefly along rocky coasts of Europe and Asia — called also *rock dove* **2 :** SANDGROUSE

**rock pile** *n* [so called fr. the custom of requiring prisoners to work at breaking rock] **:** JAIL

**rock pine** *n* **1 :** a cypress pine (*Callitris verrucosa*) **2 :** a ponderosa pine (*Pinus ponderosa scopulorum*)

**rock pink** *n* **:** a pink-flowered perennial herb (*Talinum calycinum*) of the western U. S.

**rock pipit** *n* **:** a European pipit (*Anthus spinoletta petrosus*) that frequents rocky shores — called also *rock lark*

**rock plant** *n* **:** a plant that grows on or among rocks or is suited to a rock garden

**rock plover** *n* **1 :** PURPLE SANDPIPER **2 :** TURNSTONE

**rock pool** *n* **:** a tide pool in a rocky shoreline or reef

**rock pressure** *n* **1 :** the pressure on fluids in subsurface formation **2 :** the pressure indicated in a closed well

**rock ptarmigan** *n* **:** any of various ptarmigans (esp. *Lagopus mutus*)

**rock purslane** *n* **:** a plant of the genus *Calandrinia*

**rock python** *n* **:** a very large python (*Python sebae*) of tropical and southern Africa — called also *rock snake*

**rock rabbit** *n* **1 :** 2HYRAX **2 :** PIKA

**rock rat** *n* **:** any of several African rodents of rocky uplands; *esp* **:** a small southern African hystricomorph rodent (*Petromys typicus*) having four grinding teeth on each side in each jaw

**rock-ribbed** \ˈ=¦=\ *adj* **1 :** ROCKY **2 :** firm and inflexible in doctrine or integrity ⟨a staunch, *rock-ribbed* party paper —*Omnibook*⟩ ⟨judges who stood *rock-ribbed* for legality —Zechariah Chafee⟩

**rock river** *n* **:** an exceptionally long and narrow rock stream

**rockrose** \ˈ=¦=\ *n* **1 :** a plant of the Cistaceae (esp. of the genera *Cistus*, *Helianthemum*, and *Crocanthemum*) **2 :** any of several Australian shrubs (as of the genus *Hibbertia*)

**rockrose family** *n* **:** CISTACEAE

**rocks** *pres 3d sing of* ROCK, *pl of* ROCK

**rock salmon** *n* **1 :** AMBERJACK a **2 :** a common silvery pink to bright red snapper (*Lutjanus argentimaculatus*) of the tropical Indo-Pacific highly esteemed for food and sport **3 :** any of several fishes (as the pollack, the wolffish, or the dogfish) used as food in England but not esteemed as food fishes under their usual names

**rock salt** *n* **:** common salt occurring in solid form as a mineral esp. in rocklike masses and usu. more or less colored by iron **:** HALITE; *sometimes* **:** salt artificially prepared in large crystals or masses

**rock samphire** *n* **:** SAMPHIRE 1, 2

**rock sand** *n* **:** the detritus of eroded or abraded rock commonly used for cores in casting

**rock sandwort** *n* **:** a low perennial tufted herb (*Arenaria stricta*) of northeastern No. America with subulate rigid leaves and small white flowers in dichotomous cymes

**rock saw** *n* **:** a small coarse-toothed saw that cuts into a log ahead of the main saw and protects the latter by removing small stones or pebbles embedded in the log

**rock saxifrage** *n* **:** EARLY SAXIFRAGE

**rock seal** *n* **:** HARBOR SEAL

1**rockshaft** \ˈ=,=\ *n* [1*rock* + *shaft*] **:** a shaft that oscillates on its journals instead of revolving and that usu. carries levers or projecting pieces (as arms, wipers, or tumblers) to receive and communicate reciprocating motion

2**rockshaft** \"\ *n* [4*rock* + *shaft*] **:** a shaft through which rock filling is introduced into a mine

**rock shell** *n* **:** a gastropod mollusk of the family Muricidae

**rock-shelter** \ˈ=¦==\ *n* **:** a natural shelter between or under standing rocks in which the debris and campfires of prehistoric peoples are found

**rock·skip·per** \ˈ=,==\ *n* **:** any of several blennies; *esp* **:** a small Indo-Pacific fish (*Alticops periophthalmus*) that is extremely agile in and about rocky tide pools and reefs

**rockslide** \ˈ=,=\ *n* **1 :** a usu. rapid downward movement of rock fragments that slide over an inclined surface **2 :** a rock mass moved by a rockslide — compare ROCKFALL

**rock snake** *n* **1 :** any of several large pythons: as **a :** ROCK PYTHON **b :** INDIAN PYTHON **c :** CARPET SNAKE **2 :** a snake of the genus *Bungarus* (as the krait)

**rock snipe** *n* **:** PURPLE SANDPIPER

**rock soap** *n* **:** MOUNTAIN SOAP

**rock sparrow** *n* **1 :** any of several Old World sparrows of the genus *Petronia* (as *P. petronia* and *P. superciliaris*) **2 :** a sparrow (*Aimophila ruficeps eremoeca*) of Mexico and Texas

**rock spiraea** *n* **:** a plant of the genus *Holodiscus* — compare OCEAN SPRAY

**rock spray** *n* **:** any of several plants of the genus *Cotoneaster; esp* **:** a prostrate evergreen Himalayan shrub (*C. horizontalis*) cultivated for its solitary white flowers and bright red fruits

**rock squirrel** *n* **1 :** a large ground squirrel (*Citellus variegatus grammurus*) of western No. America having better developed tail and ears than the more strictly burrowing species **2 :** any of several relatively large terrestrial squirrels (genus *Sciurotamias* or *Rupestes*) of the rocky uplands of east central Asia

**rockstaff** \ˈ=,=\ *n* [1*rock* + *staff*] **:** an oscillating bar (as the lever of a forge bellows)

**rock starling** *n* [4*rock* + *starling*] **:** RING OUZEL

**rock stream** *n* **:** a mass of rock fragments that moves or has moved slowly down a slope under its own weight usu. aided by frost action and sometimes by interstitial ice — compare ROCK GLACIER, ROCK RIVER

**rock sturgeon** *n* **:** LAKE STURGEON

**rock sucker** *n* **:** LAMPREY

**rock sunfish** *n* **:** ROCK BASS 1

**rock swallow** *n* **:** any of several swallows that nest on rocky crags; *esp* **:** a common Eurasiatic bird (*Ptyonoprogne rupestris*) — called also *crag martin, rock martin*

**rock tar** *n* **:** PETROLEUM

**rock terrace** *n* **:** a terrace of more durable bedrock left on the side of a valley cut by erosion in flat-lying sedimentary or volcanic strata of varying resistance

**rock thrush** *or* **rock shrike** *n* **:** any of various Old World thrushes of the genus *Monticola*

**rock tripe** *n* **:** a lichen of the genus *Umbilicaria* or of the related genus *Gyrophora* that has a flat coriaceous blackish thallus, is common on rocks in arctic, subarctic, and north temperate regions, and is used as food in cases of extremity

**rock trout** *n* **:** GREENLING 1a

**rock turn** *n* **:** a turn in ballroom dancing in which the couple use a rocking step

**rock turquoise** *n* **:** turquoise matrix

**rock violet** *n* **:** a green alga (*Trentepohlia iolithus*) occurring on rocks at high elevations and exhaling an odor of violets

**rock vole** *n* **:** a light-colored vole (*Microtus chrotorrhinus*) of rocky highlands of northeastern No. America

**rock wallaby** *n* **:** any of various medium-sized kangaroos of the genus *Petrogale* having a completely naked muzzle and a slender tufted tail and inhabiting rocky regions — called also *rock kangaroo*

**rock warbler** *n* **:** a small Australian singing bird (*Origma rubricata*) that frequents rocky ravines

**rock waste** *n* **:** the material resulting from the disintegration and decomposition of rock by weathering

**rockweed** \ˈ=,=\ *n* **:** a coarse seaweed of the family Fucaceae growing attached to rocks; *esp* **:** a member of the genera *Fucus* or *Ascophyllum*

**rockweed bird** *n* **:** PURPLE SANDPIPER

**rock·well hardness** \ˈrä,kwel-, -kwəl-\ *n, usu cap R* [after Stanley P. *Rockwell*, 20th cent. Am. metallurgist] **:** the hardness of a metal or alloy measured by an apparatus in which a diamond-pointed cone is pressed into the metal to a standard depth to determine the relative resistance to penetration as indicated automatically by a number on a dial

**rock whiting** *n* **:** KELPFISH b

**rock wool** *n* **:** mineral wool made by blowing a jet of steam through molten rock (as limestone or siliceous rock) or through slag and used chiefly for heat and sound insulation

**rockwork** \ˈ=,=\ *n* **1 :** a mass of rocks **2 a :** ROCK GARDEN **b :** artificial rock ledges and waterfalls in gardens **3 a :** stonework with a surface left broken and rough **b :** rock-faced masonry **4 :** ROCKCRAFT 2

**rock wren** *n* **1 :** a wren (*Salpinctes obsoletus*) of arid parts of the western U. S. and Mexico **2 :** a small short-tailed passerine bird (*Xenicus gilviventris*) of New Zealand

1**rocky** \ˈräkē, -ki\ *adj* -ER/-EST [ME *rokky*, fr. *rokke* rock, cliff + *-y*, adj. suffix] **1 :** abounding in or consisting of rocks ⟨a ~ shore⟩ **2 :** difficult to impress or affect **:** HARD, INSENSITIVE, OBDURATE ⟨may he also move my mind, and ~ heart so strike and rend —James Howell⟩ **3 :** firmly held **:** STEADFAST ⟨eccentrics . . . have their ~ rightness even when the world judges them to have been wildly wrong —*Times Lit. Supp.*⟩

2**rocky** \"\ *adj* [1*rock* + *-y*] **1 :** prone to rock or totter **:** UNSTABLE ⟨wore high ~ heels —Wright Morris⟩ **2 :** ill at ease, physically upset, or mentally confused (as from a blow, drinking excessively, or sickness) ⟨feeling pretty ~ on account of the siege I went through last night —E.A.Robinson⟩ ⟨wound up with a two-inch cut under the left eye and was ~ at the final bell —*N.Y. Times*⟩ **3 a :** appearing likely to fail **:** UNPROMISING ⟨the wedding got off to a ~ start —R.L.Taylor⟩ **b :** marked by obstacles **:** DIFFICULT ⟨eight ~ months in business —*Time*⟩ **4 :** tending towards craziness **:** DAFT ⟨a bit frisky, if indeed not slightly ~ —Alma Stone⟩ **5 :** UNCOUTH, OBSCENE ⟨a ~ story⟩

3**rocky** \"\ *n* -ES [4*rock* + *-y*, n. suffix] *Austral* **:** ROCK CRAB

**rocky ford** \¦==¦=\ *n, usu cap R&F* [fr. *Rocky Ford*, city in southeast Colorado that is the trade center for a region producing such muskmelons] **:** any of various netted muskmelons that are typically of superior shipping quality

**rocky mountain** \¦==¦==\ *adj, usu cap R&M* [fr. *Rocky mountains*, mountain system in western No. America] **:** of or relating to the Rocky mountains

**rocky mountain bee plant** *n, usu cap R&M* **:** a spiderflower (*Cleome serrulata*) of north central and western No. America sometimes used as an ornamental — called also *stinking clover*

**rocky mountain canary** *n, usu cap R&M, chiefly West* **:** BURRO

**rocky mountain elk** *n, usu cap R&M* **:** a wapiti (*Cervus canadensis nelsoni*)

**rocky mountain fir** *n, usu cap R&M* **:** ALPINE FIR

**rocky mountain garrot** *n, usu cap R&M* **:** BARROW'S GOLDENEYE

**rocky mountain goat** *n, usu cap R&M* **:** MOUNTAIN GOAT 1

**rocky mountain grape** *n, usu cap R&M* **:** OREGON GRAPE

**rocky mountain grasshopper** *or* **rocky mountain locust** *n, usu cap R&M* **:** a No. American grasshopper (*Melanoplus spretus*)

**rocky mountain jay** *n, usu cap R&M* **:** a Canada jay (*Perisoreus canadensis capitalis*) having a white head and being widely distributed in the Rocky mountain area from Montana to Arizona and New Mexico

**rocky mountain juniper** *or* **rocky mountain red cedar** *n, usu cap 1st R&M* **:** a small to medium-sized conical evergreen tree (*Juniperus scopulorum*) that is native to the Rocky mountain region, has reddish brown shreddy bark, often drooping branchlets, and gray-green foliage, and is used for hedges and other ornamental purposes

**rocky mountain maple** *n, usu cap R&1stM* **:** DWARF MAPLE

**rocky mountain oyster** *n, usu cap R&M* **:** MOUNTAIN OYSTER

**rocky mountain sheep** *n, usu cap R&M* : BIGHORN
**rocky mountain spotted fever** *n, usu cap R&M* : an acute febrile disease that is characterized by chills, fever, prostration, pains in muscles and joints, and a red to purple eruption and is caused by a microorganism (*Rickettsia rickettsii*) transmitted by the bite of the Rocky Mountain wood tick
**rocky mountain whitefish** *n, usu cap R&M* : a whitefish (*Prosopium williamsonii*) of the western U. S. and Canada
**rocky mountain white oak** *n, usu cap R&M* : any of several Rocky Mountain trees of the genus *Quercus*
**rocky mountain white pine** *n, usu cap R&M* : LIMBER PINE
**rocky mountain willow** *n, usu cap R&M* : a low much-branched shrubby willow (*Salix saximontana*) of the boreal regions of northwestern No. America, having oblong-oval to orbicular leaves
**rocky mountain wood tick** *n, usu cap R&M* : a widely distributed wood tick (*Dermacentor andersoni*) of western No. America that is a vector of Rocky Mountain spotted fever and sometimes causes tick paralysis
**¹ro·co·co** \rə'kō(,)kō, rō'k- *also* 'rōkə,kō\ *adj* [F, irreg. fr. *rocaille*; fr. the prevalence of rocaille ornamentation in 18th century France] **1** : OUTMODED, QUAINT, OLD-FASHIONED **2 a** : of, relating to, or having the characteristics of a style of artistic expression prevalent esp. during the 18th century chiefly in interior decoration, furniture, porcelain, and tapestry and characterized by an often fanciful and frivolous use of curved spatial forms, light and fantastic often flowing, reversed, or unsymmetrical curved lines, and ornament of pierced shellwork ⟨the explosive energy of the baroque . . . lessens as the ~ spirit of the new century lightens the motives it has inherited, and replaces gusto with a slighter vivacity —*History of World Art*⟩ — compare BAROQUE, LOUIS QUINZE **b** : of, relating to, or having the characteristics of a style of painting esp. prevalent during the 18th century exemplified by Watteau and often depicting scenes from classical mythology inspired by the fêtes champêtres **c** : of, relating to, or having the characteristics of a style of literature prevalent esp. in Germany in the first half of the 18th century and typified esp. by lighthearted playful lyric pieces often with suggestive erotic hints **d** : of, relating to, or having the characteristics of a style of music esp. of the 18th century marked by light gay ornamentation and the departure from thorough bass and polyphony **e** : excessively ornate or intricate ⟨his bed was covered with a lavishly embroidered velvet slip, far too ~ for any interior decorator's parlor but more like evidence of an adolescent and pathetically mistaken idea of what a prince might choose —Kay Boyle⟩ ⟨the lush and heartbreakingly ~ writings of . . . a society reporter of long ago whose prose gyrations must be read to be believed —Stanley Walker⟩ ⟨caught out with a ~ phrase or an overstuffed image —*Los Angeles (Calif.) Times*⟩ **syn** see ORNATE
**²rococo** \"\ *n* -s [F, fr. *rococo*, adj.] : rococo work or style
**rocombole** *var of* ROCAMBOLE
**rocou** *var of* ROUCOU
**rocs** *pl of* ROC
**¹rod** \'räd\ *n* -s [ME, fr. OE *rodd*; akin to ON *rudda* club and perh. to OHG *riutan* to clear land — more at RID] **1 a** (1) : a straight slender stick growing upon or cut from a tree or bush : SHOOT, WAND (2) : OSIER (3) : WALKING STICK (4) : a stick or bundle of twigs used for punishing ⟨he who spares the ~ hates his son —Prov 13:24 (RSV)⟩ (5) : a short club or stick with a bulging end used by shepherds as a cudgel to protect their flocks from wolves (6) *obs* : a stick or switch used while riding (7) : FISHING POLE (8) : a bar or staff for measuring (9) : a narrow board, lath, batten, or strip usu. cut to a fixed length and marked with feet and inches or usu. the heights and other dimensions of work to be done — called also *staff* (10) : a long wooden straightedge used with the edge against fresh plaster to bring the plaster to a true surface **b** : a slender bar resembling a wand of wood: as (1) : FISHING ROD (2) *dial Brit* : a wagon shaft (3) : RAMROD (4) : a member used in tension (as for sustaining a suspended weight) or in tension and compression (as for transmitting reciprocating motion) : CONNECTING ROD (5) : any of various parts of the metal framework below the body of a railroad car — usu. used in the phrase *ride the rods* ⟨then I rode the ~s east —Earle Birney⟩ (6) *slang* : REVOLVER, PISTOL (7) : a wood or metal often expandable bar used for hanging household items (as window or shower curtains, clothes, and towels) (8) : LIGHTNING ROD **c** (1) : SCEPTER (2) : a wand or staff carried as a badge of office by a marshal, usher, or similar official **2 a** (1) : a means of punishment (2) : punishment inflicted **b** : POWER, AUTHORITY, TYRANNY ⟨shall rule them with a ~ of iron —Rev 2:27 (RSV)⟩ **3 a** : a unit of length equal to 5½ yards or 16½ feet — see MEASURE table **b** : a square rod **4** : any of the long rod-shaped sensory bodies in the retina responsive to faint light — compare CONE 3c; see SCOTOPIA **5** : a bacterium shaped like a rod **6** : WHIP 3a **7** : FISHERMAN **8** : HOT ROD
**²rod** \"\ *vt* **rodded**; **rodded**; **rodding**; **rods 1** : to provide with lightning rods **2** : to pack tight, smooth, or pulverize (as concrete) by pounding with a rod **3** : to remove obstacles from or clean (a receptacle) by running a rod through
**rod adaptation** *n* : DARK ADAPTATION
**rod breaker** *n* : a breaker whose moldboard is replaced by bent rods to reduce friction
**rod cell** *n* : MACROSCLEREID
**rod–cone theory** *n* : DUPLICITY THEORY
**rod·der** \'rädə(r)\ *n* -s [¹*rod* + *-er*] : a textile worker who folds double-width goods
**¹rode** [ME *rood*, *rode* (past), fr. OE *rād*] *past and chiefly dial past part of* RIDE
**²rode** \'rōd\ *dial Brit var of* RUD
**³rode** \"\ *n* -s [origin unknown] : a light rope for a boat's anchor
**rode goose** \"-\ *n* [alter. of *road goose*] *Brit* : a brant (*Branta bernicla*)
**¹ro·dent** \'rōd³nt\ *adj* [L *rodent-*, *rodens*, pres. part. of *rodere* to gnaw — more at RAT] **1** : GNAWING, BITING, CORRODING **2** [NL *Rodentia*] : of or relating to the Rodentia or a rodent
**²rodent** *n* -s [NL *Rodentia*] **1** : a mammal of the order Rodentia **2** : a small mammal suggesting a member of the Rodentia (as a shrew or a pika)
**ro·den·tia** \rō'dench(ē)ə, -ntēə\ *n pl, cap* [NL, fr. L, neut. pl. of *rodent-*, *rodens*, pres. part. of *rodere* to gnaw] **1** : an order of Eutheria comprising relatively small gnawing mammals with a single pair of upper incisors that grow from persistent pulps and bear enamel chiefly in front to produce a chisel-shaped edge — compare HYSTRICOMORPHA, MYOMORPHA, SCIUROMORPHA **2** *in some classifications* : an order coextensive with Glires — **ro·den·tian** \-ənt\ *adj or n*
**ro·den·tial** \-əl\ *adj* [NL *Rodentia* + E *-al*] : of or relating to the Rodentia — **ro·den·tial·ly** \-ēlē\ *adv*
**ro·den·ti·ci·dal** \rō,dentə'sīd³l\ *adj* [²*rodent* + *-i-* + *-cidal*] **1** : destroying or controlling rodents **2** [*rodenticide* + *-al*] : of or relating to a rodenticide
**ro·den·ti·cide** \-'≈ə,sīd\ *n* -s [²*rodent* + *-i-* + *-cide*] : an agent that kills rodents; *broadly* : an agent that repels or controls rodents
**rodent ulcer** *n* : a chronic persisting ulcer of the exposed skin and esp. of the face destructive locally and spreading slowly that is usu. a basal-cell carcinoma
**ro·deo** \÷'rōdē,ō, rō'dā(,)ō *sometimes* 'rōdā,ō *or* rə'dā(,)ō; *the stress in Spanish is* ≈'≈≈\ *n* -s [Sp, roundup, action of surrounding, fr. *rodear* to surround, fr. *rueda* wheel, fr. L *rota* — more at ROLL] **1 a** : ROUNDUP **b** : a place where cattle are brought together **2 a** : a public performance that features esp. contests in bareback bronco riding, calf roping, saddle bronco riding, steer wrestling, and Brahma bull riding **b** : an assembly or contest likened to a rodeo ⟨combine forces with one or more other troops and hold a bicycle ~ —*Girl Scout Handbook*⟩ ⟨parachute ~⟩ ⟨annual sailfish ~ held each spring⟩
**²rodeo** \"\ *vi* -ED/-ING/-S : to compete in a rodeo
**rod epithelium** *n* : epithelium having the cells striated so as to appear as if divided at one end into a bundle of rods and lining parts of various glands
**rod fiber** *n* : the terminal fiber of a retinal rod
**rod granule** *n* : the cell body of a retinal rod
**rod·ham** \'räd,ham\ *n* -s [¹*rod* + *ham*] : a patch of land bearing willow trees

**rod·ing** \'rōdiŋ\ *n* -s [⁴*rode* + *-ing*] : the anchor line of a dory or similar small fishing boat
**rod in pickle** : a reproof, punishment, or penalty ready for future application
**rod·knight** \'räd,≈\ *n* [ME, fr. OE *rādcniht* — more at RADKNIGHT] : RADKNIGHT
**rod·less** \'rädləs\ *adj* : lacking a rod
**rod·let** \-dlət\ *n* -s : a small rod
**rodlike** \'≈,≈\ *adj* : resembling a rod
**rod·man** \'rädmən, -,man\ *n, pl* **rodmen 1** : CHAINMAN 4 **2** : a worker who puts reinforcing steel into concrete forms **3** : a textile worker who steams cloth in a chamber
**rod mill** *n* **1** : a mill that produces rods of steel or other metal **2** : a pulverizing machine that uses loose iron rods as the grinding media — compare BALL MILL
**rod·ney** \'rädnī\ *n* -s [prob. fr. the name *Rodney*] *dial Eng* : IDLER, BUM
**rod of cor·ti** \-'kȯrd·ē, -r,tē\ *usu cap C* [after Alfonso *Corti* †1876 Ital. anatomist] : any of the minute modified epithelial elements that rise from the basilar membrane of the organ of Corti in two spirally arranged rows so that the free ends of the members incline toward and interlock with corresponding members of the opposite row and enclose the tunnel of Corti
**ro·do·lia** \rō'dōlyə\ *n, cap* [NL] : a genus of predaceous ladybugs including the vedalia
**rod·o·mont** \'rädə,mänt, 'rōd-\ *n* -s [It *rodomonte*, fr. *Rodomonte*, *Rodamonte*, fierce and boastful Moorish king of Algiers in the epic *Orlando Innamorato* (1487) by Matteo M. Boiardo †1494 Ital. poet and in the epic *Orlando Furioso* (1516) by Lodovico Ariosto †1533 Ital. poet] : a vain or blustering boaster : BRAGGART, BRAGGADOCIO
**¹rodo·mon·tade** \¦≈≈mən·¦tād, -,män-, -tăd\ *or* **rodo·mon·ta·do** \,≈≈(,)≈'tä(,)dō\ *also* **rhodo·mon·tade** \¦rädə-, ¦rōd-\ *n* -s [MF *rodomontade*, fr. *Rodomonte*, *Rodamonte* + MF *-ade*] **1 a** : a vain exaggerated boast : a bragging speech **b** : vain boasting : empty bluster : RANT **2** : BRAGGART **syn** see BOMBAST
**²rodomontade** *also* **rhodomontade** \"\ *vi* : BOAST, BRAG, RANT
**³rodomontade** \"\ *or* **rodomontado** \"\ *also* **rhodomontade** \"\ *adj* : BOASTFUL, RANTING
**rods** *pl of* ROD, *pres 3d sing of* ROD
**rods·man** \'rädzmən\ *n, pl* **rodsmen** [*rod's* (gen. of ¹*rod*) + *man*] **1** : CHAINMAN 4 **2** : one who eases jammed oil-shale retorts by pushing with long iron rods
**rod·ster** \'rädztə(r), -dst-\ *n* -s : ANGLER
**rod weeder** *n* : an implement that destroys weeds in plowed land by means of a square rod that revolves backward as it is drawn forward across a field a few inches below the surface of the soil and lifts weeds and clods to the surface
**¹roe** \'rō\ *n, pl* **roe** *or* **roes** [ME *ro*, *roo*, fr. OE *rā*; akin to OHG *rēh* roe deer, ON *rā* roe deer, OIr *riabach* dappled, Lith *raĩbas*] **1** : ROE DEER **2 a** : HIND **b** : DOE
**²roe** \"\ *n* -s [ME *roof*, *roughe*, *row*; akin to OHG *rogo* roe, ON *hrogn* roe, Lith *kurkulaĩ* frog's eggs] **1 a** : the eggs of a fish esp. when still enclosed in the ovarian membrane ⟨shad ~⟩ — compare SOFT ROE **b** : the eggs or ovaries of an invertebrate (as the coral of a lobster) **2** : a dark mottled or flecked figure appearing esp. in quartersawed lumber of wood with an interlocked grain (as a figured mahogany)
**roe·bling·ite** \'rōbliŋ,īt\ *n* -s [Washington A. *Roebling* †1926 Am. civil engineer + E *-ite*] : a mineral supposedly $Ca_7Pb_2H_{10}(SO_4)_2(SiO_4)_6$ consisting of an acid lead calcium silicate and sulfate occurring in white crystalline masses (hardness 3, sp. gr. 3.4)
**roe·buck** \'rō,bək\ *n, pl* **roebuck** *or* **roebucks** [ME *robucke*, *roobucke*, fr. *ro*, *roo* roe deer + *buck*, *bucke* buck] : ROE DEER; *esp* : the male roe deer
**roed** \'rōd\ *adj* : filled with roe ⟨a ~ salmon⟩
**roe deer** *n* : a small European and Asiatic deer (*Capreolus capreolus*) that has erect cylindrical antlers forked at the summit and approximate at the base, is reddish brown in summer and grayish in winter, has a white rump patch, and is noted for its nimbleness and gracefulness
**roeier** *comparative of* ROEY
**roeiest** *superlative of* ROEY
**roe·mer·ite** \'rāmə,rīt, 'rərm-\ *n* -s [G *römerit*, fr. Friedrich A. *Roemer* †1869 Ger. geologist + G *-it* -ite] : a mineral $FeFe_2(SO_4)_4.14H_2O$ consisting of a hydrous sulfate of ferrous and ferric iron
**¹roent·gen** *also* **rönt·gen** \'rentgən, 'rən| *also* |chən *or* |tjən\ *adj* [ISV, fr. Wilhelm Conrad *Röntgen* †1923 Ger. physicist] : of or relating to the physicist Röntgen or to X rays ⟨~ examinations⟩ ⟨~ therapy⟩
**²roentgen** *also* **röntgen** \"\ *n* -s [ISV, fr. Wilhelm Conrad *Röntgen*] : the international unit of X radiation or gamma radiation that is the amount of radiation producing under ideal conditions in one cubic centimeter of air at 0° C and 760 millimeters mercury pressure ionization of either sign equal to one electrostatic unit of charge
**roent·gen·iza·tion** *also* **rönt·gen·iza·tion** \,≈≈ə'zāshən, -,ī'z-\ *n* -s [ISV *roentgen-*, *röntgen-* (fr. Wilhelm Conrad *Röntgen*) + *-ization*] **1** : the act or process of using X rays **2** : discoloration (as of glass) by prolonged action of X rays
**roent·gen·ize** *also* **rönt·gen·ize** \'≈≈,īz\ *vt* -ED/-ING/-S [ISV *roentgen-*, *röntgen-* (fr. Wilhelm Conrad *Röntgen*) + *-ize*] **1** : to make (air or other gas) conductive of electricity by the passage of X rays **2** : to subject to the action of X rays (as for the treatment of a tumor)
**roent·gen·kymogram** \¦≈≈+\ *n* [ISV ¹*roentgen* + *kymogram*] : a kymogram made on an X-ray film
**roent·gen·kymographic** \"+\ *adj* [ISV *roentgenkymography* + *-ic*] : of or relating to roentgenkymography
**roent·gen·kymography** \"+\ *n* [ISV ¹*roentgen* + *kymography*] : kymography on a moving X-ray film
**roentgen meter** *n* [¹*roentgen* + *meter*] : R-METER
**roent·gen·o·gram** \'≈≈ə,gram\ *n* [ISV ¹*roentgen* + *-o-* + *-gram*] : a photograph made with X rays : RADIOGRAPH
**¹roent·gen·o·graph** \-graf, -gräf\ *n* [¹*roentgen* + *-o-* + *-graph*] : ROENTGENOGRAM
**²roentgenograph** \"\ *vt* : to photograph with X rays
**roent·gen·o·graph·ic** \¦≈≈¦grafik\ *adj* [ISV *roentgenography* + *-ic*] : of or relating to roentgenography — **roent·gen·o·graph·i·cal·ly** \-fək(ə)lē\ *adv*
**roent·gen·og·ra·phy** \,≈≈'ägrəfē\ *n* -ES [ISV ¹*roentgen* + *-o-* + *-graphy*] : photography by means of X rays
**roent·gen·o·log·ic** \¦≈≈ə¦läjik\ *or* **roent·gen·o·log·i·cal** \-jəkəl\ *adj* [*roentgenologic* ISV *roentgenology* + *-ic*; *roentgenological* fr. *roentgenology* + *-ical*] : of or relating to roentgenology — **roent·gen·o·log·i·cal·ly** \-jək(ə)lē\ *adv*
**roent·gen·ol·o·gist** \,≈≈'äləjəst\ *n* -s [*roentgenology* + *-ist*] : a specialist in roentgenology
**roent·gen·ol·o·gy** \-ləjē\ *n* -ES [ISV ¹*roentgen* + *-o-* + *-logy*] : a branch of radiology that deals with the use of X rays for diagnosis or treatment of disease
**roent·gen·om·e·ter** \,≈≈'äməd·ə(r)\ *n* [¹*roentgen* + *-o-* + *-meter*] : R-METER
**roent·gen·om·e·try** \-mə·trē\ *n* -ES [¹*roentgen* + *-o-* + *-metry*] : measurement of X rays esp. of their dosage for therapeutic purposes
**roent·gen·o·scope** \'≈≈ə,skōp\ *n* [¹*roentgen* + *-o-* + *-scope*] : FLUOROSCOPE
**roent·gen·o·scop·ic** \¦≈≈ə¦skäpik\ *adj* [*roentgenoscope* + *-ic*] : FLUOROSCOPIC — **roent·gen·o·scop·i·cal·ly** \-pək(ə)lē\ *adv*
**roent·gen·os·co·py** \,≈≈'äskəpē\ *n* -ES [ISV ¹*roentgen* + *-o-* + *-scopy*] : examination by means of fluoroscopy
**roent·gen·o·ther·a·py** \¦≈≈ō¦therəpē\ *n* [ISV ¹*roentgen* + *-o-* + *therapy*] : radiotherapy by means of X rays
**roentgen ray** *n, often cap 1st R* [¹*roentgen* + *ray*] : X RAY
**roentgen-ray tube** *n* : X-RAY TUBE
**roentgen sickness** *n* [¹*roentgen* + *sickness*] : radiation sickness from overexposure to X rays
**roent·gen·ther·a·py** \¦≈≈¦therəpē\ *n* [ISV ¹*roentgen* + *therapy*] : ROENTGENOTHERAPY
**roer** \'rü(ə)r\ *n* -s [Afrik, fr. D, firelock (gun), pipe, fr. MD, firelock (gun), pipe, reed; akin to OHG *rōr* reed, ON *reyrr*, Goth *raus*] : a heavy long-barreled gun formerly used for hunting big game in southern Africa
**roes** *pl of* ROE

**roess·ler·ite** \'reslə,rīt, 'rə(r)s-\ *n* -s [G *rösslerit*, fr. Karl *Rössler*, 19th cent. resident of Hanau, Germany + G *-it* -ite] : a mineral $MgH(AsO_4).7H_2O$ consisting of a hydrous acid arsenate of magnesium
**roes·te·lia** \re'stēlyə, ,rə(r)'s-\ *n, cap* [NL, fr. *Roestel* *fl ab* 1800 Ger. pharmacist + NL *-ia*] : a form genus of rust fungi comprising forms now known to be aecial stages of fungi of the genus *Gymnosporangium*
**roestone** \'≈,≈\ *n* [²*roe* + *stone*] : OOLITE
**ro·ey** \'rōē\ *adj* **roeier**; **roeiest** [²*roe* + *-y*] : having a mottled or streaked grain ⟨~ mahogany⟩
**ROG** *abbr, often not cap* receipt of goods
**ro·ga·te sunday** \rō,gäd·ē-\ *n, usu cap R&S* [*rogate* prob. fr. L, 2d pers. pl. imper. of *rogare*] : ROGATION SUNDAY
**ro·ga·tion** \rō'gāshən\ *n* -s [ME *rogacioun*, fr. L *rogation-*, *rogatio*, fr. *rogatus* (past part. of *rogare* to ask, beg) + *-ion-*, *-io* -ion — more at RIGHT] **1 a** : LITANY, SUPPLICATION **b rogations** *pl* : the ceremonies of the Rogation Days **2 a** : the inquiry made by the consuls or tribunes of ancient Rome as to the will of the people on a proposed decree or law **b** : the consuls' or tribunes' proposal of a law or decree for passage by the people **c** : the law or decree proposed by the consuls or tribunes **3** *obs* : a formal petition : REQUEST
**rogation days** *n pl, usu cap R&D* [ME *rogacioun dayes*] : the three days before Ascension Day observed by some Christians as days of special supplication
**rogation flower** *n* [so called fr. a former practice of making it into garlands that were carried in processions on Rogation Days] **1** : a branched perennial herbaceous Old World milkwort (*Polygala vulgaris*) with pink, white, or blue flowers **2** : a pink-flowered milkwort (*Polygala incarnata*) of eastern No. America
**rogation sunday** *n, usu cap R&S* : the Sunday immediately before the three Rogation Days : the fifth Sunday after Easter
**rogationtide** \'≈≈≈,≈\ *n, usu cap* : the period of the Rogation Days
**rogation week** *n, usu cap R* : the week in which the Rogation Days occur
**ro·ga·to·ry** \'rägə,tōrē\ *adj* [F *rogatoire*, fr. ML *rogatorius* supplicatory, fr. L *rogatus* (past part. of *rogare*) + *-orius* -ory] : seeking information; *specif* : authorized to examine witnesses or ascertain facts ⟨a ~ commission⟩
**¹rog·er** \'räjə(r)\ *vb* -ED/-ING/-S [obs. E *roger*, n., penis, fr. the name *Roger*] *vt* : to copulate with — usu. considered vulgar ⟨occasionally . . . ~*ed* the lady —Ezra Pound⟩ ~ *vi* : COPULATE — usu. considered vulgar ⟨should not a half-pay officer ~ for sixpence —James Boswell⟩
**²roger** \"\ *n* -s *usu cap* [fr. the name *Roger*] : JOLLY ROGER
**³roger** \"\ *usu cap* [fr. the name *Roger*] — a communications code word for the letter *r*
**⁴roger** \"\ *interj* [fr. ³*roger* (standing for the initial letter *r* of *received*)] — used esp. in radio and signaling to indicate that a message has been received and understood or that the speaker agrees with what has been said
**roger de coverley** *or* **roger of coverley** [*roger de coverley* alter. (influenced by *Sir Roger de Coverley*, fictitious country gentleman appearing in many numbers of the daily periodical *The Spectator* conducted 1711–12 in England, fr. *roger of coverley*) of *roger of coverley*, prob. fr. *Roger* (the name) + *of* + *Coverley* (a fictitious place name)] : SIR ROGER DE COVERLEY
**rog·er·ene** \¦räjə¦rēn\ *or* **rog·er·ine** \", -ə¦rīn\ *n* -s *usu cap* [*rogerene* fr. John *Rogers* †1721 Am. religious leader + E *-ene* (as in *nazarene*); *rogerine* alter. (influenced by E *-ine*, adj. suffix) of *rogerene*] : a follower of the religious leader John Rogers holding such principles as nonparticipation in war, religious liberty, and freedom in ecclesiastical matters
**ro·get's spiral** \(')rō¦zhā-, 'rä'|\ *n, usu cap R* [after Peter M. *Roget* †1869 Eng. physician] : an open helix of elastic wire that contracts in length when an electric current passes through it and thereby demonstrates the attraction of parallel currents
**ro·gnon** \(')rōn'yō", (')rōn-\ *n* -s [F, lit., kidney, fr. (assumed) VL *renion-*, *renio*, fr. L *renes* (pl.) kidneys] : a small rounded mass of rock usu. embedded in rock of a different type
**¹rogue** \'rōg\ *n* -s [origin unknown] **1 a** : VAGRANT, TRAMP, BEGGAR **b** : a wandering, disorderly, or dissolute person formerly accountable under various vagrancy acts — usu. used in the phrase *rogues and vagabonds* **2 a** : a dishonest unprincipled person; *specif* : SWINDLER **b** : a worthless fellow : SCOUNDREL **3** : a pleasantly mischievous person ⟨tell me about . . . the dear little ~s —Walt Whitman⟩ **4 a** (1) : ROGUE ELEPHANT (2) : a large animal with habits like those of a rogue elephant **b** : a horse inclined to shirk or misbehave **5 a** : an individual exhibiting a chance biological variation or deviating from the type of a variety or breed — usu. used of an inferior, diseased, or abnormal plant **b** : a normal plant (as of a named variety) that is accidentally mixed in with plants of another kind (as a red tulip in a field of white tulips) **syn** see VILLAIN
**²rogue** \"\ *vb* **rogued**; **rogued**; **rogu·ing** *or* **rogue·ing**; **rogues** *vi* **1** : to wander or act like a rogue **2** : to weed out inferior, diseased, or abnormal individuals from a crop ⟨by careful selection and *roguing* the . . . strain was evolved —*Gardeners' Chronicle*⟩ ~ *vt* **1** : to weed out (as an inferior plant or a field) **2** : to act like a rogue toward : SWINDLE
**³rogue** \"\ *adj* **1** *of an animal* : vicious and destructive ⟨~ otter⟩ **2** : resembling a rogue elephant in being separated or vicious ⟨the ~ male self-exiled from society —E.O.Hauser⟩ ⟨wrecked by a ~ mine —Alfred Bester⟩
**rogue elephant** *n* : a vicious elephant that separates from the herd and roams alone
**rogu·er** \'rōgə(r)\ *n* -s : one that rogues
**rogu·ery** \'rōgərē, -əri\ *n* -ES **1** : the practices or conduct of a rogue ⟨more often the victim than the practitioner of ~ —S.T. Williamson⟩ **2** : an act characteristic of a rogue ⟨dismissed . . . for unspecified *rogueries* —Wolcott Gibbs⟩ **3** : mischievous play ⟨little wretches . . . stealing back through the shrubbery so as not to be seen all bedraggled from some ~ —Virginia Woolf⟩ **4** : the world of rogues ⟨a thing at which all ~ rejoiced —Walter Besant⟩
**rogue's badge** *n* **1** : a red ribbon on the tail of a hunting horse that kicks **2 a** : a hood worn by a racehorse **b** : blinkers worn by a racehorse
**rogues' gallery** *n* **1** : a collection of portraits of criminals ⟨the *rogues' gallery* in the post office⟩ **2** : a collection resembling a collection of portraits of criminals ⟨this interesting *rogues' gallery* of the insect world includes detailed snapshots of a feeding bedbug —John Pfeiffer⟩
**rogue·ship** \'rōg,ship\ *n* : the quality or state of being a rogue

rogue's badge 2

**rogue's march** *n* : a tune of English origin formerly played to accompany the expulsion of a soldier from the army
**rogue's yarn** *n* : a yarn of a different twist, material, or color inserted into navy cordage esp. to identify it if stolen or to trace the maker in case of defect
**rogu·ish** \'rōgish, -gēsh\ *adj* **1** : of, relating to, or having the characteristics of a rogue : DISHONEST, UNPRINCIPLED ⟨had some ~ intentions of his own about the money —W.M. Thackeray⟩ ⟨~ stories emphasizing ingenuity⟩ **2** : pleasantly mischievous ⟨a ~ wink⟩ — **rogu·ish·ly** *adv* — **rogu·ish·ness** *n* -ES
**roguy** \-gē, -gi\ *adj, obs* : ROGUISH
**ro·hil·la** \rō'hilə\ *n, pl* **rohilla** *or* **rohillas** *usu cap* : a member of an Afghan people settling in the district of Rohilkhand in northern India early in the 18th century
**rohr bor·dun** \¦rōr(,)bȯr¦dün\ *n* [G *rohrbordun*, fr. G *rohr* reed, pipe (fr. OHG *rōr* reed) + *bordun* bourdon, fr. F *bourdon*, fr. MF, bass horn, of imit. origin — more at ROER] : a rohrflöte of 16-foot pitch
**rohr·flö·te** \'rōr,flœtə\ *n* -s [G, fr. *rohr* reed, pipe + *flöte* flute, fr. MHG *floite*, *flöute*, fr. MD *flute*, *floyte*, fr. OF *flaute*, *flahute*, *fleute* — more at FLUTE] : a pipe-organ flute stop having closed metal pipes with chimneys
**rohr na·sat** \'rōr,nä,zät\ *or* **rohr quin·te** \'rōr,kvintə\ *n* [*rohr nasat* fr. G *rohrnasat*, fr. *rohr* reed, pipe + *nasat* nazard; *rohr quinte* fr. G *rohrquinte*, fr. *rohr* reed, pipe + *quinte* fifth

in music, fr. F, fr. MF, fem. of *quint*, adj., fifth, fr. L *quintus* — more at NASAT, QUINT] **:** a rohrflöte speaking at 2⅔-foot pitch

**ro·hu** \(ˈ)rō¦hü\ *n, pl* **rohu** *or* **rohus** [Hindi *rohū*] **:** a large small-mouthed Indian cyprinid fish (*Labeo rohita*) valued for food and sport

**ro·hun** \ˈrōən\ *or* **ro·hu·na** \-ənə\ *also* **ro·han** \-ən\ *n* -s [Hindi *rohan*, fr. Skt *rohaṇa*] **:** an East Indian tree (*Soymida febrifuga*) of the family Meliaceae having hard durable wood and tonic bark

**roi fai·né·ant** \rwȧ¦fā(,)nā'äⁿ, ¦rw-\ *n, pl* **rois fainéants** \"\ [F, faineant king] **:** a do-nothing king; *esp* **:** one who has delegated or lost his royal power while still reigning

**¹roil** \ˈrȯil, *esp before pause or consonant* -ȯiəl\ *vb* -ED/-ING/-S [origin unknown] *vt* **1 a :** to make turbid by stirring up the sediment or dregs ⟨something of the rubbery aspect of fish seen under ~*ed* water —John McCarten⟩ ⟨looked down into the ~*ed* wine —Lionel Trilling⟩ **b :** to stir up **:** DISTURB, DISORDER ⟨fine white marl which becomes . . . ~*ed* by the waves —S.E.Morison⟩ ⟨activities . . . certain to keep American politics ~*ed* —Douglass Adair⟩ **2 :** RILE 2 ⟨she's trying to be clever . . . don't let her ~ you —Frances G. Patton⟩ ~ *vi* **1 :** to move turbulently from one place to another ⟨the clouds ~*ed* up about the dome again and hid it —W.A.Dorrance⟩ ⟨the chatter of that busy little beck as it ~*ed* over its shallows —T.B.Costain⟩ **2 :** to be in a state of turbulence ⟨the air ~*ed* and eddied in the heat —Richard Thruelsen & Elliott Arnold⟩ ⟨floods from . . . ~*ing* gullies —*Time*⟩ **syn** see IRRITATE

**²roil** \"\ *n* -s **1 :** AGITATION ⟨feeling the ~ of waters on the flanks, the dangerous turbulence —Richard Eberhart⟩ **2 a :** small section of rapidly moving turbulent water ⟨the river showed steely ~*s* of slick water —H.L.Davis⟩

**³roil** \"\ *vi* -ED/-ING/-S [origin unknown] *dial Eng* **:** to romp or play esp. in a rough manner

**roily** \ˈrȯilē\ *adj* -ER/-EST [¹*roil* + -*y*] **1 :** full of sediment or dregs **:** MUDDY **2 :** TURBULENT ⟨always building higher the dams of their emotions until they broke and the ~ waters rushed out in a wasting flood —V.L.Parrington⟩ **syn** see TURBID

**roint** \ˈrȯint\ *vt* [by shortening] *dial chiefly Eng* **:** AROINT

**¹rois·ter** *also* **roys·ter** \ˈrȯistə(r)\ *n* -s [prob. fr. MF *rustre* boor, lout, alter. of *ruste*, fr. *ruste*, adj., rude, rough, fr. L *rusticus* rustic, rural — more at RUSTIC] *archaic* **:** ROISTERER

**²roister** *or* **royster** \"\ *vi* **roistered** *or* **roystered; roistered** *or* **roystered; roistering** *or* **roystering** \-t(ə)riŋ\ **roisters** *or* **roysters :** to have a noisy disorderly good time esp. under the influence of alcohol **:** CAROUSE, REVEL ⟨had gambled and ~*ed* and drunk until he dropped in his tracks —Donn Byrne⟩

**rois·ter·er** *or* **roys·ter·er** \-tərə(r)\ *n* -s **:** one that roisters

**roistering** *or* **roystering** *adj* **:** characterized by or associated with noisy revelry ⟨usual for hilarious youths to pull off the bride's garters . . . but this was no ~ wedding —Francis Hackett⟩ ⟨good rich ~ ribald words —D.W.Maurer⟩

**rois·ter·ous** *or* **roys·ter·ous** \-t(ə)rəs\ *adj* [¹*roister* + -*ous*] **:** ROISTERING ⟨take the play . . . and rush it through to a ~ conclusion —Brooks Atkinson⟩ — **rois·ter·ous·ly** *or* **roys·ter·ous·ly** *adv*

**roist·ing** *or* **royst·ing** \-tiŋ\ *adj* [fr. pres. part. of obs. E *roist*, *royst* to roister, back-formation fr. E ¹*roister*] *archaic* **:** ROISTERING

**roi·te·let** \¦rȯid·ᵊl¦et, rwä·tlā\ *n, pl* **roitelets** \-ets,-ā\ [F, fr. MF, fr. *roitel*, *roietel* petty king (fr. OF, dim. of *roi* king, fr. L *reg-*, *rex*) + -*et* — more at ROYAL] *archaic* **:** a petty king

**rok** \ˈräk\ *n* -s *usu cap* [Republic of Korea, republic constituting the southern part of Korea] **:** a member of the armed forces of the Republic of Korea

**ro·ka** \ˈrōkə\ *n* -s [Ar *ruqʻ*] **:** MAFURA

**¹roke** \ˈrōk\ *n* -s [ME, prob. fr. MD *roke*, *rooc* smoke; akin to OHG *rauh* smoke — more at REEK] **1** *dial chiefly Brit* **:** VAPOR: as **a :** FOG, MIST **b :** STEAM **2** *dial chiefly Brit* **:** SMOKE, REEK

**²roke** \"\ *vt* [origin unknown] *dial Eng* **:** to poke around **:** STIR

**rok·e·lay** \ˈräkə,lā, -ä,kʹlä, -kläˌ\ *chiefly Scot var of* ROQUELAURE

**ro·ker** \ˈrōkə(r)\ *n* -s [prob. fr. Dan *rokke*, fr. MLG *roche*, *ruche*; akin to OE *reohhe* ray and prob. to OE *rūh* rough — more at ROUGH] **1 :** any of various rays; *esp* **:** THORNBACK RAY **2** *dial Eng* **:** ROCKLING

**roky** \ˈrōki\ *adj* -ER/-EST [¹*roke* + -*y*] *dial chiefly Brit* **:** FOGGY, MISTY

**ro·lan·dic** \rō'landik\ *adj, usu cap R* [Luigi *Rolando* †1831 Ital. anatomist + E -*ic*] **:** of, relating to, or discovered by Luigi Rolando

**rolandic area** *n, usu cap R* **:** the motor area of the cerebral cortex comprising the anterior wall of the central sulcus, the anterior central gyrus, and the paracentral lobule

**rolandic fissure** *n, usu cap R* **:** CENTRAL SULCUS

**role** *also* **rôle** \ˈrōl\ *n* -s [F *rôle*, lit., roll, fr. OF *role* — more at ROLL] **1 a** (1) **:** a character assigned to or assumed by someone ⟨to prove his point he went to sea in the ~ of a castaway, on an inflated rubber raft —Walter Hayward⟩ ⟨given the ~ of peacemaker⟩ ⟨cast in the ~ of scapegoat⟩ (2) **:** a socially prescribed pattern of behavior corresponding to an individual's status in a particular society **b** (1) **:** a part played by an actor (as in a play or movie) ⟨in succeeding months played a long list of comedy and farcical ~*s* —W.P.Eaton⟩ (2) **:** a part assumed by a singer (as in an opera or oratorio) ⟨one of the most taxing tenor ~*s* in the repertoire⟩ **2 :** a function performed by someone or something in a particular situation, process, or operation ⟨the ~ of the teacher in the educational process⟩ ⟨plays an important ~ in city politics⟩ ⟨the ~ of automobiles in leisure has been significant —A.P.James⟩ ⟨the ~ of peroxidation in vitamin E deficiency —*Current Biog.*⟩

**ro·leo** \ˈrōlē,ō\ *n* -s [²*roll* + -*eo* (as in *rodeo*)] **:** a logrolling tournament

**roley-poley** *var of* ROLY-POLY

**rolfs' oak** \ˈrälfs-\ *n, cap R* [after Frederick M. *Rolfs* †1956 Am. botanist] **:** a Florida coastal scrub oak (*Quercus rolfsii*) with hard rigid branches, small leathery leaves, and acorns usu. in pairs and half-covered by the funnel-shaped cups

**¹roll** \ˈrōl\ *n* -s [ME *rolle*, fr. OF *rolle*, *role*, fr. L *rotulus*, *rotula* little wheel, dim. of *rota* wheel; akin to OFris *reth* wheel, OHG *rad* wheel, ON *röthull* halo, sun, W *rhod* wheel, Latvian *rats* wheel, Skt *ratha* wagon] **1 a** (1) **:** a written document (as on parchment or paper) that is rolled up for carrying or storing **:** SCROLL ⟨reading a certain passage from the ~ —Robert Browning⟩; *specif* **:** a written document containing an official or formal record (as of the proceedings of a court or political body) ⟨chancery ~*s*⟩ ⟨~*s* of parliament⟩ ⟨keeper of the ~*s*⟩ — compare MASTER OF THE ROLLS (2) **:** a manuscript book ⟨medieval ~*s* of arms⟩ **b :** a list of names or related items **:** CATALOG, REGISTER ⟨place at the head of the ~ of science has not been challenged —*Times Lit. Supp.*⟩ ⟨a slipshod work that hardly belongs in the ~ of his novels⟩ ⟨belongs in the ~ of great actors⟩ **c :** an official list ⟨the ~ of registered voters⟩ ⟨the public relief ~*s*⟩: as (1) **:** MUSTER ROLL (2) **:** a list of members of a school or class ⟨when students other than day students are permitted to withdraw, or are dropped from the ~ —*College of William & Mary Cat.*⟩ ⟨the teacher called the ~⟩ (3) **:** a list of members of a legislative body ⟨the clerk called the ~ and recorded the votes⟩ (4) *Brit* **:** a list of those qualified to practice as solicitors — usu. used in pl. (5) **:** a list of practitioners in a court or in the courts of a state — usu. used in pl. (6) **:** TAX LIST **2 :** something that is rolled up into or as if into a cylinder or ball ⟨great ~*s* of fat around his middle —T.B.Costain⟩ ⟨his head, which is bald on top, is outlined by a thick ~ of curly black hair —*Current Biog.*⟩ ⟨a ~ of twine⟩: as **a** (1) **:** a quantity (as of fabric or paper) rolled up to form a single package; *also* **:** a number of separate sheets or papers rolled together ⟨a ~ of wrapping paper⟩ ⟨a ~ of paper towels⟩ (2) **:** a bolt of wallpaper (3) **:** WEB **b :** a hairdo in which some or all of the hair is rolled or curled up or under ⟨pageboy *roll*⟩ **c :** a continuous strand of textile fiber (as wool) that is formed by slightly twisting, rolling, or rubbing the fibers **d :** any of

roll 2j

various food preparations rolled up for cooking or serving: as (1) **:** a small piece of yeast dough baked in any of numerous forms (2) **:** meat rolled and cooked (3) **:** JELLY ROLL (4) **:** sweet dough that is spread with a filling and then rolled up and baked ⟨a blackberry ~⟩ **e :** a rounded molding or similar architectural element (as a volute of the Ionic order) **f :** a cylindrical twist of tobacco **g :** any of a series of rounded strips of wood over which the ends of the roofing plates of a lead or other metal roof are turned and lapped **h :** BLANKET ROLL 1 **i :** MUSIC ROLL **j :** a flat flexible case (as of leather) in which articles may be rolled and fastened by straps or metal clasps; *also* **:** a cylindrical case **k** (1) **:** a number of pieces of paper money folded or rolled into a wad to be carried in the pocket ⟨a man of the world who has a ~ of bills in his pocket —Donald Windham⟩ (2) *slang* **:** BANKROLL ⟨producers themselves anxiously cast about for angels willing to shoot their ~*s* on shows —Seymour Peck⟩ **3 :** something that performs a rolling action or movement **:** a cylindrical body set in bearings and used singly or in pairs or sets to crush, flatten, shape, move, or operate something **:** ROLLER: as **a :** a roller used to break clods or level soil **b :** a metal wheel for making decorative lines on book covers; *also* **:** a design impressed by such a tool **c rolls** *pl* **:** a set of two or more similar parallel cylinders placed a small distance apart in bearings and made to rotate in opposite directions so as to draw material between them in order to crush it (as rock or ore) or compress and shape it (as malleable metal) **d :** a typewriter platen **e :** BREAK ROLL

**²roll** \"\ *vb* -ED/-ING/-S [ME *rollen*, *rolen*, fr. MF *roller*, *roler*, fr. (assumed) VL *rotulare*, fr. L *rotulus*, *rotula* small wheel] *vt* **1 a :** to impel forward by causing to turn over and over on a surface ⟨~*ed* the barrel down the hill⟩ ⟨~*ed* the hoop along the street⟩ **b :** to cause to revolve by turning over and over **:** move by turning on or as if on an axis ⟨were placed on the sheets and ~*ed* in the flour —*Amer. Guide Series: La.*⟩ **c** (1) **:** to move or cause to move in a circular manner **:** turn from one side to another ⟨already the girl was ~*ing* her eyes and giggling —Ellen Glasgow⟩ ⟨~*ed* his head round in the direction of the curtained window —Elizabeth Bowen⟩ ⟨~*ing* his shoulders —F.M.Ford⟩ (2) **:** to swing or sway from side to side ⟨~*ed* the great bomber like a jet fighter —*Time*⟩ **d :** to cause to take shape as a mass by turning over and over **:** heap up in a mass ⟨the wind blowing over the empty prairies can ~ tumbleweed as big as a bushel basket —Frances Gaither⟩ **e :** to impel forward with an easy, continuous motion ⟨the river ~*s* its waters to the ocean⟩ **f** (1) **:** to make a cast of (dice or a specified number on the dice) (2) **:** to cast dice in competition with ⟨I'll ~ you to see who pays⟩ **2 :** to reflect on **:** CONSIDER, PONDER ⟨my thoughts the matter ~, and solve and oft resolve the whole —R.W.Emerson⟩ **3 a :** to put a wrapping around **:** ENFOLD, ENVELOP ⟨very pleasant to lie snugly ~*ed* in blankets —John Seago⟩ **b :** to wrap round on itself or on something else **:** cause to take a relatively spherical or cylindrical form **:** shape into a ball or roll ⟨~*ed* his hamlike hands into fists —Irene Kuhn⟩ ⟨~*ed* his own cigarettes⟩ ⟨~*ed* up the cloth⟩ ⟨~*ed* the bandage around his leg⟩ **4 a** (1) **:** to press, spread, or level with a roller **:** make smooth, even, or compact ⟨~ steel rails⟩ ⟨~ sheet-brass⟩ ⟨~ a field⟩ ⟨~ the dough⟩ ⟨~ cracker crumbs⟩ ⟨had seen too many minds ~*ed* flat by academicism —T.M.Longstreth⟩ (2) **:** to form a screw thread on (a rod) by cold-rolling between dies or rollers having suitably shaped ridges that displace the metal from the thread space and force it up above the original surface of the work on each side **b :** to make smooth and rounded by attrition ⟨implements should be examined to see whether they are ~*ed* . . . or wind-worn, or relatively fresh —*Notes & Queries on Anthropology*⟩ **c** (1) **:** to ink with a roller or rollers ⟨~ a form⟩ (2) **:** to make (a stereotype matrix) or mold (a form) in a mangle **d :** to spread out **:** EXTEND ⟨if the weather was good we ~*ed* our beds on the ground and slept in the open —Ross Santee⟩ ⟨in the grave throw me and ~ the sod o'er me —*Western Folklore*⟩ ⟨~ out the red carpet⟩ **5 a :** to cause to move on wheels ⟨~*ed* the baby carriage to the store⟩ **b :** to transport in a wheeled vehicle ⟨loved to be ~*ed* through the park in an old-fashioned hansom cab⟩ **c :** to traverse in or by a wheeled vehicle ⟨tried to believe the hardest miles were ~*ed* —A.B. Guthrie⟩ **d :** to move or cause to be moved by means of rollers ⟨had the log house ~*ed* to its present site —*Amer. Guide Series: La.*⟩ **e :** to cause to begin operating or moving ⟨~ the cameras⟩ **6 a :** to sound with a full, reverberating tone ⟨~*ed* the psalm to wintry skies —Alfred Tennyson⟩ — often used with *out* ⟨~*ed* out the words so that everyone could hear⟩ **b :** to make a continuous beating sound upon **:** sound a roll upon ⟨local constables in remote hamlets ~*ed* their drums to bring out the villagers —*Time*⟩ **c :** to utter with a trill ⟨they might ~ their r's and use their noses as trombones of conversation —Corra Harris⟩ **d :** to play (a chord) in arpeggio style (as on a harp or piano) **7 :** to rob (a person) usu. by going through his pockets while he is drunk, asleep, or unconscious **:** JACKROLL ⟨~*ing* lushes in the subway —Wolcott Gibbs⟩ ⟨had been doped, beaten up, and ~*ed* —R.G.Martin⟩ ~ *vi* **1 a :** to move forward along a surface by rotation ⟨the ball ~*ed* along the floor⟩ **b** (1) **:** to turn over and over ⟨the children ~*ed* in the grass, or waded in the brook —Henry Adams⟩ ⟨the dog ~*ed* in the mud⟩ (2) **:** to luxuriate in an abundant supply **:** WALLOW — used with *in* ⟨tragic to think that a man may be short of money whilst his children are ~*ing* in it —J.D.Sheridan⟩ **c :** to move onward or around as if by completing a revolution ⟨the months ~ on⟩ ⟨five summers have ~*ed* round since then —Douglass Cater⟩ **:** ELAPSE, PASS ⟨the years ~ by —*Fortnight*⟩ **d :** to move in an orbit ⟨the planets ~ around the sun⟩ **2 a :** to look in one direction after another in quick succession **:** to shift the gaze continually ⟨a pair of eyes which ~*ed* with malevolent curiosity —T.B.Costain⟩ **b** *archaic* **:** to revolve in the mind **c :** to revolve on or as if on an axis ⟨long has the globe been ~*ing* round —Walt Whitman⟩ **3 :** to move about **:** ROAM, WANDER **4 a :** to flow with a rising and falling motion ⟨the waves ~ on⟩ ⟨the clouds ~ past⟩ **:** go forward in an easy, gentle, or undulating manner ⟨mists ~*ing* down the mountain —*Irish Digest*⟩ ⟨the fog, which from the foot of the lawn ~*ed* away . . . like a sea —R.M.Lovett⟩ **b :** to flow in a continuous stream **:** to arrive, become produced, or become received in abundant quantities or amount **:** POUR ⟨cars ~*ing* off the assembly line⟩ ⟨delegates ~*ed* in from all parts of the country⟩ ⟨the money was ~*ing* in⟩ **c :** to flow as part of a stream of words ⟨catchy phrases, and sharp retorts that ~ so freely from the tongues of the people he characterizes —H.H. Reichard⟩ **d :** to have an undulating contour **:** display a gently rising and falling surface ⟨most of it is prairie, but the prairie ~*s* and dips and curves —Sinclair Lewis⟩ **e :** to lie extended **:** STRETCH ⟨the flowers ~*ed* away in dizzy unbroken patterns to the horizon —Alan Moorehead⟩ ⟨to the west and south ~ the grainfields —O.A.Fitzgerald⟩ **5 a :** to become carried in a vehicle ⟨got in the car and were soon ~*ing* at high speed⟩ **b :** to become carried on a stream ⟨the scattered debris ~*ed* down the flooded river⟩ **c :** to move on wheels ⟨with a smooth hard-packed surface of snow, trucks can ~ right along —Harold Griffin⟩ **6 a :** to make a deep reverberating sound ⟨the thunder ~*s*⟩ ⟨the drums ~⟩ ⟨a roar from the crowd ~*ed* all around enveloping us —A.P.Gaskell⟩ **b :** to make a deep and sonorous sound ⟨listen to a rich voice which ~*ed* out into the dusk —Margaret Kennedy⟩ **c :** TRILL — used of a bird **7 a :** to incline first to one side and then to the other **:** swing from side to side ⟨the ship still heaved and ~*ed* on the heavy sea —C.S.Forester⟩ ⟨as he swam he ~*ed* like a sick fish —Kenneth Roberts⟩ **b :** to walk with a swinging gait **:** SWAY ⟨a heavy elderly peasant ~*ed* in his gait —F.M.Ford⟩ **c :** to move so as to cushion the impact of a blow — used with *with* ⟨~*ed* with the punch, but it caught his nose nevertheless —Edwin Corle⟩ **8 a :** to take the form of a cylinder or ball ⟨this cloth ~*s* unevenly⟩ ⟨laid my tarp on the ground and *rolled* up in every blanket I had —Ysabel Rennie⟩ **b :** to respond to rolling in a specified way **:** be in a specified condition after being rolled ⟨the tennis courts ~*ed* easily after the shower⟩ ⟨the metal ~*ed* out in flat bars⟩ **9 a :** to get under way **:** begin to move ⟨the fire engines ~*ed* while the alarm bell was still ringing⟩ ⟨the company commander gave the signal to ~ and the tanks moved out⟩ **b :** to move forward **:** develop and maintain impetus ⟨not enough real sting in demand to get business ~*ing* at the speed many steelmakers had hoped for —*Wall Street Jour.*⟩ ⟨~*ed* to a fourth term —*Time*⟩ ⟨the team was held scoreless during the third period, but in the fourth period they started to ~ again⟩ **c :** to go into action or operation ⟨the cameras were ready to ~⟩ ⟨the presses started to ~⟩ **d :** to go to press ⟨they went home after the late edition had ~*ed*⟩ **10 a :** BOWL **b :** to execute a forward or backward roll in tumbling — **roll one's hoop** *slang* **:** to attend to one's own business — often used after the verb *go* — **roll the bones :** to roll dice; *esp* **:** to shoot craps — **roll up one's sleeves :** to get to work vigorously **:** make a determined effort

**³roll** \"\ *n* -s **1 a :** a prolonged sound produced by rapid and regular strokes on a drum **b :** a sonorous and often rhythmical flow of speech ⟨no amount of circumlocution in English can do justice to the heavy ~ of the Latin periods —R.W.Southern⟩ **c :** a heavy reverberatory sound ⟨the ~ of cannon⟩ ⟨the ~ of thunder⟩ ⟨heard the slow, steady ~ of the surf —Hamilton Basso⟩ **d :** a chord in arpeggio style produced on a keyboard instrument or a harp **e :** a trill of some birds; *esp* **:** any of various trills in the song of the canary ⟨bass ~⟩ ⟨bell ~⟩ ⟨water ~⟩ **2 :** a rolling movement or an action or process involving such movement ⟨the ~ of the waves⟩ ⟨the ~ of the ball⟩ ⟨a ~ of the dice⟩ ⟨eyes with the hint of a ~ in them —Clemence Dane⟩: as **a :** a swaying movement of the body ⟨she walks slowly, easily, but with a slight ~ —Constance Walsh⟩ **b :** a side to side movement (as of a ship or train) **c** (1) **:** an angular displacement about the longitudinal axis of an airplane (2) **:** a flight maneuver in which a complete revolution about the longitudinal axis is made with the horizontal direction of flight being approximately maintained **d** (1) **:** any of several acrobatic and modern dance exercises in which the body is rotated on the floor ⟨back ~⟩ ⟨chest ~⟩ ⟨shoulder ~⟩ (2) **:** a pivot of ballroom dance partners away from or toward each other or toward a new partner **e :** a tumbling stunt in which the body is rotated in a circle on the mat either forward or backward about its lateral axis while in a tuck position **f :** the movement of a curling stone after impact with another stone **3 a :** an undulation in the roof or floor of a coal seam or in one or both walls of a mineral vein **b :** an undulation on a land surface **:** a low rounded ridge ⟨the trees around the more distant spring are hidden behind a ~ of the ground —G. R. Stewart⟩

**roll·able** \ˈrōləbəl\ *adj* **:** capable of being rolled

**roll-and-fillet molding** \¦=·=¦=-\ *n* **:** a nearly cylindrical molding that is larger than a bead and has a projecting fillet on one side

**¹rollaway** \ˈ=·=,=\ *dial var of* ROLLWAY 2

**²rollaway** \"\ *or* **rollaway bed** *n* -s [fr. *roll away*, v.] **:** a bed that can be folded and rolled away (as into a closet)

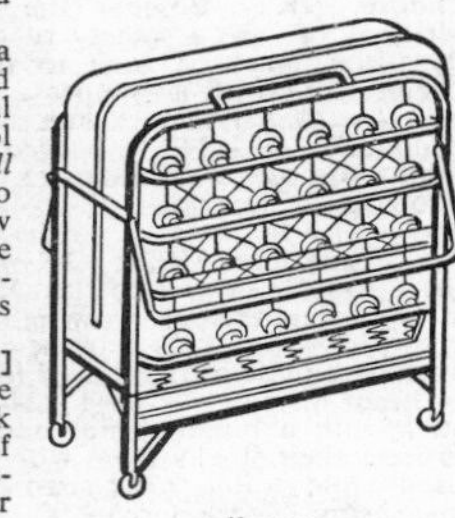
rollaway

**roll back** *vt* **1 :** to reduce (a commodity price) to or toward a previous level on a national scale by government control devices ⟨taking measures to *roll* commodity prices *back*⟩ **2 :** to cause to retreat or withdraw **:** push back ⟨confident that he could *roll back* the ragtag, disorganized force that barred his way —F.V.W.Mason⟩

**rollback** \ˈ=,=\ *n* -s [*roll back*] **1 :** the cam on the knob spindle for moving the bolt of a lock **2 :** the act or an instance of rolling back **:** a driving or forcing back to a previous level or position ⟨a ~ of prices⟩ ⟨a ~ of the invading army⟩

**roll book** *n* **:** a book in which a teacher keeps a record of the attendance or classwork of his pupils

**roll call** *n* [¹*roll* + *call*, after the phrase *call the roll*] **1 a :** the act or an instance of calling off a list of names (as for checking attendance or recording a vote) ⟨the first sergeant began the *roll call*⟩ ⟨the teacher never skips *roll call*⟩ ⟨demanded a *roll call* on the measure⟩ **b :** a regularly scheduled time for calling the roll ⟨was unable to get back before *roll call*⟩ **c :** a signal for a roll call ⟨the bugler blew *roll call*⟩ **2 :** REGISTER, ROLL ⟨in his own *roll call* of heroes —M.Y.Hughes⟩

**roll-call** \ˈ=,=\ *vt* [*roll call*] **:** to call the roll of ⟨efforts . . . to have the delegations *roll-called* —*Springfield (Mass.) Union*⟩

**roll ceiling** *n* **:** a removable stage ceiling that can be rolled up for storage

**roll-cumulus** \ˈ=,=·=·=\ *n* **:** a stratocumulus in which the clouds near the horizon resemble long bars

**rolled** \ˈrōld\ *adj* [ME, fr. past part. of *rollen*, *rolen* to roll — more at ROLL] **:** subjected to or produced by rolling

**rolled barley** *n* **:** steamed and flattened barley grains used for feeding livestock and poultry

**rolled glass** *n* **1 :** a flat glass of considerable thickness that is made by passing a roller over molten glass between thickness strips placed on the edges of the casting table **2 :** CYLINDER GLASS

**rolled gold** *or* **rolled gold plate** *n* **1 :** a base metal (as brass) with a thin plate of gold rolled over it **2 :** a gold electroplate rolled or drawn out so that the gold becomes very thin

**rolled oats** *n* **:** hulled oats steamed and then flattened by being passed between rollers

**rolled roast** *n* **:** a boned and rolled rib roast of beef — compare STANDING ROAST

**¹roll·er** \ˈrōlə(r)\ *n* -s *often attrib* [ME, fr. *rollen*, *rolen* to roll + -*er* — more at ROLL] **1 :** a revolving cylinder over or on which something is moved: as **a** (1) **:** a usu. wooden cylinder over which an endless towel passes (2) **:** any of the cylinders in a papermaking machine for carrying forward the web of paper or over and around which the machine clothing travels **b :** a hard steel cylinder used (as in a roller bearing) to reduce friction — see ROLLER BEARING illustration **c :** a cylinder on which heavy objects (as logs or steel rails) are rolled for ease in moving **d :** a wheel of a caster or roller skate **e :** ROLL 3d **f :** a disk mounted on the balance staff of a timepiece and containing the roller jewel **2 :** a revolving cylinder used alone or in pairs or sets to press, shape, or smooth something: as **a :** a device with one or more heavy broad-rimmed wheels that is pulled or driven over ground (as soil, lawn, or a macadam surface) to smooth or compact it — see BAR ROLLER, ROAD ROLLER **b :** one of a pair or set of rolls used to flatten and shape material (as metal) drawn between them **c** (1) **:** a revolving cylinder for inking or dampening a printing surface or forming one unit of the inking or dampening mechanism of a press (2) **:** PAINT ROLLER **d :** either of the hard revolving cylinders in a mangle or wringer between which material to be ironed or squeezed dry is passed **e** (1) **:** ROLLER DIE (2) **:** THREAD ROLLER **f :** MANGLE 4 **g :** BREAK ROLL **h :** a forging die fuller of such shape that the stock may be rolled on it **3 a** *or* **roller bandage :** a long rolled bandage **b :** a wide band of webbing buckled around a horse to keep his blanket in place **4 :** a cylindrical stick or rod on which something (as a map or shade) is rolled up **5 :** one that performs or supervises a rolling operation: as **a** (1) **:** one that operates a rolling mill (2) **:** one that operates a bar mill for reducing the thickness of bars of metal (as gold or silver) **b** (1) **:** one that rolls up textiles usu. by machine (2) **:** one that operates a machine for winding rolls of wallpaper **c :** one that rolls wrapper leaves around the bunches of cigars **d :** one that rolls candy centers to shape or that rolls candy in nuts **6 a :** one of a series of long heavy waves that roll in upon a coast (as after a storm) ⟨the canoe, carried helpless on the top of a big ~, grounded on the beach —A.A.Grace⟩ **b :** a tumbler pigeon; *esp* **:** one of any of several varieties in which the characteristic action is markedly developed — see ORIENTAL ROLLER **c :** a small burrowing snake of the family Aniliidae **d :** a ship that rolls ⟨a bad ~ in heavy seas⟩ **e :** a batted ball that rolls along the ground **:** a soft grounder **7 :** a woman's hat with a small crown and a narrow brim that is curved upward all around

**²roller** \"\ *n* -s [G, fr. *rollen* to roll, reverberate (fr. MHG, to roll, fr. MF *roller*, *roler*) + -*er* (fr. OHG -*āri*, fr. L -*arius*) — more at ROLL] **1 :** any of numerous mostly brightly colored nonpasserine Old World birds of the family Coraciidae that are related to the motmots and todies and include a common European bird (*Coracias garrulus*) that is chiefly blue and greenish in various shades with the back reddish brown — see

GROUND ROLLER **2 :** a canary having a song with a long rich recurrent trill in which the notes are soft and run together — distinguished from *chopper*

**roller–backer** \ˈ==,==\ *n* **:** a machine that backs a book by a roller action and forms shoulders but does not round the book except as the rollers perfect the round already imparted — compare ROUNDER AND BACKER

**roller bearing** *n* **:** a bearing in which the journal rotates in peripheral contact with a number of rollers usu. contained in a cage — compare BALL BEARING

roller bearing: *1* outer race, *2* cage, *3* roller, *4* inner race

**roller–blind shutter** *n* **:** FOCAL-PLANE SHUTTER

**roller chain** *n* **:** a block chain in which hollow transverse blocks or cylinders turning on steel pins act as rollers to lessen friction

**roll·er coaster** \ˈrōlə(r),- *also* -lē,- *or* -li,-\ *n* **1 :** an elevated railway (as in an amusement park) constructed with curves and inclines at different levels and having cars rolling upon it **2 :** a car that runs on a roller coaster

**roller–coat** \ˈ==,=\ *vt* **:** to apply (as paint or enamel) to a surface by means of a roller

**roller conveyor** *n* **:** a conveyor consisting of fixed-location rollers over which materials are moved by gravity or propulsion

**roller derby** *n* **:** a contest between two roller skating teams on a circular track in which each attempts to maneuver a skater into position to score points by circling the track and orientating one or more opponents within a given time limit

**roller die** *n* **:** one of a set of flat block or cylindrical dies used in a thread roller for rolling screw threads

**roller freight car** *n* **:** a freight car equipped with roller bearings

**roller gate** *n* **:** a hollow drum placed horizontally at the crest of a dam and rolled up or down an inclined track by pinion and rack to regulate water elevation

**roller gin** *n* **:** a cotton gin in which the lint is pulled from the seed by a roller covered with walrus hide and assisted by a fixed knife and a moving knife

**roller jewel** *n* **:** a usu. ruby or sapphire pin set upright in the roller disk and pushed by the pallet fork — called also *impulse pin*

**roller leather** *n* **:** vegetable-tanned leather from sheep, lamb, or calf skins used for covering the rollers of textile machinery

**roll·er·man** \ˈrōlə(r)mən\ *n, pl* **rollermen :** one who tends a rolling machine or performs a rolling action: as **a :** BRAKER **b :** JACKMAN **c :** a calender man who makes imitation leather **d :** a mine worker who keeps in repair the pulleys over which haulageway cables pass **e :** an auto worker who runs the motors of finished cars to check their performance, to detect unusual noises, to test parts subject to vibration, and to check the operation of gages **f :** LEVERMAN

**roller mill** *n* **:** a mill for crushing or grinding material (as grain) by passing it between rolls

**roller nest** *n* **:** a group of steel rollers assembled together in a frame and placed under the end of a bridge truss or girder and on a bearing plate to permit expansion and contraction to occur without restraint

**roller print** *n* **:** a fabric with a design made by roller printing

**roller printing** *n* **:** a method of printing textiles that uses a series of engraved metal rollers each of which contains the parts of the pattern to be printed in one color

**roller shade** *n* **:** a window shade mounted on a roller

**roller skate** *n* **:** a skate with small wheels instead of a runner for skating on a surface other than ice

**roller–skate** \ˈ==,=\ *vi* [*roller skate*] **:** to move on roller skates — **roller skater** *n*

**roller stock** *n* **:** a metal bar forming the core of a composition printing roller

**roller table** *n* **:** a double roller disk sometimes used in timepieces instead of a single roller

roller skate

**roller–top** \ˈ==,=\ *n* **:** ROLL TOP

**roller towel** *n* **:** an endless towel hung from a roller

**roller tube** *n* **:** a culture tube (as for normal or malignant tissue cells) in which the material to be cultivated is immobilized on the side of the tube by a film of serum or other medium and which is rotated (as in a water bath) to insure adequate and uniform aeration

**roller–up** \ˈ==ˈ=\ *n, pl* **rollers–up** [*roll up* + *-er*] **:** one that rolls up; *specif* **:** a textile worker who rolls skeins of yarn

**roll film** *n* **:** a strip of sensitized film for still-camera use that is wound on a spool with backing paper for light protection and daylight loading

**roll–forming machine** \ˈ=,==-\ *n* **:** a machine that shapes sheet metal to a desired curve by means of rollers

**¹rol·lick** \ˈrälik, -lēk\ *vi* -ED/-ING/-S [origin unknown] **1 :** to move or behave in a carefree joyous manner **:** FROLIC, ROMP ⟨she loved to ~; persiflage was her natural expression —W.A. White⟩ ⟨the puppies ~ about —Emily Hahn⟩ ⟨begins like an 18th century minuet and ~s suddenly into a jig —Waldo Frank⟩ **2 :** to revel in something ⟨would certainly roll and ~ in women unless there was work for him to do —H.G.Wells⟩ **syn** see PLAY

**²rollick** \"\ *n* -S **1 :** enthusiastic gaiety **:** EXUBERANCE, JOYOUSNESS ⟨filled the English theater with such ~ as it had scarcely known before —*Time*⟩ **2 :** ESCAPADE, LARK

**rol·lick·er** \-kə(r)\ *n* -S **:** one that rollicks **:** a boisterous person

**rollicking** *adj* **1 :** unrestrained in speech or behavior **:** BOISTEROUS, SWAGGERING ⟨a reckless, ~ set —Herman Melville⟩ ⟨with all his ~ rudeness, curiosity, and crudeness of dress —E.M.Coulter⟩ **2 :** light-heartedly gay **:** having or expressing a carefree joyousness ⟨the comic novels . . . are jolly, ~ affairs —John Barkham⟩ ⟨weep at the songs of sorrow, stamp their feet in joy at the ~ songs —Louise L. Davis⟩ — **rol·lick·ing·ly** *adv* — **rol·lick·ing·ness** *n* -ES

**rol·lick·some** \-ksəm\ *adj* **:** ROLLICKING — **rol·lick·some·ness** *n* -ES

**roll in** *vi* **:** to go to bed **:** turn in

**roll–in** \ˈ=,=\ *n, pl* **roll–ins** *or* **rolls–in** [fr. *roll in*, v.] **:** a play in field hockey by which a ball that has been hit out of bounds over either side line is rolled onto the field from beyond the side line by a member of the opposing team

**rol·lin film** \ˈrälən-\ *n, usu cap R* [prob. fr. the name *Rollin*] **:** a very thin film produced by capillary creeping of liquid helium II over a solid surface

**¹roll·ing** \ˈrōliŋ, -lēŋ\ *n* -S [ME, fr. gerund of *rollen, rolen* to roll — more at ROLL] **:** an act, action, or effect of one that rolls

**²rolling** \"\ *adj* [fr. pres. part. of ²*roll*] **1 a :** rotating on or as if on an axis or moving along a surface by rotation ⟨~ wheels⟩ **b :** moving on wheels or rollers ⟨this leaves only forty feet, or three lanes for ~ traffic —J.M.Lawrence⟩ **2 a :** moving from side to side or up and down ⟨~ eyes⟩ **b :** swinging from side to side **:** LURCHING, SWAYING ⟨a ~ gait⟩ **3 :** turned over upon or toward itself **:** COILING ⟨a ~ hat brim⟩ ⟨bought him a ~ Byronic collar —W.A.White⟩ **4 a :** RESOUNDING, REVERBERATING ⟨see the splintering lightning, and hear the ~ thunder —*Phoenix Flame*⟩ ⟨the traditional ~ phrases of the American declamatory style —*Time*⟩ **b :** TRILLED ⟨~ notes⟩ **5 a** (1) **:** surging on or rising upward in billows or rolls ⟨the ~ sea⟩ ⟨the ~ fog⟩ (2) **:** moving in waves **:** progressing or acting in stages **:** STAGGERED ⟨the economy was going through a ~ adjustment in which first one industry and then another was affected⟩ **b :** having gradual rounded undulations of surface ⟨ahead of us was a ~ green plain, with dark mountains beyond it —Ernest Hemingway⟩ ⟨~ hills⟩ **6 :** coming in regular rotation **:** RECURRING ⟨the ~ seasons⟩ ⟨the ~ years⟩ — **roll·ing·ly** *adv*

**rolling barrage** *n* **:** a barrage that moves forward by bounds at a fixed rate in advance of attacking infantry — called also *creeping barrage*

**rolling bridge** *n* **:** a revolving drawbridge

**rolling chair** *n* **:** a wheeled chair; *esp* **:** one adapted for recreational use and propelled by an attendant outdoors (as on a boardwalk)

**rolling chock** *n* **:** BILGE KEEL

**rolling circle** *n* **1 :** the generating circle of cycloidal and similar curves **2 :** PITCH CIRCLE

**rolling colter** *n* **:** a colter consisting of a sharp-edged steel disk

**rolling eight** *n* **:** a flight maneuver in which an airplane flies two horizontal eights side by side in immediate succession

**rolling friction** *n* **:** resistance to motion by bodies that are in rolling contact

**rolling grass** *n* **:** SPINY ROLLING GRASS

**rolling hitch** *n* **:** a hitch for fastening a line to a spar or to the standing part of another line that will not slip when the pull is parallel to the spar or line — see MAGNUS HITCH

**rolling inspection** *n* **:** a check of moving trains (as for signs of a hotbox or dragging equipment) made by track workers and the crews of passing trains

**rolling jack** *n* **:** a machine for rolling leather

**rolling key clutch** *n* **:** a friction clutch in which a set of rollers surrounding a shaft is wedged (as by a locking pawl) between this shaft and a hub on a second shaft to be connected with it

**rolling kitchen** *n* **:** a kitchen set up in a truck or trailer for cooking food and conveying it to troops in the field

**rolling landside** *n* **:** a landside consisting of a metal disk wheel that revolves on an axle

**rolling mill** *n* **1 :** an establishment where metal is rolled into plates and bars of various sections **2 :** a machine for shaping material (as heated metal, molten glass, or leather) by passing and repassing it between rolls

**rolling moment** *n* **:** a moment that tends to rotate an airplane about its longitudinal axis

**rolling pin** *n* **:** a long cylinder (as of wood or plastic) fitted with a handle or knob at each end and used for rolling out paste or dough

rolling pin

**rolling press** *n* **1 :** a calender that operates by means of rollers **2 :** a printing press with a D-shaped roller used in copperplate printing

**rolling reef** *n* **:** a reef made by rolling up the sail around a spar at the foot

**rolling road** *n* **:** a road formerly used for rolling hogsheads of tobacco to market

**rolling spar** *n* **:** BOAT BOOM

**rolling stock** *n* **1 :** the wheeled vehicles (as locomotives, passenger cars, or freight cars) owned and used by a railroad **2 :** the wheeled vehicles (as trucks or tractor-trailers) owned and used by a motor carrier

**rolling stone** *n* **:** a person who changes his habitation, business, or pursuits with great frequency **:** one who leads a wandering or unsettled life ⟨a rover perhaps, but not a thriftless *rolling stone* —*Dial*⟩

**rolling tackle** *n* **:** a tackle used to steady a yard when the ship rolls in bad weather

**rolling weed** *n* **:** TUMBLEWEED

**rol·lin·ia** \räˈlinēə\ *n, cap* [NL, fr. Charles *Rollin* †1741 Fr. educator + NL *-ia*] **:** a small genus of tropical American trees and shrubs (family Annonaceae) distinguished by the wing-appendaged petals of the flower — see BIRIBA

**roll–ins** *pl of* ROLL-IN

**roll joint** *n* **:** a joint in sheet metal made by rolling up overlapped edges and pressing flat

**roll–leaf** \ˈ=,=\ *n* **:** gold or foil laid on thin glazed paper and put up in rolls for feeding out mechanically in a stamping press

**roll·man** \ˈrōlmən\ *n, pl* **rollmen :** one who operates a rolling machine: as **a :** an operator of a power roll for smoothing sheets of metal **b :** an operator of a rolling machine for crushing already broken ore in preparation for mineral extraction **c :** an operator of a machine for cooling melted lard by contact with a refrigerated roll

**roll·mops** \ˈrōl,mäps\ *n, pl* **rollmops** \"\ *also* **rollmop·se** \-səs\ [G, fr. *rollen* to roll + *mops* simpleton, pugnosed dog, fr. LG — more at ROLLER, MOPPET] **:** a fillet of freshened salt herring rolled up with pickle or onion and skewered and then pickled in a marinade of vinegar, sliced onion, peppercorns, celery seed, bay leaves, or other spices

**rollock** *var of* ROWLOCK

**roll–off** \ˈ=,=\ *n* -S [fr. *roll off*, v.] **1 :** a tendency of an airplane esp. at high speed to lower one wing **2 :** a gradual decrease in efficiency of transmission in a sound recording system with a rise or lowering of the frequency range past a particular frequency **3 :** a play-off match in bowling

**roll–on** \ˈ=,=\ *n* -S [fr. *roll on*, v.] **:** a woman's girdle of rubber or elasticized fabric

**roll out** *vi* **:** to get out of bed ⟨*rolled out* about three o'clock in the morning to ride guard till daylight —F.B.Gipson⟩

**roll–out** \ˈ=,=\ *n* -S [fr. *roll out*, v.] **:** the rolling out to public view of a new airplane prototype

**roll over** *vt* **:** to refinance a maturing obligation (as a short-term government security) by offering a new obligation of the same type in exchange

**roll–over arm** \ˈ=,==-\ *n* **:** a fully upholstered chair or sofa arm curving outward from the seat

**roll–over plow** *n* **:** SWIVEL PLOW

**roll pass** *n* **:** ²PASS 3

**roll roofing** *n* **:** PREPARED ROOFING

**rolls** *pl of* ROLL, *pres 3d sing of* ROLL

**roll scale** *n* **:** MILL SCALE

**rolls–in** *pl of* ROLL-IN

**rolls·man** \ˈrōlzmən\ *n pl* **rollsmen :** one who passes cold steel boiler plate through a roll machine to shape it to desired curvature

**roll sulfur** *n* **:** sulfur in the form of rods or sticks made by casting molten sulfur

**roll top** *n* **1 :** the flexible cover of a rolltop desk **2 :** ROLLTOP DESK

**rolltop desk** \ˈ=,=-\ *n* **:** a writing desk having a sliding cover made of parallel slats fastened to a flexible backing

rolltop desk

**roll train** *n* **:** a set of plain or grooved rolls (as in a rolling mill) for rolling metal into various forms

**roll up** *vt* **1 :** to increase by successive accumulations **:** build up **:** ACCUMULATE ⟨*rolled up* a huge fortune⟩ ⟨*rolled up* a large majority⟩ ⟨*rolled up* a big sale⟩ **2 :** to apply developing ink to (a lithographic plate) ~ *vi* **1 :** to become larger by successive accumulations ⟨volume is expected to *roll up* as the college opening date nears —*Women's Wear Daily*⟩ **2 a :** to arrive in a vehicle ⟨turning in at the bridge, *rolled up* to the front porch —Ellen Glasgow⟩ **b** *Austral* **:** to congregate in large numbers; *esp* **:** to attend a meeting

**¹roll–up** \ˈ=,=\ *n* -S [fr. *roll up*, v.] **1 :** long hose worn by men esp. in the 18th century **2 :** a food preparation that is rolled up with or without a filling ⟨a ham *roll-up*⟩ **3** *Austral* **:** a gathering of people **4 :** a developing ink used in rolling up a lithographic plate

**²roll–up** \"\ *adj* [fr. *roll up*, v.] **:** capable of being rolled up ⟨*roll-up* blinds⟩ ⟨a *roll-up* tobacco pouch⟩

**rollway** \ˈ=,=\ *n* **1 a :** a natural or prepared slope for rolling logs into a stream **b** (1) **:** a pile of logs stored at a landing (2) **:** LANDING 2b **2 :** an outside entrance to a cellar

**roll welding** *n* **:** forge welding by pressure rolls

**rolock wall** *or* **rolok wall** *var of* ROWLOCK WALL

**rol·o·way** \ˈrälə,wā\ *n* -S [origin unknown] **:** DIANA MONKEY

**¹ro·ly–po·ly** *also* **ro·ley–po·ley** \ˈrōlēˈpōlē\ *n, pl* **roly–polys** *or* **roly–polies** [redupl. of *roly, roley*, fr. ²*roll* + *-y*] **1 :** any of various games in which a ball is rolled or thrown into holes, hats, or circles or at pins **2 :** a dessert made of rolled-out dough spread with a filling, rolled up into a cylinder shape, and baked or steamed **3 :** an Australian tumbleweed (*Bassia muricata*) that resembles the rose of Jericho **4 a :** a roly-poly person or thing **b :** a toy usu. made to resemble a person and so formed and weighted as to rock when touched and return to an erect position — called also *tumbler*

**²roly–poly** \ˈ==ˈ==\ *adj* **:** short and pudgy in stature **:** ROTUND ⟨she was so round and *roly-poly* I used to wonder how she ever moved fast enough to catch hold of a bird —Astrid Peters⟩

**rom** \ˈrōm\ *n* -S *usu cap* [Romany, married man, husband, gypsy man, fr. Skt *ḍomba, ḍoma* man of a low caste of musicians] **:** a male gypsy

**rom** *abbr* **1** roman **2** romance

**ROM** *abbr, often not cap* run of mine

**ro·ma·dur** \,rōməˈdu̇(ə)r\ *n* -S *usu cap* [G] **:** a cheese similar to Limburger in flavor and aroma

**rom·age** \ˈrəmij\ *chiefly Scot var of* RUMMAGE

**¹ro·ma·gnese** \ˌrōməˈnyēz, -ēs\ *adj, usu cap* [It, adj. & n., fr. *Romagna*, area in northern Italy + It *-ese*] **1 :** of, relating to, or characteristic of the Romagna **2 :** of, relating to, or characteristic of the people of the Romagna

**²romagnese** \"\ *n, pl* **romagnese** *cap* **:** a native or inhabitant of the Romagna

**ro·ma·gnole** *also* **ro·ma·gnol** \ˌ==ˈnyōl\ *n* -S *cap* [It *romagnolo, romagnuolo*, fr. *Romagna*] **1 :** ROMAGNESE **2 :** one who speaks an Italian dialect of the Romagna

**¹ro·maic** \rōˈmāik, -āēk\ *adj, usu cap* [NGk *Rhōmaïkos*, fr. Gk, Roman, fr. *Rhōmē, Rhōma* Rome + *-ikos* -ic] **:** of or relating to modern Greece or modern Greek

**²romaic** \"\ *n* -S *cap* **:** the modern Greek vernacular

**ro·ma·i·ka** \rōˈmāēkə\ *n* -S [NGk *rhōmaikē*, fr. fem. of *Rhōmaïkos*] **:** a modern Greek folk dance

**ro·maine** \(ˈ)rōˈmān\ *also* **romaine lettuce** *n* -S [F *romaine*, fr. fem. of *romain* Roman, fr. L *Romanus* — more at ROMAN] **:** COS LETTUCE

**ro·ma·ji** \ˈrōməjē\ *n* -S *usu cap* [Jap *rōmaji*] **:** a method of writing Japanese in Roman characters

**¹ro·mal** \rəˈmal\ *n* -S [modif. of MexSp *ramal*, fr. Sp. strand of rope, fr. *rama* branch — more at RAMADA] **:** a thong usu. braided and divided into two lashes and attached to the saddle or reins for use as a quirt

**²romal** *var of* RUMAL

**¹ro·man** \ˈrōmən\ *n* [partly fr. ME, fr. OE, fr. L *Romanus*, adj. & n., fr. *Roma* Rome + *-anus* -an; partly fr. ME *Romain*, fr. OF, fr. L *Romanus*] **1** -S *cap* **a :** a native or resident of Rome **b :** a Christian inhabitant of ancient Rome — usu. used in pl. ⟨the Epistle to the *Romans*⟩ **2** -S *usu cap* **:** ROMAN CATHOLIC — often taken to be offensive **3** -S **:** roman letters or type ⟨set this word in ~⟩ **4** -S *cap* **a** *archaic* **:** LATIN **b** *archaic* **:** ROMANCE 5 **c :** the Italian dialect of Rome **5 a** *usu cap* **:** an Italian breed of small stocky short-necked white geese **b** -S *often cap* **:** any bird of this breed **6** -S **:** a bright red sparid sea fish (*Chrysoblephus laticeps*) of southern Africa valued for sport and food — called also *red roman*

**²roman** \"\ *adj* [partly fr. ME, fr. L *Romanus*; partly fr. ME *Romain*, fr. OF, fr. L *Romanus*] **1** *usu cap* **a :** of, relating to, or characteristic of Rome, Italy, esp. ancient Rome **b :** of, relating to, or characteristic of the people of Rome; *specif* **:** having characteristics (as fortitude, courage, justice, or manliness) attributed to the ancient Romans ⟨by his *Roman* bearing in adversity, has earned a great deal of public sympathy —*Economist*⟩ **2** *usu cap* **:** of, relating to, or characteristic of the language of the ancient Romans **3 a :** UPRIGHT — used of numbers and the letters of English and other languages whose capital forms are modeled on ancient Roman inscriptions esp. as distinguished from italic, black letter, and the letters of non-Latin alphabets **b** *usu cap* **:** being round, bold, and clear — used of handwriting **4** *usu cap* **a :** of or relating to the Roman Catholic Church ⟨*Roman* practices⟩ **b :** of or relating to the Latin rite ⟨the *Roman* liturgy⟩ **5 :** having a semicircular intrados **:** ROUND ⟨a ~ arch⟩ **6** *usu cap* **:** having a prominent bridge of a slightly aquiline cast ⟨a *Roman* nose⟩ **7** *usu cap* **:** of, relating to, or constituting a mosaic formed by the ends of short slender sticks of colored glass fixed in cement **8** *usu cap* **:** of, relating to, or characteristic of the Roman ride

**ro·man à clef** \rōmäⁿnäklā\ *n, pl* **romans à clef** \"\ [F, lit., novel with a key] **:** a novel in which real persons or actual events figure under disguise ⟨a *roman à clef* of show business —Burton Rascoe⟩

**roman alphabet** *n, usu cap R* **:** LATIN ALPHABET

**roman alum** *n, usu cap R* **:** alum crystallized in cubes; *esp* **:** alum formerly made from alunite at Tolfa near Rome that was reddish because of a very small amount of iron oxide though otherwise very pure

**roman architecture** *n, usu cap R* **:** the classic architectural style of the Roman empire marked by the use of the orders, pediment, arch, dome, and vault

**roman brick** *n, often cap R* **:** a building brick having the dimensions of $1\frac{1}{2}$ in. x 4 in. x 12 in.

**roman candle** *n, usu cap R* **1 :** a firework in the form of a straight cylindrical case characterized by the continued emission of sparks and the ejection at intervals of balls or stars of fire in high arching trajectories **2 :** SPANISH DAGGER

**roman canvas** *n, usu cap R* **:** a fine linen canvas primed on one side for oil painting

**roman capital** *n, sometimes cap R* **1 :** a letter belonging to a

ROMAN CAPITALS

style of alphabet modeled upon the simple erect characters of Roman inscriptions **2 roman capitals** *pl* **:** a mode of writing consisting of roman capital letters

**¹roman catholic** *n, usu cap R&C* **:** a member of the Roman Catholic Church

**²roman catholic** *adj, usu cap R&C* **:** of, relating to, or being a Christian church with a hierarchy headed by the pope, a usu. Latin rite centering in the Mass, seven sacraments, veneration of the Virgin Mary and the saints, clerical celibacy, many religious orders, and dogma including transubstantiation and papal infallibility

**roman catholicism** *n, cap R&C* **:** the faith, doctrine, or polity of the Roman Catholic Church

**¹ro·mance** \rōˈman(t)s, -maa(ə)n-, ˈ=,=\ *n* -S [ME *romauns, romaunce*, fr. OF *romans, romanz* French, something composed in French, tale in verse, fr. L *Romanice* in the Roman manner, fr. *Romanicus* Roman, fr. *Romanus* Roman + *-icus* -ic — more at ROMAN] **1** *often cap* **a :** a tale in verse written in medieval times based chiefly on legend, chivalric love and adventure, or the supernatural — called also *metrical romance*; compare EPIC **b :** a prose tale written in medieval times and resembling a metrical romance **c :** a prose narrative having romantic qualities or characteristics: as (1) **:** one treating imaginary characters involved in events unrelated to everyday life — compare FANTASY FICTION (2) **:** one dealing with the remote in time or place, the heroic, the adventurous, and often the mysterious — compare HISTORICAL NOVEL **d :** a class or division of literature comprising romance or romantic fiction **2 :** something (as an extravagant invention or wild exaggeration) that lacks basis or foundation in fact ⟨new institutions were growing up to fight the speculation and ~ that passed for science —Mari Sandoz⟩ ⟨the critic . . . has given us what is really merely a ~ exploiting the supposed working of the mechanism, in place of an actual study that sticks close to the facts —C.I.Glicksberg⟩ **3 :** the quality or state of being romantic ⟨there is real ~ in the way words have come to have their present meanings —A.T.Weaver⟩ ⟨there is such ~ attaching to all who explore uncharted seas in cockleshell boats —*Times Lit. Supp.*⟩ ⟨~ of the pioneer⟩ ⟨~ of steel and steam⟩ ⟨~ of history⟩ ⟨~ of whaling⟩ **4 a** (1) **:** a love, love affair, or marriage of a romantic nature ⟨high school ~⟩ ⟨the ~ reportedly developed on ski jaunts —*Current Biog.*⟩ ⟨a fairy tale of love and ~ with a beautiful . . . girl —L.O.Coxe⟩ ⟨he and his wife are reported to have lived a ~ lasting almost sixty years —W.S.Rusk⟩ (2) **:** LOVEMAKING **b :** an attraction or aspiration of an emotional or romantic character ⟨the dream of travel . . . was his ~ —George Meredith⟩ ⟨the League of Nations was his first real ~ —James Cameron⟩ ⟨religion was their ~ —Van Wyck Brooks⟩ **5** *cap* **a :** the languages developed from Latin (as Portuguese, Spanish, French, Italian, Romanian) that constitute a division of the Italic branch of the Indo-European language family — see INDO-EUROPEAN LANGUAGES table **b :** any of such languages

**²romance** \(ˈ)=ˈ=\ *adj* **1** *usu cap* **:** of, relating to, or constituting the Romance languages **2 :** of or relating to the countries succeeding the Roman Empire in the medieval period **3 :** of, relating to, or characterized by romance or the romantic ⟨~ accounts of these last Gaulish invasions —Thomas Arnold⟩

**³romance** \"\ *vb* -ED/-ING/-S *vi* **1 :** to exaggerate or invent detail or incident in a romantic manner ⟨would ~ about the notables he met or the books he read —R.B.Morris⟩ ⟨the great scandal . . . was his habit of unscrupulous *romancing* —Edmund Wilson⟩ **2 :** to entertain romantic thoughts or ideas ⟨looking in at the windows . . . and *romancing* over the pictures —L.P.Smith⟩ **~** *vt* **1 :** to exaggerate or invent (as detail or incident) in a romantic manner ⟨the book exceeds and ~*s* the factual material —Donald Sutherland⟩ ⟨this *romanced* account of his wanderings, his turpitudes, and his squabbles —A.L.Guérard⟩ **2 :** to seek the favor or influence of by personal attention, flattery, or gifts ⟨was nice to the press and *romanced* the disc jockeys —*Time*⟩ **3 :** to make love to **:** carry on a love affair with ⟨a favorite spot . . . to ~ their girl friends —Budd Schulberg⟩

**⁴romance** \"\ *n* -S [F, fr. Sp, fr. OSp, Spanish, something written in Spanish, tale, ballad, fr. L *Romanice* in the Roman manner — more at ¹ROMANCE] **1 :** a short lyric tale set to music **2 :** a song or short instrumental piece in ballad style

**roman cement** *n, usu cap R* **:** a natural cement prepared by calcining septaria and grinding it dry to a fine powder

**ro·manc·er** \-sə(r)\ *n* -S [¹*romance* + *-er*] **1 :** a writer of romance or romantic fiction **2 :** one that romances

**romance stanza** *n* **:** a six-line verse stanza common in metrical romances in which lines 1, 2, 4, and 5 of 4 accents each are rhymed and lines 3 and 6 of 3 accents each are rhymed

**roman chamomile** *n, usu cap R* **:** ENGLISH CHAMOMILE

**roman chamomile oil** *n, usu cap R* **:** CHAMOMILE OIL a

**romanche** *usu cap, var of* ROMANSH

**ro·man·ci·cal** \rō'man(t)sə̇kəl\ *adj* [¹*romance* + *-ical*] **1 :** of, relating to, or consisting of romance or romantic fiction ⟨~ books⟩ **2 :** writing or inventing romance or romantic fiction ⟨~ writers⟩

**ro·manc·ist** \rō'man(t)sə̇st\ *n* -S [¹*romance* + *-ist*] **:** ROMANCER 1

**roman club** *n, usu cap R* **:** a system of bidding at contract bridge employing an artificial opening bid of one club for hands that are barely strong enough to bid or for some hands that are quite strong

**roman collar** *n, usu cap R* **:** CLERICAL COLLAR

**roman-dutch law** *n, usu cap R&D* **:** the civil-law system developed by Dutch jurists and used in So. Africa and other parts of the world colonized by the Dutch

**ro·ma·nes·ca** \,rōmə'neskə\ *n* -S [It, fr. fem. of *romanesco* Roman, fr. *romano* Roman (fr. L *Romanus*) + *-esco* -esque — more at ROMAN] **:** GALLIARD 2

**¹ro·man·esque** \¦rōmə¦nesk\ *adj, usu cap* [²*Roman* + *-esque*] **1 :** ROMANCE 1 **2 a :** of, relating to, or constructed in the Romanesque style or architecture **b :** of or relating to art contemporary with the Romanesque style and marked by religious solemnity, decorativeness, and symbolism **3 :** ROMANTIC 4 ⟨this *Romanesque* fantasy, nostalgic with adolescence and written with imagination and flourish —Janet Flanner⟩

**²romanesque** \"\ *n* -S **1** *cap* **:** ¹ROMANCE 5 **2** *usu cap* **:** the Romanesque style of art or architecture

**romanesque architecture** *or* **romanesque style** *n, usu cap R* **:** the architecture or style that developed in Italy and various parts of western Europe between the periods of the Roman and the Gothic styles: **a :** a continuation before A.D. 1000 of the Early Christian style in unvaulted basilican churches marked by the development of the cruciform plan with choirs and transepts without sculptural treatment **b :** any of several advanced and differentiated styles (as Lombard, Norman, Rhenish architecture) having as common features the use of the round arch and vault with narrowing and heightening of the nave, the substitution for columns of piers often with engaged shafts, the decorative use of arcades and colonnettes, and profuse carved ornament esp. on capitals, stringcourses, and the moldings of doorways — see ARCHITECTURE table

**romanesque revival** *n, usu cap 1st R* **:** a nostalgic stylistic return in the late 19th century to pre-Gothic architectural forms

**ro·ma·nes·ta red MT-2544** \¦rōmə¦nestə-\ *n, usu cap both Rs* [*romanesta* of unknown origin] **:** an organic pigment — see DYE table I (under *Pigment Red 15*)

**roman fern** *n, usu cap R* **:** DEER FERN

**ro·man-fleuve** \rōmäⁿflə̄v\ *n, pl* **romans-fleuves** \"\ [F, lit., river novel] **:** a distinctively French novel having the form of a long, multivolume, and usu. easygoing chronicle of persons comprising a family, community, or other social group

**roman foot** *n, usu cap R* **:** an ancient Roman unit of length equal to 11.64 English inches

**roman gold** *n, usu cap R* **:** gold having a yellow mat finish

**roman green** *n, often cap R* **:** a moderate olive color that is redder than average olive green and redder, lighter, and stronger than average olive color

**roman holiday** *n, usu cap R* [so called fr. the bloody combats staged as entertainment in ancient Rome] **1 a :** an event or occasion resembling the games or gladiatorial combats of the ancient Roman circus (as for spectacle or savagery provided or demanded as a source of sadistic pleasure for onlookers) **b :** a time of enjoyment derived from the sufferings or losses of others or the source of such enjoyment ⟨our own fliers seemed to be letting the Jerries have a *Roman holiday* at our expense —E.V.Westrate⟩ ⟨diplomats who felt themselves merely victims to be sacrificed every four years to make a *Roman holiday* for a new President —Emily Bax⟩ **2 :** a public dispute, investigation, or turmoil in which the participants inflict embarrassment, degradation, or ignominy on each other or themselves often at the direction or to the satisfaction of nonparticipants ⟨persons charging police brutality have had a *Roman holiday* in making these charges but not following them up —*Springfield (Mass.) Union*⟩ ⟨the investigation was accompanied by reams of publicity and millionaires were summoned by the score to make a *Roman holiday* —*Amer. Mercury*⟩

**roman hyacinth** *n, usu cap R* **:** a hyacinth (*Hyacinthus orientalis albulus*) with loosely flowered spikes several of which grow from one bulb

**romani** *cap, var of* ROMANY 2

**ro·ma·nia** \rō'mānēə, -nyə\ *or* **ru·ma·nia** *or* **rou·ma·nia** \rü'-\ *adj, usu cap* [fr. *Romania*, country in eastern Europe] **:** of or from Romania **:** of the kind or style prevalent in Romania **:** ROMANIAN

**¹ro·ma·nian** *or* **ru·ma·nian** *or* **rou·ma·nian** \-ən\ *adj, usu cap* [*Romania, Roumania, Rumania*, country in eastern Europe + E *-an*] **1 a :** of, relating to, or characteristic of Romania **b :** of, relating to, or characteristic of the Romanians **2 :** of, relating to, or characteristic of the Romanian language

**²romanian** *or* **rumanian** *or* **roumanian** \"\ *n* -S *cap* **1 :** a native or inhabitant of Romania; *esp* **:** one of the dominant ethnic group prob. descended from Roman provincial colonists of Dacia and Moesia **2 :** the Romance language of the Romanian people

**¹ro·man·ic** \rō'manik, -nēk\ *adj* [L *Romanicus* Roman — more at ROMANCE] **1** *usu cap* **:** ROMANCE 1 **2** *usu cap* **:** descended from the Roman people ⟨the *Romanic* races⟩ — compare LATIN, ROMANCE 2

**²romanic** \"\ *n* -S *cap* **:** ROMANCE 5

**ro·man·i·cist** \-nəsə̇st\ *n* -S *usu cap* **:** ROMANIST 3

**romanies** *pl of* ROMANY

**roman indiction** *n, usu cap R* **:** the indiction of the system that began on Dec. 25, A.D. 312 or as still used in modern chronology Jan. 1, 313 — called also *pontifical indiction*

**ro·man·ish** \'rōmənish, -nēsh\ *adj, usu cap* [²*Roman* + *-ish*] **:** of or relating to the Roman Catholic Church — usu. used disparagingly; compare ROMISH

**ro·man·ism** \-mə,nizəm\ *n* -S [²*Roman* + *-ism*] **1** *cap* **:** ROMAN CATHOLICISM **2** *usu cap* **:** the polity, institutions, or prevailing spirit of ancient Rome

**¹ro·man·ist** \-nə̇st\ *n* -S *usu cap* [NL *Romanista*, fr. L *Romanus* Roman + *-ista* -ist — more at ROMAN] **1 :** one who adheres to Roman Catholicism — usu. used disparagingly **2 :** a specialist in the language, culture, or law of ancient Rome **3 :** a person skilled or informed in Romance languages or philology — called also *Romanicist* **4 :** an historian who magnifies the influence of Roman institutions in the development of European civilization — compare GERMANIST

**²romanist** \"\ *or* **ro·man·is·tic** \¦=·=¦nistik\ *adj, usu cap* **1 :** adhering to or inclining toward Roman Catholicism **2 :** of or relating to the law of ancient Rome

**ro·man·i·ty** \rō'manəd·ē\ *n* -ES *usu cap* **:** ROMANISM

**ro·ma·ni·um** \rō'mānēəm\ *n* -S [NL, fr. R. I. *Roman*, 19th cent. metallurgist, its inventor + NL *-ium*] **:** an alloy consisting of aluminum having an admixture of less than one percent of tungsten together with a little copper, nickel, antimony, and tin

**ro·man·iza·tion** \,rōmənə̇'zāshən, -mə,nī'-\ *n* -S *usu cap* **:** the act or process of Romanizing

**ro·man·ize** \'rōmə,nīz\ *vb* -ED/-ING/-S [²*Roman* + *-ize*] *vt* **1** *often cap* **a :** to cause to acquire traits or characteristics distinctly Roman or become adapted to Roman customs or outlook **b :** to bring (as an area or people) under the political, cultural, or commercial influence of Rome **2** *sometimes cap* **a :** to write or print (as a language) in roman characters — compare ROMAJI **b :** to represent (as pagination) in roman numerals **3** *usu cap* **a :** to convert to Roman Catholicism **b** (1) **:** to give a Roman Catholic character to (2) **:** to subject to the principles and usages of the Roman Catholic Church **~** *vi, usu cap* **:** to become Roman Catholic; *also* **:** to adhere to or incline toward Roman Catholicism

**roman lake** *n, often cap R* **:** CARMINE 2

**roman law** *n, usu cap R* **:** the legal system of the ancient Romans that includes the customary or unwritten law and the written law, is based on the traditional law and the legislation of the city of Rome, and in form comprises legislation of the law-making assemblies, resolves of the senate, enactments of the emperors, the edicts or praetorian law, the writings of the jurisconsults, and the codes of the later emperors — see CIVIL LAW; compare JUS GENTIUM, NATURAL LAW

**ro·man·ly** *adv, usu cap* **:** in a manner characteristic of the ancient Romans

**roman nettle** *n, usu cap R* **:** an annual herb (*Urtica pilulifera*) with stinging foliage and small clusters of green flowers

**roman numeral** *n, often cap R* **:** one of the symbols in a system of numerical notation based upon the ancient Roman system — see NUMBER table

**ro·ma·no** \rō'mä(,)nō\ *also* **romano cheese** *n* -S *usu cap R* [It *romano* Roman, fr. L *Romanus* — more at ROMAN] **:** a sharp hard cheese of pale color and granular texture with a blackish green rind made of ewe's milk and now also of milk from cows and goats

**romano-** *comb form, usu cap* [²*Roman*] **:** Roman **:** Roman and ⟨*Romano*-Etruscan⟩ ⟨*Romano*-German⟩

**roman ocher** *n, usu cap R* **1 :** an orange-yellow ocher **2 :** OCHER BROWN

**roman order** *n, usu cap R* **1 :** the composite order in architecture **2 :** ARCH ORDER

**ro·ma·nov** \'rōmə,nȯf\ *n* [after the *Romanov* dynasty that ruled Russia 1613–1917] **1** *usu cap* **:** a Russian breed of prolific strong-wooled sheep **2** -S *often cap* **:** any sheep of the Romanov breed

**ro·ma·now·sky stain** \¦rōmə¦nȯfskē-\ *n, usu cap R* [after Dimitri L. *Romanowsky* †1921 Russ. physician] **:** a stain made from water-soluble eosin, methylene blue, and absolute methanol and used in parasitology

**roman pace** *n, usu cap R* **:** an ancient Roman unit of length that is equal to five Roman feet or 4.85 English feet and is measured in pacing from the heel of one foot to the heel of the same foot when it next touches the ground

**roman peace** *n, usu cap R* [trans. of L *pax Romana*] **:** a peace imposed and maintained by force of arms **:** PAX

**roman pearl** *n, usu cap R* **:** an imitation pearl made of a glass bulb coated with pearl essence and filled with wax

**roman plant** *n, usu cap R* **:** GOOD-KING-HENRY

**roman purple** *n, often cap R* **:** a moderate violet that is redder and deeper than Parma violet (sense 2a) and redder and stronger than damson

**roman revival** *n, usu cap 1st R* **:** a late Renaissance return to the simpler forms of classic Roman architecture

**roman ride** *n, usu cap 1st R* **:** a style of riding in which the rider stands with one foot on the back of each of two horses driven as a pair ⟨first came the *Roman ride*, a wild gallop about the ring . . . on two horses —Eduard Bass⟩

**roman rings** *n pl, usu cap 1st R* **:** large pendent rings used by an acrobat or gymnast in performing gymnastic feats in midair

**romans** *pl of* ROMAN

**roman sandal** *n, usu cap R* **:** a shoe on which the vamp is composed of a series of buckled straps equally spaced

Roman sandal

**roman sepia** *n, often cap R* **:** VANDYKE BROWN 2

**romans-fleuves** *pl of* ROMAN-FLEUVE

**ro·mansh** *or* **ro·mansch** *or* **ro·manche** \rō'manch, -mänch\ *or* **ru·mansch** \rü'-\ *n, pl* **romanshes** *or* **romansches** *or* **romanches** *or* **rumansches** *usu cap* [Romansh *rumansch, rumonsch, romonsch*] **:** the Rhaeto-Romanic dialects spoken in the Grisons, Switzerland; *esp* **:** those west of the Engadine

**roman snail** *n, usu cap R* **:** a European edible snail (*Helix pomatia*)

**roman striking** *n, usu cap R* **:** a system of striking the time in some older clocks that employs two bells of different pitch with the lower-toned bell representing the Roman figure V and the higher-toned bell the Roman figure I

**roman stripe** *n, usu cap R* **1 roman stripes** *pl* **:** bright varicolored stripes of equal or unequal widths used as a continuous textile pattern **2 :** a fabric with a pattern of Roman stripes

**¹ro·man·tic** \rō'mantik, -maan- -tēk *sometimes* rə'-\ *adj* [F *romantique*, fr. obs. *romant* romance (fr. MF, fr. OF *romans, romanz* French, something composed in French, tale in verse) + *-ique* -ic — more at ROMANCE] **1 :** consisting of or similar in form or content to a romance ⟨my advance toward ~ composition —Sir Walter Scott⟩ ⟨~ fiction⟩ **2 :** having no basis in fact **:** being the product of invention or exaggeration **:** FABULOUS, IMAGINARY ⟨liked to make observations all his own and give his characteristic ~ report afterward —Glenway Wescott⟩ ⟨treachery to the peerage was a somewhat ~ way of describing his political goings-on —Roy Lewis & Angus Maude⟩ ⟨story of drugged kidnapping and clever fencing with the . . . interrogators was deemed altogether too ~ —*Time*⟩ **3 :** impractical in conception or plan **:** UNREALISTIC, VISIONARY ⟨some ~ get-rich-quick scheme to attain a heaven-on-earth —M.R.Cohen⟩ ⟨now that the world has become more honest and less ~ —L.C.Powys⟩ ⟨was not ~ enough to assume you could reform society and get human institutions that would be perfect —Stringfellow Barr⟩ **4 :** marked by the imaginative or emotional appeal of the heroic, adventurous, remote, mysterious, or idealized characteristics of things, places, people ⟨collecting ~ articles of commerce — the pearl oyster, arrowroot, ambergris, sandalwood, coconut oil —Herman Melville⟩ ⟨a noble chase of great extent, beautifully wild and ~, well stored with game of all sorts, and abounding with excellent timber —Tobias Smollett⟩ ⟨had become so ~ a figure that his appearance on the street of any border town started lurid tales of bloodshed and sudden death —Mari Sandoz⟩ ⟨reminiscing about his childhood, he almost invariably is drawn into a nostalgic mood where events and characters assume ~ proportions —Rose Feld⟩ ⟨makes a deep impression on the mind; far deeper than the less ~, everyday thing which shows the real state of an island in the statistical sense —R.A.W.Hughes⟩ **5 :** having an inclination or desire for romance **:** responsive to the appeal of the imaginative or emotional qualities of human experience ⟨most people are ~ at 20, owing to lack of experience —E.M. Forster⟩ ⟨was once young and passionate, ~ about the schemes which he realistically carried out —Carl Van Doren⟩ ⟨children are, and ought to be, ~ —C.H.Grandgent⟩ **6 a** *often cap* **:** of, relating to, or having the characteristics of romanticism or the romantic movement ⟨the modern ~ tradition, however, can be traced to one important literary source —Mabel Elliott & Francis Merrill⟩ ⟨the generating and generic element in the *Romantic* doctrine —A.O.Lovejoy⟩ ⟨characteristic of the *Romantic* period —W.H.Auden⟩ ⟨the ~ poets⟩ — compare CLASSICAL **b** *of art, literature, or music* **:** marked by freedom, spontaneity, or freedom of conception and expression **7 a :** characterized by a strong personal sentiment, highly individualized feelings of affection, or the idealization of the beloved or the love relationship **:** ARDENT, FERVENT 2 ⟨give the impression of having married for ~ love —James Jones⟩ ⟨her first ~ admiration of his lofty bearing —George Meredith⟩ ⟨the period of ~ love among the newly married —Lewis Mumford⟩ **b :** marked chiefly by sexual passion or its gratification ⟨in popular speech, today, a ~ novel or film is one concerned . . . with sexual passion —*Times Lit. Supp.*⟩ **8 :** of, relating to, or constituting the part of the hero in a light or romantic comedy ⟨played the ~ lead⟩ **syn** see SENTIMENTAL

**²romantic** \"\ *n* -S **1 :** a characteristic or component of or suggestive of romance or romantic writing — usu. used in pl. ⟨there you are with your ~*s* again —William Black⟩ ⟨love for the banker's daughter takes care of the ~*s* —*Newsweek*⟩ **2 a :** a person of romantic temperament or disposition **:** one given to romance ⟨is still essentially a ~ — capable of seeing the world as he wishes to see it —T.R.Fyvel⟩ ⟨by temperament and training the ~ who feels first and thinks afterwards —Edward Cushing⟩ **b** *usu cap* **:** ROMANTICIST 1 ⟨the *Romantics* convert nature into a solace for the trials of civilization —Philip Rahv⟩ ⟨was characteristic of the *Romantics* to seek experience for its own sake —Edmund Wilson⟩

**ro·man·ti·cal** \-tə̇kəl\ *adj* [F *romantique* + E *-al*] **:** ROMANTIC

**ro·man·ti·cal·ly** \-tə̇k(ə)lē, -tēk-, -li\ *adv* **:** in a romantic manner ⟨~ the village fireman hangs on with one hand —S.R. Gain⟩ ⟨~ in love —W.F. De Morgan⟩ ⟨the house ~ decorated with battlemented towers and high mullioned windows —*Amer. Guide Series: Md.*⟩

**ro·man·ti·cal·ness** *n* -ES **:** the quality or state of being romantic

**romantic green** *n* **:** WARBLER GREEN

**ro·man·ti·cism** \-tə,sizəm\ *n* -S [¹*romantic* + *-ism*] **1 :** the quality or state of being romantic ⟨passed through a period of ~ when a broken love affair somehow seemed noble —G.R. Carlsen⟩ ⟨pure ~ to expect any solution of isolated issues —J.A. del Vayo⟩ ⟨no time for vague ~ in foreign policy —*New Republic*⟩ **2** *often cap* **a** (1) **:** a literary, artistic, and philosophical movement originating in Europe in the 18th century, characterized chiefly by a reaction against neoclassicism with its stress on reason and intellect and an emphasis on the imagination and emotions and their freely individualized expression or realization in all spheres of activity, and marked esp. in English literature by sensibility and the use of autobiographical material of an introspective cast, an exaltation of the primitive and the common man, an appreciation and often a worship of external nature, an interest in the remote in time and space, a predilection for melancholy, and the use in poetry of older verse forms (as the ballad stanza and the sonnet) — compare CLASSICISM 3 (2) **:** an aspect of romanticism (as sentimentalism, primitivism, or medievalism) **b :** adherence to or practice of romantic doctrine or assumptions ⟨the ~ of Byron⟩ ⟨the ~ of early 19th century music⟩ ⟨the ~ of Turner's landscapes⟩ ⟨the ~ of Rodin⟩

**¹ro·man·ti·cist** \-sə̇st\ *n* -S [¹*romantic* + *-ist*] **1** *often cap* **:** an advocate of or participant in romanticism or the romantic movement esp. in art, literature, or music **2 :** ROMANTIC 2a

**²romanticist** \"\ *also* **ro·man·ti·cis·tic** \¦=·=·=¦sistik\ *adj, often cap* **:** of, relating to, or having the characteristics of romanticism or the romantic movement ⟨is clearly of the ~ type —W.M.Wheeler⟩ ⟨built around the two most ~ nations —A.F.Buchan⟩

**ro·man·tic·i·ty** \,rō,man'tisəd·ē\ *n* -ES *archaic* **:** ROMANTICISM

**ro·man·ti·ci·za·tion** \rō,mantə̇sə̇'zāshən\ *n* -S **:** the act or process of romanticizing

**ro·man·ti·cize** \rō'mantə,sīz *sometimes* rə'-\ *vb* -ED/-ING/-S [¹*romantic* + *-ize*] *vt* **:** to make romantic **:** add romance to ⟨old forms of drudgery are *romanticized*, old forms of slavery forgotten —H.J.Muller⟩ ⟨rebuke the press for alleged *romanticizing* of gangsterism —F.L.Mott⟩ **~** *vi* **1 :** to hold romantic ideas **:** indulge in romantic fancies ⟨had *romanticized* a great deal about Indians —*Southern Observer*⟩ **2 :** to present or portray details, incidents, or people in a romantic light or manner ⟨has been . . . successful in resisting the impulse to dramatize, though she has yielded occasionally to the impulse to ~ —Howard Lindsay⟩ ⟨refuses to ~, glamorize, or otherwise adopt the strange combination of true confession and movie magazine technique —Abraham Veinus⟩

**ro·man·tic·ly** *archaic var of* ROMANTICALLY

**romantico-** *comb form* [¹*romantic*] **:** romantic and ⟨*romantico*-heroic⟩ ⟨*romantico*-literary⟩

**romantics** *pl of* ROMANTIC

**ro·man·tism** \rō'maⁿ,tizəm\ *n* -S [F *romantisme*, fr. *romantique* + *-isme* -ism] **:** ROMANTICISM ⟨moonshine ~ idealizing slave-holding aristocrats —J.F.Dobie⟩

**roman umber** *n, often cap R* **:** RAW UMBER 2

**roman violet** *n, often cap R* **:** PANSY VIOLET 3

**roman wormwood** *n, usu cap R* **1 a :** a European wormwood (*Artemisia pontica*) that is a minor source of absinthe **b :** RAGWEED 2a **2 :** a glaucous No. American corydalis (*Corydalis sempervirens*) with loose racemes of yellow-tipped pink flowers

**¹rom·a·ny** \'rämənē, 'rōm-, -ni\ *also* **rom·ma·ny** \'räm-\ *n* -ES [Romany *romano, romani*, adj., gypsy, fr. *rom* married man, husband, gypsy man — more at ROM] **1** *cap* **:** GYPSY 1 **2** *also* **rom·a·ni** \"\ *cap* **:** the Indic language of the gypsies — see INDO-EUROPEAN LANGUAGES table **3** *often cap* **:** a blackish blue that is redder and less strong than average midnight

**²romany** \"\ *also* **rommany** \"\ *adj, usu cap* [Romany *romano, romani*] **1 :** of, relating to, or characteristic of the Romanies **2 :** of, relating to, or characteristic of the Romany language

**ro·man·za** \rō'manzə\ *n* -S [It, fr. Sp *romance* — more at ROMANCE] **:** ⁴ROMANCE

**ro·maunt** \rō'mänt, -mȯnt\ *n* -S [ME, fr. MF *romant* — more at ROMANTIC] *archaic* **:** ROMANCE 1

**ro·mayne work** \(')rō¦mān-\ *n, often cap R* [prob. fr. F *romaine*, fem. of *romain* Roman — more at ROMAINE] **:** the ornamentation of furniture with carved medallions, knobs, or finials in the form of human or grotesque heads found esp. in 17th century England

**rom·berg sign** \'räm,bərg-\ *n, usu cap R* [after Moritz H. *Romberg* †1873 Ger. neurologist] **:** a diagnostic sign of locomotor ataxia and other diseases of the nervous system consisting of a swaying of the body when the feet are placed close together and the eyes are closed

**rom·bow·line** \'räm'bōlə̇n\ *or* **rum·bow·line** \,rəm-\ *n* [origin unknown] **1 :** old condemned canvas or rope unfit for use except as chafing gear aboard ship **2 :** an inferior rope used as lashing

**¹rome** \'rōm\ *n* -S *cap* [ME, fr. *Rome*, Italy] **:** ROMAN CATHOLICISM ⟨was loyal to *Rome* less because it was Catholic than because it was Roman —D.C.Williams⟩

**²rome** \"\ *adj, usu cap* [fr. *Rome*, Italy] **:** of or from Rome, capital of Italy ⟨the *Rome* correspondent⟩ **:** of the kind or style prevalent in Rome **:** ROMAN

**ro·me·ite** \'rōmē,īt\ *n* -S [modif. (influenced by *-ite*) of F *roméine*, fr. Jean B. L. *Romé* de Lisle + F *-ine*] **:** a mineral $(Ca,Fe,Mn,Na)_2(Sb,Ti)_2O_6(O,OH,F)$ consisting of a hyacinth or honey yellow oxide of calcium, iron, manganese, sodium, antimony, and titanium related to bindheimite and occurring in minute octahedrons

**rom·el·dale** \'räməl,dāl\ *n* [blend of *Romney, Rambouillet*, and *Corriedale*] **1** *usu cap* **:** an American breed of utility sheep developed by crossbreeding Romneys and Rambouillets with the intention of retaining a heavy fleece of fine wool while producing a quickly maturing high-grade market lamb **2** -S *often cap* **:** a sheep of the Romeldale breed

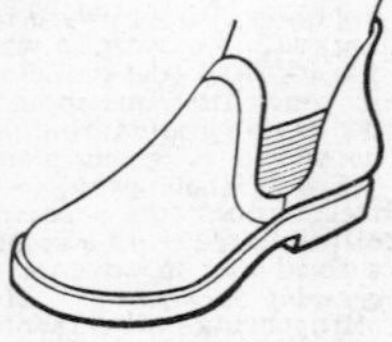

romeo 2

**¹ro·meo** \'rōmē,ō\ *n* -S [after *Romeo*, ill-fated lover in Shakespeare's *Romeo and Juliet*] **1** *usu cap* **:** one given over to a love affair or lovemaking ⟨his hair slicked down like any dance hall

*Romeo's* —*Time*⟩ ⟨deserting art and science for beauty, he became a celebrated international *Romeo* —Alva Johnston⟩ **2 :** a man's slipper or shoe with a high backing quarter, high front, and usu. U-shaped elastic gores at the sides — compare CONGRESS GAITER, GAITER, JULIET

**²romeo** \"\ *usu cap* [after *Romeo*] — a communications code word for the letter *r*

**rome penny** *n, usu cap R* **:** PETER'S PENCE

**ro·mer·il·lo** \ˌrōmə'ri(ˌ)lō\ *n* -s [AmerSp, dim. of *romero* rosemary, fr. L *ros maris*, lit., dew of the sea, fr. *ros* dew + *maris*, gen. of *mare* sea — more at RORIC, MARINE] **1 :** any of several tropical American plants with an aromatic odor most of which yield native remedies or dyes: as **a :** a So. American herb (*Heterothalamus brunioides*) of the family Compositae whose flower heads yield a yellow dye **b :** a Mexican shrubby milkweed (*Asclepias linaria*) that yields a violent purge **c :** any of several Mexican plants of the family Compositae (esp. *Porophyllum scoparium* and *Chrysactinia mexicana*) **2 :** the dye yielded by the So. American herb romerillo

**ro·me·ro** \rō'me(ˌ)rō\ *n* -s [Sp, lit., pilgrim, alter. of *romeo*, fr. ML *romaeus* Byzantine Greek, pilgrim headed for Rome, fr. MGk *rhōmaios*, fr. Gk, Roman, fr. *Rhōmē* Rome] **:** PILOT FISH 1

**rome·scot** \'rōmˌz,kät, -m,sk-\ *n, usu cap* [ME, fr. OE *Rōmescot*, fr. *Rōm* Rome + *scot*] **:** PETER'S PENCE

**rome·ward** \'rōmwə(r)d\ *adv (or adj), usu cap* [ME, fr. *Rome* + *-ward*] **:** toward Rome or Roman Catholicism ⟨the church service is oriented *Romeward*⟩ ⟨*Romeward* tendency⟩ ⟨*Romeward* doctrine⟩

**rom·ish** \'rōmish, -mēsh\ *adj, usu cap* [*Rome* + E *-ish*] **:** of or relating to the Roman Catholic Church — **rom·ish·ly** *adv* — **rom·ish·ness** *n* -ES

**rom·ist** \-məst\ *n* -s *usu cap* [*Rome* + E *-ist*] *archaic* **:** ROMAN CATHOLIC

**rom·mack** \'rämək\ *vi* [origin unknown] *dial Eng* **:** to romp or play boisterously

**rommany** *usu cap, var of* ROMANY

**rom·ney** \'rämnē\ *or* **romney marsh** *n* [fr. *Romney Marsh*, coastal pasture tract in southwestern England] **1** *usu cap R & sometimes cap M* **:** a British breed of hardy long-wooled mutton-type sheep esp. adapted to damp or marshy regions **2** -s *often cap R & sometimes cap M* **:** an animal of the Romney breed

**rom·neya** \'rämnēə, ≈'≈≈\ *n, cap* [NL, after Thomas *Romney* Robinson †1882 Brit. astronomer] **:** a genus of shrubs (family Papaveraceae) having the stigmata united in a ring at the base

**romney hut** *n, usu cap R* [fr. the name *Romney*] **:** a large strong building similar to the smaller Nissen hut

**¹romp** \'rämp *sometimes* 'rȯmp\ *n* -s [partly alter. of ⁴*ramp*; partly alter. of ²*ramp*] **1 :** one that romps; *esp* **:** a romping girl or woman **2 a :** lively, frisky, or boisterous play or sport **:** FROLIC, GAMBOL ⟨both dogs loose, it is quite possible that a joyful ~ rather than a dogfight would result —J.W.Cross⟩ ⟨students' day features a parade through town with all manner of ~ and hilarity —Ernest Stock⟩ ⟨a high-spirited ~ which is the American version of country dancing —Angelica Gibbs⟩ **b :** a romp marked by lovemaking ⟨had made a tryst for a twilight ~ —Lucy M. Montgomery⟩ ⟨the lovers . . . going out onto the porch in a ~ every little while —Elizabeth M. Roberts⟩ **3 :** a pace or rate of progress in a race or contest by which one wins easily or outdistances competitors by a large margin **:** RUNAWAY ⟨a gray colt who beat 18 other well fancied youngsters in a ~ —G.F.T.Ryall⟩ ⟨is expected to win the political race in a ~⟩ ⟨a 65-yard touchdown ~⟩ **4 :** a literary or dramatic production consisting chiefly of a series of lively fast-moving loosely organized incidents or episodes ⟨it was a semiautobiographical ~ through the sophisticated continental and domestic settings —Edward Lueders⟩ ⟨a play that begins like another ~ about a junior miss up to junior mischief —*Time*⟩ ⟨the plot is no more than an artfully regulated ~ —*Newsweek*⟩ **syn** see PLAY

**²romp** \"\ *vb* -ED/-ING/-S [alter. of ¹*ramp*] *vi* **1 a :** to play in a lively, frisky, or boisterous manner **:** FROLIC, GAMBOL ⟨found the general ~*ing* in the living room with his five children —*Newsweek*⟩ ⟨the hugest playmate that ever ~*ed* with fairies and the aery sprites of merry mischief —G.K. Chesterton⟩ **b :** to engage in lovemaking ⟨~ with one's . . . pretty serving girl when wifie's busy bathing —Robert Browning⟩ ⟨during the trial of a paternity suit it was brought out that . . . the footmen ~*ed* with the servant girls —R.D.Altick⟩ **2 a :** to proceed, move, or go in a gay, animated, or vigorous manner ⟨the wind was ~*ing* through the streets like a boisterous country visitor —Rebecca West⟩ ⟨girls . . . ~ down the stone steps with such a deafening clatter —Sam Heppner⟩ ⟨boats that ~*ed* over the bay —Jean Stafford⟩ **b :** to run or advance in a race or contest with such progress as to win easily or outdistance the competitors by a large margin ⟨~*ed* home a winner . . . in his first start —G.F.T.Ryall⟩ ⟨~*ed* for four touchdowns and three conversion points —*Newsweek*⟩ ⟨~*ing* home with 51 of the 52 seats up for election —Alex Josey⟩ **3 a :** to act a part in a play in a lively, fast, or informal manner ⟨aiming at speed, achieves it by letting his smooth cast ~ gayly and ripple off the script's cute lines at a fast rate —P.T.Hartung⟩ ⟨~ throughout the half hour flubbing and gagging, sticking to script and bouncing off into ad lib —*Newsweek*⟩ **b :** to play music in a buoyant spontaneous manner usu. with flourishes or improvisations ⟨the two ~ through chase choruses, sometimes trading every four bars, which is . . . quite exciting as they play it —Bill Simon⟩ ⟨watching the piano player take his chorus, with a fine ~*ing* offbeat in the treble —Vincent McHugh⟩ ⟨~*ed* through a few popular songs, backed up by a drummer and a bass player —Douglas Watt⟩ ~ *vt* **:** to convey or urge in a sportive or boisterous manner ⟨~ the children to bed⟩ **syn** see PLAY

**romp·er** \-pə(r)\ *n* -s **1 :** one that romps ⟨a cry like every kind of bell rang from these ~*s* as they raced —John Masefield⟩ **2 a :** a child's one-piece garment consisting of waist and short bloomers — usu. used in pl. **b :** any of various garments of somewhat similar design worn by adults — usu. used in pl.

**romping** *adj* **1 :** engaging in a romp **:** given to romps ⟨a lively ~ boy⟩ **2 :** having the characteristics of a romp ⟨had a big ~ party and ended by gathering around the piano and singing —W.A.White⟩ — **romp·ing·ly** *adv*

**romp·ish** \-pish, -pēsh\ *adj* **:** ROMPING ⟨a ~ girl⟩ ⟨a series of ~ square dances —K.M.Dodson⟩ — **romp·ish·ness** *n* -ES

**rom·pu** \'räm(ˌ)pü\ *adj* [F, past part. of *rompre* to break, fr. L *rumpere* — more at REAVE] *of a heraldic ordinary* **:** depicted as broken usu. with the broken piece pushed up — compare FRACTED 2

**rompy** \'rämpē\ *adj* -ER/-EST [²*romp* + *-y*] **:** ROMPING

**roms** *pl of* ROM

**ron·ca·dor** \ˌräŋkə'dȯ(ə)r\ *n, pl* **roncadors** \-rz\ *or* **roncado·res** \-ō,rās\ [Sp, lit., one that snores, fr. *roncado* (past part. of *roncar* to snore, fr. LL *rhonchare*, fr. *rhonchus* snore) + *-or* — more at RHONCHUS] **1 :** any of several croakers (family Sciaenidae) of the American Pacific coast (as the yellowfin croaker or the black croaker) **2 :** any of various grunts (esp. *Haemulon steindachneri*) of both the Atlantic and Pacific coasts

**ron·cet** \rän'sā\ *n* -s [F, dim. of *ronce* bramble, blackberry bush, fr. L *rumic-*, *rumex* sorrel — more at RUMEX] **:** COURT-NOUÉ

**ron·co** \'räŋ(ˌ)kō\ *n* -s [AmerSp, fr. Sp, hoarse, modif. (influenced by *roncar* to snore) of L *raucus*] **1 :** any of several grunts (genus *Haemulon*); *esp* **:** a small gray brown-streaked food fish (*H. parra*) of the tropical western Atlantic from the Florida Keys and Cuba to Brazil — called also *sailor's-choice* **2 :** ATLANTIC CROAKER

**ron·dache** \(')rän¦dash\ *n* -s [F, fr. MF *rudache*, *rondache*] **:** a small round shield carried by a foot soldier

**ron·da·vel** \'rändə,vel\ *n* -s [Afrik *rondawel*] **1 :** a round native hut of southern Africa usu. made of mud and having a thatched roof of grass **2 :** a round house resembling a native hut often used as a guesthouse or tourist dwelling in southern Africa

**rond de jambe** \ˌrändə'zhäm\ *n, pl* **ronds de jambe** \-n(z)d-\ [F, lit., circle of the leg] **:** a circular movement of the leg in ballet either par terre or en l'air

**ronde** \'ränd\ *n* -s [F, fr. fem. of *rond* round, fr. OF *roont*, *rount*, *ront* — more at ROUND] **:** script with heavy strokes nearly upright **:** ROUND HAND

**ron·deau** \'rän(ˌ)dō, ≈'≈\ *n, pl* **ron·deaux** \-ō(z)\ [MF, lit., small circle, alter. of *rondel*] **1 a :** a fixed form of verse running on two rhymes and consisting usu. of 15 lines of eight or ten syllables divided into three stanzas with the beginning of the first line of the first stanza serving as the refrain of the second and third stanzas — called also *rondel* **b :** a poem in this form **2 a :** a medieval monophonic French song characterized by the many repetitions of its two themes or sections **b :** ¹RONDO 3 **3** [LaF, fr. F] **:** ²RONDO

**rondeau re·dou·blé** \-rə,dü'blā\ *n, pl* **rondeaux redoublés** [F, lit., double rondeau] **1 :** a fixed form of verse running on two rhymes that usu. consists of five quatrains in which the lines of the first quatrain are used consecutively to end each of the remaining four quatrains and which are sometimes followed by an envoi of four lines that terminates with the opening words of the poem **2 :** a poem in the rondeau redoublé form

**ron·del** \'ränd^əl, -n,del\ *or* **ron·delle** \rän'del\ *n* -s [ME, fr. OF, lit., small circle — more at ROUNDEL] **1** *usu rondelle* **:** something that forms a circle **:** a circular object: as **a :** a tiny jeweled circle or ring-shaped bead usu. strung between larger stones or sections of a necklace **b :** a flat circular disk usu. of sapphire or ruby from which a jewel bearing is made **c :** a flat circular diamond with approximately 128 facets around the edge **2 a** *usu rondel* **:** a form of verse running on two rhymes and consisting usu. of 14 lines of eight or ten syllables divided into three stanzas with the first two lines of the first stanza serving as the refrain of the second and third stanzas **b :** a poem in this form **c :** RONDEAU 1

**ron·de·let** \ˌrändə¦let\ *n* -s [MF, dim. of *rondel*] **:** a modified rondeau running on two rhymes and consisting usu. of seven lines in which the first line of four syllables is repeated as the third line and as the final line or refrain with the remaining lines made up of eight syllables each

**ron·de·le·tia** \ˌrändə'lēshēə\ *n* [NL, fr. Guillaume *Rondelet* †1566 French naturalist + NL *-ia*] **1** *cap* **:** a genus of tropical American trees and shrubs (family Rubiaceae) having salver-shaped fragrant flowers with a long tube **2** -s **:** any plant of the genus *Rondeletia*

**ron·delle** \rän'del\ *or* **ron·dle** \'ränd^əl\ *n* -s [F *rondelle* — more at RONDEL] **:** the crust or scale on molten metal in the crucible

**ron·di·no** \rän'dē(ˌ)nō\ *or* **ron·do·let·to** \ˌrändə'led·(ˌ)ō\ *n* -s [It, dim. of *rondò*] **:** a short rondo

**¹ron·do** \'rän(ˌ)dō\ *n* -s [It *rondò*, fr. F *rondeau* — more at RONDEAU] **1 :** ⁵ROUND 3 **2 :** the musical setting of a rondeau or similar verse form **3 :** an instrumental composition or movement in which the principal theme or first subject occurs at least three times in the same key with contrasting themes or sections in between and which is often the last movement of a sonata — called also *rondeau* **4 :** a dance composition that has a recurrent movement theme alternating with new themes and is derived from a medieval round dance with singing of verse and refrain

**²rondo** \"\ *n* -s [LaF *rondeau* — more at RONDEAU] **:** a gambling game in which balls are pushed from one corner of a pocket billiard table to the opposite and bets are decided by the number of odd or even balls that remain on the table —called also *rondeau*

**ron·dure** \'ränjə(r)\ *n* -s [modif. (influenced by *-ure*) of F *rondeur* roundness, fr. MF, fr. *rond* round + *-eur* -or — more at RONDE] **1 :** ROUND 1a ⟨the whole ~ of the turning globe —J.C.Powys⟩ **2 :** gracefully rounded curvature ⟨the bare swelling ~*s* of the mountains —Meridel Le Sueur⟩ ⟨a pretty girl of agreeable ~ —Wolcott Gibbs⟩

**¹rone** \'rōn\ *n* -s [ME, prob. of Scand origin; akin to ON *runnr* bush, grove, Norw dial. *runn*, *runne* bush, *runne* twig; akin to OHG *rono* trunk of a tree, block of wood, OE *rīsan* to rise — more at RISE] *chiefly Scot* **:** BRUSHWOOD, THICKET

**²rone** \"\ *n* -s [origin unknown] *Scot* **:** a rain spout or pipe

**ro·neo** \'rōnē,ō\ *vt* -ED/-ING/-S [fr. *roneo*, a kind of duplicating machine, fr. *rotary* + *Neostyle*, a trademark for a kind of duplicating machine] **:** to produce (printed copies) on a duplicating machine that is similar in principle to the mimeograph

**ro·neo·graph** \'rōnēə,graf, -räf\ *vt* -ED/-ING/-S [*roneo*, a kind of duplicating machine + *-graph* (as in *mimeograph*)] **:** RONEO

**rong** \'räŋ\ *also* **rong–pa** \-'pä\ *n, pl* **rong** *or* **rongs** *also* **rongpa** *or* **rongpas** *usu cap* **:** LEPCHA

**ron·ga** \'räŋgə\ *n, pl* **ronga** *or* **rongas** *usu cap* **1 a :** a group of Bantu peoples chiefly of southern Mozambique **b :** a member of a Ronga people **2 :** a Bantu language of the Ronga peoples

**¹ron·geur** \rō(ⁿ)'zhər\ *n* -s [F, lit., one that gnaws, fr. MF, fr. *ronger* to gnaw (fr. — assumed — VL *rodicare*, fr. *rodere* to gnaw) + *-eur* -or — more at RAT] **:** a heavy-duty forceps for removing small pieces of bone or tough tissue

**²rongeur** \"\ *vt* -ED/-ING/-S **:** to remove (bone) with a rongeur

**rô·nier** \rō'nyā\ *n* -s [F *rondier*, *rônier*] **:** PALMYRA

**ron·quil** \'räŋkəl\ *n* -s [AmerSp *ronquillo*, dim. of *ronco* — more at RONCO] **:** any of several marine percoid fishes (family Bathymasteridae) of the northwest coast of No. America that resemble the jawfishes

**rons·dorf·er** \'ränz,dȯrfə(r)\ *also* **rons·dorf·i·an** \(')≈-'dȯrfēən\ *n* -s *usu cap* [*Ronsdorfer* fr. G, fr. *Ronsdorfer*, adj., of Ronsdorf, fr. *Ronsdorf*, city (now part of Wuppertal) in northern Germany where the sect was founded; *Ronsdorfian* fr. *Ronsdorf* + E *-ian*] **:** one of a small sect of 18th century German millenarians — called also *Zionite*

**röntgen** *var of* ROENTGEN

**ronyon** *n* -s [perh. modif. of F *rogue* scab, mange] *obs* **:** a mangy or scabby creature

**roo** \'rü\ *n* -s [by shortening] *Austral* **:** KANGAROO

**roocooyen** *usu cap, var of* RUCUYEN

**¹rood** \'rüd\ *n* -s [ME *rod*, *rood*, fr. OE *rōd* rod, cross, rood; akin to OFris *rōd*, *rōde* gallows, OHG *ruota* rod, pole, OS *rōda* gallows, ON *ræthi* oar, OSlav *ratište*, *ratovište* shaft of a lance, and perh. to L *retae* trees on a river bank or in a stream] **1 :** a cross or crucifix symbolizing the cross on which Jesus Christ died ⟨by the holy ~ —Shak.⟩; *specif* **:** a large crucifix at the entrance of the chancel of a medieval church **2 a :** any of various units of land area: as (1) **:** a unit used in England and Scotland equal to 40 square rods or ¼ acre (2) **:** a Dutch unit used in South Africa equal to 148.752 square feet **b :** any of various units of length: as (1) **:** a unit used in England and Scotland equal to 7 or 8 yards or sometimes a rod (2) **:** a Dutch unit used in South Africa equal to 12.396 feet

**rood altar** *n* **:** an altar placed against the outer side of a rood screen

**rood arch** *n* **1 :** a central arch in a rood screen above which appears the rood **2 :** an arch between the nave and the chancel immediately above the rood

**rood beam** *n* **:** the beam at the entrance of a church chancel that supports a large cross or crucifix esp. in a medieval church

**rood cloth** *n* **:** a violet or black veil used to cover the rood during Lent

**rood day** *n, usu cap R&D* **:** HOLY-ROOD DAY

**roo·de·bok** \'rüdə,bäk\ *n, pl* **roodebok** *or* **roodeboks** [Afrik *rooibok* (previously spelled *roodebok*), fr. *rooi* red (fr. MD *root*, *rood*) + *bok* male goat, male antelope, fr. MD *boc* male goat; akin to OE *rēad* red and to OE *buc*, *bucca* male goat — more at RED, BUCK] **1 :** IMPALA **2 :** a reddish duikerbok (*Cephalophus patalensis*)

**rood goose** *n* **:** BRANT

**roo·dle** \'rüd^əl\ *n* -s [G *rudel* pack, flock, troop] **:** one hand of a round of hands in poker usu. played after an esp. high hand (as four of a kind or a full house) with the special provision that the round will consist of jackpots or sometimes of stud poker or dealer's choice with the pot limit usu. doubled

**rood loft** *n* [ME *rodeloft*, fr. *rod*, *rood*, *rode* rood + *loft*] **:** a loft or gallery over the rood screen in a medieval church used for display of the rood and its appendages and for the reading of the Gospel and the Epistle

**rood screen** *n* **:** a screen separating the chancel of a church from the nave and often surmounted by a cross or crucifix — called also *jube*

**rood spire** *or* **rood steeple** *n* **:** a rood tower with a spire

**rood stair** *n* **:** a stairway leading to the rood loft

**roodstone** \'≈,≈\ *n* **:** a stone cross or crucifix

**rood tower** *n* **:** a tower at the intersection of the nave and transept of a church

**¹roof** \'rüf, 'ru̇f, *dial* 'rəf\ *n, pl* **roofs** \-fs\ *also* **rooves** \'rüvz\ *often attrib* [ME *rof*, *roof*, *rouf*, *ruf*, fr. OE *hrōf*; akin to OFris *hrōf* roof, MLG *rōf*, *rūf* cover, sheltering roof, MD *roef*, *roof* cover, roof, ON *hrōf* roof of a boathouse, boathouse, OSlav *stropŭ* roof] **1 a :** the outside cover of a building or structure including the roofing and all the materials and construction necessary to maintain the cover upon its walls or other support: (1) **:** such a cover or its inner shell on the interior of a structure; *esp* **:** a high vaulted or spacious ceiling ⟨the long interior . . . has a handsome open timber ~ decorated in polychrome —*Amer. Guide Series: Conn.*⟩ ⟨its principal room is the Livery Hall, high ceilinged, with decorated ~, chandeliers, and tall marble pillars —Gerard Foy⟩ (2) **:** such a cover of a house or home ⟨finds herself without a ~ over her head —H.M. Parshley⟩ ⟨placing . . . the most distressed families under ~ —*U. S. Code*⟩ **b :** a shelter, house, or other domicile used as a home ⟨had his ~ and taught physics in a boy's school —D. C.Peattie⟩ ⟨why not . . . share the same ~ —Virginia Woolf⟩ **c :** ROOFING ⟨the house has a slate ~⟩ ⟨slag or gravel ~⟩ ⟨coal tar, pitch, and felt ~⟩ **2 a** (1) **:** the highest point or reach of something **:** SUMMIT, CULMINATION ⟨in the desolate mountains at the ~ of the . . . world —*Newsweek*⟩ (2) **:** CEILING 7 ⟨what the nation needed . . . was a floor under some prices and a ~ over others —*Time*⟩ ⟨both wool and rubber . . . have gone through the ~ —*America*⟩ **b :** something that covers in, includes, or completes ⟨agency to put a permanent ~ over the temporary consolidation of the independent housing agencies —*Time*⟩ **c :** the vault of the heavens ⟨this majestic ~ fretted with golden fire —Shak.⟩ ⟨beneath this small blue ~ of vernal sky —S.T.Coleridge⟩ **d :** something resembling a roof in form or function: as (1) **:** the canopy of leaves and branches formed by trees or other vegetative growth ⟨from under shady arborous ~ —John Milton⟩ ⟨some do rise above the jungle ~ —C.H.Curran⟩ (2) **:** the cover of a vehicle (as a car or airplane) **:** TOP **3 a :** the vaulted upper boundary of the mouth supported largely by the palatine bones and limited anteriorly by the dental ridge and posteriorly by the uvula and upper part of the fauces **b :** TEGMENTUM **c :** a covering structure of any of various other parts of the body ⟨~ of the skull⟩ ⟨~ of a cavity⟩ **4 a** (1) **:** the rock immediately above a tabular deposit (as a coal seam or vein) (2) **:** the overhead of an excavation or tunnel in a mine (3) **:** the invaded rock above a batholith **b :** a passage excavated in quarrying slate from below upward **:** RAISE

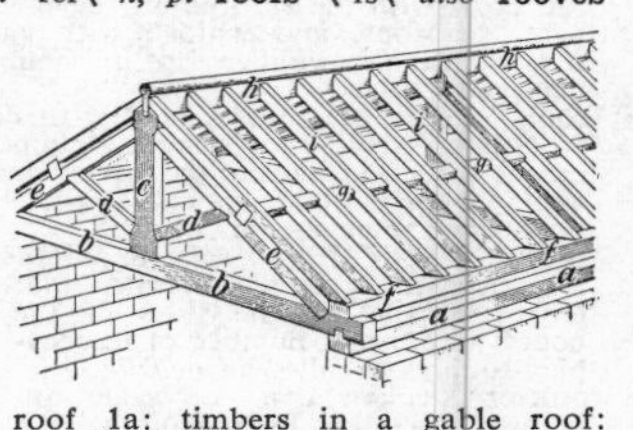

roof 1a: timbers in a gable roof: *a* wall plate; *b* tie beam; *c* king post; *d, d,* struts; *e, e,* principal rafters; *f* pole plate; *g, g,* purlins; *h* ridgepole; *i, i,* common rafters

**²roof** \"\ *vt* -ED/-ING/-S [ME *rofen*, fr. *rof*, *roof*, n.] **1 a :** to cover or provide (a structure) with a roof ⟨had the passage at the entrance of the house repaired and ~*ed* —Thomas Carlyle⟩ ⟨the thatcher mounts his ladder . . . with his burden of straw, ~*ing* the corn built to be its own storehouse —Adrian Bell⟩ **b :** to provide (a roof) with a protective or weatherproof exterior ⟨originally ~*ed* with handmade shingles —*Amer. Guide Series: La.*⟩ **2 a :** to constitute or form a roof over (something) ⟨maple trees ~*ed* every street with gold —Janet Whitney⟩ ⟨the mountains which ~ their mines —*Christian Science Monitor*⟩ **b :** to provide shelter for **:** HOUSE

**roof·age** \-fij\ *n* -s [¹*roof* + *-age*] **:** ROOFING

**roof comb** *or* **roof crest** *n* **:** a wall rising from the center line of a roof to give an appearance of greater height

**roof–deck** \'≈,≈\ *n* **:** a flat portion of a roof used as a walk or terrace

**roofed ingle** *n* **:** CHIMNEY CORNER 1

**roof·er** \-fə(r)\ *n* -s **1 :** one who builds or repairs roofs **2 :** a plank or timber used in roofing; *also* **:** a low-grade board

**roof garden** *n* **:** a restaurant at the top of a building or hotel where food and beverages are sold and facilities usu. provided for music and dancing

**roof houseleek** *n* **:** HOUSELEEK

**roof·ing** \-fiŋ, -fēŋ\ *n* -s [ME *rovyng*, fr. *rof*, *roof* roof + *-ing* — more at ROOF] **1 :** a material used or suitable for the construction of a roof; *specif* **:** a material designed for application to a roof as protection from the weather ⟨slate ~⟩ ⟨aluminum ~⟩ ⟨mineral-surfaced ~⟩ **2 :** ROOF ⟨constructing the ~ for the chicken house⟩ **3 :** the wedging (as of a horse or car) against the top of an underground passage in a mine

**roofing nail** *n* **:** a short nail usu. with a large flat head and a barbed shank used for securing roofing paper or asphalt shingles to roof boards

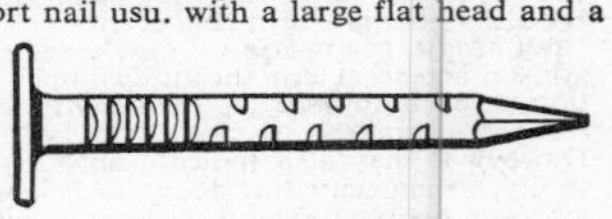

roofing nail

**roof·less** \-fləs\ *adj* **1 :** having no roof **2 :** having no house **:** HOMELESS

**roof·let** \-lət\ *n* -s **:** a small roof

**roof·man** \-fmən\ *n, pl* **roofmen :** a mine or quarry worker who inspects roofs and walls after blasting and dislodges loose blocks with a bar

**roof nucleus** *n* **:** a nucleus lying in the roof of the cerebellum

**roof pendant** *n* **:** a downward projection or sag of the roof of a batholith

**roof plate** *n* **:** PLATE 5a(1)

**roof prism** *n* **:** a glass prism used in an optical range finder and other instruments that performs the double function of changing the direction of the light rays by 90 degrees and reversing the image right to left — compare PORRO PRISM

**roof rat** *n* **:** a grayish brown rat that is a variety (*Rattus rattus alexandrinus*) of the black rat, is common in warm regions, and often nests in trees or the upper parts of buildings

**roofs** *pl of* ROOF, *pres 3d sing of* ROOF

**roof–spotter** \'≈,≈≈\ *n, Brit* **:** SPOTTER 2b(3)

**roof stay** *n* **:** a stay rod or tie rod connecting the crown sheet of a boiler with the shell

**rooftop** \'≈,≈\ *n* **:** ROOF; *esp* **:** the roof of a house ⟨every balcony and ~ on the steep hills lining the streets was crowded with spectators —*N.Y. Times*⟩

**rooftree** \'≈,≈\ *n* [ME, fr. *rof*, *roof* roof + *tre*, *tree* tree — more at TREE] **1 :** RIDGEPOLE **2 :** ROOF 1a(2) ⟨a dozen players are housed under his ~ —Nike Anderson⟩ ⟨assured of a welcome under any ~, great or humble —I.S.Cobb⟩

**roo·i·bok** *also* **roo·ye·bok** \'rüē,bäk\ *n, pl* **rooibok** *or* **rooiboks** [Afrik *rooibok* — more at ROODEBOK] **:** IMPALA

**roo·i·bos tea** \'rüē,bäs-\ *or* **roo·i·bosch tea** \-sh-\ *n* [part trans. of Afrik *rooibostee* (formerly spelled *rooiboschtee*), fr. *rooibos*, the shrub from which it is made (fr. *rooi* red + *bos* bush, fr. MD *busch*, *bosch* bush forest) + *tee* tea — more at RODEBOK, BUSH] **:** a beverage that is made from a southern African shrub (*Aspalathus cedarbergensis*) of the family Leguminosae

**roo·i·gras** \'rüē,gras\ *also* **rooi grass** \'rüē-\ *n* -ES [Afrik *rooigras*, fr. *rooi* red + *gras* grass, fr. MD; akin to OHG *gras* grass — more at GRASS] **:** an African veldt grass (*Themeda triandra*) that is valued for grazing and is represented by similar or identical grasses in parts of southern Asia and Australia — see KANGAROO GRASS

**roo·i·nek** \'rüē,nek\ *n* -s [Afrik, fr. *rooi* red + *nek* neck, nape of the neck, fr. MD *neche* nape of the neck; akin to OHG *hnac* nape of the neck — more at NECK] *southern Africa* **:** BRITISHER — usu. used disparagingly

**rooi rhebok** *or* **rooi ribbok** \'rüē-\ *n* [Afrik *rooireebok*, *rooiribbok*, fr. *rooi* red + *reebok*, *ribbok* rhebok — more at RHEBOK] **:** an African upland reedbuck (*Redunca fulvorufula*)

[1]**rook** \'ru̇k\ *n* -s [ME *rok, rook,* fr. OE *hrōc;* akin to OHG *hruoh, ruoho* rook, ON *hrōkr* rook, Goth *hrukjan* to crow, Gk *krōzein, krazein* to croak, Skt *khargalā* owl, OE *hræfn* raven — more at RAVEN] **1 a :** a common Old World gregarious bird (*Corvus frugilegus*) about the size and color of the American crow with the skin about the base of the bill becoming bare, scabrous, and whitish with age **b :** RUDDY DUCK **2 :** a cheat or swindler esp. in gaming **3** *obs* **:** one easily deceived **:** DUPE

[2]**rook** \"\ *vb* -ED/-ING/-S *vt* **1 :** to defraud by cheating or swindling ⟨arrested for ~*ing* the public in door-to-door campaigns —*Time*⟩ ⟨takes to the market and gets ~*ed* —*Commonweal*⟩ **2** *obs* **:** to take or steal (as goods or money) by cheating ~ *vi, obs* **:** to engage in cheating

[3]**rook** \"\ *n* -s [ME *rok, roke,* fr. MF *roc,* fr. Ar *rukhkh,* fr. Per] **:** a piece in a set of chessmen that moves parallel to the sides of the board across any number of unoccupied squares — called also *castle*

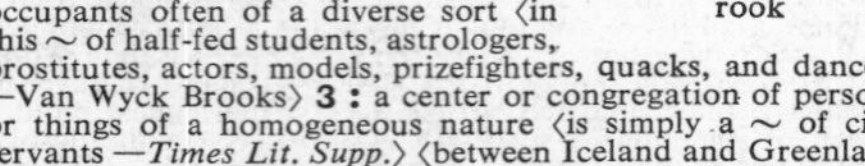

rook

**rook·er** \'ru̇kə(r)\ *n* -s [origin unknown] **:** a raker for a baker's oven

**rook·ery** \'ru̇kərē, -ri\ *n* -ES [[1]*rook* + *-ery*] **1 a :** the group of nests or the breeding place of a colony of rooks; *also* **:** a colony of rooks **b :** a breeding ground or common haunt of other gregarious birds or animals (as herons, penguins, or seals); *also* **:** a colony of such birds or animals **:** ROOST 1d **2 a :** a dilapidated tenement or run-down group of dwellings ⟨typhoid ran rampant in the *rookeries* which masqueraded as homes —*Sat. Eve. Post*⟩ **b :** a building with many rooms or occupants often of a diverse sort ⟨in this ~ of half-fed students, astrologers, prostitutes, actors, models, prizefighters, quacks, and dancers —Van Wyck Brooks⟩ **3 :** a center or congregation of persons or things of a homogeneous nature ⟨is simply a ~ of civil servants —*Times Lit. Supp.*⟩ ⟨between Iceland and Greenland are two such storm *rookeries* —P.M.Swatek⟩ **4** *chiefly dial* **:** RUMPUS **:** DISTURBANCE

**rook·ie** \'ru̇kē, -ki\ *n* -s *often attrib* [alter. (influenced by [1]*rook*) of *recruit*] **1 :** a raw recruit **:** NOVICE, BEGINNER ⟨a ~ in the army⟩ ⟨a ~ on the police force⟩ **2 :** a new member of or candidate for an athletic team; *esp* **:** a baseball player in his first season with a major league team ⟨was chosen ~ of the year⟩

**rook's tour** *n* **:** a chess problem in which a rook makes a circuit of the board touching each square once

**rookus** *var of* RUCKUS

**rooky** \'ru̇kē\ *adj* -ER/-EST [[1]*rook* + *-y*] **:** full of or containing rooks ⟨the crow makes wing to the ~ wood —Shak.⟩

[1]**room** \'rüm, 'ru̇m\ *n* -s *often attrib* [ME *roum,* fr. OE *rūm;* akin to OHG, ON, & Goth *rūm* room, space; all fr. a prehistoric Gmc n. derived fr. an adj. represented by OE *rūm* roomy, spacious, OHG *rūmi,* ON *rūmr,* Goth *rūms;* akin to L *rur-, rus* country, open land, MIr *rōe, rōi* level field, Av *ravah-* space, distance] **1 a :** unoccupied area **:** SPACE ⟨increasing population requires more ~⟩ ⟨infinity of ~ in the reaches of the universe⟩ **b :** unoccupied area or space sufficient for additional accommodation ⟨~ at the inn⟩ ⟨~ for pasture⟩ ⟨~ to swing a cat in⟩ ⟨tearing down tenements to make ~ for new building⟩ **2 a :** a particular area or limited portion of space **:** COMPASS ⟨plenty of ~ between the houses⟩ ⟨a small car requires little ~⟩ ⟨the sonnet's narrow ~ of 14 lines —O.S.J.Gogarty⟩ **b** *Scot* **:** a piece of land **:** HOLDING, FARM **3 a** *obs* **:** a place or station assigned to a person or thing **b** *obs* **:** an office or position attributed to a particular person **:** RANK, POST ⟨and therein placed a race of upstart creatures, to supply perhaps our vacant ~ —John Milton⟩ **c** (1) **:** a place or station formerly occupied by another ⟨in whose ~ I am now assuming the pen —Sir Walter Scott⟩ ⟨be thou in Adam's ~ the head of all mankind —John Milton⟩ (2) *archaic* **:** PLACE, STEAD ⟨substitute judgment in the ~ of sensation —Joseph Butler⟩ **4 a :** a part of the inside of a building, shelter, or dwelling usu. set off by a partition ⟨15 ~ colonial mansion . . . for rest or convalescent home —*advt*⟩ **:** CHAMBER; *esp* **:** such a part used as a lodging ⟨goes back to his furnished ~ —Norman Mailer⟩ ⟨the individual who actually assigns guests to their ~*s* —Don Short⟩ **b rooms** *pl* **:** a suite or set of rooms used for lodging **:** APARTMENT, FLAT ⟨sells his house and takes ~*s* in the city⟩ **c :** lodging consisting of a room usu. specifically earned or furnished ⟨~, board, and the return trip home . . . were paid for —*Newsweek*⟩ — compare ROOM AND BOARD **d :** the people or an assemblage gathered in a room ⟨attract the attention of the whole ~⟩ **5 :** the opportunity, occasion, or capacity for something (as an action, development, or mental process) ⟨~ to hope⟩ ⟨~ to improve⟩ ⟨~ for argument⟩ ⟨~ in morality for the high aspiration, the courageous decision —Havelock Ellis⟩ ⟨~ in art and in civilization for many kinds of art —Thomas Munro⟩ ⟨no ~ in his mind for that malaise —Van Wyck Brooks⟩ **6 :** a chamber in which coal is mined — called also *breast, stall*

**syn** BERTH, ELBOWROOM, CLEARANCE, LEEWAY, MARGIN, PLAY: ROOM is a general term for unfilled open space without obstruction or encumbrance to free activity ⟨space is *room* . . . and *room* is roominess, a chance to be, live and move —John Dewey⟩ It may also indicate an adequate occasion, opportunity, or capacity ⟨not alone in believing Mexico's behavior left no *room* for peaceful settlement —R.A.Billington⟩ ⟨which never arrived at so high a point of definition but that it left great *room* for disputes —G.G.Coulton⟩ BERTH, orig. maneuvering space for a ship, still indicates a separation by wide clear space in various idioms ⟨classified as the only venomous snake and is deservedly given a wide *berth* —*Amer. Guide Series: Del.*⟩ ELBOWROOM indicates adequate free space for physical activity or, by extension, freedom from cramping constraint ⟨the Swiss, who have always liked plenty of *elbowroom* in their business dealings, are considerably irked by the restrictions of postwar trading —Mollie Panter-Downes⟩ CLEARANCE as a synonym in this series stresses lack of obstruction; it is used in connection with the physical fact of a clear space around a moving object or with the indication that there is no objection, reservation, or check against free procedure ⟨the new tunnels provide *clearance* for the largest trucks⟩ ⟨the steel industry refused to make any wage proposals until it obtained federal *clearance* for higher steel prices —*Current History*⟩ LEEWAY may indicate a reserve resource or advantageous characteristic not earmarked or calculated on, an allowed tolerance, or a measure of personal discretion or freedom from restriction in activity ⟨*leeway* of a few minutes to change planes⟩ ⟨in many more or less routine matters the Union government allows them a considerable amount of *leeway* —F.A.Ogg & Harold Zink⟩ MARGIN in this sense is like LEEWAY in suggesting a reserve for contingencies and emergencies or a reserve of any sort facilitating free and easy procedure ⟨the most dogged, strong-minded ones, who find themselves with a *margin* of intellectual freshness and inquisitiveness at the end of the day —W.N.Francis⟩ PLAY applies to the fact of free movement or action without severe checks or cramping surroundings, esp. to reactions to force or stress without more than incidental suggestions about ample space or roominess ⟨the *play* of a gusty wind —Amy Lowell⟩ ⟨planning versus the *play* of the free market —*Times Lit. Supp.*⟩ ⟨a world in which affection has free *play,* in which love is purged of the instinct for domination —Bertrand Russell⟩

[2]**room** *adv, usu* -ER/-EST [obs. *room,* adj., roomy, spacious, fr. ME *roum, rom, room,* fr. OE *rūm* — more at [1]ROOM] *obs* **:** LARGE 2

[3]**room** \'rüm, 'ru̇m\ *vt* -ED/-ING/-S [ME *roumen,* fr. *roum,* adj.] *archaic* **:** to clear (a space) from encumbrance **:** make roomy or void

[4]**room** \"\ *vb* -ED/-ING/-S [[1]*room*] *vi* **:** to occupy a room **:** LODGE ⟨the students ~ together in the dormitory⟩ ~ *vt* **:** to accommodate (a guest or roomer) with lodgings; *also* **:** to convey to or install in a room ⟨a bellman ~s the guests at the hotel⟩

**room·age** \-mij\ *n* -s [[1]*room* + *-age*] **:** SPACE, ACCOMMODATION

**room and board** *n* **:** lodging and food usu. specifically earned or furnished ⟨receives wages plus *board and room*⟩ — compare ROOM 4c, BOARD 4c, FOUND

**room-and-pillar** \¦==¦==\ *adj* **:** BORD-AND-PILLAR

**room and space** *n* **:** the distance from one side of a frame of a boat to the corresponding side of the next frame

**room boss** *n* **:** one who inspects the rooms in mines to ensure that mining is done properly and safety regulations are observed

**room clerk** *n* **:** a hotel clerk who is in charge of the assignment of rooms to guests

**room divider** *n* **:** an article of furniture (as a rack, chair, or table) used to divide a room into separate areas ⟨drafts are avoided by high-backed seats that are also *room dividers* —Edgar Kaufmann⟩

**roomed** \,rümd, ¦ru̇md\ *adj* [[1]*room* + *-ed*] **:** containing or furnished with rooms — usu. used in combination ⟨a nine-*roomed* house⟩

**room·er** \'rümə(r), 'ru̇m-\ *n* -s [[4]*room* + *-er*] **:** LODGER

**room·ette** \(')rü¦met, (')ru̇¦-\ *n* -s [[1]*room* + *-ette*] **:** a small private single room on a railroad sleeping car with a folding bed and toilet facilities

**room·ful** \'rüm,fu̇l, 'ru̇m-\ *n* -s **:** as much or as many as a room will hold ⟨a ~ of men⟩; *also* **:** the persons or objects in a room ⟨the whole ~⟩ ⟨the group is one of the handsomest and most impressive ~*s* —R.M.Coates⟩

**room·ie** *also* **roomy** \'rümē, 'ru̇mē\ *n, pl* **roomies** [[1]*room* + *-ie, -y*] **:** ROOM-MATE

**room·i·ly** \'rüməlē, 'ru̇m-, -li\ *adv* **:** with ample room **:** SPACIOUSLY

**room·i·ness** \-mēnə̇s, -min-\ *n* -ES **:** the quality or state of being roomy

**rooming house** *n* **:** a house where rooms are provided and let **:** LODGING HOUSE

**rooming-in** \'==¦=\ *n* -s [fr. gerund of *room in,* v.] **:** the arrangement in a hospital whereby a newborn infant is kept in a crib at or near the mother's bedside instead of in a nursery

**roommate** \'=,=\ *n* **:** one of two or more persons occupying or sharing the same room

**rooms** *pl of* ROOM, *pres 3d sing of* ROOM

**room service** *n* **:** the service provided by a hotel or lodging house for guests in their rooms and usu. carried out by bellboys or waiters ⟨ring for *room service* and have breakfast in bed —J.R.Ullman⟩; *also* **:** the department of a hotel or lodging house responsible for room service ⟨calling *room service*⟩

**roomsome** *adj* [[1]*room* + *-some*] *obs* **:** ROOMY

**room·stead** \'rümz,ted, 'ru̇m-, -m,st-\ *n, archaic* **:** a division of space **:** COMPARTMENT

**roomth** \'rüm(p)th\ *n* -s [alter. (influenced by obs. *room,* adj., roomy, spacious) of ME *rimth,* fr. OE *rȳmth,* fr. *rūm* roomy, spacious — more at [2]ROOM] *dial chiefly Eng* **:** ROOM, PLACE

**room trader** *n* **:** FLOOR TRADER

**roomy** \'rümē, 'ru̇mē, -mi\ *adj, often* -ER/-EST [[1]*room* + *-y*] **1 :** having ample room **:** SPACIOUS, CAPACIOUS ⟨a ~ mansion⟩ ⟨a ~ ship⟩ ⟨~ pockets⟩ ⟨a ~ novel⟩ ⟨his voice . . . with its ~, rich qualities —Whitney Balliett⟩ **2** *of a female animal* **:** having a large or well-proportioned body suited for breeding ⟨a strong, healthy, ~ mare —*Horse*⟩ ⟨a ~ bitch⟩

**roon** \'ru̇n, 'rün\ *n* -s *chiefly Scot var of* ROUND

**roond** \-nd\ *Scot var of* ROUND

**roop** \'rüp\ *var of* ROUP

**roor·back** *also* **roor·bach** \'ru̇r,bak, 'ru̇(ə),-\ *n* -s [after Baron von Roorback, fictional author of *Roorback's Tour through the Western and Southern States,* an imaginary book from which an alleged passage was quoted in the Ithaca (N.Y.) *Chronicle* of 1844 that made scurrilous charges against James K. Polk, then Democratic candidate for president] **:** a defamatory falsehood published for political effect usu. before an election ⟨strategists on both sides on the alert for ~*s* —*Newsweek*⟩

**roos** *pl of* ROO

[1]**roose** \'rüz\ *n* -s [ME *ros, roos,* of Scand origin; akin to Icel *hrōs* praise, ON *hrōsa* to praise, boast; prob. akin to ON *hrōthr* praise — more at CADUCEUS] **1** *chiefly dial* **:** BOASTING, BRAGGING **2** *chiefly dial* **:** PRAISE

[2]**roose** \"\ *vt* -ED/-ING/-S [ME *rosen, rusen,* fr. ON *hrōsa* to praise, boast] *chiefly dial* **:** to commend highly **:** EXTOL, FLATTER

**roo·se·velt elk** \'rōz(ə),velt- *also* -,vəlt- *sometimes* 'rüz-\ *n, usu cap R* [after Theodore *Roosevelt*] **:** the largest of the American wapitis (*Cervus canadensis occidentalis*) now restricted to the Olympic peninsula of the state of Washington

**roo·se·velt·ian** \¦rōz(ə)¦veltēən *sometimes* ¦rüz-\ *adj, usu cap* [Theodore *Roosevelt* †1919, 26th U. S. president and Franklin Delano *Roosevelt* †1945, 32d U. S. president + E *-ian*] **1 :** of, relating to, or supporting Theodore Roosevelt or his views or policies ⟨*Rooseveltian* doctrine of speaking softly . . . and of carrying the big stick —*Nation*⟩ **2 :** of, relating to, or supporting F. D. Roosevelt or his views or policies ⟨*Rooseveltian* tendencies toward currency expansion —Jeannette P. Nichols⟩

**roo·se·velt·iana** \,=(=),veltē'anə, -'änə, -'ānə\ *n pl, usu cap* [Theodore & Franklin D. *Roosevelt* + E *-i-* + *-ana*] **:** matter (as papers, books, letters, relics) relating to Theodore Roosevelt or Franklin D. Roosevelt

**roo·se·velt·ism** \'rōz(ə),vel,tizəm *also* -,vəl- *sometimes* 'rüz-\ *n* -s *usu cap* [Theodore & Franklin D. *Roosevelt* + E *-ism*] **:** a system or views formulated by or attributed to either Theodore Roosevelt or Franklin D. Roosevelt

**roo·se·velt·ite** \-l,tīt\ *n* -s [F. D. *Roosevelt* + E *-ite*] **:** a bismuth arsenate found in Santiaguilo, Potosí, and Bolivia

**roosevelt trout** *n, usu cap R* [after Theodore *Roosevelt*] **:** a trout of western No. America prob. identical to the golden trout but often considered a separate species (*Salmo roosevelti*)

[1]**roost** \'rüst\ *n* -s [ME *rooste,* fr. OE *hrōst;* akin to MD *roest* roost, palate, OS *hrōst* framing of a roof, attic, MHG *rāz, rāze* bonfire, honeycomb, ON *hrōt* roof, Goth *hrot* roof, OSlav *krada* pile of wood, bonfire] **1 a :** a pole or other support on which birds or fowls rest esp. at night **:** PERCH **b :** a place where any birds customarily roost ⟨the starlings in these vast ~*s* —*Brit. Birds in Colour*⟩ **c :** a hen house or section of a building used for roosting ⟨barns and chicken ~*s* that have been converted into living quarters —Dwight MacDonald⟩ **d :** a group of fowls or birds roosting together ⟨alarms the whole ~ into flight⟩ **2 :** a resting place **:** LODGING ⟨the only ~ was in the garret, which . . . contained 11 double beds —J.R.Lowell⟩ **3 :** ROOKERY 3 ⟨rededicated that ~ of B-36 intercontinental bombers —*N. Y. Times*⟩ ⟨a ~ of party members and supporters —Anthony West⟩ ⟨the informal ~ for most designers —D.M.Oenslager⟩

[2]**roost** \"\ *vb* -ED/-ING/-S *vi* **1 a :** to settle down for rest or sleep **:** PERCH ⟨coveys ~ like quail on the ground during the night in stubble, under grass, and under low bushes —L.W. Wing⟩ ⟨grasshoppers have a habit of ~*ing* on sagebrush on warm nights —*Ecology*⟩ ⟨killed 90 percent of the flies that ~*ed* on the walls and ceilings overnight —*Science News Letter*⟩ ⟨chickens ~ at night⟩ **b :** to place or seat oneself as on a roost ⟨the old men ~*ed* on benches in front of the courthouse —Grace Metalious⟩ ⟨men ~*ing* on the car roofs of freight trains —A.F.Harlow⟩ ⟨flyers ~*ing* on the float of their overturned plane —E.L.Beach⟩ **2 :** to lodge or stay for a night or a period of time usu. in an informal or temporary manner ⟨vagrants wandered up and down the country, ~*ing* in hedgerows —J.A.Symonds⟩ ⟨the hotels had been abandoned, and we ~*ed* in them —A.J.Liebling⟩ ⟨planes . . . ~*ed* in the supposedly safe Inland sea —*Newsweek*⟩ ~ *vt* **:** to supply a roost for **:** put to roost ⟨so named because Indians ~*ed* their turkeys here —Cecile Johnson⟩

**roost cock** *n, archaic* **:** ROOSTER 1

**roost·er** \'rüstə(r) *sometimes* 'ru̇s-\ *n* -s **1 a :** an adult male domestic fowl **:** COCK **b :** an adult male of various other birds or fowl ⟨a ringneck pheasant ~⟩ ⟨ptarmigan ~*s*⟩ **2 :** a person having characteristics (as cockiness, pride) usu. attributed to a rooster ⟨professor who considered himself quite a ~ in his history —Jo Mora⟩ ⟨was just a young ~ then . . . breaking horses for four bits a day —F.B.Gipson⟩ **3 :** GOOSENECK b **4 :** PAPAGALLO

**roosterfish** \'==,=\ *n* **:** PAPAGALLO

**rooster heads** *n pl but sing in constr* **:** SHOOTING STAR 2

**roost·ers** \-(r)z\ *n pl but sing in constr* **1 :** a common No. American blue violet (*Viola palmata*) **2 :** WHITE ADDER'S-TONGUE

**rooster tail** *n* **:** the arching white water and spray cast up astern by a motorboat or other object moving through the water at a fast rate

[1]**root** \'rüt, 'ru̇t, *usu* |d·+V\ *n* -s *often attrib* [ME *rot, root,* fr. OE *rōt,* fr. ON; akin to OE *wyrt* herb, plant, root, OHG *wurz* herb, plant, ON *urt* herb, Goth *waurts* root, L *radix* root, Gk *rhadix* branch, *rhiza* root, Toch B *witsako,* Alb *rrānzë*]

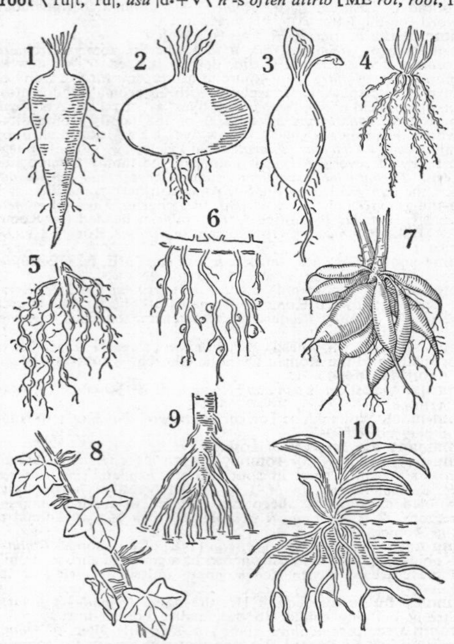


roots 1a: *1* conical, *2* napiform, *3* fusiform, *4* fibrous, *5* moniliform, *6* nodulose, *7* tuberous, *8* adventitious root, *9* prop root, *10* aerial root

**1 a :** the portion of the plant body of a seed plant that originates usu. from the radicle at the extremity of the hypocotyl, functions as an organ of absorption, aeration, and food storage or as a means of anchorage and support, and differs from a stem in lacking nodes, buds, and leaves, in possessing an endodermis and a protective cap over the apical meristem, and in producing its branches normally in acropetal succession **b** (1) **:** a subterranean part of a plant (as a true root, bulb, tuber, rootstock, or other modified stem); *specif* **:** a large fleshy edible root or similar organ (as a carrot, turnip, radish, potato) (2) **:** the substance, material, or tissue of a root — often used in combination ⟨beet*root*⟩ (3) **roots** *pl, Brit* **:** ROOT CROPS **2 :** something that resembles a root in position or function esp. as a source of nourishment or as a support: as **a :** the part of a tooth lying within the socket; *also* **:** any of the processes into which this part is often divided — see TOOTH illustration **b :** the enlarged basal part of a hair consisting of the hair follicle, papilla, and developing hair shaft that lie within the skin **c :** the proximal end of a nerve; *esp* **:** one or more bundles of nerve fibers joining the cranial and spinal nerves with their respective nuclei and gray columns — see DORSAL ROOT, VENTRAL ROOT **d :** the part of an organ or physical structure by which it is attached to the body ⟨~ of a nail⟩ **3 a** (1) **:** the origin or cause of a condition, tendency, or quality ⟨tackling not only the psychological and emotional causes of race conflicts but also their economic ~*s* —M.F.A. Montagu⟩ ⟨the ~ of civil violence lay in the unequal distribution of the land —*Current Biog.*⟩; *specif* **:** an attribute that brings about an action or condition ⟨the love of money is the ~ of all evil —1 Tim 6:10 (AV)⟩ ⟨from the ~ of hate grows war⟩ (2) **:** the line of evolutionary development of a condition, trend, or branch of human activity — usu. used in pl. ⟨although its ~*s* go back . . . before the 19th century, fascism emerged after World War I —*Collier's Yr. Bk.*⟩ **b** (1) **:** a race, family, or progenitor that is the source or beginning of a group or line of descendants ⟨should be the ~ and father of many kings —Shak.⟩ ⟨the ~*s* out of which sprang two distinct people —John Locke⟩ ⟨the ~*s* of science, however, ran deep, stretching back to the period before the appearance of civilization —S.F.Mason⟩ ⟨beginnings of these types of literature had ~*s* reaching well back —R.A.Hall b. 1911⟩ (2) *obs* **:** a descendant or offshoot of a line or family **:** SCION **c** (1) **:** the underlying support or foundation of something **:** BASIS ⟨respect for the rights and intelligence of others which is the ~ of the democratic society —*Official Register of Harvard Univ.*⟩ ⟨has loosened the ~*s* of the slave system —C.L.Carmer⟩ ⟨have created a real opposition, which is the main ~ of continued social peace —H.J.Laski⟩ ⟨nourishing a strong ~ of loyalty⟩ ⟨tear out the evil by the ~*s*⟩ (2) **:** a culture or cultural tradition underlying subsequent related cultures in a limited area **d :** the inner core or essential nature or part of something **:** HEART ⟨~ of the matter⟩ ⟨delving into the ~*s* of the inner life —R.W.Southern⟩ ⟨the two dogmas are identical at ~ —Albert Hofstadter⟩ **e :** an indigenous relationship or close and sympathetic bond usu. with or in the social environment **:** TIE — usu. used in pl. ⟨the feeling that modern life has no ~*s* —E.R.Bentley⟩ ⟨depriving youngsters of that extra stability which comes when ~*s* can grow in one place —Martha M. Eliot⟩ ⟨industrial workers who would never put their ~*s* down in the countryside —Sam Pollock⟩ **4 a :** the time (as a birth date, the position of a planet, or a point in time) from which to reckon in making astronomical or astrological calculations **b** (1) **:** a quantity that when taken as a factor the number of times indicated by the index produces another quantity ⟨either +3 or −3 is a second ~ of 9 because either taken twice as a factor produces 9⟩ (2) **:** a value that when substituted for the unknown quantity in an equation satisfies the equation **5 a** (1) **:** the base or lower part of a material thing **:** BOTTOM ⟨~ of a hill⟩ ⟨~*s* of the sea⟩ (2) **:** the basal extension of a geological formation ⟨lateral compression . . . forces the granitic part of the crust downward to form a solid ~ —W.H.Bucher⟩ **b :** the part of a material thing by which it is attached to something else: as (1) **:** the part of a weir or dam adjoining or penetrating the bank or sides of a stream or river (2) **:** the portion of an airplane wing nearest the fuselage (3) **:** the portion of the blade of a propeller or rotor nearest the hub **6 a** (1) **:** the simple element inferred as the basis from which a word is derived by phonetic change or by extension (as composition and addition of a prefix, suffix, inflectional ending, or replacive) (2) **:** the simple element (as Latin *sta*) inferred as common to all the words of a group in a language (as in Latin *stamus* "we stand" with a personal ending, *sistimus* "we place" with reduplication and personal ending, *statio* "standing place" with a suffix, and *constituere* "to establish" with a prefix) or in related languages **b :** the sequence of consonants recurring with various vowel sequences and affixes in a set of related words in Semitic **c :** a meaningful morpheme (as *hold*) esp. as recurring with various affixes or replacives in grammatically different forms (as *holds, held, beholders, withholding*) **7 a :** the musical tone from whose harmonics or overtones a chord is composed **b :** the lowest tone of a chord in its normal position **8 a :** the part of an open gear tooth between the pitch circle and the minor diameter **b** (1) **:** the surface between the threads at the minor diameter of a screw or at the major diameter of a nut — compare CREST 6 (2) **:** a similar surface on the blading of a turbine **9 :** the bottom zone of the space provided for a fusion weld **10** *slang* **:** a kick usu. delivered to the posterior ⟨caught him a great ~ with his boot on the backside —Bruce Marshall⟩ **syn** see ORIGIN

**²root** \"\ *vb* -ED/-ING/-S [ME *roten,* fr. *rot, root,* n.] *vt* **1 a :** to furnish with or enable to develop roots ⟨~ the seedlings in the hotbed⟩ ⟨two deeply ~*ed* and far-flung cultures —A.W. Hummel⟩ **b :** to fix or firmly attach by or as if by roots ⟨the lichen is ~*ed* to the rock⟩ ⟨he stands ~*ed* to the spot⟩ ⟨as firmly ~*ed* to their homesteads as the stone walls and fences —*Amer. Guide Series: N. J.*⟩ ⟨pension and seniority rights ~ workers to their jobs —Jules Abels⟩ **c :** to set firmly or establish usu. by implanting in something ⟨a peace ~*ed* in justice and law —H.S.Truman⟩ ⟨lack of a well-*rooted* tradition —R.W.Southern⟩ ⟨the ~*ed* beliefs of a lifetime are not easily shaken —T.B.Costain⟩ ⟨~*ed* in love, he grows and lives in peace⟩ ⟨wants to ~ his work in the reality of his own time —M.D.Geismar⟩ **d :** to furnish or give an origin or cause to (an action or development) ⟨a neurosis . . . is often ~*ed* in some childhood difficulty —*Irish Digest*⟩ ⟨many dental ailments are ~*ed* in psychosomatic disturbances —*Collier's Yr. Bk.*⟩ ⟨her problems are ~*ed* in temperament rather than economic handicaps —E.B.George⟩ **2 :** to pull, tear out, or remove often by force **:** root out ⟨~ these evils from the land⟩ ⟨launched his jet at the gun and tried to ~ it from its cave —J.A.Michener⟩ **~ *vi* 1 :** to grow roots in or as if in the earth **:** to strike or take root ⟨seedlings ~ quickly with plenty of water and sunlight⟩ ⟨prevent a few viruses from ~*ing* in nerve endings —*Monsanto Mag.*⟩ ⟨theories . . . ~*ing* in the savage mind, growing up strongly —Emma Hawkridge⟩ **2 :** to become fixed or firmly established **:** to establish oneself ⟨now I'll redeem my error and ~ forever here —Samuel Foote⟩ ⟨the patriots in whom the stock of freedom ~*s* —R.W.Emerson⟩ ⟨the new science of human behavior ~*s* in the study of concrete cases —H.A.Overstreet⟩ **3 :** to have or find an origin, basis, or cause in something ⟨the sin of self-righteousness which not infrequently ~*s* in sectional pride —B.G.Gallagher⟩ ⟨like everything else in human conduct, gesture ~*s* in the reactive necessities of the organism —Edward Sapir⟩

**³root** \"\ *vb* -ED/-ING/-S [alter. (influenced by ¹*root*) of earlier *wroot,* fr. ME *wroten,* fr. OE *wrōtan;* akin to MLG *wrōten* to root, MD *wroeten,* OHG *ruozzen,* ON *rōta* to root, and prob. to OE *wrītan* to incise, write — more at WRITE] *vi* **1 :** to turn up or dig in the earth with the snout **:** GRUB ⟨~, hog, or die⟩ ⟨pigs ~*ing* for truffles⟩ ⟨fish ~*ing* in the mud for food⟩ **2 :** to poke or dig down or into usu. in search of something ⟨chickens ~*ing* about in the rubbish —Alan Moorehead⟩ ⟨~*ed* in the bog and began to eat the cherries —Katherine Mansfield⟩ ⟨~*ing* about in the kitchen —Valentine Williams⟩ **~ *vt* :** root out ⟨the razor-back type was able to ~ its living and to do battle with . . . most foes —E.D.Ross⟩

**⁴root** \"\ *vi* -ED/-ING/-S [perh. alter. of ⁵*rout*] **1 :** to shout for or otherwise noisily applaud or encourage a contestant or team **:** CHEER ⟨a band of students ~*ing* for the school football team —Lucius Garvin⟩ ⟨going to the races to ~ for her brown colt —*Time*⟩ **2 :** to wish for the success of or lend support to someone or something ⟨can't be successful unless everyone loves him and ~*s* for him —Delmore Schwartz⟩ ⟨the communities which are very well ~*ing* for it —S.H.Adams⟩

**root·age** \"+ij\ *n* -S [¹*root* + *-age*] **1 :** a developed system of roots **:** a firm rooting ⟨the heavy ~ of bunchgrass necessitated ploughing the land a year in advance —*Amer. Guide Series: Wash.*⟩ ⟨it is among the ignorant that all sorts of superstitions and panaceas take ~ and flourish —*Automobilist*⟩ **2 :** the origin or beginnings of something **:** ROOT 3a(1) ⟨a man of lowly ~ —Raymond Moley⟩ ⟨all these philosophies had a Greek ~ and were developed further in the Hellenistic world —K.S.Latourette⟩ ⟨the disquiet to conscience . . . has ~ in the religious and ethical soil —B.G.Gallagher⟩ ⟨repentance has a deep ~ in the spirit of man —O.J.Raab⟩

**root beer** *n* **:** a sweetened effervescent beverage prepared by carbonating or fermenting a watery mixture of extractions from roots and herbs, natural flavoring oils (as nutmeg, cloves, anise, and wintergreen), and sugar

**root blindness** *n* **:** a lack of roots caused by disease or nematodes

**root borer** *n* **:** an insect or insect larva that bores into the roots of plants: as **a :** the large larva of a beetle (*Prionus laticollis*) of the family Cerambycidae that infests the roots of the grapevine and of various trees **b :** the larva of any of various moths (as *Paranthrene polistiformis*) that bores in grapevine roots

**root–bound** \'⸗,⸗\ *adj* **1 :** POT-BOUND **2 :** having the roots matted ⟨deep in shaggy untended lawns of old trees and ~ scented and flowering shrubs —William Faulkner⟩

**root canal** *n* **:** PULP CANAL

**root cap** *n* **:** a protective cap or thimble-shaped mass of parenchyma cells usu. irregularly arranged that covers the terminal meristem in most root tips and is constantly renewed from the meristem as the cells are sloughed off by penetration of the root apex through the soil — compare HISTOGEN

**root celery** *n* **:** CELERIAC

**root cellar** *n* **:** an underground or partly underground pit that is used for the storage of root crops, potatoes, or other vegetables and is usu. covered over with earth and entered from a stairway at one end

**root circle** *n* **:** DEDENDUM CIRCLE

**root climber** *n* **:** a plant that climbs by its adventitious roots (as the common ivy and many tropical aroids)

**root collar** *n* **:** CROWN 12a

**root crop** *n* **:** a crop grown for its enlarged roots (as turnips, mangels, sugar beets, sweet potatoes)

**root cutting** *n* **1 :** a piece of root used in propagating a plant (as blackberry, horseradish, or oriental poppy) — compare CUTTING 1a **2 :** the basal sections of jute fibers unsuitable for use in the spinning process — usu. used in pl. ⟨*root-cuttings* are separated from the other fibers⟩

**root determinative** *n* **:** DETERMINATIVE 3

**root disease** *n* **:** a disease affecting a root system or attacking a plant primarily through the roots; *esp* **:** a stunting and deterioration of sugarcane caused by unfavorable soil conditions and attacks of fungi of the genus *Pythium* (esp. *P. arrhenomanes*) — called also *Lahaina disease*

**root division** *n* **:** the propagation of plants by dividing the root stocks or the crowns

**rooted** *adj, of a tooth* **:** having a contracted root nearly closing the pulp cavity and preventing further growth

**root·ed·ly** *adv* **:** in a firm or well established manner

**root·ed·ness** *n* -ES **:** the quality or state of being rooted ⟨a ~ in his environment which made him almost immovable —Stephen Spender⟩

**¹root·er** \'rüd·ə(r), 'rů|, |tə(r)\ *n* -S [³*root* + *-er*] **:** a heavy plowing device for tearing up the ground surface esp. for a roadbed

**²rooter** \"\ *n* -S [⁴*root* + *-er*] **:** one that roots; *esp* **:** an enthusiastic supporter

**root·ery** \-ərē\ *n* -ES [¹*root* + *-ery*] **:** a pile of roots and soil set with plants

**root fly** *n* **:** CABBAGE FLY

**root fungus** *n* **:** a fungus (as a saprophyte, parasite, or symbiont) typically growing upon or associated with the roots of a plant — compare MYCORRHIZA

**root gall** *n* **1 :** an abnormal enlargement or swelling of or on the root of a plant commonly due to a parasitic organism **2 :** ROOT KNOT

**root graft** *n* **1 :** a plant graft in which the stock is a root or piece of a root ⟨whip grafts of apple are usu. *root grafts*⟩ **2 :** a natural anastomosis between roots of compatible plants growing near one another ⟨oak wilt is said to be transmitted through *root grafts*⟩

**root hair** *n* **:** one of the many hairlike tubular outgrowths of epidermal or sometimes cortical cells commonly found just behind the root apex that function in absorption and are continually replaced as the root elongates

**root–hardy** \'⸗;⸗⸗\ *adj* **:** having a hardy root or rootstock

**roothold** \'⸗,⸗\ *n* **1 :** anchorage of a plant to soil through the growth and spreading of roots ⟨the transplants should be watered carefully until they get a new ~⟩ **2 :** a place where plants may obtain a roothold ⟨the sheer face of the mountain offered scarcely a ~⟩

**root house** *n* **:** a shed or a wing of a building usu. used for the storage of foodstuffs

**rootier** *comparative of* ROOTY

**rootiest** *superlative of* ROOTY

**root in** *vi* **:** to hog in

**root knot** *n* **:** a disease of many kinds of wild or cultivated plants caused by eelworms that produce characteristic enlargements on the roots and stunt the growth of the plant — called also *root gall;* compare ROOT-KNOT NEMATODE

**root–knot nematode** *also* **root–knot eelworm** *n* **:** any of several small plant-parasitic nematodes formerly regarded as varieties of a single species (*Heterodera marioni*) but now usu. referred as separate species to the related genus *Meloidogyne,* invading roots of most cultivated and many wild plants, and inducing the formation of galls in which they live and on which they feed — compare MEADOW NEMATODE

**roo·tle** \'rüd·ᵊl\ *vi* -ED/-ING/-S [freq. of ³*root*] **:** ³ROOT ⟨lean black pigs ~ for filth —*Manchester Guardian Weekly*⟩ ⟨*rootled* at the bottom of a deep drawer —John Buchan⟩

**root·less** \'rütləs, 'rut-\ *adj* **:** having no roots: as **a :** lacking firmness or a solid basis **:** UNSTABLE ⟨this explanation we find unconvincing and biologically ~ —Weston La Barre⟩ ⟨family and environmental factors which determine the ~ behavior of adolescents —Frances Keene⟩ **b :** lacking a tie or sympathetic relationship with or in the social environment ⟨have become ~ individuals who do not find a home either with their communal environment or with a Christian atmosphere —J.M.Van der Kroef⟩ ⟨all are strangers, ~ in place or time, in the nervous new civilization —T.H.White b.1915⟩ **c** *of a tooth* **:** retaining a pulp cavity widely open at the bottom that permits an abundant supply of nutriment

**root·less·ness** *n* -ES **:** the quality or state of being rootless

**root·let** \-lət\ *or* **root·ling** \-liŋ\ *n* -S **:** a small root; *also* **:** one of the ultimate divisions of a growing root

**rootlike** \'⸗,⸗\ *adj* **:** having the appearance or acting in the manner of a root

**root line** *n* **:** DEDENDUM CIRCLE

**root maggot** *n* **:** a legless grub that is the larva of any of numerous insects (as the cabbage fly) and that feeds in roots

**root–mean–square** \'⸗,⸗'⸗\ *n* **:** the square root of the arithmetical mean of the squares of a set of numbers — abbr. *RMS, rms*

**root–mean–square deviation** *n* **:** STANDARD DEVIATION

**root metaphor** *n* **:** a fundamental perspective or viewpoint based on a supposition of similarity of form between mental concepts and external objects which though not factually supportable determines the manner in which an individual structures his knowledge — compare CATEGORY

**root nodule** *or* **root tubercle** *n* **:** NODULE 2b(3)

**root of unity :** a real or complex solution of the equation $x^n - 1 = 0$ where *n* is an integer

**¹root out** *vt* [²*root*] **:** to remove altogether **:** ERADICATE, DESTROY ⟨attempting to *root out* his mistakes —A.T.Weaver⟩ ⟨powers to *root out* organized crime and political corruption —*N.Y.Times*⟩ ⟨movement to *root* the radicals *out* of American life —Oscar Handlin⟩

**²root out** *vt* [³*root*] **:** to turn over, dig up, or discover and bring to light ⟨hogs *rooting out* truffles⟩ ⟨spent the whole of March 8 *rooting out* those treasured possessions from holes and corners —Kenneth Roberts⟩ ⟨a game which could *root* our grandfathers *out* of their beds at three o'clock in the morning —Stanislaus Lynch⟩

**root pressure** *n* **:** the chiefly osmotic pressure or force by which water rises into the stems of plants from the roots

**root–prune** \'⸗,⸗\ *vt* **:** to prune the roots of (woody plants) in order to check top growth, develop a mass of small fibrous roots, or induce flowering and fruiting

**root pulper** *n* **:** a machine used for reducing root crops to a pulp for stock feed

**root rake** *n* **:** a tree dozer or rooter with heavy teeth (attached to the front of a tractor) that is used for uprooting small trees, stumps, or brush and pushing them into piles

root rake

**root rot** *n* **:** a plant disease characterized by a decay of the roots (as those caused by fungi of the genera *Armillaria, Oozonium, Thielavia, Rhizoctonia,* or *Sphaerostilbe*) — compare ROSELLINIA

**roots–run** \'⸗,⸗\ *n* **:** a space or area for root development

**roots** *pl of* ROOT, *pres 3d sing of* ROOT

**root sheath** *n* **1 a :** a many-layered epidermal sheath surrounding an aerial root (as the velamen in an epiphytic orchid) **b :** COLEORHIZA **2 :** the epidermal lining of a hair follicle comprising two principal layers of cells that make up an inner and an outer root sheath

**rootstalk** \'⸗,⸗\ *n* **:** RHIZOME

**rootstock** \'⸗,⸗\ *n* **1 a :** a rhizomatous underground part of a plant **b :** a stock for grafting consisting of a root or a piece of root; *broadly* **:** STOCK **2 :** HYDRORHIZA **3 :** a source of offshoots **:** ORIGIN ⟨going back to one of the ~*s* of economic thought —*Times Lit. Supp.*⟩

**root sucker** *n* **:** a shoot springing from the roots of a plant (as wild plum or raspberry)

**root symbiosis** *n* **:** the mycorrhizal association of bacteria and fungi with the roots of certain plants — compare MYCORRHIZA

**root tip** *n* **:** the terminal portion of a root or root branch usu. including the root cap and the meristematic region behind it and often the regions of differentiation, elongation, and root hair formation

**root vole** *n* **:** any of various voles of the genus *Microtus; esp* **:** a Siberian vole (*M. oeconomus*) that stores up roots and tubers for future use

**root weevil** *n* **1 :** any of several Australian weevils of the genus *Baryopadus; esp* **:** a larva (*B. squalidus*) that bores in the roots of the apple and pear **2 :** WATER WEEVIL

**rootworm** \'⸗,⸗\ *n* **1 :** an insect larva (as the corn rootworm) that feeds on the roots of plants **2 :** a nematode worm that infests roots

**rooty** \'rü|d·|ē, 'rů|, |t|, |i\ *adj* -ER/-EST [ME *ruty,* fr. *rot, root, rut* root + *-y* — more at ROOT] **1 :** full or consisting of roots ⟨~ soil⟩ **2 :** similar to or of the quality of roots ⟨a ~ fragrance of pine and moss and bracken —John Buchan⟩

**roove** *var of* ROVE

**rooves** *pl of* ROOF

**rooyebok** *var of* ROOIBOK

**ROP** *abbr* **1** record of performance; record of production **2** *often not cap* run-of-paper

**rop·able** *or* **rope·able** \'rōpəbəl\ *adj* **1 :** capable of being roped **2** *Austral* **:** in a bad temper **:** ANGRY

**ropalic** *adj var of* RHOPALIC

**¹rope** \'rōp\ *n* -S *often attrib* [ME, fr. OE *rāp;* akin to OHG *reif* hoop, ON *reip* rope, Goth *skaudaraip* sandal strap] **1 a** (1) **:** a large stout cord made of strands of natural or artificial fibers (as hemp, Manila hemp, sisal, jute, flax, cotton, or nylon) twisted or braided together esp. in a thickness an inch or more in circumference or ¼ inch to 5 inches in diameter (2) **:** a large stout cord made of strands of wire twisted or braided together (3) **:** a cord having a wire core with fiber strands braided around it (4) **:** a large stout cord made of nonfibrous artificial material (as glass or a plastic) **b :** a braided or unbraided long slender strip of material used as rope ⟨rawhide ~⟩ **c :** a piece of rope cut to a suitable length for a particular function: as (1) **:** a cord for hanging a person **:** a hangman's noose (2) **:** any of various lines aboard or connected to a ship ⟨wheel ~⟩ — see SHIP illustration (3) *obs* **:** TIGHTROPE (4) **:** LASSO (5) **:** one of the usu. three cords stretched one above the other at intervals of about 18 inches that mark off a boxing or wrestling ring **2 :** a unit of length **:** ROOD **3 :** a line aboard a ship before it is used ⟨a ~ stored in a coil⟩ **4 a :** a row or string consisting of a number of things united (as by braiding, twining, or threading) ⟨a ~ of pearls⟩ ⟨a ~ of onions⟩ **b :** two or more mountain climbers fastened at intervals to a single rope for security **5 :** slimy strands in food substances (as milk, flour, or bread) caused by contamination with bacteria or fungi — compare ROPINESS, ROPY BREAD **6 :** a device usu. consisting of long streamers of aluminum foil dropped from an airplane to confuse enemy radar equipment **7 a** (1) **:** something that binds, confines, or holds in check (2) **:** a condition, event, or action that helps a person in a disadvantageous state ⟨redeemed me . . . from the ~*s* of sin —Maurice Samuel⟩ **b :** something twisted and braided like a rope ⟨the soft ~ of her hair tossed from side to side —James Joyce⟩ **c :** something long, elongated, and strung out ⟨far ahead in the dark I saw the monumental bridge, ~*s* of light across the dark river —Ralph Ellison⟩ **d :** SEQUENCE — used in panguingue and other card games of the rummy family **8 :** freedom of action esp. when likely to cause harm ⟨enough ~ to hang himself⟩ ⟨allowing himself sufficient ~ to wander beyond the city —Isolde Farrell⟩ **9 ropes** *pl* **:** the special techniques or procedures involved **:** INS AND OUTS ⟨postponed everything . . . with the excuse that he was learning the ~*s* —T.R.Ybarra⟩ — **on the ropes** *adv* (*or adj*) **1 :** in a groggy defenseless state upon the ropes of a boxing ring **2 :** in a helpless condition ⟨emotionally, physically and financially I was *on the ropes* —Polly Adler⟩

**²rope** \"\ *vb* -ED/-ING/-S *vt* **1 a :** to bind, fasten, or tie with a rope or cord ⟨I'll ~ myself here so that I won't be swept overboard —Richard Sale⟩ **b :** to partition, separate, or divide by means of a rope so as to include or exclude ⟨*roped* away from the entrance among a herd of other waiting people —J.B. Benefield⟩ ⟨to ~ off the street near the fire⟩ **c :** to capture by means of a rope **:** LASSO ⟨~ cattle⟩ ⟨~ a steer⟩ ⟨~ out a mustang⟩ **d :** to connect or fasten together (a party of mountain climbers) with a rope — usu. used with *up* **2** *of a sail* **:** to sew a boltrope on the edge of **3 :** to draw as if with a rope: **a :** to inveigle into joining an undertaking or organization ⟨the conspirators *roped* into their scheme a whole network of the magnates —Hilaire Belloc⟩ **b** *slang* **:** to take in **:** SWINDLE ⟨an old confidence man wrote with nostalgia of fat marks he had *roped* and taken for their bankrolls —R.B.Gehman⟩ — often used with *in* **c** *slang* **:** to attract by the use of sexual charms esp. into an engagement — often used with *in* **~ *vi* 1 :** to take the form of or twist in the manner of rope **:** to extend in a filament or thread (as by means of a glutinous or adhesive quality) ⟨the saliva *roping* from his jowls —Ralph Ellison⟩ **2 :** to connect or fasten together a party of mountain climbers with a rope ⟨today soft snow lay on ice . . . so we *roped up* —W.H.Murray⟩

**³rope** \"\ *n* -S [ME *rop,* fr. OE *ropp, hrop;* akin to MD *rop* animal entrails] *dial Brit* **:** ENTRAIL, INTESTINE

**ropeband** *var of* ROBAND

**ropebark** \'⸗,⸗\ *n* **:** LEATHERWOOD 1a

**rope brake** *n* **:** a band brake or absorption dynamometer in which the band is replaced by a rope — compare PRONY BRAKE

**rope brown** *n* **:** a brown paper esp. of excellent quality made from old Manila ropes

**rope clip** *n* **:** a clamp (as a U-bolt) for clamping together two ropes (as wire ropes) or two parts of a rope

rope clip

**ropedancer** \'⸗,⸗⸗\ *n* **:** one that dances, walks, or performs acrobatic feats on a rope extended through the air at some height

**ropedancing** \'⸗,⸗⸗\ *n* **:** the art of dancing, walking, or performing acrobatic feats on a rope extended through the air at some height

**rope down** *vb* **:** to make a rappel

**rope drilling** *n* [*drilling* fr. gerund of *drill*] **:** a method of sinking wells or making boreholes in which the tools are attached to the lower end of a rope or cable and lifted and dropped alternately — called also *cable drilling, cable system, percussion drilling*

**rope drive** *n* **:** one or more ropes transmitting torque from one parallel grooved pulley to another

**rope grass** *n* **:** a plant of the genus *Restio*

**rope–grass family** *n* **:** RESTIONACEAE

**rope hose tool** *n* **:** a rope having a hook and often a ring attached used by firemen esp. to hold hose in place while in use

rope hose tools

**rope house** *n* **1 :** a storehouse for rope **2 :** an open-sided shed in which salt is crystallized out from brine on ropes down which the brine trickles

**rope key** *n* **:** TENT SLIDE

**rope ladder** *n* **:** a ladder with sidepieces of rope and rungs of rope, wood, or metal

**rope–lay cable** *n* **:** a cable in which the separate wires are spirally stranded before being spiraled together

**rope molding** *n* **:** a molding in a pattern twisted like the strands of a rope

**rope of sand :** something of no cohesion or stability **:** a feeble union or tie

**rop·er** \'rōpə(r)\ *n* -S [ME *ropere* maker of ropes, fr. ¹*rope* + *-ere* -er] **1 :** a maker of ropes; *specif* **:** an operator of a machine for twisting yarn into rope **2 :** one that ropes cattle or horses **:** COWBOY **3 a :** one that entices customers to a gambling establishment esp. with a fixed game **b :** a detective who hides his identity and tries to make a suspect give himself away **c :** a strikebreaker who circulates among strikers in search of men tempted to return to work **4 :** a jockey who checks his horse to prevent it from winning **5 :** a hat blocker who forms brims

**rope race** *n* **:** a race in a pulley through which a rope runs

**rope railway** *n* **:** ROPEWAY

**¹roperipe** \'⸗,⸗\ *adj* **1** *archaic* **a** *of a deed* **:** punishable by hanging **b** *of a person* **:** deserving to be hung **2** *obs* **:** BOMBASTIC

**²roperipe** \"\ *n* -S **:** one that deserves to be hung **:** RASCAL

**rop·ery** \'rōp(ə)rē\ *n* -ES [ME *roperie,* fr. ¹*rope* + *-erie* -ery] **1 :** a place where ropes are made **2** *archaic* **:** roguish tricks or banter

**ropes** *pl of* ROPE, *pres 3d sing of* ROPE

**rope's end** *n* [ME *roppys end,* fr. *roppys, ropes* (gen. of ¹*rope*) + *end, ende* end] **1 :** a piece of rope esp. for use as a lash for punishing **2 :** a hangman's noose

**rope's–end** \'⸗,⸗\ *vt* [*rope's end*] **:** to punish with a rope's end

**rope spear** *n* **:** a spear used to recover rope lost in an oil well

**rope stitch** *n* **:** an embroidery stitch made by overlapping small slanted stitches

**rope system** *n* **:** a method of training dewberries in which the canes are tied to one or two horizontal wires strung above the plants between posts

**rope tow** *n* **:** SKI TOW 1

**ropetrick** *n, obs* **:** ROGUERY

**rope walk** *n* **1** *or* **rope yard :** a long path devoted to the manufacture of rope down which the worker carries and lays the strands **2 :** a long narrow building containing a rope walk

**ropewalker** \'⸗,⸗⸗\ *n* **:** an acrobat that walks on a rope extended through the air at some height

**ropeway** \'⸗,⸗\ *n* **1 :** a fixed cable or a pair of fixed cables suspended between supporting towers serving as a track for passenger or freight carriers that are self-propelled or move by gravity **2 :** an endless aerial cable suspended between supports that revolve, upon drums turned by a stationary engine and used to transport logs, ore, and other freight suspended free or in carriers **:** CABLEWAY

**ropework** \'⸗,⸗\ *n* **1 :** an establishment where ropes are made **2 a :** the art of tying knots **b :** work (as knots) made of entwined ropes

**rope yarn** *n* **1 a :** the yarn or thread composing the strands of a rope **b :** a yarn of fibers loosely twisted up right-handedly **2 :** something of small account **:** TRIFLE

**rope-yarn knot** *n* **:** a knot made by splitting rope yarns and joining the ends with half-knots and used to tie rope yarns together when serving

**ropeyarn sunday** \ˈ=,=-\ *n, often cap R & usu cap S* [prob. so called fr. a former practice on sailing ships of setting aside one afternoon a week for the mending of clothes] *slang* **:** an afternoon during the week in which no work is required

rope-yarn knot

**rop·i·ly** \ˈrōpəlē, -li\ *adv* **:** in a ropy manner

**rop·i·ness** \-pēnəs, -pin-\ *n* -ES **1 :** the quality or state of being ropy **2 a :** a stringy condition of milk caused by contamination with some strains of bacteria **b :** a slimy condition of flour or bread caused by bacterial or fungal contamination

**¹rop·ing** \ˈrōpiŋ\ *adj* [ME *ropinge*, fr. pres. part. of (assumed) ME *ropen* to be ropy, fr. ME ¹*rope*] *archaic* **:** ROPY

**²roping** \"\ *n* -S [¹*rope* + *-ing*] **1 :** ROPES, CORDAGE **2 :** BOLTROPE **3 :** ROVING; *specif* **:** a wool sliver delivered from the finisher card ready for spinning

**roping needle** *n* **:** a sailmaker's large needle

**ropy** *also* **rop·ey** \ˈrōpē, -pi\ *adj* **ropier**; **ropiest** [ME *ropy*, fr. ¹*rope* + *-y*] **1 a :** capable of being drawn into a thread **:** VISCOUS, GLUTINOUS ⟨a ~ froth had dried on his lips —John Bennett⟩ **b :** having a gelatinous quality (as milk) or slimy quality (as bread or flour) from bacterial or fungal contamination **c** *of a paint* **:** having a quality or characteristic that causes it to act stringy under the brush and not level out properly **2 a :** long, gnarled, and often roughly fibrous ⟨their ~ vines twisted around strands of wire strung between five-foot stakes —*Amer. Guide Series: Pa.*⟩ **b :** MUSCULAR, SINEWY ⟨~ legs⟩ ⟨in anger, ~ veins push out —Douglass Cater⟩ **3** *usu ropey, slang* **:** extremely unsatisfactory or inauspicious

**ropy bread** *n* **:** bread made slimy by overgrowth with a mucoid strain of a soil bacterium (*Bacillus subtilis*)

**ropy lava** *n* **:** lava marked with wrinkles resembling rope **:** PAHOEHOE

**roque** \ˈrōk\ *n* -S [alter. of ¹*croquet*] **:** croquet played on a hard-surfaced court having a raised border used as a cushion in bank shots

**Roque·fort** \ˈrōkfərt\ *trademark* — used for a cheese made of ewes' milk and ripened in caves

**roque·laure** \ˌräkəˌlō(ə)r, ˌrōk-\ *n* -S [F, fr. Antoine Gaston Jean Baptiste, Duc de *Roquelaure* †1738 Fr. marshal] **:** a knee-length cloak buttoned in front worn esp. in the 18th and early 19th centuries

**¹ro·quet** \(ˈ)rōˌkā\ *vt* -ED/-ING/-S [prob. alter. of ²*croquet*] **:** to hit (another's ball) — used of a croquet ball or of the player who strikes it

**²roquet** \"\ *n* -S **:** the act of roqueting

**ro·quette** \rōˈket\ *n* -S [F — more at ROCKET] **:** GARDEN ROCKET 1

**ro·ral** \ˈrōrəl\ *adj* [L *ror-, ros* dew + E *-al*] *archaic* **:** DEWY

**ro·ram hat** \ˈrōrəm-\ *n* [*roram* (of unknown origin) + *hat*] **:** a hat made of a woolen cloth with a fur face worn esp. in the 19th century

**ro·ra·te sunday** \rōˈräd·ē-\ *n, cap R&S* [*rorate* fr. L, 2d pers. pl. imper. of *rorare* to drip moisture, fr. *ror-, ros* dew; fr. the occurrence of *rorate* as the first word in the Latin form of the introit for the day in some Christian churches] **:** the fourth Sunday in Advent

**ro·ric** \ˈrōrik\ *adj* [ISV *ror-* (fr. L *ror-, ros* dew) + *-ic* — more at ROSEMARY] **:** of or relating to dew **:** DEWY

**rorid** *adj* [L *roridus*, fr. *ror-, ros* dew] *obs* **:** DEWY

**ro·rid·u·la** \rōˈrijələ\ *n, cap* [NL, prob. fr. L *roridus* dewy + *-ula*] **:** a genus of southern African insectivorous undershrubs (family Droseraceae), having entire or pinnatifid leaves and white or red flowers with a 3-celled ovary

**ro·rif·er·ous** \rōˈrif(ə)rəs\ *adj* [L *rorifer* roriferous (fr. *ror-, ros* dew + *-fer* -ferous) + E *-ous*] **:** generating dew

**ro·rip·pa** \rōˈripə\ *n, cap* [NL] **:** a large genus of chiefly weedy aquatic or marsh herbs (family Cruciferae) that have pinnate or pinnatifid leaves, yellow flowers, and terete pods with seeds in two rows in each cell and that include some forms used for salad greens or pot herbs — see MARSH CRESS

**ror·qual** \ˈrȯrkwəl\ *n* -S [F, fr. Norw *røyrhval*, fr. ON *reytharhvalr*, fr. *reythr* rorqual (fr. *rauthr* red) + *hvalr* whale — more at RED, WHALE] **:** a whalebone whale of the genus *Balaenoptera* having a small sickle-shaped dorsal fin, a rather small head, the skin of the throat marked with deep longitudinal furrows, and the forelimbs rather short and slender — see BLUE WHALE; compare FINBACK

**¹ror·schach** \ˈrō(ə)r,shäk-\ *n* -S *usu cap* [after Hermann *Rorschach* †1922 Swiss psychiatrist] **1** *or* **rorschach test :** a psychological test of personality and intelligence consisting of 10 standard black or colored inkblot designs that the subject describes in terms of what they look like to him and reveals through his selectivity the manner in which intellectual and emotional factors are integrated in his perception of environmental stimuli **2** *or* **rorschach protocol :** the data obtained by a Rorschach

**²rorschach** \"\ *vt* -ED/-ING/-S *often cap* **:** to test by means of the Rorschach

**ror·schach·er** \-kə(r)\ *or* **ror·schach·ist** \-kəst\ *n* -S *usu cap* [Hermann *Rorschach* + E *-er* or *-ist*] **:** one who is skilled in the administration, scoring, and interpretation of the Rorschach

**rort** \ˈrȯ(ə)rt\ *n* -S [perh. back-formation fr. *rorty*] *Austral* **:** a fraudulent scheme **:** TRICK

**ror·ty** \ˈrȯ(ə)rtī\ *adj* -ER/-EST [origin unknown] *slang Brit* **:** FINE, GAY, SPORTY

**rory-tory** \ˌrōriˌtōri\ *adj* [prob. alter. of *tory-rory*] *dial Eng* **:** DASHING, FLAMBOYANT, GAY

**ros** *pl of* RO

**¹ro·sa** \ˈrōzə\ *n, cap* [NL, fr. L, rose — more at ROSE] **:** a large genus of erect or sometimes climbing or creeping mostly prickly shrubs (family Rosaceae) that are widely distributed esp. in temperate regions and have compound leaves and regular 5-petaled red, white, pink, or yellow flowers with many stamens

**²rosa** \"\ *adj, usu cap* [*Rosa*, locality in north central New Mexico] **:** of or belonging to a culture in north central New Mexico A.D. 700-900 characterized by stockades and pit houses having a large and variable floor plan

**rosa americana** *n, usu cap R&A* [NL, American rose] **:** one of a series of brass coins in twopence, penny, and halfpenny denominations issued in 1722–23 for use in America that bear on the reverse a rose and an inscription containing the words *Rosa Americana*

**ro·sace** \(ˈ)rōˌzās, rōˈzäs\ *n* -S [F, fr. MF, irreg. fr. *rose*, fr. L *rosa*] **:** a circular ornamental architectural member that is usu. a panel enclosing a richly sculptured rosette

**ro·sa·cea** \rōˈzāshēə\ *n* -S [NL, fem. of *rosaceus* rose-colored, fr. L, made of roses, fr. *rosa* rose + *-aceus* -aceous] **:** ACNE ROSACEA

**ro·sa·ce·ae** \-āsē,ē\ *n pl, cap* [NL, fr. *Rosa*, type genus + *-aceae*] **:** a large family of nearly cosmopolitan trees, shrubs, and herbs (order Rosales) having alternate usu. stipulate leaves, 5-petaled regular flowers with numerous stamens, and dry fruits sometimes on pulpy receptacles — see AMYGDALACEAE

**ro·sa·ceous** \(ˈ)rōˌzāshəs\ *adj* [NL *Rosaceae* + E *-ous*] **1 a :** of or relating to the Rosaceae **b :** of, relating to, or resembling a rose esp. in having a 5-petaled regular corolla **2** [NL *rosaceus* rose-colored] **:** of the color rose **:** ROSY

**rosa-de-montana** \ˌrōzədə-ˌmänˈtän(y)ə\ *n, pl* **rosa-de-montanas** [AmerSp *rosa de montaña*] **:** PINK VINE

**rosaker** *n* -S [alter. of earlier *rosealgar*, fr. ME *rosalgere*, fr. OPg *rosalgar*, fr. Ar *rahj al-ghār* powder of the mine] *obs* **:** REALGAR

**ro·sa·les** \rōˈzā(,)lēz\ *n pl, cap* [NL, fr. *Rosa* + *-ales*] **:** an order of dicotyledonous plants having flowers with the petals separate or in some members of the family Leguminosae more or less united, a partly united calyx, epigynous or perigynous stamens, and one or more carpels

**ro·sa·lia** \rōˈzālyə\ *n* -S [It, fr. *Rosalia* (feminine name); fr. the occurrence of *Rosalia* as the first word in an old song employing such repetition] **:** a melody in which a phrase or passage is successively repeated each time a step or half step higher

**ro·sa·line** \ˈrōzə,lēn\ *n* -S [prob. irreg. fr. ²*rose*] **:** a lace with rose designs made by needlepoint or bobbin method

**ro·sa·may** \ˈrōzə,mā\ *n* -S [prob. irreg. fr. ²*rose*] **:** AUSTRALIAN ROSEWOOD 2

**ros·aniline** \(ˈ)rōz+\ *n* [ISV *ros-* (fr. L *rosa* rose) + *aniline* — more at ROSE] **1 a** *or* **rosaniline base :** a white crystalline base $H_2N(CH_3)C_6H_3C(OH)(C_6H_4NH_2)_2$ that is the methyl derivative of pararosaniline and likewise is the parent compound of many triphenylmethane dyes — see DYE table I (under *Solvent Red 41*) **b :** FUCHSINE **2 :** any of a series of bases or dyes related to rosaniline and fuchsine

**ro·sar·i·an** \rōˈza(a)rēən\ *n* -S [²*rose* + *-arian*] **:** a cultivator of roses **:** a rose fancier

**¹ro·sa·rio** \rōˈzärē,ō, -ˈsä-\ *n* -S [perh. fr. *Rosario*, municipality in southern Luzon, Republic of the Philippines] **:** ARMY BROWN

**²rosario** \"\ *adj, usu cap* [fr. *Rosario*, city in east central Argentina] **:** of or from the city of Rosario, Argentina **:** of the kind or style prevalent in Rosario

**ro·sar·i·um** \rōˈza(a)rēəm\ *n* -S [L] **:** a rose garden

**ro·sa·ry** \ˈrōz(ə)rē, -)ri\ *n* -ES [in sense 1, fr. ME *rosarie*, fr. L *rosarium* rose garden, fr. neut. of *rosarius* of roses, fr. *rosa* rose + *-arius* -ary; in other senses, fr. ML *rosarium* string of beads used in counting prayers, series of prayers, fr. L, rose garden — more at ROSE] **1 a :** a bed or bush of roses **b :** a place where roses grow **2 :** a string of beads used in counting prayers; *specif* **:** a string of beads by which the prayers of the Roman Catholic rosary are counted — compare CHAPLET **3 a** *often cap* **:** a form of devotion to the Virgin Mary in the Roman Catholic Church that consists of the recitation of usu. five decades of Ave Marias preceded each by a paternoster and ended with a gloria **b :** a devotional exercise among other religious groups marked by the use of beads ⟨a Buddhist ~⟩ **4** *med* **:** BEADING f

rosary 2

**rosary pea** *n* **1 :** INDIAN LICORICE **2 :** JEQUIRITY

**rosary vine** *n* **:** a prostrate or trailing vine (*Ceropegia woodii*) of the family Asclepiadaceae having dark green fleshy white-veined leaves and purplish flowers usu. in pairs on a long pedicel

**ro·sa·site** \ˈrōzə,sīt, -zə,zīt\ *n* -S [It, fr. *Rosas* mine, Sulcis, Sardinia, its locality + It *-ite*] **:** a mineral $(Cu,Zn)_2(OH)_2(CO_3)$ consisting of a basic carbonate of copper and zinc that is prob. a zincky malachite

**ro·sa so·lis** \ˌrōzəˈsōləs\ *n, pl* **rosa solises** [NL, alter. (influenced by L *rosa* rose) of ML *ros solis* — more at ROSOLIO] **1 :** a sundew (*Drosera rotundifolia*) **2 :** a cordial flavored with juice from the sundew or other herbs and spices

**roscher·ite** \ˈräshə,rīt, ˈrōsh-\ *n* -S [G *roscherit*, fr. Walter *Roscher*, 20th cent. Ger. mineral collector) + G *-it* -ite] **:** a mineral $(Ca,Mn,Fe)_2Al(PO_4)_2(OH).2H_2O$ consisting of a hydrous basic phosphate of aluminum, manganese, calcium, and iron and occurring in dark brown monoclinic crystals

**ros·ci·an** \ˈräsh(ē)ən\ *adj, usu cap* [L *roscianus* of Roscius, fr. *Roscius* (Roman gentile name borne by several prominent persons including Quintus Roscius) + L *-anus* -an] **:** of, relating to, or skilled in acting

**ros·cid** \ˈräsəd\ *adj* [L *roscidus*, fr. *ror-, ros* dew — more at ROSEMARY] *archaic* **:** DEWY

**ros·coe** \ˈrä(,)skō\ *n* -S [prob. fr. the name *Roscoe*] *slang* **:** PISTOL

**ros·coe·lite** \ˈrä(,)skō,līt\ *n* -S [Sir Henry E. *Roscoe* †1915 Eng. chemist + E *-lite*] **:** a mineral approximately $K_2(Mg,Fe,V,Al)_4(Si,Al)_8O_{20}(OH)_4$ consisting of a brownish mica in minute scales that contains vanadium

**ros·com·mon** \(ˈ)räˈskämən\ *adj, usu cap* [fr. *Roscommon*, county in north central Ireland] **:** of or from County Roscommon, Ireland **:** of the kind or style prevalent in County Roscommon

**¹rose** [ME *roos, rose*, fr. OE *rās*] *past of* RISE

**²rose** \ˈrōz\ *n* -S [ME, fr. OE, fr. L *rosa*, prob. fr. Gk *rhodon*,

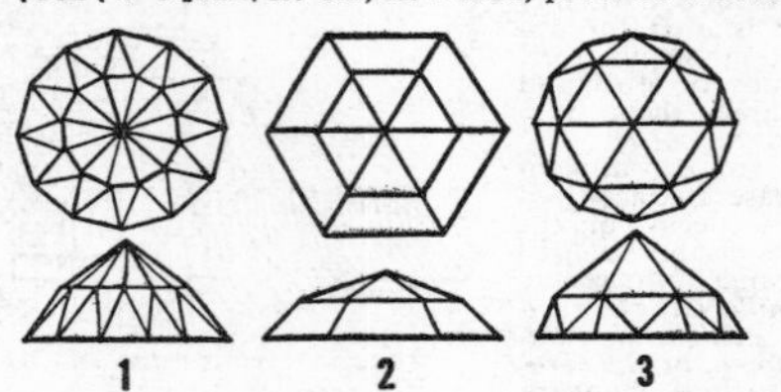

rose 2d(1): *1* rose recoupé, *2* brabant, *3* Dutch

prob. of Iranian origin; akin to the source of Per *gul* rose; akin to OE *word*, a bush] **1 :** a plant or flower of the genus *Rosa* **2 :** something resembling a rose in form: as **a :** any of various heraldic representations of a rose that usu. have five petals opened wide with barbs between and stamens or seeds in a circular center and when blazoned proper the barbs vert and the seeds or and that are often used as a cadency mark representing the seventh son **b** (1) **:** the card of the mariner's compass (2) **:** COMPASS ROSE (3) **:** a chart showing true and magnetic courses (4) **:** a circular card with radiating lines used in other instruments **c :** a rosette esp. on a shoe **d** *or* **rose cut** (1) **:** a form in which diamonds and other gems are cut that usu. has a flat circular base and facets in two ranges rising to a point and is used esp. when the loss to the stone in cutting it as a brilliant would be too great — compare BRABANT ROSE, DOUBLE ROSE, DUTCH ROSE (2) **:** a gem (as a diamond) with a rose cut (3) **:** a diamond so small that it can be cut little if at all **e** (1) **:** a perforated nozzle for delivering water in fine jets (2) **:** ROSE BOX **f :** ROSE WINDOW **g** (1) **:** an often ornamental fixture supporting or encircling a gas pipe, electric-light wire, or other conduit (as where it passes through a ceiling or wall) — called also *rosette* (2) **:** a round plate designed for attaching to a door surface and for receiving the shank of a doorknob **3 a :** a perfume having an odor like that of roses **b :** a constituent of such a perfume consisting of rose oil or a formulated preparation with a similar odor **4 a :** a person and esp. a woman of great charm, excellence, or virtue **b :** a comfortable situation or an easily accomplished task ⟨it began to look as if things might be ~*s*, ~*s* all the way —J.P.O'Donnell⟩ **5 a :** a variable color averaging a moderate purplish red that is redder and paler than violine pink, magenta rose, average fuchsia rose, or average raspberry rose, redder and stronger than mallow, and bluer and paler than solferino **b :** the hue of health **:** a pink or ruddy flush — usu. used in pl. ⟨the ~*s* in her cheeks⟩ **c :** ERYSIPELAS **6 :** the decoration of the circular sound hole in the top of a lute or similar musical instrument sometimes serving as a trademark — **under the rose** *adv* (*or adj*) **:** in secret **:** in private

**³rose** \"\ *vt* -ED/-ING/-S **:** to make of the color rose **:** FLUSH

**⁴rose** \"\ *adj* **1 a :** of or relating to a rose ⟨~ petal⟩ ⟨~ wreath⟩ **b :** bordered or overgrown with roses **:** used for roses ⟨a ~ arbor⟩ ⟨~ bower⟩ ⟨~ jar⟩ **c :** flavored, scented, or colored with or like roses ⟨~ bowl⟩ ⟨~ water⟩ **2 :** of the color rose — used esp. of gems ⟨~ opal⟩ ⟨~ topaz⟩ ⟨~ tourmaline⟩

**⁵ro·sé** \(ˈ)rōˌzā\ *n* -S [F, fr. *rosé*, adj., pink, fr. OF, fr. *rose*, n., rose, fr. L *rosa* — more at ²ROSE] **:** a table wine made from red grapes by removing the skins after fermentation has begun and thereby imparting a light pink rather than a red color to the wine — compare RED WINE, WHITE WINE

**rose acacia** *n* **:** BRISTLY LOCUST

**ro·se·al** \ˈrōzēəl\ *adj* [L *roseus* rosy (fr. *rosa* rose + *-eus* -eous) + E *-al*] *archaic* **:** resembling or suggesting a rose **:** ROSEATE

**rose alder** *n* **:** an Australian shrub (*Duboisia myoporoides*) resembling the related pituri

**rose aphid** *n* **:** any of several plant lice that feed on the foliage of the rose; *esp* **:** a green and pinkish aphid (*Macrosiphum rosae*) that feeds chiefly on new shoots and buds

**rose apple** *n* **1 :** any of several tropical plants of the genus *Eugenia* or their fruits: as **a :** a tropical tree (*E. jambos*) with large thick leaves and pink flowers; *also* **:** its large edible fleshy fruit with a woolly surface and a roselike fragrance **b :** MALAY APPLE **c :** BRUSH CHERRY **d :** JAVA PLUM **2** *Austral* **:** BURDEKIN PLUM

**rose ash** *n* **:** a grayish red that is duller and slightly bluer than bois de rose and yellower and duller than appleblossom

**ro·se·ate** \ˈrōzēə̇t, -ē,āt, *usu* |d.+V\ *adj* [L *roseus* rosy + E *-ate*] **1 a :** resembling a rose esp. in color **b :** overly optimistic or pleasing **:** viewed in or inclined to view in a favorable light ⟨the most fashionable variety of prewar liberalism was a hopeful and ~ internationalism —F.B.Millett⟩ **2** *archaic* **:** full of, consisting of, or made from roses — **ro·se·ate·ly** *adv*

**roseate spoonbill** *n* **:** a spoonbill (*Ajaia ajaja*) found from the southern U. S. to Patagonia that has the head and throat bare and chiefly pink plumage

**roseate tern** *n* **:** a cosmopolitan tern (*Sterna dougalli*) having the breast roseate in the breeding season and when adult the tail deeply forked and the cap black, mantle pearl, and feet red

**rose·bay** \ˈrōz,bā\ *n* **1 :** OLEANDER **2 :** a plant of the genus *Rhododendron*; *esp* **:** BIG LAUREL **3** *or* **rosebay willow** *or* **rosebay willow herb :** FIREWEED b

**rose beetle** *n* **1 :** ROSE CHAFER **2 :** ROSE WEEVIL

**rose beige** *n* **:** a variable color averaging a light brown that is yellower and slightly duller than alesan, paler than cork, and yellower, less strong, and slightly darker than blush

**rose bengal** \(,)rōz+ *pronunc at* BENGAL\ *also* **rose ben·gale** \-gäl,-gəl\ *n, pl* **rose bengals** *often cap R&B* [prob. fr. F *rose bengale*, fr. *rose* (fr. L *rosa*) + *Bengale* Bengal, region of the Indian subcontinent — more at ROSE] **:** either of two bluish red acid dyes that are iodinated and chlorinated derivatives of fluorescein — see DYE table I (under *Acid Red 94*)

**rose bisque** *n* **:** ROSE HORTENSIA

**rose bit** *n* **:** a rose countersink or reamer

**rose bloom** *n* **:** FALSE BLOSSOM

**rose blotch** *n* **:** BLACK SPOT 1c

**rose blush** *n* **1 :** BLUSH 4a **2 :** a light reddish brown that is redder, lighter, and slightly stronger than copper tan and slightly darker than monkey skin

**rose box** *n* **:** a strainer for the end of the suction pipe of a pump

**rose-breasted** \ˈ=;==\ *adj* **:** having the breast marked with rose

**rose-breasted cockatoo** *n* **:** GALAH 1

**rose-breasted grosbeak** *n* **:** a grosbeak (*Pheucticus ludovicianus*) found in eastern No. America that in the male is chiefly black and white with the breast and linings of the wings rose red and in the female is grayish brown streaked with paler tints with the lining of the wings orange

**rose breath** *n* **:** a pale to light pink

**rose brown** *n* **:** a variable color averaging a dark grayish red that is lighter and slightly bluer than average cordovan (sense 3b)

**rosebud** \ˈ=,=\ *n* **1 :** the flower of a rose before it opens or when but partly open **2 :** a moderate to strong purplish pink

**rosebud cherry** *n* **:** a large shrub or small shrubby tree (*Prunus subhirtella*) that is native to Japan and is often cultivated as an ornamental for the sake of its rose-pink flowers borne on long slender often drooping branches

**rosebush** \ˈ=,=\ *n* **1 :** a shrubby rose **2** *Austral* **:** a small timber tree (*Eupomatia laurina*) with soft coarse-grained yellowish brown wood

**rose cake** *n, obs* **:** rose petals pressed into a cake and used for perfume

**rose campion** *n* **1 :** MULLEIN PINK **2 :** CORN COCKLE

**rose car·o·line** \-ˈkarə,līn, -,lən\ *n, often cap C* [perh. fr. the name *Caroline*] **:** a moderate yellowish pink that is yellower and less strong than coral pink and redder and duller than peach pink

**rose car·thame** \-,kärˈtäm\ *n, often cap C* [*carthame* fr. F, fr. NL *Carthamus*] **:** CARTHAMUS RED

**rose cen·dre** \-ˈsäⁿdr(ᵊ), -d(rə)\ *n* [*cendre* fr. F, ash, ashes, fr. L *ciner-, cinis* — more at INCINERATE] **:** a moderate yellowish pink that is paler and much yellower than coral pink and yellower and less strong than peach pink

**rose chafer** *n* **1** *also* **rose bug :** a common No. American melolonthid beetle (*Macrodactylus subspinosus*) whose larva feeds on plant roots and the adults on leaves and flowers of various plants (as rosebushes, fruit trees, or grapevines) **2 :** a European Cetonian beetle (*Cetonia aurata*)

**rose-cheeked** \ˈ=;=\ *adj* [²*rose* + *-cheeked* having (such) cheeks (fr. *cheek* + *-ed*)] **:** having rose-colored cheeks

**rose chestnut** *n* **:** an East Indian timber tree (*Mesua ferrea*) that has very heavy hard wood used for railroad ties and flowers yielding a perfume

**rose clover** *n* **:** an Asiatic winter annual clover (*Trifolium hirtum*) introduced into the U.S. as a forage crop esp. on poor rangeland

**rose cold** *n* **:** ROSE FEVER

**rose-colored** \ˈ=,==\ *adj* **1 :** having a rose color **2 :** seeing or seen in a promising light **:** OPTIMISTIC ⟨delivers a final . . . talk, capping the *rose-colored* impression of life in this particular branch of the service —*Christian Science Monitor*⟩

**rose-colored spectacles** *or* **rose-colored glasses** *n* **:** optimistic eyes **:** favorably disposed opinions ⟨view the world through *rose-colored spectacles*⟩

**rose-colored starling** *or* **rose-colored pastor** *n* **:** a glossy black chiefly Asian bird (*Pastor sturnus* or *P. roseus*) of the family Sturnidae with a pink back and abdomen that is chiefly Asian though often appearing in flocks in Europe and sometimes in England

**rose comb** *n* [²*rose* + *comb*] **1 :** a flat rather broad comb of a domestic fowl that has the upper surface studded with small tubercles and terminates posteriorly in a fleshy spike — see COMB illustration **2 :** a disorder of mushrooms in which the caps are much distorted and which is prob. caused by chemical irritants (as oily sprays or heater fumes)

**rose-comb** \ˈ=,=\ *also* **rose-combed** \ˈ=;kōmd\ *adj* [*rose-comb* fr. *rose comb*; *rose-combed* fr. ²*rose* + *combed*] **:** having a rose comb

**rose coral** *n* **:** any of several corals (genus *Isophyllia*) similar to the brain corals but with deeply incised clefts which make them resemble full-blown roses

**rose countersink** *n* **:** a countersink with radial teeth on its conical end — see COUNTERSINK illustration

**rose curculio** *n* **:** a small bright red weevil (*Rhynchites bicolor*) with black snout and underside that is common on roses and produces larvae that feed on the seed pods

**rose cut** *n* **:** ROSE 2d(1)

**rose-cut** \ˈ=,=\ *adj* [*rose cut*] *of a gem* **:** cut as a rose ⟨a *rose-cut* diamond . . . is a flat, shallow stone —C.W.Dreppard⟩

**rose cutter** *n* **:** a milling cutter having a hemispherical end milling surface

**rosed** *adj* [fr. past part. of ³*rose*] **:** tinged with rose

**rose d'al·thaea** \,rōz,dalˈthēə\ *n, often cap A* [prob. fr. F] **:** a strong pink that is yellower and less strong than carnation rose, yellower and duller than coral (sense 3b), and yellower, lighter, and stronger than sea pink

**rose daphne** *n* **:** a low evergreen shrub (*Daphne cneorum*) with trailing pubescent branches and fragrant rose-pink flowers in sessile many-flowered heads

**rose de nymphe** \,rōzdəˈnim(p)f, -nam-\ *n* [prob. fr. F] **:** a pale yellow that is slightly greener and darker than average ivory and duller than cream

**rose du bar·ry** \,rōzd(y)üˈbarē\ *or* **rose pompadour** \ˈrōz + *pronunc at* POMPADOUR\ *n, usu cap B & P* [*rose du barry* prob. fr. F, fr. Marie Jeanne Bécu, Comtesse *du Barry* †1793 mistress of King Louis XV of France; *rose pompadour* prob. fr. F, fr. Jeanne Antoinette Poisson, Marquise de *Pompadour* †1764 mistress of King Louis XV of France] **:** an opaque pink ceramic overglaze color developed in France during the 18th century

**rose diamond** *n* **:** a diamond cut as a rose

**rose do·rée** \,rōzdəˈrā\ *n* [*dorée* fr. F, fr. fem. of *doré* gilded, past part. of *dorer* to gild — more at DORÉ] **:** a deep pink to moderate red that is yellower and stronger than laurel pink and yellower and less strong than watermelon

**rosedust** \ˈ=,=\ *n* **:** a grayish red to reddish brown

**rose ear** *n* **:** an ear (as of some dogs) that folds backward so as to display part of the inside

**rose end** *n* **:** the end of a potato or other tuber opposite the point of attachment

**rose engine** *n* **:** a machine or a lathe attachment for producing an eccentric relative movement between the rotating mandrel and a cutting point so as to form on the work (as paper currency) a variety of curved lines resembling a rosette — see ENGINE TURNING

**rose family** *n* **:** ROSACEAE

**rose fever** *n* **:** hay fever occurring in the spring or early summer — called also *rose cold*

**rosefish** \\'⸗,⸗\\ *n* **:** a large marine food fish (*Sebastes marinus*) of the family Scorpaenidae found on the northern coasts of Europe and America that when mature is usu. bright rose red or orange red and when young, usu. mottled with red and dusky brown — called also *ocean perch*

**rose–flowering locust** \\'⸗,⸗(⸗)⸗-\\ *n* **:** CLAMMY LOCUST

**rose france** \\⸗'⸗\\ *n, often cap F* [*France*, country of west central Europe] **:** PEACH BLOOM

**rose geranium** *n* **:** any of several southern African herbs of the genus *Pelargonium* (esp. *P. graveolens*) grown for their fragrant 3- to 5-lobed leaves and small pink flowers

**rose–geranium oil** *n* **:** geranium oil esp. when obtained by distillation of leaves to which rose petals have been added

**rose gold** *n* **:** gold with a ruddy mat surface finish

**rose gray** *n* **1 :** ASHES OF ROSE 1 **2 :** a brownish gray that is slightly less strong than mouse gray and lighter than castor

**rose gum** *n* **:** a flooded gum (*Eucalyptus grandis*)

**rosehead** \\'⸗,⸗\\ *n* **:** ROSE 2e(1)

**rosehead nail** *or* **roseheaded nail** *n* **:** a nail with a many-sided pyramidal head, used esp. as decoration in upholstery

**rose her·mo·sa** \\,rōz(,)hər'mōsə, -z,her-\\ *n* [*hermosa* fr. Sp, fem. of *hermoso* beautiful, fr. L *formosus* — more at FORMOSITY] **:** a moderate pink that is yellower and darker than arbutus pink and deeper than chalk pink or hydrangea pink — called also *pink pearl*

**rose·hill** \\'rōz,hil\\ *or* **rose·hill·er** \\-lə(r)\\ *or* **rosehill parakeet** *n* [*rosehill* fr. *Rosehill*, district near Sydney, southeast Australia; *rosehiller* fr. *Rosehill* + E *-er; rosehill parakeet* fr. *Rosehill* + E *parakeet*] **:** ROSELLA

**rose hip** *or* **rose haw** *n* **:** HIP

**rose hor·ten·sia** \\;⸗,hò(r)'ten(t)sēə, -nch(ē)ə\\ *n, often cap H* [²*rose* + NL *Hortensia* (syn. of *Hydrangea*), fr. *Hortense* van Nassau, sister of Prince Charles Henri Nicolas Othon de Nassau-Siegen †1808 military adventurer who in French service accompanied Bougainville in his voyage around the world (1766–69) + NL *-ia*] **:** a light reddish brown that is redder, lighter, and slightly stronger than copper tan and lighter than monkey skin — called also *rose bisque*

**ros·el** \\'räzəl\\ *n* -s [ME *rosell, rosyle*, alter. of *rosin, rosine* rosin] *dial Eng* **:** RESIN

**rose lake** *n* **:** a dark reddish orange that is yellower and duller than average lacquer red and redder and darker than burnt sienna or ocher red

**rose lashing** *n* **:** a lashing made by passing the parts alternately over and under and finished by securing the hauling parts over the crossing — called also *rose seizing*

rose lashing

**rose lathe** *n* **:** a lathe provided with a rose engine

**rose laurel** *n* **1 :** OLEANDER **2 :** BIG LAUREL

**roseleaf** \\'⸗,⸗\\ *n* **:** a moderate pink that is yellower and darker than arbutus pink and deeper than hydrangea pink

**rose leafhopper** *n* **:** a cicadellid bug (*Edwardsiana rosae*) native to Europe but now widespread in No. America that is a general plant feeder and is esp. injurious to roses and apples

**rose·less** \\'rōzləs\\ *adj* **:** lacking a rose

**roselike** \\'⸗,⸗\\ *adj* **:** resembling a rose

**ro·se·lite** \\'rōzə,līt\\ *n* -s [Gustav *Rose* †1873 Ger. mineralogist + E *-lite*] **:** a mineral $(Ca,Co,Mg)_3(AsO_4)_2.2H_2O$ consisting of a rose-red arsenate of calcium, cobalt, and manganese in small triclinic crystals

**ro·sel·la** \\rō'zelə\\ *n* -s [irreg. fr. *Rosehill*, district near Sydney, southeast Australia] **1 :** an Australian parrakeet (*Platycercus eximius*) often kept as a cage bird having the head and back of the neck scarlet and the cheeks white, the back dark green varied with lighter green, and the breast red and yellow; *broadly* **:** any parrakeet of the genus *Platycercus* **2** *Austral* **:** a sheep that has shed a portion of its wool

**ro·selle** \\rō'zel\\ *also* **ro·sel·la** \\-lə\\ *or* **ro·zelle** \\-l\\ *n, pl* **roselles** *also* **rosellas** *or* **rozelles** [origin unknown] **1 :** an East Indian annual herb (*Hibiscus sabdariffa*) cultivated for its fleshy calyxes that are used for making tarts and jelly and an acid drink and for its bast fiber that is used as a substitute for hemp **2 :** the fiber from the roselle

**ros·el·lin·ia** \\,räsə'linēə, -äzə-\\ *n, cap* [NL, fr. Ferdinando P. *Rosellini*, 19th cent. Ital. botanist + NL *-ia*] **:** a genus of fungi (family Xylariaceae) having smooth perithecia with dark one-celled ascospores

**rose madder** *n* **1 :** MADDER ROSE **2 :** a pale rose pigment made now usu. from alizarin and hydrated alumina — compare MADDER LAKE 2b

**rose mahogany** *n* **:** AUSTRALIAN ROSEWOOD 2

**ro·se·ma·ling** \\'rōzə,mäliŋ\\ *n* -s [Norw, fr. *rose* (fr. ON *rōs, rōsa*, fr. L *rosa*) + *maling* painting, fr. *male* to paint, fr. MLG *mālen;* akin to OHG *mālēn, mālōn* to paint, ON *mæla* to paint, Goth *meljan* to write, Gk *melas* black — more at ROSE, MULLET] **:** painted or carved decoration (as on furniture, walls, or wooden dinnerware) in Scandinavian peasant style that consists of colorful floral and other designs and inscriptions

**rose mallow** *n* **1 :** any of several plants of the genus *Hibiscus* with large rose-colored flowers; *esp* **:** a showy plant (*H. moscheutos*) of salt marshes of the eastern U.S. **2 :** HOLLYHOCK

**rose malmaison** *n* **:** MALMAISON ROSE

**rose mandarin** *n* **:** a twisted-stalk (*Streptopus roseus*) of eastern No. America with rosy purple flowers

**rose ma·rie** \\,rōzmə'rē\\ *n, often cap M* [prob. fr. the name *Marie*] **:** a deep pink that is bluer and lighter than average coral (sense 3b) and bluer and less strong than fiesta or begonia

**rose·mary** \\'rōz,merē, -,mər-\\ *n* -ES [ME, by folk etymology (influence of ME ²*rose* and of the name *Mary*) fr. *rosmarine*, fr. L *rosmarinus*, fr. *ror-, ros* dew + *marinus* of the sea; akin to Gk *exeran* to pour out, Skt *rasa* juice, ON *rās* race, course — more at RACE, MARINE] **1 :** a fragrant shrubby mint (*Rosmarinus officinalis*) of southern Europe and Asia Minor that has a warm pungent bitterish taste and is used as a culinary herb and in perfumery **2 :** COSTMARY

**rosemary oil** *n* **:** a pungent essential oil obtained from the flowering tops of rosemary and used chiefly in soaps, colognes, hair lotions, and pharmaceutical preparations

**rosemary pine** *n* **1 :** any of three common pines of the southeastern U.S. with fine-grained wood: **a :** LOBLOLLY PINE 1 **b :** LONGLEAF PINE **c :** SHORTLEAF PINE **2 :** lumber from a rosemary pine

**rose mauve** *n* **:** a variable color averaging a grayish purple that is redder and deeper than telegraph blue, mauve gray, or average orchid gray

**rose midge** *n* **:** a minute brownish gall midge (*Dasyneura rhodophaga*) whose larvae develop in the flower buds of roses

**rose mildew** *n* **:** a powdery mildew (*Sphaerotheca pannosa*) common on the foliage of cultivated roses

**rose mill** *n* **:** a milling cutter with a rounded cutting edge

**rose mist** *n* **:** a grayish to moderate pink

**rose mon·tée** \\,rōzmän·'tā\\ *n* [*montée* fr. F, fem. of *monté* mounted, set, past part. of *monter* to mount — more at MOUNT] **:** a doublet of paste

**rose morn** *n* **:** PEACH BLOOM

**rose moss** *n* **:** a portulaca (*Portulaca grandiflora*)

**rose nail** *n* **:** ROSEHEAD NAIL

**ro·sen·ber·gia** \\,rōz°n'bərgēə, -rjēə\\ [NL, perh. fr. Caroline *Rosenberg* †1902 Dan. amateur botanist + NL *-ia*] *syn of* COBAEA

**ro·sen·busch·ite** \\'rōz°n,bü,shīt\\ *n* -s [Norw *rosenbuschit*, fr. Harry *Rosenbusch* †1914 Ger. geologist + Norw *-it* -ite] **:** a mineral $(Ca,Na)_3(Zr,Ti)Si_2O_8F$ consisting of a silicate and fluoride of zirconium, titanium, sodium, and calcium

**rose ney·ron** \\,rōz,nā'rō°\\ *n, often cap N* [*neyron* perh. fr. F, variety of grape] **:** a strong red to purplish red that is lighter and stronger than spinel red

**rose nils·son** \\rōz'nilsən *also* -lts-\\ *n, often cap N* [perh. after Christine *Nilsson* †1921 Swed. soprano] **:** a deep pink that is bluer, lighter, and stronger than average coral (sense 3b) and bluer and deeper than fiesta or begonia

**rose noble** *n* [ME, fr. ²*rose* + *noble*, n.] **:** RYAL 1

**rose nude** *n* **:** a grayish yellowish pink to brownish pink

**roseo-** *comb form* [ISV, fr. L *roseus* rosy — more at ROSEAL] — specif. in names of rose-red coordination complexes (as of cobalt or chromium) containing five molecules of ammonia and one of water and also of analogous usu. yellow complexes of chromium ⟨*roseo*cobaltic chloride $[Co(H_2O)(NH_3)_5]Cl_3$⟩

**rose of china** *usu cap C* **:** CHINA ROSE 2

**rose of heaven :** an annual herb (*Lychnis coeli-rosa*) of the Mediterranean region that is cultivated for its rose-purple flowers

**rose of jer·i·cho** \\-'jerə,kō\\ *usu cap J* [ME, fr. *Jericho*, ancient city in Palestine north of the Dead sea] **1 :** an Asiatic plant (*Anastatica hierochuntica*) that rolls up when dry and expands when moistened — called also *resurrection plant* **2 :** a xerophytic plant (*Odontospermum pygmaeum*) of the family Compositae with an involucre that closes firmly over the flower when dry

**rose of shar·on** \\-'sha(a)rən, -'sher-,-'shār-\\ *n, usu cap S* [Plain of *Sharon*, coastal plain in western Palestine] **1 :** a showy flowering plant mentioned in the Bible and commonly considered to have been a tulip, narcissus, or meadow saffron **2 :** a Eurasian St.-John's-wort (*Hypericum calycinum*) often cultivated for its large yellow flowers **3 :** a commonly cultivated Asiatic shrub or small shrubby tree (*Hibiscus syriacus*) having mostly 3-lobed leaves and showy bell-shaped rose, purple, or white flowers

**rose oil** *n* **:** a fragrant essential oil obtained from roses and used chiefly in perfumery and in flavoring; *esp* **:** ATTAR OF ROSES

**ro·se·o·la** \\rō'zēələ\\ *n* -s [NL, fr. L *roseus* rosy — more at ROSEAL] **1 :** a rose-colored eruption in spots; *specif* **:** RUBELLA **2** *or* **roseola in·fan·tum** \\-lə·in'fantəm\\ [NL *roseola infantum*, lit., roseola of infants] **:** a mild disease of infants and children characterized by fever lasting three days followed by an eruption of rose-colored spots — **ro·se·o·lar** \\-lə(r)\\ *adj*

**rose parrakeet** *n* **:** ROSELLA 1

**rose pastor** *or* **rose starling** *also* **rose ouzel** *n* **:** ROSE-COLORED STARLING

**rose–petty** \\'⸗,⸗⸗\\ *n* **:** ROBIN'S PLANTAIN

**rose pink** *n* [²*rose* + *pink*, n.] **1 :** an American centaury (*Sabbatia angularis*) **2 :** a variable color averaging a moderate pink that is bluer and deeper than hydrangea pink or arbutus pink and bluer, stronger, and slightly darker than chalk pink

**rose–pink** \\'⸗;⸗\\ *adj* [²*rose* + *pink*, adj.] **:** of the color rose pink

**rose plum** *n* **:** a variable color averaging a grayish purplish red that is bluer and paler than Aztec maroon and bluer and duller than tourmaline pink or daphne pink

**rose pogonia** *n* **:** SNAKEMOUTH

**rose point** *n* **:** needlepoint lace of Venetian origin made with rose designs in low relief connected by brides

**rose purple** *n* **:** a light reddish purple that is bluer and duller than crocus (sense 3b)

**rose quartz** *n* **:** a rose-red variety of quartz

**rose reamer** *n* **:** a straight reamer that cuts on its end only and is used esp. when considerable stock is to be removed

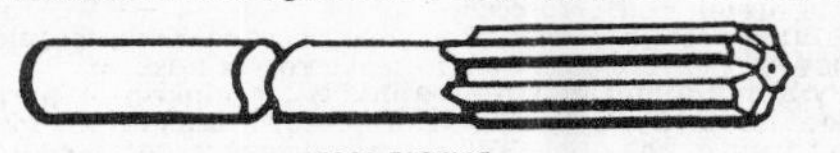

rose reamer

**rose re·cou·pé** \\-rə'küpā\\ *n* [*recoupé* fr. F, past part. of *recouper* to cut again, cut back — more at RECOUP] **:** a rose (as of a diamond or other gem) having 36 triangular facets — see ROSE illustration

**rose–red** \\'⸗;⸗\\ *adj* [ME *rose red*, fr. ²*rose* + *red*] **:** of the color rose red

**rose red** *n* [ME fr. *rose red* adj.] **:** a variable color averaging a deep red that is bluer, lighter, and stronger than cherry wine

**rose–ringed** \\'⸗;⸗\\ *adj* **:** having a red collar — used of the ring parrakeets

**roseroot** \\'⸗,⸗\\ *n* **:** a perennial fleshy herb (*Sedum rosea*) whose roots have the odor of roses

**rose rust** *n* **1 :** any of several rusts that attack roses: as **a :** a rust of the genus *Phragmidium* **b :** a rust of the genus *Earlea* **2 :** disease caused by a rose rust

**ros·ery** \\'rōz(ə)rē, -)ri\\ *n* -ES [²*rose* + *-ery*] **:** ROSARY 1

**rose ryal** *n* **:** a 30-shilling gold piece bearing the ryal design issued by James I of England

**roses** *pl of* ROSE, *pres 3d sing of* ROSE

**rosés** *pl of* ROSÉ

**rose sawfly** *n* **:** a sawfly injurious to roses: as **a :** an adult rose slug **b :** a similar European sawfly (*Hylotoma rosarum*)

**rose scale** *n* **:** a scale (*Aulacaspis rosae*) that is injurious to roses

**rose seizing** *n* **:** ROSE LASHING

**rose slug** *n* **:** either of two slimy green larval sawflies that feed on the parenchyma of and skeletonize the leaves of rosebushes: **a :** the bristly whitish green larva of a sawfly (*Cladius isomerus*) — called also *bristly rose slug* **b :** the velvety yellowish green larva of a sawfly (*Endelomyia aethiops*) that is native to Europe but now common in the eastern and central U. S.

**rose soirée** *n* **:** a deep pink that is bluer, lighter, and stronger than average coral (sense 3b), bluer and deeper than fiesta, and yellower and deeper than begonia

**rose star** *n* **:** a common usu. grayish shallow-water starfish (*Crossaster papposus*) of northern seas that is marked with two concentric rose-red bands

¹**ro·set** \\(')rō¦zet\\ *n* -s [ME, fr. MF *rosete, rosette*, lit., small rose, fr. OF — more at ROSETTE] **1** *obs* **:** a red color used by painters **2 :** BRAZIL 2

²**ros·et** \\'räzət\\ *n* -s [alter. of ME *rosin, rosine* rosin] *chiefly Scot* **:** RESIN

³**roset** \\"\\ *vt, Scot* **:** to rub with resin

**rose·tan** \\'rōz,tan, -taa(ə)n\\ *n* **:** PEARL BLUSH

**rosetangle** \\'⸗,⸗⸗\\ *n* **:** a red alga belonging to the Ceramiaceae or a related family — see CERAMIUM

**rose taupe** *n* **:** a variable color averaging a dark reddish gray that is stronger and slightly yellower and lighter than blue fox and yellower, lighter, and slightly stronger than average mauve taupe

**rose tree** *n* **:** TREE ROSE

**ro·set·ta stone** \\rō'ze|d·ə-, |tə-\\ *n, usu cap R* [*Rosetta stone*, stone found in 1799 that is celebrated for having furnished the first clue to the decipherment of Egyptian hieroglyphics since it bears an inscription in hieroglyphics, demotic characters, and Greek, fr. *Rosetta*, city in northern Egypt near which it was found] **:** something that furnishes the first clue to the decipherment of a previously incomprehensible system of ideas or state of affairs ⟨the book can be its own *Rosetta stone* and it is an interesting game to try to ferret out meanings by comparing passages till the puzzle is solved —Ellsworth Faris⟩

¹**ro·sette** \\(')rō¦zet, *usu* -ed·+V\\ *n* -s [F, lit., small rose, fr. OF *rosete, rosette*, fr. *rose* (fr. L *rosa*) + *-ete, -ette* -ette — more at ROSE] **1 :** a thin disk (as of copper) formed by chilling the surface of molten metal with water **2 :** an ornament resembling a rose usu. made of gathered or pleated material and worn as a badge of office, as evidence of having one of several decorations (as the Medal of Honor), or as trimming (as on a hat, shoe, or dress) **3 :** an ornamental disk consisting of leafage or a floral design usu. in relief used as a decorative motif — compare ROUNDEL **4 :** a structure or color marking on an animal suggestive of a rosette: as **a :** the group of five petal-shaped ambulacra on a spatangid or clypeastroid sea urchin **b :** one of the clusters of dark spots on the pelt of a leopard **5 :** a cluster of leaves developed in crowded circles or spirals from a crown either basally (as in a dandelion) or at the apex (as in many tropical palms) **6** *also* **rosette disease a** (1) **:** any of several plant diseases that are characterized by the grouping of the leaves in dense clusters and result from various causes (as the attack of fungi, virus infections, or nutritional disturbances) (2) **:** a symptom of rosette **b :** RHIZOCTONIA DISEASE **c :** a virus disease of the peanut characterized by yellowing of the leaves and extreme stunting **7 :** any of various fixtures: as **a :** ROSE 2g(1) **b :** an ornamental ring surrounding a cylinder lock **c :** an ornamental head for a screw used for fastening mirrors **d :** a ceiling device having terminals for connecting to an electric line and other terminals to which a drop cord may be attached **8 :** a small piece of boneless veal encircled by a bacon strip and skewered to be held flat for braising or frying **9 a :** an iron used with the handle of a timbale iron **b :** a pastry shell fried with a rosette

rosette 3

²**rosette** \\"\\ *vt* -ED/-ING/-S **1 :** to obtain in the form of rosettes by superficial chilling **2 :** to cause (the leaves of a plant) to form in dense clusters **3 :** to affect (a plant) with rosette

**rosette plate** *n* **:** one of the small perforated plates by which the zooecia of many marine bryozoans communicate

**ro·sett·er** \\rō'zed·ə(r)\\ *n* -s **:** one that ties ribbon bows on candy boxes

**rose water** *n* [ME, fr. ²*rose* + *water*] **:** a watery solution of the odoriferous constituents of the rose made by distilling the fresh flowers with water or steam and used as a perfume

**rosewater** *also* **rosewatered** \\'⸗,⸗⸗\\ *adj* [*rosewater* fr. *rose water; rosewatered* fr. *rose water* + *-ed*] **1 :** scented with or having the odor of rose water **2 :** affectedly nice or delicate **:** SENTIMENTAL ⟨it will take more than a ~ biography to cover up his throttling of the press, rough treatment of critics, army domination —Hubert Herring⟩

**rose water ointment** *n* **:** COLD CREAM

**rose weevil** *n* **:** a weevil (*Pantomorus godmani*) that destroys the leaves and flowers of the rose and other plants and whose larva feeds on the roots — called also *rose beetle*

**rose willow** *n* **1 :** any of several willows with purple or reddish twigs; *esp.* **:** PURPLE WILLOW **2 :** SILKY CORNEL

**rose window** *n* **:** a circular window filled with tracery — called also *rose;* compare WHEEL WINDOW

rose window

**rose wine** *n* **:** a variable color averaging a grayish red that is bluer and deeper than appleblossom, bois de rose, or Pompeian red

**rosewood** \\'⸗,⸗\\ *n* -s **1 a :** any of various tropical trees yielding valuable cabinet woods of a dark red or purplish color streaked and variegated with black: as (1) **:** BRAZILIAN ROSEWOOD (2) **:** HONDURAS ROSEWOOD — see AFRICAN ROSEWOOD, BLACKWOOD (3) **:** AMBOYNA **b :** the wood of a rosewood **2 a :** AUSTRALIAN ROSEWOOD **b :** a small Australian tree (*Heterodendron oleaefolium*) of the family Sapindaceae with very hard wood **c :** BASTARD ROSEWOOD **3 a :** a moderate reddish brown that is lighter and stronger than mahogany and yellower, lighter, and stronger than roan **b :** a light grayish reddish brown

**rosewood brown** *n* **:** a moderate reddish brown that is yellower and less strong than roan and yellower and paler than mahogany

**rosewood oil** *n* **1 :** RHODIUM OIL **2 :** BOIS DE ROSE OIL

**rosewood tan** *n* **:** a variable color averaging a light reddish brown to moderate reddish brown

**rose worm** *n* **:** the larva of a small brown tortricid moth (*Archips rosana*) that lives on the rose and various other plants, rolling up the leaves for a nest and devouring both the leaves and buds

**rosewort** \\'⸗,⸗\\ *n* **:** ROSEROOT

**ro·sha grass** \\'rōshə-\\ *n* [*rosha* fr. Hindi *rūsā*] **:** any of several Asiatic grasses of the genus *Cymbopogon* that yield pleasantly scented oils (esp. *C. martinii*)

**rosh ha·sha·nah** *or* **rosh ha·sha·na** *also* **rosh ha·sho·noh** \\,rōsh(h)ə'shōnə, ,rōsh-, ,räsh-, -'shōnə, -'shänə *also* ;r . . . sh-, ,häshə'nä\\ *n, cap R&H* [Mishnaic Heb *rōsh hashshānāh*, lit., beginning of the year] **:** Jewish New Year **:** NEW YEAR 2

**rosh ho·desh** \\⸗'kō,desh\\ *or* **rosh chodesh** *n, usu cap R&H&C* [Heb *rōsh ḥōdhesh*, lit., beginning of the new moon] **:** the beginning of each month in the Jewish calendar marked by a special liturgy

**ro·sic·ky·ite** \\rō'zitskē,īt\\ *n* -s [G *rosickýit*, fr. V. *Rosický*, 20th cent. Czechoslovak mineralogist + G *-it* -ite] **:** a mineral γ-S consisting of native sulfur in the gamma crystal form

**rosi·cru·cian** \\,rōzə'krüshən, ,räz-\\ *n* -s *usu cap, often attrib* [irreg. fr. NL Frater *Rosae Crucis* (latinization of the name of Christian *Rosenkreutz*, reputed 15th cent. founder of the secret Rosicrucian Society) + E *-an*] **1 :** one who claimed to belong to a secret society of philosophers in the 17th century and the early part of the 18th deeply versed in the secrets of nature **2 :** a member of one of several organizations held to be descended from the Rosicrucians and devoted to esoteric wisdom

**rosi·cru·cian·ism** \\-shə,nizəm\\ *n* -s *usu cap* **:** the principles, institutions, or practices of Rosicrucians

**rosied** *past of* ROSY

¹**rosier** *comparative of* ROSY

²**ro·sier** \\'rōzhər, rō'zi(ə)r\\ *n* -s [MF, rosebush, rose garden, fr. L *rosarium* rose garden — more at ROSARY] *archaic* **:** ROSEBUSH

**ro·si·er·e·site** \\,rōzē'erə,sīt\\ *n* -s [F *rosiérésite*, fr. *Rosières*, copper mine near Carmaux, southern France + F *-ite*] **:** a mineral consisting of a hydrous aluminum phosphate containing lead and copper and occurring in yellow to brown stalactitic masses (sp. gr. 2.2)

**rosies** *pres part of* ROSY

**rosiest** *superlative of* ROSY

**ro·silla** \\rō'zilə, -'silə, -'sē(y)ə\\ *n* -s [AmerSp] **1 :** a sneezeweed (*Helenium puberulum*) of southern California **2 :** a shrub or small tree (*Eysenhardtia polystachya*) of the family Leguminosae of Arizona and adjacent Mexico with small white flowers in long racemes — see NEPHRITIC WOOD

**ros·i·ly** \\'rōzəlē, -li\\ *adv* **1 :** with a rosy color or tinge **2 :** CHEERFULLY, PLEASANTLY

¹**ros·in** \\'räz°n *also* 'rōz-, *dial* 'rōzəm\\ *n* -s [ME *rosin, rosine*, modif. of MF *resine* resin] **:** a translucent pale yellow or amber to dark red or darker brittle friable resin that is obtained from the oleoresin or dead wood of pine trees by removal of the volatile turpentine or from tall oil by removal of the fatty acid components, that contains abietic acid and other resin acids as principal components, and that is used in the unmodified form, in modified form (as hydrogenated rosin or polymerized rosin), or in the form of a derivative (as a salt or ester) chiefly in making varnishes, lacquers, printing inks, driers, sizes for paper, and soaps, in adhesives, binding materials, soldering fluxes, and polishes, and for rosining bows for violins and other string instruments — called also *colophony;* see GUM ROSIN, WOOD ROSIN

²**rosin** \\"\\ *vt* **rosined; rosined; rosining** \\-z(°)niŋ, *dial* -zəmiŋ\\ **rosins** [ME *rosinen*, fr. *rosin, rosine*, n.] **1 :** to rub with rosin (as the bow of a violin) **2 :** to add rosin in some form to (as soap)

**ros·i·nan·te** \\,räz°n'antē, ,rōz-\\ *n* -s [after *Rocinante*, Don Quixote's bony horse in the novel *Don Quixote* by Miguel de Cervantes Saavedra †1616 Span. novelist] **:** a broken-down horse **:** NAG

**ros·in·ate** \'räzᵊnət, -ᵊn,āt *also* 'röz-\ *n* -s [1*rosin* + *-ate*] **:** a salt or ester or mixture of salts and esters prepared from rosin **:** RESINATE ⟨copper ~⟩

**rosinback** \'==,=\ *n* **:** a circus horse with a broad level back ridden by bareback riders and acrobats

**rosin brush** *n* **:** GREASEWOOD

**rosin cerate** *n* **:** BASILICON OINTMENT

**ros·i·ness** \'rōzēnəs, -zin-\ *n* -ES **:** the quality or state of being rosy: **a :** a rosy color or complexion **b :** a cheerful appearance or outlook ⟨there is a kind of musical-comedy bounce and ~ about the good-natured score —Douglas Watt⟩

**rosin ester** *n* **:** an ester or mixture of esters of the acid components of rosin; *esp* **:** ESTER GUM

**rosing** *pres part of* ROSE

**rosin oil** *n* **:** an oily liquid obtained by destructive distillation of rosin and composed principally of hydrocarbons with some resin acids; *esp* **:** the viscous fraction that boils higher than rosin spirit, that when crude is dark-colored and fluorescent and has a sharp odor, and that is used chiefly in making lubricating greases and printing inks, in impregnating paper coverings for electric cables, and in compounding with other oils

**ros·in·ous** \'räzᵊnəs *also* 'röz-\ *adj* **:** containing or resembling rosin

**rosin plant** *n* **:** ROSINWEED

**rosin rose** *n* **:** KLAMATH WEED

**rosin soap** *n* **1** *or* **rosined soap :** soap (as yellow soap) made from rosin as well as fat **2 a :** a resin soap made from rosin **b :** DISPROPORTIONATED ROSIN

**rosin spirit** *n, pl* **rosin spirits** *but sing or pl in constr* **:** a volatile liquid that is obtained as the first fraction in the destructive distillation of rosin, that has a sharp odor before refining, and that is used chiefly as a thinner for varnish and wood stains and as an adulterant of turpentine

**rosinweed** \'==,=\ *n* **:** any of various American plants having resinous foliage or a resinous odor: as **a :** COMPASS PLANT a **b :** GUMWEED **c :** a golden aster (*Chrysopsis villosa*) of western No. America **d :** PRAIRIE DOCK 1

**rosinwood** \'==,=\ *n* **:** ROSINWEED c

**ros·iny** \'räzᵊnē *also* 'röz-\ *adj* **:** abounding in, resembling, or having the odor of rosin

**ros·kopf** \'rä,skäpf\ *n* -s *usu cap* [after G. F. *Roskopf* †1889 Swiss watchmaker] **:** a watch with a barrel whose diameter is greater than the radius of the watch

**ros·lyn blue** \'räzlən-\ *n, often cap R* [perh. fr. the name *Roslyn*] **:** MAZARINE BLUE

**rosmarine** *n* -s [ME — more at ROSEMARY] *obs* **:** ROSEMARY

1**ros·mini·an** \(')räz¦minēən, -mēn-\ *adj, usu cap* [ISV *rosmini-* (fr. Antonio *Rosmini*-Serbati †1855 Ital. philosopher and founder of the Institute of Charity) + *-an*, adj. suffix] **:** of or relating to Antonio Rosmini-Serbati or his doctrines

2**rosminian** \"\ *n* -s *usu cap* [ISV *rosmini-* (fr. Antonio *Rosmini*-Serbati) + *-an*, n. suffix] **1 :** an adherent of Rosminianism **2 :** a member of the congregation of the Institute of Charity of the Roman Catholic Church

**ros·mini·an·ism** \-ēə,nizəm\ *n* -s *usu cap* **:** the philosophy of the Rosminian teaching that the idea of being is innate and that through it true knowledge is made possible

**ro·solic acid** \(')rō¦zälik-, -zōlik-\ *n* [*rosolic* fr. G *rosol-* (in *rosolsäure* rosolic acid) (fr. *ros-* — fr. L *rosa* rose — + *-ol-* — fr. L *oleum* oil) + E *-ic* — more at ROSE, OIL] **:** either of two phenolic quinonoid derivatives of triphenylmethane: **a :** a crystalline compound that is red by transmitted light, that is made usu. from a mixture of phenol and *ortho*-cresol or from rosaniline, and that differs from aurin in containing one or possibly two methyl groups — called also *coralline* **b :** AURIN

**ro·so·lio** *also* **ro·so·glio** \rō'zōlē,ō, -ōl(,)yō\ *n* -s [It *rosolio*, prob. fr. ML *ros solis* sundew, fr. L *ros* dew + *solis*, gen. of *sol* sun — more at ROSEMARY, SOLAR] **:** a cordial made from spirits and sugar flavored variously (as with petals of roses, orange blossom water, cinnamon, or cloves)

**ro·so·lite** \'rōzə,līt\ *n* -s [2*rose* + *-o-* + *-lite*] **:** a pink variety of garnet

**ro·so·ri·al** \rō'zōrēəl, -'sō-\ *adj* [NL *Rosores* (syn. of *Rodentia*) (fr. LL, pl. of *rosor* gnawer, fr. L *rosus* — past part. of *rodere* to gnaw — + *-or*) + E *-ial* — more at RAT] **:** of or relating to the rodents **:** GNAWING

1**ross** \'rȯs *also* 'räs\ *n* -ES [origin unknown] **:** the rough often scaly exterior of bark

2**ross** \"\ *vt* -ED/-ING/-ES **:** to remove the ross from

**ross·er** \-sə(r)\ *n* -s **:** one that rosses: **a :** a logger who peels the bark and smooths the wood on one side of logs so they can be dragged more easily — called also *barker, scalper, slipper* **b :** one who peels bark from pulpwood to save wood that would be wasted if peeling were done by machine **c :** PEELER 1b **d** (1) **:** an attachment for a circular saw to remove scaly and gritty bark ahead of the kerf (2) **:** a machine for removing bark from pulpwood

**rossi-forel scale** *n, usu cap R&F* \¦rȯ|sēfə'rel-, ¦rä|\ [after Michele Stefano De *Rossi* †1898 Ital. geologist and François Alphonse *Forel* †1912 Swiss naturalist] **:** an arbitrary numerical scale of intensity of seismic disturbances ranging from one for a barely perceptible tremor to 10 for an earthquake of the highest intensity

**ross·ite** \'rȯ,sīt\ *n* -s [Clarence S. *Ross* *b*1880 Am. geologist + E *-ite*] **:** a rare mineral $CaV_2O_6·4H_2O$ consisting of a hydrous calcium vanadate

**ros·so an·ti·co** \¦rō(,)sō,an·'tē(,)kō, ¦rȯ(-, ¦rä(-, -sō,än·-\ *n* [It] **1 a :** a deep red Grecian marble used esp. by the ancient Romans **b :** a porphyritic diorite used esp. by the ancient Egyptians and Romans **2 :** a hard red unglazed Wedgwood stoneware resembling boccaro

**ross's goose** \,rȯ|səz- *also* ,rä|\ *n, usu cap R* [after Bernard R. *Ross* †1874 Irish fur trader] **:** a very small white goose (*Chen rossii*) that breeds in arctic America and migrates through western No. America

**ross's gull** *n, usu cap R* [after Sir James Clark *Ross* †1862 Scot. polar explorer] **:** a small rare gull (*Rhodostethia rosea*) of the far north having the tail wedge-shaped and the lower parts rosy when in full plumage

**ross's seal** *n, usu cap R* [after Sir James Clark *Ross*] **:** an antarctic seal (*Ommatophoca rossi*) having but two upper incisors, very small teeth, small claws on the forefeet, and none on the hind feet

**rost** *obs var of* ROAST

**ros·tel·lar** \(')rä¦stelə(r)\ *adj* [*rostell*um + *-ar*] **:** of, relating to, or having the form of a rostellum

**ros·tel·late** \'rästə,lāt, (')rä¦stelət\ *adj* [prob. fr. (assumed) NL *rostellatus*, fr. NL *rostellum* + L *-atus* -ate] **:** having a rostellum

**ros·tel·li·form** \rä'stelə,fȯrm\ *adj* [*rostell*um + *-iform*] **:** shaped like a rostellum

**ros·tel·lum** \rä'steləm\ *n* -s [NL, fr. L, small beak, small snout, dim. of *rostrum* beak — more at ROSTRUM] **1 a :** a small process resembling a beak **:** a diminutive rostrum **b :** the apex of the gynaecium of an orchid flower that resembles a beak **2 a** (1) **:** the sucking beak of a louse (2) **:** the beak of a hemipteran **b :** an anterior prolongation of the head of a tapeworm bearing hooks — see ECHINOCOCCUS illustration

1**ros·ter** \'rästə(r) *sometimes* 'rȯs- *or* 'rōs-\ *n* -s [D *rooster* list, gridiron, fr. MD, gridiron, fr. *roosten* to roast + *-er;* fr. the parallel lines — more at ROAST] **1 :** a roll or list of officers or enlisted men; *esp* **:** a list which gives the order in which units or individuals are due to perform a prescribed duty ⟨guard ~⟩ **2 :** an itemized listing of a group or collection ⟨membership ~⟩ ⟨the season's ~ of new music by world-famous foreign masters —Virgil Thomson⟩

2**roster** \"\ *vt* -ED/-ING/-S **:** to list in a roster

**ros·tock** \'rä,stäk, 'rȯ,stȯk\ *adj, usu cap* [fr. *Rostock*, city in northern Germany] **:** of or from the city of Rostock, Germany **:** of the kind or style prevalent in Rostock

**ros·tov** \rə'stä|f, (')rä¦s-, -tȯ|, |v\ *adj, usu cap* [fr. *Rostov*-on-Don, city in the southeastern part of European Russia, U.S.S.R.] **:** of or from Rostov-on-Don, U.S.S.R. **:** of the kind or style prevalent in Rostov-on-Don

**rostr-** *or* **rostri-** *or* **rostro-** *comb form* [L *rostr-*, fr. *rostrum*] **1 :** beak **:** rostrum ⟨*rostr*ad⟩ ⟨*rostri*form⟩ **2 :** rostral and ⟨*rostro*lateral⟩

**ros·trad** \'rä,strad\ *adv* [*rostr-* + *-ad*] **:** toward a rostrum

1**ros·tral** \-‗strəl\ *adj* [NL *rostralis*, fr. L *rostrum* beak, ship's beak + *-alis* -al] **1 :** of or relating to a rostrum; *specif* **:** of, relating to, or being a scale or plate bordering the median part of the upper lip in some reptiles **2 :** adorned with rostra ⟨~ pillar⟩ **3 a** *of a part of the spinal cord* **:** SUPERIOR **b** *of a part of the brain* **:** anterior or ventral — **ros·tral·ly** \-əlē\ *adv*

2**rostral** \"\ *n* -s **:** a rostral plate or shield

**rostral column** *n* **:** a memorial column commemorating esp. a naval victory

**rostral crown** *n* **:** NAVAL CROWN 1

**ros·tralis** \rä'straləs, -strāl-,-sträl-\ *n* -ES [NL, fr. *rostralis*, adj., rostral] **:** the suctorial organ of a bug or related insect (order Hemiptera) consisting of the elongated and closely associated mandibles and maxillae

**ros·trate** \'rä,strāt, -‗strət\ *adj* [L *rostratus*, fr. *rostrum* + *-atus* -ate] **:** having a rostrum

**ros·trat·ed** \-,strād·əd\ *adj* [*rostrate* + *-ed*] **1 :** ROSTRATE **2 :** ROSTRAL 2

1**ros·tro·carinate** \¦rä(,)strō+\ *adj* [*rostr-* + *carinate*] **:** of, relating to, or constituting a chipped flint artifact shaped somewhat like an eagle's beak and found in eastern England

2**rostrocarinate** \"\ *n* -s **:** a rostrocarinate artifact

**ros·tru·lar** \'rästrələ(r)\ *adj* [*rostrul*um + *-ar*] **:** of or relating to a rostrulum

**ros·tru·lum** \-ləm\ *n, pl* **rostru·la** \-lə\ [NL, fr. L *rostrum* beak + *-ulum*] **:** a small rostrum; *specif* **:** the proboscis of a flea

**ros·trum** \'rästrəm *sometimes* 'rȯs-\ *n, pl* **rostrums** \-trəmz\ *or* **ros·tra** \-trə\ [L *rostrum* muzzle, beak, ship's beak, & L *Rostra* (fr. pl. of *rostrum*) platform for speakers in the Forum of ancient Rome decorated with the beaks of ships captured in war, fr. *rodere* to gnaw — more at RAT] **1 a** *usu rostra pl but sing in constr* **:** any of various ancient Roman platforms for public orators **b :** a stage for public speaking **:** a pulpit or platform occupied by an orator or public speaker **c :** a raised platform; *specif* **:** one upon the stage of a theater usu. with a removable top and hinged sides for flat storage and often reached by stairs or a ramp **2 :** the curved often ornamental end of a ship's prow; *esp* **:** the beak or ram of a war galley — compare ACROTERION **3 :** a part suggesting a bird's bill: as **a :** the beak, snout, or proboscis of any of various insects and arachnids **b :** the often spinelike anterior median prolongation of the carapace of a crustacean (as a lobster) **c :** the snout of a gastropod mollusk when nonretractile **d :** the grooved extension of any of many gastropod shells protecting the siphon **e :** GUARD 7c **f :** the interior median spine of the body of the basisphenoid bone articulating with the vomer **g :** the reflected anterior portion of the corpus callosum below the genu **h :** a differentiated scale forming the snout of snakes **i :** the anterior projecting element in the chondrocranium of elasmobranch fishes **4 :** a process or prolongation resembling a beak; *specif* **:** one of the inner segments of the corolla of a milkweed

**rosu·late** \'rōzələt, 'räz-\ *adj* [LL *rosula* small rose (fr. L *rosa* rose + *-ula*) + E -ate — more at ROSE] **:** arranged in the form of a rosette or in rosettes

1**rosy** \'rōzē, -zi\ *adj* -ER/-EST [ME, fr. 2*rose* + *-y*] **1 a** (1) **:** of the color rose (2) **:** having a rose-colored complexion **:** HEALTHY, BLOOMING (3) **:** suffused with blushes **:** BLUSHING **b :** perfumed with or as if with roses **c** *obs* **:** abounding in or adorned with roses **2 :** characterized by or tending to promote optimism ⟨the individual episodes are uneven in quality, but all are enveloped in a ~ romanticism —John Barkham⟩ ⟨the ~ era when men thought physical science would soon make Earth so pleasant that Heaven would no longer be desired —Webb Garrison⟩ ⟨big businessmen made their usual yearly forecasts, all of them ~ —T.W.Arnold⟩ — often used in combination ⟨*rosy*-cheeked⟩ ⟨*rosy*-fingered⟩

2**rosy** \"\ *vt* -ED/-ING/-ES **:** to make rosy **:** ROSE

**rosy apple aphid** *also* **rosy aphid** *n* **:** a pinkish or purplish plant louse (*Dysaphis plantaginea*) which feeds on the foliage and fruit of the apple and whose summer generations occur on plantain

**rosy barb** *n* **:** a small silvery green Indian cyprinid fish (*Barbus conchonius*) the male of which becomes flushed with rose during the breeding season and which is a favorite in tropical aquariums

**rosy bush** *n* **:** HARDHACK 1

**rosy finch** *n* **:** any of several finches of western No. America and eastern Asia constituting the genus *Leucosticte* and having chiefly brownish plumage suffused in the adult with rose or white on the upper tail coverts

**rosy gull** *n* **:** ROSS'S GULL

1**rot** \'rät, *usu* -äd·+V\ *vb* **rotted; rotted; rotting; rots** [ME *roten, rotien*, fr. OE *rotian;* akin to OHG *rōzzēn* to rot, ON *rotna* to rot, L *rudus* rubble, broken stone — more at RUDE] *vi* **1 a :** to undergo natural decomposition **:** decay as a result of the action of bacteria or fungi ⟨causes the bones to ~⟩ ⟨*rotting* wood⟩ **b :** to become unsound or weak (as from extended use or chemical action) ⟨the rich silk damasks . . . were the first to ~ away —Sheila O'Callaghan⟩ ⟨ships *rotting* in the harbor⟩ ⟨*rotting* ice⟩ **2 a :** to go to ruin **:** DETERIORATE ⟨sent to die on some jungle island . . . or to ~ there month after month —Irwin Shaw⟩ ⟨~ in jail⟩ **b :** to become morally corrupt **:** DEGENERATE ⟨a civilization that *rotted* and disappeared⟩ **3 :** to suffer from rot — used esp. of a plant **4** *chiefly Brit* **:** to talk nonsense **:** JOKE ⟨I know I did, silly, but I was only *rotting* —*Strand Mag.*⟩ **~** *vt* **1 :** to cause to decompose ⟨the heavy rains *rotted* the wheat⟩ ⟨dampness had *rotted* spots of the plaster —Marcia Davenport⟩ **2 :** to affect (as sheep) with rot **3 :** to cause to deteriorate **:** CORRUPT ⟨infected with the same decay as had *rotted* other great civilizations of the past —F.H.Cramer⟩ **4 :** to expose (as flax) to a process of maceration for the purpose of separating the fiber **:** RET **5** *chiefly Brit* **:** to make fun of **:** TEASE ⟨all felt that the family was being *rotted* —John Galsworthy⟩ **syn** see DECAY

2**rot** \"\ *n* -s [ME, of Scand origin; akin to Icel *rot;* akin to ON *rotna* to rot] **1 a :** the process of rotting or state of being rotten **:** DECAY, PUTREFACTION ⟨the ~ begins as soon as the fish are killed⟩ **b :** something that is rotten or rotting ⟨the moist ferny odors, the ~ and ordure . . . filled their senses —Norman Mailer⟩ **2 a** *archaic* **:** a wasting putrescent disease in people ⟨then the ~ returns to thine own lips again —Shak.⟩ **b :** any of several parasitic diseases that chiefly attack sheep and are characterized by tissue necrosis and progressive emaciation; *specif* **:** LIVER ROT **3 a :** social or spiritual deterioration or corruption ⟨the creeping ~ of the society to which he belonged —*Times Lit. Supp.*⟩ **b :** confusion or disorder esp. in a government organization ⟨organize the affairs of . . . the little state and stop the financial ~ —Stephen Spender⟩ **4 :** breakdown or decay of plant tissues caused esp. by fungi or bacteria — see BITTER ROT, BLACK ROT, DRY ROT **5 :** NONSENSE ⟨talked ~ about getting on in the world —A.H. Hawkins⟩ — often used interjectionally to express disbelief or disgust **6 :** the falling of several cricket wickets in quick succession

**rot** *abbr* **1** rotary **2** rotating; rotation **3** rotten

1**ro·ta** \'rōd·ə\ *n* -s [L, wheel — more at ROLL] **1** *chiefly Brit* **a :** a fixed order of rotation (as of persons or duties) **b :** a roll or list of persons **:** ROSTER **2** *usu cap* [ML, fr. L] **:** a tribunal of the Roman Catholic curia consisting of ten auditors exercising jurisdiction usu. of an appellate nature esp. in matrimonial cases appealed from diocesan courts **3 :** a round or other musical composition with frequent repeats or refrains

2**rota** \"\ *n* -s [ML — more at ROTE] **:** HURDY-GURDY

3**rota** *var of* ROTE

**rotacism** *var of* RHOTACISM

**ro·tal** \'rōd·ᵊl\ *adj* [LL *rotalis* wheeled, fr. L *rota* + *-alis* -al] **1 a :** of or relating to wheels **b :** of or relating to rotary motion **:** ROTARY **2** [NL *rotalis*, fr. LL] **:** of or relating to the Rota

**ro·ta·la** \rō'talə, -tälə\ *n, cap* [NL, irreg. fr. LL *rotalis*] **:** a genus of annual weedy herbs (family Lythraceae) with 4-angled stems, opposite or whorled leaves, and small, axillary, and mostly solitary flowers — see TOOTHCUP

**ro·ta·lia** \rō'tālēə\ *n, cap* [NL, fr. LL *rotalis* + NL *-ia*] **:** a genus of foraminiferans having a finely perforated test with the segments in a turbinoid spiral and with septa composed of two lamellae between which are anastomosing canals — **ro·ta·li·an** \-lēən\ *adj or n* — **ro·ta·li·form** \-lə,fȯrm\ *or* **ro·ta·li·iform** \-lēə,fȯrm\ *adj*

**ro·tame·ter** \'rōd·ə,mēd·ə(r), rō'taməd·-\ *n* [L *rota* wheel + E *-meter*] **1 :** an instrument for measuring curved lines by running over them a small wheel connected with a recording dial — compare ODOMETER, OPISOMETER **2 :** a gage that consists of a graduated glass tube containing a free float for measuring the flow of a liquid or a gas

**rotan** *var of* RATTAN

**ro·tar·i·an** \rō'terēən, -ta(a)r-, -tār-\ *n* -s *usu cap* [*Rotary* (*club*) + E *-an*] **:** a member of one of the major service clubs

**ro·tar·i·an·ism** \-ēə,nizəm\ *n* -s *usu cap* **:** the principles or practices of Rotarians

1**ro·ta·ry** \'rōd·ərē, -ōtə-, -əri *sometimes* -ō,ter-\ *adj* [ML *rotarius*, fr. L *rota* wheel + *-arius* -ary — more at ROLL] **1 a :** of, relating to, or resembling a wheel turning on its axis ⟨~ blades⟩ **b :** resembling the motion of a rotating body ⟨~ motion⟩ ⟨~ movement⟩ — compare ROTATIONAL, ROTATORY **2 :** having an important part that turns on an axis ⟨~ cutter⟩ **3 :** characterized by rotation of persons ⟨employment . . . under a ~ hiring system —Stanley Levey⟩ **4 :** produced by or used in a rotary press ⟨~ gravure⟩ ⟨~ printing⟩ ⟨~ plates⟩

2**rotary** \"\ *n* -ES **1 :** a rotary machine: as **a :** ROTARY PRESS **b :** a rig for drilling a well by the rotary method **c :** a drill-pipe turntable and the mechanical assembly for supporting and rotating it **d** *or* **rotary converter :** SYNCHRONOUS CONVERTER **2** *also* **rotary intersection :** a road junction formed around a central more or less circular plot about which traffic moves in one direction only — called also *circle, traffic circle*

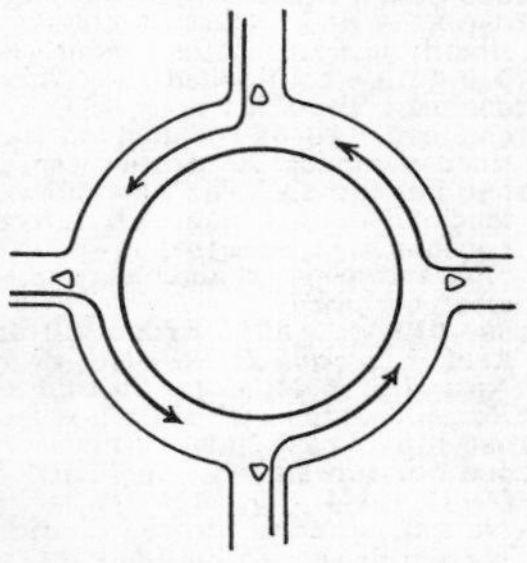

rotary 2

**rotary beater** *n* **:** a beater having single or double metal blades that rotate when a geared wheel with which they are meshed is operated by hand; *specif* **:** EGGBEATER

**rotary blower** *n* **:** a machine for producing artificial draft by centrifugal force of rotating vanes

**rotary bridge crane** *n* **:** a bridge crane that has one end of the beam or bridge pivoted and the other running on a circular track

**rotary condenser** *n* **:** SYNCHRONOUS CONDENSER

**rotary cultivator** *n* **:** a cultivator having blades or claws that revolve rapidly

**rotary-cut** \¦===¦=\ *adj* **:** spirally sliced from a log with a rotary lathe ⟨*rotary-cut* veneers⟩

**rotary discard** *n* **:** a discard from a suit in bridge or whist to denote strength in the suit next in rank (as the discard of a heart to show strength in spades)

**rotary drill** *n* **:** a rock drill that bores by a rotary action

**rotary engine** *n* **1 :** any of various engines (as a turbine) in which power is applied to vanes, disks having buckets, or similar parts constrained to move in a circular path **2 :** a radial engine in which the cylinders revolve about a stationary crankshaft

**rotary fault** *n* **:** a fracture in the earth's crust in which the displacement of rock is downward at one point and upward at another point along the strike — called also *pivotal fault*

**rotary file** *n* **:** a file of cylindrical or modified cylindrical form that is given a rotating rather than a reciprocating motion

**rotary gap** *or* **rotary spark gap** *n* **:** a spark gap in which one of the electrodes rotates thereby causing a regular change in gap length and timing the condenser discharge

**rotary hoe** *n* **:** an implement consisting essentially of a series of rotating hoe wheels each having many sharp curved steel prongs

**rotary kiln** *n* **:** a rotated cylinder lined with refractory and slightly inclined axially for manufacture of cement, gypsum plaster, and lime

**rotary microtome** *n* **:** a microtome in which the object to be cut moves vertically downward against the knife — compare SLIDING MICROTOME

**rotary milling machine** *n* **:** a milling machine having a rotary table and one or more cutters

**rotary planer** *n* **:** a machine for milling plane surfaces on large work by moving the work secured to the table of the machine past a revolving cutter

**rotary plow** *n* **1 :** a plow having a rotating propeller-shaped element for throwing snow aside **2 :** a rotary tiller **:** a plow with rapidly revolving blades or hooked fingers

**rotary press** *n* **:** a press in which paper carried by an impression cylinder is printed by rotation in contact with a curved printing surface attached to a plate cylinder or (as in photo-offset) a blanket cylinder — compare CYLINDER PRESS, PLATEN PRESS

**rotary pump** *n* **:** a valveless pump in which the fluid is positively pushed by meshing vanes on parallel revolving shafts and meshing screws into the discharge pipe

**rotary reflection axis** *n* **:** ROTOFLECTION AXIS

**rotary shear** *n* **1 :** a rotating bedplate of a lathe **2 rotary shears** *pl* **:** a machine having a pair of rotary overlapped cutter wheels for shearing sheet metal along a curved line

**rotary table oven** *n* **:** an oven comprising one or more horizontal circular tables on a vertical axis that turns so that work can be introduced at one radial position and removed at another after heat and rotation have completed the process

**rotary transformer** *n* **:** SYNCHRONOUS CONVERTER

**rotary valve** *n* **:** a valve acting by continuous or partial rotation

**rotary-wing aircraft** *n* **:** an aircraft supported in flight partially or wholly by rotating airfoils

**ro·tat·able** \'rō,tād·əbəl, -ātə-, ='===\ *adj* **:** capable of being rotated — **ro·tat·ably** \-blē,-bli\ *adv*

1**ro·tate** \'rō,tāt, *usu* -ād·+V\ *adj* [L *rota* wheel + E *-ate*] **:** having the parts flat and spreading or radiating like the spokes of a wheel ⟨~ blue flowers⟩

2**ro·tate** \'rō,tāt, *usu* -ād·+V; *chiefly Brit* ='=\ *vb* -ED/-ING/-S [L *rotatus*, past part. of *rotare*, fr. *rota* wheel — more at ROLL] *vi* **1 :** to turn about an axis or a center **:** REVOLVE ⟨the magnetic drums ~ —Magnus Pyke⟩ ⟨a pivoted seat which can ~ in an arc of 180 degrees —*Scientific American*⟩ ⟨the earth ~*s* around the sun —Hugh Odishaw⟩; *specif* **:** to move in such a way that all particles follow circles with a common angular velocity about a common axis **2 :** to perform an act, function, or operation in turn **:** pass or alternate in a series ⟨the 17 judges who ~ through the court —Marjorie Rittwagen⟩ ⟨these typewriters ~ through all the classrooms —Naomi L. Engelsman⟩ ⟨*rotating* internships⟩ **3 a :** to move a joint with a circular motion in dancing **b :** to progress in a circular path around a central axis in dancing **~** *vt* **1 :** to cause to turn about an axis or a center **:** REVOLVE ⟨the crankshaft is *rotated* —Joseph Heitner⟩ ⟨asked the patient to ~ his eyes⟩ **2 :** to cause to grow in rotation **:** vary by rotational planting ⟨~ crops⟩ **3 :** to cause to pass or act in a series **:** ALTERNATE ⟨every food used was *rotated* . . . so that each food was repeated at a specified interval —H.J.Rinkel⟩ ⟨*rotated* the honor between them so that neither should feel hurt —Ernest Beaglehole⟩ **4 :** to exchange (individuals or units) with personnel more comfortably situated ⟨a buddy of his . . . was to be *rotated* home —E.J.Kahn⟩ **5 :** to move (a joint) with a circular motion in dancing

**syn** ROTATE and ALTERNATE mean to succeed or cause to succeed each other in turn. ROTATE may apply to two or more things and implies an indefinite repetition of an order of succession, usu. a predetermined order ⟨to *rotate* crops is to grow different crops on the same land in successive seasons in an order designed to maintain soil fertility⟩ ⟨workers may *rotate* in jobs when they periodically interchange jobs according to a predetermined scheme⟩ ⟨a repertory company of veteran actors who could rotate in the playing of starring, featured, and minor roles —*Current Biography*⟩ ALTERNATE may be used interchangeably with ROTATE ⟨workers may *alternate* in their jobs⟩ but in such use it usu. puts strong stress on the succession of one upon another rather than the interchange of all even though in a given order ⟨the three plots *alternate* in the representation —L.P.Goggin⟩ ⟨a large number of vertical fountains, which *alternate* in a series of sprays —*Amer. Guide Series: Mich.*⟩ More usu. ALTERNATE applies to only two things and generally does not put strong stress on repetition or continuity ⟨a region of rich and varied productivity, in which oil fields and cultivated lands *alternate* —*Encyc. Americana*⟩ **syn** see in addition TURN

**ro·tat·ed** \'rō,tād·əd, -ātəd\ *adj* [L *rota* wheel + E *-ate* + *-ed*] : ROTATE

**ro·tat·ee** \,rō,tad·'ē, ˌ=ˈ=,=; ¦rōd·ə¦tē\ *n* -S [²*rotate* + *-ee*] : a member of the armed forces returned from combat or other arduous service because of length of stay or type of duty

**rotating band** *or* **rotating ring** *n* : a soft metal band around the lower part of a projectile to prevent the escape of gas and by fitting into the rifling to give the projectile its spin

**rotating die head** *n* : a device that revolves and chases threads on work held stationary in a machine

**rotating internship** *n* : a medical internship in which the intern works under supervision in several departments or services in succession ⟨had his *rotating internship* in medicine, surgery, obstetrics, and pediatrics⟩ — compare STRAIGHT INTERNSHIP

**rotating-wing aircraft** *n* : ROTARY-WING AIRCRAFT

**ro·ta·tion** \rō'tāshən\ *n* -S [L *rotation-, rotatio,* fr. *rotatus* (past part. of *rotare* to rotate) + *-ion-, -io* -ion] **1 a :** the act of turning about an axis or a center ⟨the ~ of a shaft⟩ ⟨the ~ of the earth about the sun⟩ ⟨body ~ in slalom skiing⟩ — see DEXTROROTATION, LEVOROTATION, SPECIFIC ROTATION; compare OPTICAL ROTATION, POLARIZATION, REVOLUTION **b :** one complete turn **:** the angular displacement required to return a rotating body or figure to its original orientation — called also *revolution* **2 a :** return or succession in a series ⟨the ~ of the seasons⟩ ⟨retired by ~⟩ **b :** the action of placing in succession in a series ⟨the resolution provided for ~ of the chairmanship —Vera M. Dean⟩ **3 :** the growing of different crops in succession on one field usu. in regular sequence **4 :** the turning of a limb or other body part about its long axis as if on a pivot ⟨~ of the head to look over the shoulder⟩ **5 :** the time required or estimated to be required to bring timber crops to a specified state of maturity **6 :** the direction in which the turn to deal, bid, and play passes from player to player in a card game **7 :** the exchange of individuals or units with personnel more comfortably situated ⟨was due for ~ back home soon —Marcus Duffield⟩ **8** *also* **rotation pool :** fifteen-ball pool in which the object balls are played upon in numerical order

**ro·ta·tion·al** \(')=¦tāshən°l, -shnəl\ *adj* **:** of, relating to, or characterized by rotation — **ro·ta·tion·al·ly** \-°l|ē, -əl , |i\ *adv*

**rotational fault** *n* : ROTARY FAULT

**rotational inertia** *n* : MOMENT OF INERTIA 1

**rotational loss** *n* : the power or energy loss incurred by friction and windage as an object is revolved

**rotational motion** *n* **1 :** motion of rotation **2 :** VORTICAL MOTION

**rotational quantum number** *n* : a vector quantum number that determines the angular momentum of a molecule rotating about an axis through its center of mass

**rotational specific heat** *n* : the contribution made to the specific heat of a substance by change in mean energy of molecular rotation with change in temperature — compare VIBRATIONAL SPECIFIC HEAT

**rotational spectrum** *n* : the part of a molecular spectrum in which the bands arise from quantized changes in the energy of molecular rotation — compare VIBRATIONAL SPECTRUM

**rotational vector** *n* : a vector field whose curl is not zero

**rotation axis** *n* : a simple axis of symmetry in a crystal about which the whole crystal configuration is brought into coincidence with its original aspect by a rotation of one half, one third, one fourth, or one sixth of a turn about the axis

**rotation crossing** *n* : a system of breeding domestic animals in which the female offspring resulting from a cross between two breeds are bred to a sire of a third breed and the female offspring resulting from the second cross are then bred to a sire of one of the two breeds used in the original cross — compare CRISSCROSSING

**rotation grazing** *n* : the shifting of livestock to different units of a pasture or range in regular sequence to permit the recovery and growth of the pasture plants after grazing

**rotation spectrum** *n* : ROTATIONAL SPECTRUM

**rotation twin** *n* : a twin crystal in which the individuals are so related that one can be made to coincide with the other by a rotation of 180 degrees or occas. 60, 90, or 120 degrees — compare REFLECTION TWIN

**ro·ta·tive** \'rō,tād·iv, rō't-\ *adj* [L *rotatus* (past part. of *rotare* to rotate) + E *-ive*] **1 :** turning like a wheel **:** ROTARY, ROTATIONAL ⟨~ velocity⟩ **2 :** occurring in a regular series **:** characterized by rotation ⟨the ~ plan of the rectorship —A. L.Vogel⟩ **3 :** causing rotation — **ro·ta·tive·ly** \-d·əvlē\ *adv*

**ro·ta·tor** \'rō,tād·ə(r) -ātə-, *chiefly Brit* =ˈ==\ *n, pl* **rotators** \-ə(r)z\ *or* **rotato·res** \,rōd·ə'tōr(,)ēz, ,rōtə-, -'tor-\ *see numbered senses* [NL, fr. L, one who rotates something, fr. *rotatus* (past part. of *rotare* to rotate) + *-or*] **1 :** a muscle that partially rotates a part on its axis; *specif* **:** any of several small muscles in the dorsal region of the spine arising from the upper and back part of a transverse process and inserted into the lamina of the vertebra above **2** *pl* **rotators :** a machine or a mechanical part that causes rotation: as **a :** the screw-shaped part of a ship's log that causes the log to rotate in the water **b :** a small fast electric motor specially adapted for rotating disks and Geissler tubes **c :** a device for rotating a television antenna

**ro·ta·to·ria** \,rōd·ə'tōrēə\ [NL, fr. neut. pl. of *rotatorius* rotatory] *syn of* ROTIFERA

¹**ro·ta·to·ri·an** \¦=ˈ=ən\ *adj* [NL *Rotatoria* + E *-an*, adj. suffix] **:** ROTIFERAL

²**rotatorian** \"\ *n* -S [NL *Rotatoria* + E *-an*, n. suffix] **:** ROTIFER

**ro·ta·to·ry** \'rōd·ə,tōrē, 'rōtə-, -,tör-, -ri\ *adj* [prob. fr. NL *rotatorius,* fr. L *rotatus* (past part. of *rotare* to rotate) + *-orius* -ory] **1 a :** of or relating to rotation **:** ROTARY ⟨~ motion⟩ **b :** producing rotation ⟨~ substances⟩ — compare DEXTROROTATORY, LEVOROTATORY **2 :** occurring in rotation ⟨become . . . wearied with the repetition of ~ acts —William Godwin⟩

**rotatory dispersion** *n* : the production of colors that results from passing white light through an optically active substance (as quartz) that causes the amount of optical rotation to vary with the wavelength

**rotatory reflection axis** *n* : ROTOFLECTION AXIS

**rotch** *or* **rotche** \'räch\ *n, pl* **rotch·es** [origin unknown] **:** DOVEKIE 2

¹**rote** \'rōt\ *also* **ro·ta** \'rōd·ə\ *or* **rot·ta** \'räd·ə\ *or* **rotte** \'rät\ *n* -S [*rote* fr. ME, fr. OF, of Gmc origin; akin to OHG *hruozza* crowd, prob. of Celt origin; akin to MIr *crott* harp; *rota, rotta, rotte* fr. ML *rota, rotta,* fr. OF *rote* — more at CROWD] **:** CRWTH

²**rote** \'rōt, *usu* -ōd·+V\ *n* -S [ME, rote, custom, perh. fr. L *rota* wheel — more at ROLL] **1 a :** the use of the memory usu. with little intelligence — usu. used in the phrase *by rote* ⟨an arrogant adolescent repeating by ~ —Harold Garfinkel⟩ **b :** something learned by memorizing ⟨the tongue in his mouth would have waggled strange ~ if they had encouraged him —Peggy Bennett⟩ **2 :** routine carried out without understanding of its meaning or purpose **:** mechanical repetition of a pattern ⟨bewildered by the entrance of science and technology into his realm where ~ had ruled so long —F.L.Paxson⟩ ⟨the champions of the liberal arts . . . have seemed content to live on ~ and reputation —A.W.Griswold⟩ ⟨unreasoning ~ learning⟩ ⟨only in the later Inca period do evidences of mass and ~ production begin to present themselves —John Collier b.1884⟩ ⟨copying their teachers by ~ —C.W.Shumaker⟩ ⟨we cannot guarantee loyalty . . . or patriotism by ~ or by oath —J.B. Oakes⟩

³**rote** \"\ *vt* -ED/-ING/-S *archaic* **:** to repeat by rote — **rot·er** \-ōd·ə(r), -ōtə-\ *n* -S

⁴**rote** \"\ *or* **rut** \'rət, *usu* -əd·+V\ *n* -S [perh. of Scand origin; akin to ON *rauta* to roar — more at ROUT] **:** the noise of the surf crashing on the shore

⁵**rote** \"\ *vi* -ED/-ING/-S [L *rotare* to rotate] *archaic* **:** to go out or change by rotation

**ro·te·noid** \'rōt°n,ȯid\ *n* -S [*rotenone* + *-oid*] **:** any of various compounds (as deguelin or toxicarol) related chemically to rotenone and usu. occurring with it

**ro·te·none** \'rōt°n,ōn\ *n* -S [ISV *roten-* (fr. Jap *roten* derris plant) + *-one*] **:** a crystalline pentacyclic compound $C_{23}H_{22}O_6$ that is related to isoflavone, found esp. in derris and cube roots, used in insecticides and in primitive fish and arrow poisons, and of low toxicity to warm-blooded animals

**rot grass** *n, dial Brit* **:** any of several marsh or bog plants believed to cause rot in sheep: as **a :** VELVET GRASS **b :** BUTTERWORT

**rotgut** \'=,=\ *n, slang* **:** bad liquor

**roth·er·ham** \'räthərəm\ *adj, usu cap* [fr. *Rotherham,* county borough in northern England] **:** of or from the county borough of Rotherham, England **:** of the kind or style prevalent in Rotherham

**roth·lie·gen·de** *or* **rot·lie·gen·de** \'rōt,lēgəndə\ *adj, usu cap* [obs. G *rothliegende* (now *rotliegende*), fr. obs. G *roth* red (now *rot*) (fr. OHG *rōt*) + G *liegende,* weak nom. sing. neut. of *liegend,* pres. part. of *liegen* to lie, fr. OHG *ligen;* fr. the red beds of sandstone near Eisenach, central Germany — more at RED, LIE] **:** of, relating to, or constituting a subdivision of the European Permian — see GEOLOGIC TIME table

**roth·rock grama** \'rä,thräk-, -,thrək-\ *n* [prob. after Joseph T. *Rothrock* †1922 Am. physician and botanist] **:** an erect perennial grass (*Bouteloua rothrockii*) with pectinately arranged spikelets

**ro·ti·fer** \'rōd·əfə(r), -ōtəf-\ *n* -S [NL *Rotifera*] **:** one of the Rotifera

**ro·tif·era** \rō'tif(ə)rə\ *n pl, cap* [NL, fr. L *rota* wheel + *-i-* + *-fera* (neut. pl. of *-fer*) — more at ROLL] **:** a class of Aschelminthes comprising minute usu. microscopic but many-celled aquatic animals having the anterior end modified into a retractile disk bearing one or two circles of strong cilia that often give the appearance of rapidly revolving wheels — **ro·tif·er·al** \-)rəl\ *adj* — **ro·tif·er·an** \-)rən\ *n or adj* — **ro·tif·er·ous** \-)rəs\ *adj*

**ro·ti·form** \'rōd·ə,fȯrm\ *adj* [NL *rotiformis,* fr. L *rota* wheel + *-iformis* -iform] **:** ROTATE

**ro·tis·ser·ie** \rō'tisərē, -əri\ *n* -S [F *rôtisserie,* fr. MF *rostisserie,* fr. *rostiss-* (stem of *rostir* to roast) + *-erie* -ery — more at ROAST] **1 a :** a shop where meats are roasted and sold **b :** a restaurant that specializes in broiled and barbecued meats **2 :** a cooking appliance fitted with a spit on which food is rotated before or over a source of heat

**rotl** \'räd·°l\ *n, pl* **rotls** \-°lz\ *also* **ar·tal** \(')är¦tal\ *or* **ar·tel** \-tel\ [Ar *raṭl, riṭl*] **:** any of various units of weight of Mediterranean and Near Eastern countries ranging from slightly less than one pound to more than six pounds

**rotn** *abbr* rotation

**ro·to** \'rōd·(,)ō, 'rō(,)tō\ *n* -S [by shortening] **:** ROTOGRAVURE

**roto-** *comb form* [L *rota* wheel + E *-o-* — more at ROLL] **:** rotary ⟨*rotospray*⟩ ⟨*roto*-planer⟩

**ro·to·beater** \'rōd·(,)ō+,-\ *n* [*roto-* + *beater*] **:** a rotating beater with flails used to macerate potato vines and weeds before digging

**ro·to·flec·tion axis** \¦rōd·ō¦flekshən-\ *n* [*rotoflection* fr. *roto-* + *flection*] **:** a compound symmetry element that requires identity of the structure and form of a crystal with its former configuration after a combination of rotation of 60, 90, 120, or 180 degrees with reflection across the plane normal to the axis

¹**ro·to·graph** \'rōd·ə,graf, -rȧf\ *n* [*roto-* + *-graph*] **:** a photographic white-on-black print (as of a manuscript or book) made directly on bromide paper by the use of a reversing prism without a negative

²**rotograph** \"\ *vt* -ED/-ING/-S **:** to make a rotograph of

**ro·to·gra·vure** \¦rōd·əgrə¦vyů(ə)r, -ōtə-, -ůə\ *n* [*roto-* + *gravure*] **1 a :** a photogravure process in which the impression is produced by a rotary press **b :** a print made by rotogravure **2 :** a section of a newspaper devoted to rotogravure pictures

**ro·tom·e·ter** \'rōd·ə,mēd·ə(r), rō'tämәd-\ *n* [*roto-* + *-meter*] **:** ROTAMETER

**ro·ton** \'rō,tän\ *n* -S [L *rotare* to rotate + E *-on*] **:** one of the hypothetical energy quanta that are concerned along with phonons in the behavior of liquid helium II — compare SECOND SOUND

**rotonda** *var of* ROTUNDA

**ro·tor** \'rōd·ə(r), -ōtə-\ *n* -S [short for *rotator*] **1 :** a part that revolves in a stationary part: as **a :** the rotating member of an electrical machine **b :** the rotating wheel or group of wheels in a steam turbine — compare STATOR **2 :** a revolving vertical cylinder of a rotor ship **3 :** a complete system of rotating airfoils that supplies all or a major part of the lift supporting an aircraft ⟨the ~ of a helicopter⟩

**rotor blade** *n* : a blade in a rotor assembly

**rotorcraft** \'==,=\ *n* : ROTARY-WING AIRCRAFT

**rotor disk** *n* : the plane circular area swept through by the blades of a helicopter rotor

**rotor plane** *n* : ROTARY-WING AIRCRAFT

**rotor ship** *n* : a ship propelled by the pressure and suction of the wind acting on one or more revolving vertical cylinders

**ro·to·till** \'rōd·ō,til\ *vt* [back-formation fr. *Rototiller*] **:** to stir with a rotary plow or a rotary tiller

**Ro·to·till·er** \-lə(r)\ *trademark* — used for a power-driven implement with a series of revolving blades or prongs that break up or pulverize the soil

**rotproof** \'=;=\ *adj* **:** proof against damage by rot

**rots** *pres 3d sing of* ROT, *pl of* ROT

**rot·se** \'rätsə\ *n, pl* **rotse** *or* **rotses** *usu cap* **:** LOZI

**rotta** *or* **rotte** *var of* ROTE

**rot·tan** *also* **rot·ten** \'rät°n\ *n* -S [ME *rotten,* alter. of *ratoun* — more at RATTON] *chiefly dial* **:** RAT

**rotted** *past of* ROT

¹**rot·ten** \'rät°n\ *adj* -ER/-EST [ME *roten,* fr. ON *rotinn;* akin to OE *rotian* to rot — more at ROT] **1 a :** having rotted **:** DECAYED, PUTRID ⟨people who are dead and ~ in their graves —Mary Deasy⟩ ⟨a ~ tomato⟩ ⟨a little paint on a ~ house —Eric Linklater⟩ ⟨some granites are exceedingly ~ —K.A. Henderson⟩ ⟨~ ice⟩ **b** *obs* **:** characterized by rot ⟨the ~ diseases of the South —Shak.⟩ **2 a :** morally corrupt ⟨people . . . have become aware of something ~ in our democracy —Garrett Mattingly⟩ ⟨his heart . . . went ~ with vanity —Maurice Cranston⟩ **b :** very badly behaved **:** SPOILED ⟨a ~ child⟩ **3 a** *of a sheep* **:** affected with rot **b :** causing or characteristic of rot in sheep **4 :** extremely unpleasant **:** DISAGREEABLE ⟨a ~ day⟩ ⟨a ~ humor⟩ ⟨soldiering is a ~ job —J.O. Hannay⟩ ⟨it's ~ waiting for things —John Galsworthy⟩ **5 :** marked by weakness or unsoundness ⟨a commando group whose special operations are canceled one after another until the group goes ~ —Curtis Bradford⟩ **6 :** very uncomfortable (as from sickness or low spirits) ⟨caught a cold and felt ~⟩ ⟨was looking ~⟩ **7 :** marked by extremely poor quality **:** ABOMINABLE ⟨a ~ book⟩ ⟨paid $50 for ~ seats —Barnaby Conrad⟩ ⟨~ luck⟩ ⟨a ~ failure⟩ — **rot·ten·ly** \-°nlē, -li\ *adv* — **rot·ten·ness** \-°n(n)əs\ *n* -ES

²**rotten** \"\ *vb* -ED/-ING/-S *chiefly dial* **:** ROT

**rotten borough** *n* : an election district that has many fewer inhabitants than other election districts with the same voting power — compare POCKET BOROUGH

**rotten-egg** \'==;=\ *vt* [fr. the phrase *rotten egg*] **:** to throw rotten eggs at

**rotten neck** *n* : rice blast

**rottenstone** \'==,=\ *n* : a friable siliceous stone that is the residue of siliceous limestone from which the calcareous matter has been removed by the action of natural waters

**rotten stop** *n* : a light temporary lashing put around a sail to hold it in a bundle while it is being hoisted

**rot·ter** \'räd·ə(r), -ätə-\ *n* -S **1 :** one that rots **2 :** an unprincipled, lazy, or weak person ⟨~s who will trip, gouge, beat, sneak, lie, cheat, and steal to win —*Emporia (Kans.) Gazette*⟩ ⟨a drunken ~⟩ ⟨the brave man's courage, the ~'s cowardice —Dixon Wecter⟩

**rot·ter·dam** \'räd·ə(r),dam, -ätə-, -,daa(ə)m\ *adj, usu cap* [fr. *Rotterdam,* city in the western Netherlands] **:** of or from the city of Rotterdam, Netherlands **:** of the kind or style prevalent in Rotterdam

**rotting** *pres part of* ROT

**rott·lera** \'rätlərə\ *n* -S [NL *Rottlera* (syn. of *Mallotus*), fr. Johann Peter *Rottler* †1836 Dan. missionary] **:** KAMALA 2

**rott·ler·in** \-lərən\ *n* -S [ISV *rottler-* (fr. NL *Rottlera*) + *-in*] **:** a salmon-colored crystalline phenolic ketone $C_{30}H_{28}O_8$ that is the active principle of kamala

**rott·wei·ler** \'rät,wīlə(r)\ *n* [G, fr. *Rottweil,* city in southwest Germany + G *-er*] **1** *usu cap* **:** a German breed of tall vigorous black cattle dogs having short hair, tan or brown marking, a short tail, small drooping ears, and a pronounced stop **2** -S *often cap* **:** a dog of the Rottweiler breed

**rot·u·la** \'rächələ\ *n, pl* **rotulas** \-ləz\ *or* **rotu·lae** \-,lē\ [in sense 1, fr. ME, fr. ML, fr. L, little wheel; in other senses, fr. NL, fr. L — more at ROLL] **1 :** PATELLA 2a **2 :** one of the five radial pieces intervening between the alveoli and extending inward toward the esophagus in the Aristotle's lantern of a sea urchin **3 :** TROCHE — **rot·u·lar** \-.lə(r)\ *adj* — **ro·tu·li·an** \rä'tülēən, rä·'tyü-, rä'chü-\ *adj*

**rot·u·lad** \'rächə,lad\ *adv* [*rotula* + *-ad*] **:** toward the patella

**rot·u·let** \'rächələt\ *n* -S [ML *rotulus* roll, register (fr. L, little wheel) + E *-et* — more at ROLL] **:** a small scroll or register

**rot·u·li·form** \'rächələ,fȯrm, rä'tü-,rä·'tyü-,rä'chü-\ *adj* [*rotula* + *-iform*] **1 :** ROTATE **2 :** PATELLIFORM

¹**ro·tund** \(')rō¦tənd\ *n* -S *archaic* [by shortening] **:** ROTUNDA

²**rotund** \"\ *adj* [L *rotundus* round — more at ROUND] **1 :** marked by roundness **:** ROUNDED ⟨no less smooth and ~ than the gorgeous melons and watermelons —George Santayana⟩ **2 :** marked by fullness **:** SONOROUS ⟨the ~ and reverberating phrase —Aldous Huxley⟩ ⟨a deep ~ voice⟩ **3 :** marked by plumpness **:** CHUBBY ⟨a ~ little man⟩ **syn** see FAT

**ro·tun·da** \rō'təndə\ *or* **ro·ton·da** \-'tän-\ *n* -S [*rotunda* alter. (influenced by L *rotundus*) of *rotonda,* fr. It, fr. L *rotunda,* fem. of *rotundus* round] **1 a :** round building; *esp* **:** one that is round both outside and inside and is covered by a dome **2 a :** a large round room **b :** a large central area in a hotel or other public building **3 :** a round script black letter type design

Rotunda

rotunda 3

**ro·tun·date** \-'təndət, -,dāt\ *adj* [L *rotundatus,* past part. of *rotundare* to make round, fr. *rotundus* round] **:** rounded at the end or corners

**ro·tun·di·ty** \-ndəd·ē, -ətē, -i\ *n* -ES [L *rotunditat-, rotunditas,* fr. *rotundus* round + *-itat-, -itas* -ity] **1 a :** the quality or state of being rotund **:** ROUNDNESS ⟨the thick ~ o' the world —Shak.⟩ **b :** a round mass or object ⟨laid his hand caressingly upon the consoling ~ of a five-gallon keg —Elinor Wylie⟩ **2 a :** rounded fullness of language ⟨scholars disputing . . . with leisured ~ of phrase —R.W.Southern⟩ **b :** a rotund phrase ⟨its adorable simplicities compensate even for its Johnsonian *rotundities* —H.J.Laski⟩ **3 a :** roundness of the body **:** PLUMPNESS ⟨a sparer diet had checked the movement towards ~ —John Buchan⟩ **b :** a rounded part of the body ⟨a cozy creased ~ between waistcoat and table —Clemence Dane⟩

**ro·tund·ly** *adv* **:** in a rotund manner

**ro·tun·do** \rō'tən(,)dō\ *n* -S [by alter.] **:** ROTUNDA

**ro·tu·ri·er** \rō'türē,ā, rō·'tyü-, *F* rōtüryā\ *n* -S [MF, fr. *roture* land tenure of a person not of noble birth, newly cleared land, action of breaking (fr. OF *routure* action of breaking, fr. L *ruptura* fracture, break) + *-ier* — more at RUPTURE] **1 :** a person not of noble birth; *specif* **:** a freeman holding land by payment of rent in money or kind without feudal duties and charges **2 :** a rich person of plebeian origin **:** NOUVEAU RICHE

**ro·ty·len·chus** \,rōd·°l'eŋkəs, ,räd-·\ *n, cap* [NL, prob. irreg. fr. *Tylenchus*] **:** a genus of plant-parasitic nematodes (family Tylenchidae) that attack plant roots and underground stems

**rou·baix** \(')rü¦be, -bā\ *adj, usu cap* [fr. *Roubaix,* city of northern France] **:** of or from the city of Roubaix, France **:** of the kind or style prevalent in Roubaix

**rouble** *var of* RUBLE

**rou·cou** \(')rü¦kü\ *also* **ro·cou** \(')rō¦-\ *n* -S [F, fr. Tupi *urucú*] **1 :** ANNATTO TREE **2 :** ANNATTO

**roucouyenne** *usu cap, var of* RUCUYEN

**roué** \(')rü¦ā\ *n* -S [F, lit. broken on the wheel, fr. past part. of *rouer* to break on the wheel, fr. ML *rotare,* fr. L, to rotate; fr. the feeling that such a person deserved this punishment — more at ROTATE] **:** a man devoted to a life of sensual pleasure esp. in his relations with women **:** DEBAUCHEE, RAKE ⟨an elderly ~ . . . had invited her to call him Daddy —Jean Stafford⟩

¹**rou·en** \(')rü¦än, -äⁿ\ *adj, usu cap* [fr. *Rouen,* city of northern France] **:** of or from the city of Rouen, France **:** of the kind or style prevalent in Rouen

²**rouen** \"\ *n* [¹*rouen*] **1** *usu cap* **:** a breed of domestic ducks resembling Pekins in form and size and wild mallards in plumage coloring **2** -S *often cap* **:** a duck of the Rouen breed

³**rouen** \"\ *or* **rouen ware** *n* -S [¹*rouen*] **:** often ornate faience and soft paste porcelain produced at Rouen, France mostly in the 17th and 18th centuries

⁴**rou·en** \'rōən\ *dial Eng var of* ROWEN

¹**rouge** \'rüzh, *esp South sometimes* 'rüj\ *n* -S [F, fr. MF, fr. *rouge* red, fr. L *rubeus* reddish; akin to L *ruber* red — more at RED] **1 :** any of various cosmetics that give a red coloring to the cheeks or lips ⟨didn't need any powder or lip ~ to make her pretty —Nora Caplan⟩ **2 a :** a red powder consisting essentially of ferric oxide and usu. prepared by calcining ferrous sulfate; *esp* **:** a comparatively light-colored form (as jewelers' rouge) used chiefly in polishing glass, metal, or gems and as a pigment — compare CROCUS 2a, IRON RED 1 **b :** any of various oxide or other materials (as black rouge or green rouge) used similarly ⟨white ~ . . . is made from pure alumina —*Materials & Methods*⟩ ⟨lampblack, known as satin ~, finds some use for polishing celluloid and bone —*Industrial Minerals & Rocks*⟩ **3 :** the red compartments in roulette when a bet is made on them ⟨played the ~ six times in a row⟩

²**rouge** \"\ *vb* -ED/-ING/-S *vt* **1 :** to apply rouge to (as the face or the cheeks) **2 :** to cause to blush **:** REDDEN ⟨lovely features, *rouged* by a hectic glow —Augusta Evans⟩ **~** *vi* **1 :** to use rouge **2 :** BLUSH ⟨you would have seen me ~ —Herbert Gold⟩

³**rouge** \"\ *adj* [F, fr. MF] **:** RED

⁴**rouge** \'rüj\ *n* -S [origin unknown] **1 a :** a scrimmage in the Eton and similar football games **b :** a one-point score in such football games made by the opponents when a defender touches the ball down behind his own goal line **2 :** CANADIAN FOOTBALL

**rouge·berry** \'=- — *see* BERRY\ *also* **rouge plant** *n* [¹*rouge*] **:** BLOODBERRY

**rouge de cui·vre** \,rüzhdə'kwēv(rə), -vr(ᵊ)\ *n* [F] **:** COPPER 5a

**rouge de feu** \-'fə̄\ *n* [F, fire red] **:** FLAME RED

**rouge et noir** \'rüzhā'nwär\ *n* [F, lit., red and black] **:** a gambling game in which two rows of cards are dealt and designated as rouge and noir and the players may bet on which row will have a count nearer 31, on whether the first card of the winning row will be of the color for that row, or on whether it will not — called also *trente-et-quarante*

**rouge flam·bé** \'rüzh,fläm'bā\ *n* [F, fr. *rouge* red + *flambé* — more at FLAMBÉ] **:** mottled purplish red

**rou·geot** \rü'zhō\ *n* -S [F, fr. *rouge* red] **:** a nonparasitic disease of the grape characterized by an arrested growth of the tips of shoots and a red discoloration of the leaves along the margin and between the main veins

**rou·get cell** \(')rü¦zhā-\ *n, usu cap R* [after Charles *Rouget* †1904 Fr. physiologist] **:** one of numerous branching cells adhering to the endothelium of capillaries and regarded as a contractile element in the capillary wall

**rouge ve·ge·tal** \'rüzh,vāzhā'tal\ *n* [F *rouge végétal,* lit., vegetable red] **:** CARTHAMUS RED

¹**rough** \'rəf\ *adj* -ER/-EST [ME, fr. OE *rūh;* akin to OHG *rūh* rough, hairy, L *runcare* to weed, *ruga* wrinkle, Gk *orychein, oryssein* to dig, *orygē* act of digging, Skt *rūksa* rough, ON *rögg* tuft, shagginess — more at RUG] **1 a :** marked by inequalities (as rises and falls, ridges, protuberances, projections, breaks, or seams) on the surface **:** not smooth or plain **:** COARSE ⟨a ~ board⟩ ⟨~ stone⟩ ⟨a tunic of ~ serge —G.B. Shaw⟩ ⟨a ~ roadway made of cinders and slag —Louis Bromfield⟩ **b :** covered with hair, fleece, or bristles **:** SHAGGY, UNSHORN ⟨~ satyrs danced —John Milton⟩ ⟨a ~ hog⟩ ⟨~ sheep⟩ ⟨a face ~ with two days' beard⟩ **c** (1) **:** having a broken, uneven, or bumpy surface ⟨~ hilly country⟩ (2) **:** difficult to

travel over or penetrate : WILD ⟨~ country . . . covered with dense jungle⟩ **2 a :** marked by turbulence or storminess : TEMPESTUOUS ⟨the ~ waters of the channel⟩ ⟨~ winds⟩ ⟨~ weather⟩ ⟨a ~ voyage⟩ ⟨airsickness brought about by flight through ~ air —H.G.Armstrong⟩ **b** (1) **:** characterized by harshness or violence : unduly or offensively forceful ⟨a ~ breed of men⟩ ⟨~ usage⟩ ⟨used ~, abusive language to the umpire⟩ ⟨a very ~ society where men . . . violated the rights of others with impunity —W.P.Webb⟩ (2) **:** marked by struggle or difficulty : TRYING ⟨a ~ day⟩ ⟨a ~ assignment⟩ ⟨things are ~ all over —Hamilton Basso⟩ ⟨she had a bit of ~ going —*Fashion Digest*⟩ **3 a :** coarse, rugged, or unpolished in character or appearance : UNREFINED: as (1) **:** lacking smoothness of outline or form ⟨a ~ landscape⟩ (2) **:** harsh or rasping to the ear ⟨a radio emitting only ~ sounds⟩ (3) **:** harsh or sharp to the taste ⟨~ whiskey⟩ ⟨a ~ red wine⟩ (4) **:** poor in quality ⟨~ food⟩ ⟨~ clothes⟩ (5) **:** crude in style or expression ⟨~ rhymes⟩ (6) **:** INDELICATE ⟨a ~ anecdote for such an audience⟩ **b** (1) **:** marked by a lack of civility, refinement, or grace : UNCOUTH, PRIMITIVE ⟨~ farm workers⟩ ⟨~ hospitality⟩ (2) **:** crudely amiable : BLUFF ⟨the ~ kindness of . . . people —Harold Griffin⟩ **4 a :** marked by crudeness or lack of finish : UNPOLISHED ⟨~ leather⟩ ⟨~ rice⟩ ⟨a ~ performance⟩ ⟨sheets of ~ . . . plate glass —Ellis Humphreys⟩ **b :** prepared or executed hastily, tentatively, or imperfectly : MAKESHIFT, APPROXIMATE ⟨a ~ draft⟩ ⟨a ~ estimate⟩ ⟨~ data⟩ ⟨~ justice⟩ ⟨a ~ idea of how a machine operates⟩ ⟨a ~ wigwam fashioned of fir boughs —F.V.W.Mason⟩ **c :** qualified for only the cruder or simpler operations of a trade ⟨a ~ carpenter⟩ **d :** demanding mainly physical force rather than intellect ⟨~ work⟩ **5 a :** pronounced with aspiration ⟨a ~ vowel⟩ **b** *of a stop consonant in ancient Greek* **:** voiceless, aspirated, and fortis — compare MEDIAL 2b **6 :** relatively poor — used esp. of a poker hand (as in lowball) — compare SMOOTH **7 :** forming rough colonies usu. made up of organisms that form chains or filaments and tend to marked decrease in capsule formation and virulence — used of dissociated strains of bacteria; compare MUCOID

**syn** UNEVEN, RUGGED, HARSH, SCABROUS: ROUGH is a general term wide in its use. In its first meaning ROUGH simply indicates noticeable inequality of surface perceptible to touch ⟨a *rough* edge⟩ ⟨a *rough* stone⟩ From this the word has spread to indicate lack of regularity, modulation, and polish, with most but not all of its suggestions unpleasant ⟨the *rough* blow of sheer force —J.R.Green⟩ ⟨the people of Teutonic speech had their *rough* verse —H.O.Taylor⟩ ⟨*rough* and graceless would be such a greeting —R.W.Emerson⟩ UNEVEN in its first uses simply indicated lack of evenness ⟨an *uneven* road⟩ ⟨an *uneven* floor⟩ In later senses it often indicates lack of uniformity or consistency of treatment ⟨the book as a whole is an *uneven* achievement; for its writing ranges from the human and impassioned to the dully academic —David Hall⟩ In its first use in reference to land surfaces RUGGED applies to land made very irregular and difficult by a series of irregularities, of hills and gullies, mountains and gorges ⟨with much labor and puffing we drew ourselves up the *rugged* declivity —John Burroughs⟩ Used in relation to style of composition, it stresses lack of smoothness and easy fluency ⟨the most *rugged*-seeming of prose dialogue, the kind of dialogue that people sometimes praise as "simply a page torn from life" —C.E.Montague⟩ In other uses it may suggest robust strength and endurance ⟨I am not of a *rugged* constitution, and it irked me to be so feeble —C.B.Nordhoff & J.N.Hall⟩ ⟨the *rugged* countenance of the stoic Julia Shane —Louis Bromfield⟩ ⟨Litchfield was as *rugged* in its faith as the hills it nestled among —V.L.Parrington⟩ Orig. meaning unpleasant to the touch because of irregularity, HARSH has come to indicate that which is strongly unpleasant to any sense ⟨the cognac was *harsh* —Winifred Bambrick⟩ ⟨that cold unfeeling prison, with the *harsh* noise of the large key and the fetters —Anthony Trollope⟩ It is never complimentary. In other senses it applies to either that which may make one physically uncomfortable or that which may offend feelings of kindliness or justice ⟨the genial influence of summer commonly prevails over the *harsh* austerity of winter —J.G. Frazer⟩ ⟨could not recall a *harsh* word that had been uttered by Amelia. She had been all sweetness and kindness —W.M. Thackeray⟩ SCABROUS orig. simply indicated presence of raised protuberances, points, or dots and had no value judgments or implications ⟨the *scabrous* leaf of the slippery elm⟩ Possibly through an imagined relation with *scabby*, the word now has often the connotation of *encrusted* and may suggest the squalid or vile ⟨tiny, *scabrous* stone cottages with squealing pigs on the ground floor —*Time*⟩ ⟨collects the scandals of the day; on these he is . . . a connoisseur who is consulted upon *scabrous* discoveries —Osbert Sitwell⟩ **syn** see in addition RUDE

[2]**rough** \"\ *n* -S [ME *ruhe, rouch,* fr. *ruhe, rough,* adj.] **1 a :** ground that is uneven and covered with high grass, brush, and stones ⟨an acre of ~ covered with . . . sumac —*Gardeners' Chronicle*⟩; *specif* **:** such ground bordering the fairway of a golf course and providing a poor lie for a golf ball ⟨the stretch of ~ for the next 15 . . . feet from the fairway is allowed to grow four or five inches high —R.T.Jones⟩ — compare FAIRWAY 3 **b** (1) **:** vegetative cover which has been undisturbed by fire or clearing (2) **:** the accumulation of underbrush, herbaceous growth, and litter characteristic of such cover **2 :** the harsh or disagreeable side or aspect of something : severe treatment ⟨learn to take the ~ with the smooth⟩ **3 a :** refuse material from mineral workings **b roughs** *pl* **:** coarse poor sands from tin dressing **4 :** something in a crude, unfinished, or preliminary state: as **a :** an uncut gem stone ⟨the huge piece of ~ was cut to a superb gem of 128 carats —*Jewelers' Circular-Keystone*⟩ **b :** broad outline : general terms — often used with *in* ⟨the question . . . has been discussed in ~ —*Manchester Guardian Weekly*⟩ **c :** a hasty preliminary drawing or layout made by an artist or designer ⟨has both ~*s* and finished work to show as samples —*Illustrator*⟩ **d :** ROUGH PROOF **e :** the state of tanned leather before it has been finished — compare CRUST 6 **5 :** a coarse uncivil person; *esp* **:** one who is disorderly or violent : ROWDY, TOUGH ⟨a gang of these ~*s* broke in —Alan Paton⟩ **6 :** a spike or calk inserted in a horseshoe to prevent the horse from slipping **7 :** the side of a tennis racket on which the binding strings form loops around the regular lengthwise strings at the top and at the throat end of the racket — **in the rough 1 :** in a crude, unfinished or uncultivated state : UNPOLISHED ⟨a diamond *in the rough*⟩ ⟨the boy will go far, but he's *in the rough* now —Agnes S. Turnbull⟩ **2 :** in the ordinary everyday state : under informal conditions ⟨you must take us *in the rough*⟩ ⟨eating fried chicken *in the rough*⟩

[3]**rough** \"\ *adv, often* -ER/-EST [[1]*rough*] **:** ROUGHLY ⟨ride ~⟩ ⟨the wood is ~ shaped —C.L.Walker⟩

[4]**rough** \"\ *vb* -ED/-ING/-S *vt* **1 a :** to make rough : ROUGHEN ⟨~ the edges of glass⟩ ⟨satin garments are very easily ~*ed* —C.B.Randall b.1901⟩ — often used with *up* ⟨a stiff breeze ~*ing* up the sea⟩ **b :** RUFFLE ⟨a bird ~*ing* his feathers⟩ **2 a :** to use physical force upon : MANHANDLE, BEAT ⟨not accustomed to being ~*ed* about —Angus Mowat⟩ — usu. used with *up* ⟨was ~*ed* up and pushed into the street —*Springfield (Mass.) Daily News*⟩ **b :** to subject (an opponent) to unnecessary and intentional violence in a sport (as football, soccer, or ice hockey) ⟨deliberately ~*ed* the . . . goalkeeper —*Newsweek*⟩ **3 a :** to calk or otherwise roughen (a horse's shoes) to prevent slipping — compare CALK **b** *chiefly Austral* **:** to break or train (a horse); *esp* **:** to partially break (a horse) that is later to be trained for some special use (as military service) — now usu. used with *off* **4 a :** to shape, make, or dress (something) in a rough or preliminary way ⟨~ the pieces of wood to approximately the size desired⟩ — often used with *down, off, out* ⟨~ down coarse iron⟩ ⟨~ off timber⟩ ⟨~ out lenses⟩ ⟨~ out disks and housings in the quantities . . . needed —*Aero Digest*⟩ **b :** to mark or indicate the outline or chief lines of — usu. used with *out,* sometimes with *in* ⟨~*ed* out the general structure —M.F.A.Montagu⟩ ⟨~*ing* out my preliminary ideas for this novel —Rex Ingamells⟩ ⟨~*ing* in the voice parts —Deems Taylor⟩ ~ *vi* **:** to subject a player to unnecessary violence in a sport ⟨sent off the field by the referee for ~*ing*⟩ — **rough it :** to endure hard or primitive living conditions : live without ordinary comforts ⟨*rough it* on a camping trip⟩

**rough·age** \-fij, -fēj\ *n* -S [[1]*rough* + *-age*] **1 :** coarse bulky food for domestic animals that is relatively high in fiber and low in digestible nutrients (as bran, hay, silage) : COARSE FODDER — opposed to *concentrate;* compare FODDER 2 **2 a :** food for humans with a considerable proportion of indigestible material that by its bulk stimulates the intestines to peristalsis **b :** the indigestible material taken in by humans as bulk; *esp* **:** CELLULOSE

**rough alpine fern** *n* **:** HOLLY FERN a

**rough amaranth** *n* **:** PIGWEED a

**rough–and–ready** \ˌ==ˈ==\ *adj* [[1]*rough*] **1** *of a thing* **:** lacking finish or polish but good enough for a temporary or limited purpose : MAKESHIFT, APPROXIMATE ⟨a *rough-and-ready* method⟩ ⟨a *rough-and-ready* estimate⟩ ⟨a *rough-and-ready* description of the development of feudalism —G.G.Coulton⟩ **2** *of a person* **:** lacking delicacy or refinement but forthright, vigorous, and roughly competent ⟨a *rough-and-ready,* loud-spoken man —Zane Grey⟩

[1]**rough–and–tumble** \ˌ==ˈ==\ *n* [prob. fr. [4]*rough*] **:** rough, disorderly, and hazardous fighting or struggling with much random knocking about and no holds barred : SCUFFLE, FREE-FOR-ALL ⟨could have handled him in a *rough-and-tumble* —Elmer Davis⟩ ⟨a *rough-and-tumble* among the boys in the playground⟩ ⟨the *rough-and-tumble* of frontier life⟩ ⟨the *rough-and-tumble* of politics⟩

[2]**rough–and–tumble** \"\ *adj* **1 :** marked by or suited for rough-and-tumble : roughly vigorous ⟨a good *rough-and-tumble* fight⟩ ⟨grew up in a *rough-and-tumble* atmosphere —E.J.Kahn⟩ ⟨stands up to *rough-and-tumble* wear —*N. Y. Times Mag.*⟩ **2 :** put together haphazardly : MAKESHIFT ⟨a *rough-and-tumble* fence⟩

**rough–bark** \ˈ=ˌ=\ *or* **rough–bark disease** *n* **1 :** any of several virus diseases of woody plants (as cherry, apple, citrus) characterized by generalized roughening and often longitudinal splitting of the bark **2 :** a disease of apples that is caused by a fungus (*Phomopsis mali*) and produces rough cankers on the twigs and branches **3 :** a nonparasitic disease of fruit trees (as apples and pears) characterized by a general roughening of the bark and not by local cankers

**rough bedstraw** *n* **:** a perennial bedstraw (*Galium asprellum*) of central and eastern No. America having stems branched below and rough with hooked bristles along the four angles

**rough bent** *or* **rough bent grass** *n* **:** a slender grass (*Agrostis scabra* or *A. hiemalis*) with widely spreading capillary panicles that is sometimes used for dried bouquets

**rough bindweed** *n* **:** a European smilax (*Smilax aspera*) the root of which yields a kind of sarsaparilla

**rough bluegrass** *or* **rough–stalked bluegrass** *n* **:** a European forage grass (*Poa trivialis*) naturalized in eastern No. America and having stems that are sometimes harsh below the panicle

**rough breathing** *n* [trans. of LL *spiritus asper*] **1 :** a mark ʽ used in Greek over some initial vowels or over ρ to show that they are aspirated (as in ὡς pronounced \ˈhōs\ or ῥήτωρ pronounced \ˈhrātōr\) **2 :** the sound indicated by a mark ʽ over a Greek vowel or ρ — called also *spiritus asper;* compare BREATHING 2, SMOOTH BREATHING

**rough buttonweed** *n* **:** BUTTONWEED 1

[1]**roughcast** \ˈ=ˌ=\ *n* [[3]*rough* + *cast,* past part. of *cast*] **1 :** the rudimentary unfinished form of something : rough model **2 :** a plastering made of lime mixed with shells or pebbles and used for covering buildings usu. by being thrown from a trowel forcibly against the wall **3 :** a rough surface finish (as of a wall made of plaster or concrete) : SPATTER DASH

[2]**roughcast** \"\ *vt* **1 :** to plaster (as a wall) with roughcast **2 :** to shape or form (something) roughly without polish, revision, or correction ⟨~ a clay model⟩ ⟨~ a poem⟩

**rough cinquefoil** *n* **:** a rough-hairy annual or biennial weed (*Potentilla norvegica*) with long-petioled usu. 3-foliolate leaves

**rough coat** *n* **:** the first coat (as of paint or plaster)

**rough–coat** \ˈ=ˌ=\ *vt* [*rough coat*] **:** to apply a rough coat of plaster to (a wall or lath)

**rough comfrey** *n* **:** PRICKLY COMFREY

**rough diamond** *n* **1 :** an uncut diamond **2 :** a person of exceptional qualities or abilities but lacking in social graces and refinement of manner : DIAMOND IN THE ROUGH

**roughdraw** \ˈ=ˌ=\ *vt* [[3]*rough* + *draw*] **:** to draw (a metal rod) into wire crudely or roughly

[1]**roughdry** \ˈ=ˈ=\ *vt* [[3]*rough* + *dry*] **:** to dry (laundry) without smoothing or ironing ⟨clothes *roughdried*⟩

[2]**roughdry** \ˈ=ˌ=\ *adj* **1 :** washed and dried but not ironed ⟨a basket of ~ laundry⟩ ⟨a pile of ~ clothes was on the bed —P.E.Green⟩ **2 :** of or relating to a laundry service in which washed articles are returned dry but not ironed ⟨has her laundry done ~⟩

**roughed** *past of* ROUGH

**rough·en** \ˈrəfən\ *vb* -ED/-ING/-S [[1]*rough* + *-en*] *vt* **:** to make (something) rough ⟨her hands were ~*ed* by work —Ellen Glasgow⟩ ~ *vi* **:** to become rough ⟨the terrain ~*s* somewhat as the watershed . . . is approached —*Amer. Guide Series: Texas*⟩

[1]**rougher** *comparative of* ROUGH

[2]**rough·er** \ˈrəfə(r)\ *n* -S [[4]*rough* + *-er*] **:** one that roughs or roughs out work: as **a :** a glass cutter that makes the first heavy incisions or grinds the edges to a rough finish **b :** one that guides heated steel bars, rods, or sheets through the roughing rolls repeatedly until steel is reduced to the desired gauge — called also *bulldogger* **c :** a poultry dresser that pulls out tail and wing feathers only

**roughest** *superlative of* ROUGH

**rough fig** *n* [[1]*rough*] *Austral* **:** PURPLE FIG

**rough file** *n* **:** a file of the grade having the coarsest cutting ridges

**rough fish** *n* **:** a fish that is neither a sport fish nor an important food for sport fishes — compare FORAGE FISH, TRASH FISH

**rough–footed** \ˈ=ˈ==\ *adj* [ME *rouh foted,* fr. *rouh, rough* rough + *foted* footed] **:** having feathered feet ⟨the *rough-footed* eagles⟩

**rough fox** *n* **:** CRAB-EATING FOX

**rough gentian** *n* **:** SOAPWORT GENTIAN

**rough–gilt** \ˈ=ˈ=\ *adj* [[3]*rough* + *gilt,* past part. of *gild*] *of a book edge* **:** gilded before sewing ⟨a ~ book⟩

**rough goldenrod** *n* **:** a very common No. American rough-stemmed herb (*Solidago rugosa*) with scabrous foliage and yellow flowers in large secund panicles

**rough grazing** *n, Brit* **:** unimproved pasture or range

**rough green snake** *n* **:** a green snake (*Ophiodrys aestivus*) of the southern and eastern U.S. having strongly keeled light to dark green scales above and smooth pale yellow to yellowish white ventral plates — see SMOOTH GREEN SNAKE

**rough hawkbit** *n* **:** a rough-hairy European weed (*Leontodon nudicaulis*) with a rosette of basal leaves and a solitary long-stalked head of yellow flowers that is adventive in No. America

**roughhearted** \ˈ=ˈ==\ *adj* [[1]*rough* + *hearted*] **:** lacking sympathy or benevolence : UNFEELING, CALLOUS, HARDHEARTED

**roughhew** \ˈ=ˈ=\ *vt* [[3]*rough* + *hew*] **1 :** to hew (as timber) coarsely without smoothing or finishing ⟨a statue out of a large block of marble⟩ **2 :** to give the first form or shape to : form crudely or roughly : ROUGHCAST ⟨~*s* his novels rapidly but then polishes them slowly over a long period⟩ ⟨a divinity that shapes our ends ~ them how we will —Shak.⟩

**roughhewn** \ˈ=ˈ=\ *adj* [[3]*rough* + *hewn*] **1 :** crudely shaped : left in a rough, unsmoothed, or unfinished state ⟨~ beams⟩ **2 :** lacking polish : UNCULTIVATED, PLAIN ⟨a ~ seaman —Francis Bacon⟩ ⟨he was rather attractive, in a ~ kind of way —Jan Speas⟩

**rough horsetail** *n* **:** a scouring rush (*Equisetum hyemale*)

[1]**rough·house** \ˈrəfˌhau̇s\ *n* [[1]*rough* + *house*] **:** an outbreak of violence or rough boisterous play esp. among occupants of a house or room ⟨the horseplay turned to a ~: snatching of trousers and smacks with the flat of hard hands, followed by clumsy steeplechases over the obstacles of beds —T.E. Lawrence⟩

[2]**rough·house** \" *also* -au̇z\ *vb* **roughhoused; roughhoused; roughhousing** \-au̇ziŋ *also* -au̇siŋ\ **roughhouses** \-au̇zəz *also* -au̇səz\ *vt* **1 :** to handle or deal with roughly often in a spirit of fun : MANHANDLE 2 ⟨intimidated and *roughhoused* their opponents⟩ ⟨young men engage in gymnastics and ~ each other —*Amer. Guide Series: N.Y.City*⟩ **2 :** to fondle (as a child) with playful roughness ⟨babies . . . tickled or *roughhoused* —Benjamin Spock⟩ ~ *vi* **:** to engage in roughhouse ⟨got to *roughhousing* in the rooms and nobody got any sleep —Henry La Cossitt⟩

[3]**rough·house** \-au̇s\ *adj* **:** of, relating to, or characterized by roughhouse ⟨~ tactics⟩

**roughies** *pl of* ROUGHY

**rough in** *vt* **:** to install in a building (the concealed part of the plumbing equipment)

**roughing** *n* -S [fr. gerund of [4]*rough*] **:** the act or process of removing (as by stippling or pebbling) a high finish on paper stock

**roughing–in** \ˈ==ˈ=\ *n* -S [fr. gerund of [4]*rough*] **1 a :** the first coat of plaster (as on brick) **b :** the act or process of applying such a coat **2 :** the installation in a building of the part of the plumbing equipment that is concealed (as in walls or under floors)

**roughing mill** *n* **1 :** a set of roughing rolls **2 :** a revolving metal disk charged with an abrasive that is used in various processes (as the grinding of gems)

**roughing rolls** *n pl* **:** a series of rolls in which wrought metal is first given the form of a bar preparatory to being reheated and finished or through which an ingot of steel or other metal first passes in the rolling process

**rough·ish** \ˈrəfish\ *adj* [[1]*rough* + *-ish*] **:** somewhat rough ⟨two ~ . . . chaps —Arnold Bennett⟩ ⟨~ spots in a summer that glided by —Booth Tarkington⟩

**rough leaf** *n* **:** ARBUTUS 3

**rough–leaf tree** *n* **:** CHAPARRO 3

**rough–leaved fig** \ˈ=ˌ=-\ *n, Austral* **:** PURPLE FIG

**rough–legged hawk** \ˈ=ˌ=(=)-\ *or* **roughleg** \ˈ=ˌ=\ *n* **:** any of several large heavily built hawks of the genus *Buteo* (as the European *B. lagopus*) that are closely related to the true buzzards but have the tarsus feathered to the base of the toes, feed chiefly on rodents (as mice), and are beneficial to the farmer — see FERRUGINOUS ROUGHLEG

**rough lemon** *n* **1 :** a hybrid lemon with a large spreading thorny tree and rough-skinned nearly globular acid fruits that prob. originated in India but has become naturalized in tropical America and southern Africa and is important chiefly as a rootstock for sweet and mandarin oranges and the grapefruit **2 :** the fruit of a rough lemon

**rough lock** *n* **1 :** a chain or rope fastened around the runner of a sled to retard its movement downhill **2 :** a chain tied around the rim of a rear wheel of a wagon and fastened to the wagon reach so that the skidding wheel will retard the movement of the wagon downhill

**rough–lock** \ˈ=ˌ=\ *vt* [*rough lock*] **:** to fasten a rough lock on ⟨*rough-locking* the wagon wheels, to keep the wagon from pushing the mules when we went down —J.H.Stuart⟩

**rough lumber** *n* **:** lumber that has not been dressed since it was sawed

**rough·ly** *adv* [ME *rohly,* fr. *roh, rough* rough + *-ly*] **:** in a rough manner: as **a :** with harshness or violence : SEVERELY ⟨women were treated ~ —Theodor Reik⟩ ⟨closed the door ~ —Marcia Davenport⟩ **b :** without finish : COARSELY ⟨local gray stone, ~ dressed —*Amer. Guide Series: Minn.*⟩ **c :** without completeness or exactness : APPROXIMATELY ⟨~ speaking⟩ ⟨in ~ chronological order⟩ ⟨must know ~ what each act will contain —John Van Druten⟩

**rough–machine** \ˈ==ˈ=\ *vt* [[3]*rough* + *machine*] **:** to machine (work) approximately to size usu. by taking heavy cuts with the object chiefly of removing excess metal rather than of obtaining a correct size and finish

**rough music** *n* [[1]*rough*] *dial Brit* **:** SHIVAREE

[1]**rough·neck** \ˈrəfˌnek\ *n* [[1]*rough* + *neck*] **1 :** a rough or uncouth person; *esp* **:** one markedly inclined to violent, quarrelsome, or mischievous behavior : ROWDY, TOUGH ⟨a gang of ~*s*⟩ ⟨stopped her boy from playing with the neighborhood ~*s*⟩ **2 :** a member of a crew that builds and repairs oil wells

[2]**roughneck** \"\ *also* **rough–necked** \-kt\ *adj* **:** having the characteristics of or suitable for a roughneck : UNCOUTH, BARBAROUS ⟨~ language⟩ ⟨the world's gone ~ —Ellen Glasgow⟩ ⟨went out to a ~ dance —Sinclair Lewis⟩

**rough·ness** *n* -ES [ME *roughnesse,* fr. [1]*rough* + *-nesse* -ness] **1 :** the quality or state of being rough: as **a :** inequality or unevenness of surface ⟨the ~ of the path⟩ ⟨place his fingers on the paper . . . to perceive ~ —R.S.Woodworth⟩ **b :** a sensation of harshness or sharpness (as to the taste or hearing) ⟨the tea . . . which sets one's teeth on edge —G.E.Fussell⟩ ⟨the ~ of their voices grating on his nerves⟩ **c :** harsh, rude, or violent speech or behavior ⟨a riverside town well known for ~ —Harvey Day⟩ **d :** violent agitation : STORMINESS ⟨the ~ of the sea⟩ ⟨the ~ of the weather⟩ **e :** lack of refinement or polish : CRUDENESS ⟨the life of the people had lost . . . its broad pioneer ~ —*Amer. Guide Series: Tenn.*⟩ **2 :** a rough place or part ⟨the ~*es* remaining after the first revision of an essay⟩ **3** *Midland* **:** roughage used as fodder

**rough·om·e·ter** \ˌrəˈfämədə(r)\ *n* [[1]*rough* + *-o-* + *-meter*] **:** an instrument for measuring the roughness of a road surface

**rough out** *vt* **:** to maintain (a horse) solely on pasture or roughage ⟨an experienced steeplechaser *roughed out* at grass —*Veterinary Record*⟩

**rough pea** *n* **:** SINGLETARY PEA

**rough pigweed** *n* **:** a pigweed (*Amaranthus retroflexus*)

**rough–point** \ˈ=ˈ=\ *vt* [[3]*rough* + *point*] **:** to point (stone) with a pick or with heavy points so as to leave projections from about half an inch to an inch in height

**rough proof** *n* **:** a printer's proof made quickly by hand without the use of special proof paper, positioning, or makeready

**rough rice** *n* **:** PADDY

**rough·ride** \ˈrəˌfrīd\ *vi* [back-formation fr. *roughrider*] **:** to ride as or in the manner of a roughrider

**rough·rid·er** \-də(r)\ *n* [[1]*rough* + *rider*] **1 :** one who breaks horses to the saddle or who is noted for or accustomed to riding little-trained horses; *specif* **:** a trooper in the British cavalry who is assigned as a horse trainer **2 a :** an irregular cavalryman **b** *usu cap* **:** an officer or enlisted man in the 1st U.S. Volunteer Cavalry regiment in the Spanish-American War composed mostly of western cowboys and hunters and eastern college athletes and sportsmen commanded by Theodore Roosevelt

**roughs** *pl of* ROUGH, *pres 3d sing of* ROUGH

**roughscuff** *also* **rough–scruff** \ˈ=ˌ=\ *n* [[1]*rough* + *scuff, scruff*] **:** RIFFRAFF ⟨the political ~ of Europe —*Atlantic*⟩

**roughseed bulrush** \ˈ=ˌ=-\ *n* [[1]*rough* + *seed*] **:** a perennial Old World rush (*Scirpus mucronatus*) that occurs as a weed in California rice fields and has seeds with barbed bristles

**roughshod** \ˈ=ˈ=\ *adj* [[3]*rough* + *shod*] **1 :** shod with shoes armed with points or calks ⟨a ~ horse⟩ **2 :** marked by inhumanity or tyranny ⟨~ condemnation proceedings⟩ ⟨~ reign⟩

**rough·some** \ˈrəfsəm\ *adj* [[1]*rough* + *-some*] *chiefly Scot* **:** ROUGH, UNCOUTH, BOORISH

**rough–spoken** \ˈ=ˈ==\ *adj* [[3]*rough* + *spoken*] **:** rough or crude in speech ⟨a ~ old sailor⟩

**rough–stalked meadow grass** \ˈ=ˌ=-\ *n* [[1]*rough*] **:** ROUGH BLUEGRASS

**rough stop** *n* **1 :** any one of the three Greek consonants φ, θ, χ that were orig. the voiceless stops \p\, \t\, \k\ followed by an \h\ sound or aspiration — called also *aspirata* **2 :** a voiceless aspirated stop in any language

**roughstring** \ˈ=ˌ=\ *n* **:** a board notched out to fit the steps and fixed to the inside of an open string to strengthen it — compare FACE STRING

[1]**roughstuff** \ˈ=ˌ=\ *n* [[1]*rough* + *stuff*] **1 :** an undercoat of paint used to level inequalities of a surface **2** *usu* **rough stuff :** boisterous behavior : violent treatment ⟨allowed no *rough stuff* in his dance hall⟩ ⟨if the fellow didn't pay off, they went in for *rough stuff* —A.J.Liebling⟩

[2]**roughstuff** \"\ *vt* **:** to paint (a surface) with roughstuff

**rought** [alter. of *raught*] *dial chiefly Brit past of* REACH

**roughtail** \ˈ=ˌ=\ *n* [[1]*rough* + *tail*] **:** a burrowing snake of the family Uropeltidae having large scales or shields on the tail

**roughtailed** \ˈ=ˌ=\ *adj* [[1]*rough* + *tailed*] **1 :** having a rough tail ⟨~ mice⟩ **2 :** having a tail that is characteristic of a roughtail

**rough–tree rail** *n* [*rough-tree* small timber used as a rail (perh. alter. of *rooftree*) + *rail*] **:** the rail at the top of a ship's main bulwarks and below the topgallant bulwarks

**rough–weed** \ˈ=ˌ=\ *n* [[1]*rough*] **:** HEDGE NETTLE

**rough whelk** *n* **:** DRILL 4

**rough–winged swallow** \ˈ=ˌ=-\ *n* **:** a swallow of the American genus *Stelgidopteryx* or of the African genus *Psalidoprocne* having the outer web of the first primary developed into a series of minute hooks

**roughy** \'rəfē\ *n* -ES [prob. fr. [1]*rough* + *-y*] **1 :** a small but highly esteemed Australian marine percoid food fish (*Arripis georgianus*) — called also *Tommy rough* **2 :** a small reddish brown Australian slime head (*Trachichthys australis*)

**rougy** \'rüzhē\ *adj* [[1]*rouge* + *-y*] **:** covered with or like rouge

**rouk** \'rōk\ *var of* ROKE

**rouky** \-ki\ *adj* -ER/-EST [*rouk* + *-y*] *chiefly Scot* **:** FOGGY, MISTY

**roul** *abbr* roulette

[1]**rou·lade** \rü'läd\ *n* -S [F, lit., act of rolling, roll, fr. *rouler* to roll (fr. MF *roller*) + *-ade* — more at ROLL] **:** a series of rapid musical notes or tones inserted in a musical composition as ornamentation; *specif* **:** a vocal ornament or coloratura (as an arpeggio or quick run) sung to one syllable

[2]**roulade** \"\ *vi* -ED/-ING/-S **:** to sing with roulades

[3]**roulade** \"\ *n* -S [F, lit., act of rolling, roll] **:** a slice of meat rolled with or without a stuffing and braised or sauteed ⟨~ of beef⟩

**roule** *obs var of* ROLL

**rou·leau** \rü'lō\ *n, pl* **rou·leaux** \-ō(z)\ *or* **rouleaus** [F, fr. MF *rolel*, dim. of *role* roll — more at ROLE] **:** a little roll: as **a :** a roll of coins put up in paper ⟨held out *rouleaux* of pennies —Richard Llewellyn⟩ **b :** a group of red blood corpuscles resembling a stack of coins **c :** a decorative piping or rolled trimming for women's clothing **d :** a bundle of fascines used in groups in siege operations

[1]**rou·lette** \rü'let, *usu* -ed·+V\ *n* -S [F, lit., small wheel, fr. OF *roelete*, dim. of *roele* small wheel, circular object, fr. LL *rotella*, dim. of L *rota* wheel — more at ROLL] **1 :** a gambling game in which players bet on which numbered red or black compartment of a revolving wheel a small ball spun in the opposite direction will come to rest in and in which the bets are placed on a table marked to correspond with the compartments of the wheel **2 :** any of various toothed wheels or disks (as for producing rows of dots on engraved plates, for roughening a plate in altering a mezzotint or for making short consecutive incisions in paper to facilitate subsequent division) **3 :** FILLET 5a **4 a :** a series of tiny slits made between rows of stamps as an aid to separation of the stamps — compare PERFORATION 2b(1) **b :** a row of teeth, scallops, or dashes along the edge of a detached stamp from a rouletted sheet **c :** one of the slits or teeth of a roulette

[2]**roulette** \"\ *vt* -ED/-ING/-S **1 :** to make roulettes in (as a sheet of stamps) or on the edge of (a stamp) **2 :** to make (a design) by rocker-stamping

**rouletting** *n* -S [fr. gerund of [2]*roulette*] **:** ROULETTE 4

**rou·man** \'rümən\ *adj or n, usu cap* [F *Roumain*, fr. Romanian *Rumân* — more at RUMAN] **:** ROMANIAN

**roumania** *usu cap, var of* ROMANIA

**roumanian** *usu cap, var of* ROMANIAN

**roumelian** *usu cap, var of* RUMELIAN

**rou·mi** \'rümē\ *n* -S [Ar *rūmīy* Roman, fr. L *Roma* + Ar *-īy* (gentilic suffix)] **:** a non-Muslim — usu. used disparagingly

**roun** \'rün\ *Scot var of* ROUND

[1]**rounce** \'raün(t)s\ *n* -S [D *rondse, rons*, prob. fr. *rond* round, fr. MF, fr. OF *roont* (fem. *roonde*) — more at ROUND] **:** a handle by which the bed of a hand printing press is run in under the platen and out again; *also* **:** the whole apparatus for moving the bed under the platen

[2]**rounce** \"\ *vi* -ED/-ING/-S [origin unknown] **:** to be agitated **:** flounce around **:** FUSS ⟨mother is kind of *rouncing* round, all right —Sinclair Lewis⟩

[1]**rounceval** *adj* [fr. *Roncesvalles, Roncevaux*, mountain pass in northern Spain; fr. the gigantic bones shown there as those of the paladins of Charlemagne slain in battle in 778] *obs* **:** HUGE, LARGE

[2]**roun·ce·val** \'raün(t)səvəl\ *n* -S **1** *obs* **a :** something very large **:** GIANT, MONSTER **b :** a big loud woman **:** VIRAGO **2 :** MARROWFAT 1

**roun·cy** \'raün(t)sē\ *n* -ES [ME, fr. MF *ronci* charger] *archaic* **:** a riding horse

[1]**round** \'raünd\ *vb* -ED/-ING/-S [ME *rounen*, fr. OE *rūnian*; akin to OHG *rūnēn* to whisper, ON *rȳna* to converse confidentially; all fr. a prehistoric NGmc-WGmc denominative verb fr. the source of OE *rūn* mystery, secret — more at RUNE] *vi, archaic* **:** WHISPER ~ *vt* **1 :** to whisper (something) **2 :** to speak to (someone) in a whisper

[2]**round** \"\ *adj, usu* -ER/-EST [ME *round, rounde*, fr. OF *roont, rount* (fem. *roonde, rounde*) fr. L *rotundus*; akin to L *rota* wheel — more at ROLL] **1 a :** having every part of the surface or of the circumference equally distant from a center within **:** SPHERICAL, CIRCULAR, ANNULAR, SPIRAL **b :** circular in cross section **:** CYLINDRICAL **c :** having a curved outline or form esp. like the arc of a circle or an ellipse or a part of the surface of a sphere **d** *of an arch* **:** having a semicircular intrados — see ARCH illustration **e** *archaic* **:** having a full or circular form — used of a garment **f** *of shoulders* **:** bent forward from the line or plane of a person's back **2 :** well fleshed **:** well filled out **:** PLUMP, SHAPELY **3 a :** COMPLETE, FULL — used of a number or quantity ⟨a ~ dozen⟩ ⟨a ~ million men⟩ ⟨a ~ ton of irreclaimable scrap⟩ **b :** approximately correct; *esp* **:** exact only to the nearest ten, hundred, or multiple of these ⟨his year's profit was about $5000 as a ~ figure⟩ **c :** substantial in amount **:** AMPLE, LARGE ⟨will be taken off our hands quickly and at a good ~ price —T.B.Costain⟩ **4 a :** showing severity or violence **:** HARSH ⟨gave him a ~ hiding —Ellery Queen⟩ **b :** marked by bluntness, directness, or forthrightness **:** BOLD, PLAIN, OUTSPOKEN ⟨asserted with a ~ oath . . . that all sergeants were liars —Haldane Macfall⟩ **c :** BRISK, FAST, VIGOROUS ⟨set a ~ pace —John Buchan⟩ **5 a :** traversing a course that ends at its starting point after retracing itself or making a circuit — used esp. in the phrase *round trip* **b :** moving in or forming a circle — compare ROUND DANCE **6 a :** brought to completion or perfection **:** thoroughly wrought **:** FINISHED **b :** imaginatively presented or drawn with lifelike fullness or vividness **:** seen from all sides or in many aspects ⟨the characters and their motives are as ~ and deep as those we might hope to find in a serious novel —*Times Lit. Supp.*⟩ **7 :** delivered with a more or less full swing of the arm ⟨a ~ blow⟩ **8 :** having full or unimpeded resonance or tone **:** MELLOW, RICH, SONOROUS **9 :** pronounced with rounded lips **:** LABIALIZED **10 :** of or relating to handwriting that is predominantly curved rather than angular ⟨a ~ schoolboy hand⟩ **11 :** of or relating to a transaction in securities that includes both buying and selling (as the sale of issues previously bought or a purchase made to cover a short sale) **12** *of a fish* **:** not gutted or dressed **:** ENTIRE

[3]**round** \"\ *adv* [ME *round, rounde*, fr. [2]*round*] **1 a :** in a circular or curved path or progression **:** in a course that follows a circle, ellipse, orbit, or spiral **:** AROUND ⟨our plane circled ~ at dusk —Noel Barber⟩ **b :** in close from all sides so as to surround, confine, or ring about ⟨walls and towers girdled ~ with radiance and splendor —Brooks Atkinson⟩ **c :** by a circuitous or curving route **:** in an indirect or roundabout way ⟨brought the milk ~ to the back door⟩ ⟨did not shine at golf but went ~ in the middle 80s⟩ **d :** to each of a group or number in succession **:** in turn **:** in rotation ⟨handed ~ water in an enamel mug —Margaret Kennedy⟩ ⟨cigars enough to go ~⟩ **2 :** on every side **:** in all or various directions from a fixed point ⟨the peasants ~ about his father's parish —O.S.J.Gogarty⟩ ⟨made frequent excursions in the country ~⟩ **3 :** with revolving or rotating motion ⟨the wheel turns ~⟩ **4** *obs* **:** DIRECTLY, OUTSPOKENLY **5 :** to a place or person either specified or understood ⟨sent ~ for the doctor⟩ ⟨invited them ~ to meet his guest⟩ ⟨called his car ~⟩ **6 :** APPROXIMATELY, NEARLY ⟨happened at the corner or ~ there⟩ **7 :** from beginning to end **:** THROUGH ⟨about 700 workers are employed at the plant the year ~ —*Amer. Guide Series: Md.*⟩ **8 a :** in the reverse or opposite direction **:** to the rear ⟨turned ~ in his chair to look⟩ **b :** from one opinion or attitude to another **:** to a different or altered position ⟨see if you can talk me ~ —Dorothy Sayers⟩ **9 a :** here and there **:** from one place to another **:** all about ⟨word got ~ quickly⟩ **b :** over a property to inspect it ⟨showed the visitors ~⟩ **10 :** back to normal health or equilibrium ⟨brought a woman ~ after a faint⟩ **11 :** in a series or progression **:** in order ⟨seemed to be going about things the wrong way ~⟩

[4]**round** \"\ *prep* **1 a :** so as to progress around or make the circuit of ⟨had the great thrill of flying ~ Africa —C.B. Randall b.1891⟩ **b :** so as to revolve or rotate about ⟨an axis or center⟩ ⟨pointed out that the planets move ~ the sun in the same direction and nearly in the same plane —H.S. Jones⟩ **c :** so as to make a partial circuit of **:** so as to reach the other side of by a curving course ⟨whether he sailed directly across the bay . . . or coasted ~ it is uncertain —Stanley Casson⟩ **d :** so as to follow the curving line of **:** along the bend of ⟨it was a mile by water, four miles ~ the shore —David Walker⟩ **e :** beyond the projection of ⟨it stood just ~ the corner from his father's house —Van Wyck Brooks⟩ **2 a :** so as to encircle or enclose **:** on all sides of ⟨the fat thus formed is to be found in large masses . . . ~ the kidneys —S.J.Watson⟩ ⟨they swarmed close ~ her to hear —C.S.Forester⟩ ⟨pulled her shawl closer ~ her —T.H.Barnardo⟩ **b :** in the vicinity of **:** adjacent to **:** NEAR ⟨the lands ~ the city —Herbert Agar⟩ **c :** so as to form a group or mass about ⟨will tend to gather ~ him the best minds in America —*New Republic*⟩ ⟨a great puddle formed ~ the hole⟩ **d** (1) **:** from point to point or from person to person in **:** here and there in ⟨took his way ~ the city, passing a discreet word here and a mere look there as he went⟩ ⟨refreshes the students' memories by asking a few simple questions ~ the class —D.H.Spencer⟩ (2) **:** throughout the extent of **:** all over **:** all through ⟨the blood circulates ~ the body⟩ **3 a :** in all directions from ⟨we cannot measure it by what we see ~ us —Lewis Galantiere⟩ **b :** so as to have a center or basis in ⟨the flame . . . was yellow on the outside, bluish in the middle, but there was no color ~ the wick —Stuart Cloete⟩ ⟨the biography is centered ~ the individual —Richard Pares⟩ **4 a :** all during a specified period of time **:** THROUGHOUT ⟨the perfect satisfaction which is one equation of love — ~ the days, the weeks —Ethel Wilson⟩ **b :** about a specified time or season ⟨~ 1900 his repute was still untarnished⟩ ⟨he had to find gunpowder and guns to keep the army from dissolving ~ Christmas —*Times Lit. Supp.*⟩

[5]**round** \"\ *n* -S [ME *rounde*, fr. [2]*round*; in some senses prob. fr. MF or F *rond, ronde*, fr. *rond* (adj.), fr. OF *roont, rount*] **1 :** something round: as **a :** a spherical object or surface **:** BALL, GLOBE **b** (1) **:** a circular area or surface or its circumference **:** CIRCLE, RING (2) *obs* **:** CROWN ⟨and wears upon his baby brow the ~ and top of sovereignty —Shak.⟩ **c :** a cylindrical object ⟨maintained a stock of bar steel that included ~s up to 2½ inches in diameter⟩ **d :** a circular building, wall, or other structure or a rounded or circular part of one (as a turret) **e :** a knot of people or a circle of things **f :** a topographical circle, bend, or curve **2 :** ROUND DANCE 1 ⟨a light fantastic ~ —John Milton⟩ **3 :** a polyphonic vocal composition in which three or four voices follow each other around in a canon at the unison or octave **:** CIRCULAR CANON **4 a :** a rung of a ladder or of a chair **b :** a round rod constituting a machine part (as a cylindrical bar of a lantern pinion) **c :** a rounded molding **5 a :** a circling or circuitous path or course **b :** motion in a circle or about a curving track ⟨won his race only with a final fast ~ of the track⟩ **6 :** a route or circuit habitually covered: as **a :** the circuit covered by a military watch at a camp or other installation; *also* **:** a military patrol that makes rounds to keep order in a community or to keep sentinels alert **b :** the beat or route regularly covered by a watchman or policeman — usu. used in pl. **c** *Brit* **:** the route of a newspaper delivery boy, milkman, or other vendor **d :** a series of professional calls on patients in a hospital made by a doctor or nurse — usu. used in pl. **e :** a series of social calls or visits **:** a routine of social activity ⟨a busy ~ of dances and parties⟩ **f :** a circuit or progression of similar calls or stops ⟨undertook a ~ of nightclubs after the play⟩ ⟨hurriedly made the ~s of his ice cream customers⟩ **g :** a line or course by which rumor, news, or other communication spreads among people — often used in pl. ⟨rumors calling his solvency in question were going the ~s of the brokerage offices⟩ ⟨knew he could expect any gossip that might be going the ~s⟩ **h rounds** *pl, Brit* **:** a circuit from farm to farm formerly followed by agricultural laborers **7** *obs* **:** a piece of sculpture modeled in full form unattached to a background **8 :** a drink of liquor apiece served at one time to each person in a group ⟨this ~ is on me⟩ **9 :** a series or sequence of actions, events, or affairs that recur in routine or repetitive manner ⟨politics exist that men may live the daily ~ in security —J.M. Cameron⟩ ⟨life for them is one ~ of committees and council meetings —Margaret Stewart⟩ **10 :** a cycle of time **:** a period that recurs in a fixed pattern ⟨the ~ of the hours⟩ ⟨the annual ~⟩ **11 a :** one shot fired by a weapon or by each man in a military unit **:** SALVO, VOLLEY **b :** a unit of ammunition consisting of all the parts (as a projectile, a propellant, an igniting charge, and a primer) necessary in the firing and functioning of one shot **12 :** a unit of card play constituted by each player's having had a turn (as in playing a card, receiving a card in the deal, dealing, or betting) **13 :** a unit or division of play in a sports contest or game which occupies a stated period of time, covers a prescribed distance, includes a specified number of moves or plays, or gives each player one turn: as **a :** any of various archery events in which a specified number of arrows are shot at prescribed distances **b :** one of the three-minute periods into which a boxing match is divided **c :** the playing of 18 holes of golf or one circuit of the course **d :** a series of 25 shots in trapshooting or skeet **e :** a match in an elimination tournament **14** *Brit* **:** a brewer's vessel in which fermentation is carried out **15 :** an outburst of applause ⟨took half a dozen curtain calls in response to repeated ~s of applause⟩ **16 a :** a hind leg of beef esp. between the rump and the lower leg ⟨a roast ~ of beef⟩ — see BEEF illustration **b :** a small beef casing **c :** a slice of food ⟨a ~ of bread⟩ ⟨a ~ of rolled dough⟩ ⟨a ~ of celeriac root⟩ **17 rounds** *pl* **:** the original striking order of a set of bells in change ringing ⟨the return to ~s concludes a set of changes⟩ **18 :** a rounded or curved part: as **a :** the shaft of a paddle **b :** the convex backbone or concave fore edge of a book **19 :** a group or series of drill holes blasted in sequence in advancing mine working places **20 :** an artist's brush having a round tapered point — compare BRIGHT, FLAT **21 :** a row in circular needlework (as kn. ting or crocheting) — **in round** *adv, of a book* **:** in the process or state of having the backbone rounded from side to side — **in the round** *adv (or adj)* **1 :** in full sculptured form unattached to a background **:** FREESTANDING ⟨an athlete superbly represented *in the round*⟩ ⟨a head shown *in the round*⟩ — distinguished from *relief* **2 :** with an inclusive or comprehensive view or representation ⟨a wise physician who saw his patients *in the round*⟩ ⟨the flat people of a novelist too little perceptive or skilled to show us humanity *in the round*⟩ **3 :** with a centered stage that is surrounded by an audience on all sides **4** *of a fish* **:** not eviscerated **:** WHOLE — **out of round :** in a distorted or imperfectly generated state of roundness ⟨great care and skill are required in machining long thin cylindrical work if it is not to be *out of round*⟩ ⟨a roll of newsprint should be stored on its end or it will get *out of round* and feed badly in the press⟩

[6]**round** \"\ *vb* -ED/-ING/-S [ME *rounden*, fr. [2]*round*] *vt* **1 a :** to make circular, spherical, or cylindrical **:** give a round or convex shape to (as the backbone of a book) **b :** to curve or curl into a ring or ball ⟨had ~*ed* her body into a little circular heap while she slept⟩ **c** (1) **:** to make (the lips) more or less round and protruded by lessening the distance between the corners of the mouth (as in the pronunciation of \ü\) (2) **:** to pronounce (a vowel or consonant) with rounding of the lips **:** LABIALIZE **2** *archaic* **a :** to trim (hair) short around the head **b :** to crop the hair of (a person) **c :** to trim the lobe of (a dog's ear) **3 a :** to go around **:** make the circuit of **b :** to pass part way around **:** reach the other side of by a curving course **:** go about (a point or corner) **:** DOUBLE ⟨whenever you ~ a turn, there's a view —E.W.Smith⟩ ⟨the railroad had ~*ed* the hill —*Amer. Guide Series: Ark.*⟩ ⟨slipped in loose dirt ~*ing* first base —Bob Broeg⟩ **4 :** to ring about **:** ENCIRCLE, ENCOMPASS, SURROUND ⟨the inclusive verge of golden metal that must ~ my brow —Shak.⟩ **5 a :** to bring to fullness or completion **:** perfect the form of **:** finish off ⟨has ~*ed* the characters by giving each a claim for sympathy —Henry Hewes⟩ **b :** to bring to perfection of style **:** POLISH ⟨music rose from paragraph after ~*ed* paragraph⟩ ⟨an epigram ~*ed* the sentence with a flourish⟩ **6 :** to cause to face about **:** turn or swing around ⟨with a dexterous swerve he ~*ed* the yawl about —Frederick Way⟩ **7 :** to express (a number) in briefer or less exact form **:** state as a round number: as **a :** to drop decimal figures to the right of a specified number of places after increasing the final remaining figure by 1 if the first digit dropped is 5 or greater ⟨11.3572 ~*ed* to three decimals becomes 11.357⟩ ⟨9.419 ~*ed* to two decimals is 9.42⟩ **b :** to express as an approximate round number rather than as the exact figure ⟨we are ~*ing* all figures to the nearest hundred million —G.V.Cox⟩ **8 a :** to cut (fleshed hides) in sections for treatment **:** TRIM **b** (1) **:** to cut (sole leather) to required shape with a knife rather than a die (2) **:** to cut (the sole of a shoe) to conform to the shape of a last after a sole has been attached ~ *vi* **1** *obs* **:** to go rounds as a guard or watchman **2 a :** to become circular or spherical **:** grow round or plump **:** attain a shapely form ⟨her body now ~s into womanhood⟩ **b :** to reach fullness, adequacy, or completion **:** DEVELOP, GROW ⟨the sales campaign he had outlined was now ~*ing* into final shape⟩ ⟨the century ~*ed* into its third decade —R.B. Fosdick⟩ **3 :** to take a curving line or direction **:** follow a winding course **:** BEND ⟨leaning wide on the turns like jockeys ~*ing* into the home stretch —H.L.Davis⟩ — **round on 1 :** to inform against **:** BETRAY **2 :** to turn against (a friend or ally) in anger or hostility **:** ASSAIL ⟨she *rounded on* him fiercely —Kathleen Freeman⟩ ⟨was always *rounding on* his own side on the eve of victory —L.B.Nicolson⟩

[1]**round about** *adv* [ME, fr. [3]*round* + *about*] **1 :** around in a circle or circular course **:** on all sides or in all directions **:** in the vicinity **:** NEARBY ⟨rows of orange trees . . . contrast pleasantly with the white walls *round about* —Samuel Van Valkenburg & Ellsworth Huntington⟩ **2 :** in an opposite direction ⟨turned *round about* and stalked off⟩ **3 :** in an indirect way ⟨came *round about* and slowly to these conclusions⟩

[2]**round about** *prep* **1 :** in an encircling course about **:** so as to move around ⟨danced lightly *round about* the maypole⟩ **2 :** in a circle about **:** so as to surround **:** here and there around **:** in the vicinity of ⟨took up positions in the desert *round about* a walled city⟩ **3 :** at approximately a specified time ⟨*round about* the turn of the century another science was lying in wait for the artist —Herbert Read⟩

[1]**roundabout** \'=,=,=\ *n* -S [[1]*round about*] **1 :** something circular: as **a** *archaic* **:** a circular course or path **b** *archaic* **:** a circular encampment **c** *chiefly dial* **:** a surrounding hedge **2 a :** a circuitous way to a destination or object **:** an indirect route **:** DETOUR ⟨the painting had reached the U. S. in the typical ~ of forgotten masterpieces, after a journey that began in 1909 —*Time*⟩ **b :** an oblique or indirect expression **:** CIRCUMLOCUTION **3** *Brit* **:** MERRY-GO-ROUND ⟨it looks like some new and terrifying ~ at a fairground —Ivor Jones⟩ ⟨what the public lose materially on the swings as consumers they will more than gain on the ~s as producers —*Economist*⟩ **4** *archaic* **:** ROUND DANCE 1 **5** *also* **roundabout jacket :** a short close-fitting jacket worn by men and boys esp. in the 19th century **6** *Brit* **:** ROTARY 2 **7 a :** ROUND TRIP **b :** a rambling excursion

[2]**roundabout** \"\ *adj* [[1]*round about*] **1 :** marked by circuitousness or indirection: as **a :** deviating from a straight line or course **:** CURVING, MEANDERING, WINDING ⟨the train has to come a ~ way —Cortland Fitzsimmons⟩ **b :** oblique or devious in speech or conduct ⟨write ~ paragraphs —C.E.Kellogg⟩ ⟨his approach to her was ~ —Jean Stafford⟩ **2 :** rounded in figure **:** PLUMP ⟨a little ~ woman with rosy cheeks —Elizabeth Goudge⟩ — **round·about·ness** *n* -ES

**roundabout chair** *n* [[2]*roundabout*] **:** CORNER CHAIR

**round angle** *n* [[2]*round*] **:** the plane angle swept through by a half line in turning positively in a plane about its extremity as a center until it returns to its original position ⟨a *round angle* is 360 degrees⟩ — compare RIGHT ANGLE, STRAIGHT ANGLE

**round-arm** \'=,=\ *adj* [[2]*round* + *arm*] **:** marked by an outward or horizontal swing of the arm ⟨a *round-arm* blow⟩

**round back** *n* [[2]*round*] **:** the backbone of a book when distinctly convex — compare SQUARE BACK

**round bale** *n* **:** a cotton bale containing a rolled-up sheet of cotton fiber wrapped in burlap and averaging 250 pounds in weight

**round-bale press** *n* **:** a hay press that binds a cylindrical bale with twine and leaves an air space running lengthwise through its center

**round barrow** *n* **:** a Neolithic British burial mound of rounded shape built by a brachycephalic people — compare LONG BARROW

**round bass** *n* **:** FLIER 3

**round bracket** *n* **:** BRACKET 4c

**round buffalo** *n* **:** BLACK BUFFALO 1

**round cell** *n* **:** a small lymphocyte or a closely related cell esp. occurring in an area of chronic infection or as the typical cell of some sarcomas

**round church** *n* **1 :** a church of circular plan usu. having a ring of columns dividing a tower nave from a surrounding aisle **2 :** a church of polygonal plan with central or radial rather than longitudinal disposition

**round clam** *n* **:** QUAHOG 1

**round dance** *n* **1 :** a folk or ritual group or couple dance in which participants form a ring and move in a prescribed direction **2 :** a ballroom dance in which couples progress around the room

**round-dealing** *adj, obs* **:** CANDID, OPEN, PLAIN DEALING

**rounded** *adj* [fr. past part. of [6]*round*] **1 a :** convex, curving, or round in shape **:** flowing rather than jagged or angular ⟨every ~ knoll was torn open in the hope of finding clues —*Amer. Guide Series: Minn.*⟩ ⟨scoop neckline; smooth, ~ shoulders —*Americana Annual*⟩ **b :** showing a norm or ideal of bodily perfection **:** SHAPELY ⟨~ like a swimmer or a wrestler —Carl Van Doren⟩ **c :** built with round rather than pointed arches **2 :** fully developed **:** COMPLETE, PERFECTED: as **a :** marked by generous attainment or developed character ⟨a ~ human being, compellingly vivid and alive —*Saturday Rev.*⟩ ⟨a mind well ~ and austere, clear with himself as with others —Robert Lawrence⟩ **b :** marked by full or many-sided perfection or excellence ⟨the ~ analysis and estimate of a great novel by a critic both firm and sensitive —E.K.Brown⟩ ⟨~ culture⟩ **c :** conceived, drawn, or presented in full form or in all aspects **:** shown perceptively or penetratingly **:** comprehensively realized ⟨a sympathetic, ~ and complete picture of a young girl growing up —*advt*⟩ **d :** polished in phrasing or style **:** deftly turned **:** FINISHED ⟨significance and effect closely mated in the telling word and the ~ period⟩ **3 a :** having full unmuted resonance **:** MELLOW, SONOROUS ⟨fine ~ sound, especially of the piano —Irving Kolodin⟩ **b :** produced with rounded lips **:** ROUND, LABIALIZED **4 :** numerically exact only to a convenient degree **:** APPROXIMATE ⟨the figures given are slightly ~ statements of the average —W.C.Allee⟩ — **round·ed·ness** *n* -ES

**roun·del** *or* **roun·dle** \'raündᵊl\ *n* -S [ME *roundel, roundell, rundel*, fr. OF *rondel, rondelle*, fr. *roont* (fem. *ronde*) round + *-el, -elle*, dim. suffix — more at ROUND] **1 :** something circular **:** a round figure: as **a** *chiefly dial* **:** a circle marked out or otherwise formed **b :** a circular group or ring of things or persons **c :** a plain or colored glass disk (as for a railway signal lamp or a theatrical lighting device) **d :** a circular tray, trencher, or small table **2 :** a circular panel, window, or niche; *esp* **:** a recessed circular niche for a bust — compare ROSETTE **3 :** any of various small circular subordinaries representing balls or plates of metal or color — compare BEZANT, GOLPE, GUZE, [4]HURT, PELLET, TORTEAU **4 :** RONDEL 1b(1) **5 a :** ROUND 3 **b :** ROUND DANCE 1 **6 a :** RONDEL 2a **b :** an English modified rondeau whose refrain comes after the first and last of three tercets and fits into the rhyme scheme *aba B, bab, aba B*

**roun·de·lay** \'raündə,lā *also* 'rän-\ *n* -S [modif. (influenced by [4]*lay*) of MF *rondelet*, dim. of *rondel* small circle, rondeau, fr. OF — more at ROUNDEL] **1 a :** RONDEAU 2a **b :** a simple lively-spirited song or air ⟨water nymphs that are singing their ~s under me —H.W.Longfellow⟩ **2 :** ROUND DANCE **3 :** a poem with a refrain that recurs frequently or at fixed intervals as in a rondel

[1]**rounder** *comparative of* ROUND

[2]**round·er** \'raündə(r)\ *n* -S [partly fr. [5]*round* + *-er*; partly fr. [6]*round* + *-er*] **1 a** *archaic* **:** a guard or watchman who makes rounds **b :** a Methodist local preacher who rides a circuit **2 :** a dissolute or rakish person **:** WASTREL ⟨nightclub ~s and pool players —*Newsweek*⟩ **3 a rounders** *pl but sing in constr*

: an English game that is played with ball and bat and somewhat resembles baseball **b :** a circuit of the bases made on a single hit in the game of rounders **4 :** one that rounds by hand or by machine: as **a :** a dividing machine operator who rolls cut pieces of dough into balls **b :** a shoe worker who trims insoles or outsoles according to a pattern **c :** one that rounds the backs of books **d :** an operator of a turning machine that rounds and trims barrel heads or basket bottoms **e :** one that cuts hat brims to prescribed width **5 :** any of various boring or shaping tools **6 :** a boxing match lasting a specified number of rounds ⟨went on to win a dull 10-*rounder* —*Sports Illustrated*⟩ **7 rounders** *pl but sing in constr* **:** ROUNDSTERS

**rounder and backer** *n* **:** a machine that accepts a book with a flat backbone, rolls it out to give concave front and convex back edges, and completes the shaping by backing — compare ROLLER-BACKER

**roundest** *superlative of* ROUND

**round–eyed** \ˈ⸗ˈ⸗\ *adj* [²*round* + *eyed*] **:** having the eyes wide open (as with astonishment)

**round file** *n* **:** a file of circular cross section used for filing round holes — compare RATTAIL FILE

**roundfish** \ˈ⸗ˌ⸗\ *n* **1 :** an ordinary fish as distinguished from a flatfish **2 :** an entire fish as distinguished from a dressed fish

**round game** *n* **:** a game usu. for four or more players in which every participant plays for himself and has no partner

**round hand** *n* **:** a bold plain handwriting ⟨write a fair *round hand* —C.S.Forester⟩

**round haul net** *or* **round haul seine** *n* **:** a fishnet (as a purse seine or a lampara) designed for surrounding a school of fishes so that they can be hauled in en masse

**roundhead** \ˈ⸗ˌ⸗\ *n* [²*round* + *head*] **1** *usu cap* **:** a Puritan or member of the Parliamentary party in England at the time of Charles I and Oliver Cromwell — compare CAVALIER **2 :** a brachycephalic person

**roundheaded** \ˈ⸗ˈ⸗⸗\ *adj* [²*round* + *headed*] **:** having a round head: as **a :** BRACHYCEPHALIC **b** *usu cap* (1) **:** having the hair closely cropped like the Roundheads (2) **:** PURITANICAL ⟨*Roundheaded* criticism —Heywood Broun⟩ **c :** rounded on the top or end ⟨a ~ screw⟩ **d :** having the head or upper part semicircular ⟨a ~ window⟩ ⟨~ door⟩ — **round·head·ed·ness** *n* -ES

**roundheaded apple tree borer** *n* **:** APPLE TREE BORER b

**roundheaded borer** *n* **:** a larval beetle (family Cerambycidae) with a small head with large strong mandibles, a large prothorax, and the legs vestigial or absent that develops and feeds in woody plant tissues — compare BARDEE, HUHU

**round–heart** \ˈ⸗ˌ⸗\ *n* [²*round* + *heart*] **:** PURPLE MEADOW PARSNIP

**round heart disease** *n* **:** an obscure disease of poultry in which affected birds often die suddenly without previous signs of illness of a dilated hypertrophied heart with fatty infiltration of its muscles and usu. passive hyperemia of the lungs and viscera

**roundheel** \ˈ⸗ˌ⸗\ *n* [²*round* + *heel*] **:** PUSHOVER ⟨a luscious ~ with a heart of gold —J.T.Latouche⟩

**round herring** *n* **:** any of numerous small mostly tropical marine fishes (family Dussumieriidae) resembling the herrings but having the belly smooth and rounded

**roundhouse** \ˈ⸗ˌ⸗\ *n* [in sense 1, fr. ⁵*round* patrol; in other senses fr. ²*round*] **1** *archaic* **:** a constable's jail **:** GUARDHOUSE, LOCKUP **2 :** a circular building for housing and repairing locomotives **3 a :** a cabin or apartment on the afterpart of a quarterdeck having the poop for its roof (as on 18th century sailing ships) **b :** a privy on deck near the bow **4 :** a meld of one king and queen of each suit scoring 240 in every form of pinochle except two-handed pinochle in which it scores at most 220 — called also *round trip* **5 :** a hook in boxing delivered with a wide or exaggerated swing **6 :** a wide slow outcurve in baseball with little or no drop

**round·house·man** \ˈ⸗ˌ⸗mən\ *n, pl* **roundhousemen :** one who is employed in a railroad roundhouse

**round in** *vt* [⁶*round*] **:** to haul in on (a rope, esp. a weather brace)

¹**rounding** *n* -S [fr. gerund of ⁶*round*] **1 a :** the act or process of making or becoming round **b :** the trimming and cutting of hides **c :** the act or result of pronouncing with rounded lips — called also *lip-rounding* **2 :** something that has been made round **:** a rounded object, surface, or corner **3 :** rope rejected for other use and wound round a ship's cable as chafing gear **4 :** the expressing of a number with only a convenient degree of exactness (as by dropping decimals beyond a stated number of places or by substituting zeros for final integers)

²**rounding** *adj* [fr. pres. part. of ⁶*round*] **1 :** ENCIRCLING, ENCOMPASSING **2 :** tending towards roundness **:** becoming round **3 :** circling round **4 :** of, relating to, or used for trimming or shaping to roundness ⟨a ~ tool⟩

**round iron** *n* [²*round*] **:** a bulbous-headed iron tool used when hot to smooth off soldered joints

**round·ish** \ˈrau̇ndish, -dēsh\ *adj* [²*round* + *-ish*] **:** somewhat round

**roundle** *var of* ROUNDEL

**round–leaved dogwood** \ˈ⸗ˌ⸗-\ *or* **round–leaf dogwood** *n* [²*round* + *leaved* or *leaf*] **:** GREEN OSIER b

**round–leaved wintergreen** *n* **:** a wintergreen (*Pyrola americana*) with small broadly elliptic or round leaves

**round·let** \ˈrau̇ndlət, rapid -nl-; *usu* -əd·+V\ *n* -S [ME *roundelet*, fr. MF *rondelet* — more at ROUNDELAY] **1 :** a little circle or round object **:** DISK **2 :** a 15th century hat for men with a round padded edge and loose drapery forming the crown and hanging over the edge **3 :** RUNDLET **4** *heraldry* **:** ROUNDEL 3

**round ligament** *n* [²*round*] **1 :** a fibrous cord resulting from the obliteration of the umbilical vein of the fetus and passing from the umbilicus to the notch in the anterior border of the liver and along the under surface of that organ **2 :** either of a pair of rounded cords arising from each side of the uterus and traceable through the inguinal canal to the tissue of the labia majora into which they merge **3 :** a triangular ligament of the hip joint implanted by its apex into a depression near the middle of the head of the femur and by its broad base into the margins of the cotyloid notch of the innominate bone

**roundline** \ˈ⸗ˌ⸗\ *n* **:** a 3-strand right-handed line used for seizings — compare HAMBROLINE

**round lot** *n* **1 :** a lot of 100 or a multiple of 100 shares of active stock traded on an exchange **2 :** a lot of 10 or a multiple of 10 shares of a few designated inactive stocks traded on an exchange — compare ODD LOT

**round·ly** \ˈrau̇ndlē, -li, *rapid* -nl-\ *adv* [ME, fr. ²*round* + *-ly*] **1 a :** COMPLETELY, FULLY, WHOLLY ⟨returned to France feeling he had been ~ snubbed —C.G.Bowers⟩ **b :** in a bold, open or plainspoken manner **:** BLUNTLY, CANDIDLY ⟨~ criticized his uncongenial master —R.A.Hall b.1911⟩ **2 a :** in a brisk or vigorous manner **:** PROMPTLY, SMARTLY **b :** BITTERLY, SCATHINGLY, SHARPLY ⟨~ denounced him for quitting —F.J. Haskin⟩ **3** *obs* **:** with ready or unimpeded speech **:** FLUENTLY **4 :** CIRCULARLY, PLUMPLY, ROTUNDLY **5 :** in a general way **:** in round numbers **:** COMPREHENSIVELY ⟨although he has some specialized knowledge, he is ~ and exhaustively general —Elizabeth Hardwick⟩

**round·man** \ˈrau̇n(d)mən\ *n, pl* **roundmen** [⁵*round* + *man*] **:** a slaughterhouse worker who cleans rounds for use as casings

**round·ness** \ˈrau̇nnəs *also* -ndnəs\ *n* -ES [ME *roundnesse*, fr. ²*round* + *-nesse* -ness] **:** the quality or state of being round

**roundnose** \ˈ⸗ˌ⸗\ *or* **roundnosed** \ˈ⸗ˈ⸗\ *adj* [²*round* + *nose* or *nosed*] **:** having a round or rounded nose **:** rounded on corners or edges; *specif* **:** having a cutting edge rounded to increase tool life ⟨a ~ turning tool⟩ or to make a curving or gouging cut ⟨a ~ chisel⟩ **:** having the working end rounded ⟨~ pliers⟩

**round of beam** [⁵*round*] **:** the camber of a ship's deck beams

**round off** *vt* [⁶*round*] **1 :** to finish off into curved or rounded form **2 :** to bring to symmetry or completion ⟨*rounded off* his property by purchase of the additional land⟩ ⟨a term in Congress *rounded off* his career⟩ **3 :** ⁶ROUND 7a ⟨*round* all decimals *off* to the nearest thousandth⟩

**roundoff** \ˈ⸗ˌ⸗\ *n* -S [*round off*] **:** a tumbling stunt in which the body makes one revolution from feet to hands to feet incorporating a half twist — compare CARTWHEEL

**round out** *vb* [⁶*round*] *vt* **:** to bring to completion or fullness **:** finish out ⟨*round out* my quartet of Americana with an autobiography —E.A.Weeks⟩ ⟨the republic had *rounded out* a century of independence —Sidney Warren⟩ **~** *vi* **:** to grow round or plump

**round pompano** *n* [²*round*] **:** a small pompano (*Trachinotus falcatus*) found from Brazil northward sometimes to Cape Cod

**round robin** *n* **1 a :** a written petition, memorial, or protest to which the signatures are affixed in a circle so as not to indicate who signed first **b :** a statement signed by several persons ⟨a *round robin* signed by 15 senators, who declared that . . . they would not vote to convict the governor —Hodding Carter⟩ **c :** a letter sent in turn to the members of a group (as a college class) each of whom signs and forwards it sometimes after adding information or comment ⟨a *round robin* letter to religious leaders in the community requesting that they pass the bibliography on to the next person on a list —*Amer. Library Assoc. Bull.*⟩ **2 :** a talk or meeting in which several participants share **:** ROUND TABLE ⟨got together on a *round robin* telephone hookup —*Newsweek*⟩ **3 :** a tournament in which every contestant meets every other contestant in turn **4 :** SERIES, SEQUENCE, ROUND ⟨another *round robin* of price boosts —*Newsweek*⟩ ⟨*round robin* of colorcasts for all the regular shows on the network —*Advertising Age*⟩ **5 :** ROUND SCAD

**round rush** *n* **:** SOFT RUSH

**rounds** *pl of* ROUND, *pres 3d sing of* ROUND

**round scad** *n* **:** a small fusiform carangid fish (*Decapterus punctatus*) of the western Atlantic related to and often included among the mackerel scads — called also *cigarfish*, *quiaquia*

**round scale** *n* **:** any of various armored scales (as the San Jose scale) that constitute the genus *Aspidiotus* and have a nearly circular covering

**rounds chef** *n* [⁵*round*] **:** ROUNDSMAN 3

**roundseam** \ˈ⸗ˌ⸗\ *n* [²*round*] **:** a seam used to join the edges of canvas without lapping (as when sewing the bottom into a sea bag)

**round–seeded spinach** \ˈ⸗ˌ⸗⸗-\ *n* **:** a spinach (*Spinacia oleracea inermis*) having the fruit without spines

**round seizing** *n* **:** a seizing in which the lines seized are parallel to each other and a double binding layer is used — compare FLAT SEIZING

**round shot** *n* **:** an obsolete spherical projectile for ordnance

**round–shouldered** \ˈ⸗ˈ⸗⸗\ *adj* **:** having the shoulders stooping or rounded

**rounds·man** \ˈrau̇n(d)zmən\ *n, pl* **roundsmen** [⁵round] **1 :** an English laborer receiving parish relief and working for various farmers in turn under a system now obsolete **2 :** one that makes rounds: as **a :** a supervisory police officer of the grade of sergeant or just below **b** *Brit* **:** ROUTE MAN ⟨a butcher's ~ in London —Flora Thompson⟩ **c :** WATCHMAN **3 :** a cook capable of substituting for or assisting any of the specialty cooks — called also *rounds chef*, *swingman*, *tournant* **4 :** one who patrols a petroleum refinery to supervise the watchmen and porters

**round splice** *n* [²*round*] **:** a long splice keeping the shape of the rope

**round stave basket** *n* **:** a basket used chiefly for fruits and vegetables that is usu. circular and of greater diameter than depth and is made in standard capacities ranging from ⅛ bushel to 2 bushels

**round steak** *n* [⁵*round*] **:** a steak cut from the whole round of beef including the bone — compare BOTTOM ROUND, TOP ROUND; see BEEF illustration

**round·sters** \ˈrau̇n(d)stə(r)z, -n(t)st-\ *n pl but sing in constr* [irreg. fr. ⁵*round*] **:** the privilege in marbles of shooting from any point on the ring line ⟨if your shooter goes outside the ring, you may take ~⟩

**round stingray** *n* [²*round*] **:** a small round-bodied stingray (*Urobatis halleri*) common in shallow water along the southern California coast — called also *stingaree*

**roundstone** \ˈ⸗ˌ⸗\ *n* **1 :** any naturally rounded stone — compare BOULDER, COBBLE, PEBBLE **2 :** a paving cobblestone

**round table** *n* [ME; fr. the Round Table of Arthurian legend] **1** *often cap* **a :** any of various knightly assemblies or tournaments modeled on King Arthur's Round Table **b :** any of various English sites, structures, or natural formations associated in legend with King Arthur's Round Table **2 a :** a conference for discussion or deliberation by several participants often seated at a round table so that no precedence in rank can be indicated **b :** the participants in such a conference **c :** the discussion carried on at a round table conference

**roundtail** \ˈ⸗ˌ⸗\ *n* [²*round* + *tail*] **:** BONYTAIL

**round–tailed muskrat** \ˈ⸗ˌ⸗-\ *n* **:** a large swamp-living vole (*Neofiber alleni*) of Florida resembling a small muskrat but having the tail cylindrical and tapering instead of keeled

**round–the–clock** *adj* **:** AROUND-THE-CLOCK

**round–the–corner** \ˈ⸗⸗ˈ⸗⸗\ *adj* **:** of or relating to a card sequence in which the king and deuce both connect with the ace

**round–the–head** \ˈ⸗⸗ˈ⸗\ *adj* **:** played forehanded on the backhand side of the body (as the left side of a right-handed player) — used of a circular stroke in badminton

**round timber** *n* [²*round*] **1 :** timber used (as for poles) without being squared by sawing or hewing **2** *South & Midland* **:** untapped turpentine-yielding pine trees

**round to** *vi* [⁶*round*] **:** to come about with head to the wind in either direction usu. preparatory to heaving to or coming to anchor

**roundtop** \ˈ⸗ˌ⸗\ *n* [²*round*] **:** a round platform at a masthead

**round tower** *n* **:** a circular stone tower ranging in height from 60 to 150 feet, having a conical cap, and built in considerable numbers in Ireland from the 9th to the 13th centuries as refuges from Viking invaders

**roundtree** \ˈ⸗ˌ⸗\ *n* [alter. of *rowan tree*] **:** AMERICAN MOUNTAIN ASH

**round trip** *n* [²*round*] **1 :** a trip to a place and back usu. over the same route **2 :** ROUNDHOUSE 4

**round turn** *n* **1 :** one turn of a rope round a timber or belaying pin or around a bollard on a pier to stop a ship suddenly **2 :** a foul hawse resulting from a 720-degree turn made by a ship riding at two anchors — compare ELBOW IN HAWSE

**round up** *vb* [⁶*round*] *vt* **1 :** to haul up (as slack rope through its leading block or a tackle by its fall) **2 a :** to collect (cattle) by riding around them and driving them in **b :** to gather in or bring together (scattered persons or things) ⟨police *rounded up* members of a gambling ring⟩ ⟨*rounds up* the news in a nightly 11 o'clock broadcast⟩ **~** *vi* **:** to collect in a group

**roundup** \ˈ⸗ˌ⸗\ *n* -S [in sense 1, fr. ⁶*round* + *up*; in other senses fr. *round up*] **1 :** an upward curvature (as in a ship's deck) **:** CAMBER **2 a :** the gathering together of cattle by riders (as for branding or for shipment to market) **b :** the men and horses engaged in a roundup **3 :** a gathering in of scattered persons or things ⟨a ~ of criminals⟩ **4 a :** a summary (as in a printed or broadcast news report) of related information of various kinds or from various sources ⟨a ~ of the year's financial news⟩ **b :** a brief résumé of late news ⟨said he heard it on the 11 o'clock news ~⟩

**roun·dure** \ˈrau̇njə(r)\ *n* [²*round* + *-ure*] *archaic* **:** ROUNDNESS

**round window** *n* **:** the cochlear fenestra of the ear

**roundwise** *adv (or adj)* [²*round* + *-wise*] *obs* **:** in a circular form or manner

**roundwood** \ˈ⸗ˌ⸗\ *n* [*round* (alter. of *rowan*) + *wood*] **1 :** AMERICAN MOUNTAIN ASH **2 :** ROUND TIMBER 1

**roundworm** \ˈ⸗ˌ⸗\ *n* [²*round*] **:** a nematode worm and sometimes also a gordian or acanthocephalan worm as distinguished from a flatworm or tapeworm

**round yam** *n* **:** BURDEKIN VINE

**roun·tree** \ˈrōn‚trē\ *Scot var of* ROWAN TREE

¹**roup** \ˈrōp, ˈrüp\ *vb* -ED/-ING/-S [ME *roupen*, fr. MD *roepen* to cry out, call; akin to OE *hrōpan* to cry out, call, OHG *hruoffan*, ON *hrōpa* to slander, Goth *hropjan* to cry out, call, and perh. to OE *hrēth* glory — more at CADUCEUS] *vi, dial chiefly Brit* **:** to call or shout hoarsely **:** CROAK **~** *vt, Scot* **:** to sell at auction

²**roup** \"\ *n* -S **1** *Scot* **:** CLAMOR, SHOUTING **2** *chiefly Scot* **:** a public auction

³**roup** \ˈrüp\ *n* -S [origin unknown] **:** any of various respiratory disorders of poultry: as **a :** coryza of chickens esp. when in an advanced stage and marked by the presence of thick cheesy mucus — compare PIP **b :** INFECTIOUS SINUSITIS **c :** FOWL POX b **d :** avitaminosis A of poultry

**roup·et** \ˈrōpət, ˈrüp-\ *adj* [Sc *roup* hoarseness + *-et* -ed] *Scot* **:** afflicted with a sore throat **:** HOARSE

**roupy** \-pi\ *adj* -ER/-EST [Sc *roup* hoarseness (prob. of imit. origin) + *-y*] *chiefly Scot* **:** HOARSE

**rous·ant** \ˈrau̇zᵊnt\ *adj* [¹*rouse* + *-ant*] **:** RISING — used of a heraldic bird, esp. a swan

¹**rouse** \ˈrau̇z\ *vb* -ED/-ING/-S [ME *rousen*, *rowsen*] *vi* **1** *obs* **a :** to erect and shake the feathers — used esp. of a hawk **b :** to stand on end ⟨my fell of hair would . . . ~, and stir as life were in't —Shak.⟩ **2 a :** to become aroused from or as if from sleep **:** AWAKEN, STIR ⟨laughed and dozed, then *roused* and read again —Vachel Lindsay⟩ ⟨before she could ~ from this insult —Grace Kinnicut⟩ — often used with *up* ⟨from under . . . ragged blankets figures *roused* up from the dirt floor —F.V.W. Mason⟩ **b :** to gather strength **:** MOUNT, INTENSIFY ⟨our indignation ~*s* —Adam Smith⟩ **3** *slang Austral* **:** to speak angrily **:** RANT, RAVE **~** *vt* **1** *archaic* **:** to cause to break from cover ⟨*roused* a hart —Charles Kingsley⟩ **2** *obs* **a :** to cause to erect and shake (the feathers) **:** RUFFLE **b :** to lift up **:** RAISE ⟨being mounted, and both *roused* in their seats —Shak.⟩ **3 a :** to call forth **:** set in motion **:** RAISE, STIMULATE ⟨names in the railway time-table . . . first ~ romantic images in the mind of the boy —Edmund Wilson⟩ ⟨these questions . . . sometimes *roused* charges and countercharges —Alan Valentine⟩ **b :** to kindle to intensity **:** EXCITE, INFLAME ⟨such wars ~ limited passions —Herbert Agar⟩ ⟨the nobility that is in us is *roused* to respond —H.A.Overstreet⟩ **c :** to arouse from sleep or torpor **:** AWAKEN, STIR ⟨use . . . histrionics to ~ her audience —Andrea Parke⟩ ⟨the government was *roused* to unparalleled activity —B.E.Supple⟩ ⟨the boat ~*s* wild ducks to flight —*Amer. Guide Series: Mich.*⟩ ⟨made an effort . . . to ~ herself from sorrow —Margaret A. Barnes⟩ — often used with *up* ⟨*roused* up his brothers, who were in bed —William Black⟩ **d** (1) **:** to alert for action — used with *out* ⟨*roused* out his anchor watch —K.M.Dodson⟩ (2) **:** to haul strongly (as on a rope or hawser) **syn** see STIR

²**rouse** \"\ *n* -S **:** an act or instance of rousing; *esp* **:** an excited stir ⟨a ~ of voices —Carl Sandburg⟩

³**rouse** \"\ *n* -S [alter. (resulting fr. incorrect division of *drink carouse*) of ¹*carouse*] **1** *obs* **:** DRINK, TOAST **2** *archaic* **:** CAROUSAL

⁴**rouse** \"\ *vt* -ED/-ING/-S [by shortening fr. earlier *arrouse* to sprinkle, bedew, fr. ME *arousen*, fr. MF *aroser*, fr. (assumed) VL *adrosare*, fr. L *ad-* + *ros* dew — more at ROSEMARY] **:** to cure (as herring) by salting

⁵**rouse** \ˈrüz\ *var of* ROOSE

**rouseabout** \ˈ⸗⸗ˌ⸗\ *n* -S [¹*rouse* + *about*] *Austral* **:** a man of all work; *specif* **:** a handyman on a sheep farm **:** KNOCKABOUT

**rouse·ment** \ˈrau̇zmənt\ *n* -S [¹*rouse* + *-ment*] **:** an act or instance of stirring up **:** AROUSAL

**rous·er** \ˈrau̇zə(r)\ *n* -S **:** one that rouses: as **a :** one that awakens or excites **b :** an implement for stirring a fermenting brew **c :** something superlative of its kind **:** HUMDINGER ⟨a real ~ of a storm —R.L.Taylor⟩

¹**rousing** *n* -S [fr. gerund of ¹*rouse*] **1 :** an act or instance of stirring up **:** AGITATION, DISTURBANCE **2** *slang Austral* **:** SCOLDING ⟨the women and the youngsters gave me a ~ —*Melbourne (Australia) Argus*⟩

²**rousing** *adj* [fr. pres. part. of ¹*rouse*] **1 a :** having the power to rouse **:** EXCITING, STIRRING ⟨a ~ speech⟩ ⟨brought the meeting to a close with a ~ hymn —Agnes S. Turnbull⟩ **b :** BRISK, LIVELY ⟨a ~ ballet about three sailors on shore leave —Walter Terry⟩ ⟨milliners doing a ~ trade at Easter⟩ **2 :** exceptional of its kind **:** SUPERLATIVE ⟨wrote three ~ best sellers in a row —Bennett Cerf⟩ — **rous·ing·ly** *adv*

**rous sarcoma** *also* **rous' sarcoma** *or* **rous's sarcoma** \ˈrau̇s(əz)-\ *n, usu cap R* [after F. Peyton *Rous* b1879 Am. physician] **:** a readily transplantable malignant spindle-cell sarcoma of chickens that is transmissible by cell-free filtrate and so is regarded as due to a specific carcinogenic virus

**rous·seau·ean** *or* **rous·seau·ian** \rüˈsōēən\ *adj, usu cap* [Jean Jacques *Rousseau* †1778 Fr. philosopher & author + E *-ean* or *-ian*] **:** ROUSSEAUISTIC

**rous·seau·esque** \ˌrüsōˈesk\ *adj, usu cap* [Jean Jacques *Rousseau* + E *-esque*] **:** ROUSSEAUISTIC

**rous·seau·ism** \rüˈsō‚izəm\ *n* -S *usu cap* [Jean Jacques *Rousseau* + E *-ism*] **:** the philosophy of Jean Jacques Rousseau or his followers and esp. the doctrines of the inherent equality of men, the general will as the basis of government, and the corruption and degradation of human nature by civilization — compare SOCIAL CONTRACT

**rous·seau·ist** \-ōəst\ *or* **rous·seau·ite** \-ō‚īt\ *n* -S *usu cap* [Jean Jacques *Rousseau* + E *-ist* or *-ite*] **:** a follower of Rousseau or adherent to Rousseauism

**rous·seau·is·tic** \ˌrüsōˈistik\ *adj, usu cap* [Jean Jacques *Rousseau* + E *-istic*] **:** of, relating to, or characteristic of Rousseau or Rousseauism

**rous·sette** \rüˈset\ *n* -S [F, fr. MF, fr. fem. of *rousset* reddish, fr. OF — more at RUSSET] **:** a small shark or dogfish of the genus *Scyliorhinus*

**rous·sin's salt** \ˈrüsᵊnz-\ *n, usu cap R* [after François Zacharie *Roussin* †1894 Fr. chemist] **:** any of two series of alkali metal salts that are nitrosyl and sulfur complexes of iron: **a :** a red unstable salt having the general formula $M[Fe(NO)_2S]$ and obtainable by reaction of nitric oxide with ferrous sulfide **b :** a black more stable salt having the general formula $M[Fe_4(NO)_7S_3]$ and obtainable (as by treatment with alkali) from a red salt

¹**roust** \ˈrau̇st\ *vb* -ED/-ING/-S [alter. of ¹*rouse*] *vt, dial* **:** to rout esp. out of bed **:** cause to appear **:** ROUSE — usu. used with *out* or *up* ⟨would roll back into his blankets . . . till the sound of another boat ~*ed* him out again —H.L.Davis⟩ ⟨the bartender ~*ed* up an odd bottle of . . . port —Jack Kerouac⟩ **~** *vi* [Sc, to shout, roar, fr. *roust* voice, shout, fr. ME *rowst*, fr. ON *raust* voice] *slang Austral* **:** ¹ROUSE 3

²**roust** \ˈrüst\ *n* -S [of Scand origin; akin to ON *rōst* current] *dial Eng* **:** a strong tide or current esp. in a narrow channel

**roustabout** \ˈ⸗⸗ˌ⸗\ *n* -S [¹*roust* + *about*] **1 a :** a dock worker or deckhand **:** and chore boy on a dirty trawler —L.C. Douglas⟩ **b :** an unskilled or semiskilled laborer; *esp* **:** one working in an oil field or refinery **:** FLOORMAN ⟨~*s* . . . maintain the oil wells once they are brought in —*Newsweek*⟩ **c :** a member of the working crew of a circus responsible for erection and dismantling of tents, care of the grounds, and handling of animals and equipment **2** *Austral* **:** ROUSEABOUT

**roust·er** \ˈrau̇stə(r)\ *n* -S [¹*roust* + *-er*] **:** ROUSTABOUT 1

¹**rout** \ˈrau̇t, *usu* -d·+V\ *vi* -ED/-ING/-S [ME *routen*, fr. OE *hrūtan*; akin to OHG *hrūzan* to snore, ON *hrjōta*, and prob. to OE *hrot* thick fluid — more at CORYZA] *archaic* **:** SNORE

²**rout** \"\ *n* -S [ME *rute*, *route*, fr. MF *route*, troop, band, defeat, fr. (assumed) VL *rupta*, fr. L, fem. of *ruptus*, past part. of *rumpere* to break — more at REAVE] **1 a :** a crowd of people **:** MOB, THRONG ⟨succeeded by a ~ of rabbis, reverends, and monsignors —Dwight MacDonald⟩; *specif* **:** RABBLE ⟨the butler, the parlormaid, and the ~ from belowstairs —J.C. Trewin⟩ **b** *or* **route** \"\ *archaic* **:** a company of animals **:** FLOCK ⟨restless ~*s* of sheep —John Clare⟩ **c :** a large number **:** MULTITUDE ⟨the ~ of series of books and pamphlets on the war —*Times Lit. Supp.*⟩ **d :** NUMBER, HERD ⟨you will not swell the ~ of lads that wore their honors out —A.E.Housman⟩ ⟨a vulgar comment . . . by the common ~ —Shak.⟩ **2 :** a disturbance of the peace by persons assembled with intent to do something and actually making a motion toward its execution which if executed would make them rioters **3** *archaic* **a :** DISTURBANCE, UPROAR **b :** FUSS ⟨make such a ~ about it —Harriet Granville⟩ **4 :** a fashionable gathering **:** RECEPTION, SOIREE ⟨foreign potentates at diplomatic ~*s* —Robert Rice⟩ **syn** see CROWD

³**rout** \"\ *vb* -ED/-ING/-S [ME *rowten*, fr. ON *rauta*; akin to OE *rēotan* to cry, weep, OHG *riozan*, L *rudere* to roar, Skt *roditi* he weeps, roars, and prob. to OE *rēon* to lament — more at RUMOR] *vi* **1** *dial chiefly Brit* **:** to low loudly **:** BAWL, BELLOW — used of cattle **2 :** to make a loud noise **:** ROAR **~** *vt, dial chiefly Brit* **:** to shout out **:** ROAR ⟨have no . . . inclination to ~ out my name to the countryside —R.L.Stevenson⟩

⁴**rout** \"\ *n* -S *dial chiefly Brit* **:** a loud noise **:** CLAMOR, UPROAR

⁵**rout** \"\ *vb* -ED/-ING/-S [alter. of ³*root*] *vi* **1 :** to poke around with the snout **:** ROOT ⟨pigs ~*ing* in the earth⟩ **2 :** to make a haphazard search **:** RUMMAGE ⟨~*ed* in a corner and came back with . . . thread and needle —G.W.Brace⟩ **3 :** to

perform a gouging operation ⟨carve, ~, shape and grind on this versatile machine —*advt*⟩ **~** *vt* **1 a** *archaic* **:** to dig up with the snout ⟨~*ing* up the moss . . . in search of acorns —Peter Beckford⟩ **b :** to gouge out or make a furrow in: as (1) **:** to scoop out or cut away (as blank parts) from a printing surface (as an engraving or electrotype) with a router (2) **:** to remove (as metal or wood) with a gouge or other hand-operated cutting tool **2 a :** to expel by force **:** EJECT — usu. used with *out* ⟨whole families are . . . ~*ed* out of house and home —Arthur Murphy⟩ **b :** to cause to emerge esp. from bed **:** drag out **:** ROUST ⟨~*ed* . . . from his garret by loud rings at the bell —Floyd Dell⟩ ⟨~*ed* me out of bed to help place the target —A.C.Fisher⟩ ⟨~ the enemies of Calvinism from the inmost keep of their stronghold —V.L.Parrington⟩ **3 :** to dig out **:** come up with **:** UNCOVER ⟨went . . . to his cellar and ~*ed* out a bottle of port —John Masefield⟩

**6rout** \"\ *n* -s **:** an act, process, or result of routing ⟨this house, with its strange clutter . . . gives the effect of ~ —Howard Griffin⟩

**7rout** \"\ *n* -s [prob. of Scand origin; akin to ON *hrota* barnacle goose] *chiefly dial* **:** BRANT

**8rout** \"\ *n* -s [MF *route* troop, band, defeat — more at 2ROUT] **1 :** a state of wild confusion or disorderly retreat ⟨charging tanks put the infantry to ~⟩ ⟨reason had been clearly put to ~ by nineteenth-century Romanticism —Edmund Wilson⟩ **2 a :** a disastrous defeat **:** DEBACLE ⟨the battle became a ~, a shambles —*Amer. Guide Series: Texas*⟩ **b :** a precipitate flight ⟨everybody was for saving his own skin in this frantic ~ —L.C.Douglas⟩ **c :** an act or instance of routing ⟨the ~ of the Democrats . . . resulted in the candidacy of Republican incumbents —V.O.Key⟩ ⟨most crushing defeat since its 61–0 ~ last year⟩ **3** *archaic* **:** a fleeing force ⟨disordered the rank . . . whereupon their men were in ~ —Mary Wroth⟩

**9rout** \"\ *vt* -ED/-ING/-S **1 a :** to disorganize completely **:** put to precipitate flight **:** DEMORALIZE, STAMPEDE ⟨the large and well-mechanized army . . . had been ~*ed* and was in part surrounded —Upton Sinclair⟩ ⟨charged the main body of Russian cavalry . . . and ~*ed* it —Al Newman⟩ **b :** to defeat decisively **:** OVERWHELM ⟨suffered the discomfiture of seeing their party ~*ed* at the polls —A.N.Holcombe⟩ ⟨the team ~*ed* their traditional Thanksgiving Day rivals 41–0⟩ **2 :** to drive out **:** cause to disappear **:** DISPEL ⟨virtues are discredited and decency is ~*ed* —Frank Mac Shane⟩ **syn** see CONQUER

**1route** \ˈrüt, ˈrau̇t, *usu* \|d·+V\ *also* **rout** \ˈrau̇t\ *n* -s [ME *rute, route*, fr. OF *route* troop, band, route, fr. (assumed) VL *rupta (via)*, lit., broken way, beaten way, fr. L *rupta*, fem. of *ruptus*, past part. of *rumpere* to break — more at REAVE] **1 a :** a traveled way **:** ROAD, HIGHWAY ⟨expressways, toll roads, turnpikes, and similar large-scale ~*s* —P.F.Griffin⟩ ⟨because of its position on a water ~, the village soon became a river-traffic center —*Amer. Guide Series: Mich.*⟩ **b :** a means of access **:** CHANNEL, PATH ⟨preparedness was offered as a ~ to peace —F.L.Paxson⟩ ⟨liberal arts courses . . . as a ~ to the graduate schools —*Univ. of Chicago Round Table*⟩ **2 a :** a regular routine **:** customary progression **b :** a method of transmitting a disease or of administering a remedy ⟨the airborne ~ of . . . infection —M.L.Furcolow⟩ ⟨may be injected into . . . patients who cannot for any reason take the material by the oral ~ —*Collier's Yr. Bk.*⟩ **3 :** a line or direction of travel **:** COURSE, TRACK ⟨bayous change their ~*s* with each flood —*Lamp*⟩ ⟨U.S. 19 follows the general ~ of the old Catawba Trail —*Amer. Guide Series: N.C.*⟩ **4 a :** an established itinerary **:** a selected or regularly traversed passage esp. between two distant points ⟨soon I'll be over the panhandle . . . if I've not drifted north of ~ —C.A.Lindbergh b.1902⟩ ⟨permission . . . for 53 new domestic air ~*s* —*Americana Annual*⟩ ⟨the preponderance of shipping traffic along the north Atlantic ~ —R.S.Thoman⟩; *specif* **:** a telephone line ⟨a new procedure . . . enables operators to use the circuits on busy ~*s* more efficiently —C.F.Craig⟩ **b :** an assigned territory to be systematically covered ⟨postal ~⟩ ⟨paper ~⟩ **c :** a prescribed manner of shipment that may include selected carriers, junctions, and delivery point ⟨inform me by what ~ they had sent an order —Georgina Grahame⟩ **5** *archaic* **:** marching orders ⟨our ~ came for a march —Robert Bage⟩ **6 :** a horse race of a mile or more ⟨a horse trained for ~*s* does not do well in sprints⟩ **syn** see WAY

**2route** \"\ *also* **rout** \"\ *vt* -ED/-ING/-S **1 a :** to plan an itinerary for **:** send by a selected route **:** DIRECT ⟨~ lines through the richest inland spots —*Amer. Guide Series: Minn.*⟩ ⟨*routed* volunteers to the guerilla frontiers —E.P.Snow⟩ **b :** to divert in a specified direction ⟨~ the high voltage to the various engine cylinders in the correct sequence —*Aircraft Power Plants*⟩ ⟨took to *routing* their business through his . . . colleague —S.H.Adams⟩ **c :** to select the course to be followed by a shipment by designating carrier, intermediate points, junctions, and final delivery **2 :** to put (the mail for a postal route) in order for delivery **3 :** to prearrange and direct the order and execution of (a series of processes or transactions) in a factory or business **:** dispatch documents or materials to appropriate destinations ⟨~ an invoice to the accounting department⟩ **syn** see SEND

**route agent** *n* [1*route*] **:** a postal employee accompanying mail being transported by train and receiving, canceling, and delivering mail along the route

**route chart** *n* **:** FLOW CHART

**route locking** *n* **:** electric locking that prevents the movement of any switch, movable point frog, or derail in advance of a train after it has passed a signal to proceed

**route·man** \ˈ=mən\ *n, pl* **routemen** [1*route* + *man*] **1 a :** a salesman or deliveryman on an assigned route **b :** the supervisor of a group of news carriers responsible for helping to establish routes, taking care of complaints, making out bills, and paying carriers **2 :** a shipyard worker who plans the most efficient routing of work through a department

**route march** *n* **:** a practice march in peacetime or one at a distance from the enemy in wartime in which troops maintain the prescribed interval and distance but are not required to keep step, maintain silence, or hold their arms in any one position

**1rout·er** \ˈrau̇d·ə(r), -au̇tə-\ *n* -s [5*rout* + *-er*] **:** one that routs: as **a :** ROUTER PLANE **b :** a machine with a rapidly revolving vertical spindle and cutter for milling out the surface of wood or metal (as in woodworking or photoengraving) **c** *or* **router-bit** \ˈ=,=\ **:** the lip on a bit (as a center bit) that cuts the radius of the nicker **d :** an aircraft worker who shapes sheet metal blanks with a routing machine **e :** an operator of a machine for cutting designs in wooden stock

**2rout·er** \ˈrü\|d·ə(r), ˈrau̇\|, \|tə(r)\ *n* -s [2*route* + *-er*] **:** one that routes: as **a :** a clerk who sorts articles according to delivery routes **b :** a floor boy who keeps shoe workers supplied with material

**3router** \"\ *n* -s [1*route* + *-er*] **:** a horse trained for distance races — compare SPRINTER

**router plane** *n* [1*router*] **:** a plane consisting of a horizontal bar with a handle at each end supporting a vertically inserted narrow cutter operated by pulling and pushing and used for cutting recesses and smoothing the bottom of grooves — see PLANE illustration

**route step** *n* [1*route*] **:** the out-of-step manner of executing a route march — used as a military command ⟨we were never given *route step* until after we'd cleared the last of the company streets —Richard Yates⟩

**route transposition** *n* **:** encipherment in which the plaintext letters are placed along a more or less complex path (as a set of lines, a zigzag, a spiral) and then copied out in order as they are found to lie along a differently defined path — compare COLUMNAR TRANSPOSITION

**routeway** \ˈ=,=\ *n* **:** ROUTE 3 ⟨the one natural ~ across the desert waste would appear to be the River Nile —L.D.Stamp⟩

**1routh** \ˈrüth, ˈrau̇th\ *n* -s [origin unknown] *chiefly Scot* **:** PLENTY, ABUNDANCE

**2routh** \"\ *also* **routhy** \-thi\ *adj* **1** *chiefly Scot* **:** PLENTIFUL, ABUNDANT **2** *chiefly Scot* **:** ABOUNDING

**1rou·tine** \(ˈ)rü¦tēn\ *n* -s [F, fr. MF, fr. *route* traveled way] **1 a :** a standard practice **:** regular course of procedure ⟨the old speakeasy ~ of having a guard inspect you with one eye through a peephole —Robert Shaplen⟩ ⟨the usual ~ of appointment: tutor, 1871–74; assistant professor, 1875–80; professor, 1880–1916 —J.M.Berdan⟩ **b :** the habitual method of performance of established procedures ⟨the matter-of-fact laconic ~ of the hospital —Leslie Rees⟩ ⟨housewives, their ~ quickened by the pace of wartime living —*Monsanto Mag.*⟩ **c :** a repetitive speech or formula ⟨that old ~ about his welfare, and what was best for it —Gregor Felsen⟩ ⟨the "visit your dentist twice a year" ~ —*Spokane (Wash.) Spokesman Rev.*⟩ **2 a :** adherence to a pattern of behavior characterized by mechanical repetition ⟨most of us are blind — made so by custom and ~ —C.S.Kilby⟩ **b :** the quality or state of being humdrum ⟨sell out quickly . . . to avoid the dull ~ of development —*Amer. Guide Series: Nev.*⟩ **3 a :** an established sequence of operations (as in a factory or business establishment) **b :** a sequence of coded instructions for an electronic computer **4 a :** a standardized piece of entertainment or showmanship **:** ACT, BIT ⟨went through the hat ~ for distinguished guests —*Time*⟩; *specif* **:** a theatrical number ⟨a breathtaking ~ on a tightrope —*New Yorker*⟩ ⟨sitting out front at rehearsals, he jots down . . . a description of each ~ —H.W.Wind⟩ **b :** a fixed series of dance steps or rhythmic movements ⟨can pick up a difficult tap ~ at a single rehearsal —Agnes de Mille⟩

**2routine** \(ˈ)=¦=\ *adj* **1 :** of a commonplace or repetitious character **:** ORDINARY, USUAL ⟨the level of artistry . . . was altogether ~ and uninspired —Winthrop Sargeant⟩ ⟨read about the spectacular flights, but . . . seldom read anything about the hundreds of ~ flights made over the same country —Harold Griffin⟩ ⟨a few phrases of ~ patriotism —James Joll⟩ ⟨the car performs well with only ~ maintenance⟩ **2 :** of, relating to, or in accordance with established procedure ⟨the ~ settlement of boundary disputes —S.F.Bemis⟩ ⟨the ~ use of the blood-pressure test —F.A.Faught⟩ ⟨the purser's ~ book . . . lists everything that has to be done —*Saturday Rev.*⟩ — **rou·tine·ly** *adv*

**3routine** \=ˈ=\ *vt* -ED/-ING/-S **:** ROUTINIZE ⟨a horse should not be *routined* in any one test —*Notes on Dressage*⟩ ⟨~*s* the sequence of dialogue —Maurice Zolotow⟩

**rou·ti·neer** \,rütə'ni(ə)r\ *n* -s [1*routine* + *-eer*] **:** one that adheres to or insists on routine ⟨hacks and ~*s* were making the fascinating game of business and finance appear endlessly dull —M.S.Rukeyser⟩

**routine orders** *n pl* **:** orders relating to military matters other than operations in the field — compare COMBAT ORDERS

**1routing** *n* -s [fr. gerund of 5*rout*] **1 :** the removal of excess material (as from a printing plate) by cutting, milling, or gouging **2 :** a groove or indentation produced by routing

**2routing** *n* -s [fr. gerund of 2*route*] **1 a :** a course of travel **:** ITINERARY **b :** transmission over a selected course **:** CIRCULATION ⟨selective ~ of messages —Eunice Cooper & Helen Dinerman⟩ **2 :** the sorting of mail into proper sequence for delivery **3 :** the scheduling or standardization of a flow of work **4 a :** the determination of a course and method of shipment (as of freight) **b :** ROUTE 4c

**rou·tin·ist** \rüˈtēnəst\ *n* -s [1*routine* + *-ist*] **:** ROUTINEER

**rou·tin·iza·tion** \rü,tēnəˈzāshən\ *n* -s **:** an act or instance of routinizing ⟨specialization and ~ have reduced the creative aspects of their work —R.K.Burns⟩

**rou·tin·ize** \rüˈtē,nīz\ *vt* -ED/-ING/-S [1*routine* + *-ize*] **:** to discipline in or reduce to a routine ⟨*routinized* assembly-line workers —J.B.Martin⟩ ⟨we can ~ this process —F.J.Gruenberger⟩

**rout·ous** \ˈrau̇d·əs\ *adj* [2*rout* + *-ous*] *archaic* **:** NOISY, UPROARIOUS

**rout·ous·ly** *adv* [*routous* + *-ly*] **1** *archaic* **:** UPROARIOUSLY, NOISILY **2 :** in violation of a law against routs

**routs** *pl of* ROUT, *pres 3d sing of* ROUT

**rout-seat** \ˈ=,=\ *n* [2*rout*] *Brit* **:** a light bench supplied for parties ⟨knocked . . . off the end of a *rout-seat* at a ball —W.F. DeMorgan⟩

**roux** \ˈrü\ *n, pl* **roux** \ˈrü(z)\ [F, fr. (*beurre*) *roux* browned butter, fr. *roux* reddish brown, russet, fr. OF *rous* — more at RUSSET] **:** a cooked mixture of flour and fat used to thicken soup and sauces, cooked sometimes until the flour browns

**1rove** [ME *roof*] *past of* RIVE

**2rove** \ˈrōv\ *n* -s [ME *rewe, rufe, rove*, fr. ON *rō*] **1** *or* **roove** \ˈrüv\ **:** BURR 3 b **2 :** the bight of a rope sling that receives the hook

**3rove** \"\ *vb* -ED/-ING/-S [ME *roven*] *vi* **1 :** to shoot at rovers in archery **2 a :** to move aimlessly **:** ROAM, STRAY ⟨criminals . . . *roving* about freely without either arrest or custodial restraint —H.E.Barnes⟩ ⟨members . . . *roved* restlessly from one committee meeting to another —Allan Nevins⟩ **b :** to follow a random course **:** RAMBLE, WANDER ⟨at first he did not follow her, his thoughts had *roved* so far —Ellen Glasgow⟩ ⟨feebly his glance *roved* over the figures by the bed —Mary Austin⟩ **3** *obs* **a :** to deviate from the point ⟨from that mark how far they ~ —John Milton⟩ **b :** to take random aim **c :** GUESS **4** *archaic* **:** to troll with live bait ⟨~ for a perch with a minnow —Izaak Walton⟩ **5** *dial Brit* **:** to be light-headed or delirious **:** RAVE **~** *vt* **:** to traverse aimlessly **:** wander through or over **:** ROAM ⟨permit their progeny . . . to ~ the forest —S.H.Adams⟩ ⟨letting her eyes ~ the room as if she were planning . . . its decoration —Jean Stafford⟩ ⟨saw the searchlights *roving* the sky —Howard Hunt⟩

**4rove** \"\ *n* -s **:** an act or instance of wandering ⟨a sidelong ~ of the eye —A.L.Kroeber⟩

**5rove** *n* -s [modif. of Sp & Pg *arroba*] *obs* **:** ARROBA

**6rove** *past of* REEVE

**7rove** \ˈrōv\ *vt* -ED/-ING/-S [origin unknown] **:** to join (textile fibers) with a slight twist and draw out into roving

**8rove** \"\ *n* -s [origin unknown] **:** 3ROVING 1

**rove beetle** \ˈrōv-\ *n* [perh. fr. 3*rove*] **:** any of numerous beetles constituting the family Staphylinidae, having a long body and very short wing covers beneath which the wings are folded transversely, often occurring on decaying animal and vegetable matter, and many of them being predatory and the larvae of some parasitic

**rove-over** \ˈ=,=\ *adj* [prob. fr. 6*rove* + *over*] **:** having an extrametrical syllable at the end of one line that forms a foot with the first syllable of the next line — used of a type of verse in sprung rhythm

**1ro·ver** \ˈrōvə(r)\ *n* -s [ME, fr. MD *rover* robber, plunderer, fr. *roven* to rob + *-er*; akin to OE *rēafian* to reave — more at REAVE] **:** PIRATE ⟨the accumulated loot of all the sea ~*s* —H.E.Rieseberg⟩

**2rov·er** \"\ *n* -s [ME, fr. *roven* to shoot at random, wander + *-er* — more at ROVE] **1 a :** a random mark at an uncertain distance used as a target in archery — usu. used in pl. ⟨in shooting at ~*s* the archer whose arrow comes nearest the mark selects the next target⟩ **b :** one of a series of fixed marks at long range **c :** a strong arrow used in shooting at rovers **d :** an archer shooting at rovers **2 :** one that wanders: as **a :** a habitual roamer **:** TRAVELER, STRAY ⟨as much night life . . . as any vacation ~ can safely stand —C.L.Biemiller⟩ ⟨cattle, some ~*s* always excepted . . . remain on a given range —J.F.Dobie⟩ **b :** FLIRT, MASHER ⟨my true love's a ~ —Edna S. V. Millay⟩ **c** *chiefly Brit* **:** a boy scout over 17 years old who takes part in advanced scouting activities **d :** an architectural molding that follows a curve **e** *usu cap* **:** COLORADAN — used as a nickname **3 a** *or* **rover ball :** a croquet ball that has been through all the wickets and would be out if it hit the stake but is continued in play **b :** the player of a rover ball — **at rovers** *adv, obs* **:** at random **:** HAPHAZARDLY ⟨speaketh not *at rovers* —Arthur Golding⟩

**3rov·er** \"\ *n* -s [7*rove* + *-er*] **:** one that makes roving

**rover bellflower** *n* [2*rover*] **:** a coarse European perennial herb (*Campanula rapunculoides*) widely naturalized esp. in eastern No. America and having racemes of nodding flowers with campanulate corollas

**rov·er boy** *n, usu cap R&B* [fr. the *Rover boys*, heroes of a series of juvenile books (1899–1925) by Edward Stratemeyer †1930 Am. writer] **:** a physically brave and morally excellent person of somewhat limited outlook and experience ⟨trying to be the *Rover Boy* of the beachhead —R.M.Ingersoll⟩

**rovescio** *adv* [by shortening] **:** a rovescio

**1roving** *n* -s [ME, fr. gerund of *roven* to shoot at random, wander — more at ROVE] **1 :** an act or instance of shooting at random archery targets and esp. at natural targets in fields or woodlands **2 :** an act or instance of roaming ⟨every year this animal's ~*s* are restricted —Washington Irving⟩ ⟨found dial ~ common in the early parts of a program —George Fisk⟩

**2roving** *adj* [fr. pres. part. of 3*rove*] **1** *obs* **:** based on guesswork **:** CONJECTURAL **2 a :** traversing a random course **:** NOMADIC, WANDERING ⟨a ~ band of gypsies⟩ ⟨a ~ vixen wanting cubs —John Masefield⟩ **b :** traversing an assigned route or capable of being shifted from place to place **:** MOBILE ⟨~ judge⟩ ⟨~ reporter⟩ ⟨serving as a ~ police force for . . . the Territory of Arizona —Ross Santee⟩ **c :** of a general nature **:** unrestricted as to location or area of concern ⟨~ envoy⟩ ⟨~ assignment⟩ **d :** DISCURSIVE, RAMBLING ⟨a ~ wit⟩ ⟨unrelated subjects that happen to strike a ~ fancy —Dorothy Sayers⟩ **3 :** inclined to travel or stray **:** PERIPATETIC, ROAMING ⟨a large and ~ cast subsidiary to the main characters —Sylvia Berkman⟩ ⟨alas for poor Madame, he had a ~ eye —H.S.Jones⟩

**3roving** *n* -s [fr. gerund of 7*rove*] **1 a :** a slightly twisted roll or strand of textile fibers **b :** material in an intermediate stage between sliver and yarn **2 :** the final process of reducing and drawing out sliver preliminary to spinning — compare SLUBBING

**roving reel** *n* [3*roving*] **:** a device for measuring the length of textile rovings

**1row** \ˈrō\ *vb* -ED/-ING/-S [ME *rowen*, fr. OE *rōwan*; akin to MHG *rüejen* to row, ON *rōa*, L *remus* oar, Gk *eressein* to row, *eretmon* oar, Skt *aritra*] *vi* **1 a :** to propel a boat by means of oars ⟨got into the dinghy and ~*ed* out to the sloop⟩ **b :** to be a member of a racing crew ⟨~*ed* on the varsity eight⟩ **c :** to take part in a rowing competition ⟨~*s* against the champions in the annual regatta⟩ **2** *archaic* **:** to struggle to advance ⟨no one shall find me ~*ing* against the stream . . . I write for general amusement —Sir Walter Scott⟩ **3 :** to move by or as if by the propulsion of oars ⟨as the boats ~*ed* in . . . we could hear groans and lamentations —Kenneth Roberts⟩ ⟨pelicans ~ by on slow, powerful wings —Juana Voyt⟩ **~** *vt* **1 a :** to propel with or as if with oars ⟨~ a boat⟩ **b :** to be equipped with (a specified number of oars) ⟨the ceremonial barge ~*ed* 14 oars⟩ **c** (1) **:** to participate in (a rowing match) ⟨~ a race⟩ (2) **:** to compete against in a rowing match ⟨~*s* the champion in the regatta⟩ (3) **:** to pull (an oar) in a crew ⟨~*ed* stroke for the class crew⟩ **2 :** to transport in or as if in a boat propelled by oars ⟨charged a small fee to ~ us across the river⟩ ⟨sailors on shore leave ~ their girls around the lake in the park⟩

**2row** \"\ *n* -s **:** an act or instance of rowing ⟨go for a ~ on the lake⟩

**3row** \ˈrau̇\ *chiefly Scot var of* RAW

**4row** \ˈrō\ *n* -s [ME *rawe, rowe*, fr. OE *rāw, rǣw*; akin to OHG *rīga* line, L *rima* slit, fissure, crack, Skt *rikhati* he scratches, *rekhā* scratch, line] **1 a :** a number of objects in an orderly series **:** STRING ⟨a double ~ of sodium vapor highway lamps —*Amer. Guide Series: Va.*⟩ **b :** an uninterrupted sequence **:** SUCCESSION ⟨utter . . . ~*s* of platitudes —Joyce Cary⟩ ⟨won the state tourney for four years in a ~ —*Bull. of Bates Coll.*⟩ **c :** an arbitrary series or arrangement of the twelve-tone chromatic scale used as a basis or organizational device for modern musical compositions **2** *archaic* **:** a homogeneous group **:** CATEGORY, SET ⟨an only daughter . . . who is, at least, approaching the old maid's ~ —Manasseh Cutler⟩ **3** *obs* **:** a written line esp. metrical ⟨the first ~ of the pious chanson —Shak.⟩ **4 a :** ROW HOUSE ⟨street after street exactly alike, lined with ~*s* —T.F.Hamlin⟩ **b :** a way for passage **:** ALLEY, STREET ⟨on Catfish ~ and down Ramcat Alley —Shelby Foote⟩ ⟨two of the island's main arteries, Royal Poinciana Way and Coconut ~ —Walter Cartwright⟩ **c :** a street or area dominated by a specific kind of enterprise or occupancy ⟨in most cities a separate automobile ~ has arisen on the edge of the central business district —C.D.Harris & E.L. Ullman⟩ ⟨rumors fly along diplomatic ~⟩ ⟨zigzag from movie house to movie house like a barfly on whiskey ~ —Nathaniel Bart⟩ **5 :** a continuous strip usu. running horizontally or parallel to a base line: as **a :** a line of seats in a theater ⟨a pair of seats in the fifth ~ center⟩ **b :** a line of cultivated plants ⟨hoe between the ~*s*⟩ **c :** a horizontal line (as of figures) — distinguished from *column* ⟨~ totals are added to get the column total⟩ **d :** a line of stitches across a piece of needlework ⟨a ~ of knitting⟩ **e** (1) **:** a line of tufts in a carpet ⟨there is usu. one ~ of pile tufts for each cycle of back weaving⟩ (2) **:** the average number of tufts per inch in a carpet counted in the direction of the warp — **a row to hoe :** a task to accomplish — usu. used with a modifying adjective ⟨have had a hard *row to hoe* —*Coast Artillery Jour.*⟩ ⟨I'd like to be a surgeon, but it's a long *row to hoe* —*Sat. Eve. Post*⟩

**5row** \"\ *vt* -ED/-ING/-S **:** to form into or furnish with rows ⟨above the . . . heads of the students ~*ed* before me —Ralph Ellison⟩ ⟨a bare room ~*ed* with dusty windows —R.M. Coates⟩

**6row** \ˈrau̇\ *n* -s [origin unknown] **1 a :** a noisy disturbance **:** BRAWL, RUCKUS ⟨a first-class ~ between a brutal ranger . . . and an inoffensive citizen —S.E.White⟩ **b :** a heated argument **:** QUARREL, SQUABBLE ⟨a terrific ~ . . . between husband and wife because the former put a 15¢ stamp too much on a letter —H.J.Laski⟩ ⟨during the recent ~ over atomic-energy legislation their feuding was epic —Alfred Friendly⟩ **2** *slang chiefly Brit* **a :** a loud sound **:** NOISE, RACKET ⟨would make a beastly ~ with that instrument —F.M. Ford⟩ **b :** MOUTH ⟨she give him a big apple to shut his ~ —Richard Llewellyn⟩ **syn** see BRAWL

**7row** \"\ *vb* -ED/-ING/-S *vt* **1** *archaic* **:** to subject to assault **:** rough up **2** *chiefly Brit* **:** to speak angrily to **:** BERATE, SCOLD ⟨~*ed* the driver about the fare —*McClure's*⟩ **~** *vi* **:** to have a quarrel **:** FIGHT, SQUABBLE ⟨wrangled and ~*ed* with . . . other editors —W.A.White⟩

**ROW** *abbr* right of way

**row·able** \ˈrōəbəl\ *adj* [1*row* + *-able*] **:** capable of being rowed or rowed upon

**row·an** \ˈrau̇ən, ˈrōən\ *n* -s [of Scand origin; akin to ON *reynir* rowan, OE *rēad* red — more at RED] **1 :** ROWAN TREE **2 :** ROWANBERRY

**row·an·berry** \ˈ=-=- — *see* BERRY\ *n* [*rowan* + *berry*] **:** the fruit of the rowan tree

**rowan tree** *n* **1 :** a Eurasian tree (*Sorbus aucuparia*) with pinnate leaves and flat corymbs of small white flowers followed by red pomes resembling berries — called also *European mountain ash* **2 :** AMERICAN MOUNTAIN ASH

**row-barge** \ˈrō,=\ *n* [1*row* + *barge*] **:** a ship's barge or a passenger boat propelled by oars

**row binder** \ˈrō,=\ *n* [4*row*] **:** CORN BINDER

**rowboat** \ˈ=,=\ *n* [1*row* + *boat*] **:** a small boat of shallow draft usu. having a flat or rounded bottom, a squared-off or V-shaped stern, cross thwarts for rowers and passengers, and rowlocks for the oars with which it is propelled

**row crop** \ˈrō-\ *n* [4*row*] **:** a crop (as corn or cotton) that is usu. planted in rows

**row culture** \ˈrō-\ *n* **:** cultivation of crops in rows

**row·di·ly** \ˈrau̇dᵊlē, -dəl\|, \|i\ *adv* **:** in a rowdy manner

**row·di·ness** \-dēnəs, -din-\ *n* -ES **:** the quality or state of being rowdy

**row down** \(ˈ)rō-\ *vt* [1*row*] **:** to overtake (as another racing shell) in a rowing match

**1row·dy** \ˈrau̇dē, -di\ *adj* -ER/-EST [perh. irreg. fr. 6*row*] **1 a :** lacking in refinement **:** noisily turbulent **:** BOISTEROUS, ROUGH ⟨a shouting ~ game —Marjory S. Douglas⟩ ⟨a ~ little girl, who gave way upon the slightest provocation to uncontrollable laughter —Scott Fitzgerald⟩ ⟨~ mountain brooks —*Amer. Guide Series: Conn.*⟩ **b :** of a disreputable character **:** RAFFISH, VULGAR ⟨lackeys, housemaids and yokels of all sorts formed the most ~, but also the most enraptured, group in the . . . theater —W.S.Clark⟩ ⟨the comedy is often broad, even ~ —Hollis Alpert⟩ **2** *Austral* **:** lacking in docility **:** STUBBORN, UNRULY — used of livestock

**2rowdy** \"\ *n* -ES **:** one that is boisterous or pugnacious ⟨a favorite pastime of these . . . *rowdies* was to ride through the town at great speed while shooting with both hands —S.H. Holbrook⟩ ⟨the tough eggs, the *rowdies* in the crew —E.L. Burdick⟩

**3rowdy** \"\ *vi* -ED/-ING/-ES **:** to behave in a rowdy manner ⟨there was a lot of gambling and *rowdying* —Bruce Siberts⟩

**row·dy·dow** *or* **row-de-dow** \ˈrau̇dē,dau̇\ *n* -s [irreg. fr. 6*row*] **1 :** noisy excitement **:** HUBBUB, TO-DO ⟨piqued by all the ruffle and ~ —M.G.Bishop⟩ **2 a :** a noisy disturbance or spirited contest **:** BRAWL, FIGHT **b :** a boisterous party **:** SPREE

**row·dy·dow·dy** \ˈrau̇dē¦dau̇dē\ *adj* [irreg. fr. *rowdydow*] **:** BOISTEROUS, VULGAR

**row·dy·ish** \'raủdēish, -di·ish\ *adj* [²*rowdy* + *-ish*] **:** tending to be crude or noisy

**row·dy·ism** \-dē,izəm, -di·iz-\ *n* -s [²*rowdy* + *-ism*] **:** rowdy character or behavior

**rowed** \ˌrōd\ *adj* [⁴*row* + *-ed*] **:** formed into or furnished with rows — often used in combination ⟨a six-*rowed* ear of corn⟩

**rowe·ite** \'rō,īt\ *n* -s [George *Rowe* 20th cent. Am. mineralogist] **:** a mineral (Mn,Mg,Zn)Ca(BO₂)₂(OH)₂, consisting of a basic borate of calcium, manganese, magnesium, and zinc

¹**row·el** \'raủ(ə)l\ *n* -s [ME *rowelle, ruel,* fr. MF *rouelle* small wheel, fr. OF *roele* — more at ROULETTE] **1 a :** a revolving disk at the end of a spur with a varying number of sharp points for goading a horse ⟨the size of the ~ and the number of spokes determine the extent of spur cruelty —N.W.McKelvey⟩ **b** *obs* **:** a small knob on a horse's bit ⟨the iron ~*s* into frothy foam he bit —Edmund Spenser⟩ **2 :** something that resembles the rowel of a spur; *specif* **:** a spiked wheel on a soil pulverizer **3 :** a roll (as of hair or silk) passed through the flesh of an animal to induce localized drainage of widespread infection — compare SETON

²**rowel** \"\ *vt* **roweled** *or* **rowelled; roweled** *or* **rowelled; roweling** *or* **rowelling; rowels 1 a :** to goad with a rowel **:** SPUR ⟨~*s* his horse to a fresh burst of speed⟩ **b** (1) **:** to rake as if with a rowel **:** dig into **:** REND ⟨bathers *rowelling* the sand with horny heels —Louis Kent⟩ ⟨screams and groans . . . ~ the air —*Time*⟩ (2) **:** to disturb or incite to action **:** TROUBLE, PRICK ⟨blurted out the question that was *roweling* each one's mind —Joseph Bryan & P.G.Reed⟩ **c :** to furnish with a rowel ⟨a *roweled* spur⟩ **2 :** to insert a rowel of hair or silk into an animal

¹**row·en** \'raủən\ *n* -s [ME *rewayn, roweyn,* fr. (assumed) ONF *rewain* (whence Picard *rouain*); akin to OF *regain* aftermath, fr. *re-* + *gaaigner* to till — more at GAIN] **1 :** a stubble field left unplowed till late in the autumn to be grazed by cattle **2 :** AFTERMATH 1 — often used in pl.

²**row·en** \'raủən\ *chiefly Scot var of* ROWAN

**row·er** \'rō(ə)r, -ōə\ *n* -s [ME, fr. *rowen* to row + *-er*] **:** one that rows a boat **:** OARSMAN

**row·et** \'raủət\ *n* -s [prob. fr. E dial. *row* rough, fr. ME, fr. OE *rūw-, rūh* rough — more at ROUGH] *dial* **:** AFTERMATH 1

**row galley** \'rō-\ *n* [¹*row*] *archaic* **:** a galley propelled by oars

**row house** *n* [⁴*row*] **:** one of a series of houses connected to other houses by common sidewalls and forming a continuous group

**row·ing** \'rōiŋ, -ōēŋ\ *n* -s *often attrib* [ME, fr. OE, fr. *rōwan* to row + *-ing*] **1 :** the propulsion of a boat by means of oars **2 :** the art or practice of racing in shells as a sport **:** CREW

**rowing boat** *n, chiefly Brit* **:** ROWBOAT

**rowing machine** *n* **:** a machine used in a gymnasium for exercising the muscles used in rowing

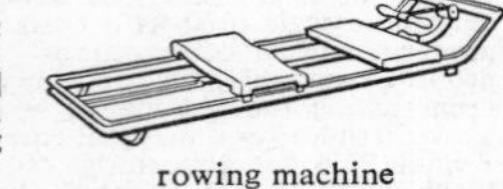

rowing machine

**row·land·ite** \'rōlən,dīt\ *n* -s [Henry A. *Rowland* †1901 Am. physicist + E *-ite*] **:** a massive grayish green yttrium silicate containing iron and fluorine

**row·lock** \'räläk, 'rələk (*usual nautical pronunciations*), 'rō,läk\ *or* **rol·lock** *or* **rul·lock** *n* [prob. alter. (influenced by ¹*row*) of *oarlock*] **1 :** OARLOCK **2 a :** a course of brick laid on edge with the ends exposed **b :** the end of a brick exposed in a rowlock

**rowlock arch** *n* **:** an arch in which voussoirs are arranged in separate concentric rings each forming an arch

**rowlock-back wall** *n* **:** a wall with a face of brick laid flat and a back of brick laid on edge

**rowlock wall** *also* **rolock wall** *or* **rolok wall** *n* **:** a hollow wall made of brick on edge placed as headers and stretchers in Flemish bond

rowlock arch

**rown** \'raủn\ *dial Brit var of* ROWAN

**row out** \(')rō-\ *vt* [¹*row*] **:** to exhaust by rowing ⟨number three had *rowed* himself *out* and was slumped over his oar at the finish line⟩

**rowport** \'rō,=\ *n* [¹*row* + *port*] **:** an opening in the side of a small sailing ship to allow for the use of sweeps in calm weather

**rows** *pres 3d sing of* ROW, *pl of* ROW

**rowse** *obs var of* ROUSE

**rowt** *dial chiefly Brit var of* ³ROUT, ⁴ROUT

**rowth** *var of* ROUTH

**rowy** \'rōē\ *adj* [⁴*row* + *-y*] **:** of uneven texture or appearance **:** STREAKED

**rox·burgh·shire** \'räks,bərə,shi(ə)r, -,b(ə)rə-, -,shər\ *or* **rox·burgh** *adj, usu cap* [fr. *Roxburgh, Roxburghshire,* county of southeast Scotland] **:** of or from the county of Roxburgh, Scotland **:** of the kind or style prevalent in Roxburgh

**rox·bury waxwork** \'räksb(ə)rē-, -,berē, |i-\ *n, usu cap R* [fr. *Roxbury,* residential district of Boston, Mass.] **:** BITTERSWEET 2 b

**rox·o·la·ni** \,räksə'lä(,)nē, -lā,nī\ *n pl* [L] **:** an ancient Sarmatian people living northeast of the Black sea, sometimes preying upon the Roman provinces, and sometimes serving as Roman auxiliaries

¹**roy·al** \'rȯi(ə)l, 'rȯ(i)yəl\ *adj* [ME, fr. MF, fr. L *regalis* of a king, royal, regal, fr. *reg-, rex* king + *-alis* -al; akin to Skt *rājan* king, OIr *rī* (gen. *rig*), L *regere* to guide, rule — more at RIGHT] **1 a :** of kingly ancestry **:** belonging to royalty ⟨English princes of the blood ~ —Virginia Cowles⟩ **b :** of, relating to, owned by, or subject to the jurisdiction of the crown ⟨the limitation of ~ power under a constitutional monarchy⟩ ⟨a special train for the queen and members of the ~ party⟩ ⟨the prince and his bride honeymooned on the ~ yacht⟩ ⟨courts had been effectively centralized under ~ control —C.H.McIlwain⟩ **c :** indicative of royalty ⟨~ title⟩ ⟨~ crown⟩ ⟨~ crest⟩ **d :** reserved for the sovereign **:** not to be hunted or captured without a license from the crown ⟨giraffes rank as ~ game —L.G.Green⟩ **e :** being in the crown's service ⟨~ prosecutor⟩ ⟨*Royal* Air Force⟩ **2 a :** of a nobility or splendor worthy of royalty **:** MAGNIFICENT, REGAL ⟨there is something . . . ~ in the stately carriage of a stag's head —R.F.Kilvert⟩ ⟨was treated with the ~ acclaim of a visiting statesman —W.A.White⟩ ⟨coffee ~ . . . with brandy or whiskey mixed up in it —J.W.Ellison b.1929⟩ **b** *archaic* **:** limited to a chosen few **:** ELITE ⟨the ~ dynasty of the apostles —J.H.Newman⟩ **c :** requiring no exertion **:** marked by special privilege **:** EASY ⟨there is no ~ road to logic and really valuable ideas can only be had at the price of close attention —Justus Buchler⟩ **3 a :** having attributes of royalty **:** MAJESTIC ⟨the lion is a ~ beast⟩ **b :** of great size or magnitude **:** BIG, IMPOSING ⟨wielded a patronage of ~ dimensions —J.H.Plumb⟩ ⟨a battle ~ that covers miles and lasts for hours —Arthur Knight⟩ ⟨stop being such a ~ pain in the neck —F.C.Thorne⟩ **c** (1) **:** of superior quality **:** EXCELLENT, SUPERB ⟨a ~ view⟩ ⟨cow of ~ breeding —*Amer. Guide Series: Minn.*⟩ (2) **:** of a highly pleasurable kind **:** GLORIOUS ⟨would have a ~ time . . . sailing the wherry —Archibald Marshall⟩ **d :** playing the part of royalty ⟨place the crowns on the ~ pair . . . elected by popular campus vote —*Springfield (Mass.) Daily News*⟩ **4 a :** established or chartered by the crown **:** enjoying the king's patronage ⟨*Royal* Academy⟩ ⟨the *Royal* Burghs of Scotland⟩ ⟨Massachusetts was once a ~ colony⟩ ⟨*Royal* Swedish Yacht Club⟩ **b** *archaic* **:** granted or performed by the king ⟨whatsoever she asked . . . Solomon gave her of his ~ bounty —1 Kings 10:13 (AV)⟩ ⟨a building . . . honored by several ~ visits —T.B.Macaulay⟩ **5 :** of, relating to, or being a part (as a mast, sail, or yard) next above the topgallant ⟨the ~ sail⟩ — see SHIP illustration **6 :** resisting chemical action **:** NOBLE ⟨~ gases⟩ ⟨~ metals⟩

²**royal** \"\ *n* -s **1 a :** ROYAL ANTLER **b :** a stag of eight years or more having antlers with at least twelve points **2 a :** RYAL 1 **b :** ⁴REAL **3 :** a small sail on the royal mast that is the highest usu. carried on a square-rigged ship and is located immediately above the topgallant sail — see SAIL illustration **4 :** a royal personage ⟨there are . . . titles for all spouses of ~*s* —V.W.Turner⟩ **5 :** a standard British size of paper usu. 20 x 25 or 19 x 24 inches **6 :** change ringing on ten bells **7 a :** a blue or green crown used as the symbol for the fifth suit in some five-suit packs of playing cards **b :** ROYAL FLUSH **c :** ROYAL SPADE **8** *or* **royal blue a :** a variable color averaging a vivid purplish blue **b** *of textiles* **:** a deep blue that is duller than Yale blue and redder and duller than imperial blue **c :** SMALT 2 **d :** PRUSSIAN BLUE 2 **9 :** ROYAL PALM ⟨mast-straight ~*s* lining the avenue —C.S.Lloyd⟩ **10** [trans. of F *royale*] **:** ROYALE 2

**royal agaric** *n* **:** a widely distributed edible mushroom (*Amanita caesarea*) resembling the poisonous fly agaric and having a smooth deep orange pileus, yellow gills, a large membranaceous annulus, and a white volva

**royal antelope** *n* **:** a tiny western African antelope (*Neotragus pygmaeus*) that is one of the smallest of ruminants standing only 12 inches high at the shoulder and has in the male short spikelike horns and bright russet above and white below — called also *kleeneboc*

**royal antler** *n* **:** the third tine above the base of a stag's antler — called also *tres-tine;* see ANTLER illustration

**royal arch mason** *n, usu cap R&A&M* **:** a member of a Royal Arch lodge

**royal assent** *n* **:** the official but purely formal approval of the sovereign required for the passage of all legislation under English parliamentary law

**royal auction bridge** *n* **:** auction bridge in which the spade suit is bid either as the lowest-ranking suit counting 2 points per odd trick or as the highest-ranking suit counting 9 points per odd trick — compare ROYAL SPADE

**royal bay** *n* **:** LAUREL 1 a

**royal casino** *n* **:** a casino in which each jack is worth 11, queen 12, and king 13 and may be so used in builds

**royal cell** *n* **:** a special chamber in most termite nests for the king and queen of the colony

**royal coachman** *n* **:** COACHMAN 2

**royal colony** *n* **:** a colony governed directly by the crown through a governor and council appointed by it — compare CHARTER COLONY, PROPRIETARY COLONY

**royal copenhagen** *n, usu cap R&C* **:** a fine Danish porcelain

**royal demesne** *n* **:** the lands belonging to the British crown including both the ancient demesne and property acquired later (as by forfeiture or gift) **:** CROWN LAND 1 ⟨the bulk of the cities were situated in the *royal demesne* —J.R.Green⟩

**royal doors** *n pl, often cap R&D* **1 :** HOLY DOORS **2 :** the central doors in some Eastern churches leading from the narthex into the nave

**royal dresden** *n, usu cap R&D* **:** a superior grade of Dresden china

**roy·ale** \(')rȯi¦al, (')rȯ(i)¦yal\ *n* -s [F, fr. fem. of *royal,* adj. — more at ROYAL] **1 :** an egg custard cooked and set in a mold, cut into various shapes when cold, and added as a garnish to clear soups **2 :** a changement de pied with a beating together of the legs while in the air

**royal eagle** *n* **:** GOLDEN EAGLE

**royal fern** *also* **royal osmund** *n* **:** a common and widely distributed fern (*Osmunda regalis*) with large bipinnate fronds bearing the panicled globose sporangia at their summit — called also *ditch fern, French bracken, king fern*

**royal fish** *n* **1** *Eng law* **:** marine animals (as whale, sturgeon or porpoises) of superior excellence that belong to the crown when cast ashore or caught in territorial waters **2** *Scots law* **a :** whales of such large size as to entitle the sovereign to claim them **b :** salmon in the sea and mussels and oysters that can be lawfully taken in public or private rivers only by license of the crown although the latter do not belong officially to the crown

**royal fizz** *n* **:** a fizz made from lemon juice, gin, a whole egg, and sugar

**royal flush** *n* **:** a straight flush in poker with the ace the highest card — see POKER illustration

**royal flycatcher** *n, usu cap R&F* **:** a small tyrant flycatcher (*Onychorhynchus coronatus*) of tropical America having a head with a large fan-shaped crest that is bright red edged with black — called also *king tody*

**royal green** *n* **1 :** LIGHT BRUNSWICK GREEN **2 :** PARIS GREEN 1

**royal hart** *n* **:** a red deer with fully developed antlers

**royal highness** *n* **1 a :** a child, brother, sister, uncle, aunt, or grandchild in the male line of the British sovereign — used as a title before 1917 **b :** a child or grandchild of the British sovereign — used as a title since 1917 **c :** someone on whom the British sovereign chooses to bestow the designation **d :** any of various members of imperial and royal families of other countries **2 :** a person properly addressed as Royal Highness ⟨eight *royal highnesses* attended the coronation⟩

**roy·al·ism** \-ə,lizəm\ *n* -s [¹*royal* + *-ism*] **:** MONARCHISM

¹**roy·al·ist** \-ələst\ *n* -s [¹*royal* + *-ist*] **1** *often cap* **:** an adherent of a king or of monarchical government: as **a :** a supporter of Charles I in his struggles with the Puritans and parliament **:** CAVALIER — compare ROUNDHEAD **b :** an adherent of George III or the British government in the American Revolution **:** TORY **c :** an adherent of the Bourbon dynasty in France during and since the French Revolution **2 :** a reactionary business tycoon or powerful trust ⟨take unwarranted power out of the hands of economic or social ~*s* —Louis Filler⟩

²**royalist** \"\ *or* **roy·al·is·tic** \¦rȯiə¦listik, ¦rȯ(i)yə¦-, -tēk\ *adj* **:** of, relating to, or characteristic of royalism or royalists

**roy·al·ize** \'==,līz\ *vb* -ED/-ING/-S *vt, archaic* **:** to make royal ⟨to ~ his blood I spilled my own —Shak.⟩ ~ *vi, obs* **:** to assume royal power

**royal jelly** *n* **:** a highly nutritious secretion of the pharyngeal glands of the honey bee that is fed to the very young larvae in a colony and to all queen larvae

**roy·al·ly** \'rȯiəlē, 'rȯ(i)yə-, -li\ *adv* [ME, fr. ¹*royal* + *-ly*] **1 a :** by the crown ⟨an edict published ~⟩ **b :** with the pomp and ceremony due a sovereign ⟨treated the ambassador ~⟩ **c :** with the utmost care and consideration **:** INDULGENTLY ⟨a small breeding stock was put inside fences and treated ~ —R.M.Yoder⟩ **2 :** in a splendid manner **:** MAGNIFICENTLY ⟨~ mounted upon one of the emperor's horses —Richard Knolles⟩ ⟨October shone ~ —George Meredith⟩ **3 :** on a large scale **:** GRANDLY, GLORIOUSLY ⟨~ duped by them and their accomplices —R.A.Hall b.1911⟩

**royal marriage** *n* **:** the king and queen of trumps in a card game (as pinochle or bezique)

**royal moth** *n* **:** any of various large handsome moths (as the regal moth and imperial moth) of *Citheronia* and related genera

**royal palm** *n* **1 :** any of several palms of the genus *Roystonea; esp* **:** a tall graceful pinnate-leaved palm (*R. regia*) of southern Florida and Cuba having a whitish trunk often enlarged or swelled out at the base and being widely planted for ornament throughout the tropical world **2 :** CABBAGE PALM 1b

**royal peculiar** *n* **:** a church or parish within the jurisdiction of the British sovereign and exempt from that of the ordinary in whose territory it is situated

**royal pendulum** *n* **:** a clock pendulum long enough to beat seconds

**royal pink** *n* **:** a deep pink that is bluer, stronger, and slightly darker than average coral (sense 3b) and bluer and deeper than fiesta or begonia

**royal poinciana** *n* **:** a showy tropical tree (*Delonix regia* syn. *Poinciana regia*) native to Madagascar but now widely planted for its immense racemes of scarlet and orange flowers, producing flat woody pods often two feet long, and having graceful twice-pinnate leaves — called also *flamboyant, flame tree, peacock flower*

**royal purple** *n* **1 :** a dark reddish purple that is redder, lighter, and stronger than average plum (sense 6a), redder and paler than imperial, and stronger than grape wine **2 :** a strong violet that is less strong and slightly lighter than pansy and bluer, less strong, and slightly darker than clematis — called also *king's purple, regal purple*

**royal python** *n* **1 :** BALL PYTHON **2 :** RETICULATED PYTHON

**royal red** *n* **1 :** VERMILIONITE **2 :** vermilion or a color resembling it

**royal rock snake** *n* **:** BALL PYTHON 2

**royals** *pl of* ROYAL

**royal scarlet** *n* **:** red mercury iodide $HgI_2$

**royal scyth** *n, usu cap R&S* **:** a member of the noble class in Scythian society acting as an integrative force for the whole nomadic group of Scythians

**royal spade** *n* **:** a spade trump in royal auction bridge when every trick over six taken by the successful bidder scores 9

**royal standard** *n* **:** an emblem of royal authority that is usu. a flag or square banner smaller than the national flag; *specif* **:** a flag bearing the arms of England quartered with those of Scotland and Ireland used as a naval flag of command or as evidence of the actual presence of the sovereign in a palace or castle or on board a ship

**royal tennis** *n* **:** COURT TENNIS

**royal tern** *n* **:** a large tern (*Thalasseus maximus*) of the southern U.S. and farther southward that is white with a black crown and crest and pearl-gray mantle

**roy·al·ty** \'rȯi(ə)ltē, 'rȯ(i)yəl-, -ti\ *n* -ES [ME *roialte,* fr. MF *roialté,* fr. OF, fr. *roial* royal (fr. L *regalis*) + *-té* -ty — more at ROYAL] **1 a :** royal status or power **:** SOVEREIGNTY ⟨gain ~ by conquest⟩ **b royalties** *pl, archaic* (1) **:** the prerogatives of sovereignty ⟨assume these *royalties,* and not refuse to reign —John Milton⟩ (2) **:** emblems of sovereignty ⟨*royalties* which he was wont to adorn himself with when he sat in state —Benjamin Church⟩ **c** *archaic* **:** KINGDOM, REALM ⟨republics were formed upon the ruin of . . . *royalties* —Thomas Carte⟩ **2 a** *obs* **:** splendid appearance **:** GLORY, MAGNIFICENCE **b :** regal character or bearing **:** MAJESTY, NOBILITY ⟨happiness depends upon the inward ~ of the spirit —W.F.Hambly⟩ **3 a** (1) **:** persons of royal lineage ⟨marriage customs among the ~ of the Peruvian Inca —Weston La Barre⟩ (2) **:** an embodiment of sovereignty ⟨she was ~ and a symbol of the British Empire —*United Press*⟩ **b :** a person of royal rank ⟨the crowd hangs about . . . in the hope of seeing a ~ or a raja's jewels —*Manchester Guardian Weekly*⟩ ⟨how to address *royalties* and persons possessing complicated titles —George Santayana⟩ **c :** a privileged class ⟨the twenty-five hundred a year that marked the economic ~ of Gopher Prairie —Sinclair Lewis⟩ **4 a :** a right delegated (as to an individual or corporation) by a sovereign ⟨the ~ is vested in the lord of the manor —M.C. Greenwell⟩ **b :** a landed estate or right of exploitation granted by a sovereign — usu. used in pl. ⟨landed proprietors . . . became anxious to lease their *royalties* —F.S.Williams⟩ **c** *Scots law* **:** a township or territory subject to royal jurisdiction **d** *Brit* **:** a tract of coal-mining land or a portion thereof **5 a :** a seigniorage on gold and silver coined at the mint **b :** a percentage paid to the British crown of gold or silver taken from mines or a tax exacted in lieu thereof **c :** a share of the product or profit of property reserved by the owner when the property is sold, leased, or used or a payment (as a percentage of the amount of property used) to the owner for permitting another to exploit, use, or market such property (as natural resources, patents, or copyrights) which is often subject to depletion with use **6 :** BONUS 4b

**royal walnut** *n* **1 :** ENGLISH WALNUT **2 :** a hybrid between two black walnuts (*Juglans nigra* and *J. californica*)

**royal water lily** *n* **1 :** a So. American water lily (*Victoria amazonia*) with large circular leaves — called also *Amazon water lily, giant water lily* **2 :** a lily (*Victoria cruziana*) of Paraguay that is closely related to the royal water lily for which it is often substituted in the horticultural trade and has flowers which turn pinkish red

**royal worcester** *n, usu cap R&W* **:** WORCESTER CHINA

**royal yellow** *n* **:** ORPIMENT 2

**royc·ean** \'rȯisēən\ *adj, cap* [Josiah *Royce* †1916 Am. philosopher + E *-an*] **:** of or relating to the American philosopher Josiah Royce or his objective idealism

**roy·e·na** \rȯi'ēnə, rȯ(i)'yē-\ *n, cap* [NL, fr. Adrian van *Royen* †1779 Du. botanist] **:** a genus of southern African shrubs or trees (family Ebenaceae) having monoclinous flowers with bell-shaped accrescent calyx and reflexed corolla lobes — see AFRICAN SNOWDROP TREE

**roy·et** \'rȯiət\ *adj* [prob. alter. of earlier *riot,* fr. ME, fr. ¹*riot*] **1** *Scot* **:** UNRULY, WILD **2** *Scot* **:** MISCHIEVOUS, ROMPING

**roy·nish** \'rȯinish\ *adj* [ME, fr. *royne* scurf, scab (fr. MF *rogne,* fr. — assumed — VL *ronea,* prob. alter. — influenced by L *rodere* to gnaw — of L *aranea* spider, spider web) + *-ish* — more at ARACHN-, RAT] **1** *archaic* **:** MANGY, SCABBY **2** *archaic* **:** BASE, COARSE

**royster** *var of* ROISTER

**roys·ton crow** \'rȯistən-\ *n, usu cap R* [fr. *Royston,* urban district of northern Hertfordshire, England] **:** HOODED CROW 1

**roy·sto·nea** \rȯi'stōnēə\ *n* [NL, fr. General *Roy Stone* †1905 Am. engineer] **1** *cap* **:** a genus of chiefly West Indian pinnate-leaved palms with smooth often spindle-shaped stems and large graceful leaves — see CABBAGE PALM, ROYAL PALM **2** -s **:** any palm of the genus *Roystonea*

**rozelle** *var of* ROSELLE

**ro·zi** \'rōzē\ *or* **roz·wi** \'räzwē\ *n, pl* **rozi** *or* **rozis** *or* **rozwi** *or* **rozwis** *usu cap* **:** LOZI

**roz·zer** \'räzə(r)\ *n* -s [origin unknown] *slang Brit* **:** POLICEMAN

**rp** *abbr* **1** rappen **2** recipe **3** *often cap R&P* reprint; reprinted; reprinting **4** rupiah

**RP** *abbr* **1** refilling point **2** regius professor **3** reply paid **4** [L *res publica*] republic **5** return of post **6** return premium **7** [L *reverendus pater*] reverend father **8** rust preventive

**RPC** *abbr* reply post card

**rpf** *abbr* reichspfennig

**RPM** *abbr, often not cap* revolutions per minute

**RPO** *abbr* railway post office

**RPP** *abbr* reply paid postcard

**RPS** *abbr, often not cap* **:** revolutions per second

**rpt** *abbr* **1** repeat **2** report; reported; reporting

**rptd** *abbr* **1** repeated **2** reported **3** reprinted **4** ruptured

**RQ** *abbr* respiratory quotient

**rqn** *abbr* requisition

**rr** *abbr* **1** [L *rarissime*] very rarely **2** rear

**RR** *abbr* **1** railroad **2** right rear **3** right reverend **4** rights reserved **5** rural route

**RRC** *abbr* regular route carrier

**-r·rha·chis** \,rəkəs\ *n comb form* -ES [NL, fr. Gk *rhachis* — more at RACHI-] **:** spine ⟨hematorrhachis⟩

**-r·rha·gia** \'rāj(ē)ə\ *n comb form* -s [NL, fr. Gk, fr. *rhēgnynai* to break, burst, rend — more at RHAGADES] **:** abnormal or excessive discharge or flow ⟨enterorrhagia⟩ ⟨metrorrhagia⟩

**-r·rha·phy** \,rəfē, -fi\ *n comb form* -ES [F *-raphie, -rrhaphie,* fr. Gk *-rrhaphia,* fr. *rhaptein* to sew together — more at RHAPSODY] **:** suture **:** sewing ⟨cardiorrhaphy⟩ ⟨nephrorrhaphy⟩

**-r·rhea** *also* **-r·rhoea** \'rēə\ *n comb form* -s [ME *-ria,* fr. LL *-rrhoea,* fr. Gk *-rrhoia,* fr. *rhoia,* fr. *rhein* to flow — more at STREAM] **:** flow **:** discharge ⟨logorrhea⟩ ⟨Melanorrhoea⟩ ⟨mucorrhea⟩

**-r·rhex·is** \'reksəs\ *n comb form, pl* **-r·rhex·es** \-k,sēz\ [NL, fr. Gk *rhēxis* action or process of breaking, fr. *rhēgnynai* to break, burst, rend] **:** rupture ⟨hysterorrhexis⟩ **:** splitting ⟨onychorrhexis⟩

**-r·rhine** *or* **-rhine** \,rīn\ *adj comb form* [ISV, fr. Gk *-rrhin-, -rrhis,* fr. *rhin-, rhis* nose — more at RHIN-] **:** having (such) a nose ⟨mesorrhine⟩ ⟨monorhine⟩ ⟨platyrrhine⟩

**-r·rhi·za** — see -RHIZA

**RRL** *abbr* regimental reserve line

**rs** *abbr, often cap* **1** reis **2** rupees

**RS** *abbr* **1** radio station **2** recording secretary **3** recruiting service; recruiting station **4** reformed spelling **5** report of survey **6** revised statutes **7** right side

**r's** *or* **rs** *pl of* R

**r salt** *n, usu cap R* **:** the disodium salt $HOC_{10}H_5(SO_3Na)_2$ of R acid

**rsi** *var of* RISHI

**RSM** *abbr* regimental sergeant major

**RSO** *abbr* **1** railway sorting office **2** railway suboffice **3** regimental supply officer

**r star** *n, usu cap R* **:** a star of spectral type R — see SPECTRAL TYPE table

**RSVP** \,ä,res,vē'pē, ,ä,es-\ *abbr* [F *répondez s'il vous plaît*] please reply

**RSWC** *abbr* right side up with care

**rt** *abbr* right

**'rt** \(ə)rt\ *vb* [by contr.] *archaic* **:** ART

**RT** *abbr* **1** radio technician **2** radio telegraphy **3** radio telephone **4** reading test **5** register ton **6** released time **7** re-

turn ticket **8** right tackle **9** room temperature **10** round trip **11** running title
**rta** *var of* RITA
**RTA** *abbr* reciprocal trade agreement
**RTC** *abbr* **1** replacement training center **2** reserve training corps
**rtd** *abbr* **1** retired **2** returned
**rte** *abbr* route
**RTN** *abbr* registered trade name
**RTO** *abbr* railroad transportation officer; railway transportation officer
**rty** *abbr* rarity
**RU** *abbr* rat unit
**Ru** *symbol* ruthenium
**ru·ade** \rü'äd\ *n* -s [F, lit., action of bucking (of a horse), fr. MF, fr. *ruer* to buck, fling, throw (fr. ML *rutare* to throw down, fr. L *rutus*, past part. of *ruere* to rush, fall) + *-ade* — more at RUG] **:** a preparatory movement for a parallel turn in skiing that consists of a bucking motion lifting the tails of the skis
**ruala** *usu cap, var of* RWALA
**ru·a·na** \rü'änə\ *n* -s [AmerSp, fr. Sp, woolen fabric] **:** a woolen covering resembling a poncho worn esp. in Colombia
**ru·an·da** \rü'ändə\ *n, pl* **ruanda** *or* **ruandas** *usu cap* **1 a :** a Bantu people in the region around the Virunga mountains in East Africa **b :** a member of such people **2 :** the Bantu language of the Ruanda people used as one of the two trade languages of Ruanda-Urundi — compare RUNDI
**ru·a·shid** \rü'äshəd\ *n, pl* **ruashid** *or* **ruashids** *usu cap* **1 :** an Arab people of inner Oman **2 :** a member of the Ruashid people
¹**rub** \'rəb\ *vb* **rubbed; rubbed; rubbing; rubs** [ME *rubben;* akin to Fris *rubben* to rub, scratch, Icel *rubba* to scrape, and prob. to OE *rēafian* to take away by stealth or force — more at REAVE] *vi* **1 a :** to move along the surface of a body with pressure **:** GRATE ⟨if the journal ~*s* against the bearing surface . . . too hard . . . the bearing surface will be scratched —H.F. Blanchard & Ralph Ritchen⟩ **b** (1) **:** to fret or chafe with friction ⟨~ upon a sore⟩ (2) **:** to cause discontent, irritation, or anger ⟨it ~*s* to be presided over by a vast . . . aggressively paternal indifference —R.W.Flint⟩ **2 :** to continue in a course, situation, or way of life usu. with slight difficulty or hindrance ⟨the great mass of modern men could ~ along happily enough without works of art —Roger Fry⟩ **3** *of a bowl* **:** to come in contact with an impediment on the green **4 :** to respond to rubbing (as for erasure or obliteration) **:** become rubbed ⟨dull inks . . . sometimes ~ off, even though the engraving is completely dry —R.N.Steffens⟩ **~** *vt* **1 a** (1) **:** to subject (as a body or a surface) to the action of something moving esp. back and forth with pressure and friction ⟨bent over and *rubbed* his sore ankle⟩ (2) **:** to scour, smooth, burnish, polish, or brighten by rubbing ⟨could see his reflection in the well *rubbed* wood⟩ — often used with *up* ⟨~ up the brass⟩ (3) **:** to spread a substance thinly over **:** SMEAR ⟨~ dressed fish generously with cut lemons —Jane Nickerson⟩ (4) **:** to roughen, wear, or make worn by the friction of rubbing **b** (1) **:** to cause (a body) to move with pressure and friction along a surface ⟨*rubbing* grubby knuckles in his eyes as he wept —T.B.Costain⟩ (2) **:** to remove, reduce to powder, spread, erase, or otherwise treat by rubbing ⟨*rubbed* the rust from old muskets —Dana Burnet⟩ ⟨the paste had hardened, and it was then vigorously *rubbed* in —H.E.Scudder⟩ (3) **:** to start (as a flame) by the friction of rubbing (4) **:** to straighten (as a wire or needle) by rubbing while hot **c :** to bring into reciprocal back and forth or rotary contact ⟨~ two sticks to make fire⟩ ⟨*rubbing* his hands in glee⟩ **d :** to take a rubbing of **2 a** *archaic* **:** to arouse a remembrance or a memory in ⟨~ him on this point, for his recollection becomes rusty —Sir Walter Scott⟩ **b :** to arouse pain, distress, or anger in **:** ANNOY, IRRITATE — **rub elbows** *or* **rub shoulders :** associate closely **:** MINGLE ⟨men and women of assorted ages and degrees of prosperity *rub elbows* and exchange opinions —Lowell Brentano⟩ ⟨reports on social products *rub shoulders* with book reviews and notes —*Friends' Intelligencer*⟩ — **rub the wrong way :** to arouse the antagonism, antipathy, or displeasure of **:** IRRITATE ⟨a knack of understanding my fellow creatures . . . and not being *rubbed the wrong way* by their faults —Max Beerbohm⟩
²**rub** \"\ *n* -s **1 a** (1) **:** an unevenness or inequality of surface of the ground in lawn bowling (2) *archaic* **:** an unevenness or inequality of surface that impedes movement ⟨there will be ~*s* in the smoothest road —Sir Walter Scott⟩ **b :** an obstruction or difficulty that hinders, stops, or alters the course of an argument, chain of thought, or action ⟨the ~ is that so few of the scholars have any sense of this truth themselves —Benjamin Farrington⟩ **c** (1) **:** something that mars the smoothness of a surface **:** ROUGHNESS ⟨leave no ~*s* nor botches in the work —Shak.⟩ (2) **:** something grating to the feelings (as a gibe, sarcasm, or harsh criticism) ⟨I got many severe ~*s*, often unconsciously given —T.B.Aldrich⟩ (3) **:** something that mars or upsets a usu. serene state of affairs or way of life ⟨even the mildest occupation produces its ~*s* and frictions —W.H. Chamberlin⟩ **2 :** the application of friction with pressure **:** RUBBING **3** *dial Eng* **:** RUBSTONE
**rub** *abbr* **1** rubbed **2** [L *ruber*] red **3** rubber
**rub-a-dub** \'rəbə,dəb\ *n* -s [imit.] **:** the sound of drumbeats
**ru·ba'i** \rü'bä,ē\ *n, pl* **ru·bai·yat** \'rübē,(y)ät, -bə,yät, -,bī-,(y)ät, *usu* -äd·+V\ *also* **rubais** [Ar *rubā'īyah*, fr. *rubā'īy* composed of four elements] **:** QUATRAIN
**rubaiyat stanza** *n, usu cap R* [*Rubáiyát*, collection of quatrains by Omar Khayyám †*ab*1123 Pers. poet and astronomer] **:** an iambic pentameter quatrain in which the first, second, and fourth lines rhyme — called also *Omar stanza*
**ru·ban** \'rübən\ *n* -s [ME (Sc), fr. MF — more at RIBBON] *archaic* **:** RIBBON
**ru·barth's disease** \'rü,bärt(h)s-\ *n, usu cap R* [after C. Sven *Rubarth b*1905 Swed. veterinarian] **:** a highly fatal febrile virus hepatitis of dogs marked by shivering, incoordination, spasms, and collapse accompanied by engorgement of visceral blood vessels and edema and cloudy swelling of liver, spleen, and lymph nodes
**ru·basse** \(')rü¦bas\ *n* -s [F *rubace*, irreg. fr. *rubis* ruby, fr. MF *rubi, rubis* — more at RUBY] **:** a quartz stained a ruby red — called also *Mont Blanc ruby*
**ru·ba·to** \rü'bäd·(,)ō, -bȧl, \|(,)tō\ *n, pl* **ruba·ti** \|d·(,)ē, \|(,)tē\ *or* **rubatos** [It, past part. of *rubare* to rob, of Gmc origin; akin to OHG *roubōn* to rob — more at REAVE] **:** fluctuation of speed within a musical phrase or measure typically against a rhythmically steady accompaniment
**rub·bage** \'rəbij\ *chiefly dial var of* RUBBISH
**rubbed brick** *n* **:** brick rubbed with sandstone to produce a smoother surface of a lighter color and used esp. in colonial Virginia
¹**rub·ber** \'rəbə(r)\ *n* -s **1 a :** one that rubs: as (1) **:** one who polishes a finish (as of wood or metal furniture) (2) **:** one that massages esp. in a public bath (3) **:** a textile worker who removes processing marks from cloth **b :** an instrument or object used in rubbing, polishing, scraping, or cleaning: as (1) **:** a towel or brush used for cleaning (2) **:** WHETSTONE, RUBSTONE (3) **:** ERASER; *esp* **:** one made of rubber (4) **:** a piece of firm cloth used in grooming a horse esp. for rubbing down the coat when wet or for giving a final gloss after brushing and currying **c :** something that operates by or is used to prevent rubbing, chafing, or friction: as (1) **:** a wooden strip protecting the outside of the gunwales of an open boat (2) **:** a rough or prepared surface to ignite a match by friction **d** (1) **:** a rough uneven place in a bowling green (2) **:** IMPEDIMENT, DIFFICULTY (3) **:** MISFORTUNE, TROUBLE **e :** a soft brick **:** CUTTER **2** [so called fr. its use in erasers] **a :** a substance that is obtained from the latex of many tropical plants esp. of the genera *Hevea* and *Ficus*, is usu. characterized by its elasticity though its properties vary widely depending upon its source and preparation, is usu. prepared by coagulating the latex (as with formic acid), collecting the sticky coagulum, and either milling into rough sheets of crepe rubber or rolling into smooth or ribbed sheets and drying often by smoking, and is used chiefly in crepe soles and rubber cements — called also *caoutchouc, india rubber, natural rubber;* see PARA RUBBER 1, PLANTATION RUBBER, WILD RUBBER **b :** any of various rubber-like substances that like natural rubber can be vulcanized **:** a vulcanizable elastomer **:** SYNTHETIC RUBBER **c :** natural or synthetic rubber that has been modified to increase its useful properties (as elasticity, toughness, resistance to abrasive wear) usu. by masticating, compounding with sulfur or other vulcanizing agents and with various chemicals (as accelerators, zinc oxide, carbon black or other reinforcing pigments, fillers, softeners, extenders, and antioxidants), forming, and vulcanizing and that is used chiefly in tires, hose, belting, friction materials, containers, electric insulation, and waterproof materials, often in combination with textile fabrics, metals, or other materials **3 :** something made of rubber or felt to resemble rubber (as in composition or elasticity): as **a :** an overshoe of rubber; *esp* **:** one having no buckles and not extending as high as the ankle — compare GALOSH, STORM RUBBER, TOE RUBBER **b :** RUBBER BAND **c** (1) **:** a rubber tire (2) **:** the set of tires on a vehicle ⟨I'll road test her for you after we get new ~ on —Gregor Felsen⟩ **d :** the puck used in ice hockey **e** (1) **:** the pitcher's plate in baseball or softball (2) **:** HOME PLATE **f :** CONDOM **4** [by shortening] **:** RUBBERNECK **5 :** a security issued by a tire and rubber company
²**rubber** \"\ *adj* **1 :** made of rubber **2 :** producing rubber
³**rubber** \"\ *vt* **rubbered; rubbered; rubbering** \-b(ə)riŋ\ **rubbers 1 :** to make of rubber **2 :** to coat with rubber **:** RUBBERIZE
⁴**rubber** \"\ *n* -s [origin unknown] **1 :** a contest consisting of a specified odd number of games so that to win one side must take a majority (as two out of three, three out of five, or four out of seven) **2 :** a victory determined by the winning of a majority of a series of games **3** *or* **rubber game :** an odd game played to determine the winner when two sides have reached a tie
⁵**rubber** \"\ *vi* -ED/-ING/-S [by shortening] **:** RUBBERNECK
**rubber band** *n* **:** an endless cord, string, or band of rubber used variously (as for holding together a sheaf of papers)
**rubber-base paint** *n* **1 :** a paint having chlorinated rubber as its binder or nonvolatile vehicle **2 :** an emulsion paint having a latex of styrene-butadiene copolymer or other synthetic resin latex as its nonvolatile vehicle
**rubber belt** *n* **:** a belt made of rubber belting
**rubber belting** *n* **:** belting made of cotton duck held together by a rubber mixture
**rubber boa** *or* **rubber snake** *n* **:** a harmless blunt-tailed snake (*Charina bottae*) of the family Boidae that is rubbery in smoothness and suppleness of appearance, usu. less than 18 inches long, and found in the moister regions of western No. America — called also *ball snake, two-headed snake*
**rubber boot** *n* **:** a boot made of fabric heavily coated with rubber
**rubber bridge** *n* **:** a form of bridge in which the cards are dealt at random and not replayed as in duplicate bridge and in which settlement is made at the end of each rubber
**rubber cement** *n* **:** an adhesive consisting typically of a dispersion of unvulcanized rubber in an organic solvent (as petroleum naphtha or benzene)
**rubber check** *n* [so called because it comes back like a bouncing rubber ball] **:** a check returned by the bank as not good because of insufficient funds in the account on which the check is drawn
**rubber dam** *n* **:** a thin sheet of rubber that is stretched around a tooth to keep it dry during dental work or is used in strips to provide drainage in surgical wounds
**rubber dog** *n* **:** PUPPY 4
**rubber-down** \'==,=\ *n, pl* **rubbers-down** [*rub down* + *-er*] **:** one that rubs down (as in smoothing leather or wood or in reducing pulp)
**rubber hydrocarbon** *n* **:** a white highly polymerized hydrocarbon $(C_5H_8)_n$ or $(C_{10}H_{16})_n$ that is amorphous at ordinary temperatures and that is stereoisomeric with gutta hydrocarbon and constitutes the principal component of natural rubber **:** a cis form of polyisoprene
**rubber hydrochloride** *n* **:** a thermoplastic substance made by treating a dispersion of natural rubber with hydrogen chloride and used chiefly in the form of thin strong stretchable moistureproof film for making raincoats, as packaging material, and as fruit wrapping — compare CHLORINATED RUBBER
**rubber ice** *n* **:** soft flexible ice on a body of water
**rub·ber·ize** \'rəbə,rīz\ *vt* -ED/-ING/-S **:** to coat or impregnate with rubber or a rubber solution ⟨~ cloth⟩
**rubber jaw** *n* **:** osteomalacia of the dog marked by softening and degenerative changes of the jaw and facial skeleton and commonly occurring in company with renal insufficiency and uremia
**rubber latex** *n* **:** a milky juice that is extracted from any of various plants and is the source of natural rubber
**rubberlike** \'==,=\ *adj* **:** resembling rubber esp. in physical properties (as elasticity and toughness)
**rubberlip perch** *or* **rubberlip sea-perch** \'==,=-\ *n* [*rubberlip* fr. ²*rubber* + *lip*] **:** a medium-sized silvery or bluish purple surf fish (*Rhacochilus toxotes*) of the California coast that is a leading market fish of the area
**rub·ber·man** \'rəbə(r)mən, -,man\ *n, pl* **rubbermen :** a worker who renews rubber tubing in electrolytic cells and purifies water for use in them
¹**rubberneck** \'==,=\ *also* **rub·ber·neck·er** \'==,=ə(r)\ *n* [*rubberneck* fr. ²*rubber* + *neck; rubbernecker* fr. ²*rubberneck* + *-er*] **1 :** an extremely inquisitive person ⟨two cars had smashed together . . . and a cluster of ~*s* had gathered around —John Brooks⟩ **2 :** TOURIST; *esp* **:** one on a guided tour
²**rubberneck** \"\ *vi* -ED/-ING/-S [¹*rubberneck*] **1 :** to look about, stare, or listen with exaggerated curiosity ⟨limping out of bed to join the ~*ing* patients at the windows —Earle Birney⟩ **2 :** to go on a tour **:** SIGHT-SEE
**rubber neck** \'==,=\ *n* [²*rubber* + *neck*] **:** CANDLEPINS
**rubbernose** \'==,=\ *or* **rubbernose sturgeon** *n* **:** LAKE STURGEON
**rubber plant** *n* **:** a plant (as the Colorado rubber plant) that yields rubber; *esp* **:** a tropical Asian tree (*Ficus elastica*) with strongly buttressed trunk that may exceed 100 feet in height, is the source of Assam rubber, and is frequently dwarfed in pots for use as an ornamental
**rubber plating** *n* **:** the deposition of rubber from rubber latex or other rubber dispersion containing negatively charged rubber particles usu. on a metal by electrophoresis or by coagulation with positively charged ions
**rubber point** *n* **:** a point credited to the side that wins a game in whist, the number of points so credited depending on the difference between the winners' and losers' scores in the game
**rubbers** *pl of* RUBBER, *pres 3d sing of* RUBBER
**rubber-seed oil** *n* **:** a fatty oil obtained esp. from the seeds of the Para rubber tree and used chiefly in soap
**rubber sheet** *n* **:** a sheet of rubber or a cloth coated with rubber for use esp. on a hospital bed or a child's crib
**rubber stamp** *n* **1 :** a stamp of rubber for making imprints **2 a :** a person who echoes the words, opinions, or mannerisms of others **:** one without originality **b :** a group (as a legislative body) or a person that approves or endorses a program or policy with little or no dissent or discussion ⟨it is probably not fair to consider the council merely a *rubber stamp* —F.A.Ogg & Harold Zink⟩ ⟨others have been more amenable *rubber stamps* for administration policy —*Economist*⟩ **3 a :** something (as an expression) that duplicates without originality a common mode or pattern **:** STEREOTYPE, CLICHÉ ⟨the usual *rubber stamps* of criticism —H.L.Mencken⟩ ⟨your windows can be . . . rich without being *rubber stamp* —*Amer. Home*⟩ **b :** an endorsement or approval esp. when given with slight study or discussion

rubber stamp 1

**rubber-stamp** \¦==¦=\ *vt* [*rubber stamp*] **1 :** to cancel, endorse, approve, or otherwise mark with a rubber stamp **2 :** to approve, endorse, or dispose of (as a document or policy) as a matter of routine usu. without the exercise of judgment or at the expressed or implied command of another person or body ⟨wanted to *rubber-stamp* the appropriations and leave —*Newsweek*⟩ ⟨citizen committees which expect the board to *rubber-stamp* their findings —*Education Digest*⟩
**rubber thread** *n* **:** a fine square or round filament of rubber used esp. for elastic and elasticized thread and fabrics
**rubber tree** *n* **:** a tree that yields rubber; *esp* **:** PARA RUBBER 2 — compare RUBBER PLANT
**rubber vine** *n* **1 :** INDIA-RUBBER VINE **2 :** MADAGASCAR RUBBER VINE **3 :** Jamaican woody vine (*Forsteronia floribunda*) of the family Apocynaceae that yields rubber
**rubberweed** \'==,=\ *n* **:** PINGUE
**rub·bery** \'rəb(ə)rē, -)ri\ *adj* **:** resembling natural rubber (as in elasticity, consistency, or texture) **:** RUBBERLIKE ⟨mud so tough and ~ that . . . it would pull the hooves off a horse —H.L.Davis⟩ ⟨had a ~ face that lent itself beautifully to mugging —E.J.Kahn⟩
**rub·bidge** \'rəbij\ *dial var of* RUBBISH
**rubbing** *n* -s [ME *rubbinge*, fr. gerund of *rubben* to rub] **1 :** the action or process of chafing, polishing, or otherwise treating or affecting a surface or body by the motion of applied pressure upon it **2 :** an image of a raised, indented, or textured surface obtained by placing paper over it and rubbing the paper (as with heelball, charcoal, graphite)
**rubbing alcohol** *n* **:** a liquid for external use containing usu. denatured alcohol or isopropyl alcohol and water
**rubbing block** *n* **1 :** an abrasive block that is commonly of sandstone and is used for cleaning, smoothing, or polishing (as marble, building stone, bricks) **2 :** the part of an electric railway plow that makes contact with a conductor rail in a conduit
**rubbing varnish** *n* **:** varnish used to form a hard surface for rubbing
**rub·bish** \'rəbish, -bēsh\ *n* -ES [ME *robous, robys, robishe;* perh. akin to ME *rubben* to rub — more at RUB] **1 a :** useless fragments of stone or other material left over in building or broken from ruined buildings **:** RUBBLE **b :** miscellaneous useless valueless waste or rejected matter **:** TRASH, DEBRIS ⟨three buildings surrounded by logs and stumps, carpenters' and masons' debris, and other ~ —*Amer. Guide Series: Mich.*⟩ ⟨letters, journals, estate accounts, locks of hair, shreds of silk, sentimental ~ of all sorts —Mollie Panter-Downes⟩ **2 :** vapid, worthless, or nonsensical writing, talk, or art ⟨of our dramatic literature few real masterpieces are forgotten and not much ~ survives —W.B.Adams⟩ ⟨it is often said that editors and publishers do not order or commission stories — which, of course, is ~ —Robert Moses⟩ **syn** see REFUSE
**rub·bish·ing** \-bəshiŋ\ *adj* **:** RUBBISHY — **rubbishingly** *adv*
**rub·bish·ly** \-bishlē\ *adj* **:** RUBBISHY
**rubbish pulley** *or* **rubbish wheel** *n* **:** GIN BLOCK
**rub·bishy** \-bəshē, -shi\ *adj* **1 :** consisting of or covered with rubbish ⟨a ~ heap of corrugated paper boxes —Berton Roueché⟩ **2 :** of the quality of rubbish **:** TRASHY, WORTHLESS ⟨the ~ newspapers which form almost the sole reading of the majority —W.R.Inge⟩
¹**rub·ble** \'rəbəl\ *n* -s [ME *robyl, rubel;* perh. akin to ME *rubben* to rub] **1 a :** broken fragments of stone and other matter resulting from the decay or destruction of a building ⟨fortifications knocked into ~ —C.S.Forester⟩ **b :** a miscellaneous confused mass, pile, or group of usu. broken or worthless things ⟨lay in a pile of ~, only this time there was more of it, additional gear having hit the deck —K.M.Dodson⟩ ⟨lonely in his box the dead man lay, with his ~ of mourners behind him —Bruce Marshall⟩ **2 a :** waterworn or rough broken stones or bricks used in coarse masonry or to fill up between the facing courses of walls **b :** masonry composed of rubble **:** RUBBLEWORK **3 a :** rough stone as it comes from the quarry **b :** the upper fragmentary and decomposed portion of a mass of stone esp. in a quarry **:** BRASH **c :** a mass or layer of fragments of rock lying under alluvium **d :** ¹TALUS 2 **4 :** floating or grounded sea ice in hard roughly rounded blocks from two to five feet in diameter
²**rubble** \"\ *vt* -ED/-ING/-S **:** to reduce to rubble **:** DESTROY ⟨the city has twice been *rubbled* in battle —H.G.Nickels⟩
**rubble ashlar** *n* **:** ashlar with rubble backing
**rubble concrete** *n* **:** concrete in which large stones are added to the freshly placed concrete while it is still soft and plastic
**rubble drain** *n* **:** FRENCH DRAIN
**rub·ble·man** \'rəbəlmən, -,man\ *n, pl* **rubblemen :** a foreman in charge of the drilling and splitting of stone
**rubble masonry** *n* **:** masonry composed of unsquared stone
**rubblestone** \'==,=\ *n* **:** RUBBLE
**rubblework** \'==,=\ *n* **:** masonry of unsquared or rudely squared stones that are irregular in size and shape

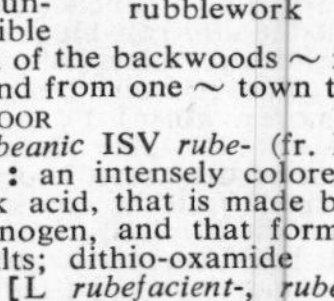

rubblework

**rub·bly** \'rəb(ə)lē\ *adj* **:** relating to, abounding in, composed of, or resembling rubble ⟨~ formation⟩ ⟨~ coal⟩
**rub down** *vt* **:** to rub from top to bottom or head to foot; *specif* **:** to dry (a horse) of sweat or rain (as with a straw wisp or a rubber)
**rubdown** \'=,=\ *n* -s [*rub down*] **:** a rubbing of the body (as after a bath) ⟨a brisk ~ with a rough towel⟩; *esp* **:** a massage given after or during the course of an athletic contest to promote the removal of fatigue products through improved circulation
**rube** \'rüb\ *n* -s [fr. *Rube*, nickname fr. the name *Reuben*] **:** an awkward unpolished unsophisticated usu. gullible rustic ignorant of urban ways ⟨the era of the backwoods ~ is gone —Jeff McDermid⟩ ⟨jumpin around from one ~ town to another —Richard Bissell⟩ **syn** see BOOR
**ru·be·an·ic acid** \¦rübē¦anik-\ *n* [*rubeanic* ISV *rube-* (fr. L *rubeus* red, reddish) + *-ane* + *-ic*] **:** an intensely colored thioamide $(CSNH_2)_2$ that is a weak acid, that is made by addition of hydrogen sulfide to cyanogen, and that forms deeply colored heat-stable nickel salts; dithio-oxamide
¹**ru·be·fa·cient** \¦rübə¦fāshənt\ *adj* [L *rubefacient-, rubefaciens*, pres. part. of *rubefacere* to make red, fr. *rubeus* red, reddish + *facere* to make — more at RUBY, DO] **:** causing redness (as of the skin)
²**rubefacient** \"\ *n* -s **:** a substance for external application that produces redness of the skin
**ru·be·faction** \-'fakshən\ *n* -s [prob. fr. (assumed) NL *rubefaction-, rubefactio*, fr. L *rubefactus* (past part. of *rubefacere*) + *-ion-, -io* -ion] **1 :** the act or process of causing redness **2 :** redness due to a rubefacient
**rube gold·berg** \rüb'gōl(d),bərg, -bōg,-bəig\ *also* **rube gold·berg·ian** \-gēən\ *adj, usu cap R&G* [*Rube Goldberg* (Reuben L. Goldberg) *b*1883 Am. cartoonist known for comic drawings of ridiculously complicated mechanical contrivances] **:** accomplishing by extremely complex roundabout means what actually or seemingly could be done simply ⟨crowded with a *Rube Goldberg* phantasmagoria of furnaces, grinders, tanks, mixers and countless unrecognizable contraptions —Webb Waldron⟩
**ru·bel·la** \rü'belə\ *n* -s [NL, fr. L, fem. of *rubellus* reddish] **:** an acute contagious disease usu. affecting children and young adults characterized by a red skin eruption, mild symptoms, and short course, but causing organic damage to the fetus in early pregnancy — called also *German measles;* see MATERNAL RUBELLA
**ru·bel·lite** \rü'be,līt, 'rübə,l-\ *n* -s [L *rubellus* reddish (fr. *ruber* red) + E *-ite* — more at RED] **1 :** a mineral consisting of a tourmaline varying from a pale rose red to a deep ruby red and found esp. in California, Brazil, and the Ural mountains **2 :** a vivid purplish red that is bluer and duller than Indiana and bluer and darker than malmaison rose
**ru·ben·esque** \¦rübə¦nesk\ *adj, usu cap* [Peter Paul *Rubens* †1640 Flem. painter + E *-esque*] **:** of, relating to, or having the characteristics of the painter Rubens or his work ⟨the high ceiling was painted blue with a sky in which floated fat *Rubenesque* cherubs discreetly veiled in wisps of cloud —Vivian Ellis⟩ ⟨the walls . . . were a blaze of magnificent form and color: a *Rubenesque* room —Hewlett Johnson⟩
**ru·ben·si·an** \(')rü¦benzēən\ *adj, usu cap* [Peter Paul *Rubens* + E *-an*] **:** RUBENESQUE
**ru·bens' madder** \'rübənz(əz)-\ *n, often cap R* **:** a dark reddish orange that is less strong and very slightly redder and lighter than average lacquer red and redder, stronger, and slightly lighter than burnt sienna

**ru·be·o·la** \rü'bēələ\ *n* -s [NL, fr. neut. pl. of (assumed) NL *rubeolus* reddish, fr. L *rubeus* red, reddish] **:** MEASLES — **ru·be·o·lar** \-lə(r)\ *adj*

**ru·ber·yth·ric acid** \¦rübə¦rithrik-\ *n* [*ruberythric* ISV *rub-* (fr. NL *Rubia*) + *erythr-* + *-ic*] **:** a yellow crystalline acidic glycoside $C_{25}H_{26}O_{13}$ occurring in madder root and yielding alizarin and primeverose on hydrolysis

**rub·eryth·rin·ic acid** \¦rübə,ri¦th¦rinik-, ¦rü,berə¦th¦\ *n* [*ruberythrinic* fr. G *ruberythrin-* (in *ruberythrinsäure* ruberythric acid) (fr. *rub-* — fr. NL *Rubia* — + *erythr-* + *-in* -ine) + E *-ic*] **:** RUBERYTHRIC ACID

**ru·bes·cence** \rü'besᵊn(t)s\ *n* -s [fr. *rubescent*, after such pairs as E *adolescent: adolescence*] **:** the quality or state of being rubescent

**ru·bes·cent** \-ᵊnt\ *adj* [L *rubescent-, rubescens*, pres. part. of *rubescere* to grow red, incho. of *rubēre* to be red; akin to L *ruber* red — more at RED] **:** growing or becoming red **:** ERUBESCENT, REDDENING, FLUSHING

**ru·bia** \'rübēə\ *n, cap* [NL, fr. L, madder; akin to L *ruber* red] **:** a genus (the type of the family Rubiaceae) of Old World herbs having pentamerous flowers and fleshy fruit — see MADDER

**ru·bi·a·ce·ae** \,rübē'āsē,ē\ *n pl, cap* [NL, fr. *Rubia*, type genus + *-aceae*] **:** a family of mostly tropical herbs, shrubs, and trees (order Rubiales) of very diverse habits having opposite stipulate leaves and regular flowers with the stamens borne on the corolla tube and a 1- to 10-celled ovary usu. with numerous ovules that becomes in fruit a capsule, a berry, or one or more distinct nutlets — **ru·bi·a·ceous** \¦rübē¦āshəs\ *adj*

**ru·bi·a·les** \,rübē'ā(,)lēz\ *n pl, cap* [NL, fr. *Rubia* + *-ales*] **:** an order of dicotyledonous plants having opposite leaves, an inferior compound ovary, and epigynous stamens equal in number to the lobes of the corolla

**ru·bi·celle** \¦rübə¦sel\ *n* -s [alter. of earlier *rubacelle*, prob. fr. F, dim. of *rubace* rubasse — more at RUBASSE] **:** a ruby spinel of a yellow or orange-red color

**¹ru·bi·con** \'rübə,kän *sometimes* -bəkən *or* -bēkən\ *n* -s [L *Rubicon-, Rubico*, small river in north central Italy which in the time of the ancient Roman republic formed part of the boundary between Cisalpine Gaul and Italy, and over which Julius Caesar crossed into Italy with his army in 49 B.C. against the orders of the government to begin the civil war in which he overthrew Pompey] **1** *usu cap* **:** a bounding or limiting line; *esp* **:** one that when crossed commits a person to an irrevocable change or decision ⟨the little lads think they have crossed the *Rubicon* when they first get trousers —Cahir Healy⟩ **2 :** the winning of a card game before the loser has reached a certain prescribed score or with a score that is at least twice as great as the loser's score and usu. with the effect that the winner's score is doubled ⟨~ bezique⟩ — compare LURCH

**²rubicon** \"\ *vt* -ED/-ING/-S **:** to defeat (as in piquet or bezique) with a score so low that it is added to the winner's

**ru·bi·cund** \'rübəkənd, -bēkə-, -bə,kə-\ *adj* [L *rubicundus*; akin to L *ruber* red — more at RED] **:** inclining to redness **:** RUDDY, RED ⟨as a result of a judicious mixture of wind, rain and beer the . . . farmer's face is ~ and jovial —S.P.B.Mais⟩

**ru·bi·cun·di·ty** \,rübə'kəndəd·ē, -ndətē, -i\ *n* -ES [ML *rubicunditat-, rubicunditas*, fr. L *rubicundus* + *-itat-, -itas* -ity] **:** the quality or state of being rubicund **:** RUDDINESS

**ru·bid·ic** \(')rü¦bidik\ *adj* [ISV *rubid-* (fr. NL *rubidium*) + *-ic*] **:** of or relating to rubidium

**ru·bid·i·um** \rü'bidēəm\ *n* -s [NL, fr. L *rubidus* red + NL *-ium*; fr. two red lines in its spectrum; akin to L *ruber* red] **:** a soft silvery metallic element of the alkali metal group that is found combined in small amounts in many minerals and mineral waters and the ashes of many plants usu. accompanied by still smaller amounts of cesium, that is produced in metallic form by electrolysis or chemical reduction of its compounds, and that decomposes water with violence and inflames spontaneously in air — symbol *Rb*; see ELEMENT table

**ru·bied** \'rübēd, -bid\ *adj* [¹*ruby* + *-ed*] **:** made like a ruby in color

**rubier** *comparative of* RUBY

**rubies** *pl of* RUBY, *pres 3d sing of* RUBY

**rubiest** *superlative of* RUBY

**ru·bi·fy** \'rübə,fī\ *vt* -ED/-ING/-ES [ME *rubifyen*, fr. MF *rubifier, rubefier*, modif. (influenced by MF *-fier* -fy) of L *rubefacere* — more at RUBEFACIENT] **:** to make red **:** REDDEN

**ru·big·i·nous** \(')rü¦bijənəs\ *also* **ru·big·i·nose** \-,nōs\ *adj* [L *robiginosus, rubiginosus* rusty, fr. *robigin-, rubigin-, robigo, rubigo* + *-osus* -ose; akin to L *ruber* red] **:** of or marked with a rusty red color **:** FERRUGINOUS

**ru·bi·jervine** \¦rübə+\ *n* [¹*ruby* + *jervine*] **:** a nonpoisonous crystalline alkaloid $C_{27}H_{43}NO_2$ found with jervine in green and white hellebore

**rub in** *vt* **:** to insist on, harp on, continue to recall, or emphasize (as something unpleasant) ⟨if they failed he never *rubbed in* their failure —F.W.Crofts⟩ ⟨trying to *rub* it *in* that they had won their freedom —J.H.Huizinga⟩

**rubine** *or* **rubin** *n* -s [ML *rubinus*, fr. L *rubeus* red, reddish — more at RUBY] *obs* **:** RUBY

**ru·bin test** \'rübən-\ *n, usu cap R* [after I.C.*Rubin* b1883 Am. gynecologist] **:** a test to determine the patency or occlusion of the fallopian tubes by insufflating them with carbon dioxide by transuterine injection

**ru·bi·ous** \'rübēəs\ *adj* [¹*ruby* + *-ous*] **:** RED, RUBY

**ru·ble** *also* **rou·ble** \'rübəl\ *n* -s [Russ *rubl'*, fr. Old Russian *rublĭ*, lit., block of wood, fr. *rubiti* to build; akin to Lith *rum̃bas* scar on a tree and perh. to MHG *rumph* trunk, torso — more at RUMP] **1 :** the basic monetary unit of the U.S.S.R. — see MONEY table **2 :** a coin representing one ruble

**rub of the green :** something happening to a golf ball in play that affects its course or status not caused by a player or caddie involved in the match

**ru·bor** \'rü,bȯ(ə)r, -,bər\ *n* -s [L, redness; akin to L *ruber* red — more at RED] **:** redness of the skin (as in inflammation or from dilated capillaries)

**rub out** *vt* **1 :** to obliterate or extinguish by rubbing ⟨*rubbed out* the shovel marks and all their tracks —W.F.Davis⟩ ⟨*rubbed out* the end of his cigarette —Kay Boyle⟩ **2 :** to destroy completely ⟨much of the older section of town was *rubbed out* in the air raids —Richard Joseph⟩; *specif* **:** MURDER, KILL ⟨somebody *rubbed* him *out* this afternoon with a twenty-two —Raymond Chandler⟩

**rub rail** *n* **:** a metal rail to protect against rubbing: as **a :** a projecting steel or aluminum strip that protects a truck or bus body against damage by gliding contact **b :** a brass rail on a boat to take wear of the lines

**ru·brene** \'rü,brēn\ *n* -s [ISV *rubr-* (fr. L *rubr-, ruber* red) + *-ene*] **:** an orange-red fluorescent crystalline polycyclic hydrocarbon $C_{42}H_{28}$ that is decolorized by oxygen with the reversible formation of a peroxide; tetraphenyl-naphthacene

**¹ru·bric** \'rü(,)brik, -,brēk\ *n* -s [ME *rubrike* red ocher, heading in red letters of a part of a book, fr. MF *rubrique*, fr. L *rubrica*, fr. *rubr-, ruber* red — more at RED] **1** *archaic* **a :** BOLE **b :** RED OCHER **2 :** a heading of a chapter, a section, or other part of a book or manuscript distinguished by being done or underlined in a color (as red) different from the rest of the text or by some other device **3 a** (1) **:** a section heading of a discourse or writing (2) **:** NAME, TITLE ⟨a variety of names . . . botany, zoology, and geography have become increasingly technical . . . they too have dropped the ~ of natural history —*Amer. Naturalist*⟩ (3) **:** something under which a thing is classed **:** CONCEPT, CLASS, CATEGORY ⟨a variety of names has been applied to the sensations falling under the general ~, "pressure" —F.A. Geldard⟩ **b** (1) **:** the title of a statute or law (2) **:** a statute, law, commandment, or dictum regarded as authoritative (3) **:** a collection or group of statutes, laws, or dicta **:** CANON; *specif* **:** a collection of ecclesiastical rules (4) **:** a rule for the conduct of a liturgical service ⟨the ~s of the Order of Confirmation⟩ (5) **:** PURITY RUBRIC **c :** a formula, commentary, or gloss that elucidates or sets within a context ⟨like accepting a fairy tale as history, through ignoring the prefatory ~ "once upon a time, in a world that never was" —A.G.N. Flew⟩; *specif* **:** an editorial interpolation ⟨clarity is promoted by the use of numbered paragraphs with marginal ~s —J.C. Stewart⟩ **4 :** a technique, custom, form, or thing established or settled (as by authority) ⟨hand engraving is an art in its own right, with its own ~s —O.L.Harvey⟩ ⟨no longer wore high laced boots, because the ~s had changed in these matters —Bruce Marshall⟩ **5** *obs* **:** a calendar of saints **6** *or* **ru·bri·ca** \-brəkə, -brēkə\ [Sp *rúbrica* paraph, heading, fr. L *rubrica*] **:** PARAPH

**²rubric** \"\ *or* **ru·bri·cal** \-brəkəl, -brēk-\ *adj* [*rubric* fr. ME *rubrike*, fr. *rubrike*, n.; *rubrical* fr. ¹*rubric* + *-al*] **1 a :** colored, written, printed in, or marked with red **b :** RED-LETTER ⟨~ day⟩ **2 :** of, relating to, or in accordance with a rubric — **ru·bri·cal·ly** \-brək(ə)lē, -brēk-, -li\ *adv*

**³rubric** \"\ *vt* -ED/-ING/-S [¹*rubric*] **:** to adorn with red **:** REDDEN

**ru·bri·cate** \'rübrə,kāt\ *vt* -ED/-ING/-S [LL *rubricatus*, past part. of *rubricare* to color red, fr. L *rubrica* red ocher] **1 a :** to write or print as a rubric ⟨*rubricated* capital letter⟩ ⟨*rubricated* title in a manuscript⟩ **b :** to add a rubric to or provide with a rubric ⟨*rubricated* manuscript⟩ ⟨*rubricated* calendar⟩ **2 :** to arrange as in a rubric **:** fix in form

**ru·bri·ca·tion** \,==ˈkāshən\ *n* -s **1 :** the act or process of rubricating **2 :** something (as a letter or word) that is rubricated

**ru·bri·ca·tor** \'==,kād·ə(r)\ *n* -s **:** one that rubricates; *esp* **:** a member of a medieval brotherhood with the duty of rubricating books and manuscripts produced in a monastery

**ru·bri·cian** \rü'brishən\ *n* -s **:** one skilled in the knowledge of or tenaciously adhering to a rubric

**ru·bric·i·ty** \rü'brisəd·ē\ *n* -ES [²*rubric* + *-ity*] **:** REDNESS

**ru·bro·cortical** \¦rü(,)brō+\ *adj* [*rubro-* (fr. L *rubr-, ruber* red + E *-o-*) + *cortical*] **:** connecting or relating to the red nucleus and the cortex of the brain

**ru·brofu·gal** \¦rübrō¦fyügəl, (')rü¦bräfyəg-\ *adj* [*rubro-* (fr. L *rubr-, ruber* red + E *-o-*) + *-fugal*] **:** passing or leading away from the red nucleus

**ru·bro·petal** \¦rübrō¦ped·ᵊl, -¦ped-, (')rü¦bräpəd·-\ *adj* [*rubro-* (fr. L *rubr-, ruber* red + E *-o-*) + *-petal*] **:** passing or leading into the red nucleus

**ru·bro·spinal** \¦rü(,)brō+\ *adj* [*rubro-* (fr. L *rubr-, ruber* red + E *-o-*) + *spinal* — more at RED] **1 :** of, relating to, or connecting the red nucleus and the spinal cord **2 :** of, relating to, or constituting a tract of crossed nerve fibers passing from the red nucleus to the spinal cord and relaying impulses from the cerebellum and corpora striata to the motor neurons of the cord

**rubs** *pres 3d sing of* RUB, *pl of* RUB

**rubstone** \'=,=\ *n* [ME *rubston*, fr. *rubben* to rub + *ston, stoon* stone] **:** a sandstone or grit for scouring, polishing, or sharpening; *esp* **:** WHETSTONE

**rub up** *vt* **1 :** to revive or refresh knowledge of **:** RECALL ⟨*rubbed up* his Latin in an epitaph for the tomb of some pet dog —Virginia Woolf⟩ **2 :** to improve the keenness of (a mental faculty) ⟨have begun a course of history . . . to *rub up* my memory before I touch on classic ground —Sydney Morgan⟩ **3 :** to daub (a lithographic stone or plate) with ink preparatory to proofing or running

**ru·bus** \'rübəs\ *n, cap* [NL, fr. L, blackberry] **:** a genus of often prickly shrubs (family Rosaceae) having 3- to 7-foliolate or simple lobed leaves, white or pink flowers with a flat persistent calyx bearing the numerous stamens, and a mass of carpels ripening into an aggregate fruit composed of many drupelets — see BLACKBERRY, DEWBERRY, RASPBERRY

**¹ru·by** \'rübē, -bi\ *n* -ES [ME, fr. MF *rubi*, fr. OF, irreg. fr. L *rubeus* red, reddish; akin to L *ruber* red — more at RED] **1 a** (1) **:** a precious stone that is a red corundum and is found esp. in Burma, Ceylon, and Thailand — see RUBY SPINEL (2) *obs* **:** any of various precious stones of red color **b :** something made of ruby; *esp* **:** a watch bearing, pin, roller, or other part made of ruby or of a substitute material **2 a** (1) *or* **ruby red :** the color of the ruby **:** a dark red that is bluer, lighter, and stronger than average garnet or average wine and less strong and very slightly yellower than cranberry (2) *of textiles* **:** a deep purplish red that is redder and paler than magenta (sense 2a) and bluer and slightly lighter than American beauty **b** (1) **:** something resembling a ruby in color (2) **:** RUBY GLASS **3** *Brit* **:** AGATE 4 **4 :** a Brazilian hummingbird of the genus *Clytolaema* whose male has a ruby-colored throat or breast

**²ruby** \"\ *adj* -ER/-EST **:** of the color ruby

**³ruby** \"\ *vt* -ED/-ING/-ES [²*ruby*] **:** to make of the color ruby **:** REDDEN

**ruby-and-topaz hummingbird** *n* **:** a showy hummingbird (*Chrysolampis mosquitus*) of northern So. America

**ruby blende** *n* **:** a red or reddish brown transparent sphalerite

**ruby copper** *or* **ruby copper ore** *n* **:** CUPRITE

**ruby-crowned kinglet** *or* **ruby-crowned wren** \'==,=-\ *n* **:** an American kinglet (*Regulus calendula*) having a notable song and in the male a bright red crown patch

**ruby glass** *n* **:** glass of a deep red color produced by the use of selenium or esp. formerly by the addition of an oxide of copper or the use of gold chloride

**ruby grass** *n* **:** NATAL GRASS

**ruby port** *n* **:** a port wine of a deep red color

**ruby silver** *or* **ruby silver ore** *n* **1 :** PYRARGYRITE **2 :** PROUSTITE

**ruby spaniel** *n* **:** an English toy spaniel of a solid red color

**ruby spinel** *n* **:** a spinel used as a gem — see BALAS, RUBICELLE, SPINEL RUBY

**rubytail** \'==,=\ *or* **ruby-tailed fly** \'==,=-\ *n* **:** any of various cuckoo wasps; *esp* **:** a common European insect (*Chrysis viridula*) having part of the abdomen metallic red

**rubythroat** \'==,=\ *n* **1 :** RUBY-THROATED HUMMINGBIRD **2 :** any of several red-throated Asiatic thrushes of the genus *Calliope*

**ruby-throated hummingbird** \¦==¦==-\ *n* **:** a hummingbird (*Archilochus colubris*) of eastern No. America having a bright bronzy green back, whitish underparts, and in the adult male a red throat with metallic reflections

**ruby wasp** *or* **ruby-tail wasp** *or* **ruby fly** *n* **:** CUCKOO WASP

**ruby wine** *n* **:** a dark red that is yellower and duller than cranberry and bluer, stronger, and slightly lighter than average garnet or average wine

**ruby wood** *n* **1 :** RED SANDALWOOD 1 b **2 :** SHEA TREE

**ruby zinc** *n* **1 :** RUBY BLENDE **2 :** ZINCITE

**ru·cer·vine** \rü'sərvən, -,vīn\ *adj* [NL *Rucervus* (fr. *Rusa* + *Cervus*) + E *-ine*] **:** of, relating to, or like a deer of a genus (*Rucervus*) that is now usu. made a subgenus of *Cervus*

**rucervine antler** *n* **:** an antler with long and simple brow tine and doubly dichotomous beam

**¹ruche** \'rüsh\ *n* -s [F, fr. ML *rusca* bark, rind, of Celt origin; akin to W *rhisgl* bark, ScGael *rùsg* rind, IrGael *rusc* bark] **:** RUCHING

**²ruche** \"\ *vt* -ED/-ING/-S **:** to trim with ruching

**ruch·ing** \'rüshiŋ\ *n* -s [¹*ruche* + *-ing*] **:** a pleated, fluted, or gathered strip of fabric (as lace, net, ribbon) used for trimming usu. in rows and esp. on women's garments

**¹ruck** \'rək\ *n* -s [ME *ruke, roke*, of Scand origin; akin to Norw dial. *rūka* heap, ON *hraukr* rick — more at RICK] **1** *chiefly dial* **:** HEAP, STACK, PILE, RICK ⟨coral ~s sticking out of the water —*Blackwood's*⟩ **2 a :** a large number or quantity taken esp. as indistinguishable in the aggregate **:** ASSEMBLAGE ⟨successes emerge from a ~ of smaller undertakings —Carl Van Doren⟩ **b :** the usual run of persons or things **:** GENERALITY, CROWD, MULTITUDE ⟨wrote the common ~ of the songs I was listening to —Max Beerbohm⟩ ⟨qualities that are bound to raise a man out of the ~ —G.W.Johnson⟩ ⟨from the ~ of routine, there arose a diversion —A.R.Griffin⟩ **c :** MASS, JUMBLE ⟨what I feel about the ~ of recent verse —J.L.Lowes⟩ ⟨a great ~ of textbooks —*Springfield (Mass.) Union*⟩ ⟨picked our way through the ~, lighting matches . . . when we found ourselves trapped in blind alleys between bales —W.D.Steele⟩ ⟨marked the land with the ~ of buffalo bones —Meridel Le Sueur⟩ **3 a :** the racehorses running in a group behind those that set the pace ⟨come up from the ~⟩ **b :** any aggregation of persons or things following the winners or vanguard ⟨finish a yacht race in the ~⟩ ⟨the ~ of wagons came after them —Irving Bacheller⟩ ⟨war and chaos in its ~ —S.L.A. Marshall⟩ **4 :** a group of players of each team in rugby that are close together but not in a set formation

**²ruck** \"\ *vt* -ED/-ING/-S *chiefly dial* **:** to rake into a heap

**³ruck** \"\ *n* -s [of Scand origin; akin to ON *hrukka* wrinkle; akin to MHG *runke* wrinkle, OE *scrincan* to shrink — more at SHRINK] **:** CREASE, PUCKER, WRINKLE

**⁴ruck** \"\ *vb* -ED/-ING/-S *vi* **:** to draw or work into wrinkles or creases **:** PUCKER ⟨more micaceous rocks may show a ~*ing* or even small folds —*Economic Geology*⟩ — often used with *up* ⟨keeping the shirt from ~*ing* up —*advt*⟩ ~ *vt* **:** CREASE, PUCKER, WRINKLE ⟨those whose natures have been ~*ed* and wrinkled with suffering —R.S.Ellery⟩ — often used with *up* ⟨page was so wet, so ~*ed* up —Elizabeth Taylor⟩ ⟨top of the world, here ~*ed* up into gleaming ridges —Phil Stong⟩

**⁵ruck** \'rək, 'ru̇k\ *n* -s [prob. fr. ³*ruck*] *dial Brit* **:** RUT, FURROW

**¹ruck·le** \'rəkəl, 'ru̇k-\ *vi* **ruckled; ruckled; ruckling** \-k(ə)liŋ\ **ruckles** [of Scand origin; akin to ON *hrygla* to rattle in the throat; akin to MHG *rückeln, rüheln* to rattle in the throat, roar, OE *hrog* mucus, phlegm, Lith *kraũkti* to croak, groan, OSlav *krukŭ* raven, L *corvus* raven, *crepare* to crack, creak — more at RAVEN] *dial Brit* **:** to make a hoarse rattling sound (as from suffocation) ⟨asses braying and camels *ruckling* —I.M.Lask⟩

**²ruck·le** \'rəkəl\ **ruckled; ruckled; ruckling** \-k(ə)liŋ\ **ruckles** *vb* [³*ruck* + *-le*] *Brit* **:** to form or work into folds **:** CRUMPLE, WRINKLE

**ruck·sack** \'rək sak, 'ru̇k-\ *n* [G, fr. *ruck-* (prob. alter. of *rücken* back, spine, fr. OHG *hrukki*) + *sack* sack, fr. OHG *sac* — more at RIDGE, SACK] **:** KNAPSACK

**rück·umlaut** \'rʊek+,-\ *n* [G lit., back umlaut, fr. *rück-* (fr. *zurück* back, backward, fr. MHG *ze rücke*, fr. *ze* to — fr. OHG *zi* — + *rücke* back, fr. OHG *hrukki*) + *umlaut* — more at TO, RIDGE, UMLAUT] **:** the absence of umlaut of the stem vowel in the past tense and past participle of some Germanic weak verbs as a result of the loss of *i* in the following syllable before the umlaut period

**ruck·us** \'rəkəs, 'ru̇k-\ *also* **roo·kus** \'rük-\ *n* -ES [*ruckus* prob. blend of *ruction* and *rumpus*; *rookus* alter. of *ruckus*] **1 :** a noisy fight; *esp* **:** one involving a number of people **:** FRACAS **2 :** CONTROVERSY, ROW, DISTURBANCE ⟨old ~*es* he stirred up among the critics —*New Yorker*⟩ ⟨political ~⟩ ⟨raise a ~⟩

**ruc·ta·tion** \,rək'tāshən\ *n* -s [LL *ructation-, ructatio*, fr. L *ructatus* (past part. of *ructare* to belch) + *-ion-, -io* -ion — more at ERUCT] *archaic* **:** BELCH

**ruc·tion** \'rəkshən\ *n* -s [perh. by shortening & alter. fr. *insurrection*] **1 :** a noisy rough-and-tumble fight **:** FREE-FOR-ALL **2 :** a heated quarrel esp. among a number of people ⟨raise a ~⟩ **3 :** a state of disturbance or uproar **:** vociferous or belligerent disagreement **:** CONTENTION, DISSENSION, FRICTION ⟨herds were pushed with constant ~ by following waves of farmers —Russell Lord⟩

**ruc·tious** \'rəkshəs\ *adj* [*ruction* + *-ious*] *dial* **:** causing a ruction **:** QUARRELSOME, CONTENTIOUS, UNRULY, VEXED ⟨~ ghosts called poltergeists —*Time*⟩

**ru·cu·yen** *also* **roo·coo·yen** *or* **rou·cou·yenne** \¦rü,kü¦yen\ *n, pl* **rucuyen** *or* **rucuyens** *usu cap* **1 a :** a Cariban people of the Tumuc-Humac mountains between Brazil and the Guianas **b :** a member of such people **2 :** a language of the Rucuyen people

**¹rud** *also* **rudd** \'rəd\ *n* -s [ME *rude, rudde, rode*, fr. OE *rudu*; akin to OE *rēad* red — more at RED] **1** *dial* **a :** a ruddy color **:** REDNESS **b :** HUE, COMPLEXION **2** *archaic* **:** RED OCHER

**²rud** *also* **rudd** \"\ *vt* **rudded; rudded; rudding; ruds** *also* **rudds** [ME *ruden, rudden, roden*, fr. *rude, rudde, rode* rud] **:** REDDEN

**rud** *abbr* rudder

**ru·das** \'rüdəs\ *n* -ES [origin unknown] *Scot* **:** an ugly foul-mouthed old hag **:** BELDAM

**rud·beck·ia** \,rəd'bekēə, rüd-\ *n* [NL, fr. Olof *Rudbeck* †1702 Swed. scientist + NL *-ia*] **1** *cap* **:** a genus of No. American perennial herbs (family Compositae) having showy pedunculate flower heads with a hemispherical involucre, mostly yellow ray flowers, and a conical chaffy receptacle — see BLACK-EYED SUSAN, GOLDEN GLOW **2** -s **:** any plant of the genus *Rudbeckia*

**rudd** \'rəd\ *n* -s [prob. fr. ¹*rud*] **:** a freshwater European cyprinid fish (*Scardinius erythrophthalmus*) resembling the roach but having the dorsal fin farther back, a stouter body, and red irises and fins — called also *redeye*

**¹rud·der** \'rədə(r)\ *n* -s *often attrib* [ME *rother*, fr. OE *rōther* paddle; akin to OHG *ruodar* rudder, ON *rōthr* act of steering; derivative fr. the root of E ¹*row*] **1 a :** a flat piece or structure of wood or metal attached upright to the sternpost or in single-screw ships to the rudderpost by hinges or by pintles and gudgeons so that it can be turned (as by a tiller) causing the ship's head to turn in the same direction because of the resistance offered to the water by the rudder **b :** a hinged or movable auxiliary airfoil usu. attached at the rear end that serves to control direction of flight in the horizontal plane by impressing yawing moments on an airplane **2 :** RUDDER ANGLE ⟨what ~, if any, the ship is carrying —*Manual of Seamanship*⟩ **3 :** one that resembles a rudder in being a guide or governor ⟨for rhyme the ~ is of verses —Samuel Butler †1680⟩ **4 :** a plate or wheel at the rear end of a lister to guide and steady the moldboards and assist in bearing the weight **5 :** a tail esp. of an otter **6 :** a swinging support for the leaf of a drop-leaf table

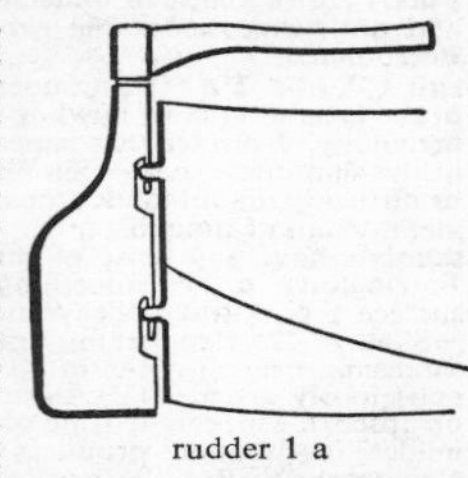
rudder 1 a

**²rudder** \"\ *vt* -ED/-ING/-S **1 :** STEER **2 :** to provide with a rudder

**rudder angle** *n* **:** the acute angle between the rudder and the fore-and-aft line of a ship or airplane

**rudder bar** *n* **:** a foot bar for operating the central cables leading to the rudder of an airplane

**rudder bird** *or* **rudder duck** *n* **:** RUDDY DUCK

**rudder brake** *n* **:** an eccentric friction band for controlling the motion of a rudder (as in a seaway)

**rudder breeching** *n* **:** a rope for lifting a rudder so as to ease the strain on the pintles

**rudder chain** *n* **:** one of a pair of loose chains or ropes that lead from a rudder to the quarters for operating it in case the tiller or rudderhead is broken

**rudder crosshead** *n* **:** an athwartship metal bar or casting which is secured to a rudderhead in lieu of a tiller and to which the connecting rods of the steering gear are secured

**rudderfish** \'==,=\ *n* [¹*rudder* + *fish*] **:** any of various fishes reputed to follow or accompany ships: as **a :** PILOT FISH 1 **b :** BANDED RUDDERFISH **c :** any of several butterfishes (family Stromateidae) **d :** any of various fishes of the family Kyphosidae; *esp* **:** BERMUDA CHUB **e :** the opaleye or other fish of the family Girellidae

**rudderhead** \'==,=\ *n* [¹*rudder* + *head*] **:** the upper end of a rudderstock to which the tiller is attached

**rudderhole** \'==,=\ *n* [¹*rudder* + *hole*] **:** a hole in a deck through which a rudderstock passes

**rudder iron** *n* **:** a pintle or gudgeon for a ship's rudder

**rud·der·less** \'rədə(r)ləs\ *adj* **:** lacking a rudder

**rudder lug** *n* **:** a projection on a rudder frame at the forward edge for taking a pintle

**rudderpost** \'==,=\ *n* [¹*rudder* + *post*] **1 :** RUDDERSTOCK **2 :** an additional sternpost in a single-screw ship to which the rudder is attached

**rudderstock** \'==,=\ *n* [¹*rudder* + *stock*] **:** the shaft of a rudder

**rudder stop** *n* **:** a fitting on the stern frame or structure of a ship to limit the swing of the rudder

**rudder tackle** *n* **:** emergency tackle for use when mechanical steering gear fails to function

**rudder torque** *n* **:** a twisting effect exerted by the rudder of an airplane on the fuselage due to the relative displacement of the center of pressure of the rudder

**rudder trunk** *n* **:** a watertight enclosure around a rudderstock

**rud·der·va·tor** *also* **rud·de·va·tor** \'rədə(r),vād·ə(r)\ *n* -s [blend of *rudder* and *elevator*] **:** a movable airfoil at the trailing edge of a vee tail designed to perform the functions of both a rudder and an elevator

**rud·di·ly** \'rədᵊlē, -dəl, ¦i\ *adv* **:** with a ruddy hue or tinge

**rud·di·ness** \'rədēnəs, -din-\ *n* -ES **:** the quality or state of being ruddy

**1rud·dle** \'rədᵊl\ *n* -s [dim. of 1*rud*] **1** *also* **red·dle** \'red-\ **:** RED OCHER **2 :** 2BOLE 3

**2ruddle** \"\ *vt* **ruddled; ruddled; ruddling** \-d(ᵊ)liŋ\ **ruddles** **1 :** to mark, paint, or color with red ocher ⟨~ sheep⟩ **2 :** ROUGE **3 :** REDDEN, FLUSH ⟨faces *ruddled* by the light of bobbing lanterns —Sinclair Lewis⟩

**rud·dle·man** \-dᵊlmən\ *also* **red·dle·man** \'red-\ *n, pl* **rud·dlemen** [1*ruddle* or *reddle* + *man*] **:** a dealer in red ocher

**rud·dock** \'rədək\ *n* -s [ME *ruddok*, fr. OE *rudduc;* akin to OE *rudu* rud] **1 :** ROBIN 1 a **2** *obs* **:** a piece of gold money

**rudds** *pl of* RUD, *pres 3d sing of* RUD

**1rud·dy** \'rədē, -di\ *adj* -ER/-EST [ME *rudi, rudie*, fr. OE *rudig*, fr. *rudu* rud + *-ig* -y — more at RUD] **1 :** having or marked by a reddish color associated with the glow of good health or a suffusion of blood (as from exercise, excitement, exposure) ⟨a ~ complexion⟩ ⟨~ face⟩ ⟨stout ~ countryman⟩ **2 a :** of the color red **b :** RED, REDDISH ⟨~ glares from the blast furnaces —D.E.Keir⟩ **3 :** GLOWING, LIVELY, VIVID ⟨~ memories⟩ **4** *Brit* — used as a generalized expression of intensification ⟨a ~ lie⟩ ⟨a ~ shame⟩ often losing all force ⟨what's the ~ matter⟩; often considered vulgar

**2ruddy** \"\ *vt* -ED/-ING/-ES **:** to make ruddy **:** REDDEN ⟨sunlight *ruddied* the windows⟩

**3ruddy** \"\ *adv, Brit* — an intensive ⟨could ~ well do as he liked⟩; often considered vulgar

**ruddy diver** *n* **:** RUDDY DUCK

**ruddy duck** *n* **:** an American duck (*Oxyura jamaicensis rubida*) having a broad bill and a wedge-shaped tail of stiff sharp feathers, the adult male having the upper parts largely rich brownish red and the female and young male being dull brown mixed with blackish on the back and grayish below

**ruddy plover** *n* **:** SANDERLING

**ruddy sheldrake** *n* **:** a sheldrake (*Tadorna ferruginea*) of southern Europe, Asia, and northern Africa that is chiefly orange-brown with the quills of the wings and tail blackish and the speculum bronzy green and with the male in summer having a black collar

**ruddy turnstone** *n* **:** an American turnstone (*Arenaria interpres morinella*) similar to the common turnstone

**rude** \'rüd\ *adj* -ER/-EST [ME, fr. MF, fr. L *rudis;* akin to L *rudus* rubble, broken stone, *rullus* coarse, rustic, MIr *rūad* ruin, MD *ruten* to tear, plunder, ON *reyta* to tear up, pluck out, L *ruere* to rush, fall, dig up — more at RUG] **1 :** being in or marked by a rough, plain, or unfinished condition: **a :** lacking in craftsmanship or artistic finish **:** UNPOLISHED ⟨a ~ sketch⟩ ⟨a few ~ benches on which the players usually sat —Edna Ferber⟩ ⟨ornate window facings had broken off, leaving ~ gaps in the design —Marcia Davenport⟩ **b :** *of sound* **:** DISCORDANT, JARRING ⟨a ~ serenade⟩ ⟨the frowning-down of ~ intonations and laughing-out of oddities —D.L.Bolinger⟩ **c :** NATURAL, RAW, UNMANUFACTURED ⟨~ cotton⟩ ⟨examines, bit by bit, the ~ material of knowledge —T.L.Peacock⟩ **d** *of land* **:** RUGGED, WILD ⟨a ~ and rocky gorge commences —Tom Marvel⟩ ⟨shelter in a ~ country of forests —*Amer. Guide Series: Va.*⟩ **e :** STORMY, TURBULENT, BITTER ⟨winter's ~ winds⟩ ⟨~ seas⟩ **f :** hastily executed and admittedly imperfect or imprecise ⟨~ estimates⟩ **g :** being in or characteristic of a primitive or undeveloped state ⟨succeeded in constructing a ~ steam engine —T.B. Macaulay⟩ ⟨peasants use ~ wooden plows —Jack Raymond⟩ ⟨idea that man has progressed from ~ beginnings to civilized society —S.F.Mason⟩ **h :** IMMODERATE, UNMITIGATED ⟨the bright ~ sun —Gordon Merrick⟩ **i :** being in the rough state **:** UNDRESSED, UNFINISHED ⟨~ monoliths⟩ **j :** SIMPLE, ELEMENTARY, ELEMENTAL, UNSUBTLE ⟨community on the outskirts of civilization which continues to maintain itself in ~ plenty and comfort —W.H.Mallock⟩ ⟨landscape done in ~ whites, blacks, deep browns —Richard Harris⟩ **2 :** lacking refinement or delicacy: **a :** lacking education **:** IGNORANT, UNLEARNED, UNTUTORED ⟨~ mountaineers⟩ **b :** lacking polish **:** INELEGANT, UNCOUTH ⟨even the ~ dialects of the illiterate began to acquire dignity —Josiah Royce⟩ ⟨gave to his historical compositions a ~ dramatic vigor —Roger Fry⟩ **c :** offensive in manner or action **:** DISCOURTEOUS, UNMANNERLY, IMPUDENT ⟨made a ~ reply⟩ ⟨his brusqueness did not make him ~ —O.S.J. Gogarty⟩ **d :** marked by a lack of gentleness or by the use of force ⟨place a ~ hand upon our little mare's bridle —Kenneth Roberts⟩ ⟨dragged him with ~ cuffs before the magistrate —A.C.Whitehead⟩ ⟨self-discipline and single-mindedness must have been needed to make this ~ initiation to the stage endurable —*Times Lit. Supp.*⟩ **e :** UNCIVILIZED, BARBAROUS, SAVAGE ⟨in the ~ ages of society —Adam Smith⟩ ⟨during ~ times no man can be useful or faithful to his tribe without courage —C.R.Darwin⟩ **f :** UNAFFECTED, GUILELESS, OPEN ⟨arguments for ~ virtue are almost inevitably less stimulating than those for sophisticated corruption —Wolcott Gibbs⟩ ⟨ought to . . . speak the ~ truth in all ways —R.W.Emerson⟩ **g :** COARSE, RIBALD, VULGAR ⟨exchanged banter in ~ phrases, which at first shocked her —Theodore Dreiser⟩ ⟨paint on which someone had scratched a ~ picture —F.D.Ommanney⟩ ⟨unimportant work with a few small, ~ words in it —Anthony West⟩ **3 :** marked by lack of training or skill **:** INEXPERIENCED, INEXPERT ⟨~ workmanship⟩ ⟨was but a ~ scholar⟩ **4 :** ROBUST, STURDY, VIGOROUS ⟨spoke of the ~ health of their children —Joseph Conrad⟩ ⟨the ~ strength of the idiom —Gilbert Millstein⟩ **5 a :** sudden and disconcerting or unpleasant **:** ABRUPT ⟨freedom that is due for a ~ awakening sooner or later —W.J.Reilly⟩ ⟨the change may not be so ~ or so sweeping —Douglas Cater⟩ **b :** GRAVE, IMPERATIVE, UNAVOIDABLE ⟨inner strength to endure in the face of ~ realities —*Americas*⟩

**syn** ILL-MANNERED, DISCOURTEOUS, IMPOLITE, UNCIVIL, UNGRACIOUS: in this set RUDE is the strongest word. It implies either a general and habitual deficiency in manners, grace, or polish or a coarse insensitivity to another's feelings or even a desire to wound them ⟨she thought he was *rude*, and so did he — and tried to philosophize himself out of his sense of social maladjustment —H.S.Canby⟩ ⟨I don't see why we should go to a house where the host apparently enjoys flatly contradicting you . . . probably he doesn't even know when he's being *rude* —Sinclair Lewis⟩ ILL-MANNERED stresses great want of knowledge of proprieties, usages, and graces of good society ⟨our Royal Family are getting a little tired of the well-meant, but at the same time *ill-mannered* homage of well-dressed crowds —*London Daily News*⟩ ⟨the pompous *ill-mannered* police —*Harper's*⟩ DISCOURTEOUS is likely to imply a consciousness of offending or wounding another if not the intent ⟨*discourteous* enough to slam the door in another's face⟩ ⟨*discourteous* in pointedly refusing to acknowledge his greeting⟩ IMPOLITE suggests less obvious and egregious departures from better conduct ⟨had been somewhat *impolite* in failing to answer her invitation as quickly as good manners demanded⟩ UNCIVIL indicates lack of decent consideration usually expected among men but not prescribed by any code of etiquette ⟨"comfortable seat, and be damned to you!" was the patient's *uncivil* reply —Anthony Trollope⟩ UNGRACIOUS may indicate lack of grace and consideration ensuing through gaucheness, callowness, surliness, irritation ⟨an interesting person, this stern Australian nurse — taciturn, suspicious, *ungracious* —A. Conan Doyle⟩

**syn** CRUDE, ROUGH, CALLOW, RAW, GREEN: except for CALLOW and GREEN, words in this series follow much the same pattern of semantic expansion. They are here compared only as indicating lack of social refinement in persons and in their actions and thoughts. RUDE may indicate complete lack of social polish or civility ⟨to be ill-bred and *rude* is intolerable, and the way to be kicked out of company —Earl of Chesterfield⟩ It may suggest intentional discourtesy or ill treatment of others ⟨I do not know whether it came from his own innate depravity or from the promptings of his master, but he was *rude* enough to set a dog at me —A. Conan Doyle⟩ CRUDE may emphasize a predisposition to the gross, simple, obvious, or primitive and an ignorance of the amenities ⟨they seem pleasant and good-humored, but a little *crude*, and lacking in the subtler forms of wit and understanding —Rose Macaulay⟩ More than others in this series, CRUDE may suggest an enduring characteristic rather than one from a passing phase ⟨the marks of the thoroughbred were simply not there. The man was blatant, *crude*, overly confidential . . . One often observed in him a certain pathetic wistfulness, a reaching out for a grand manner that was utterly beyond him —H.L.Mencken⟩ ROUGH suggests harsh, uncivil, unfeeling action or conduct, but may be concerned more with manifest conduct than inner character ⟨men of a *rough* and unsparing address should take great care that they be always in the right, the justice and propriety of their sentiments being the only tolerable apology . . . for such conduct —William Cowper⟩ It may thus suggest outer bluffness rather than inner incivility ⟨a *rough* old charitable mercifulness, better than sentimental ointment —George Meredith⟩ CALLOW, GREEN, and RAW all suggest novices' experiences and situations as causes for lack of savoir faire without indicating stupidity, truculence, or obduracy and without suggesting future inadequacy or gaucherie. CALLOW almost always denotes the immaturity of adolescence or early manhood ⟨not the aggregation of *callow* schoolboys fresh from the playing fields which in prewar times filled the academic halls, but an assemblage of men whose maturity has been forged in the holocaust of battle —Amy Loveman⟩ GREEN suggests unfamiliarity with a new environment or pursuit ⟨young men who were *green* recruits last autumn have matured into self-assured and hardened fighting men —F.D.Roosevelt⟩ It may also suggest rustic gullibility ⟨he has taken me for a *green* country girl, impressed with him because he is from the city and dressed in fine clothes —Sherwood Anderson⟩ RAW suggests outward uncertainty or awkward blundering due to lack of experience and training ⟨they think him *raw*, brusque, and uncultivated. He does not know the ritual . . . knowledge of which, acquired by long experience, is the mark of fit membership in the society —W.G. Sumner⟩

**rude·ly** *adv* [ME, fr. *rude* + *-ly* — more at RUDE] **1 :** in a rude manner ⟨spoke ~ to him⟩ ⟨laughed ~⟩ ⟨~ made⟩ ⟨~ awakened⟩ **2 :** APPROXIMATELY, IMPRECISELY ⟨estimated ~⟩ ⟨~, 75 by 125⟩

**rude·ness** *n* -ES [ME, fr. *rude* + *-ness*] **1 :** the quality or state of being rude ⟨shocked by the ~ of frontier life —*Amer. Guide Series: Tenn.*⟩ **2 :** a rude action ⟨an unpardonable ~⟩

**ru·den·ture** \(')rü¦denchə(r)\ *n* -s [F, fr. L *rudent-, rudens* ship's rope + F *-ure* — more at RHYTIDOME] *archit* **:** CABLING

**ru·dera** \'rüdərə\ *n pl* [L, pl. of *rudus* rubble, broken stone — more at RUDE] *archaic* **:** RUINS, DEBRIS

**1ru·der·al** \'rüdərəl\ *adj* [NL *ruderalis*, fr. L *rudera* + *-alis* -al] *of a plant* **:** growing in rubbish or in a waste or disturbed place

**2ruderal** \"\ *n* -s **:** a weedy and commonly introduced plant growing where the native vegetational cover has been interrupted; *esp* **:** a weed other than a grass growing where the vegetation has been disturbed by man (as in old fields or along roadsides)

**ru·der·ate** \'rüdə,rāt\ *vt* [L *ruderatus*, past part. of *ruderare* to pave with broken stone, fr. *rudus* rubble] *archaic* **:** to pave with broken stone

**ru·der·a·tion** \,rüdə'rāshən\ *n* -s [L *ruderation-, ruderatio*, fr. *ruderatus* (past part.) + *-ion-, -io* -ion] *archaic* **:** the process of paving with broken stone

**rudes·by** \'rüdzbē\ *n* -ES [*rude* + *-sby* (as in the name *Crosby*)] *archaic* **:** an uncivil turbulent person ⟨a madbrain ~ full of spleen —Shak.⟩

**rudge** \'rəj\ *chiefly dial var of* RIDGE

**ru·di·ment** \'rüdəmənt\ *n* -s [L *rudimentum* first attempt, beginning, fr. *rudis* raw, rough, rude + *-mentum* -ment — more at RUDE] **1 a :** a first principle **:** a basic element ⟨my tactics missed a ~ —Emily Dickinson⟩ ⟨the single leaf is the ~ of beauty in the landscape —Isaac Taylor⟩ — usu. used in pl. ⟨assume that the judges know the ~*s* of law —B.N.Cardozo⟩ **b rudiments** *pl* **:** fundamental skills taught or learned (as in an elementary school) ⟨carefully grounded in the ~*s* —W.B. Parker⟩ ⟨acquired the mere ~*s* of a common-school education —Edna Yost⟩ **2 a :** something that is unformed or undeveloped **:** BEGINNING ⟨must admit he had the ~ of decency —Christopher Morley⟩ — usu used in pl. ⟨experiments . . . which seem to show the ~*s* of a human type of intelligence in the chimpanzee —R.W.Murray⟩ ⟨the ~*s* of a plan⟩ ⟨gave himself the ~*s* of a wash —Maurice Walsh⟩ ⟨~*s* of a headache⟩ **b :** a body part or organ so deficient in size or in both size and structure as to entirely prevent its performing its normal function: (1) **:** an organ or part just beginning to develop **:** ANLAGE (2) **:** one whose development has been arrested at an early stage (3) **:** the remains of a part functional only in an earlier stage of the same individual or in his ancestors **:** VESTIGE

**ru·di·men·tal** \¦rüdə¦mentᵊl\ *adj* **:** RUDIMENTARY

**ru·di·men·tar·i·ly** \¦rüdə(,)men·¦terəlē, -‚mən·-, -li\ *adv* **:** in a rudimentary manner ⟨~ and geometrically Cubist —Janet Flanner⟩

**ru·di·men·ta·ri·ness** \,rüdə'mentərēnəs, -rin-\ *n* -ES **:** the quality or state of being rudimentary

**1ru·di·men·ta·ry** \¦rüdə¦mentərē, -n·trē, -ri *sometimes* -dəmən·,ter-\ *adj* [*rudiment* + *-ary*] **1 :** of or relating to rudiments: as **a :** consisting in first principles **:** BASIC, FUNDAMENTAL ⟨these ~ truths —M.R.Cohen⟩ **b :** of a primitive kind **:** UNDEVELOPED, ELEMENTARY ⟨a ~ sort of building —Henry Wynmalen⟩ ⟨man with a ~ conscience —Greer Williams⟩ ⟨conditions which do not meet ~ standards of decency —F.D. Roosevelt⟩ **c :** of or relating to the basic skills taught esp. in elementary school ⟨received four years of ~ education —*Current Biog.*⟩ **2 :** having the character of a rudiment **:** very imperfectly developed or represented only by a vestige

**2rudimentary** \"\ *n* -ES **:** RUDIMENT 2b

**ru·di·men·ta·tion** \,rüdə(,)men·'tāshən, -‚mən·-\ *n* -s [*rudiment* + *-ation*] **:** the formation of a vestigial organ by continuous lagging in development — compare APHANISIA

**rud·ish** \'rüdish\ *adj* [*rude* + *-ish*] **:** somewhat rude

**ru·dis·ta** \rü'distə\ *n pl, cap* [NL, fr. L *rudis* rude, raw + *-ista* -ist] *in some classifications* **:** a division of Eulamellibranchia comprising extinct chiefly Cretaceous bivalve mollusks with one valve elongate, conical, and thick-shelled and the other small and fitting like a lid on the first — **ru·dis·tan** \(')=-¦=stən\ *adj or n* — **ru·dis·tid** \(')=¦=stəd\ *adj or n*

**ru·dis·tae** \='=(,)stē\ [NL] *syn of* RUDISTA

**rud·mas·day** \'rədməs,dā, 'rüd-\ *n, usu cap* [alter. of earlier *roodmas day*, fr. *roodmas* (fr. *rood* + *mas* — fr. ME *masse* mass —) + *day* — more at MASS] **:** HOLY-ROOD DAY

**ru·dol·phine tables** \(')rü¦dälfən-\ *n, usu cap R* [*rudolphine* fr. *Rudolph* (Rudolf) II †1612 Holy Roman emperor + E *-ine*] **:** a set of astronomical tables computed by Kepler (1571–1630) and founded on observations by Tycho Brahe (1546–1601)

**ruds** *pl of* RUD, *pres 3d sing of* RUD

**1rue** \'rü\ *vb* -ED/-ING/-S [ME *ruen, rewen*, fr. OE *hrēowan;* akin to OHG *hriuwan* to grieve, regret, ON *hryggr* sorrowful and perh. to Gk *krouein* to strike, push & Lith *krušti* to stamp, smash] *vt* **1 a :** to repent of (wrongdoing) **:** feel penitence or remorse for **b :** to feel regret for (as an act or a choice) **:** wish undone or done differently ⟨served us unconsciously and *rued* the results —A.B.Guthrie⟩ ⟨I ~ that day —Emmett Gowen⟩ **2** *obs* **a :** to affect with pity or compassion **b :** to regard with pity or compassion ~ *vi* **1** *archaic* **:** to be repentant **:** feel contrition **2 a :** to regret an act or choice **b** *Scot* **:** to be dissatisfied with a bargain **:** try to go back on an agreement — often used with *of* **3** *obs* **:** to feel sorrow, regret, or reluctance **4** *archaic* **:** to have compassion **:** feel pity **:** show mercy — often used with *on* or *upon* — **rue back** *South & Midland* **:** to repent and try to withdraw from an agreement or bargain

**2rue** \"\ *n* -s [ME *rewe*, fr. OE *hrēow;* akin to MD *rouwe* sorrow, OHG *hriuwa* sorrow, *hriuwan* to grieve] **1 a :** REGRET, SORROW ⟨although she mocked his ~, he knew she shared it —Kathryn Grondahl⟩ **b :** REPENTANCE **2 :** COMPASSION, PITY

**3rue** \"\ *n* -s [ME *rue, ruwe, rewe*, fr. MF *rue*, fr. L *ruta*, fr. Gk *rhytē*] **:** a European strong-scented perennial woody herb (*Ruta graveolens*) having yellow flowers and decompound leaves with a bitter taste — called also *herb of grace*

**rue anemone** *n* [3*rue*] **:** a delicate vernal herb (*Anemonella thalictroides*) of the family Ranunculaceae having decompound leaves and white flowers resembling those of the wood anemone

**rue bargain** *n* **1** *dial Brit* **:** a bargain that one regrets **2** *dial Brit* **:** a forfeit (as of money) given for withdrawing from an agreement

**rue family** *n* [3*rue*] **:** RUTACEAE

**rue·ful** \'rüfəl\ *adj* [ME *rewful*, fr. *rewe* rue + *-ful*] **1 :** exciting pity or sympathy **:** PITIABLE, WOEFUL ⟨~ squalid poverty that crawled by every wayside —John Morley⟩ **2 :** feeling or expressing sorrow or pity **:** MOURNFUL, REGRETFUL, SAD ⟨troubled her with a ~ disquiet —W.M.Thackeray⟩; *often* **:** quizzically mournful ⟨looked up . . . with a ~ grin —Elmer Davis⟩

**rue·ful·ly** \-f(ə)lē, -li\ *adv* [ME *rewfully*, fr. *rewful* rueful + *-ly*] **:** in a rueful manner

**rue·ful·ness** \-fəlnəs\ *n* -ES [ME *rewfulnes*, fr. *rewful* rueful + *-nes* -ness] **:** the quality or state of being rueful

**ru·elle** \(')rü¦el\ *n* -s [ME *ruel*, fr. MF *ruele*, lit., alley, dim. of *rue* street, fr. L *ruga* wrinkle, fold — more at ROUGH] **1** *archaic* **:** the space between a bed and the wall **2 :** a morning reception held in their bedrooms by fashionable French ladies of the 17th and 18th centuries **3 :** a narrow street or alley ⟨the smaller ~*s* were in pitch-darkness —Donald Stokes⟩

**ru·el·lia** \rü'elēə\ *n* [NL, fr. Jean *Ruel* (latinized *Ruellius*) †1539 Fr. physician and botanist + NL *-ia*] **1** *cap* **:** a very large genus of chiefly tropical American herbs and shrubs (family Acanthaceae) that have showy solitary or paniculate flowers with the simple or 2-lobed style recurved at the apex and the ovary 2-celled **2** -s **:** any plant or flower of the genus *Ruellia*

**rue oil** *n* [3*rue*] **:** a colorless to yellow usu. fluorescent essential oil with an intense odor obtained from rue and other plants of the genus *Ruta* and used chiefly in perfumery and in medicine as a local irritant

**rue·ping process** \'rü|piŋ-, 'rē|\ *n, usu cap R* [after Max *Rüping* 20th cent. Ger. timber engineer, its originator] **:** a treatment for preserving wood with the use of a minimum amount of coal-tar creosote by alternating pressure and vacuum so that only the walls of the wood cells are coated and the cells themselves are not filled

**ru·fes·cence** \rü'fesᵊn(t)s\ *n* -s **:** the quality or state of being rufescent **:** a reddish or bronze color

**ru·fes·cent** \(')rü¦fesᵊnt\ *adj* [L *rufescent-, rufescens*, pres. part. of *rufescere* to become reddish, fr. *rufus* red — more at RED] **:** REDDISH

**1ruff** \'rəf\ *n* -s [ME *ruf, roffe*, prob. fr. *ruffe, rowe* sea bream, perh. fr. *row, ruh, rough*, adj., rough — more at ROUGH] **1** *also* **ruffe :** a small freshwater European perch (*Acerina cernua*) **2 :** a pumpkinseed (*Lepomis gibbosus*)

**2ruff** \"\ *n* -s [prob. back-formation fr. 1*ruffle*] **1 :** a wheel-shaped collar made of several layers of lace or lace-edged muslin or linen starched and goffered usu. in S-shaped folds and worn tied on at the front by men and women of the late 16th and early 17th centuries **2 :** RUFFLE 4a **3 :** something suggestive of a ruff: as **a :** a fringe or frill of long hairs or a set of lengthened or otherwise modified feathers around or on the neck of a mammal or bird ⟨the ~ of a Persian cat⟩ **b :** a collar to prevent endwise motion (as at either end of a shaft journal) **c :** a loose ornamented boot top common in the 17th century **4 a :** a common sandpiper (*Philomachus pugnax*) of Europe and Asia whose male during the breeding season has a large ruff of erectile feathers on the neck and yellowish naked tubercles on the face, is polygamous, and is noted for pugnacity — compare REEVE **b :** a domestic pigeon having a ruff on its neck **5** [influenced in meaning by 1*ruffle*] *obs* **a :** the highest degree (as of pride or prosperity) **:** the top extreme or limit **:** APEX, CREST, ZENITH **b :** ELATION, PRIDE **c :** fury or violence of passion

ruff 1

**3ruff** \"\ *vt* -ED/-ING/-S **1 a :** to make into a ruff **b :** 1RUFFLE 7a **2** *of a stooping falcon* **:** to strike but fail to secure (a bird) **3 :** to comb (hair) by taking hold of a strand and pushing the short hairs toward the scalp with the comb

**4ruff** \"\ *n* -s [MF *roffle, ronfle*] **1 :** a 16th century game from which whist was developed **2 :** the playing of a trump when another suit is led

**5ruff** \"\ *vb* -ED/-ING/-S **:** TRUMP

**6ruff** \"\ *n* -s [imit.] *archaic* **:** a low drumbeat **:** RUFFLE

**7ruff** \"\ *vb* -ED/-ING/-S **1** *Scot* **:** to beat a ruffle on a drum **2** *Scot* **:** to stamp with the feet in applause

**ruff and honours** *n* **:** 4RUFF 1

**ruffed** *adj* [fr. past part. of 3*ruff*] **:** having, wearing, or furnished with a ruff

**ruffed bustard** *n* **:** HOUBARA

**ruffed grouse** *n* **:** a No. American grouse (*Bonasa umbellus*) valued as a game bird in wooded parts of the U.S. and Canada whose male is about 17 inches long, is varied with rufous, black, and gray and has a dark band on the tail and tufts of large glossy black feathers on the sides of the neck, and is noted for drumming with its wings in the breeding season — compare PARTRIDGE, PHEASANT

**ruffed lemur** *n* **:** a large black-and-white lemur (*Lemur varius*) having the face framed by thick fringes of long hair on the sides of the head

**1ruf·fi·an** \'rəfēən\ *n* -s [MF *rufian*] **1 :** a coarse, brutal, or cruel fellow **:** a man of crime or violence **:** BULLY, ROWDY, TOUGH **2** *obs* **:** a keeper and companion of whores **:** PANDER, PIMP

**2ruffian** \"\ *adj* **:** of, relating to, or behaving like a ruffian **:** BRUTAL, COARSE, ROWDY

**3ruffian** \"\ *vi* -ED/-ING/-S *archaic* **:** to play the ruffian **:** act rough

**ruf·fi·an·ish** \-ēənish\ *adj* **:** RUFFIANLY

**ruf·fi·an·ism** \-ēə,nizəm\ *n* -s **:** the action, conduct, or qualities of a ruffian

**ruf·fi·an·ize** \-,nīz\ *vb* -ED/-ING/-S *vi* **:** to act in a ruffianly manner ~ *vt* **:** to make ruffianly

**ruffianlike** \'===,=\ *adj* **:** appropriate to or resembling a ruffian

**ruf·fi·an·ly** \'rəfēənlē, -li\ *adj* **:** of or relating to a ruffian **:** behaving as a ruffian **:** COARSE, ROUGH, ROWDY ⟨always appeals to the more ~ elements —A.M.Young⟩

**ruf·fi·a·no** \,rüfē'ä(,)nō\ *n, pl* **ruffia·ni** \-nē\ [It] *archaic* **:** RUFFIAN

**1ruf·fle** \'rəfəl\ *vb* **ruffled; ruffled; ruffling** \-f(ə)liŋ\ **ruffles** [ME *ruffelen;* akin to LG *ruffelen* to crumple] *vt* **1 a :** to roughen or disturb the smoothness of **:** agitate the surface of **b :** to rub (a surface) rough **:** ABRADE, GRAZE **c :** to disturb the composure of **:** DISTRACT, TROUBLE, VEX ⟨said this to try to ~ her husband —Rex Ingamells⟩ **2** *obs* **:** to throw into confusion or perplexity **3** *chiefly dial* **:** to annoy with insults **:** ATTACK, BULLY **4 :** to erect (as feathers) in or like a ruff **:** cause to rise or bristle **:** STIFFEN **5 :** to act the braggart **:** roister about **:** SWAGGER — used with *it* ⟨*ruffled* it with the other gunmen who infested the town —W.M.Raine⟩ **6 a :** to flip through (as the pages of a book) ⟨ran with it to the piano, *ruffling* the pages to find the place —Marcia Davenport⟩ **:** shuffle (playing cards) rapidly **b** *obs* **:** to rumple or tousle (a woman) familiarly or rudely **c** *obs* **:** to seize rudely **7 a :** to make into a ruffle **:** GATHER, PLEAT **b :** to finish or trim with ruffles ~ *vi* **1 a** *archaic* **:** to strive or contest against another or on behalf of another **:** engage in combat — used with *with* or *for* **b** *archaic* **:** to grow rough, boisterous, or turbulent (as the wind) **2 :** to become discomposed, irritated, or angered ⟨their dispositions ~ perceptibly —*Life*⟩ **3 :** to flutter or stir into an uneven surface **:** rise or form into folds or irregularities ⟨a flag on a tall pole *ruffled* in the breeze⟩ **4 :** to swagger arrogantly **:** act the bully or braggart **:** show bravado **:** BLUSTER ⟨gets drunk, ~*s*, and roisters —Charles Kingsley⟩ ⟨one that *ruffled* in a manly pose —W.B.Yeats⟩

**2ruffle** \"\ *n* -s **1 a :** a disturbance of calm or equanimity **:** a state of irritation, vexation, or discomposure ⟨recuperate after the ~ of breakfast —Elizabeth Taylor⟩ **b :** something that causes annoyance or vexation **2 a :** a rough brawl, fight, or dispute **:** COMMOTION, SKIRMISH ⟨all the ~ and rowdydow —M.G.Bishop⟩ **b** *obs* **:** busy ostentation **:** vainglorious pomp or display **3 :** a roughness, unevenness, or disturbance of surface **:** RIPPLE ⟨give the water a glistening ~ —Vincent McHugh⟩ **4 a :** a strip of fabric that is gathered or pleated on one edge and attached along that edge as a trimming or finish ⟨curtains with a ~ at the bottom⟩ ⟨a blouse trimmed with lace ~*s*⟩ — compare 4FLOUNCE **b :** 2RUFF 3a **c :** 2RUFF 3c **5 :** the mesentery of a slaughtered meat animal **6 :** the group of wings on a metal gudgeon for a wooden shaft

**3ruffle** \"\ *vi* -ED/-ING/-S [6*ruff* + *-le*] **1** *of a drum* **:** to beat with a ruffle **2 :** to beat a ruffle on a drum

**4ruffle** \"\ *n* -s **:** a low vibrating drumbeat less loud than a roll — compare RUFFLE AND FLOURISH

**ruffle and flourish** *n* **:** a ruffling drumbeat and fanfare played in honor of a high official at a ceremonial reception
**ruf·fled** \-fəld\ *adj* [fr. past part. of ¹*ruffle*] **1 :** having ruffles **:** trimmed with ruffles **2** *hort* **:** having a distinctly waved margin
**ruffle fat** *n* **:** the fat of the mesentery attached to the intestines of slaughtered animals
**ruf·fler** \-f(ə)lə(r)\ *n* -s [¹*ruffle* + -*er*] **1** *archaic* **:** a vagabond rogue or beggar of the 16th century often professing to be an injured soldier **2 :** a swaggering roistering fellow ⟨strut like the bold ~s they fancied themselves to be —T.B.Costain⟩ **3 :** DISTURBER ⟨a great ~ of pat orthodoxies⟩ **4 :** a sewing-machine attachment for making ruffles
**ruffling** *n* -s [fr. gerund of ¹*ruffle*] **:** fabric gathered or pleated into ruffles; *also* **:** RUFFLE
**ruf·fly** \-f(ə)lē, -li\ *adj* [²*ruff* + -*ly*] **:** having plaits, folds, or puckers **:** RUFFLED
**ruff out** *vt* **:** to establish (a bridge suit) by trumping leads on which the opponents' high cards must fall
**ruffs** *pl of* RUFF, *pres 3d sing of* RUFF
**ru·fin·ic** \(ˈ)rüˈfinik\ *adj* [L *rufus* red + -*inic* (as in *albinic*)] *biol* **:** REDDISH — **ru·fi·nism** \ˈrüfə,nizəm\ *n* -s
**ru·fos·i·ty** \rüˈfäsəd·ē\ *n* -ES [*rufous* + -*ity*] **:** the quality or state of being rufous
**ru·fous** \ˈrüfəs\ *adj* [L *rufus* red — more at RED] **1 :** of any of several colors averaging a strong yellowish pink to moderate orange **2 :** REDDISH; *esp* **:** having reddish hair and a freckling skin ⟨the ~, foxy little dentist —Nancy Hale⟩
**rufous hornbill** *n* **:** CALAO
**rufous hummingbird** *n* **:** a hummingbird (*Selasphorus rufus*) of the western U.S. with a chiefly reddish brown male
**ruf·ter hood** \ˈrəftə(r)-\ *also* **rufter** *n* -s [*rufter* prob. fr. ³*ruff*] *falconry* **:** a hood for a newly taken hawk
**ru·fus** \ˈrüfəs\ *adj* [L] **:** RUFOUS
¹**rug** \ˈrəg, ˈrüg\ *vb* **rugged; rugged; rugging; rugs** [ME *rugen, ruggen*, of Scand origin; akin to ON *rugga* to rock; akin to ON *rykkja* to jerk — more at ROCK] *dial Brit* **:** PULL, TEAR, WRENCH
²**rug** \ˈ"\ *n* -s [ME, fr. *rugen* to rug] **1** *dial Brit* **:** PULL, TUG, HAUL **2** *dial Brit* **:** a good bargain **:** FIND
³**rug** \ˈrəg\ *n* -s [of Scand origin; akin to Norw dial. *rugga* coarse rug, Sw *rugg* entangled hair, ON *rǫgg* tuft, shagginess; akin to Goth *riurs* fleeting, perishable, MIr *rūam* spade, shovel, L *ruere* to rush, fall, dig up, Gk *erysichthōn* tearing up earth, OSlav *ryti* to dig, Skt *ravate* he breaks up, smashes, *ruta* shattered, divided; basic meaning: breaking up, tearing] **1 a :** a coarse rough woolen clothing fabric of the 16th and 17th centuries **b :** a garment of this fabric **2 a :** a piece of thick heavy fabric usu. with a nap or pile and commonly of wool that is used as a floor covering, is usu. woven either in one piece of a definite shape and design or in widths so made as to form a definite design when they are united, and is not intended to cover an entire floor — compare CARPET, ORIENTAL RUG **b :** a floor mat made of an animal pelt ⟨bearskin ~⟩ **c :** a warm covering for the lap and feet (as of one riding in a sleigh or sitting on a ship's deck) **:** LAP ROBE — compare BEARSKIN, BUFFALO ROBE **3 :** a covering or blanket for an animal (as a horse or cow) **4** *slang* **:** TOUPEE 2
⁴**rug** \ˈ"\ *vt* **rugged; rugged; rugging; rugs :** to cover with a rug or blanket — often used with *up* ⟨~ up a sick goat⟩
⁵**rug** \ˈ"\ *adj* [origin unknown] *archaic* **:** COMFORTABLE, COZY, SNUG
**ru·ga** \ˈrügə\ *n, pl* **ru·gae** \-ü,gī, -ü(,)jē\ [NL, fr. L, wrinkle, fold] **:** a visceral fold or wrinkle — used chiefly in pl. — **ru·gal** \-ügəl\ *adj*
**ru·gate** \ˈrü,gāt, -gət\ *adj* [L *rugatus*, past part. of *rugare* to crease, wrinkle, fr. *ruga* wrinkle, fold — more at ROUGH] **:** WRINKLED, RUGOSE
**ru·gat·ed** \ˈrü,gād·əd\ *adj* [L *rugatus* (past part. of *rugare* to wrinkle) + E -*ed*] **:** RUGOSE
**rug·be·ian** \,rəgˈbēən, ,=ˈ==\ *n* -s *usu cap* [irreg. fr. *Rugby* School + E -*an*] **:** a pupil or alumnus of Rugby School
**rug brick** *n* [³*rug*] **:** a face brick with a surface rough like the pile of a rug
**rug·by** \ˈrəgbē, -bi\ *or* **rugby football** *n* -ES *often cap R* [fr.

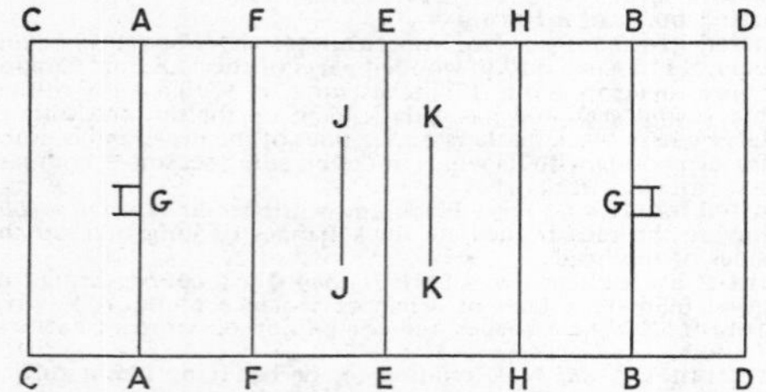


diagram of rugby field: field of play, ABBA; goal lines, AA and BB; touchlines, AB and AB; touch-in-goal lines, AC, AC, BD, and BD; in-goals, ACCA and BDDB; dead-ball lines, CC and DD; halfway line, EE; 10 yard lines, JJ and KK; 25 yard lines, FF and HH; goals, G and G

*Rugby* School, Rugby, Warwickshire, England, where it was first played] **:** an amateur football game which is played with an oval ball by teams of 15 players each and in which play is continuous, kicking, dribbling, lateral passing, tackling, and the scrum are featured, and interference and substitution are not permitted — compare RUGBY LEAGUE FOOTBALL
**rugby game** *or* **rugby fives** *n, usu cap R* **:** the game of fives played on a court having rear as well as front and side walls — compare ETON GAME
**rugby league football** *n, usu cap R&L* [*Rugby League*, unofficial name of *The Rugby Football League*, football league formed in England in 1895] **:** a modified form of rugby which is played under professional rules with 13 players to a team and in which a try counts 3 points and any goal 2 points — called also *Northern Union football*
**rugby tan** *n* **:** ARAB 4
**rugby union football** *n, usu cap R&U* [*Rugby Union*, unofficial name of *The Rugby Football League* (originally called *The Northern Rugby Football Union*), football league formed in England in 1895] **:** RUGBY
**rug-cutter** \ˈ=,==\ *n* **:** a jitterbug dancer ⟨an editorial page which will appeal primarily to *rug-cutters* and jive hounds —*Saturday Rev.*⟩
**rug-cutting** \ˈ=,==\ *n* **:** JITTERBUG
**ru·gel's plantain** \ˈrügəlz-\ *n* [after Ferdinand *Rugel* †1879 Ger. botanist, its discoverer] **:** a broad-leaved No. American plantain (*Plantago rugelii*) having reddish petioles and slender spikes of flowers — called also *broad-leaved plantain*
**rugg** *var of* RUG
**rug·ged** \ˈrəgəd\ *adj, often* -ER/-EST [ME, fr. (assumed) *rug* rag, tuft (of Scand origin) + -*ed*; akin to ON *rǫgg* tuft, shagginess — more at RUG] **1** *obs* **a :** rough with bristles or hair **:** SHAGGY **b :** having a coarse or hairy texture — used of clothing and textiles **2 :** having a rough, uneven, or irregular surface or broken jagged outline or contour ⟨a ~ mountain range⟩ ⟨a steep and ~ ascent —John Burroughs⟩ ⟨cascades, canyons, deep gorges, and ~ profiles —*Amer. Guide Series: Maine*⟩ **3 :** marked by storm or tempest **:** WILD ⟨the ~*est* weather in all No. America — dull, damp, chilly, and beset unendingly by storms —A.H.Farnsworth⟩ **4 :** rough to the ear **:** harsh-sounding ⟨a book so ~ in its style, that an attempt to polish it seemed an Herculean labor —William Cowper⟩ **5 a :** seamed with wrinkles and furrows **:** VIGOROUS, WEATHERED — used of a human face **b :** showing facial signs of physical or moral strength **:** STURDY ⟨a certain determination that was inseparable from the ~ countenance —Louis Bromfield⟩ **6 a :** austere or stern in aspect, conduct, or character **:** HARSH, UNGENTLE **b :** wanting in civility or cultivation **:** COARSE, RUDE **c :** unpolished but sturdy **7 a :** strongly built or constituted **:** HARDY, ROBUST, VIGOROUS ⟨those that survive are stalwart, ~ men —L.D.Stamp⟩ ⟨the ~ steel sections are given a heavy coating of pure zinc —*advt*⟩ **b :** presenting a severe test of ability, stamina, or resolution ⟨a ~ competitive exam⟩ ⟨the ~ conditions of frontier life⟩ **syn** see ROUGH
**rugged individualism** *n* **:** the practice or advocacy of individualism in social and economic relations emphasizing personal liberty and independence, self-reliance, resourcefulness, self-direction of the individual, and free competition in enterprise
**rug·ged·iza·tion** \,rəgədəˈzāshən, -,dīˈz-\ *n* -s **:** the act of ruggedizing or the state of being ruggedized
**rug·ged·ize** \ˈrəgə,dīz\ *vt* -ED/-ING/-S [*rugged* + -*ize*] **:** to strengthen and reinforce (as a machine, structure, instrument) for better resistance to wear, stress, and abuse ⟨the new *ruggedized* camera solves the particular problems presented by airborne applications —*Industrial Equipment News*⟩
**rug·ged·ly** *adv* **:** in a rugged manner
**rug·ged·ness** *n* -ES **:** the quality or state of being rugged
**rug·ger** \ˈrəgə(r)\ *n* -s [by alter.] *Brit* **:** RUGBY
**rug·ging** \ˈrəgiŋ\ *n* -s [³*rug* + -*ing*] **:** a coarse plainwoven woolen cloth with a thick nap used as floor covering
**rug gown** *n* **1** *obs* **:** a gown made of rug **2** *obs* **:** someone (as a watchman) wearing a rug gown
**rug·gy** \ˈrəgē\ *adj* [ME, prob. alter. (influenced by -*y*) of *rugged*] *dial* **:** RUGGED, ROUGH
**rugheaded** *adj* [³*rug* + *headed*] *obs* **:** having shaggy hair
**ru·go·sa** \rüˈgōsə\ [NL, fr. L, neut. pl. of *rugosus* wrinkled, rugose] *syn of* TETRACORALLA
**rugosa rose** *n* **:** any of various garden roses descended from a Japanese rose (*Rosa rugosa*)
**ru·gose** \ˈrü,gōs, -ōz\ *adj* [L *rugosus* wrinkled, fr. *ruga* wrinkle + -*osus* -ose — more at ROUGH] **1 :** full of wrinkles ⟨~ cheeks⟩ **2** *bot* **:** having the veinlets sunken and the spaces between elevated ⟨the ~ leaves of the sage and the horehound⟩ — compare BULLATE — **ru·gose·ly** *adv*
**rugose mosaic** *n* **:** a highly destructive virus disease of potatoes due to the combined action of the viruses responsible for veinbanding and latent virus disease and causing dwarfed, wrinkled, and mottled leaves, stunting, and premature death — compare POTATO MOSAIC
**ru·gos·i·ty** \rüˈgäsəd·ē, rəˈg-\ *n* -ES [LL *rugositat-, rugositas*, fr. L *rugosus* wrinkled + -*itat-, -itas* -ity] **:** the quality or state of being rugose **:** a wrinkled place **:** WRINKLE
**ru·gous** \ˈrügəs\ *adj* [L *rugosus*] **:** WRINKLED, RUGOSE
**rugs** *pres 3d sing of* RUG, *pl of* RUG
**ru·gu·la** \ˈrügyələ\ *n, pl* **ru·gu·lae** \-,lē\ [NL, fr. L *ruga* wrinkle, fold + -*ula* -ule] **:** a small fold
**ru·gu·lose** \-,lōs\ *adj* [prob. fr. (assumed) NL *rugulosus*, fr. NL *rugula* + L -*osus* -ose] **:** having small rugae **:** finely wrinkled **:** having rugulae
**ruhm·korff coil** \ˈrüm,kȯrf-\ *n, usu cap R* [after Heinrich *Ruhmkorff* †1877 Ger. physicist, its inventor] **:** INDUCTION COIL
¹**ru·in** \ˈrüən, ˈrü|, *also* |,in, *dial* ˈrərn\ *n* -s [ME *ruine*, fr. MF, fr. L *ruina*; akin to L *ruere* to rush, fall — more at RUG] **1 a** *archaic* **:** a falling down esp. of a building **:** COLLAPSE **b :** the decay or fall of an individual or a group **:** physical, moral, economic, or social collapse ⟨bankruptcy, dishonor, and ~ were now his lot⟩ **2 a** *archaic* **:** the condition of something that has collapsed **:** a state of destruction or abjectness **b :** the remains of something that has been destroyed **:** decayed or broken fragments — usu. used in pl. ⟨went back to the ~s of their city —Weston La Barre⟩ **3 :** a cause or agent of destruction **:** DESTROYER, WRECKER ⟨this carelessness . . . was to be his ~ —Mary A. Hamilton⟩ ⟨drink was his ~⟩ **4 a :** the destruction, laying waste, or wrecking of something **:** DEVASTATION, OVERTHROW ⟨~ can make a hideous modern building seem beautiful —Stephen Spender⟩ ⟨the ~ of modern drama —T.S.Eliot⟩ ⟨risked . . . his own political ~ —C.H.Sykes⟩ **b :** DAMAGE, INJURY, IMPAIRMENT ⟨the ~ of misspent years cannot be quickly undone⟩ **5 :** the moral or social downfall of a woman (as by vice or seduction) ⟨a daughter's ~ unhinged the old man's mind⟩ **6 :** a building, person, or other object that has tumbled down or fallen into decay ⟨a ~ that was now a home of bats and lizards⟩ ⟨should write the biography of this shambling ~ —Lee Rogow⟩
²**ruin** \ˈ"\ *vb* **ruined** \-nd, *dial* -nt\ **ruined; ruining; ruins** [MF or ML; MF *ruiner* to ruin, fr. ML *ruinare*, fr. L *ruina* ruin] *vt* **1 a :** to lay waste **:** reduce to wreckage **:** DEVASTATE, OVERTHROW ⟨~*ed* temple⟩ ⟨~*ed* city⟩ ⟨the ~*ed* land⟩ **b** *obs* **:** to root out or lay low **2 a :** to damage or destroy irredeemably **:** inflict irreparable injury on ⟨rain had ~*ed* her hat⟩ ⟨crops ~*ed* by hail⟩ ⟨a car ~*ed* in a smashup⟩ ⟨in danger of being ~*ed* by prosperity⟩ **b :** to overthrow the fortunes of **:** bring to financial ruin **:** BANKRUPT, IMPOVERISH ⟨was ~*ed* during the great crash⟩ ⟨had been ~*ed* by speculation⟩ **c :** to bring (a woman) to degradation or dishonor **3 :** to subject to entire frustration, failure, or disaster ⟨~*ed* hopes⟩ ⟨an illness that ~*ed* his chances of promotion⟩ ~ *vi* **1 a :** to crash down **:** fall headlong to destruction **b :** to become decayed or dilapidated **2 :** to come to moral, financial, or social ruin **:** be impoverished, degraded, or dishonored **syn** see DESTROY
**ruin agate** *n* **:** a usu. brown agate showing on a polished surface markings suggestive of ruined buildings
¹**ru·in·ate** \ˈrüə,nāt, ˈrüə-, *usu* -ād·+V\ *adj* [ML *ruinatus*, past part. of *ruinare* to ruin] **:** RUINED
²**ruinate** \ˈ"\ *vb* -ED/-ING/-S [ML *ruinatus*, past part. of *ruinare* to ruin] *vt* **1** *chiefly dial* **a :** to bring down **:** DEMOLISH, DESTROY, OVERTHROW **b :** to reduce to poverty or wretchedness **:** DEGRADE, DISHONOR **2** *obs* **:** to bring to nothing **:** SUBVERT ~ *vi* **1** *chiefly dial* **:** to fall into ruin **2** *obs* **:** CRASH
**ru·in·a·tion** \,==ˈnāshən\ *n* -s [²*ruinate* + -*ion*] **1 :** the act of ruining or the state of being ruined **:** DESTRUCTION **2 :** a cause of ruin **:** a destructive agent or factor ⟨the olive is the ~ of the martini —*Saturday Rev.*⟩
**ru·in·a·tor** \ˈ==,nād·ə(r), -ātə-\ *n* -s [²*ruinate* + -*or*] **:** DESTROYER, RUINER
**ru·in·er** \-nə(r)\ *n* -s [²*ruin* + -*er*] **:** one that ruins
**ruing** *pres part of* RUE
**ru·in·i·form** \ˈrüənə,fȯrm, ˈrüə-, rüˈin-\ *adj* [¹*ruin* + -*iform*] **:** having the appearance of ruins — used of minerals
**ruin marble** *n* **:** a brecciated limestone giving a mosaic effect when cut and polished that suggests a picture of ruins
**ru·in·ous** \ˈrüənəs, ˈrüə-\ *adj* [ME *ruinose*, fr. LL *ruinosus*, fr. L *ruina* ruin + -*osus* -ose — more at RUIN] **1 :** fallen into decay or dilapidation **:** RUINED ⟨the high paling was broken by the mossy and ~ posts of an old gateway —John Buchan⟩ **2 :** causing or tending to cause ruin **:** DESTRUCTIVE, DISASTROUS, PERNICIOUS ⟨the excessive wages paid for unskilled labor were ~ to the farmer —Ellen Glasgow⟩
**ru·in·ous·ly** *adv* **:** in a ruinous manner
**ru·in·ous·ness** *n* -ES **:** the quality or state of being ruinous
**rul·able** \ˈrüləbəl\ *adj* [ME *reuleable*, fr. *reule* rule + -*able*] **1** *obs* **:** capable of being ruled **2 :** permissible according to the rules
¹**rule** \ˈrül\ *n* -s [ME *riwle, reule, riule*, fr. OF *reule, riule*, fr. L *regula* straightedge, rule, fr. *regere* to lead straight, guide — more at RIGHT] **1 a :** a prescribed, suggested, or self-imposed guide for conduct or action **:** a regulation or principle ⟨his parents laid down the ~ that he must do his homework before going out to play⟩ ⟨a very sound ~ for any hiker is to mind his own business —F.D.Smith & Barbara Wilcox⟩ ⟨made it a ~ never to lose his temper⟩ **b :** the laws or regulations prescribed by the founder of a religious order for observance by its members ⟨the ~ of St. Dominic⟩ **c :** an accepted procedure, custom, or habit having the force of a regulation ⟨we are bound by the ~s of our culture to conceal such matters —Marjorie Fischer⟩ ⟨the ~ of the house was an early bedtime⟩ **d** (1) **:** a usu. written order or direction made by a court regulating court practice or the action of parties but not making a final judgment on the merits of a controversy (2) **:** a legal precept applied to a given set of facts as stating the law applicable to a case (3) **:** a statement or doctrine accepted as part of the common law — see RULE AGAINST PERPETUITIES **e :** a regulation or bylaw governing procedure in a public or private body (as a legislature or club) or controlling the conduct of its members ⟨a ~ for limiting debate⟩ ⟨a ~ against insulting language⟩ ⟨a ~ for the admission of new members⟩ **f :** one of a set of usu. official regulations by which an activity (as a sport) is governed ⟨the infield fly ~⟩ ⟨the ~s of professional basketball⟩ **2 a** (1) **:** a statement of a fact or relationship generally found to hold good **:** a usu. valid generalization ⟨the exception proves the ~⟩ (2) **:** a generally prevailing condition, quality, state, or mode of activity or behavior ⟨fair weather was the ~ yesterday afternoon over most of the nation —*N.Y. Times*⟩ ⟨persons in whose families high blood pressure was the ~ rather than the exception —Morris Fishbein⟩ **b :** a standard by which something is judged or valued **:** CRITERION ⟨"good enough" becomes the ~ and enters into the character of our theater life —Leslie Rees⟩ **c** (1) **:** a principle regulating or held to regulate the practice of an art or science ⟨the ~s of perspective⟩ ⟨the ~s of harmony⟩ ⟨the ~s of versification⟩ (2) **:** a principle regulating or held to regulate the form and use of words ⟨a knowledge of the irrefragable ~s of the comma was mistaken for a knowledge of language —Charlton Laird⟩ **d** (1) **:** a determinate method prescribed for performing a mathematical operation and attaining a certain result (2) *dial* **:** RECIPE **3 a** (1) **:** the exercise of authority or control **:** DOMINION, GOVERNMENT, SWAY ⟨under his firm ~, however, conditions quickly improved —C.M.Fuess⟩ ⟨establishing a single ~ throughout the kingdom far and wide —B.N.Cardozo⟩ (2) **:** a period during which a specified ruler or government exercises control ⟨during the ~ of the Caesars⟩ ⟨in the first year of the ~ of the republic⟩ **b :** the state of being governed **:** CONTROL ⟨to a child, winter . . . was confinement, school, ~, discipline —Henry Adams⟩ **4 a** (1) **:** an instrument for measuring or ruling off lengths that consists of a strip or strips of material (as wood, metal, or tape) marked off in units of length (as inches or centimeters) (2) **:** RULER 2a **b** (1) **:** a metal strip with a type-high face that prints a linear design (2) *Brit* **:** DASH 3e (3) **:** LINE GAUGE (4) **:** COMPOSING RULE (5) **:** MAKEUP RULE **5** *obs* **:** BEHAVIOR, CONDUCT ⟨this uncivil ~ —Shak.⟩ **6 a rules** *pl* **:** a limited area formerly established near a prison for the residence of prisoners of certain categories (as debtors) **b :** the freedom to live in such an area ⟨was a prisoner on ~⟩ **syn** see LAW — **as a rule** *adv* **:** as a general thing **:** ORDINARILY, USUALLY ⟨*as a rule* sick people recover without treatment —L.J.Henderson⟩ — **under the rule** *adv* **:** in accordance with a stock-exchange rule providing for sales or purchases to be made by an officer of the exchange for the account of members not fulfilling their contracts made on the floor
²**rule** \ˈ"\ *vb* -ED/-ING/-S [ME *riwlen, reulen, rulen*, fr. OF *reuler, riuler*, fr. L *regulare*, fr. *regula* rule] *vt* **1 a :** to control, direct, or influence the mind, character, or actions of ⟨so long as she could ~ her own mind she was not afraid of the forces without —Ellen Glasgow⟩ ⟨what ~s an Admission Dean's judgment in the midwinter heat of competition —V.S. Carruthers⟩ ⟨be *ruled* by me and have a care o' the crowd —Robert Browning⟩ **b :** to curb or moderate by the use of self-control ⟨went on a diet but found it difficult to ~ her appetite⟩ **c :** to exercise control over **:** GUIDE, MANAGE ⟨~ a horse⟩ **2 a :** to exercise authority or power over **:** GOVERN ⟨became Speaker and for nearly two years *ruled* the Assembly with a rod of iron —E.H.Collis⟩ ⟨the territory is *ruled* by a high commissioner —*Americana Annual*⟩ **b :** to hold preeminence in (as by ability, strength, or position) **:** DOMINATE ⟨an actor who ~s the Shakespearean stage⟩ ⟨*ruled* the featherweight division —*Providence (R.I.) Evening Bull.*⟩ **c :** to play a dominant role in or exert a controlling influence over ⟨profit taking *ruled* the stock market yesterday —*Wall Street Jour.*⟩ ⟨the monsoon seasons, which ~ the climate in a great part of Asia —Owen & Eleanor Lattimore⟩ **3 a :** to declare authoritatively **:** DECIDE, DECREE, DETERMINE; *specif* **:** to require or command by judicial rule **:** give as a direction, order, or determination of a court **b :** to consider as **:** JUDGE ⟨at the risk of really being *ruled* a maverick —Irving Kolodin⟩ **4 a** (1) **:** to mark with lines drawn along the straight edge of a ruler ⟨~ a sheet of paper⟩ **:** print or mark with lines by means of a rule ⟨a pad of *ruled* yellow paper⟩ (2) **:** to mark (a line) on a paper with a ruler ⟨*ruled* vertical lines on the sheet⟩ **b :** to arrange in a straight line or mark off in lines as if with a ruler ⟨nor were the eyebrows bushy like most old men's, but smoothly *ruled* —Clemence Dane⟩ ⟨flowering shrubs which *ruled* the mountain walls like a sheet of paper —John Muir †1914⟩ ~ *vi* **1 a :** to have power or command **:** exercise supreme authority ⟨*ruled* wisely over his subjects —*Time*⟩ ⟨a king who reigns but does not ~⟩ **b :** to exercise control **:** PREDOMINATE ⟨the physical did not ~ in her nature —Sherwood Anderson⟩ **2 a :** to prevail at a specified rate or level ⟨prices had *ruled* high —Robert Hunter⟩ ⟨in the offshore islands . . . temperature and humidity ~ higher than on the mainland —*Internat'l Reference Service*⟩ **b :** to exist in a specified state or condition **3 a :** to lay down a legal rule or order of court **b :** to decide an incidental legal point **c :** to enter a rule — **rule the roast** *or* **rule the roost :** to be at the head of things **:** have full authority or control ⟨wouldn't you like to *rule the roast*, and guide this university —W.S.Gilbert⟩ ⟨a little-boy school in which I and my gang had *ruled the roost* —Donald Moffat⟩ **syn** see DECIDE
**rule against perpetuities :** a rule at common law that makes void any estate so limited that it will not necessarily take effect or vest within a life or lives in being at the time of the creation of the estate and 21 years thereafter with the addition of the period of gestation in the case of a person entitled to the estate being conceived but unborn
**ruled surface** *n, math* **:** a surface generated by a moving straight line
**rule joint** *n* **:** a knuckle joint having shoulders that abut when the connected pieces are opened out fully and thus permit folding in one direction only
**rule·less** \ˈrülləs\ *adj* [ME *reweless*, fr. *rewle, riwle* rule + -*less* — more at RULE] **:** not curbed or ruled by law **:** LAWLESS
**rule nisi** *n* **:** a rule or order upon condition that is to become absolute unless cause is shown to the contrary
**rule of adjunction :** a rule in logic: if each of two statements (as *p* and *q*) has been asserted then their conjunct (as *p·q*) may be asserted
**rule of deduction :** TRANSFORMATION RULE
**rule of eleven :** a rule in bridge and whist: when a player leads his fourth-best card of a suit the number of its spots subtracted from eleven gives the number of higher cards of the same suit not in the leader's hand — called also *eleven rule*
**rule off** *vt* **:** to debar (as a horse, jockey, player) from a race or contest **:** DISQUALIFY ⟨*ruled* him *off* for rough riding⟩
**rule of faith 1 :** a standard for testing truth in religion; *esp* **:** an ultimate theological criterion **2 :** an authoritative statement of religious belief **:** a creedal formulation designed to sum up major orthodox beliefs and to exclude heresy
**rule of law 1 :** a legal rule **:** a determination of the applicable rule as distinguished from a finding of fact **2 :** adherence to due process of law **:** government by law
**rule of the air :** a provision of the code of regulations governing matters of air traffic (as the meeting and overtaking of other aircraft, the use of defined air lanes of travel, or the height of flying over cities)
**rule of the road 1 :** any of the various regulations imposed upon travelers by land or water for their mutual convenience or safety **2 :** any of the rules making up a code governing ships as to the lights to be carried, the signals to be made, and the action of one ship with respect to another when risk of collision exists
**rule of three :** a rule in mathematics: the product of the means in a proportion equals the product of the extremes — used for finding the fourth term of a proportion where three are given
**rule of thumb 1 :** a method of procedure or analysis based upon experience and common sense and intended to give generally or approximately correct or effective results ⟨seems to have run the ship by *rule of thumb* and word of mouth —William McFee⟩ **2 :** a general principle regarded as roughly correct and helpful but not intended to be scientifically accurate ⟨a good *rule of thumb* is that smart youngsters prepared to enter college at the age of 16 have not been accelerated too much —L.M.Spencer⟩
**rule of two and three :** a bidding principle in contract bridge: a player who makes a preemptive bid should not overbid by more than two tricks when vulnerable or three tricks when not vulnerable
**rule out** *vt* **1 a :** to exclude or eliminate ⟨was *ruled out* on a

technicality that required members to be experienced lawyers —*Current Biog.*⟩ ⟨*rule* such subjective and moral judgments *out* of our biology —A.L.Kroeber⟩ **b :** to eliminate as a possibility ⟨a positive diagnosis can be made only after *ruling out* gastric and duodenal ulcer —H.G.Armstrong⟩ **2 :** to make impossible **:** PREVENT ⟨heavy rain *ruled* the picnic *out* for that day⟩ **syn** see EXCLUDE

**rul·er** \ˈrülə(r)\ *n* -s [ME *reuler*, fr. *reulen* to rule + *-er* — more at RULE] **1 a :** one that exercises authority, command, or dominating influence ⟨the old male was even in captivity the undisputed guardian and ~ of all the other members —Weston La Barre⟩ ⟨the ~*s* of modern art⟩ ⟨an ambition that became the ~ of his life⟩; *specif* **:** one who rules over a nation or people ⟨an able and vigorous ~ who reunited his country⟩ ⟨their position in our democratic system as the informants of our ~*s*, the people —F.L.Mott⟩ **b :** one who exercises control in some limited field ⟨was the ~ of Admiralty Room 40 —*Brit. Book News*⟩ **2 :** one that rules lines: as **a :** a straight or curved strip (as of wood or metal) with a smooth edge usu. marked off in units (as inches or centimeters) and used for guiding a pen or pencil in drawing lines or for measuring **b :** an operator of a machine for drawing ink lines on paper

**rul·er·ship** \-ˌship\ *n* **:** the office, function, or status of a ruler **:** RULE, SOVEREIGNTY

**rules committee** *n* **:** a committee of a legislative house that determines the rules and procedure for expediting the business of the house and has the power to control the date and nature of debate of a proposed bill

**rules of court :** the regulations covering practice and procedure before a particular court

**rules of practice :** the published regulations relating to the presentation of evidence and appearance of witnesses before a particular administrative agency or regulatory body

**¹rul·ing** \ˈrüliŋ, -lēŋ\ *n* -s [ME *riwling*, fr. gerund of *riwlen* to rule] **1 :** an official or authoritative decision, decree, or statement ⟨his own experience and judgment carried more weight with him than the ~*s* of any of the surgical authorities —Harvey Graham⟩: as **a :** a decision or rule of a judge or a court **b :** an interpretation by an administrative agency of the law under which it operates applicable to a given statement of facts **2** *math* **:** a generatrix of a ruled surface

**²ruling** \"\ *adj* **1 a :** exerting power or authority ⟨~ family⟩ ⟨~ party⟩ **b :** CHIEF, PREDOMINATING ⟨a ~ passion⟩ ⟨a ~ ambition⟩ ⟨a ~ idea⟩ **2 :** generally prevailing **:** CURRENT ⟨~ prices in the world market —F.D.Smith & Barbara Wilcox⟩

**ruling elder** *n* **:** ³ELDER 4b

**ruling engine** *n* **:** an exceedingly accurate and delicately adjusted machine for ruling lines (as of a diffraction grating)

**ruling grade** *n* **:** the grade on any particular road regarded as limiting the weight of a train that can be drawn by one engine — compare PUSHER GRADE

**ruling pen** *n* **:** a draftsman's pen for ruling lines that has a pair

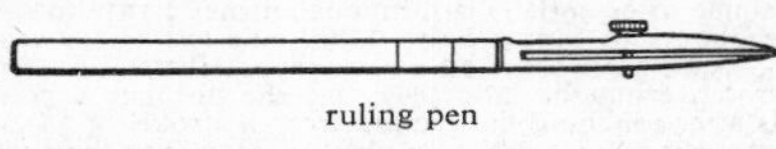

ruling pen

of adjustable metal blades or points between which the ink is contained with the thickness of the line being regulated by a screw that closes the blades or allows them to open

**rul·lion** \ˈrəlyən\ *n* -s [prob. fr. obs. E (Sc) *rullion* shoe made of untanned leather, prob. alter. of ME (Sc) *rewelin*, *rewling* shoe of rawhide, fr. OE *rifeling*; perh. akin to OE *gehriflian* to wrinkle, shrivel — more at RIVEL] *chiefly Scot* **:** a large rough-looking person or creature

**rullock** *var of* ROWLOCK

**ruly** \ˈrülē\ *adj* [back-formation fr. *unruly*] *archaic* **:** OBEDIENT, ORDERLY

**¹rum** \ˈrəm\ *adj* **rummer**; **rummest** [earlier *rome*, perh. fr. Romany *rom* married man, husband, gypsy man — more at ROM] **1** *chiefly Brit* **:** unusually fine **:** EXCELLENT **2** *chiefly Brit* **a :** characterized by queerness, peculiarity, or unusualness ⟨writing is a ~ trade . . . and what is all right one day is all wrong the next —Angela Thirkell⟩ **b :** marked by difficulty, danger, or a threatening appearance — often used as a generalized expression of disapproval ⟨had a ~ time from the weather —*Newsweek*⟩ ⟨she's ~ about the eyes —Arthur Morrison⟩

**²rum** \"\ *n* -s [prob. short for *rumbullion*] **1 :** an alcoholic liquor prepared by fermenting molasses, macerated sugarcane, or other saccharine cane product, distilling, coloring with caramel, and aging — compare RUM ESSENCE **2 :** alcoholic liquor ⟨the crimes due to ~⟩

**³rum** \"\ *var of* RUMMY

**ru·mal** \(ˈ)rüˈmäl\ *or* **ro·mal** \rōˈm-\ *n* -s [Hindi *rūmāl*, fr. Per, fr. *rū* face + *māl* wiper] **1 :** a usu. silk plainwoven Indian fabric used for dresses and handkerchiefs **2 :** an often checked cotton or silk kerchief used as a scarf and in India as a headdress by men

**¹ru·man** \ˈrümən\ *n* -s *cap* [Romanian *Rumân*, *Român*, fr. L *Romanus* Roman — more at ROMAN] **:** ROMANIAN

**²ruman** \"\ *n* -s *cap* [Romanian *rumân*] **:** WALLACHIAN

**rumania** *usu cap, var of* ROMANIA

**rumanian** *usu cap, var of* ROMANIAN

**rumansch** *usu cap, var of* ROMANSH

**rum·ba** *also* **rhum·ba** \ˈrəmbə, ˈrüm-, ˈrum-\ *n* -s [AmerSp *rumba*, fr. *rumbo* carousal, spree, fr. Sp, pomp, ostentation, looseness, perh. fr. *rumbo* bearing, course, direction, rhumb line, fr. OSp — more at RHUMB] **1 a :** a Cuban Negro dance marked by violent movements **b :** an American ballroom dance imitative of the Cuban rumba **2 :** the music for a rumba characterized by strong rhythmic syncopations

**¹rum·ble** \ˈrəmbəl\ *vb* **rumbled**; **rumbled**; **rumbling** \-b(ə)liŋ\ **rumbles** [ME *rumblen*, *romblen*; akin to MHG *rummeln* to rumble, OSw *rumbla* and prob. to ON *rymja* to roar, grumble — more at RUMOR] *vi* **1 a :** to make a low heavy rolling sound ⟨thunder which ~*s* ominously, yet, because of distance, is all but inaudible —Erle Stanley Gardner⟩ ⟨the camels' bellies *rumbling* to the water they held —I.L.Idriess⟩ ⟨the dark spaces between the walls ~ with strange and appalling noises —Sherwood Anderson⟩ **b** (1) **:** to travel as a low reverberating sound ⟨*rumbling* through the racy air — the unmistakable sound of a horn —Blanche E. Baughan⟩ (2) **:** to travel or go with an accompanying low heavy sound ⟨mule-drawn freight wagons *rumbled* through the town —*Amer. Guide Series: Texas*⟩ **c :** to speak in a low rolling tone ⟨heard him *rumbling* to himself as they went out —Grace Campbell⟩ **2 :** to constitute or create a disturbing factor **:** represent a state of unrest ⟨there had been *rumbling* in the Head Camp a controversy of no mean proportions —C.W. Ferguson⟩ **3** *slang* **:** to engage in a rumble ⟨the Cherubs are *rumbling* —Walter Bernstein⟩ ~ *vt* **1 a :** to utter or emit in a low rolling voice ⟨*rumbled* that one of his children liked frogs —*Yankee*⟩ **b** *chiefly Brit* **:** to stir up or knock about with a rumbling sound **2 a** *slang* **:** to detect or see through (as a trick, a trickster) ⟨dice are almost never gaffed so that the same numbers always come up because even the greenest mark would ~ that in short order —John Scarne & Clayton Rawson⟩ **b** *slang* **:** to give oneself away to or become detected by (as the intended victim) while in the act of committing a crime **:** excite the suspicion of ⟨I read the financial pages and the investment journals so I won't slip up and ~ the mark —D.W.Maurer⟩ **3 :** to polish or otherwise treat (metal parts) in a tumbling barrel

**²rumble** \"\ *n* -s [ME *rumbel*, fr. *rumblen*, *romblen* to rumble] **1 a :** a low heavy continuous reverberating often muffled sound (as of heavy vehicles, distant thunder) ⟨as the train lost speed the smooth ~ of wheels over rails broke into a series of rattling thumps —John Dos Passos⟩ ⟨could hear the ~ of a man's voice . . . but I couldn't hear the words —Erle Stanley Gardner⟩ **b :** low-frequency noise in disc recording or reproduction caused by low-frequency vibration mechanically transmitted to the turntable or pickup **2 a** [short for *rumble-tumble*] **:** a seat for servants behind the body of a carriage **b** [by shortening] **:** RUMBLE SEAT **3 :** TUMBLING BARREL **4 :** something that breaks in upon or upsets a peaceful state of affairs: as **a :** a generalized or widespread expression of dissatisfaction or unrest ⟨~*s* of opposition arose in the counties —J.N.Popham⟩ **b :** RUMOR, COMPLAINT ⟨picked up the ~ . . . and thought he'd pass it on just in case —P.A.Brodeur⟩ **c :** QUARREL, DISTURBANCE **d** *slang* (1) **:** detection in a criminal act (2) **:** a search by law enforcement officials of premises or a neighborhood for narcotics or narcotics peddlers **e** *slang* **:** a street fight esp. among teenage gangs ⟨down in the basement of a candy store, getting their switchblade knives, zip guns, and Molotov cocktails ready for a ~ —Marjorie Rittwagen⟩

**rumble-bumble** \ˌrəmbəlˈbəmbəl\ *n* **:** a miscellaneous mass or mixture **:** JUMBLE, HODGEPODGE

**rum·ble·ga·rie** \ˌrəm(b)əlˈgärē\ *adj* [prob. fr. ²*rumble* + connective *-g-* + *-arie* -ary] *Scot* **:** careless and disorderly in action or manner **:** HARUM-SCARUM

**rum·ble·gump·tion** *also* **rum·el·gump·tion** \ˈrəm(b)əl-ˌgəm(p)shən\ *n* [alter. (influenced by ²*rumble*) of obs. E (northern dial.) *rumgumption*, prob. fr. E ¹*rum* + *gumption*] *Scot* **:** good judgment **:** SENSE, INTELLIGENCE

**rum·bler** \ˈrəmb(ə)lə(r)\ *n* -s [¹*rumble* + *-er*] **:** one that rumbles as: **a :** TUMBLING BARREL **b :** an operator of a machine (as a tumbling barrel) that cleans small articles by tumbling them with abrasives or cleaning fluid

**rumble seat** *n* **:** a folding seat in the back of an automobile (as a coupe or roadster) not covered by the top

**rumble-tumble** \ˌrəmbəlˈtəmbəl\ *n* **1 :** RUMBLE 2a **2 :** a heavy coach or cart that moves with a deep rumbling sound

**rum·bling·ly** *adv* **:** in a rumbling manner

**rum·bly** \ˈrəmb(ə)lē, -li\ *adj* [²*rumble* + *-y*] **:** tending or causing to rumble or rattle

**rum·bo** \ˈrəm(ˌ)bō\ *n* -s [*rumb-* (fr. *rumbullion*) + *-o*] *archaic* **:** GROG

**rumbowline** *var of* ROMBOWLINE

**rum·bow·ling** \ˌrəmˈbōlən, -liŋ\ *n* -s [alter. of *rumbullion*] **:** GROG

**rumbullion** *n* -s [origin unknown] *obs* **:** RUM

**rum·bus·ti·cal** \ˌrəmˈbəstəkəl\ *adj* [*rumbustic* (prob. alter. of obs. E *robustic* robust, robustious, fr. E *robust* + *-ic*) + *-al*] **:** RAMBUNCTIOUS

**rum·bus·tious** \-schəs\ *adj* [alter. (prob. influenced by ²*rumble*) of *robustious*] **:** RAMBUNCTIOUS

**rum cherry** *n* **:** BLACK CHERRY 2a

**rum–dum** *also* **rum–dumm** \ˈrəmˌdəm\ *adj* [prob. fr. ²*rum* + G *dumm* dumb (fr. OHG *tumb* mute, stupid) — more at DUMB] **:** reeling from drunkenness **:** INTOXICATED

**rumdum** \"\ *n* -s [*rum-dum*] **:** DRUNKARD

**¹ru·me·lian** *or* **rou·me·lian** \(ˈ)rüˈmēlēən, -lyən\ *adj*, *usu cap* [*Rumelia*, former division of the Turkish empire that included Albania, Macedonia, and Thrace + E *-an*] **1 :** of, relating to, or characteristic of Rumelia, former European division of the Turkish Empire **2 :** of, relating to, or characteristic of the people of Rumelia

**²rumelian** *or* **roumelian** \"\ *n* -s *cap* [*Rumelia* + *-an* (n. suffix)] **:** a native or inhabitant of Rumelia

**ru·men** \ˈrümən\ *n, pl* **rumi·na** \-mənə\ *or* **rumens** [NL, fr. L, gullet — more at RUMINATE] **:** the large first compartment of the stomach of a ruminant from which food is regurgitated for rumination and in which cellulose is broken down by the action of bacterial and protozoan symbionts **:** PAUNCH; *broadly* **:** the first three compartments of the ruminant stomach — distinguished from *abomasum*; compare OMASUM, RETICULUM

**ru·men·itis** \ˌrüməˈnīdəs\ *n*, -ES [NL, fr. *rumen* + *-itis*] **:** inflammation of the rumen

**rumeno-** *comb form* [NL, fr. *rumen*] **:** rumen ⟨*rumeno*tomy⟩

**ru·meno·centesis** \ˈrümənō+\ *n* [NL, fr. *rumeno-* + *centesis*] **:** puncture of the rumen with a trocar and cannula to permit the escape of gas

**ru·men·ot·o·my** \ˌrüməˈnädəmē\ *n* -ES [*rumeno-* + *-tomy*] **:** incision into the rumen

**rum essence** *n* **:** ethyl butyrate or a prepared mixture of esters and oils used in the manufacture of imitation rum

**ru·mex** \ˈrüˌmeks\ *n, cap* [NL, fr. L, sorrel] **:** a genus of herbs and shrubs (family Polygonaceae) that are mainly native to north temperate regions and have small flowers in axillary clusters often aggregated in a large panicle and 3-angled wingless fruit enclosed in a persistent perianth whose inner segments often bear conspicuous tubercles — see CANAIGRE, ¹DOCK 1

**rum·fus·tian** \ˌrəmˈfəschən\ *n* [prob. fr. ²*rum* + *fustian*] **:** a hot drink composed of strong beer, wine, gin, egg yolks, sugar, and spices

**rum–hole** \ˈ=,=\ *n, slang* **:** BAR, SALOON

**ru·mi·nal** *also* **ru·men·al** \ˈrümənᵊl\ *adj* [NL *rumin-*, *rumen* + E *-al*] **:** of or relating to the rumen

**¹ru·mi·nant** \ˈrümənənt\ *n* -s [L *ruminant-*, *ruminans*, pres. part. of *ruminare*, *ruminari* to chew the cud] **:** a ruminant mammal

**²ruminant** \"\ *adj* [L *ruminant-*, *ruminans*, pres. part. of *ruminare*, *ruminari*] **1 a :** chewing the cud **:** characterized by chewing again what has been swallowed **b :** of or relating to the Ruminantia **2 :** given to or engaged in contemplation **:** MEDITATIVE — **ru·mi·nant·ly** *adv*

**ru·mi·nan·tia** \ˌrüməˈnanch(ē)ə\ *n pl, cap* [NL, fr. L *ruminant-*, *ruminans* (pres. part. of *ruminare*, *ruminari*) + NL *-ia*] **:** a suborder of Artiodactyla comprising even-toed hoofed mammals (as sheep, giraffes, deer, and camels) that chew the cud and have a complex 3- or 4-chambered stomach — compare ABOMASUM, OMASUM, RETICULUM, RUMEN; see PECORA, TRAGULINA, TYLOPODA

**¹ru·mi·nate** \ˈrüməˌnāt, *usu* -ād.+V\ *vb* -ED/-ING/-S [L *ruminatus*, past part. of *ruminare*, *ruminari* to chew the cud, think over, ruminate fr. *rumin-*, *rumen* gullet; akin to Skt *romantha* chewing the cud] *vt* **1 :** to muse upon **:** contemplate over and over **:** ponder over ⟨*ruminating* the contents of that last batch of letters she had received —Aldous Huxley⟩ ⟨*ruminating* a judgment in his solemn dull brain —Edmund Taylor⟩ **2 :** to chew repeatedly for an extended period ⟨looked over my head in a trance, occasionally *ruminating* her gum —Nathaniel Burt⟩ ~ *vi* **1 :** to chew again what has been chewed slightly and swallowed **:** chew a cud ⟨the cows . . . stood in the yards all day, *ruminating* and steaming —Adrian Bell⟩ **2 :** to consider something for a period or at intervals **:** engage in contemplation **:** REFLECT ⟨the old woman sat *ruminating* for a moment —Guy McCrone⟩ ⟨it is fascinating to ~ on what a really intelligent program might accomplish —Aaron Copland⟩ **syn** see PONDER

**²ru·mi·nate** \-nələt, -ˌnāl, *usu* |d.+V\ *adj* [L *ruminatus*, past part. of *ruminare*, *ruminari* to chew the cud] **:** mottled as if chewed — used of the endosperm of a seed (as of the nutmeg) in which the dark inner layer of the testa is infolded into the lighter endosperm

**ru·mi·nat·ing·ly** *adv* **:** in a ruminant manner

**ru·mi·na·tion** \ˌrüməˈnāshən\ *n* -s [L *rumination-*, *ruminatio* act of chewing the cud, act of thinking over, fr. *ruminatus* (past part.) + *-ion-*, *-io* -ion] **:** the act or process of ruminating: **a :** the act or process of regurgitating and rechewing previously swallowed food **b** (1) **:** the act or process of considering at more or less length **:** deliberate meditation or reflection ⟨these changes call not for argument but for ~ —Thornton Wilder⟩ (2) **:** obsessive or abnormal reflection upon an idea or deliberation over a choice

**ru·mi·na·tive** \ˈrüməˌnād|iv, -nəl, |t|, |ēv *also* |əv\ *adj* [¹*ruminate* + *-ive*] **1 :** inclined to or engaged in rumination **2 :** marked by careful consideration **:** fully meditated — **ru·mi·na·tive·ly** \|əvlē, -li\ *adv*

**ru·mi·na·tor** \-ˌnād.ə(r), -ātə-\ *n* -s [L, fr. *ruminatus* (past part.) + *-or*] **:** one that ruminates ⟨a writer who combines the beauty and precision of an artist with the wit and illumination of a ~ —E.A.Weeks⟩

**rum·kin** \ˈrəm(p)kən\ *n* -s [prob. fr. obs. D *roomerken*, prob. fr. D *roemer*, *romer* rummer + *-ken* -kin] *archaic* **:** a drinking vessel

**rum·less** \ˈrəmləs\ *adj* [²*rum* + *-less*] **:** lacking rum

**¹rum·mage** \ˈrəmij, -mēj\ *n* -s [obs. E *rummage* act of packing or arranging cargo, modif. of MF *arrimage*, fr. *arrimer*, *arimer*, *aruner* to pack or arrange cargo (fr. *a-* — fr. L *ad-* — + *-rimer*, *-rumer*, prob. of Gmc origin) + *-age*; akin to OHG *rūm* room, space — more at ROOM] **1 :** *chiefly Scot* **:** a noisy bustling turmoil **:** UPROAR **2 :** a thorough search esp. among a variety or confusion of objects or into every section of an area ⟨went off on a back-of-the-store ~ —*New Yorker*⟩ **3 a :** a confused miscellaneous collection **:** a nondescript mass or group ⟨a fabulous brown ~ of encyclopedias, world globes, maps, photographs, holy pictures, mirrors . . . and too much furniture —J.F.Powers⟩ **b** *or* **rummage goods :** the items for sale at a rummage sale **4 :** RUMMAGE SALE

**²rum·mage** \", *esp in pres part* -məj\ *vb* -ED/-ING/-S *vt* **1 a** *obs* **:** to pack or rearrange (as cargo or ballast) in the hold of a ship **b** *obs* **:** to set in order (as a ship or hold) by rearranging the cargo **2 a :** to put into confusion **:** mix up **:** DISORDER **b** *obs* **:** to mix together by stirring **:** STIR **3 a** (1) **:** to make a thorough search in **:** look through every section of **:** RANSACK ⟨one of you boys go ~ the storeroom for the corn popper —S.E.White⟩ (2) **:** to search thoroughly for contraband ⟨when the import cargo is discharged the examining officer finally ~*s* the ship —G.D.Ham⟩ **b :** to discover by or as if by a thorough search **:** produce by searching **:** hunt out ⟨*rummaged* a sword and red sash from somewhere —Mary B. Chesnut⟩ ⟨*rummaged* up his sexton and his verger as witnesses —J.C.Powys⟩ ⟨*rummaged* a conclusion from some odd corner of his soul —Samuel Butler †1902⟩ **c :** to examine minutely and completely **:** scrutinize carefully ⟨another . . . prowl through the most thoroughly *rummaged* era in our history —*New Yorker*⟩ ~ *vi* **1 :** to stow or rearrange cargo in or clean the hold of a ship **2 a :** to make a thorough search or investigation ⟨by dint of *rummaging* through various special lists and imported series, . . . it may be possible to assemble the entire series —Edward Sackville-West & Desmond Shawe-Taylor⟩ **b :** to engage in an undirected fumbling haphazard search ⟨the men ransacked the thatched huts, *rummaged* among the pots, the fishing gear, the shell ornaments —Marjory S. Douglas⟩ ⟨all my books are packed and gone and . . . I can't browse or ~ —H.J.Laski⟩ **syn** see SEEK

**rum·mag·er** \-jə(r)\ *n* -s [*rummage* + *-er*] **:** one that searches (as for contraband)

**rummage sale** *n* **1 :** a clearance sale of unclaimed or shopworn goods at a store or warehouse or of seized contraband **2 :** a sale of donated articles to raise money (as for a church)

**¹rum·mer** \ˈrəmə(r)\ *n* -s [G or D; G *römer*, fr. D *roemer*, *romer*, perh. fr. *roem* boast, praise, fr. MD; akin to OHG *hruom* honor, praise — more at BREME] **:** a large tall glass or drinking cup used esp. for wine

**²rummer** *comparative of* RUM

**rum·mery** \ˈrəmərē\ *n* -ES [²*rum* + *-ery*] **:** a commercial establishment where alcoholic beverages are sold **:** BAR, SALOON

**rummest** *superlative of* RUM

**rum–mill** \ˈ=,=\ *n, slang* **:** BAR, SALOON

**¹rum·my** \ˈrəmē, -mi\ *adj* -ER/-EST [¹*rum* + *-y*] **:** marked by oddness or idiosyncrasies **:** QUEER

**²rummy** \"\ *adj* -ER/-EST [²*rum* + *-y*] **:** of, relating to, or affected by rum ⟨~ taste⟩ ⟨his face was blotched . . . his eyes were ~, his jaw was uncertain —W.A.White⟩

**³rummy** \"\ *n* -ES [²*rum* + *-y* (n. suffix)] **1 :** one who drinks rum **:** DRUNKARD ⟨I sat at the bar along with the usual collection of winos and *rummies* —Ed Barcolo⟩ **2 :** a dealer in or distiller of intoxicating liquor

**⁴rummy** \"\ *also* **rum** \ˈrəm\ *n, pl* **rummies** *also* **rums** [*rummy* perh. fr. ¹*rummy*; *rum* back-formation fr. ⁴*rummy*] **1 :** one of numerous card games whose common essential features are that each player in turn draws one card from the stock of undealt cards or the discard of the previous player, tries to assemble in his hand groups of three or more cards of the same rank or suit usu. in order to meld them, and further tries to go out by being the first to meld all his cards **2 :** the condition of a player in rummy who has melded all his cards

**⁵rummy** \"\ *interj* — used by a player in some games of rummy to announce discovery that an opponent has neglected to take a discard he could add to a meld and to invest himself in the delinquent player's rights

**rum·ness** *n* -ES [¹*rum* + *-ness*] *chiefly Brit* **:** the quality or state of being rum **:** ODDITY, IDIOSYNCRACY

**¹ru·mor** \ˈrümə(r)\ *n* -s *see -or in Explan Notes* [ME *rumour*, fr. MF, fr. L *rumor*; akin to OE *rēon* to lament, MHG *rienen* to moan, complain, ON *rymja* to roar, grumble, *rymr* coarse voice, L *ravus* hoarse, *ravis* hoarseness, Gk *ōryesthai* to howl, roar, Skt *rauti* he roars, cries] **1 a :** common talk or opinion **:** widely disseminated belief having no discernible foundation or source **:** HEARSAY ⟨~ puts the amount at about 5000 kegs —W.Z.Ripley⟩ ⟨we make our blunders . . . as ~ has it that you make your own —B.N.Cardozo⟩ **b :** an instance of rumor **:** a statement or report current without any known authority for its truth ⟨almost every newspaper issue brought ~*s* of reduction in their salaries —V.G.Heiser⟩; *esp* **:** an unconfirmed piece of information or explanation disseminated among the public by other than formal news agencies or sources ⟨one of the community's most creative gossips begins to circulate the ~ that she is either a spy or a saboteur —Charles Lee⟩ ⟨tips and ~*s* . . . would send shares . . . up to thousands, and down again to the gutter —*Amer. Guide Series: Nev.*⟩ **c** *archaic* **:** talk or report of a notable person or event **:** FAME ⟨great is the ~ of this dreadful knight and his achievements of no less account —Shak.⟩ **2 a** *archaic* **:** a prolonged indistinct noise **:** CLAMOR, UPROAR **b :** a soft low indistinct sound **:** MURMUR ⟨a ~ of vespers in the chapel⟩

**²rumor** \"\ *vt* **rumored**; **rumored**; **rumoring** \-m(ə)riŋ\ **rumors** *see -or in Explan Notes* **:** to tell by rumor **:** give out tidings of **:** noise abroad

**ru·mor·er** \-mərə(r)\ *n* -s **:** RUMORMONGER

**rumormonger** \ˈ==,==\ *n* [¹*rumor* + *monger*] **:** one that spreads rumors

**ru·mor·ous** \ˈrümərəs\ *adj* **1 :** MURMURING **2 a :** of the nature of rumor **b :** filled with rumor

**¹rump** \ˈrəmp\ *n* -s, *often attrib* [ME *rumpe*, of Scand origin; akin to Icel *rumpr* rump, buttocks, Dan *rumpe* buttocks; akin to MHG *rumph* trunk, torso, MD *romp* trunk] **1 a :** the upper more or less rounded part of the hindquarters of a quadruped mammal — see COW illustration **b :** BUTTOCKS 1a **c :** the sacral or dorsal part of the posterior end of a bird — see BIRD illustration **d :** the hind end of the body of any of various animals in which well-defined landmarks are lacking **2 :** a cut of beef between the loin end and the round — see BEEF illustration **3 :** a small fragment or remainder: as **a :** a parliament, committee, or other group carrying on in the name of the original body after the departure or expulsion of a large number of its members ⟨the ~ of the National Assembly sits from time to time to endorse the . . . policy of the Government —*Statesman's Yr. Bk.*⟩ ⟨reduced his congregation to a determined and inveterate ~ of faithful souls —Robertson Davies⟩ ⟨~ peasant and bourgeois groups are kept in the Government as window dressing —*Economist*⟩ **b :** a small group usu. claiming to be representative of a larger whole that arises independently or breaks off from a parent body ⟨set up a ~ Government . . . with no effective authority —Sir Winston Churchill⟩ **c :** a fragment of a country left after partition or after secession, occupation, or annexation of a part ⟨this small truncated ~ of a country . . . is a viable economic unity —Edward Crankshaw⟩ ⟨partitioned into two ~ states —M.S.Handler⟩ **4 :** a geographical feature (as a ridge or a cape) resembling a rump

**²rump** \"\ *vt* -ED/-ING/-S **1 :** to turn one's back upon esp. as a sign of contempt **2 :** to remove (hide) from the hind leg of a slaughtered beef animal

**rump bone** *n* **:** SACRUM

**rumped** \ˈrəmpt\ *adj* [¹*rump* + *-ed*] **:** having a specified kind of rump — usu. used in combination ⟨white-*rumped*⟩

**rump·er** \ˈrəmpə(r)\ *n* -s [*Rump* Parliament, remnant of the Long Parliament in England after the expulsion of most of its members by the army of Cromwell in 1648 (fr. ¹*rump*) + *-er*] **1** *usu cap* **:** a member or supporter of the Rump Parliament **2** [¹*rump* + *-er*] **:** a slaughterhouse worker who removes the hide from the tail bone, rump, and hind legs

**rumpf** \ˈrüm(p)f\ *n* -s [G, trunk, torso, fr. MHG *rumph*] **:** CORE 1t

**¹rum·ple** \ˈrəmpəl\ *n* -s [dim. of ¹*rump*] *Scot* **:** RUMP, TAIL

**²rumple** \"\ *n* -s [MLG *rumpel*; akin to MD *rumpelen*, *rompelen* to rumple] **:** FOLD, WRINKLE

**³rumple** \"\ *vb* **rumpled**; **rumpled**; **rumpling** \-p(ə)liŋ\ **rumples** [D *rompelen*, fr. MD *rumpelen*, *rompelen*; akin to OE *hrympel* wrinkle, OHG *rimpfan* to crease, wrinkle, LGk *krambos* dry, withered, L *curvus* curved — more at CROWN]

*vt* **1 :** to cause to form into irregular folds **:** WRINKLE, CRUMPLE **2 :** to make unkempt **:** TOUSLE, MUSS ⟨*rumpled* hair⟩ **~** *vi* **:** to become mussed or wrinkled

**rump·less** \ˈrəmpləs\ *adj* [[1]*rump* + *-less*] **:** lacking the coccygeal vertebrae ⟨~ domestic fowls⟩ **:** TAILLESS

**rum·ply** \ˈrəmp(ə)lē\ *adj* -ER/-EST [[2]*rumple* + *-y*] **:** RUMPLED

**rumpot** \ˈ=,=\ *n* [[2]*rum* + *pot*] *slang* **:** DRUNKARD

**rump steak** *n* **:** a steak cut from the rump

[1]**rum·pus** \ˈrəmpəs\ *n* -ES [origin unknown] **1 :** a usu. noisy commotion **:** DISTURBANCE, FRACAS **2 :** a hotly debated division of opinion **syn** see BRAWL

[2]**rumpus** \"\ *vi* **rumpussed** *or* **rumpused; rumpussed** *or* **rumpused; rumpussing** *or* **rumpusing; rumpusses** *or* **rumpuses :** to cause a disturbance **:** make a rumpus

**rumpus room** *n* **:** a room usu. in the basement of a home that is set apart and furnished for games, parties, and recreation

[1]**rumpy** \ˈrəmpē\ *n* -ES [[1]*rump* + *-y* (n. suffix); fr. its rudimentary tail] **:** MANX CAT

[2]**rumpy** \"\ *adj* -ER/-EST [[1]*rump* + *-y* (adj. suffix)] **:** having a prominent rump **:** STEATOPYGOUS

**rumrunner** \ˈ=,==\ *n* [[2]*rum* + *runner*] **:** a person or ship engaged in bringing prohibited alcoholic liquor ashore or across a border

**rum-running** \ˈ=,==\ *n* **:** the act or process of bringing prohibited alcoholic liquor ashore or across a border

**rums** *pl of* RUM

**rumshop** \ˈ=,=\ *n* **:** a commercial establishment where alcoholic liquors are sold **:** BAR, SALOON

**rum sucker** *n* **:** a moss (*Polytrichum commune*)

**rum tum ditty** *also* **rum tum tiddy** *n* [origin unknown] **:** RINKTUM DITTY

[1]**run** \ˈrən\ *vb* **ran** \ˈran, ˈraa(ə)n\ *or nonstand* **run; run; running; runs** [ME *runnen, ronnen;* in intransitive senses, alter. of *rinnen, irnen,* partly fr. OE *rinnan, iernan,* partly fr. ON *rinna;* akin to OS, OHG, & Goth *rinnan* to run; in transitive senses, alter. of *rennen, ernen,* partly fr. OE *ærnan,* partly fr. ON *renna;* akin to OS *rennian* to cause to run, OHG *rennen* to cause to run, Goth ur*rannjan* to cause to rise; causatives fr. the root of OE *rinnan, iernan;* akin to OE *rīsan* to rise — more at RISE] *vi* **1 a :** to go by moving the legs quickly **:** go faster than a walk; *specif* **:** to go steadily by springing steps so that both feet leave the ground for an instant in each step **b** *of a horse* **:** to move at a fast gallop as distinguished from a canter **:** move with each leg acting in turn as a propeller and supporter and all four legs being for an instant in the air under the body **c :** FLEE, RETREAT, ESCAPE ⟨afraid to fight but ashamed to ~⟩ ⟨dropped his gun and *ran*⟩ ⟨obliged to cut and ~⟩ **d :** to make a bid in a card game in an effort to escape the consequences of a previous bid ⟨refrained from doubling four spades for fear he would ~ to five clubs⟩ — sometimes used with *out* **2 a :** to go without restraint **:** move freely about at will ⟨let his chickens ~ loose⟩ ⟨liked to ~ barefoot in the summer⟩ **b :** to keep company **:** CONSORT — used with *with* chiefly of male animals ⟨a ram *running* with his ewes⟩ **c :** to sail before the wind in distinction from reaching or sailing close-hauled **d :** ROAM, ROVE, GAD — usu. used with *about* or *around* ⟨spends his time *running* around nights and sleeping all day⟩ ⟨caught cold *running* about with no overcoat⟩ **e :** to deviate from a correct path — used of a saw cut **3 a :** to go rapidly or hurriedly **:** HASTEN ⟨~ and fetch the doctor⟩ **b :** to go in urgency or distress **:** RESORT ⟨~*s* to his mother at every little difficulty⟩ ⟨don't come *running* to me when you get in trouble⟩ **c :** to make a quick, easy, or casual trip or visit ⟨*running* up to town every week or so⟩ ⟨just *ran* over to borrow some sugar⟩ **4 a :** to contend in a race ⟨will be able to ~ tomorrow⟩; *also* **:** to finish a race in a specified place ⟨*ran* a poor third⟩ **b :** to enter into an election contest **:** become a candidate ⟨I do not choose to ~ —Calvin Coolidge⟩ **5 a :** to move on or as if on wheels **:** GLIDE ⟨the hoist ~*s* on an overhead track⟩ ⟨file drawers *running* on ball bearings⟩ ⟨the tractor ~*s* on an endless chain tread⟩ **b** (1) **:** to roll forward rapidly or freely ⟨the cue ball *ran* straight into the side pocket⟩ (2) *of a golf ball* **:** to bound or roll along after touching the ground subsequent to the carry ⟨*ran* some 10 yards onto the green⟩ **c :** to pass or slide freely along ⟨rope ~*s* through the pulley⟩ **d :** to ravel lengthwise owing to a dropped or broken stitch ⟨stockings guaranteed not to ~⟩ **6 :** to sing or play a musical passage quickly ⟨~ up the scale⟩ **7 a :** to go back and forth **:** PLY ⟨a ferry ~*s* to the island each hour⟩ **b** *of fish* **:** to migrate or move in schools; *esp* **:** to ascend a river to spawn **8 a :** TURN, ROTATE ⟨a swiftly *running* grindstone⟩ ⟨let the motor ~ until it warms up⟩ **b :** FUNCTION, OPERATE, WORK ⟨an engine that ~*s* on kerosine or gasoline⟩ ⟨things are *running* smoothly at the office now⟩ ⟨expense of keeping the old car *running*⟩ **9 a :** to continue in force or operation **:** remain effective ⟨the contract has two more years to ~⟩ ⟨six months on each charge, the sentences to ~ concurrently⟩ **b :** to accompany as a valid obligation or right ⟨covenants the rights and liabilities of which pass to assignees ~ with the land⟩ **c :** to continue to accrue or become payable in an amount increasing with the passing of time ⟨interest on the loan ~*s* from last July 1st⟩ **10 :** to pass from one state to another ⟨~ into trouble⟩ ⟨~ into debt⟩ **11 a :** to flow rapidly ⟨a brook *running* high with meltwater⟩ or under pressure ⟨someone left the hot water *running*⟩ ⟨feelings were *running* high on both sides of the dispute⟩ ⟨tide *running* out⟩ **b :** to change to a liquid state **:** MELT, FUSE ⟨heat a pipe joint until the solder ~*s*⟩ ⟨the icing had begun to ~⟩ **c :** to spread out, diffuse, or dissolve ⟨colors guaranteed not to fade or ~⟩ ⟨the writing was blurred where the ink had ~ on the wet pages⟩ **d :** to discharge pus or serum ⟨a *running* sore⟩ **e** *dial* **:** CURDLE **f** *of soil* **:** to become fluid or pasty when wet **12 a :** to develop rapidly in some specific direction; *esp* **:** to throw out an elongated and often vining shoot of growth ⟨the early squashes are beginning to ~ and flower⟩ **b :** to tend to produce or develop a specified quality or feature — usu. used with *to* ⟨they ~ to big noses in that family⟩ ⟨this tree ~*s* to quite tart fruit⟩ **13 a :** to lie in or take a certain direction ⟨the boundary line ~*s* east from the stone⟩ ⟨his action ~*s* counter to prevailing practice⟩ ⟨the printed matter on this page ~*s* the short way of the page⟩ ⟨a red thread ~*s* through the cloth⟩ **b :** to lie or extend in relation to something ⟨where the road ~*s* close to the shore⟩ ⟨a path ~*s* along the ridge⟩ ⟨the fence ~*s* along two sides of the field⟩ ⟨heating pipes *ran* overhead⟩ **c :** to go back **:** REACH ⟨a custom since the time that no man's mind ~*s* to the contrary⟩ ⟨born of a line *running* back to King Alfred⟩ **d :** to be in a certain form or expression ⟨his letter ~*s* as follows⟩ or order of succession ⟨the house numbers in this block ~ in odd numbers from 3 to 57⟩ **14 a :** to occur intermittently and persistently **:** RECUR — usu. used with *through* or *in* ⟨a note of despair ~*s* through the whole narrative⟩ ⟨musical talent seems to ~ in his family⟩ ⟨tune kept *running* in his head⟩ ⟨thoughts and memories of home kept *running* through his mind⟩ **b :** to continue to be of a specified size or character or quality ⟨peaches are *running* unusually large this year⟩ ⟨profits were *running* high⟩ **c :** to continue at a certain rate or value ⟨this ore ~*s* as high as $200 to the ton⟩ **d :** to exist or occur in a continuous range of variation ⟨guesses at his real age ~ from 39 to 45 or higher⟩ **e :** to play on a stage a number of successive days or nights ⟨the piece *ran* for six months⟩ **15 a :** to spread or pass quickly from point to point ⟨chills *ran* up his spine⟩ ⟨a whisper *ran* through the crowd⟩ ⟨a shout *ran* down the line of soldiers⟩ ⟨fire *ran* swiftly over the oily sea⟩ **b :** to be current **:** spread abroad **:** pass from mouth to mouth ⟨the story ~*s* that they have been secretly married for months⟩ ⟨speculation *ran* rife on who the candidate would be⟩ **~** *vt* **1 a :** to cause (an animal) to go at speed **:** ride or drive fast **b :** to bring to a specified condition by or as if by running ⟨he almost *ran* himself to death⟩ ⟨fie, now you ~ this humor out of breath —Shak.⟩ **c :** to go in pursuit of **:** HUNT, CHASE ⟨~ a deer⟩ ⟨the dog was caught *running* sheep and had to be shot⟩ **d :** to follow the trail of backwards **:** TRACE ⟨*ran* the rumor to its source⟩ **e :** to enter, register, or enroll as a contestant in a race ⟨*ran* the filly in the half mile⟩ **f :** to put forward as a candidate for office ⟨*ran* him for governor⟩ **2 a :** to drive (livestock) esp. to a grazing place ⟨~ cattle to pasture⟩ **b :** to provide pasturage for (livestock) ⟨land that will ~ three sheep to the acre⟩ **c :** to keep or maintain (livestock) on or as if on pasturage ⟨~ a few head of stock⟩ ⟨~ 2,000,000 chickens a year⟩ **d :** to put (a male animal) with females for breeding ⟨flush the ram before *running* him with the ewes⟩ **3 a :** to pass over, traverse, or cover by or as if by running ⟨quick at fielding and *running* bases⟩ ⟨the disease has *run* its course⟩ ⟨her acting *ran* the whole range of emotions⟩ **b :** to accomplish or perform by or as if by running ⟨*ran* a great race⟩ ⟨*running* errands for a bank⟩ **c :** to flee from ⟨*ran* the country after the robbery⟩ **d :** to slip through or past ⟨~ a blockade⟩ ⟨~ a guard⟩ ⟨~ a traffic signal⟩ **4 a :** to cause to slip into or through **:** THRUST ⟨*ran* the spear through his body⟩ ⟨*ran* a splinter into his toe⟩ ⟨*ran* his hand into his pocket⟩ **b :** STITCH; *esp* **:** to sew with running stitches ⟨~ a basting to mark the waistline⟩ ⟨~ a line of stitching⟩ **c :** to cause to pass **:** LEAD ⟨~ a rope through a pulley⟩ ⟨~ a wire in from the antenna⟩ **d :** to cause to collide ⟨*ran* his head into a post⟩ **e :** SMUGGLE **5 :** to cause to pass lightly or quickly over, along, or into something ⟨*ran* his eye down the list⟩ ⟨*ran* his fingers along the shelf⟩ ⟨~ your hand over the tabletop to see if the varnish is dry⟩ ⟨*ran* his tongue over his parched lips⟩ **6 a :** to cause or allow (as a vehicle, a vessel) to go in a specified manner or direction ⟨*ran* the ship aground on a sandbar⟩ ⟨*ran* his car off the road⟩ **b :** OPERATE ⟨~ a lawn mover⟩ ⟨~ a taxi⟩ **c :** to carry on **:** MANAGE, CONDUCT ⟨~ a factory⟩ ⟨~ a travel bureau⟩ ⟨the men who ~ things in this city⟩ **7 a :** to be full of or drenched with **:** flow with ⟨the streets *ran* blood⟩ ⟨all the brooks *ran* gold —A.E.Housman⟩ **b :** CONTAIN, ASSAY ⟨tailing ~*s* 2 percent zinc⟩ **8 a :** to cause to move or flow in a specified way or into a specified position ⟨~ sheets through a wringer⟩ ⟨~ cards into a file⟩ **b :** FAN 7b **9 a :** to melt and cast in a mold ⟨~ bullets⟩ **b :** to make (a resin) soluble in oil by subjecting to thermal processing **c :** TREAT, PROCESS, REFINE ⟨~ oil in a still⟩ **d :** to pour into the cracks and joints of a pavement ⟨~ tar⟩ or into a form ⟨~ concrete⟩ **e :** to apply (as paint) by flowing ⟨~ a wash⟩; *also* **:** to cover (a surface) by flowing on ⟨~ a wall⟩ **f :** to form (a molding) with plaster **g :** to pass (starch slurry) down a run **10 :** to make oneself liable to **:** expose oneself to **:** INCUR ⟨*ran* the risk of discovery by lighting a fire⟩ **11 :** to mark out **:** cause to be drawn ⟨~ a contour line in surveying land⟩ ⟨~ a line through the word to be deleted⟩ **12 :** to permit (as charges, accounts, bills) to accumulate before settling ⟨~ an account at the grocery⟩ **13 a :** to run off ⟨a book to be ~ on lightweight paper⟩ ⟨a job to be ~ 4-up⟩ **b :** to carry in a printed medium **:** PRINT ⟨every newspaper *ran* the story⟩ ⟨~ this advertisement for 3 days⟩ **c :** to use as a direct printing surface ⟨you may stereotype these woodcuts but do not ~ them⟩ **14 a :** to make (a series of counts) without a miss ⟨~ 19 in an inning in billiards⟩ **b** *card games* **:** to lead winning cards of (a suit) successively and usu. until no more remain **15 :** to make (a golf ball) roll forward after alighting ⟨*ran* his ball past the cup⟩ **16** *croquet* **:** to play one's ball through (a wicket) or against (a stake)

**syn** RACE, COURSE, CAREER: RUN is the general term in this set, indicating either a rapid or more-or-less normal movement or motion ⟨a halfback *running* laterally⟩ ⟨busses *running* on Elm Street⟩ ⟨the watch had stopped *running*⟩ RACE almost always indicates great speed or rapidity, often in or as though in urgent situations with freedom from normal inhibitions ⟨he *raced* for a small dune and flung himself down behind it —Irwin Shaw⟩ ⟨thoughts were under control no longer: they *raced* desperately — as she had once seen a dog *race* . . . running desperately and hopelessly from inescapable terror —Margery Sharp⟩ COURSE in this sense may indicate rapid or pulsating motion or activity, often following a definite or expected course or channel ⟨reconnaissance aircraft *coursed* North Korea —*N.Y.Times*⟩ ⟨her hand became a closer prisoner. All at once an alarming delicious shudder went through her frame. From him to her it *coursed* —George Meredith⟩ ⟨new life *coursing* through Europe's stagnant economic system —R.A.Billington⟩ CAREER is likely to indicate high speed with headlong impetus or, occas., with veering or rocking motion ⟨*careering* through the salons on a bicycle —*Time*⟩ ⟨blind historians *careering* on their juggernauts of theory —*Times Lit. Supp.*⟩ ⟨intoxicated cats *careering* through our houses —F.A.Swinnerton⟩

— **run across :** to meet with or discover by chance ⟨years later I *ran across* him in a bar in Paris⟩ — **run after 1 :** PURSUE, CHASE ⟨*running after* a pickpocket⟩; *esp* **:** to seek the company of ⟨old enough now to start *running after* the girls⟩ **2 :** to take up with **:** FOLLOW ⟨*runs after* every new fashion⟩ ⟨*run after* new theories⟩ — **run against 1 :** to meet suddenly or unexpectedly **2 :** to work or take effect unfavorably to **:** DISFAVOR, OPPOSE ⟨time is now *running against* us in this affair⟩ ⟨do nothing that would *run against* his moral principles⟩ — **run at check** *of a hunting dog* **:** to follow base game — **run a temperature :** to have a fever — **run cunning :** to run false — **run division** *obs* **:** to play variations **:** elaborate upon a theme or topic — **run down the latitude :** to sail north or south on a meridian until the latitude of the destination is reached — **run false :** to save distance by running directly for the hare or game instead of following the scent or track — **run foul of :** to collide with ⟨*ran foul* of a hidden reef⟩ **:** run into conflict with or hostility to ⟨*run foul of* the law⟩ — **run free :** to sail with the wind coming from abaft the beam **:** RUN *vi* 2 c — **run heelway :** to run the wrong way on the trail of the quarry — **run in the blood :** to be a family, national, or racial trait — **run into 1 a :** to change or transform into **:** BECOME ⟨reverence for law and prescription . . . which *runs* sometimes *into* pedantry —T.B. Macaulay⟩ **b :** to merge with ⟨little lakes that all *run into* one another⟩ ⟨a dreamy state in which one day seemed to *run into* another⟩ **c :** to mount up to ⟨keeping a boat like that one *runs into* money⟩ ⟨his yearly income often *runs into* six figures⟩ **2 a :** to collide with ⟨veered off the road and *ran into* a telephone pole⟩ **b :** ENCOUNTER, MEET ⟨*ran into* an old classmate⟩ ⟨*run into* difficulties⟩ — **run in with :** to make toward **:** NEAR ⟨*run in with* the land⟩ — **run mad :** to run wildly about under the influence of hydrophobia **:** become affected with hydrophobia — **run ragged :** to wear out **:** EXHAUST ⟨children and housework were *running* her *ragged*⟩ ⟨the word "character," meaning a person . . . of eccentricity has been *run ragged* —John McNulty⟩ — **run rings around :** to show marked superiority over **:** defeat decisively or overwhelmingly — **run riot 1 a :** to act wildly or without restraint ⟨*ran riot* with Chinese red in the living room⟩ **b :** to occur in profusion ⟨puns *ran riot* in his style⟩ **2 :** to pursue the wrong scent or base game — **run scared :** to bend every effort (as in a political campaign) through or as if through fear of defeat — **run short :** to become insufficient ⟨drinking water was *running short* before the voyage was over⟩ — **run short of :** to use up **:** become lacking in sufficient quantity of ⟨we are *running short of* time to finish the job⟩ ⟨army *ran short of* provisions⟩ — **run the cards :** to deal the requisite cards in seven-up when the eldest hand begs — **run to cover :** to flee from danger or financial risk ⟨short sellers of stock *run to cover* by buying back the stock when the market rises⟩ — **run to earth :** to hunt to its hiding place, home, starting place, or origin ⟨after much searching I *ran* him *to earth* in a dingy hotel⟩ — **run to seed 1 :** to expend or exhaust vitality in producing seed **2 :** to cease growing **:** lose vital force ⟨let his mind *run to seed*⟩ — **run track :** to compete in running events as distinguished from field events — **run upon :** to run across **:** meet with — **run wild 1 :** to go unrestrained or out of control **:** run riot ⟨prices were *running wild* all over Miami —Alva Johnston⟩ **2 :** to live or grow without cultivation or training ⟨gardens and lawns neglected and *running wild*⟩

[2]**run** \"\ *n* -S [ME *rune,* fr. *runnen, ronnen* to run — more at [1]RUN] **1 a :** an act or the action of running **:** continued and usu. rapid movement ⟨walked faster and faster finally breaking into a ~⟩ ⟨let the dogs out for a ~⟩ ⟨police arrived on the ~⟩ **b :** a quickened gallop **c** (1) **:** the act of migrating or ascending a river to spawn — used of fish (2) **:** an assemblage or school of fishes that migrate or ascend a river to spawn **d :** a running race ⟨a mile ~⟩ — distinguished from *dash* **e** (1) **:** a score made in cricket each time the batsmen safely change ends after a hit or when the ball is in play — compare BOUNDARY, EXTRA (2) **:** a score made in baseball by a runner reaching home plate safely after touching the three bases in order — compare HOME RUN **f :** strength or ability to run ⟨the first two laps took most of the ~ out of him⟩ **2 a** *chiefly Midland* **:** CREEK 2 **b :** a swift tidal current **c :** a pronounced swell or markedly choppy condition of the surface of the water ⟨there was a ~ of sea in the harbor —John Masefield⟩ **d :** something that flows in the course of a certain operation or during a certain time ⟨a ~ of must in wine making⟩ ⟨the first ~ of sap in sugar maple⟩ — compare FORERUN **3 a :** the afterpart of the underwater body of a ship from where it begins to curve or slope upward and inward to the stern — compare ENTRANCE 7; see SHIP illustration **b :** the direction in which a vein of ore lies **c :** a direction of secondary or minor cleavage **:** GRAIN ⟨~ of a mass of granite⟩ — compare RIFT 4 **d :** an irregular body of ore having an approximately horizontal direction **e :** the horizontal distance to which a mine drift is or may be carried **f** (1) **:** the length of the base of a right triangle (2) **:** the horizontal distance measured from the face of one riser to that of the next (3) **:** the horizontal distance covered by a flight of steps (4) **:** the horizontal distance from the wall plate to the center line of a building ⟨the rise of a rafter per foot of ~⟩ (5) **:** extent measured linearly ⟨the bridge carries a load of 500 pounds per foot ~⟩ **g :** the distance irrigation water must flow from the supply ditch to the end of the field or to the lower level **h :** general tendency or direction ⟨kept in touch with the general ~ of the stock market⟩ **4 :** a continuous series esp. of things of identical or similar sort ⟨a ~ of poor poker hands⟩: as **a :** a rapid scale passage in vocal or instrumental music **b** *dancing* **:** a number of rapid, small, elastic steps executed in even tempo **c :** the act of making successively a number of successful shots or strokes; *also* **:** the score thus made ⟨~ of 15 balls in pool⟩ ⟨a ~ of 20 in billiards⟩ **d :** an unbroken course of being repeated on the stage — used of a play **e** (1) **:** a set of consecutive measurements, readings, or observations (2) *math* **:** a maximal subsequence of elements of like kind in any ordered sequence of elements of two kinds **f :** a train of cars in a mine **g :** persistent and heavy demands from depositors, creditors, or customers ⟨a ~ on a bank⟩ ⟨a ~ on limited stocks of goods in a store⟩ **h :** a heavy demand for a printing sort not ordinarily needed in quantity **i :** SEQUENCE 2b **j :** a stereotyped passage of narrative or description introduced into Gaelic popular tales **5 :** the quantity of work turned out in a continuous operation: as **a :** the paper made in a continuous operation (as to fill a given order or part of an order) **b :** a single distillation of a given amount of material **c :** PIPELINE RUN **d :** the quantity of lumber cut from a log **e :** a numbering unit for woolen yarns based on the number of 1,600-yard hanks to a pound ⟨a two-*run* yarn has 3,200 yards to a pound⟩ **6 :** the usual or normal kind, character, type, or group ⟨the general ~ of modern fiction⟩ ⟨average ~ of college graduates⟩ ⟨his whole appearance was . . . out of the common ~ —Washington Irving⟩ **7 a :** a caving in of a mine working **b :** a fall of a cage in a mine shaft **c :** deviation of a tool from a correct path **8 a :** the distance covered in a period of continuous traveling or sailing ⟨betting on the day's ~ of the ship⟩ **b :** a course or route mapped out and traveled with regularity ⟨the ~ of the "Twentieth Century Limited" between New York and Chicago⟩ **c :** a single or essentially continuous journey **:** TRIP ⟨a ship on her regular ~ to Europe⟩ ⟨a 10,000 mile test ~ for gasoline mileage⟩ **d :** BOMB RUN **e :** a news reporter's regular territory **:** BEAT ⟨covering the labor ~⟩ **f :** the distance a golf ball travels after touching the ground from a stroke **g :** freedom of movement in or access to a place or area ⟨has the ~ of the whole neighborhood⟩ ⟨has the ~ of his friend's house including the kitchen⟩ **9 a :** the period during which a machine or plant is in continuous operation; *specif* **:** the period in the manufacture of water gas during which steam is admitted at the end of the blow and the gas is produced — compare BACK RUN **b :** a test or proof of a process, a material (as ore), or a machine ⟨a laboratory ~⟩ **10 a :** a way, track, or path frequented by animals ⟨a rabbit ~⟩ ⟨a beaver ~⟩ ⟨poisoning rat ~*s*⟩ **b :** an enclosure for livestock where they may feed and exercise — often used in combination ⟨fowl ~⟩ ⟨hog ~⟩ **c** *Austral* **:** a large area of land used for grazing ⟨sheep ~⟩ **:** RANCH, STATION ⟨*run*-holder⟩ **d :** the bower of a bowerbird **e :** an inclined passage between levels in a mine **f :** an inclined plane for a passageway (as in a theater) **:** RAMP **g :** the clear space not less than 15 feet in length and immediately back of the foul line from which a bowler delivers his ball **11 a :** an inclined course for coasting, skiing, or bobsledding **b :** a support (as a track, pipe, trough) on which something runs ⟨sash ~ in a window frame⟩ ⟨overhead ~ for a traveling hoist⟩ **c :** a settling trough for slimes used in working ore **d :** a long slightly inclined table used in washing starch free from gluten, fiber, and other impurities **12 a :** a ravel in a knitted fabric (as in hosiery) caused by the breaking or dropping of one or more stitches **b :** a paint defect occurring at the time of application caused by excessive flow **13 :** a pair of millstones **14 :** the distance between two degrees or assigned points on an arc or curved scale (as of a surveying instrument); *also* **:** the value of a division of the scale in seconds of arc **15 runs** *pl but sing or pl in constr* **:** DIARRHEA — not often in polite use — **by the run** *adv* **1 :** so as to run freely — used of letting go in contrast to slacking away gradually ⟨lower sail *by the run*⟩ **2 :** according to a measure of work equivalent to a linear yard of breast excavated — sometimes used in estimating the pay of miners — **in the long run :** in the course of sufficiently prolonged time, trial, or experience ⟨integrity succeeds best *in the long run*⟩

[3]**run** \"\ *adj* [fr. past part. of [1]*run*] **1 a :** MELTED ⟨~ butter⟩ ⟨~ honey⟩ **b :** made from molten material **:** cast in a mold ⟨~ metal⟩ ⟨~ joint⟩ **2 :** SMUGGLED ⟨~ diamonds⟩ **3** *Scot* **a :** THOROUGH, OUTRIGHT **b :** CONTINUOUS, RUNNING **4** *of fish* **:** having made a migration or spawning run ⟨a fresh ~ salmon⟩ **5 :** exhausted or winded from running

**runabout** \ˈ==,=\ *n* -S [fr. *run about,* v.] **1 :** a young child ⟨special problems of toddlers and ~*s* —*New Republic*⟩ **2 :** one who wanders or gads about **:** VAGABOND, STRAY, STRAGGLER **3 a :** a light uncovered wagon **b :** a light roadster **c :** a light motorboat **:** SPEEDBOAT

**run·a·gate** \ˈrənəˌgāt\ *n* -S [alter. (influenced by [1]*run*) of *renegate*] **1 :** RENEGADE **2 a :** FUGITIVE, RUNAWAY **b :** VAGABOND, WANDERER

**run along** *vi* **:** to go away **:** be on one's way **:** DEPART ⟨it's late, I must *run along*⟩

**run around** *vi* **:** to seek amusement or companionship restlessly or incessantly ⟨that crowd he used to *run around* with⟩ ⟨never home, evenings, always *running around*⟩; *specif* **:** to engage in extramarital relations ⟨suspected her husband of *running around*⟩ **~** *vt* **:** to set or arrange (type matter) as a runaround

**runaround** \ˈ==,=\ *n* -S [fr. *run around,* v.] **1 :** a whitlow encircling the fingernail **2 :** a track, way, or channel provided for bypassing an obstacle or tie-up **3 :** the distance that a scraper traverses in completing one cycle of operations (as loading, transporting, dumping, and returning to the starting point) **4 :** a passage driven in a shaft pillar to connect mine workings on opposite sides of a shaft **5 :** matter typeset in shortened measure to run down one or both sides of something (as a cut or box) inserted in running text matter **6 :** deliberately deceptive or delaying action esp. in response to a request **:** substitution of evasive or misleading replies for definite and candid refusal ⟨tried to get contracts and have been given the familiar official ~ —*New Republic*⟩

**run away** *vi* **1 :** FLEE, DESERT, ABSCOND **2 :** to leave home ⟨had *run away* twice before he was ten⟩; *esp* **:** ELOPE ⟨*ran away* with a man twice her age⟩ **3 :** to run out of control **:** STAMPEDE, BOLT ⟨realized that his horse was *running away*⟩ — **run away with 1 :** to take away in haste or secretly; *often* **:** STEAL **2 :** to take in a hauling part (as of a fall, tackle, or brace) by holding fast to it and running along the deck **3 :** to become conspicuous in or outshine the others in (a theatrical performance) ⟨in the minor role of the hero's uncle he succeeded in *running away with* the show⟩ **4 :** to carry or drive beyond prudent or reasonable limits ⟨let his imagination *run away with* him⟩

[1]**runaway** \ˈ==,=\ *n* -S [*run away*] **1 :** one that flees from danger, duty, or legal or parental restraint **:** FUGITIVE **2 :** the act of running away out of control; *also* **:** a horse that is running out of control **3 :** excessive or uncontrolled speed (as of a turbine or locomotive) or flow (as of an oil well) **4 :** a one-sided or overwhelming victory

[2]**runaway** \"\ *adj* [*run away*] **1 :** running away **:** fleeing or escaping from danger, duty, or restraint ⟨~ slave⟩ ⟨~ team⟩ ⟨~ railroad car⟩ **2 :** accomplished by elopement or during

flight ⟨a ~ marriage⟩ **3 :** won by a long lead ⟨a ~ race⟩ **:** DECISIVE **4** *of prices* **:** subject to rapid changes usu. toward higher levels ⟨~ inflation⟩

**run-away-robin** \'==,=='==\ *n* **:** GROUND IVY 1

**runaway shop** *n* **:** an industrial plant moved by its owners from one location to another to escape union labor regulations or state laws

**runback** \'=,=\ *n* -S [fr. *run back*, v.] **1 :** a run made in football after catching an opponent's kick **2 :** the area of a tennis court behind the base line **3 :** a return pipe or duct (as in a still, a heating system)

**runboard** \'=,=\ *n* **:** RUNNING BOARD

**runboat** \'=,=\ *n* **:** a boat that collects the catches of individual fishermen at prearranged points

**runby** \=,'rən,bī\ *n, pl* **runbys** \-īz\ [fr. *run by*, v.] **1 :** the clearance space between the top of the car frame and the lowest portion of the overhead work in a hoistway or elevator shaft **2 :** an extra piece of track to permit a train to back past a crossover without using it

**runcation** *n* -S [L *runcation-, runcatio*, fr. *runcatus* (past part. of *runcare* to weed) + *-ion-, -io* -ion — more at ROUGH] *obs* **:** removal of weeds

**¹runch** \'rənch\ *n* -ES [origin unknown] **1 :** CHARLOCK **2 :** JOINTED CHARLOCK

**²runch** \"\ *vb* -ED/-ING/-ES [prob. by alter.] *Scot* **:** CRUNCH

**runchweed** \'=,=\ *n* **:** CHARLOCK

**run·ci·ble spoon** \'rən(t)səbəl-\ *n* [coined with an obscure meaning in 1871 by Edward Lear †1888 Eng. landscape painter and writer of nonsense verse] **:** a fork with three broad curved prongs and a sharpened edge used with pickles or hors d'oeuvres

**run·ci·nate** \'rən(t)sənət, -sə,nāt, *usu* -d·+V\ *adj* [L *runcinatus*, past part. of *runcinare* to plane off, fr. *runcina* plane, prob. modif. (influenced by *runcare* to weed) of Gk *rhykanē*; akin to Gk *orychein, oryssein* to dig — more at ROUGH] **:** pinnately cut with the lobes pointing downward ⟨the ~ leaf of the dandelion⟩ — see LEAF illustration

**rund** \'rən(d)\ *chiefly Scot var of* RAND

**rundale** \'=,=\ *n* [¹*run* + *dale* (portion of land)] **:** a distribution of lands among tenants or owners in Scotland and Ireland by which the land is apportioned so that a single tenant's or owner's holding consists of strips lying between those of others

**run·di** \'ründē\ *n, pl* **rundi** *or* **rundis** *usu cap* **1 a :** a Bantu-speaking people of Urundi, East Africa **b :** a member of such people **2 :** a Bantu language of the Rundi people used as one of the two trade languages of Ruanda-Urundi — compare RUANDA

**¹run·dle** \'rəndᵊl\ *n* -S [ME *rundel* — more at ROUNDEL] **1** *obs* **:** CIRCLE, SPHERE **2 a :** a step of a ladder **:** RUNG **b :** one of the pins of a lantern pinion **3 :** the drum of a windlass or capstan

**²run·dle** \'rünᵊl, 'rənᵊl\ *dial var of* RUNNEL

**rund·let** \'rəndlət\ *also* **run·let** \-nl-\ *n* -S [ME *roundelet* — more at ROUNDLET] **1 :** a small barrel **:** KEG **2 :** an old unit of liquid capacity equal to 15 imperial gallons or 18 U.S. gallons

**run down** *vt* **1 a :** to collide with and knock down (as with an automobile) ⟨*ran down* an old man in the rain⟩ **b :** to run against and sink ⟨*ran* a fishing boat *down* in the harbor⟩ **2 a :** to chase until exhausted **:** pursue until overtaken or captured ⟨finally *ran* the fugitive *down* in a blind alley⟩ **b :** to find by search **:** trace the source of ⟨had quite a time *running down* the technical words —Tom Marvel⟩ **c :** to tag out (a base runner) between bases **3 :** DISPARAGE ⟨nags her husband and *runs* him *down* in company⟩ **4 :** to cause to diminish in value or quantity ⟨*run* a stock *down*⟩ ~ *vi* **1 :** to cease to operate because of the exhaustion of motive power ⟨that clock *ran down* hours ago⟩ **2 :** to decline in physical condition ⟨his health *ran down* to a dangerous level⟩ ⟨the railroads have been permitted to *run down* alarmingly⟩ **3** *Brit, of a stream* **:** to fall to normal level after a flood

**run-down** \'='=\ *adj* [fr. *run down*, past part. of *run down*] **1 :** in poor repair **:** DILAPIDATED ⟨rehabilitation of *run-down* houses and neighborhoods⟩ **2 :** in poor health or physical condition **:** worn out **:** EXHAUSTED **3 :** completely unwound **:** stopped for want of winding

**rundown** \'=,=\ *n* [*run down*] **1 :** a baseball action in which a runner is caught off base on a base path with two or more opponents throwing the ball back and forth in an attempt to tag him out **2 :** an item-by-item check, investigation, report, analysis, or summary ⟨~ of a suspect's police record⟩ ⟨gave a ~ on current foreign affairs, country by country⟩ ⟨his ~ of the kinds of people who read a newspaper —Edmund Fuller⟩

**rune** \'rün\ *n* -S [ON & OE *rūn* secret, mystery, character of the runic alphabet, writing; akin to OE *rūnian* to whisper, OHG *rūna* secret discussion, *rūnēn* to whisper, ON *reyna* to whisper, Goth *rūna* secret, mystery, and prob. to L *rumor* — more at RUMOR] **1 a :** one of the characters of the runic alphabet **b :** OGHAM **c :** one of the characters of the alphabet of the Orkhon inscriptions **d :** one of the characters of the Szekler alphabet **2 :** a magic incantation **:** CHARM, SPELL **3** [Finn *runo*, of Gmc origin; akin to ON *rūn* secret, mystery, character of the runic alphabet, writing] **a :** a Finnish poem (as the Kalevala or one of its divisions) **b (1) :** an old Norse poem **(2) :** POEM, SONG ⟨the ~s that I rehearse —R.W.Emerson⟩

**runed** \-nd\ *adj* **:** inscribed with runes ⟨~ helmet⟩

**runelike** \'=,=\ *adj* **:** resembling a rune ⟨~ symbol⟩

**rune-master** \'=,==\ *n* **:** maker of runes **:** MAGICIAN ⟨Odin was also the greatest *rune-master* of the ancient Germanic world —Anna C. Paues⟩

**runesmith** \'=,=\ *n* **:** one that writes in or deciphers runes

**rune·staff** \'rün,staf\ *n* [trans. of Sw *runstav*, fr. *runa* rune + *stav* staff] **:** CLOG ALMANAC

**run fish** *n* [*run* fr. past part. of ¹*run*] **:** a spent salmon

**¹rung** [ME *rungen* (past pl. & past part.), alter. prob. influenced by *sungen* sung) of *ringden* (past pl.), *ringed* (past part.), fr. OE *hringdon* (past pl.), *gehringed* (past part.)] *past of* RING

**²rung** \'rəŋ\ *n* -S [ME *rung, rong*, fr. OE *hrung*; akin to MLG & MHG *runge* spoke of a wagon, Goth *hrunga* staff, and perh. to OE *hring* ring — more at RING] **1** *archaic Scot* **:** a heavy stick of wood **:** a stout staff or cudgel **2 a :** a spoke of a wheel **b :** one of the radial handles projecting from the rim of a steering wheel **c :** one of the pins or trundles of a lantern pinion **d :** one of the stakes of a cart **3 a :** a crosspiece between the legs of a chair **b :** one of the crosspieces of a ladder **c :** STAIR, TREAD **4 :** a stage in an ascent **:** STEP, GRADE, DEGREE ⟨reached the top ~ of Hollywood fame —*Irish Digest*⟩ ⟨the son must rise a few ~s on the social scale by studying law —H.W. Van Loon⟩

**³rung** \"\ *adj* [fr. *rung*, obs. past part. of ²*ring*, alter. (influenced by ¹*rung*) of *ringed*] **:** RINGED ⟨fallen trunks of ~ giants have rotted —I.M.Mudie⟩ ⟨sows are ~ to prevent rooting⟩ **:** HOOPED ⟨piles with ~ heads to prevent splitting⟩

**rung·less** \-ŋləs\ *adj* **:** lacking rungs ⟨~ chair⟩

**runholder** \'=,==\ *n, Austral* **:** one that owns or leases a run

**ru·nic** \'rünik, -nēk\ *adj* [*rune* + *-ic*] **1 a :** of, relating to, or consisting of runes ⟨~ inscription⟩ ⟨~ verses⟩ **b :** having secret or magical meaning ⟨~ markings⟩ ⟨~ rhymes⟩ **2 :** of or relating to the ancient Scandinavians ⟨~ poetry⟩ ⟨~ mythology⟩ — **ru·ni·cal·ly** \-nək(ə)lē\ *adv*

**runic alphabet** *n* **1 :** an alphabet orig. of 24 and later of some 16 angular characters prob. derived from both Latin and Greek and used for inscriptions and magic signs by the Germanic peoples from about the 3d to the 13th centuries and esp. by the Scandinavians and Anglo-Saxons — called also *futhark*; compare THORN 3, WEN, YOGH **2 :** the runiform alphabet of the Orkhon inscriptions

**runic cross** *n* **:** CELTIC CROSS

**runic knot** *n* **:** an interlaced ornament found on monuments, jewelry, and metalwork of the early northern European peoples

**runic staff** *n* **:** CLOG ALMANAC

**run·i·form** \'rünə,fȯrm\ *adj* [*rune* + *-iform*] **:** resembling the ancient runes in form or appearance

**run in** *vt* **1 a :** to make (typeset matter) continuous without a paragraph or other break **b :** to insert as additional matter **c :** to give paragraph indention to (a subhead) and make part of the running text **d :** to load (matrices) into a typesetting machine in which matrix distribution is automatic **2 :** to arrest for a minor offense ⟨got drunk the other night and the coppers *run* me *in* —Carl Sandburg⟩ ⟨*run in* for speeding⟩ **3 :** to operate (a newly built machine) long enough and at the proper speeds to cause the bearing surfaces to so wear that the machine may be satisfactorily operated under service conditions ~ *vi* **1** *of typeset matter* **:** to come short of filling the estimated space **2 :** to pay a casual visit ⟨lived close by and was used to *running in* whenever he liked⟩

**run-in** \'=,=\ *n* -S [*run in*] **1 :** something inserted as a substantial addition in copy or typeset matter **2** *Brit* **:** the finish of a race or hunt **3 :** TIFF, ALTERCATION, QUARREL ⟨*run-ins* of tourists with taximen —A.D.Sheffield⟩ **4 :** the operation of running in a new engine or machine

**run-in groove** \'=,=-\ *n* **:** LEAD-IN GROOVE

**r unit** *n* **:** ROENTGEN

**ru·nite** \'rü,nīt\ *n* -S [*rune* + *-ite*] **:** GRAPHIC GRANITE

**run lace** *n* **:** needlerun lace

**run·less** \'rənləs\ *adj* **:** scoring no runs ⟨held the visiting team ~ for eight innings⟩

**¹runlet** *var of* RUNDLET

**²run·let** \'rənlət\ *n* -S [²*run* + *-let*] **:** RUNNEL

**run·na·ble** \'rənəbəl\ *adj* [¹*run* + *-able*] **:** capable of being run; *esp* **:** suitable to be hunted ⟨~ stag⟩

**run·nel** \'rənᵊl\ *n* -S [alter. (influenced by ¹*run*), of earlier *rinel*, fr. ME, fr. OE *rynel*, fr. the stem of *rinnan* to run, flow — more at RUN] **1 :** RIVULET, BROOK, STREAMLET **2 a :** the channel eroded by a small stream **b :** a small trough formed by wave or current action on a sea or lake bottom just offshore

**run·ner** \'rənə(r)\ *n* -S [ME *rinner, renner*, fr. *rinnen, rennen* to run + *-er*] **1 :** one capable of running ⟨the cheetah is the fastest ~ of all animals⟩ **:** RACER **2 a :** a horse entered in a race ⟨eight ~s in the final race of the day⟩ **b (1) :** a cricket batsman attempting to score a run; *specif* **:** a substitute allowed to run for an injured batsman **(2) :** BASE RUNNER **(3) :** a football player in possession of a live ball **c :** a man in backgammon that starts from the opponent's home table **d :** a bird that characteristically runs or scuttles along the ground; *specif* **:** WATER RAIL **e :** a wounded bird that moves fast but cannot fly **f :** a popular fast-selling item of merchandise **3 :** one whose occupation requires physical movement from place to place: as **a :** one that delivers messages, reports, materials, or products for a business organization either within the establishment or to outside locations **b :** a police officer or police detective in 18th century London — see BOW STREET RUNNER **c :** one that makes a business of running for things in return for the gratuities received ⟨a ~ called a cab for him⟩ **d :** COMMISSIONAIRE **e :** a messenger between headquarters of military units esp. during action **f :** an agent who accepts, transmits, and pays bets for a numbers game or a bookmaker **g :** one that smuggles or distributes illegal drugs ⟨dope ~⟩ **4 :** one that operates or manages something: **a :** a workman that operates a carrying vehicle (as in a mine) **:** DROPPER **b :** one that operates a machine **c :** a seaman engaged for a short single voyage **d :** the driver of a locomotive **5 a :** any of various large active carangid fishes: as **(1) :** RAINBOW RUNNER **(2) :** BLUE RUNNER **(3) :** LEATHERJACKET 1b **b** *Africa* **:** COBIA **c :** INDIAN RUNNER **d :** BLACKSNAKE 1a **6 a :** a ship of exceptional speed used for dispatches without convoy **b :** a ship that runs a blockade or carries smuggled goods **c :** RUNBOAT **7 a :** either of the longitudinal pieces on which a sled or sleigh slides **b :** the part of a skate that slides on the ice **:** BLADE **c :** ²SKATE 1a **d :** a horizontal longitudinal timber on the top of a scaffold or staging carrying a line of rails (as for a hoisting apparatus) **:** STRINGER, STRINGPIECE **e :** the support of a drawer or a sliding door **8 a :** a growth produced by a plant in running; *usu* **:** STOLON 1 **b :** a plant that forms or spreads by means of runners **c :** a twining vine — not used technically; see SCARLET RUNNER **9 a :** a rope rove through a single movable block and usu. attached to a luff tackle **b :** a backstay running from mast to rail of a sailing ship and adjustable by means of a tackle or lever **10 runners** *pl, chiefly dial* **:** the small intestine of a domestic animal **11 a :** a carpet adapted by its long and narrow shape for extending along a hall or passageway or staircase **b :** a narrow decorative cloth cover for the top of a piece of furniture (as a table, dresser) **12 a :** the rotating stone of a set of millstones **b :** a movable slab used in grinding or polishing stone or glass **13 a :** a movable pulley block running on a fall that is fixed at one end **b :** IDLER WHEEL **c :** the impeller of a pump **d :** either of the sliding centers of a watchmaker's lathe **e :** a train of wheels for regulating the speed of striking in a repeating watch **f :** the revolving part of a turbine **g :** the driven member of an automotive hydraulic coupling or transmission **h :** a rotary tool for running a nut on a bolt or screw **14 a :** the sliding piece of an umbrella to which the ribs are attached **b :** a piece bearing a hairline that slides along the outer scale of a slide rule **15 :** a channel or trough for conducting molten metal into a mold **16 :** RUN 12a **17** *Brit* **:** any of the numbers placed consecutively at the ends of lines of a printed text

**runner bean** *also* **runner** *n* -S *chiefly Brit* **:** SCARLET RUNNER

**runner peanut** *n* **:** a peanut having a low prostrate plant with pods at the base and along procumbent rooting stems — compare BUNCH PEANUT

**runner stick** *n* **:** GATE PIN

**runner-up** \'=;=\ *n, pl* **runners-up 1 :** one that raises or runs up bids at an auction **2 :** a competitor receiving a prize or special recognition but not winning first place in a contest ⟨a thousand-dollar prize for the best window display . . . "crinkly fifty-dollar bills" to the ten *runners-up* —Bennett Cerf⟩; *esp* **:** one winning second place ⟨won the conference . . . in addition to one third place, three *runners-up*, and three state championships —*Athletic Jour.*⟩

**run·net** \'rənət, 'rün-\ *dial var of* RENNET

**runnier** *comparative of* RUNNY

**runniest** *superlative of* RUNNY

**run·ni·ness** \'rənēnəs\ *n* -ES **:** the quality or state of being runny **:** FLUIDITY

**¹run·ning** \'rəniŋ, -nēŋ\ *n* -S [ME *running, ronning, rinning, renning*, fr. gerund of *runnen, ronnen, rinnen, rennen* to run — more at RUN] **1 :** the act of racing **:** RACE **2 :** strength or ability to run ⟨still had a lot of ~ left in him at the finish **3 :** the condition of a surface to be run on ⟨kept to the outside of the track where the ~ was better⟩ **4 :** the quantity of a liquid that flows (as in a certain time or during a particular operation) ⟨the first ~ of a still⟩ ⟨early ~ of sap⟩ **5 :** control of operation **:** MANAGEMENT, CARE ⟨has the ~ of two machines at the same time⟩ — **in the running 1 :** entered as a competitor in a contest **2 :** having a chance of winning a contest

**²running** \"\ *adj* [ME *running, ronning, rinning, renning*, fr. pres. part. of *runnen, ronnen, rinnen, rennen*] **1 :** FLUID, RUNNY ⟨~ bog⟩ **2 :** continuing step by step or from place to place without pause **:** CONTINUOUS ⟨~ fire of machine guns and rifles⟩ ⟨retreating troops fought a ~ battle⟩ ⟨the text forms a ~ comment on the pictures⟩ ⟨~ record of cash expenditures⟩ **3 :** measured linearly **:** LINEAR ⟨cost of lumber per ~ foot⟩ **4 :** FLOWING, EASY, CURSIVE ⟨~ hand in writing⟩ ⟨a ~ rhythm in music⟩; *specif* **:** having the flow natural to ordinary expression or statement ⟨pronunciation of a word in ~ speech⟩ **5 :** not fixed or definite in its effect or application but left open for future determination ⟨~ lease⟩ ⟨~ insurance policy⟩ ⟨~ writ⟩ **6 :** initiated or performed with impetus from running **:** executed with a running start or with emphasis on running ⟨the team's ~ plays worked better than its pass plays⟩ **7 :** fitted or trained for running rather than walking, trotting, jumping ⟨~ horse⟩

**³running** \"\ *adv* [fr. pres. part. of ¹*run*] **:** in unbroken succession **:** CONSECUTIVELY ⟨won the championship 3 years ~⟩

**running account** *n* **:** CURRENT ACCOUNT 1

**running backstay** *n* **:** RUNNER 9 b

**running bale** *n* **:** a bale of cotton as it comes from the gin weighing 500 to 508 lbs

**running birch** *n* **:** CREEPING SNOWBERRY

**running blackberry** *n* **:** DEWBERRY

**running block** *n* **:** a movable pulley block that rises or sinks with the weight that is raised or lowered — distinguished from *standing block*

**running board** *n* **:** a footboard on the side of an automobile or locomotive or on the roof of a freight car

**running bond** *n* **:** a masonry bond in which each brick is laid as a stretcher overlapping the bricks in the adjoining courses

**running bowline** *n* **:** a slip noose made by tying a bowline knot with the end of a line around its own standing part

running bowline

**running bowsprit** *n* **:** a bowsprit that can be run in or rigged in when headsails are taken off

**running brand** *n* **:** a cattle brand made by drawing a figure with a simple iron instead of stamping with a set shape

**running days** *n pl* **:** the consecutive calendar days occupied on a voyage (as under a charter party)

**running-down clause** \';==';=-\ *n* **:** COLLISION CLAUSE

**running english** *n, usu cap E* **:** side spin imparted to a cue ball so as to increase the angle of rebound — compare REVERSE ENGLISH

**running expenses** *n pl* **:** daily, current, or ordinary and necessary expenses **:** operating costs

**running fit** *n* **:** contact of mechanical parts that permits free rotation or movement

**running fits** *n pl but sing or pl in constr* **:** CANINE HYSTERIA

**running fix** *n* **:** a navigational position determined by the intersection of two or more lines of position taken at different times and then advanced to a common time

**running gate** *n* **:** a gate through which molten metal runs into a mold

**running gear** *n* **1 :** RUNNING RIGGING **2 a :** the wheels and axles of a wagon or carriage in distinction from the body **b :** the parts of an automobile chassis (as the frame, springs, axles, and wheels) not used in developing, transmitting, and controlling power **c :** the working and carrying parts of a locomotive or a machine in distinction from the framework

**running hand** *n* **:** handwriting in which the letters are usu. slanted and the words formed without lifting the pen

**running head** *or* **running headline** *n* **:** RUNNING TITLE; *also* **:** a line at the head of a page (as of a book or magazine) carrying the title or publication name and sometimes other matter (as folio, dateline, chapter number, part number)

**running inventory** *n* **:** PERPETUAL INVENTORY

**running iron** *n* **:** a branding iron with which a brand is drawn freehand on the hide of an animal

**running key** *n* **:** an unpredictable keying sequence (as a text used as a key by prearrangement)

**running knot** *n* **:** a knot that slips along the rope or line round which it is tied **:** a knot used to form a running noose; *esp* **:** an overhand slip knot

**running light** *n* **:** one of the lights carried by a ship under way at night and comprising a green light on the starboard side, a red light on the port side, and on a steamer a white light at the foremast head; *also* **:** one of a similar set of lights carried on the wingtips and fuselage of an airplane

**running line** *n* **1 :** a line carried from a ship by boat to a wharf, buoy, or other ship **:** GUESS-WARP 1 **2 :** a light line used in hauling a heavy line (as a mooring or towing cable)

**run·ning·ly** *adv* **:** in a running, rapid, or flowing manner

**running mallow** *n* **:** DWARF MALLOW

**running mate** *n* **1 :** a horse entered in a race to set the pace for a horse of the same owner or stable that is being ridden to win **2 :** a candidate running for a subordinate place on a ticket; *esp* **:** the candidate for vice-president considered in relation to the candidate for president **3 :** a staff officer's opposite on the line officers' promotion list with whose promotion the staff officer is advanced in grade on the same date **4 :** a person frequently seen in close association with another **:** COMPANION

**running milkweed** *n* **:** NEGRO VINE

**running myrtle** *n* **:** PERIWINKLE 1 a

**running oak** *n* **:** MOUNTAIN MISERY

**running ornament** *n* **:** an ornamental decoration (as on a band) formed with a continuous design **:** FRET, WAVE

**running part** *n* **:** the part of a tackle that is hauled upon — distinguished from *standing part*

**running pine** *n* **:** CORAL EVERGREEN

**running rail** *n* **:** a rail that acts as a running surface for the flanged wheels of a car or locomotive — compare GUARDRAIL, THIRD RAIL

**running rigging** *n* **:** rigging that is used primarily in setting, furling, and otherwise handling sails and movable spars or in handling cargo and that usu. runs through blocks or pulleys — compare STANDING RIGGING

**running rope** *n* **:** rope used in running rigging **:** hoisting or hauling rope — distinguished from *standing rope*

**runnings** *pl of* RUNNING

**running set** *n* **:** a folk dance of Kentucky and the Great Smoky mountains that combines couple figures of square dancing with the circular progression of a round

**running shoe** *n* **:** a soft leather shoe with spiked soles esp. designed for foot racing

**running shooting** *n* **:** shooting at a running target

**running side** *n, Brit* **:** RUNNING ENGLISH

**running spider** *n* **:** a spider that builds no web but hunts its prey by running

**running start** *n* **1 :** a start effected by setting off the competitors in a race from a point behind the starting line so that they are in rapid motion when crossing that line **2 :** a great initial impetus or advantage in carrying out a project

**running stitch** *n* **:** a small even stitch usu. run on a needle in groups (as for seaming, gathering, quilting)

**running story** *n* **1 :** a story that is continued in two or more issues of a newspaper or magazine **2 :** a newspaper story received or sent to the composing room in takes

**running strawberry-bush** *n* **:** a deciduous prostrate shrub (*Euonymus obodatus*) of eastern No. America that has rooting branches and obovate finely serrate leaves

**running text** *n* **:** straight matter

**running title** *n* **:** the title or short title of a volume printed at the top of left-hand text pages or sometimes of all text pages — called also *running head*

**running toad** *n* **:** NATTERJACK

**running track** *n* **1 :** a track reserved for movement through a railroad yard **:** a thoroughfare track **2 :** a track for running foot races

**running trap** *n* **:** a trap (as a U trap) in a pipe permitting liquid flow but forming a barrier against sewer gases

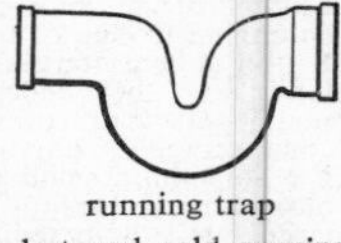
running trap

**running walk** *n* **:** a slow easy 4-beat gait of a horse in which one hindleg touches the ground just before the opposite foreleg

**running water** *n* **1 :** water flowing in a stream or river **:** water that is not stagnant or brackish **2 :** water made available through a pipe ⟨cabins with hot and cold *running water*⟩

**running wheel** *n* **:** TREADWHEEL

**run·ny** \'rənē, -ni\ *adj, sometimes* -ER/-EST [¹*run* + *-y*] **:** having a tendency to run: as **a :** excessively soft and liquid ⟨a ~ dough⟩ ⟨meringue that will not hold its shape but turns ~⟩ **b :** secreting mucus ⟨watery eyes and a ~ nose⟩

**run off** *vt* **1 a :** to recite or compose rapidly or glibly **:** dash off ⟨*run off* a letter⟩ **b :** to produce by a printing press or an analogous process ⟨*ran off* 10,000 copies of the first edition⟩ ⟨*run* a batch of mimeographed sheets *off*⟩ **c :** to cause (a race) to be run **:** cause (as a match, a tournament) to be played to a finish **d :** to decide (as a race) by a runoff **e :** to carry out (a test) **2 :** to cause (as molten metals) to flow away **:** draw off **:** drain off **3 a :** to drive off (as trespassers) or dispossess ⟨soldiers . . . raided the town's laundry, *ran off* the Chinese proprietor, and took all the clothing —*Amer. Guide Series: Wash.*⟩ **b :** to steal (as cattle) by driving away ⟨most of his stock was *run off* by Indians⟩ ~ *vi* **1 :** to run away ⟨snatched up the purse and *ran off*⟩ **2** *of bills payable* **:** to cease to exist by being paid at maturity — **run off with :** to carry off **:** STEAL

**runoff** \'=,=\ *n* -S [*run off*] **1 a :** the portion of the precipitation on the land that ultimately reaches streams and thence the sea; *esp* **:** the water from rain or melted snow that flows over the surface **b :** syrup that has been drawn off the sugar crystals **2 :** a final race, contest, or election to decide an earlier one that has not resulted in a decision in favor of any one competitor **3 :** a gradually increasing superelevation applied to a tangent on a railroad track or highway just adjacent to the easement to a curve **4** *NewZeal* **:** an area of pastureland not adjacent to the farm

**runoff primary** *n* **:** a second primary election held in some states to decide which of the two highest candidates for an office in the first primary will be awarded the party nomination

**run of mine :** ore or coal as it comes from the mine without grading or sorting for size or quality

**run-of-mine** \ˌ==ˌ=\ *or* **run-of-the-mine** \ˌ===ˌ=\ *adj* [*run of mine*] **1 :** UNGRADED, UNSORTED, CRUDE, UNREFINED **:** not ground or treated **2 :** ORDINARY, MEDIOCRE, RUN-OF-MILL ⟨*run-of-mine* college graduate⟩

**run-of-paper** \ˌ==ˌ==\ *adj* **:** to be placed anywhere in a newspaper at the option or discretion of the editor ⟨*run-of-paper* advertisement⟩ — abbr. *R.O.P.*

**run-of-river** \ˌ==ˌ==\ *adj* **:** operating on the flow of the river without modification by upstream storage ⟨*run-of-river* power plant⟩

**[1]run-of-the-mill** \ˌ===ˌ=\ *n* **:** manufactured goods not graded or sorted for quality

**[2]run-of-the-mill** *adj* **:** not outstanding in quality or rarity **:** AVERAGE, MEDIOCRE ⟨*run-of-the-mill* politician⟩ ⟨*run-of-the-mill* boxing⟩

**ru·no·log·i·cal** \ˌrünəˈläjəkəl\ *adj* **:** of or relating to runology

**ru·nol·o·gist** \rüˈnäləjəst\ *n* -s **:** a specialist in the study of runes and runic writings

**ru·nol·o·gy** \-jē\ *n* -ES [*rune* + *-o-* + *-logy*] **:** the study of runes and runic writings

**run on** *vi* **1 :** to keep going **:** CONTINUE ⟨if the disease is allowed to *run on* unchecked⟩ ⟨let an account *run on*⟩ **2 :** to talk or narrate at length ⟨*ran on* endlessly about his family⟩ ⟨apt to *run on* at the slightest provocation⟩ ~ *vt* **1 :** to carry on (matter in type) without a break or a new paragraph **:** run in **2 :** to place or add (as an entry in a dictionary) at the end of a paragraphed item

**[1]run-on** \ˈ=ˌ=\ *adj* [fr. *run on*, past part. of *run on*] **:** continuing without rhetorical pause from one line of verse into another **:** characterized by enjambment — contrasted with *end-stopped*

**[2]run-on** \ˈ=ˌ=\ *n* -s **:** something (as a dictionary entry) that is run on

**run-on couplet** *n* **:** OPEN COUPLET

**run-on sentence** *n* **1 :** a sentence formed with a comma fault **2 :** a sentence that rambles on by the slipshod adding on of clauses

**run out** *vi* **1 a :** to come to an end **:** expire ⟨the lease *runs out* next month⟩ **b :** to become exhausted or used up **:** FAIL ⟨food supplies had *run out* toward the end of the trip⟩ ⟨his patience had *run out*⟩ **c :** to come to the end of a supply ⟨have we enough milk so that we won't *run out* before the next delivery⟩ **d :** to lose distinguishing breed or varietal characters esp. as a result of inbreeding or indiscriminate breeding ⟨a herd of Herefords had been allowed to *run out*⟩ **2 :** to jut out ⟨where the land *runs out* to form a cape⟩ ~ *vt* **1 :** to finish out (as a course, a series, a contest) **:** COMPLETE; *specif* **:** *of a baseball batter* **:** to run hard to first base after (a hit) esp. when a put-out is likely ⟨the runner must *run* everything *out* if he wants the breaks —W.L.Myers⟩ **2 a :** to fill out (a line) with quads, leaders, or ornaments **b :** to set (as the first line of a paragraph) with a hanging indention **3 :** to exhaust (oneself) in running ⟨*ran* himself *out* in the first mile⟩ **4 :** FAN 7b **5 :** to put out (a cricket batsman) during an attempted run by breaking the wicket with a fielded ball **6 :** to cause to leave by force or coercion **:** EXPEL ⟨if the gamblers don't leave town they will be *run out*⟩ — **run out of :** to use up or come to the end of the available supply of ⟨*ran out of* gas a mile from home⟩ ⟨always *running out of* money before payday⟩ — **run out on :** to fail to support **:** leave in the lurch **:** DESERT ⟨his former allies *ran out on* him⟩ **:** FORSAKE ⟨if the boy senses that his girl is *running out* on him he too is hurt —Evelyn M. Duvall⟩

**runout** \ˈ=ˌ=\ *n* -s [*run out*] **1 :** the amount that one surface (as the outside surface of a cylindrical sleeve) lacks of being true with another surface of the same part (as the inside surface of the sleeve) **2 :** the greatest distance that a moving part of a machine can travel away from a fixed reference point ⟨~ of the plunger of a hydraulic press⟩ **3 :** an instance of running out a cricket batsman ⟨on no account throw hard to the bowler unless there is a good chance of a *runout* —*Calling All Cricketers*⟩ **4 :** an act of escape or desertion ⟨a divorce caused by an agrarian ~ on the partnership is labor's nightmare —*N.Y. Times*⟩

**run-out groove** \ˈ=ˌ=-\ *n* **:** a lead-out groove on a phonograph record

**runout powder** *n, slang* **:** RUNOUT, DESERTION, ESCAPE — used chiefly in the phrase *take a runout powder*

**run over** *vi* **1 :** OVERFLOW ⟨my cup *runneth over* —Ps 23:5 (AV)⟩ **2 :** to exceed a limit ⟨delay caused by the radio program *running over*⟩ **3** *of a steam engine* **:** to throw over ~ *vt* **1 :** to go over, examine, repeat, or rehearse ⟨considered all possible ways of escape, *running* them *over* swiftly in his mind⟩ ⟨let's *run* this song *over* a couple of times⟩ **2 :** to collide with, knock down, and often drive over

**run-over** \ˈ=ˌ==\ *adj* [fr. *run over*, past part. of *run over*] **1 :** extending beyond the allotted space ⟨*run-over* matter in printing⟩ **2 :** worn at one side ⟨*run-over* heels⟩

**runover** \ˈ=ˌ==\ *n* -s [in sense 1, fr. *run-over;* in sense 2, fr. *run over*] **1 :** typeset matter that exceeds the space estimated or allotted **2 :** BREAKOVER ⟨a two-column front-page lead story with a three-column ~ —A.J.Liebling⟩

**runproof** \ˈ=ˌ=\ *adj* **:** resistant to runs ⟨~ stockings⟩ ⟨~ dye⟩

**run·rig** \ˈrənˌrig\ *n* [ME *rynrig*, fr. *ryn*, *rin* run + *rig* — more at RUN] **:** RUNDALE

**runround** \ˈ=ˌ=\ *n* -s [fr. *run round*, v.] **:** RUNAROUND 1

**runs** *pres 3d sing of* RUN, *pl of* RUN

**run sheep run** *n* **:** a game in which one group of players hide and their leader tries to guide them safely home by calling "run, sheep, run" when he thinks they can escape being caught by those searching

**runt** \ˈrənt\ *n* -s *except sense 5 a* [origin unknown] **1 a** *chiefly dial* **:** the dead stump or trunk of a tree **b** *chiefly Scot* **:** a usu. hardened stalk or stem of a plant **2 :** an ox or cow belonging to one of the breeds of small British upland cattle **3 :** an animal unusually small as compared with others of its kind; *esp* **:** the smallest of a litter of pigs **4 a :** a person of small stature or stunted growth — usu. used disparagingly ⟨one scraggly, starved little ~ of a man —Ira Wolfert⟩ **b :** something small and contemptible **c** *chiefly Scot* **:** an old withered person **5 a** *usu cap* **:** an old breed of very large but slow-breeding domestic pigeons usu. white, blue, or silvery with barred wings and iridescent neck **b** *sometimes cap* **:** a bird of this breed **6 :** a poor hand in poker and some other card games; *specif* **:** a poker hand of less value than a pair

**runt·ed** \-təd\ *adj* **:** RUNTY, STUNTED ⟨discarding the ~ ears of corn⟩

**run through** *vt* **1 :** to pierce with or as if with a sword **2 :** to spend or consume wastefully ⟨inherited a fortune but *ran* it *through* in no time⟩ **3 :** to read or rehearse without pausing ⟨the cast *ran through* the whole play once without lights or scenery⟩

**run-through** \ˈ=ˌ=\ *n* -s [*run through*] **1 a :** a cursory reading **b :** a rapid or cursory summary ⟨a *run-through* of the week's events⟩ **c :** a single rehearsal of an entire piece or program **2** *Brit* **:** FOLLOW SHOT

**runt·i·ness** \ˈrəntēnəs, -tin-\ *n* -ES **:** the quality of being small or poorly developed

**runt·ish** \-tish\ *adj* **:** RUNTY, STUNTED — **runt·ish·ly** *adv* — **runt·ish·ness** *n* -ES

**runty** \-tē, -ti\ *adj* -ER/-EST **1 :** like a runt **:** UNDERSIZED **2** *dial* **:** MEAN, SURLY

**run up** *vi* **:** to grow rapidly **:** shoot up ⟨his debts *ran up* alarmingly by the week⟩ ~ *vt* **1 :** to increase by bidding **:** bid up ⟨professional traders had *run* the price *up*⟩ **2 :** to stitch quickly ⟨to *run up* a seam⟩ ⟨to *run up* a dress in a morning⟩ **3 :** to erect hastily ⟨*run up* an apartment house⟩ ⟨*run up* a circus tent⟩ **4 :** to add (a column of figures) rapidly **5 :** to shuffle (the pack) so that certain combinations of cards shall come out in desired order **6 :** to operate (an aircraft engine) at a high rate of speed either in a stationary aircraft or on a test stand in order to test, check, or warm the engine

**run-up** \ˈ=ˌ=\ *n* -s [*run up*] **:** the act of running up something ⟨a *run-up* of a golf ball to the putting green⟩ ⟨a *run-up* of a polo ball to the goal⟩ ⟨a *run-up* of prices in the stock market⟩; *specif* **:** acceleration of an aircraft engine on the ground for testing and checking

**runway** \ˈ=ˌ=\ *n* [[1]*run* + *way*] **1 :** the channel of a stream **2 :** the beaten path made by animals in passing to and from their feeding grounds **:** TRAIL, RUN **3 a :** a passageway for animals **b :** a space provided for exercise ⟨~ for chickens⟩ **4 :** a road on which logs are skidded **5 a :** a way or gauged track for wheeled vehicles, conveyors, overhead hoist **b :** an artificially surfaced or paved strip of ground on a landing field for the landing and takeoff of airplanes **6 :** a narrow platform or bridge leading from a stage into the auditorium to enable the players to perform in the midst of the audience **7 a :** a path along which a jumper or pole vaulter runs in approaching the takeoff **b :** the area behind the foul line on which a bowler makes his approach and delivers the ball

**ru·pee** \rüˈpē, ˈ=(ˌ)=\ *n* -s [Hindi *rūpaiyā*, *rupīyā*, fr. Skt *rūpya* silver, coined silver, fr. *rūpa* form, beauty] **1 a :** the basic monetary unit in India, Pakistan, Ceylon, and Nepal — see MONEY table **b :** the unit in several other territories including Mauritius, Seychelles, and some coastal areas of the Arabian peninsula **2 :** a coin representing one rupee

**ru·pert's drop** \ˈrüpərts-\ *n, usu cap R* [after Prince *Rupert* †1682 nephew of Charles I of England] **:** a congealed blob of glass formed by dropping melted glass into water and setting up such residual stresses that the globule explodes violently when the surface is scratched or a piece broken off

**ru·pes·tri·an** \rüˈpestrēən\ *or* **ru·pes·tral** \-rəl\ *adj* [NL *rupestris* rupestrian (fr. L *rupes* rock + *-estris*, as in *terrestris* terrestrial) + E *-an* or *-al;* akin to L *rumpere* to break — more at REAVE] **:** composed of rock **:** inscribed on rocks

**ru·pes·trine** \rüˈpestrən\ *adj* [L *rupes* rock + E *-trine* (as in palus*trine*)] **:** RUPICOLOUS

**[1]ru·pia** \ˈrüpēə\ *n* -s [NL, irreg. fr. Gk *rhypos* dirt, filth + NL *-ia;* perh. akin to OSlav *strupŭ* wound] **:** an eruption occurring esp. in tertiary syphilis consisting of vesicles having an inflamed base and filled with serous purulent or bloody fluid which dries up and forms large blackish conical crusts — **ru·pi·al** \-əl\ *adj*

**[2]ru·pia** \rüˈpēə\ *n* -s [Pg, fr. Hindi *rūpaiyā*, *rupīyā* rupee — more at RUPEE] **:** the rupee of Portuguese India

**ru·pi·ah** \rüˈpēə\ *n, pl* **rupiah** *or* **rupiahs** [Hindi *rūpaiyā*, *rupīyā* rupee] **1 :** the basic monetary unit of Indonesia — see MONEY table **2 :** a note representing one rupiah

**ru·pi·cap·ra** \ˌrüpəˈkaprə\ *n, cap* [NL, fr. L, chamois, fr. *rupes* rock + *-i-* + *capra* she-goat — more at RUPESTRIAN, CAPRA] **:** a genus of mammals (family Bovidae) consisting of the chamois

**ru·pi·cap·rine** \ˌ==ˈkaˌprīn, -ˌprən\ *adj* [NL *Rupicapra* + E *-ine*] **:** of or relating to the genus *Rupicapra*

**ru·pic·o·la** \rüˈpikələ\ *n, cap* [NL, fr. L *rupi-* (fr. *rupes* rock) + NL *-cola*] **:** a genus of birds (family Cotingidae) containing the cock of the rock

**ru·pic·o·lous** \-ləs\ *or* **ru·pic·o·line** \-kəˌlīn, -kələn\ *adj* [L *rupi-* + E *-colous*, *-coline*] **:** living among, inhabiting, or growing on rocks

**rup·pia** \ˈrəpēə\ *n, cap* [NL, fr. Heinrich B. *Ruppius* (Rupp) †1719 Ger. botanist + NL *-ia*] **:** a small genus of widely distributed submerged marine herbs (family Hydrocharitaceae) having capillary stems, slender alternate leaves, and monoecious flowers destitute of perianth — see DITCH GRASS

**[1]rup·ture** \ˈrəpchə(r), -psh-\ *n* -s [ME *ruptur*, fr. MF or L; MF *rupture*, fr. L *ruptura* fracture, break, fr. *ruptus* (past part. of *rumpere* to break) + *-ura* -ure — more at REAVE] **1 a :** breach of peace or concord; *specif* **:** open hostility or war between nations ⟨could not assume the responsibility of a ~ and would support the principle of arbitration —C.L. Jones⟩ **b :** a breach of the harmonious relationship between two parties ⟨mother and son avoided an open ~ —George Santayana⟩ **2 a :** the tearing apart by force, disease, or other cause of an organ or structure ⟨the ~ of the heart muscle⟩ ⟨the ~ of an intervertebral disk⟩ **b** [ML *ruptura*, fr. L, fracture, break] **:** HERNIA **3 :** a break in the earth's surface (as a gorge or ravine) **4 :** a breaking apart **:** SEPARATING **:** the state of being broken apart ⟨the last telegram sent . . . before the ~ of the wire —W.H.G.Kingston⟩ ⟨the ~ of the moral code can break down the power of principle —E.T.Thurston⟩ **syn** see BREACH

**[2]rupture** \"\ *vb* **ruptured**; **ruptured**; **rupturing** \-pchəriŋ, psh(ə)riŋ\ **ruptures** *vt* **1 a :** to part by violence **:** BREAK, BURST ⟨her nurse became alarmed and said she would ~ her stitches —Marcia Davenport⟩ **b :** to create or induce a breach of ⟨even at the expense of *rupturing* Arab unity —Denis Healey⟩ **2 :** to produce a hernia in ~ *vi* **:** to have a break or rupture

**ruptured** *adj* **1 :** torn apart **:** burst asunder **:** BROKEN ⟨~ water mains increased the misery of the flood victims⟩ ⟨beyond the ~ wire fence lay . . . cramped frame houses —W.B.Marsh⟩ **2 :** having a rupture or a hernia ⟨a ~ appendix⟩

**ruptured duck** *n, slang* **:** the symbol of an eagle with outspread wings depicted in the honorable service emblem for men and women of the U.S. armed forces

**rupturewort** \ˈ==ˌ=\ *n* **:** a plant of the genus *Herniaria; esp* **:** a common prostrate Old World herb (*H. glabra*) formerly reputed to cure ruptures and sometimes used as a ground cover

**[1]ru·ral** \ˈru̇rəl, ˈrür-\ *adj* [ME, fr. MF, fr. L *ruralis*, fr. *rur-*, *rus* country, open land + *-alis* -al — more at ROOM] **1 :** living in country areas **:** engaged in agricultural pursuits ⟨a ~ people⟩ ⟨elected by constituencies which are basically ~ —*New Republic*⟩ **2 :** characterized by simplicity **:** lacking sophistication **:** UNCOMPLICATED ⟨in search of ~ life — Christopher Rand⟩ ⟨poetry is very, very ~ —Robert Frost⟩ ⟨programs of ballads and ~ dances —Marinobel Smith⟩ **3 :** of, relating to, or characteristic of people who live in the country ⟨his long knotty ~ fingers —Edmund Wilson⟩ ⟨modern warfare no longer calls for ~ stamina —Alfred Vagts⟩ ⟨a gardener who looked excessively ~ —Rebecca West⟩ **4 :** of, relating to, associated with, or typical of the country ⟨~ architecture was reflected in houses with low, plain walls —*Amer. Guide Series: Mich.*⟩ ⟨crowds welcomed us at each ~ town —A.C.Fisher⟩ ⟨under this legislation, a ~ area includes most places with fewer than 1,500 people —J.H. Ferguson & D.E.McHenry⟩ **5 :** of, relating to, or constituting a tenement in land adapted and used for agricultural or pastoral purposes — opposed to *urban*

**[2]rural** \"\ *n* -s **:** one who lives in the country

**rural dean** *n* **:** an ecclesiastic ranking immediately under an archdeacon and appointed as a diocesan official to supervise the affairs of a group of parishes constituting a division of an archdeaconry

**rural district** *n* **:** a subdivision of an administrative county that usu. embraces several country parishes and is governed by a council — see DISTRICT COUNCIL; compare URBAN DISTRICT

**ru·ra·les** \rüˈräˌlās\ *n pl* [MexSp, fr. Sp, adj., pl. of *rural*, fr. L *ruralis* — more at RURAL] **:** the Mexican rural mounted constabulary

**rural free delivery** *also* **rural delivery** *n* **:** the free delivery of mail by the U.S. postal service usu. from the nearest post office having carrier service to a rural area not served directly by a post office or having only a small post office without carriers — abbr. *RFD*, *RD*

**ru·ral·ism** \ˈru̇rəˌlizəm, ˈrür-\ *n* -s **1 :** the quality or state of being rural **2 :** a rural idiom or expression

**ru·ral·ist** \-ˌləst\ *or* **ru·ral·ite** \-ˌlīt\ *n* -s [[1]*rural* + *-ist* or *-ite*] **1 :** an inhabitant of the country **:** FARMER **2 :** one who advocates life in the country as contrasted with life in a city

**ru·ral·i·ty** \ru̇ˈraləd·ē\ *n* -ES [[1]*rural* + *-ity*] **:** RURALISM **:** a rural place

**ru·ral·iza·tion** \ˌru̇rələˈzāshən\ *n* -s **:** the act of becoming ruralized

**ru·ral·ize** \ˈru̇rəˌlīz, ˈrür-\ *vb* -ED/-ING/-S [[1]*rural* + *-ize*] *vt* **:** to make rural **:** give a rural appearance to ~ *vi* **:** to go into the country **:** RUSTICATE ⟨*ruralizing* with my ancient cousin —*Lippincott's Mag.*⟩

**ru·ral·ly** \-əlē\ *adv* **:** in a rural manner

**rural route** *or* **rural delivery route** *n* **:** a mail-delivery route in a rural free delivery area served by a regular postal carrier and beginning and ending at the same post office — compare STAR ROUTE

**rural servitude** *n, Roman, civil, & Scots law* **:** a servitude affecting chiefly or solely the soil or land and imposed upon a rural tenement or estate — compare URBAN SERVITUDE

**rural sociology** *n* **:** a branch of sociology dealing with the study of rural communities and the rural way of life — compare URBAN SOCIOLOGY

**rur·ban** \ˈrərbən, ˈru̇r-\ *adj* [blend of [1]*rural* and *urban*] **1 :** relating to or living in a community, zone, or town which is primarily residential but where some farming is engaged in **2 :** situated or living outside the city limits but not on a farm

**ru·ri·decanal** \ˌru̇rə+\ *adj* [L *ruri-* (fr. *rur-*, *rus* country) + E *decanal* — more at ROOM] **:** of or relating to a rural dean

**ru·rig·e·nous** \ru̇ˈrijənəs\ *adj* [L *ruri-* + E *-genous*] **:** born or living in the country

**ru·ri·ta·ni·an** \ˌru̇rəˈtānēən\ *adj, usu cap* [*Ruritania*, fictional kingdom in the romantic novel *The Prisoner of Zenda* (1894) by Anthony Hope (Sir Anthony Hope Hawkins) †1933 Eng. writer + E *-an*] **:** of, relating to, or having the characteristics of an imaginary place of high romance ⟨indulged in a sort of *Ruritanian* flirtation with the Queen —H.G.Wells⟩ ⟨a *Ruritanian* existence — sumptuously gay, flitting, free of earnest obligations, infused with a fierce devotion to royalty —*Times Lit. Supp.*⟩

**ru·ru** \ˈrü(ˌ)rü\ *n* -s [Maori] **:** the New Zealand boobook owl

**ru·sa** \ˈrüsə\ *n* [Hindi *rūsā*] **1** -s **:** SAMBAR **2** *cap* [NL, fr. Hindi *rūsā*] **:** a genus of deers now usu. regarded as a subgenus of *Cervus* and comprising the sambars and related forms — **ru·sine** \ˈrüˌsīn, -üsən\ *adj*

**rus·cus** \ˈrəskəs\ *n* [NL, fr. L, butcher's-broom] **1** *cap* **:** a small genus of European evergreen shrubs (family Liliaceae) with leaflike phylloclades, small greenish flowers, and red berries — see BUTCHER'S-BROOM **2** -ES **:** any plant of the genus *Ruscus*

**ruse** \ˈrüs, ˈrüz\ *n* -s [F, fr. MF, dodging of game to evade hunters, trick, ruse, fr. MF *reuser*, *ruser* to put to flight, retreat, to dodge to evade hunters, trick, deceive — more at RUSH] **:** a stratagem or trick usu. intended to deceive **:** a wily subterfuge ⟨succeeded through a ~ in turning back an English expedition —*Amer. Guide Series: La.*⟩ ⟨has a strong bias toward ~ and cunning —G.C.Sellery⟩ **syn** see TRICK

**ru·sell** \ˈrüsᵊl, ˈrösᵊl\ *n* -s [Yiddish *rosel* pickle, broth, stew, rusell, fr. Russ *rosol*, *rossol* salt water, beef tea, broth, fr. *roz-* out of, separate from + *sol* salt; akin to L *sal* salt — more at SALT] **:** vinegar made of fermented beet juice and used during Passover

**[1]rush** \ˈrəsh\ *n* -ES *often attrib* [ME *rish*, *resh*, *rush*, fr. OE *risc*, *resc*, *rysc;* akin to MLG *risch*, *rüsch* rush, MD & MHG *rusch*, Norw *rusk*, *ryskje* hair grass, L *restis* rope, cord, Skt *rajju* rope, cord, Lith *reksti* to plait, bind, tie] **1 a :** any of various plants esp. of the genera *Juncus* and *Scirpus* the cylindrical and often hollow stems of which are used in bottoming chairs and plaiting mats and the pith of which is used in some places for wicks and rushlights **b :** any of various other plants resembling rush **c :** CATTAIL **2 :** the merest trifle **:** STRAW ⟨not even worth a ~⟩

**[2]rush** \"\ *vb* -ED/-ING/-ES [ME *russhen*, fr. *rish*, *resh*, *rush*, n.] *vt* **:** to strew with, work with, or make with rushes ~ *vi* **:** to gather rushes

**[3]rush** \"\ *vb* -ED/-ING/-ES [ME *russhen*, fr. MF *reuser*, *ruser*, to put to flight, repel, retreat, fr. L *recusare* to object to, reject, refuse — more at RECUSANT] *vi* **1 a :** to move forward or progress with speed often impetuously and sometimes with violence or tumult ⟨servants ~*ed* in and out piling up a variety of food —Heinrich Harrer⟩ ⟨the gate was open and the Indians ~*ed* in —*Amer. Guide Series: Pa.*⟩ **b :** to act with haste, precipitation, or eagerness, typically with impatience at delay or without due consideration or preparation ⟨the complaining parties . . . ~ blindly on the superficial causes of their immediate distress —J.A.Froude⟩ ⟨~*ing* in with brand-new solutions without consulting the party —Leslie Roberts⟩ ⟨men who should have known better ~*ed* into print —W.E.Swinton⟩ **2 a :** to flow or fall very rapidly and often noisily **:** dart or move quickly ⟨flames . . . ~*ing* up in long lances —John Muir †1914⟩ ⟨skim along . . . at fifty miles an hour with the air ~*ing* in —Tom Marvel⟩ ⟨the brook . . . ~*es* over a precipice in two cascades —*Amer. Guide Series: Conn.*⟩ **b :** to surge up rapidly and forcefully to a dominating degree ⟨all the horror ~*ed* over her afresh —Ellen Glasgow⟩ ⟨tenderness ~*ed* upon him —Christine Weston⟩ ⟨old times ~*ed* back upon me — the remembrance of old services —W.M.Thackeray⟩ **3 :** to act as carrier of a football in a running play ~ *vt* **1** *obs* **:** to thrust or force often ruthlessly or violently ⟨thy fault our law calls death; but the kind Prince . . . hath ~*ed* aside the law —Shak.⟩ **2 :** to cause to go forward at a high rate of speed ⟨able to guess when new gales . . . would ~ the line of snowstorms out to sea —J.A.Michener⟩ **3 a :** to move quickly and often heedlessly without thought ⟨seemed to be ~*ing* himself and others into trouble —Walter Lippmann⟩ **b :** to impel or hurry on or forward with marked speed, impetuosity, or violence ⟨was able to ~ into the field three regiments of militia —*Amer. Guide Series: N.H.*⟩ ⟨~*ed* her to the hospital —Morris Fishbein⟩ ⟨didn't want to be ~*ed* into marriage —Floyd Dell⟩ **c :** to perform, execute, or deliver in a notably short time or at high speed ⟨decided that the work . . . was to be ~*ed* —Mary Austin⟩ ⟨the same class of ambitious leaders ~*ed* it into statehood —D.Y.Thomas⟩ **4 :** to urge to an unnaturally rapid progress or pace ⟨better not to ~ young children too much, even if they are unusual —Charles Angoff⟩ ⟨the department stores always seem to ~ the season⟩ ⟨had been really ~*ed* yesterday⟩ **5 :** to run towards or against in attack **:** VANQUISH, OVERPOWER **:** break in by charge or onset ⟨~*ed* the enemy group, bayoneted their leader —H.L.Merillat⟩ ⟨if you hear three shots, ~ the door —Laura Krey⟩ **6 :** to roquet (a ball) so that it travels a considerable distance **7 a :** to carry (a ball) forward in a running play **b :** to move in quickly on (a kicker or passer) so as to hinder, prevent, or block a kick or pass **8 a :** to lavish attention on **:** court assiduously **:** have frequent dates with ⟨has been ~*ing* that girl for nearly three months⟩ **b :** to entertain esp. at parties and dances in order to secure a pledge of membership ⟨the sorority decided to ~ fewer girls this year⟩

**syn** DASH, TEAR, SHOOT, CHARGE: RUSH suggests either impetuosity or intense hurry on account of some exigency, with carelessness about the concomitant effects of the precipitate action ⟨a flying rout of suns and galaxies, *rushing* away from the solar system —E.M.Forster⟩ ⟨business *rushed* forward into the glittering years —*Amer. Guide Series: Ind.*⟩ DASH is now likely to suggest running or moving at a wild unrestrained top speed ⟨gyroscopically controlled trains that can make 150 miles an hour . . . and *dash* across an abyss on a steel cable —Waldemar Kaempffert⟩ ⟨*dash'd* on like a spurred blood-horse in a race —Lord Byron⟩ TEAR, in this sense, may suggest extreme swiftness with impetus, violence, and abandon ⟨then he *tore* out of the study —Agnes S. Turnbull⟩ ⟨disheveled atoms *tear* along at 100 miles a second —Waldemar Kaempffert⟩ SHOOT may imply the precipitate headlong rushing or darting of something impelled, as though discharged from a gun ⟨leaped to one side and out of reach of those wicked horns. The bull *shot* past —F.B.Gipson⟩ ⟨the Bridal Veil *shoots* free from the upper edge of the cliff by the velocity the stream has acquired —John Muir †1914⟩ ⟨*shooting* out in their motorcars on errands of mystery —Virginia Woolf⟩ CHARGE is likely to suggest a rapid, violent onslaught gathering forceful momentum calculated to overpower ⟨down we swept and *charged* and overthrew —Alfred Tennyson⟩ ⟨one morning he *charged* — he was a very burly man — into Rossetti's studio —Osbert Sitwell⟩ — **rush the growler :** to fetch beer from a saloon esp. in a pail or pitcher

**[4]rush** \"\ *n* -ES [ME, fr. *russhen*, v.] **1 a :** a moving forward with rapidity and force or eagerness **:** a swift sometimes violent motion or course **:** ONSET ⟨a ~ was made at the first three food-laden wagons —F.V.W.Mason〉 〈a whole load of earth fell with a ~ —Liam O'Flaherty〉 **b :** a sound or as if of swift movement 〈the idea may come with a ~ of wings —Harriet Monroe〉 〈heard the ~ of the distant waterfall〉 **c :** a surging usu. of some deeply felt emotion 〈a ~ of moral indignation —V.S.Pritchett〉 〈sat back with a curious little ~ of excitement —Ann Bridge〉 〈a quick ~ of sympathy —Gordon Cuyler〉 **2 a :** an unusual burst of activity, productivity, or speed usu. because of pressure or accumulation 〈the ~ . . . to locate and tap new and improved sources of raw materials —V.G. Iden〉 〈buy in a wild Saturday morning ~ or go without what you need —Nathaniel Peffer〉 〈the patient had peristaltic ~*es*〉 **b :** a sudden insistent and usu. eager demand 〈caused a ~ among American banking houses to retain him as their legal counsel —*Current Biog.*〉 〈was assured of a box-office ~ —*Newsweek*〉 〈the height of the Christmas ~ —Wynford Vaughan-Thomas〉 **3 :** a thronging of many people usu. to some new place; *esp* **:** GOLD RUSH 〈the second season of the great California ~ —Cliff Farrell〉 〈most men who have known the excitement of a ~ always remain prospectors at heart —*Amer. Guide Series: Nev.*〉 **4 :** the act of carrying a football during a game **:** running play 〈sped 56 yards with the kickoff and got three more on a ~ —Allison Danzig〉 **5 :** a contest or trial of strength between two classes or delegations of two classes usu. in a school or university 〈the day of the big freshman ~, in which the sophomores would . . . try to prevent the freshmen from charging —Edmund Wilson〉 **6 :** a round of assiduous attention usu. involving extensive social activity 〈seem to be giving her quite a ~ —Hamilton Basso〉 **7 :** an advance positive print of a motion-picture scene processed directly after the shooting for review by the director or producer — often used in pl. — **at a rush** *adv* **:** in a great hurry 〈victory had to be won *at a rush* or not at all —*Times Lit. Supp.*〉

**⁵rush** \"\ *adj* **1 :** involving haste **:** requiring special speed usu. in preparation, process, or action 〈~ orders for coffee and doughnuts —Robertson Davies〉 **2 :** characterized by a press of activity for students being considered for fraternity or sorority membership 〈~ week〉 **3 :** characterized by maximum activity 〈transatlantic liner business will swing into the annual ~ season —George Horne b.1902〉 〈the worst delays . . . took place not in cities but in suburban towns at the ~ commuting hours —Hal Burton〉

**rush-bearing** \ˈ=,==\ *n* **:** a festival formerly held in rural England on the anniversary of the dedication of a church and marked by the bringing of rushes by the parishioners to strew the church

**rush-bottomed** \ˈ=¦==\ *adj* **:** having a seat made of rushes 〈admired the antique *rush-bottomed* chair〉

**rush candle** *n* **:** RUSHLIGHT

**rushed** \ˈrəsht\ *adj* [¹*rush* + *-ed*] **:** overgrown or overlaid with rushes

**rush·ee** \(ˌ)rəˈshē\ *n* -s [³*rush* + *-ee*] **:** a college or university student (as a freshman) who is being rushed by a fraternity or sorority

**rush·en** \ˈrəshən, ˈrůsh-\ *adj* [ME *russchen*, fr. OE *riscen*, fr. *risc, resc, rysc* rush + *-en* — more at RUSH] *chiefly dial* **:** made of rushes

**¹rush·er** \ˈrəshə(r)\ *n* -s [³*rush* + *-er*] **:** one that rushes: as **a :** one that does things rapidly **:** a quick energetic person **b :** one that acts hastily without thought **c :** one who joins in the rush to a freshly discovered ore field **d :** a football player who carries the ball in a running play

**²rusher** \"\ *n* -s [¹*rush* + *-er*] **:** one who weaves rushes into frames of chairs

**rushes** *pl of* RUSH, *pres 3d sing of* RUSH

**rush family** *n* **:** JUNCACEAE

**rush grass** *n* **:** a grass of the genus *Sporobolus* having wiry stems and sheathed panicles

**rush hour** *n* **:** the period of the day when the demands esp. of traffic or business are at the peak 〈the rapidity of subway transit . . . outside of *rush hours* is one of the wonders of the world —Irwin Edman〉

**¹rushing** *adj* [fr. pres. part. of ³*rush*] **1 :** moving with extreme rapidity **:** IMPETUOUS, PRECIPITATE 〈give the impression that the typical mountain stream is a ~ torrent —Alexander MacDonald〉 **2 :** briskly active 〈women in shawls and boots did a ~ business in evergreen wreaths —Horace Sutton〉 — **rush·ing·ly** *adv*

**²rushing** *n* -s [fr. gerund of ³*rush*] **:** the extensive social activity characteristic of the rushes of a fraternity or sorority 〈about to ban the house from interfraternity activities, including ~ —J.D.May〉

**rush-leaved daffodil** \ˈ=,=-\ *n* **:** JONQUIL

**rushlight** \ˈ=,=\ *n* **1 :** a candle made of the pith of various rushes, peeled except on one side, and dipped in grease 〈draw the curtain, and kindle the ~ —Mary Webb〉 **2 :** one that is singularly insignificant 〈told him that good scholars were looked upon here as mere ~*s* —*Yale Literary Mag.*〉

**rushlike** \ˈ=,=\ *adj* **:** resembling a rush

**rush lily** *n* **:** a large-flowered plant of the genus *Sisyrinchium*; *esp* **:** a blue-eyed grass (*S. angustifolium*)

**rush nut** *n* **:** CHUFA

**rush pink** *n* **:** a plant of the genus *Lygodesmia* (family Compositae); *esp* **:** a No. American perennial rushlike herb (*L. juncea*) with finely grooved leaves and pink or white flowers

**rush ring** *n* **:** a ring made of plaited rushes and used as a wedding ring

**rush seat** *n* **:** a theatre or concert seat usu. in a separate section of the balcony that may be occupied by the first ticket holder securing it

**rush toad** *n* **:** NATTERJACK

**rushwork** \ˈ=,=\ *n* [¹*rush* + *work*] **:** the art or craft of weaving rushes

**rushy** \ˈrəshē\ *adj* -ER/-EST [ME *resshy, russhy*, fr. *rish, resh, rush* rush + *-y* — more at RUSH] **1 :** made of or resembling rushes **2 :** abounding with rushes

**rusine antler** *n* [*rusine* fr. NL *Rusa* + E *-ine*] **:** an antler with the brow tine simple and the beam simply forked at the tip

**¹rusk** \ˈrəsk\ *n* -s [modif. of Sp & Pg *rosca* coil, screw, twisted roll] **1 :** hard crisp bread orig. used as ship's stores **2 :** a sweet or plain twice-baked bread that is first prepared and baked and then sliced and baked a second time until it is dry and crisp

**²rusk** \"\ *vt* -ED/-ING/-S **:** to toast or crisp (bread or cake) into rusk

**ruski** *var of* RUSSKI

**rus·kin** \ˈrəskən\ *n* -s [IrGael *ruscān*, dim. of *rusc* bark — more at RUCHE] *dial Eng* **:** a receptacle for butter often made of bark

**rus·kin·ian** \ˌrəˈskinēən\ *adj, usu cap* [John *Ruskin* †1900 Eng. art critic and sociological writer + E *-ian*] **:** of, relating to, or resembling the writings of the critic Ruskin

**rus·kin·ize** \ˈrəskə,nīz\ *vb* -ED/-ING/-S *usu cap* [John *Ruskin* + E *-ize*] *vt* **:** to convert to ideas resembling those of John Ruskin 〈it is too late to *Ruskinize* our civilization —Katharine F. Gerould〉 ~ *vi* **:** to adopt or plead for the principles of Ruskin 〈don't *Ruskinize* to me —*Scribner's*〉

**rus·ot** \ˈrəsət\ *or* **rus·wut** \-swət\ *n* -s [Hindi *rasaut, raswat*] **:** an extract from the wood or roots of various shrubs of the genus *Berberis* that is used in India mixed with opium as an application to infected eyelids

**¹russ** \ˈrəs\ *n, pl* **russ** *or* **russes** *cap* [Russ *Rus'*, old name for Russia and the Russian people (first applied to the Scandinavian Varangians that settled and came to power in the Novgorod and Kiev area in the 9th cent.), of Scand origin like Finn *Ruotsi* Sweden, MGk *rhōsisti* Scandinavian, ML *Rusios* Norsemen; akin to ON *rōthr* art of rowing, *rōa* to row — more at ROW] **1 :** a native or inhabitant of Russia **2 :** the Russian language

**²russ** \"\ *adj, usu cap* **:** of or relating to the Russians

**rus·sel** \ˈrəsəl\ *n* -s [ME *ryssill*, prob. fr. *Rijssel* (Lille), city in northern France] **:** a strong twilled woolen cloth for clothing and shoes

**rus·se·lia** \ˌrəˈsēlēə, -lyə\ *n, cap* [NL, fr. Alexander *Russell* †1768 Brit. physician at Aleppo + NL *-ia*] **:** a genus of often nearly leafless Mexican shrubs (family Scrophulariaceae) having red flowers with a tubular corolla, four stamens, and a nearly globose 2-celled capsule — see CORAL PLANT 2 c

**rus·sell·ian** \ˌrəˈselēən\ *adj, usu cap* [Bertrand *Russell* b1872 Eng. mathematician and philosopher + E *-ian*] **:** of or relating to the philosopher Bertrand Russell or his theories

**rus·sell·ite** \ˈrəsə,līt\ *n* -s *usu cap* [Charles Taze *Russell* †1916 Am. religious leader + E *-ite*] **:** one of the Jehovah's Witnesses — often taken to be offensive

**rus·sell's paradox** \ˈrəsəlz-\ *n, usu cap R* [after Bertrand *Russell*] **:** a paradox that discloses itself in forming a class of all classes that are not members of themselves and in observing that the question of whether it is true or false if this class is a member of itself can be answered both ways — compare LIAR PARADOX, VICIOUS CIRCLE PRINCIPLE

**russell's viper** *n, usu cap R* [after Patrick *Russell* †1805 Brit. physician at Aleppo] **:** a strikingly marked highly venomous snake (*Vipera russellii* syn. *Daboia russelli*) of southeastern Asia that is light brown above with three longitudinal rows of black light-margined rings which sometimes encircle reddish dots — called also *daboia*

**rus·sene** *or* **ru·sin** \rüˈsēn, rů'-, ˈ=,=\ *n* -s *usu cap* [Russ *rusin*, fr. *Rus'*, old name for Russia — more at RUSS] **:** RUTHENIAN

**¹rus·set** \ˈrəsət, *usu* -əd.+V\ *n* -s [ME, fr. OF *rosset, rousset*, fr. *rosset, rousset*, adj., russet, fr. *ros, rous* russet, fr. L *russus* red; akin to L *ruber* red — more at RED] **1 :** coarse homespun cloth in reddish brown or natural colors formerly used by country people **2 :** a variable color averaging a strong brown that is duller and slightly redder than rust, paler and slightly redder than average copper brown, and redder and deeper than gold brown — compare RUSSET BROWN **3 :** any of various winter apples having rough skins of a russet color 〈the Roxbury ~〉 **4 :** russet leather **5 :** RUSSETING 3

**²russet** \"\ *adj* [ME, fr. MF *rousset*] **1 :** reddish brown or reddish gray or yellowish brown 〈the morn in ~ mantle clad —Shak.〉 **2 :** of the color russet **3 a :** made of russet **b** *obs* **:** wearing clothing made of russet **4 :** of, relating to, or constituting leather that is finished except for the coloring and polishing

**³russet** \"\ *vb* **russeted** *also* **russetted**; **russeted** *also* **russetted**; **russeting** *also* **russetting**; **russets** *vt* **1 :** to cast a russet glow over **2 :** to cause russeting ~ *vi* **1 :** to become russet in color 〈leaves ~ in autumn〉 **2 :** to become russet **:** undergo russeting

**russet-backed thrush** \ˈ==,=-\ *n* **:** a common thrush (*Hylocichla ustulata*) of the Pacific coast somewhat darker than the related olive-backed thrush of eastern No. America

**russet brown** *n* **:** a variable color averaging a moderate to strong brown that is redder and darker than oak and yellower and darker than Vassar tan or Arabian brown

**russet coat** *n* **:** a coat of russet color or russet cloth; *also* **:** a wearer of such a coat

**russet dwarf** *n* **:** a virus disease of the potato characterized by dwarfing, browning, or rusting of the leaves and leaf fall

**russet green** *n* **:** a grayish to moderate greenish yellow that is redder and darker than citron green

**rus·set·ing** *also* **rus·set·ting** \ˈrəsəd·|iŋ, -ət|, |ēŋ\ *n* -s [¹*russet* + *-ing*] **1** *obs* **:** one wearing russet **:** RUSTIC **2 :** RUSSET 3 **3 :** a brownish roughened area on the skin of fruit (as apples, pears, and citrus fruit) that resembles the normal skin of a russet apple and is caused by frost, insect or fungous injury, or spraying — compare SCURF

**rus·set·ish** \|ish\ *adj* **:** somewhat russet in color

**russet mite** *n* **:** RUST MITE

**russet orange** *n* **1 :** a variable color averaging a strong orange that is yellower and darker than pumpkin, yellower than mandarin orange, and redder and deeper than cadmium yellow **2 :** CHROME SCARLET

**russet scab** *n* [¹*russet*; fr. the roughened area on the tubers] **:** RHIZOCTONIA DISEASE 2

**russet tan** *n* **:** a moderate reddish brown that is yellower and paler than roan, mahogany, oxblood, or rustic brown

**rus·sety** \|ē\ *adj* **:** somewhat russet in color

**¹rus·sia** \ˈrəshə, *dial* ˈrüshə\ *adj, usu cap* [fr. *Russia*, country in eastern Europe] **:** of or from Russia **:** of the kind or style prevalent in Russia

**²russia** \"\ *n* -s **:** RUSSIA LEATHER

**russia duck** *or* **russian duck** *n, usu cap R* **:** a strong linen duck formerly used for summer clothing

**russia iron** *n, usu cap R* **:** a sheet iron having a lustrous blue black coating of oxide for protection against corrosion

**russia leather** *or* **russia calf** *n, usu cap R* **1 :** leather made from various skins by tanning with barks of the willow, birch, or oak and then rubbing the flesh side with birch-tar oil which imparts a peculiar odor and protects from insects **2 :** a chrome-tanned or vegetable-tanned fancy leather that resembles the original Russia leather and is generally made from calf or small cattle hides

**¹rus·sian** \-shən\ *adj, usu cap* [*Russia*, country in eastern Europe + E *-an*] **:** of or relating to Russia, its inhabitants, or their language

**²russian** \"\ *n* -s *cap* **1 a :** one of the people of Russia; *esp* **:** a member of the dominant Slavic-speaking Great Russian ethnic group of Russia **b :** one that is of Russian descent **2 a :** a Slavic language of the Russian people **:** the official language of the Soviet Union **b :** the three Slavic languages of the Russian people collectively including Belorussian and Ukrainian

**russian almond** *n, usu cap R* **:** an Asiatic dwarf almond (*Prunus tenella*) cultivated for its rosy red flowers

**russian backgammon** *n, usu cap R* **:** a variation of backgammon in which all the pieces are entered on the same table as determined by throws of the dice and proceed in the same direction around the board

**russian bagatelle** *n, usu cap R* **:** a childish variation of bagatelle employing holes, pins, arches, and bells — called also *cockamaroo*

**russian ballet** *n, usu cap R* **1 :** ballet developed early in the 20th century by teachers and students of the Russian Imperial Ballet Academy with characteristic emphasis upon the execution of dramatic, symbolic, or interpretative pantomime through rhythmic plastic movements and postures with the aid of appropriate costumes and setting **2 :** a group of dancers trained in the Russian ballet

**russian bank** *n, usu cap R* **:** a card game in its procedure similar to most forms of solitaire but always played by two persons in which each player has his own pack of cards and attempts to play all of them while impeding the opponent's plays — called also *crapette*

**russian bassoon** *n, usu cap R* **:** an obsolete brass musical instrument similar to the bass horn

**russian bath** *n, usu cap R* **:** a vapor bath variously modified consisting essentially in a prolonged exposure of the body to steam followed by washings, friction, and a cold plunge

**¹russian blue** *n, often cap R* **:** a bluish gray to pale blue

**²russian blue** *n, usu cap R & often cap B* **:** a slender long-bodied large-eared domestic cat with short silky bluish gray fur

**russian boot** *n, usu cap R* **:** a leather boot extending to the calf and having a wide cuff and sometimes a tassel

**russian cactus** *n, usu cap R* **:** RUSSIAN THISTLE

**russian calf** *n, usu cap R* **:** a moderate brown that is deeper and slightly redder than chestnut brown, deeper and yellower than auburn or bay, and redder, stronger, and slightly lighter than coffee — called also *Cappagh brown, carob brown, fudge, India tan, Kis Kilim*

**russian dandelion** *n, usu cap R* **:** KOK-SAGHYZ

**russian dressing** *n, usu cap R* **:** mayonnaise dressing with pungent additions that may include chili sauce, chopped pickles, or pimientos

**russian flax** *n, usu cap R* **:** FLAX 1

**russian fly** *n, usu cap R* **:** SPANISH FLY

**russian gray** *n, usu cap R* **:** SLATE GRAY

**russian green** *n, usu cap R* **:** a dark yellowish green to grayish green — called also *vert russe*

**rus·sian·ism** \-shə,nizəm\ *n* -s *usu cap* **1 :** a special interest in or attachment to Russia or the Russian people **2 :** a quality or group of qualities characteristic of Russia, its people, or its language

**rus·sian·iza·tion** \ˌrəshənəˈzāshən\ *n* -s *usu cap* **:** the act or process of russianizing

**rus·sian·ize** \ˈrəshə,nīz\ *vt* -ED/-ING/-S *often cap* [¹*Russian* + *-ize*] **1 a :** to cause to acquire Russian characteristics, qualities, culture, beliefs, or political practices **b** (1) **:** to bring (a region or esp. a national group) under the national control of Russia (2) **:** to force to conform to a Russian cultural pattern or political organization **2 :** to treat (leather) by a process similar to or intended to produce results similar to that used on Russia leather

**russian knapweed** *n, usu cap R* **:** a Eurasian herb (*Centaurea picris*) introduced into the central U.S. where it has become a troublesome weed

**russian mulberry** *n, usu cap R* **:** a small bushy mulberry that is a variety (*Morus alba tatarica*) of the white mulberry

**russian muskrat** *n, usu cap R* **:** DESMAN 1 a, 2

**russian olive** *n, usu cap R* **:** a large shrub or small tree (*Elaeagnus angustifolia*) that has silvery twigs, lanceolate to oblong-lanceolate leaves which are light green above and silvery below, fragrant axillary flowers which are yellow within and silvery without, and small yellow fruits covered with silvery scales and that is native to western Asia and southern Europe and is widely cultivated in arid windy regions as an ornamental, as a coarse hedge or shelterbelt plant, or for wildlife food — called also *oleaster*

**russian orthodox** *adj, usu cap R&O* **:** of, relating to, or being the autocephalous Eastern Orthodox Church of Russia headed by the Patriarch of Moscow and using an Old Church Slavonic liturgy or one of its autonomous 20th century branches chiefly outside Russia

**russian pigweed** *n, usu cap R* **:** an annual Asiatic herb (*Axyris amaranthoides*) of the family Chenopodiaceae naturalized in No. America having unisexual flowers of which the pistillate ones have a 3- or 4-parted perianth

**russian red clover** *n, usu cap 1st R* **:** a drought-resistant red clover that is usu. considered a variety (*Trifolium pratense pallidum*) of the common red clover

**russian roulette** *n, usu cap 1st R* **:** an act of bravado consisting of spinning the cylinder of a revolver loaded with one cartridge, pointing the muzzle at one's own head, and pulling the trigger

**russian sable** *n, usu cap R* **:** SIBERIAN SABLE

**russian sheet iron** *n, usu cap R* **:** RUSSIA IRON

**russian spring–summer encephalitis** *n, usu cap R* **:** a tick-borne encephalitis

**russian sunflower** *n, usu cap R* **:** a large-seeded sunflower that is a variety of the common sunflower (*Helianthus annuus*) and is used as food in Russia

**russian thistle** *or* **russian tumbleweed** *n, usu cap R* **:** a prickly European herb (*Salsola kali tenuifolia*) that is a serious pest in No. America — called also *Russian cactus*

**russian turnip** *n, usu cap R* **:** RUTABAGA

**russian turpentine** *n, usu cap R* **:** turpentine obtained chiefly from the Scotch pine

**russian walnut** *n, usu cap R* **:** ENGLISH WALNUT

**russian whist** *n, usu cap R* **:** VINT

**russian wild rye** *n, usu cap 1st R* **:** an Asiatic ryegrass (*Elymus junceus*) introduced into No. America and used as a forage grass

**russian wolfhound** *n, usu cap R* **:** BORZOI 2

**russian wormwood** *n, usu cap R* **:** an Asiatic gray-pubescent subshrub (*Artemisia sacrorum*) used as an ornamental and having nodding flower heads in slender racemes

**russia sheet iron** *n, usu cap R* **:** RUSSIA IRON

**rus·si·fi·ca·tion** \ˌrəsəfəˈkāshən\ *n* -s *sometimes cap* **:** the act or process of being russified

**rus·si·fy** \ˈrəsə,fī\ *vt* -ED/-ING/-ES *often cap* [²*Russ* + *-ify*] **1 :** RUSSIANIZE **2 :** to modify (language or a word or expression) to conform to characteristics distinctive of the Russian language 〈*Russified* more than any other of the Balto-Finnic languages —F.J.Oinas〉

**rus·sism** \ˈrə,sizəm\ *n* -s *usu cap* [²*Russ* + *-ism*] **:** a word, expression, or language characteristic or distinctive of Russian

**russ·ki** *also* **russ·ky** *or* **rus·ki** \ˈrəskē\ *n, pl* **russkies** *or* **russkis** *also* **ruskies** *or* **ruskis** *usu cap* [Russ *russkii*, adj. & n., Russian, fr. *Rus'*, old name for Russia — more at RUSS] **:** a native of Russia **:** RUSSIAN — often taken to be offensive

**russ·ni·ak** \ˈrəsnē,ak\ *n* -s *cap* [Ukr *rusnyak, rusnak*] **:** RUTHENIAN

**russo-** *comb form, usu cap* [*Russia* & ¹*Russian*] **1 :** Russia **:** Russians 〈*Russo*phobia〉 **2 :** Russian and 〈*Russo*-Japanese〉

**rus·so–byzantine** \ˌrə(ˌ)sō, -shō+\ *adj, usu cap R&B* [*Russo-* + *Byzantine*] **:** having Byzantine characteristics modified by Russian influence; *esp* **:** of or relating to the typical Russian architecture previous to 1700

**rus·so·phil** \ˈrəsə,fil\ *or* **rus·so·phile** \-fīl\ *n* -s *usu cap* [*Russo-* + *-phil, -phile*] **:** one who admires or supports Russia or Russian policy

**rus·so·pho·bia** \ˌ==ˈfōbēə\ *n, usu cap* [NL, fr. *Russo-* + *-phobia*] **:** fear or dislike of Russia or Russian policy

**rus·sud** \ˈrə,səd\ *n* -s [Hindi *rasad*, lit., income, revenue, contribution, fr. Per] **:** grain or forage provided by local Indian officers at a military camping ground

**rus·su·la** \ˈrəsyələ\ *n, cap* [NL, fr. LL, fem. of *russulus* reddish, fr. L *russus* red — more at RUSSET] **:** a large genus that comprises stout-stemmed white-spored fungi (family Agaricaceae) with neither annulus nor volva, includes some edible species, and may be distinguished from the related *Lactarius* by the absence of milky juice and by the brittle pileus of red, purple, yellow, green, or blue

**¹rust** \ˈrəst\ *n* -s [ME, fr. OE *rūst*; akin to OS, OHG, & OSw *rost* rust; derivative fr. the stem of E ¹*red*] **1 a :** the reddish porous brittle coating that is formed on iron esp. when chemically attacked by moist air and that consists essentially of hydrated ferric oxide but usu. contains some ferrous oxide and sometimes iron carbonates and iron sulfates — compare CORROSION 1a, ⁵SCALE 4a **b :** the somewhat similar coating produced on any of various other metals by corrosion — compare PATINA 2 **c :** something resembling rust **:** ACCRETION 〈this poem . . . under its accumulated ~ and dirt of five centuries is fresh and living even today —G.G.Coulton〉 **2 a** *obs* **:** corrosive or injurious accretion or influence 〈how he glisters thorough my ~ —Shak.〉 **b :** an ill effect usu. caused by idleness, inaction, or neglect 〈read to keep your mind from ~〉 〈lest through the ~ of time . . . they should be lost to the world forever —Laurence Sterne〉 **3 a** (1) *or* **rust disease :** any of numerous destructive diseases of plants produced by fungi of the order Uredinales and characterized by reddish brown pustular lesions on stems, leaves, or other plant parts — see APPLE RUST, LEAF RUST, STEM RUST, STRIPE RUST, WHEAT RUST; compare MILDEW, SMUT (2) *or* **rust fungus :** a fungus of the order Uredinales — compare PUCCINIA, UROMYCES **b :** any of several other fungus diseases of plants — usu. used with a descriptive term; see WHITE RUST **c :** an abnormal reddish or brownish discoloration of vegetation or fruit **4 :** a strong brown that is stronger and slightly yellower and lighter than average russet, lighter, stronger, and very slightly redder than average copper brown, and redder and deeper than gold brown **5 :** a composition used in making a rust joint

**²rust** \"\ *vb* -ED/-ING/-S [ME *rusten*, fr. *rust*, n.] *vi* **1 :** to form rust **:** become oxidized — compare CORRODE *vi* 2, TARNISH **2 :** to degenerate in idleness **:** become dull, slow, or impaired esp. by inaction, lack of use, or the passage of time 〈once-functioning objects now ~*ed* and moldered in this cellar —Marcia Davenport〉 〈no man to let his power ~ —*Time*〉 **3 :** to turn or become the color of rust **:** become reddish brown as if with rust 〈the leaves slowly ~〉 **4 a :** to be affected with a rust fungus **b :** to acquire a rusty appearance ~ *vt* **1 :** to cause (a metal) to form rust 〈keep up your bright swords, for the dew will ~ them —Shak.〉 — compare CORRODE *vt* 1 **2 :** to impair or corrode by or as if by time, inactivity, or deleterious use 〈a six-year layoff . . . had not ~*ed* his technique —*Newsweek*〉 **3 :** to blast or wither by or as if by the rust fungus **4 :** to turn to the color of rust **:** cause to become reddish brown 〈the wind brought salt . . . ~*ing* the crops —*N.Y.Times*〉

**rust brown** *n* **:** RUSSET 2

**rust cement** *n* **:** IRON CEMENT

**¹rus·tic** \ˈrəstik, -tēk\ *adj* [ME *rustyk*, fr. MF *rustique*, fr. L *rusticus*, fr. *rus* country, open land — more at ROOM] **1 :** of or relating to the country **:** RURAL 〈rude carts, bespattered with ~ mire —Charles Dickens〉 **2 :** of or relating to rustic work **3 a :** having an appearance or manner held to resemble country folk 〈a splendid primeval ~ figure —Osbert Lancaster〉

**b** : living in a rural area : engaged in country occupations ⟨as farming⟩ ⟨one of the few victories in all history of ~ untrained volunteers over professional soldiers —Budd Schulberg⟩ **4** : having or exhibiting qualities held to be characteristic of rural people: as **a** : marked by awkwardness : lacking polish : COARSE, RUDE ⟨~ readiness to jeer at the unusual —H.O. Taylor⟩ **b** : marked by simplicity : ARTLESS ⟨if education had not meddled with her ~ nature —Jean Stafford⟩ ⟨participating in these ~ occasions —P.L.Fermor⟩ **5** : adapted or appropriate to the country or country living : ROUGH, STURDY : lacking in ornamentation ⟨had a ~ shanty and arbor —Herman Melville⟩ ⟨dotted with tourist cabins and hotels — from the luxurious to the ~ —*Amer. Guide Series: Ariz.*⟩

**²rustic** \"\ *n* -s **1 a** : an inhabitant of a rural area ⟨new emphasis on the preciousness of the . . . soil affected both ~ and townsman —John Buchan⟩ **b** : one who is rude, coarse, or dull **c** : a rural person thought to be naturally simple in character or manners : one without sophistication ⟨where had my simple ~ procured it —Jacob Hay⟩ **2** : brick with a rough textured surface often multicolored : a style of masonry resembling rockwork **3** : RUSTIC MOTH **4** : a ceramic surface artificially roughened

**¹rus·ti·cal** \-tə̇kəl\ *adj* [ME *rusticall*, fr. MF *rustical*, fr. *rustique* rustic + *-al*] : RUSTIC

**²rustical** \"\ *n* -s : RUSTIC

**rus·ti·cal·ly** \-k(ə)lē\ *adv* : in a rustic manner

**rus·ti·cate** \ˈrəstə,kāt, *usu* -ād.+V\ *vb* -ED/-ING/-S [L *rusticatus*, past part. of *rusticari* to live in the country, fr. *rusticus* rustic] *vi* : to go into or reside in the country : pursue a rustic life ⟨*rusticating* in . . . villages off the beaten track —T.H. Fielding⟩ ~ *vt* **1** : to punish by requiring temporary absence : suspend from school or college ⟨did not stand high in the esteem of the faculty and was once *rusticated* —G.H.Genzmer⟩ **2** : to bevel or rebate (as the edges of stone blocks) to make the joints conspicuous ⟨a *rusticated* stone pavilion —H.S. Morrison⟩ **3** : to compel to reside in the country ⟨*rusticated* himself so long that he is become an absolute wild Irishman —Henry Fielding⟩ **4** : to cause to become rustic : implant rustic mannerisms in

**rus·ti·ca·tion** \,==ˈkāshən\ *n* -s [L *rustication-, rusticatio*, fr. *rusticatus* + *-ion-, -io* -ion] **1** : the act of rusticating : the state of being rusticated : retirement to or residence in the country ⟨a period of ~ before taking up his new duties⟩ **2 a** : suspension from a college, university, or professional society ⟨anything from a small fine to ~ . . . —*Time*⟩ **b** : the act of suspending or the state of being suspended **3 a** : the practice of rusticating masonry **b** : masonry having the surface textured, reticulated, or otherwise accented or the joints emphasized

**rus·ti·ca·tor** \ˈ==,kād·ə(r)\ *n* -s : one that rusticates

**rustic brown** *n* : a moderate reddish brown that is yellower and less strong than roan, yellower and slightly paler than mahogany, and yellower, less strong, and slightly lighter than oxblood — called also *casserole*, *Eskimo*, *gingerspice*

**rustic capital** *n* : a Latin book hand much used from the 1st to the 7th centuries and occas. until the 10th with the letters formed in a manner natural to the pen

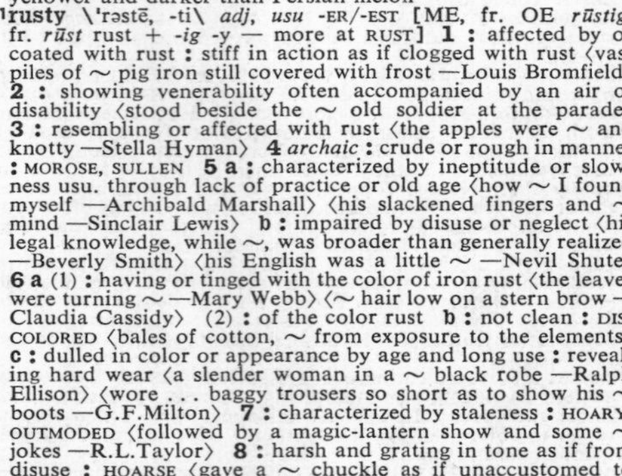

rustic capitals

**rustic drab** *n* : DRAB 2a

**rus·ti·cism** \ˈrəstə,sizəm\ *n* -s : a rustic phrase, manner of speaking, habit, or custom ⟨now and then a home ~ is fresh and startling —Charles Lamb⟩

**rus·tic·i·ty** \,rəˈstisəd·ē, -ətē, -i\ *n* -ES [MF *rusticité*, fr. L *rusticus* + MF *-ité* -ity] **1** : a lack of ease or refinement : awkwardness of manner : GAUCHERIE ⟨any little ~ of gait or pronunciation . . . was so quickly and completely lost —Samuel Butler †1902⟩ **2** : gracelessness of language : failure to reveal polish or elegance ⟨had the ~ of the average freshman theme⟩ **3** : a lack of perception or knowledge : IGNORANCE, STUPIDITY ⟨was ashamed of my own ~ in that distinguished company⟩ **4** : the quality or state of being rustic ⟨the ~ of . . . country towns —*Amer. Guide Series: Ind.*⟩

**rus·ti·cize** \ˈrəstə,sīz\ *vt* -ED/-ING/-S [*¹rustic* + *-ize*] : to give a rustic aspect to ⟨moved out . . . where accent and manner were *rusticized* —A.J.Liebling⟩

**rustic joint** *n* : a sunken joint between building stones

**rustic·ly** *adv* : RUSTICALLY

**rustic moth** *n* : any of various moths (family Noctuidae) belonging to *Agrotis* and related genera and having larvae that are cutworms

**rusti·coat** \ˈrəstē,kōt\ *adj* [*¹rusty* + *coat*] : rusty coated ⟨dine . . . upon ~ potatoes —John Quincy Adams⟩

**rustic servitude** *n* : RURAL SERVITUDE

**rustic ware** *n* : terra cotta that is light brown in color with a brown glaze and is often used in architectural work

**rustic work** *n* **1** : cut stone facing that has the joints rusticated : stone with the face cut to a rough or jagged surface in imitation of nature **2** : summerhouses or furniture for summerhouses or for outdoor use made of rough limbs of trees

chair in rustic work 2

**rustier** *comparative of* RUSTY

**rustiest** *superlative of* RUSTY

**rust·i·ly** \ˈrəstəlē\ *adv* : in a rusty manner ⟨his cart is rickety, the wheels creak —R.P. Casey⟩

**rust·i·ness** \-tēnə̇s\ *n* -ES [ME *rustynes*, fr. *rusty* + *-nes* -ness] : the quality or state of being rusty

**rust joint** *n* : a joint made with iron cement that causes the formation of rust between iron or steel surfaces

**¹rus·tle** \ˈrəsəl\ *vb* **rustled; rustled; rustling** \-s(ə)liŋ\ **rustles** [ME *rustelen, rustlen, rouschelen*, prob. of imit. origin; in some senses, influenced in meaning by *hustle*] *vi* **1 a** : to make a quick succession of small clear sounds usu. by moving ⟨the piny needles *rustled* down —Zane Grey⟩ ⟨their footsteps *rustled* in the fallen golden leaves —Anne D. Sedgwick⟩ ⟨the audience ~*s* in anticipation —Alfred Bester⟩ **b** : to wear clothing that produces soft sounds as one moves ⟨heard his wife ~⟩ **2 a** : to act or move with great energy and forthrightness ⟨the only thing to do is to ~ around —C.G. Poore⟩ ⟨as the jobs began to get scarce, he began to ~ harder —F.B.Gipson⟩ **b** : to forage food ⟨he wanted longhorns . . . they could ~ for themselves, fatten, and make a man money —F.B.Gipson⟩ **3** : to steal cattle ~ *vt* **1** : to cause to move with quick successive small clear sounds : stir with a rustling noise ⟨*rustled* the papers nervously⟩ **2 a** : to get by hustling : obtain by one's own exertions : handle actively and energetically ⟨took over all household chores, cleaning and cooking, *rustling* firewood —Bill Wolf⟩ ⟨~ some dinner together —J.B.Benefield⟩ **b** : FORAGE ⟨cows . . . died of starvation because they didn't know how to ~ a living in among the cactus —Paul Schubert⟩ **3** : to take (as cattle) feloniously : STEAL ⟨they caught him *rustling* cattle and hung him⟩

**²rustle** \"\ *n* -s **1** : a quick succession or confusion of small clear sounds ⟨a ~ of a window shade —R.P.Warren⟩ ⟨the sharp hiss and ~ of the wind —John Muir †1914⟩ ⟨heard the ~ of a newspaper —Lyle Saxon⟩ ⟨listened to the ~ of her skirts —Gilbert Parker⟩ **2** : an act of engaging actively and energetically in some pursuit : HUSTLE

**rus·tler** \ˈrəs(ə)lə(r)\ *n* -s : one that rustles: as **a** : a plant whose leaves make a rustling sound in the wind **b** : an alert energetic driving person : HUSTLER **c** : a cattle thief **d** : a domestic animal that can care for itself ⟨herefords make good ~*s*⟩ **e** : a mine worker who helps to operate the haulage system

**¹rus·tling** \ˈrəs(ə)liŋ, -lēŋ\ *n* -s [ME *rouschelynge*, fr. gerund of *rustelen, rustlen, rouschelen* to rustle — more at RUSTLE] **1** : the continuous small clear sounds made by movement ⟨the ~*s* of the birds⟩ **2** : the stealing of cattle ⟨this story of ranch life, ~ . . . and mystery —*Saturday Rev.*⟩

**²rustling** \"\ *adj* [fr. pres. part. of *¹rustle*] : making continuous small clear sounds ⟨~ silk⟩ ⟨~ leaves⟩ — **rus·tling·ly** *adv*

**rust mite** *n* : any of various small gall mites that burrow in the surface of leaves or fruits usu. producing brown or reddish patches — see CITRUS RUST MITE

**rustproof** \ˈ=,=\ *adj* : incapable of rusting ⟨the manufacture of some specialties such as ~ steel —*N.Y.Times*⟩

**rust-proof** \"\ *vt* [*rustproof*] : to make rustproof

**rust·proof·er** \"+ə(r)\ *n* : a worker who applies rust-proofing material to metal

**rus·tre** \ˈrəstə(r)\ *n* -s [F *ruste, rustre*] **1** *heraldry* : a lozenge pierced with a round opening to show the tincture of the field behind **2** : a metal scale of oval or lozenge shape used on medieval armor

rustres 1

**rus·tred** \-(r)d\ *adj* : having or composed of rustres — used of medieval armor

**rusts** *pl of* RUST, *pres 3d sing of* RUST

**rust tan** *n* : a grayish reddish orange that is yellower, darker, and slightly less strong than Etruscan red or hyacinth red and yellower and darker than Persian melon

**¹rusty** \ˈrəstē, -ti\ *adj, usu* -ER/-EST [ME, fr. OE *rūstig*, fr. *rūst* rust + *-ig* -y — more at RUST] **1** : affected by or coated with rust : stiff in action as if clogged with rust ⟨vast piles of ~ pig iron still covered with frost —Louis Bromfield⟩ **2** : showing venerability often accompanied by an air of disability ⟨stood beside the ~ old soldier at the parade⟩ **3** : resembling or affected with rust ⟨the apples were ~ and knotty —Stella Hyman⟩ **4** *archaic* : crude or rough in manner : MOROSE, SULLEN **5 a** : characterized by ineptitude or slowness usu. through lack of practice or old age ⟨how ~ I found myself —Archibald Marshall⟩ ⟨his slackened fingers and ~ mind —Sinclair Lewis⟩ **b** : impaired by disuse or neglect ⟨his legal knowledge, while ~, was broader than generally realized —Beverly Smith⟩ ⟨his English was a little ~ —Nevil Shute⟩ **6 a** (1) : having or tinged with the color of iron rust ⟨the leaves were turning ~ —Mary Webb⟩ ⟨~ hair low on a stern brow —Claudia Cassidy⟩ (2) : of the color rust **b** : not clean : DISCOLORED ⟨bales of cotton, ~ from exposure to the elements⟩ **c** : dulled in color or appearance by age and long use : revealing hard wear ⟨a slender woman in a ~ black robe —Ralph Ellison⟩ ⟨wore . . . baggy trousers so short as to show his ~ boots —G.F.Milton⟩ **7** : characterized by staleness : HOARY, OUTMODED ⟨followed by a magic-lantern show and some ~ jokes —R.L.Taylor⟩ **8** : harsh and grating in tone as if from disuse : HOARSE ⟨gave a ~ chuckle as if unaccustomed to laughing —J.H.Wheelwright⟩ ⟨a ~, willfully ancient voice —Edith Sitwell⟩

**²rusty** \ˈrùsti, ˈrəsti\ VAR OF REASTY

**³rus·ty** \ˈrəstē\ *adj* -ER/-EST [alter. (influenced by *¹rusty*) of *resty*] **1** : RESTIVE ⟨~ horses⟩ **2** *chiefly dial* : having a surly manner : ILL-TEMPERED ⟨~ ever since that business over the oil shares —John Galsworthy⟩

**rusty blackbird** *or* **rusty grackle** *n* : a blackbird (*Euphagus carolinus*) of the eastern U.S. whose adult male has a white iris and a uniformly blue-black color in spring but in the fall has the edges of the feathers become rusty

**rusty blotch** *n* : a disease of barley caused by an imperfect fungus (*Helminthosporium californicum*) characterized by irregular brown blotches on the leaves

**rusty dab** *n* : a rusty-brown yellow-tailed flatfish (*Limanda ferruginea*) of the east coast of No. America that is a small but good food fish

**rusty fig** *n* : a fig (*Ficus rubiginosa*) having rusty hairs on twigs, buds, petioles, and lower leaf surfaces

**rusty gold** *n* : native gold having on it some coating which prevents it from amalgamating readily

**rusty grain beetle** *n* : a reddish brown cucujid beetle (*Cryptolestes ferrugineus*) that is destructive to stored grain products

**rusty mottle** *n* : a virus disease of cherry characterized by retarded blossom and leaf development in spring, followed by necrotic spotting and shot-holing and frequently by yellowish rusty chlorotic spotting of leaves and considerable defoliation

**rusty plum aphid** *n* : a common plant louse (*Hysteroneura setariae*) that attacks plum, sorghum, and some other plants esp. in southwestern U.S.

**rusty tiger cat** *n* : FLATHEADED CAT

**rusty woodsia** *n* : a common rock-inhabiting fern (*Woodsia ilvensis*) of the north temperate zone with rusty-brown stipes and lanceolate pinnate fronds and with the pinnae crowded and sessile

**ruswut** *var of* RUSOT

**¹rut** \ˈrət, *usu* -d.+V\ *n* -s [ME *rutte*, fr. MF *rut, ruit* noise, roar, rut, fr. LL *rugitus* roar, fr. L, past part. of *rugire* to roar — more at BRUIT] **1** : an annually recurrent state of sexual excitement in the male deer; *broadly* : sexual excitement in a mammal esp. when recurring periodically : ESTRUS, HEAT **2** : the period during which rut occurs in most sexually mature members of a natural population — often used with *the*

**²rut** \"\ *vi* **rutted; rutted; rutting; ruts** : to be in or enter into a state of rut

**³rut** \"\ *n* -s [perh. modif. of MF *route* way, route, track of an animal — more at ROUTE] **1** : a track worn by a wheel or by habitual passage of anything : a groove in which anything runs ⟨~*s* of the wagon trains are still to be seen —Veda Conner⟩; *broadly* : CHANNEL, FURROW ⟨~*s* of old stream beds⟩ ⟨~*s* in wrinkled skin⟩ **2** : a usual or fixed practice : a regular course; *esp* : an esp. monotonous routine method of action or procedure from which one is not easily stirred ⟨shock of death had pushed men's minds out of habitual ~*s* —Dixon Wecter⟩ ⟨fall into a conversational ~⟩

**⁴rut** \"\ *vt* **rutted; rutted; rutting; ruts** : to make a rut in : FURROW ⟨wagon trains were *rutting* the prairies —*Amer. Guide Series: Texas*⟩ ⟨the *rutted* snow underfoot —I.S.Cobb⟩ ⟨*rutted* his brow⟩

**⁵rut** \"\ *var of* ROTE

**⁶rut** *or* **ruth** \"\ *n* -s [Hindi *rath*, fr. Skt *ratha* wagon, chariot — more at ROLL] **1** : a carriage drawn by a pony or by oxen **2** : a cart for carrying images in a procession

**ru·ta** \ˈrüd·ə\ *n, cap* [NL, fr. L, rue — more at RUE (herb)] : a large genus (the type of the family Rutaceae) of Eurasian strong-scented herbs and undershrubs having yellow or greenish flowers and 4- to 5-toothed petals that are borne on the receptacle — see RUE

**ru·tab** \rüˈtäb\ *adj* [Ar] : of, relating to, or constituting the third of four recognized stages in the ripening of the date in which the tip becomes soft and loses the bright color of the previous stage — compare KHALAL, KIMRI, TAMAR

**ru·ta·ba·ga** \,rüd·əˈbāgə, -ütə;-\ *n* -s [Sw dial. *rotabagge*, fr. *rot* root (fr. ON *rōt*) + *bagge* bag, ram — more at ROOT] : a turnip (*Brassica napobrassica*) commonly with a very large yellowish root that is used as food both for stock and for human beings — called also *swede*, *Swedish turnip*, *Russian turnip*

**ru·ta·ce·ae** \rüˈtāsē,ē\ *n pl, cap* [NL, fr. *Ruta*, type genus + *-aceae*] : a family of herbs, shrubs, and trees (order Geraniales) often glandular and strong scented and having flowers that are tetramerous or pentamerous with a compound ovary of four or five distinct or somewhat united carpels — **ru·ta·ceous** \-āshəs\ *adj*

**ru·tae·car·pine** *or* **ru·te·car·pine** \,rüd·ēˈkär,pēn, -,pə̇n\ *n* -s [NL *rutaecarpa* (specific epithet of *Evodia rutaecarpa*, prob. fr. L *rutae* — gen. of *ruta* rue — + *-carpa*, fr. Gk *karpos* fruit) + E *-ine* — more at RUE (herb), HARVEST] : a light yellow crystalline alkaloid $C_{18}H_{13}N_3O$ found in the fruit of an Asiatic shrub or small tree (*Evodia rutaecarpa*)

**rutch** \ˈrüch\ *vi* -ED/-ING/-ES [G *rutschen* to slide, slither, fr. MHG *rützen, rütschen*] : to move with a crunching or shuffling noise ⟨no sound except the ~*ing* of heavily loaded bare feet on the paving stones —Talbot Mundy⟩

**ru·te·li·an** \rüˈtēlēən\ *n* -s [NL *Rutela* + E *-ian*] : a beetle of the family Rutelidae

**ru·tel·id** \rüˈteləd\ *adj* [NL *Rutelidae*] : of or relating to the Rutelidae

**ru·tel·i·dae** \rüˈtelə,dē\ *n pl, cap* [NL, fr. *Rutela*, type genus (irreg. fr. L *rutilus* red) + *-idae*; prob. akin to L *ruber* red — more at RED] : a family of vegetable-feeding often brilliantly colored scarabaeoid beetles — compare GOLDSMITH BEETLE

**ru·te-mark** \ˈrüd·ə,märk\ *n* [Norw *rutemark*, fr. *rute* route + *mark*] **1** : a surface marking found in arctic regions, consisting of a row of loose stones enclosing a polygonal area, and usu. occurring in groups **2** : a mud or soil crack similar to a rute-mark in form

**ruth** \ˈrüth\ *n* -s [ME *rewthe, routhe, ruthe*, fr. *ruen, rewen* to rue — more at RUE] **1** : sorrow for the misery of another : PITY, MERCY, COMPASSION ⟨is there no pity, no relenting ~ —Robert Burns⟩ ⟨pounced on the snails without ~ and trampled them —Josephine Pinckney⟩ **2** : sorrow for one's own faults : SADNESS, DISTRESS, REMORSE ⟨I seek . . . not in ~, to curse and deny your truth —Matthew Arnold⟩ **3** : a reason or cause for ruth : a pitiful sight : a sad thing ⟨the ~ of a young man's dying in war —Bernard DeVoto⟩ **syn** see SYMPATHY

**ruthen-** *or* **ruthenio-** *or* **rutheno-** *comb form* [ISV, fr. NL *ruthenium*] : ruthenium : ruthenious ⟨*ruthen*ammines⟩ ⟨*ruthen*iopalladium⟩ ⟨*ruthen*onitrite⟩

**ru·thene** \rüˈthēn\ *n* -s *cap* [ML *Rutheni, Ruteni*, pl., Russians, modif. (influenced by L *Rutheni, Ruteni*, a people of Aquitanian Gaul) of Russ *rusin* — more at RUSSENE] : RUTHENIAN

**ru·the·ni·an** \-nēən\ *n* -s *cap* [*Ruthenia*, a part of the Ukraine + E *-an*] **1 a** : one of a branch of the Little Russians formerly chiefly of Galicia in Austria and the eastern part of Czechoslovakia and recently annexed to the Ukrainian S.S.R. along with the Ruthenian-speaking parts of former southeastern Poland **b** : the Ukrainian language as used in Galicia **2 a** : member of a former Eastern Orthodox body entering into communion with Rome at the end of the 16th century and becoming the Uniate Church of the Little Russians

**ru·then·ic** \-thenik, -thēn-\ *adj* [*ruthen-* + *-ic*] : of, relating to, or derived from ruthenium — used esp. of compounds in which this element has a relatively high valence

**ru·the·ni·ous** \rüˈthēnēəs\ *also* **ru·the·nous** \ˈrüthənəs\ *adj* [*ruthenious* fr. NL *ruthenium* + E *-ous*; *ruthenous* fr. *ruthen-* + *-ous*] : of, relating to, or derived from ruthenium — used esp. of compounds in which this element has a relatively low valence

**ru·the·ni·um** \rüˈthēnēəm\ *n* -s [NL, fr. ML *Ruthenia* Russia, where it was first found + NL *-ium*] : a hard brittle grayish white polyvalent rare metallic element that is one of the platinum metals and resembles osmium but is more resistant to corrosion (as by oxidizing acids), that occurs in platinum ores esp. in iridosmine, and that is used chiefly in hardening platinum and palladium alloys — symbol *Ru*; see ELEMENT table

**ruthenium oxide** *n* : an oxide of ruthenium: as **a** : the dark blue crystalline dioxide $RuO_2$ formed by heating ruthenium in air **b** : the explosive volatile poisonous yellow crystalline tetroxide $RuO_4$ having a disagreeable odor

**ruthenium red** *n* : an ammoniated ruthenium chloride obtained as a brownish red powder and used as a microscopic stain and as a test esp. for pectin and gums

**ruth·er·ford** \ˈrəthə(r)fə(r)d\ *n* -s [after Baron Ernest *Rutherford* †1937 Brit. physicist] : a unit strength of a radioactive source corresponding to one million disintegrations per second

**rutherford atom** *n, usu cap R* [after Baron Ernest *Rutherford*] : the atom consisting of a small dense positively charged nucleus surrounded by planetary electrons

**ruth·er·ford·ine** \-fə(r),dēn, -,də̇n\ *n* -s [G *rutherfordin*, fr. Baron Ernest *Rutherford* + G *-in* -ine] : a mineral $(UO_2)(CO_3)$ consisting of uranyl carbonate in dense yellow masses of minute fibers

**rutherford scattering** *n, usu cap R* [after Baron Ernest *Rutherford*] : a scattering of alpha particles on passage through thin metal foils in an angular distribution that indicates a concentration of positive charge at the atomic nucleus

**ruth·er·glen bug** \ˈrəthə(r),glen-\ *n, usu cap R* [fr. *Rutherglen*, Scotland] : a common Australian lygaeid bug (*Nysius vinitor*) that attacks many plants (as citrus, peach, plum, potato, and grapes)

**ruth·ful** \ˈrüthfəl\ *adj* [ME *rewtheful, routheful, rutheful*, fr. *rewthe, routhe, ruthe* pity + *-ful* — more at RUTH] **1** : full of ruth : PITIFUL, TENDER ⟨had never known a woman so ~ —Budd Schulberg⟩ **2** : full of sorrow : WOEFUL, RUEFUL ⟨a ~ smile —*Times Lit. Supp.*⟩ **3** : causing sorrow — **ruth·ful·ness** *n* -ES

**ruth·ful·ly** \-fəlē\ *adv* [ME *rewthfully, routhfully, ruthfully*, fr. *rewthful, routhful, ruthful*, adj.] : in a ruthful manner

**ruth·less** \ˈrüthlə̇s *sometimes* ˈrüth-\ *adj* [ME *rewtheles, routheles, rutheles*, fr. *rewthe, routhe, ruthe* pity, ruth + *-les* -less] : having no ruth : MERCILESS, PITILESS, RELENTLESS, UNSPARING ⟨act of savage, ~ ferocity —J.A.Froude⟩ ⟨savage and ~ energy in the shedding of innocent blood —Agnes Repplier⟩ ⟨~ enforcement of the game laws —G.B.Shaw⟩ ⟨~ disregard for the exhaustibility of the resources they exploited —J.K.Howard⟩ ⟨fearless and ~ honesty in expressing his opinions —F.W.Scott⟩

**ruth·less·ly** *adv* : in a ruthless manner : MERCILESSLY

**ruth·less·ness** *n* -ES : the quality or state of being ruthless

**ruths** *pl of* RUTH

**ru·ti·do·sis** \,rüd·əˈdōsə̇s\ *n, pl* **rutido·ses** \-ō,sēz\ [NL, irreg. fr. Gk *rhytidōsis* wrinkling, fr. *rhytidoun* to wrinkle + *-sis* — more at RHYTIDOME] : a wrinkling esp. of the cornea

**ru·ti·lant** \ˈrüd·ᵊlənt\ *adj* [ME *rutilaunt*, fr. L *rutilant-, rutilans*, pres. part. of *rutilare* to make red, fr. *rutilus* red; akin to L *ruber* red — more at RED] : having a reddish glow : SHINING ⟨sun, which put a ~ sheen on their skin —Louis Adamic⟩

**rutilate** *vi* [L *rutilatus*, past part. of *rutilare*] *obs* : SHINE

**ru·ti·lat·ed quartz** \ˈrüd·ᵊl,ād·əd-\ *n* [*rutile* + *-ate* + *-ed*] : quartz characterized by the presence of enclosed rutile needles — compare SAGENITE

**ru·tile** \ˈrü,tēl, -tīl\ *n* -s [G *rutil*, fr. L *rutilis* red — more at RUTILANT] **1** : a mineral $TiO_2$ that consists of titanium dioxide, is trimorphous with anatase and brookite, is usu. of a reddish brown color but when deep red or black is sometimes cut into a gem, has a brilliant metallic or adamantine luster, occurs in tetragonal crystals which are commonly prismatic with striations and often geniculate as a result of twinning or occas. occurs massive, and usu. contains a little iron **2** : a synthetic gem in any of several colors and of the same composition as rutile that because of its dispersion and refractive power rivals the diamond in beauty

**ru·tin** \ˈrütᵊn\ *n* -s [ISV *rut-* (fr. NL *Ruta*) + *-in*] : a yellow crystalline flavonol glycoside $C_{27}H_{30}O_{16}$ that is found in rue leaves, tobacco leaves, buckwheat, flower buds of the Japanese pagoda tree, and other plants, that yields quercetin and rutinose on hydrolysis, and that is used chiefly for strengthening capillary blood vessels (as in cases of hypertension and radiation injury)

**ru·tin·ose** \-ᵊn,ōs\ *n* -s [ISV *rutin* + *-ose*] : a hygroscopic reducing disaccharide sugar $C_{12}H_{22}O_{10}$ that is obtained from rutin and yields D-glucose and L-rhamnose on hydrolysis

**rut·i·o·don** \ˈrəd·ēə,dän\ *n, cap* [NL, irreg. fr. Gk *rhytis* wrinkle + NL *-odon* — more at RHYTIDOME] : a genus of subaquatic Triassic reptiles (order Thecodontia) with very elongate narrow skull and four or more rows of dermal scutes

**rut·land beauty** \ˈrətlənd-\ *n, usu cap R* [prob. fr. *Rutland* county, England] : HEDGE BINDWEED

**rutland leather** *n, usu cap R* [fr. *Rutland* county, England] : a high-grade flexible roan used esp. in bookbinding

**rut·land·shire** \-n(d),shi(ə)r, -,shiə, -,shə(r)\ *or* **rutland** *adj, usu cap* [fr. *Rutlandshire* or *Rutland* county, Eng.] : of or from the county of Rutland, England : of the kind or style prevalent in Rutland

**ruts** *pl of* RUT, *pres 3d sing of* RUT

**rutted** *adj* [fr. past part. of *⁴rut*] : having or marked by ruts ⟨~, odorous alleys and byways —Foster Fitz-Simons⟩

**rut·tee** *also* **rat·ti** \ˈrəd·ē\ *n* -s [Hindi *rattī*, fr. Skt *raktikā*, fr. *rakta* red, fr. *rajyati* it is dyed or colored — more at RAGA] : any of various Indian units of weight equal to around one or two grains troy

**¹rut·ter** \ˈrəd·ə(r)\ *n* -s [D *ruiter*, fr. MD *ruter, rutter, ruiter*, fr. OF *routier*, fr. *route* band, troop, route + *-ier* — more at ROUTE] *archaic* : a horseman or trooper orig. of German forces common in the 15th and 16th centuries

**²rutter** \"\ *n* -s [*⁴rut* + *-er*] **1** : one that ruts **2** : a plow for cutting ruts in a logging road for the runners of the sleds to run in

**rut·ti·ness** \ˈrəd·|ēnə̇s, -ət|, |in-\ *n* -ES : the quality or state of being rutty

**rutting** *pres part of* RUT

**rut·tish** \|ish, |ēsh\ *adj* [*²rut* + *-ish*] : inclined to rut : LUSTFUL, SALACIOUS — **rut·tish·ly** *adv* — **rut·tish·ness** *n* -ES

**[1]rut·tle** \'rət°l, 'ru̇t°l\ *vi* -ED/-ING/-S [ME *rutelen;* akin to ME *ratelen* to rattle — more at RATTLE] *dial Brit* **:** RATTLE

**[2]ruttle** \"\ *n* -S *dial Brit* **:** RATTLE; *specif* **:** DEATH RATTLE

**[1]rut·ty** \'rəd·|ē, -ət|, |i\ *adj* -ER/-EST [[3]*rut* + *-y*] **:** full of ruts ⟨lane had shriveled to a ~ track —Berton Roueché⟩

**[2]rutty** \"\ *adj* -ER/-EST [[1]*rut* + *-y*] **:** RUTTISH, LUSTFUL

**ru·tu·bu·ri** \ˌrüd·ə'bu̇rē\ *n* -S [MexSp, fr. Tarahumara] **:** a ritual round dance of the Mexican Tarahumara Indians

**rut·u·li** \'rəchəˌlī\ *n pl, cap* [L] **:** an ancient Italian people having their capital in 442 B.C. at Ardea and probably representing an early Indo-European people

**rutway** \'=ˌ=\ *n* [[3]*rut* + *way*] **:** a way for the passage and guidance of wheeled vehicles formed by stone blocks laid end to end in parallel lines

**ru·vet·tus** \rə'ved·əs\ *n, cap* [NL, fr. It *rovetto* escolar, dim. of *rovo* briar, bramble, fr. L *rubus* blackberry bush, bramble] **:** a genus of marine fishes (family Gempylidae) containing the escolars

**RV** *abbr* rendezvous

**RVA** *abbr, often not cap* reactive volt-ampere

**RVSVP** *abbr* [F *répondez vite s'il vous plaît*] please reply at once

**rw** *abbr* railway

**RW** *abbr* **1** radiological warfare **2** *often not cap* random widths **3** reverse work **4** right of way **5** right wing **6** right worshipful or worthy

**rwa·la** *or* **ru·wa·la** *or* **ru·wal·la** \rə'wälə\ *also* **ru·a·la** \rü'älə\ *n, pl* **rwala** *or* **rwalas** *or* **ruwala** *or* **ruwalas** *or* **ruwalla** *or* **ruwallas** *usu cap* **:** a member of a powerful Arabian people supposed to be descended from Abraham, regarded as the true pure Bedouins, and related to the Anezeh group of peoples

**rwan·da** \rə'wändə\ *adj, usu cap* [fr. *Rwanda*, central Africa] **:** of or from the country of Rwanda **:** of the kind or style prevalent in Rwanda

**rwan·dan** \-dən\ *n* -S *cap* [*Rwanda*, Africa + E *-an*] **:** a native or inhabitant of Rwanda — **rwandan** *adj, usu cap*

**rwy** *abbr* railway

**Rx** *n* -S [fr. *Rx*, symbol] **:** a medical prescription

**Rx** *symbol* **1** recipe **2** tens of rupees

**-ry** \rē, ri\ *n suffix* -ES [ME *-rie*, fr. OF, short for *-erie* -ery] **:** -ERY ⟨pilot*ry*⟩ ⟨wizard*ry*⟩ ⟨pheasant*ry*⟩ ⟨citizen*ry*⟩ ⟨musket*ry*⟩ ⟨ribald*ry*⟩ ⟨sloven*ry*⟩ ⟨prelat*ry*⟩ ⟨sergeant*ry*⟩ ⟨bandit*ry*⟩ ⟨peasant*ry*⟩

**ry** *abbr* **1** *often cap* railway **2** Rydberg

**ry·al** *also* **ri·al** \'rī(ə)l\ *n* -S [ME, fr. *ryal, rial* royal — more at RIAL] **1 :** an old English gold coin weighing 120 grains orig. equivalent to 10 shillings but later under Elizabeth to 15 shillings, first issued by Edward IV in place of the debased noble of Henry IV, and bearing the design of the noble with a rose added — called also *rose noble* **2 :** one of two Scottish coins: **a :** a gold coin equivalent to 60 shillings or 3 pounds issued by Mary Queen of Scots **b :** a silver coin worth 30 shillings issued by Mary and James VI

**ry·a·nia** \rī'ānēə\ *n* -S [NL *Ryania* (genus name of *Ryania speciosa*, the shrub from which it is made), fr. John *Ryan*, 18th cent. Brit. physician + NL *-ia*] **1 :** an insecticide made of a mixture of alkaloids from the ground stems of a tropical So. American shrub (*Patrisia pyrifera* syn. *Ryania speciosa*) and used esp. against the European corn borer **2 :** the plant that yields ryania

**ry·an·o·dine** \rī'anəˌdēn, -ˌdən\ *n* -S [irreg. fr. NL *Ryania* (genus name of *Ryania speciosa*) + E *-ine*] **:** a crystalline insecticidal alkaloid $C_{25}H_{35}NO_9$ that is toxic to mammals and is obtained from the root and stem of the ryania

**ryd·berg** \'ridˌbərg\ *n* -S *usu cap* [after Johannes R. *Rydberg* †1919 Swedish physicist] **:** the Rydberg constant esp. when expressed in energy terms with maximum possible value of about $2.179 \times 10^{-11}$ ergs

**rydberg constant** *or* **rydberg unit** *n, usu cap R* [after Johannes R. *Rydberg*] **:** a wave number characteristic of the atomic spectrum of each element equal to the constant factor in the wave-number formula for all the spectral series of the elements and having a value from 109,678 $cm^{-1}$ for hydrogen to 109,737 $cm^{-1}$ for the heaviest elements

**ry·der** *or* **rij·der** \'rīdə(r)\ *n* -S [*ryder* fr. ME *rydar*, fr. MD *rider*, fr. *riden* to ride + *-er; rijder* fr. D, fr. MD *rider;* akin to OHG *rītan* to ride — more at RIDE] **:** an old gold coin of the Netherlands bearing a horseman on the obverse

**[1]rye** \'rī\ *n* -S [ME, fr. OE *ryge;* akin to OFris *rogga* rye, OS *roggo*, OHG *rocko*, ON *rugr*, Russ *rozh'*, Lith *rugỹs*] **1 :** a hardy annual cereal grass (*Secale cereale*) that has loose spikes with an articulate rachis and long-awned lemmas and is widely cultivated esp. in northern continental Europe where its grain is the chief ingredient of black bread and in No. America where it is used esp. as a cover crop and for soil improvement and frequently for forage **2 :** the seeds of rye used for bread flour, whiskey manufacture, feed for poultry and other farm animals, and esp. formerly in the roasted state a coffee substitute **3 :** RYE WHISKEY **4 :** RYE BREAD ⟨ham on ~⟩

**[2]rye** \"\ *n* -S [Romany *rai*, fr. Skt *rājan* king — more at ROYAL] **:** GENTLEMAN; *specif* **:** a gypsy gentleman

**rye and indian** *n, usu cap I* **:** bread made of rye flour and corn meal and in colonial days often baked in a pot or a brick oven

**rye bread** *n* **:** any bread made wholly or in part from rye flour (as black bread, pumpernickel, knäckebröd, and a light loaf usu. containing caraway seed)

**ryecorn** \'=ˌ=\ *n, Austral* **:** [1]RYE 1

**ryegrass** \'=ˌ=\ *n* **1 :** any of several grasses of the genus *Lolium; esp* **:** PERENNIAL RYEGRASS — see ITALIAN RYEGRASS **2 :** LYME GRASS — see GIANT RYEGRASS

**rye·land** \'rīlənd\ *n* [fr. *Ryelands*, district and hamlet in Herefordshire, Eng.] **1** *usu cap* **:** an old English breed of hardy hornless white-faced sheep producing high quality wool and quick-maturing lambs of good size **2** -S *often cap* **:** an animal of the Ryeland breed

**rye rust** *n* **:** any of the several rusts of the genus *Puccinia* attacking rye

**rye smut** *n* **:** a smut (as the stem smut) attacking rye

**rye waltz** *n* **:** a ballroom dance with a waltz step alternately in duple and in triple time

**rye whiskey** *n* **:** a whiskey distilled from rye or from a mixture of rye and malt

**ryke** \'rēk\ *Scot var of* REACH

**ryme** \'rīm\ *n* -S [obs. E *ryme, rime* rim, fr. ME *rime* — more at RIM] *archaic* **:** the surface of water ⟨the gate was backed against the ~ —John Masefield⟩

**ryn·chops** \'riŋˌkäps\ *n, cap* [NL, irreg. fr. *rhynch-* + *-ops*] **:** a genus of birds consisting of the skimmers and constituting a family of the order Charadriiformes

**ryn·chos·po·ra** \riŋ'käspərə\ [NL, irreg. fr. *rhynch-* + *-spora*] *syn of* RHYNCHOSPORA

**ryn·chos·po·rous** \-rəs\ *adj* [irreg. fr. *rhynch-* + *-sporous*] **:** having a beaked fruit or seed

**rynd** *var of* RIND

**ry·o·bu** \rē'ō(ˌ)bü\ *or* **ryobu shinto** *n, cap R&S* [Jap *ryō bu*, lit., two parts] **:** a Shinto sect fostering a mixture of Shinto and Buddhism and being greatly popular in Japan between the 9th and 18th centuries

**ry·ot** *or* **rai·yat** \'rīət\ *n* -S [Hindi *raiyat, ra'īyat*, fr. Per, fr. Ar *ra'īyah* flock, herd] **:** a peasant, tenant farmer, or cultivator of the soil in India

**[1]ry·ot·war** \¦rīə·¦twär, -ət·¦w-\ *or* **ry·ot·wa·ri** *or* **ry·ot·wa·ry** *or* **rai·yat·wa·ri** \-rē\ *n, pl* **ryotwars** *or* **ryotwaris** *or* **ryotwaries** *or* **raiyatwaris** [Hindi *raiyatwār, raiyatwārī* by or with individual cultivators, fr. *raiyat, ra'īyat*] **:** a system of collecting land rent or taxes in which the government settlement is made directly with the ryots

**[2]ryotwar** \"\ *or* **ryotwari** *or* **ryotwary** *or* **raiyatwari** \"\ *adj* [Hindi *raiyatwār, raiyatwārī*] **:** of or relating to the ryotwar system

**ry·pe** \'rüēpə, 'rīp\ *n, pl* **rype** *or* **rypes** [Dan & Norw; akin to ON *rjūpa* ptarmigan, Latvian *rubenis* moorhen] **:** PTARMIGAN

**[1]ryt·i·na** \'rit°nə\ [NL, irreg. fr. *rhyt-* + *-ina*] *syn of* HYDRODAMALIS

**[2]rytina** \"\ *n* -S [NL [1]*Rytina*] **:** STELLER'S SEA COW

**ryu·kyu** \rē'(y)ü(ˌ)kyü, rə'-\ *n, usu cap* [fr. the *Ryukyu* islands, southwest of Japan] **:** the language of the Ryukyuan people that is related to Japanese

**ryu·kyu·an** \-kyüən\ *n* -S *usu cap* [*Ryukyu* islands + E *-an*] **1 :** the people of the Ryukyu islands **2 :** a member of the Ryukyuan people